2020
Harris
New England
Manufacturers Directory

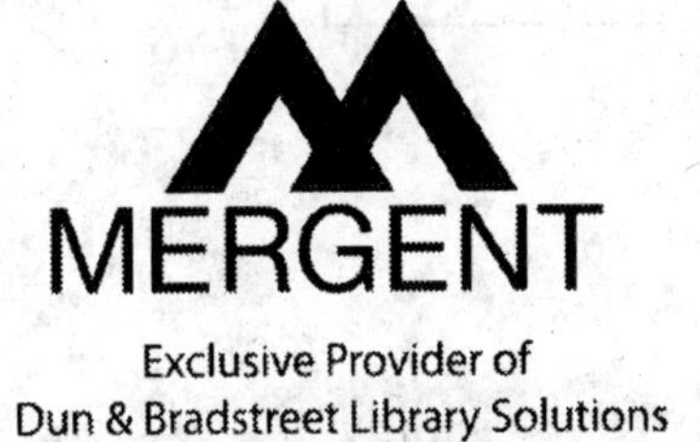

dun & bradstreet

Published April 2020 next update April 2021

Publisher

Mergent Inc.
444 Madison Ave
New York, NY 10022

2020 Mergent Business Press
ISSN 1080-2614
ISBN 978-1-64141-632-0

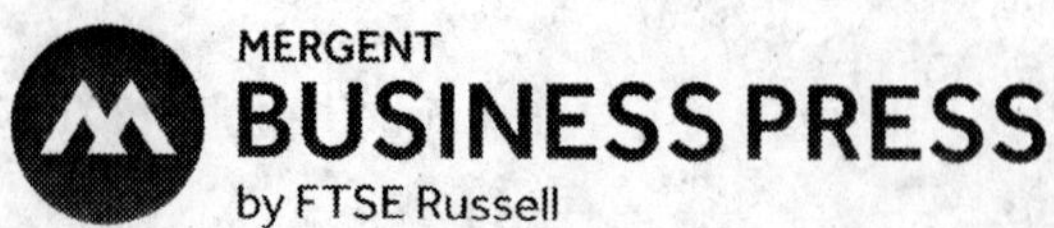

TABLE OF CONTENTS

SUMMARY OF CONTENTS

Number of Companies.. 22,743
Number of Decision Makers 46,331
Minimum Number of Employees 3

EXPLANATORY NOTES

How to Cross-Reference in This Directory

Sequential Entry Numbers. Each establishment in the Geographic Section is numbered sequentially (G-0000). The number assigned to each establishment is referred to as its "entry number." To make cross-referencing easier, each listing in the Geographic, SIC, Alphabetic and Product Sections includes the establishment's entry number. To facilitate locating an entry in the Geographic Section, the entry numbers for the first listing on the left page and the last listing on the right page are printed at the top of the page next to the city name.

Source Suggestions Welcome

Although all known sources were used to compile this directory, it is possible that companies were inadvertently omitted. Your assistance in calling attention to such omissions would be greatly appreciated. A special form on the facing page will help you in the reporting process.

Analysis

Every effort has been made to contact all firms to verify their information. The one exception to this rule is the annual sales figure, which is considered by many companies to be confidential information. Therefore, estimated sales have been calculated by multiplying the nationwide average sales per employee for the firm's major SIC/NAICS code by the firm's number of employees. Nationwide averages for sales per employee by SIC/NAICS codes are provided by the U.S. Department of Commerce and are updated annually. All sales—sales (est)—have been estimated by this method. The exceptions are parent companies (PA), division headquarters (DH) and headquarter locations (HQ) which may include an actual corporate sales figure—sales (corporate-wide) if available.

Types of Companies

Descriptive and statistical data are included for companies in the entire state. These comprise manufacturers, machine shops, fabricators, assemblers and printers. Also identified are corporate offices in the state.

Employment Data

The employment figure shown in the Geographic Section includes male and female employees and embraces all levels of the company: administrative, clerical, sales and maintenance. This figure is for the facility listed and does not include other plants or offices. It should be recognized that these figures represent an approximate year-round average. These employment figures are broken into codes A through G and used in the Product and SIC Sections to further help you in qualifying a company. Be sure to check the footnotes on the bottom of pages for the code breakdowns.

Standard Industrial Classification (SIC)

The Standard Industrial Classification (SIC) system used in this directory was developed by the federal government for use in classifying establishments by the type of activity they are engaged in. The SIC classifications used in this directory are from the 1987 edition published by the U.S. Government's Office of Management and Budget. The SIC system separates all activities into broad industrial divisions (e.g., manufacturing, mining, retail trade). It further subdivides each division. The range of manufacturing industry classes extends from two-digit codes (major industry group) to four-digit codes (product).

For example:

Industry Breakdown	Code	Industry, Product, etc.
*Major industry group	20	Food and kindred products
Industry group	203	Canned and frozen foods
*Industry	2033	Fruits and vegetables, etc.

*Classifications used in this directory

Only two-digit and four-digit codes are used in this directory.

Arrangement

1. The **Geographic Section** contains complete in-depth corporate data. This section is sorted by cities listed in alphabetical order and companies listed alphabetically within each city. A County/City Index for referencing cities within counties precedes this section.

IMPORTANT NOTICE: It is a violation of both federal and state law to transmit an unsolicited advertisement to a facsimile machine. Any user of this product that violates such laws may be subject to civil and criminal penalties, which may exceed $500 for each transmission of an unsolicited facsimile. Mergent Inc. provides fax numbers for lawful purposes only and expressly forbids the use of these numbers in any unlawful manner.

2. The **Standard Industrial Classification (SIC) Section** lists companies under approximately 500 four-digit SIC codes. An alphabetical and a numerical index precedes this section. A company can be listed under several codes. The codes are in numerical order with companies listed alphabetically under each code.

3. The **Alphabetic Section** lists all companies with their full physical or mailing addresses and telephone number.

4. The **Product Section** lists companies under unique Harris categories. An index preceding this section lists all product categories in alphabetical order. Companies can be listed under several categories.

USER'S GUIDE TO LISTINGS

GEOGRAPHIC SECTION

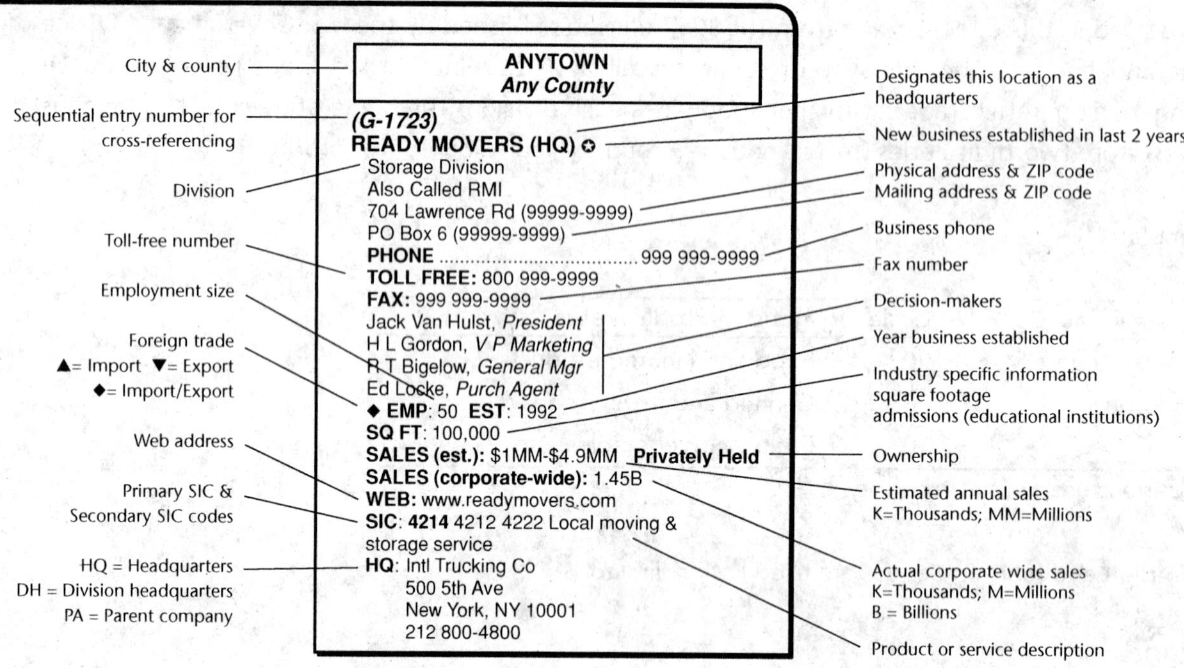

City & county
Sequential entry number for cross-referencing
Division
Toll-free number
Employment size
Foreign trade ▲= Import ▼= Export ◆= Import/Export
Web address
Primary SIC & Secondary SIC codes
HQ = Headquarters
DH = Division headquarters
PA = Parent company
ANYTOWN
Any County
(G-1723)
READY MOVERS (HQ) ✪
Storage Division
Also Called RMI
704 Lawrence Rd (99999-9999)
PO Box 6 (99999-9999)
PHONE 999 999-9999
TOLL FREE: 800 999-9999
FAX: 999 999-9999
Jack Van Hulst, President
H L Gordon, V P Marketing
R T Bigelow, General Mgr
Ed Locke, Purch Agent
◆ EMP: 50 EST: 1992
SQ FT: 100,000
SALES (est.): $1MM-$4.9MM Privately Held
SALES (corporate-wide): 1.45B
WEB: www.readymovers.com
SIC: 4214 4212 4222 Local moving & storage service
HQ: Intl Trucking Co
500 5th Ave
New York, NY 10001
212 800-4800
Designates this location as a headquarters
New business established in last 2 years
Physical address & ZIP code
Mailing address & ZIP code
Business phone
Fax number
Decision-makers
Year business established
Industry specific information square footage admissions (educational institutions)
Ownership
Estimated annual sales K=Thousands; MM=Millions
Actual corporate wide sales K=Thousands; M=Millions B = Billions
Product or service description

SIC SECTION

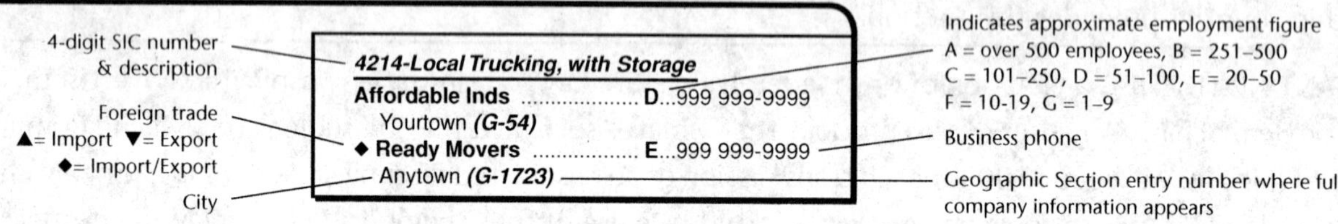

4-digit SIC number & description
Foreign trade ▲= Import ▼= Export ◆= Import/Export
City
4214-Local Trucking, with Storage
Affordable Inds .... D...999 999-9999
Yourtown (G-54)
◆ Ready Movers .... E...999 999-9999
Anytown (G-1723)
Indicates approximate employment figure A = over 500 employees, B = 251-500 C = 101-250, D = 51-100, E = 20-50 F = 10-19, G = 1-9
Business phone
Geographic Section entry number where full company information appears

ALPHABETIC SECTION

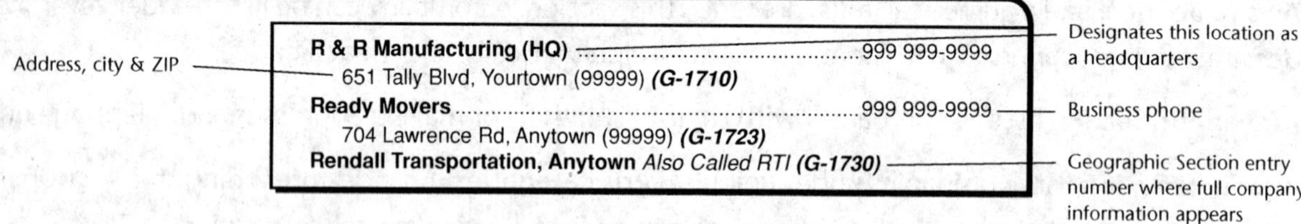

Address, city & ZIP
R & R Manufacturing (HQ) 999 999-9999
651 Tally Blvd, Yourtown (99999) (G-1710)
Ready Movers 999 999-9999
704 Lawrence Rd, Anytown (99999) (G-1723)
Rendall Transportation, Anytown Also Called RTI (G-1730)
Designates this location as a headquarters
Business phone
Geographic Section entry number where full company information appears

PRODUCTS & SERVICES SECTION

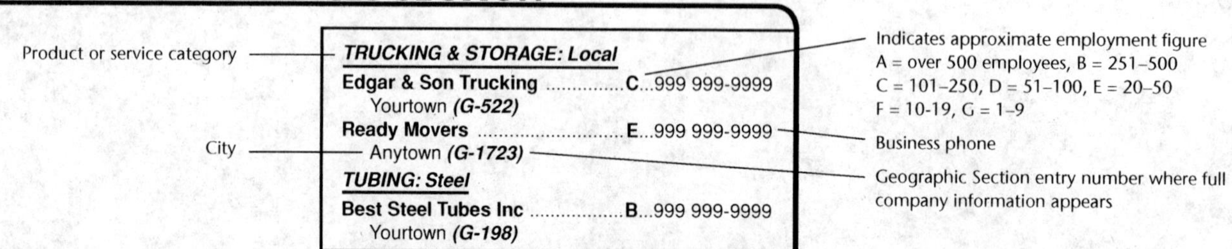

Product or service category
City
TRUCKING & STORAGE: Local
Edgar & Son Trucking ....C...999 999-9999
Yourtown (G-522)
Ready Movers ....E...999 999-9999
Anytown (G-1723)
TUBING: Steel
Best Steel Tubes Inc ....B...999 999-9999
Yourtown (G-198)
Indicates approximate employment figure A = over 500 employees, B = 251-500 C = 101-250, D = 51-100, E = 20-50 F = 10-19, G = 1-9
Business phone
Geographic Section entry number where full company information appears

GEOGRAPHIC SECTION

Companies sorted by city in alphabetical order

In-depth company data listed

STANDARD INDUSTRIAL CLASSIFICATIONS

Alphabetical index of classifcation descriptions

Numerical index of classifcation descriptions

Companies sorted by SIC product groupings

ALPHABETIC SECTION

Company listings in alphabetical order

PRODUCT INDEX

Product categories listed in alphabetical order

PRODUCT SECTION

Companies sorted by product and manufacturing service classifications

COUNTY/CITY CROSS-REFERENCE INDEX

ENTRY#

CONNECTICUT

Fairfield

Hartford

Litchfield

Middlesex

New Haven

New London

Tolland

Windham

MAINE

Androscoggin

Aroostook

Cumberland

ENTRY#

Berkshire

Adams (G-7408)
Ashley Falls (G-7672)
Becket (G-7954)
Cheshire (G-9979)
Clarksburg (G-10073)
Dalton (G-10174)
East Otis (G-10504)
Florida (G-10871)
Great Barrington (G-11232)
Hancock (G-11324)
Hinsdale (G-11520)
Housatonic (G-11742)
Lanesborough (G-11987)
Lee (G-12087)
Lenox (G-12099)
Lenox Dale (G-12104)
Monterey (G-13213)
North Adams (G-13667)
Otis (G-14250)
Pittsfield (G-14448)
Richmond (G-14779)
Sandisfield (G-14960)
Savoy (G-15003)
Sheffield (G-15059)
South Lee (G-15319)
Southfield (G-15410)
Stockbridge (G-15551)
Williamstown (G-16954)

Bristol

Acushnet (G-7396)
Assonet (G-7676)
Attleboro (G-7695)
Attleboro Falls (G-7810)
Berkley (G-8084)
Chartley (G-9857)
Dartmouth (G-10275)
Dighton (G-10335)
East Freetown (G-10452)
East Taunton (G-10509)
Easton (G-10584)
Fairhaven (G-10635)
Fall River (G-10648)
Mansfield (G-12610)
New Bedford (G-13346)
North Attleboro (G-13741)
North Dartmouth (G-13915)
North Dighton (G-13929)
North Easton (G-13940)
Norton (G-14069)
Raynham (G-14704)
Rehoboth (G-14745)
Seekonk (G-15017)
Somerset (G-15142)
South Dartmouth (G-15236)
South Easton (G-15268)
Swansea (G-15702)
Taunton (G-15719)
Westport (G-16835)
Westport Point (G-16854)

Dukes

Aquinnah (G-7620)
Chilmark (G-10072)
Edgartown (G-10585)
Oak Bluffs (G-14209)
Vineyard Haven (G-15933)

Essex

Amesbury (G-7476)
Andover (G-7532)
Beverly (G-8094)
Boxford (G-8973)
Byfield (G-9362)
Danvers (G-10188)
Essex (G-10591)
Georgetown (G-11134)
Gloucester (G-11158)
Groveland (G-11298)
Haverhill (G-11402)
Ipswich (G-11899)
Lawrence (G-11988)
Lynn (G-12487)
Lynnfield (G-12545)
Manchester (G-12601)
Marblehead (G-12673)
Merrimac (G-12999)
Methuen (G-13007)
Middleton (G-13083)
Nahant (G-13215)
Newbury (G-13462)
Newburyport (G-13467)
North Andover (G-13686)
Peabody (G-14304)
Rockport (G-14834)
Rowley (G-14846)
Salem (G-14888)
Salisbury (G-14948)
Saugus (G-14975)
South Hamilton (G-15314)
Swampscott (G-15697)
Topsfield (G-15852)
Wenham (G-16403)
West Boxford (G-16408)
West Newbury (G-16489)

Franklin

Ashfield (G-7649)
Bernardston (G-8093)
Charlemont (G-9819)
Colrain (G-10104)
Conway (G-10164)
Deerfield (G-10303)
Erving (G-10589)
Gill (G-11156)
Greenfield (G-11250)
Heath (G-11488)
Leverett (G-12198)
Millers Falls (G-13180)
Montague (G-13212)
Northfield (G-14063)
Orange (G-14213)
Shelburne Falls (G-15066)
Shutesbury (G-15140)
South Deerfield (G-15244)
Sunderland (G-15675)
Turners Falls (G-15875)
Whately (G-16905)

Hampden

Agawam (G-7415)
Bondsville (G-8325)
Brimfield (G-9109)
Chester (G-9980)
Chicopee (G-9995)
East Longmeadow (G-10464)
Feeding Hills (G-10798)
Granville (G-11230)
Hampden (G-11319)
Holland (G-11553)
Holyoke (G-11615)
Indian Orchard (G-11882)
Longmeadow (G-12331)
Ludlow (G-12452)
Monson (G-13201)
Palmer (G-14277)
Russell (G-14877)
Southwick (G-15411)
Springfield (G-15438)
Thorndike (G-15850)
Three Rivers (G-15851)
West Springfield (G-16504)
Westfield (G-16659)
Wilbraham (G-16933)

Hampshire

Amherst (G-7511)
Belchertown (G-8021)
Cummington (G-10173)
Easthampton (G-10551)
Florence (G-10864)
Goshen (G-11222)
Granby (G-11227)
Hadley (G-11305)
Hardwick (G-11371)
Hatfield (G-11400)
Haydenville (G-11487)
Leeds (G-12097)
Northampton (G-13997)
Pelham (G-14388)
South Hadley (G-15300)
Southampton (G-15337)
Ware (G-16228)
West Hatfield (G-16482)
Westhampton (G-16801)
Williamsburg (G-16946)

Middlesex

Acton (G-7333)
Arlington (G-7621)
Ashby (G-7646)
Ashland (G-7655)
Auburndale (G-7855)
Ayer (G-7905)
Bedford (G-7955)
Belmont (G-8065)
Billerica (G-8202)
Boxboro (G-8951)
Boxborough (G-8956)
Burlington (G-9227)
Cambridge (G-9366)
Carlisle (G-9797)
Chelmsford (G-9864)
Chestnut Hill (G-9981)
Concord (G-10107)
Devens (G-10316)
Dracut (G-10354)
Dunstable (G-10389)
Everett (G-10599)
Framingham (G-10914)
Groton (G-11285)
Holliston (G-11554)
Hopkinton (G-11685)
Hudson (G-11748)
Lexington (G-12199)
Lincoln (G-12285)
Littleton (G-12290)
Lowell (G-12339)
Malden (G-12556)
Marlborough (G-12708)
Maynard (G-12893)
Medford (G-12920)
Melrose (G-12973)
Natick (G-13232)
Newton (G-13550)
Newton Centre (G-13656)
Newton Upper Falls (G-13657)
North Billerica (G-13788)
North Chelmsford (G-13884)
North Reading (G-13978)
Pepperell (G-14435)
Pinehurst (G-14447)
Reading (G-14733)
Sherborn (G-15077)
Shirley (G-15080)
Somerville (G-15150)
Stoneham (G-15552)
Stow (G-15629)
Sudbury (G-15650)
Tewksbury (G-15806)
Townsend (G-15868)
Tyngsboro (G-15886)
Waban (G-15936)
Wakefield (G-15940)
Waltham (G-16019)
Watertown (G-16263)
Wayland (G-16332)
West Groton (G-16479)
West Townsend (G-16566)
Westford (G-16750)
Weston (G-16822)
Wilmington (G-16962)
Winchester (G-17083)
Woburn (G-17102)

Nantucket

Nantucket (G-13216)
Siasconset (G-15141)

Norfolk

Avon (G-7874)
Bellingham (G-8027)
Braintree (G-8984)
Brookline (G-9194)
Canton (G-9710)
Cohasset (G-10096)
Dedham (G-10279)
Dover (G-10350)
East Walpole (G-10522)
East Weymouth (G-10532)
Foxboro (G-10873)
Foxborough (G-10910)
Franklin (G-11019)
Holbrook (G-11521)
Medfield (G-12908)
Medway (G-12952)
Millis (G-13182)
Milton (G-13189)
Needham (G-13289)
Needham Heights (G-13318)
Norfolk (G-13659)
North Quincy (G-13977)
North Weymouth (G-13996)
Norwood (G-14115)
Plainville (G-14514)
Quincy (G-14612)
Randolph (G-14668)
Sharon (G-15045)
South Walpole (G-15320)
South Weymouth (G-15321)
Stoughton (G-15574)
Walpole (G-15986)
Wellesley (G-16356)
Wellesley Hills (G-16395)
Westwood (G-16855)
Weymouth (G-16883)
Wrentham (G-17513)

Plymouth

Abington (G-7319)
Bridgewater (G-9059)
Brockton (G-9112)
Carver (G-9802)
Duxbury (G-10392)
East Bridgewater (G-10405)
East Wareham (G-10530)
Halifax (G-11313)
Hanover (G-11326)
Hanson (G-11359)
Hingham (G-11489)
Hull (G-11828)
Kingston (G-11955)
Lakeville (G-11969)
Marion (G-12697)
Marshfield (G-12856)
Mattapoisett (G-12885)
Middleboro (G-13050)
Norwell (G-14094)
Pembroke (G-14389)
Plymouth (G-14539)
Plympton (G-14590)
Rochester (G-14784)
Rockland (G-14788)
Scituate (G-15004)
South Carver (G-15235)
Wareham (G-16240)
West Bridgewater (G-16428)
West Wareham (G-16567)
Whitman (G-16920)

Suffolk

Allston (G-7458)
Boston (G-8326)
Brighton (G-9092)
Charlestown (G-9823)
Chelsea (G-9943)
Dorchester (G-10339)
Hyde Park (G-11862)
Jamaica Plain (G-11940)
Mattapan (G-12883)
Revere (G-14763)
Roslindale (G-14837)
Roxbury (G-14870)
West Roxbury (G-16493)
Winthrop (G-17100)

Worcester

Ashburnham (G-7643)
Athol (G-7684)
Auburn (G-7820)
Baldwinville (G-7943)
Barre (G-7949)
Berlin (G-8090)
Blackstone (G-8311)
Bolton (G-8316)
Boylston (G-8979)
Brookfield (G-9189)
Charlton (G-9846)
Cherry Valley (G-9976)
Clinton (G-10077)
Dudley (G-10372)
East Brookfield (G-10423)
East Douglas (G-10424)
East Templeton (G-10519)
Fiskdale (G-10806)

ENTRY#

Block Island (G-20058)
Charlestown (G-20130)
Exeter (G-20450)
Hope Valley (G-20481)
Hopkinton (G-20487)
Kenyon (G-20548)
Kingston (G-20549)
Narragansett (G-20633)
North Kingstown (G-20690)
Peace Dale (G-20913)
Richmond (G-21161)
Saunderstown (G-21201)
Wakefield (G-21267)
West Kingston (G-21467)
Westerly (G-21515)
Wyoming (G-21588)

VERMONT

Addison

Bridport (G-21759)
Bristol (G-21760)
Ferrisburg (G-21986)
Ferrisburgh (G-21987)
Granville (G-22003)
Middlebury (G-22095)
New Haven (G-22184)
North Ferrisburgh (G-22224)
Orwell (G-22254)
Salisbury (G-22398)
Shoreham (G-22432)
Starksboro (G-22515)
Vergennes (G-22552)
Whiting (G-22645)

Bennington

Arlington (G-21594)
Bennington (G-21661)
Bondville (G-21697)
Dorset (G-21907)
East Arlington (G-21910)
East Dorset (G-21915)
Manchester (G-22077)
Manchester Center (G-22080)
North Bennington (G-22209)
Pownal (G-22281)
Sandgate (G-22400)
Shaftsbury (G-22402)
West Rupert (G-22614)

Caledonia

Barnet (G-21604)
Danville (G-21895)
East Ryegate (G-21920)
Groton (G-22005)
Hardwick (G-22009)
Lower Waterford (G-22060)
Lyndonville (G-22067)
Saint Johnsbury (G-22386)
South Ryegate (G-22495)
Sutton (G-22528)
West Burke (G-22604)

Chittenden

Burlington (G-21766)
Cambridge (G-21822)
Charlotte (G-21832)
Colchester (G-21855)
Essex Junction (G-21928)
Fairfax (G-21972)
Hinesburg (G-22021)
Huntington (G-22034)
Jericho (G-22048)
Milton (G-22124)
Richmond (G-22311)
Shelburne (G-22410)
South Burlington (G-22435)
St George (G-22514)
Underhill (G-22545)
Westford (G-22628)
Williston (G-22652)
Winooski (G-22716)

Essex

Canaan (G-21825)
Concord (G-21890)
Guildhall (G-22006)
Island Pond (G-22041)
Lunenburg (G-22066)
North Concord (G-22223)

Franklin

Bakersfield (G-21603)
Enosburg Falls (G-21923)
Fairfield (G-21982)
Franklin (G-21994)
Highgate Center (G-22019)
Montgomery Center (G-22141)
Richford (G-22306)
Saint Albans (G-22362)
Sheldon (G-22428)
Sheldon Springs (G-22430)
Swanton (G-22529)

Grand Isle

Alburg (G-21593)
Grand Isle (G-21997)
North Hero (G-22230)
South Hero (G-22480)

Lamoille

Belvidere Center (G-21658)
Eden (G-21921)
Elmore (G-21922)
Hyde Park (G-22035)
Jeffersonville (G-22045)
Johnson (G-22049)
Morrisville (G-22165)
North Hyde Park (G-22232)
Stowe (G-22519)
Waterville (G-22595)
Wolcott (G-22729)

Orange

Bradford (G-21698)
Brookfield (G-21765)
Chelsea (G-21837)
Corinth (G-21891)
East Corinth (G-21913)
Randolph (G-22296)
Strafford (G-22526)
Topsham (G-22540)
Tunbridge (G-22542)
Vershire (G-22558)
Washington (G-22580)
Wells River (G-22600)
West Newbury (G-22610)
West Topsham (G-22621)
Williamstown (G-22649)

Orleans

Albany (G-21592)
Barton (G-21647)
Craftsbury (G-21892)
Derby (G-21899)
Derby Line (G-21906)
Glover (G-21995)
Greensboro Bend (G-22004)
Irasburg (G-22040)
Jay (G-22044)
Lowell (G-22059)
Newport (G-22190)
Newport Center (G-22207)
North Troy (G-22240)
Orleans (G-22248)
West Glover (G-22607)
Westfield (G-22626)

Rutland

Belmont (G-21657)
Benson (G-21692)
Brandon (G-21707)
Castleton (G-21827)
Center Rutland (G-21831)
Chittenden (G-21854)
Danby (G-21893)
Fair Haven (G-21965)
Florence (G-21991)
Forest Dale (G-21993)
Hydeville (G-22039)
Killington (G-22053)
Middletown Springs (G-22123)
Mount Holly (G-22181)
N Chittenden (G-22183)
North Clarendon (G-22214)
Pawlet (G-22256)
Pittsfield (G-22262)
Pittsford (G-22263)
Poultney (G-22270)
Proctor (G-22283)
Rutland (G-22322)
Wallingford (G-22573)
Wells (G-22599)
West Pawlet (G-22611)
West Rutland (G-22615)

Washington

Barre (G-21607)
Cabot (G-21819)
Calais (G-21821)
East Barre (G-21911)
Graniteville (G-21999)
Marshfield (G-22092)
Middlesex (G-22122)
Montpelier (G-22144)
Northfield (G-22243)
Plainfield (G-22266)
Riverton (G-22314)
Waitsfield (G-22559)
Warren (G-22577)
Waterbury (G-22582)
Waterbury Center (G-22590)
Websterville (G-22596)
Woodbury (G-22734)
Worcester (G-22743)

Windham

Bellows Falls (G-21650)
Brattleboro (G-21715)
Cambridgeport (G-21824)
East Dummerston (G-21919)
Grafton (G-21996)
Guilford (G-22007)
Jacksonville (G-22043)
Londonderry (G-22057)
Newfane (G-22188)
Putney (G-22289)
Saxtons River (G-22401)
South Londonderry (G-22484)
Townshend (G-22541)
Wardsboro (G-22576)
West Dover (G-22605)
West Halifax (G-22608)
West Marlboro (G-22609)
West Townshend (G-22625)
Westminster (G-22630)
Westminster Station (G-22633)
Westminster W (G-22634)
Whitingham (G-22647)
Wilmington (G-22700)

Windsor

Bethel (G-21694)
Bridgewater (G-21757)
Bridgewater Corners (G-21758)
Chester (G-21841)
Hartland (G-22015)
Ludlow (G-22061)
North Hartland (G-22229)
North Pomfret (G-22234)
North Springfield (G-22236)
Norwich (G-22247)
Perkinsville (G-22257)
Proctorsville (G-22288)
Quechee (G-22294)
Reading (G-22305)
Rochester (G-22315)
Sharon (G-22408)
South Pomfret (G-22489)
South Royalton (G-22490)
South Woodstock (G-22497)
Springfield (G-22499)
Stockbridge (G-22518)
White River Junction (G-22635)
Wilder (G-22648)
Windsor (G-22706)
Woodstock (G-22735)

CONNECTICUT

Counties and Major Cities

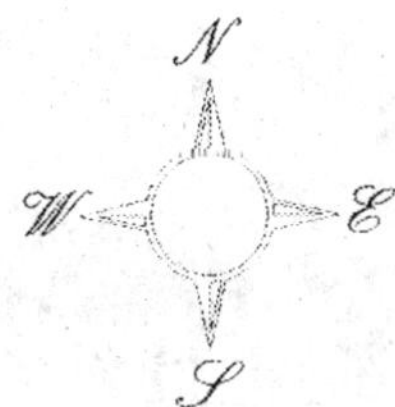

MAINE

Counties and Major Cities

N
W
E
S

MASSACHUSETTS

Counties and Major Cities

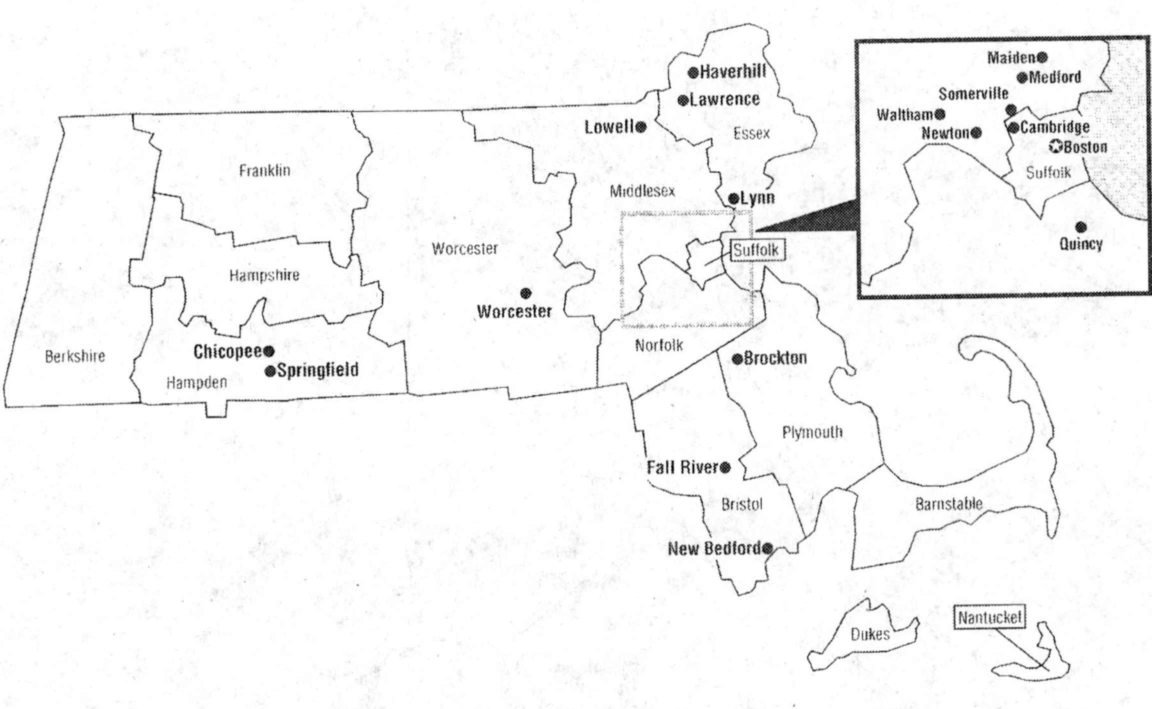

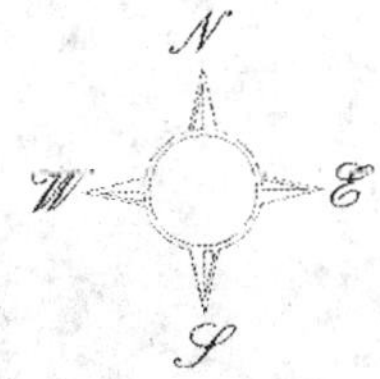

NEW HAMPSHIRE

Counties and Major Cities

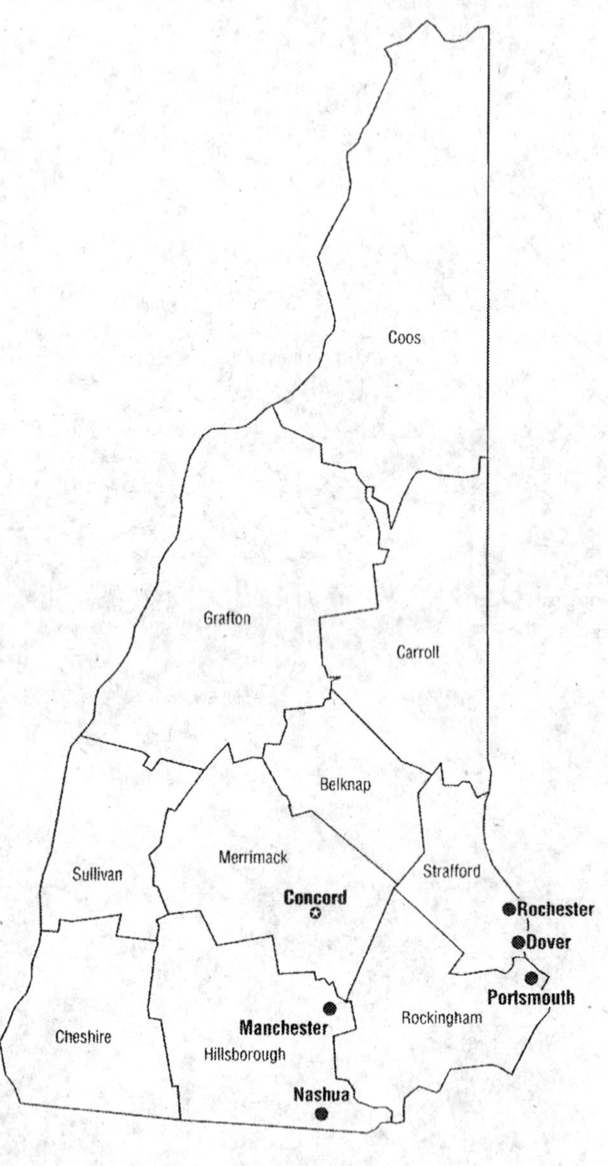

RHODE ISLAND

Counties and Major Cities

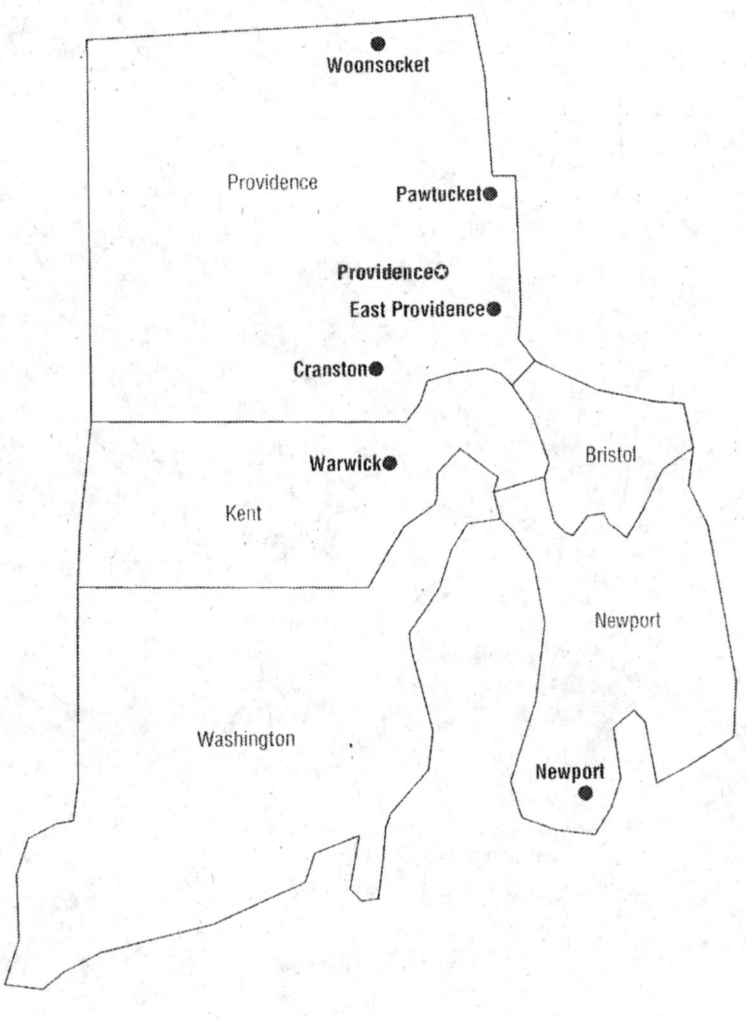

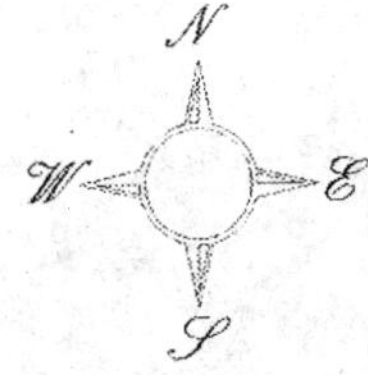

VERMONT

Counties and Major Cities

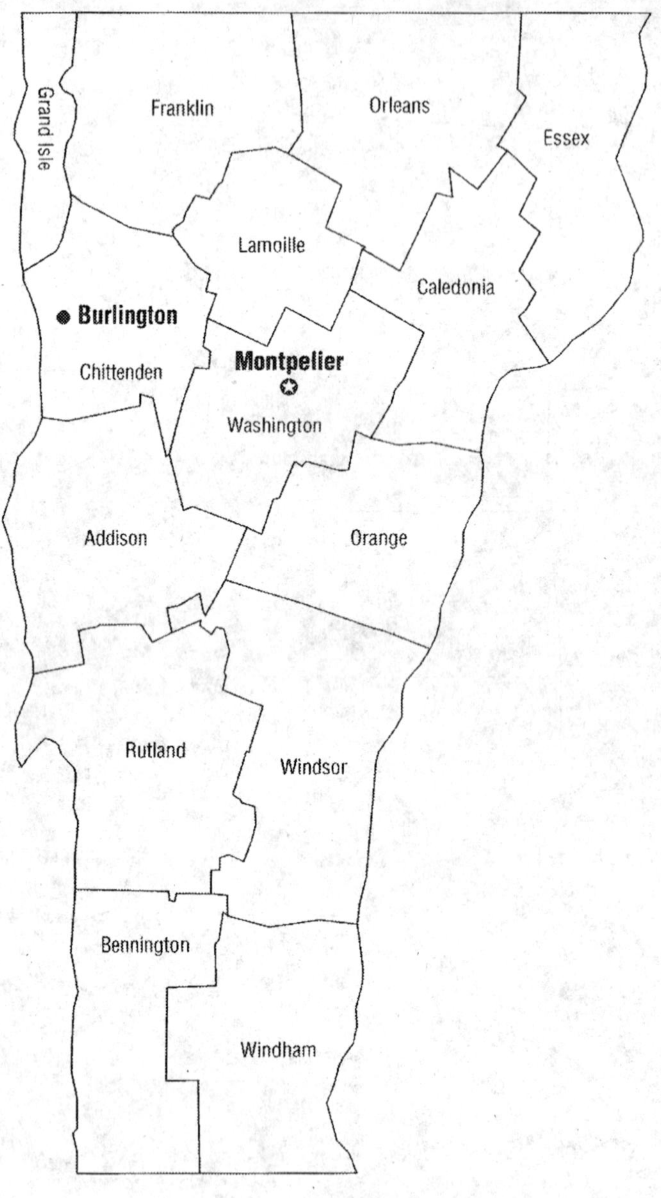

GEOGRAPHIC SECTION

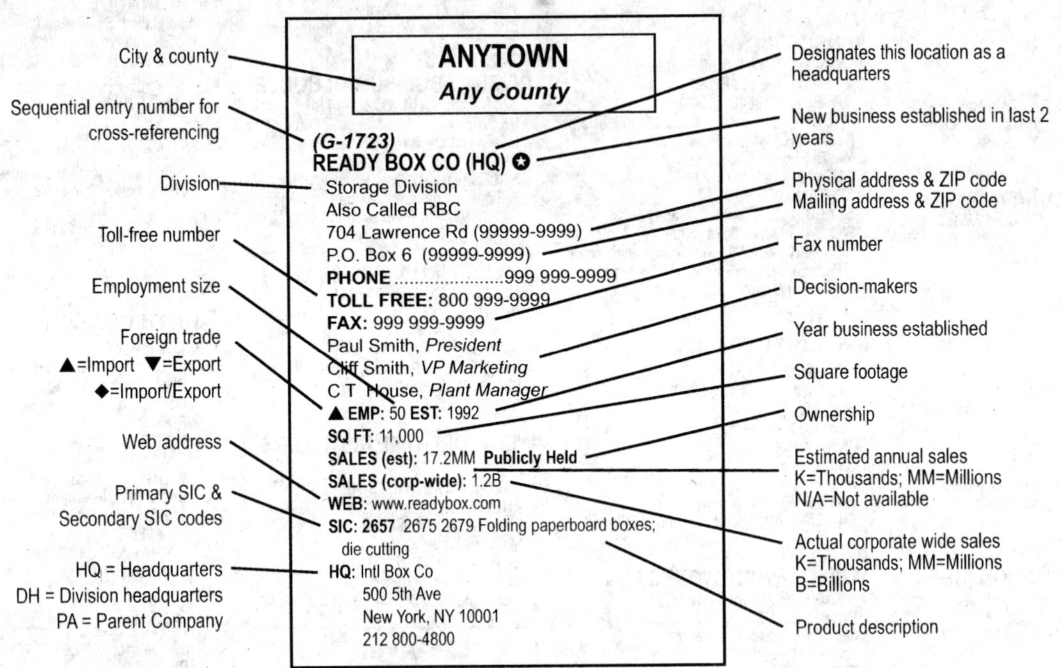

See footnotes for symbols and codes identification.

- This section is in alphabetical order by city.
- Companies are sorted alphabetically under their respective cities.
- To locate cities within a county refer to the County/City Cross Reference Index.

IMPORTANT NOTICE: It is a violation of both federal and state law to transmit an unsolicited advertisement to a facsimile machine. Any user of this product that violates such laws may be subject to civil and criminal penalties which may exceed $500 for each transmission of an unsolicited facsimile. Harris InfoSource provides fax numbers for lawful purposes only and expressly forbids the use of these numbers in any unlawful manner.

CONNECTICUT

Abington
Windham County

(G-1)
NCA INC
500 Hampton Rd (06230)
PHONE..................................860 974-2310
Richard G Whipple, *President*
Nicola Dabica, *Treasurer*
EMP: 6
SQ FT: 5,000
SALES: 1.3MM **Privately Held**
WEB: www.can.com
SIC: 2298 Mfg Cable Assemblies

Andover
Tolland County

(G-2)
AMERICAN DREAM UNLIMITED LLC
212 Gilead Rd (06232-1603)
PHONE..................................860 742-5055
Brian Fufini,
EMP: 7
SALES: 98K **Privately Held**
SIC: 3845 Mfg Electromedical Equipment

(G-3)
MTM CORPORATION
643 Route 6 (06232-1320)
P.O. Box 268 (06232-0268)
PHONE..................................860 742-9600
William Thurston Jr, *President*
EMP: 9
SQ FT: 12,000
SALES (est): 1.6MM **Privately Held**
SIC: 3728 Mfg Aircraft Parts/Equipment

Ansonia
New Haven County

(G-4)
AERO-MED MOLDING TECHNOLOGIES (PA)
50 Westfield Ave (06401-1121)
PHONE..................................203 735-2331
Lawrence Saffran, *President*
Richard Carpentiere, *Engineer*
EMP: 10
SQ FT: 30,000
SALES (est): 2MM **Privately Held**
WEB: www.aeromedmolding.com
SIC: 3089 Mfg Plastic Products

(G-5)
AMERICAN PRECISION MFG LLC
26 Beaver St Ste 1 (06401-3250)
PHONE..................................203 734-1800
Leigh Dawid, *President*
EMP: 24
SQ FT: 30,000
SALES: 2MM **Privately Held**
WEB: www.ap-mfg.com
SIC: 3599 Mfg Industrial Machinery

(G-6)
AMERICAN VETERAN TEXTILE LLC
674 Main St Fl 2 (06401-2311)
PHONE..................................203 583-0576
Yusuf Arslan, *Mng Member*
Resit Akcam, *Mng Member*
Nehmet Pehlivan, *Mng Member*
EMP: 3
SALES (est): 200.5K **Privately Held**
SIC: 2273 Mfg Carpets/Rugs

(G-7)
ANSONIA PLASTICS LLC
Also Called: Npi Medical
401 Birmingham Blvd (06401-1035)
PHONE..................................203 736-5200
Randy Ahlm, *President*
William Ball, *Project Mgr*
Edmond Meyer, *CFO*
Edmund Meyer, *CFO*
Dan Singer, *Sales Executive*
EMP: 80
SALES (est): 24.9MM **Privately Held**
SIC: 3086 Mfg Plastic Foam Products

(G-8)
CASTLE BEVERAGES INC
105 Myrtle Ave (06401-2099)
PHONE..................................203 732-0883
Kenneth Dworkin, *President*
David Pantalone, *Vice Pres*
EMP: 9
SQ FT: 96,000
SALES (est): 989K **Privately Held**
SIC: 2086 Mfg Nonalcoholic Carbonated Beverages Packaged In Bottles

(G-9)
CENTRAL MARBLE & GRANITE LLC
22 Maple St (06401-1230)
PHONE..................................203 734-4644
Naomi King,
Richard P Smeland Jr,
EMP: 4
SQ FT: 12,000
SALES (est): 466.2K **Privately Held**
SIC: 2493 3281 Mfg Stone & Granite

(G-10)
COBAL-USA ALTRNATIVE FUELS LLC
40 James St (06401-1961)
PHONE..................................203 751-1974
Petr Lisa, *Principal*
EMP: 3
SALES (est): 167K **Privately Held**
SIC: 2869 Mfg Industrial Organic Chemicals

(G-11)
CONNECTICUT METAL INDUSTRIES
1 Riverside Dr Ste G (06401-1255)
P.O. Box 234, Monroe (06468-0234)
PHONE..................................203 736-0790
Tom Mele, *Principal*
◆ **EMP:** 4
SALES (est): 323.1K **Privately Held**
SIC: 3999 Mfg Misc Products

(G-12)
DAWID MANUFACTURING INC
26 Beaver St (06401-3250)
PHONE..................................203 734-1800
Leigh Dawid, *President*
Karen Dawid, *Treasurer*
EMP: 8
SQ FT: 4,000
SALES (est): 600K **Privately Held**
SIC: 3599 5088 Mfg Industrial Machinery Whol Transportation Equipment

(G-13)
DIVERSIFIED MANUFACT
1 Riverside Dr Ste H (06401-1255)
PHONE..................................203 734-0379
Kazimierz Bialczak, *President*
EMP: 8
SALES (est): 790.9K **Privately Held**
SIC: 3999 Mfg Misc Products

(G-14)
EVER READY PRESS
78 Clifton Ave (06401-2227)
PHONE..................................203 734-5157
Frank Halpin, *Owner*
EMP: 3
SQ FT: 3,750
SALES (est): 232.5K **Privately Held**
WEB: www.everreadypress.com
SIC: 2759 Commercial Printing

(G-15)
FARREL CORPORATION (DH)
Also Called: Farrel Pomini
1 Farrel Blvd (06401-1256)
PHONE..................................203 736-5500
Mark Meulbroek, *CEO*
James Burns, *Vice Pres*
Ron Ugolik, *Engineer*
Stuart Sardinskas, *Design Engr*
Paul M Zepp, *CFO*
◆ **EMP:** 91
SQ FT: 60,000
SALES (est): 76.1MM
SALES (corp-wide): 360.4K **Privately Held**
WEB: www.farrel.com
SIC: 3559 1011 3089 Mfg Misc Industry Mach Iron Ore Mining Mfg Plastic Products
HQ: Harburg-Freudenberger Maschinenbau Gmbh
Seevestr. 1
Hamburg 21079
407 717-90

(G-16)
FUEL FIRST
575 Main St (06401-2310)
PHONE..................................203 735-5097
Brad Badel, *Owner*
EMP: 4 **EST:** 2009
SALES (est): 313.3K **Privately Held**
SIC: 2869 Mfg Industrial Organic Chemicals

(G-17)
GROHE MANUFACTURING
26 Beaver St Ste 2 (06401-3250)
PHONE..................................203 516-5536
Christian Grohe, *Owner*
EMP: 3 **EST:** 2011
SALES (est): 285K **Privately Held**
SIC: 3999 Mfg Misc Products

(G-18)
HATA HI-TECH MACHINING LLC
Also Called: Hht
1 Riverside Dr Ste E (06401-1255)
PHONE..................................203 333-9139
EMP: 28
SQ FT: 13,000
SALES: 3.7MM **Privately Held**
SIC: 3541 Mfg Machine Tools-Cutting

(G-19)
INDEPENDENT METALWORX INC
4 Hershey Dr Ste 1a (06401-2312)
PHONE..................................203 520-4089
Michael Bousquet, *President*
EMP: 5
SALES (est): 291.6K **Privately Held**
SIC: 3499 Mfg Misc Fabricated Metal Products

(G-20)
KENSCO INC (PA)
Also Called: Tub's & Stuff Plumbing Supply
41 Clifton Ave (06401-2203)
P.O. Box 43 (06401-0043)
PHONE..................................203 734-8827
Kenneth R Shortell, *President*
Yvette Shortell, *Vice Pres*
EMP: 12
SQ FT: 10,000
SALES (est): 1.5MM **Privately Held**
SIC: 3431 3089 5074 5999 Mfg Metal Sanitary Ware Mfg Plastic Products Whol Plumbing Equip/Supp Ret Misc Merchandise Ret Lumber/Building Mtrl

(G-21)
PRO COUNTERS NEW ENGLAND LLC
1 Chestnut St (06401-2300)
PHONE..................................203 347-8663
Camilla Resende, *Manager*
J V Nogueira,
Rafael Resende,
EMP: 7
SALES: 700K **Privately Held**
SIC: 2541 Mfg Wood Partitions/Fixtures

(G-22)
QUALITY WOODWORKS LLC
1 Riverside Dr (06401-1228)
PHONE..................................203 736-9200
Jack Zansardino, *President*
Jack Zanfardino,
EMP: 3
SQ FT: 2,000
SALES (est): 467.7K **Privately Held**
SIC: 2434 Mfg Wood Kitchen Cabinets

(G-23)
STELRAY PLASTIC PRODUCTS INC
50 Westfield Ave (06401-1121)
PHONE..................................203 735-2331
Mortimer Saffran, *Ch of Bd*
Lawrence David Saffran, *President*
Robert Bowns, *Mfg Mgr*
Jennifer Spaulding, *Accounting Mgr*
Sandeep Singh, *Supervisor*
▲ **EMP:** 48
SQ FT: 15,000
SALES (est): 8.6MM **Privately Held**
WEB: www.stelray.com
SIC: 3089 5031 Mfg Plastic Products Whol Lumber/Plywood/Millwork

(G-24)
VALLEY INDEPENDENT SENTINEL
158 Main St (06401-1836)
PHONE..................................203 446-2335
Eugene Driscoll, *Manager*
EMP: 3 **EST:** 2009
SALES (est): 122.2K **Privately Held**
SIC: 2711 Newspapers-Publishing/Printing

Ashford
Windham County

(G-25)
BIOFIBERS CAPITAL GROUP LLC
14 Amidon Dr (06278-2003)
PHONE..................................203 561-6133
Timothy Dowding, *Mng Member*
Eric Metz,
Richard Parnas,
EMP: 5
SALES (est): 164K **Privately Held**
SIC: 2493 7389 Mfg Reconstituted Wood Products Business Serv Non-Commercial Site

(G-26)
PITH PRODUCTS LLC
39 Nott Hwy Unit 1 (06278-1341)
PHONE..................................860 487-4859
Louis Albert,
Lance J Bouchard,
EMP: 16
SALES (est): 2.8MM **Privately Held**
WEB: www.pithproducts.com
SIC: 2449 Mfg Wood Containers

(G-27)
RIVERS EDGE SUGAR HOUSE
326 Mansfield Rd (06278-1414)
PHONE..................................860 429-1510
Bill Prulyx, *Owner*
EMP: 3
SALES (est): 177.8K **Privately Held**
WEB: www.riversedgesugarhouse.com
SIC: 2099 Mfg Food Preparations

(G-28)
WALKER INDUSTRIES LLC
464 Zaicek Rd (06278-1044)
PHONE..................................860 455-3554
Thomas Walker,
EMP: 3
SALES: 500K **Privately Held**
SIC: 2421 Sawmill/Planing Mill

(G-29)
WESTFORD HILL DISTILLERS LLC
196 Chatey Rd (06278-1007)
PHONE..................................860 429-0464
Louis Chatey, *Mng Member*
Margaret Chatey,
EMP: 6
SALES: 300K **Privately Held**
SIC: 2085 Mfg Distilled/Blended Liquor

Avon
Hartford County

(G-30)
ABBEY AESTHETICS LLC
135 Cold Spring Rd (06001-4054)
PHONE..................................860 242-0497
Rainerio J Reyes, *Principal*
EMP: 4 **EST:** 2009
SALES (est): 206.3K **Privately Held**
SIC: 3845 Mfg Electromedical Equipment

(G-31)
ADVANCED HEARING SOLUTIONS LLC
Also Called: Advance Affrdale Hring Sltions
47 W Main St (06001-4706)
PHONE..................................860 674-8558
Rich Stokes, *Mng Member*
Anne Byrnes, *Mng Member*
EMP: 10
SALES (est): 835.9K **Privately Held**
WEB: www.advancedhearingsolutions.com
SIC: 3842 Mfg Surgical Appliances/Supplies

(G-32)
BALL SUPPLY CORPORATION
52 Old Mill Rd (06001-4022)
P.O. Box 303, Riverside NJ (08075-0303)
PHONE..................................860 673-3364
Rudy Presutti, *President*
Barbara Presutti, *Corp Secy*
Leon Petersen, *Vice Pres*
EMP: 4 **EST:** 1996
SALES: 780K **Privately Held**
SIC: 3399 Mfg Primary Metal Products

(G-33)
BOSTON SCIENTIFIC CORPORATION
85 Bridgewater Dr (06001-4400)
PHONE..................................860 673-2500
Alexander Galati, *Principal*
EMP: 341
SALES (corp-wide): 9.8B **Publicly Held**
SIC: 3841 Mfg Surgical/Medical Instruments
PA: Boston Scientific Corporation
300 Boston Scientific Way
Marlborough MA 01752
508 683 4000

(G-34)
GENERAL DYNAMICS ORDNANCE
Also Called: Simunition Operations
65 Sandscreen Rd (06001-2222)
P.O. Box 576 (06001-0576)
PHONE..................................860 404-0162
Brian Berger, *Branch Mgr*
EMP: 10
SALES (corp-wide): 36.1B **Publicly Held**
SIC: 3482 8741 Mfg Small Arms Ammunition Management Services
HQ: General Dynamics Ordnance And Tactical Systems, Inc.
11399 16th Ct N Ste 200
Saint Petersburg FL 33716
727 578-8100

(G-35)
HARTFORD COURANT COMPANY
80 Darling Dr (06001-4217)
PHONE..................................860 678-1330
Bonnie Phillips, *Manager*
EMP: 7
SQ FT: 500
SALES (corp-wide): 1B **Publicly Held**
WEB: www.courantnie.com
SIC: 2711 Newspaper Publishing
HQ: The Hartford Courant Company Llc
285 Broad St
Hartford CT 06115
860 241-6200

(G-36)
IDEVICES LLC
50 Tower Ln (06001-4228)
PHONE..................................860 352-5252
Mike Daigle, *COO*
Jim Millis, *Engineer*
Kelley McIntyre, *CFO*
Sheri Yuschak, *Accounting Mgr*
Sheri Fay, *Accountant*
▲ **EMP:** 25
SALES (est): 7.8MM
SALES (corp-wide): 4.4B **Publicly Held**
SIC: 3625 Mfg Relays/Industrial Controls
PA: Hubbell Incorporated
40 Waterview Dr
Shelton CT 06484
475 882-4000

(G-37)
LEGERE GROUP LTD
Also Called: Legere Woodworking
80 Darling Dr (06001-4217)
P.O. Box 1527 (06001-1527)
PHONE..................................860 674-0392
Craig Froh, *CEO*
Ronald Legere, *President*
Bill Bruneau, *Vice Pres*
William Bruneau, *Vice Pres*
Francis Legere, *Vice Pres*
EMP: 125
SQ FT: 144,000
SALES (est): 28MM **Privately Held**
WEB: www.legeregroup.com
SIC: 2434 2431 3442 2499 Mfg Wood Kitchen Cabinet Mfg Millwork Mfg Metal Door/Sash/Trim Mfg Wood Products

(G-38)
NATURAL NUTMEG LLC
53 Mountain View Ave (06001-3813)
PHONE..................................860 206-9500
Chris Hindman, *Principal*
EMP: 3
SALES (est): 230K **Privately Held**
SIC: 2721 Periodicals-Publishing/Printing

(G-39)
OFS FITEL LLC
Also Called: Ofs Specialty Photonics Div
55 Darling Dr (06001-4273)
PHONE..................................860 678-0371
Jane Cercena, *Vice Pres*
EMP: 350 **Privately Held**
SIC: 3357 Nonferrous Wiredrawing/Insulating
HQ: Ofs Fitel Llc
2000 Northeast Expy
Norcross GA 30071
888 342-3743

▲ = Import ▼=Export
◆ =Import/Export

(G-40)
OLDCASTLE INFRASTRUCTURE INC
Also Called: Rotondo Precast
151 Old Farms Rd (06001-2253)
PHONE....................................860 673-3291
Joel Dickinson, *General Mgr*
Ronald Hoinsky, *Safety Mgr*
EMP: 23
SALES (corp-wide): 29.7B **Privately Held**
WEB: www.oldcastle-precast.com
SIC: 3272 Precast Concrete Mfg
HQ: Oldcastle Infrastructure, Inc.
7000 Cntl Prkaway Ste 800
Atlanta GA 30328
470 602-2000

(G-41)
ORAFOL AMERICAS INC
120 Darling Dr (06001-4217)
PHONE....................................860 676-7100
Bob Nielson, *President*
Steve Scott, *President*
Mike Egan, *Business Mgr*
Joseph Lupone, *COO*
David Knight, *Vice Pres*
EMP: 143
SALES (corp-wide): 642.8MM **Privately Held**
WEB: www.reflexite.com
SIC: 3081 5162 3827 Mfg Unsupported Plastic Film/Sheet Whol Plastic Materials/Shapes Mfg Optical Instruments/Lenses
HQ: Orafol Americas Inc.
1100 Oracal Pkwy
Black Creek GA 31308
912 851-5000

(G-42)
PUBLISHING DIRECTIONS LLC
Also Called: Book Mktg Works
50 Lovely St (06001-3138)
P.O. Box 715 (06001-0715)
PHONE....................................860 673-7650
Brian Jud, *Mng Member*
EMP: 3
SALES: 120K **Privately Held**
SIC: 2741 Misc Publishing

(G-43)
R R DONNELLEY & SONS COMPANY
60 Security Dr (06001-4226)
PHONE....................................860 773-6140
Steve Policks, *Manager*
EMP: 50
SALES (corp-wide): 6.8B **Publicly Held**
WEB: www.rrdonnelley.com
SIC: 2759 2752 Commercial Printing Lithographic Commercial Printing
PA: R. R. Donnelley & Sons Company
35 W Wacker Dr
Chicago IL 60601
312 326-8000

(G-44)
READYDOCK INC
46 W Avon Rd Ste 302 (06001-3679)
PHONE....................................860 523-9980
David Engelhardt, *President*
EMP: 3 **EST:** 2012
SALES (est): 306.1K **Privately Held**
SIC: 3999 3448 Mfg Misc Products Mfg Prefabricated Metal Buildings

(G-45)
SERVICETUNE INC
107 Cider Brook Rd (06001-2850)
PHONE....................................860 284-4445
David Putt, *President*
EMP: 6
SQ FT: 1,000
SALES (est): 500K **Privately Held**
SIC: 7372 Prepackaged Software Services

(G-46)
SHARI M ROTH MD
100 Simsbury Rd Ste 210 (06001-3793)
PHONE....................................860 676-2525
Shari Roth, *Owner*
EMP: 4
SALES (est): 265.8K **Privately Held**
SIC: 3851 Mfg Ophthalmic Goods

(G-47)
SILVER LITTLE SHOP INC
23 E Main St (06001-3805)
P.O. Box 100 (06001-0100)
PHONE....................................860 678-1976
Richard E Parker, *President*
D C Thompson, *Vice Pres*
M J Parker, *Admin Sec*
EMP: 4
SQ FT: 288
SALES (est): 647.3K **Privately Held**
WEB: www.littlesilvershop.com
SIC: 3911 5944 Mfg Precious Metal Jewelry Ret Jewelry

Baltic
New London County

(G-48)
AMGRAPH PACKAGING INC
90 Paper Mill Rd (06330-1436)
PHONE....................................860 822-2000
Kenneth L Fontaine, *CEO*
Michael Devlin, *Vice Pres*
Michael Drab, *Vice Pres*
Robert Guertin, *Vice Pres*
Desmond P O'Grady, *Treasurer*
▲ **EMP:** 125
SQ FT: 75,000
SALES (est): 66.4MM **Privately Held**
SIC: 2671 2759 2752 2673 Mfg Packaging Paper/Film Commercial Printing Lithographic Coml Print

(G-49)
FAILLE PRECISION MACHINING
118 W Main St (06330-1077)
P.O. Box 606 (06330-0606)
PHONE....................................860 822-1964
Alfred Faille, *Owner*
EMP: 4
SALES: 486K **Privately Held**
SIC: 3728 3599 Mfg Aircraft Parts/Equipment Mfg Industrial Machinery

(G-50)
J & D EMBROIDERING CO
26 Bushnell Hollow Rd A (06330-1364)
PHONE....................................860 822-9777
Debbie McKenzie, *Owner*
EMP: 4
SQ FT: 2,500
SALES (est): 255.9K **Privately Held**
SIC: 2395 2396 Embroidery Work On Clothing & Screen Printing

(G-51)
NUTMEG WIRE
14 Main St (06330-1443)
P.O. Box 719 (06330-0719)
PHONE....................................860 822-8616
Fred Stackpole, *President*
Sharon Stackpole, *Admin Sec*
EMP: 10
SQ FT: 15,400
SALES (est): 1.3MM **Privately Held**
SIC: 3315 Mfg Wire Products

Bantam
Litchfield County

(G-52)
BANTAM SHEET METAL
1160 Bantam Rd (06750-1406)
P.O. Box 310 (06750-0310)
PHONE....................................860 567-9690
EMP: 4
SALES (est): 306.4K **Privately Held**
SIC: 3444 Sheet Metalwork, Nsk

Beacon Falls
New Haven County

(G-53)
ANSONIA STL FABRICATION CO INC
164 Pines Bridge Rd (06403-1018)
P.O. Box 175 (06403-0175)
PHONE....................................203 888-4509
Bart Hogestyn, *President*
Debra Hogestyn, *Director*
William Hogestyn, *Director*
▲ **EMP:** 20
SQ FT: 11,000
SALES (est): 3.3MM **Privately Held**
WEB: www.ansoniasteel.com
SIC: 7692 3444 3441 Welding Repair Mfg Sheet Metalwork Structural Metal Fabrication

(G-54)
APEX TOOL & CUTTER CO INC
59 Old Turnpike Rd (06403-1310)
P.O. Box 188 (06403-0188)
PHONE....................................203 888-8970
Jim Norton, *President*
George Norton, *Treasurer*
Joseph Norton, *Admin Sec*
EMP: 4 **EST:** 1997
SALES: 300K **Privately Held**
SIC: 3599 Mfg Industrial Machinery

(G-55)
BETKOSKI BROTHERS LLC
332 Bethany Rd (06403-1404)
PHONE....................................203 723-8262
Peter Betkoski,
EMP: 5
SQ FT: 2,063
SALES (est): 632.8K **Privately Held**
SIC: 2951 Mfg Asphalt Mixtures/Blocks

(G-56)
COMMON SENSE ENGINEERED PDTS
164 Pines Bridge Rd (06403-1018)
P.O. Box 193 (06403-0193)
PHONE....................................203 888-8695
Debbie Hogeston, *Partner*
EMP: 3
SALES (est): 410.7K **Privately Held**
SIC: 2653 Mfg Corrugated/Solid Fiber Boxes

(G-57)
CONKLIN-SHERMAN COMPANY INCTHE
59 Old Turnpike Rd (06403-1310)
P.O. Box 188 (06403-0188)
PHONE....................................203 881-0190
Bernadette Norton, *President*
Janice Kopchik, *Vice Pres*
Debra Lindsay, *Admin Sec*
EMP: 3 **EST:** 1950
SQ FT: 800
SALES (est): 459.9K **Privately Held**
WEB: www.conklin-sherman.com
SIC: 3671 Mfg Electron Tubes

(G-58)
INDUSTRIAL FLAME CUTTING INC
45 Lancaster Dr (06403-1049)
P.O. Box 277 (06403-0277)
PHONE....................................203 723-4897
Michael Wassel, *President*
William Heiden, *Vice Pres*
Catherine Wassel, *Treasurer*
Cathy Wassel, *Treasurer*
EMP: 6
SQ FT: 10,000
SALES: 1.5MM **Privately Held**
SIC: 3312 Mfg Structural Shapes & Pilings Steel

(G-59)
KNAPP CONTAINER INC
17 Old Turnpike Rd (06403-1310)
PHONE....................................203 888-0511
George A Meder Jr, *President*
EMP: 4
SQ FT: 40,000
SALES (est): 551.9K **Privately Held**
SIC: 2653 Mfg Corrugated Boxes

(G-60)
LIBERTY SCREEN PRINT CO LLC
141 S Main St (06403-1469)
PHONE....................................203 632-5449
Monica Maglaris,
EMP: 16
SQ FT: 10,000
SALES: 750K **Privately Held**
SIC: 2752 2759 Lithographic Commercial Printing Commercial Printing

(G-61)
M I R INC
103 Breault Rd (06403-1033)
PHONE....................................203 888-2541
EMP: 10 **EST:** 1971
SQ FT: 30,500
SALES (est): 100.3K **Privately Held**
SIC: 3559 Rebuild Rubber & Plastic Equipment

(G-62)
MAGNA STEEL SALES INC
2 Alliance Cir (06403-1054)
PHONE....................................203 888-0300
Edward Mulligan, *President*
Patricia Mavlouganes, *Admin Sec*
EMP: 15
SQ FT: 27,000
SALES: 2MM **Privately Held**
WEB: www.magnasteel.com
SIC: 3441 5051 Structural Metal Fabrication Metals Service Center

(G-63)
O & G INDUSTRIES INC
105 Breault Rd (06403-1033)
PHONE....................................203 881-5192
EMP: 147
SALES (corp-wide): 538MM **Privately Held**
SIC: 3999 Mfg Misc Products
PA: O & G Industries, Inc.
112 Wall St
Torrington CT 06790
860 489-9261

(G-64)
O & G INDUSTRIES INC
Railroad Ave Ext (06403)
PHONE....................................203 729-4529
William Stanley, *Branch Mgr*
EMP: 10
SALES (corp-wide): 538MM **Privately Held**
WEB: www.ogind.com
SIC: 3281 1542 Mfg Cut Stone/Products Nonresidential Construction
PA: O & G Industries, Inc.
112 Wall St
Torrington CT 06790
860 489-9261

(G-65)
TRADEWINDS
274 Bethany Rd (06403-1402)
P.O. Box 2158, Bristol (06011-2158)
PHONE....................................203 723-6966
Kim Ashley, *Principal*
▲ **EMP:** 4
SALES (est): 186.9K **Privately Held**
SIC: 2711 Newspapers-Publishing/Printing

(G-66)
TRICO WELDING COMPANY LLC
84 Feldspar Ave (06403-1439)
PHONE....................................203 720-3782
Lou Poeta,
EMP: 3
SQ FT: 1,200
SALES (est): 462.1K **Privately Held**
SIC: 7692 Welding Repair

Berlin
Hartford County

(G-67)
AEROCESS INC
500 Four Rod Rd Ste 110 (06037-2282)
P.O. Box 4139, Wallingford (06492-1489)
PHONE..................................860 357-2451
William Winakor, *President*
Arthur Donorfrio, *Treasurer*
Ken Labieniec, *Admin Sec*
EMP: 12
SQ FT: 8,000
SALES (est): 880K **Privately Held**
WEB: www.aerocess.com
SIC: 3365 5088 3769 Aluminum Foundry Whol Transportation Equipment Mfg Space Vehicle Equipment

(G-68)
ALDEN TOOL COMPANY INC
199 New Park Dr (06037-3738)
PHONE..................................860 828-3556
Charles Muravnick, *President*
EMP: 30
SQ FT: 20,000
SALES (est): 5.4MM **Privately Held**
WEB: www.aldentool.com
SIC: 3545 Mfg Machine Tool Accessories

(G-69)
ALL FIVE TOOL CO INC
Also Called: North Amercn Spring Tl Co Div
169 White Oak Dr (06037-1638)
PHONE..................................860 583-1693
Joseph B Panella, *President*
▲ **EMP:** 30 **EST:** 1967
SQ FT: 18,000
SALES (est): 2.9MM
SALES (corp-wide): 6MM **Privately Held**
WEB: www.all5tool.com
SIC: 3544 3545 Mfg Dies/Tools/Jigs/Fixtures Mfg Machine Tool Accessories
PA: Sirois Tool Company, Inc.
169 White Oak Dr
Berlin CT 06037
860 828-5327

(G-70)
AMCO PRECISION TOOLS INC (PA)
Also Called: Aerospace
921 Farmington Ave (06037-2218)
P.O. Box 442 (06037-0442)
PHONE..................................860 828-5640
Aldo Zovich, *President*
Richard Zovich, *CFO*
Theresa Zovich, *Admin Sec*
EMP: 32 **EST:** 1966
SQ FT: 17,000
SALES (est): 5.5MM **Privately Held**
WEB: www.amcoprecision.com
SIC: 3845 3721 Mfg Electromedical Equipment Mfg Aircraft

(G-71)
AMERICAN SILK SCREENING LLC
386 Deming Rd (06037-1521)
PHONE..................................860 828-5486
EMP: 3 **EST:** 2008
SALES (est): 396.5K **Privately Held**
SIC: 2759 Commercial Printing

(G-72)
ANDY RAKOWICZ
Also Called: A R Tool
600 Four Rod Rd Ste 4 (06037-3665)
PHONE..................................860 828-1620
Andy Rakowicz, *Owner*
EMP: 3
SQ FT: 3,000
SALES (est): 170K **Privately Held**
SIC: 3599 Mfg Industrial Machinery Parts

(G-73)
ASSA ABLOY ACCSS & EDRSS HRDWR
Also Called: Corbin Russwin Arch Hdwr
225 Episcopal Rd (06037-1524)
P.O. Box 4004 (06037-0512)
PHONE..................................860 225-7411
Martin Huddart, *President*
John R Carlson, *Principal*
Mike Mortillaro, *Principal*
John C Davenport, *Treasurer*
John F Hannon, *Admin Sec*
◆ **EMP:** 500
SQ FT: 1,000,000
SALES (est): 98.2MM
SALES (corp-wide): 8.8B **Privately Held**
SIC: 3429 Mfg Hardware
PA: Assa Abloy Ab
Klarabergsviadukten 90
Stockholm 111 6
850 648-500

(G-74)
ASTRO INDUSTRIES INC
819 Farmington Ave Unit A (06037-1306)
P.O. Box 149 (06037-0149)
PHONE..................................860 828-6304
Edward Kasabucki, *President*
Joe Corallo, *Principal*
Kristin Kasbucki, *Purchasing*
Theresa Tierpack, *Info Tech Dir*
EMP: 6 **EST:** 1979
SQ FT: 3,600
SALES (est): 51K **Privately Held**
SIC: 3544 3469 Mfg Dies/Tools/Jigs/Fixtures Mfg Metal Stampings

(G-75)
BEES KNEES ZIPPER WAX LLC
3 Canoe Birch Ct (06037-4088)
PHONE..................................203 521-5727
Linda Mendonca, *Principal*
EMP: 5
SALES (est): 367.9K **Privately Held**
SIC: 3965 Mfg Fasteners/Buttons/Pins

(G-76)
BODYCOTE THERMAL PROC INC
675 Christian Ln (06037-1425)
PHONE..................................860 225-7691
Mike Sakelakos, *Branch Mgr*
EMP: 40
SALES (corp-wide): 960MM **Privately Held**
SIC: 3398 Metal Heat Treating
HQ: Bodycote Thermal Processing, Inc.
12700 Park Central Dr # 700
Dallas TX 75251
214 904-2420

(G-77)
BOMAR MACHINE LLC
600 Four Rod Rd Ste 7 (06037-3665)
PHONE..................................860 505-7299
Marek Szkotak, *Owner*
EMP: 3
SALES (est): 369.2K **Privately Held**
SIC: 3599 Mfg Industrial Machinery

(G-78)
BUDNEY AEROSPACE INC
131 New Park Dr (06037-3740)
PHONE..................................860 828-0585
Kevin M Budney, *President*
Lisa Budney, *Vice Pres*
Tony Biondo, *Opers Staff*
Adam Sulewski, *Engineer*
Steve Kenney, *Manager*
EMP: 75
SALES (est): 10.2MM **Privately Held**
SIC: 3728 Mfg Aircraft Parts/Equipment

(G-79)
BUDNEY OVERHAUL & REPAIR LTD
131 New Park Dr (06037-3740)
PHONE..................................860 828-0585
Kevin M Budney, *President*
Lisa Budney, *Vice Pres*
Richard Newcombe, *CFO*
Sue Elliotte, *Executive*
Richard V Newcombe, *Admin Sec*
▲ **EMP:** 160
SQ FT: 37,500
SALES (est): 30.3MM **Privately Held**
WEB: www.budneyoverhaul.com
SIC: 3599 Mfg Industrial Machinery

(G-80)
CAMBRIDGE SPECIALTY CO INC
588 Four Rod Rd (06037-2280)
PHONE..................................860 828-3579
Peter M Campanelli, *President*
Mark Labbe, *Vice Pres*
Seth Rutkowski, *Mfg Mgr*
Eric Frick, *Purchasing*
Robert Glabau, *Engineer*
EMP: 76 **EST:** 1951
SQ FT: 27,500
SALES (est): 18.3MM **Privately Held**
SIC: 3423 3728 3724 3714 Mfg Hand/Edge Tools Mfg Aircraft Parts/Equip Mfg Aircraft Engine/Part Mfg Motor Vehicle Parts Mfg Dies/Tools/Jigs/Fixt

(G-81)
COCCOMO BROTHERS DRILLING LLC
1897 Berlin Tpke (06037-3615)
PHONE..................................860 828-1632
Thomas Coccomo, *Managing Prtnr*
Michael Coccomo,
Paul Coccomo,
EMP: 12
SQ FT: 5,000
SALES (est): 1MM **Privately Held**
SIC: 1411 Limestone Quarry Drilling

(G-82)
COMPUTER EXPRESS LLC
365 New Britain Rd Ste D (06037-1366)
PHONE..................................860 829-1310
Michael Psillas, *CEO*
▲ **EMP:** 14
SQ FT: 8,500
SALES (est): 3.9MM **Privately Held**
WEB: www.computerexpressct.com
SIC: 3577 Mfg Computer Peripheral Equipment

(G-83)
FOCUS TECHNOLOGIES INC
600 Four Rod Rd Ste 5 (06037-3665)
PHONE..................................860 829-8998
Zenon Perun, *Co-Owner*
EMP: 7
SALES (est): 754.8K **Privately Held**
SIC: 3599 Mfg Industrial Machinery

(G-84)
FORREST MACHINE INC
236 Christian Ln (06037-1420)
PHONE..................................860 563-1796
David Forrest, *President*
EMP: 54 **EST:** 1973
SQ FT: 17,250
SALES: 4.8MM **Privately Held**
WEB: www.forrestmachine.com
SIC: 3469 3728 Mfg Metal Stampings Mfg Aircraft Parts/Equipment

(G-85)
FOUR TWENTY INDUSTRIES LLC
314 Deming Rd (06037-1519)
PHONE..................................860 818-3334
David Edelson, *Principal*
EMP: 3
SALES (est): 137.4K **Privately Held**
SIC: 3999 Mfg Misc Products

(G-86)
FSB INC
Also Called: Fsb North America
24 New Park Dr (06037-3741)
PHONE..................................203 404-4700
John Bergstrom, *President*
William S Ferguson, *Vice Pres*
▲ **EMP:** 11
SALES (est): 2.2MM **Privately Held**
WEB: www.fsbusa.com
SIC: 3429 Mfg Hardware

(G-87)
GRACE MACHINE COMPANY LLC
46 Woodlawn Rd Ste A (06037-1544)
PHONE..................................860 828-8789
Kazimierz Perzan, *Mng Member*
Grace Perzan,
EMP: 10
SQ FT: 5,500
SALES (est): 990K **Privately Held**
SIC: 3599 Mfg Industrial Machinery

(G-88)
H & W MACHINE LLC
37 Willow Brook Dr (06037-1533)
PHONE..................................860 828-7679
Walter Sewerniak, *President*
EMP: 8
SALES (est): 1.1MM **Privately Held**
SIC: 3599 Mfg Industrial Machinery

(G-89)
HOSOKAWA MICRON INTL INC
Also Called: Hosokawa Polymer Systems Div
63 Fuller Way (06037-1540)
PHONE..................................860 828-0541
Robert Voorhees, *President*
EMP: 20 **Privately Held**
WEB: www.hosokawa.com
SIC: 3089 Mfg Plastic Products
HQ: Hosokawa Micron International Inc.
10 Chatham Rd
Summit NJ 07901
908 273-6360

(G-90)
KENNEDY GUSTAFSON AND COLE INC
Also Called: Kgc
100 White Oak Dr (06037-1635)
PHONE..................................860 828-2594
Edward Charles Cole, *President*
Roberts T Cole, *Vice Pres*
Pierre Joseph Roy, *Vice Pres*
Ryan Cole, *Sales Engr*
Robert Thomas Cole, *Admin Sec*
EMP: 30
SQ FT: 25,000
SALES (est): 8.8MM **Privately Held**
SIC: 3564 Mfg Industrial Exhaust Systems & Dust Control Systems

(G-91)
KENSINGTON GLASS AND FRMNG CO
124 Woodlawn Rd (06037-1536)
PHONE..................................860 828-9428
Frank Carfora Jr, *President*
Frank Carfora Sr, *Treasurer*
Mary Sue Hermann, *Admin Sec*
Jennifer L Carfora, *Asst Sec*
EMP: 8 **EST:** 1976
SQ FT: 2,400
SALES (est): 750K **Privately Held**
SIC: 2499 5719 1793 Mfg Frames Medallion Mirror Photographs & Miscellaneous Ret Picture Store & Glazing Contractor

(G-92)
LLC DOW GAGE
169 White Oak Dr 6037 (06037-1638)
PHONE..................................860 828-5327
Nadeau Andre, *Cust Mgr*
Scott Brotherton, *Manager*
EMP: 35 **EST:** 1946
SQ FT: 24,000
SALES: 400K **Privately Held**
SIC: 3545 Mfg Machine Tool Accessories

(G-93)
LLC DOW GAGE
169 White Oak Dr (06037-1638)
PHONE..................................860 828-5327
Scott Brotherton, *Manager*
Alan E Ortner,
EMP: 35
SALES: 7MM **Privately Held**
SIC: 3674 Mfg Semiconductors/Related Devices

(G-94)
LORENCE SIGN WORKS LLC
Also Called: Lorence Signworks
55 Willow Brook Dr (06037-1533)
PHONE..................................860 829-9999
Michelle Lorence, *Partner*
Paul Lorence, *Vice Pres*
EMP: 4
SALES (est): 499.2K **Privately Held**
SIC: 3993 5046 Mfg Signs/Advertising Specialties Whol Commercial Equipment

(G-95)
MC KINNEY PRODUCTS COMPANY
225 Episcopal Rd 1 (06037-1524)
PHONE..................................800 346-7707

▲ = Import ▼=Export
◆ =Import/Export

Thanasis Molokotos, *President*
Jeffrey A Mereschuk, *Admin Sec*
◆ **EMP:** 219
SQ FT: 200,000
SALES (est): 39.2MM
SALES (corp-wide): 8.8B **Privately Held**
SIC: 3429 Mfg Hardware
HQ: Assa, Inc.
110 Sargent Dr
New Haven CT 06511
203 624-5225

(G-96)
MIDSUN SPECIALTY PRODUCTS INC
Also Called: Tommy Tape
378 Four Rod Rd (06037-2257)
P.O. Box 864, Southington (06489-0864)
PHONE....................................860 378-0111
Mark C Hatje, *CEO*
Robert F Vojtila, *Ch of Bd*
Michael Ossowski, *Vice Pres*
Terese Escoto, *Sales Staff*
Edward Poplawski, *Manager*
▲ **EMP:** 34
SQ FT: 16,600
SALES (est): 6.7MM **Privately Held**
WEB: www.midsunspecialtyproducts.com
SIC: 3069 Mfg Fabricated Rubber Products
PA: Midsun Group, Inc.
135 Redstone St
Southington CT 06489

(G-97)
MKB MACHINE & TOOL MFG
600 Four Rod Rd Ste 3 (06037-3665)
PHONE....................................860 828-5728
Gene Kozlowski, *Principal*
EMP: 3
SALES (est): 376K **Privately Held**
SIC: 3599 Mfg Industrial Machinery

(G-98)
NIRO COMPANIES LLC
100 Harding St (06037-5301)
PHONE....................................860 982-5645
Anthony M Niro II,
Nicholas J Niro,
Pietro A Niro,
EMP: 3
SALES (est): 91.3K **Privately Held**
SIC: 3471 Plating/Polishing Service

(G-99)
OKAY INDUSTRIES INC
Also Called: Okay Medical Products Mfg
245 New Park Dr (06037-3740)
PHONE....................................860 225-8707
EMP: 6
SALES (corp-wide): 34.9MM **Privately Held**
SIC: 3469 3542 Mfg Metal Stampings Mfg Machine Tools-Forming
PA: Okay Industries, Inc.
200 Ellis St
New Britain CT 06051
860 225-8707

(G-100)
OVL MANUFACTURING INC LLC
49 Cambridge Hts (06037-2310)
PHONE....................................860 829-0271
Craig Ogrin, *President*
Alfred Lassen, *Admin Sec*
EMP: 6
SALES (est): 96.7K **Privately Held**
SIC: 3444 3441 Mfg Sheet Metalwork Structural Metal Fabrication

(G-101)
PIONEER PRECISION PRODUCTS (PA)
2311 Chamberlain Hwy (06037-3964)
P.O. Box 396 (06037-0396)
PHONE....................................860 828-5838
Marian Rozycki, *President*
John Kumitis, *Commissioner*
Teresa Rozycki, *Admin Sec*
EMP: 12
SQ FT: 15,000
SALES (est): 1.5MM **Privately Held**
SIC: 3599 Mfg Industrial Machinery

(G-102)
POINT MACHINE COMPANY
588 Four Rod Rd (06037-2280)
P.O. Box 188 (06037-0188)
PHONE....................................860 828-6901
Peter M Campanelli, *Principal*
Peter Campanelli, *CFO*
EMP: 48
SALES (est): 6.3MM **Privately Held**
SIC: 3724 Mfg Aircraft Engines/Parts

(G-103)
PRECISION PUNCH + TOOLING CORP (PA)
304 Christian Ln (06037-1420)
PHONE....................................860 229-9902
Kevin Gregoire, *President*
Dennis Glynn, *Treasurer*
EMP: 66
SQ FT: 44,000
SALES (est): 11.8MM **Privately Held**
WEB: www.ppunch.com
SIC: 3544 Mfg Dies/Tools/Jigs/Fixtures

(G-104)
PRECISION PUNCH + TOOLING CORP
Eastern Industries
304 Christian Ln (06037-1420)
P.O. Box 7087 (06037-7087)
PHONE....................................860 225-4159
Kevin Gregoire, *Vice Pres*
EMP: 9
SALES (corp-wide): 11.8MM **Privately Held**
SIC: 3545 Mfg Machine Tool Accessories
PA: Precision Punch + Tooling Corporation
304 Christian Ln
Berlin CT 06037
860 229-9902

(G-105)
PRO TOOL AND DESIGN INC
230 Deming Rd (06037-1517)
PHONE....................................860 828-4667
Michael Bosse, *President*
Albert Gallnot, *Vice Pres*
EMP: 10
SQ FT: 2,500
SALES: 614.5K **Privately Held**
SIC: 3599 Mfg Industrial Machinery

(G-106)
PYC DEBORRING LLC F/K/A C &
500 Four Rod Rd Ste 114 (06037-2282)
PHONE....................................860 828-6806
Krzysztof Pyc, *Principal*
EMP: 3
SALES (est): 439.4K **Privately Held**
SIC: 3559 Mfg Misc Industry Machinery

(G-107)
RES-TECH CORPORATION
Also Called: Restech Plastic Molding
114 New Park Dr (06037-3741)
PHONE....................................860 828-1504
Don Caske, *Manager*
EMP: 60 **Privately Held**
SIC: 3089 Mfg Plastic Products
HQ: Res-Tech Corporation
34 Tower St
Hudson MA 01749
978 567-1000

(G-108)
ROYAL MACHINE AND TOOL CORP
4 Willow Brook Dr (06037-1534)
P.O. Box Y (06037-0505)
PHONE....................................860 828-6555
Richard Ruscio, *President*
Joseph Dibattista, *Exec VP*
Frank Biello, *QC Mgr*
William Caco, *Engineer*
John Darling, *Engineer*
EMP: 49 **EST:** 1952
SQ FT: 25,000
SALES (est): 9.2MM **Privately Held**
WEB: www.royalworkholding.com
SIC: 3545 5084 3544 Mfg Machine Tool Access Whol Industrial Equip Mfg Dies/Tools/Jigs/Fixt

(G-109)
SIROIS TOOL COMPANY INC (PA)
169 White Oak Dr (06037-1638)
PHONE....................................860 828-5327
Alan E Ortner, *President*
Marc Begin, *President*
Bruce Northrup, *Vice Pres*
Scott Horton, *Prdtn Mgr*
Barry Labarge, *Prdtn Mgr*
EMP: 52
SQ FT: 20,000
SALES: 6MM **Privately Held**
WEB: www.siroistool.com
SIC: 3544 3545 3542 3599 Mfg Dies/Tools/Jigs/Fixt Mfg Machine Tool Access Mfg Machine Tool-Forming Mfg Industrial Machinery

(G-110)
SPACE ELECTRONICS LLC
81 Fuller Way (06037-1540)
PHONE....................................860 829-0001
Kurt Wiener, *Principal*
Daniel Otlowski, *Exec VP*
Brandon Rathdun, *Exec VP*
Blair James, *Engineer*
Brandon Rathbun, *Engineer*
EMP: 22
SQ FT: 23,000
SALES (est): 6.3MM **Privately Held**
WEB: www.space-electronics.com
SIC: 3825 3545 Mfg Electrical Measuring Instruments Mfg Machine Tool Accessories

(G-111)
STEELWRIST INC
576 Christian Ln (06037-1426)
PHONE....................................225 936-1111
Stefan Stockhaus, *President*
Erik Hedenryd, *Treasurer*
EMP: 4
SALES (est): 194.2K **Privately Held**
SIC: 3531 Mfg Construction Machinery

(G-112)
TIGHITCO INC
Aerostructures Group
245 Old Brickyard Ln (06037-1423)
PHONE....................................860 828-0298
Brandi Durity, *General Mgr*
Tawne Castorina, *Vice Pres*
Nancy Castorina, *Sales Staff*
EMP: 130
SALES (corp-wide): 1.6B **Privately Held**
SIC: 3369 Nonferrous Metal Foundry
HQ: Tighitco Inc.
1375 Sboard Indus Blvd Nw
Atlanta GA 30318

(G-113)
TOMZ CORPORATION
47 Episcopal Rd (06037-1522)
PHONE....................................860 829-0670
Zbig Matulaniec, *CEO*
Tom Barwinski, *President*
Tom Matulaniec, *Vice Pres*
Mike Fries, *Engineer*
Greg Labbe, *Manager*
EMP: 130
SQ FT: 55,000
SALES (est): 24.5MM **Privately Held**
WEB: www.tomz.com
SIC: 3451 Mfg Industrial Machinery

(G-114)
TRI-STAR INDUSTRIES INC
101 Massirio Dr (06037-2311)
PHONE....................................860 828-7570
Andrew Nowakowski, *Vice Pres*
EMP: 35
SQ FT: 27,300
SALES: 8.8MM
SALES (corp-wide): 185.9MM **Privately Held**
WEB: www.tristar-inserts.com
SIC: 3451 Mfg Screw Machine Products
HQ: Mw Industries, Inc.
9501 Tech Blvd Ste 401
Rosemont IL 60018
847 349-5760

(G-115)
TRIGILA CONSTRUCTION INC
30 And A Half Ripple Ct (06037)
PHONE....................................860 828-8444
Thomas Trigila, *President*
Tina Trigila, *Vice Pres*
EMP: 20
SALES (est): 1.9MM **Privately Held**
SIC: 2452 1521 Single Family Home Contractor And Manufactures Wood Sheds

(G-116)
VAS INTEGRATED LLC
600 Four Rod Rd Ste 9 (06037-3665)
PHONE....................................860 748-4058
Chris Parzych, *President*
Jim Cox, *CFO*
EMP: 9 **EST:** 2011
SALES (est): 1.4MM **Privately Held**
SIC: 3498 Mfg Fabricated Pipe/Fittings

(G-117)
YALE SECURITY INC
Also Called: Yale Commercial Locks & Hdwr
225 Episcopal Rd (06037-1524)
P.O. Box 4004 (06037-0512)
PHONE....................................865 986-7511
Jan Mc Kenzie, *Mktg Dir*
Dick Krajewski, *Manager*
EMP: 350
SQ FT: 2,300
SALES (corp-wide): 8.8B **Privately Held**
SIC: 3429 Repair Services
HQ: Assa Abloy Accessories And Door Controls Group, Inc.
1902 Airport Rd
Monroe NC 28110
704 283-2101

Bethany
New Haven County

(G-118)
AFCON PRODUCTS INC
35 Sargent Dr (06524-3135)
PHONE....................................203 393-9301
John Mark Chayka, *President*
James Chayka, *Vice Pres*
Helen Plante, *Purchasing*
EMP: 15
SQ FT: 10,000
SALES (est): 2.9MM **Privately Held**
SIC: 3621 3563 7629 7699 Mfg Motors/Generators Mfg Air/Gas Compressors Electrical Repair Repair Services

(G-119)
CONNECTICUT ANALYTICAL CORP
696 Amity Rd Ste 13 (06524-3006)
PHONE....................................203 393-9666
Joseph Bango, *General Mgr*
Joseph J Bango Jr, *Principal*
Joseph J Bango Sr, *Treasurer*
EMP: 11
SALES (est): 1.1MM **Privately Held**
WEB: www.ctanalytical.com
SIC: 3812 5169 8731 8711 Mfg Search/Navgatn Equip Whol Chemicals/Products Coml Physical Research Engineering Services Mfg Analytical Instr

(G-120)
FAIRFIELD COUNTY MILLWORK
20 Sargent Dr (06524-3136)
PHONE....................................203 393-9751
John Ianiri, *President*
Mandy Ianiri, *Admin Sec*
EMP: 16
SQ FT: 20,000
SALES (est): 2.5MM **Privately Held**
WEB: www.fcmillwork.com
SIC: 2431 Mfg Millwork

(G-121)
FREEZER HILL MULCH COMPANY LLC
845 Carrington Rd (06524)
P.O. Box 1318, Naugatuck (06770-1318)
PHONE....................................203 758-3725
Theron Simons, *Mng Member*
EMP: 3

SALES (est): 360.8K Privately Held
SIC: 2499 Mfg Wood Products

(G-122)
LATICRETE SUPERCAP LLC
91 Amity Rd (06524-3423)
PHONE....................203 393-4558
Edward Metcalf, *President*
EMP: 3 EST: 2017
SALES (est): 131.5K Privately Held
SIC: 3823 Process Control Instruments

(G-123)
PLASTIC ASSEMBLY SYSTEMS LLC
Also Called: Pas
19 Sargent Dr (06524-3135)
PHONE....................203 393-0639
Eric Gregorich, *Vice Pres*
Kurt Fugal, *Mng Member*
Paul J Mauro,
EMP: 15
SQ FT: 9,000
SALES: 3MM Privately Held
WEB: www.heatstaking.com
SIC: 3432 Mfg Plumbing Fixture Fittings

(G-124)
RESTOPEDIC INC
695 Amity Rd (06524-3026)
PHONE....................203 393-1520
Joseph Da Silva, *President*
Joe Soares, *Corp Secy*
▲ EMP: 8
SQ FT: 18,000
SALES (est): 1.3MM Privately Held
SIC: 2515 Mfg Mattresses/Bedsprings

(G-125)
WOODWORKING PLUS LLC
375 Bethmour Rd (06524-3358)
PHONE....................203 393-1967
John J Migliaro Jr, *Manager*
EMP: 3
SALES (est): 450K Privately Held
SIC: 2431 Mfg Millwork

Bethel
Fairfield County

(G-126)
ACADEMY MARBLE & GRANITE LLC (PA)
101 Wooster St Ste C (06801-1867)
PHONE....................203 791-2956
Sinan Sepicin, *Mng Member*
▲ EMP: 4
SALES (est): 1.2MM Privately Held
SIC: 1411 Dimension Stone Quarry

(G-127)
ALL PHASE DUMPSTERS LLC
30 Wolfpits Rd (06801-2950)
PHONE....................203 778-9104
Valerie Gauthier, *Principal*
EMP: 4
SALES (est): 315.4K Privately Held
SIC: 3443 Mfg Fabricated Plate Work

(G-128)
ARTECH PACKAGING LLC
Also Called: Artech Lubricants
18 Taylor Ave Ste 2 (06801-2435)
PHONE....................845 858-8558
Thomas Arkins,
◆ EMP: 4
SALES (est): 538K Privately Held
SIC: 2992 5172 Mfg Lubricating Oils/Greases Whol Petroleum Products

(G-129)
B & R MACHINE WORKS INC
23 Henry St (06801-2405)
PHONE....................203 798-0595
Bela Zagyi, *President*
Yavette Zagyi, *Vice Pres*
EMP: 7
SQ FT: 6,500
SALES (est): 958.5K Privately Held
SIC: 3599 Mfg Industrial Machinery

(G-130)
BETHEL MAIL SERVICE
Also Called: Bethel Mail Service Center
211 Greenwood Ave Ste 2 (06801-2146)
PHONE....................203 730-1399
Sivlia Duff, *Owner*
Sivlia Guss, *Owner*
EMP: 17
SALES (est): 1.2MM Privately Held
SIC: 2542 Mfg Partitions/Fixtures-Non-wood

(G-131)
BETHEL PRINTING & GRAPHICS
81 Greenwood Ave Ste 10 (06801-2553)
PHONE....................203 748-7034
Tom Omasta, *President*
Edward Hannan, *Vice Pres*
EMP: 6
SQ FT: 2,000
SALES (est): 811.6K Privately Held
SIC: 2752 Lithographic Commercial Printing

(G-132)
BETHEL SAND & GRAVEL CO
2 Maple Avenue Ext (06801-1507)
P.O. Box 185 (06801-0185)
PHONE....................203 743-4469
Mary Nazzaro, *Partner*
EMP: 8 EST: 1956
SQ FT: 7,000
SALES (est): 642.1K Privately Held
SIC: 1442 Construction Sand/Gravel

(G-133)
BLACKSTONE INDUSTRIES LLC
Also Called: Foredom Electric Co
16 Stony Hill Rd (06801-1031)
PHONE....................203 792-8622
Richard Milici, *President*
Rob Horton, *Executive*
▲ EMP: 60 EST: 1984
SQ FT: 38,000
SALES (est): 14MM Privately Held
WEB: www.blackstoneind.com
SIC: 3546 3425 Mfg Power-Driven Handtools Mfg Saw Blades/Handsaws

(G-134)
BURNDY LLC
Also Called: Framatone Connectors USA
185 Grassy Plain St (06801-2899)
PHONE....................203 792-1115
EMP: 70
SALES (corp-wide): 4.4B Publicly Held
WEB: www.fciconnect.com
SIC: 3678 3643 Mfg Electronic Connectors Mfg Conductive Wiring Devices
HQ: Burndy Llc
47 E Industrial Park Dr
Manchester NH 03109

(G-135)
CAPITOL ELECTRONICS INC
11 Francis J Clarke Cir (06801-2872)
PHONE....................203 744-3300
Richard Warren, *President*
EMP: 10 EST: 1997
SQ FT: 7,000
SALES: 1MM Privately Held
SIC: 3613 Mfg Custom Electronic Switches

(G-136)
CFM TEST & BALANCE CORP
14 Depot Pl Ste 2 (06801-2540)
PHONE....................203 778-1900
Robert Wade, *President*
EMP: 4 EST: 1972
SALES (est): 310K Privately Held
SIC: 3821 5411 Mfg Lab Apparatus/Furniture Ret Groceries

(G-137)
CHROMATICS INC
19 Francis J Clarke Cir (06801-2847)
PHONE....................203 743-6868
Stephen Newlin, *Principal*
▲ EMP: 16
SQ FT: 10,000
SALES (est): 3.4MM Publicly Held
WEB: www.colorant-chromatics.com
SIC: 2819 Mfg Industrial Inorganic Chemicals
HQ: Colorant Chromatics Ag
Gotthardstrasse 28
Zug ZG 6302
417 410-101

(G-138)
CONNECTICUT COINING INC
10 Trowbridge Dr (06801-2858)
PHONE....................203 743-3861
Gregory J Marciano, *President*
Lisa Pittman, *Purch Mgr*
Marlene Gaberel, *Sales Staff*
Patricia R Gershwin, *Admin Sec*
Elise Marciano, *Admin Sec*
EMP: 55 EST: 1963
SQ FT: 8,500
SALES (est): 10MM Privately Held
WEB: www.ctcoining.com
SIC: 3599 3671 Mfg Industrial Machinery Mfg Electron Tubes

(G-139)
CUDZILO ENTERPRISES INC
Also Called: Tibby's Electric Motor Service
40 Taylor Ave (06801-2450)
PHONE....................203 748-4694
Gregory Cudzilo, *President*
Chris Cudzilo, *Vice Pres*
EMP: 3 EST: 1977
SQ FT: 7,000
SALES (est): 266.8K Privately Held
SIC: 7694 5065 5063 Electric Motor Repair & Whol Electric Components Parts Motors And Accessories

(G-140)
D R S DESINGS
Also Called: Lasting Impressions
217 Greenwood Ave (06801-2113)
PHONE....................203 744-2858
William Wichman, *Owner*
EMP: 6 EST: 1948
SQ FT: 2,000
SALES (est): 549.9K Privately Held
WEB: www.drs-designs.com
SIC: 3953 5945 Mfg Marking Devices Ret Hobbies/Toys/Games

(G-141)
DAILY FARE LLC
13 Durant Ave (06801-1906)
PHONE....................203 743-7300
Robin Grubard, *Principal*
EMP: 5 EST: 2008
SALES (est): 263.8K Privately Held
SIC: 2711 Newspapers-Publishing/Printing

(G-142)
DCG-PMI INC
Also Called: Dcg Precision Manufacturing
9 Trowbridge Dr (06801-2858)
PHONE....................203 743-5525
Gerald Palanzo, *CEO*
Paul Sullivan, *CFO*
EMP: 49 EST: 1943
SQ FT: 33,000
SALES (est): 11.6MM Privately Held
WEB: www.dcgprecision.com
SIC: 3499 3841 Mfg Misc Fabricated Metal Products Mfg Surgical/Medical Instruments

(G-143)
DEL-TRON PRECISION INC
5 Trowbridge Dr Ste 1 (06801-2869)
PHONE....................203 778-2727
Ralph A McIntosh Jr, *President*
Edward Keane, *Vice Pres*
Katherine Keane, *Vice Pres*
William Schule, *Engineer*
Emil Melvin, *Sales Executive*
EMP: 50 EST: 1975
SQ FT: 28,000
SALES (est): 13.2MM Privately Held
SIC: 3562 5084 3568 Mfg Ball/Roller Bearings Whol Industrial Equipment Mfg Power Transmission Equipment

(G-144)
DURACELL COMPANY (HQ)
14 Research Dr (06801-1040)
PHONE....................203 796-4000
Ron Rabinowitz, *CEO*
Paul Schacht, *Vice Pres*
Perry Peiffer, *Opers Staff*
Gail Searels, *Buyer*
Linda Jacobsen, *Purchasing*
EMP: 21
SALES (est): 5.5MM
SALES (corp-wide): 225.3B Publicly Held
SIC: 3691 Mfg Storage Batteries
PA: Berkshire Hathaway Inc.
3555 Farnam St Ste 1140
Omaha NE 68131
402 346-1400

(G-145)
DURACELL COMPANY
Duracell USA
Berkshire Corporate Bldg (06801)
PHONE....................203 796-4000
Ed Degrand, *Vice Pres*
EMP: 580
SALES (corp-wide): 225.3B Publicly Held
SIC: 3691 Mfg Akaline & Lithuim Batteries
HQ: The Duracell Company
14 Research Dr
Bethel CT 06801
203 796-4000

(G-146)
DURACELL MANUFACTURING INC
15 Research Dr (06801)
PHONE....................203 796-4000
EMP: 6
SALES (est): 185.8K Privately Held
SIC: 3691 Mfg Storage Batteries

(G-147)
DURACELL MANUFACTURING LLC
14 Research Dr (06801-1040)
PHONE....................203 796-4000
Mark Leckie, *President*
EMP: 250
SALES (est): 407.7K
SALES (corp-wide): 225.3B Publicly Held
SIC: 3692 Mfg Primary Batteries
PA: Berkshire Hathaway Inc.
3555 Farnam St Ste 1140
Omaha NE 68131
402 346-1400

(G-148)
DURACELL US HOLDING LLC (HQ)
14 Research Dr (06801-1040)
PHONE....................203 796-4000
Laura Becker, *President*
EMP: 10
SALES (est): 29.1MM
SALES (corp-wide): 225.3B Publicly Held
SIC: 3691 Mfg Storage Batteries
PA: Berkshire Hathaway Inc.
3555 Farnam St Ste 1140
Omaha NE 68131
402 346-1400

(G-149)
EAST COAST SIGN AND SUPPLY INC
11 Francis J Clarke Cir (06801-2872)
PHONE....................203 791-8326
Richard Carroll, *President*
Madeline Carroll, *Vice Pres*
EMP: 6
SQ FT: 1,800
SALES (est): 839.5K Privately Held
WEB: www.eastcoastsign.net
SIC: 3993 5084 Mfg Signs/Advertising Specialties Whol Industrial Equipment

(G-150)
EATON AEROSPACE LLC
15 Durant Ave (06801-1901)
PHONE....................203 796-6000
Mel Drummond, *Manager*
EMP: 45 Privately Held
SIC: 3679 3812 3643 3829 Mfg Elec Components Mfg Search/Navgatn Equip Mfg Conductive Wire Dvcs Mfg Measure/Control Dvcs
HQ: Eaton Aerospace Llc
1000 Eaton Blvd
Cleveland OH 44122
216 523-5000

▲ = Import ▼=Export
◆ =Import/Export

(G-151)
EATON CORPORATION
15 Durant Ave (06801-1901)
PHONE..................................203 796-6000
Jeremy Betsold, *Engineer*
Anthony D'Ostilio, *Engineer*
Mark Walter, *Project Engr*
Michael J Dodd, *Manager*
EMP: 20 **Privately Held**
WEB: www.eaton.com
SIC: 3643 Whol Electrical Equipment
HQ: Eaton Corporation
1000 Eaton Blvd
Cleveland OH 44122
440 523-5000

(G-152)
ELC ACQUISITION CORPORATION
6 Trowbridge Dr (06801-2881)
PHONE..................................203 743-4059
Bob McClernon, *President*
EMP: 5
SALES (est): 365K **Privately Held**
SIC: 3648 Mfg Lighting Equipment

(G-153)
FALLS FUEL LLC
5 Laughlin Rd (06801-1127)
PHONE..................................203 744-3835
Ed Archer, *Principal*
EMP: 3
SALES (est): 176K **Privately Held**
SIC: 2869 Mfg Industrial Organic Chemicals

(G-154)
FOCUS MEDICAL LLC
Also Called: Naturalase
23 Francis J Clarke Cir (06801-2861)
PHONE..................................203 730-8885
John B Lee Jr, *CEO*
Osmonnie Erat,
EMP: 8
SQ FT: 4,000
SALES (est): 1.7MM **Privately Held**
WEB: www.focusmedical.com
SIC: 3845 Mfg Electromedical Equipment

(G-155)
GILLETTE COMPANY
14 Research Dr (06801-1040)
PHONE..................................203 796-4000
EMP: 4
SALES (corp-wide): 67.6B **Publicly Held**
SIC: 3421 2844 3951 2899 Mfg Cutlery
HQ: The Gillette Company
1 Gillette Park
Boston MA 02127
617 421-7000

(G-156)
GRECO INDUSTRIES INC
14 Trowbridge Dr (06801-2858)
PHONE..................................203 798-7804
EMP: 7
SQ FT: 2,800
SALES: 500K **Privately Held**
SIC: 3499 Mfg Trophies Medallions And Awards

(G-157)
GREGORY WOODWORKS LLC
6 Sympaug Park Rd (06801-2838)
PHONE..................................203 794-0726
Devin P Gregory,
EMP: 9
SALES (est): 932.7K **Privately Held**
SIC: 2521 2541 Mfg Wood Office Furniture Mfg Wood Partitions/Fixtures

(G-158)
H G STEINMETZ MACHINE WORKS
2 Turnage Ln (06801-2853)
PHONE..................................203 794-1880
William Michelotti, *President*
Robert Muldoon, *Vice Pres*
EMP: 12
SQ FT: 15,000
SALES (est): 1.8MM **Privately Held**
WEB: www.steinmetzmachine.com
SIC: 3599 3499 7699 7692 Mfg Industrial Machinery Mfg Misc Fab Metal Prdts Repair Services Welding Repair

(G-159)
HIS VINEYARD INC
2 Vail Rd (06801-1138)
PHONE..................................203 790-1600
Keri Lynne Baldelli, *Principal*
EMP: 3
SALES (est): 163.9K **Privately Held**
SIC: 2084 Religious Organization

(G-160)
INSULATED WIRE INC
Iw Microwave Products Division
2c Park Lawn Dr (06801-1042)
PHONE..................................203 791-1999
John Morelli, *President*
EMP: 11
SALES (corp-wide): 9.7MM **Privately Held**
SIC: 3357 Nonferrous Wiredrawing/Insulating
PA: Insulated Wire Inc.
960 Sylvan Ave
Bayport NY 11705
631 472-4070

(G-161)
INTERSURFACE DYNAMICS INC
Also Called: Polypolish Products Div
21 Francis J Clarke Cir (06801-2847)
P.O. Box 181 (06801-0181)
PHONE..................................203 778-9995
Jonathon J Wolk, *President*
Walter Wolk Jr, *Vice Pres*
▲ **EMP:** 14
SQ FT: 20,000
SALES (est): 3.1MM **Privately Held**
WEB: www.isurface.com
SIC: 2899 Mfg Chemical Preparations

(G-162)
IR INDUSTRIES INC
21 Francis J Clarke Cir (06801-2847)
PHONE..................................203 790-8273
Eric Rothstein, *President*
Patricia Borza, *Vice Pres*
▲ **EMP:** 15
SQ FT: 25,000
SALES (est): 1.5MM **Privately Held**
SIC: 3069 5113 Mfg Fabricated Rubber Products Whol Industrial/Service Paper

(G-163)
J & B SERVICE COMPANY LLC
12 Trowbridge Dr (06801-2858)
P.O. Box 879 (06801-0879)
PHONE..................................203 743-9357
Richard D Jennings IV,
EMP: 8
SQ FT: 1,200
SALES (est): 690K **Privately Held**
SIC: 3822 1711 Mfg Environmental Controls Plumbing/Heating/Air Cond Contractor

(G-164)
J J CONCRETE FOUNDATIONS
15 Stony Hill Rd (06801-1030)
PHONE..................................203 798-8310
Rui M Ribeiro, *Principal*
EMP: 3
SALES (est): 411.3K **Privately Held**
SIC: 2515 1771 Mfg Mattresses/Bedsprings Concrete Contractor

(G-165)
JOHN J PAWLOSKI LUMBER INC
4 Pleasantview Ter (06801-2321)
PHONE..................................203 794-0737
Richard Pawloski, *President*
EMP: 3
SQ FT: 100
SALES (est): 199.6K **Privately Held**
SIC: 2421 Saw Mill

(G-166)
KELLOGG HARDWOODS INC
11 Diamond Ave (06801-1802)
PHONE..................................203 797-1992
Allen G Kellogg, *CEO*
Allen A Kellogg, *President*
Cheryl A Kellogg, *Admin Sec*
EMP: 3
SALES (est): 593.4K **Privately Held**
WEB: www.kellogghardwoods.com
SIC: 2426 Hardwood Dimension/Floor Mill

(G-167)
KINETIC INSTRUMENTS INC
17 Berkshire Blvd (06801-1095)
PHONE..................................203 743-0080
William J Becker, *President*
EMP: 20
SQ FT: 5,000
SALES (est): 3.3MM **Privately Held**
WEB: www.kineticinc.com
SIC: 3843 Mfg Dental Equipment/Supplies

(G-168)
LEADING EDGE CONCEPTS INC
15 Berkshire Blvd Ste A (06801-1052)
PHONE..................................203 797-1200
Addison Unangst, *President*
Carolyn Mc Grath, *Vice Pres*
Rosemarie Unangst, *Admin Sec*
EMP: 7
SQ FT: 6,300
SALES (est): 1MM **Privately Held**
WEB: www.leadingedgeconcepts.com
SIC: 3728 Mfg Aircraft Parts/Equipment

(G-169)
LORENCO INDUSTRIES INC
25 Henry St (06801-2405)
PHONE..................................203 743-6962
Jay Cugini, *President*
Loren Cugini, *Vice Pres*
EMP: 10
SQ FT: 6,500
SALES (est): 1.6MM **Privately Held**
WEB: www.loren.bc.ca
SIC: 2759 Commercial Printing

(G-170)
MEMRY CORPORATION (HQ)
Also Called: Saes Memry
3 Berkshire Blvd (06801-1037)
PHONE..................................203 739-1100
Dean Tulumaris, *CEO*
Nicola Dibartolomeo, *President*
Philippe Poncet, *President*
John Schosser, *Vice Pres*
Tim Wilson, *Opers Staff*
EMP: 150
SQ FT: 37,500
SALES (est): 66.4MM
SALES (corp-wide): 60.2MM **Privately Held**
WEB: www.memry.com
SIC: 3841 Mfg Surgical/Medical Instruments
PA: Saes Getters Spa
Viale Italia 77
Lainate MI 20020
029 317-81

(G-171)
MEMRY CORPORATION
8 Berkshire Blvd (06801-1001)
PHONE..................................203 739-1146
EMP: 3
SALES (corp-wide): 60.2MM **Privately Held**
SIC: 3841 Mfg Surgical/Medical Instruments
HQ: Memry Corporation
3 Berkshire Blvd
Bethel CT 06801
203 739-1100

(G-172)
MONO CRETE STEP CO OF CT LLC
12 Trowbridge Dr (06801-2858)
P.O. Box 74 (06801-0074)
PHONE..................................203 748-8419
Shawn Mc Loughlin, *Principal*
Chip McLoughin,
EMP: 10
SQ FT: 19,000
SALES: 1.3MM **Privately Held**
SIC: 3272 3446 Mfg Prefabricated Concrete Steps

(G-173)
MORRISTOWN STAR STRUCK LLC
8 Francis J Clarke Cir (06801-2850)
P.O. Box 308 (06801-0308)
PHONE..................................203 778-4925
Wesley Lang, *Principal*
Ricardo Rago, *COO*
Rose McCallum, *Manager*
Keith Sessler,
▲ **EMP:** 31
SQ FT: 20,000
SALES: 12.5MM **Privately Held**
SIC: 3873 Mfg Watches/Clocks/Parts

(G-174)
PARAMA CORP
7 Trowbridge Dr (06801-2858)
PHONE..................................203 790-8155
Aloyzas Petrikas, *President*
EMP: 15 **EST:** 1978
SQ FT: 13,500
SALES (est): 384.1K **Privately Held**
SIC: 7692 Welding Repair

(G-175)
PRECISION MANUFACTURING LLC
Also Called: Precision Mfg Tool & Tl Design
153 Gracty Plain St A12 (06801)
PHONE..................................203 790-4663
Edmond Yammine, *President*
EMP: 4
SQ FT: 2,400
SALES (est): 431.1K **Privately Held**
SIC: 3599 Machine Shop

(G-176)
RR DESIGN
13 Hearthstone Dr (06801-1208)
PHONE..................................203 792-3419
Richard Osiecki, *Owner*
EMP: 4
SALES: 15K **Privately Held**
SIC: 3999 Mfg Misc Products

(G-177)
SANDVIK WIRE AND HTG TECH CORP
119 Wooster St (06801-1837)
P.O. Box 281 (06801-0281)
PHONE..................................203 744-1440
Lars Erricson, *Branch Mgr*
EMP: 100
SALES (corp-wide): 10.5B **Privately Held**
SIC: 3357 3316 3312 3621 Nonfrs Wiredrwng/Insltng Mfg Cold-Rolled Steel Blast Furnace-Steel Work Mfg Motors/Generators Mfg Indstl Furnace/Ovens
HQ: Sandvik Wire And Heating Technology Corporation
119 Wooster St
Bethel CT 06801

(G-178)
SANDVIK WIRE AND HTG TECH CORP (DH)
Also Called: Sandvik Heating Technogy USA
119 Wooster St (06801-1837)
PHONE..................................203 744-1440
Parag Satpute, *CEO*
Nicklas Nilsson, *Ch of Bd*
Phil Yu, *President*
John Stowe, *General Mgr*
Rocky Pace, *Vice Pres*
▲ **EMP:** 82
SALES (est): 32.8MM
SALES (corp-wide): 10.5B **Privately Held**
WEB: www.kanthal.com
SIC: 3316 3357 Mfg Cold-Rolled Steel Shapes Nonferrous Wiredrawing/Insulating
HQ: Sandvik, Inc.
17-02 Nevins Rd
Fair Lawn NJ 07410
201 794-5000

(G-179)
SOLAR DATA SYSTEMS INC
23 Francis J Clarke Cir (06801-2861)
PHONE..................................203 702-7189
Guy Thouin, *CEO*
Steve Cheung, *General Mgr*
Peter Scarola, *Manager*
EMP: 12 **EST:** 2010
SALES (est): 2.4MM **Privately Held**
SIC: 3825 Mfg Electrical Measuring Instruments
HQ: Solare Datensysteme Gmbh
Fuhrmannstr. 9
Geislingen 72351
742 894-1820

(G-180)
SQUARE CREAMERY LLC
7 P T Barnum Sq (06801-1838)
PHONE..................................203 456-3490
Segundo Sanchez, *Principal*
EMP: 4 **EST:** 2013
SALES (est): 194.3K **Privately Held**
SIC: 2021 Mfg Creamery Butter

(G-181)
SUMMIT STAIR CO INC
101 Wooster St (06801-1847)
PHONE..................................203 778-2251
Al Curesky, *President*
EMP: 12
SALES (est): 1.7MM **Privately Held**
SIC: 2431 Mfg Millwork

(G-182)
SUMNER COMMUNICATIONS INC
24 Stony Hill Rd Ste 5 (06801-1166)
PHONE..................................203 748-2050
Scott Sumner, *COO*
Amber Lautier, *Sales Mgr*
Meaghan Brophy, *Manager*
Cox Jim, *CTO*
Kate Kulenski, *Executive Asst*
EMP: 20
SQ FT: 5,000
SALES (est): 3.8MM **Privately Held**
WEB: www.sumnercom.com
SIC: 2721 Magazine Publishing Not Printed On Site

(G-183)
TIBBYS ELECTRIC MOTOR SERVICE
40 Taylor Ave (06801-2450)
PHONE..................................203 748-4694
Greg Cudzilo, *President*
Chris Cudzilo, *Vice Pres*
EMP: 4
SALES: 300K **Privately Held**
SIC: 7694 Armature Rewinding

(G-184)
TRAJAN SCIENTIFIC AMERICAS INC
Also Called: Trajan Scientific and Medical
21 Berkshire Blvd (06801-1037)
PHONE..................................203 830-4910
Robert Wagner, *Branch Mgr*
EMP: 5 **Privately Held**
SIC: 3826 Mfg Analytical Instruments
HQ: Trajan Scientific Americas Inc.
1421 W Wells Branch Pkwy # 108
Pflugerville TX 78660
512 837-7190

(G-185)
TRINE ACCESS TECHNOLOGY INC
2 Park Lawn Dr (06801-1042)
PHONE..................................203 730-1756
Fred Schildwachter III, *Ch of Bd*
William Schildwachter, *Ch of Bd*
Betsy Schildwachter, *Vice Pres*
▲ **EMP:** 19
SQ FT: 12,000
SALES (est): 4MM **Privately Held**
WEB: www.trineonline.com
SIC: 3699 Mfg Electrical Equipment/Supplies

(G-186)
UNIMATION
102 Wooster St Ste 4a (06801-1862)
PHONE..................................203 792-3412
Ben Clark, *Owner*
EMP: 4
SALES (est): 220K **Privately Held**
SIC: 3535 Mfg Conveyors/Equipment

(G-187)
UNIVERSITY HLTH PUBG GROUP LLC
6 Trowbridge Dr Ste 1 (06801-2882)
PHONE..................................203 791-0101
EMP: 7
SALES: 350K **Privately Held**
SIC: 2741 Misc Publishing

(G-188)
V & V WOODWORKING LLC
107 Wooster St (06801-1837)
PHONE..................................203 740-9494
Carlos M Veloso,
EMP: 4
SALES (est): 357.7K **Privately Held**
SIC: 2431 Mfg Millwork

(G-189)
VANDERBILT CHEMICALS LLC
Also Called: Bethel Division
31 Taylor Ave (06801-2411)
PHONE..................................203 744-3900
John Eshelman, *Principal*
Jim Fernandez, *Purch Mgr*
Paul Bork, *Engineer*
Bryan Lutz, *Engineer*
Joe D'Antono, *Manager*
EMP: 42
SQ FT: 40,000
SALES (corp-wide): 272.5MM **Privately Held**
SIC: 2891 2819 2869 Mfg Industrial Inorganic Chemicals & Organic Chemicals
HQ: Vanderbilt Chemicals, Llc
30 Winfield St
Norwalk CT 06855
203 295-2141

(G-190)
VARNUM ENTERPRISES LLC
Also Called: Danbury Sheet Metal
11 Trowbridge Dr (06801-2858)
PHONE..................................203 743-4443
Richard C Varnum,
EMP: 12 **EST:** 1944
SQ FT: 14,000
SALES (est): 2.4MM **Privately Held**
WEB: www.dsmfab.com
SIC: 3441 3699 Structural Metal Fabrication Mfg Electrical Equipment/Supplies

(G-191)
VECTOR CONTROLS LLC (PA)
Also Called: Vector Contrls & Automtn Group
17 Francis J Clarke Cir (06801-2847)
PHONE..................................203 749-0883
Blake S Bonnabeau,
Markus Benzenhofer,
Rolf Schweizer,
▲ **EMP:** 10
SALES (est): 3.5MM **Privately Held**
SIC: 3585 Mfg Refrigeration/Heating Equipment

(G-192)
VITTA CORPORATION
7 Trowbridge Dr Ste 2 (06801-2864)
PHONE..................................203 790-8155
Aloyzas Petrikas, *President*
Paul Petrikas, *Admin Sec*
▼ **EMP:** 20
SQ FT: 20,000
SALES (est): 5MM **Privately Held**
WEB: www.vitta.com
SIC: 3443 Mfg Fabricated Plate Work

(G-193)
WESTROCK RKT COMPANY
Also Called: WESTROCK RKT COMPANY
2 Research Dr (06801-1040)
PHONE..................................203 739-0318
Aj Knapp, *Manager*
EMP: 12
SALES (corp-wide): 18.2B **Publicly Held**
WEB: www.rocktenn.com
SIC: 2653 Mfg Corrugated/Solid Fiber Boxes
HQ: Westrock Rkt, Llc
1000 Abernathy Rd Ste 125
Atlanta GA 30328
770 448-2193

Bethlehem
Litchfield County

(G-194)
EAGLE ELECTRIC SERVICE LLC
145 Flanders Rd (06751-2208)
PHONE..................................860 868-9898
EMP: 16
SALES (est): 1.1MM **Privately Held**
SIC: 3699 Mfg Electrical Equipment/Supplies

(G-195)
GRIFFIN GREEN
190 Hard Hill Rd N (06751-1519)
PHONE..................................203 266-5727
Kevin Griffin, *Principal*
EMP: 3
SALES (est): 188.4K **Privately Held**
SIC: 2431 Mfg Millwork

(G-196)
HERFF JONES LLC
39 Terrell Farm Rd (06751-1407)
PHONE..................................203 266-7170
Maureen Hawthorne, *Branch Mgr*
EMP: 8
SALES (corp-wide): 1.1B **Privately Held**
SIC: 2752 Lithographic Commercial Printing
HQ: Herff Jones, Llc
4501 W 62nd St
Indianapolis IN 46268
800 419-5462

(G-197)
KACERGUIS FARMS INC
78 Crane Hollow Rd (06751-1920)
PHONE..................................203 405-1202
James Kucerguis, *President*
Theresa Kacerguis, *Corp Secy*
Matthew Kacerguis, *Vice Pres*
Vincent Kacerguis, *Vice Pres*
EMP: 4
SALES (est): 400K **Privately Held**
SIC: 1442 Sand And Gravel Mining

(G-198)
PLASTIC SOLUTIONS LLC
263 Hickory Ln (06751-2313)
PHONE..................................203 266-5675
Joseph A Humenik, *Principal*
EMP: 3
SALES (est): 248.7K **Privately Held**
SIC: 3089 Mfg Plastic Products

Bloomfield
Hartford County

(G-199)
ADVANCED DEF SLUTIONS TECH LLC
23 Britton Dr (06002-3616)
P.O. Box 66 (06002-0066)
PHONE..................................860 243-1122
Steven Smith,
EMP: 4
SALES (est): 559.7K
SALES (corp-wide): 20MM **Privately Held**
SIC: 2295 3728 Mfg Coated Fabrics Mfg Aircraft Parts/Equipment
PA: Swift Textile Metalizing Llc
23 Britton Dr
Bloomfield CT 06002
860 243-1122

(G-200)
AMERICAN PREFAB WOOD PDTS CO
1217 Blue Hills Ave (06002-1955)
PHONE..................................860 242-5468
Allen Gaudet, *President*
EMP: 7 **EST:** 1976
SALES (est): 747.4K **Privately Held**
WEB: www.americanpre-fab.com
SIC: 2452 Mfg Prefabricated Wood Buildings

(G-201)
AQUA BLASTING CORP
2 Northwood Dr (06002-1911)
PHONE..................................860 242-8855
Victoria Stavola, *President*
Craig Stavola, *Vice Pres*
EMP: 12
SQ FT: 12,000
SALES: 1.4MM **Privately Held**
WEB: www.aquablasting.com
SIC: 3398 3471 7699 Metal Heat Treating Plating/Polishing Svcs Repair Services

(G-202)
ARBON EQUIPMENT CORPORATION
29 Griffin Rd S (06002-1351)
PHONE..................................410 796-5902
Jeff Friedrich, *Branch Mgr*
EMP: 3
SALES (corp-wide): 779.4MM **Privately Held**
SIC: 2431 Mfg Millwork
HQ: Arbon Equipment Corporation
8900 N Arbon Dr
Milwaukee WI 53223
414 355-2600

(G-203)
ARMOR BOX COMPANY LLC
29 Woods Rd (06002-1120)
PHONE..................................860 242-9981
Michael Swan,
Laurel Swan,
EMP: 5
SQ FT: 3,000
SALES: 200K **Privately Held**
WEB: www.armorbox.com
SIC: 3161 3089 Mfg Luggage Mfg Plastic Products

(G-204)
ARTEFFECTS INCORPORATED
Also Called: Artfx Signs
27 Britton Dr (06002-3616)
P.O. Box 804 (06002-0804)
PHONE..................................860 242-0031
Lawrin Rosen, *President*
Mel Cornette, *Corp Secy*
Paula Hansen, *Manager*
Melissa Boehm, *Director*
EMP: 26
SQ FT: 14,000
SALES (est): 4.9MM **Privately Held**
WEB: www.artfxsigns.com
SIC: 3993 7336 Mfg Signs/Advertising Specialties Commercial Art/Graphic Design

(G-205)
ASCEND ELEVATOR INC
Also Called: Cemcolift Elevator Systems
212 W Newberry Rd (06002-5305)
PHONE..................................215 703-0358
Enery Wilcox, *President*
Walter J Herrmann, *Principal*
S Choi, *Vice Pres*
H Moon, *Vice Pres*
◆ **EMP:** 205 **EST:** 1999
SQ FT: 265,000
SALES (est): 30.2MM
SALES (corp-wide): 66.5B **Publicly Held**
WEB: www.cemcolift.com
SIC: 3534 Mfg Elevators/Escalators
PA: United Technologies Corporation
10 Farm Springs Rd
Farmington CT 06032
860 728-7000

(G-206)
ASTRO AIRCOM LLC
25 Northwood Dr (06002-1908)
PHONE..................................860 688-3320
John Muth, *General Mgr*
Dariusz Demusz, *Mng Member*
EMP: 6
SQ FT: 5,000
SALES: 1MM **Privately Held**
SIC: 3599 Mfg Industrial Machinery

(G-207)
BASS PLATING COMPANY
82 Old Windsor Rd (06002-1417)
PHONE..................................860 243-2557
Rocco Mastrobattista, *President*
Peter Mastrobattista, *Vice Pres*
EMP: 33 **EST:** 1956
SQ FT: 32,000
SALES (est): 4.5MM **Privately Held**
SIC: 3471 Plating/Polishing Service

(G-208)
BECON INCORPORATED (PA)
522 Cottage Grove Rd (06002-3111)
PHONE..................................860 243-1428
Michael G Economos, *President*
Gary A Laurito, *Corp Secy*
David Archilla, *Vice Pres*
George M Economos, *Vice Pres*

Matt Smolnik, *Vice Pres*
▲ **EMP:** 80
SQ FT: 65,000
SALES (est): 31.5MM **Privately Held**
WEB: www.beconinc.com
SIC: 3511 Mfg Turbines/Generator Sets

(G-209)
BIRKEN MANUFACTURING COMPANY
3 Old Windsor Rd (06002-1397)
PHONE..................................860 242-2211
Gary Greenberg, *President*
Adam Greenberg, *Principal*
Beatrice Greenberg, *Principal*
Garry Connoly, *Plant Mgr*
Eric Schneider, *Facilities Mgr*
EMP: 92 **EST:** 1943
SQ FT: 80,000
SALES (est): 36MM **Privately Held**
WEB: www.birken.net
SIC: 3724 3728 Mfg Aircraft Engines/Parts Mfg Aircraft Parts/Equipment

(G-210)
BLASTECH OVERHAUL & REPAIR
86 W Dudley Town Rd (06002-1347)
PHONE..................................860 243-8811
Jeffrey D Wolpert, *President*
Karl D Wolpert, *Treasurer*
Abigail Saunders, *Manager*
EMP: 14
SQ FT: 15,000
SALES (est): 2.4MM **Privately Held**
WEB: www.blastechusa.com
SIC: 3511 Mfg Turbines/Generator Sets

(G-211)
BLOOMFIELD WOOD & MELAMINE INC
1 Griffin Rd S (06002-1351)
PHONE..................................860 243-3226
Eddie Leshem, *President*
Steven Leshem, *Vice Pres*
Jerry Leshem, *Admin Sec*
EMP: 10
SALES (est): 790K **Privately Held**
SIC: 2521 5072 Mfg & Whol Wood Office Furniture

(G-212)
BRICO LLC
6c Northwood Dr (06002-1911)
PHONE..................................860 242-7068
Blake Johnson, *Manager*
EMP: 3
SALES (est): 270K **Privately Held**
SIC: 2851 Mfg Paints/Allied Products

(G-213)
CATHOLIC TRANSCRIPT INC
Also Called: Catholic Transcript Online
467 Bloomfield Ave (06002-2903)
PHONE..................................860 286-2828
Henry Mansell, *President*
David Liptak, *Principal*
EMP: 11
SQ FT: 5,000
SALES (est): 713.9K **Privately Held**
WEB: www.catholictranscript.org
SIC: 2711 Newspaper

(G-214)
CLASSIC IMAGES INC
16 Walts Hl (06002-1202)
P.O. Box 7314 (06002-7314)
PHONE..................................860 243-8365
EMP: 3
SALES (est): 330K **Privately Held**
SIC: 2678 Mfg Stationery Products

(G-215)
COHERENT INC
Also Called: Coherent Bloomfield
1280 Blue Hills Ave Ste A (06002-5317)
PHONE..................................860 243-9557
Leon Newmes, *President*
Ed Clapp, *General Mgr*
Kerri Carle, *Buyer*
Alissa Karp, *Buyer*
Paulo Lopes, *Research*
EMP: 48
SALES (corp-wide): 1.4B **Publicly Held**
SIC: 3699 3845 Mfg Electrical Equipment/Supplies Mfg Electromedical Equipment
PA: Coherent, Inc.
5100 Patrick Henry Dr
Santa Clara CA 95054
408 764-4000

(G-216)
COHERENT-DEOS LLC
1280 Blue Hills Ave Ste A (06002-5317)
PHONE..................................860 243-9557
Leon Newman,
Eric R Mueller,
David Stone,
▲ **EMP:** 180
SQ FT: 50,000
SALES (est): 22.7MM
SALES (corp-wide): 1.4B **Publicly Held**
SIC: 3699 Mfg Electrical Equipment/Supplies
PA: Coherent, Inc.
5100 Patrick Henry Dr
Santa Clara CA 95054
408 764-4000

(G-217)
DERINGER-NEY INC (PA)
353 Woodland Ave (06002-1386)
PHONE..................................860 242-2281
Rod Lamm, *CEO*
Keith Kowalski, *COO*
Brett Utter, *Finance Dir*
Patricia Holton, *Human Res Mgr*
Greg Burke, *Supervisor*
▼ **EMP:** 175 **EST:** 1950
SQ FT: 100,000
SALES (est): 109.3MM **Privately Held**
WEB: www.deringerney.com
SIC: 3469 3542 3316 3452 Mfg Metal Stampings Mfg Cold-Rolled Steel Mfg Conductive Wire Dvcs Mfg Bolts/Screws/Rivets Mfg Machine Tool-Forming

(G-218)
DUCTCO LLC
13 Britton Dr (06002-3616)
PHONE..................................860 243-0350
Peter Molin, *President*
EMP: 32
SQ FT: 4,000
SALES: 6MM **Privately Held**
SIC: 3444 Mfg Sheet Metalwork

(G-219)
FMI CHEMICAL INC
4 Northwood Dr (06002-1911)
PHONE..................................860 243-3222
Harry M Fine, *President*
Christopher McCluskey, *Engineer*
Nancy Daigle, *CFO*
▼ **EMP:** 11
SQ FT: 12,000
SALES: 4.9MM **Privately Held**
WEB: www.fmipaint.com
SIC: 2822 Mfg Synthetic Rubber

(G-220)
FOILMARK INC
Also Called: ITW Foilmark
40 E Newberry Rd (06002-1441)
PHONE..................................860 243-0343
EMP: 15
SALES (corp-wide): 14.7B **Publicly Held**
SIC: 3497 3549 3544 Mfg Metal Foil/Leaf Mfg Metalworking Machinery Mfg Dies/Tools/Jigs/Fixtures
HQ: Foilmark, Inc.
5 Malcolm Hoyt Dr
Newburyport MA 01950

(G-221)
GROTE & WEIGEL INC (PA)
76 Granby St (06002-3512)
PHONE..................................860 242-8528
Michael J Greiner, *President*
▲ **EMP:** 50
SQ FT: 20,000
SALES (est): 6.3MM **Privately Held**
WEB: www.groteandweigel.com
SIC: 2013 2011 Mfg Prepared Meats Meat Packing Plant

(G-222)
GUHRING INC
121 W Ddley Town Rd Ste C (06002)
PHONE..................................860 216-5948
Debbie Wentworth, *Manager*
EMP: 135
SALES (corp-wide): 1.3B **Privately Held**
SIC: 3545 Mfg Machine Tool Accessories
HQ: Guhring, Inc.
1445 Commerce Ave
Brookfield WI 53045
262 784-6730

(G-223)
HARTFORD AIRCRAFT PRODUCTS
94 Old Poquonock Rd (06002-1427)
PHONE..................................860 242-8228
James P Griffin, *President*
Susan M Griffin, *Vice Pres*
EMP: 24
SQ FT: 13,000
SALES (est): 4.3MM **Privately Held**
SIC: 3429 3812 Mfg Hardware Mfg Search/Navigation Equipment

(G-224)
HARTFORD INDUSTRIAL FINSHG CO
25 Northwood Dr (06002-1908)
P.O. Box 313 (06002-0313)
PHONE..................................860 243-2040
Frederick C Hillier Jr, *President*
John J Ferguson, *Vice Pres*
Jeannie Ferguson, *Admin Sec*
EMP: 3 **EST:** 1947
SQ FT: 13,500
SALES (est): 271.1K **Privately Held**
SIC: 3479 Lacquering & Enameling Of Metal

(G-225)
HERMELL PRODUCTS INC
9 Britton Dr (06002-3616)
P.O. Box 7345 (06002-7345)
PHONE..................................860 242-6550
Ronald Pollack, *President*
Michelle Gladden, *General Mgr*
Lynn Polaski, *Sales Mgr*
Allie McConnell, *Marketing Staff*
▲ **EMP:** 38
SQ FT: 23,000
SALES (est): 7.4MM **Privately Held**
WEB: www.hermell.com
SIC: 3842 Mfg Surgical Appliances/Supplies

(G-226)
INQUIRING NEWS
51 Gilbert Ave (06002-3824)
PHONE..................................860 983-7587
EMP: 4 **EST:** 2013
SALES (est): 223K **Privately Held**
SIC: 2711 Newspapers-Publishing/Printing

(G-227)
JACOBS VEHICLE SYSTEMS INC
Also Called: Jake Brake
22 E Dudley Town Rd (06002-1440)
PHONE..................................860 243-5222
Sergio Sgarbi, *President*
Dennis Gallagher, *President*
Joao John Cullen, *Vice Pres*
Sam Fabian, *Vice Pres*
Bob Despres, *Facilities Mgr*
◆ **EMP:** 420
SALES (est): 125.7MM
SALES (corp-wide): 1.1B **Publicly Held**
WEB: www.jakebrake.com
SIC: 3519 Mfg Internal Combustion Engines
PA: Altra Industrial Motion Corp.
300 Granite St Ste 201
Braintree MA 02184
781 917-0600

(G-228)
JAMES L HOWARD AND COMPANY INC
10 Britton Dr (06002-3617)
PHONE..................................860 242-3581
Fred Rotondo Jr, *President*
Steven Eppler, *Vice Pres*
EMP: 30 **EST:** 1841
SQ FT: 18,300
SALES (est): 5.2MM **Privately Held**
WEB: www.jameslhowardco.com
SIC: 3429 3743 Mfg Hardware Mfg Railroad Equipment

(G-229)
JOHNSON GAGE COMPANY
534 Cottage Grove Rd (06002-3093)
PHONE..................................860 242-5541
Lowell C Johnson, *President*
David Bengtson, *Engineer*
Johnson Gage, *Personnel*
Pat Sullivan, *Sales Engr*
Michelle Sullivan, *IT/INT Sup*
▼ **EMP:** 37 **EST:** 1922
SQ FT: 15,000
SALES (est): 7.4MM **Privately Held**
WEB: www.johnsongage.com
SIC: 3545 8711 3823 Mfg Machine Tool Accessories Engineering Services Mfg Process Control Instruments

(G-230)
KAMAN AEROSPACE CORPORATION (DH)
1332 Blue Hills Ave (06002-5302)
PHONE..................................860 242-4461
Neal J Keating, *Ch of Bd*
Gregory Steiner, *President*
Alphonse J Lariviere Jr, *Division Pres*
James C Larwood Jr, *Division Pres*
Gerald C Ricketts, *Division Pres*
▲ **EMP:** 750
SQ FT: 185,000
SALES (est): 250.4MM
SALES (corp-wide): 1.8B **Publicly Held**
WEB: www.kamanaero.com
SIC: 3721 3728 Mfg Aircraft Mfg Aircraft Parts/Equipment

(G-231)
KAMAN AEROSPACE CORPORATION
Kaman Cmpsites-Connecticut Div
30 Old Windsor Rd (06002-1414)
PHONE..................................860 242-4461
EMP: 34
SALES (corp-wide): 1.8B **Publicly Held**
SIC: 3721 3728 5085 Mfg Aircraft Mfg Aircraft Parts/Equip
HQ: Kaman Aerospace Corporation
1332 Blue Hills Ave
Bloomfield CT 06002
860 242-4461

(G-232)
KAMAN AEROSPACE CORPORATION
Air Vehicles & Mro Division
30 Old Windsor Rd (06002-1414)
P.O. Box 2 (06002)
PHONE..................................860 242-4461
Salvatore Bordonaro, *Manager*
EMP: 83
SALES (corp-wide): 1.8B **Publicly Held**
WEB: www.kamanaero.com
SIC: 3728 3721 3724 Mfg Aircraft Parts/Equipment Mfg Aircraft Mfg Aircraft Engines/Parts
HQ: Kaman Aerospace Corporation
1332 Blue Hills Ave
Bloomfield CT 06002
860 242-4461

(G-233)
KAMAN AEROSPACE GROUP INC (HQ)
1332 Blue Hills Ave (06002-5302)
PHONE..................................860 243-7100
Richard R Barnhart, *President*
Gregory L Steiner, *President*
James C Larwood Jr, *Division Pres*
Dennis Elwood, *Vice Pres*
Richard C Forsberg, *Vice Pres*
◆ **EMP:** 14
SQ FT: 40,000
SALES: 702MM
SALES (corp-wide): 1.8B **Publicly Held**
SIC: 3721 3724 3728 3769 Mfg Aircraft Mfg Aircraft Engine/Part Mfg Aircraft Parts/Equip Mfg Space Vehicle Equip

PA: Kaman Corporation
1332 Blue Hills Ave
Bloomfield CT 06002
860 243-7100

(G-234)
KAMAN CORPORATION (PA)
1332 Blue Hills Ave (06002-5302)
PHONE..................................860 243-7100
Neal J Keating, *Ch of Bd*
John Blanchard, *District Mgr*
Shawn G Lisle, *Senior VP*
Paul M Villani, *Senior VP*
Robert D Starr, *CFO*
EMP: 60
SQ FT: 103,041
SALES: 1.8B **Publicly Held**
WEB: www.kaman.com
SIC: 3721 3728 5085 Mfg Aircraft Mfg Aircraft Parts/Equip

(G-235)
KAMATICS CORPORATION (DH)
1330 Blue Hills Ave (06002-5303)
PHONE..................................860 243-9704
Neal J Keating, *CEO*
Robert G Paterson, *President*
Steven J Smidler, *Exec VP*
Gregory L Steiner, *Exec VP*
Ronald M Galla, *Senior VP*
EMP: 50
SQ FT: 140,000
SALES (est): 94MM
SALES (corp-wide): 1.8B **Publicly Held**
WEB: www.kamatics.com
SIC: 3451 3562 3724 3728 Mfg Screw Machine Prdts Mfg Ball/Roller Bearings Mfg Aircraft Engine/Part Mfg Aircraft Parts/Equip

(G-236)
KAMATICS CORPORATION
1331 Blue Hills Ave (06002-1304)
PHONE..................................860 243-7230
Glen Gauvin, *General Mgr*
EMP: 5
SALES (corp-wide): 1.8B **Publicly Held**
SIC: 3562 Mfg Ball/Roller Bearings
HQ: Kamatics Corporation
1330 Blue Hills Ave
Bloomfield CT 06002
860 243-9704

(G-237)
KENNETH LEROUX
Also Called: Alrite Manufacturing Company
105 Filley St Unit C (06002-1852)
PHONE..................................860 769-9800
Ken Larue, *Owner*
EMP: 4
SQ FT: 1,200
SALES: 480K **Privately Held**
SIC: 3599 Job Shop

(G-238)
KOOL INK LLC
Also Called: Sir Speedy
21 Old Windsor Rd Ste B (06002-1362)
PHONE..................................860 242-0303
Diane Muska, *Executive*
Mark Jacobs,
EMP: 13
SQ FT: 5,000
SALES (est): 2.1MM **Privately Held**
WEB: www.sirspeedy.cc
SIC: 2752 2791 2789 2759 Lithographic Coml Print Typesetting Services Bookbinding/Related Work Commercial Printing

(G-239)
LENSES ONLY LLC
812 Park Ave (06002-2417)
PHONE..................................860 769-2020
Steven Abbate, *Mng Member*
Thomas Gonthier,
EMP: 12
SALES (est): 3MM **Privately Held**
SIC: 3841 3851 Mfg Surgical/Medical Instruments Mfg Ophthalmic Goods

(G-240)
LESRO INDUSTRIES INC
1 Griffin Rd S (06002-1351)
PHONE..................................800 275-7545
Adam Leshem, *CEO*
Jerry Leshem, *President*
Ed Leshem, *Treasurer*
Dan O'Malley, *Sales Mgr*
Erin Londen, *Office Mgr*
◆ **EMP:** 100 **EST:** 1973
SQ FT: 120,000
SALES (est): 20.6MM **Privately Held**
WEB: www.lesro.com
SIC: 2521 Mfg Wood Office Furniture

(G-241)
LIQUIDPISTON INC
1292a Blue Hills Ave (06002-1301)
PHONE..................................860 838-2677
James Norrod, *CEO*
Alexander Shkolnik, *President*
Nikolay Shkolnik, *Vice Pres*
David Habiger, *Director*
▲ **EMP:** 11
SQ FT: 6,000
SALES (est): 2.3MM **Privately Held**
WEB: www.liquidpiston.com
SIC: 3519 Mfg Internal Combustion Engines

(G-242)
LUMENTUM OPERATIONS LLC
45 Griffin Rd S (06002-1353)
PHONE..................................408 546-5483
EMP: 9
SALES (corp-wide): 1.5B **Publicly Held**
SIC: 3669 Mfg Communications Equipment
HQ: Lumentum Operations Llc
1001 Ridder Park Dr
San Jose CA 95131
408 546-5483

(G-243)
MINARIK CORPORATION
Also Called: Minarik Automation & Control
1 Vision Way (06002-5321)
P.O. Box 723 (06002-0723)
PHONE..................................860 687-5000
▲ **EMP:** 250
SQ FT: 90,000
SALES (est): 45.4MM
SALES (corp-wide): 770.7MM **Privately Held**
WEB: www.minarikdrives.com
SIC: 3625 Relays And Industrial Controls, Nsk
PA: Ruby Industrial Technologies, Llc
1 Vision Way
Bloomfield CT 06002
860 687-5000

(G-244)
MOORES SAWMILL INC
171 Mountain Ave (06002-1694)
PHONE..................................860 242-3003
Donald Moore, *President*
Douglas Moores, *Corp Secy*
EMP: 3
SALES: 160K **Privately Held**
SIC: 2421 5211 Sawmill

(G-245)
NIAGARA BOTTLING LLC
380 Woodland Ave (06002-1342)
PHONE..................................909 226-7353
EMP: 6 **EST:** 2017
SALES (est): 479.1K **Privately Held**
SIC: 2086 Mfg Bottled/Canned Soft Drinks

(G-246)
NORTHAST LGHTNING PRTCTION LLC
10 Peters Rd (06002-1333)
PHONE..................................860 243-0010
John L Barnard Jr, *Mng Member*
James G Barnard,
EMP: 15
SQ FT: 4,800
SALES: 2MM **Privately Held**
SIC: 3643 Lightning Protection Equipment

(G-247)
OLD CAMBRIDGE PRODUCTS CORP
244 Woodland Ave (06002-5318)
PHONE..................................860 243-1761
William Oneill, *Principal*
EMP: 3
SALES (est): 169.6K **Privately Held**
SIC: 3643 Mfg Conductive Wiring Devices

(G-248)
P&G METAL COMPONENTS CORP
98 Filley St (06002-1874)
PHONE..................................860 243-2220
Andrew Ponkow, *President*
Paula Marcotte, *Human Resources*
EMP: 19
SQ FT: 27,500
SALES: 900K **Privately Held**
SIC: 3469 3471 3563 4961 Mfg Metal Stampings Plating/Polishing Svcs Mfg Air/Gas Compressors Steam/Air Cond Supply Metal Heat Treating

(G-249)
P/A INDUSTRIES INC (PA)
522 Cottage Grove Rd B (06002-3111)
PHONE..................................860 243-8306
Edward Morris, *President*
Jerome Edward Finn, *Principal*
Mark Beiner, *Regional Mgr*
Gary Eschner, *Materials Mgr*
Chris Crider, *Chief Engr*
◆ **EMP:** 50 **EST:** 1953
SQ FT: 30,000
SALES: 15MM **Privately Held**
WEB: www.pa.com
SIC: 3549 3625 Mfg Metalworking Machinery Mfg Relays/Industrial Controls

(G-250)
PAXXUS INC
Also Called: Rollprint Packaging
16 Southwood Dr (06002-1952)
PHONE..................................860 242-0663
Tom Sheridan, *Manager*
EMP: 24
SQ FT: 28,000
SALES (corp-wide): 56.2MM **Privately Held**
WEB: www.rollprint.com
SIC: 3086 2671 Mfg Plastic Foam Products Mfg Packaging Paper/Film
PA: Paxxus, Inc.
320 S Stewart Ave
Addison IL 60101
630 628-1700

(G-251)
PIONEER OPTICS COMPANY INC
35 Griffin Rd S (06002-1351)
PHONE..................................860 286-0071
Ron Hille, *President*
Edward Hille, *QC Mgr*
EMP: 14
SQ FT: 8,000
SALES: 4MM **Privately Held**
WEB: www.pioneeroptics.com
SIC: 3845 3229 Mfg Electromedical Equipment Mfg Pressed/Blown Glass

(G-252)
PMD SCIENTIFIC INC
105 W Ddley Town Rd Ste F (06002)
PHONE..................................860 242-8177
Igor Abramovich, *President*
EMP: 7
SQ FT: 2,300
SALES: 1.5MM **Privately Held**
WEB: www.pmdsci.com
SIC: 3829 Develop & Mfg Geophysical Instruments

(G-253)
POINT LIGHTING CORPORATION
61-65 W Dudley Town Rd (06002)
P.O. Box 686, Simsbury (06070-0686)
PHONE..................................860 243-0600
Michael J Callahan, *President*
Christine Breton, *Vice Pres*
Robert Malley, *Vice Pres*
Ryan Pape, *Vice Pres*
Meghan Pugliese, *Admin Sec*
EMP: 32
SQ FT: 48,000
SALES (est): 4.2MM **Privately Held**
WEB: www.pointlighting.com
SIC: 3648 5063 Mfg Lighting Equipment Whol Electrical Equipment

(G-254)
PRATT WHTNEY MSUREMENT SYSTEMS
66 Douglas St (06002-3619)
PHONE..................................860 286-8181
David N Stelly, *President*
▲ **EMP:** 24
SQ FT: 20,000
SALES (est): 6MM **Privately Held**
WEB: www.prattandwhitney.com
SIC: 3829 Mfg Measuring/Controlling Devices

(G-255)
RED BULL LLC
460 Woodland Ave (06002-1342)
PHONE..................................860 519-1018
EMP: 5 **EST:** 2015
SALES (est): 377.4K **Privately Held**
SIC: 2086 Mfg Bottled/Canned Soft Drinks

(G-256)
REILLY FOAM CORP
16 Britton Dr (06002-3617)
PHONE..................................860 243-8200
Mark S Burns, *Branch Mgr*
EMP: 30
SALES (corp-wide): 33.5MM **Privately Held**
SIC: 3069 3086 Mfg Fabricated Rubber Products Mfg Plastic Foam Products
PA: Reilly Foam Corp.
751 5th Ave
King Of Prussia PA 19406
610 834-1900

(G-257)
ROMCO CONTRACTORS INC
12 E Newberry Rd (06002-1404)
PHONE..................................860 243-8872
Keith Lacourciere, *President*
Steve Hansen, *Vice Pres*
EMP: 11
SQ FT: 4,000
SALES (est): 1.1MM **Privately Held**
WEB: www.romcocontractors.com
SIC: 3441 Structural Metal Fabrication

(G-258)
RUBY AUTOMATION LLC (HQ)
Also Called: Kaman Automation, Inc.
1 Vision Way (06002-5321)
PHONE..................................860 687-5000
Steven J Smidler, *President*
Gary J Haseley, *Senior VP*
Gary Haseley, *Vice Pres*
Roger S Jorgensen, *Vice Pres*
Roger Jorgensen, *Vice Pres*
EMP: 175
SALES (est): 68.5MM
SALES (corp-wide): 770.7MM **Privately Held**
SIC: 3491 5085 Manufactures Industrial Valves Wholesales Industrial Supplies
PA: Ruby Industrial Technologies, Llc
1 Vision Way
Bloomfield CT 06002
860 687-5000

(G-259)
RUBY FLUID POWER LLC (HQ)
Also Called: Kaman Fluid Power, LLC
1 Vision Way (06002-5321)
PHONE..................................860 243-7100
Neal Keating,
James Coogan,
Richard Forsberg,
Ronald M Galla,
Patricia Goldenberg,
EMP: 25
SALES (est): 10.4MM
SALES (corp-wide): 770.7MM **Privately Held**
SIC: 3492 Mfg Fluid Power Valves/Fittings
PA: Ruby Industrial Technologies, Llc
1 Vision Way
Bloomfield CT 06002
860 687-5000

(G-260)
RUBY INDUSTRIAL TECH LLC (PA)
1 Vision Way (06002-5321)
PHONE..................................860 687-5000
Ben Mondics, *CEO*

▲ = Import ▼=Export
◆ =Import/Export

Steven J Smidler, *President*
Thomas A Weihsmann, *Vice Pres*
Shawn G Lisle, *Admin Sec*
▲ **EMP:** 100
SQ FT: 5,000
SALES (est): 770.7MM **Privately Held**
SIC: 3491 5085 Mfg Industrial Valves Whol Industrial Supplies

(G-261)
SAKLAX MANUFACTURING COMPANY
1346 Blue Hills Ave Ste B (06002-5310)
PHONE..................................860 242-2538
Dhru Bhut, *President*
Bita Bhut, *President*
Dayalal Bhut, *Vice Pres*
Kusum Bhut, *Vice Pres*
Bhanji Bhut, *Treasurer*
EMP: 6
SQ FT: 3,200
SALES: 2MM **Privately Held**
SIC: 3728 Mfg Aircraft Parts

(G-262)
SALAMANDER DESIGNS LTD
811 Blue Hills Ave (06002-3709)
PHONE..................................860 761-9500
Salvatore Carrabba, *President*
Scott Srolis, *Vice Pres*
Mario Pacheco, *Production*
Kerry Hall, *Human Resources*
Joseph Malecki, *Sales Staff*
◆ **EMP:** 22
SQ FT: 85,000
SALES (est): 6MM **Privately Held**
WEB: www.salamanderdesigns.com
SIC: 2511 2514 2521 Mfg Wood Household Furniture Mfg Metal Household Furniture Mfg Wood Office Furniture

(G-263)
SOUND CONSTRUCTION & ENGRG CO
522 Cottage Grove Rd H (06002-3111)
PHONE..................................860 242-2109
Michael G Economos, *President*
David Archilla, *Vice Pres*
George Economos, *Vice Pres*
Gary Laurito, *CFO*
EMP: 40
SQ FT: 80,000
SALES (est): 7.2MM
SALES (corp-wide): 31.5MM **Privately Held**
WEB: www.beconinc.com
SIC: 3625 Mfg Relays/Industrial Controls
PA: Becon Incorporated
522 Cottage Grove Rd
Bloomfield CT 06002
860 243-1428

(G-264)
SUBIMODS LLC
9 Old Windsor Rd Ste B (06002-1390)
PHONE..................................860 291-0015
Joseph Miller III, *Principal*
EMP: 8
SALES (est): 549.8K **Privately Held**
SIC: 3465 Ret Auto/Home Supplies

(G-265)
SWIFT TEXTILE METALIZING LLC (PA)
23 Britton Dr (06002-3616)
P.O. Box 66 (06002-0066)
PHONE..................................860 243-1122
Steven Sigmon, *CEO*
Robert Defilippe, *Engineer*
Richard Lenhardt, *CFO*
Bryan Wyrebek, *Technology*
Mary-Jane Lopa, *Executive Asst*
▲ **EMP:** 65 **EST:** 1955
SQ FT: 35,000
SALES: 20MM **Privately Held**
WEB: www.swift-textile.com
SIC: 2295 2297 2257 2221 Mfg Coated Fabrics Mfg Nonwoven Fabrics Weft Knit Fabric Mill Manmad Brdwv Fabric Mill

(G-266)
THOMAS HOOKER BREWING CO LLC
16 Tobey Rd Rear (06002-3522)
PHONE..................................860 242-3111
Curt Cameron,
▲ **EMP:** 31
SQ FT: 11,500
SALES: 2.6MM **Privately Held**
WEB: www.thomashookerbeer.com
SIC: 2082 Mfg Malt Beverages

(G-267)
TRIPLE D TRANSPORTATION INC
129 W Dudley Town Rd (06002-1379)
PHONE..................................860 243-5057
Raymond Dufresne, *President*
Lawrence Dufresne, *Corp Secy*
Charles Dufresne, *Vice Pres*
EMP: 4
SQ FT: 8,500
SALES (est): 599.9K **Privately Held**
SIC: 3711 Mfg Motor Vehicle/Car Bodies

(G-268)
TRIUMPH GROUP INC
1395 Blue Hills Ave (06002-1309)
PHONE..................................860 726-9378
Thomas Holzthum, *Exec VP*
Tom Holzthum, *Branch Mgr*
Troy Mullens, *Administration*
EMP: 8 **Publicly Held**
WEB: www.triumphgrp.com
SIC: 3728 Mfg Aircraft Parts/Equipment
PA: Triumph Group, Inc.
899 Cassatt Rd Ste 210
Berwyn PA 19312

(G-269)
TURBINE CONTROLS INC (PA)
5 Old Windsor Rd (06002-1311)
PHONE..................................860 242-0448
Glen Greenberg, *President*
Jeff Faszcza, *President*
Miriam Greenberg, *Admin Sec*
EMP: 97
SQ FT: 35,000
SALES (est): 28.5MM **Privately Held**
WEB: www.turbine-controls.com
SIC: 3541 4581 Mfg Machine Tools-Cutting Airport/Airport Services

(G-270)
UNIVERSAL FOAM PRODUCTS LLC
101 W Dudley Town Rd (06002-1319)
P.O. Box 421, Ellington (06029-0421)
PHONE..................................860 216-3015
Daniel Ekstrom,
◆ **EMP:** 12 **EST:** 2014
SQ FT: 25,000
SALES: 3.5MM **Privately Held**
SIC: 3069 3086 Mfg Fabricated Rubber Products Mfg Plastic Foam Products

(G-271)
WAYPOINT DISTILLERY
410 Woodland Ave (06002-1342)
PHONE..................................860 519-5390
EMP: 5 **EST:** 2015
SALES (est): 329.8K **Privately Held**
SIC: 2085 Mfg Distilled/Blended Liquor

(G-272)
WIRETEK INC
48 E Newberry Rd (06002-1404)
PHONE..................................860 242-9473
Kuldeep Singh Sandhu, *President*
Parminder Singh Sandhu, *Vice Pres*
Deepika K Narwan, *Director*
Sarbjeet S Narwan, *Director*
EMP: 10
SQ FT: 10,000
SALES (est): 1.7MM **Privately Held**
WEB: www.wiretek.com
SIC: 3357 3315 Nonferrous Wiredrawing/Insulating Mfg Steel Wire/Related Products

Bolton
Tolland County

(G-273)
ABLE COIL AND ELECTRONICS CO
25 Howard Rd (06043-7428)
P.O. Box 9127 (06043-9127)
PHONE..................................860 646-5686
Steven K Rockfeller, *President*
Lynn Johnson, *Purch Mgr*
Tom Revall, *CFO*
Paul Asvestas, *Info Tech Mgr*
▼ **EMP:** 30
SQ FT: 25,000
SALES (est): 6.4MM **Privately Held**
WEB: www.ablecoil.com
SIC: 3677 3679 3089 3676 Mfg Elec Coil/Transfrmrs Mfg Elec Components Mfg Plastic Products Mfg Electronic Resistors Mfg Transformers

(G-274)
BARRE PRECISION PRODUCTS INC
Also Called: Moran Tool & Die
199 Hopriver Rd (06043-7443)
PHONE..................................860 647-1913
Ted Moran, *President*
Kim Briggs, *Treasurer*
Joyce Fraietta, *Admin Sec*
EMP: 3
SQ FT: 5,000
SALES: 76.3K **Privately Held**
WEB: www.morantool.com
SIC: 3599 Machine Shop

(G-275)
BREAKAWAY BREW HAUS LLC
5 Steel Crossing Rd (06043-7622)
PHONE..................................860 647-9811
Matthew Soucy, *Principal*
EMP: 4 **EST:** 2016
SALES (est): 75.4K **Privately Held**
SIC: 2082 Mfg Malt Beverages

(G-276)
CARLYLE JOHNSON MACHINE CO LLC (PA)
Also Called: Cjmco
291 Boston Tpke (06043-7252)
P.O. Box 9546 (06043-9546)
PHONE..................................860 643-1531
Michael Gamache, *President*
Gerry Staves, *Production*
Wessell Amy, *Purchasing*
Tom Thiffault, *Marketing Staff*
Michael E Gamache,
▼ **EMP:** 46
SQ FT: 40,000
SALES (est): 9.3MM **Privately Held**
WEB: www.cjmco.com
SIC: 3568 3625 3566 5063 Mfg Power Transmsn Equip Mfg Relay/Indstl Control Mfg Speed Changer/Drives Whol Electrical Equip

(G-277)
LARCO MACHINES CO INC
239 Hopriver Rd (06043-7411)
PHONE..................................860 647-9769
Loren H Gouchoe, *President*
Bernard Gouchoe, *Vice Pres*
EMP: 3 **EST:** 1960
SALES: 150K **Privately Held**
SIC: 3599 Machine Shop

(G-278)
SIMONIZ USA INC (PA)
201 Boston Tpke (06043-7203)
PHONE..................................860 646-0172
William M Gorra, *President*
Christine Brunette-Gorra, *Vice Pres*
Christine Gorra, *Vice Pres*
William Hibbard, *Plant Mgr*
Mark Kershaw, *CFO*
▲ **EMP:** 132
SQ FT: 30,000
SALES (est): 34.2MM **Privately Held**
WEB: www.simonizusa.com
SIC: 2842 2841 Mfg Polish/Sanitation Goods Mfg Soap/Other Detergents

Bozrah
New London County

(G-279)
AEN ASPHALT INC
34 Bozrah St (06334-1304)
PHONE..................................860 885-0500
Linda Adelman, *President*
Ellen Adelman, *Admin Sec*
EMP: 4
SALES (est): 715.3K **Privately Held**
SIC: 2951 Mfg Asphalt Mixtures/Blocks

(G-280)
ELECTRO MECH SPECIALISTS LLC
6 Commerce Park Rd (06334-1122)
PHONE..................................860 887-2613
Donna Laparre, *President*
Mervin Laparre II, *COO*
Merv Laparre, *Vice Pres*
David R Weller, *Info Tech Mgr*
EMP: 8
SQ FT: 20,000
SALES (est): 2.2MM **Privately Held**
SIC: 3699 Mfg Electrical Equipment/Supplies

(G-281)
MAGIC INDUSTRIES INC
140 Bozrah St (06334-1405)
P.O. Box 158 (06334-0158)
PHONE..................................860 949-8380
Michael Krasun, *CEO*
EMP: 10
SALES (est): 560.5K **Privately Held**
SIC: 3229 3446 Mfg Pressed/Blown Glass Mfg Architectural Metalwork

(G-282)
MARTY GILMAN INCORPORATED
Also Called: Gilman Gear
1 Commerce Park Rd (06334-1122)
P.O. Box 97 (06334-0097)
PHONE..................................860 889-7334
Shirley Gilman, *Chairman*
EMP: 7
SALES (est): 694.5K
SALES (corp-wide): 6.3MM **Privately Held**
SIC: 3949 Mfg Sporting/Athletic Goods
PA: Marty Gilman, Incorporated
30 Gilman Rd
Gilman CT 06336
860 889-7334

(G-283)
NGRAVER COMPANY
Also Called: Phillips, R J Associates
67 Wawecus Hill Rd (06334-1529)
PHONE..................................860 823-1533
Ray J Phillips, *Partner*
Brian J Phillips, *Partner*
Abby Mouat, *Technology*
EMP: 3 **EST:** 1955
SALES: 250K **Privately Held**
WEB: www.ngraver.com
SIC: 3423 5961 Mfg & Ret Engraving Tools & Mail Order Services

Branford
New Haven County

(G-284)
ACE BEAUTY SUPPLY INC
937 W Main St (06405-3431)
P.O. Box 303, Monroe (06468-0303)
PHONE..................................203 488-2416
Leslie Denford, *Manager*
EMP: 4
SALES (corp-wide): 24.6MM **Privately Held**
WEB: www.acebeautysupply.com
SIC: 3999 5087 Mfg Misc Products Whol Service Establishment Equipment
PA: Ace Beauty Supply Inc
578 Pepper St
Monroe CT
203 268-6447

GEOGRAPHIC

(G-285)
AEROMICS INC
11000 Cedar Ave Ste 270 (06405)
PHONE....................216 772-1004
Marc Pelletier, *CEO*
Walter Boron, *Ch of Bd*
John Foster, *Principal*
Frederick Jones, *Principal*
Peter Longo, *Principal*
EMP: 7
SALES (est): 584.6K **Privately Held**
SIC: 2834 Mfg Pharmaceutical Preparations

(G-286)
AIRBORNE INDUSTRIES INC
6 Sycamore Way Ste 2 (06405-6528)
PHONE....................203 315-0200
Anthony Gentile, *President*
Jenny Gentile, *Vice Pres*
EMP: 10 **EST:** 1963
SQ FT: 15,000
SALES: 3MM **Privately Held**
WEB: www.airborneindustries.com
SIC: 3728 2399 Mfg Aircraft Parts/Equipment Mfg Fabricated Textile Products

(G-287)
ALACRITY SEMICONDUCTORS INC
4 Pin Oak Dr Ste B (06405-6506)
PHONE....................475 325-8435
James Lin, *President*
Francesco Annetta, *COO*
EMP: 3 **EST:** 2014
SALES (est): 224.3K **Privately Held**
SIC: 3674 8731 Semiconductors And Related Devices, Nsk

(G-288)
ALL PANEL SYSTEMS LLC
9 Baldwin Dr Unit 1 (06405-6501)
P.O. Box 804 (06405-0804)
PHONE....................203 208-3142
Venance Lafrancois, *COO*
Joe Criscuolo, *CFO*
Philip P Delise, *Mng Member*
▲ **EMP:** 67 **EST:** 2009
SQ FT: 39,000
SALES: 25.4MM **Privately Held**
SIC: 3441 Structural Metal Fabrication

(G-289)
AMERICAN POLYFILM INC (PA)
Also Called: API
15 Baldwin Dr (06405-6501)
PHONE....................203 483-9797
Victor J Cassella, *President*
Matthew V Cassella, *Vice Pres*
Paul C Cassella, *Vice Pres*
Larysa Olenska, *Treasurer*
Paul Cassella, *Sales Staff*
EMP: 8
SQ FT: 10,000
SALES (est): 3.6MM **Privately Held**
WEB: www.apiusa.com
SIC: 3081 Mfg Unsupported Plastic Film/Sheet

(G-290)
ATLAS INDUSTRIAL SERVICES LLC
30 Ne Industrial Rd (06405-2845)
PHONE....................203 315-4538
Michael C Picard, *Mng Member*
EMP: 45
SQ FT: 20,000
SALES: 12MM **Privately Held**
SIC: 3444 1611 Mfg Sheet Metalwork Highway/Street Construction

(G-291)
AUTAC INCORPORATED (PA)
25 Thompson Rd (06405-2842)
P.O. Box 306, North Branford (06471-0306)
PHONE....................203 481-3444
Marie Burkle, *CEO*
EMP: 9
SQ FT: 12,000
SALES (est): 1.9MM **Privately Held**
WEB: www.autacusa.com
SIC: 3357 5063 Nonfrs Wiredrwng/Insltng Whol Electrical Equip

(G-292)
AUTAC INCORPORATED
25 Thompson Rd (06405-2842)
PHONE....................203 481-3444
Scott Higgins, *Director*
EMP: 15
SALES (corp-wide): 1.9MM **Privately Held**
WEB: www.autacusa.com
SIC: 3621 Mfg Motors/Generators
PA: Autac, Incorporated
25 Thompson Rd
Branford CT 06405
203 481-3444

(G-293)
AXIOMX INC
688 E Main St (06405-2971)
PHONE....................203 208-1034
Christopher McLeod, *President*
Felicity Acca, *Research*
Chitra Rajagopal, *Research*
Chris Bishop, *Sales Dir*
Michael Weiner, *Security Dir*
EMP: 28
SALES (est): 2MM
SALES (corp-wide): 329.1MM **Privately Held**
SIC: 2836 Mfg Biological Products
PA: Abcam Plc
Discovery Drive
Cambridge CAMBS CB2 0
122 369-6000

(G-294)
B & B VENTURES LTD LBLTY CO
Also Called: Willoughby's Coffee & Tea
550 E Main St Ste 27 (06405-2948)
PHONE....................203 481-1700
Bob Williams, *Mng Member*
Lubna Sparks, *Manager*
▲ **EMP:** 20
SQ FT: 250,000
SALES (est): 2.4MM **Privately Held**
WEB: www.willoughbyscoffee.com
SIC: 2095 Mfg Roasted Coffee

(G-295)
BARLO MANUFACTURING
4 Beaver Rd Ste 1 (06405-3495)
PHONE....................203 481-3426
Barbara Barcsansky, *Owner*
EMP: 5
SQ FT: 5,000
SALES: 450K **Privately Held**
SIC: 3599 Cnc Precision Machine Shop

(G-296)
BETTER PALLETS INC
10 Corbin Cir (06405-6105)
PHONE....................203 230-9549
S Gordon Demetre, *Principal*
EMP: 3 **EST:** 2010
SALES (est): 164.1K **Privately Held**
SIC: 2448 Mfg Wood Pallets/Skids

(G-297)
BIG PURPLE CUPCAKE LLC
6 Conifer Dr (06405-3258)
PHONE....................203 483-8738
Regina F Criscuolo, *Owner*
EMP: 4 **EST:** 2013
SALES (est): 168.3K **Privately Held**
SIC: 2051 Mfg Bread/Related Products

(G-298)
BLAKESLEE PRESTRESS INC (PA)
At Mc Dermott Rd Rr 139 (06405)
P.O. Box 510 (06405-0510)
PHONE....................203 315-7090
Mario J Bertolini, *President*
Robert Vitelli, *Vice Pres*
Peter Bertolini, *Project Mgr*
Rick Fitzgerald, *Opers Staff*
Chris Carasone, *Engineer*
▲ **EMP:** 251
SQ FT: 165,000
SALES (est): 51.3MM **Privately Held**
SIC: 3272 Mfg Concrete Products

(G-299)
BRANFORD OPEN MRI & DIAGNOSTIC
1208 Main St (06405-3787)
PHONE....................203 481-7800
EMP: 3
SALES (est): 268.1K **Privately Held**
SIC: 2835 8011 Mfg Diagnostic Substances Medical Doctor's Office

(G-300)
BURNS WALTON
Also Called: Alphabet Publishing
29 Milo Dr (06405-6133)
PHONE....................203 422-5222
Walton Burns, *Owner*
EMP: 3
SALES (est): 45.4K **Privately Held**
SIC: 2741 2731 Misc Publishing Books-Publishing/Printing

(G-301)
CAS MEDICAL SYSTEMS INC
Also Called: Casmed
32 E Industrial Rd (06405-6532)
PHONE....................203 315-6953
EMP: 6
SALES (corp-wide): 3.7B **Publicly Held**
SIC: 3841 Mfg Surgical/Medical Instruments
HQ: Cas Medical Systems, Inc.
44 E Industrial Rd
Branford CT 06405
203 488-6056

(G-302)
CAS MEDICAL SYSTEMS INC (HQ)
44 E Industrial Rd (06405-6554)
PHONE....................203 488-6056
Thomas Patton, *President*
Paul Benni, *Security Dir*
EMP: 76
SQ FT: 24,000
SALES: 21.9MM
SALES (corp-wide): 3.7B **Publicly Held**
WEB: www.casmed.com
SIC: 3841 Mfg Surgical/Medical Instruments
PA: Edwards Lifesciences Corp
1 Edwards Way
Irvine CA 92614
949 250-2500

(G-303)
CD SOLUTIONS INC
420 E Main St Ste 16 (06405-2942)
PHONE....................203 481-5895
David Pfrommer, *President*
EMP: 20
SALES (est): 894.5K **Privately Held**
SIC: 7372 4226 Prepackaged Software Services Special Warehouse/Storage

(G-304)
CERRITO FURNITURE INDS INC
Also Called: Cerritos Upholstery Concepts
7 Venice St (06405-3111)
PHONE....................203 481-2580
Ronald Cerrito, *President*
Robert Cerrito, *Admin Sec*
EMP: 16 **EST:** 1976
SQ FT: 7,000
SALES (est): 1.5MM **Privately Held**
WEB: www.cerritofurniture.com
SIC: 2512 5712 Mfg Upholstered Household Furniture Ret Furniture

(G-305)
COMPRHNSIVE PRSTHETIC SVCS LLC
21 Business Park Dr (06405-2935)
PHONE....................203 315-1400
John Zenie, *Mng Member*
EMP: 4
SALES: 1MM **Privately Held**
WEB: www.cpsbranford.com
SIC: 3842 Mfg Surgical Appliances/Supplies

(G-306)
CONNECTICUT PARENT MAGAZINE
420 E Main St Ste 18 (06405-2942)
PHONE....................203 483-1700
Joel Macclaren, *Principal*
Lauren Piscitelle, *Accounts Exec*
EMP: 10
SALES (est): 780K **Privately Held**
SIC: 2731 Books-Publishing/Printing

(G-307)
CRYSTAL JOURNEY CANDLES LLC
69 N Branford Rd (06405-2810)
PHONE....................203 433-4735
Cosmo Coriglianao, *Owner*
Agnes Coriglianao,
▲ **EMP:** 20
SQ FT: 5,000
SALES (est): 1.9MM **Privately Held**
WEB: www.crystaljourneycandles.com
SIC: 3999 5947 Mfg Misc Products Ret Gifts/Novelties

(G-308)
CYGNUS MEDICAL LLC
965 W Main St Ste 2 (06405-3454)
PHONE....................800 990-7489
Walter L Maquire Jr,
▲ **EMP:** 8
SALES: 920K **Privately Held**
WEB: www.cygnusmedical.com
SIC: 3841 Mfg Surgical/Medical Instruments

(G-309)
DIFFERENTIAL PRESSURE PLUS
67 N Branford Rd Ste 4 (06405-2852)
PHONE....................203 481-2545
Joe Gordon, *Manager*
EMP: 7
SALES (est): 913.8K **Privately Held**
SIC: 3823 Mfg Process Control Instruments

(G-310)
DUTCH WHARF BOAT YARD & MARINA
70 Maple St (06405-3582)
PHONE....................203 488-9000
Paul Jacques, *Vice Pres*
EMP: 18
SQ FT: 5,000
SALES (est): 2.7MM **Privately Held**
SIC: 3732 Boatbuilding/Repairing

(G-311)
ECLIPSE SYSTEMS INC
14 Commercial St Ub (06405-2801)
P.O. Box 82, Guilford (06437-0082)
PHONE....................203 483-0665
William J Carroll, *President*
Nancy H Carroll, *Vice Pres*
EMP: 5
SQ FT: 6,000
SALES (est): 624.9K
SALES (corp-wide): 28MM **Privately Held**
WEB: www.eclipsesystems.com
SIC: 3845 Manufactures Electromedical Equipment
HQ: Bc Technical, Inc.
7172 S Airport Rd
West Jordan UT 84084

(G-312)
ELDORADO USA INC
322 E Main St Ste 2 (06405-3136)
PHONE....................203 208-2282
Robert B Davidson, *President*
Breanna Richardson, *Principal*
Marcos Paletta Camara, *Treasurer*
▲ **EMP:** 5
SALES: 105.4MM **Privately Held**
SIC: 2611 Pulp Mill

(G-313)
ENHANCED MFG SOLUTIONS LLC
33 Business Park Dr Ste 4 (06405-2973)
PHONE....................203 488-5796
Stephen Giardina, *Principal*
▲ **EMP:** 12
SQ FT: 2,100
SALES (est): 2.5MM **Privately Held**
SIC: 3672 Mfg Printed Circuit Boards

▲ = Import ▼=Export ◆ =Import/Export

(G-314)
EVOTEC (US) INC
33 Business Park Dr # 6 (06405-2973)
PHONE..................................650 228-1400
Werner Lanthaler, *President*
EMP: 28
SALES (corp-wide): 416.3MM **Privately Held**
SIC: 2836 2834 Mfg Biological Products Mfg Pharmaceutical Preparations
HQ: Evotec (Us) Inc.
303b College Rd E
Princeton NJ 08540

(G-315)
FABRIQUE LTD
28 School St (06405-3328)
PHONE..................................203 481-5400
Francine Farkas Sears, *President*
▲ **EMP:** 12
SALES (est): 15.5MM **Privately Held**
SIC: 3161 Mfg Luggage

(G-316)
FITZGERALD & WOOD INC
85 Rogers St Ste 3 (06405-3674)
PHONE..................................203 488-2553
Thomas J Shanley, *President*
Susan Shanley, *Manager*
EMP: 8 **EST:** 1924
SQ FT: 3,000
SALES: 500K **Privately Held**
SIC: 3432 Mfg Plumbing Fixture Fittings

(G-317)
FREETHINK TECHNOLOGIES INC
35 Ne Industrial Rd # 201 (06405-6802)
PHONE..................................860 237-5800
Kenneth C Waterman, *CEO*
K Waterman, *President*
Ken Waterman, *President*
Mark Kastan, *Vice Pres*
Butch Waterman, *CFO*
EMP: 19
SALES: 316.3K **Privately Held**
SIC: 7372 8732 Prepackaged Software Services Commercial Nonphysical Research

(G-318)
FREVVO INC
500 E Main St Ste 330 (06405-2937)
PHONE..................................203 208-3117
Ashish Desphande, *CEO*
Leandro D Costa, *President*
Leandro Dacosta, *President*
Nancy Esposito, *COO*
Eric Pias, *Vice Pres*
EMP: 11
SALES (est): 829.4K **Privately Held**
SIC: 7372 Prepackaged Software Services

(G-319)
FYC APPAREL GROUP LLC (PA)
Also Called: Allison Taylor
30 Thompson Rd (06405-2842)
P.O. Box 812 (06405-0812)
PHONE..................................203 481-2420
John Warfel, *Vice Pres*
Maia Chiat,
Sunny Leigh,
▲ **EMP:** 100
SQ FT: 42,000
SALES (est): 69.8MM **Privately Held**
WEB: www.akdesigns.net
SIC: 2331 2335 2337 5651 Mfg Women/Misses Blouses Mfg Women/Misses Dresses Mfg Women/Miss Suit/Coat Ret Family Clothing

(G-320)
GLOBE ENVIRONMENTAL CORP
131 Commercial Pkwy 1b (06405-2536)
P.O. Box 235 (06405-0235)
PHONE..................................203 481-5586
Lorraine Saputo, *Vice Pres*
Richard True, *Vice Pres*
Charles S Blaha, *CFO*
EMP: 11
SALES (est): 1.9MM **Privately Held**
SIC: 2899 Formulater & Compounder Of Water Treatment Products

(G-321)
GREG ROBBINS AND ASSOCIATES
15 Park Pl (06405-7726)
PHONE..................................888 699-8876
Gregory Robbins, *Principal*
EMP: 3
SALES (est): 155.2K **Privately Held**
SIC: 2024 Mfg Ice Cream/Frozen Desert

(G-322)
HARCOSEMCO LLC
186 Cedar St (06405-6011)
P.O. Box 10 (06405-0010)
PHONE..................................203 483-3700
Raymond Laubenthal, *CEO*
Michael Milardo, *President*
Gregory Rufus, *Corp Secy*
Jennifer Viglione, *Production*
Lester Allen, *Engineer*
EMP: 137 **EST:** 1951
SQ FT: 1,200
SALES (est): 44.7MM
SALES (corp-wide): 5.2B **Publicly Held**
WEB: www.harcolabs.com
SIC: 3829 Mfg Measuring/Controlling Devices
HQ: Transdigm, Inc.
4223 Monticello Blvd
Cleveland OH 44121

(G-323)
HOFFMANN-LA ROCHE INC
15 Commercial St (06405-2801)
PHONE..................................203 871-2303
John Waterhouse, *Branch Mgr*
EMP: 608
SALES (corp-wide): 57.7B **Privately Held**
SIC: 2834 Mfg Pharmaceutica Preps
HQ: Hoffmann-La Roche Inc.
150 Clove Rd Ste 88th
Little Falls NJ 07424
973 890-2268

(G-324)
HOUSTON WEBER SYSTEMS INC
31 Business Park Dr Ste 3 (06405-2977)
PHONE..................................203 481-0115
Via Weber, *President*
Charles Weber, *Vice Pres*
Carol Weber, *Admin Sec*
EMP: 8 **EST:** 1958
SQ FT: 13,000
SALES: 560K **Privately Held**
SIC: 3494 3599 Mfg Valves & Machine Shop

(G-325)
HOWMET CORPORATION
Howmet Trbine Cmpnents Coating
4 Commercial St (06405-2801)
PHONE..................................203 481-3451
John Schilbe, *Manager*
EMP: 331
SALES (corp-wide): 14B **Publicly Held**
SIC: 3324 Steel Investment Foundry
HQ: Howmet Corporation
1 Misco Dr
Whitehall MI 49461
231 894-5686

(G-326)
IVY BIOMEDICAL SYSTEMS INC
11 Business Park Dr # 10 (06405-2959)
PHONE..................................203 481-4183
James W Biondi, *President*
Sara Dean, *General Mgr*
Zack Curello, *Vice Pres*
Richard Kosmala, *Vice Pres*
Christopher Sheridan, *Vice Pres*
▲ **EMP:** 47
SQ FT: 14,700
SALES (est): 9.5MM **Privately Held**
WEB: www.ivybiomedical.com
SIC: 3845 Mfg Electromedical Equipment

(G-327)
J + J BRANFORD INC (PA)
Also Called: Joe's Paint Center
145 N Mn St (06405)
PHONE..................................203 488-5637
Joseph R Pagliaro, *President*
EMP: 4
SALES (est): 815K **Privately Held**
SIC: 2851 Mfg Paints/Allied Products

(G-328)
LQ MECHATRONICS INC
2 Sycamore Way (06405-6551)
PHONE..................................203 433-4430
Hans-Elmar Kessler, *President*
▲ **EMP:** 9
SQ FT: 27,900
SALES (est): 1.8MM
SALES (corp-wide): 55.4MM **Privately Held**
SIC: 3823 3824 3679 Mfg Process Control Instruments Mfg Fluid Meter/Counting Devices Mfg Electronic Components
PA: Lq Mechatronik-Systeme Gmbh
Carl-Benz-Str. 6
Besigheim 74354
714 396-830

(G-329)
MADISON COMPANY (PA)
27 Business Park Dr (06405-2954)
PHONE..................................203 488-4477
Steven Schickler, *President*
Donna Dotson, *Vice Pres*
Resha Patel, *Info Tech Mgr*
EMP: 45 **EST:** 1959
SQ FT: 20,000
SALES (est): 10.8MM **Privately Held**
SIC: 3613 3823 Mfg Switchgear/Switchboards Mfg Process Control Instruments

(G-330)
MADISON POLYMERIC ENGRG INC
Also Called: M P E
965 W Main St Ste 2 (06405-3454)
PHONE..................................203 488-4554
Walter L Maguire Jr, *President*
Robert Hojnacki, *Vice Pres*
EMP: 45
SQ FT: 50,000
SALES (est): 10.4MM **Privately Held**
WEB: www.madpoly.com
SIC: 3086 Mfg Plastic Foam Products

(G-331)
MOLD THREADS INC
21 W End Ave (06405-4549)
PHONE..................................203 483-1420
Bruce Argetsinger, *President*
EMP: 4
SQ FT: 10,000
SALES (est): 947.3K **Privately Held**
WEB: www.moldthreads.com
SIC: 3089 3544 Mfg Plastic Products Mfg Dies/Tools/Jigs/Fixtures

(G-332)
NEW ENGLAND BEVERAGES LLC
137 N Branford Rd (06405-2810)
PHONE..................................203 208-4517
Richard Hahn,
EMP: 3
SALES (est): 120.1K **Privately Held**
SIC: 2086 Mfg Bottled/Canned Soft Drinks

(G-333)
NEW ENGLAND COMPUTER SVCS INC
Also Called: Necs
322 E Main St (06405-3136)
PHONE..................................475 221-8200
Christopher Anatra, *President*
EMP: 22 **EST:** 1990
SALES (est): 2.1MM **Privately Held**
SIC: 7372 Prepackaged Software Services

(G-334)
PAPER ALLIANCE LLC
45 Ne Industrial Rd (06405-6801)
PHONE..................................203 315-3116
Paula Nancuso, *Vice Pres*
Michael Siegel, *Mng Member*
EMP: 4 **EST:** 2011
SALES (est): 522.9K
SALES (corp-wide): 74.6MM **Privately Held**
SIC: 2631 Paperboard Mill
HQ: Evergreen Fibres, Inc.
45 Ne Industrial Rd
Branford CT 06405

(G-335)
PAULS WIRE ROPE & SLING INC
4 Indian Neck Ave (06405-4616)
PHONE..................................203 481-3469
Paul Cianciola Jr, *President*
Dale Cianciola, *Admin Sec*
EMP: 10
SQ FT: 1,000
SALES (est): 1.4MM **Privately Held**
SIC: 3496 Mfg Misc Fabricated Wire Products

(G-336)
PEXAGON TECHNOLOGY INC
14 Business Park Dr Ste E (06405-2909)
PHONE..................................203 458-3364
Brian R Campbell, *President*
Albert Conte, *Vice Pres*
Tommy Fair, *Sales Mgr*
John Russo, *Mktg Dir*
Adam Jones, *Marketing Staff*
◆ **EMP:** 30
SQ FT: 10,000
SALES (est): 7MM **Privately Held**
WEB: www.pexagontech.com
SIC: 3572 Mfg Computer Storage Devices

(G-337)
PHOENIXSONGS BIOLOGICALS INC
33 Business Park Dr 1a (06405-2973)
PHONE..................................203 433-4329
Richard Malavarca, *President*
Marsha Roach, *Exec VP*
Lola Reid, *Officer*
EMP: 4 **EST:** 2012
SQ FT: 4,500
SALES (est): 576.5K **Privately Held**
SIC: 2836 Mfg Biological Products

(G-338)
PPK INC
41 Montoya Dr (06405-2516)
PHONE..................................203 376-9180
Gale Morrison, *Principal*
EMP: 3
SALES (est): 327.8K **Privately Held**
SIC: 2421 Sawmill/Planing Mill

(G-339)
PRATT-READ CORPORATION (PA)
Also Called: Cornwall & Patterson Div
193 Turtle Bay Dr (06405-4903)
PHONE..................................860 625-3620
Harwood B Comstock, *Ch of Bd*
Gordon Christie, *CFO*
EMP: 15 **EST:** 1798
SQ FT: 120,000
SALES (est): 6.2MM **Privately Held**
WEB: www.hexkeys.com
SIC: 3469 Mfg Metal Stampings

(G-340)
PROTEOWISE INC
34 Bryan Rd (06405-4504)
PHONE..................................203 430-4187
Erik Gunther, *CEO*
Mikhail Kostylev, *Principal*
Stephen Strittmatter, *Principal*
EMP: 3
SALES (est): 128K **Privately Held**
SIC: 3821 Mfg Lab Apparatus/Furniture

(G-341)
RESPOND SYSTEMS
20 Baldwin Dr (06405-6501)
PHONE..................................203 481-2810
Donald E Hudson, *President*
Dave Lantieri, *Engineer*
Doreen O Hudson, *Director*
EMP: 10 **EST:** 1981
SALES (est): 880K **Privately Held**
WEB: www.respondsystems.com
SIC: 3845 8041 Mfg Electromedical Equipment Chiropractor's Office

(G-342)
ROBINSON TAPE & LABEL INC
32 Park Dr E Ste 1 (06405-6524)
PHONE..................................203 481-5581
Edward A Pepe, *President*
Dennis Smith, *Vice Pres*
Dawn Sterns, *Shareholder*
Beth Kinney, *Administration*
EMP: 20
SQ FT: 11,000
SALES (est): 5MM **Privately Held**
WEB: www.robinsontapeandlabel.com
SIC: 2672 Mfg Coated/Laminated Paper

(G-343)
ROSTRA TOOL COMPANY
Also Called: Sargent Quality Tools
30 E Industrial Rd (06405-6507)
PHONE..................................203 488-8665
Michael Sunter, *President*
Richard A Steiner, *President*
Pat Tropeano, *Vice Pres*
▲ **EMP:** 44
SQ FT: 22,000
SALES (est): 8.9MM **Privately Held**
WEB: www.rostratool.com
SIC: 3423 Mfg Hand/Edge Tools
PA: Rostra Technologies, Inc
2519 Dana Dr
Laurinburg NC 28352

(G-344)
SANTORINI BREEZE LLC
374 E Main St (06405-2938)
PHONE..................................203 640-3431
Konstantinos Sousoulas,
EMP: 6 **EST:** 2016
SALES (est): 485.6K **Privately Held**
SIC: 2037 Mfg Frozen Fruits/Vegetables

(G-345)
SAPHLUX INC
4 Pin Oak Dr (06405-6506)
PHONE..................................475 221-8981
EMP: 6 **EST:** 2014
SQ FT: 8,000
SALES: 100K **Privately Held**
SIC: 3674 Mfg Semiconductors/Related Devices Business Serv Non-Commercial Site

(G-346)
SCHMITT REALTY HOLDINGS INC
Also Called: Acitronics
746 E Main St (06405-2918)
PHONE..................................203 488-3252
Dianne Boston, *Sales Mgr*
Stephen Sadowski, *Branch Mgr*
EMP: 35
SALES (corp-wide): 19.2MM **Privately Held**
WEB: www.georgeschmitt.com
SIC: 2754 2796 Gravure Commercial Printing Platemaking Services
PA: Schmitt Realty Holdings, Inc.
251 Boston Post Rd
Guilford CT 06437
203 453-4334

(G-347)
SEMCO INSTRUMENTS INC (DH)
Also Called: Harcosemco
186 Cedar St (06405-6011)
PHONE..................................661 257-2000
Vincent Sandoval, *CEO*
Michael G Moore, *President*
Deanne Davis, *Senior Buyer*
Matthew Pitcher, *Buyer*
EMP: 177
SQ FT: 38,000
SALES (est): 65.3MM
SALES (corp-wide): 5.2B **Publicly Held**
WEB: www.semcoinstruments.com
SIC: 3829 Mfg Measuring/Controlling Devices

(G-348)
SEMCO INSTRUMENTS INC
Also Called: Harcosemco
186 Cedar St (06405-6011)
PHONE..................................661 362-6117
Theresa V Von Szilassy, *Manager*
EMP: 3
SALES (corp-wide): 5.2B **Publicly Held**
WEB: www.semcoinstruments.com
SIC: 3829 Mfg Measuring/Controlling Devices
HQ: Semco Instruments, Inc.
186 Cedar St
Branford CT 06405
661 257-2000

(G-349)
SIGNS BY AUTOGRAFIX
7 Svea Ave (06405-3724)
PHONE..................................203 481-6502
John Miller, *Owner*
Heidi Miller, *Co-Owner*
EMP: 4
SQ FT: 3,000
SALES: 350K **Privately Held**
SIC: 3993 Mfg Signs/Advertising Specialties

(G-350)
SOUTHERN NENG ULTRAVIOLET INC
Also Called: Southern Neng Ultraviolet Co
55029 E Main St (06405)
PHONE..................................203 483-5810
Ronald Paolella, *President*
Jean Farricilli, *Admin Sec*
EMP: 6 **EST:** 1980
SQ FT: 5,000
SALES (est): 993.8K **Privately Held**
SIC: 3641 Manufactures Photochemical Equipment Which Includes Germicidal Ultraviolet Equipment

(G-351)
STAMLER PUBLISHING COMPANY
Also Called: Highway Vehicle/Safety Report
178 Thimble Island Rd (06405-5727)
P.O. Box 3367 (06405-1967)
PHONE..................................203 488-9808
S Paul Stamler, *President*
EMP: 4
SQ FT: 1,000
SALES (est): 328.3K **Privately Held**
SIC: 2741 2731 Publishing Company Of Newsletters

(G-352)
STERLING MATERIALS LLC
17 Tanglewood Dr (06405-3355)
PHONE..................................203 315-6619
Suzanne Hopkins, *Principal*
EMP: 5 **EST:** 2011
SALES (est): 363.7K **Privately Held**
SIC: 3273 Mfg Ready-Mixed Concrete

(G-353)
STONY CREEK QUARRY CORPORATION
7 Business Park Dr Ste A (06405-2926)
PHONE..................................203 483-3904
Doug Anderson, *President*
Bill Gaunt, *Treasurer*
William E Gaunt Jr, *Treasurer*
EMP: 9
SALES (est): 750K **Privately Held**
SIC: 1411 Dimension Stone Quarry

(G-354)
TANGEN BIOSCIENCES INC
20 Commercial St (06405-2801)
PHONE..................................203 433-4045
Richard C Birkmeyer, *CEO*
Richard Carroll, *Vice Pres*
Brian Chirico, *Vice Pres*
EMP: 28
SQ FT: 2,700
SALES (est): 270.2K **Privately Held**
SIC: 3841 3842 Mfg Surgical/Medical Instruments Mfg Surgical Appliances/Supplies

(G-355)
TOTAL CONCEPT TOOL INC
2 Research Dr Ste 1 (06405-2858)
PHONE..................................203 483-1130
Albert Mirto, *President*
Jennifer Mirto, *Vice Pres*
EMP: 8
SALES (est): 1MM **Privately Held**
SIC: 3544 3599 Mfg Dies/Tools/Jigs/Fixtures Mfg Industrial Machinery

(G-356)
VIBRASCIENCE INC
186 N Main St (06405-3021)
PHONE..................................203 483-6113
Joe Fattore, *President*
Martha Fattore, *Admin Sec*
EMP: 5
SQ FT: 2,500
SALES (est): 1MM **Privately Held**
WEB: www.vibrasciences.com
SIC: 3086 5033 5065 Mfg Plastic Foam Products Whol Roofing/Siding/Insulation Whol Electronic Parts/Equipment

(G-357)
VOLPE CABLE CORPORATION
201 Linden Ave (06405-5123)
PHONE..................................203 623-1818
Frank Volpe, *CEO*
▲ **EMP:** 115
SALES (est): 21.3MM **Privately Held**
WEB: www.ezform.com
SIC: 3357 Nonferrous Wiredrawing/Insulating

(G-358)
WALLINGFORD INDUSTRIES INC
31 Business Park Dr Ste 3 (06405-2977)
PHONE..................................203 481-0359
Charles Weber Jr, *President*
Vincea Weber, *Vice Pres*
Carol Weber, *Admin Sec*
EMP: 10 **EST:** 1947
SQ FT: 15,000
SALES (est): 1.7MM **Privately Held**
SIC: 3599 Mfg Industrial Machinery

(G-359)
WALLINGFORD PRTG BUS FORMS INC
758 E Main St (06405-2918)
PHONE..................................203 481-1911
Jennifer Bright, *President*
Thomas Bright, *Vice Pres*
EMP: 10
SQ FT: 5,500
SALES (est): 1.3MM **Privately Held**
WEB: www.wallprint.com
SIC: 2761 5111 2759 Mfg Manifold Business Forms Whol Printing/Writing Paper Commercial Printing

(G-360)
WEZENSKI WOODWORKING
214 Crosswoods Rd (06405-5802)
PHONE..................................203 488-3255
Paul Wezenski, *Principal*
EMP: 3
SALES (est): 241.7K **Privately Held**
SIC: 2431 Mfg Millwork

(G-361)
WFS EARTH MATERIALSI LLC
11 Business Park Dr (06405-2958)
PHONE..................................203 488-2055
Douglas Anderson, *Mng Member*
EMP: 5
SQ FT: 2,500
SALES (est): 1.5MM **Privately Held**
SIC: 1442 Construction Sand/Gravel

(G-362)
WILSON ARMS COMPANY
97 Leetes Island Rd 101 (06405-3308)
PHONE..................................203 488-7297
Hugo E Vivero, *President*
EMP: 18 **EST:** 1954
SQ FT: 15,000
SALES (est): 5MM **Privately Held**
SIC: 3484 Ret Sporting Goods/Bicycles

(G-363)
XCEL FUEL
501 Main St (06405-3526)
PHONE..................................203 481-4510
EMP: 4
SALES (est): 203.9K **Privately Held**
SIC: 2869 Mfg Industrial Organic Chemicals

Bridgeport
Fairfield County

(G-364)
A & S PHARMACEUTICAL CORP
480 Barnum Ave Ste 3 (06608-2459)
P.O. Box 2005 (06608-0005)
PHONE..................................203 368-2538
Arnold Lewis, *Ch of Bd*
Seth Lewis, *Treasurer*
◆ **EMP:** 50 **EST:** 1971
SQ FT: 40,000
SALES (est): 7.6MM **Privately Held**
SIC: 2834 Mfg Pharmaceutical Preparations

(G-365)
A J R INC
Also Called: Interface Technology
67 Poland St (06605-3266)
PHONE..................................203 384-0400
John Vaughan, *President*
Joe Saja, *Opers Mgr*
Lori Krivda, *Executive*
Lidia Sotomayor, *Admin Asst*
EMP: 10
SQ FT: 14,000
SALES (est): 1.8MM **Privately Held**
SIC: 3357 Nonferrous Wiredrawing/Insulating

(G-366)
ACCUMOLD TECHNOLOGIES INC
52 Carroll Ave (06607-2317)
PHONE..................................203 384-9256
Joseph Fiorini, *President*
Ted Deandrade, *Admin Sec*
EMP: 6
SQ FT: 5,000
SALES (est): 680K **Privately Held**
SIC: 3089 Manufactures Plastic Products Specializing In Injection Molded Finished Products

(G-367)
ACSON TOOL COMPANY
62 Carroll Ave (06607-2317)
PHONE..................................203 334-8050
David Deandrade, *President*
Antro Deandrade, *Vice Pres*
EMP: 11 **EST:** 1951
SALES (est): 1.3MM **Privately Held**
SIC: 3544 Mfg Dies/Tools/Jigs/Fixtures

(G-368)
ADVANCE HEAT TREATING CO
147 West Ave (06604)
PHONE..................................203 380-8898
EMP: 3
SQ FT: 1,250
SALES (est): 208.7K **Privately Held**
SIC: 3398 Metal Heat Treating

(G-369)
ALLOY ENGINEERING CO INC (PA)
304 Seaview Ave (06607-2434)
PHONE..................................203 366-5253
Kris Lorch, *President*
Fred Lorch, *Vice Pres*
Ken Popadic, *Traffic Dir*
▲ **EMP:** 42 **EST:** 1958
SQ FT: 28,800
SALES (est): 4.3MM **Privately Held**
WEB: www.thermowells.com
SIC: 3822 3823 Mfg Environmental Controls Mfg Process Control Instruments

(G-370)
ALTERNATIVE PROSTHETIC SVCS
Also Called: A P S
191 Bennett St (06605-2902)
PHONE..................................203 367-1212
Michael Curtin, *President*
EMP: 3
SALES: 450K **Privately Held**
SIC: 3842 Mfg Surgical Appliances/Supplies

▲ = Import ▼=Export
◆ =Import/Export

(G-371)
ALUMINUM FINISHING COMPANY INC
1575 Railroad Ave (06605-2031)
P.O. Box 3379 (06605-0379)
PHONE..................................203 333-1690
Edward Sivri, *President*
EMP: 26
SALES: 2.5MM **Privately Held**
SIC: 3471 Plating/Polishing Service

(G-372)
AMERICAN FNSHG SPECIALISTS INC
40 Cowles St (06607-2101)
PHONE..................................203 367-0663
Tim Calahan, *President*
EMP: 6
SALES (est): 733.1K **Privately Held**
SIC: 3599 Machine Shop Jobbing & Repair

(G-373)
AMERICAN HYDROGEN NORTHEAST
520 Savoy St (06606-4125)
PHONE..................................203 449-4614
Roy E McAlister, *Principal*
Daniel J Valentine, *Treasurer*
EMP: 40
SALES (est): 1.7MM **Privately Held**
SIC: 3999 Manufacturing Industries, Nec, Nsk

(G-374)
AMERICAN MOLDED PRODUCTS INC
130 Front St (06606-5109)
PHONE..................................203 333-0183
Mehmed Ramic, *President*
Paul Cipriono Taulo, *Vice Pres*
EMP: 10
SQ FT: 4,800
SALES (est): 1.3MM **Privately Held**
WEB: www.americanmoldedproducts.com
SIC: 3089 3544 Mfg Plastic Products Mfg Dies/Tools/Jigs/Fixtures

(G-375)
AMODEX PRODUCTS INC
1354 State St (06605-2003)
P.O. Box 3332 (06605-0332)
PHONE..................................203 335-1255
Sylvia Fatse, *President*
Beverlee F Dacey, *Vice Pres*
Peter Dacey, *Opers Staff*
Alexander Dacey, *Sales Staff*
Nicolas Dacey, *Info Tech Dir*
EMP: 30 **EST:** 1957
SQ FT: 1,500
SALES (est): 6.8MM **Privately Held**
SIC: 2842 2844 2841 Mfg Stain Removers Hand Cream & Soap

(G-376)
ARCADE TECHNOLOGY LLC
Also Called: A R C O
38 Union Ave (06607-2336)
PHONE..................................203 366-3871
Steve Pepe, *Mng Member*
William Rhone,
EMP: 50
SQ FT: 45,000
SALES: 5.6MM **Privately Held**
SIC: 3469 3644 3599 3544 Mfg Metal Stampings Mfg Nonconductv Wire Dvc Mfg Industrial Machinery

(G-377)
ARCHITECTURAL STONE GROUP LLC
9 Island Brook Ave (06606-5113)
PHONE..................................203 494-5451
Tom Astram, *Principal*
EMP: 6
SALES (est): 397.8K **Privately Held**
SIC: 3281 Mfg Cut Stone/Products

(G-378)
AUDUBON COPY SHPPE OF FIRFIELD
540 Barnum Ave Ste 4 (06608-2461)
PHONE..................................203 259-4311
Robert Love, *President*
Linda Love, *Vice Pres*
EMP: 5
SQ FT: 1,800
SALES (est): 636K **Privately Held**
SIC: 2752 7334 2741 Operates As Offset Printing Shop High Speed Copy Shop And Does Desktop Publishing

(G-379)
B & C SAND & GRAVEL COMPANY
412 Housatonic Ave (06604-3326)
PHONE..................................203 335-6640
Edward T Burns, *Owner*
EMP: 5
SALES (est): 525.5K **Privately Held**
SIC: 1442 Whol Brick/Stone Material

(G-380)
B & E JUICES INC
Also Called: Snapple Juices
550 Knowlton St (06608-1816)
PHONE..................................203 333-1802
Robert Clyne, *President*
Mitchell Clyne, *Vice Pres*
Rene Ferellec, *Vice Pres*
EMP: 20
SQ FT: 40,000
SALES (est): 6.7MM **Privately Held**
SIC: 2086 Mfg Bottled/Canned Soft Drinks

(G-381)
BECKSON MANUFACTURING INC (PA)
165 Holland Ave (06605-2136)
P.O. Box 3336 (06605-0336)
PHONE..................................203 366-3644
Frank Sbeckerer, *President*
Eloise Beckerer, *Vice Pres*
Frank S Beckerer Jr, *Treasurer*
◆ **EMP:** 30
SQ FT: 15,000
SALES (est): 8.3MM **Privately Held**
WEB: www.becksonmfg.com
SIC: 3561 3429 3083 Mfg Pumps/Pumping Equipment Mfg Hardware Mfg Laminated Plastic Plate/Sheet

(G-382)
BEN BAENA & SON
Also Called: Baena Ben & Matthew
218 Charles St (06606-5661)
PHONE..................................203 334-8568
Matthew Baena, *Partner*
Irene Baena Robinson, *Partner*
EMP: 6 **EST:** 1947
SQ FT: 2,400
SALES: 700K **Privately Held**
SIC: 2591 7641 Manufactures Window Swags And Custom Homefurnishings And Does Custom Upholstering Of Window Treatments

(G-383)
BL PRINTING SHOP
Also Called: Dart Products Screen Printing
3442 Fairfield Ave (06605-3226)
PHONE..................................203 334-7779
Richard L Testani, *President*
Lisa Santos, *President*
Michelle Testani, *Vice Pres*
EMP: 3 **EST:** 1972
SQ FT: 5,000
SALES: 200K **Privately Held**
SIC: 2759 Commercial Printing

(G-384)
BLACK ROCK TECH GROUP LLC
211 State St Ste 203 (06604-4824)
PHONE..................................203 916-7200
Alicen Champagne, *Accounts Mgr*
Jennifer Saccu, *Sales Staff*
John East,
EMP: 12
SQ FT: 3,000
SALES (est): 4.4MM **Privately Held**
SIC: 3571 Mfg Electronic Computers

(G-385)
BOSTON ENDO-SURGICAL TECH LLC
Also Called: Pep Be-St
1146 Barnum Ave (06610-2705)
PHONE..................................203 336-6479
Alan M Huffenus, *CEO*
Kenneth Lisk, *President*
EMP: 98 **EST:** 2012
SALES (est): 2.4MM
SALES (corp-wide): 770.6MM **Publicly Held**
SIC: 3841 5047 Mfg Surgical/Medical Instruments Whol Medical/Hospital Equipment
HQ: Precision Engineered Products Llc
110 Frank Mossberg Dr
Attleboro MA 02703
508 226-5600

(G-386)
BRI METAL WORKS INC
105 Island Brook Ave (06606-5132)
P.O. Box 5540 (06610-0540)
PHONE..................................203 368-1649
Jeffrey Mc Cathron, *President*
Joseph Mc Cathron, *Chairman*
Shirley Mc Cathron, *Treasurer*
Patricia Mc Cathron, *Admin Sec*
EMP: 6
SQ FT: 67,000
SALES (est): 799K **Privately Held**
SIC: 3441 7699 Structural Metal Fabrication Repair Services

(G-387)
BRIDGEPORT BOATWORK INC (PA)
837 Seaview Ave (06607-1607)
PHONE..................................860 536-9651
Harry Boardsen, *President*
Melissa Howard, *Bookkeeper*
EMP: 5
SQ FT: 50,000
SALES: 5MM **Privately Held**
SIC: 3731 Shipbuilding/Repairing

(G-388)
BRIDGEPORT INSULATED WIRE CO (PA)
51 Brookfield Ave (06610-3004)
P.O. Box 5217 (06610-0217)
PHONE..................................203 333-3191
Christopher Pelletier, *CEO*
Ronald A Pelletier, *Chairman*
Milton L Cohn, *Admin Sec*
EMP: 30
SQ FT: 16,000
SALES (est): 5.6MM **Privately Held**
SIC: 3357 3496 3315 Nonferrous Wire-drawing/Insulating Mfg Misc Fabricated Wire Products Mfg Steel Wire/Related Products

(G-389)
BRIDGEPORT PROC & MFG LLC
155 Davenport St (06607)
PHONE..................................203 612-7733
Moises R Prieto, *Mng Member*
Christopher J Taylor, *Manager*
EMP: 6
SALES (est): 235.9K **Privately Held**
SIC: 3999 Mfg Misc Products

(G-390)
BRIDGEPORT TL & STAMPING CORP
35 Burr Ct (06605-2204)
PHONE..................................203 336-2501
Julius Kish, *President*
Rolf Schmidt, *Vice Pres*
Sharon Kish, *Admin Sec*
Darlene Kish, *Asst Sec*
EMP: 21 **EST:** 1939
SQ FT: 14,000
SALES (est): 3.8MM **Privately Held**
SIC: 3469 3544 Mfg Metal Stampings Mfg Dies/Tools/Jigs/Fixtures

(G-391)
BRODY PRINTING COMPANY INC
265 Central Ave (06607-2495)
PHONE..................................203 384-9313
Karen Brody Collett, *CEO*
Preseo Bonacci, *President*
EMP: 18 **EST:** 1971
SQ FT: 13,500
SALES (est): 3.3MM **Privately Held**
WEB: www.brodyprinting.com
SIC: 2752 Lithographic Commercial Printing

(G-392)
BUSWELL MANUFACTURING CO INC
229 Merriam St (06604-2915)
PHONE..................................203 334-6069
Norman Buecher, *President*
Mildred Fitch, *Vice Pres*
EMP: 10
SQ FT: 9,000
SALES: 1.8MM **Privately Held**
WEB: www.buswellmfg.com
SIC: 3562 3599 Mfg Of Non Metallic Die Cutting Seals

(G-393)
BYRNE WOODWORKING INC
170 Herbert St (06604-2903)
PHONE..................................203 953-3205
Frank Byrne, *Principal*
EMP: 4
SALES (est): 486K **Privately Held**
SIC: 2431 Mfg Millwork

(G-394)
CALZONE LTD (PA)
Also Called: Calzone Case Company
225 Black Rock Ave (06605-1204)
PHONE..................................203 367-5766
Joseph Edward Calzone III, *President*
Donald Sessions, *General Mgr*
Joseph E Calzone Jr, *Corp Secy*
Vincent James Calzone, *Vice Pres*
Stephen Bajda, *Controller*
▲ **EMP:** 50
SQ FT: 26,000
SALES (est): 19.5MM **Privately Held**
WEB: www.calzonecase.com
SIC: 3161 Mfg Luggage

(G-395)
CARDINAL SHEHAN CENTER INC
1494 Main St (06604-3600)
PHONE..................................203 336-4468
Terrance O'Connor, *Director*
Christine Bianchi, *Program Dir*
Dj Ellis, *Program Dir*
Jodie Delach, *Admin Asst*
EMP: 30
SALES: 1.7MM **Privately Held**
WEB: www.shehancenter.org
SIC: 3999 Mfg Misc Products

(G-396)
CASCO PRODUCTS CORPORATION (HQ)
1000 Lafayette Blvd # 100 (06604-4725)
PHONE..................................203 922-3200
Scott Brown, *General Mgr*
Mike Dietz, *Vice Pres*
Chris Rountos, *Engrg Dir*
Walter Wood, *QC Mgr*
James Langelotti, *Treasurer*
▲ **EMP:** 15
SQ FT: 168,000
SALES (est): 21.5MM
SALES (corp-wide): 8.2B **Publicly Held**
WEB: www.cascoglobal.com
SIC: 3714 Mfg Motor Vehicle Parts/Accessories
PA: Amphenol Corporation
358 Hall Ave
Wallingford CT 06492
203 265-8900

(G-397)
CHRISTOPOULOS DESIGNS INC
195 Dewey St (06605-2114)
PHONE..................................203 576-1110
George Christopoulos, *President*
Nicholas Daniolos, *Treasurer*
EMP: 10
SQ FT: 10,000
SALES (est): 1.4MM **Privately Held**
WEB: www.christopoulosdesigns.com
SIC: 2511 2517 2434 Mfg Wood Household Furniture Mfg Wood Tv/Radio Cabinets Mfg Wood Kitchen Cabinets

(G-398)
COASTAL PALLET CORPORATION
135 E Washington Ave (06604-3607)
PHONE..................................203 333-1892
EMP: 25

SQ FT: 15,000
SALES: 3MM **Privately Held**
WEB: www.coastalpallet.com
SIC: 2448 2441 Wood Pallets And Skids, Nsk

(G-399)
COMEX MACHINERY
Also Called: Industrial Prcision Components
145 Front St (06606-5108)
PHONE..................................203 334-2196
Paul Huber, *President*
Theodore Jeffries, *Vice Pres*
EMP: 5
SQ FT: 20,000
SALES (est): 90.3K **Privately Held**
SIC: 3545 3523 Mfg Machine Tool Accessories Mfg Farm Machinery/Equipment

(G-400)
CONNECTICUT ANODIZING FINSHG
128 Logan St (06607-1930)
PHONE..................................203 367-1765
Victor Sinko II, *President*
EMP: 21
SQ FT: 24,000
SALES (est): 2.8MM **Privately Held**
SIC: 3471 Plating/Polishing Service

(G-401)
DAYBRAKE DONUTS INC
941 Madison Ave (06606-5218)
PHONE..................................203 368-4962
Thomas Devaulinius, *President*
EMP: 12
SALES (est): 1.1MM **Privately Held**
SIC: 2051 5812 Mfg Bread/Related Products

(G-402)
DECORATOR SERVICES INC
25 Wells St Ste 1 (06604-2800)
PHONE..................................203 384-8144
Charles Musante, *President*
Frances Musante, *Admin Sec*
EMP: 22
SQ FT: 9,500
SALES (est): 1.8MM **Privately Held**
SIC: 2391 2591 Mfg Drapes & Vertical Blinds

(G-403)
DELCON INDUSTRIES LLC
560 N Washington Ave # 4 (06604-2900)
PHONE..................................203 331-9720
Ronald Delmonico, *Principal*
EMP: 3
SALES (est): 200.6K **Privately Held**
SIC: 3999 Mfg Misc Products

(G-404)
DELTA-RAY INDUSTRIES INC
805 Housatonic Ave (06604-2807)
PHONE..................................203 367-9903
John M Ray, *President*
Slawek Karpinski, *Engineer*
EMP: 10
SALES (est): 2.4MM **Privately Held**
SIC: 3728 Mfg Aircraft Parts/Equipment

(G-405)
DEVAR INC
706 Bostwick Ave (06605-2396)
PHONE..................................203 368-6751
A James Ruscito, *President*
Marianne Ruscito, *Treasurer*
Anthony J Ruscito, *Director*
EMP: 30
SQ FT: 33,000
SALES (est): 5.6MM **Privately Held**
WEB: www.devarinc.com
SIC: 3625 5084 3823 Mfg Relays/Industrial Controls Whol Industrial Equipment Mfg Process Control Instruments

(G-406)
DEYULIO SAUSAGE COMPANY LLC
1501 State St (06605-2010)
PHONE..................................203 348-1863
Lauren Oxer, *Principal*
Michael Taylor, *Sales Mgr*
Nicholas J Deyulio,
EMP: 10
SQ FT: 700
SALES (est): 909.6K **Privately Held**
SIC: 2013 Mfg Prepared Meats

(G-407)
DRS NAVAL POWER SYSTEMS INC
141 North Ave (06606-5120)
PHONE..................................203 366-5211
Shaune Miller, *Purch Agent*
EMP: 300
SALES (corp-wide): 8.9B **Privately Held**
SIC: 3621 Mfg Motors/Generators
HQ: Drs Naval Power Systems, Inc
4265 N 30th St
Milwaukee WI 53216
414 875-4314

(G-408)
DRS NAVAL POWER SYSTEMS INC
206 Island Brook Ave (06606-5118)
PHONE..................................203 366-5211
Gene Frohman, *President*
Rodney Holt, *Branch Mgr*
EMP: 40
SALES (corp-wide): 8.9B **Privately Held**
WEB: www.engineeredsupport.com
SIC: 3621 Mfg Motors/Generators
HQ: Drs Naval Power Systems, Inc
4265 N 30th St
Milwaukee WI 53216
414 875-4314

(G-409)
E&S AUTOMOTIVE OPERATIONS LLC
425 Boston Ave (06610-1701)
PHONE..................................203 332-4555
Harry Gill, *Owner*
EMP: 3
SALES (est): 312.7K **Privately Held**
SIC: 2869 Mfg Industrial Organic Chemicals

(G-410)
EDCO INDUSTRIES INC
203 Dekalb Ave (06607-2492)
PHONE..................................203 333-8982
John Thomas Szalan, *President*
Anne Marie Szalan, *Vice Pres*
▲ **EMP:** 16
SQ FT: 13,500
SALES (est): 2.8MM **Privately Held**
SIC: 3089 5162 Mfg Plastic Products Whol Plastic Materials/Shapes

(G-411)
EXECUTIVE OFFICE SERVICES INC
2085 Madison Ave (06606-3234)
PHONE..................................203 373-1333
Ben Carrara, *Vice Pres*
EMP: 22
SALES (est): 2.8MM **Privately Held**
SIC: 2752 2791 2759 Lithographic Commercial Printing Typesetting Services Commercial Printing

(G-412)
EXTRA FUEL
540 Boston Ave (06610-1705)
PHONE..................................203 330-0613
Yasmin Mazick, *Principal*
EMP: 3
SALES (est): 243.2K **Privately Held**
SIC: 2869 Mfg Industrial Organic Chemicals

(G-413)
FEROLETO STEEL COMPANY INC (DH)
300 Scofield Ave (06605-2931)
P.O. Box 3344 (06605-0344)
PHONE..................................203 366-3263
Robert Siitonen, *President*
Bob Siitonen, *Principal*
Jim Hillas, *Senior VP*
Ronald Penaiti, *Senior VP*
Michael Pierson, *Vice Pres*
▲ **EMP:** 78
SQ FT: 200,000
SALES (est): 12.6MM **Privately Held**
WEB: www.feroletosteel.com
SIC: 3316 Mfg Cold-Rolled Steel Shapes
HQ: Toyota Tsusho America, Inc.
805 3rd Ave Fl 17
New York NY 10022
212 355-3600

(G-414)
FLUTED PARTITION INC (PA)
850 Union Ave (06607-1137)
PHONE..................................203 368-2548
Arthur M Vietze Jr, *President*
Rudolph Neidermeir, *Chairman*
Robert Neidermeir, *Vice Pres*
John Rainieri, *Financial Exec*
EMP: 125
SQ FT: 120,000
SALES (est): 20.9MM **Privately Held**
WEB: www.flutedpartition.com
SIC: 2671 2653 2631 Mfg Coated Or Laminated Packaging Paper Or Plastic Film Corrugated & Solid Fiber Paperboard Mill

(G-415)
FLUTED PARTITION INC
Cell Pack Div
850 Union Ave (06607-1137)
PHONE..................................203 334-3500
Robert Niedermeier, *President*
Rudy Niedermeier, *Manager*
EMP: 11
SALES (corp-wide): 20.9MM **Privately Held**
WEB: www.flutedpartition.com
SIC: 2653 Mfg Corrugated Partitions
PA: Fluted Partition, Inc.
850 Union Ave
Bridgeport CT 06607
203 368-2548

(G-416)
FRUTA JUICE BAR LLC
295 Fairfield Ave (06604-4207)
PHONE..................................203 690-9168
Christopher Jarrin, *Principal*
EMP: 9 **EST:** 2012
SALES (est): 767.8K **Privately Held**
SIC: 2037 Mfg Frozen Fruits/Vegetables

(G-417)
FULCRUM PROMOTIONS & PRINTING
75 Wheeler Ave Apt 102 (06606-5611)
PHONE..................................203 909-6362
Gia Marie Vacca, *Principal*
EMP: 4
SALES (est): 263.6K **Privately Held**
SIC: 2752 Lithographic Commercial Printing

(G-418)
GENERAL ELECTRIC COMPANY
1285 Boston Ave (06610-2693)
PHONE..................................203 396-1572
Bill O'Brien, *Plant Mgr*
Bob Landa, *Design Engr*
EMP: 100
SALES (corp-wide): 121.6B **Publicly Held**
SIC: 3625 Mfg Controls & Switches
PA: General Electric Company
5 Necco St
Boston MA 02210
617 443-3000

(G-419)
GENERAL SHEET METAL WORKS INC
120 Silliman Ave (06605-2185)
PHONE..................................203 333-6111
Jeffrey D Cibulas, *President*
EMP: 10 **EST:** 1916
SQ FT: 6,500
SALES: 780K **Privately Held**
SIC: 3444 1761 Sheet Metal Fabrication

(G-420)
GLOBAL SCENIC SERVICES INC
46 Brookfield Ave (06610-3005)
PHONE..................................203 334-2130
Warren Katz, *President*
James Malski, *Acting Pres*
John Cashman, *Project Mgr*
▲ **EMP:** 46
SQ FT: 40,000
SALES (est): 7MM **Privately Held**
WEB: www.globalscenicservices.com
SIC: 3999 Mfg Misc Products

(G-421)
GRANT MANUFACTURING & MCH CO
90 Silliman Ave (06605-2127)
P.O. Box 3345 (06605-0345)
PHONE..................................203 366-4557
Bruce W Mc Naughton, *Ch of Bd*
EMP: 20 **EST:** 1904
SQ FT: 22,000
SALES (est): 2.9MM **Privately Held**
SIC: 3542 Mfg Machine Tools-Forming

(G-422)
GRIFFITH COMPANY
239 Asylum St (06610-2103)
PHONE..................................203 333-5557
Gary Griffith, *President*
Emma Griffith, *Corp Secy*
EMP: 5 **EST:** 1936
SQ FT: 30,000
SALES (est): 915K **Privately Held**
SIC: 2842 5087 Mfg Specialty Cleaning Chemicals & Whol Cleaning Equipment

(G-423)
HARRISON ENTERPRISE LLC
Also Called: Philip Cups
237 Asylum St (06610-2103)
PHONE..................................914 665-8348
Richard Harrison,
Roxanne Gittens,
EMP: 4
SALES (est): 599.2K **Privately Held**
WEB: www.harrisonenterprise.com
SIC: 2679 Mfg Converted Paper Products

(G-424)
HARRY THOMMEN COMPANY
Also Called: Thommen, Harry Co
3404 Fairfield Ave (06605-3225)
PHONE..................................203 333-3637
Jeffrey Thommen, *President*
EMP: 4
SQ FT: 2,500
SALES (est): 561.5K **Privately Held**
SIC: 7692 3498 Welding & Fabricating

(G-425)
HISPANIC ENTERPRISES INC
Also Called: Emtec Metal Products
200 Cogswell St (06610-1941)
PHONE..................................203 588-9334
Winston A Malcolm, *President*
EMP: 20
SQ FT: 12,500
SALES (est): 2.3MM **Privately Held**
SIC: 3444 Mfg Sheet Metalwork

(G-426)
HONEY CELL INC (PA)
850 Union Ave (06607-1137)
PHONE..................................203 925-1818
Rudolph Niedermeier, *President*
Arthur Vietze Jr, *Vice Pres*
William Vietze, *Vice Pres*
Robert Niedermeier, *Treasurer*
EMP: 4
SALES: 13.9MM **Privately Held**
SIC: 2679 Mfg Converted Paper Products

(G-427)
HOPE KIT CBINETS STONE SUP LLC (PA)
1901 Commerce Dr (06605-2226)
PHONE..................................203 610-6147
Sung Young,
Ren Wu Zheng,
▲ **EMP:** 4
SALES (est): 800.6K **Privately Held**
SIC: 2434 Trade Contractor

(G-428)
HORBERG INDUSTRIES INC
19 Staples St (06604-2202)
P.O. Box 6273 (06606-0273)
PHONE..................................203 334-9444
Robert C Leety, *President*
Anita Stabler, *Executive Asst*
EMP: 10 **EST:** 1935
SQ FT: 10,000

▲ = Import ▼=Export
◆ =Import/Export

SALES (est): 1.7MM Privately Held
WEB: www.horberg.com
SIC: 3452 Mfg Industrial Machinery

(G-429)
IDENTIFICATION PRODUCTS CORP
1073 State St (06605-1504)
PHONE.................................203 334-5969
Hugh F McCann, *Manager*
EMP: 10
SALES (corp-wide): 7.4MM Privately Held
SIC: 2759 3479 2671 Commercial Printing Coating/Engraving Service Mfg Packaging Paper/Film
PA: Identification Products Corp
104 Silliman Ave
Bridgeport CT 06605
203 334-5969

(G-430)
INNOVATIVE ARC TUBES CORP
Also Called: I T C
1240 Central Ave (06607-1065)
PHONE.................................203 333-1031
Vijay Mehan, *President*
Ramesh Mehan, *Chairman*
Renee Mehan, *Treasurer*
▲ EMP: 25
SQ FT: 30,000
SALES: 3MM
SALES (corp-wide): 10MM Privately Held
WEB: www.itc-1.com
SIC: 3646 Mfg Commercial Lighting Fixtures
PA: Innovative Technologies Corp.
1020 Woodman Dr Ste 100
Dayton OH 45432
937 252-2145

(G-431)
INTEGRATED PRINT SOLUTIONS INC
Also Called: Everett Print
35 Benham Ave Ste 2 (06605-1436)
PHONE.................................203 330-0200
Philip Palmieri, *President*
Elizabeth Alesevich, *Marketing Mgr*
▲ EMP: 11
SQ FT: 40,000
SALES (est): 2.1MM Privately Held
SIC: 2759 Commercial Printing

(G-432)
J J BOX CO INC
25 Admiral St (06605-1808)
PHONE.................................203 367-1211
James Garamella, *President*
EMP: 9
SQ FT: 10,000
SALES: 1.4MM Privately Held
SIC: 2448 Mfg Wood Containers

(G-433)
JAMES IPPOLITO & CO CONN INC
1069 Conn Ave Ste 16 (06607-1228)
PHONE.................................203 366-3840
Gerald V Cavallo, *President*
EMP: 40 EST: 1995
SQ FT: 25,000
SALES (est): 7MM Privately Held
WEB: www.chinooksports.com
SIC: 3429 Mfg Hardware

(G-434)
JAMES J LICARI (PA)
Also Called: Licari Woodworking
300 N Washington Ave (06604-2810)
PHONE.................................203 333-5000
James Licari, *Owner*
EMP: 5
SALES: 600K Privately Held
SIC: 2431 Mfg Millwork

(G-435)
JERRYS PRINTING & GRAPHICS LLC
1183 Broad St (06604-4172)
PHONE.................................203 384-0015
Scott G Fisher, *President*
Barbara Fisher,
Ernest Fisher,
EMP: 3
SQ FT: 1,200
SALES: 150K Privately Held
SIC: 2752 7334 2791 2789 Lithographic Coml Print Photocopying Service Typesetting Services Bookbinding/Related Work

(G-436)
JOHN JUNE CUSTOM CABINETRY LLC
541 Fairfield Ave (06604-3904)
PHONE.................................203 334-1720
John June,
EMP: 8
SALES (est): 826.6K Privately Held
SIC: 2434 Mfg Wood Kitchen Cabinets

(G-437)
JOZEF CUSTOM IRONWORKS INC
Also Called: Aesthetic Blacksmithing
250 Smith St (06607-2219)
PHONE.................................203 384-6363
Erik Witkowski, *CEO*
Jozef Witkowski, *President*
Lidia Botero, *General Mgr*
▲ EMP: 16 EST: 1994
SQ FT: 40,000
SALES (est): 2.7MM Privately Held
WEB: www.jozef.net
SIC: 3446 Mfg Architectural Metalwork

(G-438)
KAFA GROUP LLC
800 Union Ave (06607-1422)
PHONE.................................475 275-0090
Steve McKenzie, *President*
Nicole McKenzie, *Vice Pres*
EMP: 8
SQ FT: 1,200
SALES (est): 819.4K Privately Held
SIC: 1389 1542 1541 Oil/Gas Field Services Nonresidential Construction Industrial Building Construction

(G-439)
KERIGANS FUEL INC
258 Dekalb Ave (06607-2417)
PHONE.................................203 334-3646
James W Kerigan, *President*
EMP: 4
SALES (est): 641.5K Privately Held
SIC: 3433 Mfg Heating Equipment-Non-electric

(G-440)
KEYSTONE RV COMPANY
2660 North Ave (06604-2355)
PHONE.................................203 367-9847
Stephen Holmes, *General Mgr*
Michael McGuire, *Sales Mgr*
P A Giorgio, *Manager*
EMP: 150
SALES (corp-wide): 7.8B Publicly Held
WEB: www.keystonerv.com
SIC: 3792 Mfg Travel Trailers/Campers
HQ: Keystone Rv Company
2642 Hackberry Dr
Goshen IN 46526

(G-441)
KITCHEN CAB RESURFACING LLC
136 Merriam St (06604-2912)
PHONE.................................203 334-2857
James Svab, *President*
EMP: 10
SALES (est): 929K Privately Held
WEB: www.kcrct.com
SIC: 2434 Mfg Wood Kitchen Cabinets

(G-442)
L P MACADAMS COMPANY INC
50 Austin St (06604-5437)
P.O. Box 5540 (06610-0540)
PHONE.................................203 366-3647
D Paul Macadams, *CEO*
Lawrence P Macadams, *President*
Kay Macadams, *Vice Pres*
▲ EMP: 85
SQ FT: 150,000
SALES (est): 11.8MM Privately Held
WEB: www.lpmacadams.com
SIC: 2759 7331 4225 2752 Commercial Printing Direct Mail Ad Svcs General Warehse/Storage Lithographic Coml Print

(G-443)
LACEY MANUFACTURING CO LLC
1146 Barnum Ave (06610-2794)
PHONE.................................203 336-7427
Ken Lisk, *President*
▲ EMP: 310
SQ FT: 100,000
SALES (est): 75MM
SALES (corp-wide): 770.6MM Publicly Held
WEB: www.laceymfg.com
SIC: 3841 3089 Mfg Surgical/Medical Instruments Mfg Plastic Products
HQ: Precision Engineered Products Llc
110 Frank Mossberg Dr
Attleboro MA 02703
508 226-5600

(G-444)
LAKE GRINDING COMPANY
231 Asylum St (06610-2103)
PHONE.................................203 336-3767
Marion Lake, *President*
Marian Crichton Lake, *Director*
Nancy Johnson, *Admin Sec*
EMP: 3
SQ FT: 1,500
SALES (est): 257.6K Privately Held
SIC: 3471 Finishing Metals Or Formed Products

(G-445)
LEONARD F BROOKS (PA)
Also Called: A & B Ice Co
199 Asylum St (06610-2103)
PHONE.................................203 335-4934
Leonard F Brooks, *Owner*
EMP: 5
SQ FT: 5,600
SALES (est): 600K Privately Held
SIC: 2097 Mfg Ice

(G-446)
MARKAL FINISHING CO INC
400 Bostwick Ave (06605-2407)
PHONE.................................203 384-8219
Craig Sander, *President*
Christine Royer, *Corp Secy*
Jason Sanden, *Vice Pres*
EMP: 44 EST: 1961
SQ FT: 40,000
SALES (est): 7.4MM Privately Held
SIC: 2672 Mfg Coated/Laminated Paper

(G-447)
MARS ARCHITECTURAL MILLWORK
55 Randall Ave Ste A (06606-5701)
PHONE.................................203 579-2632
Richard Marsilio, *President*
Kara Marsilio, *Vice Pres*
EMP: 4
SQ FT: 8,000
SALES (est): 338.8K Privately Held
SIC: 2431 Architectural Woodworking/Millwork

(G-448)
MASTRIANI GOURMET FOOD LLC
570 Barnum Ave (06608-2446)
PHONE.................................203 368-9556
Ralph Mastriani, *Principal*
Althea Paris,
EMP: 3
SALES (est): 199K Privately Held
SIC: 2099 Gourmet Pasta Manufacturing

(G-449)
MEDELCO INC
54 Washburn St (06605-1848)
PHONE.................................203 275-8070
Elaine Robinson, *President*
▲ EMP: 5
SQ FT: 76,000
SALES (est): 1MM Privately Held
WEB: www.medelcoinc.com
SIC: 3559 3229 3632 Mfg Misc Industry Machinery Mfg Pressed/Blown Glass Mfg Home Refrigerators/Freezers

(G-450)
MESSIAH DEVELOPMENT LLC
210 Congress St (06604-4007)
PHONE.................................203 368-2405
Collin Vice, *Mng Member*
EMP: 7
SALES (est): 539.4K Privately Held
SIC: 3271 Mfg Concrete Block/Brick

(G-451)
MILL MANUFACTURING INC
105 Willow St (06610-3220)
PHONE.................................203 367-9572
Karl E Ostberg, *President*
EMP: 8
SQ FT: 2,000
SALES (est): 1.1MM Privately Held
SIC: 3599 Mfg Industrial Machinery

(G-452)
MOHAWK TOOL AND DIE MFG CO INC
25 Wells St Ste 4 (06604-2800)
PHONE.................................203 367-2181
Vincent A Bonazzo, *President*
Lucy R Bonazzo, *Admin Sec*
▲ EMP: 13 EST: 1946
SQ FT: 8,000
SALES (est): 2MM Privately Held
SIC: 3544 3089 Mfg Dies/Tools/Jigs/Fixtures Mfg Plastic Products

(G-453)
MOORE TOOL COMPANY INC (HQ)
800 Union Ave (06607-1422)
PHONE.................................203 366-3224
Newman Marsilius III, *President*
Newman M Marsilius, *Vice Pres*
Kathie Dennis, *Purch Mgr*
Sebastian Zawadzki, *Engineer*
◆ EMP: 63
SQ FT: 334,113
SALES (est): 23.8MM
SALES (corp-wide): 65.8MM Privately Held
SIC: 3541 3544 3545 Mfg Machine Tools-Cutting Mfg Dies/Tools/Jigs/Fixtures Mfg Machine Tool Accessories
PA: Pmt Group, Inc.
800 Union Ave
Bridgeport CT 06607
203 367-8675

(G-454)
MTJ MANUFACTURING INC
127 Wilmot Ave (06607-1835)
PHONE.................................203 334-4939
Mark Carpenter, *President*
EMP: 6
SALES (est): 889.8K Privately Held
WEB: www.mtjmanufacturing.com
SIC: 3441 Steel Fabricator

(G-455)
NEUROHYDRATE LLC
4637 Main St Unit 5 (06606-1838)
PHONE.................................203 799-7900
Justin Higgins,
Hamid Sami,
EMP: 5
SQ FT: 4,500
SALES (est): 129.5K Privately Held
SIC: 2834 Mfg Pharmaceutical Preparations

(G-456)
NEW ENGLAND GRINDING AND MA
30 Radel St (06607-2113)
PHONE.................................203 333-1885
Walter Jacques,
EMP: 4
SQ FT: 30,000
SALES (est): 561.6K Privately Held
SIC: 3599 Business Services

(G-457)
NEW RESOURCES GROUP INC
955 Conn Ave Ste 1211 (06607-1246)
P.O. Box 320049, Fairfield (06825-0049)
PHONE..................................203 366-1000
William Wales, *President*
Annamari Wales, *Admin Sec*
▲ **EMP:** 4
SQ FT: 7,500
SALES: 1MM **Privately Held**
WEB: www.nrgideas.com
SIC: 3088 8748 5074 Mfg Plastic Plumbing Fixtures Business Consulting Services Whol Plumbing Equipment/Supplies

(G-458)
NNTECHNOLOGY MOORE SYSTEMS LLC
800 Union Ave (06607-1422)
P.O. Box 1381 (06601-1381)
PHONE..................................203 366-3224
Ranae Wright, *Administration*
EMP: 4
SALES (corp-wide): 65.8MM **Privately Held**
SIC: 3827 Mfg Optical Instruments/Lenses
HQ: Moore Nanotechnology Systems Llc
230 Old Homestead Hwy
Swanzey NH 03446
603 352-3030

(G-459)
O & G INDUSTRIES INC
240 Bostwick Ave (06605-2434)
P.O. Box 907, Torrington (06790-0907)
PHONE..................................203 366-4586
John Leverty, *Branch Mgr*
EMP: 50
SALES (corp-wide): 538MM **Privately Held**
WEB: www.ogind.com
SIC: 3273 1771 1794 2951 Mfg Ready-Mixed Concrete Concrete Contractor Excavation Contractor Mfg Asphalt Mixtr/Blocks Nonresidential Cnstn
PA: O & G Industries, Inc.
112 Wall St
Torrington CT 06790
860 489-9261

(G-460)
OCEAN RIGGING LLC
1 Bostwick Ave (06605-2435)
PHONE..................................800 624-2101
Ian Williams,
Rick Granville,
EMP: 6
SALES (est): 740.8K **Privately Held**
SIC: 3731 Shipbuilding/Repairing

(G-461)
ORISHA ORACLE INC
59 Regent St (06606-2332)
PHONE..................................203 612-8989
Sherwaine Mathurin, *Principal*
EMP: 4
SALES (est): 93.7K **Privately Held**
SIC: 7372 Prepackaged Software Services

(G-462)
PALMIERI INDUSTRIES INC
Also Called: Ctr
118 Burr Ct Ste 1 (06605-2210)
PHONE..................................203 384-6020
Joseph A Palmieri Jr, *President*
Robert Kellerman, *Vice Pres*
Dan Bresnahan, *Project Mgr*
Tim Firla, *Project Mgr*
EMP: 70
SALES (est): 15.8MM **Privately Held**
WEB: www.cctank.com
SIC: 1389 Oil/Gas Field Services

(G-463)
PARK DISTRIBUTORIES INC (PA)
Also Called: Universal Relay Company
347 Railroad Ave (06604-5424)
P.O. Box 1020 (06601-1020)
PHONE..................................203 579-2140
Alan Goodman, *President*
Rick Depaulis, *Principal*
Larry Depaulis, *Vice Pres*
Bill Miller, *Vice Pres*
Ricard Depaulis, *CFO*
EMP: 9 **EST:** 1966
SQ FT: 16,000
SALES (est): 3.1MM **Privately Held**
WEB: www.parkdistributors.com
SIC: 3625 5065 Mfg Relays/Industrial Controls Whol Electronic Parts/Equipment

(G-464)
PARK DISTRIBUTORIES INC
Also Called: Electronic Finishing Company
347 Railroad Ave (06604-5424)
P.O. Box 1020 (06601-1020)
PHONE..................................203 366-7200
Allan Goodman, *Manager*
EMP: 18
SALES (corp-wide): 3.1MM **Privately Held**
WEB: www.parkdistributors.com
SIC: 3625 3679 Mfg Relays/Industrial Controls Mfg Electronic Components
PA: Park Distributories Inc.
347 Railroad Ave
Bridgeport CT 06604
203 579-2140

(G-465)
PEQUONNOCK IRONWORKS INC
621 Knowlton St (06608-1536)
P.O. Box 6280 (06606-0280)
PHONE..................................203 336-2178
EMP: 15 **EST:** 1997
SALES (est): 1.8MM **Privately Held**
SIC: 3446 3312 Mfg Architectural Metalwork Blast Furnace-Steel Works

(G-466)
PEQUOT
1000 Lafayette Blvd # 1100 (06604-4710)
PHONE..................................800 620-1492
Christopher Duffy- Acevedo, *CEO*
Christopher Duffy-Acevedo, *CEO*
Stefanie Breitung Duffy, *CFO*
EMP: 5
SQ FT: 500
SALES: 2.5MM **Privately Held**
SIC: 3674 5074 1711 7382 Mfg Semiconductors/Dvcs Whol Plumbing Equip/Supp Plumbing/Heat/Ac Contr Security System Svcs

(G-467)
PEREY TURNSTILES INC
308 Bishop Ave (06610-3055)
PHONE..................................203 333-9400
M Edmund Hendrickson, *President*
Jeanne Hendrickson, *Treasurer*
EMP: 24 **EST:** 1999
SQ FT: 15,000
SALES (est): 8MM **Privately Held**
WEB: www.turnstile.com
SIC: 3829 Mfg Measuring/Controlling Devices

(G-468)
PHILLIPS FUEL SYSTEMS
109 Holland Ave (06605-2136)
PHONE..................................203 908-3323
Rodolfo Garcia, *Principal*
George Seganos, *Materials Mgr*
EMP: 6
SALES (est): 616.7K **Privately Held**
SIC: 3714 Mfg Motor Vehicle Parts/Accessories

(G-469)
PHILLIPS PUMP LLC
Also Called: Phillips Pumps
661 Lindley St (06606-5045)
P.O. Box 320742, Fairfield (06825-0742)
PHONE..................................203 576-6688
Patrick Crossin,
EMP: 10
SQ FT: 3,800
SALES: 2MM **Privately Held**
SIC: 3561 Mfg Pumps/Pumping Equipment

(G-470)
PLASTIC FACTORY LLC
678 Howard Ave (06605-1916)
P.O. Box 3111 (06605-0111)
PHONE..................................203 908-3468
Amelia Clark, *Sales Staff*
Robert J Carbone,
Barbara C Carbone,
EMP: 4
SALES (est): 697.3K **Privately Held**
SIC: 3081 3082 Mfg Unsupported Plastic Film/Sheet Mfg Plastic Profile Shapes

(G-471)
PMT GROUP INC (PA)
800 Union Ave (06607-1422)
PHONE..................................203 367-8675
Newman M Marsilius III, *President*
◆ **EMP:** 110
SQ FT: 218,000
SALES (est): 65.8MM **Privately Held**
WEB: www.producto.com
SIC: 3541 3545 3544 Mfg Machine Tool-Cutting Mfg Machine Tool Access Mfg Dies/Tools/Jigs/Fixt

(G-472)
POPLAR TOOL & MFG CO INC
420 Poplar St (06605-1644)
PHONE..................................203 333-4369
David Conroy, *President*
Rudolf Divjak, *Vice Pres*
EMP: 6 **EST:** 1951
SQ FT: 4,200
SALES (est): 450K **Privately Held**
SIC: 3599 Machine Shop

(G-473)
PRECISION ENGINEERED PDTS LLC
Also Called: Boston Endo-Surgical Tech
1146 Barnum Ave (06610-2705)
PHONE..................................203 336-6479
Alan M Huffenus, *CEO*
EMP: 7
SALES (corp-wide): 770.6MM **Publicly Held**
SIC: 3841 5047 Product Development & Contract Manufacturing Of Surgical Devices
HQ: Precision Engineered Products Llc
110 Frank Mossberg Dr
Attleboro MA 02703
508 226-5600

(G-474)
PRIME RESOURCES CORP
Also Called: Prime Line
1100 Boston Ave Bldg 1 (06610-2658)
PHONE..................................203 331-9100
Jeff Lederer, *President*
David Mercado, *Vice Pres*
Nelson Frey, *Prdtn Mgr*
Eileen Ferreira, *Purch Dir*
Michael Wiskind, *Finance Dir*
◆ **EMP:** 500
SQ FT: 128,000
SALES (est): 87.8MM
SALES (corp-wide): 3.7B **Privately Held**
WEB: www.primeworld.com
SIC: 3993 2759 Mfg Signs/Advertising Specialties Commercial Printing
PA: Broder Bros., Co.
6 Neshaminy Interplex Dr
Trevose PA 19053
215 291-0300

(G-475)
PRINT & POST SERVICES
1 Seaview Ave (06607-2400)
PHONE..................................203 336-0055
Gary Grossman, *Owner*
EMP: 6
SQ FT: 3,000
SALES (est): 421.1K **Privately Held**
SIC: 2759 Commercial Printing

(G-476)
PRODUCTO CORPORATION (HQ)
Also Called: Producto Machine Company, The
800 Union Ave (06607-1422)
PHONE..................................203 366-3224
Newman M Marsilius III, *CEO*
Joanne Clark, *Vice Pres*
Maynard Cotter, *Vice Pres*
Jon Krchnavy, *Vice Pres*
Newman Marsilius Jr, *Vice Pres*
EMP: 10
SALES (est): 37.3MM
SALES (corp-wide): 65.8MM **Privately Held**
WEB: www.ringprecision.com
SIC: 3541 3545 3544 Mfg Machine Tools-Cutting Mfg Machine Tool Accessories Mfg Dies/Tools/Jigs/Fixtures
PA: Pmt Group, Inc.
800 Union Ave
Bridgeport CT 06607
203 367-8675

(G-477)
QUALITY STAIRS INC
70 Logan St (06607-1930)
PHONE..................................203 367-8390
Lee Pereira, *President*
Jason Pereira, *Vice Pres*
Manuel Pereira, *Vice Pres*
Geomar Pereira, *Admin Sec*
EMP: 20
SQ FT: 8,000
SALES (est): 3.4MM **Privately Held**
SIC: 2431 3446 Mfg Millwork Mfg Architectural Metalwork

(G-478)
RADER INDUSTRIES INC
115 Island Brook Ave (06606-5132)
PHONE..................................203 334-6739
Sonia Halapin, *President*
Brian Halapin, *Corp Secy*
Donald S Halapin Jr, *Vice Pres*
EMP: 4
SQ FT: 10,000
SALES (est): 737.6K **Privately Held**
SIC: 3444 3471 7699 Mfg Sheet Metalwork Plating/Polishing Svcs Repair Services

(G-479)
RAYFLEX COMPANY INC
1061 Howard Ave (06605-1970)
PHONE..................................203 336-2173
Gregory Marcantonio, *President*
EMP: 4 **EST:** 1937
SQ FT: 4,000
SALES (est): 360K **Privately Held**
SIC: 3599 Machine Shop

(G-480)
READY4 PRINT LLC
2051 Main St (06604-2721)
PHONE..................................203 345-0376
Sean Reeves,
Todd Reaves,
EMP: 3
SALES (est): 338K **Privately Held**
SIC: 2752 Lithographic Commercial Printing

(G-481)
RELIABLE PLATING & POLSG CO
80 Bishop Ave (06607-1541)
PHONE..................................203 366-5261
Joseph D Bourdeau, *Ch of Bd*
James Bourdeau, *President*
Lynn Myers, *Treasurer*
EMP: 35 **EST:** 1956
SQ FT: 225,000
SALES (est): 3.6MM **Privately Held**
SIC: 3471 Metal Finishing

(G-482)
RICCO VISHNU
Also Called: Rich Snob Fashions
79 Sage Ave (06610-3061)
PHONE..................................203 449-0124
Raheem Nixon, *Owner*
EMP: 7
SALES (est): 181.7K **Privately Held**
SIC: 2389 Mfg Apparel/Accessories

(G-483)
RIVETING SYSTEMS USA LLC
Also Called: Grant Riveters USA
90 Silliman Ave (06605-2127)
PHONE..................................203 366-4557
Bruce W McNaughton, *Principal*
EMP: 6
SALES (est): 239.9K **Privately Held**
SIC: 3542 Mfg Machine Tools-Forming

(G-484)
ROTAIR AEROSPACE CORPORATION
964 Crescent Ave (06607-1066)
PHONE..............................203 576-6545
Wesley Harrington, *President*
Christine Kudravy, *Vice Pres*
EMP: 46 **EST:** 1975
SQ FT: 80,000
SALES (est): 11.5MM **Privately Held**
WEB: www.rotair.com
SIC: 3728 Mfg Aircraft Parts/Equipment

(G-485)
SASSONE LABWEAR LLC
Also Called: Labwear.com
480 Barnum Ave Ste 5 (06608-2459)
PHONE..............................860 666-4484
Robert Sassone, *Mng Member*
EMP: 5
SALES: 1.5MM **Privately Held**
SIC: 2326 2311 Mfg Men's/Boy's Work Clothing Mfg Men's/Boy's Suits/Coats

(G-486)
SAVETIME CORPORATION
2710 North Ave Ste 105b (06604-2352)
PHONE..............................203 382-2991
Donna Buckenmaier, *President*
Erwin Theodore Buckenmaier, *Chairman*
Robert Zuklie, *Vice Pres*
EMP: 14
SQ FT: 6,100
SALES (est): 1.1MM **Privately Held**
WEB: www.rainhandler.com
SIC: 3089 1761 Mfg Plastic Products Roofing/Siding Contractor

(G-487)
SCHWERDTLE STAMP COMPANY
41 Benham Ave (06605-1419)
P.O. Box 1461 (06601-1461)
PHONE..............................203 330-2750
Katherine Saint, *President*
John Schwerdtle Jr, *Treasurer*
Steve Francis, *Controller*
EMP: 35 **EST:** 1879
SQ FT: 14,000
SALES (est): 6.3MM **Privately Held**
WEB: www.schwerdtle.com
SIC: 3953 7336 Mfg Marking Devices Commercial Art/Graphic Design

(G-488)
SHARPAC LLC
Also Called: Sharpac Cutter Grinding & Sls
114 Miles St (06607-2111)
PHONE..............................203 384-0568
Kevin Foley, *Partner*
Brian Foley, *Partner*
EMP: 5
SQ FT: 3,000
SALES (est): 565.8K **Privately Held**
SIC: 3599 Tool & Cutter Grinding Service

(G-489)
SIGN MAINTENANCE SERVICE CO
Also Called: Smsc Flags and Flagpoles
24 Wallace St (06604-2733)
P.O. Box 508 (06601-0508)
PHONE..............................203 336-1051
Leonard Morano, *President*
Duke Morano, *Vice Pres*
EMP: 3
SQ FT: 5,000
SALES: 400K **Privately Held**
SIC: 3993 7699 Mfr & Service Electrical Signs

(G-490)
SIKORSKY AIRCRAFT CORPORATION
1201 South Ave (06604-5246)
PHONE..............................203 384-7532
Robert Brady, *Manager*
EMP: 500 **Publicly Held**
WEB: www.sikorsky.com
SIC: 3721 Mfg Aircraft
HQ: Sikorsky Aircraft Corporation
6900 Main St
Stratford CT 06614

(G-491)
SIKORSKY AIRCRAFT CORPORATION
1210 South Ave (06604-5243)
PHONE..............................203 386-4000
Edgar Baker, *Branch Mgr*
EMP: 138 **Publicly Held**
SIC: 3721 Mfg Aircraft
HQ: Sikorsky Aircraft Corporation
6900 Main St
Stratford CT 06614

(G-492)
SINGLE LOAD LLC
2056 Main St (06604-2720)
PHONE..............................860 944-7507
Vincent Bryant, *President*
Jack Cook, *Business Mgr*
EMP: 9 **EST:** 2012
SALES (est): 550K **Privately Held**
SIC: 3559 7389 Mfg Misc Industry Machinery Business Services At Non-Commercial Site

(G-493)
SMOKE & PRINT UNIVERSE
4106 Main St (06606-2301)
PHONE..............................203 540-5151
Syedbuali Naqvi, *Principal*
EMP: 4
SALES (est): 284.9K **Privately Held**
SIC: 2752 Lithographic Commercial Printing

(G-494)
SPEC PLATING INC
740 Seaview Ave (06607-1606)
PHONE..............................203 366-3638
Geoffrey Scott, *President*
Steve Balgach, *QC Mgr*
EMP: 14
SQ FT: 10,000
SALES (est): 1.4MM **Privately Held**
SIC: 3471 Electroplaters Of Metals

(G-495)
STERLING CUSTOM CABINETRY LLC
323 North Ave (06606-5125)
PHONE..............................203 335-5151
Charles Marsilio,
Salvatore K Dinardo,
EMP: 8
SALES (est): 72K **Privately Held**
SIC: 2434 Mfg Wood Kitchen Cabinets

(G-496)
STONE WORKSHOP LLC
1108 Railroad Ave (06605-1835)
PHONE..............................203 362-1144
Mario Muralles,
Daniel Manetta,
▲ **EMP:** 7
SQ FT: 12,000
SALES (est): 940.5K **Privately Held**
SIC: 3281 Mfg Cut Stone/Products

(G-497)
SUPERIOR FUEL CO
154 Admiral St (06605-1807)
PHONE..............................203 337-1213
EMP: 3
SALES (est): 149.4K **Privately Held**
SIC: 2869 Industrial Organic Chemicals, Nec

(G-498)
SWAGNIFICENT ENT LLC
Also Called: Ricco Vishnu Brew House
79 Sage Ave (06610-3061)
PHONE..............................203 449-0124
Raheem Nixon,
EMP: 7
SALES: 400K **Privately Held**
SIC: 2082 5813 Mfg Malt Beverages Drinking Place

(G-499)
TEES PLUS
850 Main St Fl 6 (06604-4917)
PHONE..............................800 782-8337
▲ **EMP:** 13
SALES: 38.7K **Privately Held**
SIC: 2759 Commercial Printing

(G-500)
UNGER ENTERPRISES LLC
425 Asylum St (06610-2105)
PHONE..............................203 366-4884
Rote Charles, *Vice Pres*
Peter Lupoli, *Vice Pres*
Bob Camp, *Project Mgr*
Charles Perry, *Prdtn Mgr*
Ken Paolini, *Purch Agent*
◆ **EMP:** 125 **EST:** 1975
SQ FT: 70,000
SALES (est): 29.6MM **Privately Held**
WEB: www.ungerglobal.com
SIC: 3423 Mfg Hand/Edge Tools

(G-501)
UNGER INDUSTRIAL LLC
425 Asylum St (06610-2105)
PHONE..............................203 336-3344
Hartley Cassady, *Mktg Dir*
Dane Unger,
EMP: 9
SALES (est): 1.3MM **Privately Held**
SIC: 3429 Mfg Hardware

(G-502)
US HIGHWAY PRODUCTS INC
Also Called: American Fiber Technologies
500 Bostwick Ave (06605-2440)
PHONE..............................203 336-0332
EMP: 15
SQ FT: 18,000
SALES (est): 1MM **Privately Held**
WEB: www.fiberbrite.com
SIC: 3993 5085 Mfg Signs/Advertising Specialties Whol Industrial Supplies

(G-503)
VALLEY CONTAINER INC
850 Union Ave (06607-1137)
PHONE..............................203 368-6546
Arthur Vietze Jr, *CEO*
Rudolph Neidermeir, *Ch of Bd*
Robert Neidermeir, *President*
Robert Vietze, *Vice Pres*
Dave Law, *Plant Mgr*
▲ **EMP:** 45
SQ FT: 120,000
SALES: 16.8MM **Privately Held**
WEB: www.valleycontainer.com
SIC: 2679 7319 Mfg Converted Paper Products Advertising Services

(G-504)
VINEGAR SYNDROME LLC
100 Congress St (06604-4046)
PHONE..............................212 722-9755
Joe Rubin, *Principal*
EMP: 3 **EST:** 2013
SALES (est): 218.9K **Privately Held**
SIC: 2099 Mfg Food Preparations

(G-505)
WASTE TO GREEN FUEL LLC
1376 Chopsey Hill Rd (06606-2422)
PHONE..............................203 536-5855
EMP: 4
SALES (est): 358K **Privately Held**
SIC: 2869 Mfg Industrial Organic Chemicals

(G-506)
WOODWORKERS HEAVEN INC
955 Conn Ave Ste 4106 (06607-1222)
PHONE..............................203 333-2778
John W Eskew, *President*
EMP: 10
SQ FT: 5,000
SALES: 1MM **Privately Held**
SIC: 2511 Mfg Architectural Wood Pdts

(G-507)
YANKEE METALS LLC
76 Knowlton St (06608-2105)
PHONE..............................203 612-7470
Leonard D Strocchia,
EMP: 4
SALES (est): 624.6K **Privately Held**
SIC: 3441 Structural Metal Fabrication

(G-508)
YARD STICK DECORE
145 Hart St # 1 (06606-5048)
PHONE..............................203 330-0360
Joe Costa, *Mng Member*
EMP: 10
SALES (est): 70.5K **Privately Held**
SIC: 2391 Mfg Curtains/Draperies

Bristol
Hartford County

(G-509)
A & D COMPONENTS INC
33 Stafford Ave Ste 2 (06010-4699)
PHONE..............................860 582-9541
Harold Etherington, *President*
Rita McKenzie, *Corp Secy*
Nora Etherington, *Vice Pres*
EMP: 8
SQ FT: 25,000
SALES (est): 1.2MM **Privately Held**
WEB: www.adcomponents.com
SIC: 3469 Mfg Metal Stampings

(G-510)
ABEK LLC
492 Birch St (06010-7837)
PHONE..............................860 314-3905
Alex N Beavers, *CEO*
John B Thomson Jr, *Chairman*
Robert C Magee, *Vice Chairman*
Patrick Mazzeo, *Vice Pres*
Jeffry Peterson, *Vice Pres*
▲ **EMP:** 11 **EST:** 1976
SQ FT: 12,500
SALES (est): 1.9MM
SALES (corp-wide): 19.8B **Publicly Held**
SIC: 3562 Mfg Ball/Roller Bearings
PA: Danaher Corporation
2200 Penn Ave Nw Ste 800w
Washington DC 20037
202 828-0850

(G-511)
ACCUPAULO HOLDING CORPORATION (PA)
Also Called: Accurate Threaded Products
33 Stafford Ave Ste 5 (06010-4699)
PHONE..............................860 666-5621
Jon Omichinski, *President*
Harold Etherington, *President*
EMP: 25
SALES (est): 27.9MM **Privately Held**
SIC: 3769 3599 3724 Mfg Space Vehicle Equipment Mfg Industrial Machinery Mfg Aircraft Engines/Parts

(G-512)
ACCURATE THREADED PRODUCTS CO
33 Stafford Ave Ste 5 (06010-4699)
PHONE..............................860 666-5621
Gary Fett, *President*
EMP: 40
SALES (est): 800K **Privately Held**
SIC: 3599 Mfg Industrial Machinery
PA: Atp Industries, Llc
75 Northwest Dr
Plainville CT 06062

(G-513)
ACE FINISHING CO LLC
225 Terryville Rd (06010-4010)
P.O. Box 1213 (06011-1213)
PHONE..............................860 582-4600
Nick E Phillips,
Antoni Phillips,
Edward A Phillips,
EMP: 5
SALES (est): 511.6K **Privately Held**
SIC: 2396 3542 Mfg Auto/Apparel Trimming Mfg Machine Tools-Forming

(G-514)
ADK PRESSURE EQUIPMENT CORP (DH)
745 Clark Ave (06010-4068)
PHONE..............................860 585-0050
William F Steinen, *Ch of Bd*
William F Steinen Jr, *President*
G Menninga, *Vice Pres*
Thomas Keenan, *Treasurer*
EMP: 6
SALES (est): 754K
SALES (corp-wide): 15.3MM **Privately Held**
SIC: 3564 Mfg Blowers And Fans

HQ: Mcintire Company
745 Clark Ave
Bristol CT 06010
860 585-8559

(G-515)
ADOR INC
210 Redstone Hill Rd # 5 (06010-7796)
PHONE..................................860 583-2367
Chang Lieh Hsieh, *Principal*
Pam Sokolosky, *Vice Pres*
▲ **EMP:** 3
SALES: 100K **Privately Held**
SIC: 3429 Mfg Hardware

(G-516)
AFFORDABLE CONVEYORS SVCS LLC
144 W Washington St (06010-5444)
P.O. Box 2252 (06011-2252)
PHONE..................................860 582-1800
Philip J Robotham Jr,
Karen Tibbals, *Admin Sec*
EMP: 10
SALES (est): 2MM **Privately Held**
WEB: www.affordableconveyor.com
SIC: 3535 Mfg Conveyors/Equipment

(G-517)
ALLGREENIT LLC
123 Farmington Ave # 162 (06010-4200)
PHONE..................................860 516-4948
Patrick Ouellette, *Sales Dir*
Peter Stevenson,
Bobbi Shafer, *Admin Asst*
EMP: 3
SALES (est): 492.7K **Privately Held**
SIC: 3433 Mfg Heating Equipment-Non-electric

(G-518)
ALLOY WELDING & MFG CO INC
233 Riverside Ave (06010-6319)
PHONE..................................860 582-3638
Alfred L Frechette, *President*
Darren Frechette, *General Mgr*
Alfred Frechette, *Vice Pres*
Edith Frechette, *Vice Pres*
Ken Nelson, *Sales Mgr*
EMP: 15
SQ FT: 14,000
SALES (est): 3.5MM **Privately Held**
SIC: 3441 1799 Structural Metal Fabrication Trade Contractor

(G-519)
APPSTRACT IDEAS
81 Martin Rd (06010-4020)
PHONE..................................860 857-1123
Donald McKeith, *Owner*
Jonathan Bimler,
Leo Carroll,
EMP: 3
SALES (est): 150K **Privately Held**
SIC: 7372 Prepackaged Software Services

(G-520)
ARROW MANUFACTURING COMPANY
16 Jeannette St (06010-7000)
PHONE..................................860 589-3900
Thomas E Selnau, *President*
William R Selnau, *Vice Pres*
Laurie Angers, *Safety Mgr*
Paula Green, *Bookkeeper*
Diane Kellert, *Human Res Dir*
EMP: 27 **EST:** 1951
SQ FT: 40,000
SALES (est): 5MM **Privately Held**
WEB: www.arrowmfg.com
SIC: 3469 3493 3496 Mfg Metal Stampings Mfg Steel Springs-Nonwire Mfg Misc Fabricated Wire Products

(G-521)
ARTHUR G RUSSELL COMPANY INC
750 Clark Ave (06010-4065)
P.O. Box 237 (06011-0237)
PHONE..................................860 583-4109
Robert J Ensminger, *CEO*
Mark Burzynski, *President*
William Mis, *Vice Pres*
Don Palaia, *Vice Pres*
Jim Maloney, *Project Mgr*
◆ **EMP:** 85
SQ FT: 80,000
SALES (est): 32.2MM **Privately Held**
WEB: www.arthurgrussell.com
SIC: 3569 Whol Industrial Equipment

(G-522)
ATLANTIC PRECISION SPRING INC
125 Ronzo Rd (06010-8620)
PHONE..................................860 583-1864
Neil Fries, *President*
Brian J Fries, *Vice Pres*
Michael J Fries, *Vice Pres*
Terry Fries, *Admin Sec*
EMP: 32 **EST:** 1958
SQ FT: 15,000
SALES (est): 7.9MM **Privately Held**
WEB: www.aps-ct.com
SIC: 3493 3495 3469 Mfg Steel Springs-Nonwire Mfg Wire Springs Mfg Metal Stampings

(G-523)
B & P PLATING EQUIPMENT LLC
74 Broderick Rd (06010-7736)
PHONE..................................860 589-5799
Ronald Landrette, *Mng Member*
EMP: 10
SQ FT: 10,000
SALES (est): 1.1MM **Privately Held**
SIC: 3471 3544 Plating/Polishing Service Mfg Dies/Tools/Jigs/Fixtures

(G-524)
B&T SCREW MACHINE CO INC
571 Broad St (06010-6662)
P.O. Box 431 (06011-0431)
PHONE..................................860 314-4410
Theresa Gokey, *President*
Jessica Schroder, *Opers Staff*
EMP: 12
SQ FT: 20,000
SALES (est): 2.4MM **Privately Held**
SIC: 3451 Mfg Screw Machine Products

(G-525)
BARLOW METAL STAMPING INC
2 Barlow St (06010-4001)
P.O. Box 1397 (06011-1397)
PHONE..................................860 583-1387
Peter Gaughan, *Ch of Bd*
Terry Gaughan, *President*
Norman Lazerow, *Vice Pres*
Sandy Gaughan, *Technology*
EMP: 20
SQ FT: 15,600
SALES (est): 4MM **Privately Held**
WEB: www.barlowmetalstamping.com
SIC: 3469 Mfg Metal Stampings

(G-526)
BARNES GROUP INC (PA)
123 Main St (06010-6376)
PHONE..................................860 583-7070
Thomas O Barnes, *Ch of Bd*
Patrick J Dempsey, *President*
Stephen Moule, *President*
Norbert Scheid, *President*
Murphy Kristine, *Counsel*
▲ **EMP:** 277
SALES: 1.5B **Publicly Held**
WEB: www.barnesgroupinc.com
SIC: 3724 3495 3469 Mfg Industrial Equipment & Components

(G-527)
BARNES GROUP INC
Associated Spring
18 Main St (06010-6581)
PHONE..................................860 582-9581
Stephen Connolly, *Production*
Stefanie Cooper, *Marketing Mgr*
Paulo Coit, *Branch Mgr*
Scott Litchfield, *MIS Dir*
Eric Norton, *MIS Staff*
EMP: 100
SALES (corp-wide): 1.5B **Publicly Held**
WEB: www.barnesgroupinc.com
SIC: 3469 3495 Mfg Metal Stampings And Mfg Wire Springs
PA: Barnes Group Inc.
123 Main St
Bristol CT 06010
860 583-7070

(G-528)
BARNES GROUP INC
Also Called: Barnes Aerospace W Chester Div
123 Main St (06010-6376)
PHONE..................................513 759-3503
Rick Barnhart, *General Mgr*
EMP: 3700
SALES (corp-wide): 1.5B **Publicly Held**
WEB: www.barnesgroupinc.com
SIC: 3724 Mfg Aircraft Engines And Engine Parts
PA: Barnes Group Inc.
123 Main St
Bristol CT 06010
860 583-7070

(G-529)
BARON & YOUNG CO INC
400 Middle St Ste 13 (06010-8405)
PHONE..................................860 589-3235
Donald Baron, *President*
Dennis Dutkiewicz, *Vice Pres*
Patricia Baron, *Admin Sec*
EMP: 9
SQ FT: 10,080
SALES (est): 900K **Privately Held**
SIC: 3471 3479 Buffing & Polishing Of Metals

(G-530)
BASS PRODUCTS LLC
435 Lake Ave (06010-7332)
P.O. Box 1359 (06011-1359)
PHONE..................................860 585-7923
Tony Sposato, *General Mgr*
Jesus Gonzalez, *Prdtn Mgr*
Jack Warhola, *Finance Mgr*
Kevin Warhola, *Info Tech Mgr*
Robert Sposato,
EMP: 9
SQ FT: 17,000
SALES (est): 1.5MM **Privately Held**
WEB: www.bassproducts.com
SIC: 3613 Mfg Switchgear/Switchboards

(G-531)
BAUER INC
175 Century Dr (06010-7482)
PHONE..................................860 583-9100
Lou Auletta Jr, *President*
Andy Novotny, *Principal*
Thomas Gilchrist, *Vice Pres*
Rob Michell, *Vice Pres*
Michael Auletta, *Purch Mgr*
▲ **EMP:** 58
SQ FT: 38,000
SALES (est): 17.6MM **Privately Held**
WEB: www.bauerct.com
SIC: 3829 Mfg Measuring/Controlling Devices

(G-532)
BELMONT CORPORATION
Also Called: Village Cabinets
60 Crystal Pond Pl (06010-7475)
PHONE..................................860 589-5700
David T Clark, *CEO*
Bruce L Clark, *President*
Robert L Boutot, *Exec VP*
EMP: 45
SQ FT: 41,000
SALES (est): 5.6MM **Privately Held**
WEB: www.villagecabinets.com
SIC: 2434 2521 2517 Mfg Wood Kitchen Cabinets Office Furniture Wood Tv & Radio Cabinets

(G-533)
BES CU INC
400 Middle St (06010-8405)
PHONE..................................860 582-8660
Ed O'Hannessian, *CEO*
Jay Rasmus, *President*
Karen Cunningham, *Vice Pres*
EMP: 7
SQ FT: 3,500
SALES: 500K **Privately Held**
SIC: 3496 Edm Machining

(G-534)
BETTER MOLDED PRODUCTS INC (PA)
95 Valley St Ste 2 (06010-4985)
P.O. Box 2141 (06011-2141)
PHONE..................................860 589-0066
Roy Izzo, *President*
EMP: 170
SQ FT: 60,000
SALES (est): 21.6MM **Privately Held**
WEB: www.bettermolded.com
SIC: 3089 3544 Mfg Plastic Products Mfg Dies/Tools/Jigs/Fixtures

(G-535)
BRAEMAR MACHINE CO
550 Broad St (06010-6664)
P.O. Box 207, Plantsville (06479-0207)
PHONE..................................860 585-1903
Winston Thompson, *Owner*
EMP: 4
SQ FT: 24,000
SALES (est): 220K **Privately Held**
SIC: 3599 Mfg Industrial Machinery

(G-536)
BRISTOL ADULT RESOURCE CTR INC
97 Peck Ln (06010-6163)
PHONE..................................860 583-8721
Ronnie Cassin, *Branch Mgr*
EMP: 50
SALES (corp-wide): 7.5MM **Privately Held**
SIC: 2621 Paper Mill
PA: Bristol Adult Resource Center, Inc.
195 Maltby St
Bristol CT 06010
860 261-5592

(G-537)
BRISTOL INSTRUMENT GEARS INC
164 Central St Ste 1 (06010-6778)
P.O. Box 9248 (06011-9248)
PHONE..................................860 583-1395
James Carros, *President*
David Carros, *Vice Pres*
Alex Carros, *Opers-Prdtn-Mfg*
Rosemary P Carros, *Credit Mgr*
EMP: 15 **EST:** 1951
SQ FT: 20,000
SALES (est): 2.4MM **Privately Held**
WEB: www.bristolgears.com
SIC: 3462 Mfg Iron/Steel Forgings

(G-538)
BRISTOL SIGNART INC
550 Broad St (06010-6664)
P.O. Box 9081 (06011-9081)
PHONE..................................860 582-2577
Francis Blethen, *President*
Mark Blethen, *Admin Sec*
EMP: 3
SQ FT: 2,500
SALES: 180K **Privately Held**
SIC: 3993 Mfg Signs/Advertising Specialties

(G-539)
BRISTOL TOOL & DIE COMPANY
550 Broad St Ste 13 (06010-6677)
PHONE..................................860 582-2577
Carl Guenther, *President*
EMP: 20 **EST:** 1965
SQ FT: 5,000
SALES (est): 3.1MM **Privately Held**
SIC: 3469 3599 3544 Manufactures Metal Stampings Provides Secondary Machining Operations And Manufactures Tools And Dies

(G-540)
CENTURY SPRING MFG CO INC
100 Wooster Ct (06010-6731)
P.O. Box 301 (06011-0301)
PHONE..................................860 582-3344
Walter Waseleski, *CEO*
William J Waseleski, *President*
Theresa Waseleski, *Admin Sec*
Jessica Baril, *Assistant*
EMP: 25 **EST:** 1975
SQ FT: 14,000

▲ = Import ▼=Export
◆ =Import/Export

SALES (est): 5.8MM **Privately Held**
WEB: www.centuryspringmfg.com
SIC: 3495 3493 3469 Mfg Wire Springs Mfg Steel Springs-Nonwire Mfg Metal Stampings

(G-541)
CLASSIC COIL COMPANY INC
205 Century Dr (06010-7486)
PHONE..................................860 583-7600
Rudolf Zeidler, *CEO*
James E Dowman, *President*
Nancy Matute, *Purchasing*
Richard Bisaillon, *CFO*
Heather Bauer, *Controller*
▲ **EMP:** 100 **EST:** 1976
SQ FT: 25,000
SALES (est): 29.7MM **Privately Held**
WEB: www.classic-coil.com
SIC: 3677 Mfg Electronic Coils/Transformers

(G-542)
CMI SPECIALTY PRODUCTS INC
105 Redstone Hill Rd (06010-7799)
PHONE..................................860 585-0409
Joseph A Bozzuto, *President*
▲ **EMP:** 10
SQ FT: 2,100
SALES (est): 2.2MM **Privately Held**
WEB: www.cmispecialty.com
SIC: 3312 3353 Blast Furnace-Steel Works Mfg Aluminum Sheet/Foil

(G-543)
CONNECTICUT TOOL & CUTTER CO
280 Redstone Hill Rd # 1 (06010-8624)
P.O. Box 368, Plainville (06062-0368)
PHONE..................................860 314-1740
Alfonse Skudlarek Sr, *President*
Caroline Skudlarek, *Vice Pres*
EMP: 20 **EST:** 1970
SQ FT: 16,900
SALES: 3.6MM **Privately Held**
SIC: 3541 Mfg Machine Tools-Cutting

(G-544)
CP SOLAR THERMAL LLC
210 Century Dr (06010-7477)
PHONE..................................860 877-2238
Thomas Etter, *Mng Member*
EMP: 3
SALES (est): 174.3K **Privately Held**
SIC: 3433 Mfg Heating Equipment-Nonelectric

(G-545)
CT CONVEYOR LLC
320 Terryville Rd (06010-4012)
PHONE..................................860 637-2926
Louis Labelle, *Mng Member*
EMP: 6
SQ FT: 1,000
SALES: 310K **Privately Held**
SIC: 3535 Mfg Conveyors/Equipment

(G-546)
CURTIS PRODUCTS LLC
70 Halcyon Dr (06010-7464)
PHONE..................................203 754-4155
Ronald Weintraub, *Mng Member*
EMP: 18 **EST:** 1950
SALES: 3.9MM **Privately Held**
WEB: www.curtisproducts.net
SIC: 3451 Mfg Screw Machine Products

(G-547)
DACRUZ MANUFACTURING INC
100 Broderick Rd (06010-7724)
PHONE..................................860 584-5315
Victor P Dacruz, *President*
Chelsea E Castor, *Vice Pres*
Michael Boudreau, *Purch Mgr*
Betty Dacruz, *CFO*
Don Pelletier, *Sales Executive*
EMP: 43
SQ FT: 33,000
SALES: 6MM **Privately Held**
WEB: www.cmscrew.com
SIC: 3451 Mfg Screw Machine Products

(G-548)
DAY FRED A CO LLC
Also Called: F A D C O
11 Commerce Dr (06010-8608)
PHONE..................................860 589-0531
Randy Mencil,
EMP: 4
SQ FT: 9,200
SALES (est): 611.7K **Privately Held**
SIC: 3451 Mfg Screw Machine Products

(G-549)
DI-COR INDUSTRIES INC
139 Center St (06010-5074)
P.O. Box 3128 (06011-3128)
PHONE..................................860 585-5583
Harry Vassiliou, *President*
Tom Vassiliou, *Treasurer*
▼ **EMP:** 15
SQ FT: 24,000
SALES (est): 3.8MM **Privately Held**
SIC: 3441 2542 5021 Structural Metal Fabrication Mfg Partitions/Fixtures-Nonwood Whol Furniture

(G-550)
DOUBLETREE
42 Century Dr (06010-4779)
PHONE..................................860 589-7766
EMP: 12
SALES (est): 2.4MM **Privately Held**
SIC: 2621 Paper Mills

(G-551)
DYNAMIC MANUFACTURING COMPANY
Also Called: Dymco
95 Valley St Ste 5 (06010-4985)
P.O. Box 1880 (06011-1880)
PHONE..................................860 589-2751
John Beckwith, *President*
Brian Beckwith, *Vice Pres*
Rosemary Beckwith, *Vice Pres*
▼ **EMP:** 5
SQ FT: 15,000
SALES: 750K **Privately Held**
WEB: www.dymco.com
SIC: 3493 3469 Mfg Steel Spring-Nonwire Mfg Metal Stampings

(G-552)
E P M CO INC
Also Called: Precision Swiss Screw Machine
147 Terryville Rd (06010-4010)
P.O. Box 207, Pequabuck (06781-0207)
PHONE..................................860 589-3233
Donna Patnode, *President*
EMP: 3 **EST:** 2001
SALES (est): 194.8K **Privately Held**
SIC: 3451 Mfg Screw Machine Products

(G-553)
EMME CONTROLS LLC
32 Valley St Fl C (06010-4991)
P.O. Box 2251 (06011-2251)
PHONE..................................503 793-3792
Jon Brodeur, *CEO*
David Cohen, *President*
Kim Wilson, *Sales Staff*
EMP: 8 **EST:** 2015
SQ FT: 12,000
SALES (est): 472.1K **Privately Held**
SIC: 3822 Mfg Environmental Controls

(G-554)
EMME E2MS LLC
32 Valley St Fl C (06010-4991)
P.O. Box 2251 (06011-2251)
PHONE..................................860 845-8810
Jonathan Brodeur, *CEO*
EMP: 10
SQ FT: 10,000
SALES (est): 1.4MM **Privately Held**
SIC: 3822 Mfg Environmental Controls

(G-555)
EMPCO INC (PA)
Also Called: Empco Prcision Swiss Screw Mch
147 Terryville Rd (06010-4010)
P.O. Box 207, Pequabuck (06781-0207)
PHONE..................................860 589-3233
Henry Patnode, *President*
EMP: 8 **EST:** 1969
SQ FT: 1,000
SALES (est): 874.5K **Privately Held**
SIC: 3599 Mfg Industrial Machinery

(G-556)
ENFLO CORPORATION (PA)
315 Lake Ave (06010-7397)
P.O. Box 490 (06011-0490)
PHONE..................................860 589-0014
Myron A Rudner, *President*
Robert E Dalton, *Vice Pres*
Karl Forsander, *Vice Pres*
Jonathan Stanek, *CFO*
Tasha Brown, *Sales Staff*
▲ **EMP:** 39 **EST:** 1955
SQ FT: 25,000
SALES (est): 4MM **Privately Held**
WEB: www.enflo.com
SIC: 2821 Mfg Plastic Products

(G-557)
ETHERINGTON BROTHERS INC
Also Called: E B Buffing
33 Stafford Ave Ste 2 (06010-4699)
PHONE..................................860 585-5624
Nora Etherington, *President*
Harold Etherington, *Vice Pres*
EMP: 8
SALES (est): 815.9K **Privately Held**
SIC: 3471 Plating/Polishing Service

(G-558)
EWALD INSTRUMENTS CORP
95 Wooster Ct Ste 3 (06010-6777)
P.O. Box 398, Goshen (06756-0398)
PHONE..................................860 491-9042
Richard Vreeland, *President*
Susan Vreeland, *Corp Secy*
EMP: 12 **EST:** 1954
SQ FT: 14,000
SALES (est): 2MM **Privately Held**
WEB: www.ewaldinstruments.com
SIC: 3545 3625 7699 Mfg Machine Tool Accessories Mfg Relays/Industrial Controls Repair Services

(G-559)
EXCEL SPRING & STAMPING LLC
61 E Main St Ste 2 (06010-7060)
PHONE..................................860 585-1495
John Sandstrom,
EMP: 9
SQ FT: 7,500
SALES: 1.2MM **Privately Held**
SIC: 3469 3495 3496 3493 Mfg Metal Stampings Mfg Wire Springs Mfg Misc Fab Wire Prdts Mfg Steel Spring-Nonwire

(G-560)
FAD TOOL COMPANY LLC
95 Valley St Ste 7 (06010-4985)
P.O. Box 1117 (06011-1117)
PHONE..................................860 582-7890
David Scott, *President*
Rick Miner, *Controller*
EMP: 40
SQ FT: 3,500
SALES (est): 6.1MM **Privately Held**
WEB: www.fadtool.com
SIC: 3544 Mfg Tools & Dies

(G-561)
FARMINGTON MTAL FBRICATION LLC
139 Center St Ste 2001 (06010-5082)
P.O. Box 260, Unionville (06085-0260)
PHONE..................................860 404-7415
John Cunningham, *Mng Member*
Carol Cunningham,
EMP: 6
SALES (est): 840.7K **Privately Held**
SIC: 3498 Structural Metal Fabrication

(G-562)
FASTSIGNS
1290 Farmington Ave (06010-4701)
PHONE..................................860 583-8000
Fax: 860 314-0505
EMP: 4
SALES (est): 150K **Privately Held**
SIC: 3993 Signsadv Specs

(G-563)
FOUR STAR MANUFACTURING CO
400 Riverside Ave (06010-8807)
PHONE..................................860 583-1614
Edward Plonski, *President*
Gary Plonski, *Vice Pres*
Florence Plonski, *Admin Sec*
EMP: 25 **EST:** 1961
SQ FT: 18,000
SALES (est): 3.7MM **Privately Held**
SIC: 3469 Metal Stamping Service

(G-564)
FOURSLIDE SPRING STAMPING INC
87 Cross St (06010-7434)
P.O. Box 839 (06011-0839)
PHONE..................................860 583-1688
Bryan Funk, *President*
Judy Schmidt, *Financial Exec*
Jim Richards, *Mktg Dir*
Arthur P Funk, *CIO*
Judith Schmidt, *Admin Sec*
EMP: 25 **EST:** 1962
SQ FT: 20,000
SALES (est): 6MM **Privately Held**
WEB: www.fourslide.com
SIC: 3493 3469 3495 Mfg Steel Springs-Nonwire Mfg Metal Stampings Mfg Wire Springs

(G-565)
FUTURE MANUFACTURING INC
75 Center St (06010-4979)
P.O. Box 23 (06011-0023)
PHONE..................................860 584-0685
Denis Boroski, *President*
EMP: 30
SQ FT: 10,000
SALES: 1.5MM **Privately Held**
WEB: www.futuremfg.com
SIC: 3677 Mfg Electronic Coils

(G-566)
G A INDUSTRIES
630 Emmett St Unit 1 (06010-7793)
PHONE..................................860 261-5484
EMP: 3
SALES (est): 242K **Privately Held**
SIC: 3999 Mfg Misc Products

(G-567)
GARRETT PRINTING & GRAPHICS
331 Riverside Ave (06010-8810)
PHONE..................................860 589-6710
Greg Kowalczyk, *President*
Holley Kowalczyk, *Vice Pres*
Kris Hart, *Prdtn Mgr*
Morgan Leduc, *Sales Mgr*
EMP: 6 **EST:** 1900
SQ FT: 5,000
SALES (est): 944.9K **Privately Held**
SIC: 2752 5699 7336 5043 Lithographic Coml Print Ret Misc Apparel/Access Coml Art/Graphic Design

(G-568)
GMN USA LLC
181 Business Park Dr (06010-8628)
PHONE..................................800 686-1679
Gary P Quirion, *President*
Jeffrey Lepage, *Accountant*
Don Loveless, *Sales Mgr*
▲ **EMP:** 14
SQ FT: 27,815
SALES: 6MM
SALES (corp-wide): 106.1MM **Privately Held**
WEB: www.gmnusa.com
SIC: 3541 Mfg Machine Tools-Cutting
HQ: Gmn Paul Muller Industrie Gmbh & Co. Kg
AuBere Bayreuther Str. 230
Nurnberg 90411
911 569-10

(G-569)
HRF FASTENER SYSTEMS INC
70 Horizon Dr (06010-7473)
PHONE..................................860 589-0750
Robert R Rohrs, *President*
Marsha Rohrs, *Admin Sec*
EMP: 30 **EST:** 1970

SQ FT: 5,000
SALES (est): 6.5MM **Privately Held**
SIC: 3441 3546 Structural Metal Fabrication Mfg Power-Driven Handtools

(G-570)
IDEX HEALTH & SCIENCE LLC
Also Called: Eastern Plastics
110 Halcyon Dr (06010-7487)
PHONE..................................860 314-2880
Noy Xayavong, *Buyer*
Art Bauer, *Engineer*
Daniel Rodriguez, *Engineer*
Daniel Czarnecki, *Design Engr*
Suzanne Leclair, *Human Res Mgr*
EMP: 124
SALES (corp-wide): 2.4B **Publicly Held**
SIC: 3821 3089 3494 3823 Mfg Lab Apparatus/Furn Mfg Plastic Products Mfg Valves/Pipe Fittings Mfg Process Cntrl Instr Mfg Analytical Instr
HQ: Idex Health & Science Llc
600 Park Ct
Rohnert Park CA 94928
707 588-2000

(G-571)
INSIGHT PLUS TECHNOLOGY LLC
191 Redstone Hill Rd (06010-7773)
PHONE..................................860 930-4763
Thomas J Holtz, *Principal*
EMP: 4 **EST:** 2017
SALES (est): 609.9K **Privately Held**
SIC: 3651 7382 3699 Mfg Home Audio/Video Equipment Security Systems Services Mfg Electrical Equipment/Supplies

(G-572)
JARVIS PRECISION POLISHING
190 Century Dr (06010-7491)
PHONE..................................860 589-5822
Wallace F Jarvis, *President*
EMP: 10
SALES (est): 842.1K **Privately Held**
SIC: 3471 Plating & Polishing

(G-573)
JOVEK TOOL AND DIE
474 Birch St (06010-7837)
PHONE..................................860 261-5020
Joseph Longo, *Principal*
EMP: 8
SALES: 1.7MM **Privately Held**
SIC: 3544 Mfg Dies/Tools/Jigs/Fixtures

(G-574)
KBJ MANUFACTURING INC
137 Stafford Ave (06010-4613)
PHONE..................................860 585-7257
Kenneth Beeler Jr, *President*
Kenneth Beeler Sr, *Vice Pres*
EMP: 5
SQ FT: 3,000
SALES: 700K **Privately Held**
SIC: 3599 Mfg Industrial Machinery

(G-575)
LAB SECURITY SYSTEMS CORP
Also Called: L A B
700 Emmett St (06010-7714)
PHONE..................................860 589-6037
Robert A Labbe, *President*
Gerald Roraback Jr, *Vice Pres*
▲ **EMP:** 45 **EST:** 1957
SQ FT: 36,000
SALES (est): 6.5MM **Privately Held**
WEB: www.lockpins.com
SIC: 3429 3452 Mfg Hardware Mfg Bolts/Screws/Rivets

(G-576)
LEE SPRING COMPANY LLC
245 Lake Ave (06010-7398)
P.O. Box 1038 (06011-1038)
PHONE..................................860 584-0991
Marcel Ouellette, *Plant Mgr*
EMP: 28
SALES (corp-wide): 40.6MM **Privately Held**
WEB: www.leespring.com
SIC: 3495 3493 5085 3315 Mfg Wire Springs Mfg Steel Spring-Nonwire Whol Industrial Supplies Mfg Steel Wire/Rltd Prdt
HQ: Lee Spring Company Llc
140 58th St Ste 3c
Brooklyn NY 11220
888 777-4647

(G-577)
LP HOMETOWN PIZZA LLC
90 Burlington Ave (06010-4201)
PHONE..................................860 589-1208
EMP: 3
SALES (est): 92.7K **Privately Held**
SIC: 2621 Paper Mills

(G-578)
MACKSON MFG CO INC
139 Center St Ste 2002 (06010-5082)
PHONE..................................860 589-4035
Raymond J Macklosky, *President*
EMP: 12 **EST:** 1962
SQ FT: 10,000
SALES (est): 1.6MM **Privately Held**
SIC: 3451 Mfg Screw Machine Products

(G-579)
MARTIN CABINET INC
500 Broad St (06010)
PHONE..................................860 747-5769
Dan Chamberland, *Principal*
EMP: 60
SALES (corp-wide): 6.8MM **Privately Held**
WEB: www.cabinet-mart.com
SIC: 2434 Mfg Wood Kitchen Cabinets
PA: Martin Cabinet Inc
336 S Washington St Ste 2
Plainville CT 06062
860 747-5769

(G-580)
MCINTIRE COMPANY (HQ)
Also Called: Western Progress
745 Clark Ave (06010-4068)
PHONE..................................860 585-8559
William F Steinen, *Chairman*
Thomas R Keenan, *Vice Pres*
John J Delaney Jr, *Admin Sec*
▲ **EMP:** 15
SQ FT: 12,000
SALES (est): 19MM
SALES (corp-wide): 15.3MM **Privately Held**
WEB: www.mcintireco.com
SIC: 3564 3993 3842 3634 Mfg Blowers/Fans Mfg Signs/Ad Specialties Mfg Surgical Appliances Mfg Elec Housewares/Fans Mfg Heat Equip-Nonelec
PA: Wm. Steinen Mfg. Co.
29 E Halsey Rd
Parsippany NJ 07054
973 887-6400

(G-581)
MIDCONN PRECISION MFG LLC
190 Century Dr Ste 9 (06010-7491)
PHONE..................................860 584-1340
Brent Tanguay,
EMP: 6
SALES (est): 336.6K **Privately Held**
SIC: 3469 Mfg Metal Stampings

(G-582)
MINUTEMAN PRESS OF BRISTOL
98 Farmington Ave (06010-4218)
PHONE..................................860 589-1100
EMP: 4 **EST:** 2011
SALES (est): 456.5K **Privately Held**
SIC: 2752 Comm Prtg Litho

(G-583)
MONOPOL CORPORATION
394 Riverside Ave (06010-6320)
P.O. Box 3056 (06011-3056)
PHONE..................................860 583-3852
Wesley Woisna, *President*
Lucy Woisna, *Admin Sec*
EMP: 10
SQ FT: 6,000
SALES: 450K **Privately Held**
WEB: www.monopol-colors.ch
SIC: 3841 Mfg Medical And Surgical Instruments And Parts

(G-584)
MORIN CORPORATION (DH)
Also Called: Morin East
685 Middle St (06010-8441)
P.O. Box 3028 (06011-3028)
PHONE..................................860 584-0900
Russell Shiels, *President*
Doug Matthews, *Regional Mgr*
George McDuffee, *Vice Pres*
Denise Signore, *Purchasing*
Daniel Davenport, *Sales Mgr*
▲ **EMP:** 60
SALES (est): 27.1MM **Privately Held**
WEB: www.kingspanpanels.us
SIC: 3448 Mfg Prefabricated Metal Buildings
HQ: Kingspan-Medusa Inc.
726 Summerhill Dr
Deland FL 32724
386 626-6789

(G-585)
MULTI-CABLE CORP
37 Horizon Dr (06010-7480)
P.O. Box 797 (06011-0797)
PHONE..................................860 589-9035
Patrick Joyce, *President*
Grant Campbell, *President*
Guy Campbell, *Chairman*
Emily S Joyce, *Admin Sec*
Amy Campbell, *Representative*
EMP: 15
SQ FT: 15,000
SALES (est): 3.8MM **Privately Held**
WEB: www.multicable.com
SIC: 3357 Nonferrous Wiredrawing/Insulating

(G-586)
NELSON TOOL & MACHINE CO INC
675 Emmett St (06010-7715)
PHONE..................................860 589-8004
David Florian, *Principal*
EMP: 3
SALES (est): 230K **Privately Held**
SIC: 3728 Mfg Aircraft Parts/Equipment

(G-587)
NOVO PRECISION LLC
150 Dolphin Rd (06010-8041)
PHONE..................................860 583-0517
William B Hazard,
◆ **EMP:** 22
SQ FT: 14,000
SALES (est): 6.2MM **Privately Held**
WEB: www.wirestraighteners.com
SIC: 3496 5084 Mfg Misc Fabricated Wire Products Whol Industrial Equipment

(G-588)
OSCAR JOBS
Also Called: Reliable Spring Company
165 Riverside Ave (06010-6322)
P.O. Box 1952 (06011-1952)
PHONE..................................860 583-7834
Oscar Jobs, *Owner*
EMP: 8
SQ FT: 15,000
SALES (est): 1MM **Privately Held**
WEB: www.reliablespring.net
SIC: 3469 3493 3495 Mfg Metal Stampings Mfg Steel Springs-Nonwire Mfg Wire Springs

(G-589)
P-Q CONTROLS INC (PA)
95 Dolphin Rd (06010-8000)
PHONE..................................860 583-6994
Douglas D Schumann, *President*
Bart Matthew Guthrie, *Vice Pres*
To Cheung, *Engineer*
Jake Mockler, *Engineer*
Chase Monroe, *Engineer*
▲ **EMP:** 41
SQ FT: 20,000
SALES (est): 6.7MM **Privately Held**
WEB: www.pqcontrols.com
SIC: 3625 Mfg Relays/Industrial Controls

(G-590)
PALMISANO PRINTING LLC
319 Queen St (06010-6358)
P.O. Box 372 (06011-0372)
PHONE..................................860 582-6883
Philip Palmisano, *Mng Member*
EMP: 5
SQ FT: 1,200
SALES (est): 688.8K **Privately Held**
WEB: www.palmisanoprinting.com
SIC: 2752 2791 2789 Lithographic Commercial Printing Typesetting Services Bookbinding/Related Work

(G-591)
PATRIOT MANUFACTURING LLC
Also Called: Bluewater Designs
205 Cross St (06010-7434)
PHONE..................................860 506-2213
Edward Borkoski, *President*
EMP: 3 **EST:** 1946
SQ FT: 5,000
SALES (est): 525.5K **Privately Held**
WEB: www.bluewaterdesigns.com
SIC: 3469 3544 Mfg Metal Stampings Mfg Dies/Tools/Jigs/Fixtures

(G-592)
PATTISON SIGN GROUP INC
2074 Perkins St (06010-2323)
PHONE..................................860 583-3000
Joan Pelletier, *Manager*
EMP: 7
SALES (corp-wide): 19B **Privately Held**
WEB: www.pattisonsign.com
SIC: 3993 Mfg Signs/Advertising Specialties
HQ: Pattison Sign Group Inc.
520 W Summit Hill Dr # 702
Knoxville TN 37902
865 693-1105

(G-593)
PATWIL LLC
Also Called: Amstep Products
190 Century Dr Ste 102 (06010-7491)
PHONE..................................860 589-9085
Pat Will, *Mng Member*
EMP: 8 **EST:** 1911
SQ FT: 6,400
SALES (est): 1.4MM **Privately Held**
WEB: www.amstep.com
SIC: 3446 Mfg Architectural Metalwork

(G-594)
PLAINVILLE MACHINE & TL CO INC
65 Ronzo Rd (06010-8621)
PHONE..................................860 589-5595
Lawrence M Frey, *President*
Henry R Frey Jr, *Vice Pres*
EMP: 15 **EST:** 1965
SQ FT: 9,000
SALES (est): 2.8MM **Privately Held**
WEB: www.plainvillemachinetool.com
SIC: 3544 Mfg Dies/Tools/Jigs/Fixtures

(G-595)
PLYMOUTH SPRING COMPANY INC
281 Lake Ave (06010-7322)
P.O. Box 1358 (06011-1358)
PHONE..................................860 584-0594
Richard Rubenstein, *President*
Lea Rubenstein, *Vice Pres*
Joseph Vanasse, *Foreman/Supr*
Jack Haber, *Treasurer*
Diane Gagnon, *Controller*
EMP: 63 **EST:** 1958
SQ FT: 40,000
SALES (est): 16.1MM **Privately Held**
WEB: www.plymouthspring.com
SIC: 3495 Mfg Wire Springs

(G-596)
PRECISION DEBURRING INC
139 Center St Ste 5002 (06010-5086)
PHONE..................................860 583-4662
Fax: 860 589-8658
EMP: 4
SQ FT: 2,200
SALES (est): 320K **Privately Held**
SIC: 3541 3471 Mfg Machine Tools-Cutting Plating/Polishing Service

(G-597)
PRECISION EXPRESS MFG LLC
630 Emmett St Unit 3 (06010-7793)
PHONE..................................860 584-2627
Alban Bebri, *Principal*
EMP: 10

▲ = Import ▼=Export
◆ =Import/Export

SALES (est): 1.3MM Privately Held
SIC: 3999 Mfg Misc Products

(G-598)
QUALITY COILS INCORPORATED (PA)
748 Middle St (06010-8417)
P.O. Box 1480 (06011-1480)
PHONE....860 584-0927
Keith A Gibson, *President*
Gary A Gibson, *Vice Pres*
Robert Duval, *Plant Mgr*
Jason Vallee, *Plant Mgr*
Carol Hawkins, *Prdtn Mgr*
EMP: 120 EST: 1965
SQ FT: 30,000
SALES (est): 34.5MM Privately Held
WEB: www.qualitycoils.com
SIC: 3677 Mfg Electronic Coils/Transformers

(G-599)
QUALITY WELDING LLC
61 E Main St Bldg C (06010-7060)
PHONE....860 585-1121
Peter Fortier, *Project Mgr*
Samuel Walters, *Mng Member*
EMP: 9
SQ FT: 1,800
SALES (est): 1.2MM Privately Held
WEB: www.qualityweldingllc.com
SIC: 7692 Welding Repair

(G-600)
QUALITY WIRE EDM INC
329 Redstone Hill Rd (06010-7741)
PHONE....860 583-9867
Jeffrey Rimcoski, *President*
EMP: 9
SQ FT: 2,000
SALES (est): 1.2MM Privately Held
SIC: 3599 3544 Wire Edm And Tool & Die Shop

(G-601)
R & R CORRUGATED CONTAINER INC
360 Minor St (06010-8543)
P.O. Box 399, Terryville (06786-0399)
PHONE....860 584-1194
Robert J Braverman, *President*
Roger Rainville, *Accounts Exec*
EMP: 58
SQ FT: 32,000
SALES (est): 14.4MM Privately Held
SIC: 2653 Mfg Corrugated/Solid Fiber Boxes

(G-602)
RADCLIFF WIRE INC
97 Ronzo Rd (06010-8619)
P.O. Box 603 (06011-0603)
PHONE....312 876-1754
Jean Radcliff, *CEO*
Charlie Radcliff, *President*
Donald F Radcliff, *Treasurer*
Kathy Sweetman, *Bookkeeper*
Scott Kirkpatrick, *VP Sales*
▲ EMP: 36 EST: 1959
SQ FT: 25,000
SALES (est): 9.3MM Privately Held
WEB: www.radcliffwire.com
SIC: 3357 3315 3496 Nonferrous Wire-drawing/Insulating Mfg Steel Wire/Related Products Mfg Misc Fabricated Wire Products

(G-603)
REED & STEFANOW MACHINE TL CO
165 Riverside Ave (06010-6322)
P.O. Box 1952 (06011-1952)
PHONE....860 583-7834
Joseph S Reed, *President*
Alice Reed, *Treasurer*
▲ EMP: 13 EST: 1972
SQ FT: 2,000
SALES (est): 2.2MM Privately Held
SIC: 3599 Machine Shop

(G-604)
RELIABLE SCALES & SYSTEMS LLC
150 Village St (06010-8035)
PHONE....860 380-0600
Edwin C Hollenbeck Jr,
EMP: 3
SALES (est): 305K Privately Held
SIC: 3596 Mfg Scales/Balances-Nonlaboratory

(G-605)
RGD TECHNOLOGIES CORP
Also Called: New Tech Replacement Part Co
50 Emmett St (06010-6623)
P.O. Box 9308 (06011-9308)
PHONE....860 589-0756
Robert G Dabkowski, *President*
Debra D Martin, *Corp Secy*
Cynthia D Policki, *Vice Pres*
▲ EMP: 60
SQ FT: 200,000
SALES (est): 11.4MM Privately Held
WEB: www.rgdtech.com
SIC: 3451 Mfg Screw Machine Products

(G-606)
RICHARD DAHLEN
Also Called: R & R McHy & Rebuilding Co
350 Riverside Ave (06010-6320)
P.O. Box 52, Torrington (06790-0052)
PHONE....860 584-8226
Richard Dahlen, *Owner*
EMP: 7 EST: 1973
SQ FT: 13,000
SALES (est): 721.7K Privately Held
SIC: 3599 5084 3542 Mfg Industrial Machinery Whol Industrial Equipment Mfg Machine Tools-Forming

(G-607)
RJ 15 INC
115 Cross St (06010-7434)
PHONE....860 585-0111
Joseph E Palfini, *President*
Margaret J Palfini, *Admin Sec*
EMP: 17
SQ FT: 14,500
SALES (est): 4.5MM Privately Held
WEB: www.rayjurgen.com
SIC: 3713 Mfg Truck/Bus Bodies

(G-608)
RONALD BOTTINO
Also Called: C & R Printing
381 Riverside Ave (06010-8810)
P.O. Box 9035 (06011-9035)
PHONE....860 585-9505
Chris Bottino, *Owner*
Ronald Bottino, *Owner*
EMP: 5
SQ FT: 3,000
SALES (est): 613.2K Privately Held
SIC: 2752 Offset Printing

(G-609)
ROSTRA VERNATHERM LLC
Also Called: Bilbe Controls
106 Enterprise Dr (06010-8403)
P.O. Box 3060 (06011-3060)
PHONE....860 582-6776
Kevin Lamb, *General Mgr*
Douglas Banks, *Opers Staff*
Carah Conlon, *Purch Mgr*
James Agard, *Engineer*
Alberto Medina, *Engineer*
▲ EMP: 31
SALES (est): 9.8MM Privately Held
WEB: www.rostravernatherm.com
SIC: 3491 Mfg Industrial Valves

(G-610)
ROWLEY SPRING & STAMPING CORP
210 Redstone Hill Rd # 2 (06010-7796)
PHONE....860 582-8175
John Dellalana, *President*
Barbara Tomcak, *Prdtn Mgr*
William R Joyce, *Treasurer*
Ted Sobota, *CIO*
Darlene B Krammer, *Director*
EMP: 160 EST: 1954
SQ FT: 150,000
SALES (est): 35.2MM Privately Held
WEB: www.rowleyspring.com
SIC: 3495 3621 3496 3493 Mfg Wire Springs Mfg Motors/Generators Mfg Misc Fab Wire Prdts Mfg Steel Spring-Nonwire Mfg Metal Stampings

(G-611)
ROYAL SCREW MACHINE PDTS CO
409 Lake Ave (06010-7330)
P.O. Box 1325, Waterbury (06721-1325)
PHONE....860 845-8920
Thomas H Derwin, *President*
Rory Derwin, *Info Tech Mgr*
Jason Derwin, *Information Mgr*
Lee Agostine, *Admin Sec*
EMP: 25 EST: 1940
SQ FT: 20,000
SALES (est): 5.4MM Privately Held
WEB: www.royalscrew.com
SIC: 3451 Mfg Screw Machine Products

(G-612)
SCOTTS METAL FINISHING LLC
Also Called: Scott Metal Finishing
310 Birch St (06010-7800)
P.O. Box 9091 (06011-9091)
PHONE....860 589-3778
James Barnes, *President*
Scott Barnes, *Vice Pres*
EMP: 15
SALES: 1MM Privately Held
WEB: www.scottmetalfinishing.com
SIC: 3471 5051 Plating/Polishing Service Metals Service Center

(G-613)
SOMERS MANUFACTURING INC
165 Riverside Ave (06010-6322)
PHONE....860 314-1075
Joe Fazzina, *President*
EMP: 5 EST: 1965
SQ FT: 5,000
SALES (est): 370K Privately Held
SIC: 3599 7692 3544 Mfg Industrial Machinery Welding Repair Mfg Dies/Tools/Jigs/Fixtures

(G-614)
SPRINGFIELD SPRING CORPORATION
24 Dell Manor Dr (06010-7436)
PHONE....860 584-6560
Dave Reno, *Manager*
EMP: 13
SALES (corp-wide): 9.2MM Privately Held
WEB: www.springfieldspring.com
SIC: 3495 Mfg Wire Springs
PA: Springfield Spring Corporation
311 Shaker Rd
East Longmeadow MA 01028
413 525-6837

(G-615)
SSI MANUFACTURING TECH CORP
675 Emmett St (06010-7715)
PHONE....860 589-8004
Gary Hutchison, *President*
Keith K Blethen, *Vice Pres*
Bob Peterson, *Vice Pres*
Peterson Robert, *Vice Pres*
Adam Wankier, *Vice Pres*
EMP: 36
SQ FT: 14,000
SALES (est): 8.1MM Privately Held
WEB: www.ssimanufacturing.com
SIC: 3599 Mfg Industrial Machinery

(G-616)
THEIS PRECISION STEEL USA INC (HQ)
300 Broad St (06010-6600)
PHONE....860 589-5511
Robert W Garthwait Jr, *President*
David Elliott, *COO*
David Elliot, *Vice Pres*
Thaddeus M Sendzimir, *Vice Pres*
Keith Doolittle, *Engineer*
◆ EMP: 215
SQ FT: 350,000
SALES (est): 96.4MM
SALES (corp-wide): 62.8MM Privately Held
WEB: www.theis-usa.com
SIC: 3316 Mfg Cold-Rolled Steel Shapes
PA: Tps Acquisition, Llc
151 Sharon Rd
Waterbury CT 06705
860 589-5511

(G-617)
THOMPSON AEROSPACE LLC
Also Called: Precision Threaded Products
220 Business Park Dr (06010-8629)
PHONE....860 516-0472
R Paul Nichols,
EMP: 16
SQ FT: 16,500
SALES (est): 3.2MM Privately Held
WEB: www.ptp-inc.com
SIC: 3728 Mfg Aircraft Parts/Equipment

(G-618)
TO GIVE IS BETTER
139 Center St Ste 5007 (06010-5086)
PHONE....860 261-5443
Philip Dubois, *President*
EMP: 6
SALES (est): 316.4K Privately Held
SIC: 2261 Finishing Of Cotton Broadwoven Fabrics

(G-619)
TOLLMAN SPRING COMPANY INC
560 Birch St (06010)
PHONE....860 583-4856
Chris Zink, *Branch Mgr*
EMP: 4
SALES (corp-wide): 12.5MM Privately Held
WEB: www.tollmanspring.com
SIC: 3493 Mfg Steel Springs
PA: Spring Tollman Company Incorporated
91 Enterprise Dr
Bristol CT 06010
860 583-1326

(G-620)
TRIPLE A SPRING LTD PARTNR
Also Called: Colonial Spring Company
95 Valley St Ste 1 (06010-4985)
P.O. Box 1079 (06011-1079)
PHONE....860 589-3231
William Lathrop, *Managing Prtnr*
EMP: 25 EST: 1946
SQ FT: 33,000
SALES (est): 5.3MM Privately Held
WEB: www.colonialspringco.com
SIC: 3493 Mfg Steel Springs-Nonwire

(G-621)
ULTIMATE WIREFORMS INC
200 Central St (06010-6716)
PHONE....860 582-9111
Paul Blanchette, *President*
Tom Cameron, *General Mgr*
Michael Brault, *Vice Pres*
Robert Nadeau, *Vice Pres*
Bruce Keevers, *QC Mgr*
EMP: 53
SALES (est): 7.5MM Privately Held
WEB: www.ultimateluresaver.com
SIC: 3841 8021 3843 3496 Mfg Surgical/Med Instr Dentist's Office Mfg Dental Equip/Supply Mfg Misc Fab Wire Prdts

(G-622)
VINTAGE BOAT RESTORATIONS LLC
201 Terryville Rd Ste 1 (06010-9606)
PHONE....860 582-0774
James Murdock Jr, *Mng Member*
Gail Murdock, *Manager*
EMP: 3
SALES (est): 351.3K Privately Held
SIC: 3732 Boatbuilding/Repairing

(G-623)
W M G AND SONS INC
8 Summerberry Rd (06010-2958)
PHONE....860 584-0143
William M Ghio, *President*
EMP: 5
SALES (est): 547.8K Privately Held
SIC: 1389 Construction

(G-624)
WESTFALIA INC
625 Middle St (06010-8415)
P.O. Box 9529 (06011-9529)
PHONE....860 314-2920
Stefan Hauk, *President*
Robert E Crumb, *Vice Pres*
Marc Gaudioso, *Finance Dir*

GEOGRAPHIC

Curtis Titus, *Admin Sec*
▲ **EMP:** 26
SQ FT: 35,000
SALES (est): 8.3MM
SALES (corp-wide): 563MM **Privately Held**
WEB: www.westfalia.com
SIC: 3714 Mfg Motor Vehicle Parts/Accessories
HQ: Westfalia Metallschlauchtechnik Verwaltungs-Gmbh
Konigsallee 4
Dusseldorf
273 328-3100

(G-625)
WHITMAN CONTROLS LLC
201 Dolphin Rd (06010-8000)
PHONE..................................800 233-4401
Richard Sexton, *Mng Member*
William Brame,
EMP: 13
SQ FT: 10,000
SALES (est): 565.6K **Privately Held**
SIC: 3822 Mfg Environmental Controls

(G-626)
WINCOR INC
47 Race St (06010-4906)
P.O. Box 1439 (06011-1439)
PHONE..................................860 589-5530
Kevin Likely, *President*
Carol Ann Likley, *Corp Secy*
EMP: 8 **EST:** 1978
SQ FT: 6,237
SALES (est): 820K **Privately Held**
WEB: www.wincor.com
SIC: 3451 Mfg Screw Machine Products

(G-627)
WOODWORK SPECIALTIES INC
123 New St (06010-5353)
PHONE..................................860 583-4848
Clement Letourneau, *President*
EMP: 4
SALES (est): 429.8K **Privately Held**
SIC: 2431 Mfg Millwork

Broad Brook
Hartford County

(G-628)
DC & D INC
42 Skinner Rd (06016-9694)
PHONE..................................860 623-2941
Michael Ceppetelli, *President*
EMP: 5
SALES (est): 572.2K **Privately Held**
SIC: 3699 8711 Mfg Electrical Equipment/Supplies Engineering Services

(G-629)
HARTFORD TONER & CARTRIDGE INC (PA)
6 Wapping Rd (06016-9717)
PHONE..................................860 292-1280
John Collins, *CEO*
Catherine Collins, *President*
Tim Golubeff, *Manager*
Joseph Mason, *Real Est Agnt*
EMP: 4
SQ FT: 6,000
SALES: 1MM **Privately Held**
WEB: www.hartfordtoner.com
SIC: 2759 5111 5085 5734 Commercial Printing Whol Print/Writing Paper Whol Industrial Supplies Ret Computers/Software

(G-630)
STROUTS WOODWORKING
Also Called: Strout Custom Millwork
45 Plantation Rd (06016-9551)
PHONE..................................860 623-8445
Ken Strouts, *Owner*
Cynthia Strouts, *Co-Owner*
EMP: 4
SALES (est): 292K **Privately Held**
SIC: 2499 Mfg Wood Products

Brookfield
Fairfield County

(G-631)
3T LIGHTING INC
Also Called: Nessen Lighting
20 Pocono Rd (06804-3303)
P.O. Box 165 (06804-0165)
PHONE..................................203 775-1805
Hsiaoching Yu, *Officer*
EMP: 7
SALES (est): 1.2MM **Privately Held**
SIC: 3645 3646 Mfg Residential Lighting Fixtures Mfg Commercial Lighting Fixtures

(G-632)
AB ELECTRONICS INC
61 Commerce Dr (06804-3405)
PHONE..................................203 740-2793
Armando Bernardo, *President*
Maria Bernardo, *Vice Pres*
Ncy McGuinness, *Senior Buyer*
EMP: 35
SQ FT: 13,000
SALES (est): 10.8MM **Privately Held**
WEB: www.abelectronicsinc.com
SIC: 3672 3679 8711 Mfg Printed Circuit Boards Mfg Electronic Components Engineering Services

(G-633)
AJ TUCK COMPANY
32 Tucks Rd (06804-1814)
P.O. Box 215 (06804-0215)
PHONE..................................203 775-1234
Alvin J Tuck IV, *Ch of Bd*
Lois Hunt, *Vice Pres*
Linda Pendergast, *Shareholder*
EMP: 20 **EST:** 1917
SQ FT: 8,000
SALES (est): 3.8MM **Privately Held**
WEB: www.ajtuckco.com
SIC: 3599 Mfg Industrial Machinery

(G-634)
ASTRALITE INC
20 Pocono Rd (06804)
P.O. Box 91 (06804-0091)
PHONE..................................203 775-0172
Robert Yu, *President*
Richard Yu, *Web Dvlpr*
▲ **EMP:** 6 **EST:** 2000
SQ FT: 23,988
SALES (est): 1.3MM **Privately Held**
WEB: www.astralitelighting.com
SIC: 3648 Mfg Lighting Equipment Nec

(G-635)
BOB THE BAKER LLC
594 Federal Rd (06804-2008)
P.O. Box 281 (06804-0281)
PHONE..................................203 775-1032
Frank R Labarbera, *Principal*
EMP: 10
SALES (est): 1MM **Privately Held**
SIC: 2052 Mfg Cookies/Crackers

(G-636)
BROOKFELD MDCL/SRGICAL SUP INC
Also Called: Brookfield Phrm Compounding
60 Old New Milford Rd (06804-2430)
PHONE..................................203 775-0862
James Cangelosi, *President*
Diane Cangelosi, *Corp Secy*
EMP: 10 **EST:** 1988
SALES: 1.2MM **Privately Held**
SIC: 2834 Mfg Pharmaceutical Preparations

(G-637)
CARRIER ACCESS - TRIN NETWORKS
61 Commerce Dr (06804-3405)
PHONE..................................203 778-8222
EMP: 3 **EST:** 2014
SALES (est): 117.7K **Privately Held**
SIC: 3661 Mfg Telephone/Telegraph Apparatus

(G-638)
CHANNEL SOURCES LLC
Also Called: Channel Sources Company
246 Federal Rd Ste A12-1 (06804-2635)
PHONE..................................203 775-6464
Randy Hujar, *COO*
Paul Hertz, *Vice Pres*
Tom Fitzsimmons, *Mng Member*
Phil Garel, *Director*
James Daly,
EMP: 13
SALES (est): 1.4MM **Privately Held**
WEB: www.channelsources.com
SIC: 7372 Prepackaged Software Services

(G-639)
CULTEC INC
878 Federal Rd (06804-1830)
P.O. Box 280 (06804-0280)
PHONE..................................203 775-4416
Robert Ditullio Sr, *CEO*
Gina Carolan, *President*
Robert Ditullio Jr, *Vice Pres*
Chris Ditullio, *CFO*
▼ **EMP:** 15
SQ FT: 12,000
SALES (est): 3.1MM **Privately Held**
WEB: www.cultec.com
SIC: 3089 Mfg Plastic Products

(G-640)
DAVE ROSS
Also Called: Brookfield Tractor Prfmce Eqp
92 S Lake Shore Dr (06804-1429)
PHONE..................................203 775-4327
Dave Ross, *Owner*
EMP: 4
SALES (est): 200K **Privately Held**
SIC: 3648 Mfg Lighting Equipment

(G-641)
DEFEO MANUFACTURING INC
115 Commerce Dr (06804-3400)
PHONE..................................203 775-0254
Arturo De Feo, *President*
Anthony De Feo, *Vice Pres*
◆ **EMP:** 29
SQ FT: 14,000
SALES (est): 5.9MM **Privately Held**
WEB: www.defeomfg.com
SIC: 3714 Mfg Motor Vehicle Parts/Accessories

(G-642)
DSAENCORE LLC (PA)
50 Pocono Rd (06804-3303)
PHONE..................................203 740-4200
Steve Friedman, *CEO*
Terry Algier, *Vice Pres*
Terri Winchell, *Vice Pres*
Rudolph Kraus,
EMP: 60
SQ FT: 30,000
SALES (est): 8MM **Privately Held**
SIC: 3679 Mfg Electronic Components

(G-643)
EASTERN PRECAST COMPANY INC
1 Commerce Dr (06804)
P.O. Box 5133 (06804-5133)
PHONE..................................203 775-0230
Richard G Ditullio Sr, *President*
Richard G Ditullio Jr, *Exec VP*
John J Ditullio, *Treasurer*
Judith H Ditullio, *Admin Sec*
EMP: 21
SQ FT: 3,000
SALES (est): 3.3MM **Privately Held**
WEB: www.easternprecast.com
SIC: 3272 Mfg Concrete Products

(G-644)
GK MECHANICAL SYSTEMS LLC
934 Federal Rd Ste 1b (06804-1143)
PHONE..................................203 775-4970
Keith Overthrow, *VP Opers*
Mike Dravis, *Project Engr*
Michael Barnes, *Mng Member*
Mike Sleet, *CTO*
Steve Fournier,
EMP: 8
SQ FT: 4,500
SALES (est): 3.5MM **Privately Held**
SIC: 3429 Mfg Keys Locks & Related Hardware

(G-645)
GORDON ENGINEERING CORP
67 Del Mar Dr (06804-2494)
PHONE..................................203 775-4501
Steven Weighart, *President*
Barb Baldino, *Sales Staff*
EMP: 16 **EST:** 1971
SQ FT: 3,000
SALES: 1MM **Privately Held**
WEB: www.gordoneng.com
SIC: 3823 3842 Mfg Process Control Instruments Mfg Surgical Appliances/Supplies

(G-646)
GORDON PRODUCTS INCORPORATED
67 Del Mar Dr (06804-2401)
PHONE..................................203 775-4501
Steven Weighart, *President*
Debbie Rabito, *Prdtn Mgr*
EMP: 25
SQ FT: 14,000
SALES (est): 3.6MM **Privately Held**
WEB: www.gordonproducts.com
SIC: 3625 3674 3643 Mfg Relays/Industrial Controls Mfg Semiconductors/Related Devices Mfg Conductive Wiring Devices

(G-647)
IMPERIAL ELCTRNIC ASSEMBLY INC
Also Called: I E A
1000 Federal Rd (06804-1123)
PHONE..................................203 740-8425
Tony Conte, *President*
Edward O'Donnell, *Vice Pres*
Sandy Connolly, *Purchasing*
Heather White, *Engineer*
Donna Martin, *Credit Staff*
▲ **EMP:** 93
SQ FT: 45,000
SALES (est): 34.3MM **Privately Held**
WEB: www.impea.com
SIC: 3679 Mfg Electronic Components

(G-648)
JENRAY PRODUCTS INC
4 Production Dr (06804-1156)
PHONE..................................914 375-5596
Raymond D'Urso, *President*
▲ **EMP:** 26 **EST:** 1999
SALES (est): 3.5MM **Privately Held**
SIC: 3999 Mfg Auto & Home Air Fresheners

(G-649)
JK ANTENNAS INC
72 Grays Bridge Rd Ste D (06804-2632)
PHONE..................................845 228-8700
Ken Garg, *President*
Charlisa Garg, *Vice Pres*
Ann Garg, *Director*
EMP: 5
SALES (est): 278.2K **Privately Held**
SIC: 3663 Mfg Radio/Tv Communication Equipment

(G-650)
LA PIETRA THINSTONE VENEER
Also Called: La Pietra Custom Marble & Gran
1106 Federal Rd (06804-1122)
P.O. Box 5149 (06804-5149)
PHONE..................................203 775-6162
Fabio Figueiredo, *President*
EMP: 3
SALES (est): 99.6K **Privately Held**
SIC: 3281 5211 Mfg Cut Stone/Products Ret Lumber/Building Materials

(G-651)
MCMULLIN MANUFACTURING CORP
70 Pocono Rd (06804-3303)
P.O. Box 780 (06804-0780)
PHONE..................................203 740-3360
Timothy McMullin, *President*
Kevin J McMullin, *Vice Pres*
Kevin McMullin, *Vice Pres*
Marlys J McMullin, *Director*
EMP: 31
SQ FT: 12,800

▲ = Import ▼=Export
◆ =Import/Export

SALES (est): 5.9MM Privately Held
WEB: www.mcmullinmfg.com
SIC: 3469 3444 Mfg Metal Stampings Mfg Sheet Metalwork

(G-652)
MILLBROOK PRESS INC
2 Old New Milford Rd 2e (06804-2413)
PHONE..................................203 740-2220
David Allen, *President*
EMP: 46
SALES (est): 4.8MM Privately Held
SIC: 2731 Book Publishing

(G-653)
MOONLIGHTING LLC
4 Jackson Dr (06804-1608)
PHONE..................................203 740-8964
David Morin, *Principal*
EMP: 4
SALES (est): 256.2K Privately Held
SIC: 3648 Mfg Lighting Equipment

(G-654)
PHOTRONICS INC (PA)
15 Secor Rd (06804-3937)
P.O. Box 5226 (06804-5226)
PHONE..................................203 775-9000
Peter S Kirlin, *CEO*
Richelle E Burr, *Vice Pres*
Christopher J Progler, *Vice Pres*
Rust Jay, *Traffic Mgr*
Stephen Maxwell, *Mfg Spvr*
EMP: 277
SALES: 550.6MM Publicly Held
WEB: www.photronics.com
SIC: 3674 Mfg Semiconductors/Related Devices

(G-655)
PHOTRONICS TEXAS INC
15 Secor Rd (06804-3937)
PHONE..................................203 546-3039
Sean T Smith, *Principal*
Dan Pullen, *Engineer*
EMP: 4
SALES (est): 255.4K
SALES (corp-wide): 550.6MM Publicly Held
SIC: 3674 Mfg Semiconductors/Related Devices
PA: Photronics, Inc.
15 Secor Rd
Brookfield CT 06804
203 775-9000

(G-656)
PHOTRONICS TEXAS I LLC
15 Secor Rd (06804-3937)
PHONE..................................203 775-9000
Constantine S Macricostas, *Chairman*
EMP: 4
SALES (est): 139K
SALES (corp-wide): 550.6MM Publicly Held
SIC: 3674 Mfg Semiconductors/Related Devices
PA: Photronics, Inc.
15 Secor Rd
Brookfield CT 06804
203 775-9000

(G-657)
PRECISION PLASTIC FAB
5d Del Mar Dr (06804)
PHONE..................................203 775-7047
John Clayton, *Owner*
EMP: 3
SALES (est): 377K Privately Held
SIC: 3089 Mfg Plastic Products

(G-658)
SPEEDI SIGN LLC
770 Federal Rd (06804-2026)
PHONE..................................203 775-0700
James A Myles, *Mng Member*
EMP: 3
SQ FT: 1,400
SALES (est): 272.9K Privately Held
SIC: 3993 Mfg Signs/Advertising Specialties

(G-659)
TARGET FLAVORS INC
7 Del Mar Dr (06804-2401)
PHONE..................................203 775-4727
John Maclean, *President*
John S Maclean Jr, *Vice Pres*
William Maclean, *Vice Pres*
Judy Medcalf, *Purch Agent*
▲ EMP: 12
SQ FT: 25,000
SALES (est): 2.7MM Privately Held
WEB: www.targetflavors.com
SIC: 2087 Mfg Flavor Extracts/Syrup

(G-660)
TECHNIPOWER SYSTEMS INC (HQ)
57 Commerce Dr (06804-3405)
PHONE..................................203 748-7001
EMP: 8
SQ FT: 15,000
SALES (est): 3.2MM
SALES (corp-wide): 10.4MM Privately Held
WEB: www.solomontechnologies.com
SIC: 3621 Manufacturing Of Motors And Generators
PA: Technipower Llc
3900 Coral Ridge Dr
Coral Springs FL 33071
203 748-7001

(G-661)
TOPPAN PHOTOMASKS INC
246 Federal Rd Ste C22 (06804-2647)
PHONE..................................203 775-9001
Michael G Hadsell, *Branch Mgr*
EMP: 49 Privately Held
SIC: 3559 Mfg Misc Industry Machinery
HQ: Toppan Photomasks, Inc.
131 E Old Settlers Blvd
Round Rock TX 78664
512 310-6500

(G-662)
UNIVERSAL VOLTRONICS CORP
57 Commerce Dr (06804-3405)
PHONE..................................203 740-8555
Tom Kell, *CEO*
William T Carney, *President*
Bert Yost, *Technical Staff*
EMP: 40
SQ FT: 22,000
SALES (est): 6.9MM Privately Held
WEB: www.voltronics.com
SIC: 3612 Mfg Transformers

(G-663)
VALIDUS DC SYSTEMS LLC
50 Pocono Rd (06804-3303)
PHONE..................................203 448-3600
Rudy Kraus, *CEO*
Ronald Croce, *COO*
Frank Catapano, *Vice Pres*
Al Dei Maggi, *Vice Pres*
Larry Hess,
EMP: 14
SQ FT: 29,000
SALES (est): 111.7MM Privately Held
SIC: 3679 Mfg Electronic Components

(G-664)
VISION DESIGNS LLC
1120 Federal Rd Ste 2 (06804-1122)
PHONE..................................203 778-9898
Scott D Johnson, *Managing Prtnr*
Dan Lombardo, *Partner*
Tom Seeley, *Partner*
Lenny Margiotta, *Vice Pres*
EMP: 15
SALES (est): 2.2MM Privately Held
WEB: www.visiondesignsct.com
SIC: 2759 5099 Commercial Printing Whol Durable Goods

(G-665)
WENTWORTH LABORATORIES INC (PA)
1087 Federal Rd Ste 4 (06804-1145)
PHONE..................................203 775-0448
Arthur Evans, *Ch of Bd*
Stephen AA Evans, *President*
Stephen Evans, *President*
Robert Bollo, *Vice Pres*
Sue Murphy, *Production*
EMP: 57
SQ FT: 25,000
SALES (est): 16.1MM Privately Held
WEB: www.wentworthlabs.com
SIC: 3825 Mfg Electrical Measuring Instruments

(G-666)
WENTWORTH LABORATORIES INC
500 Federal Rd (06804-2019)
P.O. Box 320 (06804-0320)
PHONE..................................203 775-9311
EMP: 4
SALES (corp-wide): 25.1MM Privately Held
SIC: 3825 3826 3823 Mfg Electrical Measuring Instruments Mfg Analytical Instruments Mfg Process Control Instruments
PA: Wentworth Laboratories, Inc.
1087 Federal Rd Ste 4
Brookfield CT 06804
203 775-0448

(G-667)
YANKEE PENNYSAVER INC
246 Federal Rd Ste D15 (06804-2649)
PHONE..................................203 775-9122
EMP: 23
SALES (est): 1MM Privately Held
WEB: www.ctpennysaver.com
SIC: 2711 Newspapers-Publishing/Printing

Brooklyn
Windham County

(G-668)
A F M ENGINEERING CORP
24 Woodward Rd (06234-1425)
PHONE..................................860 774-7518
Steven A Gilman, *President*
Lee Gilman, *Corp Secy*
EMP: 5
SQ FT: 6,600
SALES: 500K Privately Held
WEB: www.afmengineering.com
SIC: 3569 5084 Mfg General Industrial Machinery Whol Industrial Equipment

(G-669)
AD LABEL INC
59 N Society Rd (06234-2313)
PHONE..................................860 779-0513
Richard Baril, *President*
Robert Benson, *Vice Pres*
EMP: 7 EST: 1981
SQ FT: 3,200
SALES (est): 1.3MM Privately Held
SIC: 2759 Commercial Printing

(G-670)
BARRETTE MECHANICAL
36 Bush Hill Rd (06234-1400)
PHONE..................................860 774-0499
Bruce Barrette, *Principal*
EMP: 3
SALES (est): 195K Privately Held
SIC: 3999 Mfg Misc Products

(G-671)
MONOGRAMIT LLC
9 S Main St (06234-3400)
PHONE..................................860 779-0694
Georgia Ludovici, *Owner*
EMP: 3
SALES: 95K Privately Held
SIC: 2395 Pleating/Stitching Services

(G-672)
SIGFRIDSON WOOD PRODUCTS LLC
125 Fitzgerald Rd (06234-1411)
PHONE..................................860 774-2075
Kenneth Sigfridson,
Andrew Sigfridson,
EMP: 7
SQ FT: 20,000
SALES: 2MM Privately Held
WEB: www.sigfridson.com
SIC: 2421 Sawmill/Planing Mill

(G-673)
UNINSRED ALTTUDE CNNECTION INC
Also Called: Peregrine Manufacturing
330 Day St (06234-1517)
PHONE..................................860 333-1461
David Singer, *President*
Colleen Malone, *Manager*
EMP: 3
SQ FT: 3,000
SALES (est): 208.2K Privately Held
SIC: 2393 Mfg Textile Bags

(G-674)
WOLD TOOL ENGINEERING INC
7 Commonway Dr (06234-1839)
PHONE..................................860 564-8338
EMP: 7 EST: 1945
SQ FT: 3,600
SALES: 500K Privately Held
SIC: 3451 Mfg Screw Machine Products

Burlington
Hartford County

(G-675)
CEM GROUP LLC (DH)
Also Called: Chand Eisenmann Metallurgical
258 Spielman Hwy Ste 7 (06013-1723)
PHONE..................................860 675-5000
Mark Eisenmann,
EMP: 10
SQ FT: 10,000
SALES (est): 2.5MM
SALES (corp-wide): 170.1MM Privately Held
WEB: www.chandeisenmann.com
SIC: 3449 Manufactures Miscellaneous Structural Metalwork
HQ: Porvair Filtration Group, Inc.
301 Business Ln
Ashland VA 23005
804 550-1600

(G-676)
CRESCENT MNFACTURING OPERATING
700 George Wash Tpke (06013-1718)
P.O. Box 1350 (06013-0350)
PHONE..................................860 673-1921
Richard Hrinak,
Joanne Gates,
Richard V Gates,
Richard Green,
James Speck,
EMP: 34 EST: 1960
SQ FT: 18,000
SALES: 1,000K Privately Held
WEB: www.crescentmanufacturing.com
SIC: 3452 Mfg Bolts/Screws/Rivets

(G-677)
E R HINMAN & SONS INC
Also Called: Hinman Lumber
77 Milford St (06013-1722)
PHONE..................................860 673-9170
Julia Hinman, *CEO*
Michael J Hinman, *President*
Paul Hinman, *Vice Pres*
EMP: 8 EST: 1915
SQ FT: 5,000
SALES (est): 1.2MM Privately Held
SIC: 2421 2426 Sawmill/Planing Mill Hardwood Dimension/Floor Mill

(G-678)
ENERGY SAVING PRODUCTS AND SLS
713 George Washington Tpk (06013-1718)
P.O. Box 2037 (06013-1037)
PHONE..................................860 675-6443
Richard Lamothe, *President*
Susan Lamothe, *Vice Pres*
EMP: 50
SQ FT: 30,000
SALES (est): 6.8MM Privately Held
SIC: 3579 Mfg Office Machines

(G-679)
MILLER FUEL LLC
28 Monce Rd (06013-2539)
P.O. Box 1506 (06013-0506)
PHONE..................................860 675-6121
Michael J Miller, *President*
EMP: 7
SALES (est): 896.5K **Privately Held**
SIC: 2869 Mfg Industrial Organic Chemicals

(G-680)
TARGET MACHINES INC
713 George Wash Tpke (06013-1718)
PHONE..................................860 675-1539
Richard Lamothe, *President*
Susan Lamothe, *Corp Secy*
EMP: 6
SALES (est): 660K **Privately Held**
WEB: www.targetmachines.com
SIC: 3599 7389 Mfg Industrial Machinery

(G-681)
TYNE PLASTICS LLC (PA)
252 Spielman Hwy Ste B (06013-1753)
PHONE..................................860 673-7100
Wendy L Carrafa,
EMP: 4
SALES (est): 2.7MM **Privately Held**
WEB: www.tyne.com
SIC: 2821 Mfg Plastic Materials/Resins

(G-682)
W R HARTIGAN & SON INC
10 Spielman Hwy (06013-1909)
PHONE..................................860 673-9203
Gerald H Mullen, *President*
Alice I Hartigan, *Corp Secy*
Bryan Mullen, *Vice Pres*
EMP: 6 **EST:** 1869
SQ FT: 6,500
SALES (est): 200K **Privately Held**
SIC: 2541 2441 2499 7371 Industrial Woodworking And Provides Custom Application Software And Wholesales Computer Hardware

Canaan
Litchfield County

(G-683)
BECTON DICKINSON AND COMPANY
Grace Way Rr 7 (06018)
P.O. Box 749 (06018-0749)
PHONE..................................860 824-5487
Todd Zeller, *Manager*
EMP: 400
SALES (corp-wide): 15.9B **Publicly Held**
SIC: 3841 3842 Mfg Surgical/Medical Instruments Mfg Surgical Appliances/Supplies
PA: Becton, Dickinson And Company
1 Becton Dr
Franklin Lakes NJ 07417
201 847-6800

(G-684)
BONSAL AMERICAN INC
43 Clayton Rd (06018-2153)
P.O. Box 996 (06018-0996)
PHONE..................................860 824-7733
George Sperry, *Vice Pres*
EMP: 8
SALES (corp-wide): 29.7B **Privately Held**
WEB: www.bonsalamerican.com
SIC: 3272 Mfg Concrete Products
HQ: Bonsal American, Inc.
625 Griffith Rd Ste 100
Charlotte NC 28217
704 525-1621

(G-685)
BONSAL AMERICAN INC
43 Clayton Rd (06018-2153)
PHONE..................................860 824-7733
EMP: 20
SQ FT: 2,000
SALES (corp-wide): 23.5B **Privately Held**
SIC: 3273 3272 3255 Mfg Ready-Mixed Concrete Mfg Concrete Products Mfg Clay Refractories
HQ: Bonsal American, Inc.
8201 Arrowridge Blvd
Charlotte NC 28217
704 525-1621

(G-686)
CENTURY ACQUISITION
49 Clayton Rd (06018-2153)
P.O. Box 485 (06018-0485)
PHONE..................................518 758-7229
Brendan Clemente, *Owner*
EMP: 9
SALES (est): 1.3MM **Privately Held**
SIC: 3273 Mfg Ready-Mixed Concrete

(G-687)
HITBRO REALTY LLC
78 High St (06018-2535)
PHONE..................................860 824-1370
EMP: 4
SALES (est): 333.1K **Privately Held**
SIC: 2869 Mfg Industrial Organic Chemicals

(G-688)
JILL GHI
Also Called: Ghi Sign Service
532 Ashley Falls Rd (06018-2017)
P.O. Box 45 (06018-0045)
PHONE..................................860 824-7123
Jill Ghi, *Principal*
Gary Rovelto, *Prdtn Mgr*
Philip J Ghi, *Asst Treas*
EMP: 3 **EST:** 1955
SQ FT: 1,000
SALES: 150K **Privately Held**
WEB: www.ghisign.com
SIC: 3993 Mfg Signs/Advertising Specialties

(G-689)
MINTEQ INTERNATIONAL INC
Also Called: Mineral Technology
30 Daisy Hill Rd (06018-2115)
P.O. Box 667 (06018-0667)
PHONE..................................860 824-5435
Mark Lambert, *Principal*
EMP: 130 **Publicly Held**
WEB: www.minteq.com
SIC: 2851 3823 3624 Mfg Paints/Allied Products Mfg Process Control Instruments Mfg Carbon/Graphite Products
HQ: Minteq International Inc.
35 Highland Ave
Bethlehem PA 18017

(G-690)
SPECIALTY MINERALS INC
30 Daisy Hill Rd (06018-2115)
P.O. Box 667 (06018-0667)
PHONE..................................860 824-5435
Michelle Lowe, *Hum Res Coord*
Mark Lambert, *Branch Mgr*
EMP: 130 **Publicly Held**
WEB: www.specialtyminerals.com
SIC: 3297 2819 1422 Mfg Nonclay Refractories Mfg Industrial Inorganic Chemicals Crushed/Broken Limestone
HQ: Specialty Minerals Inc.
622 3rd Ave Fl 38
New York NY 10017
212 878-1800

(G-691)
TALLON LUMBER INC
2 Tallon Dr (06018)
P.O. Box 1058 (06018-1058)
PHONE..................................860 824-0733
James A Tallon, *President*
Brion Tallon, *Vice Pres*
EMP: 26
SQ FT: 1,200
SALES (est): 4.3MM **Privately Held**
WEB: www.tallonlumber.com
SIC: 2421 2426 Sawmill/Planing Mill Hardwood Dimension/Floor Mill

Canterbury
Windham County

(G-692)
BRAD KETTLE
Also Called: Brad's Logging
4 Howe Rd (06331-1919)
PHONE..................................860 546-9929
Brad Kettle, *Principal*
EMP: 3
SALES (est): 266.8K **Privately Held**
SIC: 2411 Logging

(G-693)
J D & ASSOCIATES
115 John Brook Rd (06331-1624)
PHONE..................................860 546-2112
James F Ennis III, *Managing Prtnr*
Dorothy Ennis, *Managing Prtnr*
EMP: 3 **EST:** 1987
SALES (est): 200.1K **Privately Held**
SIC: 3542 Mfg Machine Tools-Forming

(G-694)
MAURICES COUNTRY MEAT MKT LLC
155 Gooseneck Hill Rd (06331-1800)
PHONE..................................860 546-9588
Harold Levesque,
Paul Levesque,
Linda Mazur,
EMP: 3
SQ FT: 100,000
SALES (est): 209.3K **Privately Held**
SIC: 2011 2013 Meat Packing Plant Mfg Prepared Meats

Canton
Hartford County

(G-695)
ALEXIS AEROSPACE INDS LLC
Also Called: A A I
200 Smith Way (06019-2489)
P.O. Box 173, Terryville (06786-0173)
PHONE..................................860 516-4602
Frederick A Sundberg,
EMP: 5
SQ FT: 3,000
SALES: 250K **Privately Held**
SIC: 3728 Mfg Aircraft Parts/Equipment

(G-696)
CABINET RESOURCES CT INC
180 Cherry Brook Rd (06019-4510)
PHONE..................................860 352-2030
William G Trevethan, *President*
Jonathan L Fein, *Admin Sec*
EMP: 3
SALES (est): 810K **Privately Held**
SIC: 2434 Mfg Wood Kitchen Cabinets

(G-697)
DELTA ELEVATOR SERVICE CORP (DH)
Also Called: Otis Elevator Company
1 Farm Springs Rd (06019)
PHONE..................................860 676-6152
Randy Wilclx, *President*
Chris Gouyd, *Manager*
EMP: 20
SALES (est): 6MM
SALES (corp-wide): 66.5B **Publicly Held**
SIC: 3625 Mfg Relays/Industrial Controls

(G-698)
PRECISION WOODCRAFT INC
Also Called: Precision Woodcraft ME
16 Cheryl Dr (06019-2232)
PHONE..................................860 693-3641
David Byrne, *President*
Lauwrina Byrne, *Admin Sec*
EMP: 6
SQ FT: 5,000
SALES (est): 560K **Privately Held**
SIC: 2431 Mfg Millwork

(G-699)
ST PIERRE BOX AND LUMBER CO
66 Lovely St (06019-2630)
PHONE..................................860 413-9813
EMP: 5
SQ FT: 13,000
SALES (est): 625.8K **Privately Held**
SIC: 2441 2448 5211 2449 Mfg Wooden Boxes & Pallets & Ret Lumber

(G-700)
VETERINARY MEDICAL ASSOCIATES
Also Called: Roaring Brook Veterenary Hosp
60 Lovely St (06019-2630)
P.O. Box 330 (06019-0330)
PHONE..................................860 693-0214
Peter Berk, *President*
EMP: 4
SALES (est): 830.3K **Privately Held**
SIC: 2835 0742 Veterinary Services Mfg Diagnostic Substances

Centerbrook
Middlesex County

(G-701)
APCO PRODUCTS
6 Essex Industrial Park (06409)
P.O. Box 236, Essex (06426-0236)
PHONE..................................860 767-2108
Morton Reich, *President*
EMP: 25
SQ FT: 30,000
SALES (est): 4.9MM **Privately Held**
SIC: 3496 Mfg Misc Fabricated Wire Products

(G-702)
QUALITY CARE DRG/CNTRBROOK LLC
33 Main St (06409-1083)
P.O. Box 540, Higganum (06441-0540)
PHONE..................................860 767-0206
Richard Allen Olson, *Mng Member*
Mark G McKenna,
EMP: 7
SALES (est): 985.3K **Privately Held**
SIC: 2834 Mfg Pharmaceutical Preparations

(G-703)
RED ROCKET SITE 2
47 Industrial Park Rd (06409-1020)
PHONE..................................860 581-8019
EMP: 3
SALES (est): 296.2K **Privately Held**
SIC: 3577 Mfg Computer Peripheral Equipment

(G-704)
TOWER LABORATORIES LTD (PA)
Also Called: Tower Brands
8 Industrial Park Rd (06409-1019)
P.O. Box 306 (06409-0306)
PHONE..................................860 767-2127
Norman Needleman, *President*
Melissa Miles, *Buyer*
E Cook Rand, *Admin Sec*
◆ **EMP:** 95
SQ FT: 38,000
SALES (est): 30.4MM **Privately Held**
SIC: 2834 Mfg Pharmaceutical Preparations

Central Village
Windham County

(G-705)
BEAR HANDS BREWING COMPANY
13 Palmer Ct (06332-3227)
PHONE..................................860 576-5374
Matthew Trant, *Principal*
EMP: 3
SALES (est): 74.5K **Privately Held**
SIC: 2082 Mfg Malt Beverages

(G-706)
GUY RAVENELLE
Also Called: Ravco Wood Products
71 Black Hill Rd (06332)
P.O. Box 532 (06332-0532)
PHONE..................................860 564-3200
Guy Ravenelle, *Owner*
EMP: 6
SALES: 150K **Privately Held**
SIC: 2448 Mfg Wood Pallets/Skids

Cheshire
New Haven County

(G-707)
A B & F SHEET METAL
Also Called: AB&f Sheet Metal Products
327 Sandbank Rd (06410-1506)
PHONE..................................203 272-9340
Milford Armstrong, *Owner*
EMP: 7
SQ FT: 4,500
SALES (est): 915.6K **Privately Held**
SIC: 3444 Sheet Metalwork

(G-708)
AI-TEK INSTRUMENTS LLC
152 Knotter Dr (06410-1136)
P.O. Box 748 (06410-0748)
PHONE..................................203 271-6927
Peter Sandore,
David Elliott,
Leonard Mecca,
▼ **EMP:** 38
SQ FT: 18,000
SALES (est): 8.2MM **Privately Held**
WEB: www.aitekinstruments.com
SIC: 3829 Mfg Measuring/Controlling Devices

(G-709)
AIS GLOBAL HOLDINGS LLC
Also Called: Atlantic Inertial Systems
250 Knotter Dr (06410-1137)
PHONE..................................203 250-3500
Christopher Holmes, *Mng Member*
David Oldham,
EMP: 800
SALES (est): 30.7MM
SALES (corp-wide): 66.5B **Publicly Held**
SIC: 3812 Mfg Search/Navigation Equipment
HQ: Goodrich Corporation
2730 W Tyvola Rd 4
Charlotte NC 28217
704 423-7000

(G-710)
AMERICAN RUBBER STAMP COMPANY
Also Called: American Mailing Depot
35 Judson Ct (06410-2837)
PHONE..................................203 755-1135
Vincent Lentini, *President*
Elizabeth Lentini, *Treasurer*
Bryan Lentini, *Admin Sec*
EMP: 3 **EST:** 1944
SQ FT: 2,200
SALES: 195K **Privately Held**
SIC: 3953 3479 7331 Mfg Rubber Date Stamps Hand Seals Stationery Embossers Stencils And Engraving Of Name Plates & Mailing Services

(G-711)
APEX MACHINE TOOL COMPANY INC
500 Knotter Dr (06410)
PHONE..................................860 677-2884
Dominick A Pagano, *President*
Glenn L Purple, *Admin Sec*
EMP: 99 **EST:** 1944
SQ FT: 44,008
SALES (est): 16MM **Privately Held**
WEB: www.apexmachinetool.com
SIC: 3544 3545 3546 3089 Mfg Dies/Tools/Jigs/Fixt Mfg Machine Tool Access Mfg Powerdriven Handtool Mfg Plastic Products Engineering Services
HQ: Edac Technologies Llc
5 Mckee Pl
Cheshire CT 06410
203 806-2090

(G-712)
AQUACOMFORT SOLUTIONS LLC
15 Burton Dr (06410-1205)
PHONE..................................407 831-1941
EMP: 9
SALES (corp-wide): 3MM **Privately Held**
SIC: 3648 Mfg Lighting Equipment
PA: Aquacomfort Solutions Llc
950 Sunshine Ln
Altamonte Springs FL 32714
407 831-1941

(G-713)
ATLANTIC INERTIAL SYSTEMS INC (DH)
Also Called: Goodrich Sensors and Integrate
250 Knotter Dr (06410-1137)
PHONE..................................203 250-3500
Justin Robert Keppy, *President*
Zenon Melnyk, *General Mgr*
Richard S Caswell, *Vice Pres*
Kevin Swain, *Manager*
Susan Crowley, *Info Tech Mgr*
▲ **EMP:** 490 **EST:** 2000
SQ FT: 70,000
SALES (est): 110.8MM
SALES (corp-wide): 66.5B **Publicly Held**
WEB: www.condorpacific.com
SIC: 3812 Mfg Search/Navigation Equipment
HQ: Goodrich Corporation
2730 W Tyvola Rd 4
Charlotte NC 28217
704 423-7000

(G-714)
ATLANTIC INERTIAL SYSTEMS INC
Also Called: Cheshire Division
250 Knotter Dr (06410-1137)
PHONE..................................203 250-3500
Robert Nead, *Branch Mgr*
EMP: 600
SALES (corp-wide): 66.5B **Publicly Held**
SIC: 3812 3845 Mfg Search/Navigation Equipment Mfg Electromedical Equipment
HQ: Atlantic Inertial Systems Inc.
250 Knotter Dr
Cheshire CT 06410
203 250-3500

(G-715)
BOVANO INDUSTRIES INCORPORATED
Also Called: Bovano of Cheshire
830 S Main St Ofc A (06410-3474)
PHONE..................................203 272-3208
James A Flood, *President*
David Flood, *Vice Pres*
Kevin Flood, *Opers Mgr*
EMP: 15
SQ FT: 17,000
SALES (est): 1.8MM **Privately Held**
SIC: 3231 5947 3229 Mfg Products-Purchased Glass Ret Gifts/Novelties Mfg Pressed/Blown Glass

(G-716)
BRIAN SAFA
80 Royalwood Ct (06410-2242)
PHONE..................................203 271-3499
Brian Safa, *Principal*
EMP: 3 **EST:** 2010
SALES (est): 247.8K **Privately Held**
SIC: 2869 Mfg Industrial Organic Chemicals

(G-717)
BRIMATCO CORPORATION
1486 Highland Ave Ste 10 (06410-1200)
P.O. Box 88 (06410-0088)
PHONE..................................203 272-0044
James Dacunto, *President*
EMP: 3
SQ FT: 4,000
SALES (est): 513.1K **Privately Held**
WEB: www.brimatco.com
SIC: 3423 Mfg Wrenches

(G-718)
BUNTING & LYON INC
615 Broad Swamp Rd (06410-2918)
PHONE..................................203 272-4623
Peter Bunting, *President*
EMP: 6
SALES (est): 480K **Privately Held**
WEB: www.buntingandlyon.com
SIC: 2731 8748 7361 Book Publishers

(G-719)
CARTEN CONTROLS INC
604 W Johnson Ave (06410-4500)
PHONE..................................203 699-2100
Hidet S Kataoka, *CEO*
Hiroshi Ogawa, *CEO*
Kenji Yamamoto, *President*
Monty L Botkin, *Vice Pres*
Karen Dicarlo, *Sales Staff*
▲ **EMP:** 15
SQ FT: 65,000
SALES (est): 3.8MM **Privately Held**
SIC: 3592 3494 Mfg Carburetors/Pistons/Rings Mfg Valves/Pipe Fittings

(G-720)
CARTEN-FUJIKIN INCORPORATED
604 W Johnson Ave (06410-4500)
PHONE..................................203 699-2134
Seamus Sweeney, *General Mgr*
▲ **EMP:** 8
SALES (est): 770K **Privately Held**
SIC: 3674 Mfg Semiconductors/Related Devices

(G-721)
CHESHIRE MANUFACTURING CO INC
312 E Johnson Ave Ste 1 (06410-1297)
PHONE..................................203 272-3586
Joseph Whitright Jr, *President*
Dora Whitright, *Corp Secy*
EMP: 7 **EST:** 1957
SQ FT: 6,500
SALES (est): 687.5K **Privately Held**
SIC: 3714 3469 7692 Mfg Compact Heat Exchanges & Oil Coolers

(G-722)
CINTAS CORPORATION
10 Diana Ct (06410-1206)
PHONE..................................203 272-2036
Thomas Vega, *President*
EMP: 10
SALES (corp-wide): 6.8B **Publicly Held**
SIC: 2326 Mfg Men's/Boy's Work Clothing
PA: Cintas Corporation
6800 Cintas Blvd
Cincinnati OH 45262
513 459-1200

(G-723)
COLD BREW COFFEE COMPANY LLC
27 E Ridge Ct (06410-1236)
PHONE..................................860 250-4410
Gary Riccini, *Principal*
EMP: 3
SALES (est): 75.4K **Privately Held**
SIC: 2082 Mfg Malt Beverages

(G-724)
CONSOLDTED INDS ACQSITION CORP
677 Mixville Rd (06410-3836)
PHONE..................................203 272-5371
John David Wilbur, *President*
Drew Papio, *Vice Pres*
Benjamin Mark Palazzo, *Admin Sec*
▲ **EMP:** 100
SQ FT: 87,000
SALES: 30MM **Privately Held**
SIC: 3462 3369 Mfg Iron/Steel Forgings Nonferrous Metal Foundry

(G-725)
CREATIVE DIMENSIONS INC
345 Mccausland Ct (06410-1278)
PHONE..................................203 250-6500
Joel P Roy, *President*
Bill Violette, *Vice Pres*
John Stifel, *Foreman/Supr*
Nicholas Bruggeman, *Director*
Jessica Fetzer, *Director*
▲ **EMP:** 37
SQ FT: 48,000
SALES (est): 7.6MM **Privately Held**
WEB: www.creative-dimensions.com
SIC: 3993 2541 Mfg Signs/Advertising Specialties Mfg Wood Partitions/Fixtures

(G-726)
DALTON ENTERPRISES INC (PA)
131 Willow St (06410-2732)
PHONE..................................203 272-3221
John A Dalton, *President*
Barbara Alberino, *Vice Pres*
Matt Urban, *Traffic Mgr*
Darlene Stabile, *Manager*
▼ **EMP:** 100
SALES (est): 42.8MM **Privately Held**
WEB: www.latexite.com
SIC: 3272 Mfg Concrete Products

(G-727)
DANJON MANUFACTURING CORP
1075 S Main St (06410-3414)
P.O. Box 212 (06410-0212)
PHONE..................................203 272-7258
Eugene Johnson, *President*
Lorraine Johnson, *Vice Pres*
EMP: 11
SQ FT: 4,000
SALES (est): 853.9K **Privately Held**
WEB: www.danjon.com
SIC: 3545 Mfg Deep Hole Drills And Carbide Rifling Buttons

(G-728)
EDAC TECHNOLOGIES LLC (HQ)
5 Mckee Pl (06410-1119)
PHONE..................................203 806-2090
Terry Bruni, *President*
Kenneth Cook, *Opers Staff*
John Smith, *Program Mgr*
Kevin Mrozinski, *Manager*
EMP: 223
SQ FT: 19,200
SALES (est): 95.1MM **Privately Held**
WEB: www.edactechnologies.com
SIC: 3769 3541 3724 Mfg Space Vehicle Equipment Mfg Machine Tools-Cutting Mfg Aircraft Engines/Parts

(G-729)
ELECTRO-TECH INC
Also Called: E T I
408 Sandbank Rd (06410-1544)
PHONE..................................203 271-1976
Jerry F Camarota, *President*
Charles W Terry, *Vice Pres*
Kurt Puleo, *QC Mgr*
Carol Terry, *Treasurer*
April Terry, *Human Res Mgr*
EMP: 50
SQ FT: 10,000
SALES (est): 8.9MM **Privately Held**
WEB: www.eti-electrotech.com
SIC: 3451 3679 3678 Mfg Screw Machine Products Mfg Electronic Components Mfg Electronic Connectors

(G-730)
ENGINEERED POLYMERS INDS INC
726 S Main St (06410-3472)
PHONE..................................203 272-2233
Len Azzaro, *Principal*
▲ **EMP:** 5 **EST:** 2015
SALES (est): 219.3K
SALES (corp-wide): 65.5MM **Privately Held**
SIC: 2821 Mfg Plastic Materials/Resins
PA: Osterman & Company, Inc.
726 S Main St
Cheshire CT 06410
203 272-2233

(G-731)
EVERLAST PRODUCTS LLC
150 Knotter Dr (06410-1136)
P.O. Box 748 (06410-0748)
PHONE..................................203 250-7111
Anthony Tremaglio, *Partner*
Leonard Mecca, *Partner*
EMP: 3
SQ FT: 5,000

GEOGRAPHIC

SALES (est): 181.4K **Privately Held**
SIC: 3625 3643 Mfg Relays/Industrial Controls Mfg Conductive Wiring Devices

(G-732)
FIBER MOUNTAIN INC
Also Called: F M
700 W Johnson Ave Ste 100 (06410-1197)
PHONE..................................203 806-4040
M H Raza, *CEO*
Michael Lagana, *Vice Pres*
Aristito Lorenzo, *Vice Pres*
Bill Miller, *Vice Pres*
David Stone, *Vice Pres*
EMP: 40
SALES (est): 2.4MM **Privately Held**
SIC: 3674 Mfg Semiconductors/Related Devices

(G-733)
FIMOR NORTH AMERICA INC (HQ)
Also Called: Harkness Industries, Inc.
50 Grandview Ct (06410-1261)
P.O. Box 764 (06410-0764)
PHONE..................................203 272-3219
Manuel Zuckerman, *President*
Robert P Williams, *Vice Pres*
Nancy P Williams, *Executive*
David Corbin, *Admin Sec*
EMP: 24
SQ FT: 30,000
SALES (est): 3.9MM
SALES (corp-wide): 8.1MM **Privately Held**
WEB: www.harknessindustries.com
SIC: 3089 2821 Mfg Plastic Products Mfg Plastic Materials/Resins
PA: Fimor
210 Rue Du Polygone
Le Mans 72100
243 400-095

(G-734)
G SCHOEPFERINC
460 Cook Hill Rd (06410-3707)
PHONE..................................203 250-7794
James Schoepfer, *President*
David Pagado, *Principal*
Dave Pagno, *Admin Sec*
Mary Schoepfer, *Admin Sec*
EMP: 12
SQ FT: 4,000
SALES (est): 1.2MM **Privately Held**
SIC: 3229 Manufactures Glass Eyes For Stuffed Animals

(G-735)
GEOSONICS INC
416 Highland Ave Ste D (06410-2527)
PHONE..................................203 271-2504
Mohamad Sharif, *Vice Pres*
Susan Shepley, *Manager*
Mike Donahue, *Manager*
Chuck Jaworski, *Manager*
Todd Pester, *Manager*
EMP: 10
SALES (corp-wide): 5.5MM **Privately Held**
SIC: 1382 Oil/Gas Exploration Services
PA: Geosonics, Inc.
359 Northgate Dr Ste 200
Warrendale PA 15086
724 934-2900

(G-736)
GRAPHICS PRESS LLC
1161 Sperry Rd (06410-3747)
P.O. Box 430 (06410-0430)
PHONE..................................203 272-9187
Gregory Mayer, *Controller*
Edward Tufte, *Mng Member*
EMP: 7
SALES (est): 1MM **Privately Held**
SIC: 2731 Books-Publishing/Printing

(G-737)
HI-TECH FABRICATING INC
30 Knotter Dr (06410-1122)
PHONE..................................203 284-0894
John Berges, *President*
Kevin Sook, *Vice Pres*
EMP: 24
SQ FT: 18,000
SALES (est): 3.4MM **Privately Held**
WEB: www.hitechfab.com
SIC: 3444 3469 3443 2396 Mfg Sheet Metalwork Mfg Metal Stampings Mfg Fabricated Plate Wrk Mfg Auto/Apparel Trim

(G-738)
HYLIE PRODUCTS INCORPORATED
30 Grandview Ct (06410-1261)
PHONE..................................203 439-8786
Deanne C Gauya, *CEO*
Ruji Gomes, *President*
John C Gauya, *Vice Pres*
Joe Ferreira, *Engineer*
EMP: 16 **EST:** 1951
SQ FT: 10,000
SALES (est): 3.1MM **Privately Held**
WEB: www.hylie.com
SIC: 3469 Mfg Metal Stampings

(G-739)
INDIA WEEKLY CO
328 Industrial Ave (06410-1501)
PHONE..................................203 699-8419
Shivesh Kumar, *Principal*
EMP: 5
SALES (est): 192.1K **Privately Held**
SIC: 2711 Newspapers-Publishing/Printing

(G-740)
INDUSTRIAL HEATER CORP
30 Knotter Dr (06410-1122)
PHONE..................................203 250-0500
Thomas A McGwire Jr, *President*
Ted McGwire, *President*
Nancy Riel, *Controller*
James Czarzasty, *VP Sales*
Katherine McGwire, *Admin Sec*
▼ **EMP:** 80 **EST:** 1921
SALES (est): 19.3MM **Privately Held**
WEB: www.industrialheater.com
SIC: 3567 Mfg Industrial Furnaces/Ovens

(G-741)
KOVIL MANUFACTURING LLC
Also Called: Masterman & Kovil
1486 Highland Ave Ste 2 (06410-1200)
PHONE..................................203 699-9425
Vilmos Kovacs, *President*
Frank Kovacs, *Vice Pres*
Katalin Kovacs, *Treasurer*
EMP: 5
SQ FT: 1,000
SALES: 250K **Privately Held**
WEB: www.kovil.com
SIC: 3599 Mfg Industrial Machinery

(G-742)
LOU-JAN TOOL & DIE INC
161 E Johnson Ave (06410-1209)
P.O. Box 148 (06410-0148)
PHONE..................................203 272-3536
Reita Jannetty, *President*
Louis Jannetty Jr, *Vice Pres*
EMP: 15
SQ FT: 12,000
SALES (est): 800K **Privately Held**
WEB: www.lou-jan.com
SIC: 3544 3542 Mfg Dies/Tools/Jigs/Fixtures Mfg Machine Tools-Forming

(G-743)
MARION MANUFACTURING COMPANY
1675 Reinhard Rd (06410-1222)
PHONE..................................203 272-5376
Mary L Cramer, *President*
Douglas Johnson, *Vice Pres*
David Dubois, *Plant Mgr*
Patricia Stango, *QC Mgr*
Nancy Zawerton, *Sales Staff*
▼ **EMP:** 24
SQ FT: 28,000
SALES (est): 7MM **Privately Held**
WEB: www.marionmfg.com
SIC: 3469 Mfg Metal Stampings

(G-744)
MC GUIRE MANUFACTURING CO INC
60 Grandview Ct (06410-1261)
P.O. Box 746 (06410-0746)
PHONE..................................203 699-1801
Ken Byrant, *Ch of Bd*
T Michael McRoberts, *President*
▲ **EMP:** 87
SQ FT: 13,500
SALES (est): 15.6MM
SALES (corp-wide): 9.6MM **Privately Held**
WEB: www.mcguiremfg.com
SIC: 3432 Mfg Plumbing Fixture Fittings
PA: Bead Industries, Inc.
11 Cascade Blvd
Milford CT 06460
203 301-0270

(G-745)
MICROTECH INC
1425 Highland Ave (06410-1233)
PHONE..................................203 272-3234
James A McGregor III, *President*
Flavio Montiero, *Vice Pres*
Nick Petinero, *Safety Mgr*
Jennifer Danard, *Human Res Mgr*
Silva Marco, *Manager*
EMP: 83
SQ FT: 36,000
SALES (est): 13.3MM **Privately Held**
SIC: 3678 3679 3677 3663 Mfg Elec Connectors Mfg Elec Components Mfg Elec Coil/Transfrmrs Mfg Radio/Tv Comm Equip

(G-746)
NEMTEC INC
B 8 Trackside (06410)
P.O. Box 1103 (06410-5103)
PHONE..................................203 272-0788
Joe Silva, *President*
EMP: 3
SQ FT: 2,000
SALES (est): 484.7K **Privately Held**
WEB: www.nemtec.com
SIC: 3541 7699 Mfg Machine Tools-Cutting Repair Services

(G-747)
NEW DESIGNZ INC
Also Called: Ndz Performance
278 Sanbank Rd (06410)
PHONE..................................860 384-1809
Antonin Blazek, *Vice Pres*
EMP: 18
SALES: 1.2MM **Privately Held**
SIC: 3484 Mfg Small Arms

(G-748)
NUTMEG UTILITY PRODUCTS INC (PA)
1755 Highland Ave (06410-1289)
P.O. Box 723 (06410-0723)
PHONE..................................203 250-8802
Jeannine Lavallee, *CEO*
Theresa Lavallee, *President*
EMP: 35
SALES (est): 3.9MM **Privately Held**
WEB: www.nutmegutility.com
SIC: 3825 3669 3661 Mfg Elec Measuring Instr Mfg Communications Equip Mfg Telephone/Graph Eqip

(G-749)
OGS TECHNOLOGIES INC
Also Called: Waterbury Button Company
1855 Peck Ln (06410-4411)
PHONE..................................203 271-9055
Michael L Salamone, *President*
Salvatore Geraci, *Exec VP*
Chris Keenan, *Manager*
▲ **EMP:** 45
SQ FT: 40,000
SALES: 7.3MM **Privately Held**
WEB: www.waterburybutton.com
SIC: 3993 3965 Mfg Signs/Advertising Specialties Mfg Fasteners/Buttons/Pins

(G-750)
OSLO SWITCH INC
Also Called: Oslo Switches
30 Diana Ct (06410-1206)
PHONE..................................203 272-2794
Joseph Martinecz, *President*
Elizabeth Martinez, *Vice Pres*
Thomas Martinez, *Vice Pres*
Donald Lunt, *Treasurer*
Flo Sengstacken, *Sales Staff*
EMP: 31
SQ FT: 30,000
SALES (est): 4.8MM **Privately Held**
WEB: www.osloswitch.com
SIC: 3613 3825 3643 3429 Mfg Switchgear/Boards Mfg Elec Measuring Instr Mfg Conductive Wire Dvcs Mfg Hardware

(G-751)
OSTERMAN & COMPANY INC (PA)
Also Called: Osterman Trading Div
726 S Main St (06410-3472)
PHONE..................................203 272-2233
James O Dwyer, *Ch of Bd*
John Dwyer, *President*
Jennifer Vestergaard, *CFO*
Lucia De Medal, *Regl Sales Mgr*
Andrew Gorman, *Sales Staff*
◆ **EMP:** 55
SQ FT: 10,000
SALES (est): 65.5MM **Privately Held**
WEB: www.reeves.com
SIC: 2821 Mfg Plastic Materials/Resins

(G-752)
OSTERMAN & COMPANY INC
Also Called: Engineered Polymer Industries
726 S Main St (06410-3472)
PHONE..................................203 272-2233
Paul Dikan, *Manager*
EMP: 40
SALES (corp-wide): 65.5MM **Privately Held**
WEB: www.reeves.com
SIC: 2821 Manufacturer Of Engineering-Grade Compunds And Raw Materials
PA: Osterman & Company, Inc.
726 S Main St
Cheshire CT 06410
203 272-2233

(G-753)
POLYMOLD CORP
Also Called: Poly Mold Inc Building 1
951 S Meriden Rd (06410-1843)
PHONE..................................203 272-2622
Michael Chernik, *President*
Olga Chernik, *Treasurer*
EMP: 12
SQ FT: 13,000
SALES (est): 2.5MM **Privately Held**
SIC: 3089 Mfg Plastic Custom Injection Moldings

(G-754)
POWER FUELS LLC
143 Main St (06410-2408)
PHONE..................................203 699-0099
Michael Monnerat, *Principal*
EMP: 3
SALES (est): 190.4K **Privately Held**
SIC: 2869 Mfg Industrial Organic Chemicals

(G-755)
R & R PALLET CORP
120 Schoolhouse Rd (06410-1293)
PHONE..................................203 272-2784
Joseph Rizzo Jr, *President*
EMP: 12
SQ FT: 16,000
SALES (est): 1.9MM **Privately Held**
WEB: www.rr-products.com
SIC: 2448 Mfg Wood Pallets/Skids

(G-756)
RAND MACHINE & FABRICATION CO
1486 Highland Ave Ste 2 (06410-1200)
PHONE..................................203 272-1352
Donald J Ranaudo, *President*
Tom Saath, *Owner*
Connie Ranaudo, *Vice Pres*
EMP: 10
SQ FT: 4,000
SALES (est): 1.9MM **Privately Held**
WEB: www.randmachineco.com
SIC: 3599 Mfg Industrial Machinery

(G-757)
RAND SHEAVES & PULLEYS LLC
1486 Highland Ave (06410-1200)
PHONE..................................203 272-1352
Donald J Ranaudo, *Mng Member*

EMP: 9
SALES (est): 780K **Privately Held**
SIC: 3599 Mfg Industrial Machinery

(G-758)
RAYMOND J BYKOWSKI
Also Called: Dried Materials Unlimited
1685 Reinhard Rd (06410-1222)
PHONE....................203 271-2385
Raymond J Bykowski, *Owner*
EMP: 3
SQ FT: 13,000
SALES: 690K **Privately Held**
SIC: 3999 5193 Mfg Misc Products Whol Flowers/Florist Supplies

(G-759)
RIFF COMPANY INC
1484 Highland Ave Ste 7 (06410-1268)
PHONE....................203 272-4899
Daniel McCormick, *President*
Donna Mc Cormick, *Admin Sec*
◆ **EMP:** 5
SQ FT: 5,500
SALES (est): 712.1K **Privately Held**
WEB: www.riff-co.com
SIC: 3599 Machine Shop Jobbing And Repair

(G-760)
ROBERT AUDETTE (PA)
Also Called: MGA Emblem Co
1732 S Main St (06410-3539)
PHONE....................203 872-3119
Robert Audette, *Owner*
▲ **EMP:** 5
SALES (est): 282.4K **Privately Held**
SIC: 3999 3479 2759 2395 Mfg Misc Products Coating/Engraving Svcs Commercial Printing Pleating/Stitching Svcs

(G-761)
SHILOH SOFTWARE INC
718 Cortland Cir (06410-2938)
PHONE....................203 272-8456
Barbara Walkup, *Principal*
EMP: 5
SALES (est): 517.7K **Privately Held**
SIC: 7372 7379 Prepackaged Software Services Computer Related Services

(G-762)
SKY MFG COMPANY
268 Sandbank Rd (06410-1537)
PHONE....................203 439-7016
Atousa Jalayer, *President*
EMP: 5 **EST:** 1966
SQ FT: 4,000
SALES (est): 772.6K **Privately Held**
SIC: 3728 Mfg Aircraft Parts/Equipment

(G-763)
SNAPWIRE INNOVATIONS LLC
125 Commerce Ct Ste 11 (06410-1243)
PHONE....................203 806-4773
EMP: 5
SALES: 22MM **Privately Held**
SIC: 3559 Mfg Misc Industry Machinery

(G-764)
SPECIAL VHCL DEVELOPMENTS INC
337 Blacks Rd (06410-1695)
PHONE....................203 272-7928
William Mitchell, *President*
EMP: 4
SQ FT: 6,000
SALES: 600K **Privately Held**
SIC: 3711 Mfg Cars

(G-765)
SPECTRUM VIRTUAL LLC
55 Realty Dr Ste 315 (06410-4600)
PHONE....................203 303-7540
Jonathan Reeves, *Principal*
Charles Baudinet, *Principal*
Randy Geary, *VP Bus Dvlpt*
Mario Dinatale, *CIO*
Darren Reeves, *CTO*
EMP: 6
SALES (est): 381.9K **Privately Held**
SIC: 3577 7374 Mfg Computer Peripheral Equipment Data Processing/Preparation

(G-766)
TJL INDUSTRIES LLC
19 Willow St (06410-2731)
P.O. Box 837 (06410-0837)
PHONE....................203 250-2187
Tod J Lorenzen, *Principal*
EMP: 3 **EST:** 2010
SALES (est): 266.7K **Privately Held**
SIC: 3999 Mfg Misc Products

Chester
Middlesex County

(G-767)
AEROCISION LLC
12a Inspiration Ln (06412-1366)
PHONE....................860 526-9700
Andrew Gibson, *CEO*
Dan Collins, *General Mgr*
Timothy Wallace, *Materials Mgr*
Sean Morrissey, *Production*
Michele Larson, *Purch Mgr*
EMP: 70
SQ FT: 40,000
SALES: 20MM
SALES (corp-wide): 177.9K **Privately Held**
WEB: www.pyeandhogan.com
SIC: 3728 Manufacturer Of Aircraft Parts/Equipment
HQ: Bromford Industries Limited
1 Bromford Gate
Birmingham W MIDLANDS B24 8
121 683-6200

(G-768)
BLACKWOLD INC
Also Called: Greenwald Industries
212 Middlesex Ave (06412-1273)
PHONE....................860 526-0800
Leonard F Leganza, *CEO*
Leonard Samela, *President*
Jeff Carlson, *Materials Mgr*
John Caldwell, *Engineer*
Bob Gifford, *Engineer*
▲ **EMP:** 80
SQ FT: 140,000
SALES (est): 16.5MM
SALES (corp-wide): 234.2MM **Publicly Held**
WEB: www.greenwaldindustries.com
SIC: 3581 3578 Mfg Vending Machines Mfg Calculating Equipment
PA: The Eastern Company
112 Bridge St
Naugatuck CT 06770
203 729-2255

(G-769)
CHAPCO INC (PA)
10 Denlar Dr (06412-1208)
P.O. Box 378 (06412-0378)
PHONE....................860 526-9535
Robert Weinstein, *Principal*
▲ **EMP:** 70
SQ FT: 22,000
SALES (est): 18MM **Privately Held**
WEB: www.chapcoinc.com
SIC: 3444 3599 Manufacturing Sheet Metalwork And Industrial Machinery

(G-770)
CONQUIP SYSTEMS LLC
78 Turkey Hill Rd (06412-1132)
PHONE....................860 526-7883
Katherine Beaulieu, *Owner*
EMP: 4
SALES (est): 443.1K **Privately Held**
SIC: 3423 Mfg Hand/Edge Tools

(G-771)
EAST COAST PRECISION MFG
221 Middlesex Ave (06412-1221)
PHONE....................860 322-4624
Mark Rohlfs, *Principal*
EMP: 3 **EST:** 2013
SALES (est): 206.5K **Privately Held**
SIC: 3999 Mfg Misc Products

(G-772)
EASTERN COMPANY
Greenwald Industries, Inc Del
212 Middlesex Ave (06412-1273)
PHONE....................860 526-0800
Leonard Samela, *President*
EMP: 90
SALES (corp-wide): 234.2MM **Publicly Held**
WEB: www.easterncompany.com
SIC: 3581 Mfg Mechanisms For Coin-Operated Machines
PA: The Eastern Company
112 Bridge St
Naugatuck CT 06770
203 729-2255

(G-773)
NEW ENGLAND FINE WOODWORKING
37 Castle View Dr (06412-1230)
PHONE....................860 526-5799
David Strobel, *Manager*
EMP: 3
SALES (est): 231.7K **Privately Held**
SIC: 2431 Mfg Millwork

(G-774)
PURIFICATION TECHNOLOGIES LLC (DH)
67 Winthrop Rd (06412-1036)
PHONE....................860 526-7801
Gerald A Richard, *President*
James Lusis, *CFO*
James F Lusis, *Treasurer*
◆ **EMP:** 14
SQ FT: 32,000
SALES (est): 8.4MM
SALES (corp-wide): 1.4B **Publicly Held**
WEB: www.purificationtech.com
SIC: 2911 2899 Petroleum Refiner Manufacturing Chemical Preparations
HQ: Vwr Corporation
Radnor Corp Ctr 1 200
Radnor PA 19087
610 386-1700

(G-775)
ROTO-FRANK OF AMERICA INC
Also Called: Roto Hardware Systems
14 Inspiration Ln (06412-1366)
PHONE....................860 526-4996
Greg Koch, *President*
Chrissostomos Dimou, *President*
Patrick Donnelly, *Business Mgr*
Debra Wallis, *Corp Secy*
Mark Heckler, *Engineer*
◆ **EMP:** 120 **EST:** 1979
SQ FT: 64,000
SALES (est): 27.2MM
SALES (corp-wide): 750.8MM **Privately Held**
WEB: www.roto-frank.com
SIC: 2591 Mfg Drapery Hardware/Blinds
PA: Roto Frank Holding Ag
Wilhelm-Frank-Platz 1
Leinfelden-Echterdingen 70771
711 759-80

(G-776)
SAMSARA FITNESS LLC
Also Called: Trueform Runner
10 Denlar Dr (06412-1208)
PHONE....................860 895-8533
Jocelyn Coutant, *Sales Mgr*
Jeff Vernon,
EMP: 11
SALES (est): 420.5K **Privately Held**
SIC: 3949 Mfg Sporting/Athletic Goods

(G-777)
WHELEN ENGINEERING COMPANY INC (PA)
51 Winthrop Rd (06412-1036)
PHONE....................860 526-9504
John Olson, *President*
Alex Stepinski, *Division Mgr*
George Whelen IV, *Exec VP*
Charles Andrus, *Vice Pres*
Mary R Guerrera, *Vice Pres*
◆ **EMP:** 291 **EST:** 1952
SQ FT: 90,000
SALES (est): 175MM **Privately Held**
SIC: 3647 3646 3671 3651 Mfg Vehicle Light Equip Mfg Coml Light Fixtures Mfg Electron Tubes Mfg Home Audio/Video Eqp

(G-778)
WHELEN ENGINEERING COMPANY INC
Also Called: Austin Electronics
Rr 145 (06412)
PHONE....................860 526-9504
John Olson, *Branch Mgr*
EMP: 18
SALES (corp-wide): 175MM **Privately Held**
SIC: 3646 Mfg Commercial Lighting Fixtures
PA: Whelen Engineering Company, Inc.
51 Winthrop Rd
Chester CT 06412
860 526-9504

Clinton
Middlesex County

(G-779)
BAUSCH ADVANCED TECH INC (PA)
115 Nod Rd (06413-1058)
PHONE....................860 669-7380
Oliver Bausch, *President*
James Smith, *General Mgr*
Purdum Jessica, *Department Mgr*
▲ **EMP:** 49
SALES (est): 11.6MM **Privately Held**
WEB: www.bascotech.com
SIC: 3559 Mfg Misc Industry Machinery

(G-780)
CLINTON INSTRUMENT COMPANY
295 E Main St (06413-2232)
PHONE....................860 669-7548
Marianne Clinton Szreders, *President*
Donna Langley, *Vice Pres*
EMP: 23
SQ FT: 15,000
SALES (est): 5.8MM **Privately Held**
WEB: www.clintoninstrument.com
SIC: 3823 3825 3829 Mfg Electrical Measuring Instruments Mfg Measuring/Controlling Devices Mfg Process Control Instruments

(G-781)
CONNECTCUT SHRELINE DEVELOPERS
10 Long Hill Rd (06413-1824)
PHONE....................860 669-4424
Warren Shoemac, *President*
EMP: 4
SALES: 1.5MM **Privately Held**
SIC: 1389 1522 Oil/Gas Field Services Residential Construction

(G-782)
CONNELLY 3 PUBG GROUP INC
10 W Main St Fl 2 (06413-2030)
P.O. Box 920 (06413-0920)
PHONE....................860 664-4988
Rick Connelly, *President*
Sean Connelly, *Vice Pres*
Sandra Nicholas, *Vice Pres*
Darylle Connelly, *Shareholder*
EMP: 5
SALES: 1.4MM **Privately Held**
WEB: www.c3pg.com
SIC: 2741 Publishing Of Educational Materials

(G-783)
CONOPCO INC
Unilever Home & Personal Care
1 John St (06413-1753)
PHONE....................860 669-8601
Donald Wilbur, *Manager*
EMP: 325
SALES (corp-wide): 56.5B **Privately Held**
SIC: 2844 Mfg Toilet Preparations

HQ: Conopco, Inc.
700 Sylvan Ave
Englewood Cliffs NJ 07632
201 894-7760

(G-784)
CUSTOM COVERS
20 Riverside Dr (06413-2625)
P.O. Box 424 (06413-0424)
PHONE................................860 669-4169
Barbara Whiting, *Owner*
EMP: 9
SQ FT: 600
SALES (est): 502.7K **Privately Held**
SIC: 2394 Mfg Canvas Covers For Campers & Boat Interiors

(G-785)
EASTERN COMPANY
Also Called: Argo Ems
1 Heritage Park Rd (06413-1836)
PHONE................................860 669-2233
John Hughes III, *Branch Mgr*
EMP: 24
SALES (corp-wide): 234.2MM **Publicly Held**
SIC: 3672 Mfg Printed Circuit Boards
PA: The Eastern Company
112 Bridge St
Naugatuck CT 06770
203 729-2255

(G-786)
EMI INC
4 Heritage Park Rd (06413-1836)
PHONE................................860 669-1199
Sean Donkin, *President*
EMP: 8
SALES (est): 920K **Privately Held**
SIC: 3556 Mfg Food Products Machinery

(G-787)
GREENSCAPE OF CLINTON LLC
13 Janes Ln (06413-1220)
PHONE................................860 669-1880
Diane Byrne, *Principal*
Frank Byrne,
EMP: 7
SALES (est): 927.4K **Privately Held**
SIC: 3524 0782 Mfg Lawn/Garden Equipment Lawn/Garden Services

(G-788)
HELANDER PRODUCTS INC
Also Called: Tiny-Clutch
26 Knollwood Dr (06413-1606)
P.O. Box 247 (06413-0247)
PHONE................................860 669-7953
Gordon Helander, *President*
Helander Andrew, *Vice Pres*
Andrew Helander, *Treasurer*
EMP: 10 **EST:** 1964
SQ FT: 5,000
SALES: 680K **Privately Held**
WEB: www.helanderproducts.com
SIC: 3568 5084 Mfg Power Transmission Equipment Whol Industrial Equipment

(G-789)
KENYON INTERNATIONAL INC
8 Heritage Park Rd (06413-1836)
P.O. Box 925 (06413-0925)
PHONE................................860 664-4906
Phillip Williams, *President*
Mike Reischmann, *Vice Pres*
Rhonda Hooper,
◆ **EMP:** 33
SQ FT: 24,000
SALES (est): 8.8MM **Privately Held**
WEB: www.kenyonappliances.com
SIC: 3631 Mfg Household Cooking Equipment

(G-790)
NAVTEC RIGGING SOLUTIONS INC
37 Stanton Rd (06413-2733)
PHONE................................203 458-3163
Allen E Goddu, *President*
William Carson, *Vice Pres*
▲ **EMP:** 47
SQ FT: 62,000
SALES (est): 8.6MM **Privately Held**
SIC: 3731 3594 3492 Shipbuilding/Repairing Mfg Fluid Power Pumps/Motors Mfg Fluid Power Valves/Fittings

(G-791)
NINE WEST HOLDINGS INC
Also Called: Kasper
20 Killingworth Tpke # 125 (06413-1377)
PHONE................................860 669-3799
EMP: 8
SALES (corp-wide): 2.2B **Privately Held**
SIC: 2337 Mfg Women's/Misses' Suits/Coats
HQ: Nine West Holdings, Inc.
180 Rittenhouse Cir
Bristol PA 10018
215 785-4000

(G-792)
ONSITE SERVICES INC
23 Meadow Rd (06413-2211)
PHONE................................860 669-3988
Kathleen Miller, *President*
David Miller, *Vice Pres*
Jonathan Miller, *Vice Pres*
EMP: 12
SALES (est): 1.8MM **Privately Held**
WEB: www.onsiteservices.com
SIC: 3669 Mfg Communications Equipment

(G-793)
PREFERRED FOAM PRODUCTS INC
140 Killingworth Tpke (06413-1325)
P.O. Box 942 (06413-0942)
PHONE................................860 669-3626
Louis Chiocchio, *President*
Mark Richards, *Treasurer*
▲ **EMP:** 6
SQ FT: 28,000
SALES (est): 1.2MM **Privately Held**
WEB: www.prefoam.com
SIC: 3086 5162 Mfg Plastic Foam Products Whol Plastic Materials/Shapes

(G-794)
RIVER MILL CO
43 River Rd (06413-1049)
PHONE................................860 669-5915
Michael Simmons, *Owner*
EMP: 15
SQ FT: 4,000
SALES (est): 1.1MM **Privately Held**
SIC: 2599 2431 5031 Mfg Furniture/Fixtures Mfg Millwork Whol Lumber/Plywood/Millwork

(G-795)
TECHNIQUE PRINTERS INC
36 Old Post Rd (06413-1812)
PHONE................................860 669-2516
Peter Hubbard, *President*
Thomas Snelgrove, *Vice Pres*
EMP: 7
SQ FT: 2,300
SALES (est): 811K **Privately Held**
SIC: 2752 7331 Lithographic Commercial Printing Direct Mail Advertising Services

(G-796)
TOWER LABORATORIES LTD
7 Heritage Park Rd (06413-1836)
PHONE................................860 669-7078
Robin Fey, *Branch Mgr*
EMP: 40
SALES (corp-wide): 30.4MM **Privately Held**
SIC: 2834 Mfg Pharmaceutical Preparations
PA: Tower Laboratories, Ltd.
8 Industrial Park Rd
Centerbrook CT 06409
860 767-2127

(G-797)
ULTRA CLEAN EQUIPMENT INC
112 Nod Rd Ste 9 (06413-1009)
PHONE................................860 669-1354
Bill Clorite, *President*
Deborah Coe, *Office Mgr*
EMP: 8
SALES (est): 760K **Privately Held**
WEB: www.ultracleanequip.com
SIC: 3699 Mfg Electrical Equipment/Supplies

Colchester
New London County

(G-798)
ALTERNATIVE FUEL & ENERGY LLC
31 Halls Hill Rd (06415-1402)
PHONE................................860 537-5345
Bruce Hayn, *Administration*
EMP: 3
SALES (est): 87.4K **Privately Held**
SIC: 2869 Mfg Industrial Organic Chemicals

(G-799)
AVALANCHE DOWNHILL RACING INC
12 Davidson Rd (06415-1600)
PHONE................................860 537-4306
Craig Seekins, *President*
▲ **EMP:** 4
SALES (est): 405.7K **Privately Held**
WEB: www.avalanchedownhillracing.com
SIC: 3751 5941 Mfg Motorcycles/Bicycles Ret Sporting Goods/Bicycles

(G-800)
CAREFREE BUILDING CO INC (PA)
Also Called: Carefree Small Buildings
48 Westchester Rd (06415-2420)
PHONE................................860 267-7600
Norman Gustafson, *President*
Todd Gustafson, *Vice Pres*
Brian Marvin, *Vice Pres*
Reynold Marvin, *Treasurer*
Richard Eifler, *Mktg Dir*
EMP: 18
SQ FT: 20,000
SALES (est): 3.2MM **Privately Held**
WEB: www.carefreebuildings.com
SIC: 2452 2511 Mfg Prefabricated Wood Buildings Mfg Wood Household Furniture

(G-801)
EAGLE MANUFACTURING CO INC
13 Homonick Rd (06415-1911)
P.O. Box 186 (06415-0186)
PHONE................................860 537-3759
Clifton O'Donal, *President*
Jerry Risley, *Controller*
Clifton D O'Donal, *Director*
EMP: 15
SQ FT: 10,000
SALES (est): 3.7MM **Privately Held**
SIC: 3441 Steel Fabrication

(G-802)
ESSEX WOOD PRODUCTS INC
Also Called: Ewp
75 Mill St (06415-1263)
P.O. Box 513 (06415-0513)
PHONE................................860 537-3451
Stephen Lloyd Schwartz, *President*
Michael Pasternak, *Vice Pres*
EMP: 30
SQ FT: 20,000
SALES (est): 3.1MM **Privately Held**
WEB: www.ssww.com
SIC: 3944 2499 Manufactures Craft Kits And Specialty Wood Novelties

(G-803)
FINISHING SOLUTIONS LLC
28 Jurach Rd (06415-2106)
PHONE................................860 705-8231
EMP: 3
SALES (est): 268.4K **Privately Held**
SIC: 2499 Mfg Wood Products

(G-804)
INTERNATIONAL CORDAGE EAST LTD
Also Called: Baynets Safety Systems
226 Upton Rd (06415-2712)
PHONE................................860 873-5000
Chip Merritt, *CEO*
Robert T Martin, *President*
Tess Jette, *COO*
Mary Martin, *Officer*
◆ **EMP:** 70
SQ FT: 25,000
SALES (est): 15.5MM **Privately Held**
SIC: 2298 Mfg Cordage/Twine

(G-805)
PLAY-IT PRODUCTIONS INC
167b Lebanon Ave (06415-1225)
PHONE................................212 695-6530
Terri Tyler, *Vice Pres*
EMP: 10
SALES (est): 1.8MM **Privately Held**
WEB: www.play-itproductions.net
SIC: 2752 7336 7812 7819 Lithographic Coml Print Coml Art/Graphic Design Motion Pict/Video Prodtn Motion Picture Services

(G-806)
Q ALPHA INC
Also Called: Glastonbury Southern Gage Div
87 Upton Rd (06415-2712)
P.O. Box 531 (06415-0531)
PHONE................................860 357-7340
Richard Jones, *Vice Pres*
Jim Klein, *Manager*
EMP: 24
SQ FT: 25,000
SALES (corp-wide): 33.9MM **Privately Held**
SIC: 3545 Mfg Machine Tool Accessories
PA: Alpha Q, Inc.
87 Upton Rd
Colchester CT 06415
860 537-4681

(G-807)
RED ROSE DESSERTS
125 Lebanon Ave (06415-1226)
PHONE................................860 603-2670
Jacqueline Sirois, *Owner*
Rianna Merray, *Regional Mgr*
EMP: 5
SALES: 135K **Privately Held**
SIC: 2051 Mfg Bread/Related Products

(G-808)
SHAEFFER PLASTIC MFG CORP
523 Old Hartford Rd (06415-2717)
PHONE................................860 537-5524
Robert J Shaeffer, *President*
EMP: 3
SQ FT: 3,000
SALES: 300K **Privately Held**
SIC: 3089 Mfg Molded Plastics

(G-809)
SHAMROCK SHEET METAL
23 Briarwood Dr (06415-1831)
PHONE................................860 537-4282
Daniel Cavanaugh, *Principal*
EMP: 8
SALES (est): 390K **Privately Held**
SIC: 3449 Mfg Misc Structural Metalwork

(G-810)
SKYDOG KITES LLC
220 Westchester Rd (06415-2423)
PHONE................................860 365-0600
J D Christianson, *Mng Member*
▲ **EMP:** 3
SALES (est): 329.7K **Privately Held**
SIC: 3944 Mfg Games/Toys

(G-811)
SWEET COUNTRY ROADS LLC
180 Mcdonald Rd (06415-1940)
PHONE................................860 537-0069
Charlotte Abbott,
EMP: 3
SALES (est): 149.5K **Privately Held**
SIC: 2033 Mfg Canned Fruits/Vegetables

(G-812)
WESTCHESTER PET VACCINES
111 Loomis Rd Ste 1 (06415-2337)
PHONE................................860 267-4554
Lewis D Kimball Jr, *President*
EMP: 3
SALES (est): 298.3K **Privately Held**
SIC: 2836 Mfg Biological Products

▲ = Import ▼=Export
◆ =Import/Export

Colebrook
Litchfield County

(G-813)
NORTHWEST CONNECTICUT MFG CO
95 Beech Hill Rd (06021-3606)
PHONE....860 379-1553
Louis Fasano Jr, *President*
Jane Fasano, *Admin Sec*
EMP: 8 **EST:** 1974
SQ FT: 5,200
SALES (est): 760K **Privately Held**
SIC: 3599 Machine Job Shop

Collinsville
Hartford County

(G-814)
CAROL ACKERMAN DESIGNS
107 Main St (06019-3134)
PHONE....860 693-1013
Carol Ackerman, *Owner*
EMP: 3
SQ FT: 820
SALES: 500K **Privately Held**
WEB: www.carolackerman.com
SIC: 3911 Mfg Precious Metal Jewelry

(G-815)
KELYNIAM GLOBAL INC
97 River Rd Ste A (06019-3246)
PHONE....800 280-8192
Tennyson Anthony, *CEO*
Chris Breault, *COO*
Christopher Breault, *Vice Pres*
Nicholas Breault, *Vice Pres*
Chris Scrivener, *Vice Pres*
EMP: 17
SQ FT: 7,000
SALES (est): 3.1MM **Privately Held**
SIC: 3842 Mfg Surgical Appliances/Supplies

(G-816)
PURITAN INDUSTRIES INC
122 Powder Mill Rd (06019-3502)
P.O. Box 186 (06022-0186)
PHONE....860 693-0791
Andrew P Papanek, *President*
▲ **EMP:** 20
SQ FT: 10,000
SALES (est): 3MM **Privately Held**
SIC: 3559 Manufactures Industrial Sewing Machines & Components

Columbia
Tolland County

(G-817)
COLUMBIA MANUFACTURING INC
165 Route 66 E (06237-1223)
P.O. Box 368 (06237-0368)
PHONE....860 228-2259
Kimberly Bell, *President*
Lupoli Nick, *General Mgr*
Kathryn Conlon, *Vice Pres*
Kim Bell, *Export Mgr*
Emmanuel Quiles, *Mfg Spvr*
▲ **EMP:** 99
SQ FT: 100,000
SALES (est): 30.9MM **Privately Held**
SIC: 3724 5088 Mfg Aircraft Engine/Part Whol Trans Equip

(G-818)
HAWK INTEGRATED PLASTICS LLC
1 Commerce Dr (06237-1231)
PHONE....860 337-0310
Andrew Bak, *Opers Mgr*
Dana Schnabel, *Engineer*
Joseph Bak, *Mng Member*
EMP: 12 **EST:** 2000
SQ FT: 12,500
SALES (est): 2.4MM **Privately Held**
WEB: www.hawkiplas.com
SIC: 3089 Mfg Plastic Products

Cornwall
Litchfield County

(G-819)
CLOVER HILL FOREST LLC
20 Hurlburt Pl (06753)
PHONE....860 672-0394
Gary Ocain,
EMP: 6
SALES (est): 616.7K **Privately Held**
SIC: 2411 Forestry Services

Cornwall Bridge
Litchfield County

(G-820)
STATIC SAFE PRODUCTS COMPANY
8 Cook Rd (06754-1320)
P.O. Box 5346, Milford (06460-0705)
PHONE....203 937-6391
David F Greco, *President*
EMP: 10
SALES (est): 850.3K **Privately Held**
SIC: 2522 Mfg Office Furniture-Nonwood

(G-821)
STRAWBERRY RIDGE VINEYARD INC
Also Called: Vineyard At Strawberry Ridge
23 Strawbery Ridge Rd (06754)
PHONE....860 868-0730
Nick Belarge, *Manager*
EMP: 4
SALES (est): 141.2K **Privately Held**
SIC: 2084 0172 Mfg Wines/Brandy/Spirits Grape Vineyard

Cos Cob
Fairfield County

(G-822)
ARNITEX LLC
Also Called: Jagtar
110 Orchard St (06807-2010)
PHONE....203 869-1406
Bruno Garros, *Owner*
▲ **EMP:** 3
SALES (est): 425.2K **Privately Held**
SIC: 2211 8711 Wholesale And Distribution-Luxury Interior Design Furnishings

(G-823)
CHICKEN SOUP FOR SOUL LLC
132 E Putnam Ave Ste 20 (06807-2724)
P.O. Box 700 (06807-0369)
PHONE....203 861-4000
William J Rouhana Jr, *CEO*
EMP: 50
SALES (est): 1.7MM **Privately Held**
SIC: 2741 Misc Publishing

(G-824)
CHICKEN SOUP FOR SOUL ENTRMT I (HQ)
132 E Putnam Ave Fl 2w (06807-2744)
PHONE....855 398-0443
William J Rouhana Jr, *Ch of Bd*
Scott W Seaton, *Vice Ch Bd*
Elana B Sofko, *COO*
Christopher Mitchell, *CFO*
EMP: 6
SQ FT: 6,000
SALES: 26.8MM **Publicly Held**
SIC: 2741 Misc Publishing
PA: Chicken Soup For The Soul Productions, Llc
132 E Putnam Ave Ste 20
Cos Cob CT 06807
855 398-0443

(G-825)
GTRPET SMF LLC
10 Mead Ave Unit B (06807-2706)
PHONE....203 661-1229
Ajmal Khan,
Alexander Khan,
▲ **EMP:** 7
SALES (est): 845.6K **Privately Held**
WEB: www.gtrpet.com
SIC: 3565 Mfg Packaging Machinery

(G-826)
INTERNATIONAL ELEVATOR CORP
97 Valley Rd (06807-2209)
PHONE....203 302-1023
Grant Gyesky, *President*
EMP: 5
SALES (est): 419.2K **Privately Held**
SIC: 3534 Rt Elevators/Escalators

(G-827)
KWANT ELEMENTS INTL LLC
464 Valley Rd (06807-1626)
PHONE....203 625-5553
Peter Janis, *Principal*
EMP: 3
SALES (est): 260.2K **Privately Held**
SIC: 2819 Mfg Industrial Inorganic Chemicals

(G-828)
MILLBROOK DISTILLERY LLC
687 River Rd (06807-1908)
PHONE....203 637-2231
EMP: 3
SALES (est): 130.6K **Privately Held**
SIC: 2085 Mfg Distilled/Blended Liquor

(G-829)
SEAN MECESERY
Also Called: Cos Cob T V & Video
5 Strickland Rd (06807-2736)
PHONE....203 869-2277
Sean Mecesery, *Owner*
EMP: 5
SQ FT: 2,000
SALES (est): 699K **Privately Held**
SIC: 3679 7622 Mfg Elec Components Radio/Television Repair

(G-830)
SWIZZLES OF GREENWHICH
207 E Putnam Ave (06807-2734)
PHONE....917 662-0080
Nicole Cornelio, *Principal*
EMP: 4
SALES (est): 243.9K **Privately Held**
SIC: 2026 Mfg Fluid Milk

Coventry
Tolland County

(G-831)
BLACKBIRD MANUFACTURING AND DE
112 Gardner Tavern Ln (06238-6101)
PHONE....860 331-3477
William Piotroski, *Principal*
EMP: 3 **EST:** 2010
SALES (est): 253.8K **Privately Held**
SIC: 3999 Mfg Misc Products

(G-832)
CHARLES BOGGINI COMPANY LLC
Also Called: Cbc Co
733 Bread And Milk St (06238-1014)
PHONE....860 742-2652
Glen Boggini, *Partner*
Jane Boggini, *Partner*
David Boggini, *Mng Member*
◆ **EMP:** 6
SQ FT: 13,000
SALES (est): 889.5K **Privately Held**
WEB: www.bogginicola.com
SIC: 2087 Mfg Flavor Extracts/Syrup

(G-833)
ECOSYSTEM CONSULTING SVC INC
30 Mason St (06238-3121)
P.O. Box 370 (06238-0370)
PHONE....860 742-0744
Robert Kortmann, *President*
Mary S Kortmann, *Vice Pres*
EMP: 5
SQ FT: 6,600
SALES: 574.5K **Privately Held**
WEB: www.ecosystemconsulting.com
SIC: 3589 1623 8748 Mfg Service Industry Machinery Water/Sewer/Utility Construction Business Consulting Services

(G-834)
KARL STETSON ASSOCIATES LLC
Also Called: Holometrology
2060 South St (06238-2441)
PHONE....860 742-8414
Karl Stetson, *President*
EMP: 3
SALES: 100K **Privately Held**
SIC: 3827 Design & Fabricate Optical Systems

(G-835)
MIKE SADLAK
Also Called: Sadlak Innovative Design
712 Bread Milk St Unit A6 (06238-1093)
P.O. Box 207 (06238-0207)
PHONE....860 742-0227
Mike Sadlak, *Owner*
John Barrett, *Sales Staff*
EMP: 7
SQ FT: 3,000
SALES (est): 302.5K **Privately Held**
SIC: 3949 8711 3484 Mfg Sporting/Athletic Goods Engineering Services Mfg Small Arms

(G-836)
NATIONAL RIBBON LLC
1159 Main St (06238-3115)
P.O. Box 268 (06238-0268)
PHONE....860 742-6966
William Wilde, *Mng Member*
Lois Pepin,
Pamela Wilde,
EMP: 4
SQ FT: 4,000
SALES (est): 525.8K **Privately Held**
WEB: www.nationalribbon.com
SIC: 2241 Narrow Fabric Mill

(G-837)
NEW LINE USA INC
247 Brigham Tavern Rd (06238-1312)
PHONE....860 498-0347
Ilan Bartov, *President*
EMP: 3
SQ FT: 3,000
SALES: 700K **Privately Held**
WEB: www.newlineusa.com
SIC: 3699 Oem Manufacturer Of Alarm & Security Products

(G-838)
SADLAK INDUSTRIES LLC
712 Bread And Milk St A9 (06238-1093)
P.O. Box 207 (06238-0207)
PHONE....860 742-0227
Michael W Sadlak,
John Barrett,
EMP: 25
SALES: 3MM **Privately Held**
SIC: 3541 3949 Mfg Machine Tools-Cutting Mfg Sporting/Athletic Goods

(G-839)
SADLAK MANUFACTURING LLC
712 Bread And Milk St # 7 (06238-1093)
PHONE....860 742-0227
Michael Sadlak, *Mng Member*
John Barret,
EMP: 25
SALES (est): 812.7K **Privately Held**
SIC: 3999 Mfg Misc Products

(G-840)
SUM MACHINE & TOOL CO INC
156 Mark Dr (06238-1124)
PHONE....860 742-6827

GEOGRAPHIC

Donald Morris, *President*
Diana Morris, *Treasurer*
EMP: 4 **EST:** 1966
SQ FT: 5,000
SALES (est): 260K **Privately Held**
SIC: 3599 Job Shop

(G-841)
TELEFLEX INCORPORATED
1295 Main St (06238-3117)
P.O. Box 219 (06238-0219)
PHONE....................................860 742-8821
James Olson, *Technical Mgr*
Paul Jacovich, *Manager*
Debra Masso, *Manager*
EMP: 22
SALES (corp-wide): 2.4B **Publicly Held**
WEB: www.teleflex.com
SIC: 3842 Mfg Surgical Appliances/Supplies
PA: Teleflex Incorporated
550 E Swedesford Rd # 400
Wayne PA 19087
610 225-6800

Cromwell
Middlesex County

(G-842)
ACCURATE MOLD COMPANY INC
64 Nooks Hill Rd (06416-1563)
PHONE....................................860 301-1988
Nelson Dion Jr, *President*
Judith R Dion, *Director*
EMP: 3
SQ FT: 3,500
SALES (est): 389.7K **Privately Held**
SIC: 3089 Injection Molding Of Plastics

(G-843)
ACTIMUS INC
189 Coles Rd (06416-1144)
PHONE....................................617 438-9968
Ramanath Reddy Ajjagottu, *President*
EMP: 60
SALES: 1.5MM **Privately Held**
SIC: 2834 7389 Pharmaceutical Services

(G-844)
ADVANCED WINDOW SYSTEMS LLC
14 Alcap Rdg (06416-1002)
PHONE....................................800 841-6544
Joseph Lavoie, *Mng Member*
EMP: 15 **EST:** 1997
SALES (est): 2.7MM **Privately Held**
SIC: 3442 5031 Mfg Metal Doors/Sash/Trim Whol Lumber/Plywood/Millwork

(G-845)
ALBRAYCO TECHNOLOGIES INC
38 River Rd (06416-2325)
PHONE....................................860 635-3369
Allan Aylward, *President*
EMP: 8
SQ FT: 6,500
SALES: 750K **Privately Held**
SIC: 3826 Scientific Equipment Mfg Dist And Laboratory Construction

(G-846)
APOGEE CORPORATION
Also Called: Impact Plastics
154 West St Ste C (06416-4400)
PHONE....................................860 632-3550
Steven Ryan, *Manager*
EMP: 57
SALES (corp-wide): 10MM **Privately Held**
WEB: www.impactplastics-ct.com
SIC: 3081 Manufacture Unsupported Plastic Film Or Sheet
PA: Apogee Corporation
5 Highland Dr
Putnam CT 06260
860 963-1976

(G-847)
BEMAT TEC LLC
114 West St (06416-1902)
PHONE....................................860 632-0049
Brian Matyka, *Owner*
EMP: 3
SALES: 200K **Privately Held**
SIC: 7694 Armature Rewinding

(G-848)
BIOLOGICAL INDUSTRIES
100 Sebethe Dr Ste A3 (06416-1037)
PHONE....................................860 316-5197
Tanya Potcova, *Principal*
EMP: 4
SALES (est): 190.4K **Privately Held**
SIC: 3999 Mfg Misc Products

(G-849)
BOB VESS BUILDING LLC
605 Main St (06416-1433)
PHONE....................................860 729-2536
Bob Vess,
EMP: 4
SALES (est): 337.3K **Privately Held**
SIC: 3949 Mfg Sporting/Athletic Goods

(G-850)
CAREY MANUFACTURING CO INC (PA)
Also Called: Amatom Electronic Hardwares
5 Pasco Hill Rd Unit A (06416-1012)
PHONE....................................860 829-1803
John L Carey, *President*
Laure Carey, *Vice Pres*
Raymond Bedard, *Controller*
▲ **EMP:** 30
SQ FT: 25,000
SALES (est): 7.8MM **Privately Held**
WEB: www.amatom.com
SIC: 3699 Whol Hardware

(G-851)
CAREY MANUFACTURING CO INC
Also Called: Amatom Electronic Hardware
5 Pasco Hill Rd Unit B (06416-1012)
PHONE....................................860 829-1803
John L Carey, *President*
EMP: 40
SALES (corp-wide): 7.8MM **Privately Held**
SIC: 3699 Mfg Electrical Equipment/Supplies
PA: Carey Manufacturing Company, Inc.
5 Pasco Hill Rd Unit A
Cromwell CT 06416
860 829-1803

(G-852)
CRRC LLC
Also Called: Ripley
46 Nooks Hill Rd (06416-1562)
PHONE....................................860 635-2200
Kenneth Mac Cormac, *President*
David Leith, *Prdtn Mgr*
Dominic Nanci, *Opers Staff*
Barbara Aiello, *Purchasing*
Steve Parkinson, *Engineer*
EMP: 100
SALES (corp-wide): 22.9MM **Privately Held**
WEB: www.capewell.com
SIC: 3429 3423 3634 Mfg Hardware Mfg Hand/Edge Tools Mfg Electric Housewares/Fans
PA: Crrc, Llc
105 Nutmeg Rd S
South Windsor CT 06074
877 684-6464

(G-853)
GKN ARSPACE SVCS STRCTURES LLC
1000 Corporate Row (06416-2074)
PHONE....................................860 613-0236
David Olchowski, *CEO*
Alex Cassarino, *Engineer*
EMP: 135
SQ FT: 28,500
SALES (est): 39MM
SALES (corp-wide): 11.3B **Privately Held**
SIC: 3724 Mfg Aircraft Engines/Parts
HQ: Gkn Limited
Po Box 4128
Redditch WORCS
-

(G-854)
HANGER PRSTHETCS & ORTHO INC
10 Countyline Dr (06416-1175)
PHONE....................................860 667-5300
Dennis Huysman, *Branch Mgr*
EMP: 7
SALES (corp-wide): 1B **Publicly Held**
SIC: 3842 Mfg Surgical Appliances/Supplies
HQ: Hanger Prosthetics & Orthotics, Inc.
10910 Domain Dr Ste 300
Austin TX 78758
512 777-3800

(G-855)
HORTON BRASSES INC
49 Nooks Hill Rd (06416-1561)
P.O. Box 95 (06416-0095)
PHONE....................................860 635-4400
Orion Henderson, *President*
▲ **EMP:** 9
SQ FT: 21,440
SALES: 2MM **Privately Held**
WEB: www.horton-brasses.com
SIC: 3429 Mfg Hardware

(G-856)
NORTHEAST QUALITY SERVICES LLC
14 Alcap Rdg (06416-1002)
PHONE....................................860 632-7242
Ralph Coppola, *President*
Bill Hutchinson, *Sales Staff*
▲ **EMP:** 50
SQ FT: 60,000
SALES (est): 11.7MM **Privately Held**
WEB: www.northeastquality.com
SIC: 3599 Mfg Industrial Machinery

(G-857)
ONE SOURCE PRINT AND PROMO LLC
150 Salem Dr (06416-1239)
PHONE....................................860 635-3257
John Hunter, *Principal*
EMP: 4
SALES (est): 360.5K **Privately Held**
SIC: 2752 Lithographic Commercial Printing

(G-858)
R & K COOKIES LLC
9 Smith Farm Rd (06416-2492)
PHONE....................................860 613-2893
Prashant Dave, *Principal*
EMP: 4
SALES (est): 203.5K **Privately Held**
SIC: 2052 Mfg Cookies/Crackers

(G-859)
RIPLEY TOOLS LLC (PA)
46 Nooks Hill Rd (06416-1562)
PHONE....................................860 635-2200
Richard Potash, *Warehouse Mgr*
Craig Tooker, *Opers Staff*
Brian Bourgoin, *Engineer*
Richard Brooks, *Sales Staff*
Robert G McCreary III,
EMP: 27
SALES (est): 4.9MM **Privately Held**
SIC: 3643 5063 4841 Manufacturing Conductive Wiring Devices Wholesales Electrical Equipment Cable/Pay Television Service

(G-860)
RWK TOOL INC
200 Corporate Row (06416-2029)
PHONE....................................860 635-0116
William Buggie, *President*
Kenneth Buggie, *Vice Pres*
Robert V Buggie, *Director*
Donna Buggie, *Admin Sec*
EMP: 22 **EST:** 1978
SQ FT: 49,000
SALES (est): 3MM **Privately Held**
SIC: 3599 Mfg Industrial Machinery

(G-861)
SUPERIOR PLAS EXTRUSION CO INC
154 West St (06416-4400)
PHONE....................................860 234-1864
EMP: 3
SALES (est): 274.2K
SALES (corp-wide): 12.6MM **Privately Held**
SIC: 3081 Mfg Unsupported Plastic Film/Sheet
PA: Superior Plastics Extrusion Company, Inc.
5 Highland Dr
Putnam CT 06260
860 963-1976

(G-862)
UNIQUE EXTRUSIONS INCORPORATED
10 Countyline Dr (06416-1175)
PHONE....................................860 632-1314
Robert M Tabshey, *President*
John Rankin, *General Mgr*
Lauren Dalal, *Corp Secy*
Tami N Tabshey, *Vice Pres*
Kathy Ross, *Treasurer*
▲ **EMP:** 25
SQ FT: 5,600
SALES: 10MM **Privately Held**
WEB: www.uniqueextrusions.com
SIC: 3354 Mfg Aluminum Extruded Products

Danbury
Fairfield County

(G-863)
A PAPISH INCORPORATED (PA)
Also Called: Papish, Leo & Company
21 Taylor St (06810-6922)
P.O. Box 67 (06813-0067)
PHONE....................................203 744-0323
Stephen Papish, *President*
Harriet Papish, *Corp Secy*
EMP: 40 **EST:** 1900
SQ FT: 13,000
SALES: 2.5MM **Privately Held**
SIC: 3568 Manufactures Spherical And Rod End Bearings

(G-864)
ABB ENTERPRISE SOFTWARE INC
A B B Control
152 Deer Hill Ave Ste 304 (06810-7766)
PHONE....................................203 798-6210
E Santacana, *Vice Pres*
EMP: 25
SALES (corp-wide): 36.7B **Privately Held**
WEB: www.elsterelectricity.com
SIC: 3625 Mfg Relays/Industrial Controls
HQ: Abb Inc.
305 Gregson Dr
Cary NC 27511
-

(G-865)
ABB INC
24 Commerce Dr (06810-4131)
PHONE....................................203 790-8588
Tishore Sundararajan, *Manager*
EMP: 76
SALES (corp-wide): 36.7B **Privately Held**
SIC: 3612 Mfg Transformers
HQ: Abb Inc.
305 Gregson Dr
Cary NC 27511
-

(G-866)
ACCUTROL LLC
21 Commerce Dr (06810-4131)
PHONE....................................203 445-9991
Fred George, *Principal*
EMP: 31
SALES (est): 5.4MM **Privately Held**
SIC: 3599 Mfg Industrial Machinery

(G-867)
ACUREN INSPECTION INC (HQ)
Also Called: Hellier
30 Main St Ste 402 (06810-3004)
PHONE....................................203 702-8740
Peter Scannell, *President*
Peter O Scannell, *President*
John P Lockwood, *Vice Pres*
Joby Suarez, *Marketing Staff*
Jim Gustafson, *Manager*

EMP: 532 **EST:** 1976
SQ FT: 30,000
SALES (est): 1.4B
SALES (corp-wide): 1.7B **Privately Held**
WEB: www.helliernndt.com
SIC: 1389 8071 Oil/Gas Field Services Medical Laboratory
PA: Rockwood Service Corporation
43 Arch St
Greenwich CT 06830
203 869-6734

(G-868)
ALL TECH AUTO/TRUCK ELECTRIC
36 Kenosia Ave Ste B (06810-7392)
PHONE..................................203 790-8990
Joe Fiore, *President*
Bill Williams, *Vice Pres*
EMP: 4
SQ FT: 3,600
SALES (est): 664.9K **Privately Held**
SIC: 3694 7538 3714 Remanufacturers Of Automotive Industrial And Commercial Starters Alternators And Generators & Finds Shorts On Automobiles

(G-869)
ALLIED SINTERINGS INCORPORATED
29 Briar Ridge Rd (06810-7248)
PHONE..................................203 743-7502
Mark Foster, *President*
Diana Foster, *Admin Sec*
EMP: 32 **EST:** 1959
SQ FT: 15,000
SALES (est): 7.3MM **Privately Held**
WEB: www.alliedsinterings.com
SIC: 3399 Mfg Primary Metal Products

(G-870)
ALTERNATE ENERGY FUTURES
3121 Avalon Valley Dr (06810-4051)
PHONE..................................917 745-7097
Brian Kirk,
Steve Miller,
Kevin Richardson,
EMP: 5
SALES (est): 380K **Privately Held**
SIC: 1311 7389 Crude Petroleum/Natural Gas Production Business Services At Non-Commercial Site

(G-871)
AMPHENOL CORPORATION
Also Called: Amphenol Rf
4 Old Newtown Rd Ste 2 (06810-6221)
PHONE..................................203 743-9272
Mark Cunningham, *General Mgr*
Dennis Nesterov, *Business Mgr*
Sam Kom, *Mfg Staff*
Bo Chen, *Purch Agent*
Vickie Hills, *Buyer*
EMP: 150
SALES (corp-wide): 8.2B **Publicly Held**
WEB: www.amphenolrf.com
SIC: 3678 Mfg Electronic Connectors
PA: Amphenol Corporation
358 Hall Ave
Wallingford CT 06492
203 265-8900

(G-872)
APPLIED ADVERTISING INC
71 Newtown Rd Ste 5 (06810-6251)
PHONE..................................860 640-0800
Jason D Bergeron, *President*
EMP: 10
SALES (est): 1.5MM **Privately Held**
WEB: www.appliedadvertisinginc.com
SIC: 3993 7319 7311 Mfg Signs/Advertising Specialties Advertising Services Advertising Agency

(G-873)
APPLIED LASER SOLUTIONS INC
28 Commerce Dr (06810-4131)
P.O. Box 1217 (06813-1217)
PHONE..................................203 739-0179
Edward Standke, *President*
Michele Standke, *Admin Sec*
EMP: 8
SQ FT: 22,000
SALES (est): 1.6MM **Privately Held**
WEB: www.appliedlasersolutions.net
SIC: 3441 Structural Metal Fabrication

(G-874)
ARMORED AUTOGROUP INC (DH)
Also Called: Armored Auto Group
44 Old Ridgebury Rd # 300 (06810-5107)
PHONE..................................203 205-2900
Michael Klein, *CEO*
David P Lundstedt, *Ch of Bd*
Guy J Andrysick, *President*
Michael K Bauersfeld, *Exec VP*
J Andrew Bolt, *CFO*
◆ **EMP:** 60
SQ FT: 18,819
SALES: 298.1MM
SALES (corp-wide): 3.8B **Publicly Held**
SIC: 3714 Mfg Motor Vehicle Parts/Accessories

(G-875)
ARMORED AUTOGROUP PARENT INC (DH)
44 Old Ridgebury Rd # 300 (06810-5107)
PHONE..................................203 205-2900
Michael Klein, *CEO*
Andy Bolt, *CFO*
EMP: 7 **EST:** 2010
SALES (est): 149.1K
SALES (corp-wide): 3.8B **Publicly Held**
SIC: 2842 2911 2899 Manufactures Protectants Wipes Tire And Wheel Care Products Oil And Fuel Addditives Related Products

(G-876)
ARMORED AUTOGROUP SALES INC
44 Old Ridgebury Rd # 300 (06810-5107)
PHONE..................................203 205-2900
Heather Clefisch, *President*
EMP: 182 **EST:** 2010
SALES (est): 81K
SALES (corp-wide): 3.8B **Publicly Held**
SIC: 3714 Mfg Motor Vehicle Parts/Accessories
HQ: Armored Autogroup Inc.
44 Old Ridgebury Rd # 300
Danbury CT 06810

(G-877)
BEDOUKIAN RESEARCH INC (PA)
6 Commerce Dr (06810-4131)
PHONE..................................203 830-4000
Robert H Bedoukian, *President*
Izzy Heller, *General Mgr*
Ben Silidjian, *Opers Mgr*
Michael Cuan, *Production*
Caryn Hasseltine, *Human Res Mgr*
▲ **EMP:** 42
SQ FT: 44,000
SALES (est): 17.4MM **Privately Held**
WEB: www.bedoukian.com
SIC: 2844 2869 2879 Mfg Toilet Preparations Mfg Industrial Organic Chemicals Mfg Agricultural Chemicals

(G-878)
BEGELL HOUSE INC
50 North St (06810-5664)
PHONE..................................203 456-6161
Yelena Shafeyeva, *President*
Vivian Wang, *President*
Vicky Lipowski, *Vice Pres*
Lolly Madden, *Marketing Staff*
EMP: 10
SALES (est): 1.2MM **Privately Held**
SIC: 2731 Books-Publishing/Printing

(G-879)
BELIMO AIRCONTROLS (USA) INC (HQ)
Also Called: Belimo Air Controls USA
33 Turner Rd (06810-5101)
P.O. Box 2928 (06813-2928)
PHONE..................................800 543-9038
Alexander Van Der Weerd, *President*
David Hauser, *Engineer*
David Liss, *Engineer*
John Coppola, *CFO*
Roland Meyer, *Financial Analy*
◆ **EMP:** 115
SQ FT: 44,000
SALES (est): 68.8MM
SALES (corp-wide): 652MM **Privately Held**
SIC: 3822 5075 3625 Mfg Environmental Controls Whol Heat/Air Cond Equipment/Supplies Mfg Relays/Industrial Controls
PA: Belimo Holding Ag
Brunnenbachstrasse 1
Hinwil ZH
438 436-111

(G-880)
BELIMO AUTOMATION AG
33 Turner Rd (06810-5101)
PHONE..................................203 749-3319
Andreas Steiner, *President*
Brent Kidd, *Technical Staff*
Beat Trutmann, *Admin Sec*
Marie Richers,
▲ **EMP:** 13
SALES (est): 2.3MM **Privately Held**
SIC: 3822 Mfg Environmental Controls

(G-881)
BELIMO CUSTOMIZATION USA INC
33 Turner Rd (06810-5101)
PHONE..................................203 791-9915
Lars Van Der Haegen, *President*
Philip Alesi, *Production*
Beat Trutmann, *Admin Sec*
▲ **EMP:** 5
SALES (est): 1.2MM
SALES (corp-wide): 652MM **Privately Held**
SIC: 3822 5075 3625 Mfg Environmental Controls Whol Heat/Air Cond Equipment/Supplies Mfg Relays/Industrial Controls
HQ: Belimo Aircontrols (Usa), Inc.
33 Turner Rd
Danbury CT 06810
800 543-9038

(G-882)
BRANSON ULTRASONICS CORP (DH)
41 Eagle Rd Ste 1 (06810-4179)
P.O. Box 1961 (06813-1961)
PHONE..................................203 796-0400
E Joe Dillon, *President*
Jon Piasecki, *President*
Robert Tibbetts, *Vice Pres*
Louis Testa, *Engineer*
Chris Burnell, *Info Tech Dir*
▲ **EMP:** 275 **EST:** 1965
SQ FT: 200,000
SALES (est): 156.5MM
SALES (corp-wide): 18.3B **Publicly Held**
WEB: www.bransonic.com
SIC: 3699 3548 3541 Mfg Elec Mach/Equip/Supp Mfg Welding Apparatus Mfg Machine Tool-Cutting
HQ: Emerson Electric (U.S.) Holding Corporation
850 Library Ave Ste 204c
Saint Louis MO 63136
314 553-2000

(G-883)
C N C ROUTER TECHNOLOGIES
4 Barnard Dr (06810-8401)
PHONE..................................203 744-6651
Bill Lounsbury, *Owner*
Jill Lounsberg, *Owner*
EMP: 5
SALES (est): 260K **Privately Held**
SIC: 2499 Mfg Wood Products

(G-884)
CAM2 TECHNOLOGIES LLC
6 Finance Dr (06810-4132)
PHONE..................................203 456-3025
Craig Markleski, *Principal*
James Fitzpatrick, *Principal*
Jonathan Frattaroli, *Principal*
Morris Martelle, *Principal*
David Schiering, *Principal*
EMP: 4
SALES (est): 635.6K **Privately Held**
SIC: 3826 Mfg Analytical Instruments

(G-885)
CANDLEWOOD STARS INC
Also Called: Mega Resveratrol
60 Newtown Rd Ste 32 (06810-6257)
PHONE..................................203 994-8826
Doron Efrat, *President*
EMP: 7
SALES: 500K **Privately Held**
SIC: 2833 Mfg Medicinal/Botanical Products

(G-886)
CAPITAL DESIGN & ENGRG INC
Also Called: Cde
35 Eagle Rd Ste 2 (06810-4177)
PHONE..................................203 798-6027
Len Staib, *President*
Mike Staib, *Treasurer*
Anita J Staib, *Director*
Scott Staib, *Admin Sec*
EMP: 5
SQ FT: 4,200
SALES: 800K **Privately Held**
WEB: www.cdeinc.net
SIC: 3599 Mfg Industrial Machinery

(G-887)
CHEM-TRON PNTG PWDR CATING INC
92 Taylor St (06810-6986)
PHONE..................................203 743-5131
Michael Showah, *President*
EMP: 4
SALES (est): 376.4K **Privately Held**
SIC: 3479 Coating/Engraving Service

(G-888)
CHEMICAL-ELECTRIC CORPORATION
Also Called: Chem-Tron
92 Taylor St (06810-6947)
P.O. Box 303 (06813-0303)
PHONE..................................203 743-5131
Samuel P Showah, *President*
Michael Showah, *Vice Pres*
EMP: 5 **EST:** 1965
SQ FT: 9,000
SALES (est): 577.2K **Privately Held**
SIC: 3471 Mfg Of Anodizer Of Metals

(G-889)
COMENGS INC
5 Shelter Rock Rd Ste 7 (06810-7052)
PHONE..................................203 792-7306
EMP: 4
SALES (est): 399.5K **Privately Held**
SIC: 2672 Mfg Coated/Laminated Paper

(G-890)
COMMUNICATION NETWORKS LLC
3 Corporate Dr (06810-4166)
PHONE..................................203 796-5300
Andrew Acquarulo, *President*
George J Lichtblau, *Chairman*
Tony Lau, *Regional Mgr*
Jaiprakash Vappala, *Regional Mgr*
Peggy Hayes, *Vice Pres*
▲ **EMP:** 48
SALES (est): 15.9MM **Privately Held**
SIC: 3661 Communication Services

(G-891)
COMUNIDADE NEWS
4 Laurel St (06810-5321)
PHONE..................................203 730-0175
Bremo Damada, *Director*
Lucio Salsa, *Director*
EMP: 4
SALES (est): 125.3K **Privately Held**
SIC: 2711 Newspapers-Publishing/Printing

(G-892)
CONOPTICS INC
19 Eagle Rd (06810-4127)
PHONE..................................203 743-3349
Ronald Pizzo, *President*
Richard Kocka, *Exec VP*
Chay Wong, *Purch Dir*
Charles Dooley, *Senior Engr*
EMP: 15 **EST:** 1981
SQ FT: 9,000
SALES (est): 3MM **Privately Held**
WEB: www.conoptics.com
SIC: 3827 Mfg Optical Instruments/Lenses

GEOGRAPHIC

(G-893)
COOPER MARKETING GROUP INC
41 Eagle Rd Ste 2 (06810-8802)
PHONE..................................203 797-9386
David Cooper, *President*
EMP: 6
SQ FT: 4,000
SALES: 1.5MM **Privately Held**
SIC: 2053 Mfg Frozen Bakery Products

(G-894)
CTR WELDING
39 Padanaram Rd (06811-3701)
PHONE..................................704 473-1587
Rick Kaufman, *Principal*
EMP: 5
SALES (est): 89.2K **Privately Held**
SIC: 7692 Welding Repair

(G-895)
CUSTOM DESIGN SERVICE CORP
6 Ohehyahtah Pl (06810-7668)
P.O. Box 518 (06813-0518)
PHONE..................................203 748-1105
Suzanne Vetter, *President*
Sheila Vetter, *Treasurer*
EMP: 4
SALES: 1MM **Privately Held**
WEB: www.cdscorp.us
SIC: 3672 Mfg Printed Circuit Boards

(G-896)
CZITEK LLC
4 Ford Ln (06811-4614)
PHONE..................................888 326-8186
David W Schiering, *Mng Member*
EMP: 9
SALES (est): 732.7K **Privately Held**
SIC: 3826 Mfg Analytical Instruments

(G-897)
DANBURY METAL FINISHING INC
124 West St (06810-6360)
P.O. Box 1175 (06813-1175)
PHONE..................................203 748-5044
Warren Levy, *President*
Elizabeth Levy, *Corp Secy*
EMP: 6
SQ FT: 2,500
SALES (est): 651.1K **Privately Held**
SIC: 3471 Electroplating Of Metals Or Formed Products

(G-898)
DANBURY ORTHO
2 Riverview Dr (06810-6268)
PHONE..................................203 797-1500
EMP: 3 **EST:** 2017
SALES (est): 293.8K **Privately Held**
SIC: 3842 Mfg Surgical Appliances/Supplies

(G-899)
DANBURY SQUARE BOX COMPANY
1a Broad St (06810-6204)
PHONE..................................203 744-4611
Chris Ann Allen, *President*
Michael Allen, *Vice Pres*
Mike Oswald, *Representative*
EMP: 22 **EST:** 1906
SQ FT: 37,000
SALES: 5.5MM **Privately Held**
SIC: 2653 Mfg Corrugated/Solid Fiber Boxes

(G-900)
DFS IN-HOME SERVICES
15 Great Pasture Rd (06810-8127)
PHONE..................................845 405-6464
Roman Abreu, *Principal*
EMP: 4
SALES (est): 210.2K **Privately Held**
SIC: 3089 5033 Mfg Plastic Products Whol Roofing/Siding/Insulation

(G-901)
DIBA INDUSTRIES INC (HQ)
4 Precision Rd (06810-7317)
PHONE..................................203 744-0773
Charles E Dubois, *CEO*
Timothy O'Sullivan, *President*
John Cronin, *General Mgr*
John Chandler, *Materials Mgr*
Carl Gliford, *Engineer*
EMP: 103
SQ FT: 36,000
SALES (est): 19.8MM
SALES (corp-wide): 1.5B **Privately Held**
WEB: www.dibaind.com
SIC: 3823 3498 3083 Mfg Process Control Instruments Mfg Fabricated Pipe/Fittings Mfg Laminated Plastic Plate/Sheet
PA: Halma Public Limited Company
Misbourne Court
Amersham BUCKS HP7 0
149 472-1111

(G-902)
DIVERSIFIED PRINTING SOLUTIONS
128 E Liberty St (06810-6767)
PHONE..................................203 826-7198
EMP: 3 **EST:** 2015
SALES (est): 107.2K **Privately Held**
SIC: 2759 Commercial Printing

(G-903)
DMT SOLUTIONS GLOBAL CORP
Also Called: Bluecrest
37 Executive Dr (06810-4147)
PHONE..................................203 233-6231
Grant Miller, *President*
Kevin Marks, *Vice Pres*
John Capasso, *CFO*
Steve Coburn, *Director*
Mary Ann Sigler, *Director*
EMP: 1300
SALES (est): 440MM **Privately Held**
SIC: 7372 Prepackaged Software Services

(G-904)
DRS NAVAL POWER SYSTEMS INC
21 South St (06810-8147)
PHONE..................................203 798-3000
Mark Newmann, *Branch Mgr*
Bill Theobald, *Manager*
EMP: 478
SALES (corp-wide): 8.9B **Privately Held**
SIC: 3812 Mfg Search/Navigation Equipment
HQ: Drs Naval Power Systems, Inc
4265 N 30th St
Milwaukee WI 53216
414 875-4314

(G-905)
DRS NAVAL POWER SYSTEMS INC
21 South St (06810-8147)
PHONE..................................203 798-3000
EMP: 478
SALES (corp-wide): 8.9B **Privately Held**
SIC: 3823 Process Control Instruments
HQ: Drs Naval Power Systems, Inc
4265 N 30th St
Milwaukee WI 53216
414 875-4314

(G-906)
ECONOMY PRINTING & COPY CENTER (PA)
128 E Liberty St Ste 4 (06810-6682)
PHONE..................................203 792-5610
Paul Dewitt, *Owner*
EMP: 3 **EST:** 1973
SQ FT: 600
SALES (est): 989.6K **Privately Held**
SIC: 2752 7334 Lithographic Commercial Printing Photocopying Services

(G-907)
EMHART TEKNOLOGIES LLC
Heli-Coil Co
4 Shelter Rock Rd (06810)
PHONE..................................877 364-2781
John Huntley, *Branch Mgr*
EMP: 5
SALES (corp-wide): 13.9B **Publicly Held**
SIC: 3559 Whol Industrial Supplies
HQ: Emhart Teknologies Llc
480 Myrtle St
New Britain CT 06053
800 783-6427

(G-908)
EMHART TEKNOLOGIES LLC
Emhart Fastening Teknologies
Shelter Rock (06810)
PHONE..................................203 790-5000
John Carvalho, *Branch Mgr*
EMP: 30
SALES (corp-wide): 13.9B **Publicly Held**
WEB: www.helicoil.com
SIC: 3541 Whol Industrial Supplies
HQ: Emhart Teknologies Llc
480 Myrtle St
New Britain CT 06053
800 783-6427

(G-909)
EMOSYN AMERICA INC
7 Commerce Dr (06810-4131)
PHONE..................................203 794-1100
Nick Wood, *President*
EMP: 40
SALES (est): 2.3MM
SALES (corp-wide): 5.3B **Publicly Held**
SIC: 3674 Mfg Semiconductors
HQ: Silicon Storage Technology, Inc.
1020 Kifer Rd
Sunnyvale CA 94086
408 735-9110

(G-910)
ENDO GRAPHICS INC
41 Kenosia Ave Ste 102 (06810-7360)
PHONE..................................203 778-1557
EMP: 6
SQ FT: 2,500
SALES: 1.2MM **Privately Held**
SIC: 2796 Pre-Press Graphic

(G-911)
ENS MICROWAVE LLC
14 Commerce Dr (06810-4198)
PHONE..................................203 794-7940
Kristen Schretzenmayer, *Mng Member*
EMP: 3
SALES (est): 384.1K **Privately Held**
SIC: 3679 Mfg Microwave Componets

(G-912)
ENTEGRIS INC
7 Commerce Dr (06810-4131)
PHONE..................................800 766-2681
Tom Baum, *Vice Pres*
Mark Deloughy, *Manager*
EMP: 424
SALES (corp-wide): 1.5B **Publicly Held**
SIC: 3089 Mfg Plastic Products
PA: Entegris, Inc.
129 Concord Rd
Billerica MA 01821
978 436-6500

(G-913)
ENTEGRIS PROF SOLUTIONS INC (HQ)
Also Called: Atmi, Inc.
7 Commerce Dr (06810-4131)
PHONE..................................203 794-1100
Douglas A Neugold, *Ch of Bd*
Ellen T Harmon, *President*
Brian Horos, *President*
Lawrence H Dubois, *Senior VP*
Kathleen G Mincieli, *Senior VP*
◆ **EMP:** 105
SQ FT: 31,000
SALES (est): 185.7MM
SALES (corp-wide): 1.5B **Publicly Held**
WEB: www.atmi.com
SIC: 3674 Mfg Semiconductors/Related Devices
PA: Entegris, Inc.
129 Concord Rd
Billerica MA 01821
978 436-6500

(G-914)
ETHAN ALLEN INTERIORS INC (PA)
25 Lake Avenue Ext (06811-5286)
PHONE..................................203 743-8000
M Farooq Kathwari, *Ch of Bd*
Kathy Bliss, *Senior VP*
Daniel M Grow, *Senior VP*
Tracy Paccione, *Senior VP*
Holly Tedesco, *Senior VP*
EMP: 201
SQ FT: 144,000
SALES: 746.6MM **Publicly Held**
WEB: www.ethanallen.com
SIC: 2512 5712 2511 Mfg Upholstered Household Furniture Ret Furniture Mfg Wood Household Furniture

(G-915)
EXPRESSWAY LUBE CENTERS
Also Called: Lubrication Management
225 White St (06810-6827)
PHONE..................................203 744-2511
Don Daseliva, *Manager*
Vito Vontana, *Manager*
EMP: 10
SALES (est): 616.6K **Privately Held**
WEB: www.lubricationmanagement.com
SIC: 3599 3714 Mfg Industrial Machinery Mfg Motor Vehicle Parts/Accessories

(G-916)
FAG BEARINGS LLC (DH)
200 Park Ave (06810-7553)
PHONE..................................203 790-5474
Dieter Kuetemeier, *President*
Nobert Broger, *Vice Pres*
Richard Lutringer, *Admin Sec*
◆ **EMP:** 100
SQ FT: 27,000
SALES (est): 51.7MM
SALES (corp-wide): 68.1B **Privately Held**
SIC: 3562 Mfg Ball/Roller Bearings
HQ: F'ag Holding Corporation
200 Park Ave
Danbury CT 06810
203 790-5474

(G-917)
FAG HOLDING CORPORATION (DH)
200 Park Ave (06810-7553)
PHONE..................................203 790-5474
Claus Bauer, *President*
John Hess, *Info Tech Dir*
◆ **EMP:** 11
SQ FT: 27,000
SALES (est): 96.4MM
SALES (corp-wide): 68.1B **Privately Held**
SIC: 3562 Mfg Ball/Roller Bearings
HQ: Schaeffler Schweinfurt Beteiligungs Gmbh
Georg-Schafer-Str. 30
Schweinfurt 97421
972 191-0

(G-918)
FAIRFIELD PROCESSING CORP (PA)
88 Rose Hill Ave (06810-5495)
P.O. Box 1157 (06813-1157)
PHONE..................................203 744-2090
Roy Young, *Ch of Bd*
Nancy Sasso, *COO*
Jordan Young, *Exec VP*
Amy D'Alessandro, *Vice Pres*
Mahnaz Kani, *Inv Control Mgr*
▲ **EMP:** 150
SQ FT: 100,000
SALES (est): 64.6MM **Privately Held**
WEB: www.poly-fil.com
SIC: 2824 Mfg Organic Fiber-Noncellulosic

(G-919)
FEDERAL PRISON INDUSTRIES
Also Called: Unicor
Rr 37 (06811)
PHONE..................................203 743-6471
David Gold, *Superintendent*
EMP: 17 **Publicly Held**
WEB: www.unicor.gov
SIC: 3315 9223 Mfg Electronic Devices
HQ: Federal Prison Industries, Inc
320 1st St Nw
Washington DC 20534
202 305-3500

(G-920)
FLAGSHIP CONVERTERS INC
205 Shelter Rock Rd (06810-7049)
PHONE..................................203 792-0034
Frank E Gustafson, *President*
E Michael Davies, *Vice Pres*
Allan Wolfe, *Vice Pres*
James McAvoy, *CFO*
Patti Torre, *Accountant*
▲ **EMP:** 57

▲ = Import ▼=Export
◆ =Import/Export

SQ FT: 95,000
SALES (est): 10.1MM **Privately Held**
WEB: www.flagshipconverters.com
SIC: **3089** 2671 7389 3081 Mfg Plastic Products Mfg Packaging Paper/Film Business Services Mfg Unsupport Plstc Film

(G-921)
FOLEYS PUMP SERVICE INC
30 Miry Brook Rd (06810-7410)
PHONE..................................203 792-2236
James J Foley, *President*
EMP: 26
SALES (est): 4.1MM **Privately Held**
WEB: www.foleyspump.com
SIC: **3561** 1799 Mfg Pumps/Pumping Equipment Trade Contractor

(G-922)
FRAM GROUP OPERATIONS LLC
39 Old Ridgebury Rd (06810-5103)
PHONE..................................203 830-7800
Don Nelson, *Mng Member*
Guy Andrysick, *CIO*
▼ **EMP:** 27
SALES (est): 9.3MM **Privately Held**
SIC: **3714** Mfg Motor Vehicle Parts/Accessories

(G-923)
FRUITBUD JUICE LLC
131 West St (06810-6376)
P.O. Box 766 (06813-0766)
PHONE..................................203 790-8200
Fax: 203 791-2875
EMP: 30
SALES (est): 4.4MM **Privately Held**
SIC: **2037** 2033 Frozen Fruits And Vegetables, Nsk

(G-924)
G P TOOL CO INC
59 James St (06810-6196)
PHONE..................................203 744-0310
David Parille, *President*
Mark Parille, *Vice Pres*
EMP: 13 **EST:** 1947
SQ FT: 8,000
SALES (est): 2MM **Privately Held**
SIC: **3544** Mfg Special Tools Dies & Fixtures

(G-925)
GOLDWORKS
5 Locust Ave (06810-6103)
PHONE..................................203 743-9668
Emilio De Grazia, *Owner*
EMP: 3 **EST:** 1978
SQ FT: 300
SALES (est): 213.5K **Privately Held**
SIC: **3911** 5944 7631 Mfg Precious Metal Jewelry Ret Jewelry Watch/Clock/Jewelry Repair

(G-926)
GOODRICH CORPORATION
Goodrich Arospc Flight Systems
100 Wooster Hts (06810-7509)
PHONE..................................505 345-9031
Charles Laxson, *Exec VP*
Gregory Beach, *Vice Pres*
Chris Holmes, *Branch Mgr*
EMP: 460
SALES (corp-wide): 66.5B **Publicly Held**
WEB: www.bfgoodrich.com
SIC: **3679** 8711 Mfg Electronic Components Engineering Services
HQ: Goodrich Corporation
2730 W Tyvola Rd 4
Charlotte NC 28217
704 423-7000

(G-927)
GOODRICH CORPORATION
Goodrich Optical Space Systems
100 Wooster Hts (06810-7509)
PHONE..................................203 797-5000
Tom Bergeon, *President*
Jennifer Brault, *Human Res Mgr*
EMP: 500
SALES (corp-wide): 66.5B **Publicly Held**
WEB: www.bfgoodrich.com
SIC: **3728** Mfg Aircraft Parts/Equipment
HQ: Goodrich Corporation
2730 W Tyvola Rd 4
Charlotte NC 28217
704 423-7000

(G-928)
GRANTA USA LTD
62 E Starrs Plain Rd (06810-8319)
PHONE..................................440 207-6051
▲ **EMP:** 10
SALES (est): 660K **Privately Held**
WEB: www.granta.com
SIC: **2721** Periodicals-Publishing/Printing

(G-929)
GS THERMAL SOLUTIONS INC
144 Old Brookfield Rd C (06811-4071)
PHONE..................................475 289-4625
Rick Depalma, *President*
EMP: 8
SALES (est): 118.4K **Privately Held**
SIC: **3645** Mfg Residential Lighting Fixtures

(G-930)
HAT TRICK GRAPHICS LLC
Also Called: Infinity Printing
87 Sand Pit Rd Ste 1 (06810-4043)
PHONE..................................203 748-1128
Tom Tannone,
EMP: 4
SQ FT: 3,000
SALES: 450K **Privately Held**
WEB: www.infinitypcd.com
SIC: **2752** 2759 Lithographic Commercial Printing Commercial Printing

(G-931)
HI-TEMP PRODUCTS CORP
88 Taylor St (06810-6923)
PHONE..................................203 744-3025
Tony Silva, *President*
Lucy Silva, *Office Mgr*
▲ **EMP:** 6
SQ FT: 9,600
SALES (est): 1.2MM **Privately Held**
SIC: **3433** Mfg Heating Equipment-Nonelectric

(G-932)
HIGH VOLTAGE OUTSOURCING LLC
Also Called: Hvo
1 Corporate Dr (06810-4130)
PHONE..................................203 456-3101
Mariano Moran, *Branch Mgr*
EMP: 6
SALES (corp-wide): 524.8K **Privately Held**
SIC: **3629** 8711 8748 Mfg Electrical Industrial Apparatus Engineering Services Business Consulting Services
PA: High Voltage Outsourcing Llc
115 Chambers Rd
Danbury CT
203 730-2415

(G-933)
HOLOGIC INC
36 Apple Ridge Rd (06810-7301)
PHONE..................................203 790-1188
Bill Healy, *Vice Pres*
EMP: 195
SALES (corp-wide): 3.3B **Publicly Held**
WEB: www.hologic.com
SIC: **3844** 3841 Mfg Radiographic X-Ray Equip & Mammography & Breast Biopsy Products
PA: Hologic, Inc.
250 Campus Dr
Marlborough MA 01752
508 263-2900

(G-934)
IOVINO BROS SPORTING GOODS
2 Lee Mac Ave Ste 2 # 2 (06810-6999)
PHONE..................................203 790-5966
Stephen Kaplanis, *President*
Kimberly Kaplanis, *Admin Sec*
EMP: 3
SQ FT: 5,000
SALES (est): 457.4K **Privately Held**
SIC: **2759** 5941 Screen Printing And Retail Sporting Goods Store

(G-935)
ISAAC INDUSTRIES
108 Stadley Rough Rd (06811-3290)
PHONE..................................203 778-3239
Jan Angrave, *Owner*
EMP: 3
SALES (est): 190.3K **Privately Held**
SIC: **3999** Mfg Misc Products

(G-936)
ISR (NTLLGNCE SRVLLANCE RECONN
100 Wooster Hts (06810-7509)
PHONE..................................203 797-5000
Marshall O Larsen, *Principal*
EMP: 3
SALES (est): 299.2K **Privately Held**
SIC: **3728** Mfg Aircraft Parts/Equipment

(G-937)
ITHACO SPACE SYSTEMS INC
100 Wooster Hts (06810-7509)
PHONE..................................607 272-7640
Thomas C Bergeron, *Chairman*
EMP: 60 **EST:** 1996
SALES (est): 5.3MM
SALES (corp-wide): 66.5B **Publicly Held**
WEB: www.bfgoodrich.com
SIC: **3728** Mfg Aircraft Parts/Equipment
HQ: Goodrich Corporation
2730 W Tyvola Rd 4
Charlotte NC 28217
704 423-7000

(G-938)
J-TECK USA INC
50 Miry Brook Rd (06810-7411)
P.O. Box 1209, Soddy Daisy TN (37384-1209)
PHONE..................................203 791-2121
Fred Macaluso, *President*
▲ **EMP:** 4
SALES (est): 613.9K
SALES (corp-wide): 6.9B **Publicly Held**
SIC: **3555** Mfg Printing Trades Machinery
PA: Dover Corporation
3005 Highland Pkwy # 200
Downers Grove IL 60515
630 541-1540

(G-939)
JIMS WELDING SERVICE LLC
18 Finance Dr (06810-4132)
PHONE..................................203 744-2982
James E Beckman, *Owner*
EMP: 3
SQ FT: 2,000
SALES (est): 627.5K **Privately Held**
SIC: **7692** Welding Service

(G-940)
JOSEPH MERRITT & COMPANY INC
Also Called: Merritt, Joseph & Company
4c Chrstpher Columbus Ave (06810-7352)
PHONE..................................203 743-6734
Tony Texeira, *Branch Mgr*
EMP: 7
SQ FT: 10,000
SALES (corp-wide): 31.9MM **Privately Held**
SIC: **2752** 5049 2789 Lithographic Commercial Printing Whol Professional Equipment Bookbinding/Related Work
PA: Joseph Merritt & Company Incorporated
650 Franklin Ave Ste 3
Hartford CT 06114
860 296-2500

(G-941)
JOVIL UNIVERSAL LLC
10 Precision Rd (06810-7317)
PHONE..................................203 792-6700
Keith Fredlund, *President*
EMP: 25 **EST:** 2014
SQ FT: 24,000
SALES (est): 4.7MM **Privately Held**
SIC: **3549** 5084 Mfg Metalworking Machinery Whol Industrial Equipment

(G-942)
JOY CAROLE CREATIONS INC
Also Called: Pyramid Productions
42 Mill Plain Rd (06811-5140)
PHONE..................................203 794-1401
Fax: 203 740-4495
▲ **EMP:** 4
SQ FT: 5,000
SALES (est): 210K **Privately Held**
WEB: www.carolejoy.com
SIC: **2771** Mfg Greeting Cards

(G-943)
KIMCHUK INCORPORATED (PA)
1 Corporate Dr Ste 1 # 1 (06810-4139)
PHONE..................................203 790-7800
Jim Marquis, *President*
William Kimbell, *President*
James A Marquis, *Vice Pres*
Denise Jurasek, *Materials Mgr*
Vashti Sumair, *Senior Buyer*
EMP: 15
SQ FT: 10,000
SALES (est): 41.5MM **Privately Held**
WEB: www.kimchuk.com
SIC: **3625** 7389 3312 7371 Mfg Relay/Indstl Control Business Services Blast Furnace-Steel Work Computer Programming Svc Computer Systems Design

(G-944)
KIMCHUK INCORPORATED
4 Finance Dr (06810-4191)
PHONE..................................203 798-0799
Jim Maquis, *President*
EMP: 125
SALES (corp-wide): 41.5MM **Privately Held**
SIC: **3571** Mfg Electronic Computers
PA: Kimchuk, Incorporated
1 Corporate Dr Ste 1 # 1
Danbury CT 06810
203 790-7800

(G-945)
KINGSWOOD KITCHENS CO INC
70 Beaver St (06810-5497)
PHONE..................................203 792-8700
Henry Blevio, *President*
Richard Rausch, *Shareholder*
EMP: 75
SQ FT: 75,000
SALES (est): 9.1MM **Privately Held**
WEB: www.kingswoodkitchens.com
SIC: **2434** Mfg Wood Kitchen Cabinets

(G-946)
LESSER EVIL
18 Finance Dr (06810-4132)
PHONE..................................203 529-3555
Andrew Strife, *President*
EMP: 3 **EST:** 2015
SALES (est): 287.6K **Privately Held**
SIC: **2099** Mfg Food Preparations

(G-947)
LIBERTY GARAGE INC
51 Sugar Hollow Rd Ste 1 (06810-7532)
PHONE..................................203 778-0222
Anthony Sigillito, *Principal*
EMP: 4
SALES (est): 535.8K **Privately Held**
SIC: **2599** Mfg Furniture/Fixtures

(G-948)
LIGHT ROCK SPRING WATER CO
Also Called: Light Rock Beverage
9 Balmforth Ave (06810-5908)
PHONE..................................203 743-2251
George Antous, *President*
Morris Antous, *Corp Secy*
Frederick Antous, *Vice Pres*
EMP: 15 **EST:** 1905
SQ FT: 7,500
SALES (est): 2.7MM **Privately Held**
SIC: **2086** Mfg Bottled/Canned Soft Drinks

(G-949)
LO STOCCO MOTORS
19 Chestnut St (06810-6816)
PHONE..................................203 797-9618
Joe Lo Stocco, *Owner*
EMP: 6

GEOGRAPHIC

SALES (est): 412.9K **Privately Held**
SIC: 3713 5531 7538 Mfg Truck/Bus Bodies Ret Auto/Home Supplies General Auto Repair

(G-950)
LORAD CORPORATION
Also Called: Lorad Medical Systems
36 Apple Ridge Rd (06810-7301)
P.O. Box 1946 (06813-1946)
PHONE..................................203 790-5544
Raymond Calvo, *Vice Pres*
▲ **EMP:** 200
SQ FT: 63,500
SALES (est): 38.2MM
SALES (corp-wide): 3.3B **Publicly Held**
WEB: www.hologic.com
SIC: 3844 3841 Mfg X-Ray Apparatus/Tubes Mfg Surgical/Medical Instruments
PA: Hologic, Inc.
250 Campus Dr
Marlborough MA 01752
508 263-2900

(G-951)
M & M PRECAST CORP
39 Padanaram Rd (06811-3701)
PHONE..................................203 743-5559
Robert Kaufman, *President*
Todd Kaufman, *Admin Sec*
EMP: 18
SQ FT: 5,000
SALES (est): 3MM **Privately Held**
SIC: 3272 Mfg Concrete Septic Tanks & Precast Concrete Products

(G-952)
MAPLEGATE MEDIA GROUP INC
1503 Sienna Dr (06810-7156)
PHONE..................................203 826-7557
Sharon E Warner, *President*
EMP: 22
SALES (est): 3.4MM **Privately Held**
WEB: www.maplegatemedia.com
SIC: 2721 Periodicals-Publishing/Printing

(G-953)
MCM STAMPING CORPORATION
66 Beaver Brook Rd (06810-6298)
PHONE..................................203 792-3080
Arlene Mc Mullin, *President*
Kathy Timm, *Admin Sec*
EMP: 25 **EST:** 1970
SQ FT: 10,000
SALES (est): 4MM **Privately Held**
SIC: 3469 Mfg Metal Stampings

(G-954)
MGI USA INC
23 Forest Ave (06810-5706)
PHONE..................................203 312-1200
EMP: 6
SQ FT: 3,500
SALES (est): 473K
SALES (corp-wide): 0 **Privately Held**
WEB: www.maydiangusa.com
SIC: 3111 Leather Tanning/Finishing
PA: Jiangsu Maydiang Leather Goods Co., Ltd.
Meidiyang Rd., Zhaoshi Industrial Zone, Meili Town
Changshu 21551
512 523-8137

(G-955)
MINUTEMAN PRESS OF DANBURY
12 Mill Plain Rd Ste 10 (06811-5135)
PHONE..................................203 743-6755
Tom Wilson, *Partner*
EMP: 9
SQ FT: 2,450
SALES (est): 1.5MM **Privately Held**
WEB: www.minutemandanbury.com
SIC: 2752 Comm Prtg Litho

(G-956)
MOHAWK INDUSTRIES INC
4 Nabby Rd (06811-3258)
PHONE..................................203 739-0260
Bill Bitting, *Branch Mgr*
EMP: 156
SALES (corp-wide): 9.9B **Publicly Held**
SIC: 2273 3253 Mfg Tufted & Woven Carpet & Rugs & Tile Products
PA: Mohawk Industries, Inc.
160 S Industrial Blvd
Calhoun GA 30701
706 629-7721

(G-957)
MULCH FERRIS PRODUCTS LLC
6 Plumtrees Rd (06810-7023)
PHONE..................................203 790-1155
Percy Ferris, *Mng Member*
EMP: 3
SALES (est): 391.1K **Privately Held**
SIC: 2499 Mfg Wood Products

(G-958)
MWB TOY COMPANY LLC
Also Called: Luke's Toy Factory
128 E Liberty St (06810-6767)
PHONE..................................212 598-4500
James Barber, *Mng Member*
EMP: 3
SQ FT: 1,500
SALES (est): 234.6K **Privately Held**
SIC: 3944 Mfg Games/Toys

(G-959)
NEW MACHINE PRODUCTS LLC
81 Beaver Brook Rd Ste B (06810-6297)
PHONE..................................203 790-5520
Joseph Basilva,
Barry Neumann,
EMP: 3
SQ FT: 3,000
SALES: 400K **Privately Held**
SIC: 3599 Mfg Machinery Parts

(G-960)
NEWS TIMES
333 Main St (06810-5818)
PHONE..................................203 744-5100
Nicole London, *President*
Jacqueline Smith, *Principal*
Tony Fasanella, *Vice Pres*
Rich Joudy, *Info Tech Mgr*
Ron Darr, *Executive*
EMP: 4
SALES (est): 370.6K **Privately Held**
SIC: 2711 Newspapers-Publishing/Printing

(G-961)
NORDIC AMERICAN SMOKELESS INC
100 Mill Plain Rd Ste 115 (06811-5189)
PHONE..................................203 207-9977
Darren Quinn, *President*
EMP: 12
SALES (est): 1.1MM **Privately Held**
SIC: 2131 Mfg Chewing/Smoking Tobacco

(G-962)
NOVY INTERNATIONAL INC
6 Abbott St (06810-5310)
PHONE..................................203 743-7720
George Novy, *President*
EMP: 5
SALES (est): 766.1K **Privately Held**
WEB: www.novyinternational.com
SIC: 3585 Mfg Electrical Heating Systems

(G-963)
O & G INDUSTRIES INC
9 Segar St (06810-6324)
PHONE..................................203 748-5694
Drew Oneglia, *Branch Mgr*
EMP: 21
SALES (corp-wide): 538MM **Privately Held**
WEB: www.ogind.com
SIC: 3273 1542 Mfg Ready-Mixed Concrete Nonresidential Construction
PA: O & G Industries, Inc.
112 Wall St
Torrington CT 06790
860 489-9261

(G-964)
OPTINOVA AMERICAS INC
22 Shelter Rock Ln # 24 (06810-8267)
PHONE..................................203 743-0908
Robert Paltauf, *Managing Dir*
▲ **EMP:** 3
SALES (est): 468.4K **Privately Held**
WEB: www.scantube.com
SIC: 3498 Mfg Fabricated Pipe/Fittings

(G-965)
PAUL DEWITT
Also Called: Economy Printing
128 E Liberty St Ste 4 (06810-6767)
PHONE..................................203 792-5610
Paul Dewitt, *Owner*
EMP: 15
SALES (est): 1.5MM **Privately Held**
SIC: 2752 2796 2791 2789 Lithographic Coml Print Platemaking Services Typesetting Services Bookbinding/Related Work Commercial Printing

(G-966)
PEROSPHERE INC
20 Kenosia Ave (06810-7357)
PHONE..................................203 885-1111
Solomon S Steiner PHD, *CEO*
EMP: 12
SALES (est): 2.7MM **Privately Held**
SIC: 2834 7389 Mfg Pharmaceutical Preparations Business Services At Non-Commercial Site

(G-967)
PEROSPHERE TECHNOLOGIES INC
108 Mill Plain Rd Ste 301 (06811-1501)
PHONE..................................475 218-4600
Sasha Bakhru, *President*
Stefan Zappe, *Exec VP*
EMP: 3
SALES (est): 369.7K **Privately Held**
SIC: 3841 Mfg Surgical/Medical Instruments

(G-968)
PMC ENGINEERING LLC
Also Called: P.M.c
11 Old Sugar Hollow Rd (06810-7517)
PHONE..................................203 792-8686
Robert P Knowles, *President*
Ray Bartko, *Engineer*
Andrea Preftes, *Accounting Mgr*
Jim Errickson, *Manager*
Mark Knowles, *Technology*
EMP: 31 **EST:** 1963
SQ FT: 24,000
SALES: 6MM **Privately Held**
WEB: www.pmc1.com
SIC: 3823 Mfg Process Control Instruments

(G-969)
PPG INDUSTRIES INC
Also Called: PPG Painters Supply
211 White St (06810-6826)
PHONE..................................203 744-4977
Joseph Renda, *Manager*
EMP: 4
SALES (corp-wide): 15.3B **Publicly Held**
WEB: www.painterssupply.com
SIC: 2851 Mfg Paints/Allied Products
PA: Ppg Industries, Inc.
1 Ppg Pl
Pittsburgh PA 15272
412 434-3131

(G-970)
PRAXAIR INC
10 Riverview Dr (06810-6268)
PHONE..................................800 772-9247
Mike Barr, *Manager*
EMP: 80 **Privately Held**
SIC: 3842 Mfg Surgical Appliances/Supplies
HQ: Praxair, Inc.
10 Riverview Dr
Danbury CT 06810
203 837-2000

(G-971)
PRAXAIR INC (HQ)
10 Riverview Dr (06810-6268)
PHONE..................................203 837-2000
Stephen F Angel, *Ch of Bd*
Fabricio Nunes, *Counsel*
Elizabeth T Hirsch, *Vice Pres*
Riva Krut, *Vice Pres*
Michael Marino, *Vice Pres*
◆ **EMP:** 400
SALES: 11.4B **Privately Held**
SIC: 2813 3569 3471 3479 Mfg Industrial Gases Mfg General Indstl Mach

(G-972)
PRAXAIR DISTRIBUTION INC (DH)
10 Riverview Dr (06810-6268)
PHONE..................................203 837-2000
Dick Marini, *President*
James Baughman, *Vice Pres*
Barney Patel, *Opers Mgr*
Lisa Hurley, *Treasurer*
Adelino Natario, *IT/INT Sup*
▲ **EMP:** 15
SALES (est): 664.9MM **Privately Held**
WEB: www.parxair.com
SIC: 2813 5084 5999 Mfg Industrial Gases Whol Industrial Equip
HQ: Praxair, Inc.
10 Riverview Dr
Danbury CT 06810
203 837-2000

(G-973)
PRAXAIR DISTRIBUTION INC
55 Old Ridgebury Rd (06810-5121)
PHONE..................................203 837-2162
Franco Mazzali, *Managing Dir*
Don Blanchat, *Branch Mgr*
EMP: 18 **Privately Held**
SIC: 2813 Mfg Industrial Gases
HQ: Praxair Distribution, Inc.
10 Riverview Dr
Danbury CT 06810
203 837-2000

(G-974)
PREFERRED UTILITIES MFG CORP (HQ)
Also Called: Preferred Instruments
31-35 South St (06810-8147)
PHONE..................................203 743-6741
David G Bohn, *President*
David H Paddock, *Corp Secy*
Charles A White III, *Exec VP*
Chuck White, *Exec VP*
Darrel Scribner, *Vice Pres*
EMP: 60 **EST:** 1920
SQ FT: 44,000
SALES (est): 25.2MM **Privately Held**
WEB: www.preferred-mfg.com
SIC: 3829 3433 3561 8711 Mfg Measure/Control Dvcs Mfg Heat Equip-Nonelec Mfg Pumps/Pumping Equip Engineering Services
PA: Pumc Holding Corporation
31-35 South St
Danbury CT 06810
203 743-6741

(G-975)
PRESTONE PRODUCTS CORPORATION
55 Federal Rd (06810-4001)
PHONE..................................203 731-7880
Steven Clancy, *President*
EMP: 39
SALES (corp-wide): 3.2MM **Privately Held**
SIC: 2899 Mfg Chemical Preparations
HQ: Prestone Products Corporation
6250 N River Rd Ste 6000
Rosemont IL 60018

(G-976)
PUMC HOLDING CORPORATION (PA)
31-35 South St (06810-8147)
PHONE..................................203 743-6741
Robert G Bohn, *Ch of Bd*
David G Bohn, *President*
David H Paddock, *Corp Secy*
Jeff Eichenwald, *Sales Engr*
Vicky Felis, *Shareholder*
EMP: 42
SQ FT: 44,000
SALES (est): 25.2MM **Privately Held**
SIC: 3433 8711 Mfg Heating Equipment-Nonelectric Engineering Services

(G-977)
QUALITY KITCHEN CORP DELAWARE
131 West St Ste 1 (06810-6372)
PHONE..................................203 744-2000
Albert J Salame, *President*
Peter Bliss, *Vice Pres*
Mary Lou Lytle, *Manager*
EMP: 4
SQ FT: 40,000
SALES (est): 473.5K **Privately Held**
WEB: www.royalkitchens-ny.com
SIC: 2037 Mfg Frozen Fruits/Vegetables

(G-978)
RINCO ULTRASONICS USA INC
87 Sand Pit Rd Ste 1b (06810-4043)
PHONE..................................203 744-4500
J Michael Goodson, *CEO*
Anthony Hern, *Admin Sec*
▲ **EMP:** 5
SALES (est): 1MM
SALES (corp-wide): 54.7MM **Privately Held**
SIC: 3699 Mfg Electrical Equipment/Supplies
HQ: Crest Ultrasonics Corp.
18 Graphics Dr
Ewing NJ 08628
609 883-4000

(G-979)
RK MANUFACTURING CORP CONN
34 Executive Dr Ste 2 (06810-4190)
PHONE..................................203 797-8700
Donna Krebs, *President*
Richard Ponton, *VP Opers*
Josh Hubbard, *Project Engr*
Jonathan Richards, *Project Engr*
Jodi Dipreta, *Human Resources*
EMP: 83
SQ FT: 42,000
SALES (est): 15.4MM **Privately Held**
SIC: 3599 Mfg Industrial Machinery

(G-980)
RSA CORP
36 Old Sherman Tpke (06810-4124)
PHONE..................................203 790-8100
Jan S Anthony, *President*
Stephanie Weber, *Vice Pres*
▲ **EMP:** 25 **EST:** 1935
SQ FT: 20,000
SALES: 10.7MM **Privately Held**
WEB: www.rsachem.com
SIC: 2869 Mfg Industrial Organic Chemicals

(G-981)
SANDVIK PUBG INTERACTIVE INC (PA)
83 Wooster Hts Ste 208 (06810-7549)
PHONE..................................203 205-0188
Marius Sandvik, *President*
Robert Israel, *Corp Secy*
Linda Fletcher, *Accounting Mgr*
▲ **EMP:** 17
SALES (est): 5.7MM **Privately Held**
SIC: 2741 Misc Publishing

(G-982)
SANDVIKS INC (PA)
83 Wooster Hts Ste 110 (06810-7552)
PHONE..................................866 984-0188
Marius Sandvik, *President*
Robert Israel, *Treasurer*
EMP: 6 **EST:** 2010
SALES (est): 6.7MM **Privately Held**
SIC: 3542 Mfg Machine Tools-Forming

(G-983)
SANTOTO LLC
Also Called: Danbury Aviation
Danbury Municipal (06810)
P.O. Box 267, New Canaan (06840-0267)
PHONE..................................203 984-2540
Andre Bohy,
Santo Silvestro,
EMP: 4
SALES (est): 335.2K **Privately Held**
SIC: 3721 Aircraft Sales And Services

(G-984)
SCHAEFFLER AEROSPACE USA CORP (DH)
Also Called: Barden Corporation, The
200 Park Ave (06810-7553)
P.O. Box 2449 (06813-2449)
PHONE..................................203 744-2211
Peter J Enright, *CEO*
Peter Enright, *Vice Pres*
Robert Hillstrom, *Vice Pres*
Michael Palanzo, *Purch Mgr*
Gail Bardelli, *Engineer*
▲ **EMP:** 400 **EST:** 1942
SQ FT: 192,000
SALES (est): 111.3MM
SALES (corp-wide): 68.1B **Privately Held**
SIC: 3562 3469 3842 3089 Mfg Ball/Roller Bearings Mfg Metal Stampings Mfg Surgical Appliances Mfg Plastic Products Mfg Primary Metal Prdts
HQ: Schaeffler Group Usa Inc.
308 Springhill Farm Rd
Fort Mill SC 29715
803 548-8500

(G-985)
SCHAEFFLER GROUP USA INC
200 Park Ave (06810-7553)
PHONE..................................203 790-5474
Chris McAndrew, *President*
Anthony Tamburro, *Materials Mgr*
EMP: 342
SALES (corp-wide): 68.1B **Privately Held**
SIC: 3562 Mfg Ball/Roller Bearings
HQ: Schaeffler Group Usa Inc.
308 Springhill Farm Rd
Fort Mill SC 29715
803 548-8500

(G-986)
SCHOLASTIC LIBRARY PUBG INC (HQ)
90 Sherman Tpke (06816-0002)
P.O. Box 3765, Jefferson City MO (65102-3765)
PHONE..................................203 797-3500
Dominique D'Hinnin, *Ch of Bd*
Arnaud Lagardere, *Ch of Bd*
Dick Robinson, *President*
David M Arganbright, *President*
Dante Cirilli, *Exec VP*
▲ **EMP:** 790 **EST:** 1988
SQ FT: 300,836
SALES (est): 335.9MM
SALES (corp-wide): 1.6B **Publicly Held**
WEB: www.grolier.com
SIC: 2731 5963 5192 2721 Book-Publishing/Printing Direct Retail Sales
PA: Scholastic Corporation
557 Broadway Lbby 1
New York NY 10012
212 343-6100

(G-987)
SCHWING BIOSET TECHNOLOGIES
98 Mill Plain Rd Ste A (06811-6101)
PHONE..................................203 744-2100
Thomas Anderson, *President*
EMP: 50
SALES (est): 4MM **Privately Held**
WEB: www.schwing.com
SIC: 3592 Mfg Carburetors/Pistons/Rings
HQ: Schwing America, Inc.
5900 Centerville Rd
Saint Paul MN 55127
651 429-0999

(G-988)
SEALED AIR CORPORATION
10 Old Sherman Tpke (06810-4159)
PHONE..................................203 791-3648
Randy Gouveia, *Vice Pres*
EMP: 120
SALES (corp-wide): 4.7B **Publicly Held**
WEB: www.sealedair.com
SIC: 3086 2671 Mfg Plastic Foam Products Mfg Packaging Paper/Film
PA: Sealed Air Corporation
2415 Cascade Pointe Blvd
Charlotte NC 28208
980 221-3235

(G-989)
SI GROUP USA (USAA) LLC (DH)
Also Called: Addivant Usa, LLC
4 Mountainview Ter (06810-4116)
PHONE..................................203 702-6140
John Steitz, *CEO*
Peter R Smith, *President*
Paul Trimble, *Vice Pres*
Patrick Weinberg, *CFO*
Jeff Kennel, *Treasurer*
◆ **EMP:** 150
SALES (est): 84.1MM **Privately Held**
SIC: 2869 2822 Mfg Industrial Organic Chemicals Mfg Synthetic Rubber
HQ: Si Group Usa Holdings (Usha) Corp.
4 Mountainview Ter
Danbury CT 06810
203 702-6140

(G-990)
SI GROUP USA HLDINGS USHA CORP (HQ)
Also Called: Addivant USA Holdings Corp.
4 Mountainview Ter (06810-4116)
PHONE..................................203 702-6140
Peter R Smith, *CEO*
◆ **EMP:** 31
SALES (est): 1.1B **Privately Held**
SIC: 2869 Mfg Industrial Organic Chemicals

(G-991)
SIGMUND SOFTWARE LLC
83 Wooster Hts Ste 210 (06810-7549)
PHONE..................................800 448-6975
Angelyn Spada, *Human Resources*
Bethany Irish, *Consultant*
Joseph Santoro,
Marcus Sharpe,
EMP: 18
SALES (est): 2.7MM **Privately Held**
SIC: 7372 Prepackaged Software Services

(G-992)
SIGN A RAMA
Also Called: Sign-A-Rama
35 Eagle Rd (06810-4187)
PHONE..................................203 792-4091
Robert Morris, *President*
EMP: 7
SQ FT: 1,250
SALES (est): 400K **Privately Held**
SIC: 3993 Signsadv Specs

(G-993)
SIGN LANGUAGE LLC
71 Newtown Rd Ste 6 (06810-6258)
PHONE..................................203 778-2250
Ira Rubinstein, *Mng Member*
Joyce Rubinstein, *Mng Member*
EMP: 3
SALES: 190K **Privately Held**
WEB: www.signlanguagesigns.com
SIC: 3993 Mfg Signs/Advertising Specialties

(G-994)
SIMMONDS PRECISION PDTS INC
Also Called: UTC Aerospace Systems
100 Wooster Hts (06810-7509)
PHONE..................................203 797-5000
Justin Robert Keppy, *CEO*
Dwayne Baker, *Senior Buyer*
Eric Hansell, *Engineer*
Jonathan Vena, *Engineer*
Linda Kelly, *Accountant*
EMP: 36
SALES (corp-wide): 66.5B **Publicly Held**
SIC: 3829 3694 3724 3728 Mfg Measure/Control Dvcs Mfg Engine Elec Equip Mfg Aircraft Engine/Part Mfg Aircraft Parts/Equip
HQ: Simmonds Precision Products, Inc.
100 Panton Rd
Vergennes VT 05491
802 877-4000

(G-995)
SOVIPE FOOD DISTRIBUTORS LLC
87 E Liberty St (06810-3237)
PHONE..................................203 648-2781
John C Pinto, *Principal*
EMP: 3
SALES (est): 86K **Privately Held**
SIC: 2099 Mfg Food Preparations

(G-996)
SPECTRUM BRANDS INC
Armored Autogroup
44 Old Ridgebury Rd # 300 (06810-5107)
PHONE..................................203 205-2900
Guy J Andrysick, *Exec VP*
EMP: 8
SALES (corp-wide): 3.8B **Publicly Held**
SIC: 3714 Mfg Motor Vehicle Parts/Accessories
HQ: Spectrum Brands, Inc.
3001 Deming Way
Middleton WI 53562
608 275-3340

(G-997)
STP PRODUCTS MANUFACTURING CO (DH)
44 Old Ridgebury Rd # 300 (06810-5107)
PHONE..................................203 205-2900
Guy Andrysic, *President*
▼ **EMP:** 16 **EST:** 1994
SALES (est): 7.3MM
SALES (corp-wide): 3.8B **Publicly Held**
WEB: www.clorox.com
SIC: 2911 Petroleum Refiner

(G-998)
TARRY MEDICAL PRODUCTS INC
Also Called: Tarry Manufacturing
22 Shelter Rock Ln Unit 7 (06810-8268)
PHONE..................................203 794-1438
Scott Bell, *President*
Don Mortifoglio, *Vice Pres*
George Quatropanni, *Vice Pres*
EMP: 15
SQ FT: 4,500
SALES (est): 3.3MM **Privately Held**
WEB: www.tarrymfg.com
SIC: 3841 5047 Mfg Surgical/Medical Instruments Whol Medical/Hospital Equipment

(G-999)
TOPEX INC
10 Precision Rd Fl 2 (06810-7317)
PHONE..................................203 748-5918
Anthony Pellegrino, *CEO*
John Brenna, *President*
EMP: 10
SALES: 3MM **Privately Held**
SIC: 3844 3679 Mfg X-Ray Apparatus/Tubes Mfg Electronic Components

(G-1000)
TP CYCLE & ENGINEERING INC
Also Called: T P Engineering
4 Finance Dr (06810-4191)
PHONE..................................203 744-4960
Thomas A Pirone, *President*
EMP: 25
SQ FT: 63,000
SALES (est): 4.9MM **Privately Held**
WEB: www.tpeng.com
SIC: 3599 8711 Mfg Industrial Machinery Engineering Services

(G-1001)
TRIBUNA NEWSPAPER LLC
32 Farview Ave 3 (06810-5533)
PHONE..................................203 730-0457
Celia Becelar,
Emmanuela Leaf,
EMP: 4
SALES (est): 326.8K **Privately Held**
SIC: 2711 Newspapers-Publishing/Printing

(G-1002)
TROPAX PRECISION MANUFACTURING
10 Precision Rd (06810-7317)
PHONE..................................203 794-0733
Bruno Tropeano, *President*
Elio Tropeano, *Corp Secy*
Mike Tropeano, *Vice Pres*
EMP: 10
SQ FT: 6,000
SALES: 1.2MM **Privately Held**
SIC: 3599 Mfg Industrial Machinery

GEOGRAPHIC

(G-1003)
VANGUARD PRODUCTS CORPORATION
87 Newtown Rd (06810-4199)
PHONE..................................203 744-7265
Robert C Benn Sr, *Ch of Bd*
Robert C Benn Jr, *President*
Lisa Golino, *Purchasing*
Mark S Hansen, *Sales Mgr*
Merima Trako, *Program Mgr*
▲ **EMP:** 75 **EST:** 1965
SQ FT: 51,000
SALES (est): 16MM **Privately Held**
WEB: www.vanguardproducts.com
SIC: **3053** 3061 Mfg Gaskets/Packing/Sealing Devices Mfg Mechanical Rubber Goods

(G-1004)
VILLARINA PASTA & FINE FOODS (PA)
22 Shelter Rock Ln Unit 4 (06810-8268)
PHONE..................................203 917-4463
Joseph Filc, *President*
Joseph M Filc, *President*
Joseph W Filc, *Vice Pres*
EMP: 7
SALES: 1.2MM **Privately Held**
SIC: **2098** 2038 Mfg Macaroni/Spaghetti Mfg Frozen Specialties

(G-1005)
VISUAL IMPACT LLC
Also Called: Memory Lane Collections
12 Finance Dr (06810-4132)
PHONE..................................203 790-9650
William McCann,
EMP: 6
SALES: 575K **Privately Held**
SIC: **2759** Mfg Signs/Advertising Specialties

(G-1006)
WARMUP INC
52 Federal Rd Ste 1b (06810-6162)
PHONE..................................203 791-0072
Charles Mathias, *President*
Zoe Bean, *Human Res Mgr*
Martha Henry, *Sales Staff*
Keith Knorps, *Sales Staff*
Emily Leidlein, *Technician*
▲ **EMP:** 10
SALES (est): 2.1MM **Privately Held**
SIC: **3567** Mfg Industrial Furnaces/Ovens

(G-1007)
WATER WORKS
60 Backus Ave (06810-7329)
PHONE..................................203 546-6000
Shanon McAvoy, *Manager*
◆ **EMP:** 5
SALES (est): 310K **Privately Held**
WEB: www.thewwwbeds.com
SIC: **3261** Whol Plumbing Equipment/Supplies

(G-1008)
WESCONN STAIRS INC
Also Called: A-1 Stairs By Wesconn Stairs
2 Mill Plain Rd (06811-5141)
P.O. Box 2148 (06813-2148)
PHONE..................................203 792-7367
Danna Mackey, *President*
EMP: 7 **EST:** 1974
SQ FT: 3,500
SALES (est): 1MM **Privately Held**
SIC: **2431** Mfg Millwork

(G-1009)
WESTCHESTER PUBG SVCS LLC (PA)
Also Called: Westchester Book Group
4 Old Newtown Rd (06810-4200)
PHONE..................................203 791-0080
Dennis J Pistone, *CEO*
Susan Baker, *Director*
Tyler M Carey, *Director*
Terry Colosimo, *Director*
Michael Jon Jensen, *Director*
EMP: 8
SALES (est): 1.1MM **Privately Held**
SIC: **2791** Typesetting Services

(G-1010)
WESTCHSTER BK/RNSFORD TYPE INC
4 Old Newtown Rd (06810-4200)
PHONE..................................203 791-0080
Dennis J Pistone, *President*
Nancy Rainsford-Pistone, *Vice Pres*
EMP: 104
SALES (est): 15.1MM **Privately Held**
SIC: **2791** Typesetting Services

(G-1011)
WESTCONN ORTHOPEDIC LABORATORY
52 Federal Rd Ste 2 (06810-6162)
PHONE..................................203 743-4420
Robert Foster, *President*
Elizabeth Foster, *Corp Secy*
EMP: 4
SQ FT: 1,000
SALES (est): 240K **Privately Held**
SIC: **3842** Mfg Orthopedic Appliances

Danielson
Windham County

(G-1012)
BROOKLYN SAND & GRAVEL LLC
42 Junior Ave (06239-4217)
PHONE..................................860 779-3980
Wayne L Jolley,
EMP: 4
SALES (est): 284K **Privately Held**
SIC: **1442** Construction Sand/Gravel

(G-1013)
HUTCHINSON PRECISION SS INC
39 Wauregan Rd (06239-3714)
PHONE..................................860 779-0300
James Basque, *Controller*
▼ **EMP:** 180 **EST:** 1957
SQ FT: 51,000
SALES (est): 44.4MM
SALES (corp-wide): 8.1B **Publicly Held**
WEB: www.nnbr.com
SIC: **3069** Mfg Fabricated Rubber Products
HQ: Hutchinson
2 Rue Balzac
Paris 8e Arrondissement 75008
140 748-300

(G-1014)
JOLLEY PRECAST INC
463 Putnam Rd (06239-2041)
PHONE..................................860 774-9066
Clarence Jolley, *President*
David Jolley, *Vice Pres*
Eleanor Jolley, *Vice Pres*
Stacie Jolley, *Bookkeeper*
EMP: 21
SQ FT: 1,080
SALES (est): 3.6MM **Privately Held**
SIC: **3272** 5074 Mfg Concrete Products Whol Plumbing Equip/Supp

(G-1015)
MARC JOHNSON
16 Depot Rd (06239-2019)
PHONE..................................860 774-3315
Marc Johnson, *Principal*
EMP: 5
SALES (est): 538.5K **Privately Held**
SIC: **3161** Mfg Luggage

(G-1016)
PELLETIER MILLWRIGHTS LLC
161 Moosup Pond Rd (06239-2015)
PHONE..................................860 564-8936
Debra Pelletier,
Marc Pelletier,
EMP: 5
SALES (est): 600.4K **Privately Held**
SIC: **2041** Mfg Flour/Grain Mill Prooducts

(G-1017)
SIRI MANUFACTURING COMPANY
90 Wauregan Rd (06239-3712)
PHONE..................................860 236-5901
Roger Bond, *President*
Robert Bond, *Co-President*
Craig Bond, *Manager*
Tim Bollinger, *Supervisor*
Ruth Bond, *Admin Sec*
▲ **EMP:** 23
SQ FT: 100,000
SALES (est): 5.8MM **Privately Held**
WEB: www.siriwire.com
SIC: **3315** Mfg Steel Wire/Related Products

(G-1018)
SPIROL INTERNATIONAL CORP (HQ)
30 Rock Ave (06239-1434)
PHONE..................................860 774-8571
William R Hunt, *President*
Jeffrey F Koehl, *Chairman*
Hans H Koehl, *Chairman*
James C Shaw, *Chairman*
Peter Omalley, *Engineer*
▲ **EMP:** 150
SQ FT: 120,000
SALES (est): 69.1MM **Privately Held**
WEB: www.spirol.com
SIC: **3452** 3499 3469 3053 Mfg Bolts/Screws/Rivets Mfg Misc Fab Metal Prdts Mfg Metal Stampings
PA: Spirol International Holding Corporation
30 Rock Ave
Danielson CT 06239
860 774-8571

(G-1019)
SPIROL INTL HOLDG CORP (PA)
30 Rock Ave (06239-1425)
PHONE..................................860 774-8571
Jeffrey F Koehl, *CEO*
Hans Koehl, *Chairman*
▲ **EMP:** 150 **EST:** 1979
SQ FT: 100,000
SALES (est): 69.1MM **Privately Held**
SIC: **3452** 3499 3469 Mfg Bolts/Screws/Rivets Mfg Misc Fab Metal Prdts Mfg Metal Stampings

(G-1020)
VEGWARE US INC
90 Wauregan Rd (06239-3712)
PHONE..................................860 779-7970
Robert A Bond, *President*
Craig A Bond, *Vice Pres*
▲ **EMP:** 8 **EST:** 2008
SALES (est): 969.7K **Privately Held**
SIC: **2836** Mfg Biological Products

Darien
Fairfield County

(G-1021)
CECELIA NEW YORK LLC
23 Chestnut St (06820-4209)
PHONE..................................917 392-4536
Ashley N Cole, *Principal*
EMP: 6
SQ FT: 530
SALES (est): 594.7K **Privately Held**
SIC: **3144** Mfg Women's Footwear

(G-1022)
DP2 LLC HEAD
25 Old Kings Hwy N (06820-4608)
PHONE..................................203 655-0747
Peter Dan Winkle,
EMP: 12
SALES (est): 679K **Privately Held**
SIC: **3433** 3585 Mfg Heating Equipment-Nonelectric Mfg Refrigeration/Heating Equipment

(G-1023)
EXECUTIVE PRINTING DARIEN LLC
1082 Post Rd (06820-5441)
PHONE..................................203 655-4691
J Trask Pfeifle, *Mng Member*
EMP: 6
SALES (est): 879.3K **Privately Held**
SIC: **2752** Offset Printing

(G-1024)
FERGTECH INC
28 Thorndal Cir Ste 1 (06820-5429)
PHONE..................................203 656-1139
Bruce Ferguson, *Branch Mgr*
EMP: 6
SALES (corp-wide): 1.9MM **Privately Held**
SIC: **7372** Prepackaged Software Services
PA: Fergtech Inc
19 Wilson Ridge Rd
Darien CT 06820
203 656-1139

(G-1025)
FERGTECH INC (PA)
19 Wilson Ridge Rd (06820-5133)
PHONE..................................203 656-1139
Bruce S Ferguson, *President*
EMP: 6
SQ FT: 4,000
SALES (est): 1.9MM **Privately Held**
WEB: www.fergtech.com
SIC: **7372** 7371 Prepackaged Software Services Custom Computer Programing

(G-1026)
FLAVRZ ORGANIC BEVERAGES LLC
25 Hamilton Ln (06820-2810)
PHONE..................................203 716-8082
Valli Stavros-Baker, *President*
Steven E Baker, *Mng Member*
EMP: 3
SALES (est): 219.7K **Privately Held**
SIC: **2087** Mfg Flavor Extracts/Syrup

(G-1027)
JAM COMPANY
1770 Post Rd (06820-5802)
P.O. Box 3425 (06820-8425)
PHONE..................................203 655-3260
Jeffrey Mc Clure, *Owner*
EMP: 5
SALES (est): 463.7K **Privately Held**
SIC: **3599** Mfg Precision Machine Parts

(G-1028)
LIFE STUDY FLLWSHIP FOUNDATION
90 Heights Rd (06820-4129)
PHONE..................................203 655-1436
Michael Keane, *CEO*
John J Keane Jr, *Vice Pres*
EMP: 26
SQ FT: 10,000
SALES: 1.3MM **Privately Held**
WEB: www.lifestudyfellowship.org
SIC: **2731** 7331 2741 Book-Publishing/Printing Direct Mail Ad Svcs Misc Publishing

(G-1029)
MOBILE SENSE TECHNOLOGIES INC
24 Cliff Ave (06820-4914)
PHONE..................................203 914-5375
Justin Chickles, *CEO*
Ki Chon, *Vice Pres*
EMP: 6
SALES (est): 424.8K **Privately Held**
SIC: **3845** Mfg Electromedical Equipment

(G-1030)
NTECO INC
10 Center St (06820-4500)
PHONE..................................203 656-1154
Kevin Ohara, *Director*
EMP: 30 **EST:** 2013
SALES (est): 1.4MM **Privately Held**
SIC: **3272** Mfg Concrete Products

(G-1031)
SCHMITT REALTY HOLDINGS INC
Also Called: Image Processing
1082 Post Rd (06820-5441)
PHONE..................................203 662-6661
Craig Goodrow, *Branch Mgr*
EMP: 4
SALES (corp-wide): 19.2MM **Privately Held**
WEB: www.georgeschmitt.com
SIC: **2796** Platemaking Services

PA: Schmitt Realty Holdings, Inc.
251 Boston Post Rd
Guilford CT 06437
203 453-4334

(G-1032)
SMOKEY MOUNTAIN CHEW INC (PA)
1 Center St Fl 2 (06820-4503)
PHONE..................................203 656-1088
David Savoca, *President*
EMP: 3
SQ FT: 2,500
SALES (est): 23.8MM **Privately Held**
WEB: www.smokeysnuff.com
SIC: 2131 Mfg Chewing/Smoking Tobacco

(G-1033)
TELLUS TECHNOLOGY INC (PA)
10 Corbin Dr Ste 210 (06820-5403)
PHONE..................................646 265-7960
Sanford Ewing, *CEO*
Kenneth Hamby, *President*
James Kelly, *Chairman*
Cosmin Negulescu, *Vice Pres*
EMP: 4
SALES (est): 324.2K **Privately Held**
SIC: 3069 Mfg Fabricated Rubber Products

(G-1034)
TOPS MANUFACTURING CO INC (PA)
83 Salisbury Rd (06820-2225)
PHONE..................................203 655-9367
Mitchell A Himmel, *President*
Patricia Himmel, *Vice Pres*
▲ **EMP:** 4 **EST:** 1964
SALES (est): 1.3MM **Privately Held**
SIC: 3089 3469 3229 Mfg Plastic Glass & Metal Kitchenware & Accessories

(G-1035)
UBM LLC
Also Called: Cliggott Publishing
330 Post Rd Fl 2 (06820-3600)
PHONE..................................203 662-6501
Gary Marshal, *CEO*
EMP: 5
SALES (corp-wide): 1.3B **Privately Held**
WEB: www.cmp.com
SIC: 2721 2741 2731 8748 Book-Publishing/Printing Misc Publishing Periodical-Publish/Print Business Consulting Svcs
HQ: Ubm, Llc
1983 Marcus Ave Ste 250
New Hyde Park NY 11042
516 562-7800

(G-1036)
UNIWORLD BUS PUBLICATIONS INC
35 Kensett Ln (06820-2438)
PHONE..................................201 384-4900
Michael Shimkin, *Ch of Bd*
Barbara Fiorito, *CFO*
EMP: 7
SALES: 275K **Privately Held**
WEB: www.uniworldbp.com
SIC: 7372 7389 Prepackaged Software Services Business Serv Non-Commercial Site

(G-1037)
ZIGA MEDIA LLC
5 Overbrook Ln (06820-2819)
PHONE..................................203 656-0076
Laura Livingston, *Prdtn Dir*
Charles J Ziga, *Mng Member*
▲ **EMP:** 3
SALES (est): 267.7K **Privately Held**
WEB: www.newyorklandmarks.com
SIC: 2752 2731 2741 Lithographic Commercial Printing Books-Publishing/Printing Misc Publishing

Dayville
Windham County

(G-1038)
ALL STATES ASPHALT INC
Also Called: Killingly Asphalt Products
127 Attwaugan Crossing Rd (06241-1601)
PHONE..................................860 774-7550
Todd Larkin, *Branch Mgr*
EMP: 6
SALES (corp-wide): 202.2MM **Privately Held**
WEB: www.allstatesasphalt.com
SIC: 2951 Highway/Street Construction
PA: All States Asphalt, Inc.
325 Amherst Rd
Sunderland MA 01375
413 665-7021

(G-1039)
BOLLORE INC
60 Louisa Viens Dr (06241-1106)
P.O. Box 530 (06241-0530)
PHONE..................................860 774-2930
Steve Brunetti, *President*
Bernard Jean-Luc, *General Mgr*
Xavier Cys, *Opers Staff*
Rob Caron, *Engineer*
Tracy Lefebvre, *Human Res Mgr*
▲ **EMP:** 80
SQ FT: 62,000
SALES (est): 20.5MM **Privately Held**
WEB: www.bolloreinc.com
SIC: 2671 Mfg Packaging Paper/Film
HQ: Bollore Se
Odet
Ergue-Gaberic 29500
298 667-200

(G-1040)
BOUDREAUS WELDING CO INC
1029 N Main St (06241-2170)
P.O. Box 339 (06241-0339)
PHONE..................................860 774-2771
Ronald Jussaume, *President*
Julie Jussaume, *Vice Pres*
Monique Jussaume, *Admin Sec*
Randall Jussaume, *Admin Sec*
EMP: 25 **EST:** 1957
SQ FT: 20,600
SALES: 2.4MM **Privately Held**
SIC: 3446 3312 Blast Furnace-Steel Work Mfg Architectural Mtlwrk

(G-1041)
CENTRAL ELECTRIC INC
364 Putnam Pike (06241-1621)
P.O. Box 34 (06241-0034)
PHONE..................................860 774-3054
EMP: 3 **EST:** 1996
SQ FT: 3,000
SALES: 250K **Privately Held**
SIC: 7694 Electric Motor Repair Services

(G-1042)
COLTS PLASTICS COMPANY INC
969 N Main St (06241-2123)
P.O. Box 429 (06241-0429)
PHONE..................................860 774-2277
Charles W Bentley Jr, *President*
Mark Egan, *Vice Pres*
Pat Garrity, *Vice Pres*
Patrick Garrity, *Vice Pres*
Chris Lepine, *Engineer*
▲ **EMP:** 125 **EST:** 1936
SQ FT: 80,000
SALES (est): 24.7MM **Privately Held**
WEB: www.coltsplastics.com
SIC: 3089 Mfg Plastic Products

(G-1043)
FERRON MOLD AND TOOL LLC
154 Louisa Viens Dr (06241-1133)
P.O. Box 144 (06241-0144)
PHONE..................................860 774-5555
Norman Ferron, *Partner*
Beverly Ferron, *Partner*
EMP: 8
SQ FT: 6,500
SALES (est): 1.4MM **Privately Held**
SIC: 3544 Mfg Dies/Tools/Jigs/Fixtures

(G-1044)
FILMX TECHNOLOGIES
20 Louisa Viens Dr (06241-1106)
PHONE..................................860 779-3403
Donald Romine, *President*
◆ **EMP:** 5
SALES (est): 551K **Privately Held**
SIC: 3081 Mfg Unsupported Plastic Film/Sheet

(G-1045)
FRITO-LAY NORTH AMERICA INC
1886 Upper Maple St (06241-1555)
PHONE..................................860 412-1000
Kevin Richardson, *Opers Staff*
Bob Shrek, *Manager*
EMP: 600
SALES (corp-wide): 64.6B **Publicly Held**
WEB: www.fritolay.com
SIC: 2096 Whol Confectionery
HQ: Frito-Lay North America, Inc.
7701 Legacy Dr
Plano TX 75024

(G-1046)
MIYOSHI AMERICA INC (HQ)
110 Louisa Viens Dr (06241-1132)
PHONE..................................860 779-3990
Kaoru Takagi, *President*
Taizo Miyoshi, *Chairman*
Brian Grossguth, *Opers Mgr*
▲ **EMP:** 67
SQ FT: 82,000
SALES (est): 21.1MM **Privately Held**
WEB: www.us-cosm.com
SIC: 2844 5169 Mfg Toilet Preparations Whol Chemicals/Products

(G-1047)
MIYOSHI AMERICA INC
313 Lake Rd (06241-1551)
P.O. Box 859 (06241-0859)
PHONE..................................860 779-3990
Kaoru Takagi, *President*
EMP: 11 **Privately Held**
SIC: 3295 5169 2844 Mfg Minerals-Ground/Treated Whol Chemicals/Products Mfg Toilet Preparations
HQ: Miyoshi America, Inc.
110 Louisa Viens Dr
Dayville CT 06241
860 779-3990

(G-1048)
MIYOSHI AMERICA INC
90 Louisa Viens Dr (06241-1106)
P.O. Box 859 (06241-0859)
PHONE..................................860 779-3990
Kaoru Takagi, *President*
EMP: 6 **Privately Held**
SIC: 3295 5169 2844 Mfg Minerals-Ground/Treated Whol Chemicals/Products Mfg Toilet Preparations
HQ: Miyoshi America, Inc.
110 Louisa Viens Dr
Dayville CT 06241
860 779-3990

(G-1049)
NORTHEAST FOODS INC
Also Called: Automatic Rolls of New England
328 Lake Rd (06241-1537)
PHONE..................................860 779-1117
John Denitti, *Engineer*
Fred Sexton, *Branch Mgr*
EMP: 100
SALES (corp-wide): 335.5MM **Privately Held**
SIC: 2051 Mfg Bread/Related Products
PA: Northeast Foods, Inc.
601 S Caroline St
Baltimore MD 21231
410 276-7254

(G-1050)
PEPSI-COLA BTLG OF WRCSTER INC
Also Called: Pepsico
135 Louisa Viens Dr (06241-1105)
P.O. Box 736 (06241-0736)
PHONE..................................860 774-4007
Tim Brown, *Branch Mgr*
EMP: 30
SALES (corp-wide): 16.5MM **Privately Held**
WEB: www.pepsiworcester.com
SIC: 2086 Carb Sft Drnkbtlcn
PA: Pepsi-Cola Bottling Co., Of Worcester, Inc.
90 Industrial Dr
Holden MA 01520
508 829-6551

(G-1051)
PUTNAM PLASTICS CORPORATION
40 Louisa Viens Dr (06241-1106)
PHONE..................................860 774-1559
James Binch, *President*
Jim Dandeneau, *Co-CEO*
Lawrence Acquarulo Jr, *Co-CEO*
William Appling, *Engineer*
Darko Krsulic, *Engineer*
EMP: 150
SQ FT: 40,000
SALES (est): 30.8MM **Privately Held**
WEB: www.putnamplastics.com
SIC: 3082 Mfg Plastic Profile Shapes

(G-1052)
ROL-VAC LIMITED PARTNERSHIP
207 Tracy Rd (06241-1123)
P.O. Box 777 (06241-0777)
PHONE..................................860 928-9929
Ron Jones, *General Ptnr*
▲ **EMP:** 12 **EST:** 1998
SQ FT: 45,000
SALES (est): 292.5K **Privately Held**
WEB: www.rolvac.com
SIC: 2671 Mfg Packaging Paper/Film

(G-1053)
SYMBOL MATTRESS OF NEW ENGLAND
312 Lake Rd (06241-1537)
P.O. Box 6689, Richmond VA (23230-0689)
PHONE..................................860 779-3112
Gordon Wallace, *CEO*
Charles Neal, *President*
Ronald Clevenger, *Vice Pres*
EMP: 450
SALES (est): 26.2MM
SALES (corp-wide): 96.2MM **Privately Held**
WEB: www.symbolmattress.com
SIC: 2515 Mfg Mattresses/Bedsprings
PA: Eastern Sleep Products Company
4901 Fitzhugh Ave
Richmond VA 23230
804 254-1711

(G-1054)
UNIVERSITY OPTICS LLC
Also Called: University Opticians
791 Hartford Pike (06241-1715)
P.O. Box 450, Wasco IL (60183-0450)
PHONE..................................860 779-6123
Aarlan Acepo,
EMP: 3
SALES (est): 329.2K **Privately Held**
SIC: 3851 Mfg Ophthalmic Goods

(G-1055)
WEB INDUSTRIES HARTFORD INC (HQ)
20 Louisa Viens Dr (06241-1106)
PHONE..................................860 779-3197
Robert Fulton, *Ch of Bd*
Donald Romine, *President*
Steve Sherburne, *Controller*
James Hanrahan, *Admin Sec*
▲ **EMP:** 32 **EST:** 1982
SQ FT: 40,000
SALES (est): 4.7MM
SALES (corp-wide): 117.8MM **Privately Held**
WEB: www.primastrip.com
SIC: 3082 5162 Mfg Plastic Profile Shapes Whol Plastic Materials/Shapes
PA: Web Industries Inc.
700 Nickerson Rd Ste 250
Marlborough MA 01752
508 898-2988

Deep River
Middlesex County

(G-1056)
ABSTRACT TOOL INC
500 Main St Ste 15 (06417-2000)
PHONE..................................860 526-4635
Ken Hallden, *President*
Glenn Guggenheim, *Vice Pres*
Janet Hallden, *Treasurer*
Diane Guggenheim, *Admin Sec*
EMP: 10
SQ FT: 6,000
SALES (est): 660K **Privately Held**
SIC: 3599 Tool & Die Machine Shop

(G-1057)
APS ROBOTICS & INTEGRATION LLC
500 Main St Ste 9 (06417-2000)
P.O. Box 245 (06417-0245)
PHONE..................................860 526-1040
Charles M Chadwick,
EMP: 3 **EST:** 1997
SQ FT: 5,000
SALES: 250K **Privately Held**
SIC: 3599 Machine Shop Jobbing Equip Intergrator

(G-1058)
BELL AND HOWELL LLC
6 Winter Ave (06417-1813)
PHONE..................................860 526-9561
EMP: 27 **Privately Held**
SIC: 3579 Mfg Office Machines
PA: Bell And Howell, Llc
3791 S Alston Ave
Durham NC 27713
-

(G-1059)
CHESTER BOATWORKS
444 Main St (06417-2034)
PHONE..................................860 526-2227
Gil Bartlett, *Owner*
EMP: 3 **EST:** 2014
SALES (est): 263.3K **Privately Held**
SIC: 3732 Boatbuilding/Repairing

(G-1060)
FLEXO LABEL SOLUTIONS LLC
500 Main St Ste 6 (06417-2000)
PHONE..................................860 243-9300
Rod Milligan, *Owner*
EMP: 9
SALES (est): 1.4MM **Privately Held**
SIC: 2679 Mfg Converted Paper Products

(G-1061)
GROVE SYSTEMS INC
572 Route 148 (06419-1107)
PHONE..................................860 663-2555
Jennifer Luzietti, *President*
EMP: 4
SALES (est): 984.1K **Privately Held**
WEB: www.grovesystems.com
SIC: 3822 Mfg Environmental Controls

(G-1062)
INTERPRO LLC
Also Called: Interpro Rapid Technology
630 Industrial Park Rd (06417-1600)
PHONE..................................860 526-5869
Dan Straka, *Opers Mgr*
Kevin Dyer,
EMP: 15
SQ FT: 7,500
SALES: 2MM **Privately Held**
SIC: 3555 Mfg Printing Trades Machinery

(G-1063)
INVENTEC PRFMCE CHEM USA LLC
500 Main St Ste 18 (06417-2000)
P.O. Box 989 (06417-0989)
PHONE..................................860 526-8300
Jean-Noel Poirier, *CEO*
David Reitz, *CFO*
Tina Williams, *Executive*
EMP: 20
SQ FT: 12,000
SALES (est): 3.9MM
SALES (corp-wide): 12.6MM **Privately Held**
SIC: 2899 Mfg Chemical Preparations
PA: Dehon
4 Rue De La Croix Faubin
Paris 11e Arrondissement
143 987-584

(G-1064)
PARASON MACHINE INC
1000 Industrial Park Rd (06417)
P.O. Box 292 (06417-0292)
PHONE..................................860 526-3565
Charles Paradis, *President*
Janice Paradis, *Vice Pres*
EMP: 18
SQ FT: 10,000
SALES (est): 2.5MM **Privately Held**
WEB: www.parasonmachine.com
SIC: 3599 Mfg Industrial Machinery

(G-1065)
SCHAEFER MACHINE COMPANY INC
200 Commercial Dr (06417-1682)
PHONE..................................860 526-4000
Robert C Gammons, *President*
Virginia Gammons, *Admin Sec*
▼ **EMP:** 6
SQ FT: 10,000
SALES (est): 1.3MM **Privately Held**
SIC: 3569 Mfg General Industrial Machinery

(G-1066)
SILGAN PLASTICS LLC
38 Bridge St (06417-1731)
P.O. Box 405 (06417)
PHONE..................................860 526-6300
Steve Monahan, *Engineer*
Jim Worthington, *Senior Engr*
Jim Leardi, *Manager*
Dave McLaughlin, *Supervisor*
Rosemary Grispino, *Executive*
EMP: 170
SALES (corp-wide): 4.4B **Publicly Held**
WEB: www.silganplastics.com
SIC: 3089 Mfg Plastic Products
HQ: Silgan Plastics Llc
14515 North Outer 40 Rd # 210
Chesterfield MO 63017
800 274-5426

(G-1067)
SWPC PLASTICS LLC
Also Called: Tri Town Precision Plastics
12 Bridge St (06417-1704)
PHONE..................................860 526-3200
Jeffrey Buchanan, *CFO*
James Debney, *Mng Member*
EMP: 112
SALES (est): 36.7MM
SALES (corp-wide): 638.2MM **Publicly Held**
SIC: 3089 Mfg Plastic Products
HQ: American Outdoor Brands Sales Company
2100 Roosevelt Ave
Springfield MA 01104
413 781-8300

Derby
New Haven County

(G-1068)
BEARD CONCRETE CO DERBY INC
37 Main St (06418-1932)
P.O. Box 590, Milford (06460-0590)
PHONE..................................203 735-4641
James Beard, *Vice Pres*
EMP: 13
SALES (corp-wide): 1.1MM **Privately Held**
SIC: 3241 5211 Mfg Hydraulic Cement Ret Lumber/Building Materials
PA: Beard Concrete Co. Of Derby, Inc.
127 Boston Post Rd
Milford CT 06460
203 874-2533

(G-1069)
BP COUNTERTOP DESIGN CO LLC
101 Elizabeth St Ste 1 (06418-1835)
PHONE..................................203 732-1620
EMP: 5
SQ FT: 7,000
SALES (est): 360K **Privately Held**
SIC: 2434 2541 Mfg Wood Kitchen Cabinets Mfg Wood Partitions/Fixtures

(G-1070)
EARTH ENGINEERED SYSTEMS
630 Hawthorne Ave (06418-1022)
P.O. Box 159, East Haddam (06423-0159)
PHONE..................................203 231-4614
Jim Lindner, *Owner*
EMP: 3
SALES (est): 163.3K **Privately Held**
SIC: 3567 Mfg Industrial Furnaces/Ovens

(G-1071)
EMPIRE TOOL LLC
259 Roosevelt Dr (06418-1653)
PHONE..................................203 735-7467
Joe Sender,
Mark Banyacski,
EMP: 3
SALES (est): 240K **Privately Held**
SIC: 3089 Mfg Plastic Products

(G-1072)
GORDON RUBBER AND PKG CO INC
10 Cemetery Ave (06418-1604)
P.O. Box 298 (06418-0298)
PHONE..................................203 735-7441
John A Mazur, *President*
EMP: 33 **EST:** 1948
SQ FT: 20,000
SALES (est): 6.4MM **Privately Held**
SIC: 3069 5085 3544 Mfg Fabricated Rubber Products Whol Industrial Supplies Mfg Dies/Tools/Jigs/Fixtures

(G-1073)
HESSEL INDUSTRIES INC
95 Roosevelt Dr (06418-1648)
PHONE..................................203 736-2317
Willie Krutoholow, *President*
EMP: 4 **EST:** 1960
SQ FT: 10,000
SALES (est): 592.6K **Privately Held**
WEB: www.hesselsindustries.com
SIC: 3496 3469 3452 Mfg Misc Fabricated Wire Products Mfg Metal Stampings Mfg Bolts/Screws/Rivets

(G-1074)
IDA INTERNATIONAL INC
200 Roosevelt Dr (06418-1625)
P.O. Box 284 (06418-0284)
PHONE..................................203 736-9249
Norman M Harbinson, *President*
Thomas Harbinson, *Principal*
Aldi Bylyku, *Project Mgr*
Mike Potkay, *Technology*
Robin Moscato, *Administration*
EMP: 45
SQ FT: 124,581
SALES (est): 10.6MM **Privately Held**
WEB: www.ida-intl.com
SIC: 3446 Mfg Architectural Metalwork

(G-1075)
M & B ENTERPRISE LLC
Also Called: Wholesale Poster Frames
155 New Haven Ave (06418-2161)
PHONE..................................203 298-9781
Michael J Klein,
Basile Tzovolos,
EMP: 12 **EST:** 2004
SQ FT: 20,000
SALES: 1.5MM **Privately Held**
SIC: 3499 Mfg Misc Fabricated Metal Products

(G-1076)
ON TIME SCREEN PRINTING & EMBR
155 New Haven Ave (06418-2161)
PHONE..................................203 874-4581
Michael J Klein, *Owner*
EMP: 15
SALES (est): 1.4MM **Privately Held**
SIC: 2399 2759 Mfg Fabricated Textile Products Commercial Printing

(G-1077)
PETER TASI
Also Called: P T Tool & Machine
10 Francis St (06418-1506)
PHONE..................................203 732-6540
Peter Tasi, *Owner*
EMP: 3
SALES (est): 410.1K **Privately Held**
WEB: www.pttool.com
SIC: 3599 Mfg Industrial Machinery

(G-1078)
RSS ENTERPRISES LLC
Also Called: City Stitchers
101 Elizabeth St Ste 7 (06418-1835)
PHONE..................................203 736-6220
Ron Bartone, *Owner*
EMP: 5
SALES (est): 443.7K **Privately Held**
SIC: 2395 Pleating/Stitching Services

(G-1079)
RUBBER SUPPLIES COMPANY INC
1 Park Ave Ste 1 # 1 (06418-1650)
P.O. Box 378 (06418-0378)
PHONE..................................203 736-9995
Edward Manion Jr, *President*
Michael Manion, *Treasurer*
EMP: 3
SQ FT: 11,000
SALES (est): 636.8K **Privately Held**
WEB: www.list-link.net
SIC: 3053 Mfg Gaskets/Packing/Sealing Devices

(G-1080)
SIGNS UNLIMITED INC
2 Francis St (06418-1552)
PHONE..................................203 734-7446
Allan Esposito, *President*
EMP: 5
SQ FT: 13,000
SALES (est): 810.3K **Privately Held**
SIC: 3993 3089 7389 Fabricators Of Backlit Awnings Made Of Fiberglass And Plastic And A Custom Sign Shop

(G-1081)
VALLEY PUBLISHING COMPANY INC
Also Called: Valley Times
7 Francis St (06418-1597)
PHONE..................................203 735-6696
Blaze A Garbatini, *President*
Irene Garbatini, *Corp Secy*
Romolo Garbatini, *Vice Pres*
EMP: 10
SALES (est): 928.4K **Privately Held**
WEB: www.thevalleytimes.com
SIC: 2711 Newspapers-Publishing/Printing

(G-1082)
WEIMANN BROTHERS MFG CO
247 Roosevelt Dr (06418-1626)
P.O. Box 333 (06418-0333)
PHONE..................................203 735-3311
James A Fair Sr, *President*
Jeff Fair, *Vice Pres*
James A Fair Jr, *Treasurer*
Marion Neville, *Admin Sec*
EMP: 15
SQ FT: 12,000
SALES (est): 2.5MM **Privately Held**
SIC: 3469 3544 Mfg Metal Stampings Mfg Dies/Tools/Jigs/Fixtures

(G-1083)
WHALLEY GLASS COMPANY (PA)
Also Called: Curved Glass Distributors
72 Chapel St (06418-2130)
PHONE..................................203 735-9388
Mark S Vece, *President*
Corinne V Cacopardo, *Vice Pres*
Blaise L Vece, *Treasurer*
Joyce Gaul, *Admin Sec*
▲ **EMP:** 100
SQ FT: 50,000

SALES (est): 2.7MM **Privately Held**
SIC: 3229 5023 Mfg Pressed/Blown Glass Whol Homefurnishings

(G-1084)
WILSON ANCHOR BOLT SLEEVE
259 Roosevelt Dr (06418-1653)
PHONE..................................203 516-5260
Theresa Somo Passander, *Principal*
EMP: 4
SALES (est): 256.1K **Privately Held**
SIC: 3452 Mfg Bolts/Screws/Rivets

(G-1085)
YANKEE SCREEN PRINTING
15 Kings Ct (06418-2241)
PHONE..................................203 924-9926
Daniel L Blackwell, *Owner*
EMP: 3
SQ FT: 3,500
SALES (est): 192.3K **Privately Held**
SIC: 2759 2752 2262 5699 Silk Screen Printing

Durham
Middlesex County

(G-1086)
APPLIED DIAMOND COATINGS LLC
30 Ozick Dr (06422-1022)
PHONE..................................860 349-3133
John J Ozycz,
EMP: 4
SALES (est): 360K **Privately Held**
SIC: 3312 Blast Furnace-Steel Works

(G-1087)
ASCT LLC
30 Ozick Dr (06422-1022)
PHONE..................................860 349-1121
Tom Ozycz,
John Ozycz,
▲ **EMP:** 3
SQ FT: 7,000
SALES (est): 684.9K **Privately Held**
WEB: www.asct.com
SIC: 3674 Mfg Semiconductors/Related Devices

(G-1088)
CHEMOTEX PROTECTIVE COATINGS (PA)
15 Commerce Cir (06422-1002)
PHONE..................................860 349-0144
Kevin Wise, *President*
EMP: 11
SQ FT: 10,000
SALES (est): 1.1MM **Privately Held**
WEB: www.cpc-corp.com
SIC: 2899 Mfg Automotive Chemicals

(G-1089)
CLAREMONT SALES CORPORATION
35 Winsome Rd (06422-1315)
P.O. Box 430 (06422-0430)
PHONE..................................860 349-4499
Keith Williams, *President*
Dave Coutts, *Treasurer*
David Coutts, *Admin Sec*
▼ **EMP:** 30
SQ FT: 32,000
SALES (est): 8.2MM **Privately Held**
WEB: www.claremontcorporation.com
SIC: 3086 2221 Mfg Plastic Foam Products Manmade Broadwoven Fabric Mill

(G-1090)
DURHAM MANUFACTURING COMPANY (PA)
201 Main St (06422-2108)
P.O. Box 230 (06422-0230)
PHONE..................................860 349-3427
Richard Patterson, *CEO*
Francis Korn, *Senior VP*
John Patterson, *Vice Pres*
John Gowac, *CFO*
◆ **EMP:** 99 **EST:** 1922
SQ FT: 120,000
SALES: 55MM **Privately Held**
WEB: www.durhammfg.com
SIC: 3469 2542 2522 2514 Mfg Metal Stampings Mfg Nonwd Partition/Fixt Mfg Nonwood Office Furn Mfg Metal Household Furn

(G-1091)
GRAPHITE DIE MOLD INC
18 Airline Rd (06422-1000)
PHONE..................................860 349-4444
Don Klas, *President*
Don Ozycz, *General Mgr*
▲ **EMP:** 5 **EST:** 1977
SQ FT: 60,000
SALES (est): 1.3MM
SALES (corp-wide): 1.3B **Privately Held**
WEB: www.graphitediemold.com
SIC: 3624 Manufacturing Carbon/Graphite Products
HQ: Morgan Advanced Materials And Technology, Inc.
441 Hall Ave
Saint Marys PA 15857

(G-1092)
HOBSON AND MOTZER INCORPORATED (PA)
30 Airline Rd (06422-1000)
PHONE..................................860 349-1756
Frank W Dworak, *President*
James O'Brien, *Vice Pres*
Donald Zak, *Vice Pres*
Michael Manna, *Supervisor*
EMP: 113 **EST:** 1912
SQ FT: 52,000
SALES (est): 26MM **Privately Held**
WEB: www.hobsonmotzer.com
SIC: 3469 3544 Mfg Metal Stampings Mfg Dies/Tools/Jigs/Fixtures

(G-1093)
PRAXAIR DISTRIBUTION INC
89 Commerce Cir (06422-1002)
PHONE..................................860 349-0305
Ron Caselino, *General Mgr*
EMP: 42 **Privately Held**
SIC: 2813 Whol Industrial Equipment
HQ: Praxair Distribution, Inc.
10 Riverview Dr
Danbury CT 06810
203 837-2000

(G-1094)
TECHNICAL MANUFACTURING CORP
Also Called: T M C
645 New Haven Rd (06422-2512)
P.O. Box 306 (06422-0306)
PHONE..................................860 349-1735
Mary Lou Bonito, *President*
Marylou Bonito, *President*
Fred Bonito, *Vice Pres*
Tony Calabrese, *VP Opers*
Catherine Bender, *Production*
EMP: 30
SQ FT: 70,000
SALES (est): 6.3MM **Privately Held**
SIC: 3672 3679 Mfg Printed Circuit Boards Mfg Electronic Components

(G-1095)
TRANSFORMER TECHNOLOGY INC
60 Commerce Cir (06422-1001)
P.O. Box 436 (06422-0436)
PHONE..................................860 349-1061
Bruce M Gueble Jr, *President*
Suzanne M Gueble, *Treasurer*
▲ **EMP:** 12
SQ FT: 20,000
SALES: 2MM **Privately Held**
SIC: 3679 3612 Mfg Electronic Components Mfg Transformers

(G-1096)
WELDER REPAIR & RENTAL SVC INC
37 Commerce Cir (06422-1002)
P.O. Box 659 (06422-0659)
PHONE..................................203 238-9284
Bruce J Dowd, *Owner*
EMP: 4 **EST:** 1979
SQ FT: 16,000
SALES (est): 404.9K **Privately Held**
SIC: 7692 7359 Welding Repair Equipment Rental/Leasing

East Berlin
Hartford County

(G-1097)
ASI SIGN SYSTEMS INC
100 Clark Dr (06023-1172)
PHONE..................................860 828-3331
Doden Hoff, *Manager*
EMP: 8
SALES (corp-wide): 20.7MM **Privately Held**
SIC: 3993 Mfg Signs/Advertising Specialties
PA: Asi Sign Systems, Inc.
8181 Jetstar Dr Ste 110
Irving TX 75063
214 352-9140

(G-1098)
DEBURRING HOUSE INC
230 Berlin St (06023-1032)
PHONE..................................860 828-0889
David Durity, *Vice Pres*
Steven Cyr, *Vice Pres*
Kevin Cyr, *Admin Sec*
EMP: 50
SQ FT: 10,000
SALES (est): 5.8MM **Privately Held**
WEB: www.deburringhouse.com
SIC: 3471 3484 3724 Plating/Polishing Svcs Mfg Small Arms Mfg Aircraft Engine/Part

(G-1099)
EDRO CORPORATION
Also Called: Dynawash
37 Commerce St (06023-1106)
P.O. Box 308 (06023-0308)
PHONE..................................860 828-0311
Barbara Kirejczyk, *Ch of Bd*
Edward S Kirejczyk III, *President*
Edward S Kirejczyk Jr, *President*
Scott Kirejczyk, *Managing Dir*
Caroline Wojcicki, *Vice Pres*
▲ **EMP:** 34
SQ FT: 45,000
SALES (est): 8.4MM **Privately Held**
WEB: www.edrodynawash.com
SIC: 3582 Mfg Commercial Laundry Equipment

(G-1100)
FENN LLC
80 Clark Dr Unit 5d (06023-1157)
PHONE..................................860 259-6600
David Somers, *CEO*
Ryan Cutter, *President*
Mike Geiger, *Sales Mgr*
Kevin Campion, *Accounts Mgr*
Weylin Trombley, *Sales Staff*
▲ **EMP:** 30
SQ FT: 22,000
SALES (est): 4.9MM
SALES (corp-wide): 24MM **Privately Held**
SIC: 3542 Mfg Machine Tools-Forming
PA: Quality Products, Inc.
1 Air Cargo Pkwy E
Swanton OH 43558
614 228-0185

(G-1101)
FINISHERS TECHNOLOGY CORP
Also Called: Kelsey Mfg Division
319 Main St (06023)
PHONE..................................860 829-1000
EMP: 18
SQ FT: 14,500
SALES (est): 229.9K **Privately Held**
SIC: 3541 5084 Mfg Machine Tools-Cutting Whol Industrial Equipment

(G-1102)
FLETCHER-TERRY COMPANY LLC (PA)
91 Clark Dr (06023-1104)
PHONE..................................860 828-3400
John Peterson, *President*
Blair Tomalonis, *President*
Brian M Johnson,
◆ **EMP:** 90
SALES (est): 21.9MM **Privately Held**
SIC: 3423 3541 6512 3549 Mfg Hand/Edge Tools Mfg Machine Tool-Cutting Nonresdentl Bldg Operatr Mfg Metalworking Mach Mfg Machine Tool Access

(G-1103)
HEISE INDUSTRIES INC
196 Commerce St (06023-1105)
PHONE..................................860 828-6538
Brooks B Heise Sr, *CEO*
Brooks B Heise Jr, *President*
Carrie Milslagle, *Purchasing*
Michael Cesario, *Treasurer*
Carol Obrien, *Controller*
EMP: 54 **EST:** 1965
SQ FT: 25,000
SALES (est): 10.1MM **Privately Held**
WEB: www.heiseindustries.com
SIC: 3544 Mfg Dies/Tools/Jigs/Fixtures

(G-1104)
K & K PRECISION MANUFACTURING
54 Clark Dr Ste F (06023-1150)
PHONE..................................860 828-7681
Peter Kiss, *President*
Darlene Kiss, *Vice Pres*
EMP: 3
SALES: 220K **Privately Held**
SIC: 3599 Mfg Industrial Machinery

(G-1105)
PARADIGM PRCISION HOLDINGS LLC
Also Called: Berlin Operations
134 Commerce St (06023-1105)
PHONE..................................860 829-3663
Lester Karolek, *Branch Mgr*
EMP: 70
SALES (corp-wide): 368.2MM **Privately Held**
SIC: 3545 Mfg Machine Tool Accessories
HQ: Paradigm Precision Holdings, Llc
404 W Guadalupe Rd
Tempe AZ 85283

(G-1106)
PRECISION GRAPHICS INC
10 Clark Dr (06023-1103)
P.O. Box 248 (06023-0248)
PHONE..................................860 828-6561
Burton Johnson, *President*
Eric Johnson, *Vice Pres*
Ross Johnson, *Vice Pres*
Karen Johnson, *Admin Sec*
EMP: 25
SQ FT: 13,000
SALES (est): 4.9MM **Privately Held**
WEB: www.frontpanels.com
SIC: 3613 3993 Mfg Switchgear/Switchboards Mfg Signs/Advertising Specialties

(G-1107)
S D & D INC
Also Called: Sign Design & Display
99 Clark Dr 1 (06023-1104)
PHONE..................................860 357-2603
EMP: 15
SQ FT: 7,000
SALES (est): 1.9MM **Privately Held**
WEB: www.sdd.com
SIC: 3993 Mfg Signs/Advertising Specialties

(G-1108)
SMS MACHINE INC
54 Clark Dr Ste A (06023-1150)
PHONE..................................860 829-0813
Scott Steele, *President*
Sandra Steele, *Admin Sec*
EMP: 4
SQ FT: 2,000
SALES (est): 620.4K **Privately Held**
WEB: www.smsmachine.com
SIC: 2821 3471 Mfg Plastic Materials/Resins Plating/Polishing Service

(G-1109)
T M INDUSTRIES INC
134 Commerce St (06023-1105)
P.O. Box 278 (06023-0278)
PHONE..................................860 828-0344
Rosemarie Fischer, *CEO*
Anthony Micacci, *President*
Lucia Micacci Bantle, *Principal*
Vincent Micacci, *Principal*
Lucille Micacci, *Chairman*
▲ **EMP:** 75
SQ FT: 70,000
SALES (est): 9.7MM **Privately Held**
WEB: www.tmindustries.com
SIC: 3599 Jobbing & Repair Shop

(G-1110)
WAD INC
Also Called: Asi Modulex
100 Clark Dr (06023-1172)
P.O. Box 504 (06023-0504)
PHONE..................................860 828-3331
William Dodenhoff, *President*
Cindy Dodenhoff, *Vice Pres*
EMP: 25
SQ FT: 9,000
SALES (est): 3.5MM **Privately Held**
SIC: 3993 1799 Mfg Signs/Advertising Specialties Trade Contractor

East Canaan
Litchfield County

(G-1111)
ALLYNDALE CORPORATION
40 Allyndale Rd (06024)
P.O. Box 265 (06024-0265)
PHONE..................................860 824-7959
Louis C Allyn II, *President*
Brian Allyn, *General Mgr*
Steven Allyn, *Vice Pres*
Leonard Allyn, *Treasurer*
EMP: 15
SQ FT: 450
SALES (est): 3.6MM **Privately Held**
SIC: 1422 Limestone Quarry

(G-1112)
LAND OF NOD WINERY LLC
99 Lower Rd (06024-2624)
PHONE..................................860 824-5225
William S Adam, *Principal*
EMP: 7
SALES (est): 404.1K **Privately Held**
SIC: 2084 Mfg Wines/Brandy/Spirits

(G-1113)
LAURELBROOK NTRAL RSOURCES LLC
12 Casey Hill Rd (06024-2638)
P.O. Box 431, Norfolk (06058-0431)
PHONE..................................860 824-5843
Robert Jacquie,
James Jacquier,
EMP: 19 **EST:** 1926
SALES (est): 2.5MM **Privately Held**
SIC: 1442 Sand & Gravel Pit

East Glastonbury
Hartford County

(G-1114)
QUALITY NAME PLATE INC
Also Called: Qnp Technologies
22 Fisher Hill Rd (06025)
P.O. Box 308 (06025-0308)
PHONE..................................860 633-9495
Craig O Garneau, *President*
Barry B Ralston, *Vice Pres*
Andrew Adams, *Engineer*
▲ **EMP:** 95 **EST:** 1946
SQ FT: 40,000
SALES (est): 20.4MM **Privately Held**
WEB: www.qnp.com
SIC: 3625 3613 2759 3083 Mfg Switchgear/Boards Mfg Relay/Indstl Control Mfg Lamnatd Plstc Plates Commercial Printing Mfg Auto/Apparel Trim

East Granby
Hartford County

(G-1115)
ACCELERON INC
21 Lordship Rd Ste 1 (06026-9589)
PHONE..................................860 651-9333
Donald Montano, *CEO*
Rory Montano, *President*
Donald Christensen, *Vice Pres*
Lance Montano, *Vice Pres*
Scott Dawick, *Engineer*
EMP: 46 **EST:** 1974
SQ FT: 60,000
SALES (est): 10.3MM **Privately Held**
WEB: www.acceleron-enbeam.com
SIC: 3629 Mfg Electrical Industrial Apparatus

(G-1116)
AMERICAN CLADDING TECHNOLOGIES
15 International Dr (06026-9718)
PHONE..................................860 413-3098
Scott Poeppel, *Vice Pres*
EMP: 3
SALES (est): 297.2K **Privately Held**
SIC: 3444 Mfg Sheet Metalwork

(G-1117)
APPLETON GRP LLC
Also Called: Egs Electrcl Grp Nelson Heat T
2 Connecticut South Dr (06026-9738)
PHONE..................................860 653-1603
Lynn Avers, *Manager*
EMP: 40
SALES (corp-wide): 18.3B **Publicly Held**
SIC: 3823 Mfg Process Control Instruments
HQ: Appleton Grp Llc
9377 W Higgins Rd
Rosemont IL 60018
847 268-6000

(G-1118)
BROOME & CO LLC
62 Turkey Hills Rd (06026-9572)
PHONE..................................860 653-2106
Christopher Broome,
EMP: 5
SALES (est): 519.6K **Privately Held**
SIC: 3931 Mfg Musical Instruments

(G-1119)
BURKE PRECISION MACHINE CO INC
7 Hatchett Hill Rd (06026-9526)
P.O. Box 329 (06026-0329)
PHONE..................................860 408-1394
Peter Burke, *President*
EMP: 9
SQ FT: 10,000
SALES (est): 1.1MM **Privately Held**
WEB: www.burkeprecision.com
SIC: 3599 Mfg Industrial Machinery

(G-1120)
CBS MANUFACTURING COMPANY
35 Kripes Rd (06026-9644)
PHONE..................................860 653-8100
John James Lawton, *CEO*
Clifford James Lawton, *President*
Kevin Lawton, *General Mgr*
Robert Bruce Lawton, *Vice Pres*
Vince Klezos, *Engineer*
EMP: 39 **EST:** 1972
SQ FT: 16,000
SALES (est): 8MM **Privately Held**
WEB: www.cbsmfg.com
SIC: 3724 3728 Mfg Aircraft Engines/Parts Mfg Aircraft Parts/Equipment

(G-1121)
COLOR CRAFT LTD
Also Called: Createx Colors
14 Airport Park Rd (06026-9523)
P.O. Box 120 (06026-0120)
PHONE..................................800 509-6563
Vincent H Kennedy, *President*
Craig Kenndey, *Treasurer*
EMP: 13
SQ FT: 10,000
SALES (est): 2.2MM **Privately Held**
WEB: www.autoaircolors.com
SIC: 3952 5199 5198 5961 Mfg Lead Pencils/Art Sup Whol Nondurable Goods Whol Paints/Varnishes Ret Mail-Order House Ret Paint/Glass/Wallppr

(G-1122)
COMMAND CORPORATION
59 Rainbow Rd (06026-9763)
P.O. Box 832 (06026-0832)
PHONE..................................800 851-6012
Robert Bazyk, *President*
John Bazyk, *Sales Staff*
EMP: 14
SQ FT: 1,150
SALES (est): 2.2MM **Privately Held**
WEB: www.commandco.com
SIC: 3699 1731 Mfg & Install Electronic Surveillance Systems

(G-1123)
COMPUTER COMPONENTS INC
Also Called: Relays Unlimited
18 Kripes Rd (06026-9645)
P.O. Box 1378 (06026-1378)
PHONE..................................860 653-9909
Gary Flor, *President*
EMP: 15 **EST:** 1959
SQ FT: 6,000
SALES: 1.8MM **Privately Held**
WEB: www.relays-unlimited.com
SIC: 3625 Mfgs Relays For Electronic Use

(G-1124)
COORSTEK INC
Also Called: Coorstek East Granby
10 Airport Park Rd (06026-9523)
PHONE..................................860 653-8071
Roman Czarniecki, *Engineer*
Janis Hunter, *Admin Sec*
EMP: 25
SALES (corp-wide): 407.6MM **Privately Held**
SIC: 3264 Mfg Porcelain Electrical Supplies
HQ: Coorstek, Inc.
14143 Denver West Pkwy # 400
Lakewood CO 80401
303 271-7000

(G-1125)
DAYTON BAG & BURLAP CO
10 Hazelwood Rd Ste A5 (06026-9670)
PHONE..................................860 653-8191
Mark Lundin, *Manager*
EMP: 3
SALES (corp-wide): 45.3MM **Privately Held**
SIC: 2393 5085 Mfg Textile Bags Whol Industrial Supplies
PA: The Dayton Bag & Burlap Co
322 Davis Ave
Dayton OH 45403
937 258-8000

(G-1126)
ENERGY BEAM SCIENCES INC
Also Called: Labpulse Medical
29 Kripes Rd Ste B (06026-9669)
PHONE..................................860 653-0411
Michael Nesta, *President*
Gary Braga, *Materials Mgr*
Paul Kenney, *Treasurer*
Cindy McMurray, *Asst Controller*
Mike Whittlesy, *Admin Sec*
EMP: 17
SQ FT: 18,000
SALES (est): 4.3MM **Privately Held**
WEB: www.ebsciences.com
SIC: 3826 Mfg Analytical Instruments

(G-1127)
FUNKHOUSER INDUSTRIAL PRODUCTS
10 Hazelwood Rd Ste 3b (06026-9670)
P.O. Box 1153 (06026-1153)
PHONE..................................860 653-1972
Robert Funkhouser III, *President*
Kimberly Minch, *Vice Pres*
EMP: 3
SQ FT: 4,800
SALES: 800K **Privately Held**
SIC: 3492 Mfg Fluid Power Valves/Fittings

(G-1128)
GALASSO MATERIALS LLC
60 S Main St (06026-9550)
P.O. Box 1776 (06026-0676)
PHONE..................................860 527-1825
Timoth McAvoy,
Emil J Galasso,
Martin A Galasso,
Craig C Timpson,
EMP: 160
SQ FT: 7,000
SALES (est): 38.6MM **Privately Held**
WEB: www.galassomaterials.com
SIC: 1499 1429 1442 Nonmetallic Mineral Mining Crushed/Broken Stone Construction Sand/Gravel

(G-1129)
GULFSTREAM AEROSPACE CORP
95 Old County Rd (06026-9754)
PHONE..................................912 965-3000
Scott McDougall, *Branch Mgr*
EMP: 3
SALES (corp-wide): 36.1B **Publicly Held**
SIC: 3721 Mfg Aircraft
HQ: Gulfstream Aerospace Corporation
500 Gulfstream Rd
Savannah GA 31408
912 965-3000

(G-1130)
JOINING TECHNOLOGIES INC
17 Connecticut South Dr B (06026-9671)
PHONE..................................860 653-0111
David Hudson, *President*
Greg Miller, *General Mgr*
Michael Francoeur, *Chairman*
Gary Francoeur, *Vice Pres*
Scott Poeppel, *Vice Pres*
EMP: 75
SQ FT: 27,578
SALES: 14MM **Privately Held**
WEB: www.joiningtech.com
SIC: 7692 Welding Repair

(G-1131)
MAGNATECH LLC
Also Called: Magnatech Dsd Co, The
6 Kripes Rd (06026-9645)
P.O. Box 260 (06026-0260)
PHONE..................................860 653-2573
Scott Wright, *Production*
John G Emmerson, *Mng Member*
▼ **EMP:** 54
SQ FT: 24,000
SALES (est): 14.4MM **Privately Held**
SIC: 3548 3699 Mfg Welding Apparatus Mfg Electrical Equipment/Supplies

(G-1132)
MARK V LABORATORY INC
18 Kripes Rd (06026-9645)
P.O. Box 540 (06026-0540)
PHONE..................................860 653-7201
Norman Villeneuve, *President*
Mark Villeneuve, *Vice Pres*
Karen Cox, *Marketing Staff*
Mark Vanata, *Executive*
EMP: 4
SQ FT: 10,000
SALES (est): 832.2K **Privately Held**
WEB: www.markvlab.com
SIC: 3821 Mfg Lab Apparatus/Furniture

(G-1133)
MB AEROSPACE
99 Rainbow Rd (06026-9400)
PHONE..................................860 653-0569
William Kircher, *COO*
Bill Evans, *Vice Pres*
Scott Truehart, *Foreman/Supr*
Pete Tsilimingras, *Program Mgr*
Robin Gamble, *Manager*
EMP: 4
SALES (est): 335K **Privately Held**
SIC: 3721 Mfg Aircraft

(G-1134)
MP SYSTEMS INC
34 Bradley Park Rd (06026-9789)
PHONE..................................860 687-3460
Bradley Morris, *President*
Graham Noake, *President*
EMP: 12

SALES (est): 3.3MM **Privately Held**
SIC: 3443 5078 Mfg Fabricated Plate Work Whol Refrigeration Equipment/Supplies
PA: Morris Group, Inc.
910 Day Hill Rd
Windsor CT 06095

(G-1135)
NATIONAL CONVEYORS COMPANY INC
33 Nicholson Rd Ste 2 (06026-9304)
PHONE....................................860 653-0374
Donald B Brant Jr, *CEO*
Arnold Serenkin, *President*
James Dumaine-Savage, *Vice Pres*
Brian Smith, *Vice Pres*
Darryl Beech, *Sales Staff*
▲ **EMP:** 25 **EST:** 1933
SQ FT: 17,500
SALES (est): 6.5MM **Privately Held**
WEB: www.nationalconveyors.com
SIC: 3535 Mfg Conveyors/Equipment

(G-1136)
NIDEC AMERICA CORPORATION
16 International Dr (06026-9718)
PHONE....................................860 653-2144
EMP: 10 **Privately Held**
SIC: 3564 Mfg Blowers/Fans
HQ: Nidec America Corporation
50 Braintree Hill Park # 110
Braintree MA 02184
781 848-0970

(G-1137)
NUFERN
7 Airport Park Rd (06026-9523)
PHONE....................................860 408-5000
Martin Seifert, *President*
Bryce Samson, *Vice Pres*
Dr Kanishka Tankala, *Vice Pres*
Jeff Wojtkiewicz, *Vice Pres*
Jarek Abramczyk, *Technical Mgr*
▲ **EMP:** 68
SQ FT: 57,000
SALES (est): 11.6MM
SALES (corp-wide): 1.4B **Publicly Held**
WEB: www.nufern.com
SIC: 3229 Mfg Pressed/Blown Glass
PA: Coherent, Inc.
5100 Patrick Henry Dr
Santa Clara CA 95054
408 764-4000

(G-1138)
OSHKOSH CORPORATION
35 Nicholson Rd (06026)
P.O. Box 1126 (06026-1126)
PHONE....................................860 653-5548
Bruce Anderson, *Manager*
EMP: 18
SALES (corp-wide): 8.3B **Publicly Held**
WEB: www.oshkoshtruck.com
SIC: 3711 Mfg Motor Vehicle/Car Bodies
PA: Oshkosh Corporation
1917 Four Wheel Dr
Oshkosh WI 54902
920 502-3000

(G-1139)
OVENTROP CORP
29 Kripes Rd (06026-9669)
P.O. Box 789 (06026-0789)
PHONE....................................860 413-9173
Joe Walsh, *CEO*
Sunil Anand, *Manager*
Sigmund Michel, *Director*
▲ **EMP:** 26
SALES (est): 5MM
SALES (corp-wide): 272.2MM **Privately Held**
SIC: 3491 Valve Controls System
HQ: Oventrop Gmbh & Co.Kg.
Paul-Oventrop-Str. 1
Olsberg 59939
296 282-0

(G-1140)
OVERHAUL SUPPORT SERVICES LLC
18 Connecticut South Dr (06026-9738)
PHONE....................................860 653-1980
David Dulude, *Branch Mgr*
EMP: 4
SQ FT: 15,820 **Privately Held**
WEB: www.overhaulsupportservices.com
SIC: 3728 Mfg Aircraft Parts/Equipment
PA: Overhaul Support Services, Llc
5 Connecticut South Dr
East Granby CT 06026

(G-1141)
OVERHAUL SUPPORT SERVICES LLC (PA)
5 Connecticut South Dr (06026-9738)
PHONE....................................860 264-2101
Ken O'Connor, *Vice Pres*
Brett Gillespie, *Prdtn Mgr*
Debbie Mlinek, *Safety Mgr*
Ana Langevin, *Purchasing*
Ken Oconnor, *Mng Member*
EMP: 47
SQ FT: 10,000
SALES (est): 9.9MM **Privately Held**
SIC: 3728 Mfg Aircraft Parts/Equipment

(G-1142)
R G L INC
121 Rainbow Rd (06026-9795)
P.O. Box 1051 (06026-1051)
PHONE....................................860 653-7254
Rocco G Lapenta, *President*
EMP: 46
SQ FT: 6,000
SALES (est): 3.4MM **Privately Held**
SIC: 2731 2721 2741 Publishes Books Periodicals & Programs

(G-1143)
RSCC WIRE & CABLE LLC (DH)
20 Bradley Park Rd (06026-9789)
PHONE....................................860 653-8300
Gary J Gagnon, *Vice Pres*
Mike St Jean, *Engineer*
Frederick Schwelm Jr, *Mng Member*
R C Gluth,
Wayne Yakich,
▲ **EMP:** 263
SQ FT: 140,000
SALES (est): 143.5MM
SALES (corp-wide): 225.3B **Publicly Held**
SIC: 3357 3315 Nonferrous Wiredrawing/Insulating Mfg Steel Wire/Related Products
HQ: Marmon Holdings, Inc.
181 W Madison St Ste 2600
Chicago IL 60602
312 372-9500

(G-1144)
SIGNS PLUS INC (PA)
3 Turkey Hills Rd (06026-9564)
P.O. Box 560 (06026-0560)
PHONE....................................860 653-0547
Christopher Aubin, *President*
Barbara A Aubin, *Admin Sec*
EMP: 7
SQ FT: 3,000
SALES (est): 853.6K **Privately Held**
SIC: 3993 Mfg Signs/Advertising Specialties

(G-1145)
SPECIALTY STEEL TREATING INC
Also Called: Heat Treating
12 Kripes Rd (06026-9645)
PHONE....................................860 653-0061
Dennis Kollmorgen, *Principal*
EMP: 40
SALES (corp-wide): 49.4MM **Privately Held**
WEB: www.sstfraser.com
SIC: 3398 Metal Heat Treating
PA: Specialty Steel Treating, Inc.
34501 Commerce
Fraser MI 48026
586 293-5355

(G-1146)
UNITED TECHNOLOGIES CORP
200 Signature Way (06026-2510)
PHONE....................................860 292-3270
Scott E Ashton, *Manager*
EMP: 14
SALES (corp-wide): 66.5B **Publicly Held**
SIC: 3534 4581 Mfg Elevators/Escalators
PA: United Technologies Corporation
10 Farm Springs Rd
Farmington CT 06032
860 728-7000

East Haddam
Middlesex County

(G-1147)
ALL PHASE HTG COOLG CONTR LLC
500 Tater Hill Rd (06423-1636)
P.O. Box 577, Moodus (06469-0577)
PHONE....................................860 873-9680
Maryjane Fay,
EMP: 3
SALES: 250K **Privately Held**
SIC: 3585 Mfg Refrigeration/Heating Equipment

(G-1148)
BEST MANAGEMENT PRODUCTS INC
Also Called: Best Manager Products
9 Matthews Dr Unit A1-A2 (06423-1350)
PHONE....................................860 434-0277
Judith H Duran, *Principal*
EMP: 4
SALES (est): 695.8K **Privately Held**
SIC: 3589 Mfg Service Industry Machinery

(G-1149)
C SHERMAN JOHNSON COMPANY
Also Called: Johnson Marine
1 Matthews Dr (06423-1350)
P.O. Box L (06423-0296)
PHONE....................................860 873-8697
Burton Johnson, *CEO*
Curtiss Johnson III, *President*
Elsie Johnson, *Admin Sec*
◆ **EMP:** 14
SQ FT: 5,200
SALES (est): 3.1MM **Privately Held**
WEB: www.csjohnson.com
SIC: 3429 Mfg Hardware

(G-1150)
CUSTOM HOUSE LLC
8 Matthews Dr Ste 3 (06423-1350)
PHONE....................................860 873-1259
Robert Finch, *President*
EMP: 10
SALES (est): 1.4MM **Privately Held**
SIC: 3315 5731 Mfg Steel Wire/Related Products Ret Radio/Tv/Electronics

(G-1151)
MARK G CAPPITELLA (PA)
Also Called: Mgc's Cstm Made Wooden
31 Bogue Ln (06423-1442)
PHONE....................................860 873-3093
Mark Cappitella, *Owner*
EMP: 3
SQ FT: 2,300
SALES: 150K **Privately Held**
WEB: www.ctrivervalley.com
SIC: 3944 Mfg Games/Toys

(G-1152)
PINE RIDGE GRAVEL LLC
24 Mount Parnassus Rd (06423-1475)
PHONE....................................860 873-2500
EMP: 3
SALES (est): 180K **Privately Held**
SIC: 1442 Construction Sand/Gravel

(G-1153)
TEX ELM INC
136 Town St (06423-1423)
PHONE....................................860 873-9715
Luella A Lyman, *President*
Emmett J Lyman, *Treasurer*
William B Harmon, *Clerk*
EMP: 15
SQ FT: 10,000
SALES (est): 1.1MM **Privately Held**
WEB: www.texas-relocation.org
SIC: 2759 Textile Engraving

East Hampton
Middlesex County

(G-1154)
4 D TECHNOLOGY CORPORATION
91 Daniel St (06424-1806)
PHONE....................................860 365-0420
James Wyant, *Branch Mgr*
EMP: 3
SALES (corp-wide): 324.5MM **Publicly Held**
SIC: 3827 Mfg Optical Instruments/Lenses
HQ: 4d Technology Corporation
3280 E Hmshre Loop Ste 14
Tucson AZ 85706
520 294-5600

(G-1155)
AMERICA EXTRACT CORPORATION
31 E High St (06424-1021)
PHONE....................................860 267-4444
Edward Jackowitz, *President*
EMP: 16
SQ FT: 65,000
SALES (est): 1MM **Privately Held**
SIC: 2087 Mfg Flavoring Extracts

(G-1156)
AMERICAN DISTILLING INC (PA)
31 E High St (06424-1021)
P.O. Box 319 (06424-0319)
PHONE....................................860 267-4444
Edward C Jackowitz, *President*
Kevin R Jackowitz, *Vice Pres*
George Perham, *Lab Dir*
▼ **EMP:** 75
SQ FT: 65,000
SALES (est): 15.9MM **Privately Held**
SIC: 2085 2833 2844 2087 Mfg Distilled Liquors Mfg Medicinal/Botanicals Mfg Toilet Preparations Mfg Flavor Extracts

(G-1157)
AMERICAN PRECISION MOLD INC
58 E High St (06424-1052)
P.O. Box 22 (06424-0022)
PHONE....................................860 267-1356
Richard Erlandson, *President*
EMP: 4
SQ FT: 3,000
SALES (est): 570.6K **Privately Held**
SIC: 3544 Mfg Plastic Injection Molds

(G-1158)
BEVIN BROS MANUFACTURING CO
Also Called: Bevin Bells
17 Watrous St (06424-1234)
P.O. Box 60 (06424-0060)
PHONE....................................860 267-4431
Stanley R Bevin, *President*
Alison Bevinlove, *Vice Pres*
EMP: 40
SALES (est): 7.1MM **Privately Held**
WEB: www.bevinbells.com
SIC: 3699 Mfg Electrical Equipment/Supplies

(G-1159)
HUMPHREYS PHARMACAL INC
31 E High St (06424-1021)
P.O. Box 317 (06424-0317)
PHONE....................................860 267-8710
Tom Shultz, *President*
▼ **EMP:** 10 **EST:** 1854
SALES (est): 1MM
SALES (corp-wide): 4.9MM **Privately Held**
WEB: www.humphreysusa.com
SIC: 2834 Mfg Pharmaceutical Preparations
PA: Dickinson Brands Inc.
31 E High St
East Hampton CT 06424
860 267-2279

GEOGRAPHIC

(G-1160)
INTEGRITY CYLINDER SALES LLC
17 Watrous St (06424-1234)
P.O. Box 60 (06424-0060)
PHONE..................................860 267-6667
Doug Dilla, *Mng Member*
Matthew Dedin,
Jeff True,
EMP: 3 **EST:** 2012
SALES: 89K **Privately Held**
SIC: 3479 Gas Cylinder Coating

(G-1161)
JOHNSON MILLWORK INC
222 Quarry Hill Rd (06424-3054)
PHONE..................................860 267-4693
Robert W Johnson, *President*
EMP: 3
SALES (est): 359.9K **Privately Held**
SIC: 2431 Whol Lumber/Plywood/Millwork

(G-1162)
NAUTA ROLL CORPORATION
7 Whippoorwill Hollow Rd (06424-1830)
PHONE..................................860 267-2027
Robert Hilton, *President*
Cheryl Hilton, *Vice Pres*
EMP: 3
SQ FT: 6,000
SALES (est): 270K **Privately Held**
SIC: 3069 Mfg Silicone Rubber Rolls

(G-1163)
POST & BEAM HOMES INC
4 Sexton Hill Rd (06424-1817)
PHONE..................................860 267-2060
Natale Malatesta, *President*
EMP: 3
SALES (est): 415.2K **Privately Held**
WEB: www.postandbeamhomes.com
SIC: 2452 1521 Mfg Prefabricated Wood Buildings Single-Family House Construction

(G-1164)
PSI PLUS INC
17 Watrous St (06424-1234)
P.O. Box 147 (06424-0147)
PHONE..................................860 267-6667
Douglas Dilla, *President*
Stanley R Bevin, *Director*
EMP: 15
SQ FT: 14,000
SALES: 875K **Privately Held**
SIC: 3443 Mfg Fabricated Plate Work

(G-1165)
STICKLER MACHINE COMPANY LLC
4 N Main St Ste 1 (06424-1048)
PHONE..................................860 267-8246
EMP: 4
SQ FT: 3,500
SALES (est): 27K **Privately Held**
SIC: 3599 Machine Shop

(G-1166)
T N DICKINSON COMPANY
Also Called: Dickinson's Cosmetics
31 E High St (06424-1021)
PHONE..................................860 267-2279
Edward C Jackowitz, *President*
Bryan E Jackowitz, *Corp Secy*
Kevin R Jackowitz, *Vice Pres*
EMP: 10
SALES (est): 1.1MM **Privately Held**
SIC: 2844 5122 Mfg Toilet Preparations Whol Drugs/Sundries

(G-1167)
VENTURE TOOL AND MANUFACTURING
12 Summit St (06424-1242)
P.O. Box 343 (06424-0343)
PHONE..................................860 267-9647
Daniel Woodis, *President*
Gary Woodis, *Corp Secy*
EMP: 3
SALES: 100K **Privately Held**
SIC: 3599 Mfg Industrial Machinery

(G-1168)
ZATORSKI COATING COMPANY INC
77 Wopowog Rd (06424-1674)
PHONE..................................860 267-9889
Diane A Zatorski, *President*
Diane Achenbach-Zatorski, *President*
Raymond Zatorski, *Admin Sec*
EMP: 14
SALES (est): 1.8MM **Privately Held**
SIC: 3554 Mfg Coating Service & Equipment

East Hartford
Hartford County

(G-1169)
ACTUALMEDS CORPORATION
222 Pitkin St Ste 107 (06108-3261)
PHONE..................................888 838-9053
Patricia Meisner, *CEO*
Ann Marie Biernacki, *Vice Pres*
John Wagner, *VP Bus Dvlpt*
EMP: 5
SALES (est): 315.3K **Privately Held**
SIC: 7372 Prepackaged Software Services

(G-1170)
ADAPTIVE OPTICS ASSOCIATES INC
Also Called: Aoa Xinetics
121 Prestige Park Cir (06108-1908)
PHONE..................................860 282-4401
Rick Little, *Manager*
EMP: 18 **Publicly Held**
WEB: www.adaptiveoptics.org
SIC: 3827 Mfg Optical Instruments/Lenses
HQ: Adaptive Optics Associates, Inc.
115 Jackson Rd
Devens MA 01434
978 757-9600

(G-1171)
AERO COMPONENT SERVICES LLC
781 Goodwin St (06108-1202)
PHONE..................................860 291-0417
Kirk Morris, *Mng Member*
EMP: 5
SQ FT: 3,000
SALES (est): 605K **Privately Held**
SIC: 3724 Mfg Aircraft Engines/Parts

(G-1172)
AMERICAN RAILWAY TECHNOLOGIES
61 Alna Ln Ste 1 (06108-1160)
P.O. Box 312, Glastonbury (06033-0312)
PHONE..................................860 291-1170
Donald Schucht, *President*
EMP: 5
SQ FT: 5,000
SALES (est): 526.4K **Privately Held**
WEB: www.americanrailwaytechnologies.com
SIC: 3571 1731 Mfg Electronic Computers Electrical Contractor

(G-1173)
ARDENT INC (PA)
Also Called: Ardent Displays & Packaging
95 Leggett St (06108-1167)
PHONE..................................860 528-6000
Donald Budnick, *President*
Matthew Pope, *Vice Pres*
Terri Serafin, *Project Mgr*
Megan Arcari, *Buyer*
Jake Thibault, *Natl Sales Mgr*
▲ **EMP:** 27
SQ FT: 55,000
SALES (est): 6.1MM **Privately Held**
WEB: www.ardentdisplays.com
SIC: 2542 5046 Mfg Partitions/Fixtures-Nonwood Whol Commercial Equipment

(G-1174)
ATI LADISH MACHINING INC (DH)
Also Called: ATI Forged Products
311 Prestige Park Rd (06108-1928)
PHONE..................................860 688-3688
John Delaney, *President*
Jeff Cebula, *General Mgr*
John S Minich, *Principal*
Dale G Reid, *Exec VP*
Susan Campbell, *Vice Pres*
EMP: 51 **EST:** 1946
SQ FT: 40,000
SALES (est): 17.6MM **Publicly Held**
WEB: www.stowemachine.com
SIC: 3724 Mfg Aircraft Engines/Parts
HQ: Ati Ladish Llc
5481 S Packard Ave
Cudahy WI 53110
414 747-2611

(G-1175)
ATI LADISH MACHINING INC
Also Called: East Hartford Operations
311 Prestige Park Rd (06108-1928)
PHONE..................................860 688-3688
Richard Cleary, *Branch Mgr*
Erika Pafford, *Manager*
EMP: 100 **Publicly Held**
SIC: 3724 Used For Registration With Samgov
HQ: Ati Ladish Machining, Inc.
311 Prestige Park Rd
East Hartford CT 06108
860 688-3688

(G-1176)
BESSETTE HOLDINGS INC
Also Called: Connecticut Die Cutting Svc
95 Leggett St (06108-1167)
PHONE..................................860 289-6000
Ken Besset, *Principal*
Gary R Bessette, *Vice Pres*
Raymond J Gruzas, *Treasurer*
Donald Budnick, *Mng Member*
Carmen Bessette, *Admin Sec*
EMP: 35
SQ FT: 25,000
SALES (est): 5.8MM **Privately Held**
WEB: www.connecticutdiecutting.com
SIC: 3544 3469 3423 Mfg Dies/Tools/Jigs/Fixtures Mfg Metal Stampings Mfg Hand/Edge Tools

(G-1177)
BRESCIAS PRINTING SERVICES INC
66 Connecticut Blvd (06108-3013)
PHONE..................................860 528-4254
William G Brescia, *President*
William Brescia, *President*
Laura Bolduc, *Associate*
EMP: 7
SQ FT: 5,000
SALES (est): 1MM **Privately Held**
WEB: www.brescias.com
SIC: 2752 7334 2791 7331 Offset Printing Hi-Speed Copying Color Copying Typesetting & Mailing Service

(G-1178)
BURNSIDE SUPERMARKET LLC
Also Called: Connecticut Dist Svcs Ltd
1150 Burnside Ave (06108-1508)
PHONE..................................860 291-9965
Dereck Singh,
▲ **EMP:** 5 **EST:** 2010
SQ FT: 11,026
SALES (est): 378.4K **Privately Held**
SIC: 2099 5411 Mfg Food Preparations Ret Groceries

(G-1179)
CARDINAL HEALTH 414 LLC
131 Hartland St Ste 8 (06108-3229)
PHONE..................................860 291-9135
Arshad Mehmood, *Principal*
EMP: 9
SALES (corp-wide): 145.5B **Publicly Held**
SIC: 2835 2834 Mfg Pharmaceutical Preparations Mfg Diagnostic Substances
HQ: Cardinal Health 414, Llc
7000 Cardinal Pl
Dublin OH 43017
614 757-5000

(G-1180)
CENTRAL CONNECTICUT COATING
52 Village St (06108-3904)
PHONE..................................860 528-8281
Gene Schaeffer, *President*
EMP: 11
SALES (est): 1.6MM **Privately Held**
SIC: 3479 Coating/Engraving Service

(G-1181)
CENTRITEC SEALS LLC
222 Pitkin St Ste 104 (06108-3261)
PHONE..................................860 594-7183
Douglas Rode,
EMP: 3
SALES (est): 207.9K **Privately Held**
SIC: 3399 Mfg Primary Metal Products

(G-1182)
CLARCOR ENG MBL SOLUTIONS LLC (DH)
Also Called: Parker
60 Prestige Park Rd (06108-1919)
PHONE..................................860 920-4200
Christopher Conway, *CEO*
Stephen S Langin, *CFO*
◆ **EMP:** 58
SQ FT: 571,000
SALES (est): 127.9MM
SALES (corp-wide): 14.3B **Publicly Held**
SIC: 3492 3714 Mfg Fluid Power Valves/Fittings Mfg Motor Vehicle Parts/Accessories
HQ: Clarcor Inc.
840 Crescent Centre Dr # 600
Franklin TN 37067
615 771-3100

(G-1183)
COMPANY OF COCA-COLA BOTTLING
471 Main St 471 # 471 (06118-1402)
PHONE..................................860 569-0037
Jody Lemay, *Branch Mgr*
EMP: 58 **Privately Held**
WEB: www.coke.com
SIC: 2086 Carb Sft Drnkbtlcn
HQ: Coca-Cola Bottling Company Of Southeastern New England, Inc.
150 Waterford Parkway S
Waterford CT 06385
860 443-2816

(G-1184)
COVALENT COATING TECH LLC
222 Pitkin St (06108-3261)
PHONE..................................860 214-6452
Orville Dialey, *Principal*
EMP: 3
SALES: 30K **Privately Held**
SIC: 3479 Coating/Engraving Service

(G-1185)
DECO PRODUCTS INC
34 Nelson St Ste C (06108-3930)
P.O. Box 482, Bloomfield (06002-0482)
PHONE..................................860 528-4304
Gary A Dellorso, *President*
Shirley Dellorso, *Shareholder*
EMP: 4 **EST:** 1965
SQ FT: 2,400
SALES: 150K **Privately Held**
SIC: 3451 Mfg Screw Machine Products

(G-1186)
DEMUSZ MFG CO INC
303 Burnham St (06108-1183)
PHONE..................................860 528-9845
Waldemar Demusz, *President*
Wieslaw Demusz, *Vice Pres*
Alexander Demusz, *Engineer*
Roma Demusz, *VP Finance*
EMP: 27
SQ FT: 12,000
SALES (est): 5.2MM **Privately Held**
WEB: www.demusz.com
SIC: 3724 Mfg Aircraft Engines/Parts

(G-1187)
DIGNIFIED ENDINGS LLC
15 Stanley St (06108-1662)
PHONE..................................860 291-0575
David Hurovite, *Principal*
Michelle Hurovite,
EMP: 65
SQ FT: 2,400
SALES (est): 4.3MM **Privately Held**
SIC: 3995 7261 Mfg Burial Caskets Funeral Service/Crematory

▲ = Import ▼=Export
◆ =Import/Export

(G-1188)
DUNN PAPER HOLDINGS INC
2 Forbes St (06108-3727)
PHONE..................................860 289-7496
Chris Fedler, *Plant Mgr*
EMP: 85
SALES (corp-wide): 139.6MM **Privately Held**
SIC: 2621 Paper Mill
PA: Dunn Paper Holdings, Inc.
218 Riverview St
Port Huron MI 48060
810 984-5521

(G-1189)
DUNN PAPER LLC
2 Forbes St (06108-3727)
PHONE..................................860 466-4141
James Dickerson,
EMP: 80
SALES (est): 13.8MM **Privately Held**
SIC: 2676 Mfg Sanitary Paper Products

(G-1190)
EBL PRODUCTS INC
22 Prestige Park Cir (06108-1917)
PHONE..................................860 290-3737
Joseph Zarrelli, *President*
Andrew Tremblay, *President*
EMP: 13
SALES (est): 1.8MM **Privately Held**
WEB: www.eblproducts.com
SIC: 3679 Mfg Electronic Components

(G-1191)
ELJEN CORPORATION
125 Mckee St (06108-4018)
PHONE..................................860 610-0426
Joseph Glasser, *CEO*
EMP: 28
SALES (corp-wide): 24.7MM **Privately Held**
SIC: 3259 Mfg Structural Clay Products
PA: Eljen Corporation
10 N Main St Ste 216
West Hartford CT
860 232-0077

(G-1192)
EMR GLOBAL INC
265 Prestige Park Rd (06108-1939)
PHONE..................................203 452-8166
William Rudolph, *President*
Mark Mascheck, *Vice Pres*
Brian McHugh, *Treasurer*
EMP: 4
SALES (est): 282.6K **Privately Held**
SIC: 3053 Packaging Materials

(G-1193)
ENDOTO CORP
43 Franklin St (06108-1723)
PHONE..................................860 289-8033
Guy J Bolduc, *President*
▲ **EMP:** 3
SALES (est): 568.4K **Privately Held**
SIC: 3669 Mfg Communications Equipment

(G-1194)
ENDURO WHEELCHAIR COMPANY
750 Tolland St (06108-2727)
PHONE..................................860 289-0374
Kenneth J Messier, *Principal*
EMP: 3 **EST:** 2010
SALES (est): 185.4K **Privately Held**
SIC: 3842 Mfg Surgical Appliances/Supplies

(G-1195)
FLUOROPOLYMER RESOURCES LLC (PA)
99 Erver Dr Rvrview Sq Ii Riverview (06108)
P.O. Box 875, Old Lyme (06371-0875)
PHONE..................................860 423-7622
Kevin F Buchanan, *President*
Julie A Buchanan, *Vice Pres*
Mike Wilosko, *Vice Pres*
John Ieronimo, *Controller*
Denise Coyle, *Sales Mgr*
EMP: 7
SQ FT: 2,000
SALES (est): 8MM **Privately Held**
WEB: www.friusa.net
SIC: 3089 Mfg Plastic Products

(G-1196)
FMI PAINT & CHEMICAL INC
14 Eastern Park Rd (06108-1105)
PHONE..................................860 218-2210
Harry Fine, *President*
EMP: 12
SQ FT: 10,000
SALES (est): 1.5MM **Privately Held**
SIC: 2851 Manufactures Paint & Stain

(G-1197)
GARDEN OF LIGHT INC
Also Called: Garden Light Natural Foods Mkt
127 Park Ave Ste 100 (06108-4012)
PHONE..................................860 895-6622
Michael Smulders, *President*
EMP: 80
SQ FT: 110,000
SALES: 20MM **Privately Held**
SIC: 2043 Mfg Cereal Breakfast Food

(G-1198)
GOONG
798 Silver Ln (06118-1228)
PHONE..................................860 216-3041
Numi Hwang, *Principal*
EMP: 4
SALES (est): 357.4K **Privately Held**
SIC: 3421 Mfg Cutlery

(G-1199)
HORST ENGRG DE MEXICO LLC
36 Cedar St (06108-2003)
PHONE..................................860 289-8209
Lynn Livingston, *Human Res Mgr*
Scott Livingston,
EMP: 35
SQ FT: 18,000
SALES (est): 3.6MM **Privately Held**
SIC: 3452 3451 3724 Mfg Bolts/Screws/Rivets Mfg Screw Machine Products Mfg Aircraft Engines/Parts

(G-1200)
HYDRO HONING LABORATORIES INC (PA)
Also Called: Peening Technologies Conn
8 Eastern Park Rd (06108-1105)
P.O. Box 280306 (06128-0306)
PHONE..................................860 289-4328
Thomas Beach, *President*
Scott Rossignol, *Mfg Staff*
Walter Beach Jr, *Treasurer*
Richard Brooks, *Admin Sec*
EMP: 45 **EST:** 1966
SQ FT: 24,000
SALES (est): 4.6MM **Privately Held**
WEB: www.hydro-honing.com
SIC: 3398 Shot Peening Services

(G-1201)
IAE INTERNATIONAL AERO ENGS AG
400 Main St Ms121-10 (06108-0968)
PHONE..................................860 565-1773
Jon Beatty, *President*
Rick Deurloo, *Senior VP*
Jim Guiliano, *Senior VP*
Steve Burrill, *Vice Pres*
Dave Avery, *CFO*
EMP: 150
SQ FT: 34,900
SALES (est): 52.8MM
SALES (corp-wide): 66.5B **Publicly Held**
WEB: www.iaev2500.com
SIC: 3724 Mfg Aircraft Engines/Parts
PA: United Technologies Corporation
10 Farm Springs Rd
Farmington CT 06032
860 728-7000

(G-1202)
IMAGE INSIGHT INC
87 Church St (06108-3720)
PHONE..................................860 528-9806
Eric Rubenstein, *President*
Gordon Drukier, *Vice Pres*
EMP: 3
SALES (est): 382.9K **Privately Held**
SIC: 3829 Mfg Measuring/Controlling Devices

(G-1203)
INTERNATIONAL AERO ENGINES LLC
Also Called: Iae
400 Main St (06108-0968)
PHONE..................................860 565-5515
Karen C McCusker, *Vice Pres*
EMP: 37
SALES (est): 26.4MM
SALES (corp-wide): 66.5B **Publicly Held**
SIC: 3724 Mfg Aircraft Engines/Parts
PA: United Technologies Corporation
10 Farm Springs Rd
Farmington CT 06032
860 728-7000

(G-1204)
INTLAERO BETA CORP
400 Main St (06108-0968)
PHONE..................................317 821-2000
David J Avery, *Principal*
EMP: 3
SALES (est): 279.5K **Privately Held**
SIC: 3724 Mfg Aircraft Engines/Parts

(G-1205)
MARENA INDUSTRIES INC
Also Called: Marena Machinery Sales Div
433 School St (06108-1162)
PHONE..................................860 528-9701
Teodoro Marena, *President*
John Salisbury, *Superintendent*
Fran Marena, *Admin Sec*
EMP: 15
SQ FT: 19,000
SALES (est): 3.2MM **Privately Held**
WEB: www.championsaw.com
SIC: 3545 3541 Mfg Machine Tool Accessories Mfg Machine Tools-Cutting

(G-1206)
NEW ENGLAND CHROME PLATING
63 Thomas St (06108-2056)
PHONE..................................860 528-7176
David Malinguaggio, *President*
Peter Brown, *General Mgr*
Dean Malinguaggio, *Vice Pres*
EMP: 6
SQ FT: 6,800
SALES (est): 846.7K **Privately Held**
WEB: www.newenglandchrome.com
SIC: 3471 Mfg Of Chrome Plating Shop

(G-1207)
NORTHROP GRUMMAN CORPORATION
121 Prestige Park Cir (06108-1908)
PHONE..................................860 282-4461
EMP: 80 **Publicly Held**
SIC: 3812 Mfg Search/Navigation Equipment
PA: Northrop Grumman Corporation
2980 Fairview Park Dr
Falls Church VA 22042

(G-1208)
OLDE BURNSIDE BREWING CO LLC
780 Tolland St (06108-2727)
PHONE..................................860 528-2200
▲ **EMP:** 8
SALES (est): 718.2K **Privately Held**
WEB: www.oldeburnsidebrewing.com
SIC: 2097 Mfg Ice

(G-1209)
PEENING TECHNOLOGIES EQP LLC
8 Eastern Park Rd (06108-1105)
PHONE..................................860 289-4328
Thomas Beach,
Walter Beach Jr,
Richard Brooks,
EMP: 50
SALES (est): 5MM **Privately Held**
SIC: 3398 Metal Heat Treating

(G-1210)
PICTURE THIS HARTFORD INC
Also Called: Hartford Fine Art & Framing Co
80 Pitkin St (06108-3318)
PHONE..................................860 528-1409
William Plage, *President*
Lauren Plage, *Vice Pres*
EMP: 7
SQ FT: 9,500
SALES (est): 887.1K **Privately Held**
WEB: www.hartfordfineart.com
SIC: 3993 5719 3999 Mfg Signs/Ad Specialties Ret Misc Homefurnishings Mfg Misc Products

(G-1211)
POPCORN MOVIE POSTER CO LLC
1 Cherry St (06108-3922)
P.O. Box 1121, Glastonbury (06033-6121)
PHONE..................................860 610-0000
David Graveen,
Annette Daniels,
EMP: 14
SQ FT: 4,500
SALES (est): 1.9MM **Privately Held**
SIC: 2759 Commercial Printing

(G-1212)
PRATT & WHITNEY COMPANY INC (HQ)
Also Called: Middletown Engine Center
400 Main St (06108-0968)
PHONE..................................860 565-4321
Scott M Lewis, *President*
Laura Austin, *General Mgr*
Michael Mahonski, *General Mgr*
Buddy Remington, *General Mgr*
Todd Shields, *General Mgr*
EMP: 143 **EST:** 1986
SALES (est): 129.6MM
SALES (corp-wide): 66.5B **Publicly Held**
SIC: 3724 Mfg Aircraft Engines/Parts
PA: United Technologies Corporation
10 Farm Springs Rd
Farmington CT 06032
860 728-7000

(G-1213)
PRATT & WHITNEY ENG SVCS INC
126 Silver Ln Apt 19 (06118-1013)
PHONE..................................860 610-2631
Lagoy Christine, *Engineer*
Beach Eric, *Engineer*
Al Hunter, *Manager*
Dube Robert, *Technical Staff*
Cerasoli Lorraine, *Executive Asst*
EMP: 212
SALES (corp-wide): 66.5B **Publicly Held**
SIC: 3724 Mfg Aircraft Engines/Parts
HQ: Pratt & Whitney Engine Services, Inc.
1525 Midway Park Rd
Bridgeport WV 26330
304 842-5421

(G-1214)
PRATT & WHITNEY ENGINE SVCS
Also Called: Pratt Whtney Cstmer Trning Ctr
400 Main St Ste 1 (06118-1888)
PHONE..................................860 565-4321
Lisa Madsen, *Business Mgr*
Ivan Rojas, *Electrical Engi*
Joseph Oconnell, *HR Admin*
Brian Lammers, *Manager*
Joseph Hillmon, *Info Tech Mgr*
EMP: 27
SALES (corp-wide): 66.5B **Publicly Held**
SIC: 3724 Mfg Aircraft Engines/Parts
HQ: Pratt & Whitney Engine Services, Inc.
1525 Midway Park Rd
Bridgeport WV 26330
304 842-5421

(G-1215)
PRATT & WHITNEY SERVICES INC
400 Main St (06108-0968)
PHONE..................................860 565-5489
Paul Adams, *President*
EMP: 24 **EST:** 2007
SALES (est): 3.8MM
SALES (corp-wide): 66.5B **Publicly Held**
SIC: 3724 Mfg Aircraft Engines/Parts
PA: United Technologies Corporation
10 Farm Springs Rd
Farmington CT 06032
860 728-7000

GEOGRAPHIC

(G-1216)
PRECISION OPTICAL CO
351 Burnham St (06108-1159)
P.O. Box 280023 (06128-0023)
PHONE..................................860 289-6023
Richard J Welch, *President*
Dan O'Brien, *Vice Pres*
Annemarie O'Brien, *Treasurer*
Dan O' Brein, *VP Sales*
Doreen Dias, *Manager*
EMP: 47
SQ FT: 8,000
SALES: 5MM
SALES (corp-wide): 1.4MM **Privately Held**
WEB: www.precision-optical-co.com
SIC: 3851 5048 Mfg Ophthalmic Goods Whol Ophthalmic Goods
HQ: Perferx Optical Co., Inc.
25 Downing Three Park
Pittsfield MA 01201
413 358-9020

(G-1217)
REGIONAL STAIRS LLC
183 Prestige Park Rd (06108-1923)
PHONE..................................860 290-1242
Jake Streceyko,
Andrew Dobranski,
EMP: 5
SQ FT: 5,000
SALES (est): 1MM **Privately Held**
WEB: www.regionalstairs.com
SIC: 2499 Mfg Wood Products

(G-1218)
RSL FIBER SYSTEMS LLC
473 Silver Ln (06118-1152)
PHONE..................................860 282-4930
Giovanni P Tomasi,
EMP: 13 **EST:** 2001
SALES: 2.2MM **Privately Held**
SIC: 3648 Mfg Lighting Equipment

(G-1219)
SEALPRO LLC
721 Burnham St (06108-1307)
PHONE..................................860 289-0804
David Lombardo, *Owner*
EMP: 4
SALES (est): 480.5K **Privately Held**
SIC: 2891 Mfg Adhesives/Sealants

(G-1220)
SIGN STOP INC
657 Main St (06108-3320)
PHONE..................................860 721-1411
John Oudheusden, *President*
EMP: 3
SQ FT: 1,900
SALES (est): 190K **Privately Held**
SIC: 3993 Mfg Signs

(G-1221)
SMARTER SEALANTS LLC
14 Eastern Park Rd (06108-1105)
PHONE..................................860 218-2210
▲ **EMP:** 4
SALES (est): 240K **Privately Held**
SIC: 2891 Mfg Adhesives/Sealants

(G-1222)
STANDARD WELDING COMPANY INC
212 Prospect St (06108-1653)
PHONE..................................860 528-9628
Richard Ashlaw, *President*
Clifford Wayner, *Treasurer*
EMP: 9
SQ FT: 7,000
SALES (est): 560.7K **Privately Held**
SIC: 7692 7549 7513 Welding Repair Automotive Services Truck Rental/Leasing

(G-1223)
STP BINDERY SERVICES INC
265 Prestige Park Rd # 2 (06108-1939)
PHONE..................................860 528-1430
Steven Pensiero, *President*
EMP: 30
SQ FT: 25,000
SALES (est): 4.2MM **Privately Held**
SIC: 2789 Bookbinding Service

(G-1224)
STRYKER CORPORATION
155 Founders Plz (06108-8313)
PHONE..................................860 528-1111
Vince Morgera, *Branch Mgr*
EMP: 11
SALES (corp-wide): 13.6B **Publicly Held**
SIC: 3841 Mfg Surgical/Medical Instruments
PA: Stryker Corporation
2825 Airview Blvd
Portage MI 49002
269 389-4934

(G-1225)
SUEZ WTS SERVICES USA INC
405 School St (06108-1135)
PHONE..................................860 291-9660
Lyman B Dickerson, *President*
EMP: 26
SALES (corp-wide): 91.7MM **Privately Held**
WEB: www.ecolochem.com
SIC: 3589 2899 Mfg Service Industry Machinery Mfg Chemical Preparations
HQ: Suez Wts Services Usa, Inc.
4545 Patent Rd
Norfolk VA 23502
757 855-9000

(G-1226)
SURE INDUSTRIES INC
122 Park Ave Ste C (06108-4045)
PHONE..................................860 289-2522
Reese Korman, *Principal*
Mark Peters, *Principal*
EMP: 6
SALES (est): 684.6K **Privately Held**
SIC: 3713 Mfg Truck Cabs

(G-1227)
TAYLOR COMMUNICATIONS INC
800 Connecticut Blvd (06108-7303)
PHONE..................................860 290-6851
Thomas Bareline, *Branch Mgr*
EMP: 11
SALES (corp-wide): 2.8B **Privately Held**
WEB: www.stdreg.com
SIC: 2761 Manifold Business Forms
HQ: Taylor Communications, Inc.
1725 Roe Crest Dr
North Mankato MN 56003
866 541-0937

(G-1228)
THEBEAMER LLC
87 Church St (06108-3720)
PHONE..................................860 212-5071
Peter Solomon, *CEO*
EMP: 17 **EST:** 2014
SQ FT: 400
SALES (est): 200K **Privately Held**
SIC: 7372 Prepackaged Software Services

(G-1229)
THREAD ROLLING INC
41 Cedar St (06108-2051)
PHONE..................................860 528-1515
Steve Livingston, *President*
EMP: 10
SQ FT: 7,000
SALES: 600K
SALES (corp-wide): 22.3MM **Privately Held**
WEB: www.threadrolling.com
SIC: 3452 Mfg Bolts/Screws/Rivets Mfg Bolts/Screws/Rivets
PA: Horst Engineering & Manufacturing Co
36 Cedar St
East Hartford CT 06108
860 289-8209

(G-1230)
TOTAL COMMUNICATIONS INC (PA)
333 Burnham St (06108-1183)
PHONE..................................860 282-9999
Richard Lennon, *President*
Linda Lennon, *Admin Sec*
EMP: 100
SQ FT: 24,000
SALES: 20.9MM **Privately Held**
SIC: 3661 5065 7629 Mfg Telephone/Telegraph Apparatus Whol Electronic Parts/Equipment Electrical Repair

(G-1231)
UNAS GRINDING CORPORATION
28 Cherry St (06108-2010)
P.O. Box 280535 (06128-0535)
PHONE..................................860 289-1538
John Orzech, *President*
Greg Endrelunas, *Vice Pres*
Kyle Endrelunas, *Manager*
Scott Petrarca, *Manager*
EMP: 30 **EST:** 1952
SQ FT: 18,500
SALES (est): 4.6MM **Privately Held**
WEB: www.unasgrinding.com
SIC: 3599 Mfg Industrial Machinery

(G-1232)
UNITED STEEL INC
164 School St (06108-1867)
PHONE..................................860 289-2323
Keith Corneau, *President*
Glen Corneau, *Vice Pres*
John Gagas, *Vice Pres*
Skip Henderson, *Safety Dir*
Joshua Messier, *Project Mgr*
EMP: 150 **EST:** 1979
SQ FT: 122,500
SALES (est): 67.8MM **Privately Held**
WEB: www.unitedsteel.com
SIC: 3441 3443 3446 3444 Structural Metal Fabrctn Mfg Fabricated Plate Wrk Mfg Architectural Mtlwrk Mfg Sheet Metalwork Structural Steel Erectn

(G-1233)
UNITED TECHNOLOGIES CORP
Also Called: Pratt & Whitney
400 Main St (06118-1873)
PHONE..................................860 565-4321
Jon Forrest, *General Mgr*
Polis Vrionides, *General Mgr*
Qwandrell Banks, *Project Mgr*
Kelly Boerenko, *Project Mgr*
Deborah Mattia, *Buyer*
EMP: 5
SALES (corp-wide): 66.5B **Publicly Held**
WEB: www.utc.com
SIC: 3724 Mfg Aircraft Engines/Parts
PA: United Technologies Corporation
10 Farm Springs Rd
Farmington CT 06032
860 728-7000

(G-1234)
UNITED TECHNOLOGIES CORP
400 Main St (06108-0968)
PHONE..................................860 565-7622
Rick Silva, *President*
Nathan Sebastiao, *Engineer*
EMP: 214
SALES (corp-wide): 66.5B **Publicly Held**
WEB: www.utc.com
SIC: 3585 Manufactures Industrial Machinery & Equipment
PA: United Technologies Corporation
10 Farm Springs Rd
Farmington CT 06032
860 728-7000

(G-1235)
UNITED TECHNOLOGIES CORP
Also Called: Pratt & Whitney
400 Main St (06108-0968)
PHONE..................................860 565-4321
Rick Silva, *President*
EMP: 100
SALES (corp-wide): 66.5B **Publicly Held**
SIC: 3724 Mfg Aircraft Engines/Parts
PA: United Technologies Corporation
10 Farm Springs Rd
Farmington CT 06032
860 728-7000

(G-1236)
UNITED TECHNOLOGIES CORP
Also Called: Pratt Whitney-Spare Parts Div
400 Main St (06118-1873)
PHONE..................................860 565-4321
William Pursell, *Manager*
EMP: 6
SALES (corp-wide): 66.5B **Publicly Held**
WEB: www.utc.com
SIC: 3724 Mfg Aircraft Engines/Parts
PA: United Technologies Corporation
10 Farm Springs Rd
Farmington CT 06032
860 728-7000

(G-1237)
UNITED TECHNOLOGIES CORP
Also Called: Utrc
411 Silver Ln (06118-1127)
PHONE..................................860 610-7000
Leslie Doody, *Branch Mgr*
EMP: 500
SALES (corp-wide): 66.5B **Publicly Held**
SIC: 3699 Mfg Electrical Equipment/Supplies
PA: United Technologies Corporation
10 Farm Springs Rd
Farmington CT 06032
860 728-7000

(G-1238)
UNITED TECHNOLOGIES CORP
Also Called: Pratt & Whitneys Repair &
400 Main St (06108-0968)
PHONE..................................860 557-3333
EMP: 77
SALES (corp-wide): 66.5B **Publicly Held**
SIC: 3728 Mfg Aircraft Parts/Equipment
PA: United Technologies Corporation
10 Farm Springs Rd
Farmington CT 06032
860 728-7000

(G-1239)
UNITED THREAD ROLLING LLC
25 Rosenthal St (06108-3429)
PHONE..................................860 290-9349
EMP: 3
SALES (est): 156K **Privately Held**
SIC: 3452 Mfg Bolts/Screws/Rivets

East Hartland
Hartford County

(G-1240)
TR LANDWORKS LLC
36 Kensington Acres Rd (06027-1110)
PHONE..................................860 402-6177
Theodore R Donofrio Jr,
EMP: 8
SALES (est): 699.8K **Privately Held**
SIC: 2411 Logging

East Haven
New Haven County

(G-1241)
A B C PRINTING INC
Also Called: A B C Printing & Mailing
875 Foxon Rd (06513-1837)
PHONE..................................203 468-1245
Salvatore L Vadala, *President*
Salvatore A Vadala Jr, *Vice Pres*
Randy Carmona, *Graphic Designe*
Josh Coyne, *Graphic Designe*
Renee Domian, *Graphic Designe*
EMP: 10
SQ FT: 3,200
SALES: 400K **Privately Held**
SIC: 2752 Offset Printers

(G-1242)
BARDELL PRINTING CORP
Also Called: Bardell Office Sty & Sups
42 Michael St (06513-1811)
PHONE..................................203 469-2441
Frank Gambardella, *President*
Adeline Gambardella, *Vice Pres*
Anthony Gambardella, *Vice Pres*
Gary Gambardella, *CFO*
EMP: 7 **EST:** 1978
SQ FT: 6,000
SALES (est): 1MM **Privately Held**
SIC: 2759 Commercial Printing

(G-1243)
BIG PRINTS LLC
15 Baer Cir Ste 2 (06512-4100)
PHONE..................................203 469-1100
Mark Azzolina, *Mng Member*
Bob Garbo,
EMP: 3
SALES: 180K **Privately Held**
WEB: www.bigprintsct.com
SIC: 3993 Mfg Signs/Advertising Specialties

▲ = Import ▼=Export
◆ =Import/Export

(G-1244)
CIRILLO MANUFACTURING GROUP
34 Panagrosi St (06512-4143)
PHONE....203 484-5010
Bob Cirillo, *President*
Joanne Cirillo, *Admin Sec*
EMP: 4
SALES (est): 580.3K **Privately Held**
SIC: 3599 3441 Machine Shop Welding And Steel Fabrication

(G-1245)
CLAYTON OFFROAD MANUFACTURER
99 Commerce St (06512-4146)
PHONE....475 238-8251
Clayton Walters, *Principal*
EMP: 4 **EST:** 2013
SALES (est): 509.8K **Privately Held**
SIC: 3714 Mfg Motor Vehicle Parts/Accessories

(G-1246)
CREATIVE STONE LLC
Also Called: Creative Stone & Tile
42 Vista Dr (06512-3433)
PHONE....203 624-1882
Keith D Kronberg,
Andrew Donsiglio,
EMP: 10 **EST:** 1998
SALES (est): 1.2MM **Privately Held**
WEB: www.creativestonetile.com
SIC: 3281 Mfg Cut Stone/Products

(G-1247)
EAST SHORE WIRE ROPE
5 Old Bradley St (06512-2344)
P.O. Box 308, North Haven (06473-0308)
PHONE....203 469-5204
Gary Lipkvich, *Owner*
EMP: 7
SALES: 950K **Privately Held**
SIC: 3462 Mfg Iron/Steel Forgings

(G-1248)
EDAL INDUSTRIES INC
51 Commerce St (06512-4113)
PHONE....203 467-2591
Andrew Esposito, *President*
Pat Lauria, *Vice Pres*
▲ **EMP:** 23 **EST:** 1958
SQ FT: 14,000
SALES (est): 3.7MM **Privately Held**
SIC: 3679 3674 Mfg Electronic Components Mfg Semiconductors/Related Devices

(G-1249)
F J WEIDNER INC
34 Tyler Street Ext (06512-3033)
PHONE....203 469-4202
John Weidner, *President*
Randy Weidner, *Corp Secy*
EMP: 4
SQ FT: 2,200
SALES (est): 405.5K **Privately Held**
WEB: www.zero-altitude-flight.com
SIC: 3544 3479 Mfg Dies/Tools/Jigs/Fixtures Coating/Engraving Service

(G-1250)
FOXON PARK BEVERAGES INC
103 Foxon Blvd (06513-1871)
PHONE....203 467-7874
Anthony M Naclerio, *President*
Jay Brancati, *COO*
Raymond Naclerio, *Admin Sec*
EMP: 8
SQ FT: 6,500
SALES (est): 1MM **Privately Held**
WEB: www.foxonpark.com
SIC: 2086 Mfg Soft Drinks

(G-1251)
FUCHS LUBRICANTS CO
Also Called: Fuchs Northeast Division
281 Silver Sands Rd (06512-4140)
PHONE....203 469-2336
Cris Licursi, *Branch Mgr*
EMP: 24
SQ FT: 35,000
SALES (corp-wide): 2.8B **Privately Held**
WEB: www.fuchs.com
SIC: 2992 5172 Mfg Lubricating Oils/Greases Whol Petroleum Products
HQ: Fuchs Lubricants Co.
17050 Lathrop Ave
Harvey IL 60426
708 333-8901

(G-1252)
FYC APPAREL GROUP LLC
Donno Ricco
158 Commerce St (06512-4145)
PHONE....203 466-6525
Maia Chiatt, *President*
EMP: 30 **Privately Held**
WEB: www.akdesigns.net
SIC: 2331 Mfg Women's/Misses' Blouses
PA: Fyc Apparel Group, Llc
30 Thompson Rd
Branford CT 06405

(G-1253)
KAPCOM LLC
86 John St (06513-2612)
PHONE....203 891-5112
David Kaplan, *Partner*
EMP: 4
SALES (est): 324.5K **Privately Held**
SIC: 3823 7812 Mfg Process Control Instruments Motion Picture/Video Production

(G-1254)
MACKENZIE MCH & MAR WORKS INC
36 Morgan Ter (06512-4501)
PHONE....203 777-3479
Kenneth Mackenzie Jr, *President*
Dana Mackenzie, *Vice Pres*
EMP: 6
SQ FT: 7,500
SALES (est): 852.9K **Privately Held**
WEB: www.mackenziemachine.com
SIC: 3599 7692 7378 Mfg Industrial Machinery Welding Repair Computer Maintenance/Repair

(G-1255)
MILBAR LABS INC
20 Commerce St (06512-4145)
PHONE....203 467-1577
Mary Ann Emswiler, *CEO*
Susan S Lamar, *Treasurer*
Edward A Zelinsky, *Admin Sec*
▲ **EMP:** 15
SQ FT: 36,000
SALES (est): 4.4MM
SALES (corp-wide): 8.4MM **Privately Held**
SIC: 2844 Mfg Toilet Preparations
PA: Dermatologic Cosmetic Laboratories Ltd.
20 Commerce St
East Haven CT 06512
800 552-5060

(G-1256)
NATIONAL SCREW MANUFACTURING
259 Commerce St (06512-4147)
PHONE....203 469-7109
Cahrles Hirsch, *President*
William Feingold, *Vice Pres*
Joan Hirsch, *Admin Sec*
EMP: 12 **EST:** 1970
SALES (est): 1.1MM **Privately Held**
SIC: 3541 Machine Tools, Metal Cutting Type

(G-1257)
NEW HAVEN COMPANIES INC
41 Washington Ave (06512-3768)
PHONE....203 469-6421
EMP: 15
SALES (corp-wide): 65.2MM **Privately Held**
SIC: 2299 3625 5012 3537 Mfg Textile Goods Mfg Relay/Indstl Control Whol Auto/Motor Vehicles Mfg Indstl Truck/Tractor Mfg Canvas/Related Prdts
PA: The New Haven Companies Inc
4820 Suthpoint Dr Ste 102
Fredericksburg VA 22407
540 898-2354

(G-1258)
POINT VIEW DISPLAYS LLC
200 Morgan Ave (06512-4519)
PHONE....203 468-0887
Cynthia Sedelmeyer,
EMP: 4
SALES: 700K **Privately Held**
WEB: www.pointviewdisplays.com
SIC: 3993 Mfg Signs/Advertising Specialties

(G-1259)
PSD INC
80 Caroline Rd (06512-4651)
PHONE....860 305-6346
EMP: 3
SALES (est): 251.4K **Privately Held**
SIC: 2759 Commercial Printing

(G-1260)
SABAR GRAPHICS LLC (PA)
Also Called: Minuteman Press
330 Main St (06512-2920)
P.O. Box 120541 (06512-0541)
PHONE....203 467-3016
Ronald S Burlakoff, *Mng Member*
Sandra T Burlakoff,
EMP: 4
SALES (est): 833K **Privately Held**
SIC: 2752 Comm Prtg Litho

(G-1261)
SHORELINE METAL SERVICES LLC
250 Dodge Ave (06512-3360)
PHONE....203 466-7372
Jennifer Tower,
Mark Tower,
EMP: 8
SQ FT: 10,000
SALES (est): 1MM **Privately Held**
SIC: 3444 Mfg Sheet Metalwork

(G-1262)
SIMKINS INDUSTRIES
317 Foxon Rd Ste 3 (06513-2038)
PHONE....203 787-7171
EMP: 3 **EST:** 2010
SALES (est): 160K **Privately Held**
SIC: 3999 Mfg Misc Products

(G-1263)
SPECIAL EVENTS SCREEN PRTG LLC
35 Washington Ave (06512-3768)
PHONE....203 468-5453
Scott Seward, *Mng Member*
EMP: 5
SALES: 300K **Privately Held**
SIC: 2759 Commercial Printing

(G-1264)
THERMATOOL CORP (HQ)
31 Commerce St (06512-4172)
PHONE....203 468-4100
Michael A Nallen, *President*
Elizabeth Baleck, *Regional Mgr*
Michael Didonato, *Business Mgr*
Ray Cagganello, *Plant Mgr*
David Patrick, *Purch Mgr*
◆ **EMP:** 65
SQ FT: 75,000
SALES (est): 18.4MM
SALES (corp-wide): 1B **Privately Held**
WEB: www.thermatool.com
SIC: 3599 Mfg Industrial Machinery
PA: Rowan Technologies, Inc.
10 Indel Ave
Rancocas NJ 08073
609 267-9000

(G-1265)
THOMSON REUTERS CORPORATION
250 Dodge Ave (06512-3360)
PHONE....203 466-5055
Estim Pop Lazarov, *Branch Mgr*
EMP: 15
SALES (corp-wide): 10.6B **Publicly Held**
SIC: 2741 Provider Of Business Information/News Agency
HQ: Thomson Reuters Corporation
3 Times Sq
New York NY 10036
646 223-4000

(G-1266)
TOTAL FAB LLC
140 Commerce St (06512-4145)
PHONE....475 238-8176
Fred Moore Jr, *Mng Member*
EMP: 10
SQ FT: 3,500
SALES (est): 1.2MM **Privately Held**
SIC: 3441 7692 Structural Metal Fabrication Welding Repair

(G-1267)
UNIVERSAL COMPONENT CORP
193 Silver Sands Rd (06512-4124)
PHONE....203 481-8787
Tom Mort, *President*
EMP: 25
SALES (est): 3.4MM **Privately Held**
SIC: 2439 Mfg Structural Wood Members

East Lyme
New London County

(G-1268)
ACE SAILMAKERS
3 Colton Rd (06333-1453)
PHONE....860 739-5999
Dave Pelissier, *Principal*
EMP: 4
SALES (est): 238.1K **Privately Held**
SIC: 2394 Mfg Canvas/Related Products

(G-1269)
BIRK MANUFACTURING INC
14 Capitol Dr (06333-1452)
PHONE....800 531-2070
Norman Birk, *President*
▲ **EMP:** 95
SQ FT: 32,000
SALES (est): 10.8MM **Privately Held**
WEB: www.birkmfg.com
SIC: 3567 Mfg Industrial Furnaces/Ovens

(G-1270)
FIVES N AMERCN COMBUSTN INC
287 Boston Post Rd (06333-1554)
P.O. Box 160 (06333-0160)
PHONE....860 739-3466
Ted Jablkowski, *Regional Mgr*
Philip Daigle, *Sales Executive*
EMP: 3
SALES (corp-wide): 843.9K **Privately Held**
SIC: 3433 Mfg Heating Equipment-Non-electric
HQ: Fives North American Combustion, Inc.
4455 E 71st St
Cleveland OH 44105
216 271-6000

(G-1271)
PAW PRINT PANTRY LLC (PA)
33 Gurley Rd (06333-1713)
PHONE....860 447-8442
Jennifer Mohr, *Owner*
EMP: 3 **EST:** 2013
SALES (est): 782.3K **Privately Held**
SIC: 2752 Lithographic Commercial Printing

(G-1272)
PRE -CLINICAL SAFETY INC
69 Quarry Dock Rd (06333)
PHONE....860 739-9797
Ricardo Ochoa, *President*
EMP: 4
SALES (est): 305.8K **Privately Held**
SIC: 2834 Child Day Care Services

(G-1273)
R-D MFG INC
6 Colton Rd (06333-1435)
PHONE....860 739-3986
Louis N Tashash, *President*
Connelly Richard, *Vice Pres*
Nancy A Tashash, *Treasurer*
EMP: 12
SQ FT: 13,000
SALES (est): 2.4MM **Privately Held**
WEB: www.rdmfginc.com
SIC: 3444 Mfg Sheet Metalwork

East Windsor
Hartford County

(G-1274)
A HARDIMAN MACHINE CO INC
94 Newberry Rd (06088-9544)
PHONE..................................860 623-8133
John Gould, *President*
Suzanne J Barstis, *Vice Pres*
EMP: 8
SALES (est): 647.5K **Privately Held**
SIC: 3599 Machine Shop

(G-1275)
AEROCOR INC
59 Newberry Rd (06088-9631)
PHONE..................................860 281-9274
Marc Corallo, *Principal*
Daniel Corallo, *Principal*
Erica Poulin, *Principal*
EMP: 12
SALES (est): 789.9K **Privately Held**
SIC: 3444 Mfg Sheet Metalwork

(G-1276)
ALS BEVERAGE COMPANY INC
13 Revay Rd (06088-9688)
PHONE..................................860 627-7003
Gerald E Martin, *President*
Marjorie Feldman, *President*
EMP: 20 **EST:** 1955
SQ FT: 11,000
SALES (est): 4.2MM
SALES (corp-wide): 24.2MM **Privately Held**
WEB: www.fallonreynolds.com
SIC: 2086 2095 Mfg Bottled/Canned Soft Drinks Mfg Roasted Coffee
PA: Al's Holding Inc
13 Revay Rd
East Windsor CT 06088
860 627-7003

(G-1277)
AVALON ADVANCED TECH REPR INC
Also Called: Avatar
59 Newberry Rd (06088-9631)
PHONE..................................860 254-5442
Vinod Franklin, *CEO*
Donald Ball, *President*
EMP: 24
SALES (est): 4.9MM **Privately Held**
SIC: 3728 Mfg Aircraft Parts/Equipment

(G-1278)
BLUE BELL MATTRESS COMPANY LLC
Also Called: King Koil Northeast
24 Thompson Rd (06088-9698)
PHONE..................................860 292-6372
Mark J Kolovson, *Ch of Bd*
Derek Ritzel, *President*
Steve Buyer, *Vice Pres*
◆ **EMP:** 220
SQ FT: 100,000
SALES (est): 35.8MM
SALES (corp-wide): 117.1K **Privately Held**
SIC: 2515 Mfg Mattresses/Bedsprings
PA: Landon Capital Partners, Llc
21 Custom House St # 700
Boston MA 02110
617 412-2700

(G-1279)
BOEING COMPANY
1 Hartfield Blvd Ste 112 (06088-9582)
PHONE..................................860 627-9393
George Buswell, *Manager*
EMP: 6
SALES (corp-wide): 101.1B **Publicly Held**
SIC: 3812 Mfg Search/Navigation Equipment
PA: The Boeing Company
100 N Riverside Plz
Chicago IL 60606
312 544-2000

(G-1280)
BROOK BROAD BREWING LLC
122 Prospect Hill Rd (06088-9546)
PHONE..................................860 623-1000
Robert Muska, *Owner*
EMP: 14 **EST:** 2015
SALES (est): 2MM **Privately Held**
SIC: 2082 Mfg Malt Beverages

(G-1281)
CA INC
160 Bridge St Ste 300 (06088)
PHONE..................................800 225-5224
Art Cartier, *Manager*
EMP: 45
SALES (corp-wide): 22.6B **Publicly Held**
WEB: www.cai.com
SIC: 7372 8742 Prepackaged Software Services Management Consulting Services
HQ: Ca, Inc.
520 Madison Ave
New York NY 10022
800 225-5224

(G-1282)
DRI-AIR INDUSTRIES INC
16 Thompson Rd (06088-9696)
P.O. Box 1020 (06088-1020)
PHONE..................................860 627-5110
Charles F Sears Jr, *President*
Jo-Ann Macfarlane, *Purchasing*
Steve Corcoran, *Natl Sales Mgr*
Herb Wischow, *Sales Mgr*
Jim Poglitsch, *Manager*
EMP: 23
SQ FT: 20,000
SALES (est): 7MM **Privately Held**
WEB: www.dri-air.com
SIC: 3567 3537 Mfg Industrial Furnaces/Ovens Mfg Industrial Trucks/Tractors

(G-1283)
EDAC TECHNOLOGIES LLC
68 Prospect Hill Rd (06088-9667)
PHONE..................................860 789-2511
EMP: 10 **Privately Held**
SIC: 3769 3541 3724 Mfg Space Vehicle Equipment Mfg Machine Tools-Cutting Mfg Aircraft Engines/Parts
HQ: Edac Technologies Llc
5 Mckee Pl
Cheshire CT 06410
203 806-2090

(G-1284)
FSM PLASTICOID MFG INC
32 North Rd (06088-9607)
P.O. Box 1036, Ada MI (49301-1036)
PHONE..................................860 623-1361
David Facchini, *President*
▲ **EMP:** 17
SALES (est): 2.5MM **Privately Held**
SIC: 3089 Mfg Plastic Products

(G-1285)
HERMTECH INC
8 Thompson Rd Ste 9 (06088-6902)
PHONE..................................860 758-7528
John Griffin, *President*
Kevin Griffin, *Director*
EMP: 4 **EST:** 2011
SQ FT: 2,000
SALES: 90K **Privately Held**
SIC: 3812 Mfg Search/Navigation Equipment

(G-1286)
HOMELAND FUNDRAISING
Also Called: Kelleher Marketing
38 Borrup Rd (06088-9605)
PHONE..................................860 386-6698
Kevin Kelleher, *Owner*
EMP: 7
SQ FT: 2,300
SALES: 525K **Privately Held**
WEB: www.homelandfundraising.com
SIC: 3949 Sports Fundraising Products Distributor

(G-1287)
INTEGRATED PACKG SYSTEMS INC
256 Main St Ste D (06088-9558)
PHONE..................................860 623-2623
Lee Kelting, *President*
Carl Fossum, *Admin Sec*
EMP: 5
SQ FT: 2,000
SALES (est): 950.4K **Privately Held**
WEB: www.intpacsys.com
SIC: 3565 7629 Mfg Custom Automation Machinery Electrical Repair

(G-1288)
JMF GROUP LLC
Also Called: Al's Beverage Company
13 Revay Rd (06088-9688)
PHONE..................................860 627-7003
Toll Free:..................................888 -
Marjorie Feldman,
EMP: 55
SALES (est): 7.4MM **Privately Held**
SIC: 2087 5149 Mfg Flavor Extracts/Syrup Whol Groceries

(G-1289)
K F MACHINING
36 Newberry Rd (06088-9544)
PHONE..................................860 292-6466
EMP: 3
SQ FT: 1,000
SALES (est): 100K **Privately Held**
WEB: www.kfmachining.com
SIC: 3999 Mfg Misc Products

(G-1290)
K T I TURBO-TECH INC
3 Thompson Rd (06088-9695)
P.O. Box 658 (06088-0658)
PHONE..................................860 623-2511
Howard Orr, *Principal*
John Minges, *Admin Sec*
EMP: 16
SALES (est): 342K
SALES (corp-wide): 2.4MM **Privately Held**
SIC: 7692 Welding Repair
HQ: Kti Inc
3 Thompson Rd
East Windsor CT 06088
860 623-2511

(G-1291)
KIN-THERM INC
Also Called: K T I
3 Thompson Rd (06088-9695)
P.O. Box 658 (06088-0658)
PHONE..................................860 623-2511
Howard Orr, *President*
Warren H Reid Jr, *Vice Pres*
John Minges, *Admin Sec*
EMP: 15
SQ FT: 30,000
SALES (est): 986.4K
SALES (corp-wide): 2.4MM **Privately Held**
WEB: www.ktiinc.com
SIC: 7692 Electron Beam Welding
HQ: Kti Inc
3 Thompson Rd
East Windsor CT 06088
860 623-2511

(G-1292)
KINETIC TOOL CO INC
5 Craftsman Rd Ste 7 (06088-9617)
PHONE..................................860 627-5882
Jonathan Cherpak, *President*
EMP: 13
SQ FT: 4,000
SALES (est): 1.4MM **Privately Held**
SIC: 3545 Mfg Machine Tool Accessories

(G-1293)
KTI BI-METALLIX INC
Also Called: Bi-Metalix
3 Thompson Rd (06088-9695)
P.O. Box 658 (06088-0658)
PHONE..................................860 623-2511
Howard Orr, *President*
Wasseluk Steve, *CTO*
John Minges, *Admin Sec*
EMP: 17
SQ FT: 30,000
SALES (est): 1MM
SALES (corp-wide): 2.4MM **Privately Held**
SIC: 7692 Electron Beam Welding
HQ: Kti Inc
3 Thompson Rd
East Windsor CT 06088
860 623-2511

(G-1294)
KTI INC (HQ)
Also Called: K T I Kin Therm
3 Thompson Rd (06088-9695)
P.O. Box 658 (06088-0658)
PHONE..................................860 623-2511
Howard Orr, *Chairman*
EMP: 18
SQ FT: 30,000
SALES (est): 2.4MM **Privately Held**
SIC: 7692 Electron Beam Welding
PA: Applied Energy Corporation
33 East St Ste 4
Winchester MA
781 756-1216

(G-1295)
METAL IMPROVEMENT COMPANY LLC
Curtiss-Wright Surface Tech
12 Thompson Rd (06088-9696)
PHONE..................................860 523-9901
EMP: 70
SALES (corp-wide): 2.4B **Publicly Held**
SIC: 3398 Metal Heat Treating
HQ: Metal Improvement Company, Llc
80 E Rte 4 Ste 310
Paramus NJ 07652
201 843-7800

(G-1296)
MLS ACQ INC
32 North Rd (06088-9607)
P.O. Box 390 (06088-0390)
PHONE..................................860 386-6878
John Stack, *CEO*
EMP: 10
SALES (est): 327.7K **Privately Held**
SIC: 3999 Mfg Misc Products

(G-1297)
NOBLE FIRE BRICK COMPANY INC (PA)
Also Called: Noble Industrial Furnace Co
40 Woolam Rd (06088-9707)
PHONE..................................860 623-9256
Raymond G Noble, *President*
Raymond Dan Noble, *Vice Pres*
Jennifer Fahey, *Office Mgr*
EMP: 5
SQ FT: 14,000
SALES (est): 668.6K **Privately Held**
SIC: 3567 Mfg Industrial Furnaces/Ovens

(G-1298)
PLASTICOID MANUFACTURING INC
Also Called: P M I
32 North Rd Rear (06088-9607)
P.O. Box 450 (06088-0450)
PHONE..................................860 623-1361
Jonathan Shoham, *President*
Robert Shoham, *President*
Daniel Shoham, *Vice Pres*
Jim Downey, *CFO*
▲ **EMP:** 25
SQ FT: 16,200
SALES (est): 3.7MM **Privately Held**
WEB: www.plasticoidmfg.com
SIC: 3089 Mfg Plastic Products

(G-1299)
R&R TOOL & DIE LLC
94 Newberry Rd (06088-9544)
PHONE..................................860 627-9197
Rolland Cote III,
EMP: 8
SQ FT: 2,000
SALES: 300K **Privately Held**
SIC: 3545 3544 Injection Molds And Diamond Cutting Tools

(G-1300)
ROTO-DIE COMPANY INC
Also Called: Preston Engravers
7d Pasco Dr (06088-1707)
PHONE..................................860 292-7030
Naomi Hamad, *Principal*
EMP: 10
SALES (corp-wide): 190.8MM **Privately Held**
WEB: www.rotometrics.com
SIC: 3944 2759 3544 Mfg Games/Toys Commercial Printing Mfg Dies/Tools/Jigs/Fixtures
PA: Roto-Die Company, Inc.
800 Howerton Ln
Eureka MO 63025
636 587-3600

(G-1301)
SIFCO APPLIED SRFC CNCEPTS LLC
Sifco Selective Plating Div
22 Thompson Rd Ste 2 (06088-9616)
PHONE..................................860 623-6006
David Parmenter, *Sales/Mktg Mgr*
EMP: 5
SALES (corp-wide): 7.6MM **Privately Held**
WEB: www.sifco.com
SIC: 3471 Plating/Polishing Service
PA: Sifco Applied Surface Concepts, Llc
5708 E Schaaf Rd
Cleveland OH 44131
216 524-0099

(G-1302)
SPECIALTY PRINTING LLC
15 Thompson Rd (06088-9697)
PHONE..................................860 654-1850
William Bailey,
EMP: 10
SALES (est): 700K
SALES (corp-wide): 52.5MM **Privately Held**
SIC: 2752 Lithographic Commercial Printing
PA: Specialty Printing, Llc
4 Thompson Rd
East Windsor CT 06088
860 623-8870

(G-1303)
SPECIALTY PRINTING LLC (PA)
Also Called: S P
4 Thompson Rd (06088-9626)
PHONE..................................860 623-8870
Fred Bailey, *Vice Pres*
Tom Costella, *Vice Pres*
Roger Reed, *Vice Pres*
Anil Selby, *Vice Pres*
Alex Bellamy, *Production*
EMP: 100 **EST:** 1977
SQ FT: 40,000
SALES (est): 52.5MM **Privately Held**
WEB: www.specialtyprinting.net
SIC: 2679 2759 2672 Mfg Converted Paper Products Commercial Printing Mfg Coated/Laminated Paper

(G-1304)
STACY B GOFF
Also Called: Stace Welding
100 Newberry Rd (06088-9544)
PHONE..................................860 623-2547
Stacy B Goff, *Owner*
EMP: 5
SQ FT: 10,000
SALES: 275K **Privately Held**
SIC: 3599 Mfg Industrial Machinery

(G-1305)
STAKE COMPANY LLC
22 Thompson Rd Ste 7 (06088-9616)
P.O. Box 528 (06088-0528)
PHONE..................................860 623-2700
Donna Charette,
EMP: 4
SALES: 256K **Privately Held**
SIC: 2426 Hardwood Dimension/Floor Mill

(G-1306)
SUOMINEN US HOLDING INC (HQ)
1 Hartfield Blvd Ste 101 (06088-9500)
PHONE..................................860 386-8001
Lynn Hotchkiss, *Accountant*
John Bigos, *Director*
▼ **EMP:** 15
SALES (est): 139.5MM
SALES (corp-wide): 493.5MM **Privately Held**
SIC: 2297 Mfg Nonwoven Fabrics
PA: Suominen Oyj
Karvaamokuja 2b
Helsinki 00380
102 143-00

(G-1307)
TITANIUM METALS CORPORATION
Also Called: Timet
7 Craftsman Rd (06088-9685)
PHONE..................................860 627-7051
Phil Macvain, *Manager*
EMP: 13
SQ FT: 22,000
SALES (corp-wide): 225.3B **Publicly Held**
WEB: www.timet.com
SIC: 3356 5051 Nonferrous Rolling/Drawing Metals Service Center
HQ: Titanium Metals Corporation
4832 Richmond Rd Ste 100
Warrensville Heights OH 44128
610 968-1300

(G-1308)
TRENTO GROUP LLC
Also Called: Plastech Manufacturing
32 North Rd (06088-9607)
P.O. Box 997 (06088-0997)
PHONE..................................860 623-1361
Emanuele Mangiafico,
EMP: 3
SALES (est): 177.4K **Privately Held**
SIC: 3089 Mfg Plastic Products

(G-1309)
VOYTEKS INC
7 Thompson Rd (06088-9614)
P.O. Box 479, Suffield (06078-0479)
PHONE..................................860 967-6558
Wojciech Skoczylas, *President*
EMP: 3
SALES (est): 232.4K **Privately Held**
SIC: 3599 Mfg Industrial Machinery

(G-1310)
WEBBERS TRUCK SERVICE INC
27 Depot Hill Rd (06088)
P.O. Box 702 (06088-0702)
PHONE..................................860 623-4554
Hartson Webber, *President*
EMP: 13
SQ FT: 2,500
SALES (est): 2.3MM **Privately Held**
SIC: 3715 Mfg Truck Trailers

(G-1311)
WINDSOR LOCKS NONWOVENS INC (DH)
Also Called: Suominen Nonwoven
1 Hartfield Blvd Ste 101 (06088-9500)
PHONE..................................860 292-5600
Nina Kopola, *CEO*
Petri Rolig, *Vice Pres*
John Bigos, *Finance*
◆ **EMP:** 30
SQ FT: 312,000
SALES (est): 67.9MM
SALES (corp-wide): 493.5MM **Privately Held**
SIC: 2297 Mfg Nonwoven Fabrics
HQ: Suominen Us Holding, Inc.
1 Hartfield Blvd Ste 101
East Windsor CT 06088
860 386-8001

Eastford
Windham County

(G-1312)
ANDERT INC
39 Boston Tpke (06242)
P.O. Box 372 (06242-0372)
PHONE..................................860 974-3893
Michael Andert, *President*
▲ **EMP:** 5
SQ FT: 5,000
SALES (est): 885.4K **Privately Held**
SIC: 3441 Structural Metal Fabrication

(G-1313)
INDUSTRIAL PALLET LLC
27 Chaplin Rd (06242-9439)
P.O. Box 389 (06242-0389)
PHONE..................................860 974-0093
Jayson Tanner, *Vice Pres*
Joe O'Brien,
▲ **EMP:** 46
SQ FT: 51,000
SALES (est): 6.7MM **Privately Held**
WEB: www.industrialpallet.com
SIC: 2448 Mfg Wood Pallets/Skids

(G-1314)
S S FABRICATIONS INC
82 County Rd (06242-7700)
P.O. Box 37 (06242-0037)
PHONE..................................860 974-1910
David Buchholz Jr, *President*
EMP: 8 **EST:** 1976
SQ FT: 3,000
SALES (est): 245.2K **Privately Held**
SIC: 7692 3599 Welding Repair & Machine Shop/Jobbing & Repair

(G-1315)
WHITCRAFT LLC (PA)
76 County Rd (06242-7700)
P.O. Box 128 (06242-0128)
PHONE..................................860 974-0786
Colin Cooper, *CEO*
Jeff Paul, *President*
Steve Ruggiero, *VP Opers*
Brian Carlin, *Production*
Kurt Texiera, *Senior Buyer*
▲ **EMP:** 183 **EST:** 1960
SQ FT: 63,200
SALES (est): 115MM **Privately Held**
WEB: www.whitcraft.com
SIC: 3443 3444 3728 Mfg Fabricated Plate Work Mfg Sheet Metalwork Mfg Aircraft Parts/Equipment

(G-1316)
WHITCRAFT SCRBOROUGH/TEMPE LLC (HQ)
76 County Rd (06242-7700)
PHONE..................................860 974-0786
Colin Cooper, *CEO*
EMP: 200
SALES (est): 5MM
SALES (corp-wide): 115MM **Privately Held**
SIC: 3728 3443 3444 Aircraft Parts And Equipment, Nec, Nsk
PA: Whitcraft Llc
76 County Rd
Eastford CT 06242
860 974-0786

Easton
Fairfield County

(G-1317)
EASTON BREWING COMPANY LLC
53 Ridgeway Rd (06612-1717)
PHONE..................................203 921-7263
John Cavallero, *Principal*
EMP: 3
SALES (est): 75K **Privately Held**
SIC: 2082 Mfg Malt Beverages

(G-1318)
ECCLES-LEHMAN INC
Also Called: Eccles Carleton
44 Sanford Dr (06612-1423)
PHONE..................................203 268-0605
Rosemarie Lehman, *President*
Rosemary Lehman, *President*
EMP: 5
SQ FT: 6,000
SALES (est): 340K **Privately Held**
SIC: 2759 2752 5943 2796 Commercial Printing Lithographic Coml Print Ret Stationery Platemaking Services Typesetting Services

(G-1319)
HENRY THAYER COMPANY
Also Called: Thayers Natural Remedies
65 Adams Rd (06612-1355)
PHONE..................................203 226-0940
Karen Clarke, *CEO*
John Reppucci, *Vice Pres*
Helen Kaufman, *Treasurer*
EMP: 3
SQ FT: 3,500
SALES (est): 511.1K **Privately Held**
WEB: www.thayers.com
SIC: 2834 Mfg Pharmaceutical Preparations

(G-1320)
INSIGHT ENTERPRISES INC
78 Gate Ridge Rd (06612-1838)
PHONE..................................203 374-2013
Jason Cavanaugh, *Branch Mgr*
EMP: 3 **Publicly Held**
SIC: 7372 Prepackaged Software Services
PA: Insight Enterprises, Inc.
6820 S Harl Ave
Tempe AZ 85283

(G-1321)
MODEAN INDUSTRIES INC
15 Lucielle Dr (06612-1819)
P.O. Box 275 (06612-0275)
PHONE..................................203 371-6625
Dean Azzam, *President*
Haney Azzam, *Chairman*
EMP: 3
SALES: 900K **Privately Held**
WEB: www.modeanindustries.com
SIC: 3567 Mfg Industrial Furnaces/Ovens

(G-1322)
POLARIS MANAGEMENT INC
30 Silver Hill Rd (06612-1114)
PHONE..................................203 261-6399
Robert G George, *President*
Matthew Simpson, *Vice Pres*
EMP: 4
SALES (est): 208.7K **Privately Held**
SIC: 3621 Mfg Motors/Generators

(G-1323)
ROCKET BOOKS INC
34 Ridgeway Rd (06612-1718)
PHONE..................................203 372-1818
Steven Loo, *President*
▲ **EMP:** 5
SALES (est): 400.7K **Privately Held**
WEB: www.rocketbooks.com
SIC: 2731 Books-Publishing/Printing

Ellington
Tolland County

(G-1324)
ACCU-TIME SYSTEMS INC (DH)
Also Called: A T S
420 Somers Rd (06029-2629)
PHONE..................................860 870-5000
James McHale, *CEO*
David Hopkins, *Senior VP*
Phillip SIS, *Opers Staff*
Thomas Benton, *Treasurer*
Renee Vollrath, *Accountant*
▲ **EMP:** 36
SQ FT: 23,500
SALES (est): 16.7MM **Privately Held**
WEB: www.accu time.com
SIC: 3579 3873 Mfg Office Machines Mfg Watches/Clocks/Parts
HQ: Amano Usa Holdings, Inc.
140 Harrison Ave
Roseland NJ 07068
973 403-1900

(G-1325)
ACTION PACKAGING SYSTEMS INC (PA)
372 Somers Rd (06029)
PHONE..................................860 222-9510
Douglas E Rice, *President*
Gordon E Rice, *Vice Pres*
▲ **EMP:** 5

SALES (est): 1MM **Privately Held**
WEB: www.actionpkg.com
SIC: 2631 Paperboard Mill

(G-1326)
ADVANCE MOLD MFG INC
15 Teaberry Ridge Rd (06029-2726)
PHONE....................................860 783-5024
Doug Schneider, *President*
EMP: 4
SALES (est): 296.1K **Privately Held**
SIC: 3089 Mfg Plastic Products

(G-1327)
ADVANCED MACHINE TECHNOLOGY
5 Industrial Dr (06029-2632)
P.O. Box 95 (06029-0095)
PHONE....................................860 872-2664
Gary Hublard, *President*
Dorothy Hublard, *Admin Sec*
EMP: 3
SQ FT: 2,000
SALES (est): 390.9K **Privately Held**
SIC: 3599 Mfg Industrial Machinery

(G-1328)
ALL STEEL LLC
240 Crystal Lake Rd (06029-3406)
PHONE....................................860 871-6023
Eben J Holmes, *Mng Member*
EMP: 3
SALES (est): 279.2K **Privately Held**
SIC: 3334 Primary Aluminum Producer

(G-1329)
ARROW DIVERSIFIED TOOLING INC
17 Pinney St (06029-3812)
P.O. Box 508 (06029-0508)
PHONE....................................860 872-9072
David Trench, *President*
EMP: 22
SQ FT: 13,000
SALES: 3.3MM **Privately Held**
WEB: www.arrowdiversified.com
SIC: 3544 3363 3542 3543 Mfg Dies/Tools/Jigs/Fixt Mfg Aluminum Die-Casting Mfg Machine Tool-Forming Mfg Industrial Patterns Mfg Aircraft Parts/Equip

(G-1330)
BRYMILL CORPORATION (PA)
Also Called: Brymill Cryogenic Sys
105 Windermere Ave Ste 3b (06029-3858)
PHONE....................................860 875-2460
M Gail Bryne, *President*
Claudio Russo, *General Mgr*
Sheryl Thibeault, *General Mgr*
Mike Bryne, *Vice Pres*
EMP: 10 **EST:** 1966
SQ FT: 10,000
SALES (est): 1.1MM **Privately Held**
WEB: www.brymill.com
SIC: 3842 Mfg Surgical/Medical Instruments

(G-1331)
COUNTRY PURE FOODS INC
58 West Rd (06029-4200)
PHONE....................................330 753-2293
Kim Wilford, *Manager*
EMP: 106 **Privately Held**
WEB: www.countrypurefoods.com
SIC: 2033 Mfg Canned Fruits/Vegetables
PA: Country Pure Foods, Inc.
222 W Main St Ste 401
Akron OH 44308
-

(G-1332)
DESIGN IDEA PRINTING
344 Somers Rd (06029)
P.O. Box 2215, Vernon Rockville (06066-1615)
PHONE....................................860 896-0103
David Pinkham, *Owner*
Irene Pinkham, *Owner*
EMP: 3
SALES (est): 254.1K **Privately Held**
SIC: 2752 Lithographic Commercial Printing

(G-1333)
DYMOTEK CORPORATION
7 Main St (06029-3317)
PHONE....................................860 875-2868
Steven R Trueb, *President*
Thomas W Trueb, *Vice Pres*
Robert Perkins, *Technician*
◆ **EMP:** 50
SQ FT: 35,000
SALES (est): 18.5MM **Privately Held**
WEB: www.dymotek.net
SIC: 3089 Mfg Plastic Products

(G-1334)
ELLINGTON PRINTERY INC
Also Called: Med Print
25 West Rd Ste B (06029-4260)
P.O. Box 219 (06029-0219)
PHONE....................................860 875-3310
Carol White, *President*
EMP: 7
SQ FT: 2,000
SALES (est): 950.2K **Privately Held**
SIC: 2752 Lithographic Commercial Printing

(G-1335)
MAYARC INDUSTRIES INC
54 Minor Hill Rd (06029-3107)
PHONE....................................860 871-1872
Matthew Minor, *President*
Mark Minor, *Principal*
EMP: 7
SALES (est): 380K **Privately Held**
WEB: www.midiaclick.net
SIC: 3441 Structural Metal Fabrication

(G-1336)
MERRILL INDUSTRIES INC
26 Village St (06029-3815)
P.O. Box 150 (06029-0150)
PHONE....................................860 871-1888
Merrill Lieberman, *President*
EMP: 38
SQ FT: 80,000
SALES (est): 8.2MM **Privately Held**
SIC: 2653 2441 3086 Mfg Corrugated/Solid Fiber Boxes Mfg Wood Boxes/Shook Mfg Plastic Foam Products

(G-1337)
MERRILL INDUSTRIES LLC
26 Village St (06029-3815)
P.O. Box 150 (06029-0150)
PHONE....................................860 871-1888
Albert Gardiner, *Vice Pres*
EMP: 25
SQ FT: 82,000
SALES (est): 5.2MM **Privately Held**
SIC: 2653 Mfg Corrugated/Solid Fiber Boxes

(G-1338)
RICE PACKAGING INC
356 Somers Rd (06029-2628)
PHONE....................................860 870-7057
William A Rice, *Ch of Bd*
Clifford Rice, *President*
Debra Dubois, *Manager*
Ranee O'Neill, *Manager*
▲ **EMP:** 100 **EST:** 1964
SQ FT: 95,000
SALES (est): 27.3MM **Privately Held**
WEB: www.ricepackaging.com
SIC: 2657 2653 2652 2631 Mfg Folding Paperbrd Box Mfg Corrugated/Fiber Box Mfg Setup Paperboard Box Paperboard Mill

(G-1339)
SHAWS PUMP COMPANY INC
37 Windermere Ave (06029-3840)
PHONE....................................860 872-6891
George Shaw, *President*
Joanne Shaw, *Corp Secy*
EMP: 4
SALES: 120K **Privately Held**
SIC: 3589 Mfg Service Industry Machinery

(G-1340)
SJM PROPERTIES INC
164 Maple St (06029-3330)
PHONE....................................860 979-0060
Stanley E Matczak, *President*
Stanley Matczak, *President*
Joseph Matczak, *Vice Pres*
EMP: 9
SQ FT: 12,000
SALES (est): 793.1K **Privately Held**
WEB: www.sjmproperties.com
SIC: 3545 Mfg Machine Tool Accessories

(G-1341)
SYN-MAR PRODUCTS INC
5 Nutmeg Dr (06029-3899)
P.O. Box 333 (06029-0333)
PHONE....................................860 872-8505
Tim Hill, *President*
Ken Hill, *Marketing Staff*
EMP: 16
SALES (est): 3.3MM **Privately Held**
WEB: www.syn-marproducts.com
SIC: 3088 3261 Mfg Plastic Plumbing Fixtures Mfg Vitreous Plumbing Fixtures

(G-1342)
TOY PALLET
11 Rothe Ln (06029-3847)
PHONE....................................860 803-9838
Benjamin Priest, *Principal*
EMP: 3
SALES (est): 248.8K **Privately Held**
SIC: 2448 Mfg Wood Pallets/Skids

(G-1343)
TRANS-TEK INC
10 Industrial Dr (06029-2632)
P.O. Box 338 (06029-0338)
PHONE....................................860 872-8351
Nancy Hamilton, *President*
James L Waters, *Admin Sec*
EMP: 25
SQ FT: 14,000
SALES (est): 5.8MM **Privately Held**
WEB: www.transtekinc.com
SIC: 3825 3669 3829 Mfg Electrical Measuring Instruments Mfg Communications Equipment Mfg Measuring/Controlling Devices

(G-1344)
YELLOWFIN HOLDINGS INC
Yellowfin Distribution
160 West Rd (06029-3723)
P.O. Box 83 (06029-0083)
PHONE....................................866 341-0979
Joseph Teixeira, *Manager*
EMP: 46 **Privately Held**
SIC: 3577 Mfg Computer Peripheral Equipment
PA: Yellowfin Holdings, Inc.
26 Main St
Ellington CT 06029
-

Enfield
Hartford County

(G-1345)
ADAMCZYK ENTERPRISES INC
Also Called: Enfield Collision
3 Palomba Dr (06082-3823)
P.O. Box 1143 (06083-1143)
PHONE....................................860 745-9830
Robert P Adamczyk, *President*
Thomas Adamczyk, *Admin Sec*
EMP: 9
SALES (est): 331.4K **Privately Held**
SIC: 3549 Mfg Metalworking Machinery

(G-1346)
ANDERSON DAVID C & ASSOC LLC (PA)
Also Called: Anderson Group
9 Moody Rd Ste 1 (06082-3120)
PHONE....................................860 749-7547
Chris Anderson, *Vice Pres*
David C Anderson,
Christopher Anderson,
EMP: 10
SQ FT: 7,200
SALES (est): 1.4MM **Privately Held**
SIC: 3089 8742 7389 8748 Mfg Plastic Products Mgmt Consulting Svcs Business Services Business Consulting Svcs

(G-1347)
ATLANTIC WOODCRAFT INC
Also Called: B&C Kitchen and Bath
199 Moody Rd (06082-3209)
PHONE....................................860 749-4887
Michael St Germain, *President*
Genevieve St Germain, *Admin Sec*
EMP: 15
SALES (est): 3.3MM **Privately Held**
SIC: 3423 2431 Mfg Hand/Edge Tools Mfg Millwork

(G-1348)
CARRIS REELS CONNECTICUT INC
11 Randolph St (06082-4724)
P.O. Box 1104 (06083-1104)
PHONE....................................860 749-8308
Dave Ferraro, *President*
David Ferraro, *Vice Pres*
Frank Donovan, *Maint Spvr*
David Fitz-Gerald, *CFO*
Linda Gallipo, *Asst Treas*
▲ **EMP:** 64 **EST:** 1868
SQ FT: 116,640
SALES (est): 9.2MM **Privately Held**
WEB: www.carris.net
SIC: 2499 Mfg Wood Products
PA: Carris Financial Corp.
49 Main St
Proctor VT 05765
-

(G-1349)
CIRTEC MEDICAL CORP
99 Print Shop Rd (06082-3211)
PHONE....................................860 814-3973
EMP: 120
SALES (corp-wide): 53.4MM **Privately Held**
SIC: 3841 Mfg Surgical/Medical Instruments
PA: Cirtec Medical Corp.
9200 Xylon Ave N
Brooklyn Park MN 55445
763 493-8556

(G-1350)
COLLINS COMPOST
11 Powder Hill Rd (06082-5212)
PHONE....................................860 749-3416
Jack Collins, *Principal*
EMP: 3 **EST:** 1998
SALES (est): 219.7K **Privately Held**
SIC: 2875 Mfg Fertilizers-Mix Only

(G-1351)
COLONIAL IRON SHOP INC
15 Dust House Rd (06082-4650)
P.O. Box 1116 (06083-1116)
PHONE....................................860 763-0659
Anthony Leno, *President*
Daniel Swenson, *Vice Pres*
EMP: 4
SQ FT: 6,000
SALES: 750K **Privately Held**
SIC: 3441 1791 Mfg Fabricated Structural Steel & Iron & Structural Steel Erection

(G-1352)
COMVAC SYSTEMS INC
3 Peerless Way Ste U (06082-2388)
PHONE....................................860 265-3658
Daniel W Lawrence, *Principal*
▲ **EMP:** 3
SALES (est): 442.2K **Privately Held**
SIC: 3563 Mfg Air/Gas Compressors

(G-1353)
CONVAL INC
96 Phoenix Ave (06082-4408)
PHONE....................................860 749-0761
Frank A Siver, *Principal*
Gene McNamara, *Regional Mgr*
Mike Hendrick, *Vice Pres*
▲ **EMP:** 105
SALES: 23MM **Privately Held**
WEB: www.conval.com
SIC: 3491 Mfg Industrial Valves

(G-1354)
CUSTOM PRINTING & COPY INC (PA)
16 Debra St (06082-5031)
P.O. Box 280745, East Hartford (06128-0745)
PHONE..................................860 290-6890
Martin Madeux, *President*
Bedilea Bodo, *Vice Pres*
EMP: 11
SQ FT: 1,200
SALES (est): 1.4MM **Privately Held**
WEB: www.customprintingct.com
SIC: 2752 7334 Lithographic Commercial Printing Photocopying Services

(G-1355)
EAST LONGMEADOW BUSINESS SVCS
Also Called: Priority Press
25 Lake Dr (06082-2336)
PHONE..................................413 525-6111
Patricia Mance, *President*
Eric Mance, *President*
EMP: 5
SALES: 450K **Privately Held**
WEB: www.prioritypress.com
SIC: 2752 7334 Offset Job Printing & Photocopying

(G-1356)
EASTERN METAL TREATING INC
28 Bacon Rd (06082-2302)
PHONE..................................860 763-4311
Maureen R Lyman, *President*
Bob Lyman, *General Mgr*
EMP: 10
SQ FT: 20,000
SALES (est): 1.5MM **Privately Held**
SIC: 3398 Metal Heat Treating

(G-1357)
ENFIELD TRANSIT MIX INC
84 Broadbrook Rd (06082-5303)
P.O. Box 376 (06083-0376)
PHONE..................................860 763-0864
Zigmund Kertenis Jr, *President*
EMP: 16
SALES (est): 3MM **Privately Held**
SIC: 3273 Mfg Ready-Mixed Concrete

(G-1358)
EPPENDORF INC (DH)
175 Freshwater Blvd (06082-4444)
PHONE..................................732 287-1200
Lisa Kendzlic, *CEO*
William Dunne, *Vice Pres*
Dr Lee Eppstein, *Vice Pres*
Martin Axelsson, *Engineer*
Thomas Bocchino, *CFO*
▲ **EMP:** 350 **EST:** 1946
SQ FT: 243,000
SALES (est): 67.1MM
SALES (corp-wide): 177.9K **Privately Held**
WEB: www.nbsc.com
SIC: 3821 Mfg Lab Apparatus/Furn

(G-1359)
EPPENDORF HOLDING INC (DH)
175 Freshwater Blvd (06082-4444)
PHONE..................................860 253-3417
Martin Farb, *CEO*
Christian Jaaks, *CFO*
Klaus U Theidmann, *Admin Sec*
▲ **EMP:** 25
SALES (est): 62MM
SALES (corp-wide): 177.9K **Privately Held**
SIC: 3821 Mfg Lab Apparatus/Furniture
HQ: Eppendorf Ag
Barkhausenweg 1
Hamburg 22339
405 380-10

(G-1360)
EPPENDORF MANUFACTURING CORP
175 Freshwater Blvd (06082-4444)
PHONE..................................860 253-3400
Kirti Patel, *CEO*
Perry Aschenbrand, *Controller*
◆ **EMP:** 170
SALES (est): 37MM
SALES (corp-wide): 177.9K **Privately Held**
SIC: 3841 Mfg Surgical/Medical Instruments
HQ: Eppendorf Ag
Barkhausenweg 1
Hamburg 22339
405 380-10

(G-1361)
EVSE LLC
89 Phoenix Ave (06082-4439)
PHONE..................................860 745-2433
James S Bianco, *Principal*
EMP: 3
SALES (est): 178.9K
SALES (corp-wide): 11.3MM **Privately Held**
SIC: 3699 Mfg Electrical Equipment/Supplies
PA: Control Module, Inc.
89 Phoenix Ave
Enfield CT 06082
860 745-2433

(G-1362)
FALCON PRESS
13 Rockland Dr (06082-5815)
P.O. Box 142 (06083-0142)
PHONE..................................860 763-2293
Peter Sarno, *Owner*
EMP: 3
SQ FT: 5,800
SALES: 200K **Privately Held**
SIC: 2759 2789 2752 Commercial Printing Bookbinding/Related Work Lithographic Commercial Printing

(G-1363)
FLEET MANAGEMENT LLC
89 Phoenix Ave (06082-4439)
PHONE..................................800 722-6654
James Bianco,
EMP: 3
SALES (est): 169.2K
SALES (corp-wide): 11.3MM **Privately Held**
SIC: 3823 Mfg Process Control Instruments
PA: Control Module, Inc.
89 Phoenix Ave
Enfield CT 06082
860 745-2433

(G-1364)
HIGH GRADE FINISHING CO LLC
Also Called: High Grade Furnishing
6 Print Shop Rd (06082-3212)
PHONE..................................860 749-8883
Valarie Ainsworth, *Vice Pres*
Russell Ainsworth,
EMP: 3 **EST:** 1959
SQ FT: 5,400
SALES: 140K **Privately Held**
SIC: 3479 7641 Coating/Engraving Service Reupholstery/Furniture Repair

(G-1365)
I Q TECHNOLOGY LLC
9 Moody Rd Ste 18 (06082-3120)
PHONE..................................860 749-7255
Peter Hasiuk,
EMP: 12
SQ FT: 10,000
SALES: 2MM **Privately Held**
WEB: www.iqtechnology.com
SIC: 3555 Mfg Printing Trades Machinery

(G-1366)
INTEGRAL TECHNOLOGIES INC (DH)
120 Post Rd (06082-5690)
PHONE..................................860 741-2281
Gottfried Keusters, *President*
Paul Lettieri, *Admin Sec*
▲ **EMP:** 6
SQ FT: 75,000
SALES (est): 6.8MM
SALES (corp-wide): 101.5K **Privately Held**
SIC: 3699 3599 8731 Mfg Electrical Equipment/Supplies Mfg Industrial Machinery Commercial Physical Research
HQ: Ptr Strahltechnik Gmbh
Am Erlenbruch 9
Langenselbold 63505
618 420-550

(G-1367)
JANIK SAUSAGE CO INC
136 Hazard Ave (06082-4520)
P.O. Box 751 (06083-0751)
PHONE..................................860 749-4661
Diane Prokop, *President*
Raymond Prokop, *Vice Pres*
EMP: 3
SQ FT: 1,900
SALES (est): 242K **Privately Held**
SIC: 2013 Mfg Kielbasa Links Polish & Italian Sausage & Pressed-Ham

(G-1368)
LEGO SYSTEMS INC (DH)
Also Called: Lego Brand Retail
555 Taylor Rd (06082-2372)
PHONE..................................860 749-2291
Soren Torp Laursen, *President*
Rachel Wendt, *General Mgr*
Chad Ketterling, *Store Mgr*
Marjorie Lao, *CFO*
Sarah Rhodes, *Executive Asst*
◆ **EMP:** 1350
SQ FT: 1,000,000
SALES (est): 559.6MM
SALES (corp-wide): 1.5B **Privately Held**
SIC: 3944 5092 Mfg Games/Toys Whol Toys/Hobby Goods
HQ: Lego A/S
Astvej 1
Billund 7190
795 060-70

(G-1369)
MACALA TOOL INC
7 Moody Rd Bldg 5 (06082-3123)
P.O. Box 765, Vernon (06066-0765)
PHONE..................................860 763-2580
Ian Macala, *President*
EMP: 5
SQ FT: 2,000
SALES: 250K **Privately Held**
SIC: 3599 Machine Shop Jobbing & Repair

(G-1370)
MRND LLC
75 Hazard Ave Ste 1 (06082-3866)
PHONE..................................860 749-0256
Larry Vertefeuille, *Manager*
EMP: 7
SQ FT: 6,000
SALES (corp-wide): 2.5MM **Privately Held**
WEB: www.mrnd.com
SIC: 3444 Mfg Sheet Metalwork
PA: Mrnd Llc
4418 Louisburg Rd
Raleigh NC
919 862-8480

(G-1371)
NEW BRITAIN HEAT TREATING CORP
5 Grant Ave (06082-3611)
PHONE..................................860 223-0684
Daniel Audet, *President*
Joan Litteral, *Manager*
Diane Audet, *Admin Sec*
EMP: 15
SALES: 1.1MM **Privately Held**
SIC: 3398 Metal Heat Treating

(G-1372)
NEW ENGLAND PRINTING LLC
1 Anngina Dr (06082-3222)
PHONE..................................860 745-3600
Lindsey Weber, *Principal*
Gail Weber, *Principal*
EMP: 6
SALES (est): 182.6K **Privately Held**
SIC: 2759 Commercial Printing

(G-1373)
P & M INVESTMENTS LLC
Also Called: Minuteman Press
1 Anngina Dr (06082-3222)
PHONE..................................860 745-3600
Paul Mazzaccaro,
EMP: 3
SALES (est): 411.7K **Privately Held**
SIC: 2752 Comm Prtg Litho

(G-1374)
PHOENIX POULTRY CORPORATION
8 Wheeler Dr (06082-2227)
PHONE..................................413 732-1433
EMP: 20
SQ FT: 12,000
SALES (est): 2.4MM **Privately Held**
SIC: 2015 Poultry Processing

(G-1375)
POLYMERIC CONVERTING LLC
5 Old Depot Hill Rd (06082-6040)
PHONE..................................860 623-1335
Frank Magnani,
Alan Gervais,
▲ **EMP:** 20
SQ FT: 56,000
SALES (est): 4.6MM **Privately Held**
SIC: 2671 3089 Mfg Packaging Paper/Film Mfg Plastic Products

(G-1376)
PTI INDUSTRIES INC (HQ)
Also Called: P T I
2 Peerless Way (06082-2371)
PHONE..................................800 318-8438
Ronald Lalli, *CEO*
Harley Delude, *President*
Ed Moreau, *Facilities Mgr*
Eric Payette, *Facilities Mgr*
Spencer Roy, *QA Dir*
EMP: 42
SQ FT: 19,000
SALES (est): 6.1MM
SALES (corp-wide): 39.1MM **Privately Held**
WEB: www.ptiwebsite.com
SIC: 3479 8734 Coating/Engraving Svcs Testing Laboratory
PA: Iss 2, Llc
10070 Daniels Interstate
Fort Myers FL 33913
239 244-2244

(G-1377)
PULVER PRECISION LLC
38 Bacon Rd (06082-2302)
PHONE..................................860 763-0763
Brian Pulver,
EMP: 4
SALES (est): 552.4K **Privately Held**
SIC: 3599 Mfg Industrial Machinery

(G-1378)
QG PRINTING II CORP
96 Phoenix Ave (06082-4408)
PHONE..................................860 741-0150
Ron Amarante, *Sales Staff*
EMP: 519
SALES (corp-wide): 4.1B **Publicly Held**
WEB: www.qwdys.com
SIC: 2752 Lithographic Commercial Printing
HQ: Qg Printing Ii Corp.
N61w23044 Harrys Way
Sussex WI 53089

(G-1379)
RELIABLE WELDING & SPEED LLC
85 North St (06082-3933)
PHONE..................................860 749-3977
Brad Hietala, *Mng Member*
Linda Hietala,
EMP: 6
SQ FT: 2,500
SALES (est): 800K **Privately Held**
SIC: 7692 5531 3444 3441 Welding Repair Metal Fabricator Retail Auto Racing Parts Truck Accs

(G-1380)
SCHRADER BELLOWS
80 Shaker Rd (06082-3106)
PHONE..................................860 749-2215
EMP: 25
SALES (est): 895.4K **Privately Held**
SIC: 2796 Platemaking Services

(G-1381)
SCREENING INK LLC
39 Celtic Ct (06082-5778)
PHONE..................................860 212-0475
Brett Silva, *Principal*
EMP: 3
SALES (est): 224.6K **Privately Held**
SIC: 3952 Mfg Lead Pencils/Art Goods

(G-1382)
SENIOR OPERATIONS LLC
Also Called: Senior Aerospace Connecticut
4 Peerless Way (06082-2371)
PHONE..................................860 741-2546
Michael Lang, *CEO*
David Squires, *President*
Ken Bernier, *QC Mgr*
Jeffrey Audet, *Engineer*
Donald Caravella, *Engineer*
EMP: 95 **EST:** 1992
SQ FT: 55,000
SALES (est): 22.2MM **Privately Held**
WEB: www.sterlingmachineco.com
SIC: 3728 Mfg Aircraft Parts/Equipment

(G-1383)
SENIOR OPERATIONS LLC
Also Called: Sterling Machine Division
4 Peerless Way (06082-2371)
PHONE..................................860 741-2546
Robert Segal, *CEO*
EMP: 80
SALES (corp-wide): 1.4B **Privately Held**
SIC: 3599 Mfg Industrial Machinery
HQ: Senior Operations Llc
300 E Devon Ave
Bartlett IL 60103
630 372-3500

(G-1384)
SIGN FACTORY
Also Called: Little John's Sign Factory
25 Dust House Rd (06082-4650)
PHONE..................................860 763-1085
Little John, *Owner*
EMP: 10
SQ FT: 7,000
SALES (est): 782.8K **Privately Held**
SIC: 3993 Mfg Signs/Advertising Specialties

(G-1385)
SIMPSON STRONG-TIE COMPANY INC
7 Pearson Way (06082-2655)
PHONE..................................860 741-8923
John Adkins, *Manager*
EMP: 16
SALES (corp-wide): 1B **Publicly Held**
SIC: 3449 Whol Construction Materials
HQ: Simpson Strong-Tie Company Inc.
5956 W Las Positas Blvd
Pleasanton CA 94588
925 560-9000

(G-1386)
STR HOLDINGS INC (PA)
1559 King St (06082-5844)
PHONE..................................860 272-4235
Robert S Yorgensen, *Ch of Bd*
Thomas D Vitro, *CFO*
EMP: 19
SQ FT: 69,500
SALES: 10.8MM **Publicly Held**
WEB: www.strus.com
SIC: 3081 Unsupported Plastics Film & Sheet

(G-1387)
SWEETHEART FLUTE COMPANY LLC
32 S Maple St (06082-4653)
PHONE..................................860 749-8514
Ralph Sweet,
Walter D Sweet,
EMP: 3
SALES (est): 333.7K **Privately Held**
WEB: www.sweetheartflute.com
SIC: 3931 5736 Mfg Musical Instruments Ret Musical Instruments

(G-1388)
TURNING STONE SAND & GRAV LLC
128 Moody Rd (06082-3202)
PHONE..................................413 519-1560
Anna L Lincoln, *Principal*
EMP: 3
SALES (est): 92K **Privately Held**
SIC: 1442 Construction Sand/Gravel

(G-1389)
VERICO TECHNOLOGY LLC (HQ)
230 Shaker Rd (06082-2385)
PHONE..................................800 492-7286
Yuval Dubois, *President*
Rebecca Itkin Duffy, *CFO*
▲ **EMP:** 45
SQ FT: 11,500
SALES (est): 112.4MM **Privately Held**
WEB: www.presstek.com
SIC: 3577 3861 3555 Mfg Computer Peripheral Equipment Mfg Photographic Equipment/Supplies Mfg Printing Trades Machinery

(G-1390)
WEST SHORE METALS LLC
28 W Shore Dr (06082-2223)
PHONE..................................860 749-8013
Bruce Bouchard, *Principal*
EMP: 4
SALES (est): 199.1K **Privately Held**
SIC: 3469 Mfg Metal Stampings

(G-1391)
WORLD CORD SETS INC
210 Moody Rd (06082-3206)
P.O. Box 1111 (06083-1111)
PHONE..................................860 763-2100
Edward C Smith, *President*
Ed Smith, *Info Tech Mgr*
▲ **EMP:** 8
SALES (est): 1.4MM **Privately Held**
WEB: www.worldcordsets.com
SIC: 3699 3643 Mfg Appliance Cords & Current Carrying Devices

(G-1392)
YANKEE CASTING CO INC
243 Shaker Rd (06082-2327)
P.O. Box 813 (06083-0813)
PHONE..................................860 749-6171
Mark Vecchiarelli, *President*
Timothy Vecchiarelli, *Corp Secy*
Brian Vecchiarelli, *Vice Pres*
Kevin Vecchiarelli, *Vice Pres*
Madaline Vecchiarelli, *Executive*
EMP: 55 **EST:** 1961
SQ FT: 51,000
SALES: 5.3MM **Privately Held**
WEB: www.yankeecasting.com
SIC: 3369 Nonferrous Metal Foundry

Essex
Middlesex County

(G-1393)
BELL POWER SYSTEMS LLC
Also Called: John Deere Authorized Dealer
34 Plains Rd (06426-1501)
P.O. Box 980 (06426-0980)
PHONE..................................860 767-7502
Michael J Hucovski,
▲ **EMP:** 60
SALES: 11.4MM **Privately Held**
SIC: 3519 5082 Mfg Internal Combustion Engines Whol Construction/Mining Equipment

(G-1394)
BROCKWAY FERRY CORPORATION (PA)
Also Called: Leather Man Limited
59 Plains Rd (06426-1504)
P.O. Box 57 (06426-0057)
PHONE..................................860 767-8231
W Cecil Lyon, *President*
Cecil Lyon, *Chancellor*
Tina Beaulac, *Sales Staff*
Linda B Lyon, *Admin Sec*
◆ **EMP:** 4
SQ FT: 15,000
SALES (est): 597.6K **Privately Held**
WEB: www.leathermanlimited.com
SIC: 3199 2241 3172 Mfg Leather Goods Narrow Fabric Mill Mfg Personal Leather Goods

(G-1395)
CONNECTICUT SIGN SERVICE LLC
25 Saybrook Rd Ste 6 (06426)
P.O. Box 645, Old Saybrook (06475-0645)
PHONE..................................860 767-7446
Arlene Fernandes,
John Morrison,
EMP: 5
SALES (est): 900K **Privately Held**
WEB: www.ctsign.com
SIC: 2499 3993 Mfg Wood Products Mfg Signs/Advertising Specialties

(G-1396)
ESSEX CONCRETE PRODUCTS INC
141 Westbrook Rd (06426-1512)
PHONE..................................860 767-1768
Robert Vitari, *President*
Ruth Vitari, *Admin Sec*
EMP: 10 **EST:** 1958
SQ FT: 5,000
SALES (est): 1.6MM **Privately Held**
SIC: 3273 3272 Mfg Ready-Mixed Concrete Mfg Concrete Products

(G-1397)
HI-REL GROUP LLC
16 Plains Rd (06426-1501)
PHONE..................................860 767-9031
William Hubbard, *President*
EMP: 7 **EST:** 2013
SALES (est): 973.6K
SALES (corp-wide): 67.1MM **Privately Held**
SIC: 3674 Mfg Semiconductors/Related Devices
PA: Hermetic Solutions Group Inc.
4000 State Route 66 # 310
Tinton Falls NJ 07753
732 722-8780

(G-1398)
HI-REL PRODUCTS LLC
16 Plains Rd (06426-1501)
PHONE..................................860 767-9031
William Hubbard, *President*
EMP: 40 **EST:** 2013
SQ FT: 16,500
SALES (est): 6.2MM
SALES (corp-wide): 67.1MM **Privately Held**
WEB: www.hi-rel.net
SIC: 3674 Mfg Semiconductors/Related Devices
PA: Hermetic Solutions Group Inc.
4000 State Route 66 # 310
Tinton Falls NJ 07753
732 722-8780

(G-1399)
JACKSON CORRUGATED CONT CORP
45 River Rd (06426-1302)
PHONE..................................860 767-3373
William P Herlihy, *President*
Paula Bingham, *Admin Sec*
EMP: 40 **EST:** 1949
SQ FT: 60,000
SALES (est): 7.1MM **Privately Held**
WEB: www.jacksonbox.com
SIC: 2653 Mfg Corrugated/Solid Fiber Boxes

(G-1400)
JB FILTRATION LLC
18 River Road Dr (06426-1377)
P.O. Box 793 (06426-0793)
PHONE..................................860 333-7962
Matthew F Winkler IV, *Mng Member*
Judith B Winkler, *Mng Member*
EMP: 3
SALES: 1.3MM **Privately Held**
SIC: 3677 Mfg Electronic Coils/Transformers

(G-1401)
LEE COMPANY
55 Bokum Rd (06426-1506)
PHONE..................................860 399-6281
Steve Hanssen, *Senior Buyer*
Dave Schweitzer, *Chief Engr*
Joseph Blazevich, *Engineer*
Robert Lee, *Branch Mgr*
EMP: 120
SALES (corp-wide): 207.5MM **Privately Held**
WEB: www.eeco.com
SIC: 3823 Mfg Fluid Process Control Devices
PA: The Lee Company
2 Pettipaug Rd
Westbrook CT 06498
860 399-6281

(G-1402)
LIGHTING EDGE INC
50 West Ave Ste 4 (06426-1163)
P.O. Box 925 (06426-0925)
PHONE..................................860 767-8968
William Barber, *President*
Scott Thompson, *Admin Sec*
EMP: 5
SQ FT: 8,000
SALES: 540K **Privately Held**
WEB: www.lightingedge.com
SIC: 3646 5063 Mfg Commercial Lighting Fixtures Whol Electrical Equipment

(G-1403)
LIMB-IT-LESS LOGGING LLC
182 Saybrook Rd (06426-1414)
PHONE..................................860 227-0987
Andrew Clark, *CEO*
EMP: 3
SALES (est): 132.5K **Privately Held**
WEB: www.limbitlesslogging.com
SIC: 2411 Logging

(G-1404)
NEW ENGLAND JOINERY WORKS INC
19 Bokum Rd (06426-1506)
PHONE..................................860 767-3377
Matthew Ouellette, *President*
Peter Leffingwell, *Admin Sec*
EMP: 5
SQ FT: 8,600
SALES (est): 1MM **Privately Held**
SIC: 2431 2499 Mfg Millwork Mfg Wood Products

(G-1405)
SMITH HILL OF DELAWARE INC
34 Plains Rd (06426-1501)
P.O. Box 980 (06426-0980)
PHONE..................................860 767-7502
Martin A Bell, *President*
John Jackson, *Area Mgr*
Bob Jones, *Area Mgr*
Bill Rockelmann, *Area Mgr*
Jerry Stewart, *COO*
▲ **EMP:** 32
SQ FT: 52,000
SALES (est): 5.3MM **Privately Held**
WEB: www.bellpower.com
SIC: 3519 Mfg Internal Combustion Engines

(G-1406)
SOUNDINGS PUBLICATIONS LLC
Also Called: Woodshop News Magazine
10 Bokum Rd (06426-1500)
PHONE..................................860 767-8227
Mary Beth Morrissey, *Marketing Mgr*
Glen Mallory, *Supervisor*
EMP: 22
SALES (est): 2.8MM **Privately Held**
WEB: www.soundingspub.com
SIC: 2721 Periodicals-Publishing/Printing

(G-1407)
UNITED TECHNOLOGIES CORP
10 Curiosity Ln (06426-1356)
PHONE..................................860 767-9592
Richard Gilliland, *Branch Mgr*
EMP: 268
SALES (corp-wide): 66.5B **Publicly Held**
SIC: 3585 Mfg Refrigeration/Heating Equipment

▲ = Import ▼=Export
◆ =Import/Export

PA: United Technologies Corporation
10 Farm Springs Rd
Farmington CT 06032
860 728-7000

(G-1408)
WILT PRUF PRODUCTS INC
132 River Rd (06426-1306)
P.O. Box 469 (06426-0469)
PHONE..................................860 767-7033
Robert B Nichols Jr, *President*
Constance Casey, *Vice Pres*
EMP: 3 **EST:** 1976
SALES (est): 250K **Privately Held**
WEB: www.wiltpruf.com
SIC: 2879 Mfg Agricultural Chemicals

(G-1409)
WINTHROP TOOL LLC
55 Plains Rd (06426-1504)
PHONE..................................860 526-9079
Frederick J Malcarne,
EMP: 7
SQ FT: 2,500
SALES: 800K **Privately Held**
WEB: www.tmarksman.com
SIC: 3599 3544 Mfg Industrial Machinery Mfg Dies/Tools/Jigs/Fixtures

Fabyan
Windham County

(G-1410)
SCOTS LANDING
929 Riverside Dr (06245)
PHONE..................................860 923-0437
EMP: 3
SALES (est): 207K **Privately Held**
SIC: 3826 Mfg Analytical Instruments

Fairfield
Fairfield County

(G-1411)
200 MILL PLAIN ROAD LLC
1411 Cross Hwy (06824-1706)
PHONE..................................203 254-0113
Terrence Keegan, *Principal*
EMP: 3
SALES (est): 76.2K **Privately Held**
SIC: 2711 Newspapers-Publishing/Printing

(G-1412)
ACME UNITED CORPORATION (PA)
55 Walls Dr Ste 201 (06824-5163)
PHONE..................................203 254-6060
Walter C Johnsen, *Ch of Bd*
Brian S Olschan, *President*
Paul G Driscoll, *CFO*
◆ **EMP:** 221
SQ FT: 15,400
SALES: 137.3MM **Publicly Held**
WEB: www.acmeunited.com
SIC: 3421 2499 3842 3579 Mfg Cutting Measuring And Safety Products

(G-1413)
ADVANCED PHOTONICS INTL INC
96 Lamplighter Ln (06825-2321)
PHONE..................................203 259-0437
Dorothy Zweibaum, *President*
Frederic Zweibaum, *Vice Pres*
EMP: 3
SALES (est): 527.2K **Privately Held**
WEB: www.advancedphotonicsintl.com
SIC: 3699 3827 Mfg Electrical Equipment/Supplies

(G-1414)
ARCAT INC
173 Sherman St (06824-5823)
PHONE..................................203 929-9444
F P Jannott, *President*
Kathy Madigan, *District Mgr*
Leslie L Jannott, *Vice Pres*
Carla Nash, *Mktg Dir*
Roger Johnson, *Manager*
EMP: 8
SQ FT: 1,600
SALES (est): 958.6K **Privately Held**
WEB: www.arcat.com
SIC: 2752 2741 Lithographic Commercial Printing Misc Publishing

(G-1415)
BABCOCK & KING INCORPORATED (PA)
750 Commerce Dr (06825-5519)
PHONE..................................203 336-7989
David S Babcock, *President*
Mary K Babcock, *Chairman*
Brian Feidt, *Treasurer*
EMP: 7
SALES (est): 1MM **Privately Held**
SIC: 2891 5032 Mfg Adhesives/Sealants Whol Brick/Stone Material

(G-1416)
BEEHIVE HEAT TREATING SVCS INC
373 Katona Dr (06824-4047)
PHONE..................................203 866-1635
Barry Brown, *President*
EMP: 8
SALES (est): 629.4K **Privately Held**
SIC: 3398 Metal Heat Treating

(G-1417)
CALMARE THERAPEUTICS INC (PA)
1375 Kings Hwy Ste 400 (06824-5380)
PHONE..................................203 368-6044
Peter Brennan, *Ch of Bd*
Conrad F Mir, *President*
Thomas P Richtarich, *CFO*
Stephen J D'Amato, *Chief Mktg Ofcr*
Donna Mays, *Info Tech Mgr*
EMP: 7
SQ FT: 2,700
SALES: 1.1MM **Publicly Held**
WEB: www.competitivetech.net
SIC: 3841 Mfg Surgical & Medical Instruments

(G-1418)
CIMBALI USA INC
418 Meadow St Ste 203 (06824-5365)
PHONE..................................203 254-6046
Erwin Pas, *President*
Assaad Benabid, *Vice Pres*
Darcy Simonis, *Admin Sec*
▲ **EMP:** 5
SQ FT: 2,500
SALES: 500K
SALES (corp-wide): 159.1MM **Privately Held**
WEB: www.cimbali.com
SIC: 3556 Mfg Food Products Machinery
PA: Gruppo Cimbali Spa
Via Alessandro Manzoni 17
Binasco MI 20082
029 004-91

(G-1419)
CLARKTRON PRODUCTS INC
1525 Kings Hwy Ste 7 (06824-5321)
PHONE..................................203 333-6517
William F Mason Jr, *President*
EMP: 8 **EST:** 1950
SQ FT: 5,000
SALES (est): 1.1MM **Privately Held**
WEB: www.clarktron.com
SIC: 3625 Mfg Industrial Control Systems

(G-1420)
CLEAN AIR GROUP INC
Also Called: Atmosair
418 Meadow St Ste 204 (06824-5365)
PHONE..................................203 335-3700
Steve Levine, *President*
Carlos Gendron, *Vice Pres*
Tony Abate, *Purch Agent*
Michael Herz, *CFO*
James McManus, *CFO*
EMP: 21
SQ FT: 1,500
SALES (est): 2.4MM **Privately Held**
SIC: 3564 Mfg Blowers/Fans

(G-1421)
COASTAL SEAFOODS INC (PA)
35 Brentwood Ave Ste 4 (06825-5443)
P.O. Box 455, Ridgefield (06877-0455)
PHONE..................................203 431-0453
Robert Iseley, *President*
Linda Iseley, *Corp Secy*
EMP: 12
SQ FT: 5,000
SALES (est): 1.3MM **Privately Held**
SIC: 2092 5146 Mfg Fresh/Frozen Fish Whol Fish/Seafoods

(G-1422)
COMMAND CHEMICAL CORPORATION
2490 Black Rock Tpke # 359 (06825-2400)
PHONE..................................203 319-1857
Robert Lesko, *President*
Lori Ann Lesko, *Vice Pres*
◆ **EMP:** 9
SQ FT: 15,000
SALES (est): 3.6MM **Privately Held**
SIC: 2899 Mfg Chemical Preparations

(G-1423)
CONNECTICUT GREENSTAR INC
1157 Melville Ave (06825-2057)
P.O. Box 921, Los Olivos CA (93441-0921)
PHONE..................................203 368-1522
Val Luca, *President*
Olga Luca, *Admin Sec*
▲ **EMP:** 3
SALES (est): 210K **Privately Held**
SIC: 3429 Mfg Hardware

(G-1424)
CONNECTICUT TRADE COMPANY INC
1157 Melville Ave (06825-2057)
P.O. Box 921, Los Olivos CA (93441-0921)
PHONE..................................203 368-0398
Val Luca, *President*
▲ **EMP:** 3
SALES: 5MM **Privately Held**
SIC: 3429 7389 Mfg Hardware Business Services At Non-Commercial Site

(G-1425)
CONVEXITY SCIENTIFIC LLC
418 Meadow St (06824-5364)
PHONE..................................949 637-1216
Ralph Mng, *Principal*
Ralph Finger, *Mng Member*
James Benjamin,
EMP: 3
SALES (est): 95.3K **Privately Held**
SIC: 3841 Mfg Surgical/Medical Instruments

(G-1426)
DIRECT SALES LLC (PA)
440 Sky Top Dr (06825-1219)
PHONE..................................203 371-2373
Anthony Reis,
EMP: 5
SQ FT: 8,200
SALES (est): 531.9K **Privately Held**
SIC: 3272 Building Materials Wholesale

(G-1427)
DOMESTIC KITCHENS INC
515 Commerce Dr (06825-5541)
PHONE..................................203 368-1651
Pasquale Staltaro, *President*
Frank Staltaro, *Corp Secy*
EMP: 27
SALES (est): 4.2MM **Privately Held**
SIC: 2434 Mfg Wood Kitchen Cabinets

(G-1428)
EARLY ADVANTAGE LLC
426 Mine Hill Rd (06824-2151)
PHONE..................................203 259-6480
David Ward, *Mng Member*
▲ **EMP:** 10
SALES (est): 1.2MM **Privately Held**
WEB: www.early-advantage.com
SIC: 2731 Books-Publishing/Printing

(G-1429)
EMC CORPORATION
2150 Post Rd Fl 5 (06824-5669)
PHONE..................................203 418-4500
Dave Sheehan, *General Mgr*
Nicholas Giudice, *Engineer*
EMP: 65
SALES (corp-wide): 90.6B **Publicly Held**
SIC: 3572 Mfg Computer Storage Devices
HQ: Emc Corporation
176 South St
Hopkinton MA 01748
508 435-1000

(G-1430)
EMC7 LLC
149 Brookview Ave (06825-1867)
PHONE..................................203 429-4355
Rebecca Ryan, *Principal*
Curt Kibbe, *Principal*
David Orloff, *Principal*
EMP: 4
SALES (est): 170.2K **Privately Held**
SIC: 3572 Mfg Computer Storage Devices

(G-1431)
FAIRFIELD POOL & EQUIPMENT CO (PA)
278 Meadow St (06824-5353)
PHONE..................................203 334-3600
Jeromy Luem, *President*
EMP: 6
SQ FT: 11,000
SALES (est): 1.9MM **Privately Held**
WEB: www.fairfieldpool.com
SIC: 3949 5999 1799 Mfg Sporting/Athletic Goods Ret Misc Merchandise Trade Contractor

(G-1432)
FOCUS NOW SOLUTIONS LLC
Also Called: Nootelligence
1140 Post Rd (06824-6020)
PHONE..................................203 247-9038
Ian O'Connell, *Mng Member*
Tyler Debussy,
Parjer Klingerman,
EMP: 3
SALES (est): 239.2K **Privately Held**
SIC: 2087 Mfg Flavor Extracts/Syrup

(G-1433)
FRESCOBENE FOODS LLC
185 Red Oak Rd (06824-1898)
PHONE..................................203 610-4688
Lisa Maute, *CEO*
Ann Riffice, *Principal*
EMP: 3
SALES (est): 206.1K **Privately Held**
SIC: 2099 Mfg Food Preparations

(G-1434)
GE ENRGY PWR CNVERSION USA INC
3135 Eon Tpke (06828)
PHONE..................................203 373-2211
EMP: 3
SALES (corp-wide): 121.6B **Publicly Held**
SIC: 3629 Mfg Electrical Industrial Apparatus
HQ: Ge Energy Power Conversion Usa Inc.
100 E Kensinger Dr
Cranberry Township PA 16066
412 967-0765

(G-1435)
GE TRANSPORTATION PARTS LLC
3135 Easton Tpke (06828-0002)
P.O. Box 60320, Fort Myers FL (33906-6320)
PHONE..................................816 650-6171
EMP: 8 **EST:** 2001
SALES (est): 386.8K
SALES (corp-wide): 121.6B **Publicly Held**
SIC: 3511 Turbines And Turbine Generator Sets, Nsk
PA: General Electric Company
5 Necco St
Boston MA 02210
617 443-3000

(G-1436)
GRAYBARK ENTERPRISES LLC
20 Governors Ln (06824-2106)
PHONE..................................203 255-4503
Mark Grayson,
EMP: 9

GEOGRAPHIC

SALES (est): 439.6K **Privately Held**
SIC: 7372 Prepackaged Software Services

(G-1437)
IPC SYSTEMS INC
Also Called: IPC Information Systems
777 Commerce Dr Ste 100 (06825-5500)
PHONE..................................860 271-4100
Tim Bachmann, *Senior Engr*
Peter Gyurko, *Branch Mgr*
Diane Lonigro, *Senior Mgr*
Ann Everett, *Analyst*
Tim Curran, *Recruiter*
EMP: 135
SALES (corp-wide): 490.9MM **Privately Held**
SIC: 3661 Mfg Telephone/Telegraph Apparatus
PA: I.P.C. Systems, Inc.
3 2nd St Fl Plz10
Jersey City NJ 07311
201 253-2000

(G-1438)
JK MOTORSPORTS
500 Grasmere Ave (06824-6146)
PHONE..................................203 255-9120
Jerome Kozera, *Principal*
EMP: 4
SALES (est): 270K **Privately Held**
SIC: 3714 Mfg Motor Vehicle Parts/Accessories

(G-1439)
JOLEN CREAM BLEACH CORP
25 Walls Dr (06824-5156)
P.O. Box 458 (06824-0458)
PHONE..................................203 259-8779
Evelyn Kossak, *President*
Melissa Flores, *Publications*
EMP: 15 **EST:** 1964
SQ FT: 8,000
SALES (est): 1.5MM **Privately Held**
SIC: 2844 Mfg Cosmetic Cream

(G-1440)
KATONA BAKERY LLC
1189 Post Rd Ste 3b (06824-6046)
PHONE..................................203 337-5349
Ken Kleban,
EMP: 22
SALES (est): 727.4K **Privately Held**
SIC: 2051 Mfg Bread/Related Products

(G-1441)
L R K COMMUNICATIONS INC
Also Called: American Litho
96 Toll House Ln (06825-1030)
PHONE..................................203 372-1456
Lionel Ketchian, *President*
Lionel R Ketchian, *President*
Barbara E Ketchian, *Corp Secy*
Glen L Ketchian, *Vice Pres*
EMP: 4
SQ FT: 1,000
SALES (est): 497.9K **Privately Held**
WEB: www.lrkcommunications.com
SIC: 2759 Commercial Printing

(G-1442)
LIFETIME ACRYLIC SIGNS INC
593 Cascade Dr (06825-2300)
PHONE..................................203 255-6751
Joel Bernstein, *President*
EMP: 8 **EST:** 1957
SQ FT: 8,000
SALES (est): 591K **Privately Held**
SIC: 3993 Mfg Signs/Advertising Specialties

(G-1443)
MET TECH INC
1901 Post Rd (06824-5721)
PHONE..................................203 254-9319
Thomas Quick, *President*
Thomas Qucik, *President*
EMP: 3 **EST:** 1993
SALES: 500K **Privately Held**
WEB: www.mettech.com
SIC: 3449 Mfg Misc Structural Metalwork

(G-1444)
MICKEY HERBST
Also Called: Quality Printing & Graphics
32 Laurel St (06825-4218)
PHONE..................................203 993-5879
Ryan Zygmont, *Owner*
EMP: 5
SALES (est): 234K **Privately Held**
SIC: 2759 Commercial Printing

(G-1445)
MODERN ELECTRONIC FAX & CMPT
Also Called: Modern Elec Fax & Computers
65 Milton St (06824-6921)
PHONE..................................203 292-6520
Naresh Doshi, *President*
EMP: 5
SQ FT: 2,000
SALES (est): 729.3K **Privately Held**
WEB: www.mecdot.com
SIC: 3571 7373 1731 7378 Computer Assembly System Integration Lan Install & Service Computers Faxes Copiers Printers & Other Office Equipment

(G-1446)
MOHICAN VALLEY CONCRETE CORP
195 Ardmore St (06824-6127)
PHONE..................................203 254-7133
Mark Greenawalt, *CEO*
Thomas Greenawalt II, *Vice Pres*
Donna Sedgewick, *Treasurer*
Thomas Greenawalt Sr, *Shareholder*
EMP: 20
SQ FT: 2,700
SALES (est): 3.9MM **Privately Held**
WEB: www.mohicanvalley.com
SIC: 3273 Mfg Ready-Mixed Concrete

(G-1447)
MOHICAN VLY SAND & GRAV CORP
195 Ardmore St (06824-6127)
PHONE..................................203 254-7133
Mark Greenawalt Jr, *President*
Donna Sedgewick, *Corp Secy*
Thomas Greenawalt Jr, *Vice Pres*
Thomas Greenawalt Sr, *Shareholder*
EMP: 15
SQ FT: 2,500
SALES (est): 5MM **Privately Held**
SIC: 3273 Mfg Ready-Mixed Concrete

(G-1448)
PARISH ASSOCIATES INC
1383 Kings Hwy (06824-5312)
P.O. Box 2543, Bridgeport (06608-0543)
PHONE..................................203 335-4100
Paul C Zec, *President*
▲ **EMP:** 5
SQ FT: 3,600
SALES (est): 613.3K **Privately Held**
SIC: 2511 Garden And Building Equipment Distributors

(G-1449)
POWER STRATEGIES LLC
2384 Redding Rd (06824-1760)
PHONE..................................203 254-9926
J Norman Allen, *Principal*
EMP: 3
SALES (est): 176.1K **Privately Held**
SIC: 3621 Mfg Motors/Generators

(G-1450)
RBC LINEAR PRECISION PDTS INC
60 Round Hill Rd (06824-5172)
PHONE..................................203 255-1511
EMP: 4
SALES (est): 347K
SALES (corp-wide): 702.5MM **Publicly Held**
SIC: 3562 Mfg Ball/Roller Bearings
PA: Rbc Bearings Incorporated
102 Willenbrock Rd
Oxford CT 06478
203 267-7001

(G-1451)
RC BIGELOW INC (PA)
Also Called: Bigelow Tea
201 Black Rock Tpke (06825-5512)
PHONE..................................888 244-3569
David C Bigelow, *Ch of Bd*
Cindi Bigelow, *President*
Cynthia Bigelow, *Co-President*
Lori Bigelow, *Co-President*
Eunice Bigelow, *Co-COB*
◆ **EMP:** 170 **EST:** 1945
SQ FT: 113,000
SALES (est): 94.8MM **Privately Held**
WEB: www.rcbigelow.com
SIC: 2099 Ret Misc Foods

(G-1452)
RIVERSIDE BAKING COMPANY LLC
1891 Post Rd (06824-5742)
PHONE..................................203 451-0331
Richard Schneider, *Principal*
EMP: 4
SALES (est): 99.1K **Privately Held**
SIC: 2051 Mfg Bread/Related Products

(G-1453)
SABON INDUSTRIES INC
150 Jennie Ln (06824-1914)
PHONE..................................203 255-8880
Leslie N Wilder, *President*
Leslie Wilder, *Owner*
EMP: 6
SQ FT: 6,000
SALES (est): 550K **Privately Held**
WEB: www.sabonindustries.com
SIC: 2522 Mfg Office Furniture-Nonwood

(G-1454)
SANCO ENERGY
41 Riders Ln (06824-1940)
PHONE..................................203 259-5914
EMP: 12
SALES (est): 637.5K **Privately Held**
SIC: 2869 Ethanol Manufacturing

(G-1455)
SCHINDLER COMBUSTION LLC
159 Tahmore Dr (06825-2513)
PHONE..................................203 371-5068
Edmund G Schindler,
EMP: 3 **EST:** 2015
SALES (est): 288.3K **Privately Held**
SIC: 3433 Mfg Heating Equipment-Nonelectric

(G-1456)
SIXFURLONGS LLC
382 Round Hill Rd (06824-5116)
PHONE..................................203 255-8553
John Short, *Principal*
EMP: 4
SALES (est): 239.3K **Privately Held**
SIC: 2721 7313 Periodicals-Publishing/Printing Advertising Representative

(G-1457)
TECHNISONIC RESEARCH INC
328 Commerce Dr (06825-5560)
PHONE..................................203 368-3600
Kenneth Thompson, *President*
Joseph Di Blasi, *Vice Pres*
Tony Ruiz, *Sales Staff*
EMP: 9
SQ FT: 3,000
SALES (est): 2MM **Privately Held**
SIC: 3829 Mfr Ultrasonic Testing Equipment

(G-1458)
UNCLE WILEYS INC
1220 Post Rd Ste 2 (06824-6027)
PHONE..................................203 256-9313
Wiley Mullins, *President*
Greg Hill, *Admin Sec*
EMP: 16 **EST:** 1992
SQ FT: 6,000
SALES (est): 2.4MM **Privately Held**
WEB: www.unclewileys.com
SIC: 2099 Mfg Food Preparations

(G-1459)
UNIVERSAL THREAD GRINDING CO
30 Chambers St (06825-5594)
PHONE..................................203 336-1849
William H Everett Jr, *President*
Carl Linley, *Treasurer*
EMP: 15 **EST:** 1947
SQ FT: 10,000
SALES (est): 2.7MM **Privately Held**
WEB: www.universal-thread.com
SIC: 3452 Mfg Bolts/Screws/Rivets

(G-1460)
VENU MAGAZINE LLC
840 Reef Rd (06824-6540)
PHONE..................................203 259-2075
Tracey Alison Thomas, *Principal*
▲ **EMP:** 3
SALES (est): 195.7K **Privately Held**
SIC: 2721 Periodicals-Publishing/Printing

(G-1461)
VOICE EXPRESS CORP
1525 Kings Hwy Ste 1 (06824-5321)
PHONE..................................203 221-7799
Geoffrey Stern, *President*
Rick Rubin, *Vice Pres*
▲ **EMP:** 3
SQ FT: 1,000
SALES: 1.5MM **Privately Held**
WEB: www.voice-express.com
SIC: 3669 Mfg Communications Equipment

Falls Village
Litchfield County

(G-1462)
CROSSROADS DELI & FUEL LLC
123 Johnson Rd (06031-1618)
PHONE..................................860 824-8474
Michael Hodgkins, *Principal*
EMP: 6
SALES (est): 823.7K **Privately Held**
SIC: 2869 Mfg Industrial Organic Chemicals

(G-1463)
HAMILTONBOOKCOM LLC
147 Route 7 S (06031-1603)
P.O. Box 5007 (06031-5007)
PHONE..................................860 824-0275
John J Tuozzolo, *Principal*
EMP: 3
SALES (est): 179.1K **Privately Held**
SIC: 2711 Newspapers-Publishing/Printing

Farmington
Hartford County

(G-1464)
AGENCYPORT SOFTWARE CORP
Also Called: Sword-Agencyport
190 Farmington Ave (06032-1713)
PHONE..................................860 674-6135
EMP: 3
SALES (corp-wide): 21MM **Privately Held**
SIC: 7372 Software Solutions
HQ: Agencyport Software Corporation
22 Boston Wharf Rd 10
Boston MA 02210
866 539-6623

(G-1465)
ANAPO PLASTICS CORP
222 Main St 214 (06032-3623)
PHONE..................................860 874-8174
Carmelo Piraneo, *President*
EMP: 3
SALES (est): 319.6K **Privately Held**
SIC: 2821 Mfg Plastic Materials/Resins

(G-1466)
AVITUS ORTHOPAEDICS INC
400 Farmington Ave R2826 (06032-1913)
PHONE..................................860 637-9922
Neil Shah, *President*
EMP: 10
SALES (est): 1.3MM **Privately Held**
SIC: 3842 Mfg Surgical Appliances/Supplies

(G-1467)
BARNES GROUP INC
Barnes Aerospace
80 Scott Swamp Rd (06032-2847)
PHONE..................................860 298-7740
Scott Mayo, *Vice Pres*
Joel Rafaniello, *Vice Pres*

Gregory Milzcik, *Manager*
Robert Dutton, *Manager*
EMP: 8
SALES (corp-wide): 1.5B **Publicly Held**
WEB: www.barnesgroupinc.com
SIC: 3495 3469 Mfg Wire Springs Mfg Metal Stampings
PA: Barnes Group Inc.
123 Main St
Bristol CT 06010
860 583-7070

(G-1468)
BIOARRAY GENETICS INC
400 Farmington Ave (06032-1913)
PHONE..................................508 577-0205
EMP: 3
SALES (est): 182.9K **Privately Held**
SIC: 2835 Diagnostic Substances, Nsk

(G-1469)
BREACH INTELLIGENCE INC
Also Called: Polarity
6 S Ridge Rd (06032-3021)
PHONE..................................844 312-7001
Paul Battista, *CEO*
Edmund Dorsey, *Treasurer*
Joseph Rivela, *Admin Sec*
EMP: 20
SALES (est): 171.6K **Privately Held**
SIC: 7372 Prepackaged Software Services

(G-1470)
BROADCASTMED INC
Also Called: Or-Live, Inc.
195 Farmington Ave (06032-1700)
PHONE..................................860 953-2900
Ross J Joel, *CEO*
Peter Gailey, *President*
Joslyn Dalton, *Vice Pres*
Richard Meyer, *CFO*
Denise Callan, *Producer*
EMP: 22
SQ FT: 5,000
SALES: 5.1MM **Privately Held**
SIC: 2741 Internet Publishing And Broadcasting

(G-1471)
CARRIER CORPORATION
426 Colt Hwy (06032-2587)
PHONE..................................860 728-7000
Allen Johnson, *Principal*
Bryan Mitchell, *Advt Staff*
EMP: 4
SALES (corp-wide): 66.5B **Publicly Held**
SIC: 3585 Plumbing/Heating/Air Cond Contractor
HQ: Carrier Corporation
13995 Pasteur Blvd
Palm Beach Gardens FL 33418
800 379-6484

(G-1472)
CISCO SYSTEMS INC
50 Stanford Dr (06032-2474)
PHONE..................................860 284-5500
Daniel Johnson, *Engineer*
Tim Jahrling, *Sales Staff*
Dave Chalfon, *Branch Mgr*
Mike Saviano, *Manager*
Bob Williston, *Executive*
EMP: 691
SALES (corp-wide): 51.9B **Publicly Held**
WEB: www.cisco.com
SIC: 3577 Mfg Computer Peripheral Equipment
PA: Cisco Systems, Inc.
170 W Tasman Dr
San Jose CA 95134
408 526-4000

(G-1473)
CONNECTCUT SPRING STMPING CORP
Also Called: Connecticut Spring & Stamping
48 Spring Ln (06032-3140)
PHONE..................................860 677-1341
William Stevenson, *President*
Shawn Gibbons, *President*
Steve Dicke, *Vice Pres*
David Fischler, *Vice Pres*
Chuck Thomas, *Vice Pres*
▲ **EMP:** 500 **EST:** 1939
SQ FT: 150,000
SALES (est): 123.6MM **Privately Held**
SIC: 3469 3495 3493 Mfg Metal Stampings Mfg Wire Springs Mfg Steel Spring-Nonwire

(G-1474)
CONNECTICUT CONCRETE FORM INC
168 Brickyard Rd (06032-1202)
PHONE..................................860 674-1314
Richard N Dahle, *President*
EMP: 18
SQ FT: 12,000
SALES (est): 3.4MM **Privately Held**
SIC: 3271 Mfg Concrete Block/Brick

(G-1475)
COROTEC CORP
145 Hyde Rd (06032-2846)
PHONE..................................860 678-0038
Bruce D Stobbe, *President*
Thomas Ignatowski, *Managing Dir*
David Dufourny, *Engineer*
Steve Easterday, *Treasurer*
Ronald Seaman, *VP Sales*
EMP: 13
SQ FT: 16,000
SALES (est): 2.8MM
SALES (corp-wide): 1B **Privately Held**
WEB: www.corotec.com
SIC: 3613 Mfg Switchgear/Switchboards
HQ: Indel, Inc.
10 Indel Ave
Rancocas NJ 08073
609 267-9000

(G-1476)
DAYON MANUFACTURING INC
1820 New Britain Ave (06032-3114)
P.O. Box 588 (06034-0588)
PHONE..................................860 677-8561
Leslie R Dayon, *President*
Rose Dayon Sonstroem, *Vice Pres*
Kim Sonstroem, *Treasurer*
▲ **EMP:** 32 **EST:** 1957
SQ FT: 17,000
SALES (est): 5.6MM **Privately Held**
WEB: www.dayonmfg.com
SIC: 3495 3493 Mfg Wire Springs Mfg Steel Springs-Nonwire

(G-1477)
DUNDEE HOLDING INC (DH)
36 Spring Ln (06032-3140)
PHONE..................................860 677-1376
EMP: 8
SALES (est): 24MM **Privately Held**
SIC: 3324 3599 Steel Investment Foundry Mfg Industrial Machinery
HQ: Doncasters 456 Limited
Millennium Court
Burton-On-Trent STAFFS
133 286-4900

(G-1478)
DUNNING SAND & GRAVEL COMPANY
105 Brickyard Rd (06032-1236)
PHONE..................................860 677-1616
Benjamin Dunning, *President*
EMP: 12
SQ FT: 900
SALES (est): 4.6MM **Privately Held**
WEB: www.dunningsand.com
SIC: 1442 Construction Sand/Gravel

(G-1479)
EAST COAST PACKAGING LLC (PA)
210 Main St Unit 1182 (06034-7047)
P.O. Box 1182 (06034-1182)
PHONE..................................860 675-8500
Laura Lachance, *Mng Member*
Michael Lachance,
EMP: 3
SQ FT: 5,000
SALES (est): 1.1MM **Privately Held**
WEB: www.eastcoastpkg.com
SIC: 2752 7389 Lithographic Commercial Printing Business Services

(G-1480)
EDMUNDS MANUFACTURING COMPANY (PA)
Also Called: Edmunds Gages
45 Spring Ln (06032-3139)
P.O. Box 385 (06034-0385)
PHONE..................................860 677-2813
Robert F Edmunds Sr, *Ch of Bd*
Robert F Edmunds Jr, *Chairman*
Robert F Edmunds III, *Vice Pres*
Gary A Hutchinson, *Engineer*
Scott Sokolik, *Engineer*
EMP: 100
SQ FT: 43,000
SALES (est): 13.6MM **Privately Held**
WEB: www.edmundsgages.com
SIC: 3829 3545 Mfg Measuring/Controlling Devices Mfg Machine Tool Accessories

(G-1481)
FARMINGTON DISPLAYS INC
Also Called: F D I
21 Hyde Rd Ste 2 (06032-2859)
PHONE..................................860 677-2497
Sabastian Ditomosso, *President*
Robert Ditommaso, *General Mgr*
Maria Fabrizi, *Corp Secy*
Paul F Ditomaso Jr, *Vice Pres*
Salvatore Ditomaso, *Vice Pres*
▲ **EMP:** 45
SQ FT: 130,000
SALES (est): 7.6MM **Privately Held**
WEB: www.fdi-group.com
SIC: 3993 Mfg Signs/Advertising Specialties

(G-1482)
FORMATRON LTD
21 Hyde Rd (06032-2859)
PHONE..................................860 676-0227
Salvatore Ditommaso, *President*
Paul Ditommaso Jr, *Principal*
EMP: 18
SQ FT: 25,000
SALES (est): 2.6MM **Privately Held**
WEB: www.formatron.com
SIC: 2541 3999 Mfg Wood Partitions/Fixtures Mfg Misc Products

(G-1483)
FREDERICKS JF AERO LLC
25 Spring Ln (06032-3128)
PHONE..................................860 677-2646
Robert Mongell, *Mng Member*
Stephen Gabbert, *Officer*
Jerry Sirois,
▼ **EMP:** 92
SQ FT: 25,000
SALES (est): 21.9MM
SALES (corp-wide): 19.7MM **Privately Held**
WEB: www.jfftool.com
SIC: 3724 Mfg Aircraft Engines/Parts
PA: Wentworth Manufacturing Llc
1102 Windham Rd
South Windham CT 06266
860 423-4575

(G-1484)
FREQUENCY THERAPEUTICS INC
400 Farmington Ave (06032-1913)
PHONE..................................978 436-0704
David L Lucchino, *President*
EMP: 26
SALES (corp-wide): 471.6K **Publicly Held**
SIC: 2834 Mfg Pharmaceutical Preparations
PA: Frequency Therapeutics, Inc.
19 Presidential Way Fl 2
Woburn MA 01801
866 389-1970

(G-1485)
FUEL LAB
20 Burnt Hill Rd (06032-2039)
PHONE..................................860 677-4987
Shashi Bansal, *Owner*
EMP: 5 **EST:** 2011
SALES (est): 266.5K **Privately Held**
SIC: 2869 Mfg Industrial Organic Chemicals

(G-1486)
INNOVATION GROUP
76 Batterson Park Rd (06032-2571)
PHONE..................................860 674-2900
Euan King, *CEO*
Chris Benecick, *Exec VP*
Mitch Letho, *Exec VP*
Andrew Peet, *Exec VP*
Stacie Wolf, *CFO*
EMP: 22
SALES (est): 4.3MM **Privately Held**
SIC: 7372 7371 Prepackaged Software Services Custom Computer Programing
HQ: The Innovation Group Limited
Yarmouth House
Fareham HANTS
148 989-8300

(G-1487)
INTEGRITY MANUFACTURING LLC
1451 New Britain Ave # 1 (06032-3348)
PHONE..................................860 678-1599
James Gadoury, *Mng Member*
EMP: 6
SQ FT: 3,200
SALES (est): 679.2K **Privately Held**
SIC: 3423 Mfg Hand/Edge Tools

(G-1488)
KIP INC
Also Called: Norgren
72 Spring Ln (06032-3140)
PHONE..................................860 677-0272
Nick Testanero, *President*
Nicholas Testanero, *President*
Gary Fett, *Vice Pres*
James Etter, *Treasurer*
Donald McMahan, *Admin Sec*
▲ **EMP:** 189
SALES (est): 53.4K
SALES (corp-wide): 2.5B **Privately Held**
SIC: 3491 Mfg Industrial Valves
HQ: Norgren Limited
Blenheim Way
Lichfield STAFFS WS13
154 326-5000

(G-1489)
LAMBDAVISION INCORPORATED
400 Farmington Ave Mc6409 (06032-1913)
PHONE..................................860 486-6593
Nicole Wagner, *CEO*
Mark Van Allen, *President*
EMP: 3
SALES (est): 269.9K **Privately Held**
SIC: 3841 Mfg Surgical/Medical Instruments

(G-1490)
LIPID GENOMICS INC
400 Farmington Ave R1718 (06032-1913)
PHONE..................................443 465-3495
Annabelle Rodriguez-Oquendo, *President*
Eric Oquendo, *Business Mgr*
Debora Wilder, *Accountant*
EMP: 4 **EST:** 2014
SALES (est): 351.9K **Privately Held**
SIC: 2834 Mfg Pharmaceutical Preparations

(G-1491)
LITHOGRAPHICS INC
55 Spring Ln (06032-3139)
P.O. Box 767 (06034-0767)
PHONE..................................860 678-1660
Judith A Wilson, *President*
Thomas R Smith, *Vice Pres*
Glenn H Wilson, *Treasurer*
Twyla Lambert, *Sales Staff*
Jill W Kijanka, *Admin Sec*
EMP: 54
SQ FT: 31,800
SALES (est): 9.4MM **Privately Held**
WEB: www.litholand.com
SIC: 2752 Lithographic Commercial Printing

(G-1492)
MICROSOFT CORPORATION
74 Batterson Park Rd # 100 (06032-2591)
PHONE..................................860 678-3100
Bernie Odoy, *Principal*
Anissa Battaglino, *Manager*

GEOGRAPHIC

EMP: 45
SQ FT: 14,000
SALES (corp-wide): 125.8B **Publicly Held**
WEB: www.microsoft.com
SIC: 7372 Prepackaged Software Services
PA: Microsoft Corporation
1 Microsoft Way
Redmond WA 98052
425 882-8080

(G-1493)
MOTT CORPORATION (PA)
84 Spring Ln (06032-3142)
PHONE..................................860 793-6333
Boris F Levin, *CEO*
David Allen, *Vice Pres*
Jamie Stringer, *Mfg Mgr*
Robert Sjogren, *Opers Staff*
Aravind Mohanram, *Research*
◆ **EMP:** 189 **EST:** 1959
SQ FT: 50,000
SALES (est): 58.5MM **Privately Held**
WEB: www.mottcorp.com
SIC: 3569 Mfg General Industrial Machinery

(G-1494)
MOTT CORPORATION
75 Spring Ln (06032-3139)
PHONE..................................800 289-6688
Roger Klene, *Manager*
EMP: 180
SQ FT: 36,000
SALES (est): 18.2MM
SALES (corp-wide): 58.5MM **Privately Held**
WEB: www.mottcorp.com
SIC: 3312 Mfg Tool & Die Steel & Alloys
PA: Mott Corporation
84 Spring Ln
Farmington CT 06032
860 793-6333

(G-1495)
NATIONAL INTEGRATED INDS INC (PA)
Also Called: American Electro Products
322 Main St (06032-2961)
P.O. Box 4129, Waterbury (06704-0129)
PHONE..................................860 677-7995
Dennis M Burke, *President*
EMP: 135
SQ FT: 100,000
SALES (est): 15MM **Privately Held**
SIC: 3471 3312 Plating/Polishing Svcs Blast Furnace-Steel Work

(G-1496)
NATURAL POLYMER DEVICES INC
400 Farmington Ave Mc6409 (06032-1913)
PHONE..................................860 679-7894
EMP: 3
SALES (est): 184.2K **Privately Held**
SIC: 3841 Surgical And Medical Instruments

(G-1497)
NELSON STUD WELDING INC
36 Spring Ln (06032-3140)
PHONE..................................800 635-9353
Ken Caratelli, *President*
EMP: 3
SALES (corp-wide): 13.9B **Publicly Held**
SIC: 3452 3548 Mfg Bolts/Screws/Rivets Mfg Welding Apparatus
HQ: Nelson Stud Welding, Inc.
7900 W Ridge Rd
Elyria OH 44035
440 329-0400

(G-1498)
NEW ENGLAND AIRFOIL PDTS INC
36 Spring Ln (06032-3140)
PHONE..................................860 677-1376
Stefano Rosa Uliana, *President*
EMP: 25
SQ FT: 100,000
SALES (est): 2.1MM
SALES (corp-wide): 347.8K **Privately Held**
SIC: 3721 3724 3795 Mfg Aircraft Mfg Aircraft Engines/Parts Mfg Tanks/Tank Components
HQ: Pietro Rosa T.B.M. Srl
Via Francesco Petrarca 7
Maniago PN 33085
042 771-503

(G-1499)
NEW ENGLAND SHOULDER ELBOW SOC
Also Called: Neses
232 Farmington Ave (06030-0001)
PHONE..................................860 679-6600
Jon JP Warner, *President*
Ben Banister, *Instructor*
EMP: 3
SALES (est): 124.5K **Privately Held**
SIC: 3842 Surgical Appliances And Supplies, Nsk

(G-1500)
NORGREN INC
Also Called: IMI Precision Engineering
72 Spring Ln (06032-3140)
P.O. Box 468 (06034-0468)
PHONE..................................860 677-0272
Nick Testanero, *Branch Mgr*
EMP: 200
SALES (corp-wide): 2.5B **Privately Held**
WEB: www.norgren.com
SIC: 3492 Mfg Fluid Power Valves/Fittings
HQ: Norgren, Inc.
5400 S Delaware St
Littleton CO 80120
303 794-5000

(G-1501)
NORTHEAST PANEL CO LLC
325 Main St Ste 3 (06032-2977)
PHONE..................................860 678-9078
Bert Rompre, *Principal*
EMP: 5
SALES (est): 430K **Privately Held**
SIC: 3444 Manufactures Sheet Metalwork Specializing In Metal Roofing

(G-1502)
ORAL FLUID DYNAMICS LLC
400 Farmington Ave R1844 (06032-1913)
PHONE..................................860 561-5036
J Robert Kelly DDS, *Manager*
J Robert Kelly DDS PHD, *Manager*
EMP: 4
SALES: 240K **Privately Held**
SIC: 3841 Mfg Surgical/Medical Instruments

(G-1503)
OTIS ELEVATOR COMPANY (HQ)
1 Carrier Pl (06032-2562)
PHONE..................................860 674-3000
Judith F Marks, *President*
Mario Abajo, *President*
Todd M Bluedorn, *President*
Bruno Grob, *President*
Angelo J Messina, *President*
◆ **EMP:** 277
SQ FT: 200,000
SALES (est): 9.3B
SALES (corp-wide): 66.5B **Publicly Held**
WEB: www.otis.com
SIC: 3534 7699 1796 Mfg Elevators/Escalators Repair Services Building Equipment Installation
PA: United Technologies Corporation
10 Farm Springs Rd
Farmington CT 06032
860 728-7000

(G-1504)
OTIS ELEVATOR COMPANY
5 Farm Springs Rd (06032-2575)
PHONE..................................860 290-3318
Jenna Parezo, *Sales Mgr*
Henry Sosa, *Accounts Mgr*
Lianne Mason, *Manager*
EMP: 8
SALES (corp-wide): 66.5B **Publicly Held**
SIC: 3534 Mfg Elevators/Escalators
HQ: Otis Elevator Company
1 Carrier Pl
Farmington CT 06032
860 674-3000

(G-1505)
PANELOC CORPORATION
142 Brickyard Rd (06032-1202)
P.O. Box 547 (06034-0547)
PHONE..................................860 677-6711
Courtney Crocker III, *President*
Michele Anstett, *Purch Mgr*
Liza Rioux, *Director*
Sarah Horner, *Admin Sec*
EMP: 32
SQ FT: 13,000
SALES (est): 5.3MM **Privately Held**
SIC: 3429 3965 Mfg Hardware Mfg Fasteners/Buttons/Pins

(G-1506)
PAR MANUFACTURING INC
Also Called: Par Thread Grinding
1824 New Britain Ave (06032-3114)
PHONE..................................860 677-1797
Ken Dimauro, *President*
John Vasellina Jr, *President*
Sal Dimauro, *Vice Pres*
EMP: 8 **EST:** 1951
SQ FT: 5,000
SALES (est): 580K **Privately Held**
WEB: www.parmfg.com
SIC: 3599 Machine Shop

(G-1507)
POLYMER RESOURCES LTD (PA)
656 New Britain Ave (06032-2146)
PHONE..................................203 324-3737
Leslie M Klein, *Ch of Bd*
William R Feldman, *President*
Robert Borrello, *Vice Pres*
William Galla, *Vice Pres*
Stephanie Vollono, *Controller*
▲ **EMP:** 60
SALES (est): 25.6MM **Privately Held**
WEB: www.polymerresources.com
SIC: 2821 Mfg Plastic Materials/Resins

(G-1508)
POST MORTEM SERVICES LLC
82 Knollwood Rd (06032-1029)
PHONE..................................860 675-1103
Paul Marduson, *Owner*
EMP: 4
SALES (est): 267.6K **Privately Held**
SIC: 3444 Mfg Sheet Metalwork

(G-1509)
PROGRESSIVE STAMPING CO DE INC
36 Spring Ln (06032-3140)
PHONE..................................248 299-7100
Doug Shantz, *General Mgr*
▲ **EMP:** 45
SQ FT: 65,000
SALES (est): 4.6MM
SALES (corp-wide): 604.8MM **Privately Held**
WEB: www.progressivestamping.com
SIC: 3465 3452 Mfg Automotive Stampings Mfg Bolts/Screws/Rivets
HQ: Fastentech, Inc.
8500 Normandale Lake Blvd
Minneapolis MN 55437
952 921-2090

(G-1510)
RAYM-CO INC
62 Spring Ln (06032-3140)
PHONE..................................860 678-8292
Sarah Artibani, *President*
Karen Motta, *General Mgr*
Brandon Artibani, *Vice Pres*
Earl Reilly, *Opers Mgr*
EMP: 43 **EST:** 1980
SQ FT: 35,000
SALES: 4.3MM **Privately Held**
SIC: 3599 Mfg Industrial Machinery

(G-1511)
SAAR CORPORATION
81 Spring Ln (06032-3139)
PHONE..................................860 674-9440
Mariusz Saar, *President*
Krystyna Saar, *Vice Pres*
Luke Saar, *Vice Pres*
Angela Gladding, *Office Mgr*
Kurt Stephens, *Director*
EMP: 13
SQ FT: 8,000
SALES (est): 3.1MM **Privately Held**
WEB: www.saarmed.com
SIC: 3841 3724 Mfg Surgical/Medical Instruments Mfg Aircraft Engines/Parts

(G-1512)
SHOCK SOCK INC LLC
409 Colt Hwy (06032-2535)
PHONE..................................860 680-7252
James M Manning, *Principal*
EMP: 4
SALES (est): 345.9K **Privately Held**
SIC: 2252 Mfg Hosiery

(G-1513)
SIKORSKY AIRCRAFT CORPORATION
9 Farm Springs Rd Ste 3 (06032-2576)
P.O. Box 766, Windsor (06095-0766)
PHONE..................................610 644-4430
Eugene Buckley, *President*
EMP: 25 **Publicly Held**
WEB: www.sikorsky.com
SIC: 3721 Mfg Helicopters
HQ: Sikorsky Aircraft Corporation
6900 Main St
Stratford CT 06614
-

(G-1514)
STANLEY BLACK & DECKER INC
65 Spot Swamp Rd (06032)
PHONE..................................860 225-5111
Vito Spinelli, *Engineer*
John F Lundgren, *Branch Mgr*
EMP: 11
SALES (corp-wide): 13.9B **Publicly Held**
WEB: www.stanleyworks.com
SIC: 3423 Mfg Hand/Edge Tools
PA: Stanley Black & Decker, Inc.
1000 Stanley Dr
New Britain CT 06053
860 225-5111

(G-1515)
TAYLOR COML FOODSERVICE INC
Taylor Company
3 Farm Glen Blvd Ste 301 (06032-1981)
P.O. Box 410, Rockton IL (61072-0410)
PHONE..................................336 245-6400
Clark Wangaard, *President*
Larry Vondran, *Data Proc Exec*
Melissa McCormick, *Director*
Allan Stabenow, *Director*
EMP: 627
SQ FT: 100,000
SALES (corp-wide): 2.7B **Publicly Held**
WEB: www.ccr.carrier.com
SIC: 3556 Mfg Food Products Machinery
HQ: Taylor Commercial Foodservice Inc.
750 N Blackhawk Blvd
Rockton IL 61072
815 624-8333

(G-1516)
TRANE US INC
135 South Rd Ste 1 (06032-2570)
P.O. Box 977 (06034-0977)
PHONE..................................860 470-3901
Kevin McNamara, *Branch Mgr*
EMP: 60 **Privately Held**
SIC: 3585 Mfg Refrigeration/Heating Equipment
HQ: Trane U.S. Inc.
3600 Pammel Creek Rd
La Crosse WI 54601
608 787-2000

(G-1517)
TRUMPF INC (DH)
111 Hyde Rd (06032-2851)
P.O. Box 105 (06034-0105)
PHONE..................................860 255-6000
Nicola Leibinger-Kammuller, *Ch of Bd*
Peter Hoecklin, *President*
Christof Lehner, *General Mgr*
Yessica Chavez, *Regional Mgr*
Robert Leahy, *Regional Mgr*

◆ **EMP:** 277 **EST:** 1969
SQ FT: 160,000
SALES (est): 206.9MM
SALES (corp-wide): 4.2B **Privately Held**
WEB: www.us.trumpf.com
SIC: **3542** 3423 3546 Mfg Machine Tools-Forming Mfg Hand/Edge Tools Mfg Power-Driven Handtools
HQ: Trumpf International Beteiligungs-Gmbh
Johann-Maus-Str. 2
Ditzingen 71254
715 630-30

(G-1518)
TRUMPF INC
1 Johnson Ave (06032-2842)
PHONE..................................860 255-6000
Rolf Biekert, *CEO*
Wendy Nadeau, *Senior Buyer*
Jeff Curtis, *Engineer*
Jeff McQuarrie, *Engineer*
Paul Vetre, *Engineer*
EMP: 500
SALES (corp-wide): 4.2B **Privately Held**
SIC: **3542** 3423 3546 Mfg Machine Tools-Forming Mfg Hand/Edge Tools Mfg Power-Driven Handtools
HQ: Trumpf, Inc.
111 Hyde Rd
Farmington CT 06032
860 255-6000

(G-1519)
TRUMPF PHOTONICS INC
111 Hyde Rd (06032-2834)
PHONE..................................860 255-6000
Nicola Leibinger-Kammuller, *CEO*
Heinz-Jurgen Prokop, *CEO*
Christian Schmitz, *CEO*
Lars Grunert, *CFO*
Peter Leibinger, *CTO*
EMP: 8
SALES (est): 1.2MM **Privately Held**
SIC: **3444** Mfg Sheet Metalwork

(G-1520)
TRYCYCLE DATA SYSTEMS US INC
400 Farmington Ave # 1844 (06032-1913)
PHONE..................................860 558-1148
Kenneth House, *President*
John Macbeth, *President*
EMP: 4
SALES (est): 98.3K
SALES (corp-wide): 1.7MM **Privately Held**
SIC: **7372** Prepackaged Software Services
PA: Trycycle Data Systems Inc
1296 Carling Ave Suite 300
Ottawa ON K1Z 7
613 274-0001

(G-1521)
TURBINE TECHNOLOGIES INC (PA)
126 Hyde Rd (06032-2866)
P.O. Box 1267 (06034-1267)
PHONE..................................860 678-1642
Tyler J Burke, *President*
John A Guyette, *COO*
Brittany M Bowie, *Vice Pres*
Justin H Lamprey, *Vice Pres*
Fred Fitzgerald, *Plant Engr*
EMP: 80
SALES: 20MM **Privately Held**
WEB: www.omegact.com
SIC: **3724** 3714 Mfg Aircraft Engines/Parts Mfg Motor Vehicle Parts/Accessories

(G-1522)
UNITED TECHNOLOGIES CORP (PA)
Also Called: UTC
10 Farm Springs Rd (06032-2577)
PHONE..................................860 728-7000
Gregory J Hayes, *Ch of Bd*
David L Gitlin, *President*
Robert F Leduc, *President*
▼ **EMP:** 430 **EST:** 1934
SALES: 66.5B **Publicly Held**
WEB: www.utc.com
SIC: **3724** 3585 3721 3534 Provides Technology Products & Services To Building Systems & Aerospace Industries

(G-1523)
UNITED TECHNOLOGIES CORP
Also Called: UTC Climate Controls & SEC
9 Farm Springs Rd Ste 3 (06032-2576)
PHONE..................................954 485-6501
William Brown, *President*
Scott Sullivan, *Sales Mgr*
Danny Loggins, *Sales Staff*
Lorraine Smith, *Sales Staff*
Rich Johnston, *Technology*
EMP: 500
SALES (corp-wide): 66.5B **Publicly Held**
SIC: **3699** 3669 Mfg Electrical Equipment/Supplies Mfg Communications Equipment
PA: United Technologies Corporation
10 Farm Springs Rd
Farmington CT 06032
860 728-7000

(G-1524)
ZERO HAZARD LLC
38 Pembroke Hl (06032-1461)
P.O. Box 767 (06034-0767)
PHONE..................................860 561-9879
Carlos M Rosales, *Principal*
EMP: 8
SALES (est): 539.1K **Privately Held**
SIC: **3292** Mfg Asbestos Products

Gales Ferry
New London County

(G-1525)
B&R SAND AND GRAVEL
1358 Baldwin Hill Rd (06335-1856)
PHONE..................................860 464-5099
EMP: 5 **EST:** 2016
SALES (est): 481.8K **Privately Held**
SIC: **3273** Mfg Ready-Mixed Concrete

(G-1526)
CALVIN BROWN
Also Called: Cal Brown Paving
259 Gallup Hill Rd (06339-2010)
PHONE..................................860 536-6178
Calvin Brown, *Owner*
EMP: 5
SALES (est): 191.8K **Privately Held**
WEB: www.calvinbrown.com
SIC: **3531** Mfg Construction Machinery

(G-1527)
KAPPA SAILS LLC
25 Whippoorwill Dr (06335-2029)
PHONE..................................860 399-8899
Clark Basset, *President*
Kathryn Bassett,
EMP: 6
SALES (est): 514.7K **Privately Held**
WEB: www.kappasails.com
SIC: **2394** Mfg Canvas/Related Products

(G-1528)
TRINSEO LLC
1761 Route 12 Bldg 21 (06335-1213)
PHONE..................................860 447-7298
Celso Goncalves, *CFO*
EMP: 20 **Publicly Held**
SIC: **2821** Mfg Plastic Materials/Resins
HQ: Trinseo Llc
1000 Chesterbrook Blvd # 300
Berwyn PA 19312

Gaylordsville
Litchfield County

(G-1529)
CANDLEWOOD TOOL & MACHINE SHOP
24 Martha Ln (06755-1501)
PHONE..................................860 355-1892
George Christophersen, *President*
James Jacques, *Vice Pres*
Amy Jacques, *Treasurer*
Joan B Christophersen, *Admin Sec*
EMP: 10
SQ FT: 5,300
SALES: 1MM **Privately Held**
SIC: **3599** 3544 Mfg Industrial Machinery Mfg Dies/Tools/Jigs/Fixtures

(G-1530)
CONWAY HARDWOOD PRODUCTS LLC
Also Called: Conway, Jeremiah
37 Gaylord Rd (06755-1518)
PHONE..................................860 355-4030
Jeremiah C Conway, *Mng Member*
Mike Artese, *Manager*
▲ **EMP:** 25
SQ FT: 9,000
SALES (est): 3MM **Privately Held**
SIC: **2426** 2434 2431 5211 Hdwd Dimension/Flr Mill Mfg Wood Kitchen Cabinet Mfg Millwork Ret Lumber/Building Mtrl

(G-1531)
GAIA CHEMICAL CORPORATION
23 George Washington Plz (06755)
PHONE..................................860 355-2730
A Kodylinsky, *Director*
EMP: 4
SALES (est): 262.9K **Privately Held**
SIC: **2834** Research Compounds

(G-1532)
MICRO SOURCE DISCOVERY SYSTEMS
11 George Washington Plz (06755)
PHONE..................................860 350-8078
John Devlin, *President*
Mary Ortner, *Vice Pres*
EMP: 7
SQ FT: 2,000
SALES (est): 1.1MM **Privately Held**
WEB: www.msdiscovery.com
SIC: **2834** Pharmaceutical Preparations

Georgetown
Fairfield County

(G-1533)
TRASSIG CORP
65 Redding Rd Unit 874 (06829-7735)
P.O. Box 874 (06829-0874)
PHONE..................................203 659-0456
Khalid Gourad, *President*
▲ **EMP:** 5 **EST:** 2007
SALES: 1MM **Privately Held**
SIC: **3949** Mfg Sporting/Athletic Goods

Gilman
New London County

(G-1534)
GILMAN CORPORATION
1 Polly Ln (06336)
P.O. Box 68 (06336-0068)
PHONE..................................860 887-7080
Richard Gilman, *CEO*
Elizabeth Gilman, *President*
George Warner, *MIS Dir*
▼ **EMP:** 30
SQ FT: 32,000
SALES (est): 7MM **Privately Held**
WEB: www.gilmancorp.com
SIC: **3086** 3949 Mfg Plastic Foam Products Mfg Sporting/Athletic Goods

(G-1535)
MARTY GILMAN INCORPORATED (PA)
Also Called: Gilman Gear
30 Gilman Rd (06336-1006)
P.O. Box 97 (06336-0097)
PHONE..................................860 889-7334
Shirley Gilman, *Ch of Bd*
Neil Gilman, *President*
Geoffrey Gilman, *Admin Sec*
EMP: 55 **EST:** 1929
SQ FT: 20,000
SALES (est): 6.3MM **Privately Held**
WEB: www.magipotholders.com
SIC: **3949** Mfg Sporting/Athletic Goods

Glastonbury
Hartford County

(G-1536)
AIRFLO INSTRUMENT COMPANY
53 Addison Rd (06033-1601)
P.O. Box 192 (06033-0192)
PHONE..................................860 633-9455
William Lajewski, *President*
Anthony Coiro, *Shareholder*
EMP: 5 **EST:** 1948
SQ FT: 7,500
SALES: 490.7K **Privately Held**
SIC: **3648** 3829 3812 3625 Mfg Lighting Equipment Mfg Measure/Control Dvcs Mfg Search/Navgatn Equip Mfg Relay/Indstl Control

(G-1537)
AM MANUFACTURING LLC
278 Oakwood Dr Ste 6 (06033-5019)
PHONE..................................860 573-1987
Michael Karwowski, *Mng Member*
EMP: 4
SALES (est): 401.1K **Privately Held**
SIC: **3599** Mfg Industrial Machinery

(G-1538)
ARRAY TECHNOLOGIES INC
21 Sequin Dr (06033-2443)
PHONE..................................860 657-8086
David Loos, *CEO*
David Pirie, *President*
EMP: 5
SQ FT: 1,551
SALES (est): 927.7K **Privately Held**
WEB: www.arraytechnologies.com
SIC: **7372** Prepackaged Software Services

(G-1539)
BAGEL BOYS INC (PA)
85 Nutmeg Ln (06033-2314)
PHONE..................................860 657-4400
Wes Becher, *President*
Michael Bellobuono, *Vice Pres*
EMP: 14
SALES (est): 2.4MM **Privately Held**
SIC: **2051** Retail Bakery

(G-1540)
BIOMED HEALTH INC
70 Oakwood Dr Ste 8 (06033-2459)
P.O. Box 911 (06033-0911)
PHONE..................................860 657-2258
M E Sherman, *President*
Generosa Mendez, *Corp Secy*
EMP: 12
SALES (est): 1.9MM **Privately Held**
WEB: www.biomed-health.com
SIC: **2833** 2834 Mfg Medicinal/Botanical Products Mfg Pharmaceutical Preparations

(G-1541)
BRITISH PRECISION INC
20 Sequin Dr (06033-2475)
PHONE..................................860 633-3343
Ralph Naylor, *President*
David Ouelette, *Purchasing*
Mary Naylor, *Treasurer*
EMP: 30
SQ FT: 11,000
SALES (est): 5.2MM **Privately Held**
WEB: www.britishprecision.com
SIC: **3599** Mfg Industrial Machinery

(G-1542)
C & W MANUFACTURING CO INC
74 Eastern Blvd (06033-4304)
PHONE..................................860 633-4631
Myles Covey, *President*
Scott Miller, *Vice Pres*
EMP: 20
SQ FT: 19,000
SALES: 2.3MM **Privately Held**
SIC: **3599** 3841 3728 Mfg Industrial Machinery Mfg Surgical/Medical Instruments Mfg Aircraft Parts/Equipment

GEOGRAPHIC

(G-1543)
CAMERON INTERNATIONAL CORP
Also Called: Measurement Systems
256 Oakwood Dr Ste 1 (06033-2465)
PHONE..................................860 633-0277
Kim Giansianti, *Manager*
EMP: 10 **Publicly Held**
SIC: 1389 Oil/Gas Field Services
HQ: Cameron International Corporation
4646 W Sam Houston Pkwy N
Houston TX 77041

(G-1544)
CONARD CORPORATION
101 Commerce St (06033-2312)
P.O. Box 676 (06033-0676)
PHONE..................................860 659-0591
William J Fox, *President*
Tom Odea, *Engineer*
▲ **EMP:** 23 **EST:** 1965
SQ FT: 12,000
SALES (est): 3.9MM **Privately Held**
WEB: www.conardcorp.com
SIC: 3479 Coating/Engraving Service

(G-1545)
CONNECTICUT ADVANCED PRODUCTS
41c New London Tpke (06033-4206)
PHONE..................................860 659-2260
Jeffrey Kretzmer, *President*
Cynthia Kretzmer, *Vice Pres*
EMP: 4
SQ FT: 1,500
SALES (est): 429.3K **Privately Held**
WEB: www.capcad.com
SIC: 3728 5599 5088 5961 Mfg Ret And Whol Heat Shields For Airplanes Through Mail-Order

(G-1546)
CUSSON SASH COMPANY
128 Addison Rd (06033-1605)
PHONE..................................860 659-0354
Walter Cusson, *President*
Richard Cusson, *Corp Secy*
Charles Cusson, *Vice Pres*
Howard Rath, *Vice Pres*
EMP: 5 **EST:** 1946
SQ FT: 10,000
SALES (est): 570K **Privately Held**
WEB: www.cussonssash.com
SIC: 3442 1521 1751 5211 Mfg Aluminum Products General Remodeling Install Ret & Whol Doors & Windows & Screens

(G-1547)
EAST HARTFORD LAMINATION CO
Also Called: Ehl Kitchens
110 Commerce St (06033-2369)
P.O. Box 22 (06033-0022)
PHONE..................................860 633-4637
Mario Disomma, *Owner*
EMP: 4 **EST:** 1967
SQ FT: 10,000
SALES (est): 410K **Privately Held**
WEB: www.ehlkitchens.com
SIC: 2541 5211 2434 Mfg Wood Partitions/Fixt Ret Lumber/Building Mtrl Mfg Wood Kitchen Cabinet

(G-1548)
EDAC ND INC
Also Called: Flanagan Brothers, Inc
81 National Dr (06033-1211)
P.O. Box 396 (06033-0396)
PHONE..................................860 633-9474
Terry Bruni, *CEO*
EMP: 100
SQ FT: 55,000
SALES (est): 19.1MM **Privately Held**
WEB: www.fillc.com
SIC: 3728 3812 3721 Mfg Aircraft Parts/Equipment Mfg Search/Navigation Equipment Mfg Aircraft
HQ: Edac Technologies Llc
5 Mckee Pl
Cheshire CT 06410
203 806-2090

(G-1549)
EMPIRE PRINTING SYSTEMS LLC
Also Called: Signal Graphics Printing
63 Hebron Ave Ste C (06033-2078)
PHONE..................................860 633-3333
Phillip Bombart,
Maydie Bombart,
▲ **EMP:** 5
SQ FT: 2,080
SALES: 660K **Privately Held**
SIC: 2752 Offset Printing

(G-1550)
ENGINE ALLIANCE LLC
124 Hebron Ave Ste 200 (06033-2063)
PHONE..................................860 565-2239
Dean Athans, *President*
Chip Blankenship, *President*
Jonathan Lynch, *General Mgr*
Melissa Argiro, *Info Tech Mgr*
Willam Fehling,
EMP: 400
SALES: 26.1MM
SALES (corp-wide): 66.5B **Publicly Held**
SIC: 3724 Mfg Aircraft Engines/Parts
PA: United Technologies Corporation
10 Farm Springs Rd
Farmington CT 06032
860 728-7000

(G-1551)
FLANAGAN BROTHERS INC
25 Mill St (06033-1209)
PHONE..................................860 633-3558
EMP: 4
SALES (corp-wide): 146.8MM **Privately Held**
SIC: 3728 Mfg Aircraft Assemblies Subassemblies & Parts
HQ: Flanagan Brothers, Inc.
25 Mill St
Glastonbury CT 06033
860 633-9474

(G-1552)
FREEDOM TECHNOLOGIES LLC
80 Timrod Trl (06033-1937)
P.O. Box 117, East Glastonbury (06025-0117)
PHONE..................................860 633-0452
Mary Ellen Gatti, *President*
Suzanne Gatti,
Victor Gatti,
EMP: 8
SQ FT: 5,000
SALES: 3MM **Privately Held**
WEB: www.freedomlaser.com
SIC: 3661 Mfg Of Optical Electronic Products

(G-1553)
GAC INC
Also Called: New England Traffic Solutions
160 Oak St Ste 412 (06033-2376)
PHONE..................................860 633-1768
Amy Vecchiarino, *President*
Claudio Vecchiarino, *Vice Pres*
Kevin Cramer, *Technician*
EMP: 5
SQ FT: 16,000
SALES (est): 1MM **Privately Held**
SIC: 3669 Mfg Communications Equipment

(G-1554)
GENERAL ELECTRO COMPONENTS
Also Called: Line Electric
122 Naubuc Ave Ste A7 (06033-4226)
PHONE..................................860 659-3573
Bill Harris, *President*
Billy D Harris, *Director*
◆ **EMP:** 8
SQ FT: 5,000
SALES (est): 943K **Privately Held**
WEB: www.lineelectric.com
SIC: 3679 3625 3613 Mfg Elec Components Mfg Relay/Indstl Control Mfg Switchgear/Boards

(G-1555)
GLASTONBURY CITIZEN INC
87 Nutmeg Ln (06033-2353)
P.O. Box 373 (06033-0373)
PHONE..................................860 633-4691
Jane Hallas, *President*
Jason Baran, *Editor*
Marian Hallas, *Corp Secy*
James Hallas, *Vice Pres*
EMP: 25
SQ FT: 3,200
SALES (est): 1.4MM **Privately Held**
WEB: www.glcitizen.com
SIC: 2711 Newspapers-Publishing/Printing

(G-1556)
HABCO INDUSTRIES LLC
172 Oak St (06033-2318)
PHONE..................................860 682-6800
Brian Montnari, *CEO*
Scott Brown, *Vice Pres*
Jeff Kretzmer, *Vice Pres*
James Maynard, *Vice Pres*
Nick Zandonella, *Vice Pres*
EMP: 32 **EST:** 2013
SQ FT: 50,000
SALES: 8.6MM **Privately Held**
SIC: 3824 3825 3829 Mfg Fluid Meter/Counting Devices Mfg Electrical Measuring Instruments Mfg Measuring/Controlling Devices

(G-1557)
HARPOON ACQUISITION CORP
455 Winding Brook Dr (06033-4315)
PHONE..................................860 815-5736
Louis Hernandez Jr, *CEO*
EMP: 1700
SALES (est): 43.4MM
SALES (corp-wide): 5.8B **Publicly Held**
SIC: 7372 7373 Prepackaged Software Services Computer Systems Design
PA: Fiserv, Inc.
255 Fiserv Dr
Brookfield WI 53045
262 879-5000

(G-1558)
HIGHWAY SAFETY CORP (PA)
Also Called: Connecticut Galvanizing
239 Commerce St Ste C (06033-2448)
P.O. Box 358 (06033-0358)
PHONE..................................860 659-4330
W Patric Gregory, *CEO*
Robert West, *CFO*
Jean Naan, *Accounts Mgr*
▼ **EMP:** 100
SQ FT: 83,000
SALES: 50.4MM **Privately Held**
SIC: 3444 3479 Mfg Sheet Metalwork Coating/Engraving Service

(G-1559)
HORIZON SOFTWARE INC
148 Eastern Blvd Ste 208 (06033-4321)
P.O. Box 735 (06033-0735)
PHONE..................................860 633-2090
Thomas Riley, *Owner*
EMP: 5
SALES (est): 421.2K **Privately Held**
SIC: 7372 Prepackaged Software Services

(G-1560)
JEM PRECISION GRINDING INC
35 Nutmeg Ln (06033-2363)
PHONE..................................860 633-0152
Michael Pare, *President*
Ronald Bourbau, *Vice Pres*
EMP: 4
SQ FT: 7,000
SALES (est): 582.7K **Privately Held**
SIC: 3599 Precision Grinding

(G-1561)
KENT BILLINGS LLC
320 Spring Street Ext (06033-1240)
PHONE..................................860 659-1104
Kent Billings, *Managing Prtnr*
EMP: 3
SALES: 200K **Privately Held**
SIC: 3999 Mfg Misc Products

(G-1562)
KINDERMA LLC
55 Village Pl (06033-1677)
PHONE..................................860 796-5503
David Thompson,
Todd Calder,
EMP: 5
SALES (est): 282.8K **Privately Held**
SIC: 2834 Mfg Pharmaceutical Preparations

(G-1563)
MAURER & SHEPHERD JOYNERS
122 Naubuc Ave Ste B4 (06033-4271)
PHONE..................................860 633-2383
Galen Shepherd, *President*
Donna Shepherd, *Vice Pres*
EMP: 10 **EST:** 1973
SQ FT: 3,000
SALES (est): 1.2MM **Privately Held**
SIC: 2431 Mfg Millwork

(G-1564)
MEPP TOOL CO INC
81 Commerce St (06033-2312)
P.O. Box 97, South Windsor (06074-0097)
PHONE..................................860 289-8230
Edward Pacholski, *President*
EMP: 4
SQ FT: 6,600
SALES: 461K **Privately Held**
SIC: 3599 Machine Shop Jobbing & Repair

(G-1565)
NAP BROTHERS PARLOR FRAME INC
122 Naubuc Ave Ste B3 (06033-4291)
PHONE..................................860 633-9998
Stephen Napoletano, *President*
Mike Napoletano, *Vice Pres*
EMP: 10 **EST:** 1948
SQ FT: 25,000
SALES (est): 1.4MM **Privately Held**
SIC: 2511 5712 Mfg Wood Household Parlor Frame Furniture

(G-1566)
NEW ENGLAND BORING CONTRACTORS
129 Kreiger Ln Ste A (06033-2392)
PHONE..................................860 633-4649
Steven Preli, *President*
Edward Preli, *Vice Pres*
Janis Preli, *Treasurer*
EMP: 18
SQ FT: 6,000
SALES (est): 4MM **Privately Held**
WEB: www.newenglandboring.com
SIC: 1481 Water Well Drilling

(G-1567)
NORTHEAST CIRCUIT TECH LLC
112 Sherwood Dr (06033-3724)
PHONE..................................860 633-1967
George R Willis, *Principal*
EMP: 7
SALES (est): 883.4K **Privately Held**
SIC: 3672 Mfg Printed Circuit Boards

(G-1568)
NORTONLIFELOCK INC
Also Called: Symantec
200 Glastonbury Blvd # 30 (06033-4418)
PHONE..................................860 652-6600
Dave Bourgoin, *Principal*
EMP: 62
SALES (corp-wide): 4.7B **Publicly Held**
WEB: www.symantec.com
SIC: 7372 Computer Software Development
PA: Nortonlifelock Inc.
60 E Rio Salado Pkwy # 1
Tempe AZ 85281
650 527-8000

(G-1569)
OPEN SOLUTIONS LLC (HQ)
455 Winding Brook Dr # 101 (06033-4351)
PHONE..................................860 815-5000
Stephen J Cameron, *President*
Ken Boin, *Vice Pres*
Jan Frymyer, *Vice Pres*
Kelly Gardner, *Vice Pres*
Mike Gatesman, *Vice Pres*
EMP: 200
SQ FT: 66,000

SALES (est): 2MM
SALES (corp-wide): 5.8B Publicly Held
WEB: www.imagicsystems.com
SIC: 7372 7373 Prepackaged Software Services Computer Systems Design
PA: Fiserv, Inc.
255 Fiserv Dr
Brookfield WI 53045
262 879-5000

(G-1570)
PARMACO LLC
111 Warner Ct (06033-5011)
PHONE..............................860 573-7118
Paul Marchinetti,
EMP: 3
SALES: 1.8MM Privately Held
SIC: 3629 Mfg Electrical Industrial Apparatus

(G-1571)
PINTO MANUFACTURING LLC
122 Naubuc Ave Ste A6 (06033-4298)
PHONE..............................860 659-9543
Robert Pinto, *Owner*
EMP: 8
SQ FT: 3,000
SALES (est): 938.5K Privately Held
WEB: www.pintodesigns.com
SIC: 3599 Machine Job Shop

(G-1572)
PLASTICS AND CONCEPTS CONN INC
101 Laurel Trl (06033-4055)
PHONE..............................860 657-9655
Kathleen Harris, *President*
Tom Harris, *Vice Pres*
Harold Harris, *Admin Sec*
EMP: 11
SQ FT: 3,000
SALES: 100K Privately Held
WEB: www.plasticsandconcepts.com
SIC: 3089 3498 Mfg Plastic Products Mfg Fabricated Pipe/Fittings

(G-1573)
PRINT HOUSE LLC
22 Kreiger Ln Ste 6 (06033-2371)
PHONE..............................860 652-0803
Laura Danaher, *Manager*
EMP: 4
SALES (est): 481.5K Privately Held
SIC: 2752 Lithographic Commercial Printing

(G-1574)
PROJECTS INC
65 Sequin Dr (06033-2484)
P.O. Box 190 (06033-0190)
PHONE..............................860 633-4615
Adelle Kenyon, *Ch of Bd*
F Michael Kenyon, *President*
Edwin Rodriguez, *Opers Mgr*
John Bannon, *Mfg Spvr*
Alicia Corson, *Production*
EMP: 102
SQ FT: 36,000
SALES (est): 41.6MM Privately Held
WEB: www.projectsinc.com
SIC: 3829 3599 7699 3823 Mfg Measure/Control Dvcs Mfg Industrial Machinery Repair Services Mfg Process Cntrl Instr

(G-1575)
PROLINK INC
148 Eastern Blvd Ste 104 (06033-4368)
PHONE..............................860 659-5928
Bruce Brigham, *President*
Gene Vanpatten, *Sales Dir*
Thomas Wrinkle, *Software Dev*
Barbara Brigham, *Admin Sec*
EMP: 6
SQ FT: 3,000
SALES (est): 786.9K Privately Held
WEB: www.prolinksoftware.com
SIC: 7372 Development Of Computer Software

(G-1576)
PW POWER SYSTEMS LLC (HQ)
628 Hebron Ave Ste 400 (06033-5018)
PHONE..............................860 368-5900
Raul Pereda, *CEO*
Moraith Macrae, *President*
Paul Coderre, *General Mgr*
Maurice Gabbidon, *Project Mgr*
Joseph Jaworski, *Project Mgr*
◆ EMP: 52
SQ FT: 120,000
SALES (est): 52.6MM Privately Held
WEB: www.utc.com
SIC: 3511 Mfg Turbines/Generator Sets

(G-1577)
SAS INSTITUTE INC
95 Glastonbury Blvd # 301 (06033-4447)
PHONE..............................860 633-4119
Linda Admin, *Branch Mgr*
EMP: 30
SALES (corp-wide): 3B Privately Held
WEB: www.sas.com
SIC: 7372 Prepackaged Software Svc Subdivider/Developer
PA: Sas Institute Inc.
100 Sas Campus Dr
Cary NC 27513
919 677-8000

(G-1578)
SURFACE PLATE CO
23 Pearl St (06033-1013)
P.O. Box 135, Middle Haddam (06456-0135)
PHONE..............................860 652-8905
David Baribault, *President*
Walter Baribault, *Vice Pres*
EMP: 3 EST: 1989
SALES (est): 195.6K Privately Held
SIC: 3281 Mfg Cut Stone/Products

(G-1579)
TIMKEN COMPANY
701 Hebron Ave Ste 2 (06033-2489)
PHONE..............................860 652-4630
Raymond Buckno, *Manager*
EMP: 11
SQ FT: 2,000
SALES (corp-wide): 3.5B Publicly Held
SIC: 3562 Mfg Ball/Roller Bearings
PA: The Timken Company
4500 Mount Pleasant St Nw
North Canton OH 44720
234 262-3000

(G-1580)
TURBINE KINETICS INC
60 Sequin Dr Ste 2 (06033-5042)
PHONE..............................860 633-8520
Mike Siegel, *CEO*
Bryan Peters, *Senior VP*
EMP: 11
SALES (est): 3.9MM Publicly Held
SIC: 3724 Mfg Aircraft Engines/Parts
HQ: Heico Aerospace Holdings Corp.
3000 Taft St
Hollywood FL 33021
954 987-4000

(G-1581)
WALKER PRODUCTS INCORPORATED
80 Commerce St Ste C (06033-2385)
PHONE..............................860 659-3781
Bernadine A Brock, *President*
Charles Y Brock Jr, *Admin Sec*
▲ EMP: 14
SQ FT: 25,000
SALES (est): 3.4MM Privately Held
SIC: 2675 Mfg Marker Boards

Goshen
Litchfield County

(G-1582)
COUNTRY LOG HOMES INC
27 Rockwall Ct (06756-1714)
PHONE..............................413 229-8084
Ivan Chassie, *President*
Doreen Chassie, *Corp Secy*
EMP: 12
SQ FT: 12,000
SALES (est): 1.7MM Privately Held
WEB: www.countryloghomes.com
SIC: 2452 1521 Manufacture Prefabricated Wood Buildings Single-Family House Construction

(G-1583)
DESJARDINS WOODWORKING INC
211 East St N (06756-1120)
PHONE..............................860 491-9972
Peter E Desjardins, *President*
EMP: 6
SALES (est): 520K Privately Held
SIC: 2499 Wood Products

(G-1584)
KORNER KARE
175 North St (06756-1204)
P.O. Box 291 (06756-0291)
PHONE..............................860 491-3731
Jim Korner, *Owner*
Antonette Korner, *Partner*
EMP: 4
SALES (est): 228.3K Privately Held
SIC: 2842 Mfg Polish/Sanitation Goods

(G-1585)
L & L MECHANICAL LLC
28 Pie Hill Rd (06756-2024)
PHONE..............................860 491-4007
Lisa Lillis,
Charles Lillis,
EMP: 11
SALES (est): 1.1MM Privately Held
SIC: 3443 1711 Mfg Fabricated Plate Work Plumbing/Heating/Air Cond Contractor

(G-1586)
MIRANDA VINEYARD LLC
42 Ives Rd (06756-2118)
PHONE..............................860 491-9906
Manuel D Miranda, *Principal*
EMP: 4
SALES (est): 326.7K Privately Held
SIC: 2084 Mfg Wines/Brandy/Spirits

(G-1587)
SOFTWARE CNSLTING RSOURCES INC
9 Valcove Ct (06756-1913)
PHONE..............................860 491-2689
Stanley J Detwiler, *Owner*
Amanda Canon, *Partner*
EMP: 3
SALES (est): 220.4K Privately Held
WEB: www.scrinc.net
SIC: 7372 Prepackaged Software Services

Granby
Hartford County

(G-1588)
ARROW CONCRETE PRODUCTS INC (PA)
560 Salmon Brook St (06035-1100)
PHONE..............................860 653-5063
Kurt A Burkhart, *President*
Ronald Burkhart Sr, *Vice Pres*
Susan Burkhart, *Vice Pres*
Jon Maxwell, *Plant Mgr*
Pat Ditullio, *Sales Staff*
▲ EMP: 32 EST: 1953
SALES (est): 14.4MM Privately Held
WEB: www.arrow-concrete.com
SIC: 3272 Mfg Concrete Products

(G-1589)
GRASS ROOTS CREAMERY
4 Park Pl (06035-2300)
PHONE..............................860 653-6303
Elizabeth Florian, *Principal*
EMP: 6
SALES (est): 169.6K Privately Held
SIC: 2021 Mfg Creamery Butter

(G-1590)
MONARCH PLASTIC LLC
514r Salmon Brook St (06035-1425)
PHONE..............................860 653-2000
Michael Guarco Jr,
EMP: 10
SQ FT: 10,000
SALES (est): 1.3MM Privately Held
SIC: 3084 3089 Manufactures Plastic Pipe & Fittings

(G-1591)
SINGULARITY SPACE SYSTEMS LLC
Also Called: SSS
33 Wolcott Dr (06035-1320)
PHONE..............................860 713-3626
William Hosack, *CEO*
EMP: 4 EST: 2014
SALES (est): 190.3K Privately Held
SIC: 3761 4789 3823 Mfg Missiles/Space Vehcl Transportation Services Mfg Process Cntrl Instr

Greenwich
Fairfield County

(G-1592)
ACUREN INSPECTION INC
43 Arch St (06830-6512)
PHONE..............................203 869-6734
Peter Scannell, *Branch Mgr*
EMP: 52
SALES (corp-wide): 1.7B Privately Held
SIC: 1389 Oil/Gas Field Services
HQ: Acuren Inspection, Inc.
30 Main St Ste 402
Danbury CT 06810
203 702-8740

(G-1593)
APRICOT HOME LLC
15 Sheffield Way (06831-3725)
PHONE..............................203 552-1791
Abby Pillari, *Mng Member*
▲ EMP: 7
SALES (est): 355.7K Privately Held
SIC: 2273 Mfg Carpets/Rugs

(G-1594)
ATLAS AGI HOLDINGS LLC
Also Called: Agi-Shorewood U.S.
100 Northfield St (06830-4618)
PHONE..............................203 622-9138
Larry Hall, *Asst Controller*
Andrew M Bursky, *Mng Member*
Troy Schirk, *Info Tech Dir*
Sam G Astor,
Daniel E Cromie,
▼ EMP: 3860 EST: 2010
SALES (est): 228.8MM Privately Held
SIC: 2671 Mfg Packaging Paper/Film

(G-1595)
AXELS CUSTOM WOODWORKING LLC
45 Rodwell Ave (06830-6170)
PHONE..............................203 869-1317
James Decarlo, *Principal*
EMP: 4
SALES (est): 247.6K Privately Held
SIC: 2431 Mfg Millwork

(G-1596)
B H SHOE HOLDINGS INC (HQ)
124 W Putnam Ave Ste 1 (06830-5317)
PHONE..............................203 661-2424
James Issler, *President*
Marc Hamburg, *Vice Pres*
J Scott Bohling, *Admin Sec*
◆ EMP: 50
SALES (est): 365.1MM
SALES (corp-wide): 225.3B Publicly Held
SIC: 3143 Mfg Men's Footwear
PA: Berkshire Hathaway Inc.
3555 Farnam St Ste 1140
Omaha NE 68131
402 346-1400

(G-1597)
BAOBAB ASSET MANAGEMENT LLC
2 Greenwich Office Park # 300 (06831-5155)
PHONE..............................203 340-5700
Russell Fryer, *Portfolio Mgr*
EMP: 3
SALES: 922.3K Privately Held
SIC: 1021 Copper Ore Mining

GEOGRAPHIC

(G-1598)
BAXTER BROS INC
Also Called: Baxter Investment Management
1030 E Putnam Ave (06830)
PHONE..................................203 637-4559
William J Baxter Jr, *President*
John Baxter, *Director*
EMP: 5
SQ FT: 2,000
SALES (est): 675.9K **Privately Held**
SIC: 2721 6282 Periodicals-Publishing/Printing Investment Advisory Service

(G-1599)
BAYER CLOTHING GROUP INC (PA)
Also Called: Hyde Clothes Div
503 Riversville Rd (06831-2914)
PHONE..................................203 661-4140
Robert Bayer, *President*
Philip P Looby, *COO*
Kathy Jo Corry, *Purch Mgr*
▼ **EMP:** 59 **EST:** 1951
SQ FT: 40,000
SALES (est): 44.6MM **Privately Held**
SIC: 2311 2337 2325 Mfg Mens/Boys Suit/Coats Mfg Women/Miss Suit/Coat Mfg Mens/Boys Trousers

(G-1600)
BLUE SKY STUDIOS INC
Also Called: Blue Sky/Vifx
1 American Ln Ste 301 (06831-2563)
PHONE..................................203 992-6000
Robert Cohen, *Ch of Bd*
Brian Keane, *CFO*
EMP: 200 **EST:** 1987
SALES (est): 24.5MM
SALES (corp-wide): 69.5B **Publicly Held**
WEB: www.blueskystudios.com
SIC: 7372 7812 Prepackaged Software Services Motion Picture/Video Production
HQ: Fox Entertainment Group, Llc
1211 Ave Of The Americas
New York NY 10036
212 852-7000

(G-1601)
BRANT INDUSTRIES INC (PA)
Also Called: White Birch Paper Company
80 Field Point Rd Ste 3 (06830-6416)
PHONE..................................203 661-3344
Peter M Brant, *CEO*
Christopher Brant, *President*
Bruno Antonios, *Senior VP*
Jean Blais, *Senior VP*
Russell Lowder, *Senior VP*
◆ **EMP:** 18
SQ FT: 4,500
SALES (est): 257.7MM **Privately Held**
SIC: 2621 Paper Mill

(G-1602)
CAPRICORN INVESTORS II LP
30 E Elm St (06830-6529)
PHONE..................................203 861-6600
Herbert Winokur Jr, *General Ptnr*
James M Better, *General Ptnr*
Nathaniel A Gregory, *General Ptnr*
Dudley C Mecum, *General Ptnr*
EMP: 5953
SALES: 3.3MM **Privately Held**
WEB: www.capricornholdings.com
SIC: 2676 5461 6794 Investment Holding Company

(G-1603)
CONNECTICUT IRON WORKS INC
59 Davenport Ave (06830-7105)
PHONE..................................203 869-0657
Albert Margenot, *President*
John R Margenot, *Vice Pres*
EMP: 8 **EST:** 1921
SQ FT: 8,800
SALES: 750K **Privately Held**
SIC: 3441 3446 Structural Metal Fabrication Mfg Architectural Metalwork

(G-1604)
COUPONZ DIRECT LLC
25 Lewis St Ste 303 (06830-5537)
PHONE..................................212 655-9615
Penny Oloughnane,
EMP: 3
SALES (est): 71.1K **Privately Held**
SIC: 7372 Prepackaged Software Services

(G-1605)
CUSTOM FOOD PDTS HOLDINGS LLC
411 W Putnam Ave (06830-6261)
PHONE..................................310 637-0900
Ervin J Hickerson, *President*
EMP: 55
SALES (est): 16.3MM **Privately Held**
SIC: 2013 Mfg Prepared Meats
PA: Contrarian Capital Management Llc
411 W Putnam Ave Ste 425
Greenwich CT 06830

(G-1606)
DELANY & LONG LTD
41 Chestnut St (06830-5969)
PHONE..................................203 532-0010
Jack Flynn, *President*
EMP: 3
SALES (est): 290K **Privately Held**
SIC: 3441 Structural Metal Fabrication

(G-1607)
DELFIN MARKETING INC
500 W Putnam Ave Ste 400 (06830-6096)
PHONE..................................203 554-2707
Aki Immonen, *Principal*
Heikki Meriranta, *Engineer*
EMP: 8
SALES (est): 723.1K
SALES (corp-wide): 511.1K **Privately Held**
SIC: 3841 Mfg Surgical/Medical Instruments
PA: Delfin Technologies Oy
Microkatu 1
Kuopio 70210
509 111-199

(G-1608)
DESROSIER OF GREENWICH INC
Also Called: Lighthouse Technology Partners
103 Mason St (06830-6605)
PHONE..................................203 661-2334
Brian Desrosier, *President*
Jon Gould, *General Mgr*
EMP: 15
SQ FT: 8,000
SALES (est): 1.3MM **Privately Held**
WEB: www.computersupercenter.com
SIC: 7372 7371 7373 Prepackaged Software Services Custom Computer Programing Computer Systems Design

(G-1609)
EASY GRAPHICS INC
Also Called: Minuteman Press
31 Saint Roch Ave Ste 1 (06830-6775)
PHONE..................................203 622-0001
David Goldvug, *President*
▲ **EMP:** 3
SQ FT: 1,100
SALES (est): 572.5K **Privately Held**
SIC: 2752 Comm Prtg Litho

(G-1610)
FAIRFIELD COUNTY LOOK
6 Wyckham Hill Ln (06831-3049)
PHONE..................................203 869-0077
Elaine Ubina, *Principal*
EMP: 3
SALES (est): 312.7K **Privately Held**
SIC: 2721 Periodicals-Publishing/Printing

(G-1611)
FINE PETS LLC
229 Stanwich Rd (06830-3501)
PHONE..................................203 833-1517
Janette Souliere,
EMP: 5
SALES: 100K **Privately Held**
SIC: 2047 Mfg Dog/Cat Food

(G-1612)
FISHER FOOTWEAR LLC
777 W Putnam Ave (06830-5091)
PHONE..................................203 302-2800
Marc Fisher, *CEO*
Roger Ho, *Vice Pres*
▲ **EMP:** 10
SQ FT: 45,000
SALES (est): 1.2MM **Privately Held**
SIC: 3143 3144 Mfg Men's Footwear Mfg Women's Footwear

(G-1613)
FISHER SIGERSON MORRISON LLC
777 W Putnam Ave (06830-5091)
PHONE..................................203 302-2800
▲ **EMP:** 30
SQ FT: 1,600
SALES: 4.6MM
SALES (corp-wide): 120.9MM **Privately Held**
SIC: 3144 Womens Footwear, Except Athletic, Nsk
PA: Marc Fisher Llc
777 W Putnam Ave
Greenwich CT 06830
203 302-2800

(G-1614)
FLANGE LOCK LLC
57 Old Post Rd No 2 Ste 3 (06830-6786)
PHONE..................................203 861-9400
Arnold Frumin, *Mng Member*
EMP: 6
SALES (est): 457.9K **Privately Held**
SIC: 3462 Mfg Iron/Steel Forgings

(G-1615)
FMP PRODUCTS
100 Melrose Ave Ste 206 (06830-6277)
PHONE..................................203 422-0686
Thomas Friedlander, *Principal*
EMP: 4
SALES: 50K **Privately Held**
SIC: 3821 Laboratory Equipment Manufacturer

(G-1616)
FRESHIANA LLC
375 Greenwich Ave Apt 6 (06830-6545)
PHONE..................................800 301-8071
John Stewart, *Principal*
EMP: 3
SALES (est): 76.2K **Privately Held**
SIC: 2711 Newspapers-Publishing/Printing

(G-1617)
GRADUATION SOLUTIONS LLC
Also Called: Graduation Source
200 Pemberwick Rd (06831-4236)
PHONE..................................914 934-5991
Jessie Alexander, *Mng Member*
Matthew Gordon, *Mng Member*
◆ **EMP:** 30
SQ FT: 3,600
SALES: 6.1MM **Privately Held**
SIC: 2384 Mfg Robes/Dressing Gowns

(G-1618)
GREEN RAY LED INTL LLC (PA)
115 E Putnam Ave Ste 3 (06830-5643)
PHONE..................................203 485-1435
Tony Allan, *President*
Rey Norat, *CFO*
EMP: 5
SALES (est): 11.2MM **Privately Held**
SIC: 3646 Mfg Commercial Lighting Fixtures

(G-1619)
GREENWICH SENTINEL
28 Bruce Park Ave (06830-2728)
PHONE..................................203 883-1430
Beth Barhydt, *Owner*
EMP: 4 **EST:** 2017
SALES (est): 169.6K **Privately Held**
SIC: 2711 Newspapers-Publishing/Printing

(G-1620)
HH BROWN SHOE COMPANY INC (DH)
Also Called: Cove Shoe Company Division
124 W Putnam Ave Ste 1a (06830-5317)
PHONE..................................203 661-2424
J E Issler, *CEO*
Francis C Rooney Jr, *Ch of Bd*
James Issler, *President*
J Scott Bohling, *Exec VP*
◆ **EMP:** 50 **EST:** 1927
SQ FT: 13,000
SALES (est): 298.5MM
SALES (corp-wide): 225.3B **Publicly Held**
WEB: www.coveshoe.com
SIC: 3143 3144 Mfg Men's Footwear Mfg Women's Footwear

(G-1621)
IDA PUBLISHING CO INC
Also Called: Total Food Service
282 Railroad Ave Ste 4 (06830-6382)
P.O. Box 2507 (06836-2507)
PHONE..................................203 661-9090
Leslie Klashman, *President*
Michael Scinto, *Director*
EMP: 6
SALES (est): 909.4K **Privately Held**
SIC: 2721 Publisher Of A Trade Newspaper

(G-1622)
INDUSTRIAL FORREST PRODUCTS LL
21 Stanwich Rd (06830-4840)
PHONE..................................203 863-9486
EMP: 3
SALES (est): 185.2K **Privately Held**
SIC: 2411 Logging

(G-1623)
INTERSTATE + LAKELAND LBR CORP
184 S Water St (06830-6849)
PHONE..................................203 531-8050
Sheldon Kahan, *Owner*
Richard Rose, *Sales Staff*
EMP: 15
SALES (corp-wide): 24.8MM **Privately Held**
SIC: 2421 Sawmill/Planing Mill
PA: Interstate + Lakeland Lumber Corporation
247 Mill St
Greenwich CT 06830
203 531-8885

(G-1624)
JACOBSEN WOODWORKING CO INC
3 Oak St W (06830-6885)
P.O. Box 4422 (06831-0408)
PHONE..................................203 531-9050
EMP: 3
SALES (est): 223.3K **Privately Held**
SIC: 2431 Mfg Millwork

(G-1625)
JOHN M KRISKEY CARPENTRY
129 N Water St (06830-5816)
PHONE..................................203 531-0194
John Kriskey, *Partner*
Scott Kriskey, *Partner*
EMP: 3
SALES (est): 288.9K **Privately Held**
SIC: 2499 2541 2434 2431 Mfg Wood Products Mfg Wood Partitions/Fixt Mfg Wood Kitchen Cabinet Mfg Millwork

(G-1626)
LGL GROUP INC
140 Greenwich Ave Ste 4 (06830-6560)
PHONE..................................407 298-2000
EMP: 3
SALES (est): 265.9K **Privately Held**
SIC: 2672 Mfg Coated/Laminated Paper

(G-1627)
LYNCH CORP
140 Greenwich Ave Ste 3 (06830-6560)
PHONE..................................203 452-3007
Ralph Papitto, *Principal*
EMP: 3
SALES (est): 314.3K **Privately Held**
SIC: 3559 Mfg Misc Industry Machinery

(G-1628)
MAINE POWER EXPRESS LLC
485 W Putnam Ave (06830-6060)
PHONE..................................203 661-0055
Joseph Cotter, *Mng Member*
EMP: 3
SALES (est): 95.3K **Privately Held**
SIC: 1382 8731 Oil/Gas Exploration Services Commercial Physical Research

▲ = Import ▼=Export
◆ =Import/Export

(G-1629)
MBF HOLDINGS LLC
777 W Putnam Ave (06830-5091)
PHONE..................................203 302-2812
Roger Ho, *VP Finance*
Marc Fisher, *Mng Member*
▲ **EMP:** 10
SQ FT: 70,000
SALES: 100MM **Privately Held**
SIC: 3143 Mfg Men's Footwear

(G-1630)
MERCURIA ENERGY TRADING INC
33 Benedict Pl Ste 1 (06830-5323)
PHONE..................................203 413-3355
Joseph Donner, *Branch Mgr*
Scot Lilly, *Officer*
EMP: 8 **Privately Held**
SIC: 1381 Oil/Gas Well Drilling
HQ: Mercuria Energy Trading, Inc.
20 Greenway Plz Ste 650
Houston TX 77046

(G-1631)
MILLBRAE ENERGY LLC (PA)
500 W Putnam Ave Ste 400 (06830-6096)
PHONE..................................203 742-2800
Stewart Mills Reid, *CEO*
Robert E King Jr, *President*
Charles R Boyce, *COO*
Ryburn McCullough, *Senior VP*
Gary A Watson, *Senior VP*
EMP: 10
SALES (est): 960.3K **Privately Held**
SIC: 1381 Oil/Gas Well Drilling

(G-1632)
MUNK PACK INC
222 Railroad Ave Ste 2 (06830-2711)
PHONE..................................203 769-5005
Michelle Leutzinger, *CEO*
Tobias Glienke, *President*
EMP: 10
SALES: 361.9K **Privately Held**
SIC: 2043 Mfg Cereal Breakfast Food

(G-1633)
NEW ENGLAND FILTER COMPANY INC (PA)
21 S Water St Ste 2a (06830-6822)
P.O. Box 31111 (06831-0811)
PHONE..................................203 531-0500
Thomas H James, *President*
William James, *Vice Pres*
Diane James, *Treasurer*
Joan James, *Admin Sec*
▼ **EMP:** 6
SALES (est): 707.6K **Privately Held**
SIC: 3677 Mfg Electronic Coils/Transformers

(G-1634)
NEXTEC APPLICATIONS INC (PA)
Also Called: Epic By Nextec
11 Turner Dr (06831-4415)
P.O. Box 150, Bonsall CA (92003-0150)
PHONE..................................203 661-1484
Peter Santoro, *Ch of Bd*
Bill McCabe, *Co-CEO*
Jamie Henderson, *Opers Staff*
▲ **EMP:** 4
SALES (est): 1.1MM **Privately Held**
WEB: www.nextec.com
SIC: 2262 2295 2221 Manmade Fiber & Silk Finishing Plant Mfg Coated Fabrics Manmade Broadwoven Fabric Mill

(G-1635)
NORFOLK INDUSTRIES LLC
Also Called: Husky Meadows Farm
21 Deer Park Dr (06830-4602)
PHONE..................................860 618-8822
Tracy Hayhurst,
EMP: 6
SALES (est): 200.3K **Privately Held**
SIC: 3999 Mfg Misc Products

(G-1636)
ONCOSYNERGY INC
380 Greenwich Ave (06830-6523)
PHONE..................................617 755-9156
Shawn Carbonell, *CEO*
EMP: 3
SALES (est): 290.2K **Privately Held**
SIC: 2836 Mfg Biological Products

(G-1637)
PINNACLE AEROSPACE MFG LLC
361 Field Point Rd (06830-7054)
PHONE..................................203 258-3398
Deb Husti, *Principal*
EMP: 15
SALES (est): 1MM **Privately Held**
SIC: 3724 Mfg Aircraft Engines/Parts

(G-1638)
POOF-ALEX HOLDINGS LLC (PA)
Also Called: Slinky
10 Glenville St Ste 1 (06831-3680)
PHONE..................................203 930-7711
John Belniak,
Michael Cornell,
EMP: 9
SALES (est): 11.7MM **Privately Held**
SIC: 3944 Mfg Games/Toys

(G-1639)
PUPPY HUGGER
Also Called: Hugger Design
121 North St (06830-4722)
PHONE..................................203 661-4858
Elaine Doran, *Managing Prtnr*
Judy McAuliff, *Managing Prtnr*
EMP: 8
SALES (est): 513.7K **Privately Held**
SIC: 2399 Mfg Fabricated Textile Products

(G-1640)
RAY GREEN CORP
115 E Putnam Ave Ste 1 (06830-5643)
PHONE..................................707 544-2662
EMP: 13
SALES (est): 1.8MM **Privately Held**
SIC: 3674 Mfg Semiconductors/Related Devices

(G-1641)
REMOTE TECHNOLOGIES INC (PA)
57 Old Mill Rd (06831-3344)
P.O. Box 1185 (06836-1185)
PHONE..................................203 661-2798
Cheryl Makrinos, *President*
EMP: 4
SQ FT: 300
SALES (est): 733K **Privately Held**
WEB: www.remotetechnologies.com
SIC: 3844 Mfg X-Ray Medical Equipment

(G-1642)
RHINO ENERGY HOLDINGS LLC
411 W Putnam Ave Ste 125 (06830-6294)
PHONE..................................203 862-7000
Arthur Amron, *Mng Member*
EMP: 860
SALES (est): 11.3MM **Privately Held**
SIC: 1222 1221 Bituminous Coal-Underground Mining Bituminous Coal/Lignite Surface Mining
PA: Wexford Capital, L.P.
411 W Putnam Ave Ste 125
Greenwich CT 06830

(G-1643)
RITCH HERALD & LINDA
10 Fort Hill Ln (06831-3719)
PHONE..................................203 661-8634
Herald Ritch, *Principal*
EMP: 3
SALES (est): 118K **Privately Held**
SIC: 2711 Newspapers-Publishing/Printing

(G-1644)
RJTB GROUP LLC
253 Mill St (06830-5806)
PHONE..................................203 531-7216
Ana Bangay, *CFO*
Thomas Butkiewicz,
EMP: 4
SQ FT: 400
SALES: 8MM **Privately Held**
SIC: 2844 Mfg Toilet Preparations

(G-1645)
ROCKWOOD SERVICE CORPORATION (PA)
43 Arch St (06830-6512)
PHONE..................................203 869-6734
Peter Scannell, *President*
Don Thomas, *Opers Mgr*
John Lockwood, *Treasurer*
Dennis Nolan, *Human Res Dir*
Bonnie Pace, *Hum Res Coord*
EMP: 9
SALES (est): 1.7B **Privately Held**
SIC: 1389 Oil/Gas Field Services

(G-1646)
SASC LLC (PA)
Also Called: Sangari Active Science
44 Amogerone Crossway (06830-9993)
PHONE..................................203 846-2274
Eric Johnson, *CEO*
Dan Toberman, *Regional Mgr*
Tom Pence, *Exec VP*
Tom Laster, *Senior VP*
Benjamin Reynolds, *Production*
EMP: 9
SALES (est): 2MM **Privately Held**
SIC: 2731 Books-Publishing/Printing

(G-1647)
SAXONY WOOD PRODUCTS INC
18 Beech St (06830-5945)
PHONE..................................203 869-3717
John Giagnorio, *President*
EMP: 5 **EST:** 1955
SQ FT: 5,000
SALES (est): 401.2K **Privately Held**
SIC: 2431 Mfg Millwork

(G-1648)
SDA LABORATORIES INC
280 Railroad Ave Ste 207 (06830-6338)
PHONE..................................203 861-0005
Sheldon Davis, *President*
EMP: 8
SQ FT: 1,200
SALES (est): 1.1MM **Privately Held**
SIC: 2834 Mfg Pharmaceutical Preparations

(G-1649)
SILVERSMITH INC
392 W Putnam Ave (06830-6215)
PHONE..................................203 869-4244
Mark Fakundiny, *President*
Jennifer Fakundiny, *Vice Pres*
EMP: 3
SQ FT: 2,000
SALES (est): 307.1K **Privately Held**
SIC: 3471 3479 5944 3914 Polishing Plating & Ret Silverware

(G-1650)
SIMON PEARCE US INC
125 E Putnam Ave (06830-5612)
PHONE..................................203 861-0780
Nancy Defillippo, *Branch Mgr*
EMP: 6
SALES (corp-wide): 64.2MM **Privately Held**
WEB: www.simonpearce.com
SIC: 3229 Ret Gifts/Novelties
PA: Simon Pearce U.S., Inc.
109 Park Rd
Windsor VT 05089
802 674-6280

(G-1651)
SONITOR TECHNOLOGIES INC
37 Brookside Dr (06830-6422)
PHONE..................................727 466-4557
Arvid Gomez, *President*
Erik Fausa Olsen, *CFO*
EMP: 6 **EST:** 2005
SALES (est): 965.4K **Privately Held**
SIC: 3663 Mfg Radio/Tv Communication Equipment
PA: Sonitor Ips Holding As
Drammensveien 288
Oslo 0283

(G-1652)
SOUNDVIEW PAPER MILLS LLC (DH)
1 Sound Shore Dr Ste 203 (06830-7251)
PHONE..................................201 796-4000
George Wurtz, *CEO*
Karl Meyers, *President*
Tim Crawford, *Senior VP*
John McLean, *Vice Pres*
Kimberly Knotts, *CFO*
EMP: 7 **EST:** 2012
SALES (est): 477.6MM
SALES (corp-wide): 2.9B **Privately Held**
SIC: 2676 Mfg Sanitary Paper Products
HQ: Soundview Paper Holdings Llc
1 Market St
Elmwood Park NJ 07407
201 796-4000

(G-1653)
STELLA PRESS LLC
58 Brookridge Dr (06830-4830)
PHONE..................................203 661-2735
Irving Schwartz, *Principal*
EMP: 3 **EST:** 2016
SALES (est): 81.4K **Privately Held**
SIC: 2711 Newspapers-Publishing/Printing

(G-1654)
TEED OFF PUBLISHING INC
48 Nicholas Ave (06831-4924)
PHONE..................................561 266-0872
EMP: 4 **EST:** 2009
SALES (est): 277.5K **Privately Held**
SIC: 2741 Misc Publishing

(G-1655)
TIMER DIGEST PUBLISHING INC
268 Round Hill Rd (06831-3359)
P.O. Box 1688 (06836-1688)
PHONE..................................203 629-2589
Jim Schmidt, *President*
EMP: 5
SALES (est): 429.1K **Privately Held**
WEB: www.timerdigest.com
SIC: 2721 6282 Periodicals-Publishing/Printing Investment Advisory Service

(G-1656)
TMS INTERNATIONAL LLC
165 W Putnam Ave (06830-5222)
PHONE..................................203 629-8383
EMP: 3 **Privately Held**
SIC: 3312 Blast Furnace-Steel Works
HQ: Tms International, Llc
Southside Wrks Bldg 1 3f
Pittsburgh PA 15203
412 678-6141

(G-1657)
TRI-STATE LED INC
255 Mill St (06830-5806)
PHONE..................................203 813-3791
Ron Young, *President*
Mike Forlivio, *Regional Mgr*
Sam Thompson, *Opers Staff*
Bob Ostrander, *Admin Sec*
EMP: 14 **EST:** 2010
SALES (est): 3.7MM
SALES (corp-wide): 99.9MM **Publicly Held**
SIC: 3646 Mfg Commercial Lighting Fixtures
PA: Revolution Lighting Technologies, Inc.
177 Broad St Fl 12
Stamford CT 06901
203 504-1111

(G-1658)
TURNSTONE INC
Also Called: AlphaGraphics
154 Prospect St (06830-6130)
PHONE..................................203 625-0000
Karen Brinker, *President*
EMP: 15
SALES (est): 2.2MM **Privately Held**
SIC: 2752 Comm Prtg Litho

(G-1659)
UST
100 W Putnam Ave (06830-5361)
PHONE..................................203 661-1100
Vincent Gierer, *Chairman*
EMP: 15

GEOGRAPHIC

SALES (est): 2.2MM **Privately Held**
SIC: 2141 Tobacco Stemming/Redrying

(G-1660)
VCS GROUP LLC
Vincent Camuto LLC-Mens
411 W Putnam Ave Fl 2 (06830-6261)
PHONE..................................203 413-6500
Alex Delcielo, *Branch Mgr*
EMP: 3 **Privately Held**
SIC: 3143 Mens Footwear, Except Athletic
HQ: Vcs Group Llc
411 W Putnam Ave Ste 210
Greenwich CT 06830
203 413-6500

(G-1661)
WESTCHESTER INDUSTRIES INC
485 W Putnam Ave (06830-6060)
PHONE..................................203 661-0055
Joe Cotter, *Ch of Bd*
EMP: 18
SALES (est): 3.6MM **Privately Held**
SIC: 2951 1611 Mfg Asphalt Mixtures/Blocks Highway/Street Construction

(G-1662)
XMI CORPORATION
140 Greenwich Ave (06830-6556)
PHONE..................................800 838-0424
Elizabeth Pulitzer, *Manager*
EMP: 3
SALES (est): 154.6K
SALES (corp-wide): 6.8MM **Privately Held**
WEB: www.xmi.com
SIC: 2323 Mfg Men's/Boy's Neckwear
PA: Xmi Corporation
8296 Commerce Pkwy Ste 2
Chippewa Falls WI 54729
715 723-1999

Griswold
New London County

(G-1663)
GRACIE MAES KITCHEN LLC
383 Bethel Rd (06351-8802)
PHONE..................................860 885-8250
Jennifer Chominski,
Betty Kubica,
EMP: 5
SALES (est): 277.9K **Privately Held**
SIC: 2051 Mfg Bread/Related Products

Groton
New London County

(G-1664)
210 INNOVATIONS
210 Leonard Dr (06340-5334)
PHONE..................................860 445-0210
James Marquis, *Partner*
▲ **EMP:** 6
SALES (est): 515K **Privately Held**
SIC: 3999 Mfg Misc Products

(G-1665)
CASE PATTERNS INC
Also Called: Case Patterns & Wood Products
257 South Rd (06340-4611)
P.O. Box 666 (06340-0666)
PHONE..................................860 445-6722
James Case, *President*
Carol Case, *Vice Pres*
EMP: 3 **EST:** 1975
SQ FT: 3,500
SALES: 350K **Privately Held**
SIC: 3543 3999 Mfg Industrial Patterns Mfg Misc Products

(G-1666)
CASHON
Also Called: Alue Optics
350 W Shore Ave (06340-8843)
PHONE..................................786 325-4144
John X Watson, *Principal*
EMP: 3
SALES (est): 224.3K **Privately Held**
SIC: 3851 Mfg Ophthalmic Goods

(G-1667)
CATELECTRIC CORP (PA)
33 Island Cir S (06340-8823)
PHONE..................................860 912-0800
Robert M Furek, *CEO*
Peter D Pappas, *President*
EMP: 3
SQ FT: 400
SALES (est): 432.9K **Privately Held**
WEB: www.catelectric.biz
SIC: 3567 Mfg Industrial Furnaces & Ovens

(G-1668)
COMPONENTS FOR MFG LLC
26 High St (06340-5752)
PHONE..................................860 572-1671
Tracey Jacey, *Branch Mgr*
EMP: 3
SALES (corp-wide): 1.4MM **Privately Held**
SIC: 3999 Mfg Misc Products
PA: Components For Manufacturing Llc
800 Flanders Rd Unit 3-5
Mystic CT 06355
860 245-5326

(G-1669)
CUSTOM MARINE CANVAS LLC
Also Called: Hood Sailmakers
71 Marsh Rd (06340-5619)
PHONE..................................860 572-9547
Katharine Bradford,
EMP: 6
SQ FT: 3,000
SALES: 330K **Privately Held**
SIC: 2211 2394 Cotton Broadwoven Fabric Mill Mfg Canvas/Related Products

(G-1670)
DONCASTERS INC
Also Called: Doncasters Precision Castings-
835 Poquonnock Rd (06340-4537)
PHONE..................................860 446-4803
Bruce Ebright, *Manager*
Richard Brown, *Manager*
EMP: 84
SALES (corp-wide): 604.8MM **Privately Held**
SIC: 3356 3369 3324 Nonferrous Rolling/Drawing Nonferrous Metal Foundry Steel Investment Foundry
HQ: Doncasters Inc.
835 Poquonnock Rd
Groton CT 06340
-

(G-1671)
DONCASTERS INC (HQ)
835 Poquonnock Rd (06340-4537)
P.O. Box 1146 (06340-1146)
PHONE..................................860 449-1603
David Smoot, *CEO*
Christian Garcia, *General Mgr*
Tim Martin, *Vice Pres*
Peter Rowe, *Vice Pres*
Jim Bonny, *Safety Dir*
◆ **EMP:** 60
SQ FT: 100,000
SALES (est): 126MM
SALES (corp-wide): 604.8MM **Privately Held**
SIC: 3356 3728 7699 3511 Nonferrous Rollng/Drawng Mfg Aircraft Parts/Equip Repair Services Mfg Turbine/Genratr Sets
PA: Doncasters Group Limited
Repton House
Burton-On-Trent STAFFS
133 286-4900

(G-1672)
DONCASTERS US HLDINGS 2018 INC
835 Poquonnock Rd (06340-4537)
PHONE..................................860 677-1376
Ian Molyneux, *President*
Duncan Hinks, *Treasurer*
EMP: 10
SALES (est): 390.1K **Privately Held**
SIC: 3324 Steel Investment Foundry

(G-1673)
ELECTRIC BOAT CORPORATION
210 Mitchell St (06340-4046)
P.O. Box 949 (06340-0949)
PHONE..................................860 433-0503
Ellen Mathews, *Principal*
William Jones, *Purch Mgr*
Philip Kiley, *Senior Buyer*
Michelle Sottile Hoyt, *Buyer*
Scott Fermeglia, *Engineer*
EMP: 91
SALES (corp-wide): 36.1B **Publicly Held**
SIC: 3731 Shipbuilding/Repair Ing Engineering Services
HQ: Electric Boat Corporation
75 Eastern Point Rd
Groton CT 06340
-

(G-1674)
ELECTRIC BOAT CORPORATION
Also Called: Electric Boat Fairwater Div
75 Eastern Point Rd (06340-4905)
PHONE..................................860 433-3000
Susan Williams, *Branch Mgr*
EMP: 91
SALES (corp-wide): 36.1B **Publicly Held**
SIC: 3731 8711 Design/Build Submarines Engineering Svcs
HQ: Electric Boat Corporation
75 Eastern Point Rd
Groton CT 06340
-

(G-1675)
ELECTRIC BOAT CORPORATION (HQ)
Also Called: General Dynamics Electric Boat
75 Eastern Point Rd (06340-4905)
P.O. Box 1327 (06340-1327)
PHONE..................................860 433-3000
John P Casey, *President*
Craig Sipe, *General Mgr*
Lew Clark, *Editor*
Paul Ramsey, *Editor*
Greg Haines, *Division VP*
◆ **EMP:** 6399
SQ FT: 2,600,000
SALES (est): 2.4B
SALES (corp-wide): 36.1B **Publicly Held**
WEB: www.gdeb.com
SIC: 3731 8711 Shipbuilding/Repairing Engineering Services
PA: General Dynamics Corporation
11011 Sunset Hills Rd
Reston VA 20190
703 876-3000

(G-1676)
FINE FOOD SERVICES INC
Also Called: Paul's Pasta Shop
223 Thames St (06340-3955)
PHONE..................................860 445-5276
Paul Fidrych, *President*
Dorothy P Fidrych, *Principal*
Edward J Planeta Jr, *Principal*
Edward J Planeta, *Senior VP*
Paul T Fidrych, *Treasurer*
EMP: 24
SQ FT: 2,000
SALES (est): 1.8MM **Privately Held**
WEB: www.paulspasta.com
SIC: 2099 5812 Mfg Fresh Pasta And Pasta Restaurant

(G-1677)
HBI BOAT LLC
145 Pearl St (06340-5773)
PHONE..................................860 536-7776
William Reed,
EMP: 4
SALES: 82K **Privately Held**
SIC: 3732 Boatbuilding/Repairing

(G-1678)
KONGSBERG DGTAL SIMULATION INC
170 Leonard Dr (06340-5320)
P.O. Box 180, West Mystic (06388-0180)
PHONE..................................860 405-2300
Geir Haoy, *President*
Erich Stritzel, *President*
Herbert Taylor, *General Mgr*
David Meers, *Vice Pres*
▲ **EMP:** 18
SQ FT: 10,000
SALES (est): 3.4MM
SALES (corp-wide): 1.5B **Privately Held**
WEB: www.navpac.com
SIC: 3824 Mfg Fluid Meter/Counting Devices
HQ: Kongsberg Maritime As
Strandpromenaden 50
Horten 3183
-

(G-1679)
LARRYS AUTO MACHINE LLC
Also Called: Larry's Auto Machine & Supply
175 Leonard Dr (06340-5320)
PHONE..................................860 449-9112
Gary Espinosa,
EMP: 3
SQ FT: 2,000
SALES (est): 492.5K **Privately Held**
SIC: 3599 Mfg Industrial Machinery

(G-1680)
LEGNOS MEDICAL INC
973 North Rd (06340-3272)
PHONE..................................860 446-8058
Peter J Legnos, *President*
EMP: 10
SALES (est): 399.6K **Privately Held**
SIC: 3845 Mfg Electromedical Equipment

(G-1681)
OUTER LIGHT BREWING CO LLC
266 Bridge St Ste 1 (06340-3739)
PHONE..................................475 201-9972
Matthew Ferrucci,
Tom Drejer,
EMP: 3
SALES: 500K **Privately Held**
SIC: 2082 Mfg Malt Beverages

(G-1682)
PCC STRUCTURALS GROTON (DH)
839 Poquonnock Rd (06340-4537)
PHONE..................................860 405-3700
William C McCormick, *Ch of Bd*
Joseph B Cox, *President*
▲ **EMP:** 175 **EST:** 1990
SALES (est): 301MM
SALES (corp-wide): 225.3B **Publicly Held**
SIC: 3364 Mfg Nonferrous Die-Castings
HQ: Wyman-Gordon Company
244 Worcester St
North Grafton MA 01536
508 839-8252

(G-1683)
PEL ASSOCIATES LLC (PA)
187 Ledgewood Rd Apt 407 (06340-6627)
PHONE..................................860 446-9921
Morton L Wallach, *Owner*
EMP: 4 **EST:** 1990
SQ FT: 2,000
SALES (est): 729K **Privately Held**
WEB: www.pelassociates.com
SIC: 3089 Mfg Plastic Products

(G-1684)
PFIZER INC
100 Eastern Point Rd (06340-4950)
PHONE..................................860 441-4100
Gerardo Ortiz, *General Mgr*
Lori Siller, *Purchasing*
Cheryl Tow-Keogh, *QC Mgr*
Iasson Mustakis, *Research*
Jeff Ballachino, *Senior Mgr*
EMP: 146
SALES (corp-wide): 53.6B **Publicly Held**
WEB: www.pfizer.com
SIC: 2834 Mfg Pharmaceutical Preparations
PA: Pfizer Inc.
235 E 42nd St Rm 107
New York NY 10017
212 733-2323

(G-1685)
R & B APPAREL PLUS LLC
78 Plaza Ct (06340-4223)
PHONE..................................860 333-1757
Connie Flynn, *Finance*
Richard P Bernardo Sr, *Mng Member*
Patricia Jullarine,

▲ = Import ▼=Export
◆ =Import/Export

EMP: 4
SQ FT: 1,000
SALES (est): 522.6K Privately Held
SIC: 2759 7389 5199 Commercial Printing Business Services Whol Nondurable Goods

(G-1686)
SKYLINE VET PHARMA INC
37 Skyline Dr (06340-5427)
PHONE..................................860 625-0424
Serge Martinod, *CEO*
George Murphy, *Vice Pres*
EMP: 3
SALES (est): 123.2K Privately Held
SIC: 2834 Mfg Pharmaceutical Preparations

(G-1687)
SYSTAMEDIC INC
1084 Shennecossett Rd (06340-6061)
PHONE..................................860 912-6101
Robert A Volkmann, *President*
EMP: 4
SALES (est): 291.4K Privately Held
SIC: 2834 Mfg Pharmaceutical Preparations

(G-1688)
THAYERMAHAN INC
120b Leonard Dr (06340-5336)
PHONE..................................860 785-9994
Michael Connor, *CEO*
Richard Hine, *CFO*
EMP: 32
SALES (est): 3.9MM Privately Held
SIC: 3812 8731 Mfg Search/Navigation Equipment Commercial Physical Research

(G-1689)
UNITED STATES DEPT OF NAVY
Also Called: D L A Disposition Services
33 Grayback Ave Bldg 33 (06349)
P.O. Box 12 (06349-5012)
PHONE..................................860 694-3524
Michael Efstathiou, *Director*
EMP: 6 Publicly Held
SIC: 3812 Mfg Search/Navigation Equipment
HQ: United States Department Of The Navy
1200 Navy Pentagon
Washington DC 20350

(G-1690)
YOURMEMBERSHIPCOM INC
Also Called: Your Membership.com
541 Eastern Point Rd (06340-5158)
PHONE..................................860 271-7241
EMP: 7
SALES (corp-wide): 2B Privately Held
SIC: 7372 Prepackaged Software Services
HQ: Yourmembership.Com, Inc.
9620 Exec Ctr N 200
Saint Petersburg FL 33702
727 827-0046

Guilford
New Haven County

(G-1691)
ADVANCE DEVELOPMENT & MFG
325 Soundview Rd (06437-2970)
P.O. Box 396 (06437-0396)
PHONE..................................203 453-4325
John F Fisher, *President*
Robert Fisher, *Chairman*
EMP: 10 EST: 1956
SQ FT: 12,000
SALES (est): 2.2MM Privately Held
SIC: 3599 Mfg Industrial Machinery

(G-1692)
ALGONQUIN INDUSTRIES INC (HQ)
129 Soundview Rd (06437-2943)
PHONE..................................203 453-4348
Kamesh Chivukula, *President*
John Bielot, *Administration*
◆ EMP: 54
SQ FT: 104,000
SALES (est): 18.9MM
SALES (corp-wide): 400MM Privately Held
WEB: www.reawire.com
SIC: 3357 Nonferrous Wiredrawing/Insulating
PA: Rea Magnet Wire Company, Inc.
3400 E Coliseum Blvd # 200
Fort Wayne IN 46805
260 421-7321

(G-1693)
BIO-MED DEVICES INC
Also Called: Bmd
61 Soundview Rd (06437-2937)
PHONE..................................203 458-0202
Dean J Bennett Jr, *Ch of Bd*
Dean J Bennett III, *President*
Doris A Bennett, *Admin Sec*
▼ EMP: 67
SQ FT: 20,000
SALES (est): 14.1MM Privately Held
WEB: www.biomeddevices.com
SIC: 3845 3841 Mfg Electromedical Equipment Mfg Surgical/Medical Instruments

(G-1694)
BREAKFAST WOODWORKS INC
135 Leetes Island Rd (06437-3027)
PHONE..................................203 458-8888
Louis Mackall, *President*
Ken Field, *Vice Pres*
EMP: 6
SQ FT: 9,000
SALES: 1.1MM Privately Held
WEB: www.breakfastwoodworks.com
SIC: 2431 Millwork

(G-1695)
BROOK & WHITTLE LIMITED (HQ)
20 Carter Dr (06437-2125)
P.O. Box 409, North Branford (06471-0409)
PHONE..................................203 483-5602
Simon Grimes, *Vice Pres*
Richard Marsie, *Plant Mgr*
Roberto Santos, *Plant Mgr*
Bob Bovee, *Prdtn Mgr*
Sean Kerr, *Prdtn Mgr*
▲ EMP: 130
SALES (est): 39.1MM
SALES (corp-wide): 7.8MM Privately Held
WEB: www.bwhittle.com
SIC: 2754 Gravure Commercial Printing
PA: Brook & Whittle Holding Corp.
20 Carter Dr
Guilford CT 06437
203 483-5602

(G-1696)
BRUSHFOIL LLC
1 Shoreline Dr Ste 6 (06437-2978)
PHONE..................................203 453-7403
Fax: 203 453-7408
EMP: 12
SALES (est): 4.7MM
SALES (corp-wide): 267.2MM Privately Held
SIC: 3081 Unsupported Plastics Film And Sheet, Nsk
HQ: Transilwrap Company, Inc.
127 Turningstone Ct
Greenville SC 60067
864 269-4690

(G-1697)
COMPETITION ENGINEERING INC
80 Carter Dr (06437-2125)
PHONE..................................203 453-5200
Richard B Moroso, *President*
Pamela Kiss, *Admin Sec*
EMP: 140
SQ FT: 70,000
SALES (est): 8MM
SALES (corp-wide): 38MM Privately Held
WEB: www.competitionengineering.com
SIC: 3714 Mfg Motor Vehicle Parts/Accessories
PA: Moroso Performance Products, Inc.
80 Carter Dr
Guilford CT 06437
203 453-6571

(G-1698)
CONNECTICUT LAW BOOK CO INC
39 Chaffinch Island Rd (06437-3244)
P.O. Box 575 (06437-0575)
PHONE..................................203 458-8000
Eugene Oleary, *President*
EMP: 15
SALES (est): 1.4MM Privately Held
WEB: www.lawreporter.com
SIC: 2731 Books-Publishing/Printing

(G-1699)
COOPERSURGICAL INC
Also Called: Lifeglobal Group, The
393 Soundview Rd (06437-2970)
PHONE..................................203 453-1700
Monica Mezezi, *Manager*
EMP: 40
SALES (corp-wide): 2.6B Publicly Held
SIC: 2836 Mfg Biological Products
HQ: Coopersurgical, Inc.
95 Corporate Dr
Trumbull CT 06611

(G-1700)
DEFIBTECH LLC (PA)
741 Boston Post Rd # 201 (06437-2714)
PHONE..................................866 333-4248
Robert Reinhardt, *CEO*
Glenn W Laub, *CEO*
Scott Smallshaw, *Info Tech Mgr*
EMP: 57
SQ FT: 10,850
SALES: 24.4MM Privately Held
WEB: www.defibtech.com
SIC: 3845 Mfg Electromedical Equipment

(G-1701)
DONALI SYSTEMS INTEGRATION INC
128 Tanner Marsh Rd (06437-2203)
PHONE..................................860 715-5432
Donald Ludington, *President*
EMP: 3
SALES (est): 395.8K Privately Held
SIC: 3699 7389 Mfg Electrical Equipment/Supplies

(G-1702)
DONNIN PUBLISHING INC
Also Called: The Real Estate Book
800 Village Walk (06437-2762)
PHONE..................................203 453-8866
Robert Schmidt, *President*
Glen Ramsteck, *Vice Pres*
EMP: 3
SQ FT: 350
SALES: 1.5MM Privately Held
SIC: 2721 Real Estate Magazine Publisher

(G-1703)
ENTERPLAY LLC
800 Village Walk Ste 307 (06437-2762)
PHONE..................................203 458-1128
Dean E Irwin, *Mng Member*
▲ EMP: 10 EST: 2007
SALES (est): 770K Privately Held
SIC: 3944 Mfg Games/Toys

(G-1704)
FITZHUGH ELECTRICAL CORP
Also Called: Timco Instruments Div
361 Long Hill Rd (06437-1827)
P.O. Box 100, Rockville RI (02873-0100)
PHONE..................................203 453-3171
EMP: 5
SALES (est): 39.7K Privately Held
SIC: 3825 Manufactures Electronic Test Equipment

(G-1705)
GENX INTERNATIONAL INC (PA)
Also Called: Life Global
393 Soundview Rd (06437-2970)
PHONE..................................203 453-1700
Fax: 203 453-1769
EMP: 30 EST: 1996
SQ FT: 18,000
SALES (est): 4MM Privately Held
WEB: www.ivfonline.com
SIC: 2836 Mfg Biological Products

(G-1706)
INTERNATIONAL COMM SVCS INC
Also Called: Ics
2 Burgis Ln (06437-2286)
PHONE..................................401 580-8888
Steven Lee, *President*
EMP: 3
SALES: 1.5MM Privately Held
SIC: 2759 Commercial Printing

(G-1707)
LAM THERAPEUTICS INC
530 Old Whitfield St (06437-3441)
PHONE..................................203 458-7100
Marylens Hernandez, *Research*
Wes Conard, *Marketing Staff*
Henri Lichenstein, *Officer*
Elizabeth Whayland, *Admin Sec*
EMP: 12
SALES (est): 1.9MM Privately Held
SIC: 2835 Mfg Diagnostic Substances

(G-1708)
LEWMAR INC (DH)
Also Called: Lewmar Marine
351 New Whitfield St (06437-3400)
PHONE..................................203 458-6200
Peter Tierney, *CEO*
Harcourt Schutz, *General Mgr*
Stacy Richards, *Business Mgr*
Kevin Donahue, *COO*
Monica Gilhuly, *Accountant*
▲ EMP: 20
SQ FT: 2,500
SALES (est): 4.1MM
SALES (corp-wide): 74MM Privately Held
WEB: www.lewmarusa.com
SIC: 3423 3429 3714 Mfg Hand/Edge Tools Mfg Hardware Mfg Motor Vehicle Parts/Accessories
HQ: Lewmar Limited
Southmoor Lane
Havant HANTS PO9 1
239 247-1841

(G-1709)
MATTHEW FISEL ND
20 Dunk Rock Rd (06437-2509)
PHONE..................................203 453-0122
Matthew Fisel, *Principal*
EMP: 3 EST: 2010
SALES (est): 196.4K Privately Held
SIC: 3221 Mfg Glass Containers

(G-1710)
MCBOOKS PRESS INC
246 Goose Ln Ste 200 (06437-2186)
PHONE..................................607 272-2114
Alexander Skutt, *President*
Panda Musgrove, *Publisher*
▲ EMP: 5
SALES (est): 1.2MM
SALES (corp-wide): 293.8MM Privately Held
WEB: www.mcbooks.com
SIC: 2731 Books-Publishing/Printing
PA: The Rowman & Littlefield Publishing Group Inc
4501 Forbes Blvd Ste 200
Lanham MD 20706
301 459-3366

(G-1711)
MOROSO PERFORMANCE PDTS INC (PA)
80 Carter Dr (06437-2116)
PHONE..................................203 453-6571
Richard B Moroso, *President*
Gary Burkel, *Opers Dir*
James Knudsen, *Buyer*
Phil Tulli, *QC Mgr*
John Galayda, *Engineer*
▲ EMP: 190
SQ FT: 70,000
SALES (est): 38MM Privately Held
WEB: www.moroso.com
SIC: 3714 Mfg Motor Vehicle Parts/Accessories

GEOGRAPHIC

(G-1712)
MORRIS COMMUNICATIONS CO LLC
Also Called: Globe Pequot Press
246 Goose Ln Ste 200 (06437-2186)
P.O. Box 480 (06437-0480)
PHONE..................................203 458-4500
Scott Watrous, *General Mgr*
Lynn Zelem, *Production*
Bounthavy Soukthideth, *Human Res Mgr*
Mark Carbray, *Sales Staff*
Shana Capozza, *Mktg Dir*
EMP: 90 **Privately Held**
WEB: www.morris.com
SIC: 2711 Newspapers-Publishing/Printing
HQ: Morris Communications Company Llc
725 Broad St
Augusta GA 30901
706 724-0851

(G-1713)
NORTHSTAR BIOSCIENCES LLC
2514 Boston Post Rd 4r (06437-1338)
PHONE..................................203 689-5399
Mike Vitagliano, *COO*
EMP: 3
SALES (est): 162K **Privately Held**
SIC: 2834 Mfg Pharmaceutical Preparations

(G-1714)
PEACEFUL DAILY INC
800 Village Walk Ste 103 (06437-2762)
PHONE..................................203 909-2961
Sandra Corso, *CEO*
EMP: 6
SALES (est): 445.8K **Privately Held**
SIC: 2711 Newspapers-Publishing/Printing

(G-1715)
RAM TECHNOLOGIES LLC
29 Soundview Rd Ste 12 (06437-2997)
PHONE..................................203 453-3916
Richard Mentelos, *President*
Nancy Degray, *Mfg Staff*
Susan Senter, *CFO*
▲ **EMP:** 10 **EST:** 1992
SQ FT: 3,000
SALES (est): 4MM **Privately Held**
SIC: 3845 Mfg Electromedical Equipment

(G-1716)
REA MAGNET WIRE COMPANY INC
Algonquin Industries Division
129 Soundview Rd (06437-2972)
PHONE..................................203 738-6100
Kamesh Chivukula, *President*
Rodney Goodman, *Sales Mgr*
EMP: 90
SQ FT: 104,000
SALES (corp-wide): 400MM **Privately Held**
WEB: www.reawire.com
SIC: 3357 Drawing & Insulating Of Nonferrous Wire
PA: Rea Magnet Wire Company, Inc.
3400 E Coliseum Blvd # 200
Fort Wayne IN 46805
260 421-7321

(G-1717)
SAYBROOK PRESS INCORPORATED
39 Chaffinch Island Rd (06437-3244)
P.O. Box 575 (06437-0575)
PHONE..................................203 458-3637
Eugene O Leary, *President*
Jean Oleary, *Treasurer*
EMP: 15
SALES (est): 926.3K **Privately Held**
SIC: 2791 2789 2759 Typesetting Services Bookbinding/Related Work Commercial Printing

(G-1718)
SCHMITT REALTY HOLDINGS INC (PA)
251 Boston Post Rd (06437-2904)
P.O. Box 448 (06437-0448)
PHONE..................................203 453-4334
William G Gunther, *CEO*
Lisa Sutherland, *Technology*
◆ **EMP:** 59 **EST:** 1874
SQ FT: 48,000
SALES (est): 19.2MM **Privately Held**
WEB: www.georgeschmitt.com
SIC: 2759 Commercial Printing

(G-1719)
SCHMITT REALTY HOLDINGS INC
Also Called: George Schmithet and Company
251 Boston Post Rd (06437-2904)
PHONE..................................203 453-4334
Gunther William, *President*
EMP: 5
SALES (corp-wide): 19.2MM **Privately Held**
SIC: 2759 Commercial Printing
PA: Schmitt Realty Holdings, Inc.
251 Boston Post Rd
Guilford CT 06437
203 453-4334

(G-1720)
SOLAR GENERATIONS LLC
741 Podunk Rd (06437-2217)
PHONE..................................203 453-3920
Daphne Byrne, *Mng Member*
▲ **EMP:** 3
SALES (est): 350K **Privately Held**
SIC: 3823 Mfg Process Control Instruments

(G-1721)
T KEEFE AND SONS
1790 Little Meadow Rd (06437-1620)
PHONE..................................203 457-0267
Thomas Keefe, *Partner*
Jason Keefe, *Partner*
Regina Keefe, *Partner*
EMP: 3
SALES (est): 472.9K **Privately Held**
SIC: 3441 Structural Metal Fabrication

(G-1722)
TAKE CAKE LLC
2458 Boston Post Rd Ste 2 (06437-1398)
PHONE..................................203 453-1896
Nancy Purcell, *Owner*
EMP: 8
SQ FT: 1,200
SALES (est): 410K **Privately Held**
WEB: www.originaltakethecake.com
SIC: 2051 Mfg Bread/Related Products

(G-1723)
UP WITH PAPER
34 York St Ste 3 (06437-2473)
PHONE..................................203 453-3300
Monika Brandrup, *General Mgr*
Brandrup Monika, *Vice Pres*
EMP: 6
SALES (est): 616K **Privately Held**
SIC: 2621 Paper Mill

(G-1724)
WALSTON INC
131 Nut Plains Rd (06437-2135)
PHONE..................................203 453-5929
Richard Walston, *President*
Marie Walston, *Vice Pres*
EMP: 9
SQ FT: 4,500
SALES (est): 1.1MM **Privately Held**
SIC: 2431 Mfg Millwork

(G-1725)
ZUSE INC
727 Boston Post Rd Ste 1 (06437-2793)
PHONE..................................203 458-3295
Ted Zuse, *President*
Skip Zuse, *Vice Pres*
Thatcher Zuse, *Shareholder*
EMP: 11
SQ FT: 6,000
SALES (est): 1.2MM **Privately Held**
SIC: 2396 2395 Mfg Auto/Apparel Trimming Pleating/Stitching Services

Haddam
Middlesex County

(G-1726)
ENERGY TECH LLC
63 Church Hill Rd (06438-1124)
PHONE..................................860 345-3993
Joseph L Brasky,
Diane Brasky,
EMP: 6
SALES (est): 949.5K **Privately Held**
WEB: www.energytech-brasky.com
SIC: 3825 Mfg Electrical Measuring Instruments

(G-1727)
MOONLIGHT MEDIA LLC
Also Called: Koolart USA
95 Bridge Rd Bldg 4b (06438-1354)
PHONE..................................860 345-3595
Valerie Cox,
Kristopher Cox,
EMP: 6 **EST:** 1996
SQ FT: 5,600
SALES: 250K **Privately Held**
WEB: www.storesign.com
SIC: 2759 Commerical Printing

Hamden
New Haven County

(G-1728)
A & K RAILROAD MATERIALS INC
200 Benton St (06517-3907)
PHONE..................................203 495-8790
Ronald Johnson, *Manager*
EMP: 6
SALES (corp-wide): 150.1MM **Privately Held**
WEB: www.akrailroad.com
SIC: 3531 5211 5088 Mfg Construction Machinery Ret Lumber/Building Materials Whol Transportation Equipment
PA: A & K Railroad Materials, Inc.
1505 S Redwood Rd
Salt Lake City UT 84104
801 974-5484

(G-1729)
ABBOTT PRINTING COMPANY INC
912 Dixwell Ave (06514-5014)
PHONE..................................203 562-5562
Nancy B Mellone, *President*
David Mellone, *Vice Pres*
EMP: 5
SQ FT: 5,000
SALES (est): 696.8K **Privately Held**
SIC: 2752 Lithographic Commercial Printing

(G-1730)
ADVANCED PRODUCT SOLUTIONS LLC
555 Sherman Ave Unit C16 (06514-1152)
PHONE..................................203 745-4225
Rick Palmeri, *Partner*
Jim Beveridge, *Partner*
EMP: 6
SQ FT: 3,000
SALES: 350K **Privately Held**
SIC: 3672 5063 Mfg Printed Circuit Boards Whol Electrical Equipment

(G-1731)
ALPHAGRAPHICS LLC
24 Rossotto Dr (06514-1335)
PHONE..................................203 230-0018
Jerry Kenney, *Vice Pres*
EMP: 4 **EST:** 2010
SALES (est): 428.4K **Privately Held**
SIC: 2752 Comm Prtg Litho

(G-1732)
AMPHENOL CORPORATION
Amphenol Spctr-Strip Oprations
720 Sherman Ave (06514-1146)
P.O. Box 4340 (06514-0340)
PHONE..................................203 287-2272
Eric Juntwait, *General Mgr*
Dennis Lynn, *Controller*
Denise Masulli, *Human Res Mgr*
EMP: 72
SALES (corp-wide): 8.2B **Publicly Held**
SIC: 3678 Mfg Electronic Connectors
PA: Amphenol Corporation
358 Hall Ave
Wallingford CT 06492
203 265-8900

(G-1733)
B-P PRODUCTS INC
100 Sanford St (06514-1775)
PHONE..................................203 288-0200
Dorothy R Podgwaite, *CEO*
Bruce Giannetti, *Administration*
EMP: 28
SQ FT: 32,000
SALES: 2.3MM **Privately Held**
WEB: www.b-pproducts.com
SIC: 2657 2675 2679 2631 Mfg Folding Paperbrd Box Mfg Die-Cut Paper/Board Mfg Converted Paper Prdt Paperboard Mill Mfg Dies/Tools/Jigs/Fixt

(G-1734)
BAR-PLATE MANUFACTURING CO
1180 Sherman Ave (06514-1300)
P.O. Box 185470 (06518-0470)
PHONE..................................203 397-0033
Brian Garrity, *President*
▲ **EMP:** 10 **EST:** 1985
SQ FT: 17,000
SALES (est): 973.4K
SALES (corp-wide): 360.9MM **Privately Held**
WEB: www.barplate.com
SIC: 3554 Mfg Paper Industrial Machinery
PA: R.A.F. Industries, Inc.
165 Township Line Rd # 2100
Jenkintown PA 19046
215 572-0738

(G-1735)
BEVERAGE PUBLICATIONS INC
Also Called: Connecticut Beverage Journal
2508 Whitney Ave Apt N (06518-3042)
P.O. Box 185159 (06518-0159)
PHONE..................................203 288-3375
Gerald Slone, *President*
EMP: 3 **EST:** 1949
SQ FT: 2,000
SALES (est): 357.6K **Privately Held**
WEB: www.ctbeveragejournal.com
SIC: 2721 Periodicals-Publishing/Printing

(G-1736)
CARLTON INDUSTRIES CORP
33 Rossotto Dr (06514-1336)
PHONE..................................203 288-5605
Brad Carlton, *President*
Weston See, *Vice Pres*
Beverly Kempa, *Purch Agent*
Donna Conklin, *Buyer*
Susan Stone, *Purchasing*
◆ **EMP:** 49
SQ FT: 27,000
SALES (est): 11.8MM **Privately Held**
WEB: www.carltonindustriesonline.com
SIC: 3672 Mfg Printed Circuit Boards

(G-1737)
CENTURY SIGN LLC
2666 State St (06517-2232)
PHONE..................................203 230-9000
Bill Lynch,
EMP: 3
SQ FT: 3,600
SALES (est): 386K **Privately Held**
SIC: 3993 7389 Mfg Signs/Advertising Specialties Business Services

(G-1738)
COPY STOP INC
Also Called: Printing Store, The
2371 Whitney Ave (06518-3206)
PHONE..................................203 288-6401
Joyce Curran, *President*
Robert Curran, *Vice Pres*
Margaret Curran, *Treasurer*
Christopher Curran, *Director*
Jacob Curran, *Director*
EMP: 4 **EST:** 1974
SQ FT: 6,000
SALES (est): 39.9K **Privately Held**
SIC: 2752 5943 2791 Lithographic Commercial Printing Ret Stationery Typesetting Services

(G-1739)
CROWN MOLDING ETC LLC
148 Gillies Rd (06517-2116)
PHONE..................................203 287-9424
Jefrey B Agli, *Principal*
EMP: 3

▲ = Import ▼=Export
◆ =Import/Export

SALES (est): 216.8K **Privately Held**
SIC: 3089 Mfg Plastic Products

(G-1740)
CUSTOM & PRECISION PDTS INC
2893 State St Rear (06517-1712)
P.O. Box 5446 (06518-0446)
PHONE..................................203 281-0818
Diamante Dente, *President*
Gregory Dente, *Admin Sec*
EMP: 9
SQ FT: 12,000
SALES (est): 1.4MM **Privately Held**
WEB: www.injection-moldings.com
SIC: 3444 Mfg Sheet Metalwork

(G-1741)
CYCLONE MICROSYSTEMS INC
25 Marne St (06514-3610)
PHONE..................................203 786-5536
Joel Zackin, *President*
George Tafuto, *Opers Mgr*
Scott Coulter, *Engineer*
Szeming Leung, *Human Res Dir*
EMP: 38
SALES (est): 7.3MM **Privately Held**
WEB: www.cyclone.com
SIC: 3571 3672 Mfg Electronic Computers Mfg Printed Circuit Boards

(G-1742)
CYCLONE PCIE SYSTEMS LLC
25 Marne St (06514-3610)
PHONE..................................203 786-5536
George Tafuto,
EMP: 5
SQ FT: 4,000
SALES (est): 210.9K **Privately Held**
SIC: 3577 Mfg Computer Peripheral Equipment

(G-1743)
DAILY IMPRESSIONS LLC
Also Called: Janitorial Commercial Gen Svc
60 Village Cir (06514-3342)
PHONE..................................203 508-5305
Tommie Shields, *Mng Member*
EMP: 4
SALES: 50K **Privately Held**
SIC: 2711 Newspapers-Publishing/Printing

(G-1744)
DUROL COMPANY
2580 State St (06517-3009)
P.O. Box 4141 (06514-0141)
PHONE..................................203 288-3383
Cynthia Civitello, *President*
Carol D Newman, *Vice Pres*
EMP: 15 **EST:** 1962
SQ FT: 9,000
SALES (est): 2.6MM **Privately Held**
WEB: www.durol.com
SIC: 3599 Mfg Industrial Machinery

(G-1745)
ELECTRONIC SPC CONN INC
19 Hamden Park Dr (06517-3151)
PHONE..................................203 288-1707
William Kovacs, *President*
Duc Huu Nguyen, *Vice Pres*
EMP: 24
SQ FT: 12,500
SALES (est): 4.7MM **Privately Held**
SIC: 3672 Mfg Printed Circuit Boards

(G-1746)
ELM CITY CHEESE COMPANY INC
2240 State St (06517-3798)
PHONE..................................203 865-5768
Marjorie Weinstein-Kowal, *President*
Suzanne Weinstein, *Admin Sec*
EMP: 10 **EST:** 1896
SQ FT: 12,000
SALES (est): 1.5MM **Privately Held**
SIC: 2022 Mfg Cheese

(G-1747)
ELM CITY MFG JEWELERS INC
29 Marne St (06514)
PHONE..................................203 248-2195
Anthony Cuomo, *President*
Marianne Cuomo, *Treasurer*
Rosemarie Cuomo, *Admin Sec*
EMP: 6 **EST:** 1927
SQ FT: 2,000
SALES (est): 670.5K **Privately Held**
SIC: 3911 5094 5944 Mfg Whol & Ret Jewelry

(G-1748)
ENERGYBLOX INC
21 Overlook Dr (06514-1140)
PHONE..................................203 230-3000
Stephen Young, *CEO*
Peter Knudsen, *Chairman*
EMP: 6
SALES (est): 251.5K **Privately Held**
SIC: 3621 Mfg Motors/Generators

(G-1749)
FARMINGTON RIVER HOLDINGS LLC
Also Called: Earmark
1125 Dixwell Ave (06514-4735)
PHONE..................................203 777-2130
Andrew Cowell, *Mng Member*
EMP: 5
SQ FT: 11,000
SALES (est): 334.9K **Privately Held**
SIC: 3669 Mfg Communications Equipment

(G-1750)
FURS BY PREZIOSO LTD
Also Called: Prezioso Furs
2969 Whitney Ave Ste 201 (06518-2556)
PHONE..................................203 230-2930
Tom Prezioso, *President*
EMP: 3
SQ FT: 2,800
SALES (est): 344.2K **Privately Held**
SIC: 2221 Manmade Broadwoven Fabric Mill

(G-1751)
GOLDSLAGER CONVEYOR COMPANY
73 Fernwood Rd (06517-2915)
P.O. Box 6326 (06517-0326)
PHONE..................................203 795-9886
Bruce Goldslager, *CEO*
Ralph Gould, *Shareholder*
Sharon Goldslager, *Admin Sec*
EMP: 3
SALES (est): 557.4K **Privately Held**
SIC: 3535 Whol Industrial Equipment

(G-1752)
GUTKIN ENTERPRISES LLC
Also Called: First Place USA
1349 Dixwell Ave Ste 1 (06514-4124)
PHONE..................................203 777-5510
Carol Gutkin, *CFO*
Howard Gutkin,
EMP: 6
SALES (est): 544.3K **Privately Held**
SIC: 3999 3953 Mfg Trophies & Awards

(G-1753)
HAMDEN GRINDING
555 Sherman Ave Ste 11 (06514-1154)
PHONE..................................203 288-2906
Joe Nuzzo, *Owner*
EMP: 5
SALES (est): 190K **Privately Held**
SIC: 3999 Mfg Misc Products

(G-1754)
HAMDEN JOURNAL LLC
99 Burke St (06514-4819)
P.O. Box 187101 (06518-7019)
PHONE..................................203 668-6307
Shala Latorraca, *Sales Staff*
EMP: 3
SALES (est): 189.9K **Privately Held**
SIC: 2711 Newspapers-Publishing/Printing

(G-1755)
HAMDEN METAL SERVICE COMPANY
2 Broadway (06518-2629)
PHONE..................................203 281-1522
Jay Hirsch, *President*
Edward Hirsch III, *Vice Pres*
Martha Hirsch, *Admin Sec*
EMP: 15 **EST:** 1976
SALES (est): 2.1MM **Privately Held**
WEB: www.hamdenmetal.com
SIC: 3315 3357 Mfg Steel Wire/Related Products Nonferrous Wiredrawing/Insulating

(G-1756)
HAMDEN PRESS INC
1054 Dixwell Ave (06514-4912)
PHONE..................................203 624-0554
Phillip Costanzo, *President*
Jerome Constanzo, *Treasurer*
Robert Costanzo, *Admin Sec*
EMP: 3
SQ FT: 2,700
SALES (est): 326.7K **Privately Held**
SIC: 2752 Lithographic Commercial Printing

(G-1757)
HAMDEN SHEET METAL INC
1079 Dixwell Ave (06514-4718)
PHONE..................................203 776-1472
Michael Soufrine, *President*
Samford Soufrine, *Vice Pres*
Wayne Soufrine, *Vice Pres*
Betty Soufrine, *Admin Sec*
EMP: 4
SQ FT: 5,000
SALES: 200K **Privately Held**
SIC: 3444 1711 1799 Sheet Metal Heating Air Conditioning Welding & Conveyor Work

(G-1758)
HAMDEN SPORTS CENTER INC
2858 Whitney Ave (06518-2554)
PHONE..................................203 248-9898
Robert Bush, *President*
Dan Bush, *Vice Pres*
EMP: 3
SALES (est): 256K **Privately Held**
SIC: 3949 Ret Sporting Goods/Bicycles

(G-1759)
HERRICK & COWELL COMPANY INC
839 Sherman Ave (06514-1132)
P.O. Box 4332 (06514-0332)
PHONE..................................203 288-2578
EMP: 9 **EST:** 1874
SQ FT: 16,000
SALES (est): 1.1MM **Privately Held**
SIC: 3599 3549 Mfg Industrial Machinery Mfg Metalworking Machinery

(G-1760)
HPI MANUFACTURING INC
375 Morse St (06517-3133)
PHONE..................................203 777-5395
Glenn M Ayer, *Principal*
EMP: 4 **EST:** 2016
SALES (est): 344.8K **Privately Held**
SIC: 3999 Mfg Misc Products

(G-1761)
INSULPANE CONNECTICUT INC
Also Called: Solar Seal of Connecticut
30 Edmund St (06517-3914)
PHONE..................................800 922-3248
Paul Cody, *CEO*
Frederick Federico Sr, *Principal*
Frederick Federico Jr, *Vice Pres*
Beth Lesniak, *Vice Pres*
Rick Shaw, *Vice Pres*
▲ **EMP:** 62
SQ FT: 12,000
SALES (est): 10.5MM
SALES (corp-wide): 462.1MM **Privately Held**
SIC: 3211 3469 Mfg Flat Glass Mfg Metal Stampings
PA: Grey Mountain Partners, Llc
1470 Walnut St Ste 400
Boulder CO 80302
303 449-5692

(G-1762)
JEFFREY GOLD
Also Called: Laser Body Solutions
2440 Whitney Ave Ste 6 (06518-3268)
PHONE..................................203 281-5737
Jeffrey Gold, *Owner*
Vicki Gold, *Co-Owner*
EMP: 7
SALES (est): 1MM **Privately Held**
WEB: www.laserbody.com
SIC: 3845 8011 Mfg Electromedical Equipment Medical Doctor's Office

(G-1763)
JFD TUBE & COIL PRODUCTS INC
7 Hamden Park Dr (06517-3151)
P.O. Box 6309 (06517-0309)
PHONE..................................203 288-6941
Joseph Orlowski, *Founder*
Diane Orlowski, *Corp Secy*
Daniel Orlowski, *Vice Pres*
Thomas Orlowski, *Vice Pres*
EMP: 34
SQ FT: 14,200
SALES: 7.3MM **Privately Held**
WEB: www.jfdcoil.com
SIC: 3443 3498 Mfg Fabricated Plate Wrk Mfg Fabrctd Pipe/Fitting

(G-1764)
JOSEPH A CNTE MFG JEWELERS INC
2582 Whitney Ave (06518-3032)
PHONE..................................203 248-9853
Joseph A Conte, *President*
EMP: 4
SALES (est): 423K **Privately Held**
SIC: 3911 5944 Mfg Precious Metal Jewelry Ret Jewelry

(G-1765)
KTT ENTERPRISES LLC
15 Marne St (06514)
PHONE..................................203 288-7883
Richard J Coffey, *Mng Member*
Nancy J Coffey,
▲ **EMP:** 5
SQ FT: 15,000
SALES: 1MM **Privately Held**
WEB: www.kttenterprises.com
SIC: 3069 Mfg Fabricated Rubber Products

(G-1766)
LEED - HIMMEL INDUSTRIES INC
75 Leeder Hill Dr (06517-2731)
PHONE..................................203 288-8484
Howard B Goldfarb, *President*
Larry Himmel, *Exec VP*
Shadi Goldslager, *Credit Mgr*
Nancy Chovitz, *Human Res Mgr*
Adam Stern, *Chief Mktg Ofcr*
EMP: 70 **EST:** 1945
SQ FT: 120,000
SALES (est): 24.5MM **Privately Held**
WEB: www.leed-himmel.com
SIC: 3446 Mfg Architectural Metalwork

(G-1767)
LEGAL AFFAIRS INC
Also Called: LEGAL AFFAIRS MAGAZINE
115 Blake Rd (06517-3405)
PHONE..................................203 865-2520
Lincoln Caplan, *President*
EMP: 9
SALES: 0 **Privately Held**
WEB: www.legalaffairs.com
SIC: 2721 Magazine Publisher

(G-1768)
M G M INSTRUMENTS INC (PA)
925 Sherman Ave (06514-1171)
PHONE..................................203 248-4008
George Mismas, *President*
Murray Dennis, *Mfg Mgr*
Steve Meyer, *QC Mgr*
Janice Mismas, *Treasurer*
Kris Schied, *Financial Exec*
EMP: 30
SQ FT: 12,000
SALES (est): 2.7MM **Privately Held**
WEB: www.mgminstruments.com
SIC: 3841 Mfg Surgical/Medical Instruments

(G-1769)
MEDIA ONE LLC
44 Hawley Rd (06517-2128)
PHONE..................................203 745-5825
Saad Mobarak, *CEO*
Muhd Molla, *President*

EMP: 50
SALES (est): 1.7MM **Privately Held**
SIC: 3559 Mfg Misc Industry Machinery

(G-1770)
MERRITT EXTRUDER CORP
15 Marne St (06514)
PHONE..................................203 230-8100
Lucien D Yokana, *Ch of Bd*
Alexander Guthrie, *President*
Thomas J Oravits, *Vice Pres*
Mark Roland, *Controller*
Charles Jaffin, *Admin Sec*
EMP: 50
SQ FT: 45,000
SALES (est): 9.8MM **Privately Held**
WEB: www.merrittdavis.com
SIC: 3559 3089 3549 3542 Mfg Misc Industry Mach Mfg Plastic Products Mfg Metalworking Mach Mfg Machine Tool-Forming

(G-1771)
MEYER WIRE & CABLE COMPANY LLC
1072 Sherman Ave (06514-1337)
PHONE..................................203 281-0817
Laura N Comen, *Sales Mgr*
Karen Meyer,
Brian Meyer,
EMP: 21
SQ FT: 2,000
SALES (est): 3.7MM **Privately Held**
SIC: 3496 Mfg Misc Fabricated Wire Products

(G-1772)
MINUTE MAN PRESS
Also Called: Minuteman Press
5 Hamden Park Dr (06517-3150)
PHONE..................................203 891-6251
EMP: 4
SALES (est): 234.6K **Privately Held**
SIC: 2752 Comm Prtg Litho

(G-1773)
MOON CUTTER CO INC
2969 State St (06517-1712)
PHONE..................................203 288-9249
Eleanor Moon, *President*
Charles Moon, *Vice Pres*
Matt Rome, *Engineer*
Lenore Capasso, *Asst Sec*
EMP: 45
SQ FT: 54,000
SALES (est): 7MM **Privately Held**
SIC: 3541 3545 Mfg Machine Tools-Cutting Mfg Machine Tool Accessories

(G-1774)
NDR LIUZZI INC
Also Called: Liuzzi Cheese
86 Rossotto Dr (06514-1335)
PHONE..................................203 287-8477
Nicola Liuzzi, *President*
▲ **EMP:** 48
SALES (est): 4.7MM **Privately Held**
SIC: 2022 5143 Mfg Cheese Whol Dairy Products

(G-1775)
NEW ENGLAND CNC INC
46 Manila Ave (06514-4107)
PHONE..................................203 288-8241
Ronald Krutz, *Vice Pres*
EMP: 15
SALES (est): 1.7MM **Privately Held**
SIC: 3599 Mfg Industrial Machinery

(G-1776)
NEW ENGLAND ORTHO NEURO LLC
2080 Whitney Ave Ste 290 (06518-3604)
PHONE..................................203 200-7228
James Yue, *Principal*
EMP: 3
SALES (est): 168.2K **Privately Held**
SIC: 2813 Mfg Industrial Gases

(G-1777)
POROBOND PRODUCTS LLC
80 Sanford St (06514-1707)
P.O. Box 5, North Haven (06473-0005)
PHONE..................................203 234-7747
Wayne Paulsen,
◆ **EMP:** 10
SQ FT: 25,000
SALES (est): 1.5MM **Privately Held**
SIC: 3443 Mfg Fabricated Plate Work

(G-1778)
QUINNIPIAC VALLEY TIMES
2301 State St (06517-3721)
PHONE..................................203 675-9483
Fred Nevin, *Principal*
EMP: 3 **EST:** 2009
SALES (est): 114.3K **Privately Held**
SIC: 2711 Newspapers-Publishing/Printing

(G-1779)
RAYMON TOOL LLC
79 Rossotto Dr (06514-1336)
PHONE..................................203 248-2199
Vincent Palumbo, *Mng Member*
Paul Derenzo,
EMP: 12 **EST:** 1997
SQ FT: 10,000
SALES (est): 2.5MM **Privately Held**
WEB: www.raymontool.com
SIC: 3542 Mfg Machine Tools-Forming

(G-1780)
RHODE ISLAND BEVERAGE JOURNAL
2508 Whitney Ave (06518-3040)
PHONE..................................203 288-3375
Gerald Slone, *Principal*
EMP: 3
SALES (est): 176.7K **Privately Held**
SIC: 2711 Newspapers-Publishing/Printing

(G-1781)
ROLLINS PRINTING INCORPORATED
3281 Whitney Ave (06518-1923)
PHONE..................................203 248-3200
Carl F De Rosa, *President*
Patricia De Rosa, *Admin Sec*
EMP: 6
SQ FT: 5,000
SALES: 750K **Privately Held**
WEB: www.rollinsprintingusa.com
SIC: 2752 Commercial Offset Printing

(G-1782)
SCREEN TEK PRINTING CO INC
130 Welton St (06517-3930)
PHONE..................................203 248-6248
Robert Mastriano, *President*
Paul Mastriano, *Vice Pres*
EMP: 3
SQ FT: 6,000
SALES: 1.1MM **Privately Held**
WEB: www.screentek.net
SIC: 2752 Lithographic Commercial Printing

(G-1783)
SECONDARY OPERATIONS INC
46 Manila Ave (06514-4107)
PHONE..................................203 288-8241
Lawrence Carrignan, *President*
Ronald Krutz, *Vice Pres*
EMP: 10 **EST:** 1960
SQ FT: 6,600
SALES (est): 910K **Privately Held**
WEB: www.secondaryoperations.com
SIC: 3599 3541 Mfg Industrial Machinery Mfg Machine Tools-Cutting

(G-1784)
SKICO MANUFACTURING CO LLC
3 Industrial Cir (06517-3153)
PHONE..................................203 230-1305
Daniel D Skibitcky, *Partner*
Dan Skibitcky,
EMP: 9
SQ FT: 7,200
SALES (est): 788.3K **Privately Held**
SIC: 3599 3545 3544 7699 Precision C & C Machining

(G-1785)
SPECIALTY WIRE & CORD SETS
Also Called: SWC
1 Gallagher Rd (06517-3171)
PHONE..................................203 498-2932
Lynn Campo, *President*
Liborio Campo, *Vice Pres*
EMP: 18
SQ FT: 12,000
SALES: 2.2MM **Privately Held**
WEB: www.specialtywire.com
SIC: 3351 Mfg Misc Fabricated Wire Products

(G-1786)
SUPERIOR PRINTING INK CO INC
750 Sherman Ave (06514-1191)
PHONE..................................203 281-1921
Andrew Anselmo, *Branch Mgr*
EMP: 45
SQ FT: 5,200
SALES (corp-wide): 151.6MM **Privately Held**
SIC: 2893 Mfg Printing Ink
PA: Superior Printing Ink Co Inc
100 North St
Teterboro NJ 07608
201 478-5600

(G-1787)
TACHWA ENTERPRISES INC
4 Industrial Cir (06517-3152)
PHONE..................................203 691-5772
James White Jr, *President*
Andrew Wilkes, *Vice Pres*
EMP: 7
SQ FT: 7,200
SALES (est): 1.5MM **Privately Held**
WEB: www.tachwa.com
SIC: 3728 Mfg Aircraft Parts/Equipment

(G-1788)
TL WOODWORKING
299 Welton St (06517-3900)
PHONE..................................203 787-9661
Thomas Leary, *Principal*
EMP: 4 **EST:** 2011
SALES (est): 304.2K **Privately Held**
SIC: 2431 Mfg Millwork

(G-1789)
TLC MEDIA LLC
900 Mix Ave Apt 22 (06514-5107)
PHONE..................................203 980-1361
EMP: 6
SALES (est): 229.3K **Privately Held**
SIC: 2711 Newspapers

(G-1790)
TOMTEC INC
1000 Sherman Ave (06514-1358)
PHONE..................................203 281-6790
Tom Astle, *CEO*
Gade Ajeigbe, *CEO*
Joan Astle, *Corp Secy*
Ted Miller, *Technology*
John Daddio, *Software Engr*
▲ **EMP:** 68
SQ FT: 70,000
SALES (est): 11.9MM **Privately Held**
WEB: www.tomtec.com
SIC: 3845 3826 3821 Mfg Electromedical Equipment Mfg Analytical Instruments Mfg Lab Apparatus/Furniture

(G-1791)
TRANSACT TECHNOLOGIES INC (PA)
2319 Whitney Ave Ste 3b (06518-3534)
PHONE..................................203 859-6800
Bart C Shuldman, *Ch of Bd*
Steven A Demartino, *President*
Lindsay Nix, *COO*
Donald E Brooks, *Senior VP*
Tracey S Chernay, *Senior VP*
EMP: 123
SQ FT: 11,100
SALES: 54.5MM **Publicly Held**
WEB: www.transact-tech.com
SIC: 3577 7378 Mfg Specialty Printers & Terminals

(G-1792)
TUDOR HOUSE FURNITURE CO INC
929 Sherman Ave (06514-1150)
PHONE..................................203 288-8451
Harold Margolies, *President*
EMP: 28 **EST:** 1963
SQ FT: 20,000
SALES (est): 4.1MM **Privately Held**
SIC: 2512 2511 Mfg Upholstered Household Furniture Mfg Wood Household Furniture

(G-1793)
ULTRAMATIC WEST
87 Beechwood Ave (06514-2913)
PHONE..................................203 745-4688
Richard Golia, *Owner*
EMP: 3
SQ FT: 1,000
SALES: 350K **Privately Held**
SIC: 3552 Mfg Textile Machinery

(G-1794)
W AND G MACHINE COMPANY INC
4 Hamden Park Dr (06517-3149)
P.O. Box 6187 (06517-0187)
PHONE..................................203 288-8772
Jay Kroopnick, *President*
Gene Borysewicz, *VP Engrg*
Robin Kroopnick, *Treasurer*
Sheree A Napolitan, *Admin Sec*
EMP: 36 **EST:** 1952
SQ FT: 12,000
SALES (est): 8.1MM **Privately Held**
SIC: 3728 Mfg Aircraft Parts/Equipment

(G-1795)
WESTFORT CONSTRUCTION CORP
3000 Whitney Ave (06518-2353)
PHONE..................................860 833-7970
Erica Morizio, *Principal*
EMP: 3
SALES (est): 148.1K **Privately Held**
SIC: 2952 7389 Mfg Asphalt Felts/Coatings Business Serv Non-Commercial Site

Hampton
Windham County

(G-1796)
BURELL BROS INC
Rr 97 (06247)
PHONE..................................860 455-9681
Frances Burell, *President*
Francis Burell, *President*
John Burell, *Vice Pres*
Carol Burell, *Admin Sec*
EMP: 7
SQ FT: 10,000
SALES (est): 957.4K **Privately Held**
SIC: 2421 Sawmill/Planing Mill

(G-1797)
CHARLES PIKE & SONS
311 Providence Tpke (06247-1433)
PHONE..................................860 455-9968
Charles Pike, *Owner*
Virginia Pike, *Co-Owner*
EMP: 4
SALES (est): 150K **Privately Held**
SIC: 2421 Sawmill/Planing Mill

(G-1798)
NEW ENGLAND CTR FOR HRING RHAB
Also Called: N E C H E A R
354 Hartford Tpke (06247-1320)
PHONE..................................860 455-1404
Diane Brackett, *Director*
EMP: 6
SALES (est): 836.2K **Privately Held**
SIC: 3842 8099 Mfg Surgical Appliances/Supplies Health/Allied Services

Hartford
Hartford County

(G-1799)
A & P COAT APRON & LIN SUP INC
Also Called: Unitex Textile Rental Service
420 Ledyard St (06114-3207)
PHONE..................................914 840-3200
Raymond Neal, *Plant Mgr*

▲ = Import ▼=Export
◆ =Import/Export

Raymon Neal, *Branch Mgr*
EMP: 60
SALES (corp-wide): 70.3MM **Privately Held**
WEB: www.rent-a-uniform.com
SIC: 2299 7213 7218 Mfg Textile Goods Linen Supply Services Industrial Launderer
PA: A & P Coat, Apron, & Linen Supply, Inc.
565 Taxter Rd Ste 620
Elmsford NY 10523
914 840-3200

(G-1800)
A G RUSSELL COMPANY INC
60 George St (06114-2915)
P.O. Box 1685 (06144-1685)
PHONE....................................860 247-9093
Francis Fertera, *President*
Leroy Lowe, *Vice Pres*
Douglas Lowe, *Treasurer*
EMP: 5
SQ FT: 3,900
SALES: 425K **Privately Held**
WEB: www.stampitmarkit.com
SIC: 3469 3953 3542 Mfg Steel Stamps Marking Dies & Marking Machinery

(G-1801)
ACE TECHNICAL PLASTICS INC
122 Park Ave J (06108-4036)
P.O. Box 4519 (06147-4519)
PHONE....................................860 278-2444
EMP: 6
SALES (est): 812K **Privately Held**
SIC: 3089 Mfg Plastic Products

(G-1802)
ADAMSAHERN SIGN SOLUTIONS INC
30 Arbor St Unit 208 (06106-1238)
PHONE....................................860 523-8835
Diane Ahern, *President*
Chris Adams, *Admin Sec*
EMP: 14
SALES (est): 700K **Privately Held**
SIC: 3993 1799 Mfg Signs/Advertising Specialties Trade Contractor

(G-1803)
AEROSPACE METALS INC
Also Called: Suisman & Blumenthal
239 W Service Rd (06120-1205)
PHONE....................................860 522-3123
Paul Haveson, *President*
Michael Suisman, *Principal*
Robert Kaseta, *CFO*
EMP: 112
SQ FT: 225,000
SALES (est): 13.2MM **Privately Held**
WEB: www.mtlm.com
SIC: 3356 Nonferrous Rolling/Drawing
HQ: Metal Management, Inc.
200 W Madison St Ste 3600
Chicago IL 60606
312 645-0700

(G-1804)
ALBERT KEMPERLE INC
141 Locust St (06114-1504)
PHONE....................................860 727-0933
Ronald Kemperle, *President*
EMP: 19
SALES (corp-wide): 163.8MM **Privately Held**
SIC: 2851 Mfg Paints/Allied Products
PA: Albert Kemperle, Inc.
8400 New Horizons Blvd
Amityville NY 11701
631 841-1241

(G-1805)
ALM MEDIA LLC
Also Called: The Connecticut Law Tribune
201 Ann Uccello St Fl 4 (06103-2000)
PHONE....................................860 527-7900
Jeffrey Forte, *Branch Mgr*
EMP: 22
SALES (corp-wide): 181.8MM **Privately Held**
WEB: www.alm.com
SIC: 2711 Newspapers-Publishing/Printing
HQ: Alm Media, Llc
150 E 42nd St
New York NY 10017
212 457-9400

(G-1806)
APPELS PRINTING & MAILING BUR
307 Homestead Ave (06112-2155)
P.O. Box 512, East Windsor (06088-0512)
PHONE....................................860 522-8189
Joel Appelbaum, *President*
EMP: 10
SQ FT: 5,000
SALES (est): 600K **Privately Held**
SIC: 2752 2791 Lithographic Commercial Printing Typesetting Services

(G-1807)
AQUILINE DRONES LLC
750 Main St Ste 319 (06103-2706)
PHONE....................................860 361-7958
Barry Alexander, *Mng Member*
EMP: 15
SALES: 5K **Privately Held**
SIC: 3721 Mfg Aircraft

(G-1808)
AUSTIN ORGANS INCORPORATED
156 Woodland St (06105-1284)
P.O. Box 355, Chester (06412-0355)
PHONE....................................860 522-8293
Richard G Taylor, *CEO*
Michael B Fazio, *President*
EMP: 25 **EST:** 1893
SQ FT: 35,000
SALES (est): 3.4MM **Privately Held**
WEB: www.austinorgans.com
SIC: 3931 Mfg Musical Instruments

(G-1809)
CABLE ELECTRONICS INC
221 Newfield Ave Ste 2 (06106-3662)
P.O. Box 330326, West Hartford (06133-0326)
PHONE....................................860 953-0300
David H Farrah, *President*
Florence Farrah, *Vice Pres*
EMP: 5
SQ FT: 3,500
SALES (est): 555.1K **Privately Held**
SIC: 3679 5084 7622 Mfg Electronic Components Whol Industrial Equipment Radio/Television Repair

(G-1810)
CAPITOL PRINTING CO INC
Also Called: Minuteman Press
52 Pratt St (06103-1601)
PHONE....................................860 522-1547
Joel Steinman, *President*
Steve Weber, *Vice Pres*
Amy Steinman, *Director*
Gail Weber, *Director*
EMP: 8
SQ FT: 1,500
SALES (est): 1.3MM **Privately Held**
SIC: 2752 Comm Prtg Litho

(G-1811)
CAPITOL SAUSAGE & PROVS INC
101 Reserve Rd Bldg 14 (06114-1608)
PHONE....................................860 527-5510
William Driscoll, *CEO*
Sandra Driscoll, *Admin Sec*
EMP: 7
SQ FT: 10,000
SALES (est): 959.1K **Privately Held**
SIC: 2013 Mfg Sausage & Prepared Meats

(G-1812)
CAT LLC
819 N Mountain Rd (06111-1414)
PHONE....................................860 953-1807
Daniel Bourget,
▼ **EMP:** 4
SALES (est): 464.9K **Privately Held**
WEB: www.billetcats.com
SIC: 3751 Mfg Motorcycles Accessories

(G-1813)
CITY SIGN
1811 Park St (06106-2121)
PHONE....................................860 232-4803
Martin Glennie, *Mng Member*
Carol Glennie, *Mng Member*
EMP: 4 **EST:** 1977
SQ FT: 8,400
SALES (est): 455.1K **Privately Held**
SIC: 3993 Mfg & Install Signs & Advertising Specialties

(G-1814)
CITY WELDING
84 Wellington St (06106-2952)
PHONE....................................860 951-4714
Frank Serrao, *Owner*
EMP: 3
SALES: 200K **Privately Held**
SIC: 7692 Welding Repair

(G-1815)
CONNECTCUT HSPNIC YELLOW PAGES
2074 Park St Ste 2 (06106-2055)
PHONE....................................860 560-8713
Hector Torres, *President*
Angel Funtes, *Principal*
▲ **EMP:** 10
SALES (est): 879.9K **Privately Held**
SIC: 2741 Misc Publishing

(G-1816)
COURANT SPECIALTY PRODUCTS INC
285 Broad St (06115-3785)
PHONE....................................860 241-3795
Stephen D Carver, *President*
Richard S Feeney, *Vice Pres*
David P Eldersveld, *Admin Sec*
EMP: 30
SALES (est): 120.6K
SALES (corp-wide): 2.7B **Publicly Held**
WEB: www.tribune.com
SIC: 2711 Newspapers-Publishing/Printing
HQ: Tribune Media Company
515 N State St Ste 2400
Chicago IL 60654
312 222-3394

(G-1817)
DE MUERTE USA LLC
73 Morningside St W (06112-1142)
PHONE....................................860 331-7085
Kevin Dumont, *Principal*
Josh Jenkins, *Principal*
EMP: 3
SALES (est): 139.8K **Privately Held**
SIC: 2389 Mfg Apparel/Accessories

(G-1818)
DLZ ARCHITECTURAL MILL WORK
510 Ledyard St (06114-3213)
PHONE....................................860 883-7562
David L Zavarella, *President*
EMP: 4
SALES (est): 246K **Privately Held**
SIC: 2431 Mfg Millwork

(G-1819)
EL PASO PROD OIL GAS TEXAS LP
490 Capitol Ave (06106-1354)
PHONE....................................860 293-1990
Tom Starr, *Manager*
EMP: 11 **Publicly Held**
SIC: 1382 1311 Oil & Gas Exploration & Production
HQ: El Paso Production Oil & Gas Texas, L.P.
1001 Louisiana St
Houston TX 77002
713 997-1000

(G-1820)
ENVIRONMANTAL SYSTEMS COR
18 Jansen Ct (06110-1913)
PHONE....................................860 953-5167
Donald McCurdy, *Principal*
EMP: 10
SALES (est): 2.4MM **Privately Held**
SIC: 3569 Mfg General Industrial Machinery

(G-1821)
FIDELUX LIGHTING LLC (HQ)
100 Great Meadow Rd # 600 (06109-2355)
PHONE....................................860 436-5000
Suzanne Templeton, *Office Mgr*
Jay Jayanthan,
▲ **EMP:** 12
SALES (est): 4MM
SALES (corp-wide): 5.6MM **Privately Held**
SIC: 3674 3648 7371 Mfg Semiconductors/Related Devices Mfg Lighting Equipment Custom Computer Programing
PA: Prime Ae Group
100 Great Meadow Rd # 600
Wethersfield CT 06109
203 269-2993

(G-1822)
G & R ENTERPRISES INCORPORATED
Also Called: Heritage Printers
101 Kinsley St (06103-1813)
PHONE....................................860 549-6120
Ron Miller, *President*
J Duff Miller, *Vice Pres*
EMP: 3
SQ FT: 1,200
SALES: 500K **Privately Held**
SIC: 2759 7334 2791 2789 Commercial Printing Photocopying Service Typesetting Services Bookbinding/Related Work Lithographic Coml Print

(G-1823)
G&K SERVICES LLC
Also Called: G K Services
96 Murphy Rd (06114-2103)
PHONE....................................860 856-4400
EMP: 7
SALES (corp-wide): 6.8B **Publicly Held**
SIC: 2326 Mfg Men's/Boy's Work Clothing
HQ: G&K Services, Llc
6800 Cintas Blvd
Mason OH 45040
952 912-5500

(G-1824)
GAMUT PUBLISHING
Also Called: Southside Media
563 Franklin Ave (06114-3019)
PHONE....................................860 296-6128
Jon Harden, *Owner*
EMP: 20
SALES (est): 840.5K **Privately Held**
SIC: 2711 2721 2731 Newspapers-Publishing/Printing Periodicals-Publishing/Printing Books-Publishing/Printing

(G-1825)
GG SPORTSWEAR INC
241 Ledyard St Ste B10 (06114-2029)
PHONE....................................860 296-4441
Roberto Giansiracusa, *President*
George Marinelli, *Treasurer*
Gina Karavetsos, *Controller*
Inez Giansiracusa, *Admin Sec*
EMP: 30
SQ FT: 14,000
SALES (est): 3MM **Privately Held**
SIC: 2329 2339 5136 5137 Mfg & Whol Men's & Women's Sportswear & Embroidery

(G-1826)
GIMA LLC
Also Called: Gimasport
241 Ledyard St Ste B10 (06114-2029)
PHONE....................................860 296-4441
Roberto Giansiracusa, *Principal*
George Marinelli, *Principal*
Gina Karavetsos, *Controller*
EMP: 20
SQ FT: 20,000
SALES (est): 2.3MM **Privately Held**
WEB: www.gimasport.com
SIC: 2329 5136 Whol Sportswear

(G-1827)
GOVERNMENT SURPLUS SALES INC
Also Called: Government Sales
69 Francis Ave (06106-2102)
PHONE....................................860 247-7787
Eric L Schweitzer, *President*
David H Schweitzer, *Vice Pres*
EMP: 7
SQ FT: 15,000
SALES: 1.3MM **Privately Held**
WEB: www.aviationhelmets.com
SIC: 3469 5571 Mfg Metal Stampings Ret Motorcycles

(G-1828)
GREEN EGG DESIGN LLC
750 Main St Ste 506 (06103-2709)
PHONE..................................860 541-5411
Samuel McGee,
EMP: 3
SALES (est): 121.7K **Privately Held**
SIC: 3085 Mfg Plastic Bottles

(G-1829)
HANGER PRSTHETCS & ORTHO INC
282 Washington St 1b (06106-3322)
PHONE..................................860 545-9050
James Fezio, *Manager*
EMP: 10
SALES (corp-wide): 1B **Publicly Held**
SIC: 3842 Mfg Surgical Appliances/Supplies
HQ: Hanger Prosthetics & Orthotics, Inc.
10910 Domain Dr Ste 300
Austin TX 78758
512 777-3800

(G-1830)
HARTFORD BUSINESS SUPPLY INC
Also Called: Printers
1718 Park St (06106-2132)
PHONE..................................860 233-2138
Susan Falotico, *President*
Daniel J Falotico, *Vice Pres*
Carole Becker, *Sales Staff*
EMP: 26
SQ FT: 12,050
SALES: 3.1MM **Privately Held**
SIC: 2752 5943 Lithographic Commercial Printing Ret Stationery

(G-1831)
HARTFORD COURANT COMPANY LLC (HQ)
285 Broad St (06115-3785)
PHONE..................................860 241-6200
Rick Daniels, *CEO*
Nancy Schoeffler, *Editor*
Mary Lou Stoneburner, *Vice Pres*
Andrea Pape, *Prdtn Dir*
Antonio Pereira, *Opers Staff*
EMP: 700 **EST:** 1764
SQ FT: 293,792
SALES (est): 115.6MM
SALES (corp-wide): 1B **Publicly Held**
WEB: www.courantnie.com
SIC: 2711 Newspapers-Publishing/Printing
PA: Tribune Publishing Company
160 N Stetson Ave
Chicago IL 60601
312 222-9100

(G-1832)
HARTFORD COURANT COMPANY LLC
Also Called: Hartford Courant South BR Off
121 Wawarme Ave (06114-1507)
PHONE..................................860 525-5555
George Sassano, *Branch Mgr*
EMP: 15
SALES (corp-wide): 1B **Publicly Held**
SIC: 2711 Newspapers-Publishing/Printing
HQ: The Hartford Courant Company Llc
285 Broad St
Hartford CT 06115
860 241-6200

(G-1833)
HARTFORD CPL CO-OP INC
75 Airport Rd (06114-2004)
PHONE..................................860 296-5636
William Galatis, *Ch of Bd*
William Ghio, *Treasurer*
Thomas Brazel, *Admin Sec*
EMP: 110
SALES (est): 17.4MM **Privately Held**
SIC: 2051 Retail Bakery

(G-1834)
HARTFORD FLAVOR COMPANY LLC
30 Arbor St Unit 107 (06106-1238)
PHONE..................................860 604-9767
Tom Dubay, *Manager*
Lelaneia Dubay,
EMP: 5
SALES (est): 209.9K **Privately Held**
SIC: 2085 Mfg Distilled/Blended Liquor

(G-1835)
HARTFORD JET CENTER LLC
20 Lindbergh Dr (06114-2132)
PHONE..................................860 548-9334
Arian Prevalla,
Robert J Morande,
EMP: 7 **EST:** 2015
SALES (est): 138.6K **Privately Held**
SIC: 3721 Mfg Aircraft

(G-1836)
HYDROCHEMICAL TECHNIQUES INC
Also Called: Hydroclean Rstrtn Clng Systms
253 Locust St (06114-2008)
P.O. Box 2078 (06145-2078)
PHONE..................................860 527-6350
Thomas Rudder, *President*
Linda Clerget, *Corp Secy*
C Scott Rudder, *Vice Pres*
Chris Penny, *Finance Mgr*
EMP: 3
SQ FT: 2,300
SALES (est): 439.5K **Privately Held**
SIC: 2842 5169 Mfg Polish/Sanitation Goods Whol Chemicals/Products

(G-1837)
INFORMATION BUILDERS INC
100 Pearl St Fl 14 (06103-4500)
PHONE..................................860 249-7229
EMP: 12
SALES (corp-wide): 176MM **Privately Held**
SIC: 7372 Prepackaged Software Services
PA: Information Builders, Inc.
2 Penn Plz Fl 28
New York NY 10121
212 736-4433

(G-1838)
INTERNTONAL MBL GRAN ENTPS INC
110 Airport Rd (06114-2005)
PHONE..................................860 296-0741
Adrian R Costa, *President*
Brian Costa, *Sales Mgr*
EMP: 6
SALES (est): 646.4K **Privately Held**
SIC: 3281 1752 1522 Mfg Cut Stone/Products Floor Laying Contractor Residential Construction

(G-1839)
L & P GATE COMPANY INC
83 Meadow St (06114-1526)
PHONE..................................860 296-8009
Bolivar Jimenez, *President*
EMP: 6
SQ FT: 1,800
SALES (est): 1MM **Privately Held**
SIC: 3548 Mfg Welding Apparatus

(G-1840)
LOAVES & FISHES MINISTRIES
646 Prospect Ave (06105-4203)
PHONE..................................860 524-1730
Alyce Hild, *Exec Dir*
EMP: 4
SALES: 256.5K **Privately Held**
SIC: 2099 Soup Kitchen

(G-1841)
MAGNANI PRESS INCORPORATED
120 New Park Ave (06106-2185)
PHONE..................................860 236-2802
EMP: 5
SQ FT: 5,000
SALES (est): 460K **Privately Held**
SIC: 2752 2791 Lithographic Commercial Printing Typesetting Services

(G-1842)
MALTA FOOD PANTRY INC
19 Woodland St Ste 37 (06105-2335)
PHONE..................................860 725-0944
Scott Muryasz, *Principal*
EMP: 3
SALES (est): 196.9K **Privately Held**
SIC: 2099 Mfg Food Preparations

(G-1843)
MANCHESTER TL & DESIGN ADP LLC
Also Called: ADP Rivet
465 Ledyard St (06114-3211)
PHONE..................................860 296-6541
Joe Derosie, *COO*
Peter Depaola, *Mng Member*
EMP: 7 **EST:** 1951
SQ FT: 12,000
SALES (est): 1.1MM **Privately Held**
WEB: www.adprivet.com
SIC: 3965 3599 Mfg Fasteners/Buttons/Pins Mfg Industrial Machinery

(G-1844)
MARK KAROTKIN
17 Grassmere Ave (06110-1216)
PHONE..................................860 202-7821
Mark Karotkin, *Owner*
EMP: 4
SALES: 500K **Privately Held**
SIC: 3715 Mfg Truck Trailers

(G-1845)
MASSACHUSETTS ENVELOPE CO INC
General Business Envelope Co
10 Midland St (06120-1118)
P.O. Box 750 (06142-0750)
PHONE..................................860 727-9100
Emilie Camarco, *Div Sub Head*
Doug Smith, *CFO*
Bruce Newell, *Sales Staff*
Thomas Cummings, *Business Anlyst*
Maralyn Dolan, *Business Anlyst*
EMP: 30
SQ FT: 34,000
SALES (corp-wide): 12.1MM **Privately Held**
WEB: www.massenvplus.com
SIC: 2754 2752 5112 Gravure Commercial Printing Lithographic Commercial Printing Whol Stationery/Office Supplies
PA: Massachusetts Envelope Company, Inc.
30 Cobble Hill Rd
Somerville MA 02143
617 623-8000

(G-1846)
MERRILL CORPORATION
100 Pearl St Fl 14 (06103-4500)
PHONE..................................860 249-7220
Summa Josepha, *Manager*
EMP: 87
SALES (corp-wide): 566.6MM **Privately Held**
WEB: www.merrillcorp.com
SIC: 2759 Commercial Printing
PA: Merrill Corporation
1 Merrill Cir
Saint Paul MN 55108
651 646-4501

(G-1847)
METAL INDUSTRIES INC
806r Wethersfield Ave (06114-3197)
PHONE..................................860 296-6228
Vincent M Zito, *President*
EMP: 5
SQ FT: 8,000
SALES (est): 1MM **Privately Held**
SIC: 7692 3599 Metallizing And Welding Repair Mfg Industrial Machinery

(G-1848)
METALLIZING SERVICE CO INC (PA)
11 Cody St (06110-1949)
PHONE..................................860 953-1144
David S Gollob, *President*
Rona B Gollob, *Vice Pres*
EMP: 43
SQ FT: 14,000
SALES (est): 7.4MM **Privately Held**
WEB: www.mscplasma.com
SIC: 3479 Coating/Engraving Service

(G-1849)
NANOCAP TECHNOLOGIES LLC (PA)
17 Morningcrest Dr (06117-2906)
PHONE..................................860 521-9743
Arthur S Kesten, *President*
Jack N Blechner, *President*
EMP: 3
SALES (est): 776.4K **Privately Held**
SIC: 3585 Mfg Refrigeration/Heating Equipment

(G-1850)
NELSON APOSTLE INC
11 Sherman St (06110-1914)
P.O. Box 330147, West Hartford (06133-0147)
PHONE..................................860 953-4633
William Lyth, *President*
EMP: 6
SQ FT: 5,000
SALES (est): 540K **Privately Held**
SIC: 3545 7699 5085 Mfg Machine Tool Accessories Repair Services Whol Industrial Supplies

(G-1851)
NEW ENGLAND FOAM PRODUCTS LLC (PA)
760 Windsor St (06120-1918)
P.O. Box 583, Windsor (06095-0583)
PHONE..................................860 524-0121
Nicholas Elia, *General Mgr*
Krisandra Elia, *Controller*
Tammy Nefoam, *Office Mgr*
Anthony D Elia,
EMP: 49
SQ FT: 80,000
SALES (est): 11.3MM **Privately Held**
WEB: NewEnglandFoam.com
SIC: 3069 3086 Mfg Fabricated Rubber Products Mfg Plastic Foam Products

(G-1852)
NEW MASS MEDIA INC
Also Called: Hartford Advocate
285 Broad St (06115-3785)
PHONE..................................860 241-3617
Josh Mamis, *Publisher*
EMP: 50
SALES (est): 2MM **Privately Held**
SIC: 2711 Newspapers-Publishing/Printing

(G-1853)
NORTHEAST MINORITY NEWS INC
3580 Main St Ste 1 (06120-1131)
P.O. Box 4159 (06147-4159)
PHONE..................................860 249-6065
Eugene Monroe, *President*
EMP: 4
SALES (est): 50K **Privately Held**
SIC: 2711 Newspapers-Publishing/Printing

(G-1854)
NORTHEND AGENTS LLC
150 Trumbull St Fl 4 (06103-2446)
P.O. Box 2308 (06146-2308)
PHONE..................................860 244-2445
Sasha Allen Walton, *Principal*
EMP: 3
SALES (est): 132.7K **Privately Held**
SIC: 2711 Newspapers-Publishing/Printing

(G-1855)
NRG CONNECTICUT LLC
Also Called: Jewish Ledger
36 Woodland St Ste 1 (06105-2328)
PHONE..................................860 231-2424
N Richard Greenfield, *Principal*
Joan Gaffin, *Accounts Exec*
EMP: 25 **EST:** 1929
SQ FT: 2,000
SALES (est): 1.4MM **Privately Held**
WEB: www.jewishledger.com
SIC: 2711 8661 Newspapers-Publishing/Printing Religious Organization

(G-1856)
PERMATEX INC (PA)
Also Called: Permatex, Inc./ A Division ITW
10 Columbus Blvd Ste 1 (06106-2069)
PHONE..................................860 543-7500
Harry Blake, *President*
Andy Robinson, *General Mgr*
Wayne Gibson, *Buyer*
Felix L Rodriguez, *Director*
◆ **EMP:** 50
SQ FT: 19,424

SALES (est): 71MM **Privately Held**
WEB: www.notouch.com
SIC: 2891 2899 2992 Mfg Adhesives/Sealants Mfg Chemical Preparations Mfg Lubricating Oils/Greases

(G-1857)
PISTRITTO MARBLE IMPORTS INC
97 Airport Rd (06114-2004)
PHONE..................................860 296-5263
Joseph Pistritto, *CEO*
Sabrina Pistritto, *Vice Pres*
Luciano Pistritto, *Treasurer*
Mariella Pistritto, *Sales Staff*
▲ **EMP:** 5
SQ FT: 7,000
SALES (est): 741.3K **Privately Held**
WEB: www.pistrittomarble.com
SIC: 3281 5999 5032 Mfg Cut Stone/Products Ret Misc Merchandise Whol Brick/Stone Matrls

(G-1858)
PLAINVILLE ELECTRO PLATING CO
21 Forest Hills Dr (06117-1112)
PHONE..................................860 525-5328
Jerry Glassman, *Owner*
EMP: 5
SALES (est): 465.6K **Privately Held**
SIC: 3471 Plating/Polishing Service

(G-1859)
PLASTONICS INC
230 Locust St (06114-2081)
PHONE..................................860 249-5455
Robert B Zimmerli Jr, *President*
Brian Zimmerli, *Sales Executive*
EMP: 28
SQ FT: 32,000
SALES (est): 4.6MM **Privately Held**
WEB: www.plastonics.com
SIC: 3479 Coating/Engraving Service

(G-1860)
POPPYS LLC
Also Called: Emilee's Italian Ice
260 Steele Rd (06117-2743)
PHONE..................................860 778-9044
Michele Tabora, *Sales Staff*
Christopher L Tabora,
Janet Davis,
EMP: 15
SQ FT: 3,000
SALES (est): 680K **Privately Held**
SIC: 2024 Mfg Ice Cream/Frozen Desert

(G-1861)
PPG INDUSTRIES INC
Also Called: PPG 9431
292 Murphy Rd (06114-2107)
PHONE..................................860 522-9544
Mike King, *Manager*
EMP: 5
SALES (corp-wide): 15.3B **Publicly Held**
WEB: www.ppg.com
SIC: 2851 Mfg Paints/Allied Products
PA: Ppg Industries, Inc.
1 Ppg Pl
Pittsburgh PA 15272
412 434-3131

(G-1862)
PYNE-DAVIDSON COMPANY
237 Weston St (06120-1209)
PHONE..................................860 522-9106
Harry H Davidson, *CEO*
Daniel J Davidson, *President*
Jeff Milliard, *Vice Pres*
Diane Davidson, *Admin Sec*
EMP: 28
SQ FT: 12,500
SALES (est): 4MM **Privately Held**
WEB: www.pyne-davidson.com
SIC: 2752 Lithographic Commercial Printing

(G-1863)
QSR STEEL CORPORATION LLC
121 Elliott St E (06114-1515)
PHONE..................................860 548-0248
Ulysses Garcia, *Director*
David Rusconi,
Marc Mantia,
Glen Salamone,
EMP: 20
SALES (est): 6MM **Privately Held**
SIC: 3441 Structural Metal Fabrication

(G-1864)
QUATUM INC
43 Maselli Rd (06111-5520)
PHONE..................................860 666-3464
Manuel Inacio, *President*
Maria J Inacio, *Treasurer*
EMP: 4
SQ FT: 2,400
SALES (est): 534.4K **Privately Held**
SIC: 3089 Mfg Plastic Products

(G-1865)
R L FISHER INC
Also Called: Rlf Homes
30 Bartholomew Ave (06106-2201)
PHONE..................................860 951-8110
Robin Fisher, *President*
Philip Sarrantonio, *Vice Pres*
EMP: 99
SQ FT: 36,000
SALES (est): 11.6MM **Privately Held**
WEB: www.rlfhome.com
SIC: 2391 2392 Mfg Curtains/Draperies Mfg Household Furnishings

(G-1866)
RAMDIAL PARTS AND SERVICES LLC
18 Adelaide St (06114-1801)
PHONE..................................860 296-5175
Chunilall Ramdial, *Mng Member*
EMP: 3
SALES (est): 145.5K **Privately Held**
SIC: 2515 Mfg Mattresses/Bedsprings

(G-1867)
ROYAL WELDING LLC
50 Francis Ave Ste 4 (06106-2183)
PHONE..................................860 232-5255
David Pronovost, *Owner*
Francesco Formica, *Co-Owner*
Alicia Formica, *Admin Sec*
EMP: 4
SALES (est): 607.6K **Privately Held**
SIC: 3499 Mfg Misc Fabricated Metal Products

(G-1868)
SEVERANCE FOODS INC
Also Called: Pan De Oro Brand
3478 Main St (06120-1138)
PHONE..................................860 724-7063
Richard Stevens, *President*
Kim Huynh, *Plant Mgr*
Leif Dana, *Director*
EMP: 45
SQ FT: 40,400
SALES (est): 9.5MM **Privately Held**
WEB: www.severancefoods.com
SIC: 2096 Mfg Potato Chips/Snacks

(G-1869)
SHEPARD STEEL CO INC (PA)
110 Meadow St (06114-1598)
PHONE..................................860 525-4446
George R Beckerman, *President*
Brian Ritchie, *Exec VP*
Elaine Anderson, *Purch Mgr*
Jeff Parnell, *Engineer*
Keith F Wolf, *CFO*
▲ **EMP:** 65
SQ FT: 100,000
SALES (est): 19.4MM **Privately Held**
WEB: www.shepardsteel.com
SIC: 3441 3446 Structural Metal Fabrication Mfg Architectural Metalwork

(G-1870)
SIGN WIZARD
1 Union Pl (06103-1490)
PHONE..................................860 525-7729
Joseph Coppola, *Owner*
John Schmid, *Partner*
EMP: 4
SALES (est): 221.4K **Privately Held**
SIC: 3993 Mfg Signs

(G-1871)
SLEEP MANAGEMENT SOLUTIONS LLC (HQ)
20 Church St Ste 900 (06103-1248)
PHONE..................................888 497-5337
Sam Helmick, *CEO*
EMP: 10
SALES (est): 1.4MM **Privately Held**
SIC: 3841 8741 Mfg Surgical/Medical Instruments Management Services

(G-1872)
STATE AWNING COMPANY
100 Cedar St (06106-1622)
P.O. Box 261010 (06126-1010)
PHONE..................................860 246-2575
James Fitzgerald, *President*
Susan Adams, *Corp Secy*
Patricia La Barron, *Vice Pres*
EMP: 8 **EST:** 1928
SQ FT: 10,000
SALES: 400K **Privately Held**
SIC: 2394 Mfg Canvas/Related Products

(G-1873)
STONEGATE CAPITAL GROUP
100 Pearl St Fl 12 (06103-4511)
PHONE..................................860 899-1181
Allen Mendelson, *Principal*
EMP: 3 **EST:** 2009
SALES (est): 296.7K **Privately Held**
SIC: 3721 Mfg Aircraft

(G-1874)
SWING BY SWING GOLF INC
80 State House Sq # 158 (06123-7701)
PHONE..................................310 922-8023
Charles A Cox, *CEO*
James Reid Gorman, *CFO*
EMP: 7
SQ FT: 2,000
SALES (est): 362.6K **Privately Held**
SIC: 7372 Prepackaged Software Services

(G-1875)
SYCAST INC
148 Bartholomew Ave (06106-2903)
PHONE..................................860 308-2122
Anhared Stowe, *CEO*
John W Stowe, *President*
EMP: 6
SALES (est): 885.5K **Privately Held**
SIC: 3369 Nonferrous Metal Foundry

(G-1876)
TEES & MORE LLC
306 Murphy Rd (06114-2127)
PHONE..................................860 244-2224
Marco Venditti,
EMP: 9
SALES (est): 1MM **Privately Held**
WEB: www.teesandmore1.com
SIC: 2262 Manmade Fiber & Silk Finishing Plant

(G-1877)
TEREX UTILITIES INC
Also Called: Hartford Division
61 Arrow Rd Ste 12 (06109-1357)
PHONE..................................860 436-3700
Tom Ofleherty, *Branch Mgr*
EMP: 5
SALES (corp-wide): 5.1B **Publicly Held**
SIC: 3531 Mfg Construction Machinery
HQ: Terex Utilities, Inc.
12805 Sw 77th Pl
Tigard OR 97223
503 620 0611

(G-1878)
THE SMITH WORTHINGTON SAD CO
275 Homestead Ave (06112-2183)
PHONE..................................860 527-9117
Curtis C Hanks, *President*
Ruth Hanks, *Vice Pres*
▲ **EMP:** 6
SQ FT: 14,000
SALES (est): 1MM **Privately Held**
WEB: www.smithworthington.com
SIC: 3199 Mfg Leather Goods

(G-1879)
THOMAS W RAFTERY INC
1055 Broad St (06106-2310)
PHONE..................................860 278-9870
Gary Rigoletti, *CEO*
Robert O'Connor, *President*
Irena D Santos, *VP Opers*
Johnny Castro, *Prdtn Mgr*
EMP: 45
SQ FT: 60,000
SALES (est): 7.7MM **Privately Held**
WEB: www.thomaswraftery.com
SIC: 2391 2392 5131 2591 Mfg Curtains/Drapery Mfg Household Furnishing Whol Piece Goods/Notions Mfg Drape Hardware/Blind

(G-1880)
THREE SUNS LTD
157 Robin Rd (06119-1242)
PHONE..................................860 233-7658
John Flattery Jr, *President*
EMP: 4
SALES (est): 159.1K **Privately Held**
SIC: 2084 Mfg Wines/Brandy/Spirits

(G-1881)
TRANE US INC
485 Ledyard St (06114-3211)
PHONE..................................860 541-1721
Beth Florian, *Vice Pres*
Lori Meany, *Sales Staff*
Tim Chamberlain, *Branch Mgr*
EMP: 4 **Privately Held**
SIC: 3585 Mfg Refrigeration/Heating Equipment
HQ: Trane U.S. Inc.
3600 Pammel Creek Rd
La Crosse WI 54601
608 787-2000

(G-1882)
TRUTH TRCKG EXPEDITED SVCS LLC
2015 Main St (06120-2316)
P.O. Box 2261 (06146-2261)
PHONE..................................860 306-5630
Akwan Shabazz,
Ahmad Compton,
Justin Marshall,
EMP: 4
SALES (est): 176.5K **Privately Held**
SIC: 3537 Mfg Industrial Trucks/Tractors

(G-1883)
UNITED STATES FIRE ARMS MFG CO
445 Ledyard St Ste 453 (06114-3211)
PHONE..................................860 296-7441
EMP: 23
SALES (est): 1.7MM **Privately Held**
WEB: www.usfirearms.com
SIC: 3489 3484 3471 Mfg Ordnance/Accessories Mfg Small Arms Plating/Polishing Service

(G-1884)
US FIREARMS MANUFACTURING CO
453 Ledyard St (06114-3211)
P.O. Box 1901 (06144-1901)
PHONE..................................860 296-7441
EMP: 4
SALES (est): 501K **Privately Held**
SIC: 3484 Mfg Small Arms

(G-1885)
WILD CARD GOLF LLC
222 Murphy Rd (06114-2107)
PHONE..................................860 296-1661
Mike Blair, *Mng Member*
▲ **EMP:** 3
SALES (est): 28.3K **Privately Held**
SIC: 3949 5091 Mfg Sporting/Athletic Goods Whol Sporting/Recreational Goods

Harwinton
Litchfield County

(G-1886)
ADVANCED RECEIVER RESEARCH
Also Called: Arr
535 Burlington Rd (06791-1505)
P.O. Box 1242, Burlington (06013-0242)
PHONE..................................860 485-0310
Jay Rusgrove, *Owner*
EMP: 3
SQ FT: 3,000
SALES (est): 326.4K **Privately Held**
WEB: www.advancedreceiver.com
SIC: 3663 Mfg Radio/Tv Communication Equipment

(G-1887)
BRYAN HEAVENS LOGGING & FIREWO
50 Shingle Mill Rd (06791-2310)
PHONE..................................860 485-1712
Gene A Heavens, *Manager*
EMP: 6
SALES (est): 449.6K **Privately Held**
SIC: 2411 Logging

(G-1888)
DURSTIN MACHINE & MFG
57 Westleigh Dr (06791-1107)
PHONE..................................860 485-1257
Michael Durstin, *President*
Elizabeth Durstin, *Admin Sec*
EMP: 4
SALES: 350K **Privately Held**
SIC: 3599 Custom Machine Work And Robotic Accessories

(G-1889)
EASTERN ELECTRIC CNSTR CO
75 North Rd (06791-1902)
PHONE..................................860 485-1100
Thomas Simko, *Principal*
David Pallanck, *Vice Pres*
EMP: 7 **EST:** 2010
SALES (est): 821.5K **Privately Held**
SIC: 3699 1731 1521 Mfg Electrical Equipment/Supplies Electrical Contractor Single-Family House Construction

(G-1890)
EASTSIDE ELECTRIC INC
178 Birge Park Rd (06791-1909)
PHONE..................................860 485-0700
Gregory L Mele, *Principal*
EMP: 19
SALES (est): 3.6MM **Privately Held**
SIC: 3699 1731 Mfg Electrical Equipment/Supplies Electrical Contractor

(G-1891)
O & G INDUSTRIES INC
255 Lower Bogue Rd (06791-1626)
PHONE..................................860 485-6600
Bob Oneglia, *Vice Pres*
Carol Lucia, *Associate*
EMP: 110
SALES (corp-wide): 538MM **Privately Held**
SIC: 3999 Mfg Misc Products
PA: O & G Industries, Inc.
112 Wall St
Torrington CT 06790
860 489-9261

(G-1892)
PRECISION WIRE CUTTING
9 Windmill Rd (06791-1116)
PHONE..................................860 485-1494
John Corey, *Owner*
EMP: 3
SQ FT: 1,500
SALES (est): 170K **Privately Held**
SIC: 3599 Mfg Industrial Machinery

(G-1893)
SPRING COMPUTERIZED INDS LLC
Also Called: Csi
93 Oakwood Dr (06791-1307)
PHONE..................................860 605-9206
Elliot Cyr, *Owner*
Janice Syr -Ofc, *Manager*
EMP: 8
SQ FT: 1,500
SALES (est): 630K **Privately Held**
WEB: www.csi-springs.com
SIC: 3495 3493 Mfg Wire Springs Mfg Steel Springs-Nonwire

Hawleyville
Fairfield County

(G-1894)
MISSION ALLERGY INC
28 Hawleyville Rd (06440)
P.O. Box 45 (06440-0045)
PHONE..................................203 364-1570
Jeffrey Miller, *President*
EMP: 6
SQ FT: 13,959
SALES (est): 1.1MM **Privately Held**
WEB: www.missionallergy.com
SIC: 3822 Mfg Environment Control Products

Hebron
Tolland County

(G-1895)
BENNETTSVILLE HOLDINGS LLC
Also Called: Bennettsville Printing
33 Pendleton Dr A (06248-1512)
PHONE..................................860 444-9400
Victor Winogradrow, *Mng Member*
Carol Winogradrow,
EMP: 85
SALES (est): 6.2MM **Privately Held**
SIC: 2396 Printing Textile Manufacture

(G-1896)
COUNTRY CARPENTERS INC
326 Gilead St (06248-1347)
PHONE..................................860 228-2276
Roger G Barrett Jr, *President*
Lois M Barrett, *Vice Pres*
Mark Coppinger, *Finance Mgr*
Paul Baker, *Finance*
EMP: 8
SALES (est): 1.5MM **Privately Held**
WEB: www.carriagesheds.com
SIC: 2491 1521 2452 2439 Wood Preserving Single-Family House Cnst Mfg Prefabrcatd Wd Bldgs Mfg Structural Wd Member

(G-1897)
INNOVATIVE SOFTWARE LLC
94 Country Ln (06248-1400)
PHONE..................................860 228-4144
Fred W Knapp Jr, *Mng Member*
EMP: 5
SALES (est): 346.6K **Privately Held**
SIC: 7372 Prepackaged Software Services

(G-1898)
TEK ARMS INC
282 Jagger Ln (06248-1122)
PHONE..................................860 748-6289
Mark Matheny, *Principal*
Alaina Matheny, *Officer*
EMP: 5
SALES (est): 355.1K **Privately Held**
SIC: 3489 Ordnance And Accessories, Nec

Higganum
Middlesex County

(G-1899)
APERTURE OPTICAL SCIENCES INC
23 Soobitsky Rd (06441-4476)
PHONE..................................860 301-2589
Flemming Tinker, *Principal*
EMP: 3
SALES (est): 236.1K **Privately Held**
SIC: 3827 Mfg Optical Instruments/Lenses

(G-1900)
B&B LOGGING LLC
298 Brainard Hill Rd (06441-4070)
PHONE..................................860 982-2425
Robert F Mesick,
EMP: 3
SALES: 180K **Privately Held**
SIC: 2411 0851 Logging Forestry Services

(G-1901)
BIZCARD XPRESS LLC
26 Killingworth Rd (06441-9995)
PHONE..................................860 324-6840
Daniela M Morello, *Principal*
EMP: 3
SALES (est): 173.8K **Privately Held**
SIC: 2752 Lithographic Commercial Printing

(G-1902)
BURDON ENTERPRISES LLC
20 Reisman Trl (06441-4360)
PHONE..................................860 345-4882
Gayle Burdon, *Principal*
EMP: 8 **EST:** 1995
SALES (est): 443.2K **Privately Held**
SIC: 3446 Mfg Architectural Metalwork

(G-1903)
KENYON LABORATORIES LLC
Also Called: Ken-Labs
12 Scovil Rd (06441-4218)
PHONE..................................860 345-2097
Ron Denman,
Bobbie Kenyon,
EMP: 7
SQ FT: 17,000
SALES: 1MM **Privately Held**
WEB: www.ken-lab.com
SIC: 3861 Mfg Photographic Equipment/Supplies

(G-1904)
N EXCELLENCE WOOD INC
Also Called: Wood N Excellence Cab Refacing
323 Hidden Lake Rd (06441-4528)
PHONE..................................860 345-2050
Paul Gregaitis, *President*
Karen Gregaitis, *Admin Sec*
EMP: 4
SALES (est): 363.4K **Privately Held**
WEB: www.woodnexcellence.com
SIC: 2434 Mfg Wood Kitchen Cabinets

(G-1905)
PW PRECISION MACHINE LLC
12 Scovil Rd Unit B (06441-4218)
PHONE..................................203 889-8615
Philip Warner, *Principal*
EMP: 4
SALES (est): 139.1K **Privately Held**
SIC: 3599 Mfg Industrial Machinery

(G-1906)
SOJA WOODWORKING LLC
548 Killingworth Rd (06441-4310)
PHONE..................................860 345-3909
Bryan Soja, *Principal*
EMP: 4
SALES (est): 240.8K **Privately Held**
SIC: 2431 Mfg Millwork

Ivoryton
Middlesex County

(G-1907)
MOELLER INSTRUMENT COMPANY INC
126 Main St (06442-1102)
P.O. Box 668 (06442-0668)
PHONE..................................800 243-9310
Jeff Murtz, *President*
Darla Allen, *Purchasing*
Thomas Janet, *Executive*
Janet Thomas, *Executive*
Darcy Murtz, *Admin Sec*
EMP: 20
SQ FT: 5,000
SALES: 1.8MM **Privately Held**
WEB: www.moellerinstrument.com
SIC: 3823 Mfg Process Control Instruments

(G-1908)
ORTRONICS LEGRAND
14 Windermere Way (06442-1275)
PHONE..................................860 767-3515
Mike Hines, *Principal*
EMP: 3
SALES (est): 199.8K **Privately Held**
SIC: 3577 Mfg Computer Peripheral Equipment

(G-1909)
THE L C DOANE COMPANY (PA)
110 Pond Meadow Rd (06442-1121)
PHONE..................................860 767-8295
Margaret P Eagan, *President*
William Psillos, *Vice Pres*
Steven Shapiro, *Vice Pres*
Rose Sypher, *Purch Mgr*
Ryan Gallacher, *Engineer*
EMP: 15 **EST:** 1947
SQ FT: 140,000
SALES (est): 14.2MM **Privately Held**
SIC: 3646 3647 Mfg Commercial Lighting Fixtures Mfg Vehicle Lighting Equipment

Jewett City
New London County

(G-1910)
CLINT S CUSTOM WOODWORKIN
628 River Rd (06351-3230)
P.O. Box 250, Ledyard (06339-0250)
PHONE..................................860 887-1476
Clinton Babcock, *Principal*
EMP: 8
SALES (est): 829.4K **Privately Held**
SIC: 2499 Mfg Wood Products

(G-1911)
DANTE LTD
633 Plainfield Rd (06351-1025)
PHONE..................................860 376-0204
Dante L Grassi, *President*
EMP: 5
SQ FT: 6,000
SALES: 1.5MM **Privately Held**
SIC: 2434 2431 2499 Manufacturing Kitchen & Bathroom Cabinetry

(G-1912)
GEER CONSTRUCTION CO INC
Also Called: Geer Sand & Gravel
852 Voluntown Rd (06351-3315)
PHONE..................................860 376-5321
H David Geer, *President*
Barbara Geer, *Vice Pres*
Richard B Geer, *Vice Pres*
Thomas D Geer, *Vice Pres*
EMP: 4
SALES (est): 693.4K **Privately Held**
WEB: www.geersfamilytree.com
SIC: 1442 0811 Sand & Gravel Pit

(G-1913)
GRISWOLD MACHINE & FABRICATION
8 Sheldon Rd (06351-3622)
PHONE..................................860 376-9891
Richard Farina Jr, *Owner*
EMP: 4
SQ FT: 16,000
SALES: 220K **Privately Held**
SIC: 3599 Mfg Industrial Machinery

(G-1914)
K & D BUSINESS VENTURES LLC
39 1/2 Wedgewood Dr (06351-2439)
P.O. Box 199 (06351)
PHONE..................................860 237-1458
Michael Giacobbe, *Branch Mgr*
EMP: 3
SALES (corp-wide): 20K **Privately Held**
SIC: 3949 Mfg Sporting/Athletic Goods
PA: K & D Business Ventures, Llc
4322 Carrollwood Vlg Dr
Tampa FL 33618
321 474-5948

(G-1915)
MAPLE PRINT SERVICES INC
39 Wedgewood Dr (06351-2437)
PHONE..........860 381-5470
Mike Johnson, *President*
EMP: 4
SALES (est): 179.8K **Privately Held**
SIC: 2752 Lithographic Commercial Printing

Kensington
Hartford County

(G-1916)
ACADEMY PRINTING SERVICE
Also Called: Austin Rubber Stamps
900 Farmington Ave Ste 2 (06037-2219)
PHONE..........860 828-5549
Timothy J Mc Mullen, *Owner*
EMP: 3
SQ FT: 1,950
SALES (est): 276.6K **Privately Held**
SIC: 2752 5999 Lithographic Commercial Printing Ret Misc Merchandise

(G-1917)
ALINABAL INC
Also Called: Sterling Screw Machine Pdts
384 Christian Ln (06037-1424)
PHONE..........860 828-9933
Larry Desimone, *Manager*
EMP: 16
SALES (corp-wide): 57MM **Privately Held**
WEB: www.dacoinstrument.com
SIC: 3451 Mfg Screw Machine Products
HQ: Alinabal, Inc.
28 Woodmont Rd
Milford CT 06460
203 877-3241

(G-1918)
KENSINGTON WELDING & TRLR CO
1114 Farmington Ave (06037-2245)
PHONE..........860 828-3564
Jerry Marcoux, *President*
EMP: 5 **EST:** 1947
SQ FT: 7,500
SALES (est): 710.6K **Privately Held**
SIC: 7692 3715 5013 Welding Repair Mfg Truck Trailers Whol Auto Parts/Supplies Mfg Indstl Truck/Tractor Mfg Sheet Metalwork

(G-1919)
MEADOW MANUFACTURING INC
120 Old Brickyard Ln (06037-1437)
PHONE..........860 357-3785
Mark Gregoretti, *President*
Patrick D Temme, *Principal*
Heidi Pascucci, *Controller*
EMP: 15
SALES (est): 2.6MM **Privately Held**
SIC: 3545 Mfg Machine Tool Accessories

(G-1920)
ROTATING COMPOSITE TECH LLC
49 Cambridge Hts (06037-2310)
PHONE..........860 829-6809
John Violette, *President*
Jacob Virkler, *Engineer*
Christopher Aliapoulios, *Webmaster*
EMP: 8 **EST:** 2007
SALES: 1.6MM **Privately Held**
SIC: 3728 Mfg Aircraft Parts/Equipment

(G-1921)
TELKE TOOL & DIE MFG CO
47 Cambridge Hts (06037-2310)
P.O. Box 97 (06037-0097)
PHONE..........860 828-9955
Bruce Telke, *President*
Steve Telke, *Vice Pres*
Lynn Telke, *Treasurer*
EMP: 4 **EST:** 1950
SQ FT: 2,500
SALES: 150K **Privately Held**
SIC: 3544 3469 Tool & Die Shop & Metal Stamping

Kent
Litchfield County

(G-1922)
INDIGO COAST INC
Also Called: Trailheads
17 Meadow St (06757-1329)
PHONE..........860 592-0088
Stephanie Raftery, *President*
Karen Dignacco, *Sales Staff*
Lorienne Cote, *Admin Sec*
▲ **EMP:** 8
SALES: 994K **Privately Held**
SIC: 2353 7389 Mfg Hats/Caps/Millinery Business Services At Non-Commercial Site

(G-1923)
KENT FALLS BREWING COMPANY
33 Camps Rd (06757-1901)
PHONE..........860 398-9645
Barry Labendz, *Founder*
EMP: 3
SALES (est): 68.6K **Privately Held**
SIC: 2082 Mfg Malt Beverages

Killingworth
Middlesex County

(G-1924)
ANDERSON TECHNOLOGIES INC
243 Roast Meat Hill Rd (06419-2346)
P.O. Box 643, Guilford (06437-0643)
PHONE..........860 663-2100
Andy Anderson, *President*
Lawrence Anderson, *Vice Pres*
◆ **EMP:** 4
SQ FT: 2,500
SALES (est): 722K **Privately Held**
SIC: 3564 5084 Mfg Air Or Gas Purification Equipment & Whol Spare Parts

(G-1925)
COASTAL GROUP INC
Also Called: Coastal Tooling
145 Chestnut Hill Rd (06419-1300)
PHONE..........860 452-4148
Martha Springer, *CEO*
Jeff Springer, *President*
Shane Springer, *Director*
EMP: 3
SQ FT: 500
SALES: 100K **Privately Held**
SIC: 3545 Mfg Machine Tool Accessories

(G-1926)
EAST COAST PRECISION MFG LLC
63 Pond Meadow Rd (06419-1136)
P.O. Box 294, Boxford MA (01921-0294)
PHONE..........978 887-5920
Chris Marchand, *Engineer*
Mark Rohlfs, *Associate Dir*
EMP: 4
SALES: 190K **Privately Held**
WEB: www.eastcoastmfg.com
SIC: 3082 Mfg Plastic Profile Shapes

(G-1927)
MARTIN MFG SERVICES LLC
96 Cow Hill Rd (06419-2402)
PHONE..........860 663-1465
Paul J Martin, *Mng Member*
EMP: 4
SALES (est): 57.9K **Privately Held**
SIC: 3999 Mfg Misc Products

(G-1928)
NEW ENGLAND TOOLING INC
145 Chestnut Hill Rd (06419-1300)
PHONE..........800 866-5105
Shane Springer, *President*
Jeff Springer, *Vice Pres*
Gary Beeman, *Technical Staff*
Tom Bittner, *Technical Staff*
EMP: 10
SALES (est): 952.8K **Privately Held**
SIC: 3541 Mfg Machine Tools-Cutting

(G-1929)
SEXTANT BTSLLC
166 Route 81 (06419-1481)
PHONE..........203 500-3245
EMP: 3
SALES (est): 251.9K **Privately Held**
SIC: 3812 Mfg Search/Navigation Equipment

Lakeville
Litchfield County

(G-1930)
ILLINOIS TOOL WORKS INC
ITW Impro Lakeville Operations
14 Brook St (06039-1104)
P.O. Box 1570 (06039-1570)
PHONE..........860 435-2574
Bill Thurston, *Manager*
EMP: 50
SQ FT: 20,000
SALES (corp-wide): 14.7B **Publicly Held**
SIC: 3089 Mfg Plastic Products
PA: Illinois Tool Works Inc.
155 Harlem Ave
Glenview IL 60025
847 724-7500

(G-1931)
LAKEVILLE JOURNAL COMPANY LLC (PA)
Also Called: Lakeville Journal, The
33 Bissell St (06039)
P.O. Box 1688 (06039-1688)
PHONE..........860 435-9873
Will Little, *President*
Cynthia Hochswender, *Editor*
EMP: 51
SQ FT: 10,000
SALES (est): 3.1MM **Privately Held**
WEB: www.lakevillejournal.com
SIC: 2711 Newspapers-Publishing/Printing

Lebanon
New London County

(G-1932)
ANN S DAVIS
Also Called: Recognition Products
754 Exeter Rd (06249-1735)
P.O. Box 1980 (06249-1980)
PHONE..........860 642-7228
Ann S Davis, *Owner*
EMP: 10
SALES (est): 771.5K **Privately Held**
WEB: www.rproducts.com
SIC: 3999 3479 7389 Mfg Misc Products Coating/Engraving Service Business Services

(G-1933)
C AND B WELDING LLC
20 Hillside Dr (06249-1017)
PHONE..........860 423-9047
Chris Pearl, *Owner*
EMP: 6
SALES (est): 224.4K **Privately Held**
SIC: 7692 Welding Repair

(G-1934)
DENS SAND & GRAVEL
970 Goshen Hill Rd Ext (06249-2303)
PHONE..........860 642-6478
EMP: 3
SALES (est): 166.4K **Privately Held**
SIC: 1442 Construction Sand/Gravel

(G-1935)
INDARS STAIRS LLC
39 W Town St (06249-1536)
P.O. Box 87, Willimantic (06226-0087)
PHONE..........860 208-3826
Albert Manning, *Mng Member*
Kellie Monroe, *Manager*
EMP: 4
SALES: 730K **Privately Held**
SIC: 2431 Mfg Millwork

(G-1936)
MIRACLE INSTRUMENTS CO
1667 Exeter Rd (06249-1904)
PHONE..........860 642-7745
John Ryan, *President*
EMP: 11
SQ FT: 3,000
SALES (est): 1.7MM **Privately Held**
WEB: www.miracleinstrument.com
SIC: 3545 3829 3699 Mfg Chuck Keys Levels And Garage Door Openers

(G-1937)
SCOTTS COMPANY LLC
20 Industrial Rd (06249-1326)
P.O. Box 143 (06249-0143)
PHONE..........860 642-7591
Mark Kulling, *Manager*
EMP: 70
SALES (corp-wide): 3.1B **Publicly Held**
WEB: www.scottscompany.com
SIC: 2875 Mfg Natural & Organic Soils
HQ: The Scotts Company Llc
14111 Scottslawn Rd
Marysville OH 43040
937 644-0011

(G-1938)
WASTE RESOURCE RECOVERY INC (PA)
505 Exeter Rd (06249-1544)
PHONE..........860 287-3332
Richard N Madrak, *President*
Richard Madrak, *President*
EMP: 3 **EST:** 2014
SQ FT: 5,000
SALES (est): 331.3K **Privately Held**
SIC: 2869 Mfg Industrial Organic Chemicals

Ledyard
New London County

(G-1939)
BAA CREATIONS
13 Lambtown Rd (06339-1925)
PHONE..........860 464-1339
Elizabeth Macleod, *Owner*
EMP: 3
SALES: 85K **Privately Held**
SIC: 2395 Pleating/Stitching Services

(G-1940)
CLARIOS
Also Called: Johnson Controls
39 Route 2 (06339-1128)
PHONE..........860 886-9021
Tom Oneil, *Manager*
EMP: 94 **Privately Held**
SIC: 2531 Mfg Automotive Seating & Interior Systems
HQ: Johnson Controls Inc
5757 N Green Bay Ave
Milwaukee WI 53209
414 524-1200

(G-1941)
FORTE RTS INC
Also Called: Forte Carbon Fiber Products
14 Lorenz Industrial Pkwy (06339-1946)
PHONE..........860 464-5221
Anthony F Delima, *President*
Clint Rand, *Marketing Mgr*
▼ **EMP:** 8
SALES (est): 1.3MM **Privately Held**
WEB: www.fortecarbon.com
SIC: 3825 Mfg Electrical Measuring Instruments

(G-1942)
MANAGEMENT SOFTWARE INC
Also Called: MSI
547 Colonel Ledyard Hwy (06339-1611)
PHONE..........860 536-5177
Frank Thompson, *President*
Margaret Thompson, *CFO*
EMP: 4
SALES (est): 340.8K **Privately Held**
WEB: www.managementsoftware.com
SIC: 7372 7379 7373 Prepackaged Software Computer System Integration Computer Maint & Consulting Services

GEOGRAPHIC

Lisbon
New London County

(G-1943)
JUST BREAKFAST & THINGS
15 River Rd (06351-3035)
PHONE.................................860 376-4040
Mary Thompson, *Owner*
EMP: 4
SALES (est): 264.5K **Privately Held**
SIC: 2038 Mfg Frozen Specialties

(G-1944)
OMNI MOLD SYSTEMS LLC
21 Kimball Heights Ln (06351-2833)
PHONE.................................888 666-4755
Gaston Cyr, *Principal*
EMP: 5
SALES (est): 606K **Privately Held**
SIC: 3544 Mfg Dies/Tools/Jigs/Fixtures

Litchfield
Litchfield County

(G-1945)
BEARICUDA INC
Also Called: Bearicuda Bins
3 West St Ste 3e (06759-3501)
P.O. Box 56 (06759-0056)
PHONE.................................860 361-6860
Kevin Lacilla, *President*
EMP: 5 **EST:** 2008
SALES (est): 323.6K **Privately Held**
SIC: 3469 Mfg Metal Stampings

(G-1946)
CONCRETE SUPPLEMENT CO
272 Norfolk Rd (06759-2517)
P.O. Box 501 (06759-0501)
PHONE.................................860 567-5556
Alan Landau, *President*
Christopher Krone, *Vice Pres*
EMP: 9
SQ FT: 36,000
SALES (est): 2.8MM **Privately Held**
WEB: www.consupco.com
SIC: 2899 Mfg Chemical Preparations

(G-1947)
CUSTOM FURNITURE & DESIGN LLC
601 Bantam Rd (06759)
P.O. Box 1533 (06759-1533)
PHONE.................................860 567-3519
Mike Moskowitz, *Mng Member*
Robert Paradis,
EMP: 11
SQ FT: 6,000
SALES (est): 1.5MM **Privately Held**
SIC: 2434 2511 Mfg Wood Kitchen Cabinets Mfg Wood Household Furniture

(G-1948)
ENGINEERED COATINGS INC
272 Norfolk Rd (06759-2517)
P.O. Box 501 (06759-0501)
PHONE.................................860 567-5556
Jack Walnes, *President*
Alfred Matarese, *Vice Pres*
Richard Novak, *Vice Pres*
EMP: 32
SQ FT: 21,200
SALES (est): 3.1MM **Privately Held**
SIC: 3479 Coating/Engraving Service

(G-1949)
GRAPHIC PACKAGING INTL LLC
133 Goodhouse Rd (06759-2216)
PHONE.................................860 567-4196
Tom Binstadt, *Manager*
EMP: 3
SQ FT: 1,500 **Publicly Held**
SIC: 2631 Whol Nondurable Goods
HQ: Graphic Packaging International, Llc
1500 Riveredge Pkwy # 100
Atlanta GA 30328

(G-1950)
JAMIESON LASER LLC
50 Thomaston Rd (06759)
P.O. Box 1531 (06759-1531)
PHONE.................................860 482-3375
Wolfgang Kesselring, *General Mgr*
Wolfgang Kesserling, *Mng Member*
Rory Shepherd, *Technician*
▲ **EMP:** 5
SQ FT: 12,000
SALES: 500K **Privately Held**
SIC: 3699 Mfg Electrical Equipment/Supplies

(G-1951)
LITCHFIELD INTERNATIONAL INC
457 Bantam Rd Ste 12 (06759-3225)
PHONE.................................860 567-8824
C Stuart Hungerford, *President*
Kate Hungerford, *Vice Pres*
Charles Hungerford, *Shareholder*
▲ **EMP:** 5
SQ FT: 4,000
SALES (est): 1MM **Privately Held**
SIC: 3317 Mfg Steel Pipe/Tubes

(G-1952)
SPACE SWISS MANUFACTURING INC
428 Maple St (06759-2100)
PHONE.................................860 567-4341
EMP: 10 **EST:** 1963
SQ FT: 18,000
SALES (est): 720K **Privately Held**
SIC: 3451 Mfg Screw Machine Products

(G-1953)
SWEET PEET NORTH AMERICA INC
3 West St Ste 3 (06759-3501)
P.O. Box 56 (06759-0056)
PHONE.................................860 361-6444
EMP: 3
SALES (est): 160K **Privately Held**
SIC: 2499 Mfg Wood Products

Lyme
New London County

(G-1954)
DEBRASONG PUBLISHING LLC
82-3 Mount Archer Rd (06371-3158)
PHONE.................................413 204-4682
Debra L Alt, *Principal*
EMP: 3
SALES (est): 107.3K **Privately Held**
SIC: 2741 Misc Publishing

(G-1955)
LIMBKEEPERS LLC
25 Joshuatown Rd (06371-3119)
PHONE.................................860 304-3250
Deborah Vezan, *Principal*
EMP: 3 **EST:** 2013
SALES (est): 195.6K **Privately Held**
SIC: 3842 Mfg Surgical Appliances/Supplies

(G-1956)
SUNSET HILL VINEYARD
5 Elys Ferry Rd (06371-3406)
PHONE.................................860 598-9427
Salvatore A Caruso, *Principal*
EMP: 3
SALES (est): 151.6K **Privately Held**
SIC: 2084 Mfg Wines/Brandy/Spirits

Madison
New Haven County

(G-1957)
CR-TEC ENGINEERING INC
15 Orchard Park Rd A20 (06443-2268)
PHONE.................................203 318-9500
Charles W Lehberger, *President*
EMP: 4
SALES (est): 474.7K **Privately Held**
WEB: www.crtec.com
SIC: 3491 Mfg Industrial Valves

(G-1958)
CRANIAL TECHNOLOGIES INC
1343 Boston Post Rd (06443-3481)
PHONE.................................203 318-8739
Lynne Ball, *Branch Mgr*
EMP: 17 **Privately Held**
SIC: 3842 Mfg Surgical Appliances/Supplies
PA: Cranial Technologies, Inc.
1395 W Auto Dr
Tempe AZ 85284

(G-1959)
D P ENGINEERING INC
211 Summer Hill Rd (06443-1850)
PHONE.................................203 421-7965
David Penniman, *President*
EMP: 3
SQ FT: 2,000
SALES: 200K **Privately Held**
WEB: www.polyhangers.com
SIC: 3589 5082 Mfg & Whol Asbestos Removing Specialty Products

(G-1960)
E M M INC
8 Bishop Ln (06443-3367)
PHONE.................................203 245-0306
Herbert D'Alo, *President*
Melissa D'Alo, *Vice Pres*
Melissa Dalo, *Sales Mgr*
EMP: 20
SALES (est): 1.9MM **Privately Held**
SIC: 3841 Mfg Surgical/Medical Instruments

(G-1961)
GRAYFIN SECURITY LLC
Also Called: Grayfin Micro
82 Bradley Rd (06443-2684)
P.O. Box 1333 (06443-1333)
PHONE.................................203 800-6760
Benjamin Gray, *Mng Member*
EMP: 6 **EST:** 2012
SQ FT: 1,320
SALES: 1.5MM **Privately Held**
SIC: 7372 7373 7371 5065 Prepackaged Software Svc Computer Systems Design Computer Programming Svc Whol Electronic Parts Security System Svcs

(G-1962)
HARBOR PUBLICATIONS INC
Also Called: Mail-A-Map
1 Orchard Park Rd Ste 8 (06443-2272)
P.O. Box 883 (06443-0883)
PHONE.................................203 245-8009
Matt Holmes, *President*
EMP: 4
SQ FT: 1,400
SALES: 1.3MM **Privately Held**
SIC: 2741 Misc Publishing

(G-1963)
HEALTHY HARVEST INC
42 Godman Rd (06443-2033)
PHONE.................................203 245-3786
David Roach, *President*
Russell Phillips, *Vice Pres*
EMP: 5
SQ FT: 5,000
SALES (est): 477.2K **Privately Held**
SIC: 2879 8732 Mfg Fruit And Vegetable Rinse

(G-1964)
IMAGINE 8 LLC
26 Eagle Meadow Rd (06443-8123)
PHONE.................................203 421-0905
Michael Mazzaferro,
◆ **EMP:** 4
SALES (est): 225.3K **Privately Held**
WEB: www.imagine8.com
SIC: 3944 Designs/Mfr Premium Toys

(G-1965)
INDEPENDENCE PARK
38 Sheffield Ln (06443-1770)
PHONE.................................203 421-9396
Tom Burke, *President*
EMP: 3
SALES (est): 252.8K **Privately Held**
SIC: 3625 Mfg Relays/Industrial Controls

(G-1966)
INDUSTRIAL ANALYTICS CORP
1 Orchard Park Rd Ste 10 (06443-2272)
PHONE.................................203 245-0380
Nicholas J Afragola, *President*
Ann Afragola, *Admin Sec*
EMP: 3
SALES: 1MM **Privately Held**
SIC: 3826 Whol Professional Equipment

(G-1967)
KIRCHOFF WOHLBERG INC
897 Boston Post Rd (06443-3155)
PHONE.................................212 644-2020
Morris Kirchoff, *President*
Mary Jane Martin, *Vice Pres*
Ronald Zollshan, *Treasurer*
EMP: 13 **EST:** 1974
SQ FT: 8,000
SALES (est): 3MM **Privately Held**
WEB: www.kirchoffwohlberg.com
SIC: 2731 7389 Educational Publishing Services & Artists' Representatives

(G-1968)
MENTAL CANVAS LLC
61 Hartford Ave (06443-2743)
PHONE.................................475 329-0515
Julie Dorsey,
EMP: 5
SALES (est): 179.1K **Privately Held**
SIC: 7372 Prepackaged Software Services

(G-1969)
NEW PRECISION TECHNOLOGY LLC
Also Called: USI Education & Government Sls
98 Fort Path Rd Ste B (06443-2264)
PHONE.................................800 243-4565
Nicholas Gianacoplos, *Owner*
Sherri Montminy, *Principal*
Frederick Franco, *Info Tech Mgr*
EMP: 7
SQ FT: 14,000
SALES (est): 630K **Privately Held**
WEB: www.np-tek.com
SIC: 3083 Mfg Laminated Plastic Plate/Sheet

(G-1970)
NO BUTTS BIN COMPANY INC
16 Birch Ln (06443-2535)
P.O. Box 1065 (06443-1065)
PHONE.................................203 245-5924
Martyn A Bright, *President*
Greg Burke, *General Mgr*
▲ **EMP:** 4
SQ FT: 5,000
SALES: 900K **Privately Held**
SIC: 3469 Manufacturer Of Smoking Control Products

(G-1971)
ONCOARENDI THERAPEUTICS LLC
125 Devonshire Ln (06443-8124)
PHONE.................................609 571-0306
Stanislaw Pikul,
Adam Golebiowski,
EMP: 4 **EST:** 2014
SALES (est): 211.5K **Privately Held**
SIC: 2834 Mfg Pharmaceutical Preparations

(G-1972)
PUCUDA INC
Also Called: Leading Edge Safety Systems
14 New Rd (06443-2507)
P.O. Box 471 (06443-0471)
PHONE.................................860 526-8004
John Rexroad, *President*
Jason Lawlor, *Vice Pres*
Philipp Paragrin, *Manager*
Drew Bishop, *Graphic Designe*
◆ **EMP:** 15
SQ FT: 12,500
SALES: 5MM **Privately Held**
WEB: www.netting.com
SIC: 3089 Mfg Plastic Products

(G-1973)
RWT CORPORATION
Also Called: Welding Works
32 New Rd (06443-2507)
PHONE.....203 245-2731
Ross E McCartney, *President*
Maria Teixeira, *Office Mgr*
Laurie McCartney, *Admin Sec*
EMP: 24
SQ FT: 22,000
SALES: 5MM **Privately Held**
SIC: 3441 3448 Structural Metal Fabrication Mfg Prefabricated Metal Buildings

(G-1974)
SCOTT WOODFORD
817 Boston Post Rd (06443-3155)
PHONE.....203 245-4266
Scott Woodford, *Principal*
EMP: 4
SALES (est): 348.1K **Privately Held**
SIC: 3843 Mfg Dental Equipment/Supplies

(G-1975)
SHORE PUBLISHING LLC
724 Boston Post Rd (06443-3039)
P.O. Box 1010 (06443-1010)
PHONE.....203 245-1877
Robyn Wolcott, *Publisher*
Lee Howard, *Editor*
Chris Negrini, *Editor*
Andrea J Simeone, *Credit Mgr*
James Warner,
EMP: 45 **EST:** 1994
SQ FT: 2,500
SALES (est): 2.6MM **Privately Held**
WEB: www.shorepublishing.com
SIC: 2711 Newspapers-Publishing/Printing

(G-1976)
SHORELINE VINE
724 Boston Post 105a (06443)
PHONE.....203 779-5331
Dawn Schwab, *Principal*
EMP: 3
SALES (est): 237.9K **Privately Held**
SIC: 2079 Mfg Edible Fats/Oils

(G-1977)
SPECTROGRAM CORPORATION
287 Boston Post Rd (06443-2938)
PHONE.....203 245-2433
Herbert R Gram, *President*
Joan Friborg, *Vice Pres*
Geoffery A Gram, *Director*
EMP: 3
SQ FT: 6,000
SALES: 100K **Privately Held**
WEB: www.spectrogram.com
SIC: 3826 8731 3812 Mfg Analytical Instruments Commercial Physical Research Mfg Search/Enviromental Research Equipment

(G-1978)
TANGO MODEM LLC
303 Race Hill Rd (06443-1628)
PHONE.....203 421-2245
Robert Allen, *Principal*
Michael Borsari, *Opers Staff*
EMP: 5
SALES (est): 381.9K **Privately Held**
SIC: 3661 Mfg Telephone/Telegraph Apparatus

(G-1979)
WIRE JOURNAL INC
71 Bradley Rd Unit 9 (06443-2662)
P.O. Box 578, Guilford (06437-0578)
PHONE.....203 453-2777
Sanford May, *Exec Dir*
EMP: 20
SQ FT: 10,000
SALES: 1.9MM
SALES (corp-wide): 988.9K **Privately Held**
WEB: www.wirenet.org
SIC: 2721 Periodicals-Publishing/Printing
PA: The Wire Association International Inc
71 Bradley Rd Unit 9
Madison CT 06443
203 453-2777

Manchester
Hartford County

(G-1980)
ABA-PGT INC (PA)
Also Called: A B A Tool & Die Div
10 Gear Dr (06042-8907)
PHONE.....860 649-4591
Samuel D Pierson, *CEO*
Michael J Rice, *Corp Secy*
Thomas R Peck, *Vice Pres*
Frankie Lee, *Mfg Mgr*
Paul Caswell, *Maint Spvr*
EMP: 104 **EST:** 1944
SQ FT: 67,000
SALES (est): 30.5MM **Privately Held**
WEB: www.abapgt.com
SIC: 3089 3544 Mfg Plastic Products Mfg Dies/Tools/Jigs/Fixtures

(G-1981)
ACCURATE BRAZING CORPORATION
4 Progress Dr (06042)
PHONE.....860 432-1840
Bob Sartori, *Manager*
Waleska Laureano, *Assistant*
EMP: 18
SALES (corp-wide): 3B **Privately Held**
SIC: 3398 Metal Heat Treating
HQ: Accurate Brazing Corporation
36 Cote Ave Ste 5
Goffstown NH 03045

(G-1982)
ACMT INC
369 Progress Dr (06042-2296)
PHONE.....860 645-0592
Michael G Polo, *President*
Dan Polo, *General Mgr*
Paul Polo Sr, *Vice Pres*
Michael Cyr, *Facilities Mgr*
Bob Coulombe, *Purchasing*
EMP: 100
SQ FT: 48,000
SALES (est): 17.9MM **Privately Held**
WEB: www.acmtct.com
SIC: 3728 3061 3724 Mfg Aircraft Parts/Equipment Mfg Mechanical Rubber Goods Mfg Aircraft Engines/Parts

(G-1983)
ADVANCE MOLD & MFG INC
Also Called: Vision Technical Molding
71 Utopia Rd (06042-2192)
PHONE.....860 432-5887
Douglas Schneider, *President*
Kate Gihon, *Supervisor*
EMP: 150 **EST:** 1959
SQ FT: 28,500
SALES (est): 34.9MM
SALES (corp-wide): 26.2B **Privately Held**
WEB: www.advancemold.com
SIC: 3544 3089 Mfg Dies/Tools/Jigs/Fixtures Mfg Plastic Products
HQ: Flextronics International Usa, Inc.
6201 America Center Dr
San Jose CA 95002

(G-1984)
ALLIED PRINTING SERVICES INC (PA)
1 Allied Way (06042-8933)
P.O. Box 850 (06045-0850)
PHONE.....860 643-1101
John G Sommers, *President*
Chuck Samar, *Business Mgr*
Elyse Mahoney, *COO*
Bettina Sommers, *Exec VP*
Gerald Sommers, *Exec VP*
▲ **EMP:** 350 **EST:** 1950
SALES (est): 80.8MM **Privately Held**
SIC: 2396 2752 2759 2789 Mfg Auto/Apparel Trim Lithographic Coml Print Commercial Printing Bookbinding/Related Work Typesetting Services

(G-1985)
ALLOY SPECIALTIES INCORPORATED
110 Batson Dr (06042-1694)
PHONE.....860 646-4587
Richard Ramondetta, *President*
Dennis P Dimauro, *Vice Pres*
Rob Siggia, *Production*
Jim Thurston, *Purchasing*
Steve Bissell, *Engineer*
EMP: 40
SQ FT: 14,500
SALES (est): 9MM **Privately Held**
WEB: www.alloysp.com
SIC: 3724 5051 Mfg Aircraft Engines/Parts Metals Service Center

(G-1986)
AMERICAN REFACING CSTM CAB LLC
1 Mitchell Dr (06042-2394)
PHONE.....860 647-0868
George Warner,
EMP: 5
SQ FT: 1,800
SALES (est): 537.5K **Privately Held**
SIC: 2434 Mfg Wood Kitchen Cabinets

(G-1987)
BAKELITE N SUMITOMO AMER INC (DH)
24 Mill St (06042-2316)
PHONE.....860 645-3851
Henny Van Dijk, *President*
Shintaro Ishiwata, *Chairman*
Alan Houghton, *Admin Sec*
▲ **EMP:** 85 **EST:** 2002
SALES (est): 16MM **Privately Held**
WEB: www.sumitomobakelite.com
SIC: 2821 Mfg Plastic Materials/Resins

(G-1988)
BRAVO LLC (PA)
Also Called: Bravo Pet Store
349 Wetherell St (06040-6349)
PHONE.....866 922-9222
David J Bogner,
EMP: 17
SALES (est): 5.6MM **Privately Held**
WEB: www.bravo.com
SIC: 2047 Mfg Dog/Cat Food

(G-1989)
BREAD AND WINE PUBLISHING LLC
220 Charter Oak St (06040-6213)
PHONE.....860 649-3109
Frank Bausola,
EMP: 3
SQ FT: 1,500
SALES (est): 224.8K **Privately Held**
SIC: 2759 Commercial Printing

(G-1990)
CAM GROUP LLC
130 Chapel Rd (06042-1625)
PHONE.....860 646-2378
Charles Joseph Angle,
EMP: 10
SQ FT: 2,000
SALES: 2.5MM **Privately Held**
WEB: www.camgroup.com
SIC: 3519 Mfg Internal Combustion Engines

(G-1991)
CAMETOID TECHNOLOGIES INC
150 Colonial Rd (06042-2306)
P.O. Box 130 (06045-0130)
PHONE.....860 646-4667
John W Adams, *President*
Robert Sanderson, *Vice Pres*
Ray Berasi, *Controller*
Keith Kevorkian, *Manager*
Susanne Hilbert, *Officer*
EMP: 19
SQ FT: 18,000
SALES (est): 2.8MM **Privately Held**
WEB: www.cametoid.com
SIC: 3479 Coating/Engraving Service

(G-1992)
CARRIAGE HOUSE COMPANIES INC
42 Steeplechase Dr (06040-7067)
PHONE.....860 647-1909
EMP: 472
SALES (corp-wide): 15.4B **Publicly Held**
SIC: 2099 Mfg Syrups Mfg
HQ: The Carriage House Companies Inc
196 Newton St
Fredonia NY 14063
716 673-1000

(G-1993)
CHAMPLIN-PACKRITE INC
151 Batson Dr (06042-1624)
PHONE.....860 951-9217
Rory T Poole, *President*
Christine E Poole, *Corp Secy*
Sean T Poole, *Director*
EMP: 44
SQ FT: 75,000
SALES (est): 7.9MM **Privately Held**
SIC: 2441 2449 2653 3412 Mfg Wood Boxes/Shooks Mfg Wood Containers Mfg Corrugated/Fiber Box Mfg Metal Barrels/Pails

(G-1994)
CHARLES J ANGELO MFG GROUP LLC
130 Chapel Rd (06042-1625)
PHONE.....860 646-2378
Charles J Angelo,
EMP: 10 **EST:** 2003
SQ FT: 12,000
SALES: 1.7MM **Privately Held**
SIC: 3544 Mfg Dies/Tools/Jigs/Fixtures

(G-1995)
CLAY FURNITURE INDUSTRIES INC
41 Chapel St (06042-7340)
PHONE.....860 643-7580
Julie Clay, *President*
Richard F Clay Jr, *Vice Pres*
EMP: 10
SQ FT: 15,000
SALES (est): 1.2MM **Privately Held**
WEB: www.clayfurniture.com
SIC: 2521 Mfg Custom Cabinetry Wood Veneers

(G-1996)
CONNECTCUT CRNIAL FCIAL IMGERY
483 Middle Tpke W Ste 102 (06040-3864)
PHONE.....860 643-2940
Joel Rosenlicht, *Principal*
EMP: 3
SALES (est): 302.4K **Privately Held**
SIC: 2844 Mfg Toilet Preparations

(G-1997)
CREATIVE MOBILE SYSTEMS INC
189 Adams St (06042-1919)
P.O. Box 8198 (06040-0198)
PHONE.....860 649-6272
Dominic Acquarulo Jr, *President*
Edward Izzo, *President*
Richard Lumpkin, *Vice Pres*
Brian L Smith, *Vice Pres*
EMP: 6
SQ FT: 8,000
SALES (est): 1.2MM **Privately Held**
WEB: www.cmssystem.com
SIC: 3589 Mfg Service Industry Machinery

(G-1998)
DAVID DEREWIANKA
459 Dennison Rdg (06040-6839)
PHONE.....860 649-1983
David Derewianka, *Principal*
EMP: 3
SALES (est): 114.3K **Privately Held**
SIC: 3451 Mfg Screw Machine Products

(G-1999)
DAWN ENTERPRISES LLC
275 Progress Dr Ste B (06042-2211)
PHONE.....860 646-8200
Richard Sheldon,
Mike Bergeron,

GEOGRAPHIC

(PA)=Parent Co (HQ)=Headquarters (DH)=Div Headquarters
✪ = New Business established in last 2 years

Chad Glucksman,
◆ **EMP:** 9 **EST:** 1978
SALES (est): 1.7MM **Privately Held**
WEB: www.godawn.com
SIC: 3272 Mfg Concrete Products

(G-2000)
DEROSA PRINTING COMPANY INC
485 Middle Tpke E (06040-3735)
P.O. Box 1567 (06045-1567)
PHONE....................................860 646-1698
Richard De Rosa, *President*
EMP: 15 **EST:** 1980
SQ FT: 7,000
SALES (est): 2.1MM **Privately Held**
SIC: 2752 7334 Offset Printing High Speedy Copying And Four Color Process

(G-2001)
DIVINE TREASURE
404 Middle Tpke W (06040-3824)
PHONE....................................860 643-2552
Diane Wagemann, *Owner*
EMP: 5
SALES (est): 566.1K **Privately Held**
SIC: 2066 Mfg Chocolate/Cocoa Products

(G-2002)
DONWELL COMPANY
130 Sheldon Rd (06042-2388)
P.O. Box 906 (06045-0906)
PHONE....................................860 649-5374
Tracey B Sherman, *President*
Jeffrey Sherman, *Treasurer*
Dean A Sherman, *Director*
EMP: 44 **EST:** 1957
SQ FT: 23,000
SALES (est): 5.3MM **Privately Held**
WEB: www.donwell.com
SIC: 3479 Coating/Engraving Service

(G-2003)
DREAMER SOFTWARE LLC
17 Mckinley St (06040-4813)
PHONE....................................860 645-1240
Christopher A Walnum, *Manager*
EMP: 5
SALES (est): 348.3K **Privately Held**
SIC: 7372 Prepackaged Software Services

(G-2004)
EA PATTEN CO LLC
303 Wetherell St (06040-6349)
PHONE....................................860 649-2851
David W Pinette, *President*
Forest E Patten, *Chairman*
Lisa Rinn, *Purch Mgr*
Guscyna Davila, *Controller*
Rauls Ramans, *Marketing Mgr*
▼ **EMP:** 95 **EST:** 1945
SQ FT: 40,000
SALES (est): 28.7MM **Privately Held**
WEB: www.eapatten.com
SIC: 3498 3599 Mfg Fabricated Pipe/Fittings Mfg Industrial Machinery

(G-2005)
EMPIRE INDUSTRIES INC
180 Olcott St (06040-2647)
PHONE....................................860 647-1431
Mark Schauster, *President*
John Feeney, *Vice Pres*
Richard Schauster, *Treasurer*
Drew Mercure, *Sales Staff*
▲ **EMP:** 37
SQ FT: 55,000
SALES (est): 10.2MM **Privately Held**
WEB: www.copperguard.com
SIC: 3469 Mfg Metal Stampings

(G-2006)
FLUID DYNAMICS LLC (PA)
192 Sheldon Rd (06042-2319)
P.O. Box 2468 (06045-2468)
PHONE....................................860 791-6325
Tom Plourde, *General Mgr*
Krista Cooper, *Opers Mgr*
Jeremy Bride, *Sales Staff*
Russ Neale, *Sales Executive*
Paul J Cooper,
EMP: 5
SQ FT: 9,000
SALES (est): 2.3MM **Privately Held**
WEB: www.flddyn.com
SIC: 3492 5085 Whol Industrial Supplies Mfg Fluid Power Valves

(G-2007)
GREEN MANOR CORPORATION (PA)
Also Called: Journal Inquirer
306 Progress Dr (06042-9011)
PHONE....................................860 643-8111
Neil H Ellis, *President*
Chapman Jennifer, *Editor*
Elizabeth Ellis, *Treasurer*
Rudy Rudewicz, *VP Finance*
Deborah J Ellis, *Director*
EMP: 280 **EST:** 1950
SQ FT: 36,000
SALES (est): 34.8MM **Privately Held**
SIC: 2711 Newspapers-Publishing/Printing

(G-2008)
HHC LLC
Also Called: Hydrofera
340 Progress Dr (06042-2280)
PHONE....................................860 456-0677
Tom Rallo,
Thomas Drury,
EMP: 20
SQ FT: 10,000
SALES (est): 4.5MM **Privately Held**
WEB: www.hydrofera.com
SIC: 3086 Mfg Plastic Foam Products

(G-2009)
HIGHLAND MANUFACTURING INC
5 Glen Rd Ste 4 (06040-6793)
PHONE....................................860 646-5142
Christian Wqueen, *President*
EMP: 28
SQ FT: 16,000
SALES (est): 6MM **Privately Held**
SIC: 3545 3544 Mfg Machine Tool Access Mfg Dies/Tools/Jigs/Fixt

(G-2010)
HYDROFERA LLC
340 Progress Dr (06042-2280)
PHONE....................................860 456-0677
Tom Drury, *Principal*
EMP: 65
SALES (est): 103K **Privately Held**
SIC: 3086 Mfg Plastic Foam Products

(G-2011)
ILLINOIS TOOL WORKS INC
ITW Graphics
375 New State Rd (06042-1818)
PHONE....................................860 646-8153
Joe Tetrault, *Opers Staff*
Amy Velasquez, *Accounting Mgr*
Karl Kisselle, *Sales Mgr*
James Moore, *Technical Staff*
EMP: 145
SALES (corp-wide): 14.7B **Publicly Held**
SIC: 2672 Mfg Coated/Laminated Paper
PA: Illinois Tool Works Inc.
155 Harlem Ave
Glenview IL 60025
847 724-7500

(G-2012)
INFORMATION TECH INTL CORP
440 Oakland St (06042-5102)
PHONE....................................860 648-2570
Clive Thomas, *President*
Kenneth Koos, *Admin Sec*
EMP: 7
SQ FT: 5,000
SALES (est): 370.9K **Privately Held**
SIC: 7372 7379 Prepackaged Software & Information Technology Consulting

(G-2013)
J & L MACHINE CO INC
62 Batson Dr (06042-1657)
PHONE....................................860 649-3539
Marian Jusko, *President*
Joann Rund, *General Mgr*
Barbara Jusko, *Admin Sec*
EMP: 49
SQ FT: 30,000
SALES (est): 10.8MM **Privately Held**
WEB: www.jlmachineco.com
SIC: 3599 Mfg Industrial Machinery

(G-2014)
JOURNAL PUBLISHING COMPANY INC
Also Called: Journal Inquirer
306 Progress Dr (06042-9011)
P.O. Box 510 (06045-0510)
PHONE....................................860 646-0500
Elizabeth Ellis, *President*
EMP: 560
SQ FT: 36,000
SALES (est): 34.8MM **Privately Held**
SIC: 2711 Newspapers-Publishing/Printing
PA: Green Manor Corporation
306 Progress Dr
Manchester CT 06042
860 643-8111

(G-2015)
K & G CORP
Also Called: R T G
219 Adams St (06042-1985)
P.O. Box 8267 (06040-0267)
PHONE....................................860 643-1133
Kenneth Wolf, *President*
Gail Wolf, *Vice Pres*
EMP: 10 **EST:** 1955
SQ FT: 6,000
SALES (est): 1.1MM **Privately Held**
WEB: www.kgcorp.com
SIC: 3479 3251 Metal & Ceramic Protective Coatings For Heat Resistance & Wear

(G-2016)
KENNETH R CARSON
34 Cole St (06042-3621)
PHONE....................................860 247-2707
Fax: 860 247-2707
EMP: 4
SALES: 250K **Privately Held**
SIC: 3911 Mfg Precious Metal Jewelry

(G-2017)
L M GILL WELDING AND MFR LLC (PA)
Also Called: Bhs-Torin
1422 Tolland Tpke (06042-1636)
PHONE....................................860 647-9931
Richard A Brink, *President*
Gale Brink, *Admin Sec*
EMP: 14 **EST:** 1978
SALES (est): 8.3MM **Privately Held**
SIC: 3542 5084 3549 Mfg Machine Tools-Forming Whol Industrial Equipment Mfg Metalworking Machinery

(G-2018)
L M GILL WELDING AND MFR LLC
Also Called: Lm Gill Welding & Mfg
1422 Tolland Tpke (06042-1636)
P.O. Box 8185 (06040-0185)
PHONE....................................860 647-9931
Gale Brink, *Admin Sec*
EMP: 20
SALES (corp-wide): 8.3MM **Privately Held**
SIC: 7692 3728 Welding Repair Mfg Aircraft Parts/Equipment
PA: L M Gill Welding And Manufacturer Llc
1422 Tolland Tpke
Manchester CT 06042
860 647-9931

(G-2019)
LINGARD CABINET CO LLC
540 N Main St Ste 2 (06042-1998)
PHONE....................................860 647-9886
Dan Lingard,
Carol Lingard, *Admin Sec*
EMP: 3
SALES: 300K **Privately Held**
SIC: 2541 2431 5211 Mfg Custom Made Cabinets Counters And Millwork

(G-2020)
LM GILL WELDING & MFG LLC
1422 Tolland Tpke (06042-1636)
PHONE....................................860 647-9931
Richard A Brink, *Owner*
Harry Saddack,
EMP: 21
SQ FT: 25,000
SALES: 3MM **Privately Held**
SIC: 7692 3728 3731 Welding Repair Mfg Aircraft Parts/Equip Shipbuilding/Repairing

(G-2021)
LYDALL INC (PA)
1 Colonial Rd (06042-2307)
P.O. Box 151 (06045-0151)
PHONE....................................860 646-1233
Marc T Giles, *Ch of Bd*
Dale G Barnhart, *President*
Diane Beaudoin, *President*
Robert Junker, *President*
David Glenn, *Vice Pres*
EMP: 50
SALES: 785.9MM **Publicly Held**
WEB: www.lydall.com
SIC: 2297 3053 2899 2631 Mfg Thermal Acoustical And Filtration Separation Products

(G-2022)
LYDALL THERMAL ACOUSTICAL INC
1 Colonial Rd (06042-2307)
P.O. Box 151 (06045-0151)
PHONE....................................860 646-1233
Dale G Barnhart, *CEO*
Robert K Julian, *President*
William M Lachenmeyer, *Vice Pres*
James Laughlan, *Vice Pres*
Chad McDaniel, *Vice Pres*
EMP: 6
SALES (est): 1.8MM **Privately Held**
SIC: 2297 Mfg Nonwoven Fabrics

(G-2023)
MANCHESTER MOLDING AND MFG CO
96 Sheldon Rd (06042-2399)
PHONE....................................860 643-2141
Allan Griffin, *President*
Joseph Nadeau, *Owner*
Joanne Scanlon, *Vice Pres*
EMP: 50
SQ FT: 27,500
SALES (est): 9.5MM **Privately Held**
SIC: 3089 3544 Mfg Plastic Products Mfg Dies/Tools/Jigs/Fixtures

(G-2024)
MANCHESTER PACKING COMPANY INC
Also Called: Bogner's
349 Wetherell St (06040-6349)
PHONE....................................860 646-5000
Robert E Bogner, *President*
Kurt Bogner, *Vice Pres*
David Bogner, *Admin Sec*
▲ **EMP:** 60
SQ FT: 19,000
SALES (est): 10.7MM **Privately Held**
WEB: www.manchestersilkworms.org
SIC: 2011 5147 5421 2013 Meat Packing Plant Whol Meats/Products Ret Meat/Fish Mfg Prepared Meats

(G-2025)
NETSOURCE INC (PA)
260 Progress Dr (06042-9001)
PHONE....................................860 649-6000
Thor Swanson, *President*
Shannon Spence, *Financial Exec*
Tracy Burch, *Sales Staff*
Larry Englisby, *Sales Staff*
Joline Swanson, *Admin Sec*
EMP: 55
SALES (est): 10.7MM **Privately Held**
WEB: www.netsource-inc.com
SIC: 3496 Mfg Misc Fabricated Wire Products

(G-2026)
NOVEL TEES SCREEN PRTG EMB LLC
81 Tolland Tpke (06042-1737)
PHONE....................................860 643-6008
Connie Vandermyn,
EMP: 10 **EST:** 2016
SALES (est): 479.6K **Privately Held**
SIC: 2759 Commercial Printing

▲ = Import ▼=Export
◆ =Import/Export

(G-2027)
NOVEL-TEES UNLIMITED LLC
81 Tolland Tpke (06042-1737)
PHONE..................................860 643-6008
Chet Dimovski, *President*
EMP: 3
SALES: 200K **Privately Held**
SIC: 2759 Commercial Printing

(G-2028)
NZYMSYS INC
642 Hilliard St Ste 1208 (06042-2700)
P.O. Box 840, Glastonbury (06033-0840)
PHONE..................................877 729-4190
John Fantry, *Vice Pres*
David Bloom, *Manager*
EMP: 3 **EST:** 2008
SALES: 200K **Privately Held**
SIC: 2833 Mfg Medicinal/Botanical Products

(G-2029)
PARADIGM MANCHESTER INC
Also Called: Paradigm Precision
203 Sheldon Rd Bldg 2 (06042-2318)
PHONE..................................860 646-4048
Tom Polo, *Manager*
EMP: 100
SQ FT: 17,000
SALES (corp-wide): 368.2MM **Privately Held**
WEB: www.dgtmfg.com
SIC: 3444 3728 Mfg Sheet Metalwork Mfg Aircraft Parts/Equipment
HQ: Manchester Paradigm Inc
967 Parker St
Manchester CT 06042
860 646-4048

(G-2030)
PARADIGM MANCHESTER INC
Also Called: Paradigm Precision
186 Adams St S Bldg 3 (06040)
PHONE..................................860 646-4048
Howard Miller, *CEO*
EMP: 191
SQ FT: 59,000
SALES (corp-wide): 368.2MM **Privately Held**
WEB: www.dgtmfg.com
SIC: 3444 3728 Mfg Sheet Metalwork Mfg Aircraft Parts/Equipment
HQ: Manchester Paradigm Inc
967 Parker St
Manchester CT 06042
860 646-4048

(G-2031)
PARADIGM MANCHESTER INC (DH)
Also Called: Paradigm Precision
967 Parker St (06042-2208)
PHONE..................................860 646-4048
Michael Grunza, *President*
James Donahu, *President*
William W Booth, *Vice Pres*
Steve Lindsey, *Vice Pres*
Rita Lei, *CFO*
▲ **EMP:** 500
SQ FT: 66,000
SALES (est): 172.7MM
SALES (corp-wide): 368.2MM **Privately Held**
WEB: www.dgtmfg.com
SIC: 3728 Mfg Aircraft Parts/Equipment

(G-2032)
PARADIGM MANCHESTER INC
Also Called: Dynamic Gunver Technologies
255 Sheldon Rd Bldg 4 (06042-2322)
P.O. Box 240 (06045-0240)
PHONE..................................860 649-2888
Howard Miller, *Ch of Bd*
EMP: 247
SALES (corp-wide): 368.2MM **Privately Held**
WEB: www.dgtmfg.com
SIC: 3444 3462 3429 3398 Mfg Sheet Metalwork Mfg Iron/Steel Forgings Mfg Hardware Metal Heat Treating Secndry Nonfrs Mtl Prdcr
HQ: Manchester Paradigm Inc
967 Parker St
Manchester CT 06042
860 646-4048

(G-2033)
PARADIGM MANCHESTER INC
151 Sheldon Rd (06042-2318)
PHONE..................................860 646-4048
Howard Miller, *Ch of Bd*
EMP: 7
SALES (corp-wide): 368.2MM **Privately Held**
WEB: www.dgtmfg.com
SIC: 3444 Manufactures Precision Parts In The Gas Turbine Industies
HQ: Manchester Paradigm Inc
967 Parker St
Manchester CT 06042
860 646-4048

(G-2034)
PARADIGM PRCISION HOLDINGS LLC
967 Parker St (06042-2208)
PHONE..................................860 649-2888
EMP: 4
SALES (corp-wide): 368.2MM **Privately Held**
SIC: 3469 Mfg Metal Stampings
HQ: Paradigm Precision Holdings, Llc
404 W Guadalupe Rd
Tempe AZ 85283

(G-2035)
PARAGON TOOL COMPANY INC
121 Adams St S (06040)
P.O. Box 8168 (06040-0168)
PHONE..................................860 647-9935
Valdis Klavins, *President*
John Zemzars, *Vice Pres*
Lorraine Amaio, *Manager*
EMP: 8
SQ FT: 7,400
SALES (est): 1.4MM **Privately Held**
SIC: 3544 3728 Mfg Dies/Tools/Jigs/Fixtures Mfg Aircraft Parts/Equipment

(G-2036)
PARAMOUNT MACHINE COMPANY INC
138 Sanrico Dr (06042-9008)
PHONE..................................860 643-5549
Andrew Djiounas, *CEO*
Nick Djiounas, *President*
Steve Djiounas, *Vice Pres*
Ken Alexander, *Mfg Spvr*
Leah Farren, *Purchasing*
EMP: 50 **EST:** 1976
SQ FT: 46,000
SALES: 5.4MM **Privately Held**
WEB: www.paramountmachineco.com
SIC: 3599 Mfg Industrial Machinery

(G-2037)
PAS TECHNOLOGIES INC
Also Called: Bolton Aerospace
321 Progress Dr (06042-2296)
PHONE..................................860 649-2727
EMP: 26 **Privately Held**
SIC: 3728 Mfg Aircraft Parts/Equipment
HQ: Pas Technologies Inc.
1234 Atlantic Ave
North Kansas City MO 64116

(G-2038)
PERISTERE LLC
Also Called: Recovery Zone
95 Hilliard St (06042-3001)
PHONE..................................860 783-5301
Bruce Peristere, *Mng Member*
EMP: 4
SALES (est): 383.7K **Privately Held**
SIC: 2221 2522 Manmade Broadwoven Fabric Mill Mfg Office Furniture-Nonwood

(G-2039)
PRAXAIR SURFACE TECH INC
1366 Tolland Tpke (06042-8903)
PHONE..................................860 646-0700
John Whalen, *Manager*
EMP: 80 **Privately Held**
WEB: www.sermatech.com
SIC: 3479 3548 Coating/Engraving Svcs Mfg Welding Apparatus
HQ: Praxair Surface Technologies, Inc.
1500 Polco St
Indianapolis IN 46222
317 240-2500

(G-2040)
R R DONNELLEY & SONS COMPANY
151 Redstone Rd (06042-8754)
PHONE..................................860 649-5570
Mark Angelson, *CEO*
EMP: 17
SALES (corp-wide): 6.8B **Publicly Held**
SIC: 2759 2752 2732 7331 Commercial Printing Lithographic Coml Print Book Printing Direct Mail Ad Svcs
PA: R. R. Donnelley & Sons Company
35 W Wacker Dr
Chicago IL 60601
312 326-8000

(G-2041)
R WOODWORKING LARSON INC
192 Sheldon Rd (06042-2319)
PHONE..................................860 646-7904
EMP: 20
SQ FT: 10,000
SALES (est): 1.6MM **Privately Held**
SIC: 2431 Millwork, Nsk

(G-2042)
RAINBOW GRAPHICS INC
118 Adams St S (06040)
PHONE..................................860 646-8997
Fred Cask, *President*
Lisa Evans, *Sales Staff*
EMP: 6
SQ FT: 5,000
SALES: 600K **Privately Held**
SIC: 2396 2759 2395 Mfg Auto/Apparel Trimming Commercial Printing Pleating/Stitching Services

(G-2043)
ROYAL ICE CREAM COMPANY INC (PA)
27 Warren St (06040-6500)
PHONE..................................860 649-5358
James S Orfitelli, *President*
Cynthia L Orfitelli, *Admin Sec*
▲ **EMP:** 11
SQ FT: 12,000
SALES (est): 1.7MM **Privately Held**
WEB: www.royalicecream.com
SIC: 2024 Mfg Ice Cream/Frozen Desert

(G-2044)
SATELLITE AEROSPACE INC
240 Chapel Rd (06042-1629)
P.O. Box 1077 (06045-1077)
PHONE..................................860 643-2771
Mark Knec, *President*
Frances Lynch, *Corp Secy*
John Lynch, *Prdtn Mgr*
EMP: 22 **EST:** 1975
SQ FT: 13,000
SALES (est): 4.7MM **Privately Held**
SIC: 3469 Mfg Metal Stampings

(G-2045)
SAZACKS INC
Also Called: PIP Printing
520 Center St (06040-3936)
PHONE..................................860 647-8367
Larry Schwartz, *President*
Bernice Schwartz, *Vice Pres*
EMP: 5
SQ FT: 4,000
SALES (est): 1.1MM **Privately Held**
WEB: www.pipmanchester.com
SIC: 2752 7334 Lithographic Commercial Printing Photocopying Services

(G-2046)
SCAN-OPTICS LLC
169 Progress Dr (06042-2242)
PHONE..................................860 645-7878
Thomas Rice, *CEO*
Jerry D Thomas, *President*
Paul Yantus,
EMP: 99
SALES (est): 13MM **Privately Held**
SIC: 3577 Mfg Computer Peripheral Equipment

(G-2047)
SEMIOTICS LLC
Also Called: FASTSIGNS
1540 Pleasant Valley Rd D (06042-8760)
PHONE..................................860 644-5700
Michael Melillo, *Owner*
EMP: 4
SALES: 757.4K **Privately Held**
SIC: 3993 Signsadv Specs

(G-2048)
SIGNS OF ALL KINDS
227 Progress Dr Ste A (06042-2278)
PHONE..................................860 649-1989
John Prusak, *Owner*
EMP: 4
SALES (est): 485.6K **Privately Held**
SIC: 3993 Mfg Signs/Advertising Specialties

(G-2049)
SPARTAN AEROSPACE LLC
41 Progress Dr (06042-2293)
PHONE..................................860 533-7500
Allan Lehrer, *President*
Jaime Miller, *Vice Pres*
Wayne Thibodeau, *Vice Pres*
Victoria Zita, *Purch Mgr*
Bryan Linberk, *Engineer*
EMP: 89
SQ FT: 69,000
SALES (est): 13.8MM **Privately Held**
SIC: 3724 3544 3469 3769 Mfg Aircraft Engines Jigs And Fixtures Metal Stampings & Auxiliary Equipment

(G-2050)
SPECIALTY SHOP INC
18 Sanrico Dr (06042-2225)
PHONE..................................860 647-1477
Hector Alzugaray Jr, *President*
Manny Rodrigues, *Vice Pres*
Hector Alzugaray Sr, *Treasurer*
EMP: 7
SQ FT: 15,000
SALES (est): 1.2MM **Privately Held**
WEB: www.gacoast.com
SIC: 2434 2541 Mfg Wood Kitchen Cabinets Mfg Wood Partitions/Fixtures

(G-2051)
STANDARD WASHER & MAT INC
299 Progress Dr (06042-2211)
P.O. Box 368 (06045-0368)
PHONE..................................860 643-5125
Carl Eckblom, *President*
Brian Eckblom, *Vice Pres*
Robyn Willmore, *Purch Mgr*
Linda Lestini, *Sales Mgr*
Richard Rosinald, *Supervisor*
EMP: 20
SQ FT: 15,000
SALES: 2.5MM **Privately Held**
WEB: www.standardwasher.com
SIC: 3069 3089 3053 Manufacturer Of Rubber And Plastic Washers And Gaskets

(G-2052)
STERLING JEWELERS INC
194 Buckland Hills Dr # 1 (06042-8705)
PHONE..................................860 644-7207
Jeff Majka, *Branch Mgr*
EMP: 6 **Privately Held**
SIC: 3423 Mfg Hand/Edge Tools
HQ: Sterling Jewelers Inc.
375 Ghent Rd
Fairlawn OH 44333
330 668-5000

(G-2053)
STETSON BREWING CO INC
22 Fleming Rd (06042-2918)
PHONE..................................860 643-0257
Christopher J Stetson, *Principal*
EMP: 3 **EST:** 1998
SALES (est): 125.4K **Privately Held**
SIC: 2082 Mfg Malt Beverages

(G-2054)
STITCHERS HIDEAWAY LLC
172 Birch St (06040-5461)
PHONE..................................860 268-4741
Susan L Donnelly, *Principal*
EMP: 3

SALES (est): 140.2K Privately Held
SIC: 2395 Pleating/Stitching Services

(G-2055)
TIMKEN AROSPC DRV SYSTEMS LLC
586 Hilliard St (06042-2879)
PHONE....860 649-0000
Richard G Kyle, *President*
William R Burkhart, *Exec VP*
Christopher A Coughlin, *Exec VP*
Philip D Fracassa, *CFO*
Bruce Angell, *Program Mgr*
EMP: 120
SQ FT: 18,700
SALES (est): 49MM
SALES (corp-wide): 3.5B Publicly Held
SIC: 3724 3728 Mfg Aircraft Engines/Parts Mfg Aircraft Parts/Equipment
HQ: Mpb Corporation
7 Optical Ave
Keene NH 03431
603 352-0310

(G-2056)
TOWN FAIR TIRE CENTERS INC
328 Middle Tpke W (06040-3842)
PHONE....860 646-2807
William Rivera, *Manager*
EMP: 15
SALES (corp-wide): 288.7MM Privately Held
WEB: www.townfair.com
SIC: 3011 Mfg Tires/Inner Tubes
PA: Town Fair Tire Centers, Inc.
460 Coe Ave
East Haven CT 06512
203 467-8600

(G-2057)
VISION TECHNICAL MOLDING
20 Utopia Rd (06042-2191)
PHONE....860 783-5050
EMP: 4
SALES (est): 218.1K Privately Held
SIC: 3089 Mfg Plastic Products

(G-2058)
WHITELEDGE INC
Also Called: C B Enterprises Division
134 Pine St (06040-5831)
PHONE....860 647-1883
Robert Blass, *President*
Pamela Blass, *Admin Sec*
EMP: 5
SQ FT: 5,500
SALES (est): 623K Privately Held
SIC: 3451 Corrosion Resistant Bearing Mfg Precision Machining

(G-2059)
WILLSON MANUFACTURING OF CONN
71 Batson Dr (06042-1657)
P.O. Box 8020 (06040-0020)
PHONE....860 643-8182
Donald Willson, *President*
EMP: 4
SALES (est): 300K Privately Held
SIC: 3599 Machine Shop

(G-2060)
WINDHAM SAND AND STONE INC
60 Adams St S (06040-2604)
P.O. Box 133, Willimantic (06226-0133)
PHONE....860 643-5578
Fax: 860 423-0300
EMP: 100
SQ FT: 2,000
SALES (est): 12MM
SALES (corp-wide): 28.8MM Privately Held
SIC: 3273 Mfg Ready-Mixed Concrete
PA: Windham Materials Llc
79 Boston Post Rd
Willimantic CT 06226
860 456-4111

Mansfield Center
Tolland County

(G-2061)
AFFORDABLE WATER TRTMNT
498 Stafford Rd (06250-1425)
PHONE....860 423-3147
Douglas Lohman, *Owner*
EMP: 4
SALES (est): 548.4K Privately Held
SIC: 3589 Mfg Service Industry Machinery

(G-2062)
BOMBADILS SPIRIT SHOP INC
135 Storrs Rd 8 (06250-1638)
PHONE....860 423-9661
Roger Gagne, *President*
EMP: 5
SALES (est): 310.5K Privately Held
SIC: 2086 Mfg Bottled/Canned Soft Drinks

Marlborough
Hartford County

(G-2063)
AMERICAN DISTILLING INC
380 N Main St (06447-1346)
P.O. Box 319, East Hampton (06424-0319)
PHONE....860 267-4444
Matthew McArthur, *Exec Dir*
EMP: 5
SALES (est): 433.6K
SALES (corp-wide): 15.9MM Privately Held
SIC: 2085 2833 2844 2087 Mfg Distilled Liquors Mfg Medicinal/Botanicals Mfg Toilet Preparations Mfg Flavor Extracts
PA: American Distilling Inc.
31 E High St
East Hampton CT 06424
860 267-4444

(G-2064)
ESSENTIAL TRADING SYSTEMS CORP
Also Called: Etc
9 Austin Dr Ste 3 (06447-1375)
PHONE....860 295-8100
Gilbert M Smith, *CEO*
David Harding, *President*
Jeffrey Hasbargen, *Vice Pres*
▲ EMP: 14
SQ FT: 10,000
SALES (est): 1.4MM Privately Held
WEB: www.essentialtel.com
SIC: 3669 Mfg Communications Equipment

(G-2065)
HEARTWOOD CABINETRY
345 N Main St (06447-1315)
PHONE....860 295-0304
EMP: 8
SALES (est): 420K Privately Held
SIC: 2434 Wood Kitchen Cabinets

(G-2066)
MARLBOROUGH PLASTICS INC
350 N Main St (06447-1346)
PHONE....860 295-9124
Joseph J Asklar, *President*
Corrine Machowski, *Treasurer*
▲ EMP: 8
SQ FT: 11,250
SALES (est): 1.5MM Privately Held
WEB: www.marlplastics.com
SIC: 3089 Plastic Molding

(G-2067)
MPS PLASTICS INCORPORATED
351 N Main St (06447-1315)
P.O. Box 59 (06447-0059)
PHONE....860 295-1161
Knut Imshaug, *President*
Dave Nickolonko, *Vice Pres*
Mike Griffin, *Engineer*
▲ EMP: 27
SQ FT: 18,000
SALES (est): 4.6MM Privately Held
WEB: www.mpsplastics.com
SIC: 3089 Mfg Plastic Products

(G-2068)
PFD STUDIOS
213 Flood Rd (06447-1545)
PHONE....860 295-8500
Paul Drexler, *Owner*
EMP: 3
SALES: 250K Privately Held
SIC: 3949 Specialty Games Manufacturer

Meriden
New Haven County

(G-2069)
3M COMPANY
400 Research Pkwy (06450-7172)
PHONE....203 237-5541
WEI Moline, *President*
Christine Wetzel, *Research*
Paul Moore, *Engineer*
Dian Zheng, *Senior Engr*
Matt Kachur, *Human Res Mgr*
EMP: 80
SALES (corp-wide): 32.7B Publicly Held
SIC: 3465 Industrial And Transportation Business
PA: 3m Company
3m Center
Saint Paul MN 55144
651 733-1110

(G-2070)
3M PURIFICATION INC (HQ)
400 Research Pkwy (06450-7172)
P.O. Box 1018 (06450-1018)
PHONE....203 237-5541
Inge Thulin, *Ch of Bd*
Mark G Kachur, *Ch of Bd*
Timothy B Carney, *President*
David Schaeffer, *General Mgr*
Frederick C Flynn Jr, *CFO*
▲ EMP: 300
SQ FT: 189,000
SALES (est): 454.4MM
SALES (corp-wide): 32.7B Publicly Held
WEB: www.cuno.com
SIC: 3589 3569 Mfg Svc Industry Mach Mfg General Indstl Mach
PA: 3m Company
3m Center
Saint Paul MN 55144
651 733-1110

(G-2071)
A & M AUTO MACHINE INC
711 E Main St (06450-6018)
PHONE....203 237-3502
Ernie Adduci, *President*
David Maniscalco, *Vice Pres*
EMP: 3
SQ FT: 2,200
SALES: 300K Privately Held
SIC: 3599 7539 7538 Mfg Industrial Machinery Automotive Repair General Auto Repair

(G-2072)
A G C INCORPORATED (PA)
106 Evansville Ave (06451-5135)
PHONE....203 235-3361
R Bruce Andrews, *President*
Walter Layman, *President*
Doris D Harms, *Principal*
Shelly Anderson, *Treasurer*
Rhoda Hurwitz, *Admin Sec*
EMP: 160
SQ FT: 110,000
SALES (est): 28.3MM Privately Held
WEB: www.agcincorporated.com
SIC: 3728 3444 3398 3053 Mfg Aircraft Parts/Equip Mfg Sheet Metalwork Metal Heat Treating Mfg Gasket/Packing/Seals Mfg Paints/Allied Prdts

(G-2073)
ACCEL INTL HOLDINGS INC
508 N Colony St (06450-2246)
PHONE....203 237-2700
Anthony OH, *President*
Kyle Senk, *VP Sales*
Kyle Scott Senk, *Chief Mktg Ofcr*
Jodi Lynn OH, *Admin Sec*
▲ EMP: 30
SQ FT: 150,000
SALES (est): 11.6MM Privately Held
SIC: 3315 Mfg Steel Wire/Related Products

(G-2074)
AEROSWISS LLC
20 Powers Dr (06451-5556)
PHONE....203 634-4545
John Daniel Gullo,
EMP: 19 EST: 2000
SQ FT: 1,000
SALES (est): 3.8MM Privately Held
WEB: www.aeroswiss.com
SIC: 3599 Mfg Industrial Machinery

(G-2075)
AGC ACQUISITION LLC
106 Evansville Ave (06451-5135)
PHONE....203 639-7125
Doris D Harms, *President*
Michael Doolan, *Vice Pres*
Glenn Dalessandro, *CFO*
EMP: 112
SALES (est): 22.9MM Privately Held
SIC: 3724 Mfg Aircraft Engines/Parts

(G-2076)
APERTURE OPTICAL SCIENCES INC
170 Pond View Dr (06450-7142)
PHONE....860 301-2372
Flemming Tinker, *President*
Kai Xin, *Principal*
Joann Fazekas, *Bookkeeper*
Jennifer Buell, *Human Res Mgr*
EMP: 4 EST: 2010
SALES: 380K Privately Held
SIC: 3827 Mfg Optical Instruments/Lenses

(G-2077)
APLICARE PRODUCTS LLC (HQ)
550 Research Pkwy (06450-7172)
PHONE....203 630-0500
Charlie Mills, *CEO*
EMP: 198
SQ FT: 55,416
SALES (est): 7.8MM
SALES (corp-wide): 5.5B Privately Held
SIC: 2834 3841 Manufacture Medicinal Antiseptics Surgical/Medical Instruments
PA: Medline Industries, Inc.
3 Lakes Dr
Northfield IL 60093
847 949-5500

(G-2078)
B & G FORMING TECHNOLOGY INC
956 Old Colony Rd (06451-7921)
PHONE....203 235-2169
Elizabeth Gassman,
Arthur A Bell,
Louis Bell,
Garrett Gassman,
EMP: 4
SALES (est): 418K Privately Held
WEB: www.bgforming.com
SIC: 3469 Mfg Metal Stampings

(G-2079)
BENNICE MOLDING CO
184 Gravel St Apt 42 (06450-4661)
PHONE....203 440-2543
EMP: 3
SALES (est): 151.4K Privately Held
SIC: 3089 Mfg Plastic Products

(G-2080)
BRAND-NU LABORATORIES INC (PA)
Also Called: Biosolutions
377 Research Pkwy Ste 2 (06450-7155)
PHONE....203 235-7989
John J Gorman III, *President*
Carol A Shea, *Vice Pres*
Eric Tranquist, *Prdtn Mgr*
Giovanna Coppola, *Technical Staff*
Wayne A Huskes, *Admin Sec*
◆ EMP: 35 EST: 1955
SQ FT: 80,000

SALES (est): 13MM **Privately Held**
WEB: www.brandnu.com
SIC: 2899 Mfg Chemical Preparations

(G-2081)
BUSHWICK METALS LLC
130 Research Pkwy Ste 203 (06450-7152)
PHONE..............................203 630-2459
EMP: 4
SALES (corp-wide): 194.6B **Publicly Held**
SIC: 3312 5051 Blast Furnace-Steel Works Metals Service Center
HQ: Bushwick Metals, Llc
560 N Washington Ave # 2
Bridgeport CT 06484
203 576-1800

(G-2082)
C & S ENGINEERING INC
956 Old Colony Rd (06451-7921)
PHONE..............................203 235-5727
Alfred L Cavallo, *President*
Michael Cavallo, *Vice Pres*
EMP: 29
SQ FT: 20,000
SALES (est): 3.6MM **Privately Held**
WEB: www.csengineering.com
SIC: 3449 3562 3471 Mfg Misc Structural Metalwork Mfg Ball/Roller Bearings Plating/Polishing Service

(G-2083)
CABLE MANAGEMENT LLC
290 Pratt St Ste 1108 (06450-8600)
P.O. Box 2719 (06450-1788)
PHONE..............................860 670-1890
Josue Loic Trudeau, *Owner*
Josh Loic Trudeau, *Owner*
▲ **EMP:** 30
SALES (est): 1.2MM **Privately Held**
SIC: 3569 Mfg General Industrial Machinery

(G-2084)
CENTER BROACH & MACHINE CO
525 N Colony St (06450-2287)
P.O. Box 2 (06450-0002)
PHONE..............................203 235-6329
William Phillips IV, *Vice Pres*
EMP: 9
SQ FT: 13,000
SALES: 500K **Privately Held**
SIC: 3545 Mfg Broaches

(G-2085)
CHERISE CPL LLC
57 S Broad St (06450-6544)
PHONE..............................203 238-3482
EMP: 3
SALES (est): 207.3K **Privately Held**
SIC: 2052 Mfg Cookies/Crackers

(G-2086)
CLARIOS
Also Called: Johnson Controls
71 Deerfield Ln (06450-7151)
PHONE..............................678 297-4040
EMP: 94 **Privately Held**
SIC: 2531 3714 3691 3822 Mfg Automotive Seating & Interior Systems And Installs & Svcs Facility Control Systems
HQ: Johnson Controls Inc
5757 N Green Bay Ave
Milwaukee WI 53209
414 524-1200

(G-2087)
CLEAN UP GROUP
82 Jodi Dr (06450-3569)
PHONE..............................203 668-8323
Maurice Langlois, *Owner*
Donna Langlois, *Co-Owner*
EMP: 3
SALES (est): 110K **Privately Held**
SIC: 2851 Mfg Paints/Allied Products

(G-2088)
CONNECTICUT CARPENTRY LLC
290 Pratt St Ofc (06450-8603)
PHONE..............................203 639-8585
Leo Dufour, *Owner*
EMP: 40
SALES: 1MM **Privately Held**
SIC: 2431 Millwork

(G-2089)
COUTURIER INO
Also Called: Ogle Specialty
5 Cross St (06451-3201)
PHONE..............................203 238-4555
Ino Couturier, *Owner*
EMP: 6
SALES (est): 350K **Privately Held**
SIC: 3599 Machine Shop

(G-2090)
CRC CHROME CORPORATION
169 Pratt St R (06450-4250)
PHONE..............................203 630-1008
Frank Ciarcia, *President*
Michael Ciarcia, *Corp Secy*
EMP: 10
SQ FT: 8,000
SALES (est): 1.4MM **Privately Held**
WEB: www.crcchrome.com
SIC: 3471 Plating/Polishing Service

(G-2091)
DI-EL TOOL & MANUFACTURING
69 Research Pkwy Ste 1 (06450-7178)
PHONE..............................203 235-2169
Arthur A Bell Jr, *President*
Louis Bell, *Vice Pres*
Arthur B Bell, *Admin Sec*
EMP: 4 **EST:** 1956
SQ FT: 7,000
SALES (est): 641.7K **Privately Held**
SIC: 3469 Mfg Dies/Tools/Jigs/Fixtures

(G-2092)
DRT AEROSPACE LLC
620 Research Pkwy (06450-7127)
PHONE..............................203 781-8020
Gary Van Gundy, *CEO*
EMP: 38 **Privately Held**
SIC: 3724 Mfg Aircraft Engines/Parts
HQ: Drt Aerospace, Llc
8694 Rite Track Way
West Chester OH 45069
937 298-7391

(G-2093)
FORM-ALL PLASTICS CORPORATION
104 Gracey Ave (06451-2295)
PHONE..............................203 634-1137
Tim Jennings, *President*
EMP: 7 **EST:** 1963
SQ FT: 7,000
SALES (est): 1.4MM **Privately Held**
WEB: www.form-all.com
SIC: 3089 Mfg Plastic Products

(G-2094)
HINT PERIPHERALS CORP
46 Gracey Ave (06451-2249)
PHONE..............................203 634-4468
Oscar Gimenez, *President*
EMP: 9
SALES (est): 1.9MM **Privately Held**
WEB: www.hintperipherals.com
SIC: 3577 Manufactuers Mobile Unit Peripherals

(G-2095)
J M COMPOUNDS INC
290 Pratt St Ofc (06450-8603)
PHONE..............................203 376-9854
John Guida, *President*
Mary Dunkovich, *Vice Pres*
EMP: 6
SQ FT: 3,000
SALES (est): 716.3K **Privately Held**
WEB: www.jmcompounds.com
SIC: 3471 Production Of Buffing Compounds For All Metal Types

(G-2096)
J T FANTOZZI CO INC
95 Fair St (06451-2005)
PHONE..............................203 238-7018
John T Fantozzi, *President*
EMP: 3
SALES (est): 200K **Privately Held**
SIC: 7692 1799 Welding Repair Trade Contractor

(G-2097)
JONAL LABS LOGISTICS LLC
468 Center St (06450)
PHONE..............................203 634-4444
Ralph Bonczewski, *Engineer*
Haley Nemeth, *Mng Member*
EMP: 3 **EST:** 2016
SQ FT: 1,000
SALES (est): 127.7K **Privately Held**
SIC: 3728 Mfg Aircraft Parts/Equipment

(G-2098)
L SUZIO ASPHALT CO INC
975 Westfield Rd (06450-2553)
P.O. Box 748 (06450-0748)
PHONE..............................203 237-8421
Leonardo C Suzio, *President*
Scott P Suzio, *Vice Pres*
Leonardo H Suzio, *Admin Sec*
EMP: 12 **EST:** 1957
SQ FT: 10,000
SALES (est): 1.8MM **Privately Held**
WEB: www.suzioyorkhill.com
SIC: 2951 Mfg Ready-Mixed Concrete

(G-2099)
LEGACY WOODWORKING LLC
912 Old Colony Rd (06451-7921)
PHONE..............................203 440-9710
Steven Pelczar,
EMP: 4 **EST:** 2008
SALES: 1MM **Privately Held**
SIC: 2431 Mfg Millwork Mfg Household Furniture

(G-2100)
LYONS TOOL AND DIE COMPANY
185 Research Pkwy (06450-7124)
PHONE..............................203 238-2689
William Lyons III, *CEO*
William Lyons IV, *President*
David Brown, *Vice Pres*
Gini Selvaggi, *Treasurer*
Neal Lyons, *Admin Sec*
EMP: 38 **EST:** 1951
SQ FT: 32,000
SALES (est): 8.9MM **Privately Held**
WEB: www.lyons.com
SIC: 3469 3544 3545 Mfg Metal Stampings Mfg Dies/Tools/Jigs/Fixt Mfg Machine Tool Access

(G-2101)
MAINVILLE WELDING CO INC
55 Goffe St (06451-1899)
PHONE..............................203 237-3103
Jack Mainville, *President*
Carmel Mainville, *Admin Sec*
EMP: 4
SQ FT: 4,500
SALES (est): 270K **Privately Held**
SIC: 7692 Welding Shop

(G-2102)
MEB ENTERPRISES INC
496 S Broad St (06450-6662)
PHONE..............................203 599-0273
EMP: 8
SALES (est): 945.7K **Privately Held**
SIC: 2819 Industrial Inorganic Chemicals, Nec

(G-2103)
MERIDEN ELECTRONICS CORP
Also Called: Melco
1777 N Colony Rd (06450-1964)
P.O. Box 139 (06450-0139)
PHONE..............................203 237-8811
Mark R Merliss, *President*
EMP: 4
SQ FT: 12,000
SALES (est): 130K **Privately Held**
SIC: 3812 Whol Electronic Parts/Equipment

(G-2104)
MERIDEN MANUFACTURING INC
230 State Street Ext (06450-3205)
P.O. Box 694 (06450-0694)
PHONE..............................203 237-7481
Lester Maloney, *Ch of Bd*
Lester G Maloney, *Ch of Bd*
Sharon M Fox, *President*
James Muller, *President*
Aedra Baston, *Admin Sec*
EMP: 86
SQ FT: 27,000
SALES (est): 18.7MM **Privately Held**
WEB: www.meridenmfg.com
SIC: 3469 3769 3812 Mfg Metal Stampings Mfg Space Vehicle Equipment Mfg Search/Navigation Equipment

(G-2105)
MERIDEN PRECISION PLASTICS LLC
290 Pratt St Ste 18 (06450-8601)
PHONE..............................203 235-3261
Fax: 203 237-8627
EMP: 9
SQ FT: 8,500
SALES (est): 780K **Privately Held**
WEB: www.meridenprecision.com
SIC: 3089 Mfg Toilet Repair Parts

(G-2106)
MERL INC
1777 N Colony Rd (06450-1964)
P.O. Box 188 (06450-0188)
PHONE..............................203 237-8811
Mark R Merliss, *President*
EMP: 9 **EST:** 1978
SQ FT: 12,000
SALES (est): 1MM **Privately Held**
SIC: 3694 3663 Mfg Engine Electrical Equipment Mfg Radio/Tv Communication Equipment

(G-2107)
MID STATE ASSEMBLY & PACKG INC
604 Pomeroy Ave (06450-4872)
PHONE..............................203 634-8740
Daniel Nichols, *President*
▲ **EMP:** 6
SALES (est): 930.9K **Privately Held**
SIC: 2671 3569 7389 Mfg Packaging Paper/Film Mfg General Industrial Machinery Business Services

(G-2108)
MILLER COMPANY
275 Pratt St (06450-4251)
PHONE..............................203 235-4474
Michael Rodgers, *Principal*
Erich Graf, *Vice Pres*
Timo Strobel, *Vice Pres*
Josue Diaz, *Project Mgr*
Claudia Baraglia, *Finance Mgr*
▲ **EMP:** 35
SALES (est): 10.6MM
SALES (corp-wide): 472MM **Privately Held**
WEB: www.themillerco.com
SIC: 3351 Copper Rolling/Drawing
PA: Diehl Metall Stiftung & Co. Kg
Heinrich-Diehl-Str. 9
Rothenbach A.D.Pegnitz 90552
911 570-40

(G-2109)
MIRION TECH CANBERRA INC (HQ)
Also Called: Canberra Industries, Inc.
800 Research Pkwy (06450-7127)
PHONE..............................203 238-2351
Jean Bernard Koehl, *CEO*
Barre Bertrand, *Vice Pres*
Jesse Tyler, *Senior Buyer*
David Smith, *Senior Engr*
Fabrice Burtin, *CFO*
▲ **EMP:** 277
SQ FT: 170,000
SALES (est): 97.8MM **Privately Held**
SIC: 3829 4813 Manufactures Measuring/Controlling Devices Telephone Communications

(G-2110)
MISTER BS JERKY CO
25 Harness Dr (06450-6922)
PHONE..............................203 631-2758
Daniel Baril, *Principal*
EMP: 3 **EST:** 2017
SALES (est): 104.3K **Privately Held**
SIC: 2013 Mfg Prepared Meats

(G-2111)
MULTIPRINTS INC
Also Called: Barker Screen Printers
812 Old Colony Rd (06451-7929)
P.O. Box 834 (06450-0834)
PHONE.................................203 235-4409
Amy J P Barker, *President*
Susan Dunphy, *Admin Sec*
EMP: 12
SQ FT: 12,000
SALES (est): 1.2MM **Privately Held**
WEB: www.multiprints.necoxmail.com
SIC: 2759 Commercial Printing

(G-2112)
NEW ENGLAND ORTHOTIC & PROST
61 Pomeroy Ave Unit 2a (06450-7483)
PHONE.................................203 634-7566
EMP: 3
SALES (corp-wide): 25.6MM **Privately Held**
SIC: 3842 Mfg Surgical Appliances/Supplies
PA: New England Orthotic And Prosthetic Systems, Llc
33 Business Park Dr Ste 3
Branford CT 06405
203 483-8488

(G-2113)
OMERIN USA INC
Also Called: Qs Tehcnoligies Divison
95 Research Pkwy (06450-7124)
PHONE.................................475 343-3450
Aurelien Paumier, *President*
Xavier Omerin, *Director*
EMP: 30
SALES: 6MM **Privately Held**
SIC: 3357 Nonferrous Wiredrawing/Insulating
HQ: Omerin Sas
Omerin Div Silisol & Div Principale
Zone Industrielle
Ambert 63600
473 824-436

(G-2114)
ORBIT DESIGN LLC
290 Pratt St (06450-8600)
PHONE.................................203 393-0171
Ron Oren, *Mng Member*
Melba Oren,
EMP: 10
SQ FT: 4,000
SALES: 900K **Privately Held**
SIC: 3089 Mfg Plastic Products

(G-2115)
PASTRY SHOP
31 Main St (06451)
PHONE.................................203 238-0483
Freddy Gillette, *Partner*
EMP: 4
SALES (est): 174.8K **Privately Held**
SIC: 2051 Mfg Bread/Related Products

(G-2116)
PERFORMANCE CONNECTION SYSTEMS
599 W Main St (06451-2751)
P.O. Box 556, Marion (06444-0556)
PHONE.................................203 868-5517
John Keefe, *Owner*
EMP: 8
SALES (est): 602K **Privately Held**
WEB: www.keefeperformance.com
SIC: 3499 Mfg Misc Fabricated Metal Products

(G-2117)
PRENTIS PRINTING SOLUTIONS INC
35 Pratt St (06450-4241)
P.O. Box 126 (06450-0126)
PHONE.................................203 634-1266
Bruce Burchsted, *Principal*
EMP: 4
SALES (est): 473.6K **Privately Held**
SIC: 2752 Lithographic Commercial Printing

(G-2118)
PRODUCTION EQUIPMENT COMPANY
401 Liberty St (06450-4500)
PHONE.................................800 758-5697
Rebecca Davis, *President*
Roswell Davis Sr, *Treasurer*
Stephanie Jordan, *Admin Sec*
EMP: 25
SQ FT: 10,000
SALES (est): 6.3MM **Privately Held**
WEB: www.peco1938.com
SIC: 3536 3535 Mfg Hoists/Cranes/Monorails Mfg Conveyors/Equipment

(G-2119)
PROTEIN SCIENCES CORPORATION (HQ)
1000 Research Pkwy (06450-7149)
PHONE.................................203 686-0800
Elaine O'Hara, *President*
Mireli Fino, *Vice Pres*
Chan Lee, *Vice Pres*
Douglas McCormack, *Vice Pres*
Zhimin Zhou, *Project Mgr*
EMP: 89
SQ FT: 26,000
SALES (est): 22.2MM **Privately Held**
WEB: www.proteinsciences.com
SIC: 2834 2836 8733 Mfg Pharmaceutical Preparations Mfg Biological Products Noncommercial Research Organization

(G-2120)
PYRAMID TIME SYSTEMS LLC
45 Gracey Ave (06451-2284)
PHONE.................................203 238-0550
John Augustyn, *President*
George Bucci, *Vice Pres*
Bob Lennon, *Vice Pres*
Anne Galanto, *Purch Agent*
Virginia Hutnik, *Cust Mgr*
▲ **EMP:** 50
SQ FT: 70,000
SALES (est): 13.2MM **Privately Held**
WEB: www.pyramidtech.com
SIC: 3579 3873 Mfg Office Machines Mfg Watches/Clocks/Parts

(G-2121)
QUICK MACHINE SERVICES LLC
290 Pratt St Ste 4 (06450-8601)
PHONE.................................203 634-8822
Danny Demerchant,
EMP: 7
SQ FT: 5,600
SALES (est): 994.2K **Privately Held**
SIC: 3599 7699 Mfg Industrial Machinery Repair Services

(G-2122)
RADIO FREQUENCY SYSTEMS INC (DH)
200 Pond View Dr (06450-7195)
PHONE.................................203 630-3311
William Bayne, *President*
Suzanne Kasai, *Business Mgr*
Rick Kluesner, *Corp Secy*
Steve Hull, *Vice Pres*
J RG Springer, *Vice Pres*
◆ **EMP:** 30
SQ FT: 380,000
SALES (est): 259.4MM
SALES (corp-wide): 25B **Privately Held**
WEB: www.rfsworld.com
SIC: 3663 3661 5045 5065 Mfg Radio/Tv Comm Equip Mfg Telephone/Graph Eqip Whol Computer/Peripheral

(G-2123)
RAGOZZINO FOODS INC (PA)
10 Ames Ave (06451-2912)
P.O. Box 116 (06450-0116)
PHONE.................................203 238-2553
Gloria A Ragozzino, *CEO*
Nancy Ragozzino, *President*
Susan Darin, *Vice Pres*
Ellen Sattler, *Vice Pres*
John Ragozzino, *CFO*
EMP: 15
SQ FT: 71,000
SALES: 35.7MM **Privately Held**
SIC: 2038 2033 Mfg Frozen Specialties Mfg Canned Fruits/Vegetables

(G-2124)
RECORD-JOURNAL NEWSPAPER (PA)
Also Called: Town Times
500 S Broad St Ste 2 (06450-6643)
PHONE.................................203 235-1661
Eliot C White, *Owner*
Liz White, *Exec VP*
John Ausanka, *Senior VP*
Pam Adamski, *Vice Pres*
Ralph Tomaselli, *Vice Pres*
▲ **EMP:** 175 **EST:** 1867
SALES (est): 49.4MM **Privately Held**
SIC: 2711 2752 Newspapers-Publishing/Printing Lithographic Commercial Printing

(G-2125)
RFS AMERICAS
Also Called: Radio Frequency Systems
175 Corporate Ct (06450-7180)
PHONE.................................203 630-3311
◆ **EMP:** 4 **EST:** 2010
SALES (est): 449K **Privately Held**
SIC: 3663 Whol Electronic Parts/Equipment

(G-2126)
RICH PLASTIC PRODUCTS INC
57 High St (06450-5739)
PHONE.................................203 235-4241
Daniel J Rich, *President*
Denise Rivard, *Admin Sec*
EMP: 7
SQ FT: 10,000
SALES (est): 1.4MM **Privately Held**
WEB: www.richplastics.com
SIC: 3822 Mfg Environmental Controls

(G-2127)
SAF INDUSTRIES LLC
Also Called: General Pneumatics
106 Evansville Ave (06451-5135)
PHONE.................................203 729-4900
EMP: 28
SALES (corp-wide): 23.6MM **Privately Held**
WEB: www.gpcvalves.com
SIC: 3491 3592 3559 3492 Mfg Industrial Valves Mfg Carburetors/Pistons
HQ: Saf Industries Llc
106 Evansville Ave
Meriden CT 06451

(G-2128)
SAF INDUSTRIES LLC (HQ)
Also Called: Gar Kenyon Aerospace & Defense
106 Evansville Ave (06451-5135)
PHONE.................................203 729-4900
Shelly Anderson, *President*
Brian D Archangelo, *General Mgr*
Jonathan Fournier, *Vice Pres*
EMP: 28
SQ FT: 44,000
SALES (est): 5.6MM
SALES (corp-wide): 23.6MM **Privately Held**
WEB: www.garkenyon.com
SIC: 3728 3812 Mfg Aircraft Parts/Equipment Mfg Search/Navigation Equipment
PA: Loar Group Inc.
450 Lexington Ave Fl 31
New York NY 10017
212 210-9348

(G-2129)
SAFE-T-TANK CORP
25 Powers Dr (06451-5578)
PHONE.................................203 237-6320
Sheila R Bartis, *President*
Peter A Bartis, *Vice Pres*
EMP: 5
SQ FT: 5,000
SALES (est): 1.1MM **Privately Held**
SIC: 3443 Mfg Fuel Tanks (Oil Gas Etc) Metal Plate

(G-2130)
SHINER SIGNS INC
Also Called: Signage US
38 Elm St Ste 3 (06450-5704)
PHONE.................................203 634-4331
Robert Laurencelle, *President*
Irwin Laurencelle, *Treasurer*
EMP: 20 **EST:** 1904
SQ FT: 10,000
SALES (est): 3.2MM **Privately Held**
WEB: www.signageus.com
SIC: 3993 Mfg Signs/Advertising Specialties

(G-2131)
SO AND SEW PLUSHIES
104 Elm St (06450-5708)
PHONE.................................860 916-2918
Jessy Hart, *Principal*
EMP: 3
SALES (est): 168.3K **Privately Held**
SIC: 3566 Mfg Speed Changers/Drives

(G-2132)
SOUTHINGTON CITIZEN
Also Called: Record Journal, The
500 S Broad St Ste 1 (06450-6643)
PHONE.................................860 620-5960
Elliot White, *President*
EMP: 6
SALES (est): 250K **Privately Held**
SIC: 2711 Newspapers-Publishing/Printing

(G-2133)
SOUTHWICK & MEISTER INC
Also Called: Innovative Systems
1455 N Colony Rd (06450-1979)
P.O. Box 725 (06450-0725)
PHONE.................................203 237-0000
Robert A Meister, *President*
Ernest M Meister, *President*
Lynn M Papale, *Vice Pres*
Barbara Meister, *Admin Sec*
EMP: 105
SQ FT: 45,000
SALES (est): 19.1MM **Privately Held**
WEB: www.s-mcollets.com
SIC: 3545 Mfg Machine Tool Accessories

(G-2134)
STONEHOUSE FINE CAKES
61 N 1st St (06451-4018)
PHONE.................................203 235-5091
Susan Stone, *Mng Member*
Armand Stone,
EMP: 10 **EST:** 1997
SALES (est): 550.8K **Privately Held**
WEB: www.cakelady.com
SIC: 2051 Bakery

(G-2135)
SULZER PUMP SOLUTIONS US INC (PA)
140 Pond View Dr (06450-7142)
PHONE.................................203 238-2700
John Everhart, *Principal*
Stefan Baumgaertner, *Vice Pres*
▲ **EMP:** 25
SALES (est): 16.1MM **Privately Held**
SIC: 3561 5251 5084 Mfg Pumps/Pumping Equip Ret Hardware Whol Industrial Equip

(G-2136)
T D I ENTERPRISES LLC
22 Gypsy Ln (06451-7910)
PHONE.................................203 630-1268
Tim Isyk, *Owner*
EMP: 5 **EST:** 1982
SALES (est): 410.2K **Privately Held**
SIC: 2951 Mfg Asphalt Mixtures/Blocks

(G-2137)
T G INDUSTRIES INC
361 S Colony St Ste 1 (06451-6280)
PHONE.................................203 235-3239
Anthony Gullo, *President*
Bob Kowalski, *Vice Pres*
Helen Gullo, *Admin Sec*
EMP: 15
SQ FT: 10,000
SALES (est): 2.4MM **Privately Held**
WEB: www.tgimachine.com
SIC: 3599 Precision Machine Shop

(G-2138)
TEAM DESTINATION INC
Also Called: Instant Imprints
477 S Broad St Ste 14 (06450-6660)
PHONE.................................203 235-6000
Vandan Divatia, *President*
Deepan Divatia, *Vice Pres*
Rudra Divatia, *Admin Sec*

▲ = Import ▼=Export
◆ =Import/Export

EMP: 3
SQ FT: 1,566
SALES (est): 330K **Privately Held**
SIC: **2752** 5699 Lithographic Commercial Printing Ret Misc Apparel/Accessories

(G-2139)
TGS CABLES
290 Pratt St (06450-8600)
P.O. Box 7174 (06450-7637)
PHONE..................................203 668-6568
James Tyrrel, *General Ptnr*
EMP: 4
SQ FT: 2,500
SALES (est): 260K **Privately Held**
SIC: **3679** Mfg Electronic Components

(G-2140)
THE L SUZIO CONCRETE CO INC (PA)
975 Westfield Rd (06450-2553)
P.O. Box 748 (06450-0748)
PHONE..................................203 237-8421
Leonardo H Suzio, *Vice Pres*
Cheryl Suzio, *Vice Pres*
Henry E Suzio, *Vice Pres*
Scott P Suzio, *Vice Pres*
Henrietta R Suzio, *Admin Sec*
EMP: 37
SQ FT: 10,000
SALES (est): 5.4MM **Privately Held**
WEB: www.lsuzio.com
SIC: **3273** Mfg Ready-Mixed Concrete

(G-2141)
THOMPSON BRANDS LLC
80 S Vine St (06451-3823)
PHONE..................................203 235-2541
William H Thompson, *Founder*
Bob Lis, *Plant Mgr*
Kristen Sullivan, *QC Mgr*
Joseph Ciullo, *CFO*
Pam Parrot, *Accountant*
▲ **EMP:** 85
SQ FT: 114,000
SALES (est): 15.4MM **Privately Held**
SIC: **2064** 5441 2066 5145 Mfg Candy/Confectionery Ret Candy/Confectionery Mfg Chocolate/Cocoa Prdt Whol Confectionery

(G-2142)
THOMPSON CANDY COMPANY
80 S Vine St (06451-3823)
PHONE..................................203 235-2541
Jeffrey H White, *President*
William Walsh, *Vice Pres*
Allan E White, *Vice Pres*
Susan Giddix, *Purch Mgr*
Joanne Giddix, *Buyer*
EMP: 70
SQ FT: 114,000
SALES (est): 26.9K **Privately Held**
WEB: www.thompsoncandy.com
SIC: **2064** 5441 Mfg Candy/Confectionery Ret Candy/Confectionery

(G-2143)
TIMS SIGN & LIGHTING SERVICE
38 Elm St Ste 2 (06450-5704)
PHONE..................................203 634-8840
Timothy G Walsh, *Principal*
EMP: 8
SQ FT: 4,500
SALES: 950K **Privately Held**
SIC: **3993** 1799 7389 Sign Installation Mfg Signs/Advertising Specialties Business Services

(G-2144)
UNITED OPHTHALMICS LLC
430 Smith St (06451)
PHONE..................................203 745-8399
Gaston S Levesque, *Principal*
EMP: 3
SALES (est): 377.4K **Privately Held**
SIC: **3841** Mfg Surgical/Medical Instruments

(G-2145)
UNIVERSAL BUILDING CONTRLS INC
170 Research Pkwy Ste 1 (06450-7144)
PHONE..................................203 235-1530
Andrew Divicino, *President*
Michael Poplawski, *Treasurer*
Diana Poplawski, *Admin Sec*
EMP: 13
SQ FT: 2,000
SALES (est): 3.1MM **Privately Held**
WEB: www.universalbuildingcontrols.com
SIC: **3491** 3822 1731 7373 Mfg Industrial Valves Electrical Contractor Plumbing/Heat/Ac Contr Computer Systems Design Mfg Environmntl Controls

(G-2146)
UPC LLC
170 Research Pkwy (06450-7144)
PHONE..................................877 466-1137
Andy Divicino,
EMP: 4
SALES (est): 32.8K **Privately Held**
SIC: **3089** Mfg Plastic Products

(G-2147)
USA WOOD INCORPORATED
998 N Colony Rd (06450-2372)
PHONE..................................203 238-4285
Dominick A Derobertis Jr, *President*
▲ **EMP:** 4
SALES (est): 380K **Privately Held**
SIC: **2511** Mfg Wood Household Furniture

(G-2148)
VICTOR TOOL CO INC
290 Pratt St Ste 7 (06450-8601)
PHONE..................................203 634-8113
David Victor, *President*
Travis Vumback, *Vice Pres*
EMP: 6
SQ FT: 9,500
SALES (est): 1.4MM **Privately Held**
SIC: **3544** 3545 Mfg Dies Or Tools & Machine Tool Accessories

(G-2149)
WASHER TECH INC
956 Old Colony Rd (06451-7921)
PHONE..................................203 886-0054
Garret Gassman, *President*
Elizabeth Gassman, *Vice Pres*
Don Clark, *Treasurer*
Don N Clark, *Treasurer*
EMP: 4
SQ FT: 4,000
SALES (est): 440K **Privately Held**
SIC: **3469** Mfg Metal Stampings

(G-2150)
WESS TOOL & DIE COMPANY INC
140 Research Pkwy Ste 2 (06450-7162)
PHONE..................................203 237-5277
Robert Wisniewski, *President*
Richard Wisniewski, *Vice Pres*
Tim Wisniewski, *Administration*
EMP: 5 **EST:** 1960
SALES: 400K **Privately Held**
WEB: www.wesstoolanddie.com
SIC: **3544** Mfg Tools & Dies

(G-2151)
WILLIES WELDING INC
313 Spring St (06451-5318)
P.O. Box 1744 (06450-8844)
PHONE..................................203 237-6235
William Davis Phillips Jr, *President*
Franklin Phillips, *Vice Pres*
Catherine Phillips, *Admin Sec*
EMP: 3
SQ FT: 8,400
SALES: 190K **Privately Held**
SIC: **7692** Welding Fabrication Job Shop

(G-2152)
YORK HILL TRAP ROCK QUARRY CO
975 Westfield Rd (06450-2553)
P.O. Box 748 (06450-0748)
PHONE..................................203 237-8421
Leonardo C Suzio, *President*
Cheryl Suzio, *Vice Pres*
Henry E Suzio, *Vice Pres*
Scott P Suzio, *Vice Pres*
EMP: 16
SQ FT: 16,000
SALES (est): 1.7MM **Privately Held**
SIC: **1429** Mfg Ready-Mixed Concrete

Middlebury
New Haven County

(G-2153)
AECC/PEARLMAN BUYING GROUP LLC
1255 Middlebury Rd (06762-2333)
P.O. Box 809 (06762-0809)
PHONE..................................203 598-3200
Norman S Drubner,
AP LLC,
EMP: 10
SALES (est): 1.6MM **Privately Held**
SIC: **3827** Mfg Optical Instruments/Lenses

(G-2154)
AMERICAN ROLLER COMPANY LLC
Also Called: Plasma Coatings
84 Turnpike Dr (06762-1819)
P.O. Box 10006, Waterbury (06725-0006)
PHONE..................................203 598-3100
Gary Carlo, *Plant Mgr*
EMP: 18
SALES (corp-wide): 102MM **Privately Held**
WEB: www.plasmacoatings.com
SIC: **3069** 3479 Mfg Fabricated Rubber Products Coating/Engraving Service
PA: American Roller Company, Llc
1440 13th Ave
Union Grove WI 53182
262 878-8665

(G-2155)
JMS GRAPHICS INC
Also Called: Velocity Print Solution
850 Straits Tpke Ste 204 (06762-2843)
PHONE..................................203 598-7555
James Stiles, *CEO*
Mike Mello, *CFO*
Lori Vilela, *Sales Staff*
EMP: 3
SQ FT: 300
SALES (est): 3.6MM
SALES (corp-wide): 34.3MM **Privately Held**
WEB: www.sm-pm.com
SIC: **2752** 2759 Lithographic Commercial Printing Commercial Printing
PA: Shipmates/Printmates Holding Corp.
705 Corporation Park # 2
Scotia NY 12302
518 370-1158

(G-2156)
MIDDLBURY BEE-INTELLIGENCER-CT
2030 Straits Tpke (06762-1831)
P.O. Box 10 (06762-0010)
PHONE..................................203 577-6800
EMP: 6
SALES (est): 190.4K **Privately Held**
SIC: **2711** Newspapers-Publishing/Printing

(G-2157)
ROLLER BEARING CO AMER INC
Pic Design
86 Benson Rd (06762-3215)
P.O. Box 1004 (06762-1004)
PHONE..................................203 758-8272
Michael J Hartnett, *President*
Andrew Frisbie, *General Mgr*
John Queenen, *VP Finance*
Canio Tortora, *VP Finance*
EMP: 50
SALES (corp-wide): 702.5MM **Publicly Held**
SIC: **3568** 3566 3535 3462 Mfg Power Transmsn Equip Mfg Speed Changer/Drives Mfg Conveyors/Equipment Mfg Iron/Steel Forgings Mfg Hardware
HQ: Roller Bearing Company Of America, Inc.
102 Willenbrock Rd
Oxford CT 06478
203 267-7001

(G-2158)
SIR SPEEDY PRINTING
199 Park Road Ext Ste D (06762-1833)
PHONE..................................203 346-0716
EMP: 20
SALES (est): 1.8MM **Privately Held**
SIC: **2752** Commercial Printing, Lithographic

(G-2159)
STRIDE INC
80 Turnpike Dr Ste 1 (06762-1830)
PHONE..................................203 758-8307
Roberta Nole, *President*
EMP: 13
SALES: 610.5K **Privately Held**
WEB: www.stride.com
SIC: **3842** Mfg Surgical Appliances/Supplies

(G-2160)
TIMEX GROUP USA INC (DH)
555 Christian Rd (06762-3206)
PHONE..................................203 346-5000
Paolo Marai, *CEO*
Jeff Grosberg, *Counsel*
Benjamin Abitbol, *Senior VP*
Robert Butler, *Senior VP*
Greg Miller, *Senior VP*
◆ **EMP:** 230 **EST:** 1857
SQ FT: 81,000
SALES (est): 486.5MM
SALES (corp-wide): 571.8MM **Privately Held**
SIC: **3873** Mfg Watches/Clocks/Parts
HQ: Tanager Group B.V.
Herengracht 466
Amsterdam 1017
235 563-660

Middlefield
Middlesex County

(G-2161)
ADVANCED SHEETMETAL ASSOC LLC
52 Indstrial Pk Access Rd (06455-1263)
PHONE..................................860 349-1644
Joseph Cohn, *General Mgr*
Kevin Thibodeau, *Manager*
EMP: 20
SALES (est): 4.6MM **Privately Held**
SIC: **3444** Mfg Sheet Metalwork

(G-2162)
COOPER-ATKINS CORPORATION (HQ)
33 Reeds Gap Rd (06455-1138)
PHONE..................................860 349-3473
Carol P Wallace, *President*
Robert Nerbonne, *Treasurer*
Carol Duplessis, *Admin Sec*
▲ **EMP:** 115 **EST:** 1885
SQ FT: 40,000
SALES (est): 20.5MM
SALES (corp-wide): 18.3B **Publicly Held**
WEB: www.cooper-atkins.com.com
SIC: **3829** Manufacture Measuring/Controlling Devices
PA: Emerson Electric Co.
8000 West Florissant Ave
Saint Louis MO 63136
314 553-2000

(G-2163)
POWERHOLD INC
63 Old Indian Trl (06455-1248)
P.O. Box 447 (06455-0447)
PHONE..................................860 349-1044
Richard C Spooner, *CEO*
R Chadwick Spooner, *President*
Marilyn D Harris, *Corp Secy*
William T Spooner, *Vice Pres*
Will Spooner, *VP Mfg*
EMP: 24 **EST:** 1958
SQ FT: 14,900
SALES (est): 5.4MM **Privately Held**
WEB: www.powerholdinc.com
SIC: **3545** Mfg Machine Tool Access

GEOGRAPHIC

(G-2164)
R E F MACHINE COMPANY INC
24 West St (06455-1150)
P.O. Box 54 (06455-0054)
PHONE..................................860 349-9344
Robert Fowler, *President*
Lorraine Fowler, *Vice Pres*
EMP: 4
SQ FT: 5,000
SALES: 700K **Privately Held**
SIC: 3599 Machine Shop

(G-2165)
RAMAR-HALL INC
26 Old Indian Trl (06455-1200)
P.O. Box 218 (06455-0218)
PHONE..................................860 349-1081
David Ferraguto, *President*
Tom Varricchio, *Vice Pres*
John Dockendorff, *Engineer*
EMP: 28 **EST:** 1956
SQ FT: 9,000
SALES (est): 7.2MM **Privately Held**
WEB: www.ramarhall.com
SIC: 3728 3544 3769 Mfg Aircraft Parts/Equip Mfg Dies/Tools/Jigs/Fixt Mfg Space Vehicle Equip

(G-2166)
TET MFG CO INC
Also Called: Tet Mfg Co/Machine Shop
2 Old Indian Trl (06455-1200)
PHONE..................................860 349-1004
Thomas H Cady Jr, *President*
Virginia F Cady, *Vice Pres*
John Scholten, *Plant Mgr*
Dennis Brault, *Director*
EMP: 22
SQ FT: 10,000
SALES (est): 3.8MM **Privately Held**
SIC: 3599 Mfg Industrial Machinery

(G-2167)
TIMES PUBLISHING LLC
Also Called: Antiqueweb.com
491 Main St (06455-1205)
P.O. Box 333 (06455-0333)
PHONE..................................860 349-8532
Robert G Ahlgren, *President*
EMP: 8
SALES (est): 339.5K **Privately Held**
WEB: www.monkeytv.com
SIC: 2741 Misc Publishing

(G-2168)
WEPCO PLASTICS INC
27 Indstrial Pk Access Rd (06455-1263)
P.O. Box 182 (06455-0182)
PHONE..................................860 349-3407
Waldo Parmelee Jr, *President*
David Parmelee, *Vice Pres*
Charles Daniels, *CFO*
EMP: 21
SQ FT: 10,350
SALES (est): 3.5MM **Privately Held**
WEB: www.wepcoplastics.com
SIC: 3089 3544 Mfg Plastic Products Mfg Dies/Tools/Jigs/Fixtures

(G-2169)
ZYGO CORPORATION (HQ)
21 Laurel Brook Rd (06455-1291)
PHONE..................................860 347-8506
Gary K Willis, *President*
▲ **EMP:** 8 **EST:** 1970
SQ FT: 153,500
SALES (est): 141.3MM
SALES (corp-wide): 4.8B **Publicly Held**
WEB: www.zygo.com
SIC: 3827 Mfg Optical Instruments/Lenses
PA: Ametek, Inc.
1100 Cassatt Rd
Berwyn PA 19312
610 647-2121

Middletown
Middlesex County

(G-2170)
AMERICAN LIBRARY ASSOCIATION
Also Called: Choice Magazine
575 Main St Ste 300 (06457-2845)
PHONE..................................860 347-6933
Ervin E Rockwood, *Branch Mgr*
EMP: 25
SALES (corp-wide): 49MM **Privately Held**
WEB: www.alawash.org
SIC: 2721 Periodicals-Publishing/Printing
PA: American Library Association
50 E Huron St
Chicago IL 60611
800 545-2433

(G-2171)
AMERICAN OVERHEAD RET DIV INC
1885 S Main St (06457-6149)
PHONE..................................860 876-4552
Michael Misenti, *President*
EMP: 4
SQ FT: 500
SALES (est): 168.9K **Privately Held**
SIC: 2431 3442 Mfg Millwork Mfg Metal Doors/Sash/Trim

(G-2172)
ARMETTA LLC
Also Called: Copar Industries
90 Industrial Park Rd (06457-1521)
P.O. Box 236, East Berlin (06023-0236)
PHONE..................................860 788-2369
Kimberley Ponticelli, *Accounting Mgr*
Antonia Armetta,
EMP: 29
SALES (est): 6.2MM **Privately Held**
SIC: 1411 Dimension Stone Quarry

(G-2173)
AUBURN MANUFACTURING COMPANY
29 Stack St (06457-2274)
PHONE..................................860 346-6677
Gary Mittelman, *President*
Ronald Carta Jr, *Plant Mgr*
Robert L Mittelman, *Treasurer*
Mary Banker, *Bookkeeper*
Rob Mittelman, *Manager*
▲ **EMP:** 23
SQ FT: 40,000
SALES (est): 4.8MM **Privately Held**
WEB: www.auburn-mfg.com
SIC: 3053 5169 3069 Mfg Gaskets/Packing/Sealing Devices Whol Chemicals/Products Mfg Fabricated Rubber Products

(G-2174)
AUTOMATIC MACHINE PRODUCTS
40 Liberty St (06457-2724)
P.O. Box 548 (06457-0548)
PHONE..................................860 346-7064
John Houston, *President*
Catherine Houston, *Treasurer*
EMP: 6 **EST:** 1949
SQ FT: 4,200
SALES (est): 490K **Privately Held**
SIC: 3451 3599 Mfg Screw Machine Products & Machine Shop

(G-2175)
AZTEC INDUSTRIES LLC
Also Called: American Metalcrafters
695 High St (06457-2288)
PHONE..................................860 343-1960
Donna Noonan, *Mng Member*
Ken Pearson,
EMP: 50
SQ FT: 60,000
SALES (est): 9.8MM **Privately Held**
SIC: 3339 Primary Nonferrous Metal Producer

(G-2176)
BALDWIN LAWN FURNITURE LLC
440 Middlefield St Ste 1 (06457-3551)
PHONE..................................860 347-1306
Max Baldwin, *Partner*
Sherry Baldwin, *Mng Member*
EMP: 18
SQ FT: 30,000
SALES (est): 900K **Privately Held**
WEB: www.baldwinfurniture.com
SIC: 2511 5021 Mfg & Whol Furniture

(G-2177)
BERGAN ARCHITECTURAL WDWKG INC
55 N Main St (06457-2228)
PHONE..................................860 346-0869
Richard Bergan, *President*
Maria Bergan, *Vice Pres*
EMP: 20 **EST:** 1976
SQ FT: 16,000
SALES (est): 3.6MM **Privately Held**
WEB: www.berganwood.com
SIC: 2431 2521 2435 2434 Mfg Millwork Mfg Wood Office Furn Mfg Hrdwd Veneer/Plywood Mfg Wood Kitchen Cabinet

(G-2178)
BIDWELL INDUSTRIAL GROUP INC (PA)
Also Called: Rapidprint
2055 S Main St (06457-6151)
PHONE..................................860 346-9283
Donald Bidwell, *CEO*
Donald Bidwell Jr, *Vice Pres*
Michael M Bidwell, *Vice Pres*
Eleni Gabrysiak, *Controller*
Michael Bidwell, *Officer*
EMP: 50 **EST:** 1969
SQ FT: 40,000
SALES (est): 11.7MM **Privately Held**
WEB: www.bidwellinc.com
SIC: 3824 3579 3089 3861 Mfg Fluid Meters/Devices Mfg Office Machines Mfg Plastic Products Mfg Photo Equip/Supplies Mfg X-Ray Apparatus/Tube

(G-2179)
BOURDON FORGE CO INC
99 Tuttle Rd (06457-1827)
PHONE..................................860 632-2740
Peter Bourdon, *President*
▲ **EMP:** 145
SQ FT: 50,000
SALES (est): 33.5MM **Privately Held**
WEB: www.bourdonforge.com
SIC: 3429 3462 Mfg Hardware Mfg Iron/Steel Forgings

(G-2180)
BULL METAL PRODUCTS INC
Also Called: Bull Display
191 Saybrook Rd (06457-4714)
P.O. Box 738 (06457-0738)
PHONE..................................860 346-9691
Steven Z Bull, *President*
Lawrence J Malone, *Admin Sec*
EMP: 40
SQ FT: 40,000
SALES (est): 7.5MM **Privately Held**
WEB: www.bullmetal.com
SIC: 2542 3444 Mfg Partitions/Fixtures-Nonwood Mfg Sheet Metalwork

(G-2181)
CARL PERRY
Also Called: Inotec
91 Highview Ter (06457-2431)
PHONE..................................860 834-4459
Carl Perry, *Owner*
EMP: 3
SALES (est): 341.6K **Privately Held**
SIC: 3812 Mfg Precision Aerospace Components And Sensors

(G-2182)
CONTEMPORARY PRODUCTS LLC
2055 S Main St (06457-6151)
PHONE..................................860 346-9283
Eleni Gabrysiak, *Controller*
Susan Barton, *Sales Staff*
Donald Bidwell Sr,
Robert T Johnson,
EMP: 25
SQ FT: 40,000
SALES (est): 1.6MM **Privately Held**
SIC: 3842 3491 5047 Mfg Surgical Appliances Mfg Industrial Valves Whol Med/Hospital Equip

(G-2183)
DISCO CHICK
170 Main St (06457-3466)
PHONE..................................860 788-6203
Michael Boney, *President*
EMP: 3
SALES (est): 109.8K **Privately Held**
SIC: 2711 Newspapers-Publishing/Printing

(G-2184)
DU-LITE CORPORATION
171 River Rd (06457-3917)
PHONE..................................860 347-2505
Walter Smith, *President*
Patrick Smith, *Treasurer*
Amy Strickland, *Manager*
EMP: 4 **EST:** 1985
SQ FT: 7,500
SALES: 1MM **Privately Held**
SIC: 2911 2841 Petroleum Refiner Mfg Soap/Other Detergents

(G-2185)
E-B MANUFACTURING COMPANY INC
825 Middle St (06457-1524)
PHONE..................................860 632-8563
Edward A Billings, *President*
Andrew Downs, *Engineer*
Chris Webber, *Office Mgr*
Mark Billings, *Supervisor*
Linda H Billings, *Admin Sec*
EMP: 26
SQ FT: 15,000
SALES (est): 5.2MM **Privately Held**
WEB: www.ebmanufacturing.com
SIC: 3599 Mfg Industrial Machinery

(G-2186)
GARBECK AIRFLOW INDUSTRIES
442 Arbutus St (06457-5121)
PHONE..................................860 301-5032
Michael Garofalo, *Owner*
EMP: 3
SALES (est): 81.3K **Privately Held**
SIC: 3999 Mfg Misc Products

(G-2187)
GORILLA GRAPHICS INC
52 N Main St (06457-2269)
PHONE..................................860 704-8208
Geoff Konstan, *President*
Geoffrey Konstan, *Sales Executive*
EMP: 10
SQ FT: 13,000
SALES (est): 1MM **Privately Held**
WEB: www.gorillagraphics.com
SIC: 2269 Finishing Plant

(G-2188)
HABASIT ABT INC
150 Industrial Park Rd (06457-1521)
PHONE..................................860 632-2211
Harry Cardillo, *CEO*
Chad Gibbs, *Controller*
Matthew Etherington, *Manager*
Steve Venice, *Info Tech Mgr*
▲ **EMP:** 140
SQ FT: 78,000
SALES (est): 24.1MM
SALES (corp-wide): 708MM **Privately Held**
WEB: www.habasitabt.com
SIC: 3496 Mfg Misc Fabricated Wire Products
HQ: Habasit America, Inc.
805 Satellite Blvd Nw
Suwanee GA 30024
678 288-3600

(G-2189)
HABASIT AMERICA INC
150 Industrial Park Rd (06457-1521)
PHONE..................................860 632-2211
Mike Kuba, *Finance Mgr*
Gary Peterson, *Branch Mgr*
EMP: 100

SALES (corp-wide): 708MM Privately Held
WEB: www.habasit.com
SIC: 3496 Mfg Misc Fabricated Wire Products
HQ: Habasit America, Inc.
805 Satellite Blvd Nw
Suwanee GA 30024
678 288-3600

(G-2190)
HYDRO SERVICE & SUPPLIES INC
975 Middle St Ste K (06457-7572)
PHONE....203 265-3995
Wes Robbins, *Vice Pres*
Richard Desrosiers, *Manager*
EMP: 9
SALES (corp-wide): 18.7MM Privately Held
SIC: 3589 7699 Mfg Service Industry Machinery Repair Services
PA: Hydro Service & Supplies, Inc.
513 United Dr
Durham NC 27713
919 544-3744

(G-2191)
HYPACK INC (PA)
56 Bradley St (06457-1513)
PHONE....860 635-1500
Patrick Sanders, *President*
John D Marinuzzi, *VP Human Res*
Lourdes Evans, *Sales Staff*
Christine Hypack, *Sales Staff*
Brittany Danek, *Marketing Staff*
EMP: 15
SALES (est): 1.9MM Privately Held
WEB: www.hypack.com
SIC: 7372 Prepackaged Software Services

(G-2192)
J ARNOLD MITTLEMAN
29 Stack St (06457-2265)
PHONE....860 346-6562
J Arnold Mittleman, *Owner*
EMP: 22
SALES (est): 1MM Privately Held
SIC: 2284 Thread Mill

(G-2193)
JARVIS PRODUCTS CORPORATION (HQ)
33 Anderson Rd (06457-4926)
PHONE....860 347-7271
Vincent R Volpe, *President*
Michael Abdul, *Opers Mgr*
Penfield Jarvis, *Treasurer*
Robert Cornelius Danaher, *Admin Sec*
◆ EMP: 10
SQ FT: 54,800
SALES (est): 22.8MM
SALES (corp-wide): 23.6MM Privately Held
WEB: www.jarvisproducts.com
SIC: 3556 Mfg Food Products Machinery
PA: Penco Corporation
229 Buckingham St
Hartford CT
860 278-2345

(G-2194)
JJ PORTLAND NEWS LLC
264 Main St (06457)
PHONE....860 342-1432
EMP: 4
SALES (est): 213K Privately Held
SIC: 2711 Newspapers-Publishing/Printing

(G-2195)
KAMAN AEROSPACE CORPORATION
Precision Products Division
217 Smith St (06457-8750)
PHONE....860 632-1000
Gerald C Ricketts, *Manager*
EMP: 234
SALES (corp-wide): 1.8B Publicly Held
WEB: www.kamanaero.com
SIC: 3489 3572 3823 Mfg Ordnance/Accessories Mfg Computer Storage Devices Mfg Process Control Instruments
HQ: Kaman Aerospace Corporation
1332 Blue Hills Ave
Bloomfield CT 06002
860 242-4461

(G-2196)
KAMAN CORPORATION
217 Smith St (06457-8750)
PHONE....860 632-1000
EMP: 152
SALES (corp-wide): 1.8B Publicly Held
SIC: 3812 Mfg Search/Navigation Equipment
PA: Kaman Corporation
1332 Blue Hills Ave
Bloomfield CT 06002
860 243-7100

(G-2197)
KAMAN PRECISION PRODUCTS INC
217 Smith St (06457-8750)
PHONE....860 632-1000
EMP: 20
SALES (corp-wide): 1.8B Publicly Held
SIC: 3812 Mfg Search/Navigation Equipment
HQ: Kaman Precision Products, Inc.
6655 E Colonial Dr
Orlando FL 32807
407 282-1000

(G-2198)
KIWANIS FNDTION MIDDLETOWN INC
340 Chamberlain Hill Rd (06457-7200)
PHONE....860 638-8135
David Darling, *Principal*
Lyn Baldoni, *Vice Pres*
EMP: 4
SALES: 82.2K Privately Held
SIC: 3732 Boatbuilding And Repairing, Nsk

(G-2199)
L&P AEROSPACE ACQUISITION LLC
Also Called: Pegasus Manufacturing
422 Timber Ridge Rd (06457-7540)
P.O. Box 501, East Berlin (06023-0501)
PHONE....860 635-8811
Chris Dipentima, *President*
Todd Dipentima, *Vice Pres*
EMP: 82
SALES (corp-wide): 4.2B Publicly Held
SIC: 3498 Manufacturing Fabricated Pipe/Fittings
HQ: L&P Aerospace Acquisition Company, Llc
1 Leggett Rd
Carthage MO 64836
417 358-8131

(G-2200)
LABCO WELDING INC
129 Industrial Park Rd (06457-1520)
PHONE....860 632-2625
Vincent La Bella, *President*
Susan M La Bella, *Admin Sec*
EMP: 5
SQ FT: 15,000
SALES (est): 1MM Privately Held
WEB: www.labcowelding.com
SIC: 3444 3599 7692 Metal Fabricator Specializing In Sheet Metal Work Welding & Machine Shop

(G-2201)
LORD & HODGE INC
362 Industrial Park Rd # 4 (06457-1548)
P.O. Box 737 (06457-0737)
PHONE....860 632-7006
Gary Lord, *President*
EMP: 10
SQ FT: 9,000
SALES (est): 1.4MM Privately Held
WEB: www.lordandhodge.com
SIC: 3965 3069 3545 Mfg Fasteners/Buttons/Pins Mfg Fabricated Rubber Products Mfg Machine Tool Accessories

(G-2202)
LYMAN PRODUCTS CORPORATION (PA)
Also Called: Raytech Industries Div
475 Smith St (06457-1529)
PHONE....860 632-2020
Richard Ranzinger, *President*
Thomas Andersen, *Vice Pres*
Luke Fichthorn III, *Treasurer*
Karl Oberg, *Controller*
Edward W Wytrych, *Admin Sec*
◆ EMP: 100 EST: 1876
SQ FT: 100,000
SALES (est): 21.5MM Privately Held
WEB: www.lymanproducts.com
SIC: 3559 Mfg Misc Industry Machinery

(G-2203)
LYMAN PRODUCTS CORPORATION
Raytech Industries
475 Smith St (06457-1529)
PHONE....860 632-2020
Miles Herrick, *Branch Mgr*
EMP: 20
SALES (corp-wide): 21.5MM Privately Held
SIC: 3559 Mfg Misc Industry Machinery
PA: Lyman Products Corporation
475 Smith St
Middletown CT 06457
860 632-2020

(G-2204)
METAL IMPROVEMENT COMPANY LLC
20 Tuttle Pl Ste 6 (06457-1870)
PHONE....860 635-9994
Paul Dimatti, *Manager*
EMP: 25
SALES (corp-wide): 2.4B Publicly Held
SIC: 3398 Metal Heat Treating
HQ: Metal Improvement Company, Llc
80 E Rte 4 Ste 310
Paramus NJ 07652
201 843-7800

(G-2205)
MICROSPECIALITIES INC
430 Smith St (06457-1531)
PHONE....203 874-1832
Gaston Levesque, *CEO*
EMP: 10 EST: 1997
SQ FT: 5,200
SALES (est): 1.6MM Privately Held
WEB: www.microspecialties.com
SIC: 3841 Mfg Surgical/Medical Instruments

(G-2206)
MIDDLETOWN PRINTING CO INC
Also Called: Minuteman Press
512 Main St (06457-2810)
PHONE....860 347-5700
Charlie Lazich, *President*
EMP: 10
SALES (est): 1.2MM Privately Held
SIC: 2752 Comm Prtg Litho

(G-2207)
MOHAWK MANUFACTURING COMPANY
1270 Newfield St (06457-1842)
PHONE....860 632-2345
William W Ferguson Jr, *President*
William P Ferguson, *Vice Pres*
Sal M Marino, *Purch Mgr*
Debra J Ferguson, *Admin Sec*
EMP: 18 EST: 1921
SQ FT: 32,000
SALES (est): 3.4MM Privately Held
WEB: www.mohawk-mfg.com
SIC: 3469 Mfg Metal Stampings

(G-2208)
ORACLE CORPORATION
54 Shady Hill Ln (06457-1786)
PHONE....860 632-8329
Nancy Marx, *Branch Mgr*
EMP: 302
SALES (corp-wide): 39.5B Publicly Held
SIC: 7372 Prepackaged Software Services
PA: Oracle Corporation
500 Oracle Pkwy
Redwood City CA 94065
650 506-7000

(G-2209)
PENCO CORPORATION
Also Called: Jarvis Products
33 Anderson Rd (06457-4901)
PHONE....860 347-7271
Vincent Volpe, *President*
Daniel Burr, *Technician*
John Sadlowski, *Technician*
EMP: 130
SALES (corp-wide): 23.6MM Privately Held
SIC: 3556 Mfg Food Products Machinery
PA: Penco Corporation
229 Buckingham St
Hartford CT
860 278-2345

(G-2210)
PLASTIC DESIGN INTL INC (PA)
Also Called: PDI
111 Industrial Park Rd (06457-1520)
PHONE....860 632-2001
Donald A Bergeron, *President*
Suzette Gaudet, *Safety Mgr*
Kim Guillemin, *Purch Agent*
Roman Suski, *Engineer*
Thomas McMellon, *Manager*
▲ EMP: 46 EST: 1977
SQ FT: 30,000
SALES: 5.9MM Privately Held
WEB: www.plasticdesign.com
SIC: 3089 3544 Mfg Plastic Products Mfg Dies/Tools/Jigs/Fixtures

(G-2211)
POWER-DYNE LLC
Also Called: Power-Dyne LLC/Bidwll Indstrl
2055 S Main St (06457-6151)
PHONE....860 346-9283
Susan Barton, *Chief Mktg Ofcr*
Donald Bidwell Jr, *CIO*
EMP: 25
SQ FT: 40,000
SALES (est): 2.6MM Privately Held
SIC: 3423 3829 7699 Mfg Hand/Edge Tools Mfg Measuring/Controlling Devices Repair Services

(G-2212)
PRATT & WHITNEY ENGINE SVCS
1 Aircraft Rd (06457-5723)
P.O. Box 611 (06457-0611)
PHONE....860 344-4000
Roger Cherichoni, *Vice Pres*
Wayne Carney, *Engineer*
Michael Coonan, *Engineer*
Brian Neiberg, *Engineer*
Mike Parkin, *Engineer*
EMP: 500
SALES (corp-wide): 66.5B Publicly Held
SIC: 3728 3724 3714 Mfg Aircraft Parts/Equipment Mfg Aircraft Engines/Parts Mfg Motor Vehicle Parts/Accessories
HQ: Pratt & Whitney Engine Services, Inc.
1525 Midway Park Rd
Bridgeport WV 26330
304 842-5421

(G-2213)
PRECISION SPEED MFG LLC
422 Timber Ridge Rd (06457-7540)
P.O. Box 501, East Berlin (06023-0501)
PHONE....860 635-8811
Todd Dipentima,
Chris Dipentima,
Vincent Dipentima,
EMP: 30 EST: 2004
SQ FT: 21,000
SALES (est): 5.3MM Privately Held
WEB: www.precisionspeedmfg.com
SIC: 3724 3728 Mfg Aircraft Engine Parts & Aircraft Parts & Equipments

(G-2214)
PROTOTYPE PLASTIC MOLD CO INC
35 Industrial Park Pl (06457-1501)
PHONE....860 632-2800
Victor De Jong, *President*

GEOGRAPHIC

Victor Feldesy, *QC Mgr*
Brian Smith, *Manager*
Murray A Gerber, *Admin Sec*
EMP: 46
SQ FT: 27,000
SALES (est): 10.2MM **Privately Held**
WEB: www.prototypeplastic.net
SIC: 3089 3544 Mfg Plastic Products Mfg Dies/Tools/Jigs/Fixtures

(G-2215)
QUEMERE INTERNATIONAL LLC
234 Middle St (06457-7517)
PHONE..................................914 934-8366
Celine Quemere, *Owner*
EMP: 8 **EST:** 1999
SALES (est): 706K **Privately Held**
SIC: 3253 Mfg Ceramic Wall/Floor Tile

(G-2216)
RA SMYTHE LLC
439 Higby Rd (06457-2383)
PHONE..................................860 398-5764
Catherine L Smythe, *Principal*
EMP: 4
SALES (est): 235.2K **Privately Held**
SIC: 3823 Mfg Process Control Instruments

(G-2217)
RAYCO METAL FINISHING INC
134 Mill St (06457-3749)
P.O. Box 177 (06457-0177)
PHONE..................................860 347-7434
Louise Goldreich, *Ch of Bd*
Mark Goldreich, *Vice Pres*
George Goldreich, *Treasurer*
EMP: 18
SQ FT: 7,500
SALES: 1MM **Privately Held**
SIC: 3471 Electroplating Of Metals

(G-2218)
REAL-TIME ANALYZERS INC
362 Industrial Park Rd # 8 (06457-1548)
PHONE..................................860 635-9800
Stuart Farquharson, *President*
David Hamblen, *Corp Secy*
Chetan Shende, *Research*
EMP: 8
SQ FT: 3,000
SALES (est): 1.6MM **Privately Held**
WEB: www.rta.biz
SIC: 3826 Mfg Analytical Instruments

(G-2219)
RISHA RISHI LLC
Also Called: West and Package
596 Washington St (06457-2513)
PHONE..................................860 346-7645
Risha Rishi, *Owner*
EMP: 3
SALES (est): 207.3K **Privately Held**
SIC: 2631 Paperboard Mill

(G-2220)
SECURITY SYSTEMS INC
1125 Middle St (06457-1526)
PHONE..................................800 833-3211
David G Roman, *Principal*
EMP: 3
SALES (est): 142.3K **Privately Held**
SIC: 3699 Security Systems Services

(G-2221)
SILICONE CASTING TECHNOLOGIES
9 Red Orange Rd (06457-4916)
PHONE..................................860 347-5227
EMP: 3
SALES (est): 181.6K **Privately Held**
SIC: 3325 Steel Foundry

(G-2222)
SKYLINE EXHIBITS & GRAPHICS
362 Industrial Park Rd # 6 (06457-1548)
PHONE..................................860 635-2400
Larry Zollo, *President*
Sal Randazzo, *Buyer*
EMP: 10
SQ FT: 12,500
SALES (est): 1.7MM **Privately Held**
WEB: www.skyline-ct.com
SIC: 2653 Mfg Corrugated/Solid Fiber Boxes

(G-2223)
SMILING DOG
77 Arbutus St (06457-5118)
PHONE..................................860 344-0707
Kimberly Barcello, *Principal*
EMP: 3
SALES (est): 158.6K **Privately Held**
SIC: 2393 3961 2771 Mfg Textile Bags Mfg Costume Jewelry Mfg Greeting Cards

(G-2224)
SOMERSET PLASTICS COMPANY
454 Timber Ridge Rd (06457-7540)
P.O. Box 8446, Berlin (06037-8446)
PHONE..................................860 635-1601
Clifford F White Jr, *President*
Clifford White Jr, *President*
Lois White, *Vice Pres*
Kim White, *Admin Sec*
EMP: 20
SQ FT: 10,000
SALES: 2MM **Privately Held**
SIC: 3544 3089 Mfg Dies/Tools/Jigs/Fixtures Mfg Plastic Products

(G-2225)
SPERIAN PROTECTN INSTRUMENTATN
651 S Main St (06457-4252)
PHONE..................................860 344-1079
Jerry Mc Gurkin,
Jeffrey Brown,
EMP: 146
SQ FT: 75,000
SALES (est): 14.7MM
SALES (corp-wide): 41.8B **Publicly Held**
WEB: www.posichek.com
SIC: 3829 3812 3823 Mfg Measuring/Controlling Devices Mfg Search/Navigation Equipment Mfg Process Control Instruments
HQ: Honeywell Analytics Inc.
405 Barclay Blvd
Lincolnshire IL 60069
847 955-8200

(G-2226)
T & J MANUFACTURING LLP
Also Called: T&J Manufacturing
1385 Newfield St (06457-1819)
PHONE..................................860 632-8655
Mark Jablonski, *Owner*
Chris Targanski, *Partner*
EMP: 25
SALES (est): 3.7MM **Privately Held**
SIC: 3599 Mfg Industrial Machinery

(G-2227)
TEST LOGIC INC
17 Kenneth Dooley Dr (06457-7530)
PHONE..................................860 347-8378
Rod Gwillam, *President*
Kwok Wong, *Exec VP*
Amanda Hartwig, *Purchasing*
Rachel Woolley, *Executive Asst*
EMP: 14
SQ FT: 9,000
SALES (est): 3.7MM **Privately Held**
WEB: www.testlogic.com
SIC: 3825 Mfg Electrical Measuring Instruments

(G-2228)
TINNY CORPORATION
Also Called: Shelco Filters Division
100 Bradley St (06457-1513)
PHONE..................................860 854-6121
Robert Leconche Jr, *President*
Debra A Leconche, *Vice Pres*
Darin Dockter, *Sales Dir*
Bruce Hafner, *Sales Dir*
▲ **EMP:** 25
SQ FT: 40,000
SALES (est): 7.4MM **Privately Held**
WEB: www.shelco.com
SIC: 3569 5074 5085 Mfg General Industrial Machinery Whol Plumbing Equipment/Supplies Whol Industrial Supplies

(G-2229)
TRIUMPH MANUFACTURING CO INC
422 Timber Ridge Rd (06457-7540)
P.O. Box 501, East Berlin (06023-0501)
PHONE..................................860 635-8811
Vincent Dipentima, *President*
EMP: 15
SQ FT: 7,100
SALES (est): 1.8MM **Privately Held**
SIC: 3599 Machine Shop

(G-2230)
WESLEYAN UNIVERSITY
Also Called: Wes Press
110 Mount Vernon St (06457-3289)
PHONE..................................860 685-2980
Suzanna Tamminen, *Director*
EMP: 8
SALES (corp-wide): 231.5MM **Privately Held**
WEB: www.wesleyan.edu
SIC: 2731 8221 Books-Publishing/Printing College/University
PA: Wesleyan University
45 Wyllys Ave
Middletown CT 06459
860 685-2000

(G-2231)
YOUNGS COMMUNICATIONS INC
Also Called: Youngs Printing
182 Court St (06457-3357)
PHONE..................................860 347-8567
Daniel Litwin, *President*
Georgia Chu, *Vice Pres*
EMP: 10
SQ FT: 12,000
SALES (est): 1.9MM **Privately Held**
SIC: 2752 Lithographic Commercial Printing

Milford
New Haven County

(G-2232)
A L C INOVATORS INC
230 Pepes Farm Rd Ste C (06460-8611)
PHONE..................................203 877-8526
Scott Brown, *President*
Carol Musante, *Admin Sec*
◆ **EMP:** 6
SQ FT: 4,800
SALES (est): 748K **Privately Held**
WEB: www.alc-inovators.com
SIC: 2047 2048 3999 Mfg Dog/Cat Food Mfg Prepared Feeds Mfg Misc Products

(G-2233)
ABBOTT ASSOCIATES INC
261a Pepes Farm Rd (06460-3671)
P.O. Box 5405 (06460-0706)
PHONE..................................203 878-2370
John Winfield, *President*
EMP: 15 **EST:** 1968
SQ FT: 10,000
SALES (est): 2.7MM **Privately Held**
WEB: www.goabbott.com
SIC: 3841 Mfg Medical Device Components

(G-2234)
ABET TECHNOLOGIES INC
168 Old Gate Ln (06460-3651)
PHONE..................................203 540-9990
Zbigniew Drozdowicz, *CEO*
Allen Smith, *President*
EMP: 5
SQ FT: 2,900
SALES: 1.6MM **Privately Held**
WEB: www.abet-technologies.com
SIC: 3827 Mfg Optical Instruments/Lenses

(G-2235)
ACME PRESS INC
95 Erna Ave (06461-3119)
P.O. Box 344 (06460-0344)
PHONE..................................203 334-8221
Bruce Riso, *President*
Tom Riso, *Vice Pres*
EMP: 3 **EST:** 1925
SQ FT: 1,500
SALES (est): 330K **Privately Held**
SIC: 2752 Lithographic Commercial Printing

(G-2236)
ADVANCED LINEN GROUP
215 Pepes Farm Rd (06460-3626)
P.O. Box 3608 (06460-0945)
PHONE..................................203 877-3896
Joel B Gorkowski, *Principal*
EMP: 10
SALES (est): 1.3MM **Privately Held**
SIC: 2299 Mfg Textile Goods

(G-2237)
ADVANCED PRCSION CASTINGS CORP
120 Pullman Dr (06461-2058)
PHONE..................................203 736-9452
George Taylor Middleton, *President*
George M Middleton, *Vice Pres*
Maryann Middleton, *Vice Pres*
EMP: 4
SALES (est): 531.6K **Privately Held**
SIC: 3363 Manufactures Prototype Specialty Aluminum Castings

(G-2238)
AIR-LOCK INCORPORATED
108 Gulf St (06460-4859)
PHONE..................................203 878-4691
Michael H McCarthy, *President*
John W Bassick, *President*
Robert A Vincent, *Chairman*
Lois Hetherington, *Vice Pres*
David A Sweet, *Treasurer*
EMP: 25
SQ FT: 27,000
SALES (est): 5.3MM
SALES (corp-wide): 68.7MM **Privately Held**
WEB: www.airlockinc.com
SIC: 3728 3429 Mfg Aircraft Parts/Equipment Mfg Hardware
PA: David Clark Company Incorporated
360 Franklin St
Worcester MA 01604
508 756-6216

(G-2239)
ALC SALES COMPANY LLC (PA)
230 Pepes Farm Rd Ste C (06460-8611)
PHONE..................................203 877-8526
Scott Brown, *Mng Member*
Carol Reitenbach, *Admin Asst*
EMP: 3
SQ FT: 6,000
SALES (est): 512.9K **Privately Held**
SIC: 2048 Mfg Prepared Feeds

(G-2240)
ALCAT INCORPORATED
116 W Main St (06460-3310)
PHONE..................................203 878-0648
James Edwards, *President*
▲ **EMP:** 32
SQ FT: 31,000
SALES: 4MM **Privately Held**
WEB: www.alcat.com
SIC: 3083 Mfg Laminated Plastic Plate/Sheet

(G-2241)
ALFA NOBEL LLC
94 Utica St (06461-2347)
PHONE..................................203 876-2823
EMP: 5
SQ FT: 11,770
SALES: 1.5MM **Privately Held**
SIC: 2676 Mfg Wet Wipes

(G-2242)
ALINABAL INC (HQ)
Also Called: Sterling Screw Machine Div
28 Woodmont Rd (06460-2872)
PHONE..................................203 877-3241
Samuel S Bergami Jr, *President*
Luigi Cazzaniga, *General Mgr*
Tom Crowley, *General Mgr*
Kevin Conlisk, *Vice Pres*
Paul Kelley, *Vice Pres*
▲ **EMP:** 243
SQ FT: 110,000

▲ = Import ▼=Export
◆ =Import/Export

SALES (est): 33.2MM
SALES (corp-wide): 57MM **Privately Held**
WEB: www.dacoinstrument.com
SIC: 3469 3399 3625 3728 Mfg Metal Stampings Mfg Primary Metal Prdts Mfg Relay/Indstl Control Mfg Aircraft Parts/Equip Mfg Motor Vehicle Parts
PA: Alinabal Holdings Corporation
28 Woodmont Rd
Milford CT 06460
203 877-3241

(G-2243)
ALINABAL HOLDINGS CORPORATION (PA)
28 Woodmont Rd (06460-2872)
PHONE..................................203 877-3241
Samuel Bergami, *President*
Robert Pentino, *Chief Engr*
Greg Humphries, *Project Engr*
Kevin M Conlisk, *CFO*
Rick Williams, *Executive*
▲ **EMP:** 300
SQ FT: 147,000
SALES: 57MM **Privately Held**
WEB: www.alinabal.com
SIC: 3714 3577 3399 3469 Mfg Motor Vehicle Parts Mfg Computer Peripherals Mfg Primary Metal Prdts Mfg Metal Stampings Mfg Fluid Meters/Devices

(G-2244)
ANNA M CHISILENCO-RAHO
67 Cherry St Ste 2 (06460-8904)
PHONE..................................203 877-0377
Anna M Chisilenco-Raho, *Principal*
EMP: 8
SALES (est): 784.1K **Privately Held**
SIC: 3843 Dentist's Office

(G-2245)
ARGYLE OPTICS LLC
28 Tower St (06460-3213)
PHONE..................................203 451-3320
Eric Stanley, *Principal*
EMP: 3 **EST:** 2010
SALES (est): 258.1K **Privately Held**
SIC: 3827 Mfg Optical Instruments/Lenses

(G-2246)
ATLANTIC SENSORS & CONTRLS LLC
301 Brewster Rd (06460-3700)
PHONE..................................203 878-8118
Peter Terek,
EMP: 4
SALES (est): 627.5K **Privately Held**
SIC: 3829 Mfg Measuring/Controlling Devices

(G-2247)
AUDIOWORKS INC
260 Old Gate Ln (06460-8621)
PHONE..................................203 876-1133
Frank A Ventresca, *President*
EMP: 5
SQ FT: 5,600
SALES (est): 1MM **Privately Held**
WEB: www.audioworksct.com
SIC: 3651 Ret Musical Instruments

(G-2248)
B & A COMPANY INC
160 Wampus Ln (06460-4861)
PHONE..................................203 876-7527
Richard Schwarz, *President*
Ronald Schwartz, *Vice Pres*
EMP: 20
SALES (est): 3.8MM **Privately Held**
SIC: 3599 Mfg Industrial Machinery

(G-2249)
B L C INVESTMENTS INC
Also Called: Gradar Metals
228a Rowe Ave (06461-3031)
PHONE..................................203 877-1888
Barry Chuba, *Vice Pres*
EMP: 4
SQ FT: 5,000 **Privately Held**
SIC: 3444 1799 Mfg Sheet Metalwork Trade Contractor

(G-2250)
BALDING PRECISION INC
61 Woodmont Rd (06460-2840)
PHONE..................................203 878-9135
Mike Goodman, *President*
EMP: 8
SQ FT: 5,000
SALES (est): 1.2MM **Privately Held**
SIC: 3599 Mfg Industrial Machinery

(G-2251)
BEAD INDUSTRIES INC (PA)
Also Called: Bead Electronics
11 Cascade Blvd (06460-2849)
PHONE..................................203 301-0270
Jill Bryant Mayer, *CEO*
Lou Guerci, *President*
James Balazsi, *Senior Engr*
Kristen Sawyer, *CFO*
Michelle Mackeil, *Human Resources*
◆ **EMP:** 50 **EST:** 1914
SQ FT: 75,000
SALES (est): 9.6MM **Privately Held**
WEB: www.beadindustries.com
SIC: 3432 3679 3678 3643 Mfg Plumbing Fxtr Fittng Mfg Elec Components Mfg Elec Connectors Mfg Conductive Wire Dvcs Mfg Power Transmsn Equip

(G-2252)
BEARD CONCRETE CO DERBY INC (PA)
Also Called: Beard Concrete Company
127 Boston Post Rd (06460-3104)
PHONE..................................203 874-2533
Robert Beard, *President*
James R Beard, *Vice Pres*
EMP: 4 **EST:** 1957
SQ FT: 9,600
SALES (est): 1.1MM **Privately Held**
SIC: 3273 Mfg Ready-Mixed Concrete

(G-2253)
BETZ TOOL COMPANY INC
70 Raton Rd Ste K (06461-1768)
PHONE..................................203 878-1187
George Betz, *President*
Sharon Betz, *Vice Pres*
EMP: 3
SQ FT: 2,400
SALES: 250K **Privately Held**
WEB: www.betztool.com
SIC: 3544 3089 Mfr Tool Molds Tool Builder

(G-2254)
BIC CONSUMER PRODUCTS MFG CO
565 Bic Dr (06461-1769)
PHONE..................................203 783-2000
Mario Guevara, *President*
Ken Brannin, *Vice Pres*
Thomas M Kelleher, *Vice Pres*
James V Dipietro, *Treasurer*
Lisa Palladino, *Manager*
▲ **EMP:** 120
SALES (est): 18.3MM
SALES (corp-wide): 766.4MM **Privately Held**
WEB: www.biceveryday.com
SIC: 3951 2899 Mfg Pens/Mechanical Pencils Mfg Chemical Preparations
HQ: Bic Usa Inc.
1 Bic Way Ste 1 # 1
Shelton CT 06484
203 783-2000

(G-2255)
BOJAK COMPANY
152 Old Gate Ln D (06460-3651)
PHONE..................................203 378-5086
Carl Johansson, *President*
EMP: 7
SALES (est): 1MM **Privately Held**
SIC: 3829 Mfg Fire Detection Systems

(G-2256)
BOMAN PRECISION TECH INC
67 Erna Ave (06461-3118)
PHONE..................................203 415-8350
Allen Godman, *President*
Robert Godman, *Admin Sec*
EMP: 6
SQ FT: 5,000
SALES (est): 1MM **Privately Held**
WEB: www.bomantool.com
SIC: 3599 Mfg Industrial Machinery

(G-2257)
BUCKS SPUMONI COMPANY INC
Also Called: Buck's Ice Cream
229 Pepes Farm Rd (06460-3671)
PHONE..................................203 874-2007
Charles Buck Jr, *President*
Lois Gosselin, *Admin Sec*
EMP: 15
SQ FT: 14,000
SALES (est): 2.5MM **Privately Held**
SIC: 2024 Mfg Ice Cream/Frozen Desert

(G-2258)
CAAP CO INC
152 Pepes Farm Rd (06460-3670)
P.O. Box 2066, Shelton (06484-1066)
PHONE..................................203 877-0375
James F Moraveck, *President*
Christopher J Moraveck, *Vice Pres*
Charles Scheidler Jr, *Vice Pres*
Christine L Sledge, *Vice Pres*
Kim Loomis, *Bookkeeper*
▲ **EMP:** 20
SQ FT: 10,000
SALES (est): 4.9MM **Privately Held**
WEB: www.caapco.com
SIC: 2899 Mfg Chemical Preparations

(G-2259)
CADCOM INC
110 Raton Rd (06461-1779)
PHONE..................................203 877-0640
Richard Meisenheimer, *President*
Daniel Meisenheimer, *Vice Pres*
Maria Sabina, *Controller*
EMP: 10
SQ FT: 3,500
SALES (est): 1.5MM **Privately Held**
WEB: www.spectrumct.com
SIC: 3451 Mfg Screw Machine Products

(G-2260)
CANEVARI PLASTICS INC
10 Furniture Row (06460-3607)
P.O. Box 464 (06460-0464)
PHONE..................................203 878-4319
George Canevari, *President*
Kevin Callahan, *Vice Pres*
Janice Canevari, *Admin Sec*
EMP: 9
SQ FT: 1,200
SALES (est): 1.8MM **Privately Held**
WEB: www.canevariplastics.com
SIC: 3089 Mfg Plastic Products

(G-2261)
CARDIOPULMONARY CORP
200 Cascade Blvd Ste B (06460-8515)
PHONE..................................203 877-1999
Dr James Biondi, *Ch of Bd*
Joseph McGuire, *Vice Pres*
Michael Bowering, *Engineer*
Nick Snow, *CFO*
Jay McGuire, *CTO*
▲ **EMP:** 45
SQ FT: 25,000
SALES (est): 5.8MM **Privately Held**
WEB: www.cardiopulmonarycorp.com
SIC: 3842 Mfg Surgical Appliances/Supplies

(G-2262)
CARRUBBA INCORPORATED
70 Research Dr (06460-8523)
PHONE..................................203 878-0605
Duane Carrubba, *President*
▲ **EMP:** 55 **EST:** 1976
SQ FT: 15,000
SALES (est): 11MM **Privately Held**
WEB: www.carrubba.com
SIC: 2869 2844 2087 Mfg Industrial Organic Chemicals Mfg Toilet Preparations Mfg Flavor Extracts/Syrup

(G-2263)
CET INC
270 Rowe Ave Ste D (06461-3085)
PHONE..................................203 882-8057
John Breger, *President*
Janelle Stauffer, *Principal*
EMP: 8
SQ FT: 5,000
SALES (est): 1.1MM **Privately Held**
SIC: 3625 Mfg Industrial Electrical Controls

(G-2264)
CHARGE SOLUTIONS INC
Also Called: C S I
205 Research Dr Unit 1011 (06460-8531)
PHONE..................................203 871-7282
Marc Karpel, *President*
EMP: 4 **EST:** 2015
SALES: 1.5MM **Privately Held**
SIC: 3629 Mfg Electrical Industrial Apparatus

(G-2265)
COLONIAL COATINGS INC
66 Erna Ave (06461-3115)
PHONE..................................203 783-9933
Russell A Colon, *President*
Richard S Castorina, *Vice Pres*
Richard Castorina, *Vice Pres*
Patrick Rossomando, *Production*
Jessica Tobin, *Production*
EMP: 45
SQ FT: 17,000
SALES (est): 7.6MM **Privately Held**
WEB: www.colonialcoatings.com
SIC: 3479 3471 2851 Coating/Engraving Svcs Plating/Polishing Svcs Mfg Paints/Allied Prdts

(G-2266)
COMFORTABLE ENVIRONMENTS
11 Terrell Dr (06461-2037)
PHONE..................................203 876-2140
Joshua Miller,
EMP: 6
SALES: 800K **Privately Held**
SIC: 3585 Mfg Refrigeration/Heating Equipment

(G-2267)
CONNECTICUT DIESEL AND MARINE
287 Woodmont Rd (06460-2847)
PHONE..................................203 481-1010
Marla Walker, *Owner*
EMP: 3
SALES (est): 273.7K **Privately Held**
SIC: 3731 Shipbuilding/Repairing

(G-2268)
CONNECTICUT FABRICATING CO INC
15 Warfield St (06461-2930)
PHONE..................................203 878-3465
Thomas Wirkus, *President*
Richard T Wirkus, *Vice Pres*
Rosemarie Wirkus, *Admin Sec*
EMP: 6
SQ FT: 2,600
SALES: 400K **Privately Held**
SIC: 3444 Mfg Sheet Metal Products

(G-2269)
CONNECTICUT MCH TOOLING & CAST
93 Research Dr (06460-8525)
PHONE..................................203 874-8300
George Paulis Jr, *President*
Marolyn Paulis, *Treasurer*
EMP: 12
SQ FT: 8,000
SALES (est): 1.6MM **Privately Held**
SIC: 3599 Contract Machine Shop Jobbing & Repair

(G-2270)
CONNECTICUT STONE SUPPLIES INC (PA)
138 Woodmont Rd (06460-2832)
PHONE..................................203 882-1000
Joseph Dellacroce, *President*
Lance Dellacroce, *Sales Dir*
Ed Mish, *Sr Project Mgr*
Jim Williamson, *Sr Project Mgr*
Jeff Abeling, *Manager*
▲ **EMP:** 83
SALES (est): 11.6MM **Privately Held**
SIC: 3281 5032 1411 Mfg Cut Stone/Products Whol Brick/Stone Material Dimension Stone Quarry

GEOGRAPHIC

(G-2271)
CT DUMPSTER LLC
32 Birch Ave (06460-5301)
PHONE..................................203 521-0779
Saulo Silva, *Principal*
EMP: 3 **EST:** 2017
SALES (est): 147.8K **Privately Held**
SIC: 3443 Mfg Fabricated Plate Work

(G-2272)
D & B TOOL CO LLC
83 Erna Ave (06461-3118)
PHONE..................................203 878-6026
John Butka, *Owner*
EMP: 8
SALES (est): 125K **Privately Held**
SIC: 3429 Mfg Dies/Tools/Jigs/Fixtures

(G-2273)
DATA SIGNAL CORPORATION
16 Higgins Dr (06460-2853)
PHONE..................................203 882-5393
Lynda Kilgore, *President*
Gerard Kilgore, *Admin Sec*
EMP: 20
SQ FT: 15,900
SALES (est): 3.5MM **Privately Held**
SIC: 3679 Mfg Electronic Components

(G-2274)
DEL ARBOUR LLC
152 Old Gate Ln (06460-3651)
PHONE..................................203 882-8501
Ruzdi Muaremi,
EMP: 10
SQ FT: 2,500
SALES: 750K **Privately Held**
WEB: www.delarbour.com
SIC: 2329 2339 5136 5137 Mfg Mens/Boys Clothing Mfg Women/Miss Outerwear Whol Mens/Boys Clothing Whol Women/Child Clothng Ret Mail-Order House

(G-2275)
DELLTECH INC
175 Buckingham Ave (06460-4842)
PHONE..................................203 878-8266
Tom Dellipoali, *President*
Dolores Dellipoali, *Admin Sec*
EMP: 3
SQ FT: 3,000
SALES: 380K **Privately Held**
SIC: 3599 Machine Job Shop

(G-2276)
DPC QUALITY PUMP SERVICE
544 Bridgeport Ave (06460-4202)
PHONE..................................203 874-6877
Dean Cyr, *Owner*
EMP: 3
SALES: 220K **Privately Held**
SIC: 3561 5084 5074 Mfg Pumps/Pumping Equipment Whol Industrial Equipment Whol Plumbing Equipment/Supplies

(G-2277)
DUMOND CHEMICALS INC
695 West Ave (06461-3003)
PHONE..................................609 655-7700
Mohamad Ajjan, *General Mgr*
EMP: 9
SALES (corp-wide): 1.3MM **Privately Held**
WEB: www.dumondchemicals.com
SIC: 2851 Whol Chemicals/Products
PA: Dumond Chemicals, Inc.
1475 Phnxvlle Pike Ste 18
West Chester PA 19380
609 655-7700

(G-2278)
DUZ MANUFACTURING INC
87 Opal St (06461-3029)
PHONE..................................203 874-1032
Janusz Duz, *President*
Aneta Duz, *Vice Pres*
EMP: 5
SALES (est): 550K **Privately Held**
SIC: 3086 Mfg Plastic Foam Products

(G-2279)
E-Z SWITCH MANUFACTURING INC
463 Naugatuck Ave (06460-5048)
PHONE..................................203 874-7766
Elizabeth G Bradley, *President*
▲ **EMP:** 15
SALES (est): 1.7MM **Privately Held**
SIC: 3625 Mfg Switchgear/Switchboards

(G-2280)
EASTERN MARBLE & GRANITE LLC
201 Buckingham Ave (06460-4842)
PHONE..................................203 882-8221
Michael Ballaro, *Mng Member*
▲ **EMP:** 10
SALES (est): 366K **Privately Held**
SIC: 3281 Mfg Cut Stone/Products

(G-2281)
EASTERN METAL WORKS INC
333 Woodmont Rd (06460-2847)
PHONE..................................203 878-6995
Raymond J Weiner, *President*
Christopher J Weiner, *Corp Secy*
▼ **EMP:** 22
SQ FT: 15,000
SALES: 10MM **Privately Held**
WEB: www.easternmetalworks.com
SIC: 3449 3446 5051 Mfg Misc Structural Mtl Mfg Architectural Mtlwrk Metals Service Center

(G-2282)
EDGEWELL PER CARE BRANDS LLC
10 Leighton Rd (06460-3552)
PHONE..................................203 882-2300
Joseph Lynch, *Branch Mgr*
EMP: 98
SALES (corp-wide): 2.1B **Publicly Held**
WEB: www.eveready.com
SIC: 3421 Mfg Cutlery
HQ: Edgewell Personal Care Brands, Llc
6 Research Dr
Shelton CT 06484
203 944-5500

(G-2283)
EDGEWELL PERSONAL CARE COMPANY
10 Leighton Rd (06460-3552)
PHONE..................................203 882-2308
Lisa Geronimo, *Business Mgr*
Terry Schulke, *Exec VP*
Jeffrey Garrant, *Senior Buyer*
Lucy Vano, *Senior Buyer*
Doyle Tim, *Research*
EMP: 29
SALES (corp-wide): 2.1B **Publicly Held**
SIC: 3421 Mfg Cutlery
PA: Edgewell Personal Care Company
1350 Tmberlake Manor Pkwy
Chesterfield MO 63017
314 594-1900

(G-2284)
ELECTRODES INCORPORATED
160 Cascade Blvd (06460-2848)
PHONE..................................203 878-7400
Michael Dudas, *Manager*
EMP: 25
SALES (corp-wide): 23.3MM **Privately Held**
WEB: www.electrodes-inc.com
SIC: 3699 Mfg Electrical Equipment/Supplies
PA: Electrodes, Incorporated
260a Quarry Rd
Milford CT 06460
954 803-4736

(G-2285)
ENGINEERED INSERTS & SYSTEMS (PA)
Also Called: Eis
26 Quirk Rd (06460-3745)
P.O. Box 610, Watertown (06795-0610)
PHONE..................................203 301-3334
Teri Cook, *President*
EMP: 15
SALES (est): 2.1MM **Privately Held**
WEB: www.eisinserts.com
SIC: 3429 Mfg & Design Metal Inserts

(G-2286)
ENGINUITY PLM LLC (HQ)
Also Called: IMS
440 Wheelers Farms Rd (06461-9133)
PHONE..................................203 218-7225
John P Sottery, *CEO*
Donald F Logan Jr, *COO*
EMP: 19
SQ FT: 6,600
SALES (est): 2.5MM
SALES (corp-wide): 1.7B **Privately Held**
SIC: 7372 7373 8734 8742 Prepackaged Software Svc Computer Systems Design Testing Laboratory Mgmt Consulting Svcs
PA: Dassault Systemes
10 Rue Marcel Dassault
Velizy Villacoublay 78140
161 623-000

(G-2287)
EXCELLO TOOL ENGRG & MFG CO
37 Warfield St (06461-2930)
PHONE..................................203 878-4073
Michael Zahornacky Jr, *President*
Jeff Solomon, *Vice Pres*
EMP: 25 **EST:** 1960
SALES (est): 4.4MM **Privately Held**
WEB: www.excellotool.com
SIC: 3599 Mfg Industrial Machinery

(G-2288)
FASTSIGNS
1015 Bridgeport Ave (06460-3160)
PHONE..................................203 298-4075
Brian Reeves, *Owner*
EMP: 5 **EST:** 2008
SALES (est): 617.5K **Privately Held**
SIC: 3993 Signsadv Specs

(G-2289)
FERRARO CUSTOM WOODWORK LLC
29 Eastern Steel Rd (06460-2837)
PHONE..................................203 876-1280
Joseph Ferraro, *Owner*
EMP: 5
SALES (est): 575.9K **Privately Held**
SIC: 2431 Mfg Millwork

(G-2290)
FLOWSERVE CORPORATION
408 Woodmont Rd (06460-3789)
PHONE..................................203 877-4252
Robert Emerling, *Office Mgr*
David Krupp, *Manager*
EMP: 20
SALES (corp-wide): 3.8B **Publicly Held**
SIC: 3561 Mfg Pumps/Pumping Equipment
PA: Flowserve Corporation
5215 N Ocnnor Blvd Ste 23 Connor
Irving TX 75039
972 443-6500

(G-2291)
FORCE3 PRO GEAR LLC
45 Banner Dr 1 (06460-2859)
PHONE..................................315 367-2331
James Evans, *Partner*
Cole Flowers, *Partner*
Michael Klein, *Partner*
Jason Klein, *General Ptnr*
Lisa Franco, *Comms Dir*
EMP: 4 **EST:** 2017
SALES (est): 146K **Privately Held**
SIC: 3949 Mfg Sporting/Athletic Goods

(G-2292)
GALAXY FUEL LLC
180 New Haven Ave (06460-4829)
PHONE..................................203 878-8173
Mustafa Bayram, *Principal*
EMP: 3
SALES (est): 204.1K **Privately Held**
SIC: 2869 Mfg Industrial Organic Chemicals

(G-2293)
GRAPHIC IMAGE INC
561 Boston Post Rd (06460-2676)
PHONE..................................203 877-8787
Leigh Danenberg, *President*
Silvano Stasolla, *President*
Lynn Tedler, *Pub Rel Mgr*
Carole Norman, *Accounts Exec*
Jose Ortiz,
EMP: 25
SQ FT: 11,000
SALES: 3.5MM **Privately Held**
WEB: www.graphicimage.net
SIC: 2752 Lithographic Commercial Printing

(G-2294)
GRILLO SERVICES LLC
1183 Oronoque Rd (06461-1714)
PHONE..................................203 877-5070
John Michael Grillo, *President*
Lawrence Grillo, *Vice Pres*
Mark Mumich, *Administration*
EMP: 25
SALES (est): 1MM **Privately Held**
SIC: 2875 4213 4953 5191 Mfg Fertilizer Truck Operator-Nonlocal Refuse Systems Whol Farm Supplies
PA: Grillo Organic Inc
1183 Oronoque Rd
Milford CT 06461

(G-2295)
GYBENORTH INDUSTRIES LLC
Also Called: American Dry Stripping
80 Wampus Ln Ste 13 (06460-4856)
PHONE..................................203 876-9876
Roger F Van Brussel, *Principal*
Roger Vanbrussel,
EMP: 12
SALES (est): 919.4K **Privately Held**
SIC: 3479 3471 Coating/Engraving Service Plating/Polishing Service

(G-2296)
HAYWARD TURNSTILES INC
160 Wampus Ln (06460-4861)
PHONE..................................203 877-7096
Richard Schwarz, *CEO*
Ronald B Schwarz, *President*
EMP: 6
SQ FT: 6,000
SALES (est): 1.2MM **Privately Held**
SIC: 3829 Mfg Measuring/Controlling Devices

(G-2297)
HUBBELL WIRING DEVICE
185 Plains Rd (06461-2473)
P.O. Box 1000, Shelton (06484-1000)
PHONE..................................203 882-4800
◆ **EMP:** 15
SALES (est): 3.1MM
SALES (corp-wide): 4.4B **Publicly Held**
WEB: www.hubbell.com
SIC: 3643 Mfg Conductive Wiring Devices
PA: Hubbell Incorporated
40 Waterview Dr
Shelton CT 06484
475 882-4000

(G-2298)
I & J MACHINE TOOL COMPANY
230 Woodmont Rd Ste V (06460-2845)
PHONE..................................203 877-5376
Ivan Jukic, *Partner*
Jure Jukic, *Partner*
▼ **EMP:** 15
SQ FT: 7,200
SALES (est): 3.1MM **Privately Held**
SIC: 3728 3724 Mfg Aircraft Parts/Equipment Mfg Aircraft Engines/Parts

(G-2299)
IDEAS INC
Also Called: Connecticut Engravers
80a Rowe Ave (06461-3031)
PHONE..................................203 878-9686
Paul Mangels, *President*
Marcia Mangels, *Admin Sec*
EMP: 4
SQ FT: 2,000
SALES (est): 300K **Privately Held**
SIC: 2754 2759 Gravure Commercial Printing Commercial Printing

(G-2300)
IEMCT
Also Called: International Energy MGT
205 Research Dr Ste 8 (06460-2874)
PHONE....................................203 683-4382
EMP: 4 **EST:** 2007
SALES: 500K **Privately Held**
SIC: 3699 Mfg Electrical Equipment/Supplies

(G-2301)
IMPERIAL GRPHIC CMMNCTIONS INC
Also Called: Imperial Graphics
22 Way St (06460-4200)
PHONE....................................203 650-3478
David Emery, *President*
Robert Emery, *Vice Pres*
EMP: 23
SQ FT: 20,000
SALES (est): 5.7MM **Privately Held**
WEB: www.imperialgraphics.com
SIC: 2752 2789 2759 Lithographic Commercial Printing Bookbinding/Related Work Commercial Printing

(G-2302)
INDECO NORTH AMERICA INC
135 Research Dr (06460-2839)
PHONE....................................203 713-1030
Michael Fischer, *CEO*
Charles Ameer, *CFO*
Carole Funk, *Administration*
◆ **EMP:** 28
SQ FT: 77,000
SALES (est): 8.7MM
SALES (corp-wide): 34MM **Privately Held**
WEB: www.indeco-breakers.com
SIC: 3531 Mfg Construction Machinery
PA: Indeco Ind Spa
Viale Guglielmo Lindemann 10
Bari BA 70132
080 531-3340

(G-2303)
INTERFACE DEVICES INCORPORATED
Also Called: IDI
230 Depot Rd (06460-3813)
PHONE....................................203 878-4648
Mark Robinson, *President*
Mike Hotchkiss, *Vice Pres*
Roger Dennis, *Treasurer*
EMP: 8
SQ FT: 10,000
SALES: 1.9MM **Privately Held**
WEB: www.interfacedevices.com
SIC: 3599 5084 Mfg Industrial Machinery Whol Industrial Equipment

(G-2304)
JOE PASSARELLI & CO
67 Andrews Ave (06460-5815)
PHONE....................................203 877-1434
Jo-Anne Urena, *Manager*
EMP: 3
SALES (est): 167.9K **Privately Held**
SIC: 1429 Crushed/Broken Stone

(G-2305)
JOHN RAWLINSON JOHN LEARY
316 Boston Post Rd (06460-2527)
PHONE....................................203 882-8484
John Rawlinson, *Partner*
John Leary, *Partner*
EMP: 5
SALES: 750K **Privately Held**
SIC: 3993 Mfg Signs/Advertising Specialties

(G-2306)
KBC ELECTRONICS INC
273 Pepes Farm Rd (06460-3671)
PHONE....................................203 298-9654
Kue Choi, *Owner*
Cheryl Burke, *Materials Mgr*
EMP: 10
SQ FT: 7,500
SALES (est): 2.2MM **Privately Held**
WEB: www.kbcelectronics.com
SIC: 3679 3841 3842 Mfg Electronic Components Mfg Surgical/Medical Instruments Mfg Surgical Appliances/Supplies

(G-2307)
KILO AMPERE SWITCH CORPORATION
Also Called: K A Switch
230 Woodmont Rd Ste 27 (06460-2845)
PHONE....................................203 877-5994
Ann Impellitteri, *President*
Thomas Impellitteri, *Treasurer*
EMP: 4
SQ FT: 2,750
SALES: 330K **Privately Held**
WEB: www.kaswitch.com
SIC: 3613 Mfr Of High Current Switches & Jumpers

(G-2308)
LAC LANDSCAPING LLC
60 Country Ln (06461-1943)
PHONE....................................203 807-1067
Luis A Castro,
EMP: 10
SALES (est): 1.3MM **Privately Held**
SIC: 3714 Mfg Motor Vehicle Parts/Accessories

(G-2309)
LIGHT SOURCES INC
70 Cascade Blvd (06460-2848)
P.O. Box 3010 (06460-0810)
PHONE....................................203 799-7877
EMP: 101
SALES (corp-wide): 37.4MM **Privately Held**
SIC: 3645 Mfg Residential Lighting Fixtures
PA: Light Sources, Inc.
37 Robinson Blvd
Orange CT 06477
203 799-7877

(G-2310)
LIVING MAGAZINE
162 Bridgeport Ave (06460-3935)
PHONE....................................203 283-5290
Suzanne Cahill, *President*
EMP: 3
SALES (est): 173.4K **Privately Held**
SIC: 2721 Periodicals-Publishing/Printing

(G-2311)
LYON MANUFACTURING LLC
215 Research Dr Ste 4 (06460-8554)
PHONE....................................203 876-7386
Gary Lyon, *Owner*
EMP: 4
SQ FT: 1,600
SALES: 500K **Privately Held**
SIC: 3444 Mfg Sheet Metalwork

(G-2312)
MADDOG LLC
33 Tall Pine Rd (06461-1951)
PHONE....................................203 878-0147
Michael Garvey,
EMP: 3
SALES (est): 166K **Privately Held**
SIC: 2431 Mfg Millwork

(G-2313)
MAGNA STANDARD MFG CO INC
122 Cascade Blvd (06460-2848)
PHONE....................................203 874-0444
Carl G Swebilius, *President*
George Adams, *Vice Pres*
EMP: 6
SQ FT: 7,000
SALES: 1MM **Privately Held**
WEB: www.magnastandard.com
SIC: 3599 Machine Shop Services

(G-2314)
MDM PRODUCTS LLC
Also Called: Rhino Shelters
105 Woodmont Rd (06460-2840)
PHONE....................................203 877-7070
Michael Skoldberg,
Don Skoldberg,
◆ **EMP:** 11
SQ FT: 65,000
SALES (est): 2.1MM **Privately Held**
WEB: www.mdmproducts.org
SIC: 3448 3089 Mfg Prefabricated Metal Buildings Mfg Plastic Products

(G-2315)
MIDGET LOUVER COMPANY INC
671 Naugatuck Ave (06461-4064)
PHONE....................................203 783-1444
Michael Vignola, *President*
Paul Creatore, *Principal*
Delores Creatore, *Admin Sec*
EMP: 8 **EST:** 1948
SQ FT: 3,300
SALES (est): 1.2MM **Privately Held**
WEB: www.midgetlouver.com
SIC: 3444 Mfg Sheet Metalwork

(G-2316)
MORNING STAR TOOL LLC
Also Called: D&B Tool Co.
83 Erna Ave (06461-3118)
PHONE....................................203 878-6026
Leon Tyrrell, *President*
Rebekah Butler, *Business Mgr*
Alan Vensel, *Plant Mgr*
EMP: 5
SALES (est): 289.5K **Privately Held**
SIC: 3724 3429 3728 Mfg Aircraft Parts/Equip Mfg Aircraft Engine/Part Mfg Hardware

(G-2317)
MRH TOOL LLC
124 Research Dr Ste A (06460-8571)
PHONE....................................203 878-3359
George Scobie,
EMP: 4
SALES: 200K **Privately Held**
SIC: 3545 3599 Mfg Machine Tool Accessories Mfg Industrial Machinery

(G-2318)
NEATO PRODUCTS LLC
37 Eastern Steel Rd (06460-2837)
PHONE....................................203 466-5170
John Blakeslee, *President*
EMP: 4
SQ FT: 20,000
SALES (est): 544.2K **Privately Held**
SIC: 2672 Mfg Coated/Laminated Paper

(G-2319)
NEOPOST USA INC (DH)
478 Wheelers Farms Rd (06461-9105)
PHONE....................................203 301-3400
Dennis P Lestrange, *President*
Austin Maddox, *General Mgr*
Jim Owens, *General Mgr*
Jim Gray, *Business Mgr*
Jason Tyson, *Business Mgr*
▲ **EMP:** 250
SQ FT: 62,000
SALES (est): 339.7MM
SALES (corp-wide): 38.4MM **Privately Held**
WEB: www.neopostinc.com
SIC: 3579 7359 7629 Mfg Office Machines Equipment Rental/Leasing Electrical Repair

(G-2320)
NEW ENGLAND STANDARD CORP
16 Honey St (06461-3122)
PHONE....................................203 876-7733
Bill Marston, *Branch Mgr*
EMP: 8
SALES (corp-wide): 3.1MM **Privately Held**
SIC: 2431 Mfg Millwork
PA: New England Standard Corporation
323 Boston Post Rd
Old Saybrook CT 06475
860 388-0438

(G-2321)
NEWHART PLASTICS INC
10 Furniture Row (06460-3607)
P.O. Box 3386 (06460-0942)
PHONE....................................203 877-5367
Frank A Canevari, *President*
Pamela Zimmerman, *Admin Sec*
EMP: 5
SQ FT: 12,000
SALES (est): 727.9K **Privately Held**
SIC: 3089 Mfg Plastic Products

(G-2322)
NOREASTER YACHTS INC
29 Roselle St (06461-3165)
PHONE....................................203 877-4339
Hugh Whitman Jr, *President*
Steven Whitman, *Vice Pres*
EMP: 3
SQ FT: 2,050
SALES: 500K **Privately Held**
WEB: www.noreasteryachts.com
SIC: 2221 Manmade Broadwoven Fabric Mill

(G-2323)
NORTH SAILS GROUP LLC (DH)
Also Called: North Technology Group
125 Old Gate Ln Ste 7 (06460-3611)
PHONE....................................203 874-7548
Thomas A Whidden, *CEO*
Jay Hansen, *Exec VP*
Dan Neri, *Vice Pres*
Brian Engel, *Export Mgr*
Travers Blossom, *Mfg Staff*
◆ **EMP:** 70
SQ FT: 3,000
SALES (est): 83.4MM **Privately Held**
WEB: www.northsails.com
SIC: 2394 2211 Mfg Canvas/Related Products Cotton Broadwoven Fabric Mill
HQ: Tehnology North Group Llc
125 Old Gate Ln Ste 7
Milford CT 06460
203 877-7621

(G-2324)
NORTHEAST ELECTRONICS CORP
455 Bic Dr (06461-1735)
PHONE....................................203 878-3511
Armand J Cantafio, *President*
Timothy A Cantafio, *Vice Pres*
Timothy Cantafio, *Vice Pres*
Frank Gaudiano, *Vice Pres*
John Short, *Vice Pres*
▲ **EMP:** 100 **EST:** 1961
SQ FT: 36,000
SALES (est): 18.3MM **Privately Held**
WEB: www.northeast.com
SIC: 3679 Mfg Electronic Components

(G-2325)
OEM SOURCES LLC
214 Broadway (06460-5858)
PHONE....................................203 283-5415
Thomas Bach, *President*
Tom Bach, *Vice Pres*
▲ **EMP:** 9
SALES (est): 1.4MM **Privately Held**
WEB: www.oemsources.com
SIC: 3542 3462 3469 3451 Mfg Machine Tool-Forming Mfg Iron/Steel Forgings Mfg Metal Stampings Mfg Screw Machine Prdts

(G-2326)
ORANGE RESEARCH INC
140 Cascade Blvd (06460-2893)
PHONE....................................203 877-5657
Leslie Hoffman, *Ch of Bd*
Paul A Hoffman, *President*
Don Malizia, *General Mgr*
Mike Donovan, *Vice Pres*
Ed Wilson, *Mfg Mgr*
EMP: 53
SQ FT: 10,000
SALES (est): 13.7MM **Privately Held**
SIC: 3823 Mfg Process Cntrl Instr

(G-2327)
OSDA CONTRACT SERVICES INC
291 Pepes Farm Rd (06460-3671)
P.O. Box 3048 (06460-0848)
PHONE....................................203 878-2155
David H Ingraham, *President*
Mark Forcier, *Manager*
EMP: 25
SQ FT: 14,000
SALES (est): 6.8MM **Privately Held**
WEB: www.osda.com
SIC: 3679 Mfg Electronic Components

GEOGRAPHIC

(G-2328)
OSDA INC
98 Quirk Rd (06460-3763)
P.O. Box 3048 (06460-0848)
PHONE..................................203 878-2155
David Ingraham, *Principal*
Mark Haskins, *Human Resources*
EMP: 5
SALES (est): 736.8K **Privately Held**
SIC: 3679 Mfg Electronic Components

(G-2329)
OUTLAND ENGINEERING INC
167 Cherry St Pmb 280 (06460-3466)
PHONE..................................800 797-3709
Stewart Burton, *President*
Grace Burton, *Admin Sec*
▲ **EMP:** 19
SQ FT: 54,000
SALES (est): 2.3MM **Privately Held**
WEB: www.ac-safe.com
SIC: 3429 5075 Mfg Hardware Whol Heat/Air Cond Equipment/Supplies

(G-2330)
P&P TOOL & DIE CORP
72 Erna Ave (06461-3115)
PHONE..................................203 874-2571
Gabor Pernyeszi, *President*
EMP: 3
SALES: 250K **Privately Held**
SIC: 3599 Mfg Industrial Machinery

(G-2331)
PARIDISE FOODS LLC
828 New Haven Ave (06460-3675)
P.O. Box 5178 (06460-0709)
PHONE..................................203 283-3903
Hristos Paridis, *Principal*
EMP: 3 **EST:** 2010
SALES (est): 246.2K **Privately Held**
SIC: 2099 Mfg Food Preparations

(G-2332)
PENNY PRESS INC
185 Plains Rd Ste 100e (06461-2480)
PHONE..................................203 866-6688
Vincent Petrecca, *Principal*
EMP: 20
SALES (corp-wide): 12.7MM **Privately Held**
SIC: 2721 Misc Publishing
PA: Penny Press, Inc.
6 Prowitt St
Norwalk CT 06855
203 866-6688

(G-2333)
PENNY PUBLICATIONS LLC
185 Plains Rd Ste 201e (06461-2474)
PHONE..................................203 866-6688
Peter Kanter, *Branch Mgr*
EMP: 29
SALES (corp-wide): 16MM **Privately Held**
SIC: 2741 Misc Publishing
PA: Penny Publications Llc
6 Prowitt St
Norwalk CT 06855
203 866-6688

(G-2334)
PERFECT INFINITY INC
167 Cherry St Ste 145 (06460-3466)
PHONE..................................203 906-0442
Winston Phillips, *Principal*
Desiree Mullins, *Treasurer*
EMP: 5
SQ FT: 2,400
SALES (est): 305.8K **Privately Held**
SIC: 2899 Chemical Preparations, Nec, Nsk

(G-2335)
POPS DONUTS
587 New Haven Ave (06460-3619)
PHONE..................................203 876-1210
Gus Grigo Riabis, *President*
EMP: 5
SALES (est): 270K **Privately Held**
SIC: 2051 5461 Mfg Bread/Related Products Retail Bakery

(G-2336)
PRACTICAL AUTOMATION INC (HQ)
45 Woodmont Rd (06460-2883)
P.O. Box 3028 (06460-0828)
PHONE..................................203 882-5640
Samuel Bergami, *President*
Luigi Cazzaniga, *General Mgr*
Dave Petreycik, *Purch Mgr*
John Prokop, *Purchasing*
Chris Mitchell, *Engineer*
▲ **EMP:** 52
SQ FT: 35,000
SALES (est): 9.8MM
SALES (corp-wide): 57MM **Privately Held**
WEB: www.practicalautomation.com
SIC: 2759 Commercial Printing
PA: Alinabal Holdings Corporation
28 Woodmont Rd
Milford CT 06460
203 877-3241

(G-2337)
PRECISION METAL PRODUCTS INC
307 Pepes Farm Rd (06460-8605)
PHONE..................................203 877-4258
William O'Brien, *President*
EMP: 196
SQ FT: 36,000
SALES (est): 51.9MM **Privately Held**
WEB: www.pmpinc.biz
SIC: 3841 Mfg Surgical/Medical Instruments

(G-2338)
PRECISION SENSORS INC
340 Woodmont Rd (06460-3702)
P.O. Box 509 (06460-0509)
PHONE..................................203 877-2795
Robert D Reis, *Ch of Bd*
David A Reis, *President*
R Tim Straub, *Vice Pres*
Ann Patry, *Purchasing*
Derek Dewitt, *Engineer*
▼ **EMP:** 39 **EST:** 1962
SQ FT: 10,000
SALES (est): 6.5MM
SALES (corp-wide): 39.4MM **Privately Held**
SIC: 3823 Mfg Process Control Instruments
PA: United Electric Controls Company
180 Dexter Ave
Watertown MA 02472
617 923-6900

(G-2339)
PRECISION TOOL & COMPONENTS
195 Rock Ln (06460-3831)
PHONE..................................203 874-9215
Joseph Reilly, *President*
Michael Yevich, *Treasurer*
EMP: 5 **EST:** 1977
SQ FT: 1,700
SALES: 450K **Privately Held**
SIC: 3599 Machine Shop

(G-2340)
PRESTIGE TOOL MFG LLC
154 Old Gate Ln (06460-3651)
P.O. Box 5241 (06460-0702)
PHONE..................................203 874-0360
Kenneth E Dugan,
Cindy Dugan,
EMP: 6
SQ FT: 6,600
SALES (est): 770K **Privately Held**
WEB: www.prestigetoolmfg.com
SIC: 3599 Mfg Industrial Machinery

(G-2341)
PRINT SOURCE LTD
116a Research Dr Ste D (06460-2838)
P.O. Box 5214 (06460-0701)
PHONE..................................203 876-1822
Douglas Hecker, *President*
EMP: 3
SALES (est): 329.9K **Privately Held**
SIC: 2759 7336 Commercial Printing Coml Art/Graphic Design

(G-2342)
PROBATTER SPORTS LLC
49 Research Dr Ste 1 (06460-2864)
PHONE..................................203 874-2500
Timothy Oreilly, *Engineer*
Wesley Hurty, *Sales Staff*
Greg Battersby, *Mng Member*
Adam Battersby,
EMP: 8
SALES (est): 1.1MM **Privately Held**
WEB: www.probatter.com
SIC: 3949 5941 Mfg Sporting/Athletic Goods Ret Sporting Goods/Bicycles

(G-2343)
PUCKS PUTTERS & FUEL LLC
10 Robert Dennis Dr (06461-2267)
PHONE..................................203 877-5457
Steven Genova, *Branch Mgr*
EMP: 11
SALES (corp-wide): 871.9K **Privately Held**
SIC: 2869 Mfg Industrial Organic Chemicals
PA: Pucks Putters & Fuel Llc
784 River Rd
Shelton CT 06484
203 494-3952

(G-2344)
QTRAN INC
155 Hill St Ste 3 (06460-3192)
PHONE..................................203 367-8777
John Tremaine, *CEO*
Susan Cutler Tremaine, *President*
Jordan Nodelman, *Vice Pres*
Elizabeth Pisano, *Vice Pres*
Alex Fiorelli, *Opers Mgr*
▲ **EMP:** 40
SQ FT: 10,000
SALES (est): 12.2MM **Privately Held**
WEB: www.q-tran.com
SIC: 3679 3677 Mfg Electronic Components Mfg Electronic Coils/Transformers

(G-2345)
QUALEDI INC (PA)
121 W Main St Ste 4 (06460-9201)
PHONE..................................203 874-4334
Stephen Morocco, *President*
EMP: 5
SALES (est): 1.2MM **Privately Held**
WEB: www.qualedi.com
SIC: 7372 Prepackaged Software Services

(G-2346)
R A TOOL CO
230 Woodmont Rd Ste Y (06460-2845)
PHONE..................................203 877-2998
Diane Andrews, *Owner*
EMP: 4
SQ FT: 1,800
SALES (est): 399K **Privately Held**
SIC: 3544 3469 Mfg Dies/Tools/Jigs/Fixtures Mfg Metal Stampings

(G-2347)
REL-TECH ELECTRONICS INC
215 Pepes Farm Rd (06460-3626)
P.O. Box 3111 (06460-0911)
PHONE..................................203 877-8770
Ralph L Palumbo, *President*
Noreen C Palumbo, *Admin Sec*
EMP: 85
SQ FT: 12,000
SALES (est): 9.6MM
SALES (corp-wide): 55.3MM **Publicly Held**
WEB: www.rel-tech.com
SIC: 3679 5063 Manufacturing Electronic Components Wholesales Electrical Equipment
PA: Rf Industries, Ltd.
7610 Miramar Rd Ste 6000
San Diego CA 92126
858 549-6340

(G-2348)
RELIABLE TOOL & DIE INC
435 Woodmont Rd (06460-3703)
PHONE..................................203 877-3264
Russell J Vecsey, *President*
Agail Reese, *Admin Sec*
EMP: 26 **EST:** 1978
SQ FT: 27,000
SALES (est): 6MM **Privately Held**
WEB: www.reliabletooling.com
SIC: 3544 Mfg Metal Stampings

(G-2349)
RICHARD BREAULT
Also Called: Datex Microcomputer Service
117 North St (06460-3443)
P.O. Box 5094 (06460-1494)
PHONE..................................203 876-2707
Richard Breault, *Owner*
EMP: 3
SALES (est): 200.9K **Privately Held**
SIC: 7372 5045 Prepackaged Software Services Whol Computers/Peripherals

(G-2350)
RICHARD MANUFACTURING CO INC
250 Rock Ln (06460-3853)
PHONE..................................203 874-3617
James F Steponavich, *President*
EMP: 35 **EST:** 1957
SQ FT: 13,000
SALES (est): 8MM **Privately Held**
WEB: www.rmcoonline.com
SIC: 3728 Mfg Aircraft Parts/Equipment

(G-2351)
RIDGE VIEW ASSOCIATES INC
Also Called: J Burdon Division
122 Cascade Blvd (06460-2848)
PHONE..................................203 878-8560
William B Maley Jr, *President*
Peter Murray, *Opers Spvr*
▲ **EMP:** 70
SQ FT: 55,000
SALES (est): 14.5MM **Privately Held**
WEB: www.trans-liteinc.com
SIC: 3647 3546 Mfg Vehicle Light Equip Mfg Powerdriven Handtool

(G-2352)
RINGS WIRE INC (PA)
257 Depot Rd (06460-3804)
P.O. Box 3013 (06460-0813)
PHONE..................................203 874-6719
Stanley Reiter, *President*
Howard J Reiter, *Vice Pres*
EMP: 45
SQ FT: 300,000
SALES (est): 2.4MM **Privately Held**
SIC: 3965 Manufactures Metal Snap Fasteners Belt Buckles & Wire Formings

(G-2353)
RITAS OF MILFORD
175 Boston Post Rd (06460-3104)
PHONE..................................203 301-4490
Michael Guerino, *Owner*
EMP: 10
SALES (est): 491.3K **Privately Held**
SIC: 2024 Mfg Ice Cream/Frozen Desert

(G-2354)
ROME FASTENER CORPORATION
257 Depot Rd (06460-3804)
P.O. Box 3013 (06460-0813)
PHONE..................................203 874-6719
Stanley F Reiter, *President*
Howard J Reiter, *Vice Pres*
Marcia W Reiter, *Director*
▲ **EMP:** 50
SQ FT: 75,000
SALES (est): 5.7MM **Privately Held**
WEB: www.romefast.com
SIC: 3999 3965 Mfg Misc Products Mfg Fasteners/Buttons/Pins

(G-2355)
ROME FASTENER SALES CORP
257 Depot Rd (06460-3804)
P.O. Box 3013 (06460-0813)
PHONE..................................203 874-6719
Stanley F Reiter, *Manager*
EMP: 16
SALES (corp-wide): 4MM **Privately Held**
SIC: 3965 Whol Hardware
PA: Rome Fastener Sales Corporation
246 W 38th St Rm 501
New York NY 10018
212 741-9779

(G-2356)
ROSS MFG & DESIGN LLC
124 Research Dr Ste A (06460-8571)
PHONE..............................203 878-0187
Christopher Ross, *Managing Prtnr*
Donald Ross, *Partner*
EMP: 12
SQ FT: 4,200
SALES (est): 998.7K **Privately Held**
SIC: 3599 Machine Shop

(G-2357)
RUBBER LABELS USA LLC
500 Bic Dr Bldg 2 (06461-1777)
PHONE..............................203 713-8059
Robert Vero, *Mng Member*
EMP: 5
SALES (est): 171.1K **Privately Held**
SIC: 2754 Gravure Commercial Printing

(G-2358)
S AND Z GRAPHICS LLC
Also Called: Minuteman Press
415 Boston Post Rd Ste 7 (06460-2578)
PHONE..............................203 783-9675
Kevin M Mola,
EMP: 4
SQ FT: 1,000
SALES (est): 715K **Privately Held**
WEB: www.ambyth.com
SIC: 2752 7336 Lithographic Commercial Printing Commercial Art/Graphic Design

(G-2359)
SANTEC CORPORATION
84 Old Gate Ln (06460-8622)
PHONE..............................203 878-1379
Laura Lombardo, *Vice Pres*
Laurajane Uruza, *Vice Pres*
Vito J Lombardo, *Opers Mgr*
EMP: 12
SQ FT: 14,000
SALES (est): 3.5MM **Privately Held**
WEB: www.santec-corp.com
SIC: 3555 Mfg Printing Press Parts

(G-2360)
SCHICK MANUFACTURING INC (HQ)
Also Called: Schick-Wilkinson Sword
10 Leighton Rd (06460-3552)
PHONE..............................203 882-2100
David Hatfield, *President*
Joseph Lynch, *Principal*
Daniel J Sescleifer, *Exec VP*
William C Fox, *Vice Pres*
Mark S Lavigne, *Vice Pres*
◆ **EMP:** 55
SALES (est): 108.8MM
SALES (corp-wide): 2.1B **Publicly Held**
WEB: www.energizer.com
SIC: 3421 Mfg Cutlery
PA: Edgewell Personal Care Company
1350 Tmberlake Manor Pkwy
Chesterfield MO 63017
314 594-1900

(G-2361)
SCHMIDT TOOL MANUFACTURING
76 Finch St Ste D (06461-3042)
P.O. Box 2391 (06460-0876)
PHONE..............................203 877-8149
George Schmidt, *Vice Pres*
EMP: 3
SQ FT: 2,600
SALES (est): 220K **Privately Held**
SIC: 3544 3599 Mfg Dies/Tools/Jigs/Fixtures Mfg Industrial Machinery

(G-2362)
SHOW MOTION INC
1034 Bridgeport Ave (06460-3167)
PHONE..............................203 866-1866
William Mensching Sr, *President*
William Mensching, *President*
▲ **EMP:** 50
SQ FT: 30,000
SALES (est): 7.3MM **Privately Held**
WEB: www.showmotion.com
SIC: 3999 3531 1799 Mfg Misc Products Mfg Construction Machinery Trade Contractor

(G-2363)
SIGNCENTER LLC
333 Quarry Rd (06460-8574)
PHONE..............................800 269-2130
Michael Oliveras, *Principal*
Jimmy Whitehill, *Production*
▲ **EMP:** 6
SALES (est): 895.5K **Privately Held**
SIC: 3993 Mfg Signs/Advertising Specialties

(G-2364)
SONITEK CORPORATION
84 Research Dr (06460-8523)
PHONE..............................203 878-9321
Robert James Bishop, *President*
Cheryl Ann Bishop, *Corp Secy*
Harry Crease, *Vice Pres*
Paul Denton, *Design Engr*
Linda Pereira, *Office Mgr*
EMP: 30
SQ FT: 7,500
SALES (est): 7.8MM **Privately Held**
WEB: www.plasticassembly.com
SIC: 3548 3541 Mfg Welding Apparatus Mfg Machine Tools-Cutting

(G-2365)
SOUTHPORT BREWING CO
33 New Haven Ave (06460-3308)
PHONE..............................203 874-2337
William Dasilva, *Owner*
EMP: 35
SALES (est): 2.3MM **Privately Held**
SIC: 2082 5812 Mfg Malt Beverages Eating Place

(G-2366)
SPECIALTY TOOL COMPANY USA LLC
61 Erna Ave (06461-3118)
PHONE..............................203 874-2009
Richard E Fisk, *Manager*
EMP: 13 **EST:** 1968
SQ FT: 5,000
SALES: 1.8MM **Privately Held**
SIC: 3724 Mfg Aircraft Engines/Parts

(G-2367)
SPECTRUM ASSOCIATES INC
440 New Haven Ave Ste 1 (06460-3629)
P.O. Box 470 (06460-0470)
PHONE..............................203 878-4618
Richard Meisenheimer, *President*
Daniel Meisenheimer III, *Vice Pres*
Thomas Casolino, *Engineer*
Peter Jackson, *Engineer*
Linda Meisenheimer, *Admin Sec*
EMP: 10
SALES (est): 1.3MM **Privately Held**
SIC: 3643 5084 5085 Mfg Conductive Wiring Devices Whol Industrial Equipment Whol Industrial Supplies

(G-2368)
SPECTRUM PRESS
Also Called: Spectrum Graphix
354 Woodmont Rd Ste 15 (06460-3766)
PHONE..............................203 878-9090
Peter J Bonaventure, *Partner*
Kim Bonaventure, *Partner*
EMP: 15
SQ FT: 8,000
SALES (est): 1.6MM **Privately Held**
WEB: www.spectrumgraphix.com
SIC: 2752 Lithographic Commercial Printing

(G-2369)
STEVENS MANUFACTURING CO INC
220 Rock Ln (06460-3853)
PHONE..............................203 878-2328
Stephen Fogler, *President*
Elizabeth Fogler, *Vice Pres*
Chester Pyzik, *Train & Dev Mgr*
Vartika Kumar, *Info Tech Mgr*
Susan Capozzo, *Admin Asst*
▲ **EMP:** 32 **EST:** 1957
SQ FT: 34,000
SALES (est): 12.8MM **Privately Held**
WEB: www.stevensmfgco.com
SIC: 3599 Mfg Industrial Machinery

(G-2370)
SUMMIT ORTHOPEDIC TECH INC
294 Quarry Rd (06460-2851)
PHONE..............................203 693-2727
Adam Ferrell, *President*
Jason Blake, *COO*
Ron Dunn, *Vice Pres*
EMP: 45 **EST:** 2014
SALES (est): 5.1MM **Privately Held**
SIC: 3841 Mfg Surgical/Medical Instruments

(G-2371)
SUMMIT SCREW MACHINE CORP
49 Research Dr Ste 3 (06460-2864)
PHONE..............................203 693-2727
EMP: 3
SALES (est): 385.4K **Privately Held**
SIC: 3599 Mfg Industrial Machinery

(G-2372)
SUN FARM CORPORATION
75 Woodmont Rd (06460-2840)
PHONE..............................203 882-8000
Linus Sun, *President*
Alexander S Sun, *President*
EMP: 7
SALES (est): 840K **Privately Held**
SIC: 3556 Mfg Food Products Machinery

(G-2373)
SURGIQUEST INC
488 Wheelers Farms Rd # 3 (06461-5801)
PHONE..............................203 799-2400
Kourosh Azabarzin, *CEO*
Kurt Azarbarzin, *CEO*
Christine Antalik, *CFO*
Erik Anderson, *Sales Staff*
Carlos Babini, *Sales Staff*
EMP: 83
SALES (est): 11.6MM
SALES (corp-wide): 859.6MM **Publicly Held**
SIC: 3841 Manufacturer Of Surgical/Medical Instruments
PA: Conmed Corporation
525 French Rd
Utica NY 13502
315 797-8375

(G-2374)
SYNECTIC ENGINEERING INC
60 Commerce Park Ste 1 (06460-3513)
PHONE..............................203 877-8488
Adam Lehman, *President*
EMP: 18 **EST:** 2013
SALES (est): 3.2MM
SALES (corp-wide): 432.8MM **Privately Held**
SIC: 3841 Catheter-Based And Minimally Invasive Surgical Devices For Orthopedic Cardiac Gynecological/Urological
HQ: Mack Molding Company, Inc.
608 Warm Brook Rd
Arlington VT 05250
802 375-2511

(G-2375)
THOMAS SPRING CO OF CONNENICUT
29 Seemans Ln (06460-4338)
PHONE..............................203 874-7030
Peter Tessitore, *President*
Gerry Tessitore, *Vice Pres*
EMP: 8
SALES (est): 1MM **Privately Held**
SIC: 3495 Mfg Mechanical Springs

(G-2376)
TINSLEY GROUP-PS&W INC (HQ)
Also Called: Olympic STEel-Ps&w
1 Eastern Steel Rd (06460-2837)
PHONE..............................919 742-5832
Michael Siegal, *CEO*
David A Wolfort, *President*
Richard T Marabito, *CFO*
▲ **EMP:** 53
SQ FT: 70,000
SALES (est): 23.1MM
SALES (corp-wide): 1.7B **Publicly Held**
SIC: 3531 7692 3441 Mfg Construction Machinery Welding Repair Structural Metal Fabrication
PA: Olympic Steel, Inc.
22901 Millcreek Blvd # 650
Cleveland OH 44122
216 292-3800

(G-2377)
UNITED ELECTRIC CONTROLS CO
Also Called: Precision Sensors
340 Woodmont Rd (06460-3702)
PHONE..............................203 877-2795
Timothy R Straub, *Manager*
EMP: 55
SQ FT: 6,372
SALES (corp-wide): 39.4MM **Privately Held**
WEB: www.ueonline.com
SIC: 3823 3674 3643 3625 Mfg Process Cntrl Instr Mfg Semiconductors/Dvcs Mfg Conductive Wire Dvcs Mfg Relay/Indstl Control
PA: United Electric Controls Company
180 Dexter Ave
Watertown MA 02472
617 923-6900

(G-2378)
UNIVERSE PUBLISHING CO LLC
167 Cherry St Ste 261 (06460-3466)
PHONE..............................203 283-5201
Ioana Crupenschi, *President*
EMP: 3
SQ FT: 1,000
SALES (est): 130.2K **Privately Held**
SIC: 2741 Misc Publishing

(G-2379)
VARSITY IMPRINTS
22 Roller Ter (06461-2643)
PHONE..............................203 354-4371
Richard Kurtzman, *Principal*
EMP: 3 **EST:** 2013
SALES (est): 225.9K **Privately Held**
SIC: 2759 Commercial Printing

(G-2380)
VITRO TECHNOLOGY LTD
205 Research Dr Ste 12 (06460-8552)
PHONE..............................203 783-9566
George Davis, *President*
EMP: 6
SALES (est): 166.8K **Privately Held**
SIC: 3229 Mfg Pressed/Blown Glass

(G-2381)
W&R MANUFACTURING INC
230 Woodmont Rd Ste U (06460-2845)
P.O. Box 191, Stratford (06615-0191)
PHONE..............................203 877-5955
Elizabeth Butrymowicz, *President*
Rose Zimnoch, *Vice Pres*
EMP: 4
SQ FT: 3,500
SALES (est): 456K **Privately Held**
SIC: 3728 Mfg Aircraft Parts/Equipment

(G-2382)
WINE WELL CHILLER COMP INC
301 Brewster Rd Ste 3 (06460-3700)
PHONE..............................203 878-2465
Anna Bell Fisher, *President*
James Fisher, *Chairman*
Robert Hewson, *Director*
EMP: 3
SQ FT: 2,000
SALES: 300K **Privately Held**
WEB: www.wine-well.com
SIC: 3585 Mfg Specialized Refrigeration Equipment

GEOGRAPHIC

Milldale
Hartford County

(G-2383)
CENTURY TOOL AND DESIGN INC
260 Canal St (06467)
P.O. Box 545 (06467-0545)
PHONE..................................860 621-6748
Michael Aldi, *President*
Ray Koontz, *Vice Pres*
Raymond Koontz, *Vice Pres*
Charles Maxfield, *Treasurer*
EMP: 14 **EST:** 1975
SQ FT: 5,000
SALES: 2MM **Privately Held**
WEB: www.centool.com
SIC: 3545 7389 Mfg Machine Tool Accessories Business Services

(G-2384)
JAY SONS SCREW MCH PDTS INC
197 Burritt St (06467)
P.O. Box 674 (06467-0674)
PHONE..................................860 621-0141
David Tellerico, *President*
John Spinello, *Vice Pres*
Joseph Tellerico III, *Admin Sec*
EMP: 18 **EST:** 1945
SQ FT: 12,000
SALES (est): 3.5MM **Privately Held**
WEB: www.jaysons.com
SIC: 3451 Mfg Screw Machine Products

(G-2385)
MICRO INSERT INC
183 Clark St (06467)
P.O. Box 673 (06467-0673)
PHONE..................................860 621-5789
James Deangelo, *President*
Keith Smith, *Vice Pres*
Kenneth Nelson, *Treasurer*
Fred Douglas Smith, *Admin Sec*
EMP: 9
SQ FT: 15,000
SALES (est): 1.3MM **Privately Held**
SIC: 3545 Mfg Tool Holders & Carbide Inserts

(G-2386)
MID-STATE MANUFACTURING INC
1610 Mriden Waterburytpke (06467)
P.O. Box 585 (06467-0585)
PHONE..................................860 621-6855
Robert Pisko, *President*
Dennis Pisko, *Shareholder*
EMP: 15
SQ FT: 5,000
SALES: 1MM **Privately Held**
WEB: www.midstatemfg.com
SIC: 3544 3599 3545 3541 Mfg Dies/Tools/Jigs/Fixt Mfg Industrial Machinery Mfg Machine Tool Access Mfg Machine Tool-Cutting

(G-2387)
STEEL RULE DIE CORP AMERICA
289 Clark Street Ext (06467)
P.O. Box 546 (06467-0546)
PHONE..................................860 621-5284
Thomas Brandt, *President*
Theresa Brandt, *Vice Pres*
EMP: 5
SQ FT: 2,600
SALES: 270K **Privately Held**
SIC: 3544 Mfg Tools & Dies

(G-2388)
TOFF INDUSTRY INC
323 Clark St (06467-6503)
P.O. Box 579 (06467-0579)
PHONE..................................860 378-0532
Harold Toffey, *President*
Dori Tapineau, *Office Mgr*
▲ **EMP:** 7
SQ FT: 5,000
SALES (est): 1MM **Privately Held**
WEB: www.toffindustries.com
SIC: 2394 Mfg Canvas/Related Products

Monroe
Fairfield County

(G-2389)
AAPI
593 M St (06468)
PHONE..................................203 268-2450
Bill Harris, *Principal*
EMP: 3
SALES (est): 211.4K **Privately Held**
SIC: 2721 Periodicals-Publishing/Printing

(G-2390)
AMERICAN HEAT TREATING INC
16 Commerce Dr (06468-2601)
PHONE..................................203 268-1750
Peter J Wolcott, *President*
Charles Polatsek, *Vice Pres*
John H Weiland, *Treasurer*
EMP: 45 **EST:** 1969
SQ FT: 32,000
SALES (est): 8.6MM **Privately Held**
SIC: 3398 Metal Heat Treating

(G-2391)
AMERICAN IMEX CORPORATION
57 Maryanne Dr (06468-3209)
PHONE..................................203 261-5200
Yogesh Mehrotra, *President*
Patrice Green, *Vice Pres*
EMP: 5
SALES (est): 500K **Privately Held**
WEB: www.imex-co.com
SIC: 3357 Nonferrous Wiredrawing/Insulating

(G-2392)
AXEL PLASTICS RES LABS INC
50 Cambridge Dr (06468-2661)
PHONE..................................718 672-8300
Franklin Bk Axel, *CEO*
Jake Axel, *President*
Barbara Axel, *Corp Secy*
Zachary Wilde, *Research*
◆ **EMP:** 32
SQ FT: 4,500
SALES (est): 9MM **Privately Held**
WEB: www.axelplast.com
SIC: 2821 2992 Mfg Plastic Materials/Resins Mfg Lubricating Oils/Greases

(G-2393)
B-SWEET LLC
444 Main St Ste C (06468-1112)
PHONE..................................203 452-0499
EMP: 4
SALES (est): 248.7K **Privately Held**
SIC: 2024 Mfg Ice Cream/Frozen Desert

(G-2394)
BAUER COMPRESSORS INC
Also Called: Bauer Compressor North East
60 Twin Brook Ter (06468-1808)
PHONE..................................203 445-9514
Tom Liscinski, *Manager*
EMP: 5
SALES (corp-wide): 65MM **Privately Held**
WEB: www.bauersf.com
SIC: 3563 Mfg Air/Gas Compressors
PA: Bauer Compressors, Inc.
1328 Azalea Garden Rd
Norfolk VA 23502
757 855-6006

(G-2395)
BML TOOL & MFG CORP
67 Enterprise Dr (06468-2674)
PHONE..................................203 880-9485
Philip Battaglia, *President*
Vincent Battaglia, *Vice Pres*
EMP: 60
SQ FT: 38,000
SALES: 11MM **Privately Held**
WEB: www.boottrac.com
SIC: 3469 3544 Mfg Metal Stampings Mfg Dies/Tools/Jigs/Fixtures

(G-2396)
BOBBEX INC
523 Pepper St Ste B (06468-2676)
PHONE..................................800 792-4449
Robert Ecsedy, *President*
Greg Ecsedy, *Vice Pres*
Betty K Ecsedy, *Director*
EMP: 3
SQ FT: 3,000
SALES (est): 564.4K **Privately Held**
WEB: www.bobbex.com
SIC: 2873 5261 Mfg Nitrogenous Fertilizers Ret Nursery/Garden Supplies

(G-2397)
BUDRAD ENGINEERING CO LLC
26 Patmar Cir (06468-1545)
PHONE..................................203 452-7310
Radoslaw Szawiola,
EMP: 3
SALES (est): 330.4K **Privately Held**
WEB: www.budrad.com
SIC: 3599 Mfg Industrial Machinery

(G-2398)
CONNECTICUT PRECAST CORP
Also Called: CT Precast
555 Fan Hill Rd (06468-1336)
PHONE..................................203 268-8688
Stephen Domizio, *President*
George T Domizio, *Vice Pres*
EMP: 23 **EST:** 1952
SQ FT: 20,000
SALES (est): 5.3MM **Privately Held**
WEB: www.ctprecast.com
SIC: 3272 Mfg Concrete Products

(G-2399)
CORNELL-CARR CO INC
626 Main St (06468-2808)
P.O. Box 253 (06468-0253)
PHONE..................................203 261-2529
Anton S Cornell, *President*
Philip H Gangnath, *Vice Pres*
Stan Szarek, *Treasurer*
Margaret Carr, *Shareholder*
▲ **EMP:** 35 **EST:** 1955
SQ FT: 22,000
SALES (est): 10.7MM **Privately Held**
WEB: www.cornell-carr.com
SIC: 3442 3647 3429 Mfg Metal Door/Sash/Trim Mfg Vehicle Light Equip Mfg Hardware

(G-2400)
CUSTOM CRFT KTCHNS BY RIZIO BR
8 Maple Dr (06468-1603)
PHONE..................................203 268-0271
Ralph Rizio, *President*
Mario E Rizio, *Vice Pres*
Millie B Rizio, *Treasurer*
Angelina Rizio, *Admin Sec*
EMP: 12
SQ FT: 18,000
SALES: 3MM **Privately Held**
WEB: www.enkeboll.com
SIC: 2541 1799 1751 Mfg Cabinetry Installs Kitchen Formica Counter Tops Wood Cabinetry And Entertainment Units

(G-2401)
DYNAMIC FLIGHT SYSTEMS
303 Stanley Rd (06468-1526)
PHONE..................................203 449-7211
Linda Harrington, *Owner*
EMP: 5
SALES: 1,000K **Privately Held**
SIC: 3728 Mfg Aircraft Parts/Equipment

(G-2402)
ENTREES MADE EASY
100 Cross Hill Rd (06468-2318)
PHONE..................................203 261-5777
Cathy Hayden, *Principal*
EMP: 3
SALES (est): 165.4K **Privately Held**
SIC: 2099 Mfg Food Preparations

(G-2403)
FSNB ENTERPRISES INC
Also Called: Minuteman Press
12 Woodacre Ln (06468-1125)
PHONE..................................203 254-1947
Frank V Giacalone, *President*
Frank Giacalone, *President*
EMP: 4
SQ FT: 3,500
SALES (est): 643.4K **Privately Held**
SIC: 2752 Comm Prtg Litho

(G-2404)
IMAGE ONE PRTG & GRAPHICS INC
838 Main St Ste L (06468-2834)
PHONE..................................203 459-1880
Edward Mathey, *President*
Marcel Leroux, *Admin Sec*
EMP: 3
SQ FT: 2,400
SALES (est): 307.1K **Privately Held**
SIC: 2759 Commercial Printing

(G-2405)
JURMAN METRICS INC
555 Hammertown Rd (06468-1310)
P.O. Box 223 (06468-0223)
PHONE..................................203 261-9388
David R Jurman, *President*
Rudolf Jurman, *Vice Pres*
Regina Vey, *Office Admin*
Jeannette Jurman, *Admin Sec*
EMP: 13
SQ FT: 5,000
SALES: 3.3MM **Privately Held**
WEB: www.jurmanmetrics.com
SIC: 3829 Mfg Mechanical Analytical Equipment Parts

(G-2406)
LD ASSOC LLC
16 Georges Ln (06468-3136)
PHONE..................................203 452-9393
Leon Barnaby, *Vice Pres*
EMP: 5
SALES (est): 339.1K **Privately Held**
SIC: 3442 Mfg Metal Doors/Sash/Trim

(G-2407)
M CUBED TECHNOLOGIES INC
921 Main St (06468-2811)
PHONE..................................203 452-2333
Mark Meiberger, *President*
EMP: 20
SALES (corp-wide): 1.3B **Publicly Held**
SIC: 3599 Mfg Industrial Machinery
HQ: M Cubed Technologies, Inc.
31 Pecks Ln Ste 8
Newtown CT 06470
203 304-2940

(G-2408)
MAGCOR INC
14 Wrabel Cir (06468-2669)
PHONE..................................203 445-0302
John Torrielli, *President*
EMP: 4
SALES (est): 467.8K **Privately Held**
SIC: 3291 3541 Mfg Abrasive Products Mfg Machine Tools-Cutting

(G-2409)
MUMM ENGINEERING INC
57 Wells Rd (06468-1266)
PHONE..................................203 445-9777
EMP: 4
SALES (est): 280K **Privately Held**
SIC: 3577 Mfg Industrial Parts

(G-2410)
NEW AGE MOTORSPORTS LLC
Also Called: Uh Motor Sports
501 Pepper St (06468-2670)
PHONE..................................203 268-1999
Edward C Ostrosky, *Partner*
Christopher Ostrosky, *Partner*
Ed Ostrosky, *Partner*
EMP: 3
SALES: 500K **Privately Held**
WEB: www.newage-motorsports.com
SIC: 2519 5521 Mfg Household Furniture Ret Used Automobiles

(G-2411)
NEW ENGLAND KITCHEN DESIGN CTR
401 Monroe Tpke Ste 4 (06468-2200)
PHONE..................................203 268-2626
F Scott Johnson, *President*
Nancy A Johnson, *Vice Pres*
EMP: 5
SALES (est): 676.7K **Privately Held**
WEB: www.newenglandkitchen.com
SIC: 2434 Mfg Wood Kitchen Cabinets

(G-2412)
NEW ENGLAND MATERIALS LLC
64 Cambridge Dr (06468-2661)
PHONE..................................203 261-5500
John Kimball, *Mng Member*
EMP: 3 **EST:** 2004
SALES (est): 512.9K **Privately Held**
SIC: 3281 Mfg Cut Stone/Products

(G-2413)
PRECISION ELECTRONIC ASSEMBLY
133 Bart Rd (06468-1108)
PHONE..................................203 452-1839
William Romaniello, *President*
EMP: 12
SQ FT: 5,000
SALES: 1MM **Privately Held**
SIC: 3679 3575 Mfg Electronic Components Mfg Computer Terminals

(G-2414)
PRO-LOCK USA LLC
62 Church St (06468-1819)
PHONE..................................203 382-3428
Noel Mara, *Mng Member*
Susan Mara, *Manager*
Neil Blair,
Susan Blair,
Susan F Mara,
EMP: 7
SALES (est): 460K **Privately Held**
SIC: 3429 Mfg/Ret Reusable Cable Locks

(G-2415)
PROLUME INC
525 Fan Hill Rd Ste E (06468-1346)
P.O. Box 444, Randolph VT (05060-0444)
PHONE..................................203 268-7778
Robert Johnstone, *Co-President*
James Carson, *Co-President*
EMP: 7
SQ FT: 4,000
SALES (est): 900K **Privately Held**
WEB: www.prolumeled.com
SIC: 3646 Mfg Commercial Lighting Fixtures

(G-2416)
PROUDFOOT COMPANY INC
588 Pepper St (06468-2672)
P.O. Box 276 (06468-0276)
PHONE..................................203 459-0031
EMP: 14 **EST:** 1965
SQ FT: 1,800
SALES: 350K **Privately Held**
SIC: 3275 Mfg Gypsum Products

(G-2417)
TAG PROMOTIONS INC
500 Purdy Hill Rd Ste 9 (06468-1661)
PHONE..................................800 909-4011
Chris Zinkel, *President*
▲ **EMP:** 4
SALES (est): 541.8K **Privately Held**
SIC: 3999 Mfg Misc Products

(G-2418)
TEK-AIR SYSTEMS INC
600 Pepper St (06468-2671)
PHONE..................................203 791-1400
Arnold B Siemer, *Ch of Bd*
Joseph Colletti Jr, *President*
Roger Bailey, *Corp Secy*
John Lombardi, *Engineer*
▲ **EMP:** 45
SALES (est): 7.4MM **Privately Held**
WEB: www.tek-air.com
SIC: 3829 3823 3822 Mfg Measuring/Controlling Devices Mfg Process Control Instruments Mfg Environmental Controls

(G-2419)
TELENITY INC
755 Main St Ste 7 (06468-2830)
PHONE..................................203 445-2000
Ilhan Bagoren, *CEO*
Esref Ozulkulu, *Corp Secy*
Yogesh S Bijlani, *Vice Pres*
EMP: 185 **EST:** 2000
SQ FT: 3,000
SALES (est): 13.4MM **Privately Held**
WEB: www.telenity.com
SIC: 7372 Prepackaged Software Services
PA: I3g Llc
755 Main St Ste 7
Monroe CT 06468
203 445-2000

(G-2420)
WHITE HILLS TOOL
8 Maple Dr (06468-1603)
PHONE..................................203 590-3143
Lou Havanich, *Owner*
EMP: 5
SALES: 125K **Privately Held**
SIC: 3545 7389 Mfg Machine Tool Accessories Business Services

Montville
New London County

(G-2421)
ALL-TIME MANUFACTURING CO INC
Bridge St (06353)
P.O. Box 37 (06353-0037)
PHONE..................................860 848-9258
David Brodie, *President*
EMP: 18 **EST:** 1946
SQ FT: 36,000
SALES (est): 3.4MM **Privately Held**
WEB: www.alltimemfg.com
SIC: 3442 1751 3089 Mfg Metal Doors/Sash/Trim Carpentry Contractor Mfg Plastic Products

(G-2422)
RAND-WHITNEY RECYCLING LLC
370 Route 163 (06353)
PHONE..................................860 848-1900
Robert Kraft, *President*
▲ **EMP:** 100
SALES (est): 31.6MM **Privately Held**
SIC: 2679 Mfg Converted Paper Products
PA: Kraft Group Llc
1 Patriot Pl
Foxboro MA 02035

Moodus
Middlesex County

(G-2423)
BROWNELL & COMPANY INC (PA)
423 E Haddam Moodus Rd (06469)
P.O. Box 362 (06469-0362)
PHONE..................................860 873-8625
Anthony A Ferraz, *President*
Cynthia Stackowitz, *Admin Sec*
▲ **EMP:** 12 **EST:** 1844
SQ FT: 100,000
SALES (est): 1.6MM **Privately Held**
WEB: www.brownellco.com
SIC: 2298 Mfg Cordage/Twine

(G-2424)
CARLTON FORGE WORKS
37 Eli Chapman Rd (06469-1403)
PHONE..................................860 873-9730
EMP: 20
SALES (corp-wide): 210.8B **Publicly Held**
SIC: 3462 Mfg Iron/Steel Forgings
HQ: Carlton Forge Works
7743 Adams St
Paramount CA 90723
562 633-1131

Moosup
Windham County

(G-2425)
DETOTEC NORTH AMERICA INC
363 Ekonk Hill Rd (06354-2215)
PHONE..................................860 230-0078
Timothy J O'Brien, *President*
Martha M O'Brien, *Admin Sec*
EMP: 3
SALES (est): 326.5K **Privately Held**
SIC: 2298 Mfg Cordage/Twine

(G-2426)
GRISWOLD LLC
Also Called: Griswold Rubber Company
1 River St (06354-1309)
P.O. Box 638 (06354-0638)
PHONE..................................860 564-3321
David Natorski, *CEO*
Jerald Esrick, *Admin Sec*
▼ **EMP:** 60 **EST:** 1949
SQ FT: 200,000
SALES (est): 15.1MM
SALES (corp-wide): 879MM **Publicly Held**
WEB: www.griswoldrubber.com
SIC: 3069 Manufacturing Fabricated Rubber Products
PA: Rogers Corporation
2225 W Chandler Blvd
Chandler AZ 85224
480 917-6000

(G-2427)
INNER OFFICE INC
49 Daggett St (06354-1236)
P.O. Box 847 (06354-0847)
PHONE..................................860 564-6777
Joy Johnson, *President*
EMP: 4
SALES (est): 360.7K **Privately Held**
WEB: www.inneroffice.com
SIC: 7372 7291 Business Support Services Taxes Bookkeeping Payroll Advertising Website Design

(G-2428)
TYPEISRIGHT
Also Called: Type Is Right The
11 E Main St (06354)
PHONE..................................860 564-0537
Shirley Hattayer, *Owner*
EMP: 3
SALES (est): 218.4K **Privately Held**
SIC: 2752 Commercial Printing

(G-2429)
VAPORIZER LLC
245 Main St (06354-1249)
PHONE..................................860 564-7225
Gunther Bowerman, *Mng Member*
Neil Cohen, *Mng Member*
Joseph Ducci, *Mng Member*
Kerri Frenette,
◆ **EMP:** 20
SALES (est): 4MM
SALES (corp-wide): 787.2MM **Privately Held**
SIC: 2097 Mfg Ice
PA: American Rock Salt Company Llc
3846 Retsof Rd
Retsof NY 14539
585 991-6878

Morris
Litchfield County

(G-2430)
AMERICAN BACKPLANE INC
355 Bantam Lake Rd (06763-1102)
PHONE..................................860 567-2360
Thomas L Zampini, *President*
Marie Zampini, *Admin Sec*
EMP: 35
SQ FT: 85,000
SALES (est): 5.4MM **Privately Held**
WEB: www.americanbackplane.com
SIC: 3672 Mfg Printed Circuit Boards

(G-2431)
BIRKETT WOODWORKING LLC
14 Benedict Rd (06763-1134)
PHONE..................................860 361-9142
Tobylynne C Birkett,
EMP: 3
SALES (est): 209.4K **Privately Held**
SIC: 2431 Mfg Millwork

(G-2432)
SUN CORP
27 Anderson Road Ext (06763-1910)
PHONE..................................860 567-0817
Edwin H Nearing III, *President*
EMP: 7
SQ FT: 3,000
SALES: 954K **Privately Held**
SIC: 3451 Mfg Screw Machine Products

Mystic
New London County

(G-2433)
ACME WIRE PRODUCTS CO INC
1 Broadway Ave (06355-2752)
P.O. Box 218 (06355-0218)
PHONE..................................860 572-0511
Mary P Fitzgerald, *President*
Michael A Planeta, *CFO*
Shelley Williams, *Data Proc Staff*
Edward Planeta Jr, *Admin Sec*
▲ **EMP:** 50
SQ FT: 73,000
SALES (est): 14.4MM **Privately Held**
WEB: www.acmewire.com
SIC: 3496 Mfg Misc Fabricated Wire Products

(G-2434)
AQUA MASSAGE INTERNATIONAL INC
Also Called: A M I
1101 Noank Ledyard Rd (06355-1318)
P.O. Box 808, Groton (06340-0808)
PHONE..................................860 536-3735
David Cote, *President*
Hilaire Cote, *Vice Pres*
▲ **EMP:** 17
SQ FT: 29,000
SALES (est): 2.5MM **Privately Held**
WEB: www.amiaqua.com
SIC: 3949 Mfg Sporting/Athletic Goods

(G-2435)
C J BRAND & SON
9 Overlook Ave (06355-2232)
PHONE..................................860 536-9266
Muriel Brand, *Owner*
Pam Green Brand, *Co-Owner*
Peter Grand, *Co-Owner*
EMP: 4
SALES: 210K **Privately Held**
SIC: 2434 1521 Mfg Wood Kitchen Cabinets Single-Family House Construction

(G-2436)
COMPANY OF CRAFTSMEN
43 W Main St (06355-2545)
PHONE..................................860 536-4189
Jack Steel, *Owner*
EMP: 3
SQ FT: 1,000
SALES (est): 203.4K **Privately Held**
SIC: 3269 3446 2499 5947 Mfg Pottery Products Mfg Architectural Metalwork Mfg Wood Products Ret Gifts/Novelties

(G-2437)
COMPONENTS FOR MFG LLC (PA)
800 Flanders Rd Unit 3-5 (06355-1347)
PHONE..................................860 245-5326
Tracey Jacey, *Owner*
EMP: 9
SALES (est): 1.4MM **Privately Held**
SIC: 3999 Mfg Misc Products

(G-2438)
DURANT MACHINE INC (PA)
Also Called: Dur-Mate
664 Noank Rd (06355-2119)
PHONE..................................860 536-7698
Walter F Durant, *President*
Russell Holly, *Vice Pres*
EMP: 6
SQ FT: 3,000
SALES: 600K **Privately Held**
WEB: www.duramate.com
SIC: 7692 3593 Mfg Fluid Power Cylinders Welding Repair

GEOGRAPHIC

(G-2439)
HUBBELL PREMISE WIRING INC
23 Clara Dr Ste 103 (06355-1959)
PHONE..................................860 535-8326
Gary Amato, *Principal*
Naved Khan, *Design Engr*
Bob Holder, *Sales Mgr*
Rafael Vale, *Sales Mgr*
Mark Bart, *Regl Sales Mgr*
EMP: 12
SALES (est): 34.9K
SALES (corp-wide): 4.4B **Publicly Held**
WEB: www.hubbell-premise.com
SIC: 3661 Mfg Telephone/Telegraph Apparatus
PA: Hubbell Incorporated
40 Waterview Dr
Shelton CT 06484
475 882-4000

(G-2440)
JENNINGS YACHT SERVICES
800 Flanders Rd (06355-1331)
P.O. Box 159, West Mystic (06388-0159)
PHONE..................................860 625-1368
Bill Jennings, *Owner*
EMP: 5
SQ FT: 800
SALES (est): 501.1K **Privately Held**
SIC: 3732 Boatbuilding/Repairing

(G-2441)
MACRIS INDUSTRIES INC
8 Summit St (06355-2722)
PHONE..................................860 514-7003
Harrison Macris, *President*
EMP: 4
SALES (est): 424.5K **Privately Held**
SIC: 3648 Mfg Lighting Equipment

(G-2442)
MADISON TECHNOLOGY INTL
Also Called: M T I
375 Allyn St Unit 1 (06355-1665)
PHONE..................................860 245-0245
George C Connolly, *President*
EMP: 6
SALES (est): 742.5K **Privately Held**
SIC: 3826 8731 Mfg Analytical Instruments Commercial Physical Research

(G-2443)
MCCLAVE PHILBRICK & GIBLIN
929 Flanders Rd (06355-1313)
PHONE..................................860 572-7710
Andrew Giblin, *Mng Member*
Benjamin Philbrick,
Edward McClave,
EMP: 5
SQ FT: 1,152
SALES (est): 692.1K **Privately Held**
SIC: 3732 Boatbuilding/Repairing

(G-2444)
MYSTIC KNOTWORK LLC
25 Cottrell St Ste 1 (06355-2668)
PHONE..................................860 889-3793
Matthew Beaudoin,
EMP: 12
SALES: 585K **Privately Held**
SIC: 3961 Mfg Costume Jewelry

(G-2445)
MYSTIC RIVER FOUNDRY LLC
2 Broadway Ave (06355-2702)
P.O. Box 121 (06355-0121)
PHONE..................................860 536-7634
Sharon E Hertxler, *Owner*
EMP: 3
SALES: 250K **Privately Held**
SIC: 3366 Copper Foundry

(G-2446)
MYSTIC STAINLESS & ALUM INC
23 Jackson Ave (06355-2824)
P.O. Box 282, West Mystic (06388-0282)
PHONE..................................860 536-2236
Charles Marques, *President*
Ann-Marie Pals, *Admin Sec*
EMP: 4
SALES: 469.8K **Privately Held**
WEB: www.mysticstainless.com
SIC: 3441 Fabricated Structural Metal

(G-2447)
ORION MANUFACTURING LLC
800 Flanders Rd Unit 4-8 (06355-1349)
PHONE..................................860 572-2921
Byron N Foote, *Founder*
Chris Foote, *Project Mgr*
Byron Foote,
Geoff Foote,
EMP: 8
SQ FT: 6,000
SALES (est): 915.2K **Privately Held**
SIC: 2431 Mfg Millwork

(G-2448)
PERENNIAL ELEMENTS LLC
15 Mystic Hill Rd (06355-3071)
PHONE..................................860 536-8593
EMP: 3
SALES (est): 246.6K **Privately Held**
SIC: 2819 Mfg Industrial Inorganic Chemicals

(G-2449)
RAYTHEON COMPANY
11 Main St Ste 3 (06355-3654)
PHONE..................................860 446-4900
Jeffrey Mazurek, *Manager*
EMP: 25
SALES (corp-wide): 27B **Publicly Held**
SIC: 3812 Mfg Search/Navigation Equipment
PA: Raytheon Company
870 Winter St
Waltham MA 02451
781 522-3000

(G-2450)
RECORD-JOURNAL NEWSPAPER
Also Called: Mystic River Press
15 Holmes St Ste 3 (06355-2659)
PHONE..................................860 536-9577
Peter Griggs, *Manager*
EMP: 4
SALES (corp-wide): 49.4MM **Privately Held**
SIC: 2711 Newspapers-Publishing/Printing
PA: Record-Journal Newspaper
500 S Broad St Ste 2
Meriden CT 06450
203 235-1661

(G-2451)
SHUTTERS & SAILS LLC
31 Water St (06355-2568)
PHONE..................................860 331-1510
EMP: 3 **EST:** 2015
SALES (est): 235.6K **Privately Held**
SIC: 3442 Mfg Metal Doors/Sash/Trim

(G-2452)
SWIFT INNOVATIONS LLC
800 Flanders Rd Bldg 5 (06355-1331)
PHONE..................................860 572-8322
Wade A Swift, *Principal*
EMP: 4
SALES (est): 413K **Privately Held**
SIC: 3441 Structural Metal Fabrication

(G-2453)
THOMAS S KLISE CO
42 Denison Ave (06355-2728)
PHONE..................................860 536-4200
Margaret Mary Klise, *President*
Elizabeth Klise, *Vice Pres*
EMP: 7
SQ FT: 10,000
SALES (est): 648.3K **Privately Held**
WEB: www.klise.com
SIC: 3999 Mfg Misc Products

(G-2454)
TRADE LABELS INC
28 Cottrell St Ste 28e (06355-2650)
P.O. Box 879, Stonington (06378-0879)
PHONE..................................860 535-4828
Lynn Rajewski, *General Mgr*
EMP: 3
SALES (est): 376.7K **Privately Held**
WEB: www.tradelabels.com
SIC: 2754 Gravure Commercial Printing

(G-2455)
VECTOR ENGINEERING INC
Also Called: Tylaska Marine Hardware
800 Flanders Rd Unit 1-4 (06355-1341)
PHONE..................................860 572-0422
Tim Tylaska, *President*
▼ **EMP:** 19 **EST:** 1993
SQ FT: 70,000
SALES: 1.5MM **Privately Held**
WEB: www.tylaska.com
SIC: 3429 8711 Mfg Hardware Engineering Services

(G-2456)
VOICE GLANCE LLC
12 Roosevelt Ave (06355-2809)
PHONE..................................800 260-3025
Chandrasekhar Naik, *President*
Richard Durishin, *Vice Pres*
EMP: 15
SALES: 600K **Privately Held**
SIC: 7372 Prepackaged Software Services

Naugatuck
New Haven County

(G-2457)
ADVANTAGE SHEET METAL MFG LLC
Also Called: Micro Matic
51 Elm St (06770-4157)
PHONE..................................203 720-0929
Tom Britton, *Opers Mgr*
Jon Hare, *Sls & Mktg Exec*
EMP: 46
SALES (est): 8MM **Privately Held**
SIC: 3444 Mfg Sheet Metalwork

(G-2458)
AHEAD COMMUNICATIONS SYSTEMS
6 Rubber Ave (06770-4117)
PHONE..................................203 720-0227
Anton Kaeslin, *CEO*
Linda Pagona, *Finance*
EMP: 72
SALES (est): 5.1MM **Privately Held**
WEB: www.aheadcomusa.com
SIC: 3661 4812 4813 Broadband Network

(G-2459)
AIRGAS USA LLC
Also Called: Tech Air
120 Rado Dr (06770-2211)
PHONE..................................203 729-2159
Kevin Haley, *Manager*
EMP: 6
SALES (corp-wide): 121.9MM **Privately Held**
WEB: www.techair.com
SIC: 2813 Whol Industrial Equipment
HQ: Airgas Usa, Llc
259 N Radnor Chester Rd
Radnor PA 19087
610 687-5253

(G-2460)
ANDREWS ARBORICULTURE LLC
860 Andrew Mountain Rd (06770-3621)
PHONE..................................203 565-8570
Russell Andrew, *Principal*
EMP: 4 **EST:** 2009
SALES (est): 426.3K **Privately Held**
SIC: 2879 Mfg Agricultural Chemicals

(G-2461)
ANOMATIC CORPORATION
50 Rado Dr Unit B (06770-2254)
PHONE..................................203 720-2367
Nick Sicilian, *Mfg Staff*
Mark Krin, *Branch Mgr*
EMP: 9
SALES (corp-wide): 620MM **Privately Held**
SIC: 3471 Plating/Polishing Service
HQ: Anomatic Corporation
8880 Innvation Campus Way
Johnstown OH 43031
740 522-2203

(G-2462)
BALTASAR & SONS INC
186 Sheridan Dr (06770-2033)
PHONE..................................203 723-0425
Jack Baltasar, *President*
Arthur Aniceto, *Admin Sec*
EMP: 3
SQ FT: 4,300
SALES: 200K **Privately Held**
SIC: 2013 5812 Mfg Prepared Meats Eating Place

(G-2463)
BRASS CITY TECHNOLOGIES LLC (PA)
1344 New Haven Rd (06770-5038)
PHONE..................................203 723-7021
Frank Testa,
Joe Testa,
EMP: 3
SQ FT: 5,000
SALES (est): 250K **Privately Held**
WEB: www.brasscitytech.com
SIC: 3545 3451 Mfg Of Cutting Tools For Machine Tools & Screw Machine Products

(G-2464)
BUSINESS CARDS TOMORROW INC
Also Called: B C T
69 Raytkwich Rd (06770-2223)
PHONE..................................203 723-5858
Jim Redwanz, *Branch Mgr*
EMP: 6
SALES (corp-wide): 1.2MM **Privately Held**
SIC: 2752 Comm Prtg Litho
PA: Business Cards Tomorrow, Inc.
3000 Ne 30th Pl Fl 5
Fort Lauderdale FL 33306
954 563-1224

(G-2465)
CADI CO INC (PA)
Also Called: Cadi Company
60 Rado Dr (06770-2211)
P.O. Box 1127 (06770-1127)
PHONE..................................203 729-1111
Rocco Capozzi, *President*
Dana M Capozzi, *Vice Pres*
Dana Capozzi, *Controller*
Peter Tatalias, *Admin Sec*
▲ **EMP:** 35
SQ FT: 33,000
SALES (est): 8.4MM **Privately Held**
WEB: www.cadicompany.com
SIC: 3548 Mfg Welding Apparatus

(G-2466)
CKS PACKAGING INC
10 Great Hill Rd (06770-2224)
P.O. Box 979 (06770-0979)
PHONE..................................203 729-0716
Bill Padgett, *Manager*
EMP: 100
SALES (corp-wide): 496.3MM **Privately Held**
SIC: 3089 Whol Nondurable Goods
PA: C.K.S. Packaging, Inc.
350 Great Sw Pkwy
Atlanta GA 30336
404 691-8900

(G-2467)
CON-TEC INC
41 Raytkwich Rd (06770-2223)
PHONE..................................203 723-8942
Craig Corbett, *President*
EMP: 12
SQ FT: 5,000
SALES (est): 1.8MM **Privately Held**
WEB: www.con-tecinc.com
SIC: 3599 Mfg Industrial Machinery

(G-2468)
CONNECTICUT SIGN CRAFT INC
47 Cherry St (06770-4109)
PHONE..................................203 729-0706
David Dunn, *President*
Robert Nepe, *Vice Pres*
Bill Dunn, *Admin Sec*
EMP: 4
SQ FT: 2,500

SALES (est): 320K **Privately Held**
SIC: 3993 Mfg Electric And Non-Electric Signs

(G-2469)
CONVERTER CONSULTANTS LLC
1058 Rubber Ave (06770-1501)
PHONE..............................203 729-1031
Alec Wargo,
Ilse Wargo,
EMP: 5
SQ FT: 4,000
SALES: 650K **Privately Held**
WEB: www.converterconsultants.com
SIC: 3568 Power Electronic Equipment & Components

(G-2470)
EAST COAST METAL HOSE INC
41 Raytkwich Rd (06770-2223)
P.O. Box 978 (06770-0978)
PHONE..............................203 723-7459
Lloyd Corbett, *President*
Michelle Baranoski, *Vice Pres*
▼ **EMP:** 7
SALES (est): 934.2K **Privately Held**
WEB: www.eastcoastmetalhose.com
SIC: 3599 Mfg Flexible Metal Hose

(G-2471)
EASTERN COMPANY (PA)
112 Bridge St (06770-2903)
P.O. Box 460 (06770-0460)
PHONE..............................203 729-2255
James A Mitarotonda, *Ch of Bd*
August M Vlak, *President*
Angelo M Labbadia, *Vice Pres*
Carmen Mitcho, *Vice Pres*
John L Sullivan III, *CFO*
EMP: 40 **EST:** 1912
SQ FT: 8,000
SALES: 234.2MM **Publicly Held**
WEB: www.easterncompany.com
SIC: 3452 3316 2439 3429 Mfg Bolts/Screws/Rivets Mfg Cold-Rolled Steel Mfg Structural Wd Member Mfg Hardware

(G-2472)
ELECTRIC CABLE COMPOUNDS INC
108 Rado Dr (06770-2211)
PHONE..............................203 723-2590
Ida L Fridland, *CEO*
Eugene Fridland, *President*
◆ **EMP:** 60
SQ FT: 60,000
SALES: 55MM **Privately Held**
WEB: www.electriccablecompounds.com
SIC: 3087 Custom Compounding-Purchased Resins

(G-2473)
FLABEG TECHNICAL GLASS US CORP
451 Church St (06770-2834)
PHONE..............................203 729-5227
Patrick McGinley, *President*
Michael Priga, *CFO*
▲ **EMP:** 35 **EST:** 1928
SQ FT: 50,000
SALES (est): 6.2MM
SALES (corp-wide): 177.9K **Privately Held**
WEB: www.flabeg.com
SIC: 3231 3229 3827 Mfg Products-Purchased Glass Mfg Pressed/Blown Glass Mfg Optical Instruments/Lenses
HQ: Flabeg Us Holding Inc.
1000 Church St
Naugatuck CT 06770

(G-2474)
FREIHOFER CHARLES BAKING CO
1041 New Haven Rd (06770-4746)
PHONE..............................203 729-4545
Dennis Brown, *Manager*
EMP: 4
SALES (est): 197K **Privately Held**
SIC: 2051 Mfg Bread/Related Products

(G-2475)
GARMAC SCREW MACHINE INC
70 Great Hill Rd (06770-2224)
P.O. Box 1338 (06770-1338)
PHONE..............................203 723-6911
Gerald Gardino, *President*
James Mac Burney, *Vice Pres*
Anthony Gardino, *Admin Sec*
EMP: 16
SQ FT: 5,000
SALES (est): 2.8MM **Privately Held**
SIC: 3451 Mfg Screw Machine Parts

(G-2476)
H BARBER & SONS INC
15 Raytkwich Rd (06770-2223)
PHONE..............................203 729-9000
John H Barber, *President*
James P Barber, *Vice Pres*
Chris Kelly, *Sls & Mktg Exec*
◆ **EMP:** 20
SQ FT: 5,000
SALES (est): 6.4MM **Privately Held**
WEB: www.hbarber.com
SIC: 3531 Mfg Construction Machinery

(G-2477)
HG TECH LLC
162 Spencer St (06770-4552)
PHONE..............................203 632-5946
Henry Garcia,
EMP: 4 **EST:** 2009
SALES (est): 250K **Privately Held**
SIC: 3571 Mfg Electronic Computers

(G-2478)
HOWARD ENGINEERING LLC
687 Wooster St (06770-3135)
P.O. Box 6211, Wolcott (06716-0211)
PHONE..............................203 729-5213
Lesley H Swirski, *CEO*
Brian N Howard, *President*
Holley E Duffy, *Asst Sec*
EMP: 44
SQ FT: 32,840
SALES (est): 8.4MM **Privately Held**
WEB: www.howardengineering.com
SIC: 3469 3452 Mfg Metal Stampings Mfg Bolts/Screws/Rivets

(G-2479)
ILLINOIS TOOL WORKS INC
Also Called: ITW Nutmeg
29 Rado Dr (06770-2220)
PHONE..............................203 720-1676
EMP: 33
SQ FT: 24,470
SALES (corp-wide): 14.7B **Publicly Held**
SIC: 3965 3469 3444 Mfg Fastener/Button/Pins Mfg Metal Stampings Mfg Sheet Metalwork
PA: Illinois Tool Works Inc.
155 Harlem Ave
Glenview IL 60025
847 724-7500

(G-2480)
ITW POWERTRAIN FASTENING
29 Rado Dr (06770-2220)
PHONE..............................203 720-1676
Jim Dara, *President*
EMP: 4
SALES (est): 78.2K **Privately Held**
SIC: 3965 Mfg Fasteners/Buttons/Pins

(G-2481)
K & E AUTO MACHINE L L C
Also Called: Mike's Engine Stand
628 Prospect St (06770-3120)
PHONE..............................203 723-7189
Michael Adomaitis,
EMP: 3
SALES (est): 283.4K **Privately Held**
SIC: 3599 Mfg Industrial Machinery

(G-2482)
KAMMETAL INC (PA)
300 Great Hill Rd (06770-2000)
PHONE..............................718 722-9991
Samuel Kusack, *President*
Alastair Kusack, *Vice Pres*
EMP: 28
SALES (est): 8.1MM **Privately Held**
SIC: 3446 Mfg Architectural Metalwork

(G-2483)
LANXESS SOLUTIONS US INC
400 Elm St (06770-4556)
P.O. Box 490 (06770-0490)
PHONE..............................203 723-2237
Richard Hooper, *Manager*
Susan V Bryan, *Manager*
EMP: 75
SALES (corp-wide): 7.9B **Privately Held**
WEB: www.cromptoncorp.com
SIC: 2879 Mfg Agricultural Chemicals
HQ: Lanxess Solutions Us Inc.
2 Armstrong Rd Ste 101
Shelton CT 06484
203 573-2000

(G-2484)
MINI LLC
66 Church St (06770-4112)
PHONE..............................203 464-5495
Derrick Lee,
John Migliore,
EMP: 6
SALES (est): 152.3K **Privately Held**
SIC: 3572 Mfg Computer Storage Devices

(G-2485)
MJM MARGA LLC
28 Raytkwich Rd (06770-2222)
PHONE..............................203 729-0600
Mario Mazzettini, *Mng Member*
Joe Mazzettini,
EMP: 7
SALES (est): 993.1K **Privately Held**
SIC: 3469 Mfg Metal Stampings

(G-2486)
NAUGATUCK ELEC INDUS SUP LLC
68 Radnor Ave (06770-2006)
PHONE..............................203 723-1082
Robert M Schmidt,
Robert F Schmidt,
EMP: 3
SALES: 250K **Privately Held**
SIC: 3699 Mfg Electrical Equipment/Supplies

(G-2487)
NAUGATUCK RECOVERY INC (HQ)
300 Great Hill Rd (06770-2000)
PHONE..............................203 723-1122
Fax: 203 729-4977
▲ **EMP:** 35
SALES (est): 4.5MM
SALES (corp-wide): 7.8MM **Privately Held**
WEB: www.lavatec.com
SIC: 3582 Mfg Commercial Laundry Equipment
PA: Lavatec Laundry Technology Gmbh
Wannenackerstr. 53
Heilbronn 74078
713 129-80

(G-2488)
NAUGATUCK STAIR COMPANY INC
51 Elm St (06770-4157)
P.O. Box 384 (06770-0384)
PHONE..............................203 729-7134
Henry Carrier, *President*
Ginette Carrier, *Vice Pres*
EMP: 16
SQ FT: 7,000
SALES (est): 2.1MM **Privately Held**
SIC: 2431 3446 Mfg Millwork Mfg Architectural Metalwork

(G-2489)
PHOENIX COMPANY OF CHICAGO INC (PA)
22 Great Hill Rd (06770-2224)
PHONE..............................630 595-2300
Bernard C Machura, *Ch of Bd*
Michael B Machura, *President*
Doris G Machura, *Corp Secy*
▲ **EMP:** 60 **EST:** 1969
SQ FT: 550,000
SALES: 16MM **Privately Held**
WEB: www.mil-coninc.com
SIC: 3678 5063 5065 Mfg Electronic Connectors Whol Electrical Equipment Whol Electronic Parts/Equipment

(G-2490)
PISANI STEEL FABRICATION INC
360 Prospect St Ste 1 (06770-3196)
P.O. Box 2612, Waterbury (06723-2612)
PHONE..............................203 720-0679
Joseph Pisani, *President*
Frank Pisani, *Vice Pres*
Maryjean Pisani, *Admin Sec*
EMP: 5
SQ FT: 10,000
SALES (est): 769.7K **Privately Held**
SIC: 3441 Structural Steel Fabrication For Construction Industry

(G-2491)
PRAXAIR INC
120 Rado Dr (06770-2211)
PHONE..............................203 720-2477
Dennis Reilley, *President*
EMP: 20 **Privately Held**
SIC: 2813 Mfg Industrial Gases
HQ: Praxair, Inc.
10 Riverview Dr
Danbury CT 06810
203 837-2000

(G-2492)
QUALITY SHEET METAL INC
17 Clark Rd (06770-5097)
PHONE..............................203 729-2244
Lawrence H Torto Jr, *President*
EMP: 17 **EST:** 1976
SQ FT: 10,000
SALES (est): 3.3MM **Privately Held**
WEB: www.qualitysheetmetal.com
SIC: 3444 Mfg Sheet Metalwork

(G-2493)
RELIABLE SILVER CORPORATION
302 Platts Mill Rd (06770-2036)
P.O. Box 750, Waterbury (06720-0750)
PHONE..............................203 574-7732
Arlo Ellison, *President*
EMP: 11
SQ FT: 13,000
SALES (est): 3.1MM **Privately Held**
WEB: www.reliablesilver.com
SIC: 3339 Primary Nonferrous Metal Producer

(G-2494)
RONDO AMERICA INCORPORATED
Also Called: Rondo Packaging Systems
209 Great Hill Rd (06770-2096)
PHONE..............................203 723-5831
James M Simkins, *President*
Morton H Simkins, *Treasurer*
Stephanie Simkins, *Admin Sec*
EMP: 200 **EST:** 1949
SQ FT: 55,000
SALES (est): 37.4MM **Privately Held**
WEB: www.rondopackaging.com
SIC: 2652 3569 Mfg Setup Paperboard Boxes Mfg General Industrial Machinery
PA: Simkins Corporation
1636 Valley Rd
Jenkintown PA 19046
215 739-4033

(G-2495)
SEMCO TOOL MANUFACTURING CO
30 Naugatuck Dr (06770-2094)
PHONE..............................203 723-7411
Thomas Semeraro, *President*
Rose Semeraro, *Vice Pres*
EMP: 5
SQ FT: 10,000
SALES (est): 634.1K **Privately Held**
SIC: 3469 Mfg Metal Stampings

(G-2496)
SPECIALTY METALS AND FAB
51 Elm St (06770-4157)
PHONE..............................203 509-5028
EMP: 4
SALES (est): 433.6K **Privately Held**
SIC: 3499 Mfg Misc Fabricated Metal Products

GEOGRAPHIC

(G-2497)
SPERRY AUTOMATICS CO INC
1372 New Haven Rd (06770-5039)
P.O. Box 717 (06770-0717)
PHONE....................................203 729-4589
Charles A Pugliese, *President*
David A Pugliese, *Vice Pres*
Richard Pugliese, *Treasurer*
EMP: 20 **EST:** 1963
SQ FT: 12,000
SALES (est): 3.5MM **Privately Held**
WEB: www.sperryautomatics.com
SIC: 3451 5085 3541 Mfg Screw Machine Products Whol Industrial Supplies Mfg Machine Tools-Cutting

(G-2498)
UNIMETAL SURFACE FINISHING LLC
Also Called: Donham Crafts
15 E Waterbury Rd (06770-2138)
P.O. Box 1187 (06770-1187)
PHONE....................................203 729-8244
Pat Hayden, *President*
Jim Murphy, *Manager*
EMP: 30
SALES (corp-wide): 22.7MM **Privately Held**
SIC: 3471 Plating/Polishing Service
PA: Unimetal Surface Finishing, Llc
135 S Main St
Thomaston CT 06787
860 283-0271

(G-2499)
UNITED AVIONICS INC
Also Called: Ua
38 Great Hill Rd (06770-2224)
PHONE....................................203 723-1404
Richard F Nicolari, *President*
Thomas D Bunk, *President*
Joseph Cardella Sr, *Vice Pres*
Louis Nicoletti, *Vice Pres*
William Nicoletti, *Vice Pres*
EMP: 48
SQ FT: 22,000
SALES (est): 10.5MM **Privately Held**
WEB: www.unitedavionicsinc.com
SIC: 3728 Mfg Aircraft Parts/Equipment

(G-2500)
VITEK RESEARCH CORPORATION
33 Sheridan Dr (06770-2039)
P.O. Box 315, Derby (06418-0315)
PHONE....................................203 735-1813
Robert Evans, *President*
EMP: 13 **EST:** 1968
SQ FT: 10,000
SALES: 1.1MM **Privately Held**
WEB: www.vitekres.com
SIC: 3479 8732 Coating/Engraving Service Commercial Nonphysical Research

New Britain
Hartford County

(G-2501)
A-1 MACHINING CO
235 John Downey Dr (06051-2905)
PHONE....................................860 223-6420
David S Bovenizer, *CEO*
Thomas Daily, *President*
Tom Stanger, *Engineer*
Van H MAI, *Admin Sec*
▼ **EMP:** 52
SQ FT: 36,800
SALES (est): 9.9MM
SALES (corp-wide): 31.3MM **Privately Held**
WEB: www.a1machining.com
SIC: 3724 3728 3621 Mfg Aircraft Engines/Parts Mfg Aircraft Parts/Equipment Mfg Motors/Generators
PA: Lionheart Holdings Llc
54 Friends Ln Ste 125
Newtown PA 18940
215 283-8400

(G-2502)
ACE CABINET COMPANY
321 Ellis St Ste 18 (06051-3504)
PHONE....................................860 225-6111
EMP: 3 **EST:** 1981
SALES (est): 200K **Privately Held**
SIC: 2541 Mfg Wood Partitions/Fixtures

(G-2503)
ACME MONACO CORPORATION (PA)
75 Winchell Rd (06052-1097)
PHONE....................................860 224-1349
Michael J Karabin, *CEO*
Thomas Sebastian, *President*
Mark Jarrett, *General Mgr*
Lucas Karabin, *Exec VP*
Rebecca Karabin-Ahern, *Exec VP*
▲ **EMP:** 125
SQ FT: 37,520
SALES (est): 24.4MM **Privately Held**
WEB: www.acmemonaco.com
SIC: 3841 3843 3469 3493 Mfg Surgical/Med Instr Mfg Dental Equip/Supply Mfg Metal Stampings Mfg Steel Spring-Nonwire Mfg Misc Fab Wire Prdts

(G-2504)
ADAM Z GOLAS (PA)
Also Called: Zag Machine & Tool Co
99 John Downey Dr (06051-2916)
P.O. Box 1120 (06050-1120)
PHONE....................................860 224-7178
Adam Z Golas, *Owner*
EMP: 8
SQ FT: 50,000
SALES (est): 2.1MM **Privately Held**
SIC: 3547 Mfg Rolling Mill Machinery

(G-2505)
ADDITIVE EXPERTS LLC
1 Liberty Sq (06051-2637)
PHONE....................................860 351-3324
Geza Czako III, *Mng Member*
EMP: 5
SALES (est): 150.7K **Privately Held**
SIC: 3999 Mfg Misc Products

(G-2506)
ADKINS PRINTING COMPANY
40 South St Ste 2 (06051-3574)
P.O. Box 2440 (06050-2440)
PHONE....................................800 228-9745
Scott Pechout, *President*
EMP: 21 **EST:** 1880
SQ FT: 18,000
SALES (est): 3.1MM **Privately Held**
SIC: 2752 5943 5112 2789 Lithographic Coml Print Ret Stationery Whol Stationery/Offc Sup Bookbinding/Related Work

(G-2507)
AK STUCCO LLC
47 Hatch St (06053-2534)
PHONE....................................860 832-9589
Alfred Kania, *Principal*
EMP: 4
SALES (est): 306.5K **Privately Held**
SIC: 3299 Mfg Nonmetallic Mineral Products

(G-2508)
ALVARIUM BEER COMPANY LLC
30 Biltmore St (06053-2133)
PHONE....................................860 306-3857
Christopher Degasero, *Principal*
Brain Bugnacki, *Co-Owner*
Chris Degasero, *Co-Owner*
Michael Larson, *Co-Owner*
EMP: 3
SALES (est): 125.5K **Privately Held**
SIC: 2082 5921 5963 Mfg Malt Beverages Ret Alcoholic Beverages Direct Retail Sales

(G-2509)
AMMUNITION STOR COMPONENTS LLC
206 Newington Ave (06051-2130)
PHONE....................................860 225-3548
Paul Sliwinski, *VP Opers*
Barry Bergen, *Manager*
EMP: 8 **EST:** 2011
SALES (est): 1MM **Privately Held**
SIC: 3949 Mfg Sporting/Athletic Goods

(G-2510)
ATLAS METALLIZING INC
5 East St (06051-3609)
PHONE....................................860 827-9777
Elizabeth Mierkiewicz, *President*
Tom Mierkiewicz, *Vice Pres*
▲ **EMP:** 13
SQ FT: 16,000
SALES (est): 1.8MM **Privately Held**
WEB: www.atlasmetallizing.com
SIC: 3081 Mfg Unsupported Plastic Film/Sheet

(G-2511)
AVERYS BEVERAGE LLC
520 Corbin Ave (06052-1606)
PHONE....................................860 224-0830
Rob Metz, *General Mgr*
EMP: 5
SALES (est): 520K **Privately Held**
WEB: www.averysoda.com
SIC: 2086 5963 Mfg Soft Drinks/Bottled Water Delivery

(G-2512)
B & F MACHINE CO INC
145 Edgewood Ave (06051-4154)
PHONE....................................860 225-6349
Federico Bragoni, *President*
Carl Francalangia, *Vice Pres*
Robert Riccini, *Project Mgr*
Tom Blade, *Engineer*
Gene Coburn, *Engineer*
▲ **EMP:** 100
SQ FT: 37,400
SALES (est): 32.2MM **Privately Held**
WEB: www.bfmachine.com
SIC: 3599 7692 Mfg Industrial Machinery Welding Repair

(G-2513)
BARILE PRINTERS LLC
43 Viets St (06053-3988)
P.O. Box 2628 (06050-2628)
PHONE....................................860 224-0127
Joseph Barile, *Mng Member*
EMP: 6
SQ FT: 3,000
SALES: 500K **Privately Held**
SIC: 2752 5999 5099 Lithographic Commercial Printing Ret Misc Merchandise Whol Durable Goods

(G-2514)
BLACK & DECKER (US) INC
Also Called: Stanley Black and Decker
700 Stanley Dr (06053-1679)
PHONE....................................860 225-5111
EMP: 7
SALES (corp-wide): 13.9B **Publicly Held**
SIC: 3546 3634 Mfg Powerdriven Handtool Mfg Elec Housewares/Fans
HQ: Black & Decker (U.S.) Inc.
1000 Stanley Dr
New Britain CT 06053
860 225-5111

(G-2515)
BLACK & DECKER (US) INC (HQ)
1000 Stanley Dr (06053-1675)
PHONE....................................860 225-5111
Nolan D Archibald, *President*
Charles E Fenton, *Senior VP*
Barbara B Lucas, *Senior VP*
Michael D Mangan, *Senior VP*
Mark M Rothleitner, *Senior VP*
◆ **EMP:** 3
SQ FT: 100,000
SALES (est): 1.3B
SALES (corp-wide): 13.9B **Publicly Held**
WEB: www.dewalt.com
SIC: 3546 3634 Mfg Powerdriven Handtool Mfg Elec Housewares/Fans
PA: Stanley Black & Decker, Inc.
1000 Stanley Dr
New Britain CT 06053
860 225-5111

(G-2516)
BRYT MANUFACTURING
23 John St (06051-2724)
PHONE....................................860 224-4772
Stanley Szylobryt, *Owner*
Matthew Szylobryt, *Partner*
EMP: 4
SQ FT: 3,500
SALES: 150K **Privately Held**
SIC: 3599 Mfg Industrial Machinery

(G-2517)
CARRIER MANUFACTURING INC
70a Saint Claire Ave (06051-1631)
PHONE....................................860 223-2264
Michael Carrier, *President*
EMP: 6
SQ FT: 3,000
SALES (est): 1MM **Privately Held**
SIC: 3369 Mfg Aerospace Parts

(G-2518)
CCC MEDIA LLC
1 Court St (06051-2262)
P.O. Box 1090 (06050-1090)
PHONE....................................860 225-4601
Michael Schroeder, *President*
Harry J Binder, *Principal*
EMP: 5 **EST:** 2014
SQ FT: 1,500
SALES (est): 163.6K **Privately Held**
SIC: 2711 Newspapers-Publishing/Printing

(G-2519)
CENTRAL CONN CMMUNICATIONS LLC
Also Called: New Britain Herald , The
1 Court St Fl 4 (06051-2259)
P.O. Box 1090 (06050-1090)
PHONE....................................860 225-4601
Janet Schroeder, *Controller*
Michael Schroeder,
EMP: 80
SALES: 950K **Privately Held**
SIC: 2711 Newspapers-Publishing/Printing

(G-2520)
CENTRAL PALLET & BOX
271 John Downey Dr (06051-2905)
PHONE....................................860 224-4416
Michael T Hannifan, *Owner*
EMP: 13
SQ FT: 12,000
SALES: 1.2MM **Privately Held**
SIC: 2448 Mfg Wooden Pallets

(G-2521)
CONNECTICUT VALLEY BINDERY
1 Hartford Sq Ste 28w (06052-1179)
PHONE....................................860 229-7637
Kevin Hubert, *President*
Dan Valente, *Vice Pres*
Tracey Hubert, *Treasurer*
Tracy Hubert, *Treasurer*
▼ **EMP:** 30 **EST:** 1980
SQ FT: 37,598
SALES (est): 3.1MM **Privately Held**
WEB: www.connvalleybindery.com
SIC: 2789 Bookbinding/Related Work

(G-2522)
CONTINENTAL MACHINE TL CO INC
533 John Downey Dr (06051-2435)
PHONE....................................860 223-2896
Tadeusz Malkowski, *President*
Wanda Malkowski, *Corp Secy*
EMP: 97 **EST:** 1983
SQ FT: 24,800
SALES (est): 16.8MM **Privately Held**
WEB: www.continentalmachinetool.com
SIC: 3599 3714 3728 3484 Mfg Industrial Machinery Mfg Motor Vehicle Parts Mfg Aircraft Parts/Equip Mfg Small Arms

(G-2523)
CONTORQ COMPONENTS LLC
433 John Downey Dr (06051-2909)
PHONE....................................860 225-3366
John McCarthy Jr, *President*
EMP: 11
SALES (est): 2.7MM **Privately Held**
SIC: 3452 Mfg Bolts/Screws/Rivets

(G-2524)
CREED-MONARCH INC
1 Pucci Park (06051)
P.O. Box 550 (06050-0550)
PHONE....................................860 225-7884
Richard Creed, *President*
Deborah Boynton, *Corp Secy*
David Creed, *Vice Pres*

▲ = Import ▼=Export
◆ =Import/Export

Don Creed, *Vice Pres*
Jim Lundebjerg, *Engineer*
▲ **EMP:** 275 **EST:** 1952
SQ FT: 150,000
SALES (est): 62.4MM **Privately Held**
WEB: www.creedmonarch.com
SIC: 3451 Mfg Screw Machine Products

(G-2525)
D B F INDUSTRIES INC
Also Called: DB&f Industries
145 Edgewood Ave (06051-4109)
PHONE..................................860 827-8283
Carl Francalangia, *President*
Federico Bragoni, *Vice Pres*
EMP: 40
SQ FT: 7,000
SALES (est): 1.5MM **Privately Held**
SIC: 7692 Fabrication And Welding Service

(G-2526)
DAY MACHINE SYSTEMS INC
221 South St Bldg F2 (06051-3650)
P.O. Box 2667 (06050-2667)
PHONE..................................860 229-3440
Jim Kostin, *President*
Gary Goen, *Plant Mgr*
EMP: 13 **EST:** 1984
SQ FT: 14,500
SALES (est): 2MM **Privately Held**
SIC: 3451 3559 Mfg Screw Machine Products Mfg Misc Industry Machinery

(G-2527)
DECKS R US
35 Carlton St Fl 2 (06053-3101)
PHONE..................................860 505-0726
Vasyl Dyakun, *Principal*
EMP: 3
SALES (est): 242.9K **Privately Held**
SIC: 2421 Sawmill/Planing Mill

(G-2528)
DSO MANUFACTURING COMPANY INC
390 John Downey Dr (06051-2932)
PHONE..................................860 224-2641
Carl Bernard Deleo, *President*
Tina Joan Deleo, *Vice Pres*
EMP: 25 **EST:** 1947
SQ FT: 35,000
SALES (est): 5.7MM **Privately Held**
WEB: www.dsomfg.com
SIC: 3599 Mfg Industrial Machinery

(G-2529)
E R HITCHCOCK COMPANY
Also Called: Hitchcock Printers
191 John Downey Dr (06051-2945)
PHONE..................................860 229-2024
Edward R Young, *President*
Dane Baclaski, *Vice Pres*
Melissa Ramos, *Accounts Mgr*
Constance M Young, *Shareholder*
Pat Cote, *Admin Asst*
EMP: 33 **EST:** 1895
SQ FT: 22,000
SALES (est): 6.3MM **Privately Held**
SIC: 2752 2791 2789 Lithographic Commercial Printing Typesetting Services Bookbinding/Related Work

(G-2530)
EK-RIS CABLE COMPANY INC
503 Burritt St Apt 7 (06053-3627)
PHONE..................................860 223-4327
Gary J Robinson, *President*
Charles Wusterbarth, *Treasurer*
Dolores M Robinson, *Admin Sec*
EMP: 45
SALES (est): 7.6MM **Privately Held**
WEB: www.ekriscable.com
SIC: 3643 Mfg Conductive Wiring Devices

(G-2531)
ENJET AERO NEW BRITAIN LLC
150 John Downey Dr (06051-2904)
PHONE..................................860 356-0330
Bruce Breckenridge, *CEO*
Christopher Ferraro, *CFO*
EMP: 134
SQ FT: 63,000
SALES (est): 4MM
SALES (corp-wide): 42.7MM **Privately Held**
SIC: 3728 Mfg Aircraft Parts/Equipment
PA: Enjet Aero, Llc
9401 Indian Creek Pkwy
Overland Park KS 66210
913 717-7396

(G-2532)
EVERYTHING 2 WHEELS LLC
230 South St (06051-3637)
PHONE..................................860 225-2453
Mark Furrow, *Principal*
EMP: 5
SALES (est): 476K **Privately Held**
SIC: 3312 Blast Furnace-Steel Works

(G-2533)
EZ WELDING LLC
244 Garry Dr (06052-1106)
PHONE..................................860 707-3100
EMP: 8
SALES (est): 88.7K **Privately Held**
SIC: 7692 Welding Repair

(G-2534)
FITNESS ELEMNET
267 Chapman St (06051-4805)
PHONE..................................860 670-2855
EMP: 3
SALES (est): 171.6K **Privately Held**
SIC: 2819 Industrial Inorganic Chemicals, Nec

(G-2535)
GLOBAL PALLET SOLUTIONS LLC
271 John Downey Dr (06051-2905)
PHONE..................................860 826-5000
Michael T Hannifan, *Manager*
EMP: 3
SALES (est): 226.3K **Privately Held**
SIC: 2448 Mfg Wood Pallets/Skids

(G-2536)
GRIMCO INC
221 South St Unit G1 (06051-3650)
PHONE..................................800 542-9941
Sarah Monestero, *Branch Mgr*
EMP: 5
SALES (corp-wide): 97.5MM **Privately Held**
WEB: www.grimco.com
SIC: 3081 Mfg Signs/Advertising Specialties
PA: Grimco, Inc.
11745 Sppngton Brracks Rd
Saint Louis MO 63127
636 305-0088

(G-2537)
GUIDA-SEIBERT DAIRY COMPANY (PA)
Also Called: Guida's Milk & Ice Cream
433 Park St (06051-2700)
P.O. Box 2110 (06050-2110)
PHONE..................................860 224-2404
Pat Panko, *CEO*
Michael Young, *President*
Alex Bachelor, *Vice Pres*
Joel Clark, *Vice Pres*
James Guida, *Vice Pres*
EMP: 225
SQ FT: 70,000
SALES (est): 74.2MM **Privately Held**
WEB: www.supercow.com
SIC: 2026 2033 5143 5149 Mfg Fluid Milk Mfg Canned Fruits/Vegtbl Whol Dairy Products Whol Groceries

(G-2538)
HAJAN LLC
788 W Main St (06053-3856)
PHONE..................................860 223-2005
Mukhtar Ahmed, *Principal*
EMP: 5
SALES (est): 484.9K **Privately Held**
SIC: 2869 Mfg Industrial Organic Chemicals

(G-2539)
HSB AIRCRAFT COMPONENTS LLC
80 Production Ct (06051-2917)
P.O. Box 342, East Berlin (06023-0342)
PHONE..................................860 505-7349
Henry Wasik, *Mng Member*
Henry W Wasik Jr,
EMP: 12
SQ FT: 5,000
SALES (est): 1.6MM **Privately Held**
SIC: 3724 Mfg Aircraft Engines/Parts

(G-2540)
INCURE INC
1 Hartford Sq Ste 16w (06052-1175)
P.O. Box 16 (06050-0016)
PHONE..................................860 748-2979
William Tan, *President*
EMP: 3 **Privately Held**
SIC: 2891 3648 Mfg Adhesives/Sealants Mfg Lighting Equipment

(G-2541)
INTEGRA-CAST INC
265 Newington Ave (06051-2129)
PHONE..................................860 225-7600
David Arcesi, *President*
Lori Theriault, *Safety Dir*
Matt Smith, *Executive*
EMP: 62
SQ FT: 30,000
SALES: 11MM **Privately Held**
WEB: www.integracast.com
SIC: 3365 3599 3364 3324 Aluminum Foundry Mfg Industrial Machinery Mfg Nonfrs Die-Castings Steel Investment Foundry

(G-2542)
INTEGRO LLC
30 Peter Ct (06051-3545)
PHONE..................................860 832-8960
Tara Stewart, *President*
Jessica Otero, *Purchasing*
Paul Kish, *Engineer*
Kimberly Czarnecki, *Accountant*
Carmen Duffy, *Accountant*
▲ **EMP:** 40 **EST:** 1971
SQ FT: 4,000
SALES (est): 9.7MM **Privately Held**
WEB: www.integro-usa.com
SIC: 3648 Mfg Lighting Equipment

(G-2543)
INTERNATIONAL AUTOMOBILE ENTPS (PA)
Also Called: ERA Replica Automobiles
608 E Main St Ste 612 (06051-2074)
PHONE..................................860 224-0253
Philip R Gaudette, *President*
Thomas Portante, *Vice Pres*
Robert Putnam, *CFO*
EMP: 13
SQ FT: 4,000
SALES (est): 2.1MM **Privately Held**
WEB: www.erareplicas.com
SIC: 3714 5531 Mfg Motor Vehicle Parts/Accessories Ret Auto/Home Supplies

(G-2544)
INTERNATIONAL AUTOMOBILE ENTPS
608 E Main St (06051-2074)
PHONE..................................860 224-0253
Phillip Glenda, *Manager*
EMP: 15
SALES (corp-wide): 2.1MM **Privately Held**
WEB: www.erareplicas.com
SIC: 3714 Mfg Auto Body Parts
PA: International Automobile Enterprises, Inc
608 E Main St Ste 612
New Britain CT 06051
860 224-0253

(G-2545)
J H METAL FINISHING INC (PA)
1146 East St (06051-1619)
PHONE..................................860 223-6412
John Helenek Sr, *President*
Jeanne Helenek, *Admin Sec*
EMP: 5 **EST:** 1953
SQ FT: 7,200
SALES (est): 1.5MM **Privately Held**
SIC: 3471 Plating/Polishing Service

(G-2546)
K & K BLACK OXIDE LLC
50 Peter Ct (06051-3545)
P.O. Box 1856 (06050-1856)
PHONE..................................860 223-1805
Marilyn Jester, *Manager*
EMP: 3
SALES (est): 283.6K **Privately Held**
SIC: 3471 Plating/Polishing Service

(G-2547)
K AND R PRECISION GRINDING
39 John St (06051-2724)
PHONE..................................860 505-8030
Marc W Begin, *Administration*
EMP: 8 **EST:** 2017
SALES (est): 836.5K **Privately Held**
SIC: 3999 Mfg Misc Products

(G-2548)
LEOS KITCHEN & STAIR CORP
48 John St (06051-2725)
PHONE..................................860 225-7363
Jean-Paul Ayotte, *President*
EMP: 8 **EST:** 1950
SQ FT: 2,000
SALES: 660K **Privately Held**
SIC: 2434 2541 2431 Mfg Wooden Custom Kitchen Cabinets Laminated Counter Tops & Stairs

(G-2549)
MAKINO INC
Also Called: Global E.D.M. Supplies
255 Myrtle St (06053-4161)
PHONE..................................860 223-0236
Thomas Kucharski, *Principal*
EMP: 12 **Privately Held**
SIC: 2675 Mfg Die-Cut Paper/Paperboard
HQ: Makino Inc.
7680 Innovation Way
Mason OH 45040
513 573-7200

(G-2550)
MARSAM METAL FINISHING CO
206 Newington Ave (06051-2130)
P.O. Box 1975 (06050-1975)
PHONE..................................860 826-5489
Jonathan Scalise, *President*
EMP: 25
SALES (est): 3.6MM **Privately Held**
WEB: www.marsammetalfinishing.com
SIC: 3471 Plating/Polishing Service

(G-2551)
MARTIN ROSOLS INC
45 Grove St (06053-4198)
PHONE..................................860 223-2707
Robert C Rosol, *Ch of Bd*
Karen M Rosol, *Vice Pres*
EMP: 25 **EST:** 1929
SQ FT: 85,000
SALES (est): 3.8MM **Privately Held**
WEB: www.martinrosols.com
SIC: 2011 5421 2013 Meat Packing Plant Ret Meat/Fish Mfg Prepared Meats

(G-2552)
METAL IMPROVEMENT COMPANY LLC
E/M Coatings Solutions
1 John Downey Dr (06051-2901)
PHONE..................................860 224-9148
Tony Cummings, *Prdtn Mgr*
Tom Gambino, *Engineer*
Eric Altomare, *Manager*
Dale Minor, *Technical Staff*
EMP: 28
SQ FT: 10,000
SALES (corp-wide): 2.4B **Publicly Held**
SIC: 3398 Metal Heat Treating
HQ: Metal Improvement Company, Llc
80 E Rte 4 Ste 310
Paramus NJ 07652
201 843-7800

(G-2553)
METALFORM ACQUISITION LLC (PA)
Also Called: Metalform Company
555 John Downey Dr (06051-2435)
PHONE..................................860 224-2630
Martin C McCarthy, *Ch of Bd*
John P McCarthy, *Principal*
EMP: 34
SQ FT: 15,000

SALES (est): 4MM **Privately Held**
WEB: www.metalformcompany.com
SIC: 3965 3469 3452 Mfg Fasteners/Buttons/Pins Mfg Metal Stampings Mfg Bolts/Screws/Rivets

(G-2554)
MICRO CARE CORPORATION (PA)
Also Called: Micro Care Marketing Svcs Div
595 John Downey Dr (06051-2435)
PHONE.................................860 827-0626
Christopher A Jones, *President*
Michael D Jones, *Vice Pres*
Jay S Tourigny, *Vice Pres*
Clarence P Clapp, *Treasurer*
John Farris, *Director*
▲ **EMP:** 15
SQ FT: 12,000
SALES (est): 5.4MM **Privately Held**
WEB: www.microcare.com
SIC: 2842 Mfg Polish/Sanitation Goods

(G-2555)
NEW ENGLAND CABINET CO INC
580 E Main St (06051-2042)
PHONE.................................860 747-9995
Joel Salwocki, *President*
EMP: 12
SQ FT: 20,000
SALES (est): 1.8MM **Privately Held**
SIC: 2541 2431 Mfg Wood Partitions/Fixtures Mfg Millwork

(G-2556)
NEW ENGLAND TOOL & AUTOMTN INC
321 Ellis St Ste 17 (06051-3504)
PHONE.................................860 827-9389
Yola Noga, *President*
John Noga, *Vice Pres*
EMP: 5
SALES: 350K **Privately Held**
SIC: 3599 Machine Shop

(G-2557)
NEW ENGLAND TRAVELING WIRE LLC
Also Called: Netw
162 Whiting St (06051-3132)
PHONE.................................860 223-6297
Vincent Savulis, *Mng Member*
EMP: 4
SALES (est): 330K **Privately Held**
SIC: 3599 Mfg Industrial Machinery

(G-2558)
ORCA INC
199 Whiting St (06051-3146)
PHONE.................................860 223-4180
Gregory P Goguen, *Principal*
Kathleen Goguen, *Admin Sec*
EMP: 30
SQ FT: 60,000
SALES (est): 6.7MM **Privately Held**
WEB: www.orca-mfg.com
SIC: 3466 Mfg Crowns/Closures

(G-2559)
OXFORD INDUSTRIES CONN INC
Also Called: Oxford Polymers
221 South St Bldg H (06051-3627)
PHONE.................................860 225-3700
Nicholas L Defelice, *President*
David Gambardella, *CFO*
John Oconnor, *VP Sales*
Karen Defelice, *Director*
▲ **EMP:** 24 **EST:** 1980
SQ FT: 100,000
SALES (est): 9.2MM **Privately Held**
WEB: www.oxfordpolymers.com
SIC: 2821 Mfg Plastic Materials/Resins

(G-2560)
PAINT & POWDER WORKS LLC
35 M And S Ct (06051-2320)
PHONE.................................860 225-2019
Fred H Sillner, *Manager*
EMP: 10
SALES (est): 1.1MM **Privately Held**
WEB: www.paintandpowderworks.com
SIC: 3479 Coating/Engraving Service

(G-2561)
PARKER-HANNIFIN CORPORATION
Also Called: Fluid Controls Division
95 Edgewood Ave (06051-4151)
P.O. Box 1450 (06050-1450)
PHONE.................................860 827-2300
Steve Sawczuk, *Purch Mgr*
Peter Lennon, *Engineer*
Michael Williams, *Engineer*
Michael Valenches, *Project Engr*
Larry Ryba, *Branch Mgr*
EMP: 250
SALES (corp-wide): 14.3B **Publicly Held**
WEB: www.parker.com
SIC: 3491 3492 Mfg Industrial Valves & Fluid Power Valves/Fittings & Controls
PA: Parker-Hannifin Corporation
6035 Parkland Blvd
Cleveland OH 44124
216 896-3000

(G-2562)
PETER PAUL ELECTRONICS CO INC
480 John Downey Dr (06051-2910)
P.O. Box 1180 (06050-1180)
PHONE.................................860 229-4884
Paul S Mangiafico, *President*
Michael Mangiafico II, *President*
Mark Mangiafico, *Vice Pres*
Shelly Cyr, *Marketing Staff*
▲ **EMP:** 140 **EST:** 1947
SQ FT: 77,000
SALES (est): 34.9MM **Privately Held**
WEB: www.peterpaul.com
SIC: 3491 Mfg Industrial Valves

(G-2563)
POLAMER PRECISION INC
105 Alton Brooks Way (06053-3359)
PHONE.................................860 259-6200
Chris Galik, *President*
Andrew Dulnik, *Exec VP*
Joanna Lutrzykowski, *QC Mgr*
Jeff Weston, *Engineer*
Mario Gioco, *CFO*
EMP: 145
SQ FT: 3,200
SALES (est): 58.8MM **Privately Held**
WEB: www.polamer.us
SIC: 3728 Mfg Aircraft Parts/Equipment

(G-2564)
POLAR CORPORATION
59 High St Ste 11 (06051-2279)
PHONE.................................860 223-7891
Andrew Kowalski, *President*
Lou Melluzzo, *General Mgr*
Kazimiera Zamojska Kowalski, *Admin Sec*
EMP: 25
SQ FT: 15,000
SALES (est): 6.4MM **Privately Held**
WEB: www.polaraircraft.com
SIC: 3724 3812 3728 Mfg Aircraft Engines/Parts Mfg Search/Navigation Equipment Mfg Aircraft Parts/Equipment

(G-2565)
PRECISION GRINDING COMPANY
33 Charles St (06051-2162)
PHONE.................................860 229-9652
James Weber, *President*
EMP: 12 **EST:** 1957
SQ FT: 4,000
SALES (est): 1.5MM **Privately Held**
SIC: 3599 Mfg Industrial Machinery

(G-2566)
PROMAN INC
60 Saint Claire Ave Ste 2 (06051-1665)
PHONE.................................860 827-8778
Ted Jastrzebski, *President*
EMP: 3
SALES: 250K **Privately Held**
SIC: 3599 3544 Mfg Industrial Machinery Mfg Dies/Tools/Jigs/Fixtures

(G-2567)
R K MACHINE COMPANY LLC
Also Called: Rk Machine
200 Myrtle St (06053-4160)
P.O. Box 1958 (06050-1958)
PHONE.................................860 224-7545
Rishard Kanar,
EMP: 6
SQ FT: 1,600
SALES (est): 177.1K **Privately Held**
SIC: 3599 Mfg Industrial Machinery

(G-2568)
RAM BELTING COMPANY INC
100 Production Ct Ste 3 (06051-2914)
PHONE.................................860 438-7029
Rocco A Montano, *President*
Joyce L Montano, *Vice Pres*
EMP: 5 **EST:** 1980
SQ FT: 5,200
SALES: 1MM **Privately Held**
WEB: www.rambelting.com
SIC: 3052 8611 Mfg Rubber/Plastic Hose/Belting Business Association

(G-2569)
RAYCO INC
206 Newington Ave Fl 2 (06051-2130)
PHONE.................................860 357-4693
Jose Fontanez, *President*
Judith Emanuelson, *Office Mgr*
EMP: 8
SALES (est): 2MM **Privately Held**
SIC: 3471 Plating/Polishing Service

(G-2570)
RICH PRODUCTS CORPORATION
263 Myrtle St (06053-4161)
PHONE.................................866 737-8884
EMP: 750
SALES (corp-wide): 3.8B **Privately Held**
SIC: 2053 Manufacturing Frozen Bakery Products Fresh/Frozen Fish
PA: Rich Products Corporation
1 Robert Rich Way
Buffalo NY 14213
716 878-8000

(G-2571)
RICH PRODUCTS CORPORATION
263 Myrtle St (06053-4161)
P.O. Box 649, Burlington NJ (08016-0649)
PHONE.................................800 356-7094
EMP: 750
SALES (corp-wide): 3.8B **Privately Held**
SIC: 2053 Mfg Frozen Bakery Products
PA: Rich Products Corporation
1 Robert Rich Way
Buffalo NY 14213
716 878-8000

(G-2572)
RICH PRODUCTS CORPORATION
1 Celebration Way (06053-1480)
PHONE.................................860 827-8000
EMP: 450
SALES (corp-wide): 3.8B **Privately Held**
SIC: 2024 5143 Mfg Ice Cream/Frozen Desert Whol Dairy Products
PA: Rich Products Corporation
1 Robert Rich Way
Buffalo NY 14213
716 878-8000

(G-2573)
RICH PRODUCTS CORPORATION
Also Called: Mother's Kitchen
263 Myrtle St (06053-4161)
PHONE.................................609 589-3049
Admir Mumic, *Principal*
EMP: 173
SALES (corp-wide): 3.8B **Privately Held**
WEB: www.richs.com
SIC: 2092 Mfg Fresh/Frozen Packaged Fish
PA: Rich Products Corporation
1 Robert Rich Way
Buffalo NY 14213
716 878-8000

(G-2574)
ROMAN WOODWORKING
1181 East St (06051-1666)
PHONE.................................860 490-5989
Roman Szewczak, *Owner*
EMP: 4
SALES: 400K **Privately Held**
SIC: 2431 1799 Mfg Millwork Trade Contractor

(G-2575)
SALAMON INDUSTRIES LLC
250 John Downey Dr (06051-2906)
PHONE.................................860 612-8420
Andrew Salamon, *Principal*
EMP: 4
SALES (est): 277.1K **Privately Held**
SIC: 3599 Mfg Industrial Machinery

(G-2576)
SEABOARD METAL FINISHING CO
Also Called: Seaboard Plating
410 John Downey Dr (06051-2910)
PHONE.................................203 933-1603
Steven D Tarantino, *President*
Karen A Tarantino, *Corp Secy*
EMP: 26
SQ FT: 25,000
SALES: 3.9MM **Privately Held**
WEB: www.seaboardmetalfin.com
SIC: 3471 Plating/Polishing Service

(G-2577)
SOUTHPACK LLC
1 Hartford Sq (06052-1161)
PHONE.................................860 224-2242
Lynn Mogielnicki,
Kurt Mogielnicki,
EMP: 25
SQ FT: 20,000
SALES (est): 4.8MM **Privately Held**
WEB: www.southpack.com
SIC: 3089 Mfg Plastic Products

(G-2578)
STAG ARMS LLC
515 John Downey Dr (06051-2435)
PHONE.................................860 229-9994
▲ **EMP:** 8
SALES (est): 1.7MM **Privately Held**
SIC: 3484 Mfg Small Arms

(G-2579)
STAG ARMS LLC
515 John Downey Dr (06051-2435)
PHONE.................................860 229-9994
Chad Larsen, *President*
Kalani Laker,
Jesse Tischauser,
EMP: 8
SALES (est): 402.2K **Privately Held**
SIC: 3484 Manufactures Small Arms

(G-2580)
STANLEY BLACK & DECKER INC (PA)
1000 Stanley Dr (06053-1675)
P.O. Box 7000 (06050-7000)
PHONE.................................860 225-5111
James M Loree, *President*
Keith Eisenhut, *Regional Mgr*
Jonathan Bush, *Counsel*
Donald J Riccitelli, *Counsel*
Janet M Link, *Senior VP*
EMP: 200
SALES: 13.9B **Publicly Held**
WEB: www.stanleyworks.com
SIC: 3429 3546 3423 3452 Mfg Power & Hand Tools Mechanical Access Solutions & Electronic Security & Monitoring Systems

(G-2581)
STANLEY BLACK & DECKER INC
100 Curtis St (06052-1326)
P.O. Box 1308 (06050-1308)
PHONE.................................860 225-5111
Patrick Egan, *Branch Mgr*
EMP: 100
SALES (corp-wide): 13.9B **Publicly Held**
WEB: www.stanleyworks.com
SIC: 3429 Mfg Engineered Components
PA: Stanley Black & Decker, Inc.
1000 Stanley Dr
New Britain CT 06053
860 225-5111

(G-2582)
STANLEY BLACK & DECKER INC
480 Myrtle St (06053-4018)
PHONE....................................860 225-5111
Yolanda Costantini, *Vice Pres*
Joe Voelker, *Branch Mgr*
EMP: 220
SALES (corp-wide): 13.9B **Publicly Held**
SIC: 3699 3429 Mfg Electrical Equipment/Supplies Mfg Hardware
PA: Stanley Black & Decker, Inc.
1000 Stanley Dr
New Britain CT 06053
860 225-5111

(G-2583)
STANLEY BLACK & DECKER INC
Stanley Tools
480 Myrtle St (06053-4018)
P.O. Box 1308 (06050-1308)
PHONE....................................860 225-5111
Thomas E Mahoney, *Branch Mgr*
EMP: 46
SALES (corp-wide): 13.9B **Publicly Held**
WEB: www.stanleyworks.com
SIC: 3429 5085 3546 3423 Mfg Hardware Whol Industrial Supplies Mfg Power-driven Handtool Mfg Hand/Edge Tools
PA: Stanley Black & Decker, Inc.
1000 Stanley Dr
New Britain CT 06053
860 225-5111

(G-2584)
STANLEY FASTENING SYSTEMS LP
Also Called: Stanley-Bostitch
480 Myrtle St (06053-4018)
PHONE....................................860 225-5111
Bruce Behnke, *President*
EMP: 5
SALES (corp-wide): 13.9B **Publicly Held**
SIC: 3579 Mfg Office Machines
HQ: Stanley Fastening Systems Lp
2 Briggs Dr
East Greenwich RI 02818
401 884-2500

(G-2585)
STANLEY INDUSTRIAL & AUTO LLC
Also Called: Proto Industrial Tools
480 Myrtle St (06053-4018)
PHONE....................................800 800-8005
Kate White, *Director*
EMP: 46
SALES (corp-wide): 13.9B **Publicly Held**
SIC: 3429 Manufacturing Hardware
HQ: Stanley Industrial & Automotive, Llc
505 N Cleveland Ave
Westerville OH 43082
614 755-7000

(G-2586)
TDY INDUSTRIES LLC
Also Called: ATI Specialty Materials
33 John St Ste 39 (06051-2748)
PHONE....................................860 259-6346
EMP: 4 **Publicly Held**
SIC: 3724 Mfg Aircraft Engines/Parts
HQ: Tdy Industries, Llc
1000 Six Ppg Pl
Pittsburgh PA 15222
412 394-2800

(G-2587)
ULTRA FOOD AND FUEL
788 W Main St (06053-3856)
PHONE....................................860 223-2005
Mukhtar Ahmed, *Principal*
EMP: 4 **EST:** 2010
SALES (est): 275.3K **Privately Held**
SIC: 2869 Mfg Industrial Organic Chemicals

(G-2588)
UNITED PLASTICS TECHNOLOGIES
163 John Downey Dr (06051-2903)
PHONE....................................860 224-1110
Vincent Dicioccio Jr, *President*
Anthony Straska, *Vice Pres*
John Shurkus, *Treasurer*
EMP: 12
SQ FT: 28,000
SALES (est): 2MM **Privately Held**
SIC: 3089 Mfg Plastic Novelties & Displays

(G-2589)
WENTWORTH MANUFACTURING LLC
623 E Main St (06051-2032)
PHONE....................................860 205-6437
Kevin McDermott,
EMP: 4
SALES: 950K **Privately Held**
SIC: 3724 Mfg Aircraft Engines/Parts

(G-2590)
WESTBROOK PRODUCTS LLC
623 E Main St (06051-2032)
PHONE....................................860 205-6437
Kevin McDermott,
EMP: 3
SALES (est): 600K **Privately Held**
SIC: 3724 Mfg Aircraft Engines/Parts

(G-2591)
WINSLOW AUTOMATICS INC
23 Saint Claire Ave (06051-1630)
PHONE....................................860 225-6321
Janusz Podlasek, *CEO*
Walter Borysewicz, *Vice Pres*
J George Podlasek, *Vice Pres*
Wendi P Scata, *Vice Pres*
Rick Milka, *Purch Mgr*
EMP: 91
SQ FT: 70,000
SALES (est): 18.9MM **Privately Held**
WEB: www.winslowautomatics.com
SIC: 3841 3724 3843 3743 Mfg Surgical/Med Instr Mfg Aircraft Engine/Part Mfg Dental Equip/Supply Mfg Railroad Equipment

New Canaan
Fairfield County

(G-2592)
ADVANTAGE COMMUNICATIONS LLC
43 Pine St (06840-5409)
P.O. Box 757 (06840-0757)
PHONE....................................203 966-8390
Maria Crocitto,
EMP: 20 **EST:** 1997
SQ FT: 10,000
SALES (est): 1.6MM **Privately Held**
SIC: 2721 Trade Journals

(G-2593)
CHARLES CLAY LTD
149 Cherry St (06840-5525)
PHONE....................................203 662-0125
Gordon Smith, *President*
▲ **EMP:** 3
SALES (est): 92.8K **Privately Held**
SIC: 2396 Mfg Auto/Apparel Trimming

(G-2594)
CONTEK INTERNATIONAL CORP
93 Cherry St (06840)
PHONE....................................203 972-3406
John J C Chen, *Principal*
EMP: 4
SALES (est): 123.5K **Privately Held**
SIC: 3577 Mfg Computer Peripheral Equipment

(G-2595)
CONTEK INTERNATIONAL CORP
Also Called: Century Products
60 Field Crest Rd (06840-6328)
PHONE....................................203 972-7330
John Chen, *President*
Alice Chen, *Vice Pres*
▲ **EMP:** 15
SQ FT: 5,000
SALES (est): 1.8MM **Privately Held**
WEB: www.contek.net
SIC: 3577 Mfg Personal Computer Peripherals

(G-2596)
CSC COCOA LLC
36 Grove St (06840-5329)
PHONE....................................203 846-5611
Paul Farmer, *COO*
EMP: 5 **EST:** 2017
SALES (est): 139.9K **Privately Held**
SIC: 2066 Mfg Chocolate/Cocoa Products

(G-2597)
EASTERN INC
Also Called: Taroli Chris
95 Locust Ave (06840-4727)
PHONE....................................203 563-9535
Chris Taroli, *Principal*
EMP: 9
SALES (est): 1.6MM **Privately Held**
SIC: 3441 Structural Metal Fabrication

(G-2598)
GREEK ELEMENTS LLC
49 Journeys End Rd (06840-2414)
PHONE....................................203 594-2022
Athanasios Damis, *Principal*
EMP: 3 **EST:** 2014
SALES (est): 157K **Privately Held**
SIC: 2819 Mfg Industrial Inorganic Chemicals

(G-2599)
GRIDIRON CAPITAL LLC (PA)
220 Elm St Fl 2 (06840-5322)
PHONE....................................203 972-1100
Thomas A Burger, *Managing Prtnr*
Scott Harrison, *COO*
Donald E Cihak,
Timothy W Clark,
Eugene P Conese Jr,
EMP: 53
SALES (est): 306.4MM **Privately Held**
WEB: www.gridironcapital.com
SIC: 2434 Mfg Wood Kitchen Cabinets

(G-2600)
HEARST CORPORATION
Also Called: New Canaan Advertiser
42 Vitti St (06840-4823)
P.O. Box 605 (06840-0605)
PHONE....................................203 438-6544
V Donald Hersam, *Manager*
EMP: 40
SALES (corp-wide): 8.3B **Privately Held**
WEB: www.acorn-online.com
SIC: 2711 2741 Newspaper Publisher & Corporate Publishing
PA: The Hearst Corporation
300 W 57th St Fl 42
New York NY 10019
212 649-2000

(G-2601)
HERSAM PUBLISHING COMPANY
Also Called: Darien Times
42 Vitti St (06840-4823)
P.O. Box 605 (06840-0605)
PHONE....................................203 966-9541
Martin Hersam, *CEO*
Donald V Hersam Jr, *President*
V Hersham, *Publisher*
Eric Gatten, *Technology*
EMP: 300
SQ FT: 6,000
SALES (est): 11.7MM **Privately Held**
SIC: 2711 2741 Newspapers-Publishing/Printing Misc Publishing

(G-2602)
JOR SERVICES LLC
4 Parting Brook Rd (06840-2827)
PHONE....................................203 594-7774
Joachim Roesler, *Principal*
EMP: 3
SALES (est): 300.3K **Privately Held**
SIC: 3089 Mfg Plastic Products

(G-2603)
LITURGICAL PUBLICATIONS INC
Also Called: Parish Publishing
87 Lambert Rd (06840-3631)
PHONE....................................203 966-6470
Ken Pranger, *Manager*
EMP: 12
SALES (corp-wide): 103.5MM **Privately Held**
WEB: www.mylpi.com
SIC: 2721 2741 Periodicals-Publishing/Printing Misc Publishing
PA: Liturgical Publications, Inc.
2875 S James Dr
New Berlin WI 53151
262 785-1188

(G-2604)
MAGNELI MATERIALS LLC
33 Weeburn Dr (06840-5228)
P.O. Box 9 (06840-0009)
PHONE....................................203 644-8560
Robert Sterner, *Principal*
EMP: 5 **EST:** 2014
SALES (est): 362K **Privately Held**
SIC: 2816 Mfg Inorganic Pigments

(G-2605)
MB SPORT LLC (PA)
31 Grove St (06840-5324)
PHONE....................................203 966-1985
Alfred Lam, *Vice Pres*
Michael Buscher, *Mng Member*
Sonia Lamp, *Mng Member*
Joseph Bove, *Info Tech Dir*
▲ **EMP:** 19 **EST:** 1998
SQ FT: 5,500
SALES (est): 1.3MM **Privately Held**
WEB: www.mbsport.com
SIC: 2321 2337 Mfg Men's/Boy's Furnishings Mfg Women's/Misses' Suits/Coats

(G-2606)
MECHANCAL ENGNERED SYSTEMS LLC
180 Jonathan Rd (06840-2116)
PHONE....................................203 400-4658
Matthew Farrell,
EMP: 7 **EST:** 2012
SQ FT: 2,000
SALES: 1.1MM **Privately Held**
SIC: 3564 3585 Mfg Blowers/Fans Mfg Refrigeration/Heating Equipment

(G-2607)
MEGASONICS INC
205 Benedict Hill Rd (06840-2913)
PHONE....................................203 966-3404
Chan Kob Chung, *President*
EMP: 3
SALES (est): 507.8K **Privately Held**
SIC: 3829 Mfg Measuring/Controlling Devices

(G-2608)
MR SKYLIGHT LLC
411 South Ave (06840-6316)
PHONE....................................203 966-6005
John A Cole, *Manager*
EMP: 3
SALES (est): 320.2K **Privately Held**
SIC: 3993 Mfg Signs/Advertising Specialties

(G-2609)
MRK FINE ARTS LLC
65 Locust Ave Ste 301 (06840-4753)
PHONE....................................203 972-3115
Christina Usher, *Production*
Rod Kosann,
Monica Kosann,
▲ **EMP:** 5
SALES (est): 683.8K **Privately Held**
SIC: 3911 Mfg Precious Metal Jewelry

(G-2610)
NEW CANAAN FORGE LLC (PA)
26 Burtis Ave (06840-5503)
PHONE....................................203 966-3858
Joseph Haas, *Mng Member*
EMP: 3
SQ FT: 3,235
SALES: 400K **Privately Held**
SIC: 7692 1791 Welding Repair Structural Steel Erection

(G-2611)
NEWSBANK INC
58 Pine St Ste 1 (06840-5426)
PHONE....................................203 966-1100
John McDowell, *Vice Pres*
EMP: 3

GEOGRAPHIC

SALES (corp-wide): 77.3MM Privately Held
WEB: www.newsbank.com
SIC: 2741 Electronic Publishing
PA: Newsbank, Inc.
5801 Pelican Bay Blvd
Naples FL 34108
800 762-8182

(G-2612)
OOMPH LLC
5 Elm St (06840-5502)
PHONE....203 216-9848
Katherine Urban, *Opers Staff*
Jeffrey Johnston, *Marketing Mgr*
Patty Hopple,
Louise Brooks,
Amy Rice,
▼ EMP: 6
SALES (est): 1.1MM Privately Held
SIC: 2519 2511 Mfg Household Furniture Mfg Wood Household Furn

(G-2613)
PUTU LLC
Also Called: Lolo Bags
48 Elm St (06840-5501)
PHONE....203 594-9700
Bruce McLaire, *Mng Member*
▲ EMP: 3
SALES (est): 419.5K Privately Held
SIC: 3172 Mfg Personal Leather Goods

(G-2614)
SLOGIC HOLDING CORP (PA)
36 Grove St (06840-5329)
PHONE....203 966-2800
James Kelly, *Sales Mgr*
Christa Spry, *Director*
EMP: 7 EST: 2016
SALES (est): 121.5MM Privately Held
SIC: 2394 5091 Canvas And Related Products

(G-2615)
SONG BATH LLC
146 Old Kings Hwy (06840-6415)
PHONE....800 353-0313
Peter Nemiroff, *Principal*
▲ EMP: 3
SALES (est): 232.3K Privately Held
SIC: 2434 Mfg Wood Kitchen Cabinets

(G-2616)
STRUCTURED SOLUTIONS II LLC
55 Saint Johns Pl Ste 201 (06840-4530)
PHONE....203 972-5717
Mark Noonan, *President*
Alexandria Lawer,
Hank Pohl,
▲ EMP: 6
SQ FT: 2,500
SALES (est): 1.1MM Privately Held
WEB: www.structuredsolutionsii.com
SIC: 3711 Mfg Motor Vehicle/Car Bodies

(G-2617)
SUPERNOVA DIAGNOSTICS INC
36 Richmond Hill Rd (06840-5301)
PHONE....301 792-4345
Neil J Campbell, *CEO*
Hans-Georg Eisenwiener, *Ch of Bd*
Dr Christopher M Ball, *Exec VP*
Dane Saglio, *CFO*
George W H Cautherley, *Director*
EMP: 7
SALES (est): 510K Privately Held
SIC: 3841 Mfg Surgical/Medical Instruments

(G-2618)
TRIPLE CLOVER PRODUCTS LLC
4 Smith Ridge Ln (06840-3217)
PHONE....475 558-9503
Joanne Grasso, *Mng Member*
Michael Kirby,
Tricia O'Connor,
EMP: 3
SALES: 250K Privately Held
SIC: 3423 7389 Mfg Hand/Edge Tools Business Serv Non-Commercial Site

(G-2619)
UNIMIN LIME CORPORATION (DH)
258 Elm St (06840-5309)
PHONE....203 966-8880
Joseph Shapiro, *President*
EMP: 11
SALES (est): 14MM
SALES (corp-wide): 138.1MM Publicly Held
SIC: 1446 Industrial Sand Mining
HQ: Covia Holdings Corporation
3 Summit Park Dr Ste 700
Independence OH 44131
440 214-3284

(G-2620)
US CHEMICALS INC
280 Elm St (06840-5313)
PHONE....203 655-8878
H T Von Oehsen, *CEO*
EMP: 3
SALES (est): 202.1K Privately Held
SIC: 2911 5169 Petroleum Refiner Whol Chemicals/Products

(G-2621)
WESTCHESTER FORGE INC
28 Benedict Hill Rd (06840-2903)
PHONE....914 584-2429
EMP: 3
SALES (est): 243.7K Privately Held
SIC: 2721 Periodicals-Publishing/Printing

New Fairfield
Fairfield County

(G-2622)
CABIN CRITTERS INC
3 Dunham Dr Ste A (06812-4055)
PHONE....203 778-4552
David Smith, *President*
▲ EMP: 4
SALES: 200K Privately Held
WEB: www.cabincrittersinc.com
SIC: 3942 Whol Stuffed Animals

(G-2623)
CITIZEN NEWS
Candle Wood Cor Rm 39 (06812)
P.O. Box 8048 (06812-8048)
PHONE....203 746-4669
Ellen Burnett, *Owner*
EMP: 6
SALES: 362K Privately Held
SIC: 2711 Newspaper Publisher

(G-2624)
INTEGRITY INDUSTRIES INC
1 Saw Mill Rd Ste 7 (06812-4045)
PHONE....203 312-9788
EMP: 6
SALES (corp-wide): 225.3B Publicly Held
SIC: 2841 Mfg Soap/Other Detergent
HQ: Integrity Delaware, Llc
2710 E Corral Ave
Kingsville TX 78363
361 595-5561

(G-2625)
MATRIX APPAREL GROUP LLC
29 Candlewood Dr (06812-5111)
PHONE....203 740-7837
James Mager, *Mng Member*
James K Mager, *Mng Member*
EMP: 3 EST: 2002
SQ FT: 2,500
SALES: 2.5MM Privately Held
SIC: 2389 Mfg Apparel/Accessories

(G-2626)
NEW FAIRFIELD PRESS INC
3 Dunham Dr (06812-4055)
P.O. Box 8864 (06812-8864)
PHONE....203 746-2700
John Paul Parille, *President*
Arlene Pugliatti, *Vice Pres*
EMP: 15 EST: 1965
SQ FT: 5,000
SALES (est): 2.1MM Privately Held
WEB: www.nfpress.com
SIC: 2759 2752 Commercial Printing Lithographic Commercial Printing

(G-2627)
STAR TECH INSTRUMENTS INC
3 State Route 39 (06812-4000)
P.O. Box 1822 (06812-1822)
PHONE....203 312-0767
William C Fricke, *President*
EMP: 4
SALES (est): 496.8K Privately Held
SIC: 3845 Mfg Electromedical Equipment

(G-2628)
SWANHART WOODWORKING
5 Bayberry Ln (06812-2565)
PHONE....203 746-1184
Kenneth Swanhart, *Principal*
EMP: 4
SALES (est): 388.5K Privately Held
SIC: 2431 Mfg Millwork

(G-2629)
TOWN TRIBUNE LLC
10 Sleepy Hollow Rd (06812-5102)
PHONE....203 648-6085
Marylou Schirmer, *Principal*
EMP: 4
SALES (est): 216.5K Privately Held
SIC: 2711 Newspapers-Publishing/Printing

(G-2630)
VIDEO AUTOMATION SYSTEMS INC
13 Arrow Meadow Rd (06812-3901)
PHONE....203 312-0152
Thorsten Cook, *President*
EMP: 3 EST: 1976
SALES: 216.4K Privately Held
WEB: www.videoautomation.com
SIC: 3663 8748 Mfg Radio/Tv Communication Equipment Business Consulting Services

(G-2631)
WESTERN CONN CRAFTSMEN LLC
246 Pine Hill Rd (06812-2209)
PHONE....203 312-8167
A Nicholas Kaplanis,
EMP: 5
SALES: 500K Privately Held
SIC: 2511 Mfg Wood Household Furniture

New Hartford
Litchfield County

(G-2632)
BETX LLC
440 Cedar Ln (06057-2403)
PHONE....860 459-1681
Krish Dasgupta, *CEO*
EMP: 3
SALES (est): 86.5K Privately Held
SIC: 2741 7371 Internet Publishing And Broadcasting Custom Computer Programing

(G-2633)
CONNECTICUT VALLEY WINERY LLC
1480 Litchfield Tpke (06057-3210)
PHONE....860 489-9463
Anthony Ferraro,
EMP: 3
SALES: 147K Privately Held
SIC: 2084 Mfg Wines

(G-2634)
CTECH ADHESIVES
39 Maple Hollow Rd (06057-3020)
PHONE....860 482-5947
Wells Cunningham, *Principal*
EMP: 3
SALES (est): 206.4K Privately Held
SIC: 2891 Mfg Adhesives/Sealants

(G-2635)
CUNNINGHAM TECH LLC (PA)
39 Maple Hollow Rd (06057-3020)
PHONE....860 738-8759
Wells Cunningham, *Owner*
Robin Cunningham,
EMP: 4
SALES: 200K Privately Held
SIC: 2891 Mfg Adhesives/Sealants

(G-2636)
EXECUTIVE GREETINGS INC (HQ)
Also Called: Baldwin Cooke
120 Industrial Park Rd (06057-2308)
P.O. Box 3669, Mankato MN (56002-3669)
PHONE....860 379-9911
Dan RAO, *President*
Stephen D Roberts, *CFO*
▼ EMP: 450
SQ FT: 140,000
SALES (est): 49.1MM
SALES (corp-wide): 2.8B Privately Held
WEB: www.executivegreetings.com
SIC: 2741 5112 5199 2759 Misc Publishing Whol Stationery/Offc Sup Whol Nondurable Goods Commercial Printing
PA: Taylor Corporation
1725 Roe Crest Dr
North Mankato MN 56003
507 625-2828

(G-2637)
FENDER MUSICAL INSTRS CORP
37 Greenwoods Rd (06057-2207)
PHONE....860 379-7575
Bob Saunders, *Branch Mgr*
EMP: 6
SALES (corp-wide): 711.9MM Privately Held
SIC: 3931 Ret Musical Instruments
PA: Fender Musical Instruments Corporation
17600 N Perimeter Dr # 100
Scottsdale AZ 85255
480 596-9690

(G-2638)
HURLEY MANUFACTURING COMPANY
37 Greenwoods Rd (06057-2207)
P.O. Box 366 (06057-0366)
PHONE....860 379-8506
David J Hurley, *President*
Thomas P Hurley, *Vice Pres*
EMP: 30
SQ FT: 22,600
SALES (est): 5.8MM Privately Held
WEB: www.hurleyspring.com
SIC: 3493 3469 Mfg Steel Springs-Nonwire Mfg Metal Stampings

(G-2639)
INERTIA DYNAMICS LLC
31 Industrial Park Rd (06057-2310)
PHONE....860 379-1252
Csceve Myquist,
▲ EMP: 110
SQ FT: 32,000
SALES (est): 20.8MM
SALES (corp-wide): 1.1B Publicly Held
WEB: www.inertiadynamics.com
SIC: 3625 3568 Mfg Relays/Industrial Controls Mfg Power Transmission Equipment
PA: Altra Industrial Motion Corp.
300 Granite St Ste 201
Braintree MA 02184
781 917-0600

(G-2640)
INERTIA DYNAMICS INC
31 Industrial Park Rd (06057-2310)
P.O. Box 641, South Beloit IL (61080-0641)
PHONE....860 379-1252
Steve Nyquist, *Principal*
Oliwer Janiec, *Engineer*
Adam Krukar, *Technician*
EMP: 18
SALES (est): 3.2MM Privately Held
SIC: 3465 Mfg Automotive Stampings

(G-2641)
INJECTECH ENGINEERING LLC (PA)
19 Pioneer Rd (06057-4235)
PHONE..................................860 379-9781
Kenneth Heyse, *Mng Member*
Robert Risbridger,
EMP: 7
SQ FT: 7,000
SALES (est): 1.8MM **Privately Held**
SIC: **3089** Mfg Special Injection Machinery & Automation Equipment

(G-2642)
L & M MANUFACTURING CO INC
37 Greenwoods Rd (06057-2207)
PHONE..................................860 379-2751
Maurice J La Brecque, *President*
Joseph J Mangiome, *Vice Pres*
EMP: 20
SQ FT: 24,000
SALES (est): 2.8MM **Privately Held**
WEB: www.lmmfg.com
SIC: **3452** Mfg Bolts/Screws/Rivets

(G-2643)
NEW HARTFORD INDUSTRIAL PARK
Also Called: Hurley Manufacturing
37 Greenwoods Rd (06057-2207)
P.O. Box 366 (06057-0366)
PHONE..................................860 379-8506
David Hurley, *President*
Thomas Hurley, *Vice Pres*
EMP: 30
SQ FT: 30,000
SALES (est): 2.4MM **Privately Held**
WEB: www.hurleymfg.com
SIC: **3469** Mfg Metal Stampings

(G-2644)
PERRY TECHNOLOGY CORPORATION
120 Industrial Park Rd (06057-2308)
P.O. Box 21 (06057-0021)
PHONE..................................860 738-2525
Lansford Perry, *President*
Bernie Levesque, *Purch Agent*
Jason Ferree, *Engineer*
Mark Goddard, *Engineer*
Jesus Penaranda, *Supervisor*
EMP: 85 **EST**: 1938
SQ FT: 55,000
SALES (est): 28.5MM **Privately Held**
WEB: www.perrygear.com
SIC: **3545** 3728 3568 3462 Mfg Machine Tool Access Mfg Aircraft Parts/Equip Mfg Power Transmsn Equip Mfg Iron/Steel Forgings Mfg Hardware

(G-2645)
PROSPECT DESIGNS INC
11 Prospect St (06057-2223)
P.O. Box 62, Pine Meadow (06061-0062)
PHONE..................................860 379-7858
Ann Evans, *President*
Marshall Janes, *General Mgr*
EMP: 5
SQ FT: 2,000
SALES (est): 591.1K **Privately Held**
WEB: www.prospectdesigns.com
SIC: **3842** Manufactures Furniture

(G-2646)
R L TURICK CO INC
186 Main St (06057-2746)
PHONE..................................860 693-2230
David R Turick, *President*
Richard Turick, *Vice Pres*
▼ **EMP**: 7 **EST**: 1961
SQ FT: 3,200
SALES (est): 900K **Privately Held**
SIC: **3599** Mfg Industrial Machinery

(G-2647)
SCP MANAGEMENT LLC
Also Called: Syntac Coated Products
29 Industrial Park Rd (06057-2310)
PHONE..................................860 738-2600
Aaron Rutsky, *Vice Pres*
Curt Rutsky, *Mng Member*
▲ **EMP**: 45
SALES (est): 21.5MM **Privately Held**
SIC: **3312** Blast Furnace-Steel Works

(G-2648)
SHURTAPE SPECIALTY COATING LLC (DH)
29 Industrial Park Rd (06057-2310)
PHONE..................................860 738-2600
Curt Rutsky, *CEO*
EMP: 50
SQ FT: 60,000
SALES (est): 7MM
SALES (corp-wide): 691.3MM **Privately Held**
SIC: **2891** Manufactures Adhesives/Sealants

(G-2649)
WAYNE HORN
308 Cedar Ln (06057-2907)
PHONE..................................860 491-3315
Wayne Horn, *Principal*
EMP: 3
SALES (est): 279.3K **Privately Held**
SIC: **2411** Logging

New Haven
New Haven County

(G-2650)
109 DESIGN LLC (PA)
55 Whitney Ave Fl 2 (06510-1301)
PHONE..................................203 941-1812
Sebastian Monzon, *Principal*
Levi Deluke, *Principal*
Ellen Su, *Principal*
Elliot Swart, *Director*
EMP: 3
SALES (est): 434.5K **Privately Held**
SIC: **3841** 8711 Mfg Surgical/Medical Instruments Engineering Services

(G-2651)
A D PERKINS COMPANY
43 Elm St (06510-2032)
PHONE..................................203 777-3456
Kirk Schroff, *President*
Nancy Schroff, *Corp Secy*
Jay Smilovich, *Vice Pres*
EMP: 9
SQ FT: 1,200
SALES: 200K **Privately Held**
WEB: www.adperkins.com
SIC: **3953** 3993 7389 Mfg Rubber Stamps & Advertising Specialties & Does Sign Engraving

(G-2652)
ACHILLION PHARMACEUTICALS INC
300 George St Ste 801 (06511-6656)
PHONE..................................203 624-7000
Milind S Deshpande, *President*
EMP: 80
SQ FT: 38,632
SALES (est): 22.3MM **Privately Held**
WEB: www.achillion.com
SIC: **2834** 8731 Mfg Pharmaceutical Preparations Commercial Physical Research

(G-2653)
ALEXION PHARMA LLC (HQ)
100 College St (06510-3210)
PHONE..................................203 272-2596
Nikhil Jayaram, *Regional Mgr*
Nick Gurreri, *Vice Pres*
Todd Spalding, *Vice Pres*
Martine Zimmermann, *Vice Pres*
Patricia Bento, *Research*
EMP: 45 **EST**: 2015
SALES (est): 36.9MM **Publicly Held**
SIC: **2834** 8733 Pharmaceutical Preparations & Medical Research

(G-2654)
ALL PHASE STEEL WORKS LLC
57 Trumbull St (06510-1004)
PHONE..................................203 375-8881
Paul J Pinto, *Principal*
EMP: 55 **EST**: 2012
SQ FT: 30,000
SALES (est): 14.6MM **Privately Held**
SIC: **3441** 1791 Structural Metal Fabrication Structural Steel Erection

(G-2655)
ALLIANCE ENERGY LLC
Also Called: Connecticut Refining Co
Merritt Pkwy (06535)
P.O. Box 9545 (06535-0545)
PHONE..................................203 933-2511
Rich Hyland, *Manager*
EMP: 4
SALES (corp-wide): 12.6B **Publicly Held**
SIC: **1389** Oil/Gas Field Services
HQ: Alliance Energy Llc
800 South St Ste 500
Waltham MA 02453

(G-2656)
AMIUS PARTNERS LLC
180 E Rock Rd (06511-1326)
PHONE..................................203 526-5926
Bruce Benson, *Owner*
EMP: 5
SALES (est): 342.4K **Privately Held**
SIC: **3812** Mfg Search/Navigation Equipment

(G-2657)
ANDERSON TOOL COMPANY INC
85 Willow St Ste 3 (06511-2694)
PHONE..................................203 777-4153
David Christensen, *President*
Thomas Christensen, *Vice Pres*
Harold Christensen, *Shareholder*
EMP: 5 **EST**: 1957
SQ FT: 4,500
SALES: 335.2K **Privately Held**
SIC: **3544** 7692 Mfg Dies Tools Jigs & Fixtures And Special Machinery

(G-2658)
ARVINAS INC (PA)
Also Called: Protac
395 Winchester Ave (06511)
PHONE..................................203 535-1456
John Dombrosky, *CEO*
Timothy Shannon, *Ch of Bd*
John Houston, *President*
Angela Cacace, *Vice Pres*
John Grosso, *Vice Pres*
EMP: 15
SQ FT: 34,000
SALES: 7.5MM **Publicly Held**
SIC: **2834** 8731 Pharmaceutical Preparations Biotechnical Research

(G-2659)
ASSA INC (HQ)
Also Called: Assa Abloy Inc.
110 Sargent Dr (06511-5918)
PHONE..................................203 624-5225
Thanasis Molokotos, *President*
Cris Davidson, *Vice Pres*
Kelly Bowers, *Opers Staff*
Jeff Mereschuk, *CFO*
Joseph P Hurley, *Treasurer*
◆ **EMP**: 400
SQ FT: 325,000
SALES (est): 2B
SALES (corp-wide): 8.8B **Privately Held**
WEB: www.assaabloy.com
SIC: **3429** 3699 Mfg Hardware Mfg Electrical Equipment/Supplies
PA: Assa Abloy Ab
Klarabergsviadukten 90
Stockholm 111 6
850 648-500

(G-2660)
ASSA INC
Also Called: Assa High Security Locks
110 Sargent Dr (06511-5918)
P.O. Box 9453 (06534-0453)
PHONE..................................800 235-7482
Lance Berger, *Opers-Prdtn-Mfg*
Edmond Dorne, *Sales/Mktg Mgr*
Richard Eisen, *Director*
L Page Heslin, *Admin Sec*
▲ **EMP**: 4
SQ FT: 5,000
SALES: 7.5MM
SALES (corp-wide): 8.8B **Privately Held**
SIC: **3429** High Security Lock Cylinder Mfg
HQ: Assa, Inc.
110 Sargent Dr
New Haven CT 06511
203 624-5225

(G-2661)
ATTICUS BAKERY LLC
Also Called: Chabaso Bakery
360 James St (06513-3013)
PHONE..................................203 562-9007
Charles J Negaro, *CEO*
EMP: 110
SALES (est): 22.2MM **Privately Held**
WEB: www.chabaso.com
SIC: **2051** Retail Bakery

(G-2662)
AU NEW HAVEN LLC
30 Lenox St (06513-4419)
PHONE..................................203 468-0342
Rick Landau, *General Mgr*
Brian Lathrop, *VP Engrg*
Milton Berlinski, *Mng Member*
Stuart Press,
◆ **EMP**: 102
SQ FT: 65,000
SALES (est): 31.5MM **Privately Held**
WEB: www.uretek.com
SIC: **2295** Mfg Coated Fabrics

(G-2663)
B AND G ENTERPRISE LLC (PA)
Also Called: New Haven Awning Co
178 Chapel St (06513-4209)
PHONE..................................203 562-7232
Dan Barnick, *Mng Member*
Tom Gumkowski, *Mng Member*
EMP: 4
SQ FT: 4,500
SALES (est): 343.2K **Privately Held**
WEB: www.nhawning.com
SIC: **2394** Mfg & Installation Of Awnings & Canopies

(G-2664)
BARNES TECHNICAL PRODUCTS LLC
15 High St (06510-2304)
PHONE..................................203 931-8852
Aaron Frazier, *Engineer*
Russell Barnes, *Mng Member*
EMP: 7
SALES (est): 680K **Privately Held**
SIC: **3599** Mfg Industrial Machinery

(G-2665)
BECAID LLC
Also Called: C8 Sciences
5 Science Park Ste 29 (06511-1967)
PHONE..................................203 915-6914
Ken Coleman, *Director*
Kenneth Coleman,
EMP: 8
SALES (est): 699.5K **Privately Held**
SIC: **7372** Prepackaged Software Services

(G-2666)
BIOHAVEN PHARMACEUTICALS INC
215 Church St (06510-1803)
PHONE..................................203 404-0410
Robert Berman, *CEO*
Clifford Bechtold, *COO*
Kimberly Gentile, *Vice Pres*
Jim Engelhart, *CFO*
EMP: 65 **EST**: 2013
SALES (est): 676.3K
SALES (corp-wide): 1MM **Privately Held**
SIC: **2834** Mfg Pharmaceutical Preparations
HQ: Biohaven Pharmaceutical Holding Company Ltd.
C/O Maples Corporate Services (Bvi) Limited
Road Town

(G-2667)
BIOHAVEN PHRM HOLDG CO LTD
Also Called: Biohaven Pharmaceuticals
215 Church St (06510-1803)
PHONE..................................203 404-0410
Vlad Coric, *CEO*
Declan Doogan, *Ch of Bd*
Alex Deboissiere, *Vice Pres*
James Engelhart, *CFO*
William Jones, *Ch Credit Ofcr*
EMP: 42
SQ FT: 4,240

GEOGRAPHIC

SALES (est): 8.2MM **Privately Held**
SIC: 2834 Pharmaceutical Preparations

(G-2668)
BIOXCEL THERAPEUTICS INC
555 Long Wharf Dr (06511-6107)
PHONE..................................475 238-6837
Peter Mueller, *Ch of Bd*
Vimal Mehta, *President*
Richard Steinhart, *CFO*
Vincent O'Neill, *Chief Mktg Ofcr*
Frank Yocca, *Security Dir*
EMP: 15
SQ FT: 11,040
SALES (est): 950.5K
SALES (corp-wide): 3MM **Publicly Held**
SIC: 2834 Pharmaceutical Preparations
PA: Bioxcel Corporation
780 E Main St
Branford CT 06405
203 433-4086

(G-2669)
BIRDTRACK PRESS
26 Mckinley Ave (06515-2732)
PHONE..................................203 389-7789
David Goodrich, *Owner*
EMP: 3 **EST:** 1990
SALES (est): 158.5K **Privately Held**
WEB: www.birdtrack.com
SIC: 2791 2731 Typesetting Services Books-Publishing/Printing

(G-2670)
BOLD WOOD INTERIORS LLC
138 Haven St (06513-3522)
PHONE..................................203 907-4077
Robert Bolduc, *Mng Member*
▲ **EMP:** 15
SQ FT: 8,500
SALES (est): 1MM **Privately Held**
WEB: www.boldwoodinteriors.com
SIC: 2521 Mfg Wood Office Furniture

(G-2671)
BOSTON MODEL BAKERY
Also Called: Lupi-Marchigiano Bakery
169 Washington Ave (06519-1618)
PHONE..................................203 562-9491
Peter Luppi, *President*
EMP: 20
SALES (est): 1.3MM **Privately Held**
SIC: 2051 Mfg Bread/Related Products

(G-2672)
BROADSTRIPES LLC
129 Church St Ste 805 (06510-2005)
PHONE..................................203 350-9824
Timothy C Holahan, *Mng Member*
EMP: 3
SALES: 500K **Privately Held**
SIC: 3599 7371 Mfg Industrial Machinery Custom Computer Programing

(G-2673)
CAPITAL CITIES COMMUNICATIONS
8 Elm St (06510-2006)
PHONE..................................203 784-8800
Hank Yaggi, *Principal*
EMP: 3
SALES (est): 111.8K **Privately Held**
SIC: 2711 Newspapers-Publishing/Printing

(G-2674)
CARESTREAM HEALTH MOLECULAR
Also Called: Carestream Molecular Imaging
4 Science Park (06511-1962)
PHONE..................................888 777-2072
Stephanie Chiang, *Principal*
Shahram Hejazi, *Principal*
Sindy Woodhams, *Principal*
EMP: 50
SALES (est): 1.3MM **Privately Held**
SIC: 3826 Mfg Analytical Instruments

(G-2675)
CARIGENT THERAPEUTICS INC
5 Science Park Ste 10 (06511-1989)
PHONE..................................203 887-2873
Peter Fong, *Principal*
EMP: 3
SALES (est): 234.8K **Privately Held**
WEB: www.carigent.com
SIC: 2834 Mfg Pharmaceutical Preparations

(G-2676)
CHIP IN A BOTTLE LLC
837 Whalley Ave Ste 1 (06515-1794)
PHONE..................................203 460-0665
Darrell Nurse, *Mng Member*
EMP: 3 **EST:** 2016
SQ FT: 1,400
SALES: 60K **Privately Held**
SIC: 2024 5441 2066 Mfg Ice Cream/Desserts Ret Candy/Confectionery Mfg Chocolate/Cocoa Prdt

(G-2677)
CONNECTICUT LAMINATING CO INC
162 James St (06513-3845)
PHONE..................................203 787-2184
Henry S Snow, *President*
Steven M Snow, *Vice Pres*
Henry Snow, *Info Tech Dir*
Sandra Snow, *Admin Sec*
▲ **EMP:** 100
SQ FT: 55,000
SALES (est): 11.3MM **Privately Held**
WEB: www.ctlaminating.com
SIC: 3089 Mfg Plastic Products

(G-2678)
CONTINUITY ENGINE INC
59 Elm St (06510-2047)
PHONE..................................866 631-5556
Andy Greenawalt, *CEO*
Noel May, *Mktg Dir*
EMP: 3
SQ FT: 10,000
SALES (est): 229.9K **Privately Held**
SIC: 3599 7372 Mfg Industrial Machinery Prepackaged Software Services

(G-2679)
CORBIN RUSSWIN
110 Sargent Dr (06511-5918)
PHONE..................................860 225-7411
Douglas Millikan, *Principal*
EMP: 9
SALES (est): 710.8K **Privately Held**
SIC: 3429 Hardware, Nec

(G-2680)
COVIDIEN LP
Also Called: Surgical Devices
555 Long Wharf Dr Fl 4 (06511-6102)
PHONE..................................781 839-1722
Scott Riley, *Branch Mgr*
EMP: 430 **Privately Held**
SIC: 3841 Mfg Surgical/Medical Instruments
HQ: Covidien Lp
15 Hampshire St
Mansfield MA 02048
763 514-4000

(G-2681)
CUSTOM TEES PLUS
365 Whalley Ave (06511-3044)
PHONE..................................203 752-1071
William Gibbs, *Owner*
EMP: 25
SALES (est): 1.4MM **Privately Held**
SIC: 2759 Commercial Printing

(G-2682)
DOCUPRINT & IMAGING INC
Also Called: Docuprintnow
27 Whitney Ave (06510-1219)
PHONE..................................203 776-6000
Anthony Colasanto, *President*
EMP: 8 **EST:** 1972
SQ FT: 4,000
SALES (est): 1.4MM **Privately Held**
WEB: www.docuprintandimaging.com
SIC: 2752 Lithographic Commercial Printing

(G-2683)
DOW COVER COMPANY INCORPORATED
Also Called: Dcci
373 Lexington Ave (06513-4061)
PHONE..................................203 469-5394
Mark Steinhardt, *President*
Barry Konet, *Admin Sec*
▲ **EMP:** 68 **EST:** 1947
SQ FT: 38,000
SALES (est): 7.8MM **Privately Held**
WEB: www.dowcover.com
SIC: 2393 Mfg Textile Bags

(G-2684)
EAST ROCK BREWING COMPANY LLC
285 Nicoll St (06511-2625)
PHONE..................................203 530-3484
Tim Wilson, *Mng Member*
Christopher J Wilson,
Shaun M Wilson,
EMP: 3
SALES (est): 73.1K **Privately Held**
SIC: 2082 Mfg Malt Beverages

(G-2685)
EDSAN CHEMICAL COMPANY INC
150 Whittier Rd (06515-2474)
PHONE..................................203 624-3123
Susan Fewes, *President*
EMP: 110 **EST:** 1948
SQ FT: 10,000
SALES (est): 11.5MM **Privately Held**
SIC: 2842 5087 Mfg Polish/Sanitation Goods Whol Service Establishment Equipment

(G-2686)
ELECTRIX LLC
45 Spring St (06519-2340)
P.O. Box 9575 (06535-0575)
PHONE..................................203 776-5577
Haim Swisha, *Ch of Bd*
Daniel Swisha, *Vice Pres*
Gordon Swisha, *Vice Pres*
David Michaud, *Senior Buyer*
Armando Abrina, *Engineer*
▲ **EMP:** 54 **EST:** 1961
SQ FT: 84,000
SALES (est): 13.1MM **Privately Held**
WEB: www.electrix.com
SIC: 3648 Mfg Lighting Equipment

(G-2687)
F & L IRON WORK INC
105 Barclay St (06519-2032)
PHONE..................................203 777-0751
Lorraine Pizzola, *President*
Frank Pizzola, *Treasurer*
EMP: 5
SQ FT: 4,000
SALES (est): 789K **Privately Held**
SIC: 3446 Mfg Architectural Metalwork

(G-2688)
F W WEBB COMPANY
Also Called: Johnson Contrls Authorized Dlr
650 Boulevard (06519-1810)
PHONE..................................203 865-6124
Michael Sewell, *Manager*
EMP: 10
SALES (corp-wide): 1B **Privately Held**
SIC: 3432 5074 5251 Mfg Plumbing Fixture Fittings Whol Plumbing Equipment/Supplies Ret Hardware
PA: F. W. Webb Company
160 Middlesex Tpke
Bedford MA 01730
781 272-6600

(G-2689)
GE ENGINE SVCS UNC HOLDG I INC
71 Shelton Ave (06511)
Rural Route R 1 Ive D, Schenectady NY (12345-0001)
PHONE..................................518 380-0767
Randall McAlister, *President*
Jonathan Goodman, *Vice Pres*
Doriann Salisbury, *Treasurer*
EMP: 3
SALES (est): 201.2K
SALES (corp-wide): 121.6B **Publicly Held**
SIC: 3511 Mfg Turbines/Generator Sets
PA: General Electric Company
5 Necco St
Boston MA 02210
617 443-3000

(G-2690)
GELATO GIULIANA LLC
240 Sargent Dr Ste 9 (06511-6108)
PHONE..................................203 772-0607
Giuliana Maravalle,
EMP: 9
SALES (est): 1MM **Privately Held**
SIC: 2024 Mfg Ice Cream/Frozen Desert

(G-2691)
GOODCOPY PRINTING CENTER INC
Also Called: Goodcopy Printing & Graphics
110 Hamilton St (06511-5813)
P.O. Box 8088 (06530-0088)
PHONE..................................203 624-0194
Louis Goldberg, *President*
Edith Goldberg, *Vice Pres*
Corey Greco, *Prdtn Mgr*
Dave Signore, *Prdtn Mgr*
Arleen Claudio-Gore, *Sales Staff*
EMP: 20
SQ FT: 10,000
SALES (est): 5MM **Privately Held**
WEB: www.goodcopy.com
SIC: 2752 Lithographic Commercial Printing

(G-2692)
GREENLEAF BFUELS NEW HAVEN LLC
100 Waterfront St (06512-1713)
PHONE..................................203 672-9028
Mark McCall, *Mng Member*
Augustus G Kellogg, *Manager*
EMP: 10
SALES (est): 3MM **Privately Held**
SIC: 2869 Mfg Industrial Organic Chemicals

(G-2693)
GREY WALL SOFTWARE LLC
Also Called: Veoci.com
195 Church St Fl 14 (06510-2009)
PHONE..................................203 782-5944
Drew Mazurek, *Partner*
Ken Moon, *Project Mgr*
Tamas Simon, *Engineer*
Vincent Jessel, *Accounts Exec*
Sukh Greywal, *Mng Member*
EMP: 15 **EST:** 2011
SQ FT: 5,600
SALES (est): 1.8MM **Privately Held**
SIC: 7372 Prepackaged Software Services

(G-2694)
H KREVIT AND COMPANY INC
73 Welton St (06511-1523)
PHONE..................................203 772-3350
Thomas Ross, *President*
Donald Dechello, *Vice Pres*
Carolyn Dechello, *Admin Sec*
EMP: 44
SQ FT: 45,000
SALES (est): 26.1MM **Privately Held**
WEB: www.hkrevit.com
SIC: 2869 2819 3589 Mfg Industrial Organic Chemicals Mfg Industrial Inorganic Chemicals Mfg Service Industry Machinery

(G-2695)
HARTY PRESS INC
Also Called: Harty Integrated Solutions
25 James St (06513-4218)
P.O. Box 324 (06513-0324)
PHONE..................................203 562-5112
George Platt, *President*
Bill Nims, *Vice Pres*
Kevin Platt, *Vice Pres*
Henry Gargiulo, *Traffic Mgr*
Michael Platt, *Treasurer*
EMP: 86 **EST:** 1957
SQ FT: 68,000
SALES (est): 25.1MM **Privately Held**
WEB: www.hartynet.com
SIC: 2752 Lithographic Commercial Printing

(G-2696)
HISPANIC COMMUNICATIONS LLC
Also Called: La Voz Hispana De Connecticut
51 Elm St (06510-2049)
PHONE..................................203 624-8007

Norma R Reyes,
EMP: 8
SQ FT: 2,000
SALES (est): 568.3K **Privately Held**
WEB: www.lavozhispanact.com
SIC: 2711 Newspapers-Publishing/Printing

(G-2697)
HUMMEL BROS INC
180 Sargent Dr (06511-5919)
PHONE..................................203 787-4113
William F Hummel, *President*
Kurt Hummel, *Corp Secy*
Robert W Hummel Jr, *Vice Pres*
Mary Ellen Hummel, *CFO*
EMP: 70 **EST:** 1933
SQ FT: 42,000
SALES (est): 11.7MM **Privately Held**
WEB: www.hummelbros.com
SIC: 2099 2013 Mfg Food Preparations Mfg Prepared Meats

(G-2698)
IDEAL PRINTING CO INC
228 Food Terminal Plz (06511-5910)
P.O. Box 8488 (06531-0488)
PHONE..................................203 777-7626
Jim Cohane, *President*
Rocco Candela, *Treasurer*
EMP: 7 **EST:** 1920
SQ FT: 7,920
SALES (est): 1MM **Privately Held**
SIC: 2759 2752 Commercial Printing Lithographic Commercial Printing

(G-2699)
JOSHUA LLC (PA)
Also Called: Unicast Development Co.
90 Hamilton St (06511-5920)
PHONE..................................203 624-0080
Chris Syvertsen, *General Mgr*
Christopher Syvertsen,
Tanya Cunningham,
Joshua H Meshiach,
EMP: 35
SQ FT: 8,600
SALES (est): 4.3MM **Privately Held**
WEB: www.unicastdev.com
SIC: 3542 2819 3297 3624 Mfg Indstl Inorgan Chem Mfg Machine Tool-Forming Mfg Nonclay Refractories Mfg Carbon/Graphite Prdt Mfg Indstl Furnace/Ovens

(G-2700)
K H CORNELL INTERNATIONAL INC
59 Amity Rd (06515-1407)
PHONE..................................203 392-3660
K H Maeng, *President*
Emil Brown, *Manager*
EMP: 4
SQ FT: 1,500
SALES: 700K **Privately Held**
WEB: www.cornellkh.com
SIC: 3442 Exporting Agent Of Manufactured Doors

(G-2701)
KNB DESIGN LLC
91 Shelton Ave (06511-1811)
PHONE..................................203 777-6661
Nir Bongart, *Principal*
EMP: 3
SALES (est): 359.8K **Privately Held**
SIC: 2434 Mfg Wood Kitchen Cabinets Mfg Wood Kitchen Cabinets

(G-2702)
KOLLTAN PHARMACEUTICALS INC (HQ)
300 George St Ste 530 (06511-6624)
PHONE..................................203 773-3000
Gerald McMahon, *President*
Theresa M Lavallee, *Vice Pres*
Jane Henderson, *CFO*
Ronald A Peck, *Chief Mktg Ofcr*
Rich Gedrich, *Director*
EMP: 25
SALES (est): 1.9MM
SALES (corp-wide): 9.5MM **Publicly Held**
SIC: 2834 Mfg Pharmaceutical Preparations
PA: Celldex Therapeutics, Inc.
53 Frontage Rd Ste 220
Hampton NJ 08827
908 200-7500

(G-2703)
KUEHNE NEW HAVEN LLC
71 Welton St (06511)
PHONE..................................203 508-6703
William Paulin,
Bill Paulin,
EMP: 23
SALES: 10MM
SALES (corp-wide): 107.9MM **Privately Held**
SIC: 2812 2899 Mfg Alkalies/Chlorine Mfg Chemical Preparations
PA: Kuehne Chemical Company, Inc.
86 N Hackensack Ave
Kearny NJ 07032
973 589-0700

(G-2704)
LAFARGE NORTH AMERICA INC
410 Waterfront St (06512-1717)
PHONE..................................203 468-6068
Gerald Muscad, *Manager*
EMP: 3
SALES (corp-wide): 4.5B **Privately Held**
WEB: www.lafargenorthamerica.com
SIC: 3241 5032 Mfg Hydraulic Cement Whol Brick/Stone Material
HQ: Lafarge North America Inc.
8700 W Bryn Mawr Ave
Chicago IL 60631
773 372-1000

(G-2705)
LAMBERTI PACKING COMPANY
207 Food Terminal Plz # 207 (06511-5911)
PHONE..................................203 562-0436
Joseph Kelley, *President*
Jean Lamberti, *Admin Sec*
EMP: 8
SALES (est): 932.1K **Privately Held**
SIC: 2013 Mfg Prepared Meats

(G-2706)
LISA LEE CREATIONS INC
10 Selden St (06525-2218)
PHONE..................................203 479-4462
EMP: 3 **EST:** 2010
SALES (est): 150K **Privately Held**
SIC: 3399 Mfg Primary Metal Products

(G-2707)
LONGHINI LLC
41 Longhini Ln (06519-1820)
PHONE..................................212 219-1230
Richard Longhini Jr, *President*
David Kemp, *Mng Member*
EMP: 22
SQ FT: 7,500
SALES (est): 834.2K
SALES (corp-wide): 22.3MM **Privately Held**
SIC: 2013 Mfg Prepared Meats
PA: 3 Little Pigs, Llc
4223 1st Ave Fl 2
Brooklyn NY 11232
212 219-1230

(G-2708)
LOUIS RODRIGUZ
Also Called: Sofrito Ponce
145 Adeline St (06519-2037)
PHONE..................................203 777-6937
Louie Rodriguz, *Owner*
EMP: 3
SALES (est): 244.7K **Privately Held**
SIC: 2032 Mfg Canned Specialties

(G-2709)
LUCKEY LLC
184 Chapel St (06513)
PHONE..................................203 285-3819
Nancy Bradley,
Dana M Peterson,
EMP: 10 **EST:** 2008
SALES (est): 1.2MM **Privately Held**
SIC: 3299 3446 2431 Mfg Nonmetallic Mineral Products Mfg Architectural Metalwork Mfg Millwork

(G-2710)
LUPIS INC
169 Washington Ave (06519-1618)
PHONE..................................203 562-9491
Peter P Lupi, *President*
Ellen Lupi, *Admin Sec*
EMP: 25 **EST:** 1935
SQ FT: 10,000
SALES (est): 3.1MM **Privately Held**
WEB: www.lupis.com
SIC: 2051 5461 Mfg Bread/Related Products Retail Bakery

(G-2711)
MECHA NOODLE BAR
201 Crown St (06510-2701)
PHONE..................................203 691-9671
Tony Pham, *President*
EMP: 5
SALES (est): 110.5K **Privately Held**
SIC: 2098 Mfg Macaroni/Spaghetti

(G-2712)
MLK BUSINESS FORMS INC
25 James St (06513-4218)
P.O. Box 383 (06513-0383)
PHONE..................................203 624-6304
Gene Booth, *President*
Fred Levesh, *Vice Pres*
Craig Levesh, *Admin Sec*
EMP: 13
SQ FT: 12,500
SALES (est): 1.8MM **Privately Held**
SIC: 2759 2761 Commercial Printing Mfg Manifold Business Forms

(G-2713)
NEW ENGLAND DRMTLGCAL SOC BRET
333 Cedar St (06510-3206)
PHONE..................................203 432-0092
Tania Phillips, *Principal*
EMP: 4 **EST:** 2017
SALES: 1MM **Privately Held**
SIC: 2834 Mfg Pharmaceutical Preparations

(G-2714)
NEW HAVEN CHLOR-ALKALI LLC
Also Called: H.krevit
73 Welton St (06511-1523)
PHONE..................................203 772-3350
Nalluru C Murthy, *Mng Member*
EMP: 70
SALES (est): 3.8MM **Privately Held**
SIC: 2819 Mfg Industrial Inorganic Chemicals

(G-2715)
NEW HAVEN NATUROPATHIC CENTER
14 Judwin Ave (06515-2313)
PHONE..................................203 387-8661
Jennifer Botwick, *Principal*
EMP: 3
SALES (est): 285.6K **Privately Held**
SIC: 2834 Mfg Pharmaceutical Preparations

(G-2716)
NEW HAVEN REGISTER LLC
100 Gando Dr (06513-1014)
PHONE..................................203 789-5200
Kevin F Walsh, *President*
Paul Barbetta, *Publisher*
Thomas Rice, *Senior VP*
John Collins, *CFO*
Angel Diggs, *Librarian*
▲ **EMP:** 590 **EST:** 1915
SQ FT: 250,000
SALES (est): 32.7MM
SALES (corp-wide): 8.3B **Privately Held**
WEB: www.journalregister.com
SIC: 2711 2752 Newspapers-Publishing/Printing Lithographic Commercial Printing
PA: The Hearst Corporation
300 W 57th St Fl 42
New York NY 10019
212 649-2000

(G-2717)
NEW HAVEN SHEET METAL CO
42 Foxon St (06513-2320)
PHONE..................................203 468-0341
EMP: 6 **EST:** 1975
SQ FT: 5,000
SALES (est): 360K **Privately Held**
SIC: 3443 Mfg Fabricated Plate Work

(G-2718)
NEW WAVE SURGICAL CORP
555 Long Wharf Dr Fl 2 (06511-6102)
PHONE..................................954 796-4126
Andrew Widmark, *Ch of Bd*
R Alexander Gomez, *President*
Matt Sokany, *Vice Pres*
Michael Lpez, *Admin Sec*
▲ **EMP:** 45
SQ FT: 2,700
SALES (est): 11.3MM **Privately Held**
SIC: 3841 Mfg Surgical/Medical Instruments

(G-2719)
NOFET LLC
227 Church St Apt 5j (06510-1825)
P.O. Box 466, Shelton (06484-0466)
PHONE..................................203 848-9064
Idit Hoter-Ishay, *Owner*
Idit Hoter- Ishay, *Owner*
Ran Assaf,
EMP: 10 **EST:** 2013
SALES: 3MM **Privately Held**
SIC: 3691 7389 Mfg Storage Batteries Business Services At Non-Commercial Site

(G-2720)
NOLAN INDUSTRIES INC
67 Mill River St (06511-3907)
PHONE..................................203 865-8160
Mark Nolan, *President*
Dan Nolan, *Treasurer*
EMP: 4
SQ FT: 8,000
SALES (est): 477K **Privately Held**
SIC: 3599 General Machine Shop

(G-2721)
ONOFRIOS ULTIMATE FOODS INC
35 Wheeler St (06512-1632)
PHONE..................................203 469-4014
John Astarita, *Buyer*
Richard Onofrio, *Mng Member*
EMP: 10
SALES (est): 1.6MM **Privately Held**
SIC: 2033 2035 Mfg Canned Fruits/Vegtbl Mfg Pickles/Sauces

(G-2722)
PEMKO MANUFACTURING CO
110 Sargent Dr (06511-5918)
PHONE..................................901 365-2160
EMP: 4
SALES (est): 121.1K **Privately Held**
SIC: 3429 Mfg Hardware

(G-2723)
PEPSICO
150 Munson St (06511-3572)
PHONE..................................203 974-8912
Magdalena Mackay, *District Mgr*
EMP: 10
SALES (est): 1.4MM **Privately Held**
SIC: 2086 Carb Sft Drnkbtlcn

(G-2724)
PFIZER INC
1 Howe St (06511-5473)
PHONE..................................203 401-0100
Subhashis Banerjee MD, *Manager*
Patricia Gallipoli, *Manager*
EMP: 9
SALES (corp-wide): 53.6B **Publicly Held**
WEB: www.pfizer.com
SIC: 2834 Mfg Pharmaceutical Preparations
PA: Pfizer Inc.
235 E 42nd St Rm 107
New York NY 10017
212 733-2323

GEOGRAPHIC

(G-2725)
PGXHEALTHHOLDING INC (PA)
5 Science Park (06511-1966)
PHONE..................................203 786-3400
Kevin Rakin, *President*
Gerald F Vovis, *Exec VP*
EMP: 164
SQ FT: 72,000
SALES (est): 17.1MM **Privately Held**
WEB: www.genaissance.com
SIC: 2834 Mfg Pharmaceutical Preparations

(G-2726)
PHOENIX PRESS INC
15 James St (06513-4253)
P.O. Box 347 (06513-0347)
PHONE..................................203 865-5555
Brian Driscoll, *President*
Troy Jasaitis, *Accounts Exec*
EMP: 30
SQ FT: 56,000
SALES (est): 3.5MM **Privately Held**
WEB: www.phoenixpressinc.com
SIC: 2752 2791 2789 Lithographic Commercial Printing Typesetting Services Bookbinding/Related Work

(G-2727)
PLATT BROTHERS REALTY II LLC
25 James St (06513-4218)
PHONE..................................203 562-5112
George Platt,
EMP: 3 **EST:** 1982
SALES: 60K **Privately Held**
SIC: 2759 Commercial Printing

(G-2728)
PPG INDUSTRIES INC
Also Called: PPG Painters Supply
390 East St (06511-5018)
PHONE..................................203 562-5173
Don Bradford, *Branch Mgr*
EMP: 5
SALES (corp-wide): 15.3B **Publicly Held**
SIC: 2851 Mfg Paints/Allied Products
PA: Ppg Industries, Inc.
1 Ppg Pl
Pittsburgh PA 15272
412 434-3131

(G-2729)
QUANTUM CIRCUITS INC
25 Science Park Ste 203 (06511-1984)
PHONE..................................203 891-6216
Martin Mengwall, *CEO*
EMP: 18
SALES (est): 94.5K **Privately Held**
SIC: 3572 Mfg Computer Storage Devices

(G-2730)
REACTEL INC
315 Peck St Fl 3 (06513-2933)
PHONE..................................203 773-0135
EMP: 3
SQ FT: 2,000
SALES (est): 463.5K **Privately Held**
SIC: 3613 Mfg Automatic Meter Reading Systems

(G-2731)
RENETX BIO INC
157 Church St Fl 19 (06510-2100)
PHONE..................................203 444-6642
Erika Smith, *CEO*
EMP: 5
SALES (est): 688.8K **Privately Held**
SIC: 2834 Mfg Pharmaceutical Preparations

(G-2732)
SAINT JOSEPHS WOOD PDTS LLC
80 Middletown Ave (06513-2101)
PHONE..................................203 787-5746
Andrew Anastasia Sr,
Barbara Anastasia,
EMP: 4
SALES (est): 315K **Privately Held**
SIC: 2499 Wood Products, Nec, Nsk

(G-2733)
SAME DAY DUMPSTERS LLC
225 Quinnipiac Ave (06513-4574)
PHONE..................................203 676-1219
Fabricio Freitas, *Principal*
EMP: 3 **EST:** 2014
SALES (est): 159.5K **Privately Held**
SIC: 3443 Mfg Fabricated Plate Work

(G-2734)
SAMMI SLEEPING SYSTEMS LLC
5 Science Park (06511-1966)
PHONE..................................203 684-3131
Carlton Chen, *Mng Member*
Vivian Jiang, *Mng Member*
Allen Weng, *Mng Member*
EMP: 3
SALES (est): 91.1K **Privately Held**
SIC: 2392 5719 Mfg Household Furnishings Ret Misc Homefurnishings

(G-2735)
SARGENT MANUFACTURING COMPANY
Also Called: Assa Abloy USA
100 Sargent Dr (06511-5943)
P.O. Box 9725 (06536-0915)
PHONE..................................203 562-2151
Thanasis Molokotos, *CEO*
Michael Vigneux, *Engineer*
David M Ambrosini, *Treasurer*
Carol Brustman, *Executive Asst*
Jeffrey Mereschuk, *Admin Sec*
◆ **EMP:** 900
SQ FT: 344,000
SALES (est): 120.3MM
SALES (corp-wide): 8.8B **Privately Held**
SIC: 3429 Mfg Hardware
HQ: Assa, Inc.
110 Sargent Dr
New Haven CT 06511
203 624-5225

(G-2736)
SECOND WIND MEDIA LIMITED
Also Called: Business New Haven
315 Front St (06513-3200)
PHONE..................................203 781-3480
Michael Bingham, *President*
EMP: 10
SQ FT: 1,200
SALES (est): 912.8K **Privately Held**
WEB: www.conntact.com
SIC: 2711 Newspaper Publication

(G-2737)
SENSOR SWITCH INC (DH)
265 Church St Fl 15 (06510-7003)
PHONE..................................203 265-2842
Vernon J Nagel, *President*
Brian Platner, *President*
Richard K Reece, *Exec VP*
Beverly Platner, *Vice Pres*
C Dan Smith, *Vice Pres*
EMP: 29
SQ FT: 36,000
SALES (est): 13.8MM
SALES (corp-wide): 3.6B **Publicly Held**
WEB: www.sensorswitch.com
SIC: 3812 3648 Mfg Search/Navigation Equipment Mfg Lighting Equipment

(G-2738)
SOMETHING SWEET INC (PA)
724 Grand Ave (06511-5006)
P.O. Box 8238 (06530-0238)
PHONE..................................203 603-9766
Greg Menke, *CEO*
Joseph Montesano, *Principal*
Brian Murray, *COO*
Mark Cohen, *CFO*
EMP: 30
SQ FT: 35,000
SALES (est): 17.2MM **Privately Held**
SIC: 2053 Mfg Frozen Bakery Products

(G-2739)
SOTO HOLDINGS INC
300 East St (06511-5801)
PHONE..................................203 781-8020
John Soto, *President*
Azizul Quaderi, *Purch Agent*
Selvan Candron, *Manager*
Tim Evans, *Manager*
Adrienne Montano, *Admin Sec*
EMP: 43
SQ FT: 44,000
SALES (est): 11.6MM **Privately Held**
WEB: www.space-craft.com
SIC: 3724 Mfg Aircraft Engines/Parts

(G-2740)
STUART HARDWOOD CORP
Also Called: Stuart Xlan
32 Old Amity Rd (06524-3418)
PHONE..................................203 376-0036
Stuart Paley, *President*
Diego Fernandez, *Admin Sec*
EMP: 6
SQ FT: 14,000
SALES: 900K **Privately Held**
SIC: 2421 Sawmill/Planing Mill

(G-2741)
SURACI CORP
Also Called: Suraci Paint & Powder Coating
90 River St Ste 2 (06513-4382)
PHONE..................................203 624-1345
Bruno F Suraci, *CEO*
Bruno Suraci Jr, *Founder*
EMP: 60
SALES (est): 6.7MM **Privately Held**
SIC: 3444 Mfg Sheet Metalwork

(G-2742)
SURACI METAL FINISHING LLC
90 River St Ste 2 (06513-4382)
PHONE..................................203 624-1345
Bruno F Suraci Jr, *CEO*
Marc Suraci, *COO*
EMP: 24
SQ FT: 26,000
SALES (est): 4MM **Privately Held**
WEB: www.suracicorp.com
SIC: 3471 Plating/Polishing Service

(G-2743)
TECHNOLUTIONS INC
234 Church St Fl 15 (06510-1800)
PHONE..................................203 404-4835
Alexander Grant Clark, *CEO*
EMP: 35
SALES: 286.8K **Privately Held**
WEB: www.technolutions.com
SIC: 7372 Prepackaged Software Services

(G-2744)
TOTO LLC
27 Whitney Ave (06510-1219)
PHONE..................................203 776-6000
Antonio Colasanto, *Mng Member*
EMP: 10
SALES: 400K **Privately Held**
SIC: 2752 Lithographic Commercial Printing

(G-2745)
TRACK180 LLC
900 Chapel St Fl 10 (06510-2806)
P.O. Box 574, Old Saybrook (06475-0574)
PHONE..................................203 605-3540
EMP: 6
SALES (est): 373.3K **Privately Held**
SIC: 2711 Newspapers

(G-2746)
TRANE INC
Also Called: Trane Supply
178 Wallace St (06511-5032)
PHONE..................................860 437-6208
EMP: 100 **Privately Held**
SIC: 3585 Mfg Refrigeration/Heating Equipment
HQ: Trane Inc.
1 Centennial Ave Ste 101
Piscataway NJ 08854
732 652-7100

(G-2747)
TRELLEBORG CTD SYSTEMS US INC
Also Called: Uretek
30 Lenox St (06513-4419)
PHONE..................................203 468-0342
Paolo Astarita, *Vice Pres*
Patrik Romberg, *Vice Pres*
Kurt Rutt, *Safety Mgr*
Brian Lathrop, *VP Engrg*
Sarah McGuire, *Branch Mgr*
EMP: 180
SALES (corp-wide): 3.5B **Privately Held**
SIC: 2295 Mfg Coated Fabrics
HQ: Trelleborg Coated Systems Us, Inc.
715 Railroad Ave
Rutherfordton NC 28139
828 286-9126

(G-2748)
TREVI THERAPEUTICS INC
195 Church St Fl 14 (06510-2009)
PHONE..................................203 304-2499
David Meeker, *Ch of Bd*
Jennifer Good, *President*
Christopher Seiter, *CFO*
Yann Mazabraud, *Ch Credit Ofcr*
Thomas Sciascia, *Chief Mktg Ofcr*
EMP: 16
SQ FT: 5,600
SALES (est): 3.2MM **Privately Held**
SIC: 2834 Pharmaceutical Preparations

(G-2749)
TRINITY MOBILE NETWORKS INC
770 Chapel St Ste 2 (06510-3101)
PHONE..................................301 332-6401
Tyler Reynolds, *CEO*
Stephen Hall, *Chief Engr*
EMP: 4
SALES (est): 204.7K **Privately Held**
SIC: 7372 Prepackaged Software Services

(G-2750)
UNITED STATES SURGICAL CORP (HQ)
Also Called: U.s Surgical
555 Long Wharf Dr Fl 4 (06511-6102)
PHONE..................................203 845-1000
John W Kapples, *President*
Gregory Andrulonis, *Vice Pres*
▲ **EMP:** 1000
SALES (est): 160.9MM **Privately Held**
SIC: 3841 3845 3842 Mfg Surgical/Med Instr Mfg Electromedical Equip

(G-2751)
VESPOLI USA INC
385 Clinton Ave (06513-4812)
PHONE..................................203 773-0311
Michael Vespoli, *President*
Nancy P Vespoli, *Principal*
Walter Torres, *Opers Staff*
Jeff Border, *Sales Staff*
John Monaghan, *Manager*
◆ **EMP:** 45
SQ FT: 32,000
SALES (est): 8.1MM **Privately Held**
WEB: www.vespoli.com
SIC: 3732 5551 Boatbuilding/Repairing Ret Boats

(G-2752)
VIOLA AUDIO LABORATORIES INC
446a Blake St Ste 220 (06515)
PHONE..................................203 772-0435
Paul Jayson, *President*
EMP: 9
SQ FT: 5,000
SALES (est): 1.5MM **Privately Held**
WEB: www.violalabs.com
SIC: 3651 Mfg Home Audio/Video Equipment

(G-2753)
WELLINKS INC
770 Chapel St Ste 2d (06510-3101)
PHONE..................................650 704-0714
Ellen Su, *CEO*
EMP: 3
SQ FT: 1,200
SALES (est): 261.9K **Privately Held**
SIC: 3842 Mfg Surgical Appliances/Supplies

(G-2754)
WHOLE GERMAN BREADS LLC
85 Willow St (06511-2668)
PHONE..................................203 507-0663
Andrea Corazzini, *Mng Member*
EMP: 9
SALES (est): 1MM **Privately Held**
SIC: 2051 Mfg Bread/Related Products

(G-2755)
XIJET CORP
8 Lunar Dr Ste 3 (06525-2352)
PHONE....203 397-2800
Scott Snietka, *President*
Philip Black, *Vice Pres*
EMP: 10
SALES (est): 1.7MM **Privately Held**
WEB: www.xijet.com
SIC: 3577 7389 Mfg Computer Peripheral Equipment Business Services

(G-2756)
YALE ALUMNI PUBLICATIONS INC
149 York St Fl 2 (06511-8923)
PHONE....203 432-0645
J Weili Cheng, *Chairman*
EMP: 9
SALES: 1.9MM **Privately Held**
WEB: www.yalealumnimagazine.com
SIC: 2721 Periodicals-Publishing/Printing

(G-2757)
YALE DAILY NEWS PUBLISHING CO
212 York St (06511-8925)
P.O. Box 209007 (06520-9007)
PHONE....203 432-2400
Kimberly Schramberg, *President*
EMP: 4
SQ FT: 5,000
SALES: 424.9K **Privately Held**
WEB: www.yaledailynews.com
SIC: 2711 2731 Newspapers-Publishing/Printing Books-Publishing/Printing

(G-2758)
YALE UNIVERSITY
Also Called: Printing & Graphic Services
149 York St (06511-8923)
P.O. Box 208227 (06520-8227)
PHONE....203 432-2880
Joseph Maynard, *Branch Mgr*
Melissa Fournier, *Manager*
Peter Yacono, *Supervisor*
EMP: 7
SALES (corp-wide): 4.1B **Privately Held**
WEB: www.yale.edu
SIC: 2711 8221 Newspapers-Publishing/Printing College/University
PA: Yale University
105 Wall St
New Haven CT 06511
203 432-2550

(G-2759)
YALE UNIVERSITY
Also Called: Kline Chemistry Laboratory
225 Prospect St Rm 1 (06511-8499)
PHONE....203 432-3916
Kerri Sancomb, *Production*
Joanne Bentley, *Manager*
Bonnie Aniballi, *Assistant*
EMP: 4
SALES (corp-wide): 4.1B **Privately Held**
WEB: www.yale.edu
SIC: 2869 8221 Mfg Industrial Organic Chemicals College/University
PA: Yale University
105 Wall St
New Haven CT 06511
203 432-2550

(G-2760)
YALE UNIVERSITY
Also Called: Yale Daily News
202 York St (06511-4804)
P.O. Box 209007 (06520-9007)
PHONE....203 432-2424
Lewis York, *Branch Mgr*
EMP: 5
SALES (corp-wide): 4.1B **Privately Held**
WEB: www.yale.edu
SIC: 2621 8221 Paper Mill College/University
PA: Yale University
105 Wall St
New Haven CT 06511
203 432-2550

(G-2761)
YALE UNIVERSITY
Also Called: Marsh Botanical Garden
285 Mansfield St (06511)
PHONE....203 432-6320
Eric Warson, *Manager*
EMP: 4
SALES (corp-wide): 4.1B **Privately Held**
WEB: www.yale.edu
SIC: 2833 8221 Mfg Medicinal/Botanical Products College/University
PA: Yale University
105 Wall St
New Haven CT 06511
203 432-2550

(G-2762)
YALE UNIVERSITY
Also Called: Yale Herald
305 Crown St (06511-6612)
PHONE....203 432-7494
Alexis Peter, *Branch Mgr*
EMP: 5
SALES (corp-wide): 4.1B **Privately Held**
WEB: www.yale.edu
SIC: 2621 8221 Paper Mill College/University
PA: Yale University
105 Wall St
New Haven CT 06511
203 432-2550

(G-2763)
ZENITH-OMNI HEARING CENTER (PA)
Also Called: Zenith Hearing Aid
111 Park St Ste 1k (06511-5472)
PHONE....203 624-9857
David Mc Mahon, *President*
Richard Mc Mahon, *Owner*
Susan Mc Mahon, *Vice Pres*
EMP: 3
SQ FT: 1,000
SALES (est): 437.1K **Privately Held**
SIC: 3842 5999 7629 Manufactures Retails And Services Hearing Aids

New London
New London County

(G-2764)
A CAPELA DO SANTO ANTONIO INC
35 Henry St (06320-3311)
PHONE....860 447-3329
Roberta Vincent, *Director*
Brenda Delgado, *Director*
Alfred Gonsalves, *Director*
EMP: 3
SALES (est): 130K **Privately Held**
SIC: 3961 Mfg Costume Jewelry

(G-2765)
BAYARD INC (DH)
Also Called: Creative Communications
1 Montauk Ave Ste 3 (06320-4967)
PHONE....860 437-3012
Richard Johnson, *President*
Didier Remiot, *Director*
Guylene Dumais, *Admin Sec*
Lise Marie C Zanghetti, *Admin Sec*
EMP: 40
SALES (est): 18.1MM
SALES (corp-wide): 40K **Privately Held**
WEB: www.bayard-inc.com
SIC: 2759 Misc Publishing
HQ: Bayard Presse
18 Rue Barbes
Montrouge 92120
174 316-060

(G-2766)
BIOCLINICA INC
234 Bank St (06320-6070)
PHONE....860 701-0082
Michaelanne Hussey, *Manager*
Jesse Mazarelli, *Manager*
EMP: 6
SALES (corp-wide): 89MM **Privately Held**
SIC: 3821 Medical Laboratory
HQ: Bioclinica, Inc.
211 Carnegie Ctr
Princeton NJ 08540

(G-2767)
BUON APPETITO FROM ITALY LLC
15 Shaw St (06320-4939)
PHONE....860 437-3668
Petrit Marku,
Sander Marku,
EMP: 8 **EST:** 2010
SALES (est): 381.6K **Privately Held**
SIC: 1389 Oil/Gas Field Services

(G-2768)
CARWILD CORPORATION (PA)
3 State Pier Rd (06320-5817)
PHONE....860 442-4914
Joel S Wildstein, *Ch of Bd*
Heather Schryver, *Controller*
Ryan Schryver, *Supervisor*
Thomas McDonald, *Director*
◆ **EMP:** 32
SQ FT: 40,000
SALES: 20MM **Privately Held**
WEB: www.carwild.net
SIC: 3842 3841 Mfg Surgical Appliances/Supplies Mfg Surgical/Medical Instruments

(G-2769)
CLARK MANNER MARGUARITE
Also Called: Leon's Upholstery
601 Broad St (06320-2544)
PHONE....860 444-7679
EMP: 7
SALES: 350K **Privately Held**
SIC: 2512 Mfg Upholstered Household Furniture

(G-2770)
DAY PUBLISHING COMPANY (HQ)
Also Called: Day, The
47 Eugene Oneill Dr (06320-6351)
P.O. Box 1231 (06320-1231)
PHONE....860 701-4200
Gary Farrugia, *President*
Bob Tousignant, *CFO*
Lisa Brown, *Sales Staff*
David J Glaski, *Sales Staff*
Jaclyn Nardone, *Marketing Mgr*
EMP: 352
SQ FT: 20,000
SALES (est): 33.4MM **Privately Held**
WEB: www.marianireck.com
SIC: 2711 Newspapers-Publishing/Printing
PA: The Day Trust
47 Eugene Oneill Dr
New London CT 06320
860 442-2200

(G-2771)
EPATH LEARNING INC
300 State St Ste 400 (06320-6115)
PHONE....860 444-7900
Dudley Molina, *President*
Steve Morse, *Vice Pres*
Steven Morse, *Vice Pres*
Carol Wojtkun, *Vice Pres*
Donna Lord, *Production*
▼ **EMP:** 32
SQ FT: 3,457
SALES (est): 3.9MM **Privately Held**
WEB: www.epathcampus.com
SIC: 7372 Prepackaged Software Services

(G-2772)
FARRAR SAILS INC
6 Union St Ste 6 # 6 (06320-6107)
PHONE....860 447-0382
Kevin Farrar, *President*
William Reed, *Corp Secy*
John Lucey, *Vice Pres*
EMP: 4
SQ FT: 12,000
SALES (est): 399.6K **Privately Held**
WEB: www.farrarsails.com
SIC: 2394 7699 Mfg Sails From Purchased Materials Sail Repair Shop & Ret Yachting Accessories

(G-2773)
FIRST AID BANDAGE CO INC
Also Called: Fabco Wrap
3 State Pier Rd (06320-5817)
PHONE....860 443-8499
Joel S Wildstein, *President*
EMP: 15 **EST:** 1932
SQ FT: 4,000
SALES (est): 1.6MM **Privately Held**
WEB: www.fabco.net
SIC: 3842 5122 Mfg Bandages & Whol First Aid Supplies

(G-2774)
JEWISH LEADER NEWSPAPER
28 Channing St (06320-5756)
PHONE....860 442-7395
Jerome Fischer, *Exec Dir*
EMP: 3 **EST:** 2016
SALES (est): 74K **Privately Held**
SIC: 2711 Newspapers-Publishing/Printing

(G-2775)
NEW LONDON PRINTING CO LLC
Also Called: Minuteman Press
147 State St Ste 1 (06320-6353)
PHONE....860 701-9171
Gail Weber,
EMP: 4
SALES (est): 501K
SALES (corp-wide): 23.4MM **Privately Held**
SIC: 2752 Comm Prtg Litho
PA: Minuteman Press International, Inc.
61 Executive Blvd
Farmingdale NY 11735
631 249-1370

(G-2776)
ORTRONICS INC (DH)
125 Eugene Oneill Dr # 140 (06320-6417)
PHONE....860 445-3900
Mark Panico, *President*
Halsey Cook, *President*
Doug Fikse, *President*
Jerry Mix, *President*
Larry Giles, *Partner*
▲ **EMP:** 60
SALES (est): 108.2MM
SALES (corp-wide): 20.6MM **Privately Held**
WEB: www.ortronics.com
SIC: 3577 3357 Mfg Computer Peripheral Equipment Nonferrous Wiredrawing/Insulating
HQ: Legrand Holding, Inc.
60 Woodlawn St
West Hartford CT 06110
860 233-6251

(G-2777)
QDISCOVERY LLC (HQ)
Also Called: Forensicon
125 Eugene Oneill Dr # 140 (06320-6430)
PHONE....860 271-7080
Robert Polus, *President*
Dana Conneally, *Managing Prtnr*
Don Elliott, *Vice Pres*
Arjuna Reddy, *VP Finance*
James Norman, *Sales Mgr*
EMP: 28 **EST:** 2011
SALES (est): 5.5MM **Privately Held**
SIC: 7372 Prepackaged Software Services

(G-2778)
QUALITY PRINTERS INC
141 Shaw St (06320-4930)
P.O. Box 749 (06320-0749)
PHONE....860 443-2800
Faye Vathauer, *President*
Brenda Vathauer, *Vice Pres*
Chad Waterman, *Info Tech Mgr*
Frank Londregan, *Admin Sec*
EMP: 9
SQ FT: 4,800
SALES (est): 1.5MM **Privately Held**
WEB: www.qualityprintersct.com
SIC: 2752 Commercial Offset Printer Including Advertising Layouts

(G-2779)
SHEFFIELD PHARMACEUTICALS LLC (PA)
170 Broad St (06320-5313)
PHONE..................................860 442-4451
Jeffrey Davis, *President*
Roland Hernandez, *Exec VP*
Ana De Oliveira, *Vice Pres*
Anthony Sollima, *Vice Pres*
James Congdon, *VP Opers*
◆ **EMP:** 135
SQ FT: 113,618
SALES (est): 35.4MM **Privately Held**
WEB: www.sheffield-labs.com
SIC: 2844 5122 Mfg Toilet Preparations Whol Drugs/Sundries

(G-2780)
SIGN A RAMA
Also Called: Sign-A-Rama
365 Broad St (06320-3726)
PHONE..................................860 443-9744
Bill Shaw, *Owner*
EMP: 5
SQ FT: 2,500
SALES (est): 240K **Privately Held**
SIC: 3993 Signsadv Specs

(G-2781)
T L S DESIGN & MANUFACTURING
100 Blinman St (06320-5646)
PHONE..................................860 439-1414
Thomas L Smith II, *President*
EMP: 5
SQ FT: 6,600
SALES (est): 616.7K **Privately Held**
SIC: 3599 8711 Custom Machine Shop

(G-2782)
THAMES SHIPYARD & REPAIR CO
50 Farnsworth St (06320-4104)
P.O. Box 791 (06320-0791)
PHONE..................................860 442-5349
John P Wronowski, *President*
Richard Macmurray, *Vice Pres*
Thomas Tyreseck, *Vice Pres*
Adam C Wronowski, *Vice Pres*
EMP: 100
SQ FT: 6,000
SALES (est): 19.1MM **Privately Held**
SIC: 3731 Shipbuilding/Repairing

(G-2783)
TIMES COMMUNITY NEWS GROUP
47 Eugene Oneill Dr (06320-6306)
PHONE..................................860 437-1150
Howard Lee, *Principal*
EMP: 3
SALES (est): 138.8K **Privately Held**
SIC: 2711 Newspapers-Publishing/Printing

(G-2784)
TRANE US INC
571 Broad St (06320-2517)
PHONE..................................860 437-6208
Chuck Mrowka, *Branch Mgr*
EMP: 62 **Privately Held**
SIC: 3585 Mfg Refrigeration/Heating Equipment
HQ: Trane U.S. Inc.
3600 Pammel Creek Rd
La Crosse WI 54601
608 787-2000

New Milford
Litchfield County

(G-2785)
3 STORY SOFTWARE LLC
63 Bridge St (06776-3527)
PHONE..................................203 530-3224
Darren Reid, *Mng Member*
EMP: 8 **EST:** 2007
SALES (est): 819.7K
SALES (corp-wide): 7.6B **Privately Held**
SIC: 7372 Prepackaged Software Services
PA: Hays Plc
250 Euston Road
London NW1 2
-

(G-2786)
71 PICKETT DISTRICT ROAD LLC
71 Pickett District Rd (06776-4412)
PHONE..................................860 350-5964
Hector Reyes, *Technology*
Antonio Capanna Jr,
EMP: 3
SALES (est): 243.1K **Privately Held**
SIC: 3612 3677 3679 Mfg Transformers Mfg Electronic Coils/Transformers Mfg Electronic Components

(G-2787)
BALL & ROLLER BEARING CO LLC
46 Old State Rd Ste 4 (06776-4330)
PHONE..................................860 355-4161
David Nohe, *President*
Mike Smith, *Mktg Dir*
EMP: 10
SALES (est): 1.7MM **Privately Held**
WEB: www.bandrb.com
SIC: 3568 3562 3312 Mfg Power Transmission Equipment Mfg Ball/Roller Bearings Blast Furnace-Steel Works

(G-2788)
BOOK AUTOMATION INC
458 Danbury Rd Ste B10 (06776-4380)
PHONE..................................860 354-7900
Manrico Caglioni, *President*
Giovanna Meratti, *Admin Sec*
▲ **EMP:** 4 **EST:** 1975
SQ FT: 3,000
SALES: 1.9MM
SALES (corp-wide): 4.6MM **Privately Held**
WEB: www.bookautomation.com
SIC: 2789 3541 Bookbinding/Related Work Mfg Machine Tools-Cutting
PA: Cofint Sa
Avenue Pasteur 3
Luxembourg 2311
-

(G-2789)
CALCULATOR TRAINING
94 Buckingham Rd (06776-2235)
PHONE..................................860 355-8255
T Patrick Burke, *Owner*
EMP: 3
SALES (est): 100K **Privately Held**
SIC: 2731 Books-Publishing/Printing

(G-2790)
CANDLEWOOD MACHINE PDTS LLC
46 Old State Rd Ste 6 (06776-4330)
P.O. Box 262, Brookfield (06804-0262)
PHONE..................................860 350-2211
EMP: 3
SQ FT: 1,000
SALES (est): 210K **Privately Held**
SIC: 3599 Machine Shop

(G-2791)
CARLSON SHEET METAL
24 Bostwick Pl (06776-3510)
PHONE..................................860 354-4660
Craig R Carlson, *Principal*
EMP: 3
SALES (est): 287.3K **Privately Held**
SIC: 3444 Mfg Sheet Metalwork

(G-2792)
CHEMESSENCE INC
180 Sunny Valley Rd # 15 (06776-3393)
PHONE..................................860 355-4108
Michael Lavelle, *President*
Robert W Booth Jr, *Treasurer*
George Whitmeyer, *Sales Staff*
EMP: 4 **EST:** 1964
SQ FT: 4,000
SALES (est): 470.9K **Privately Held**
WEB: www.chemessence.com
SIC: 2844 Mfg Perfume Bases

(G-2793)
COL-LAR ENTERPRISES INC (PA)
37 S End Plz (06776-4243)
PHONE..................................203 798-1786
Lawrence Prockter, *President*
Collen G Prockter, *Vice Pres*
▲ **EMP:** 11
SQ FT: 1,000
SALES (est): 2MM **Privately Held**
SIC: 3944 Games Toys And Children's Vehicles

(G-2794)
COMPUCISION LLC
29 S End Plz (06776-4235)
PHONE..................................860 355-9790
George Blass,
Eve Sturdevant,
EMP: 4
SQ FT: 3,600
SALES (est): 688.7K **Privately Held**
SIC: 3599 Mfg Industrial Machinery

(G-2795)
CRYSTAL FAIRFIELD TECH LLC
8 S End Plz (06776-4200)
PHONE..................................860 354-2111
Andrew Timmerman,
▼ **EMP:** 11
SQ FT: 6,500
SALES (est): 1.5MM **Privately Held**
WEB: www.fairfieldcrystal.com
SIC: 3679 Mfg Electronic Components

(G-2796)
D F & B PRECISION MFG INC
180 Sunny Valley Rd Ste 3 (06776-3361)
PHONE..................................860 354-5663
Domenico Franciamore, *President*
Domingo Franciamore, *Vice Pres*
EMP: 6
SQ FT: 18,000
SALES (est): 862.6K **Privately Held**
SIC: 3599 Mfg Industrial Machinery

(G-2797)
DYNAMIC LASERS LLC
324 Candlewood Mtn Rd (06776-5802)
PHONE..................................866 731-9610
EMP: 5 **EST:** 2011
SALES: 2MM **Privately Held**
WEB: www.dynamiclasers.com
SIC: 3845 Mfg Electromedical Equipment

(G-2798)
EAST BRANCH ENGRG & MFG INC
57 S End Plz (06776-4244)
PHONE..................................860 355-9661
Paul Guidotti, *President*
Chris Guidotti, *Principal*
Linda Guidotti, *Admin Sec*
EMP: 16
SQ FT: 1,500
SALES (est): 2.5MM **Privately Held**
WEB: www.eastbrancheng.com
SIC: 3089 Mfg Plastic Products

(G-2799)
FARRELL PRCSION MTALCRAFT CORP
192 Danbury Rd (06776-4311)
PHONE..................................860 355-2651
Michael Tkacs, *President*
William Farrell, *Vice Pres*
Terrance Farrell, *Treasurer*
EMP: 40
SQ FT: 17,500
SALES (est): 8.8MM **Privately Held**
SIC: 3444 3479 7692 Mfg Sheet Metalwork Coating/Engraving Service Welding Repair

(G-2800)
GLACIER COMPUTER LLC (PA)
46 Bridge St Ste 1 (06776-3531)
PHONE..................................860 355-7552
Daniel Poisson, *Vice Pres*
Ronald D'Ambrosio, *Mng Member*
Brian Wallace, *Info Tech Mgr*
EMP: 4
SQ FT: 2,500
SALES (est): 2.9MM **Privately Held**
WEB: www.glaciercomputer.com
SIC: 3571 Mfg Electronic Computers

(G-2801)
GO GREEN INDUSTRIES LLC
23 Meredith Ln (06776-3723)
PHONE..................................914 772-0026
EMP: 3
SALES (est): 127.4K **Privately Held**
SIC: 3999 Mfg Misc Products

(G-2802)
GUARDIAN ENVMTL TECH INC
208 Sawyer Hill Rd (06776-2018)
P.O. Box 2344, New Preston (06777-0344)
PHONE..................................860 350-2200
William Litwin, *President*
Patricia Garland, *Marketing Staff*
James McKeon, *Technical Staff*
EMP: 18
SQ FT: 800
SALES (est): 2.4MM **Privately Held**
WEB: www.guardianenvironmental.com
SIC: 3589 3564 Mfg Service Industry Machinery Mfg Blowers/Fans

(G-2803)
GULFSTREAM AEROSPACE CORP
142 Second Hill Rd (06776-3138)
PHONE..................................860 210-1469
EMP: 4
SALES (corp-wide): 36.1B **Publicly Held**
SIC: 3721 4581 Mfg Aircraft/Airport Services
HQ: Gulfstream Aerospace Corporation
500 Gulfstream Rd
Savannah GA 31408
912 965-3000

(G-2804)
GWILLIAM COMPANY INC
46 Old State Rd (06776-4330)
PHONE..................................860 354-2884
David Nohe, *President*
Margaret Nohe, *Admin Sec*
▲ **EMP:** 12 **EST:** 1929
SALES (est): 3.2MM **Privately Held**
SIC: 3562 3568 Mfg Ball/Roller Bearings Mfg Power Transmission Equipment

(G-2805)
H & S WOODWORKS L T D
161 Merryall Rd (06776-5226)
PHONE..................................914 391-3926
Howard Senior, *Principal*
EMP: 4 **EST:** 2009
SALES (est): 502.2K **Privately Held**
SIC: 2431 Mfg Millwork

(G-2806)
IT HELPS LLC
54 Boxwood Ln (06776-4673)
PHONE..................................860 799-8321
Weimin LI, *Principal*
Xueyan Dong, *Principal*
EMP: 5 **EST:** 2016
SALES (est): 115.2K **Privately Held**
SIC: 7372 Prepackaged Software Services

(G-2807)
JB MUZE ENTERPRISES
Also Called: Fat City Sports
180 Sunny Valley Rd Ste 9 (06776-3361)
PHONE..................................860 355-5949
Jill Weiss, *Owner*
EMP: 4
SALES (est): 321.7K **Privately Held**
SIC: 2759 Commercial Printing

(G-2808)
JOSEPH J MCFADDEN JR
Also Called: Quality Machine
87 Danbury Rd (06776-3413)
PHONE..................................860 354-6794
Joseph J McFadden Jr, *Owner*
Edwin Estinal, *Manager*
EMP: 6
SQ FT: 4,500
SALES (est): 466.8K **Privately Held**
SIC: 3599 Machine Job Shop

(G-2809)
KARAS ENGINEERING CO INC
20 Old Route 7 Plz (06776-4339)
PHONE..................................860 355-3153
Denny Karas, *President*
Andrea Karas, *COO*
Shane Karas, *Engineer*
Lisa Karas, *Admin Sec*
EMP: 8
SQ FT: 5,000
SALES (est): 1.3MM **Privately Held**
WEB: www.karaseng.com
SIC: **3599** Mfg Industrial Machinery

(G-2810)
KILCOURSE SPECIALTY PRODUCTS
46 Old State Rd Ste 3 (06776-4330)
PHONE..................................860 210-2075
David Kilcourse, *Principal*
EMP: 6
SQ FT: 6,000
SALES (est): 968K **Privately Held**
SIC: **2591** 7389 Mfg Drapery Hardware/Blinds Business Services

(G-2811)
KIMBERLY-CLARK CORPORATION
58 Pickett District Rd (06776-4493)
PHONE..................................860 210-1602
Marvin Prewitt, *Warehouse Mgr*
Tom Condon, *Engineer*
Scott Hamylak, *Engineer*
Wayne Sanders, *Manager*
Daphy Mc Kay, *Technician*
EMP: 600
SALES (corp-wide): 18.4B **Publicly Held**
WEB: www.kimberly-clark.com
SIC: **2621** 2676 Paper Mill Mfg Sanitary Paper Products
PA: Kimberly-Clark Corporation
351 Phelps Dr
Irving TX 75038
972 281-1200

(G-2812)
LABLITE LLC
8 S Main St (06776-3508)
P.O. Box 1206 (06776-1206)
PHONE..................................860 355-8817
Randy Bell, *COO*
Curtis Read, *Executive*
EMP: 10
SQ FT: 1,400
SALES (est): 953.9K **Privately Held**
WEB: www.lablite.com
SIC: **7372** Prepackaged Software Services

(G-2813)
LOCAL MEDIA GROUP INC
Also Called: Greater New Milford Spectrum
45 Main St (06776-2807)
PHONE..................................860 354-2273
Deborah Rose, *Principal*
EMP: 4
SALES (corp-wide): 1.5B **Publicly Held**
WEB: www.ottaway.com
SIC: **2711** Newspapers-Publishing/Printing
HQ: Local Media Group, Inc.
40 Mulberry St
Middletown NY 10940
845 341-1100

(G-2814)
MODELVISION INC
566 Danbury Rd Ste 4 (06776-4331)
PHONE..................................860 355-3884
David Spiegel, *President*
Laura Spiegel, *Corp Secy*
EMP: 7
SQ FT: 7,500
SALES (est): 829.3K **Privately Held**
SIC: **3999** Mfg Misc Products

(G-2815)
NEELTRAN INC
71 Pickett District Rd (06776-4412)
PHONE..................................860 350-5964
Antonio Capanna Jr, *President*
Dave Franco, *Owner*
◆ **EMP:** 117
SQ FT: 45,000
SALES (est): 36.2MM **Privately Held**
WEB: www.neeltran.com
SIC: **3612** 3677 3679 Mfg Transformers Mfg Electronic Coils/Transformers Mfg Electronic Components

(G-2816)
NEW MILFORD BLOCK & SUPPLY
574 Danbury Rd (06776-4341)
PHONE..................................860 355-1101
Jay Montfort, *President*
John Montfort, *Admin Sec*
EMP: 15
SQ FT: 25,000
SALES (est): 2.3MM **Privately Held**
SIC: **3271** 5032 5211 5039 Mfg Concrete Block/Brick Whol Brick/Stone Matrls Ret Lumber/Building Mtrl

(G-2817)
NEW MILFORD COMMISSION
Also Called: New Milfrd Water Pollutn Cntrl
123 West St (06776-3540)
P.O. Box 178 (06776-0178)
PHONE..................................860 354-3758
Ken Bailey, *Superintendent*
EMP: 11
SQ FT: 3,652
SALES (est): 1.3MM **Privately Held**
SIC: **3589** Mfg Service Industry Machinery

(G-2818)
NEW MILFORD FARMS INC
60 Boardman Rd (06776-5516)
PHONE..................................860 210-0250
Walter Carey, *President*
EMP: 12
SALES (est): 1.4MM
SALES (corp-wide): 14.9B **Publicly Held**
WEB: www.garick.com
SIC: **2875** Mfg Fertilizers-Mix Only
HQ: Garick, Llc
13600 Broadway Ave Ste 1
Cleveland OH 44125
216 581-0100

(G-2819)
NUTEK AEROSPACE CORP
180 Sunny Valley Rd Ste 2 (06776-3361)
PHONE..................................860 355-3169
Joseph Di Candido, *President*
Eloise Di Candido, *Treasurer*
EMP: 7
SQ FT: 7,000
SALES (est): 1.2MM **Privately Held**
WEB: www.nutekaerospace.com
SIC: **3592** Mfg Aerospace Valves

(G-2820)
O & G INDUSTRIES INC
271 Danbury Rd (06776-4313)
PHONE..................................860 354-4438
Bill Eayrs, *Branch Mgr*
EMP: 53
SQ FT: 7,465
SALES (corp-wide): 538MM **Privately Held**
WEB: www.ogind.com
SIC: **2951** 1542 Mfg Asphalt Mixtures/Blocks Nonresidential Construction
PA: O & G Industries, Inc.
112 Wall St
Torrington CT 06790
860 489-9261

(G-2821)
OLIVE NUTMEG OIL ✪
25 Main St (06776-2807)
PHONE..................................860 354-7300
EMP: 3 **EST:** 2019
SALES (est): 91.3K **Privately Held**
SIC: **2079** Mfg Edible Fats/Oils

(G-2822)
PARKER MEDICAL INC
5 Old Town Park Rd # 34 (06776-4212)
PHONE..................................860 350-3446
Tony Szklany, *Manager*
EMP: 4
SALES (corp-wide): 6.4MM **Privately Held**
SIC: **3844** Mfg X-Ray Apparatus
PA: Parker Medical Inc.
137 New Milford Rd E
Bridgewater CT 06752
860 350-4304

(G-2823)
PATRICIA POKE
Also Called: Patricias Presents
20 Maple Ln (06776-4021)
P.O. Box 1449 (06776-1449)
PHONE..................................860 354-4193
Patricia Poke, *Owner*
EMP: 6
SALES (est): 420.9K **Privately Held**
WEB: www.patriciaspresents.com
SIC: **3111** Mfg Accessories

(G-2824)
QUALITY MACHINE INC
87 Danbury Rd (06776-3413)
PHONE..................................860 354-6794
Joseph John McFadden Jr, *Principal*
EMP: 3
SALES (est): 260.6K **Privately Held**
SIC: **3599** Mfg Industrial Machinery

(G-2825)
RAND WHITNEY
7 Nutmeg Dr (06776-4113)
PHONE..................................860 354-6063
Elmer Burkey, *Principal*
EMP: 3 **EST:** 2009
SALES (est): 215.2K **Privately Held**
SIC: **3131** Mfg Footwear Cut Stock

(G-2826)
S M CHURYK IRON WORKS INC
Also Called: Churyk, Stefan M
539 Danbury Rd (06776-4304)
PHONE..................................860 355-1777
Stefan Churyk, *President*
Wayne Churyk, *Vice Pres*
EMP: 5
SQ FT: 10,000
SALES (est): 713.2K **Privately Held**
SIC: **3446** Manufactures Structural Steelwork

(G-2827)
SEGA READY MIX INCORPORATED (PA)
519 Danbury Rd (06776-4392)
PHONE..................................860 354-3969
Roderic Oneglia, *President*
EMP: 10
SQ FT: 8,000
SALES (est): 2MM **Privately Held**
SIC: **3273** Mfg Ready-Mixed Concrete

(G-2828)
SETMA INC
458 Danbury Rd Ste A2 (06776-4381)
PHONE..................................409 833-9797
Joseph Duchon, *President*
Margaret Ross, *Admin Sec*
EMP: 4 **EST:** 1975
SQ FT: 2,000
SALES: 300K **Privately Held**
WEB: www.setma.com
SIC: **3599** Machine Shop

(G-2829)
TIMBERCRAFT LLC
70 S End Plz (06776-4245)
PHONE..................................860 355-5538
James McGough,
EMP: 5
SALES (est): 762.5K **Privately Held**
SIC: **3731** Shipbuilding/Repairing

(G-2830)
TLC ULTRASOUND INC
143 West St Ste V (06776-3525)
PHONE..................................860 354-6333
Thomas Leveille, *President*
Joan F Leveille, *Admin Sec*
EMP: 5
SQ FT: 2,500
SALES (est): 1MM **Privately Held**
SIC: **3829** Mfg Measuring/Controlling Devices

(G-2831)
TOTAL REGISTER INC
180 Sunny Valley Rd Ste 1 (06776-3361)
PHONE..................................860 210-0465
Terence Gallagher, *President*
Daniel J Gallagher, *Vice Pres*
John Gallagher, *Vice Pres*
▲ **EMP:** 10
SALES (est): 870K **Privately Held**
WEB: www.totalregister.com
SIC: **3699** Mfg Laser Systems & Equipment Specializing In Holography And Rotary Die-Cutting Holograms

(G-2832)
TRI STATE CHOPPERS LLC
30 Old Route 7 Plz (06776-4340)
PHONE..................................860 210-1854
Carl J Lindstrom, *Manager*
EMP: 3
SALES (est): 329.5K **Privately Held**
SIC: **3751** Ret Motorcycles

(G-2833)
YORK STREET STUDIO INC
Also Called: Yorkstreet.com
143 West St Ste Y (06776-3525)
PHONE..................................203 266-9000
Linda Zelenko, *CEO*
Stephen Piscuskas, *Vice Pres*
EMP: 6
SALES: 1.4MM **Privately Held**
WEB: www.yorkstreet.com
SIC: **3429** 3648 Mfg Hardware Mfg Lighting Equipment

New Preston
Litchfield County

(G-2834)
D K SCHULMAN
239 New Milford Tpke (06777-1604)
P.O. Box 2325 (06777-0325)
PHONE..................................860 868-4300
Dana Schulman, *Owner*
EMP: 3
SALES (est): 338.4K **Privately Held**
SIC: **2621** Paper Mill

(G-2835)
STUDIO STEEL INC
159 New Milford Tpke (06777-1603)
PHONE..................................860 868-7305
Spencer Hardy, *President*
Matt Archer, *Manager*
EMP: 9
SQ FT: 10,000
SALES (est): 1.3MM **Privately Held**
WEB: www.studiosteel.com
SIC: **3648** Mfg Lighting

Newington
Hartford County

(G-2836)
A-1 CHROME AND POLISHING CORP
125 Stamm Rd (06111-3619)
PHONE..................................860 666-4593
Claudio Spada, *President*
Joseph Spada, *Vice Pres*
EMP: 14 **EST:** 1980
SQ FT: 2,400
SALES (est): 1.6MM **Privately Held**
WEB: www.a1chrome.com
SIC: **3471** Plating/Polishing Service

(G-2837)
ADDAMO MANUFACTURING INC
360 Stamm Rd (06111-3627)
PHONE..................................860 667-2601
Sebastian Addamo, *President*
Paul Addamo, *Vice Pres*
Sevvy Addamo, *Vice Pres*
Lucy Addamo, *Admin Sec*
EMP: 7
SQ FT: 15,000
SALES (est): 1MM **Privately Held**
SIC: **3469** 3599 Mfg Machine Parts & Machine Shop

(G-2838)
ADVANCED ADHESIVE SYSTEMS INC
Also Called: A A S
681 N Mountain Rd (06111-1349)
PHONE..................................860 953-4100
Robert Batson, *CEO*
Andy Batson, *President*
Carol Batson, *Treasurer*
Fred Caputo, *Technical Staff*
EMP: 28
SALES (est): 6.9MM **Privately Held**
WEB: www.advancedadhesivesystems.com
SIC: 2891 Mfg Adhesives/Sealants

(G-2839)
ADVANCED TORQUE PRODUCTS LLC
56 Budney Rd (06111-5132)
P.O. Box 7241, Berlin (06037-7241)
PHONE..................................860 828-1523
Dan Castle, *Mng Member*
George L Castle,
EMP: 8
SQ FT: 12,146
SALES (est): 1.6MM **Privately Held**
WEB: www.advancedtorque.com
SIC: 3545 Mfg Machine Tool Accessories

(G-2840)
ALLIANCE GRAPHICS INC
16 Progress Cir Bldg 3 (06111-5545)
PHONE..................................860 666-7992
Mark Bruks, *CEO*
EMP: 10
SQ FT: 4,200
SALES (est): 1.9MM **Privately Held**
WEB: www.aginK.com
SIC: 2752 7334 Lithographic Commercial Printing Photocopying Services

(G-2841)
ALLIED MACHINING CO INC
Also Called: Allied Engineering
50 Progress Cir Ste 3 (06111-5547)
PHONE..................................860 665-1228
Katherine Jankowski, *President*
Peter Jankowski, *Corp Secy*
Chris Jankowski, *Vice Pres*
EMP: 9
SQ FT: 9,600
SALES (est): 2MM **Privately Held**
SIC: 3599 Mfg Industrial Machinery

(G-2842)
AMERICAN TOOL & MFG CORP
125 Rockwell Rd (06111-5535)
PHONE..................................860 666-2255
Grzegorz Wolanin, *CEO*
EMP: 11
SQ FT: 6,000
SALES: 1.5MM **Privately Held**
SIC: 3599 Mfg Industrial Machinery

(G-2843)
ANCHOR RUBBER PRODUCTS LLC
152 Rockwell Rd Ste C9 (06111-5554)
PHONE..................................860 667-2628
Michael Shannon, *General Mgr*
Robert Shannon,
▲ **EMP:** 6 **EST:** 1996
SQ FT: 5,000
SALES (est): 938.9K **Privately Held**
WEB: www.anchorrubber.com
SIC: 3069 Mfg Fabricated Rubber Products

(G-2844)
ATLAS STAMPING & MFG CORP
729 N Mountain Rd (06111-1424)
PHONE..................................860 757-3233
Kenneth Prigodich, *President*
EMP: 30
SQ FT: 13,500
SALES (est): 6MM **Privately Held**
WEB: www.asm.necoxmail.com
SIC: 3469 3544 Mfg Metal Stampings Mfg Dies/Tools/Jigs/Fixtures

(G-2845)
B&N AEROSPACE INC
44 Rockwell Rd (06111-5526)
PHONE..................................860 665-0134
Dennis Blaszko, *President*
Walter Blaszko, *Principal*
Donna Blaszko, *Corp Secy*
Gary Klinsman Sr, *Vice Pres*
Gary Klinzmann, *Vice Pres*
EMP: 45
SQ FT: 15,000
SALES (est): 10MM **Privately Held**
WEB: www.bntool.com
SIC: 3728 Mfg Aircraft Parts/Equipment

(G-2846)
BEACON GROUP INC (PA)
549 Cedar St (06111-1814)
PHONE..................................860 594-5200
Suresh Mirchandani, *President*
Karishma Mirchandani, *Vice Pres*
Robert Sarkisian, *Vice Pres*
Ajoy Alphonso, *Production*
Nishita Mirchandani, *Human Resources*
EMP: 135
SQ FT: 100,000
SALES (est): 23.4MM **Privately Held**
WEB: www.thebeacongroup.com
SIC: 3724 3812 3053 3714 Mfg Aircraft Engine/Part Mfg Search/Navgatn Equip Mfg Gasket/Packing/Seals Mfg Motor Vehicle Parts

(G-2847)
BEACON INDUSTRIES INC
549 Cedar St (06111-1814)
PHONE..................................860 594-5200
Suresh Mirchandani, *CEO*
Robert S Sarkisian, *Vice Pres*
Mietek Kostaniak, *Technology*
▲ **EMP:** 122 **EST:** 1948
SQ FT: 300,000
SALES: 18MM
SALES (corp-wide): 23.4MM **Privately Held**
WEB: www.beacongp.com
SIC: 3728 Mfg Aircraft Parts/Equipment
PA: The Beacon Group Inc
549 Cedar St
Newington CT 06111
860 594-5200

(G-2848)
BEN & JERRYS HOMEMADE INC
120 Northwood Rd (06111-3152)
PHONE..................................203 488-9666
EMP: 3
SALES (corp-wide): 67.1B **Privately Held**
SIC: 2024 Mfg Ice Cream/Frozen Desert
HQ: Ben & Jerry's Homemade, Inc.
30 Community Dr Ste 1
South Burlington VT 05403
802 846-1500

(G-2849)
BRAMPTON TECHNOLOGY LTD
61 Maselli Rd (06111-5520)
PHONE..................................860 667-7689
Shaun Wheatley, *Principal*
EMP: 5 **EST:** 1996
SALES (est): 568.1K **Privately Held**
WEB: www.bramptontechnology.com
SIC: 3949 Mfg Sporting/Athletic Goods

(G-2850)
BRYKA SKYSTOCKS LLC
549 Cedar St (06111-1814)
PHONE..................................845 507-8200
Suresh Mirchandani,
Karishma Mirchandani,
EMP: 5
SQ FT: 1,700
SALES: 2MM **Privately Held**
SIC: 3728 Mfg Aircraft Parts/Equipment

(G-2851)
C & A MACHINE CO INC
49 Progress Cir (06111-5532)
PHONE..................................860 667-0605
Joe Milluzzo, *President*
Andre Senteio, *QC Mgr*
John Marut, *Admin Sec*
EMP: 43
SQ FT: 16,000
SALES: 10MM **Privately Held**
SIC: 3451 3599 Mfg Screw Machine Products Mfg Industrial Machinery

(G-2852)
CATSKILL GRAN COUNTERTOPS INC
Also Called: Counters
156 Pane Rd Ste A (06111-5557)
PHONE..................................860 667-1555
Nicacio F Pinho, *President*
EMP: 12
SALES (est): 1.8MM **Privately Held**
SIC: 3131 Mfg Footwear Cut Stock

(G-2853)
CEDA COMPANY INC
36 Holmes Rd (06111-1787)
PHONE..................................860 666-1593
Donald Morander, *President*
Derek Morander, *Software Dev*
EMP: 6
SQ FT: 8,750
SALES: 1MM **Privately Held**
WEB: www.cedacompany.com
SIC: 3541 8711 Mfg & Design Machine Tools

(G-2854)
CENTRAL CONNECTICUT SLS & MFG
37 Stanwell Rd (06111-4531)
PHONE..................................860 667-1411
Paul Campbell, *President*
Cindy Campbell, *Principal*
Richard Campbell, *Vice Pres*
EMP: 7
SQ FT: 6,000
SALES (est): 860.1K **Privately Held**
WEB: www.walbernprecision.com
SIC: 3599 Machine Job Shop

(G-2855)
COMPONENT TECHNOLOGIES INC (PA)
Also Called: CTI
68 Holmes Rd (06111-1708)
PHONE..................................860 667-1065
Fred Viggiano, *President*
Fred Viggiano Jr, *President*
Larry Hutnick, *Vice Pres*
EMP: 22
SQ FT: 24,000
SALES (est): 3.1MM **Privately Held**
WEB: www.componenttechnologiesinc.com
SIC: 3471 Plating/Polishing Service

(G-2856)
CONVERTING MCHY ADHESIVES LLC
50 Sleepy Hollow Rd (06111-1034)
PHONE..................................860 561-0226
Vincent J Barresi, *Principal*
EMP: 4
SALES (est): 293.8K **Privately Held**
SIC: 2891 Mfg Adhesives/Sealants

(G-2857)
CUSTOM METAL CRAFTERS INC
Also Called: Custom Metal Crafters CMC
815 N Mountain Rd (06111-1489)
PHONE..................................860 953-4210
Daniel F Bourget, *President*
Stephen Rosner, *President*
Jean Bourget, *Chairman*
Lynn M Clemente, *Vice Pres*
▲ **EMP:** 56
SQ FT: 55,000
SALES (est): 10.6MM **Privately Held**
WEB: www.custom-metal.com
SIC: 3364 3369 3363 Mfg Nonferrous Die-Castings Nonferrous Metal Foundry Mfg Aluminum Die-Castings

(G-2858)
CYR WOODWORKING INC
139 Summit St (06111-1715)
PHONE..................................860 232-1991
Roderique Cyr, *President*
Lisa Salvini, *Sales Executive*
EMP: 7 **EST:** 1966
SALES (est): 900K **Privately Held**
WEB: www.cyrwoodworking.com
SIC: 2521 2434 Mfg Office & Kitchen Cabinets

(G-2859)
DATA-GRAPHICS INC
240 Hartford Ave (06111-2077)
PHONE..................................860 667-0435
Andrew Mandell, *President*
Bruce Mandell, *Vice Pres*
Joyce Mandell, *Admin Sec*
▲ **EMP:** 74
SQ FT: 15,000
SALES (est): 22.6MM **Privately Held**
SIC: 2752 Lithographic Commercial Printing

(G-2860)
EDAC TECHNOLOGIES LLC
Edac Aero
275 Richard St (06111-5046)
PHONE..................................860 667-2134
Tom Mosdale, *General Mgr*
EMP: 120 **Privately Held**
WEB: www.edactechnologies.com
SIC: 3728 Mfg Aircraft Parts/Equipment
HQ: Edac Technologies Llc
5 Mckee Pl
Cheshire CT 06410
203 806-2090

(G-2861)
EDRIVE ACTUATORS INC
385 Stamm Rd (06111-3628)
PHONE..................................860 953-0588
Richard Swanson, *President*
James Haury, *Vice Pres*
EMP: 8
SQ FT: 3,600
SALES (est): 1.4MM
SALES (corp-wide): 2.7B **Publicly Held**
WEB: www.edriveactuators.com
SIC: 3545 Mfg Machine Tool Accessories
HQ: Joyce/Dayton Corp.
3300 S Dixie Dr Ste 101
Dayton OH 45439
937 294-6261

(G-2862)
ENVELOPES & MORE INC
124 Francis Ave (06111-1216)
PHONE..................................860 286-7570
Mike Sullivan, *President*
John Sullivan, *President*
Michael Sullivan, *President*
Tim Sullivan, *Treasurer*
EMP: 15
SALES: 2.5MM **Privately Held**
WEB: www.envmore.com
SIC: 2759 Printing Of Envelopes

(G-2863)
FINE PRINT NEW ENGLAND INC
711 N Mountain Rd (06111-1424)
PHONE..................................860 953-0660
James Weber Jr, *President*
EMP: 8
SQ FT: 7,200
SALES (est): 495K **Privately Held**
SIC: 2752 Lithographic Commercial Printing

(G-2864)
FLOW RESOURCES INC (HQ)
Also Called: Wolf Colorprint
135 Day St Ste 1 (06111-1200)
PHONE..................................860 666-1200
John W Meier, *CEO*
Glenn Basale, *Vice Pres*
EMP: 25
SQ FT: 20,000
SALES (est): 4.7MM
SALES (corp-wide): 35MM **Privately Held**
WEB: www.wolfcolorprint.com
SIC: 2752 Lithographic Commercial Printing
PA: J.S. Mccarthy Co., Inc.
15 Darin Dr
Augusta ME 04330
207 622-6241

(G-2865)
FRASAL TOOL CO INC
14 Foster St (06111-4906)
PHONE..................................860 666-3524
Frank Giangrave, *President*
Pierrette Giangrave, *Corp Secy*
Paul Giangrave, *Vice Pres*
▲ **EMP:** 10

SALES (est): 1.5MM Privately Held
WEB: www.frasaltool.com
SIC: 3599 3546 Machine Shop

(G-2866)
GKN AEROSPACE NEWINGTON LLC
183 Louis St (06111)
PHONE..........800 667-8502
EMP: 3
SALES (est): 180K Privately Held
SIC: 3724 Aircraft Engines And Engine Parts

(G-2867)
GKN AEROSPACE NEWINGTON LLC (DH)
183 Louis St (06111)
PHONE..........860 667-8502
Lauren Bukowski, *Human Res Mgr*
Martin Thorden,
▲ EMP: 146
SQ FT: 43,000
SALES (est): 37.3MM
SALES (corp-wide): 11.3B Privately Held
SIC: 3724 3728 Mfg Aircraft Engines/Parts Mfg Aircraft Parts/Equipment
HQ: Gkn Aerospace Sweden Ab
Flygmotorvagen 1m
Trollhattan 461 3
520 940-00

(G-2868)
GRANITE LLC
116 Willard Ave (06111-1125)
PHONE..........860 586-8132
Luiz C Ribeiro, *Principal*
EMP: 6
SALES (est): 455.9K Privately Held
SIC: 3281 Trade Contractor

(G-2869)
HANGER PRSTHETCS & ORTHO INC
181 Patricia M Genova Dr (06111-1500)
PHONE..........860 667-5370
Patricia Havens, *Manager*
EMP: 5
SALES (corp-wide): 1B Publicly Held
SIC: 3842 Mfg Surgical Appliances/Supplies
HQ: Hanger Prosthetics & Orthotics, Inc.
10910 Domain Dr Ste 300
Austin TX 78758
512 777-3800

(G-2870)
HI-TECH POLISHING INC
50 Progress Cir Ste 3 (06111-5547)
PHONE..........860 665-1399
Pasquale Griffo, *President*
Frances Griffo, *Vice Pres*
EMP: 13
SQ FT: 1,600
SALES (est): 1.5MM Privately Held
SIC: 3471 Precision Polishing

(G-2871)
IMAGE INK INC
102 Pane Rd Ste A (06111-5561)
PHONE..........860 665-9792
Jeff Gambino, *President*
Scott Skates, *Vice Pres*
EMP: 5
SQ FT: 2,200
SALES (est): 700.5K Privately Held
SIC: 2752 Lithographic Commercial Printing

(G-2872)
INTEGRAL INDUSTRIES INC
111 Holmes Rd (06111-1714)
PHONE..........860 953-0686
Edward R Mascolo, *President*
Joann Mascolo, *Corp Secy*
Edward Mark Mascolo, *Vice Pres*
EMP: 17
SQ FT: 8,000
SALES (est): 4.6MM Privately Held
WEB: www.integralind.com
SIC: 3545 Mfg Machine Tool Accessories

(G-2873)
J OCONNOR LLC
Also Called: Connecticut Metalworks
309 Pane Rd Ste 1 (06111-5500)
PHONE..........860 665-7702
Jim Oconnor, *Principal*
James O' Connor,
EMP: 15
SQ FT: 12,000
SALES (est): 2.4MM Privately Held
SIC: 3499 3444 Mfg Misc Fabricated Metal Products Mfg Sheet Metalwork

(G-2874)
JENSEN MACHINE CO
721 Russell Rd (06111-1527)
PHONE..........860 666-5438
John Andrew Jensen Jr, *President*
Alice Jensen, *Treasurer*
EMP: 9
SQ FT: 15,000
SALES: 1MM Privately Held
WEB: www.jensenmachine.com
SIC: 3599 Mfg Industrial Machinery

(G-2875)
KELLOGG COMPANY
52 Hollow Tree Ln (06111)
PHONE..........860 665-9920
EMP: 699
SALES (corp-wide): 13.5B Publicly Held
WEB: www.kelloggs.com
SIC: 2043 Mfg Cereals
PA: Kellogg Company
1 Kellogg Sq
Battle Creek MI 49017
269 961-2000

(G-2876)
KOHLER MIX SPECIALTIES LLC
100 Milk Ln (06111-2242)
PHONE..........860 666-1511
Rachel A Gonzalez,
Midd McManus,
EMP: 132 EST: 2001
SQ FT: 70,000
SALES (est): 13.7MM Publicly Held
SIC: 2099 2038 2026 2023 Mfg Food Preparations Mfg Frozen Specialties Mfg Fluid Milk Mfg Dry/Evap Dairy Prdts
HQ: Dean Holding Company
2711 N Haskell Ave # 340
Dallas TX 75204
214 303-3400

(G-2877)
LYNN WELDING CO INC
75 Rockwell Rd Ste 1 (06111-5564)
PHONE..........860 667-4400
Jan Kania, *President*
James Inglis Sr, *President*
Ricardo Kimball, *General Mgr*
Joseph Inglis, *Treasurer*
Regina Kania, *Admin Sec*
EMP: 13
SQ FT: 13,900
SALES (est): 2.4MM Privately Held
SIC: 3599 7692 Mfg Industrial Machinery Welding Repair

(G-2878)
M & R MANUFACTURING INC
Also Called: National Tool & CAM
111 Carr Ave (06111-4331)
PHONE..........860 666-5066
Joseph Wieter, *President*
EMP: 6
SQ FT: 3,200
SALES (est): 894.5K Privately Held
SIC: 3544 3545 Mfg Dies/Tools/Jigs/Fixtures Mfg Machine Tool Accessories

(G-2879)
MACRISTY INDUSTRIES INC (PA)
610 N Mountain Rd (06111-1347)
PHONE..........860 225-4637
Jeff Barlow, *President*
Jon Brad Barlow, *Asst Sec*
Kristin Barlow, *Asst Sec*
▲ EMP: 247
SQ FT: 150,000
SALES (est): 31MM Privately Held
WEB: www.macristyindustries.com
SIC: 3498 3432 3433 4226 Mfg Fabrctd Pipe/Fitting Mfg Plumbing Fxtr Fittng Mfg Heat Equip-Nonelec Special Warehse/Storage General Crop Farm

(G-2880)
MATIAS IMPORTING & DISTRG CORP
Also Called: Matias Importing & Distrg Co
135 Fenn Rd (06111-2250)
PHONE..........860 666-5544
Ernest Matias, *President*
Mary L Matias, *Director*
▲ EMP: 3
SQ FT: 1,200
SALES (est): 250K Privately Held
SIC: 3443 7692 5181 5182 Mfg Fabricated Plate Wrk Welding Repair Whol Beer/Ale Whol Wine/Distilled Bev

(G-2881)
MEGA MANUFACTURING LLC
115 Pane Rd (06111-5522)
PHONE..........860 666-5555
EMP: 7
SALES: 300K Privately Held
SIC: 3599 Mfg Industrial Machinery

(G-2882)
MICROTRAIN INC
23 Judge Ln (06111-4224)
PHONE..........860 666-7890
Michale Domdek, *President*
EMP: 5
SALES (est): 440K Privately Held
SIC: 7372 Prepackaged Software Services

(G-2883)
MINIATURE NUT & SCREW CORP
820 N Mountain Rd (06111-1415)
PHONE..........860 953-4490
Pauline Smith, *President*
Keith Smith, *Vice Pres*
Mark Smith, *Vice Pres*
EMP: 6 EST: 1963
SQ FT: 10,000
SALES (est): 788.9K Privately Held
SIC: 3452 Mfg Bolts/Screws/Rivets

(G-2884)
MUIR ENVELOPE PLUS INC
Also Called: Muir Envelope Div
124 Francis Ave (06111-1216)
PHONE..........860 953-6847
Paul Klett, *President*
Jack Muir, *Corp Secy*
EMP: 12
SQ FT: 40,000
SALES (est): 1.4MM Privately Held
SIC: 2759 2752 Prints Trade Envelopes

(G-2885)
N & B MANUFACTURING CO INC
215 Pascone Pl (06111-4524)
PHONE..........860 667-3204
Miroslaw Boksz, *President*
Krzysztos Nowakowski, *Corp Secy*
Jesse Boksz, *Vice Pres*
EMP: 4
SQ FT: 7,000
SALES (est): 499.9K Privately Held
SIC: 3724 Mfg Aircraft Engines/Parts

(G-2886)
NCT INC
Also Called: Numerical Control Technology
20 Holmes Rd (06111-1708)
PHONE..........860 666-8424
Volodmyr Drobockyi, *President*
Adam Jarzebowski, *President*
Elizabeth Jarzebowski, *Vice Pres*
Walter Jarzebowski, *Vice Pres*
EMP: 15
SQ FT: 12,500
SALES: 700K Privately Held
WEB: www.nctfrictionwelding.com
SIC: 7692 7629 7389 Welding Repair Electrical Repair Business Services

(G-2887)
NOWAK PRODUCTS INC
101 Rockwell Rd (06111-5535)
PHONE..........860 666-9685
Gary Nowak, *President*
Jay Giblin, *Corp Secy*
Florian Nowak, *Director*
EMP: 9
SQ FT: 20,000
SALES: 1.5MM Privately Held
WEB: www.nowakproducts.com
SIC: 3541 Mfg Machine Tools-Cutting

(G-2888)
OMAR COFFEE COMPANY
41 Commerce Ct (06111-2246)
PHONE..........860 667-8889
Steve Costas, *Ch of Bd*
Diane C Bokron, *President*
Joann Lemnior, *Vice Pres*
Greg Dadinos, *Plant Mgr*
Daniel Dimauro, *Sales Staff*
EMP: 50 EST: 1937
SQ FT: 30,000
SALES (est): 9.4MM Privately Held
WEB: www.omarcoffeecompany.com
SIC: 2095 5149 Mfg Roasted Coffee Whol Groceries

(G-2889)
PAL CORPORATION
Also Called: Model Works
45 Maselli Rd (06111-5520)
PHONE..........860 666-9211
Timothy Dostie, *President*
Julia R Dostie, *Vice Pres*
Alice Dostie, *Treasurer*
EMP: 6
SQ FT: 2,500
SALES (est): 568.3K Privately Held
SIC: 3599 Machine Shop

(G-2890)
PALADIN COMMERCIAL PRTRS LLC
300 Hartford Ave (06111-1501)
PHONE..........860 953-4900
William Saunders, *Owner*
Sean Coane, *Sales Staff*
George Feisthamel, *Program Mgr*
EMP: 27
SQ FT: 13,000
SALES (est): 5MM Privately Held
SIC: 2752 Lithographic Commercial Printing

(G-2891)
PAUL WELDING COMPANY INC
157 Kelsey St (06111-5419)
PHONE..........860 229-9945
Michael Paul, *President*
Terese Seidl, *Corp Secy*
David Paul, *Vice Pres*
Jeffrey Paul, *Vice Pres*
Michael J Paul, *Director*
EMP: 13
SQ FT: 5,000
SALES: 500K Privately Held
SIC: 7692 Welding Repair

(G-2892)
PCX AEROSTRUCTURES LLC
300 Fenn Rd (06111-2277)
PHONE..........860 666-2471
EMP: 40
SALES (corp-wide): 100MM Privately Held
WEB: www.cpx.com
SIC: 3441 Structural Metal Fabrication
PA: Pcx Aerostructures, Llc
300 Fenn Rd
Newington CT 06111
860 666-2471

(G-2893)
PCX AEROSTRUCTURES LLC (PA)
300 Fenn Rd (06111-2277)
PHONE..........860 666-2471
Jeff Frisby, *President*
Tim Fagan, *CFO*
▲ EMP: 200
SQ FT: 145,000
SALES: 100MM Privately Held
SIC: 3728 Mfg Aircraft Parts/Equipment

(G-2894)
PROMISE PROPANE
110 Holmes Rd (06111-1713)
PHONE..................................860 685-0676
Justin Kovalcek, *Principal*
EMP: 3
SALES (est): 112.1K **Privately Held**
SIC: 1311 Crude Petroleum/Natural Gas Production

(G-2895)
PRONTO PRINTER OF NEWINGTON
2406 Berlin Tpke (06111-4105)
PHONE..................................860 666-2245
Robert Sander, *President*
Holly H Sander, *Vice Pres*
EMP: 5
SQ FT: 2,700
SALES (est): 746.3K **Privately Held**
WEB: www.prontoprinterofnewington.com
SIC: 2752 Lithographic Commercial Printing

(G-2896)
PROSPECT PRODUCTS INCORPORATED
43 Kelsey St (06111-5415)
PHONE..................................860 666-0323
Richard E Carlson, *President*
Jerry Johnson, *General Mgr*
Liza Bang, *Office Mgr*
EMP: 26 **EST:** 1950
SQ FT: 4,000
SALES (est): 18.9MM **Privately Held**
WEB: www.prospectproducts.com
SIC: 3559 3826 3089 Mfg Misc Industry Machinery Mfg Analytical Instruments Mfg Plastic Products

(G-2897)
RADICAL COMPUTING CORPORATION
705 N Mountain Rd A210 (06111-1432)
PHONE..................................860 953-0240
Timur Y Ruban, *President*
EMP: 5
SQ FT: 1,500
SALES (est): 328.8K **Privately Held**
WEB: www.radicalcomputing.com
SIC: 7372 Prepackaged Software Services

(G-2898)
RENO MACHINE COMPANY INC
170 Pane Rd Ste 1 (06111-5537)
PHONE..................................860 666-5641
Antonio Occhialini, *Ch of Bd*
Mark Occhialini, *President*
Art Santos, *Production*
Carroll Bouchard, *QC Mgr*
David Occhialini, *Treasurer*
▲ **EMP:** 65 **EST:** 1956
SQ FT: 68,000
SALES (est): 13.3MM **Privately Held**
SIC: 3599 7692 3544 Mfg Industrial Machinery Welding Repair Mfg Dies/Tools/Jigs/Fixtures

(G-2899)
RICHARDS MACHINE TOOL CO INC
187 Stamm Rd (06111-3619)
PHONE..................................860 436-2938
Lillian Bartkowicz, *President*
Dorothy Bartkowicz Weber, *Vice Pres*
EMP: 12 **EST:** 1978
SQ FT: 7,000
SALES (est): 2.1MM **Privately Held**
SIC: 3599 3544 Mfg Industrial Machinery Mfg Dies/Tools/Jigs/Fixtures

(G-2900)
SACCUZZO COMPANY INC
149 Louis St (06111-4517)
PHONE..................................860 665-1101
Vincent Saccuzzo, *President*
Marco Saccuzzo, *Senior VP*
Vincenzo Saccuzzo, *Engineer*
▲ **EMP:** 7
SQ FT: 16,000
SALES (est): 1MM **Privately Held**
WEB: www.icaffe.com
SIC: 2095 5046 5149 Mfg Roasted Coffee Whol Commercial Equipment Whol Groceries

(G-2901)
SCHUCO USA LLLP (HQ)
Also Called: Schuco International
240 Pane Rd (06111-5527)
PHONE..................................860 666-0505
Thomas Knobloch, *CEO*
Dirk U Hindrichs, *President*
Edgar Freind, *Partner*
Dana Grant, *Facilities Mgr*
Andreas Gursch, *Sales Dir*
◆ **EMP:** 56 **EST:** 1997
SQ FT: 90,000
SALES (est): 14.4MM
SALES (corp-wide): 1B **Privately Held**
WEB: www.schuco-usa.com
SIC: 2431 Mfg Millwork
PA: SchUco International Kg
Karolinenstr. 1-15
Bielefeld 33609
521 783-0

(G-2902)
SHEPARD STEEL CO INC
55 Shepard Dr (06111-1159)
PHONE..................................860 525-4446
Allen Shilosky, *Branch Mgr*
EMP: 30
SALES (corp-wide): 19.4MM **Privately Held**
WEB: www.shepardsteel.com
SIC: 3316 3446 3441 Mfg Cold-Rolled Steel Shapes Mfg Architectural Metalwork Structural Metal Fabrication
PA: Shepard Steel Co. Inc.
110 Meadow St
Hartford CT 06114
860 525-4446

(G-2903)
SIGNS NOW LLC
2434 Berlin Tpke Ste 14 (06111-4122)
PHONE..................................860 667-8339
Susan Hamilton, *Principal*
Randy Hamilton,
EMP: 6
SALES: 390K **Privately Held**
SIC: 3993 2759 Mfr Signs & Screen Printing

(G-2904)
SOUSA CORP
565 Cedar St (06111-1814)
PHONE..................................860 523-9090
Norman W Sousa Jr, *President*
EMP: 11
SQ FT: 37,000
SALES (est): 2.4MM **Privately Held**
SIC: 3398 3471 8734 Metal Heat Treating Plating/Polishing Service Testing Laboratory

(G-2905)
SYCHRON INC
683 N Mountain Rd (06111-1350)
PHONE..................................860 953-8157
EMP: 3
SALES (est): 153.4K **Privately Held**
SIC: 2861 Mfg Gum/Wood Chemicals

(G-2906)
THE KEENEY MANUFACTURING CO (PA)
Also Called: Plumb Pak Medical
1170 Main St (06111-3098)
PHONE..................................603 239-6371
Robert S Holden, *CEO*
Jean Hanna Holden, *Chairman*
James H Holden, *Exec VP*
Edwin F Atkins, *Vice Pres*
Stephen A Cooke, *Vice Pres*
▲ **EMP:** 200
SQ FT: 150,000
SALES: 132MM **Privately Held**
WEB: www.keeneymfg.com
SIC: 3432 5074 Mfg Plumbing Fixture Fittings Whol Plumbing Equipment/Supplies

(G-2907)
TILCON CONNECTICUT INC
301 Harford Ave Unit 301 (06111)
P.O. Box 310903 (06131-0903)
PHONE..................................860 756-8016
Tim Marti, *Manager*
EMP: 3
SALES (corp-wide): 29.7B **Privately Held**
WEB: www.tilconct.com
SIC: 1442 Gravel Pit
HQ: Tilcon Connecticut Inc.
642 Black Rock Ave
New Britain CT 06052
860 224-6010

(G-2908)
TRUSS MANUFACTURING INC
97 Stanwell Rd (06111-4531)
PHONE..................................860 665-0000
Lawrence Vernon, *President*
Aurelien Giguere, *Vice Pres*
EMP: 13
SQ FT: 8,000
SALES (est): 2.3MM **Privately Held**
WEB: www.trussmfg.com
SIC: 2439 Mfg Structural Wood Members

(G-2909)
U S STUCCO LLC
28 Costello Pl (06111-5146)
PHONE..................................860 667-1935
Beata Pszczola, *Principal*
EMP: 9
SALES (est): 792.8K **Privately Held**
SIC: 3299 Mfg Nonmetallic Mineral Products

(G-2910)
U-SEALUSA LLC
56 Fenn Rd (06111-2212)
PHONE..................................860 667-0911
Ilran Kim,
EMP: 90 **EST:** 2011
SQ FT: 20,000
SALES (est): 8.9MM **Privately Held**
SIC: 3444 Mfg Sheet Metalwork

(G-2911)
VN MACHINE CO
57 Maselli Rd (06111-5520)
PHONE..................................860 666-8797
Lan Psam, *Owner*
EMP: 3
SQ FT: 2,000
SALES (est): 267K **Privately Held**
SIC: 3599 Mfg Industrial Machinery

(G-2912)
WEST HRTFORD STIRS CBINETS INC
17 Main St (06111-1314)
P.O. Box 330118, West Hartford (06133-0118)
PHONE..................................860 953-9151
Andre Letourneau, *President*
EMP: 85 **EST:** 1937
SQ FT: 68,000
SALES (est): 11.6MM **Privately Held**
SIC: 2431 2434 Mfg Millwork Mfg Wood Kitchen Cabinets

(G-2913)
ZAVARELLA WOODWORKING INC
48 Commerce Ct (06111-2246)
PHONE..................................860 666-6969
Bruno Zavarella, *President*
EMP: 9
SALES (est): 1.9MM **Privately Held**
WEB: www.zavarellawoodworking.com
SIC: 2431 Mfg Millwork

Newtown
Fairfield County

(G-2914)
AMERICAN ALLOY WIRE CORP
1 Wire Rd (06470-1613)
P.O. Box 667, Sandy Hook (06482-0667)
PHONE..................................203 426-3133
William J McCarthy, *President*
James Dyke, *Vice Pres*
EMP: 4
SALES: 500K **Privately Held**
SIC: 3357 Nonferrous Wiredrawing/Insulating

(G-2915)
AMERICAN WIRE CORPORATION
1 Wire Rd (06470-1613)
P.O. Box 667, Sandy Hook (06482-0667)
PHONE..................................203 426-3133
William J McCarthy, *President*
William J Mc Carthy, *President*
William Dyke, *Vice Pres*
EMP: 15 **EST:** 1928
SQ FT: 40,000
SALES: 1.5MM **Privately Held**
SIC: 3357 Mfg Copper Magnet Wire

(G-2916)
BETLAN CORPORATION
31 Pecks Ln Ste 7 (06470-5312)
PHONE..................................203 270-7898
Thomas A Polchowski, *President*
EMP: 10
SQ FT: 6,000
SALES (est): 980K **Privately Held**
WEB: www.betlan.com
SIC: 3634 1711 Mfg & Installs Kitchen Hood Exhaust & Ventilating Systems

(G-2917)
CAD/CAM DNTL STDIO MIL CTR INC
184 Mount Pleasant Rd (06470-1408)
PHONE..................................203 733-3069
Bernt Balke,
EMP: 3 **EST:** 2017
SALES (est): 83.9K **Privately Held**
SIC: 3999 Mfg Misc Products

(G-2918)
CASCADES HOLDING US INC
Cascades Cntnrbard Pckg Nwtown
1 Edmund Rd (06470-1632)
PHONE..................................203 426-5871
Geoff Schiffenhaus, *Plant Mgr*
EMP: 61
SALES (corp-wide): 3.5B **Privately Held**
SIC: 2653 Mfg Corrugated/Solid Fiber Boxes
HQ: Cascades Holding Us Inc.
4001 Packard Rd
Niagara Falls NY 14303
716 285-3681

(G-2919)
CHASE MEDIA GROUP
31 Pecks Ln Ste 3 (06470-5312)
PHONE..................................914 962-3871
Dave Fitzmorris, *Manager*
EMP: 14
SALES (est): 619.6K **Privately Held**
SIC: 2711 Newspapers-Publishing/Printing

(G-2920)
EDELMAN METALWORKS INC
36 Butterfield Rd (06470-1009)
PHONE..................................203 744-7331
David Edelman, *President*
Dana Edelman, *Vice Pres*
EMP: 6
SALES (est): 1MM **Privately Held**
SIC: 3446 Mfg Architectural Metalwork

(G-2921)
FLAGPOLE SOFTWARE LLC
19 Scudder Rd (06470-1769)
PHONE..................................203 426-5166
EMP: 4
SALES: 400K **Privately Held**
SIC: 7372 Prepackaged Software Services

(G-2922)
FORECAST INTERNATIONAL INC
22 Commerce Rd Ste 1 (06470-1643)
PHONE..................................203 426-0800
Edward M Nebinger, *CEO*
Douglas A Nebinger, *President*
Margaret G Nebinger, *Vice Pres*
Monty Nebinger, *Vice Pres*
Marge Nebinger, *VP Finance*
EMP: 57
SQ FT: 15,600
SALES (est): 7.6MM **Privately Held**
WEB: www.forecastinternational.com
SIC: 2731 8742 Books-Publishing/Printing Management Consulting Services

▲ = Import ▼=Export
◆ =Import/Export

(G-2923)
HELIUM PLUS INC
17 Pebble Rd (06470-2229)
PHONE..................................203 304-1880
Rose Mary Savo, *President*
EMP: 5
SALES (est): 682.1K **Privately Held**
SIC: 2813 Mfg Industrial Gases

(G-2924)
HOPP COMPANIES INC
3 Simm Ln Ste 2 (06470-2393)
PHONE..................................800 889-8425
Robert Hopp, *President*
EMP: 12
SQ FT: 5,000
SALES (est): 2MM **Privately Held**
WEB: www.hoppcompanies.com
SIC: 3578 3086 Mfg Calculating Equipment Mfg Plastic Foam Products

(G-2925)
HP HOOD LLC
153 S Main St (06470-2791)
PHONE..................................203 304-9151
Matthew J D Amico, *President*
EMP: 296
SALES (corp-wide): 2.2B **Privately Held**
SIC: 2026 Mfg Fluid Milk
PA: Hp Hood Llc
6 Kimball Ln Ste 400
Lynnfield MA 01940
617 887-8441

(G-2926)
HUBBELL INCORPORATED
14 Prospect Dr (06470-2338)
PHONE..................................203 426-2555
Michael O'Connor, *Vice Pres*
Robert Khansen, *Branch Mgr*
EMP: 20
SALES (corp-wide): 4.4B **Publicly Held**
WEB: www.hubbell.com
SIC: 3643 Mfg Conductive Wiring Devices
PA: Hubbell Incorporated
40 Waterview Dr
Shelton CT 06484
475 882-4000

(G-2927)
L M T COMMUNICATIONS INC
Also Called: L M T Magazine
84 S Main St (06470-2356)
PHONE..................................203 426-4568
Judy Fishman, *President*
Kate Conetta, *Production*
Zhane Cardenas, *Sales Staff*
Susan Poitras, *Office Mgr*
Lauren Meehan, *Manager*
EMP: 11
SQ FT: 1,600
SALES: 1.2MM **Privately Held**
WEB: www.lmtcommunications.com
SIC: 2721 7389 Periodical-Publish/Print Business Services

(G-2928)
M CUBED TECHNOLOGIES INC (HQ)
31 Pecks Ln Ste 8 (06470-5312)
PHONE..................................203 304-2940
Randall Price Sr, *President*
Jai Singh, *Exec VP*
Mike Aghajanian, *Vice Pres*
Lori Capomolla, *Vice Pres*
Sean Mulhall, *Senior Buyer*
▲ **EMP:** 45 **EST:** 1993
SQ FT: 110,000
SALES (est): 773.2K
SALES (corp-wide): 1.3B **Publicly Held**
WEB: www.mmmt.com
SIC: 3444 5051 3599 Mfg Sheet Metalwork Metals Service Center Mfg Industrial Machinery
PA: Ii-Vi Incorporated
375 Saxonburg Blvd
Saxonburg PA 16056
724 352-4455

(G-2929)
NATIONAL SHOOTING SPORTS FOUND
11 Mile Hill Rd Ste A (06470-2328)
PHONE..................................203 426-1320
Steve Sanetti, *President*
Bill Dunn, *Managing Dir*
Lawrence Keane, *Senior VP*
Nancy Coburn, *Vice Pres*
Chris Dolnack, *Vice Pres*
EMP: 44
SQ FT: 20,000
SALES: 44MM **Privately Held**
WEB: www.nssf.org
SIC: 2721 8611 2741 Periodicals-Publishing/Printing Business Association Misc Publishing

(G-2930)
NEW LEAF PHARMACEUTICAL
77 S Main St (06470-2388)
P.O. Box 735 (06470-0735)
PHONE..................................203 270-4167
Paul Carpenter, *CEO*
EMP: 17
SALES (est): 763.3K **Privately Held**
SIC: 2834 Mfg Pharmaceutical Preparations

(G-2931)
NEWTOWN SPORTS GROUP
15 Anthony Ridge Rd (06470-1344)
PHONE..................................508 341-1238
Robert Burbank, *Principal*
EMP: 3
SALES (est): 112K **Privately Held**
SIC: 2711 Newspapers-Publishing/Printing

(G-2932)
OLD CASTLE FOODS LLC
13 Old Castle Dr (06470-1783)
PHONE..................................203 426-1344
William Meier, *Principal*
EMP: 3 **EST:** 2012
SALES (est): 182.4K **Privately Held**
SIC: 2099 Mfg Food Preparations

(G-2933)
QSONICA LLC
Also Called: Sonicators
53 Church Hill Rd (06470-1614)
PHONE..................................203 426-0101
Lauren Soloff, *President*
Robert Soloff, *Vice Pres*
Steven A Bowen, *CFO*
Ronald Verrilli, *Admin Sec*
EMP: 8
SALES (est): 544.3K
SALES (corp-wide): 19.6MM **Publicly Held**
WEB: www.Sonicator.com
SIC: 3569 Mfg General Industrial Machinery
PA: Sonics & Materials, Inc.
53 Church Hill Rd
Newtown CT 06470
203 270-4600

(G-2934)
RAND-WHITNEY GROUP LLC
Also Called: Rand-Whitney Container Newtown
1 Edmund Rd (06470-1600)
P.O. Box 498 (06470-0498)
PHONE..................................203 426-5871
Dick Minton, *Manager*
EMP: 75 **Privately Held**
SIC: 2653 Mfg Corrugated & Solid Fiber Boxes
HQ: Rand-Whitney Group Llc
1 Rand Whitney Way
Worcester MA 01607
508 791-2301

(G-2935)
ROBERT LOUIS COMPANY INC
31 Shepard Hill Rd (06470-1936)
PHONE..................................203 270-1400
Robert Foege, *President*
EMP: 3
SALES (est): 270K **Privately Held**
SIC: 3949 Manufacturing Sporting/Athletic Goods

(G-2936)
SHOP SMART CENTRAL INC
Also Called: Chase Press
31 Pecks Ln (06470-5312)
PHONE..................................914 962-3871
Carla Chase, *President*
EMP: 7 **EST:** 2005
SALES (est): 659.4K **Privately Held**
SIC: 2741 Misc Publishing

(G-2937)
SINOL USA INC
77 S Main St (06470-2388)
P.O. Box 735 (06470-0735)
PHONE..................................203 470-7404
Paul Carpenter, *CEO*
EMP: 10
SALES (est): 1.6MM **Privately Held**
WEB: www.sinolusa.com
SIC: 2834 Mfg Pharmaceutical Preparations

(G-2938)
SONICS & MATERIALS INC (PA)
Also Called: Ultra Sonic Seal Co
53 Church Hill Rd (06470-1699)
PHONE..................................203 270-4600
Robert Soloff, *CEO*
Lauren H Soloff, *Vice Pres*
Lauren Soloff, *Vice Pres*
Steven Bowen, *CFO*
▲ **EMP:** 75 **EST:** 1969
SQ FT: 44,000
SALES (est): 19.6MM **Publicly Held**
WEB: www.Sonics.com
SIC: 3548 3569 Mfg Welding Apparatus Mfg General Industrial Machinery

(G-2939)
STANDARD PNEUMATIC PRODUCTS
31 Shepard Hill Rd (06470-1936)
PHONE..................................203 270-1400
Robert Foege, *President*
Jeanne Foege, *Corp Secy*
EMP: 3 **EST:** 1992
SQ FT: 2,600
SALES: 500K **Privately Held**
WEB: www.stdpneumatics.com
SIC: 3563 Manufactures Autodual

(G-2940)
SWIVEL MACHINE WORKS INC
11 Monitor Hill Rd (06470-2242)
PHONE..................................203 270-6343
Glen Ekstrom, *President*
EMP: 3
SALES: 250K **Privately Held**
WEB: www.swivelmachine.com
SIC: 3949 5941 Mfg Sporting/Athletic Goods Ret Sporting Goods/Bicycles

(G-2941)
TAUNTON INC
Also Called: Taunton Press
63 S Main St (06470-2355)
P.O. Box 5506 (06470-0921)
PHONE..................................203 426-8171
Daniel R McCarthy, *CEO*
Andrea Roman, *Ch of Bd*
Timothy Rahr, *President*
Jeffrey Roos, *Manager*
Justin Fink, *Assoc Editor*
EMP: 844
SQ FT: 70,000
SALES (est): 76.7MM **Privately Held**
SIC: 2721 2731 7812 5963 Periodical-Publish/Print Book-Publishing/Printing Motion Pict/Video Prodtn Direct Retail Sales

(G-2942)
TAUNTON PRESS INC
191 S Main St (06470-2733)
PHONE..................................203 426-8171
John Lively, *CEO*
EMP: 285
SALES (corp-wide): 72MM **Privately Held**
WEB: www.taunton.com
SIC: 2721 Publisher Of Magazines Books & Video's
PA: The Taunton Press Inc
63 S Main St
Newtown CT 06470
203 426-8171

(G-2943)
THE BEE PUBLISHING COMPANY (PA)
Also Called: Health Monitor
5 Church Hill Rd (06470-1605)
P.O. Box 5503 (06470-5503)
PHONE..................................203 426-8036
R Scudder Smith, *President*
Scott Baggett, *General Mgr*
Helen Smith, *Vice Pres*
Kim Smith, *Controller*
Sandra Morici, *Credit Mgr*
▼ **EMP:** 50 **EST:** 1877
SQ FT: 20,000
SALES (est): 3.7MM **Privately Held**
WEB: www.thebee.com
SIC: 2711 Newspapers-Publishing/Printing

(G-2944)
THE BEE PUBLISHING COMPANY
17 Commerce Rd (06470-1607)
PHONE..................................203 426-0178
James Busby, *Manager*
EMP: 4
SALES (est): 251.9K
SALES (corp-wide): 3.7MM **Privately Held**
WEB: www.thebee.com
SIC: 2711 Newspapers-Publishing/Printing
PA: The Bee Publishing Company
5 Church Hill Rd
Newtown CT 06470
203 426-8036

(G-2945)
TIER ONE LLC
31 Pecks Ln Ste 1 (06470-5312)
PHONE..................................203 426-3030
Terry Toth, *Engineer*
Linda Iassogna, *CFO*
Richard A Hall,
EMP: 67
SQ FT: 35,000
SALES (est): 12.7MM **Privately Held**
WEB: www.tieronemachining.com
SIC: 3599 Mfg Industrial Machinery

(G-2946)
TUDOR CONVERTED PRODUCTS INC (PA)
22 Main St Unit 1b (06470-2106)
PHONE..................................203 304-1875
Richard P Cuminale Jr, *President*
Debbie T Cuminale, *Admin Sec*
▲ **EMP:** 20
SQ FT: 34,000
SALES (est): 2.7MM **Privately Held**
SIC: 2679 Mfg Converted Paper Products

(G-2947)
UTC FIRE SEC AMERICAS CORP INC
Fiber Options Division
16 Commerce Rd (06470-1607)
PHONE..................................203 426-1180
EMP: 120
SALES (corp-wide): 59.8B **Publicly Held**
SIC: 3669 3827 Mfg Communications Equipment Mfg Optical Instruments/Lenses
HQ: Utc Fire & Security Americas Corporation, Inc.
8985 Town Center Pkwy
Lakewood Ranch FL 34202

(G-2948)
WILD RVER CSTM SCREEN PRTG LLC
3 Simm Ln Ste 2e1 (06470-2300)
PHONE..................................203 426-1500
EMP: 4
SALES: 200K **Privately Held**
SIC: 2752 Lithographic Commercial Printing

(G-2949)
WIND CORPORATION
Also Called: Wind Hardware & Engineering
30 Pecks Ln (06470-2361)
PHONE..................................203 778-1001
Patrick E Wind, *President*
Kevin Houlihan, *Vice Pres*

GEOGRAPHIC

Matthews Brian, *Warehouse Mgr*
Dave Carlson, *Opers Staff*
Mike Gallo, *Engineer*
◆ **EMP:** 28
SQ FT: 60,000
SALES (est): 7.4MM **Privately Held**
WEB: www.windcorp.com
SIC: 3429 Whol Hardware

(G-2950)
ZEPHYR LOCK LLC
30 Pecks Ln (06470-2361)
PHONE..................................866 937-4971
Patrick Wind,
Kevin Houlihan,
▲ **EMP:** 12
SQ FT: 20,000
SALES (est): 1.3MM **Privately Held**
WEB: www.zephyrlock.com
SIC: 3429 Mfg Hardware

Niantic
New London County

(G-2951)
HAYLONS MARKET LLC
157 W Main St Ste 1 (06357-1057)
PHONE..................................860 739-9509
David Haylon, *Principal*
EMP: 3 **EST:** 2015
SALES (est): 110K **Privately Held**
SIC: 2051 Mfg Bread/Related Products

(G-2952)
HEATERS INC
11 Freedom Way Unit D5 (06357-1041)
PHONE..................................860 739-5477
Debra Thurlow, *President*
EMP: 5 **EST:** 1945
SQ FT: 5,000
SALES: 450K **Privately Held**
WEB: www.heatincorp.com
SIC: 2822 Mfg Synthetic Rubber

(G-2953)
JAMMAR MFG CO INC
26 Industrial Park Rd (06357-1209)
P.O. Box 392, Uncasville (06382-0392)
PHONE..................................866 848-1113
James Bliss, *President*
Marian Bliss, *Admin Sec*
EMP: 5
SALES (est): 607.9K **Privately Held**
WEB: www.jammarmfg.com
SIC: 3949 Mfg Athletic Goods

(G-2954)
NIANTIC AWNING COMPANY
Also Called: Niantic Awning & Sunroom Co
193 Pennsylvania Ave (06357-1927)
PHONE..................................860 739-0161
Edwin Franklin, *President*
Karen Franklin, *Vice Pres*
EMP: 3 **EST:** 1995
SQ FT: 800
SALES (est): 453.1K **Privately Held**
WEB: www.nianticawning.com
SIC: 2431 2591 3444 3448 Mfg Millwork Mfg Drape Hardware/Blind Mfg Sheet Metalwork Mfg Prefab Metal Bldgs

(G-2955)
NIANTIC TOOL INC
Also Called: Machine Shop
32 Industrial Park Rd (06357-1209)
P.O. Box 205, East Lyme (06333-0205)
PHONE..................................860 739-2182
David Nelson, *President*
Robert W Nelson, *Vice Pres*
Joanne Nelson, *Admin Sec*
EMP: 6
SQ FT: 8,500
SALES: 839.9K **Privately Held**
WEB: www.niantictoolinc.com
SIC: 3599 Mfg Industrial Machinery

(G-2956)
PAW PRINT PANTRY LLC
214 Flanders Rd Ste A (06357-1260)
PHONE..................................860 447-8442
Jennifer Mohr, *Branch Mgr*
EMP: 9
SALES (corp-wide): 782.3K **Privately Held**
SIC: 2752 Lithographic Commercial Printing
PA: Paw Print Pantry Llc
33 Gurley Rd
East Lyme CT 06333
860 447-8442

Norfolk
Litchfield County

(G-2957)
KINGSLAND CO
7 Colebrook Rd (06058-1332)
P.O. Box 594 (06058-0594)
PHONE..................................860 542-6981
Luke K Burke, *President*
Liane Burke, *Corp Secy*
Mark K Burke, *Vice Pres*
Matthew K Burke, *Vice Pres*
EMP: 8
SQ FT: 7,200
SALES (est): 1MM **Privately Held**
WEB: www.kingsland-shutters.com
SIC: 2431 Millwork

(G-2958)
LOUIS E ALLYN SONS INC
270 Ashpohtag Rd (06058-1007)
P.O. Box 217, East Canaan (06024-0217)
PHONE..................................860 542-5741
Walter Allyn, *President*
Lisa Allen, *Manager*
EMP: 4
SALES (est): 251.4K **Privately Held**
SIC: 1381 Oil/Gas Well Drilling

North Branford
New Haven County

(G-2959)
BRIAN BERLEPSCH
Also Called: Imposition Graphics
21 Commerce Dr Ste 2 (06471-3204)
PHONE..................................203 484-9799
Brian Berlepsch, *Owner*
EMP: 4
SQ FT: 2,000
SALES (est): 220K **Privately Held**
SIC: 2752 Color Seperation & Digital Pre-Press Services

(G-2960)
CONCORDIA LTD
Also Called: J B Silk Screen Printing
5 Enterprise Dr (06471-1324)
P.O. Box 130 (06471-0130)
PHONE..................................203 483-0221
Rocco Esposito, *President*
Christopher Esposito, *Vice Pres*
EMP: 5
SQ FT: 4,000
SALES: 350K **Privately Held**
WEB: www.concordia-iye.org.uk
SIC: 2759 2396 Commercial Printing Mfg Auto/Apparel Trimming

(G-2961)
DICON CONNECTIONS INC
33 Fowler Rd (06471-1519)
P.O. Box 190 (06471-0190)
PHONE..................................203 481-8080
Jeffrey Williams, *President*
Timothy Williams, *Vice Pres*
Buzz Johnson, *Sales Staff*
EMP: 50
SQ FT: 18,000
SALES (est): 11.7MM **Privately Held**
WEB: www.diconconnections.com
SIC: 3643 Mfg Conductive Wiring Devices

(G-2962)
DWYER ALUMINUM MAST COMPANY
2 Commerce Dr Ste 1 (06471-1200)
PHONE..................................203 484-0419
Robert Dwyer, *President*
Andrew Dwyer, *Admin Sec*
◆ **EMP:** 10 **EST:** 1963
SQ FT: 10,500
SALES (est): 1.8MM **Privately Held**
WEB: www.dwyermast.com
SIC: 3365 3429 Aluminum Foundry Mfg Hardware

(G-2963)
DYNAMIC RACING TRANSM LLC
104-5 Enterprise Dr (06471)
PHONE..................................203 315-0138
Harold Miller,
EMP: 4
SALES (est): 800K **Privately Held**
WEB: www.dynamicracingtrans.com
SIC: 3714 Mfg Motor Vehicle Parts/Accessories

(G-2964)
GOODYFAB LLC
88 Totoket Rd (06471-1031)
PHONE..................................203 927-3059
Matt Goodwin,
EMP: 5
SALES (est): 667.8K **Privately Held**
SIC: 3446 7389 7692 Mfg Architectural Metalwork Metal Slitting And Shearing Welding Repair

(G-2965)
HALL MACHINE SYSTEMS INC (HQ)
Also Called: Hall Industries
8c Commerce Dr (06471-1250)
P.O. Box 647, Branford (06405-0647)
PHONE..................................203 481-4275
Robert Johnson, *President*
William Gurecki, *Vice Pres*
Douglas Hall, *Vice Pres*
Thomas McComiskey, *Vice Pres*
EMP: 9
SQ FT: 20,000
SALES (est): 2.1MM
SALES (corp-wide): 18MM **Privately Held**
SIC: 3549 5084 Mfg Metalworking Machinery Whol Industrial Equipment
PA: M.G.S. Manufacturing Inc.
122 Otis St
Rome NY 13441
315 337-3350

(G-2966)
HALLS RENTAL SERVICE LLC
Also Called: D C Hall Rental Service
45 Cedar Lake Rd (06471-1247)
PHONE..................................203 488-0383
David Hall, *Mng Member*
Catherine Hall,
EMP: 4
SALES: 290K **Privately Held**
SIC: 2531 Mfg Public Building Furniture

(G-2967)
HONEYWELL INTERNATIONAL INC
12 Clintonville Rd (06471)
PHONE..................................203 484-7161
EMP: 657
SALES (corp-wide): 41.8B **Publicly Held**
WEB: www.honeywell.com
SIC: 3724 Mfg Aircraft Engines/Parts
PA: Honeywell International Inc.
300 S Tryon St
Charlotte NC 28202
973 455-2000

(G-2968)
HYDROGEN HIGHWAY LLC
242 Branford Rd (06471-1303)
PHONE..................................203 871-1000
Terri S Alpert, *Manager*
EMP: 3
SALES (est): 146.1K **Privately Held**
SIC: 2813 Mfg Industrial Gases

(G-2969)
INTERNATIONAL PIPE & STL CORP
4 Enterprise Dr (06471-1354)
PHONE..................................203 481-7102
W A Lalani, *President*
Sada Lalani, *Admin Sec*
▼ **EMP:** 10
SQ FT: 25,000
SALES (est): 1.9MM **Privately Held**
WEB: www.internationalpipe.net
SIC: 3446 5051 3496 3315 Mfg Architectural Mtlwrk Metals Service Center Mfg Misc Fab Wire Prdts Mfg Steel Wire/Rltd Prdt

(G-2970)
MGS MANUFACTURING INC
Also Called: Mgs Group-Hall Industries The
8c Commerce Dr (06471-1250)
PHONE..................................203 481-4275
EMP: 4
SALES (corp-wide): 18MM **Privately Held**
SIC: 3549 Mfg Metalworking Machinery
PA: M.G.S. Manufacturing Inc.
122 Otis St
Rome NY 13441
315 337-3350

(G-2971)
PENNSYLVANIA GLOBE GASLIGHT CO
300 Shaw Rd (06471-1061)
PHONE..................................203 484-7749
Marcia Lafemina, *President*
Mark Lahner, *Vice Pres*
EMP: 20
SQ FT: 16,000
SALES (est): 4.7MM **Privately Held**
WEB: www.penglobe.com
SIC: 3648 5063 Mfg Lighting Equipment Whol Electrical Equipment

(G-2972)
PRECISION X-RAY INC
15 Commerce Dr (06471-1251)
PHONE..................................203 484-2011
William McLaughlin, *President*
Paul Murtagh, *Vice Pres*
Chris Carrano, *Prdtn Mgr*
Lori Rubin, *Office Mgr*
Amy Bradley, *Admin Sec*
EMP: 17
SALES (est): 3MM **Privately Held**
SIC: 3844 Mfg X-Ray Apparatus/Tubes

(G-2973)
PRECISION X-RAY INC
15 Comm Dr Unit 1 (06471)
PHONE..................................203 484-2011
Brian P Dermott, *President*
Michael Aiello CPA, *Vice Pres*
Donald Santacroce, *Treasurer*
▲ **EMP:** 15
SQ FT: 16,500
SALES (est): 3MM **Privately Held**
WEB: www.pxinc.com
SIC: 3844 Mfg X-Ray Apparatus/Tubes

(G-2974)
PRIME TECHNOLOGY LLC
344 Twin Lakes Rd (06471-1220)
P.O. Box 185 (06471-0185)
PHONE..................................203 481-5721
Raymon S Sterman, *Mng Member*
▲ **EMP:** 150
SQ FT: 38,000
SALES (est): 27.8MM **Privately Held**
WEB: www.primetechnology.com
SIC: 3676 3825 3823 3679 Mfg Electronic Resistors Mfg Elec Measuring Instr Mfg Process Cntrl Instr Mfg Elec Components

(G-2975)
S A CANDELORA ENTERPRISES
Also Called: Taconic Wire
250 Totoket Rd (06471-1035)
PHONE..................................203 484-2863
Angela Watrous, *President*
Salvatore Candelora, *Chairman*
Anthony Candelora, *Vice Pres*
Joseph Candelora, *Admin Sec*
◆ **EMP:** 19
SQ FT: 30,000
SALES (est): 5.8MM **Privately Held**
WEB: www.taconicwire.com
SIC: 3315 Mfg Steel Wire/Related Products

(G-2976)
SHORELINE COATINGS LLC
14 Commerce Dr Ste 1 (06471-1240)
PHONE..................................203 213-3471

Trevor King, *Principal*
EMP: 4
SALES (est): 388.7K **Privately Held**
SIC: 3479 Coating/Engraving Service

(G-2977)
SOURCE INC (PA)
101 Fowler Rd (06471-1556)
PHONE..................................203 488-6400
Susan Domizi, *President*
◆ **EMP:** 9 **EST:** 1975
SQ FT: 18,000
SALES (est): 848.3K **Privately Held**
WEB: www.4source.com
SIC: 2048 2099 Mfg Prepared Feeds Mfg Food Preparations

(G-2978)
STREAMLINE PRESS
21 Commerce Dr Ste 2 (06471-3204)
PHONE..................................203 484-9799
Brian Berlepsch, *Partner*
Holly Berlepsch, *Partner*
EMP: 6
SALES (est): 651.5K **Privately Held**
WEB: www.streamline-press.com
SIC: 2752 Lithographic Commercial Printing

(G-2979)
STREAMLINE PRESS LLC
21 Commerce Dr Ste 2 (06471-3204)
PHONE..................................203 484-9799
Elizabeth Detmers,
EMP: 4
SQ FT: 5,000
SALES (est): 230.5K **Privately Held**
SIC: 2752 Lithographic Commercial Printing

(G-2980)
T WOODWARD STAIR BUILDING LLC
10 Bailey Dr (06471-1447)
PHONE..................................860 664-0515
Woodward Tom, *Principal*
EMP: 3
SALES (est): 312.2K **Privately Held**
SIC: 3446 Mfg Architectural Metalwork

(G-2981)
TIM WELDING
107 W Pond Rd (06471-1587)
PHONE..................................203 488-3486
Timothy Buravski, *Principal*
EMP: 6
SALES (est): 107.3K **Privately Held**
SIC: 7692 Welding Repair

(G-2982)
TRANSMONDE USA INC
Also Called: Transmode USA
100 Shaw Rd (06471-1062)
PHONE..................................203 484-1528
Carol Mansfield, *President*
Marcella Sheridan, *President*
Mark Tracey, *President*
Marcella Walten-Sherdon, *President*
James M Foley, *Vice Pres*
▲ **EMP:** 60
SALES (est): 8.3MM **Privately Held**
SIC: 2752 7331 Lithographic Commercial Printing Direct Mail Advertising Services

(G-2983)
WALSH CLAIM SERVICES
6 Enterprise Dr (06471-1354)
P.O. Box 439 (06471-0439)
PHONE..................................203 481-0680
Kevin Walsh, *Owner*
EMP: 3
SALES (est): 434.8K **Privately Held**
SIC: 3553 Mfg Woodworking Machinery

(G-2984)
WEST END AUTO PARTS
797 Foxon Rd (06471-1107)
P.O. Box 151 (06471-0151)
PHONE..................................203 453-9009
Roman Dzruba, *Owner*
EMP: 3
SALES (est): 259.6K **Privately Held**
SIC: 3694 Mfg Engine Electrical Equipment

(G-2985)
WITKOWSKY JOHN
73 Branford Rd (06471-1323)
PHONE..................................203 483-0152
Tiffanie Witkowsky, *Principal*
EMP: 3
SALES (est): 225.6K **Privately Held**
SIC: 2411 Logging

North Franklin
New London County

(G-2986)
ADVANCED FUEL CO LLC
126 Pleasure Hill Rd (06254-1007)
PHONE..................................860 642-4817
Richard Williams, *Principal*
EMP: 3 **EST:** 2010
SALES (est): 245.3K **Privately Held**
SIC: 2869 Mfg Industrial Organic Chemicals

(G-2987)
ARICO ENGINEERING INC
841 Route 32 Ste 19 (06254-1132)
PHONE..................................860 642-7040
John Arico, *President*
Mary Ann Arico, *Vice Pres*
EMP: 7
SQ FT: 5,000
SALES (est): 1.2MM **Privately Held**
WEB: www.aricoengineering.com
SIC: 3555 7699 Mfg Retrofits For Printing Press Folders & Services & Rebuilds Printing Press Folders & Printing Presses

(G-2988)
CT WOODWORKING LLC
438 Route 32 (06254-1322)
PHONE..................................860 884-9586
James B Crofts, *Principal*
EMP: 4 **EST:** 2008
SALES (est): 368K **Privately Held**
SIC: 2431 Mfg Millwork

(G-2989)
MILLER CASTINGS INC
30 Pautipaug Hill Rd (06254-1210)
PHONE..................................860 822-9991
William Smith, *Branch Mgr*
EMP: 234
SALES (corp-wide): 76.1MM **Privately Held**
SIC: 3324 Steel Investment Foundry
PA: Miller Castings, Inc.
2503 Pacific Park Dr
Whittier CA 90601
562 695-0461

(G-2990)
PRECISION MACHINE AND GEARS
21 Country Club Dr (06254-1202)
PHONE..................................860 822-6993
Michael Earling, *Principal*
EMP: 3 **EST:** 2001
SALES (est): 232.3K **Privately Held**
SIC: 3599 Mfg Industrial Machinery

(G-2991)
QMDI PRESS
841 Route 32 Ste 19 (06254-1132)
PHONE..................................860 642-8074
EMP: 4
SALES (est): 66.5K **Privately Held**
SIC: 2741 Misc Publishing

(G-2992)
U T Z
140 Route 32 (06254-1811)
PHONE..................................860 383-4266
Cory Gervais, *Manager*
EMP: 3
SALES (est): 143.3K **Privately Held**
SIC: 2096 Mfg Potato Chips/Snacks

North Granby
Hartford County

(G-2993)
AEROTEK WELDING CO INC
51 Loomis St (06060-1205)
PHONE..................................860 653-0120
Robert W Fusick, *President*
Elizabeth L Fusick, *Admin Sec*
EMP: 4
SQ FT: 1,200
SALES (est): 450K **Privately Held**
SIC: 7692 Welding Service

North Grosvenordale
Windham County

(G-2994)
FRENCH RIVER MTLS THOMPSON LLC
307 Reardon Rd (06255)
PHONE..................................860 450-9574
Harold Hopkins, *Owner*
EMP: 3
SALES (est): 262.9K **Privately Held**
SIC: 3281 Mfg Cut Stone/Products

(G-2995)
G THOMAS AND SONS INC
573 Fabyan Rd (06255-1514)
P.O. Box 807 (06255-0807)
PHONE..................................860 935-5174
David Thomas, *President*
EMP: 3 **EST:** 1948
SALES: 700K **Privately Held**
SIC: 2221 Manmade Broadwoven Fabric Mill

(G-2996)
IRON CRAFT FABRICATING LLC
34 Corttiss Rd (06255-1102)
PHONE..................................860 923-9869
Lewis Bunker,
EMP: 6
SQ FT: 17,500
SALES (est): 1.1MM **Privately Held**
SIC: 3441 Structural Metal Fabrication

(G-2997)
LIBERTY GLASS AND MET INDS INC
339 Riverside Dr (06255-2160)
PHONE..................................860 923-3623
Donna Esposito, *President*
Edward Esposito Sr, *Vice Pres*
Daniel Marschat, *Admin Sec*
EMP: 32
SQ FT: 52,000
SALES (est): 3.6MM **Privately Held**
WEB: www.libertywindowsystems.com
SIC: 3229 3442 1793 5039 Mfg Pressed/Blown Glass Mfg Metal Door/Sash/Trim Glass/Glazing Contractor Whol Cnstn Materials

(G-2998)
LITTLE BITS MANUFACTURING INC
694 Riverside Dr (06255-2170)
P.O. Box 215 (06255-0215)
PHONE..................................860 923-2772
Charles T Skowron, *President*
EMP: 6 **EST:** 1966
SQ FT: 6,000
SALES (est): 396K **Privately Held**
SIC: 3089 Mfg Plastic Products

(G-2999)
LORIC TOOL INC
95 Gaumond Rd (06255-2011)
PHONE..................................860 928-0171
Ricky Smith, *President*
Lorraine Smith, *Admin Sec*
EMP: 10
SQ FT: 3,000
SALES (est): 810K **Privately Held**
SIC: 3599 Mfg Industrial Machinery

North Haven
New Haven County

(G-3000)
A & A MANUFACTURING CO INC
Polyclutch Division
457 State St (06473-3019)
PHONE..................................262 786-1500
EMP: 20
SALES (corp-wide): 2.3B **Privately Held**
SIC: 3495 Wire Springs, Nsk
HQ: Dynatect Manufacturing, Inc.
2300 S Calhoun Rd
New Berlin WI 53151
262 786-1500

(G-3001)
ACM WAREHOUSE & DISTRIBUTION
77 Sackett Point Rd (06473-3211)
PHONE..................................203 239-9557
Steve Andreucci, *Partner*
EMP: 3
SALES (est): 250K **Privately Held**
SIC: 2448 Mfg Wood Pallets/Skids

(G-3002)
ADVISOR
83 State St (06473-2208)
P.O. Box 460 (06473-0460)
PHONE..................................203 239-4121
Patricia Flagg, *Owner*
EMP: 14 **EST:** 1965
SALES (est): 400K **Privately Held**
SIC: 2711 Newspapers-Publishing/Printing

(G-3003)
AER CONTROL SYSTEMS LLC
36 Nettleton Ave (06473-3619)
PHONE..................................203 772-4700
John Dixon, *President*
EMP: 6
SALES: 1.2MM **Privately Held**
WEB: www.aercontrolsystems.com
SIC: 3677 Mfg Electronic Coils/Transformers

(G-3004)
ALARM ONE
142 Maple Ave (06473-2606)
P.O. Box 307 (06473-0307)
PHONE..................................203 239-1714
Roger Bailey, *Owner*
EMP: 3
SALES (est): 323.6K **Privately Held**
SIC: 3669 5063 Mfg Communications Equipment Whol Electrical Equipment

(G-3005)
ALDLAB CHEMICALS LLC
410 Sackett Point Rd (06473-3168)
P.O. Box 465, Branford (06405-0465)
PHONE..................................203 589-4934
EMP: 3
SALES (est): 143.6K **Privately Held**
SIC: 2813 Mfg Industrial Gases

(G-3006)
AMERICAN STITCH & PRINT INC
222 Elm St Ste 9 (06473-3260)
PHONE..................................203 239-5383
Alan V Golia, *President*
Vincent J Golia, *Director*
EMP: 9
SALES (est): 909.5K **Privately Held**
WEB: www.american-stitch.com
SIC: 2395 2759 Embroidery Screen Printing Advertising Specialties Wearable Products

(G-3007)
AMERICAN WOOD PRODUCTS
Also Called: Bar Co American
301 State St (06473-6104)
PHONE..................................203 248-4433
Valerie Galleuba, *CEO*
EMP: 7
SALES (est): 748.9K **Privately Held**
SIC: 2511 Mfg Wood Household Furniture

GEOGRAPHIC

(G-3008)
ANDERSON STAIR & RAILING
348 Sackett Point Rd (06473-3103)
PHONE..................................203 288-0117
Art Anderson, *Owner*
EMP: 10
SALES (est): 852.6K **Privately Held**
SIC: 2431 Mfg Millwork

(G-3009)
AQUALOGIC INC
30 Devine St (06473-2236)
PHONE..................................203 248-8959
Nicholas Papa, *President*
Dorothy F Papa, *Corp Secy*
Lisa Papa, *Finance*
Maryann Papa, *Director*
EMP: 20
SQ FT: 6,000
SALES (est): 4.4MM **Privately Held**
WEB: www.aqualogic.com
SIC: 3589 Mfg Service Industry Machinery

(G-3010)
BAY CRANE SERVICE CONN INC
37 Nettleton Ave (06473-3618)
PHONE..................................203 785-8000
Kenneth Bernardo, *President*
Joe Zils, *Manager*
EMP: 6
SALES (est): 990.2K **Privately Held**
SIC: 3531 Mfg Construction Machinery

(G-3011)
BONITO MANUFACTURING INC
Also Called: New England Clock
445 Washington Ave (06473-1320)
PHONE..................................203 234-8786
Fax: 203 248-6399
EMP: 61
SQ FT: 70,000
SALES (est): 6.9MM **Privately Held**
WEB: www.bonitogroup.com
SIC: 2429 7641 2522 2511 Special Product Sawmill Reupholstery/Furn Repair Mfg Nonwood Office Furn Mfg Wood Household Furn Mfg Wood Kitchen Cabinet

(G-3012)
C COWLES & COMPANY (PA)
Also Called: Hydrolevel Div
126 Bailey Rd (06473-2612)
PHONE..................................203 865-3117
Lawrence C Moon Jr, *Ch of Bd*
Richard Lyons, *President*
Robert Gaura, *CFO*
Nicole Tanner, *CFO*
Russell Spector, *VP Finance*
▲ **EMP:** 75
SQ FT: 170,000
SALES (est): 43.4MM **Privately Held**
WEB: www.ccowles.com
SIC: 3089 3465 3443 3646 Mfg Plastic Products Mfg Automotive Stampings Mfg Fabricated Plate Wrk Mfg Coml Light Fixtures

(G-3013)
CARLIN COMBUSTION TECH INC
126 Bailey Rd (06473-2612)
PHONE..................................413 525-7700
EMP: 4
SALES (corp-wide): 43.4MM **Privately Held**
SIC: 3433 Mfg Heating Equipment-Non-electric
HQ: Carlin Combustion Technology, Inc.
126 Bailey Rd
North Haven CT 06473

(G-3014)
CARLIN COMBUSTION TECH INC (HQ)
126 Bailey Rd (06473-2612)
PHONE..................................203 680-9401
Lawrence C Moon Jr, *President*
Richard Lyons, *Vice Pres*
Russell Spector, *Treasurer*
▲ **EMP:** 75
SALES (est): 15.5MM
SALES (corp-wide): 43.4MM **Privately Held**
SIC: 3433 Mfg Heating Equipment-Non-electric
PA: C. Cowles & Company
126 Bailey Rd
North Haven CT 06473
203 865-3117

(G-3015)
CLOPAY CORPORATION
285 State St Ste 4 (06473-2170)
PHONE..................................203 230-9116
Joel Eberlein, *Vice Pres*
EMP: 231
SALES (corp-wide): 2.2B **Publicly Held**
SIC: 3081 Mfg Unsuppor Plstc Film
HQ: Clopay Corporation
8585 Duke Blvd
Mason OH 45040
800 282-2260

(G-3016)
COLE S CREW MACHINE PRODUCTS
69 Dodge Ave (06473-1119)
PHONE..................................203 723-1418
David F Calabrese, *President*
Patricia Calabrese, *Admin Sec*
EMP: 22
SQ FT: 6,500
SALES (est): 3.5MM **Privately Held**
SIC: 3451 3542 Mfg Screw Machine Products Mfg Machine Tools-Forming

(G-3017)
COMPOSITE MCHINING EXPERTS LLC
222 Universal Dr Bldg 1 (06473-3658)
PHONE..................................203 624-0664
Rose Tomaszewski, *General Mgr*
Frank Tomaszewski,
EMP: 5
SQ FT: 19,100
SALES (est): 266.2K **Privately Held**
SIC: 3429 Mfg Hardware

(G-3018)
CONNECTICUT CONTAINER CORP (PA)
Also Called: Unicorr Group
455 Sackett Point Rd (06473-3199)
PHONE..................................203 248-2161
Harry A Perkins, *President*
Louis Ceruzzi, *Vice Pres*
Jeffrey Hopkins, *Plant Mgr*
Gerry Earnshaw, *CFO*
Susan Damato, *Controller*
◆ **EMP:** 132 **EST:** 1946
SQ FT: 160,000
SALES (est): 121.1MM **Privately Held**
WEB: www.unicorr.com
SIC: 2653 3993 3412 2631 Mfg Corrugated/Fiber Box Mfg Signs/Ad Specialties Mfg Metal Barrels/Pails Paperboard Mill

(G-3019)
COVIDIEN HOLDING INC
195 Mcdermott Rd (06473-3665)
PHONE..................................203 492-5000
Stan Malinowski, *Manager*
EMP: 5 **Privately Held**
SIC: 3841 Mfg Surgical/Medical Instruments
HQ: Covidien Holding Inc.
710 Medtronic Pkwy
Minneapolis MN 55432

(G-3020)
COVIDIEN LP
195 Mcdermott Rd (06473-3665)
PHONE..................................203 492-6332
Paul Landino, *Maint Spvr*
Mike Prescott, *Engineer*
Darcy Phabmixay, *Supervisor*
Kenneth Niehoff, *Director*
EMP: 430 **Privately Held**
SIC: 3841 Mfg Surgical/Medical Instruments
HQ: Covidien Lp
15 Hampshire St
Mansfield MA 02048
763 514-4000

(G-3021)
COVIDIEN LP
Also Called: Surgical Devices
60 Middletown Ave (06473-3908)
PHONE..................................203 492-5000
Armand Lacombe, *Project Mgr*
Arthur Hislop, *Research*
John Skala, *Research*
Kevin Golebieski, *Engineer*
Pat Julian, *Engineer*
EMP: 521 **Privately Held**
SIC: 3841 Mfg Surgical/Medical Instruments
HQ: Covidien Lp
15 Hampshire St
Mansfield MA 02048
763 514-4000

(G-3022)
COWLES PRODUCTS COMPANY INC
126 Bailey Rd (06473-2612)
PHONE..................................203 865-3110
Lawrence Moon, *President*
Arturo Moreno, *Business Mgr*
Anthony Amenta, *Vice Pres*
Sylvia Bonilla, *Sales Staff*
Barbara Gratchian, *Marketing Staff*
▲ **EMP:** 100
SALES (est): 14.5MM
SALES (corp-wide): 43.4MM **Privately Held**
WEB: www.ccowles.com
SIC: 3089 Mfg Extruded Plastics Moldings
PA: C. Cowles & Company
126 Bailey Rd
North Haven CT 06473
203 865-3117

(G-3023)
COWLES STAMPING INC
126 Bailey Rd (06473-2612)
PHONE..................................203 865-3117
Lawrence C Moon Jr, *President*
Rich McElwee, *Vice Pres*
Whyn Pelkey, *Engineer*
Russell Spector, *VP Finance*
▲ **EMP:** 40
SQ FT: 64,000
SALES (est): 5.4MM
SALES (corp-wide): 43.4MM **Privately Held**
WEB: www.ccowles.com
SIC: 3469 Mfg Metal Stampings
PA: C. Cowles & Company
126 Bailey Rd
North Haven CT 06473
203 865-3117

(G-3024)
ELM CITY MANUFACTURING LLC
Also Called: Atlantic Millwork
370 Sackett Point Rd (06473-3106)
PHONE..................................203 248-1969
Paul McKechnie, *Vice Pres*
Mark Bolling, *Mng Member*
Paul W McKechnie,
EMP: 12
SQ FT: 13,000
SALES (est): 1.9MM **Privately Held**
SIC: 2499 Mfg Wood Products

(G-3025)
EPICUREAN FEAST MEDTRON O
195 Mcdermott Rd (06473-3665)
PHONE..................................203 492-5000
EMP: 3
SALES (est): 95.3K **Privately Held**
SIC: 3845 Mfg Electromedical Equipment

(G-3026)
F D GRAVE & SON INC
85 State St Ste C (06473-2240)
P.O. Box 2085 (06473-8285)
PHONE..................................203 239-9394
Frederick D Grave Jr, *President*
EMP: 8
SQ FT: 25,000
SALES (est): 982.5K **Privately Held**
SIC: 2121 Mfg Cigars

(G-3027)
FARMINGTON ENGINEERING INC
73 Defco Park Rd (06473-1135)
PHONE..................................800 428-7584
Bob Adelson, *Principal*
▲ **EMP:** 7
SALES (est): 800.5K **Privately Held**
SIC: 3499 Fabricated Metal Products Nec

(G-3028)
FLIGHT SUPPORT INC
101 Sackett Point Rd (06473-3211)
P.O. Box 498 (06473-0498)
PHONE..................................203 562-1415
Wayne Blake, *CEO*
Bernadette Blake, *Admin Sec*
EMP: 50
SQ FT: 17,200
SALES (est): 8.3MM **Privately Held**
WEB: www.flightsupport.net
SIC: 3728 Mfg Aircraft Parts/Equipment

(G-3029)
HANGER PRSTHETCS & ORTHO INC
260 State St (06473-2135)
PHONE..................................203 230-0667
David Knatt, *Manager*
EMP: 5
SALES (corp-wide): 1B **Publicly Held**
SIC: 3842 Mfg Surgical Appliances/Supplies
HQ: Hanger Prosthetics & Orthotics, Inc.
10910 Domain Dr Ste 300
Austin TX 78758
512 777-3800

(G-3030)
HYDROLEVEL COMPANY
126 Bailey Rd (06473-2612)
PHONE..................................203 776-0473
Alan C Bennett, *Ch of Bd*
John Downs, *President*
Russell Specter, *CFO*
T Richard Coss, *Treasurer*
Lawrence Moon, *Executive*
▲ **EMP:** 10 **EST:** 1979
SQ FT: 5,000
SALES: 2MM
SALES (corp-wide): 43.4MM **Privately Held**
SIC: 3494 Mfr High & Low Water Controls For Boilers
PA: C. Cowles & Company
126 Bailey Rd
North Haven CT 06473
203 865-3117

(G-3031)
INTELLGENT CLEARING NETWRK INC
110 Washington Ave (06473-1723)
PHONE..................................203 972-0861
Gary Oakley, *CEO*
Jon Robertson, *Exec VP*
Rich Thibedeau, *Exec VP*
Ron Schulte, *Sr Software Eng*
EMP: 8
SALES (est): 533.6K **Privately Held**
SIC: 7372 Prepackaged Software Services

(G-3032)
INTERACTIVE MARKETING CORP
Also Called: IMC Internet
399 Sackett Point Rd (06473-3105)
PHONE..................................203 248-5324
Robert Caldarella, *President*
EMP: 7
SQ FT: 6,000
SALES (est): 1.2MM **Privately Held**
WEB: www.imcinternet.net
SIC: 3571 7373 Mfg Electronic Computers Computer Systems Design

(G-3033)
JENSEN INDUSTRIES INC (PA)
Also Called: Jensen Dental
50 Stillman Rd (06473-1622)
P.O. Box 514 (06473-0514)
PHONE..................................203 285-1402
David J Stine, *President*
Peter Kouvaris, *Vice Pres*
Kevin Mahan, *Vice Pres*

▲ = Import ▼=Export
◆ =Import/Export

Ray McTeague, *Opers Mgr*
Anthony M Schittina, *CFO*
▲ **EMP:** 60
SQ FT: 25,000
SALES (est): 30.8MM **Privately Held**
WEB: www.jensenindustries.com
SIC: 3843 Mfg Dental Equipment/Supplies

(G-3034)
JESKEY LLC
Also Called: James Manufacturing
69 Dodge Ave (06473-1119)
PHONE..................................203 772-6675
Adam Jeskey, *Mng Member*
EMP: 23 **EST:** 1946
SQ FT: 29,000
SALES (est): 2.7MM **Privately Held**
WEB: www.jamesscrew.com
SIC: 3451 Mfg S Crew Machine Products

(G-3035)
JET PROCESS CORPORATION
57 Dodge Ave (06473-1119)
PHONE..................................203 985-6000
Richard Hart, *Ch of Bd*
Bret Halpern, *Engineer*
Krista Hart, *Bookkeeper*
EMP: 8
SQ FT: 16,000
SALES (est): 1.1MM **Privately Held**
WEB: www.jetprocess.com
SIC: 3559 3479 8731 2851 Manufactures Misc Industry Mach Coating/Engraving Svcs Coml Physical Research Mfg Paints/Allied Prdts

(G-3036)
JOHNSTONE COMPANY INC
222 Sackett Point Rd (06473-3160)
P.O. Box 472 (06473-0472)
PHONE..................................203 239-5834
David R Johnstone Jr, *President*
Michael Johnstone, *Vice Pres*
Tonya Johnstone, *Admin Sec*
▼ **EMP:** 26 **EST:** 1941
SQ FT: 20,000
SALES (est): 9.8MM **Privately Held**
WEB: www.johnstonecompany.com
SIC: 3398 3559 3443 Metal Heat Treating Mfg Misc Industry Machinery Mfg Fabricated Plate Work

(G-3037)
KB CUSTOM STAIR BUILDERS INC
101 Powdered Metal Rd # 1 (06473-3280)
PHONE..................................203 234-0836
Kevin P Boyle, *President*
EMP: 6 **EST:** 2001
SALES: 500K **Privately Held**
SIC: 2431 Mfg Millwork

(G-3038)
MAVERICK ARMS INC
7 Grasso Ave (06473-3237)
PHONE..................................203 230-5300
A Iver Mossberg Jr, *Principal*
EMP: 3
SALES (est): 227.2K **Privately Held**
SIC: 3484 Mfg Small Arms

(G-3039)
MEDTRONIC INC
60 Middletown Ave (06473-3908)
PHONE..................................203 492-5764
Holly Donahue, *Principal*
Dasarathy Chakravarthi, *Engineer*
Rosanne Barbieri, *Manager*
EMP: 35 **Privately Held**
SIC: 3841 Mfg Surgical/Medical Instruments
HQ: Medtronic, Inc.
710 Medtronic Pkwy
Minneapolis MN 55432
763 514-4000

(G-3040)
MILLTURN MANUFACTURING CO
1203 Ridge Rd (06473-4437)
PHONE..................................203 248-1602
Rudy Krizan, *Owner*
EMP: 3
SQ FT: 1,500
SALES (est): 170K **Privately Held**
SIC: 3599 Mfg Industrial Machinery

(G-3041)
MILLWOOD INC
33 Stiles Ln (06473-2133)
PHONE..................................203 248-7902
Edwin Melendez, *Branch Mgr*
EMP: 17 **Privately Held**
SIC: 3565 5084 Mfg & Whol Packging And Material Handling Machinery
PA: Millwood, Inc.
3708 International Blvd
Vienna OH 44473

(G-3042)
MOSSBERG CORPORATION (PA)
7 Grasso Ave (06473-3259)
PHONE..................................203 230-5300
Alan Iver Mossberg, *Ch of Bd*
Paul Chartier, *Vice Pres*
Dan Jean, *Plant Mgr*
Alain Leyva, *Project Mgr*
Mike Anastasio, *Buyer*
▲ **EMP:** 5
SQ FT: 80,000
SALES: 41.9MM **Privately Held**
SIC: 3484 Mfg Small Arms

(G-3043)
NEU SPCLTY ENGINEERED MTLS LLC
15 Corporate Dr (06473-3255)
PHONE..................................203 239-9629
Mark Crist, *Vice Pres*
Isaac Deluca, *Vice Pres*
Giuseppe Di Salvo, *Vice Pres*
Michael A Garratt, *Vice Pres*
EMP: 12
SALES (est): 2.7MM **Publicly Held**
SIC: 2821 3087 5162 Mfg Plstc Material/Resin Custm Cmpnd Prchsd Resin
PA: Polyone Corporation
33587 Walker Rd
Avon Lake OH 44012

(G-3044)
NOVA DENTAL LLC (PA)
41 Middletown Ave Ste 2 (06473-3940)
PHONE..................................203 234-3900
Asma Ijaz, *Manager*
EMP: 4
SALES (est): 563.2K **Privately Held**
SIC: 3843 Mfg Dental Equipment/Supplies

(G-3045)
O F MOSSBERG & SONS INC (HQ)
7 Grasso Ave (06473-3237)
P.O. Box 497 (06473-0497)
PHONE..................................203 230-5300
A Iver Mossberg Jr, *Ch of Bd*
Alan I Mossberg, *President*
Joseph H Bartozzi, *Senior VP*
John Maclellan, *Vice Pres*
Christopher Orlando, *Vice Pres*
▲ **EMP:** 160 **EST:** 1919
SQ FT: 80,000
SALES (est): 38MM **Privately Held**
WEB: www.mossberg.com
SIC: 3484 Ret Sporting Goods/Bicycles

(G-3046)
OSKR INC
14a Buell St (06473-4311)
PHONE..................................475 238-2634
Tony Lawlor, *President*
EMP: 8
SQ FT: 1,800
SALES: 2.4MM **Privately Held**
SIC: 3942 Mfg Dolls/Stuffed Toys

(G-3047)
PACTIV CORPORATION
458 Sackett Point Rd (06473-3111)
PHONE..................................203 288-7722
Ed Sidlowsky, *Branch Mgr*
EMP: 45
SALES (corp-wide): 14.1MM **Privately Held**
WEB: www.pactiv.com
SIC: 2679 5199 Mfg Converted Paper Products Whol Nondurable Goods
HQ: Pactiv Llc
1900 W Field Ct
Lake Forest IL 60045
847 482-2000

(G-3048)
PALLET GUYS LLC
102 Bailey Rd (06473-2611)
PHONE..................................203 691-6716
David Schneider, *Principal*
EMP: 4
SALES (est): 222.1K **Privately Held**
SIC: 2448 Mfg Wood Pallets/Skids

(G-3049)
PARKER-HANNIFIN CORPORATION
Also Called: Advanced Products Operation
33 Defco Park Rd (06473-1129)
PHONE..................................203 239-3341
Robert Akumbak, *Project Engr*
Jim Randall, *Branch Mgr*
EMP: 100
SALES (corp-wide): 14.3B **Publicly Held**
WEB: www.parker.com
SIC: 3053 Mfg Gaskets/Packing/Sealing Devices Engineering Services
PA: Parker-Hannifin Corporation
6035 Parkland Blvd
Cleveland OH 44124
216 896-3000

(G-3050)
PEPSI-COLA METRO BTLG CO INC
Also Called: Pepsico
27 Leonardo Dr (06473-2528)
P.O. Box 690 (06473-0690)
PHONE..................................203 234-9014
Mat Karl, *Manager*
EMP: 115
SALES (corp-wide): 64.6B **Publicly Held**
WEB: www.pbg.com
SIC: 2086 5149 Mfg Bottled/Canned Soft Drinks Whol Groceries
HQ: Pepsi-Cola Metropolitan Bottling Company, Inc.
1111 Westchester Ave
White Plains NY 10604
914 767-6000

(G-3051)
PLATT & LABONIA COMPANY LLC
70-80 Stoddard Ave (06473)
PHONE..................................800 505-9099
Guy A Ferraiolo, *President*
EMP: 45 **EST:** 2015
SALES (est): 1.7MM **Privately Held**
SIC: 3441 Metal Products Fabrication

(G-3052)
PLATT-LABONIA OF N HAVEN INC
Also Called: Craftline
70 Stoddard Ave (06473-2524)
P.O. Box 398 (06473-0398)
PHONE..................................203 239-5681
Guy Ferraiolo, *President*
Vincent Labonia Jr, *President*
Vincent Ferraiolo, *COO*
Elizabeth Labonia, *Vice Pres*
Peter Corrado, *Prdtn Mgr*
▲ **EMP:** 65 **EST:** 1953
SQ FT: 110,000
SALES (est): 11MM **Privately Held**
WEB: www.plattlabonia.com
SIC: 2542 3714 Mfg Partitions/Fixtures-Nonwood Mfg Motor Vehicle Parts/Accessories

(G-3053)
PRATT & WHITNEY ENGINE SVCS
415 Washington Ave (06473)
PHONE..................................203 934-2806
Bob Winer, *Branch Mgr*
EMP: 500
SALES (corp-wide): 66.5B **Publicly Held**
SIC: 3724 Mfg Aircraft Engine Parts
HQ: Pratt & Whitney Engine Services, Inc.
1525 Midway Park Rd
Bridgeport WV 26330
304 842-5421

(G-3054)
PREFERRED MANUFACTURING CO
68 Old Broadway E (06473-1605)
P.O. Box 279 (06473-0279)
PHONE..................................203 239-0727
Brian D Vanacore, *President*
EMP: 6
SQ FT: 13,000
SALES (est): 863.2K **Privately Held**
SIC: 3599 Machine Shop Jobbing & Repair

(G-3055)
PROFLOW INC
Also Called: Proflow Process Equipment
303 State St (06473-6104)
P.O. Box 748 (06473-0748)
PHONE..................................203 230-4700
Kurt Uihlein, *President*
William Iaai-Fit, *COO*
Lawrence Bee Jr, *Vice Pres*
Susan Sargeant, *Vice Pres*
Jonathan Montague, *Project Mgr*
EMP: 47
SQ FT: 18,000
SALES (est): 13.4MM **Privately Held**
SIC: 3823 5084 5251 3561 Mfg Process Cntrl Instr Whol Industrial Equip Ret Hardware Mfg Pumps/Pumping Equip Mfg Meas/Dispensing Pump

GEOGRAPHIC

(G-3056)
Q-JET DSI INC
303 State St (06473-6104)
PHONE..................................203 230-4700
Kurt Uihlein, *President*
EMP: 7
SALES (est): 578.3K **Privately Held**
WEB: www.q-jet.com
SIC: 3556 Manufacture Food Process Machines

(G-3057)
QUAD/GRAPHICS INC
291 State St (06473-2131)
P.O. Box 860 (06473-0860)
PHONE..................................203 288-2468
Marc Shapiro, *Branch Mgr*
EMP: 509
SALES (corp-wide): 4.1B **Publicly Held**
SIC: 2752 2754 3823 2721 Lithographic Coml Print Gravure Coml Printing Mfg Process Cntrl Instr Periodical-Publish/Print
PA: Quad/Graphics Inc.
N61w23044 Harrys Way
Sussex WI 53089
414 566-6000

(G-3058)
RELIANCE BUSINESS SYSTEMS INC
420 Sackett Point Rd # 8 (06473-3171)
PHONE..................................203 281-4407
William K Rothfuss, *President*
Christine Nastri, *Admin Sec*
EMP: 5
SQ FT: 2,400
SALES (est): 807.7K **Privately Held**
SIC: 3861 Mfg Photographic Equipment/Supplies

(G-3059)
RUSSELL PARTITION CO INC
20 Dodge Ave (06473-1124)
PHONE..................................203 239-5749
Jim Bango, *President*
EMP: 9 **EST:** 1969
SQ FT: 25,000
SALES (est): 2.6MM **Privately Held**
SIC: 2653 2631 Mfg Corrugated/Solid Fiber Boxes Paperboard Mill

(G-3060)
S CAMEROTA & SONS INC
Also Called: Camerota Truck Parts
166 Universal Dr Unit 2 (06473-3630)
P.O. Box 1134, Enfield (06083-1134)
PHONE..................................203 782-0360
Tom Antonioli, *General Mgr*
EMP: 6

SALES (corp-wide): 111MM **Privately Held**
WEB: www.camerota.com
SIC: 3714 5531 Mfg Motor Vehicle Parts/Accessories Ret Auto/Home Supplies
PA: S. Camerota & Sons, Inc.
245 Shaker Rd
Enfield CT 06082
860 763-0896

(G-3061)
SAFT AMERICA INC
3 Powdered Metal Rd (06473-3209)
PHONE..................................203 234-8333
Ivor Hay, *Marketing Staff*
David Cox, *Manager*
Sara Lopofsky, *Info Tech Mgr*
EMP: 35
SALES (corp-wide): 8.1B **Publicly Held**
SIC: 3691 Mfg Storage Batteries
HQ: Saft America Inc
13575 Waterworks St
Jacksonville FL 32221
904 861-1501

(G-3062)
SIKORSKY AIRCRAFT CORPORATION
1 N Frontage Rd (06473)
PHONE..................................516 228-2000
Kevin Doheny, *Manager*
EMP: 18 **Publicly Held**
WEB: www.sikorsky.com
SIC: 3721 Mfg Helicopters
HQ: Sikorsky Aircraft Corporation
6900 Main St
Stratford CT 06614

(G-3063)
THE E J DAVIS COMPANY
10 Dodge Ave (06473-1140)
P.O. Box 326 (06473-0326)
PHONE..................................203 239-5391
Gregory J Godbout, *President*
Evelyn Davis Edwards, *Treasurer*
Barbara D Godbout, *Admin Sec*
EMP: 30 **EST:** 1953
SQ FT: 62,000
SALES (est): 5MM **Privately Held**
WEB: www.ejdavis.com
SIC: 3296 3083 2672 Mfg Mineral Wool Mfg Coated/Laminated Paper Mfg Laminated Plastic Plate/Sheet

(G-3064)
TRI STATE MAINTENANCE SVCS LLC
356 Old Maple Ave (06473-3248)
P.O. Box 180 (06473-0180)
PHONE..................................203 691-1343
Thomas Giuliano,
EMP: 11 **EST:** 2006
SALES (est): 1.3MM **Privately Held**
SIC: 1389 1731 Oil/Gas Field Services Electrical Contractor

(G-3065)
U-TECH WIRE ROPE & SUPPLY LLC
222 Universal Dr Bldg 9 (06473-3659)
PHONE..................................203 865-8885
Igor Ursini,
▲ **EMP:** 6
SQ FT: 8,000
SALES (est): 890K **Privately Held**
WEB: www.utechwirerope.com
SIC: 3496 Mfg Misc Fabricated Wire Products

(G-3066)
ULBRICH OF GEORGIA INC
153 Washington Ave (06473-1710)
PHONE..................................203 239-4481
EMP: 3
SALES (est): 139.4K **Privately Held**
SIC: 3495 Mfg Wire Springs

(G-3067)
ULBRICH STNLESS STELS SPCIAL M (PA)
153 Washington Ave (06473-1710)
P.O. Box 294 (06473-0294)
PHONE..................................203 239-4481
Frederick C Ulbrich III, *CEO*
Cesar Medellin, *General Mgr*
John J Cei, *COO*
Rich Papeika, *Vice Pres*
Arnie Muniz, *Plant Mgr*
▲ **EMP:** 60 **EST:** 1955
SQ FT: 25,000
SALES (est): 208.4MM **Privately Held**
WEB: www.ulbrich.com
SIC: 3316 3356 5051 3341 Mfg Cold-Rolled Steel Nonferrous Rollng/Drawng Metals Service Center Secndry Nonfrs Mtl Prdcr

(G-3068)
VEROTEC INC
473e Washington Ave (06473)
PHONE..................................603 821-9921
Marc Harvey, *President*
EMP: 5
SALES: 125K **Privately Held**
SIC: 3679 Mfg Electronic Components

(G-3069)
WMB INDUSTRIES LLC
62 Pool Rd (06473-2733)
PHONE..................................203 927-2822
William M Bakutis, *Principal*
EMP: 3
SALES (est): 152.7K **Privately Held**
SIC: 3999 Mfg Misc Products

(G-3070)
ZP COUTURE LLC
410 State St Rm 6 (06473-3149)
PHONE..................................888 697-7239
Zeb Powell,
EMP: 4
SQ FT: 900
SALES (est): 291.3K **Privately Held**
SIC: 2731 7336 7389 Book-Publishing/Printing Coml Art/Graphic Design Business Services

North Stonington
New London County

(G-3071)
BEEDE ELECTRICAL INSTR CO INC
75 Frontage Rd 106 (06359-1769)
PHONE..................................603 753-6362
Walter Pelletier, *Ch of Bd*
Robert Janisch, *President*
David Curdie, *Treasurer*
Cathy Wagenrener, *Treasurer*
▲ **EMP:** 110
SALES (est): 20.2MM **Privately Held**
WEB: www.beede.com
SIC: 3694 Mfg Engine Electrical Equipment

(G-3072)
DYNAMIC BLDG ENRGY SLTIONS LLC (PA)
183 Provdnc New London (06359-1721)
PHONE..................................860 599-1872
Julia Discuillo, *Principal*
Craig Olisky,
EMP: 10
SQ FT: 5,000
SALES: 2MM **Privately Held**
WEB: www.dynasys.org
SIC: 3599 3625 Mfg Industrial Machinery Mfg Relays/Industrial Controls

(G-3073)
EDWARDS WINES LLC
Also Called: Edwards, Jonathan Winery
74 Chester Maine Rd (06359-1303)
PHONE..................................860 535-0202
Jonathan Edwards,
Karen Edwards,
Robert Edwards,
▲ **EMP:** 3
SALES (est): 220K **Privately Held**
SIC: 2084 Mfg Wines

(G-3074)
FARIA BEEDE INSTRUMENTS INC
Also Called: Faria Marine Instruments
75 Frontage Rd Ste 106 (06359-1711)
PHONE..................................860 848-9271
Pam Meissner, *President*
Jason Blackburn, *Vice Pres*
Bill Randall, *Vice Pres*
Kevin Terry, *Vice Pres*
Cassie Daniels, *Senior Buyer*
▲ **EMP:** 165
SALES (est): 64.8MM **Privately Held**
WEB: www.faria-instruments.com
SIC: 3824 3825 3823 3643 Mfg Fluid Meters/Devices Mfg Elec Measuring Instr Mfg Process Cntrl Instr

(G-3075)
FISHER CONTROLS INTL LLC
95 Pendleton Hill Rd (06359)
PHONE..................................860 599-1140
John Wells, *Marketing Staff*
Bill Quernemoen, *Manager*
EMP: 170
SALES (corp-wide): 18.3B **Publicly Held**
WEB: www.emersonprocess.com/fisher
SIC: 3491 3494 Mfg Industrial Valves Mfg Valves/Pipe Fittings
HQ: Fisher Controls International Llc
205 S Center St
Marshalltown IA 50158
641 754-3011

(G-3076)
ISOPUR FLUID TECHNOLOGIES INC
183 Provi New Londo Tpke (06359)
PHONE..................................860 599-1872
Jason Lin, *CEO*
James V Gibbons, *General Mgr*
EMP: 10
SQ FT: 7,000
SALES: 1.3MM **Privately Held**
WEB: www.isopurfluid.com
SIC: 3569 Mfg General Industrial Machinery
PA: Dynamic Building & Energy Solutions Llc
183 Provdnc New London
North Stonington CT 06359

(G-3077)
WILKINSON TOOL & DIE CO
55 Stillman Rd (06359-1734)
PHONE..................................860 599-5821
Fax: 860 599-5821
EMP: 5 **EST:** 1978
SQ FT: 1,800
SALES: 1.2MM **Privately Held**
SIC: 3544 3089 Mfg Special Dies & Tools & Injection Molding Of Plastics

North Windham
Windham County

(G-3078)
BOLDUCS MACHINE WORKS INC
207 Miller Rd (06235-2649)
PHONE..................................860 455-1232
John F Bolduc, *President*
Doreen L Bolduc, *Treasurer*
EMP: 4
SALES: 530K **Privately Held**
WEB: www.icegroup.com
SIC: 3724 Machine Shop

(G-3079)
BUILDERS CONCRETE EAST LLC
79 Boston Post Rd (06256-1302)
P.O. Box 133, Willimantic (06226-0133)
PHONE..................................860 456-4111
Kevin Jones, *QC Mgr*
Thomas Fricchione, *Sales Mgr*
Steven E Aiudi, *Mng Member*
Steve Aiudi, *Executive*
Harold Hopkins,
EMP: 25
SQ FT: 12,000
SALES (est): 6.1MM **Privately Held**
SIC: 3273 Mfg Ready-Mixed Concrete

(G-3080)
COLD RIVER LOGGING LLC
195 Tuckie Rd (06256-1317)
PHONE..................................860 334-9506
David J Labombard, *Principal*
EMP: 3
SALES (est): 108.7K **Privately Held**
SIC: 2411 Logging

(G-3081)
CONCRETE PRODUCTS
356 Tuckie Rd (06256-1329)
PHONE..................................860 423-4144
William Hamill, *President*
EMP: 6
SALES (est): 718.2K **Privately Held**
SIC: 3272 Mfg Concrete Products

(G-3082)
HITECH CHROME PLTG & POLSG LC
30 Baker Rd (06256)
P.O. Box 204 (06256-0204)
PHONE..................................860 456-8070
Fabrizio Chiulli, *Managing Prtnr*
Lisa Krukoff, *Mng Member*
EMP: 4
SQ FT: 1,500
SALES: 176.1K **Privately Held**
SIC: 3471 Plating/Polishing Service

(G-3083)
MOTIVE INDUSTRIES LLC
356 Tuckie Rd (06256-1329)
PHONE..................................860 423-2064
Steven Gould,
EMP: 3
SALES (est): 266.6K **Privately Held**
SIC: 3999 Mfg Misc Products

(G-3084)
UNITED ABRASIVES INC (PA)
185 Boston Post Rd (06256-1302)
PHONE..................................860 456-7131
Aris Marziali, *Ch of Bd*
Michael Smyth, *Plant Mgr*
Michael Smardon, *Opers Mgr*
Scott Lavallie, *Purch Agent*
Carolyn Houlihan, *Purchasing*
◆ **EMP:** 280 **EST:** 1969
SQ FT: 300,000
SALES (est): 52.9MM **Privately Held**
SIC: 3291 3553 2296 Mfg Abrasive Products Mfg Woodworking Machinery Mfg Tire Cord/Fabrics

(G-3085)
WILLIAMS PRINTING GROUP LLC
387 Tuckie Rd Ste G (06256-1330)
P.O. Box 121201, Clermont FL (34712-1201)
PHONE..................................860 423-8779
L Franklin Williams Jr, *Principal*
EMP: 4
SALES (est): 386.5K **Privately Held**
SIC: 2752 Lithographic Commercial Printing

Northford
New Haven County

(G-3086)
BRASCO TECHNOLOGIES LLC
76 Woodland Dr (06472-1206)
PHONE..................................203 484-4291
David Winchell,
EMP: 3 **EST:** 1998
SQ FT: 1,000
SALES: 360K **Privately Held**
WEB: www.brascotech.com
SIC: 3589 Industrial Water Treatement

(G-3087)
HONEYWELL INTERNATIONAL INC
12 Clintonville Rd (06472-1610)
PHONE..................................203 484-7161
Dan Corbett, *Marketing Mgr*

▲ = Import ▼=Export
◆ =Import/Export

Andrew Nolan, *Branch Mgr*
EMP: 60
SALES (corp-wide): 41.8B **Publicly Held**
SIC: 3724 Mfg Aircraft Engines/Parts
PA: Honeywell International Inc.
300 S Tryon St
Charlotte NC 28202
973 455-2000

(G-3088)
HONEYWELL INTERNATIONAL INC
12 Clintonville Rd (06472-1610)
PHONE..................................203 484-7161
Mike Lynch, *President*
Paul Stone, *Branch Mgr*
EMP: 450
SALES (corp-wide): 41.8B **Publicly Held**
WEB: www.honeywell.com
SIC: 3724 Mfg Aircraft Engines/Parts
PA: Honeywell International Inc.
300 S Tryon St
Charlotte NC 28202
973 455-2000

(G-3089)
HONEYWELL INTERNATIONAL INC
12 Clintonville Rd (06472-1610)
PHONE..................................203 484-6202
Abraham William, *President*
EMP: 500
SALES (corp-wide): 41.8B **Publicly Held**
WEB: www.honeywell.com
SIC: 3724 Mfg Aircraft Engines/Parts
PA: Honeywell International Inc.
300 S Tryon St
Charlotte NC 28202
973 455-2000

(G-3090)
HONEYWELL INTERNATIONAL INC
1 Fire Lite Pl 4 (06472-1662)
PHONE..................................203 484-7161
Ed Busch, *Engineer*
Steven Chow, *Branch Mgr*
EMP: 48
SALES (corp-wide): 41.8B **Publicly Held**
SIC: 3724 Mfg Aircraft Engines/Parts
PA: Honeywell International Inc.
300 S Tryon St
Charlotte NC 28202
973 455-2000

(G-3091)
NEW HAVEN SIGN COMPANY
1831 Middletown Ave (06472-1167)
P.O. Box 4187, Hamden (06514-0187)
PHONE..................................203 484-2777
Peter L Deyo, *Principal*
EMP: 3
SALES (est): 267.3K **Privately Held**
SIC: 3993 Mfg Signs/Advertising Specialties

(G-3092)
SOLIDIFICATION PDTS INTL INC
524 Forest Rd (06472-1485)
P.O. Box 35 (06472-0035)
PHONE..................................203 484-9494
William Gannon, *President*
Bill Gannon, *President*
EMP: 7
SALES (est): 1MM **Privately Held**
SIC: 2843 2819 3999 Mfg Surface Active Agents Mfg Industrial Inorganic Chemicals Mfg Misc Products

(G-3093)
SOLIDIFICATION PRODUCTS INTL
Also Called: Solidification Products Intl
215 Village St (06472-1405)
P.O. Box 35 (06472-0035)
PHONE..................................203 484-9494
William J Gannon Jr, *President*
EMP: 12
SALES (est): 2.2MM **Privately Held**
WEB: www.oilbarriers.com
SIC: 2819 Mfg Industrial Inorganic Chemicals

Norwalk
Fairfield County

(G-3094)
420 SIGN DESIGN INC
25 Commerce St (06850-4111)
PHONE..................................203 852-1255
John Malagisi, *President*
Mary Malagisi, *Corp Secy*
EMP: 3 **EST:** 1996
SQ FT: 2,500
SALES (est): 499.3K **Privately Held**
WEB: www.signdesignct.com
SIC: 3993 Mfg Signs/Advertising Specialties

(G-3095)
ABB FINANCE (USA) INC
501 Merritt 7 Ste 2 (06851-7001)
PHONE..................................919 856-2360
EMP: 4
SALES (est): 23.3K
SALES (corp-wide): 36.7B **Privately Held**
SIC: 3613 Mfg Switchgear/Switchboards
PA: Abb Ltd
Affolternstrasse 44
ZUrich ZH 8050
433 177-111

(G-3096)
ACCESS INTELLIGENCE
761 Main Ave Ste 2 (06851-1080)
PHONE..................................203 854-6730
EMP: 5
SALES (est): 497.6K **Privately Held**
SIC: 2721 Periodicals-Publishing/Printing

(G-3097)
AIRPOT CORPORATION
35 Lois St (06851-4405)
PHONE..................................800 848-7681
Mark Gaberman, *President*
Barbara Cohen, *Principal*
Tom Lee, *Vice Pres*
Robert M Cohen, *Director*
▲ **EMP:** 26
SQ FT: 12,000
SALES (est): 5.7MM **Privately Held**
WEB: www.airpot.com
SIC: 3499 3714 3593 Mfg Misc Fabricated Metal Products Mfg Motor Vehicle Parts/Accessories Mfg Fluid Power Cylinders

(G-3098)
AJ CASEY LLC
Also Called: Beverly Feldman
597 Westport Ave C363 (06851-4440)
PHONE..................................203 226-5961
Anthony J Casey, *Mng Member*
▲ **EMP:** 7
SQ FT: 2,100
SALES: 6.8MM **Privately Held**
SIC: 3144 Mfg Women's Footwear

(G-3099)
ALVARADO CUSTOM CABINETRY LLC
51 Midrocks Dr (06851-1623)
PHONE..................................203 831-0181
EMP: 12
SALES (est): 1.4MM **Privately Held**
SIC: 2431 Mfg Millwork

(G-3100)
AMBIANCE PAINTING LLC
67 Murray St (06851-3307)
PHONE..................................203 354-8689
Douglas Kitchen,
EMP: 13
SALES (est): 1.7MM **Privately Held**
WEB: www.ambiancepainting.com
SIC: 2679 Painting/Paper Hanging Contractor

(G-3101)
ANSA COMPANY INC
130 Water St (06854-3140)
PHONE..................................203 687-1664
Austin Iodice, *Manager*
EMP: 11
SQ FT: 34,000
SALES (corp-wide): 2.6MM **Privately Held**
SIC: 3085 Mfg Plastic Bottles
PA: Ansa Company, Inc
1200 S Main St
Muskogee OK 74401
918 687-1664

(G-3102)
APPLIED BIOSYSTEMS LLC
301 Merritt 7 Ste 23 (06851-1062)
PHONE..................................781 271-0045
Tony L White, *Principal*
EMP: 9
SALES (corp-wide): 24.3B **Publicly Held**
WEB: www.applera.com
SIC: 3826 Mfg Analytical Instruments
HQ: Applied Biosystems, Llc
5791 Van Allen Way
Carlsbad CA 92008

(G-3103)
ARTISAN BREAD & PRODUCTS LLC
13 Dry Hill Rd (06851-4002)
PHONE..................................914 843-4401
Diego Perez,
EMP: 8
SALES (est): 607K **Privately Held**
SIC: 2051 Mfg Bread/Related Products

(G-3104)
ARTISTIC IRON WORKS LLC
11 Reynolds St (06855-1014)
PHONE..................................203 838-9200
Maciej Jankowski, *Prdtn Mgr*
Edward Jankowski, *Mng Member*
Renata Singh, *Mng Member*
EMP: 9
SALES: 350K **Privately Held**
SIC: 3446 Mfg Architectural Mtlwrk

(G-3105)
ASEA BROWN BOVERI INC (DH)
Also Called: A B B Power Transmission
501 Merritt 7 (06851-7000)
PHONE..................................203 750-2200
Donald Aiken, *President*
J P Brett, *Senior VP*
Jeff Halsey, *Senior VP*
Han-Anders Nilsson, *Senior VP*
Julie Guarino, *Vice Pres*
EMP: 8 **EST:** 1978
SQ FT: 36,000
SALES (est): 456.4MM
SALES (corp-wide): 36.7B **Privately Held**
SIC: 3612 3613 5063 3511 Holding Company
HQ: Abb Holdings Inc.
305 Gregson Dr
Cary NC 27511
919 856-2360

(G-3106)
AUTO SUTURE COMPANY AUSTRALIA
150 Glover Ave (06850-1308)
PHONE..................................203 845-1000
EMP: 3
SALES (est): 17.1K **Publicly Held**
SIC: 3841 3842 Surgical And Medical Instruments
PA: Medtronic Public Limited Company
20 Lower Hatch Street
Dublin

(G-3107)
AUTO SUTURE COMPANY UK
150 Glover Ave (06850-1308)
PHONE..................................203 845-1000
EMP: 500
SALES (est): 16.7MM **Publicly Held**
SIC: 3841 3842 Surgical And Medical Instruments
PA: Medtronic Public Limited Company
20 Lower Hatch Street
Dublin

(G-3108)
AUTO SUTURE RUSSIA INC
150 Glover Ave (06850-1308)
PHONE..................................203 845-1000
EMP: 3
SALES (est): 138.1K **Publicly Held**
SIC: 3841 Surgical And Medical Instruments
PA: Medtronic Public Limited Company
20 Lower Hatch Street
Dublin

(G-3109)
AVARA PHARMACEUTICAL SVCS INC (HQ)
401 Merritt 7 (06851-1000)
PHONE..................................203 918-1659
Leonard Levi, *Ch of Bd*
Andy Glanville, *Exec VP*
Keith A Lyon, *CFO*
EMP: 31
SALES (est): 39.3MM
SALES (corp-wide): 39.8MM **Privately Held**
SIC: 2834 Mfg Pharmaceutical Preparations
PA: Avara Us Holdings Llc
101 Merritt 7
Norwalk CT 06851
203 655-1333

(G-3110)
BEIERSDORF INC
360 Dr Martin Luther King (06854-4648)
P.O. Box 5529 (06856)
PHONE..................................203 854-8000
Kathleen Shea, *Vice Pres*
EMP: 500
SALES (corp-wide): 11.5B **Privately Held**
WEB: www.bdfusa.com
SIC: 2844 5122 3842 2841 Mfg & Whol Skin Care Products Surgical Bandages Dressings And Wound Care Prod Specialty Soaps And Compression Stockings
HQ: Beiersdorf, Inc.
45 Danbury Rd
Wilton CT 06897
203 563-5800

(G-3111)
BELVOIR MEDIA GROUP LLC
535 Cnncticut Ave Ste 100 (06854)
PHONE..................................203 857-3128
Jared Max Hendler, *Principal*
EMP: 4
SALES (est): 238.4K **Privately Held**
SIC: 2721 Periodicals

(G-3112)
BELVOIR PUBLICATIONS INC (PA)
Also Called: Belvoir Media Group
800 Connecticut Ave 4w02 (06854-1631)
P.O. Box 5656 (06856-5656)
PHONE..................................203 857-3100
Robert Englander, *CEO*
Ron Goldberg, *CFO*
EMP: 50
SQ FT: 11,000
SALES (est): 61.6MM **Privately Held**
WEB: www.belvoir.com
SIC: 2731 Books-Publishing/Printing

(G-3113)
BIO MED PACKAGING SYSTEMS INC
100 Pearl St (06850-1629)
PHONE..................................203 846-1923
James B Brown, *President*
Janet Kaufman, *Vice Pres*
▼ **EMP:** 25
SQ FT: 50,000
SALES (est): 4MM **Privately Held**
SIC: 3842 Mfg Surgical Appliances/Supplies

(G-3114)
BITE TECH INC
20 Glover Ave Ste 1 (06850-1234)
PHONE..................................203 987-6898
Jeff Padovan, *CEO*
James Meyers, *Vice Pres*
▼ **EMP:** 27 **EST:** 1995
SQ FT: 3,500
SALES (est): 5.6MM **Privately Held**
SIC: 3069 Mfg Fabricated Rubber Products

GEOGRAPHIC

(G-3115)
BRUCE PARK SPORTS EMB LLC
20 Chatham Dr (06854-2528)
PHONE..................................203 853-4488
John Mackenzie, *Mng Member*
EMP: 3
SQ FT: 1,800
SALES (est): 257.4K **Privately Held**
SIC: 2395 Pleating/Stitching Services

(G-3116)
BUCK SCIENTIFIC INC
58 Fort Point St (06855-1097)
PHONE..................................203 853-9444
Robert Anderson, *President*
Edward Nadeau, *Vice Pres*
John Mellor, *Prdtn Mgr*
Eric Anderson, *Admin Sec*
Theresa Perkins, *Contractor*
EMP: 55
SQ FT: 10,000
SALES (est): 11.6MM **Privately Held**
WEB: www.bucksci.com
SIC: 3826 3823 Mfg Analytical Instr Mfg Process Cntrl Instr

(G-3117)
BUSINESS JOURNALS INC (PA)
Also Called: Travel Wear
50 Day St Fl 3 (06854-3100)
PHONE..................................203 853-6015
EMP: 55
SQ FT: 20,000
SALES (est): 5.6MM **Privately Held**
WEB: www.breweryage.com
SIC: 2721 2741 Periodicals

(G-3118)
CANTATA MEDIA LLC
Also Called: Daily Voice
132b Water St (06854-3140)
P.O. Box 464 (06856-0464)
PHONE..................................203 951-9885
Travis Hardman, *Mng Member*
EMP: 12
SALES (est): 227.1K **Privately Held**
SIC: 2711 7371 Newspapers-Publishing/Printing Custom Computer Programing

(G-3119)
CARNEGIE TOOL INC
25 Perry Ave Ste 12 (06850-1655)
PHONE..................................203 866-0744
Paul C Stratton, *President*
Phyllis Stratton, *Vice Pres*
EMP: 10
SALES (est): 1.4MM **Privately Held**
SIC: 3544 3599 Mfg Tools And Dies & Proto-Type Machining

(G-3120)
CB SEATING ETC LLC (PA)
324 Strawberry Hill Ave (06851-4328)
PHONE..................................203 359-3880
Carol Bruno, *Principal*
EMP: 4
SALES (est): 767.1K **Privately Held**
SIC: 2511 5021 Mfg Wood Household Furniture Whol Furniture

(G-3121)
CEBAL AMERICAS (PA)
Also Called: Alcan Packaging
101 Merritt 7 Ste 2 (06851-1060)
PHONE..................................203 845-6356
Christel Bories, *CEO*
EMP: 7
SALES: 200MM **Privately Held**
WEB: www.cebalamerica.com
SIC: 3082 Manufactures Plasctic Packaging Tubes 100

(G-3122)
CELLMARK PULP & PAPER INC
80 Washington St Ste 1 (06854-3049)
PHONE..................................203 299-5050
Johan Rafstedt, *President*
Andreas Ceder, *Vice Pres*
EMP: 19
SALES (est): 4.8MM
SALES (corp-wide): 2.9B **Privately Held**
SIC: 2611 Pulp Mill
HQ: Cellmark Ab
Lilla Bommen 3c
Goteborg 411 0
311 900-07

(G-3123)
CHANNEL ALLOYS
301 Merritt 7 Ste 1 (06851-1051)
PHONE..................................203 975-1404
Chris Howard, *President*
▲ **EMP:** 5 **EST:** 2015
SALES (est): 228.4K **Privately Held**
SIC: 3316 2041 Mfg Cold-Rolled Steel Shapes Mfg Flour/Grain Mill Prooducts

(G-3124)
CHRISTOPHER CONDORS
Also Called: Condor Press
23 1st St Ste 1 (06855-2333)
PHONE..................................203 852-8181
Christopher Condors, *Owner*
EMP: 4 **EST:** 1992
SQ FT: 2,500
SALES: 200K **Privately Held**
SIC: 2759 Commercial Printing

(G-3125)
CISCO SYSTEMS INC
383 Main Ave Ste 7 (06851-1544)
PHONE..................................203 229-2300
Jeff Distasio, *Regional Mgr*
Paul La Croix, *Engineer*
Mark King, *Marketing Mgr*
Greg Prindel, *Manager*
Karen Lemire, *Director*
EMP: 40
SALES (corp-wide): 51.9B **Publicly Held**
WEB: www.cisco.com
SIC: 3577 5045 Mfg Computer Peripheral Equipment Whol Computers/Peripherals
PA: Cisco Systems, Inc.
170 W Tasman Dr
San Jose CA 95134
408 526-4000

(G-3126)
CLARKE DISTRIBUTION CORP
64 S Main St (06854-2934)
PHONE..................................203 838-9385
Thomas Clarke, *President*
EMP: 7
SQ FT: 14,894 **Privately Held**
SIC: 3639 5722 Mfg Household Appliances Ret Household Appliances
PA: Clarke Distribution Corporation
393 Fortune Blvd
Milford MA 01757

(G-3127)
COCCHIA NORWALK GRAPE CO
Also Called: Homemade Lbtons By Ccchia Sons
25 Ely Ave (06854-2995)
PHONE..................................203 855-7911
Fax: 203 866-4690
EMP: 10
SQ FT: 3,000
SALES (est): 620K **Privately Held**
SIC: 2084 5149 5084 Winery & Whol Wine Makers' Equipment & Brewery Products Machinery

(G-3128)
COLONIAL WOODWORKING INC
145 Water St (06854-3129)
PHONE..................................203 866-5844
Frank Carlucci, *President*
Nancy Carlucci, *Vice Pres*
Peter Carlucci, *Vice Pres*
Veronica Mahan, *Admin Sec*
EMP: 18 **EST:** 1975
SQ FT: 13,000
SALES (est): 1.6MM **Privately Held**
WEB: www.colonialwoodworking.com
SIC: 2431 Mfg Millwork

(G-3129)
COLOR FILM MEDIA GROUP LLC (PA)
45 Keeler Ave (06854-2307)
PHONE..................................203 202-2929
J Bradford Lareau,
EMP: 8
SALES (est): 942.2K **Privately Held**
SIC: 3651 Mfg Home Audio/Video Equipment

(G-3130)
COMPUTER TECH EXPRESS LLC
95 New Canaan Ave (06850-2620)
PHONE..................................203 810-4932
Mohammad Ghazi, *Principal*
EMP: 5
SALES (est): 369.7K
SALES (corp-wide): 118.4K **Privately Held**
SIC: 7372 7379 Prepackaged Software Services Computer Related Services
PA: Computer Tech Express Llc
912 Hope St
Stamford CT 06907
203 817-0100

(G-3131)
CONCORD INDUSTRIES INC
Also Called: Concord Distributing
19 Willard Rd (06851-4414)
PHONE..................................203 750-6060
Karen Muller Condron, *President*
▲ **EMP:** 45
SQ FT: 27,000
SALES (est): 5.7MM **Privately Held**
WEB: www.concordind.com
SIC: 3499 5199 3993 Manufactures Misc Fabricated Metal Products Signs/Advertising Specialties Wholesales Nondurable Goods

(G-3132)
CORR/DIS INCORPORATED
Also Called: Fastserv/Northeast
38 Burchard Ln (06853-1105)
P.O. Box 125 (06853-0125)
PHONE..................................203 838-6075
Jeffrey Gerwig, *President*
Christopher Gerwig, *Vice Pres*
Norma Gerwig, *Treasurer*
EMP: 3
SALES: 250K **Privately Held**
WEB: www.fastservnortheast.com
SIC: 2653 3993 Mfg Corrugated/Solid Fiber Boxes Mfg Signs/Advertising Specialties

(G-3133)
CRITERION INC
Also Called: Perfectsoftware
501 Merritt 7 Ste 1 (06851-7001)
PHONE..................................203 703-9000
Sunil Reddy, *CEO*
EMP: 25
SALES (est): 2.3MM **Privately Held**
SIC: 7372 Prepackaged Software Services

(G-3134)
DESIGNING ELEMENT
6 Barnum Ave (06851-4111)
PHONE..................................203 849-3076
EMP: 3
SALES (est): 189.2K **Privately Held**
SIC: 2819 Industrial Inorganic Chemicals, Nec

(G-3135)
DIAGEO AMERICAS INC
801 Main Ave (06851-1127)
PHONE..................................203 229-2100
Deirdre Mahlan, *CEO*
James Thompson, *President*
Elizabeth Tong, *Vice Pres*
Corinn Williams, *Manager*
Gabriel Bisio, *Admin Sec*
EMP: 8
SALES (est): 658.4K
SALES (corp-wide): 16.3B **Privately Held**
SIC: 2084 Mfg Wines/Brandy/Spirits
PA: Diageo Plc
Lakeside Drive Park Royal
London NW10
208 978-6000

(G-3136)
DIAGEO AMERICAS SUPPLY INC
801 Main Ave (06851-1127)
PHONE..................................203 229-2100
Paul Gallagher, *President*
Dan Russo, *Vice Pres*
Aren Korte, *CFO*
Claire Macintyre, *VP Human Res*
Gabriel Bisio, *Director*
◆ **EMP:** 4 **EST:** 2008
SALES (est): 806.5K **Privately Held**
SIC: 2084 Mfg Wines/Brandy/Spirits

(G-3137)
DIAGEO INVESTMENT CORPORATION
801 Main Ave (06851-1127)
PHONE..................................203 229-2100
Michael Fernandez, *General Mgr*
Jeff Millstein, *Exec VP*
Scott Barnhart, *Vice Pres*
Harry Bigelow, *Vice Pres*
Gary Galanis, *Vice Pres*
◆ **EMP:** 12
SALES (est): 1.3MM
SALES (corp-wide): 16.3B **Privately Held**
SIC: 2082 Mfg Malt Beverages
PA: Diageo Plc
Lakeside Drive Park Royal
London NW10
208 978-6000

(G-3138)
DIAGEO NORTH AMERICA INC (HQ)
801 Main Ave (06851-1127)
PHONE..................................203 229-2100
Ivan Menezes, *CEO*
Thomas Day, *Vice Pres*
Gerald Dinallo, *Vice Pres*
Susan Jones, *Vice Pres*
Robert Moore, *Vice Pres*
◆ **EMP:** 3500
SALES (est): 2.6B
SALES (corp-wide): 16.3B **Privately Held**
SIC: 2084 2085 Mfg Wines/Brandy/Spirits Mfg Distilled/Blended Liquor
PA: Diageo Plc
Lakeside Drive Park Royal
London NW10
208 978-6000

(G-3139)
DIAGEO PLC
Joseph E Seagram & Sons
801 Main Ave (06851-1127)
PHONE..................................203 229-2100
Edgar M Bronfman Jr, *President*
Jennifer Van Ness, *VP Mktg*
Cody Hickok, *Marketing Staff*
EMP: 100
SALES (corp-wide): 16.3B **Privately Held**
SIC: 2085 2084 Mfg Distilled/Blended Liquor Mfg Wines/Brandy/Spirits
PA: Diageo Plc
Lakeside Drive Park Royal
London NW10
208 978-6000

(G-3140)
DICKSON PRODUCT DEVELOPMENT
14 Perry Ave (06850-1623)
PHONE..................................203 846-2128
Maurice Bennett, *President*
Margaret Bennett, *Vice Pres*
EMP: 7
SQ FT: 6,000
SALES (est): 725.4K **Privately Held**
WEB: www.dicksonconsulting.biz
SIC: 3599 Machine Shop

(G-3141)
DOMINICS DECORATING INC
6 Allen Ct (06851-2306)
PHONE..................................203 838-1827
Michael Nardella, *President*
Peter Murphy, *Vice Pres*
EMP: 6
SQ FT: 4,000
SALES (est): 730.6K **Privately Held**
SIC: 2211 2231 2391 2392 Mfr Cotton And Wool Upholstery Draperies & Slipcovers

(G-3142)
DOONEY & BOURKE INC (PA)
1 Regent St (06855-1405)
P.O. Box 841 (06856-0841)
PHONE..................................203 853-7515
H Peter Dooney, *President*
Philip R Kinsley, *Vice Pres*

▲ = Import ▼=Export
◆ =Import/Export

Frederick A Bourke Jr, *Treasurer*
Palmer Chiappetta, *Accountant*
▲ **EMP:** 38
SQ FT: 56,000
SALES (est): 26.1MM **Privately Held**
SIC: 3171 2387 3161 3172 Mfg Womens Handbag/Purse Mfg Apparel Belts Mfg Luggage Mfg Personal Leather Gds

(G-3143)
DORADO TANKERS POOL INC
20 Glover Ave (06850-1219)
PHONE..................................203 662-2600
Mark La Monte, *President*
John Greenwood, *Admin Sec*
EMP: 20
SALES (est): 3.8MM **Privately Held**
SIC: 3731 Shipbuilding/Repairing

(G-3144)
DOUGLAS MOSS
Also Called: E Magazine
28 Knight St Ste 5 (06851-4719)
P.O. Box 5098, Westport (06881-5098)
PHONE..................................203 854-5559
EMP: 9
SALES (est): 510K **Privately Held**
WEB: www.emagazine.com
SIC: 2721 Periodicals-Publishing/Printing

(G-3145)
DULCE DOMUM LLC
Also Called: Cottages & Grdns Publications
40 Richards Ave Ste 4 (06854-2320)
PHONE..................................203 227-1400
Mary A Howatson,
EMP: 22
SQ FT: 3,225
SALES (est): 3MM **Privately Held**
WEB: www.cottages-gardens.com
SIC: 2721 Whol Books/Newspapers

(G-3146)
E-Z TOOLS INC
5 Poplar St (06855-2108)
PHONE..................................203 838-2102
Fax: 203 855-9965
EMP: 5
SALES: 100K **Privately Held**
SIC: 3423 Mfg Hand/Edge Tools

(G-3147)
EC HOLDINGS INC
2 Muller Ave (06851)
PHONE..................................203 846-1651
EMP: 9
SQ FT: 40,000
SALES (est): 1.7MM **Privately Held**
SIC: 3613 5063 Mfg Switchgear/Switchboards Whol Electrical Equipment

(G-3148)
ECOMETICS INC
19 Concord St (06854-3706)
P.O. Box 179 (06856-0179)
PHONE..................................203 853-7856
Mark Lowenstein, *President*
Michael Lowenstein, *Vice Pres*
Judith Lowenstein, *Admin Sec*
▲ **EMP:** 30
SQ FT: 25,000
SALES (est): 6.8MM **Privately Held**
SIC: 2844 Mfg Toilet Preparations

(G-3149)
ELEMENT ONE LLC
1 N Water St Ste 100 (06854-2260)
PHONE..................................203 344-1553
EMP: 4
SALES (est): 338.2K **Privately Held**
SIC: 2819 Industrial Inorganic Chemicals, Nec

(G-3150)
FC MEYER PACKAGING LLC (HQ)
108 Main St Ste 3 (06851-4640)
PHONE..................................203 847-8500
Steve Gilliand, *CFO*
Kenneth Schulman, *Mng Member*
Steven Schulman,
EMP: 60
SQ FT: 12,000
SALES (est): 42.4MM
SALES (corp-wide): 100.3MM **Privately Held**
SIC: 3086 Paper Mill
PA: Mafcote, Inc.
108 Main St Ste 3
Norwalk CT 06851
203 847-8500

(G-3151)
FCA LLC
26 2nd St (06855-2316)
PHONE..................................203 857-0825
Frank C Arcamone Jr, *Principal*
EMP: 4
SALES (est): 283.7K **Privately Held**
SIC: 2448 Mfg Wood Pallets/Skids

(G-3152)
FIRE PREVENTION SERVICES
13 Winfield St (06855-1307)
PHONE..................................203 866-6357
Andrew Delcarmine, *Owner*
Julio Delcarmine, *Co-Owner*
Andrew Carmine, *Vice Pres*
EMP: 10
SALES (est): 1.1MM **Privately Held**
SIC: 3999 Mfg Misc Products

(G-3153)
FITZGERALD-NORWALK AWNING CO
Also Called: Norwalk Awning Company
131 Main St (06851-4628)
PHONE..................................203 847-5858
EMP: 7
SALES (est): 682.1K **Privately Held**
SIC: 2394 1799 Canvas And Related Products

(G-3154)
FOUNDRY FOODS INC
383 Main Ave Fl 5 (06851-1586)
PHONE..................................314 982-3204
EMP: 4
SALES (est): 155.1K
SALES (corp-wide): 92.8B **Privately Held**
SIC: 2052 2032 2095 2086 Mfg Cookies/Crackers Mfg Canned Specialties Mfg Roasted Coffee Mfg Soft Drinks Mgmt Consulting Svcs
PA: Nestle S.A.
Avenue Nestle 55
Vevey VD 1800
219 242-111

(G-3155)
G M F WOODWORKING LLC
22 Sunset Hill Ave (06851-5828)
PHONE..................................203 788-8979
George Farrington, *Principal*
EMP: 4
SALES (est): 192.2K **Privately Held**
SIC: 2431 Mfg Millwork

(G-3156)
G WOODCRAFT
11 Ruby St (06850-1614)
PHONE..................................203 846-4168
Gary Cimino, *Managing Prtnr*
EMP: 3
SALES (est): 279.6K **Privately Held**
SIC: 2521 Mfg Wood Office Furniture

(G-3157)
GATEWAY DIGITAL INC
16 Testa Pl (06854-4638)
PHONE..................................203 853-4929
Van David Cudiner, *President*
Ray Compagna, *General Mgr*
Tom Steele, *Vice Pres*
Bill Bepko, *Accounts Exec*
Taylor McIntosh, *Sales Staff*
EMP: 19
SQ FT: 13,000
SALES (est): 3MM **Privately Held**
WEB: www.gwayonline.com
SIC: 2796 2752 2791 2759 Platemaking Services Lithographic Coml Print Typesetting Services Commercial Printing

(G-3158)
GCN PUBLISHING INC
Also Called: Gcn Media Services
194 Main St Ste 2nw (06851-3502)
PHONE..................................203 665-6211
Joanne Persico, *Principal*
Elaine Goncalves, *Accounts Exec*
EMP: 13
SALES (est): 1.1MM **Privately Held**
SIC: 2741 Internet Publishing And Broadcasting

(G-3159)
GENERAL ELECTRIC COMPANY
901 Main Ave Ste 103 (06851-1187)
PHONE..................................518 385-7164
Don Kesterson, *Engineer*
Mark Robson, *Sales Mgr*
Matthew Chriss, *Accounts Mgr*
Kurt Wildermuth, *Regl Sales Mgr*
David Kohl, *Sales Staff*
EMP: 65
SALES (corp-wide): 121.6B **Publicly Held**
SIC: 3825 Mfg Electrical Measuring Instruments
PA: General Electric Company
5 Necco St
Boston MA 02210
617 443-3000

(G-3160)
GENERAL PACKAGING PRODUCTS INC
3 Valley View Rd Apt 9 (06851-1033)
PHONE..................................203 846-1340
Peter D Schonberg, *President*
Anthony Lorenzo, *Admin Sec*
EMP: 9
SQ FT: 1,400
SALES (est): 1.4MM **Privately Held**
SIC: 3086 2653 2671 Mfg Plastic Foam Prdts Mfg Corrugated/Fiber Box Mfg Packaging Paper/Film

(G-3161)
GENVARIO AWNING CO
131 Main St (06851-4628)
PHONE..................................203 847-5858
George Genvario, *CEO*
EMP: 4
SALES (est): 156.2K **Privately Held**
SIC: 2394 Mfg Canvas/Related Products

(G-3162)
GOLF GALAXY LLC
Also Called: Golfsmith
595 Connecticut Ave Ste 4 (06854-1734)
PHONE..................................203 855-0500
Steve Partin, *Principal*
EMP: 5
SALES (corp-wide): 8.4B **Publicly Held**
SIC: 3949 5091 5941 Mfg Sporting/Athletic Goods Whol Sporting/Recreational Goods Ret Sporting Goods/Bicycles
HQ: Golf Galaxy, Llc
345 Court St
Coraopolis PA 15108

(G-3163)
GOTHAM CHEMICAL COMPANY INC
21 South St (06854-2602)
PHONE..................................203 854-6644
Richard Zane Elkin, *President*
Ernest Elkin, *President*
Richard Elkin, *Vice Pres*
EMP: 100
SQ FT: 10,000
SALES (est): 17.4MM **Privately Held**
SIC: 2899 Mfg Water Treating Chemicals

(G-3164)
GUASA SALSA VZLA
9 Rainbow Rd (06851-2806)
PHONE..................................203 981-7011
Maria Quiroga, *Principal*
EMP: 3
SALES (est): 139.1K **Privately Held**
SIC: 2099 Mfg Food Preparations

(G-3165)
GUINNESS AMERICA INC
801 Main Ave (06851-1127)
PHONE..................................203 229-2100
Chuck Phillips, *Principal*
▼ **EMP:** 5
SALES (est): 325.3K
SALES (corp-wide): 16.3B **Privately Held**
SIC: 2082 Mfg Malt Beverages
PA: Diageo Plc
Lakeside Drive Park Royal
London NW10
208 978-6000

(G-3166)
HANNES PRECISION INDUSTRY INC
74 Fort Point St (06855-1210)
PHONE..................................203 853-7276
Jean Schaer, *President*
EMP: 12
SALES (corp-wide): 700K **Privately Held**
SIC: 3999 Mfg Misc Products
PA: Hannes Precision Industry Inc
12 Pleasant St
Norwalk CT
203 853-7276

(G-3167)
HEARST CORPORATION
Also Called: Greenwich Time
301 Merritt 7 Ste 1 (06851-1051)
PHONE..................................203 625-4445
EMP: 25
SALES (corp-wide): 6.6B **Privately Held**
SIC: 2711 Newspapers-Publishing/Printing
PA: The Hearst Corporation
300 W 57th St Fl 42
New York NY 10019
212 649-2000

(G-3168)
HICKS AND OTIS PRINTS INC
9 Wilton Ave (06851-4515)
PHONE..................................203 846-2087
Harold Kaplan, *President*
Linwood Wade, *Vice Pres*
Steven Crovatto, *Admin Sec*
▲ **EMP:** 32 **EST:** 1939
SQ FT: 45,000
SALES (est): 5.8MM **Privately Held**
WEB: www.dorrie.com
SIC: 3083 3429 Mfg Laminated Plastic Plate/Sheet Mfg Hardware

(G-3169)
HOLLAND & SHERRY INC (PA)
Also Called: Elizabeth Eakins
5 Taft St (06854-4201)
PHONE..................................212 628-1950
Elizabeth Eakins, *President*
Scott Lethbridge, *Vice Pres*
▲ **EMP:** 10
SALES (est): 1.9MM **Privately Held**
WEB: www.elizabetheakins.com
SIC: 2273 5713 5023 Mfg Carpets/Rugs Ret Floor Covering Whol Homefurnishings

(G-3170)
HOLLY PRESS INC
8 College St (06851-4006)
PHONE..................................203 846-1720
EMP: 3 **EST:** 1962
SQ FT: 1,500
SALES (est): 330K **Privately Held**
SIC: 2752 Commercial Offset Printers

(G-3171)
IHS HEROLD INC (DH)
200 Connecticut Ave Ste 8 (06854-1907)
PHONE..................................203 857-0215
Christin Juneau, *CEO*
Gilbert Baliki, *Senior VP*
Lysle Brinker, *Vice Pres*
John Parry, *Vice Pres*
Donald Whelley, *CFO*
▼ **EMP:** 66
SQ FT: 16,000
SALES (est): 5.6MM **Privately Held**
WEB: www.herold.com
SIC: 3826 6282 8742 Mfg Analytical Instruments Investment Advisory Service Management Consulting Services
HQ: Ihs Global Inc.
15 Inverness Way E
Englewood CO 80112
303 790-0600

(G-3172)
INDUSTRIAL PRESS INC
32 Haviland St 3 (06854-3005)
PHONE..................................212 889-6330
Michael A Backer, *Ch of Bd*
Alex Luchars, *President*

GEOGRAPHIC

Judy Bass, *Editor*
▲ **EMP:** 11 **EST:** 1894
SQ FT: 3,400
SALES (est): 1.5MM **Privately Held**
WEB: www.industrialpress.com
SIC: 2731 Books-Publishing/Printing

(G-3173)
INFORMATION RESOURCES INC
383 Main Ave Ste 20 (06851-1582)
PHONE..................................203 845-6400
Samantha Desrancesco, *Principal*
EMP: 70
SALES (corp-wide): 364.2MM **Privately Held**
WEB: www.infores.com
SIC: 7372 8732 Prepackaged Software Services Commercial Nonphysical Research
PA: Information Resources, Inc
150 N Clinton St
Chicago IL 60661
312 726-1221

(G-3174)
INSIGHT MEDIA LLC
Also Called: Microdisplay Report
3 Morgan Ave Ste 2 (06851-5018)
PHONE..................................203 831-8464
Chris Chinnock, *Mng Member*
EMP: 4 **EST:** 1998
SQ FT: 4,452
SALES (est): 295.1K **Privately Held**
WEB: www.mdreport.com
SIC: 2741 Misc Publishing

(G-3175)
INSYS MICRO INC
40 Richards Ave Ste 3 (06854-2320)
PHONE..................................917 566-5045
Yuriy Kartoshkin, *President*
EMP: 7
SALES (est): 632.7K **Privately Held**
SIC: 3679 7373 Mfg Electronic Components Computer Systems Design

(G-3176)
INTERSTATE TAX CORPORATION
83 East Ave Ste 110 (06851-4902)
PHONE..................................203 854-0704
Carol Sheiber, *President*
Harvey Sheiber, *Treasurer*
EMP: 3
SALES (est): 304.7K **Privately Held**
WEB: www.interstatetaxcorp.com
SIC: 2721 Periodicals-Publishing/Printing

(G-3177)
IZZI BS ALLERGY FREE LLC
Also Called: Izzi B'S Allergen Free Cupcake
22 Knight St (06851-4707)
PHONE..................................203 810-4378
Pamela G Nicholas, *Mng Member*
EMP: 4
SALES (est): 220K **Privately Held**
SIC: 2051 Mfg Bakery Products

(G-3178)
JAIME M CAMACHO
Also Called: Sign-A-Rama
345 Main Ave (06851-1547)
PHONE..................................203 846-8221
Jamie M Camacho, *Owner*
EMP: 4
SQ FT: 1,400
SALES: 185K **Privately Held**
SIC: 3993 Signsadv Specs

(G-3179)
JARDEN LLC
301 Merritt 7 Ste 5 (06851-1051)
PHONE..................................203 845-5300
James Lillie, *President*
EMP: 21
SALES (corp-wide): 8.6B **Publicly Held**
SIC: 3089 3634 Mfg Plastic Products Wood Products Electronic Products Consumer Products
HQ: Jarden Llc
221 River St
Hoboken NJ 07030

(G-3180)
JARED MANUFACTURING CO INC
25 Perry Ave (06850-1655)
P.O. Box 266 (06850)
PHONE..................................203 846-1732
Timothy C Frate, *President*
Tim Frate, *CFO*
EMP: 15
SQ FT: 11,000
SALES (est): 3.2MM **Privately Held**
WEB: www.jaredmfg.com
SIC: 3444 3599 3699 Mfg Sheet Metalwork Mfg Industrial Machinery Mfg Electrical Equipment/Supplies

(G-3181)
JENKINS SUGAR GROUP INC
16 S Main St Ste 202 (06854-2981)
PHONE..................................203 853-3000
Frank Jenkins, *President*
Eric Bergman, *Broker*
EMP: 10
SALES (est): 710.8K **Privately Held**
SIC: 2062 Cane Sugar Refining

(G-3182)
JKB DAIRA INC (PA)
22 S Smith St (06855-1018)
PHONE..................................203 642-4824
Yoichi Ota, *CEO*
Joan Brakeley, *President*
▲ **EMP:** 7
SQ FT: 4,800
SALES (est): 959.7K **Privately Held**
WEB: www.jkbdaira.com
SIC: 3482 3484 Mfg Small Arms Ammunition Mfg Small Arms

(G-3183)
K W GRIFFEN COMPANY
Also Called: Biomed Packing Systems
100 Pearl St (06850-1629)
PHONE..................................203 846-1923
James B Brown, *President*
Rosemary Brown, *Treasurer*
EMP: 40
SQ FT: 32,000
SALES (est): 7.1MM **Privately Held**
SIC: 3842 Mfg Surgical Scrub Brushes And Dressings

(G-3184)
KARAVAS FASHIONS LTD
17 Wall St (06850-3413)
PHONE..................................203 866-4000
Stelios Paraskevas, *President*
Carol Paraskevas, *Admin Sec*
EMP: 10 **EST:** 1979
SALES (est): 1.2MM **Privately Held**
SIC: 3911 Mfg Precious Metal Jewelry

(G-3185)
LEEK BUILDING PRODUCTS INC
205 Wilson Ave Ste 3 (06854-5025)
PHONE..................................203 853-3883
William A Leek Jr, *President*
Martha K Leek, *Corp Secy*
▲ **EMP:** 20
SQ FT: 10,000
SALES (est): 4.3MM **Privately Held**
SIC: 3446 3444 3296 5211 Mfg Architectural Mtlwrk Mfg Sheet Metalwork Mfg Mineral Wool Ret Lumber/Building Mtrl

(G-3186)
LONZA WOOD PROTECTION
501 Merritt 7 (06851-7000)
PHONE..................................203 229-2900
Steven Wisnewski, *Principal*
EMP: 3 **EST:** 2013
SALES (est): 323.4K **Privately Held**
SIC: 2899 Mfg Chemical Preparations

(G-3187)
LOOKOUT SOLUTIONS LLC
Also Called: Shelfgenie
7 Lookout Rd (06850-1035)
PHONE..................................203 750-0307
Alejandro Modica, *Principal*
EMP: 5 **EST:** 2009
SALES (est): 714.5K **Privately Held**
SIC: 2511 Mfg Wood Household Furniture

(G-3188)
LOREX PLASTICS CO INC
221 Wilson Ave (06854-5026)
PHONE..................................203 286-0020
Ed Abdelnour, *Owner*
EMP: 7
SALES (est): 791.6K **Privately Held**
SIC: 3089 Mfg Plastic Products

(G-3189)
MAFCOTE INTERNATIONAL INC (HQ)
108 Main St Ste 3 (06851-4640)
PHONE..................................203 644-1200
Steven A Schulnan, *President*
Miles Hisiger, *Treasurer*
EMP: 11
SALES (est): 1.8MM
SALES (corp-wide): 100.3MM **Privately Held**
WEB: www.mafcote.com
SIC: 2621 Paper Mill
PA: Mafcote, Inc.
108 Main St Ste 3
Norwalk CT 06851
203 847-8500

(G-3190)
MANGO DSP INC
Also Called: Mango Intllgent Vdeo Solutions
83 East Ave Ste 115 (06851-4902)
PHONE..................................203 857-4008
Edward Czernik, *President*
EMP: 24
SQ FT: 2,554
SALES (est): 4.4MM
SALES (corp-wide): 1.7MM **Privately Held**
WEB: www.mangodsp.com
SIC: 3663 Mfg Radio/Tv Communication Equipment
PA: Mango D.S.P. Ltd
250 Emek Haela
Modiin-Maccabim-Reut 71779
258 850-00

(G-3191)
MAX PRODUCTIONS LLC
Also Called: Minuteman Press
167 Main St Ste 1 (06851-3757)
PHONE..................................203 838-2795
Greg Duffey, *Mng Member*
Joe Brenneis,
EMP: 5
SQ FT: 1,800
SALES (est): 693.6K **Privately Held**
SIC: 2752 Comm Prtg Litho

(G-3192)
MAYAN CORPORATION
79 Day St (06854-3733)
PHONE..................................203 854-4711
Luis M Huerta, *President*
Ronald E Pair, *Vice Pres*
EMP: 15
SQ FT: 6,800
SALES: 1.4MM **Privately Held**
WEB: www.mayanet.net
SIC: 3172 Mfg Personal Leather Goods

(G-3193)
MBM SALES
Also Called: Bank Sails
40 Quintard Ave (06854-3735)
PHONE..................................203 866-3674
Steven Benjaman, *President*
Park Benjiman, *Treasurer*
EMP: 12
SQ FT: 6,000
SALES (est): 750K **Privately Held**
SIC: 2394 Mfg Sails For Sail Boats

(G-3194)
MEDIA VENTURES INC
200 Connecticut Ave # 23 (06854-1971)
PHONE..................................203 852-6570
David Persson, *President*
Benson Briggs, *Vice Pres*
EMP: 24
SQ FT: 6,000
SALES (est): 2.4MM **Privately Held**
WEB: www.mediaventuresinc.com
SIC: 2741 2721 Misc Publishing Periodicals-Publishing/Printing

(G-3195)
MEDIANEWS GROUP INC
Also Called: Connecticut Post
301 Merritt 7 Ste 1 (06851-1051)
PHONE..................................203 333-0161
Erin Walsh, *Opers Staff*
Lauren Corbo, *Human Res Mgr*
Robert Laska, *Branch Mgr*
Chuck Northrup, *Info Tech Mgr*
EMP: 10
SALES (corp-wide): 4.2B **Privately Held**
SIC: 2711 Newspaper Publishing
HQ: Medianews Group, Inc.
101 W Colfax Ave Ste 1100
Denver CO 80202

(G-3196)
METSA BOARD AMERICAS CORP
301 Merritt 7 Ste 2 (06851-1051)
PHONE..................................203 229-0037
Lasse Wikstrom, *CEO*
Mika Paljakka, *Ch of Bd*
Jorma Sahlstedt, *President*
Paul Zelinsky, *COO*
◆ **EMP:** 69
SQ FT: 12,000
SALES (est): 22.4MM
SALES (corp-wide): 2.1B **Privately Held**
SIC: 2631 Paperboard Mill
PA: Metsa Board Oyj
Revontulentie 6
Espoo 02100
104 611-

(G-3197)
MIAMI WABASH PAPER LLC (HQ)
108 Main St Ste 3 (06851-4640)
PHONE..................................203 847-8500
Steven D Schulman,
Miles Hisiger,
Miles E Misiger,
Kenneth B Schulman,
EMP: 20
SQ FT: 12,000
SALES (est): 13.1MM
SALES (corp-wide): 100.3MM **Privately Held**
WEB: www.miamiwabashpaper.com
SIC: 2671 Paper Mill
PA: Mafcote, Inc.
108 Main St Ste 3
Norwalk CT 06851
203 847-8500

(G-3198)
MILLEN INDUSTRIES INC (PA)
108 Main St Ste 4 (06851-4640)
PHONE..................................203 847-8500
Steven A Schulman, *President*
Miles E Hisiger, *Vice Pres*
Kenneth B Schulman, *Vice Pres*
▲ **EMP:** 3
SQ FT: 11,000
SALES (est): 19.3MM **Privately Held**
WEB: www.millenindustries.com
SIC: 2652 2631 Mfg Setup Paperboard Boxes Paperboard Mill

(G-3199)
MIMFORMS LLC
50 Washington St Fl 7 (06854-2751)
PHONE..................................800 445-1245
Robert C Linke, *Mng Member*
◆ **EMP:** 6
SALES: 5MM **Privately Held**
SIC: 3443 Mfg Fabricated Plate Work

(G-3200)
MODERN DISTILLERY AGE
228 Silvermine Ave (06850-2032)
PHONE..................................203 971-8710
Gregg Glaser, *President*
EMP: 3
SALES (est): 134.3K **Privately Held**
SIC: 2085 Mfg Distilled/Blended Liquor

(G-3201)
MODERN OBJECTS INC
5 River Dr (06855-2505)
PHONE..................................203 378-5785
Michael Aguero, *President*
EMP: 4

SALES (est): 491.1K Privately Held
SIC: 2514 5023 Designs & Whol Metal Home Furnishings

(G-3202)
MY SLIDE LINES LLC
173 Main St (06851-3606)
PHONE..................................203 324-1642
Michael Keating,
EMP: 5
SALES (est): 502.1K Privately Held
SIC: 1389 Oil/Gas Field Services

(G-3203)
NANO PET PRODUCTS LLC
Also Called: Dog Gone Smart
10 Hoyt St (06851-4605)
PHONE..................................203 345-1330
Chris Onthank, *CEO*
▲ EMP: 3
SALES (est): 435.6K Privately Held
SIC: 3999 Mfg Misc Products

(G-3204)
NC BRANDS LP
40 Richards Ave Ste 2 (06854-2320)
PHONE..................................203 295-2300
Robert Kulperger, *CEO*
Mark Munford, *President*
Debra Gordon, *CFO*
EMP: 85
SQ FT: 3,500
SALES (est): 20.6MM
SALES (corp-wide): 3.2MM Privately Held
SIC: 2842 Mfg Polish/Sanitation Goods
HQ: Bio-Lab, Inc.
1725 N Brown Rd
Lawrenceville GA 30043
678 502-4000

(G-3205)
NCI HOLDINGS INC (PA)
40 Richards Ave Ste 2 (06854-2320)
PHONE..................................203 295-2300
Robert J Kulperger, *CEO*
Debbie Gordon, *Treasurer*
▲ EMP: 43
SALES (est): 21.7MM Privately Held
SIC: 2842 Mfg Polish/Sanitation Goods

(G-3206)
NEASI-WEBER INTERNATIONAL
17 Little Fox Ln (06850-2317)
PHONE..................................203 857-4404
Michael Brier, *Senior VP*
EMP: 3
SALES (est): 126.6K
SALES (corp-wide): 5.5MM Privately Held
WEB: www.nwintl.com
SIC: 7372 Prepackaged Software Services
PA: Neasi-Weber International
25115 Ave Stnford Ste 220
Valencia CA 91355
818 895-6900

(G-3207)
NEW ENGLAND FIBERGLASS REPAIR (PA)
144 Water St (06854-3191)
PHONE..................................203 866-1690
Bob Mills, *Owner*
EMP: 3
SALES (est): 314.2K Privately Held
SIC: 3732 Boatbuilding/Repairing

(G-3208)
NEWS 12 CONNECTICUT
28 Cross St (06851-4632)
PHONE..................................203 849-1321
Erin Colton, *General Mgr*
Charles F Dolan, *Principal*
Lori Golias, *Editor*
Frank Bruce, *Manager*
Adam Jenkins, *Asst Mgr*
EMP: 26
SALES (est): 1.3MM Privately Held
SIC: 2711 Newspapers-Publishing/Printing

(G-3209)
NEWSPAPER SPACE BUYERS
149 Rowayton Ave Ste 2 (06853-1460)
PHONE..................................203 967-6452
Gerry Walsh, *Principal*
EMP: 5
SALES (est): 263.4K Privately Held
SIC: 2711 Newspapers-Publishing/Printing

(G-3210)
OASIS COFFEE CORP
327 Main Ave (06851-6156)
PHONE..................................203 847-0554
Ralph Sandolo, *President*
Veronica Rondini, *Vice Pres*
Joseph Sandolo, *Vice Pres*
EMP: 20
SQ FT: 6,000
SALES (est): 2.5MM Privately Held
SIC: 2095 2098 5461 Mfg Roasted Coffee Mfg Macaroni/Spaghetti Retail Bakery

(G-3211)
OMEGA ENGINEERING INC (HQ)
Also Called: Omegadyne
800 Connecticut Ave 5n01 (06854-1696)
P.O. Box 4047, Stamford (06907-0047)
PHONE..................................203 359-1660
James R Dale, *President*
Dewana Harris, *Materials Mgr*
Suzanne Babic, *Purch Mgr*
Joseph Aiello, *Engineer*
Ed Corella, *Engineer*
◆ EMP: 233 EST: 1962
SALES (est): 138.4MM
SALES (corp-wide): 2.1B Privately Held
WEB: www.omega.com
SIC: 3823 3575 3577 3433 Mfg Process Cntrl Instr Mfg Computer Terminals
PA: Spectris Plc
Heritage House
Egham TW20
178 447-0470

(G-3212)
OMEGA ENGINEERING INC
Also Called: Newport Electronics
800 Cnncticut Ave Ste 5n1 (06854)
PHONE..................................714 540-4914
Bill Keating, *General Mgr*
EMP: 70
SALES (corp-wide): 2.1B Privately Held
SIC: 3559 3829 3822 3825 Mfg Misc Industry Mach Mfg Measure/Control Dvcs Mfg Environmntl Controls Mfg Elec Measuring Instr Mfg Switchgear/Boards
HQ: Omega Engineering, Inc.
800 Connecticut Ave 5n01
Norwalk CT 06854
203 359-1660

(G-3213)
PACO ASSENSIO WOODWORKING LLC
15 Meadow St (06854-4504)
PHONE..................................203 536-2608
Francisco Paco Fernandez, *Principal*
EMP: 5
SALES (est): 471.7K Privately Held
SIC: 2431 Mfg Millwork

(G-3214)
PALMERS ELC MTRS & PUMPS INC
40 Osborne Ave (06855-1021)
PHONE..................................203 348-7378
Michael Vigneault, *President*
Carlton Brown, *Vice Pres*
Clive Hyde, *Vice Pres*
Lorraine Vigneault, *Treasurer*
EMP: 7
SQ FT: 6,600
SALES: 1.2MM Privately Held
WEB: www.palmerselectric.com
SIC: 7694 5063 5999 Armature Rewinding Whol Electrical Equipment Ret Misc Merchandise

(G-3215)
PDC INTERNATIONAL CORP (PA)
8 Sheehan Ave (06854-4659)
P.O. Box 492 (06856-0492)
PHONE..................................203 853-1516
Neal Konstantin, *President*
Neal A Konstantin, *Principal*
Gary Tantimonico, *Vice Pres*
Dave Guzowski, *Engineer*
Anthony Caccamo, *Manager*
EMP: 55 EST: 1968
SQ FT: 19,000
SALES (est): 11.4MM Privately Held
WEB: www.pdc-corp.com
SIC: 3565 Mfg Packaging Machinery

(G-3216)
PEACOCK CABINETRY
9 Bettswood Rd (06851-5103)
PHONE..................................203 862-9333
Kathy Conroy, *Vice Pres*
Julie Sabbagh, *Technical Mgr*
Christopher L Peacock, *Manager*
EMP: 4
SALES (est): 360K Privately Held
SIC: 2434 Mfg Wood Kitchen Cabinets

(G-3217)
PENNY MARKETING LTD PARTNR (PA)
6 Prowitt St (06855-1204)
PHONE..................................203 866-6688
Cathrine Cappellini, *Partner*
EMP: 21
SALES (est): 1.2MM Privately Held
WEB: www.dellmagazines.com
SIC: 2721 Periodicals-Publishing/Printing

(G-3218)
PENNY PRESS INC (PA)
6 Prowitt St (06855-1220)
PHONE..................................203 866-6688
William E Kanter, *Ch of Bd*
Peter A Kanter, *President*
Selma Kanter, *Admin Sec*
EMP: 130
SQ FT: 20,000
SALES (est): 12.7MM Privately Held
WEB: www.pennypress.com
SIC: 2721 Periodicals-Publishing/Printing

(G-3219)
PENNY PUBLICATIONS LLC (PA)
6 Prowitt St (06855-1204)
PHONE..................................203 866-6688
Peter Kanter,
EMP: 100
SALES (est): 16MM Privately Held
SIC: 2721 Misc Publishing

(G-3220)
PILOT MACHINE DESIGNERS INC
32 Hemlock Pl (06854-4331)
PHONE..................................203 866-2227
James Cobb, *President*
EMP: 5
SQ FT: 4,800
SALES (est): 250K Privately Held
SIC: 3599 Mfg Industrial Machinery

(G-3221)
PIXELS 2 PRESS LLC
26 Pearl St Ste 8 (06850-1647)
PHONE..................................203 642-3740
EMP: 4
SALES (est): 300.1K Privately Held
SIC: 2741 Miscellaneous Publishing, Nsk

(G-3222)
PORTFOLIO ARTS GROUP LTD
Also Called: New York Graphic Society
129 Glover Ave (06850-1345)
PHONE..................................203 661-2400
Richard Fleischmann, *President*
EMP: 18 EST: 2007
SALES (est): 1.9MM Privately Held
SIC: 2741 Misc Publishing

(G-3223)
PPG INDUSTRIES INC
Also Called: PPG Painters Supply
106 Main St (06851-4648)
PHONE..................................203 750-9553
Charles E Bunch, *Ch of Bd*
EMP: 3
SALES (corp-wide): 15.3B Publicly Held
SIC: 2851 Mfg Paints/Allied Products
PA: Ppg Industries, Inc.
1 Ppg Pl
Pittsburgh PA 15272
412 434-3131

(G-3224)
PRICED RIGHT FUEL LLC
29 Golden Hill St (06854-2031)
PHONE..................................203 856-7031
Jaime Chetta, *Principal*
EMP: 3 EST: 2009
SALES (est): 166.9K Privately Held
SIC: 2869 Mfg Industrial Organic Chemicals

(G-3225)
PROFESSIONAL GRAPHICS INC
25 Perry Ave (06850-1655)
PHONE..................................203 846-4291
Thomas Bumbolow, *President*
Anthony Federici, *Vice Pres*
EMP: 12
SQ FT: 9,000
SALES (est): 1.9MM Privately Held
WEB: www.progi.net
SIC: 2752 2791 Lithographic Commercial Printing Typesetting Services

(G-3226)
R F H COMPANY INC
79 Rockland Rd Ste 3 (06854-4628)
PHONE..................................203 853-2863
Pamela Falcone, *President*
Blake Billmeyer, *Vice Pres*
EMP: 10
SQ FT: 5,000
SALES (est): 643.9K Privately Held
WEB: www.rfhcompany.com
SIC: 2395 2396 Pleating/Stitching Services Mfg Auto/Apparel Trimming

(G-3227)
RED 7 MEDIA LLC (HQ)
10 Norden Pl Ste 202 (06855-1445)
PHONE..................................203 853-2474
Kerry Smith, *President*
EMP: 38
SQ FT: 5,000
SALES (est): 2.7MM
SALES (corp-wide): 77.7MM Privately Held
WEB: www.red7media.com
SIC: 2721 Periodicals-Publishing/Printing
PA: Access Intelligence Llc
9211 Corporate Blvd Fl 4
Rockville MD 20850
301 354-2000

(G-3228)
REEDS INC
201 Merritt 7 (06851-1056)
PHONE..................................203 890-0557
John Bello, *CEO*
Stefan Freeman, *COO*
Norman E Snyder Jr, *COO*
Thomas J Spisak, *CFO*
Christopher J Reed, *CIO*
◆ EMP: 22
SQ FT: 76,000
SALES: 38.1MM Privately Held
WEB: www.reedsgingerbrew.com
SIC: 2086 2064 2024 Mfg Natural Non-Alcoholic & New Age Beverages Candies & Ice Creams

(G-3229)
RELOCATION INFORMATION SVC INC
Also Called: National Relocation & RE Mag
69 East Ave Ste 4 (06851-4904)
PHONE..................................203 855-1234
John Featherston, *President*
Suzanne Vita, *Editor*
Darryl McPherson, *Exec VP*
Anne Kraft, *Senior VP*
John Scully, *Vice Pres*
EMP: 23
SALES (est): 3.5MM Privately Held
SIC: 2721 2741 8742 Magazine & Directory Publishing Spec In Relocation Communication & Long Distance Services For Real Estate & Relocation Industry

(G-3230)
RELX INC
Reed Exhibitions
383 Main Ave Fl 3 (06851-1544)
PHONE..................................203 840-4800
Charlie Acquisto, *President*
Christine Flanagan, *Opers Mgr*
Jacqueline Boswick, *Sales/Mktg Mgr*
Joann Bottoni-Jepsen, *VP Human Res*
Larry Settembrini, *Sales Staff*
EMP: 4000
SQ FT: 238,000

GEOGRAPHIC

SALES (corp-wide): 9.8B **Privately Held**
WEB: www.lexis-nexis.com
SIC: 2721 Periodicals-Publishing/Printing
HQ: Relx Inc.
230 Park Ave Ste 700
New York NY 10169
212 309-8100

(G-3231)
REMA DRI-VAC CORP
45 Ruby St (06850-1614)
P.O. Box 86 (06852-0086)
PHONE..................................203 847-2464
F W Petri, *President*
Barry Gunterson, *Vice Pres*
James J Reed Jr, *Vice Pres*
James Flynn, *Treasurer*
▲ **EMP:** 15
SQ FT: 9,300
SALES (est): 4MM **Privately Held**
WEB: www.remadrivac.com
SIC: 3582 5084 Mfg Commercial Laundry Equipment Whol Industrial Equipment

(G-3232)
RINDLE LLC
3 Richards Ave (06854-2309)
PHONE..................................551 482-2037
Brian Faust, *Mng Member*
EMP: 5
SALES (est): 232.6K **Privately Held**
SIC: 7372 Prepackaged Software Services

(G-3233)
RISING SIGN COMPANY INC
50 Commerce St Ste 1 (06850-4141)
PHONE..................................203 853-4155
EMP: 5
SQ FT: 2,500
SALES: 225K **Privately Held**
SIC: 3993 Mfg Signs

(G-3234)
ROYAL CONSUMER PRODUCTS LLC (HQ)
Also Called: Geographics Australia
108 Main St Ste 3 (06851-4640)
P.O. Box 25118 Network Pl, Chicago IL (60673-0001)
PHONE..................................203 847-8500
Nona Nicau, *Accounts Mgr*
Baciu Irina, *Manager*
Steven A Schulman,
Steve Gilliland,
Kenneth B Schulman,
▲ **EMP:** 40
SQ FT: 1,000
SALES (est): 16.9MM
SALES (corp-wide): 100.3MM **Privately Held**
SIC: 2679 2621 Mfg Converted Paper Prdt Paper Mill
PA: Mafcote, Inc.
108 Main St Ste 3
Norwalk CT 06851
203 847-8500

(G-3235)
SAFE HARBOUR PRODUCTS INC
1 Selleck St Ste 3e (06855-1126)
PHONE..................................203 295-8377
Adam Stolpen, *Principal*
EMP: 3
SALES (est): 388.2K **Privately Held**
SIC: 2992 Mfg Lubricating Oils/Greases

(G-3236)
SAM & TY LLC (PA)
Also Called: Tailor Vintage
12 S Main St Ste 403 (06854-2980)
PHONE..................................212 840-1871
Robyn Shapiro, *Cust Mgr*
Richard Rosenthal, *Mng Member*
Joy Rosenthal,
◆ **EMP:** 8
SALES (est): 2.4MM **Privately Held**
SIC: 2396 Mfg Auto/Apparel Trimming

(G-3237)
SEAFARER CANVAS (PA)
144 Water St (06854-3191)
PHONE..................................203 853-2624
William Ashley, *Principal*
EMP: 10
SALES (est): 1.1MM **Privately Held**
SIC: 2394 Mfg Canvas/Related Products

(G-3238)
SEBASTIAN KITCHEN CABINETS
4 Taft St Ste B1 (06854-4252)
PHONE..................................203 853-4411
Sebastian Tornatore, *Owner*
EMP: 7
SQ FT: 5,000
SALES (est): 604.8K **Privately Held**
WEB: www.sebastiancorealestate.com
SIC: 2434 Mfg Kitchen Cabinets

(G-3239)
SECOND LAC INC (PA)
401 Merritt 7 Ste 1 (06851-1069)
PHONE..................................203 321-1221
James W Hart Jr, *Principal*
Douglas B Hart, *COO*
▲ **EMP:** 5
SALES (est): 39.2MM **Privately Held**
SIC: 2221 2295 2394 2396 Manmad Brdwv Fabric Mill Mfg Coated Fabrics Mfg Canvas/Related Prdts Mfg Auto/Apparel Trim

(G-3240)
SELECT PLASTICS LLC
219 Liberty Sq (06855-1029)
PHONE..................................203 866-3767
Anthony G D'Andrea, *Mng Member*
Gary Simmers, *Director*
EMP: 5
SQ FT: 6,000
SALES (est): 716K **Privately Held**
WEB: www.selectplastics.com
SIC: 3089 Mfg Plastic Products

(G-3241)
SERVERS STORAGE NETWORKING LLC
25 Perry Ave (06850-1655)
PHONE..................................203 433-0808
Justin Samuels,
EMP: 8
SALES (est): 295.3K **Privately Held**
SIC: 3674 5065 Mfg Semiconductors/Related Devices Whol Electronic Parts/Equipment

(G-3242)
SHIBUMICOM INC
50 Washington St Ste 302e (06854-2792)
PHONE..................................855 744-2864
Robert Nahmias, *CEO*
EMP: 10 **EST:** 2011
SQ FT: 6,000
SALES (est): 789.8K **Privately Held**
SIC: 7372 7374 Prepackaged Software Services Data Processing/Preparation

(G-3243)
SIGGPAY INC
50 Water St Rear B (06854-3061)
PHONE..................................203 957-8261
Brian Fuller, *CEO*
Carlyn Martino, *Vice Pres*
Shae Morris, *Vice Pres*
EMP: 5
SALES: 6K **Privately Held**
SIC: 7372 Prepackaged Software Services

(G-3244)
SIGMA TANKERS INC
20 Glover Ave Ste 5 (06850-1234)
PHONE..................................203 662-2600
Ben Ognibene, *CEO*
John Greenwood, *Principal*
Kathleen Haines, *CFO*
EMP: 16
SALES (est): 3.5MM
SALES (corp-wide): 1.1MM **Privately Held**
SIC: 1389 Oil/Gas Field Services
HQ: Heidmar Inc.
20 Glover Ave
Norwalk CT 06850

(G-3245)
SIGNS BY ANTHONY INC
19 Fitch St (06855-1308)
PHONE..................................203 866-1744
Anthony Masi, *President*
EMP: 3
SALES: 90K **Privately Held**
SIC: 3993 Mfg Signs/Advertising Specialties

(G-3246)
SILVERMINE PRESS INC
4 Van Tassell Ct (06851-3504)
PHONE..................................203 847-4368
Louis H Brehm, *President*
Helen Brehm, *Admin Sec*
EMP: 5 **EST:** 1947
SQ FT: 880
SALES (est): 451.4K **Privately Held**
WEB: www.adeleart.com
SIC: 2759 Commercial Printing

(G-3247)
SIMPLY ORIGINALS LLC
14 Crest Rd (06853-1207)
PHONE..................................203 273-3523
Renato Varas, *Principal*
EMP: 4
SALES (est): 204.5K **Privately Held**
SIC: 2086 Mfg Bottled/Canned Soft Drinks

(G-3248)
SOUND CONTROL TECHNOLOGIES
Also Called: S C T
22 S Smith St (06855-1018)
PHONE..................................203 854-5701
David Neaderland, *President*
Chris Audette, *Natl Sales Mgr*
Leslie Ward, *Technical Staff*
▲ **EMP:** 7
SQ FT: 5,000
SALES (est): 1.3MM **Privately Held**
WEB: www.soundcontrol.net
SIC: 3661 Mfr Teleconference Systems & Voice Reinforcement System

(G-3249)
SPRAY FOAM OUTLETS LLC
30 Muller Ave Unit 19 (06851)
P.O. Box 1182, New Canaan (06840-1182)
PHONE..................................631 291-9355
Anthony Brezac, *COO*
EMP: 25
SQ FT: 5,000
SALES: 40MM **Privately Held**
SIC: 3531 Mfg Construction Machinery

(G-3250)
STATHAM WOODWORK
38 Hemlock Pl (06854-4331)
PHONE..................................203 831-0629
Gary Statham, *President*
Emily Statham, *Vice Pres*
Andrew Catron, *Project Mgr*
EMP: 7
SQ FT: 7,000
SALES (est): 684.3K **Privately Held**
SIC: 2521 Mfg Wood Office Furniture

(G-3251)
STEPPING STONES MBL & GRAN LLC (PA)
4 Taft St Ste D1 (06854-4280)
PHONE..................................203 854-0552
Dale Hamman, *Mng Member*
EMP: 9
SALES (est): 1.2MM **Privately Held**
WEB: www.classicstones.com
SIC: 2493 Stone Fabrication

(G-3252)
SUCCESS PRINTING & MAILING INC
10 Pearl St (06850-1629)
PHONE..................................203 847-1112
Robert Hurwitz, *President*
William Roos, *Vice Pres*
EMP: 12
SQ FT: 15,000
SALES (est): 2.6MM **Privately Held**
WEB: www.successprint.com
SIC: 2752 2796 7336 Lithographic Commercial Printing Platemaking Services Commercial Art/Graphic Design

(G-3253)
SWEDISH NEWS INC
Also Called: North Shannon
268 Fillow St (06850-2215)
P.O. Box 1710, New Canaan (06840-1710)
PHONE..................................203 299-0380
Ulf Martensson, *CEO*
▲ **EMP:** 5
SALES (est): 407.7K **Privately Held**
SIC: 2711 Newspaper Publisher

(G-3254)
TAM COMMUNICATIONS INC
Also Called: Road Bike
37 North Ave Ste 208 (06851-3827)
PHONE..................................203 425-8777
John D Kanter, *President*
Buzz Kanter, *Publisher*
Marjorie Kleiman, *Editor*
Chuck Queener, *Creative Dir*
EMP: 20
SALES (est): 2.5MM **Privately Held**
WEB: www.roadbike.com
SIC: 2721 2741 Periodicals-Publishing/Printing Misc Publishing

(G-3255)
TCC MULTI KARGO
349 Dr Mrtin L King Jr Dr (06854-4691)
PHONE..................................203 803-1462
EMP: 4 **EST:** 2012
SALES (est): 268.3K **Privately Held**
SIC: 2448 Mfg Wood Pallets/Skids

(G-3256)
TICK BOX TECHNOLOGY CORP
15 Chapel St (06850-4113)
P.O. Box 1439 (06856-1439)
PHONE..................................203 852-7171
David Whitman, *President*
Richard Whitman, *Vice Pres*
EMP: 4
SALES (est): 442K **Privately Held**
SIC: 2879 Mfg Agricultural Chemicals

(G-3257)
TM WARD CO OF CONNECTICUT LLC
5 Wilbur St (06854-4112)
PHONE..................................203 866-9203
Jeffrey Sommer, *Mng Member*
EMP: 7
SALES: 1.4MM **Privately Held**
SIC: 2095 Mfg Roasted Coffee

(G-3258)
TOOL LOGISTICS II
46 Chestnut St (06854-3623)
PHONE..................................203 855-9754
Cawthon Smith, *Owner*
EMP: 10
SALES (est): 800.7K **Privately Held**
SIC: 3599 3315 Mfg Industrial Machinery Mfg Steel Wire/Related Products

(G-3259)
TOPAZ ENTERPRISE SAND PUBG
304 Main Ave (06851-6167)
PHONE..................................203 449-1903
Harry Francois, *Principal*
EMP: 6
SALES (est): 60.5K **Privately Held**
SIC: 2741 Misc Publishing

(G-3260)
TOWER OPTICAL COMPANY INC
275 East Ave Fl 2 (06855-1924)
P.O. Box 251 (06856-0251)
PHONE..................................203 866-4535
Bonnie Rising, *President*
Gregory Rising, *Admin Sec*
EMP: 7
SQ FT: 4,000
SALES (est): 650K **Privately Held**
WEB: www.toweropticalco.com
SIC: 3827 5049 Mfg & Dist Binocular Viewing Machines

(G-3261)
TRANE INC
145 Main St (06851-3709)
PHONE..................................203 866-7115
EMP: 100 **Privately Held**
SIC: 3585 Mfg Refrig/Heat

HQ: Trane Inc.
1 Centennial Ave Ste 101
Piscataway NJ 08854
732 652-7100

(G-3262)
TUCCI LUMBER CO LLC
227 Wilson Ave (06854-5026)
PHONE..................................203 956-6181
Peter Tucci, *Mng Member*
Sean Mathews,
Pablo Sandoval,
Amy Tucci,
Troy Tulowitzki,
EMP: 8
SQ FT: 10,300
SALES (est): 762.3K **Privately Held**
SIC: 3949 5941 Mfg Sporting/Athletic Goods Ret Sporting Goods/Bicycles

(G-3263)
TWENTY FIVE COMMERCE INC
Also Called: Cico
25 Commerce St (06850-4111)
P.O. Box 146 (06852-0146)
PHONE..................................203 866-0540
Robert Slapin, *President*
EMP: 8 **EST:** 1924
SALES (est): 761.2K **Privately Held**
WEB: www.cico.com
SIC: 2097 Mfg Ice

(G-3264)
VALORE INC
Also Called: Grannick's Bitter Apple Co
2 Academy St (06850-4015)
PHONE..................................203 854-4799
Valerie Cohen, *President*
Harrie J Grannick, *Vice Pres*
Jack Cohen, *Treasurer*
▲ **EMP:** 9
SQ FT: 50,000
SALES (est): 2MM **Privately Held**
SIC: 3999 Mfg Pet Supplies

(G-3265)
VANDERBILT CHEMICALS LLC (HQ)
30 Winfield St (06855-1329)
P.O. Box 5150 (06856-5150)
PHONE..................................203 295-2141
Roger Burtraw, *President*
Stephen Turbak, *Corp Secy*
Paul Graves, *Vice Pres*
Vncent Gatto, *Research*
Daniel Gershon, *Engineer*
◆ **EMP:** 67
SALES (est): 90.1MM
SALES (corp-wide): 272.5MM **Privately Held**
SIC: 2819 2869 5169 Mfg Industrial Inorganic Chemicals Mfg Industrial Organic Chemicals Whol Chemicals/Products
PA: R.T. Vanderbilt Holding Company, Inc.
30 Winfield St
Norwalk CT 06855
203 295-2141

(G-3266)
VANDERBILT MINERALS LLC (HQ)
33 Winfield St (06855)
P.O. Box 5150 (06856-5150)
PHONE..................................203 295-2140
James Ian Begley, *President*
Jeffrey Brohel, *Corp Secy*
Peter Ciullo, *Treasurer*
Elizabeth Slaby, *Manager*
Matt Stewart, *Director*
◆ **EMP:** 20
SALES (est): 77.7MM
SALES (corp-wide): 272.5MM **Privately Held**
SIC: 1459 Clay/Related Mineral Mining
PA: R.T. Vanderbilt Holding Company, Inc.
30 Winfield St
Norwalk CT 06855
203 295-2141

(G-3267)
VETO PRO PAC LLC
3 Morgan Ave Ste 4 (06851-5018)
P.O. Box 2072 (06852-2072)
PHONE..................................203 847-0297
Roger Brouard, *Partner*
Jill Flint, *Vice Pres*
▲ **EMP:** 3
SALES (est): 537K **Privately Held**
WEB: www.vetopropac.com
SIC: 3111 Leather Tanning/Finishing

(G-3268)
VITAL STRETCH LLC
112 Main St (06851-4617)
PHONE..................................203 847-4477
Melissa Goldring, *Mng Member*
EMP: 3
SALES: 300K **Privately Held**
SIC: 3542 Mfg Machine Tools-Forming

(G-3269)
WDSS CORPORATION
7 Old Well Ct (06855-2014)
PHONE..................................203 854-5930
Wayne Nasution, *President*
EMP: 10 **EST:** 2009
SALES: 150K **Privately Held**
SIC: 3599 Mfg Industrial Machinery

(G-3270)
WESPORT SIGNS
17 Linden St (06851-1506)
PHONE..................................203 286-7710
Jeremias Refosco, *Principal*
EMP: 3
SALES (est): 158.7K **Privately Held**
SIC: 3993 Mfg Signs/Advertising Specialties

(G-3271)
WINCHESTER INTERCONNECT CORP (HQ)
68 Water St (06854-3071)
PHONE..................................203 741-5400
Kevin S Perhamus, *President*
Beth Beadle, *General Mgr*
Stephen Eccles, *General Mgr*
Roger Rawlins, *General Mgr*
Mac Robinson, *General Mgr*
EMP: 45
SALES (est): 440.7MM
SALES (corp-wide): 16.6B **Privately Held**
SIC: 3678 Mfg Electronic Connectors
PA: Aptiv Plc
Queensway House Hilgrove Street
Jersey JE1 1
163 422-4000

(G-3272)
WINDHOVER INFORMATION INC (DH)
Also Called: Windhver Rvw-Emerging Med Vent
383 Main Ave (06851-1543)
PHONE..................................203 838-4401
Roger Longman, *President*
David Cassak, *Vice Pres*
▼ **EMP:** 30
SQ FT: 5,000
SALES (est): 4MM
SALES (corp-wide): 9.8B **Privately Held**
WEB: www.windhover.com
SIC: 2721 2731 7375 Periodicals-Publishing/Printing Books-Publishing/Printing Information Retrieval Services
HQ: Elsevier Inc.
230 Park Ave Fl 8
New York NY 10169
212 989-5800

(G-3273)
WOODWORKERS CLUB LLC
215 Westport Ave (06851-4310)
PHONE..................................203 847 9663
John Matchack, *President*
Tom Matchak,
Virgina Matchak,
EMP: 3
SALES (est): 456K **Privately Held**
WEB: www.woodworkersclubnorwalk.com
SIC: 2431 Mfg Millwork

(G-3274)
XEROX CORPORATION (HQ)
201 Merritt 7 (06851-1056)
P.O. Box 4505 (06856-4505)
PHONE..................................203 968-3000
Giovanni Visentin, *CEO*
Keith Cozza, *Ch of Bd*
Louis J Pastor, *Exec VP*
Stephen P Hoover, *Senior VP*
Brian Cannatelli, *Vice Pres*
EMP: 475
SALES: 9.8B **Publicly Held**
WEB: www.xerox.com
SIC: 3577 3861 3579 7629 Mfg Computer Equipment Mfg Photo Equip/Supplies Mfg Office Machines Electrical Repair Computer Maint/Repair
PA: Xerox Holdings Corporation
201 Merritt 7
Norwalk CT 06851
203 968-3000

(G-3275)
ZILLION GROUP INC
501 Merritt 7 (06851-7000)
PHONE..................................203 810-5400
James R Boyle, *Ch of Bd*
William Van Wyck, *President*
Brent Wilkinson, *COO*
Gregg Tavolacci, *Opers Staff*
Andy Brooks, *CFO*
EMP: 18
SALES (est): 2.9MM **Privately Held**
SIC: 7372 Prepackaged Software Services

Norwich
New London County

(G-3276)
AP DISPOSITION LLC
387 N Main St (06360-3917)
PHONE..................................860 889-1344
Paul Siefert,
James Brown,
Doreen Sylvistre,
▼ **EMP:** 55 **EST:** 2004
SALES (est): 5.7MM **Privately Held**
WEB: www.atlanticpackaginggroup.com
SIC: 2653 Mfg Corrugated/Solid Fiber Boxes

(G-3277)
CHARLES RIVER LABORATORIES INC
Charles Rver Avian Vccine Svcs
1 Wisconsin Ave Ste 100 (06360-1515)
PHONE..................................860 889-1389
Joan Johnson, *Human Res Mgr*
Kevin White, *Manager*
EMP: 35
SALES (corp-wide): 2.2B **Publicly Held**
SIC: 2836 Testing Laboratory
HQ: Charles River Laboratories, Inc.
251 Ballardvale St
Wilmington MA 01887
781 222-6000

(G-3278)
DERRICK MASON (PA)
Also Called: Sign-Grafx Group
2 Nelson St (06360-1336)
PHONE..................................413 527-4282
Derrick Mason, *Owner*
Wife Mason, *Vice Pres*
EMP: 6
SQ FT: 3,800
SALES (est): 313.5K **Privately Held**
WEB: www.sign-grafx.com
SIC: 3993 5046 1799 Mfg Signs/Advertising Specialties Whol Commercial Equipment Trade Contractor

(G-3279)
E B ASPHALT & LANDSCAPING LLC
60 Terminal Way (06360-6760)
PHONE..................................860 639-1921
Rickie Emmons Jr, *Mng Member*
EMP: 10
SQ FT: 80,000
SALES: 1.5MM **Privately Held**
SIC: 2951 0781 Mfg Asphalt Mixtures/Blocks Landscape Services

(G-3280)
GATEHOUSE MEDIA LLC
Norwich Bulletin, The
10 Railroad Ave (06360-5829)
PHONE..................................860 886-0106
Nadine McBride, *Opers Staff*
Dan Graziano, *Adv Dir*
Ellen Lind, *Branch Mgr*
EMP: 150
SALES (corp-wide): 1.5B **Publicly Held**
WEB: www.gatehousemedia.com
SIC: 2711 Newspapers-Publishing/Printing
HQ: Gatehouse Media, Llc
175 Sullys Trl Fl 3
Pittsford NY 14534
585 598-0030

(G-3281)
GATEHOUSE MEDIA CONN HOLDINGS
Also Called: Colchester Bulletin Bulletin
10 Railroad Ave (06360-5829)
PHONE..................................860 887-9211
Michael E Reed, *Ch of Bd*
Kirk A Davis, *President*
Melinda Ajanik Sr, *Senior VP*
Polly Grunfeld Sack Sr, *Senior VP*
EMP: 39
SALES (est): 2.4MM
SALES (corp-wide): 1.5B **Publicly Held**
SIC: 2711 Newspapers-Publishing/Printing
PA: Gannett Co., Inc.
7950 Jones Branch Dr
Mc Lean VA 22102
703 854-6000

(G-3282)
HIGGS ENERGY LLC
66 Franklin St (06360-5806)
P.O. Box 172 (06360-0172)
PHONE..................................860 213-5561
Eddie Oquendo,
EMP: 3
SALES (est): 121.7K **Privately Held**
SIC: 3812 Mfg Search/Navigation Equipment

(G-3283)
INCJET INC
31 Clinton Ave Ste 2 (06360-2165)
PHONE..................................860 823-3090
Marc Perkins, *President*
EMP: 13
SALES (est): 1.5MM
SALES (corp-wide): 2.6MM **Privately Held**
WEB: www.guntherintl.com
SIC: 3229 Mfg Pressed/Blown Glass
PA: Inc.Jet Holding, Inc.
1 Winnenden Rd
Norwich CT 06360
860 823-1427

(G-3284)
J & M PLUMBING & CNSTR LLC
16 West St (06360-6120)
PHONE..................................860 319-3082
Michael Watkinson,
EMP: 12 **EST:** 2015
SALES (est): 825.5K **Privately Held**
SIC: 1389 1799 1711 Oil/Gas Field Services Trade Contractor Plumbing/Heating/Air Cond Contractor

(G-3285)
LAUREL TOOL & MANUFACTURING
177 Franklin St (06360-4516)
PHONE..................................860 889-5354
Dennis Moran, *Owner*
EMP: 3
SALES (est): 216K **Privately Held**
SIC: 3544 Mfg Tools & Dies

(G-3286)
NALAS ENGINEERING SERVICES
1 Winnenden Rd (06360-1513)
PHONE..................................860 861-3691
Jerry Salan, *CEO*
David AM Ende, *President*
Shilpa Amato, *Exec VP*
Kerri Salan, *Vice Pres*
EMP: 52
SALES (est): 1.8MM **Privately Held**
SIC: 2869 Mfg Industrial Organic Chemicals

(G-3287)
NUTRON MANUFACTURING INC
5 Wisconsin Ave (06360-1515)
P.O. Box 314, Waterford (06385-0314)
PHONE..................................860 887-4550

GEOGRAPHIC

Jack Edward Feinberg, *President*
Mark L Favalora, *Vice Pres*
Joseph L Feinberg, *Treasurer*
Mark Feinberg, *Treasurer*
Michael J Feinberg, *Treasurer*
▲ **EMP:** 24
SQ FT: 95,000
SALES (est): 4.6MM **Privately Held**
WEB: www.nutron-mfg.com
SIC: 3646 Mfg Commercial Lighting Fixtures

(G-3288)
ONE AND CO INC
Also Called: Eon Designs
154 N Main St (06360-5121)
PHONE..................................860 892-5180
Gordon Kyle, *President*
Mark Stasko, *Vice Pres*
EMP: 12
SQ FT: 16,000
SALES (est): 1.7MM **Privately Held**
WEB: www.eondesigns.com
SIC: 2522 2541 Mfg Office Furniture-Nonwood Mfg Wood Partitions/Fixtures Mfg Office Furniture-Nonwood

(G-3289)
ROSS CURTIS PRODUCT INC
Also Called: Ross Custom Switches
45 Church St (06360-5001)
PHONE..................................860 886-6800
Steven Ross Brenneisen, *President*
Thomas Monroe, *Vice Pres*
Heidi Fields Revocable Trust, *Shareholder*
EMP: 6
SALES: 750K **Privately Held**
WEB: www.rossswitches.com
SIC: 3944 Mfg Accessories For Lionel Trains

(G-3290)
SHEFFIELD PHARMACEUTICALS LLC
9 Wisconsin Ave (06360-1562)
PHONE..................................860 442-4451
Jeffrey Davis, *President*
EMP: 10
SALES (corp-wide): 35.4MM **Privately Held**
SIC: 2834 Mfg Pharmaceutical Preparations
PA: Sheffield Pharmaceuticals, Llc
170 Broad St
New London CT 06320
860 442-4451

(G-3291)
SIGN PROFESSIONALS
303 W Main St (06360-5430)
PHONE..................................860 823-1122
Scott Lawrence, *Partner*
David McDowell, *Partner*
EMP: 4
SQ FT: 5,000
SALES: 350K **Privately Held**
SIC: 3993 Mfg Signs/Advertising Specialties

(G-3292)
VERMONT PALLET & SKID SHOP
104 Baltic Rd (06360-9409)
P.O. Box 646, Baltic (06330-0646)
PHONE..................................860 822-6949
James Adams, *President*
Dave Renfahw, *Vice Pres*
Inez Urso, *Treasurer*
EMP: 9
SQ FT: 3,200
SALES (est): 605K **Privately Held**
SIC: 2448 2441 2449 Mfg Wood Pallets Skids Boxes And Crates

(G-3293)
XUARE LLC
471 N Main St (06360-3923)
PHONE..................................860 383-8863
Peter Obuchowski, *Principal*
EMP: 3
SQ FT: 4,000
SALES (est): 336K **Privately Held**
SIC: 3599 Mfg Industrial Machinery

Oakdale
New London County

(G-3294)
NORTHMEN DEFENSE LLC
24 Old Colchester Rd Ext (06370-1031)
PHONE..................................860 908-9308
Brent Walker, *Principal*
EMP: 3
SALES (est): 210.1K **Privately Held**
SIC: 3812 Mfg Search/Navigation Equipment

Oakville
Litchfield County

(G-3295)
A&R PLATING SERVICES LLC
147 Riverside St (06779-1537)
PHONE..................................860 274-9562
Robert Rose, *President*
EMP: 5
SALES (est): 446.8K **Privately Held**
SIC: 3471 Plating/Polishing Service

(G-3296)
B T S GRAPHICS LLC
36 Zoar Ave Ste 2 (06779-1651)
P.O. Box 86 (06779-0086)
PHONE..................................860 274-6422
Tom Taylor,
EMP: 6
SALES (est): 560K **Privately Held**
SIC: 2759 Lithographic Commercial Printing

(G-3297)
BANNER WORKS
Also Called: Banner & Awning Works
15 Rockland Ave (06779-1611)
P.O. Box 3115, Waterbury (06705-0115)
PHONE..................................203 597-9999
Jennifer Nelson, *Owner*
EMP: 3
SALES (est): 136.1K **Privately Held**
SIC: 2399 Mfg Banner Blanks For The Sign Industry & Commercial Sewing

(G-3298)
FERRE FORM METAL PRODUCTS
25 Falls Ave (06779-1807)
P.O. Box 109, Waterbury (06720-0109)
PHONE..................................860 274-3280
Thomas Boileau, *President*
Jeff Valentine, *Vice Pres*
EMP: 10
SQ FT: 5,900
SALES (est): 1.4MM **Privately Held**
SIC: 3469 Mfg Metal Stampings

(G-3299)
M T S TOOL LLC
27 Main St Ste 2 (06779-1703)
PHONE..................................860 945-0875
Christopher McKenna,
Robert McCarthy,
EMP: 4
SQ FT: 1,000
SALES (est): 399.3K **Privately Held**
WEB: www.mtstool.com
SIC: 3545 Mfg Tools

(G-3300)
QUALITY AUTOMATICS INC (PA)
15 Mclennan Dr (06779-1428)
P.O. Box 11190, Waterbury (06703-0190)
PHONE..................................860 945-4795
Stephen White, *President*
Robert Cermola, *Vice Pres*
EMP: 40
SQ FT: 25,000
SALES (est): 6.7MM **Privately Held**
WEB: www.qualityautomatics.com
SIC: 3451 Mfg S'crew Machine Products

(G-3301)
RAMDY CORPORATION
40 Mclennan Dr (06779-1429)
P.O. Box 834, Watertown (06795-0834)
PHONE..................................860 274-3713
Richard Jklipp, *President*
John Mendicino, *President*
Allen Thornberg, *President*
Mark Pavao, *Vice Pres*
Paul Thornberg, *Vice Pres*
EMP: 45
SQ FT: 10,000
SALES (est): 9MM **Privately Held**
SIC: 3541 Mfg Machine Tools-Cutting

(G-3302)
RINTEC CORPORATION
30 Mclennan Dr (06779-1429)
PHONE..................................860 274-3697
Antonio F Rinaldi, *President*
Veronica S Rinaldi, *Vice Pres*
EMP: 10
SQ FT: 5,500
SALES: 930K **Privately Held**
SIC: 3544 Tool & Die Shop

(G-3303)
T & J SCREW MACHINE PDTS LLC
27 Main St (06779-1703)
PHONE..................................860 417-3801
Anthony P Troisi, *Principal*
EMP: 3
SALES (est): 413K **Privately Held**
SIC: 3451 Mfg Screw Machine Products

(G-3304)
UNIVERSAL BODY & EQP CO LLC
17 Di Nunzio Rd (06779-1407)
PHONE..................................860 274-7541
Todd Richards, *Mng Member*
John Dufour,
Nick Nicol,
EMP: 16
SQ FT: 6,000
SALES (est): 3.3MM **Privately Held**
SIC: 3713 3711 Mfg Truck/Bus Bodies Mfg Motor Vehicle/Car Bodies

(G-3305)
WATERTOWN CANVAS AND AWNG LLC
98 Falls Ave (06779-1810)
PHONE..................................860 274-0933
Fax: 860 274-8519
EMP: 5
SQ FT: 4,000
SALES (est): 330K **Privately Held**
SIC: 2394 Mfg Canvas/Related Products

Old Greenwich
Fairfield County

(G-3306)
CLANOL SYSTEMS INC
Also Called: Colonial Print & Imaging
1374 E Putnam Ave (06870-1308)
P.O. Box 416, Riverside (06878-0416)
PHONE..................................203 637-9909
Samantha Carter, *CEO*
Benjamin Carter, *President*
EMP: 5 **EST:** 1973
SQ FT: 2,750
SALES (est): 607.5K **Privately Held**
SIC: 2759 2752 Offset Printingcopying And Digital

(G-3307)
COSS SYSTEMS INC (NOT INC)
26 Arcadia Rd (06870-1721)
PHONE..................................732 447-7724
Antonia Spitzer, *Principal*
EMP: 7
SALES (est): 436.6K **Privately Held**
SIC: 7372 Prepackaged Software Services

(G-3308)
ELOT INC (PA)
Also Called: Elottery
51 Forest Ave Apt 117 (06870-1529)
PHONE..................................203 388-1808
Edwin J McGuinn Jr, *President*
EMP: 4
SALES (est): 537.8K **Privately Held**
WEB: www.elottery.com
SIC: 3661 8741 Mfg Telephone/Telegraph Apparatus Management Services

(G-3309)
GREENWICH GOFER
56 Halsey Dr (06870-1225)
PHONE..................................203 637-8425
Lisa Gapp Palmer, *Principal*
EMP: 3
SALES (est): 109K **Privately Held**
SIC: 2711 Newspapers-Publishing/Printing

(G-3310)
GRILL DADDY BRUSH COMPANY
29 Arcadia Rd (06870-1701)
PHONE..................................888 840-7552
Michael A Wales, *President*
Grace L Wales, *Admin Sec*
▲ **EMP:** 30
SQ FT: 2,000
SALES: 10MM **Privately Held**
SIC: 2842 Mfg Polish/Sanitation Goods

(G-3311)
JUDITH JACKSON INC
1535 E Putnam Ave Apt 406 (06870-1356)
PHONE..................................203 698-3011
Judith Jackson, *President*
EMP: 3
SALES (est): 340.5K **Privately Held**
WEB: www.judithjackson.com
SIC: 2844 Mfg Cosmetics

(G-3312)
NAVTECH SYSTEMS INC
322 Sound Beach Ave (06870-1931)
PHONE..................................203 661-7800
Sushil Advaney, *President*
EMP: 4
SALES (est): 246.7K **Privately Held**
WEB: www.navtechsys.com
SIC: 7372 Prepackaged Software Services

(G-3313)
OPEN WATER DEVELOPMENT LLC
Also Called: Speakeasy Ai
14 Cove Ridge Ln (06870-1903)
PHONE..................................646 883-2062
Richard Simons,
EMP: 5
SALES (est): 117.2K **Privately Held**
SIC: 7372 Prepackaged Software Services

(G-3314)
YORK MILLWORK LLC
210 Sound Beach Ave (06870-1600)
PHONE..................................203 698-3460
Nicholas Barile, *Manager*
EMP: 4
SALES (est): 386K **Privately Held**
SIC: 2431 Mfg Millwork

Old Lyme
New London County

(G-3315)
BYRON LORD INC
18 Bailey Rd (06371-1701)
PHONE..................................203 287-9881
James Byron, *President*
George Byron, *Vice Pres*
Erna Byron, *Admin Sec*
EMP: 5 **EST:** 1978
SQ FT: 2,400
SALES: 1MM **Privately Held**
WEB: www.lordbyron.on.ca
SIC: 2396 2391 3545 Mfg Fender Covers Drapes & Tool Pouches

(G-3316)
CALLAWAY CARS INC
3 High St (06371-1529)
PHONE..................................860 434-9002
E Reeves Callaway III, *President*
Joanne Mercer, *Engineer*
Michael Zoner, *Admin Sec*
EMP: 18 **EST:** 1976

SQ FT: 10,000
SALES (est): 4.6MM
SALES (corp-wide): 6.2MM Privately Held
SIC: 3714 Mfg Motor Vehicle Parts/Accessories
PA: The Callaway Companies Inc
3 High St
Old Lyme CT 06371
860 434-9002

(G-3317)
CALLAWAY COMPANIES INC (PA)
3 High St (06371-1529)
PHONE..........860 434-9002
E Reeves Callaway III, *President*
▲ EMP: 15
SQ FT: 16,300
SALES (est): 6.2MM Privately Held
SIC: 3714 8732 Holding Company

(G-3318)
CUSHS HOMEGROWN LLC
4 Green Valley Lake Rd (06371-1524)
PHONE..........860 739-7373
Elizabeth Cushing, *President*
James C Cushing, *Treasurer*
Christopher J Cushing, *Mng Member*
Phyllis P Cushing, *Admin Sec*
EMP: 4 EST: 2009
SALES: 135K Privately Held
SIC: 2032 Mfg Canned Specialties

(G-3319)
CUSTOM DESIGN WOODWORKS LLC
10 Maywood Dr (06371-1523)
P.O. Box 376 (06371-0376)
PHONE..........860 434-0515
Christopher Defiore, *Principal*
EMP: 4
SALES (est): 444.2K Privately Held
SIC: 2431 Mfg Millwork

(G-3320)
DAVID SHUCK
Also Called: Advanced Precast Concrete
Hatchetts Hill Rd (06371)
P.O. Box 492 (06371-0492)
PHONE..........860 434-8562
David Shuck, *Owner*
EMP: 3
SALES (est): 342.8K Privately Held
SIC: 3272 Mfg Concrete Products

(G-3321)
DESIGN LABEL MANUFACTURING INC (PA)
12 Nottingham Dr (06371-1820)
PHONE..........860 739-6266
Jeff Paul Dunphy, *President*
Paul Dunphy, *Chairman*
Kim D Eaton, *CFO*
Scott J Dunphy, *Shareholder*
Gene Toombs, *Shareholder*
EMP: 38 EST: 1963
SQ FT: 15,000
SALES (est): 7.1MM Privately Held
SIC: 2672 2759 Mfg Coated/Laminated Paper Commercial Printing

(G-3322)
ECOFLIK LLC
1 Old Bridge Rd (06371-1425)
P.O. Box 966 (06371-0999)
PHONE..........860 460-4419
Duane W Buckingham, *Mng Member*
Samantha W Noonan,
EMP: 5
SALES: 1.2MM Privately Held
SIC: 3172 Manufactures And Markets Cigarette Butt Receptacle

(G-3323)
GENERATORS ON DEMAND LLC
61-1 Buttonball Rd (06371-1761)
PHONE..........860 662-4090
Ronald J Swaney,
EMP: 13
SALES (est): 2.1MM Privately Held
SIC: 3621 Mfg Motors/Generators

(G-3324)
KEELING COMPANY INC
Also Called: Keeling's
107 Shore Dr (06371-1209)
PHONE..........860 349-0916
John Keeling, *President*
Avelina Broekstra, *Treasurer*
Pamela Keeling, *Admin Sec*
EMP: 4
SQ FT: 4,500
SALES (est): 422.9K Privately Held
WEB: www.keelinglamps.com
SIC: 3645 5719 Mfg Residential Lighting Fixtures Ret Misc Homefurnishings

(G-3325)
NANCY LARSON PUBLISHERS INC
27 Talcott Farm Rd (06371-1474)
P.O. Box 688 (06371-0688)
PHONE..........860 434-0800
Nancy A Larson, *President*
Margaret Heisserer, *Editor*
Leann Harmon, *Marketing Staff*
Pam Winkle, *Marketing Staff*
Madon Dailey, *Manager*
EMP: 30
SALES: 1.1MM Privately Held
SIC: 2741 Misc Publishing

(G-3326)
PATRICIA SPRATT FOR HOME LLC
60 Lyme St (06371-2332)
PHONE..........860 434-9291
Patricia Spratt,
Emily Spratt,
John Patrick Spratt,
Lilliane Spratt,
Meredith Spratt,
EMP: 10
SQ FT: 1,000
SALES (est): 1MM Privately Held
WEB: www.patriciasprattforthehome.com
SIC: 2392 5131 Mfg Household Furnishings Whol Piece Goods/Notions

Old Saybrook
Middlesex County

(G-3327)
ALL-TEST PRO LLC (PA)
20 Research Pkwy Unit G&H (06475-4214)
P.O. Box 1139 (06475-5139)
PHONE..........860 399-4222
Tim Scully, *General Mgr*
Jorgen Bjorkman, *Treasurer*
Mike Schneider, *Regl Sales Mgr*
Mike Bjorkman, *Marketing Staff*
Aaron Schnelle, *Technical Staff*
◆ EMP: 10
SQ FT: 10,000
SALES: 3MM Privately Held
WEB: www.alltestpro.com
SIC: 3825 Mfg Electrical Measuring Instruments

(G-3328)
BFF HOLDINGS INC (HQ)
Also Called: B L R
141 Mill Rock Rd E (06475-4217)
PHONE..........860 510-0100
Robert L Brady, *President*
Matthew Humphrey, *President*
Brian E Gurnham, *COO*
Amy Wieman, *Vice Pres*
Brian Toney, *Plant Mgr*
EMP: 175
SQ FT: 75,000
SALES (est): 15.3MM Privately Held
WEB: www.blr.com
SIC: 2721 2731 7812 3652 Periodical-Publish/Print Book-Publishing/Printing Motion Pict/Video Prodtn Mfg Recorded Record/Tape Misc Publishing

(G-3329)
BJM PUMPS LLC
123 Spencer Plain Rd # 1 (06475-4051)
P.O. Box 1138 (06475-5138)
PHONE..........860 399-5937
Ron Woodward, *President*
▲ EMP: 35
SALES (est): 6.7MM
SALES (corp-wide): 27.3MM Privately Held
SIC: 3561 5084 Mfg Pumps/Pumping Equipment Whol Industrial Equipment
PA: Industrial Flow Solutions Holdings Llc
1 N Wacker Dr Ste 1920
Chicago IL 60606
312 750-1771

(G-3330)
BRANNKEY INC
137 Mill Rock Rd E (06475-4217)
PHONE..........860 510-0501
Anthony Carambot, *Branch Mgr*
EMP: 38
SALES (corp-wide): 10.6MM Privately Held
SIC: 3911 Mfg Precious Metal Jewelry
PA: Brannkey Inc.
1385 Broadway Fl 14
New York NY 10018
212 371-1515

(G-3331)
COMPUTER SGNS OLD SAYBROOK LLC
460 Boston Post Rd (06475-1550)
PHONE..........860 388-9773
Maura Vercillo, *General Ptnr*
Andrew J Vercillo,
Craig Rahemba, *Graphic Designe*
EMP: 5
SALES: 750K Privately Held
SIC: 3993 Mfg Signs/Advertising Specialties

(G-3332)
CONNECTICUT VALLEY INDS LLC
8 Center Rd (06475-4012)
PHONE..........860 388-0822
Timothy P Johnson,
▲ EMP: 5 EST: 1976
SQ FT: 10,000
SALES (est): 857.7K Privately Held
SIC: 3648 3613 Mfg Lighting Equipment Mfg Switchgear/Switchboards

(G-3333)
CRYSTAL TOOL LLC
50 Connally Dr (06475-1162)
PHONE..........860 510-0113
Lisa Fitzsimmons,
Scott Fitzsimmons,
EMP: 4
SQ FT: 700
SALES (est): 485.5K Privately Held
WEB: www.crystaltool.com
SIC: 3629 Mfg Electrical Components

(G-3334)
EZFLOW LIMITED PARTNERSHIP (DH)
4 Business Park Rd (06475-4238)
P.O. Box 768 (06475-0768)
PHONE..........860 577-7064
Roy E Moore, *CEO*
Bryan Coppes, *Vice Pres*
James Bransfield, *Manager*
EMP: 50
SALES (est): 8.2MM
SALES (corp-wide): 1.3B Publicly Held
SIC: 3531 Mfg Construction Machinery
HQ: Infiltrator Water Technologies, Llc
4 Business Park Rd
Old Saybrook CT 06475
860 577 7000

(G-3335)
FOUR COLOR INK LLC
2 Business Park Rd (06475-4206)
PHONE..........860 395-5471
Paul Ross,
William Argyle,
EMP: 3
SQ FT: 2,200
SALES: 200K Privately Held
SIC: 2796 Image Assembly And Color Separation

(G-3336)
GUNWORKS INTERNATIONAL L L C
4 Center Rd (06475-4007)
P.O. Box 252 (06475-0252)
PHONE..........860 388-4591
Chris Gosselin, *Principal*
EMP: 3
SQ FT: 3,000
SALES (est): 183K Privately Held
SIC: 3484 5941 Mfg Small Arms Ret Sporting Goods/Bicycles

(G-3337)
HANFORD CABINET & WDWKG CO
102 Ingham Hill Rd (06475-4115)
PHONE..........860 388-5055
Steve Hanford, *President*
Lane T Hanford, *Director*
EMP: 7 EST: 1969
SQ FT: 6,000
SALES (est): 862K Privately Held
WEB: www.hanfordcabinet.com
SIC: 2434 1521 Mfg Wood Kitchen Cabinets Single-Family House Construction

(G-3338)
IPC SYSTEMS INC
Also Called: IPC Information Systems
8 Custom Dr (06475-4008)
PHONE..........203 339-7000
Antoine Verzilli, *Branch Mgr*
EMP: 15
SALES (corp-wide): 490.9MM Privately Held
SIC: 3661 Mfg Telephone/Telegraph Apparatus
PA: I.P.C. Systems, Inc.
3 2nd St Fl Plz10
Jersey City NJ 07311
201 253-2000

(G-3339)
ITERUM THERAPEUTICS INC
20 Research Pkwy (06475-4214)
PHONE..........860 391-8349
Jeff Schaffnit, *Ch Credit Ofcr*
EMP: 4 EST: 2016
SALES (est): 284.4K Privately Held
SIC: 2834 Mfg Pharmaceutical Preparations

(G-3340)
JFJ SERVICES LLC
17 Forest Glen Rd (06475-2605)
PHONE..........860 395-1922
Beverly Johnson, *Owner*
EMP: 4
SALES (est): 337.9K Privately Held
SIC: 3589 Mfg Service Industry Machinery

(G-3341)
KNOLL INC
5 Connolly Dr (06475-1163)
PHONE..........860 395-2093
EMP: 50
SALES (corp-wide): 887.5MM Publicly Held
SIC: 2521 Mfg Wood Office Furniture
PA: Knoll, Inc.
1235 Water St
East Greenville PA 18041
215 679-7991

(G-3342)
LIFTLINE CAPITAL LLC
Also Called: Stencil Ease
7 Center Rd W (06475-4053)
P.O. Box 1127 (06475-5127)
PHONE..........860 395-0150
Milissa Brigante, *Office Mgr*
James Randolph,
John Helm,
▼ EMP: 18
SQ FT: 30,000
SALES (est): 4.4MM Privately Held
WEB: www.stencilease.com
SIC: 2675 3991 3953 Mfg Custom Stencils

GEOGRAPHIC

(G-3343)
LIGHTHOUSE PRINTING LLC
315 Boston Post Rd Ste 3 (06475-1544)
P.O. Box 1158 (06475-5158)
PHONE..................................860 388-2677
Bill Dempsey, *Mng Member*
EMP: 4
SALES: 300K **Privately Held**
SIC: 2752 Lithographic Commercial Printing

(G-3344)
METALPRO INC
50 School House Rd (06475-4029)
PHONE..................................860 388-1811
Thomas Wright, *President*
Elizabeth Wright, *Vice Pres*
EMP: 50
SQ FT: 45,000
SALES (est): 4.6MM **Privately Held**
SIC: 3599 Mfg Industrial Machinery

(G-3345)
MOLDING TECHNOLOGIES LLC
304 Boston Post Rd Ste 1 (06475-1561)
PHONE..................................860 395-3230
William Stoner, *Owner*
EMP: 3
SQ FT: 5,000
SALES: 600K **Privately Held**
WEB: www.ttkbox.com
SIC: 3089 Mfg Plastic Products

(G-3346)
PARAGON PRODUCTS INC
175 Elm St Ste 1 (06475-4109)
P.O. Box 747 (06475-0747)
PHONE..................................860 388-1363
John Schutz, *President*
John Contreras, *Executive*
EMP: 3
SQ FT: 5,000
SALES: 150K **Privately Held**
SIC: 3089 Injection Molding Of Plastics

(G-3347)
PATHWAY LIGHTING PRODUCTS INC
Also Called: Pathway The Lighting Source
175 Elm St 5 (06475-4109)
P.O. Box 591 (06475-0591)
PHONE..................................860 388-6881
Frederick W Stark III, *President*
Jill Elizabeth Coan, *Corp Secy*
Johnna Maynard, *Purch Agent*
Kenton Baker, *Technical Mgr*
Russell Budzilek, *Engineer*
▲ **EMP:** 85
SALES (est): 12.7MM **Privately Held**
WEB: www.pathwaylighting.com
SIC: 3646 3648 5063 Mfg Commercial Lighting Fixtures Mfg Lighting Equipment Whol Electrical Equipment

(G-3348)
PAUL H GESSWEIN & COMPANY INC
40 River St (06475)
PHONE..................................860 388-0652
John Hoadley, *Manager*
EMP: 8
SALES (corp-wide): 593.1K **Privately Held**
SIC: 3281 Stone Processing
PA: Paul H. Gesswein & Company, Inc.
201 Hancock Ave
Bridgeport CT 06605
203 366-5400

(G-3349)
PRIVATEER LTD
Also Called: Label One
5 Center Rd W (06475-4053)
PHONE..................................860 526-1837
Richard Wilczewski, *President*
Gregg Viebranz, *General Mgr*
EMP: 18
SQ FT: 10,000
SALES (est): 2.7MM **Privately Held**
WEB: www.privateerusa.com
SIC: 2759 Commercial Printing

(G-3350)
SOUND MANUFACTURING INC
1 Williams Ln (06475-4233)
PHONE..................................860 388-4466
Kelli Valleries, *CEO*
Marco Piacenti, *Production*
Laura Young, *Purch Mgr*
Glen Guidi, *Engineer*
Brian E Cote, *Director*
▲ **EMP:** 81
SALES (est): 16.6MM **Privately Held**
SIC: 3444 Mfg Sheet Metalwork

(G-3351)
TANTOR MEDIA INCORPORATED
6 Business Park Rd (06475-4238)
PHONE..................................860 395-1155
Kevin Colebank, *CEO*
Melanie Bodin, *Editor*
Amanda Currier, *Prdtn Mgr*
Hilary Eurich, *Production*
Sandy Vasmatics, *Production*
▼ **EMP:** 164
SALES (est): 18.3MM **Privately Held**
WEB: www.tantor.com
SIC: 2731 Books-Publishing/Printing
PA: Recorded Books, Inc.
270 Skipjack Rd
Prince Frederick MD 20678

(G-3352)
TARGET CUSTOM MANUFACTURING CO
164 Old Boston Post Rd (06475-2230)
PHONE..................................860 388-5848
Neil Gallagher, *President*
Christine Gallagher, *Vice Pres*
Vanessa Braig, *Admin Sec*
EMP: 9
SQ FT: 7,500
SALES (est): 1.1MM **Privately Held**
SIC: 3444 3469 Mfg Sheet Metalwork Mfg Metal Stampings

(G-3353)
VIJON STUDIOS INC
97a Spencer Plain Rd (06475-4001)
PHONE..................................860 399-7440
Vincent F Yannone, *President*
EMP: 3
SALES (est): 184K **Privately Held**
SIC: 2515 Mfg Mattresses/Bedsprings

(G-3354)
VIJON STUDIOS INC
Also Called: Vijon Stdios Stined GL Sup Ctr
97 Spencer Plain Rd Ste A (06475-4001)
PHONE..................................860 399-7440
Vincent Yannone, *President*
EMP: 3
SALES: 150K **Privately Held**
SIC: 3231 5719 5231 5961 Mfg Prdt-Purchased Glass Ret Misc Homefurnishings Ret Paint/Glass/Wallppr Ret Mail-Order House

(G-3355)
VITA PASTA INC
225 Elm St (06475-4135)
P.O. Box 523 (06475-0523)
PHONE..................................860 395-1452
Richard Cersosimo, *President*
Luis A Castanho, *Vice Pres*
EMP: 7
SQ FT: 3,000
SALES (est): 400K **Privately Held**
WEB: www.nottapasta.com
SIC: 2099 5149 Mfg Food Preparations Whol Groceries

Orange
New Haven County

(G-3356)
ACE SERVICING CO INC
340 Edward Ct (06477-2526)
PHONE..................................203 795-1400
Christopher Prisco, *Principal*
EMP: 3 **EST:** 2016
SALES (est): 108.8K **Privately Held**
SIC: 1389 Oil/Gas Field Services

(G-3357)
ADVANCED DECISIONS INC
350 Woodland Ln (06477-3038)
PHONE..................................203 402-0603
Michael R Landino, *President*
Gary Felberbaum, *Treasurer*
EMP: 16
SALES (est): 1MM **Privately Held**
WEB: www.advanceddecisions.com
SIC: 7372 7379 Consultants For Computer Software & Hardware Systems

(G-3358)
AMERICAN SEAL AND ENGRG CO INC (DH)
Also Called: Ase
295 Indian River Rd (06477-3609)
PHONE..................................203 789-8819
Thomas Kinisky, *President*
Joseph Kedues, *Vice Pres*
Todd Stockwell, *Engineer*
Terri Doughty, *Sales Staff*
Joe Kedves, *Sales Executive*
EMP: 40
SQ FT: 30,000
SALES (est): 5.3MM
SALES (corp-wide): 209.1MM **Privately Held**
WEB: www.ameriseal.com
SIC: 3053 Mfg Gaskets/Packing/Sealing Devices

(G-3359)
ATECH INDUSTRIES LLC
879 Robert Treat Ext (06477-1649)
PHONE..................................203 887-4900
Michael Micheli, *Principal*
EMP: 6 **EST:** 2016
SALES (est): 458.9K **Privately Held**
SIC: 3999 Mfg Misc Products

(G-3360)
BIMBO BAKERIES USA INC
Also Called: Best Foods Baking Co. Now.
284 Bull Hill Ln (06477-3211)
PHONE..................................203 932-1000
John Payne, *Manager*
EMP: 58 **Privately Held**
WEB: www.englishmuffin.com
SIC: 2051 2052 Mfg Cakes Pies & Cookies
HQ: Bimbo Bakeries Usa, Inc
255 Business Center Dr # 200
Horsham PA 19044
215 347-5500

(G-3361)
CHRIS & ZACK LLC
385 Boston Post Rd (06477-3507)
PHONE..................................203 298-0742
Kam Jhilal, *Principal*
EMP: 3
SALES (est): 167.5K **Privately Held**
SIC: 2015 2022 Poultry Processing Mfg Cheese

(G-3362)
CTI INDUSTRIES INC (HQ)
283 Indian River Rd (06477-3609)
PHONE..................................203 795-0070
Perry Tallman, *President*
Jake Bajko, *Treasurer*
Peter Mace Tallman, *Admin Sec*
▲ **EMP:** 25
SQ FT: 22,000
SALES: 6.1MM
SALES (corp-wide): 21MM **Privately Held**
SIC: 3443 Mfg Fabricated Plate Work
PA: Rocore Thermal Systems, Llc
2401 Directors Row Ste R
Indianapolis IN 46241
317 227-2929

(G-3363)
CYRO INDUSTRIES
25 Executive Blvd 1 (06477-3659)
P.O. Box 425, Wallingford (06492-7050)
PHONE..................................203 269-4481
Fax: 203-795-5800
EMP: 8 **EST:** 2007
SALES (est): 430K **Privately Held**
SIC: 3999 Mfg Misc Products

(G-3364)
DATAPREP INC
109 Boston Post Rd Ste 2 (06477-3235)
PHONE..................................203 795-2095
Fax: 203 795-2096
EMP: 30
SQ FT: 1,500
SALES (corp-wide): 5.2MM **Privately Held**
SIC: 7372 7374 7371 Prepackaged Software Services Data Processing/Preparation Custom Computer Programing
PA: Dataprep Inc
97 South St Ste 105
West Hartford CT 06611
860 728-5224

(G-3365)
EXPRESS CNTERTOPS KIT FLRG LLC
303 Boston Post Rd (06477-3520)
PHONE..................................203 283-4909
Roger Mehta, *Branch Mgr*
EMP: 3
SALES (corp-wide): 5.2MM **Privately Held**
SIC: 3263 Mfg Semivetreous China Tableware
PA: Express Countertops, Kitchen & Flooring, Llc
231 Weston St
Hartford CT 06120
860 247-1000

(G-3366)
F & W RENTALS INC
164 Boston Post Rd (06477-3234)
PHONE..................................203 795-0591
Harold R Funk, *President*
Jenn Kellogg, *Parts Mgr*
EMP: 15
SQ FT: 15,000
SALES (est): 1.2MM **Privately Held**
SIC: 7692 5084 Welding Repair Whol Industrial Equipment

(G-3367)
KCO NUMET INC
235 Edison Rd (06477-3603)
PHONE..................................203 375-4995
Mark Roscio, *CEO*
Andrew Gale, *CEO*
Joseph Sartori, *COO*
Antonio Neto, *Vice Pres*
Scott Kokosa, *CFO*
EMP: 15
SQ FT: 40,000
SALES (est): 9MM **Privately Held**
SIC: 3519 6719 Mfg Internal Combustion Engines Holding Company

(G-3368)
KI INC
342 Cedarwood Dr (06477-1665)
PHONE..................................203 641-5492
Rondi D'Agostino, *President*
David Goodman, *Engineer*
▲ **EMP:** 20
SALES (est): 1.3MM **Privately Held**
SIC: 3651 Mfg Home Audio/Video Equipment

(G-3369)
KRELL INDUSTRIES LLC
45 Connair Rd Ste 1 (06477-3681)
PHONE..................................203 298-4000
Rondi D'Agostino, *Mng Member*
EMP: 16
SQ FT: 10,000
SALES: 1.2MM **Privately Held**
SIC: 3651 Mfg Home Audio/Video Equipment

(G-3370)
LCD LIGHTING INC
Also Called: Voltarc
37 Robinson Blvd (06477-3623)
P.O. Box 948 (06477-0948)
PHONE..................................203 799-7877
Christian L Sauska, *CEO*
Bruce Kingsley, *Chief*
Arpad Pirovic, *Vice Pres*
Karl Platzer, *Sales Staff*
Graham Foster, *Manager*
▲ **EMP:** 110
SQ FT: 75,000

SALES (est): 21.3MM Privately Held
WEB: www.lcdl.com
SIC: 3641 3646 Mfg Electric Lamps Mfg Commercial Lighting Fixtures

(G-3371)
LIGHT SOURCES INC (PA)
Also Called: L S I
37 Robinson Blvd (06477-3623)
P.O. Box 948 (06477-0948)
PHONE..................................203 799-7877
Christian Sauska, *President*
Ula Kret, *Purchasing*
Anrui Zhu, *Electrical Engi*
Mohamed Maklad, *VP Finance*
Raymond Panther, *Accounting Mgr*
▲ **EMP:** 129
SQ FT: 150,000
SALES (est): 37.4MM **Privately Held**
WEB: www.light-sources.com
SIC: 3641 Mfg Electric Lamps

(G-3372)
MARENNA AMUSEMENTS LLC
88 Marsh Hill Rd (06477-3625)
P.O. Box 788 (06477-0788)
PHONE..................................203 623-4386
George J Marenna Jr,
EMP: 10
SALES: 333K **Privately Held**
SIC: 3599 Carnival Machines & Equipment Amusement Park

(G-3373)
MCWEENEY MARKETING GROUP INC
53 Robinson Blvd (06477-3623)
P.O. Box 989 (06477-0989)
PHONE..................................203 891-8100
George E McWeeney Jr, *President*
John Kelly, *Vice Pres*
George Mc Weeney, *Manager*
EMP: 9
SQ FT: 3,000
SALES (est): 966.6K **Privately Held**
WEB: www.mcweeneymarketing.com
SIC: 2759 5199 Commercial Printing Whol Nondurable Goods

(G-3374)
NATURES FIRST INC (PA)
58 Robinson Blvd Ste C (06477-3647)
PHONE..................................203 795-8400
Harjit Singh, *President*
▼ **EMP:** 8
SQ FT: 12,000
SALES (est): 1MM **Privately Held**
WEB: www.naturesfirst.com
SIC: 2023 Mfg Dry/Evaporated Dairy Products

(G-3375)
NORTH HAVEN EQP & LSG LLC
212 Argyle Rd (06477-2914)
P.O. Box 943 (06477-0943)
PHONE..................................203 795-9494
John Pritchard, *Manager*
EMP: 4 **EST:** 2001
SALES (est): 100K **Privately Held**
SIC: 3569 Mfg General Industrial Machinery

(G-3376)
NUMET MACHINING TECHNIQUES LLC
235 Edison Rd (06477-3603)
PHONE..................................203 375-4995
Tim Ullos, *CEO*
Joseph Satori, *COO*
Anthony Guarascio, *CFO*
▲ **EMP:** 32
SQ FT: 40,000
SALES (est): 9.5MM
SALES (corp-wide): 177.9K **Privately Held**
WEB: www.numetmachining.com
SIC: 3724 Mfg Aircraft Engines/Parts
HQ: Bromford Industries Limited
1 Bromford Gate
Birmingham W MIDLANDS B24 8
121 683-6200

(G-3377)
ORANGE CHEESE COMPANY
5 Hampton Close (06477-1934)
PHONE..................................917 603-4378
Hangyu Liu, *Principal*
EMP: 4
SALES (est): 191.7K **Privately Held**
SIC: 2022 2038 Mfg Cheese Mfg Frozen Specialties

(G-3378)
ORANGE DEMOCRAT
297 Boston Post Rd (06477-3537)
PHONE..................................203 298-4575
EMP: 3 **EST:** 2009
SALES (est): 102.5K **Privately Held**
SIC: 2711 Newspapers-Publishing/Printing

(G-3379)
PEZ CANDY INC (HQ)
35 Prindle Hill Rd (06477-3616)
PHONE..................................203 795-0531
Christian Jegen, *CEO*
Pat Early, *Vice Pres*
Steve Rowe, *Plant Mgr*
Brian Fry, *CFO*
Jeanine Santana, *Accounting Mgr*
▲ **EMP:** 61 **EST:** 1953
SALES (est): 25.3MM
SALES (corp-wide): 355.8K **Privately Held**
WEB: www.pezcandyinc.com
SIC: 2064 Mfg Candy/Confectionery
PA: Pez Inter Holding Ag
C/O Globaltax Gmbh
ZUrich ZH
432 550-816

(G-3380)
PEZ MANUFACTURING CORP
35 Prindle Hill Rd (06477-3616)
PHONE..................................203 795-0531
Christian Jegen, *CEO*
Brian Fry, *CFO*
Peter Graf, *Admin Sec*
▲ **EMP:** 100 **EST:** 1973
SQ FT: 50,000
SALES (est): 14.3MM
SALES (corp-wide): 355.8K **Privately Held**
SIC: 2064 Mfg Candy/Confectionery
HQ: Pez Candy, Inc.
35 Prindle Hill Rd
Orange CT 06477
203 795-0531

(G-3381)
RESAVUE INC
Also Called: Resavue Exhibits
48 Grannis Rd (06477-1908)
PHONE..................................203 878-0944
John B Kelman, *CEO*
Christine Kelman, *Admin Sec*
◆ **EMP:** 10
SALES (est): 2.2MM **Privately Held**
WEB: www.resavue.com
SIC: 3577 7319 Mfg Graphic Displays Advertising Services

(G-3382)
ROEBIC LABORATORIES INC (PA)
Also Called: Roetech
25 Connair Rd (06477-3601)
P.O. Box 927 (06477-0927)
PHONE..................................203 795-1283
Stuart J Bush, *CEO*
Derek J Bush, *President*
Hedy S Bush, *COO*
John Peters, *COO*
Steven Smith, *Vice Pres*
EMP: 5 **EST:** 1959
SQ FT: 30,000
SALES (est): 4MM **Privately Held**
WEB: www.roebic.com
SIC: 2842 Mfg Polish/Sanitation Goods

(G-3383)
SALLY CONANT
Also Called: Orange Restoration Labs
454 Old Cellar Rd (06477-3707)
PHONE..................................203 878-3005
Sally Conant, *President*
EMP: 12
SALES (est): 78.8K **Privately Held**
WEB: www.gownrestoration.com
SIC: 2221 7212 7211 Manmade Broadwoven Fabric Mill Garment Press/Cleaner's Agent Power Laundry

(G-3384)
SIGN A RAMA
Also Called: Sign-A-Rama
553 Boston Post Rd (06477-3331)
PHONE..................................203 795-5450
Barbara Metzger, *Partner*
David Metzger, *Mng Member*
EMP: 5
SALES (est): 368K **Privately Held**
SIC: 3993 Signsadv Specs

(G-3385)
TOMTEC
607 Harborview Rd (06477-2031)
PHONE..................................203 795-5030
Fax: 203 248-5724
EMP: 3 **EST:** 2010
SALES (est): 259K **Privately Held**
SIC: 3841 Mfg Surgical/Medical Instruments

(G-3386)
VALLEY TOOL AND MFG LLC (HQ)
Also Called: Milford Fabricating Co.
22 Prindle Hill Rd (06477-3615)
P.O. Box 564 (06477-0564)
PHONE..................................203 799-8800
Phillip C Freidman, *CEO*
Howard Turner, *President*
Gary Greco, *Exec VP*
Constantine Demos, *Vice Pres*
Kurt Maurer, *CFO*
EMP: 72 **EST:** 2017
SQ FT: 36,000
SALES: 12MM
SALES (corp-wide): 118.6MM **Privately Held**
SIC: 3728 Manufacture Aircraft Parts/Equipment
PA: Harlow Aerostructures Llc
1501 S Mclean Blvd
Wichita KS 67213
316 265-5268

Oxford
New Haven County

(G-3387)
ADVANCED SONICS LLC
Also Called: Advanced Sonic Proc Systems
324 Christian St (06478-1023)
PHONE..................................203 266-4440
David Hunicke, *Mng Member*
EMP: 7
SQ FT: 17,500
SALES (est): 1.3MM **Privately Held**
WEB: www.advancedsonics.com
SIC: 3629 7379 Mfg Electrical Industrial Apparatus Computer Related Services

(G-3388)
AEROTURN LLC
115 Hurley Rd Ste 2c (06478-1047)
PHONE..................................203 262-8309
Robert R Hellman Jr,
EMP: 6
SALES (est): 998.2K **Privately Held**
WEB: www.aeroturn.com
SIC: 3699 Mfg Electrical Equipment/Supplies

(G-3389)
ALL POWER MANUFACTURING CO (HQ)
1 Tribiology Ctr (06478-1035)
PHONE..................................562 802-2640
Michael J Hartnett, *CEO*
▲ **EMP:** 130
SQ FT: 40,000
SALES (est): 22.1MM
SALES (corp-wide): 702.5MM **Publicly Held**
WEB: www.allpowermfg.com
SIC: 3728 2899 Mfg Aircraft Parts/Equipment Mfg Chemical Preparations
PA: Rbc Bearings Incorporated
102 Willenbrock Rd
Oxford CT 06478
203 267-7001

(G-3390)
ALTERIO TRACTOR PULLING LLC
37 Cold Spring Dr (06478-1903)
PHONE..................................203 305-9812
Matthew Alterio, *Principal*
EMP: 5
SALES (est): 310.7K **Privately Held**
SIC: 1389 Oil/Gas Field Services

(G-3391)
BALFOR INDUSTRIES INC
327 Riggs St (06478-1129)
PHONE..................................203 828-6473
Richard Ballot, *President*
Felice Ballot, *Manager*
EMP: 15 **EST:** 1955
SQ FT: 17,500
SALES (est): 4.4MM **Privately Held**
WEB: www.cmail.cz
SIC: 3089 Mfg Plastic Products

(G-3392)
BRIGHTON & HOVE MOLD LTD
115 Hurley Rd Ste 2c (06478-1047)
PHONE..................................203 264-3013
Robert Hellman Jr, *President*
Michael A Stoll, *CFO*
EMP: 6
SQ FT: 6,000
SALES (est): 805.9K **Privately Held**
SIC: 3089 5162 Product Design And Manufacturer

(G-3393)
CAST GLOBAL MANUFACTURING CORP
Also Called: Met-Craft
66 Prokop Rd (06478-1107)
PHONE..................................203 828-6147
Chung Hsuen Hu, *President*
EMP: 11
SALES (est): 1.4MM **Privately Held**
SIC: 3452 Mfg Bolts/Screws/Rivets

(G-3394)
CATACHEM INC
353 Christian St Ste 2 (06478-1053)
PHONE..................................203 262-0330
Luis P Leon, *President*
David Templeton, *COO*
Erik Eskind, *Manager*
▲ **EMP:** 7
SQ FT: 3,500
SALES: 500K **Privately Held**
SIC: 3841 Manufactures Clinical Diagnostic Reagents

(G-3395)
CD RACING PRODUCTS
91 Willenbrock Rd Ste B3 (06478-1036)
PHONE..................................203 264-7822
Michael Paquette, *Owner*
EMP: 3
SALES (est): 303.8K **Privately Held**
SIC: 3711 Mfg Race Cars

(G-3396)
CHASSIS DYNAMICS INC
91 Willenbrock Rd Ste A1 (06478-1036)
PHONE..................................203 262-6272
Robert Cuneo, *President*
EMP: 3 **EST:** 1974
SQ FT: 3,800
SALES: 220K **Privately Held**
SIC: 3711 Fabrication Of Custom Made Race Car Chassis

(G-3397)
COLORGRAPHIX LLC
91 Willenbrock Rd Ste B5 (06478-1036)
P.O. Box 545, Southbury (06488-0545)
PHONE..................................203 264-5212
Jeff Jones, *Mng Member*
EMP: 8
SQ FT: 4,500
SALES (est): 1MM **Privately Held**
WEB: www.colorgraphix.com
SIC: 2759 Commercial Printing

GEOGRAPHIC

(G-3398)
CONSULTING ENGRG DEV SVCS INC
Also Called: C E D
3 Fox Hollow Rd (06478-3162)
PHONE..................................203 828-6528
Steven G Meyer, *President*
Lisa Brayall, *QC Mgr*
David Keckley, *Info Tech Mgr*
Christopher Defusco, *Technology*
EMP: 55
SQ FT: 20,000
SALES (est): 15MM **Privately Held**
WEB: www.cedservicesinc.com
SIC: 3599 3469 Mfg Industrial Machinery Mfg Metal Stampings

(G-3399)
DEWEY J MANUFACTURING COMPANY
112 Willenbrock Rd (06478-1031)
PHONE..................................203 264-3064
George Dewey, *President*
Brian Dewey, *Vice Pres*
EMP: 6
SQ FT: 2,500
SALES (est): 460K **Privately Held**
WEB: www.deweyrods.com
SIC: 3484 3949 Mfg Small Arms Mfg Sporting/Athletic Goods

(G-3400)
ENVAX PRODUCTS INC
349 Christian St (06478-1023)
PHONE..................................203 264-8181
Michael Tarby, *President*
EMP: 3
SQ FT: 2,000
SALES (est): 542.5K **Privately Held**
SIC: 3567 Mfg Vacuum Furnaces & Ovens

(G-3401)
FLIGHT ENHANCEMENTS CORP
47 Oakcrest Rd (06478-1247)
PHONE..................................912 257-0440
Robert Steven Takacs, *CEO*
EMP: 3
SALES (est): 179K **Privately Held**
SIC: 3728 Mfg Aircraft Parts/Equipment

(G-3402)
FRYER CORPORATION
43 Old State Road 67 (06478-1978)
P.O. Box 565 (06478-0565)
PHONE..................................203 888-9944
Tracy Fryer, *President*
George Fryer, *Admin Sec*
EMP: 5 **EST:** 1952
SQ FT: 5,500
SALES (est): 500K **Privately Held**
SIC: 3599 Mfg Industrial Machinery

(G-3403)
GEN-EL-MEC ASSOCIATES INC
2 Fox Hollow Rd (06478-3161)
PHONE..................................203 828-6566
Dean Contaxis, *President*
Theresa Contaxis, *Corp Secy*
Tom Villano, *Vice Pres*
EMP: 24 **EST:** 1961
SQ FT: 30,000
SALES (est): 4.4MM **Privately Held**
SIC: 3599 Mfg Industrial Machinery

(G-3404)
GENERAL DATACOMM INC (HQ)
353 Christian St Ste 4 (06478-1053)
PHONE..................................203 729-0271
Howard S Modlin, *President*
Mark Johns, *COO*
Bill Henry, *Sr Corp Ofcr*
George Gray, *Vice Pres*
Jeff Turner, *Opers Staff*
◆ **EMP:** 50
SQ FT: 360,000
SALES (est): 7.5MM
SALES (corp-wide): 12.9MM **Publicly Held**
SIC: 3661 1731 7629 Mfg Telephone/Telegraph Apparatus Electrical Contractor Electrical Repair
PA: General Datacomm Industries, Inc.
353 Christian St Ste 4
Oxford CT 06478
203 729-0271

(G-3405)
GENERAL DATACOMM INDS INC (PA)
353 Christian St Ste 4 (06478-1053)
PHONE..................................203 729-0271
Howard S Modlin, *Ch of Bd*
George M Gray, *Vice Pres*
William G Henry, *CFO*
EMP: 25 **EST:** 1969
SQ FT: 360,000
SALES (est): 12.9MM **Publicly Held**
WEB: www.gdc.com
SIC: 3661 Mfg Telephone/Telegraph Apparatus

(G-3406)
GRAND EMBROIDERY INC
Also Called: Grand Imprints
225 Christian St (06478-1252)
PHONE..................................203 888-7484
Joseph Grandieri, *President*
Patricia Grandieri, *Vice Pres*
EMP: 11
SQ FT: 6,300
SALES (est): 838.3K **Privately Held**
WEB: www.grandembroidery.com
SIC: 2395 2269 Pleating/Stitching Services Finishing Plant

(G-3407)
HART TOOL & ENGINEERING
339 Christian St (06478-1023)
PHONE..................................203 264-9776
Gilbert Hart, *Owner*
EMP: 7 **EST:** 1975
SQ FT: 2,500
SALES (est): 811.3K **Privately Held**
SIC: 3545 Mfg Machine Tool Accessories

(G-3408)
HUSKY FUEL
62 Larkey Rd (06478-3149)
PHONE..................................203 783-0783
Robert James Hofmiller, *Principal*
EMP: 3
SALES (est): 88.3K **Privately Held**
SIC: 2869 Mfg Industrial Organic Chemicals

(G-3409)
HYDROTEC INC
115 Hurley Rd Ste 7a (06478-1037)
PHONE..................................203 264-6700
Kjell D Oloffsson, *President*
EMP: 5
SQ FT: 5,000
SALES (est): 1.3MM **Privately Held**
WEB: www.hydrotec-inc.com
SIC: 3621 Mfg Motors/Generators

(G-3410)
JARDEN CORPORATION
288 Christian St Ste 11 (06478-1038)
PHONE..................................203 264-9717
EMP: 3
SALES (est): 180.3K **Privately Held**
SIC: 3089 Mfg Plastic Products

(G-3411)
KENNETH LYNCH & SONS INC
114 Willenbrock Rd (06478-1031)
PHONE..................................203 762-8363
Melody Sonntag, *Sales Mgr*
Timothy A Lynch, *Manager*
▲ **EMP:** 9 **EST:** 1946
SQ FT: 30,000
SALES (est): 1.4MM **Privately Held**
WEB: www.klynchandsons.com
SIC: 3446 3281 Mfg Architectural Metalwork Mfg Cut Stone/Products

(G-3412)
LEWIS R MARTINO
328 Oxford Rd (06478-1617)
PHONE..................................203 463-4430
Lewis R Martino, *Principal*
EMP: 4
SALES (est): 189.5K **Privately Held**
SIC: 3433 Mfg Heating Equipment-Nonelectric

(G-3413)
MACTON CORPORATION
116 Willenbrock Rd (06478-1031)
PHONE..................................203 267-1500
Peter McGonagle, *President*
Steve Schumacher, *Vice Pres*
John C Shepherd, *Vice Pres*
Paul Spicer, *Vice Pres*
Thomas E Young Sr, *Vice Pres*
▼ **EMP:** 60
SQ FT: 27,000
SALES: 20MM **Privately Held**
WEB: www.macton.com
SIC: 3537 Mfg Industrial Trucks/Tractors

(G-3414)
MODERN METAL FINISHING INC
110 Willenbrock Rd (06478-1031)
PHONE..................................203 267-1510
Russell Peterson, *President*
David Murelli, *Treasurer*
Bruno Perin, *Admin Sec*
EMP: 18
SQ FT: 6,300
SALES (est): 2.3MM **Privately Held**
WEB: www.mmfinc.com
SIC: 3479 Aluminum Coating Of Metal Products And Phosphates On Steel

(G-3415)
MORSE WATCHMANS INC
2 Morse Rd (06478-1040)
PHONE..................................203 264-1108
Manuel Pires, *President*
Joe Granitto, *General Mgr*
Fernando Pires, *Vice Pres*
W Schr Eyer, *Engineer*
Tim Purpura, *VP Sls/Mktg*
▲ **EMP:** 50
SQ FT: 20,000
SALES (est): 11MM **Privately Held**
WEB: www.morsewatchman.com
SIC: 3699 3577 Mfg Electrical Equipment/Supplies Mfg Computer Peripheral Equipment

(G-3416)
NXTID INC
288 Christian St (06478-1038)
PHONE..................................203 266-2103
Gino M Pereira, *Principal*
Vincent Miceli, *Vice Pres*
Bonnie Bartosiak, *Controller*
EMP: 10
SALES (est): 1.9MM **Privately Held**
SIC: 7372 Prepackaged Software Services

(G-3417)
OXFORD SCIENCE INC
178 Christian St (06478-1239)
PHONE..................................203 881-3115
Edward L Carver Jr, *President*
EMP: 18
SQ FT: 18,000
SALES (est): 3.3MM **Privately Held**
WEB: www.oxfordscienceinc.com
SIC: 3841 Mfg Surgical And Medical Instruments

(G-3418)
OXFORD SCIENCE CENTER LLC
Also Called: O S C
Iii One American Way (06478)
PHONE..................................203 751-1912
Tanya G Carver,
EMP: 4
SALES (est): 278.3K **Privately Held**
SIC: 3841 Mfg Medical Instrument

(G-3419)
POWER TRANS CO INC
Also Called: Meritronics
315 Riggs St Ste 2 (06478-1176)
PHONE..................................203 881-0314
Paul Zaloumis, *President*
Shirley Zaloumis, *Vice Pres*
▼ **EMP:** 5 **EST:** 1976
SQ FT: 7,000
SALES (est): 1.5MM **Privately Held**
SIC: 3612 3679 3672 Mfg Transformers Mfg Electronic Components Mfg Printed Circuit Boards

(G-3420)
PRO SCIENTIFIC INC
99 Willenbrock Rd (06478-1032)
P.O. Box 448, Monroe (06468-0448)
PHONE..................................203 267-4600
Richard Yacko, *President*
Patricia Yacko, *Vice Pres*
Holly Yacko-Archibald, *Sales Dir*
Holly Yacko, *Sales Mgr*
Ray Pistey, *Info Tech Mgr*
EMP: 10
SALES (est): 2MM **Privately Held**
WEB: www.proscientific.com
SIC: 3556 Mfg Food Products Machinery

(G-3421)
RBC BEARINGS INCORPORATED (PA)
102 Willenbrock Rd (06478-1033)
PHONE..................................203 267-7001
Michael J Hartnett, *Ch of Bd*
Daniel A Bergeron, *COO*
Patrick S Bannon, *Vice Pres*
Patrick Bannon, *Vice Pres*
Richard Edwards, *Vice Pres*
EMP: 277 **EST:** 1919
SALES: 702.5MM **Publicly Held**
WEB: www.rbcbearings.com
SIC: 3562 Mfg Ball/Roller Bearings

(G-3422)
RBC PRCISION PDTS - BREMEN INC (DH)
102 Willenbrock Rd (06478-1033)
PHONE..................................203 267-7001
George Viering, *General Mgr*
▲ **EMP:** 42 **EST:** 1971
SQ FT: 50,000
SALES (est): 11.5MM
SALES (corp-wide): 702.5MM **Publicly Held**
SIC: 3452 Mfg Bolts/Screws/Rivets
HQ: Roller Bearing Company Of America, Inc.
102 Willenbrock Rd
Oxford CT 06478
203 267-7001

(G-3423)
ROLLER BEARING CO AMER INC (HQ)
Also Called: R B C
102 Willenbrock Rd (06478-1033)
PHONE..................................203 267-7001
Michael J Harnett, *Ch of Bd*
Thomas Williams, *Counsel*
Michael S Gostomski, *Exec VP*
Richard J Edwards, *Vice Pres*
Christopher Thomas, *Vice Pres*
◆ **EMP:** 155 **EST:** 1934
SQ FT: 40,000
SALES (est): 507MM
SALES (corp-wide): 702.5MM **Publicly Held**
SIC: 3562 Mfg Ball/Roller Bearings
PA: Rbc Bearings Incorporated
102 Willenbrock Rd
Oxford CT 06478
203 267-7001

(G-3424)
ROLLER BEARING CO AMER INC
1 Tribiology Ctr (06478-1035)
PHONE..................................203 267-7001
Anthony Cavalieri, *Principal*
Kimberly Veal, *Controller*
EMP: 20
SALES (est): 4.4MM
SALES (corp-wide): 702.5MM **Publicly Held**
SIC: 3562 Ball And Roller Bearings
PA: Rbc Bearings Incorporated
102 Willenbrock Rd
Oxford CT 06478
203 267-7001

(G-3425)
STIHL INCORPORATED
Also Called: Northeast Stihl
2 Patriot Way (06478-1274)
PHONE..................................203 929-8488
Nick Jiannas, *Branch Mgr*
EMP: 50
SALES (corp-wide): 4B **Privately Held**
WEB: www.stihlusa.com
SIC: 3546 5083 Mfg Power-Driven Handtools Whol Farm/Garden Machinery

▲ = Import ▼=Export
◆ =Import/Export

HQ: Stihl Incorporated
536 Viking Dr
Virginia Beach VA 23452
757 486-9100

(G-3426)
SUSAN MARTOVICH
Also Called: Ms Design CT
118 Bowers Hill Rd (06478-1757)
PHONE....................203 881-1848
Susan Martovich, *Owner*
EMP: 4
SALES: 900K **Privately Held**
SIC: 3728 3446 Mfg Aircraft Parts/Equipment Mfg Architectural Metalwork

(G-3427)
TEXTRON AVIATION INC
Also Called: Cessna Aircraft
288 Christian St (06478-1038)
PHONE....................203 262-9366
EMP: 697
SALES (corp-wide): 13.9B **Publicly Held**
SIC: 3721 Mfg Aircraft
HQ: Textron Aviation Inc.
1 Cessna Blvd
Wichita KS 67215
316 517-6000

(G-3428)
VANGOR ENGINEERING CORPORATION
115 Hurley Rd Ste 7f (06478-1046)
PHONE....................203 267-4377
Greg Van Gor, *President*
Greg Vangor, *President*
EMP: 4
SQ FT: 5,000
SALES: 500K **Privately Held**
SIC: 3549 Mfg Specialized Machinery Assembly Systems

(G-3429)
WALZ & KRENZER INC (PA)
Also Called: Mapeco Products
91 Willenbrock Rd Ste B4 (06478-1036)
PHONE....................203 267-5712
Benjamin Rising, *President*
Tom Themel, *Vice Pres*
▲ **EMP:** 13
SQ FT: 3,750
SALES (est): 2.4MM **Privately Held**
WEB: www.wkdoors.com
SIC: 3429 Mfg Hardware

(G-3430)
WALZ & KRENZER INC
Also Called: Pilgrim Nuts
91 Willenbrock Rd Ste B4 (06478-1036)
PHONE....................203 267-5712
Benjamin Rising, *President*
EMP: 9
SALES (est): 343.9K
SALES (corp-wide): 2.4MM **Privately Held**
WEB: www.wkdoors.com
SIC: 3443 Mfg Fabricated Plate Work
PA: Walz & Krenzer, Inc.
91 Willenbrock Rd Ste B4
Oxford CT 06478
203 267-5712

(G-3431)
ZACKIN PUBLICATIONS INC
Also Called: Alternative Energy Retailer
100 Willenbrock Rd (06478-1044)
P.O. Box 2180, Waterbury (06722-2180)
PHONE....................203 262-4670
EMP: 24 **EST:** 1967
SQ FT: 2,000
SALES (est): 3.4MM **Privately Held**
WEB: www.zackin.com
SIC: 2721 Periodicals-Publishing/Printing

Pawcatuck
New London County

(G-3432)
DAVIS-STANDARD LLC (HQ)
Also Called: Harrel
1 Extrusion Dr (06379-2327)
PHONE....................860 599-1010
James Murphy, *President*
Charles Buckley, *Chairman*
Bob Preston, *Vice Chairman*
Robert Armstrong, *Vice Pres*
Kevin Coghlan, *CFO*
◆ **EMP:** 398
SALES (est): 152.5MM **Privately Held**
SIC: 3089 Mfg Plastic Products

(G-3433)
DAVIS-STANDARD HOLDINGS INC (PA)
Also Called: Egan, Sterling, Nrm, Brookes
1 Extrusion Dr (06379-2327)
PHONE....................860 599-1010
James Murphy, *President*
Charles Buckley, *President*
Hassan Helmy, *Exec VP*
Mark Panozzo, *Exec VP*
Ernest Plasse, *Exec VP*
◆ **EMP:** 400
SQ FT: 170,000
SALES (est): 262.2MM **Privately Held**
WEB: www.davis-standard.com
SIC: 3559 Mfg Misc Industry Machinery

(G-3434)
DESCHENES & COOPER ARCHITECTUR
25 White Rock Bridge Rd (06379-1312)
P.O. Box 9222, Groton (06340-9222)
PHONE....................860 599-2481
Brian Cooper, *President*
EMP: 8
SQ FT: 10,000
SALES (est): 928.6K **Privately Held**
SIC: 2431 1521 Mfg Millwork Single-Family House Construction

(G-3435)
FREEDOM PRESS
30 Sunrise Ave (06379-2006)
P.O. Box 1213 (06379-0213)
PHONE....................860 599-5390
Jeffrey Tebbets, *Owner*
EMP: 3 **EST:** 2002
SALES (est): 123.9K **Privately Held**
WEB: www.freedompress.org
SIC: 2741 Misc Publishing

(G-3436)
GUIDERA MARKETING SERVICES
Also Called: Fabricgraphics
21 Pawcatuck Ave (06379-2421)
P.O. Box 108, Stonington (06378-0108)
PHONE....................860 599-8880
Timothy Guidera, *President*
Pamela Guidera, *Vice Pres*
EMP: 20
SQ FT: 2,500
SALES: 800K **Privately Held**
WEB: www.embroiderygiant.com
SIC: 2395 Pleating/Stitching Services

(G-3437)
HOMEWOOD CABINET CO INC
262 S Broad St (06379-1922)
PHONE....................860 599-2441
James Varas, *President*
Michael Varas, *Vice Pres*
EMP: 3
SQ FT: 1,000
SALES (est): 351.6K **Privately Held**
SIC: 2434 5211 Mfg Wood Kitchen Cabinets Ret Lumber/Building Materials

(G-3438)
LEHVOSS NORTH AMERICA LLC
185 S Broad St Ste 2b (06379-1997)
PHONE....................860 495-2046
Crystal Wang, *General Mgr*
Robert Healy, *Managing Dir*
Jim Meegan, *Business Mgr*
Meghan Moore, *Office Mgr*
Ted Sidoriak, *Manager*
▲ **EMP:** 10
SALES (est): 1.4MM
SALES (corp-wide): 247.5MM **Privately Held**
SIC: 3089 Nonclassified Establishment
PA: Lehmann & Voss & Co. Kg
Alsterufer 19
Hamburg 20354
404 419-70

(G-3439)
OLIVE CAPIZZANO OILS & VINEGAR
5 Coggswell St Ste 1 (06379-1672)
PHONE....................860 495-2187
Stephen Capizzano, *Principal*
EMP: 5
SALES (est): 326.6K **Privately Held**
SIC: 2079 Mfg Edible Fats/Oils

(G-3440)
PERFORMANCE COMPOUNDING INC
185 S Broad St Ste 2a (06379-1997)
PHONE....................860 599-5616
Michael Valsamis, *CEO*
Dr Lefteris Valsamis, *General Mgr*
Hubertus Richert, *Admin Sec*
EMP: 6
SQ FT: 40,000
SALES (est): 1.5MM
SALES (corp-wide): 247.5MM **Privately Held**
WEB: www.performancecompounding.com
SIC: 3087 Custom Compounding-Purchased Resins
PA: Lehmann & Voss & Co. Kg
Alsterufer 19
Hamburg 20354
404 419-70

(G-3441)
PRESCOTT CABINET CO
31 Buckingham St (06379-2524)
PHONE....................860 495-0176
Gary Prescott, *Owner*
EMP: 8 **EST:** 1980
SQ FT: 6,000
SALES (est): 479.4K **Privately Held**
SIC: 2434 2431 5072 Cabinet Maker

(G-3442)
THAVENET MACHINE COMPANY INC
12 Chase St Ste 14 (06379-2127)
PHONE....................860 599-4495
Fax: 860 599-4495
EMP: 8
SQ FT: 4,000
SALES (est): 720K **Privately Held**
SIC: 3599 5084 Machine Shop & Whol Welding Supplies

(G-3443)
VACCA ARCHITECTURAL WOODWORKIN
9 Coggswell St (06379-1626)
PHONE....................860 599-3677
Annette Vacca,
EMP: 8
SQ FT: 6,958
SALES (est): 842.5K **Privately Held**
SIC: 2499 Mfg Wood Products

(G-3444)
WESCON CORP OF CONN
Elmata Ave (06379)
P.O. Box 296, Westerly RI (02891-0296)
PHONE....................860 599-2500
Paul Lynch, *President*
Steven Lynch, *Corp Secy*
EMP: 8
SQ FT: 1,200
SALES (est): 1.2MM
SALES (corp-wide): 95.6MM **Privately Held**
WEB: www.wesconco.com
SIC: 2951 Mfg Asphalt Mixtures/Blocks Mfg Construction Machinery
PA: J.H. Lynch & Sons, Inc.
50 Lynch Pl
Cumberland RI 02864
401 333-4300

(G-3445)
WESTERLY SUN
99 Mechanic St Ste C (06379-2189)
PHONE....................401 348-1000
David Lucey, *Publisher*
Bob Laux-Bachand, *Editor*
John Layton, *Sales Staff*
Kathy Enders, *Advt Staff*
Alex Walker, *Consultant*
EMP: 8 **EST:** 2015
SALES (est): 395.8K **Privately Held**
SIC: 2711 Newspapers-Publishing/Printing

Pine Meadow
Litchfield County

(G-3446)
TRD SPECIALTIES INC
Also Called: T R D Specialities
8 Wickett St (06061-2039)
P.O. Box 80 (06061-0080)
PHONE....................860 738-4505
Thomas Reading, *President*
Albert De Gaeta, *Treasurer*
▲ **EMP:** 8
SQ FT: 7,500
SALES (est): 1.2MM **Privately Held**
WEB: www.trdspecialties.com
SIC: 3399 Mfg Primary Metal Products

Plainfield
Windham County

(G-3447)
AMTEC CORPORATION
30 Center Pkwy (06374-2051)
PHONE....................860 230-0006
David E Fallon, *President*
Donna M Hunt, *Admin Sec*
EMP: 30
SQ FT: 15,000
SALES (est): 5.8MM **Privately Held**
WEB: www.amtecgrips.com
SIC: 3496 Mfg Misc Fabricated Wire Products

(G-3448)
APCM MANUFACTURING LLC
Also Called: Adhesives Prepregs
1366 Norwich Rd (06374-1931)
P.O. Box 264 (06374-0264)
PHONE....................860 564-7817
David L Young, *CEO*
Rj Young, *Marketing Mgr*
EMP: 3
SQ FT: 7,000
SALES (est): 556.9K **Privately Held**
WEB: www.prepregs.com
SIC: 2891 Mfg Adhesives/Sealants

(G-3449)
ARS PRODUCTS LLC
43 Lathrop Road Ext (06374-1965)
P.O. Box 288 (06374-0288)
PHONE....................860 564-0208
Theodore A Coppola,
EMP: 43
SALES (est): 953.6K **Privately Held**
WEB: www.arsproducts.com
SIC: 3825 Mfg Electrical Measuring Instruments

(G-3450)
ASAP MACHINE SP & FABRICATION
89 Mill Brook Rd (06374-1967)
PHONE....................860 564-4114
Earl Starks, *Principal*
EMP: 7
SALES (est): 1.1MM **Privately Held**
SIC: 3599 Mfg Industrial Machinery

(G-3451)
B S T SYSTEMS INC
78 Plainfield Pike (06374-1700)
PHONE....................860 564-4078
Kenneth P Avery, *President*
Thomas T Terjesen, *President*
Edward J Mulvey, *Director*
Michael A Solis, *Director*
▲ **EMP:** 55
SQ FT: 27,000
SALES (est): 13.6MM **Privately Held**
WEB: www.bstsys.com
SIC: 3692 3691 3629 Mfg Primary Batteries Mfg Storage Batteries Mfg Electrical Industrial Apparatus

GEOGRAPHIC

(G-3452)
BAY STATE MACHINE INC
21 Center Pkwy (06374-2054)
PHONE..................................860 230-0054
Robert Stafford, *President*
Pamela Stafford, *Corp Secy*
EMP: 8 **EST:** 1970
SQ FT: 2,000
SALES: 500K **Privately Held**
SIC: 3599 Mfg Industrial Machinery

(G-3453)
LINEMASTER SWITCH CORPORATION
16 Center Pkwy (06374-2051)
PHONE..................................860 564-7713
▲ **EMP:** 3
SALES (est): 364.4K **Privately Held**
SIC: 3679 Mfg Electronic Components

(G-3454)
MERIDIAN OPERATIONS LLC
1414 Norwich Rd (06374-1931)
PHONE..................................860 564-8811
EMP: 10
SALES (est): 720K **Privately Held**
SIC: 3069 Mfg Fabricated Rubber Products

(G-3455)
PRO-MANUFACTURED PRODUCTS INC
29 Center Pkwy (06374-2054)
PHONE..................................860 564-2197
Ward E Walker, *President*
Kristin D Walker, *Corp Secy*
EMP: 8
SQ FT: 5,250
SALES (est): 1.5MM **Privately Held**
WEB: www.pro-equine.com
SIC: 3451 Mfg Screw Machine Products

(G-3456)
RADECO OF CT INC
17 West Pkwy (06374-2048)
P.O. Box 1304, Forestdale MA (02644-0715)
PHONE..................................860 564-1220
Paul Lovendale, *President*
Keith Lovendale, *Vice Pres*
Brad Lovendale, *VP Sales*
Ann Lovendale, *Admin Sec*
▼ **EMP:** 12
SQ FT: 6,000
SALES: 1.6MM **Privately Held**
WEB: www.radecoinc.com
SIC: 3674 Manufactures Radiation Detection Devices

(G-3457)
SCOPE TECHNOLOGY INC
8 Center Pkwy (06374-2051)
PHONE..................................860 963-1141
Ronald Green, *President*
Monty Nussbaum, *Director*
EMP: 10
SQ FT: 4,000
SALES (est): 968K **Privately Held**
WEB: www.scopetech.com
SIC: 3827 Mfg Optical Instruments/Lenses

(G-3458)
THELEMIC PRINTSHOP
13 West Pkwy (06374-2048)
PHONE..................................860 383-4014
Eric Ross, *President*
EMP: 4
SALES (est): 217.3K **Privately Held**
SIC: 2752 Lithographic Commercial Printing

(G-3459)
WESTMINSTER TOOL INC
5 East Pkwy (06374-2046)
PHONE..................................860 564-6966
Raymond S Coombs Jr, *President*
Paul L Szydlo, *Vice Pres*
Jason Eliasson, *Production*
Michael Belmont, *Sales Staff*
Nicholas Stein, *Manager*
▲ **EMP:** 30 **EST:** 1997
SQ FT: 4,500
SALES: 6MM **Privately Held**
WEB: www.westminstertool.com
SIC: 3599 Mfg Industrial Machinery

Plainville
Hartford County

(G-3460)
A D GRINDING
54 Lewis St (06062-2049)
PHONE..................................860 747-6630
Anthony Loumbard, *President*
Dan Haag, *Admin Sec*
EMP: 13
SALES (est): 1.6MM **Privately Held**
SIC: 3599 Mfg Industrial Machinery

(G-3461)
ABB ENTERPRISE SOFTWARE INC
Also Called: GE
41 Woodford Ave (06062-2372)
PHONE..................................860 747-7111
Gary Arnott, *General Mgr*
Steven Meiners, *General Mgr*
Scott P Parent, *General Mgr*
Thomas Henning, *Project Mgr*
Carlos Sanabria, *Project Mgr*
EMP: 900
SALES (corp-wide): 36.7B **Privately Held**
SIC: 3613 7361 3643 Mfg Switchgear/Boards Employment Agency Mfg Conductive Wire Dvcs
HQ: Abb Inc.
305 Gregson Dr
Cary NC 27511

(G-3462)
ACCU-MILL TECHNOLOGIES LLC
161 Woodford Ave Ste 39 (06062-2369)
PHONE..................................860 747-3921
Wojciech Wojtak, *Principal*
Artur Wojtak,
EMP: 3
SQ FT: 5,000
SALES: 400K **Privately Held**
SIC: 3365 7539 Mfg Aerospace Components Automotive Repair

(G-3463)
ACCURATE BURRING COMPANY
161 Woodford Ave Ste 19 (06062-2368)
PHONE..................................860 747-8640
Robert Beaudoin, *Owner*
EMP: 12
SQ FT: 20,000
SALES (est): 1.1MM **Privately Held**
SIC: 3471 Plating/Polishing Service

(G-3464)
ALPHA PLATING AND FINISHING CO
169 W Main St (06062-1925)
P.O. Box 89 (06062-0089)
PHONE..................................860 747-5002
Rafael Bawabe, *President*
EMP: 12
SQ FT: 15,000
SALES: 960K **Privately Held**
SIC: 3471 Plating/Polishing Service

(G-3465)
ALTO PRODUCTS CORP AL
Also Called: Plainville Special Tool
63 N Washington St (06062-1972)
P.O. Box 160 (06062-0160)
PHONE..................................860 747-2736
Rick Statchen, *Manager*
EMP: 38 **Privately Held**
WEB: www.altousa.com
SIC: 3469 3599 Mfg Metal Stampings Mfg Industrial Machinery
PA: Alto Products Corp. Al
1 Alto Way
Atmore AL 36502

(G-3466)
ATLANTIC PIPE CORPORATION
60 N Washington St (06062-1994)
PHONE..................................860 747-5557
Fax: 860 793-2477
EMP: 75 **EST:** 1962
SQ FT: 60,000
SALES (est): 8.5MM **Privately Held**
WEB: www.apartmentcities.com
SIC: 3272 Mfg Concrete Products

(G-3467)
ATP INDUSTRIES LLC (PA)
75 Northwest Dr (06062-1101)
PHONE..................................860 479-5007
Gary Fett, *Mng Member*
Mariusz Saar,
EMP: 14
SQ FT: 20,000
SALES: 1MM **Privately Held**
SIC: 3541 3492 8711 3451 Mfg Machine Tool-Cutting Mfg Fluid Power Valves Engineering Services Mfg Screw Machine Prdts

(G-3468)
B & L TOOL AND MACHINE COMPANY
76 Northwest Dr (06062-1164)
P.O. Box 308 (06062-0308)
PHONE..................................860 747-2721
Joseph Berarducci, *President*
Peter Berarducci, *Vice Pres*
EMP: 3 **EST:** 1948
SQ FT: 10,000
SALES (est): 400K **Privately Held**
SIC: 3544 3541 Mfg Dies/Tools/Jigs/Fixtures Mfg Machine Tools-Cutting

(G-3469)
BCT REPORTING LLC
55 Whiting St Ste 1a (06062-2262)
P.O. Box 1774, Bristol (06011-1774)
PHONE..................................860 302-1876
Brenda Lafleur, *Mng Member*
EMP: 6
SALES (est): 293.5K **Privately Held**
SIC: 2752 Lithographic Commercial Printing

(G-3470)
BRIARWOOD PRINTING COMPANY INC
301 Farmington Ave (06062-1398)
PHONE..................................860 747-6805
David M Drew, *President*
Brian Kupchik, *Vice Pres*
EMP: 12 **EST:** 1960
SQ FT: 10,000
SALES (est): 2.1MM **Privately Held**
WEB: www.briarwoodprinting.com
SIC: 2752 Lithographic Commercial Printing

(G-3471)
CAD CAM MACHINE LLC
150 Robert Jackson Way (06062-2651)
PHONE..................................860 410-9788
Darek Tuczapski, *General Mgr*
Malgorzata Zbrzeski, *Technology*
EMP: 6
SQ FT: 8,775
SALES (est): 1MM **Privately Held**
SIC: 3599 Mfg Industrial Machinery

(G-3472)
CAPITOL MACHINE INC PRECI
30 Hayden Ave Ste B (06062-2872)
PHONE..................................860 410-0758
Joseph Szabo, *Owner*
EMP: 3
SALES (est): 316.9K **Privately Held**
SIC: 3599 Mfg Industrial Machinery

(G-3473)
CARLING TECHNOLOGIES INC (PA)
Also Called: Carlingswitch
60 Johnson Ave (06062-1181)
PHONE..................................860 793-9281
Richard W Sorenson, *President*
Jen Buddenhagen, *Exec VP*
Jennifer Buddenhagen, *Exec VP*
Edward Rosenthal, *Exec VP*
Richard Sorenson Jr, *Exec VP*
▲ **EMP:** 175 **EST:** 1920
SQ FT: 135,000
SALES (est): 34.8MM **Privately Held**
SIC: 3643 3613 3612 Mfg Conductive Wiring Devices Mfg Switchgear/Switchboards Mfg Transformers

(G-3474)
COMPU-SIGNS LLC
105 E Main St (06062-1992)
PHONE..................................860 747-1985
Vincent J Zavarella, *Mng Member*
EMP: 3
SALES (est): 246.9K **Privately Held**
SIC: 3993 Mfg Signs/Advertising Specialties

(G-3475)
CONDOMDEPOT CO
186 Camp St (06062-1612)
PHONE..................................860 747-1338
John Fidi, *Principal*
Jennifer Amato, *Mktg Dir*
EMP: 3
SALES (est): 218K **Privately Held**
SIC: 2834 Mfg Pharmaceutical Preparations

(G-3476)
CONNECTICUT HONE INCORPORATED
9 Grace Ave (06062-2849)
P.O. Box 263 (06062-0263)
PHONE..................................860 747-3884
Bert Simard, *President*
Bertrand Simard, *President*
Douglas Simard, *Vice Pres*
Gregory Simard, *Vice Pres*
Doug Simard, *Opers Staff*
EMP: 7
SQ FT: 2,500
SALES (est): 724.7K **Privately Held**
SIC: 3599 Mfg Industrial Machinery

(G-3477)
CONNECTICUT SOLID SURFACE LLC
361 East St (06062-3260)
PHONE..................................860 410-9800
Steven Roux, *Mng Member*
Raymond Roux, *Mng Member*
Jaclyn Roux,
EMP: 40
SQ FT: 36,000
SALES: 5.9MM **Privately Held**
WEB: www.ctsolidsurface.com
SIC: 2434 2511 3281 Mfg Cut Stone/Products Mfg Wood Kitchen Cabinets Mfg Wood Household Furniture

(G-3478)
CONNECTICUT TOOL & MFG CO LLC
Also Called: CT Tool
35 Corp Ave (06062)
PHONE..................................860 846-0800
Sadik Lilaporia, *Engineer*
Collin Cooper, *Mng Member*
▲ **EMP:** 70
SQ FT: 29,000
SALES (est): 26.4MM
SALES (corp-wide): 115MM **Privately Held**
WEB: www.cttool.com
SIC: 3728 Mfg Aircraft Parts/Equipment
PA: Whitcraft Llc
76 County Rd
Eastford CT 06242
860 974-0786

(G-3479)
D & M SCREW MACHINE PDTS LLC
Also Called: Lowe Manufacturing
97 Forestville Ave (06062-2149)
PHONE..................................860 410-9781
Dennis Morin, *President*
Gerry Glass, *Sales Executive*
EMP: 5
SALES (est): 370K **Privately Held**
SIC: 3429 3451 Mfg Hardware Mfg Screw Machine Products

(G-3480)
DELL ACQUISITION LLC
Also Called: Dell Manufacturing
35 Corporate Ave (06062-1194)
PHONE..................................860 677-8545
Joe Maisto, *Principal*
EMP: 40 **EST:** 2011
SALES: 6MM **Privately Held**
SIC: 3728 Mfg Aircraft Parts/Equipment

▲ = Import ▼=Export
◆ =Import/Export

(G-3481)
DISPLAYCRAFT INC
335 S Washington St (06062-2729)
PHONE..................................860 747-9110
Richard Seigars, *President*
Rui Carvalho, *Exec VP*
▲ **EMP:** 20
SQ FT: 80,000
SALES (est): 2.6MM **Privately Held**
WEB: www.displaycraft.com
SIC: 3993 2542 Mfg Signs & Advertising Specialties Non-Wood Partitions & Fixtures

(G-3482)
DR TEMPLEMAN COMPANY
1 Northwest Dr (06062-1340)
PHONE..................................860 747-2709
Richard Williams, *President*
Arthur Williams, *Vice Pres*
David Williams, *Vice Pres*
Anita Williams, *Bookkeeper*
▼ **EMP:** 18 **EST:** 1938
SQ FT: 15,000
SALES (est): 3.6MM **Privately Held**
WEB: www.drtempleman.com
SIC: 3495 Mfg Wire Springs

(G-3483)
EASTERN BROACH INC
10 Sparks St (06062-2052)
PHONE..................................860 828-4800
Robert Tarver, *President*
Ivor Tarver, *President*
Patricia Tarver, *Corp Secy*
Charles H Tarver, *Shareholder*
Malcolm Tarver, *Admin Sec*
EMP: 15
SQ FT: 6,000
SALES (est): 2.5MM **Privately Held**
WEB: www.easternbroach.com
SIC: 3545 7699 Mfg Broaches

(G-3484)
EDISON COATINGS INC
3 Northwest Dr (06062-1336)
PHONE..................................860 747-2220
Michael Edison, *President*
Leya Edison, *Vice Pres*
Chad Lausberg, *Engineer*
◆ **EMP:** 13
SQ FT: 20,000
SALES (est): 2.8MM **Privately Held**
WEB: www.edisoncoatings.com
SIC: 2891 Mfg Adhesives/Sealants

(G-3485)
ELLIS MANUFACTURING LLC
161 Woodford Ave Ste 62 (06062-2374)
PHONE..................................865 518-0531
Robert Knowlton, *Principal*
EMP: 3
SALES (est): 164.8K **Privately Held**
SIC: 3999 Mfg Misc Products

(G-3486)
ENGINERING COMPONENTS PDTS LLC
Also Called: Industrial Automation
35 Forshaw Ave (06062-2555)
PHONE..................................860 747-6222
Robert Reeve, *President*
John Nejfelt,
EMP: 5 **EST:** 1970
SQ FT: 11,000
SALES (est): 400K **Privately Held**
SIC: 3441 3541 Structural Metal Fabrication Mfg Machine Tools Cutting

(G-3487)
EXECUTIVE PRESS INC
27 East St (06062-2308)
PHONE..................................860 793-0060
Robert Crago, *President*
John Crago, *President*
EMP: 3
SALES (est): 491.5K **Privately Held**
SIC: 2752 Lithographic Commercial Printing

(G-3488)
FLEETWOOD INDUSTRIES INC
4 Northwest Dr (06062-1311)
P.O. Box 862 (06062-0862)
PHONE..................................860 747-6750
Harry G Raymond, *President*
Darren Raymond, *Vice Pres*
EMP: 6
SQ FT: 2,500
SALES (est): 1MM **Privately Held**
SIC: 3451 Mfg Screw Machine Products

(G-3489)
FONDA FABRICATING & WELDING CO
50 Milford Street Ext (06062-2494)
PHONE..................................860 793-0601
Edward J Zakowski, *President*
Vallarie A Zakowski, *Admin Sec*
EMP: 5 **EST:** 1981
SQ FT: 20,000
SALES (est): 420K **Privately Held**
SIC: 3444 7692 3479 Mfg Of Sheet Metal & Welding Repair

(G-3490)
FORESTVILLE MACHINE CO INC
355 S Washington St (06062-2742)
PHONE..................................860 747-6000
Jeffrey Paul Hamel, *President*
Peter Lionell Vigue, *Vice Pres*
▲ **EMP:** 45 **EST:** 1945
SQ FT: 28,000
SALES (est): 9MM **Privately Held**
WEB: www.forestvillemachine.com
SIC: 3451 Mfg Screw Machine Products

(G-3491)
GEMS SENSORS INC (HQ)
Also Called: Gems Sensors & Controls
1 Cowles Rd (06062-1107)
PHONE..................................860 747-3000
Anne N De Greeg-Sasst, *President*
Muriel Bras-Jorge, *President*
Bryan Labarge, *Research*
Michael Riddell, *Chief Engr*
Terry Andreoli, *Engineer*
▲ **EMP:** 325
SALES (est): 93.9MM
SALES (corp-wide): 6.4B **Publicly Held**
SIC: 3824 5084 3812 3625 Mfg Fluid Meters/Devices Whol Industrial Equip Mfg Search/Navgatn Equip Mfg Relay/Indstl Control Mfg Switchgear/Boards
PA: Fortive Corporation
6920 Seaway Blvd
Everett WA 98203
425 446-5000

(G-3492)
GEMS SENSORS INC
1 Cowles Rd (06062-1107)
PHONE..................................800 378-1600
Tom Kepler, *Controller*
EMP: 12
SALES (corp-wide): 6.4B **Publicly Held**
SIC: 3829 5099 Mfg Measuring/Controlling Devices Whol Durable Goods
HQ: Gems Sensors Inc.
1 Cowles Rd
Plainville CT 06062
860 747-3000

(G-3493)
GERDAU AMERISTEEL US INC
75 Neal Ct (06062-1622)
PHONE..................................860 351-9029
EMP: 5 **Privately Held**
SIC: 3312 Blast Furnace- Steel Work
HQ: Gerdau Ameristeel Us Inc.
4221 W Boy Scout Blvd # 600
Tampa FL 33607
813 286-8383

(G-3494)
GPA
10 Farmington Valley Dr # 5 (06062-1182)
PHONE..................................860 410-0624
Greg Kuns, *Principal*
EMP: 6
SALES (est): 317.6K **Privately Held**
SIC: 2711 Newspapers-Publishing/Printing

(G-3495)
H & B WOODWORKING CO
105 E Main St (06062-1992)
PHONE..................................860 793-6991
Matthew Malley, *President*
EMP: 3
SALES (est): 397.6K **Privately Held**
SIC: 2434 Mfg Wood Kitchen Cabinets

(G-3496)
HYGRADE PRECISION TECH INC
329 Cooke St (06062-1448)
PHONE..................................860 747-5773
John A Salce, *CEO*
Richard J Cleary, *President*
Stephen Lsaltzman, *Admin Sec*
EMP: 28 **EST:** 1962
SQ FT: 40,000
SALES (est): 6.6MM **Privately Held**
WEB: www.hygrade.com
SIC: 3599 Mfg Industrial Machinery

(G-3497)
INDUSTRIAL CNNCTONS SLTONS LLC
41 Woodford Ave (06062-2372)
PHONE..................................860 747-7677
EMP: 20
SALES (corp-wide): 36.7B **Privately Held**
SIC: 3613 Mfg Switchgear/Switchboards
HQ: Industrial Connections & Solutions Llc
4200 Wildwood Pkwy
Atlanta GA 30339
678 844-6000

(G-3498)
J M SHEET METAL LLC
161 Woodford Ave Ste 11 (06062-2336)
PHONE..................................860 747-5537
Juan Marimon, *Mng Member*
EMP: 4 **EST:** 2001
SQ FT: 4,954
SALES (est): 575.7K **Privately Held**
SIC: 3444 Mfg Sheet Metalwork

(G-3499)
J&P MFG LLC
125 Robert Jackson Way F (06062-2663)
PHONE..................................860 747-4790
Pawel Surowaniec, *Owner*
EMP: 4
SALES (est): 279K **Privately Held**
SIC: 3999 Mfg Misc Products

(G-3500)
LASSY TOOLS INC
96 Bohemia St (06062-2122)
P.O. Box G (06062-0956)
PHONE..................................860 747-2748
William Lassy, *President*
Dave Lassy, *Vice Pres*
Marc Lassy, *Vice Pres*
Lassy Marc, *Vice Pres*
Gail Sjogren, *Admin Sec*
EMP: 7 **EST:** 1938
SQ FT: 10,000
SALES: 800K **Privately Held**
WEB: www.lassytools.com
SIC: 3429 3544 Mfg Machine Tools Including Dies Tools Jigs And Fixtures And Clamps

(G-3501)
LOGIC SEAL LLC
10 Sparks St (06062-2052)
PHONE..................................203 598-3400
Gary Rogers, *Prdtn Mgr*
Gregory Guay, *Mng Member*
EMP: 6 **EST:** 2011
SQ FT: 1,800
SALES (est): 1MM **Privately Held**
SIC: 3491 Mfg Industrial Valves

(G-3502)
LPG METAL CRAFTS LLC
54 Carol Dr (06062-3206)
PHONE..................................860 982-3573
Leonard Gale, *Mng Member*
EMP: 3
SALES (est): 260K **Privately Held**
SIC: 3446 Mfg Architectural Metalwork

(G-3503)
MARETRON LLP
60 Johnson Ave (06062-1181)
PHONE..................................602 861-1707
Saguaro Marine LLC, *Partner*
Mark Biegel, *Vice Pres*
▲ **EMP:** 14
SALES (est): 3.4MM **Privately Held**
SIC: 3531 Mfg Construction Machinery

(G-3504)
MARK DZIDZK
Also Called: Continental Marble & Granite
20k Hultenius St (06062-2848)
PHONE..................................860 793-2767
Mark Dzidzk, *Owner*
EMP: 20 **EST:** 1999
SALES (est): 1.8MM **Privately Held**
SIC: 3281 Mfg Marble And Granite Products

(G-3505)
MARTIN CABINET INC (PA)
336 S Washington St Ste 2 (06062-2752)
PHONE..................................860 747-5769
Jean Martin, *President*
Brian Martin, *Admin Sec*
EMP: 26 **EST:** 1971
SQ FT: 5,000
SALES (est): 6.8MM **Privately Held**
WEB: www.cabinet-mart.com
SIC: 2434 5211 Mfg Wood Kitchen Cabinets Ret Lumber/Building Materials

(G-3506)
MASTER TOOL & MACHINE INC
13 Grace Ave (06062-2849)
PHONE..................................860 747-2581
Robert William Mastrianni, *President*
Alfred James Mastrianni, *Vice Pres*
EMP: 6
SQ FT: 2,000
SALES: 3.5MM **Privately Held**
SIC: 3599 Machine Shop Jobbing And Repair

(G-3507)
MICRODYNE TECHNOLOGIES
64 Neal Ct (06062-1606)
PHONE..................................860 747-9473
David J Sperduti, *Partner*
Alexander J Sperduti, *Partner*
EMP: 4
SQ FT: 3,200
SALES (est): 528.4K **Privately Held**
WEB: www.microdynetech.com
SIC: 3312 Mfg Steel Wire Products/Cnc Servo Control Programing

(G-3508)
MODERN WOODCRAFTS LLC
72 Northwest Dr (06062-1164)
PHONE..................................860 677-7371
Gerald L Pelletier, *Founder*
John Lapre, *Vice Pres*
Philip Shuman, *CFO*
Lisa Fekete, *VP Sales*
Philip W Shuman,
EMP: 70
SQ FT: 65,000
SALES: 15MM **Privately Held**
WEB: www.modernwoodcrafts.com
SIC: 2541 2431 Mfg Wood Partitions/Fixtures Mfg Millwork

(G-3509)
NICKSON INDUSTRIES INC
336 Woodford Ave (06062-2487)
PHONE..................................860 747-1671
Ilan Ginga, *President*
Tasdelen Ozlem, *Controller*
▲ **EMP:** 48 **EST:** 1968
SQ FT: 100,000
SALES (est): 10.8MM
SALES (corp-wide): 30.1MM **Privately Held**
WEB: www.nickson.com
SIC: 3714 Mfg Motor Vehicle Parts/Accessories
PA: Metapoint Partners, A Limited Partnership
108 Beach St
Manchester MA 01944
978 531-1398

(G-3510)
OLSON BROTHERS COMPANY
272 Camp St (06062-1612)
P.O. Box 188 (06062-0188)
PHONE..................................860 747-6844
Robert R Carroll, *CEO*
Christopher Carroll, *President*
EMP: 16
SQ FT: 7,000

GEOGRAPHIC

SALES (est): 1.9MM **Privately Held**
WEB: www.obcinc.net
SIC: 3451 Mfg Screw Machine Products

(G-3511)
PLAINVILLE PLATING COMPANY INC
21 Forestville Ave (06062-2159)
P.O. Box 219 (06062-0219)
PHONE..................................860 747-1624
Gerald Glassman, *Ch of Bd*
Charles L Pratt, *President*
Roy Manzie, *Opers Staff*
Jay R Fienman, *Treasurer*
Richard Bochenek, *Director*
EMP: 60 **EST:** 1920
SQ FT: 23,000
SALES (est): 7.5MM **Privately Held**
WEB: www.plainvilleplating.com
SIC: 3471 Plating/Polishing Service

(G-3512)
PRALINES OF PLAINVILLE
107 New Britain Ave (06062-2073)
PHONE..................................860 410-1151
Jim Scarfo, *Owner*
EMP: 4
SALES (est): 167.7K **Privately Held**
SIC: 2024 Mfg Ice Cream/Frozen Desert

(G-3513)
R J BRASS INC
26 Ashford Rd (06062-1236)
PHONE..................................860 793-2336
EMP: 10
SQ FT: 15,000
SALES (est): 700K **Privately Held**
SIC: 3471 Buffing & Polishing

(G-3514)
ROAD-FIT ENTERPRISES LLC
98 Whiting St (06062-2881)
PHONE..................................860 371-5137
James A Cole,
EMP: 3
SALES (est): 120.5K **Privately Held**
SIC: 3949 Mfg Sporting/Athletic Goods

(G-3515)
STYLAIR LLC
161 Woodford Ave (06062-2370)
P.O. Box 7014 (06062-7014)
PHONE..................................860 747-4588
Roger Kidwell,
Pelly Esposito,
EMP: 14
SQ FT: 8,000
SALES (est): 3.6MM **Privately Held**
WEB: www.stylair.com
SIC: 3564 3563 Mfg Blowers/Fans Mfg Air/Gas Compressors

(G-3516)
SUPERIOR ELC HOLDG GROUP LLC (HQ)
1 Cowles Rd (06062-1107)
PHONE..................................860 582-9561
Julian Watt, *COO*
Pam Metzer, *CFO*
Michael Miga, *Sales Dir*
Ted Gladis, *Marketing Mgr*
James Greeno, *Manager*
▲ **EMP:** 34
SQ FT: 27,000
SALES (est): 3.9MM
SALES (corp-wide): 19.8B **Publicly Held**
SIC: 3612 Mfg Transformers
PA: Danaher Corporation
2200 Penn Ave Nw Ste 800w
Washington DC 20037
202 828-0850

(G-3517)
SYMAN MACHINE LLC
161 Woodford Ave Ste 5b (06062-2336)
PHONE..................................860 747-8337
EMP: 3
SALES (est): 330K **Privately Held**
SIC: 3541 Mfg Machine Tools-Cutting

(G-3518)
TACO FASTENERS INC
71 Northwest Dr (06062-1101)
P.O. Box 338 (06062-0338)
PHONE..................................860 747-5597
Arnold Finn, *President*
Marguerite Finn, *Admin Sec*
EMP: 10
SQ FT: 10,000
SALES (est): 1.5MM **Privately Held**
SIC: 3469 3544 Mfg Metal Stampings Mfg Dies/Tools/Jigs/Fixtures

(G-3519)
TETCO INC
4 Northwest Dr (06062-1311)
PHONE..................................860 747-1280
Sandra T Simmons, *President*
Sandra Thibault, *President*
George Simmons, *Vice Pres*
EMP: 15
SQ FT: 14,000
SALES: 1MM **Privately Held**
SIC: 3541 Manufacturer Of & Reconditions Centerless Grinding Work Rest Blades

(G-3520)
TOP FLIGHT MACHINE TOOL LLC
Also Called: Aircraft
90 Robert Jackson Way (06062-2650)
PHONE..................................860 747-4726
Stanley Kusmider,
EMP: 9
SALES (est): 1.7MM **Privately Held**
SIC: 3599 Manufacturing Aircraft Medical & Ind

(G-3521)
TRANSIT SYSTEMS INC
161 Woodford Ave Ste 34 (06062-2369)
PHONE..................................860 747-3669
Jeffrey Yost, *President*
Walter J Lappen, *Treasurer*
Walter Lappen, *CTO*
Fred Weingarten, *Technology*
EMP: 7
SQ FT: 8,000
SALES (est): 1.2MM **Privately Held**
SIC: 3743 Mfg Railroad Equipment

(G-3522)
TRUMPF INC
3 Johnson Ave (06062)
PHONE..................................860 255-6000
Shelia Lamothe, *Manager*
EMP: 262
SALES (corp-wide): 4.2B **Privately Held**
SIC: 3542 3546 3423 Mfg Machine Tools-Forming Mfg Power-Driven Handtools Mfg Hand/Edge Tools
HQ: Trumpf, Inc.
111 Hyde Rd
Farmington CT 06032
860 255-6000

(G-3523)
VAB INC
49 Johnson Ave (06062-1155)
P.O. Box 349, New Hartford (06057-0349)
PHONE..................................860 793-0246
Victor Tomasso Sr, *President*
Victor F Tomass0, *Director*
EMP: 5
SALES (est): 356.3K **Privately Held**
WEB: www.vytas.net
SIC: 1382 Oil/Gas Exploration Services

(G-3524)
ZEECO INC
80 Spring Ln (06062-1151)
PHONE..................................860 479-0999
EMP: 5 **Privately Held**
SIC: 3433 Mfg Heating Equipment-Non-electric
HQ: Zeeco, Inc.
22151 E 91st St S
Broken Arrow OK 74014
918 258-8551

Plantsville
Hartford County

(G-3525)
ACCUBEND LLC
1657 Mrden Wtrbury Tpke (06479)
P.O. Box 532 (06479-0532)
PHONE..................................860 378-0303
Ron Dehnel,
EMP: 3
SALES: 200K **Privately Held**
SIC: 3542 Mfg Machine Tools-Forming

(G-3526)
AMERICAN METAL MASTERS LLC
Also Called: American Metal Master Mch Tl
141 Summer St (06479-1156)
PHONE..................................860 621-6911
Frank Carbone,
Doreen Sward,
EMP: 3
SQ FT: 7,000
SALES (est): 145.7K **Privately Held**
SIC: 3599 3511 3492 Mfg Industrial Machinery Mfg Turbines/Generator Sets Mfg Fluid Power Valves/Fittings

(G-3527)
ATHENS INDUSTRIES INC
220 West St (06479-1145)
P.O. Box 487, Southington (06489-0487)
PHONE..................................860 621-8957
Richard Emmings Sr, *President*
EMP: 9
SQ FT: 5,000
SALES (est): 1.7MM **Privately Held**
SIC: 3728 Mfg Aircraft Parts/Equipment

(G-3528)
CLINICAL DYNAMICS CONN LLC
1210 Mrden Waterbury Tpke (06479-2024)
PHONE..................................203 269-0090
Joe Rebot,
EMP: 9
SALES (est): 1.1MM **Privately Held**
SIC: 3841 Mfg Surgical/Medical Instruments

(G-3529)
DEBURR CO
201 Atwater St (06479-1653)
P.O. Box 24 (06479-0024)
PHONE..................................860 621-6634
Ben Divalentino, *President*
Gino Brino, *Vice Pres*
EMP: 27
SQ FT: 6,500
SALES (est): 2.1MM **Privately Held**
WEB: www.deburr.com
SIC: 3471 Plating/Polishing Service

(G-3530)
FORRATI MANUFACTURING & TL LLC
411 Summer St (06479-1122)
PHONE..................................860 426-1105
Mark Forauer, *Mng Member*
EMP: 7
SALES (est): 997.4K **Privately Held**
SIC: 3599 Mfg Industrial Machinery

(G-3531)
G M T MANUFACTURING CO INC
Also Called: Gmt Mfg
220 West St (06479-1145)
P.O. Box 324 (06479-0324)
PHONE..................................860 628-6757
Guy Touma, *President*
EMP: 8 **EST:** 1947
SQ FT: 11,000
SALES: 500K **Privately Held**
SIC: 3451 Mfg Screw Machine Products

(G-3532)
GRANITECH LLC
409 Canal St Ste 4 (06479-1751)
PHONE..................................860 620-1733
Brendan O'Connor,
Brendan O Connor,
EMP: 6
SALES (est): 641.4K **Privately Held**
SIC: 3281 Mfg Cut Stone/Products

(G-3533)
INNOVATIVE COMPONENTS LLC
635 Old Turnpike Rd (06479-1608)
PHONE..................................860 621-7220
Michael Meade, *Mng Member*
EMP: 6
SQ FT: 3,200
SALES (est): 859K **Privately Held**
WEB: www.innovativecomponents.com
SIC: 3823 Mfg Process Control Instruments

(G-3534)
J J RYAN CORPORATION
Also Called: Rex Forge Div
355 Atwater St (06479-1653)
P.O. Box 39 (06479-0039)
PHONE..................................860 628-0393
Ronald Fontanella, *President*
Mark Dudzinski, *Manager*
Joseph P Polzella, *Admin Sec*
EMP: 170 **EST:** 1975
SQ FT: 150,000
SALES (est): 43.2MM **Privately Held**
WEB: www.jjryanradio.com
SIC: 3312 3423 3451 3462 Blast Furnace-Steel Work Mfg Hand/Edge Tools Mfg Screw Machine Prdts Mfg Iron/Steel Forgings

(G-3535)
KC CRAFTS LLC
384 Old Turnpike Rd (06479-1566)
PHONE..................................860 426-9797
Normand Charette,
EMP: 6
SQ FT: 8,000
SALES (est): 830.5K **Privately Held**
WEB: www.kccrafts.com
SIC: 3625 Mfg Relays/Industrial Controls

(G-3536)
LADRDEFENSE LLC
Also Called: Krav Maga Southington
243 Canal St (06479-1734)
PHONE..................................860 637-8488
Robert Rand, *Principal*
EMP: 3
SALES (est): 176.3K **Privately Held**
SIC: 3812 7371 Mfg Search/Navigation Equipment Custom Computer Programing

(G-3537)
NATIONAL MAGNETIC SENSORS INC
141 Summer St Ste 3 (06479-1154)
P.O. Box 64 (06479-0064)
PHONE..................................860 621-6816
Robert J Bardoorian, *President*
Margaret Bardoorian, *Corp Secy*
Michael Bardoorian, *Vice Pres*
EMP: 6
SQ FT: 3,000
SALES (est): 510K **Privately Held**
WEB: www.nationalmagnetic.com
SIC: 3823 Mfg Process Control Instruments

(G-3538)
RM PRINTING
384 Old Turnpike Rd (06479-1566)
P.O. Box 485 (06479-0485)
PHONE..................................860 621-0498
Bill Trainor, *Partner*
James Mac Donald, *Partner*
EMP: 5 **EST:** 1977
SQ FT: 6,000
SALES: 390K **Privately Held**
WEB: www.rmprinting.com
SIC: 2752 Lithographic Commercial Printing

(G-3539)
SIGN PRO INC
60 Westfield Dr (06479-1753)
PHONE..................................860 229-1812
Peter Rappoccio, *President*
Keith Dubois, *General Mgr*
Chelseah Carroll, *Project Mgr*
Rob Mulcunry, *Prdtn Mgr*
Suzanne Rappoccio, *Admin Sec*
EMP: 15
SQ FT: 16,000
SALES (est): 349.2K **Privately Held**
WEB: www.signpro-usa.com
SIC: 3993 Mfg Signs/Advertising Specialties

(G-3540)
SOUTHINGTON TOOL & MFG CORP
Also Called: Stmc
300 Atwater St (06479-1643)
P.O. Box 595, Southington (06489-0595)
PHONE..................................860 276-0021
Lynette Nadeau, *President*
Edward Kalat, *Principal*
Arthur Pfaff, *Sales Staff*
EMP: 37
SQ FT: 25,000
SALES (est): 5MM **Privately Held**
WEB: www.stmc.com
SIC: 3841 3469 3495 Mfg Surgical/Medical Instruments Mfg Metal Stampings Mfg Wire Springs

(G-3541)
SUPREME-LAKE MFG INC
455 Atwater St (06479-1666)
P.O. Box 19 (06479-0019)
PHONE..................................860 621-8911
Gary N Dobrindt, *President*
Richard L Fazzone, *General Mgr*
Dave Cano, *Vice Pres*
David A Cano, *Vice Pres*
Troy Fazzone, *Vice Pres*
▲ **EMP:** 85
SQ FT: 42,739
SALES (est): 35MM **Privately Held**
SIC: 3451 Mfg Sc Rew Machine Products

(G-3542)
TIGER ENTERPRISES INC
379 Summer St (06479-1149)
PHONE..................................860 621-9155
Rex Florian, *President*
Lance Florian, *Corp Secy*
EMP: 28
SQ FT: 30,000
SALES: 3.2MM **Privately Held**
WEB: www.tigerstamping.com
SIC: 3469 3496 3429 3423 Mfg Metal Stampings Mfg Misc Fab Wire Prdts Mfg Hardware Mfg Hand/Edge Tools

(G-3543)
TORREY S CRANE COMPANY
492 Summer St (06479-1123)
P.O. Box 374 (06479-0374)
PHONE..................................860 628-4778
David Baker, *President*
Barbara Baker, *Vice Pres*
▲ **EMP:** 25
SQ FT: 10,000
SALES (est): 4.9MM **Privately Held**
SIC: 3356 Nonferrous Rolling/Drawing

(G-3544)
UNITED STATES CHEMICAL CORP
609 Old Turnpike Rd (06479-1664)
P.O. Box 293 (06479-0293)
PHONE..................................860 621-6831
Jim Rawn, *President*
David Govoni, *Exec VP*
Coral Rawn, *Admin Sec*
▲ **EMP:** 6
SQ FT: 6,000
SALES: 1.5MM **Privately Held**
SIC: 2899 2841 Mfg Metal Finishing Compounds & Detergent Metal Cleaners

Pleasant Valley
Litchfield County

(G-3545)
GOULET ENTERPRISES INC
Also Called: Goulet Printery
115 New Hartford Rd (06063-3350)
PHONE..................................860 379-0793
Paul Goulet, *President*
Barbara Goulet, *Corp Secy*
Dennis M Goulet, *Vice Pres*
Richard Goulet, *Asst Treas*
Cyril Goulet, *Asst Sec*
EMP: 16
SQ FT: 10,000
SALES (est): 2.3MM **Privately Held**
SIC: 2752 Lithographic Commercial Printing

(G-3546)
PLEASANT VALLEY FENCE CO INC
Also Called: Bazzano, J Cedar Products
Rr 181 (06063)
P.O. Box 153 (06063-0153)
PHONE..................................860 379-0088
Katherine Bazzano, *President*
Richard Bazzano, *Vice Pres*
Pat Bazzano, *Treasurer*
Pasquale Bazzano, *Admin Sec*
EMP: 12
SQ FT: 1,115
SALES (est): 1.6MM **Privately Held**
WEB: www.pleasantvalleyfence.com
SIC: 2499 3999 Mfg Wood Products Mfg Misc Products

(G-3547)
STERLING ENGINEERING CORP
236 New Hartford Rd (06063-3345)
P.O. Box 559, Winsted (06098-0559)
PHONE..................................860 379-3366
John N Lavieri, *President*
Bob Emerson, *Software Dev*
Judy Boyle, *Director*
Patricia L Minton, *Admin Sec*
▲ **EMP:** 105
SQ FT: 75,000
SALES (est): 17.6MM **Publicly Held**
WEB: www.sterlingeng.com
SIC: 3599 3769 Mfg Industrial Machinery Mfg Space Vehicle Equipment
PA: Air Industries Group
1460 5th Ave
Bay Shore NY 11706

(G-3548)
TRU HITCH INC
16 W West Hill Rd (06063-3221)
PHONE..................................860 379-7772
Martin Marola, *President*
Anthony Cuozzo, *Corp Secy*
EMP: 12
SQ FT: 13,000
SALES (est): 2.4MM **Privately Held**
SIC: 3714 Mfg Fifth Wheel Towing Hitches

Plymouth
Litchfield County

(G-3549)
WASP ARCHERY PRODUCTS INC
707 Main St (06782-2243)
P.O. Box 303 (06782-0303)
PHONE..................................860 283-0246
Richard C Maleski, *President*
Karen Maleski, *Admin Sec*
EMP: 5 **EST:** 1972
SQ FT: 11,000
SALES (est): 1.5MM **Privately Held**
WEB: www.wasparchery.com
SIC: 3949 Mfg Archery Arrowheads

Pomfret
Windham County

(G-3550)
FIBEROPTICS TECHNOLOGY INC (PA)
1 Quasset Rd (06258)
P.O. Box 286 (06258-0286)
PHONE..................................860 928-0443
Joan Loos, *Chairman*
Tim Chiou, *CFO*
Richard Griswold, *Treasurer*
Steve Giamundo, *Chief Mktg Ofcr*
Stan Chmura, *Info Tech Mgr*
▲ **EMP:** 110 **EST:** 1977
SQ FT: 62,000
SALES (est): 17.6MM **Privately Held**
WEB: www.fiberoptix.com
SIC: 3357 Nonferrous Wiredrawing/Insulating

(G-3551)
FIBEROPTICS TECHNOLOGY INC
1 Fiber Rd (06258-8003)
PHONE..................................860 928-0443
August Loos, *Branch Mgr*
EMP: 100
SALES (corp-wide): 17.6MM **Privately Held**
WEB: www.fiberoptix.com
SIC: 3229 Mfg Pressed/Blown Glass
PA: Fiberoptics Technology, Inc.
1 Quasset Rd
Pomfret CT 06258
860 928-0443

(G-3552)
LOOS & CO INC (PA)
Also Called: Wire Rope Div
16b Mashamoquet Rd (06258)
P.O. Box 98 (06258-0098)
PHONE..................................860 928-7981
William Loos, *President*
Richard Griswold, *President*
Russ Cox, *Vice Pres*
Alan Jaaskela, *VP Opers*
Richard Graham, *Production*
◆ **EMP:** 300 **EST:** 1989
SQ FT: 175,000
SALES: 60MM **Privately Held**
WEB: www.loosnaples.com
SIC: 3357 3315 5051 2298 Nonfrs Wire-drwng/Insltng Mfg Steel Wire/Rltd Prdt Metals Service Center Mfg Cordage/Twine

(G-3553)
LOOS & CO INC
Jewel Wire Company
Rr 101 (06258)
P.O. Box 282 (06258-0282)
PHONE..................................860 928-6681
Samuel Dixon, *General Mgr*
EMP: 13
SALES (corp-wide): 60MM **Privately Held**
WEB: www.loosnaples.com
SIC: 3315 3991 Mfg Steel Wire/Related Products Mfg Brooms/Brushes
PA: Loos & Co., Inc.
16b Mashamoquet Rd
Pomfret CT 06258
860 928-7981

(G-3554)
SHARPE HILL VINEYARD INC
108 Wade Rd (06258)
P.O. Box 1 (06258-0001)
PHONE..................................860 974-3549
Steven Vollweiler, *President*
Catherine Vollweiler, *Co-President*
Jill R Vollweiler, *Treasurer*
EMP: 30
SQ FT: 11,000
SALES (est): 4.1MM **Privately Held**
WEB: www.sharpehill.com
SIC: 2084 5812 Mfg Wines/Brandy/Spirits Eating Place

Pomfret Center
Windham County

(G-3555)
JAKES JR LAWRENCE
Also Called: J & J Moulding
405 Brooklyn Rd (06259-2403)
PHONE..................................860 974-3744
Lawrence Jakes Jr, *Owner*
EMP: 22
SALES (est): 1.2MM **Privately Held**
SIC: 2431 Custom Wood Moldings

(G-3556)
LLC GLASS HOUSE
Also Called: Glasshouse
50 Swedetown Rd (06259-1014)
PHONE..................................860 974-1665
James Potrezeba,
EMP: 5
SALES (est): 524.1K **Privately Held**
SIC: 3448 Mfg Prefabricated Aluminum Clad & Wood Buildings

(G-3557)
MTR PRECISION MACHINING INC
60a Bradley Rd (06259-1501)
PHONE..................................860 928-9440
Michael E Gibeault, *President*
Thomas St Jean, *Vice Pres*
EMP: 4
SQ FT: 864
SALES: 218K **Privately Held**
SIC: 3599 Mfg Industrial Machinery

(G-3558)
NESTLE USA INC
151 Mashamoquet Rd (06259)
PHONE..................................860 928-0082
Peter Argentine, *Branch Mgr*
EMP: 139
SALES (corp-wide): 92.8B **Privately Held**
WEB: www.nestleusa.com
SIC: 2023 Mfg Dry/Evaporated Dairy Products
HQ: Nestle Usa, Inc.
1812 N Moore St Ste 118
Rosslyn VA 22209
818 549-6000

(G-3559)
TONMAR LLC
Also Called: Majilly
56 Babbitt Hill Rd (06259-1700)
PHONE..................................860 974-3714
Tony Emilio,
Martha Emilio,
▲ **EMP:** 3
SALES: 990K **Privately Held**
WEB: www.majilly.com
SIC: 3269 Design & Mfg Of Ceramic Wear

Poquonock
Hartford County

(G-3560)
PREVENTATIVE MAINTENANCE CORP
55 Tunxis St (06064)
PHONE..................................860 683-1180
Richard Rzasa, *President*
Pamela Rzasa, *Treasurer*
▲ **EMP:** 10
SQ FT: 3,000
SALES: 200K **Privately Held**
WEB: www.presat.com
SIC: 3471 Mfg Cleaning Cards

Portland
Middlesex County

(G-3561)
AMERICAN MACHINING TECH INC
141 Pickering St (06480-1961)
PHONE..................................860 342-0005
Craig Gervais, *President*
Tracy Gervais, *Admin Sec*
EMP: 5
SQ FT: 2,500
SALES: 475K **Privately Held**
SIC: 3599 Mfg Industrial Machinery

(G-3562)
ARRIGONI WINERY
209 Sand Hill Rd (06480-1774)
PHONE..................................860 342-1999
Edward B Manner, *Principal*
EMP: 3
SALES (est): 248.3K **Privately Held**
SIC: 2084 Mfg Wines/Brandy/Spirits

(G-3563)
B & B EQUIPMENT LLC
80 Main St Ste D (06480-4825)
PHONE..................................860 342-5773
Stephen J Bankowski,
Peter J Bankowski,
EMP: 8
SQ FT: 45,000
SALES (est): 1.2MM **Privately Held**
SIC: 3565 Mfg Packaging Machinery

GEOGRAPHIC

(G-3564)
BIMBO BAKERIES USA INC
9 Freedom Way (06480-1058)
PHONE.................................860 691-1180
EMP: 23 **Privately Held**
SIC: 2051 Mfg Bread/Related Products
HQ: Bimbo Bakeries Usa, Inc
255 Business Center Dr # 200
Horsham PA 19044
215 347-5500

(G-3565)
CLONDALKIN PHARMA & HEALTHCARE
264 Freestone Ave (06480-1640)
PHONE.................................860 342-1987
EMP: 27
SALES (corp-wide): 1.3B **Privately Held**
SIC: 2657 Mfg Folding Paperboard Boxes
HQ: Clondalkin Pharma & Healthcare, Inc
1072 Boulder Rd
Greensboro NC 46268
336 292-4555

(G-3566)
DEEP RIVER FUEL TERMINALS LLC
29 Myrtle Rd (06480-1643)
P.O. Box 32 (06480-0032)
PHONE.................................860 342-4619
David J Daniels, *Principal*
EMP: 3
SALES (est): 350.5K **Privately Held**
SIC: 2869 Mfg Industrial Organic Chemicals

(G-3567)
DURBIN MACHINE INC
101 Airline Ave (06480-1908)
P.O. Box 237, Bombay NY (12914-0237)
PHONE.................................860 342-1602
Gil Durbin Jr, *President*
EMP: 5
SQ FT: 2,600
SALES: 250K **Privately Held**
SIC: 3599 Machine Shop

(G-3568)
JARVIS AIRFOIL INC
528 Glastonbury Tpke (06480-1099)
PHONE.................................860 342-5000
Wal Jarvis, *President*
Elaine Nichols, *Production*
Thomas Flanagan, *QC Mgr*
Greg Terwilliger, *QC Mgr*
Michael Hrubiec, *Engineer*
▲ **EMP:** 88 **EST:** 1954
SQ FT: 50,000
SALES (est): 16.3MM
SALES (corp-wide): 20.4MM **Privately Held**
WEB: www.jarvisairfoil.com
SIC: 3728 Mfg Aircraft Parts/Equipment
PA: Jarvis Group, Inc.
229 Buckingham St
Hartford CT
860 278-2353

(G-3569)
LA CHANCE CONTROLS
175 Penfield Hill Rd (06480-1352)
PHONE.................................860 342-2212
Ronald Lachance, *Owner*
Ronald La Chance, *Owner*
EMP: 3
SALES: 400K **Privately Held**
SIC: 3613 Mfg Switchgear/Switchboards

(G-3570)
PORTLAND SLITTING CO INC
193 Pickering St (06480-1961)
PHONE.................................860 342-1500
James Riotte, *President*
EMP: 3
SALES (est): 290K **Privately Held**
SIC: 3312 Blast Furnace-Steel Works

(G-3571)
PRECISION PLASTIC PRODUCTS INC
151 Freestone Ave (06480-1641)
PHONE.................................860 342-2233
Edward Organek Sr, *President*
Edward Organek Jr, *Vice Pres*
Rosemarie Organek, *Admin Sec*
▲ **EMP:** 14 **EST:** 1981
SQ FT: 17,000
SALES (est): 2.5MM **Privately Held**
SIC: 3089 Mfg Plastic Products

(G-3572)
QUALITY WELDING SERVICE LLC
265 Brownstone Ave (06480-1803)
PHONE.................................860 342-7202
James Vacca, *Mng Member*
Joy Vacca,
EMP: 3
SALES (est): 374.7K **Privately Held**
SIC: 7692 3548 Welding Repair Mfg Welding Apparatus

(G-3573)
REDIFOILS LLC
193 Pickering St (06480-1961)
PHONE.................................860 342-1500
Ketan Patel, *Mng Member*
Tushar Patel,
▲ **EMP:** 10
SQ FT: 10,000
SALES (est): 3.3MM **Privately Held**
WEB: www.redifoilsllc.com
SIC: 3312 Blast Furnace-Steel Works

(G-3574)
RIVER VALLEY OIL SERVICE LLC
695 Portland Cobalt Rd (06480-1725)
P.O. Box 866, Middletown (06457-0866)
PHONE.................................860 342-5670
John Dimauro, *Mng Member*
Michael Dimauro,
EMP: 3
SALES (est): 302.5K **Privately Held**
SIC: 1311 Crude Petroleum/Natural Gas Production

(G-3575)
STANDARD-KNAPP INC
63 Pickering St (06480-1957)
PHONE.................................860 342-1100
James Michael Weaver, *President*
Mark Jehinges, *COO*
Tara Bogucki, *Accountant*
Edward Bartus, *Marketing Mgr*
Bob Otfinoski, *Manager*
▲ **EMP:** 55 **EST:** 1893
SQ FT: 50,000
SALES (est): 21.4MM
SALES (corp-wide): 355.8K **Privately Held**
WEB: www.standard-knapp.com
SIC: 3565 Mfg Packaging Machinery
PA: Eol Packaging Experts Gmbh
Industriestr. 11-13
Kirchlengern

(G-3576)
SUPERIOR CONCRETE PRODUCTS LLC
830 Portland Cobalt Rd (06480-1731)
P.O. Box 17 (06480-0017)
PHONE.................................860 342-0186
Joseph Labbadia, *Partner*
William Buggie, *Partner*
EMP: 3 **EST:** 1952
SQ FT: 3,200
SALES (est): 505.8K **Privately Held**
SIC: 3272 Manufactures Concrete Septic Tanks And Steps From Prefabricated Concrete

(G-3577)
TILCON CONNECTICUT INC
Also Called: Tilcon Bituminous Concrete
231 Airline Ave (06480-1926)
PHONE.................................860 342-6157
Ben Norris, *Manager*
EMP: 4
SALES (corp-wide): 29.7B **Privately Held**
WEB: www.tilconct.com
SIC: 2951 Mfg Asphalt Mixtures/Blocks
HQ: Tilcon Connecticut Inc.
642 Black Rock Ave
New Britain CT 06052
860 224-6010

(G-3578)
TILCON CONNECTICUT INC
Also Called: Tilcon Connecticut Portland
Black Rock Ave (06480)
P.O. Box 311228, Newington (06131-1228)
PHONE.................................860 342-1096
Joel Edman, *Manager*
EMP: 8
SALES (corp-wide): 29.7B **Privately Held**
WEB: www.tilconct.com
SIC: 3273 Mfg Ready-Mixed Concrete
HQ: Tilcon Connecticut Inc.
642 Black Rock Ave
New Britain CT 06052
860 224-6010

(G-3579)
TRANSPORTATION CONN DEPT
Also Called: Portland Connecticut Mch Sp
263 Freestone Ave (06480-1641)
PHONE.................................860 342-5996
Peter Mrowka, *Manager*
EMP: 7 **Privately Held**
WEB: www.grotonnewlondonairport.com
SIC: 3599 9621 Mfg Industrial Machinery Regulation/Administrative Transportation
HQ: Connecticut Department Of Transportation
2800 Berlin Tpke
Newington CT 06111

Preston
New London County

(G-3580)
FINANCIAL PRTG SOLUTIONS LLC
21a River Rd (06365-8024)
PHONE.................................860 886-9931
Stephen C Behrens, *Principal*
EMP: 4
SALES (est): 550.2K **Privately Held**
SIC: 2752 Lithographic Commercial Printing

(G-3581)
HYTEK PLUMBING AND HEATING LLC
241 Krug Rd (06365-8004)
PHONE.................................860 389-1122
Thomas Kaiser, *CEO*
EMP: 6
SALES (est): 250.1K **Privately Held**
SIC: 3494 Mfg Valves/Pipe Fittings

(G-3582)
PRESTON RIDGE VINEYARD LLC
26 Miller Rd (06365-8515)
PHONE.................................860 383-4278
Stephen J Sawyer, *Principal*
EMP: 6
SALES (est): 600.7K **Privately Held**
SIC: 2084 Mfg Wines/Brandy/Spirits

Prospect
New Haven County

(G-3583)
BEN ART MANUFACTURING CO INC
109 Waterbury Rd (06712-1295)
PHONE.................................203 758-4435
Benny A Paventy, *President*
Albert M Paventy, *Vice Pres*
Robert Paventy, *Treasurer*
EMP: 7 **EST:** 1952
SQ FT: 9,900
SALES: 800K **Privately Held**
SIC: 3469 Mfg Metal Stampings

(G-3584)
C F D ENGINEERING COMPANY (PA)
194 Cook Rd (06712-1899)
PHONE.................................203 758-4148
William Flaherty, *President*
William A Finn III, *Vice Pres*
EMP: 20
SQ FT: 2,400
SALES (est): 1.5MM **Privately Held**
WEB: www.naugatuckmfg.com
SIC: 3469 Mfg Stamped Metal Products

(G-3585)
COMMSCOPE TECHNOLOGIES LLC
33 Union City Rd Ste 2 (06712-1550)
PHONE.................................203 699-4100
Peter Sandore, *Branch Mgr*
EMP: 10 **Publicly Held**
WEB: www.andrew.com
SIC: 3663 Mfg Radio/Tv Communication Equipment
HQ: Commscope Technologies Llc
1100 Commscope Pl Se
Hickory NC 28602
708 236-6600

(G-3586)
CURTISS WOODWORKING INC
123 Union City Rd (06712-1030)
PHONE.................................203 527-9305
Dale R Curtiss, *President*
Lisa Curtiss, *Vice Pres*
Isabelle Curtiss, *Admin Sec*
EMP: 12
SQ FT: 10,000
SALES (est): 2.3MM **Privately Held**
WEB: www.curtisswoodworking.com
SIC: 2599 2431 Mfg Furniture/Fixtures Mfg Millwork

(G-3587)
DAVES PAVING AND CONSTRUCTION
105 Waterbury Rd Ste 5 (06712-1233)
PHONE.................................203 753-4992
David Coretto, *Owner*
EMP: 3
SQ FT: 2,000
SALES: 200K **Privately Held**
SIC: 3531 Paving Driveways

(G-3588)
MARC TOOL & DIE INC
23 Oak Ln (06712-1315)
PHONE.................................203 758-5933
Gaetan Marcoux, *President*
Marie Marcoux, *Principal*
Bart Marcoux, *Vice Pres*
EMP: 3
SALES (est): 150K **Privately Held**
SIC: 3544 Mfg Dies/Tools/Jigs/Fixtures

(G-3589)
MARIO PRECISION PRODUCTS
19 Wihbey Dr (06712-1466)
PHONE.................................203 758-3101
Mario Dias, *Owner*
EMP: 3
SALES: 50K **Privately Held**
SIC: 3451 Mfg Screw Machine Products

(G-3590)
OXFORD GENERAL INDUSTRIES INC
3 Gramar Ave (06712-1017)
P.O. Box 7033 (06712-0033)
PHONE.................................203 758-4467
D L Carnaroli, *Vice Pres*
Brian Barrett, *Vice Pres*
Donna L Carnaroli, *Vice Pres*
Gordon Eckman, *Vice Pres*
EMP: 11
SQ FT: 25,000
SALES (est): 1.8MM **Privately Held**
SIC: 3499 3544 3542 Mfg Misc Fabricated Metal Products Mfg Dies/Tools/Jigs/Fixtures Mfg Machine Tools-Forming

(G-3591)
PACKARD INC
Also Called: Packard Specialties
6 Industrial Rd (06712-1018)
P.O. Box 7238 (06712-0238)
PHONE.................................203 758-6219
John F Jones, *President*
Carol Jones, *Vice Pres*
Paul Bird, *Engineer*
EMP: 20 **EST:** 1980
SQ FT: 15,000

SALES (est): 4.4MM Privately Held
WEB: www.packardinc.com
SIC: 3565 3569 Mfg Packaging Machinery Mfg General Industrial Machinery

(G-3592)
POLAR INDUSTRIES INC (PA)
32 Gramar Ave (06712-1016)
P.O. Box 7075 (06712-0075)
PHONE....................203 758-6651
Eugene R Lewis, *Ch of Bd*
David L Lewis, *President*
Mike Accuosti, *Controller*
▲ EMP: 35
SALES (est): 6.4MM Privately Held
WEB: www.polarcentral.com
SIC: 2821 Mfg Plastic Materials/Resins

(G-3593)
PROSPECT MACHINE PRODUCTS INC
139 Union City Rd (06712-1031)
P.O. Box 7016 (06712-0016)
PHONE....................203 758-4448
Richard Laurenzi, *President*
David Boiano, *Engineer*
EMP: 23
SQ FT: 20,000
SALES (est): 6.8MM Privately Held
SIC: 3469 8711 Mfg Metal Stampings Engineering Services

(G-3594)
PROSPECT PRINTING LLC
16 Waterbury Rd (06712-1255)
P.O. Box 7242 (06712-0242)
PHONE....................203 758-6007
Angela Halloran, *Cust Mgr*
Mark Deloia,
Mike Ambrose,
Anthony Bracco,
EMP: 10
SQ FT: 5,500
SALES (est): 1.8MM Privately Held
SIC: 2752 Lithographic Commercial Printing

(G-3595)
RED BARN INNOVATIONS
Also Called: Friction Force
8 Tress Rd (06712-1727)
PHONE....................203 393-0778
Thomas Allen, *Owner*
EMP: 5
SALES: 0 Privately Held
SIC: 3569 Mfg General Industrial Machinery

(G-3596)
SGA COMPONENTS GROUP LLC
13 Gramar Ave (06712-1017)
PHONE....................203 758-3702
Robert N Morin,
EMP: 8
SQ FT: 5,000
SALES (est): 600K Privately Held
WEB: www.sgalt.com
SIC: 3451 Mfg Screws Machine Products

(G-3597)
SHELDON PRECISION LLC
10 Industrial Rd (06712-1018)
PHONE....................203 758-4441
John Hoskins Jr, *CEO*
EMP: 50
SQ FT: 17,500
SALES: 12MM Privately Held
SIC: 3451 Mfg Screw Machine Products

(G-3598)
THERMO CONDUCTOR SERVICES INC
3 Industrial Rd (06712-1039)
P.O. Box 7191 (06712-0191)
PHONE....................203 758-6611
Mark Baker, *President*
▲ EMP: 5
SALES (est): 1MM Privately Held
SIC: 3312 Blast Furnace-Steel Works

(G-3599)
TSS & A INC
Also Called: Triple Stitch Sportswear
115 Waterbury Rd (06712-1254)
P.O. Box 7036 (06712-0036)
PHONE....................800 633-3536
Joseph Commendatore, *President*
Nicholas D'Eramo, *Vice Pres*
EMP: 13
SQ FT: 3,000
SALES (est): 1.5MM Privately Held
WEB: www.triplestitch.com
SIC: 2395 7336 Pleating/Stitching Services Commercial Art/Graphic Design

Putnam
Windham County

(G-3600)
AEROTECH FASTENERS INC
1 Ridge Rd (06260-3034)
PHONE....................860 928-6300
Erik Sandberg-Diment, *President*
Frank Di Rienzo, *Vice Pres*
EMP: 13
SQ FT: 18,000
SALES (est): 2MM Privately Held
WEB: www.aerotechfasteners.com
SIC: 3452 Mfg Bolts/Screws/Rivets

(G-3601)
APOGEE CORPORATION (PA)
Also Called: Impact Plastics
5 Highland Dr (06260-3010)
PHONE....................860 963-1976
Christopher L Ryan, *Principal*
David Kingeter, *Chairman*
Steven M Ryan, *Treasurer*
▲ EMP: 60 EST: 1970
SALES (est): 10MM Privately Held
WEB: www.impactplastics-ct.com
SIC: 3081 Mfg Unsupported Plastic Film/Sheet

(G-3602)
BARNES CONCRETE CO INC
873 Providence Pike (06260-2606)
PHONE....................860 928-7242
David Barnes, *President*
Bruce Barnes, *Vice Pres*
EMP: 20
SQ FT: 2,500
SALES: 4MM Privately Held
SIC: 3273 Mfg Ready-Mixed Concrete

(G-3603)
CASTROL INDUSTRIAL N AMER INC
251 Kennedy Dr (06260-1628)
PHONE....................860 928-5100
Dan Caissie, *Branch Mgr*
EMP: 5
SALES (corp-wide): 298.7B Privately Held
SIC: 2992 Automotive Services
HQ: Castrol Industrial North America Inc.
150 W Warrenville Rd
Naperville IL 60563
877 641-1600

(G-3604)
CENTRAL CONSTRUCTION INDS LLC
Also Called: CCI
30 Harris St (06260-1907)
P.O. Box 229 (06260-0229)
PHONE....................860 963-8902
Llyod Frink,
Bruce A Richards,
EMP: 20 EST: 1996
SALES (est): 5.6MM Privately Held
WEB: www.ccict.com
SIC: 3441 1542 1521 Structural Metal Fabrication Nonresidential Construction Single-Family House Construction

(G-3605)
CHASE GRAPHICS INC
124 School St (06260-1613)
PHONE....................860 315-9006
James St Jean, *President*
Debra St Jean, *Vice Pres*
Jennifer Beckett, *Executive*
Nadeau Carolyn, *Graphic Designe*
Kathleen Guertin, *Graphic Designe*
EMP: 11
SQ FT: 4,500
SALES (est): 1.8MM Privately Held
WEB: www.chasegraphics.com
SIC: 2752 Lithographic Commercial Printing

(G-3606)
CONNECTICUT TOOL CO INC
6 Highland Dr (06260-3007)
PHONE....................860 928-0565
Philip Durand, *Chairman*
Stephen Durand, *Vice Pres*
EMP: 24
SQ FT: 13,500
SALES (est): 4.4MM Privately Held
WEB: www.conntool.com
SIC: 3089 3544 Mfg Plastic Products Mfg Dies/Tools/Jigs/Fixtures

(G-3607)
CONNTROL INTERNATIONAL INC
135 Park Rd (06260-3032)
P.O. Box 645 (06260-0645)
PHONE....................860 928-0567
Ronald Braaten, *President*
Willie O Pritchard, *Admin Sec*
EMP: 12
SQ FT: 13,000
SALES (est): 1.4MM Privately Held
WEB: www.conntrol.com
SIC: 3625 Mfg Relays/Industrial Controls

(G-3608)
CONTROL CONCEPTS INC (PA)
Also Called: Merlyn
100 Park St (06260-2332)
PHONE....................860 928-6551
Henry D Tiffany III, *President*
Gerry Knowles, *Purch Mgr*
Jonathan Larrabee, *Admin Sec*
◆ EMP: 12
SQ FT: 8,200
SALES: 3.5MM Privately Held
WEB: www.speedswitch.com
SIC: 3625 3613 3566 Mfg Relays & Industrial Controls Electric Power Switches Speed Changers Drives & Gears

(G-3609)
CREATIVE ENVELOPE INC
26 Highland Dr (06260-3007)
P.O. Box 588 (06260-0588)
PHONE....................860 963-1231
Richard A Sherman, *President*
▲ EMP: 4
SQ FT: 5,000
SALES (est): 843K Privately Held
WEB: www.creativeenvelope.com
SIC: 2759 Commercial Printing

(G-3610)
DIMENSION-POLYANT INC
78 Highland Dr (06260-3037)
PHONE....................860 928-8300
John E Gluek Jr, *President*
Kenneth Madsen, *Vice Pres*
Andrew McNulty, *Plant Mgr*
Karin Ruckwardt, *Treasurer*
Don Swanson, *Controller*
◆ EMP: 35
SQ FT: 50,000
SALES (est): 7MM Privately Held
WEB: www.dimension-polyant.com
SIC: 2211 2221 2394 Cotton Broadwoven Fabric Mill Manmade Broadwoven Fabric Mill Mfg Canvas/Related Products

(G-3611)
ENSINGER PRCSION CMPONENTS INC
Also Called: Plastock
11 Danco Rd (06260-3001)
PHONE....................860-928-7911
Matt McKenney, *General Mgr*
Michele Kowal, *QC Mgr*
Christine Campbell, *Sales Staff*
▲ EMP: 65
SQ FT: 66,000
SALES (est): 7MM
SALES (corp-wide): 533.1MM Privately Held
WEB: www.putnamprecisionmolding.com
SIC: 3089 Mfg Plastic Products
HQ: Ensinger Industries, Inc.
365 Meadowlands Blvd
Washington PA 15301
724 746-6050

(G-3612)
FLUID COATING TECHNOLOGY INC
48 Industrial Park Rd (06260-3003)
PHONE....................860 963-2505
Nathan Rosebrooks, *President*
Roger De Bruyn, *Vice Pres*
Janet Hill, *Technology*
EMP: 5
SQ FT: 5,500
SALES (est): 806.3K Privately Held
WEB: www.fct-inc.com
SIC: 3229 Mfg Pressed/Blown Glass

(G-3613)
FOSTER CORPORATION (HQ)
Also Called: Foster Delivery Science
45 Ridge Rd (06260-3034)
PHONE....................860 928-4102
Larry Acquarulo, *CEO*
Carmella Robles, *Prdtn Mgr*
Art Beshaw, *Production*
Carol-Lynn Maynard, *Buyer*
Carol Beauchesne, *QC Mgr*
▲ EMP: 65
SQ FT: 43,000
SALES (est): 14.3MM Privately Held
SIC: 3087 Custom Compounding-Purchased Resins

(G-3614)
FOSTER DELIVERY SCIENCE INC (DH)
36 Ridge Rd (06260-3035)
PHONE....................860 928-4102
Hank Hague, *CFO*
EMP: 12
SALES (est): 1.6MM Privately Held
SIC: 2834 Mfg Pharmaceutical Preparations
HQ: Foster Corporation
45 Ridge Rd
Putnam CT 06260
860 928-4102

(G-3615)
FOSTER DELIVERY SCIENCE INC
45 Ridge Rd (06260-3034)
PHONE....................860 630-4515
Lawrence Acquarulo, *CEO*
EMP: 12 Privately Held
SIC: 2834 Mfg Pharmaceutical Preparations
HQ: Foster Delivery Science, Inc.
36 Ridge Rd
Putnam CT 06260
860 928-4102

(G-3616)
INTERNATIONAL PAPER COMPANY
175 Park Rd (06260-3040)
PHONE....................860 928-7901
Anita Santerre, *Human Res Mgr*
Don Davis, *Manager*
Kevin Shead, *Manager*
EMP: 130
SALES (corp-wide): 23.3B Publicly Held
WEB: www.internationalpaper.com
SIC: 2621 Paper Mill
PA: International Paper Company
6400 Poplar Ave
Memphis TN 38197
901 419-9000

(G-3617)
J B CONCRETE PRODUCTS INC
1 Arch St (06260)
P.O. Box 387 (06260-0387)
PHONE....................860 928-9365
John W Barnes Sr, *President*
Heather Barnes, *Admin Sec*
EMP: 5 EST: 1969
SQ FT: 9,000

GEOGRAPHIC

SALES (est): 883.4K **Privately Held**
SIC: 3272 Mfg Concrete Products

(G-3618)
JAMES WRIGHT PRECISION PDTS
20 Mechanics St (06260-1315)
P.O. Box 924 (06260-0924)
PHONE..........860 928-7756
Robert A Main Jr, *President*
Susan Main, *Corp Secy*
William Main, *Vice Pres*
EMP: 12 **EST:** 1975
SQ FT: 7,500
SALES (est): 1.9MM
SALES (corp-wide): 35.5MM **Privately Held**
WEB: www.jwpp.com
SIC: 3451 Mfg Screw Machine Products
PA: Main, Robert A & Sons Holding Company Inc
555 Goffle Rd
Wyckoff NJ 07481
201 447-3700

(G-3619)
KAPSTONE PAPER AND PACKG CORP
25 Intervale St (06260-1312)
PHONE..........860 928-2211
EMP: 3
SALES (corp-wide): 18.2B **Publicly Held**
SIC: 2653 Mfg Corrugated/Solid Fiber Boxes
HQ: Kapstone Paper And Packaging Corporation
1000 Abernathy Rd
Atlanta GA 30328
770 448-2193

(G-3620)
NATIONAL CHROMIUM COMPANY INC
10 Senexet Rd (06260-1039)
PHONE..........860 928-7965
John Miller, *President*
Whitby K Ellsworth, *Admin Sec*
EMP: 11 **EST:** 1941
SQ FT: 9,000
SALES (est): 1.4MM **Privately Held**
WEB: www.nationalchromium.com
SIC: 3471 Chromium Nickel And Electrolyses Nickel Plating

(G-3621)
NEW ENGLAND PLASMA DEV CORP
14 Highland Dr (06260-3007)
P.O. Box 369 (06260-0369)
PHONE..........860 928-6561
Peter J Olshewski, *President*
Maureen Olshewski, *Vice Pres*
EMP: 10
SQ FT: 3,800
SALES (est): 1.9MM **Privately Held**
WEB: www.neplasma.com
SIC: 3541 Mfg Machine Tools-Cutting

(G-3622)
NUTMEG CONTAINER CORPORATION (HQ)
100 Canal St (06260-1912)
PHONE..........860 963-6727
Harry A Perkins, *CEO*
Charles Pious, *President*
James Pious, *Exec VP*
Jeff Hopkins, *Human Res Dir*
Mike Deubel, *Director*
EMP: 100
SQ FT: 25,000
SALES (est): 15.9MM
SALES (corp-wide): 121.1MM **Privately Held**
SIC: 2653 Mfg Corrugated/Solid Fiber Boxes
PA: Connecticut Container Corp.
455 Sackett Point Rd
North Haven CT 06473
203 248-2161

(G-3623)
OMNICRON ELECTRONICS
554 Liberty Hwy Ste 2 (06260-2728)
P.O. Box 623 (06260-0623)
PHONE..........860 928-0377
William Jones, *Owner*
EMP: 6 **EST:** 1976
SQ FT: 4,000
SALES (est): 200K **Privately Held**
SIC: 3651 3677 Mfg Home Audio/Video Equipment Mfg Electronic Coils/Transformers

(G-3624)
OPTICONX INC
45 Danco Rd (06260-3001)
PHONE..........888 748-6855
Patricia Doherty, *President*
Paul Doherty, *Vice Pres*
Paul Langlois, *VP Mfg*
EMP: 25
SQ FT: 16,000
SALES (est): 5.8MM **Privately Held**
WEB: www.opticonx.com
SIC: 3661 Mfg Telephone/Telegraph Apparatus

(G-3625)
PALLFLEX PRODUCTS COMPANY
125 Kennedy Dr (06260-1945)
PHONE..........860 928-7761
Lawrence D Kingsley, *President*
Ronald Hoffman, *Chairman*
Joseph Doherty, *Vice Pres*
Lisa McDermott, *CFO*
▲ **EMP:** 50 **EST:** 1990
SALES (est): 11.4MM
SALES (corp-wide): 19.8B **Publicly Held**
WEB: www.pall.com
SIC: 3569 Mfg General Industrial Machinery
HQ: Pall Corporation
25 Harbor Park Dr
Port Washington NY 11050
516 484-5400

(G-3626)
PARK-PMC LIQUIDATION CORP
Also Called: Phillips-Moldex Company
161 Park Rd (06260-3032)
PHONE..........860 928-0401
Lawrence C Moon Jr, *President*
Robert Gaura, *Vice Pres*
Gregory Mickelson, *Vice Pres*
Jennifer Lyons, *Admin Sec*
EMP: 25
SALES (est): 5.9MM
SALES (corp-wide): 43.4MM **Privately Held**
SIC: 3089 Mfg Plastic Products
PA: C. Cowles & Company
126 Bailey Rd
North Haven CT 06473
203 865-3117

(G-3627)
POLYMEDEX DISCOVERY GROUP INC (PA)
45 Ridge Rd (06260-3034)
PHONE..........860 928-4102
Lawrence A Acquarulo Jr, *President*
Hank Hague, *COO*
James V Dandeneau, *Vice Pres*
EMP: 15
SALES (est): 17.7MM **Privately Held**
SIC: 3082 3083 6719 Mfg Plastic Profile Shapes Mfg Laminated Plastic Plate/Sheet

(G-3628)
R W E INC
91 Highland Dr (06260-3010)
P.O. Box 431 (06260-0431)
PHONE..........860 974-1101
Eric Whittenburg, *President*
Robin Whittenburg, *Vice Pres*
Bob Laroche, *Engineer*
Betsey Kuhn, *Manager*
EMP: 34
SQ FT: 15,000
SALES: 5MM **Privately Held**
WEB: www.erwinc.com
SIC: 3444 Mfg Sheet Metalwork

(G-3629)
RAWSON DEVELOPMENT INC
205 Munyan Rd (06260-2508)
PHONE..........860 928-4536
Allan Rawson, *President*
Harold Hopkins, *Vice Pres*
Richard A Rawson, *Vice Pres*
Kathleen Rawson, *Treasurer*
EMP: 15
SQ FT: 1,500
SALES (est): 1.1MM **Privately Held**
SIC: 1442 5032 5211 Sand & Gravel Pit & A Whol & Ret Of Sand & Gravel

(G-3630)
RAWSON MANUFACTURING INC (PA)
99 Canal St (06260-1909)
PHONE..........860 928-4458
James Rawson, *President*
Ben Rawson, *Vice Pres*
Jim Rawson, *Branch Mgr*
EMP: 17
SQ FT: 24,299
SALES (est): 3MM **Privately Held**
WEB: www.rawsonscreens.com
SIC: 3531 Structural Metal Fabrication

(G-3631)
RENCHEL TOOL INC
51 Ridge Rd (06260-3034)
PHONE..........860 315-9017
Ronald Williams, *President*
Brenda Williams, *Corp Secy*
Robert McCurry, *Vice Pres*
Shane Szall, *Vice Pres*
EMP: 12
SQ FT: 3,000
SALES (est): 2.6MM **Privately Held**
WEB: www.rencheltoolinc.com
SIC: 3599 Mfg Industrial Machinery

(G-3632)
SHOPPERS-TURNPIKE CORPORATION
Also Called: Shoppers Guide
70 Main St (06260-1918)
P.O. Box 529 (06260-0529)
PHONE..........860 928-3040
Dennis E Neumann, *President*
Wilbur D Neumann, *President*
EMP: 18
SQ FT: 2,000
SALES (est): 1.5MM **Privately Held**
WEB: www.shopperturnpike.com
SIC: 2741 Misc Publishing

(G-3633)
SLATER HILL TOOL LLC
77 Industrial Park Rd (06260-3013)
PHONE..........860 963-0415
Josh W Nason, *Principal*
EMP: 3
SALES (est): 220K **Privately Held**
SIC: 3599 3546 Mfg Industrial Machinery Mfg Power-Driven Handtools

(G-3634)
SONOCO PRTECTIVE SOLUTIONS INC
29 Park Rd (06260-3044)
PHONE..........860 928-7795
Emil Castagna, *Prdtn Mgr*
Ken Blandina, *Foreman/Supr*
EMP: 48
SQ FT: 80,000
SALES (corp-wide): 5.3B **Publicly Held**
WEB: www.tuscarora.com
SIC: 3086 2821 2671 Mfg Plastic Foam Products Mfg Plastic Materials/Resins Mfg Packaging Paper/Film
HQ: Sonoco Protective Solutions, Inc.
1 N 2nd St
Hartsville SC 29550
843 383-7000

(G-3635)
SPECTRAL LLC (PA)
Also Called: Spectral Products
111 Highland Dr (06260-3010)
PHONE..........860 928-7726
Sheila Dupre, *Manager*
Yu H Hahn,
▲ **EMP:** 5
SALES: 1.5MM **Privately Held**
SIC: 3826 Mfg Analytical Instruments

(G-3636)
SUPERIOR PLAS EXTRUSION CO INC (PA)
Also Called: Town of Putnam
5 Highland Dr (06260-3010)
PHONE..........860 963-1976
David P Kingeter, *President*
Steven Ryan, *Vice Pres*
Steven M Ryan, *Treasurer*
Stephen Stedioso, *Controller*
Denis A Chaves, *Admin Sec*
▲ **EMP:** 44
SQ FT: 50,000
SALES (est): 12.6MM **Privately Held**
WEB: www.impactputnam.com
SIC: 3081 Mfg Unsupported Plastic Film/Sheet

(G-3637)
UNIBOARD CORP
Also Called: Teleboardusa.com
570 River Rd (06260-2929)
P.O. Box 2 (06260-0002)
PHONE..........860 428-5979
Martin Fey, *President*
Bill Butler, *Vice Pres*
Erik Fey, *Director*
EMP: 6
SALES (est): 380K **Privately Held**
SIC: 3949 Manufacturer Of Ski Boards

(G-3638)
US BUTTON CORPORATION
328 Kennedy Dr (06260-1629)
PHONE..........860 928-2707
Larry Jacobs, *President*
◆ **EMP:** 140
SQ FT: 100,000
SALES (est): 21.1MM **Privately Held**
WEB: www.usbutton.com
SIC: 3965 Mfg Fasteners/Buttons/Pins

(G-3639)
VILLAGER NEWSPAPERS
107 Providence St (06260-1542)
PHONE..........860 928-1818
Ron Tremblay, *Principal*
EMP: 5
SALES (est): 157.9K **Privately Held**
SIC: 2711 Newspapers-Publishing/Printing

(G-3640)
WINDHAM CONTAINER CORPORATION
30 Park Rd (06260-3030)
P.O. Box 944 (06260-0944)
PHONE..........860 928-7934
Gordie Mauer, *President*
Jeanine Mauer, *Treasurer*
EMP: 20 **EST:** 1958
SQ FT: 45,000
SALES (est): 4MM **Privately Held**
WEB: www.windhamcontainer.com
SIC: 2653 2671 Mfg Corrugated Boxes & Specialty Packaging Paper Inserts

(G-3641)
WOODSTOCK LINE CO
91 Canal St (06260-1947)
PHONE..........860 928-6557
Bernard Phaneuf, *President*
▲ **EMP:** 15 **EST:** 1946
SQ FT: 22,000
SALES (est): 2.1MM **Privately Held**
WEB: www.woodstockline.com
SIC: 2298 Mfg Cordage/Twine

(G-3642)
WOOLWORKS LTD
154 Main St B (06260-1932)
PHONE..........860 963-1228
Jennifer Ruggirello, *Principal*
EMP: 3
SALES (est): 160K **Privately Held**
SIC: 3229 Mfg Pressed/Blown Glass

Quaker Hill
New London County

(G-3643)
RHODE ISLAND RACEWAY LLC
846 Vauxhall Street Ext (06375-1031)
PHONE..................................860 701-0192
Jonathan Avery, *Principal*
EMP: 3
SALES (est): 160.7K **Privately Held**
SIC: 3644 Mfg Nonconductive Wiring Devices

(G-3644)
USES MFG INC
152 Old Colchester Rd (06375-1025)
P.O. Box 156 (06375-0156)
PHONE..................................860 443-8737
Brian Wohlforth, *President*
Edmund Wohlforth, *Vice Pres*
Doris Wohlforth, *Treasurer*
EMP: 4
SQ FT: 2,500
SALES (est): 450.6K **Privately Held**
WEB: www.usesmfg.com
SIC: 3825 Mfg Energy Saving Controls

Redding
Fairfield County

(G-3645)
AMERICAN ACTUATOR CORPORATION
292 Newtown Tpke (06896-2418)
P.O. Box 113096, Stamford (06911-3096)
PHONE..................................203 324-6334
Joseph Fowler, *President*
Evelyn Fowler, *Corp Secy*
EMP: 14
SQ FT: 1,800
SALES (est): 1.5MM **Privately Held**
SIC: 3542 Mfg Automation Equipment For Metal Fabricating Industry

(G-3646)
ARMORED SHIELD TECHNOLOGIES
Also Called: Cable Manufacturing Business
3655 W Mcfadden Ave (06896)
PHONE..................................714 848-5796
Christopher Badinelli, *President*
▲ **EMP:** 15
SQ FT: 10,000
SALES (est): 2.3MM **Privately Held**
WEB: www.cablemanufacturing.com
SIC: 3496 Mfg Misc Fabricated Wire Products

(G-3647)
GE OIL & GAS ESP INC
78 Black Rock Tpke (06896-3010)
PHONE..................................405 670-1431
EMP: 30
SALES (corp-wide): 121.6B **Publicly Held**
WEB: www.woodgroup-esp.com
SIC: 1389 Oil/Gas Field Services
HQ: Ge Oil & Gas Esp, Inc.
5500 Se 59th St
Oklahoma City OK 73135
405 670-1431

(G-3648)
GOLD LINE CONNECTOR INC (PA)
40 Great Pasture Rd (06896-2303)
P.O. Box 500 (06896-0500)
PHONE..................................203 938-2588
Martin Miller, *President*
Marjorie Miller, *Vice Pres*
EMP: 30 **EST:** 1961
SALES (est): 2.2MM **Privately Held**
WEB: www.gold-line.com
SIC: 3825 3663 3643 3829 Mfg Elec Measuring Instr Mfg Radio/Tv Comm Equip Mfg Conductive Wire Dvcs Mfg Measure/Control Dvcs

(G-3649)
LOLLIPOP KIDS LLC
13 Woodland Drive Ext (06896-3407)
PHONE..................................203 664-1799
EMP: 3
SALES (est): 111.3K **Privately Held**
SIC: 2064 Mfg Candy/Confectionery

(G-3650)
M P ROBINSON PRODUCTION
77 Topstone Rd (06896-1816)
PHONE..................................203 938-1336
Martin Robinson, *Owner*
Lore K Wright, *Nurse*
EMP: 20 **EST:** 1994
SALES (est): 613.3K **Privately Held**
SIC: 3999 3569 Mfg Misc Products Mfg General Industrial Machinery

(G-3651)
REDDING CREAMERY LLC
2 Marli Ln (06896-1919)
P.O. Box 4137, Stamford (06907-0137)
PHONE..................................203 938-2766
Maya Curto, *Principal*
EMP: 3
SALES (est): 111.3K **Privately Held**
SIC: 2021 Mfg Creamery Butter

(G-3652)
SHAWNEE CHEMICAL
429 Rock House Rd (06896-3401)
PHONE..................................203 938-3003
Richard Bradley, *Principal*
EMP: 4
SALES (est): 149.8K **Privately Held**
SIC: 3795 Mfg Tanks/Tank Components

Ridgefield
Fairfield County

(G-3653)
283 INDUSTRIES INC
3 Mallory Hill Rd (06877-6302)
PHONE..................................203 276-8956
Marjory Savino, *Principal*
EMP: 3 **EST:** 2012
SALES (est): 191.8K **Privately Held**
SIC: 3999 Mfg Misc Products

(G-3654)
ACE TIRE & AUTO CENTER INC
861 Ethan Allen Hwy (06877-2801)
PHONE..................................203 438-4042
Richard Desrochers, *Administration*
EMP: 11
SALES (est): 1MM **Privately Held**
SIC: 3011 Mfg Tires/Inner Tubes

(G-3655)
API WIZARD LLC
10 Hamilton Rd (06877-4320)
PHONE..................................914 764-5726
Richard Volpitta, *Mng Member*
EMP: 9 **EST:** 2016
SALES (est): 204.2K **Privately Held**
SIC: 7372 7389 Prepackaged Software Services Business Serv Non-Commercial Site

(G-3656)
BAILEY AVENUE KITCHENS
904 Ethan Allen Hwy (06877-2826)
PHONE..................................203 438-4868
David Adams, *Owner*
EMP: 6
SALES (est): 367.5K **Privately Held**
WEB: www.baileyavenuekitchens.com
SIC: 2434 Mfg Wood Kitchen Cabinets

(G-3657)
BOEHRINGER INGELHEIM CORP (DH)
900 Ridgebury Rd (06877-1058)
P.O. Box 368 (06877-0368)
PHONE..................................203 798-9988
Hans-Peter Grau, *President*
Paul Fonteyne, *Principal*
Philip I Datlow, *Counsel*
Albert Ros, *Exec VP*
Kathleen Hirst, *Vice Pres*
◆ **EMP:** 1500
SQ FT: 266,000
SALES (est): 1.2B
SALES (corp-wide): 19.4B **Privately Held**
WEB: www.us.boehringer-ingelheim.com
SIC: 2834 6221 Mfg Pharmaceutical Preparations Commodity Contract Broker

(G-3658)
BOEHRINGER INGELHEIM PHARMA (DH)
900 Ridgebury Rd (06877-1058)
P.O. Box 368 (06877-0368)
PHONE..................................203 798-9988
Paul Fonteyne, *CEO*
Andreas Barner, *President*
Jay Fine, *Vice Pres*
Graham Goodrich, *Vice Pres*
Stefan Rinn Sr, *Vice Pres*
▲ **EMP:** 1300
SQ FT: 1,326,000
SALES (est): 293.6MM
SALES (corp-wide): 19.4B **Privately Held**
SIC: 2834 Mfg Pharmaceutical Preparations
HQ: Boehringer Ingelheim Corporation
900 Ridgebury Rd
Ridgefield CT 06877
203 798-9988

(G-3659)
BOEHRINGER INGELHEIM USA CORP (DH)
900 Ridgebury Rd (06877-1058)
P.O. Box 368 (06877-0368)
PHONE..................................203 798-9988
Paul Fonteyne, *CEO*
Andreas Barner, *Ch of Bd*
Marla S Persky, *Senior VP*
Genevieve Faith, *Project Mgr*
Stefan Rinn, *CFO*
▲ **EMP:** 102
SALES (est): 1.2B
SALES (corp-wide): 19.4B **Privately Held**
SIC: 2834 Mfg Pharmaceutical Preparations
HQ: Boehringer Ingelheim Auslandsbeteiligungs Gmbh
Binger Str. 173
Ingelheim Am Rhein 55218
613 277-0

(G-3660)
BOEHRNGER INGELHEIM ROXANE INC
175 Briar Ridge Rd (06877)
PHONE..................................203 798-5555
EMP: 32
SALES (corp-wide): 16.5B **Privately Held**
SIC: 2834 Manufactures Pharmaceutical Preparations
HQ: Boehringer Ingelheim Roxane, Inc.
1809 Wilson Rd
Columbus OH 43228
614 276-4000

(G-3661)
BRANDSTROM INSTRUMENTS INC
85 Ethan Allen Hwy (06877-6226)
PHONE..................................203 544-9341
Arvid A Brandstrom, *CEO*
Thomas Allard, *Vice Pres*
▼ **EMP:** 25
SQ FT: 5,000
SALES (est): 4.8MM **Privately Held**
WEB: www.brandstrominstruments.com
SIC: 3728 3812 Mfg Aircraft Parts/Equipment Mfg Search/Navigation Equipment

(G-3662)
CHERNER CHAIR COMPANY LLC
218 North St (06877-2538)
P.O. Box 509 (06877-0509)
PHONE..................................203 894-4702
Thomas Cherner,
Ben Cherner,
▲ **EMP:** 5
SQ FT: 5,000
SALES (est): 557.5K **Privately Held**
WEB: www.chernerchair.com
SIC: 2511 Mfg Furniture Office And Residential

(G-3663)
CITRA SOLV LLC
188 Shadow Lake Rd (06877-1032)
P.O. Box 2597, Danbury (06813-2597)
PHONE..................................203 778-0881
Sherrill Tedino, *Accounting Mgr*
Eric Zeitler, *Regl Sales Mgr*
Cindy Howley, *Sales Staff*
Steven Zeitler,
Melissa Zeitler,
EMP: 7
SALES (est): 1.5MM **Privately Held**
WEB: www.citrasolv.com
SIC: 2842 Mfg Polish/Sanitation Goods

(G-3664)
CURBSIDE COMPOST LLC
65 Spring Valley Rd (06877-1218)
P.O. Box 188 (06877-0188)
PHONE..................................914 646-6890
Nicholas Skeadas, *Principal*
EMP: 4
SALES (est): 159.5K **Privately Held**
SIC: 2875 Mfg Fertilizers-Mix Only

(G-3665)
CUSTOM TS N MORE LLC
135 Ethan Allen Hwy (06877-6207)
PHONE..................................203 438-1592
Arthur F Crabtree, *Owner*
EMP: 3
SALES (est): 333K **Privately Held**
SIC: 2759 Commercial Printing

(G-3666)
ECONOMY PRINTING & COPY CENTER
Also Called: Village Printer
971 Ethan Allen Hwy (06877-2802)
PHONE..................................203 438-7401
Lisa D Witt, *Manager*
EMP: 4
SALES (corp-wide): 989.6K **Privately Held**
SIC: 2752 7334 Offset Printing & Photocopying
PA: Economy Printing & Copy Center
128 E Liberty St Ste 4
Danbury CT 06810
203 792-5610

(G-3667)
HAMLETHUB LLC
37 Danbury Rd Ste 202 (06877-4079)
PHONE..................................203 431-6400
Steven Blackburn, *Editor*
Peter Flier, *Editor*
Rachel Lampen, *Editor*
Lauterborn Mike, *Editor*
Sandy Vas, *Editor*
EMP: 5 **EST:** 2011
SALES: 450K **Privately Held**
SIC: 2711 Online Publishing Only

(G-3668)
HERSAM ACORN CMNTY PUBG LLC (HQ)
16 Bailey Ave (06877-4512)
PHONE..................................203 438-6544
Martin Hersam,
EMP: 16
SALES (est): 3.7MM
SALES (corp-wide): 5.3MM **Privately Held**
SIC: 2711 Engaged In Newspapers Publishing And Printing
PA: Hersam Acorn Newspapers, Llc
16 Bailey Ave
Ridgefield CT
203 438-6000

(G-3669)
J S DENTAL MANUFACTURING INC
Also Called: J S Dental
196 N Salem Rd (06877-3127)
P.O. Box 904 (06877-8904)
PHONE..................................203 438-8832
Inga Engstrom, *CEO*
Mats Engstrom, *President*
Gerhard Kiklas, *Sales Mgr*
EMP: 7
SQ FT: 6,000

GEOGRAPHIC

SALES (est): 1.4MM **Privately Held**
WEB: www.jsdental.com
SIC: 3843 Whol Medical/Hospital Equipment

(G-3670)
JAMES CALLAHAN
55 Buck Hill Rd (06877-2702)
PHONE..................................914 641-2852
James Callahan, *Principal*
EMP: 3
SALES (est): 195.5K **Privately Held**
SIC: 2411 Logging

(G-3671)
KIELO AMERICA INC
163 Branchville Rd (06877-5127)
PHONE..................................203 431-3999
EMP: 3 **EST:** 1984
SALES (est): 270K **Privately Held**
SIC: 2253 5632 Mfgs & Ret Hand Knit Women's Clothing

(G-3672)
MODERN NUTRITION & BIOTECH
61 Overlook Dr (06877-3711)
PHONE..................................203 244-5830
Jan Dong, *Vice Pres*
EMP: 4
SALES (est): 250K **Privately Held**
SIC: 2833 Nutrition And Bio-Tech

(G-3673)
NORILSK NICKEL USA INC
3 Turtle Ridge Ct (06877-1060)
PHONE..................................203 730-0676
EMP: 3 **EST:** 2011
SALES (est): 171.6K **Privately Held**
SIC: 3356 Nonferrous Rolling/Drawing

(G-3674)
NORTHEAST CABINET DESIGN
18 Bailey Ave (06877-4512)
PHONE..................................203 438-1709
Simon Johnson, *Principal*
Kimberly Jonson, *Principal*
EMP: 4
SALES (est): 543.9K **Privately Held**
WEB: www.northeastcabinetdesign.com
SIC: 2434 Mfg Wood Kitchen Cabinets

(G-3675)
PICKADENT INC
196 N Salem Rd Ste 2 (06877-3127)
P.O. Box 4185, Danbury (06813-4185)
PHONE..................................203 431-8716
Mats Engstrom, *President*
Inga Engstrom, *Vice Pres*
▼ **EMP:** 3
SQ FT: 3,000
SALES: 301.1K **Privately Held**
SIC: 3843 Distributor Dental Equipment/Supplies

(G-3676)
PILLA INC
908 Ethan Allen Hwy (06877-2826)
PHONE..................................203 894-3265
Phillip Pilla, *President*
Carlo Pilla, *Adv Board Mem*
Ryan Carey, *Sales Staff*
Dan Fireman, *Director*
EMP: 4
SALES (est): 509.6K **Privately Held**
SIC: 3851 5941 Mfg Ophthalmic Goods

(G-3677)
PINNACLE POLYMERS LLC
31 Bailey Ave Ste 4 (06877-4533)
PHONE..................................203 313-4116
EMP: 3
SALES (corp-wide): 44.9MM **Privately Held**
SIC: 2821 Mfg Plastic Materials/Resins
PA: Pinnacle Polymers, Llc
1 Pinnacle Ave
Garyville LA 70051
985 535-2000

(G-3678)
PLANET TECHNOLOGIES INC
96 Danbury Rd (06877-4069)
PHONE..................................800 255-3749
Scott L Glenn, *Ch of Bd*
Edward J Steube, *President*
Bret Megargel, *Vice Pres*
Francesca Dinota, *CFO*
EMP: 11
SQ FT: 13,317
SALES: 8MM **Privately Held**
SIC: 3564 Mfg Blowers/Fans

(G-3679)
RIDGEFIELD OVERHEAD DOOR LLC
703 Danbury Rd Ste 4 (06877-2737)
P.O. Box 928 (06877-8928)
PHONE..................................203 431-3667
Paul Peloquin,
Nancy Peloquin,
EMP: 7
SALES: 1.1MM **Privately Held**
SIC: 2431 Ret Lumber/Building Materials

(G-3680)
RUSSELL AMY KAHN (PA)
225 S Salem Rd (06877-4832)
PHONE..................................203 438-2133
Amy Kahn Russell, *Owner*
EMP: 10
SALES (est): 1.5MM **Privately Held**
WEB: www.supplementsny.net
SIC: 3911 Mfg Precious Metal Jewelry

(G-3681)
RX ANALYTIC INC
6 Bob Hill Rd (06877-2006)
PHONE..................................203 733-0837
Michael Goldstein, *Ch of Bd*
Joan Goldstein, *Vice Pres*
EMP: 6
SALES (est): 397.2K **Privately Held**
SIC: 2834 Mfg Pharmaceutical Preparations

(G-3682)
SAFETY DISPATCH INC
57 Jefferson Dr (06877-5919)
PHONE..................................203 885-5722
Carrie Shields, *President*
John Shields, *Sales Staff*
EMP: 3
SALES: 120K **Privately Held**
SIC: 3842 Mfg Surgical Appliances/Supplies

(G-3683)
SEWN IN AMERICA INC (PA)
Also Called: Sia
54 Danbury Rd Ste 240 (06877-4019)
PHONE..................................203 438-9149
John Mc Loughlin, *President*
▲ **EMP:** 80
SALES (est): 6MM **Privately Held**
WEB: www.sewninamerica.com
SIC: 2326 Mfg Men's/Boy's Work Clothing

(G-3684)
SILICON CATALYST LLC
258 W Mountain Rd (06877-2917)
PHONE..................................203 240-0499
Daniel J Armbrust,
Daniel Armbrust,
Rick Lazansky,
EMP: 3
SALES (est): 167.3K **Privately Held**
SIC: 3674 Mfg Semiconductors/Related Devices

(G-3685)
SONIAS CHOCOLATERIE INC
6 Ascot Way (06877-5503)
PHONE..................................203 438-5965
EMP: 10
SALES (est): 400K **Privately Held**
SIC: 2064 Mfg Candy/Confectionery

(G-3686)
TRITON THALASSIC TECH INC (PA)
241 Ethan Allen Hwy (06877-6208)
PHONE..................................203 438-0633
Barry Ressler, *President*
Stephenson Ward, *CFO*
EMP: 5
SQ FT: 40,000
SALES (est): 474.2K **Privately Held**
WEB: www.t3i-uv.com
SIC: 3641 Mfg Electric Lamps

(G-3687)
ULLMAN DEVICES CORPORATION
664 Danbury Rd (06877-2720)
P.O. Box 398 (06877-0398)
PHONE..................................203 438-6577
Steve Gorden, *CEO*
Edward Coleman, *President*
Benjamin Ungar, *Vice Pres*
Bernard Jaffe, *Treasurer*
Janet Lemma, *Admin Sec*
▲ **EMP:** 70 **EST:** 1935
SQ FT: 15,000
SALES (est): 12.1MM **Privately Held**
SIC: 3423 Mfg Hand/Edge Tools

(G-3688)
VITAL HEALTH PUBLISHING INC
149 Old Branchville Rd (06877-6013)
PHONE..................................203 438-3229
David Richard, *President*
EMP: 3 **EST:** 1998
SALES (est): 220.9K **Privately Held**
SIC: 2731 Books-Publishing/Printing

(G-3689)
WALPOLE WOODWORKERS INC
Also Called: Walpole Fence Company
346 Ethan Allen Hwy (06877-4722)
PHONE..................................508 668-2800
Robert Booth, *Branch Mgr*
EMP: 30
SQ FT: 1,000
SALES (corp-wide): 83.9MM **Privately Held**
WEB: www.walpolewoodworkers.com
SIC: 2499 5211 5712 2452 Mfg Wood Products Ret Lumber/Building Mtrl Ret Furniture Mfg Prefabrcatd Wd Bldgs Mfg Prefab Metal Bldgs
PA: Walpole Outdoors Llc
100 Rver Ridge Dr Ste 302
Norwood MA 02062
508 668-2800

Riverside
Fairfield County

(G-3690)
DP MARINE LLC
34 Lockwood Ln (06878-1708)
PHONE..................................917 705-7435
Jacques Guillet,
Pierre Guillet,
EMP: 5 **EST:** 2017
SALES (est): 253.7K **Privately Held**
SIC: 3531 Mfg Construction Machinery

(G-3691)
TRIBAL WEAR
27 Summit Rd (06878-2104)
PHONE..................................203 637-7884
David Fescier, *Owner*
EMP: 3
SALES (est): 50K **Privately Held**
SIC: 2329 2339 Mfg Men's/Boy's Clothing Mfg Women's/Misses' Outerwear

(G-3692)
TURQ LLC
123 Lockwood Rd (06878-1827)
PHONE..................................203 344-1257
Susan White, *CEO*
▲ **EMP:** 5
SALES (est): 299.2K **Privately Held**
SIC: 2329 Mfg Men's/Boy's Clothing

(G-3693)
WEIGH & TEST SYSTEMS INC
Also Called: Wagner Instruments
17 Wilmot Ln Ste 2 (06878-1633)
P.O. Box 1217, Greenwich (06836-1217)
PHONE..................................203 698-9681
William B Wagner, *President*
Pierrette Wagner, *Vice Pres*
▲ **EMP:** 10
SQ FT: 2,000
SALES: 1MM **Privately Held**
WEB: www.wagnerforce.com
SIC: 3829 Mfg Measuring/Controlling Devices

Riverton
Litchfield County

(G-3694)
DURALITE INCORPORATED
15 School St (06065-1013)
PHONE..................................860 379-3113
Elliott E Jessen, *Ch of Bd*
Mark Jessen, *President*
Dale L Smith, *Vice Pres*
Jeanette Smith, *Treasurer*
Vickie Clarke, *Sales Staff*
▲ **EMP:** 10 **EST:** 1946
SQ FT: 5,500
SALES (est): 2MM **Privately Held**
WEB: www.duralite.com
SIC: 3567 Mfg Industrial Furnaces/Ovens

(G-3695)
LEE BROWN CO LLC
91 Old Forge Rd (06065-1213)
P.O. Box 263 (06065-0263)
PHONE..................................860 379-4706
Peter Lee Brown, *Owner*
EMP: 10
SALES (est): 1.1MM **Privately Held**
SIC: 3442 Mfg Metal Doors/Sash/Trim

Rockfall
Middlesex County

(G-3696)
AIRCRAFT FORGED TOOL COMPANY
98 Cedar St (06481-2038)
PHONE..................................860 347-3778
William Piantek, *President*
EMP: 3 **EST:** 1957
SQ FT: 1,200
SALES (est): 340.1K **Privately Held**
SIC: 3545 Mfg High Speed Steel Cutting Tools

(G-3697)
J F TOOL INC
205 Main St Ste C (06481-2081)
P.O. Box 158 (06481-0158)
PHONE..................................860 349-3063
Rebeca Meadows, *President*
John Meadows Jr, *President*
EMP: 9
SQ FT: 12,000
SALES (est): 760K **Privately Held**
WEB: www.jftool.com
SIC: 3544 3545 Mfg Dies/Tools/Jigs/Fixtures Mfg Machine Tool Accessories

(G-3698)
LOYAL FENCE COMPANY LLC
1 Lorraine Ter (06481-2067)
PHONE..................................203 530-7046
Frank Garcia,
EMP: 7 **EST:** 2013
SALES (est): 386.1K **Privately Held**
SIC: 3446 Architectural Metalwork

(G-3699)
ROGERS MANUFACTURING COMPANY
Also Called: Mery Manufacturing
72 Main St (06481-2001)
P.O. Box 155 (06481-0155)
PHONE..................................860 346-8648
Vincent J Bitel Jr, *President*
Elaine B Cunningham, *Vice Pres*
▲ **EMP:** 100 **EST:** 1891
SQ FT: 65,000
SALES (est): 21.4MM **Privately Held**
SIC: 3089 Mfg Plastic Products

Rocky Hill
Hartford County

(G-3700)
A-1 ASPHALT PAVING
925 New Britain Ave (06067-1707)
P.O. Box 274 (06067-0274)
PHONE..................................860 436-6085
Gabby Thompson, *Owner*
EMP: 5 **EST:** 2011
SALES (est): 393.8K **Privately Held**
SIC: 2951 Mfg Asphalt Mixtures/Blocks

(G-3701)
ADVANCED DRAINAGE SYSTEMS INC
520 Cromwell Ave (06067-1864)
PHONE..................................860 529-8188
Ron Vitarelli, *Branch Mgr*
EMP: 32
SALES (corp-wide): 1.3B **Publicly Held**
SIC: 3272 3084 Pipe Concrete Or Lined With Concrete Plastic Pipe
PA: Advanced Drainage Systems, Inc.
4640 Trueman Blvd
Hilliard OH 43026
614 658-0050

(G-3702)
ARC DYNAMICS INC
28 Belamose Ave Ste C (06067-3795)
P.O. Box 656 (06067-0656)
PHONE..................................860 563-1006
Dave Pracon, *President*
Virginia Pracon, *Vice Pres*
EMP: 5
SQ FT: 4,000
SALES (est): 920.7K **Privately Held**
WEB: www.arcdynamics.com
SIC: 3441 Fabricator Of Structural Metal

(G-3703)
BINGHAM & TAYLOR CORP (HQ)
1022 Elm St (06067-1809)
P.O. Box 939, Culpeper VA (22701-0939)
PHONE..................................540 825-8334
Laura T Grondin, *CEO*
Lincoln Thompson, *Vice Pres*
Phil Ferrari, *CFO*
John Gould, *Controller*
Jay Corazza, *Sales Staff*
▲ **EMP:** 3
SALES (est): 20.8MM
SALES (corp-wide): 51.9MM **Privately Held**
WEB: www.binghamandtaylor.com
SIC: 3321 Gray/Ductile Iron Foundry
PA: Virginia Industries, Inc.
1022 Elm St
Rocky Hill CT 06067
860 571-3600

(G-3704)
BIZ WIZ PRINT & COPY CTR LLC (PA)
781 Cromwell Ave Ste E (06067-3000)
PHONE..................................860 721-0040
Kelly Dotson,
Chris Dotson,
EMP: 5
SALES (est): 638.5K **Privately Held**
SIC: 2759 Commercial Printing

(G-3705)
CROMWELL CHRONICLE
222 Dividend Rd (06067-3740)
P.O. Box 289 (06067-0289)
PHONE..................................860 257-8715
Ralph Rarey, *Principal*
EMP: 4
SALES (est): 138.4K **Privately Held**
SIC: 2711 Newspapers-Publishing/Printing

(G-3706)
CUSTOM PUBLISHING DESIGN GROUP
35 Cold Spring Rd Ste 321 (06067-3163)
PHONE..................................860 513-1213
Douglas Hatch, *President*
EMP: 18
SALES (est): 1.6MM **Privately Held**
WEB: www.mycompanymagazine.com
SIC: 2741 Misc Publishing

(G-3707)
DAILY MART
2204 Silas Deane Hwy (06067-2315)
PHONE..................................860 529-5210
EMP: 6
SALES (est): 210K **Privately Held**
SIC: 2711 Newspapers-Publishing/Printing

(G-3708)
DRAGONLAB LLC
1275 Cromwell Ave Ste C6 (06067-3430)
PHONE..................................860 436-9221
Michael Williams, *President*
▲ **EMP:** 3 **EST:** 2008
SALES (est): 360.6K **Privately Held**
SIC: 2869 3821 Mfg Industl Organic Chem Mfg Lab Apparatus/Furn

(G-3709)
FRONTIER VISION TECH INC
Also Called: Evogence
2080 Silas Deane Hwy # 203 (06067-2334)
PHONE..................................860 953-0240
Timur Y Ruban, *President*
Thomas Jacob, *Vice Pres*
Yury Ruban, *Treasurer*
EMP: 43
SQ FT: 5,000
SALES: 2.9MM **Privately Held**
SIC: 3571 3577 7378 5045 Mfg Electronic Computers Mfg Computer Peripherals Computer Maint/Repair Whol Computer/Peripheral

(G-3710)
GULF MANUFACTURING INC
645 Cromwell Ave (06067)
P.O. Box 430 (06067-0430)
PHONE..................................860 529-8601
James Murphy, *President*
Julie Murphy, *Admin Sec*
EMP: 23
SQ FT: 8,000
SALES (est): 2.4MM **Privately Held**
SIC: 3441 3599 Structural Metal Fabrication Mfg Industrial Machinery

(G-3711)
HARTFORD ELECTRIC SUP CO INC
ASG
70 Inwood Rd (06067-3441)
PHONE..................................860 760-4887
Bill Thompson, *Division Mgr*
EMP: 11
SALES (corp-wide): 38.5MM **Privately Held**
SIC: 3679 Mfg Electronic Components
PA: The Hartford Electric Supply Company Inc
30 Inwood Rd Ste 1
Rocky Hill CT 06067
860 236-6363

(G-3712)
HARTFORD TECHNOLOGIES INC
1022 Elm St (06067-1809)
PHONE..................................860 571-3602
Laura T Grondin, *President*
Lincoln Thomson, *Vice Pres*
Christopher Cowles, *CFO*
Lori Landry, *Human Res Mgr*
Vickie Brown, *Sales Staff*
▲ **EMP:** 27
SALES (est): 7.9MM
SALES (corp-wide): 51.9MM **Privately Held**
WEB: www.hartfordtechnologies.com
SIC: 3562 3399 Mfg Ball/Roller Bearings Mfg Primary Metal Products
PA: Virginia Industries, Inc.
1022 Elm St
Rocky Hill CT 06067
860 571-3600

(G-3713)
HBL AMERICA INC (HQ)
Also Called: Hbl Batteries
712 Brook St Ste 107 (06067-3447)
PHONE..................................860 257-9800
James McAuliffe, *President*
Robert Herritty, *Director*
◆ **EMP:** 8
SQ FT: 10,000
SALES (est): 1.3MM **Privately Held**
SIC: 3691 Mfg Storage Batteries

(G-3714)
HENKEL LOCTITE CORPORATION (DH)
1 Henkel Way (06067-3581)
PHONE..................................860 571-5100
Jerry Perkins, *President*
◆ **EMP:** 40
SQ FT: 500,000
SALES (est): 50.7MM
SALES (corp-wide): 22B **Privately Held**
SIC: 2891 3677 8731 8711 Mfg Adhesives/Sealants Mfg Elec Coil/Transfrmrs Coml Physical Research Engineering Services
HQ: Henkel Us Operations Corporation
1 Henkel Way
Rocky Hill CT 06067
860 571-5100

(G-3715)
HENKEL OF AMERICA INC (HQ)
1 Henkel Way (06067-3581)
PHONE..................................860 571-5100
Dr Lothar Steinebach, *Ch of Bd*
Nicole Bernabo, *Counsel*
William B Read III, *Senior VP*
Frederic Chupin, *Vice Pres*
Patrick Courtney, *Vice Pres*
▲ **EMP:** 421 **EST:** 1979
SQ FT: 60,000
SALES (est): 1.7B
SALES (corp-wide): 22B **Privately Held**
SIC: 2843 2821 2833 2899 Mfg Surface Active Agent Mfg Plstc Material/Resin Mfg Medicinal/Botanicals
PA: Henkel Ag & Co. Kgaa
Henkelstr. 67
Dusseldorf 40589
211 797-0

(G-3716)
HENKEL US OPERATIONS CORP (DH)
1 Henkel Way (06067-3581)
PHONE..................................860 571-5100
Hans Van Bylen, *CEO*
Dr Jochen Krautter, *Ch of Bd*
Stephan Fuesti-Molnar, *President*
Chris Hallsey, *President*
Jeffrey C Piccolomini, *President*
◆ **EMP:** 400
SQ FT: 60,000
SALES (est): 1.7B
SALES (corp-wide): 22B **Privately Held**
WEB: www.handheld.com
SIC: 2843 2821 2833 2899 Mfg Surface Active Agent Mfg Plstc Material/Resin Mfg Medicinal/Botanicals
HQ: Henkel Of America, Inc.
1 Henkel Way
Rocky Hill CT 06067
860 571-5100

(G-3717)
IDEMIA IDENTITY & SEC USA LLC
101 Hammer Mill Rd (06067-3771)
PHONE..................................860 529-2559
Jim Lyons, *Branch Mgr*
EMP: 6
SALES (corp-wide): 3.5B **Privately Held**
SIC: 3089 Mfg Plastic Products
HQ: Idemia Identity & Security Usa Llc
11951 Freedom Dr Fl 18
Reston VA 20190

(G-3718)
INTERSEC LLC
1275 Cromwell Ave Ste B3 (06067-3421)
PHONE..................................860 985-3158
Peter Sywenkyj, *Mng Member*
EMP: 5 **EST:** 2015
SALES (est): 423.2K **Privately Held**
SIC: 3949 8742 Mfg Sporting/Athletic Goods Management Consulting Services

(G-3719)
JAMES J SCOTT LLC
38 New Britain Ave Ste 3 (06067-1197)
PHONE..................................860 571-9200
Scott Mokoski, *CFO*
James J Mokoski,
James F Mokoski,
James Mokoski,
Scott P Mokoski,
◆ **EMP:** 6
SQ FT: 6,800
SALES (est): 1.1MM **Privately Held**
SIC: 3592 5088 3545 Mfg Carburetors/Pistons/Rings Whol Transportation Equipment Mfg Machine Tool Accessories

(G-3720)
JOHNSON CONTROLS INC
27 Inwood Rd (06067-3412)
PHONE..................................860 571-3300
Dave Clark, *Vice Pres*
EMP: 9 **Privately Held**
SIC: 2531 Mfg Automotive Seating & Interior Systems
HQ: Johnson Controls Inc
5757 N Green Bay Ave
Milwaukee WI 53209
414 524-1200

(G-3721)
LINVAR LLC
2189 Silas Deane Hwy # 15 (06067-2324)
PHONE..................................860 951-3818
Joseph Ramondetta, *President*
EMP: 5
SALES (est): 486.8K **Privately Held**
SIC: 3443 5084 Mfg Fabricated Plate Work Whol Industrial Equipment

(G-3722)
LUXPOINT INC
101 Hammer Mill Rd Ste K (06067-3771)
PHONE..................................860 982-9588
Paul Sanders, *Director*
EMP: 6
SQ FT: 10,000
SALES (est): 319.8K **Privately Held**
SIC: 3829 Mfg Measuring/Controlling Devices

(G-3723)
MERRIFIELD PAINT COMPANY INC
47 Inwood Rd (06067-3412)
PHONE..................................860 529-1583
John Merrifield Jr, *President*
Douglas A Merrifield, *Vice Pres*
Paige M Merrifield, *Admin Sec*
EMP: 3 **EST:** 1946
SQ FT: 3,000
SALES (est): 615.5K **Privately Held**
WEB: www.merrifieldpaint.com
SIC: 2851 5231 Mfg & Ret Paint

(G-3724)
MTU AERO ENGINES N AMER INC
795 Brook St 5 (06067-3403)
PHONE..................................860 258-9700
Alarm Eerube, *President*
EMP: 3
SALES (corp-wide): 5B **Privately Held**
SIC: 3812 Mfg Rotating Parts Of Aero Engine
HQ: Mtu Aero Engines North America Inc.
795 Brook St Bldg 5
Rocky Hill CT 06067
860 258-9700

(G-3725)
NQ INDUSTRIES INC
1275 Cromwell Ave Ste A9 (06067-3428)
PHONE..................................860 258-3466
William Carey, *CEO*
▲ **EMP:** 7
SQ FT: 3,000
SALES (est): 700K **Privately Held**
SIC: 3564 Mfg Air Cleaning Systems

(G-3726)
OLIVE OILS AND BALSAMICS LLC
35 New Rd (06067-1703)
PHONE..................................860 563-0105

GEOGRAPHIC

Anna Flynn, *Principal*
EMP: 3
SALES (est): 110.5K **Privately Held**
SIC: 2079 Mfg Edible Fats/Oils

(G-3727)
PDQ INC (PA)
24 Evans Rd (06067-3734)
PHONE..................................860 529-9051
Ronald Gronback Sr, *President*
Ronald G Gronback Jr, *President*
Jeffrey W Gronback, *Admin Sec*
EMP: 25
SQ FT: 6,000
SALES (est): 4.7MM **Privately Held**
WEB: www.pdqcorp.com
SIC: 3724 Mfg Aircraft Engines/Parts

(G-3728)
RARE REMINDER INCORPORATED
222 Dividend Rd (06067-3740)
P.O. Box 289 (06067-0289)
PHONE..................................860 563-9386
Kevin Rarey, *President*
Greg Barden, *General Mgr*
James Klatt, *Vice Pres*
Rob Zappulla, *Accounts Exec*
Libby Lord, *Consultant*
EMP: 50 **EST:** 1953
SQ FT: 14,300
SALES (est): 5.4MM **Privately Held**
WEB: www.rarereminder.com
SIC: 2741 2752 Misc Publishing Lithographic Commercial Printing

(G-3729)
SYSTEMATICS INC
1275 Cromwell Ave Ste B1 (06067-3429)
PHONE..................................860 721-0706
EMP: 11
SALES (corp-wide): 11.6MM **Privately Held**
SIC: 3572 Mfg Computer Storage Devices
PA: Systematics, Inc.
238 Cherry St Ste C
Shrewsbury MA 01545
508 366-1306

(G-3730)
TARGET MARKETING ASSOC INC
35 Cold Spring Rd Ste 224 (06067-3162)
P.O. Box 566 (06067-0566)
PHONE..................................860 571-7294
Gregory Reynolds, *President*
EMP: 3
SALES (est): 303.8K **Privately Held**
WEB: www.targetmarketingreps.com
SIC: 3721 Mfg Aircraft

(G-3731)
TORNIK INC
16 Old Forge Rd B (06067-3729)
PHONE..................................860 282-6081
Edward S Stephens, *President*
▲ **EMP:** 110
SQ FT: 21,000
SALES (est): 29.1MM **Privately Held**
WEB: www.tornik.com
SIC: 3679 8711 Mfg Electronic Components Engineering Services

(G-3732)
UNITED SEATING & MOBILITY LLC (PA)
Also Called: Numotion
1111 Cromwell Ave (06067-3449)
PHONE..................................860 761-0700
Mike Swinford, *CEO*
EMP: 8
SALES (est): 947.7K **Privately Held**
SIC: 3842 Mfg Surgical Appliances/Supplies

(G-3733)
VIRGINIA INDUSTRIES INC (PA)
1022 Elm St (06067-1809)
PHONE..................................860 571-3600
Laura T Grondin, *President*
Douglas Ericson, *Project Engr*
Lincoln L Thompson Jr, *Shareholder*
▲ **EMP:** 5
SQ FT: 128,000
SALES: 51.9MM **Privately Held**
WEB: www.virginiaindustries.com
SIC: 3562 3084 3321 3568 Mfg Ball/Roller Bearings Mfg Plastic Pipe Gray/Ductile Iron Fndry Mfg Power Transmsn Equip

(G-3734)
WETHERSFIELD OFFSET INC
1795 Silas Deane Hwy (06067-1305)
PHONE..................................860 721-8236
Joseph P Amaio, *President*
EMP: 5
SALES (est): 531.2K **Privately Held**
SIC: 2752 Lithographic Commercial Printing

(G-3735)
WETHERSFIELD PRINTING CO INC
1795 Silas Deane Hwy (06067-1305)
PHONE..................................860 721-8236
Joseph Amaio, *President*
Barbara Amaio, *Corp Secy*
EMP: 12
SQ FT: 7,500
SALES (est): 1.4MM **Privately Held**
WEB: www.wethersfieldoffset.com
SIC: 2752 Lithographic Commercial Printing

Roxbury
Litchfield County

(G-3736)
MINE HILL DISTILLERY
5 Mine Hill Rd (06783-1323)
PHONE..................................860 210-1872
Elliott B Davis, *President*
EMP: 4
SALES (est): 265.2K **Privately Held**
SIC: 2085 Mfg Distilled/Blended Liquor

Salem
New London County

(G-3737)
CARLI FARM & EQUIPMENT LLC
40 Mill Ln (06420-3519)
PHONE..................................860 908-3227
Victor Carli,
Rance V Carli,
EMP: 5 **EST:** 2009
SQ FT: 5,500
SALES (est): 34.3K **Privately Held**
SIC: 3498 Mfg Fabricated Pipe/Fittings

(G-3738)
DUNDORF DESIGNS USA INC
Also Called: Distinctive Designs USA
426 Forsyth Rd (06420-4018)
PHONE..................................860 859-2955
David Dundorf, *President*
EMP: 4
SALES (est): 320K **Privately Held**
SIC: 3993 2499 Mfg Signs/Advertising Specialties Mfg Wood Products

(G-3739)
SALEM VLY FARMS ICE CREAM INC
20 Darling Rd (06420-3906)
PHONE..................................860 859-2980
David Bingham, *President*
Tiffany B Cunningham, *Vice Pres*
Anne W Bingham, *Admin Sec*
EMP: 8
SALES (est): 695.4K **Privately Held**
SIC: 2024 Mfg Ice Cream/Frozen Desert

(G-3740)
STEED READ HORSEMANS CLASSIFIE
16b Mill Ln (06420-3539)
PHONE..................................860 859-0770
Dana Stillwell,
EMP: 3
SALES: 350K **Privately Held**
WEB: www.steedread.com
SIC: 2721 0752 Periodicals-Publishing/Printing Animal Services

Sandy Hook
Fairfield County

(G-3741)
CONN ENGINEERING ASSOC CORP
Also Called: Ceac
27 Philo Curtis Rd (06482-1245)
P.O. Box 656 (06482-0656)
PHONE..................................203 426-4733
Gregory Jossick, *President*
Sandra Jossick, *Corp Secy*
Ziad Fakhoury, *Exec VP*
Jeffrey Jossick, *Vice Pres*
Nick Sopchak, *Manager*
▲ **EMP:** 14 **EST:** 1967
SQ FT: 6,000
SALES (est): 2.5MM **Privately Held**
WEB: www.ceacpowder.com
SIC: 3399 Mfg Primary Metal Products

(G-3742)
CURTIS CORPORATION A DEL CORP
44 Berkshire Rd (06482-1499)
PHONE..................................203 426-5861
Donald Droppo, *President*
William Peck, *Corp Secy*
Susan Smith, *Admin Sec*
EMP: 155
SQ FT: 112,000
SALES (est): 24.8MM **Privately Held**
SIC: 2657 Mfg Folding Paperboard Boxes

(G-3743)
CURTIS PACKAGING CORPORATION
44 Berkshire Rd (06482-1428)
PHONE..................................203 426-5861
Donald R Droppo Jr, *Ch of Bd*
Donald Droppo Jr, *President*
William F Peck, *Senior VP*
Kerry Brown, *Safety Mgr*
Jon Porter, *Production*
▲ **EMP:** 130
SQ FT: 150,000
SALES: 13.8K **Privately Held**
WEB: www.curtispackaging.com
SIC: 2657 Mfg Folding Paperboard Boxes

(G-3744)
MAPLE CRAFT FOODS LLC
6 Cider Mill Rd (06482-1587)
PHONE..................................203 913-7066
EMP: 4
SALES (est): 99.1K **Privately Held**
SIC: 2099 Mfg Food Preparations

(G-3745)
Q-LANE TURNSTILES LLC
52 Riverside Rd (06482-1213)
PHONE..................................860 410-1801
Ed Jacobsen, *Manager*
EMP: 11 **EST:** 2016
SALES (est): 619.9K **Privately Held**
SIC: 3829 7382 1731 3669 Measuring And Controlling Devices, Nec

(G-3746)
USA CIRCUITS LLC
114 Lakeview Ter (06482-1482)
PHONE..................................203 364-1378
Thomas Cheung, *Principal*
EMP: 3 **EST:** 2010
SALES (est): 208.9K **Privately Held**
SIC: 3679 Mfg Electronic Components

Scotland
Windham County

(G-3747)
SCOTLAND HARDWOODS LLC
117 Ziegler Rd (06264)
P.O. Box 328 (06264-0328)
PHONE..................................860 423-1233
Peter J Rossi, *Mng Member*
Andrew Becker,
▼ **EMP:** 34
SQ FT: 45,000
SALES (est): 5.6MM **Privately Held**
SIC: 2421 Sawmill/Planing Mill
PA: New England Timber Resources Inc
162 West St Ste A
Cromwell CT
860 632-3505

Seymour
New Haven County

(G-3748)
AIR-VAC ENGINEERING CO INC (PA)
30 Progress Ave Ste 2 (06483-3935)
P.O. Box 216 (06483-0216)
PHONE..................................203 888-9900
Clifford S Lasto, *President*
Jeffrey S Duhaime, *Vice Pres*
Howard C Lasto, *Treasurer*
Gary R Duhaime, *Admin Sec*
EMP: 22 **EST:** 1959
SQ FT: 25,000
SALES (est): 4.8MM **Privately Held**
SIC: 3548 Mfg Welding Apparatus

(G-3749)
CANOGA PERKINS CORPORATION
100 Bank St (06483-2806)
PHONE..................................203 888-7914
Steve Hannay, *Branch Mgr*
EMP: 3
SALES (corp-wide): 1B **Privately Held**
WEB: www.canoga.com
SIC: 3661 Mfg Telephone/Telegraph Apparatus
HQ: Canoga Perkins Corporation
20600 Prairie St
Chatsworth CA 91311
818 718-6300

(G-3750)
CASPARI INC (PA)
99 Cogwheel Ln (06483-3900)
PHONE..................................203 888-1100
Douglas H Stevens, *Ch of Bd*
Lisa Fingeret, *Vice Pres*
Caralyn Stevens, *Vice Pres*
Steve Shellnutt, *Prdtn Mgr*
Gloria Finkenauer, *CFO*
◆ **EMP:** 16
SQ FT: 35,000
SALES (est): 36.3MM **Privately Held**
SIC: 2771 Mfg Greeting Cards

(G-3751)
G & M TOOL COMPANY
45 Highland Rd (06478-1694)
PHONE..................................203 888-9354
George Maciulewski, *Owner*
EMP: 3
SQ FT: 1,200
SALES (est): 308.2K **Privately Held**
SIC: 3599 Mfg Industrial Machinery

(G-3752)
HOUSATONIC WIRE CO
109 River St (06483-2639)
PHONE..................................203 888-9670
EMP: 12 **EST:** 1972
SQ FT: 65,000
SALES (est): 132.2K **Privately Held**
SIC: 3315 Mfg Steel Wire/Related Products

(G-3753)
JV PRECISION MACHINE CO
71 Cogwheel Ln (06483-3919)
PHONE..................................203 888-0748
Josef Visinski Jr, *President*
Andrew Visinski, *Treasurer*
EMP: 30
SQ FT: 42,000
SALES (est): 5.3MM **Privately Held**
WEB: www.jvprecision.net
SIC: 3599 Mfg Industrial Machinery

(G-3754)
KINETIC DEVELOPMENT GROUP LLC
Also Called: Kdg
71 Cogwheel Ln (06483-3919)
PHONE..................................203 888-4321
Darren Mellors, *Mng Member*
Charles Lafferty, *Mng Member*
Josef Visinski, *Administration*
EMP: 5
SQ FT: 72,000
SALES (est): 527.1K **Privately Held**
SIC: 3484 Guns (Firearms) Or Gun Parts 30 Mm And Below

(G-3755)
MARMON UTILITY LLC
Also Called: Kerite
49 Day St (06483-3401)
PHONE..................................203 881-5358
Edmund Sleight, *President*
Wayne Yakich, *Mng Member*
Michael Garratt, *Mng Member*
Craig Phelon, *Mng Member*
Robert W Webb, *Mng Member*
◆ **EMP:** 31 **EST:** 1996
SALES (est): 10.6MM
SALES (corp-wide): 225.3B **Publicly Held**
SIC: 3315 3357 Mfg Steel Wire/Related Products Nonferrous Wiredrawing/Insulating
HQ: The Marmon Group Llc
181 W Madison St Ste 2600
Chicago IL 60602

(G-3756)
MATTHEW WARREN INC
Also Called: Raf Electronic Hardware
95 Silvermine Rd Ste 1 (06483-3915)
PHONE..................................203 888-2133
Nick Russo, *Vice Pres*
Brian Stach, *Plant Mgr*
Mark Kulinski, *Engineer*
David Granger, *Sales Staff*
Mike Heywosz, *Sales Staff*
EMP: 8
SALES (corp-wide): 185.9MM **Privately Held**
SIC: 3451 3452 Mfg Screw Machine Products Mfg Bolts/Screws/Rivets
HQ: Matthew Warren, Inc.
9501 Tech Blvd Ste 401
Rosemont IL 60018
847 349-5760

(G-3757)
MICROBOARD PROCESSING INC
Also Called: M P I
36 Cogwheel Ln (06483-3922)
PHONE..................................203 881-4300
Craig Hoekenga, *Ch of Bd*
Nicole Russo, *President*
Bryan Brady, *Vice Pres*
Ted Labowski, *Vice Pres*
Tyler Allen, *Production*
▲ **EMP:** 105
SQ FT: 60,000
SALES (est): 35.5MM **Privately Held**
WEB: www.microboard.com
SIC: 3672 7629 Mfg Printed Circuit Boards Electrical Repair

(G-3758)
NEW ENGLAND CAP COMPANY
Also Called: Om Cass Swiss
756 Derby Ave (06483-2412)
PHONE..................................203 736-6184
Mike Murjani, *Mng Member*
EMP: 16
SQ FT: 16,000
SALES: 600K **Privately Held**
WEB: www.newenglandcap.com
SIC: 2353 Whol Men's/Boy's Clothing

(G-3759)
PHOENIX MACHINE INC
279 Pearl St (06483-3719)
PHONE..................................203 888-1135
Al Pokrywka, *President*
EMP: 5
SQ FT: 3,500
SALES: 390K **Privately Held**
SIC: 3599 7692 Mfg Industrial Machinery Welding Repair

(G-3760)
PLASTIC MOLDING TECHNOLOGY
92 Cogwheel Ln (06483-3923)
PHONE..................................203 881-1811
Charles Sholtis, *Principal*
EMP: 4
SALES (est): 310.9K **Privately Held**
SIC: 3089 Mfg Plastic Products

(G-3761)
PORTA DOOR CO
65 Cogwheel Ln (06483-3919)
PHONE..................................203 888-6191
Peter Romanos, *President*
Chris Malizia, *Vice Pres*
EMP: 31
SQ FT: 20,000
SALES (est): 3.8MM **Privately Held**
WEB: www.portadoor.com
SIC: 2434 5712 2431 Mfg Wood Kitchen Cabinets Ret Furniture Mfg Millwork

(G-3762)
PRECISION AEROSPACE INC
88 Cogwheel Ln (06483-3923)
PHONE..................................203 888-3022
Jack E Hillman Sr, *CEO*
Jack E Hillman Jr, *President*
Jeffrey W Hillman, *Vice Pres*
Janice Hillman Frost, *Admin Sec*
Dorothy Hillman, *Admin Sec*
EMP: 40
SQ FT: 16,000
SALES (est): 8.1MM **Privately Held**
SIC: 3728 Mfg Industrial Machinery

(G-3763)
RETINA SYSTEMS INC
146 Day St (06483-3403)
PHONE..................................203 881-1311
Floyd Moir, *President*
George Wixon, *Engineer*
Billie Guliuzza, *Accountant*
Karl Cressotti, *Director*
Floyd William Moir, *Director*
▲ **EMP:** 25
SQ FT: 14,000
SALES (est): 5.5MM **Privately Held**
WEB: www.retinasystems.com
SIC: 3827 Mfg Optical Instruments/Lenses

(G-3764)
SAFE WATER
371 Roosevelt Dr (06483-2120)
PHONE..................................203 732-4806
Vincent Vecchiarelli, *Owner*
EMP: 3 **EST:** 1999
SALES (est): 142.9K **Privately Held**
WEB: www.safewater.com
SIC: 3589 Mfg Service Industry Machinery

(G-3765)
THULE INC (DH)
42 Silvermine Rd (06483-3928)
PHONE..................................203 881-9600
Fred Clark, *President*
Kajsa Von Geijer, *Senior VP*
Maureen Murphy-Parente, *Vice Pres*
Fred Wyckoff, *Vice Pres*
Mike Rak, *Safety Mgr*
◆ **EMP:** 157
SALES (est): 120.4MM **Privately Held**
WEB: www.karriteus.com
SIC: 3714 5021 Mfg Motor Vehicle Parts/Accessories Whol Furniture

(G-3766)
THULE HOLDING INC (DH)
42 Silvermine Rd (06483-3928)
PHONE..................................203 881-9600
Fred Clark, *President*
Moreen Parente, *Vice Pres*
Patrick Monahan, *VP Opers*
Tami Wiesniak, *Accountant*
Erin Reilly, *Sales Staff*
EMP: 13
SALES (est): 120.4MM **Privately Held**
SIC: 3792 3714 Mfg Travel Trailers/Campers Mfg Motor Vehicle Parts/Accessories
HQ: Thule Holding Ab
Fosievagen 13
Malmo
406 359-000

(G-3767)
VERNIER METAL FABRICATING INC
Also Called: V M F
26 Progress Ave (06483-3921)
PHONE..................................203 881-3133
Edward Zerjav, *President*
John J Zerjav, *Vice Pres*
Robert Zerjav, *Treasurer*
Barbara Zerjav, *Admin Sec*
EMP: 70
SQ FT: 54,000
SALES (est): 15.7MM **Privately Held**
WEB: www.vmf.com
SIC: 3441 3444 Structural Metal Fabrication Mfg Sheet Metalwork

(G-3768)
WILDFLOUR CUPCAKES SWEETS LLC
18 Bank St (06483-2802)
PHONE..................................203 828-6576
Alyssa Dematteo, *Principal*
EMP: 4
SALES (est): 193.6K **Privately Held**
SIC: 2051 Mfg Bread/Related Products

(G-3769)
XAMAX INDUSTRIES INC
63 Silvermine Rd (06483-3915)
PHONE..................................203 888-7200
Martin J Weinberg, *President*
Robert Markowski, *Vice Pres*
Margaret Pederson, *Admin Sec*
▲ **EMP:** 50
SQ FT: 36,000
SALES (est): 21.8MM **Privately Held**
WEB: www.xamax.com
SIC: 2621 2297 Paper Mill Mfg Nonwoven Fabrics

Sharon
Litchfield County

(G-3770)
TCG GREEN TECHNOLOGIES INC
Also Called: Turtle Clan Global
1 Skiff Mountain Rd (06069-2224)
P.O. Box 861 (06069-0861)
PHONE..................................860 364-4694
Albert Snow, *President*
Lesley Burton-Dallas, *Chairman*
▲ **EMP:** 10 **EST:** 2013
SALES (est): 601.5K **Privately Held**
SIC: 3291 2851 Mfg Abrasive Products Mfg Paints/Allied Products

Shelton
Fairfield County

(G-3771)
A & I CONCENTRATE LLC
2 Corporate Dr Ste 136 (06484-6274)
PHONE..................................203 447-1938
Don Vultaggio, *Mng Member*
EMP: 10
SALES: 9.9MM **Privately Held**
SIC: 3556 5181 Mfg Food Products Machinery Whol Beer/Ale

(G-3772)
ABC SIGN CORPORATION
30 Controls Dr Ste 1 (06484-6157)
PHONE..................................203 513-8110
Gus De Santy, *CEO*
Greg De Santy, *President*
EMP: 25 **EST:** 1955
SQ FT: 20,000
SALES (est): 4.6MM **Privately Held**
WEB: www.abcsigncorp.com
SIC: 3993 Mfg Signs/Advertising Specialties

(G-3773)
ALPHA-CORE INC
6 Waterview Dr (06484-4300)
PHONE..................................203 954-0050
Peder Ulrik Poulsen, *President*
Sandu Pescaru, *Vice Pres*
◆ **EMP:** 20
SQ FT: 25,000
SALES (est): 2.8MM **Privately Held**
SIC: 3679 5731 3612 3549 Mfg Elec Components Ret Radio/Tv/Electronics Mfg Transformers Mfg Metalworking Mach Nonfrs Wiredrwng/Insltng

(G-3774)
AMERICAN SPECIALTY CO INC
762 River Rd (06484-5465)
P.O. Box 670, Northford (06472-0670)
PHONE..................................203 929-5324
James W Monde, *President*
Emil J Monde, *Vice Pres*
EMP: 10 **EST:** 1957
SQ FT: 12,000
SALES (est): 956.1K **Privately Held**
SIC: 3493 Mfg Steel Springs-Nonwire

(G-3775)
ANCO ENGINEERING INC
217 Long Hill Cross Rd (06484-6145)
PHONE..................................203 925-9235
Lucian S Leszczynski, *President*
Daniel Leszczynski, *Vice Pres*
Lucian Leszczynski Jr, *Vice Pres*
Ann Leszczynski, *Treasurer*
EMP: 85 **EST:** 1981
SQ FT: 100,000
SALES (est): 22MM **Privately Held**
WEB: www.ancoeng.com
SIC: 3441 3444 Structural Metal Fabrication Mfg Sheet Metalwork

(G-3776)
ANTHONY S FUEL
56 Great Oak Rd (06484-5208)
PHONE..................................203 513-7400
Anthony Frank Mobilio, *Principal*
EMP: 3
SALES (est): 433K **Privately Held**
SIC: 2869 Mfg Industrial Organic Chemicals

(G-3777)
BAGELA USA LLC
70 Platt Rd (06484-5339)
PHONE..................................203 944-0525
Gregory Harla,
▲ **EMP:** 5
SALES (est): 959K **Privately Held**
SIC: 3531 Mfg Construction Machinery

(G-3778)
BAINGAN LLC
94 River Rd (06484-5618)
PHONE..................................203 924-2626
Shrijana Kandel, *Principal*
EMP: 4
SALES (est): 384.2K **Privately Held**
SIC: 3421 Mfg Cutlery

(G-3779)
BAKERY ENGINEERING/WINKLER INC
Also Called: Winkler USA
2 Trap Falls Rd Ste 105 (06484-4670)
PHONE..................................203 929-8630
EMP: 19
SQ FT: 15,000
SALES (est): 3.4MM **Privately Held**
WEB: www.krausectp.com
SIC: 3556 Food Products Machinery, Nsk

(G-3780)
BETA PHARMA INC
1 Enterprise Dr Ste 408 (06484-7624)
PHONE..................................203 315-5062
Don Zhang, *President*
Mehrnaz Kamal, *Exec VP*
Michael Costanzo, *Director*
Jidong Liu, *Director*
◆ **EMP:** 12
SQ FT: 4,800

SALES (est): 2.6MM **Privately Held**
WEB: www.betapharma.com
SIC: 2834 8731 Mfg Pharmaceutical Preparations Commercial Physical Research

(G-3781)
BETA SHIM CO
11 Progress Dr (06484-6218)
PHONE..................................203 926-1150
John P McCue, *President*
Mark Lovallo, *Vice Pres*
Scott McCue, *Vice Pres*
Zach Pratt, *Vice Pres*
John McCue, *Info Tech Mgr*
EMP: 47
SQ FT: 21,000
SALES (est): 12.5MM **Privately Held**
WEB: www.betashim.com
SIC: 3499 3469 Mfg Misc Fabricated Metal Products Mfg Metal Stampings

(G-3782)
BIC CORPORATION (HQ)
Also Called: Bic Graphic USA
1 Bic Way Ste 1 # 1 (06484-6223)
PHONE..................................203 783-2000
Mario Guevara, *CEO*
Bruno Bich, *Ch of Bd*
Pauline Dantas, *President*
Nikita Minchenko, *Business Mgr*
Ed Shea, *Business Mgr*
▲ **EMP:** 900 **EST:** 1958
SQ FT: 800,000
SALES (est): 1.4B
SALES (corp-wide): 766.4MM **Privately Held**
WEB: www.biclink.com
SIC: 3951 2899 3999 3421 Mfg Pens/Mechncl Pencils Mfg Chemical Preparation Mfg Misc Products Mfg Cutlery Whol Sporting Goods/Supp
PA: Societe Bic
14 Rue Jeanne D Asnieres
Clichy 92110
800 101-214

(G-3783)
BIC USA INC (DH)
1 Bic Way Ste 1 # 1 (06484-6223)
PHONE..................................203 783-2000
Kazufumi Ikeda, *Ch of Bd*
Don Cummins, *President*
Steven A Burkhart, *Vice Pres*
Barry Johnson, *Vice Pres*
David T Kimball, *Vice Pres*
▲ **EMP:** 200
SQ FT: 15,000
SALES (est): 133.1MM
SALES (corp-wide): 766.4MM **Privately Held**
WEB: www.biceveryday.com
SIC: 3951 2899 3999 3421 Mfg Pens/Mechncl Pencils Mfg Chemical Preparation Mfg Misc Products Mfg Cutlery
HQ: Bic Corporation
1 Bic Way Ste 1 # 1
Shelton CT 06484
203 783-2000

(G-3784)
BRIDGEPORT MAGNETICS GROUP INC
6 Waterview Dr (06484-4300)
PHONE..................................203 954-0050
Ulrik Poulsen, *President*
Sandu Pescaru, *Vice Pres*
Charlotte Poulsen, *Admin Sec*
▲ **EMP:** 27
SALES (est): 6.3MM **Privately Held**
SIC: 3357 3679 3612 Nonferrous Wire-drawing/Insulating Mfg Electronic Components Mfg Transformers

(G-3785)
CCL INDUSTRIES CORPORATION (DH)
Also Called: CCL Label
15 Controls Dr (06484-6111)
PHONE..................................203 926-1253
Geoffrey T Martin, *CEO*
Wayne M E McLeod, *President*
Dominic Castor, *General Mgr*
Peter Fleissner, *Vice Pres*
Lalitha Vaidyanathan, *Vice Pres*
▲ **EMP:** 85
SQ FT: 38,000
SALES (est): 1B
SALES (corp-wide): 3.9B **Privately Held**
SIC: 2759 2992 3411 2819 Commercial Printing Mfg Lubrictng Oil/Grease Mfg Metal Cans Mfg Indstl Inorgan Chem
HQ: Ccl International Inc
105 Gordon Baker Rd Suite 800
North York ON
416 756-8500

(G-3786)
CCL LABEL INC
15 Controls Dr (06484-6111)
PHONE..................................203 926-1253
EMP: 190
SALES (corp-wide): 3.9B **Privately Held**
SIC: 2759 3411 2671 Commercial Printing Mfg Metal Cans Mfg Packaging Paper/Film
HQ: Ccl Label, Inc.
161 Worcester Rd Ste 603
Framingham MA 01701
508 872-4511

(G-3787)
CCL LABEL (DELAWARE) INC (DH)
15 Controls Dr (06484-6111)
PHONE..................................203 926-1253
Serge De Paoli, *President*
Ronald Perin, *Vice Pres*
Victor Theriault, *Vice Pres*
David Blackwell, *Production*
▲ **EMP:** 4
SQ FT: 30,000
SALES (est): 197.1MM
SALES (corp-wide): 3.9B **Privately Held**
SIC: 2759 Commercial Printing
HQ: Ccl Label, Inc.
161 Worcester Rd Ste 603
Framingham MA 01701
508 872-4511

(G-3788)
CENTRIX INC
770 River Rd (06484-5430)
PHONE..................................203 929-5582
William B Dragan, *President*
John J Discko Jr, *Vice Pres*
John Discko, *Vice Pres*
Hank Buddrus, *Manager*
Paul Fattibene, *Admin Sec*
▲ **EMP:** 103
SQ FT: 50,000
SALES (est): 21.5MM **Privately Held**
SIC: 3843 Mfg Dental Equipment/Supplies

(G-3789)
CHROMALLOY COMPONENT SVCS INC
415 Howe Ave (06484-3166)
PHONE..................................203 924-1666
Dan Martin, *Branch Mgr*
EMP: 8
SALES (corp-wide): 2.4B **Publicly Held**
SIC: 3471 Plating/Polishing Service
HQ: Chromalloy Component Services, Inc.
303 Industrial Park Rd
San Antonio TX 78226
210 331-2300

(G-3790)
COMET TECHNOLOGIES USA INC (DH)
Also Called: Yxlon International
100 Trap Falls Road Ext (06484-4646)
PHONE..................................203 447-3200
Robert Jardim, *President*
Rebecca Rudolph, *Vice Pres*
Paul Wade, *Engineer*
Noah Fredette, *Sales Staff*
Corey Gordon, *Manager*
◆ **EMP:** 30
SQ FT: 16,421
SALES (est): 139.5MM
SALES (corp-wide): 442.9MM **Privately Held**
WEB: www.yxlon.com
SIC: 3844 3829 Mfg X-Ray Apparatus/Tubes Mfg Measuring/Controlling Devices
HQ: Comet Ag
Herrengasse 10
Flamatt FR 3175
317 449-000

(G-3791)
CTS SERVICES LLC
15 Rayo Dr (06484-2450)
PHONE..................................203 268-5865
Daryl D Bouchard, *Mng Member*
EMP: 4 **EST:** 2012
SALES (est): 216.6K **Privately Held**
SIC: 2869 Mfg Industrial Organic Chemicals

(G-3792)
CYA TECHNOLOGIES INC
3 Enterprise Dr Ste 408 (06484-4696)
PHONE..................................203 513-3111
Wayne Crandall, *President*
Uma Annareddy, *Consultant*
Clint Karlin, *Info Tech Dir*
Brian Roberts, *Technology*
Scott Young, *Software Engr*
EMP: 50
SALES (est): 3.8MM **Privately Held**
WEB: www.cya.com
SIC: 7372 Prepackaged Software Services

(G-3793)
DAC SYSTEMS INC
4 Armstrong Rd Ste 12 (06484-4721)
PHONE..................................203 924-7000
Mark G Nickson, *President*
EMP: 10
SQ FT: 4,000
SALES (est): 1.6MM **Privately Held**
WEB: www.dacsystems.com
SIC: 3661 Mfg Telephone Voice Automation Response Systems

(G-3794)
DAN BEARD INC
Also Called: Island Sand & Gravel Pit
64 Hawthorne Ave (06484-4437)
P.O. Box 71 (06484-0071)
PHONE..................................203 924-4346
Jeff Rhodes, *Manager*
EMP: 15
SALES (corp-wide): 3.2MM **Privately Held**
WEB: www.danbeard.com
SIC: 3281 5032 1442 Mfg Cut Stone/Products Whol Brick/Stone Material Construction Sand/Gravel
PA: Dan Beard Inc
Mary St
Shelton CT 06484
203 924-1575

(G-3795)
DERBY CELLULAR PRODUCTS INC
680 Bridgeport Ave Ste 3 (06484-4705)
PHONE..................................203 735-4661
Frank Osak Jr, *President*
Allan Cribbines, *President*
Charles Drabek, *Vice Pres*
Michael Osak, *Vice Pres*
EMP: 145
SQ FT: 161,000
SALES (est): 20.3MM **Privately Held**
WEB: www.derbycellularproducts.com
SIC: 3053 Mfg Gaskets/Packing/Sealing Devices

(G-3796)
DIGATRON POWER ELECTRONICS INC
50 Waterview Dr (06484-4376)
PHONE..................................203 446-8000
Mark Clark, *Engineer*
Paula Fernandes, *Finance*
▲ **EMP:** 35
SQ FT: 16,000
SALES (est): 9.1MM
SALES (corp-wide): 177.9K **Privately Held**
SIC: 3629 3625 3825 Mfg Electrical Industrial Apparatus Mfg Relays/Industrial Controls Mfg Electrical Measuring Instruments
HQ: Digatron Power Electronics Gmbh
Tempelhofer Str. 12-14
Aachen 52068
241 168-090

(G-3797)
DONUT STOP
368 Howe Ave (06484-3127)
PHONE..................................203 924-7133
Maria Bobotsis, *Owner*
EMP: 5
SALES (est): 160K **Privately Held**
SIC: 2051 5461 Mfg Bread/Related Products Retail Bakery

(G-3798)
EBEAM FILM LLC
240 Long Hill Cross Rd (06484-6161)
PHONE..................................203 926-0100
EMP: 12
SALES (est): 820.5K **Privately Held**
SIC: 3861 3577 7374 8731 Mfg Photo Equip/Supplies Mfg Computer Peripherals Data Processing/Prep Coml Physical Research Commercial Photography

(G-3799)
EDGEWELL PER CARE BRANDS LLC (HQ)
Also Called: Energizer
6 Research Dr (06484-6228)
PHONE..................................203 944-5500
Ward Klein, *Ch of Bd*
Sean Salvarezza, *Counsel*
Corey Barrette, *Vice Pres*
Stephanie Lynn, *Vice Pres*
Glen Dupuis, *Research*
◆ **EMP:** 370
SALES (est): 3.5B
SALES (corp-wide): 2.1B **Publicly Held**
WEB: www.eveready.com
SIC: 3421 2844 2676 Mfg Cutlery Mfg Toilet Preparations Mfg Sanitary Paper Products
PA: Edgewell Personal Care Company
1350 Tmberlake Manor Pkwy
Chesterfield MO 63017
314 594-1900

(G-3800)
ELVEX CORPORATION
2 Mountain View Dr (06484-6419)
PHONE..................................203 743-2488
Jeffrey Begoon, *President*
Walter Fred Ravetto, *Vice Pres*
Richard Sustello, *Vice Pres*
▲ **EMP:** 15
SQ FT: 12,000
SALES (est): 3.3MM **Privately Held**
WEB: www.elvex.com
SIC: 3842 5099 Mfg Surgical Appliances/Supplies Whol Durable Goods

(G-3801)
ENFIELD TECHNOLOGIES LLC
50 Waterview Dr Ste 120 (06484-4377)
PHONE..................................203 375-3100
Ken Barbee, *Engineer*
Alady Cubas, *Info Tech Mgr*
R Edwin Howe,
Rosa Trombetta, *Admin Asst*
Vince McCarroll,
▼ **EMP:** 10
SQ FT: 6,000
SALES (est): 2.2MM **Privately Held**
WEB: www.enfieldtech.com
SIC: 3492 3494 Mfg Fluid Power Valves/Fittings Mfg Valves/Pipe Fittings

(G-3802)
FIVE STAR PRODUCTS INC
60 Parrott Dr (06484-4733)
PHONE..................................203 336-7900
Wilfred A Martinez, *CEO*
David Babcock, *President*
David S Babcock, *Chairman*
Brian R Feidt, *Vice Pres*
Terry Stysly, *Vice Pres*
▲ **EMP:** 30
SALES (est): 11.3MM **Privately Held**
SIC: 3273 2891 2899 2851 Mfg Ready-Mixed Concrete Mfg Adhesives/Sealants Mfg Chemical Preparation Mfg Paints/Allied Prdts

(G-3803)
FLEXIINTERNATIONAL SFTWR INC (PA)
2 Trap Falls Rd Ste 501 (06484-7623)
PHONE..................................203 925-3040

Stefan R Bothe, *Ch of Bd*
Maureen M Okerstrom, *President*
Dmitry G Trudov, *President*
EMP: 34
SQ FT: 25,000
SALES (est): 9.9MM **Publicly Held**
SIC: 7372 Prepackaged Software Services

(G-3804)
GELDER AEROSPACE LLC
Also Called: United Aero Group
12 Commerce Dr (06484-6202)
PHONE..................................203 283-9524
Kurt Gelder, *Sales Mgr*
Joshua Gelder,
EMP: 8
SQ FT: 81,000
SALES (est): 3.2MM **Privately Held**
SIC: 3728 Mfg Aircraft Parts/Equipment

(G-3805)
GRAYWOLF SENSING SOLUTIONS LLC (PA)
6 Research Dr Ste 110 (06484-6228)
PHONE..................................203 402-0477
Richard T Stonier, *President*
Juan Irizarry-Hernan, *Engineer*
Randy Nunley, *Regl Sales Mgr*
Erik Anderson, *Sales Staff*
EMP: 9
SALES (est): 2.3MM **Privately Held**
WEB: www.wolfsense.com
SIC: 3822 Mfg Environmental Controls

(G-3806)
GREAT LAKES CHEMICAL CORP (DH)
2 Armstrong Rd Ste 101 (06484-4735)
PHONE..................................203 573-2000
Craig Rogerson, *CEO*
Anne Noonan, *President*
◆ **EMP:** 50 **EST:** 1932
SALES (est): 668.9MM
SALES (corp-wide): 7.9B **Privately Held**
WEB: www.glcc.com
SIC: 2899 2842 Mfg Chemical Preparation Mfg Polish/Sanitation Gd
HQ: Lanxess Solutions Us Inc.
2 Armstrong Rd Ste 101
Shelton CT 06484
203 573-2000

(G-3807)
HAMDEN BREWING COMPANY LLC
819 Bridgeport Ave (06484-4714)
PHONE..................................203 247-4677
EMP: 3 **EST:** 2008
SALES (est): 134.2K **Privately Held**
SIC: 2082 Mfg Malt Beverages

(G-3808)
HAMWORTHY PEABODY COMBUSTN INC (DH)
Also Called: John Zink Company
6 Armstrong Rd Ste 2 (06484-4722)
PHONE..................................203 922-1199
Lawrence Berry, *President*
Anthony R Baker, *Vice Pres*
▲ **EMP:** 23 **EST:** 1920
SALES (est): 5.9MM
SALES (corp-wide): 40.6B **Privately Held**
WEB: www.hamworthy-peabody.com
SIC: 3433 3567 3561 Mfg Heat Equip-Nonelec Mfg Indstl Furnace/Ovens Mfg Pumps/Pumping Equip
HQ: John Zink Company, Llc
11920 E Apache St
Tulsa OK 74116
918 234-1800

(G-3809)
HARD-CORE SELF DEFENSE
500 River Rd (06484-4540)
PHONE..................................203 231-2344
EMP: 3
SALES (est): 206.5K **Privately Held**
SIC: 3812 Mfg Search/Navigation Equipment

(G-3810)
HASLER INC
19 Forest Pkwy (06484-6135)
P.O. Box 858 (06484-0903)
PHONE..................................203 301-3400
John Vavra, *Principal*
EMP: 3
SALES (est): 322.9K **Privately Held**
SIC: 3579 Mfg Office Machines

(G-3811)
HEARST CORPORATION
Also Called: Milford Mirror, The
1000 Bridgeport Ave (06484-4660)
PHONE..................................203 926-2080
Jill Dion, *Principal*
EMP: 3
SALES (corp-wide): 8.3B **Privately Held**
SIC: 2711 Newspapers-Publishing/Printing
PA: The Hearst Corporation
300 W 57th St Fl 42
New York NY 10019
212 649-2000

(G-3812)
HJ BAKER & BRO LLC (PA)
2 Corporate Dr Ste 545 (06484-6279)
PHONE..................................203 682-9200
Christopher Smith, *CEO*
David Smith, *President*
Jack L Williams, *Exec VP*
Kevin Courtney, *Plant Mgr*
Ray McElhaney, *Export Mgr*
◆ **EMP:** 40 **EST:** 1850
SQ FT: 12,500
SALES (est): 135.8MM **Privately Held**
SIC: 2048 5191 5052 Mfg Prepared Feeds Whol Farm Supplies Whol Coal/Minerals/Ores

(G-3813)
HUBBELL INCORPORATED (PA)
40 Waterview Dr (06484-4300)
PHONE..................................475 882-4000
David G Nord, *Ch of Bd*
Gerben W Bakker, *President*
Mike Overstreet, *Regional Mgr*
Jacqueline Donnelly, *District Mgr*
Gary Daviau, *Counsel*
EMP: 65 **EST:** 1888
SALES: 4.4B **Publicly Held**
WEB: www.hubbell.com
SIC: 3699 3678 Mfg Electrical And Electronic Products

(G-3814)
HUBBELL INCORPORATED DELAWARE
Hubbell Wiring Device-Kellems
40 Waterview Dr (06484-4300)
P.O. Box 1000 (06484-1000)
PHONE..................................475 882-4800
Gary Amato, *Vice Pres*
James Landolina, *Vice Pres*
Mark Bart, *Regl Sales Mgr*
Brad Fuller, *Manager*
EMP: 200
SQ FT: 21,600
SALES (corp-wide): 4.4B **Publicly Held**
SIC: 3643 Mfg Conductive Wiring Devices
HQ: Hubbell Incorporated (Delaware)
40 Waterview Dr
Shelton CT 06484
475 882-4000

(G-3815)
HUBBELL INCORPORATED DELAWARE (HQ)
40 Waterview Dr (06484-4300)
PHONE..................................475 882-4000
Gary Amato, *CEO*
Rex Daenzer, *Manager*
Chris Kyle, *Director*
Javier Piraneque, *Director*
Jim Putnam, *Training Spec*
EMP: 88
SALES (est): 59MM
SALES (corp-wide): 4.4B **Publicly Held**
WEB: www.hubbell.com
SIC: 3643 Mfg Conductive Wiring Devices
PA: Hubbell Incorporated
40 Waterview Dr
Shelton CT 06484
475 882-4000

(G-3816)
IKIGAI FOODS LLC
19 Beverly Hill Dr (06484-5105)
PHONE..................................203 954-8083
Richard B Harvey, *Principal*
EMP: 3
SALES (est): 145.9K **Privately Held**
SIC: 2099 Mfg Food Preparations

(G-3817)
INDUSTRIAL WOOD PRODUCT CO
84 Platt Rd (06484-5340)
PHONE..................................203 735-2374
H William Karcher, *President*
William H Karcher, *Trustee*
Susanne Karcher, *Vice Pres*
William Karcher, *VP Mfg*
EMP: 5
SALES: 500K **Privately Held**
SIC: 2431 2511 2434 1751 Mfg Millwork Mfg Wood Household Furniture Mfg Wood Kitchen Cabinets Carpentry Contractor

(G-3818)
INFORM INC
Also Called: Visible Record Systems
25 Brook St Ste 200 (06484-2332)
P.O. Box 785 (06484-0785)
PHONE..................................203 924-9929
Bill Carlson, *President*
David Carlson, *Corp Secy*
Greg Mattei, *Accounts Exec*
EMP: 8
SQ FT: 10,000
SALES (est): 1.4MM **Privately Held**
WEB: www.informprinting.com
SIC: 2752 Lithographic Commercial Printing

(G-3819)
INLINE PLASTICS CORP (PA)
Also Called: Surelock Division
42 Canal St (06484-3265)
PHONE..................................203 924-5933
Thomas Orkisz, *President*
Paul Bertuglia, *Vice Pres*
Augie Lanzetta, *Vice Pres*
Sam Maida, *Plant Mgr*
Shane Woodall, *Prdtn Mgr*
◆ **EMP:** 190
SQ FT: 312,000
SALES (est): 68.5MM **Privately Held**
WEB: www.inlineplastics.com
SIC: 3089 Mfg Plastic Products

(G-3820)
ITT WATER & WASTEWATER USA INC (HQ)
1 Greenwich Pl Ste 2 (06484-7603)
PHONE..................................262 548-8181
Ron Port, *President*
Frank Oliveira, *Vice Pres*
Jonny Sandstedt, *Vice Pres*
◆ **EMP:** 70 **EST:** 1957
SQ FT: 35,000
SALES (est): 52.9MM **Publicly Held**
WEB: www.flygtus.com
SIC: 3561 Whol Industrial Equipment

(G-3821)
JOHN ZINK COMPANY LLC
Also Called: John Zink -Todd Combustn Group
2 Armstrong Rd Fl 3 (06484-4735)
PHONE..................................203 925-0380
Andrew Darrieau, *Principal*
Timothy Webster, *Plant Mgr*
EMP: 100
SQ FT: 45,000
SALES (est): 6.1MM **Privately Held**
SIC: 3433 8711 5074 Mfg Heat Equip-Nonelec Engineering Services Whol Plumbing Equip/Supp

(G-3822)
KENO GRAPHIC SERVICES INC
1 Parrott Dr Ste 100 (06484-4853)
PHONE..................................203 925-7722
Daniel Kennedy, *President*
Bill Kennedy Jr, *Vice Pres*
William Kennedy Jr, *Treasurer*
Barbara Steadman, *Office Mgr*
Thomas Kennedy, *Admin Sec*
EMP: 27
SALES (est): 3.9MM **Privately Held**
SIC: 2759 Lithographic Commercial Printing

(G-3823)
LAMOR USA CORPORATION
2 Enterprise Dr Ste 404 (06484-4657)
PHONE..................................203 888-7700
Daniel Beyer, *General Mgr*
Stephen J Reilly, *Vice Pres*
Juri Tubashov, *Export Mgr*
Annika Blomqvist, *Controller*
Stuart Duncanson, *Sales Mgr*
◆ **EMP:** 4 **EST:** 1960
SQ FT: 30,000
SALES (est): 4.8MM **Privately Held**
SIC: 3559 Mfg Misc Industry Machinery

(G-3824)
LANXESS SOLUTIONS US INC (DH)
Also Called: Chemtura USA
2 Armstrong Rd Ste 101 (06484-4735)
PHONE..................................203 573-2000
Antonis Papadourakis, *President*
EMP: 22
SALES (est): 1.1B
SALES (corp-wide): 7.9B **Privately Held**
WEB: www.cromptoncorp.com
SIC: 2869 2843 2821 2911 Mfg Industl Organic Chem Mfg Surface Active Agent Mfg Plstc Material/Resin
HQ: Lanxess Deutschland Gmbh
Kennedyplatz 1
Koln 50679
221 888-50

(G-3825)
LATEX FOAM INTERNATIONAL LLC (HQ)
Also Called: Latex Foam Products
510 River Rd (06484-4517)
PHONE..................................203 924-0700
Joanne Osmolik, *VP Human Res*
Robert L Jenkins, *Mng Member*
Dave Fisher,
Steven Russo,
◆ **EMP:** 87
SALES (est): 39.1MM **Privately Held**
SIC: 2392 3069 Mfg Household Furnishings Mfg Fabricated Rubber Products
PA: Latex Foam International Holdings, Inc.
510 River Rd
Shelton CT 06484
203 924-0700

(G-3826)
LATEX FOAM INTL HOLDINGS INC (PA)
Also Called: Talalay Global
510 River Rd (06484-4517)
PHONE..................................203 924-0700
Marc Navarre, *CEO*
David T Fisher, *President*
Steve Turner, *Vice Pres*
Steve Tolmich, *Purch Mgr*
Steven Watson, *Treasurer*
◆ **EMP:** 200 **EST:** 1975
SQ FT: 284,000
SALES (est): 39.1MM **Privately Held**
SIC: 3069 Mfg Fabricated Rubber Products

(G-3827)
LECLAIRE FUEL OIL LLC
97 Unit 3 Bridgeport Ave (06484)
PHONE..................................203 922-1512
Richard Leclaire, *Principal*
EMP: 3
SALES (est): 310K **Privately Held**
SIC: 2911 Petroleum Refining

(G-3828)
LEX PRODUCTS LLC (PA)
15 Progress Dr (06484-6218)
PHONE..................................203 363-3738
Robert R Luther, *CEO*
Dawn Tuthill, *Vice Pres*
Doreen Cordeiro, *Senior Buyer*
Liz Luther, *Treasurer*
Jim Clausi, *Human Res Mgr*
▲ **EMP:** 150
SQ FT: 18,000
SALES (est): 54MM **Privately Held**
WEB: www.lex-mps.com
SIC: 3829 3315 3643 3613 Mfg Measure/Control Dvcs Mfg Steel Wire/Rltd Prdt Mfg Conductive Wire Dvcs Mfg Switchgear/Boards

GEOGRAPHIC

(G-3829)
LOANWORKS SERVICING LLC
3 Corporate Dr Ste 208 (06484-6278)
PHONE..................................203 402-7304
Joe Caravetta, *Director*
EMP: 6 **EST:** 2009
SALES (est): 431.7K **Privately Held**
SIC: 1389 Oil/Gas Field Services

(G-3830)
MACRO SYSTEMS INC
20 Hubbell Ln (06484-2166)
PHONE..................................203 225-6266
John Tokarczyk, *President*
Sandra Tokarczyk, *Vice Pres*
EMP: 3
SQ FT: 1,600
SALES: 230K **Privately Held**
WEB: www.macrosystemsinc.com
SIC: 3827 Manufactures Measuring Equipment

(G-3831)
MARSARS WATER RESCUE SYSTEMS
8 Algonkin Rd (06484-4903)
PHONE..................................203 924-7315
Robert E Davis, *President*
Michelle Davis, *Vice Pres*
EMP: 8
SQ FT: 2,000
SALES (est): 717K **Privately Held**
WEB: www.marsars.com
SIC: 3561 Mfg Pumps/Pumping Equipment

(G-3832)
MERCANTILE DEVELOPMENT INC
10 Waterview Dr (06484-4300)
P.O. Box 825 (06484-0825)
PHONE..................................203 922-8880
F Alan Fankhanel, *President*
Tim Miller, *General Mgr*
Frank Digiovanni, *COO*
Lucia Furman, *Vice Pres*
Alan Sankhanel, *Purch Agent*
◆ **EMP:** 38 **EST:** 1947
SQ FT: 138,960
SALES (est): 12.7MM **Privately Held**
WEB: www.mdiwipers.com
SIC: 2679 Mfg Converted Paper Products

(G-3833)
MICROPHASE CORPORATION
100 Trap Falls Road Ext # 400 (06484-4646)
PHONE..................................203 866-8000
Amos Kohn, *CEO*
Necdet F Ergul, *President*
Jeffrey R F Peterson, *Corp Secy*
Jorge Lopez, *Production*
Bob Pasciucco, *QA Dir*
EMP: 26
SQ FT: 23,898
SALES: 9.1MM
SALES (corp-wide): 27.1MM **Publicly Held**
WEB: www.microphase.com
SIC: 3663 3677 3674 3661 Manufactures Radio Frequency And Microwave Equipment
HQ: Digital Power Corporation
48430 Lakeview Blvd
Fremont CA 94538
510 657-2635

(G-3834)
MILITARYLIFE PUBLISHING LLC
4 Research Dr (06484-6280)
PHONE..................................203 402-7234
Vincent Santoro,
EMP: 4
SALES: 700K **Privately Held**
SIC: 2741 Misc Publishing

(G-3835)
MOTORCYCLISTS POST
11 Haven Ln (06484-2017)
PHONE..................................203 929-9409
Leo Castell, *Owner*
EMP: 4
SALES (est): 180.7K **Privately Held**
SIC: 2721 Periodicals-Publishing/Printing

(G-3836)
NAIAD DYNAMICS US INC (HQ)
Also Called: Naiad Marine Systems
50 Parrott Dr (06484-4733)
PHONE..................................203 929-6355
John D Venables, *President*
Dave Archambault, *General Mgr*
Steve Colliss, *General Mgr*
Charlotte Gore, *Vice Pres*
Roger Pelzer, *Engineer*
▲ **EMP:** 50
SQ FT: 26,500
SALES (est): 16.9MM **Privately Held**
WEB: www.naiad.com
SIC: 3531 3625 3569 3599 Mfg Construction Mach Mfg Relay/Indstl Control Mfg General Indstl Mach Mfg Industrial Machinery Mfg Aircraft Parts/Equip

(G-3837)
NEVAMAR COMPANY LLC (HQ)
Also Called: Nevamar Distributors
1 Corporate Dr Ste 725 (06484-6230)
PHONE..................................203 925-1556
Jeffrey Muller, *Mng Member*
Jim Tees,
▲ **EMP:** 300
SALES (est): 82.1MM **Privately Held**
SIC: 3089 5162 Mfg Plastic Products Whol Plastic Materials/Shapes

(G-3838)
NEW ENGLAND STAIR COMPANY INC
1 White St (06484-3117)
P.O. Box 763 (06484-0763)
PHONE..................................203 924-0606
William J Sylvia, *President*
Matthew Sylvia, *Admin Sec*
EMP: 21
SQ FT: 25,000
SALES (est): 4.3MM **Privately Held**
WEB: www.newenglandstair.com
SIC: 2431 Mfg Millwork

(G-3839)
NEWCO CONDENSER INC
40 Waterview Dr (06484-4300)
PHONE..................................475 882-4000
EMP: 4 **EST:** 2007
SALES (est): 187.4K
SALES (corp-wide): 4.4B **Publicly Held**
SIC: 3264 3699 3675 3674 Mfg Porcelain Elc Supply Mfg Elec Mach/Equip/Supp Mfg Electronic Capacitor Mfg Semiconductors/Dvcs Mfg Switchgear/Boards
PA: Hubbell Incorporated
40 Waterview Dr
Shelton CT 06484
475 882-4000

(G-3840)
NEWCO LIGHTING INC (HQ)
40 Waterview Dr (06484-4300)
PHONE..................................475 882-4000
David G Nord, *President*
EMP: 5
SALES (est): 46MM
SALES (corp-wide): 4.4B **Publicly Held**
SIC: 3646 Mfg Commercial Lighting Fixtures
PA: Hubbell Incorporated
40 Waterview Dr
Shelton CT 06484
475 882-4000

(G-3841)
NORCELL INC (DH)
2 Corporate Dr Fl 5 (06484-6238)
PHONE..................................203 254-5292
Mark Cassidy, *President*
Leslie Santore, *CFO*
Sperre Lars, *Human Res Mgr*
Michael Cross, *Manager*
Stig Stene, *Representative*
▲ **EMP:** 15
SQ FT: 3,600
SALES (est): 3.1MM
SALES (corp-wide): 2.9B **Privately Held**
WEB: www.norske-skog-utmark.com
SIC: 2621 Paper Mill
HQ: Cellmark Ab
Lilla Bommen 3c
Goteborg 411 0
311 900-07

(G-3842)
NOVAMONT NORTH AMERICA INC
1000 Bridgeport Ave # 304 (06484-4676)
PHONE..................................203 744-8801
Alessandro Ferlito, *President*
Gaetano Lo Monaco, *Principal*
Paul Darby, *Manager*
EMP: 13 **EST:** 2010
SALES (est): 2.5MM **Privately Held**
SIC: 3821 Mfg Lab Apparatus/Furniture
HQ: Novamont Spa
Via Giacomo Fauser 8
Novara NO 28100
032 169-9611

(G-3843)
NUTMEG BREWING REST GROUP LLC
Also Called: Southport Brewing Company
819 Bridgeport Ave (06484-4714)
PHONE..................................203 256-2337
William Dasilva,
David Rutigliano,
EMP: 50
SQ FT: 3,200
SALES (est): 4.2MM **Privately Held**
SIC: 2082 Mfg Malt Beverages

(G-3844)
O C TANNER COMPANY
2 Corporate Dr Ste 935 (06484-6250)
PHONE..................................203 944-5430
Christopher Osinski, *Manager*
EMP: 3
SALES (corp-wide): 378.7MM **Privately Held**
WEB: www.octanner.com
SIC: 3911 Mfg Precious Metal Jewelry
PA: O. C. Tanner Company
1930 S State St
Salt Lake City UT 84115
801 486-2430

(G-3845)
O E M CONTROLS INC (PA)
10 Controls Dr (06484-6100)
P.O. Box 894 (06484-0894)
PHONE..................................203 929-8431
S Brian Simons, *President*
Keith T Simons, *Vice Pres*
Robert D Rose, *Plant Mgr*
Diane Clifford, *Purch Mgr*
Ken Pontbriant, *Electrical Engi*
EMP: 200 **EST:** 1966
SQ FT: 56,000
SALES (est): 34.2MM **Privately Held**
WEB: www.oemcontrols.com
SIC: 3625 3229 3577 Mfg Relay/Indstl Control Mfg Pressed/Blown Glass Mfg Computer Peripherals

(G-3846)
OERLIKON AM MEDICAL INC
Also Called: (PARENT IS OERLIKON USA HOLDING INC, TRAFFORD, PA.)
10 Constitution Blvd S (06484-4302)
PHONE..................................203 712-1030
Ottavio Disanto, *CEO*
Thomas Barret, *President*
Nancy Theodorides, *Treasurer*
Mark Zembrzuski, *Admin Sec*
Adreana Di Santo, *Assistant*
EMP: 75
SQ FT: 30,000
SALES (est): 14.3MM
SALES (corp-wide): 2.6B **Privately Held**
WEB: www.disanto.com
SIC: 3841 Mfg Surgical/Medical Instruments
PA: Oc Oerlikon Corporation Ag, Pfaffikon
Churerstrasse 120
PfAffikon SZ 8808
583 609-696

(G-3847)
OPEL CONNECTICUT SOLAR LLC
3 Corporate Dr Ste 204 (06484-6210)
P.O. Box 555, Storrs Mansfield (06268-0555)
PHONE..................................203 612-2366
Robert G Pico, *President*
France Pagnot, *General Mgr*
Susanne Schaefer, *General Mgr*
Johan Brusing, *District Mgr*
Andrew Carlson, *Engineer*
▲ **EMP:** 27
SQ FT: 5,500
SALES (est): 3.4MM **Privately Held**
SIC: 3674 Mfg Semiconductors/Related Devices

(G-3848)
PANOLAM INDUSTRIES INC (HQ)
Also Called: Panolam Surface System
1 Corporate Dr Ste 725 (06484-6230)
PHONE..................................203 925-1556
Robert Muller, *President*
Alan S Kabus, *President*
Lawrence Grossman, *Exec VP*
Vincent Miceli, *CFO*
Jeffery Muller, *Admin Sec*
▲ **EMP:** 40
SALES (est): 265.6MM **Privately Held**
WEB: www.panolam.com
SIC: 3089 3083 Mfg Plastic Products Mfg Laminated Plastic Plate/Sheet

(G-3849)
PANOLAM INDUSTRIES INTL INC (PA)
Also Called: Panolam Surface Systems
1 Corporate Dr Ste 725 (06484-6230)
PHONE..................................203 925-1556
Peter Jones, *President*
Robert Vail, *Research*
Marc Deraps, *Engineer*
Barbara Chernesky, *Controller*
Lisa Bentham, *Credit Mgr*
▲ **EMP:** 40
SALES (est): 550.9MM **Privately Held**
SIC: 2493 3089 Mfg Reconstituted Wood Products Mfg Plastic Products

(G-3850)
PERIODIC TABLEWARE LLC
415 Howe Ave Ste 110 (06484-3182)
PHONE..................................310 428-4250
Marshall Jamshidi, *Principal*
EMP: 10 **EST:** 2013
SALES (est): 1MM **Privately Held**
SIC: 3229 3231 Mfg Pressed/Blown Glass Mfg Products-Purchased Glass

(G-3851)
PERKINELMER INC
Perkinelmer Life and Analytic
710 Bridgeport Ave (06484-4794)
PHONE..................................203 925-4600
Vinod Aliminate, *Project Mgr*
Erika Garrison, *Project Mgr*
James Haydu, *Mfg Mgr*
Richard Franklin, *Purch Mgr*
Leslie Siwakoski, *Buyer*
EMP: 8
SALES (corp-wide): 2.7B **Publicly Held**
WEB: www.perkinelmer.com
SIC: 3826 Mfg Analytical Instruments
PA: Perkinelmer, Inc.
940 Winter St
Waltham MA 02451
781 663-6900

(G-3852)
PERKINELMER HLTH SCIENCES INC
710 Bridgeport Ave (06484-4794)
PHONE..................................203 925-4600
EMP: 135
SALES (corp-wide): 2.7B **Publicly Held**
SIC: 3826 Mfg Analytical Instruments
HQ: Perkinelmer Health Sciences, Inc.
940 Winter St
Waltham MA 02451
781 663-6900

(G-3853)
PIONEER PLASTICS CORPORATION (HQ)
Also Called: Pionite Decorative Surfaces
1 Corporate Dr Ste 725 (06484-6230)
PHONE..................................203 925-1556
Alan S Kabus, *President*
Robert Muller, *President*
Jeffrey Muller, *COO*
Larry Grossman, *CFO*
Vincent Miceli, *CFO*
◆ **EMP:** 89

SQ FT: 560,000
SALES (est): 204MM **Privately Held**
SIC: 3083 3087 Mfg Laminated Plastic Plate/Sheet Custom Compounding-Purchased Resins

(G-3854)
PITNEY BOWES INC
27 Waterview Dr (06484-4301)
PHONE..................................203 922-4000
Barret S Johnson, *President*
EMP: 35
SALES (corp-wide): 3.5B **Publicly Held**
SIC: 3579 7359 Mfg Office Machines Equipment Rental/Leasing
PA: Pitney Bowes Inc.
3001 Summer St Ste 3
Stamford CT 06905
203 356-5000

(G-3855)
PITNEY BOWES INC
27 Waterview Dr (06484-4301)
PHONE..................................203 356-5000
EMP: 35
SALES (corp-wide): 3.5B **Publicly Held**
SIC: 3579 7359 3661 8744 Mfg Office Machines Equipment Rental/Leasing Mfg Telephone/Graph Eqip
PA: Pitney Bowes Inc.
3001 Summer St Ste 3
Stamford CT 06905
203 356-5000

(G-3856)
PLAYTEX PRODUCTS LLC (HQ)
6 Research Dr Ste 400 (06484-6228)
P.O. Box 889 (06484-0889)
PHONE..................................203 944-5500
Thomas Schultz, *Development*
Neil P Defeo, *Mng Member*
Perry R Beadon,
James S Cook,
Kris Kelley,
▼ **EMP:** 100
SQ FT: 59,100
SALES (est): 473.3MM
SALES (corp-wide): 2.1B **Publicly Held**
WEB: www.playtexproductsinc.com
SIC: 2676 3069 2844 3842 Mfg Sanitary Paper Prdts
PA: Edgewell Personal Care Company
1350 Tmberlake Manor Pkwy
Chesterfield MO 63017
314 594-1900

(G-3857)
PR-MX HOLDINGS COMPANY LLC (HQ)
Also Called: Precision Resource Mexico
25 Forest Pkwy (06484-6122)
PHONE..................................203 925-0012
Peter Wolcott,
Scott Fabricant,
Charles Polatsek,
John Weiland,
EMP: 15
SQ FT: 70,000
SALES (est): 1.7MM
SALES (corp-wide): 260.1MM **Privately Held**
WEB: www.precisionresource.com
SIC: 3469 Mfg Metal Stampings
PA: Precision Resource, Inc.
25 Forest Pkwy
Shelton CT 06484
203 925-0012

(G-3858)
PRECISE CIRCUIT COMPANY INC
155 Myrtle St (06484-4062)
PHONE..................................203 924-2512
Thomas Misencik, *President*
Roseann Misencik, *Admin Sec*
EMP: 25
SQ FT: 15,000
SALES (est): 3.4MM **Privately Held**
WEB: www.precisecircuit.com
SIC: 3672 Mfg Printed Circuit Boards

(G-3859)
PRECISION RESOURCE INC (PA)
25 Forest Pkwy (06484-6122)
PHONE..................................203 925-0012
Peter Wolcott, *CEO*
Charles Polatsek, *Vice Pres*
Mony Singh, *Engineer*
Gregory Chvirko, *Design Engr*
Dan Bazar, *Manager*
▲ **EMP:** 176 **EST:** 1953
SQ FT: 100,000
SALES (est): 260.1MM **Privately Held**
WEB: www.precisionresource.com
SIC: 3469 Mfg Metal Stampings

(G-3860)
PREFERRED PDT & MKTG GROUP LLC
415 Howe Ave Ste 103 (06484-3174)
PHONE..................................203 567-0221
Celeste S McGorty,
EMP: 3
SALES: 80K **Privately Held**
WEB: www.ppmgllc.com
SIC: 3679 Electronic Supplies

(G-3861)
PREFERRED TOOL & DIE INC (PA)
Also Called: Preferred Precision
30 Forest Pkwy (06484-6122)
PHONE..................................203 925-8525
Michael Fortin, *President*
Virginia Fortin, *Principal*
Wayne Fortin, *Vice Pres*
Kim Oconnor, *Office Mgr*
EMP: 82
SQ FT: 26,000
SALES (est): 17.2MM **Privately Held**
SIC: 3469 3544 Mfg Metal Stampings Mfg Dies/Tools/Jigs/Fixtures

(G-3862)
PREFERRED TOOL & DIE INC
Preferred Precision
19 Forest Pkwy (06484-6135)
PHONE..................................203 925-8525
Mark Testani, *Branch Mgr*
EMP: 40
SALES (est): 5.2MM
SALES (corp-wide): 17.2MM **Privately Held**
SIC: 3545 Mfg Machine Tool Accessories
PA: Preferred Tool & Die, Inc.
30 Forest Pkwy
Shelton CT 06484
203 925-8525

(G-3863)
PREMIER MFG GROUP INC
Also Called: Electri-Cable Assemblies
10 Mountain View Dr (06484-6403)
PHONE..................................203 924-6617
Russell Hayden, *President*
David Black, *Treasurer*
EMP: 60
SALES (est): 15.5MM
SALES (corp-wide): 2.7B **Publicly Held**
SIC: 3645 2541 Mfg Residential Lighting Fixtures Mfg Wood Partitions/Fixtures
HQ: Group Dekko, Inc.
2505 Dekko Dr
Garrett IN 46738

(G-3864)
PUCKS PUTTERS & FUEL LLC (PA)
784 River Rd (06484-5430)
PHONE..................................203 494-3952
Steven Genova, *Principal*
EMP: 3 **EST:** 2012
SALES (est): 871.9K **Privately Held**
SIC: 2869 Mfg Industrial Organic Chemicals

(G-3865)
QDS LLC
120 Long Hill Cross Rd (06484-6180)
PHONE..................................203 338-9668
Paul Christian, *Principal*
Dave Christian, *Technical Staff*
EMP: 3
SALES (est): 278.6K **Privately Held**
SIC: 3999 Mfg Misc Products

(G-3866)
QUALEDI INC
1 Trap Falls Rd Ste 206 (06484-4672)
P.O. Box 623, Stratford (06615-0623)
PHONE..................................203 538-5320
Stephen A Morocco, *Branch Mgr*
EMP: 9
SALES (corp-wide): 1.2MM **Privately Held**
SIC: 7372 Prepackaged Software Services
PA: Qualedi Inc
121 W Main St Ste 4
Milford CT 06460
203 874-4334

(G-3867)
SAFETY BAGS INC
2 Corporate Dr Ste 250 (06484-6239)
P.O. Box 553 (06484-0553)
PHONE..................................203 242-0727
Dori Decarlo, *CEO*
EMP: 3
SALES: 500K **Privately Held**
SIC: 2673 Mfg Bags-Plastic/Coated Paper

(G-3868)
SATIN AMERICAN CORPORATION
40 Oliver Ter (06484-5384)
P.O. Box 619 (06484-0619)
PHONE..................................203 929-6363
Joseph Satin, *President*
Leo Disorbo, *Vice Pres*
Anthony Ciccaglione, *VP Sales*
EMP: 35
SQ FT: 55,000
SALES (est): 7.6MM **Privately Held**
WEB: www.satinamerican.com
SIC: 3613 Mfg Switchgear/Switchboards

(G-3869)
SHEAFFER PEN CORP
1 Bic Way Ste 1 (06484-6223)
PHONE..................................203 783-2894
EMP: 300 **EST:** 1960
SALES (est): 18.8MM **Privately Held**
SIC: 2621 Paper Mill

(G-3870)
SIGN IN SOFT INC
1 Waterview Dr (06484-4368)
PHONE..................................203 216-3046
Peter Pynadath, *President*
Sridhar Rapelli, *Principal*
EMP: 4
SALES (est): 98.6K **Privately Held**
SIC: 3993 5045 5049 Mfg Signs/Advertising Specialties Whol Computers/Peripherals Whol Professional Equipment

(G-3871)
SIKORSKY AIRCRAFT CORPORATION
1 Far Mill Xing (06484-6121)
PHONE..................................203 386-7861
Filmson Alexander, *Branch Mgr*
EMP: 715 **Publicly Held**
SIC: 3721 Mfg Aircraft
HQ: Sikorsky Aircraft Corporation
6900 Main St
Stratford CT 06614

(G-3872)
SORGE INDUSTRIES INC
289 Coram Rd (06484-4529)
PHONE..................................203 924-8900
Thomas Sorge, *President*
Susan K Sorge, *Corp Secy*
EMP: 6
SQ FT: 3,000
SALES (est): 973.8K **Privately Held**
SIC: 7692 3446 Welding Shop

(G-3873)
SPINE WAVE INC
3 Enterprise Dr Ste 210 (06484-4696)
PHONE..................................203 944-9494
Mark Loguidice, *President*
Hal Jungerheld, *Exec VP*
Ronnie Smith, *Vice Pres*
Tom Wilson, *Vice Pres*
Beth Stuart, *Research*
EMP: 100
SALES (est): 21MM **Privately Held**
SIC: 3841 Mfg Surgical/Medical Instruments

(G-3874)
STONEAGE LLC
36 Narragansett Trl (06484-4911)
PHONE..................................203 926-1133
EMP: 3
SALES: 180K **Privately Held**
SIC: 3281 Mfg Cut Stone/Products

(G-3875)
SYFERLOCK TECHNOLOGY CORP
917 Bridgeport Ave Ste 5 (06484-4679)
PHONE..................................203 292-5441
Robert D Russo, *President*
Francis Laplante, *Technology*
Abu Marcose, *Technology*
EMP: 7 **EST:** 2008
SALES (est): 876.4K **Privately Held**
SIC: 3577 5045 Mfg Computer Peripheral Equipment Whol Computers/Peripherals

(G-3876)
SYSTEM INTGRTION CNSULTING LLC
Also Called: Allegra Print & Imaging
1000 Bridgeport Ave 1-3 (06484-4660)
PHONE..................................203 926-9599
Gary Bean, *CEO*
EMP: 5
SQ FT: 300
SALES: 900K **Privately Held**
SIC: 2752 Lithographic Commercial Printing

(G-3877)
TANGOE US INC
1 Waterview Dr Ste 200 (06484-4368)
PHONE..................................203 859-9300
Robert Irwin, *CEO*
Christine Foster, *Vice Pres*
Jonathan Ladov, *Vice Pres*
Bill Lynch, *Vice Pres*
Chris Newman, *Vice Pres*
EMP: 300
SALES (corp-wide): 491.5MM **Privately Held**
SIC: 7372 Prepackaged Software Services
HQ: Tangoe Us, Inc.
1 Waterview Dr Ste 200
Shelton CT 06484
973 257-0300

(G-3878)
TANGOE US INC (HQ)
1 Waterview Dr Ste 200 (06484-4368)
PHONE..................................973 257-0300
Robert Irwin, *CEO*
Marc Culver, *Vice Pres*
Chris Taylor, *CFO*
Rick Young, *CFO*
Sidra Berman, *Chief Mktg Ofcr*
EMP: 120
SQ FT: 66,000
SALES (est): 491.5MM **Privately Held**
WEB: www.tangoe.com
SIC: 7372 Prepackaged Software Services
PA: Tangoe, Llc
6410 Poplar Ave Ste 200
Memphis TN 38119
901 752-6200

(G-3879)
THREADS OF EVIDENCE LLC
52 Oronoque Trl (06484-4949)
PHONE..................................203 929-5209
Mary McQullan, *Mng Member*
EMP: 4
SALES: 220K **Privately Held**
SIC: 2391 Mfg Curtains/Draperies

(G-3880)
TIGER-SUL PRODUCTS LLC
4 Armstrong Rd Ste 220 (06484-4721)
P.O. Box 5, Atmore AL (36504-0005)
PHONE..................................251 202-3850
Don Cherry, *President*
▼ **EMP:** 50

SALES (est): 12.6MM
SALES (corp-wide): 74.2MM **Privately Held**
SIC: 2819 Mfg Industrial Inorganic Chemicals
PA: Platte River Equity Iii, L.P.
200 Fillmore St Ste 200 # 200
Denver CO 80206
303 292-7300

(G-3881)
TREIF USA INC
50 Waterview Dr Ste 130 (06484-4377)
PHONE..................................203 929-9930
Guenter Becker, *President*
Cornelia Bischoff, *Sales Staff*
Roger Costello, *Sales Staff*
Alicia Clayton, *Office Mgr*
Carmen Diaz, *Manager*
◆ **EMP:** 15
SQ FT: 12,000
SALES (est): 3.4MM
SALES (corp-wide): 62.6MM **Privately Held**
SIC: 3556 5046 Mfg Food Products Machinery Whol Commercial Equipment
PA: T R E I F - Maschinenbau Gesellschaft Mit Beschrankter Haftung
Toni-Reifenhauser-Str. 1
Oberlahr 57641
268 594-40

(G-3882)
TRI SOURCE INC
84 Platt Rd (06484-5340)
PHONE..................................203 924-7030
Edward Hyland, *President*
Anita Hampel, *Corp Secy*
EMP: 12
SQ FT: 17,000
SALES: 1.5MM **Privately Held**
WEB: www.trisourceinc.com
SIC: 3679 8732 Mfg Electronic Components Commercial Nonphysical Research

(G-3883)
TRYON MANUFACTURING COMPANY
30 Oliver Ter (06484-5336)
P.O. Box 242 (06484-0242)
PHONE..................................203 929-0464
George Fairbanks Jr, *Owner*
EMP: 6 **EST:** 1917
SQ FT: 4,000
SALES (est): 686.4K **Privately Held**
SIC: 3451 Mfg Screw Machine Products

(G-3884)
UNILEVER ASCC AG
3 Corporate Dr (06484-6222)
PHONE..................................203 381-2482
EMP: 300
SALES (corp-wide): 56.5B **Privately Held**
SIC: 2841 2099 Mfg Food And Soap
HQ: Unilever Ascc Ag
Spitalstrasse 5
Schaffhausen SH
526 315-000

(G-3885)
VIKING TOOL COMPANY
435 Access Rd (06484)
P.O. Box 808 (06484-0808)
PHONE..................................203 929-1457
Ole C Severson Jr, *President*
Ole C Severson III, *Treasurer*
James J Severson, *Admin Sec*
EMP: 35 **EST:** 1946
SQ FT: 10,000
SALES (est): 5MM **Privately Held**
WEB: www.vikingtool.com
SIC: 3541 5084 3545 Mfg Machine Tools-Cutting Whol Industrial Equipment Mfg Machine Tool Accessories

(G-3886)
VISHAY AMERICAS INC (HQ)
1 Greenwich Pl (06484-7603)
PHONE..................................203 452-5648
Gerald Paul, *CEO*
Marc Zandman, *Ch of Bd*
EMP: 500
SALES (est): 363.2MM
SALES (corp-wide): 3B **Publicly Held**
SIC: 3676 3674 Mfg Electronic Resistors Mfg Semiconductors/Related Devices
PA: Vishay Intertechnology, Inc.
63 Lancaster Ave
Malvern PA 19355
610 644-1300

(G-3887)
VITEC PRODUCTION SOLUTIONS INC (HQ)
14 Progress Dr (06484-6216)
PHONE..................................203 929-1100
Dan Fitzpatrick, *President*
Michael Accardi, *Vice Pres*
Curt Dann, *Treasurer*
Penny Lock, *Sales Staff*
Matthew Danilowicz, *Director*
▲ **EMP:** 100 **EST:** 1970
SALES (est): 31.1MM
SALES (corp-wide): 507.8MM **Privately Held**
WEB: www.antonbauer.com
SIC: 3861 3692 Mfg Photographic Equipment/Supplies Mfg Primary Batteries
PA: The Vitec Group Plc.
Bridge House
Richmond TW9 1
208 332-4600

(G-3888)
WEST-CONN TOOL AND DIE INC
128 Long Hill Cross Rd (06484-6169)
PHONE..................................203 538-5081
David Marasco, *President*
Laura Pinciaro, *Vice Pres*
Dave Zell, *Opers Staff*
Shelley Schneider, *Administration*
EMP: 11 **EST:** 1983
SQ FT: 15,900
SALES (est): 2.2MM **Privately Held**
SIC: 3544 Mfg Dies/Tools/Jigs/Fixtures

(G-3889)
WICKS BUSINESS INFORMATION LLC (PA)
Also Called: Treasury & Risk Management
4 Research Dr Ste 402 (06484-6242)
PHONE..................................203 334-2002
Douglas J Manoni,
EMP: 10 **EST:** 1999
SALES: 20MM **Privately Held**
WEB: www.assetnews.com
SIC: 2721 2711 Periodicals-Publishing/Printing Newspapers-Publishing/Printing

(G-3890)
WIFFLE BALL INCORPORATED
275 Bridgeport Ave (06484-3827)
P.O. Box 193 (06484-0193)
PHONE..................................203 924-4643
David J Mullany, *President*
Stephen A Mullany, *Vice Pres*
EMP: 15 **EST:** 1953
SQ FT: 20,000
SALES (est): 2.5MM **Privately Held**
WEB: www.wiffle.com
SIC: 3949 Mfg Sporting/Athletic Goods

(G-3891)
XYLEM WATER SOLUTIONS USA INC
1000 Bridgeport Ave # 402 (06484-4660)
PHONE..................................203 450-3715
EMP: 25 **Publicly Held**
SIC: 3561 Mfg Pumps/Pumping Equipment
HQ: Xylem Water Solutions U.S.A., Inc.
4828 Prkwy Plz Blvd 200
Charlotte NC 28217

Sherman
Fairfield County

(G-3892)
ALPHA 1C LLC
3 Leach Hollow Rd (06784-2302)
PHONE..................................860 354-7979
Al Kenney, *Mng Member*
EMP: 6
SALES (est): 464.4K **Privately Held**
SIC: 3826 Mfg Analytical Instruments

(G-3893)
CLANCY WOODWORKING LLC
12 Anderson Rd E (06784-1014)
PHONE..................................860 355-3655
Brian Clancy, *Principal*
EMP: 4
SALES (est): 357.6K **Privately Held**
SIC: 2431 Mfg Millwork

(G-3894)
JAMES M MUNCH
Also Called: JM Logging Forestry
48 Route 37 S (06784-1529)
PHONE..................................802 353-3114
James Munch, *Principal*
EMP: 3
SALES (est): 212.2K **Privately Held**
SIC: 2411 Logging

(G-3895)
P L WOODWORKING
4 Deer Hill Rd (06784-2321)
PHONE..................................860 354-6855
Paul Levine, *President*
EMP: 6
SALES: 100K **Privately Held**
SIC: 2434 Mfg Wood Kitchen Cabinets

(G-3896)
PRIVATE COMMUNICATIONS CORP
Also Called: Private Wifi
39 Holiday Point Rd (06784-1628)
P.O. Box 159 (06784-0159)
PHONE..................................860 355-2718
Kent Lawson, *President*
EMP: 12
SQ FT: 4,000
SALES (est): 1.2MM **Privately Held**
WEB: www.privatewifi.com
SIC: 7372 Prepackaged Software Services

Simsbury
Hartford County

(G-3897)
BMI CAD SERVICES INC
8a Herman Dr (06070-1404)
P.O. Box 522 (06070-0522)
PHONE..................................860 658-0808
Bradford T Martin, *President*
Karen A Martin, *Vice Pres*
Karen Martin, *Vice Pres*
EMP: 10
SALES (est): 1.6MM **Privately Held**
SIC: 3599 Mfg Industrial Machinery

(G-3898)
CONTAINMENT SOLUTIONS INC
35 Ichabod Rd (06070-2812)
PHONE..................................860 651-4371
Scott Knake, *Branch Mgr*
EMP: 128
SALES (corp-wide): 8.4B **Publicly Held**
WEB: www.containmentsolutions.com
SIC: 3443 Mfg Fabricated Plate Work
HQ: Containment Solutions, Inc.
333 N Rivershire Dr # 190
Conroe TX 77304

(G-3899)
DESIGNS & PROTOTYPES LTD
Also Called: D & P Instruments
1280 Hopmeadow St Ste E (06070-1425)
PHONE..................................860 658-0458
Winthrop Wadsworth, *Branch Mgr*
EMP: 3
SALES (est): 416.9K **Privately Held**
WEB: www.dpinstruments.com
SIC: 3826 Mfg Analytical Instruments
PA: Designs & Prototypes, Ltd.
10 White Oak Dr Apt 113
Exeter NH 03833

(G-3900)
DYNO NOBEL INC
660 Hopmeadow St (06070-2420)
P.O. Box 2006 (06070-7603)
PHONE..................................860 843-2000
Dave Mains, *Engineer*
Jock Muir, *Branch Mgr*
Rudy Maurer, *Manager*
Robert Cooper, *Technology*
EMP: 150 **Privately Held**
SIC: 2892 Industrial Services
HQ: Dyno Nobel Inc.
2795 E Cottonwood Pkwy # 500
Salt Lake City UT 84121
801 364-4800

(G-3901)
ENSIGN BICKFORD INDUSTRIES
100 Grist Mill Ln (06070-2484)
P.O. Box 7 (06070-0007)
PHONE..................................203 843-2126
EMP: 13
SALES (est): 301K **Privately Held**
SIC: 3999 Mfg Misc Products

(G-3902)
ENSIGN-BCKFORD RNWBLE ENRGIES
125 Powder Forest Dr (06070)
PHONE..................................860 843-2000
Caleb E White, *President*
Scott M Deakin, *Treasurer*
Musa Elsir, *Accountant*
Dorothy Hammett, *Admin Sec*
EMP: 20
SALES (est): 2.1MM
SALES (corp-wide): 193.7MM **Privately Held**
SIC: 2421 Sawmill/Planing Mill
PA: Ensign-Bickford Industries, Inc.
999 17th St Ste 900
Denver CO 80202
860 843-2000

(G-3903)
ENSIGN-BICKFORD AROSPC DEF CO (HQ)
Also Called: EBA&d
640 Hopmeadow St (06070-2420)
P.O. Box 429 (06070-0429)
PHONE..................................860 843-2289
Brendan Walsh, *President*
Brendan M Walsh, *President*
Jeremy Stewart, *General Mgr*
Catherine Russo, *Executive Asst*
Dorothy T Hammett, *Admin Sec*
▲ **EMP:** 273
SQ FT: 150,000
SALES (est): 138.1MM
SALES (corp-wide): 193.7MM **Privately Held**
WEB: www.eba-d.com
SIC: 2892 Mfg Explosives
PA: Ensign-Bickford Industries, Inc.
999 17th St Ste 900
Denver CO 80202
860 843-2000

(G-3904)
ENSIGN-BICKFORD COMPANY (HQ)
125 Powder Forest Dr (06070)
P.O. Box 711 (06070-0711)
PHONE..................................860 843-2001
Scott M Deakin, *President*
Charles Difatta, *President*
Anna Fusari, *Accountant*
Rich Stewart, *Technical Staff*
Dorothy T Hammett, *General Counsel*
◆ **EMP:** 7
SQ FT: 11,000
SALES (est): 11.1MM
SALES (corp-wide): 193.7MM **Privately Held**
SIC: 2892 Mfg Explosives
PA: Ensign-Bickford Industries, Inc.
999 17th St Ste 900
Denver CO 80202
860 843-2000

(G-3905)
ENSIGN-BICKFORD INDUSTRIES INC
630 Hopmeadow St Rm 20 (06070-2420)
PHONE..................................860 658-4411
Michael Long, *Vice Pres*
EMP: 35

SALES (corp-wide): 193.7MM **Privately Held**
WEB: www.e-bind.com
SIC: 3089 8742 3613 3489 Mfg Plastic Products Mgmt Consulting Svcs Mfg Switchgear/Boards Mfg Ordnance/Accessories Mfg Ammo-Ex Small Arms
PA: Ensign-Bickford Industries, Inc.
999 17th St Ste 900
Denver CO 80202
860 843-2000

(G-3906)
INTEGRITY GRAPHICS INC
42 Carver Cir (06070-2020)
PHONE..................................800 343-1248
Joseph E La Valla, *President*
Michael Hart, *Exec VP*
Tom Shaw, *Vice Pres*
Walter August, *VP Opers*
Tanya Hughes, *Project Mgr*
EMP: 62
SALES: 17MM **Privately Held**
WEB: www.integrity-usa.com
SIC: 2752 Lithographic Commercial Printing

(G-3907)
J FOSTER ICE CREAM
894 Hopmeadow St (06070-1825)
PHONE..................................860 651-1499
John Darcangelo, *Branch Mgr*
EMP: 5
SALES (est): 268.1K **Privately Held**
SIC: 2024 5812 Mfg Ice Cream/Frozen Desert Eating Place
PA: J Foster Ice Cream
4 Bailey Rd
Avon CT 06001

(G-3908)
MJ TOOL & MANUFACTURING INC
11 Herman Dr Ste B (06070-1463)
P.O. Box 13 (06070-0013)
PHONE..................................860 352-2688
Gustav Jaeggi, *President*
Marie Jaeggi, *Admin Sec*
EMP: 3 **EST:** 1981
SALES: 250K **Privately Held**
SIC: 3599 Mfg Industrial Machinery

(G-3909)
PHARMAVITE CORP
10 Station St (06070-2258)
PHONE..................................860 651-1885
Thomas Leloup, *Principal*
Federico Troiani, *Mktg Dir*
Erez Levy, *Manager*
John Newcomb, *Manager*
Juan Rodriguez, *Manager*
EMP: 6 **EST:** 1997
SALES (est): 533K **Privately Held**
SIC: 2834 Mfg Pharmaceutical Preparations

(G-3910)
RE-STYLE YOUR CLOSETS LLC
86 E Weatogue St (06070-2525)
PHONE..................................860 658-9450
Heather Feinsinger, *Principal*
EMP: 4
SALES (est): 287.4K **Privately Held**
SIC: 2673 Mfg Bags-Plastic/Coated Paper

(G-3911)
SIMSBURY PRECISION PRODUCTS
11 Herman Dr Ste C (06070-1463)
PHONE..................................860 658-6909
Bruce Staubley, *President*
EMP: 8 **EST:** 1966
SQ FT: 4,800
SALES: 1.2MM **Privately Held**
SIC: 3599 Machine Shop

(G-3912)
SPECIALTY SAW INC
30 Wolcott Rd (06070-1445)
PHONE..................................860 658-4419
David Bryan Nagy, *President*
Beverly Stillbach Nagy, *Admin Sec*
▲ **EMP:** 25
SQ FT: 11,000
SALES (est): 6.5MM **Privately Held**
WEB: www.specialtysaw.com
SIC: 3425 Mfg Saw Blades/Handsaws

(G-3913)
TALCOTT MOUNTAIN ENGINEERING
22 Talcott Mountain Rd (06070-2515)
PHONE..................................860 651-3141
James Miller, *President*
▲ **EMP:** 12 **EST:** 1997
SALES (est): 1.7MM **Privately Held**
SIC: 3561 Mfg Pumps/Pumping Equipment

(G-3914)
VALLEY PRESS INC
540 1/2 Hopmeadow St (06070)
PHONE..................................860 651-4700
Keith Turley, *Mng Member*
EMP: 25 **EST:** 2009
SALES (est): 241K **Privately Held**
SIC: 2741 Misc Publishing

Somers
Tolland County

(G-3915)
CT FIBEROPTICS INC
64 Field Rd Ste 11 (06071-2043)
PHONE..................................860 763-4341
John Plocharczyk, *President*
EMP: 10
SQ FT: 4,500
SALES (est): 1.1MM **Privately Held**
WEB: www.ctfiberoptics.com
SIC: 3827 Mfg Fiber Optic Devices

(G-3916)
DYMOTEK CORPORATION
24 Scitico Rd (06071)
PHONE..................................800 788-1984
EMP: 6
SALES (est): 427.3K **Privately Held**
SIC: 3089 Mfg Plastic Products

(G-3917)
FILTER FAB INC
Also Called: Filter Fabrication
23b Eleanor Rd (06071-1632)
PHONE..................................860 749-6381
David Marini, *President*
Catherine Marini, *Vice Pres*
EMP: 5 **EST:** 1992
SALES (est): 275K **Privately Held**
SIC: 3599 Mfg Industrial Machinery

(G-3918)
FOREST REMODELING
122 Hampden Rd (06071-1270)
PHONE..................................413 222-7953
Edward J Forest, *Owner*
EMP: 5
SALES: 500K **Privately Held**
SIC: 2434 Mfg Wood Kitchen Cabinets

(G-3919)
OLIVE SABOR OIL CO
22 Brookford Rd (06071-1253)
PHONE..................................860 922-7483
Luis Valentin, *Principal*
EMP: 3
SALES (est): 91.3K **Privately Held**
SIC: 2079 Mfg Edible Fats/Oils

(G-3920)
STAR STEEL STRUCTURES INC
392 Four Bridges Rd (06071-1107)
P.O. Box 535 (06071-0535)
PHONE..................................860 763-5681
Kurt Knoefel, *President*
Karl Milikowski, *Chairman*
Mark Milikowski, *Corp Secy*
Neal Farnham, *Vice Pres*
EMP: 9
SQ FT: 9,000
SALES (est): 1.2MM **Privately Held**
SIC: 3448 Mfg Prefabricated Metal Buildings

(G-3921)
VORTEX MANUFACTURING
60 Sunshine Farms Dr (06071-2028)
PHONE..................................860 749-9769
George Gergely, *Owner*
EMP: 3
SQ FT: 4,000
SALES (est): 250K **Privately Held**
SIC: 3599 Mfg Industrial Machinery

(G-3922)
WINK INK LLC
Also Called: Sue's Shirt Creations
154 Main St (06071)
PHONE..................................860 202-8709
Chad Wink,
Susan Janssen,
EMP: 4 **EST:** 2016
SQ FT: 1,700
SALES: 343K **Privately Held**
SIC: 2759 Commercial Printing

Somersville
Tolland County

(G-3923)
CARBON PRODUCTS INC
40 Scitico Rd (06072)
P.O. Box N (06072-0914)
PHONE..................................860 749-0614
Peter Ouellet, *President*
◆ **EMP:** 9
SQ FT: 18,000
SALES (est): 1.2MM **Privately Held**
SIC: 3624 Mfg Carbon/Graphite Products

South Glastonbury
Hartford County

(G-3924)
O W HEAT TREAT INC
77 Great Pond Rd (06073-3104)
PHONE..................................860 430-6709
EMP: 4 **EST:** 2016
SALES (est): 347.5K **Privately Held**
SIC: 3398 Metal Heat Treating

South Windham
Windham County

(G-3925)
HARWEST HOLDINGS ONE INC
1102 Windham Rd (06266)
P.O. Box 96 (06266-0096)
PHONE..................................860 423-8334
Robert Mongell, *President*
Anthony Williams, *Chairman*
Joseph Loffredo, *Vice Pres*
Catherine Salemma, *Sales Mgr*
Stuart Alexander, *CTO*
EMP: 35
SALES (est): 3.8MM **Privately Held**
SIC: 3599 Mfg Industrial Machinery

(G-3926)
MICRO PRECISION LLC
1102 Windham Rd (06266)
P.O. Box 96 (06266-0096)
PHONE..................................860 423-4575
Robert Mongell,
John Desrosier,
Hadley Mongell,
EMP: 29
SALES (est): 6.2MM **Privately Held**
SIC: 3599 Mfg Industrial Machinery

(G-3927)
NATHAN AIRCHIME INC
1102 Windham Rd (06266)
P.O. Box 96 (06266-0096)
PHONE..................................860 423-4575
▲ **EMP:** 8
SALES (est): 1.3MM **Privately Held**
SIC: 3714 Mfg Motor Vehicle Parts/Accessories

(G-3928)
WENTWORTH MANUFACTURING LLC (PA)
1102 Windham Rd (06266-1131)
P.O. Box 96 (06266-0096)
PHONE..................................860 423-4575
Joseph Loffredo,
EMP: 35 **EST:** 1981
SQ FT: 7,000
SALES (est): 19.7MM **Privately Held**
WEB: www.microprecisiongroup.com
SIC: 3599 Machine Shop

(G-3929)
WINDHAM AUTOMATED MACHINES INC
Also Called: W A M
1102 Windham Rd (06266)
PHONE..................................860 208-5297
Christopher H Ramm, *President*
EMP: 19
SALES (est): 2.5MM **Privately Held**
WEB: www.windhamautomated.com
SIC: 3559 Mfg Misc Industry Machinery

South Windsor
Hartford County

(G-3930)
A C T MANUFACTURING LLC
Also Called: Act Manufacturing
55 Glendale Rd (06074-2415)
PHONE..................................860 289-8837
Richard Rondinone, *Owner*
EMP: 3
SQ FT: 2,600
SALES: 200K **Privately Held**
SIC: 3599 Machine Shop

(G-3931)
ACCUTURN MFG CO LLC
100 Commerce Way (06074-1151)
PHONE..................................860 289-6355
Hasu Viroja,
Sunny Viroja,
EMP: 10
SQ FT: 2,000
SALES (est): 781.8K **Privately Held**
SIC: 3812 Mfg Industrial Machinery

(G-3932)
AERO TUBE TECHNOLOGIES LLC
425 Sullivan Ave Ste 8 (06074-1947)
PHONE..................................860 289-2520
Dean Tulamaris,
Juan Agreda,
EMP: 25
SALES (est): 6.2MM **Privately Held**
SIC: 3728 Mfg Aircraft Parts/Equipment

(G-3933)
AERO-MED LTD
571 Nutmeg Rd N (06074-2461)
PHONE..................................860 659-2270
Daniel Del Mastro, *Branch Mgr*
EMP: 8
SALES (corp-wide): 145.5B **Publicly Held**
SIC: 3843 Mfg Dental Equipment/Supplies
HQ: Aero-Med, Ltd.
85 Commerce St
Glastonbury CT 06033
860 659-0602

(G-3934)
ALLIED METAL FINISHING L L C
379 Chapel Rd (06074-4104)
P.O. Box 26 (06074-0026)
PHONE..................................860 290-8865
Joseph A Toce,
EMP: 8
SALES (est): 1MM **Privately Held**
WEB: www.alliedmetalfinishing.com
SIC: 3471 Plating/Polishing Service

(G-3935)
AMERICAN DESIGN & MFG INC
145 Commerce Way (06074-1152)
PHONE..................................860 282-2719
Adam Vyskocil, *Principal*
Daniel Lessard, *Vice Pres*
Daniel W Jordan, *Vice Pres*
Amanda Trudeau, *Purch Agent*
EMP: 35
SQ FT: 33,000

SALES (est): 13.1MM **Privately Held**
WEB: www.americandes-mfg.com
SIC: 3829 3724 Mfg Measuring/Controlling Devices Mfg Aircraft Engines/Parts

(G-3936)
AMERICAN METALLIZING
401 Governors Hwy (06074-2510)
PHONE.................................860 289-1677
Paul Oliva, *CEO*
EMP: 3
SALES (est): 341.7K **Privately Held**
WEB: www.americanmetallizing.com
SIC: 3479 3599 Coating/Engraving Service Mfg Industrial Machinery

(G-3937)
AMK WELDING INC (HQ)
Also Called: Amk Technical Services
283 Sullivan Ave (06074-1914)
PHONE.................................860 289-5634
Daniel R Godin, *President*
EMP: 28 **EST:** 2009
SALES (est): 3.4MM
SALES (corp-wide): 358.7MM **Privately Held**
SIC: 7692 3398 7699 Welding Repair Metal Heat Treating Repair Services
PA: Meyer Tool, Inc.
3055 Colerain Ave
Cincinnati OH 45225
513 681-7362

(G-3938)
ANDRE FURNITURE INDUSTRIES
55 Sandra Dr Ste 1 (06074-1039)
PHONE.................................860 528-8826
Andre K Charbonneau, *Owner*
EMP: 8
SQ FT: 12,000
SALES: 800K **Privately Held**
SIC: 2511 Mfg Plastic Laminate Wood Furniture

(G-3939)
ATI LADISH MACHINING INC
Also Called: Aerex Manufacturing
34 S Satellite Rd (06074-3445)
PHONE.................................860 688-3688
Richard Cleary, *Branch Mgr*
EMP: 95 **Publicly Held**
SIC: 3724 Mfg Aircraft Engines/Parts
HQ: Ati Ladish Machining, Inc.
311 Prestige Park Rd
East Hartford CT 06108
860 688-3688

(G-3940)
ATLANTIC FABRICATING CO INC
71 Edwin Rd (06074-2476)
P.O. Box 433 (06074-0433)
PHONE.................................860 291-9882
William S Johnson, *President*
Susan Johnson, *Admin Sec*
EMP: 10
SQ FT: 7,500
SALES (est): 1.5MM **Privately Held**
WEB: www.atlfab.com
SIC: 3441 Structural Metal Fabrication

(G-3941)
ATLAS METAL WORKS LLC
48 Commerce Way (06074-1151)
PHONE.................................860 282-1030
Peter Saxon, *Opers Mgr*
Shaun Miller, *Prdtn Mgr*
Gary Allard, *Mng Member*
Dennis Larose,
EMP: 12
SALES: 1.9MM **Privately Held**
WEB: www.atlasmetalworksllc.com
SIC: 3441 Structural Metal Fabrication

(G-3942)
ATLAS PRECISION MFG LLC
508 Burnham St (06074-4102)
PHONE.................................860 290-9114
Waclaw Dybinski, *Mng Member*
EMP: 25
SQ FT: 20,000
SALES: 3MM **Privately Held**
SIC: 3599 Mfg Industrial Machinery

(G-3943)
BARKER STEEL LLC
30 Talbot Ln (06074-5401)
PHONE.................................860 282-1860
Raymond Kandolin, *Branch Mgr*
EMP: 30
SALES (corp-wide): 25B **Publicly Held**
WEB: www.barker.com
SIC: 3449 5085 Mfg Misc Structural Metalwork Whol Industrial Supplies
HQ: Barker Steel Llc
55 Sumner St Ste 1
Milford MA 01757
800 363-3953

(G-3944)
BODYCOTE THERMAL PROC INC
45 Connecticut Ave (06074-3475)
PHONE.................................860 282-1371
Mike Sakelakos, *Branch Mgr*
EMP: 40
SALES (corp-wide): 960MM **Privately Held**
SIC: 3398 Metal Heat Treating
HQ: Bodycote Thermal Processing, Inc.
12700 Park Central Dr # 700
Dallas TX 75251
214 904-2420

(G-3945)
C & T PRINT FINISHING INC
67 Commerce Way (06074-1152)
PHONE.................................860 282-0616
Jeffrey Cole, *President*
Mary Ann Cole, *Treasurer*
EMP: 10
SQ FT: 9,500
SALES (est): 4.9MM **Privately Held**
WEB: www.ctpf.com
SIC: 2675 Mfg Die-Cut Paper/Paperboard

(G-3946)
C MATHER COMPANY INC
Also Called: Mathertops
339 Chapel Rd (06074-4104)
PHONE.................................860 528-5667
Thomas Mather, *President*
James Fromerth, *Vice Pres*
Clayton D Mather, *Shareholder*
Richard Mather, *Admin Sec*
EMP: 9
SQ FT: 10,000
SALES (est): 1.3MM **Privately Held**
WEB: www.mathertops.com
SIC: 2542 2821 2541 Mfg Partitions/Fixtures-Nonwood Mfg Plastic Materials/Resins Mfg Wood Partitions/Fixtures

(G-3947)
CAPEWELL AERIAL SYSTEMS LLC (PA)
105 Nutmeg Rd S (06074-5400)
PHONE.................................860 610-0700
Richard Wheeler, *Mng Member*
▲ **EMP:** 100
SALES: 45.4MM **Privately Held**
SIC: 3531 Mfg Construction Machinery

(G-3948)
CARL ASSOCIATES INC
1257 John Fitch Blvd 3 (06074-2431)
PHONE.................................860 749-7620
Susan Carl, *President*
EMP: 4
SALES (est): 516K **Privately Held**
WEB: www.carl-associates.com
SIC: 3599 Mfg Industrial Machinery

(G-3949)
CARLAS PASTA INC
50 Talbot Ln (06074-5401)
PHONE.................................860 436-4042
Carla Squatrito, *President*
Keith Branham, *Regional Mgr*
John Koch, *Regional Mgr*
Dawn Iannacone, *Business Mgr*
Sandro Squatrito, *Vice Pres*
▲ **EMP:** 145
SQ FT: 13,000
SALES: 72MM **Privately Held**
WEB: www.carlaspasta.com
SIC: 2098 Mfg Food Preparations

(G-3950)
CLEARLY CLEAN PRODUCTS LLC (PA)
225 Oakland Rd Ste 401 (06074-2896)
PHONE.................................860 646-1040
Gary D Colby, *General Counsel*
Jeffrey Maguire,
EMP: 17
SALES (est): 8.7MM **Privately Held**
WEB: www.peelatray.com
SIC: 3089 Mfg Plastic Products

(G-3951)
COBURN TECHNOLOGIES INC (PA)
83 Gerber Rd W (06074-3230)
PHONE.................................860 648-6600
Edward G Jepsen, *CEO*
Alex Incera, *President*
Michael Dolen, *Vice Pres*
Mike Dolen, *Vice Pres*
Wayne Labrecque, *Vice Pres*
◆ **EMP:** 141
SALES (est): 48MM **Privately Held**
SIC: 3851 3827 Mfg Ophthalmic Goods Mfg Optical Instruments/Lenses

(G-3952)
COMPETITIVE EDGE COATINGS LLC
185 Nutmeg Rd S (06074-3461)
PHONE.................................860 882-0762
Damon Schuster,
Christopher Scutnik,
EMP: 3
SQ FT: 5,000
SALES (est): 263.9K **Privately Held**
SIC: 3479 Coating/Engraving Service

(G-3953)
CONNECTICUT PLASMA TECH LLC
273 Chapel Rd (06074-4104)
P.O. Box 58 (06074-0058)
PHONE.................................860 289-5500
James J Jasmin, *Mng Member*
Robert Lempicki, *Mng Member*
EMP: 13
SALES (est): 1.2MM **Privately Held**
SIC: 3479 Coating/Engraving Service

(G-3954)
CRAMER COMPANY
105 Nutmeg Rd S (06074-5400)
PHONE.................................860 291-8402
Kenneth Mac Cormac, *President*
EMP: 5
SALES (est): 374.6K **Privately Held**
SIC: 3621 Mfg Motors/Generators

(G-3955)
CT COMPOSITES & MARINE SVC LLC
620 Sullivan Ave (06074-1919)
PHONE.................................860 282-0100
Tom Krivickas,
EMP: 8
SALES (est): 473.4K **Privately Held**
SIC: 3083 Mfg Laminated Plastic Plate/Sheet

(G-3956)
DOOSAN FUEL CELL AMERICA INC (HQ)
195 Governors Hwy (06074-2419)
PHONE.................................860 727-2200
Jeff Hyungrak Chung, *President*
Chankyo Chung, *General Mgr*
Michael Coskun, *General Mgr*
Minchul Kim, *Corp Secy*
Tiffany Eisenbise, *Counsel*
◆ **EMP:** 150
SQ FT: 238,711
SALES (est): 57.1MM **Privately Held**
SIC: 3674 7629 Mfg Semiconductors/Related Devices Electrical Repair

(G-3957)
DST OUTPUT EAST LLC (DH)
125 Ellington Rd (06074-4112)
PHONE.................................816 221-1234
Steven J Towle, *CEO*
Tebbetts Al, *Opers Staff*
Jasmin Hrnjic, *Production*
Michael Ponting, *Financial Analy*
Bill Hankard, *Sr Software Eng*
EMP: 20
SQ FT: 30,000
SALES (est): 8.1MM
SALES (corp-wide): 4.3B **Publicly Held**
WEB: www.output.net
SIC: 2759 Commercial Printing

(G-3958)
DYCO INDUSTRIES INC
229 S Satellite Rd (06074-3474)
PHONE.................................860 289-4957
David Dyke, *President*
Barbara Dyke, *Senior VP*
Chris Van Dyke, *Vice Pres*
Paul Socolosky, *Opers Mgr*
Kaylin S Dyke, *Admin Sec*
EMP: 30
SQ FT: 24,000
SALES (est): 6.7MM **Privately Held**
SIC: 3446 7692 3444 Mfg Architectural Metalwork Welding Repair Mfg Sheet Metalwork

(G-3959)
EAGLE TISSUE LLC
70 Bidwell Rd (06074-2412)
PHONE.................................860 282-2535
Robert E Costa, *President*
Dan Sforza, *Vice Pres*
Richard Costa,
▲ **EMP:** 14
SQ FT: 21,000
SALES (est): 3.5MM **Privately Held**
WEB: www.eagletissue.com
SIC: 2679 Mfg Converted Paper Products

(G-3960)
EAST COAST STAIRS CO INC
125 Bidwell Rd (06074-2443)
PHONE.................................860 528-7096
Richard Hall, *President*
EMP: 6
SALES (est): 1.8MM **Privately Held**
SIC: 2431 Mfg Millwork

(G-3961)
EAST WINDSOR METAL FABG INC
91 Glendale Rd (06074-2415)
P.O. Box 357, East Windsor Hill (06028-0357)
PHONE.................................860 528-7107
Peter Hughes, *President*
Mary Ellen Brennan, *Vice Pres*
James Hughes, *Vice Pres*
Josephine Hughes, *Admin Sec*
EMP: 11
SQ FT: 20,000
SALES (est): 1MM **Privately Held**
WEB: www.eastwindsor-ct.gov
SIC: 3444 7692 3446 3441 Mfg Sheet Metalwork Welding Repair Mfg Architectural Mtlwrk Structural Metal Fabrctn

(G-3962)
ELECTRO-METHODS INC (PA)
330 Governors Hwy (06074-2422)
P.O. Box 54 (06074-0054)
PHONE.................................860 289-8661
Randall Fries, *President*
William W Soucy, *Vice Pres*
Dani Stephens, *Vice Pres*
William Soucy, *VP Mfg*
Jeff Paradis, *Foreman/Supr*
EMP: 121 **EST:** 1965
SQ FT: 101,000
SALES (est): 40.6MM **Privately Held**
WEB: www.electro-methods.com
SIC: 3724 7629 3728 3829 Mfg Aircraft Engine/Part Electrical Repair Mfg Aircraft Parts/Equip Mfg Measure/Control Dvcs Mfg Search/Navgatn Equip

(G-3963)
ELECTRO-METHODS INC
525 Nutmeg Rd N (06074-2461)
P.O. Box 54 (06074-0054)
PHONE.................................860 289-8661
Randall Fries, *Branch Mgr*
EMP: 79
SALES (corp-wide): 40.6MM **Privately Held**
WEB: www.electro-methods.com
SIC: 3724 Mfg Aircraft Engines/Parts

▲ = Import ▼=Export
◆ =Import/Export

PA: Electro-Methods, Inc.
330 Governors Hwy
South Windsor CT 06074
860 289-8661

(G-3964)
ENCORE OPTICS
140 Commerce Way (06074-1151)
PHONE..................................860 282-0082
Paul Zito, *Owner*
▲ **EMP:** 15
SALES (est): 2.2MM **Privately Held**
SIC: 3851 Mfg Ophthalmic Goods

(G-3965)
ENGINEERING SERVICES & PDTS CO (PA)
Also Called: Clearspan
1395 John Fitch Blvd (06074-1029)
PHONE..................................860 528-1119
Barry Goldsher, *President*
Lynn Walters, *Business Mgr*
Charles R Clark Jr, *Corp Secy*
Matthew K Niaura, *Vice Pres*
Matthew Niaura, *Vice Pres*
◆ **EMP:** 88
SQ FT: 51,281
SALES (est): 73.6MM **Privately Held**
WEB: www.esapco.com
SIC: 3523 5083 3081 Mfg Farm Machinery/Equip Whol Farm/Garden Mach

(G-3966)
ESTEEM MANUFACTURING CORP
175 S Satellite Rd (06074-3474)
PHONE..................................860 282-9964
David Kostyk, *President*
Shawn Dietz, *Vice Pres*
Keith Maciolek, *QA Dir*
Joel Newcomb, *Director*
Suzanne Kostyk, *Admin Sec*
EMP: 35
SQ FT: 10,000
SALES (est): 6.5MM **Privately Held**
WEB: www.esteemmfg.com
SIC: 3599 Mfg Industrial Machinery

(G-3967)
EVOAERO INC
425 Sullivan Ave Ste 5 (06074-1947)
PHONE..................................860 289-2520
Pedro J Agreda, *President*
Tom Ferreira, *Sales Dir*
Juan C Agreda, *Admin Sec*
EMP: 65
SALES (est): 17.3MM **Privately Held**
WEB: www.candpmachine.com
SIC: 3728 Mfg Aircraft Parts/Equipment

(G-3968)
EVOQUA WATER TECHNOLOGIES LLC
88 Nutmeg Rd S (06074-3469)
PHONE..................................860 528-6512
Robert Rohan, *Manager*
EMP: 26
SALES (corp-wide): 1.4B **Publicly Held**
SIC: 3589 Mfg Service Industry Machinery
HQ: Evoqua Water Technologies Llc
210 6th Ave Ste 3300
Pittsburgh PA 15222
724 772-0044

(G-3969)
EXPERIMENTAL PROTOTYPE PDTS CO
248 Chapel Rd (06074-4103)
PHONE..................................860 289-4948
Robert H Ainsworth Jr, *President*
William Ainsworth Sr, *Vice Pres*
Robert Ainsworth Sr, *Admin Sec*
EMP: 10
SQ FT: 2,500
SALES (est): 1.7MM **Privately Held**
SIC: 3599 General Machine Shop

(G-3970)
FIBRE OPTIC PLUS INC
585 Nutmeg Rd N (06074-2461)
PHONE..................................860 646-3581
Donald E Ballsieper, *President*
Sylvia Ballsieper, *Vice Pres*
Greg Brown, *Manager*
EMP: 13
SQ FT: 2,400
SALES (est): 3.2MM **Privately Held**
WEB: www.fibreopticplus.com
SIC: 3661 Water/Sewer/Utility Construction

(G-3971)
GENERAL SEATING SOLUTIONS LLC
45 S Satellite Rd Ste 5 (06074-5407)
PHONE..................................860 242-3307
Anthony Nash,
Antonio Medina,
EMP: 10
SALES (est): 1.1MM **Privately Held**
WEB: www.generalseatingsolutions.com
SIC: 2599 7641 Mfg & Reupholsters Commercial Seating

(G-3972)
GERBER COBURN OPTICAL INC (HQ)
55 Gerber Rd E (06074-3244)
PHONE..................................800 843-1479
Alex Incera, *President*
Wayne Labrecque, *Vice Pres*
◆ **EMP:** 120
SQ FT: 60,000
SALES (est): 11MM **Privately Held**
SIC: 3851 3827 Mfg Ophthalmic Goods Mfg Optical Instruments/Lenses

(G-3973)
GLOBAL TRBINE CMPNENT TECH LLC
125 S Satellite Rd (06074-3474)
PHONE..................................860 528-4722
William W Baker, *Opers Staff*
Brian Fielding, *QC Mgr*
Edmund Autuori, *Executive*
Carla Diniz, *Executive*
EMP: 35
SQ FT: 20,000
SALES (est): 6.6MM **Privately Held**
WEB: www.globalturbine.com
SIC: 3728 3724 Mfg Aircraft Parts/Equipment Mfg Aircraft Engines/Parts

(G-3974)
GOLIK MACHINE CO
154 Commerce Way (06074-1151)
PHONE..................................860 610-0095
Chris Golik, *Owner*
EMP: 4
SQ FT: 2,000
SALES (est): 750K **Privately Held**
SIC: 3599 Mfg Industrial Machinery

(G-3975)
GRANITE & KITCHEN STUDIO LLC
313 Pleasant Valley Rd (06074-5411)
PHONE..................................860 290-4444
Ahmed Eldirany, *Mng Member*
▲ **EMP:** 5 **EST:** 2012
SQ FT: 8,000
SALES (est): 542.7K **Privately Held**
SIC: 3281 Trade Contractor

(G-3976)
H & B TOOL & ENGINEERING CO
481 Sullivan Ave (06074-1942)
P.O. Box 717 (06074-0717)
PHONE..................................860 528-9341
Michael Gennelli, *Ch of Bd*
Janice Proll, *President*
Michael Giannelli, *Vice Pres*
Darlene Parker, *Purch Mgr*
Randy Poulin, *Purch Mgr*
EMP: 50 **EST:** 1960
SQ FT: 33,000
SALES (est): 8.6MM **Privately Held**
SIC: 3599 3823 3728 3545 Mfg Industrial Machinery Mfg Process Cntrl Instr Mfg Aircraft Parts/Equip Mfg Machine Tool Access

(G-3977)
HERMAN SCHMIDT PRECISION WORKH
26 Sea Pave Rd (06074-4155)
PHONE..................................860 289-3347
Thomas Duff III, *President*
EMP: 8
SALES (est): 351.8K **Privately Held**
SIC: 3544 Mfg Dies/Tools/Jigs/Fixtures

(G-3978)
HERMANN SCHMIDT COMPANY INC
26 Sea Pave Rd (06074-4155)
PHONE..................................860 289-3347
Peter Schmidt, *President*
EMP: 10
SALES (est): 1.5MM **Privately Held**
SIC: 3545 Mfg Machine Tool Accessories

(G-3979)
HEXCEL CORPORATION
250 Nutmeg Rd S (06074-3498)
PHONE..................................925 520-3232
Jason Eddy, *President*
Nick Stanage, *President*
EMP: 99
SALES (est): 9.6MM
SALES (corp-wide): 2.1B **Publicly Held**
SIC: 3324 Steel Investment Foundry
PA: Hexcel Corporation
281 Tresser Blvd Ste 1503
Stamford CT 06901
203 969-0666

(G-3980)
HGH INDUSTRIES LLC
43 Sally Dr (06074-3500)
PHONE..................................860 644-1150
Herbert Hoyne, *Mng Member*
John Hoyne,
EMP: 3
SALES: 240K **Privately Held**
SIC: 3545 Mfg Industrial Machinery

(G-3981)
HI HEAT COMPANY INC
32 Glendale Rd (06074-2416)
PHONE..................................860 528-9315
Leonard Werner, *President*
Prairie Brown, *Vice Pres*
EMP: 3
SQ FT: 22,000
SALES: 1MM **Privately Held**
WEB: www.hi-heat.com
SIC: 3567 Mfg Industrial Furnaces/Ovens

(G-3982)
HOYA CORPORATION
Also Called: Hoya Optcal Labs Amrc-Hartford
580 Nutmeg Rd N (06074-2458)
PHONE..................................860 289-5379
Joe Bassler, *Branch Mgr*
EMP: 252 **Privately Held**
SIC: 3851 5049 Mfg Ophthalmic Goods Whol Professional Equipment
HQ: Hoya Corporation
651 E Corporate Dr
Lewisville TX 75057
972 221-4141

(G-3983)
JAD LLC
Also Called: Industronics Service
489 Sullivan Ave (06074-1942)
P.O. Box 649 (06074-0649)
PHONE..................................860 289-1551
James L Wyse, *President*
George Shaw, *QC Mgr*
EMP: 25
SQ FT: 14,000
SALES (est): 6.2MM **Privately Held**
WEB: www.industronics.com
SIC: 3823 3567 5084 3433 Mfg Process Cntrl Instr Mfg Indstl Furnace/Ovens Whol Industrial Equip Mfg Heat Equip-Nonelec

(G-3984)
JHS RESTORATION INC
170 Strong Rd (06074-1013)
PHONE..................................860 757-3870
Bonnie M Snyder, *President*
John Snyder, *Vice Pres*
EMP: 10
SALES: 600K **Privately Held**
SIC: 3444 1761 Mfg Sheet Metalwork Roofing/Siding Contractor

(G-3985)
JL AEROTECH INC
475 Buckland Rd Ste 103 (06074-3738)
PHONE..................................860 248-8628
Brian Sohn, *President*
Kangho Son, *Director*
EMP: 3 **EST:** 2016
SALES (est): 1.5MM **Privately Held**
SIC: 3324 Steel Investment Foundry

(G-3986)
JONES METAL PRODUCTS CO INC
22 Schwier Rd Ste 1 (06074-1940)
PHONE..................................860 289-8023
Kevin R Jones, *President*
EMP: 5 **EST:** 1964
SQ FT: 11,000
SALES: 750K **Privately Held**
SIC: 3444 Mfg Sheet Metalwork

(G-3987)
KASHETA POWER EQUIPMENT
1275 John Fitch Blvd (06074-2431)
PHONE..................................860 528-8421
Edward Kasheta Jr, *President*
Susan Kasheta, *Admin Sec*
EMP: 5
SQ FT: 2,400
SALES (est): 977.3K **Privately Held**
SIC: 3568 Mfg Power Transmission Equipment

(G-3988)
KEYSTONE PAPER & BOX CO INC
31 Edwin Rd (06074-2413)
P.O. Box 355, East Windsor Hill (06028-0355)
PHONE..................................860 291-0027
James Rutt, *President*
John Goodenow, *Admin Sec*
EMP: 52
SQ FT: 61,000
SALES (est): 17.7MM **Privately Held**
WEB: www.keystonepaperbox.com
SIC: 2657 2631 Mfg Folding Paperboard Boxes Paperboard Mill

(G-3989)
L T A GROUP INC
Also Called: Argix Direct
694 Nutmeg Rd N (06074-2433)
PHONE..................................860 291-9911
EMP: 25
SALES (est): 2.5MM **Privately Held**
WEB: www.ltagroup.com
SIC: 3743 Mfg Railroad Equipment

(G-3990)
LIGHTHOUSE INTERNATIONAL LLC
125 S Satellite Rd (06074-3474)
PHONE..................................860 528-4722
Edmond Autuori,
EMP: 20
SALES (est): 1.5MM **Privately Held**
SIC: 3724 Mfg Aircraft Engines/Parts

(G-3991)
MARKOW RACE CARS
701 Nutmeg Rd N Ste 1 (06074-2437)
PHONE..................................860 610-0776
Ronald Siemienski, *Principal*
EMP: 3
SALES (est): 380.5K **Privately Held**
SIC: 3711 Mfg Motor Vehicle/Car Bodies

(G-3992)
MASSCONN DISTRIBUTE CPL
12 Commerce Way (06074-1151)
PHONE..................................860 882-0717
Brian Hastings, *Director*
EMP: 85
SALES (est): 11.7MM **Privately Held**
SIC: 2051 Mfg Bread/Related Products

(G-3993)
MEYER GAGE CO INC
230 Burnham St (06074-4193)
PHONE..................................860 528-6526
John Meyer, *CEO*
James Meyer, *Vice Pres*
Stephanie Antrum, *Sales Mgr*
▲ **EMP:** 18
SQ FT: 28,000
SALES: 3.6MM **Privately Held**
WEB: www.meyergage.com
SIC: 3545 Mfg Measuring/Controlling Devices

GEOGRAPHIC

(G-3994)
MH RHODES CRAMER LLC
105 Nutmeg Rd S (06074-5400)
PHONE..................................860 291-8402
Robert G McCreary III,
▲ **EMP:** 3
SALES (est): 260K **Privately Held**
SIC: 3613 5012 Manufacturing Switchgear/Switchboards Wholesales Autos/Motor Vehicles

(G-3995)
NEYRA INDUSTRIES INC
239 Sullivan Ave (06074-1914)
P.O. Box 588 (06074-0588)
PHONE..................................860 289-4359
Randy Lee, *Regional Mgr*
EMP: 6
SQ FT: 4,000
SALES (corp-wide): 15.2MM **Privately Held**
WEB: www.neyra.com
SIC: 2952 Mfg Asphalt Felts/Coatings
PA: Neyra Industries, Inc.
10700 Evendale Dr
Cincinnati OH 45241
513 733-1000

(G-3996)
NUWAY TOBACCO COMPANY
200 Sullivan Ave Ste 2 (06074-1953)
P.O. Box 415, East Windsor Hill (06028-0415)
PHONE..................................860 289-6414
Raymond A Voorhies, *CEO*
Anne S King, *Vice Pres*
Thomas Kirby, *CFO*
Jean E Shepard III, *Asst Treas*
James T Farrell, *Admin Sec*
◆ **EMP:** 85 **EST:** 1951
SQ FT: 65,000
SALES (est): 28.4MM **Privately Held**
SIC: 2131 5159 Mfg Chewing/Smoking Tobacco Whol Farm Product Raw Materials

(G-3997)
OXFORD PERFORMANCE MTLS INC
30 S Satellite Rd (06074-3445)
PHONE..................................860 698-9300
Scott Defelice, *President*
Paul Martin, *President*
Severine Valdant Zygmont, *President*
Severine Zygmont, *President*
Lawrence Varholak, *Vice Pres*
◆ **EMP:** 35
SQ FT: 16,000
SALES (est): 253K **Privately Held**
SIC: 2821 Mfg Plastic Materials/Resins

(G-3998)
OXPEKK PERFORMANCE MTLS INC
30 S Satellite Rd (06074-3445)
PHONE..................................860 698-9300
Scott Defelice, *President*
Bernard Plishtin, *Officer*
EMP: 15
SALES (est): 1.8MM **Privately Held**
SIC: 2821 Mfg Plastic Materials/Resins

(G-3999)
P & M WELDING CO LLC
Also Called: P&M Welding
38 Edwin Rd (06074-2414)
PHONE..................................860 528-2077
John Chesanek, *Mng Member*
Cynthia Chesanek,
EMP: 3
SQ FT: 10,000
SALES (est): 350K **Privately Held**
SIC: 7692 Welding Repair

(G-4000)
PLAS-TEC COATINGS INC
68 Mascolo Rd (06074-3312)
PHONE..................................860 289-6029
Richard Cyr, *President*
Brian Cyr, *Vice Pres*
Sandra Cyr, *Treasurer*
EMP: 10
SQ FT: 10,000
SALES (est): 1.5MM **Privately Held**
WEB: www.plas-teccoatings.com
SIC: 3479 Coating/Engraving Service

(G-4001)
PLASMA TECHNOLOGY INCORPORATED
70 Rye St (06074-1218)
PHONE..................................860 282-0659
Richard Petersen, *Branch Mgr*
EMP: 35
SQ FT: 12,000
SALES (corp-wide): 17.4MM **Privately Held**
SIC: 2836 3471 Mfg Biological Products Plating/Polishing Service
PA: Plasma Technology Incorporated
1754 Crenshaw Blvd
Torrance CA 90501
310 320-3373

(G-4002)
PODUNK POPCORN
245 Barber Hill Rd (06074-1659)
PHONE..................................860 648-9565
EMP: 3
SALES (est): 131.9K **Privately Held**
SIC: 2099 Mfg Food Preparations

(G-4003)
POWERSCREEN CONNECTICUT INC
Also Called: Powerscreen England
140 Nutmeg Rd S (06074-3468)
PHONE..................................860 627-6596
Michael Sheelan, *President*
Bernadette Sheelan, *CFO*
Sean Clifford, *Sales Staff*
Jeff Morrow, *Sales Staff*
▲ **EMP:** 10
SQ FT: 11,000
SALES (est): 2.8MM **Privately Held**
SIC: 3532 Mfg Mining Machinery

(G-4004)
PRESSURE BLAST MFG CO INC
205 Nutmeg Rd S Ste E (06074-5406)
PHONE..................................800 722-5278
Lowell W Mc Mullen III, *Ch of Bd*
Ted Clifford, *Treasurer*
Stephen Zavarella, *Admin Sec*
EMP: 15 **EST:** 1958
SQ FT: 25,000
SALES: 2MM **Privately Held**
SIC: 3629 3469 3291 Mfg Electrical Industrial Apparatus Mfg Metal Stampings Mfg Abrasive Products

(G-4005)
PRINTED COMMUNICATIONS
400 Chapel Rd Ste L1 (06074-4159)
PHONE..................................860 436-9619
Wayne Egienbaum, *Manager*
EMP: 7
SALES (est): 201.6K **Privately Held**
SIC: 2711 Newspapers-Publishing/Printing

(G-4006)
PROGRESSIVE SHEETMETAL LLC
36 Mascolo Rd (06074-3312)
PHONE..................................860 436-9884
Keith Beaulieu, *Mng Member*
Andrea Beaulieu,
EMP: 36
SQ FT: 13,600
SALES: 5MM **Privately Held**
SIC: 3444 Mfg Sheet Metalwork

(G-4007)
REDLAND BRICK INC
Also Called: K F Brick Plant
1440 John Fitch Blvd (06074-1036)
PHONE..................................860 528-1311
Simon Whalley, *Director*
EMP: 130
SALES (corp-wide): 8.1MM **Privately Held**
WEB: www.redlandbrick.com
SIC: 3255 3251 Mfg Clay Refractories Mfg Brick/Structural Tile
HQ: Redland Brick Inc.
15718 Clear Spring Rd
Williamsport MD 21795
301 223-7700

(G-4008)
SATELLITE TOOL & MCH CO INC
185 Commerce Way Ste 1 (06074-1154)
PHONE..................................860 290-8558
J Mark Lukasik, *CEO*
Jack Lukasik, *President*
Jan Lukasik, *President*
Monica Marselli, *Vice Pres*
EMP: 50 **EST:** 1975
SQ FT: 10,000
SALES (est): 15.7MM **Privately Held**
SIC: 3728 Mfg Aircraft Parts/Equipment

(G-4009)
SIFTEX EQUIPMENT COMPANY
Also Called: American Pulley Cover
52 Connecticut Ave Ste D (06074-3484)
PHONE..................................860 289-8779
Steven Weil, *President*
◆ **EMP:** 25
SQ FT: 12,000
SALES: 4.5MM **Privately Held**
WEB: www.siftex.com
SIC: 3089 Mfg Plastic Products

(G-4010)
SKILLCRAFT MACHINE TOOL CO
255 Nutmeg Rd S (06074-5403)
PHONE..................................860 953-1246
Thomas Litke, *President*
Todd Koplin, *Engineer*
Jacob Litke, *Engineer*
Jim Bailey, *Info Tech Mgr*
Salvatore Di Fabio, *Admin Sec*
EMP: 15 **EST:** 1946
SALES (est): 4.2MM **Privately Held**
SIC: 3423 3544 Mfg Hand/Edge Tools Mfg Dies/Tools/Jigs/Fixtures

(G-4011)
SMR METAL TECHNOLOGY
524 Sullivan Ave Ste 15 (06074-1946)
PHONE..................................860 291-8259
Sharon M Riley, *Owner*
EMP: 7
SALES (est): 972.6K **Privately Held**
SIC: 3443 Mfg Fabricated Plate Work

(G-4012)
SOURCE LOUDSPEAKERS
Also Called: Source Technologies
701 Nutmeg Rd N Ste 2 (06074-2437)
PHONE..................................860 918-3088
John Sollecito, *Owner*
◆ **EMP:** 3
SQ FT: 3,000
SALES: 300K **Privately Held**
SIC: 3651 Mfg Home Audio/Video Equipment

(G-4013)
SPACE TOOL & MACHINE CO INC
130 Commerce Way Ste 1 (06074-1151)
PHONE..................................860 290-8599
Thomas Luaasik, *President*
EMP: 5 **EST:** 1975
SALES (est): 440K **Privately Held**
SIC: 3599 Mfg Industrial Machinery

(G-4014)
STEELTECH BUILDING PDTS INC
636 Nutmeg Rd N (06074-2433)
PHONE..................................860 290-8930
J Robert Denton, *Chairman*
Steve Iacino, *Vice Pres*
Steve Rich, *Vice Pres*
EMP: 51 **EST:** 1965
SQ FT: 38,000
SALES (est): 19.1MM **Privately Held**
WEB: www.econstructionspecialties.com
SIC: 3441 1791 5072 5031 Structural Metal Fabrctn Structural Steel Erectn Whol Hardware Whol Lumber/Plywd/Millwk

(G-4015)
STONEWALL KITCHEN LLC
400 Evergreen Way # 408 (06074-6967)
PHONE..................................860 648-9215
Silvester Linda, *Branch Mgr*
EMP: 120 **Privately Held**
SIC: 2514 Mfg Metal Household Furniture
PA: Stonewall Kitchen, Llc
2 Stonewall Ln
York ME 03909

(G-4016)
TELEFUNKEN USA LLC
Also Called: Telefunken Elektro Acoustic
300 Pleasant Valley Rd E (06074-5408)
PHONE..................................860 882-5919
Toni Fishman,
▲ **EMP:** 15
SQ FT: 10,000
SALES: 2MM **Privately Held**
WEB: www.telefunkenusa.com
SIC: 3651 Mfg Home Audio/Video Equipment

(G-4017)
TRUE POSITION MFG LLC
40 Sandra Dr Ste 3 (06074-1043)
PHONE..................................860 291-2987
Richard Stathers,
Jeffrey Stathers,
EMP: 8
SQ FT: 2,000
SALES (est): 1MM **Privately Held**
SIC: 3549 Mfg Metal Machine Parts

(G-4018)
UNITED TECHNOLOGIES CORP
Also Called: Power Systems Division
Governors Hwy (06074)
PHONE..................................860 727-2200
Jan Vandokkum, *Branch Mgr*
EMP: 255
SALES (corp-wide): 66.5B **Publicly Held**
WEB: www.utc.com
SIC: 3724 Mfg Aircraft Engines/Parts
PA: United Technologies Corporation
10 Farm Springs Rd
Farmington CT 06032
860 728-7000

(G-4019)
US AVIONICS INC / SUPERABR
Also Called: US Avionics
1265 John Fitch Blvd # 3 (06074-2456)
P.O. Box 599 (06074-0599)
PHONE..................................860 528-1114
Sari Alt, *Principal*
EMP: 5
SALES (est): 480.9K **Privately Held**
SIC: 3541 Mfg Machine Tools-Cutting

(G-4020)
WAYBEST FOODS INC
1510 John Fitch Blvd (06074-1019)
PHONE..................................860 289-7948
Stanley Karasinski, *President*
S Karasinski, *Office Mgr*
EMP: 9
SALES (est): 859.3K **Privately Held**
SIC: 2015 Poultry Processing

Southbury
New Haven County

(G-4021)
ABSOLUTE PRECISION CO
234 Bates Rock Rd (06488-3216)
PHONE..................................203 767-9066
James Muller, *Owner*
EMP: 4
SALES (est): 220.1K **Privately Held**
SIC: 3724 Mfg Aircraft Engines/Parts

(G-4022)
ADVANCED PROTOTYPE DEVELOPMENT
7 Stiles Rd (06488-1241)
PHONE..................................203 267-1262
Robert Bedard, *Owner*
Bob Bedard, *Engineer*
EMP: 3
SALES: 190K **Privately Held**
SIC: 2514 Mfg Metal Household Furniture

(G-4023)
ALFRO CUSTOM MANUFACTURING CO
99 Old Woodbury Rd (06488-1933)
PHONE..................................203 264-6246

EMP: 6
SQ FT: 5,000
SALES (est): 280K Privately Held
SIC: 3469 Mfg Machine Parts

(G-4024)
CAREY AUTOMATIC DOOR LLC
35 Forest Rd (06488-2405)
PHONE..................................203 267-4278
Lisa M Carey,
EMP: 3
SALES: 500K Privately Held
SIC: 3442 Mfg Metal Doors/Sash/Trim

(G-4025)
COMSAT INC
2120 River Rd (06488-1147)
PHONE..................................203 264-4091
Guy White, *Branch Mgr*
EMP: 14
SALES (corp-wide): 20.8MM Privately Held
SIC: 3663 Mfg Radio/Tv Communication Equipment
HQ: Comsat, Inc.
2550 Wasser Ter Ste 600
Herndon VA 20171
571 599-3600

(G-4026)
GLAXOSMITHKLINE LLC
186 Beecher Dr (06488-1942)
PHONE..................................203 232-5145
EMP: 26
SALES (corp-wide): 40.6B Privately Held
SIC: 2834 Mfg Pharmaceutical Preparations
HQ: Glaxosmithkline Llc
5 Crescent Dr
Philadelphia PA 19112
215 751-4000

(G-4027)
HISTORICAL ART PRINTS
464 Burr Rd (06488-2788)
P.O. Box 660 (06488-0660)
PHONE..................................203 262-6680
Don Troiani, *Owner*
Donna O'Brien, *Office Mgr*
EMP: 3
SALES: 1MM Privately Held
WEB: www.historicalartprints.com
SIC: 2741 Misc Publishing

(G-4028)
INTERNATIONAL CONTACT TECH
Also Called: I C T
1432 Old Waterbury Rd # 6 (06488-3905)
PHONE..................................203 264-5757
Joseph Baker, *President*
Paul J Geary, *Vice Pres*
▲ EMP: 20 EST: 1993
SALES (est): 3.2MM Privately Held
SIC: 3825 Mfg Electrical Measuring Instruments

(G-4029)
KAN PAK LLC
425 Main St N (06488-3804)
PHONE..................................203 933-6631
Art Mc Farrin, *Manager*
EMP: 5
SALES (corp-wide): 1.3B Privately Held
WEB: www.mixology.com
SIC: 2024 Mfg Ice Cream/Frozen Desert
HQ: Kan. Pak, Llc
151 S Whittier Rd
Wichita KS 67207
620 442-6820

(G-4030)
MBSIINET INC
194 Main St N (06488-3806)
P.O. Box 425 (06488-0425)
PHONE..................................888 466-2744
Tim Thomas, *President*
Carolyn Thomas, *CFO*
EMP: 12 EST: 1992
SALES (est): 1MM Privately Held
WEB: www.proflc.com
SIC: 7372 Prepackaged Software Services

(G-4031)
MICRO-PROBE INCORPORATED
Also Called: Form Factor
2 Pomperaug Office Park # 103 (06488-2288)
PHONE..................................203 267-6446
Todd Martin, *Branch Mgr*
EMP: 3 Publicly Held
SIC: 3674 Mfg Semiconductors/Related Devices
HQ: Micro-Probe Incorporated
617 River Oaks Pkwy
San Jose CA 95134
408 457-3900

(G-4032)
REAL WOMEN INTERNATIONAL LLC
Also Called: Jolie Montre
385 Main St S Ste 404 (06488-4247)
PHONE..................................212 719-3130
Mark Levine, *President*
Rundah Arafat, *Manager*
EMP: 3
SALES: 500K Privately Held
SIC: 3873 Mfg Watches/Clocks/Parts

(G-4033)
SOUTHBURY PRINTING CENTRE INC
385 Main St S Ste 107 (06488-4292)
PHONE..................................203 264-0102
Fredrick Plescia Jr, *President*
EMP: 9
SQ FT: 1,500
SALES (est): 1.6MM Privately Held
SIC: 2752 Lithographic Commercial Printing

(G-4034)
TMF INCORPORATED
1266 Main St S Ste 3 (06488-2136)
PHONE..................................203 267-7364
Todd Decater, *President*
EMP: 4
SQ FT: 4,000
SALES: 1MM Privately Held
WEB: www.tmslitho.com
SIC: 3549 3544 Mfg Metalworking Machinery Mfg Dies/Tools/Jigs/Fixtures

(G-4035)
TRAP ROCK QUARRY
236 Roxbury Rd (06488-1234)
PHONE..................................203 263-2195
John Jenkins, *Principal*
EMP: 3 EST: 1994
SALES (est): 136.1K Privately Held
SIC: 1422 Crushed/Broken Limestone

Southington
Hartford County

(G-4036)
ACUCUT INC
200 Town Line Rd (06489-1145)
PHONE..................................860 793-7012
Scott Barmore, *CEO*
Judith Barmore, *Ch of Bd*
Michael Barmore, *President*
Larry Mc Nellis, *President*
Ray Lemay, *Vice Pres*
EMP: 48 EST: 1978
SQ FT: 30,000
SALES (est): 9.2MM Privately Held
WEB: www.acucut.com
SIC: 3599 Mfg Industrial Machinery

(G-4037)
AMERICAN STANDARD COMPANY
Also Called: Florian Tools
157 Water St (06489-3018)
PHONE..................................860 628-9643
▲ EMP: 25 EST: 1937
SQ FT: 20,000
SALES (est): 4.2MM Privately Held
WEB: www.ratchetcut.com
SIC: 3469 3312 5261 Mfg Metal Stampings Blast Furnace-Steel Works Ret Nursery/Garden Supplies

(G-4038)
ANDERSON PUBLISHING LLC
24 Mooreland Dr (06489-2900)
P.O. Box 786 (06489-0786)
PHONE..................................860 621-2192
Joan Anderson, *Mng Member*
Anderson Publishing, *E-Business*
EMP: 3
SALES (est): 308.5K Privately Held
WEB: www.andersonpublish.com
SIC: 2752 Lithographic Commercial Printing

(G-4039)
APAROS ELECTRIC MOTOR SERVICE
Also Called: Aparo's Electric Motor Repair
134 Industrial Dr (06489-1182)
PHONE..................................860 276-2044
Steven Aparo, *President*
Stephen Aparo, *President*
Daniel Aparo, *Treasurer*
Marie Aparo, *Admin Sec*
EMP: 5
SQ FT: 2,400
SALES: 500K Privately Held
SIC: 7694 5063 5999 Repair Wholesale & Retail Electric Motors

(G-4040)
AZ COPY CENTER INC
Also Called: A Z Copy Center
298 Captain Lewis Dr (06489-1153)
PHONE..................................860 621-7325
Steven J Adduci, *President*
EMP: 4
SQ FT: 1,200
SALES (est): 61.3K Privately Held
SIC: 2759 Commercial Printing

(G-4041)
BRACONE METAL SPINNING INC
39 Depaolo Dr (06489-1021)
PHONE..................................860 628-5927
Christina Bracone, *President*
EMP: 20
SQ FT: 15,000
SALES (est): 3.3MM Privately Held
SIC: 3599 3469 Mfg Industrial Machinery Mfg Metal Stampings

(G-4042)
C V TOOL COMPANY INC (PA)
44 Robert Porter Rd (06489-1159)
PHONE..................................978 353-7901
Carmine Votino, *President*
Assunta Votino, *Corp Secy*
Kenneth Mattson, *Plant Mgr*
Filomena Maria Hurley, *Manager*
John Votino, *Manager*
EMP: 32 EST: 1980
SQ FT: 35,000
SALES (est): 10MM Privately Held
WEB: www.cvtool.com
SIC: 3599 3728 7692 3544 Mfg Industrial Machinery Mfg Aircraft Parts/Equip Welding Repair Mfg Dies/Tools/Jigs/Fixt Mfg Machine Tool-Cutting

(G-4043)
CARBIDE TECHNOLOGY INC
55 Captain Lewis Dr (06489-1148)
PHONE..................................860 621-8981
Robert Burz, *President*
Judith Burz, *Shareholder*
EMP: 5
SQ FT: 6,000
SALES: 500K Privately Held
WEB: www.carbidetechnology.net
SIC: 2819 Mfg Industrial Inorganic Chemicals

(G-4044)
CLEAR AUTOMATION LLC
85 Robert Porter Rd (06489-1152)
PHONE..................................860 621-2955
Ronald McCleary, *President*
Bruce Barnes, *Engineer*
Steve Serina, *Engineer*
Brian Stearns, *Engineer*
Thomas Genovese, *Design Engr*
▲ EMP: 27
SQ FT: 31,000
SALES: 5.7MM Privately Held
WEB: www.clearautomation.com
SIC: 3549 Mfg Metalworking Machinery

(G-4045)
COMPANION INDUSTRIES INC
891 W Queen St (06489-1094)
PHONE..................................860 628-0504
Ken Paul, *President*
Vinny Roy, *Opers Mgr*
Steve Tosta, *Admin Sec*
EMP: 70
SQ FT: 34,000
SALES (est): 12.9MM Privately Held
WEB: www.companionind.com
SIC: 3469 Mfg Metal Stampings

(G-4046)
DEE ZEE ICE LLC
93 Industrial Dr (06489-1181)
PHONE..................................860 276-3500
Robert L Rogers, *Mng Member*
Carl Verderame III, *Info Tech Mgr*
EMP: 15
SQ FT: 2,000
SALES (est): 2.2MM Privately Held
SIC: 2097 Mfg Ice

(G-4047)
DENCO COUNTER-BORE LLC
30 Peters Cir (06489-3713)
P.O. Box 875 (06489-0875)
PHONE..................................860 276-0782
Dennis Glatz,
Chris Glatz,
Patricia Glatz,
EMP: 3
SALES: 100K Privately Held
SIC: 3541 Mfg Machine Tools-Cutting

(G-4048)
ETHICON INC
Also Called: Ethicon Endo - Surgery
201 W Queen St (06489-1138)
PHONE..................................860 621-9111
John Callen, *Manager*
EMP: 300
SALES (corp-wide): 81.5B Publicly Held
WEB: www.ethiconinc.com
SIC: 3842 Mfg Surgical Appliances/Supplies
HQ: Ethicon Inc.
Us Route 22
Somerville NJ 08876
732 524-0400

(G-4049)
F F SCREW PRODUCTS INC
Also Called: Ff Screw Products
888 W Queen St (06489-1033)
PHONE..................................860 621-4567
Frank Fragola, *President*
Mary Fragola, *Vice Pres*
▲ EMP: 25
SQ FT: 15,000
SALES (est): 6MM Privately Held
SIC: 3089 3451 Mfg Plastic Products Mfg Screw Machine Products

(G-4050)
FIRE TECHNOLOGY INC
122 Spring St (06489-1534)
PHONE..................................860 276-2181
Benjamin S Wysocki Jr, *Principal*
EMP: 4
SALES (est): 689.8K Privately Held
SIC: 3569 Mfg General Industrial Machinery

(G-4051)
FIVES N AMERCN COMBUSTN INC
999 Andrews St (06489-2911)
PHONE..................................216 271-6000
EMP: 43
SALES (corp-wide): 843.9K Privately Held
SIC: 3433 Mfg Heating Equipment-Non-electric
HQ: Fives North American Combustion, Inc.
4455 E 71st St
Cleveland OH 44105
216 271-6000

GEOGRAPHIC

(G-4052)
GEMCO MANUFACTURING CO INC
555 W Queen St (06489-1178)
PHONE..................................860 628-5529
Mark Divenere, *President*
Annmarie Johnson, *Business Mgr*
Andrew White, *VP Mfg*
EMP: 21 **EST:** 1943
SQ FT: 40,000
SALES (est): 4.7MM **Privately Held**
WEB: www.gemcomfg.com
SIC: 3469 3495 3496 Mfg Metal Stampings Mfg Wire Springs Mfg Misc Fabricated Wire Products

(G-4053)
GENERAL MACHINE COMPANY INC
1223 Mount Vernon Rd (06489-2116)
PHONE..................................860 426-9295
Mary Grzegorzk, *President*
Walentyn Grzegorzk, *Vice Pres*
EMP: 10
SQ FT: 2,500
SALES (est): 930K **Privately Held**
SIC: 3599 Mfg Industrial Machinery

(G-4054)
GLOBE TOOL & MET STAMPG CO INC
95 Robert Porter Rd (06489-1161)
PHONE..................................860 621-6807
Reginald J Cote, *CEO*
Michelle Cote Knuth, *President*
Paul Cote, *Vice Pres*
Phyllis B Cote, *Admin Sec*
EMP: 35 **EST:** 1945
SQ FT: 31,000
SALES (est): 7.2MM **Privately Held**
WEB: www.globe-tool.com
SIC: 3469 3544 Mfg Metal Stampings Mfg Dies/Tools/Jigs/Fixtures

(G-4055)
GORDON CORPORATION
170 Spring St Unit 3 (06489-1532)
PHONE..................................860 628-4775
Anthony Prepiatti, *President*
David Gross, *Vice Pres*
Sue Devine, *Administration*
EMP: 79
SQ FT: 50,000
SALES (est): 15.5MM **Privately Held**
WEB: www.gordoncelladoor.com
SIC: 3317 3442 Mfg Steel Pipe/Tubes Mfg Metal Doors/Sash/Trim

(G-4056)
HANDYSCAPE LLC
43 Sandy Pine Dr (06489-6016)
PHONE..................................860 318-1067
Alan Seibert, *Principal*
EMP: 3
SALES (est): 261.8K **Privately Held**
SIC: 2851 Mfg Paints/Allied Products

(G-4057)
HIGH TECH PRECISION MFG L L C
43 Aircraft Rd (06489-1402)
P.O. Box 709 (06489-0709)
PHONE..................................860 621-7242
Stanley Maciorowski,
EMP: 3 **EST:** 2000
SQ FT: 5,000
SALES: 325K **Privately Held**
SIC: 3599 Mfg Industrial Machinery

(G-4058)
HOLM CORRUGATED CONTAINER INC
Metals Dr (06489)
P.O. Box 477 (06489-0477)
PHONE..................................860 628-5559
Robert E Holm, *President*
Francine Holm, *Admin Sec*
EMP: 26
SQ FT: 25,000
SALES (est): 6MM **Privately Held**
SIC: 2653 Mfg Corrugated/Solid Fiber Boxes

(G-4059)
HOYT MANUFACTURING CO INC
37 W Center St Ste Ll1 (06489-3501)
PHONE..................................860 628-2050
Carl H Schmidt, *Vice Pres*
Jason David Hoyt, *Vice Pres*
EMP: 6
SALES (est): 625.6K **Privately Held**
SIC: 3469 Mfg Metal Stampings

(G-4060)
J J INDUSTRIES CONN INC
125 W Queen St (06489-1126)
PHONE..................................860 628-4655
Todd Sanzone, *President*
Kathleen Sanzone, *Vice Pres*
Jon Salvitti, *Sales Mgr*
Pete Wallace, *Sales Staff*
Wendy Perkins, *Office Mgr*
EMP: 14
SQ FT: 2,000
SALES (est): 2.8MM **Privately Held**
WEB: www.jjindustries.com
SIC: 3545 Mfg Machine Tool Accessories

(G-4061)
JET TOOL & CUTTER MFG INC
125 W Queen St (06489-1126)
PHONE..................................860 621-5381
Ronald Sanzone, *CEO*
Todd Sanzone, *President*
Thomas Albert, *Shareholder*
Christy Sanzone, *Admin Sec*
EMP: 24
SQ FT: 3,400
SALES (est): 4.6MM **Privately Held**
WEB: www.jettool.com
SIC: 3545 Mfg Machine Tool Accessories

(G-4062)
LIGHT METALS COLORING CO INC
Also Called: L M C
270 Spring St (06489-1589)
PHONE..................................860 621-0145
Richard William Fleet, *President*
Mark Thomas, *Admin Sec*
EMP: 100 **EST:** 1945
SQ FT: 27,000
SALES (est): 14.8MM **Privately Held**
WEB: www.lightmetalscoloring.com
SIC: 3471 Plating/Polishing Service

(G-4063)
M & M CARBIDE INC
290 Center St (06489-3112)
PHONE..................................860 628-2002
Marcial Mendez, *President*
Carmen Mendez, *Vice Pres*
EMP: 5
SQ FT: 1,500
SALES: 400K **Privately Held**
SIC: 3545 7699 Mfg Machine Tool Accessories Repair Services

(G-4064)
MASTERCRAFT TOOL AND MCH CO
100 Newell St (06489-1123)
PHONE..................................860 628-5551
Stephen Lassy, *President*
Brian J Lassy, *Vice Pres*
Brian Lassy, *Vice Pres*
Michael Lassy, *Vice Pres*
Alec Konovalov, *QC Mgr*
EMP: 19
SALES (est): 3.5MM **Privately Held**
WEB: www.mastercrafttool-mach.com
SIC: 3469 3443 3544 Mfg Metal Stampings Mfg Fabricated Plate Work Mfg Dies/Tools/Jigs/Fixtures

(G-4065)
MATTHEW WARREN INC
Also Called: Economy Spring
29 Depaolo Dr (06489-1021)
PHONE..................................860 621-7358
Leonide Charette, *Branch Mgr*
EMP: 89
SALES (corp-wide): 185.9MM **Privately Held**
SIC: 3495 3493 Mfg Wire Springs Mfg Steel Spring-Nonwire
HQ: Matthew Warren, Inc.
9501 Tech Blvd Ste 401
Rosemont IL 60018
847 349-5760

(G-4066)
MILL MACHINE TOOL & DIE CO
280 Mill St (06489-4715)
PHONE..................................860 628-6700
John D'Angelo, *Owner*
EMP: 3
SQ FT: 6,000
SALES (est): 228.3K **Privately Held**
SIC: 3599 Machine Shop

(G-4067)
NEWCOMB SPRING CORP
235 Spring St (06489-1542)
PHONE..................................860 621-0111
George D Jacobson, *Manager*
EMP: 27
SALES (corp-wide): 71.2MM **Privately Held**
WEB: www.newcombspring.com
SIC: 3495 3493 Mfg Wire Springs Mfg Steel Springs-Nonwire
PA: Spring Newcomb Corp
5408 Panola Indus Blvd
Decatur GA 30035
770 981-2803

(G-4068)
NEWCOMB SPRINGS CONNECTICUT
235 Spring St (06489-1542)
PHONE..................................860 621-0111
Robert Jacobson, *President*
Kurt Tonhaeuser, *General Mgr*
Donald Jacobson, *Chairman*
Jason Wargo, *Info Tech Dir*
EMP: 50
SQ FT: 80,000
SALES (est): 8.2MM **Privately Held**
SIC: 3495 Mfg Wire Springs

(G-4069)
NORTHEAST CARBIDE INC
Also Called: Springs Manufacturer Supply Co
525 W Queen St (06489-1192)
PHONE..................................860 628-2515
William Lyons III, *President*
Ralph Parlado, *Vice Pres*
Marianne Caiaze, *Office Mgr*
EMP: 15
SQ FT: 10,000
SALES (est): 2.1MM **Privately Held**
WEB: www.springmfrssupply.com
SIC: 3544 Mfg Dies/Tools/Jigs/Fixtures

(G-4070)
OWEN TOOL AND MFG CO INC
149 Aircraft Rd (06489-1404)
P.O. Box 8, Plainville (06062-0008)
PHONE..................................860 628-6540
Thomas Owen, *President*
EMP: 8 **EST:** 1941
SQ FT: 10,000
SALES (est): 1.1MM **Privately Held**
WEB: www.owen-tool.com
SIC: 3469 Mfg Dies/Tools/Jigs/Fixtures

(G-4071)
QUANTUM BPOWER SOUTHINGTON LLC
49 Depaolo Dr (06489-1021)
PHONE..................................860 201-0621
Mike Curtis, *Director*
Kevin J Boucher,
EMP: 4 **EST:** 2016
SALES (est): 104K **Privately Held**
SIC: 3572 Mfg Computer Storage Devices

(G-4072)
R & D SERVICES LLC
45 Old Turnpike Rd (06489-3633)
PHONE..................................860 628-5205
Kevin Johnston, *CEO*
Dan Mac Kenzie, *Manager*
Stan Mac Kenzie, *Manager*
Linda Johnston,
Donald Mac Kenzie,
EMP: 5
SQ FT: 1,400
SALES (est): 680.3K **Privately Held**
SIC: 2026 Mfg Fluid Milk

(G-4073)
RECOR WELDING CENTER INC
86 Gannet Dr (06489-1758)
PHONE..................................860 573-1942
Sonia Bourget, *Admin Sec*
EMP: 3
SALES: 394K **Privately Held**
SIC: 7692 Welding Repair

(G-4074)
REM CHEMICALS INC (PA)
Also Called: R E M
325 W Queen St (06489-1177)
PHONE..................................860 621-6755
Mark D Michaud, *President*
Lori Bailey, *Facilities Mgr*
Justin Michaud, *Opers Staff*
Vincent Cline, *Project Engr*
Louise B Michaud, *Treasurer*
▲ **EMP:** 17 **EST:** 1965
SQ FT: 14,500
SALES (est): 7.1MM **Privately Held**
WEB: www.remchem.com
SIC: 2899 Mfg Chemical Preparations

(G-4075)
SAUCIERS MISC METAL WORKS LLC
89 Birch St (06489-1120)
P.O. Box 1040 (06489-5040)
PHONE..................................860 747-4577
Clayton Saucier,
Clayton R Saucier,
EMP: 4
SQ FT: 2,400
SALES (est): 362K **Privately Held**
SIC: 7692 Welding Repair Services

(G-4076)
SENS ALL INC
85 Water St (06489-3017)
P.O. Box 626 (06489-0626)
PHONE..................................860 628-8379
Walter E Jacobson Sr, *President*
Walter E Jacobson Jr, *Vice Pres*
EMP: 4 **EST:** 1982
SALES (est): 516.6K **Privately Held**
SIC: 3829 Mfg Of Transducers

(G-4077)
SMARTPAY SOLUTIONS
200 Executive Blvd Ste 3a (06489-1042)
PHONE..................................860 986-7659
Gavin Forrester, *Principal*
EMP: 3
SALES (est): 235.5K **Privately Held**
SIC: 7372 Prepackaged Software Services

(G-4078)
SMITHS MEDICAL ASD INC
Also Called: Medex Southington
201 W Queen St (06489-1194)
PHONE..................................860 621-9111
Darren Hodkinson, *Opers Staff*
Harsh Chheda, *Research*
Massimo Castaldi, *Engineer*
John Hemsted, *Branch Mgr*
Andrea Alexander, *Senior Mgr*
EMP: 341
SALES (corp-wide): 3.1B **Privately Held**
SIC: 3841 Mfg Surgical/Medical Instruments
HQ: Smiths Medical Asd, Inc.
6000 Nathan Ln N Ste 100
Plymouth MN 55442
763 383-3000

(G-4079)
SOUTHINGTON METAL FABG CO
95 Corporate Dr (06489-1085)
P.O. Box 456 (06489-0456)
PHONE..................................860 621-0149
John Brunalli, *President*
James Needham, *Corp Secy*
EMP: 10 **EST:** 1967
SQ FT: 17,500
SALES (est): 1.9MM **Privately Held**
SIC: 3446 Mfg Architectural Metalwork

(G-4080)
SOUTHINGTON TRANSM AUTO REPR
1900 West St (06489-1030)
PHONE..................................860 329-0381
Richard Singer, *Principal*

EMP: 4
SALES (est): 463.5K Privately Held
SIC: 3714 Mfg Motor Vehicle Parts/Accessories

(G-4081)
SPECIALTY PRODUCTS MFG LLC
251 Captain Lewis Dr (06489-1155)
PHONE..................................860 621-6969
David Randall, Mng Member
EMP: 6
SQ FT: 6,000
SALES (est): 929.7K Privately Held
SIC: 3429 3451 Mfg Hardware Mfg Screw Machine Products

(G-4082)
STEP SAVER INC
Also Called: Observer, The
213 Spring St (06489-1530)
P.O. Box 648 (06489-0648)
PHONE..................................860 621-6751
William B Pape, President
Douglas Guersney, Exec VP
Kevin Smalley, Prdtn Mgr
EMP: 45
SQ FT: 17,000
SALES (est): 3.2MM
SALES (corp-wide): 24MM Privately Held
WEB: www.stepsaver.com
SIC: 2741 2752 2791 2789 Misc Publishing Lithographic Coml Print Typesetting Services Bookbinding/Related Work
PA: American-Republican, Incorporated
389 Meadow St
Waterbury CT 06702
203 574-3636

(G-4083)
SUPREME STORM SERVICES LLC
49 Depaolo Dr (06489-1021)
PHONE..................................860 201-0642
Ronald Wuennemann,
Kevin Boucher,
Joseph Calvanese,
EMP: 3 EST: 2016
SALES (est): 91.3K Privately Held
SIC: 2099 4222 5149 8744 Mfg Food Preparations Refrig Warehouse/Storage Whol Groceries Facilities Support Svcs

(G-4084)
THADIEO LLC
405 Queen St Ste M (06489-1823)
PHONE..................................860 621-4500
Michael Thadieo, Principal
EMP: 4 EST: 2008
SALES (est): 154K Privately Held
SIC: 2051 Mfg Bread/Related Products

(G-4085)
THOMAS PRODUCTS LTD
987 West St (06489-1023)
PHONE..................................860 621-9101
Thomas Duksa, President
Paul Cameron, Controller
EMP: 20
SQ FT: 20,000
SALES (est): 3.8MM Privately Held
WEB: www.thomasprod.com
SIC: 3625 3643 Mfg Relays/Industrial Controls Mfg Conductive Wiring Devices

(G-4086)
THORNTON AND COMPANY INC
132 Main St Ste 2a 3 (06489-2561)
PHONE..................................860 628-6771
Paul P Thornton, President
Nate Deangelis, Vice Pres
Jake Thornton, Vice Pres
Lisa Vaccaro, Admin Sec
◆ EMP: 10
SQ FT: 3,000
SALES (est): 4.3MM Privately Held
SIC: 2821 5162 Whol Plastic Materials/Shapes Mfg Plastic Materials/Resins

(G-4087)
TOOL 2000
327 Captain Lewis Dr (06489-1170)
PHONE..................................860 620-0020
Andrzej Siwek, Owner
EMP: 4
SALES (est): 328.1K Privately Held
SIC: 3423 7389 Mfg Hand/Edge Tools Business Services

(G-4088)
TRI MAR MANUFACTURING COMPAN
191 Captain Lewis Dr (06489-1144)
PHONE..................................860 628-4791
Keith Martinelli, President
Martin Martinelli, Corp Secy
Kevin Martinelli, Vice Pres
David Martinelli, Asst Treas
EMP: 13
SQ FT: 6,000
SALES (est): 2.1MM Privately Held
WEB: www.marathonrecruiters.com
SIC: 3599 General Machine Shop

(G-4089)
VANGUARD PLASTICS CORPORATION
100 Robert Porter Rd (06489-1160)
PHONE..................................860 628-4736
Lawrence J Budnick Jr, CEO
Christopher Budnick, President
Marsha A Budnick, Vice Pres
Daren Fippinger, Vice Pres
Kimberly Lagace, Vice Pres
▲ EMP: 45
SQ FT: 22,500
SALES (est): 9.3MM Privately Held
WEB: www.vanguardplastics.com
SIC: 3089 Mfg Plastic Products

(G-4090)
VERZATEC INC
119 Sabina Dr (06489-2449)
PHONE..................................860 628-0511
Darryl Upson, Director
EMP: 3
SALES (est): 335.2K Privately Held
SIC: 3599 Mfg Industrial Machinery

(G-4091)
WELD-ALL INC
987 West St (06489-1023)
PHONE..................................860 621-3156
Thomas R Duksa, President
Clara Duksa, Admin Sec
EMP: 15
SQ FT: 10,000
SALES (est): 1.7MM Privately Held
SIC: 3599 7692 Mfg Industrial Machinery Welding Repair

(G-4092)
YARDE METALS INC (HQ)
45 Newell St (06489-1424)
PHONE..................................860 406-6061
William K Sales Jr, CEO
Matthew L Smith, President
Carla Lewis, Vice Pres
Douglas Candreva, Opers Staff
George D'Addario, Opers Staff
◆ EMP: 425
SQ FT: 500,000
SALES (est): 240.1MM
SALES (corp-wide): 11.5B Publicly Held
WEB: www.yarde.com
SIC: 3499 5051 Mfg Misc Fabricated Metal Products Metals Service Center
PA: Reliance Steel & Aluminum Co.
350 S Grand Ave Ste 5100
Los Angeles CA 90071
213 687-7700

Southport
Fairfield County

(G-4093)
ASYLUM DISTILLERY
105 Waterville Rd (06890-1056)
PHONE..................................203 209-0146
Robert Schulten, Principal
EMP: 3
SALES (est): 111.3K Privately Held
SIC: 2085 Mfg Distilled/Blended Liquor

(G-4094)
C O JELLIFF CORPORATION (PA)
354 Pequot Ave Ste 300 (06890-1485)
PHONE..................................203 259-1615
Wilmot F Wheeler Jr, Ch of Bd
Geoffrey Wheeler, President
Rand Glucroft, Vice Pres
Halsted W Wheeler, Treasurer
▲ EMP: 62
SQ FT: 40,000
SALES (est): 12.8MM Privately Held
WEB: www.jelliff.com
SIC: 3496 Mfg Misc Fabricated Wire Products

(G-4095)
CENTER FOR DISCOVERY
1320 Mill Hill Rd (06890-3017)
PHONE..................................203 955-1381
Alyse Peekman, Principal
EMP: 50 EST: 2012
SALES (est): 3.7MM Privately Held
SIC: 3822 Mfg Environmental Controls

(G-4096)
INTERNATIONAL SOCCER & RUGBY
3683 Post Rd (06890-1113)
PHONE..................................203 254-1979
Gus Avalos, Branch Mgr
EMP: 5 Privately Held
SIC: 3949 Mfg Sporting/Athletic Goods
PA: International Soccer & Rugby Imports, Llc
3683 Post Rd Unit 1
Fairfield CT 06430

(G-4097)
RESOLUTE FP US INC
97 Village Ln (06890-1149)
PHONE..................................203 292-6560
Breen Blaine, Branch Mgr
EMP: 438
SALES (corp-wide): 3.7B Privately Held
SIC: 2621 Mfg Newsprint
HQ: Resolute Fp Us Inc.
5300 Cureton Ferry Rd
Catawba SC 29704
803 981-8000

(G-4098)
SIGN CREATIONS
89 Arbor Dr (06890-1190)
PHONE..................................203 259-8330
Mark Milosky, Owner
EMP: 3
SALES (est): 180.8K Privately Held
WEB: www.signcreations.com
SIC: 3993 Mfg Signs/Advertising Specialties

(G-4099)
STURM RUGER & COMPANY INC (PA)
1 Lacey Pl (06890-1207)
PHONE..................................203 259-7843
C Michael Jacobi, Ch of Bd
Michael O Fifer, Vice Ch Bd
Christopher J Killoy, President
Thomas P Sullivan, Senior VP
Steve Maynard, Vice Pres
▲ EMP: 277 EST: 1949
SQ FT: 25,000
SALES: 495.6MM Publicly Held
WEB: www.ruger-firearms.com
SIC: 3484 3324 Mfg Firearms And Precision Investment Castings

(G-4100)
SUPERIOR PLATING COMPANY
2 Lacey Pl (06890-1241)
PHONE..................................203 255-1501
John L Raymond, President
EMP: 75
SQ FT: 20,000
SALES (est): 9.2MM
SALES (corp-wide): 6.7MM Privately Held
WEB: www.superiorplatingco.com
SIC: 3471 Plating/Polishing Service
PA: Superior Technology Corp.
Lacey Pl
Southport CT 06890
203 255-1501

(G-4101)
SUPERIOR TECHNOLOGY CORP (PA)
Lacey Pl (06890)
PHONE..................................203 255-1501
John L Raymond, President
EMP: 120 EST: 1974
SQ FT: 30,000
SALES (est): 6.7MM Privately Held
SIC: 3471 Plating/Polishing Service

(G-4102)
THOMAS BERNHARD BUILDING SYS
Also Called: B T Building Systems
281 Pequot Ave (06890-1360)
PHONE..................................203 925-0414
Harold C Thomas, Principal
Bryan Maloney, CFO
Van H Bernhard,
EMP: 35
SQ FT: 110,000
SALES (est): 3.3MM Privately Held
WEB: www.btbuildingsystems.com
SIC: 2439 5211 2435 Mfg Structural Wood Members Ret Lumber/Building Materials Mfg Hardwood Veneer/Plywood

Stafford Springs
Tolland County

(G-4103)
3M PURIFICATION INC
32 River Rd (06076-1500)
PHONE..................................860 684-8628
Michael Bristol, Opers-Prdtn-Mfg
EMP: 150
SALES (corp-wide): 32.7B Publicly Held
WEB: www.cuno.com
SIC: 3677 Mfg Disposable Filter Devices
HQ: 3m Purification Inc.
400 Research Pkwy
Meriden CT 06450
203 237-5541

(G-4104)
AMERICAN SLEEVE BEARING LLC
1 Spring St (06076-1504)
PHONE..................................860 684-8060
Howard Buckland,
▲ EMP: 35 EST: 1982
SQ FT: 60,000
SALES (est): 9.4MM Privately Held
WEB: www.asbbearings.com
SIC: 3568 3366 Mfg Power Transmission Equipment Copper Foundry

(G-4105)
AMERICAN WOOLEN COMPANY INC
8 Furnace Ave (06076-1223)
PHONE..................................860 684-2766
Jacob Harrison Long, CEO
Katherine J Knight, President
Michael Fournier, Opers Staff
Giuseppe Monteleone, Opers Staff
Lisa Cornish, Treasurer
EMP: 3
SALES (est): 701.1K Privately Held
SIC: 2211 7389 Cotton Broadwoven Fabric Mill Business Services

(G-4106)
BALSAM WOODS FARM
Also Called: Realmaplesyrup.com
4 Clinton St (06076-1106)
PHONE..................................860 265-1800
David Broer, Owner
EMP: 3
SALES (est): 78K Privately Held
SIC: 2099 Mfg Food Preparations

GEOGRAPHIC

(G-4107)
CROTEAU DEVELOPMENT GROUP INC
25 West St (06076-1325)
P.O. Box 150 (06076-0150)
PHONE..................................860 684-3605
Jim Croteau, *President*
EMP: 3
SQ FT: 11,000
SALES: 600K **Privately Held**
SIC: 3444 3585 Product Development Of Service Machines & Light Sheet Metal Fabrication

(G-4108)
DALLA CORTE LUMBER
12 Minor Rd (06076-4215)
PHONE..................................860 875-9480
Keven Dallacorte, *President*
EMP: 3
SALES (est): 296.5K **Privately Held**
SIC: 2421 Sawmill/Planing Mill

(G-4109)
DIVISION 5 LLC
99 Cooper Ln (06076-1312)
PHONE..................................860 752-4127
Conrad Barker, *Business Mgr*
EMP: 7
SALES: 2.2MM **Privately Held**
SIC: 3441 Micellaneous Metal Fabrication & Installation Company

(G-4110)
EDGEWATER INTERNATIONAL LLC
Also Called: Rec Components
17 Middle River Dr (06076-1034)
PHONE..................................860 851-9014
Bill Purtill, *Controller*
Alan Gnann,
Linda L Gnann,
▲ **EMP:** 15
SQ FT: 15,000
SALES (est): 2MM **Privately Held**
WEB: www.recoilguides.com
SIC: 3949 Mfg Sporting/Athletic Goods

(G-4111)
HOBBS MEDICAL INC
8 Spring St (06076-1505)
PHONE..................................860 684-5875
Joanna Warner, *President*
Wayne Singer, *Purchasing*
Edward Page, *Engineer*
EMP: 22
SQ FT: 10,000
SALES (est): 4.6MM **Privately Held**
WEB: www.hobbsmedical.com
SIC: 3841 3845 Mfg Surgical/Medical Instruments Mfg Electromedical Equipment

(G-4112)
LUCHON CABINET WOODWORK
140 Buckley Hwy (06076-4407)
PHONE..................................860 684-5037
Jeff Luchon, *Owner*
EMP: 3
SALES (est): 411.4K **Privately Held**
WEB: www.luchoncabinet.com
SIC: 2434 Mfg Wood Kitchen Cabinets

(G-4113)
MSJ INVESTMENTS INC
Also Called: Rmi
72 W Stafford Rd Ste 3 (06076-1000)
PHONE..................................860 684-9956
Mark S Jewson, *President*
EMP: 10
SQ FT: 4,000
SALES: 5MM **Privately Held**
WEB: www.msjinvestments.com
SIC: 3724 3812 Manufactures Aircraft Jet Engine Components

(G-4114)
SERAFIN SULKY CO
65 Buckley Hwy (06076-4426)
PHONE..................................860 684-2986
Elmo Serafin, *President*
Michael Serafin, *Treasurer*
Marjorie Serafin, *Admin Sec*
EMP: 5
SQ FT: 5,000
SALES (est): 694.8K **Privately Held**
SIC: 3799 7699 Mfg Transportation Equipment Repair Services

(G-4115)
SKYLINE QUARRY
110 Conklin Rd (06076-4204)
PHONE..................................860 875-3580
Wayne C Williams, *Partner*
Carolyn Williams, *Partner*
EMP: 25
SQ FT: 1,500
SALES (est): 2.9MM **Privately Held**
SIC: 3281 1442 1423 5032 Mfg Cut Stone/Products Construction Sand/Gravel Crushed/Broken Granite Whol Brick/Stone Matrls

(G-4116)
TE CONNECTIVITY CORPORATION
Tyco Elec Stafford Sprng Div
15 Tyco Dr (06076)
PHONE..................................860 684-8000
Robert Peirce, *General Mgr*
EMP: 110
SALES (corp-wide): 13.9B **Privately Held**
WEB: www.raychem.com
SIC: 3549 3672 Mfg Metalworking Machinery Mfg Printed Circuit Boards
HQ: Te Connectivity Corporation
1050 Westlakes Dr
Berwyn PA 19312
610 893-9800

(G-4117)
TETRAULT & SONS INC
Also Called: Awnair
75 Tetrault Rd (06076-3134)
PHONE..................................860 872-9187
Alan Tetrault, *President*
Jayne Tetrault, *Treasurer*
Joan Beaudet, *Admin Sec*
EMP: 6
SALES (est): 925.1K **Privately Held**
SIC: 3444 2394 1799 1751 Mfg & Installs Aluminum & Canvas Awnings Installs Custom Doors Windows Vertical & Custom Pleated Drapes & Patio Enclosures

(G-4118)
TTM PRINTED CIRCUIT GROUP INC
15 Industrial Park Dr (06076-3612)
PHONE..................................860 684-8000
Bob Pierce, *General Mgr*
EMP: 165
SALES (corp-wide): 2.8B **Publicly Held**
WEB: www.printedcircuits.tycoelectronics.com
SIC: 3672 Mfg Printed Circuit Boards & Assembles Backplanes
HQ: Ttm Printed Circuit Group, Inc.
2630 S Harbor Blvd
Santa Ana CA 92704

(G-4119)
TTM TECHNOLOGIES INC
4 Old Monson Rd (06076-3319)
PHONE..................................860 684-5881
Phil Titterton, *General Mgr*
EMP: 400
SALES (corp-wide): 2.8B **Publicly Held**
WEB: www.ttmtechnologies.com
SIC: 3672 Mfg Printed Circuit Boards
PA: Ttm Technologies, Inc.
200 Sandpointe Ave # 400
Santa Ana CA 92707
714 327-3000

(G-4120)
TTM TECHNOLOGIES INC
20 Industrial Park Dr (06076-3613)
PHONE..................................860 684-8000
Keith Wood, *Branch Mgr*
Jim Blair, *Info Tech Dir*
EMP: 100
SALES (corp-wide): 2.8B **Publicly Held**
WEB: www.ttmtechnologies.com
SIC: 3672 Mfg Printed Circuit Board
PA: Ttm Technologies, Inc.
200 Sandpointe Ave # 400
Santa Ana CA 92707
714 327-3000

(G-4121)
URG GRAPHICS INC (PA)
12 Fox Hill Dr (06076-3742)
PHONE..................................860 928-0835
Arthur Etchells, *CEO*
Rennie Cercone, *President*
Helen R Etchells, *Vice Pres*
J Paul Etchells, *Admin Sec*
EMP: 24
SQ FT: 19,000
SALES (est): 1.6MM **Privately Held**
SIC: 2796 Platemaking Services

Stamford
Fairfield County

(G-4122)
20/20 SOFTWARE INC
2001 W Main St Ste 270 (06902-4540)
PHONE..................................203 316-5500
Donald Resnick, *President*
Sheron Resnick, *Vice Pres*
EMP: 8
SQ FT: 1,200
SALES (est): 994.2K **Privately Held**
WEB: www.2020soft.net
SIC: 3695 7389 4813 Mfg Computer Software And Provides Website Design & Host Services

(G-4123)
A GERBER CORP
110 Idlewood Dr (06905-2406)
PHONE..................................203 918-1913
Akemi Gerber Stuart, *President*
EMP: 3
SALES: 200K **Privately Held**
SIC: 2326 Mfg Men's/Boy's Work Clothing Mfg Misc Products

(G-4124)
A S FINE FOODS
Also Called: A-S Catering
856 High Ridge Rd (06905-1911)
PHONE..................................203 322-3899
Jack Marnaia, *President*
EMP: 65
SALES (est): 5.2MM **Privately Held**
SIC: 2032 Mfg Canned Specialties

(G-4125)
ABB ENTERPRISE SOFTWARE INC
900 Long Ridge Rd (06902-1139)
PHONE..................................203 329-8771
Nils Leffler, *Vice Pres*
Gregory E Sages, *CFO*
R Norton, *Treasurer*
John W Cutler Jr, *Branch Mgr*
Eugene E Madara, *Director*
EMP: 10
SALES (corp-wide): 36.7B **Privately Held**
WEB: www.elsterelectricity.com
SIC: 3612 Mfg Transformers
HQ: Abb Inc.
305 Gregson Dr
Cary NC 27511

(G-4126)
ACCENT SIGNS LLC
130 Lenox Ave Ste 21 (06906-2337)
PHONE..................................203 975-8688
John Massari,
Jill Massari,
EMP: 4
SQ FT: 2,000
SALES: 500K **Privately Held**
WEB: www.accent-signs.com
SIC: 3993 Mfg Signs/Advertising Specialties

(G-4127)
ACCURATE TOOL & DIE INC
16 Leon Pl (06902-5508)
PHONE..................................203 967-1200
Jeffrey Salvatore, *President*
▲ **EMP:** 22 **EST:** 1956
SQ FT: 14,500
SALES (est): 3.6MM **Privately Held**
SIC: 3599 3544 Mfg Industrial Machinery Mfg Dies/Tools/Jigs/Fixtures

(G-4128)
ACME SIGN CO (PA)
12 Research Dr (06906-1419)
P.O. Box 2345 (06906-0345)
PHONE..................................203 324-2263
Stephen Trell, *President*
Jeff Trell, *Vice Pres*
EMP: 18
SQ FT: 7,000
SALES (est): 2.3MM **Privately Held**
WEB: www.acmesignco.com
SIC: 3993 3953 5099 5719 Mfg Signs/Ad Specialties Mfg Marking Devices Whol Durable Goods Ret Misc Homefurnishings

(G-4129)
ACQUISITIONS CONTROLLED SVCS
55 Woodland Pl Apt 4 (06902-6962)
P.O. Box 106, Riverside (06878-0106)
PHONE..................................203 327-6364
Kenneth Thron, *President*
Deborah Thron, *Admin Sec*
EMP: 3
SQ FT: 6,000
SALES: 1.5MM **Privately Held**
SIC: 3441 Structural Metal Fabrication

(G-4130)
AG JEWELRY DESIGNS LLC (PA)
1 Stamford Plz (06901-3271)
PHONE..................................800 643-0978
Michael Soutar,
Mary K Soutar,
EMP: 4
SQ FT: 3,600
SALES: 1MM **Privately Held**
SIC: 3911 5094 Mfg Precious Metal Jewelry Whol Jewelry/Precious Stones

(G-4131)
AG SEMICONDUCTOR SERVICES LLC
1111 Summer St Fl 4 (06905-5511)
PHONE..................................203 322-5300
Albert P Vasquez,
Joshua Brain,
Julian Gates,
▼ **EMP:** 30
SQ FT: 10,000
SALES: 15MM **Privately Held**
SIC: 3674 Mfg Semiconductors/Related Devices

(G-4132)
AGI-SHOREWOOD GROUP US LLC
300 Atlantic St Ste 206 (06901-3514)
PHONE..................................203 324-4839
Timothy J Facio, *Vice Pres*
Jacob D Hudson, *Vice Pres*
Donald K Eldert, *CFO*
Philip E Schuch, *Treasurer*
◆ **EMP:** 1005 **EST:** 1966
SALES (est): 70.1K
SALES (corp-wide): 2.9B **Privately Held**
WEB: www.shorepak.com
SIC: 2671 2652 2657 Mfg Packaging Paper/Film Mfg Setup Paperboard Boxes Mfg Folding Paperboard Boxes
PA: Atlas Holdings, Llc
100 Northfield St
Greenwich CT 06830
203 622-9138

(G-4133)
ALLIANCE WATER TREATMENT CO
28 Coachlamp Ln (06902-2005)
P.O. Box 3036 (06905-0036)
PHONE..................................203 323-9968
John F Piatek, *President*
Laure Kovacs, *Office Mgr*
EMP: 6
SALES (est): 550K **Privately Held**
WEB: www.allianceh2o.com
SIC: 3589 Mfg Service Industry Machinery

(G-4134)
ALLIED CONTROLS INC
25 Forest St Apt 14a (06901-1860)
PHONE..................................860 628-8443
EMP: 11
SQ FT: 25,000

▲ = Import ▼=Export
◆ =Import/Export

SALES: 596.6K **Privately Held**
WEB: www.alliedcontrols.com
SIC: **3643** 3613 3625 Current-Carrying Wiring Devices

(G-4135)
AMERICAN BANKNOTE CORPORATION (PA)
Also Called: Abcorp
1055 Washington Blvd Fl 6 (06901-2216)
PHONE.................................203 941-4090
Steven G Singer, *CEO*
Jack Barnett, *Vice Pres*
David Kober, *Vice Pres*
Steve Andrews, *CFO*
◆ **EMP**: 6
SQ FT: 8,020
SALES (est): 292.8MM **Privately Held**
WEB: www.americanbanknote.com
SIC: **2759** 2752 2621 Commercial Printing Lithographic Commercial Printing Paper Mill

(G-4136)
AMERICAN UNMANNED SYSTEMS LLC
460 Summer St (06901-1301)
PHONE.................................203 406-7611
Dorothea Smith, *Vice Pres*
Peter Muhlrad, *Marketing Staff*
EMP: 5
SALES (est): 370.8K **Privately Held**
SIC: **3519** 3724 5088 Mfg Internal Combustion Engines Mfg Aircraft Engines/Parts Whol Transportation Equipment

(G-4137)
AMPCO PUBLISHING & PRTG CORP
130 Lenox Ave Ste 32 (06906-2337)
P.O. Box 8239 (06905-8239)
PHONE.................................203 325-1509
Daniel Sposi Sr, *President*
Maryann Sposi, *Vice Pres*
EMP: 4
SQ FT: 3,000
SALES: 526.1K **Privately Held**
SIC: **2752** Commercial Offset Printers

(G-4138)
AMPHENOL CORPORATION
Amphenol Nexus Technologies
50 Sunnyside Ave (06902-7641)
PHONE.................................203 327-7300
Fereidoun A Farahani, *Manager*
EMP: 60
SALES (corp-wide): 8.2B **Publicly Held**
SIC: **3643** Mfg Conductive Wiring Devices
PA: Amphenol Corporation
358 Hall Ave
Wallingford CT 06492
203 265-8900

(G-4139)
AMPHENOL NEXUS TECHNOLOGIES
50 Sunnyside Ave (06902-7641)
PHONE.................................203 327-7300
Fereidoun A Farahani, *General Mgr*
EMP: 60 **EST**: 1961
SQ FT: 16,000
SALES (est): 11.6MM
SALES (corp-wide): 8.2B **Publicly Held**
WEB: www.nexus.com
SIC: **3643** Mfg Conductive Wiring Devices
PA: Amphenol Corporation
358 Hall Ave
Wallingford CT 06492
203 265-8900

(G-4140)
ANJAR CO
42 Russet Rd (06903-1822)
PHONE.................................203 321-1023
James Becker, *Partner*
Jonathan Becker, *Partner*
David Schlatter, *Manager*
EMP: 5
SQ FT: 1,000
SALES (est): 340K **Privately Held**
WEB: www.anjar.com
SIC: **3944** 3942 Mfg Designs Develops & Licenses Toys Dolls & Games

(G-4141)
APIJECT SYSTEMS CORP (PA)
2 High Ridge Park (06905-1350)
PHONE.................................203 461-7121
Jay Walker, *CEO*
EMP: 5
SALES: 500K **Privately Held**
SIC: **3999** Mfg Misc Products

(G-4142)
ARCADIA ARCHITECTURAL PDTS INC
110 Viaduct Rd (06907-2707)
PHONE.................................203 316-8000
Robert Sayour, *President*
◆ **EMP**: 25
SALES (est): 5.9MM **Privately Held**
WEB: www.arcadiaproducts.com
SIC: **3442** Mfg Metal Doors/Sash/Trim

(G-4143)
ARCCOS GOLF LLC
700 Canal St Ste 19 (06902-5921)
PHONE.................................844 692-7226
Sal Syed, *Owner*
Ammad Faisal, *COO*
Stephanie Boms, *Vice Pres*
Ryan Smith, *Opers Staff*
Jared Rapoport, *Sales Mgr*
EMP: 28
SQ FT: 4,500
SALES (est): 2.5MM **Privately Held**
SIC: **3679** Mfg Electronic Components

(G-4144)
ART OF WELLBEING LLC
230 Saddle Hill Rd (06903-2301)
PHONE.................................917 453-3009
Michiel Nolet, *CEO*
Igor Shindel, *COO*
EMP: 5
SALES: 80K **Privately Held**
SIC: **7372** 7389 Prepackaged Software Services Business Serv Non-Commercial Site

(G-4145)
ATACCAMA CORP US
263 Tresser Blvd Fl 9 (06901-3236)
PHONE.................................203 564-1488
Michal Klaus, *CEO*
Marek Ovcacek, *Engineer*
Sona Gajova, *Mktg Dir*
Radek Doubrava, *Consultant*
David Vanek, *Software Engr*
EMP: 12
SALES (est): 698.4K **Privately Held**
SIC: **7372** Prepackaged Software Services

(G-4146)
AVOLON AEROSPACE NEW YORK INC
700 Canal St 2nd (06902-5921)
PHONE.................................203 663-5490
Lisa Janiga, *Vice Pres*
Debbie McAdam, *Vice Pres*
EMP: 7
SALES (est): 246.3K **Privately Held**
SIC: **3721** Mfg Aircraft
PA: Avolon Aerospace Leasing Limited
Building 1
Dublin

(G-4147)
BAL INTERNATIONAL INC
281 Tresser Blvd Fl 12 (06901-3238)
PHONE.................................203 359-6775
Emilio Galetzki, *President*
Elliott Levy, *Vice Pres*
Edward Thomas Jr, *Treasurer*
Richard Southey, *Director*
EMP: 25
SALES (est): 2.1MM **Privately Held**
SIC: **3339** Primary Nonferrous Metal Producer

(G-4148)
BELDOTTI BAKERIES
Also Called: Cerbone Bakery
605 Newfield Ave (06905-3302)
PHONE.................................203 348-9029
James Beldotti Jr, *Partner*
Michael Beldotti, *Partner*
EMP: 15
SQ FT: 3,000
SALES (est): 903.5K **Privately Held**
SIC: **2051** 2052 Mfg Bread/Related Products Mfg Cookies/Crackers

(G-4149)
BELLA CASA ROOFING LLC
585 Cove Rd Apt 2 (06902-6186)
PHONE.................................475 619-0393
Evelyn A Segura, *Mng Member*
EMP: 5
SALES: 180K **Privately Held**
SIC: **2952** Mfg Asphalt Felts/Coatings

(G-4150)
BIROTECH INC
29 Sunnyside Ave Ste 4 (06902-7607)
PHONE.................................203 968-5080
Maria Szebeni, *President*
Larry Szebeni, *Exec VP*
EMP: 4
SQ FT: 1,750
SALES: 425K **Privately Held**
SIC: **3469** 3724 Mfg Metal Stampings Mfg Aircraft Engines/Parts

(G-4151)
BOTTOM LINE INC (PA)
Also Called: Bottom Line Publications
3 Landmark Sq Ste 230 (06901-2501)
PHONE.................................203 973-5900
Margie Abramas, *President*
Martin Edelston, *Chairman*
Rita Edelston, *Vice Pres*
Sam Edelston, *Vice Pres*
Marilyn Knowlton, *Research*
EMP: 80
SQ FT: 22,000
SALES (est): 21.4MM **Privately Held**
WEB: www.bottomlinepublications.com
SIC: **2721** Periodicals-Publishing/Printing

(G-4152)
BROOKSIDE FLVORS INGRDENTS LLC (HQ)
201 Tresser Blvd Ste 320 (06901-3435)
PHONE.................................203 595-4520
Donald L Hawks III, *President*
Richard Nikola, *COO*
William Gambrell, *Vice Pres*
Gaetan Sourceau, *CFO*
EMP: 88
SALES (est): 19.2MM **Privately Held**
SIC: **2087** Mfg Flavor Extracts/Syrup
PA: Bep Flavor Holdings Llc
201 Tresser Blvd Ste 320
Stamford CT 06901
203 595-4520

(G-4153)
C J S MILLWORK INC
425 Fairfield Ave Ste 12 (06902-7588)
PHONE.................................203 708-0080
Chris Sculti, *President*
Steve Scenna, *Manager*
EMP: 10 **EST**: 1996
SALES (est): 1.2MM **Privately Held**
WEB: www.cjsmillwork.com
SIC: **2431** Mfg Millwork

(G-4154)
CADMUS
200 1st Stamford Pl Fl 2 (06902-6753)
PHONE.................................203 595-3000
Scott J Goodwin, *CFO*
Scott Grant, *Manager*
John Lindquist, *Technology*
EMP: 6
SALES (est): 461K **Privately Held**
SIC: **2752** Lithographic Commercial Printing

(G-4155)
CARA THERAPEUTICS INC
107 Elm St Fl 9 (06902-3834)
PHONE.................................203 406-3700
Derek Chalmers, *President*
Frederique Menzaghi, *Senior VP*
Mani Mohindru, *CFO*
Richard Makara, *Controller*
Scott M Terrillion, *Ch Credit Ofcr*
EMP: 37
SQ FT: 24,000
SALES: 13.4MM **Privately Held**
WEB: www.caratherapeutics.com
SIC: **2834** 8731 Pharmaceutical Preparations & Commercial Physical Research

(G-4156)
CASARO LABS LTD
1100 Summer St Ste 203 (06905-5520)
PHONE.................................203 353-8500
Ron Viccari, *President*
Sam Lubliner, *Vice Pres*
▲ **EMP**: 7
SQ FT: 2,200
SALES (est): 1MM **Privately Held**
SIC: **2844** Mfg Toilet Preparations

(G-4157)
CASE CONCEPTS INTL LLC (PA)
112 Prospect St Unit A (06901-1207)
PHONE.................................203 883-8602
Ed Bell, *Vice Pres*
Raul Riveros,
▲ **EMP**: 16
SQ FT: 7,500
SALES: 2.2MM **Privately Held**
WEB: www.caseconcepts.com
SIC: **3161** Mfg Luggage

(G-4158)
CCI CORPUS CHRISTI LLC
2200 Atlantic St Ste 800 (06902-6834)
PHONE.................................203 564-8100
Michale Dowling, *President*
EMP: 4
SALES (est): 260.3K **Privately Held**
SIC: **2911** Petroleum Refiner
PA: Castleton Commodities International Llc
2200 Atlantic St Ste 800
Stamford CT 06902

(G-4159)
CCI CYRUS RIVER TERMINAL LLC
2200 Atlantic St Ste 800 (06902-6834)
PHONE.................................203 761-8000
William C Reed II, *President*
EMP: 9 **EST**: 2008
SALES (est): 800.4K **Privately Held**
SIC: **3999** Mfg Misc Products
HQ: Cci Us Asset Holdings Llc
2200 Atlantic St Ste 800
Stamford CT 06902
203 564-8100

(G-4160)
CCI ROBINSONS BEND LLC
2200 Atlantic St Ste 800 (06902-6834)
PHONE.................................203 564-8571
Craig Jarchow, *President*
EMP: 4
SALES (est): 172.6K **Privately Held**
SIC: **1311** Crude Petroleum/Natural Gas Production
PA: Castleton Commodities International Llc
2200 Atlantic St Ste 800
Stamford CT 06902

(G-4161)
CENVEO INC
200 1st Stamford Pl (06902-6753)
PHONE.................................203 595-3000
EMP: 7300
SALES (est): 1.6B **Privately Held**
WEB: www.mail-well.com
SIC: **2677** 2679 Mfg Envelopes Mfg Converted Paper Products

(G-4162)
CENVEO ENTERPRISES INC (PA)
200 First Stamford Pl # 2 (06902-6753)
PHONE.................................203 595-3000
Robert G Burton Jr, *Ch of Bd*
Mike Burton, *COO*
Colin Christ, *Exec VP*
Atul Goel, *Exec VP*
Andy Johnson, *Exec VP*
EMP: 5
SALES (est): 2.8B **Privately Held**
SIC: **2677** 2679 Mfg Envelopes Mfg Converted Paper Products

(G-4163)
CENVEO WORLDWIDE LIMITED (DH)
Also Called: Lightninglabel.com
200 First Stamford Pl # 2 (06902-6753)
PHONE..................................203 595-3000
Robert G Burton Jr, *CEO*
Michael G Burton, *President*
Glenn Eddleman, *General Mgr*
Alex Orbanowski, *Vice Pres*
Robert Rossato, *Vice Pres*
EMP: 11
SALES (est): 2.8B **Privately Held**
SIC: 2677 2679 Mfg Envelopes Mfg Converted Paper Products
HQ: Cwl Enterprises, Inc.
200 First Stamford Pl # 2
Stamford CT 06902
303 790-8023

(G-4164)
CHIEF EXECUTIVE GROUP LLC (PA)
9 W Broad St Ste 430 (06902-3764)
PHONE..................................785 832-0303
Marshall Cooper, *CEO*
Wayne Cooper, *Chairman*
Melanie Haniph, *Vice Pres*
Gabriella Kallay, *Vice Pres*
Robert Dudley, *Data Proc Staff*
EMP: 14
SQ FT: 4,200
SALES: 6MM **Privately Held**
SIC: 2721 2741 7319 8611 Periodical-Publish/Print Misc Publishing Advertising Services Business Association Mgmt Consulting Svcs

(G-4165)
CHIEF EXECUTIVE GROUP LP (PA)
Also Called: Chief Executive Magazine
9 W Broad St Ste 430 (06902-3764)
PHONE..................................203 930-2700
Edward Kopko, *CEO*
EMP: 23 **EST:** 1972
SQ FT: 6,600
SALES (est): 2.5MM **Privately Held**
SIC: 2721 8742 Periodicals-Publishing/Printing Management Consulting Services

(G-4166)
CITY DATA CABLE CO
34 Parker Ave (06906-1712)
PHONE..................................203 327-7917
Greg Burns, *President*
EMP: 3
SALES (est): 197.3K **Privately Held**
SIC: 3315 Mfg Steel Wire/Related Products

(G-4167)
COMANCHE CLEAN ENERGY CORP
1 Dock St Ste 101 (06902-5872)
PHONE..................................203 326-4570
EMP: 3 **EST:** 2007
SALES (est): 170K **Privately Held**
SIC: 2842 Mfg Polish/Sanitation Goods

(G-4168)
COMICANA INC
61 Studio Rd (06903-4724)
PHONE..................................203 968-0748
Mort Walker, *President*
Greg Walker, *Vice Pres*
Brian Walker, *Admin Sec*
EMP: 9
SALES: 1.2MM **Privately Held**
SIC: 2721 2731 Produces Comic Strips & Publishes Books

(G-4169)
COMPANY OF COCA-COLA BOTTLING
333 Ludlow St Ste 8 (06902-6991)
PHONE..................................203 905-3900
Ann Ellam, *Manager*
EMP: 80 **Privately Held**
WEB: www.coke.com
SIC: 2086 Carb Sft Drnkbtlcn
HQ: Coca-Cola Bottling Company Of Southeastern New England, Inc.
150 Waterford Parkway S
Waterford CT 06385
860 443-2816

(G-4170)
COMPUTER PRGRM & SYSTEMS INC (PA)
Also Called: Actuaries Division
1011 High Ridge Rd # 208 (06905-1604)
PHONE..................................203 324-9203
Samuel Urda, *President*
Allan Aferrone, *Vice Pres*
Peter O'Karma, *Vice Pres*
Peter Okarma, *Vice Pres*
Gabriela Solis, *Office Mgr*
EMP: 7
SQ FT: 3,000
SALES (est): 2.2MM **Privately Held**
WEB: www.cccdinc.org
SIC: 7372 8742 8999 Prepackaged Software Management Consulting & Actuarial Service

(G-4171)
CONAIR CORPORATION (PA)
Also Called: Personal Care Appliances Div
1 Cummings Point Rd (06902-7901)
PHONE..................................203 351-9000
James M Dubin, *Ch of Bd*
Ronald T Diamond, *President*
Julianne Bochinski, *Counsel*
Lawrence Cruz, *Counsel*
Michael Baldino, *Vice Pres*
◆ **EMP:** 366 **EST:** 1959
SALES: 2B **Privately Held**
WEB: www.conair.com
SIC: 3634 3631 3639 3999 Mfg Elec Housewares/Fans Mfg Household Cook Equip

(G-4172)
CONNECTICUT NEWSPAPERS INC
75 Tresser Blvd (06901-3329)
PHONE..................................203 964-2200
Durham Monsma, *Principal*
EMP: 6
SALES (est): 279.2K **Privately Held**
SIC: 2711 Newspapers-Publishing/Printing

(G-4173)
CONTINENTAL FRAGRANCES LTD
Also Called: Continental Consumer Products
333 Ludlow St 2nd (06902-6987)
PHONE..................................800 542-5903
M Benjamin Jones, *Principal*
EMP: 12
SQ FT: 56,000
SALES (est): 2.8MM
SALES (corp-wide): 52.9MM **Privately Held**
WEB: www.petchul.com
SIC: 2844 Mfg Toilet Preparations
HQ: High Ridge Brands Co.
333 Ludlow St Ste 2
Stamford CT 06902
-

(G-4174)
CORINTH ACQUISITION CORP (PA)
Also Called: United Pioneer Company
2777 Summer St Ste 206 (06905-4383)
PHONE..................................203 504-6260
Bernard Braverman, *President*
Michael Braverman, *Vice Pres*
▲ **EMP:** 5
SQ FT: 3,000
SALES: 22.4MM **Privately Held**
SIC: 2311 Mfg Men's/Boy's Suits/Coats

(G-4175)
CRAFTSMEN PRINTING GROUP INC
104 Lincoln Ave (06902-3121)
PHONE..................................203 327-2817
James Zygmont, *President*
Marcia Gogliettino, *Treasurer*
EMP: 7
SQ FT: 1,600
SALES (est): 759.9K **Privately Held**
SIC: 2752 Offset Printing

(G-4176)
CRANE AEROSPACE INC (DH)
100 Stamford Pl (06902-6740)
PHONE..................................203 363-7300
Max H Mitchell, *CEO*
Curtis A Baron Jr, *Vice Pres*
EMP: 137
SALES (est): 441.4MM
SALES (corp-wide): 3.3B **Publicly Held**
SIC: 3492 3728 Mfg Fluid Power Valves/Fittings Mfg Aircraft Parts/Equipment

(G-4177)
CRANE CO (PA)
100 1st Stamford Pl # 300 (06902-6740)
PHONE..................................203 363-7300
Robert S Evans, *Ch of Bd*
Max H Mitchell, *President*
Lee-Ann Etter, *President*
Alan N Howell, *Principal*
Jim Whitelock, *Principal*
▲ **EMP:** 56 **EST:** 1855
SALES: 3.3B **Publicly Held**
WEB: www.craneco.com
SIC: 3492 3494 3594 3589 Mfg Fluid Power Valves/Pipe Fittings Fluid Power Pump/Meters & Vending Machinery

(G-4178)
CRANE CONTROLS INC (DH)
100 Stamford Pl (06902-6740)
PHONE..................................203 363-7300
Andrew Krawitt, *Principal*
EMP: 5
SALES (est): 29.3MM
SALES (corp-wide): 3.3B **Publicly Held**
SIC: 3492 Mfg Fluid Power Valves/Fittings

(G-4179)
CRANE INTL HOLDINGS INC (HQ)
100 Stamford Pl (06902-6740)
PHONE..................................203 363-7300
Max H Mitchell, *CEO*
EMP: 9
SALES (est): 1.2B
SALES (corp-wide): 3.3B **Publicly Held**
SIC: 3492 Mfg Fluid Power Valves/Fittings
PA: Crane Co.
100 1st Stamford Pl # 300
Stamford CT 06902
203 363-7300

(G-4180)
CUNNINGHAM INDUSTRIES INC
102 Lincoln Ave Ste 3 (06902-3103)
PHONE..................................203 324-2942
Frederick E Cunningham, *President*
EMP: 3 **EST:** 1953
SQ FT: 2,000
SALES: 250K **Privately Held**
WEB: www.cunningham-ind.com
SIC: 3566 5734 3462 Mfg Speed Changer/Drives Ret Computers/Software Mfg Iron/Steel Forgings

(G-4181)
CWL ENTERPRISES INC (HQ)
200 First Stamford Pl # 2 (06902-6753)
PHONE..................................303 790-8023
Robert G Burton Jr, *Ch of Bd*
EMP: 4
SALES (est): 1.9B
SALES (corp-wide): 2.8B **Privately Held**
SIC: 2677 2679 Mfg Envelopes Mfg Converted Paper Products
PA: Cenveo Enterprises, Inc.
200 First Stamford Pl # 2
Stamford CT 06902
203 595-3000

(G-4182)
CYLINDER VODKA INC
101 Washington Blvd # 1223 (06902-7061)
PHONE..................................203 979-0792
Stylianos D Stavrianos, *President*
Alexis M Navarro, *Admin Sec*
EMP: 3
SALES (est): 122K **Privately Held**
SIC: 2085 Mfg Distilled/Blended Liquor

(G-4183)
CYTEC INDUSTRIES INC
1937 W Main St Ste 1 (06902-4578)
P.O. Box 60 (06904-0060)
PHONE..................................203 321-2200
Qi Dai, *Research*
William Haseltine, *Research*
Philip D Kutzenco, *Research*
Min Wang, *Research*
Bill Moore, *Manager*
EMP: 78
SALES (corp-wide): 12.4MM **Privately Held**
SIC: 2899 8731 Mfg Chemical Preparations Commercial Physical Research
HQ: Cytec Industries Inc.
4500 Mcginnis Ferry Rd
Alpharetta GA 30005
-

(G-4184)
DANONE HOLDINGS INC
208 Harbor Dr Fl 3 (06902-7467)
PHONE..................................203 229-7000
Jim Stevens, *CEO*
EMP: 1300
SALES (est): 21.7K
SALES (corp-wide): 738.6MM **Privately Held**
SIC: 2086 Mfg & Distributor Of Bottled Mineral & Spring Water
HQ: Danone Us, Llc
1 Maple Ave
White Plains NY 10605
914 872-8400

(G-4185)
DASCO SUPPLY LLC
Also Called: Dunphey Associates Supply Co
43 Homestead Ave (06902-7262)
PHONE..................................203 388-0095
Gene Brown, *Manager*
EMP: 4
SALES (corp-wide): 4.5B **Publicly Held**
SIC: 3585 Whol Heat/Air Cond Equipment/Supplies
HQ: Dasco Supply, Llc
9 Whippany Rd Bldngd
Whippany NJ 07981
973 884-1390

(G-4186)
DATAQUEST KOREA INC
56 Top Gallant Rd (06902-7747)
PHONE..................................239 561-4862
Christopher J Lafond, *Principal*
EMP: 3 **EST:** 2001
SALES (est): 207K **Privately Held**
SIC: 3695 Mfg Magnetic/Optical Recording Media

(G-4187)
DAVID WEISMAN LLC
30 Mill Valley Ln (06903-1642)
PHONE..................................203 322-9978
David W Weisman,
EMP: 6
SALES (est): 779.1K **Privately Held**
SIC: 3567 Mfg Industrial Furnaces/Ovens

(G-4188)
DEER CREEK FABRICS INC
509 Glenbrook Rd (06906-1825)
PHONE..................................203 964-0922
Steven Lucier, *President*
Jill Cooper, *Vice Pres*
Mary Ann Lucier, *Vice Pres*
EMP: 7
SQ FT: 3,000
SALES (est): 2.2MM **Privately Held**
WEB: www.deercreekfabrics.com
SIC: 2221 Manmade Broadwoven Fabric Mill

(G-4189)
DIY AWARDS LLC (PA)
1 Atlantic St Ste 705 (06901-2402)
PHONE..................................800 810-1216
Daniel WEI Xu,
EMP: 5
SALES: 700K **Privately Held**
SIC: 2499 Mfg Wood Products

(G-4190)
EARTH ANIMAL VENTURES INC
49 John St (06902-5845)
PHONE..................................717 271-6393
EMP: 8 **EST:** 2011
SALES (est): 673.1K **Privately Held**
SIC: 2048 Mfg Prepared Feeds

(G-4191)
ECOLOGIC ENERGY SOLUTIONS LLC
48 Union St Ste 14 (06906-1342)
PHONE..................................203 889-0505
Justin Breiner,
Brian Bodell,
Jeremy Klein,
EMP: 25
SALES (est): 2.9MM
SALES (corp-wide): 1.3B **Publicly Held**
SIC: 3296 1742 Installs Spray Foam And Fiberglass Insulation Products
PA: Installed Building Products, Inc.
495 S High St Ste 50
Columbus OH 43215
614 221-3399

(G-4192)
EFFIHEALTH LLC
259 Main St Apt 3 (06901-2933)
PHONE..................................888 435-3108
Jack Nail,
EMP: 5
SALES (est): 278K **Privately Held**
SIC: 2833 Mfg Medicinal/Botanical Products

(G-4193)
EMSC LLC
2009 Summer St Ste 201 (06905-5023)
PHONE..................................203 268-5101
Andrew Krzywosz, *President*
Cathie Krzywosz, *General Mgr*
EMP: 6 **EST:** 1987
SALES (est): 299.4K **Privately Held**
WEB: www.emsc-llc.com
SIC: 3612 Mfg Transformers

(G-4194)
EOWS MIDLAND INC
1 Landmark Sq Fl 11 (06901-2603)
PHONE..................................203 358-5705
Charles Drimal, *President*
EMP: 32
SALES: 1.8MM **Privately Held**
SIC: 1381 Oil/Gas Well Drilling

(G-4195)
EVERCEL INC (PA)
1055 Washington Blvd Fl 8 (06901-2251)
PHONE..................................781 741-8800
James D Gerson, *Ch of Bd*
Garry A Prime, *President*
Daniel J McCarthy, *COO*
Anthony P Kiernan, *CFO*
EMP: 77
SALES (est): 6.2MM **Publicly Held**
SIC: 3691 Manufactures Rechargeable Nickel-Zinc Batteries

(G-4196)
FPR PINEDALE LLC
58 Commerce Rd (06902-4506)
PHONE..................................203 542-6000
Centaurus Capital LP,
Freepoint Resources LLC,
EMP: 5
SALES: 14.9MM **Privately Held**
SIC: 1311 Crude Petroleum/Natural Gas Production

(G-4197)
FREDERICK PURDUE COMPANY INC (PA)
Also Called: Purdue Pharma
201 Tresser Blvd (06901-3435)
PHONE..................................203 588-8000
John H Stewart, *President*
Stuart D Baker, *Exec VP*
Jim Dolan, *Senior VP*
David Long, *Senior VP*
Martimer D Sackler, *Vice Pres*
▲ **EMP:** 310
SQ FT: 90,000
SALES (est): 88.5MM **Privately Held**
SIC: 2834 5122 Mfg Pharmaceutical Preparations Wnol Drugs/Sundries

(G-4198)
GENESIS ALKALI LLC
1 Stamford Plz 263 (06901-3271)
PHONE..................................215 299-6773
Kathy Harper, *Manager*
EMP: 60 **Publicly Held**
SIC: 2812 Mfg Alkalies/Chlorine
HQ: Genesis Alkali, Llc
919 Milam St Ste 2100
Houston TX 77002
713 860-2500

(G-4199)
GENEVE HOLDINGS INC (PA)
96 Cummings Point Rd (06902-7919)
PHONE..................................203 358-8000
Edward Netter, *Ch of Bd*
F Peter Zoch II, *President*
Robert Keiser, *Vice Pres*
◆ **EMP:** 5
SQ FT: 15,000
SALES (est): 269.1MM **Privately Held**
WEB: www.ihc-geneve.com
SIC: 3462 6331 Mfg Iron/Steel Forgings Fire/Casualty Insurance Carrier

(G-4200)
GOLDEN SUN INC
Also Called: Newhall Labs
5 High Ridge Park Ste 200 (06905-1326)
PHONE..................................800 575-7960
Jon Achenbaum, *CEO*
Dario Margve, *Chairman*
Ian Mactaggart, *Vice Pres*
Chris Conley, *CFO*
▲ **EMP:** 19
SQ FT: 20,000
SALES (est): 2.8MM **Privately Held**
WEB: www.goldensun.com
SIC: 2844 Mfg Toilet Preparations
HQ: Golden Sun Holdings, Inc.
5 High Ridge Park Ste 100
Stamford CT 06905
203 595-5228

(G-4201)
GOLF RESEARCH ASSOCIATES
Also Called: Shotbyshop.com
2810 High Ridge Rd (06903-1808)
PHONE..................................203 968-1608
Peter Sanders, *Managing Prtnr*
Molly Sanders, *Partner*
EMP: 3
SALES: 125K **Privately Held**
WEB: www.shotbyshot.com
SIC: 7372 Prepackaged Software Services

(G-4202)
GRANATA SIGNS LLC
Also Called: Granata Sign Co
80 Lincoln Ave 90 (06902-3102)
PHONE..................................203 358-0780
John Granata, *Owner*
EMP: 6
SQ FT: 6,000
SALES (est): 626K **Privately Held**
WEB: www.granatasigns.com
SIC: 3993 Mfg Signs/Advertising Specialties

(G-4203)
GREENWICH TIME
44 Columbus Pl Apt 9 (06907-1614)
PHONE..................................203 253-2922
Katelyn L Imbornoni, *Principal*
EMP: 4
SALES (est): 117K **Privately Held**
SIC: 2711 Newspapers-Publishing/Printing

(G-4204)
HALLS EDGE INC
420 Fairfield Ave Ste 3 (06902-7550)
PHONE..................................203 653-2281
David Hall, *President*
EMP: 3
SQ FT: 2,500
SALES: 500K **Privately Held**
WEB: www.hallsedge.com
SIC: 3429 Mfg Cabinet Parts

(G-4205)
HARMAN BECKER AUTOMOTIVE SYSTE
400 Atlantic St Ste 15 (06901-3533)
PHONE..................................203 328-3501
EMP: 3
SALES (est): 151.4K **Privately Held**
SIC: 3651 Mfg Home Audio/Video Equipment
HQ: Harman International Industries Incorporated
400 Atlantic St Ste 15
Stamford CT 06901
203 328-3500

(G-4206)
HARMAN CONSUMER INC
Also Called: Jbl
400 Atlantic St Ste 1500 (06901-3512)
PHONE..................................203 328-3500
Dinesh Paliwal, *CEO*
Jennifer Peter, *Vice Pres*
Chet Simon, *Vice Pres*
EMP: 5 **EST:** 1979
SALES (est): 555.4K **Privately Held**
SIC: 3651 Mfg Home Audio/Video Equipment

(G-4207)
HARMAN INTERNATIONAL INDS INC (DH)
400 Atlantic St Ste 15 (06901-3533)
PHONE..................................203 328-3500
Dinesh C Paliwal, *President*
Michael Mauser, *President*
Mike Peters, *President*
Valerie Freeman, *Business Mgr*
Sanjay Dhawan, *Exec VP*
▲ **EMP:** 277
SALES (est): 5B **Privately Held**
WEB: www.harman.com
SIC: 3651 Mfg Home Audio/Video Equipment
HQ: Samsung Electronics America, Inc.
85 Challenger Rd Fl 7
Ridgefield Park NJ 07660
201 229-4000

(G-4208)
HARMAN INTERNATIONAL INDS INC
Also Called: Harman Consumer Group Division
400 Atlantic St Ste 15 (06901-3533)
PHONE..................................203 328-3500
EMP: 3 **Privately Held**
SIC: 3651 Mfg Home Audio/Video Equipment
HQ: Harman International Industries Incorporated
400 Atlantic St Ste 15
Stamford CT 06901
203 328-3500

(G-4209)
HARMAN INTERNATIONAL INDS INC
400 Atlantic St Fl 5 (06901-3519)
PHONE..................................203 328-3500
EMP: 130
SALES (corp-wide): 6.1B **Publicly Held**
SIC: 3651 Household Audio And Video Equipment
PA: Harman International Industries Incorporated
400 Atlantic St Ste 15
Stamford CT 06901
203 328-3500

(G-4210)
HARMAN KG HOLDING LLC (DH)
400 Atlantic St Ste 1500 (06901-3512)
PHONE..................................203 328-3500
Dinesh C Paliwal, *Ch of Bd*
EMP: 13
SALES (est): 504.9MM **Privately Held**
SIC: 3651 Mfg Home Audio/Video Equipment
HQ: Harman International Industries Incorporated
400 Atlantic St Ste 15
Stamford CT 06901
203 328-3500

(G-4211)
HARVEST HILL HOLDINGS LLC (PA)
1 High Ridge Park Fl 2 (06905-1330)
PHONE..................................203 914-1620
Tim Voelkerding, *President*
Michael McNiff, *Vice Pres*
EMP: 14
SALES (est): 1.2B **Privately Held**
SIC: 2086 5499 Mfg Bottled/Canned Soft Drinks Ret Misc Foods

(G-4212)
HENKEL CONSUMER GOODS INC (DH)
200 Elm St (06902-3800)
PHONE..................................475 210-0230
Norbert Koll, *President*
Donna Yarnal, *Chairman*
Joseph Debiase, *Vice Pres*
Steven Essick, *Vice Pres*
Brad A Gazaway, *Vice Pres*
◆ **EMP:** 600
SALES (est): 1.2B
SALES (corp-wide): 22B **Privately Held**
SIC: 2841 Mfg Soap/Other Detergents
HQ: Henkel Us Operations Corporation
1 Henkel Way
Rocky Hill CT 06067
860 571-5100

(G-4213)
HEXCEL CORPORATION (PA)
281 Tresser Blvd Ste 1503 (06901-3261)
PHONE..................................203 969-0666
Nick L Stanage, *Ch of Bd*
Colleen Pritchett, *President*
Brett Schneider, *President*
Timothy Swords, *President*
Robert G Hennemuth, *Exec VP*
EMP: 26
SALES: 2.1B **Publicly Held**
WEB: www.hexcel.com
SIC: 3728 3089 3624 2891 Mfg Aircraft Parts/Equip Mfg Plastic Products Mfg Carbon/Graphite Prdt

(G-4214)
HEXCEL POTTSVILLE CORPORATION
2 Stamford Plz 16thf (06901-3263)
PHONE..................................203 969-0666
Wayne C Pensky, *President*
EMP: 4 **EST:** 1998
SALES (est): 82.4K
SALES (corp-wide): 2.1B **Publicly Held**
SIC: 3728 Mfg Aircraft Parts/Equipment
PA: Hexcel Corporation
281 Tresser Blvd Ste 1503
Stamford CT 06901
203 969-0666

(G-4215)
HIGH RIDGE BRANDS CO (HQ)
333 Ludlow St Ste 2 (06902-6991)
PHONE..................................203 674-8080
Patricia Lopez, *CEO*
Amanda Allen, *CFO*
David Anthony, *Sales Dir*
Maria Segura, *Sales Staff*
Pam Collins, *Manager*
EMP: 65
SALES (est): 52.8MM
SALES (corp-wide): 52.9MM **Privately Held**
WEB: www.highridgebrands.com
SIC: 2844 Mfg Toilet Preparations

(G-4216)
HIGH RIDGE COPY INC
Also Called: High Ridge Printing & Copy Ctr
1009 High Ridge Rd (06905-1602)
PHONE..................................203 329-1889
Jon De Crescenzo, *President*
Christine De Crescenzo, *Corp Secy*
EMP: 10
SQ FT: 25,000
SALES (est): 1.4MM **Privately Held**
WEB: www.highridgecapital.com
SIC: 2752 Lithographic Commercial Printing

GEOGRAPHIC

(G-4217)
HILLSIDE CAPITAL INC DE CORP (HQ)
201 Tresser Blvd Ste 200 (06901-3435)
PHONE..................................203 618-0202
John N Irwin III, *President*
EMP: 12
SQ FT: 7,000
SALES (est): 1.7MM
SALES (corp-wide): 7.3MM **Privately Held**
WEB: www.hillsidecapital.com
SIC: 2711 A Stockholding Company
PA: Brookside International Inc
201 Tresser Blvd Ste 200
Stamford CT 06901
203 595-4500

(G-4218)
HISPANIC COMMUNICATIONS LLC
400 Main St (06901-3004)
PHONE..................................203 674-6793
Norma Rodriguez, *President*
EMP: 4
SALES (est): 149.6K **Privately Held**
SIC: 2711 Newspapers-Publishing/Printing

(G-4219)
ICT BUSINESS
17 Bridge St (06905-4501)
PHONE..................................203 595-9452
EMP: 3
SALES (est): 140K **Privately Held**
SIC: 3842 Mfg Surgical Appliances/Supplies

(G-4220)
IMPERIAL METALWORKS LLC
92 Coolidge Ave (06906-2406)
P.O. Box 2761 (06906-0761)
PHONE..................................203 791-8567
Harry Van Dyke, *Principal*
EMP: 3
SALES (est): 290.9K **Privately Held**
SIC: 3446 Mfg Architectural Metalwork

(G-4221)
IMPRESSION POINT INC
500 West Ave Ste 4 (06902-6360)
PHONE..................................203 353-8800
Robert Labanca, *CEO*
Mary Labanca, *Treasurer*
EMP: 15
SQ FT: 5,000
SALES (est): 1.6MM **Privately Held**
WEB: www.impressionpt.com
SIC: 2752 Lithographic Commercial Printing

(G-4222)
INDUSTRIAL SHIPG ENTPS MGT LLC
2187 Atlantic St (06902-6880)
PHONE..................................203 504-5800
EMP: 5
SALES (est): 393.2K **Privately Held**
SIC: 3429 Mfg Hardware

(G-4223)
INFORMA BUSINESS MEDIA INC
Also Called: Electronic Magazine
11 Riverbend Dr S (06907-2524)
P.O. Box 4232 (06907-0232)
PHONE..................................203 358-9900
Frank L Hajdu, *Pub Rel Mgr*
Charles Usher, *Branch Mgr*
EMP: 100
SALES (corp-wide): 3.1B **Privately Held**
SIC: 2721 Periodicals-Publishing/Printing
HQ: Informa Business Media, Inc.
605 3rd Ave
New York NY 10158
212 204-4200

(G-4224)
INFORMA BUSINESS MEDIA INC
National Ctr For Database Mktg
11 River Band Dry S (06906)
P.O. Box 4949 (06907-0949)
PHONE..................................203 358-9900
Ryan Heart, *Director*
EMP: 110
SALES (corp-wide): 3.1B **Privately Held**
SIC: 2721 Marketing Logistics And Conference Coordination
HQ: Informa Business Media, Inc.
605 3rd Ave
New York NY 10158
212 204-4200

(G-4225)
INSTALLED BUILDING PDTS INC
43 Crescent St Apt 19 (06906-1853)
PHONE..................................203 889-0505
Justin Breiner, *Branch Mgr*
EMP: 5
SALES (corp-wide): 1.3B **Publicly Held**
SIC: 3296 Mfg Mineral Wool
PA: Installed Building Products, Inc.
495 S High St Ste 50
Columbus OH 43215
614 221-3399

(G-4226)
INTERNATIONAL MKTG STRATEGIES
Also Called: Marine Money
1 Stamford Lndg (06902-7229)
PHONE..................................203 406-0106
James Lawrence, *Chairman*
Jill Lawrence, *Vice Pres*
Gail Karlshoej, *Marketing Staff*
EMP: 11
SQ FT: 4,000
SALES: 1MM **Privately Held**
WEB: www.intmarketingstrategies.com
SIC: 2721 Publisher Of Trade Journals

(G-4227)
INTERNATIONAL PAPER - 16 INC (HQ)
281 Tresser Blvd (06901-3284)
PHONE..................................203 329-8544
Robert Amen, *President*
Charles Greenberg, *Vice Pres*
Syvert Nerheim, *Vice Pres*
Donald Folley, *Treasurer*
EMP: 4
SQ FT: 50,000
SALES (est): 5.9MM
SALES (corp-wide): 23.3B **Publicly Held**
SIC: 2621 2611 Paper Mill Pulp Mill
PA: International Paper Company
6400 Poplar Ave
Memphis TN 38197
901 419-9000

(G-4228)
INTERNATIONAL ROBOTICS INC
761 Stillwater Rd (06902-1726)
P.O. Box 11474, Naples FL (34101-1474)
PHONE..................................914 630-1060
Robert Doornic, *CEO*
EMP: 10
SALES (est): 1MM **Privately Held**
SIC: 3535 Mfg Conveyors/Equipment

(G-4229)
IPSOGEN
700 Canal St Ste 5 (06902-5921)
PHONE..................................203 504-8583
Susan Hertzberg, *Principal*
EMP: 4
SALES (est): 321.8K **Privately Held**
SIC: 3841 Mfg Surgical/Medical Instruments

(G-4230)
JKL SPECIALTY FOODS INC
417 Shippan Ave Ste 2 (06902-6189)
P.O. Box 4607 (06907-0607)
PHONE..................................203 541-3990
Ken Liu, *President*
Judy Chan, *Vice Pres*
▼ **EMP:** 10
SALES (est): 1.4MM **Privately Held**
WEB: www.asianmenusauces.com
SIC: 2035 Mfg Pickles/Sauces/Dressing

(G-4231)
JOE VALENTINE MACHINE COMPANY
77 Southfield Ave Ste 2 (06902-7690)
PHONE..................................203 356-9776
Joseph Valentine, *President*
Patricia Valentine, *Vice Pres*
EMP: 5
SALES (est): 600.8K **Privately Held**
SIC: 3599 Machine Shop

(G-4232)
JORNIK MAN CORP
652 Glenbrook Rd Ste 2 (06906-1410)
PHONE..................................203 969-0500
Jacqueline Herz, *President*
Jordie Freedman, *VP Sls/Mktg*
Elyse Strauss, *Sales Executive*
Peter Herz, *Admin Sec*
▲ **EMP:** 19
SQ FT: 7,500
SALES (est): 3.1MM **Privately Held**
WEB: www.jornik.com
SIC: 3993 2396 Mfg Signs/Advertising Specialties Mfg Auto/Apparel Trimming

(G-4233)
JS MCCARTHY CO INC
Also Called: Printech
652 Glenbrook Rd 4-101 (06906-1410)
PHONE..................................203 355-7600
EMP: 50
SALES (corp-wide): 35MM **Privately Held**
SIC: 2752 Lithographic Commercial Printing
PA: J.S. Mccarthy Co., Inc.
15 Darin Dr
Augusta ME 04330
207 622-6241

(G-4234)
K A F MANUFACTURING CO INC
14 Fahey St (06907-2216)
PHONE..................................203 324-3012
John Feighery, *President*
Sharon Feighery, *Admin Sec*
EMP: 22 **EST:** 1971
SQ FT: 11,500
SALES: 5MM **Privately Held**
WEB: www.kaf.com
SIC: 3826 3562 Mfg Analytical Instruments Mfg Ball/Roller Bearings

(G-4235)
KIEFFER ASSOCIATES INC
Also Called: Betoel Publishers
86 Wallacks Dr (06902-7125)
PHONE..................................203 323-3437
EMP: 3
SALES: 35K **Privately Held**
SIC: 2731 Books-Publishing/Printing

(G-4236)
LAYLAS FALAFEL
936 High Ridge Rd (06905-1601)
PHONE..................................203 685-2830
Imad Sakakini, *Principal*
EMP: 4
SALES (est): 268.1K **Privately Held**
SIC: 3421 Mfg Cutlery

(G-4237)
LEISURE LEARNING PRODUCTS INC
Also Called: Leisure Group
652 Glenbrook Rd Bldg 8 (06906-1410)
P.O. Box 2697 (06906-0697)
PHONE..................................203 325-2800
Richard Bendett, *President*
Christine Binsteiner, *Vice Pres*
▲ **EMP:** 18
SQ FT: 15,000
SALES: 5MM **Privately Held**
WEB: www.mightymind.com
SIC: 3999 5092 Mfg Educational Learning Products & Imports Educational Products Including Toys And Games

(G-4238)
LOCALLIVE NETWORKS INC
175 Atlantic St Ste 2 (06901-3530)
PHONE..................................877 355-6225
Nelson Santos, *CEO*
EMP: 5
SALES (est): 339.6K **Privately Held**
SIC: 7372 Prepackaged Software Services

(G-4239)
LONGFORDS ICE CREAM LTD
Also Called: Longford's Own
425 Fairfield Ave Ste 25 (06902-7547)
PHONE..................................914 935-9469
Nolan West, *President*
Patricia Sudbay West, *Vice Pres*
EMP: 12
SQ FT: 3,000
SALES: 1.2MM **Privately Held**
WEB: www.longfordsicecream.com
SIC: 2024 5143 Mfg Ice Cream/Frozen Desert Whol Dairy Products

(G-4240)
LOS ANGLES TMES CMMNCTIONS LLC
Also Called: Outdoor Life Channel
250 Harbor Dr (06902-7444)
PHONE..................................203 965-6434
Peter Englehart, *Vice Pres*
EMP: 149
SALES (corp-wide): 846.2MM **Privately Held**
SIC: 2711 Newspapers-Publishing/Printing
PA: Los Angeles Times Communications, Llc
2300 E Imperial Hwy
El Segundo CA 90245
213 237-5000

(G-4241)
LOXO ONCOLOGY INC (HQ)
281 Tresser Blvd Fl 9 (06901-3238)
PHONE..................................203 653-3880
Joshua H Bilenker MD, *President*
James Pierson, *Vice Pres*
Michael Rothenberg MD, *Vice Pres*
Sara Slifka, *Vice Pres*
Jennifer Burstein, *Finance*
EMP: 50
SQ FT: 36,400
SALES: 21.3MM
SALES (corp-wide): 24.5B **Publicly Held**
SIC: 2834 Pharmaceutical Preparations
PA: Eli Lilly And Company
Lilly Corporate Ctr
Indianapolis IN 46285
317 276-2000

(G-4242)
M & B AUTOMOTIVE MACHINE SHOP
443 Elm St (06902-5112)
P.O. Box 2336 (06906-0336)
PHONE..................................203 348-6134
Michael Lessard, *President*
EMP: 4
SQ FT: 800
SALES (est): 481.4K **Privately Held**
SIC: 3599 5531 7539 Machine Shop

(G-4243)
MALABAR BAY LLC
Also Called: Jaye's Studio
1127 High Ridge Rd # 159 (06905-1203)
PHONE..................................203 359-9714
Lalan K Shrikam, *Mng Member*
EMP: 7
SQ FT: 4,000
SALES (est): 1.8MM **Privately Held**
SIC: 2389 5632 Mfg Apparel/Accessories Ret Women's Accessories

(G-4244)
MARINERO EXPRESS 809 EAST
809 E Main St (06902-3807)
PHONE..................................203 487-0636
Jose L Marinero, *Principal*
EMP: 7 **EST:** 2009
SALES (est): 887.5K **Privately Held**
SIC: 3578 Mfg Calculating Equipment

(G-4245)
MAYBORN USA INC
Also Called: Mayborn Group
1010 Washington Blvd # 11 (06901-2202)
P.O. Box 5003, Westport (06881-5003)
PHONE..................................781 269-7490
Steve Parkin, *CEO*
Brenda O'Grady Liistro, *President*
Chris Parsons, *General Mgr*
George Idicula, *Corp Secy*
Sean Neasham, *QC Mgr*
▲ **EMP:** 13
SQ FT: 3,000

▲ = Import ▼=Export
◆ =Import/Export

SALES (est): 32.5MM
SALES (corp-wide): 244.1MM **Privately Held**
WEB: www.maws-usa.com
SIC: 3069 3085 3634 3821 Manufactures Baby Goods
HQ: Mayborn Group Limited
Northumberland Business Park West
Cramlington NORTHD NE23
191 250-1864

(G-4246)
MCINNIS USA INC
850 Canal St (06902-6943)
PHONE..................................203 890-9950
Herve Mallet, *CEO*
James Braselton, *Senior VP*
Claude Ferland, *CFO*
EMP: 40 **EST:** 2013
SALES (est): 5.6MM
SALES (corp-wide): 28.4MM **Privately Held**
SIC: 3241 Mfg Hydraulic Cement
PA: Ciment Mcinnis Inc
1350 Boul Rene-Levesque O Bureau 205
Montreal QC H3G 2
438 382-3331

(G-4247)
MD SOLARSCIENCES CORPORATION
9 W Broad St Ste 320 (06902-3758)
PHONE..................................203 857-0095
Robert Friedman, *CEO*
Paul Ainsworth, *President*
Scott Friedman, *Vice Pres*
▲ **EMP:** 12
SQ FT: 2,500
SALES (est): 713.1K **Privately Held**
SIC: 2834 Mfg Pharmaceutical Preparations

(G-4248)
MEDITERRANEAN SNACK FD CO LLC
1111 Summer St Ste 5a (06905-5511)
PHONE..................................973 402-2644
Vincent James,
◆ **EMP:** 12
SQ FT: 2,500
SALES (est): 3.8MM
SALES (corp-wide): 10.4MM **Privately Held**
WEB: www.mediterraneansnackfoods.com
SIC: 2096 Manufacturer Potato Chips And Snacks Items
PA: American Halal Company, Inc
1111 Summer St Fl 5
Stamford CT 06905
203 961-1954

(G-4249)
MELEGA INC
Also Called: AlphaGraphics
47 W Main St (06902-5030)
PHONE..................................203 961-8703
Fax: 203 961-8715
EMP: 6
SQ FT: 2,000
SALES (est): 1.2MM **Privately Held**
SIC: 2752 Comm Prtg Litho

(G-4250)
MIND2MIND EXCHANGE LLC
32 Mill Brook Rd (06902-1018)
PHONE..................................203 856-0981
Faisal Hoque, *Principal*
Edward Burke,
EMP: 4
SALES (est): 276K **Privately Held**
SIC: 7372 Prepackaged Software Services

(G-4251)
MINDTRAINR LLC
107 Revonah Cir (06905-4026)
PHONE..................................914 799-1515
Marvin Schildkraut, *Mng Member*
EMP: 5 **EST:** 2015
SALES (est): 58K **Privately Held**
SIC: 7372 7389 Prepackaged Software Services

(G-4252)
MOSAIC RECORDS INC
425 Fairfield Ave Ste 1 (06902-7533)
PHONE..................................203 327-7111
Michael Cuscuna, *President*
Frances Lourie, *Treasurer*
EMP: 7
SQ FT: 4,000
SALES (est): 1.2MM **Privately Held**
WEB: www.truebluemusic.com
SIC: 3652 7922 Mfg Prerecorded Records/Tapes Theatrical Producers/Services

(G-4253)
NELSON & MILLER ASSOCIATES
5 Hillandale Ave Ste F (06902-2843)
PHONE..................................203 356-9694
Denis O'Malley, *Owner*
EMP: 3
SALES (est): 227.8K **Privately Held**
SIC: 2741 Misc Publishing

(G-4254)
NERJAN DEVELOPMENT COMPANY
101 West Ave (06902-4696)
PHONE..................................203 325-3228
Blake Zizzi, *President*
Robert Zizzi, *Vice Pres*
Cynthia Zizzi, *Admin Sec*
EMP: 6
SQ FT: 3,300
SALES (est): 956.6K **Privately Held**
WEB: www.nerjan.com
SIC: 3599 Mfg Industrial Machinery

(G-4255)
NEW CANAAN OLIVE OIL LLC
47 Blachley Rd (06902-4318)
PHONE..................................845 240-3294
Heidi Lindblad Burrows, *Principal*
EMP: 3 **EST:** 2013
SALES (est): 202.5K **Privately Held**
SIC: 2079 Mfg Edible Fats/Oils

(G-4256)
NEW ENGLAND TILE & STONE INC
85 Old Long Ridge Rd # 2 (06903-1641)
PHONE..................................914 481-4488
EMP: 10
SALES (est): 1.3MM **Privately Held**
SIC: 2499 Wood Products, Nec, Nsk

(G-4257)
NEW HORIZON MACHINE CO INC
36 Ludlow St (06902-6914)
PHONE..................................203 316-9355
Antoinette Balbi, *President*
Carmello Balbi, *Vice Pres*
EMP: 8 **EST:** 1978
SQ FT: 5,500
SALES (est): 1.2MM **Privately Held**
WEB: www.newhorizonmachine.com
SIC: 3599 Mfg Industrial Machinery

(G-4258)
NEWTEC AMERICA INC
1055 Washington Blvd Fl 6 (06901-2216)
PHONE..................................203 323-0042
Emmanuel Schellekens, *CEO*
Serge Van Herck, *CEO*
Raymond Pieck, *President*
Timy Abraham, *Engineer*
Geert Tackaert, *CFO*
EMP: 11 **EST:** 1997
SQ FT: 3,700
SALES (est): 2.7MM **Privately Held**
WEB: www.newtecamerica.com
SIC: 3663 Mfg Radio/Tv Communication Equipment
HQ: St Engineering Idirect (Europe) Cy
Laarstraat 5
Sint-Niklaas 9100
378 065-00

(G-4259)
NEXVUE INFORMATION SYSTEMS INC
65 Broad St (06901-2374)
PHONE..................................203 327-0800
Dan Schwartz, *President*
Gary Frey, *Vice Pres*
EMP: 15
SALES (est): 1.8MM **Privately Held**
WEB: www.nexvue.com
SIC: 7372 Prepackaged Software Services

(G-4260)
NON-INVASIVE MED SYSTEMS LLC
1 Harbor Point Rd # 2050 (06902-7352)
PHONE..................................914 462-0701
Arthur Rappaport, *President*
EMP: 3
SALES (est): 207K **Privately Held**
SIC: 3845 Mfg Electromedical Equipment

(G-4261)
NORTHEASTERN METALS CORP
130 Lenox Ave Ste 23 (06906-2337)
PHONE..................................203 348-8088
Charles Schemera, *President*
Fred Lorenzen, *Treasurer*
EMP: 7
SQ FT: 2,500
SALES: 9MM **Privately Held**
SIC: 3339 5094 5084 Sells & Refines Precious Metals & Distributes Ultrasonic Cleaning Equipment

(G-4262)
NOVAERUS US INC (PA)
35 Melrose Pl (06902-7516)
PHONE..................................813 304-2468
Kevin Maughan, *President*
Eric Murphy, *Treasurer*
EMP: 10
SALES (est): 2.3MM **Privately Held**
SIC: 3564 Mfg Blowers/Fans

(G-4263)
NOVATEK MEDICAL INC
Also Called: Cloodloc
1 Strawberry Hill Ave (06902-2609)
P.O. Box 4963, Greenwich (06831-0419)
PHONE..................................203 356-0156
Gail Kirhoffer, *President*
EMP: 3
SALES (est): 206K **Privately Held**
SIC: 3841 3845 Mfg Surgical/Medical Instruments Mfg Electromedical Equipment

(G-4264)
NUTMEG ARCHITECTURAL WDWRK INC
48 Union St Ste 14 (06906-1342)
PHONE..................................203 325-4434
Tito Cerretani, *President*
Glenn Silkman, *Vice Pres*
EMP: 20
SQ FT: 22,300
SALES (est): 2.7MM **Privately Held**
SIC: 2522 Mfg Office Furniture-Nonwood

(G-4265)
O & G INDUSTRIES INC
686 Canal St (06902-5904)
PHONE..................................203 977-1618
Ray Oneglia, *Branch Mgr*
EMP: 28
SALES (corp-wide): 538MM **Privately Held**
WEB: www.ogind.com
SIC: 2951 Mfg Asphalt Mixtures/Blocks
PA: O & G Industries, Inc.
112 Wall St
Torrington CT 06790
860 489-9261

(G-4266)
ODOROX IAQ INC
1266 E Main St Ste 700r (06902-3507)
PHONE..................................203 541-5577
Harry Hirschfeld, *Principal*
EMP: 3
SALES (est): 209.1K **Privately Held**
SIC: 3442 Mfg Metal Doors/Sash/Trim

(G-4267)
OLD NI INCORPORATED
50 Sunnyside Ave (06902-7641)
PHONE..................................203 327-7300
EMP: 3
SALES (est): 160.5K **Privately Held**
SIC: 3643 Current-Carrying Wiring Devices

(G-4268)
OLIVE CHIAPPETTA OIL LLC
50 Mathews St (06902-4434)
PHONE..................................203 223-3655
Pat Chiappetta, *Principal*
EMP: 3
SALES (est): 186.9K **Privately Held**
SIC: 2079 Mfg Edible Fats/Oils

(G-4269)
OMEGA ENGINEERING INC
1 Omega Dr (06907-2336)
P.O. Box 2699 (06906-0699)
PHONE..................................203 359-7922
Dewana Harris, *Materials Mgr*
Weidong Tao, *Purch Agent*
Jennifer Obrien, *Purchasing*
James Bizak, *Engineer*
Ed Corella, *Engineer*
EMP: 5
SALES (corp-wide): 2.1B **Privately Held**
WEB: www.omega.com
SIC: 3823 Mfg Process Control Instruments
HQ: Omega Engineering, Inc.
800 Connecticut Ave 5n01
Norwalk CT 06854
203 359-1660

(G-4270)
OPTAMARK CT LLC
15 Bank St Ste 1 (06901-3037)
PHONE..................................203 325-1180
Tarang Gosalia,
EMP: 3 **EST:** 2017
SALES (est): 58.5K
SALES (corp-wide): 320.5K **Privately Held**
SIC: 2752 Lithographic Commercial Printing
PA: Optamark Llc
865 E Washington St
North Attleboro MA 02760
508 643-1017

(G-4271)
OPTICAL DESIGN ASSOCIATES
600 Summer St (06901-4404)
PHONE..................................203 249-6408
Lev Sakim, *Owner*
EMP: 3
SALES (est): 245.8K **Privately Held**
SIC: 3827 Mfg Optical Instruments/Lenses

(G-4272)
OPTICAL ENERGY TECHNOLOGIES
472 Westover Rd (06902-1930)
PHONE..................................203 357-0626
Gerald Felbel, *President*
Gerald Falbel, *President*
Judith Falbel, *Admin Sec*
EMP: 5
SALES: 200K **Privately Held**
WEB: www.opticalenergy.com
SIC: 3433 8742 Mfg Solar Energy & Electro-Optical Equipment & Consulting

(G-4273)
ORACLE AMERICA INC
900 Long Ridge Rd Bldg 1 (06902-1139)
PHONE..................................203 703-3000
Lou Cusano, *Sales Staff*
Steven McLaughlin, *Branch Mgr*
Larry Obrien, *Manager*
Diane Reichert, *Manager*
Zoe Wagner, *Manager*
EMP: 51
SALES (corp-wide): 39.5B **Publicly Held**
SIC: 3571 7379 7373 7372 Mfg Electronic Computers Computer Related Svcs Computer Systems Design Prepackaged Software Svc Mfg Semiconductors/Dvcs
HQ: Oracle America, Inc.
500 Oracle Pkwy
Redwood City CA 94065
650 506-7000

(G-4274)
ORTHOZON TECHNOLOGIES LLC
175 Atlantic St Ste 206 (06901-3500)
PHONE..................................203 989-4937
Joshua Aferzon,
EMP: 5

GEOGRAPHIC

SQ FT: 1,000
SALES (est): 420K **Privately Held**
SIC: 3841 Mfg Surgical/Medical Instruments

(G-4275)
P & S PRINTING LLC
Also Called: Minuteman Press
513 Summer St (06901-1314)
PHONE..................................203 327-9818
Peter Sandler,
EMP: 5
SQ FT: 2,000
SALES (est): 839.4K **Privately Held**
SIC: 2752 Comm Prtg Litho

(G-4276)
P C I GROUP
652 Glenbrook Rd 3-201 (06906-1443)
PHONE..................................203 327-0410
Mary Ferrara, *President*
Anne Chiapetta, *Vice Pres*
EMP: 10
SQ FT: 4,500
SALES (est): 1.7MM **Privately Held**
WEB: www.pcigroup.net
SIC: 2752 7336 Lithographic Commercial Printing Commercial Art/Graphic Design

(G-4277)
PARFUMS DE COEUR LTD (PA)
Also Called: PDC Brands
750 E Main St (06902-3831)
PHONE..................................203 655-8807
James Stammer, *President*
Mark A Laracy, *Chairman*
James E Rogers, *COO*
John F Owen, *CFO*
Edward Kaminski, *Treasurer*
◆ **EMP:** 30
SQ FT: 13,000
SALES (est): 29.2MM **Privately Held**
WEB: www.pdcpm.com
SIC: 2844 Mfg Toilet Preparations

(G-4278)
PASSUR AEROSPACE INC (PA)
1 Landmark Sq Ste 1900 (06901-2671)
PHONE..................................203 622-4086
James T Barry, *President*
Keith D Wichman, *General Mgr*
G S Beckwith Gilbert, *Chairman*
Timothy Campbell, *Exec VP*
Tim Cinello, *Vice Pres*
EMP: 44
SQ FT: 5,300
SALES: 14.8MM **Publicly Held**
WEB: www.passur.com
SIC: 3812 Provides Predictive Analytics & Decision Support Technology

(G-4279)
PAULS MARBLE DEPOT LLC
Also Called: Extile.com
40 Warshaw Pl Ste 1 (06902-6354)
PHONE..................................203 978-0669
Parag Adalja, *Mng Member*
▲ **EMP:** 13
SQ FT: 28,000
SALES (est): 2.8MM **Privately Held**
SIC: 3272 5032 Mfg Concrete Products Whol Brick/Stone Material

(G-4280)
PEANUT BUTTER AND JELLY
500 Bedford St Apt 227 (06901-1513)
PHONE..................................203 504-2280
EMP: 3
SALES (est): 83K **Privately Held**
SIC: 2099 Mfg Food Preparations

(G-4281)
PEERLESS SYSTEMS CORPORATION (DH)
1055 Washington Blvd Fl 8 (06901-2251)
PHONE..................................203 350-0040
Anthony Bonid, *CEO*
Lodovico De Visconti, *President*
EMP: 11
SQ FT: 1,200
SALES: 3.6MM
SALES (corp-wide): 4.6MM **Privately Held**
SIC: 7372 7371 Licenses Software-Based Imaging And Networking Technology For Controllers
HQ: Mobius Acquisition, Llc
1000 Mcknight Park Dr
Pittsburgh PA 15237
412 281-7000

(G-4282)
PEGASUS CAPITAL ADVISORS LP (PA)
750 E Main St (06902-3831)
PHONE..................................203 869-4400
Craig Cogut, *Managing Prtnr*
Greg Gish, *Managing Prtnr*
Daniel Stencel, *Managing Prtnr*
Brian Friedman, *Vice Pres*
John Dolan, *Office Mgr*
EMP: 24
SALES (est): 54.6MM **Publicly Held**
SIC: 3646 3648 Mfg Commercial Lighting Fixtures Mfg Lighting Equipment

(G-4283)
PF LABORATORIES INC (HQ)
201 Tresser Blvd Ste 324 (06901-3435)
PHONE..................................973 256-3100
John Stewart, *President*
David Long, *Senior VP*
Russ Gasdia, *Vice Pres*
Edward Mahony, *CFO*
EMP: 150
SQ FT: 300,000
SALES (est): 16.9MM **Privately Held**
SIC: 2834 Mfg Pharmaceutical Preparations

(G-4284)
PHARMACEUTICAL RES ASSOC INC (HQ)
201 Tresser Blvd (06901-3435)
PHONE..................................203 588-8000
Stuart Baker, *Vice Pres*
Howard Udell, *Vice Pres*
EMP: 3
SQ FT: 90,000
SALES (est): 60.6MM **Privately Held**
SIC: 2834 5122 Mfg Pharmaceutical Preparations Whol Drugs/Sundries

(G-4285)
PITNEY BOWES INC (PA)
3001 Summer St Ste 3 (06905-4321)
PHONE..................................203 356-5000
Michael I Roth, *Ch of Bd*
Marc B Lautenbach, *President*
Jason C Dies, *President*
Robert Guidotti, *President*
Lila Snyder, *President*
◆ **EMP:** 3500 **EST:** 1920
SALES: 3.5B **Publicly Held**
WEB: www.pb.com
SIC: 3579 7359 3661 8744 Mfg & Leases Mailing & Postage Equip Facsimile Machines Facilities Management Services

(G-4286)
PITNEY BOWES INC
300 Stamford Pl Ste 200 (06902-6735)
PHONE..................................203 356-5000
Mark Flynn, *Branch Mgr*
EMP: 35
SALES (corp-wide): 3.5B **Publicly Held**
SIC: 3579 7359 Mfg Office Machines Equipment Rental/Leasing
PA: Pitney Bowes Inc.
3001 Summer St Ste 3
Stamford CT 06905
203 356-5000

(G-4287)
POLYMER ENGINEERED PDTS INC (PA)
595 Summer St Ste 2 (06901-1407)
PHONE..................................203 324-3737
Leslie Klein, *CEO*
Sheila Klein, *Director*
▲ **EMP:** 100 **EST:** 1970
SQ FT: 8,500
SALES (est): 13.9MM **Privately Held**
SIC: 3089 Mfg Plastic Products

(G-4288)
POLYONE CORPORATION
70 Carlisle Pl (06902-7630)
PHONE..................................203 327-6010
Julie A McAlindon, *Manager*
EMP: 9 **Publicly Held**
SIC: 2821 Mfg Plastic Materials/Resins
PA: Polyone Corporation
33587 Walker Rd
Avon Lake OH 44012
-

(G-4289)
POZZI FMLY WINE & SPIRITS LLC
37 Old Well Rd (06907-1128)
PHONE..................................646 422-9134
Daniele Pozzi,
Barbara Pozzi,
EMP: 3
SALES: 3MM **Privately Held**
SIC: 2084 Mfg Wines/Brandy/Spirits

(G-4290)
PRA HOLDINGS INC
1 Stamford Forum (06901-3516)
PHONE..................................203 853-0123
Stuart Baker, *President*
Howard Udell, *Vice Pres*
EMP: 3
SQ FT: 90,000
SALES (est): 61.2MM
SALES (corp-wide): 2.8B **Publicly Held**
SIC: 2834 5122 8742 Mfg Pharmaceutical Preparations Whol Drugs/Sundries Management Consulting Services
PA: Pra Health Sciences, Inc.
4130 Parklake Ave Ste 400
Raleigh NC 27612
919 786-8200

(G-4291)
PRESIDIUM USA INC
100 Stamford Pl (06902-6740)
PHONE..................................203 674-9374
EMP: 3
SALES (est): 306.9K **Privately Held**
SIC: 2821 Mfg Plastic Materials/Resins

(G-4292)
PROTEGRITY USA INC (PA)
333 Ludlow St Ste 8 (06902-6991)
PHONE..................................203 326-7200
Rick Farnell, *CEO*
MA Hui, *Engineer*
Pramod Nair, *Engineer*
Jay Wolf, *Controller*
Eileen Garry, *Chief Mktg Ofcr*
EMP: 22
SQ FT: 8,000
SALES (est): 18.3MM **Privately Held**
WEB: www.protegrity.com
SIC: 7372 Prepackaged Software Services

(G-4293)
PURDUE PHARMA LP
201 Tresser Blvd Fl 1 (06901-3432)
PHONE..................................203 588-8000
EMP: 3 **Privately Held**
SIC: 2834 Mfg Pharmaceutical Preparations
PA: Purdue Pharma L.P.
201 Tresser Blvd Fl 1
Stamford CT 06901
-

(G-4294)
PURDUE PHARMA LP (PA)
201 Tresser Blvd Fl 1 (06901-3432)
PHONE..................................203 588-8000
Craig Landau, *President*
Steve Miller, *Partner*
Stuart D Baker, *Exec VP*
Alan W Dunton, *Senior VP*
Raul Damas, *Vice Pres*
▲ **EMP:** 256
SQ FT: 500,000
SALES (est): 484.4MM **Privately Held**
SIC: 2834 5122 Mfg Pharmaceutical Preparations Whol Drugs/Sundries

(G-4295)
PURDUE PHARMA MANUFACTURING LP
201 Tresser Blvd Fl 1 (06901-3432)
PHONE..................................252 265-1924
David Lundie, *Senior VP*
Stuart D Baker, *Vice Pres*
Edward Mahony, *Vice Pres*
Phillip Strassburger, *Vice Pres*
▲ **EMP:** 32 **EST:** 2013
SALES (est): 2.6MM **Privately Held**
SIC: 2834 Mfg Pharmaceutical Preparations
PA: Purdue Pharma L.P.
201 Tresser Blvd Fl 1
Stamford CT 06901
-

(G-4296)
RAIN CARBON INC (HQ)
10 Signal Rd (06902-7909)
PHONE..................................203 406-0535
Jagan Nellore, *CEO*
Gerard Sweeney, *President*
Gunther Weymans, *COO*
Paul Francese, *CFO*
Matthew Scott Hansen,
EMP: 6 **EST:** 2010
SALES (est): 192.7K **Privately Held**
SIC: 3624 Mfg Carbon/Graphite Products

(G-4297)
RAIN CII CARBON LLC
10 Signal Rd (06902-7909)
PHONE..................................203 406-0535
Gerard Sweeney, *Branch Mgr*
EMP: 15 **Privately Held**
SIC: 2999 8741 8748 Mfg Petroleum/Coal Products Management Services Business Consulting Services
HQ: Rain Cii Carbon Llc
2627 Chestnut Ridge Dr # 200
Kingwood TX 77339
281 318-2400

(G-4298)
RESINALL CORP (DH)
3065 High Ridge Rd (06903-1301)
P.O. Box 195, Severn NC (27877-0195)
PHONE..................................203 329-7100
Elaine Godina, *President*
Harry Anderson, *Project Mgr*
Joyce Sullivan, *Buyer*
Lee T Godina, *Treasurer*
▼ **EMP:** 10 **EST:** 1979
SQ FT: 4,000
SALES (est): 65.3MM
SALES (corp-wide): 997.6MM **Privately Held**
WEB: www.resinall.com
SIC: 2821 Manufactures Plastic Materials/Resins
HQ: Ergon Chemicals, Llc
2829 Lakeland Dr Ste 2000
Flowood MS 39232
601 933-3000

(G-4299)
REVOLUTION LIGHTING (HQ)
177 Broad St Fl 12 (06901-5002)
PHONE..................................203 504-1111
Robert V Lapenta, *President*
EMP: 3 **EST:** 2016
SQ FT: 6,625
SALES (est): 1.3MM
SALES (corp-wide): 99.9MM **Publicly Held**
SIC: 3674 3641 3993 Manufacturer Of Semiconductors/Related Devices Electric Lamps And Signs/Advertising Specialties
PA: Revolution Lighting Technologies, Inc.
177 Broad St Fl 12
Stamford CT 06901
203 504-1111

(G-4300)
REVOLUTION LIGHTING TECH INC (PA)
177 Broad St Fl 12 (06901-5002)
PHONE..................................203 504-1111
Robert V Lapenta, *Ch of Bd*
Richard Hanlon, *COO*
Jon Barker, *Vice Pres*
Joe Herbst, *Vice Pres*
John Poerstel, *Vice Pres*
EMP: 111
SQ FT: 16,626
SALES (est): 99.9MM **Publicly Held**
WEB: www.nexxuslighting.com
SIC: 3674 3641 3993 Led & Lighting Products

(G-4301)
REVOLUTION LIGHTING TECH INC
177 Broad St Fl 12 (06901-5002)
PHONE.................................203 504-1111
Susan Knox, *Branch Mgr*
EMP: 14
SALES (corp-wide): 99.9MM **Publicly Held**
WEB: www.nexxuslighting.com
SIC: 3993 Mfg Fiber Optic Displays And Signs
PA: Revolution Lighting Technologies, Inc.
177 Broad St Fl 12
Stamford CT 06901
203 504-1111

(G-4302)
RISEANDSHINE CORPORATION (PA)
Also Called: Rise Brewing Co
425 Fairfield Ave 1a11 (06902-7538)
PHONE.................................917 599-7541
Grant Gyesky, *CEO*
EMP: 18
SALES (est): 2.8MM **Privately Held**
SIC: 2095 Mfg Roasted Coffee

(G-4303)
RLP INC
Also Called: Amusements Unlimited
12 Magee Ave (06902-5907)
PHONE.................................203 359-2504
Richard Preli, *President*
▲ **EMP:** 3
SQ FT: 3,000
SALES: 500K **Privately Held**
SIC: 3999 Distributor Of Coin Operated Amusement Games

(G-4304)
ROBERT L LOVALLO
Also Called: Roblo Woodworks
127 Myrtle Ave (06902-3906)
PHONE.................................203 324-6655
Robert L Lovallo, *Owner*
EMP: 7 **EST:** 1956
SQ FT: 2,500
SALES (est): 551K **Privately Held**
WEB: www.sallylamb.com
SIC: 2434 2541 2431 Mfg Wood Kitchen Cabinets Mfg Wood Partitions/Fixtures Mfg Millwork

(G-4305)
ROLLEASE ACMEDA INC (PA)
750 E Main St 7 (06902-3831)
PHONE.................................203 964-1573
Derick Marsch, *President*
Greg Farr, *Senior VP*
Thomas Gilboy, *Vice Pres*
Tom Gilboy, *CFO*
Kevin Leon, *Human Res Mgr*
◆ **EMP:** 88 **EST:** 1980
SQ FT: 54,000
SALES (est): 26.9MM **Privately Held**
WEB: www.rollease.com
SIC: 3568 2591 Mfg Power Transmsn Equip Mfg Drape Hardware/Blind

(G-4306)
ROSCO HOLDINGS INC (PA)
52 Harbor View Ave (06902-5914)
PHONE.................................203 708-8900
Stanford Miller, *President*
Mark Engel, *COO*
Stan Schwartz, *Exec VP*
Maria Szots, *Office Mgr*
▲ **EMP:** 60
SQ FT: 20,000
SALES (est): 7.7MM **Privately Held**
SIC: 3861 Mfg Photographic Equipment/Supplies

(G-4307)
ROSCO LABORATORIES INC (HQ)
52 Harbor View Ave (06902-5947)
PHONE.................................203 708-8900
Stanford Miller, *Ch of Bd*
Mark Engel, *President*
Stan Schwartz, *Exec VP*
Lauren Deluca, *Purchasing*
Rich Luce, *CFO*
▲ **EMP:** 25 **EST:** 1921
SQ FT: 40,000
SALES (est): 7.6MM **Privately Held**
WEB: www.rosco.com
SIC: 3861 Mfg Photographic Equipment/Supplies

(G-4308)
SAFE LASER THERAPY LLC
1747 Summer St Ste 4 (06905-5144)
PHONE.................................203 261-4400
Malti G Gupta, *President*
EMP: 4 **EST:** 2008
SALES (est): 274K **Privately Held**
SIC: 3845 8093 7999 Mfg Electromedical Equipment Specialty Outpatient Clinic Amusement/Recreation Services

(G-4309)
SANFORD REDMOND INC
746 Riverbank Rd (06903-3514)
PHONE.................................203 351-9800
EMP: 8 **EST:** 1953
SALES (est): 1.5MM **Privately Held**
WEB: www.sanfordredmond.com
SIC: 3565 Packaging Machinery, Nsk

(G-4310)
SCINETX LLC
Also Called: Capital Venture
1836 Long Ridge Rd (06903-3234)
PHONE.................................203 355-3676
Louis G Cornacchia, *Mng Member*
EMP: 4 **EST:** 2009
SALES: 100K **Privately Held**
SIC: 3663 Mfg Radio/Tv Communication Equipment

(G-4311)
SCITECH INTERNATIONAL LLC
Also Called: Scitech Ingredients
50 Soundview Dr (06902-7113)
PHONE.................................203 967-8502
John Sbordone,
Steve Carlin,
William Gambrell,
Jack Manno,
Carlos Mendez,
EMP: 7
SQ FT: 1,800
SALES (est): 279.1K **Privately Held**
WEB: www.scitech1.com
SIC: 2087 Mfg Flavor Extracts/Syrup

(G-4312)
SEESMART INC
Also Called: Revolution Lighting
177 Broad St Fl 12 (06901-5002)
PHONE.................................203 504-1111
James Depalma, *President*
Ken Ames, *Vice Pres*
Jonathan Miller, *CFO*
Patrick Doehner, *Treasurer*
▲ **EMP:** 27
SALES (est): 6.1MM
SALES (corp-wide): 99.9MM **Publicly Held**
SIC: 3645 3646 Mfg Residential Lighting Fixtures Mfg Commercial Lighting Fixtures
PA: Revolution Lighting Technologies, Inc.
177 Broad St Fl 12
Stamford CT 06901
203 504-1111

(G-4313)
SEKISUI DIAGNOSTICS LLC
500 West Ave (06902-6360)
PHONE.................................203 602-7777
Adele Ozanne, *Branch Mgr*
Les Deluca, *Director*
EMP: 7 **Privately Held**
SIC: 3841 Mfg Surgical/Medical Instruments
HQ: Sekisui Diagnostics, Llc
1 Wall St Ste 301
Burlington MA 01803

(G-4314)
SENIOR NETWORK INC
777 Summer St Ste 103 (06901-1085)
PHONE.................................203 969-2700
Frederick Adler, *President*
Larry Brown, *Exec VP*
Darren Galazin, *Manager*
EMP: 34
SALES (est): 3.3MM **Privately Held**
WEB: www.seniornetwork.com
SIC: 2741 Misc Publishing

(G-4315)
SHENONDAH VLY SPECIALTY FOODS
Also Called: Valley of Mexico
28 Intervale Rd (06905-1308)
PHONE.................................203 348-0402
Stephen Bowling, *President*
EMP: 3
SALES (est): 190K **Privately Held**
WEB: www.valleyofmexico.com
SIC: 2032 Mfg Canned Specialties

(G-4316)
SHORE THERAPEUTICS INC
177 Broad St Ste 1101 (06901-2048)
PHONE.................................646 562-1243
EMP: 4
SALES (est): 140K **Privately Held**
SIC: 2834 Mfg Pharmaceutical Preparations

(G-4317)
SIGG SWITZERLAND (USA) INC
1177 High Ridge Rd (06905-1221)
PHONE.................................203 321-1232
Daniel McNamara, *Vice Pres*
▲ **EMP:** 9
SALES (est): 1.1MM **Privately Held**
SIC: 2086 Sigg Bottles And Accessories

(G-4318)
SIGNCRAFTERS INC
874 E Main St (06902-3926)
PHONE.................................203 353-9535
Paul D Muenzen, *President*
EMP: 5
SALES (est): 374.4K **Privately Held**
SIC: 3993 Mfg Signs/Advertising Specialties

(G-4319)
SIGNS OF SUCCESS INC
1084 Hope St (06907-1823)
PHONE.................................203 329-3374
Richard Farber, *President*
EMP: 3
SALES (est): 395.2K **Privately Held**
SIC: 3993 Mfg Signs/Advertising Specialties

(G-4320)
SILGAN CONTAINERS CORPORATION
4 Landmark Sq (06901-2502)
PHONE.................................203 975-7110
Debbie Turziano, *Human Res Mgr*
Peter Willumsen, *Manager*
EMP: 12
SALES (corp-wide): 4.4B **Publicly Held**
SIC: 3411 Mfg Metal Cans
HQ: Silgan Containers Corporation
21600 Oxnard St Ste 1600
Woodland Hills CA 91367
818 348-3700

(G-4321)
SILGAN HOLDINGS INC (PA)
4 Landmark Sq Ste 400 (06901-2502)
PHONE.................................203 975-7110
Anthony J Allott, *Ch of Bd*
Adam J Greenlee, *President*
Thomas J Snyder, *President*
Frank W Hogan III, *Senior VP*
B Frederik Prinzen, *Senior VP*
EMP: 108
SALES: 4.4B **Publicly Held**
WEB: www.silgan.com
SIC: 3411 3085 3089 Mfg Fabricated Metal Products Rubber & Miscellaneous Plastic Products

(G-4322)
SMART POLISHING
24 Betts Ave (06902-6465)
PHONE.................................203 559-1541
Edgar Cavero, *Principal*
EMP: 3 **EST:** 2010
SALES (est): 134K **Privately Held**
SIC: 3471 Plating/Polishing Service

(G-4323)
SOLAIS LIGHTING INC
650 West Ave (06902-6325)
PHONE.................................203 683-6222
James Leahy, *President*
Glenn Bordfeld, *Vice Pres*
Colleen Kelly Kishore, *Controller*
Steve Johnson, *CTO*
Scott Frazier, *Director*
EMP: 10
SALES (est): 161.3K
SALES (corp-wide): 23.5B **Publicly Held**
SIC: 3648 Mfg Lighting Equipment
HQ: Powersecure, Inc.
1609 Heritage Commerce Ct
Wake Forest NC 27587
919 556-3056

(G-4324)
SOLDIER SOCKS
90 Fairfield Ave (06902-5021)
PHONE.................................203 832-2005
EMP: 4 **EST:** 2011
SALES (est): 324.9K **Privately Held**
SIC: 2252 Mfg Hosiery

(G-4325)
SOUTH BEND ETHANOL LLC
107 Elm St (06902-3834)
PHONE.................................203 326-8132
Bill Bronin,
EMP: 50
SALES (est): 56.8MM
SALES (corp-wide): 1.5B **Privately Held**
SIC: 1311 Crude Petroleum/Natural Gas Production
HQ: Vitol Americas Corp.
2925 Richmond Ave Ste 11
Houston TX 77098

(G-4326)
SOUTHWIRE COMPANY LLC
Also Called: Seatek Wireless
392 Pacific St (06902-5816)
PHONE.................................203 324-0067
EMP: 19
SALES (corp-wide): 2.2B **Privately Held**
SIC: 3423 Mfr Hand Tools
PA: Southwire Company, Llc
1 Southwire Dr
Carrollton GA 30119
770 832-4242

(G-4327)
SPARTECH LLC
Also Called: Polycast
69 Southfield Ave (06902-7614)
PHONE.................................203 327-6010
Julie A McAlindon, *Manager*
EMP: 185
SALES (corp-wide): 961.3MM **Privately Held**
WEB: www.spartech.com
SIC: 3089 3081 2821 Mfg Plastic Products Mfg Unsupported Plastic Film/Sheet Mfg Plastic Materials/Resins
PA: Spartech Llc
11650 Lkeside Crossing Ct
Saint Louis MO 63146
314 569-7400

(G-4328)
SPEED PRINTING & GRAPHICS INC
Also Called: S P & G
330 Fairfield Ave Ste 3 (06902-7248)
PHONE.................................203 324-4000
Steven Seifert, *President*
John Schnefke, *Sales Staff*
EMP: 6
SQ FT: 2,800
SALES (est): 927K **Privately Held**
WEB: www.sp-g.com
SIC: 2752 2759 Offset Printing

(G-4329)
STAMFORD CAPITAL GROUP INC (PA)
1266 E Main St (06902-3546)
PHONE.................................800 977-7837
Patton Corrigan, *President*
Evan Tessler, *Vice Pres*
EMP: 1675

GEOGRAPHIC

SALES (est): 52.8MM **Privately Held**
SIC: 2741 6211 Misc Publishing Security Broker/Dealer

(G-4330)
STAMFORD FORGE & METAL CFT INC
63 Victory St (06902-5614)
PHONE..................................203 348-8290
Chris Salvator, *President*
EMP: 3 **EST:** 1970
SQ FT: 3,500
SALES: 500K **Privately Held**
SIC: 3446 Ornamental Iron Works

(G-4331)
STAMFORD IRON & STL WORKS INC
347 Courtland Ave (06906-2201)
P.O. Box 2190 (06906-0190)
PHONE..................................203 324-6751
Joseph Fuss Jr, *President*
Thomas Pettit Jr, *Vice Pres*
EMP: 15 **EST:** 1957
SQ FT: 4,500
SALES (est): 4MM **Privately Held**
WEB: www.clcstamford.org
SIC: 3441 Structural Metal Fabrication

(G-4332)
STAMFORD RISK ANALYTICS LLC
263 Tresser Blvd Fl 9 (06901-3236)
PHONE..................................203 559-0883
Ali Samad-Khan, *President*
EMP: 11
SALES (est): 669.2K **Privately Held**
WEB: www.opriskadvisory.com
SIC: 7372 Prepackaged Software Services

(G-4333)
STAMFORD RPM RACEWAY LLC
600 West Ave (06902-6325)
PHONE..................................203 323-7223
Eyal Farage, *Principal*
EMP: 3
SALES (est): 106.9K **Privately Held**
SIC: 3644 Mfg Nonconductive Wiring Devices

(G-4334)
STORA ENSO N AMERCN SLS INC (HQ)
201 Broad St (06901-2004)
PHONE..................................203 541-5178
Peter Mersmann, *President*
Brent Saunders, *Vice Pres*
Reto Leuenberger, *Admin Sec*
Robert Zitnay, *Admin Sec*
▲ **EMP:** 5
SQ FT: 5,000
SALES (est): 2MM **Privately Held**
SIC: 2671 Mfg Packaging Paper/Film

(G-4335)
SUMMER STREET PRESS LLC
460 Summer St (06901-1301)
PHONE..................................203 978-0098
Judy Glickman, *Co-Founder*
Nicolas Mandelkern,
EMP: 12
SQ FT: 3,500
SALES (est): 1MM **Privately Held**
WEB: www.summerstreetpress.com
SIC: 2731 Book Publishing

(G-4336)
SURFACE MOUNT DEVICES LLC
Also Called: S M D
16 Acre View Dr (06903-2507)
PHONE..................................203 322-8290
Douglas Muller, *President*
EMP: 3
SQ FT: 4,000
SALES: 100K **Privately Held**
SIC: 3679 3678 Mfg Electronic Components Mfg Electronic Connectors

(G-4337)
SWAROVSKI NORTH AMERICA LTD
100 Greyrock Pl (06901-3118)
PHONE..................................203 462-3357
Jose Melendez, *Branch Mgr*
EMP: 7
SALES (corp-wide): 4.7B **Privately Held**
SIC: 3961 Mfg Costume Jewelry
HQ: Swarovski North America Limited
1 Kenney Dr
Cranston RI 02920
401 463-6400

(G-4338)
SWEET LEAF TEA COMPANY (DH)
900 Long Ridge Rd Bldg 2 (06902-1140)
PHONE..................................203 863-0263
Dan Costello, *CEO*
Clayton Christopher, *President*
David Smith, *Vice Pres*
Brian Goldberg, *CFO*
▲ **EMP:** 12
SQ FT: 2,000
SALES (est): 10.1MM
SALES (corp-wide): 92.8B **Privately Held**
WEB: www.sweetleaftea.com
SIC: 2086 Mfg Bottled/Canned Soft Drinks

(G-4339)
SYSDYNE TECHNOLOGIES LLC
9 Riverbend Dr S (06907-2524)
PHONE..................................203 327-3649
Derek Dukes, *Office Mgr*
Jill Zhang,
▲ **EMP:** 10
SQ FT: 3,500
SALES (est): 2.2MM **Privately Held**
WEB: www.sysdyne.com
SIC: 3679 Mfg Electronic Components

(G-4340)
T-S DISPLAY SYSTEMS INC
Also Called: Tele-Spot Systems
76 Progress Dr (06902-3600)
PHONE..................................203 964-0575
John J Mauro, *President*
Darrell Schneider, *Vice Pres*
▼ **EMP:** 6
SQ FT: 3,700
SALES: 7MM **Privately Held**
SIC: 3669 7629 Mfg Electronic Traffic Signs

(G-4341)
TAGETIK NORTH AMERICA LLC
Also Called: Cch Tagetik
9 W Broad St Ste 400 (06902-3764)
PHONE..................................203 391-7520
Pierluigi Pierallini, *President*
Marco Pierallini, *Exec VP*
Nicola Pierallini, *CFO*
EMP: 5
SALES (est): 1.1MM
SALES (corp-wide): 4.7B **Privately Held**
SIC: 7372 Prepackaged Software Services
HQ: Tagetik Software Srl
Via Franklyn Delano Roosevelt 103
Lucca LU 55100
058 396-811

(G-4342)
TAVISCA LLC
6 High Ridge Park (06905-1327)
PHONE..................................203 956-1000
Priyanka Ratnacarkhi, *Managing Prtnr*
EMP: 5
SALES (est): 180.8K
SALES (corp-wide): 699.8MM **Privately Held**
SIC: 7372 Prepackaged Software Services
PA: Cxloyalty
6 High Ridge Park
Stamford CT 06905
203 956-1000

(G-4343)
TECLENS LLC
9 Riverbend Dr S Ste C (06907-2524)
PHONE..................................919 824-5224
David Acker, *CEO*
Patrick Lopath, *COO*
EMP: 3
SALES (est): 160.7K **Privately Held**
SIC: 3845 Mfg Electromedical Equipment

(G-4344)
THIS OLD HOUSE VENTURES LLC
2 Harbor Dr (06902)
PHONE..................................475 209-8665
Eric Thorkilsen, *CEO*
EMP: 50
SALES (est): 1.5MM **Privately Held**
SIC: 2721 7299 Periodicals-Publishing And Printing Misc Personal Services

(G-4345)
THOMAS DESIGN GROUP LLC
Also Called: Peekaboopumpkin.com
360 Fairfield Ave (06902-7249)
PHONE..................................203 588-1910
Alexander M Thomas,
Alex Thomas,
Kimberly Thomas,
EMP: 6
SQ FT: 3,000
SALES (est): 914.7K **Privately Held**
SIC: 2621 Paper Mill

(G-4346)
THOMSON REUTERS US LLC (DH)
1 Station Pl Ste 6 (06902-6893)
PHONE..................................203 539-8000
Dick Harington, *CEO*
Patrick Naughton, *Business Mgr*
Darren B Pocsik, *Counsel*
Edward Friedland, *Vice Pres*
Michael Moore, *Vice Pres*
EMP: 46
SALES (est): 405.3MM
SALES (corp-wide): 10.6B **Publicly Held**
SIC: 2711 Newspapers-Publishing/Printing
HQ: Thomson Reuters Corporation
3 Times Sq
New York NY 10036
646 223-4000

(G-4347)
TORQMASTER INC
Also Called: Torqmaster International
200 Harvard Ave (06902-6351)
PHONE..................................203 326-5945
Garrett Bebell, *President*
Dr Martin Waine, *Vice Pres*
Victor A Ceci, *Engineer*
Rob Mozdzer, *Project Engr*
Andy Macdowell, *CFO*
◆ **EMP:** 45
SQ FT: 20,000
SALES (est): 7.5MM **Privately Held**
WEB: www.torqmaster.com
SIC: 3499 Mfg Misc Fabricated Metal Products

(G-4348)
TRADEWINDS
1010 Washington Blvd # 3 (06901-2202)
PHONE..................................203 324-2994
Aase Jakobsen, *Manager*
V Tricolo, *Manager*
EMP: 4
SALES (corp-wide): 739.8MM **Privately Held**
SIC: 2711 Newspapers-Publishing/Printing
HQ: Nhst Global Publications As
Christian Krohgs Gate 16
Oslo 0186
755 449-00

(G-4349)
TRI LLC
34 Crescent St Apt 1i (06906-1840)
PHONE..................................203 353-8418
Glenn Wecker, *Principal*
EMP: 3 **EST:** 2008
SALES (est): 183.6K **Privately Held**
SIC: 3281 Mfg Cut Stone/Products

(G-4350)
TRONOX INCORPORATED (DH)
1 Stamford Plz (06901-3271)
PHONE..................................203 705-3800
Thomas Casey, *Ch of Bd*
John D Romano, *Exec VP*
Michael J Foster, *Vice Pres*
Daniel Greenwell, *CFO*
Edward G Ritter,
◆ **EMP:** 200
SALES (est): 378.5MM **Privately Held**
WEB: www.tieandtimber.com
SIC: 2421 2819 Sawmill/Planing Mill Mfg Industrial Inorganic Chemicals
HQ: Tronox Us Holdings Inc.
3301 Nw 150th St
Oklahoma City OK 73134
405 775-5000

(G-4351)
TRONOX LIMITED
1 Stamford Plz (06901-3271)
PHONE..................................203 705-3800
EMP: 4 **Privately Held**
SIC: 1099 Metal Ore Mining
PA: Tronox Limited
Lot 22 Mason Rd
Kwinana WA 6167

(G-4352)
TRONOX LLC (PA)
263 Tresser Blvd Ste 1100 (06901-3227)
PHONE..................................203 705-3800
Tom Casey, *CEO*
Daniel Blue, *Bd of Directors*
EMP: 26 **EST:** 2012
SALES (est): 26.5MM **Privately Held**
SIC: 1241 1442 Coal Mining Services Construction Sand/Gravel

(G-4353)
US GAMES SYSTEMS INC
Also Called: Cove Press
179 Ludlow St (06902-6900)
PHONE..................................203 353-8400
Stuart R Kaplan, *Ch of Bd*
Ricardo Cruz, *Treasurer*
Luis Cardez, *Manager*
Paula Palmer, *Creative Dir*
Marilyn Kaplan, *Admin Sec*
◆ **EMP:** 20
SQ FT: 22,000
SALES (est): 2.5MM **Privately Held**
WEB: www.usgamesinc.com
SIC: 2741 5092 3944 2752 Misc Publishing Whol Toys/Hobby Goods Mfg Games/Toys Lithographic Coml Print

(G-4354)
US SMOKELESS TOBACCO CO LLC
6 High Ridge Park Bldg A (06905-1327)
P.O. Box 85107, Richmond VA (23285-5107)
PHONE..................................203 661-1100
EMP: 61
SALES (est): 15.4MM
SALES (corp-wide): 25.4B **Publicly Held**
SIC: 2131 Chewing And Smoking Tobacco
HQ: Ust Llc
6 High Ridge Park Bldg A
Stamford CT 06905
203 817-3000

(G-4355)
UST LLC (HQ)
6 High Ridge Park Bldg A (06905-1327)
P.O. Box 85107, Richmond VA (23285-5107)
PHONE..................................203 817-3000
Rich A Kohlberger, *Exec VP*
Richard A Kohlberger, *Exec VP*
Richard Kohlberger, *Exec VP*
Raymond Silcock, *Senior VP*
Gary B Glass, *Vice Pres*
◆ **EMP:** 9
SALES (est): 43.6MM
SALES (corp-wide): 25.3B **Publicly Held**
WEB: www.ustshareholder.com
SIC: 2131 2084 2621 3999 Mfg Chew/Smoking Tobacco Mfg Wines/Brandy/Spirits Paper Mill Mfg Misc Products
PA: Altria Group, Inc.
6601 W Broad St
Richmond VA 23230
804 274-2200

(G-4356)
WAGZ INC
Also Called: Link AKC
1 Landmark Sq Ste 505 (06901-2632)
PHONE..................................203 553-9336
Herbie Calves, *Branch Mgr*
EMP: 6
SALES (corp-wide): 1.5MM **Privately Held**
SIC: 3663 Retails Gps Collars
PA: Wagz, Inc.
230 Commerce Way Ste 325
Portsmouth NH 03801
603 570-6015

▲ = Import ▼=Export
◆ =Import/Export

(G-4357)
WENDON COMPANY INC
17 Irving Ave (06902-6622)
PHONE..................................203 348-6272
Michael Montanaro, *President*
Donald Bosak, *Vice Pres*
EMP: 18 **EST:** 1961
SQ FT: 13,000
SALES (est): 7.2MM **Privately Held**
WEB: www.wendon.net
SIC: 3599 Mfg Industrial Machinery

(G-4358)
WENDON TECHNOLOGIES INC
Also Called: Stamford Fabricating
17 Irving Ave (06902-6622)
P.O. Box 112875 (06911-2875)
PHONE..................................203 348-6271
Julius Bogdan, *President*
EMP: 60
SQ FT: 20,000
SALES (est): 8.7MM **Privately Held**
SIC: 3444 Mfg Sheet Metalwork

(G-4359)
WESTROCK COMMERCIAL LLC
1635 Coining Dr (06902)
PHONE..................................203 595-3130
EMP: 4 **EST:** 2013
SALES (est): 381.7K **Privately Held**
SIC: 2752 Lithographic Commercial Printing

(G-4360)
WILSON PARTITIONS INC
Also Called: Arcadia
120 Viaduct Rd (06907-2707)
PHONE..................................203 316-8033
Jim Schladen, *Owner*
Sean Boylan, *General Mgr*
▼ **EMP:** 13
SALES (est): 1.1MM **Privately Held**
SIC: 3334 Primary Aluminum Producer

(G-4361)
WOODWAY PRINT INC
48 Union St Ste 21 (06906-1342)
PHONE..................................203 323-6423
Arnold Feintuck, *President*
EMP: 3 **EST:** 1961
SALES (est): 355.2K **Privately Held**
SIC: 2752 Offset Printing

(G-4362)
XINTEKIDEL INC
Also Called: Intelvideo
56 W Broad St (06902-3715)
PHONE..................................203 348-9229
John Rossi, *President*
Marie Rossi, *Admin Sec*
EMP: 5
SQ FT: 2,000
SALES: 1MM **Privately Held**
WEB: www.xintekvideo.com
SIC: 3663 3651 Mfg Radio/Tv Communication Equipment Mfg Home Audio/Video Equipment

(G-4363)
YUMMYEARTH LLC (PA)
Also Called: Yumearth
9 W Broad St Ste 440 (06902-3764)
PHONE..................................203 276-1259
Sergio Bicas, *CEO*
Rob Wunder, *CFO*
▲ **EMP:** 4
SQ FT: 400
SALES (est): 7.2MM **Privately Held**
WEB: www.yummyearth.com
SIC: 2064 Mfg Candy/Confectionery

(G-4364)
Z-LODA SYSTEMS INC
111 Prospect St (06901-1221)
PHONE..................................203 359-2991
Clifford Mollo, *President*
EMP: 4
SALES (est): 471.9K **Privately Held**
WEB: www.z-loda.com
SIC: 3535 Mfg Vertical Conveyor Material Handling Equipment

Sterling
Windham County

(G-4365)
AUSTIN POWDER COMPANY
332 Ekonk Hill Rd (06377)
PHONE..................................860 564-5466
William Schappert, *Manager*
EMP: 26
SALES (corp-wide): 567.4MM **Privately Held**
SIC: 2892 Mfg Explosives
HQ: Austin Powder Company
25800 Science Park Dr # 300
Cleveland OH 44122
216 464-2400

(G-4366)
DETOTEC NORTH AMERICA INC
401 Snake Meadow Hill Rd (06377-1713)
P.O. Box 276 (06377-0276)
PHONE..................................860 564-1012
Tim Obrien, *President*
Martha Obrien, *Admin Sec*
▲ **EMP:** 9
SQ FT: 100
SALES (est): 1.6MM **Privately Held**
WEB: www.detotec.com
SIC: 2298 Mfg Cordage & Twine

(G-4367)
JORDAN SAW MILL L L C
Also Called: Jordan Sawmill
201 Saw Mill Hill Rd (06377-1405)
PHONE..................................860 774-0247
Kevin Jordan, *Mng Member*
EMP: 10
SQ FT: 20,000
SALES (est): 1.3MM **Privately Held**
SIC: 2421 Sawmill/Planing Mill

(G-4368)
MAXAM INITIATION SYSTEMS LLC
74 Dixon Rd (06377-1503)
PHONE..................................860 774-3507
Pierre Labelle, *General Mgr*
◆ **EMP:** 12
SALES (est): 2.3MM **Privately Held**
SIC: 2892 Mfg Explosives

(G-4369)
MAXAM NORTH AMERICA INC
74 Dixon Rd (06377-1503)
PHONE..................................860 774-2333
EMP: 3
SALES (corp-wide): 48.6MM **Privately Held**
SIC: 2892 Mfg Explosives
HQ: Maxam North America, Inc.
433 Las Colinas Blvd E # 900
Irving TX 75039
801 233-6000

(G-4370)
NU-STONE MFG & DISTRG LLC
160 Sterling Rd (06377-2006)
PHONE..................................860 564-6555
Charlie Corson, *Owner*
EMP: 7
SALES (est): 397.5K **Privately Held**
SIC: 1429 Crushed/Broken Stone

(G-4371)
OLD COACH HOME SALES
242 Harris Rd (06377-1508)
PHONE..................................860 774-1379
Michael Angelo, *Owner*
Gerry Scott, *Owner*
EMP: 22
SQ FT: 3,600
SALES: 22MM **Privately Held**
SIC: 2451 Mfg Mobile Homes

(G-4372)
STERLING PRECISION MACHINING
112 Industrial Park Rd (06377)
P.O. Box 236 (06377-0236)
PHONE..................................860 564-4043
Carmine Demarco, *President*
Ellen W De Marco, *Vice Pres*
Rick Demarco, *Treasurer*
Dave Demarco, *Admin Sec*
EMP: 13
SQ FT: 12,000
SALES (est): 1.8MM **Privately Held**
WEB: www.spmachining.com
SIC: 3599 Contract Machine Shop

(G-4373)
STERLING SAND AND GRAVEL LLC
485 Saw Mill Hill Rd (06377-1407)
PHONE..................................860 774-3985
Erick E Smith, *Manager*
EMP: 6
SALES (est): 303K **Privately Held**
SIC: 1442 Construction Sand/Gravel

Stevenson
Fairfield County

(G-4374)
ANODIC INCORPORATED
1480 Monroe Tpke (06491)
P.O. Box 52 (06491-0052)
PHONE..................................203 268-9966
Ronald Buttner, *President*
EMP: 19 **EST:** 1951
SQ FT: 16,000
SALES (est): 2.4MM **Privately Held**
WEB: www.anodic.com
SIC: 3471 Plating-Polishing Service

Stonington
New London County

(G-4375)
BEERD BREWING CO LLC
22 Bayview Ave (06378-1142)
PHONE..................................585 771-7428
Aaron Simon Cini, *Mng Member*
EMP: 15
SALES (est): 1.7MM **Privately Held**
SIC: 2082 Mfg Malt Beverages

(G-4376)
GREENHAVEN CABINETRY & MILLWOR
338 Elm St (06378-2926)
PHONE..................................860 535-1106
Robert D Wood, *Principal*
EMP: 3
SALES (est): 391.4K **Privately Held**
SIC: 2434 Mfg Wood Kitchen Cabinets

(G-4377)
JAW PRECISION MACHINING LLC
44 Taugwonk Spur Rd # 1 (06378-2035)
PHONE..................................860 535-0615
Jeff Washburn, *Owner*
EMP: 3
SALES (est): 290.2K **Privately Held**
SIC: 3599 Mfg Industrial Machinery

(G-4378)
STONINGTON VINEYARDS INC
523 Taugwonk Rd (06378-1805)
P.O. Box 463 (06378-0463)
PHONE..................................860 535-1222
Cornelius H Smith, *President*
Harriet Smith, *Admin Sec*
EMP: 9
SQ FT: 11,000
SALES (est): 825K **Privately Held**
WEB: www.stoningtonvineyards.com
SIC: 2084 Vineyard & Winery

(G-4379)
ZUCKERMAN HRPSICHORDS INTL LLC
65 Cutler St (06378-1004)
P.O. Box 151 (06378-0151)
PHONE..................................860 535-1715
Richard Auber, *Owner*
David Jacques Way,
EMP: 6
SQ FT: 10,000
SALES (est): 814.8K **Privately Held**
WEB: www.zhi.net
SIC: 3931 Mfg Harpsichords Pianos & Pipe Organs

Storrs
Tolland County

(G-4380)
BIORASIS INC
23 Fellen Rd (06268-2520)
PHONE..................................860 429-3592
Malti Jain, *President*
EMP: 4
SALES (est): 292.6K **Privately Held**
SIC: 3841 Mfg Surgical/Medical Instruments

(G-4381)
CHARLES RIVER LABORATORIES INC
67 Baxter Rd (06268-1109)
PHONE..................................860 429-7261
Seador Girshick, *Manager*
EMP: 25
SALES (corp-wide): 2.2B **Publicly Held**
WEB: www.criver.com
SIC: 2836 8731 2835 Mfg Biological Products Commercial Physical Research Mfg Diagnostic Substances
HQ: Charles River Laboratories, Inc.
251 Ballardvale St
Wilmington MA 01887
781 222-6000

(G-4382)
ORTEOPONIX LLC
22 Scottron Dr (06268)
PHONE..................................203 804-9775
Michael Zilm, *CEO*
EMP: 3
SALES (est): 155.3K **Privately Held**
SIC: 3842 Mfg Surgical Appliances/Supplies

Storrs Mansfield
Tolland County

(G-4383)
AQUATIC SENSOR NETWRK TECH LLC
Also Called: Aquasent
30 Beacon Hill Dr (06268-2756)
PHONE..................................860 429-4303
Jun Hong Cui, *Principal*
▲ **EMP:** 10 **EST:** 2012
SALES (est): 1.2MM **Privately Held**
SIC: 3669 Mfg Communications Equipment

(G-4384)
CONN DAILY CAMPUS
Also Called: Daily Campus, The
11 Dog Ln (06268-2206)
PHONE..................................860 486-3407
Jim Acton, *Principal*
EMP: 4
SALES (est): 269.6K **Privately Held**
SIC: 2711 Newspapers-Publishing/Printing

(G-4385)
ODIS INC
22 Quail Run Rd (06268-2768)
P.O. Box 555 (06268-0555)
PHONE..................................860 450-8407
Lee Pierhal, *President*
◆ **EMP:** 4
SALES: 1MM **Privately Held**
SIC: 3827 Optoelectronics Manufacturing Research And Design

(G-4386)
SANDBALLZ INTERNATIONAL LLC
832 Stafford Rd (06268-2023)
PHONE..................................860 465-9628
George Kronen, *Principal*
EMP: 3
SALES (est): 154K **Privately Held**
SIC: 1455 Kaolin/Ball Clay Mining

GEOGRAPHIC

(G-4387)
WILLARD J STEARNS & SONS INC
Also Called: Mountain Dairy
50 Stearns Rd (06268-2701)
PHONE..................................860 423-9289
Willard C Stearns, *CEO*
David Stearns, *Vice Pres*
Arthur B Stearns, *Treasurer*
Leslie H Stearns, *Director*
James W Stearns, *Admin Sec*
EMP: 35
SALES: 4MM **Privately Held**
WEB: www.mountaindairy.com
SIC: 2026 0241 Mfg Fluid Milk Dairy Farm

Stratford
Fairfield County

(G-4388)
ADVANCED GRAPHICS INC
55 Old South Ave (06615-7368)
P.O. Box 656 (06615-0656)
PHONE..................................203 378-0471
John Alesevich, *President*
Kim Auten, *Office Mgr*
Bonnie Alesevich, *Admin Sec*
EMP: 24 **EST:** 1976
SQ FT: 11,000
SALES (est): 3.4MM **Privately Held**
WEB: www.advanced-graphics.com
SIC: 3479 2759 2396 Coating/Engraving Svcs Commercial Printing Mfg Auto/Apparel Trim

(G-4389)
AGISSAR CORPORATION
526 Benton St (06615-7351)
PHONE..................................203 375-8662
James Foley, *President*
Suzanne Rassiga, *Vice Pres*
EMP: 64
SQ FT: 15,500
SALES (est): 13.5MM **Privately Held**
WEB: www.agissar.com
SIC: 3579 7629 5044 Mfg & Service Mail Handling Equipment & Sales Representative Of Mail Handling Equipment & Check Handling Equipment

(G-4390)
ALBERT E ERICKSON CO
1111 Honeyspot Rd Ste 1 (06615-7144)
PHONE..................................203 386-8931
Donald Erickson, *Vice Pres*
Mary Erickson, *Treasurer*
EMP: 15 **EST:** 1952
SQ FT: 15,000
SALES (est): 2.1MM **Privately Held**
SIC: 3599 Mfg Industrial Machinery

(G-4391)
APTARGROUP INC
Aptar Stratford
125 Access Rd (06615-7414)
PHONE..................................203 377-8100
Phil Miller, *Vice Pres*
John Sullo, *Opers Staff*
Anthony Mancini, *Mfg Staff*
Amy Flood, *Human Res Mgr*
Melissa Bopko, *Marketing Staff*
EMP: 350 **Publicly Held**
SIC: 3089 3499 Mfg Plastic Products Mfg Misc Fabricated Metal Products
PA: Aptargroup, Inc.
265 Exchange Dr Ste 100
Crystal Lake IL 60014

(G-4392)
ASHCROFT INC (DH)
250 E Main St (06614-5145)
PHONE..................................203 378-8281
Steven Culmone, *CEO*
◆ **EMP:** 450
SQ FT: 325,000
SALES (est): 195.7MM **Privately Held**
SIC: 3823 3679 3663 3625 Mfg Process Cntrl Instr Mfg Elec Components Mfg Radio/Tv Comm Equip Mfg Relay/Indstl Control
HQ: Ashcroft-Nagano Keiki Holdings, Inc.
250 E Main St
Stratford CT 06614
203 378-8281

(G-4393)
ASHCROFT INC
Heise
250 E Main St (06614-5145)
PHONE..................................203 378-8281
Gene Urbinati, *Branch Mgr*
EMP: 35 **Privately Held**
SIC: 3825 Manufacturing Pressure Measurement Devices
HQ: Ashcroft Inc.
250 E Main St
Stratford CT 06614
203 378-8281

(G-4394)
B/E AEROSPACE INC
Also Called: Klx Aerospace Solutions
650 Long Beach Blvd (06615-7168)
PHONE..................................203 380-5000
Jason Lewis, *Branch Mgr*
EMP: 4
SALES (corp-wide): 66.5B **Publicly Held**
WEB: www.beaerospace.com
SIC: 3728 Mfg Aircraft Parts/Equipment
HQ: B/E Aerospace, Inc.
1400 Corporate Center Way
Wellington FL 33414
561 791-5000

(G-4395)
BARGAIN NEWS FREE CLASSIFIED A
720 Barnum Avenue Cutoff (06614-5037)
PHONE..................................203 377-3000
Carol Leach, *Manager*
EMP: 80
SALES (est): 2.1MM **Privately Held**
SIC: 2711 2721 Newspapers-Publishing/Printing Periodicals-Publishing/Printing

(G-4396)
BARNEYS SIGN SERVICE INC
Also Called: A Barney's Sign
45 Seymour St Ste 3 (06615-6170)
PHONE..................................203 878-3763
Charles Barnes Jr, *President*
Amelia Barnes, *Admin Sec*
EMP: 5
SALES (est): 396.1K **Privately Held**
SIC: 3993 Mfg Signs/Advertising Specialties

(G-4397)
BLASE MANUFACTURING COMPANY (PA)
Also Called: Blase Tool & Manufacturing Co
60 Watson Blvd Ste 3 (06615-7165)
PHONE..................................203 375-5646
John Blase, *President*
EMP: 55
SQ FT: 60,000
SALES (est): 9.4MM **Privately Held**
WEB: www.blasemfg.com
SIC: 3469 Mfg Metal Stampings

(G-4398)
BREMSER TECHNOLOGIES INC
305 Sniffens Ln (06615-7558)
PHONE..................................203 378-8486
Helma Chartier, *President*
Eric Chartier, *Vice Pres*
Eric Helma, *Vice Pres*
EMP: 10 **EST:** 1949
SQ FT: 5,000
SALES: 500K **Privately Held**
WEB: www.bremsertech.com
SIC: 3544 5084 Mfg Dies/Tools/Jigs/Fixtures Whol Industrial Equipment

(G-4399)
BRIDGEPORT BURIAL VAULT CO
544 Surf Ave (06615-6725)
PHONE..................................203 375-7375
Dennis McNamara, *President*
Carla Mc Namara, *Corp Secy*
EMP: 3 **EST:** 1946
SQ FT: 12,000
SALES: 500K **Privately Held**
SIC: 3272 Mfg Concrete Burial Vaults

(G-4400)
BRIDGEPORT FITTINGS LLC
705 Lordship Blvd (06615-7313)
P.O. Box 619, Bridgeport (06601-0619)
PHONE..................................203 377-5944
Paul Suzio, *President*
▲ **EMP:** 200
SQ FT: 135,000
SALES (est): 46.3MM **Privately Held**
WEB: www.bptfittings.com
SIC: 3644 Mfg Nonconductive Wiring Devices
PA: Nsi Industries, Llc
9730 Northcross Center Ct
Huntersville NC 28078

(G-4401)
BRIDGEPORT INSULATED WIRE CO
514 Surf Ave (06615-6725)
PHONE..................................203 375-9579
Wayne Gombar, *Opers-Prdtn-Mfg*
EMP: 25
SQ FT: 2,200
SALES (corp-wide): 5.6MM **Privately Held**
SIC: 3357 3496 Nonferrous Wiredrawing/Insulating Mfg Misc Fabricated Wire Products
PA: The Bridgeport Insulated Wire Company
51 Brookfield Ave
Bridgeport CT 06610
203 333-3191

(G-4402)
CARALA VENTURES LTD
Also Called: Classics of Golf
120 Research Dr (06615-7126)
PHONE..................................800 483-6449
Michael P Beckerich, *President*
EMP: 28
SQ FT: 10,000
SALES (est): 2.3MM **Privately Held**
WEB: www.classicsofgolf.com
SIC: 2731 Books-Publishing

(G-4403)
CARBTROL CORPORATION
200 Benton St (06615-7330)
PHONE..................................203 337-4340
Chris Rotondo, *President*
Kenneth Lanouette, *President*
Heather Mroz, *Vice Pres*
Austin Shepherd, *Vice Pres*
Mary Nelson, *Purch Agent*
EMP: 20
SALES (est): 5.3MM **Privately Held**
WEB: www.carbtrol.com
SIC: 2819 Mfg Industrial Inorganic Chemicals

(G-4404)
CHRIS CROSS LLC
Also Called: Prestige Remodeling
294 Benton St (06615-7330)
P.O. Box 321135, Fairfield (06825-6135)
PHONE..................................203 386-8426
John Cross, *Manager*
EMP: 4
SALES (est): 403.6K **Privately Held**
SIC: 2434 Mfg Wood Kitchen Cabinets

(G-4405)
COATING DESIGN GROUP INC
430 Sniffens Ln (06615-7559)
PHONE..................................203 878-3663
William L Roy, *President*
Kathryn G Cunningham, *Corp Secy*
Kathryn Cunningham-Roy, *Vice Pres*
Kevin Joseph, *Exec Dir*
EMP: 20
SQ FT: 11,500
SALES (est): 4.2MM **Privately Held**
WEB: www.coatingdesigngroup.com
SIC: 3827 3089 Mfg Optical Instruments/Lenses Mfg Plastic Products

(G-4406)
CONNECTICUT MACHINE & WELDING
Also Called: Rollins Transmission Service
425 Harding Ave (06615-7248)
P.O. Box 249 (06615-0249)
PHONE..................................203 502-2605
Wayne J Rollins, *President*
Gary Rollins, *Treasurer*
Glenn A Rollins, *Admin Sec*
EMP: 20
SQ FT: 7,000
SALES: 965K **Privately Held**
WEB: www.rollinstransmission.com
SIC: 3599 Welding Repair

(G-4407)
CUESCRIPT INC
555 Lordship Blvd Unit F (06615-7156)
PHONE..................................203 763-4030
Michael Accardi, *President*
EMP: 7 **EST:** 2014
SALES (est): 658.4K **Privately Held**
SIC: 3663 Mfg Radio/Tv Communication Equipment

(G-4408)
D & L ENGINEERING COMPANY
564 Surf Ave (06615-6725)
PHONE..................................203 375-5856
Judith Di Libro, *President*
Judith M Delibro, *Director*
EMP: 5
SQ FT: 3,000
SALES: 200K **Privately Held**
SIC: 3599 Mfg Industrial Machinery

(G-4409)
DICTAPHONE CORPORATION (HQ)
3191 Broadbridge Ave (06614-2559)
PHONE..................................203 381-7000
Robert Schwager, *Ch of Bd*
Daniel P Hart, *Senior VP*
Joseph Delaney, *Senior VP*
Thomas C Hodge, *Senior VP*
Ed Rucinski, *Senior VP*
▲ **EMP:** 200 **EST:** 1881
SQ FT: 100,000
SALES (est): 225.5MM **Publicly Held**
WEB: www.dictaphone.com
SIC: 3579 3825 3695 3577 Mfg Office Machines Mfg Elec Measuring Instr Mfg Magnetic Disks/Tapes Mfg Computer Peripherals

(G-4410)
ELECTRIC ENTERPRISE INC
1410 Stratford Ave (06615-6417)
PHONE..................................203 378-7311
Raymond S Sierakowski, *President*
Mary Jo Sierakowski, *Admin Sec*
EMP: 11
SQ FT: 3,200
SALES (est): 2MM **Privately Held**
WEB: www.electricenterprise.com
SIC: 7694 5063 Armature Rewinding Whol Electrical Equipment

(G-4411)
FAIRFIELD WOODWORKS LLC
Also Called: Fairfield Wood Works
365 Sniffens Ln (06615-7558)
PHONE..................................203 380-9842
David Evans,
Mark Bento,
EMP: 18
SQ FT: 10,500
SALES (est): 2.4MM **Privately Held**
SIC: 2431 Mfg Millwork

(G-4412)
FOOD ATMTN - SVC TCHNIQUES INC (PA)
Also Called: Fast
905 Honeyspot Rd (06615-7140)
PHONE..................................203 377-4414
Timothy Lane, *CEO*
Bernard G Koether II, *Ch of Bd*
George F Koether, *President*
Reza Khani, *COO*
John Balkonis, *Vice Pres*
◆ **EMP:** 130
SQ FT: 100,000

▲ = Import ▼=Export
◆ =Import/Export

SALES (est): 28.2MM **Privately Held**
WEB: www.fastinc.com
SIC: 3823 3822 Mfg Process Control Instruments Mfg Environmental Controls

(G-4413)
FRANK ROTH CO INC
1795 Stratford Ave (06615-6442)
PHONE..................................203 377-2155
Walker Woodworth, *President*
Cornelia Toffolo, *Corp Secy*
Marissa Woodworth, *Treasurer*
EMP: 60 **EST:** 1934
SQ FT: 14,000
SALES (est): 9MM **Privately Held**
WEB: www.frankroth.com
SIC: 3599 3325 3841 3751 Mfg Industrial Machinery Steel Foundry Mfg Surgical/Med Instr Mfg Motorcycles/Bicycles

(G-4414)
GARY TOOL COMPANY
26 Grant St (06615-6188)
PHONE..................................203 377-3077
Raymond Anderson Jr, *President*
Cristine Ansder, *President*
EMP: 7
SQ FT: 10,000
SALES (est): 1.2MM **Privately Held**
SIC: 3541 3544 Mfg Machine Tools-Cutting Mfg Dies/Tools/Jigs/Fixtures

(G-4415)
GLYNE MANUFACTURING CO INC
380 E Main St (06614-5145)
PHONE..................................203 375-4495
Bruce McGalliard, *President*
Thomas Frei, *Vice Pres*
Tom Frei, *Vice Pres*
Ben McGalliard, *Vice Pres*
EMP: 16
SQ FT: 9,600
SALES (est): 3.7MM **Privately Held**
WEB: www.glyne.com
SIC: 3728 Mfg Aircraft Parts/Equipment

(G-4416)
GRAFTED COATINGS INC
Also Called: We Make Paint
400 Surf Ave (06615-6723)
PHONE..................................203 377-9979
James A Bolton, *President*
Joanne M Young, *Treasurer*
Alice Irene Bolton, *Admin Sec*
EMP: 15
SQ FT: 12,000
SALES (est): 2.4MM **Privately Held**
WEB: www.graftedcoatings.com
SIC: 2891 5198 Mfg Water Based Paint Whol Paints/Varnishes

(G-4417)
HAMPFORD RESEARCH INC (PA)
54 Veterans Blvd (06615-5111)
PHONE..................................203 375-1137
Clare C Hampford Donahue, *President*
Timothy Hampford, *Executive*
Steve Finson, *Admin Sec*
Anne B Hampford, *Admin Sec*
Anne Hampford, *Admin Sec*
▲ **EMP:** 34
SQ FT: 100,000
SALES (est): 3.8MM **Privately Held**
WEB: www.hampfordresearch.com
SIC: 2869 8731 Mfg Industrial Organic Chemicals Commercial Physical Research

(G-4418)
HANGER PRSTHETCS & ORTHO INC
1985 Barnum Ave (06615-5512)
PHONE..................................203 377-8820
Nathan Seversky, *Manager*
Morris Cohen, *Manager*
EMP: 7
SALES (corp-wide): 1B **Publicly Held**
SIC: 3842 Ret Misc Merchandise
HQ: Hanger Prosthetics & Orthotics, Inc.
10910 Domain Dr Ste 300
Austin TX 78758
512 777-3800

(G-4419)
HERFF JONES LLC
71 Vought Pl (06614-2949)
PHONE..................................203 368-9344
Herff Jones, *Branch Mgr*
EMP: 10
SALES (corp-wide): 1.1B **Privately Held**
SIC: 3911 Mfg Precious Metal Jewelry
HQ: Herff Jones, Llc
4501 W 62nd St
Indianapolis IN 46268
800 419-5462

(G-4420)
HI-TECH PACKAGING INC
1 Bruce Ave (06615-6102)
PHONE..................................203 378-2700
Michael Rappa, *President*
Alfred Thibault, *Senior VP*
EMP: 28
SQ FT: 40,000
SALES (est): 5.4MM **Privately Held**
SIC: 2448 2653 3086 Mfg Wood Pallets/Skids Mfg Corrugated/Solid Fiber Boxes Mfg Plastic Foam Products

(G-4421)
HYDRO-FLEX INC
Also Called: Necs
534 Surf Ave (06615-6725)
PHONE..................................203 269-5599
James William, *President*
Chester Cornacchia, *Principal*
Eileen Kelly, *Principal*
EMP: 4
SQ FT: 20,000
SALES (est): 250K **Privately Held**
SIC: 3999 Mfg Misc Products

(G-4422)
IMPERIAL METAL FINISHING INC
920 Honeyspot Rd (06615-7112)
PHONE..................................203 377-1229
Vincent Bevacqua, *President*
Frank Bevacqua, *Vice Pres*
John Bevacqua Jr, *Vice Pres*
EMP: 9
SQ FT: 13,000
SALES: 850K **Privately Held**
SIC: 3479 Industrial Spray Painting And Powder Coating Of Manufactured Metal Formed Procucts

(G-4423)
INNARAH INC
838 Woodend Rd (06615-7324)
P.O. Box 335 (06615-0335)
PHONE..................................203 873-0015
Manozoor Jaffery, *President*
▲ **EMP:** 5
SALES (est): 473.3K **Privately Held**
SIC: 2844 Mfg Toilet Preparations

(G-4424)
INNOTEQ INC (PA)
555 Lordship Blvd (06615-7156)
P.O. Box 1640, Pleasantville NJ (08232-6640)
PHONE..................................203 659-4444
Craig J Berry, *President*
Laurie Koppe, *General Mgr*
John Ledonne, *Director*
▼ **EMP:** 40
SQ FT: 25,000
SALES (est): 8.9MM **Privately Held**
SIC: 2834 Mfg Pharmaceutical Preparations

(G-4425)
JGS PROPERTIES LLC
Also Called: R A Lalli
1805 Stratford Ave (06615-6426)
PHONE..................................203 378-7508
Geza Scap, *Owner*
Julie Scap, *Vice Pres*
EMP: 30 **EST:** 1953
SQ FT: 25,000
SALES (est): 5.6MM **Privately Held**
SIC: 3444 Mfg Sheet Metalwork

(G-4426)
JUDGE TOOL & GAGE INC
Also Called: Judge Tool Sales Company
555 Lordship Blvd Unit A (06615-7156)
PHONE..................................800 214-5990
Joseph Palmer, *CEO*
Bob Ratzenberger, *Sales Staff*
Gwen Palmer, *Admin Sec*
EMP: 4 **EST:** 1958
SQ FT: 1,800
SALES (est): 765.3K **Privately Held**
WEB: www.judgetool.com
SIC: 3829 Mfg Measuring/Controlling Devices

(G-4427)
KIMBERLY-CLARK CORPORATION
137 Ryegate Ter (06615-7659)
PHONE..................................973 986-8454
Ryan Wagner, *Branch Mgr*
EMP: 202
SALES (corp-wide): 18.4B **Publicly Held**
SIC: 2621 2676 Paper Mill Mfg Sanitary Paper Products
PA: Kimberly-Clark Corporation
351 Phelps Dr
Irving TX 75038
972 281-1200

(G-4428)
KIMS NAIL CORPORATION
Also Called: Kim's Nail Salon
7365 Main St Ste 11 (06614-1300)
PHONE..................................203 380-8608
Euneui Jo, *Principal*
EMP: 3
SALES: 30K **Privately Held**
SIC: 2844 Beauty Shop

(G-4429)
KUB TECHNOLOGIES INC
Also Called: Kubtec
111 Research Dr (06615-7126)
PHONE..................................203 364-8544
Vikram Butani, *President*
Preeti Butani, *Vice Pres*
▼ **EMP:** 28
SQ FT: 10,000
SALES (est): 4.3MM **Privately Held**
WEB: www.kubtec.com
SIC: 3844 Mfg X-Ray Apparatus/Tubes

(G-4430)
M & D COATINGS LLC
167 Avon St (06615-6744)
PHONE..................................203 380-9466
Jeffrey Dumas, *Manager*
▲ **EMP:** 8
SALES (est): 948.5K **Privately Held**
SIC: 2851 Mfg Paints/Allied Products

(G-4431)
MCMELLON BROS INCORPORATED
915 Honeyspot Rd (06615-7192)
PHONE..................................203 375-5685
Thomas Miller, *President*
Hans Hanshaffner, *Vice Pres*
Reberta Miller, *Vice Pres*
Alan Brown, *Marketing Staff*
Thomas Kaskie, *Director*
EMP: 27 **EST:** 1951
SQ FT: 20,000
SALES (est): 6.3MM **Privately Held**
WEB: www.mcmellonbros.com
SIC: 3728 3452 Mfg Aircraft Parts/Equipment Mfg Bolts/Screws/Rivets

(G-4432)
NATURE PLUS INC
55 Rachel Dr (06615-6411)
PHONE..................................203 380-0316
Jon Sedgwick, *President*
EMP: 7
SQ FT: 5,100
SALES (est): 834K **Privately Held**
SIC: 2842 Natural Cleaning And Deodorizing Products

(G-4433)
NORWALK COMPRESEER COMPANY
1650 Stratford Ave (06615-6419)
PHONE..................................203 386-1234
Arthur McCauley, *Ch of Bd*
Jeff Barker, *Sales Staff*
▼ **EMP:** 45
SQ FT: 33,000
SALES (est): 9MM **Privately Held**
SIC: 3563 Mfg Air/Gas Compressors

(G-4434)
NORWALK COMPRESSOR INC
1650 Stratford Ave (06615-6419)
PHONE..................................203 386-1234
Arthur Cauley, *Principal*
Chris McCauley, *Executive*
▲ **EMP:** 6
SALES (est): 1.9MM **Privately Held**
SIC: 3563 Mfg Air/Gas Compressors

(G-4435)
NORWALK POWDERED METALS INC
Also Called: Npm
30 Moffitt St (06615-6718)
PHONE..................................203 338-8000
Thomas A Blumenthal, *President*
Ann Blumenthal, *Vice Pres*
Richard Webb, *Vice Pres*
Henry Adams, *VP Sales*
EMP: 70 **EST:** 1957
SQ FT: 34,000
SALES (est): 14.4MM **Privately Held**
SIC: 3399 Mfg Primary Metal Products

(G-4436)
NUANCE COMMUNICATIONS INC
3191 Broadbridge Ave Fl 2 (06614-2566)
PHONE..................................781 565-5000
Ed Rucinski, *Exec VP*
Simon Howes, *Vice Pres*
Betsy Hipp, *Senior Mgr*
EMP: 4 **Publicly Held**
SIC: 7372 Prepackaged Software Services
PA: Nuance Communications, Inc.
1 Wayside Rd
Burlington MA 01803

(G-4437)
NUOVO PASTA PRODUCTIONS LTD
1330 Honeyspot Road Ext (06615-7115)
PHONE..................................203 380-4090
Carl L Zuanelli, *President*
Tom Quinn, *Exec VP*
Kevin Sterner, *Regl Sales Mgr*
Michael Voelker, *Manager*
Christine Calabrese, *Executive Asst*
◆ **EMP:** 150
SQ FT: 40,000
SALES: 36MM **Privately Held**
SIC: 2099 Mfg Food Preparations

(G-4438)
PALMERO HEALTHCARE LLC
120 Goodwin Pl (06615-6790)
PHONE..................................203 377-6424
Karen Neiner, *President*
Bernie Dutton, *COO*
Beth Wade, *Sales Staff*
EMP: 13
SALES (est): 3.6MM **Privately Held**
SIC: 3843 Mfg Dental Equipment/Supplies

(G-4439)
PEPSI-COLA METRO BTLG CO INC
Also Called: Pepsico
355 Benton St (06615-7329)
PHONE..................................203 375-2484
Spencer Bresette, *Sales Staff*
Todd Bixby, *Manager*
EMP: 400
SALES (corp-wide): 64.6B **Publicly Held**
WEB: www.pbg.com
SIC: 2086 Carb Sft Drnkbtlcn
HQ: Pepsi-Cola Metropolitan Bottling Company, Inc.
1111 Westchester Ave
White Plains NY 10604
914 767-6000

(G-4440)
PREMIER GRAPHICS LLC
Also Called: Premier Prtg Mailing Solutions
860 Honeyspot Rd Ste 1 (06615-7159)
PHONE..................................800 414-1624
Tim Chiccese, *President*
Michael Fatse, *Partner*
EMP: 55
SQ FT: 33,000

GEOGRAPHIC

SALES (est): 13.3MM **Privately Held**
SIC: 2721 Lithographic Commercial Printing

(G-4441)
REDCO AUDIO INC
1701 Stratford Ave (06615-6421)
PHONE..................................203 502-7600
David Berliner, *President*
Peter Greenwood, *Engineer*
Marc Lelyveld, *Sales Staff*
▲ **EMP**: 14
SQ FT: 6,000
SALES (est): 2.9MM **Privately Held**
WEB: www.redco.com
SIC: 3496 3651 1761 Mfg Misc Fabricated Wire Products Mfg Home Audio/Video Equipment Roofing/Siding Contractor

(G-4442)
SAUGATUCK KITCHENS LLC
125 Bruce Ave (06615-6102)
PHONE..................................203 334-1099
Sonia Fernandez-Wells,
David Wells,
Nicolas Wells,
Oliver Wells,
EMP: 5 **EST**: 1998
SQ FT: 20,000
SALES (est): 118.7K **Privately Held**
SIC: 2092 Mfg Fresh/Frozen Packaged Fish

(G-4443)
SIKORSKY AIRCRAFT CORPORATION
1825 Main St (06615-6528)
P.O. Box 9729 (06615-9129)
PHONE..................................203 386-4000
Steven Finger, *President*
EMP: 600 **Publicly Held**
WEB: www.sikorsky.com
SIC: 3724 Mfg Aircraft Engines/Parts
HQ: Sikorsky Aircraft Corporation
6900 Main St
Stratford CT 06614

(G-4444)
SIKORSKY AIRCRAFT CORPORATION (HQ)
6900 Main St (06614-1385)
P.O. Box 9729 (06615-9129)
PHONE..................................203 386-4000
Daniel Schultz, *President*
John Palumbo, *Senior VP*
Judith E Bankowski, *Vice Pres*
Chris Buiten, *Vice Pres*
Stephen B Estill, *Vice Pres*
◆ **EMP**: 2093
SALES (est): 2.9B **Publicly Held**
WEB: www.sikorsky.com
SIC: 3721 4581 5599 Mfg Aircraft Airport/Airport Services Ret Misc Vehicles

(G-4445)
SIKORSKY EXPORT CORPORATION
6900 Main St (06614-1378)
PHONE..................................203 386-4000
Mick Maurer, *President*
▼ **EMP**: 300
SALES (est): 19MM **Publicly Held**
WEB: www.sikorskyarchives.com
SIC: 3721 Mfg Aircraft
HQ: Sikorsky Aircraft Corporation
6900 Main St
Stratford CT 06614

(G-4446)
SKYTECH MACHINING INC
765 Woodend Rd (06615-7323)
PHONE..................................203 378-9994
Carlos Lobo, *President*
Antonio Da Silva, *Vice Pres*
EMP: 5
SQ FT: 3,200
SALES: 650K **Privately Held**
WEB: www.skytechmachining.com
SIC: 3599 Mfg Industrial Machinery

(G-4447)
SNEHAM MANUFACTURING INC
727 Honeyspot Rd Ste 99 (06615-7172)
PHONE..................................203 610-6669
Suja Thomas, *President*
Saji Thomas, *Principal*
EMP: 4
SQ FT: 4,000
SALES (est): 370K **Privately Held**
SIC: 3599 Mfg Industrial Machinery

(G-4448)
SONIC CORP
1 Research Dr (06615-7184)
PHONE..................................203 375-0063
Robert Brakeman III, *President*
Richard Cizik, *Purch Mgr*
Bill Brakeman, *Engineer*
Claire C Skidd, *Admin Sec*
EMP: 12
SQ FT: 10,000
SALES (est): 3MM **Privately Held**
WEB: www.sonicmixing.com
SIC: 3556 3561 3552 3554 Mfg Food Prdts Mach Mfg Pumps & Pumping Equip Mfg Textile Machinery Mfg Paper Indstl Mach

(G-4449)
STRATFORD STEEL LLC
185 Masarik Ave (06615)
PHONE..................................203 612-7350
Michael Matkovic, *Mng Member*
EMP: 40
SQ FT: 13,000
SALES: 5MM **Privately Held**
SIC: 3441 Structural Metal Fabrication

(G-4450)
STRATON INDUSTRIES INC
180 Surf Ave (06615-7137)
PHONE..................................203 375-4488
Edward J Cremin, *CEO*
David E Cremin, *President*
James Jarusinsky, *Engineer*
Kathleen McCann, *VP Sls/Mktg*
Marie Brackett, *Accounting Mgr*
EMP: 52 **EST**: 1961
SQ FT: 12,000
SALES (est): 14MM **Privately Held**
WEB: www.straton.com
SIC: 3544 3599 3721 3728 Mfg Dies/Tools/Jigs/Fixt Mfg Industrial Machinery Mfg Aircraft Mfg Aircraft Parts/Equip

(G-4451)
SUPER SEAL CORP
45 Seymour St (06615-6170)
P.O. Box 394 (06615-0394)
PHONE..................................203 378-5015
William Newbauer Jr, *President*
Einer Dineson, *Admin Sec*
▲ **EMP**: 10
SQ FT: 12,000
SALES (est): 1.2MM **Privately Held**
SIC: 3089 Mfg Plastic Molded Products

(G-4452)
SURF METAL CO INC
460 Lordship Blvd (06615-7123)
PHONE..................................203 375-2211
James Chacho Jr, *President*
Dorie Chacho, *Admin Sec*
EMP: 5
SQ FT: 4,000
SALES (est): 450K **Privately Held**
SIC: 3341 5093 Refiner Of White Metals

(G-4453)
THE MERRILL ANDERSON CO INC
1166 Barnum Ave (06614-5427)
PHONE..................................203 377-4996
Samuel H Heitzman, *Ch of Bd*
Thomas Gerrity, *President*
Samuel Simpson, *Treasurer*
Paula Tkacs, *Art Dir*
Jim Gust, *Senior Editor*
EMP: 12
SQ FT: 7,500
SALES (est): 1.4MM **Privately Held**
WEB: www.merrillanderson.com
SIC: 2741 8742 Misc Publishing Management Consulting Services

(G-4454)
TOTAL PTRCHEMICALS REF USA INC
125 Ontario St (06615-7135)
PHONE..................................203 375-0668
Donna Kovac, *Branch Mgr*
EMP: 30
SALES (corp-wide): 8.1B **Publicly Held**
SIC: 2821 Mfg Plastic Materials/Resins
HQ: Total Petrochemicals & Refining Usa, Inc.
1201 La St Ste 1800
Houston TX 77002
713 483-5000

(G-4455)
TYGER TOOL INC
45 Sperry Ave (06615-7317)
PHONE..................................203 375-4344
Mark Bracchi, *President*
Darrell Ingram, *Corp Secy*
Paul Ferencz, *Vice Pres*
Kimberly Smircich, *Office Mgr*
EMP: 10
SQ FT: 4,800
SALES: 1MM **Privately Held**
WEB: www.tygertool.com
SIC: 3469 3549 Manufactures Machine Parts & Automated Hardware Machinery

(G-4456)
USC TECHNOLOGIES LLC
175 Garfield Ave (06615-7103)
PHONE..................................203 378-9622
Robert Reath, *Manager*
EMP: 4
SALES (est): 133.8K **Privately Held**
SIC: 3471 Plating/Polishing Service

(G-4457)
WESTPORT PRECISION LLC
280 Hathaway Dr (06615-7344)
PHONE..................................203 378-2175
Carlos Mora, *Purch Mgr*
Tom Fischetti, *Sales Engr*
Judd Mellott,
Robert Zawadski,
EMP: 53
SQ FT: 25,000
SALES (est): 12.2MM **Privately Held**
WEB: www.westportprecision.com
SIC: 3599 Mfg Industrial Machinery

(G-4458)
WJ KETTLEWORKS LLC
55 Sperry Ave (06615-7317)
PHONE..................................203 377-5000
William J Kettles,
EMP: 3
SALES (est): 220K **Privately Held**
SIC: 3272 Mfg Concrete Products

(G-4459)
XG INDUSTRIES LLC
53 Hancock St (06615-6204)
PHONE..................................475 282-4643
Marx Bowens,
EMP: 11 **EST**: 2016
SALES (est): 2.6MM **Privately Held**
SIC: 2891 Mfg Additives/Sealants

Suffield
Hartford County

(G-4460)
BLESSED CREEK
908 Overhill Dr (06078-1944)
PHONE..................................860 416-3692
Jean Wild, *President*
EMP: 4
SALES (est): 308.8K **Privately Held**
SIC: 2844 Mfg Toilet Preparations

(G-4461)
CADENCE CT INC
4 Kenny Roberts Mem Dr (06078-2529)
PHONE..................................860 370-9780
Alan Connor, *President*
EMP: 75
SQ FT: 30,000
SALES: 10MM
SALES (corp-wide): 55MM **Privately Held**
SIC: 3699 Manufacture Electrical Equipment/Supplies
PA: Cadence, Inc.
9 Technology Dr
Staunton VA 24401
540 248-2200

(G-4462)
EVANS COOLING SYSTEMS INC (PA)
1 Mountain Rd Ste 1 # 1 (06078-2163)
PHONE..................................860 668-1114
John W Evans, *President*
Catherine Wright, *General Mgr*
Jeffrey Bye, *COO*
Jeff Bye, *Vice Pres*
Andy Barbieri, *Sales Staff*
▼ **EMP**: 7
SALES (est): 1.5MM **Privately Held**
SIC: 3559 3724 Mfg Misc Industry Machinery Mfg Aircraft Engines/Parts

(G-4463)
HP HOOD LLC
Ice Cream Division
1250 East St S (06078-2498)
PHONE..................................860 623-4435
Rick Kovarik, *Opers Mgr*
Scott Whitman, *Engineer*
Dana Johnson, *Sales Staff*
Joseph McFadden, *Sales Staff*
Joe Uchneat, *Manager*
EMP: 225
SQ FT: 147,000
SALES (corp-wide): 2.2B **Privately Held**
WEB: www.hphood.com
SIC: 2024 Mfg Ice Cream/Frozen Desert
PA: Hp Hood Llc
6 Kimball Ln Ste 400
Lynnfield MA 01940
617 887-8441

(G-4464)
KONGSBERG ACTUATION (HQ)
Also Called: Kongsberg Automotive
1 Firestone Dr (06078-2611)
PHONE..................................860 668-1285
Hennings Jensen, *CEO*
Jonathan Day, *President*
James Fuda, *Treasurer*
John Gibbs, *Sales Mgr*
Charles Lu, *Manager*
▲ **EMP**: 6
SALES (est): 20.7MM **Privately Held**
SIC: 3052 Mfg Motor Vehicle Parts/Accessories

(G-4465)
MOBILE MINI INC
911 S St Mach 1 Indus Par 1 Mach (06078)
PHONE..................................860 668-1888
Brian Lowder, *Manager*
EMP: 20
SALES (corp-wide): 593.2MM **Publicly Held**
SIC: 3448 3441 3412 7359 Mfg Prefab Metal Bldgs Structural Metal Fabrctn Mfg Metal Barrels/Pails Equipment Rental/Leasing
PA: Mobile Mini, Inc.
4646 E Van Buren St # 400
Phoenix AZ 85008
480 894-6311

(G-4466)
PRAXAIR INC
1 U Car St (06078-2454)
PHONE..................................860 292-5400
Jim Bozzone, *Opers-Prdtn-Mfg*
EMP: 64
SQ FT: 4,832 **Privately Held**
SIC: 2813 Whol Industrial Equipment
HQ: Praxair, Inc.
10 Riverview Dr
Danbury CT 06810
203 837-2000

(G-4467)
ROAMING RACEWAY AND RR LLC
755 Sheldon St (06078-2052)
PHONE..................................413 531-3390
Danny Decosmo, *Principal*

▲ = Import ▼=Export
◆ =Import/Export

EMP: 4
SALES (est): 266.6K **Privately Held**
SIC: 3644 Mfg Nonconductive Wiring Devices

(G-4468)
STONE IMAGE CUSTOM CONCRETE
1186 Old Coach Xing (06078-1538)
PHONE..................................860 668-2434
Robert Heim, *Principal*
EMP: 3
SALES (est): 228.8K **Privately Held**
SIC: 3272 Mfg Concrete Products

(G-4469)
UNITED GEAR & MACHINE CO INC
1087 East St S (06078-2405)
PHONE..................................860 623-6618
William J Malec, *President*
Genevieve Malec, *Corp Secy*
Kurt Malec, *Vice Pres*
EMP: 10 **EST:** 1955
SALES (est): 1.5MM **Privately Held**
SIC: 3599 3462 Machine Shop Manufactures Gear

Taftville
New London County

(G-4470)
GP INDUSTRIES
500 Norwich Ave Ste 7 (06380-1335)
PHONE..................................860 859-9938
Vesselin Zaprianov, *President*
EMP: 7
SALES (est): 552.6K **Privately Held**
SIC: 3089 Mfg Plastic Products

(G-4471)
PROKOP SIGN CO
Also Called: Prokop Signs & Graphics
338 Norwich Ave Ste 1 (06380-1254)
PHONE..................................860 889-6265
Francis Houle, *Owner*
Karen Houle, *Co-Owner*
EMP: 3
SALES (est): 283K **Privately Held**
WEB: www.prokopsigns.com
SIC: 3993 Mfg Signs/Advertising Specialties

Tariffville
Hartford County

(G-4472)
APPLIED POROUS TECH INC
2 Tunxis Rd Ste 103 (06081-9687)
P.O. Box 569 (06081-0569)
PHONE..................................860 408-9793
Edward Swiniarski, *President*
Heidi Eisenhaure, *Vice Pres*
▲ **EMP:** 12
SQ FT: 7,500
SALES: 1.8MM **Privately Held**
WEB: www.appliedporous.com
SIC: 3569 Mfg General Industrial Machinery

Terryville
Litchfield County

(G-4473)
ADVANCED MICRO CONTROLS INC
Also Called: Amci
20 Gear Dr (06786-7314)
PHONE..................................860 585-1254
William Erb, *President*
Richard Eykelhoff, *General Mgr*
Stancho Djiev, *Engineer*
Stanko Mantchev, *Design Engr*
Bob Alesio, *Sales Dir*
◆ **EMP:** 38
SQ FT: 16,000
SALES: 10.3MM **Privately Held**
WEB: www.amciworld.com
SIC: 3625 Mfg Relays/Industrial Controls

(G-4474)
ALLREAD PRODUCTS CO LLC
22 S Main St (06786-6212)
PHONE..................................860 589-3566
William Allread,
EMP: 19
SQ FT: 8,000
SALES: 1MM **Privately Held**
WEB: www.allreadproducts.com
SIC: 3399 2821 Mfr Powdered Metal And Powdered Teflon Products

(G-4475)
C-B MANUFACTURING & TOOL CO
118 Napco Dr (06786-7309)
P.O. Box 61 (06786-0061)
PHONE..................................860 583-5402
Bruce Czaplicki, *President*
Sally Czaplicki, *Vice Pres*
EMP: 4 **EST:** 1963
SQ FT: 4,000
SALES: 240K **Privately Held**
WEB: www.rimfg.com
SIC: 3599 Mfg Industrial Machinery

(G-4476)
DRILL RITE CARBIDE TOOL CO
6 Orchard St (06786-6017)
PHONE..................................860 583-3200
Donald Tanguay, *President*
EMP: 5
SALES (est): 403.8K **Privately Held**
SIC: 3545 Mfg Machine Tool Accessories

(G-4477)
ELM PRESS INCORPORATED
16 Tremco Dr (06786-7312)
PHONE..................................860 583-3600
Victor L Losure, *President*
Dennis Martel, *Mfg Staff*
Joel A Zinn, *Admin Sec*
EMP: 40 **EST:** 1961
SQ FT: 13,200
SALES (est): 7.6MM **Privately Held**
WEB: www.elmpress.com
SIC: 2752 2791 2789 2759 Lithographic Coml Print Typesetting Services Bookbinding/Related Work Commercial Printing

(G-4478)
ES METAL FABRICATIONS INC
11 Allread Dr (06786-7300)
PHONE..................................860 585-6067
Eric Schleich, *President*
Russell Schleich, *Vice Pres*
Ruth E Schleich, *Director*
▲ **EMP:** 17
SQ FT: 6,000
SALES (est): 3.6MM **Privately Held**
WEB: www.esmetal.com
SIC: 3441 Structural Metal Fabrication

(G-4479)
FURNACE SOURCE LLC
99 Agney Ave (06786-6224)
PHONE..................................860 582-4201
Marshall Klimasewiski,
EMP: 18
SALES (est): 4.2MM **Privately Held**
WEB: www.thefurnacesource.com
SIC: 3567 3841 Mfg Industrial Furnaces/Ovens Mfg Surgical/Medical Instruments

(G-4480)
FX MODELS LLC
111 Seymour Rd (06786-4512)
PHONE..................................860 589-5279
Marc L Dantonio, *Principal*
Jodi D Antonio,
Ed Miarecki,
EMP: 4
SALES: 80K **Privately Held**
WEB: www.fxmodels.com
SIC: 3999 7812 Design & Mfg Industrial Models

(G-4481)
GENOVESE MANUFACTURING CO
8 Bombard Ct (06786-4403)
P.O. Box 2112, Bristol (06011-2112)
PHONE..................................860 582-9944
Mike Genovese, *Vice Pres*
Vincent Genovese Jr, *Shareholder*
EMP: 10
SQ FT: 15,000
SALES (est): 1.7MM **Privately Held**
SIC: 3599 Machine Shop Jobbing & Repair

(G-4482)
GRAHAM TOOL AND MACHINE LLC
9 Container Dr (06786-7302)
PHONE..................................860 585-1261
Michael Graham, *Mng Member*
EMP: 6
SQ FT: 3,300
SALES (est): 869.6K **Privately Held**
SIC: 3599 Mfg Industrial Machinery

(G-4483)
KEMBY MANUFACTURING
56 E Orchard St (06786-6113)
P.O. Box 116 (06786-0116)
PHONE..................................860 582-2850
EMP: 3
SQ FT: 2,400
SALES: 100K **Privately Held**
SIC: 3451 Mfg Screw Machine Products

(G-4484)
LAURETANO SIGN GROUP INC
1 Tremco Dr (06786-7311)
PHONE..................................860 582-0233
Michael Lauretano, *President*
Patrick Byrne, *President*
Joanne West, *Corp Secy*
EMP: 50
SQ FT: 28,000
SALES (est): 9.3MM **Privately Held**
WEB: www.lauretano.com
SIC: 3993 Mfg Signs/Advertising Specialties

(G-4485)
MALCO INC
Also Called: Brass Traditions
38 Napco Dr (06786-7307)
P.O. Box 326 (06786-0326)
PHONE..................................860 584-0446
Michael L Theriault, *President*
Allen J Theriault, *Vice Pres*
Allen Theriault, *Vice Pres*
EMP: 11 **EST:** 1972
SQ FT: 8,000
SALES (est): 1.8MM **Privately Held**
WEB: www.malco.com
SIC: 3648 Mfg Lighting Equipment

(G-4486)
MICHAUD TOOL CO INC
122 Napco Dr (06786-7309)
P.O. Box 430 (06786-0430)
PHONE..................................860 582-6785
Roy Michaud, *President*
Darlene Michaud, *Corp Secy*
James Michaud, *Vice Pres*
EMP: 5
SQ FT: 4,500
SALES (est): 623.9K **Privately Held**
SIC: 3599 3544 Electrical Discharge Machining & Mfg Cutting Tools Machine Tools Accessories & Machinists' Precision Measuring Devices

(G-4487)
NEW ENGLAND FUELS & ENERGY LLC
86 Allen St (06786-6403)
PHONE..................................860 585-5917
James Schultz, *Principal*
EMP: 3 **EST:** 2010
SALES (est): 168.9K **Privately Held**
SIC: 2869 Mfg Industrial Organic Chemicals

(G-4488)
NORTH EAST FASTENERS CORP
8 Tremco Dr (06786-7312)
P.O. Box 322 (06786-0322)
PHONE..................................860 589-3242
Eric Webster, *President*
Diane Webster, *Vice Pres*
Joseph Longo, *QC Mgr*
▲ **EMP:** 22
SQ FT: 9,000
SALES (est): 3.7MM **Privately Held**
WEB: www.nef1.com
SIC: 3452 3316 Mfg Bolts/Screws/Rivets Mfg Cold-Rolled Steel Shapes

(G-4489)
R & I MANUFACTURING CO
118 Napco Dr (06786-7309)
PHONE..................................860 589-6364
Bruce Czatlicki, *Owner*
EMP: 10 **EST:** 1968
SQ FT: 2,400
SALES (est): 1.1MM **Privately Held**
SIC: 3535 Mfg Conveyors/Equipment

(G-4490)
RAY MACHINE CORPORATION
84 Town Hill Rd (06786-5802)
P.O. Box 47 (06786-0047)
PHONE..................................860 582-8202
Raymond Lassy, *President*
Brian Lassy, *Vice Pres*
EMP: 20 **EST:** 1955
SQ FT: 15,000
SALES: 700K **Privately Held**
WEB: www.raymachinecorp.com
SIC: 3545 3544 Mfg Precision Machined Components Cnc And Conventional Machining Swiss Type Screw Machining

(G-4491)
SNOWATHOME LLC
84 Napco Dr Ste 6 (06786-7315)
PHONE..................................860 584-2991
Matt Pittman, *Principal*
Alissa Pittman, *COO*
▲ **EMP:** 3
SALES (est): 401.8K **Privately Held**
SIC: 3585 Mfg Refrigeration/Heating Equipment

(G-4492)
SPARGO MACHINE PRODUCTS INC
6 Gear Dr (06786-7314)
PHONE..................................860 583-3925
Randy Spargo, *President*
Carole Spargo, *Admin Sec*
EMP: 11
SALES (est): 1.9MM **Privately Held**
SIC: 3599 Job Shop

(G-4493)
TECHNOLOGY PLASTICS LLC
75 Napco Dr (06786-7305)
PHONE..................................806 583-1590
Tom Fernandes, *CEO*
Edward Butkevich,
▲ **EMP:** 15
SQ FT: 46,000
SALES (est): 2.2MM **Privately Held**
SIC: 3089 Mfg Plastic Products

(G-4494)
TRIEM INDUSTRIES LLC
105 Napco Dr (06786-7310)
PHONE..................................203 888-1212
Douglas A Mola, *Mng Member*
Lea A Mola, *Mng Member*
Robert D Mola,
▲ **EMP:** 28
SQ FT: 23,000
SALES (est): 5.8MM **Privately Held**
WEB: www.triemindustries.com
SIC: 3452 Mfg Bolts/Screws/Rivets

(G-4495)
UNIPRISE INTERNATIONAL INC
Also Called: Uniprise Sales
50 Napco Dr (06786-7307)
P.O. Box 369 (06786-0369)
PHONE..................................860 589-7262
Philip Porter, *President*
Douglas Porter, *Vice Pres*

EMP: 24
SQ FT: 10,000
SALES (est): 4.7MM **Privately Held**
SIC: 3599 3423 Mfg Flexible Metal Tubing & Soldering Tools

(G-4496)
VICTORY FUEL LLC
248 Main St (06786-5901)
PHONE....860 585-0532
Samuel J Gizzie Jr, *Owner*
EMP: 8
SALES (est): 903.6K **Privately Held**
SIC: 2869 Mfg Industrial Organic Chemicals

Thomaston
Litchfield County

(G-4497)
ALBEA THOMASTON INC
60 Electric Ave (06787-1617)
PHONE....860 283-2000
Francois Luscan, *CEO*
▲ **EMP:** 370
SQ FT: 150,000
SALES (est): 121.4MM **Privately Held**
SIC: 2844 Mfg Toilet Preparations
HQ: Albea Americas, Inc.
191 State Route 31 N
Washington NJ 07882

(G-4498)
BEARDSWORTH GROUP INC
1085 Waterbury Rd (06787-2028)
P.O. Box 358, Woodbury (06798-0358)
PHONE....860 283-4014
Douglas Beardsworth, *President*
Carrie Beardsworth, *Admin Sec*
▲ **EMP:** 5
SALES (est): 885.2K **Privately Held**
WEB: www.beardsworthgroup.com
SIC: 3565 5084 Mfg Packaging Machinery Whol Industrial Equipment

(G-4499)
BIEDERMANN MFG INDS INC
Also Called: B M I South
135 S Main St (06787-1754)
PHONE....860 283-8268
Fax: 860 283-5222
EMP: 50
SALES (corp-wide): 5.7MM **Privately Held**
SIC: 3451 Mfr Screw Machine Products
PA: Biedermann Manufacturing Industries Incorporated
4500 Preslyn Dr
Raleigh NC
919 878-7776

(G-4500)
BROOKFIELD INDUSTRIES INC
99 W Hillside Ave (06787-1433)
PHONE....860 283-6211
Karl P Kinzer, *President*
Chris S Kinzer, *Vice Pres*
EMP: 25
SQ FT: 10,000
SALES: 4.7MM **Privately Held**
WEB: www.brookfieldindustries.com
SIC: 3699 3429 Mfg Electrical Equipment/Supplies Mfg Hardware

(G-4501)
DON S SCREW MACHINE PDTS LLC
247 Old Northfield Rd (06787-1140)
PHONE....860 283-6448
Donald Carl Schlicher,
EMP: 3
SALES (est): 114.3K **Privately Held**
SIC: 3451 Mfg Screw Machine Products

(G-4502)
EDWARD SEGAL INC
360 Reynolds Bridge Rd (06787-1914)
P.O. Box 429 (06787-0429)
PHONE....860 283-5821
David Segal, *President*
Margaret Bartone, *Purchasing*
Tommy Trufan, *Engineer*
Fred Nadeau, *Marketing Mgr*
Richard Segal, *Shareholder*
▲ **EMP:** 20 **EST:** 1942
SQ FT: 20,000
SALES (est): 4.5MM **Privately Held**
SIC: 3559 Mfg Misc Industry Machinery

(G-4503)
ELEMENT 119 LLC
296 Reynolds Bridge Rd (06787-1996)
PHONE....860 358-0119
Andrew Zeppa, *President*
EMP: 10
SQ FT: 4,000
SALES (est): 4MM **Privately Held**
SIC: 2851 Mfg Paints/Allied Products

(G-4504)
INTRASONICS INC
1401 Waterbury Rd (06787-2030)
P.O. Box 186 (06787-0186)
PHONE....860 283-8040
Keith Rogozinski, *President*
Peter Rogozinski, *President*
Donald Charette, *Admin Sec*
EMP: 5
SALES (est): 726.2K **Privately Held**
WEB: www.intrasonics.com
SIC: 3599 Machine Shop

(G-4505)
J & J PRECISION EYELET INC
116 Waterbury Rd (06787-1829)
PHONE....860 283-8243
John Stephen Maxwell, *President*
EMP: 70
SQ FT: 3,000
SALES: 13.7MM **Privately Held**
WEB: www.jjprecision.com
SIC: 3965 2834 3469 Mfg Fasteners/Buttons/Pins Mfg Pharmaceutical Preparations Mfg Metal Stampings

(G-4506)
JFS INDUSTRIES
90 Walnut St Apt B (06787-1553)
PHONE....203 592-0754
EMP: 3
SALES (est): 146.3K **Privately Held**
SIC: 3999 Mfg Misc Products

(G-4507)
K-TEC LLC
33 River St Ste 2 (06787-1714)
PHONE....860 283-8875
Milan Keklak,
EMP: 4
SALES: 175K **Privately Held**
WEB: www.ktecmolding.com
SIC: 3089 Mfg Plastic Products

(G-4508)
LASER TOOL COMPANY INC
98 N Main St (06787-1654)
P.O. Box 278 (06787-0278)
PHONE....860 283-8284
Faye Duquette, *President*
EMP: 15
SQ FT: 4,840
SALES (est): 2MM **Privately Held**
SIC: 3541 Mfg Machine Tools-Cutting

(G-4509)
METALLON INC
1415 Waterbury Rd (06787-2030)
PHONE....860 283-8265
Paul P Ayoub, *Principal*
Dennis Hayes, *Project Mgr*
Susan Ackers, *Human Res Mgr*
John Zoldy, *Manager*
Sarkis Balikian, *Supervisor*
EMP: 50
SQ FT: 30,000
SALES (est): 11.6MM **Privately Held**
WEB: www.metallon.com
SIC: 3469 3728 Mfg Metal Stampings Mfg Aircraft Parts/Equipment

(G-4510)
NATIONAL SPRING & STAMPING INC
135 S Main St Ste 8 (06787-1754)
P.O. Box 369 (06787-0369)
PHONE....860 283-0203
Walter Janczyk, *President*
William Yeske III, *Corp Secy*
Raymond Kowalec, *Vice Pres*
EMP: 22
SQ FT: 8,000
SALES (est): 4.3MM **Privately Held**
WEB: www.nationalsprings.com
SIC: 3495 3469 Mfg Wire Springs Mfg Metal Stampings

(G-4511)
QUALITY ROLLING DEBURRING INC
135 S Main St Ste 3 (06787-1754)
P.O. Box 128 (06787-0128)
PHONE....860 283-0271
George Lacapra, *Ch of Bd*
George Lacapra Jr, *President*
Ronald Stango, *Director*
EMP: 90 **EST:** 1949
SQ FT: 110,000
SALES (est): 8.6MM **Privately Held**
WEB: www.qualityrolling.com
SIC: 3471 Plating/Polishing Service

(G-4512)
REYNOLDS CARBIDE DIE CO INC
27 Reynolds Bridge Rd (06787-1910)
P.O. Box 326 (06787-0326)
PHONE....860 283-8246
James Zaccaria, *President*
Michael Masi Jr, *Vice Pres*
EMP: 35 **EST:** 1971
SQ FT: 12,000
SALES (est): 5.9MM **Privately Held**
WEB: www.rcdinc.com
SIC: 3552 3544 Mfg Textile Machinery Mfg Dies/Tools/Jigs/Fixtures

(G-4513)
S & M SWISS PRODUCTS INC
135 S Main St Ste 7 (06787-1754)
PHONE....860 283-4020
Gerald Maccione, *President*
EMP: 4 **EST:** 1978
SQ FT: 5,400
SALES (est): 552.4K **Privately Held**
SIC: 3451 Mfg Swiss Screw Machine Products

(G-4514)
SELECTIVES LLC
166 Litchfield St (06787-1427)
P.O. Box 336 (06787-0336)
PHONE....860 585-1956
EMP: 5
SALES (est): 475.2K **Privately Held**
SIC: 3089 Mfg Plastic Products

(G-4515)
STEVENS COMPANY INCORPORATED
1085 Waterbury Rd 1 (06787-2028)
P.O. Box 428 (06787-0428)
PHONE....860 283-8201
Doug Stevens, *President*
Jannette Stevens, *President*
Michele Caulfield, *Admin Sec*
▲ **EMP:** 65
SQ FT: 40,000
SALES: 5.1MM **Privately Held**
WEB: www.stevenscompanyinc.com
SIC: 3469 3965 Manufacturing Metal Stampings Manufacturing Fasteners/Buttons/Pins

(G-4516)
STEWART EFI LLC (PA)
45 Old Waterbury Rd (06787-1903)
PHONE....860 283-8213
Mike Morrissey, *President*
Angel Sanchez, *Plant Mgr*
Debbie Eckert, *Buyer*
Chris Carey, *Engineer*
Marty Dionne, *Engineer*
EMP: 105
SQ FT: 98,000
SALES (est): 64.6MM **Privately Held**
WEB: www.stewartefi.com
SIC: 3469 Mfg Metal Stampings

(G-4517)
STEWART EFI LLC
332 Reynolds Bridge Rd (06787-1914)
PHONE....860 283-2523
Daniel Stokes, *Manager*
EMP: 25
SALES (corp-wide): 64.6MM **Privately Held**
WEB: www.stewartefi.com
SIC: 3469 Mfg Metal Stampings
PA: Stewart Efi, Llc
45 Old Waterbury Rd
Thomaston CT 06787
860 283-8213

(G-4518)
STEWART EFI CONNECTICUT LLC
45 Old Waterbury Rd (06787-1903)
PHONE....860 283-8213
Steve Sauvron, *Purch Mgr*
Daniel Stokes, *Mng Member*
Phillip Rejeski,
Bernie Rosselli,
EMP: 110
SQ FT: 98,000
SALES (est): 18.7MM
SALES (corp-wide): 64.6MM **Privately Held**
WEB: www.stewartefi.com
SIC: 3469 Mfg Metal Stampings
PA: Stewart Efi, Llc
45 Old Waterbury Rd
Thomaston CT 06787
860 283-8213

(G-4519)
SUMMIT CORPORATION OF AMERICA
Also Called: Summit Finishing Division
1430 Waterbury Rd (06787-2098)
PHONE....860 283-4391
Harry M Scoble, *Principal*
Larry Buhl, *Director*
Daniel Stokes, *Director*
Linda L Scapellati, *Admin Sec*
▲ **EMP:** 83
SQ FT: 140,000
SALES (est): 23.7MM **Privately Held**
WEB: www.scact.com
SIC: 3471 3479 Plating/Polishing Service Coating/Engraving Service

(G-4520)
THOMASTN-MDTOWN SCREW MCH PDTS
550 N Main St (06787-1315)
P.O. Box 249 (06787-0249)
PHONE....860 283-9796
Robert P Lyman, *President*
Celeste Parsons, *Vice Pres*
EMP: 15 **EST:** 1963
SQ FT: 7,500
SALES (est): 2.2MM **Privately Held**
WEB: www.mypww.com
SIC: 3451 Mfg Screw Machine Products

(G-4521)
THOMASTON INDUSTRIES INC
41 Electric Ave (06787-1651)
P.O. Box 308 (06787-0308)
PHONE....860 283-4358
Dennis Diemand, *President*
EMP: 10
SALES (est): 1.7MM **Privately Held**
SIC: 3451 3999 Mfg Screw Machine Products Mfg Misc Products

(G-4522)
TREADWELL CORPORATION
341 Railroad St (06787-1667)
P.O. Box 458 (06787-0458)
PHONE....860 283-7600
John A Johnson, *CEO*
Robert Johnson, *COO*
Steven Malaspina, *Exec VP*
Michael Patruski, *Vice Pres*
EMP: 33
SQ FT: 30,000
SALES (est): 16.3MM **Privately Held**
WEB: www.treadwellcorp.com
SIC: 3564 Mfg Blowers/Fans

(G-4523)
TYLER AUTOMATICS INCORPORATED
Also Called: Thomaston Swiss
437 S Main St (06787-1816)
P.O. Box 247 (06787-0247)
PHONE....860 283-5878

George Kowaleski, *President*
EMP: 20 **EST:** 1947
SQ FT: 20,000
SALES (est): 5.9MM **Privately Held**
SIC: 3451 Mfg Screw Machine Products

(G-4524)
UNIMETAL SURFACE FINISHING LLC (PA)
135 S Main St (06787-1754)
P.O. Box 902 (06787-0902)
PHONE..................................860 283-0271
Armand Deangelis, *Plant Mgr*
Ron Stango, *Facilities Mgr*
Marco Quintana, *Engineer*
Michele Sovia, *Sales Staff*
George Lacapra Jr, *Mng Member*
EMP: 50 **EST:** 2011
SALES (est): 22.7MM **Privately Held**
SIC: 2843 Mfg Surface Active Agents

(G-4525)
WARD LEONARD CT LLC (DH)
401 Watertown Rd (06787-1990)
PHONE..................................860 283-5801
Jon Carter, *CEO*
Mike Clute, *President*
Bill Berger, *Business Mgr*
David Michelin, *Senior Buyer*
Ed Iulo, *Buyer*
◆ **EMP:** 199
SQ FT: 135,000
SALES (est): 49.5MM
SALES (corp-wide): 49.5MM **Privately Held**
SIC: 3621 3625 Mfg Motors/Generators Mfg Relays/Industrial Controls
HQ: Ward Leonard Operating Llc
401 Watertown Rd
Thomaston CT 06787
860 283-5801

(G-4526)
WARD LEONARD CT LLC
401 Watertown Rd (06787-1990)
PHONE..................................860 283-2294
Jon Carter, *President*
EMP: 56
SQ FT: 150,000
SALES (corp-wide): 49.5MM **Privately Held**
SIC: 3621 Mfg Motor Generator Sets & Specialty Motors
HQ: Ward Leonard Ct Llc
401 Watertown Rd
Thomaston CT 06787
860 283-5801

(G-4527)
WHYCO FINISHING TECH LLC
670 Waterbury Rd (06787-2099)
PHONE..................................860 283-5826
William Nicholas Post, *Mng Member*
EMP: 47
SQ FT: 100,000
SALES (est): 6MM **Privately Held**
SIC: 3471 Plating/Polishing Service

(G-4528)
WTM COMPANY
135 S Main St Ste 12 (06787-1754)
P.O. Box 226 (06787-0226)
PHONE..................................860 283-5871
Stanley E Mossey, *President*
John R Laone, *President*
EMP: 5
SQ FT: 7,500
SALES (est): 880K **Privately Held**
SIC: 3429 Mfg Hardware

(G-4529)
ZERO CHECK LLC
297 Reynolds Bridge Rd (06787-1974)
P.O. Box 903 (06787-0903)
PHONE..................................860 283-5629
James Upton,
EMP: 8 **EST:** 1983
SQ FT: 8,600
SALES (est): 1.3MM **Privately Held**
WEB: www.zerocheck.com
SIC: 3545 Mfg Machine Tool Accessories

Thompson
Windham County

(G-4530)
AJ MFG
999 Quaddick Town Farm Rd (06277-2918)
P.O. Box 435 (06277-0435)
PHONE..................................860 963-7622
Pamela Bellavance, *Owner*
EMP: 5
SALES (est): 547.1K **Privately Held**
SIC: 2273 Mfg Carpets/Rugs

(G-4531)
B H DAVIS CO
227 Riverside Dr (06277-2713)
P.O. Box 70, Grosvenor Dale (06246-0070)
PHONE..................................860 923-2771
Bernard Davis, *Owner*
EMP: 3
SQ FT: 3,000
SALES: 100K **Privately Held**
SIC: 2431 5712 Mfg Millwork Ret Furniture

(G-4532)
BEN BARRETTS LLC
129 Robbins Rd (06277-2846)
PHONE..................................860 928-9373
Bernard Barrett, *President*
EMP: 5
SALES (est): 371.8K **Privately Held**
SIC: 2426 5031 5023 5211 Hardwood Dimension/Floor Mill Whol Lumber/Plywood/Millwork Whol Homefurnishings Ret Lumber/Building Mtrl

(G-4533)
CENTURY TOOL CO INC
753 Thompson Rd (06277-1939)
P.O. Box 314 (06277-0314)
PHONE..................................860 923-9523
Joseph Simonelli, *President*
EMP: 18
SQ FT: 8,000
SALES: 1.5MM **Privately Held**
WEB: www.centurytoolco.com
SIC: 3544 Mfg Dies/Tools/Jigs/Fixtures

(G-4534)
JS INDUSTRIES
526 Quaddick Rd (06277-2911)
PHONE..................................860 928-0786
Joe Suich, *Principal*
EMP: 3 **EST:** 2017
SALES (est): 174.5K **Privately Held**
SIC: 3999 Mfg Misc Products

(G-4535)
LINCOLN PRECISION MACHINE INC
923 Thompson Rd (06277-1909)
PHONE..................................860 923-9358
Ronald Lincoln, *President*
Todd Lincoln, *Vice Pres*
EMP: 5 **EST:** 1997
SALES: 400K **Privately Held**
SIC: 3599 Mfg Industrial Machinery

(G-4536)
MOLDVISION LLC
316 County Home Rd (06277-2845)
PHONE..................................860 315-1025
John Carpenter, *President*
EMP: 3
SALES (est): 175.5K **Privately Held**
SIC: 3544 Mfg Dies/Tools/Jigs/Fixtures

(G-4537)
NUMA TOOL COMPANY (PA)
646 Thompson Rd (06277-2252)
P.O. Box 348 (06277-0348)
PHONE..................................860 923-9551
Ralph H Leonard, *President*
Laurene Darling, *Purch Mgr*
Mark Stickney, *CFO*
Dena Dugas, *Info Tech Mgr*
Wendy Bouchey, *Administration*
▼ **EMP:** 80
SQ FT: 52,000
SALES: 16MM **Privately Held**
WEB: www.numadth.com
SIC: 3532 3531 3533 5082 Mfg Mining Machinery Mfg Construction Mach Mfg Oil/Gas Field Mach Whol Cnstn/Mining Mach

Tolland
Tolland County

(G-4538)
ACCU-RITE TOOL & MFG CO
23 Industrial Park Rd W B (06084-2861)
PHONE..................................860 688-4844
Steve Gessay, *President*
Christophe Gessay, *Vice Pres*
Benjamin Wells, *Engineer*
EMP: 11 **EST:** 1956
SQ FT: 6,500
SALES: 1.1MM **Privately Held**
SIC: 3545 Mfg Machine Tool Accessories

(G-4539)
B & D MACHINE INC
30 Industrial Park Rd E (06084-2805)
P.O. Box 791 (06084-0791)
PHONE..................................860 871-9226
Robert Stutz, *President*
Donald Gagnon, *Vice Pres*
Kenneth Gibbons, *Treasurer*
EMP: 12
SQ FT: 9,000
SALES: 1.5MM **Privately Held**
WEB: www.bdmachine.net
SIC: 3544 Mfg Dies/Tools/Jigs/Fixtures

(G-4540)
BLUE CHIP TOOL
40 Tolland Stage Rd D4 (06084-2341)
PHONE..................................860 875-7999
Fred Bulach, *Owner*
EMP: 3
SALES: 250K **Privately Held**
SIC: 3545 Mfg Machine Tool Accessories

(G-4541)
CONNECTICUT COMPONENTS INC
Also Called: Cciyes
60 Industrial Park Rd W # 2 (06084-2838)
PHONE..................................860 633-0277
Kimberly Jean Giansanti, *President*
▲ **EMP:** 6 **EST:** 1973
SALES: 3MM **Privately Held**
WEB: www.cciyes.com
SIC: 3999 Mfg Misc Products

(G-4542)
D D M METAL FINISHING CO INC
25 Industrial Park Rd W (06084-2806)
P.O. Box 687 (06084-0687)
PHONE..................................860 872-4683
Daniel R Castonguay, *President*
EMP: 8
SQ FT: 2,500
SALES (est): 1MM **Privately Held**
SIC: 3471 Plating/Polishing Service

(G-4543)
DALBERGIA LLC (PA)
58 Gerber Dr (06084-2851)
PHONE..................................860 870-2500
Charles E Wilson, *Manager*
EMP: 3
SALES (est): 343.2K **Privately Held**
SIC: 2431 Mfg Millwork

(G-4544)
DARI-FARMS ICE CREAM CO INC
55 Gerber Dr (06084-2851)
PHONE..................................860 872-8313
EMP: 13
SALES (est): 1.9MM **Privately Held**
SIC: 2024 Mfg Ice Cream/Frozen Desert

(G-4545)
DATA TECHNOLOGY INC
24 Industrial Park Rd W (06084-2806)
PHONE..................................860 871-8082
David Buckley, *President*
Leonard Marano, *Vice Pres*
Terry Grainger, *Engineer*
Lidia Mireles, *Finance Dir*
Erica Clendening, *Manager*
EMP: 25 **EST:** 1960
SQ FT: 29,000
SALES (est): 2.8MM
SALES (corp-wide): 258.7MM **Privately Held**
WEB: www.data-technology.com
SIC: 3577 3829 3827 Mfg Computer Peripherals Mfg Measure/Control Dvcs Mfg Optical Instr/Lens
PA: Gerber Scientific Llc
24 Indl Pk Rd W
Tolland CT 06084
860 871-8082

(G-4546)
E AND S GAGE INC
Also Called: E & S Gauge Company
38 Gerber Dr (06084-2851)
PHONE..................................860 872-5917
Kevin S Hilinski, *President*
EMP: 12 **EST:** 1953
SQ FT: 2,500
SALES: 1.6MM **Privately Held**
SIC: 3545 3544 Mfg Machine Tool Accessories Mfg Dies/Tools/Jigs/Fixtures

(G-4547)
ENVIRONICS INC
69 Industrial Park Rd E (06084-2873)
PHONE..................................860 872-1111
Catherine S Dunn, *CEO*
Terrence P Dunn, *President*
Cathy Dunnn, *Vice Pres*
Rachel M Stansel, *Vice Pres*
Karl Sentivany, *Production*
EMP: 20
SQ FT: 15,000
SALES: 4.1MM **Privately Held**
WEB: www.environics.com
SIC: 3823 3821 Mfg Process Control Instruments Mfg Lab Apparatus/Furniture

(G-4548)
GERBER SCIENTIFIC LLC (PA)
24 Indl Pk Rd W (06084)
PHONE..................................860 871-8082
Michael Elia, *President*
Patti Burmahl, *Vice Pres*
Steven Gore, *Vice Pres*
John Henderson, *Vice Pres*
James Martin, *Vice Pres*
◆ **EMP:** 200 **EST:** 1948
SQ FT: 250,000
SALES: 258.7MM **Privately Held**
WEB: www.gerberscientific.com
SIC: 3993 7336 3851 7372 Mfg Signs/Ad Specialties Coml Art/Graphic Design Mfg Ophthalmic Goods Prepackaged Software Svc Mfg Computer Peripherals

(G-4549)
GERBER TECHNOLOGY LLC (HQ)
24 Industrial Park Rd W (06084-2806)
PHONE..................................860 871-8082
Mohit Uberoi, *CEO*
Scott Schinlever, *President*
Patricia L Burmahl, *Senior VP*
Steven Gore, *Senior VP*
Peter Morrissey, *Senior VP*
◆ **EMP:** 344
SQ FT: 260,000
SALES (est): 239MM
SALES (corp-wide): 283.5MM **Privately Held**
SIC: 3559 7371 Mfg Misc Industry Machinery Custom Computer Programing
PA: American Industrial Partners, L.P.
1 Maritime Plz Ste 1925
San Francisco CA 94111
415 788-7354

(G-4550)
LOON MEDICAL INC
1 Technology Dr (06084-3902)
PHONE..................................860 373-0217
Kevin Miller, *President*
EMP: 5
SALES (est): 373.7K **Privately Held**
SIC: 3845 Electromedical Equipment

GEOGRAPHIC

(G-4551)
NORTHEAST STAIR COMPANY LLC
185 Buff Cap Rd (06084-2613)
PHONE....................860 875-3358
William Drzyzga,
Pat Drzyzga,
EMP: 6
SALES: 650K **Privately Held**
WEB: www.northeasttimes.com
SIC: 2431 Mfg Millwork

(G-4552)
SOLDREAM SPCIAL PROCESS - WLDG
203 Hartford Tpke (06084-2821)
PHONE....................860 858-5247
Maggie Pytel, *Purch Mgr*
EMP: 3
SALES (est): 165.2K **Privately Held**
SIC: 3599 Mfg Industrial Machinery

(G-4553)
SYSTEMS AND TECH INTL INC
24 Goose Ln Ste 5 (06084-3417)
PHONE....................860 871-0401
Joseph J Mahar, *President*
EMP: 5
SQ FT: 1,500
SALES (est): 690.5K **Privately Held**
SIC: 3548 5065 Mfg Soldering & Curing Systems Imports Surface Mount Electronic Equip & Exports Semiconductors

(G-4554)
TITANIUM INDUSTRIES INC
362 Mile Hill Rd (06084-3605)
PHONE....................860 870-3939
Brett Paddock, *CEO*
EMP: 3 **Privately Held**
SIC: 3356 Nonferrous Rolling/Drawing
PA: Titanium Industries, Inc.
18 Green Pond Rd Ste 1
Rockaway NJ 07866

(G-4555)
TOOLMAX DESIGNING TOOLING INC
69 Industrial Park Rd E A (06084-2873)
P.O. Box 103 (06084-0103)
PHONE....................860 871-7265
Michael A Tyler, *President*
Sally A Tyler, *Corp Secy*
EMP: 4
SALES (est): 501.8K **Privately Held**
SIC: 3423 Mfg Hand/Edge Tools

Torrington
Litchfield County

(G-4556)
ALPHA MAGNETICS & COILS INC
527 Westledge Dr (06790-4490)
PHONE....................860 496-0122
Shiban Qasba, *President*
▲ **EMP:** 4
SALES: 250K **Privately Held**
SIC: 3677 5731 Mfg Elec Coil/Transfrmrs Ret Radio/Tv/Electronics

(G-4557)
ALTEK COMPANY
89 Commercial Blvd Ste 1 (06790-7215)
P.O. Box 1128 (06790-1128)
PHONE....................860 482-7626
Stephen Altschuler, *President*
Joan Altschuler, *Admin Sec*
EMP: 180
SALES (est): 909.6K **Privately Held**
WEB: www.altekcompany.com
SIC: 3625 Mfg Relays/Industrial Controls

(G-4558)
ALTEK ELECTRONICS INC
89 Commercial Blvd (06790-7215)
P.O. Box 1128 (06790-1128)
PHONE....................860 482-7626
David Altschuler, *CEO*
Stephen Altschuler, *Ch of Bd*
Sabrina Beck, *Vice Pres*
▲ **EMP:** 170
SQ FT: 65,000
SALES: 27.8MM **Privately Held**
WEB: www.electronics.altekcompany.com
SIC: 3825 3599 3625 3672 Mfg Elec Measuring Instr Mfg Industrial Machinery Mfg Relay/Indstl Control Mfg Printed Circuit Brds Nonfrs Wiredrwng/Insltng

(G-4559)
AMERICAN-REPUBLICAN INC
122 Franklin St (06790-5508)
PHONE....................860 496-9301
Brigitte Ruthman, *Branch Mgr*
EMP: 107
SALES (corp-wide): 24MM **Privately Held**
SIC: 2711 Newspapers-Publishing/Printing
PA: American-Republican, Incorporated
389 Meadow St
Waterbury CT 06702
203 574-3636

(G-4560)
AN DESIGNS INC
111 Putter Ln (06790-2360)
PHONE....................860 618-0183
Robert Nilsson, *President*
EMP: 5
SALES (est): 570K **Privately Held**
SIC: 3423 Mfg Tools For Auto Industry

(G-4561)
ANDRITZ SHW INC
90 Commercial Blvd (06790-3097)
P.O. Box 238 (06790-0238)
PHONE....................860 496-8888
George Shank, *CEO*
George L Shank, *CEO*
Ulrich Severing, *President*
▲ **EMP:** 30
SQ FT: 50,000
SALES: 8.1MM
SALES (corp-wide): 416.3MM **Privately Held**
WEB: www.shwinc.com
SIC: 3554 Mfg Paper Industrial Machinery
HQ: Shw Casting Technologies Gmbh
Stiewingstr. 101
Aalen 73433
736 137-0239

(G-4562)
APTAR INC
301 Ella Grasso Ave (06790-2346)
PHONE....................860 489-6249
Wayne Maw, *Principal*
Lise Fitzpatrick, *Office Mgr*
EMP: 3
SALES (est): 717.7K **Privately Held**
SIC: 3083 Mfg Laminated Plastic Plate/Sheet

(G-4563)
ASTI COMPANY INC
953 S Main St (06790-6941)
PHONE....................860 482-2675
Americo Marola, *President*
Edna Marola, *Vice Pres*
EMP: 3 **EST:** 1977
SQ FT: 2,400
SALES: 85K **Privately Held**
SIC: 3089 Mfg Plastic Products

(G-4564)
BETTER BAKING BY BETH
270 W Hill Rd (06790-2337)
PHONE....................860 482-4706
Beth Zukowski, *Principal*
EMP: 8
SALES (est): 721.6K **Privately Held**
SIC: 2051 Mfg Bread/Related Products

(G-4565)
BEY-LOW MOLDS
80 Sunrise Dr (06790-5848)
PHONE....................860 482-6561
Alan Beyer, *Owner*
EMP: 3
SALES (est): 159.7K **Privately Held**
SIC: 3089 Mfg Plastic Products

(G-4566)
BICRON ELECTRONICS COMPANY (PA)
427 Goshen Rd (06790-2601)
PHONE....................860 482-2524
Chris Skomorowski, *President*
Ron Flores, *Business Mgr*
William J Zeronsa, *Treasurer*
Lisa Skomorowski, *Admin Sec*
◆ **EMP:** 79 **EST:** 1964
SQ FT: 30,000
SALES (est): 13.3MM **Privately Held**
WEB: www.bicronusa.com
SIC: 3612 3679 3677 Mfg Transformers Mfg Electronic Components Mfg Electronic Coils/Transformers

(G-4567)
BRICINS INC
347 Technology Park Dr (06790-2594)
P.O. Box 162, Harwinton (06791-0162)
PHONE....................860 482-0250
EMP: 10
SQ FT: 16,000
SALES (est): 1.4MM **Privately Held**
SIC: 2051 Mfg Bread/Related Products

(G-4568)
BRISTOL PRESS
Also Called: Thomaston Express, The Div
188 Main St (06790)
P.O. Box 2158, Bristol (06011-2158)
PHONE....................860 584-0501
Robert Jelenic, *President*
Jazzya Coakley, *Opers Staff*
Bradford Carroll, *Manager*
EMP: 100 **EST:** 1871
SQ FT: 24,000
SALES (est): 4.1MM
SALES (corp-wide): 693.9MM **Privately Held**
WEB: www.journalregister.com
SIC: 2711 Newspapers-Publishing/Printing
PA: Journal Register Company
5 Hanover Sq Fl 25
New York NY 10004

(G-4569)
BROTHERS & SONS SUGAR HOUSE
998 Saw Mill Hill Rd (06790-2121)
PHONE....................860 489-2719
Frances Schoonmaker, *Owner*
EMP: 4 **EST:** 1992
SALES (est): 241K **Privately Held**
SIC: 2099 Mfg Food Preparations

(G-4570)
COLONIAL BRONZE COMPANY
511 Winsted Rd (06790-2932)
P.O. Box 207 (06790-0207)
PHONE....................860 489-9233
Jamie V Gregg, *CEO*
▲ **EMP:** 55
SQ FT: 50,000
SALES (est): 10.7MM **Privately Held**
WEB: www.colonialbronze.com
SIC: 3429 3432 Mfg Hardware Mfg Plumbing Fixture Fittings

(G-4571)
COMMERCIAL SEWING INC
65 Grant St (06790-6899)
P.O. Box 1173 (06790-1173)
PHONE....................860 482-5509
Samuel G Mazzarelli, *CEO*
Greg Perosino, *President*
David Mazzarelli, *Vice Pres*
Stephen Mazzarelli, *Vice Pres*
▲ **EMP:** 140 **EST:** 1967
SQ FT: 30,000
SALES (est): 26.7MM **Privately Held**
WEB: www.commercialsewing.com
SIC: 3161 2394 Mfg Luggage Mfg Canvas/Related Products

(G-4572)
CONAIR CORPORATION
Also Called: Waring Products Division
314 Ella Grasso Ave (06790-2345)
P.O. Box 3201 (06790-8181)
PHONE....................800 492-7464
Dave Kayser, *Engineer*
Fran Ney, *Marketing Staff*
Richard Dombroski, *Manager*
EMP: 66
SALES (corp-wide): 2B **Privately Held**
WEB: www.conair.com
SIC: 3634 5064 8741 7629 Mfg Elec Housewares/Fans Whol Appliances/Tv/Radio Management Services Electrical Repair Mfg Food Prdts Mach
PA: Conair Corporation
1 Cummings Point Rd
Stamford CT 06902
203 351-9000

(G-4573)
CONNECTCUT PRCSION CMPNNTS LLC
Also Called: CP
588 S Main St Rear (06790-6944)
PHONE....................860 489-8621
Deb Guilmart,
Mike S Pierre,
EMP: 6
SQ FT: 4,200
SALES (est): 588.3K **Privately Held**
SIC: 3965 Mfg Needles

(G-4574)
DESIGN ENGINEERING INC
245 E Elm St (06790-5059)
PHONE....................860 482-4120
Charles H Gumbert, *President*
Terrance R Bell, *Vice Pres*
Dawn Florio, *Admin Sec*
EMP: 5
SALES: 500K **Privately Held**
SIC: 3089 7389 Plastics Fabricator

(G-4575)
DYMAX CORPORATION
Also Called: Dymax Oligomers & Coatings
51 Greenwoods Rd (06790-2349)
PHONE....................860 626-7006
Yamaira Rodriguez, *Production*
Colleen Rood, *Administration*
EMP: 9
SALES (corp-wide): 103.6MM **Privately Held**
SIC: 2869 Mfg Industrial Organic Chemicals
PA: Dymax Corporation
318 Industrial Ln Ste 1
Torrington CT 06790
860 482-1010

(G-4576)
DYMAX MATERIALS INC (HQ)
51 Greenwoods Rd (06790-2349)
PHONE....................860 482-1010
Andrew Bachman, *President*
Jane Bachman, *Vice Pres*
EMP: 3
SQ FT: 20,000
SALES (est): 2.5MM
SALES (corp-wide): 103.6MM **Privately Held**
SIC: 2869 Mfg Industrial Organic Chemicals
PA: Dymax Corporation
318 Industrial Ln Ste 1
Torrington CT 06790
860 482-1010

(G-4577)
DYMAX OLIGOMERS & COATINGS
318 Industrial Ln (06790-7709)
PHONE....................860 626-7006
Roberta E Hagstrom, *President*
Greg Bachmann, *Chairman*
▲ **EMP:** 10
SQ FT: 15,000
SALES (est): 2.5MM
SALES (corp-wide): 103.6MM **Privately Held**
WEB: www.bomarspecialties.com
SIC: 2869 Mfg Industrial Organic Chemicals
HQ: Dymax Materials, Inc.
51 Greenwoods Rd
Torrington CT 06790

▲ = Import ▼=Export
◆ =Import/Export

(G-4578)
FRANKLIN PRINT SHOPPE INC
48 Main St (06790-5303)
PHONE..............................860 496-9516
Jean Murphy, *President*
EMP: 4
SQ FT: 1,000
SALES (est): 314.6K **Privately Held**
WEB: www.franklinprintshoppe.com
SIC: 2752 2791 Lithographic Commercial Printing Typesetting Services

(G-4579)
FUELCELL ENERGY INC
Also Called: Fuel Cell Manufacturing
539 Technology Park Dr (06790-2594)
PHONE..............................860 496-1111
Christopher R Bentley, *President*
Tom Lucas, *Engineer*
Jill Crossman, *Executive*
Rebecca Budny, *Technician*
EMP: 35
SALES (corp-wide): 89.4MM **Publicly Held**
WEB: www.fuelcellenergy.com
SIC: 3674 3621 3699 Mfg Semiconductors/Related Devices Mfg Motors/Generators Mfg Electrical Equipment/Supplies
PA: Fuelcell Energy, Inc.
3 Great Pasture Rd
Danbury CT 06810
203 825-6000

(G-4580)
GREGOR TECHNOLOGIES LLC
529 Technology Park Dr (06790-2594)
PHONE..............................860 482-2569
David H Hannah,
Janice Gregorich,
John Gregorich,
EMP: 49
SQ FT: 40,000
SALES (est): 11.7MM
SALES (corp-wide): 11.5B **Publicly Held**
WEB: www.gregortech.com
SIC: 3599 Mfg Industrial Machinery
HQ: Metals Usa Holdings Corp.
4901 Nw 17th Way Ste 405
Fort Lauderdale FL 33309
954 202-4000

(G-4581)
HANGER PRSTHETCS & ORTHO INC
811 E Main St Ste B (06790-3930)
PHONE..............................860 482-5611
Scott Greenstein, *Branch Mgr*
EMP: 7
SALES (corp-wide): 1B **Publicly Held**
SIC: 3842 Ret Misc Merchandise
HQ: Hanger Prosthetics & Orthotics, Inc.
10910 Domain Dr Ste 300
Austin TX 78758
512 777-3800

(G-4582)
JEFF MANUFACTURING CO INC
679 Riverside Ave (06790-4535)
PHONE..............................860 482-8845
Jeff Roesing, *President*
Jeff Currier, *Vice Pres*
EMP: 10
SQ FT: 2,000
SALES: 1.4MM **Privately Held**
SIC: 7692 3599 Welding And Machine Work

(G-4583)
JONMANDY CORPORATION
151 Ella Grasso Ave Ste 3 (06790-2351)
P.O. Box 324, Goshen (06756-0324)
PHONE..............................860 482-2354
Donald Nardozzi, *President*
Marilyn Nardozzi, *Vice Pres*
Tom Nardozzi, *Admin Sec*
EMP: 3
SQ FT: 4,000
SALES: 300K **Privately Held**
WEB: www.jonmandy.com
SIC: 3479 Coating/Engraving Service

(G-4584)
K-TECH INTERNATIONAL
56 Ella Grasso Ave (06790-2341)
PHONE..............................860 489-9399
Samuel J Massameno, *President*
Samuel Massameno, *President*
Kay E Massameno, *Vice Pres*
Michelle Allen, *Purch Mgr*
Jim Cateno, *Marketing Mgr*
EMP: 25
SQ FT: 10,800
SALES (est): 6.8MM **Privately Held**
WEB: www.ktechonline.com
SIC: 3534 3661 3499 Mfg Elevators/Escalators Mfg Telephone/Telegraph Apparatus Mfg Misc Fabricated Metal Products

(G-4585)
M & Z ENGINEERING INC
643 Riverside Ave (06790-4535)
PHONE..............................860 496-0282
Michael Dedkiewicz, *President*
Zbigniew Dedkiewicz, *Corp Secy*
EMP: 6
SQ FT: 10,000
SALES (est): 730K **Privately Held**
SIC: 3599 3471 Mfg Industrial Machinery Plating/Polishing Service

(G-4586)
M-FAB LLC
52 Norwood St (06790-4632)
PHONE..............................860 496-0055
Andre Cloutier, *President*
James Dion, *CFO*
EMP: 8
SQ FT: 35,000
SALES: 961.1K **Privately Held**
SIC: 3599 Mfg Industrial Machinery

(G-4587)
MILLWORK SHOP LLC
39 Putter Ln (06790-2360)
PHONE..............................860 489-8848
Jonathan Dowd, *Mng Member*
James Dowd,
EMP: 3
SQ FT: 3,000
SALES: 300K **Privately Held**
WEB: www.millworkshop.com
SIC: 2431 Mfg Millwork

(G-4588)
MOHAWK INDUSTRIES INC
180 Church St (06790-5225)
PHONE..............................706 629-7721
Tina Dileo, *Principal*
Tommy Woods, *Manager*
EMP: 3
SALES (est): 80.7K **Privately Held**
SIC: 2273 Mfg Carpets/Rugs

(G-4589)
NORSE INC
100 South Rd (06790-2441)
PHONE..............................860 482-1532
Alfred C Langer, *President*
Christopher Langer, *Treasurer*
Karen Langer, *Sales Staff*
EMP: 6
SQ FT: 8,800
SALES: 1.5MM **Privately Held**
WEB: www.norse.net
SIC: 3429 Mfg Metal Fasteners

(G-4590)
ODDO PRINT SHOP INC
Also Called: Oddo Print Shop & Copy Center
142 E Main St (06790-5429)
PHONE..............................860 489-6585
Patricia Meneguzzo, *President*
Lisa Meneguzzo, *Admin Sec*
EMP: 8 **EST:** 1946
SALES (est): 1.1MM **Privately Held**
WEB: www.oddoprint.com
SIC: 2752 7334 2791 7331 Lithographic Coml Print Photocopying Service Typesetting Services Direct Mail Ad Svcs

(G-4591)
PACKAGING CONCEPTS ASSOC LLC
Also Called: PCA
230 Ella Grasso Ave (06790-8513)
PHONE..............................860 489-0480
Guy Ferrelli, *Opers Mgr*
Lori Holbrook, *VP Human Res*
Emil Meshberg, *Mng Member*
David Meshberg,
▲ **EMP:** 5
SQ FT: 1,500
SALES (est): 1MM **Privately Held**
SIC: 3085 Mfg Plastic Bottles

(G-4592)
PANACOL-USA INC
142 Industrial Ln (06790-2325)
PHONE..............................860 738-7449
Gary Grosclaude, *President*
Richard Wick, *Vice Pres*
Susan Beckwith, *Office Mgr*
EMP: 15
SQ FT: 34,000
SALES (est): 2.2MM **Privately Held**
WEB: www.tangentindinc.com
SIC: 2891 Mfg Adhesives/Sealants

(G-4593)
PRINT MASTER LLC
1219 E Main St (06790-3963)
PHONE..............................860 482-8152
Judy McKay, *Partner*
Tom McKay,
EMP: 4 **EST:** 1974
SQ FT: 3,600
SALES: 500K **Privately Held**
SIC: 2752 Offset Printing

(G-4594)
PULP PAPER PRODUCTS INC
30 Norwood St (06790-4632)
PHONE..............................860 806-0143
Eric Haggard, *President*
▲ **EMP:** 4
SALES (est): 587.4K **Privately Held**
WEB: www.pulpproducts.com
SIC: 2678 Paper Mill

(G-4595)
QUEST PLASTICS INC
89 Commercial Blvd Ste 3 (06790-7215)
PHONE..............................860 489-1404
James A Bean, *President*
Jim Bean, *President*
Starzky Ron, *Plant Mgr*
Alan Bean, *Admin Sec*
EMP: 17
SQ FT: 26,000
SALES (est): 3.5MM **Privately Held**
SIC: 3089 3559 Mfg Plastic Products Mfg Misc Industry Machinery

(G-4596)
REIDVILLE HYDRAULICS & MFG INC
175 Industrial Ln (06790-2326)
PHONE..............................860 496-1133
Larry J Becker, *President*
Kevin Becker, *Manager*
Jeanette Becker, *Admin Sec*
▲ **EMP:** 25 **EST:** 1955
SQ FT: 23,000
SALES (est): 5.6MM **Privately Held**
WEB: www.reidvillehydraulics.com
SIC: 3594 3599 Mfg Fluid Power Pumps/Motors Mfg Industrial Machinery

(G-4597)
RUBCO PRODUCTS COMPANY
1697 E Main St (06790-3520)
PHONE..............................860 496-1178
Glenn Rubenoff, *Owner*
EMP: 4 **EST:** 1939
SQ FT: 11,000
SALES (est): 343.9K **Privately Held**
SIC: 3052 Mfg Rubber/Plastic Hose/Belting

(G-4598)
SCOTT OLSON ENTERPRISES LLC
Also Called: CT Pellet
1707 E Main St (06790-3520)
PHONE..............................860 482-4391
Scott Olson, *Mng Member*
EMP: 4
SQ FT: 65,000
SALES (est): 550.1K **Privately Held**
SIC: 3484 Mfg Small Arms

(G-4599)
SCREEN-TECH INC
230 Ella Grasso Ave (06790-2343)
PHONE..............................860 496-8016
EMP: 6
SQ FT: 5,700
SALES (est): 490K **Privately Held**
WEB: www.screen-tech.com
SIC: 3552 Mfg Textile Machinery

(G-4600)
TECHNICAL INDUSTRIES INC (PA)
336 Pinewoods Rd (06790-2350)
PHONE..............................860 489-2160
Susan O Parent, *President*
R Dale Smith, *Vice Pres*
EMP: 52
SQ FT: 25,000
SALES (est): 19.7MM **Privately Held**
WEB: www.technicalindustriesinc.com
SIC: 3089 Mfg Plastic Products

(G-4601)
THOMAS LA GANGA
Also Called: Colonial Welding Service
612 S Main St (06790-6920)
PHONE..............................860 489-0920
Thomas La Ganga, *Owner*
EMP: 5
SQ FT: 8,000
SALES (est): 294.1K **Privately Held**
SIC: 7692 7699 3444 3441 Welding Repair Repair Services Mfg Sheet Metalwork Structural Metal Fabrctn

(G-4602)
TORRINGTON BRUSH WORKS INC
63 Avenue A (06790-6519)
P.O. Box 56 (06790-0056)
PHONE..............................860 482-3517
Sidney Fitzgerald, *Principal*
Richard McKenna, *Materials Mgr*
EMP: 3
SQ FT: 12,750
SALES (corp-wide): 1.4MM **Privately Held**
WEB: www.brusheswholesale.com
SIC: 3991 Brooms And Brushes
PA: Torrington Brush Works Inc
4377 Independence Ct
Sarasota FL 34234
941 355-1499

(G-4603)
TORRINGTON DIESEL CORPORATION
287 Old Winsted Rd (06790-2420)
PHONE..............................860 496-9948
Pierre Bauchiero, *President*
EMP: 5
SQ FT: 2,400
SALES (est): 821.6K **Privately Held**
SIC: 7692 7538 Welding Repair General Auto Repair

(G-4604)
TORRINGTON DISTRIBUTORS INC (PA)
Also Called: Tdi
43 Norfolk St (06790-4825)
PHONE..............................860 482-4464
James A Mazzarelli, *President*
Teresa L Asklar, *Vice Pres*
David Holtman, *Research*
Katie Theriault,
▲ **EMP:** 25 **EST:** 1974
SQ FT: 17,000
SALES (est): 6.1MM **Privately Held**
WEB: www.torringtondistributors.com
SIC: 2531 Mfg Public Building Furniture

(G-4605)
TORRINGTON LUMBER COMPANY
281 Church St (06790-5208)
PHONE..............................860 482-3529
Donna Fabro, *President*
Eugene Farely, *Vice Pres*
Eugene Farley, *Vice Pres*
Daniel T Farley, *Admin Sec*
EMP: 6
SQ FT: 49,800
SALES: 804.9K **Privately Held**
WEB: www.tlcdoor.com
SIC: 2431 Mfg - Windows Doors

(G-4606)
UPPER VALLEY MOLD LLC
481 Guerdat Rd (06790-2846)
PHONE..................................860 489-8282
Teofilo M Pleil, *Principal*
EMP: 3
SALES (est): 197.8K **Privately Held**
SIC: 3544 Mfg Dies/Tools/Jigs/Fixtures

(G-4607)
WHITE DOG WOODWORKING LLC
199 W Pearl Rd (06790-3026)
PHONE..................................860 482-3776
Thomas C Officer, *Manager*
EMP: 4
SALES (est): 417.7K **Privately Held**
SIC: 2431 Mfg Millwork

(G-4608)
WITTMANN BATTENFELD INC (DH)
1 Technology Park Dr (06790-2594)
PHONE..................................860 496-9603
Michael Wittmann, *CEO*
David C Preusse, *President*
Markus Klaus, *Division Mgr*
Duane Royce, *Vice Pres*
Dave Cantey, *Safety Mgr*
▲ **EMP:** 80
SQ FT: 40,000
SALES (est): 98.7MM
SALES (corp-wide): 2.6MM **Privately Held**
WEB: www.wittmann-ct.com
SIC: 3559 5084 Mfg Misc Industry Machinery Whol Industrial Equipment
HQ: Wittmann Kunststoffgerate Gesellschaft M.B.H.
LichtblaustraBe 10
Wien 1220
125 039-0

(G-4609)
WRITE WAY SIGNS & DESIGN INC
73 Migeon Ave (06790-4813)
PHONE..................................860 482-8893
Jeremy Schaller, *President*
Kelly Lund, *Graphic Designe*
EMP: 6
SQ FT: 3,800
SALES (est): 919.6K **Privately Held**
WEB: www.writewaysigns.com
SIC: 3993 Mfg Signs

Trumbull
Fairfield County

(G-4610)
5N PLUS WISCONSIN INC
120 Corporate Dr (06611-1387)
PHONE..................................203 384-0331
Teri Beckoff, *Principal*
Paul Tancell, *Vice Pres*
Jason Merrell, *Research*
Richard Perron, *CFO*
▲ **EMP:** 16 **EST:** 1969
SQ FT: 40,000
SALES (est): 7.5MM
SALES (corp-wide): 218MM **Privately Held**
SIC: 3341 Secondary Nonferrous Metal Producer
PA: 5n Plus Inc
4385 Rue Garand
Saint-Laurent QC H4R 2
514 856-0644

(G-4611)
AMERICAN GRIPPERS INC
Also Called: A G I Automation
171 Spring Hill Rd (06611-1327)
PHONE..................................203 459-8345
Peter Farkas, *President*
John Barnes, *Vice Pres*
EMP: 23
SALES (est): 3MM **Privately Held**
WEB: www.agi-automation.com
SIC: 3545 Mfg Machine Tool Accessories

(G-4612)
ANSEL LABEL AND PACKAGING CORP
204 Spring Hill Rd Ste 3 (06611-1356)
PHONE..................................203 452-0311
William San Fan Andre, *Ch of Bd*
Jeff San Fan Andre, *President*
Harold Smyth, *Treasurer*
Clifford Albers, *VP Sales*
EMP: 22
SQ FT: 13,364
SALES (est): 3MM **Privately Held**
SIC: 2759 2671 Commercial Printing Mfg Packaging Paper/Film

(G-4613)
AVERY ABRASIVES INC
2225 Reservoir Ave Ste 1 (06611-4795)
PHONE..................................203 372-3513
Craig F Avery, *President*
Ray Soto, *Opers Mgr*
Robert J Berta, *Admin Sec*
▲ **EMP:** 35 **EST:** 1960
SQ FT: 42,000
SALES (est): 6.2MM **Privately Held**
SIC: 3291 Mfg Abrasive Products

(G-4614)
BARON TECHNOLOGY INC
62 Spring Hill Rd (06611-1328)
PHONE..................................203 452-0515
David Baron, *President*
Frank Baron, *Chairman*
Ruth Baron, *Corp Secy*
Karlo Glad, *Vice Pres*
Karla Glad, *Office Mgr*
EMP: 45
SQ FT: 5,300
SALES (est): 9.9MM **Privately Held**
WEB: www.baronengraving.com
SIC: 2759 3231 2796 Commercial Printing Mfg Products-Purchased Glass Platemaking Services

(G-4615)
BIOMETRICS INC (PA)
115 Technology Dr Cp102 (06611-6342)
PHONE..................................203 261-1162
David Rooney, *President*
Robert Dzurenda, *President*
Ian Engelman, *Shareholder*
EMP: 8
SALES (est): 862.9K **Privately Held**
WEB: www.biometricsct.com
SIC: 3842 Mfg Orthotic & Prosthetic Devices

(G-4616)
BLAIRDEN PRECISION INSTRS INC
Also Called: Cooper Surgical
95 Corporate Dr (06611-1350)
PHONE..................................203 799-2000
▲ **EMP:** 9
SQ FT: 13,000
SALES (est): 2MM **Privately Held**
WEB: www.coopersurgical.com
SIC: 3841 Surgical And Medical Instruments

(G-4617)
CADESK COMPANY LLC (PA)
88 Cottage St (06611-2830)
PHONE..................................203 268-8083
Michael G Pagett, *Principal*
Robert Hutcheon, *Director*
EMP: 3
SALES (est): 302.2K **Privately Held**
SIC: 3577 Mfg Computer Furniture

(G-4618)
CAR BUYERS MARKET
30 Nutmeg Dr Ste B (06611-5453)
P.O. Box 110317 (06611-0317)
PHONE..................................516 482-0292
John Roy, *President*
Robert Fitting, *Treasurer*
EMP: 30 **EST:** 1958
SQ FT: 1,800
SALES (est): 1.6MM **Privately Held**
SIC: 2711 5521 Newspapers-Publishing/Printing Ret Used Automobiles

(G-4619)
COACH INC
5065 Main St Ste P2114 (06611-4223)
PHONE..................................203 372-0208
EMP: 15
SALES (corp-wide): 4.4B **Publicly Held**
SIC: 3171 Mfg Women's Handbags/Purses
PA: Coach, Inc.
10 Hudson Yards
New York NY 10001
212 594-1850

(G-4620)
CONOPCO INC
Also Called: Thomas J Lipton
75 Merritt Blvd (06611-5435)
PHONE..................................708 606-0540
Andrea Misek, *Administration*
EMP: 50
SALES (corp-wide): 56.5B **Privately Held**
SIC: 2099 2034 2033 2098 Mfg Food Preparations Mfg Dhydrtd Fruit/Vegtbl
HQ: Conopco, Inc.
700 Sylvan Ave
Englewood Cliffs NJ 07632
201 894-7760

(G-4621)
CONOPCO INC
Also Called: Slim-Fast Foods Company
75 Merritt Blvd (06611-5435)
PHONE..................................203 381-3557
Eric Walsh, *President*
EMP: 99
SALES (corp-wide): 56.5B **Privately Held**
SIC: 2037 Services-Misc
HQ: Conopco, Inc.
700 Sylvan Ave
Englewood Cliffs NJ 07632
201 894-7760

(G-4622)
DELCON INDUSTRIES
31 Frenchtown Rd (06611-4729)
PHONE..................................203 371-5711
EMP: 3
SALES (est): 190.1K **Privately Held**
SIC: 3999 Mfg Misc Products

(G-4623)
E-LITE TECHNOLOGIES INC
2285 Reservoir Ave (06611-4752)
PHONE..................................203 371-2070
Mark Appelberg, *President*
Gustaf T Appelberg, *Chairman*
EMP: 11
SQ FT: 10,600
SALES (est): 1.9MM **Privately Held**
WEB: www.e-lite.com
SIC: 3645 Mfg Residential Lighting Fixtures

(G-4624)
HERSAM ACORN CMNTY PUBG LLC
Also Called: Trumbull Printing
205 Spring Hill Rd (06611-1327)
PHONE..................................203 261-2548
Gus Semon, *Manager*
EMP: 15
SALES (corp-wide): 5.3MM **Privately Held**
SIC: 2711 Newspapers-Publishing/Printing
HQ: Hersam Acorn Community Publishing, Llc
16 Bailey Ave
Ridgefield CT 06877

(G-4625)
HOME DIAGNOSTICS CORP
1 Trefoil Dr (06611-6352)
PHONE..................................203 445-1170
George Holley, *President*
Donald Parson, *Admin Sec*
EMP: 200
SQ FT: 20,000
SALES (est): 11.1MM **Privately Held**
SIC: 3845 8731 3841 Mfg Electromedical Equip Coml Physical Research Mfg Surgical/Med Instr

(G-4626)
LADY ANNE COSMETICS INC
Also Called: Ecogenics
78 Russ Rd (06611-3434)
PHONE..................................203 372-6972
Ann McDonnell, *President*
▲ **EMP:** 5
SQ FT: 1,500
SALES (est): 865.1K **Privately Held**
WEB: www.ecogenics.com
SIC: 2844 5122 5999 Mfg Whol & Ret Cosmetics

(G-4627)
LRP CONFERENCES LLC
Also Called: Professional Media Group
35 Nutmeg Dr (06611-5431)
PHONE..................................203 663-0100
Joseph Hanson, *Mng Member*
EMP: 42
SALES (corp-wide): 106.4MM **Privately Held**
SIC: 2759 Commercial Printing
HQ: Lrp Conferences, Llc
360 Hiatt Dr
Palm Beach Gardens FL 33418
215 784-0860

(G-4628)
M T D CORPORATION
171 Spring Hill Rd (06611-1327)
PHONE..................................203 261-3721
Dorothy Bertini, *President*
Milo Bertini, *Vice Pres*
EMP: 15
SQ FT: 9,000
SALES (est): 1MM **Privately Held**
SIC: 3599 Mfg Industrial Machinery

(G-4629)
ORIGIO MIDATLANTIC DEVICES INC
75 Corporate Dr (06611-1350)
PHONE..................................856 762-2000
Paul Rennell, *CEO*
Terrance J Fortino, *CEO*
◆ **EMP:** 22
SQ FT: 11,000
SALES (est): 3.8MM **Privately Held**
WEB: www.midatlanticdiagnostics.com
SIC: 3821 5047 Mfg Lab Apparatus/Furniture Whol Medical/Hospital Equipment
HQ: Origio Inc.
2400 Hunters Way
Charlottesville VA 22911

(G-4630)
RAMPAGE LLC
38 Palisade Ave (06611-3040)
PHONE..................................203 930-1022
EMP: 12
SALES: 745K **Privately Held**
WEB: www.rampag.com
SIC: 3949 Mfg Sporting/Athletic Goods

(G-4631)
SCAN TOOL & MOLD INC
2 Trefoil Dr (06611-1330)
PHONE..................................203 459-4950
John F Gotch Jr, *President*
Joe Heeran, *QC Mgr*
Jan Gallagher, *Bookkeeper*
Nancy Ares, *Supervisor*
Lynn Tomas, *Admin Asst*
▲ **EMP:** 26
SQ FT: 32,500
SALES (est): 6.1MM **Privately Held**
WEB: www.scantoolinc.com
SIC: 3089 3544 Mfg Plastic Products Mfg Dies/Tools/Jigs/Fixtures

(G-4632)
SECUREMARK DECAL CORP
20 Nutmeg Dr (06611-5414)
PHONE..................................773 622-6815
Norman Hoffderg, *President*
Jim Chmura, *General Mgr*
Paul Choiniere, *Opers Mgr*
George Houston, *QC Dir*
EMP: 15
SALES (est): 2.1MM **Privately Held**
SIC: 2672 Mfg Coated/Laminated Paper

(G-4633)
SURYS INC
20 Nutmeg Dr (06611-5414)
PHONE..................................203 333-5503
Fabio Tremolada, *President*
▲ **EMP:** 202
SALES (est): 17.3MM
SALES (corp-wide): 4.2MM **Privately Held**
SIC: 2679 2759 Mfg Converted Paper Products Commercial Printing
HQ: Surys
Parc D Activite G Eiffel
Bussy-Saint-Georges 77600
164 763-100

(G-4634)
SWAROVSKI NORTH AMERICA LTD
5065 Main St (06611-4204)
PHONE..................................203 372-0336
White Thayer, *Branch Mgr*
EMP: 4
SALES (corp-wide): 4.7B **Privately Held**
SIC: 3961 Mfg Costume Jewelry
HQ: Swarovski North America Limited
1 Kenney Dr
Cranston RI 02920
401 463-6400

(G-4635)
THOMAS J LIPTON INC
Also Called: Unilever Foods Chill
75 Merritt Blvd (06611-5435)
PHONE..................................206 381-3500
◆ **EMP:** 2200 **EST:** 2006
SALES (est): 18.5K **Privately Held**
SIC: 2099 2034 2035 2033 Mfg Food Preparations Mfg Dhydrtd Fruit/Vegtbl

(G-4636)
TRUMBULL PRINTING INC
205 Spring Hill Rd (06611-1327)
PHONE..................................203 261-2548
Steve Huhta, *President*
Tiberio Moniz, *President*
William McCann, *CFO*
Walter Cooper, *Manager*
Sharon Esares,
EMP: 150
SQ FT: 80,000
SALES (est): 32.6MM **Privately Held**
SIC: 2752 Offset Printing Service

(G-4637)
UNILEVER HOME AND PER CARE NA
Also Called: Unilever Hpc NA
75 Merritt Blvd (06611-5435)
PHONE..................................203 502-0086
Frederick Baumer, *Principal*
◆ **EMP:** 78
SALES (est): 37.5MM **Privately Held**
SIC: 2841 2844 Mfg Soap/Other Detergents Mfg Toilet Preparations

(G-4638)
UNILEVER HPC USA
45 Commerce Dr (06611-5403)
PHONE..................................203 381-3311
Richard McNabb, *Director*
EMP: 4 **EST:** 2010
SALES (est): 342.6K **Privately Held**
SIC: 2844 Mfg Toilet Preparations

(G-4639)
UNILEVER TRUMBULL RES SVCS INC (HQ)
Also Called: Unilever Hpc USA
40 Merritt Blvd (06611-5413)
PHONE..................................203 502-0086
Peter Gallagher, *President*
Anthony K Mills, *President*
Jason Harcup, *Vice Pres*
John Weir, *Vice Pres*
Christine Koch, *Treasurer*
◆ **EMP:** 3
SALES (est): 1.7MM
SALES (corp-wide): 56.5B **Privately Held**
SIC: 2844 Mfg Toilet Preparations
PA: Unilever N.V.
Weena 455
Rotterdam
102 174-000

(G-4640)
UNITED STTS SGN & FBRCTION
Also Called: US Sign
1 Trefoil Dr Ste 2 (06611-6352)
PHONE..................................203 601-1000
George Holley, *Ch of Bd*
Ron Eppert, *Vice Pres*
Alan Posner, *CFO*
Eppert Diane, *Office Mgr*
EMP: 40
SQ FT: 40,000
SALES (est): 7.1MM **Privately Held**
WEB: www.ussign.com
SIC: 3953 3993 3444 3356 Mfg Marking Devices Mfg Signs/Ad Specialties Mfg Sheet Metalwork Nonferrous Rollng/Drawng

(G-4641)
UNIVERSAL PRECISION MFG
21 Leffert Rd (06611-4949)
PHONE..................................203 374-9809
Ron Bouffard, *Owner*
EMP: 3
SQ FT: 600
SALES (est): 254.7K **Privately Held**
SIC: 3545 3546 Mfg Machine Tool Accessories Mfg Power-Driven Handtools

(G-4642)
VIGIRODA ENTERPRISES INC
104 Garwood Rd (06611-2231)
PHONE..................................203 268-6117
Frank Ferraro, *President*
Edward J Cremin, *Mfg Mgr*
EMP: 5
SQ FT: 6,000
SALES (est): 427.3K **Privately Held**
SIC: 3631 Mfg Barbecue Grills

(G-4643)
W S POLYMERS
93 Calhoun Ave (06611-2455)
PHONE..................................203 268-1557
Wayne D Stokes, *Owner*
EMP: 6
SALES (est): 428K **Privately Held**
SIC: 2821 Mfg Plastic Materials/Resins

(G-4644)
WALLACH SURGICAL DEVICES INC (PA)
75 Corporate Dr (06611-1350)
PHONE..................................203 799-2000
Nicholas J Pichotta, *CEO*
Paul L Remmell, *President*
Tina Allan, *Business Mgr*
Carol R Kaufman, *Vice Pres*
Dan Wallach, *Admin Sec*
▲ **EMP:** 31
SQ FT: 40,000
SALES (est): 2.5MM **Privately Held**
SIC: 3841 Mfg Surgical/Medical Instruments

(G-4645)
WALLACH SURGICAL DEVICES INC
95 Corporate Dr (06611-1350)
PHONE..................................800 243-2463
Nicholas J Pichotta, *Branch Mgr*
EMP: 14
SALES (corp-wide): 2.5MM **Privately Held**
SIC: 3841 Mfg Surgical/Medical Instruments
PA: Wallach Surgical Devices, Inc.
75 Corporate Dr
Trumbull CT 06611
203 799-2000

Uncasville
New London County

(G-4646)
BOCCELLI
1 Mohegan Sun Blvd 621c (06382-1355)
PHONE..................................860 862-9300
Linda Nelson, *Manager*
EMP: 5
SALES (est): 290.5K **Privately Held**
SIC: 3172 Mfg Personal Leather Goods

(G-4647)
NORTHEAST WOOD PRODUCTS LLC
Also Called: Thermaglo
13 Crow Hill Rd (06382-1118)
PHONE..................................860 862-6350
Guy J Mozzicato, *President*
Michael D Reid, *Senior VP*
Kenneth N Wycherley, *Senior VP*
EMP: 25
SQ FT: 20,000
SALES (est): 2.3MM **Privately Held**
SIC: 3999 Mfg Misc Products

(G-4648)
PEPSI-COLA METRO BTLG CO INC
260 Gallivan Ln (06382-1121)
PHONE..................................860 848-1231
Paul Andreotta, *Manager*
EMP: 40
SALES (corp-wide): 64.6B **Publicly Held**
WEB: www.joy-of-cola.com
SIC: 2086 Mfg Bottled/Canned Soft Drinks
HQ: Pepsi-Cola Metropolitan Bottling Company, Inc.
1111 Westchester Ave
White Plains NY 10604
914 767-6000

(G-4649)
TECH-AIR INCORPORATED
152 Route 163 (06382-2118)
P.O. Box 363 (06382-0363)
PHONE..................................860 848-1287
Richard Hubbert, *President*
Donald L Hubbert, *Vice Pres*
Michael F Hubbert, *Vice Pres*
Jeanette B Hubbert, *Admin Sec*
EMP: 34 **EST:** 1978
SQ FT: 13,000
SALES (est): 6.3MM **Privately Held**
SIC: 3444 1761 Mfg Sheet Metalwork Roofing/Siding Contractor

(G-4650)
TOWN OF MONTVILLE
Also Called: Montville Sewer Plant
83 Pink Row (06382-2427)
PHONE..................................860 848-3830
Mike Didato, *Manager*
EMP: 13 **Privately Held**
SIC: 3589 Mfg Service Industry Machinery
PA: Town Of Montville
310 Nrwich New Lndon Tpke
Uncasville CT 06382
860 848-3030

(G-4651)
WESTROCK CP LLC
125 Depot Rd (06382-2441)
PHONE..................................860 848-1500
Paul Hayes, *Branch Mgr*
EMP: 115
SALES (corp-wide): 18.2B **Publicly Held**
WEB: www.sto.com
SIC: 2631 Mfg Corrugated/Solid Fiber Boxes
HQ: Westrock Cp, Llc
1000 Abernathy Rd
Atlanta GA 30328

Unionville
Hartford County

(G-4652)
AIR TOOL SALES & SERVICE CO (PA)
1 Burnham Ave (06085-1225)
P.O. Box 218 (06085-0218)
PHONE..................................860 673-2714
Niles O Lindstedt, *President*
EMP: 9
SQ FT: 15,000
SALES (est): 1.5MM **Privately Held**
SIC: 3546 5084 5072 7699 Mfg Whol & Repair Construction & Industrial Air & Power Hand Tools Ret Work Clothing & Electric Tool Repair

(G-4653)
AUTOMATECH INC
21 Westview Ter (06085-1459)
PHONE..................................860 673-5940
John Murry, *Manager*
EMP: 10 **Privately Held**
SIC: 7372 Prepackages Software
PA: Automatech, Inc.
138 Industrial Park Rd
Plymouth MA 02360

(G-4654)
CHAS W HOUSE & SONS INC
19 Perry St (06085-1021)
PHONE..................................860 673-2518
Matthew Bristiw, *President*
Patricia Burwood, *Vice Pres*
EMP: 65
SQ FT: 140,000
SALES (est): 4.7MM **Privately Held**
SIC: 2231 3053 Mfg Wool Woven Felts Woolen Blankets Billiard Cloths & Gaskets

(G-4655)
DATA MANAGEMENT INCORPORATED
Also Called: Threshold
557 New Britain Ave (06085)
P.O. Box 789, Farmington (06034-0789)
PHONE..................................860 677-8586
Daniel A Hincks, *CEO*
Brian Gallagher, *President*
EMP: 45 **EST:** 1961
SQ FT: 6,000
SALES: 7.2MM **Privately Held**
WEB: www.checksforms.com
SIC: 2752 2782 Lithographic Commercial Printing Mfg Blankbooks/Binders

(G-4656)
FIREHOUSE DISCOUNT OIL LLC (PA)
17 Depot Pl Ste C (06085-6202)
PHONE..................................860 404-1827
Brian C Damato,
Robert E Lavoie,
EMP: 3 **EST:** 2008
SALES (est): 374.2K **Privately Held**
SIC: 2869 Mfg Industrial Organic Chemicals

(G-4657)
KARGER S PUBLISHERS INC
26 W Avon Rd (06085-1162)
PHONE..................................860 675-7834
EMP: 5
SALES (est): 528.7K **Privately Held**
SIC: 2721 Periodicals Publishing/Printing
PA: S. Karger Ag
Allschwilerstrasse 10
Basel BS 4055
613 061-111

(G-4658)
MADIGAN MILLWORK INC
150 New Britain Ave (06085-1221)
PHONE..................................860 673-7601
James Madigan, *President*
Regina Madigan, *Admin Sec*
EMP: 9
SQ FT: 20,000
SALES (est): 1.5MM **Privately Held**
SIC: 2431 2511 Mfg Millwork Mfg Wood Household Furniture

(G-4659)
MVP SYSTEMS SOFTWARE INC
29 Mill St Ste 8 (06085-1484)
PHONE..................................860 269-3112
EMP: 11
SQ FT: 2,200
SALES (est): 900.3K **Privately Held**
SIC: 7372 Prepackaged Software Services

(G-4660)
NOVA MACHINING LLC
16 E Shore Blvd (06085-1510)
PHONE..................................860 675-8131
Mariusz Wroblewski, *Manager*
EMP: 3
SALES (est): 180K **Privately Held**
SIC: 3599 Mfg Industrial Machinery

GEOGRAPHIC

(G-4661)
S KARGER PUBLISHERS INC
26 W Avon Rd (06085-1162)
P.O. Box 529 (06085-0529)
PHONE..................................860 675-7834
Petra Schlegel, *Managing Dir*
Iola Gulijew, *Business Mgr*
Cristina Baptista, *Accounts Mgr*
Thomas Nold, *Marketing Mgr*
Monika Brendel, *Manager*
EMP: 5
SALES (est): 448.8K
SALES (corp-wide): 51.6MM **Privately Held**
SIC: 2731 2721 Books-Publishing/Printing Periodicals-Publishing/Printing
PA: S. Karger Ag
Allschwilerstrasse 10
Basel BS 4055
613 061-111

Vernon
Tolland County

(G-4662)
AMERICAN SPECIALTY PDTS LLC
101 Industrial Park Rd (06066-5538)
PHONE..................................860 871-2279
Bob Morton, *General Mgr*
Andrew Robinson,
EMP: 6
SQ FT: 4,000
SALES (est): 1MM **Privately Held**
WEB: www.aspusaonline.com
SIC: 3599 8711 3643 Mfg Industrial Machinery Engineering Services Mfg Conductive Wiring Devices

(G-4663)
BNL INDUSTRIES INC
30 Industrial Park Rd (06066-5523)
PHONE..................................860 870-6222
Leonard Bosh Jr, *President*
Dennis Grogan, *General Mgr*
Rick Rasimas, *Plant Mgr*
Jason Gonzalez, *Purch Mgr*
John Browne, *Purch Agent*
EMP: 40
SQ FT: 27,000
SALES (est): 10.6MM **Privately Held**
WEB: www.valves.net
SIC: 3491 Mfg Industrial Valves

(G-4664)
BRAVO LLC
Also Called: Manchester Packing
1084 Hartford Tpke (06066-4413)
PHONE..................................860 896-1899
David Bogner, *Manager*
EMP: 20
SALES (est): 2.4MM
SALES (corp-wide): 5.6MM **Privately Held**
SIC: 2047 Mfg Dog/Cat Food
PA: Bravo , Llc
349 Wetherell St
Manchester CT 06040
866 922-9222

(G-4665)
CONNECTICUT MILLWORK INC
80 Spring St (06066-3452)
P.O. Box 71 (06066-0071)
PHONE..................................860 875-2860
Gregory A Stewart, *President*
EMP: 9
SQ FT: 6,000
SALES (est): 1.4MM **Privately Held**
SIC: 2431 Manufactures Wooden Millwork

(G-4666)
CRYSTAL TOOL AND MACHINE CO
Also Called: Ridgeway Racing
114 Brooklyn St (06066-6708)
P.O. Box 504 (06066-0504)
PHONE..................................860 870-7431
John D Yedziniak Jr, *Owner*
EMP: 6
SQ FT: 4,000
SALES (est): 450K **Privately Held**
SIC: 3599 Machine Shop

(G-4667)
FAMILY RACEWAY LLC
11 Earl St (06066-3734)
PHONE..................................860 896-0171
Kimberly Cavaliere, *Principal*
EMP: 3
SALES (est): 157.7K **Privately Held**
SIC: 3644 Mfg Nonconductive Wiring Devices

(G-4668)
HANGER PRSTHETCS & ORTHO INC
428 Hartford Tpke Ste 103 (06066-4841)
PHONE..................................860 871-0905
Paul Armstrong, *Manager*
EMP: 4
SALES (corp-wide): 1B **Publicly Held**
SIC: 3842 Mfg Surgical Appliances/Supplies
HQ: Hanger Prosthetics & Orthotics, Inc.
10910 Domain Dr Ste 300
Austin TX 78758
512 777-3800

(G-4669)
MILLER PROFESSIONAL TRANS SVC
8 Bancroft Rd (06066-3506)
PHONE..................................860 871-6818
Samuel Miller, *Principal*
EMP: 4
SALES (est): 230K **Privately Held**
SIC: 3715 Logistical Transportation

(G-4670)
MYCO TOOL & MANUFACTURING INC
176 Bolton Rd Ste 6 (06066-5527)
PHONE..................................860 875-7340
Michael Simard, *President*
Linda Simard, *Corp Secy*
EMP: 3
SQ FT: 4,000
SALES: 400K **Privately Held**
WEB: www.manufacturingworkers.com
SIC: 3599 Machine Shop

(G-4671)
NEISS CORP
29 Naek Rd (06066-3942)
PHONE..................................860 872-8528
John Cratty, *President*
Bonnie Cratty, *Admin Sec*
EMP: 10
SQ FT: 8,000
SALES (est): 916.8K **Privately Held**
SIC: 2521 Mfg Wood Office Furniture

(G-4672)
REMINDER BROADCASTER
Also Called: Reminder Media
130 Old Town Rd (06066-2322)
P.O. Box 27 (06066-0027)
PHONE..................................860 875-3366
Ken Hovland, *President*
EMP: 99
SALES (est): 2.8MM **Privately Held**
SIC: 2711 Newspapers-Publishing/Printing

(G-4673)
TEK INDUSTRIES INC
48 Hockanum Blvd Unit 1 (06066-7048)
PHONE..................................860 870-0001
Mark Matheny, *President*
Deborah Gordon, *Vice Pres*
EMP: 32
SALES (est): 7.1MM **Privately Held**
WEB: www.tekind.com
SIC: 3672 7373 8711 Mfg Printed Circuit Boards Computer Systems Design Engineering Services

(G-4674)
TOLLAND MACHINE COMPANY LLC
1050 Hartford Tpke (06066-4487)
P.O. Box 82 (06066-0082)
PHONE..................................860 872-4863
Lance Shackway, *Manager*
EMP: 6
SQ FT: 7,500
SALES: 1MM **Privately Held**
WEB: www.tollandmachine.com
SIC: 3599 Machine Shop

(G-4675)
TOWN OF VERNON
Also Called: Water Treatment Plant
100 Windsorville Rd (06066-2315)
PHONE..................................860 870-3545
Robert Grasis, *General Mgr*
EMP: 17 **Privately Held**
WEB: www.vernonctpolice.com
SIC: 3589 Mfg Service Industry Machinery
PA: Town Of Vernon
14 Park Pl
Vernon CT 06066
860 870-3690

(G-4676)
VENTURES LLC DOT COM LLC
35-31 Tlcottville Rd 23 (06066)
PHONE..................................203 930-8972
Leonard Wells,
EMP: 5
SALES (est): 535.4K **Privately Held**
SIC: 3556 Mfg Food Products Machinery

Vernon Rockville
Tolland County

(G-4677)
ABA-PGT INC
140 Bolton Rd (06066-5512)
PHONE..................................860 872-2058
Sam Pierson, *Branch Mgr*
EMP: 4
SALES (est): 250.5K
SALES (corp-wide): 30.5MM **Privately Held**
WEB: www.abapgt.com
SIC: 3089 Mfg Plastic Products
PA: Aba-Pgt Inc.
10 Gear Dr
Manchester CT 06042
860 649-4591

(G-4678)
ATLAS HOBBING AND TOOL CO INC
Also Called: American Molding Product
20 Mountain St (06066-3310)
PHONE..................................860 870-9226
Mehmed Ramic, *President*
Supie Polo, *Corp Secy*
Raum Bombard, *Vice Pres*
EMP: 17
SQ FT: 2,400
SALES (est): 2.3MM **Privately Held**
SIC: 3089 Mfg Plastic Products

(G-4679)
B & A DESIGN INC
255 Bamforth Rd (06066-5629)
P.O. Box 3153 (06066-2053)
PHONE..................................860 871-0134
Robert E Triggs Jr, *President*
Ann Triggs, *Vice Pres*
EMP: 3
SALES (est): 40K **Privately Held**
SIC: 3559 3613 Builds Special Industrial Machinery And Control Panels

(G-4680)
CLEMSON SHEET METAL LLC
344 Somers Rd Unit 1 (06066)
PHONE..................................860 871-9369
Alan Clemson, *Owner*
EMP: 3 **EST:** 2007
SALES (est): 318.4K **Privately Held**
SIC: 3444 Mfg Sheet Metalwork

(G-4681)
RMI INC
Also Called: Stafford Reminder
130 Old Town Rd (06066-2322)
P.O. Box 27 (06066-0027)
PHONE..................................860 875-3366
Kenneth A Hovland Jr, *President*
George Cunningham, *Corp Secy*
Keith A Hovland, *Vice Pres*
EMP: 200
SQ FT: 30,000
SALES (est): 10.3MM **Privately Held**
SIC: 2711 2752 Newspapers-Publishing/Printing Lithographic Commercial Printing

(G-4682)
SIGN CONNECTION INC
101 West St (06066-2954)
PHONE..................................860 870-8855
Bodin Muschinsky, *President*
Evon Muschinsky, *Vice Pres*
EMP: 6
SQ FT: 2,900
SALES: 200K **Privately Held**
SIC: 3993 Graphics And Signs

(G-4683)
SOLDREAM INC
129 Reservoir Rd (06066-5705)
PHONE..................................860 871-6883
Jarek Kalecinski, *President*
Jadwiga Kalecinski, *President*
Anthony Steullet, *Vice Pres*
Richard Letellier, *QC Mgr*
Rob Renaud, *QC Mgr*
▼ **EMP:** 49
SQ FT: 20,000
SALES (est): 15.3MM **Privately Held**
WEB: www.soldream.com
SIC: 3829 Mfg Measuring/Controlling Devices

(G-4684)
THERMA-SCAN INC
43 Claire Rd (06066-4821)
P.O. Box 121, Ellington (06029-0121)
PHONE..................................860 872-9770
Gayle Carroll, *CEO*
George Carroll, *President*
EMP: 3
SALES (est): 253.7K **Privately Held**
SIC: 2759 Infrared Thermography

(G-4685)
TIM POLOSKI
38 Risley Rd (06066-5923)
PHONE..................................860 508-6566
Timothy Poloski, *Owner*
EMP: 4
SALES (est): 182.7K **Privately Held**
SIC: 3479 Coating/Engraving Service

(G-4686)
TOWN OF VERNON
Also Called: Water Pollution Control Dept
5 Park St Fl 2 (06066-3211)
P.O. Box 147 (06066-0147)
PHONE..................................860 870-3699
David Ignatowicz, *Director*
EMP: 4 **Privately Held**
WEB: www.vernonctpolice.com
SIC: 3589 Mfg Service Industry Machinery
PA: Town Of Vernon
14 Park Pl
Vernon CT 06066
860 870-3690

(G-4687)
UNITED PHOTONICS LLC
42 Diane Dr (06066-6237)
PHONE..................................617 752-2073
Scott Nelson, *Principal*
EMP: 4 **EST:** 2016
SALES (est): 285.6K **Privately Held**
SIC: 3661 Mfg Telephone/Telegraph Apparatus

(G-4688)
VERNON PRINTING CO INC
Also Called: Minuteman Press
352 Hartford Tpke Ste 9 (06066-4733)
PHONE..................................860 872-1826
Amy Steiman, *President*
Joel Steinman, *Exec VP*
EMP: 8
SALES (est): 176.3K **Privately Held**
SIC: 2752 2791 2789 Lithographic Commercial Printing Typesetting Services Bookbinding/Related Work

Voluntown
New London County

(G-4689)
CHARLES RIVER LABORATORIES INC
425 Pendleton Hill Rd (06384-2107)
PHONE..................................860 376-1240

▲ = Import ▼=Export
◆ =Import/Export

Lydia Cary, *Administration*
EMP: 30
SALES (corp-wide): 2.2B **Publicly Held**
WEB: www.criver.com
SIC: 2836 Testing Laboratory
HQ: Charles River Laboratories, Inc.
251 Ballardvale St
Wilmington MA 01887
781 222-6000

(G-4690)
COLEMAN DRILLING & BLASTING
1458 Hopeville Rd (06384)
PHONE....................................860 376-3813
Robert Coleman, *President*
EMP: 5
SALES (est): 2MM **Privately Held**
WEB: www.colemandrillingandblasting.com
SIC: 1381 1629 Drilling & Blasting

Wallingford
New Haven County

(G-4691)
A LINE DESIGN INC
18 Martin Trl (06492-2622)
PHONE....................................203 294-0080
John Arrigoni, *President*
EMP: 5
SALES (est): 525.1K **Privately Held**
WEB: www.alinedesign.com
SIC: 3423 Mfg Hand/Edge Tools

(G-4692)
A S J SPECIALTIES LLC
2 Toms Dr (06492-2558)
PHONE....................................203 284-8650
Anthony Savo Jr,
Sheila Savo,
EMP: 3
SALES: 80K **Privately Held**
SIC: 2541 2434 Mfg Counter Tops & Cabinets

(G-4693)
ACCENT SCREENPRINTING
186 Center St (06492-4142)
PHONE....................................203 284-8601
EMP: 3 **EST:** 2010
SALES (est): 255.1K **Privately Held**
SIC: 2759 Commercial Printing

(G-4694)
AERO PRECISION MFG LLC
71 S Turnpike Rd (06492-3421)
PHONE....................................203 675-7625
Frank Jukic, *Principal*
EMP: 8 **EST:** 2007
SALES (est): 853.8K **Privately Held**
SIC: 3999 Mfg Misc Products

(G-4695)
ALLNEX USA INC
Also Called: Evonic Cyro
528 S Cherry St (06492-4458)
PHONE....................................203 269-4481
Linda Harroch, *CEO*
Benoit Debecker, *Vice Pres*
Robert Wood, *Engineer*
Duncan Taylor, *CFO*
Bob Logano, *Maintence Staff*
EMP: 99
SALES (corp-wide): 177.9K **Privately Held**
SIC. 2821 Mfg Plastic Materials/Resins
HQ: Allnex Usa Inc.
9005 Westside Pkwy
Alpharetta GA
800 433-2873

(G-4696)
ALLOY METALS INC (PA)
34b Barnes Indus Rd S (06492-2438)
P.O. Box 336, Roseville MI (48066-0336)
PHONE....................................203 774-3270
John Melanson, *President*
Erin St Thomas, *Manager*
▲ **EMP:** 13
SALES (est): 1.3MM **Privately Held**
SIC: 3351 Copper Rolling/Drawing

(G-4697)
AMERICAN PERFORMANCE PDTS LLC
7 Atwater Pl (06492-1774)
PHONE....................................203 269-4468
Ronald P Normandin, *Mng Member*
Andrew Debaise,
EMP: 6
SQ FT: 13,000
SALES: 350K **Privately Held**
SIC: 3444 Mfg Sheet Metalwork

(G-4698)
AMERICAN STONECRAFTERS INC
Also Called: A American Stone & Countertop
224 S Whittlesey Ave (06492-4511)
PHONE....................................203 514-9725
Fax: 203 269-7471
EMP: 5
SALES (est): 510K **Privately Held**
SIC: 2542 3281 5999 5032 Mfg Nonwd Partition/Fixt Mfg Cut Stone/Products Ret Misc Merchandise Whol Brick/Stone Matrls

(G-4699)
AMETEK INC
Also Called: Ametek Specialty Metal Pdts
21 Toelles Rd (06492-4456)
P.O. Box 5807 (06492-7607)
PHONE....................................203 265-6731
David Jenkins, *President*
Brian McConnell, *Project Mgr*
Andrew Vidmar, *Project Mgr*
Robert Kowalczyk, *Opers Staff*
John Lalena, *Buyer*
EMP: 105
SALES (corp-wide): 4.8B **Publicly Held**
SIC: 3452 3823 3399 3331 Mfg Bolts/Screws/Rivets Mfg Process Cntrl Instr Mfg Primary Metal Prdts Primary Copper Producer Mfg Steel Wire/Rltd Prdt
PA: Ametek, Inc.
1100 Cassatt Rd
Berwyn PA 19312
610 647-2121

(G-4700)
AMPHENOL CORPORATION (PA)
358 Hall Ave (06492-3574)
P.O. Box 5030 (06492-7530)
PHONE....................................203 265-8900
Martin H Loeffler, *Ch of Bd*
R Adam Norwitt, *President*
Lance E D'Amico, *Senior VP*
Zachary W Raley, *Senior VP*
David Silverman, *Senior VP*
▼ **EMP:** 85
SALES: 8.2B **Publicly Held**
SIC: 3678 3643 3661 Mfg Electronic Connectors Conductive Wiring Devices And Telephone/Telegraph Apparatus

(G-4701)
AMPHENOL INTERNATIONAL LTD (HQ)
358 Hall Ave (06492-3574)
PHONE....................................203 265-8900
EMP: 3
SALES (est): 1.8MM
SALES (corp-wide): 8.2B **Publicly Held**
SIC: 3678 Mfg Electronic Connectors
PA: Amphenol Corporation
358 Hall Ave
Wallingford CT 06492
203 265-8900

(G-4702)
APCT-CT INC
Also Called: Apct Global
340 Quinnipiac St Unit 25 (06492-4050)
P.O. Box 309 (06492-0309)
PHONE....................................203 284-1215
Steve Robinson, *President*
Tracy Conway, *Controller*
▲ **EMP:** 5
SQ FT: 2,500
SALES (est): 2.5MM
SALES (corp-wide): 25.5MM **Privately Held**
SIC: 3672 Mfg Printed Circuit Boards
PA: Apct, Inc.
3495 De La Cruz Blvd
Santa Clara CA 95054
408 727-6442

(G-4703)
APCT-WALLINGFORD INC
Also Called: Tech Circuits
340 Quinnipiac St Unit 25 (06492-4050)
P.O. Box 309 (06492-0309)
PHONE....................................203 269-3311
Steve Robinson, *President*
Greg Elder, *CFO*
Kimberly Johnson, *Sales Staff*
Pat Fusco, *Department Mgr*
EMP: 45
SQ FT: 46,000
SALES (est): 8MM
SALES (corp-wide): 25.5MM **Privately Held**
WEB: www.techcircuits.com
SIC: 3672 Mfg Printed Circuit Boards
PA: Apct, Inc.
3495 De La Cruz Blvd
Santa Clara CA 95054
408 727-6442

(G-4704)
ARRIS TECHNOLOGY INC
15 Sterling Dr (06492-1843)
PHONE....................................678 473-8493
EMP: 10
SALES (est): 1.1MM **Privately Held**
SIC: 3661 Mfg Telephone/Telegraph Apparatus

(G-4705)
ATLANTIC EQP INSTALLERS INC
55 N Plains Industrial Rd (06492-5841)
P.O. Box 547 (06492-0547)
PHONE....................................203 284-0402
Robert J Huelsman, *President*
Bill Bohne, *CFO*
William E Bohne, *CFO*
Robert K Huelsman, *Shareholder*
EMP: 22 **EST:** 1981
SQ FT: 12,000
SALES (est): 6.8MM **Privately Held**
SIC: 3441 1796 Structural Metal Fabrication Building Equipment Installation

(G-4706)
ATLAS FILTRI NORTH AMERICA LLC
1068 N Farms Rd Ste 3 (06492-5939)
PHONE....................................203 284-0080
Gary Fappino, *CEO*
Daniele Costantini, *Vice Pres*
EMP: 12
SQ FT: 24,000
SALES: 1.5MM **Privately Held**
SIC: 3589 Mfg Service Industry Machinery

(G-4707)
AXIS LASER
7 Atwater Pl (06492-1774)
PHONE....................................203 284-9455
Paul Best, *Owner*
EMP: 4 **EST:** 2007
SALES (est): 349.1K **Privately Held**
SIC: 3444 Structural Metal Fabrication

(G-4708)
B H S INDUSTRIES LTD
23 N Plains Industrial Rd # 3 (06492-2345)
PHONE....................................203 284-9764
Fax: 203 265-5999
EMP: 8
SQ FT: 3,600
SALES (est): 490K **Privately Held**
SIC: 3369 Manufactures Industrial And Giftware Castings

(G-4709)
BEI HOLDINGS INC
6 Capital Dr (06492-2318)
PHONE....................................203 741-9300
EMP: 15
SALES (est): 587.6K **Privately Held**
SIC: 3695 Magnetic And Optical Recording Media

(G-4710)
BOARDMAN SILVERSMITHS INC
22 N Plains Industrial Rd 6c (06492-2341)
PHONE....................................203 265-9978
Burton Boardman, *President*
EMP: 15
SALES (est): 2.3MM **Privately Held**
WEB: www.boardmansilversmiths.com
SIC: 3914 Manufactures Silver And Pewter Products

(G-4711)
BOND-BILT GARAGES INC
30 N Plains Industrial Rd # 16 (06492-2357)
PHONE....................................203 269-3375
Kenneth Kaye, *President*
Arlene Kaye, *Admin Sec*
EMP: 6 **EST:** 1961
SQ FT: 2,400
SALES: 1.9MM **Privately Held**
SIC: 2452 Mfr Prefabricated Wood Buildings

(G-4712)
BRITTANY COMPANY INC
193 S Cherry St (06492-4017)
P.O. Box 221 (06492-0221)
PHONE....................................203 269-7859
Thaddeus Swierczynski, *President*
Thaddeau Siviernyznski, *President*
EMP: 5
SQ FT: 7,500
SALES: 1MM **Privately Held**
WEB: www.brittanycompany.com
SIC: 3444 1761 Mfg Sheet Metalwork Roofing/Siding Contractor

(G-4713)
BROAD PEAK MANUFACTURING LLC
10 Beaumont Rd Ste 1 (06492-2455)
PHONE....................................203 678-4664
Levi Citarella,
EMP: 20 **EST:** 2015
SALES (est): 1.7MM **Privately Held**
SIC: 3471 Engaged In Metal Plating And Polishing Specializing In Hand Finishing Medical Implants

(G-4714)
BROWNE HANSEN LLC
44 School House Rd (06492-3434)
PHONE....................................203 269-0557
Ronald Hansen Jr, *Mng Member*
Frederick Browne, *Mng Member*
Steven Browne,
Kelly O Neil,
EMP: 6
SQ FT: 50,000
SALES (est): 521.2K **Privately Held**
SIC: 2844 Mfg Toilet Preparations

(G-4715)
CARDIOXYL PHARMACEUTICALS INC
5 Research Pkwy (06492-1951)
PHONE....................................919 869-8586
Christopher A Kroeger, *President*
Doug Cowart, *Exec VP*
EMP: 7
SALES (est): 785.2K
SALES (corp-wide): 22.5B **Publicly Held**
WEB: www.cardioxyl.com
SIC: 2834 Mfg Pharmaceutical Preparations
PA: Bristol-Myers Squibb Company
430 E 29th St Fl 14
New York NY 10016
212 546-4000

(G-4716)
CHARTER OAK AUTOMATION LLC
340 Quinnipiac St Ste 19 (06492-4050)
PHONE....................................203 562-0699
Randall Betta,
Mark Herman,
Loudon Page,
▲ **EMP:** 4
SALES (est): 563.2K **Privately Held**
SIC: 3541 3549 Mfg Machine Tools-Cutting Mfg Metalworking Machinery

(G-4717)
CIDRA CHEMICAL MANAGEMENT INC (HQ)
50 Barnes Park Rd N # 103 (06492-5920)
PHONE....................................203 265-0035

GEOGRAPHIC

F Kevin Didden, *President*
Michael Grillo, *Vice Pres*
John Viega, *Opers Mgr*
Gary Hokunson, *CFO*
EMP: 70
SALES (est): 8.7MM **Privately Held**
WEB: www.cidra.com
SIC: 3823 Mfg Process Control Instruments

(G-4718)
CIDRA CORPORATE SERVICES INC
50 Barnes Park Rd N (06492-5920)
PHONE.................................203 265-0035
Kevin Didden, *President*
F Kevin Didden, *President*
John Viega, *COO*
Gary Hokunson, *Treasurer*
EMP: 70
SALES (est): 15.6MM **Privately Held**
WEB: www.cidra.com
SIC: 3823 Mfg Process Control Instruments
PA: Cidra Holdings Llc
50 Barnes Park Rd N # 103
Wallingford CT 06492

(G-4719)
CIDRA CORPORATION
50 Barnes Park Rd N # 103 (06492-5920)
PHONE.................................203 265-0035
F Kevin Didden, *CEO*
Patrick Curry, *President*
Martin Putnam, *President*
Marc Grammatico, *Vice Pres*
John Viega, *Vice Pres*
▼ **EMP:** 95
SALES (est): 22MM **Privately Held**
SIC: 3823 Mfg Process Control Instruments

(G-4720)
CIDRA MINERAL PROCESSING INC
50 Barnes Park Rd N (06492-5920)
PHONE.................................203 265-0035
F Kevin Didden, *President*
Michael Grillo, *Vice Pres*
John Viega, *Opers Mgr*
Gary Hokunson, *CFO*
EMP: 70
SALES (est): 527.4K **Privately Held**
WEB: www.cidra.com
SIC: 3823 Mfg Process Control Instruments
PA: Cidra Holdings Llc
50 Barnes Park Rd N # 103
Wallingford CT 06492

(G-4721)
CIDRA OILSANDS INC (HQ)
50 Barnes Park Rd N (06492-5920)
PHONE.................................203 265-0035
F Kevin Didden, *President*
Michael Grillo, *Vice Pres*
Gary Hokunson, *CFO*
EMP: 6
SALES (est): 4.9MM **Privately Held**
WEB: www.cidra.com
SIC: 3823 Mfg Process Control Instruments

(G-4722)
COLORS INK
40 Capital Dr (06492-2318)
PHONE.................................203 269-4000
Sema Sargin, *President*
Oguc Sargin, *Vice Pres*
EMP: 4
SQ FT: 4,000
SALES (est): 800K **Privately Held**
SIC: 3952 5084 Mfg Lead Pencils/Art Goods Whol Industrial Equipment

(G-4723)
COMPONENT ENGINEERS INC
Also Called: C E I
108 N Plains Indus Rd (06492-2334)
PHONE.................................203 269-0557
Ronald Hansen Jr, *CEO*
Anthony Bracale, *Vice Pres*
Clayton Oliver, *CFO*
Brittany Ryan, *Human Resources*
◆ **EMP:** 95
SQ FT: 52,000
SALES (est): 27.6MM **Privately Held**
WEB: www.componenteng.com
SIC: 3469 Mfg Metal Stampings

(G-4724)
CONFORMIS INC
10 Beaumont Rd Ste 4 (06492-2455)
PHONE.................................203 793-7178
Mark Augusti, *CEO*
EMP: 3 **Publicly Held**
SIC: 3996 Mfg Surface Active Agents
PA: Conformis, Inc.
600 Technology Park Dr # 3
Billerica MA 01821

(G-4725)
CONNECTICUT HYPODERMICS INC
519 Main St (06492-1723)
PHONE.................................203 265-4881
Leonard Tutolo, *Ch of Bd*
Steven Tutolo, *President*
Mark Tutolo, *Treasurer*
Kerri Tutolo, *Office Mgr*
Chris Tutolo, *Admin Sec*
◆ **EMP:** 90
SQ FT: 30,000
SALES (est): 21MM **Privately Held**
WEB: www.connhypo.com
SIC: 3841 Mfg Surgical/Medical Instruments

(G-4726)
CONNECTICUT SCREEN WORKS INC
Also Called: Csw
121 N Plains Indus Rd (06492-2352)
P.O. Box 4578 (06492-7566)
PHONE.................................203 269-4499
Sharon A Caruso, *President*
Michael J Caruso, *Vice Pres*
Mario A Caruso Jr,
EMP: 6
SQ FT: 5,000
SALES (est): 780K **Privately Held**
WEB: www.ctscreen.com
SIC: 3448 3442 Mfg Prefabricated Metal Buildings Mfg Metal Doors/Sash/Trim

(G-4727)
COOL-IT LLC
340 Quinnipiac St (06492-4050)
P.O. Box 309 (06492-0309)
PHONE.................................203 284-4848
Gregory Peterson,
Ashley Dean, *Admin Sec*
Randy Peterson,
EMP: 4 **EST:** 2012
SALES (est): 190K **Privately Held**
SIC: 3089 Mfg Plastic Products

(G-4728)
CORRU SEALS INC
Also Called: Nicholsons
24 Capital Dr (06492-2318)
PHONE.................................203 284-0319
T P Nicholson, *CEO*
William Warner, *President*
EMP: 19
SQ FT: 8,000
SALES (est): 3.6MM **Privately Held**
WEB: www.corru-seals.com
SIC: 3053 Manufactures Metal Gaskets

(G-4729)
CRUSH CLUB LLC
65 S Colony St (06492-4150)
P.O. Box 1827 (06492-7127)
PHONE.................................203 626-9545
Frank Martone, *President*
EMP: 3
SALES (est): 268.1K **Privately Held**
SIC: 2084 Mfg Wines/Brandy/Spirits

(G-4730)
CT ACQUISITIONS LLC
Also Called: Danver
1 Grand St (06492-3509)
PHONE.................................888 441-0537
Alex Drozd, *Plant Mgr*
Denise Litchfield, *Sales Associate*
Phil Zaleon, *Mktg Dir*
Linda Colon, *Marketing Staff*
Mitchell Slater, *Mng Member*
EMP: 50 **EST:** 1998
SQ FT: 52,000
SALES: 8.5MM **Privately Held**
WEB: www.danver.com
SIC: 2514 Mfg Metal Household Furniture

(G-4731)
CUSTOM CHROME PLATING
400 S Orchard St (06492-4500)
PHONE.................................203 265-5667
Jerry Sofocli, *Manager*
EMP: 3
SALES (est): 115.8K **Privately Held**
SIC: 3471 Plating/Polishing Service

(G-4732)
DANAHER TOOL GROUP
61 Barnes Industrial Park (06492-1845)
PHONE.................................203 284-7000
Lawrence Culp Jr, *CEO*
EMP: 15
SALES (est): 2.2MM **Privately Held**
SIC: 3823 Mfg Process Control Instruments

(G-4733)
DEMARTINO FIXTURE CO INC
Also Called: Chefs Equipment Emporium
920 S Colony Rd (06492-5263)
PHONE.................................203 269-3971
Dominick Demartino, *President*
Michele Salvatore, *Corp Secy*
Pasquale Salvatore, *Vice Pres*
EMP: 40
SQ FT: 150,000
SALES (est): 9.4MM **Privately Held**
WEB: www.chefsequip.com
SIC: 3585 Mfg Refrigeration/Heating Equipment

(G-4734)
DEXMET CORPORATION
22 Barnes Industrial Rd S (06492-2462)
PHONE.................................203 294-4440
Tim Poor, *CEO*
▲ **EMP:** 65
SALES (est): 12.5MM **Privately Held**
SIC: 3497 Mfg Metal Foil/Leaf

(G-4735)
DOCTOR STUFF LLC
20 N Plains Industrial Rd # 1 (06492-2300)
PHONE.................................203 785-8475
Kathleen Bouvier, *Principal*
Nora Laverty,
EMP: 6
SALES (est): 643.8K **Privately Held**
SIC: 2759 8711 Commercial Printing Engineering Services

(G-4736)
E & A ENTERPRISES INC
Also Called: Northeast Thermography
10 Capital Dr A (06492-2318)
PHONE.................................203 250-8050
EMP: 20
SQ FT: 10,000
SALES (est): 2MM **Privately Held**
SIC: 2759 Mfg Thermographically Printed Items Including Business Cards Stationery Envelopes & Social Announcements

(G-4737)
E-J ELECTRIC T & D LLC
53 N Plains Industrial Rd (06492-5808)
PHONE.................................203 626-9625
Joe Rubino, *General Mgr*
Anthony Edward Mann,
EMP: 80 **EST:** 2009
SALES (est): 25MM **Privately Held**
SIC: 3699 1731 Mfg Electrical Equipment/Supplies Electrical Contractor

(G-4738)
ETHOSENERGY COMPONENT REPR LLC
Also Called: Wood Group Component Repair
34 Capital Dr (06492-2318)
PHONE.................................203 949-8144
Bert Voisine, *President*
EMP: 35
SQ FT: 15,000
SALES (est): 388.8K
SALES (corp-wide): 10B **Privately Held**
WEB: www.woodgroupgts.com
SIC: 3724 Mfg Aircraft Engines/Parts
HQ: Ethosenergy Gts Holdings (Us), Llc
2800 North Loop W # 1100
Houston TX 77092

(G-4739)
EVEREST ISLES LLC
616 N Elm St (06492-3270)
PHONE.................................203 561-5128
Jeffrey Hladky, *President*
Ross Fenton, *Comms Dir*
EMP: 5
SALES (est): 608.3K **Privately Held**
SIC: 2329 Mfg Men's/Boy's Clothing

(G-4740)
EXOCETUS AUTONOMOUS SYSTEMS
7 Laser Ln (06492-1928)
PHONE.................................860 512-7260
William Turner, *CEO*
Joseph Turner, *COO*
EMP: 5 **EST:** 2017
SALES (est): 348.3K **Privately Held**
SIC: 3731 3812 Shipbuilding/Repairing

(G-4741)
EXPERT EMBROIDERY
121 N Plains Indus Ste G (06492-5883)
PHONE.................................203 269-9675
Chris Fjuer, *President*
EMP: 15
SALES (est): 870.3K **Privately Held**
SIC: 2395 Pleating/Stitching Services

(G-4742)
EYLWARD TIMBER CO
13 Quince St (06492-2964)
PHONE.................................203 265-4276
Mike Eylward, *Owner*
EMP: 9
SALES (est): 806.7K **Privately Held**
SIC: 2421 5099 Sawmill/Planing Mill Whol Durable Goods

(G-4743)
FIBERGLASS ENGR & DESIGN CO
Also Called: Fedco
25 N Plains Industrial Hw (06492-6804)
PHONE.................................203 265-1644
Dave Papoosha, *President*
EMP: 4
SQ FT: 13,000
SALES: 500K **Privately Held**
SIC: 3089 3792 Mfg Plastic Products Mfg Travel Trailers/Campers

(G-4744)
FISHER MFG SYSTEMS INC (PA)
Also Called: Fisher Products
20 N Plains Industrial Rd # 12
(06492-6811)
PHONE.................................203 269-3846
Curtis Fisher, *President*
Sharon Fisher, *Admin Sec*
EMP: 10
SQ FT: 10,000
SALES: 1MM **Privately Held**
WEB: www.fishermfgsystems.com
SIC: 3599 Mfg Industrial Machinery

(G-4745)
FOUGERA PHARMACEUTICALS INC
Byk-Chemie USA
524 S Cherry St (06492-4453)
P.O. Box 5670 (06492-7651)
PHONE.................................203 265-2086
Darryl Jackson, *Publisher*
Wolfgang Zinnert, *Manager*
EMP: 69
SALES (corp-wide): 51.9B **Privately Held**
SIC: 2851 Mfg Chemicals
HQ: Fougera Pharmaceuticals Inc.
60 Baylis Rd
Melville NY 11747
631 454-7677

▲ = Import ▼=Export
◆ =Import/Export

(G-4746)
FRANK PRINTING CO R
184 Center St (06492-4142)
PHONE..............................203 265-6152
Richard Frank, *Owner*
EMP: 3
SQ FT: 1,300
SALES (est): 265.5K **Privately Held**
SIC: 2759 Lithographic Commercial Printing

(G-4747)
FRONT PORCH BREWING
226 N Plins Ind Rd Unit 4 (06492-2397)
PHONE..............................203 679-1096
James Flynn, *Owner*
EMP: 5
SALES (est): 139.9K **Privately Held**
SIC: 2082 Mfg Malt Beverages

(G-4748)
GEORGE S PREISNER JEWELERS
Also Called: Preisner, George S Pewter Co
150 Center St (06492-4114)
P.O. Box 460 (06492-0460)
PHONE..............................203 265-0057
George S Preisner, *President*
Erna Damm, *Vice Pres*
EMP: 5
SQ FT: 5,280
SALES (est): 280K **Privately Held**
SIC: 3914 3911 Mfg Silverware/Plated Ware Mfg Silverware/Plated Ware Mfg Precious Metal Jewelry

(G-4749)
GLASS INDUSTRIES AMERICA LLC
340 Quinnipiac St Unit 9 (06492-4050)
PHONE..............................203 269-6700
Livia Liburdi, *Manager*
George Sutherland,
EMP: 15
SALES (est): 1.7MM **Privately Held**
SIC: 3231 5023 Mfg Glass

(G-4750)
HERBASWAY LABORATORIES LLC
101 N Plains Indstrl Rd (06492-2360)
PHONE..............................203 269-6991
Lou St John, *Controller*
Franklin M Saintjohn,
▲ **EMP:** 49
SALES (est): 6.1MM **Privately Held**
WEB: www.herbasway.com
SIC: 2099 8731 2087 5149 Mfg Food Preparations Coml Physical Research Mfg Flavor Extracts Whol Groceries

(G-4751)
HIGH ENERGY X-RAYS INTL CORP
Also Called: Hexi
57 N Plains Industrial Rd B (06492-5841)
P.O. Box 457 (06492-0457)
PHONE..............................203 909-9777
Sereymeth Kong, *Vice Pres*
EMP: 3
SALES (est): 175.3K **Privately Held**
SIC: 3844 Mfg X-Ray Apparatus/Tubes

(G-4752)
HITACHI ALOKA MEDICAL LTD
10 Fairfield Blvd (06492-5903)
PHONE..............................203 269-5088
Minoru Yoshizumi, *President*
EMP: 99
SALES (est): 8.5MM **Privately Held**
SIC: 3841 5047 3829 Mfg Surgical/Medical Instruments Whol Medical/Hospital Equipment Mfg Measuring/Controlling Devices

(G-4753)
HITACHI ALOKA MEDICAL AMER INC
10 Fairfield Blvd (06492-5903)
PHONE..............................203 269-5088
David R Famiglietti, *President*
Randy R Baraso, *Business Mgr*
Angela Van Arsdale, *QC Mgr*
Ray Koba, *Treasurer*
EMP: 99
SALES (est): 19.7MM **Privately Held**
WEB: www.aloka.com
SIC: 3841 5047 3829 Mfg Surgical/Medical Instruments Whol Medical/Hospital Equipment Mfg Measuring/Controlling Devices
PA: Hitachi, Ltd.
1-6-6, Marunouchi
Chiyoda-Ku TKY 100-0

(G-4754)
HOLO-KROME USA
61 Barnes Industrial Park (06492-1845)
PHONE..............................800 879-6205
Mary Raymond, *Purch Agent*
Orlando Castaneda, *Manager*
EMP: 30 **EST:** 2018
SALES (est): 2.2MM **Privately Held**
SIC: 3452 Mfg Bolts/Screws/Rivets

(G-4755)
IMAGE360
Also Called: Signs By Tomorrow
163 N Plains Indus Rd (06492-2332)
PHONE..............................203 949-0726
Tim Keogh, *President*
EMP: 14
SQ FT: 5,600
SALES: 700K **Privately Held**
SIC: 3993 Signsadv Specs

(G-4756)
ITS NEW ENGLAND INC
8 Capital Dr (06492-2318)
PHONE..............................203 265-8100
Brian Russell, *President*
EMP: 4 **EST:** 2010
SALES (est): 467.9K **Privately Held**
SIC: 3579 Mfg Office Machines

(G-4757)
J & L TOOL COMPANY INC
368 N Cherry Street Ext (06492-2309)
PHONE..............................203 265-6237
Leonard Rossicone Sr, *President*
Leonard Rossicone Jr, *Vice Pres*
Nancy Rossicone, *Vice Pres*
Sheri Lynn Rossicone, *Vice Pres*
EMP: 25
SQ FT: 12,000
SALES (est): 3.4MM **Privately Held**
SIC: 3544 Mfg Prototype Plastic Molds

(G-4758)
J&L PLASTIC MOLDING LLC
368 N Cherry Street Ext (06492-2309)
PHONE..............................203 265-6237
Al Kunst, *Production*
Michael Griglun, *QC Mgr*
Marty Kellaher, *VP Sales*
Leonard Rossicone,
Leonard Rossicone Jr,
▲ **EMP:** 7
SQ FT: 12,000
SALES (est): 1.4MM **Privately Held**
WEB: www.jlmolding.com
SIC: 3089 Mfg Plastic Products

(G-4759)
JEM MANUFACTURING INC
Also Called: American Industrial Rbr Pdts
20 N Plains Industrial Rd # 12 (06492-6811)
PHONE..............................203 250-9404
Ian Robinson, *President*
EMP: 6
SALES (est): 652.2K **Privately Held**
SIC: 3061 Mfg Mechanical Rubber Goods

(G-4760)
KINAMOR INCORPORATED
Also Called: Kinamor Plastics
63 N Plains Industrial Rd (06492-5841)
PHONE..............................203 269-0380
John Romanik Sr, *CEO*
John Romanik Jr, *Vice Pres*
Mary Romanik, *Vice Pres*
▲ **EMP:** 29
SQ FT: 15,000
SALES (est): 5.2MM **Privately Held**
WEB: www.kinamorinc.com
SIC: 3089 3441 2396 Mfg Plastic Products Structural Metal Fabrication Mfg Auto/Apparel Trimming

(G-4761)
KOVACS MACHINE AND TOOL CO
50 N Plains Industrial Rd (06492-2372)
PHONE..............................203 269-4949
Allen Cuccaro, *President*
Peter Albrycht, *Vice Pres*
Michael Frank, *Vice Pres*
EMP: 37 **EST:** 1967
SQ FT: 8,000
SALES (est): 5.4MM **Privately Held**
SIC: 3599 3544 Mfg Industrial Machinery Mfg Dies/Tools/Jigs/Fixtures

(G-4762)
KRAFTY KAKES INC
39 N Plains Industrial Rd E (06492-2346)
PHONE..............................203 284-0299
Tom Conlon, *President*
EMP: 4
SALES (est): 355.7K **Privately Held**
SIC: 2051 Mfg Bread/Related Products

(G-4763)
L R BROWN MANUFACTURING CO
53 Prince St (06492-4119)
P.O. Box 282 (06492-0282)
PHONE..............................203 265-5639
Charles Liedke Sr, *President*
Charles Liedke Jr, *Vice Pres*
Robert Liedke, *Vice Pres*
Frances Liedke, *Admin Sec*
EMP: 8 **EST:** 1949
SQ FT: 5,000
SALES (est): 300K **Privately Held**
SIC: 3599 3542 Mfg Custom Machinery & Machine Tool Rebuilding

(G-4764)
LAWRENCE HOLDINGS INC (PA)
34b Barnes Indus Rd S (06492-2438)
P.O. Box 336, Roseville MI (48066-0336)
PHONE..............................203 949-1600
Lawrence Buhl III, *CEO*
K C Jones, *CFO*
EMP: 17
SALES (est): 37.7MM **Privately Held**
SIC: 3469 3089 3544 Mfg Metal Stampings Mfg Plastic Products Mfg Dies/Tools/Jigs/Fixtures

(G-4765)
LEE MANUFACTURING INC
46 Barnes Industrial Rd S (06492-2438)
P.O. Box 758 (06492-0758)
PHONE..............................203 284-0466
George M Eames IV, *President*
George M Eames III, *Director*
EMP: 60
SQ FT: 40,000
SALES (est): 10.9MM **Privately Held**
WEB: www.leemanufacturing.com
SIC: 3444 Mfg Sheet Metalwork

(G-4766)
LINGOL CORPORATION
415 S Cherry St (06492-4428)
P.O. Box 791 (06492-0791)
PHONE..............................203 265-3608
Peter W Lindenfelser, *Vice Pres*
Ruth B Lindenfelser, *Admin Sec*
EMP: 10
SALES (est): 1.4MM **Privately Held**
SIC: 3089 Mfg Plastic Products

(G-4767)
LOGO SPORTSWEAR INC
12 Beaumont Rd (06492-2402)
PHONE..............................203 678-4700
Patrick Cerreta, *CEO*
Tom Kordik, *Opers Staff*
Josh Ferguson, *Sales Mgr*
Terry Halloran, *Sales Staff*
Frederick Swan, *Sales Staff*
EMP: 6 **EST:** 2015
SQ FT: 15,000
SALES (est): 617.7K
SALES (corp-wide): 851.2K **Privately Held**
SIC: 2759 5699 Commercial Printing Ret Misc Apparel/Accessories
PA: Digital Room Llc
8000 Haskell Ave
Van Nuys CA 91406
310 575-4440

(G-4768)
MAGNETEC CORPORATION
Also Called: Ithaca Peripherals Div
7 Laser Ln (06492-1928)
PHONE..............................203 949-9933
Bart C Shuldman, *President*
David Ritchie, *President*
John Cygielnik, *Senior VP*
Michael Kumpf, *Senior VP*
Lucy H Staley, *Senior VP*
EMP: 100 **EST:** 1973
SQ FT: 44,000
SALES (est): 47MM **Publicly Held**
WEB: www.magnetec.com
SIC: 3577 Mfg Transaction Based Printers & Printer Peripherals
PA: Transact Technologies Incorporated
2319 Whitney Ave Ste 3b
Hamden CT 06518

(G-4769)
MATERIALS PROC DEV GROUP LLC
7 Swan Ave (06492-1624)
PHONE..............................203 269-6617
Robert Hancock, *Owner*
EMP: 3
SALES (est): 241.5K **Privately Held**
SIC: 2851 Mfg Paints/Allied Products

(G-4770)
MATTHEWS PRINTING CO
10 Marshall St (06492-4097)
P.O. Box 456 (06492-0456)
PHONE..............................203 265-0363
Dean De Negris, *President*
Gail De Negris, *Admin Sec*
EMP: 10
SQ FT: 4,000
SALES (est): 1.5MM **Privately Held**
SIC: 2752 2759 Commercial Offset & Letter Printing

(G-4771)
MAX-TEK LLC
Also Called: Max-Tek Ue Superabrasive Mch
48 N Plains Industrial Rd # 1 (06492-2351)
PHONE..............................860 372-4900
Edward Elie, *President*
▲ **EMP:** 10
SALES (est): 2MM **Privately Held**
SIC: 3541 Mfg Machine Tools-Cutting

(G-4772)
MEASUREMENT SYSTEMS INC
Also Called: Ultra Elec Measurement Systems
50 Barnes Park Rd N # 102 (06492-5940)
PHONE..............................203 949-3500
Peter Crawford, *President*
Ken L Tasch, *President*
Rick Blais, *Purch Mgr*
EMP: 42
SQ FT: 19,500
SALES (est): 13.5MM
SALES (corp-wide): 1B **Privately Held**
WEB: www.ultra-msi.com
SIC: 3625 3577 Mfg Relays/Industrial Controls Mfg Computer Peripheral Equipment
PA: Ultra Electronics Holdings Plc
417 Bridport Road
Greenford MIDDX UB6 8
208 813-4567

(G-4773)
MICHELE SCHIANO DI COLA INC
11 S Colony St (06492-4150)
PHONE..............................203 265-5301
Cindy Fiorentino, *President*
EMP: 3
SALES (est): 273.1K **Privately Held**
SIC: 2041 3531 Mfg Flour/Grain Mill Prooducts Mfg Construction Machinery

(G-4774)
MICROMOD AUTOMATION & CONTROLS
10 Capital Dr (06492-2318)
PHONE..............................585 321-9209

GEOGRAPHIC

Eric Vangellow, *President*
Jeffrey Galvin, *Sales Engr*
EMP: 16
SALES: 3MM **Privately Held**
SIC: 3823 Mfg Process Control Instruments

(G-4775)
MICROMOD AUTOMTN & CONTRLS LLC
10 Capital Dr (06492-2318)
PHONE..................................585 321-9200
Sohil Patel, *President*
Wayne France, *General Mgr*
Robert Shaffer, *Vice Pres*
EMP: 20
SALES (est): 4MM **Privately Held**
WEB: www.micmod.com
SIC: 3625 Mfg Relays/Industrial Controls

(G-4776)
MIKCO MANUFACTURING INC
14 Village Ln (06492-2427)
P.O. Box 764 (06492-0764)
PHONE..................................203 269-2250
Michael J Boissy, *President*
Michael S Boissy, *Vice Pres*
Betty Boissy, *Executive*
Betty J Boissy, *Shareholder*
EMP: 14 **EST:** 1977
SQ FT: 9,000
SALES (est): 2.5MM **Privately Held**
SIC: 3599 Mfg Industrial Machinery

(G-4777)
NATIONAL FILTER MEDIA CORP
9 Fairfield Blvd (06492-1828)
PHONE..................................203 741-2225
Denis Charest, *Branch Mgr*
EMP: 40
SQ FT: 32,745
SALES (corp-wide): 922.9MM **Privately Held**
WEB: www.nfm-filter.com
SIC: 3569 Mfg General Industrial Machinery
HQ: The National Filter Media Corporation
691 N 400 W
Salt Lake City UT 84103
801 363-6736

(G-4778)
NOMIS ENTERPRISES
90 Northford Rd (06492-5519)
PHONE..................................631 821-3120
Susan Simon, *Owner*
EMP: 3
SALES: 40K **Privately Held**
SIC: 2329 3993 5999 2399 Mfg Mens/Boys Clothing Mfg Signs/Ad Specialties Ret Misc Merchandise Mfg Fabrctd Textile Pdts Business Services

(G-4779)
NU LINE DESIGN LLC
Also Called: Nu Line Signs
21 N Plains Industrial Rd (06492-2382)
PHONE..................................203 949-0726
Susan Keogh,
Tim Keogh,
EMP: 4
SQ FT: 2,600
SALES: 190K **Privately Held**
SIC: 3993 7389 4493 Mfg Signs/Advertising Specialties Business Services Marina Operation

(G-4780)
NUCOR STEEL CONNECTICUT INC
Also Called: Nucor Bar Mill Group
35 Toelles Rd (06492-4419)
P.O. Box 928 (06492-0928)
PHONE..................................203 265-0615
Mark Brando, *Principal*
▲ **EMP:** 157
SQ FT: 227,120
SALES (est): 71.8MM
SALES (corp-wide): 25B **Publicly Held**
WEB: www.nucor.com
SIC: 3312 3449 3496 Blast Furnace-Steel Works Mfg Misc Structural Metalwork Mfg Misc Fabricated Wire Products
PA: Nucor Corporation
1915 Rexford Rd Ste 400
Charlotte NC 28211
704 366-7000

(G-4781)
ON TRACK KARTING INC (PA)
984 N Colony Rd (06492-1860)
PHONE..................................203 626-0464
Martin Tyrrel, *Principal*
▲ **EMP:** 15
SALES (est): 2.2MM **Privately Held**
SIC: 3799 Mfg Transportation Equipment

(G-4782)
PARADISE HLLS VNYRD WINERY LLC
15 Windswept Hill Rd (06492-2755)
PHONE..................................203 284-0123
Albert Ruggiero,
EMP: 6
SALES (est): 532.4K **Privately Held**
SIC: 2084 Mfg Wines/Brandy/Spirits

(G-4783)
PAUWAY CORP
63 N Cherry St Ste 2 (06492-2363)
PHONE..................................203 265-3939
Wayne Rydzy, *President*
Paulette Rydzy, *Admin Sec*
EMP: 15
SALES (est): 1.9MM **Privately Held**
WEB: www.pauwaycorp.com
SIC: 3479 Industrial Spray Painting Of Metal Products

(G-4784)
POWER CONTROLS INC
801 N Main Street Ext (06492-2463)
PHONE..................................203 284-0235
Ronald Nash, *President*
Karen Nash, *Admin Sec*
EMP: 14
SQ FT: 7,500
SALES (est): 2.4MM **Privately Held**
WEB: www.powercontrols.com
SIC: 3679 Mfg Electronic Components

(G-4785)
PPG INDUSTRIES INC
22 Barnes Industrial Rd S (06492-2462)
PHONE..................................203 294-4440
Michael McGarry, *Branch Mgr*
EMP: 65
SALES (corp-wide): 15.3B **Publicly Held**
SIC: 3497 Mfg Metal Foil/Leaf
PA: Ppg Industries, Inc.
1 Ppg Pl
Pittsburgh PA 15272
412 434-3131

(G-4786)
PRALINES INC
Also Called: Pralines Central
30 N Plains Industrial Rd # 12
(06492-2357)
PHONE..................................203 284-8847
Dana Torre, *President*
EMP: 11
SQ FT: 1,900
SALES (est): 1.3MM **Privately Held**
WEB: www.pralines.com
SIC: 2024 Mfg Ice Cream/Frozen Desert

(G-4787)
PRAXAIR INC
10 Research Pkwy (06492-1963)
PHONE..................................203 793-1200
Lori M Lieser, *Vice Pres*
Steven Christie, *Treasurer*
Maria Scarpa, *Director*
Robert S Zuccaro, *Director*
Stephen Sonnone, *Admin Sec*
EMP: 20 **Privately Held**
SIC: 2813 Mfg Industrial Gases
HQ: Praxair, Inc.
10 Riverview Dr
Danbury CT 06810
203 837-2000

(G-4788)
PRECISION DEVICES INC (PA)
55 N Plains Industrial Rd (06492-5841)
PHONE..................................203 265-9308
William P Bacha Jr, *President*
Mark Hoover, *Vice Pres*
Christine Bacha, *Admin Sec*
EMP: 17 **EST:** 1981
SQ FT: 8,000
SALES (est): 4MM **Privately Held**
SIC: 7694 5063 Armature Rewinding Whol Electrical Equipment

(G-4789)
PRECISION ENGINEERED PDTS LLC
Also Called: Pep Connecticut Plastics
6 Northrop Indus Pk Rd W (06492-1962)
PHONE..................................203 265-3299
Claire Webb, *Manager*
EMP: 40
SALES (corp-wide): 770.6MM **Publicly Held**
SIC: 3089 Mfg Plastic Products
HQ: Precision Engineered Products Llc
110 Frank Mossberg Dr
Attleboro MA 02703
508 226-5600

(G-4790)
PROTON ENERGY SYSTEMS INC
Also Called: Proton Onsite
10 Technology Dr (06492-1955)
PHONE..................................203 678-2000
Anders Soreng, *CEO*
David T Bow, *Senior VP*
John A Zagaja III, *Senior VP*
Everett Anderson, *Vice Pres*
Sheldon A Paul, *CFO*
▲ **EMP:** 90
SQ FT: 98,703
SALES (est): 33.6MM **Privately Held**
WEB: www.protonenergy.com
SIC: 3569 Mfg General Industrial Machinery
PA: Nel Asa
Karenslyst Alle 20
Oslo 0278

(G-4791)
PROTRONIX INC
28 Parker St (06492-2320)
PHONE..................................203 269-5858
Don Rosadini Jr, *President*
Janis Rosadini, *Admin Sec*
EMP: 10
SQ FT: 3,500
SALES (est): 1.6MM **Privately Held**
SIC: 3679 Electro Mechanical Component Assembly

(G-4792)
R & D PRECISION INC
63 N Cherry St Ste 1 (06492-2363)
PHONE..................................203 284-3396
William D Harkness, *President*
Robin Harkness, *Admin Sec*
EMP: 19
SQ FT: 14,000
SALES (est): 3.5MM **Privately Held**
SIC: 3444 Mfg Sheet Metalwork

(G-4793)
RACING TIMES
428 Main St (06492-2275)
PHONE..................................203 298-2899
Alan Joseph Piquette, *Partner*
EMP: 25
SQ FT: 2,300
SALES: 98K **Privately Held**
SIC: 2721 Periodicals-Publishing/Printing

(G-4794)
RADIALL USA INC
777 Northrop Rd (06492-1954)
P.O. Box 510, New Haven (06513-0510)
PHONE..................................203 776-2813
Jolanda Meinen, *General Mgr*
Bill Neale, *COO*
Gary Ramadei, *Facilities Mgr*
Claude Brocheton, *Engineer*
Janice Martin, *Human Res Mgr*
EMP: 190
SQ FT: 65,000
SALES (corp-wide): 160.1MM **Privately Held**
SIC: 3678 Mfg Electronic Connectors
PA: Radiall Usa, Inc.
8950 S 52nd St Ste 401
Tempe AZ 85284
480 682-9400

(G-4795)
RESPIRONICS INC
5 Technology Dr (06492-1942)
PHONE..................................203 697-6490
Dorita A Pishko, *Branch Mgr*
EMP: 164
SALES (corp-wide): 20.1B **Privately Held**
SIC: 3842 Mfg Surgical Appliances
HQ: Respironics, Inc.
1001 Murry Ridge Ln
Murrysville PA 15668
724 387-5200

(G-4796)
RESPIRONICS NOVAMETRIX LLC
5 Technology Dr (06492-1942)
PHONE..................................203 697-6475
Philip F Nuzzo, *Plant Mgr*
▲ **EMP:** 150 **EST:** 1978
SQ FT: 53,000
SALES (est): 15.4MM
SALES (corp-wide): 20.1B **Privately Held**
SIC: 3841 3845 Mfg Surgical/Medical Instruments Mfg Electromedical Equipment
HQ: Respironics, Inc.
1001 Murry Ridge Ln
Murrysville PA 15668
724 387-5200

(G-4797)
RF PRINTING LLC
Also Called: AlphaGraphics
200 Church St Ste 5 (06492-2274)
P.O. Box 302, Guilford (06437-0302)
PHONE..................................203 265-9939
Richard W Fuhrman, *Mng Member*
EMP: 6
SALES: 500K **Privately Held**
SIC: 2752 Comm Prtg Litho

(G-4798)
ROEHM AMERICA LLC
528 S Cherry St (06492-4458)
PHONE..................................203 269-4481
Peter Stein, *Manager*
Jeffrey Zgorski, *Manager*
EMP: 50
SALES (corp-wide): 195.2MM **Privately Held**
SIC: 2821 Mfg Plastic Materials/Resins
PA: Roehm America Llc
299 Jefferson Rd
Parsippany NJ 07054
973 929-8000

(G-4799)
ROKAP INC
Also Called: Sign Stop
1002 Yale Ave (06492-5923)
PHONE..................................203 265-6895
Rosalind Kaplan, *President*
Seth Kaplan, *Vice Pres*
Russ Kaplan, *Admin Sec*
EMP: 7
SQ FT: 4,200
SALES (est): 1MM **Privately Held**
WEB: www.signstopsigns.com
SIC: 3993 7699 7532 7389 Mfg Signs/Ad Specialties Repair Services Auto Body Repair/Paint Business Services

(G-4800)
ROODLE RICE & NOODLE BAR
1263 S Broad St (06492-1737)
PHONE..................................203 269-9899
EMP: 4 **EST:** 2016
SALES (est): 218.6K **Privately Held**
SIC: 2098 Mfg Macaroni/Spaghetti

(G-4801)
ROWLAND TECHNOLOGIES INC
320 Barnes Rd (06492-1804)
PHONE..................................203 269-9500
Stephen J Dimugno, *President*
Peter J Connerton Jr, *Exec VP*
Michael A Iovene, *Admin Sec*
◆ **EMP:** 75
SQ FT: 40,000

▲ = Import ▼=Export
◆ =Import/Export

SALES (est): 27.4MM **Privately Held**
WEB: www.rowlandtechnologies.com
SIC: 3081 Mfg Unsupported Plastic Film/Sheet

(G-4802)
RUCKUS WIRELESS INC
Also Called: Broadband Communication Div
15 Sterling Dr (06492-1843)
PHONE..................................203 303-6400
John Caezza, *Division Pres*
EMP: 20 **Privately Held**
WEB: www.c-cor.net
SIC: 3661 Mfg Telephone/Telegraph Apparatus
HQ: Ruckus Wireless, Inc.
350 W Java Dr
Sunnyvale CA 94089
650 265-4200

(G-4803)
RUSSELL ORGANICS LLC
329 Main St Ste 208 (06492-2273)
PHONE..................................203 285-6633
Richard Russell, *CEO*
◆ **EMP:** 7
SALES: 3MM **Privately Held**
SIC: 2844 Mfg Toilet Preparations

(G-4804)
S & S SEALCOATING LLC
5 Barker Dr (06492-1773)
PHONE..................................203 284-0054
Gary Stanley, *Principal*
EMP: 4
SALES (est): 421.6K **Privately Held**
SIC: 2891 Mfg Adhesives/Sealants

(G-4805)
SHIRT GRAPHIX
198 Center St (06492-4142)
PHONE..................................203 294-1656
Ed Zielinski, *Owner*
EMP: 3
SALES (est): 334.5K **Privately Held**
SIC: 2759 2395 Commercial Printing Pleating/Stitching Services

(G-4806)
SIAM VALEE
20 Ives Rd (06492-2484)
PHONE..................................203 269-6888
EMP: 3 **EST:** 2007
SALES (est): 224.3K **Privately Held**
SIC: 3993 Mfg Signs/Advertising Specialties

(G-4807)
SIMSON PRODUCTS CO INC
50 N Plains Industrial Rd (06492-2333)
PHONE..................................203 265-9882
Allen Cuccaro, *President*
Michael Frank, *Admin Sec*
EMP: 12
SALES (est): 1.3MM **Privately Held**
SIC: 3599 Machine Shop

(G-4808)
SOUTHERN CONN PALLET CO INC
346 Quinnipiac St (06492-4053)
P.O. Box 4566 (06492-7566)
PHONE..................................203 265-1313
James Waldeck, *President*
EMP: 7
SQ FT: 10,000
SALES (est): 1.3MM **Privately Held**
SIC: 2448 Mfg Wood Pallets/Skids

(G-4809)
SPECIALTY CABLE CORP
2 Tower Dr (06492-1877)
P.O. Box 50 (06492-0050)
PHONE..................................203 265-7126
Kim Bowen, *CEO*
Carl Shanahan, *President*
Christopher Lambert, *Purch Mgr*
Wayne Davis, *Info Tech Dir*
Carl Shanahan Jr, *Admin Sec*
EMP: 70
SQ FT: 65,000
SALES (est): 30.1MM **Privately Held**
SIC: 3357 3315 5063 Nonferrous Wiredrawing/Insulating Mfg Steel Wire/Related Products Whol Electrical Equipment

(G-4810)
SPECIALTY COMPONENTS INC (PA)
14 Village Ln Ste 1 (06492-2459)
PHONE..................................203 284-9112
Marc Hadarik, *President*
Amy Hadarik, *Admin Sec*
EMP: 5 **EST:** 1975
SQ FT: 17,000
SALES (est): 1.3MM **Privately Held**
WEB: www.specialtycomponents.com
SIC: 3599 Mfg Industrial Machinery

(G-4811)
SPECIALTY COMPONENTS INC
14 Village Ln (06492-2459)
PHONE..................................203 284-9112
Jam Hadararick, *Owner*
EMP: 4
SALES (corp-wide): 1.3MM **Privately Held**
WEB: www.specialtycomponents.com
SIC: 3829 Mfg Industrial Machinery
PA: Specialty Components, Inc.
14 Village Ln Ste 1
Wallingford CT 06492
203 284-9112

(G-4812)
STABAN ENGINEERING CORP
65 N Plains Industrial Rd (06492-5832)
P.O. Box 8 (06492-0008)
PHONE..................................203 294-1997
Dennis Bandecchi, *President*
Todd Widener, *Vice Pres*
EMP: 14
SQ FT: 16,500
SALES (est): 4.2MM **Privately Held**
SIC: 3565 Automated Equipment Designers & Manufacturers

(G-4813)
STATE WELDING & FABG INC
107 N Cherry St (06492-2305)
PHONE..................................203 294-4071
Charles Mascola, *President*
EMP: 7
SQ FT: 18,000
SALES (est): 1.5MM **Privately Held**
SIC: 3441 7692 Structural Metal Fabrication Welding Repair

(G-4814)
STRAIN MEASUREMENT DEVICES INC
55 Barnes Park Rd N (06492-1883)
PHONE..................................203 294-5800
Frederick E Jackson, *President*
Daniel Shapiro, *Vice Pres*
Linda Anderson, *Production*
Eduard Krutyanskiy, *Engineer*
Jason Michaud, *Controller*
EMP: 25
SQ FT: 14,000
SALES (est): 6.3MM **Privately Held**
WEB: www.smdsensors.com
SIC: 3829 3674 Mfg Measuring/Controlling Devices Mfg Semiconductors/Related Devices

(G-4815)
TECHNICAL METAL FINISHING INC
Also Called: T M F
29 Capital Dr (06492-5818)
PHONE..................................203 284-7825
Levi Citarella, *President*
Alfred Malarese, *Principal*
John Helm, *Vice Pres*
Phillip Milidaneri, *Vice Pres*
EMP: 23
SALES (est): 2.8MM **Privately Held**
SIC: 3471 Plating/Polishing Service

(G-4816)
TEE-IT-UP LLC
21 N Plains Industrial Rd (06492-2382)
PHONE..................................203 949-9455
Dan Sullivan, *Principal*
EMP: 3
SALES (est): 280K **Privately Held**
SIC: 2759 2395 Commercial Printing Pleating/Stitching Services

(G-4817)
THERMOSPAS HOT TUB PRODUCTS
10 Research Pkwy Ste 300 (06492-1963)
PHONE..................................203 303-0005
Andrew Tournas, *President*
Paul Anderson, *Sales Staff*
EMP: 35
SALES (est): 5.2MM **Privately Held**
SIC: 3999 Mfg Misc Products
HQ: Sundance Spas, Inc.
13925 City Center Dr # 200
Chino Hills CA 91709
909 606-7733

(G-4818)
TIMES FIBER COMMUNICATIONS INC (HQ)
358 Hall Ave (06492-3574)
P.O. Box 384 (06492-7006)
PHONE..................................203 265-8500
Adam R Norwitt, *President*
Greg Lamto, *CFO*
◆ **EMP:** 54
SQ FT: 15,000
SALES (est): 166.5MM
SALES (corp-wide): 8.2B **Publicly Held**
WEB: www.timesfiber.com
SIC: 3357 Nonferrous Wiredrawing/Insulating
PA: Amphenol Corporation
358 Hall Ave
Wallingford CT 06492
203 265-8900

(G-4819)
TIMES MICROWAVE SYSTEMS INC (HQ)
358 Hall Ave (06492-3574)
P.O. Box 5039 (06492-7539)
PHONE..................................203 949-8400
Bill Callahan, *General Mgr*
Warren Lucid, *Controller*
Timothy Smith, *Manager*
▲ **EMP:** 300
SQ FT: 154,000
SALES (est): 62.9MM
SALES (corp-wide): 8.2B **Publicly Held**
WEB: www.timesmicrowave.com
SIC: 3679 3357 3678 Mfg Electronic Components Nonferrous Wiredrawing/Insulating Mfg Electronic Connectors
PA: Amphenol Corporation
358 Hall Ave
Wallingford CT 06492
203 265-8900

(G-4820)
TIMES WIRE AND CABLE COMPANY (HQ)
Also Called: Amphenol
358 Hall Ave (06492-3574)
PHONE..................................203 949-8400
Mark St Hilaire, *General Mgr*
EMP: 7
SALES (est): 1.9MM
SALES (corp-wide): 8.2B **Publicly Held**
SIC: 3643 5063 Mfg Conductive Wiring Devices Whol Electrical Equipment
PA: Amphenol Corporation
358 Hall Ave
Wallingford CT 06492
203 265-8900

(G-4821)
TIMNA MANUFACTURING INC
204 N Plains Indus Rd (06492-2358)
PHONE..................................203 265-4656
Sharon A Nagy, *President*
Frank A Nagy, *Treasurer*
EMP: 9
SQ FT: 5,000
SALES (est): 1.2MM **Privately Held**
SIC: 3599 Machine Shop

(G-4822)
TOTAL CONTROL INC
130 S Turnpike Rd (06492-4320)
PHONE..................................203 269-4749
Peter Kulak, *President*
EMP: 8
SALES (est): 2.2MM **Privately Held**
WEB: www.totalcontrol-online.com
SIC: 7694 Whol Electrical Equipment

(G-4823)
TRUE PUBLISHING COMPANY
Also Called: Cheshire Herald
125 Grandview Ave (06492-5157)
P.O. Box 247, Cheshire (06410-0247)
PHONE..................................203 272-5316
Joseph Jakubisyn, *Owner*
Maureen Jakubisyn, *Treasurer*
Debbie Eckert, *Representative*
EMP: 13 **EST:** 1953
SALES: 1MM **Privately Held**
WEB: www.cheshireherald.com
SIC: 2711 Publishes A Weekly Newspaper

(G-4824)
ULBRICH STAINLESS STEELS
Also Called: Ulbrich Steel
1 Dudley Ave (06492-4457)
P.O. Box 610 (06492-0610)
PHONE..................................203 269-2507
Mike Marzik, *Opers Mgr*
Lisa Aurora, *Purch Mgr*
Bob Ferguson, *Inv Control Mgr*
Theresa Schneider, *Purchasing*
Rob Giapponi, *Sales/Mktg Mgr*
EMP: 180
SALES (corp-wide): 208.4MM **Privately Held**
WEB: www.ulbrich.com
SIC: 3316 3547 3356 3339 Mfg Cold-Rolled Steel Mfg Rolling Mill Mach Nonferrous Rollng/Drawng Primary Nonfrs Mtl Prdcr Blast Furnace-Steel Work
PA: Ulbrich Stainless Steels & Special Metals, Inc.
153 Washington Ave
North Haven CT 06473
203 239-4481

(G-4825)
UNHOLTZ-DICKIE CORPORATION (PA)
6 Brookside Dr (06492-1893)
PHONE..................................203 265-9875
Michael K Reen, *President*
Gerald K Reen, *Corp Secy*
▲ **EMP:** 44 **EST:** 1958
SQ FT: 40,000
SALES (est): 12.4MM **Privately Held**
WEB: www.udco.com
SIC: 3829 Mfg Measuring/Controlling Devices

(G-4826)
VALUE PRINT INCORPORATED
34 Mellor Dr (06492-4953)
PHONE..................................203 265-1371
John L Kastukevich, *President*
Mary R Kastukevich, *Admin Sec*
EMP: 11
SQ FT: 5,000
SALES (est): 1MM **Privately Held**
SIC: 2752 Offset Printers

(G-4827)
VERTIV CORPORATION
8 Fairfield Blvd Ste 4 (06492-1890)
PHONE..................................203 294-6020
Bob Paradiso, *Manager*
EMP: 10
SALES (corp-wide): 2.9B **Privately Held**
WEB: www.liebert.com
SIC: 3823 Mfg Process Control Instruments
HQ: Vertiv Corporation
1050 Dearborn Dr
Columbus OH 43085
614 888-0246

(G-4828)
WEATHERFORD INTERNATIONAL LLC
8 Enterprise Rd (06492-1835)
PHONE..................................203 294-0190
Christopher McDowell, *Engineer*
Kevin Didden, *Branch Mgr*
EMP: 25 **Privately Held**
WEB: www.weatherford.com
SIC: 1389 Oil/Gas Field Services
HQ: Weatherford International, Llc
2000 Saint James Pl
Houston TX 77056
713 693-4000

GEOGRAPHIC

(G-4829)
WINSLOW MANUFACTURING INC
68 N Plains Indus Hwy (06492-2331)
PHONE....................203 269-1977
EMP: 15
SQ FT: 13,000
SALES (est): 2.1MM **Privately Held**
SIC: 3451 Mfg Screw Machine Products

Washington
Litchfield County

(G-4830)
AMERICAN CT RNG BNDER INDEX &
42 Sabbaday Ln (06793-1305)
PHONE....................860 868-7900
Peter Tagley, *President*
Diana Tagley, *Corp Secy*
EMP: 17
SQ FT: 14,000
SALES: 1MM **Privately Held**
WEB: www.ringbinders.com
SIC: 2782 2678 2675 Mfg Blankbooks/Binders Mfg Stationery Products Mfg Die-Cut Paper/Paperboard

(G-4831)
WASHINGTON COPPER WORKS INC
49 South St (06793-1516)
PHONE....................860 868-7637
Serge L Miller, *President*
EMP: 3
SALES (est): 288.5K **Privately Held**
WEB: www.washingtoncopperworks.com
SIC: 3645 5719 5063 Mfg Ret & Whol Copper Lighting Fixtures

Washington Depot
Litchfield County

(G-4832)
BERKSHIRE PHOTONICS LLC
88 Bee Brook Rd (06794-1202)
P.O. Box 595 (06794-0595)
PHONE....................860 868-0412
Michael Windebank, *Engineer*
Jeffrey Miller, *Admin Asst*
EMP: 8
SQ FT: 2,200
SALES: 1.2MM **Privately Held**
WEB: www.berkshirephotonics.com
SIC: 3559 Mfg Misc Industry Machinery

(G-4833)
NICHOLS WOODWORKING LLC (PA)
136 Walker Brook Rd S (06794)
PHONE....................860 350-4223
Franklin Nichols, *Principal*
EMP: 3
SALES (est): 782.3K **Privately Held**
SIC: 2431 Mfg Millwork

Waterbury
New Haven County

(G-4834)
77 MATTATUCK HEIGHTS LLC
77 Mattatuck Heights Rd (06705-3832)
PHONE....................203 597-9338
Jim Xhema,
▲ **EMP:** 20
SALES (est): 2.3MM **Privately Held**
SIC: 2431 Mfg Millwork

(G-4835)
ABAIR MANUFACTURING COMPANY
Also Called: Abair Assemblies
250 Mill St Ste 2 (06706-1209)
PHONE....................203 757-0112
EMP: 19
SQ FT: 10,000
SALES: 720K **Privately Held**
SIC: 3711 Automobile Component Assembly

(G-4836)
ADVANCED MACHINE SERVICES LLC (PA)
2056 Thomaston Ave (06704-1038)
PHONE....................203 888-6600
Christopher G Mackenzie,
Chris Mackenzie,
EMP: 4
SQ FT: 3,100
SALES (est): 711.2K **Privately Held**
WEB: www.precisionspindle.com
SIC: 3552 3542 7389 Mfg Textile Machinery Mfg Machine Tools-Forming Business Services

(G-4837)
AI DIVESTITURES INC
245 Freight St (06702-1818)
PHONE....................203 575-5727
Stuart L Daniels, *Director*
EMP: 4
SALES (est): 228.4K
SALES (corp-wide): 1.9B **Publicly Held**
SIC: 2869 Mfg Industrial Organic Chemicals
PA: Element Solutions Inc
500 E Broward Blvd # 1860
West Palm Beach FL 33394
561 207-9600

(G-4838)
ALENT INC
245 Freight St (06702-1818)
PHONE....................203 575-5727
Allan Macdonald, *Principal*
EMP: 70
SALES (est): 1.1MM
SALES (corp-wide): 1.9B **Publicly Held**
SIC: 3699 Mfg Electrical Equipment/Supplies
HQ: Macdermid, Incorporated
245 Freight St
Waterbury CT 06702
203 575-5700

(G-4839)
ALENT USA HOLDING INC
245 Freight St (06702-1818)
PHONE....................203 575-5727
Steven Corbett, *President*
William Gorgone, *Vice Pres*
Robert Landry, *Vice Pres*
Allan Macdonald, *Vice Pres*
Joseph M Creighton, *Treasurer*
EMP: 279
SALES (est): 230.9K
SALES (corp-wide): 1.9B **Publicly Held**
SIC: 3699 3356 3341 3313 Holding Company
PA: Element Solutions Inc
500 E Broward Blvd # 1860
West Palm Beach FL 33394
561 207-9600

(G-4840)
AMERICAN ELECTRO PRODUCTS INC
1358 Thomaston Ave (06704-1791)
P.O. Box 4129 (06704-0129)
PHONE....................203 756-7051
Dennis Burke, *President*
John Krin, *CFO*
EMP: 135 **EST:** 1950
SALES (est): 19.1MM
SALES (corp-wide): 15MM **Privately Held**
SIC: 3471 Plating/Polishing Service
PA: National Integrated Industries, Inc.
322 Main St
Farmington CT 06032
860 677-7995

(G-4841)
AMERICAN PLASTIC PRODUCTS INC
2114 Thomaston Ave (06704-1013)
P.O. Box 4429 (06704-0429)
PHONE....................203 596-2410
Dennis M Burke, *President*
EMP: 135
SQ FT: 5,000
SALES (est): 34.9MM
SALES (corp-wide): 15MM **Privately Held**
WEB: www.amerplastic.com
SIC: 3089 Mfg Plastic Products
PA: National Integrated Industries, Inc.
322 Main St
Farmington CT 06032
860 677-7995

(G-4842)
AMERICAN-REPUBLICAN INC (PA)
Also Called: Republican-American
389 Meadow St (06702-1808)
P.O. Box 2090 (06722-2090)
PHONE....................203 574-3636
William B Pape, *President*
Jennine Goldenberg, *Human Res Mgr*
Daniel Wheeler, *Manager*
Ed Winters, *Director*
EMP: 79
SQ FT: 110
SALES: 24MM **Privately Held**
WEB: www.rep-am.com
SIC: 2711 2752 Newspapers-Publishing/Printing Lithographic Commercial Printing

(G-4843)
AMODIOS INC (PA)
Also Called: Pilot Seasonings
40 Falls Ave Ste 4 (06708-1054)
PHONE....................203 573-1229
Joseph R Summa, *President*
Fred Schnaars Jr, *Corp Secy*
Richard Rogers, *Vice Pres*
EMP: 12 **EST:** 1981
SQ FT: 12,000
SALES (est): 1.3MM **Privately Held**
WEB: www.pilotseasoning.com
SIC: 2099 2051 Mfg Food Preparations Mfg Bread/Related Products

(G-4844)
ANGEL FUEL LLC
56 Knoll St (06705-1813)
PHONE....................203 597-8759
Angel L Morales, *Manager*
EMP: 7
SALES (est): 656.1K **Privately Held**
SIC: 3443 Mfg Fabricated Plate Work

(G-4845)
ARCHITECTURAL SUPPLEMENTS LLC
567 S Leonard St Bldg 1b (06708-4300)
PHONE....................203 591-5505
Phil Feinman, *Ch of Bd*
Steven C Decker, *Partner*
▲ **EMP:** 18
SQ FT: 50,000
SALES (est): 4.2MM **Privately Held**
SIC: 3089 3412 Mfg Plastic Products Mfg Metal Barrels/Pails

(G-4846)
ARMED & READY ALARM SYSTEM
112 Fieldwood Rd (06704-1107)
P.O. Box 591, Oxford (06478-0591)
PHONE....................203 596-0327
Shawn Burch, *Owner*
EMP: 15
SALES (est): 1.2MM **Privately Held**
SIC: 3273 Mfg Ready-Mixed Concrete

(G-4847)
ATI FLAT RLLED PDTS HLDNGS LLC
271 Railroad Hill St (06708-4306)
PHONE....................203 756-7414
Jose Reyes, *Manager*
EMP: 10 **Publicly Held**
WEB: www.alleghenyludlum.com
SIC: 3312 5051 Blast Furnace-Steel Works Metals Service Center
HQ: Ati Flat Rolled Products Holdings, Llc
1000 Six Ppg Pl
Pittsburgh PA 15222
412 394-3047

(G-4848)
BAR WORK MANUFACTURING CO INC
1198 Highland Ave (06708-4911)
PHONE....................203 753-4103
William Steinen Jr, *President*
John J Scopelliti, *Vice Pres*
Jr C Jung, *Executive*
John B Dangler, *Admin Sec*
EMP: 14 **EST:** 1951
SQ FT: 24,000
SALES (est): 2.3MM
SALES (corp-wide): 15.3MM **Privately Held**
WEB: www.bar-work.com
SIC: 3451 Mfg Screw Machine Products
PA: Wm. Steinen Mfg. Co.
29 E Halsey Rd
Parsippany NJ 07054
973 887-6400

(G-4849)
BERNELL TOOL & MFG CO
181 Mulloy Rd (06705-3439)
PHONE....................203 756-4405
Charles Famiglietti, *President*
Margaret Famiglietti, *Corp Secy*
EMP: 5
SQ FT: 3,400
SALES (est): 200K **Privately Held**
SIC: 3541 5084 Mfg Machine Tools-Cutting Whol Industrial Equipment

(G-4850)
BOBKEN AUTOMATICS INC
1495 Thomaston Ave Ste 2 (06704-1744)
P.O. Box 131, Oakville (06779-0131)
PHONE....................203 757-5525
Bob Piazzaroli, *President*
Ursula Piazzaroli, *Admin Sec*
EMP: 6
SALES (est): 821.5K **Privately Held**
SIC: 3451 Mfg Screw Machine Products

(G-4851)
BPREX HALTHCARE BROOKVILLE INC
574 E Main St (06702-1706)
P.O. Box 808 (06720-0808)
PHONE....................203 754-4141
Kevin Edwards, *Opers-Prdtn-Mfg*
EMP: 195
SQ FT: 100,000 **Publicly Held**
SIC: 3089 Manufactures Plastics Closures
HQ: Bprex Healthcare Brookville Inc.
1899 N Wilkinson Way
Perrysburg OH 43551

(G-4852)
BYRNE GROUP INC
Also Called: Minuteman Tress
170 Grand St (06702-1909)
PHONE....................203 573-0100
Matt Byrne, *President*
Tiffany Byrne, *Vice Pres*
EMP: 3
SALES (est): 114.2K **Privately Held**
SIC: 2752 Lithographic Commercial Printing

(G-4853)
C F D ENGINEERING COMPANY
Naugatuck Manufacturing Div
105 Avenue Of Industry (06705-3902)
P.O. Box 3175 (06705-0175)
PHONE....................203 754-2807
Chuck Adminson, *Manager*
EMP: 17
SALES (corp-wide): 1.5MM **Privately Held**
WEB: www.naugatuckmfg.com
SIC: 3823 Industrial Floats Liquid Level Cont Ornamental Assemblies Commercial Flagpole Ornamental Balls
PA: The C F D Engineering Company
194 Cook Rd
Prospect CT 06712
203 758-4148

(G-4854)
CARPIN MANUFACTURING INC
411 Austin Rd (06705-3763)
P.O. Box 471 (06720-0471)
PHONE....................203 574-2556

Ralph H Carpinella, *Ch of Bd*
Ralph Carpinella, *Chairman*
Rachel Albanese, *Controller*
James Bachis, *Sales Staff*
David Ferraro, *Officer*
▲ **EMP:** 90
SQ FT: 60,000
SALES (est): 24.8MM **Privately Held**
WEB: www.carpin.com
SIC: **3469** 3089 3441 Mfg Metal Stampings Mfg Plastic Products Structural Metal Fabrication

(G-4855)
CAVTECH INDUSTRIES
217 Interstate Ln (06705-2642)
PHONE.................................203 437-8764
Sam Cavallo, *Owner*
EMP: 4
SQ FT: 6,500
SALES: 500K **Privately Held**
SIC: **3599** Mfg Industrial Machinery

(G-4856)
CHEMTURA RECEIVABLES LLC
199 Benson Rd (06749-0001)
PHONE.................................203 573-3327
EMP: 5 **EST:** 2008
SALES (est): 20.6K **Privately Held**
SIC: **2879** Mfg Agricultural Chemicals

(G-4857)
CLASSIC TOOL & MFG INC
112 Porter St (06708-3819)
PHONE.................................203 755-6313
Robert Druan, *President*
EMP: 4
SALES (est): 329.8K **Privately Held**
SIC: **3544** Mfg Dies/Tools/Jigs/Fixtures

(G-4858)
CLASSIC TOOL & MFG LLC
112 Porter St (06708-3819)
PHONE.................................203 755-6313
Robert J Druan, *Manager*
EMP: 3
SALES (est): 264.4K **Privately Held**
SIC: **3999** Mfg Misc Products

(G-4859)
CLY-DEL MANUFACTURING COMPANY
151 Sharon Rd (06705-4041)
P.O. Box 1367 (06721-1367)
PHONE.................................203 574-2100
Robert W Garthwait Jr, *President*
Robert W Garthwait, *Chairman*
Bruce Weingart, *Plant Mgr*
Charles W Henry, *Admin Sec*
▲ **EMP:** 210
SQ FT: 185,000
SALES (est): 56.4MM **Privately Held**
WEB: www.cly-del.com
SIC: **3469** Mfg Metal Stampings

(G-4860)
COLONIAL CORRUGATED PDTS INC
118 Railroad Hill St (06708-4320)
P.O. Box 2753 (06723-2753)
PHONE.................................203 597-1707
Jack Bair, *President*
Angela Derkins, *Admin Sec*
EMP: 40
SALES (est): 6.1MM **Privately Held**
WEB: www.colonialcorrugated.com
SIC: **2653** Mfg Corrugated/Solid Fiber Boxes

(G-4861)
CREATIVE RACK SOLUTIONS INC
365 Thomaston Ave (06702-1024)
P.O. Box 750, Southington (06489-0750)
PHONE.................................203 755-2102
EMP: 4
SQ FT: 1,000
SALES (est): 582.7K **Privately Held**
WEB: www.crea-sol.com
SIC: **3498** Mfg Fabricated Pipe/Fittings

(G-4862)
CUSTOMIZED FOODS MFG LLC
8 S Commons Rd (06704-1035)
PHONE.................................203 759-1645
Al Poe, *Principal*
EMP: 8
SALES (est): 518.8K **Privately Held**
SIC: **3999** Mfg Misc Products

(G-4863)
DA SILVA KLANKO LTD
Also Called: Love 'n Herbs
70 Deerwood Ln Unit 8 (06704-1665)
PHONE.................................203 756-4932
Maria B Klanko, *President*
Donald Klanko, *Corp Secy*
Peter J Klanko, *Vice Pres*
EMP: 3
SALES: 850K **Privately Held**
SIC: **2035** Mfg Pickles/Sauces/Dressing

(G-4864)
DASCO WELDED PRODUCTS INC
2038 Thomaston Ave (06704-1036)
PHONE.................................203 754-9353
Daren Edward Thornberg, *President*
Patrick Hale, *Vice Pres*
EMP: 11
SQ FT: 3,000
SALES: 1.2MM **Privately Held**
SIC: **3444** Welding Repair

(G-4865)
DURCO MANUFACTURING CO INC
493 S Leonard St (06708-4315)
PHONE.................................203 575-0446
F Donald Ek, *CEO*
Sabastian Corona, *President*
EMP: 8
SQ FT: 5,000
SALES (est): 1.4MM **Privately Held**
WEB: www.durcomfg.com
SIC: **3451** Mfg Screw Machine Products

(G-4866)
E & J PARTS CLEANING INC
1669 Thomaston Ave (06704-1026)
P.O. Box 4250 (06704-0250)
PHONE.................................203 757-1716
Everett Hardick, *President*
EMP: 11
SALES (est): 1.1MM **Privately Held**
WEB: www.ejpartscleaning.com
SIC: **3471** 7349 Cleaning Of Manufactured Parts

(G-4867)
EEMAX INC (DH)
400 Captain Neville Dr (06705-3811)
PHONE.................................203 267-7890
Kevin M Ruppelt, *President*
Jens Bolleyer, *Vice Pres*
Mike Burns, *Plant Mgr*
Mark Smola, *QC Mgr*
Chris Hayden, *Engineer*
▲ **EMP:** 80
SQ FT: 16,000
SALES (est): 14.2MM **Privately Held**
WEB: www.eemax.com
SIC: **3639** Manufacturing Household Appliances Specializing In Hot Water Heaters
HQ: Rheem Manufacturing Company Inc
1100 Abernathy Rd # 1700
Atlanta GA 30328
770 351-3000

(G-4868)
ELECTRONIC CONNECTION CORP
112 Porter St (06708-3819)
PHONE.................................860 243-3356
Ray Gorski Jr, *President*
Ronald Gorski, *Vice Pres*
Melinda Farley, *Manager*
EMP: 20
SQ FT: 8,000
SALES (est): 3.3MM **Publicly Held**
WEB: www.eccwire.com
SIC: **3679** Mfg Processed Wire Electrical Harnesses
PA: Air Industries Group
1460 5th Ave
Bay Shore NY 11706

(G-4869)
ELECTRONIC FILM CAPACITORS
Also Called: EFC
41 Interstate Ln (06705-2639)
PHONE.................................203 755-5629
Jay Weiner, *President*
Leonard Gelonese, *Engineer*
Bob Fountain, *Sales Executive*
Jessica Gadzik, *Marketing Staff*
Anglea Sousa, *Admin Sec*
EMP: 47
SQ FT: 15,000
SALES (est): 7MM **Privately Held**
WEB: www.filmcapacitors.com
SIC: **3675** Mfg Electronic Capacitors

(G-4870)
ELEMENT SOLUTIONS INC
245 Freight St (06702-1818)
PHONE.................................203 575-5850
EMP: 25
SALES (corp-wide): 1.9B **Publicly Held**
SIC: **2899** 2869 Mfg Chemical Preparations Mfg Industrial Organic Chemicals
PA: Element Solutions Inc
500 E Broward Blvd # 1860
West Palm Beach FL 33394
561 207-9600

(G-4871)
EYELET CRAFTERS INC
2712 S Main St (06706-2647)
P.O. Box 2542 (06723-2542)
PHONE.................................203 757-9221
Robert A Finkenzeller, *President*
William E Finkenzeller, *Vice Pres*
Harriet Finkenzeller, *Admin Sec*
Frank T Healey, *Asst Sec*
EMP: 65
SQ FT: 30,000
SALES (est): 16.6MM **Privately Held**
WEB: www.eyeletcrafters.com
SIC: **3469** 3471 Mfg Metal Stampings Plating/Polishing Service

(G-4872)
EYELET DESIGN INC
574 E Main St (06702-1706)
P.O. Box 808 (06720-0808)
PHONE.................................203 754-4141
Robert L Hughes, *President*
Card Chris, *Safety Mgr*
Ken Schoppmann, *QC Mgr*
Craig Parker, *Engineer*
Claudia M Hughes, *Treasurer*
EMP: 100
SQ FT: 130,000
SALES (est): 15.5MM **Privately Held**
WEB: www.eyeletdesign.com
SIC: **3469** 3466 Mfg Metal Stampings Mfg Crowns/Closures

(G-4873)
FABOR FOURSLIDE INC
44 Railroad Hill St (06708-4320)
P.O. Box 2420 (06722-2420)
PHONE.................................203 753-4380
EMP: 5
SQ FT: 6,000
SALES (est): 400K **Privately Held**
WEB: www.faborfourslideinc.com
SIC: **3469** Manufacturer Of Metal Stampings

(G-4874)
FOAM PLASTICS NEW ENGLAND INC
32 Gramar Ave (06712-1016)
P.O. Box 7075, Prospect (06712-0075)
PHONE.................................203 758-6651
David L Lewis, *President*
Eugene R Lewis, *Admin Sec*
EMP: 4
SQ FT: 96,000
SALES (est): 570K **Privately Held**
SIC: **3086** Mfg Plastic Foam Products

(G-4875)
FORUM PLASTICS LLC
105 Progress Ln (06705-3830)
PHONE.................................203 754-0777
Joseph Pasqualucci, *Principal*
EMP: 44
SALES (est): 15.8MM **Privately Held**
SIC: **2821** Manufacturer Of Plastic Products

(G-4876)
G F GRINDING TOOL MFG CO INC
649 Captain Neville Dr (06705-3826)
PHONE.................................203 757-6244
John Fratamico, *President*
EMP: 3 **EST:** 1968
SALES: 175K **Privately Held**
SIC: **3599** Machine Shop

(G-4877)
GEM MANUFACTURING CO INC (PA)
78 Brookside Rd (06708-1402)
P.O. Box 4550 (06704-0550)
PHONE.................................203 574-1466
Robert C Caulfield Jr, *President*
Gerard Berthiaume, *Vice Pres*
Mark G Caulfield, *Vice Pres*
Christopher C Gemino, *Admin Sec*
◆ **EMP:** 90 **EST:** 1943
SQ FT: 84,000
SALES (est): 19.5MM **Privately Held**
WEB: www.gemmfg.com
SIC: **3469** Mfg Metal Stampings

(G-4878)
GENERAL HEAT TREATING CO
80 Fulkerson Dr (06708-1409)
PHONE.................................203 755-5441
Larry Maknis, *President*
Tracy Maknis, *Treasurer*
Tracey Maknis, *Admin Sec*
EMP: 6
SQ FT: 7,000
SALES (est): 911.5K **Privately Held**
SIC: **3398** Metal Heat Treating Ferrous & Nonferrous Metals

(G-4879)
GLOBAL BRASS & COPPER LLC (PA)
Also Called: Somers Thin Strip
215 Piedmont St (06706-2152)
PHONE.................................203 597-5000
Tom Werner, *Vice Pres*
William M Fautch, *Vice Pres*
Mike Houston, *Vice Pres*
Dale R Taylor, *Vice Pres*
Brian Weyel, *Supervisor*
▲ **EMP:** 5 **EST:** 2010
SQ FT: 150,000
SALES (est): 2.1MM **Privately Held**
SIC: **3351** Metals Service Center

(G-4880)
H&T WATERBURY INC
Also Called: Bouffard Metal Goods
984 Waterville St (06710-1015)
P.O. Box 4700 (06704-0700)
PHONE.................................203 574-2240
Reinhard S Scholle, *General Mgr*
Ronald Turmel, *General Mgr*
Christian Diemer, *Principal*
Daniel D Moffa, *Vice Pres*
Ronald T Turmel, *Vice Pres*
▲ **EMP:** 150
SQ FT: 128,000
SALES (est): 39.3MM
SALES (corp-wide): 125.1K **Privately Held**
SIC: **3469** Mfg Metal Stampings
PA: Sdruzeni Firem Heitkamp&Thumann Group
Havlickova 540/28
Hustopece

(G-4881)
HALCO INC
Also Called: Waterbury Plating
114 Porter St (06708-3819)
P.O. Box 2545 (06723-2545)
PHONE.................................203 575-9450
Glen Harper, *President*
Bob Lanz, *Vice Pres*
EMP: 75 **EST:** 1941
SQ FT: 55,000

GEOGRAPHIC

SALES (est): 10.1MM **Privately Held**
WEB: www.waterburyplating.com
SIC: 3471 3479 Plating/Polishing Service Coating/Engraving Service

(G-4882)
HARDCORE SWEET CUPCAKES LLC
784 Cooke St (06710-1112)
PHONE..................................203 808-5547
Danette McEvoy, *Principal*
EMP: 4
SALES (est): 166.6K **Privately Held**
SIC: 2051 Mfg Bread/Related Products

(G-4883)
HAYDON KERK MTION SLUTIONS INC
1500 Meriden Rd (06705-3982)
P.O. Box 3329 (06705-0329)
PHONE..................................203 756-7441
John P Norris, *President*
Robert S Feit, *Vice Pres*
James Bostwick, *Engineer*
William J Burke, *Treasurer*
Kathryn E Sena, *Admin Sec*
▲ **EMP:** 140 **EST:** 1963
SQ FT: 42,000
SALES (est): 39.3MM
SALES (corp-wide): 4.8B **Publicly Held**
WEB: www.hsi-inc.com
SIC: 3823 Mfg Process Control Instruments
PA: Ametek, Inc.
1100 Cassatt Rd
Berwyn PA 19312
610 647-2121

(G-4884)
HOTSEAT CHASSIS INC
Also Called: Semipilot
20 S Commons Rd (06704-1035)
PHONE..................................860 582-5031
Jay Leboff, *President*
EMP: 6
SALES: 750K **Privately Held**
WEB: www.hotseatinc.com
SIC: 7372 5999 Prepackaged Software Services Ret Misc Merchandise

(G-4885)
HOUSTON MACDERMID INC
245 Freight St (06702-1818)
PHONE..................................203 575-5700
EMP: 3
SALES (est): 123.2K
SALES (corp-wide): 1.9B **Publicly Held**
SIC: 2869 Mfg Industrial Organic Chemicals
PA: Element Solutions Inc
500 E Broward Blvd # 1860
West Palm Beach FL 33394
561 207-9600

(G-4886)
I AND U LLC
Also Called: Pan Del Cielo
66 Mattatuck Heights Rd (06705-3831)
PHONE..................................860 803-1491
Tony Tasilva, *President*
Ivania Lorenzo, *Vice Pres*
EMP: 6
SQ FT: 2,500
SALES: 600K **Privately Held**
SIC: 2051 Mfg Bread/Related Products

(G-4887)
ILLINOIS TOOL WORKS INC
ITW Drawform Waterbury
1240 Wolcott St (06705-1320)
PHONE..................................203 574-2119
Mark Milo, *Opers Mgr*
Rob Webber, *Branch Mgr*
EMP: 140
SALES (corp-wide): 14.7B **Publicly Held**
SIC: 3482 3469 3448 Mfg Small Arms Ammunition
PA: Illinois Tool Works Inc.
155 Harlem Ave
Glenview IL 60025
847 724-7500

(G-4888)
INFINITY STONE INC
1261 Meriden Rd (06705-3637)
PHONE..................................203 575-9484
Michael Amendola, *President*
Ellen Labriola, *Sales Staff*
EMP: 10 **EST:** 2014
SALES (est): 290.3K **Privately Held**
SIC: 1411 3944 Dimension Stone Quarry Mfg Games/Toys

(G-4889)
ITW DRAWFORM INC
1240 Wolcott St (06705-1320)
PHONE..................................203 574-3200
Gills Boehm, *Principal*
Burt Hanson, *Foreman/Supr*
EMP: 29
SALES (est): 5.9MM **Privately Held**
SIC: 3469 Mfg Metal Stampings

(G-4890)
J & R PROJECTS
1509 Wolcott Rd (06716-1321)
PHONE..................................203 879-2347
James F Rideout Sr, *Partner*
James Rideout Jr, *Partner*
EMP: 3
SQ FT: 1,600
SALES (est): 323K **Privately Held**
SIC: 3451 Mfg Screw Machine Products

(G-4891)
JL LUCAS MACHINERY CO INC
429 Brookside Rd (06708-1418)
P.O. Box 4220 (06704-0220)
PHONE..................................203 597-1300
John Pelletier, *President*
Judy Pelletier, *Admin Sec*
▲ **EMP:** 18
SQ FT: 20,000
SALES (est): 3.3MM **Privately Held**
WEB: www.jllucas.com
SIC: 3541 5084 Whol Industrial Equipment Mfg Machine Tools-Cutting

(G-4892)
JO VEK TOOL AND DIE MFG CO
2121 Thomaston Ave (06704)
PHONE..................................203 755-1884
Frank Longo, *President*
Chris Longo, *Corp Secy*
EMP: 6 **EST:** 1953
SQ FT: 10,200
SALES (est): 1MM **Privately Held**
SIC: 3469 3965 3312 Mfg Metal Stampings Mfg Fasteners/Buttons/Pins Blast Furnace-Steel Works

(G-4893)
JOHN HYCHKO
Also Called: Valley Truckstop
299 Sheffield St (06704-1010)
PHONE..................................203 757-3458
John Hychko, *Owner*
EMP: 4
SQ FT: 14,400
SALES (est): 526.9K **Privately Held**
SIC: 1442 1794 Sand & Gravel Pit And Excavation Contractor

(G-4894)
JOMA INCORPORATED
185 Interstate Ln (06705-2640)
PHONE..................................203 759-0848
Francis X Macary, *President*
▲ **EMP:** 20 **EST:** 1953
SQ FT: 20,000
SALES (est): 4MM **Privately Held**
SIC: 3469 Mfg Metal Stampings

(G-4895)
KNIGHT INC
Also Called: Knight Manufacturing
47 Stevens St (06704-1020)
P.O. Box 4343 (06704-0343)
PHONE..................................203 754-6502
Jim Troland, *President*
EMP: 5
SQ FT: 12,000
SALES (est): 750.7K **Privately Held**
SIC: 3965 Manufacturer Of Eyelet Stampings

(G-4896)
L C M TOOL CO
68 Diane Ter (06705-3523)
P.O. Box 3245 (06705-0245)
PHONE..................................203 757-1575
Dante Carrafa, *President*
Michele Longo, *Vice Pres*
Sebastian Longo, *Treasurer*
Mario Longo, *Admin Sec*
EMP: 9 **EST:** 1966
SALES: 1.1MM **Privately Held**
WEB: www.lcmtool.com
SIC: 3541 Mfg Screw Machine Tools

(G-4897)
LEELYND CORP
546 S Main St (06706-1015)
PHONE..................................203 753-9137
Thomas Deleon, *President*
EMP: 3
SQ FT: 3,500
SALES (est): 448.9K **Privately Held**
SIC: 3469 Mfg Metal Stampings

(G-4898)
LUIS PRESSURE WASHER
47 Esther Ave (06708-4818)
PHONE..................................203 706-7399
Luis Rodriguez, *Principal*
EMP: 3 **EST:** 2011
SALES (est): 188.8K **Privately Held**
SIC: 3452 Mfg Bolts/Screws/Rivets

(G-4899)
LUVATA WATERBURY INC
2121 Thomaston Ave Ste 1 (06704)
PHONE..................................203 753-5215
James C Lajewski, *President*
Gwen Gilbert, *Director*
Pekka Kleemola, *Admin Sec*
▲ **EMP:** 66
SQ FT: 210,000
SALES (est): 27.7MM **Privately Held**
SIC: 3357 Nonferrous Wiredrawing/Insulating
HQ: Luvata Pori Oy
Kuparitie 5
Pori 28330
262 661-11

(G-4900)
MACDERMID INCORPORATED (HQ)
Also Called: Macdermid Prfmce Solutions
245 Freight St (06702-1818)
P.O. Box 671 (06720-0671)
PHONE..................................203 575-5700
Scot Benson, *President*
Frank J Monteiro, *COO*
Nicholas Banis, *Vice Pres*
Patricia Gaglione, *Vice Pres*
Steve Racca, *Vice Pres*
◆ **EMP:** 200 **EST:** 1922
SQ FT: 51,700
SALES (est): 437MM
SALES (corp-wide): 1.9B **Publicly Held**
WEB: www.macdermid.com
SIC: 2842 2992 2752 3577 Mfg Polish/Sanitation Gd Mfg Lubrictng Oil/Grease Lithographic Coml Print Mfg Computer Peripherals Mfg Chemical Preparation
PA: Element Solutions Inc
500 E Broward Blvd # 1860
Fort Lauderdale FL 33394
561 207-9600

(G-4901)
MACDERMID INCORPORATED
Also Called: Mac Dermid Elec Solution
245 Freight St (06702-1818)
PHONE..................................203 575-5700
Richard A Nave, *Branch Mgr*
EMP: 38
SALES (corp-wide): 1.9B **Publicly Held**
WEB: www.macdermid.com
SIC: 2899 Mfg Chemical Preparations
HQ: Macdermid, Incorporated
245 Freight St
Waterbury CT 06702
203 575-5700

(G-4902)
MACDERMID ACUMEN INC
245 Freight St (06702-1818)
PHONE..................................203 575-5700
EMP: 4 **EST:** 1997
SALES (est): 232.8K
SALES (corp-wide): 1.9B **Publicly Held**
SIC: 2899 Mfg Chemical Preparations
PA: Element Solutions Inc
500 E Broward Blvd # 1860
West Palm Beach FL 33394
561 207-9600

(G-4903)
MACDERMID AG SOLUTIONS INC
Also Called: Agriphar Crop Solutions
245 Freight St (06702-1818)
PHONE..................................203 575-5727
Frank Monteiro, *President*
Michael Kennedy, *Treasurer*
John Cordani, *Admin Sec*
EMP: 15 **EST:** 2014
SQ FT: 50,000
SALES (est): 35.6MM
SALES (corp-wide): 1.9B **Publicly Held**
SIC: 2879 Mfg Agricultural Chemicals
HQ: Macdermid, Incorporated
245 Freight St
Waterbury CT 06702
203 575-5700

(G-4904)
MACDERMID ANION INC
245 Freight St (06702-1818)
PHONE..................................203 575-5700
EMP: 3 **EST:** 2002
SALES (est): 123.2K
SALES (corp-wide): 1.9B **Publicly Held**
SIC: 2869 Mfg Industrial Organic Chemicals
PA: Element Solutions Inc
500 E Broward Blvd # 1860
West Palm Beach FL 33394
561 207-9600

(G-4905)
MACDERMID BRAZIL INC
245 Freight St (06702-1818)
PHONE..................................203 575-5700
EMP: 3
SALES (est): 123.2K
SALES (corp-wide): 1.9B **Publicly Held**
SIC: 2869 Mfg Industrial Organic Chemicals
PA: Element Solutions Inc
500 E Broward Blvd # 1860
West Palm Beach FL 33394
561 207-9600

(G-4906)
MACDERMID OVERSEAS ASIA LTD (HQ)
245 Freight St (06702-1818)
PHONE..................................203 575-5799
EMP: 5 **EST:** 1983
SALES (est): 8MM
SALES (corp-wide): 1.9B **Publicly Held**
SIC: 2899 Mfg Chemical Preparations
PA: Element Solutions Inc
500 E Broward Blvd # 1860
West Palm Beach FL 33394
561 207-9600

(G-4907)
MACDERMID PRINTING SOLUTIONS
245 Freight St (06702-1818)
PHONE..................................203 575-5727
Ted Antonellis, *Research*
Matti Lilback, *Engineer*
Eric Wetmore, *Engineer*
Deborah Gorzelany, *Credit Staff*
Holly Delaurentis, *Financial Analy*
EMP: 6
SALES (est): 488K
SALES (corp-wide): 1.9B **Publicly Held**
SIC: 2899 Mfg Chemical Preparations
PA: Element Solutions Inc
500 E Broward Blvd # 1860
Fort Lauderdale FL 33394
561 207-9600

(G-4908)
MACDERMID SOUTH AMERICA INC
245 Freight St (06702-1818)
PHONE..................................203 575-5700
EMP: 3
SALES (est): 123.2K
SALES (corp-wide): 1.9B **Publicly Held**
SIC: 2869 Mfg Industrial Organic Chemicals

▲ = Import ▼=Export
◆ =Import/Export

PA: Element Solutions Inc
500 E Broward Blvd # 1860
West Palm Beach FL 33394
561 207-9600

(G-4909)
MACDERMID SOUTH ATLANTIC INC
245 Freight St (06702-1818)
PHONE..................................203 575-5700
EMP: 3
SALES (est): 150.1K
SALES (corp-wide): 1.9B **Publicly Held**
SIC: 2869 Mfg Industrial Organic Chemicals
PA: Element Solutions Inc
500 E Broward Blvd # 1860
West Palm Beach FL 33394
561 207-9600

(G-4910)
MARJAN INC
44 Railroad Hill St (06708-4320)
P.O. Box 2420 (06722-2420)
PHONE..................................203 573-1742
George Strobel Sr, *President*
William C Strobel, *Vice Pres*
George Strobel Jr, *Treasurer*
Richard Strobel, *Admin Sec*
▲ **EMP:** 19
SQ FT: 17,000
SALES (est): 2MM **Privately Held**
WEB: www.marjaninc.com
SIC: 3479 Coating/Engraving Service

(G-4911)
MASTER ENGRV & PRINTERY INC (PA)
Also Called: Waterbury Printing
45 Westridge Dr (06708-3336)
PHONE..................................203 723-2779
Rocco Corso, *President*
Roselyn Goldman, *Bookkeeper*
EMP: 8
SQ FT: 4,800
SALES (est): 844.3K **Privately Held**
SIC: 2759 2791 2789 2752 Commercial Printing Typesetting Services Bookbinding/Related Work Lithographic Coml Print

(G-4912)
MATERIAL PROMOTIONS INC
145 Railroad Hill St (06708-4306)
PHONE..................................203 757-8900
Peter Bove, *President*
EMP: 4 **EST:** 2007
SALES (est): 550.6K **Privately Held**
SIC: 2752 Lithographic Commercial Printing

(G-4913)
MCLEOD OPTICAL COMPANY INC
451 Meriden Rd Ste 3 (06705-2248)
PHONE..................................203 754-2187
Daniel Mattaboni, *Manager*
EMP: 7
SALES (corp-wide): 5.8MM **Privately Held**
SIC: 3851 Whol Professional Equipment
PA: Mcleod Optical Company, Inc.
50 Jefferson Park Rd
Warwick RI 02888
401 467-3000

(G-4914)
MEXI-GRILL LLC
495 Union St (06706-1292)
PHONE..................................203 574-2127
EMP: 4 **EST:** 2011
SALES (est): 180K **Privately Held**
SIC: 3421 Mfg Cutlery

(G-4915)
MICROBEST INC
670 Captain Neville Dr # 1 (06705-3855)
PHONE..................................203 597-0355
Steven Griffin, *President*
Edward McNerney, *President*
Michael Altberg, *Vice Pres*
Paul Lemay, *Vice Pres*
Elaine M Studwell, *Vice Pres*
EMP: 135
SQ FT: 43,000
SALES (est): 41.7MM **Privately Held**
WEB: www.microbest.com
SIC: 3451 3541 Mfg Screw Machine Products Mfg Machine Tools-Cutting

(G-4916)
MILITE BAKERY
Also Called: Arturo Milite and Spinella Bky
53 Interstate Ln (06705-2658)
PHONE..................................203 753-9451
Ralph Spinella, *Owner*
EMP: 8 **EST:** 1932
SALES (est): 468.2K **Privately Held**
SIC: 2051 5461 Mfg Bread/Related Products Retail Bakery

(G-4917)
MIRROR POLISHING & PLTG CO INC
346 Huntingdon Ave (06708-1430)
PHONE..................................203 574-5400
Gary Nalband, *President*
Glenn Geddis, *Engineer*
Kurt Stronk, *Engineer*
Penny Nalband, *Human Res Mgr*
◆ **EMP:** 40
SQ FT: 85,000
SALES (est): 6.3MM **Privately Held**
WEB: www.mpp.net
SIC: 3471 5719 Plating/Polishing Service Ret Misc Homefurnishings

(G-4918)
MITCHELL-BATE COMPANY
365 Thomaston Ave (06702-1024)
P.O. Box 1707 (06721-1707)
PHONE..................................203 233-0862
Donald C Lang Jr, *President*
Scott Lang, *Vice Pres*
Peter Dimaria, *Representative*
EMP: 30 **EST:** 1955
SQ FT: 15,000
SALES (est): 5.8MM **Privately Held**
SIC: 2542 3479 3443 Mfg Partitions/Fixtures-Nonwood Coating/Engraving Service Mfg Fabricated Plate Work

(G-4919)
MY CITIZENS NEWS
389 Meadow St (06702-1808)
PHONE..................................203 729-2228
Paul Roth, *Publisher*
EMP: 5
SALES (est): 194.2K **Privately Held**
SIC: 2711 Newspapers-Publishing/Printing

(G-4920)
MY TOOL COMPANY INC
1212 S Main St (06706-1747)
PHONE..................................203 755-2333
Fax: 203 755-4744
EMP: 4
SQ FT: 5,000
SALES: 500K **Privately Held**
SIC: 3599 3544 Mfg Industrial Machinery Mfg Dies/Tools/Jigs/Fixtures

(G-4921)
NAPP PRINTING PLATE DIST INC
245 Freight St (06702-1818)
PHONE..................................203 575-5727
Frank Monteiro, *Principal*
EMP: 7
SALES (est): 913.6K
SALES (corp-wide): 1.9B **Publicly Held**
SIC: 2752 Lithographic Commercial Printing
PA: Element Solutions Inc
500 E Broward Blvd # 1860
Fort Lauderdale FL 33394
561 207-9600

(G-4922)
NATIONAL INTEGRATED INDS INC
Also Called: American Electro Products Div
1358 Thomaston Ave (06704-1791)
P.O. Box 4129 (06704-0129)
PHONE..................................203 756-7051
Dennis Burke, *President*
James Moore, *Plant Mgr*
Joseph Gannon, *Purchasing*
John Krin, *Controller*
Angela Ciccone, *Human Res Dir*
EMP: 100
SALES (est): 9.2MM
SALES (corp-wide): 15MM **Privately Held**
SIC: 3471 Plating/Polishing Service
PA: National Integrated Industries, Inc.
322 Main St
Farmington CT 06032
860 677-7995

(G-4923)
NATURES VIEW INC
15 Maplerow Ave Ste A (06705-1731)
PHONE..................................800 506-5307
Miguel Rivera, *President*
EMP: 6
SALES (est): 602.8K **Privately Held**
SIC: 3599 7335 Mfg Industrial Machinery Commercial Photography

(G-4924)
NAUGATUCK VLY PHOTO ENGRV INC
2148 S Main St (06706-2639)
PHONE..................................203 756-7345
Daniel Semeraro, *President*
Frank Semeraro, *Vice Pres*
Nancy Semeraro, *Admin Sec*
EMP: 4
SALES (est): 544.3K **Privately Held**
SIC: 2754 2752 Manufactures Printing Plates

(G-4925)
NELSON HEAT TREATING CO INC
2046 N Main St (06704-2365)
PHONE..................................203 754-0670
James La France, *President*
James Lafrance, *President*
EMP: 11
SQ FT: 6,000
SALES (est): 1.5MM **Privately Held**
SIC: 3398 Metal Heat Treating

(G-4926)
NEOPERL INC
171 Mattatuck Heights Rd (06705-3832)
PHONE..................................203 756-8891
Frederic Fraisse, *Managing Dir*
Michael Moraniec, *Senior VP*
Marie Helene Pernin, *Vice Pres*
Chris Manning, *QC Mgr*
David Davino, *Engineer*
▲ **EMP:** 60 **EST:** 1927
SQ FT: 60,000
SALES (est): 11.1MM
SALES (corp-wide): 355.8K **Privately Held**
WEB: www.neoperl.com
SIC: 3432 5074 3088 Mfg Plumbing Fixture Fittings Whol Plumbing Equipment/Supplies Mfg Plastic Plumbing Fixtures
PA: Neoperl Holding Ag
Pfeffingerstrasse 21
Reinach BL
617 167-411

(G-4927)
NEW ENGLAND DIE CO INC
48 Ford Ave (06708-1408)
PHONE..................................203 574-5140
Joseph Almeida, *President*
Joseph Almeida Jr, *President*
Shelly Almeida, *Admin Sec*
EMP: 12 **EST:** 1941
SQ FT: 10,000
SALES (est): 1.8MM **Privately Held**
WEB: www.newenglanddie.com
SIC: 3541 Mfg Machine Tools-Cutting

(G-4928)
NEWMARK MEDICAL COMPONENTS INC
2670 S Main St (06706-2616)
P.O. Box 1030 (06721-1030)
PHONE..................................203 753-1158
James Behuniak, *Ch of Bd*
David W Mieczkowski, *President*
Thomas Tassis, *Corp Secy*
EMP: 14 **EST:** 2010
SQ FT: 15,000
SALES (est): 1.9MM
SALES (corp-wide): 20.2MM **Privately Held**
SIC: 3841 Mfg Surgical/Medical Instruments
PA: The Platt Brothers & Company
2670 S Main St
Waterbury CT 06706
203 753-4194

(G-4929)
NOUJAIM TOOL CO INC
412 Chase River Rd (06704-1401)
PHONE..................................203 753-4441
Joseph Noujaim, *President*
Selim G Noujaim, *President*
Joseph Noujaim, *Owner*
Naim Noujaim, *Vice Pres*
Daad Noujaim, *Treasurer*
EMP: 23
SQ FT: 5,500
SALES (est): 4.4MM **Privately Held**
WEB: www.noujaimtools.com
SIC: 3599 3544 Mfg Industrial Machinery Mfg Dies/Tools/Jigs/Fixtures

(G-4930)
NYLO METAL FINISHING LLC
730 N Main St Ste 1 (06704-3510)
P.O. Box 4960 (06704-0960)
PHONE..................................203 574-5477
Olyn Jaboin,
▲ **EMP:** 6 **EST:** 2000
SALES (est): 689.3K **Privately Held**
WEB: www.nylometalfinishing.com
SIC: 3471 Plating/Polishing Service

(G-4931)
OAKVILLE QUALITY PRODUCTS LLC
Also Called: Bobken Automatics
1495 Thomaston Ave Ste 2 (06704-1744)
PHONE..................................203 757-5525
Mark Newton,
EMP: 10
SALES (est): 1.4MM **Privately Held**
SIC: 3599 Mfg Industrial Machinery

(G-4932)
OIL PURIFICATION SYSTEMS INC
2176 Thomaston Ave (06704-1013)
PHONE..................................203 346-1800
Greg Slawson, *CEO*
William F Esposito, *President*
Mark Smith, *CFO*
Beth Muller, *Software Dev*
▲ **EMP:** 15
SQ FT: 1,200
SALES (est): 3.4MM **Privately Held**
WEB: www.oilpursys.com
SIC: 3533 Mfg Oil/Gas Field Machinery

(G-4933)
PACKAGING AND CRATING TECH LLC
150 Mattatuck Heights Rd (06705-3893)
PHONE..................................203 759-1799
David Goodrich,
Claude Michael Jackson,
EMP: 6
SALES (est): 903.9K **Privately Held**
SIC: 2671 3089 Mfg Packaging Paper/Film Mfg Plastic Products

(G-4934)
PACT INC
150 Mattatuck Heights Rd (06705 3893)
PHONE..................................203 759-1799
Rodger Mort, *President*
David Goodrich, *President*
EMP: 17
SALES (est): 2.8MM **Privately Held**
SIC: 2631 Paperboard Mill

(G-4935)
PALLADIN PRECISION PDTS INC
57 Bristol St (06708-4901)
PHONE..................................203 574-0246
Anthony Palladino, *President*
Dean Palladino, *Vice Pres*
Gary Wininger, *QC Dir*
Lynne R Palladino, *Treasurer*
Dannielle Gonzalez, *Admin Asst*
EMP: 25

GEOGRAPHIC

SQ FT: 20,000
SALES (est): 5.9MM **Privately Held**
WEB: www.palladin.com
SIC: 3451 Mfg Screw Machine Products

(G-4936)
PARK ADVNCED CMPOSITE MTLS INC
172 E Aurora St Ste A (06708-2048)
PHONE..................................203 755-1344
John Jongebloed, *President*
Steven Peake, *Manager*
▲ **EMP:** 53
SQ FT: 100,000
SALES (est): 433.1K
SALES (corp-wide): 51.1MM **Publicly Held**
WEB: www.fibercote.com
SIC: 2295 Mfg Coated Fabrics
PA: Park Aerospace Corp.
1400 Old Country Rd # 409
Westbury NY 11590
631 465-3662

(G-4937)
PHARMACAL RESEARCH LABS INC
562 Captain Neville Dr # 1 (06705-3875)
P.O. Box 369, Naugatuck (06770-0369)
PHONE..................................203 755-4908
Kenneth Shapiro, *President*
Jerry Shapiro, *CFO*
◆ **EMP:** 34
SQ FT: 14,500
SALES (est): 8.5MM **Privately Held**
WEB: www.pharmacal.com
SIC: 2841 Mfg Soap/Other Detergents

(G-4938)
PHILIPS ULTRASOUND INC
Igc Advanced Superconductors
1875 Thomaston Ave Ste 5 (06704-1034)
PHONE..................................203 753-5215
Richard Lenharbt, *Manager*
EMP: 95
SALES (corp-wide): 20.1B **Privately Held**
SIC: 3845 Mfg Electromedical Equipment
HQ: Philips Ultrasound, Inc.
22100 Bothell Everett Hwy
Bothell WA 98021
800 982-2011

(G-4939)
PLASMA COATINGS INC
758 E Main St (06702-1712)
P.O. Box 10006 (06725-0006)
PHONE..................................203 598-3100
Gary Carlo, *President*
Jody Leblanc, *Sales Staff*
EMP: 3
SALES (est): 405.5K **Privately Held**
SIC: 2836 Mfg Biological Products

(G-4940)
PLATT BROTHERS & COMPANY (PA)
2670 S Main St (06706-2616)
PHONE..................................203 753-4194
Milton Grile, *Ch of Bd*
James P Behuniak, *President*
David W Mieczkowski, *President*
James J Goggins, *Corp Secy*
John Greaney, *Vice Pres*
EMP: 98 **EST:** 1830
SQ FT: 120,000
SALES (est): 20.2MM **Privately Held**
WEB: www.plattbros.com
SIC: 3356 3357 3965 3272 Nonferrous Rollng/Drawng Nonfrs Wiredrwng/Insltng Mfg Fastener/Button/Pins Mfg Concrete Products Mfg Metal Stampings

(G-4941)
PORTER PRESTON INC
61 Mattatuck Heights Rd # 2 (06705-3854)
PHONE..................................203 753-1113
John P Birtwell, *President*
Steven P Gilmore, *Vice Pres*
Michelle Clark, *Accountant*
EMP: 29
SALES: 6MM **Privately Held**
WEB: www.porterpreston.com
SIC: 2591 Mfg Drapery Hardware/Blinds

(G-4942)
POWER COVER USA LLC
37 Commons Ct Ste 3 (06704-1400)
PHONE..................................203 755-2687
Erik Noeding,
Jill Noeding,
EMP: 4
SALES (est): 1MM **Privately Held**
SIC: 2399 3537 Mfg Hydraulic Tarping Systems For Transportation Industry

(G-4943)
PRECISION DIP COATING LLC
176 Chase River Rd (06704-1441)
PHONE..................................203 805-4564
Gary Santoro,
Charlene Santoro,
EMP: 5
SALES (est): 630K **Privately Held**
WEB: www.precisiondipcoating.com
SIC: 3291 2821 Plastic Coating And Molding

(G-4944)
PREMIERE PACKG PARTNERS LLC
197 Huntingdon Ave (06708-1413)
PHONE..................................203 694-0003
Michael O'Gorman,
EMP: 25
SALES (est): 809.2K **Privately Held**
SIC: 2099 Mfg Food Preparations

(G-4945)
PREYCO MFG CO INC
1184 N Main St (06704-3114)
P.O. Box 4057 (06704-0057)
PHONE..................................203 574-4545
Dennis Laperrierre, *President*
Susan Laperriere, *Director*
EMP: 3 **EST:** 1960
SQ FT: 8,000
SALES (est): 450K **Privately Held**
WEB: www.preyco.com
SIC: 3469 Mfg Metal Stampings

(G-4946)
PRODUCTION DECORATING CO INC
184 Railroad Hill St (06708-4307)
PHONE..................................203 574-2975
Frank Hartnett, *President*
Brendan Hartnett, *Vice Pres*
EMP: 20
SQ FT: 11,000
SALES (est): 2.5MM **Privately Held**
SIC: 2759 Commercial Printing

(G-4947)
PROXTALKERCOM LLC (PA)
Also Called: Logantech
327 Huntingdon Ave (06708-1413)
PHONE..................................203 721-6074
Mary Wyatt, *General Mgr*
Gary Taulbee, *Manager*
Glen Dobbs,
Kevin Miller,
EMP: 7
SALES (est): 570.3K **Privately Held**
SIC: 3651 Mfg Home Audio/Video Equipment

(G-4948)
QSCEND TECHNOLOGIES INC
231 Bank St (06702-2213)
PHONE..................................203 757-6000
Keith Lebeau, *President*
Irene Lebeau, *Comptroller*
Jessica Chase, *VP Sales*
Kristee Trelli, *Mktg Coord*
Sean Williams, *Bd of Directors*
EMP: 21
SALES (est): 2.9MM **Privately Held**
WEB: www.qscend.com
SIC: 7372 Prepackaged Software Services

(G-4949)
RAYPAX MANUFACTURING CO INC
21 Tremont St (06708-2217)
PHONE..................................203 758-7416
EMP: 8 **EST:** 1960
SQ FT: 17,370
SALES (est): 65.1K **Privately Held**
SIC: 3451 Mfg Screw Machine Products

(G-4950)
RICHARD DUDGEON INC
24 Swift Pl (06710-2026)
PHONE..................................203 336-4459
Allen D Haight, *Ch of Bd*
Allen Haight, *Ch of Bd*
EMP: 6 **EST:** 1849
SQ FT: 19,000
SALES: 2MM **Privately Held**
WEB: www.dudgeonjacks.com
SIC: 3569 7353 Mfg General Industrial Machinery Heavy Construction Equipment Rental

(G-4951)
SALESCHAIN LLC
61 Mattatuck Heights Rd # 201 (06705-3839)
PHONE..................................203 262-1611
Tim Szczygiel, *President*
EMP: 10
SALES (est): 1.6MM **Privately Held**
WEB: www.saleschain.com
SIC: 7372 Prepackaged Software Services

(G-4952)
SANDUR TOOL CO
853 Hamilton Ave (06706-1998)
PHONE..................................203 753-0004
Anthony Durso Jr, *President*
Jean Gaudiosi, *Finance Mgr*
EMP: 7 **EST:** 1955
SQ FT: 5,000
SALES: 1.5MM **Privately Held**
SIC: 3544 Mfg Dies/Tools/Jigs/Fixtures

(G-4953)
SEGA READY MIX INCORPORATED
310 Chase River Rd (06704-1401)
PHONE..................................203 465-1052
Mark Whitlock, *Manager*
EMP: 8
SALES (corp-wide): 2MM **Privately Held**
SIC: 3273 Mfg Ready-Mixed Concrete
PA: Sega Ready Mix, Incorporated
519 Danbury Rd
New Milford CT 06776
860 354-3969

(G-4954)
SEIDEL INC
Also Called: Anodizing
1883 Thomaston Ave (06704-1039)
P.O. Box 4727 (06704-0727)
PHONE..................................203 757-7349
Michael Ritzenhoff, *Vice Pres*
Donna Van Nostrand, *Purchasing*
EMP: 95
SALES (corp-wide): 83.7MM **Privately Held**
SIC: 3471 Plating/Polishing Service
PA: Seidel Gmbh & Co. Kg
Rosenstr. 8
Marburg 35037
642 160-40

(G-4955)
SEIDEL INC
2223 Thomaston Ave (06704-1000)
PHONE..................................203 757-7349
Michael Ritzenhoff, *President*
▲ **EMP:** 70
SQ FT: 75,000
SALES (est): 12.1MM **Privately Held**
WEB: www.seidel.com
SIC: 3471 Plating/Polishing Service

(G-4956)
SHEILA P PATRICK
Also Called: Printing Plus
179 Dwight St (06704-1816)
PHONE..................................203 575-1716
Sheila P Patrick, *Owner*
EMP: 5
SALES (est): 306.6K **Privately Held**
SIC: 2759 Commercial Printing

(G-4957)
SHELDON PRECISION LLC
10 Industrial Rd (06712-1018)
PHONE..................................203 758-4441
EMP: 3
SALES (est): 430.7K **Privately Held**
SIC: 3451 Mfg Screw Machine Products

(G-4958)
SPECIALTY POLYMERS INC
245 Freight St (06702-1818)
PHONE..................................203 575-5727
John Cordani, *President*
EMP: 4 **EST:** 2017
SALES (est): 232.2K
SALES (corp-wide): 1.9B **Publicly Held**
SIC: 2822 Mfg Synthetic Rubber
PA: Element Solutions Inc
500 E Broward Blvd # 1860
Fort Lauderdale FL 33394
561 207-9600

(G-4959)
SPINELLA BAKERY
53 Interstate Ln (06705-2658)
PHONE..................................203 753-9451
Ralph Spinella Jr, *Owner*
EMP: 12 **EST:** 1934
SQ FT: 4,000
SALES (est): 964.5K **Privately Held**
SIC: 2051 Mfg Bread/Related Products

(G-4960)
STATELY STAIR CO INC
3810 E Main St (06705-3853)
PHONE..................................203 575-1966
Nick Pennacchio, *President*
Elizabeth Adams, *General Mgr*
EMP: 23
SQ FT: 12,000
SALES (est): 3.3MM **Privately Held**
WEB: www.touristnetuk.com
SIC: 2431 3446 Mfg Millwork Mfg Architectural Metalwork

(G-4961)
TECHNO MTAL POST WATERTOWN LLC
88 Meadowbrook Dr (06706-2722)
PHONE..................................203 755-6403
Sylvain Halle,
EMP: 3 **EST:** 2007
SALES (est): 391.3K **Privately Held**
SIC: 3272 2491 Mfg Concrete Products Wood Preserving

(G-4962)
TESCO RESOURCES INC
170 Freight St (06702-1804)
PHONE..................................203 754-3900
Hank Berberat, *President*
Delores Marino, *Corp Secy*
Tammy Berberat, *Vice Pres*
EMP: 4
SQ FT: 4,000
SALES: 1.8MM **Privately Held**
WEB: www.tescotank.com
SIC: 3443 Mfg Of Environmental Tank Systems

(G-4963)
TOOL THE SOMMA COMPANY
109 Scott Rd (06705-3202)
P.O. Box 2559 (06723-2559)
PHONE..................................203 753-2114
Eric A Somma, *President*
Thomas R Minuto, *Vice Pres*
Gerard H Somma, *Vice Pres*
Jerry Somma, *Vice Pres*
Dick Noti, *Purch Agent*
EMP: 25 **EST:** 1939
SQ FT: 27,000
SALES (est): 5.3MM **Privately Held**
WEB: www.somma.com
SIC: 3545 Mfg Machine Tool Accessories

(G-4964)
TOP SOURCE INC
490 S Main St (06706-1018)
PHONE..................................203 753-6490
Danna M Gizzie, *President*
EMP: 3
SALES: 800K **Privately Held**
SIC: 3131 Mfg Counter Tops

(G-4965)
TPS ACQUISITION LLC (PA)
151 Sharon Rd (06705-4044)
PHONE..................................860 589-5511
Robert W Garthwait Jr,
David Elliot,
Peter K Gersky,
Thaddeus M Sendzimir,

EMP: 5 EST: 2013
SALES (est): 62.8MM **Privately Held**
SIC: 3324 Steel Investment Foundry

(G-4966)
TRAVER ELECTRIC MOTOR CO INC
151 Homer St (06704-1729)
PHONE....203 753-5103
Jack E Traver, *President*
Elaine Traver, *Admin Sec*
EMP: 25
SQ FT: 14,000
SALES (est): 5.3MM **Privately Held**
WEB: www.traveridc.com
SIC: 7694 5063 Armature Rewinding Whol Electrical Equipment

(G-4967)
TRITEX CORPORATION
Also Called: Haydon Motion Europe
1500 Meriden Rd (06705-3982)
P.O. Box 3329 (06705-0329)
PHONE....203 756-7441
John Norris, *President*
▲ EMP: 250
SQ FT: 42,000
SALES (est): 31.2MM **Privately Held**
SIC: 3679 3621 Mfg Electronic Components Mfg Motors/Generators

(G-4968)
TRUELINE CORPORATION
196 Mill St Ste 1 (06706-1208)
PHONE....203 757-0344
Roger Pegolo, *President*
Paul Pegolo, *Vice Pres*
John Gadjue, *Office Mgr*
Vivian Pegolo, *Admin Sec*
EMP: 5
SQ FT: 6,000
SALES: 500K **Privately Held**
WEB: www.trueline.us
SIC: 3545 3544 Mfg Machine Tool Accessories Mfg Dies/Tools/Jigs/Fixtures

(G-4969)
VIKING PLATINUM LLC
46 Municipal Rd (06708-4305)
PHONE....203 574-7979
EMP: 14
SQ FT: 21,500
SALES (est): 1.1MM **Privately Held**
SIC: 3341 Secondary Nonferrous Metal Producer

(G-4970)
VILLE SWISS AUTOMATICS INC
205 Cherry St (06702-1610)
P.O. Box 4068 (06704-0068)
PHONE....203 756-2825
John Petro, *President*
Miriam Hernandez, *Corp Secy*
EMP: 14
SQ FT: 7,800
SALES (est): 2.5MM **Privately Held**
WEB: www.villeswiss.com
SIC: 3451 Mfg Screw Machine Products

(G-4971)
W CANNING INC
245 Freight St (06702-1818)
PHONE....203 575-5727
EMP: 4
SALES (est): 217.9K
SALES (corp-wide): 1.9B **Publicly Held**
SIC: 2899 Mfg Chemical Preparations
PA: Element Solutions Inc
500 E Broward Blvd # 1860
West Palm Beach FL 33394
561 207-9600

(G-4972)
WATERBURY LEATHERWORKS CO
1691 Thomaston Ave Ste 3 (06704-1044)
PHONE....203 755-7789
Ernest Bentley, *President*
Russ Kaye, *Vice Pres*
EMP: 12
SQ FT: 14,000
SALES (est): 1.1MM **Privately Held**
SIC: 3172 Mfg Leather Goods

(G-4973)
WATERBURY ROLLING MILLS INC
215 Piedmont St (06706-2152)
PHONE....203 597-5000
Pat Kelly, *General Mgr*
EMP: 95 EST: 1906
SQ FT: 100,000
SALES: 18.5MM
SALES (corp-wide): 6.9B **Publicly Held**
WEB: www.olin.com
SIC: 3351 3312 3356 Copper Rolling/Drawing Blast Furnace-Steel Work Nonferrous Rollng/Drawng
PA: Olin Corporation
190 Carondelet Plz # 1530
Saint Louis MO 63105
314 480-1400

(G-4974)
WATERBURY SCREW MACHINE
319 Thomaston Ave (06702-1024)
PHONE....203 756-8084
Matt Corcoran, *Principal*
Matthew Corcoran, *Principal*
EMP: 6
SALES (est): 637.7K **Privately Held**
SIC: 3451 Mfg Screw Machine Products

(G-4975)
WATERBURY SCREW MCH PDTS CO
311 Thomaston Ave Ste 319 (06702-1024)
P.O. Box 2576 (06723-2576)
PHONE....203 756-8084
Matthew Corcoran, *President*
EMP: 30 EST: 1938
SQ FT: 13,500
SALES (est): 5.2MM **Privately Held**
SIC: 3451 Mfg Screw Machine Products

(G-4976)
WATERBURY SWISS AUTOMATICS
43 Mattatuck Heights Rd (06705-3832)
P.O. Box 3128 (06705-0128)
PHONE....203 573-8584
Neil Tremaglio Jr, *President*
Jerry Beaudoin, *General Mgr*
Alba Tremaglio, *Vice Pres*
EMP: 27 EST: 1950
SQ FT: 11,500
SALES (est): 5.5MM **Privately Held**
SIC: 3451 Mfg Screw Machine Products

(G-4977)
WCES INC
Also Called: Inc, Waterbury
225 S Leonard St (06708-4247)
P.O. Box 33 (06720-0033)
PHONE....203 573-1325
Lisa Meyer, *President*
Donald Martelli, *General Mgr*
EMP: 14
SQ FT: 18,000
SALES: 1.6MM **Privately Held**
WEB: www.wces.com
SIC: 3469 Mfg Metal Stampings

(G-4978)
WHITE WELDING COMPANY INC
44 N Elm St (06702-1512)
PHONE....203 753-1197
Leo Tomaiolo, *Corp Secy*
Robert Tomaiolo, *Vice Pres*
Mark Krause, *Treasurer*
EMP: 8
SQ FT: 10,000
SALES: 1MM **Privately Held**
WEB: www.whitewelding.com
SIC: 3444 7692 Mfg Sheet Metalwork Welding Repair

(G-4979)
WOODFREE CRATING SYSTEMS INC
150 Mattatuck Heights Rd (06705-3893)
PHONE....203 759-1799
David Goodrich, *President*
Michael Jackson, *Admin Sec*
EMP: 12
SQ FT: 17,900
SALES: 2.8MM **Privately Held**
WEB: www.woodfreecrating.com
SIC: 2449 Manufacture All Types Of Crates

Waterford
New London County

(G-4980)
ADVANCED REASONING
82 Boston Post Rd Ste 3 (06385-2425)
P.O. Box 41 (06385-0041)
PHONE....860 437-0508
John Lehet, *President*
EMP: 5
SALES: 480K **Privately Held**
WEB: www.advreason.com
SIC: 7372 Prepackaged Software Services

(G-4981)
BESTWAY FOOD AND FUEL
6 Boston Post Rd (06385-2402)
PHONE....860 447-0729
Chirag Patel, *Owner*
EMP: 5
SALES (est): 235.5K **Privately Held**
SIC: 2869 Mfg Industrial Organic Chemicals

(G-4982)
COASTAL STEEL CORPORATION
10 Mallard Ln (06385-1110)
PHONE....860 443-4073
Glenn Ahnert, *President*
Susan Ahnert, *Treasurer*
EMP: 20
SQ FT: 22,000
SALES (est): 2.3MM **Privately Held**
SIC: 3441 Structural Metal Fabrication

(G-4983)
COCA-COLA COMPANY
150 Parkway S (06385)
PHONE....860 443-2816
Steven K Perrelli, *Treasurer*
EMP: 3
SALES (corp-wide): 31.8B **Publicly Held**
WEB: www.cocacola.com
SIC: 2086 Carb Sft Drnkbtlcn
PA: The Coca-Cola Company
1 Coca Cola Plz Nw
Atlanta GA 30313
404 676-2121

(G-4984)
HARJANI HITESH
Also Called: In Style Fragrances
850 Hartford Tpke H109 (06385-4238)
PHONE....860 913-6032
Hitesh Harjani, *Owner*
EMP: 3
SALES: 84K **Privately Held**
WEB: www.instylefragrances.com
SIC: 2844 Mfg Toilet Preparations

(G-4985)
HARSHA INC
850 Hartford Tpke (06385-4238)
PHONE....860 439-1466
Dinesh Vachhani, *Vice Pres*
EMP: 4
SALES (est): 264.3K **Privately Held**
SIC: 2052 Mfg Cookies/Crackers

(G-4986)
JAYPRO SPORTS LLC
Also Called: US Athletic Equipment
976 Hartford Tpke Ste B (06385-4044)
PHONE....860 447-3001
Michael J Ferrara,
Mark Ferrara,
▲ EMP: 50 EST: 1953
SALES (est): 3.7MM **Privately Held**
WEB: www.jaypro.com
SIC: 3949 5091 Mfg Sporting/Athletic Goods Whol Sporting/Recreational Goods

(G-4987)
KOBYLUCK READY-MIX INC
24 Industrial Dr (06385-4026)
PHONE....860 444-9604
Matthew T Kobyluck, *President*
Daniel W Kobyluck, *Vice Pres*
Joshua E Kobyluck, *Vice Pres*
Mark N Kobyluck, *Vice Pres*
Maureen A Kobyluck, *Vice Pres*
EMP: 10 EST: 1995
SALES (est): 2.5MM **Privately Held**
SIC: 3271 Mfg Concrete Block/Brick

(G-4988)
KOBYLUCK SAND AND GRAVEL INC
24 Industrial Dr (06385-4026)
PHONE....860 444-9600
Daniel W Kobyluck, *President*
Maureen Kobyluck, *Admin Sec*
EMP: 15
SALES (est): 3.8MM **Privately Held**
SIC: 1442 Construction Sand/Gravel

(G-4989)
MISTRAS GROUP INC
6 Mill Ln (06385-2616)
PHONE....860 447-2474
Alfonso Gianfanti, *General Mgr*
EMP: 40 **Publicly Held**
SIC: 3829 Testing Laboratory
PA: Mistras Group, Inc.
195 Clarksville Rd Ste 2
Princeton Junction NJ 08550

(G-4990)
NOVELTY TEXTILE MILLS LLC
24 Spithead Rd (06385-1917)
PHONE....860 774-5000
Allan Taylor, *President*
EMP: 4
SALES (est): 310K **Privately Held**
SIC: 2258 Lace/Warp Knit Fabric Mill

(G-4991)
PRICE-DRISCOLL CORPORATION
17 Industrial Dr (06385-4010)
PHONE....860 442-3575
Philip C Barth, *President*
Nancy Arzamarski, *Accounts Exec*
Robert Walter, *Manager*
Jessica Kelliher, *Administration*
EMP: 8 EST: 1947
SQ FT: 12,000
SALES (est): 2MM **Privately Held**
WEB: www.price-driscoll.com
SIC: 2992 Mfg Lubricating Oils/Greases

(G-4992)
SECONN AUTOMATION SOLUTIONS
147 Cross Rd (06385-1216)
P.O. Box 294 (06385-0294)
PHONE....860 442-4325
Robert Mareli, *CEO*
EMP: 16 EST: 1956
SQ FT: 2,600
SALES: 10.3MM **Privately Held**
SIC: 3444 Mfg Sheet Metalwork

(G-4993)
SECONN FABRICATION LLC
180 Cross Rd (06385-1215)
PHONE....860 443-0000
Lisa Robison, *Mfg Staff*
Robert J Marelli Jr,
EMP: 65
SQ FT: 60,000
SALES (est): 15.3MM **Privately Held**
WEB: www.seconn.com
SIC: 3444 Mfg Sheet Metalwork

(G-4994)
SPORTEES LLC
262 Boston Post Rd Unit 8 (06385-2053)
PHONE....860 440-3922
Thomas J Harrington,
EMP: 3
SQ FT: 1,000
SALES (est): 205.7K **Privately Held**
SIC: 2759 Commercial Printing

(G-4995)
VIKING ENTERPRISES INC
41 Millstone Rd (06385-3116)
PHONE....860 440-0728
David Engdall, *President*
William Engdall, *Director*
EMP: 4
SALES: 175K **Privately Held**
SIC: 3441 Steel Fabrication And Acoustical Installation

GEOGRAPHIC

(G-4996)
YOST MANUFACTURING & SUPPLY
1018 Hartford Tpke (06385-4032)
P.O. Box 263 (06385-0263)
PHONE..................................860 447-9678
George P Yost, *President*
Andrew Saad, *General Mgr*
Albert G Yost Jr, *Vice Pres*
EMP: 10
SQ FT: 5,000
SALES (est): 710K **Privately Held**
SIC: 3444 Mfg Rain Gutters

Watertown
Litchfield County

(G-4997)
ADVANCED SPECIALIST LLC
162 Commercial St (06795-3309)
PHONE..................................860 945-9125
Gardner W Gage, *Principal*
Steve Gage, *VP Mfg*
▲ **EMP:** 8
SALES (est): 796.2K **Privately Held**
SIC: 3999 Mfg Misc Products

(G-4998)
AMRO TOOL CO
127 Echo Lake Rd Ste 26 (06795-2657)
PHONE..................................860 274-9766
Robert Valunas, *Owner*
EMP: 3
SALES (est): 386.6K **Privately Held**
SIC: 3546 Mfg Power-Driven Handtools

(G-4999)
BEANS INC
2213 Litchfield Rd (06795-1006)
PHONE..................................860 945-9234
Danielle Brennan, *President*
EMP: 4
SALES (est): 189K **Privately Held**
SIC: 2051 Mfg Bread/Related Products

(G-5000)
BRAXTON MANUFACTURING CO INC
858 Echo Lake Rd (06795-1636)
P.O. Box 429 (06795-0429)
PHONE..................................860 274-6781
Thomas Ordway, *President*
Shirley Bridge, *Production*
Robert G Dionne, *Treasurer*
Joseph E Triano, *Admin Sec*
EMP: 170
SQ FT: 60,000
SALES (est): 30.7MM **Privately Held**
WEB: www.braxtonmfg.com
SIC: 3965 3769 3577 Mfg Fastener/Button/Pins Mfg Space Vehicle Equip Mfg Computer Peripherals

(G-5001)
BRISTOL INC (HQ)
Also Called: Emerson Rmote Automtn Solution
1100 Buckingham St (06795-6602)
P.O. Box 36911, Saint Louis MO (63136-9011)
PHONE..................................860 945-2200
Craig T Llewlyn, *President*
Craig Llewlyn, *President*
Warren Howard, *Vice Pres*
Teresa A Burnett, *Treasurer*
▲ **EMP:** 300 **EST:** 1980
SQ FT: 190,000
SALES (est): 113.9MM
SALES (corp-wide): 18.3B **Publicly Held**
WEB: www.bristolbabcock.com
SIC: 3823 Mfg Process Control Instruments
PA: Emerson Electric Co.
8000 West Florissant Ave
Saint Louis MO 63136
314 553-2000

(G-5002)
CGL INC
Also Called: Anco Tool & Manufacturing
1094 Echo Lake Rd (06795-1635)
P.O. Box 698 (06795-0698)
PHONE..................................860 945-6166
Charles G Lacombe, *President*
Charles J Lacombe, *Vice Pres*
Donald Melason, *Vice Pres*
Nicholas Meglio, *QC Mgr*
EMP: 12 **EST:** 1956
SALES (est): 3.1MM **Privately Held**
WEB: www.ancotool.com
SIC: 3544 3599 3469 Mfg Dies/Tools/Jigs/Fixtures Mfg Industrial Machinery Mfg Metal Stampings

(G-5003)
CLICK BOND INC
18 Park Rd (06795-1618)
PHONE..................................860 274-5435
Charles G Hutter III, *CEO*
EMP: 50
SALES (corp-wide): 59.8MM **Privately Held**
SIC: 3452 Mfg Bolts Rivets & Screws
HQ: Click Bond, Inc.
2151 Lockheed Way
Carson City NV 89706
775 885-8000

(G-5004)
COVIT AMERICA INC
Also Called: Albea Metal Americas
1 Seemar Rd (06795-1638)
PHONE..................................860 274-6791
Henry F Seebach Jr, *President*
John Spino, *General Mgr*
▲ **EMP:** 375
SALES (est): 84.9MM **Privately Held**
SIC: 3086 Mfg Plastic Foam Products
HQ: Albea Services
Zac Des Barbanniers Le Signac
Gennevilliers 92230
181 932-000

(G-5005)
CRYSTAL ROCK HOLDINGS INC (HQ)
1050 Buckingham St (06795-6602)
PHONE..................................860 945-0661
Peter K Baker, *President*
Jack Baker, *Exec VP*
John B Baker, *Exec VP*
David Jurasek, *CFO*
Brandon Sereni, *Sales Staff*
▲ **EMP:** 41
SQ FT: 67,000
SALES: 59MM
SALES (corp-wide): 2.2B **Privately Held**
SIC: 2086 3589 Mfg Bottled/Canned Soft Drinks Mfg Service Industry Machinery
PA: Cott Corporation
6525 Viscount Rd
Mississauga ON L4V 1
905 672-1900

(G-5006)
DEMSEY MANUFACTURING CO INC
78 New Wood Rd (06795-3339)
PHONE..................................860 274-6209
Richard A Demsey, *President*
Scott Demsey, *General Mgr*
EMP: 35 **EST:** 1954
SQ FT: 35,000
SALES (est): 8.7MM **Privately Held**
WEB: www.demseyelets.com
SIC: 3469 Mfg Metal Stampings

(G-5007)
DISTINCTIVE STEERING WHEELS
189 Chimney Rd (06795-1682)
PHONE..................................860 274-9087
EMP: 3
SALES (est): 165.2K **Privately Held**
SIC: 3465 Mfg Automotive Stampings

(G-5008)
ECI SCREEN PRINT INC
15 Mountain View Rd (06795-1648)
P.O. Box 116, Thomaston (06787-0116)
PHONE..................................860 283-9849
Edward Cook, *President*
Eleanor Maynard, *COO*
Irma Diaz, *Vice Pres*
Girolimon Mark, *Opers Mgr*
Brett Owen, *Sales Staff*
EMP: 12
SQ FT: 13,000
SALES (est): 2.5MM **Privately Held**
WEB: www.eciscreenprint.com
SIC: 2759 Commercial Printing

(G-5009)
EYELET TOOLMAKERS INC
40 Callender Rd (06795-1628)
P.O. Box 402 (06795-0402)
PHONE..................................860 274-5423
Albinas Rickevicius, *President*
Linda Rickevicius, *Vice Pres*
Anna Rickevicius, *Admin Sec*
EMP: 40
SQ FT: 30,000
SALES (est): 5.2MM **Privately Held**
WEB: www.eyelettoolmakers.com
SIC: 3469 Mfg Metal Stampings

(G-5010)
GENERAL WLDG & FABRICATION INC
977 Echo Lake Rd (06795-1639)
PHONE..................................860 274-9668
Holly A Herbert, *President*
Jay N Herbert, *Corp Secy*
EMP: 13
SQ FT: 12,400
SALES (est): 3.7MM **Privately Held**
SIC: 7692 Welding Repair

(G-5011)
GLOBAL STEERING SYSTEMS LLC (PA)
Also Called: G S S
156 Park Rd (06795-1616)
P.O. Box 210 (06795-0210)
PHONE..................................860 945-5400
Larry Finnell, *CEO*
Julio Costa, *Vice Pres*
Scott Filion, *Vice Pres*
Gabe Rosa, *Vice Pres*
Eileen Meade, *Purch Mgr*
◆ **EMP:** 131
SQ FT: 180,000
SALES (est): 54.6MM **Privately Held**
SIC: 3714 Mfg Motor Vehicle Parts/Accessories

(G-5012)
KOSTER KEUNEN INC
1021 Echo Lake Rd (06795-1639)
PHONE..................................860 945-3333
John Koster, *Ch of Bd*
Henry Muschio, *Vice Pres*
Michael Samson, *Sales Mgr*
EMP: 3
SALES (est): 209.9K **Privately Held**
SIC: 2911 Petroleum Refiner

(G-5013)
KOSTER KEUNEN LLC (PA)
1021 Echo Lake Rd (06795-1639)
PHONE..................................860 945-3333
Joe Iorfino, *Opers Staff*
John Koster,
Joanna Koster,
◆ **EMP:** 14
SALES (est): 9.3MM **Privately Held**
SIC: 2999 2834 2671 2842 Mfg Petroleum/Coal Prdts Mfg Pharmaceutical Preps Mfg Packaging Paper/Film

(G-5014)
KOSTER KEUNEN MFG INC
1021 Echo Lake Rd (06795-1639)
P.O. Box 69 (06795-0069)
PHONE..................................860 945-3333
John F Koster, *President*
Robert Behrer, *Vice Pres*
Henry Muschio, *VP Opers*
Jessica Dynda, *Sales Staff*
◆ **EMP:** 60
SQ FT: 100,000
SALES (est): 13.1MM **Privately Held**
WEB: www.kosterkeunen.com
SIC: 2911 Petroleum Refiner

(G-5015)
PEACHWAVE OF WATERTOWN
1156 Main St (06795-2918)
PHONE..................................203 942-4949
Kelly Dun, *Managing Prtnr*
EMP: 4 **EST:** 2012
SALES (est): 218.3K **Privately Held**
SIC: 2026 Mfg Fluid Milk

(G-5016)
PETRON AUTOMATION INC
65 Mountain View Rd (06795-1648)
P.O. Box 399 (06795-0399)
PHONE..................................860 274-9091
Michael Petro Jr, *President*
Patricia Petro, *Vice Pres*
EMP: 24
SQ FT: 7,500
SALES (est): 5.1MM **Privately Held**
WEB: www.petronautomation.com
SIC: 3451 Mfg Screw Machine Products

(G-5017)
PRIME ENGNEERED COMPONENTS INC
1012 Buckingham St (06795-6602)
PHONE..................................860 274-6773
Dennis J Izzo, *President*
Mark Izzo, *Vice Pres*
EMP: 3
SALES (est): 295.4K **Privately Held**
SIC: 3451 Mfg Screw Machine Products

(G-5018)
PRIME PUBLISHERS INC
Also Called: Town Times
449 Main St (06795-2628)
P.O. Box 1 (06795-0001)
PHONE..................................860 274-6721
Annette Linster, *CFO*
Walter Mazurosky, *Adv Mgr*
Terry Pfeifer, *Manager*
EMP: 6
SALES (corp-wide): 5MM **Privately Held**
SIC: 2711 Newspapers-Publishing/Printing
PA: Prime Publishers Inc
90 Middle Quarter Rd
Woodbury CT
203 263-2116

(G-5019)
PRIME SCREW MACHINE PDTS INC (PA)
Also Called: Prime Engineered Components
1012 Buckingham St (06795-1667)
P.O. Box 359 (06795-0359)
PHONE..................................860 274-6773
Dennis Izzo, *President*
Mark Izzo, *Vice Pres*
Prima Izzo, *Admin Sec*
EMP: 61
SQ FT: 32,000
SALES (est): 12.5MM **Privately Held**
WEB: www.primesmp.com
SIC: 3451 Mfg Screw Machine Products

(G-5020)
PROTOPAC INC
Also Called: Protopac Printing Services
120 Echo Lake Rd (06795-2664)
PHONE..................................860 274-6796
Hugh J Langin, *President*
Stephen Langin, *Treasurer*
Hugh F Langin, *Controller*
Susan Langin, *Admin Sec*
EMP: 9 **EST:** 1979
SQ FT: 3,000
SALES: 900K **Privately Held**
WEB: www.protopac.com
SIC: 3496 2752 Mfg Misc Fabricated Wire Products Lithographic Commercial Printing

(G-5021)
RED APPLE CHEESE LLC (PA)
27 Siemon Co Dr Ste 231w (06795-2654)
PHONE..................................203 755-5579
Paul Brzezienski,
Salvatore Distasio,
▲ **EMP:** 9
SQ FT: 700
SALES (est): 2.4MM **Privately Held**
WEB: www.redapplecheese.com
SIC: 2022 Mfg Cheese

(G-5022)
RTC MFG CO INC
1094 Echo Lake Rd (06795-1635)
P.O. Box 698 (06795-0698)
PHONE..................................800 888-3701
Carolyn A Locombe, *President*
Charles Lacombe, *General Mgr*
Charles J Lacombe, *Vice Pres*
Charles G Lacombe, *Treasurer*

Gene Mc Redmond, *Accountant*
EMP: 5
SQ FT: 3,000
SALES: 160K **Privately Held**
SIC: 3469 Mfg Metal Stampings

(G-5023)
SHELTERLOGIC CORP (HQ)
150 Callender Rd (06795-1628)
PHONE..................................860 945-6442
James Raymond, *CEO*
Rob Silinski, *President*
Jon Slaughter, *Vice Pres*
Ken Smith, *Vice Pres*
Joann Trezza, *Vice Pres*
◆ **EMP:** 151
SALES (est): 121.5MM **Privately Held**
SIC: 2394 5091 Mfg Canvas/Related Products Whol Sporting/Recreational Goods
PA: Slogic Holding Corp.
36 Grove St
New Canaan CT 06840
203 966-2800

(G-5024)
SIEMON COMPANY (PA)
Also Called: Siemon Global Project Services
101 Siemon Company Dr (06795-2651)
PHONE..................................860 945-4200
Carl N Siemon, *President*
CK Siemon, *President*
John Siemon, *Vice Pres*
Brian Wheelock, *Plant Mgr*
Lance Lorusso, *Senior Buyer*
◆ **EMP:** 537
SQ FT: 200,000
SALES (est): 156.3MM **Privately Held**
SIC: 3643 3089 3679 3469 Mfg Conductive Wire Dvcs Mfg Plastic Products Mfg Elec Components Mfg Metal Stampings Mfg Switchgear/Boards

(G-5025)
SIEMON COMPANY
Siemon Electronics Co
101 Siemon Company Dr (06795-2651)
PHONE..................................860 945-4218
Carl Siemon, *President*
Carly Achenbach, *Sales Staff*
EMP: 22
SALES (corp-wide): 156.3MM **Privately Held**
SIC: 3643 Mfg Conductive Wiring Devices
PA: The Siemon Company
101 Siemon Company Dr
Watertown CT 06795
860 945-4200

(G-5026)
SOLLA EYELET PRODUCTS INC
50 Seemar Rd (06795-1638)
PHONE..................................860 274-5729
Louis Solla, *CEO*
Salvatore L Solla, *Vice Pres*
EMP: 20
SQ FT: 9,000
SALES (est): 3.2MM **Privately Held**
SIC: 3469 Mfg Metal Stampings

(G-5027)
SUMAL ENTERPRISES LLC
Also Called: Town & Country Cleaners & Tlrs
620 Main St (06795-2614)
PHONE..................................860 945-3337
Malini S Jadav,
EMP: 5
SALES (est): 488K **Privately Held**
SIC: 3582 Dry Cleaning Laundry Linnen Supplies

(G-5028)
THREE KINGS PRODUCTS LLC
1021 Echo Lake Rd (06795-1639)
P.O. Box 69 (06795-0069)
PHONE..................................860 945-5294
John Coster, *Owner*
▲ **EMP:** 3
SALES (est): 317.9K **Privately Held**
WEB: www.threekingsproducts.com
SIC: 2899 3999 Mfg Chemical Preparations Mfg Misc Products

(G-5029)
TIMBER-TOP INC
210 Hopkins Rd (06795-1549)
P.O. Box 517 (06795-0517)
PHONE..................................860 274-6706
Jay P Fischer, *President*
Justin T Fischer, *General Mgr*
Nancy Fischer, *Info Tech Mgr*
EMP: 3 **EST:** 1957
SALES: 500K **Privately Held**
SIC: 3965 3399 5072 Mfg Fasteners/Buttons/Pins Mfg Primary Metal Products Whol Hardware

(G-5030)
TRIPLE PLAY SPORTS
16 Straits Tpke (06795-3119)
PHONE..................................860 417-2877
Tom Daddona, *Partner*
EMP: 10
SALES (est): 926K **Privately Held**
SIC: 2599 Mfg Furniture/Fixtures

(G-5031)
TRUELOVE & MACLEAN INC
57 Callender Rd (06795-1627)
P.O. Box 268 (06795-0268)
PHONE..................................860 274-9600
Richard L Bouffard, *President*
Grant Demerchant, *Vice Pres*
Mario Lambiase, *Vice Pres*
Dan Moffa, *Finance Dir*
Charles Henry, *Admin Sec*
▲ **EMP:** 124 **EST:** 1998
SQ FT: 105,000
SALES (est): 28.3MM **Privately Held**
WEB: www.trueloveandmaclean.com
SIC: 3469 Mfg Metal Stampings

(G-5032)
UTITEC INC (HQ)
169 Callender Rd (06795-1627)
P.O. Box 370 (06795-0370)
PHONE..................................860 945-0605
Carl Contadini, *President*
EMP: 65
SALES (est): 13.6MM
SALES (corp-wide): 13.9MM **Privately Held**
SIC: 3841 3341 3469 Mfg Surgical/Medical Instruments Secondary Nonferrous Metal Producer Mfg Metal Stampings
PA: Utitec Holdings, Inc.
169 Callender Rd
Watertown CT 06795
860 945-0601

(G-5033)
UTITEC HOLDINGS INC (PA)
169 Callender Rd (06795-1627)
P.O. Box 370 (06795-0370)
PHONE..................................860 945-0601
Bob Oppici, *Principal*
Ronald Lipeika, *COO*
EMP: 8
SALES (est): 13.9MM **Privately Held**
SIC: 3841 3469 Manufacturer Of Precision Miniature Drawn Metal Components For The Medical And Electronics Industries

(G-5034)
WATERTOWN JIG BORE SERVICE INC
29 New Wood Rd (06795-3314)
PHONE..................................860 274-5898
Fax: 860 274-7830
EMP: 16
SQ FT: 7,000
SALES (est): 1.4MM **Privately Held**
SIC: 3544 3541 Mfg Dies/Tools/Jigs/Fixtures Mfg Machine Tools-Cutting

(G-5035)
WATERTOWN PLASTICS INC
830 Echo Lake Rd (06795-1636)
P.O. Box 309 (06795-0309)
PHONE..................................860 274-7535
Jonathan Andrew, *President*
Diane Andrew, *Corp Secy*
Mike Andrew, *Vice Pres*
Edward Nickles, *Vice Pres*
Laurie Smith, *Office Mgr*
EMP: 36
SQ FT: 15,000
SALES (est): 9.3MM **Privately Held**
WEB: www.watertownplastics.com
SIC: 3089 3544 Mfg Plastic Products Mfg Dies/Tools/Jigs/Fixtures

(G-5036)
WIRE TECH LLC
1094 Echo Lake Rd (06795-1635)
PHONE..................................860 945-9473
Charles G Lacompe,
Charles J Lacompe,
EMP: 6
SQ FT: 3,000
SALES (est): 558.7K **Privately Held**
SIC: 3599 Mfg Industrial Machinery

(G-5037)
WORLDSCREEN INC
843 Echo Lake Rd (06795-1637)
PHONE..................................860 274-9218
Stephen P Lukos, *President*
Carol Anne Lukos, *Manager*
EMP: 3
SALES (est): 258.7K **Privately Held**
SIC: 3851 Mfg Ophthalmic Goods

Wauregan
Windham County

(G-5038)
BROOKWOOD LAMINATING INC
Also Called: Brookwood Roll Goods Group
275 Putnam Rd (06387)
PHONE..................................860 774-5001
Amber M Brookman, *President*
Robert Vander Meulen, *Vice Pres*
Joseph Trumpetto, *Treasurer*
▲ **EMP:** 53
SQ FT: 50,000
SALES (est): 12.8MM **Privately Held**
SIC: 2295 2269 Mfg Coated Fabrics Finishing Plant
HQ: Brookwood Companies Incorporated
485 Madison Ave Ste 500
New York NY 10022
212 551-0100

(G-5039)
FORTERRA PIPE & PRECAST LLC
174 All Hallows Rd (06387)
PHONE..................................860 564-9000
George Stevens, *General Mgr*
EMP: 19
SALES (corp-wide): 1.4B **Publicly Held**
SIC: 3272 Mfg Concrete Products
HQ: Forterra Pipe & Precast, Llc
511 E John Carpenter Fwy
Irving TX 75062
469 458-7973

(G-5040)
WAUREGAN MACHINE SHOP
51 S Walnut St (06387-8700)
P.O. Box 212 (06387-0212)
PHONE..................................860 774-0686
EMP: 3
SQ FT: 4,800
SALES: 120K **Privately Held**
SIC: 3599 Mfg Industrial Machinery

Weatogue
Hartford County

(G-5041)
BIOMASS ENERGY LLC
125 Powder Forest Dr (06089-7943)
PHONE..................................540 872-3300
Mark Boivin, *Principal*
EMP: 20 **EST:** 2007
SALES (est): 2.2MM **Privately Held**
SIC: 2421 Sawmill/Planing Mill

(G-5042)
ENSIGN-BICKFORD INDUSTRIES INC
Also Called: Human Resources
175 Powder Forest Dr (06089-7902)
P.O. Box 7, Simsbury (06070-0007)
PHONE..................................860 843-2000
Andres Kukk, *Branch Mgr*
EMP: 125
SALES (corp-wide): 193.7MM **Privately Held**
WEB: www.e-bind.com
SIC: 2892 2891 3081 3357 Mfg Explosives Mfg Adhesives/Sealants Mfg Unsupported Plastic Film/Sheet Nonfrs Wiredrwng/Insltng Real Estate Agent/Mgr
PA: Ensign-Bickford Industries, Inc.
999 17th St Ste 900
Denver CO 80202
860 843-2000

(G-5043)
LEATHERBY
19 Deer Park Rd (06089-9703)
PHONE..................................860 658-6166
Richard Goldberg, *Owner*
EMP: 3
SALES: 75K **Privately Held**
SIC: 3171 3161 5948 3172 Mfg Small Leather Goods & Ret Leather Goods Such As Belts Key Rings Wallets Handbags Purses & Backpacks

(G-5044)
RC CONNECTORS LLC
146 Hopmeadow St (06089-7908)
PHONE..................................860 413-2196
John D Ritson, *Principal*
EMP: 3
SALES (est): 289K **Privately Held**
SIC: 3678 Mfg Electronic Connectors

(G-5045)
VEEDER-ROOT COMPANY (HQ)
125 Powder Forest Dr Fl 1 (06089-7943)
P.O. Box 2003, Simsbury (06070-7684)
PHONE..................................860 651-2700
Brian Burnett, *President*
Gaston Berrio, *President*
Dick Lucas, *President*
Martin Gafinowitz, *Vice Pres*
Don Murashima, *Vice Pres*
◆ **EMP:** 80
SQ FT: 25,000
SALES (est): 115MM
SALES (corp-wide): 6.4B **Publicly Held**
SIC: 3823 3824 Mfg Process Control Instruments Mfg Fluid Meter/Counting Devices
PA: Fortive Corporation
6920 Seaway Blvd
Everett WA 98203
425 446-5000

West Cornwall
Litchfield County

(G-5046)
CLOVERDALE INC
Also Called: Cloverdale Cleaner
5 Smith Pl (06796-1116)
P.O. Box 268 (06796-0268)
PHONE..................................860 672-0216
Harry L Colley II, *President*
EMP: 5
SALES (est): 390K **Privately Held**
WEB: www.cloverdale.com
SIC: 2842 5169 4959 Mfg Polish/Sanitation Gd Whol Chemicals/Products Sanitary Services

(G-5047)
TIM PRENTICE
129 Lake Rd (06796-1402)
PHONE..................................860 672-6728
Tim Prentice, *Owner*
EMP: 3 **EST:** 1989
SQ FT: 576
SALES (est): 140K **Privately Held**
WEB: www.timprentice.com
SIC: 3299 Mfg Nonmetallic Mineral Products

GEOGRAPHIC

West Granby
Hartford County

(G-5048)
BELMEADE GROUP LLC
Also Called: Belmeade Signs
46 Simsbury Rd (06090-1401)
PHONE....860 413-3569
Jean-Luc Godard,
EMP: 3
SALES (est): 121K **Privately Held**
SIC: 3993 Mfg Signs/Advertising Specialties

(G-5049)
JEROME RIDEL
Also Called: R S Enterprise
15 Hampsted Rd (06090)
PHONE....860 379-1774
Jerome Ridel, *Owner*
EMP: 4
SALES (est): 189.7K **Privately Held**
SIC: 3599 Machine Shop

West Hartford
Hartford County

(G-5050)
ABBOTT BALL COMPANY
19 Railroad Pl (06110-2384)
P.O. Box 330100 (06133-0100)
PHONE....860 236-5901
Craig W Bond, *President*
Patricia Dacunha, *Human Res Mgr*
Ted Oblon, *Info Tech Mgr*
Joanne Thorpe, *Director*
▲ **EMP:** 75
SALES (est): 21.5MM **Privately Held**
WEB: www.abbottball.com
SIC: 3399 Mfg Primary Metal Products

(G-5051)
ABBYDABBY
2523 Albany Ave (06117-2308)
PHONE....860 586-8832
Andrea Matteson, *Manager*
EMP: 6 **EST:** 2010
SALES (est): 280.7K **Privately Held**
SIC: 2024 Mfg Ice Cream/Frozen Desert

(G-5052)
ACME TYPESETTING SERVICE CO
47 Cody St (06110-1901)
PHONE....860 953-1470
Jeffrey F Lewis, *Owner*
EMP: 5
SALES: 220K **Privately Held**
SIC: 2791 2759 Typesetting Services Commercial Printing

(G-5053)
ANDERSON SPECIALTY COMPANY
81 Custer St (06110-1908)
PHONE....860 953-6630
Kenneth Swanson, *President*
EMP: 6 **EST:** 1940
SQ FT: 5,600
SALES (est): 935.1K **Privately Held**
SIC: 3398 Metal Heat Treating

(G-5054)
AUTOMATION INC
707 Oakwood Ave (06110-1508)
P.O. Box 330346 (06133-0346)
PHONE....860 236-5991
Ronald D Hall, *President*
Robert C Dodge, *Vice Pres*
Alice L Hall, *Admin Sec*
EMP: 11 **EST:** 1963
SQ FT: 5,000
SALES: 2.3MM **Privately Held**
WEB: www.automationincct.com
SIC: 3569 5085 Mfg General Industrial Machinery Whol Industrial Supplies

(G-5055)
BERTRAM SIRKIN
Also Called: Photobert Cheatsheets
200 Mohegan Dr (06117-1426)
PHONE....860 656-7446
Bertram Sirkin, *Owner*
EMP: 3
SALES: 140K **Privately Held**
SIC: 2741 Misc Publishing

(G-5056)
CABINET HARWARD SPECIALTI
50 Chelton Ave (06110-1205)
PHONE....860 231-1192
Art Roth, *Owner*
EMP: 7
SALES (est): 555.5K **Privately Held**
SIC: 2434 Mfg Wood Kitchen Cabinets

(G-5057)
CAMPUS YELLOW PAGES LLC
Also Called: High School Counselor Connect
79 High Wood Rd (06117-1117)
P.O. Box 270071 (06127-0071)
PHONE....860 523-9909
Gary Dinowitz,
Heather Dinowitz,
Glen Hauser,
EMP: 5
SALES: 1MM **Privately Held**
WEB: www.campusyellowpages.com
SIC: 2741 7374 Misc Publishing Data Processing/Preparation

(G-5058)
CCR PRODUCTS LLC
167 South St (06110-1928)
P.O. Box 330186 (06133-0186)
PHONE....860 953-0499
Jim Augelli, *Sales Staff*
Craig Bond,
▲ **EMP:** 20
SQ FT: 14,000
SALES (est): 4.4MM **Privately Held**
WEB: www.ccrproducts.com
SIC: 3312 3399 Blast Furnace-Steel Works Mfg Primary Metal Products

(G-5059)
CHROMATIC PRESS US INC
84 Woodrow St (06107-2729)
P.O. Box 270138 (06127-0138)
PHONE....860 796-7667
Magda Erik-Soussi, *Director*
Lianne Sentar, *Director*
EMP: 5
SALES (est): 101.4K **Privately Held**
SIC: 2711 Newspapers-Publishing/Printing

(G-5060)
COLT DEFENSE LLC (HQ)
Also Called: Colt Defense Holding
547 New Park Ave (06110-1336)
PHONE....860 232-4489
Dennis Veilleux, *CEO*
Richard Harris, *CFO*
Mike Holmes, *CIO*
Arthur Daigle, *IT/INT Sup*
EMP: 380
SQ FT: 250,000
SALES: 277.9MM
SALES (corp-wide): 110.2MM **Privately Held**
WEB: www.colt.com
SIC: 3484 Mfg Small Arms
PA: Colt Defense Holding Llc
547 New Park Ave
West Hartford CT 06110
860 232-4489

(G-5061)
COLTS MANUFACTURING CO LLC (DH)
547 New Park Ave (06110-1336)
P.O. Box 1868, Hartford (06144-1868)
PHONE....860 236-6311
Dennis Veilleux, *CEO*
Donald E Zilkha, *Ch of Bd*
William M Keys, *President*
Franck Legendre, *Partner*
Ronald Belcourt, *Vice Pres*
EMP: 160
SQ FT: 300,000
SALES (est): 53.1MM
SALES (corp-wide): 110.2MM **Privately Held**
SIC: 3484 Mfg Small Arms

(G-5062)
COMPONENT CONCEPTS INC
Also Called: Celtic Co
26 Hammick Rd (06107-1221)
PHONE....860 523-4066
Michael Clifford, *President*
Michael David Clifford, *Director*
EMP: 5
SALES: 3.2MM **Privately Held**
WEB: www.comcpt.com
SIC: 3678 3679 3625 5065 Mfg & Whol Of Electronic Components

(G-5063)
CRICKET PRESS INC
236 Park Rd (06119-2018)
PHONE....860 521-9279
Michelle Confessore, *President*
Michelle T Confessore, *Treasurer*
Carol Teasdale, *Treasurer*
EMP: 6
SQ FT: 2,000
SALES (est): 525.1K **Privately Held**
WEB: www.cricketpress.net
SIC: 2752 Lithographic Commercial Printing

(G-5064)
D & M TOOL COMPANY INC
17 Grassmere Ave (06110-1216)
P.O. Box 330631 (06133-0631)
PHONE....860 236-6037
Elmer Dakin, *President*
James Dakin, *General Mgr*
EMP: 5 **EST:** 1966
SQ FT: 4,000
SALES: 300K **Privately Held**
SIC: 3544 3724 3545 Mfg Dies Tools Jigs Aircraft Parts & Gauges

(G-5065)
DELTA-SOURCE LLC
138 Beacon Hill Dr (06117-1006)
PHONE....860 461-1600
Daniel Barash, *Principal*
EMP: 10 **EST:** 2010
SALES (est): 408.9K **Privately Held**
SIC: 3999 Mfg Misc Products

(G-5066)
DOOR STEP PREP LLC
51 Thomson Rd (06107-2535)
PHONE....860 550-0460
Linda Houde,
EMP: 3
SALES (est): 266.4K **Privately Held**
SIC: 3845 Mfg Electromedical Equipment

(G-5067)
EFITZGERALD PUBLISHING LLC
319 Ridgewood Rd (06107-3515)
PHONE....860 904-7250
Patrice Fitzgerald, *Principal*
EMP: 3
SALES (est): 87.9K **Privately Held**
SIC: 2711 Newspapers-Publishing/Printing

(G-5068)
EL MAR INC
Also Called: Uncle Bill's Tweezers
38 Cody St 2 (06110-1904)
P.O. Box 925, Avon (06001-0925)
PHONE....860 729-7232
Glen Baron, *President*
EMP: 9
SQ FT: 5,000
SALES: 700K **Privately Held**
SIC: 3599 Tweezer Manufacturing & Prototype Machining

(G-5069)
ELEMENTS LLC
945 Farmington Ave (06107-2203)
PHONE....860 231-8011
EMP: 3
SALES (est): 193K **Privately Held**
SIC: 2819 Mfg Industrial Inorganic Chemicals

(G-5070)
ELM-CAP INDUSTRIES INC
111 South St (06110-1928)
P.O. Box 330099 (06133-0099)
PHONE....860 953-1060
R Thomas Abbate, *President*
EMP: 45 **EST:** 1914
SALES (est): 6.1MM **Privately Held**
SIC: 3272 Mfg Concrete Burial Vaults & Precast Concrete Products

(G-5071)
EYELASH EXTENSIONS AND MORE
998 Farmington Ave (06107-2162)
PHONE....860 951-9355
Esther Nicholls, *Owner*
EMP: 12
SQ FT: 900
SALES (est): 330.1K **Privately Held**
SIC: 3999 Mfg Misc Products

(G-5072)
GREENMAKER INDUSTRIES CONN LLC
697 Oakwood Ave (06110-1506)
PHONE....860 761-2830
John Di Stefano, *Mfg Staff*
Mike Jalbert, *Sales Staff*
Sarah Beatty, *Mng Member*
Cheryl Buller,
John Distefano,
EMP: 16
SALES (est): 2.2MM **Privately Held**
SIC: 2851 Mfg Paints/Allied Products

(G-5073)
HAR-CONN CHROME COMPANY (PA)
603 New Park Ave (06110-1380)
P.O. Box 330189 (06133-0189)
PHONE....860 236-6801
Kent N Backus, *CEO*
Tim Backus, *President*
Fred Gariepy, *General Mgr*
Daniel Backus, *Vice Pres*
Scherry Rowland, *Purchasing*
EMP: 70 **EST:** 1948
SQ FT: 40,000
SALES (est): 17.2MM **Privately Held**
WEB: www.har-conn.com
SIC: 3471 Plating/Polishing Service

(G-5074)
HARTFORD COURANT COMPANY
141 South St Ste E (06110-1963)
PHONE....860 560-3747
George Madera, *Branch Mgr*
EMP: 15
SALES (corp-wide): 1B **Publicly Held**
WEB: www.courantnie.com
SIC: 2711 Newspapers-Publishing/Printing
HQ: The Hartford Courant Company Llc
285 Broad St
Hartford CT 06115
860 241-6200

(G-5075)
HARTFORD GAUGE CO
23 Brook St (06110-2350)
P.O. Box 1975, Boerne TX (78006-6975)
PHONE....860 233-9619
EMP: 4 **EST:** 1941
SQ FT: 6,000
SALES: 500K **Privately Held**
WEB: www.hartfordgage.com
SIC: 3545 3544 Mfg Gages Jigs & Tools

(G-5076)
HARTFORD MONTHLY MEETING
144 Quaker Ln S (06119-1636)
PHONE....860 232-3631
EMP: 4 **EST:** 2015
SALES (est): 141.3K **Privately Held**
SIC: 2711 Newspapers-Publishing/Printing

(G-5077)
IMPACT SALES & MARKETING LLC
48 Carlyle Rd (06117-1325)
PHONE....860 523-5366
Ira Gold, *Owner*
EMP: 4

SALES (est): 327K **Privately Held**
SIC: 3651 Mfg Home Audio/Video Equipment

(G-5078)
INITIAL STEP MONOGRAMMING
635 New Park Ave Ste 2a (06110-1338)
PHONE..................................860 665-0542
Michael Reddy, *Partner*
Joan Maradie, *Partner*
Gloria Reddy, *Partner*
EMP: 3
SQ FT: 1,000
SALES (est): 301.7K **Privately Held**
SIC: 2395 Pleating/Stitching Services

(G-5079)
JOBIN MACHINE INC
37 Custer St (06110-1907)
PHONE..................................860 953-1631
George Kiss, *President*
Barry Kalin, *General Mgr*
Erica Kiss Ames, *Treasurer*
EMP: 28
SQ FT: 9,500
SALES (est): 7MM **Privately Held**
SIC: 3728 3714 Mfg Aircraft Parts/Equipment Mfg Motor Vehicle Parts/Accessories

(G-5080)
LEGRAND HOLDING INC (DH)
60 Woodlawn St (06110-2326)
PHONE..................................860 233-6251
John P Selldorff, *CEO*
Giles Schnep, *President*
Jim Waddell, *President*
Kenneth Ruh, *General Mgr*
Lori Kelly, *District Mgr*
▲ **EMP**: 30
SALES (est): 1.8B
SALES (corp-wide): 20.6MM **Privately Held**
SIC: 3643 6719 Mfg Conductive Wiring Devices
HQ: Legrand France
128 Av Du Mal De Lattre De Tassigny
Limoges 87000
555 067-272

(G-5081)
LEMAC IRON WORKS INC
18 Brainard Rd (06117-2201)
PHONE..................................860 232-7380
Michael Levy, *President*
Max Levy, *Vice Pres*
EMP: 3 **EST**: 1963
SQ FT: 10,000
SALES (est): 242.3K **Privately Held**
SIC: 7692 3441 5032 Welding Shop & Miscellaneous Steel Fabricator

(G-5082)
LEWTAN INDUSTRIES CORPORATION
Also Called: Abbott Manufacturing
57 Loomis Dr Apt A1 (06107-2035)
P.O. Box 4694, Greenwich (06831-0412)
PHONE..................................860 278-9800
Marvin Lewtan, *Ch of Bd*
Douglas Lewtan, *President*
▲ **EMP**: 75 **EST**: 1947
SQ FT: 35,000
SALES (est): 8MM **Privately Held**
WEB: www.lewtan8.com
SIC: 3993 Mfg Signs/Advertising Specialties

(G-5083)
LIFE PUBLICATIONS
Also Called: White Publishing
106 South St Ste 5 (06110-1965)
PHONE..................................860 953-0444
Christopher White, *Owner*
Chris White, *Opers Dir*
EMP: 30
SALES (est): 1.6MM **Privately Held**
SIC: 2711 Newspapers-Publishing/Printing

(G-5084)
MANUFACTURERS COML FIN LLC
Also Called: Electro-Flex Heat
1022 Boulevard (06119-1801)
P.O. Box 88, Bloomfield (06002-0088)
PHONE..................................860 242-6287
Matt Byrne, *Engineer*
Delly Lugo, *Finance Mgr*
Sandy Tetreault, *Sales Executive*
EMP: 31
SALES (est): 8.6MM **Privately Held**
SIC: 3567 Mfg Industrial Furnaces/Ovens

(G-5085)
MARKETING SLTONS UNLIMITED LLC
109 Talcott Rd (06110-1228)
PHONE..................................860 523-0670
Heidi Anderson Buckley, *President*
EMP: 22
SALES (est): 4.9MM **Privately Held**
SIC: 2752 Lithographic Commercial Printing

(G-5086)
MBSW INC
41 Plainfield Rd (06117-1936)
PHONE..................................860 243-0303
Theodore L Zachs, *President*
Jed Zachs, *Vice Pres*
Ross Zachs, *Treasurer*
▲ **EMP**: 75 **EST**: 1939
SQ FT: 45,000
SALES (est): 9MM **Privately Held**
WEB: www.cthruruler.com
SIC: 3089 3953 2782 Mfg Plastic Products Mfg Marking Devices Mfg Blankbooks/Binders Specializing In Scrapbooks

(G-5087)
NEW ENGLAND GRAN CABINETS LLC
8 Cody St (06110-1903)
PHONE..................................860 310-2981
Wenbo MA, *Mng Member*
EMP: 6
SALES (est): 546K **Privately Held**
SIC: 3281 Mfg Cut Stone/Products

(G-5088)
ORTRONICS INC
Also Called: Legrand
60 Woodlawn St (06110-2326)
PHONE..................................877 295-3472
Kirsten Mathis, *Regional Mgr*
Jeff Thompson, *District Mgr*
Ken Freeman, *Vice Pres*
Harold Jepsen, *Vice Pres*
Steve Killius, *Vice Pres*
EMP: 7
SALES (corp-wide): 20.6MM **Privately Held**
SIC: 3577 3357 Computer Peripheral Equipment, Nec
HQ: Ortronics, Inc.
125 Eugene Oneill Dr # 140
New London CT 06320
860 445-3900

(G-5089)
PAL TECHNOLOGIES LLC
9 Tolles St (06110-1504)
PHONE..................................860 953-1984
EMP: 3
SQ FT: 6,000
SALES: 600K **Privately Held**
SIC: 3599 Mfg Industrial Machinery

(G-5090)
PETRUNTI DESIGN & WDWKG LLC
23c Andover Dr (06110-1502)
PHONE..................................860 953-5332
William Petrunti, *Owner*
Bill Petrunti,
EMP: 4
SALES (est): 476.6K **Privately Held**
SIC: 2431 Mfg Millwork

(G-5091)
PICK & MIX CORP
1234 Farmington Ave Ste 3 (06107-2670)
PHONE..................................860 521-1521
Ho Y Joo, *Principal*
EMP: 4
SALES (est): 233.4K **Privately Held**
SIC: 3273 Mfg Ready-Mixed Concrete

(G-5092)
RBF FROZEN DESSERTS LLC
240 Park Rd Ste 3 (06119-2040)
PHONE..................................516 474-6488
Thomas Marshall, *Mng Member*
EMP: 12
SQ FT: 20,000
SALES (est): 605K **Privately Held**
SIC: 2024 Mfg Ice Cream/Frozen Desert

(G-5093)
READY TOOL COMPANY (HQ)
1 Carney Rd (06110-1937)
PHONE..................................860 524-7811
Joseph Wagner, *President*
Daniel Piendak, *Engineer*
Dave Brunette, *Mktg Dir*
EMP: 20 **EST**: 1908
SQ FT: 40,000
SALES (est): 1.6MM
SALES (corp-wide): 43.9MM **Privately Held**
WEB: www.readytool.com
SIC: 3541 Mfg Machine Tools-Cutting Whol Industrial Equipment
PA: The United Tool And Die Company
1 Carney Rd
West Hartford CT 06110
860 246-6531

(G-5094)
RUGSALECOM LLC
17 S Main St (06107-2407)
PHONE..................................860 756-0959
Charles Kaoud,
EMP: 5
SALES (est): 598.9K **Privately Held**
SIC: 2273 5713 Mfg Carpets/Rugs Ret Floor Covering

(G-5095)
SORENSON LIGHTED CONTROLS INC (PA)
Also Called: Solico
100 Shield St (06110-1920)
PHONE..................................860 527-3092
Robert C Sorenson Jr, *President*
John D Gallery, *Exec VP*
Fred Kundahl, *Exec VP*
Wesley T Sorenson II, *Vice Pres*
Suzanne Ferguson, *Sales Staff*
▲ **EMP**: 62 **EST**: 1960
SQ FT: 25,000
SALES (est): 18.7MM **Privately Held**
WEB: www.solico.com
SIC: 3648 Mfg Lighting Equipment

(G-5096)
SPV INDUSTRIES LLC
9 Tolles St (06110-1504)
PHONE..................................860 953-5928
Wendy Palacios,
EMP: 3
SALES (est): 261.9K **Privately Held**
SIC: 3999 Mfg Misc Products

(G-5097)
SWANSON TOOL MANUFACTURING INC
71 Custer St (06110-1908)
P.O. Box 330318 (06133-0318)
PHONE..................................860 953-1641
Kenneth Swanson Jr, *CEO*
Kenneth W Swanson Sr, *CEO*
Annlouise Swanson, *Treasurer*
Merle Nicoletta, *Technology*
EMP: 25
SQ FT: 19,000
SALES (est): 6.5MM **Privately Held**
WEB: www.swansongage.com
SIC: 3545 5084 5251 Mfg Machine Tool Access Whol Industrial Equip Ret Hardware

(G-5098)
THINK AHEAD SOFTWARE LLC (PA)
30 Wardwell Rd (06107-2734)
PHONE..................................860 463-9786
Richard M Spear, *Principal*
EMP: 3
SALES (est): 1.1MM **Privately Held**
SIC: 7372 Prepackaged Software Services

(G-5099)
TRIATIC INCORPORATED
22 Grassmere Ave (06110-1215)
PHONE..................................860 236-2298
William Plourd, *President*
Bill Kauffman, *Admin Sec*
EMP: 11
SQ FT: 10,000
SALES: 1.3MM **Privately Held**
WEB: www.triaticinc.com
SIC: 3291 Plating Facility Specializing In Abrasives And Grinding Wheels

(G-5100)
TRIUMPH ENG CTRL SYSTEMS LLC
Also Called: Goodrich
1 Charter Oak Blvd (06110-1328)
PHONE..................................860 236-0651
Alec Searle, *Vice Pres*
Scott Maze, *Business Anlyst*
Don Fortier, *Business Dir*
EMP: 560 **EST**: 2013
SALES (est): 200.8MM **Publicly Held**
SIC: 3728 3724 3812 Mfg Aircraft Parts/Equipment Mfg Aircraft Engines/Parts Mfg Search/Navigation Equipment
PA: Triumph Group, Inc.
899 Cassatt Rd Ste 210
Berwyn PA 19312

(G-5101)
TRIUMPH ENG CTRL SYSTEMS LLC
1 Talcott Rd (06110)
PHONE..................................860 236-0651
EMP: 14
SALES (est): 2.4MM **Privately Held**
SIC: 3812 Mfg Search/Navigation Equipment

(G-5102)
UNITED TOOL AND DIE COMPANY (PA)
1 Carney Rd (06110-1982)
PHONE..................................860 246-6531
Julie Susan Wagner, *CEO*
Joseph Wagner, *President*
Charles Zien, *Vice Pres*
Sheila Suchecki, *Purch Mgr*
Francis Charest, *Engineer*
EMP: 115 **EST**: 1925
SQ FT: 150,000
SALES (est): 43.9MM **Privately Held**
WEB: www.utdco.com
SIC: 3724 3541 3769 Mfg Aircraft Engines/Parts Mfg Machine Tools-Cutting Mfg Space Vehicle Equipment

(G-5103)
WEST HARTFORD STONE MULCH LLC
154 Reed Ave (06110-1510)
PHONE..................................860 461-7616
Robert Dignoti, *Mng Member*
EMP: 3
SALES (est): 144.7K **Privately Held**
SIC: 1411 3272 1442 0782 Dimension Stone Quarry Mfg Concrete Products Construction Sand/Gravel Lawn/Garden Services

(G-5104)
WIREMOLD COMPANY (DH)
60 Woodlawn St (06110-2383)
PHONE..................................860 233-6251
John P Selldorff, *CEO*
Brian Dibella, *President*
Kim Moore, *Project Mgr*
Robert Blanchard, *Engineer*
Joe Pisarski, *Engineer*
◆ **EMP**: 750 **EST**: 1919
SQ FT: 226,000
SALES (est): 387.7MM
SALES (corp-wide): 20.6MM **Privately Held**
SIC: 3643 3496 3315 3644 Mfg Conductive Wire Dvcs Mfg Misc Fab Wire Prdts Mfg Steel Wire/Rltd Prdt Mfg Nonconductv Wire Dvc

HQ: Legrand Holding, Inc.
60 Woodlawn St
West Hartford CT 06110
860 233-6251

(G-5105)
WIREMOLD COMPANY
21 Railroad Pl (06110-2344)
PHONE..................................860 263-3115
John P Selldorff, *CEO*
EMP: 15
SALES (corp-wide): 20.6MM **Privately Held**
SIC: 3644 Mfg Nonconductive Wiring Devices
HQ: Wiremold Company
60 Woodlawn St
West Hartford CT 06110
860 233-6251

(G-5106)
WIREMOLD LEGRAND CO CENTEREX
60 Woodlawn St (06110-2326)
PHONE..................................877 295-3472
Amy Gerakos, *Principal*
Joe Milheiro, *Engineer*
EMP: 37
SALES (est): 6.5MM **Privately Held**
SIC: 3644 Mfg Nonconductive Wiring Devices

West Haven
New Haven County

(G-5107)
AA & B CO
284 2nd Ave (06516-5126)
PHONE..................................203 933-9110
Alex Borodkin, *Owner*
Eugene Borodkin, *Corp Secy*
Mark Borodkin, *Vice Pres*
EMP: 6
SALES (est): 250.6K **Privately Held**
SIC: 3089 Mfg Plastic Products

(G-5108)
AMERIFIX LLC
278 Washington Ave (06516-5327)
PHONE..................................203 931-7290
Richard L Moore Jr,
Ellen L Manning-Moore,
EMP: 9
SQ FT: 22,000
SALES (est): 960K **Privately Held**
SIC: 2491 Millwork Treated Wood

(G-5109)
AMPOL TOOL INC
44 Hamilton St (06516-2321)
PHONE..................................203 932-3161
Jerzy Kozlowski, *President*
EMP: 5
SQ FT: 4,500
SALES: 500K **Privately Held**
SIC: 3423 Mfg Hand/Edge Tools

(G-5110)
CANNELLI PRINTING CO INC
39 Wood St (06516-3843)
PHONE..................................203 932-1719
Victor Cannelli, *President*
Rose Cannelli, *Vice Pres*
EMP: 9
SALES (est): 1.5MM **Privately Held**
WEB: www.cannelli.com
SIC: 2752 2759 Lithographic Coml Print Commercial Printing

(G-5111)
CODEBRIDGE SOFTWARE INC
91 Honor Rd (06516-6837)
PHONE..................................203 535-0517
Pedro Rodriguez Jr, *Principal*
EMP: 3
SALES (est): 165.3K **Privately Held**
SIC: 7372 Prepackaged Software Services

(G-5112)
COLONIAL WOOD PRODUCTS INC
250 Callegari Dr (06516-6234)
PHONE..................................203 932-9003
Kevin Donovan, *President*
William Donovan Jr, *Vice Pres*
EMP: 15 **EST:** 1938
SQ FT: 10,000
SALES: 2MM **Privately Held**
SIC: 2431 2441 Mfg Millwork Mfg Wood Boxes/Shook

(G-5113)
CONCO WOOD WORKING INC
755 1st Ave (06516-2712)
P.O. Box 17176, Stamford (06907-7176)
PHONE..................................203 934-9665
Louis M Cutaneo, *President*
EMP: 9
SQ FT: 27,000
SALES (est): 1MM **Privately Held**
WEB: www.concowoodworking.com
SIC: 2521 2522 Mfg Wood Office Furniture Mfg Office Furniture-Nonwood

(G-5114)
COSMOS FOOD PRODUCTS INC
200 Callegari Dr (06516-6234)
PHONE..................................800 942-6766
Cosmo N Laudano, *President*
Lisa L Laudano, *Vice Pres*
Mario Laudano, *Treasurer*
Mark C Laudano, *Treasurer*
Lauren N Laudano, *Admin Sec*
▲ **EMP:** 40
SQ FT: 25,000
SALES (est): 9.1MM **Privately Held**
WEB: www.cosmosfoods.com
SIC: 2033 Mfg Canned Fruits/Vegetables

(G-5115)
DEITSCH PLASTIC COMPANY INC
14 Farwell St (06516-1717)
P.O. Box 26005 (06516-8005)
PHONE..................................203 934-6601
Mordecoi Deitsch, *President*
Bob Frank, *Purchasing*
Moti Sandman, *Asst Controller*
Mendel Deitsch, *Manager*
Joshua Sandman, *Admin Sec*
◆ **EMP:** 68 **EST:** 1954
SQ FT: 200,000
SALES (est): 13.8MM **Privately Held**
WEB: www.deitschplastic.com
SIC: 2221 2295 Manmade Broadwoven Fabric Mill Mfg Coated Fabrics

(G-5116)
DEVICE42 INC
600 Saw Mill Rd (06516-4007)
PHONE..................................203 409-7242
Raj Jalen, *CEO*
Damian Roskill, *VP Mktg*
Jacques Wagemaker, *Marketing Staff*
Stephen Timms, *Risk Mgmt Dir*
EMP: 14
SALES (est): 564.9K **Privately Held**
SIC: 7372 Prepackaged Software Services

(G-5117)
DL DISTRIBUTORS LLC
343 Beach St (06516-6176)
PHONE..................................203 931-1724
EMP: 4
SALES (est): 254.6K **Privately Held**
SIC: 2051 Mfg Bread/Related Products

(G-5118)
DURANTES PASTA INC
78 Fenwick St (06516-1120)
PHONE..................................203 387-5560
Amedeo Durante, *President*
EMP: 3
SALES (est): 275.2K **Privately Held**
SIC: 2099 5149 Mfg Food Preparations Whol Groceries

(G-5119)
DUROL LABORATORIES LLC
Also Called: Durol Cosmetic Laboratories
5 Knight Ln (06516-2940)
PHONE..................................866 611-9694
Ade Aminu, *CEO*
EMP: 10 **EST:** 2010
SQ FT: 11,000
SALES (est): 720K **Privately Held**
SIC: 2844 Mfg Toilet Preparations

(G-5120)
E O MANUFACTURING COMPANY INC
474 Frontage Rd (06516-4154)
PHONE..................................203 932-5981
Peter Lemere Jr, *President*
EMP: 23 **EST:** 1945
SQ FT: 8,748
SALES: 1MM **Privately Held**
SIC: 3599 Mfg Industrial Machinery

(G-5121)
ERA WIRE INC
19 Locust St (06516-2022)
PHONE..................................203 933-0480
Richard T Rae, *President*
Katherine Rae, *Vice Pres*
EMP: 11
SQ FT: 5,000
SALES (est): 2MM **Privately Held**
WEB: www.erawire.com
SIC: 3496 Mfg Misc Fabricated Wire Products

(G-5122)
FAGAN DESIGN & FABRICATION
44 Railroad Ave (06516-4132)
PHONE..................................203 937-1874
Jay Fagan, *President*
Lisa Spetrini, *Office Mgr*
EMP: 4
SQ FT: 20,000
SALES (est): 600K **Privately Held**
SIC: 2431 2499 Mfg Millwork Mfg Wood Products

(G-5123)
FIRE & IRON
298 Platt Ave (06516-4837)
PHONE..................................203 934-3756
EMP: 3
SALES (est): 130K **Privately Held**
SIC: 3842 Mfg Surgical Appliances/Supplies

(G-5124)
GHP MEDIA INC (PA)
475 Heffernan Dr (06516-4151)
PHONE..................................203 479-7500
John Robinson, *CEO*
Fred Hoxsie, *Managing Prtnr*
Scott Carter, *Exec VP*
Dave Sweet, *Vice Pres*
Andy Robinson, *Plant Mgr*
EMP: 109
SQ FT: 11,000
SALES (est): 21.2MM **Privately Held**
WEB: www.gist-image.com
SIC: 2752 2796 Lithographic Commercial Printing Platemaking Services

(G-5125)
HARBISONWALKER INTL INC
163 Boston Post Rd (06516-2038)
PHONE..................................203 934-7960
Robert Murray, *Branch Mgr*
EMP: 4
SALES (corp-wide): 633.5MM **Privately Held**
WEB: www.hwr.com
SIC: 3255 Mfg Clay Refractories
HQ: Harbisonwalker International, Inc.
1305 Cherrington Pkwy # 100
Moon Township PA 15108

(G-5126)
IMANI MAGAZINE/FMI
15 Boylston St (06516-3383)
PHONE..................................203 809-2565
Corrine Thomas, *Principal*
EMP: 3
SALES (est): 161.7K **Privately Held**
SIC: 2721 Periodicals-Publishing/Printing

(G-5127)
JUPITER COMMUNICATIONS LLC
755 1st Ave (06516-2712)
PHONE..................................475 238-7082
Ethan Odin, *Mng Member*
Rose Mannon, *Admin Sec*
EMP: 12
SQ FT: 16,000
SALES (est): 3.9MM **Privately Held**
WEB: www.jupitercommunications.net
SIC: 2752 2791 Lithographic Commercial Printing Typesetting Services

(G-5128)
KEMPER MANUFACTURING CORP
5 Clinton Pl (06516-2808)
PHONE..................................203 934-1600
Cathy Harter, *President*
▲ **EMP:** 20
SQ FT: 10,000
SALES (est): 2.4MM **Privately Held**
WEB: www.straplady.com
SIC: 2399 Mfg Fabricated Textile Products

(G-5129)
KRAMER PRINTING COMPANY INC
270 Front Ave (06516-2800)
PHONE..................................203 933-5416
Richard Kramer, *President*
Don Schmitz, *Manager*
Ilene J Kramer, *Director*
Marcy Kramer-Ide, *Admin Sec*
EMP: 13
SQ FT: 7,800
SALES: 700K **Privately Held**
SIC: 2752 2759 Lithographic Commercial Printing Commercial Printing

(G-5130)
KX TECHNOLOGIES LLC (DH)
55 Railroad Ave (06516-4143)
PHONE..................................203 799-9000
John J Goody, *Mng Member*
Bruce R Belcher,
Frank A Brigano PHD,
Leon R Drake II,
▲ **EMP:** 12
SQ FT: 67,000
SALES (est): 27.8MM
SALES (corp-wide): 225.3B **Publicly Held**
SIC: 3589 Mfg Service Industry Machinery

(G-5131)
LIGHT FANTASTIC REALTY INC
Also Called: Fraqtir
114 Boston Post Rd (06516-2043)
PHONE..................................203 934-3441
Allison K Schieffelin, *CEO*
David R Pfund, *President*
Suzanne Carroll, *Exec VP*
Joseph R Zaharewicz, *Vice Pres*
Cynthia Hoboken, *CFO*
▲ **EMP:** 125
SQ FT: 100,000
SALES (est): 16.3MM **Privately Held**
WEB: www.elliptipar.com
SIC: 3647 3645 Mfg Residential Lighting Fixtures Mfg Vehicle Lighting Equipment

(G-5132)
MACDERMID ENTHONE INC (HQ)
350 Frontage Rd (06516-4130)
PHONE..................................203 934-8611
Scott Benson, *President*
Emmanuel Colchen, *President*
Robert Collin, *Technical Mgr*
Pingping Ye, *Research*
Rachel Falcon, *Engineer*
◆ **EMP:** 158
SALES (est): 152MM
SALES (corp-wide): 1.9B **Publicly Held**
WEB: www.enthone.com
SIC: 2899 Mfg Chemical Preparations
PA: Element Solutions Inc
500 E Broward Blvd # 1860
Fort Lauderdale FL 33394
561 207-9600

(G-5133)
MAD SPORTSWEAR LLC
100 Putney Dr (06516-2931)
PHONE..................................203 932-4868
David Ruotolo,
Anthony Mantone,
Michael Volpe,
EMP: 3
SQ FT: 3,000
SALES (est): 154.9K **Privately Held**
WEB: www.madsportswear.com
SIC: 2395 2759 Screen Printing/Embroidery Services

▲ = Import ▼=Export
◆ =Import/Export

(G-5134)
MANUFACTURERS ASSOCIATES INC
45 Railroad Ave (06516-4143)
P.O. Box 4419, Hamden (06514-0419)
PHONE..............................203 931-4344
Lonnie Parillo, *President*
EMP: 20
SQ FT: 25,000
SALES (est): 1.8MM **Privately Held**
SIC: 3451 Mfg Screw Machine Products

(G-5135)
MAREL CORPORATION
5 Saw Mill Rd (06516-4111)
PHONE..............................203 934-8187
John Rice, *President*
Tim McNeil, *Vice Pres*
Elizabeth Rice, *Admin Sec*
EMP: 11
SALES (est): 1.4MM **Privately Held**
SIC: 3841 5047 Mfg Surgical/Medical Instruments Whol Medical/Hospital Equipment

(G-5136)
MCNEIL HEALTHCARE INC
5 Saw Mill Rd (06516-4111)
PHONE..............................203 934-8187
Tim McNeil, *President*
EMP: 3
SALES (est): 14.2K **Privately Held**
SIC: 3842 Mfg Surgical Appliances/Supplies

(G-5137)
NEW ENGLAND NONWOVENS LLC
283 Dogburn Rd (06516)
PHONE..............................203 891-0851
John Guchmanowicz, *Mng Member*
Alan Lapoint,
EMP: 19 **EST:** 2008
SALES (est): 4MM **Privately Held**
SIC: 2297 Mfg Nonwoven Fabrics

(G-5138)
OMI INTERNATIONAL CORPORATION
350 Frontage Rd (06516-4130)
PHONE..............................203 575-5727
EMP: 4
SALES (est): 212.4K
SALES (corp-wide): 1.9B **Publicly Held**
SIC: 2899 Mfg Chemical Preparations
PA: Element Solutions Inc
500 E Broward Blvd # 1860
Fort Lauderdale FL 33394
561 207-9600

(G-5139)
PANAGRAFIX INC
Also Called: USA Notepads
50 Fresh Meadow Rd (06516-1445)
PHONE..............................203 691-5529
EMP: 28
SALES (corp-wide): 3.8MM **Privately Held**
SIC: 2678 Mfg Stationery Products
PA: Panagrafix, Inc.
75 Cascade Blvd
Milford CT

(G-5140)
PANZA WOODWORK & SUPPLY LLC
4 Hugo St (06516-1308)
PHONE..............................203 934-3430
John Panza, *Principal*
Ed Panza,
EMP: 5 **EST:** 1994
SQ FT: 2,700
SALES: 550K **Privately Held**
SIC: 3429 Mgf Cabinets

(G-5141)
PINPOINT PROMOTIONS & PRTG LLC
45 Railroad Ave (06516-4143)
PHONE..............................203 301-4273
Steve Gentile, *Managing Prtnr*
Tj Andrews, *Managing Prtnr*
Jillian Putterman, *Project Mgr*
EMP: 17
SALES: 3MM **Privately Held**
SIC: 2752 Lithographic Commercial Printing

(G-5142)
POLYMER FILMS INC
301 Heffernan Dr (06516-4151)
PHONE..............................203 932-3000
John Watson, *President*
Mary Watson, *Corp Secy*
Robert Watson, *Vice Pres*
James Watson, *CFO*
Kimberly Imbimbo, *Manager*
EMP: 25 **EST:** 1963
SQ FT: 88,000
SALES (est): 271.1K **Privately Held**
WEB: www.watsonfoods.com
SIC: 3081 2671 Mfg Unsupported Plastic Film/Sheet Mfg Packaging Paper/Film

(G-5143)
PROIRON LLC
1 Calgery Dr (06516)
PHONE..............................203 934-7967
James Charbonneau, *General Mgr*
Stephanie Siclari, *Vice Pres*
Mary F Charbonneau,
EMP: 4
SALES (est): 698.7K **Privately Held**
SIC: 3542 Mfg Machine Tools-Forming

(G-5144)
SABATINO NORTH AMERICA LLC (PA)
Also Called: Speedy Food Group USA
135 Front Ave (06516-2811)
PHONE..............................718 328-4120
Vincent Jeanseaume, *Vice Pres*
Andrea Casali, *Sales Staff*
Federico Balestra,
▲ **EMP:** 25
SQ FT: 42,000
SALES (est): 13.6MM **Privately Held**
SIC: 2033 Mfg Canned Fruits/Vegetables

(G-5145)
SCHRAFEL PAPERBOARD CONVERTING
82 W Clark St Ste 1 (06516-3559)
PHONE..............................203 931-1700
Richard B Schrafel, *President*
Robert Schrafel, *Treasurer*
EMP: 25
SQ FT: 101,000
SALES (est): 4.8MM **Privately Held**
SIC: 2679 2631 Mfg Converted Paper Products Paperboard Mill

(G-5146)
SUBURBAN VOICES PUBLISHING LLC
Also Called: West Haven Voice
840 Boston Post Rd Ste 2 (06516-1848)
PHONE..............................203 934-6397
William Riccio, *President*
Maurizio Girotto, *Prdtn Mgr*
EMP: 4
SALES: 100K **Privately Held**
WEB: www.whvoice.com
SIC: 2711 Newspapers-Publishing/Printing

(G-5147)
SYLVAN R SHEMITZ DESIGNS LLC
Also Called: Lighting Quotient, The
114 Boston Post Rd (06516-2043)
PHONE..............................203 934-3441
Allison K Schieffelin, *President*
Eric Henault, *Engineer*
Ken Pask, *Design Engr*
Cindy Hoboken, *CFO*
Gene Mingrone, *Technology*
▲ **EMP:** 102 **EST:** 2014
SALES (est): 22MM **Privately Held**
SIC: 3646 Mfg Commercial Lighting Fixtures

(G-5148)
THERMAXX LLC (PA)
14 Farwell St (06516-1717)
PHONE..............................203 672-1021
Mike Bannon, *Mng Member*
EMP: 7
SALES (est): 60.5K **Privately Held**
SIC: 3443 Mfg Insulated Jakts

(G-5149)
WATSON LLC (DH)
301 Heffernan Dr (06516-4151)
PHONE..............................203 932-3000
James Watson, *President*
Gavin Watson, *COO*
Moira Watson, *Vice Pres*
Philip Lee, *Plant Mgr*
Gary Wada, *Prdtn Mgr*
◆ **EMP:** 277
SQ FT: 220,000
SALES (est): 76.1MM **Privately Held**
SIC: 2045 2833 2087 2051 Manufactures Prepared Flour Mixes Medicinal/Botanicals Flavor Extracts And Bread/Related Prdts

(G-5150)
WEST MONT GROUP
14 Gilbert St Ste 202 (06516-1639)
PHONE..............................203 931-1033
Jeff Carter, *Owner*
EMP: 6
SALES (est): 408.2K **Privately Held**
SIC: 2434 7389 Mfg Wood Kitchen Cabinets Business Services

(G-5151)
WESTMOUNT GROUP LLC
14b Gilbert St M202 (06516)
PHONE..............................203 931-1033
Jeffrey H Carter, *Principal*
EMP: 5
SALES (est): 539.1K **Privately Held**
SIC: 2599 Mfg Furniture/Fixtures

(G-5152)
WOODLAND POWER PRODUCTS INC
72 Acton St (06516-1704)
PHONE..............................888 531-7253
James C Whitney PHD, *President*
Matthew Coz, *General Mgr*
Ethan Hershman, *Vice Pres*
Dave Troop, *Mfg Mgr*
Kenneth Rowe, *Accounts Mgr*
▲ **EMP:** 25
SQ FT: 15,000
SALES (est): 9.4MM **Privately Held**
WEB: www.cyclonerake.com
SIC: 3524 Mfg Lawn/Garden Equipment

(G-5153)
YOLANDA DUBOSE RECORDS AND
105 W Prospect St (06516-3540)
P.O. Box 5034, Milford (06460-1434)
PHONE..............................203 823-6699
Yolanda Dubose, *Mng Member*
EMP: 10
SALES (est): 275K **Privately Held**
SIC: 2782 7929 7389 Mfg Record Albums & Entertainment Srvc

West Simsbury
Hartford County

(G-5154)
CTL CORPORATION
10 Rocklyn Ct (06092-2623)
PHONE..............................860 651-9173
Carl Fink, *President*
Lynn Fink, *Chairman*
EMP: 4
SALES (est): 363.2K **Privately Held**
WEB: www.glovebags.com
SIC: 3842 Imports And Manuf Fire Resistant And Protective Clothing

Westbrook
Middlesex County

(G-5155)
AIUDI CONCRETE INC
129 Norris Ave (06498)
PHONE..............................860 399-9289
Elmo Aiudi, *President*
EMP: 8
SQ FT: 1,939
SALES (est): 1.4MM **Privately Held**
WEB: www.aiudiconcrete.com
SIC: 3273 Mfg Ready-Mixed Concrete

(G-5156)
INNOPHASE CORP
18 Sea Scape Dr (06498-1969)
P.O. Box 755 (06498-0755)
PHONE..............................860 399-2269
EMP: 3
SALES: 100K **Privately Held**
SIC: 2819 8732 8999 Mfg Industrial Inorganic Chemicals Commercial Nonphysical Research Services-Misc

(G-5157)
LEE COMPANY (PA)
2 Pettipaug Rd (06498-1500)
P.O. Box 424 (06498-0424)
PHONE..............................860 399-6281
William W Lee, *President*
Leighton Lee III, *Chairman*
Jeff Svadlenak, *District Mgr*
Robert M Lee, *Exec VP*
Thomas Lee, *Exec VP*
▲ **EMP:** 775 **EST:** 1949
SQ FT: 365,000
SALES (est): 207.5MM **Privately Held**
WEB: www.eeco.com
SIC: 3823 3841 3812 3728 Mfg Process Cntrl Instr Mfg Surgical/Med Instr Mfg Search/Navgatn Equip Mfg Aircraft Parts/Equip Mfg Motor Vehicle Parts

(G-5158)
LEE COMPANY
22 Pequot Park Rd (06498-1466)
PHONE..............................860 399-6281
Ed Jones, *Branch Mgr*
EMP: 20
SALES (corp-wide): 207.5MM **Privately Held**
SIC: 3823 Mfg Process Control Instruments
PA: The Lee Company
2 Pettipaug Rd
Westbrook CT 06498
860 399-6281

(G-5159)
LIBERTY SERVICES LLC
Also Called: Canvas and Sail Repair Company
790 Boston Post Rd Ste 2 (06498-2189)
PHONE..............................860 399-0077
Billy Liberty, *Manager*
Debbie Liberty,
EMP: 4
SALES (est): 379.8K **Privately Held**
SIC: 2394 Mfg Canvas/Related Products

(G-5160)
MEADE DAILY GROUP LLC
103 Cold Spring Dr (06498-3511)
PHONE..............................860 399-7342
Eileen M Daily, *Manager*
EMP: 3
SALES (est): 116.8K **Privately Held**
SIC: 2711 Newspapers-Publishing/Printing

(G-5161)
PURFX INC
51 Brookwood Dr (06498-1576)
P.O. Box 227 (06498-0227)
PHONE..............................860 399-4045
Arno Utegg, *President*
EMP: 3
SALES: 2.4MM **Privately Held**
SIC: 3677 Mfg Electronic Coils/Transformers

(G-5162)
SCRAPBOOK CLUBHOUSE
20 Westbrook Pl (06498-3902)
PHONE..............................860 399-4443
Sharon Cooke, *Owner*
EMP: 10
SALES (est): 659.5K **Privately Held**
SIC: 2782 Mfg Blankbooks/Binders

GEOGRAPHIC

(G-5163)
SSHC INC
Also Called: Solid State Heating
1244 Old Clinton Rd (06498-1871)
P.O. Box 769, Old Saybrook (06475-0769)
PHONE..................................860 399-5434
Richard Watson, *President*
Susan Watson, *Vice Pres*
William C Bieluch Jr, *Admin Sec*
EMP: 15
SALES (est): 3MM **Privately Held**
WEB: www.heatnow.net
SIC: 3567 1711 Mfg Industrial Furnaces/Ovens Plumbing/Heating/Air Cond Contractor

(G-5164)
TOPSIDE CANVAS UPHOLSTERY
768 Boston Post Rd (06498-1846)
PHONE..................................860 399-4845
Robert Ramsdell, *President*
Maureen Ramsdell, *President*
EMP: 7
SQ FT: 2,400
SALES: 150K **Privately Held**
SIC: 2394 Mfg Canvas/Related Products

(G-5165)
WATERSIDE VENDING LLC
643 Old Clinton Rd (06498-1760)
PHONE..................................860 399-6039
EMP: 3
SALES: 180K **Privately Held**
SIC: 3581 Vending Machines

(G-5166)
WESTBROOK CON BLOCK CO INC
Cold Spring Brook Ind Par (06498)
PHONE..................................860 399-6201
Rose Maksin, *Manager*
EMP: 25
SALES (corp-wide): 3.6MM **Privately Held**
WEB: www.westbrookblock.com
SIC: 3271 Mfg Concrete Block/Brick
PA: Westbrook Concrete Block Company, Inc.
439 Spencer Plains Rd
Westbrook CT
860 399-6201

Weston
Fairfield County

(G-5167)
360ALUMNI INC
1 Norfield Rd (06883-2111)
PHONE..................................203 253-5860
Christina Balotescu, *CEO*
EMP: 7
SQ FT: 1,200
SALES (est): 328.6K **Privately Held**
SIC: 7372 Prepackaged Software Services

(G-5168)
AMT MICROPURE INC
14 Mountain View Dr (06883-1306)
P.O. Box 904, Georgetown (06829-0904)
PHONE..................................203 226-7938
B Anthony McNulty, *President*
EMP: 3
SALES (est): 28.6K **Privately Held**
SIC: 3556 D&D Of Microwave Purification Systems

(G-5169)
AUTOMOTIVE COOP COUPONING INC
Also Called: Auto Merchandising Depot
27 Cardinal Rd (06883-2448)
PHONE..................................203 227-2722
Peter D Shafer, *President*
Janica Shafer, *Admin Sec*
EMP: 5 **EST:** 1992
SALES: 1MM **Privately Held**
SIC: 3993 7331 7311 8742 Mfg Signs/Ad Specialties Direct Mail Ad Svcs Advertising Agency Mgmt Consulting Svcs

(G-5170)
CELL NIQUE
12 Old Stage Coach Rd (06883-1908)
P.O. Box 1131 (06883-0131)
PHONE..................................888 417-9343
EMP: 3
SALES (est): 146.7K **Privately Held**
SIC: 2086 Mfg Bottled/Canned Soft Drinks

(G-5171)
CREATIVE MEDIA APPLICATIONS
22 Old Orchard Dr (06883-1309)
PHONE..................................203 226-0544
Barbara Stewart, *President*
Daniel Oelsen, *Vice Pres*
Lary Rosenblatt, *Vice Pres*
EMP: 15
SQ FT: 1,500
SALES: 800K **Privately Held**
WEB: www.cmacontent.com
SIC: 2731 Books-Publishing/Printing

(G-5172)
PMC TECHNOLOGIES LLC
31 Glenwood Rd (06883-2310)
PHONE..................................203 222-0000
Patrick Chila,
EMP: 7
SALES: 500K **Privately Held**
SIC: 3651 Mfg Home Audio/Video Equipment

(G-5173)
PUBLISHING DIMENSIONS LLC
15 Treadwell Ln (06883-1949)
PHONE..................................203 856-7716
Ken Brooks,
EMP: 4
SALES (est): 134.2K **Privately Held**
SIC: 2741 Misc Publishing

(G-5174)
US-MALABAR COMPANY INC
25 Timber Mill Ln (06883-2727)
PHONE..................................203 226-1773
Matthew Mathai, *President*
Claudia Young, *Director*
▲ **EMP:** 6
SALES (est): 484.8K **Privately Held**
SIC: 3365 7389 Aluminum Foundry

(G-5175)
VAN DEUSEN & LEVITT ASSOC INC
14 Wood Hill Rd (06883-1603)
PHONE..................................203 445-6244
Glenn C Van Deusen, *President*
EMP: 40
SALES (est): 2.1MM **Privately Held**
SIC: 3953 Mfg Marking Devices

(G-5176)
WOODS END INC
Also Called: Bee-Commerce.com
11 Lilac Ln (06883-3032)
PHONE..................................203 226-6303
Howland Blackiston, *President*
Ed Weiss, *Vice Pres*
EMP: 8
SALES (est): 749.9K **Privately Held**
SIC: 2842 7379 Mfg Polish/Sanitation Goods Computer Related Services

Westport
Fairfield County

(G-5177)
8 TIMES LLC
12 Juniper Rd (06880-2535)
PHONE..................................203 227-7575
EMP: 4
SALES (est): 164.3K **Privately Held**
SIC: 2711 Newspapers-Publishing/Printing

(G-5178)
AFFICIENCY INC
606 Post Rd E (06880-4540)
PHONE..................................718 496-9071
Mark Scafaro, *CEO*
EMP: 5
SALES: 500K **Privately Held**
SIC: 7372 Prepackaged Software Services

(G-5179)
AIRTIME PUBLISHING INC
191 Post Rd W (06880-4625)
PHONE..................................203 454-4773
▲ **EMP:** 30
SALES (est): 1.9MM **Privately Held**
SIC: 2721 Periodicals-Publishing/Printing

(G-5180)
ALPINE MANAGEMENT GROUP LLC
Also Called: Alpine Art & Mirror
25 Sylvan Rd S Ste B (06880-4637)
PHONE..................................954 531-1692
Jeffrey Spitzer, *Mng Member*
EMP: 5 **EST:** 2011
SALES (est): 294.4K **Privately Held**
SIC: 3999 2499 Mfg Misc Products Mfg Wood Products

(G-5181)
AMERICAN NATURAL SODA ASH CORP (PA)
Also Called: Ansac
15 Riverside Ave Ste 2 (06880-4245)
PHONE..................................203 226-9056
John M Andrews, *President*
Janice Osullivan, *President*
Samuel R Blood, *Vice Pres*
Ravi Kuruppu, *Vice Pres*
Daniel Martinez, *Vice Pres*
◆ **EMP:** 20
SQ FT: 9,000
SALES (est): 49.5MM **Privately Held**
WEB: www.ansac.com
SIC: 1474 Potash/Soda/Borate Mining

(G-5182)
AMERICAN TRADE FAIRS ORG
Also Called: Atfo
250 Main St Ste 101 (06880-2431)
P.O. Box 489 (06881-0489)
PHONE..................................203 221-0114
Michael Montanaro, *Partner*
EMP: 3
SALES (est): 137.8K **Privately Held**
SIC: 2741 Misc Publishing

(G-5183)
CHESSCO INDUSTRIES INC (PA)
1330 Post Rd E Ste 2 (06880-5539)
PHONE..................................203 255-2804
Jeffrey Radler, *President*
Louis Radler, *Vice Pres*
Shaun Daly, *Plant Mgr*
Michael J Daly, *Treasurer*
Albert J Kleban, *Admin Sec*
▲ **EMP:** 41
SQ FT: 2,000
SALES (est): 8.5MM **Privately Held**
WEB: www.processresearch.com
SIC: 3291 2911 2992 2899 Mfg Abrasive Products Petroleum Refining Mfg Lubrictng Oil/Grease Mfg Chemical Preparation Mfg Adhesives/Sealants

(G-5184)
COMMERCE CONNECT MEDIA INC
Also Called: Cygnus Business Media
830 Post Rd E Fl 2 (06880-5222)
PHONE..................................800 547-7377
Paul Mackler, *CEO*
EMP: 2188
SALES (est): 66.9MM **Privately Held**
WEB: www.abry.com
SIC: 2721 Periodicals-Publishing/Printing
PA: Abry Partners, Inc.
888 Boylston St Ste 1600
Boston MA 02199

(G-5185)
COMMUNITY BRANDS HOLDINGS LLC
Also Called: Tripbuilder Media
180 Post Rd E Ste 200 (06880-3414)
PHONE..................................203 227-1255
EMP: 15
SALES (corp-wide): 13.5MM **Privately Held**
SIC: 7372 Prepackaged Software Services
PA: Community Brands Holdings, Llc
9620 Executive Center Dr
Saint Petersburg FL 33702
727 827-0046

(G-5186)
CONVERGENT SOLUTIONS LLC
3 Baywood Ln (06880-4036)
PHONE..................................203 293-3534
Nancy Mahmoud, *Principal*
EMP: 3
SALES (est): 108.9K **Privately Held**
SIC: 3674 Mfg Semiconductors/Related Devices

(G-5187)
CUERO OPERATING
Also Called: Quero Shoes
34 Meeker Rd (06880-1708)
PHONE..................................203 253-8651
Randy Shuken,
EMP: 4
SALES: 1.5MM **Privately Held**
SIC: 3111 5661 Leather Tanning/Finishing Ret Shoes

(G-5188)
DOMINO MEDIA GROUP INC
Also Called: Domino.com
16 Taylor Pl (06880-4313)
PHONE..................................877 223-7844
Cliff Sirlin, *CEO*
Andy Appelbaum, *Principal*
Aaron Wallace, *Treasurer*
Lily Sullivan, *Assistant*
EMP: 30 **EST:** 2012
SQ FT: 1,500
SALES (est): 3MM **Privately Held**
SIC: 2721 5712 Periodicals-Publishing/Printing Ret Furniture

(G-5189)
EARNIX INC
191 Post Rd W (06880-4625)
PHONE..................................203 557-8077
Meryl Golden, *Branch Mgr*
EMP: 10 **Privately Held**
SIC: 7372 Prepackaged Software Services
PA: Earnix Ltd
4 Ariel Sharon
Givataim
375 382-92

(G-5190)
ELLIPSON DATA LLC
21 Bridge Sq (06880-5900)
PHONE..................................203 227-5520
Bernhard Keppler,
EMP: 3
SALES: 500K **Privately Held**
SIC: 3577 Mfg Computer Peripheral Equipment

(G-5191)
FENTON CORP
191 Post Rd W (06880-4625)
PHONE..................................203 221-2788
Harrison Kwan, *President*
Florence Lee, *Bookkeeper*
Michael Brown, *Senior Mgr*
EMP: 10 **EST:** 1993
SALES (est): 910.2K **Privately Held**
SIC: 3663 5065 Mfg Radio/Tv Communication Equipment Whol Electronic Parts/Equipment

(G-5192)
FIRST AVIATION SERVICES INC (PA)
15 Riverside Ave (06880-4245)
PHONE..................................203 291-3300
Aaron P Hollander, *President*
Joshua Krotec, *Senior VP*
Janelle Miller, *CFO*
Joy Sideleau, *Executive Asst*
Larissa Strautman, *Admin Sec*
EMP: 4
SQ FT: 3,000
SALES (est): 31.7MM **Privately Held**
SIC: 3728 3724 Mfg Aircraft Parts/Equipment Mfg Aircraft Engines/Parts

(G-5193)
FIRST EQUITY GROUP INC (PA)
15 Riverside Ave Ste 1 (06880-4245)
PHONE..................................203 291-7700

Aaron Hollander, *CEO*
Larissa Strautman, *Admin Sec*
EMP: 15
SQ FT: 3,000
SALES (est): 17.9MM **Privately Held**
SIC: 3724 7389 Mfg Aircraft Engines/Parts Business Services

(G-5194)
FJB AMERICA LLC
8 Wright St Ste 107 (06880-3114)
PHONE..................................203 682-2424
Francisco Barreto, *Mng Member*
Jacqueline Barreto,
▲ **EMP:** 3
SALES (est): 3MM **Privately Held**
SIC: 2095 Mfg Roasted Coffee

(G-5195)
FLOTTEC INTERNATIONAL SLS CORP
Also Called: Fife
3 Meeker Rd (06880-1704)
PHONE..................................973 588-4717
John E Tober, *President*
Frank R Cappuccitti, *Director*
EMP: 4 **EST:** 2014
SQ FT: 800
SALES: 4MM
SALES (corp-wide): 1MM **Privately Held**
SIC: 2899 Mfg Agricultural Chemicals
PA: Flottec Llc
5 Hillcrest Rd
Boonton NJ 07005
973 588-4717

(G-5196)
FUEL FOR HUMANITY INC
11 Hedley Farms Rd (06880-6335)
PHONE..................................203 255-5913
Jerid O'Connell, *Principal*
EMP: 3
SALES (est): 174.5K **Privately Held**
SIC: 2869 Mfg Industrial Organic Chemicals

(G-5197)
GEMMA ORO INC
2 Coach Ln (06880-2107)
PHONE..................................203 227-0774
Perry Gandelman, *President*
Nanette Gandelman, *Vice Pres*
EMP: 5
SQ FT: 850
SALES (est): 486.8K **Privately Held**
SIC: 3911 Mfg Precious Metal Jewelry

(G-5198)
GLOBAL PALATE FOODS LLC
161 Cross Hwy (06880-2245)
PHONE..................................203 543-3028
Craig Kyzar, *Principal*
EMP: 3 **EST:** 2011
SALES (est): 187.9K **Privately Held**
SIC: 2099 Mfg Food Preparations

(G-5199)
GREENPORT FOODS LLC
191 Post Rd W (06880-4625)
PHONE..................................203 221-2673
Eduardo Bembibre, *General Mgr*
Carlos Grego, *Principal*
◆ **EMP:** 11 **EST:** 2011
SALES (est): 3.1MM **Privately Held**
SIC: 2091 Mfg Canned/Cured Fish/Seafood

(G-5200)
HILLS POINT INDUSTRIES LLC (PA)
191 Post Rd W (06880-4625)
PHONE..................................917 515-8650
Marissa Saporta,
Jennifer Richter,
▼ **EMP:** 3
SALES: 2MM **Privately Held**
SIC: 2392 Mfg Household Furnishings Business Serv Non-Commercial Site

(G-5201)
IN STORE EXPERIENCE INC
49 Richmondville Ave # 102 (06880-2050)
PHONE..................................203 221-4777
Christopher S Anderson, *CEO*
Deborah Anderson, *Vice Pres*
Frank Cirillo, *Vice Pres*
Greg Cuccinello, *Vice Pres*
George Martocchio, *Vice Pres*
▲ **EMP:** 26
SALES (est): 4.7MM **Privately Held**
SIC: 2542 Mfg Partitions/Fixtures-Nonwood

(G-5202)
INDUSTRIAL SALES CORP (PA)
Also Called: Industrial Sales Supply
727 Post Rd E (06880-5219)
PHONE..................................203 227-5988
James Hornung, *President*
Robert Hornung, *Vice Pres*
▲ **EMP:** 11
SALES (est): 2.1MM **Privately Held**
SIC: 2431 Whol Distributor & Manufacturer's Rep Of Window And Insulating Glass Components

(G-5203)
INFIRST HEALTHCARE INC
8 Church Ln (06880-3508)
PHONE..................................203 222-1300
Manfred Scheske, *CEO*
James Barickman, *President*
Philip Lindsell, *CFO*
John Linderman, *Director*
EMP: 7
SQ FT: 5,000
SALES: 22.8MM
SALES (corp-wide): 19.2MM **Privately Held**
SIC: 2834 Mfg Pharmaceutical Preparations
PA: Infirst Healthcare Limited
Central Point
London EC2Y
207 153-6600

(G-5204)
INSTINCTIVE WORKS LLC
5 Spicer Ct (06880-4527)
PHONE..................................203 434-8094
Stuart David Farnworth,
Tony Yao,
EMP: 5 **EST:** 2013
SQ FT: 1,000
SALES: 250K **Privately Held**
SIC: 3633 Mfg Home Laundry Equipment

(G-5205)
KERRY R WOOD
2 Hideaway Ln (06880-6115)
PHONE..................................203 221-7780
Kerry Wood, *Owner*
EMP: 7
SALES (est): 419.8K **Privately Held**
SIC: 2035 2099 Mfg Pickles/Sauces/Dressing Mfg Food Preparations

(G-5206)
KNOX ENTERPRISES INC (PA)
830 Post Rd E Ste 205 (06880-5222)
PHONE..................................203 226-6408
Paul K Kelly, *CEO*
Frederick A Rossetti, *COO*
Jeffrey B Gaynor, *Exec VP*
◆ **EMP:** 3
SQ FT: 2,500
SALES (est): 10.6MM **Privately Held**
SIC: 2671 3496 Manufactures Rolled Paper Products & Fabricated Steel Products

(G-5207)
KNOX INDUSTRIES INC
830 Post Rd E Ste 205 (06880-5222)
PHONE..................................203 226-6408
Frederick Rossetti, *President*
Jeffrey B Gaynor, *Admin Sec*
◆ **EMP:** 142
SQ FT: 860
SALES (est): 8.1MM
SALES (corp-wide): 10.6MM **Privately Held**
SIC: 2679 Mfg Converted Paper Products
PA: Knox Enterprises Inc
830 Post Rd E Ste 205
Westport CT 06880
203 226-6408

(G-5208)
KTCR HOLDING
4 Pheasant Ln (06880-1709)
PHONE..................................203 227-4115
Joshua Rizack, *Owner*
EMP: 8
SALES (est): 327.1K **Privately Held**
SIC: 3621 Mfg Motors/Generators

(G-5209)
LH GAULT & SON INCORPORATED
11 Ferry Ln W (06880-5808)
P.O. Box 2030 (06880-0030)
PHONE..................................203 227-5181
Samuel M Gault, *President*
William L Gault, *Chairman*
Debbie Finan, *Controller*
Clay Bassett, *Sales Staff*
Megan Donaher, *Sales Staff*
▲ **EMP:** 65
SQ FT: 40,000
SALES (est): 41.5MM **Privately Held**
SIC: 1411 5032 3441 5211 Dimension Stone Quarry Whol Brick/Stone Matrls

(G-5210)
LUMENDI LLC
253 Post Rd W (06880-4737)
PHONE..................................203 528-0316
Michael Parrilla, *COO*
Michael R Thomas, *VP Sales*
EMP: 7
SQ FT: 4,000
SALES (est): 1.3MM **Privately Held**
SIC: 3841 Mfg Surgical/Medical Instruments

(G-5211)
MAGNESIUM INTERACTIVE LLC
171 Roseville Rd (06880-2618)
PHONE..................................917 609-1306
John C Dodd, *Principal*
EMP: 4
SALES (est): 120.9K **Privately Held**
SIC: 3356 Nonferrous Rolling/Drawing

(G-5212)
MANTROSE-HAEUSER CO INC (HQ)
100 Nyala Farms Rd (06880-6266)
PHONE..................................203 454-1800
William J Barrie, *President*
Stephen A Santos, *Senior VP*
Susan Wahler, *Export Mgr*
Xiangdong Gan, *Research*
Arun Uppalanchi, *Research*
▲ **EMP:** 29
SALES (est): 24.2MM
SALES (corp-wide): 5.5B **Publicly Held**
WEB: www.mantrose.com
SIC: 2064 2066 2851 0723 Mfg Candy/Confectionery Mfg Chocolate/Cocoa Prdt Mfg Paints/Allied Prdts Crop Marketing Prep Mfg Medicinal/Botanicals
PA: Rpm International Inc.
2628 Pearl Rd
Medina OH 44256
330 273-5090

(G-5213)
MASON MEDICAL COMMUNICATIONS
10 Covlee Dr (06880-6405)
P.O. Box 216, Greens Farms (06838-0216)
PHONE..................................203 227-9252
Howard Mason, *President*
Jacqueline Mason, *Corp Secy*
EMP: 5
SQ FT: 1,000
SALES (est): 405.3K **Privately Held**
SIC: 2721 Medical Publishing Company

(G-5214)
MINUTEMAN NEWSPAPER (PA)
1175 Post Rd E Ste 3e (06880-5400)
PHONE..................................203 226-8877
Paula Walsh, *Manager*
EMP: 24 **Privately Held**
SIC: 2711 Holding Company For Newspaper Publisher Not Printed On Site

(G-5215)
MOFFLY PUBLICATIONS INC
Also Called: Westport Magazine
205 Main St Ste 1 (06880-3206)
PHONE..................................203 222-0600
John W Moffly, *Branch Mgr*
EMP: 11
SALES (corp-wide): 4.4MM **Privately Held**
WEB: www.mofflypub.com
SIC: 2721 Periodicals-Publishing/Printing
PA: Moffly Publications Inc
205 Main St Ste 1
Westport CT 06880
203 222-0600

GEOGRAPHIC

(G-5216)
MOFFLY PUBLICATIONS INC (PA)
Also Called: Greenwich Magazine
205 Main St Ste 1 (06880-3206)
PHONE..................................203 222-0600
Jonathan Moffly, *CEO*
John W Moffly IV, *Chairman*
Pete Michalsky, *Vice Pres*
Elena Moffly, *Treasurer*
EMP: 23
SQ FT: 4,500
SALES (est): 4.4MM **Privately Held**
WEB: www.mofflypub.com
SIC: 2721 Magazine Publisher

(G-5217)
MR BOLTONS MUSIC INC
31 Kings Hwy N (06880-3002)
PHONE..................................646 578-8081
Micheal Bolotin, *President*
EMP: 3
SALES (est): 229.1K **Privately Held**
SIC: 2741 Music Publishing

(G-5218)
NEWMANS OWN INC (PA)
Also Called: Newman's Own Organics
1 Morningside Dr N Ste 1 # 1 (06880-3847)
PHONE..................................203 222-0136
Thomas Indoe, *President*
Tom Indoe, *COO*
Lori Dibiase, *Vice Pres*
William Lee, *Vice Pres*
Jeffrey Smith, *VP Opers*
▼ **EMP:** 28
SQ FT: 4,200
SALES (est): 19MM **Privately Held**
WEB: www.newmansown.com
SIC: 2035 2086 Mfg Pickles/Sauces/Dressing Mfg Bottled/Canned Soft Drinks

(G-5219)
ONE KID LLC (PA)
188 Compo Rd S (06880-5019)
PHONE..................................203 254-9978
Eric Autard,
▲ **EMP:** 3 **EST:** 1998
SALES (est): 342.8K **Privately Held**
WEB: www.onekid.com
SIC: 2369 Mfg Girl/Youth Outerwear

(G-5220)
OUR TOWN CRIER
36 Lyons Plains Rd (06880-1305)
PHONE..................................203 400-5000
EMP: 3
SALES (est): 126.9K **Privately Held**
SIC: 2711 Newspapers-Publishing/Printing

(G-5221)
OWLSTONE INC (PA)
19 Ludlow Rd Ste 202 (06880-3040)
PHONE..................................203 908-4848
Bret Bader, *CEO*
Andrew Koehl, *President*
Thomas Finn, *CFO*
EMP: 6
SQ FT: 2,771
SALES (est): 4.6MM **Privately Held**
SIC: 3826 3829 Mfg Analytical Instruments Mfg Measuring/Controlling Devices

(G-5222)
PALLET INC LLC
41 Charcoal Hill Rd (06880-1635)
PHONE..................................203 227-8148
Mark Ancona, *Principal*

EMP: 3
SALES (est): 156.7K **Privately Held**
SIC: 2448 Mfg Wood Pallets/Skids

(G-5223)
PENINSULA PUBLISHING
1630 Post Rd E Unit 312 (06880-5647)
PHONE..................................203 292-5621
Charles Wiseman, *Owner*
EMP: 3
SALES: 50K **Privately Held**
SIC: 2731 Books-Publishing/Printing

(G-5224)
PPC BOOKS LTD
Also Called: Publishing Packagers
335 Post Rd W (06880)
PHONE..................................203 226-6644
Christopher Watson, *President*
EMP: 4
SQ FT: 1,200
SALES: 200K **Privately Held**
SIC: 2732 2731 2721 Book Printing Books-Publishing/Printing Periodicals-Publishing/Printing

(G-5225)
RAND MEDIA CO LLC
265 Post Rd W (06880-4746)
PHONE..................................203 226-8727
EMP: 4
SALES: 100K **Privately Held**
SIC: 2741 Misc Publishing

(G-5226)
RJ CABINETRY LLC
943 Post Rd E (06880-5362)
PHONE..................................203 515-8401
Ruben Reinoso, *Principal*
EMP: 3
SALES (est): 187.7K **Privately Held**
SIC: 2434 Mfg Wood Kitchen Cabinets

(G-5227)
ROBERT WARREN LLC (PA)
Also Called: Lance International
1 Sprucewood Ln (06880-4022)
PHONE..................................203 247-3347
Murray Doscher,
Ed Diamond,
EMP: 50 **EST:** 1974
SQ FT: 18,000
SALES (est): 9.8MM **Privately Held**
WEB: www.lanceintl.com
SIC: 3679 Mfg Electronic Components

(G-5228)
SAATVA INC
8 Wright St Ste 108 (06880-3114)
PHONE..................................877 672-2882
Ron Rudzin, *CEO*
Edward Seidner, *Vice Pres*
Robin Belliveau, *Human Res Dir*
Robert Kramer, *Business Anlyst*
Nicolle Hiddleston, *Marketing Staff*
EMP: 34
SALES (est): 4.1MM **Privately Held**
SIC: 2515 Mfg Mattresses/Bedsprings

(G-5229)
SATORI AUDIO LLC
Also Called: Satori Nyc
180 Post Rd E Ste 201 (06880-3414)
PHONE..................................203 571-6050
Jeffrey Warshaw, *Mng Member*
EMP: 4
SALES (est): 146.9K **Privately Held**
SIC: 7372 Prepackaged Software Services

(G-5230)
SHELL SHOCK TECHNOLOGIES LLC
38 Owenoke Park (06880-6833)
PHONE..................................203 557-3256
Andrew Vallance, *Vice Pres*
Craig F Knight, *Mng Member*
EMP: 6 **EST:** 2015
SALES: 1MM **Privately Held**
SIC: 3482 Mfg Small Arms Ammunition

(G-5231)
SHIRE RGENERATIVE MEDICINE INC (DH)
36 Church Ln (06880-3505)
PHONE..................................877 422-4463
Kevin Rakin, *President*
Kathy McGee, *Senior VP*
Charles E Hart PHD, *Vice Pres*
Kevin C O'Boyle, *CFO*
Jan Lessem MD PHD, *Officer*
EMP: 4
SALES (est): 15.4MM
SALES (corp-wide): 15.1B **Privately Held**
WEB: www.advancedtissue.com
SIC: 2834 Mfg Pharmaceutical Preparations
HQ: Shire Us Holdings Llc
9200 Brookfield Ct # 108
Florence KY 41042
859 669-8000

(G-5232)
STYLE AND GRACE LLC
101 Franklin St Ste 3 (06880-5966)
PHONE..................................917 751-2043
Paris Gordon, *CEO*
EMP: 3
SQ FT: 1,000
SALES: 900K **Privately Held**
SIC: 2389 Mfg Apparel/Accessories

(G-5233)
TEREX CORPORATION (PA)
200 Nyala Farms Rd Ste 2 (06880-6261)
PHONE..................................203 222-7170
John L Garrison Jr, *Ch of Bd*
James Barr, *General Mgr*
Terri Paynter, *Editor*
Robert Brown, *Vice Pres*
Damian Kitson, *Vice Pres*
◆ **EMP:** 15
SALES: 5.1B **Publicly Held**
WEB: www.terex.com
SIC: 3537 3531 Mfg Indstl Truck/Tractor Mfg Construction Mach

(G-5234)
TEREX USA LLC (HQ)
Also Called: Cedarapids
200 Nyala Farms Rd (06880-6265)
PHONE..................................203 222-7170
Gary Pils, *Credit Staff*
Ethan Waller, *Regl Sales Mgr*
Jodi Robledo, *Sales Staff*
Gerald Corder, *Marketing Mgr*
Ronald M Defeo, *Mng Member*
◆ **EMP:** 335 **EST:** 1923
SQ FT: 61,700
SALES (est): 232.9MM
SALES (corp-wide): 5.1B **Publicly Held**
SIC: 3532 Mfg Construction Machinery
PA: Terex Corporation
200 Nyala Farms Rd Ste 2
Westport CT 06880
203 222-7170

(G-5235)
THT INC
33 Riverside Ave Ste 506 (06880-4223)
PHONE..................................203 226-6408
Paul K Kelly, *CEO*
EMP: 3
SALES (est): 196.7K **Privately Held**
SIC: 2671 Mfg Packaging Paper/Film

(G-5236)
VARPRO INC
4 Shadbush Ln Pmb 2224 (06880-1838)
P.O. Box 2224 (06880-0224)
PHONE..................................203 227-6876
Peter Brink, *President*
Sandra Brink, *Treasurer*
EMP: 20
SQ FT: 2,000
SALES (est): 1.2MM **Privately Held**
SIC: 2371 8742 Mfg Apparel And Management Consulting Srvcs

(G-5237)
WALPOLE WOODWORKERS INC
Also Called: Walpole Outdoors
1835 Post Rd E Ste 6 (06880-5678)
PHONE..................................203 255-9010
Linda Bartlle, *Manager*
EMP: 4
SALES (corp-wide): 83.9MM **Privately Held**
WEB: www.walpolewoodworkers.com
SIC: 2499 5211 5712 2452 Mfg Wood Products Ret Lumber/Building Mtrl Ret Furniture Mfg Prefabrcatd Wd Bldgs Mfg Wood Household Furn
PA: Walpole Outdoors Llc
100 Rver Ridge Dr Ste 302
Norwood MA 02062
508 668-2800

(G-5238)
WIZARD TOO LLC
34 Little Fox Ln (06880-1403)
PHONE..................................203 984-7180
Ronald Leong,
EMP: 3
SALES (est): 129.4K **Privately Held**
SIC: 2741 Misc Publishing

Wethersfield
Hartford County

(G-5239)
A HELIUM PLUS BALLOONS LLC
94 Albert Ave (06109-1057)
PHONE..................................860 833-1761
Diaram T Gopaul, *Principal*
EMP: 3 **EST:** 2018
SALES (est): 123.2K **Privately Held**
SIC: 2813 Mfg Industrial Gases

(G-5240)
ARROW WINDOW SHADE MFG CO
1252 Berlin Tpke (06109-1004)
PHONE..................................860 956-3570
Kris T Hoskins, *Principal*
Madelyn A Hoskins, *Vice Pres*
Donald B Hoskins, *Treasurer*
EMP: 3
SQ FT: 2,200
SALES: 350K **Privately Held**
SIC: 2591 5719 7699 Mfg Drape Hardware/Blind

(G-5241)
ARROW WINDOW SHADE MFG CO MRDN
47 Oxford St (06109-1724)
PHONE..................................860 563-4035
Oscar Laraia, *President*
EMP: 12
SALES (est): 930K **Privately Held**
SIC: 2591 5719 Mfg Drapery Hardware/Blinds Ret Misc Homefurnishings

(G-5242)
BLACK & DECKER (US) INC
Also Called: Dewalt Service Center 050
662 Silas Deane Hwy (06109-3053)
PHONE..................................860 563-5800
John Walls, *Manager*
EMP: 6
SQ FT: 4,000
SALES (corp-wide): 13.9B **Publicly Held**
WEB: www.dewalt.com
SIC: 3546 Mfg Power-Driven Handtools
HQ: Black & Decker (U.S.) Inc.
1000 Stanley Dr
New Britain CT 06053
860 225-5111

(G-5243)
CAP-TECH PRODUCTS INC
61 Arrow Rd Ste 11 (06109-1301)
P.O. Box 290123 (06129-0123)
PHONE..................................860 490-5078
EMP: 10
SQ FT: 4,500
SALES (est): 954K **Privately Held**
WEB: www.captechproducts.com
SIC: 2399 2221 Mfg Sewn Textile Products

(G-5244)
CKH INDUSTRIES INC
365 Silas Deane Hwy Ste 1 (06109-2121)
PHONE..................................860 563-2999
Kenneth Cline, *Branch Mgr*
EMP: 71
SALES (corp-wide): 14.6MM **Privately Held**
SIC: 3442 Mfg Metal Doors/Sash/Trim
PA: Ckh Industries Inc
520 Temple Hill Rd
New Windsor NY 12553
845 561-9000

(G-5245)
CLEAR WATER MANUFACTURING CORP (PA)
900 Wells Rd (06109-2417)
PHONE..................................860 372-4907
Patrick Sullivan, *President*
Mike Cackowski, *VP Mfg*
Kelly Thompson, *CFO*
Penny Harris, *Sales Staff*
Laketa Bobbitt, *Asst Mgr*
EMP: 8
SALES (est): 1.9MM **Privately Held**
SIC: 3498 Mfg Fabricated Pipe/Fittings

(G-5246)
CORPORATE CONNECTICUT MAG LLC
912 Silas Deane Hwy (06109-3434)
PHONE..................................860 257-0500
Anders G Helm, *Principal*
EMP: 3
SALES (est): 197.6K **Privately Held**
SIC: 2721 Periodicals-Publishing/Printing

(G-5247)
DOSS CORPORATION
102 Orchard Hill Dr (06109-2420)
PHONE..................................860 721-7384
Vijaya L Murthy, *President*
Mal V Murthy, *Vice Pres*
EMP: 3
SQ FT: 2,000
SALES: 300K **Privately Held**
SIC: 3089 Mfg Custom Plastic Injection Molding Tooling And Rubber Products

(G-5248)
EASTWOOD PRINTING INC
501 Middletown Ave (06109-3809)
P.O. Box 290271 (06129-0271)
PHONE..................................860 529-6673
Lewis Eastwood, *President*
Ellen Eastwood, *Admin Sec*
EMP: 10
SQ FT: 2,500
SALES (est): 1MM **Privately Held**
WEB: www.eastwoodprinting.com
SIC: 2759 Commercial Printing

(G-5249)
INDUSTRIAL PRSSURE WASHERS LLC
500 Ridge Rd (06109-1925)
PHONE..................................860 608-6153
Richard Senokosoff,
Patti Senokosoff,
EMP: 3 **EST:** 2011
SALES (est): 335.4K **Privately Held**
SIC: 3452 3548 Mfg Bolts/Screws/Rivets Mfg Welding Apparatus

(G-5250)
J & T PRINTING LLC
46 2 Silas Deane Hwy (06109)
PHONE..................................860 529-4628
Jeffrey W Foley, *Principal*
EMP: 3
SALES (est): 262.5K **Privately Held**
SIC: 2752 Lithographic Commercial Printing

(G-5251)
JOHN OLDHAM STUDIOS INC
888 Wells Rd (06109-2417)
PHONE..................................860 529-3331
John W Oldham Jr, *President*
Mark Oldham, *Vice Pres*
Jennifer Jenkins, *Office Mgr*
Patrica Oldham, *Admin Sec*
▲ **EMP:** 24 **EST:** 1931
SQ FT: 86,000
SALES (est): 3.3MM **Privately Held**
WEB: www.oldhamstudios.com
SIC: 3993 7389 Mfg Signs/Advertising Specialties Business Services

▲ = Import ▼=Export
◆ =Import/Export

(G-5252)
KAHN INDUSTRIES INC
885 Wells Rd (06109-2499)
PHONE....860 529-8643
Jeffrey S Kahn, *President*
Gerhard Merkle, *Vice Pres*
David Kahn, *Admin Sec*
▼ **EMP:** 20
SQ FT: 50,000
SALES (est): 7MM **Privately Held**
SIC: 3829 Mfg Measuring/Controlling Devices

(G-5253)
KELL-STROM TOOL CO INC (PA)
214 Church St (06109-2397)
PHONE....860 529-6851
Francis P Kelly, *President*
Robert Kelly, *Vice Pres*
Jerry Edison, *Production*
Gary Viola, *Purch Mgr*
Don Blais, *Research*
EMP: 39
SALES (est): 9.1MM **Privately Held**
SIC: 3429 3599 3423 Mfg Hardware Mfg Industrial Machinery Mfg Hand/Edge Tools

(G-5254)
KELL-STROM TOOL INTL INC
214 Church St (06109-2316)
PHONE....860 529-6851
Francis P Kelly, *President*
Robert M Kelly, *Vice Pres*
Thomas J Kelly, *Treasurer*
Peter J Kelly, *Admin Sec*
EMP: 39 **EST:** 1942
SQ FT: 30,000
SALES (est): 7.1MM **Privately Held**
SIC: 3429 3599 5072 5085 Mfg Hardware Mfg Industrial Machinery Whol Hardware Whol Industrial Supplies Welding Repair
PA: The Kell-Strom Tool Co Incorporated
214 Church St
Wethersfield CT 06109

(G-5255)
KEYWAY INC
3 Wells Rd (06109-3041)
PHONE....860 571-9181
EMP: 3
SQ FT: 2,400
SALES: 300K **Privately Held**
WEB: www.keyway.com
SIC: 3599 Machine Shop

(G-5256)
LEONA CORP
Also Called: Altman Orthotics & Prosthetics
638 Silas Deane Hwy (06109-3053)
PHONE....860 257-3840
John Miller, *President*
Kim Miller, *Vice Pres*
EMP: 3
SALES (est): 230K **Privately Held**
SIC: 3842 Mfg Surgical Appliances/Supplies

(G-5257)
MERRITT MACHINE COMPANY
Also Called: Arrow Tool Division
61 Arrow Rd Ste 5 (06109-1358)
PHONE....860 257-4484
Fax: 860 529-2509
EMP: 3
SQ FT: 40,000
SALES: 400K **Privately Held**
SIC: 3599 Machine Shop

(G-5258)
MINUTEMAN PRESS
462 Silas Deane Hwy (06109-2104)
PHONE....860 529-4628
Taunya Foley, *Owner*
EMP: 4
SALES (est): 351.4K **Privately Held**
SIC: 2752 Comm Prtg Litho

(G-5259)
MOZZICATO FMLY INVESTMENTS LLC
Also Called: Sam Maulucci & Sons
631 Ridge Rd (06109-2617)
PHONE....860 296-0426
Rino Mozzicato, *Mng Member*
EMP: 7
SQ FT: 1,200
SALES (est): 656.2K **Privately Held**
SIC: 2022 5143 Mfg Cheese Whol Dairy Products

(G-5260)
PATRIOT ENVELOPE LLC
501 Middletown Ave (06109-3809)
PHONE....860 529-1553
Lewis Eastwood,
EMP: 3
SALES (est): 210K **Privately Held**
SIC: 2759 Lithographic Commercial Printing

Willimantic
Windham County

(G-5261)
ARCH PARENT INC
82 Storrs Rd (06226-4001)
PHONE....860 336-4856
EMP: 3 **Privately Held**
SIC: 2752 Lithographic Commercial Printing
HQ: Arch Parent Inc.
9 W 57th St Fl 31
New York NY 10019
212 796-8500

(G-5262)
CHRONICLE PRINTING COMPANY
Also Called: Chronicle, The
1 Chronicle Rd (06226-1932)
P.O. Box 229 (06226-0229)
PHONE....860 423-8466
Lucy B Crosbie, *President*
Jean Beckley, *Director*
EMP: 86 **EST:** 1877
SQ FT: 22,000
SALES (est): 6MM **Privately Held**
WEB: www.thechronicle.com
SIC: 2711 Newspapers-Publishing/Printing

(G-5263)
EASTERN CONNECTICUT
42 Boston Post Rd (06226-2920)
PHONE....860 423-1972
William Soucy, *Branch Mgr*
EMP: 10
SALES (est): 480K **Privately Held**
SIC: 1389 7389 Oil/Gas Field Services Business Services

(G-5264)
GENERAL CABLE INDUSTRIES INC
Also Called: Willimantic, CT Plant
1600 Main St (06226-1128)
PHONE....860 456-8000
Jim Barney, *President*
Jim Charron, *Vice Pres*
Edward Aberbach, *Engineer*
Stew Later, *VP Sales*
EMP: 148 **Privately Held**
WEB: www.generalcable.com
SIC: 3496 3357 Mfg Misc Fabricated Wire Products Nonferrous Wiredrawing/Insulating
HQ: General Cable Industries, Inc.
4 Tesseneer Dr
Highland Heights KY 41076

(G-5265)
GULEMO INC
Also Called: Willimatic Instant Print
2 Birch St (06226-2103)
P.O. Box 467 (06226-0467)
PHONE....860 456-1151
Gunnel Stenberg, *President*
Lena Fontaine, *Admin Sec*
EMP: 8
SALES (est): 1.2MM **Privately Held**
WEB: www.gulemo.com
SIC: 2752 Lithographic Commercial Printing

(G-5266)
HORIZONS UNLIMITED INC
Also Called: Quality Sign Crafters
90 S Park St Ste 1 (06226-3336)
P.O. Box 35 (06226-0035)
PHONE....860 423-1931
Richard Napolitano, *President*
Lisa Napolitano, *Admin Sec*
EMP: 12 **EST:** 1995
SQ FT: 15,000
SALES: 1MM **Privately Held**
WEB: www.qscct.com
SIC: 3993 Mfg Signs/Advertising Specialties

(G-5267)
MARC BOULEY
Also Called: M B Machine
28 Young St (06226-3333)
PHONE....860 450-1713
Marc Bouley, *Owner*
EMP: 6
SQ FT: 1,500
SALES (est): 29.3K **Privately Held**
SIC: 3599 7692 Mfg Industrial Machinery Welding Repair

(G-5268)
POLYMATH SOFTWARE
42 Carey St (06226-2622)
P.O. Box 523 (06226-0523)
PHONE....860 423-5823
Michael Cutlip, *Owner*
EMP: 4
SALES (est): 304.9K **Privately Held**
WEB: www.polymath-software.com
SIC: 7372 Prepackaged Software Services

(G-5269)
SIGNS PLUS LLC
700 Main St (06226-2651)
PHONE....860 423-3048
Joseph Duvall,
EMP: 3
SALES (est): 273.2K **Privately Held**
SIC: 3993 5999 Mfg Signs/Advertising Specialties Ret Misc Merchandise

Willington
Tolland County

(G-5270)
CABLE TECHNOLOGY INC
73 River Rd (06279-1830)
PHONE....860 429-7889
Michael Cariglia, *President*
Carl Beyor, *Vice Pres*
EMP: 25 **EST:** 1982
SQ FT: 35,000
SALES (est): 4.5MM **Privately Held**
SIC: 3677 3357 Mfg Electronic Coils/Transformers Nonferrous Wiredrawing/Insulating

(G-5271)
TRUMBULL RECREATION SUPPLY CO
148 River Rd (06279-1629)
P.O. Box 109 (06279-0109)
PHONE....860 429-6604
Francis Kosowicz Sr, *President*
EMP: 7
SALES (est): 1MM **Privately Held**
SIC: 3088 Mfg Plastic Plumbing Fixtures

Wilton
Fairfield County

(G-5272)
2 GIRL A TRUNK
35 Dudley Rd (06897-3508)
PHONE....203 762-0360
Carol Schuler, *Principal*
EMP: 3
SALES (est): 231.4K **Privately Held**
SIC: 3161 Mfg Luggage

(G-5273)
21ST CENTURY FOX AMERICA INC
20 Westport Rd (06897-4549)
PHONE....203 563-6600
Ralph Masiello, *President*
Carey Chase, *Chairman*
Linda Campbell, *Area Mgr*
Paul Schmidt, *Vice Pres*
Joe Poulos, *Engineer*
EMP: 8
SALES (corp-wide): 69.5B **Publicly Held**
SIC: 2711 Newspapers-Publish/Print
HQ: 21st Century Fox America, Inc.
1211 Ave Of The Americas
New York NY 10036
212 852-7000

(G-5274)
AIR AGE INC
88 Danbury Rd Ste 2b (06897-4423)
PHONE....203 431-9000
Louis Defrancesco Jr, *President*
Louis De Francesco Jr, *President*
Yvonne De Francesco, *Exec VP*
Carol Shepherd, *CFO*
Yelena Trakht, *Accounting Mgr*
EMP: 27 **EST:** 1929
SQ FT: 9,675
SALES (est): 5MM **Privately Held**
WEB: www.airage.com
SIC: 2721 2731 Periodicals-Publishing/Printing Books-Publishing/Printing

(G-5275)
ASML US LLC
77 Danbury Rd (06897-4407)
PHONE....203 761-4000
Noreen Harned, *Vice Pres*
Gary Zhang, *Vice Pres*
Terry Blakeslee, *Engineer*
David Calabro, *Engineer*
Chris Delangis, *Engineer*
EMP: 800
SALES (corp-wide): 12.1B **Privately Held**
SIC: 3555 Mfg Printing Trades Machinery
HQ: Asml Us, Llc
2650 W Geronimo Pl
Chandler AZ 85224
480 696-2888

(G-5276)
BEIERSDORF INC (DH)
45 Danbury Rd (06897-4405)
PHONE....203 563-5800
Amy Nenner, *Vice Pres*
Kathy Shea, *Vice Pres*
Mauricio Valdes, *Vice Pres*
Joerg Disseld, *CFO*
Alex Lund, *Marketing Staff*
▲ **EMP:** 9
SQ FT: 300,000
SALES (est): 223.4MM
SALES (corp-wide): 11.5B **Privately Held**
WEB: www.bdfusa.com
SIC: 2844 Mfg Toilet Preparations
HQ: Beiersdorf North America Inc.
45 Danbury Rd
Wilton CT 06897
203 563-5800

(G-5277)
BEIERSDORF NORTH AMERICA INC (DH)
45 Danbury Rd (06897-4405)
PHONE....203 563-5800
James A Kenton, *CEO*
Bill Graham, *President*
Stefan Heidenreich, *Chairman*
Sarah Simpson, *Business Mgr*
Jorg Diesfeld, *Vice Pres*
▲ **EMP:** 10
SALES (est): 223.4MM
SALES (corp-wide): 11.5B **Privately Held**
SIC: 2844 5122 3842 2841 Mfg Toilet Preparations Whol Drugs/Sundries Mfg Surgical Appliances Mfg Soap/Other Detergent
HQ: Beiersdorf Ag
Unnastr. 48
Hamburg 20253
404 909-0

GEOGRAPHIC

(G-5278)
BIOWAVE INNOVATIONS LLC
274 Ridgefield Rd (06897-2335)
PHONE..................................203 982-8157
Donald Rabinovitch, *President*
EMP: 191
SALES (est): 8.5MM **Privately Held**
SIC: **3844** Designs Manufactures And Distributes X-Ray Apparatus And Radiographic Equipment

(G-5279)
BLUE BUFFALO COMPANY LTD (DH)
11 River Rd Ste 200 (06897-6011)
PHONE..................................203 762-9751
Kurt Schmidt, *CEO*
William Bishop, *Principal*
Bill Bishop, *Chairman*
Brenda Gonzalez, *Regional Mgr*
Debbie Skibo, *Regional Mgr*
EMP: 277
SALES (est): 441.6MM
SALES (corp-wide): 16.8B **Publicly Held**
SIC: **2047** 5149 Mfg Dog/Cat Food Whol Groceries
HQ: Blue Buffalo Pet Products, Inc.
11 River Rd Ste 103
Wilton CT 06897
203 762-9751

(G-5280)
BLUE BUFFALO PET PRODUCTS INC (HQ)
11 River Rd Ste 103 (06897-6011)
P.O. Box 770 (06897-0770)
PHONE..................................203 762-9751
William Bishop Jr, *President*
Kathryn K Garrison, *Vice Pres*
Gerald J Morris, *Vice Pres*
Mike Nathenson, *Treasurer*
Christian Setterlund, *Marketing Staff*
EMP: 47
SQ FT: 41,000
SALES: 1.2B
SALES (corp-wide): 16.8B **Publicly Held**
SIC: **2048** Mfg Prepared Feeds
PA: General Mills, Inc.
1 General Mills Blvd
Minneapolis MN 55426
763 764-7600

(G-5281)
BUCHANAN MINERALS LLC (DH)
57 Danbury Rd Ste 201 (06897-4439)
PHONE..................................304 392-1000
Arold R Spindler, *CEO*
Garold Spindler, *CEO*
James Campbell, *COO*
Robert Cline, *Vice Pres*
EMP: 53
SALES (est): 5.3MM
SALES (corp-wide): 1.9B **Privately Held**
SIC: **1241** Coal Mining Services
HQ: Coronado Coal Llc
57 Danbury Rd Ste 201
Wilton CT 06897
203 761-1291

(G-5282)
BUFFALO INDUSTRIAL FABRICS INC
372 Danbury Rd Ste 199 (06897-2523)
P.O. Box 607 (06897-0607)
PHONE..................................203 553-9400
Stewart Ehrenhaus, *President*
EMP: 5
SQ FT: 1,500
SALES (est): 702.8K **Privately Held**
SIC: **2281** Yarn Spinning Mill

(G-5283)
CHILDRENS HEALTH MARKET INC
27 Cannon Rd Ste 1b (06897-2627)
P.O. Box 7294 (06897-7294)
PHONE..................................203 762-2938
Nancy M Grace, *President*
Timothy C Grace, *Principal*
James C Grace, *Admin Sec*
EMP: 7
SQ FT: 1,400
SALES (est): 782.3K **Privately Held**
WEB: www.thegreatbodyshop.net
SIC: **2741** 8748 Publisher And Business Consultants

(G-5284)
CORONADO GROUP LLC (PA)
57 Danbury Rd Ste 201 (06897-4439)
PHONE..................................203 761-1291
Jeff Bitzer, *Vice Pres*
Garold R Spindler, *Mng Member*
EMP: 6 **EST**: 2015
SALES (est): 1.9B **Privately Held**
SIC: **1241** Coal Mining Services

(G-5285)
CORTINA LEARNING INTL INC (PA)
Also Called: Cortina Famous Schools
33 Catalpa Rd (06897-2002)
PHONE..................................800 245-2145
Robert E Livesey, *President*
Robert Ellis, *Vice Pres*
Magdalen B Livesey, *Admin Sec*
EMP: 12 **EST**: 1882
SALES (est): 1.6MM **Privately Held**
WEB: www.cortina-french.com
SIC: **2731** 8249 Books Publishing Only & Correspondence School

(G-5286)
CYCLING SPORTS GROUP INC (HQ)
Also Called: Cannondale Sports Group
1 Cannondale Way (06897-4319)
PHONE..................................608 268-8916
Peter Woods, *President*
Joshua Richman, *Business Mgr*
Peter Scannell, *Project Mgr*
Sean Jacobs, *CFO*
Dan Fiengo, *Credit Mgr*
◆ **EMP**: 70
SQ FT: 32,500
SALES (est): 112.7MM
SALES (corp-wide): 2.6B **Privately Held**
SIC: **3751** 2329 Mfg Motorcycles/Bicycles Mfg Men's/Boy's Clothing
PA: Industries Dorel Inc, Les
1255 Av Greene Bureau 300
Westmount QC H3Z 2
514 934-3034

(G-5287)
DAMPITS LLC
98 Ridgefield Rd (06897-2427)
PHONE..................................203 210-7946
David Hollander, *Principal*
EMP: 3
SALES (est): 296.3K **Privately Held**
SIC: **3634** Mfg Electric Housewares/Fans

(G-5288)
DIETZE & ASSOCIATES LLC
Also Called: Dietze Associates
88 Danbury Rd Ste 1a (06897-4423)
PHONE..................................203 762-3500
Herlof Sorensen, *Branch Mgr*
EMP: 14
SALES (est): 621K
SALES (corp-wide): 2.4MM **Privately Held**
SIC: **1311** Crude Petroleum/Natural Gas Production
PA: Dietze & Associates Llc
88 Danbury Rd Ste 1a
Wilton CT 06897
203 762-3500

(G-5289)
FEDERICI BRANDS LLC
195 Danbury Rd (06897-4075)
PHONE..................................203 762-7667
Jeff Livingston, *President*
James Federici, *Principal*
Lynn Federici, *VP Opers*
Joseph Cincotta, *Research*
John Roth, *CFO*
▲ **EMP**: 19
SALES (est): 3.3MM **Privately Held**
SIC: **3273** Mfg Ready-Mixed Concrete

(G-5290)
GROUP WORKS
50 Powder Horn Hill Rd (06897-3123)
P.O. Box 7269 (06897-7269)
PHONE..................................203 834-7905
Shane Scott, *Owner*
EMP: 4
SALES (est): 266.9K **Privately Held**
WEB: www.groupworksllc.com
SIC: **3949** 1799 Mfg Sporting/Athletic Goods Trade Contractor

(G-5291)
INFORMATION TODAY INC
Online
88 Danbury Rd Ste 2c (06897-4423)
PHONE..................................203 761-1466
John Sculley, *Partner*
Adam Pemberton, *Manager*
EMP: 14
SALES (corp-wide): 20.3MM **Privately Held**
WEB: www.infotoday.com
SIC: **2721** 2731 7389 Periodicals-Publishing/Printing Books-Publishing/Printing Business Services
PA: Information Today, Inc.
143 Old Marlton Pike
Medford NJ 08055
609 654-6266

(G-5292)
JPG CONSULTING INC
65 Heather Ln (06897-4130)
PHONE..................................203 247-2730
Johnathan P Griep, *President*
Jonathan P Griep, *President*
Joseph Griep, *Vice Pres*
Mark Griep, *Treasurer*
Martha E Griep, *Admin Sec*
EMP: 3
SALES (est): 199K **Privately Held**
SIC: **7372** Prepackaged Software Services

(G-5293)
M&G BERMAN INC
67 Pond Rd (06897-3226)
PHONE..................................203 834-8754
Murray Berman, *Owner*
EMP: 4
SALES (est): 210.8K **Privately Held**
SIC: **2711** Newspapers-Publishing/Printing

(G-5294)
MKRS CORPORATION
32 Blueberry Hill Pl (06897-1406)
PHONE..................................203 762-2662
Rohit Sharma, *Principal*
EMP: 6
SALES (est): 101.4K **Privately Held**
SIC: **2711** Newspapers-Publishing/Printing

(G-5295)
MPI SYSTEMS INC
28 Powder Horn Hill Rd (06897-3121)
PHONE..................................203 762-2260
Richard Kaye, *President*
Annette G Kaye, *Vice Pres*
EMP: 5
SALES (est): 487.5K **Privately Held**
WEB: www.mpisystems.com
SIC: **7372** Prepackaged Software Services

(G-5296)
OPTICAL RESEARCH TECHNOLOGIES
310 Hurlbutt St (06897-2605)
P.O. Box 398 (06897-0398)
PHONE..................................203 762-9063
John Wilson, *Owner*
EMP: 3
SALES: 1.5MM **Privately Held**
WEB: www.wiltonsingers.com
SIC: **3827** Mfg Optical Instruments/Lenses

(G-5297)
OUTPOST EXPLORATION LLC
7 Broad Axe Ln (06897-3904)
PHONE..................................203 762-7206
Paul Mazzarulli, *Principal*
EMP: 3 **EST**: 2015
SALES (est): 127K **Privately Held**
SIC: **1311** Crude Petroleum/Natural Gas Production

(G-5298)
PATHFINDER SOLUTIONS GROUP LLC
116 Danbury Rd Unit 5232 (06897-4467)
PHONE..................................203 247-2479
Sean Drake, *Principal*
Brooks Bash, *Principal*
Keith Burge, *Principal*
EMP: 3
SALES (est): 71.1K **Privately Held**
SIC: **7372** Prepackaged Software

(G-5299)
POLSTAL CORPORATION
10 Admiral Ln (06897-4710)
PHONE..................................203 849-7788
Peter Wycislo, *President*
Danuta Wycislo, *Vice Pres*
▲ **EMP**: 4
SALES (est): 302K **Privately Held**
SIC: **3325** 3295 3315 Steel Foundry Mfg Minerals-Ground/Treated Mfg Steel Wire/Related Products

(G-5300)
PROSPEROUS PRINTING LLC
Also Called: Paul's Prosperous Printing
35 Danbury Rd Ste 4 (06897-4428)
PHONE..................................203 834-1962
Paul Hafter, *Mng Member*
EMP: 3
SQ FT: 1,700
SALES (est): 352.4K **Privately Held**
SIC: **2752** 2791 2789 Lithographic Commercial Printing Typesetting Services Bookbinding/Related Work

(G-5301)
RAVAGO AMERICAS LLC
Muehlstein
10 Westport Rd (06897-4543)
PHONE..................................203 855-6000
David Roesner, *Plant Mgr*
Margarita Salazar, *Export Mgr*
EMP: 50
SALES (corp-wide): 1.9MM **Privately Held**
SIC: **2821** Mfg Plastic Materials/Resins
HQ: Ravago Americas Llc
1900 Summit Tower Blvd
Orlando FL 32810
407 875-9595

(G-5302)
ROCKWELL ART & FRAMING LLC (PA)
Also Called: Wilton Art Framing
151 Old Ridgefield Rd # 101 (06897-3058)
PHONE..................................203 762-8311
Hector Rosario, *Owner*
EMP: 6
SQ FT: 1,500
SALES (est): 700.9K **Privately Held**
SIC: **2499** Picture Framing Retail

(G-5303)
SHILLER AND COMPANY INC
Also Called: Shillermath
258 Thunder Lake Rd (06897-1339)
PHONE..................................203 210-5208
Larry Shiller, *President*
EMP: 90
SALES: 1,000K **Privately Held**
SIC: **2741** Montessori-Based Curriculum Publishing

(G-5304)
SPRAYFOAMPOLYMERSCOM LLC
134 Old Ridgefield Rd # 3 (06897-3048)
P.O. Box 1182, New Canaan (06840-1182)
PHONE..................................800 853-1577
Richard Ettinger, *President*
EMP: 3
SALES (est): 870.6K **Privately Held**
SIC: **3086** 5199 Mfg Plastic Foam Products Whol Nondurable Goods

(G-5305)
STARTECH ENVIRONMENTAL CORP (PA)
88 Danbury Rd Ste 2b (06897-4423)
PHONE..................................203 762-2499
Joseph F Longo, *Ch of Bd*
Ralph N Dechiaro, *Vice Pres*
Peter J Scanlon, *CFO*
EMP: 14
SQ FT: 5,612

SALES: 157.4K **Privately Held**
WEB: www.startech.net
SIC: **3559** Mfg Misc Industry Machinery

(G-5306)
SYNERGY SOLUTIONS LLC
276 Newtown Tpke (06897-4715)
PHONE....................203 762-1153
Barney Stevenson,
EMP: 5
SALES (est): 400K **Privately Held**
WEB: www.solves-it.com
SIC: **7372** Prepackaged Software Services

(G-5307)
SYZYGY HALTHCARE SOLUTIONS LLC
33 Cannon Rd (06897-2619)
P.O. Box 588, Westport (06881-0588)
PHONE....................203 226-4449
John Linderman, *Mng Member*
EMP: 4
SQ FT: 5,000
SALES: 300K **Privately Held**
SIC: **2834** Mfg Pharmaceutical Preparations

(G-5308)
TOWN OF WILTON
Also Called: Public Works Dept
238 Danbury Rd (06897-4058)
PHONE....................203 563-0152
Thomas Therkepple, *Director*
EMP: 4 **Privately Held**
SIC: **3531** Mfg Construction Machinery
PA: Town Of Wilton
238 Danbury Rd
Wilton CT 06897
203 563-0100

(G-5309)
ULTIMATE INK LLC
681 Danbury Rd Ste 1 (06897-5024)
PHONE....................203 762-0602
James Gerwect,
EMP: 5
SQ FT: 500
SALES: 100K **Privately Held**
SIC: **2261** Cotton Finishing Plant

Winchester Center
Litchfield County

(G-5310)
CUSTOM INTERIORS
152 Colebrook River Rd (06098-2205)
PHONE....................860 738-8754
Glen Lauzier, *Principal*
EMP: 4
SALES (est): 658K **Privately Held**
SIC: **2434** Mfg Wood Kitchen Cabinets

Windham
Windham County

(G-5311)
E & J ANDRYCHOWSKI FARMS
257 Brick Top Rd (06280-1006)
PHONE....................860 423-4124
Robert Andrychowski, *Owner*
EMP: 3
SALES: 75K **Privately Held**
SIC: **2011** Meat Packing Plant

Windsor
Hartford County

(G-5312)
A & A PRODUCTS AND SERVICES
610 Hayden Station Rd (06095-1338)
PHONE....................860 683-0879
Fred Saleh, *Owner*
EMP: 3
SALES (est): 201.7K **Privately Held**
SIC: **3471** Servicing And Mfg

(G-5313)
A&S INNERSPRINGS USA LLC
4 Market Cir (06095-1422)
PHONE....................860 298-0401
Deborah Covey, *Mng Member*
EMP: 4 **EST**: 2016
SALES (est): 237.5K
SALES (corp-wide): 162.3MM **Privately Held**
SIC: **2515** Mfg Mattresses/Bedsprings
PA: Agro Holding Gmbh
Senfdamm 21
Bad Essen 49152
547 294-200

(G-5314)
ABB ENTERPRISE SOFTWARE INC
Also Called: Corporate
5 Waterside Xing Fl 3-2 (06095-1577)
PHONE....................860 285-0183
Steve Alger, *Branch Mgr*
EMP: 76
SALES (corp-wide): 36.7B **Privately Held**
WEB: www.elsterelectricity.com
SIC: **3612** Mfg Transformers
HQ: Abb Inc.
305 Gregson Dr
Cary NC 27511

(G-5315)
ACCUTRON INC
149 Addison Rd (06095-2102)
PHONE....................860 683-8300
Vijay R Faldu, *President*
Bhagwati Faldu, *COO*
Bharat R Faldu, *Vice Pres*
Bhagwati R Faldu, *Treasurer*
Parin Patel, *CTO*
▲ **EMP**: 110
SQ FT: 55,000
SALES: 25MM **Privately Held**
WEB: www.accutroninc.com
SIC: **3672** 3613 3441 Mfg Printed Circuit Boards Mfg Switchgear/Switchboards Structural Metal Fabrication

(G-5316)
AERO GEAR INCORPORATED
1050 Day Hill Rd (06095-4728)
PHONE....................860 688-0888
Douglas B Rose, *President*
Roger Burdick, *COO*
◆ **EMP**: 140
SQ FT: 78,000
SALES (est): 40.5MM **Privately Held**
WEB: www.aerogear.com
SIC: **3728** Mfg Aircraft Parts/Equipment

(G-5317)
AKO INC
Also Called: Torque Specialties
50 Baker Hollow Rd (06095-2133)
P.O. Box 1283, Enfield (06083-1283)
PHONE....................860 298-9765
Patrick Pierce, *CEO*
Doris Leclerc, *President*
Rachel Leclerc, *Admin Sec*
EMP: 20
SQ FT: 17,800
SALES (est): 4.6MM **Privately Held**
WEB: www.akotorque.com
SIC: **3825** 3545 3621 3823 Mfg Elec Measuring Instr Testing Laboratory Mfg Machine Tool Access Mfg Process Cntrl Instr Mfg Motors/Generators

(G-5318)
ALSTOM POWER CO
175 Addison Rd (06095-2178)
PHONE....................860 688-1911
EMP: 10
SALES (est): 650K
SALES (corp-wide): 121.6B **Publicly Held**
SIC: **3569** 8711 Mfg General Industrial Machinery Engineering Services
PA: General Electric Company
5 Necco St
Boston MA 02210
617 443-3000

(G-5319)
ALSTOM RENEWABLE US LLC
Also Called: GE Renewable Energy USA
200 Great Pond Dr (06095-1564)
PHONE....................860 688-1911
Teresa Rivera, *Technology*
Kevin Hulse, *Director*
EMP: 3
SALES (corp-wide): 121.6B **Publicly Held**
SIC: **3621** Mfg Motors/Generators
HQ: Alstom Renewable Us Llc
8000 E Maplewood Ave # 105
Greenwood Village CO 80111
303 730-4000

(G-5320)
ALVEST (USA) INC (HQ)
812 Bloomfield Ave (06095-2340)
PHONE....................860 602-3400
Mark Garlasco, *CEO*
Shaun Doyle, *Technician*
EMP: 29
SALES (est): 331MM
SALES (corp-wide): 28.3MM **Privately Held**
WEB: www.tldusa.com
SIC: **3585** 3535 Mfg Refrigeration/Heating Equipment Mfg Conveyors/Equipment
PA: Lbo France Gestion
148 Rue De L Universite
Paris 7e Arrondissement 75007
140 627-767

(G-5321)
APPLIED RUBBER & PLASTICS INC
100 Skitchewaug St (06095-4605)
PHONE....................860 987-9018
Brendan Ward Farrell, *President*
Patricia C Farrell, *Admin Sec*
Crystal Vono, *Admin Asst*
▲ **EMP**: 15
SQ FT: 20,000
SALES (est): 2.6MM **Privately Held**
WEB: www.appliedrubber-plastics.com
SIC: **3061** 5085 Mfg Mechanical Rubber Goods Whol Industrial Supplies

(G-5322)
BARNES GROUP INC
Also Called: Barnes Aerospace
169 Kennedy Rd (06095-2043)
PHONE....................860 298-7740
Jannett Williams, *President*
Dawn Johnson, *Division Mgr*
David Brunner, *Business Mgr*
Michael Beck, *Vice Pres*
Becky Newton, *Materials Mgr*
EMP: 1434
SQ FT: 160,000
SALES (corp-wide): 1.5B **Publicly Held**
WEB: www.barnesgroupinc.com
SIC: **3724** Mfg Aircraft Engines/Parts
PA: Barnes Group Inc.
123 Main St
Bristol CT 06010
860 583-7070

(G-5323)
C & C LOGGING
416 Pigeon Hill Rd (06095-2157)
PHONE....................860 683-0071
Grace Cranouski, *Principal*
EMP: 8
SALES (est): 723.1K **Privately Held**
SIC: **2411** Logging

(G-5324)
CARBIDE SOLUTIONS LLC
800 Marshall Phelps Rd (06095-2143)
PHONE....................860 515-8665
Alan M Stanek, *Principal*
EMP: 4 **EST**: 2015
SALES (est): 213K **Privately Held**
SIC: **2819** Mfg Industrial Inorganic Chemicals

(G-5325)
CHROMALLOY COMPONENT SVCS INC
Chromalloy Connecticuit
601 Marshall Phelps Rd (06095-5716)
PHONE....................860 688-7798
Robert Jones, *Manager*
EMP: 140
SQ FT: 50,000
SALES (corp-wide): 2.4B **Publicly Held**
WEB: www.chromalloysatx.com
SIC: **3724** 3812 2851 Mfg Aircraft Engines/Parts Mfg Search/Navigation Equipment Mfg Paints/Allied Products
HQ: Chromalloy Component Services, Inc.
303 Industrial Park Rd
San Antonio TX 78226
210 331-2300

(G-5326)
CHROMALLOY GAS TURBINE LLC
Also Called: Chromalloy Connecticut
601 Marshall Phelps Rd (06095-5716)
P.O. Box 748, Wallingford (06492-0748)
PHONE....................860 688-7798
Clive Bailey, *Principal*
Darlene Reedy, *Controller*
Miguel Acevedo, *Manager*
EMP: 77
SALES (corp-wide): 2.4B **Publicly Held**
SIC: **3724** Mfg Aircraft Engines/Parts
HQ: Chromalloy Gas Turbine Llc
3999 Rca Blvd
Palm Beach Gardens FL 33410
561 935-3571

(G-5327)
COOPER CROUSE-HINDS LLC
Airport Lighting Division
1200 Kennedy Rd (06095-1384)
PHONE....................860 683-4300
Mike West, *Sales Mgr*
Jason Smith, *Manager*
Gerald Smith, *Bd of Directors*
Jacob Hicock, *Technician*
EMP: 92
SQ FT: 66,000 **Privately Held**
SIC: **3069** 3648 Mfg Fabricated Rubber Products Mfg Lighting Equipment
HQ: Cooper Crouse-Hinds, Llc
1201 Wolf St
Syracuse NY 13208
315 477-7000

(G-5328)
DARLY CUSTOM TECHNOLOGY INC
276 Addison Rd (06095-2334)
P.O. Box 527 (06095-0527)
PHONE....................860 298-7966
Yimou Yang, *President*
Stanley J Misunas, *Vice Pres*
Yao Kuang Yang, *Treasurer*
HEI-Ju Yang, *Shareholder*
Li-Chiung CHI Yang, *Shareholder*
▲ **EMP**: 12
SQ FT: 15,000
SALES (est): 1.8MM **Privately Held**
WEB: www.darlytech.com
SIC: **3599** Mfg Industrial Machinery

(G-5329)
DOW DIV OF UTC
360 Bloomfield Ave (06095-2700)
PHONE....................860 683-7340
EMP: 3
SALES (est): 208.5K **Privately Held**
SIC: **3613** Mfg Switchgear/Switchboards

(G-5330)
EATON ELECTRIC HOLDINGS LLC
Crouse-Hinds Airport Lighting
1200 Kennedy Rd (06095-1304)
PHONE....................860 683-4300
Kurt Foster, *Senior Engr*
Jack BAC, *Branch Mgr*
Dan Flanagan, *Manager*
Raymond Doyle, *Representative*
EMP: 16 **Privately Held**
SIC: **3648** Mfg Lighting Equipment
HQ: Eaton Electric Holdings Llc
1000 Eaton Blvd
Cleveland OH 44122
440 523-5000

(G-5331)
EMHART GLASS INC (DH)
123 Great Pond Dr (06095-1569)
P.O. Box 220 (06095-0220)
PHONE....................860 298-7340

GEOGRAPHIC

Joseph Laundry, *President*
Xu Ding, *Senior Engr*
Paula Messier, *Human Res Mgr*
Alan Batchelor, *Manager*
Walter E Lovell, *Info Tech Mgr*
◆ **EMP:** 65
SALES (est): 41.1MM
SALES (corp-wide): 3.1B **Privately Held**
SIC: 3559 Mfg Misc Industry Machinery
HQ: Emhart Glass Sa
Hinterbergstrasse 22
Steinhausen ZG 6312
417 494-200

(G-5332)
EMHART GLASS MANUFACTURING INC (DH)
123 Great Pond Dr (06095-1569)
P.O. Box 220 (06095-0220)
PHONE..................................860 298-7340
Martin Jetter, *President*
William Grninger, *Vice Pres*
Jeffrey D Hartung, *Vice Pres*
Christer Hermansson, *Vice Pres*
Matthias Kmmerle, *Vice Pres*
▲ **EMP:** 20
SALES (est): 32.3MM
SALES (corp-wide): 3.1B **Privately Held**
WEB: www.emhartglass.com
SIC: 3221 Mfg Glass Containers
HQ: Emhart Glass Inc.
123 Great Pond Dr
Windsor CT 06095
860 298-7340

(G-5333)
EUROPA SPORTS PRODUCTS INC
755 Rainbow Rd (06095-1024)
PHONE..................................860 688-1110
Stan Schapp, *Manager*
EMP: 8
SALES (corp-wide): 296.1MM **Privately Held**
SIC: 3949 Mfg Sporting/Athletic Goods
PA: Europa Sports Products, Inc.
11401 Granite St Ste H
Charlotte NC 28273
704 405-2022

(G-5334)
FOUNDATION CIGAR COMPANY LLC
110 Day Hill Rd (06095-2296)
PHONE..................................203 738-9377
Michael Hyatt, *Opers Dir*
Nicholas Melillo, *Mng Member*
EMP: 11
SALES (est): 1.5MM **Privately Held**
SIC: 2121 5194 5993 Mfg Cigars Whol Tobacco Products Ret Tobacco Products

(G-5335)
GE GRID SOLUTIONS LLC
175 Addison Rd (06095-2178)
PHONE..................................425 250-2695
EMP: 3 **EST:** 2017
SALES (est): 267.4K **Privately Held**
SIC: 3613 Mfg Switchgear/Switchboards

(G-5336)
GE STEAM POWER INC (HQ)
Also Called: Alstom Power Co
175 Addison Rd (06095-2178)
PHONE..................................866 257-8664
Conor Begley, *President*
Jonathan Wenger, *General Mgr*
Richard D Austin, *Vice Pres*
Francois Berthiaume, *Vice Pres*
Jorge Cavazos, *Vice Pres*
◆ **EMP:** 1200
SQ FT: 286,000
SALES (est): 838.7MM
SALES (corp-wide): 121.6B **Publicly Held**
WEB: www.boilerperformance.com
SIC: 3621 3823 8711 4931 Mfg Motors/Generators Mfg Process Cntrl Instr Engineering Services Electric/Other Services Electric Services
PA: General Electric Company
5 Necco St
Boston MA 02210
617 443-3000

(G-5337)
HFO CHICAGO LLC
910 Day Hill Rd (06095-5727)
PHONE..................................860 285-0709
Bradley R Morris, *Manager*
EMP: 7
SALES (est): 994.4K **Privately Held**
SIC: 3599 Mfg Industrial Machinery

(G-5338)
HUBERGROUP USA INC
147 Addison Rd (06095-2102)
PHONE..................................860 687-1617
Jeffrey Sorensen, *Manager*
EMP: 12
SALES (corp-wide): 355.8K **Privately Held**
WEB: www.hostmann-steinberg.com
SIC: 2893 Mfg Printing Ink
HQ: Hubergroup Usa, Inc.
1701 Golf Rd Ste 3-201
Rolling Meadows IL 60008
815 929-9293

(G-5339)
HW GRAPHICS
92 Wyndemere Ln (06095-1178)
PHONE..................................860 278-2338
Hector V Webb, *Owner*
EMP: 3
SALES: 82K **Privately Held**
SIC: 2759 Lithographic Commercial Printing

(G-5340)
ITT STANDARD
1036 Poquonock Ave (06095-1860)
PHONE..................................860 683-2144
Debra Avenali, *Principal*
EMP: 3
SALES (est): 162.1K **Privately Held**
SIC: 3443 Mfg Fabricated Plate Work

(G-5341)
JOHNSON CONTROLS INC
21 Griffin Rd N Ste 4 (06095-1512)
PHONE..................................860 688-7151
Donna Biaggiotti, *Manager*
EMP: 120 **Privately Held**
SIC: 3822 Mfg Environmental Controls Whol Heat Air Conditioner Equipment And Supplies
HQ: Johnson Controls Inc
5757 N Green Bay Ave
Milwaukee WI 53209
414 524-1200

(G-5342)
JPSEXTON LLC
460 Hayden Station Rd (06095-1367)
PHONE..................................860 748-2048
Davis Perlroth,
Davis B Perlroth,
EMP: 4 **EST:** 2012
SALES (est): 416K **Privately Held**
SIC: 3714 Mfg Motor Vehicle Parts/Accessories

(G-5343)
KITCHEN KRAFTSMEN
77 Pierson Ln Ste A (06095-2000)
PHONE..................................860 616-1240
EMP: 3 **EST:** 2013
SALES (est): 190K **Privately Held**
SIC: 2434 Wood Kitchen Cabinets

(G-5344)
LEIPOLD INC
545 Marshall Phelps Rd (06095-1702)
PHONE..................................860 298-9791
Pascal Schiefer, *President*
Thomas Fees, *Vice Pres*
Ewa Boucher, *QC Mgr*
Lydia Blanche, *Sales Mgr*
Christoph Lange, *Admin Sec*
▲ **EMP:** 30 **EST:** 1997
SALES (est): 6.9MM
SALES (corp-wide): 775.7K **Privately Held**
WEB: www.leipold-inc.com
SIC: 3451 M F G Screw Machine Products
HQ: Carl Leipold Gmbh
Schiltacher Str. 5
Wolfach 77709
783 483-950

(G-5345)
LONG ISLAND PIPE SUPPLY INC
Also Called: LONG ISLAND PIPE SUPPLY OF ALBANY, INC.
1220 Kennedy Rd (06095-1328)
PHONE..................................860 688-1780
Mark Krause, *Manager*
EMP: 6
SALES (corp-wide): 2.6B **Privately Held**
WEB: www.lipipe.com
SIC: 3498 Mfg Fabricated Pipe/Fittings
HQ: Miles Moss Of Albany, Inc.
586 Commercial Ave
Garden City NY 11530
516 222-8008

(G-5346)
MANUFACTURING PRODUCTIVI
910 Day Hill Rd (06095-5727)
PHONE..................................860 916-8189
Lee Morris, *Principal*
EMP: 3 **EST:** 2009
SALES (est): 196.7K **Privately Held**
SIC: 3999 Mfg Misc Products

(G-5347)
MATERION LRGE AREA CATINGS LLC (DH)
300 Lamberton Rd (06095-2131)
PHONE..................................216 486-4200
Michael Giuliana, *CFO*
Lee Donohue, *Technology*
▲ **EMP:** 53
SQ FT: 30,000
SALES (est): 15MM
SALES (corp-wide): 1.2B **Publicly Held**
WEB: www.techni-met.com
SIC: 3479 Coating/Engraving Service
HQ: Materion Advanced Materials Technologies And Services Inc.
2978 Main St
Buffalo NY 14214
800 327-1355

(G-5348)
MEDIA LINKS INC
431-C Hayden Station Rd (06095)
PHONE..................................860 206-9163
Takatsugu Ono, *CEO*
John Dale III, *Vice Pres*
EMP: 14
SQ FT: 10,000
SALES: 24.4MM **Privately Held**
SIC: 3663 Mfg Radio/Tv Communication Equipment
PA: Media Links Co., Ltd.
580-16, Horikawacho, Saiwai-Ku
Kawasaki KNG 212-0
-

(G-5349)
METAL IMPROVEMENT COMPANY LLC
145 Addison Rd (06095-2102)
PHONE..................................860 688-6201
Cesar Gonzales, *QC Mgr*
Kelly Hoffman, *Manager*
Nikia Wallace, *Executive*
EMP: 28
SALES (corp-wide): 2.4B **Publicly Held**
SIC: 3398 Metal Heat Treating
HQ: Metal Improvement Company, Llc
80 E Rte 4 Ste 310
Paramus NJ 07652
201 843-7800

(G-5350)
NEL GROUP LLC
154 Broad St (06095-2944)
PHONE..................................860 683-0190
EMP: 10
SALES (corp-wide): 6MM **Privately Held**
SIC: 2066 5149 5441 5199 Mfg Chocolate/Cocoa Prdt Whol Groceries Ret Candy/Confectionery Whol Nondurable Goods Ret Gifts/Novelties
PA: Nel Group Llc
32 Rainbow Rd
East Granby CT 06026
860 413-9042

(G-5351)
O S WALKER COMPANY INC (DH)
600 Day Hill Rd (06095-1703)
PHONE..................................508 853-3232
Richard Longo, *President*
Debra Krikorian, *Corp Secy*
Ken Wanko, *Director*
▲ **EMP:** 70
SALES (est): 15.5MM
SALES (corp-wide): 116.9MM **Privately Held**
WEB: www.speckvc.com
SIC: 3545 Mfg Machine Tool Accessories
HQ: Walker Magnetics Group, Inc.
600 Day Hill Rd
Windsor CT 06095
508 853-3232

(G-5352)
OSF FLAVORS INC (PA)
40 Baker Hollow Rd (06095-2133)
P.O. Box 591 (06095-0591)
PHONE..................................860 298-8350
Olivier De Botton, *CEO*
Eduardo De Botao, *President*
Jim Bartlein, *Accounts Mgr*
Alan Ladd, *Manager*
▲ **EMP:** 15
SQ FT: 18,000
SALES (est): 4.2MM **Privately Held**
WEB: www.osfflavors.com
SIC: 2087 Mfg Flavor Extracts/Syrup

(G-5353)
PEPSI-COLA METRO BTLG CO INC
Also Called: Pepsico
55 International Dr (06095-1062)
PHONE..................................860 688-6281
Mario Ramirez, *Project Mgr*
Doug Lord, *Opers Mgr*
Matt Karl, *Finance Mgr*
David Cronin, *Manager*
EMP: 125
SALES (corp-wide): 64.6B **Publicly Held**
WEB: www.pbg.com
SIC: 2086 Carb Sft Drnkbtlcn
HQ: Pepsi-Cola Metropolitan Bottling Company, Inc.
1111 Westchester Ave
White Plains NY 10604
914 767-6000

(G-5354)
PIONEER CAPITAL CORP
651 Day Hill Rd (06095-1798)
PHONE..................................860 683-2005
John Ferraro, *President*
Robert Lerman, *Treasurer*
EMP: 4 **EST:** 1988
SALES (est): 206.9K **Privately Held**
SIC: 3443 Mfg Of Heat Exchangers

(G-5355)
POLYTRONICS CORPORATION
800 Marshall Phelps Rd 1hi (06095-2143)
PHONE..................................860 683-2442
Michael Serrano, *President*
▲ **EMP:** 5
SQ FT: 10,000
SALES (est): 248.9K **Privately Held**
SIC: 3089 Mfg Of Injection Molding Of Plastics

(G-5356)
PRECISION FINISHING SVCS INC
60 Ezra Silva Ln (06095-2122)
P.O. Box 189, North Granby (06060-0189)
PHONE..................................860 882-1073
Arthur French, *President*
Linda Clark, *Executive Asst*
EMP: 20
SQ FT: 33,000
SALES (est): 2.2MM **Privately Held**
WEB: www.precisionfinishingservices.com
SIC: 3471 Metal Finishing

(G-5357)
RAPIDEX
875 Marshall Phelps Rd (06095-2108)
PHONE..................................860 285-8818
Darek Luciarz, *Owner*
EMP: 6
SQ FT: 16,324

SALES (est): 721.6K **Privately Held**
SIC: 3599 Machine Shop

(G-5358)
RELX INC
15 Cobbler Way (06095-1747)
PHONE.................................860 219-0733
EMP: 5
SALES (corp-wide): 9.8B **Privately Held**
SIC: 3541 Mfg Machine Tools-Cutting
HQ: Relx Inc.
230 Park Ave Ste 700
New York NY 10169
212 309-8100

(G-5359)
SCA PHARMACEUTICALS LLC
755 Rainbow Rd Bldg 1 (06095-1024)
PHONE.................................501 312-2800
Roy Graves, *President*
Matthew Graves, *COO*
EMP: 7
SQ FT: 75,000
SALES (est): 1MM
SALES (corp-wide): 11.7MM **Privately Held**
SIC: 2834 Pharmaceutical Preparations
PA: Sca Pharmaceuticals, Llc
8821 Knoedl Ct
Little Rock AR 72205
501 312-2800

(G-5360)
SCAPA HOLDINGS INC (HQ)
111 Great Pond Dr (06095-1527)
PHONE.................................860 688-8000
Steve Lennon, *Chief*
EMP: 300
SALES (est): 91.9MM
SALES (corp-wide): 401.1MM **Privately Held**
SIC: 2672 Paper Coated And Laminated
PA: Scapa Group Public Limited Company
994 Manchester Road
Ashton-Under-Lyne LANCS OL7 0
161 301-7400

(G-5361)
SCAPA TAPES NORTH AMERICA LLC (DH)
Also Called: Finite Industries
111 Great Pond Dr (06095-1527)
PHONE.................................860 688-8000
Heejae Chae, *CEO*
Eric Springer, *President*
Margaret Gilmartin, *Vice Pres*
Michael Muchin, *Vice Pres*
Santos Mendez, *Supervisor*
◆ **EMP:** 138
SQ FT: 112,000
SALES (est): 61.1MM
SALES (corp-wide): 401.1MM **Privately Held**
WEB: www.scapa.com
SIC: 3842 Mfg Surgical Appliances/Supplies
HQ: Scapa North America Inc
111 Great Pond Dr
Windsor CT 06095
860 688-8000

(G-5362)
SECURITIES SOFTWARE & CONSULTI
80 Lamberton Rd (06095-2136)
PHONE.................................860 298-4500
William C Stone, *Principal*
EMP: 9
SALES (est): 704.7K **Privately Held**
SIC: 7372 Prepackaged Software Services

(G-5363)
SPENCER TURBINE COMPANY (HQ)
600 Day Hill Rd (06095-4706)
PHONE.................................860 688-8361
Antonio Mancini, *Exec VP*
Tony Mancini, *Exec VP*
Patti Mullins, *Plant Mgr*
Earle Fredericksen, *Buyer*
Jim Burns, *Engineer*
◆ **EMP:** 146
SQ FT: 200,000
SALES (est): 51.6MM
SALES (corp-wide): 116.9MM **Privately Held**
SIC: 3589 3564 3498 5084 Mfg Svc Industry Mach Mfg Blowers/Fans Mfg Fabrctd Pipe/Fitting Whol Industrial Equip
PA: Alliance Holdings, Inc.
100 Witmer Rd Ste 170
Horsham PA 19044
215 706-0873

(G-5364)
SS&C TECHNOLOGIES INC
261 Broad St (06095-2906)
PHONE.................................860 930-5882
EMP: 3
SALES (corp-wide): 3.4B **Publicly Held**
SIC: 7372 Prepackaged Software Services
HQ: Ss&C Technologies, Inc.
80 Lamberton Rd
Windsor CT 06095
860 298-4500

(G-5365)
SS&C TECHNOLOGIES INC (HQ)
80 Lamberton Rd (06095-2136)
PHONE.................................860 298-4500
William C Stone, *Ch of Bd*
Normand A Boulanger, *President*
Campbell R Dyer, *Principal*
Marshall Pimenta, *Principal*
Claudius E Watts IV, *Principal*
EMP: 200
SQ FT: 73,000
SALES (est): 335.3MM
SALES (corp-wide): 3.4B **Publicly Held**
WEB: www.ssctech.com
SIC: 7372 7371 8741 Prepackaged Software Services Custom Computer Programing Management Services
PA: Ss&C Technologies Holdings, Inc.
80 Lamberton Rd
Windsor CT 06095
860 298-4500

(G-5366)
SS&C TECHNOLOGIES HOLDINGS INC (PA)
Also Called: SS&c Holdings
80 Lamberton Rd (06095-2136)
PHONE.................................860 298-4500
William C Stone, *Ch of Bd*
Normand A Boulanger, *Vice Ch Bd*
Laton Spahr, *President*
Craig Schachter, *Managing Dir*
Christy Bremner, *Vice Pres*
EMP: 68
SQ FT: 93,500
SALES: 3.4B **Publicly Held**
SIC: 7372 7371 Prepackaged Software Services Custom Computer Programing

(G-5367)
STANADYNE INTRMDATE HLDNGS LLC (HQ)
92 Deerfield Rd (06095-4200)
PHONE.................................860 525-0821
David P Galuska, *CEO*
John A Pinson, *President*
Stephen S Langin, *CFO*
Steve Rodgers, *Treasurer*
▲ **EMP:** 250
SQ FT: 662,000
SALES: 210MM **Privately Held**
SIC: 3714 3492 Mfg Motor Vehicle Parts/Accessories Mfg Fluid Power Valves/Fittings
PA: Stanadyne Parent Holdings, Inc.
92 Deerfield Rd
Windsor CT 06095
860 525-0821

(G-5368)
STANADYNE LLC (DH)
92 Deerfield Rd (06095-4200)
PHONE.................................860 525-0821
David P Galuska, *CEO*
John A Pinson, *President*
Terrence Gilbert, *General Mgr*
David Galuska, *COO*
Jesse Palermo, *Project Mgr*
◆ **EMP:** 950
SQ FT: 642,000
SALES (est): 209.8MM
SALES (corp-wide): 210MM **Privately Held**
SIC: 3714 Mfg Motor Vehicle Parts/Accessories
HQ: Stanadyne Intermediate Holdings, Llc
92 Deerfield Rd
Windsor CT 06095
860 525-0821

(G-5369)
STAUFFER SHEET METAL LLC
56 Depot St (06006-0001)
PHONE.................................860 623-0518
Kenneth Stauffer, *Owner*
EMP: 9
SQ FT: 10,400
SALES (est): 961.5K **Privately Held**
SIC: 3444 Mfg Sheet Metalwork

(G-5370)
SUBINAS USA LLC
4 Market Cir (06095-1422)
PHONE.................................860 298-0401
Daniel Herran, *Mng Member*
▲ **EMP:** 10
SALES (est): 1.9MM **Privately Held**
SIC: 2515 Mfg Mattresses/Bedsprings

(G-5371)
T & T AUTOMATION INC
88 Pierson Ln (06095-2049)
PHONE.................................860 683-8788
Ben Terkildsen, *President*
EMP: 12
SQ FT: 8,000
SALES: 1.2MM **Privately Held**
SIC: 3625 Mfg Relays/Industrial Controls

(G-5372)
TAYLOR & FENN COMPANY
22 Deerfield Rd (06095-4237)
PHONE.................................860 219-9393
Edgar B Butler Jr, *Vice Ch Bd*
Brian Butler, *Chairman*
◆ **EMP:** 100 **EST:** 1834
SQ FT: 130,000
SALES (est): 12.2MM **Privately Held**
WEB: www.taylorfenn.com
SIC: 3321 Gray/Ductile Iron Foundry

(G-5373)
TIMBER FRAME BARN CONVERSIONS
226 Rollingbrook (06095-1364)
PHONE.................................860 219-0519
Brian P Cigal, *Principal*
EMP: 4
SALES (est): 382.4K **Privately Held**
SIC: 2439 Mfg Structural Wood Members

(G-5374)
TLD ACE CORPORATION
805 Bloomfield Ave (06095-2341)
PHONE.................................860 602-3300
Mark Garlasco, *CEO*
Antoine Maguin, *President*
Peter Owitz, *COO*
Herve Criquillion, *Vice Pres*
Julian Stinton, *Vice Pres*
◆ **EMP:** 300 **EST:** 1953
SQ FT: 75,000
SALES: 165MM
SALES (corp-wide): 28.3MM **Privately Held**
WEB: www.tld-group.com
SIC: 3585 Mfg Refrigeration/Heating Equipment
HQ: Alvest (Usa) Inc.
812 Bloomfield Ave
Windsor CT 06095

(G-5375)
TOMMY LLC SOCK IT
4 Walters Way (06095-1071)
PHONE.................................860 688-2019
Thomas Defranzo, *Principal*
EMP: 3
SALES (est): 162.3K **Privately Held**
SIC: 2252 Mfg Hosiery

(G-5376)
TRIUMPH ACTUATION SYSTEMS - CO (HQ)
175 Addison Rd Ste 4 (06095-2179)
PHONE.................................860 687-5412
Daniel Crowley, *CEO*
Richard C Ill, *Ch of Bd*
Jeffry D Frisby, *President*
Tom Holtzum, *President*
Tony Leblanc, *General Mgr*
▲ **EMP:** 85
SALES (est): 31.4MM **Publicly Held**
WEB: www.htdaerospace.com
SIC: 3728 Mfg Aircraft Parts/Equipment

(G-5377)
VULCAN INDUSTRIES INC
651 Day Hill Rd (06095-1798)
PHONE.................................860 683-2005
Robert Lerman, *CEO*
Keith Briggs, *General Mgr*
John Ferarro, *Chairman*
John Hughes, *Director*
Fred Samuelson, *Director*
EMP: 142
SQ FT: 33,000
SALES (est): 12.1MM
SALES (corp-wide): 7.4MM **Publicly Held**
WEB: www.thermodynetics.com
SIC: 3714 3444 3443 Mfg Motor Vehicle Parts/Accessories Mfg Sheet Metalwork Mfg Fabricated Plate Work
PA: Thermodynetics, Inc.
651 Day Hill Rd
Windsor CT 06095
860 683-2005

(G-5378)
WALKER MAGNETICS GROUP INC (HQ)
600 Day Hill Rd (06095-1703)
PHONE.................................508 853-3232
John Morissette, *President*
Patricia Mullins, *Prdtn Mgr*
Debra Krikorian, *CFO*
◆ **EMP:** 45
SQ FT: 89,000
SALES: 20MM
SALES (corp-wide): 116.9MM **Privately Held**
WEB: www.walkermagnet.com
SIC: 3545 3559 3845 3535 Mfg Machine Tool Access Mfg Misc Industry Mach Mfg Electromedical Equip Mfg Conveyors/Equipment
PA: Alliance Holdings, Inc.
100 Witmer Rd Ste 170
Horsham PA 19044
215 706-0873

(G-5379)
WILSON WOODWORKS INC
100 Lamberton Rd (06095-2124)
PHONE.................................860 870-2500
Jonathan Boullay, *President*
EMP: 18
SALES (est): 3.2MM **Privately Held**
SIC: 2426 Hardwood Dimension/Floor Mill

Windsor Locks
Hartford County

(G-5380)
ACCURATE WELDING SERVICES LLC
7 Industrial Rd (06096-1101)
PHONE.................................860 623-9500
Edward Loiseau, *Mng Member*
EMP: 10
SALES (est): 488K **Privately Held**
SIC: 7692 Welding Repair

(G-5381)
AHLSTROM WINDSOR LOCKS LLC
3 Chirnside Rd (06096-1142)
PHONE.................................860 654-8629
◆ **EMP:** 11
SALES (est): 2.4MM **Privately Held**
SIC: 2621 Paper Mill

GEOGRAPHIC

(G-5382)
AHLSTROM-MUNKSJO NONWOVENS LLC (DH)
2 Elm St (06096-2335)
P.O. Box 270 (06096-0270)
PHONE....860 654-8300
Gary Blevins, *President*
Donna Decoteau, *Treasurer*
Leonard Mirahver, *Asst Treas*
Matthew Spaulding, *Asst Treas*
David Pluta, *Admin Sec*
◆ **EMP:** 264
SALES (est): 322.3MM
SALES (corp-wide): 2.7B **Privately Held**
SIC: 2591 3291 Mfg Drapery Hardware/Blinds Mfg Abrasive Products

(G-5383)
AHLSTROM-MUNKSJO USA INC (HQ)
2 Elm St (06096-2335)
P.O. Box 270 (06096-0270)
PHONE....860 654-8300
William Casey, *President*
Christopher Coates, *Vice Pres*
David T Pluta, *Vice Pres*
Leonard H Mirahver, *Treasurer*
Gustav Adlercreutz, *Asst Sec*
▼ **EMP:** 11
SALES (est): 461.7MM
SALES (corp-wide): 2.7B **Privately Held**
SIC: 2621 Paper Mill
PA: Ahlstrom-Munksjo Oyj
Alvar Aallon Katu 3c
Helsinki 00100
108 880-

(G-5384)
ALLEN PRECISION LLC
1 Northgate Dr (06096-1206)
PHONE....860 370-9881
Thomas A Pouliot, *Mng Member*
EMP: 3
SALES (est): 445.4K **Privately Held**
SIC: 3599 Mfg Industrial Machinery

(G-5385)
ALTHOR PRODUCTS LLC
200 Old County Cir # 116 (06096-1599)
PHONE....860 386-6700
Matthew Anderson, *Mng Member*
Kelly E Anderson,
EMP: 3
SQ FT: 5,000
SALES: 750K **Privately Held**
WEB: www.althor.com
SIC: 3089 Mfg Plastic Products

(G-5386)
AWM LLC
Also Called: American Molding
100 D Neil Hagen Dr (06096-1595)
PHONE....860 386-1000
EMP: 55
SALES (corp-wide): 155.7MM **Privately Held**
SIC: 3089 5031 Mfg Plastic Products Whol Lumber/Plywood/Millwork
PA: Awm, Llc
1800 Washington Blvd # 140
Baltimore MD 21230
410 694-6802

(G-5387)
BROOME & COMPANY LLC
12 Copper Dr (06096-2624)
PHONE....860 623-0254
David A Broome,
Caroline Broome,
Catherine Broome,
Christopher Broome,
EMP: 4
SALES (est): 190K **Privately Held**
SIC: 3931 Mfg Musical Instruments

(G-5388)
CHARLIES RIDE
389 North St (06096-1204)
PHONE....860 916-3637
Beth Hensel, *Principal*
EMP: 3 **EST:** 2011
SALES (est): 179.6K **Privately Held**
SIC: 3845 Mfg Electromedical Equipment

(G-5389)
COLONIAL PRINTERS OF WINDSOR
1 Concorde Way (06096-1533)
PHONE....860 627-5433
Gary Christensen, *President*
Margaret Christensen, *President*
Robert B Christensen, *Director*
EMP: 4
SQ FT: 3,200
SALES (est): 497.8K **Privately Held**
SIC: 2752 2759 Offset & Letterpress Printing Service

(G-5390)
DARCY SAW LLC
10 Canal Bank Rd (06096-2329)
PHONE....800 569-1264
John D'Arcy,
EMP: 3
SQ FT: 5,000
SALES: 1.2MM **Privately Held**
SIC: 3425 3546 Mfg Saw Blades/Handsaws Mfg Power-Driven Handtools

(G-5391)
DYNAMIC CONTROLS HS INC
1 Hamilton Rd (06096-1000)
PHONE....860 654-6000
EMP: 4
SALES (est): 252.4K
SALES (corp-wide): 66.5B **Publicly Held**
WEB: www.utc.com
SIC: 3812 3724 Search And Navigation Equipment, Nsk
PA: United Technologies Corporation
10 Farm Springs Rd
Farmington CT 06032
860 728-7000

(G-5392)
EMBRAER EXECUTIVE JET SVCS LLC
Also Called: Embraer Executive Jets
41 Perimeter Rd (06096-1069)
PHONE....860 804-4600
Eric Pettersen, *Manager*
EMP: 8 **Privately Held**
SIC: 3721 Mfg Aircraft
HQ: Embraer Executive Jet Services, Llc
2008 General Aviation Dr
Melbourne FL 32935
321 751-5050

(G-5393)
GIRARDIN MOULDING INC
564 Halfway House Rd (06096-1500)
P.O. Box 577 (06096-0577)
PHONE....860 623-4486
Gaston Girardin, *President*
Daniel Girardin, *Vice Pres*
Gail Girardin, *Admin Sec*
EMP: 15 **EST:** 1952
SQ FT: 55,000
SALES (est): 3MM **Privately Held**
WEB: www.girardinmoulding.com
SIC: 3442 Mfg Metal Doors/Sash/Trim

(G-5394)
GREIF INC
491 North St (06096-1140)
PHONE....740 549-6000
Miles Withington, *Purchasing*
Dinal Patel, *Engineer*
Cristina Gonzalez, *Personnel*
David Russolski, *Manager*
Steve Gendreau, *Maintence Staff*
EMP: 70
SALES (corp-wide): 4.6B **Publicly Held**
WEB: www.greif.com
SIC: 2655 Mfg Fiber Cans & Drums
PA: Greif, Inc.
425 Winter Rd
Delaware OH 43015
740 549-6000

(G-5395)
HAMILTON SNDSTRND SPACE
1 Hamilton Rd (06096-1000)
PHONE....860 654-6000
Edward Francis, *President*
Lawrence McNamara, *General Mgr*
Daneil Lee, *Dir Ops-Prd-Mfg*
Michael Randall, *Treasurer*
Paul Carew, *Asst Treas*
▲ **EMP:** 700
SQ FT: 230,000
SALES (est): 163MM **Privately Held**
SIC: 3841 3826 Mfg Surgical/Medical Instruments Mfg Analytical Instruments

(G-5396)
HAMILTON STANDARD SPACE
1 Hamilton Rd (06096-1010)
PHONE....860 654-6000
Harry Garfinkel, *President*
Annemarie Orange, *General Mgr*
David Rovazzini, *Engineer*
Brian Shannon, *Engineer*
Steve Ash, *Manager*
EMP: 24
SALES (est): 3.6MM **Privately Held**
SIC: 3822 3728 3842 3569 Mfg Environmental Control Life Support Systems Space Suits & Oxygen And Hydrogen Generation Units

(G-5397)
HAMILTON SUNDSTRAND CORP (HQ)
Also Called: UTC Aerospace Systems
1 Hamilton Rd (06096-1000)
PHONE....860 654-6000
Kelly Ortberg, *CEO*
Robert Schechtman, *Business Mgr*
Usman Toor, *Project Mgr*
Tim Topitzer, *Opers Mgr*
Michael Cicero, *Engineer*
◆ **EMP:** 800 **EST:** 1910
SALES (est): 3.4B
SALES (corp-wide): 66.5B **Publicly Held**
WEB: www.hamilton-standard.com
SIC: 3621 3625 3728 3594 Mfg Motors/Generators Mfg Relay/Indstl Control Mfg Aircraft Parts/Equip Mfg Fluid Power Pump/Mtr
PA: United Technologies Corporation
10 Farm Springs Rd
Farmington CT 06032
860 728-7000

(G-5398)
PINE MEADOW MACHINE CO INC
5 Webb St (06096-2500)
PHONE....860 623-4494
Thomas Bernadz, *President*
Paul Bernardz, *Vice Pres*
EMP: 6 **EST:** 1950
SQ FT: 35,000
SALES: 310K **Privately Held**
SIC: 3599 3545 Aerospace Machine Shop

(G-5399)
QUICK TURN MACHINE COMPANY INC
1000 Old County Cir # 105 (06096-1570)
PHONE....860 623-2569
Maria Rafalowski, *President*
Stanley Rafalowski, *Vice Pres*
Jessica Viggiano, *Sales Staff*
EMP: 15
SQ FT: 21,000
SALES (est): 3MM **Privately Held**
WEB: www.quickturnmfg.com
SIC: 3599 Mfg Industrial Machinery

(G-5400)
SPECTRUM MACHINE & DESIGN LLC
800 Old County Cir (06096-1575)
P.O. Box 4144 (06096-4144)
PHONE....860 386-6490
Gary Poesnecker,
Connie Poesnecker,
EMP: 8
SQ FT: 4,000
SALES: 810K **Privately Held**
WEB: www.smd-llc.com
SIC: 3599 Mfg Industrial Machinery

(G-5401)
STANDARD BELLOWS CO (PA)
375 Ella Grasso Tpke (06096-1003)
PHONE....860 623-2307
Stanley E Tkacz Jr, *President*
Thomas J Tkacz, *Corp Secy*
Stanley Tkacz, *CFO*
Thomas Tkacz, *CPA*
EMP: 20 **EST:** 1961
SQ FT: 18,400
SALES (est): 3.5MM **Privately Held**
WEB: www.std-bellows.com
SIC: 3599 Mfg Industrial Machinery

(G-5402)
TWC TRANS WORLD CONSULTING
Also Called: Drainage Products
383 S Main St (06096-2839)
PHONE....860 668-5108
Paul Tarko Jr, *President*
Paul Tarko Sr, *CTO*
EMP: 5
SQ FT: 10,000
SALES: 500K **Privately Held**
WEB: www.drainaway.com
SIC: 3089 Mfg Plastic Products

Winsted
Litchfield County

(G-5403)
AMERICAN COLLARS COUPLINGS INC
88 Hubbard St (06098-1025)
PHONE....860 379-7043
Shirley A Clarke, *President*
Michael A Clarke, *Vice Pres*
Linda Stommel, *Vice Pres*
▲ **EMP:** 12
SQ FT: 8,000
SALES (est): 930K **Privately Held**
SIC: 3568 Mfg Shaft Collars

(G-5404)
ARCONIC INC
145 Price Rd (06098-2237)
PHONE....860 379-3314
Richard Dellagnese, *Engineer*
Paul Masucci, *Engineer*
Klaus Kleinfield, *Branch Mgr*
EMP: 9
SALES (corp-wide): 14B **Publicly Held**
SIC: 3334 Primary Aluminum Producer
PA: Arconic Inc.
201 Isabella St Ste 200
Pittsburgh PA 15212
412 553-1950

(G-5405)
BKMFG CORP
Also Called: Broil King
200 International Way (06098-2252)
PHONE....860 738-2200
Michael Shanahan, *President*
Michael Bosson, *Vice Pres*
▲ **EMP:** 35
SQ FT: 30,000
SALES (est): 7.3MM
SALES (corp-wide): 12.7MM **Privately Held**
WEB: www.broilking.com
SIC: 3634 Mfg Electric Housewares/Fans
PA: Cadco, Ltd.
200 International Way
Winsted CT 06098
860 738-2500

(G-5406)
BROWSER DAILY
211 Spencer Hill Rd (06098-2214)
PHONE....860 469-5534
Jon Bishop, *Principal*
EMP: 5
SALES (est): 257.9K **Privately Held**
SIC: 2711 Newspapers-Publishing/Printing

(G-5407)
CAINE MACHINING INC
43 Meadow St (06098-1419)
P.O. Box 293 (06098-0293)
PHONE....860 738-1619
Michael Sultaire, *President*
Robert Carpenter, *Admin Sec*
EMP: 4
SALES: 400K **Privately Held**
SIC: 3451 Mfg Screw Machine Products

(G-5408)
DRT AEROSPACE LLC
Also Called: Drt Power Systems
200 Price Rd (06098-2236)
PHONE..................................860 379-0783
Gary Van Gundy, *CEO*
EMP: 16 **Privately Held**
SIC: 3728 5013 Mfg Aircraft Parts/Equipment Whol Auto Parts/Supplies
HQ: Drt Aerospace, Llc
8694 Rite Track Way
West Chester OH 45069
937 298-7391

(G-5409)
E & E TOOL & MANUFACTURING CO
100 International Way (06098-2251)
PHONE..................................860 738-8577
Edward Clark, *Partner*
Bill Clark, *Partner*
EMP: 10
SQ FT: 6,000
SALES: 1MM **Privately Held**
SIC: 3544 Mfg Dies/Tools/Jigs/Fixtures

(G-5410)
EAST COAST LIGHTNING EQP INC
Also Called: East Coast Roof Specialties
24 Lanson Dr (06098-2072)
PHONE..................................860 379-9072
Mark P Morgan, *President*
Jennifer Morgan, *Corp Secy*
EMP: 24
SQ FT: 20,000
SALES (est): 5.9MM **Privately Held**
WEB: www.eastcoastlightning.com
SIC: 3643 5072 Mfg Conductive Wiring Devices Whol Hardware

(G-5411)
FAIRCHILD AUTO-MATED PARTS INC
10 White St (06098-2132)
PHONE..................................860 379-2725
Norman F Thompson, *Ch of Bd*
Jonathan P Thompson, *President*
EMP: 22 **EST:** 1944
SQ FT: 16,500
SALES (est): 3.9MM **Privately Held**
WEB: www.fairchildparts.com
SIC: 3599 Mfg Industrial Machinery

(G-5412)
H-O PRODUCTS CORPORATION
12 Munro St (06098-1423)
PHONE..................................860 379-9875
Chris Olson, *President*
Robert Carfiro, *Controller*
EMP: 26
SQ FT: 50,000
SALES (est): 4.7MM **Privately Held**
WEB: www.h-oproducts.com
SIC: 3069 3086 3053 2672 Mfg Fabrcatd Rubber Prdt Mfg Plastic Foam Prdts Mfg Gasket/Packing/Seals Mfg Coat/Laminated Paper

(G-5413)
HOWMET CASTINGS & SERVICES INC
Alcoa Howmet, Winsted
145 Price Rd (06098-2240)
PHONE..................................860 379-3314
Elmer Miller, *General Mgr*
Robert Beckquist, *Branch Mgr*
EMP: 270
SQ FT: 63,000
SALES (corp-wide): 14B **Publicly Held**
SIC: 3324 Mfg Machining Precision Airfoils
HQ: Howmet Castings & Services, Inc.
1616 Harvard Ave
Newburgh Heights OH 44105
216 641-4400

(G-5414)
J & G MACHINING COMPANY INC
100 Whiting St Ste 1 (06098-1878)
PHONE..................................860 379-7038
Robert Goulet, *President*
Lillian Goulet, *Treasurer*
Bob Goulet, *Data Proc Dir*
EMP: 6 **EST:** 1978
SQ FT: 1,500
SALES: 491K **Privately Held**
SIC: 3599 Mfg Industrial Machinery

(G-5415)
KING OF COVERS INC (PA)
154 Torrington Rd (06098-2085)
PHONE..................................860 379-2427
Linwood Quinn, *President*
Constance Quinn, *Vice Pres*
EMP: 5 **EST:** 1970
SALES: 500K **Privately Held**
WEB: www.thekingofcovers.com
SIC: 3714 Mfg Dump Truck Covers

(G-5416)
METAL PLUS LLC
214 Wallens Hill Rd (06098-1378)
PHONE..................................860 379-1327
Mario Lallier, *Principal*
EMP: 4
SALES (est): 609.4K **Privately Held**
SIC: 3531 Mfg Construction Machinery

(G-5417)
METAMORPHIC MATERIALS INC
122 Colebrook River Rd (06098)
PHONE..................................860 738-8638
Jay K Martin, *President*
▲ **EMP:** 10
SALES (est): 1.3MM **Privately Held**
SIC: 2819 2891 3479 Mfg Industrial Inorganic Chemicals Mfg Adhesives/Sealants Coating/Engraving Service

(G-5418)
NARRAGANSETT SCREW CO
119 Rowley St (06098-2068)
PHONE..................................860 379-4059
Charlie Rhoades, *President*
Charles Rhoades, *Info Tech Mgr*
EMP: 13 **EST:** 1960
SQ FT: 27,000
SALES (est): 1.3MM **Privately Held**
WEB: www.narragansettscrew.com
SIC: 3452 3364 3354 Mfg Bolts/Screws/Rivets Mfg Nonferrous Die-Castings Mfg Aluminum Extruded Products

(G-5419)
PRECISION METALS AND PLASTICS
Also Called: Precision Metals and Plas Mfg
118 Colebrook River Rd # 7 (06098-2241)
P.O. Box 7264, Berlin (06037-7264)
PHONE..................................860 238-4320
William Bonk, *Principal*
EMP: 9
SALES (est): 1.1MM **Privately Held**
SIC: 3728 Mfg Aircraft Parts/Equipment

(G-5420)
RED BARN WOODWORKERS
118 Laurel Way (06098-2532)
PHONE..................................860 379-3158
Waldo Placo, *Owner*
EMP: 3 **EST:** 1962
SALES (est): 170K **Privately Held**
SIC: 2431 Mfg Millwork

(G-5421)
SCHAEFFLER AEROSPACE USA CORP
Also Called: Winsted Precision Ball
159 Colebrook River Rd (06098-2203)
PHONE..................................860 379-7558
Roman Czarniecki, *General Mgr*
EMP: 71
SALES (corp-wide): 68.1B **Privately Held**
SIC: 3562 3399 3229 Mfg Ball/Roller Bearings Mfg Primary Metal Products Mfg Pressed/Blown Glass
HQ: Schaeffler Aerospace Usa Corporation
200 Park Ave
Danbury CT 06810
203 744-2211

(G-5422)
SKF SPECIALTY BALLS
149 Colebrook River Rd (06098-2203)
PHONE..................................860 379-8511
EMP: 3
SALES (est): 170.3K **Privately Held**
SIC: 3562 Mfg Ball/Roller Bearings

(G-5423)
SKF USA INC
149 Colebrook River Rd (06098-2203)
PHONE..................................860 379-8511
Frank Baker, *Branch Mgr*
EMP: 35
SALES (corp-wide): 9B **Privately Held**
WEB: www.skfusa.com
SIC: 3562 3053 Mfg Anti Friction Bearings & Seals
HQ: Skf Usa Inc.
890 Forty Foot Rd
Lansdale PA 19446
267 436-6000

(G-5424)
SONCHIEF ELECTRICS INC
Also Called: Son-Chief Stampings
41 Meadow St Ste 1 (06098-1438)
P.O. Box 204, Harwinton (06791-0204)
PHONE..................................860 379-2741
Donal F Fitzgerald, *President*
Barbara Fitzgerald, *Admin Sec*
EMP: 5
SQ FT: 120,000
SALES (est): 727.2K **Privately Held**
SIC: 3469 Mfg Metal Stampings

(G-5425)
SOUTHPORT PRODUCTS LLC
157 Colebrook River Rd (06098-2203)
PHONE..................................860 379-0761
John Auclair, *President*
Randolph Auclair,
EMP: 6
SQ FT: 10,000
SALES (est): 914.1K **Privately Held**
WEB: www.southportindustries.com
SIC: 3643 Mfg Conductive Wiring Devices

(G-5426)
STERLING NAME TAPE COMPANY
9 Willow St (06098-2009)
P.O. Box 939 (06098-0939)
PHONE..................................860 379-5142
James P Barrett, *President*
Jonathan Ryan, *Vice Pres*
Paula Ryan-Richard, *Treasurer*
Daniel Barrett, *Admin Sec*
Virginia D Barrett, *Admin Sec*
EMP: 4 **EST:** 1901
SQ FT: 12,000
SALES (est): 639.8K **Privately Held**
WEB: www.sterlingtape.com
SIC: 2269 Mfg Name Tapes & Garment Labels

(G-5427)
VIZ-PRO LLC
120 Colebrook River Rd (06098-2205)
PHONE..................................860 379-0055
Pan Haipo, *President*
EMP: 3
SQ FT: 4,000
SALES: 4MM **Privately Held**
SIC: 3931 Mfg Musical Instruments

(G-5428)
WESTWOOD PRODUCTS INC
167 Torrington Rd (06098-2087)
P.O. Box 933 (06098-0933)
PHONE..................................860 379-9401
Brian Tarbox, *President*
Sara Westervelt, *Office Mgr*
EMP: 16
SQ FT: 8,000
SALES: 2.3MM **Privately Held**
SIC: 2441 2448 2449 Mfg Wood Boxes/Shook Mfg Wood Pallets/Skids Mfg Wood Containers

(G-5429)
WINCHESTER INDUSTRIES INC
106 Groppo Dr (06098)
P.O. Box 917 (06098-0917)
PHONE..................................860 379-5336
John Devanney, *President*
Damien Devanney, *Vice Pres*
Linda Devanney, *Treasurer*
EMP: 7
SQ FT: 17,800
SALES (est): 1MM **Privately Held**
WEB: www.railroadgage.com
SIC: 3743 Mfg Railroad Equipment

(G-5430)
WINCHESTER PRODUCTS INC
22 Lanson Dr (06098-2072)
PHONE..................................860 379-8590
Charles H Ackerman, *President*
Judy B Ackerman, *Vice Pres*
EMP: 6 **EST:** 1994
SQ FT: 5,000
SALES: 600K **Privately Held**
SIC: 3369 Manufacturer Of Metal Castings

(G-5431)
WINCHESTER WOODWORKS LLC
12 Munro St (06098-1423)
PHONE..................................860 379-9875
Chris Olson, *President*
EMP: 4
SALES (est): 327.5K **Privately Held**
SIC: 2431 Mfg Millwork

Wolcott
New Haven County

(G-5432)
ALDEN CORPORATION
Also Called: Drill-Out
1 Hillside Dr (06716-2403)
P.O. Box 6262 (06716-0262)
PHONE..................................203 879-8830
Yvon J Desaulniers, *President*
▲ **EMP:** 60
SQ FT: 40,000
SALES (est): 10.3MM **Privately Held**
WEB: www.aldencorporation.com
SIC: 3545 3546 Mfg Machine Tool Accessories Mfg Power-Driven Handtools

(G-5433)
C & G PRECISIONS PRODUCTS INC
Also Called: C&G Precision Parts
14 Venus Dr (06716-2608)
PHONE..................................203 879-6989
Pat Guerrera, *President*
EMP: 5
SQ FT: 1,400
SALES: 600K **Privately Held**
SIC: 3549 Mfg Metalworking Machinery

(G-5434)
CHILD EVNGELISM FELLOWSHIP INC
730 Bound Line Rd (06716-1556)
PHONE..................................203 879-2154
Daniel Guido, *Branch Mgr*
EMP: 41
SALES (corp-wide): 24.4MM **Privately Held**
SIC: 2752 Lithographic Commercial Printing
PA: Child Evangelism Fellowship Incorporated
17482 Highway M
Warrenton MO 63383
636 456-4321

(G-5435)
CLEAR & COLORED COATINGS LLC (PA)
222 Spindle Hill Rd (06716-1729)
PHONE..................................203 879-1379
Steven Chares Bosse, *Principal*
EMP: 8 **EST:** 2001
SALES (est): 680.6K **Privately Held**
SIC: 3479 Coating/Engraving Service

(G-5436)
COILS PLUS INC
30 Town Line Rd (06716-2624)
PHONE..................................203 879-0755
Michael Mennillo, *President*
Daniel J Mennillo Jr, *Vice Pres*
EMP: 28
SQ FT: 13,000

GEOGRAPHIC

SALES (est): 4.5MM **Privately Held**
WEB: www.coilsplus.com
SIC: 3621 3677 Mfg Motors/Generators Mfg Electronic Coils/Transformers

(G-5437)
CUSTOM SPORTSWEAR MFG
Also Called: Teta Actvwear By Cstm Sprtwear
14 Town Line Rd (06716-2635)
PHONE..................................203 879-4420
Mario Teta Jr, *President*
Sharon Gibson, *Corp Secy*
EMP: 6 **EST:** 1996
SQ FT: 3,500
SALES (est): 614.4K **Privately Held**
SIC: 2329 2339 Mfg Men's/Boy's Clothing Mfg Women's/Misses' Outerwear

(G-5438)
DEVON PRECISION INDUSTRIES INC
Also Called: Devon Precision Industries.
251 Munson Rd (06716-2728)
P.O. Box 6555 (06716-0555)
PHONE..................................203 879-1437
Yvon J Desaulniers, *CEO*
David J Desaulniers, *President*
Lorraine Desaulniers, *Corp Secy*
Donald J Desaulniers, *Vice Pres*
John Trusch, *Project Mgr*
EMP: 65 **EST:** 1967
SQ FT: 55,000
SALES: 4.5MM **Privately Held**
WEB: www.devonp.com
SIC: 3451 Mfg Screw Machine Products

(G-5439)
DIECRAFT COMPACTING TOOL INC
36 James Pl (06716-1017)
PHONE..................................203 879-3019
EMP: 5 **EST:** 1952
SQ FT: 6,800
SALES (est): 469.4K **Privately Held**
SIC: 3544 Mfg Dies/Tools/Jigs/Fixtures

(G-5440)
DRAHER MACHINE COMPANY
30 Tosun Rd (06716-2629)
PHONE..................................203 753-0179
Robert Maton, *President*
Barbara Maton, *Admin Sec*
EMP: 6 **EST:** 1930
SQ FT: 9,000
SALES (est): 1.1MM **Privately Held**
SIC: 3599 Machine Shop

(G-5441)
EDSON MANUFACTURING INC
10 Venus Dr (06716-2627)
P.O. Box 6211 (06716-0211)
PHONE..................................203 879-1411
Lee Gaw, *President*
John Famiglietti, *Admin Sec*
▲ **EMP:** 10
SQ FT: 6,200
SALES (est): 3.1MM **Privately Held**
WEB: www.edsonmfg.com
SIC: 3452 Mfg Bolts/Screws/Rivets

(G-5442)
EYELET TECH LLC
10 Venus Dr (06716-2627)
PHONE..................................203 879-5306
Scott Allen, *Mng Member*
EMP: 48
SALES (est): 5.3MM **Privately Held**
WEB: www.eyelettech.com
SIC: 3542 3965 3469 Mfg Machine Tools-Forming Mfg Fasteners/Buttons/Pins Mfg Metal Stampings

(G-5443)
GRANNYS GOT IT
724 Wolcott Rd Ste 3 (06716-2448)
PHONE..................................203 879-0042
Raeann Gugliotti, *Owner*
Regina Enbardo, *Office Mgr*
EMP: 3
SQ FT: 590
SALES (est): 275.8K **Privately Held**
SIC: 2782 5945 Mfg Blankbooks/Binders Ret Hobbies/Toys/Games

(G-5444)
HOB INDUSTRIES INC
750 Bound Line Rd (06716-1556)
PHONE..................................203 879-3028
Francis X Macary Jr, *CEO*
Raymond R Macary, *Vice Pres*
Sarah Macary, *Treasurer*
Peter Macary, *Admin Sec*
EMP: 40 **EST:** 1975
SQ FT: 15,000
SALES (est): 7.6MM **Privately Held**
WEB: www.hobindustries.com
SIC: 3469 Mfg Metal Stampings

(G-5445)
JAN MANUFACTURING INC
Also Called: Connecticut Cue Parts
14 Town Line Rd Ste 8 (06716-2635)
PHONE..................................203 879-0580
John Ciavarella Jr, *President*
Nancy Ciavarella, *Vice Pres*
EMP: 7
SQ FT: 3,500
SALES (est): 1.1MM **Privately Held**
WEB: www.janmfg.com
SIC: 3599 7694 Mfg Industrial Machinery Armature Rewinding

(G-5446)
JOVAN MACHINE CO INC
1133 Wolcott Rd Ste A (06716-1514)
P.O. Box 6171 (06716-0171)
PHONE..................................203 879-2855
Daniel Brewster, *President*
EMP: 5
SQ FT: 5,000
SALES: 350K **Privately Held**
SIC: 3599 General Machine Shop Jobbing & Repair

(G-5447)
LOUIS ELECTRIC CO INC
1584 Wolcott Rd (06716-1327)
P.O. Box 1781, Bristol (06011-1781)
PHONE..................................203 879-5483
Louis R Duguette, *President*
Linda Duguette, *Vice Pres*
Louis R Duquette, *Director*
EMP: 3 **EST:** 1972
SALES (est): 450.3K **Privately Held**
SIC: 3823 1731 Manufactures Electrical Controls & Electrical Contractor

(G-5448)
MAILLY MANUFACTURING COMPANY
54 Wakelee Rd (06716-2620)
P.O. Box 6143 (06716-0143)
PHONE..................................203 879-1445
John Mailly, *President*
Richard Mailly, *President*
Janet Corden, *Admin Sec*
EMP: 7 **EST:** 1945
SQ FT: 8,000
SALES (est): 1.2MM **Privately Held**
SIC: 3451 Mfg Screw Machine Products

(G-5449)
NATIONAL DIE COMPANY
64 Wolcott Rd (06716-2612)
P.O. Box 6281 (06716-0281)
PHONE..................................203 879-1408
John J Ernst, *CEO*
Paul Cote, *President*
EMP: 9 **EST:** 1945
SQ FT: 15,000
SALES (est): 1.8MM **Privately Held**
SIC: 3469 Mfg Metal Stampings

(G-5450)
NUCAP US INC (DH)
238 Wolcott Rd (06716-2617)
PHONE..................................203 879-1423
Roman Arbesman, *President*
John Diniz, *CFO*
Rick Tibau, *Marketing Mgr*
▲ **EMP:** 30
SQ FT: 56,000
SALES (est): 18.3MM
SALES (corp-wide): 95MM **Privately Held**
WEB: www.anstroinc.com
SIC: 3965 3452 3469 3714 Mfg Fastener/Button/Pins Mfg Bolts/Screws/Rivets Mfg Metal Stampings Mfg Motor Vehicle Parts
HQ: Nucap Industries Inc
3370 Pharmacy Ave
Scarborough ON M1W 3
416 494-1444

(G-5451)
P-A-R PRECISION INC
15 Town Line Rd (06716-2625)
P.O. Box 6127 (06716-0127)
PHONE..................................860 491-4181
Robert L Clement, *President*
Alex Zambetti, *Treasurer*
Patrick Galvin, *Admin Sec*
EMP: 30
SQ FT: 8,000
SALES (est): 4.5MM **Privately Held**
WEB: www.p-a-r.com
SIC: 3451 3541 Mfg Screw Machine Products Mfg Machine Tools-Cutting

(G-5452)
PRECISION METHODS INCORPORATED
Also Called: PMI
40 North St (06716-1332)
P.O. Box 6445 (06716-0445)
PHONE..................................203 879-1429
C Thomas Accuosti, *President*
Thomas D Accuosti, *Vice Pres*
EMP: 19
SQ FT: 10,000
SALES: 1.5MM **Privately Held**
WEB: www.precisionmethods.com
SIC: 3451 Mfr Screw Machine Products

(G-5453)
PRINT SHOP OF WOLCOTT LLC
450 Wolcott Rd (06716-2639)
PHONE..................................203 879-3353
Scott Little,
EMP: 3
SQ FT: 600
SALES (est): 379.4K **Privately Held**
SIC: 2752 7336 2759 Lithographic Commercial Printing Commercial Art/Graphic Design Commercial Printing

(G-5454)
RICHARDS METAL PRODUCTS INC
14 Swiss Ln (06716-2622)
P.O. Box 6290 (06716-0290)
PHONE..................................203 879-2555
Christopher Cobb, *President*
Vezir Memeti, *Mfg Staff*
EMP: 12 **EST:** 1965
SQ FT: 10,000
SALES (est): 2.5MM **Privately Held**
WEB: www.richardsmetalproducts.com
SIC: 3469 Mfg Metal Stampings

(G-5455)
SCHAEFER ROLLS INC
32 Bolduc Ct (06716-3146)
PHONE..................................203 910-0224
EMP: 3
SALES (est): 148.8K **Privately Held**
SIC: 3724 Mfg Aircraft Engines/Parts

(G-5456)
SEAFOOD GOURMET INC
264 Lyman Rd Apt 3-13 (06716-2335)
PHONE..................................203 272-1544
James L Romano, *President*
James Romano, *President*
Deborah Romano, *Vice Pres*
EMP: 12
SALES (est): 860K **Privately Held**
SIC: 2092 Mfg Fresh/Frozen Packaged Fish

(G-5457)
SECONDARIES INC
19 Venus Dr (06716-2695)
PHONE..................................203 879-4633
Robert A Ferry, *President*
John A Karas, *Vice Pres*
EMP: 7 **EST:** 1962
SQ FT: 6,400
SALES: 1MM **Privately Held**
WEB: www.secondariesinc.com
SIC: 3599 3462 Mfg Industrial Machinery Mfg Iron/Steel Forgings

(G-5458)
SELECTCOM MFG CO INC
29 Nutmeg Valley Rd (06716-2621)
PHONE..................................203 879-9900
Brian Lanese, *President*
Arthur Lanese Jr, *Treasurer*
Sheila Lanese, *Admin Sec*
EMP: 7 **EST:** 1970
SQ FT: 7,500
SALES: 430K **Privately Held**
SIC: 3451 Mfg Screw Machine Products

(G-5459)
SEQUEL SPECIAL PRODUCTS LLC
1 Hillside Dr (06716-2403)
PHONE..................................203 759-1020
Adan Hernandez, *Buyer*
Scott Debisschop,
EMP: 25
SQ FT: 20,000
SALES (est): 5.8MM **Privately Held**
WEB: www.sequelmail.com
SIC: 3841 Mfg Surgical/Medical Instruments

(G-5460)
SILKSCREEN PLUS LLC
413 Wolcott Rd (06716-2613)
P.O. Box 6104 (06716-0104)
PHONE..................................203 879-0345
James Briglia, *President*
EMP: 3
SALES (est): 290K **Privately Held**
WEB: www.silkscreenplus.com
SIC: 2759 Commercial Printing

(G-5461)
TETA ACTIVEWEAR BY CUSTOM
14 Town Line Rd Ste 1 (06716-2635)
PHONE..................................203 879-4420
Mario Teta Jr, *President*
EMP: 3
SALES (est): 490K **Privately Held**
WEB: www.tetawear.com
SIC: 2339 Retail Men's And Women's Sportswear

(G-5462)
YANKEE STEEL SERVICE LLC
9 Venus Dr (06716-2607)
PHONE..................................203 879-5707
Fax: 203 879-5704
EMP: 4
SQ FT: 12,000
SALES: 500K **Privately Held**
SIC: 3312 Mfg Stainless Steel

Woodbridge
New Haven County

(G-5463)
BUNSEN RUSH LABORATORIES INC
270 Amity Rd Ste 124 (06525-2236)
PHONE..................................203 397-0820
Michael R Lerner, *President*
EMP: 6
SQ FT: 1,000
SALES (est): 616.4K **Privately Held**
SIC: 2844 Develops Sells & Markets Pigment Cell Based Technologies & Products For The Skin

(G-5464)
CHASE CORPORATION
149 Amity Rd (06525-2244)
PHONE..................................203 285-1244
EMP: 11
SALES (corp-wide): 281.3MM **Publicly Held**
SIC: 3644 Mfg Nonconductive Wiring Devices
PA: Chase Corporation
295 University Ave
Westwood MA 02090
781 332-0700

(G-5465)
CHEMIN PHARMA LLC
4 Research Dr (06525-2347)
PHONE..................................203 208-2811

Uday R Khire, *Principal*
EMP: 6 **EST:** 2014
SALES (est): 579.1K **Privately Held**
SIC: 2834 Mfg Pharmaceutical Preparations

(G-5466)
CLASSIC LABEL INC
10 Research Dr (06525-2347)
PHONE..................................203 389-3535
Louis Fantarella, *President*
Dean J Fantarella, *Vice Pres*
Laura Fantarella, *Admin Sec*
▲ **EMP:** 9
SQ FT: 10,000
SALES (est): 1.8MM **Privately Held**
SIC: 2759 Commercial Printing

(G-5467)
GR ENTERPRISES AND TECH
Also Called: Great
3 Penny Ln (06525-1531)
PHONE..................................203 387-1430
Mark Gerber, *Partner*
Manny Ratafia,
EMP: 4 **EST:** 2013
SALES (est): 222.2K **Privately Held**
SIC: 3841 Mfg Surgical/Medical Instruments

(G-5468)
INTRACRANIAL BIOANALYTICS LLC
22 Richard Sweet Dr (06525-1126)
PHONE..................................914 490-1524
Thomas Jasinski, *Mng Member*
Konstantine Drakonakis,
Mark Reed,
Dennise Spencer,
Hitten Zaveri,
EMP: 5
SALES (est): 198.4K **Privately Held**
SIC: 3845 Mfg Electromedical Equipment

(G-5469)
JOYCE PRINTERS INC
16 Research Dr (06525-2355)
PHONE..................................203 389-4452
James F Scott, *President*
EMP: 3 **EST:** 1962
SQ FT: 4,000
SALES (est): 328.1K **Privately Held**
SIC: 2759 Lithographic Commercial Printing

(G-5470)
KOL LLC
12 Cassway Rd (06525-1215)
PHONE..................................203 393-2924
Christopher Neumann, *Mng Member*
Mark Schleimer, *Prgrmr*
Michael Toscani, *Director*
EMP: 25
SQ FT: 3,000
SALES (est): 2MM **Privately Held**
SIC: 7372 Prepackaged Software Services

(G-5471)
MANUFACTURERS SERVICE CO INC
Also Called: Air Handling Systems
5 Lunar Dr (06525-2320)
PHONE..................................203 389-9595
David Edward Scott, *President*
Jamison Scott, *Vice Pres*
Patricia Scott, *Treasurer*
▼ **EMP:** 8
SQ FT: 12,800
SALES (est): 1.3MM **Privately Held**
WEB: www.airhand.com
SIC: 3444 Mfg Sheet Metalwork

(G-5472)
MERRILL OIL LLC
517 Amity Rd (06525-1603)
PHONE..................................203 387-1130
Christian Merrill, *Principal*
EMP: 3 **EST:** 2015
SALES (est): 99.1K **Privately Held**
SIC: 1311 Crude Petroleum/Natural Gas Production

(G-5473)
NEW ENGLAND BREWING CO LLC
175 Amity Rd (06525-2201)
PHONE..................................203 387-2222
Robert Leonard,
William Pastyrnak,
Matthew Westfall,
EMP: 6
SQ FT: 20,000
SALES: 1.1MM **Privately Held**
WEB: www.newenglandbrewing.com
SIC: 2082 Mfg Beer

(G-5474)
ODD JOBS HANDYMAN SERVICE LLC
19 Grouse Ln (06525-1452)
PHONE..................................203 397-5275
Liliana Lara,
Alfonso Lara,
EMP: 4
SALES: 300K **Privately Held**
SIC: 2842 Cleaning Service

(G-5475)
P2 SCIENCE INC
4 Research Dr (06525-2347)
PHONE..................................203 821-7457
Neil Burns, *CEO*
Patrick Foley, *Principal*
Rob Bettigole, *Chairman*
EMP: 4
SALES (est): 670K **Privately Held**
SIC: 2879 3532 7353 Mfg Agricultural Chemicals Mfg Mining Machinery Heavy Construction Equipment Rental

(G-5476)
PLASTIC FORMING COMPANY INC (PA)
20 S Bradley Rd (06525-2330)
PHONE..................................203 397-1338
John Womer, *President*
Peter T Schurman, *President*
Gary Amatrudo, *Vice Pres*
Mike Warth, *Vice Pres*
Patrick Pietrantonio, *Design Engr*
▲ **EMP:** 25 **EST:** 1966
SQ FT: 60,000
SALES (est): 7.4MM **Privately Held**
WEB: www.plasticformingcompany.com
SIC: 3089 3086 Mfg Plastic Products

(G-5477)
PRESCO INCORPORATED
Also Called: Presco Engineering
8 Lunar Dr Ste 4 (06525-2366)
PHONE..................................203 397-8722
Phil Black, *President*
Jeff Gates, *Vice Pres*
Alan Katze, *Vice Pres*
Dan Kohler, *Vice Pres*
Daniel Kohler, *Vice Pres*
EMP: 12 **EST:** 1971
SQ FT: 5,000
SALES (est): 2.8MM **Privately Held**
WEB: www.prescoinc.com
SIC: 3699 7389 7371 Mfg Electrical Equipment & Supplies Design Services Computer Software Development

(G-5478)
SCRY HEALTH INC
1 Bradley Rd Ste 404 (06525-2235)
PHONE..................................203 936-8244
Kirk Mettler, *Principal*
EMP: 10
SALES (est): 432.4K **Privately Held**
SIC: 7372 8999 Prepackaged Software Services Services-Misc

(G-5479)
SHELTERS OF AMERICA LLC
73 Ford Rd (06525-1721)
P.O. Box 3792, New Haven (06525-0792)
PHONE..................................203 397-1037
Norm Schaaf, *Mng Member*
EMP: 3
SALES (est): 374.5K **Privately Held**
WEB: www.sheltersofamerica.com
SIC: 3448 Mfg Prefabricated Metal Buildings

Woodbury
Litchfield County

(G-5480)
A X M S INC
27 Woodside Cir (06798-1528)
PHONE..................................203 263-5046
Emilia Corey, *President*
▲ **EMP:** 7
SALES (est): 672.8K **Privately Held**
SIC: 3199 Mfg Leather Goods

(G-5481)
ANDERSON MANUFACTURING COMPANY
337 Quassapaug Rd (06798-2306)
PHONE..................................203 263-2318
Karen Anderson-Crimmins, *President*
Charles Whitcomb, *Vice Pres*
Denny Manders, *Engineer*
Mike Brady, *Director*
EMP: 4 **EST:** 1945
SQ FT: 5,000
SALES (est): 392.1K **Privately Held**
SIC: 3469 3728 Mfg Metal Stampings Mfg Aircraft Parts/Equipment

(G-5482)
AXERRA NETWORKS INC
Also Called: Axerra Networks Limited
30 Bear Run (06798-3334)
PHONE..................................203 906-3570
Hezi Lapid, *President*
EMP: 5
SALES (est): 422.8K **Privately Held**
SIC: 3663 Mfg Radio/Tv Communication Equipment
PA: Axerra Networks Ltd
24 Wallenberg Raul
Tel Aviv-Jaffa
376 599-84

(G-5483)
BEARDSLEY PUBLISHING CORP
Also Called: Ski Area Management
45 Main St N (06798-2915)
P.O. Box 644 (06798-0644)
PHONE..................................203 263-0888
Jennifer Rowan, *President*
Olivia Rowan, *Marketing Staff*
EMP: 6
SALES: 900K **Privately Held**
WEB: www.stablemanagement.com
SIC: 2741 Misc Publishing

(G-5484)
COGZ SYSTEMS LLC
58 Steeple View Ln (06798-3300)
PHONE..................................203 263-7882
Jay Ambrose, *Owner*
EMP: 10
SALES (est): 1.4MM **Privately Held**
SIC: 3695 5961 Retail/Mfr Software

(G-5485)
DENOMINATOR COMPANY INC
744 Main St S (06798-3732)
P.O. Box 5004 (06798-5004)
PHONE..................................203 263-3210
Thomas C Clark, *President*
EMP: 15 **EST:** 1961
SALES (est): 2.5MM **Privately Held**
WEB: www.denominatorcompany.com
SIC: 3824 Mfg Manual Mechanical Tally Counters And Tabulating Machines

(G-5486)
DUDA AND GOODWIN INC
Also Called: Dg Precision Manufacturing
90 Washington Rd (06798-2804)
P.O. Box 349 (06798-0349)
PHONE..................................203 263-4353
David S Duda, *President*
Brian P Duda, *Vice Pres*
Peggy Nelson, *Bookkeeper*
Patricia Sugden, *Office Mgr*
EMP: 10 **EST:** 1945
SQ FT: 8,000
SALES (est): 1.9MM **Privately Held**
WEB: www.dgprecision.com
SIC: 3451 Mfr Screw Machine Products

(G-5487)
EYE EAR IT LLC
19 Pomperaug Rd (06798-3714)
PHONE..................................203 487-8949
EMP: 18
SALES (est): 758.9K **Privately Held**
SIC: 2731 3577 5999 Books-Publishing Printing Mfg Education Supplies & Computer Peripheral Equipment

(G-5488)
FOUR SEASONS COOLER EQP LLC
150 Brushy Hill Rd (06798-1606)
PHONE..................................203 263-0705
Toll Free:..................................877
Cheryl Korowotny,
EMP: 6
SALES (est): 470.7K **Privately Held**
SIC: 3585 Mfg Refrigeration/Heating Equipment

(G-5489)
MIDDLE QUARTER ANIMAL HOSPITAL
726 Main St S (06798-3701)
PHONE..................................203 263-4772
Jill Bogdan, *Principal*
EMP: 4
SALES (est): 613.3K **Privately Held**
SIC: 3131 Veterinary Services

(G-5490)
TOTAL PARTS SERVICES LLC
97 S Pomperaug Ave (06798-3711)
P.O. Box 696 (06798-0696)
PHONE..................................203 263-5619
Fred Plumb, *Principal*
EMP: 6
SALES (est): 1MM **Privately Held**
SIC: 3599 Mfg Industrial Machinery

(G-5491)
WINDING DRIVE CORPORATION
744 Main St S (06798-3732)
PHONE..................................203 263-6961
Fran Adams, *Principal*
EMP: 3
SALES (est): 179.2K **Privately Held**
SIC: 2033 Mfg Canned Fruits/Vegetables

(G-5492)
WOODBURY PEWTERERS INC
860 Main St S (06798-3706)
P.O. Box 482 (06798-0482)
PHONE..................................203 263-2668
Paul Titcomb, *President*
Linda Charbonneau, *Vice Pres*
Brooks T Titcomb, *Plant Supt*
EMP: 32 **EST:** 1952
SQ FT: 10,000
SALES (est): 4.8MM **Privately Held**
WEB: www.woodburypewter.com
SIC: 3914 Mfg Pewterware

Woodstock
Windham County

(G-5493)
AARDVARK POLYMERS
Also Called: Gapolymer
73 Underwood Rd Ste 13 (06281)
PHONE..................................609 483-1013
Mike Gehrig, *Owner*
EMP: 9
SQ FT: 14,000
SALES: 6MM **Privately Held**
SIC: 2822 Mfg Synthetic Rubber

(G-5494)
BRIGHTSIGHT LLC
9 Hebert Ln (06281-3502)
PHONE..................................860 208-0222
Heather Plummer, *President*
Scott Plummer, *Plant Mgr*
EMP: 3 **EST:** 2017
SALES (est): 154.9K **Privately Held**
SIC: 3827 Mfg Optical Instruments/Lenses

GEOGRAPHIC

(G-5495)
BROOKE TAYLOR WINERY LLC (PA)
848 Route 171 (06281-2930)
PHONE..................................860 974-1263
Richard Auger,
EMP: 4
SALES: 370K **Privately Held**
SIC: 2084 Mfg Wines/Brandy/Spirits

(G-5496)
CEDAR SWAMP LOG & LUMBER
45 Hager Rd (06281-1718)
PHONE..................................860 974-2344
John Rucki, *Owner*
EMP: 3
SALES (est): 260.4K **Privately Held**
SIC: 2421 Sawmill/Planing Mill

(G-5497)
HOLLOW FROST PUBLISHERS
411 Barlow Cemetery Rd (06281-2706)
PHONE..................................860 974-2081
Leslie Roberts Holland, *Principal*
EMP: 4
SALES (est): 241.9K **Privately Held**
WEB: www.frosthollowpub.com
SIC: 2741 Misc Publishing

(G-5498)
LINEMASTER SWITCH CORPORATION
29 Plaine Hill Rd (06281-2913)
P.O. Box 238 (06281-0238)
PHONE..................................860 630-4920
Joseph J Carlone, *President*
Jason Barnes, *Production*
Tammy Flores, *Purchasing*
Richard Poinatale, *Purchasing*
Edward Ursillo, *QA Dir*
▲ **EMP:** 160 **EST:** 1952
SQ FT: 55,000
SALES (est): 45MM **Privately Held**
WEB: www.linemaster.com
SIC: 3625 Mfg Relays/Industrial Controls

(G-5499)
OAK TREE MOULDING LLC
7 Pole Bridge Rd (06281-1203)
PHONE..................................860 455-3056
Ranier E Landry,
Lorraine E Landry,
EMP: 3
SALES (est): 92.3K **Privately Held**
SIC: 3999 Mfg Misc Products

(G-5500)
QBA INC
24 Woodland Dr (06281-3032)
PHONE..................................860 963-9438
Neil Brown, *President*
EMP: 6
SALES (est): 556.6K **Privately Held**
SIC: 2952 5033 7349 Mfg Asphalt Felts/Coatings Whol Roofing/Siding/Insulation Building Maintenance Services

(G-5501)
ROGERS CORPORATION
High Performance Foams Div
245 Woodstock Rd (06281-1815)
P.O. Box 188 (06281-0188)
PHONE..................................860 928-3622
Peter Kaczmarek, *President*
EMP: 103
SALES (corp-wide): 879MM **Publicly Held**
WEB: www.rogers-corp.com
SIC: 3069 Mfg Fabricated Rubber Products
PA: Rogers Corporation
2225 W Chandler Blvd
Chandler AZ 85224
480 917-6000

(G-5502)
SKYKO INTERNATIONAL LLC (PA)
243 New Sweden Rd (06281-3216)
P.O. Box 704, Putnam (06260-0704)
PHONE..................................860 928-5170
Krista O Shultz, *Mng Member*
Preston Shultz,
EMP: 9
SALES (est): 2.8MM **Privately Held**
SIC: 3613 Mfg Switchgear/Switchboards

Woodstock Valley
Windham County

(G-5503)
BAY TACT CORPORATION
440 Route 198 (06282-2427)
PHONE..................................860 315-7372
O Henry Grinde, *President*
Diane G Patterson, *Admin Sec*
EMP: 25
SQ FT: 9,000
SALES (est): 2.5MM **Privately Held**
WEB: www.prars.com
SIC: 2741 2721 2731 Misc Publishing Periodicals-Publishing/Printing Books-Publishing/Printing

(G-5504)
PRESTIGE METAL FINISHING LLC
44 Bradford Corner Rd (06282-2001)
P.O. Box 97, Eastford (06242-0097)
PHONE..................................860 974-1999
Cheryl Gillmore,
EMP: 3
SALES: 100K **Privately Held**
SIC: 3471 Plating/Polishing Service

Yalesville
New Haven County

(G-5505)
JOVAL MACHINE CO INC
Also Called: Pac Products
515 Main St (06492-1736)
PHONE..................................203 284-0082
Gerald A Chase, *President*
Joyce Chase, *Corp Secy*
Jeffrey Chase, *Vice Pres*
Karen Madonna, *Bookkeeper*
EMP: 25
SQ FT: 25,000
SALES (est): 4.4MM **Privately Held**
WEB: www.jovalmachine.com
SIC: 3469 Mfg Industrial Machinery

Yantic
New London County

(G-5506)
AC/DC INDUSTRIAL ELECTRIC LLC
44 Yantic Flats Rd Ste 2 (06389-1005)
PHONE..................................860 886-2232
Charles Carroll, *Mng Member*
EMP: 8
SALES (est): 770K **Privately Held**
SIC: 3621 1731 5063 Mfg Motors/Generators Electrical Contractor Whol Electrical Equipment

(G-5507)
AMERICAN VEHICLES SALES LLC
58 Yantic Flats Rd (06389-1020)
PHONE..................................860 886-0327
Scott Davis,
EMP: 3
SQ FT: 9,600
SALES: 1.5MM **Privately Held**
WEB: www.americanvehiclesales.com
SIC: 3711 5012 Mfg/Dist Speciality Motor Vehicle Bodies

(G-5508)
CAMARO SIGNS INC (PA)
58 Yantic Flats Rd Unit 1 (06389-1019)
PHONE..................................860 886-1553
John Hansen, *President*
Erica Hansen, *Admin Sec*
Wayland James, *Graphic Designe*
EMP: 7
SQ FT: 5,000
SALES (est): 1MM **Privately Held**
WEB: www.camarosigns.com
SIC: 3993 Mfg Signs/Advertising Specialties

MAINE

Acton
York County

(G-5509)
SCOTT STANTON
Also Called: Dasco Signs
654 County Rd (04001-4802)
PHONE..................................207 477-2956
Scott Stanton, *Owner*
EMP: 6
SALES (est): 697.2K **Privately Held**
SIC: 3993 Mfg Signs/Advertising Specialties

Addison
Washington County

(G-5510)
R&R LOGGING FOREST MANAGEMENT
Ridge Rd (04606)
P.O. Box 110 (04606-0110)
PHONE..................................207 483-4612
Robert Ramsey, *Owner*
EMP: 4
SALES (est): 292.4K **Privately Held**
SIC: 2411 Logging

(G-5511)
SUNRISE COMPOSTING
444 E Side Rd (04606-3218)
PHONE..................................207 483-4081
Elliott Batson, *Owner*
EMP: 6
SALES: 189K **Privately Held**
SIC: 2879 5191 Mfg & Whol Organic Compost

Albany Twp
Oxford County

(G-5512)
CITIZEN PRINTERS INCORPORATED
Also Called: Bethel Citizen
19 Crooked River Cswy (04217-6300)
P.O. Box 109, Bethel (04217-0109)
PHONE..................................207 824-2444
Edward Snook, *President*
Michael Daniels, *Manager*
EMP: 7 **EST:** 1927
SQ FT: 4,900
SALES (est): 454.7K **Privately Held**
WEB: www.bethelcitizen.com
SIC: 2711 Newspapers-Publishing/Printing

Albion
Kennebec County

(G-5513)
UNIQUE SPIRAL STAIRS INC
117 Benton Rd (04910-6164)
PHONE..................................207 437-2415
Cliffard Dumont, *President*
Darren Dumont, *Vice Pres*
▼ **EMP:** 8
SQ FT: 6,000
SALES (est): 300K **Privately Held**
WEB: www.uniquespiralstairs.com
SIC: 2431 Mfg Millwork

Alfred
York County

(G-5514)
ALFREDS UPHOLSTERING & CUSTOM
Also Called: Alfred's Upholstrey and Co.
181 Waterboro Rd (04002)
P.O. Box 1065 (04002-1065)
PHONE..................................207 536-5565
Troy Delano, *President*
Rebecca Delano, *Officer*
EMP: 12
SQ FT: 8,000
SALES: 1.3MM **Privately Held**
SIC: 2512 2431 2211 Mfg Uphls Household Furn Mfg Millwork Cotton Brdwv Fabric Mill

(G-5515)
ARK PLASMA
9 Mountain Rd (04002-3301)
PHONE..................................207 332-6999
Kevin Strout, *Partner*
EMP: 3
SALES (est): 122.5K **Privately Held**
SIC: 3541 Mfg Machine Tools-Cutting

(G-5516)
NICMAR INDUSTRIES
Also Called: George R Roberts Company
192 Biddeford Rd (04002-3211)
PHONE..................................207 324-6571
Tim Cook, *President*
Allan L Martin, *Chairman*
Todd Meserve, *QC Mgr*
Ron Cormier, *Controller*
Kevin Murphy, *Human Res Mgr*
EMP: 50 **EST:** 1962
SQ FT: 24,000
SALES (est): 10MM **Privately Held**
WEB: www.stepguys.com
SIC: 3272 Mfg Concrete Products

(G-5517)
PRO-VAC INC
342 Jordan Springs Rd (04002-3532)
PHONE..................................207 324-1846
Daniel Payeur, *President*
Joanne Payeur, *Vice Pres*
EMP: 6
SQ FT: 10,000
SALES (est): 660K **Privately Held**
WEB: www.pro-vac.com
SIC: 3441 Structural Metal Fabrication

Allagash
Aroostook County

(G-5518)
BROOK WILES LOGGING INC
209 Allagash Rd (04774-4002)
PHONE..................................207 398-4105
EMP: 3 **EST:** 2009
SALES (est): 276.8K **Privately Held**
SIC: 2411 Logging

(G-5519)
OTIS GAZETTE
14 Dickey Rd (04774-4107)
PHONE..................................207 398-9001
Angelina Dubourg, *Principal*
EMP: 3 **EST:** 2015
SALES (est): 76.2K **Privately Held**
SIC: 2711 Newspapers-Publishing/Printing

(G-5520)
SYL VER LOGGING INC
206 Allagash Rd (04774-4014)
PHONE..................................207 398-3158
Sylvia Pelletier, *Owner*
EMP: 6
SALES (est): 526.7K **Privately Held**
SIC: 2411 Logging

Amherst
Hancock County

(G-5521)
HERB ALLURE INC
201 Tannery Loop (04605-8320)
PHONE..................................207 584-3550
Russ Tanner, *President*
Laura Clement, *Vice Pres*
EMP: 3 **EST:** 2000
SALES (est): 75K **Privately Held**
WEB: www.herballure.com
SIC: 2731 Books-Publishing/Printing

Amity
Aroostook County

(G-5522)
B & R BARTLETT ENTERPRISES
592 Us Route One (04471)
PHONE..................................207 448-7060
EMP: 10
SALES (est): 922.7K **Privately Held**
SIC: 2411 Logging

(G-5523)
COLIN BARTLETT & SONS INC
592 Us Route One (04471)
PHONE..................................207 532-2214
EMP: 40
SQ FT: 350
SALES (est): 5.2MM **Privately Held**
SIC: 2411 Pulpwood Contractor

(G-5524)
RON LEDGER SON LOGGING
81 Lycette Rd (04471-5113)
PHONE..................................207 532-2423
Ron Ledger, *Owner*
EMP: 6
SALES (est): 509.9K **Privately Held**
SIC: 2411 Logging

Anson
Somerset County

(G-5525)
LUCES PURE MAPLE SYRUP
54 Sugar Maple Dr (04911-3038)
PHONE..................................207 696-3732
Arnold Luce, *Owner*
EMP: 3
SALES: 400K **Privately Held**
SIC: 2087 Mfg Flavor Extracts/Syrup

Appleton
Knox County

(G-5526)
JOHN FANCY INC
118 Jones Hill Rd (04862-6232)
PHONE..................................207 785-3610
John Fancy, *Owner*
EMP: 3
SALES (est): 281.2K **Privately Held**
SIC: 3826 Mfg Analytical Instruments

Arundel
York County

(G-5527)
AMMO AND BULLET MANUFACTURING
2210 Portland Rd (04046-7930)
PHONE..................................978 807-7681
Ed Berman, *CEO*
EMP: 5
SALES (est): 175K **Privately Held**
SIC: 3482 Mfg Small Arms Ammunition

(G-5528)
ARUNDEL MACHINE TOOL CO
20 Technology Dr (04046-7979)
PHONE..................................207 985-8555
Ray Bertrand, *Vice Pres*
Veronica Stover, *Human Resources*
Joe Fournier, *Accounts Mgr*
Mike Paquette, *Supervisor*
William Plamondon, *Maintence Staff*
EMP: 53
SQ FT: 30,000
SALES: 13.4MM **Privately Held**
WEB: www.arundelmachine.com
SIC: 3451 3599 Mfg Screw Machine Products Mfg Industrial Machinery

(G-5529)
C B P CORP (PA)
Also Called: Port Canvas Company
39 Limerick Rd Unit 2 (04046-8158)
PHONE..................................207 985-9767
Margot L Thompson, *President*
Ned Thompson, *President*
Scott Phillips, *Prdtn Mgr*
Kathy Stearns, *Production*
Kathy Streans, *CFO*
EMP: 10
SQ FT: 3,200
SALES: 350K **Privately Held**
WEB: www.portcanvas.com
SIC: 2211 3161 2394 2393 Cotton Brdwv Fabric Mill Mfg Luggage Mfg Canvas/Related Prdts Mfg Textile Bags

(G-5530)
CHARLIE HORSE SCREEN PRINTING/
1468 Portland Rd (04046-8171)
PHONE..................................207 985-3293
Michael McCurry, *Principal*
EMP: 4
SALES (est): 311.3K **Privately Held**
SIC: 2752 Lithographic Commercial Printing

(G-5531)
DREAM SPIRIT PUBLISHERS
17 Alpine Ln (04046-8527)
PHONE..................................207 283-0667
Kevin Patt, *Owner*
EMP: 3 **EST:** 2015
SALES (est): 107.1K **Privately Held**
SIC: 2721 Periodicals-Publishing/Printing

(G-5532)
HUSTON & COMPANY WOOD DESIGN
226 Log Cabin Rd (04046-7703)
PHONE..................................207 967-2345
Bill Huston, *President*
Mia Millesoglie, *Owner*
EMP: 7
SQ FT: 4,600
SALES: 400K **Privately Held**
WEB: www.hustonandcompany.com
SIC: 2511 5712 Mfg Wood Household Furniture Ret Furniture

(G-5533)
LANK MACHINING CO LLC
113 Mountain Rd (04046-8330)
PHONE..................................207 286-9549
Lucille Lank, *Treasurer*
Delvern Lank,
EMP: 7
SQ FT: 6,000
SALES (est): 977.4K **Privately Held**
SIC: 3599 Mfg Machinery Machine Metal Parts

(G-5534)
MOUNTAIN TOPS CUSTOM T-SHIRTS (PA)
39 Limerick Rd Unit 6 (04046-8158)
PHONE..................................207 985-1919
Diane Frazier, *Vice Pres*
Jayne Coy, *Vice Pres*
Robert E Frazier, *Vice Pres*
EMP: 5
SQ FT: 1,800
SALES (est): 2.1MM **Privately Held**
WEB: www.mountaintops.com
SIC: 2321 Mfg Men's/Boy's Furnishings

(G-5535)
SLACKTIDE CAFE LLC
1697 Portland Rd (04046-7937)
PHONE..................................207 467-3822
EMP: 4
SALES (est): 279.6K **Privately Held**
SIC: 2038 5812 Mfg Frozen Specialties Eating Place

Ashland
Aroostook County

(G-5536)
ECOSHEL INC (PA)
Also Called: Mars Associates
126 Clark Siding Rd (04732)
P.O. Box 2530, South Portland (04116-2530)
PHONE..................................207 274-3508
Bryan Kirkey, *CEO*
EMP: 6
SALES: 1.1MM **Privately Held**
SIC: 3089 Mfg Plastic Products

(G-5537)
MOOSEWOOD MILLWORKS LLC
42 American Realty Rd (04732)
PHONE..................................207 435-4950
John McNulty, *Mng Member*
Tim Kelly,
EMP: 16 **EST:** 2012
SALES (est): 2.1MM
SALES (corp-wide): 5.4MM **Privately Held**
SIC: 2426 Hardwood Flooring Manufacturer
HQ: Seven Islands Land Company
112 Broadway
Bangor ME 04401
207 947-0541

(G-5538)
NORTHEAST PELLETS LLC
53 Realty Rd (04732-3101)
P.O. Box 19 (04732-0019)
PHONE..................................207 435-6230
Matthew Bell, *Owner*
EMP: 13
SQ FT: 10,000
SALES: 100K **Privately Held**
SIC: 3532 Mfg Wood Pellets

(G-5539)
P M KELLY INC
27 Clark Rd (04732)
P.O. Box 288 (04732-0288)
PHONE..................................207 435-6654
EMP: 14
SQ FT: 1,000
SALES: 2.5MM **Privately Held**
SIC: 2431 Operates As A Plaining Mill

(G-5540)
ROXANNE L TARDIE
Also Called: Aroostook Fiber Works
918 Presque Isle Rd (04732-3424)
PHONE..................................207 540-4945
Roxanne L Tardie, *Owner*
▲ **EMP:** 5
SALES (est): 170K **Privately Held**
SIC: 2299 Textile Goods, Nec, Nsk

Athens
Somerset County

(G-5541)
LINKLETTER AND SONS INC
115 Harmony Rd (04912-4629)
P.O. Box 135 (04912-0135)
PHONE..................................207 654-2301
Richard Linkletter, *President*
Bruce Linkletter, *Vice Pres*
Robert Linkletter, *Vice Pres*
Sandra Linkletter, *Admin Sec*
EMP: 32 **EST:** 1961
SALES (est): 4.4MM **Privately Held**
SIC: 2421 Biomass Chip Production

(G-5542)
MAINE WOODS PELLET COMPANY LLC
164 Harmony Rd (04912)
PHONE..................................207 654-2237
Scot Linkletter, *Plant Mgr*
Kathy York, *Human Res Mgr*
George Rybarczyk, *Mng Member*
Robert Linkletter, *Mng Member*
▲ **EMP:** 47
SALES (est): 10.3MM **Privately Held**
SIC: 2499 Mfg Wood Products

(G-5543)
PINE STATE DRILLING INC
Also Called: Pine State Drilling & Hardware
Rr 150 (04912)
P.O. Box 196 (04912-0196)
PHONE..................................207 654-2771
Rebbecca Sanford, *President*
Chad Grignon, *Manager*
Barry Sandford, *Shareholder*
EMP: 4
SQ FT: 2,640
SALES: 400K **Privately Held**
WEB: www.pinestatedrilling.com
SIC: 1381 1781 5251 Water Well Drilling Hardware Store Ret Pump & Installation

Atkinson
Piscataquis County

(G-5544)
NORTHWOOD CANOE CO
336 Range Rd (04426-6001)
PHONE..................................207 564-3667
Rollin Thurlow, *Managing Prtnr*
Peter Wallace, *Partner*
EMP: 3
SALES (est): 370.3K **Privately Held**
WEB: www.woodencanoes.com
SIC: 3732 Boatbuilding/Repairing

Auburn
Androscoggin County

(G-5545)
AC ELECTRIC CORP (PA)
Also Called: AC
120 Merrow Rd (04210-8896)
P.O. Box 1508 (04211-1508)
PHONE..................................207 784-7341
Dan Parsons, *President*
Brian Curit, *Engineer*
Marcia Clark, *Treasurer*
▲ **EMP:** 27
SQ FT: 17,000
SALES (est): 7.2MM **Privately Held**
WEB: www.acelec.com
SIC: 7694 5063 7629 Armature Rewinding Whol Electrical Equipment Electrical Repair

(G-5546)
ACUREN INSPECTION INC
264 Merrow Rd Ste 3 (04210-8995)
PHONE..................................207 786-7884
Shane Hodgson, *Branch Mgr*
EMP: 15
SALES (corp-wide): 1.7B **Privately Held**
SIC: 1389 1541 Oil/Gas Field Services Industrial Building Construction
HQ: Acuren Inspection, Inc.
30 Main St Ste 402
Danbury CT 06810
203 702-8740

(G-5547)
AFFORDABLE EXHIBIT DISPLAYS
142 Turner St (04210-5956)
PHONE..................................207 782-6175
Dena Wing, *President*
Jeffrey Wing, *Vice Pres*
Elissa Viscarelli, *Sales Associate*
▲ **EMP:** 6
SQ FT: 11,000

SALES (est): 614K Privately Held
WEB: www.affordabledisplays.com
SIC: 3999 3993 7389 Mfg Displays And Provides Trade Show Services

(G-5548)
AFFORDABLE EXHIBIT DISPLAYS
142 Turner St (04210-5956)
PHONE..................................207 782-6175
Jeffrey E Wing, *Principal*
EMP: 3
SALES (est): 190.6K Privately Held
SIC: 3993 Mfg Signs/Advertising Specialties

(G-5549)
ALBARRIE TECHNICAL FABRICS INC
Also Called: Albarrie Environmental Svcs
195 Center St (04210-5284)
P.O. Box 1226, Lewiston (04243-1226)
PHONE..................................207 786-0424
Reginald Driscoll, *President*
EMP: 5
SQ FT: 16,000
SALES (est): 932.1K Privately Held
WEB: www.albarrie.com
SIC: 3569 7699 Mfg General Industrial Machinery Repair Services

(G-5550)
AMERICAN CONCRETE INDS INC (PA)
982 Minot Ave (04210-3719)
PHONE..................................207 947-8334
Shawn Macdonald, *President*
Dan Sinclair, *Purchasing*
Kimberly Macdonald, *Treasurer*
EMP: 20
SQ FT: 82,000
SALES: 10MM Privately Held
WEB: www.americanconcrete.com
SIC: 3272 Mfg Concrete Products

(G-5551)
ANGOSTURA INTERNATIONAL LTD
176 First Flight Dr (04210-9055)
PHONE..................................207 786-3200
Steve Angostura, *President*
▲ EMP: 3
SALES (est): 213.4K Privately Held
SIC: 2013 Mfg Prepared Meats

(G-5552)
CASCADES AUBURN FIBER INC
586 Lewiston Junction Rd (04210-8847)
PHONE..................................207 753-5300
Paul Deraich, *Principal*
EMP: 40
SALES (est): 11.1MM
SALES (corp-wide): 3.5B Privately Held
SIC: 2621 8711 Paper Mill Engineering Services
PA: Cascades Inc
404 Boul Marie-Victorin
Kingsey Falls QC J0A 1
819 363-5100

(G-5553)
COASTAL T SHIRTS INC
205 Washington St S (04210-4814)
PHONE..................................207 784-4184
Mike Wise, *President*
EMP: 5
SALES (est): 742.9K Privately Held
WEB: www.coastaltshirts.com
SIC: 2759 Commercial Printing

(G-5554)
COMPUTECH INC
Also Called: Curry Printing & Marketing
31 Mill St (04210-6837)
P.O. Box 202, Lewiston (04243-0202)
PHONE..................................207 777-7468
Armand Girard, *President*
Rachel Duquette, *Opers Mgr*
Rose Girard, *Treasurer*
Robert Couturier, *Clerk*
EMP: 8 EST: 1977
SQ FT: 6,000
SALES (est): 1.3MM Privately Held
WEB: www.curryonline.com
SIC: 2752 2759 Lithographic Commercial Printing Commercial Printing

(G-5555)
CONFORM GISSING INTL LLC
Also Called: Formed Fiber Technologies, LLC
125 Allied Rd (04210-7985)
P.O. Box 1300 (04211-1300)
PHONE..................................207 784-1118
◆ EMP: 160
SQ FT: 129,000
SALES (est): 100MM Privately Held
WEB: www.formedfiber.com
SIC: 2824 3089 2823 Mfg Organic Fiber-Noncellulosic Mfg Plastic Products Mfg Cellulosic Manmade Fibers
PA: Detroit Technologies, Inc.
32500 Telg Rd Ste 207
Bingham Farms MI 48025

(G-5556)
CREATIVE EMBROIDERY LLC
213 Washington St S (04210-4814)
PHONE..................................207 777-6300
EMP: 3
SALES (est): 178.8K Privately Held
SIC: 2395 Pleating/Stitching Services

(G-5557)
CRESCENT INDUSTRIES COMPANY
191 Washington St S (04210-4821)
PHONE..................................207 777-3500
Rex Bradbury, *President*
Mark Hewes,
EMP: 8
SQ FT: 3,500
SALES (est): 700K Privately Held
WEB: www.crescentindustries.com
SIC: 3714 Mfg Motor Vehicle Parts/Accessories

(G-5558)
CRYSTAL SPRING WATER CO INC (PA)
24 Brickyard Cir (04210-4853)
P.O. Box 1450 (04211-1450)
PHONE..................................207 782-1521
Peter Bornstein, *President*
Derek Laliberta, *General Mgr*
Richard Bornstein, *Treasurer*
EMP: 17
SQ FT: 10,000
SALES (est): 1.8MM Privately Held
SIC: 2086 5499 Mfg Bottled/Canned Soft Drinks Ret Misc Foods

(G-5559)
DESIGN FAB INC
928 Minot Ave (04210-3719)
PHONE..................................207 786-2446
Leo Roche, *President*
EMP: 3 EST: 2012
SALES (est): 207.5K Privately Held
SIC: 3441 Structural Metal Fabrication

(G-5560)
DETROIT TECHNOLOGIES INC
Also Called: Conform Automotive
125 Allied Rd (04210-7985)
P.O. Box 1300 (04211-1300)
PHONE..................................207 784-1118
Steven Philips, *Principal*
EMP: 900 Privately Held
SIC: 2823 2824 3089 Mfg Cellulosic Manmade Fibers Mfg Organic Fiber-Noncellulosic Mfg Plastic Products
PA: Detroit Technologies, Inc.
32500 Telg Rd Ste 207
Bingham Farms MI 48025

(G-5561)
ENEFCO INTERNATIONAL INC (PA)
Also Called: Globaldie
1130 Minot Ave (04210-3739)
P.O. Box 1120 (04211-1120)
PHONE..................................207 514-7218
Marc Fontaine, *Ch of Bd*
Peter Klein, *President*
Timothy Smith, *CFO*
▲ EMP: 60
SQ FT: 78,000
SALES (est): 7.7MM Privately Held
WEB: www.enefco.com
SIC: 3131 7389 5999 5719 Mfg Footwear Cut Stock Business Services Ret Misc Merchandise Ret Misc Homefurnishings

(G-5562)
ENERCON
234 First Flight Dr (04210-9056)
P.O. Box 665, Gray (04039-0665)
PHONE..................................207 657-7001
Roger Wincox, *Branch Mgr*
Garrett Vanatta, *Director*
EMP: 25
SALES (corp-wide): 25.7MM Privately Held
WEB: www.enerconmaine.com
SIC: 3672 5063 Mfg Printed Circuit Boards Whol Electrical Equipment
PA: Enercon
25 Northbrook Dr
Gray ME 04039
207 657-7000

(G-5563)
EVERGREEN CUSTOM PRINTING INC
63 Broad St (04210-6814)
PHONE..................................207 782-2327
Donald Cote, *President*
Laurie Hickot, *Production*
Laurie Hiscock, *Production*
EMP: 8
SQ FT: 3,000
SALES: 200K Privately Held
WEB: www.evergreencustomprinting.com
SIC: 2752 2759 Lithographic Commercial Printing Commercial Printing

(G-5564)
FALCON PERFORMANCE FTWR LLC
27 Wrights Lndg (04210-8308)
PHONE..................................207 784-9186
Carl Spang, *President*
▲ EMP: 58
SALES (est): 4.9MM Privately Held
SIC: 3143 Mfg Men's Footwear

(G-5565)
FUTUREGUARD BUILDING PDTS INC (PA)
Also Called: Nuimage Awnings
101 Merrow Rd (04210-8319)
P.O. Box 2030 (04211-2030)
PHONE..................................800 858-5818
Donald Buteau, *President*
Thomas J Dean, *CFO*
Tom Dean, *CFO*
Brenda Buteau, *Treasurer*
Diane Rogers, *Human Res Dir*
▲ EMP: 68
SQ FT: 163,000
SALES (est): 18.8MM Privately Held
WEB: www.futureguard.net
SIC: 3444 3479 Mfg Sheet Metalwork Coating/Engraving Svcs

(G-5566)
GAGNE & SON CON BLOCKS INC
270 Riverside Dr (04210-9629)
PHONE..................................207 495-3313
George Allen, *Manager*
EMP: 7
SALES (corp-wide): 12.6MM Privately Held
SIC: 3271 5211 5039 3444 Mfg Concrete Block/Brick/Products Sheet Metalwork Ret Lumber/Building Mtrl Whol Cnstn Materials
PA: Gagne & Son Concrete Blocks, Inc.
28 Old Rte 27 Rd
Belgrade ME 04917
207 495-3313

(G-5567)
GENERAL ELECTRIC COMPANY
135 Rodman Rd (04210-3831)
PHONE..................................207 786-5100
Fletch Rickman, *Manager*
Judy White, *Manager*
Kendall Keniston, *Data Proc Staff*
EMP: 255
SALES (corp-wide): 121.6B Publicly Held
SIC: 3613 3643 Mfg Switchgear/Switchboards Mfg Conductive Wiring Devices
PA: General Electric Company
5 Necco St
Boston MA 02210
617 443-3000

(G-5568)
GLOBE FOOTWEAR LLC
Also Called: Falcon Performance Footwear
27 Wrights Lndg (04210-8308)
PHONE..................................207 784-9186
EMP: 50
SALES (corp-wide): 1.3B Publicly Held
SIC: 3143 Mfg Men's Footwear
HQ: Globe Footwear, Llc
27 Wrights Lndg
Auburn ME 04210

(G-5569)
GLOBE FOOTWEAR LLC (HQ)
27 Wrights Lndg (04210-8308)
PHONE..................................207 784-9186
Tom Vetras, *President*
Rob Freese, *Vice Pres*
Donald D Welch, *Administration*
Janet Sleeper, *Receptionist*
◆ EMP: 9
SALES (est): 3.3MM
SALES (corp-wide): 1.3B Publicly Held
SIC: 3842 Mfg Surgical Appliances/Supplies
PA: Msa Safety Incorporated
1000 Cranberry Woods Dr
Cranberry Township PA 16066
724 776-8600

(G-5570)
GUY LITTLE PRESS INC (PA)
235 N River Rd (04210-9479)
P.O. Box 891, Lewiston (04243-0891)
PHONE..................................207 795-0650
Aaron S White, *President*
EMP: 3
SQ FT: 1,500 Privately Held
WEB: www.littleguypress.com
SIC: 2759 Commercial Printing

(G-5571)
HANGER PRSTHETCS & ORTHO INC
600 Turner St Ste 2b (04210-5093)
PHONE..................................207 782-6907
Walt Meffert, *Branch Mgr*
EMP: 7
SALES (corp-wide): 1B Publicly Held
SIC: 3842 Mfg Surgical Appliances/Supplies
HQ: Hanger Prosthetics & Orthotics, Inc.
10910 Domain Dr Ste 300
Austin TX 78758
512 777-3800

(G-5572)
INTERNATIONAL PAPER COMPANY
175 Allied Rd (04210-7985)
P.O. Box 238 (04212-0238)
PHONE..................................207 784-4051
Benjamin Foster, *Engineer*
Bob Ritter, *Manager*
EMP: 130
SALES (corp-wide): 23.3B Publicly Held
WEB: www.internationalpaper.com
SIC: 2621 Paper Mill
PA: International Paper Company
6400 Poplar Ave
Memphis TN 38197
901 419-9000

(G-5573)
JFM NO 3 CORP
800 Center St (04210-6404)
PHONE..................................207 782-2726
Peter A Kowalski, *President*
Scott Sawyer, *CFO*
EMP: 20
SALES: 84.9K Privately Held
SIC: 2834 Mfg Pharmaceutical Preparations

(G-5574)
KICTEAM INC
1130 Minot Ave (04210-3739)
P.O. Box 1120 (04211-1120)
PHONE....................207 514-7030
Peter Klein, *President*
Timothy S Smith, *COO*
▲ **EMP:** 20
SQ FT: 20,000
SALES (est): 5.4MM
SALES (corp-wide): 7.7MM **Privately Held**
WEB: www.cleanteam.com
SIC: 2842 Mfg Polish/Sanitation Goods
PA: Enefco International, Inc.
1130 Minot Ave
Auburn ME 04210
207 514-7218

(G-5575)
LAPOINT INDUSTRIES INC (PA)
65 First Flight Dr (04210-9049)
P.O. Box 1970 (04211-1970)
PHONE....................207 777-3100
Alan Lapoint, *President*
EMP: 80 **EST:** 1998
SQ FT: 820,000
SALES (est): 21.9MM **Privately Held**
SIC: 3569 2393 2655 5085 Mfg General Indstl Mach Mfg Textile Bags Mfg Fiber Can/Drums Whol Industrial Supplies

(G-5576)
LEPAGE BAKERIES PARK ST LLC
Also Called: Green Mountain Baking Co
11 Adamian Dr (04210)
PHONE....................207 783-9161
EMP: 39
SALES (corp-wide): 3.9B **Publicly Held**
SIC: 2051 5461 Mfg Bread/Related Prdts Retail Bakery
HQ: Lepage Bakeries Park Street Llc
11 Adamian Dr
Auburn ME 04210
207 783-9161

(G-5577)
LEPAGE BAKERIES PARK ST LLC (HQ)
11 Adamian Dr (04210-8304)
P.O. Box 1900 (04211-1900)
PHONE....................207 783-9161
Andrew Barowsky,
Albert Lepage,
EMP: 40
SQ FT: 20,000
SALES (est): 61.6MM
SALES (corp-wide): 3.9B **Publicly Held**
SIC: 2051 5461 Mfg Bread/Related Products Retail Bakery
PA: Flowers Foods, Inc.
1919 Flowers Cir
Thomasville GA 31757
229 226-9110

(G-5578)
MAINE SCALE LLC
4 Washington St N Ste 1 (04210-4859)
PHONE....................207 777-9500
Thomas A Boughter Jr, *Principal*
EMP: 10
SALES: 2MM **Privately Held**
SIC: 3545 Mfg Machine Tool Accessories

(G-5579)
MANAGEMENT CONTROLS LLC
Also Called: Dough Masters
265 Rodman Rd (04210-3829)
P.O. Box 2058 (04211-2058)
PHONE....................207 753-6844
Don Buteau, *Owner*
Tom Dean, *CFO*
Pat Nash, *Sales Mgr*
EMP: 5
SQ FT: 5,000
SALES (est): 493K **Privately Held**
SIC: 2041 Mfg Flour/Grain Mill Products

(G-5580)
METAL SPECIALTIES INC
300 Rodman Rd (04210-3898)
PHONE....................207 786-4268
Mark Hodsdon, *President*
Irving Isaacson, *Clerk*
EMP: 11 **EST:** 1968
SQ FT: 13,000
SALES: 811K **Privately Held**
SIC: 3599 Mfg Industrial Machinery

(G-5581)
MILOR CORPORATION INC
Also Called: Vipi
120 Center St Ste 204 (04210-6340)
PHONE....................207 783-4226
Amy Plummer, *President*
EMP: 5 **EST:** 2006
SALES: 280K **Privately Held**
SIC: 3851 Ophthalmic Goods, Nsk

(G-5582)
MOUNTAIN MACHINE WORKS
Also Called: Mountain Fluid Power
2589 Hotel Rd (04210-8822)
PHONE....................207 783-6680
Bruce R Tisdale, *President*
Rebecca Cote, *Vice Pres*
Scott Pelchat, *Vice Pres*
Charles Gillis, *Treasurer*
EMP: 24
SQ FT: 5,500
SALES (est): 4.6MM **Privately Held**
WEB: www.mountainfluidpower.com
SIC: 3599 Mfg Industrial Machinery

(G-5583)
NORTH E WLDG & FABRICATION INC
Also Called: Newfab
928 Minot Ave (04210-3719)
PHONE....................207 786-2446
Leo Roche, *President*
Leon V White, *Vice Pres*
EMP: 25
SQ FT: 29,400
SALES (est): 3.8MM **Privately Held**
SIC: 7692 3441 3531 3444 Welding Repair Structural Metal Fabrctn Mfg Construction Mach Mfg Sheet Metalwork

(G-5584)
NORTHAST EMRGNCY APPARATUS LLC
Also Called: Nea
440 Washington St N (04210-3806)
PHONE....................207 753-0080
Susan Lake, *Treasurer*
Scott Lake,
Randall Cousineau,
EMP: 10
SALES: 1.7MM **Privately Held**
SIC: 3569 Mfg General Industrial Machinery

(G-5585)
PAINE PRODUCTS INC
Also Called: Paine Incense Co
17 Sunset Ave (04210-4127)
P.O. Box 1056 (04211-1056)
PHONE....................207 782-0931
Ann Loomis, *President*
John Vigue, *Vice Pres*
David Vigue, *Treasurer*
▲ **EMP:** 14 **EST:** 1931
SQ FT: 10,000
SALES (est): 2.4MM **Privately Held**
SIC: 2899 Mfg Incense Products

(G-5586)
PANOLAM INDUSTRIES INTL INC
Also Called: Pionite Decorative Surfaces
1 Pionite Rd (04210-3800)
P.O. Box 1014 (04211-1014)
PHONE....................207 784-9111
Betty Dwyer, *Branch Mgr*
John Hickey, *Manager*
EMP: 20 **Privately Held**
SIC: 2493 3083 2821 2672 Mfg Reconstd Wood Prdts Mfg Lamnatd Plstc Plates Mfg Plstc Material/Resin Mfg Coat/Laminated Paper
PA: Panolam Industries International, Inc.
1 Corporate Dr Ste 725
Shelton CT 06484

(G-5587)
PANOLAM SURFACE SYSTEMS
1 Pionite Rd (04210-3800)
PHONE....................203 925-1556
EMP: 5
SALES (est): 441.4K **Privately Held**
SIC: 3089 Mfg Plastic Products

(G-5588)
PEPSI-COLA METRO BTLG CO INC
191 Merrow Rd (04210-8319)
P.O. Box 1090 (04211-1090)
PHONE....................207 784-5791
Tressa Meiser, *Opers Staff*
Brian Garrison, *Branch Mgr*
EMP: 142
SALES (corp-wide): 64.6B **Publicly Held**
SIC: 2086 Mfg Bottled/Canned Soft Drinks
HQ: Pepsi-Cola Metropolitan Bottling Company, Inc.
1111 Westchester Ave
White Plains NY 10604
914 767-6000

(G-5589)
PERFORMANCE PRODUCTS PAINTING
63 Omni Cir (04210)
P.O. Box 2030 (04211-2030)
PHONE....................207 783-4222
David Sullivan, *President*
Paul Lavoie, *Admin Sec*
EMP: 20
SQ FT: 20,000
SALES (est): 2MM **Privately Held**
WEB: www.powderpaintme.com
SIC: 3479 Coating/Engraving Service
PA: Futureguard Building Products, Inc.
101 Merrow Rd
Auburn ME 04210

(G-5590)
PINE STATE PEST SOLUTIONS INC
546 Poland Rd (04210-3819)
P.O. Box 1480 (04211-1480)
PHONE....................207 795-1100
Parker Adams, *Principal*
EMP: 3
SALES (est): 555.3K **Privately Held**
SIC: 2879 0971 7342 4959 Disinfect/Pest Cntrl Svc Mfg Agricultural Chemcl Wildlife/Game Management Sanitary Services Pest Control Services

(G-5591)
PIONEER PLASTICS CORPORATION
1 Pionite Rd (04210-3840)
P.O. Box 1014 (04211-1014)
PHONE....................207 784-9111
Joe Dambrosio, *Owner*
Jeffrey O'Hearn, *Corp Comm Staff*
EMP: 209
SQ FT: 500,000 **Privately Held**
SIC: 3083 Mfg Laminated Plastic Sheets
HQ: Pioneer Plastics Corporation
1 Corporate Dr Ste 725
Shelton CT 06484
203 925-1556

(G-5592)
PIONEER PLASTICS CORPORATION
1 Pionite Rd (04210-3840)
PHONE....................207 784-9111
Pete Roseno, *Manager*
EMP: 500 **Privately Held**
SIC: 3083 3087 Mfg High And Low Pressure Industrial And Decorative Laminates & Mfg Specialty Resins
HQ: Pioneer Plastics Corporation
1 Corporate Dr Ste 725
Shelton CT 06484
203 925-1556

(G-5593)
PROCTER & GAMBLE COMPANY
2879 Hotel Rd (04210-8823)
PHONE....................207 753-4000
Jordan Carr, *Engineer*
Mike Caron, *Branch Mgr*
Todd Edwards, *Info Tech Mgr*
EMP: 150
SALES (corp-wide): 67.6B **Publicly Held**
SIC: 2844 Mfg Toilet Preparations
PA: The Procter & Gamble Company
1 Procter And Gamble Plz
Cincinnati OH 45202
513 983-1100

(G-5594)
R A CUMMINGS INC
82 Goldthwaite Rd (04210-3812)
P.O. Box 1747 (04211-1747)
PHONE....................207 777-7100
Rodney Cummings, *President*
Joel Cummings, *Vice Pres*
Lori Cummings, *Vice Pres*
EMP: 20
SQ FT: 3,000
SALES (est): 7.7MM **Privately Held**
WEB: www.auburnconcrete.com
SIC: 3273 Mfg Ready Mix Concrete

(G-5595)
RJF - MORIN BRICK LLC
Also Called: La Chance Brick
130 Morin Brick Rd (04210)
PHONE....................207 784-9375
Norman Davis, *President*
▲ **EMP:** 89 **EST:** 1934
SQ FT: 44,000
SALES (est): 10.9MM **Privately Held**
SIC: 3271 5032 3251 5211 Mfg Concrete Block/Brick Whol Brick/Stone Matrls Mfg Brick/Structrl Tile Ret Lumber/Building Mtrl

(G-5596)
S & D SHEET METAL INC
945 Washington St N (04210-3863)
PHONE....................207 777-7338
Toll Free:....................888 -
Diana Oemieux, *President*
Steve Lemieux, *Vice Pres*
Steven Oemieux, *Vice Pres*
EMP: 7
SQ FT: 3,000
SALES: 1MM **Privately Held**
SIC: 3444 Mfg Sheet Metalwork

(G-5597)
S&S EXCAVATION AND LOGGING LLC
447 Danville Corner Rd (04210-8610)
PHONE....................207 312-5590
Sheldon Stanley, *Principal*
EMP: 3 **EST:** 2013
SALES (est): 200.4K **Privately Held**
SIC: 2411 Logging

(G-5598)
SCOTT-LYNN MFG
Also Called: Maine Cage Factory
45 Hutchins St (04210-5718)
PHONE....................207 784-3372
Timothy Bouche, *President*
Debra Bouche, *Corp Secy*
EMP: 3
SQ FT: 7,200
SALES (est): 500K **Privately Held**
WEB: www.mainecagefactory.com
SIC: 3496 5199 Mfg Misc Fabricated Wire Products Whol Nondurable Goods

(G-5599)
THOS MOSER CABINETMAKERS INC (PA)
72 Wrights Lndg (04210-8307)
PHONE....................207 753-9834
Thomas Moser, *President*
Mary Moser, *Principal*
Colleen McCracken, *COO*
Darrell Pardy, *Vice Pres*
Cindy Joy, *Cust Mgr*
▲ **EMP:** 100 **EST:** 1972
SQ FT: 89,000
SALES (est): 19.4MM **Privately Held**
SIC: 2511 Mfg Wood Household Furniture

(G-5600)
UNITED FBRCNTS STRAINRITE CORP (HQ)
65 First Flight Dr (04210-9049)
P.O. Box 1970 (04211-1970)
PHONE....................207 376-1600
Alan Lapoint, *President*
Mike Gousse, *COO*
Karen Freeman, *Mfg Staff*
Riley Mattor, *Engineer*

GEOGRAPHIC

Donna Greenlaw, *Human Res Mgr*
▲ **EMP:** 75
SQ FT: 82,000
SALES (est): 21.7MM
SALES (corp-wide): 21.9MM **Privately Held**
WEB: www.ufstrainrite.com
SIC: 3569 5078 Mfg General Industrial Machinery Whol Refrigeration Equipment/Supplies
PA: Lapoint Industries, Inc.
65 First Flight Dr
Auburn ME 04210
207 777-3100

(G-5601)
WORLD HARBORS INC
176 First Flight Dr (04210-9055)
PHONE..................................207 786-3200
Steven Arthurs, *President*
Karen Foust, *Vice Pres*
EMP: 25
SQ FT: 40,000
SALES (est): 2.2MM **Privately Held**
WEB: www.worldharbors.com
SIC: 2035 Mfg Pickles/Sauces/Dressing
HQ: Mizkan America, Inc.
1661 Feehanville Dr # 200
Mount Prospect IL 60056
847 590-0059

(G-5602)
ZAMPELL REFRACTORIES INC
192 First Flight Dr (04210-9055)
PHONE..................................207 786-2400
Sean Case, *Manager*
EMP: 20
SALES (corp-wide): 52.1MM **Privately Held**
WEB: www.zampellrefractories.com
SIC: 3255 1742 Mfg Clay Refractories Drywall/Insulating Contractor
PA: Zampell Refractories, Inc.
3 Stanley Tucker Dr
Newburyport MA 01950
978 465-0055

Augusta
Kennebec County

(G-5603)
ALBISONS PRINTING INC
124 Riverside Dr (04330-4384)
P.O. Box 4622 (04330-1622)
PHONE..................................207 622-1941
Stephen W Albison, *President*
Susan Albison, *Treasurer*
EMP: 4
SQ FT: 4,000
SALES: 1MM **Privately Held**
WEB: www.albisonsprinting.com
SIC: 2759 2752 Commercial Printing Lithographic Commercial Printing

(G-5604)
BULZEYEPRO
1069 S Belfast Ave (04330-0319)
PHONE..................................207 626-0000
William Rocque, *Owner*
EMP: 3
SQ FT: 6,000
SALES (est): 156.1K **Privately Held**
SIC: 3827 Mfg Optical Instruments/Lenses

(G-5605)
CIVES CORPORATION
Also Called: Cives Steel
103 Lipman Rd (04330-8322)
P.O. Box 1077 (04332-1077)
PHONE..................................207 622-6141
Lawrence J Morgan, *President*
Darrin Wood, *Prdtn Mgr*
Travis Wing, *Safety Mgr*
Eric Corrow, *Purch Mgr*
Martin Keniston, *Controller*
EMP: 140
SALES (corp-wide): 651.3MM **Privately Held**
WEB: www.cives.com
SIC: 3441 3446 Structural Metal Fabrication Mfg Architectural Metalwork
PA: Cives Corporation
3700 Mansell Rd Ste 500
Alpharetta GA 30022
770 993-4424

(G-5606)
CPK MANUFACTURING LLC
Also Called: Kenway Composites
681 Riverside Dr (04330-8300)
PHONE..................................207 622-6229
Ian Kopp, *Branch Mgr*
EMP: 35
SALES (corp-wide): 840.5MM **Privately Held**
SIC: 3089 Mfg Plastic Products
HQ: Cpk Manufacturing, Llc
214 Industrial Ln
Alum Bank PA 15521
814 839-4186

(G-5607)
ELECTRNIC MOBILITY CONTRLS LLC
Also Called: EMC
26 Gabriel Dr (04330-7853)
PHONE..................................207 512-8009
Scott A Bolduc,
Kay Braud,
EMP: 16
SQ FT: 12,000
SALES (est): 3.6MM **Privately Held**
SIC: 3714 3845 3625 Mfg Motor Vehicle Parts/Accessories Mfg Electromedical Equipment Mfg Relays/Industrial Controls

(G-5608)
HANGER PRSTHETCS & ORTHO INC
24 Stone St (04330-5298)
PHONE..................................207 622-9792
Scott Hubert, *Branch Mgr*
EMP: 7
SALES (corp-wide): 1B **Publicly Held**
SIC: 3842 Ret Misc Merchandise
HQ: Hanger Prosthetics & Orthotics, Inc.
10910 Domain Dr Ste 300
Austin TX 78758
512 777-3800

(G-5609)
JS MCCARTHY CO INC (PA)
Also Called: J.S. McCarthy Printers
15 Darin Dr (04330-7815)
PHONE..................................207 622-6241
Toll Free:..................................888 -
Jonathan Tardiff, *President*
Phil Germain, *Business Mgr*
Phil St Germain, *Business Mgr*
Bill White, *COO*
Roger Schutte, *Production*
EMP: 88 **EST:** 1960
SQ FT: 90,000
SALES: 35MM **Privately Held**
WEB: www.jsmccarthy.com
SIC: 2791 2752 2789 2759 Typesetting Services Lithographic Coml Print Bookbinding/Related Work Commercial Printing

(G-5610)
KENNEBEC TECHNOLOGIES
150 Church Hill Rd (04330-8261)
P.O. Box 470, Auburn (04212-0470)
PHONE..................................207 626-0188
Charles Johnson, *President*
Bart Haley, *Vice Pres*
Steve Lee, *Vice Pres*
Richard L Trafton, *Clerk*
▲ **EMP:** 65
SQ FT: 25,000
SALES: 10MM **Privately Held**
SIC: 3544 3599 Mfg Dies/Tools/Jigs/Fixtures Mfg Industrial Machinery

(G-5611)
KENT NUTRITION GROUP INC
10 Dalton Rd (04330-8326)
P.O. Box 980 (04332-0980)
PHONE..................................207 622-1530
John Hanson, *Branch Mgr*
EMP: 11
SALES (corp-wide): 449.1MM **Privately Held**
WEB: www.blueseal.com
SIC: 2048 5999 Mfg Prepared Feeds Ret Misc Merchandise
HQ: Kent Nutrition Group, Inc.
1600 Oregon St
Muscatine IA 52761
866 647-1212

(G-5612)
KW BOATS (DH)
Also Called: Harbor Technologies
681 Riverside Dr (04330-8300)
PHONE..................................207 622-6229
Kenneth G Priest II, *CEO*
Ian D Kopp, *President*
Ian Kopp, *Branch Mgr*
◆ **EMP:** 5 **EST:** 1957
SQ FT: 40,000
SALES (est): 16.5MM
SALES (corp-wide): 840.5MM **Privately Held**
WEB: www.kenway.com
SIC: 3089 Mfg Plastic Products
HQ: Cpk Manufacturing, Llc
214 Industrial Ln
Alum Bank PA 15521
814 839-4186

(G-5613)
LETTER SYSTEMS INC (PA)
Also Called: J S McCarthy Printing
15 Darin Dr (04330-7815)
PHONE..................................207 622-7126
Richard Tardiff, *President*
Conrad Ayotte, *CFO*
Matthew Tardiff, *Controller*
Sandy Rines, *Cust Svc Dir*
EMP: 160
SQ FT: 90,000
SALES (est): 42.7MM **Privately Held**
SIC: 2752 Lithographic Commercial Printing

(G-5614)
MCLEOD OPTICAL COMPANY INC
179 Mount Vernon Ave (04330-4233)
PHONE..................................207 623-3841
Donald J McLeod, *President*
EMP: 12
SQ FT: 1,300
SALES (corp-wide): 5.8MM **Privately Held**
SIC: 3851 5048 Mfg Ophthalmic Goods Whol Ophthalmic Goods
PA: Mcleod Optical Company, Inc.
50 Jefferson Park Rd
Warwick RI 02888
401 467-3000

(G-5615)
MINUTEMAN SIGN CENTERS INC (PA)
297 State St (04330-7036)
PHONE..................................207 622-4171
William C McKeen, *President*
Kevin McKeen, *Vice Pres*
EMP: 9
SQ FT: 3,000
SALES: 450K **Privately Held**
SIC: 3993 Mfg Signs/Advertising Specialties

(G-5616)
PEPSI-COLA METRO BTLG CO INC
80 Anthony Ave (04330-7882)
PHONE..................................207 623-1313
EMP: 77
SALES (corp-wide): 64.6B **Publicly Held**
SIC: 2086 Mfg Bottled/Canned Soft Drinks
HQ: Pepsi-Cola Metropolitan Bottling Company, Inc.
1111 Westchester Ave
White Plains NY 10604
914 767-6000

(G-5617)
PURBECK ISLE INC (PA)
36 Anthony Ave Ste 104 (04330-7891)
PHONE..................................207 623-5119
David Hinson, *President*
Eric Dick, *Admin Sec*
▼ **EMP:** 32
SQ FT: 20,000
SALES: 18MM **Privately Held**
SIC: 2037 Pet Food Distributor

(G-5618)
SANMINA CORPORATION
500 Civic Center Dr (04330)
PHONE..................................207 623-6511
Larry Chadwick, *Purch Mgr*
Pat Barry, *Manager*
Bill Morgan, *Manager*
EMP: 70 **Publicly Held**
WEB: www.sci.com
SIC: 3672 Mfg Printed Circuit Boards
PA: Sanmina Corporation
2700 N 1st St
San Jose CA 95134

(G-5619)
SEATTLE TIMES COMPANY
Also Called: Blethen Maine Newspapers
274 Western Ave (04330)
PHONE..................................207 623-3811
John Christie, *Manager*
EMP: 160
SALES (corp-wide): 226.3MM **Privately Held**
WEB: www.seattletimes.nwsource.com
SIC: 2711 Newspapers-Publishing/Printing
HQ: Seattle Times Company
1000 Denny Way Ste 501
Seattle WA 98109
206 464-2111

(G-5620)
SPB LLC
Also Called: Maritime Marine Group
681 Riverside Dr (04330-8300)
PHONE..................................207 620-7998
Mark E Levey,
Ken Pierce,
◆ **EMP:** 5
SALES (est): 1.3MM **Privately Held**
SIC: 3732 Boatbuilding/Repairing

(G-5621)
SPINDOC INC
126 Western Ave Ste 147 (04330-7249)
PHONE..................................207 689-7010
Susan Thomas, *CEO*
EMP: 3
SALES (est): 86K **Privately Held**
SIC: 7372 Prepackaged Software Services

(G-5622)
TRANQUILITEES
139 Northern Ave (04330-4214)
PHONE..................................207 441-8058
Kimberly Bard, *Principal*
EMP: 3
SALES (est): 163.3K **Privately Held**
SIC: 2759 Commercial Printing

Avon
Franklin County

(G-5623)
GCA LOGGING INC
118 River Rd (04966-3040)
PHONE..................................207 639-3941
Greg Adams, *President*
Andrea Adams, *Treasurer*
EMP: 4
SALES (est): 667.6K **Privately Held**
SIC: 2411 Timber Logging

Baileyville
Washington County

(G-5624)
DOMTAR PAPER COMPANY LLC
144 Main St (04694-3529)
PHONE..................................207 427-6400
James Oliver, *Business Anlyst*
Mona W Moorman, *Branch Mgr*
EMP: 650
SALES (corp-wide): 264.5MM **Privately Held**
SIC: 2621 Paper Mill
HQ: Domtar Paper Company, Llc
234 Kingsley Park Dr
Fort Mill SC 29715

(G-5625)
FULGHUM FIBRES INC
224 Main St (04694)
P.O. Box 727 (04694-0727)
PHONE..................................207 427-6560
Mark Seaby, *Manager*
EMP: 42
SALES (corp-wide): 150.7MM **Privately Held**
WEB: www.fulghumfibres.com
SIC: 2421 Sawmill/Planing Mill
HQ: Fulghum Fibres, Inc.
3604 Wheeler Rd Ste C
Augusta GA 30909
706 651-1000

(G-5626)
GEORGIA-PACIFIC LLC
144 Main St (04694-3545)
P.O. Box 759 (04694-0759)
PHONE..................................207 427-4077
Jim Runyan, *Manager*
EMP: 8
SALES (corp-wide): 40.6B **Privately Held**
WEB: www.gp.com
SIC: 2431 2621 2631 2421 Mfg Pulp And Paper Products
HQ: Georgia-Pacific Llc
133 Peachtree St Nw
Atlanta GA 30303
404 652-4000

(G-5627)
WOODLAND PULP LLC (PA)
144 Main St (04694-3529)
PHONE..................................207 427-3311
Randy Raditya, *Engineer*
Berk Martin,
▲ **EMP:** 300
SALES (est): 187.7MM **Privately Held**
SIC: 2611 Paper Mill

Bangor
Penobscot County

(G-5628)
AC ELECTRIC CORP
Also Called: AC Electric
40 Target Industrial Cir (04401-5798)
PHONE..................................207 945-9487
Dan Parsons, *President*
EMP: 13
SALES (corp-wide): 7.2MM **Privately Held**
WEB: www.acelec.com
SIC: 7694 5085 Armature Rewinding Whol Industrial Supplies
PA: A.C. Electric Corp.
120 Merrow Rd
Auburn ME 04210
207 784-7341

(G-5629)
AMERICAN CONCRETE INDS INC
Also Called: Shawnee Steps
1717 Stillwater Ave (04401-2671)
PHONE..................................207 947-8334
Shawn McDonald, *Branch Mgr*
EMP: 70
SALES (est): 8.4MM
SALES (corp-wide): 10MM **Privately Held**
WEB: www.americanconcrete.com
SIC: 3272 5211 Mfg Concrete Products Ret Lumber/Building Materials
PA: American Concrete Industries, Inc.
982 Minot Ave
Auburn ME 04210
207 947-8334

(G-5630)
BAFS INC (PA)
61 Florida Ave Ste 101 (04401-3005)
PHONE..................................207 942-5226
Allon R Fish Jr, *President*
EMP: 18 **EST:** 1999
SQ FT: 36,000
SALES (est): 8MM **Privately Held**
WEB: www.bafsinc.com
SIC: 2038 Mfg Frozen Specialties

(G-5631)
BANGOR NEON INC
1567 Hammond St (04401-5793)
PHONE..................................207 947-2766
Gayle Treworgy Hansen, *President*
Joel Hansen, *Vice Pres*
Grace C Treworgy, *Director*
Lee White, *Graphic Designe*
EMP: 10 **EST:** 1948
SQ FT: 5,000
SALES: 1.1MM **Privately Held**
WEB: www.bangorneon.com
SIC: 3993 7389 Mfg Signs/Advertising Specialties Business Services

(G-5632)
BANGOR PUBLISHING COMPANY (PA)
Also Called: Bangor Daily News
1 Merchants Plz (04401-8302)
P.O. Box 1329 (04402-1329)
PHONE..................................207 990-8000
Todd Benoit, *President*
Arthur E Mc Kenzie, *Treasurer*
Tim Reynolds, *Asst Treas*
Susan Coffman, *Admin Sec*
▲ **EMP:** 200
SQ FT: 60,000
SALES (est): 74MM **Privately Held**
WEB: www.bangornews.com
SIC: 2711 Newspapers-Publishing/Printing

(G-5633)
C & L AVIATION GROUP (PA)
40 Wyoming Ave (04401-3068)
PHONE..................................207 217-6050
Chris Kilgour, *CEO*
Tom Chapman, *Senior VP*
Warrick Hood, *Senior VP*
Donald Kamenz, *Vice Pres*
Todd Williams, *Opers Mgr*
EMP: 20
SALES (est): 8.1MM **Privately Held**
SIC: 3728 Mfg Aircraft Parts/Equipment

(G-5634)
C&L ENGINE SOLUTIONS LLC
40 Wyoming Ave (04401-3068)
PHONE..................................307 217-6050
Christopher Kilgour, *Mng Member*
EMP: 3
SALES: 10.8MM **Privately Held**
SIC: 3724 Mfg Aircraft Engines/Parts

(G-5635)
CENTRAL STREET CORPORATION
Also Called: Northeast Reprographics
80 Central St (04401-5110)
P.O. Box 2008 (04402-2008)
PHONE..................................207 947-8049
Vernon Haynes, *President*
Ken Rogers Jr, *Treasurer*
Paul Weeks, *Clerk*
EMP: 10
SQ FT: 3,500
SALES (est): 1.3MM **Privately Held**
WEB: www.nerepro.com
SIC: 2741 2752 7334 Misc Publishing Lithographic Commercial Printing Photocopying Services

(G-5636)
CINTAS CORPORATION
293 Target Cir (04401-5719)
PHONE..................................207 307-2448
EMP: 6
SALES (corp-wide): 6.8B **Publicly Held**
SIC: 2326 Ret Misc Apparel/Accessories
PA: Cintas Corporation
6800 Cintas Blvd
Cincinnati OH 45262
513 459-1200

(G-5637)
COCA-COLA BOTTLING COMPANY
91 Dowd Rd (04401-6733)
PHONE..................................207 942-5546
Patrick Conley, *Sales Mgr*
Russell Perry, *Branch Mgr*
Brian Hanlon, *Manager*
David Page, *Manager*
Mark Brown, *IT/INT Sup*
EMP: 71 **Privately Held**
SIC: 2086 Carb Sft Drnkbtlcn
HQ: Coca-Cola Beverages Northeast, Inc.
1 Executive Park Dr # 330
Bedford NH 03110
603 627-7871

(G-5638)
COFFEE NEWS USA INC (PA)
1 Cumberland Pl Ste 102 (04401-5087)
PHONE..................................207 941-0860
William Buckley, *President*
Sue-Ann Buckley, *Vice Pres*
Peter Philbrick, *Officer*
Melissa Wildes, *Executive Asst*
EMP: 3 **EST:** 1994
SALES (est): 322.2K **Privately Held**
WEB: www.coffeenewsusa.com
SIC: 2711 Newspapers-Publishing/Printing

(G-5639)
COMMERCIAL SCREENPRINT EMB INC
130 Thatcher St (04401-6829)
PHONE..................................207 942-2862
David Berry, *President*
Eleanor Berry, *Vice Pres*
Audrey Robinson Blakeman, *Shareholder*
Sabra Robinson, *Shareholder*
EMP: 6
SQ FT: 4,300
SALES (est): 332.7K **Privately Held**
SIC: 2262 2395 Manmade Fiber & Silk Finishing Plant Pleating/Stitching Services

(G-5640)
CREATIVE DIGITAL IMAGING
24 Dowd Rd (04401-6700)
P.O. Box 1296 (04402-1296)
PHONE..................................207 973-0500
Micheal Bazinet, *CEO*
EMP: 36
SALES (est): 7MM **Privately Held**
WEB: www.creativedi.com
SIC: 2759 Commercial Printing

(G-5641)
DOWN E EMULSIONS LTD LBLTY CO
58 Bennett St (04401-5702)
PHONE..................................207 947-8624
Steve Ford, *Mng Member*
Ron Simbari,
EMP: 3
SALES (est): 537.6K
SALES (corp-wide): 80.9MM **Privately Held**
SIC: 2951 Mfg Asphalt Mixtures/Blocks
HQ: Barrett Paving Materials Inc.
3 Becker Farm Rd Ste 307
Roseland NJ 07068
973 533-1001

(G-5642)
ELDUR CORPORATION
Also Called: Eldur AG
448 Griffin Rd (04401-3031)
PHONE..................................207 942-6592
Werner Dietze, *President*
Rick Starbird, *Prdtn Mgr*
Joe Hornyak, *Manager*
▲ **EMP:** 21
SQ FT: 33,000
SALES (est): 4.8MM
SALES (corp-wide): 52.1MM **Privately Held**
SIC: 3357 Nonferrous Wiredrawing/Insulating
PA: Eldur Ag, Maienfeld
Industriestrasse 4
Maienfeld GR 7304
813 004-848

(G-5643)
EZTOUSECOM DIRECTORIES
592 Hammond St (04401-4545)
PHONE..................................207 974-3171
Nicole Lozier, *Principal*
EMP: 7
SALES (est): 336.8K **Privately Held**
SIC: 2741 Misc Publishing

(G-5644)
FIORE ARTISAN OLIVE OILS
86 Hammond St (04401-4915)
PHONE..................................207 801-8549
Pat O'Brien, *Principal*
EMP: 3
SALES (est): 100.5K **Privately Held**
SIC: 2079 Mfg Edible Fats/Oils

(G-5645)
FOAM PRO INC
6 State St (04401-5112)
P.O. Box 458, Greene (04236-0458)
PHONE..................................207 212-9657
Anthony Michaud, *President*
EMP: 5
SALES (est): 900K **Privately Held**
SIC: 2899 Mfg Chemical Preparations

(G-5646)
FREIHOFER BAKING CO
1172 Hammond St (04401-5756)
PHONE..................................207 947-2387
Kirby Astbury, *Branch Mgr*
EMP: 5 **EST:** 2010
SALES (est): 209.7K **Privately Held**
SIC: 2051 Mfg Bread/Related Products

(G-5647)
FURBUSH ROBERTS PRTG CO INC
435 Odlin Rd (04401-6705)
PHONE..................................207 945-9409
Thomas C Roberts, *President*
Caitline Sullivan, *Vice Pres*
Ron Crane, *Prdtn Mgr*
Frances Kelly, *CFO*
EMP: 9
SQ FT: 12,700
SALES: 955.3K **Privately Held**
WEB: www.furbushroberts.com
SIC: 2752 Lithographic Commercial Printing

(G-5648)
GENERAL ELECTRIC COMPANY
534 Griffin Rd (04401-3086)
PHONE..................................207 941-2500
Jonathan Hatch, *Opers Staff*
Brackett Denniston, *Branch Mgr*
EMP: 500
SALES (corp-wide): 121.6B **Publicly Held**
SIC: 3511 3563 Mfg Turbines/Generator Sets Mfg Air/Gas Compressors
PA: General Electric Company
5 Necco St
Boston MA 02210
617 443-3000

(G-5649)
HENDERSONS REDWARE
53 Downing Rd (04401-2716)
PHONE..................................207 942-9013
Kenneth J Henderson, *Owner*
EMP: 3
SQ FT: 2,000
SALES: 75K **Privately Held**
WEB: www.hendersonsredware.com
SIC: 3269 Mfg Pottery Products

(G-5650)
HIGGINS FABRICATION LLC
40 Johnson St Ste 5 (04401-3391)
PHONE..................................719 930-6437
Keven Higgins, *Mng Member*
EMP: 5
SALES (est): 533.3K **Privately Held**
SIC: 2599 5021 5712 Mfg Furniture/Fixtures Whol Furniture Ret Furniture

(G-5651)
HOWARD TOOL COMPANY
547 Odlin Rd (04401-6707)
PHONE..................................207 942-1203
Marty H Arsenault, *Owner*
EMP: 20
SQ FT: 5,000
SALES (est): 5.2MM **Privately Held**
WEB: www.howardtool.com
SIC: 3469 Mfg Metal Stampings

(G-5652)
JIFFY PRINT INC
494 Broadway (04401-3468)
PHONE..................................207 947-4490
Mark D Grandchamp, *President*
EMP: 9
SQ FT: 6,000

SALES: 1MM **Privately Held**
SIC: 2752 Lithographic Commercial Printing

(G-5653)
LEES CONCRETE INC
974 Odlin Rd (04401-6716)
PHONE..................................207 974-4936
Margaret Lee, *Principal*
Darin Lee, *Co-Owner*
EMP: 3
SALES (est): 110.5K **Privately Held**
SIC: 3273 Mfg Ready-Mixed Concrete

(G-5654)
NAUTEL MAINE INC
201 Target Industrial Cir (04401-5799)
PHONE..................................207 947-8200
Peter Conlon, *Ch of Bd*
Darlene Fowlow, *President*
Doreen Commeau, *Treasurer*
▼ **EMP:** 175
SQ FT: 24,000
SALES (est): 27.8MM
SALES (corp-wide): 1.3MM **Privately Held**
WEB: www.nautel.com
SIC: 3663 Mfg Radio/Tv Communication Equipment
HQ: Nautel Limited
10089 Peggys Cove Rd Hwy 333
Hacketts Cove NS B3Z 3
902 823-3900

(G-5655)
NEW ENGLAND DENTURE CNTR BANGR (PA)
Also Called: Empire Denture Center
58 Fruit St (04401-5522)
PHONE..................................207 941-6550
William Buxton, *Principal*
EMP: 15
SALES (est): 2.2MM **Privately Held**
WEB: www.nedenturecenter.com
SIC: 3843 Retail Dental Supplies

(G-5656)
NEW ENGLAND SALT CO LLC
500 Odlin Rd (04401-6708)
P.O. Box 352, Winterport (04496-0352)
PHONE..................................207 262-9779
Steven Clisham, *Principal*
EMP: 4
SALES (est): 673.6K **Privately Held**
SIC: 2899 Mfg Chemical Preparations

(G-5657)
PATRICKS INC
629 Broadway (04401-3339)
PHONE..................................207 990-9303
Pat Smith, *President*
EMP: 3
SALES (est): 429.7K **Privately Held**
SIC: 2771 Mfg Greeting Cards

(G-5658)
SALIBAS RUG & UPHOLSTERY CLRS
Also Called: A & A Products
59 May St (04401-6437)
PHONE..................................207 947-8876
Tom Gagne, *President*
EMP: 3
SALES (est): 388.5K **Privately Held**
SIC: 3589 Cleaning Supplies

(G-5659)
TERESA BURGESS
11 Bond Rd (04401-0840)
PHONE..................................207 848-5697
Teresa Burgess, *Principal*
EMP: 3
SALES (est): 198.1K **Privately Held**
SIC: 2411 Logging

(G-5660)
TRIO SOFTWARE CORP
56 Banair Rd (04401-8712)
P.O. Box 407, Hampden (04444-0407)
PHONE..................................207 942-6222
Ronald Wentworth, *President*
James Philips, *Vice Pres*
EMP: 10
SALES (est): 763.7K **Privately Held**
WEB: www.triosoftwarecorp.com
SIC: 7372 Prepackaged Software Services

(G-5661)
TWISTED
663 Stillwater Ave (04401-3680)
PHONE..................................207 942-9530
EMP: 4 **EST:** 2010
SALES (est): 140.2K **Privately Held**
SIC: 2052 Mfg Cookies/Crackers

(G-5662)
UMAMI NOODLE
1 Main St (04401-6303)
PHONE..................................207 947-9991
Thinda Cristana, *Owner*
EMP: 10
SALES (est): 121.3K **Privately Held**
SIC: 2098 Mfg Macaroni/Spaghetti

(G-5663)
WATERWORKS
Also Called: Bed Works, The
25 Dowd Rd (04401-6733)
PHONE..................................207 941-8306
Stephen Hammann, *President*
EMP: 14
SALES (corp-wide): 2.8MM **Privately Held**
SIC: 2511 Mfg Wood Furniture
PA: The Waterworks
270 State St
Brewer ME 04412
207 989-3233

(G-5664)
WILD COW CREAMERY LLC
28 Broad St (04401-6645)
PHONE..................................207 907-0301
EMP: 5 **EST:** 2013
SQ FT: 2,830
SALES (est): 186.7K **Privately Held**
SIC: 2052 Mfg Cookies/Crackers

Bar Harbor
Hancock County

(G-5665)
FABRICATE LLC
64 Mount Desert St (04609-1324)
PHONE..................................207 288-5113
Erin Early Ward, *Principal*
EMP: 4
SALES (est): 409.6K **Privately Held**
SIC: 2782 Mfg Blankbooks/Binders

(G-5666)
MOUNT DESERT ISLAND ICE CREAM
325 Main St (04609-1640)
PHONE..................................207 460-5515
EMP: 8
SALES (est): 646.4K **Privately Held**
SIC: 2024 Ice Cream And Frozen Desserts, Nsk

(G-5667)
MOUNT DESERT ISLANDER
310 Main St (04609-1638)
P.O. Box 900 (04609-0900)
PHONE..................................207 288-0556
Earl Brechlin, *CEO*
EMP: 7
SALES (est): 372.3K **Privately Held**
WEB: www.mdislander.com
SIC: 2711 Newspapers-Publishing/Printing

(G-5668)
ROBERT GAYNOR
Also Called: Screen Printery Downeast Maine
758 Norway Dr (04609-7921)
PHONE..................................207 288-4398
Toll Free:..877 -
Robert Gaynor, *Owner*
EMP: 5
SALES (est): 150K **Privately Held**
WEB: www.screenprintery.com
SIC: 2396 7389 Mfg Auto/Apparel Trimming Business Services

(G-5669)
SALISBURY COVE ASSOCIATES INC
Also Called: Atlantic Brewing Company
15 Knox Rd (04609-7770)
PHONE..................................207 288-2337
Alex Maffucci, *President*
Doug Maffucci, *Vice Pres*
▲ **EMP:** 20
SALES (est): 829.9K **Privately Held**
WEB: www.atlanticbrewing.com
SIC: 2082 Mfg Malt Beverages

(G-5670)
SOYATECH INC
Also Called: Soya Techcom
1369 State Highway 102 (04609-7019)
P.O. Box 1307, Southwest Harbor (04679-1307)
PHONE..................................207 288-4969
▲ **EMP:** 6
SQ FT: 2,000
SALES (est): 484.6K **Privately Held**
WEB: www.soyatech.com
SIC: 2741 2721 8731 Publishing Of Directories & Magazines & Provides R & D Services For New Food Products & Markets

(G-5671)
WILLIS & SONS INC
Also Called: Rock Shop
69 Main St 73 (04609-1844)
PHONE..................................207 288-4935
Roger Willis, *President*
Weston Willis, *Vice Pres*
Cheryl Willis, *Treasurer*
EMP: 5
SQ FT: 1,200
SALES (est): 655.4K **Privately Held**
SIC: 3911 5944 5947 Mfg Precious Metal Jewelry Ret Jewelry Ret Gifts/Novelties

Bass Harbor
Hancock County

(G-5672)
MORRIS YACHT INC (PA)
53 Granville Rd (04653-3233)
P.O. Box 395 (04653-0395)
PHONE..................................207 667-6235
Doug Metchick, *CEO*
Cuyler Morris, *President*
Dewitt C Morris, *President*
Justine M Morris, *Treasurer*
▼ **EMP:** 26
SALES (est): 5.6MM **Privately Held**
WEB: www.morrisyachts.com
SIC: 3732 Boatbuilding/Repairing

Bath
Sagadahoc County

(G-5673)
BAE SYSTEMS TECH SOL SRVC INC
149 Front St (04530-2672)
PHONE..................................207 449-3577
Steve Frye, *Branch Mgr*
EMP: 3
SALES (corp-wide): 22.1B **Privately Held**
SIC: 3812 Mfg Search/Navigation Equipment
HQ: Bae Systems Technology Solutions & Services Inc.
520 Gaither Rd
Rockville MD 20850
703 847-5820

(G-5674)
BATH IRON WORKS CORPORATION (HQ)
700 Washington St Stop 1 (04530-2556)
PHONE..................................207 443-3311
Phebe N Novakovic, *President*
Tom Stevens, *Superintendent*
Cindy Osgood, *Principal*
Jay L Johnson, *Chairman*
Thomas A Brown, *Vice Pres*
▲ **EMP:** 277
SALES (est): 286.3MM
SALES (corp-wide): 36.1B **Publicly Held**
WEB: www.gdbiw.com
SIC: 3731 8711 Shipbuilding/Repairing Engineering Services Structural Metal Fabrication
PA: General Dynamics Corporation
11011 Sunset Hills Rd
Reston VA 20190
703 876-3000

(G-5675)
CUSTOM COMPOSITE TECHNOLOGIES
15 Wing Farm Pkwy (04530-1515)
PHONE..................................207 442-7007
Toll Free:..866 -
Stephen Hassett, *President*
Maurine Hassett, *Treasurer*
EMP: 6 **EST:** 1999
SQ FT: 7,500
SALES: 950K **Privately Held**
WEB: www.customcomposite.com
SIC: 3732 Boatbuilding/Repairing

(G-5676)
DIRECT DISPLAY PUBLISHING INC
765 High St Ste 5 (04530-2459)
P.O. Box 451 (04530-0451)
PHONE..................................207 443-4800
Spencer Richie, *President*
Bebera Mosher, *Manager*
EMP: 8
SALES (est): 1MM **Privately Held**
WEB: www.direct-display.com
SIC: 2741 Misc Publishing

(G-5677)
GENERAL DYNAMICS CORPORATION
700 Washington St (04530-2574)
PHONE..................................207 442-3245
Jerry Cashman, *President*
Tim Glinatsis, *Engineer*
Chris Waaler, *Engineer*
Dan Provencher, *Design Engr*
Jeff Geiger, *Branch Mgr*
EMP: 25
SALES (corp-wide): 36.1B **Publicly Held**
SIC: 3731 Shipbuilding/Repairing
PA: General Dynamics Corporation
11011 Sunset Hills Rd
Reston VA 20190
703 876-3000

(G-5678)
KENNEBEC CABINETRY INC
Also Called: Kennebec Company, The
37 Wing Farm Pkwy (04530-1515)
PHONE..................................207 442-0813
James Stewart, *Principal*
EMP: 18
SQ FT: 15,651
SALES (est): 1MM **Privately Held**
SIC: 2434 Mfg Wood Kitchen Cabinets

(G-5679)
KENNEBEC COMPANY
Also Called: Kennebec Cabinet Company
1 Front St Ste 3 (04530-2562)
PHONE..................................207 443-2131
J D Leonard, *Owner*
EMP: 40
SQ FT: 16,000
SALES (est): 4.7MM **Privately Held**
WEB: www.kennebeccompany.com
SIC: 2434 Mfg Wood Kitchen Cabinets

(G-5680)
LOCKHEED MARTIN CORPORATION
Also Called: Lockheed Martin Rso
590 Washington St (04530-1934)
P.O. Box 269 (04530-0269)
PHONE..................................207 442-1112
Timothy Kemstra, *Manager*
EMP: 50 **Publicly Held**
WEB: www.lockheedmartin.com
SIC: 3812 Mfg Search/Navigation Equipment
PA: Lockheed Martin Corporation
6801 Rockledge Dr
Bethesda MD 20817

▲ = Import ▼=Export
◆ =Import/Export

(G-5681)
SUPERVISOR OF SHIPBUILDING
Also Called: C & R Usn
574 Washington St (04530-1905)
PHONE..................................207 442-2520
Robert Crowe, *President*
EMP: 4
SALES (est): 628.1K **Privately Held**
SIC: 3731 Shipbuilding/Repairing

(G-5682)
ZEN BEAR HONEY TEA LLC
114 Old Brunswick Rd (04530-4219)
P.O. Box 554 (04530-0554)
PHONE..................................207 449-1553
Elise Ferrel, *Mng Member*
Frank Ferrel, *Manager*
EMP: 4 **EST:** 2014
SALES: 190K **Privately Held**
SIC: 2099 Mfg Food Preparations

Beals
Washington County

(G-5683)
DENNIS WELDING & MARINE INC
179 Alley Bays Rd (04611)
P.O. Box 193 (04611-0193)
PHONE..................................207 497-5998
Dennis Smorch, *President*
EMP: 5
SALES (est): 500.1K **Privately Held**
SIC: 7692 1799 Welding Repair Trade Contractor

(G-5684)
LIBBYS BOAT SHOP
12 Hixey Head Rd (04611)
P.O. Box 154 (04611-0154)
PHONE..................................207 497-5487
Ernest Libby, *Partner*
Glenn Libby, *Partner*
Ivan Libby, *Partner*
Lavaron Libby, *Partner*
EMP: 4
SALES (est): 250.1K **Privately Held**
SIC: 3732 Boatbuilding/Repairing

Belfast
Waldo County

(G-5685)
BANGOR PUBLISHING COMPANY
Also Called: Bangor Daily News
26 Spring St (04915-6817)
PHONE..................................207 338-3034
Walter Griffin, *Manager*
EMP: 3
SALES (corp-wide): 74MM **Privately Held**
WEB: www.bangornews.com
SIC: 2711 Newspapers-Publishing/Printing
PA: Bangor Publishing Company
1 Merchants Plz
Bangor ME 04401
207 990-8000

(G-5686)
BELFAST BAY BREWING COMPANY
14 Cliff Ln (04915-7245)
PHONE..................................866 338-5722
John Mullen, *President*
EMP: 4
SQ FT: 5,000
SALES: 160K **Privately Held**
SIC: 2082 Mfg Malt Beverages

(G-5687)
CHASE S DAILY LLC
Also Called: Chase's Daily
96 Main St (04915-6533)
PHONE..................................207 338-0555
Penny Aster, *Owner*
EMP: 5
SALES (est): 226.4K **Privately Held**
SIC: 2052 2599 Mfg Cookies/Crackers Mfg Furniture/Fixtures

(G-5688)
DUCKTRAP RIVER OF MAINE LLC
57 Little River Dr (04915-6035)
PHONE..................................207 338-6280
Gian Franco Nattero, *President*
◆ **EMP:** 130 **EST:** 1978
SQ FT: 70,000
SALES (est): 27MM
SALES (corp-wide): 3.9B **Privately Held**
WEB: www.ducktrap.com
SIC: 2091 2092 Mfg Canned/Cured Fish/Seafood Mfg Fresh/Frozen Packaged Fish
HQ: Marine Harvest Usa Holding, Llc
57 Little River Dr
Belfast ME 04915
207 338-6280

(G-5689)
FRENCH WEBB & CO INC
21 Front St (04915-6836)
PHONE..................................207 338-6706
Todd French, *President*
Peter C Webb, *Vice Pres*
EMP: 15
SALES (est): 2.2MM **Privately Held**
WEB: www.frenchwebb.com
SIC: 3732 Custom Wooden Boat Building/Yacht Joinery

(G-5690)
HOLLANDS BOAT SHOP INC
7 Mill Ln (04915-7240)
PHONE..................................207 338-3155
Glenn C Holland, *President*
Cathy Holland, *Admin Sec*
EMP: 9
SQ FT: 4,200
SALES: 200K **Privately Held**
SIC: 3732 Boatbuilding/Repairing

(G-5691)
J A BLACK COMPANY
Also Called: Printing Brokersof Maine
3 Blacks Lndg (04915-7225)
P.O. Box 214 (04915-0214)
PHONE..................................207 338-4040
James A Black, *Owner*
EMP: 3
SQ FT: 2,800
SALES (est): 234.6K **Privately Held**
SIC: 2752 2761 2759 2791 Lithographic Coml Print Mfg Manifold Bus Forms Commercial Printing Typesetting Services

(G-5692)
MARKS PRINTING HOUSE INC
17 Main St (04915-6821)
PHONE..................................207 338-5460
Russell Prace, *President*
Jayme Okmalee, *Director*
EMP: 3
SALES: 200K **Privately Held**
WEB: www.marksprinting.com
SIC: 2752 8111 2791 Lithographic Commercial Printing Legal Services Office Typesetting Services

(G-5693)
MATHEWS BROTHERS COMPANY (PA)
22 Perkins Rd (04915-6034)
P.O. Box 345 (04915-0345)
PHONE..................................207 338-3360
John Hawthorne, *CEO*
Scott Hawthorne, *President*
Kyle Hawthorne, *Vice Pres*
Ryan Harnden, *Project Mgr*
Ralph McDermott, *Engineer*
▲ **EMP:** 130 **EST:** 1854
SQ FT: 100,000
SALES (est): 22.6MM **Privately Held**
WEB: www.mathewsbrothers.com
SIC: 2431 3089 Mfg Millwork Mfg Plastic Products

(G-5694)
MINUTEMAN SIGN CENTERS
171 High St Ste 1 (04915-6571)
PHONE..................................207 338-2299
Bill McKeen, *Owner*
EMP: 3
SALES (est): 135K **Privately Held**
WEB: www.minutemansigns.com
SIC: 3993 Mfg Signs/Advertising Specialties

(G-5695)
MOONBAT CITY BAKING CO LLC
129 Main St Apt 3 (04915-6560)
PHONE..................................207 323-4955
Michelle Berry, *Principal*
EMP: 4
SALES (est): 233.6K **Privately Held**
SIC: 2051 Mfg Bread/Related Products

(G-5696)
PENOBSCOT MCCRUM LLC
28 Pierce St (04915-6648)
P.O. Box 229 (04915-0229)
PHONE..................................207 338-4360
Jay McCrum, *CEO*
Gordon Pow, *CFO*
Jennifer Hartley, *Accounting Mgr*
Tammy Colbert, *Human Res Mgr*
Christine Whitmore, *Cust Mgr*
EMP: 175
SQ FT: 56,000
SALES: 24MM **Privately Held**
SIC: 2037 Mfg Frozen Fruits/Vegetables

(G-5697)
TINCANPALLY LLC
84 Miller St (04915-6411)
PHONE..................................732 485-5636
Richard Green, *Principal*
EMP: 3
SALES (est): 205.3K **Privately Held**
SIC: 3411 Mfg Metal Cans

(G-5698)
VILLAGE NETMEDIA INC
Also Called: Republican Journal
156 High St (04915-6581)
PHONE..................................207 338-3333
Richard Anderson, *Owner*
EMP: 6
SALES (corp-wide): 9.6MM **Privately Held**
WEB: www.jobsformaine.com
SIC: 2711 Newspapers-Publishing/Printing
PA: Village Netmedia, Inc.
91 Camden St Ste 403
Rockland ME 04841
207 594-4401

Belgrade
Kennebec County

(G-5699)
RON LAVALLEE
Also Called: You Know Solutions
27 Campground Rd (04917)
PHONE..................................248 705-3231
Ron Lavallee, *Owner*
EMP: 3
SALES (est): 118.7K **Privately Held**
SIC: 3571 3674 Mfg Electronic Computers Mfg Semiconductors/Related Devices

(G-5700)
TUKEY BROTHERS INC
460 Smithfield Rd (04917-3230)
PHONE..................................207 465-3570
Leroy J Tukey, *President*
Daniel E Tukey, *Vice Pres*
EMP: 15 **EST:** 1947
SQ FT: 9,600
SALES: 450K **Privately Held**
SIC: 2421 5211 Sawmill & Retail Lumber

Belmont
Waldo County

(G-5701)
BELMONT BOATWORKS LLC
163 Augusta Rd (04952-3005)
PHONE..................................207 342-2885
Daniel Miller, *Owner*
EMP: 12
SQ FT: 144
SALES (est): 1.6MM **Privately Held**
SIC: 3732 Boatbuilding/Repairing

(G-5702)
CREATIVE APPAREL ASSOC LLC (HQ)
318 Augusta Rd (04952-3015)
P.O. Box 301, Princeton (04668-0301)
PHONE..................................207 342-2814
Sharon Rybarczyk, *Managing Dir*
▲ **EMP:** 45
SQ FT: 15,000
SALES (est): 30.4MM **Privately Held**
SIC: 2339 2329 Mfg Women's/Misses' Outerwear Mfg Men's/Boy's Clothing
PA: Passamaquoddy Tribe At Indian Township
8 Kennabasis Rd
Princeton ME 04668
207 796-5004

Benton
Kennebec County

(G-5703)
ALLAN FULLER
Also Called: Fuller Allan Analytical Instrs
304 Unity Rd (04901-3820)
PHONE..................................603 886-5555
Allan Fuller, *Owner*
▼ **EMP:** 3
SQ FT: 3,500
SALES: 1MM **Privately Held**
WEB: www.allanfuller.com
SIC: 3826 5049 Mfg & Whol Analytical Instruments

(G-5704)
BROCHU LOGGING INC
178 E Benton Rd (04901-2842)
PHONE..................................207 453-2982
Mark Brochu, *Principal*
EMP: 3
SALES (est): 237K **Privately Held**
SIC: 2411 Logging

(G-5705)
FTIRCOM LLC
304 Unity Rd (04901-3820)
PHONE..................................603 886-5555
Allan Fuller, *Mng Member*
EMP: 3 **EST:** 2015
SALES (est): 218.8K **Privately Held**
SIC: 3825 Mfg Electrical Measuring Instruments

Bernard
Hancock County

(G-5706)
CLASSIC BOAT SHOP INC
Rr 102 (04612)
P.O. Box 74 (04612-0074)
PHONE..................................207 244-3374
Jean Beaulieu, *President*
EMP: 5
SALES (est): 660K **Privately Held**
WEB: www.classicboatshop.com
SIC: 3732 Marina Operation

(G-5707)
JAMES H RICH BOATYARD
Main St Rr 102 (04612)
PHONE..................................207 244-3208
Nancy Thurlow, *Owner*
EMP: 8
SALES (est): 768.3K **Privately Held**
SIC: 3732 4493 Boat Building & Boat Yard

Berwick
York County

(G-5708)
COLLINS SHEET METAL INC
510 Portland St (03901-2873)
P.O. Box 1248 (03901-1248)
PHONE..................................207 384-4428
Gary Collins Sr, *President*
Pat Collins, *Vice Pres*
Brian Collins, *Contractor*
EMP: 10

SQ FT: 5,000
SALES: 1MM **Privately Held**
SIC: 3444 Mfg Sheet Metalwork

(G-5709)
EVERGREEN LANDSCAPING INC
Ledge Ln (03901)
P.O. Box 59, South Berwick (03908-0059)
PHONE..................................207 451-5007
Nick Curtis, *President*
Vicki Curtis, *Treasurer*
EMP: 5 **EST:** 2008
SALES (est): 685.3K **Privately Held**
SIC: 3531 Mfg Construction Machinery

(G-5710)
LITTLE HARBOR WINDOW CO INC
Also Called: Little Harbor Window Company
11 Little Harbor Rd (03901-2456)
P.O. Box 1188 (03901-1188)
PHONE..................................207 698-1332
James Eaton, *President*
Marcia Wadsworth, *Vice Pres*
John Royal, *CFO*
Michael Eaton, *Analyst*
EMP: 25
SQ FT: 6,000
SALES (est): 3.9MM **Privately Held**
WEB: www.littleharborwindow.com
SIC: 2431 Mfg Millwork

(G-5711)
MBW TRACTOR SALES LLC
540 Route 4 (03901)
PHONE..................................207 384-2001
David Mick,
EMP: 10 **EST:** 2005
SALES (est): 710K **Privately Held**
SIC: 3471 7532 Plating/Polishing Service Auto Body Repair/Painting

(G-5712)
SPIN ANALYTICAL INC
468 Portland St (03901-2819)
P.O. Box 865, Durham NH (03824-0865)
PHONE..................................207 704-0160
J Brett Austin, *President*
Thomas M Laue, *Treasurer*
◆ **EMP:** 5
SQ FT: 1,800
SALES (est): 641.2K **Privately Held**
SIC: 3841 Mfg Surgical/Medical Instruments

(G-5713)
TRADITIONAL WOOD WORKS INC
27 Commercial Dr (03901-2833)
PHONE..................................207 676-9668
Michael Pouliotte, *Principal*
EMP: 4 **EST:** 2013
SALES (est): 594.3K **Privately Held**
SIC: 2431 Mfg Millwork

Bethel
Oxford County

(G-5714)
CHAPMAN & WHEELER INC
Mason St (04217)
P.O. Box 478 (04217-0478)
PHONE..................................207 824-2224
Howard V Chapman, *President*
EMP: 4
SALES (est): 310K **Privately Held**
SIC: 2411 6799 Logging Investor

(G-5715)
MAYVILLE HOUSE
Also Called: Timberlake and Compny
158 Mayville Rd (04217-4442)
P.O. Box 24 (04217-0024)
PHONE..................................207 824-6545
Ross Timberlake, *Owner*
EMP: 4
SALES: 2MM **Privately Held**
WEB: www.stimberlake.com
SIC: 2511 5712 Mfg Wood Household Furniture Ret Furniture

Biddeford
York County

(G-5716)
32 NORTH CORPORATION
Also Called: Stabil
16 Pomerleau St (04005-9457)
PHONE..................................207 284-5010
John Milburn, *President*
Dan Theberge, *Mfg Staff*
Anne Gould, *CFO*
Shayna Haigh, *Bookkeeper*
▲ **EMP:** 8
SQ FT: 10,000
SALES (est): 6MM
SALES (corp-wide): 300MM **Privately Held**
WEB: www.32north.com
SIC: 3021 Manufactures Rubber/Plastic Footwear
HQ: Implus Llc
2001 Tw Alexander Dr
Durham NC 27709
919 544-7900

(G-5717)
AMERICAN RHEINMETALL DEF INC (PA)
15 Morin St Ste B (04005-4403)
PHONE..................................207 571-5850
Stephen Hedger, *President*
EMP: 3
SALES (est): 9MM **Privately Held**
SIC: 3827 Optical Instruments And Lenses

(G-5718)
AMERICAN RHNMETALL SYSTEMS LLC
Also Called: Vingtech
15 Morin St Ste B (04005-4403)
PHONE..................................207 571-5850
Torgrim Jorgensen, *Vice Pres*
Brad Hittle, *Engineer*
Eileen Stone, *Office Admin*
James Lebel,
EMP: 40
SQ FT: 35,000
SALES (est): 9MM **Privately Held**
WEB: www.vingtech.com
SIC: 3827 Mfg Optical Instruments/Lenses
PA: American Rheinmetall Defense, Inc.
15 Morin St Ste B
Biddeford ME 04005
207 571-5850

(G-5719)
ATLANTIC COASTAL PRINTING INC
321 Elm St Ste 1 (04005-3034)
PHONE..................................207 284-4328
Ron Nevers, *President*
Peter Mela, *Treasurer*
EMP: 3
SALES (est): 272.8K **Privately Held**
WEB: www.atlanticcoastalprinting.com
SIC: 2752 Lithographic Commercial Printing

(G-5720)
AVX TANTALUM CORPORATION
Also Called: A V X
401 Hill St (04005-4335)
PHONE..................................207 282-5111
John Gilbertson, *CEO*
Mark Arsenault, *Engineer*
Betsy Smith, *Engineer*
Bill Richards, *Design Engr*
Richard King, *Info Tech Dir*
▲ **EMP:** 135
SQ FT: 75,000
SALES (est): 24.6MM **Publicly Held**
WEB: www.avxtantalum.com
SIC: 3629 3675 Mfg Electrical Industrial Apparatus Mfg Electronic Capacitors
HQ: Avx Corporation
1 Avx Blvd
Fountain Inn SC 29644
864 967-2150

(G-5721)
BARRETTE OUTDOOR LIVING INC
8 Morin St (04005-4413)
PHONE..................................800 866-8101
Steve Hanscom, *Manager*
EMP: 35
SALES (corp-wide): 1.5MM **Privately Held**
SIC: 2411 Logging
HQ: Barrette Outdoor Living, Inc.
7830 Freeway Cir
Middleburg Heights OH 44130
440 891-0790

(G-5722)
BEACON PRESS INC
Also Called: Northern Light
457 Alfred St (04005-9447)
P.O. Box 627 (04005-0627)
PHONE..................................207 282-1535
George Sample, *President*
Dayle Pennell, *General Mgr*
EMP: 35
SALES (est): 2.4MM **Privately Held**
WEB: www.journaltribune.com
SIC: 2711 Newspapers-Publishing/Printing

(G-5723)
BRADY SCREENPRINT INC
464 Elm St (04005-4126)
PHONE..................................207 284-8531
Toll Free:..888 -
Paul Brady, *President*
Theresa Brady, *Corp Secy*
Theresa Tarboz, *Corp Secy*
Michael Brady, *Vice Pres*
EMP: 5
SALES (est): 639.3K **Privately Held**
WEB: www.bradyscreenprint.com
SIC: 2759 Commercial Printing

(G-5724)
CAKES FOR ALL SEASONS LLC
10 W Point Ln Ste 206 (04005-3770)
PHONE..................................207 432-9192
Lisa Parker, *Mng Member*
EMP: 4
SQ FT: 1,200
SALES: 60K **Privately Held**
SIC: 2051 Mfg Bread/Related Products

(G-5725)
COUNTRYSIDE BUTCHERS
50 Washington St (04005-2523)
PHONE..................................207 282-2882
Christopher Hoglund, *Principal*
EMP: 4 **EST:** 2009
SALES (est): 354.2K **Privately Held**
SIC: 3421 Ret Meat/Fish

(G-5726)
CRI-SIL LLC
Also Called: Cri-Sil Silicone Technologies
359 Hill St (04005-3949)
PHONE..................................207 283-6422
Mark S Stevens, *CEO*
Barbara Lavigne, *Materials Mgr*
Susan Dewitz, *Controller*
Mary Emmons, *Bookkeeper*
Michael Hirschy,
▲ **EMP:** 32 **EST:** 1994
SQ FT: 35,000
SALES (est): 13MM **Privately Held**
WEB: www.crisil-silicones.com
SIC: 2822 Mfg Synthetic Rubber

(G-5727)
DALY BROS BEDDING CO INC
25 Edwards Ave (04005-3709)
PHONE..................................207 282-9583
Donald Shuris, *President*
Betty Lou Shuris, *Treasurer*
EMP: 6
SQ FT: 17,000
SALES: 530K **Privately Held**
SIC: 2515 5712 Mfg Mattresses/Bedsprings Ret Furniture

(G-5728)
DEEPWATER BUOYANCY INC
394 Hill St (04005-4341)
P.O. Box 2190 (04005-8190)
PHONE..................................207 468-2565
David Capotosto, *President*
Dan Cote, *Sales Mgr*
EMP: 10 **EST:** 2013
SQ FT: 35,000
SALES (est): 2.4MM **Privately Held**
SIC: 3086 5085 3533 Mfg Plastic Foam Products Whol Industrial Supplies Mfg Oil/Gas Field Machinery

(G-5729)
DSM METAL FABRICATION INC
Also Called: Metal Fabrications
129 Precourt St (04005-4343)
P.O. Box 404 (04005-0404)
PHONE..................................207 282-6740
Bob Standard, *Owner*
Paula Hayward, *Human Res Dir*
Tom Hopkins, *Director*
William Cain, *Clerk*
EMP: 45
SQ FT: 30,000
SALES (est): 9.6MM **Privately Held**
WEB: www.donssheetmetal.com
SIC: 3444 1711 Mfg Sheet Metalwork Plumbing/Heating/Air Cond Contractor

(G-5730)
EAMI INC
Also Called: E A M
19 Pomerleau St (04005-9457)
P.O. Box 519 (04005-0519)
PHONE..................................207 283-3001
Stephen G Swinburne, *CEO*
Thomas Messer, *Purch Mgr*
Jim Robinson, *CFO*
EMP: 18
SQ FT: 15,000
SALES (est): 3.2MM
SALES (corp-wide): 6.8MM **Privately Held**
WEB: www.eaminc.com
SIC: 3699 3565 Mfg Electrical Equipment/Supplies Mfg Packaging Machinery
PA: Prescott Metal
565 Elm St
Biddeford ME 04005
207 283-0115

(G-5731)
ELM STREET VAULT INC
38 Landry St (04005-4310)
PHONE..................................207 284-4855
Donald Daigle, *President*
Christiane Daigle, *Corp Secy*
David Daigle, *Manager*
EMP: 8 **EST:** 1971
SQ FT: 5,000
SALES: 1.1MM **Privately Held**
SIC: 3272 5039 Mfg Concrete Products Whol Cnstn Materials

(G-5732)
FAUCHER ORGAN COMPANY INC
31 Sokokis Rd (04005-9521)
P.O. Box 1222 (04005-1222)
PHONE..................................207 283-1420
Robert R Faucher, *President*
EMP: 4
SQ FT: 5,000
SALES (est): 445.6K **Privately Held**
WEB: www.faucherorgan.com
SIC: 3931 7699 Mfg Musical Instruments Repair Services

(G-5733)
FIBER MATERIALS INC (HQ)
5 Morin St (04005-4414)
PHONE..................................207 282-5911
Rob Pierson, *President*
Mark Lippold, *Project Mgr*
Jeanne Kramer, *Production*
Noyes Christopher, *Manager*
Godbout Dan, *Manager*
EMP: 32 **EST:** 2011
SQ FT: 40,000
SALES (est): 67.6MM
SALES (corp-wide): 79.6MM **Privately Held**
WEB: www.fibermaterialsinc.com
SIC: 3769 2299 7389 5131 Manufactures Space Vehicle Equip And Textile Goods Business Services Wholesales Piece Goods/Notions

PA: Edgewater Capital Partners, L.P.
5005 Rockside Rd Ste 840
Independence OH 44131
216 292-3838

(G-5734)
FOOTWEAR SPECIALTIES INC
16 Pomerleau St (04005-9457)
PHONE....................207 284-5003
Dan Theberge, *President*
Anne Gould, *Vice Pres*
David Gould, *Treasurer*
EMP: 15
SQ FT: 10,000
SALES: 400K **Privately Held**
SIC: 3143 3144 Mfg Footwear

(G-5735)
G PRO INDUSTRIAL SERVICES
5 Drapeau St (04005-4411)
P.O. Box 1362 (04005-1362)
PHONE....................207 766-1671
EMP: 4 **EST:** 2013
SALES (est): 362.4K **Privately Held**
SIC: 3089 Mfg Plastic Products

(G-5736)
GARTLAND DISTRIBUTORS LLC
4 Dusty Acres (04005-8509)
PHONE....................207 282-9456
Bob Scottland, *Owner*
Bob Gartland, *Mng Member*
EMP: 5
SALES (est): 90.8K **Privately Held**
SIC: 2064 Mfg Candy/Confectionery

(G-5737)
GENERAL MARINE INC
56 Landry St (04005-4321)
PHONE....................207 284-7517
Stacey Raymond, *President*
▲ **EMP:** 7
SQ FT: 6,000
SALES (est): 640K **Privately Held**
WEB: www.generalmarine.com
SIC: 3732 Boatbuilding/Repairing

(G-5738)
HIGHTECH EXTRACTS LLC
5 Drapeau St (04005-4411)
PHONE....................207 590-3251
Paul Gelardi, *Principal*
Martha Dempsey, *Sales Staff*
Norman Olson, *Marketing Staff*
EMP: 3
SALES (est): 81.8K **Privately Held**
SIC: 2836 Mfg Biological Products

(G-5739)
HOY PRINTING CORP
120 Main St (04005)
P.O. Box 1597 (04005-1597)
PHONE....................207 284-5531
Frank Hoy, *President*
Pricilla Hoy Baker, *Treasurer*
EMP: 3
SQ FT: 2,000
SALES: 225K **Privately Held**
SIC: 2752 Lithographic Commercial Printing

(G-5740)
INTEGRITY COMPOSITES LLC
8 Morin St (04005-4413)
PHONE....................207 571-0743
Andrea Herr, *Office Mgr*
Matt Bevin, *Mng Member*
EMP: 15 **EST:** 2012
SQ FT: 100,000
SALES (est): 2.6MM **Privately Held**
SIC: 2491 1521 Wood Preserving Single-Family House Construction

(G-5741)
JUNORA LTD
16 Pomerleau St (04005-9457)
PHONE....................207 284-4900
Dean Plaisted, *CEO*
EMP: 7
SALES (est): 646.4K **Privately Held**
SIC: 2295 Mfg Coated Fabrics

(G-5742)
LAKONIA GREEK PRODUCTS LLC
10 W Point Ln Unit 202 (04005-3770)
PHONE....................207 282-4002
Melissa Rioux, *Owner*
EMP: 3
SALES (est): 267.9K **Privately Held**
SIC: 2079 Mfg Edible Fats/Oils

(G-5743)
LAUZON GILLES
Also Called: Affordable Kitchen and Baths
428 Elm St (04005-4116)
PHONE....................207 286-0600
Gilles Lauzon, *Owner*
EMP: 3
SQ FT: 4,000
SALES (est): 270.7K **Privately Held**
SIC: 2434 Mfg Wood Kitchen Cabinets

(G-5744)
LUKAS FOODS INC
Also Called: Great Atlantic Seafood
64 Landry St (04005-4321)
P.O. Box 1952 (04005-1952)
PHONE....................207 284-7052
Gregory J Willoughby, *President*
Geoffrey Willoughby, *Treasurer*
EMP: 22
SQ FT: 10,000
SALES (est): 1.9MM **Privately Held**
WEB: www.lukasfoods.com
SIC: 2099 Mfg Food Preparations

(G-5745)
MAINE LURE COMPANY LLC
Also Called: Al's Goldfish Lure Co.
40 Main St Ste 13-114 (04005-5178)
P.O. Box 193, Eliot (03903-0193)
PHONE....................413 543-1524
Michael Lee, *President*
EMP: 4
SQ FT: 2,400
SALES (est): 255.3K **Privately Held**
SIC: 3949 Mfg Sporting/Athletic Goods

(G-5746)
MAINELY NEWSPAPERS INC
Also Called: Biddeford Saco Courier
180 Main St (04005-2410)
P.O. Box 1894 (04005-1894)
PHONE....................207 282-4337
David Flood, *President*
Carolyn Flood, *Treasurer*
EMP: 17
SQ FT: 11,000
SALES (est): 760K **Privately Held**
WEB: www.biddefordsacooobcourier.com
SIC: 2711 Newspapers-Publishing

(G-5747)
MAXYM TECHNOLOGIES INC
17 Landry St (04005-4309)
PHONE....................207 283-8601
Tom Bryand, *President*
EMP: 6
SQ FT: 5,000
SALES: 650K **Privately Held**
WEB: www.maxymtech.com
SIC: 3553 Mfg Woodworking Machinery

(G-5748)
MCALLISTER MACHINE INC
7 Pomerleau St 102 (04005-9457)
PHONE....................207 282-8655
James A McAllister, *President*
Donna McAllister, *Treasurer*
EMP: 20
SALES: 1.8MM **Privately Held**
WEB: www.mcallistermachine.com
SIC: 3599 Machine Job Shop

(G-5749)
ME INDUSTRIES
Also Called: Donovan Marine-Atlantic
19 Pomerleau St (04005-9457)
PHONE....................207 286-2030
Thomas Norton, *Manager*
▲ **EMP:** 8
SALES: 2.2MM **Privately Held**
SIC: 3462 Mfg Iron/Steel Forgings

(G-5750)
MOLDING TOOLING AND DESIGN
64 Landry St (04005-4321)
PHONE....................207 247-4077
Dan Hutchens, *President*
Kathleen Hutchens, *Vice Pres*
EMP: 15
SQ FT: 8,000
SALES (est): 1.8MM **Privately Held**
WEB: www.mtdplastics.com
SIC: 3089 Mfg Plastic Injection Molds & Plastic Injection Molding

(G-5751)
NATURALLY MAINE
1 Parkview Ct Ste 132 (04005-9625)
PHONE....................207 423-6443
EMP: 3 **EST:** 2010
SALES (est): 241.5K **Privately Held**
SIC: 2834 Mfg Pharmaceutical Preparations

(G-5752)
NIBMOR INC
10 W Point Ln (04005-3770)
P.O. Box 6, Kennebunk (04043-0006)
PHONE....................207 502-7540
Heather K Terry, *Principal*
Jennifer Love, *Principal*
Marcia Bell, *Manager*
EMP: 5
SALES: 57.9K **Privately Held**
SIC: 2066 Mfg Chocolate/Cocoa Products

(G-5753)
NIKEL PRECISION GROUP LLC
Also Called: Precision Mfg Solutions
419 Hill St (04005-4336)
P.O. Box 974 (04005-0974)
PHONE....................207 282-6080
John Strautnieks, *President*
Jamie Bell, *Opers Mgr*
Wesley Bisson, *Engineer*
Shaun McAlevey, *Engineer*
Laurie Letourneau, *Accountant*
▲ **EMP:** 70
SQ FT: 30,000
SALES: 9MM **Privately Held**
WEB: www.precision-mfg.com
SIC: 3599 7389 Mfg Industrial Machinery Business Services

(G-5754)
PAUL ISRAELSON
Also Called: Ideal Packaging Solutions
14 Sky Oaks Dr (04005-9280)
PHONE....................512 574-4737
Paul Israelson, *Owner*
EMP: 3
SALES (est): 246.3K **Privately Held**
SIC: 3565 Mfg Packaging Machinery

(G-5755)
PLASTICS SUPPLY OF MAINE INC
6 Pomerleau St (04005-9406)
PHONE....................207 775-7778
Ed Vetrone, *President*
▼ **EMP:** 3
SALES (est): 366.9K **Privately Held**
SIC: 3993 7699 Mfg Signs/Advertising Specialties Repair Services

(G-5756)
PORTLAND MATTRESS MAKERS INC (PA)
25 Edwards Ave (04005-3709)
PHONE....................207 772-2276
George Samaras, *President*
Scott Trefethen, *Sales Staff*
Catherine Sullivan, *Manager*
EMP: 10 **EST:** 1938
SALES (est): 1MM **Privately Held**
WEB: www.portlandmattressmakers.com
SIC: 2515 5712 Mfg & Ret Mattresses & Furniture

(G-5757)
PRAXAIR SURFACE TECH INC
24 Landry St (04005-4310)
PHONE....................207 282-3787
Roger Dumas, *Ltd Ptnr*
Patrick Mahony, *QC Mgr*
EMP: 100 **Privately Held**
WEB: www.sermatech.com
SIC: 3479 7692 Coating/Engraving Service Welding Repair
HQ: Praxair Surface Technologies, Inc.
1500 Polco St
Indianapolis IN 46222
317 240-2500

(G-5758)
PRECISION SCREW MCH PDTS INC
Also Called: P S M P
30 Gooch St (04005-2015)
P.O. Box 1944 (04005-1944)
PHONE....................207 283-0121
Joseph Moreshead, *President*
Andrea C Moreshead, *Vice Pres*
Andrea Moreshead, *Vice Pres*
Tom Katon, *Plant Mgr*
Higgins Lawrence, *Engineer*
EMP: 30 **EST:** 1961
SQ FT: 28,000
SALES (est): 5.9MM **Privately Held**
WEB: www.psmp.com
SIC: 3599 Mfg Industrial Machinery

(G-5759)
PRESCOTT METAL (PA)
565 Elm St (04005-4324)
P.O. Box 519 (04005-0519)
PHONE....................207 283-0115
John Grondin, *President*
Gary Dumas, *Prdtn Mgr*
Steve St Ours, *Prdtn Mgr*
Cosmo Dipierro, *CFO*
Mark Whitmore, *Sales Mgr*
EMP: 42
SQ FT: 30,000
SALES (est): 6.8MM **Privately Held**
WEB: www.prescottmetal.com
SIC: 3441 3444 Structural Metal Fabrication Mfg Sheet Metalwork

(G-5760)
R & W ENGRAVING INC
Also Called: Quick Copy Center
30 Morin St (04005-4413)
PHONE....................207 286-3020
Roger Bastarache, *President*
EMP: 3
SALES: 125K **Privately Held**
WEB: www.rwengraving.com
SIC: 2752 2791 2789 2672 Lithographic Coml Print Typesetting Services Bookbinding/Related Work Mfg Coat/Laminated Paper

(G-5761)
RICHARDSON-ALLEN INC
38 Pearl St (04005)
P.O. Box 236, Saco (04072-0236)
PHONE....................207 284-8402
Samuel R Butler, *President*
Rebecca Butler, *Treasurer*
EMP: 14
SQ FT: 9,000
SALES (est): 800K **Privately Held**
SIC: 2511 Manufacture Furniture

(G-5762)
SALO BAY TRADING CO
Also Called: Harbor House Cottages
40 Granite Point Rd (04005-9262)
PHONE....................207 283-4732
Dennis Tallagnon, *Partner*
Bonnie Tallagnon, *Partner*
EMP: 4
SALES (est): 236.1K **Privately Held**
SIC: 2391 Mfg Curtains/Draperies

(G-5763)
SOLERAS ADVANCED COATINGS LTD (PA)
589 Elm St (04005-4417)
P.O. Box 1867 (04005-1867)
PHONE....................207 282-5699
Jason Bergquist, *President*
Dean Plaisted, *President*
Jim Burns, *Accountant*
Ramiro Lopez, *Technician*
▲ **EMP:** 48
SQ FT: 25,000
SALES (est): 15.8MM **Privately Held**
WEB: www.soleras.com
SIC: 3599 Mfg Industrial Machinery

(G-5764)
SPEED MAT INC
374 South St (04005-9397)
PHONE.................................207 294-4358
Peter Boutet, *President*
EMP: 3
SALES: 974.9K **Privately Held**
WEB: www.speedmat.com
SIC: 3541 Mfg Machine Tools-Cutting

(G-5765)
STERLING ROPE COMPANY INC
26 Morin St (04005-4413)
PHONE.................................207 885-0033
Tripp Wyckoff, *President*
◆ **EMP:** 8
SALES (est): 1.7MM
SALES (corp-wide): 25.5MM **Privately Held**
WEB: www.sterlingrope.com
SIC: 2298 Mfg Cordage/Twine
HQ: Sherrill, Inc.
496 Gallimore Dairy Rd C
Greensboro NC 27409
336 378-0444

(G-5766)
THERMOFORMED PLASTICS NENG LLC
362 Hill St (04005-4341)
PHONE.................................207 286-1775
Paul Tyson, *Mng Member*
EMP: 12
SALES (est): 2.3MM **Privately Held**
WEB: www.tpne.com
SIC: 3089 Mfg Plastic Products

(G-5767)
VALMET INC
516 Alfred St (04005-9432)
P.O. Box 502 (04005-0502)
PHONE.................................207 282-1521
Jack Barbaro, *Buyer*
Elizabeth Belliveau, *Marketing Staff*
Jt Pineau, *Manager*
Donald Beaumont, *MIS Mgr*
Judy Lamontagne, *Personnel Assit*
EMP: 150
SALES (corp-wide): 3.6B **Privately Held**
WEB: www.metso.com
SIC: 3567 3554 Mfg Industrial Furnaces/Ovens Mfg Paper Industrial Machinery
HQ: Valmet, Inc.
2425 Commerce Ave Ste 100
Duluth GA 30096
770 263-7863

(G-5768)
VOLK PACKAGING CORPORATION
11 Morin St (04005-4498)
P.O. Box 1011 (04005-1011)
PHONE.................................207 282-6151
Douglas A Volk, *CEO*
Rich Wills, *General Mgr*
Gerk Volk, *Vice Pres*
Neil Browne, *Design Engr*
Kevin Shea, *Design Engr*
EMP: 74 **EST:** 1967
SQ FT: 140,000
SALES (est): 20.5MM **Privately Held**
WEB: www.volkboxes.com
SIC: 2653 2657 2652 Mfg Corrugated/Solid Fiber Boxes Mfg Folding Paperboard Boxes Mfg Setup Paperboard Boxes

Bingham
Somerset County

(G-5769)
ANDYS SILKSCREEN
322 Main St (04920-4034)
P.O. Box 184 (04920-0184)
PHONE.................................207 672-3302
Andrew Jacques, *Owner*
Andrew Jacquesowner, *Vice Pres*
EMP: 5
SQ FT: 1,500
SALES (est): 451.9K **Privately Held**
WEB: www.logologic.com
SIC: 2759 Commercial Printing

Blue Hill
Hancock County

(G-5770)
BLUE HILL CABINET & WOODWORK
517 Pleasant St (04614-5103)
PHONE.................................207 374-2260
Richard Sawyer, *Business Mgr*
EMP: 5
SALES: 750K **Privately Held**
SIC: 2431 2426 Mfg Millwork Hardwood Dimension/Floor Mill

(G-5771)
BOREALIS PRESS INC
35 Tenney Hl (04614-5948)
P.O. Box 230, Surry (04684-0230)
PHONE.................................207 370-6020
Mark Baldwin, *President*
Dede Johnson, *Manager*
EMP: 9
SALES (est): 999.5K **Privately Held**
WEB: www.borealispress.com
SIC: 2771 Publisher Of Greeting Cards

(G-5772)
PENOBSCOT BAY PRESS INC
Also Called: Weekly Packet, The
13 Main St (04614-5985)
P.O. Box 646 (04614-0646)
PHONE.................................207 374-2341
Sandye Alexander, *Manager*
EMP: 6
SQ FT: 5,000
SALES (corp-wide): 1.6MM **Privately Held**
SIC: 2711 Newspaper Publishing
PA: Penobscot Bay Press Inc
138 Main St
Stonington ME 04681
207 367-2200

(G-5773)
RACKLIFFE POTTERY INC
Ellsworth Rd Rr 172 (04614)
P.O. Box 393 (04614-0393)
PHONE.................................207 374-2297
Dennis Rackliffe, *President*
David Rackliffe, *Principal*
EMP: 3 **EST:** 1966
SQ FT: 1,500
SALES (est): 298.6K **Privately Held**
SIC: 3269 5719 Mfg Pottery Products Ret Misc Homefurnishings

(G-5774)
SISTERS SALSA INC
689 Hinckley Ridge Rd (04614-5701)
PHONE.................................207 374-2170
James Buddington, *Principal*
EMP: 8
SALES (est): 864K **Privately Held**
SIC: 2033 Mfg Food Preparations

(G-5775)
WISE-ACRE INC
9 Tradewinds Ln (04614-6029)
PHONE.................................207 374-5400
Jim Picariello, *President*
EMP: 6
SQ FT: 3,000
SALES (est): 435.6K **Privately Held**
SIC: 2038 Mfg Frozen Specialties

Boothbay
Lincoln County

(G-5776)
CREATIVE CANVAS
514 Wiscasset Rd (04537-4627)
P.O. Box 365, Southport (04576-0365)
PHONE.................................207 633-2056
Sarah H Conner, *Partner*
EMP: 3
SALES (est): 303.1K **Privately Held**
WEB: www.clinic.net
SIC: 3089 Mfg Plastic Products

(G-5777)
ELKINS & CO INC
103 Industrial Park Rd (04537-4670)
PHONE.................................207 633-0109
Michael R Elkins, *President*
Jennifer B Elkins, *Treasurer*
EMP: 10
SQ FT: 7,700
SALES: 480K **Privately Held**
SIC: 2426 Mfg Hardwood Furniture Stock & Parts

(G-5778)
HARBOR PRINT SHOP
59 Corey Ln (04537-4101)
P.O. Box 243 (04537-0243)
PHONE.................................207 633-4176
EMP: 4
SQ FT: 2,500
SALES (est): 310.4K **Privately Held**
SIC: 2752 2759 Lithographic Commercial Printing Commercial Printing

(G-5779)
ME TOMACELLI INC
Also Called: Mid-Coast Machine
55 Industrial Park Rd (04537-4667)
P.O. Box 483, Boothbay Harbor (04538-0483)
PHONE.................................207 633-7553
Michael Tomacelli, *President*
EMP: 3
SQ FT: 2,500
SALES: 200K **Privately Held**
SIC: 3441 3599 1799 Structural Metal Fabrication Mfg Industrial Machinery Trade Contractor

(G-5780)
PRINTS CHARMING PRINTERS INC
1036b Wiscasset Rd (04537-4641)
P.O. Box 750 (04537-0750)
PHONE.................................207 633-6663
Jimmy Hanna, *President*
Peggy Hanna, *Vice Pres*
Sam Cohen, *Admin Sec*
EMP: 3
SQ FT: 2,000
SALES (est): 353.7K **Privately Held**
WEB: www.printscharmingprinters.com
SIC: 2752 7389 Lithographic Commercial Printing Business Services

Boothbay Harbor
Lincoln County

(G-5781)
ALLEY ROAD LLC
120 Commercial St (04538-1823)
P.O. Box 462 (04538-0462)
PHONE.................................207 633-3171
Terrance McClinch,
EMP: 20
SALES (est): 4.2MM **Privately Held**
SIC: 3732 Boatbuilding/Repairing

(G-5782)
B MARINE CORP
Also Called: Samples Shipyard
120 Commercial St (04538-1823)
P.O. Box 462 (04538-0462)
PHONE.................................207 633-3171
Robert J Braga, *President*
Chris Braga, *Vice Pres*
EMP: 12
SALES: 1.2MM **Privately Held**
SIC: 3732 7699 Boatbuilding/Repairing Repair Services

(G-5783)
BBH APPARREL
45 Commercial St (04538-1826)
PHONE.................................207 633-0601
Den Rankins, *President*
EMP: 10
SQ FT: 1,300
SALES: 300K **Privately Held**
WEB: www.harborembroidery.com
SIC: 2395 7336 7389 Pleating/Stitching Services Commercial Art/Graphic Design Business Services

(G-5784)
MAINE-OK ENTERPRISES INC
Also Called: Wiscasset Newspaper
97 Townsend Ave (04538-1843)
P.O. Box 357 (04538-0357)
PHONE.................................207 633-4620
A R Tandy, *President*
Kevin Burnham, *Editor*
Mary Dodge Brewer, *Manager*
EMP: 25
SALES (est): 1.5MM **Privately Held**
WEB: www.boothbayregister.com
SIC: 2711 Newspapers-Publishing/Printing

(G-5785)
MCDONALD STAIN GLASS LTD
7 Wall Point Rd (04538-2308)
PHONE.................................207 633-4815
Richard Macdonald, *President*
EMP: 7
SALES: 200K **Privately Held**
WEB: www.macdonaldglass.com
SIC: 3229 3231 Mfg Pressed/Blown Glass Mfg Products-Purchased Glass

(G-5786)
RIDGETOP CABINETRY
26 Carter Ridge Rd (04538)
P.O. Box 54, Newcastle (04553-0054)
PHONE.................................207 563-8249
Randall Wade, *Owner*
EMP: 3
SALES (est): 154.6K **Privately Held**
SIC: 2434 Mfg Wood Kitchen Cabinets

Bowdoin
Sagadahoc County

(G-5787)
FHC INC (PA)
1201 Main St (04287-7302)
PHONE.................................207 666-8190
Frederick Haer, *CEO*
Andrei Barborica, *Vice Pres*
Kristina Reeher, *Prdtn Mgr*
Kathy Albasini, *Opers Staff*
Matthew Hillery, *Opers Staff*
EMP: 90
SQ FT: 35,000
SALES (est): 11.6MM **Privately Held**
WEB: www.fh-co.com
SIC: 3845 3826 Mfg Electromedical Equipment Mfg Analytical Instruments

Bowdoinham
Sagadahoc County

(G-5788)
BANANA BANNERS
160 Main St (04008-4215)
PHONE.................................207 666-3951
Robin Riendeau, *President*
EMP: 4
SALES: 250K **Privately Held**
WEB: www.bananabanners.com
SIC: 3993 7532 Mfg Signs/Advertising Specialties Auto Body Repair/Painting

(G-5789)
LONG LIFE SAUNAS
112 Pond Rd Ste G (04008-4247)
P.O. Box 315 (04008-0315)
PHONE.................................802 349-0501
Michael Goldstein, *President*
EMP: 3
SALES (est): 250.9K **Privately Held**
SIC: 3826 Mfg Analytical Instruments

(G-5790)
RICHMOND CONTRACT MFG
85 White Rd (04008-5422)
P.O. Box 247, Richmond (04357-0247)
PHONE.................................207 737-4385
Wayne Bodge, *President*
Jim Margette, *Principal*
Linda Douglass, *Vice Pres*
Jim Margetts, *Vice Pres*
EMP: 25
SQ FT: 27,500

▲ = Import ▼=Export
◆ =Import/Export

SALES: 550K **Privately Held**
WEB: www.richmond-contract-mfg.com
SIC: 3625 Mfg Relays/Industrial Controls

Bremen
Lincoln County

(G-5791)
ECOHOUSE LLC
45 Cora Cressy Rd (04551)
P.O. Box 106 (04551-0106)
PHONE..................................207 529-2700
Gary Worthley, *Principal*
Carolyn Butler, *QC Mgr*
EMP: 6
SALES (est): 280.8K **Privately Held**
SIC: 2091 Mfg Canned/Cured Fish/Seafood

(G-5792)
MAINE CAT CO INC
300 Waldoboro Rd (04551-3306)
P.O. Box 205, Medomak (04551-0205)
PHONE..................................207 529-6500
Dick Vermeulen, *President*
EMP: 14
SQ FT: 30,000
SALES (est): 2.7MM **Privately Held**
SIC: 3732 Boatbuilding/Repairing

Brewer
Penobscot County

(G-5793)
AMERICAN NAMEPLATE
103 Center St (04412-2603)
P.O. Box 291 (04412-0291)
PHONE..................................207 848-7187
EMP: 3
SALES (est): 190.8K
SALES (corp-wide): 454.8K **Privately Held**
WEB: www.amernameplate.com
SIC: 3993 Mfg Signs/Advertising Specialties
PA: American Nameplate
21 White Pine Rd Ste 1
Hermon ME 04401
207 848-7187

(G-5794)
BACKWASH BREW HOLDINGS LLC
Also Called: Mason's Brewing
15 Hardy St (04412-2207)
PHONE..................................207 659-2300
Christopher Morley,
EMP: 11
SALES (est): 814.3K **Privately Held**
SIC: 2085 Drinking Place

(G-5795)
DOWN EAST SHTMTL & CERTIF WLDG
19 Sparks Ave (04412-1446)
P.O. Box 332 (04412-0332)
PHONE..................................207 989-3443
James Hillman, *President*
EMP: 9
SALES (est): 1.3MM **Privately Held**
SIC: 3444 7692 Mfg Sheet Metalwork Welding Repair

(G-5796)
GREGG STEWART
Also Called: Sardine Can Giftware
17 Doughty Dr Ste 106 (04412-2278)
P.O. Box 283 (04412-0283)
PHONE..................................207 989-0903
Gregg Stewart, *President*
EMP: 3
SQ FT: 5,000
SALES (est): 310.7K **Privately Held**
SIC: 3949 Mfg Sporting/Athletic Goods

(G-5797)
L H THOMPSON INC
Also Called: Thompson Printing
54 Wilson St (04412-2024)
PHONE..................................207 989-3280
Paul Kenneth Smith, *President*
Thomas E Needham, *Clerk*
EMP: 14 **EST:** 1902
SALES (est): 1.8MM **Privately Held**
SIC: 2752 Offset Printing & Lithographed Letters Circular Or Form

(G-5798)
M DRUG LLC
Also Called: Miller Drug Whiting Hill Phrm
33 Whiting Hill Rd Ste 4 (04412-1022)
PHONE..................................207 973-9444
Bill Miller,
EMP: 8
SALES (est): 854.8K **Privately Held**
SIC: 2834 Mfg Pharmaceutical Preparations

(G-5799)
NYLE SYSTEMS LLC
12 Stevens Rd Unit B (04412-4700)
PHONE..................................207 989-4335
Nathan Cyr, *Opers Staff*
Antonius Mathissen, *Mng Member*
◆ **EMP:** 35
SQ FT: 35,000
SALES: 62MM **Privately Held**
SIC: 3585 Mfg Refrigeration/Heating Equipment

(G-5800)
OWEN GRAY & SON
Also Called: Owen Gray and Son
300 Chamberlain St (04412-1409)
PHONE..................................207 989-3575
Richard Gray, *Owner*
Mark Gray, *Systems Mgr*
EMP: 5
SQ FT: 3,600
SALES: 300K **Privately Held**
SIC: 2431 1751 Mfg Millwork Carpentry Contractor

(G-5801)
SOMIC AMERICA INC
6 Baker Blvd (04412-2253)
PHONE..................................207 989-1759
Scott Young, *Mfg Mgr*
Michelle Braley, *Opers-Prdtn-Mfg*
Pasco Grove, *QC Mgr*
Ken Albert, *Engineer*
Amanda Martin, *Human Res Mgr*
EMP: 100 **Privately Held**
SIC: 3714 Mfg Motor Vehicle Parts/Accessories
HQ: Somic America, Inc.
343 E Lee Trinkle Dr
Wytheville VA 24382
276 228-4307

(G-5802)
TURBINE SPECIALISTS LLC
55 Baker Blvd (04412-2200)
PHONE..................................207 947-9327
Chad Walton,
▲ **EMP:** 12
SQ FT: 5,000
SALES (est): 1MM **Privately Held**
WEB: www.turbinespecialists.com
SIC: 3471 Plating/Polishing Service

(G-5803)
W S EMERSON COMPANY INC (PA)
15 Acme Rd (04412-1500)
P.O. Box 10 (04412-0010)
PHONE..................................207 989-3410
John A Vickery, *President*
Russel M Vicery, *Vice Pres*
John A Vickery Jr, *Vice Pres*
John Vickery, *CFO*
Laurie Baughman, *Controller*
EMP: 45 **EST:** 1921
SQ FT: 35,000
SALES (est): 8.2MM **Privately Held**
SIC: 2759 Commercial Printing

(G-5804)
WESTMOR INDUSTRIES LLC
42 Coffin Ave (04412-2271)
PHONE..................................207 989-0100
Kenneth Peters, *President*
EMP: 50
SALES (corp-wide): 37.2MM **Privately Held**
SIC: 3443 Mfg Fabricated Plate Work
PA: Westmor Industries, Llc
7 Industrial Blvd
Morris MN 56267
320 589-2100

Bridgewater
Aroostook County

(G-5805)
E G W BRADBURY ENTERPRISES
Also Called: Bradbury Barrel Co
100 Main Rd (04735-3011)
P.O. Box 129 (04735-0129)
PHONE..................................207 429-8141
Adelle F Bradbury, *President*
William Yerxa, *Div Sub Head*
D Wayne Bradbury, *Vice Pres*
EMP: 12 **EST:** 1974
SQ FT: 12,000
SALES (est): 1.8MM **Privately Held**
SIC: 2541 2542 2449 Mfg Wood Partitions/Fixt Mfg Nonwd Partition/Fixt Mfg Wood Containers

Bridgton
Cumberland County

(G-5806)
BRIDGTON NEWS CORP
Also Called: Bridgton News The
118 Main St (04009-1127)
P.O. Box 244 (04009-0244)
PHONE..................................207 647-2851
Stephen Shorey, *President*
Eric Gulberndsen, *Administration*
EMP: 12
SQ FT: 3,000
SALES: 600K **Privately Held**
WEB: www.bridgton.com
SIC: 2711 Newspapers-Publishing/Printing

(G-5807)
DOWN EAST INC
Also Called: Magic Lantern Movie Theatre
11 Depot St (04009-1211)
P.O. Box 328 (04009-0328)
PHONE..................................207 647-5443
Frank Howell, *President*
EMP: 11
SQ FT: 26,500
SALES (est): 1MM **Privately Held**
WEB: www.downeastinc.com
SIC: 3599 Mfg Industrial Machinery

(G-5808)
J D PAULSEN
Also Called: Rigby Precision Products
249 Portland Rd (04009)
PHONE..................................207 647-5679
J David Paulsen, *Owner*
EMP: 3
SQ FT: 1,000
SALES (est): 183K **Privately Held**
SIC: 3599 3552 3541 Mfg Industrial Machinery Mfg Textile Machinery Mfg Machine Tools-Cutting

(G-5809)
MERRIMACK MANUFACTURING CO
217 Harrison Rd (04009-4731)
PHONE..................................207 647-3566
Robert Plame, *President*
Mark Gilmore, *Vice Pres*
EMP: 3
SQ FT: 5,500
SALES: 1MM **Privately Held**
WEB: www.merrimackmfg.com
SIC: 3452 Mfr Metal Screws

(G-5810)
ROD JAKES SHOP LLC
400 N Bridgton Rd Ste A (04009-4620)
PHONE..................................207 595-0677
Charles F Parrott III,
Kelley Parrot,
Charles Parrott,
EMP: 3
SALES (est): 373.5K **Privately Held**
SIC: 3711 Mfg Motor Vehicle/Car Bodies

(G-5811)
SCOTT DOCKS INC
Rr 302 (04009)
P.O. Box 37, Denmark (04022-0037)
PHONE..................................207 647-3824
Kevin Whitney, *President*
EMP: 6
SQ FT: 864
SALES: 250K **Privately Held**
SIC: 2499 4491 4959 Mfg Temporary Docks Service & Snowplowing

Bristol
Lincoln County

(G-5812)
GRAVEL DOCTOR MIDCOAST MAINE
15 Halls Ln (04539)
PHONE..................................207 633-1099
Jonathan Ludwick, *Principal*
EMP: 3
SALES (est): 145.9K **Privately Held**
SIC: 1442 Construction Sand/Gravel

Brooklin
Hancock County

(G-5813)
ATLANTIC BOAT COMPANY
Flye Point Rd (04616)
P.O. Box 217 (04616-0217)
PHONE..................................207 664-2900
O D Hopkins, *CEO*
EMP: 45
SALES (est): 6.8MM **Privately Held**
WEB: www.atlanticboat.com
SIC: 3732 Boatbuilding/Repairing

(G-5814)
BENJAMIN RIVER MARINE INC
64 Benjamin River Dr (04616-3553)
P.O. Box 58 (04616-0058)
PHONE..................................207 359-2244
John Dunbar, *President*
EMP: 4
SALES (est): 392.4K **Privately Held**
SIC: 3732 Boatbuilding/Repairing

(G-5815)
BRIDGES POINT BOAT YARD INC
23 Bridges Point Ln (04616-3558)
PHONE..................................207 359-2713
Wade Dow, *President*
Forrest Dow, *Treasurer*
EMP: 3
SALES (est): 354.3K **Privately Held**
WEB: www.bridgespoint.com
SIC: 3732 4493 Boatbuilding/Repairing Marina Operation

(G-5816)
BRION RIEFF BOATBUILDER INC
130 Reach Rd (04616-3517)
PHONE..................................207 359-4455
Brion Reiff, *President*
Elaine Reiff, *Vice Pres*
EMP: 6
SQ FT: 4,000
SALES (est): 550K **Privately Held**
WEB: www.brionrieffboatbuilder.com
SIC: 3732 Boatbuilding/Repairing

(G-5817)
BROOKLIN BOAT YARD INC (PA)
44 Center Hbr Rd Ste 44 (04616)
P.O. Box 143 (04616-0143)
PHONE..................................207 359-2236
J Steven White, *President*
Frank C Hull, *Vice Pres*
Brent Morey, *Opers Mgr*
John Maxwell, *Sales Staff*
EMP: 51 **EST:** 1960
SQ FT: 15,000

GEOGRAPHIC

SALES (est): 10.2MM **Privately Held**
WEB: www.brooklinboatyard.com
SIC: 3732 4493 Boatbuilding/Repairing Marina Operation

(G-5818)
CENTER HARBOR SAILS LLC
Reach Rd (04616)
P.O. Box 32 (04616-0032)
PHONE..................................207 359-2003
Martha Seibert,
EMP: 3
SALES (est): 237.3K **Privately Held**
SIC: 2394 2211 Mfg Canvas/Related Products Cotton Broadwoven Fabric Mill

(G-5819)
D N HYLAN ASSOCIATES INC
53 Benjamin River Dr (04616-3551)
PHONE..................................207 359-9807
Douglas N Hylan, *President*
Ellery Brown, *Business Mgr*
EMP: 5
SALES: 500K **Privately Held**
WEB: www.dhylanboats.com
SIC: 3732 Boatbuilding/Repairing

(G-5820)
ERIC DOW BOATBUILDER
71 Reach Rd (04616-3500)
P.O. Box 7 (04616-0007)
PHONE..................................207 359-2277
Eric Dow, *Owner*
EMP: 3
SALES (est): 175.9K **Privately Held**
WEB: www.dowboats.com
SIC: 3732 5551 Boatbuilding/Repairing Ret Boats

(G-5821)
NOAH PUBLICATIONS
Also Called: Benjamin Mndlowitz Photography
751 Rich Rd (04616)
P.O. Box 14 (04616-0014)
PHONE..................................207 359-2131
Benjamin Mendlowitz, *Owner*
Lorna Grant, *Principal*
EMP: 3
SQ FT: 1,600
SALES (est): 153.3K **Privately Held**
WEB: www.noahpublications.com
SIC: 2741 5961 5199 7221 Publishing Of A Calendar Entitled "the Calendar Of Wooden Boats" And Marine Photography

(G-5822)
WOODENBOAT PUBLICATIONS INC
Also Called: Professional Boat Builder
41 Wooden Boat Ln (04616-3371)
P.O. Box 78 (04616-0078)
PHONE..................................207 359-4651
Jonathan A Wilson, *Ch of Bd*
James Miller, *President*
Kim Patten, *Business Mgr*
Justin Jamison, *CFO*
Todd Richardson, *Adv Dir*
▲ **EMP:** 45 **EST:** 1974
SQ FT: 12,000
SALES (est): 6.5MM **Privately Held**
WEB: www.woodenboat.com
SIC: 2721 Periodicals-Publishing/Printing

Brooks
Waldo County

(G-5823)
DALE A THOMAS AND SONS INC
Also Called: Thomas Barn Equipment
148 Moosehead Trail Hwy (04921-3407)
P.O. Box 95 (04921-0095)
PHONE..................................207 722-3505
Jonathan Thomas, *President*
Dale A Thomas, *Vice Pres*
Beatrice Thomas, *Treasurer*
EMP: 5
SQ FT: 4,500
SALES: 500K **Privately Held**
WEB: www.thomasbandsawmills.com
SIC: 3523 Mfg Farm Machinery & Equipment

Brooksville
Hancock County

(G-5824)
BROWNS GREENS
715 Coastal Rd (04617-3604)
P.O. Box 40 (04617-0040)
PHONE..................................207 326-4636
Nancy Brown, *Owner*
Robert Brown, *Co-Owner*
EMP: 3
SQ FT: 1,200
SALES (est): 66.5K **Privately Held**
SIC: 3331 3399 Mfg Specialty Copper Products

Brownfield
Oxford County

(G-5825)
LAWRENCE PARSON
Also Called: Parson's Kitchen
510 Hampshire Rd (04010-4031)
PHONE..................................207 935-3737
Lawrence Parson, *Owner*
EMP: 9
SQ FT: 3,000
SALES (est): 1.1MM **Privately Held**
WEB: www.parsonskitchens.com
SIC: 2434 Mfg Wood Kitchen Cabinets

Brownville
Piscataquis County

(G-5826)
EARL W GERRISH & SONS INC
2 Charlottes Rd (04414)
P.O. Box 630 (04414-0630)
PHONE..................................207 965-2171
Earl W Gerrish Jr, *President*
Daniel Gerrish Sr, *Vice Pres*
Peter Gerrish, *Vice Pres*
Ronald Gerrish, *Vice Pres*
Kevin Stitham, *Admin Sec*
EMP: 11
SALES (est): 1.1MM **Privately Held**
SIC: 1442 4212 0711 1711 Sand Gravel And Stone Construction Wood Trucking Snow Plowing And Septic System Installation

(G-5827)
SEAL 1 LLC
193 Davis St (04414-3716)
PHONE..................................207 965-8860
Scott Lee, *Opers Staff*
Kathie Lee, *Director*
Anthony Paen,
EMP: 4
SALES (est): 490.5K **Privately Held**
SIC: 3586 5172 7699 7389 Mfg & Whol Petroleum Products Repair Services

Brunswick
Cumberland County

(G-5828)
ALLIANCE PRINTERS LLC
Also Called: Alliance Press, The
3 Business Pkwy Ste 1 (04011-7549)
PHONE..................................207 504-8200
Chris P Mile, *CEO*
▲ **EMP:** 19 **EST:** 2012
SALES (est): 2.4MM **Privately Held**
SIC: 2752 Lithographic Commercial Printing

(G-5829)
ARTFORMS (PA)
128 Maine St (04011-2011)
PHONE..................................800 828-8518
Michelle Fish, *Cust Mgr*
Chris McGough, *Sales Staff*
Joanne Malia, *Director*
◆ **EMP:** 24
SALES (est): 3.4MM **Privately Held**
SIC: 2759 Commercial Printing

(G-5830)
BATH IRON WORKS CORPORATION
Mallet Park (04011)
PHONE..................................207 442-1266
Chris Marco, *Branch Mgr*
EMP: 80
SALES (corp-wide): 36.1B **Publicly Held**
WEB: www.gdbiw.com
SIC: 3731 Shipbuilding/Repairing
HQ: Bath Iron Works Corporation
700 Washington St Stop 1
Bath ME 04530
207 443-3311

(G-5831)
BLUSHIFT AEROSPACE INC
74 Orion St 116 (04011-5031)
PHONE..................................207 619-1703
Sascha Deri, *CEO*
EMP: 4
SALES (est): 292.1K **Privately Held**
SIC: 3764 3761 Mfg Space Propulsion Units/Parts Mfg Guided Missiles/Space Vehicles

(G-5832)
BRUNSWICK INSTANT PRINTING INC
44 Cushing St (04011-1815)
PHONE..................................207 729-6854
Pamela J Wright, *President*
John Moncure, *Clerk*
EMP: 6
SQ FT: 1,500
SALES (est): 803.1K **Privately Held**
WEB: www.bipprint.com
SIC: 2752 Lithographic Commercial Printing

(G-5833)
BRUNSWICK PUBLISHING LLC
3 Business Pkwy (04011-7549)
P.O. Box 10 (04011-1302)
PHONE..................................207 729-3311
Christopher Miles,
EMP: 87
SALES (est): 4.1MM **Privately Held**
SIC: 2711 Newspapers-Publishing/Printing

(G-5834)
CARROT SIGNS
6 Bay Bridge Rd (04011-9100)
PHONE..................................207 725-0769
Allan Buonaiuto, *Owner*
EMP: 3
SALES (est): 235.5K **Privately Held**
WEB: www.carrotsigns.com
SIC: 3993 2399 Mfg Signs/Advertising Specialties Mfg Fabricated Textile Products

(G-5835)
EAST COAST WOODWORKING INC
6 Crooker Rd (04011)
P.O. Box 453, Bath (04530-0453)
PHONE..................................207 442-0025
Thomas Gilbert, *President*
EMP: 6
SQ FT: 6,000
SALES: 500K **Privately Held**
SIC: 2431 Mfg Millwork

(G-5836)
FUJI CLEAN USA LLC
41 Greenwood Rd Ste 2 (04011-7499)
PHONE..................................207 406-2927
Scott Samuelson, *Mng Member*
▲ **EMP:** 3
SQ FT: 1,360
SALES (est): 481.1K **Privately Held**
SIC: 3589 Mfg Service Industry Machinery
PA: Fuji Clean Co.,Ltd.
4-1-4, Imaike, Chikusa-Ku
Nagoya AIC 464-0

(G-5837)
IDENTITY GROUP HOLDINGS CORP
Also Called: Allen Screen Printing
43 Bibber Pkwy (04011-7357)
PHONE..................................207 510-6800
Josh Wolfgram, *Branch Mgr*
EMP: 40
SALES (corp-wide): 259.3MM **Privately Held**
SIC: 2759 Commercial Printing
PA: Identity Group Holdings Corp.
1480 Gould Dr
Cookeville TN 38506
931 432-4000

(G-5838)
INSPHERO INC
74 Orion St (04011-5031)
PHONE..................................800 779-7558
Jan Lichtenberg, *President*
David Fluri, *Principal*
Brian Manning, *Director*
EMP: 5
SQ FT: 500
SALES: 2MM
SALES (corp-wide): 1.4MM **Privately Held**
SIC: 3841 Mfg Surgical/Medical Instruments
PA: Insphero Ag
Wagistrasse 27
Schlieren ZH 8952
442 517-469

(G-5839)
INVISION INC
48 Melden Dr (04011-9553)
PHONE..................................207 725-7123
EMP: 4
SALES (est): 200K **Privately Held**
WEB: www.mainerentals.com
SIC: 2731 7812 Medical And Dental Publishing And Video Production

(G-5840)
L L BEAN INC
Also Called: LL Bean Mfg Bus
8 Industrial Pkwy (04011-7314)
PHONE..................................207 725-0300
Mike Laflamme, *Director*
EMP: 475
SALES (corp-wide): 893MM **Privately Held**
SIC: 3143 3144 3161 2384 Mfg Men's Footwear Mfg Women's Footwear Mfg Luggage Mfg Robes/Dressing Gowns Mfg Women/Miss Underwear
PA: L. L. Bean, Inc.
15 Casco St
Freeport ME 04033
207 552-2000

(G-5841)
MAINE WOOLENS LLC
15 Paul St (04011-2807)
PHONE..................................207 725-7900
Jo Miller, *Mng Member*
EMP: 30
SALES (est): 4.3MM **Privately Held**
SIC: 2211 Cotton Broadwoven Fabric Mill

(G-5842)
MEDICAL RESOURCES INC
Also Called: Inside Premier Health
11 Medical Center Dr # 1 (04011-3061)
PHONE..................................207 721-1110
Cristy Joubert, *Exec Dir*
EMP: 37
SALES (corp-wide): 22.8MM **Privately Held**
SIC: 3841 Mfg Surgical/Medical Instruments
PA: Medical Resources, Inc.
1455 Broad St Ste 4
Bloomfield NJ 07003
973 707-1100

(G-5843)
NORTHERN TURF PRFESSIONALS INC
251 Old Portland Rd (04011-7273)
P.O. Box 285 (04011-0285)
PHONE..................................207 522-8598
EMP: 4

SALES (est): 505K Privately Held
SIC: 2879 0782 Mfg Agricultural Chemcl Lawn/Garden Services

(G-5844)
RAVEN TECHNOLOGY LLC
14 Industrial Pkwy (04011-7358)
PHONE..................................207 729-7904
Christopher Tupper, *Director*
Duncan Wood,
EMP: 10
SQ FT: 3,600
SALES: 269.4K Privately Held
SIC: 3621 Mfg Generators Electric

(G-5845)
SOURCE INC
Also Called: Source Maine
7 Industrial Pkwy (04011-7315)
PHONE..................................207 729-1107
Susan Domizi, *President*
Gavin Hood, *Manager*
EMP: 3
SALES (corp-wide): 848.3K Privately Held
WEB: www.4source.com
SIC: 2048 Mfg Prepared Feeds
PA: Source Inc
101 Fowler Rd
North Branford CT 06471
203 488-6400

(G-5846)
STARC SYSTEMS INC
166 Orion St (04011-5032)
PHONE..................................844 596-1784
Timothy Hebert, *CEO*
Bruce Bickford, *COO*
Chris Mackenzie, *Exec VP*
EMP: 3
SALES (est): 270K Privately Held
SIC: 2542 Mfg Partitions/Fixtures-Non-wood

(G-5847)
STERIZIGN PRECISION TECH LLC
74 Orion St (04011-5031)
PHONE..................................888 234-3074
Sonia Lutarewych, *President*
EMP: 5 EST: 2016
SALES (est): 304.8K Privately Held
SIC: 3841 Mfg Surgical/Medical Instruments

(G-5848)
SYLVIA WYLER POTTERY INC (PA)
Also Called: Wyler Gallery
150 Maine St (04011-2010)
PHONE..................................207 729-1321
Sylvia Wyler, *President*
John Faulkner, *Shareholder*
EMP: 6
SALES (est): 772.9K Privately Held
SIC: 3269 5023 5719 5331 Mfg Pottery Products Whol Homefurnishings Ret Misc Homefurnishings Variety Store Ret Women's Clothing

(G-5849)
TIMES RECORD MAIN OFC
3 Business Pkwy (04011-7549)
PHONE..................................207 729-3311
Christopher Miles, *Principal*
EMP: 6
SALES (est): 478.6K Privately Held
SIC: 2711 Newspapers Publishing/Printing

(G-5850)
VACUUM PRESSING SYSTEMS INC
553 River Rd (04011-7116)
PHONE..................................207 725-0935
Darryl Keil, *President*
Annabelle Keil, *General Mgr*
EMP: 3
SQ FT: 3,000
SALES: 1MM Privately Held
WEB: www.vacupress.com
SIC: 3553 5085 5251 Mfg Woodworking Machinery Whol Industrial Supplies Ret Hardware

(G-5851)
WESTCON MFG INC
Also Called: Theam
22 Bibber Pkwy (04011-7357)
PHONE..................................207 725-5537
John Garrec, *President*
▲ EMP: 25
SALES (est): 6.4MM Privately Held
WEB: www.theamconveyors.com
SIC: 3555 Mfg Printing Trades Machinery

Buckfield
Oxford County

(G-5852)
MCCAFFERTY LOGGING LLC
243 N Buckfield Rd (04220-4536)
P.O. Box 395 (04220-0395)
PHONE..................................207 212-8600
EMP: 5 EST: 2012
SALES (est): 296.2K Privately Held
SIC: 2411 Logging

(G-5853)
TURNING ACQUISITIONS LLC
Also Called: Wells Wood Turning & Finishing
46 John Ellingwood Rd (04220-4360)
P.O. Box 220 (04220-0220)
PHONE..................................207 336-2400
Tom Wallace, *CFO*
Christian Chandler,
EMP: 40
SALES (est): 5.5MM Privately Held
WEB: www.wellswoodturning.com
SIC: 2426 2499 Hardwood Dimension/Floor Mill Manufacture Wood Products

Bucksport
Hancock County

(G-5854)
CENTRAL MAINE COLD STORAGE
Also Called: Totally Maine Lobster
84 Heritage Park Rd (04416-4664)
PHONE..................................419 215-7955
Brian McCarthy, *CEO*
Tony Kelley, *President*
Tina Kelley, *Vice Pres*
EMP: 9 EST: 2013
SALES (est): 1.1MM Privately Held
SIC: 2092 Mfg Fresh/Frozen Packaged Fish

Burnham
Waldo County

(G-5855)
PRIDE MANUFACTURING CO LLC (PA)
Also Called: Pride Sports
10 N Main St (04922-3300)
PHONE..................................207 487-3322
Joe Zeller, *President*
Richard Dupont, *CFO*
Sara Doyon, *Asst Treas*
Jeremy Boutot, *CIO*
Heather McKinzie, *Executive*
▲ EMP: 120
SQ FT: 87,000
SALES (est): 89.2MM Privately Held
WEB: www.pridemfg.com
SIC: 2411 3949 Logging Mfg Sporting/Athletic Goods

Buxton
York County

(G-5856)
GALAXIE SALSA CO
62 Webster Rd (04093-3744)
PHONE..................................207 939-3392
EMP: 3
SALES (est): 133.1K Privately Held
SIC: 2099 Mfg Food Preparations

(G-5857)
HIGH PINE WELL DRILLING INC
116 Webster Rd (04093-3745)
PHONE..................................207 929-4122
Arthur Tompson, *President*
Deborah Dyer, *President*
Arthur Thompson, *Owner*
Glenn L Dyer Sr, *Partner*
EMP: 5
SALES: 150K Privately Held
SIC: 1381 Oil/Gas Well Drilling

(G-5858)
MC FAULKNER & SONS INC
28 Hague Rd (04093-3611)
PHONE..................................207 929-4545
Mark C Faulkner, *President*
Susan Williams, *Vice Pres*
EMP: 11
SQ FT: 7,040
SALES (est): 1.2MM Privately Held
WEB: www.mcfaulkner.com
SIC: 3444 Mfg Sheet Metalwork

(G-5859)
NANOSPIRE INC
25 Jesse Daniel Dr (04093-6565)
P.O. Box 734, Gorham (04038-0734)
PHONE..................................207 929-6226
Mark Le Clair, *President*
Serge Lebid, *Vice Pres*
EMP: 6
SALES (est): 421.8K Privately Held
WEB: www.nanotechnology.com
SIC: 3541 Cavitation Nanotechnology Tools Fabrication And Process Technology Nanophase Materials Solar Biodiesel

(G-5860)
SACO BAY MILLWORK CO
20 Tory Hill Dr (04093-6155)
PHONE..................................207 929-8400
Tim Flynn, *President*
Dave Durrell, *Vice Pres*
Dave Burrell, *Vice Pres*
EMP: 18
SALES (est): 2.1MM Privately Held
SIC: 2431 Mfg Millwork

(G-5861)
TEM INC
Also Called: T E M
8 Pierce Dr (04093-6018)
PHONE..................................207 929-8700
Eric Nelson, *President*
▲ EMP: 29 EST: 1976
SQ FT: 26,000
SALES (est): 6.2MM Privately Held
SIC: 3724 3462 3463 Mfg Aircraft Engines/Parts Mfg Iron/Steel Forgings Mfg Nonferrous Forgings

(G-5862)
TYLERS SHEET METAL SHOP INC
1126 Long Plains Rd lr3 (04093-6050)
PHONE..................................207 929-6912
Charles Tyler, *Owner*
Patricia Tyler, *Treasurer*
EMP: 4
SQ FT: 2,000
SALES: 175K Privately Held
SIC: 3444 Mfg Sheet Metalwork

(G-5863)
VITAMINSEA LLC
369 Beech Plain Rd (04093-6320)
PHONE..................................207 671-0955
Kelly Roth,
EMP: 8
SALES (est): 686.8K Privately Held
SIC: 3519 Mfg Internal Combustion Engines

Calais
Washington County

(G-5864)
CALAIS PRESS INC
23 Washington St Ste 1 (04619-1689)
P.O. Box 424 (04619-0424)
PHONE..................................207 454-8613
Eric Hinson, *President*
EMP: 5
SQ FT: 3,000
SALES (est): 74.9K Privately Held
SIC: 2752 Lithographic Commercial Printing

(G-5865)
NORTHERN TACK
4 River Rd (04619-4042)
PHONE..................................207 217-7584
Rob Diadone, *Business Mgr*
EMP: 5
SALES (est): 313.6K Privately Held
SIC: 2048 5941 5661 5139 Mfg Prepared Feeds Ret Sport Goods/Bicycles Ret Shoes Whol Footwear

Camden
Knox County

(G-5866)
C W PAINE YACHT DESIGN INC
59 Sea St (04843-1731)
PHONE..................................207 236-2166
Charles W Paine, *President*
EMP: 5
SALES: 400K Privately Held
SIC: 3732 Boatbuilding/Repairing

(G-5867)
LULLA SMITH
44 Timbercliffe Dr Camden Me (04843-4525)
P.O. Box 409 (04843-0409)
PHONE..................................207 230-0832
Carol Smith, *Owner*
EMP: 5
SALES (est): 252.4K Privately Held
WEB: www.lullasmith.com
SIC: 2392 Mfg Household Furnishings

(G-5868)
MAINE BATS HRBORS PUBLICATIONS
Also Called: Maine Boats Homes & Harbors
218 Main St (04847-3434)
P.O. Box 566, Rockland (04841-0566)
PHONE..................................207 594-8622
John K Hanson Jr, *President*
Laurel Frye, *Finance*
Julie Corcoran, *Advt Staff*
Leila Murphy, *Manager*
Gretchen Ogden, *Manager*
EMP: 6
SQ FT: 1,000
SALES: 500K Privately Held
WEB: www.maineboats.com
SIC: 2721 Publish Magazines

(G-5869)
PIG + POET RESTAURANT
52 High St (04843-1735)
PHONE..................................207 236-3391
EMP: 3
SALES (est): 125K Privately Held
SIC: 2011 5812 Meat Packing Plant Eating Place

(G-5870)
THOMAS MICHAELS DESIGNERS INC
Also Called: Thomas Michaels USA
11 Elm St (04843-1902)
PHONE..................................207 236-2708
Thomas C Michaels, *President*
Nora Michaels, *Corp Secy*
EMP: 5
SQ FT: 1,600

GEOGRAPHIC

SALES: 1MM **Privately Held**
WEB: www.thomasmichaels.com
SIC: 3911 5944 7389 6531 Mfg Precious Mtl Jewelry Ret Jewelry Business Services Real Estate Agent/Mgr

(G-5871)
WARNER GRAPHICS INC
22 Washington St (04843-1711)
PHONE..................................207 236-2065
Richard Warner, *President*
Rendel Jones, *Agent*
EMP: 3 **EST:** 2000
SALES (est): 386K **Privately Held**
WEB: www.warnergraphics.com
SIC: 3663 Lithographic Commercial Printing

Canaan
Somerset County

(G-5872)
DADDYS PRIVATE STOCK LLC
185 Whitten Rd (04924-3712)
P.O. Box 253 (04924-0253)
PHONE..................................207 399-7154
Julianna L Thrasher,
EMP: 3
SALES (est): 73.3K **Privately Held**
SIC: 2052 Mfg Cookies/Crackers

(G-5873)
OLSON S LOGGING LLC
15 Strickland Rd (04924-3032)
PHONE..................................207 474-8835
Daim Meyer, *Principal*
EMP: 6
SALES (est): 531.1K **Privately Held**
SIC: 2411 Logging

Cape Elizabeth
Cumberland County

(G-5874)
BARNEY & CO CALIFORNIA LLC
4 Belfield Rd (04107-1612)
PHONE..................................559 442-1752
EMP: 3
SALES (est): 194.7K **Privately Held**
SIC: 2099 Mfg Food Preparations

(G-5875)
DARBY POP LLC
66 Cross Hill Rd (04107-5116)
PHONE..................................207 799-4202
Jessy Kline,
EMP: 4
SALES (est): 210.7K **Privately Held**
SIC: 2741 Misc Publishing

(G-5876)
EAT DRINK LUCKY
10 Fieldstone Rd (04107-2309)
P.O. Box 2809, South Portland (04116-2809)
PHONE..................................207 450-9060
Kevin Phelan, *President*
EMP: 3 **EST:** 2014
SALES (est): 110.9K **Privately Held**
SIC: 2741 Misc Publishing

(G-5877)
LILYPAD LLC
17 Cole Field Rd (04107-9676)
PHONE..................................207 200-0221
Gregory Wolf,
Stephen Blattner,
David Rodgers,
EMP: 3
SALES (est): 130.2K **Privately Held**
SIC: 7372 7389 Prepackaged Software Services

Cape Neddick
York County

(G-5878)
EVERLASTING IMAGES INC
1272 Us Route 1 (03902-7451)
P.O. Box 830 (03902-0830)
PHONE..................................207 351-3277
Rob Arra, *President*
Loring Wetherholtz, *Vice Pres*
EMP: 7
SQ FT: 8,000
SALES: 2.4MM **Privately Held**
SIC: 2752 Lithographic Commercial Printing

(G-5879)
FERNWOOD INC (PA)
24 Logging Rd (03902-7442)
PHONE..................................207 363-7891
Mike Fernald, *President*
EMP: 9
SALES (est): 1.2MM **Privately Held**
WEB: www.fernwood.com
SIC: 2431 Mfg Millwork

(G-5880)
KNIGHT UNDERWATER BEARING LLC
Also Called: Kub
2 Knight Ln (03902-7468)
P.O. Box 944, Ogunquit (03907-0944)
PHONE..................................207 251-0001
John Knight, *Co-Owner*
Richard Knight Knight, *Co-Owner*
Rick Knight, *Co-Owner*
EMP: 3
SALES (est): 156.6K **Privately Held**
SIC: 3429 Mfg Hardware

Caratunk
Somerset County

(G-5881)
DENNIS FRIGON
Also Called: Frigon, Dennis Logging
Rr 201 (04925)
P.O. Box 99, Rockwood (04478-0099)
PHONE..................................207 672-4076
Dennis Frigon, *President*
EMP: 14
SALES (est): 1.2MM **Privately Held**
SIC: 2411 Logging

Cardville
Penobscot County

(G-5882)
MARTIN CARMICHAEL
Also Called: Martin Carmichael Hvy Eqp Repr
1095 Main Rd (04418)
P.O. Box 163, Greenbush (04418-0163)
PHONE..................................207 827-2858
Martin Carmichael, *Owner*
EMP: 13
SALES (est): 1.1MM **Privately Held**
SIC: 3561 Mfg Pumps/Pumping Equipment

(G-5883)
MC CROSSINS LOGGING INC
549 E Ridge Rd (04418-3106)
PHONE..................................207 826-2225
Steve McCroosings, *President*
EMP: 4
SALES: 250K **Privately Held**
SIC: 2411 Logging

(G-5884)
STEPHEN F MADDEN
183 Greenfield Rd (04418-3501)
P.O. Box 59 (04418-0059)
PHONE..................................207 827-5737
Stephen Madden, *Owner*
EMP: 12
SALES: 60K **Privately Held**
SIC: 2411 Logging

Caribou
Aroostook County

(G-5885)
LEON MERCHANT SIGNS (PA)
Also Called: Lee Merchant Signs
72 Madawaska Rd (04736-4076)
P.O. Box 634 (04736-0634)
PHONE..................................207 498-2475
Leon Merchant, *Owner*
EMP: 5
SALES (est): 380.3K **Privately Held**
SIC: 3993 Mfg Signs/Advertising Specialties

(G-5886)
MAINE POTATO GROWERS INC
Also Called: Maine Bag Co
56 Sincock St (04736-2344)
PHONE..................................207 764-3131
Lester Hersey, *Opers-Prdtn-Mfg*
EMP: 20
SALES (corp-wide): 28MM **Privately Held**
WEB: www.mpgco-op.com
SIC: 2674 5199 Mfg Bags-Uncoated Paper Whol Nondurable Goods
PA: Maine Potato Growers, Inc.
261 Main St
Presque Isle ME 04769
207 764-3131

(G-5887)
MARTIN FOREST PRODUCTS
369 Albair Rd (04736-4009)
PHONE..................................207 498-6723
Norman Martin, *Owner*
EMP: 4
SALES (est): 351K **Privately Held**
SIC: 2411 7389 Logging

(G-5888)
NORTHEAST PACKAGING CO
56 Sincock St (04736-2344)
PHONE..................................207 496-3141
Art Crouse, *Branch Mgr*
EMP: 4
SALES (corp-wide): 7.8MM **Privately Held**
SIC: 2673 Mfg Bags-Plastic/Coated Paper
PA: Northeast Packaging Co.
875 Skyway St
Presque Isle ME 04769
207 764-6271

(G-5889)
ONIX CORPORATION
71 Main St (04736-4159)
P.O. Box 270 (04736-0270)
PHONE..................................866 290-5362
Charles Verhoff, *President*
Janet Marr, *Vice Pres*
Chris Osborne, *Vice Pres*
EMP: 35
SQ FT: 100,000
SALES: 6MM **Privately Held**
WEB: www.theonixcorp.com
SIC: 3567 3433 3443 Mfg Industrial Furnaces/Ovens Mfg Heating Equipment-Nonelectric Mfg Fabricated Plate Work

(G-5890)
PORVAIR FILTRATION GROUP INC
15 Armco Ave (04736-1601)
PHONE..................................207 493-3027
EMP: 9
SALES (corp-wide): 170.1MM **Privately Held**
SIC: 3677 Mfg Electronic Coils/Transformers
HQ: Porvair Filtration Group, Inc.
301 Business Ln
Ashland VA 23005
804 550-1600

(G-5891)
TYLER R HEWS
309 Fort Fairfield Rd (04736-3603)
PHONE..................................207 272-9273
Tyler R Hews, *Principal*
EMP: 3
SALES (est): 106.7K **Privately Held**
SIC: 2099 Mfg Food Preparations

(G-5892)
VC PRINT
9 Vesta Dr (04736-2217)
PHONE..................................207 492-1919
Vickie Cummings, *Principal*
EMP: 4 **EST:** 2010
SALES (est): 401.3K **Privately Held**
SIC: 2752 Lithographic Commercial Printing

Carmel
Penobscot County

(G-5893)
R & R LUMBER COMPANY INC
1435 Fuller Rd (04419)
PHONE..................................207 848-3726
Robert G Noyes, *President*
Janice L Noyes, *Treasurer*
Brent Slater, *Clerk*
EMP: 4
SALES (est): 330K **Privately Held**
SIC: 2421 4959 0781 Sawmill/Planing Mill Sanitary Services Landscape Services

Carroll Plt
Penobscot County

(G-5894)
TRAVIS WORSTER
528 Brown Rd (04487-5524)
PHONE..................................207 738-3792
Travis Worster, *Principal*
EMP: 3
SALES (est): 257.3K **Privately Held**
SIC: 2411 Logging

Casco
Cumberland County

(G-5895)
RED MILL
46 Red Mill Rd (04015-3544)
P.O. Box 1000, South Casco (04077-1000)
PHONE..................................207 655-7520
Kermit A Schott, *President*
EMP: 7
SQ FT: 4,000
SALES (est): 1.8MM **Privately Held**
SIC: 2421 Sawmill/Planing Mill

(G-5896)
RIDLONS METAL SHOP
627 Roosevelt Trl (04015-3509)
PHONE..................................207 655-7997
Mike Ridlon, *Owner*
EMP: 3 **EST:** 2000
SALES (est): 369.6K **Privately Held**
SIC: 3444 Mfg Sheet Metalwork

(G-5897)
RUBY MOON LLC
7 Fieldcrest Dr (04015-3254)
PHONE..................................207 200-3242
Douglas Sanborn, *Principal*
Lyndsey Snteusanio,
◆ **EMP:** 5 **EST:** 2010
SALES (est): 460K **Privately Held**
SIC: 2841 Mfg Soap/Other Detergents

(G-5898)
YANKEE MACHINE INC
1300 Poland Spring Rd # 11 (04015-3226)
P.O. Box 10 (04015-0010)
PHONE..................................207 627-4277
Phillip N Hanson, *President*
Richard Thompson, *Clerk*
EMP: 25
SQ FT: 8,600
SALES (est): 1.8MM **Privately Held**
SIC: 3599 Mfg Industrial Machinery

Charleston
Penobscot County

(G-5899)
BURROUGHS MACHINE TOOL PDTS
1 Isthmus Rd (04422)
PHONE..................................207 745-5558
Alan B Clemence, *Owner*
EMP: 3
SALES: 115K **Privately Held**
WEB: www.burroughsmtp.com
SIC: 3599 Mfg Industrial Machinery

Charlotte
Washington County

(G-5900)
GEM CREATIONS OF MAINE
14 Sherrard Ln (04666-6618)
PHONE..................................207 454-2139
Harold Hawkes, *Owner*
Jane Hawkes, *Co-Owner*
EMP: 4 **EST:** 1996
SALES (est): 195.3K **Privately Held**
WEB: www.gemcreationsofmaine.com
SIC: 3911 Mfg Precious Metal Jewelry

Chelsea
Kennebec County

(G-5901)
MARSHALL SPECIALTY GRINDING
40 Beech St (04330-1047)
PHONE..................................207 623-3700
Craig A Marshall, *Owner*
EMP: 3
SALES (est): 310.3K **Privately Held**
SIC: 3599 Mfg Industrial Machinery

Cherryfield
Washington County

(G-5902)
CHERRYFIELD FOODS INC (DH)
320 Ridge Rd (04622-4030)
P.O. Box 128 (04622-0128)
PHONE..................................207 546-7573
John Bragg, *President*
Ragnar Kamp, *COO*
Matthew Bragg, *Vice Pres*
Melissa Beal, *CFO*
Peter Durand, *CFO*
◆ **EMP:** 73 **EST:** 1991
SQ FT: 35,000
SALES (est): 11MM
SALES (corp-wide): 3.3MM **Privately Held**
SIC: 2033 Mfg Canned Fruits/Vegetables
HQ: Oxford Frozen Foods Limited
4881 Main St
Oxford NS B0M 1
902 447-2320

(G-5903)
JASPER WYMAN & SON
Rr 193 (04622)
P.O. Box 100, Milbridge (04658-0100)
PHONE..................................207 546-3381
Ellen Rossi, *Project Mgr*
Homer Woodward, *Branch Mgr*
EMP: 30
SALES (corp-wide): 18.8MM **Privately Held**
SIC: 2033 Mfg Canned Fruits/Vegetables
PA: Jasper Wyman & Son
280 Main St
Milbridge ME 04658
207 546-3800

(G-5904)
JASPER WYMAN & SON
178 Main St (04622-4212)
PHONE..................................207 546-3381
Fred Robinson, *Executive*
EMP: 20
SALES (corp-wide): 18.8MM **Privately Held**
SIC: 2033 Mfg Canned Fruits/Vegetables
PA: Jasper Wyman & Son
280 Main St
Milbridge ME 04658
207 546-3800

Chester
Penobscot County

(G-5905)
GARDNER CHIPMILLS MILLINOCKET
820 S Chester Rd (04457-5521)
P.O. Box 189, Lincoln (04457-0189)
PHONE..................................207 794-2223
Tom Gardner, *Principal*
EMP: 10
SALES (est): 1.1MM **Privately Held**
SIC: 3999 Mfg Misc Products

(G-5906)
TROY VOISINE LOGGING INC
60 N Chester Rd (04457-5735)
PHONE..................................207 794-6301
Troy Voisine, *President*
Lori Voisine, *Vice Pres*
EMP: 4
SALES (est): 410.7K **Privately Held**
SIC: 2411 Logging Contractor

(G-5907)
VOISINE & SON LOGGING INC
1094 N Chester Rd (04457-5747)
PHONE..................................207 794-3336
Eugene Voisine, *President*
Travis Voisine, *President*
EMP: 5
SQ FT: 3,960
SALES (est): 530.9K **Privately Held**
SIC: 2411 Logging Contractor

(G-5908)
WALPOLE WOODWORKERS INC
235 N Chester Rd (04457-5725)
PHONE..................................207 794-2248
Barry Spegenga, *Branch Mgr*
EMP: 44
SALES (corp-wide): 83.9MM **Privately Held**
WEB: www.walpolewoodworkers.com
SIC: 2499 5211 5712 2452 Mfg Wood Products Ret Lumber/Building Mtrl Ret Furniture Mfg Prefabrcatd Wd Bldgs Mfg Prefab Metal Bldgs
PA: Walpole Outdoors Llc
100 Rver Ridge Dr Ste 302
Norwood MA 02062
508 668-2800

Chesterville
Franklin County

(G-5909)
WOOD-MIZER HOLDINGS INC
Also Called: Pine Tree Lumber
541 Borough Rd (04938-3301)
PHONE..................................207 645-2072
Ross Clair, *Owner*
EMP: 10
SALES (corp-wide): 133.2MM **Privately Held**
SIC: 2421 Sawmill/Planing Mill
PA: Wood-Mizer Holdings, Inc.
8180 W 10th St
Indianapolis IN 46214
317 271-1542

China
Kennebec County

(G-5910)
M A HASKELL & SONS LLC
174 Mann Rd (04358-4435)
PHONE..................................207 993-2265
William R Peebles, *Principal*
EMP: 12
SALES (est): 2.3MM **Privately Held**
SIC: 2869 Mfg Industrial Organic Chemicals

(G-5911)
MA HASKELL FUEL CO LLC
1166 Route 3 (04358-5519)
PHONE..................................207 993-2265
Maurice Haskel, *CEO*
Haskell Dawn, *CEO*
Heather Haskell,
EMP: 4 **EST:** 2011
SALES (est): 29.8K **Privately Held**
SIC: 2869 Mfg Industrial Organic Chemicals

Clinton
Kennebec County

(G-5912)
A W CHAFFEE
163 Hinckley Rd (04927-3601)
P.O. Box 69, Oakland (04963-0069)
PHONE..................................207 426-8588
Lowell Hall, *Manager*
EMP: 35
SALES (corp-wide): 3.3MM **Privately Held**
SIC: 2421 Sawmill/Planing Mill
PA: A W Chaffee
164 Belgrade Rd
Oakland ME 04963
207 465-3234

(G-5913)
BLACK DOG SCREEN PRINTING
27 Main St (04927)
P.O. Box 621 (04927-0621)
PHONE..................................207 426-9041
Jeff Lucas, *Owner*
EMP: 3
SALES (est): 199.2K **Privately Held**
WEB: www.blackdogshirts.com
SIC: 2759 Commercial Printing

(G-5914)
CLARKS MACHINE SHOP
Also Called: Clarks Machine Shop
58 Pleasant St (04927-3124)
P.O. Box 15 (04927-0015)
PHONE..................................207 426-8977
George Dewey Clark III, *Owner*
EMP: 5
SQ FT: 7,000
SALES (est): 330K **Privately Held**
SIC: 3599 Mfg Industrial Machinery

(G-5915)
K M MORIN LOGGING INC
749 Hinckley Rd (04927-3704)
PHONE..................................207 399-8835
Kevin Morin, *Principal*
EMP: 6
SALES (est): 544.5K **Privately Held**
SIC: 2411 Logging

(G-5916)
MESTEK INC
Cooper-Weymouth, Peterson
76 Hinckley Rd (04927-3611)
PHONE..................................207 426-2351
Robert Mallia, *Principal*
Matt Watson, *Vice Pres*
Robert Evans, *Vice Pres*
Donna Kelso, *Buyer*
Susan Nelson, *Executive*
EMP: 102
SALES (corp-wide): 629.1MM **Privately Held**
SIC: 3545 3585 3433 Mfg Of Machine Tool Accessories Refrigeration/Heating Equipment Heating Equipment-Nonelectric
PA: Mestek, Inc.
260 N Elm St
Westfield MA 01085
470 898-4533

(G-5917)
WEYMOUTHS INC
121 Mutton Ln (04927-3301)
PHONE..................................207 426-3211
Lindell A Weymouth, *President*
Timothy Weymouth, *Vice Pres*
Terry Weymouth, *Treasurer*
Pearl J Weymouth, *Clerk*
EMP: 3
SALES (est): 412.3K **Privately Held**
SIC: 1389 1711 5983 5172 Oil/Gas Field Services Plumbing/Heat/Ac Contr Ret Fuel Oil Dealer Whol Petroleum Products

Columbia
Washington County

(G-5918)
MAINE BLUEBERRY EQUIPMENT CO
250 Epping Rd (04623-3007)
P.O. Box 2, Columbia Falls (04623-0002)
PHONE..................................207 483-4156
Zane Emerson, *Principal*
EMP: 4
SALES (est): 436.2K **Privately Held**
SIC: 3523 Mfg Farm Machinery/Equipment

Columbia Falls
Washington County

(G-5919)
COUNTY CONCRETE & CNSTR CO
125 Pit Rd (04623-5116)
PHONE..................................207 483-4409
Morrill Worcester, *President*
EMP: 27
SQ FT: 3,360
SALES (est): 2.1MM **Privately Held**
SIC: 3273 3531 1611 3275 Mfg Ready-Mixed Concrete & Asphalt Plant Including Travel-Mix Type

(G-5920)
EPPING VOLUNTEER FIRE DISTRICT
Also Called: EPPING VFD
392 Us Rte 1 (04623)
P.O. Box 204 (04623-0204)
PHONE..................................207 483-2036
Mark Howe, *President*
David Perham,
EMP: 19
SALES: 75.1K **Privately Held**
SIC: 3711 Mfg Motor Vehicle/Car Bodies

Corinna
Penobscot County

(G-5921)
MCKENNEY MACHINE & TOOL CO
Also Called: Mc Kenney Machine & Tool Co
400 Exeter Rd (04928-3514)
PHONE..................................207 278-7091
Galen Mc Kenney, *Owner*
EMP: 15
SQ FT: 5,000
SALES (est): 750.2K **Privately Held**
WEB: www.mckenneymachine.com
SIC: 3599 Machine Shop

GEOGRAPHIC

(G-5922)
MELVIN L YODER
16 Bolstridge Rd (04928-3209)
PHONE....................................207 278-3539
Melvin L Yoder, *Principal*
EMP: 9
SALES (est): 920K **Privately Held**
SIC: 2421 Sawmill/Planing Mill

(G-5923)
PERFECT FIT
39 Stetson Rd (04928-3617)
P.O. Box 439 (04928-0439)
PHONE....................................207 278-3333
Paul Levesque, *Mfg Staff*
Michael C Levesque,
▲ **EMP:** 18
SQ FT: 13,000
SALES: 2.1MM **Privately Held**
SIC: 3172 3199 Mfg Personal Leather Goods Mfg Leather Goods

Corinth
Penobscot County

(G-5924)
NEON PIPE
313 Main St Ste C (04427-3024)
PHONE....................................207 285-7420
Kevin Kneeland, *Principal*
EMP: 3
SALES (est): 123.2K **Privately Held**
SIC: 2813 Ret Tobacco Products

Cornish
York County

(G-5925)
HELI MODIFIED INC
20 Industrial Way (04020-3247)
P.O. Box 638 (04020-0638)
PHONE....................................207 625-4642
Harry Eddy, *President*
Cindy Eddy, *Vice Pres*
Cynthia Eddy, *CFO*
Jennifer Pettengill, *Sales Mgr*
EMP: 15
SQ FT: 8,000
SALES (est): 2.4MM **Privately Held**
WEB: www.helibars.com
SIC: 3751 Mfg Motorcycles/Bicycles

Cornville
Somerset County

(G-5926)
A S & C B GOULD & SONS INC
9 Walton Mills Rd (04976-6338)
PHONE....................................207 474-3930
Arthur Gould, *President*
Michael Gould, *Vice Pres*
Linda Gould, *Treasurer*
EMP: 33
SQ FT: 500
SALES: 1.2MM **Privately Held**
SIC: 2411 Logging

(G-5927)
D F MOODY LLC
1284 E Ridge Rd (04976-6517)
PHONE....................................207 474-6029
David Moody, *Owner*
David F Moody,
EMP: 3
SALES (est): 381.3K **Privately Held**
SIC: 2411 Logging

Crystal
Aroostook County

(G-5928)
ANDERSON FAMILY TREE FARM INC
244 Winding Hill Rd (04747-3127)
PHONE....................................207 463-2843
Vernon Anderson Jr, *President*
Rebecca Anderson, *Vice Pres*
EMP: 3
SALES: 190K **Privately Held**
SIC: 2411 Logging

Cumberland Center
Cumberland County

(G-5929)
MAINE TURNPIKE AUTHORITY
108 Blackstrap Rd (04021-3030)
PHONE....................................207 829-4531
Greg Hinds, *Director*
EMP: 13
SALES (corp-wide): 127MM **Privately Held**
WEB: www.maineturnpike.com
SIC: 2499 7349 Sign Shop And Building Maintenance
PA: Maine Turnpike Authority
2360 Congress St Ste 1
Portland ME 04102
207 842-4030

(G-5930)
NEW GEN INDUSTRIES
10 Native Way (04021-3456)
PHONE....................................207 400-1928
Dan Herman, *Principal*
EMP: 3
SALES (est): 157.9K **Privately Held**
SIC: 3999 Mfg Misc Products

(G-5931)
PORTLAND SAND & GRAVEL INC
61 Rose Dr (04021-3242)
PHONE....................................207 829-2196
Anthony Mancini, *Principal*
EMP: 3 **EST:** 2013
SALES (est): 227.6K **Privately Held**
SIC: 1442 Construction Sand/Gravel

Cumberland Foreside
Cumberland County

(G-5932)
PORT CY LF COMMUNICATIONS INC
9 Ocean Ter (04110-1217)
PHONE....................................207 781-4644
Laurie Hyndman, *President*
Thomas Hyndman, *Vice Pres*
EMP: 4
SQ FT: 1,500
SALES: 750K **Privately Held**
WEB: www.portcitylife.com
SIC: 2721 Periodicals Publishing Work

(G-5933)
VICTORIA ANN VARGA INC
21 Foreside Rd (04110-1403)
PHONE....................................207 781-4050
Victoria Ann Varga, *President*
Daniel Brouder, *Corp Secy*
EMP: 3
SQ FT: 1,800
SALES (est): 352.9K **Privately Held**
SIC: 3961 Designs & Mfg Costume Jewelry

Cushing
Knox County

(G-5934)
PJ SCHWALBENBERG & ASSOC
26 Spear Mill Rd (04563-3144)
PHONE....................................207 354-0700
Peter Schwalbenberg, *President*
EMP: 9
SQ FT: 3,200
SALES (est): 1.5MM **Privately Held**
SIC: 3511 Mfg Turbines/Generator Sets

Damariscotta
Lincoln County

(G-5935)
DARMARISCOTTA POTTERY INC
Northey Sq (04543)
P.O. Box 211 (04543-0211)
PHONE....................................207 563-8843
Rhonda Friedman, *President*
EMP: 6
SQ FT: 1,200
SALES: 230K **Privately Held**
SIC: 3269 5719 Mfg Pottery Products Ret Misc Homefurnishings

(G-5936)
HODGDON SHIPBUILDING LLC
6 Angell Ln (04543-4507)
PHONE....................................207 563-7033
EMP: 4
SALES (corp-wide): 25.2MM **Privately Held**
SIC: 3732 Boatbuilding/Repairing
HQ: Hodgdon Shipbuilding, Llc
14 School St
East Boothbay ME 04544

(G-5937)
N C HUNT INC
237 Route One (04543)
PHONE....................................207 563-8503
David Smith, *Branch Mgr*
EMP: 40
SALES (corp-wide): 21.4MM **Privately Held**
SIC: 2421 5211 Sawmill/Planing Mill Ret Lumber/Building Materials
PA: N. C. Hunt, Inc.
200 S Clary Rd
Jefferson ME 04348
207 549-0922

(G-5938)
OYSTER CREEK MUSHROOMS COMPANY
61 Standpipe Rd (04543-4241)
P.O. Box 1 (04543-0001)
PHONE....................................207 563-1076
Candice M Heydon, *President*
Daniel Heydon, *Vice Pres*
EMP: 4
SALES: 350K **Privately Held**
WEB: www.oystercreekmushroom.com
SIC: 2033 Mfg Canned Fruits/Vegetables

(G-5939)
ROUND TOP ICE CREAM INC
526 Main St (04543-4680)
PHONE....................................207 563-5307
Gary Woodcock, *President*
Brenda Woodcock, *Vice Pres*
Rob Gregory, *Admin Sec*
EMP: 25 **EST:** 1924
SQ FT: 4,000
SALES: 400K **Privately Held**
SIC: 2024 5812 Mfg Ice Cream/Frozen Desert Eating Place

(G-5940)
SUPPLIES UNLIMITED
47 School St (04543-4617)
PHONE....................................207 563-7010
Jane Gravel, *Owner*
EMP: 5
SQ FT: 1,240
SALES (est): 530.4K **Privately Held**
SIC: 2752 Lithographic Commercial Printing

Danforth
Washington County

(G-5941)
GILLIS LUMBER INC
231 Maple St (04424-3102)
P.O. Box 114 (04424-0114)
PHONE....................................207 448-2218
Fred R Gillis, *President*
EMP: 4 **EST:** 1969
SQ FT: 3,800
SALES (est): 464.1K **Privately Held**
SIC: 2421 Sawmill/Planing Mill

(G-5942)
PFC LOGGING INC
46 Snow Farm Rd (04424-3129)
PHONE....................................207 448-7998
Patrick Cowger, *Principal*
EMP: 3
SALES (est): 254.6K **Privately Held**
SIC: 2411 Logging

(G-5943)
THERIAULT JR PETER INC
264 Calais Rd (04424-3020)
P.O. Box 133 (04424-0133)
PHONE....................................207 446-9441
Peter Theriault Jr, *President*
EMP: 3
SALES (est): 315.7K **Privately Held**
SIC: 2411 Logging Service

Dayton
York County

(G-5944)
DAYTON SAND & GRAVEL INC
928 Goodwins Mills Rd (04005-7352)
PHONE....................................207 499-2306
Russell Keene, *President*
EMP: 75 **EST:** 1966
SQ FT: 1,200
SALES (est): 12.5MM **Privately Held**
WEB: www.daytonsand.com
SIC: 3273 2951 1442 Mfg Ready-Mixed Concrete Mfg Asphalt Mixtures/Blocks Construction Sand/Gravel

(G-5945)
FINEST KIND
975 South St (04005-7701)
PHONE....................................207 499-7176
Dana Googins, *Owner*
EMP: 6 **EST:** 1995
SALES (est): 50K **Privately Held**
SIC: 2499 Mfg Wood Products

Deblois
Washington County

(G-5946)
JASPER WYMAN & SON
Also Called: C & D
601 Rte 193 (04622-3507)
PHONE....................................207 638-2201
Darren Hammen, *Manager*
EMP: 20
SALES (corp-wide): 18.8MM **Privately Held**
SIC: 2033 0171 Mfg Canned Fruits/Vegetables Berry Crop Farm
PA: Jasper Wyman & Son
280 Main St
Milbridge ME 04658
207 546-3800

Deer Isle
Hancock County

(G-5947)
COMPASS PUBLICATIONS INC
Also Called: Commercial Fisheries News
161 Perez Xrd (04627-3843)
P.O. Box 600 (04627-0600)
PHONE....................................207 348-1057
Rick Martin, *Systems Mgr*
EMP: 4
SQ FT: 2,000
SALES (est): 399.2K
SALES (corp-wide): 987.5K **Privately Held**
WEB: www.sea-technology.com
SIC: 2721 Periodicals-Publishing/Printing
PA: Compass Publications Inc
4600 Fairfax Dr Ste 304
Arlington VA 22203
703 524-3136

Denmark
Oxford County

(G-5948)
CARDINAL PRINTING CO INC
33 E Main St (04022-5500)
P.O. Box 115 (04022-0115)
PHONE..................................207 452-2931
James Stacy, *President*
EMP: 5 **EST:** 1946
SQ FT: 1,400
SALES (est): 510K **Privately Held**
SIC: 2752 Lithographic Commercial Printing

(G-5949)
JOHN KHIEL III LOG CHPPING INC
65 Bull Ring Rd (04022-5300)
P.O. Box 85 (04022-0085)
PHONE..................................207 452-2157
John Khiel III, *President*
Travis Khiel, *Vice Pres*
EMP: 40 **EST:** 1994
SALES (est): 2.1MM **Privately Held**
SIC: 2411 1794 Logging Excavation Contractor

(G-5950)
K W AGGREGATES
65 Bull Ring Rd (04022-5300)
PHONE..................................207 452-8888
EMP: 3
SALES (est): 99.6K **Privately Held**
SIC: 1442 Construction Sand/Gravel

(G-5951)
MOIR COMPANY INC
67 E Main St (04022-5501)
PHONE..................................207 452-2000
Douglas Bauer, *President*
Margaret H Bauer, *Vice Pres*
EMP: 10
SQ FT: 3,000
SALES (est): 993.5K **Privately Held**
WEB: www.moirco.com
SIC: 7694 Armature Rewinding

Detroit
Somerset County

(G-5952)
NORTHEAST AGRICULTURAL SLS INC
36 North Rd (04929)
PHONE..................................207 487-6273
Aaron Bell, *Branch Mgr*
EMP: 6
SALES (corp-wide): 4MM **Privately Held**
SIC: 2873 5599 5261 Mfg Nitrogenous Fertilizers Ret Misc Vehicles Ret Nursery/Garden Supplies
PA: Northeast Agricultural Sales, Incorporated
205 East St
Lyndonville VT 05851
802 626-3351

(G-5953)
SOMATEX INC
70 North Rd (04929-3227)
P.O. Box 487, Pittsfield (04967-0487)
PHONE..................................207 487-6141
Laurie Ferland, *CEO*
Jason Kamara, *President*
▼ **EMP:** 26
SQ FT: 12,000
SALES (est): 10.5MM **Privately Held**
WEB: www.somatexinc.com
SIC: 3531 3536 5084 7389 Mfg Construction Mach Mfg Hoist/Crane/Monorail Whol Industrial Equip Business Services

(G-5954)
WALPOLE WOODWORKERS INC
88 Main St (04929-3236)
PHONE..................................207 368-4302
Robert Hayes, *Branch Mgr*
EMP: 50
SALES (corp-wide): 83.9MM **Privately Held**
WEB: www.walpolewoodworkers.com
SIC: 2499 5211 5712 2452 Mfg Wood Products Ret Lumber/Building Mtrl Ret Furniture Mfg Prefabrcatd Wd Bldgs Mfg Prefab Metal Bldgs
PA: Walpole Outdoors Llc
100 Rver Ridge Dr Ste 302
Norwood MA 02062
508 668-2800

Dexter
Penobscot County

(G-5955)
ADVANCED CONCEPTS & ENGRG LLC
9 Zions Hill Rd (04930-1117)
PHONE..................................207 270-3025
Joel Costonis, *President*
EMP: 6
SALES (est): 550.9K **Privately Held**
SIC: 3821 3531 5049 Mfg Lab Apparatus/Furn Mfg Construction Mach Whol Professional Equip

(G-5956)
RFI INDUSTRIES
32 Main St (04930-1346)
PHONE..................................443 255-8767
Chris Rickel, *Executive Asst*
EMP: 3
SALES (est): 184.6K **Privately Held**
SIC: 3999 Mfg Misc Products

Dixfield
Oxford County

(G-5957)
IRVING WOODLANDS LLC
24 Hall Hill Rd (04224-9571)
PHONE..................................207 562-4400
Jim Irving, *President*
EMP: 125
SALES (corp-wide): 2.8B **Privately Held**
SIC: 2421 Saw Mill
HQ: Irving Woodlands Llc
1798 St John Rd
St John Plt ME 04743
207 834-5767

(G-5958)
ROLAND H TYLER LOGGING INC
Canton Point Rd (04224)
P.O. Box 818 (04224-0818)
PHONE..................................207 562-7282
Roland H Tyler, *President*
George A Hess, *Clerk*
EMP: 9 **EST:** 1960
SALES (est): 901.1K **Privately Held**
SIC: 2411 4212 Logging Contractor

Dover Foxcroft
Piscataquis County

(G-5959)
AMB SIGNS INC (PA)
Also Called: Amb Audio-Video
25 North St Ste D (04426-1159)
PHONE..................................207 564-3633
Carl Brackett, *President*
Victoria M Brackett, *Treasurer*
EMP: 3 **EST:** 1979
SQ FT: 1,800
SALES (est): 344.8K **Privately Held**
SIC: 3993 7384 5731 7359 Mfg Signs/Ad Specialties Photofinish Laboratory Ret Radio/Tv/Electronics Equipment Rental/Leasing

(G-5960)
CREATIVE APPAREL ASSOC LLC
62 Engdahl Dr (04426-3652)
PHONE..................................207 564-0235
Fax: 207 564-0234
EMP: 40
SALES (corp-wide): 33.3MM **Privately Held**
SIC: 2311 Mfg Men's/Boy's Suits/Coats
HQ: Creative Apparel Associates, Llc
318 Augusta Rd
Belmont ME 04952
207 342-2814

(G-5961)
NORTHEAST PUBLISHING COMPANY
Also Called: Piscataquis Observer
12 E Main St Ste A (04426-1414)
P.O. Box 30 (04426-0030)
PHONE..................................207 564-8355
Roger Tremblay, *Director*
EMP: 4
SALES (corp-wide): 74MM **Privately Held**
SIC: 2752 7334 7313 4822 Lithographic Coml Print Photocopying Service Advertising Rep Telegraph Communications Commercial Printing
HQ: Northeast Publishing Company Inc
260 Missile St
Presque Isle ME 04769
207 764-4471

(G-5962)
P-Q CONTROLS INC
64 Park St (04426-1000)
PHONE..................................207 564-7141
Jody Knowles, *Branch Mgr*
Brian Church, *Technical Staff*
EMP: 8
SALES (est): 954.1K
SALES (corp-wide): 6.7MM **Privately Held**
SIC: 3625 Mfg Relays/Industrial Controls
PA: P-Q Controls, Inc.
95 Dolphin Rd
Bristol CT 06010
860 583-6994

(G-5963)
PIKE INDUSTRIES INC
53 Spaulding Rd (04426-4006)
PHONE..................................207 564-8444
Andy Brewer, *Principal*
EMP: 3
SALES (corp-wide): 29.7B **Privately Held**
SIC: 3999 Highway/Street Construction
HQ: Pike Industries, Inc.
3 Eastgate Park Dr
Belmont NH 03220
603 527-5100

(G-5964)
PLEASANT RIVER LUMBER COMPANY (PA)
432 Milo Rd (04426-3339)
P.O. Box 68 (04426-0068)
PHONE..................................207 564-8520
Luke Brochu, *President*
Christopher Brochu, *Vice Pres*
Jason Brochu, *Vice Pres*
Stephanie Smith, *Controller*
Sandy Leavitt, *Technology*
EMP: 98
SQ FT: 100,000
SALES (est): 19.8MM **Privately Held**
WEB: www.pleasantriverlumber.com
SIC: 2421 Sawmill/Planing Mill

Dresden
Lincoln County

(G-5965)
CHRISTMAS COVE DESIGNS INC
Also Called: Cotton's Woolens
438 Middle Rd (04342-3645)
PHONE..................................207 350-1035
Jefferson Cotton, *President*
Kamala Grohman, *Vice Pres*
EMP: 5
SQ FT: 5,000
SALES (est): 407.7K **Privately Held**
WEB: www.christmascovedesigns.com
SIC: 3999 Mfg Christmas Tree Ornaments

(G-5966)
FARM TRUCK INSTITUTE
1265 Middle Rd (04342-4027)
PHONE..................................207 400-2242
Walter Loeman, *Principal*
EMP: 3
SALES (est): 91.3K **Privately Held**
SIC: 2033 Mfg Canned Fruits/Vegetables

(G-5967)
MAINE MEDICINALS INC
555 Gardiner Rd (04342-3032)
PHONE..................................207 737-8717
Edie Johnston, *President*
Geo Johnston, *Opers Staff*
EMP: 4
SALES (est): 333.6K **Privately Held**
SIC: 2099 Mfg Food Preparations

Durham
Androscoggin County

(G-5968)
BSD SOFT WARE
Also Called: BSD Software
10 Brookside Dr (04222-5314)
PHONE..................................207 522-5881
EMP: 3 **EST:** 1986
SALES (est): 270K **Privately Held**
WEB: www.bsdsoftware.com
SIC: 7372 Prepackaged Software Services

(G-5969)
CHURCHS WELDING & FAB INC
103 Old Brunswick Rd (04222-5303)
PHONE..................................207 353-4249
EMP: 5 **EST:** 1983
SALES: 100K **Privately Held**
SIC: 7692 Steel Erection / Crane Rental

(G-5970)
COPP EXCAVATING INC
190 Pinkham Brook Rd (04222-5429)
PHONE..................................207 926-4988
Micheal S Copp, *President*
EMP: 13
SALES (est): 1.3MM **Privately Held**
SIC: 1389 4959 Oil/Gas Field Services Sanitary Services

(G-5971)
MAINE CUSTOM WOODLANDS LLC
1326 Hallowell Rd (04222-5376)
PHONE..................................207 353-9020
Thomas Cushman, *Principal*
EMP: 12
SALES (est): 1.6MM **Privately Held**
SIC: 2411 Logging

Dyer Brook
Aroostook County

(G-5972)
DANA HARDY
1285 Dyer Brook Rd (04747-5015)
PHONE..................................207 757-8445
Dana Hardy, *Owner*
Kirby Hardy, *Co-Owner*
EMP: 5
SALES (est): 309.1K **Privately Held**
WEB: www.danahardyconsulting.com
SIC: 2411 Logging

Eagle Lake
Aroostook County

(G-5973)
CHOPPER ONE INC
215 Old Main St (04739-3304)
P.O. Box 396 (04739-0396)
PHONE..................................207 444-5476
Reynold Blair, *President*
Jeff Blair, *Vice Pres*
Mary Blair, *Treasurer*
EMP: 7

SALES (est): 750K Privately Held
SIC: 2411 Logging

East Baldwin
Cumberland County

(G-5974)
LIMINGTON LUMBER COMPANY
411 Pequawket Trl (04024)
P.O. Box 47 (04024-0047)
PHONE....207 625-3286
Winthrop N Smith, *President*
James Henderson, *Opers Mgr*
EMP: 40 EST: 1961
SQ FT: 700
SALES (est): 6.6MM Privately Held
WEB: www.limingtonlumber.com
SIC: 2421 Sawmill/Planing Mill

East Blue Hill
Hancock County

(G-5975)
WEBBERS COVE BOAT YARD INC
Also Called: Storage and Repair
Morgan Bay Rd (04629)
P.O. Box 364, Blue Hill (04614-0364)
PHONE....207 374-2841
John D Cousins, *President*
EMP: 5
SALES (est): 609.9K Privately Held
SIC: 3732 4493 Boatbuilding/Repairing Marina Operation

East Boothbay
Lincoln County

(G-5976)
HODGDON SHIPBUILDING LLC (HQ)
14 School St (04544-6029)
P.O. Box 505 (04544-0505)
PHONE....207 633-4194
Timothy Hodgdon, *President*
Chad Jones, *QA Dir*
Don O'Grady, *CFO*
EMP: 15
SQ FT: 60,000
SALES (est): 7.2MM
SALES (corp-wide): 25.2MM Privately Held
SIC: 3732 Boatbuilding/Repairing
PA: Hodgdon Yachts, Inc.
14 School St
East Boothbay ME 04544
207 737-2802

(G-5977)
HODGDON YACHTS INC (PA)
14 School St (04544-6029)
PHONE....207 737-2802
Timothy S Hodgdon, *President*
Andrew Wright, *COO*
Nate Thompson, *Design Engr*
Don O Grady, *CFO*
Christina Flood, *Office Mgr*
▲ EMP: 120
SALES (est): 25.2MM Privately Held
WEB: www.hodgdonyachts.com
SIC: 3732 Boatbuilding/Repairing

(G-5978)
NATHANIEL S WILSON SAILMAKER
15 Lincoln St (04544-6035)
P.O. Box 71 (04544-0071)
PHONE....207 633-5071
Nathaniel S Wilson, *President*
Clayton Howard, *Principal*
EMP: 3
SALES: 250K Privately Held
SIC: 2394 Mfg Canvas/Related Products

(G-5979)
PAUL E LUKE INC
15 Lukes Gulch (04544-6229)
PHONE....207 633-4971
A Franklin Luke, *President*
Nora Luke, *Vice Pres*
EMP: 6
SQ FT: 9,757
SALES: 1MM Privately Held
WEB: www.peluke.com
SIC: 3429 4493 Mfg Marine Hardware Supplies & Boat Yard

(G-5980)
WASHBURN & DOUGHTY ASSOC INC
7 Enterprise St (04544-6045)
P.O. Box 296 (04544-0296)
PHONE....207 633-6517
Bruce H Doughty, *CEO*
Bruce D Washburn, *Vice Pres*
Justin Clark, *Production*
Matt Maddox, *CFO*
▲ EMP: 55
SQ FT: 50,000
SALES (est): 14.4MM Privately Held
WEB: www.washburndoughty.com
SIC: 3731 3732 Shipbuilding/Repairing Boatbuilding/Repairing

(G-5981)
WILLIAMS PARTNERS LTD
Also Called: Sullivan Associates
29 Lincoln St (04544-6035)
P.O. Box 514 (04544-0514)
PHONE....207 633-3111
Pete Williams, *President*
EMP: 7
SQ FT: 1,200
SALES (est): 1.3MM Privately Held
WEB: www.williamspartners.net
SIC: 3589 Mfg Service Industry Machinery

East Machias
Washington County

(G-5982)
ASHLEY & HARMON LOGGING INC
230 Chases Mill Rd (04630-3804)
PHONE....207 259-2043
George Harmon, *President*
Thomas Ashley, *Vice Pres*
Kathy Harmon, *Treasurer*
EMP: 10
SALES (est): 1MM Privately Held
SIC: 2411 Logging

(G-5983)
BRUCE DENNISON
Also Called: Roytoy
599 Jacksonville Rd (04630-3611)
P.O. Box 660 (04630-0660)
PHONE....207 255-0954
Bruce W Dennison, *Owner*
Sue Dennison, *Owner*
EMP: 6
SQ FT: 4,000
SALES (est): 751.5K Privately Held
SIC: 3944 Mfg Games/Toys

(G-5984)
TRP LOGGING
9 Dike Gaddis Loop (04630-4223)
P.O. Box 178 (04630-0178)
PHONE....207 263-6425
Todd R Purington, *Owner*
EMP: 7
SALES (est): 25.2K Privately Held
SIC: 2411 4959 Logging Sanitary Services

East Waterboro
York County

(G-5985)
NORTHPORT LLC
Also Called: Northport Wood Products
61 Sokokis Trl (04030-5400)
P.O. Box 186 (04030-0186)
PHONE....207 247-7600
Cory Ericson, *Mng Member*
EMP: 6
SALES (est): 493.4K Privately Held
SIC: 2434 Mfg Wood Kitchen Cabinets

(G-5986)
R S D GRAPHICS INC
158 Main St (04030)
P.O. Box 390 (04030-0390)
PHONE....207 247-6430
Todd Abbott, *President*
Jennifer Abbott, *Vice Pres*
EMP: 5
SQ FT: 2,200
SALES: 200K Privately Held
SIC: 3993 Mfg Signs/Advertising Specialties

East Wilton
Franklin County

(G-5987)
JARDEN LLC
Also Called: Unimark Plastics
5 Mill St (04234)
PHONE....207 645-2574
John Beach, *Manager*
EMP: 220
SALES (corp-wide): 8.6B Publicly Held
WEB: www.jarden.com
SIC: 2033 3089 3356 3479 Mfg Canned Fruits/Vegtbl Mfg Plastic Products Nonferrous Rollng/Drawng Coating/Engraving Svcs
HQ: Jarden Llc
221 River St
Hoboken NJ 07030

Eastbrook
Hancock County

(G-5988)
INDIAN MEADOW HERBALS LLC
1284 Macomber Mill Rd (04634-4319)
PHONE....207 565-3010
Nancy Lowry,
Roseanna Rich,
EMP: 4
SALES (est): 467.2K Privately Held
WEB: www.imherbal.com
SIC: 2833 Medicinals And Botanicals, Nsk

Easton
Aroostook County

(G-5989)
HUBER ENGINEERED WOODS LLC
333 Station Rd (04740-4005)
P.O. Box 69 (04740-0069)
PHONE....207 488-6700
Kevin Kearney, *Purch Mgr*
John Goding, *Manager*
Christopher Washburn, *Exec Dir*
EMP: 92
SALES (corp-wide): 826.6MM Privately Held
SIC: 2493 3613 Mfg Reconstituted Wood Products Mfg Switchgear/Switchboards
HQ: Huber Engineered Woods Llc
10925 David Taylor Dr # 3
Charlotte NC 28262
800 933-9220

(G-5990)
JM HUBER CORPORATION
333 Station Rd (04740-4005)
P.O. Box 69 (04740-0069)
PHONE....207 488-2051
Dragan Kornicer, *Branch Mgr*
EMP: 112
SALES (corp-wide): 826.6MM Privately Held
SIC: 2819 Mfg Industrial Inorganic Chemicals
PA: J.M. Huber Corporation
499 Thornall St Ste 8
Edison NJ 08837
732 549-8600

(G-5991)
MCCAIN FOODS USA INC
319 Richardson Rd (04740-4056)
P.O. Box 159 (04740-0159)
PHONE....207 488-2561
Kevin Nichols, *Opers Mgr*
Darren Goulet, *Production*
John Johnston, *Production*
Timothy Embelton, *Buyer*
Conrad Caron, *Manager*
EMP: 500
SALES (corp-wide): 19.5B Privately Held
WEB: www.mccainusa.com
SIC: 2037 2038 2033 Mfg Frozen Fruits/Vegetables Mfg Frozen Specialties Mfg Canned Fruits/Vegetables
HQ: Mccain Foods Usa, Inc.
1 Tower Ln Ste Uppr
Oakbrook Terrace IL 60181
630 955-0400

(G-5992)
MCCAIN FOODS USA INC
Station Rd (04740)
PHONE....207 488-2561
William Voss, *Principal*
EMP: 520
SALES (corp-wide): 19.5B Privately Held
WEB: www.mccainusa.com
SIC: 2037 Processes Frozen Foods
HQ: Mccain Foods Usa, Inc.
1 Tower Ln Ste Uppr
Oakbrook Terrace IL 60181
630 955-0400

(G-5993)
MIKE MAINE PICKLE
46 White Rd (04740)
P.O. Box 284 (04740-0284)
PHONE....207 488-6881
Mike Henderson, *Owner*
EMP: 3
SALES: 225K Privately Held
SIC: 2035 Mfg Gourmet Pickles

Eastport
Washington County

(G-5994)
ENGELHARD CORP SCALES
30 Staniels Rd (04631-3017)
PHONE....207 853-2501
Barbara Cummings, *Principal*
EMP: 3 EST: 2011
SALES (est): 208.5K Privately Held
SIC: 2816 Mfg Inorganic Pigments

(G-5995)
QUODDY TIDES INC
Also Called: Quoddy Tides Newspaper
123 Water St (04631-1333)
P.O. Box 213 (04631-0213)
PHONE....207 853-4806
Edward French, *President*
EMP: 7
SQ FT: 1,800
SALES: 414K Privately Held
WEB: www.quoddytides.com
SIC: 2711 Newspapers-Publishing/Printing

(G-5996)
RAYES MUSTARD MILL
83 Washington St (04631-1226)
P.O. Box 2 (04631-0002)
PHONE....207 853-4451
Nancy Raye, *President*
Karen Raye, *President*
Donald Raye, *Treasurer*
Gerald Greenlaw, *Director*
Caroline Raye, *Clerk*
EMP: 6
SQ FT: 5,000
SALES (est): 672.4K Privately Held
WEB: www.rayesmustard.com
SIC: 2035 Mfg Pickles/Sauces/Dressing

▲ = Import ▼=Export
◆ =Import/Export

Eddington
Penobscot County

(G-5997)
PEAVEY MANUFACTURING COMPANY
526 Main Rd (04428-3211)
P.O. Box 129 (04428-0129)
PHONE....207 843-7861
Raymond F Delano, *President*
Rodney Buswell, *Vice Pres*
Rena Delano, *Treasurer*
▲ **EMP:** 45
SALES (est): 6.3MM **Privately Held**
WEB: www.peaveymfg.com
SIC: 2499 3545 3423 Mfg Wood Products Mfg Machine Tool Access Mfg Hand/Edge Tools

(G-5998)
PORTABLE SAWMILL
218 Blackcap Rd (04428-3447)
PHONE....207 843-7216
John Weed, *Principal*
EMP: 3
SALES (est): 245.7K **Privately Held**
SIC: 2421 Sawmill/Planing Mill

Edgecomb
Lincoln County

(G-5999)
BLEVINS COMPANY
178 Boothbay Rd (04556-3020)
PHONE....207 882-6396
EMP: 3
SALES (est): 169.6K **Privately Held**
SIC: 3732 2431 Boatbuilding/Repairing Mfg Millwork

(G-6000)
CHASE ASSOCIATES INC
304 Boothbay Rd (04556-3240)
P.O. Box 75 (04556-0075)
PHONE....207 882-7526
John Allan, *President*
EMP: 5 **EST:** 1979
SQ FT: 5,000
SALES (est): 987.5K **Privately Held**
WEB: www.manways.com
SIC: 3312 Steel Fabrication

(G-6001)
CONTACT INC
788 Boothbay Rd (04556-3330)
PHONE....207 882-6116
Richard D Reid II, *President*
Alvin G Reid, *Director*
EMP: 3
SQ FT: 3,200
SALES (est): 310.4K **Privately Held**
WEB: www.contact-contact.com
SIC: 3548 3823 3255 Mfg Welding Apparatus Mfg Process Control Instruments Mfg Clay Refractories

(G-6002)
EDGECOMB BOAT WORKS
957 Boothbay Rd (04556-3320)
PHONE....207 882-5038
Michael Mayne, *President*
EMP: 7
SALES (est): 746.8K **Privately Held**
SIC: 3732 Boatbuilding/Repairing

(G-6003)
OPCO INC
916 Cross Point Rd (04556-3516)
PHONE....207 882-6783
Gary Woods, *Principal*
EMP: 4
SALES (est): 301.6K **Privately Held**
SIC: 2836 Mfg Biological Products

(G-6004)
SWEENEY RIDGE
186 River Rd (04556-3434)
PHONE....207 482-0499
Mary Underwood, *Owner*
EMP: 4
SALES (est): 295K **Privately Held**
SIC: 3444 Mfg Sheet Metalwork

Edmunds Twp
Washington County

(G-6005)
D M G ENTERPRISES
160 Belyea Rd (04628-5330)
PHONE....207 726-4603
Dale Griffin, *President*
Michael Griffin, *Vice Pres*
Shelly Griffin, *Treasurer*
Dennis L Mahar, *Clerk*
EMP: 4
SALES: 500K **Privately Held**
WEB: www.dmg-enter.com
SIC: 2411 1542 Logging & Construction

(G-6006)
TIDE MILL ENTERPRISES
40 Tide Mill Rd (04628-5502)
PHONE....207 733-4425
Terry A Bell, *President*
EMP: 5
SALES: 975.7K **Privately Held**
SIC: 2411 Logging

Eliot
York County

(G-6007)
JOHNSON PRINTING & GRAPHICS
384 Harold L Dow Hwy # 15 (03903-1411)
PHONE....207 439-2567
Donald Johnson, *Owner*
EMP: 3
SALES (est): 282K **Privately Held**
SIC: 2752 Offset Printer

(G-6008)
MODERNIST PANTRY LLC
25 Harold L Dow Hwy (03903-2081)
PHONE....207 200-3817
Jieming Wang, *Mng Member*
▲ **EMP:** 9
SALES (est): 1.2MM **Privately Held**
SIC: 2099 5499 Mfg Food Preparations Ret Misc Foods

(G-6009)
NATURAL ROCKS SPRING WATER ICE
299 Harold L Dow Hwy (03903-1443)
PHONE....207 451-2110
Stephen Tischner, *President*
EMP: 4
SQ FT: 5,000
SALES (est): 519.3K **Privately Held**
SIC: 2097 Mfg Ice

(G-6010)
STERLING POWER USA LLC
406 Harold L Dow Hwy # 6 (03903-1452)
PHONE....207 226-3500
Charles Sterling,
◆ **EMP:** 4
SALES: 500K **Privately Held**
WEB: www.sterling-power-usa.com
SIC: 3629 Mfg Electrical Industrial Apparatus

(G-6011)
TIN CAN SALLY
50 Russell Rd (03903-1333)
PHONE....207 651-6188
Sarah Kilvert, *Principal*
EMP: 4
SALES (est): 242K **Privately Held**
SIC: 3411 Mfg Metal Cans

(G-6012)
VENTECH INDUSTRIES INC
384 Harold L Dw Hwy (03903)
PHONE....207 439-0069
Michael A Varney, *President*
EMP: 8
SQ FT: 6,000
SALES: 2MM **Privately Held**
WEB: www.ventechindustries.com
SIC: 3251 3253 3585 Mfg Brick/Structural Tile Mfg Ceramic Wall/Floor Tile Mfg Refrigeration/Heating Equipment

Ellsworth
Hancock County

(G-6013)
ALLENS BLUEBERRY FREEZER INC (PA)
244 Main St (04605-1698)
P.O. Box 536 (04605-0536)
PHONE....207 667-5561
Roy Allen, *President*
▼ **EMP:** 25 **EST:** 1956
SQ FT: 18,000
SALES (est): 3.8MM **Privately Held**
WEB: www.allensblueberries.com
SIC: 2037 Mfg Frozen Blueberries

(G-6014)
BANGOR PUBLISHING COMPANY
Also Called: Bangor Daily News Hancock Bur
98 Main St Ste B (04605-1930)
PHONE....207 667-9393
Kathy Cook, *Manager*
EMP: 7
SALES (corp-wide): 74MM **Privately Held**
WEB: www.bangornews.com
SIC: 2711 Newspapers-Publishing/Printing
PA: Bangor Publishing Company
1 Merchants Plz
Bangor ME 04401
207 990-8000

(G-6015)
C&C MACHINE SHOP INC
328 Bucksport Rd Ste 1 (04605-2893)
PHONE....207 667-6910
Glenn Crawford, *President*
Donna Crawford, *Treasurer*
EMP: 4
SQ FT: 20,000
SALES (est): 586.9K **Privately Held**
SIC: 3599 Mfg Industrial Machinery

(G-6016)
DOWNEAST GRAPHICS & PRTG INC
477 Washington Jct Rd (04605)
P.O. Box 1103 (04605-1103)
PHONE....207 667-5582
Charles E Ferden, *President*
EMP: 12
SQ FT: 16,500
SALES: 1.1MM **Privately Held**
WEB: www.downeastgraphics.com
SIC: 2752 2759 Lithographic Commercial Printing Commercial Printing

(G-6017)
E SKIP GRINDLE & SONS
485 North St (04605-3454)
PHONE....207 460-0334
E Grindle, *Owner*
EMP: 7 **EST:** 2014
SALES (est): 159.7K **Privately Held**
SIC: 3949 5932 4959 Mfg Sporting/Athletic Goods Ret Used Merchandise Sanitary Services

(G-6018)
ELLSWORTH AMERICAN INC
30 Water St (04605-2033)
P.O. Box 509 (04605-0509)
PHONE....207 667-2576
Alan Baker, *President*
Terry Carlisle, *Vice Pres*
Kathy Cook, *Accounting Mgr*
Wendy Ward, *Officer*
Barbara Tedesco, *Graphic Designe*
EMP: 60 **EST:** 1851
SQ FT: 25,000
SALES (est): 3.9MM **Privately Held**
WEB: www.ellsworthmaine.com
SIC: 2711 7375 Newspapers-Publishing/Printing Information Retrieval Services

(G-6019)
H W DUNN & SON INC
Also Called: Darlene Springo
146 Water St (04605-2051)
P.O. Box 306 (04605-0306)
PHONE....207 667-8121
H Howard Dunn, *President*
Reta Dunn, *Vice Pres*
EMP: 3
SALES (est): 220K **Privately Held**
SIC: 3272 5999 Mfg Concrete Products Ret Misc Merchandise

(G-6020)
PYRAMID STUDIOS
10 State St (04605-1938)
PHONE....207 667-3321
David Herrington, *President*
Donald Herrington, *Vice Pres*
Denise Hue, *Officer*
EMP: 4
SQ FT: 2,500
SALES (est): 499.3K **Privately Held**
WEB: www.pyramidjewelry.com
SIC: 3911 5094 5944 Mfg Whol Ret Jewelry

(G-6021)
REGAL PRESS INC
265 Water St (04605-2048)
PHONE....207 667-5227
Scott Vicnaire, *President*
EMP: 5 **EST:** 1979
SQ FT: 2,500
SALES (est): 530.7K **Privately Held**
SIC: 2752 Lithographic Commercial Printing

(G-6022)
SUPERIOR WLDG FABRICATION INC
Also Called: Superior Docks
420 Christian Ridge Rd (04605-3218)
PHONE....207 664-2121
Richard Newman, *President*
▲ **EMP:** 14
SQ FT: 3,600
SALES: 800K **Privately Held**
WEB: www.lakedocks.com
SIC: 3479 Mfg Aluminum Die-Castings Welding Repair

(G-6023)
WINKUMPAUGH LINE CONSTRUCTION
233 Thorsen Rd (04605)
PHONE....207 667-2962
Carlton L Morse Jr, *President*
EMP: 6
SALES (est): 630K **Privately Held**
SIC: 3612 Mfg Transformers

(G-6024)
WOODLAND STUDIOS INC
406 State St (04605-3331)
PHONE....207 667-3286
Chris Feldkamp, *President*
Cathy Feldkamp, *Corp Secy*
Thomas Feldkamp, *Vice Pres*
EMP: 10
SQ FT: 5,000
SALES (est): 1MM **Privately Held**
WEB: www.woodlandstudios.com
SIC: 2395 5136 2759 Mfg Embroidered Emblems & Whol Men's & Boys' Outerwear

Etna
Penobscot County

(G-6025)
FAMILY YARNS INC
15 Family Cir (04434-3448)
PHONE....207 269-3852
Joe Marchelletta, *President*
Gary Marchelletta, *Vice Pres*
Antonio Marchelletta, *Shareholder*
Michael Marchelletta, *Admin Sec*
EMP: 8
SQ FT: 26,000
SALES: 400K **Privately Held**
SIC: 2281 Yarn Spinning Mill

Fairfield
Somerset County

(G-6026)
DISTANCE RACING PRODUCTS
441 Center Rd (04937-3221)
P.O. Box 342 (04937-0342)
PHONE..................................207 453-2644
Jeff Taylor, *Owner*
EMP: 4
SALES (est): 343.5K **Privately Held**
SIC: 3714 Mfg Motor Vehicle Parts/Accessories

(G-6027)
J & M ENTERPRISES INC
Also Called: Superior Fire Services
33 Howe Rd (04937-3419)
PHONE..................................207 968-2729
Michael Dawes, *CEO*
Jon Cochran, *President*
EMP: 6
SALES (est): 914.8K **Privately Held**
SIC: 3589 Mfg Service Industry Machinery

(G-6028)
NORTHERN SIGNS
105 Martin Stream Rd (04937-3011)
P.O. Box 1475, Waterville (04903-1475)
PHONE..................................207 465-2399
Mark Atework, *Principal*
EMP: 3
SALES (est): 329.5K **Privately Held**
SIC: 3993 Mfg Signs/Advertising Specialties

(G-6029)
SOYAZ
7 Truss Ln (04937-1180)
P.O. Box 377 (04937-0377)
PHONE..................................207 453-4911
Michael Boulet, *President*
EMP: 35
SQ FT: 19,000
SALES (est): 5.2MM **Privately Held**
WEB: www.mainelytrusses.com
SIC: 2439 Mfg Structural Wood Members

Falmouth
Cumberland County

(G-6030)
CURRENT PUBLISHING LLC
Also Called: American Journal
5 Fundy Rd Ste 1 (04105-1771)
PHONE..................................207 854-2577
Lee Hews Casler, *Mng Member*
Amy Canfield, *Manager*
EMP: 50 **EST:** 1950
SALES (est): 2.7MM **Privately Held**
WEB: www.americanjournal.com
SIC: 2711 Newspapers-Publishing/Printing

(G-6031)
LIGHTING SOLUTIONS INC
52 Middle Rd (04105-1892)
PHONE..................................207 772-2738
Steven K Grimshaw, *President*
EMP: 4
SALES (est): 370K **Privately Held**
WEB: www.lightingsolutionsinc.us
SIC: 3645 3646 Mfg Residential Lighting Fixtures Mfg Commercial Lighting Fixtures

(G-6032)
MCGUIRE & CO INC
Also Called: McGuire Controls
27 Gray Rd (04105-2027)
PHONE..................................207 797-3323
Ken McGuire, *President*
EMP: 4
SALES: 600K **Privately Held**
WEB: www.mcguirecontrols.com
SIC: 3829 1731 3491 3625 Mfg Measure/Control Dvcs Electrical Contractor Mfg Industrial Valves Mfg Relay/Indstl Control

(G-6033)
SOUTHWORTH INTL GROUP INC (PA)
11 Gray Rd (04105-2027)
P.O. Box 1380, Portland (04104-1380)
PHONE..................................207 878-0700
Lewis Cabot, *CEO*
Brian E Mc Namara, *President*
Misty Martin, *Buyer*
Ian Macleod, *Engineer*
Michael Nordman, *CFO*
◆ **EMP:** 65
SQ FT: 15,000
SALES (est): 81.4MM **Privately Held**
SIC: 3537 3625 3554 2822 Mfg Indstl Truck/Tractor Mfg Relay/Indstl Control Mfg Paper Indstl Mach Mfg Synthetic Rubber

(G-6034)
SOUTHWORTH PRODUCTS CORP (HQ)
11 Gray Rd (04105-2027)
P.O. Box 1380, Portland (04104-1380)
PHONE..................................207 878-0700
Brian E McNamara, *President*
Katherine Jensen, *Vice Pres*
John Harguess, *Plant Mgr*
Kerry Pugh, *Plant Mgr*
Allison Shea, *Safety Mgr*
▲ **EMP:** 40
SQ FT: 15,000
SALES: 40MM
SALES (corp-wide): 81.4MM **Privately Held**
SIC: 3537 5084 Mfg Industrial Trucks/Tractors Whol Industrial Equipment
PA: Southworth International Group, Inc.
11 Gray Rd
Falmouth ME 04105
207 878-0700

(G-6035)
TOZIER GROUP INC
Also Called: Tozier Group, The
185 Mountain Rd (04105-2573)
PHONE..................................207 838-7939
Ronald R Tozier, *President*
Leonard Nelson, *Clerk*
EMP: 21
SALES (est): 2.8MM **Privately Held**
WEB: www.toziergroup.com
SIC: 2541 1521 Mfg Wood Partitions/Fixtures Single-Family House Construction

(G-6036)
UPSTAIRS
Also Called: Cape Courier
251 Us Route 1 Ste 11 (04105-1322)
P.O. Box 6242, Cape Elizabeth (04107-0042)
PHONE..................................207 799-2217
Elizabeth Brogan, *Principal*
EMP: 8
SALES (est): 251.5K **Privately Held**
WEB: www.capecourier.com
SIC: 2711 Newspapers-Publishing/Printing

(G-6037)
WB ENGINEERING INC (HQ)
Also Called: Presto Lifts
11 Gray Rd (04105-2027)
PHONE..................................207 878-0700
Brian McNamara, *President*
EMP: 50
SALES (est): 22.7MM
SALES (corp-wide): 81.4MM **Privately Held**
WEB: www.lifttable.com
SIC: 3537 Mfg Industrial Trucks/Tractors
PA: Southworth International Group, Inc.
11 Gray Rd
Falmouth ME 04105
207 878-0700

Farmingdale
Kennebec County

(G-6038)
COMMUNITY ADVERTISER
20 Peter Path (04344-2930)
PHONE..................................207 582-8486
Keith Peters, *President*
EMP: 4
SALES (est): 251K **Privately Held**
WEB: www.comadvertiser.com
SIC: 2711 Newspapers-Publishing/Printing

(G-6039)
KENOCO INC
347 Maine Ave (04344-2900)
P.O. Box 99, Oakland (04963-0099)
PHONE..................................207 620-7260
Donn Gifford, *President*
EMP: 5
SALES (est): 662.6K **Privately Held**
SIC: 2911 Petroleum Refiner

Farmington
Franklin County

(G-6040)
ALICE JAMES POETRY COOP INC
Also Called: ALICE JAMES BOOKS
114 Prescott St (04938-6801)
PHONE..................................207 778-7071
Rachel Eliza Griffiths, *Treasurer*
Carey Salerno, *Exec Dir*
April Ossmann, *Director*
EMP: 4
SALES: 236.1K **Privately Held**
WEB: www.alicejamesbooks.org
SIC: 2731 Books-Publishing/Printing

(G-6041)
BLACK BEAR GRAPHICS INC
805 Farmington Falls Rd # 8 (04938-6454)
PHONE..................................207 778-9715
Amy Morin, *Treasurer*
EMP: 4
SALES (est): 310K **Privately Held**
SIC: 2759 Screen Printing & Embroidery

(G-6042)
CORN SNOW LLC
161 Maple Ave (04938-6704)
PHONE..................................603 684-2427
John Cook, *Mng Member*
Bill Dodge, *Mng Member*
Mike McChesney, *Mng Member*
EMP: 5
SALES (est): 145.4K **Privately Held**
SIC: 3949 Mfg Sporting/Athletic Goods

(G-6043)
DONALD MCINTIRE
Also Called: Heritage Printing Co
300 Porter Hill Rd (04938-5026)
P.O. Box 792 (04938-0792)
PHONE..................................207 778-3581
Donald McIntire, *Owner*
Tyla McIntire, *Co-Owner*
EMP: 4
SQ FT: 3,500
SALES: 500K **Privately Held**
SIC: 2752 Lithographic Commercial Printing

(G-6044)
DRAMATIC DFFRENCE PUBLICATIONS
139 Adams Cir (04938-5501)
PHONE..................................207 778-9696
Brian Rebert, *Principal*
EMP: 3 **EST:** 2008
SALES (est): 167.2K **Privately Held**
SIC: 2741 Misc Publishing

(G-6045)
DYEABLES INC
374 High St (04938-6748)
PHONE..................................207 778-9871
EMP: 3
SALES (est): 121.7K **Privately Held**
SIC: 3021 Mfg Rubber/Plastic Footwear

(G-6046)
FARMINGTON CHIPPING ENTERPRISE
Town Farm Rd (04938)
P.O. Box 488, Jackman (04945-0488)
PHONE..................................207 778-4888
Ecland Carrier, *President*
Richard Carrier, *Vice Pres*
EMP: 9
SALES (est): 1.1MM **Privately Held**
SIC: 2411 Logging

(G-6047)
FARMINGTON COCA COLA BTLG DSTR
Also Called: Coca-Cola
282 Farmington Falls Rd (04938-6434)
PHONE..................................207 778-4733
Allen Trask, *President*
Jim Sweet, *Vice Pres*
Sherry Walker, *Treasurer*
Jill Gray, *Corp Comm Staff*
Penny Camfferman,
EMP: 21 **EST:** 1922
SQ FT: 6,000
SALES (est): 2.5MM **Privately Held**
SIC: 2086 Carb Sft Drnkbtlcn

(G-6048)
FRANKLIN GROUP
Also Called: Franklin Journal, The
187 Wilton Rd (04938-6120)
P.O. Box 750 (04938-0750)
PHONE..................................207 778-2075
Barbara Zelasko, *Principal*
Sandi Grondin,
EMP: 20
SALES (est): 1.3MM **Privately Held**
SIC: 2711 Newspapers-Publishing/Printing

(G-6049)
HALEY CONSTRUCTION INC
116 Pierpole Rd (04938-5517)
PHONE..................................207 778-9990
Jan Carter, *Branch Mgr*
EMP: 7
SALES (corp-wide): 3.6MM **Privately Held**
WEB: www.haleyconstructioninc.com
SIC: 3273 Mfg Ready-Mixed Concrete
PA: Haley Construction, Inc.
165 Main Rd
Sangerville ME 04479
207 876-4412

(G-6050)
HOLLAND DRUG INC
624 Wilton Rd (04938-6138)
PHONE..................................207 778-5419
Kevin Holland, *Principal*
EMP: 6
SALES (est): 809.3K **Privately Held**
SIC: 2834 Mfg Pharmaceutical Preparations

(G-6051)
KIRKLAND NEWSPAPER INC
Also Called: Livermall Falls Advertiser
187 Wilton Rd (04938-6120)
PHONE..................................207 778-2075
EMP: 15
SALES (est): 650K **Privately Held**
SIC: 2711 Newspaper Publishing Not Printed On Site

(G-6052)
NEMI PUBLISHING INC
Also Called: Franklin's Printing
553 Wilton Rd (04938-6126)
P.O. Box 568 (04938-0568)
PHONE..................................207 778-4801
Gregory Nemi, *President*
Richard Nemi, *Vice Pres*
Patrick Joyce, *Admin Sec*
Travis Melcher, *Technician*
EMP: 49 **EST:** 1948
SQ FT: 28,000
SALES (est): 194.8K **Privately Held**
WEB: www.franklinprinting.com
SIC: 2752 Lithographic Commercial Printing

(G-6053)
SIGNWORKS INC
680 Farmington Falls Rd (04938-6440)
P.O. Box 389 (04938-0389)
PHONE..................................207 778-3822
Michael Monahan, *President*
EMP: 5
SALES (est): 563.2K **Privately Held**
SIC: 3993 Mfg Signs/Advertising Specialties

▲ = Import ▼=Export
◆ =Import/Export

(G-6054)
W A MITCHELL INC
Also Called: W A Mitchell Chair Makers
710 Wilton Rd (04938-6140)
P.O. Box 432 (04938-0432)
PHONE..................................207 778-5212
Dan Maxham, *Owner*
EMP: 7
SQ FT: 4,000
SALES (est): 1.2MM **Privately Held**
WEB: www.wamitchell.com
SIC: 3553 Ret Furniture

Fayette
Kennebec County

(G-6055)
MAINE MARKET REFRIGERATION LLC (PA)
98 Morris Springer Rd (04349-3709)
PHONE..................................207 685-3504
Mike Reeve, *Mng Member*
EMP: 49
SQ FT: 3,200
SALES (est): 9.4MM **Privately Held**
SIC: 3585 Mfg Refrigeration/Heating Equipment

Fort Fairfield
Aroostook County

(G-6056)
LUCERNE FARMS
40 Easton Line Rd (04742)
P.O. Box 510 (04742-0510)
PHONE..................................207 488-2520
George James, *President*
Allen White, *Principal*
Hannah Eaton, *Sales Staff*
H Allen White, *Shareholder*
EMP: 20
SQ FT: 500
SALES (est): 3.5MM **Privately Held**
WEB: www.lucernefarms.com
SIC: 2048 2499 Mfg Horse Feed & Mulch

(G-6057)
WESTERN POLYMER CORPORATION
145 Presque Isle St (04742-1074)
PHONE..................................207 472-1250
Richard Pfeffer, *Branch Mgr*
EMP: 33
SALES (corp-wide): 5.8B **Publicly Held**
SIC: 2046 Wet Corn Milling
HQ: Western Polymer Llc
32 Road R Se
Moses Lake WA 98837
509 765-1803

Fort Kent
Aroostook County

(G-6058)
BOUCHARD FAMILY FARM PRODUCTS
3 Strip Rd (04743-1550)
PHONE..................................207 834-3237
Joseph Bouchard, *President*
Aldan Bouchard, *Treasurer*
Elaine Mininger, *Manager*
Jane Crawford, *Director*
EMP: 5
SALES: 125K **Privately Held**
SIC: 2045 Mfg Prepared Flour Mixes/Doughs

(G-6059)
FIDDLEHEAD FOCUS
90 E Main St 1 (04743-1436)
PHONE..................................207 316-2243
Andrew Birden, *Principal*
EMP: 5
SALES (est): 284.9K **Privately Held**
SIC: 2711 Newspapers-Publishing/Printing

(G-6060)
GUIMOND LOGGING
Also Called: Diamond Trucking
760 Aroostook Rd (04743-2113)
PHONE..................................207 834-6329
Larry Guimond, *Owner*
Debby Guimond, *Co-Owner*
EMP: 3
SALES: 100K **Privately Held**
SIC: 2411 Logging

(G-6061)
J VOISINE & SON LOGGING INC
771 Aroostook Rd (04743-2106)
PHONE..................................207 436-0932
Justin Voisine, *Principal*
EMP: 5
SALES (est): 420.8K **Privately Held**
SIC: 2411 Logging

(G-6062)
MJB LOGGING INC
1139 St John Rd (04743-2248)
PHONE..................................207 231-1376
Heather Berube, *Principal*
EMP: 3
SALES (est): 201.1K **Privately Held**
SIC: 2411 Logging

(G-6063)
MORIN BROTHERS
41 Charette Hill Rd (04743-1438)
P.O. Box 68, Fort Kent Mills (04744-0068)
PHONE..................................207 834-5361
Robbie Morin, *Partner*
EMP: 8
SALES (est): 1.1MM **Privately Held**
SIC: 2951 Asphalt Paving

(G-6064)
MORRIS LOGGING
158 Volette Settlement Rd (04743-2225)
PHONE..................................207 834-6210
Sherbey Morris, *Owner*
EMP: 6
SALES (est): 498.5K **Privately Held**
SIC: 2411 Logging

(G-6065)
NADEAU LOGGING INC
48 Summer Ave (04743-1619)
P.O. Box 106 (04743-0106)
PHONE..................................207 834-6338
Paul J Nadeau Jr, *President*
EMP: 15
SALES (est): 1.4MM **Privately Held**
SIC: 2411 Logging

(G-6066)
PELLETIER & PELLETIER
14 E Main St (04743-1305)
PHONE..................................207 834-2296
James Pelletier, *President*
Keith Pelletier, *Vice Pres*
Steven Pelletier, *Treasurer*
Rina Pelletier, *Clerk*
EMP: 35
SALES: 3MM **Privately Held**
SIC: 2411 Logging Contractor

(G-6067)
ROLAND LEVESQUE
185 Volette Settlement Rd (04743-2217)
PHONE..................................207 834-6244
Roland Levesque, *Principal*
EMP: 6
SALES (est): 510.8K **Privately Held**
SIC: 2411 Logging

(G-6068)
UP NORTH CORP INC
185 Pleasant St (04743-1502)
P.O. Box 200, Fort Kent Mills (04744-0200)
PHONE..................................207 834-6178
Leroy R Martin, *President*
Mary L Martin, *Treasurer*
EMP: 25
SQ FT: 2,925
SALES (est): 3MM **Privately Held**
SIC: 2411 0722 Logging Crop Harvesting Services

Franklin
Hancock County

(G-6069)
SEA & REEF AQUACULTURE LLC
33 Salmon Farm Rd (04634-3144)
PHONE..................................207 422-2422
Soren Hansen, *CEO*
EMP: 7
SALES (est): 733.9K **Privately Held**
SIC: 2092 0273 Mfg Fresh/Frozen Packaged Fish Fish/Shellfish Farm

Freedom
Waldo County

(G-6070)
CHASES DAILY LLC
623 N Palermo Rd (04941-3518)
PHONE..................................207 930-0464
EMP: 3
SALES (est): 113K **Privately Held**
SIC: 2711 Newspapers-Publishing/Printing

Freeport
Cumberland County

(G-6071)
AEC ENGINEERING
172 Lower Main St (04032-1001)
PHONE..................................207 865-4190
David A Audesse, *President*
Robert Renton, *COO*
Roberta J Audesse, *Treasurer*
David Kew, *Marketing Mgr*
John Kraus, *Program Mgr*
EMP: 10
SQ FT: 4,800
SALES (est): 1.5MM **Privately Held**
WEB: www.aecmaine.com
SIC: 3823 Engineering Services

(G-6072)
BETTY REEZ WHOOPIEZ
67 Carter Rd (04032-6889)
PHONE..................................207 865-1735
Betty Ree Zolla, *Principal*
EMP: 8
SALES (est): 605.3K **Privately Held**
SIC: 2051 Mfg Bread/Related Products

(G-6073)
CASCO BAY FIBERS
15 Main St (04032-1100)
PHONE..................................207 869-5429
Karen Minott, *Principal*
EMP: 4
SALES (est): 259.7K **Privately Held**
SIC: 2823 2824 Mfg Cellulosic Manmade Fibers Mfg Organic Fiber-Noncellulosic

(G-6074)
CHILTON PAINT CO INC ME
Also Called: Chilton Furniture and Paint
184 Lower Main St (04032-1008)
PHONE..................................207 865-4443
Todd Davis, *Manager*
EMP: 8
SALES (corp-wide): 4.3MM **Privately Held**
SIC: 2851 5198 5712 Mfg Paints/Allied Products Whol Paints/Varnishes Ret Furniture
PA: Chilton Paint Co Inc Me
410 Payne Rd
Scarborough ME 04074
207 883-3366

(G-6075)
CORNINGWARE CORELLE & MORE
1 Freeport Village Sta (04032-1563)
PHONE..................................207 865-3942
EMP: 3
SALES (est): 202.2K **Privately Held**
SIC: 3643 Mfg Conductive Wiring Devices

(G-6076)
DOWNEAST WOODWORKS
9 Lavers Pond Rd (04032-6211)
PHONE..................................207 781-4800
Sean Dunfey, *Principal*
EMP: 6
SALES (est): 800.6K **Privately Held**
SIC: 2431 Mfg Millwork

(G-6077)
ELTEC INDUSTRIES INC (PA)
171 Wardtown Rd (04032-6847)
P.O. Box 2586, South Portland (04116-2586)
PHONE..................................207 541-9085
Michael Letarte, *President*
Lars Larsen, *Vice Pres*
Dana Moore, *Vice Pres*
EMP: 6
SQ FT: 2,600
SALES (est): 584.4K **Privately Held**
SIC: 3599 3559 3569 3535 Mfg Industrial Machinery Mfg Misc Industry Mach Mfg General Indstl Mach Mfg Conveyors/Equipment

(G-6078)
FLAVOR UNLIMITED INC
Also Called: Flavor & The Menu
5 Brook Hill Rd (04032-6265)
PHONE..................................207 865-4432
Cathy N Holley, *President*
Cathy Holley, *Chief*
Lex Holley, *Business Mgr*
Julie Tobias, *Manager*
EMP: 5 **EST:** 2006
SALES: 800K **Privately Held**
SIC: 2721 Magazines Publishing Only

(G-6079)
FREEPORT MANUFACTURING COMPANY
89 Wardtown Rd (04032-6845)
P.O. Box 236 (04032-0236)
PHONE..................................207 865-9340
EMP: 3
SQ FT: 2,100
SALES (est): 397.6K **Privately Held**
SIC: 3599 Machine Shop

(G-6080)
HINDSIGHT IMAGING INC
23 Staples Point Rd (04032)
PHONE..................................607 793-3762
Arsen Hajian, *CEO*
EMP: 4
SALES (est): 240K **Privately Held**
SIC: 3826 Mfg Analytical Instruments

(G-6081)
L L BEAN INC
5 Campus Dr Desert (04033-0001)
PHONE..................................207 552-2000
EMP: 700
SALES (corp-wide): 893MM **Privately Held**
WEB: www.llbean.com
SIC: 2621 Paper Mill
PA: L. L. Bean, Inc.
15 Casco St
Freeport ME 04033
207 552-2000

(G-6082)
MAINE BEER COMPANY LLC
525 Us Route 1 (04032-7009)
PHONE..................................207 221-5711
Peter Walker, *Principal*
Cole Corbin, *Opers Staff*
Eben Joslyn, *Opers Staff*
EMP: 15
SALES (est): 2.7MM **Privately Held**
SIC: 2082 Mfg Malt Beverages

(G-6083)
MAINE DISTILLERIES LLC
437 Us Route 1 (04032-7008)
PHONE..................................207 865-4828
Christopher Dowe,
Bob Harkins,
Don Thibodeau,
Lee Thibodeau,
EMP: 4
SQ FT: 4,000

GEOGRAPHIC

SALES (est): 410K **Privately Held**
WEB: www.coldrivervodka.com
SIC: 2085 Mfg Distilled/Blended Liquor

(G-6084)
MOMS ORGANIC MUNCHIES
174 Lower Main St Ste 21 (04032-1001)
PHONE..................................207 869-4078
Betty Crush, *Owner*
EMP: 7
SALES: 650K **Privately Held**
SIC: 2052 Mfg Cookies/Crackers

(G-6085)
R F CONSULTING LLC (PA)
192 Lower Flying Point Rd (04032-6385)
PHONE..................................207 233-8846
Robert R Fuller,
Rob Fuller,
▲ **EMP:** 4
SALES (est): 497.5K **Privately Held**
WEB: www.smile.ch
SIC: 2655 8748 Mfg Fiber Cans/Drums Business Consulting Services

(G-6086)
SEA BAGS INC
6 Bow St (04032-1515)
PHONE..................................207 939-3679
Sokunthy Yean, *Branch Mgr*
EMP: 6
SALES (corp-wide): 1.7MM **Privately Held**
SIC: 3161 5948 Mfg Luggage Ret Luggage/Leather Goods
PA: Sea Bags, Llc
25 Custom House Wharf
Portland ME 04101
207 780-0744

(G-6087)
THOS MOSER CABINETMAKERS INC
Also Called: Moser Thos Cabinetmakers
149 Main St (04032-1353)
PHONE..................................207 865-4519
Scott McCurdy, *Senior Engr*
Thomas Moser, *Branch Mgr*
EMP: 5
SALES (corp-wide): 19.4MM **Privately Held**
SIC: 2511 Mfg Household Furniture
PA: Thos. Moser Cabinetmakers, Inc.
72 Wrights Lndg
Auburn ME 04210
207 753-9834

(G-6088)
VINTAGE MAINE KITCHEN LLC
491 Us Route 1 Ste 10 (04032-7022)
PHONE..................................207 317-2536
Kelly Brodeur, *Mng Member*
EMP: 4 **EST:** 2018
SALES (est): 275K **Privately Held**
SIC: 2096 Mfg Potato Chips/Snacks

(G-6089)
WAYSIDE PUBLISHING
262 Us Route 1 Ste 2 (04032-7015)
PHONE..................................888 302-2519
Greg Greuel, *President*
EMP: 11
SQ FT: 5,000
SALES (est): 1MM **Privately Held**
SIC: 2731 Books-Publishing

Frenchville
Aroostook County

(G-6090)
AUTOTRONICS LLC (PA)
129 Us Route 1 (04745-6106)
P.O. Box 535, Madawaska (04756-0535)
PHONE..................................207 543-6262
Paul Daigle, *Principal*
EMP: 8 **EST:** 2011
SALES (est): 1.3MM **Privately Held**
SIC: 3711 Mfg Motor Vehicle/Car Bodies

(G-6091)
MK LOGGING
38 Cleveland Ave (04745-6032)
P.O. Box 192 (04745-0192)
PHONE..................................207 436-1809
EMP: 3 **EST:** 2016
SALES (est): 98.8K **Privately Held**
SIC: 2411 Logging

Friendship
Knox County

(G-6092)
BARTLETTS BENCH AND WIRE INC (PA)
574 Cushing Rd (04547-4146)
P.O. Box 274, Howland (04448-0274)
PHONE..................................207 354-0138
John Pike Bartlett Jr, *President*
Elizabeth Ann Bartlette, *Vice Pres*
EMP: 3
SQ FT: 12,000
SALES (est): 511.4K **Privately Held**
WEB: www.bbwire.com
SIC: 3496 Mfg Misc Fabricated Wire Products

(G-6093)
FTC INC (PA)
570 Cushing Rd (04547-4146)
PHONE..................................207 354-2545
Chris Anderson, *President*
J Pike Bartlett Jr, *President*
▲ **EMP:** 40
SQ FT: 16,000
SALES (est): 4.1MM **Privately Held**
WEB: www.friendshiptrap.com
SIC: 3496 5051 Mfg Misc Fabricated Wire Products Metals Service Center

(G-6094)
WESLEY LASH
Also Called: Lash Boat Yard
31 Harbor Rd (04547-4450)
P.O. Box 177 (04547-0177)
PHONE..................................207 832-7807
Wesley Lash, *Owner*
EMP: 6 **EST:** 1948
SQ FT: 2,400
SALES: 600K **Privately Held**
SIC: 3732 Boatbuilding/Repairing

Fryeburg
Oxford County

(G-6095)
BEAR PAW LUMBER CORP (PA)
103 Main St (04037-1154)
P.O. Box 522 (04037-0522)
PHONE..................................207 935-3052
Dennis Keaten, *President*
Gregory Kellough, *Vice Pres*
Lisa Lovejoy, *Treasurer*
EMP: 10
SQ FT: 3,600
SALES (est): 2.6MM **Privately Held**
SIC: 2426 5031 2435 Hdwd Dimension/Flr Mill Whol Lumber/Plywd/Millwk Mfg Hrdwd Veneer/Plywood

(G-6096)
COLD RIVER STITCHING LLC
89 Lovell Rd (04037-4600)
P.O. Box 426 (04037-0426)
PHONE..................................207 515-0039
Janice Purslow, *President*
EMP: 3
SALES (est): 124.6K **Privately Held**
SIC: 2381 Mfg Fabric Gloves

(G-6097)
DEARBORN BORTEC INC
12 Budrich Dr (04037-1287)
P.O. Box 310 (04037-0310)
PHONE..................................207 935-2502
Deborah Kelly, *President*
Agnes Irving, *Principal*
Joseph Keaney, *Treasurer*
EMP: 12 **EST:** 2010
SALES (est): 1.2MM **Privately Held**
SIC: 3599 Mfg Industrial Machinery

(G-6098)
HARMAC REBAR & STEEL CORP
103 Corn Shop Rd (04037-4302)
P.O. Box 142 (04037-0142)
PHONE..................................207 935-3531
Gary Mac Farlane, *President*
Patrick Maillett, *Exec VP*
Robert W Parsons, *Treasurer*
Cathy Sampson, *Credit Mgr*
Julie Davis, *Executive*
EMP: 50 **EST:** 2002
SALES (est): 11.3MM **Publicly Held**
SIC: 3441 Structural Metal Fabrication
HQ: Hds Ip Holding, Llc
3100 Cumberland Blvd Se
Atlanta GA 30339

(G-6099)
HUNTING DEARBORN INC
6 Dearborn Dr (04037-1609)
PHONE..................................207 935-2171
Bill Findeisen, *President*
Matt Fortin, *Opers Mgr*
Kendra Kincaid, *Safety Mgr*
Robert F Newton, *CFO*
Robert Newton, *CFO*
▲ **EMP:** 150
SQ FT: 212,000
SALES (est): 62.9MM
SALES (corp-wide): 911.4MM **Privately Held**
WEB: www.dearbornprecision.com
SIC: 3599 1382 3812 Mfg Industrial Machinery Oil/Gas Exploration Services Mfg Search/Navigation Equipment
PA: Hunting Plc
5 Hanover Square
London W1S 1
207 321-0123

(G-6100)
MAINE PURE
37 W View Dr (04037-1516)
P.O. Box 603 (04037-0603)
PHONE..................................207 256-8111
Richard H Eastman, *Principal*
EMP: 3
SALES (est): 171.2K **Privately Held**
SIC: 2086 Mfg Bottled/Canned Soft Drinks

(G-6101)
PHYSICIAN ENGINEERED PRODUCTS
Also Called: P E P
103 Smith St (04037-1182)
PHONE..................................207 935-1256
Robert Rose, *President*
Sam Lennon-Rose, *Prdtn Mgr*
Tony Martineau, *VP Sales*
▲ **EMP:** 8
SQ FT: 15,000
SALES (est): 1.2MM **Privately Held**
WEB: www.peponline.com
SIC: 3841 3845 Mfg Surgical/Medical Instruments Mfg Electromedical Equipment

(G-6102)
R H WALES & SON INC
376 Mcneil Rd (04037-4711)
P.O. Box 116, Lovell (04051-0116)
PHONE..................................207 925-1363
R H Wales, *CEO*
Randolph H Wales, *President*
EMP: 4 **EST:** 1955
SALES (est): 634.2K **Privately Held**
SIC: 2421 2411 Sawmill/Planing Mill Logging

(G-6103)
WESTERN MAINE TIMBERLANDS
278 Mcneil Rd (04037-4709)
PHONE..................................207 925-1138
Marc Graney, *President*
Jennifer Graney, *Corp Secy*
EMP: 10 **EST:** 2001
SALES (est): 1.2MM **Privately Held**
SIC: 2411 Logging

Gardiner
Kennebec County

(G-6104)
ANTHONY AUTOMOTIVE
810 Brunswick Ave (04345-6219)
P.O. Box 223 (04345-0223)
PHONE..................................207 582-7105
Jason McMaster, *Owner*
EMP: 3
SALES (est): 192.2K **Privately Held**
SIC: 3423 Mfg Hand/Edge Tools

(G-6105)
SEBAGO LAKE DISTILLERY LLC
463 Water St (04345)
PHONE..................................207 557-0557
David Tomer, *President*
Dan Davis, *Vice Pres*
Brock Tredway, *Vice Pres*
Allen Tait, *Treasurer*
EMP: 4 **EST:** 2014
SALES (est): 140.5K **Privately Held**
SIC: 2085 Distilled And Blended Liquors

Georgetown
Sagadahoc County

(G-6106)
GEORGETOWN POTTERY
755 Five Islands Rd (04548-3304)
P.O. Box 151 (04548-0151)
PHONE..................................207 371-2801
Jeffrey Peters, *Owner*
▲ **EMP:** 9
SQ FT: 4,500
SALES (est): 683.4K **Privately Held**
SIC: 3269 5719 Mfg Pottery Products Ret Misc Homefurnishings

(G-6107)
WOODEX BEARING COMPANY INC
216 Bay Point Rd (04548-3509)
PHONE..................................207 371-2210
Glenn R Irish, *President*
Stephen Williams, *Treasurer*
EMP: 28
SQ FT: 28,390
SALES (est): 5.5MM **Privately Held**
WEB: www.woodex-meco.com
SIC: 3053 3568 2499 Mfg Gaskets/Packing/Sealing Devices Mfg Power Transmission Equipment Mfg Wood Products

Glenburn
Penobscot County

(G-6108)
TODDS ORIGINALS LLC
Also Called: Todd's Salsa
51 Aa Landing Rd (04401-1235)
P.O. Box 1674, Bangor (04402-1674)
PHONE..................................844 328-7257
Erik Zola,
John Simcox,
Todd Simcox,
EMP: 6
SALES: 136K **Privately Held**
SIC: 2033 Management Consulting Services

Gorham
Cumberland County

(G-6109)
B & T MILLWORKS
Also Called: New England Trads Cstm Mllwrks
62 Sanford Dr (04038-2646)
PHONE..................................207 591-5740
William Benson, *CEO*
Tara Benson, *Shareholder*
▲ **EMP:** 6

▲ = Import ▼=Export
◆ =Import/Export

SALES (est): 600K Privately Held
SIC: 3446 Mfg Custom Treads Molding And Hardwood Floors

(G-6110)
BELOIT PTRY JRNL FUNDATION INC
271 N Gorham Rd (04038-2449)
PHONE 207 522-1303
Elizabeth Gray, President
Melissa Crowe, Principal
Rachel Flynn, Principal
Lee Sharkey, Principal
Jessica Jacobs, Senior Editor
EMP: 4
SALES (est): 218.3K Privately Held
SIC: 2721 Periodicals-Publishing/Printing

(G-6111)
EMERSON APPARATUS COMPANY
59 Sanford Dr Unit 12 (04038-2667)
PHONE 207 856-0055
Kimberly Miller, President
Jack Miller, Vice Pres
EMP: 15
SQ FT: 7,500
SALES (est): 660.7K Privately Held
SIC: 3821 Mfg Industrial Machinery

(G-6112)
GORHAM GROWL
2 Main St (04038-1302)
PHONE 207 839-4795
EMP: 4
SALES (est): 210.1K Privately Held
SIC: 2711 Newspapers-Publishing/Printing

(G-6113)
HELICAL SOLUTIONS LLC
29 Sanford Dr (04038-2647)
PHONE 866 543-5422
Laurie Hooker, Vice Pres
▲ EMP: 5
SQ FT: 5,000
SALES (est): 1.5MM
SALES (corp-wide): 2.6MM Privately Held
SIC: 3541 Mfg Machine Tools-Cutting
PA: Harvey Tool Company, Llc
428 Newburyport Tpke
Rowley MA 01969
978 948-8555

(G-6114)
HILL TIM FINE WOODWORKING
11 Little Wing Ln (04038-1884)
PHONE 207 854-1387
Tim Hill, Owner
EMP: 5 EST: 1997
SALES (est): 329.9K Privately Held
SIC: 2431 Mfg Millwork

(G-6115)
IRWIN INDUSTRIAL TOOL COMPANY
37 Bartlett Rd (04038-2642)
PHONE 207 856-6111
David Tweedt, Branch Mgr
EMP: 200
SQ FT: 20,000
SALES (corp-wide): 13.9B Publicly Held
WEB: www.americantool.com
SIC: 3423 3545 Mfg Hand/Edge Tools Mfg Machine Tool Accessories
HQ: Irwin Industrial Tool Company
8935 N Pointe Exec Pk Dr
Huntersville NC 28078
704 987-4555

(G-6116)
JOTUL NORTH AMERICA INC
55 Hutcherson Dr (04038-2644)
PHONE 207 797-5912
Bret Watson, President
Jim Merkel, VP Sales
▲ EMP: 85
SQ FT: 117,000
SALES (est): 20.2MM Privately Held
WEB: www.jotuluk.com
SIC: 3433 Mfg Heating Equipment-Non-electric
HQ: Jotul As
Langoyveien
Krakeroy 1679
693 590-00

(G-6117)
KNOWLTON MACHINE COMPANY
Also Called: Knowlton Machine Engineering
5 Sanford Dr (04038-2647)
P.O. Box 190 (04038-0190)
PHONE 207 854-8471
Normand R Trudel, President
David Miller, Treasurer
EMP: 40 EST: 1864
SQ FT: 25,000
SALES (est): 5.1MM Privately Held
WEB: www.kmaine.com
SIC: 3599 7699 8711 3444 Mfg Industrial Machinery Repair Services Engineering Services Mfg Sheet Metalwork Mfg Fabricated Plate Wrk

(G-6118)
MAINE CONVEYOR INC (PA)
259 New Portland Rd (04038-1867)
PHONE 207 854-5661
Scott Winslow, President
Zilpha Weeman, Corp Secy
Lisa McDermott, Vice Pres
EMP: 3
SALES: 1.9MM Privately Held
SIC: 3535 Mfg Conveyors/Equipment

(G-6119)
MAINE FABRICATORS INC
18 Mitchell Hill Rd (04038-2378)
PHONE 207 839-8555
Raymond Kirkpatrick, President
Dale Kirkpatrick, President
George Burns, Principal
EMP: 3 EST: 1978
SQ FT: 6,000
SALES (est): 505.7K Privately Held
SIC: 3441 3599 Mfg Fabricated Structural Metal & Machine Shop Jobbing & Repair

(G-6120)
MARCA MANUFACTURING LLC
Also Called: Marca Machine Engineering
5 Sanford Dr (04038-2647)
PHONE 207 854-8471
Frederick Veitch, CEO
John Shaw, General Mgr
EMP: 19
SALES (est): 2.5MM Privately Held
SIC: 3999 Mfg Misc Products

(G-6121)
MEDRHYTHMS INC
4 Old Dynamite Way (04038-1575)
PHONE 207 447-2177
Owen McCarthy, President
EMP: 6
SALES (est): 230.9K Privately Held
SIC: 3845 Mfg Electromedical Equipment

(G-6122)
MONTALVO CORPORATION
50 Hutcherson Dr (04038-2645)
PHONE 207 856-2501
Margaret B Montalvo, CEO
Edwin J Montalvo Jr, President
Margaret M Denham, Vice Pres
Chris Osgood, Engineer
Heidi Morrill, Asst Controller
▲ EMP: 32 EST: 1947
SQ FT: 25,000
SALES (est): 6.9MM Privately Held
WEB: www.montalvo.com
SIC: 3599 3568 3625 3823 Mfg Industrial Machinery Mfg Power Transmsn Equip Mfg Relay/Indstl Control

(G-6123)
ODAT MACHINE INC
20 Sanford Dr (04038-2646)
PHONE 207 854-2455
Richard C Pratt, President
Roxana E Pratt, Vice Pres
Roxana Pratt, VP Accounting
EMP: 40
SQ FT: 10,000
SALES (est): 7MM Privately Held
WEB: www.odatmachine.com
SIC: 3599 Mfg Industrial Machinery

(G-6124)
PHINNEY LUMBER CO
519 Fort Hill Rd (04038-2270)
PHONE 207 839-3336
Michael J Phinney, President
EMP: 31 EST: 1928
SQ FT: 5,000
SALES (est): 4.4MM Privately Held
SIC: 2421 5211 Sawmill/Planing Mill Ret Lumber/Building Materials

(G-6125)
PLAS-TECH INC
22 Bartlett Rd (04038-2600)
PHONE 207 854-8324
Terry A Webber Jr, President
EMP: 5
SQ FT: 5,000
SALES (est): 990.9K Privately Held
SIC: 3089 Mfg Plastic Products

(G-6126)
POOL ENVIRONMENTS INC
10 Elm St (04038-1506)
PHONE 207 839-8225
William Chase, President
EMP: 15
SALES (est): 2.1MM Privately Held
SIC: 3585 Mfg Pool Dehumidifiers

(G-6127)
PORT CITY GRAPHICS INC
664a Main St (04038-2621)
P.O. Box 586, Westbrook (04098-0586)
PHONE 207 450-6299
Paul Gore, President
Joseph Mazzone, Treasurer
EMP: 5
SALES: 500K Privately Held
WEB: www.portcitygraphics.com
SIC: 2759 Commercial Printing

(G-6128)
PRIME ELECTRIC MOTORS
72 Sanford Dr (04038-2646)
PHONE 207 591-7800
Daniel Furrow, President
EMP: 10
SALES (est): 2.8MM Privately Held
WEB: www.primeelectricmotor.com
SIC: 7694 Armature Rewinding

(G-6129)
SEBAGO BREWING CO (PA)
616 Main St (04038-2620)
P.O. Box 1054, Scarborough (04070-1054)
PHONE 207 856-2537
Brad Monarch, President
Kai Adams, Vice Pres
Tim Haines, Treasurer
Brandon Libby, Manager
Mike McElroy, Manager
EMP: 50
SQ FT: 7,700
SALES (est): 16.2MM Privately Held
WEB: www.sebagobrewing.com
SIC: 2082 Mfg Malt Beverages

(G-6130)
SEBAGO BREWING CO
616 Main St (04038-2620)
PHONE 207 856-2537
EMP: 45
SALES (corp-wide): 16.1MM Privately Held
SIC: 2082 Mfg Malt Beverages
PA: Sebago Brewing Co
150 Philbrook Ave
South Portland ME 04038

(G-6131)
TOWN AND COUNTRY CABINETS INC
420 Fort Hill Rd (04038-2257)
PHONE 207 839-2709
Ronald Smith, President
David Smith, Vice Pres
Grace Smith, Treasurer
EMP: 4
SQ FT: 8,880
SALES (est): 280K Privately Held
SIC: 2511 5712 2434 Mfg Wood Household Furniture Ret Furniture Mfg Wood Kitchen Cabinets

(G-6132)
TOWN OF GORHAM (PA)
75 South St Ste 1 (04038-1737)
PHONE 207 222-1610
Sharon Laflamme, General Mgr
David O Cole, Manager
Benjamin Hartwell, Council Mbr
Ronald Shepard, Council Mbr
Robert Burns, Director
EMP: 50
SQ FT: 3,000
SALES: 64.5MM Privately Held
WEB: www.gorhammeusa.org
SIC: 2741 Misc Publishing

(G-6133)
TOWN OF GORHAM
Also Called: Town Planner
270 Main St (04038-1312)
PHONE 207 839-5555
Debra Fossum, Director
EMP: 3
SALES (corp-wide): 64.5MM Privately Held
WEB: www.gorhammeusa.org
SIC: 2741 Misc Publishing
PA: Town Of Gorham
75 South St Ste 1
Gorham ME 04038
207 222-1610

(G-6134)
TWIN CITY TIMES
10 Valley View Dr (04038-2545)
PHONE 207 795-5017
Peter A Steele, Owner
Laurie Steele, Co-Owner
EMP: 7
SALES (est): 411.5K Privately Held
SIC: 2711 Newspapers-Publishing/Printing

Gouldsboro
Hancock County

(G-6135)
BARTLETT MAINE ESTATE WINERY
Also Called: Bartlett Winery
175 Chicken Mill Pond Rd (04607-3213)
P.O. Box 275 (04607-0275)
PHONE 207 546-2408
Bob Bartlett, President
Kathe Bartlett, Treasurer
EMP: 4
SQ FT: 4,500
SALES (est): 416.1K Privately Held
WEB: www.bartlettmaineestatewinery.com
SIC: 2084 5182 5921 Mfg Whol & Ret Wine

(G-6136)
ELSCOTT MANUFACTURING LLC (PA)
38 Route 1 (04607-3015)
PHONE 207 422-6747
Leah Hurlburt, President
Will Taylor, President
Amber Newenham, Purchasing
Paul Hurlburt, Sales Staff
EMP: 80
SQ FT: 6,000
SALES (est): 15.5MM Privately Held
WEB: www.elscott.com
SIC: 3672 3625 Mfg Printed Circuit Boards Mfg Relays/Industrial Controls

(G-6137)
OFFSHORE FUEL
130 Route 1 (04607-3017)
PHONE 207 963-7068
Jamie R Watson, Principal
EMP: 3
SALES (est): 236.2K Privately Held
SIC: 2869 Mfg Industrial Organic Chemicals

GEOGRAPHIC

Gray
Cumberland County

(G-6138)
DYNAMIC URETHANES INC
42 Yarmouth Rd (04039-9601)
P.O. Box 1025 (04039-1025)
PHONE..................................207 657-3770
EMP: 3
SQ FT: 4,000
SALES (est): 250.7K **Privately Held**
SIC: 3089 Plastics Products, Nec, Nsk

(G-6139)
ENERCON (PA)
Also Called: Enercon Technologies
25 Northbrook Dr (04039-9451)
P.O. Box 665 (04039-0665)
PHONE..................................207 657-7000
Ronald Marcotte, *President*
Walter Hebold, *Vice Pres*
Paul Adams, *Safety Mgr*
Roger Wilcox, *Mfg Spvr*
Debbie Gates, *Mfg Staff*
▲ **EMP:** 106
SQ FT: 32,000
SALES (est): 25.7MM **Privately Held**
WEB: www.enerconmaine.com
SIC: 3672 5063 3699 3545 Mfg Printed Circuit Brds Whol Electrical Equip Mfg Elec Mach/Equip/Supp Mfg Machine Tool Access Engineering Services

(G-6140)
LOVETT & HALL WOODWORKS
77 Egypt Rd (04039-9646)
PHONE..................................207 650-5139
EMP: 4
SALES (est): 126K **Privately Held**
SIC: 2431 Mfg Millwork

(G-6141)
PEMBERTONS FOOD INC
Also Called: Pemberton's Gourmet
32 Lewiston Rd Bldg 1b (04039-7583)
P.O. Box 1405 (04039-1405)
PHONE..................................207 657-6446
David Fillinger, *President*
▼ **EMP:** 8
SQ FT: 3,500
SALES (est): 750K **Privately Held**
WEB: www.pembertonsgourmet.com
SIC: 2033 Mfg Canned Fruits/Vegetables

(G-6142)
STEPHEN E WITHAM
31 Weymouth Rd (04039-9542)
PHONE..................................207 657-3410
Stephen E Witham, *Principal*
EMP: 3
SALES (est): 188.1K **Privately Held**
SIC: 2024 Mfg Ice Cream/Frozen Desert

(G-6143)
VUETEK SCIENTIFIC LLC
Also Called: Spirometrics
22 Shaker Rd (04039-6702)
P.O. Box 680 (04039-0680)
PHONE..................................207 657-6565
Amy Pierce, *Accounting Mgr*
Ronald P Marcotte, *Mng Member*
Walter Hebold,
EMP: 15
SALES (est): 1.4MM **Privately Held**
SIC: 3845 Mfg Electromedical Equipment

(G-6144)
WOODEN THINGS INC
85 Egypt Rd (04039-9646)
PHONE..................................207 712-4654
Danny W Holmquist, *Principal*
EMP: 4
SALES (est): 346.3K **Privately Held**
SIC: 2511 Mfg Wood Household Furniture

Great Pond
Hancock County

(G-6145)
NORTH COUNTRY COMFORTERS
912 Great Pond Rd (04408-3011)
PHONE..................................207 584-2196
EMP: 3
SALES: 5K **Privately Held**
SIC: 2392 Mfg Household Furnishings

Greenbush
Penobscot County

(G-6146)
COREY MADDEN LOGGING INC
6 Madden Ln (04418-3539)
P.O. Box 116 (04418-0116)
PHONE..................................207 827-1632
Corey Madden, *Principal*
EMP: 4
SALES (est): 235.1K **Privately Held**
SIC: 2411 Logging

Greene
Androscoggin County

(G-6147)
BASS CABINETRY AND MLLWK LLC
228 Sawyer Rd (04236-3201)
P.O. Box 446, Sabattus (04280-0446)
PHONE..................................207 754-0087
Rosaire R Anctil,
EMP: 4
SALES (est): 166.3K **Privately Held**
SIC: 2431 Mfg Millwork

(G-6148)
BUBIERS MEATS
Also Called: Bubier Meats
194 Sprague Mills Rd (04236-3218)
PHONE..................................207 946-7761
Clayton F Bubier, *Owner*
EMP: 4 **EST:** 1953
SALES: 140K **Privately Held**
SIC: 2011 Meat Packing Plant

(G-6149)
IN YOUR OWN WORDS LLC
582 Quaker Ridge Rd (04236-3604)
PHONE..................................207 946-5049
Lewis Alessio, *Principal*
EMP: 4
SALES (est): 260K **Privately Held**
SIC: 2771 7389 Mfg Greeting Cards

(G-6150)
MAINE POLY AQUISITION CORP
Also Called: Mpac
933 Route 202 (04236-3466)
PHONE..................................207 946-7000
Kimball H Dunton, *President*
EMP: 31
SQ FT: 64,000
SALES (est): 2.5MM **Privately Held**
SIC: 2759 Commercial Printing

(G-6151)
TECHNICAL SALES & SVC OF NENG
Also Called: Tne
170 N Daggett Hill Rd (04236-4123)
PHONE..................................207 946-5506
William George, *President*
EMP: 10
SQ FT: 12,000
SALES: 1MM **Privately Held**
WEB: www.tneinc.com
SIC: 3599 Machine Shop

Greenfield Twp
Penobscot County

(G-6152)
ALEXANDERS WELDING & MCH INC
Also Called: Alexanders Mech Solutions
79 Alexander Way (04418-7200)
PHONE..................................207 827-3300
James E Alexander Jr, *President*
EMP: 8
SALES (est): 1.1MM **Privately Held**
WEB: www.alexandersmechanicalsolutions.com
SIC: 3599 Welding Repair

Greenville
Piscataquis County

(G-6153)
MOOSEHEAD COUNTRY LOG HOMES
Greenville Industral Park (04441)
P.O. Box 1285 (04441-1285)
PHONE..................................207 695-3730
Randall E Comber, *President*
Lucille Comber, *Vice Pres*
EMP: 24
SALES (est): 2.8MM **Privately Held**
SIC: 2452 Mfg Prefabricated Wood Buildings

Greenville Junction
Piscataquis County

(G-6154)
MOOSEHEAD WOOD COMPONENTS INC
Also Called: Moosehead Cedar Log Homes
441 Pritham Ave (04442)
P.O. Box 1285, Greenville (04441-1285)
PHONE..................................207 695-3730
Randy Comber, *President*
Lucy Comber, *Vice Pres*
EMP: 13
SALES: 2MM **Privately Held**
SIC: 2452 Mfg Prefabricated Wood Buildings

Greenwood
Oxford County

(G-6155)
RICKIE D OSGOOD SR
8 Osgood Ln (04255-3928)
PHONE..................................207 674-3529
Rickie Osgood, *Owner*
EMP: 3 **EST:** 2010
SALES (est): 204.5K **Privately Held**
SIC: 2411 Logging

(G-6156)
SAUNDERS AT LOCKE MILLS LLC
256 Main St (04255)
PHONE..................................207 875-2853
Louise Jonatis, *Mng Member*
EMP: 14
SALES (est): 1.1MM **Privately Held**
SIC: 2493 Mfg Wood Products

Guilford
Piscataquis County

(G-6157)
DUVALTEX (US) INC (DH)
9 Oak St (04443-6367)
P.O. Box 179 (04443-0179)
PHONE..................................207 873-3331
Alain Duval, *CEO*
Douglas Warren, *Opers Staff*
Sue Hicks, *Engineer*
Chris Ayer, *Human Res Mgr*
Joanie Currier, *Manager*
▲ **EMP:** 205
SQ FT: 290,000
SALES (est): 126.9MM
SALES (corp-wide): 300K **Privately Held**
WEB: www.interfacefabricsgroup.com
SIC: 2221 Manmade Broadwoven Fabric Mill
HQ: Duvaltex Inc
2805 90e Rue
Saint-Georges QC G6A 1
418 227-9897

(G-6158)
HARDWOOD PRODUCTS COMPANY LP
Also Called: Puritan Medical Products
31 School St (04443-6388)
P.O. Box 149 (04443-0149)
PHONE..................................207 876-3311
Timothy Templet, *Partner*
Terry Young, *General Mgr*
Lori Armstrong, *Vice Pres*
Heidi Corkery, *Vice Pres*
Elaine Maliff, *Vice Pres*
◆ **EMP:** 382
SQ FT: 482,000
SALES: 48.9MM **Privately Held**
WEB: www.puritanmedproducts.com
SIC: 3842 2499 Mfg Surgical Appliances/Supplies Mfg Wood Products

(G-6159)
PRIDE MANUFACTURING CO LLC
Also Called: Pride Manufacturing Machine Sp
169 Water St (04443-6333)
PHONE..................................207 876-2719
Brad Coburn, *Branch Mgr*
EMP: 10
SALES (corp-wide): 89.2MM **Privately Held**
WEB: www.pridemfg.com
SIC: 2411 2426 Logging Hardwood Dimension/Floor Mill
PA: Pride Manufacturing Company Llc
10 N Main St
Burnham ME 04922
207 487-3322

(G-6160)
PURITAN MEDICAL PDTS CO LLC
31 School St (04443-6388)
P.O. Box 149 (04443-0149)
PHONE..................................207 876-3311
Paul Dube, *QC Dir*
Terry Young, *Mng Member*
EMP: 470
SALES (est): 153.5K **Privately Held**
SIC: 3842 Mfg Surgical Appliances/Supplies

(G-6161)
R A THOMAS LOGGING INC
58 Butter St (04443-6039)
PHONE..................................207 876-2722
Richard Thomas, *President*
Roberta Thomas, *Treasurer*
Phyllis Dyer, *Admin Sec*
EMP: 7
SALES: 1.7MM **Privately Held**
SIC: 2411 1611 Logging Highway/Street Construction

(G-6162)
TRUE GUILFORD INC
9 Oak St (04443-6367)
P.O. Box 179 (04443-0179)
PHONE..................................207 876-3331
Alain Duval, *President*
Denis Chabot, *Treasurer*
Tom Olive, *Manager*
EMP: 3
SALES (est): 778.7K **Privately Held**
SIC: 2299 Mfg Textile Goods

Hallowell
Kennebec County

(G-6163)
MELTON SALES AND SERVICE INC
Also Called: Butler & Macmaster Engines
323 Water St (04347-1341)
PHONE..................................207 623-8895
John F Melton, *President*
EMP: 15 **EST:** 2012
SQ FT: 50,000
SALES (est): 1.6MM **Privately Held**
SIC: **3519** 3599 7538 5084 Mfg Intrnl Cmbstn Engine Mfg Industrial Machinery General Auto Repair Whol Industrial Equip Automotive Services

(G-6164)
QUARRY TAP ROOM LLC
122 Water St (04347-1313)
PHONE..................................207 213-6173
Chris Vallee, *Mng Member*
EMP: 4
SALES (est): 194.6K **Privately Held**
SIC: **2599** Mfg Furniture/Fixtures

Hampden
Penobscot County

(G-6165)
EXTREME DIM WILDLIFE CALLS LLC
208 Kennebec Rd (04444-1318)
P.O. Box 220 (04444-0220)
PHONE..................................207 862-2825
Peter M Brown,
Melvin Brown,
▲ **EMP:** 6
SQ FT: 6,000
SALES (est): 359.2K **Privately Held**
SIC: **3949** Mfg Sporting/Athletic Goods

(G-6166)
PENTA-TECH COATED PRODUCTS LLC (PA)
58 Main Rd N (04444-1307)
P.O. Box 697, Bangor (04402-0697)
PHONE..................................207 862-3105
Nick Collins, *Mng Member*
◆ **EMP:** 17 **EST:** 1998
SALES (est): 6.3MM **Privately Held**
WEB: www.ptcp.net
SIC: **2671** Mfg Packaging Paper/Film

(G-6167)
PEPSI-COLA METRO BTLG CO INC
19 Penobscot Meadow Dr (04444-1933)
PHONE..................................207 973-2217
Bob Bates, *Manager*
EMP: 65
SALES (corp-wide): 64.6B **Publicly Held**
WEB: www.joy-of-cola.com
SIC: **2086** Mfg Bottled/Canned Soft Drinks
HQ: Pepsi-Cola Metropolitan Bottling Company, Inc.
1111 Westchester Ave
White Plains NY 10604
914 767-6000

(G-6168)
PINE TREE GRAVEL INC
436 Meadow Rd (04444-3223)
PHONE..................................207 862-4983
David Lachance, *Principal*
EMP: 6 **EST:** 2008
SALES (est): 493.4K **Privately Held**
SIC: **1442** Construction Sand/Gravel

(G-6169)
WISEMAN & SPAULDING DESIGNS
Also Called: Antiquity Tile
12 Shaw Hill Rd (04444-3402)
PHONE..................................207 862-3513
Brad Wiseman, *President*
Paul Spaulding, *Vice Pres*
EMP: 24
SQ FT: 1,500
SALES (est): 2.2MM **Privately Held**
WEB: www.antiquitytile.com
SIC: **3253** Mfg Ceramic Wall/Floor Tile

Hancock
Hancock County

(G-6170)
MERRILL BLUEBERRY FARMS INC
63 Thorsen Rd (04640-3141)
P.O. Box 149, Ellsworth (04605-0149)
PHONE..................................207 667-2541
Todd Merrill, *President*
Richard O Merrill, *Vice Pres*
EMP: 12 **EST:** 1946
SQ FT: 50,000
SALES (est): 2.3MM **Privately Held**
SIC: **2037** 4222 Blueberry Freezing Cold Storage Plant

(G-6171)
PRL HANCOCK LLC
Also Called: Pleasant River Pine
71 Salems Rd Washington J Washington Jctn (04640)
PHONE..................................207 564-8520
Jason Brochu, *Partner*
EMP: 25
SALES (est): 2MM **Privately Held**
SIC: **2421** Sawmill/Planing Mill

Harmony
Somerset County

(G-6172)
TRACY J MORRISON
Also Called: Morrison's Forest Products
26 Wellington Rd (04942-7600)
PHONE..................................207 683-2371
Tracy J Morrison, *President*
EMP: 8
SALES (est): 795K **Privately Held**
SIC: **2411** 4212 Logging Contractor Local & Log Hauling

Harpswell
Cumberland County

(G-6173)
MAINE SAILING PARTNERS LLC
111 Reach Rd (04079-2245)
PHONE..................................207 865-0850
J Fowler, *Owner*
EMP: 6
SALES (est): 422.1K **Privately Held**
SIC: **2394** Mfg Canvas/Related Products

(G-6174)
PAMS WREATHS
46 Clark Shore Rd (04079-3128)
PHONE..................................207 751-7234
Pam Douglas, *Owner*
Sterling Douglas, *Co-Owner*
EMP: 4 **EST:** 2011
SALES (est): 278.7K **Privately Held**
SIC: **3999** 3229 Mfg Misc Products Mfg Pressed/Blown Glass

(G-6175)
WILD DUCK BOAT WORKS LLC
1444 Harpswell Neck Rd (04079-3221)
PHONE..................................207 837-2920
John Moore, *President*
Mary B Moore, *Principal*
Mary Moore, *Vice Pres*
EMP: 5
SQ FT: 7,000
SALES: 110K **Privately Held**
SIC: **3732** Boatbuilding/Repairing

Harrison
Cumberland County

(G-6176)
ELMS PUZZLES INC
Hobbs Hill Ln (04040)
P.O. Box 537 (04040-0537)
PHONE..................................207 583-6262
Elizabeth Stuart, *President*
Frederick E Stuart Jr, *Vice Pres*
Patricia Peard, *Clerk*
EMP: 10
SALES: 500K **Privately Held**
SIC: **3944** Mfg Jigsaw Puzzles

Hartford
Oxford County

(G-6177)
MAINE MOLD & MACHINE INC
208 Town Farm Rd (04220-5160)
PHONE..................................207 388-2732
David Bullecks, *President*
Colleen Bullecks, *Office Mgr*
EMP: 7
SALES: 750K **Privately Held**
SIC: **3544** 3089 Mfg Dies/Tools/Jigs/Fixtures Mfg Plastic Products

(G-6178)
TERRENCE L HAYFORD
74 Moses Young Rd (04220-5012)
PHONE..................................207 357-0142
Terry Hayford, *Principal*
EMP: 3
SALES (est): 108.7K **Privately Held**
SIC: **2411** Logging

Hartland
Somerset County

(G-6179)
TASMAN INDUSTRIES INC
Also Called: Prime Tanning Compan
9 Main St (04943-3759)
PHONE..................................207 938-4491
EMP: 50
SALES (corp-wide): 75.9MM **Privately Held**
SIC: **3111** 5199 Leather Tanning/Finishing Whol Nondurable Goods
PA: Tasman Industries, Inc.
930 Geiger St
Louisville KY 40206
502 785-7477

Hebron
Oxford County

(G-6180)
JAMES M DUNN
45 Ledge Hill Rd (04238-3544)
PHONE..................................207 212-2963
James Dunn, *Principal*
EMP: 3
SALES (est): 281.6K **Privately Held**
SIC: **2411** Logging

Hermon
Penobscot County

(G-6181)
ALBERT M M JOHNSTON IV
Also Called: Johnston Logging
527 Fuller Rd (04401-0403)
PHONE..................................207 848-2561
Albert M M Johnston IV, *Principal*
EMP: 3
SALES (est): 188.8K **Privately Held**
SIC: **2411** Logging

(G-6182)
AMERICAN NAMEPLATE (PA)
21 White Pine Rd Ste 1 (04401-0267)
PHONE..................................207 848-7187
EMP: 5 **EST:** 2011
SALES (est): 454.8K **Privately Held**
SIC: **3993** Mfg Signs/Advertising Specialties

(G-6183)
ARMSTRONG FAMILY INDS INC
Also Called: Snowman's Printing & Stamps
1 Printers Dr (04401-1333)
PHONE..................................207 848-7300
Edward J Armstrong, *President*
Mark Armstrong, *Vice Pres*
Richard G Armstrong, *Vice Pres*
Mary Armstrong, *Shareholder*
▲ **EMP:** 30
SQ FT: 17,000
SALES (est): 4.8MM **Privately Held**
WEB: www.snowprint.com
SIC: **2752** 3953 2759 Lithographic Commercial Printing Mfg Marking Devices Commercial Printing

(G-6184)
CARON SIGNS CO INC
41 Daves Way (04401-1341)
PHONE..................................207 848-7889
Lisa Caron, *President*
Peter Caron, *Vice Pres*
EMP: 4
SQ FT: 2,000
SALES (est): 419.5K **Privately Held**
WEB: www.caronsigns.com
SIC: **3993** 7389 Mfg Signs/Ad Specialties Business Services

(G-6185)
DYSARTS
Also Called: Cold Brook Energy
530 Coldbrook Rd (04401-1314)
P.O. Box 1689, Bangor (04402-1689)
PHONE..................................207 947-8649
Ed Dysart, *Owner*
EMP: 4
SALES (est): 659.8K **Privately Held**
SIC: **1389** Oil/Gas Field Services

(G-6186)
FAST FORMS PRINTING & PAPER
229 Swan Rd (04401-0344)
PHONE..................................207 941-8383
EMP: 5
SALES (est): 512.1K **Privately Held**
SIC: **2752** Lithographic Commercial Printing

(G-6187)
GARY M POMEROY LOGGING INC
1909 Hammond St (04401-1116)
PHONE..................................207 848-3171
Gary M Pomeroy, *President*
Gayle M Pomeroy, *Vice Pres*
EMP: 16
SALES (est): 2.2MM **Privately Held**
SIC: **2411** Logging

(G-6188)
HERBERT C HAYNES INC
40 Freedom Pkwy (04401-1105)
P.O. Box 41, Bangor (04402-0041)
PHONE..................................207 848-5930
Fax: 207 848-5744
EMP: 3
SALES (corp-wide): 6.2MM **Privately Held**
SIC: **2411** Logging
PA: Herbert C Haynes Inc
40 Route 168
Winn ME 04495
207 736-3412

(G-6189)
HERMON SAND & GRAVEL LLC
23 Timberview Dr (04401-0460)
P.O. Box 6003, Bangor (04402-6003)
PHONE..................................207 848-5977
Maury Thayer, *Mng Member*
Mary Thayer,
EMP: 8

GEOGRAPHIC

SALES (est): 858.3K Privately Held
SIC: 1442 Construction Sand/Gravel

(G-6190)
MGI INC
21 White Pine Rd Ste 7 (04401-0267)
PHONE.....207 817-3280
EMP: 5
SALES (est): 626.6K Privately Held
SIC: 3399 Weapons Manufacture

(G-6191)
NAHEKS INC
15 Elaine Dr (04401-1129)
PHONE.....207 848-7770
Robert Skehan, *Principal*
EMP: 4
SALES (est): 422.2K Privately Held
SIC: 2434 Mfg Wood Kitchen Cabinets

(G-6192)
ORONO SPECTRAL SOLUTIONS INC
25 Freedom Pkwy (04401-1100)
PHONE.....866 269-8007
Carl Tripp, *President*
EMP: 3
SALES (est): 311.2K Privately Held
WEB: www.ossmaine.com
SIC: 1389 Oil/Gas Field Services

Hiram
Oxford County

(G-6193)
ALFRED ST GERMAIN
Also Called: Kezaer Trailbrakers
38 Shotgun Gulch Rd (04041-3549)
PHONE.....207 925-1135
Alfred St Germain, *Owner*
EMP: 30
SALES (est): 1.6MM Privately Held
SIC: 3799 Snow Club

Hodgdon
Aroostook County

(G-6194)
TRUSS WORTHY TRUSS
217 Lincoln Rd (04730-4410)
PHONE.....207 532-3200
Ernest Kauffman, *Mng Member*
EMP: 3
SALES (est): 225.9K Privately Held
SIC: 2439 Mfg Structural Wood Members

(G-6195)
WA LOGGING LLC
634 White Settlement Rd (04730-4434)
PHONE.....207 694-2921
Weldon L Willette, *Owner*
EMP: 6
SALES (est): 629.9K Privately Held
SIC: 2411 Logging

Holden
Penobscot County

(G-6196)
CONNECTIVITY WORKS INC
182 Bagaduce Rd (04429-7246)
PHONE.....207 843-0854
Daniel Smith, *President*
Heather Smith, *Treasurer*
EMP: 6
SALES: 789.3K Privately Held
SIC: 3651 1623 7382 5999 Home Audio/Video Eqp Ret Misc Merchandise Security System Svcs Water/Sewer/Utility Cnst

(G-6197)
FABULA NEBULAE LLC
31 Gilmore Ln (04429-7271)
PHONE.....917 545-9049
EMP: 4
SALES (est): 306.7K Privately Held
SIC: 2844 Mfg Toilet Preparations

Hollis Center
York County

(G-6198)
BEAR HILL LUMBER CO
668 Hollis Rd (04042-3913)
P.O. Box 41 (04042-0041)
PHONE.....207 929-5225
Jeanette Decker, *President*
Fred Decker, *Vice Pres*
EMP: 11
SQ FT: 3,000
SALES: 2.7MM Privately Held
SIC: 2421 Sawmill

(G-6199)
EAGLE INDUSTRIES INC
118 Hollis Rd (04042-4010)
P.O. Box 179 (04042-0179)
PHONE.....207 929-3700
Jon Sjulander, *President*
▼ EMP: 25
SQ FT: 27,000
SALES (est): 5.2MM Privately Held
WEB: www.eagleinds.com
SIC: 3444 Mfg Sheet Metalwork

(G-6200)
MID CAPE RESTORATION
335 Cape Rd (04042-3703)
PHONE.....207 929-4759
Lloyd Bradbury, *President*
Cathy Bradbury, *Treasurer*
EMP: 11
SALES (est): 1.5MM Privately Held
WEB: www.midcaperestoration.com
SIC: 3559 Mfg Misc Industry Machinery

Hope
Knox County

(G-6201)
STATE MAINE CHEESE COMPANY LLC
341 Gillette Rd (04847-3239)
PHONE.....207 236-8895
Cathy Morrill,
Frank Morrill,
EMP: 7
SALES: 350K Privately Held
WEB: www.cheese-me.com
SIC: 2022 Mfg Cheese

Houlton
Aroostook County

(G-6202)
AMERICAN OUTDOOR BRANDS SLS CO
19 Aviation Dr (04730-3308)
PHONE.....207 532-7966
Terry Wade, *Manager*
EMP: 85
SALES (corp-wide): 638.2MM Publicly Held
SIC: 3484 Mfg Small Arms
HQ: American Outdoor Brands Sales Company
2100 Roosevelt Ave
Springfield MA 01104
413 781-8300

(G-6203)
CHAMBERS LEASING
Also Called: Houlton Powers Boards
381 North St (04730-3547)
PHONE.....207 532-4381
Ben Adams, *Manager*
EMP: 4
SALES (corp-wide): 5MM Privately Held
WEB: www.scottsrecreation.com
SIC: 3949 Mfg Sporting/Athletic Goods
PA: Chambers Leasing
746 Western Ave
Manchester ME 04351
207 622-0672

(G-6204)
CHUTE CHEMICAL AGENCY
11 Putnam Ave (04730-1874)
P.O. Box 891 (04730-0891)
PHONE.....207 532-4370
Gary Dwyer, *Owner*
EMP: 6
SALES (est): 719.4K Privately Held
SIC: 2899 Mfg Chemical Preparations

(G-6205)
DARRELL C MCGUIRE & SONS INC
1157 Hodgdon Corner Rd (04730)
PHONE.....207 532-0511
Brent McGuire, *Corp Secy*
Jonathan McGuire, *Vice Pres*
Douglas McGuire, *Shareholder*
EMP: 12
SALES: 2.5MM Privately Held
SIC: 2411 Logging

(G-6206)
HOULTON FARMS DAIRY INC (PA)
Commonwealth Ave (04730)
P.O. Box 429 (04730-0429)
PHONE.....207 532-3170
Alice M Lincoln, *President*
Leonard Lincoln, *Vice Pres*
Eric Lincoln, *Asst Treas*
James Lincoln, *Asst Sec*
EMP: 15
SQ FT: 8,400
SALES (est): 5.8MM Privately Held
SIC: 2026 Mfg Fluid Milk Mfg Fluid Milk

(G-6207)
MCQUADE TIDD INDUSTRIES
Also Called: Steelstone Industries
154 Steelstone St (04730)
P.O. Box 746 (04730-0746)
PHONE.....207 532-2675
Blake McQuade, *President*
EMP: 51
SALES: 950K Privately Held
SIC: 1442 Construction Sand/Gravel

(G-6208)
NORTHEAST PUBLISHING COMPANY
Also Called: Houlton Pioneer Times
23 Court St (04730-1745)
P.O. Box 456 (04730-0456)
PHONE.....207 532-2281
Mark Putman, *Manager*
EMP: 6
SALES (corp-wide): 74MM Privately Held
SIC: 2711 Newspapers-Publishing/Printing
HQ: Northeast Publishing Company Inc
260 Missile St
Presque Isle ME 04769
207 764-4471

(G-6209)
QED OPTICAL INC
2 Washburn St (04730-2212)
PHONE.....207 532-6772
Willard Hamilton, *President*
EMP: 4
SALES (est): 360K Privately Held
SIC: 3827 Mfg Optical Lenses

(G-6210)
SABIAN LTD
91 Airport Dr (04730-3303)
P.O. Box 693 (04730-0693)
PHONE.....506 272-2199
Luis Sabian, *Branch Mgr*
EMP: 9
SALES (corp-wide): 39.1MM Privately Held
SIC: 3399 Mfg Primary Metal Products
PA: Sabian Ltd
219 Main St
Meductic NB E6H 2
506 272-2019

(G-6211)
TATE LYLE INGRDNTS AMRICAS LLC
48 Morningstar Rd (04730-3039)
PHONE.....207 532-9523
Kevin King, *Mfg Staff*
Thomas Strong, *Opers-Prdtn-Mfg*
Lisa Lapointe, *Purch Dir*
EMP: 50
SALES (corp-wide): 3.5B Privately Held
WEB: www.aestaley.com
SIC: 2046 Wet Corn Milling
HQ: Tate & Lyle Ingredients Americas Llc
2200 E Eldorado St
Decatur IL 62521
217 423-4411

(G-6212)
WLHC INC (PA)
Also Called: Ward Cedar Log Homes
37 Bangor St (04730-1739)
P.O. Box 72 (04730-0072)
PHONE.....207 532-6531
Jay McLaughlin, *President*
Dana Delano, *Vice Pres*
Ron Silliboy, *Sales Staff*
EMP: 7 EST: 1923
SQ FT: 3,200
SALES (est): 2.2MM Privately Held
SIC: 2452 1521 Mfg Prefabricated Wood Buildings Single-Family House Construction

Howland
Penobscot County

(G-6213)
A & G DIRTWORKS INC
22 Caron Dr (04448)
P.O. Box 50 (04448-0050)
PHONE.....207 290-5054
Glenn Brawn, *President*
Laurie Brawn, *Treasurer*
EMP: 3
SALES (est): 543.1K Privately Held
SIC: 1442 Construction Sand/Gravel

(G-6214)
TDF INCORPORATED
63 Water St (04448-3704)
PHONE.....207 631-4325
Thane D Ferguson, *President*
EMP: 3
SALES (est): 270K Privately Held
SIC: 2411 Logging

Islesboro
Waldo County

(G-6215)
DARK HARBOR BOATYARD CORP
700 Acre Is (04848)
P.O. Box 25, Lincolnville (04849-0025)
PHONE.....207 734-2246
Ethan Emery, *President*
EMP: 10
SQ FT: 5,000
SALES (est): 1.2MM Privately Held
WEB: www.darkharborboatyard.com
SIC: 3732 4493 5541 5551 Boatbuilding/Repairing Marina Operation Gasoline Service Station Ret Boats

Jackman
Somerset County

(G-6216)
E J CARRIER INC
Rr 201 (04945)
P.O. Box 489 (04945-0489)
PHONE.....207 668-4457
Jacquelin Carrier, *President*
EMP: 65
SQ FT: 10,000
SALES (est): 11MM Privately Held
SIC: 2411 Logging

(G-6217)
JACKMAN LUMBER INC (PA)
Also Called: Jackman Cash Fuel
548 Main St (04945-5222)
P.O. Box 425 (04945-0425)
PHONE.....207 668-4407

Reginald Griffin, *President*
Russell Griffin, *Vice Pres*
Linda Griffin, *Treasurer*
EMP: 30
SQ FT: 500
SALES: 3MM **Privately Held**
SIC: 2411 2421 Logging Sawmill/Planing Mill

Jackson
Waldo County

(G-6218)
BOLINDA PUBLISHING INC
186 S Long Swamp Rd (04921-3154)
PHONE....207 722-3185
Karen J Heysser, *President*
EMP: 4
SALES (est): 247.4K **Privately Held**
WEB: www.bolinda.com
SIC: 2741 Wholesaler Of Audio Books

Jay
Franklin County

(G-6219)
ANTOINE MECHANICAL INC
Also Called: Memco
102 Main St (04239-1660)
P.O. Box 60 (04239-0060)
PHONE....207 897-4100
Antoine St Pierre, *President*
EMP: 3
SQ FT: 13,000
SALES (est): 477.4K **Privately Held**
SIC: 3433 5074 Mfg Heating Equipment-Nonelectric Whol Plumbing Equipment/Supplies

(G-6220)
HOWIES WLDG & FABRICATION INC
1148 Main St (04239-4220)
PHONE....207 645-2581
Mary Howes, *President*
EMP: 9
SQ FT: 9,200
SALES: 1.9MM **Privately Held**
SIC: 7692 3441 Welding Repair Structural Metal Fabrication

(G-6221)
SPECIALTY MINERALS INC
Riley Rd Gate 15 (04239)
P.O. Box 329 (04239-0329)
PHONE....207 897-4492
Robert Door, *Manager*
EMP: 11 **Publicly Held**
WEB: www.specialtyminerals.com
SIC: 2819 Mfg Industrial Inorganic Chemicals
HQ: Specialty Minerals Inc.
622 3rd Ave Fl 38
New York NY 10017
212 878-1800

(G-6222)
VERSO PAPER HOLDING LLC
300 Riley Rd (04239-4840)
P.O. Box 20 (04239-0020)
PHONE....207 897-3431
James Bailey, *Principal*
Anthony Bolanger, *COO*
Connie Pentti, *Purchasing*
Mark Lake, *Engineer*
Rick Schneider, *VP Mktg*
EMP: 800 **Publicly Held**
WEB: www.versopaper.com
SIC: 2671 2672 2621 Mfg Packaging Paper/Film Mfg Coated/Laminated Paper Paper Mill
HQ: Verso Paper Holding Llc
8540 Gander Creek Dr
Miamisburg OH 45342
877 855-7243

(G-6223)
VERSO PAPER HOLDING LLC
21 Riley Rd (04239)
PHONE....207 897-3431
Dick Jackson, *Branch Mgr*
EMP: 976 **Publicly Held**
SIC: 2671 Mfg Packaging Paper/Film
HQ: Verso Paper Holding Llc
8540 Gander Creek Dr
Miamisburg OH 45342
877 855-7243

Jonesboro
Washington County

(G-6224)
DOWNEAST WIRE TRAP COMPANY
141 Evergreen Point Rd (04648-3127)
PHONE....207 434-5791
Donna Alley, *Partner*
Mark Alley, *Partner*
EMP: 5
SALES: 310K **Privately Held**
SIC: 3496 Mfg Misc Fabricated Wire Products

(G-6225)
STORED SOLAR J&WE LLC
Rr Box 1a (04648)
PHONE....207 434-6500
Anthony Orlando, *CEO*
EMP: 25
SALES (corp-wide): 15.2MM **Privately Held**
SIC: 2869 Mfg Industrial Organic Chemicals
PA: Stored Solar J&We, Llc
1231 Main Rd
West Enfield ME 04493
219 712-4764

Jonesport
Washington County

(G-6226)
HUBBARD RAKE CO
1561 Mason Bay Rd (04649-3007)
PHONE....207 497-5949
Harold L Hubbard, *Owner*
Lois Hubbard, *Office Mgr*
EMP: 3
SQ FT: 2,500
SALES: 70K **Privately Held**
WEB: www.hubbardrakes.com
SIC: 3523 Mfg Farm Machinery/Equipment

(G-6227)
LARRY BALCHEN
Also Called: Balchen Tool & Machine
1834 Mason Bay Rd (04649-3038)
PHONE....207 497-5621
Larry Balchen, *Owner*
EMP: 3
SALES (est): 171.9K **Privately Held**
SIC: 3599 3544 Mfg Industrial Machinery Mfg Dies/Tools/Jigs/Fixtures

Kennebunk
York County

(G-6228)
ASHLEIGH INC (PA)
Also Called: Kennebunkport Brewing Company
8 Western Ave Ste 6 (04043-7756)
PHONE....207 967-4311
Fred Frosley, *President*
EMP: 28
SQ FT: 2,000
SALES (est): 11.8MM **Privately Held**
WEB: www.federaljacks.com
SIC: 2082 5813 5812 Mfg Malt Beverages Drinking Place Eating Place

(G-6229)
BEER SAVER USA
16 Sylvan Cir (04043-6917)
PHONE....207 299-2826
Larry Gumb, *CEO*
EMP: 10
SALES (est): 950K **Privately Held**
SIC: 3585 Mfg Refrigeration/Heating Equipment

(G-6230)
CANVASWORKS INC
8 Bragdon Ln (04043-7230)
PHONE....207 985-2419
Stephen R Eberle, *President*
EMP: 7
SQ FT: 3,500
SALES: 525K **Privately Held**
WEB: www.canvasworksinc.com
SIC: 2394 Mfg Canvas/Related Prdts

(G-6231)
CORNING INCORPORATED
2 Alfred Rd (04043-6266)
PHONE....207 985-3111
Ken Walker, *Principal*
Anne Patterson, *Safety Mgr*
Kevin Cavanaugh, *Engineer*
Paul Gagnon, *Engineer*
John Graham, *Engineer*
EMP: 60
SQ FT: 90,000
SALES (corp-wide): 11.2B **Publicly Held**
WEB: www.corning.com
SIC: 3229 Mfg Pressed/Blown Glass
PA: Corning Incorporated
1 Riverfront Plz
Corning NY 14831
607 974-9000

(G-6232)
DIRIGO ANALYTICS LLC
14 Oak Bluff Rd (04043-6847)
PHONE....978 376-5522
Brian Desmarais,
EMP: 3
SALES (est): 224K **Privately Held**
SIC: 3826 Mfg Analytical Instruments

(G-6233)
EXPANDED RUBBER PRODUCTS INC
62 Portland Rd Ste 9 (04043-6650)
P.O. Box 889 (04043-0889)
PHONE....207 985-4141
EMP: 9
SALES (corp-wide): 4.5MM **Privately Held**
SIC: 3069 Mfg Fabricated Rubber Products
PA: Expanded Rubber Products Inc
41 Industrial Ave
Sanford ME 04073
207 324-8226

(G-6234)
G & G PRODUCTS LLC
70 Twine Mill Rd Ste 1 (04043-6359)
PHONE....207 985-9100
Gary Gagnon, *Mng Member*
▲ **EMP:** 27
SQ FT: 23,000
SALES: 1.5MM **Privately Held**
SIC: 3089 2821 Mfg Plastic Products Mfg Plastic Materials/Resins

(G-6235)
HAIR STUDIO AT LAFAYETTE
2 Storer St Ste 105 (04043-6862)
PHONE....207 604-5005
EMP: 4
SALES (est): 183.1K **Privately Held**
SIC: 2299 Mfg Textile Goods

(G-6236)
JAK DESIGNS LLC
2 Sayward St (04043-6829)
PHONE....330 689-6849
Tanya M Alsberg, *Principal*
EMP: 22
SALES (corp-wide): 6.4MM **Privately Held**
SIC: 2678 5699 Mfg Stationery Products Ret Misc Apparel/Accessories
PA: Jak Designs Llc
24 Ocean Ave
Kennebunkport ME 04046
207 204-0396

(G-6237)
JOHN COSTIN STUDIO
Also Called: Veneer Services Unlimited
1 Colonel Gelardi Dr # 104 (04043-7024)
P.O. Box 969, Sanford (04073-0969)
PHONE....207 985-7221
John Costin, *Owner*
EMP: 4
SQ FT: 6,900
SALES: 138K **Privately Held**
SIC: 2541 2431 Mfg Wood Partitions/Fixtures Mfg Millwork

(G-6238)
LIMMER EDUCATION LLC
1 Sayward St (04043-6828)
PHONE....207 482-0622
Stephanie Limmer, *CEO*
Daniel Limmer, *Officer*
EMP: 6
SALES: 162K **Privately Held**
SIC: 7372 7389 Prepackaged Software Services

(G-6239)
NORTHEAST COATING TECH INC
Also Called: Nct
105 York St (04043-7104)
P.O. Box 539 (04043-0539)
PHONE....207 985-3232
Shawn P Spencer, *President*
Gil Cole, *QC Dir*
Scott Johnson, *Engineer*
Mary E Noel, *Sales Staff*
Stevens Charlie, *Manager*
▲ **EMP:** 50
SQ FT: 30,000
SALES (est): 7.5MM
SALES (corp-wide): 257.2K **Privately Held**
WEB: www.northeastcoating.com
SIC: 3479 Coating/Engraving Service
PA: Hef M&S Services
Avenue Benoit Fourneyron
Andrezieux Boutheon
477 555-222

(G-6240)
RAMBLERS WAY FARM INC
6 Commerce Dr (04043-6501)
PHONE....888 793-9665
Robert Hamblen, *Branch Mgr*
EMP: 47 **Privately Held**
SIC: 2231 Wool Broadwoven Fabric Mill
PA: Rambler's Way Farm, Inc.
2 Storer St Ste 207
Kennebunk ME

(G-6241)
TOMS OF MAINE INC
1 Trackside Dr (04043-7048)
PHONE....207 985-2944
EMP: 150
SALES (corp-wide): 15.4B **Publicly Held**
SIC: 2844 Mfg Deodorant Toothpaste & Other Health & Beauty
HQ: Tom's Of Maine, Inc.
2 Storer St Ste 302
Kennebunk ME 04043
207 985-2944

(G-6242)
TOMS OF MAINE INC (HQ)
Also Called: Tom's Natural Soap
2 Storer St Ste 302 (04043-6883)
PHONE....207 985-2944
Tom Obrien, *CEO*
Joanne Murphy, *Mktg Dir*
Brendan Murphy, *Manager*
Rob Robinson, *Manager*
▲ **EMP:** 95 **EST:** 1970
SQ FT: 20,000
SALES (est): 49.7MM
SALES (corp-wide): 15.5B **Publicly Held**
WEB: www.tomsofmaine.com
SIC: 2844 Mfg Toilet Preparations
PA: Colgate-Palmolive Company
300 Park Ave Fl 3
New York NY 10022
212 310-2000

GEOGRAPHIC

(G-6243)
YORK COUNTY COAST STAR INC
39 Main St (04043-7081)
P.O. Box 979 (04043-0979)
PHONE.................................207 985-5901
Dan King, *Principal*
Brian Hewett, *Manager*
EMP: 13
SALES (est): 422.2K **Privately Held**
SIC: 2711 Newspapers-Publishing/Printing

Kennebunkport
York County

(G-6244)
FINE PRINT BOOKSELLERS
28 Dock Sq (04046-6011)
P.O. Box 1860 (04046-4860)
PHONE.................................207 967-9989
EMP: 3 **EST:** 2017
SALES (est): 132K **Privately Held**
SIC: 2752 Lithographic Commercial Printing

(G-6245)
JAK DESIGNS LLC (PA)
24 Ocean Ave (04046-6141)
PHONE.................................207 204-0396
Tanya M Alsberg, *Principal*
Jennifer K Armstrong,
EMP: 10
SALES (est): 6.4MM **Privately Held**
SIC: 2678 5699 Mfg Stationery Products Ret Misc Apparel/Accessories

(G-6246)
KATES HOMEMADE BUTTER INC
Also Called: Kate's Creamery
24 Dairy Ln (04046-8795)
P.O. Box 79, Old Orchard Beach (04064-0079)
PHONE.................................207 934-5134
Karen Patry, *President*
Dan Patry, *Treasurer*
Harold Arsenault, *Admin Sec*
Daniel F Barret,
▲ **EMP:** 6
SALES (est): 1.1MM **Privately Held**
WEB: www.kateshomemadebutter.com
SIC: 2021 Mfg Creamery Butter

(G-6247)
KENNEBUNKPORT PIE COMPANY LLC
Also Called: Maine Cookie Co., The
40 Maine St Ste 124 (04046)
PHONE.................................207 205-4466
McKay Ashleigh, *Prdtn Mgr*
Jill Miller,
Louise Miller,
EMP: 4
SQ FT: 3,500
SALES (est): 311.9K **Privately Held**
SIC: 2051 Mfg Bread/Related Products

(G-6248)
ULTIMATE INDUSTRIES
6 Clark Rd (04046-7208)
PHONE.................................617 923-1568
EMP: 3 **EST:** 2015
SALES (est): 123.5K **Privately Held**
SIC: 3999 Mfg Misc Products

Kezar Falls
York County

(G-6249)
JORDAN FAMILY CHIPPING INC
Rr 160 (04047)
P.O. Box 121 (04047-0121)
PHONE.................................207 625-8890
Gerald Jordan, *President*
Margaret Jordan, *Admin Sec*
EMP: 3
SALES: 200K **Privately Held**
SIC: 2411 2421 Logging Contractor & Chipper Mill

(G-6250)
JORDAN TREE HARVESTERS INC (PA)
River St (04047)
P.O. Box 186 (04047-0186)
PHONE.................................207 625-4378
Michael Jordan II, *President*
Cory Jordan, *Vice Pres*
EMP: 4
SALES (est): 343.2K **Privately Held**
SIC: 2411 Logging

Kingfield
Franklin County

(G-6251)
ADVANCED RESOURCES & CONSTRUCT
Also Called: ARC Enterprises
27 Commercial Rd (04947)
P.O. Box 120 (04947-0120)
PHONE.................................207 265-2646
Walter P Kilbreth, *President*
Jake Kilbreth, *Vice Pres*
EMP: 25
SQ FT: 18,000
SALES (est): 6.7MM **Privately Held**
SIC: 3441 Structural Metal Fabrication

(G-6252)
BLACK BEAR GRAPHICS
51 W Kingfield Rd (04947-4252)
PHONE.................................207 265-4593
James A Grant, *Owner*
EMP: 4
SALES: 230K **Privately Held**
SIC: 2759 2395 2396 Commercial Printing Pleating/Stitching Services Mfg Auto/Apparel Trimming

(G-6253)
FRONTIER FORGE INC
Also Called: Kingfield Wood Products
37 Depot St (04947-4208)
PHONE.................................207 265-2151
Phillip Kennedy, *President*
Marilyn Niles, *Office Mgr*
EMP: 38
SQ FT: 35,000
SALES (est): 5.4MM **Privately Held**
WEB: www.kingfieldwood.com
SIC: 2499 Mfg Custom Wood Turnings & Novelties

(G-6254)
ORIGINAL IRREGULAR
239 Main St Ste 1 (04947-4233)
P.O. Box 616 (04947-0616)
PHONE.................................207 265-2773
Heidi Murphy, *Owner*
EMP: 4
SALES (est): 325.4K **Privately Held**
SIC: 2711 2741 Newspapers-Publishing/Printing Misc Publishing

Kittery
York County

(G-6255)
EDWARDS LTD
9 Ranger Dr (03904-1055)
PHONE.................................207 439-2400
Steve Bays, *Manager*
EMP: 3
SALES (est): 123.2K **Privately Held**
SIC: 2813 Mfg Industrial Gases

(G-6256)
GOOD TO-GO LLC
484 Us Route 1 (03904-5507)
PHONE.................................207 451-9060
Jennifer Scism, *President*
David Koorits, *Vice Pres*
EMP: 10
SQ FT: 3,000
SALES (est): 283.4K **Privately Held**
SIC: 2034 Mfg Dehydrated Fruits/Vegetables

(G-6257)
MESSER LLC
9 Ranger Dr (03904-1055)
PHONE.................................207 475-3102
Daryl Souzer, *Branch Mgr*
Darrell Souzer, *Manager*
Ted Shufelt, *Technical Staff*
EMP: 30
SALES (corp-wide): 1.4B **Privately Held**
SIC: 2813 Mfg Nitrogen/ Oxygen
HQ: Messer Llc
200 Somerset Corp Blvd # 7000
Bridgewater NJ 08807
908 464-8100

(G-6258)
RON-BET COMPANY INC
99 State Rd Ste 1 (03904-1516)
PHONE.................................207 439-5868
Andrew Chick, *President*
EMP: 6 **EST:** 1947
SQ FT: 2,400
SALES (est): 500K **Privately Held**
SIC: 3442 Mfg Metal Doors/Sash/Trim

(G-6259)
VILLEROY & BOCH USA INC
Also Called: House of Villeroy & Boch
360 Us Route 1 (03904-6502)
PHONE.................................207 439-6440
Mary Hui, *Manager*
EMP: 10
SALES (corp-wide): 946.1MM **Privately Held**
WEB: www.villeroy-boch.com
SIC: 3089 Mfg Plastic Products
HQ: Villeroy & Boch Usa, Inc.
3a S Middlesex Ave
Monroe Township NJ 08831
800 536-2284

(G-6260)
YORK HARBOR BREWING COMPANY
8 Blueberry Ln (03904-5453)
PHONE.................................207 703-8060
David Albert Dauteuil, *President*
EMP: 6 **EST:** 2015
SALES (est): 91.3K **Privately Held**
SIC: 2082 Mfg Malt Beverages

Kittery Point
York County

(G-6261)
SEA POINT CHANDLERS LLC
76 Brave Boat Harbor Rd (03905-5232)
PHONE.................................207 703-2395
Mary Loring, *Principal*
EMP: 3 **EST:** 2012
SALES (est): 246.6K **Privately Held**
SIC: 3999 Mfg Misc Products

Knox
Waldo County

(G-6262)
CENTER POINT INC
Also Called: Center Point Publishing
600 Brooks Rd (04986-4210)
P.O. Box 1, Thorndike (04986-0001)
PHONE.................................207 568-3717
Paul Garelli, *President*
Ken Larrbee, *Manager*
Michelle Larrabee, *Admin Mgr*
◆ **EMP:** 22
SALES (est): 1.1MM **Privately Held**
WEB: www.centerpointlargeprint.com
SIC: 2741 2732 Misc Publishing Book Printing

Lamoine
Hancock County

(G-6263)
CRANES CONTRACT CUTTING INC
350 Douglas Hwy (04605-4248)
PHONE.................................207 667-9008
David Crane, *President*
Kathy Crane, *Vice Pres*
EMP: 6
SALES (est): 410K **Privately Held**
SIC: 2411 Logging

(G-6264)
SW BOATWORKS
358 Douglas Hwy (04605-4248)
PHONE.................................207 667-7427
Stewart Workman, *Owner*
EMP: 6
SALES (est): 1MM **Privately Held**
SIC: 3732 Boatbuilding/Repairing

Lebanon
York County

(G-6265)
GREAT BROOK LUMBER INC
766 Upper Guinea Rd (04027-4417)
P.O. Box 400 (04027-0400)
PHONE.................................207 457-1063
Christopher Sewell, *President*
Janel Sewell, *Treasurer*
EMP: 6
SQ FT: 18,000
SALES (est): 745.8K **Privately Held**
SIC: 2421 5211 Sawmill And Planing Mill Including Retail Lumber Yard

Lee
Penobscot County

(G-6266)
T RAYMOND FOREST PRODUCTS INC
260 Arab Rd (04455-4519)
PHONE.................................207 738-2313
Terry R Raymond, *President*
Paula Raymonds, *Vice Pres*
EMP: 30
SALES (est): 3.6MM **Privately Held**
SIC: 2411 Logging Contractor

(G-6267)
YATES LUMBER INC
137 Winn Rd (04455-4202)
P.O. Box 137 (04455-0137)
PHONE.................................207 738-2331
Scott Yates, *President*
Alton Yates, *Vice Pres*
EMP: 16
SALES (est): 1.7MM **Privately Held**
SIC: 2421 Sawmill/Planing Mill

Leeds
Androscoggin County

(G-6268)
BRUCE A PETTENGILL
Also Called: Pettengill Printing
129 Bog Rd (04263-3732)
PHONE.................................207 933-2578
Bruce A Pettengill, *Owner*
Jean Pettengill, *Co-Owner*
EMP: 4
SALES (est): 322.2K **Privately Held**
SIC: 2759 2752 2791 2789 Commercial Printing Lithographic Coml Print Typesetting Services Bookbinding/Related Work

▲ = Import ▼=Export
◆ =Import/Export

(G-6269)
GERRITY COMPANY INCORPORATED
Also Called: Dayken Pallet
152 Bog Rd (04263-3736)
P.O. Box 121, Monmouth (04259-0121)
PHONE....207 933-2804
Toll Free:....877 -
Peter F Gerrity, *President*
J F Gerrity III, *Treasurer*
Peter J Young, *Admin Sec*
EMP: 40
SQ FT: 40,000
SALES (est): 6.8MM
SALES (corp-wide): 36.4MM **Privately Held**
WEB: www.gerrityco.com
SIC: 2448 2421 Mfg Wood Pallets/Skids Sawmill/Planing Mill
PA: Gerrity Enterprises, Incorporated
63b Bedford St
Lakeville MA 02347
617 916-0776

(G-6270)
M & C POWERSPORTS
443 Church Hill Rd (04263-3409)
PHONE....207 713-3128
Michael Bell, *Owner*
EMP: 4
SALES (est): 309.9K **Privately Held**
SIC: 3799 Mfg Transportation Equipment

Levant
Penobscot County

(G-6271)
KEVIN CALL
Also Called: Call Construction
4206 Union St (04456-4308)
PHONE....207 884-7786
Kevin Call, *Owner*
EMP: 3
SALES (est): 411K **Privately Held**
SIC: 3531 Groundwork Construction

Lewiston
Androscoggin County

(G-6272)
ACTION SCREEN PRINTING
41 Chestnut St Ste 5 (04240-7779)
PHONE....207 795-7786
Phil Giogetti, *Owner*
EMP: 7
SALES: 1MM **Privately Held**
WEB: www.actionscreenprinting.net
SIC: 2759 Commercial Printing

(G-6273)
ALLEN MANUFACTURING INC
41 Canal St (04240-7764)
PHONE....207 333-3385
David Allen, *President*
▲ **EMP:** 20
SALES (est): 2MM **Privately Held**
SIC: 2399 Fabricated Textile Products, Nec, Nsk

(G-6274)
ALMANAC PUBLISHING CO
Also Called: Farmers Almanac
70 Mount Hope Ave (04240-1021)
P.O. Box 1609 (04241-1609)
PHONE....207 755-2000
Gene Geiger, *President*
Darrell Smith, *Partner*
Peter Geiger, *Exec VP*
Ashley Duffy, *Sales Staff*
Renee Richardson, *Office Mgr*
▲ **EMP:** 5
SALES (est): 1.3MM **Privately Held**
WEB: www.farmersalmanac.com
SIC: 2741 Misc Publishing

(G-6275)
B & T PALLET RECYCLING INC
13 Fireslate Pl (04240)
P.O. Box 1120 (04243-1120)
PHONE....207 784-9048
Ronald Tierney, *President*
EMP: 7
SQ FT: 45,000
SALES: 500K **Privately Held**
SIC: 2448 Mfg Wood Pallets/Skids

(G-6276)
BELL MANUFACTURING CO
Also Called: Bell Label Co.
777 Main St (04240-5803)
P.O. Box 196 (04243-0196)
PHONE....207 784-2961
Tom Seder, *President*
Don Bradman, *Mfg Dir*
◆ **EMP:** 60 **EST:** 1947
SQ FT: 30,000
SALES (est): 7.1MM
SALES (corp-wide): 13.1MM **Privately Held**
WEB: www.belllabel.com
SIC: 2241 2759 Mfg Woven & Printed Labels
PA: Sml Usa Inc.
1 Harmon Plz Fl 6
Secaucus NJ 07094
212 736-8800

(G-6277)
BRAVA ENTERPRISES LLC
86 Main St (04240)
PHONE....207 241-2420
Scott Demers, *Mng Member*
EMP: 5 **EST:** 2007
SALES: 1.5MM **Privately Held**
SIC: 2013 5812 Mfg Prepared Meats Eating Place

(G-6278)
BRETTUNSVILLAGECOM
Also Called: Brettuns Village.com
557 Lincoln St (04240-6159)
PHONE....207 782-7863
Churchill Barton, *Owner*
Clinton Trunk, *Technology*
▲ **EMP:** 16
SALES (est): 470K **Privately Held**
WEB: www.brettunsvillage.com
SIC: 3111 Mfg Leather Products

(G-6279)
CARBONITE INC
18 Mollison Way (04240-5811)
PHONE....617 927-3521
Brett Siedman, *Principal*
EMP: 8
SALES (est): 1MM **Privately Held**
SIC: 7372 Prepackaged Software Services

(G-6280)
CLARIANT PLAS COATINGS USA LLC
17 Foss Rd (04240-1303)
PHONE....207 784-0733
Russ Neal, *General Mgr*
Eric Dann, *QC Mgr*
Larry Poulin, *Manager*
EMP: 24
SALES (corp-wide): 6.7B **Privately Held**
WEB: www.myclariant.com
SIC: 2865 5169 Mfg Cyclic Crudes/Intermediates/Dyes Whol Chemicals/Products
HQ: Clariant Plastics & Coatings Usa Llc
4000 Monroe Rd
Charlotte NC 28205
704 331-7000

(G-6281)
CUSTOM CANVAS & UPHOLSTERY LLC
134 Main St Ste 8 (04240-8006)
PHONE....207 241-8518
Simon I Graham,
EMP: 15
SQ FT: 4,000
SALES: 3.2MM **Privately Held**
SIC: 2512 2394 5999 5714 Mfg Uphls Household Furn Mfg Canvas/Related Prdts Ret Misc Merchandise Ret Draperies/Upholstery

(G-6282)
CUSTOM WINDOW DECORATORS
1486 Lisbon St (04240)
P.O. Box 1802 (04241-1802)
PHONE....207 784-4113
Mike Favreau, *Owner*
EMP: 5
SQ FT: 2,500
SALES (est): 462.2K **Privately Held**
WEB: www.customwindowdecorators.com
SIC: 2591 5714 Mfg Drapery Hardware/Blinds Ret Draperies/Upholstery

(G-6283)
DESIGN ARCHITECTURAL HEATING
141 Howe St (04240-6422)
P.O. Box 7110 (04243-7110)
PHONE....207 784-0309
Paul Roy, *President*
▲ **EMP:** 10
SQ FT: 8,000
SALES (est): 865.6K **Privately Held**
SIC: 3699 Mfg Commercial And Residential Electric And Hydronic Heating Products

(G-6284)
DVE MANUFACTURING INC
550 Lisbon St (04240-6580)
P.O. Box 2005 (04241-2005)
PHONE....207 783-9895
Donald Loiselle, *President*
EMP: 35
SQ FT: 49,000
SALES (est): 2.9MM **Privately Held**
WEB: www.dvemfg.com
SIC: 2353 7336 2396 Mfg Hats/Caps/Millinery Commercial Art/Graphic Design Mfg Auto/Apparel Trimming

(G-6285)
ELCO INC (PA)
Also Called: Elco Precision Machining
9 Enterprise St (04240-3503)
PHONE....207 784-3996
Daniel Guerette, *President*
Joel Guerette, *Vice Pres*
Claire Guerette, *Treasurer*
EMP: 5
SQ FT: 6,000
SALES (est): 1MM **Privately Held**
SIC: 3599 Machine Shop Jobbing & Repair

(G-6286)
ELEMENT ALL STARS
746 Main St (04240-5807)
PHONE....207 576-6931
EMP: 3 **EST:** 2018
SALES (est): 190.3K **Privately Held**
SIC: 2819 Industrial Inorganic Chemicals, Nec

(G-6287)
ELMET TECHNOLOGIES LLC
1560 Lisbon St (04240-3519)
PHONE....207 333-6100
Andrew D R Nichols, *CEO*
John Johnson, *Vice Pres*
Marc Lamare, *Vice Pres*
Jon Adams, *Opers Mgr*
Michael Ducharme, *Engineer*
◆ **EMP:** 207
SQ FT: 220,000
SALES (est): 74.7MM **Privately Held**
SIC: 3356 3499 3769 3599 Nonferrous Rollng/Drawng Mfg Misc Fab Metal Prdts Mfg Space Vehicle Equip Mfg Industrial Machinery Mfg Aircraft Parts/Equip

(G-6288)
ENTERPRISE CASTINGS LLC
Also Called: Enterprise Foundry
40 South Ave (04240-5756)
PHONE....207 782-5511
Paul R Legendre, *President*
EMP: 4 **EST:** 2015
SALES (est): 90K **Privately Held**
SIC: 2899 2891 5084 3398 Mfg Chemical Preparation Mfg Adhesives/Sealants Whol Industrial Equip Metal Heat Treating

(G-6289)
GRAPHIC EXPLOSION INC
41 Delcliffe Ln (04240-4001)
P.O. Box 2404 (04241-2404)
PHONE....207 576-3210
Jim Berube, *Principal*
EMP: 3
SALES (est): 257.7K **Privately Held**
SIC: 2759 Commercial Printing

(G-6290)
HUHTAMAKI INC
11 Fireslate Pl (04240-2310)
PHONE....207 795-6000
EMP: 34
SALES (corp-wide): 3.4B **Privately Held**
SIC: 2671 Mfg Packaging Paper/Film
HQ: Huhtamaki, Inc.
9201 Packaging Dr
De Soto KS 66018
913 583-3025

(G-6291)
INFAB REFRACTORIES INC
150 Summer St (04240-7532)
PHONE....207 783-2075
David Collins, *CEO*
Jean Bergeron, *Vice Pres*
Richard Marston, *Treasurer*
EMP: 8
SQ FT: 12,600
SALES (est): 1.3MM **Privately Held**
WEB: www.infabrefractories.com
SIC: 3297 Mfg Nonclay Refractories

(G-6292)
INSULSAFE TEXTILES INC
55 Holland St (04240-7515)
P.O. Box 149, Greene (04236-0149)
PHONE....207 782-7011
Charles Gillis, *President*
Bruce Bubier, *Vice Pres*
Joyce Graham, *Vice Pres*
▲ **EMP:** 28
SQ FT: 45,000
SALES (est): 4MM **Privately Held**
WEB: www.insulsafe.com
SIC: 2297 2211 Mfg Nonwoven Fabrics Cotton Broadwoven Fabric Mill

(G-6293)
ITALIAN BAKERY PRODUCTS CO
225 Bartlett St (04240-6502)
PHONE....207 782-8312
Frank Chiaravelotti, *Owner*
EMP: 10 **EST:** 1959
SQ FT: 2,400
SALES (est): 716.7K **Privately Held**
SIC: 2051 5461 Mfg Bread/Related Products Retail Bakery

(G-6294)
JOHNS MANVILLE CORPORATION
51 Lexington St (04240-3529)
PHONE....207 784-0123
Tim Olehowski, *Manager*
EMP: 25
SALES (corp-wide): 225.3B **Publicly Held**
WEB: www.jm.com
SIC: 3296 Mfg Mineral Wool
HQ: Johns Manville Corporation
717 17th St Ste 800
Denver CO 80202
303 978-2000

(G-6295)
JONES & VINING INCORPORATED
765 Webster St (04240-1600)
P.O. Box 1903 (04241-1903)
PHONE....207 784-3547
Rejean Tremblay, *Manager*
EMP: 50
SQ FT: 8,000
SALES (corp-wide): 71.5MM **Privately Held**
WEB: www.jvmaine.com
SIC: 3089 3131 3061 Mfg Plastic Products Mfg Footwear Cut Stock Mfg Mechanical Rubber Goods

GEOGRAPHIC

PA: Jones & Vining, Incorporated
1115 W Chestnut St Ste 2
Brockton MA 02301
508 232-7470

(G-6296)
KULLSON HOLDING COMPANY INC
Also Called: Purestat Engineered Tech
21 Old Farm Rd (04240-2302)
PHONE....................207 783-3442
Richard Kullson, *President*
Keith Donaldson, *Vice Pres*
▼ **EMP:** 29
SALES: 5MM **Privately Held**
SIC: 2671 6719 Mfg Packaging Paper/Film Holding Company

(G-6297)
LASERWORDS MAINE
1775 Lisbon St (04240-3523)
PHONE....................207 782-9595
Vellayan Subbiah, *President*
Daniel Boilard, *Vice Pres*
EMP: 25 **EST:** 1973
SQ FT: 5,000
SALES (est): 2.1MM **Privately Held**
WEB: www.pinetreecomposition.com
SIC: 2791 Computerized Book Typesetting Service

(G-6298)
LEPAGE BAKERIES PARK ST LLC
Also Called: Country Kitchen
354 Lisbon St (04240-7306)
P.O. Box 1900, Auburn (04211-1900)
PHONE....................207 783-9161
Thomas Mato, *Manager*
EMP: 100
SALES (corp-wide): 3.9B **Publicly Held**
WEB: www.lbck.com
SIC: 2051 Mfg Bread/Related Products
HQ: Lepage Bakeries Park Street Llc
11 Adamian Dr
Auburn ME 04210
207 783-9161

(G-6299)
LEWISTON DAILY SUN (PA)
Also Called: Sun Journal
104 Park St (04240-7202)
P.O. Box 4400 (04243-4400)
PHONE....................207 784-3555
James R Costello, *President*
Lee Horton, *Editor*
David Costello, *Vice Pres*
Stephen Costello, *Vice Pres*
James Thornton, *Vice Pres*
EMP: 245 **EST:** 1898
SQ FT: 16,000
SALES: 12.9MM **Privately Held**
WEB: www.sunjournal.com
SIC: 2711 Newspapers-Publishing/Printing

(G-6300)
LEWISTON DAILY SUN
Also Called: Sun Journal
104 Park St (04240-7202)
PHONE....................207 784-5411
Deb Vines, *Manager*
EMP: 5
SALES (corp-wide): 12.9MM **Privately Held**
WEB: www.sunjournal.com
SIC: 2711 Newspapers-Publishing/Printing
PA: Daily Lewiston Sun
104 Park St
Lewiston ME 04240
207 784-3555

(G-6301)
LEWISTON-AUBURN TENT & AWNG CO
Also Called: L & A Tent Awning
240 River Rd (04240)
PHONE....................207 784-7353
Barry Richardson, *President*
Malcolm W Philbrook, *Clerk*
EMP: 8
SQ FT: 5,000
SALES (est): 563.4K **Privately Held**
SIC: 2394 Mfg Canvas Products

(G-6302)
LIFELINE SYSTEMS COMPANY
100 Campus Ave Ste G1 (04240-6040)
PHONE....................207 777-8827
Cathy White, *Principal*
EMP: 150
SALES (corp-wide): 20.1B **Privately Held**
SIC: 3669 Mfg Communications Equipment
HQ: Lifeline Systems Company
111 Lawrence St
Framingham MA 01702
508 988-1000

(G-6303)
MAINE BARREL & DISPLAY COMPANY
Also Called: Bench Systems
21 Fireslate Pl (04240-2310)
P.O. Box 1908 (04241-1908)
PHONE....................207 784-6700
Michael Morin, *President*
EMP: 25
SQ FT: 27,000
SALES (est): 4.1MM **Privately Held**
SIC: 2541 3524 3535 Mfg Wood Partitions/Fixtures Mfg Lawn/Garden Equipment Mfg Conveyors/Equipment

(G-6304)
MAINELINE INDUSTRIES INC
Also Called: Maine-Line Leather
850 Main St Ste 3 (04240-5187)
PHONE....................207 782-6622
James Custeau, *President*
▲ **EMP:** 6
SQ FT: 5,000
SALES: 220K **Privately Held**
SIC: 3199 3172 Mfg Leather Goods

(G-6305)
MICRONETIXX MICROWAVE LLC
1 Gendron Dr (04240-1036)
P.O. Box 2114 (04241-2114)
PHONE....................207 786-2000
Peter Robicheau,
George Harris,
EMP: 12
SQ FT: 2,000
SALES: 1MM **Privately Held**
SIC: 3679 Mfg Electronic Components

(G-6306)
MICRONETIXX TECHNOLOGIES LLC
70 Commercial St Ste 1 (04240-3958)
P.O. Box 2114 (04241-2114)
PHONE....................207 786-2000
Peter Robicheau, *VP Mfg*
George M Harris, *Mng Member*
▼ **EMP:** 9
SQ FT: 8,500
SALES: 650K **Privately Held**
SIC: 3589 3825 Mfg Service Industry Machinery Mfg Electrical Measuring Instruments

(G-6307)
MOLDS PLUS INC
41 Chestnut St Ste 1a (04240-7779)
PHONE....................207 795-0000
Greg Gagnier, *President*
Tee Tardif, *Vice Pres*
EMP: 3
SALES: 350K **Privately Held**
SIC: 3089 Mfg Plastic Products

(G-6308)
MR BOSTON BRANDS LLC (HQ)
Also Called: Boston Brands of Maine
21 Saratoga St (04240-3527)
P.O. Box 2359 (04241-2359)
PHONE....................207 783-1433
William Goldring, *CEO*
▲ **EMP:** 32
SALES (est): 8.1MM
SALES (corp-wide): 306.3MM **Privately Held**
SIC: 2085 2084 Mfg Distilled/Blended Liquor Mfg Wines/Brandy/Spirits
PA: Sazerac Company, Inc.
3850 N Causeway Blvd # 1695
Metairie LA 70002
504 831-9450

(G-6309)
NEAL SPECIALTY COMPOUNDING LLC
Also Called: COMPOUNDING SOLUTIONS
258 Goddard Rd (04240-1000)
PHONE....................207 777-1122
Toll Free:....................877 -
Robert Neal, *Sales Staff*
Scott Neal, *Mng Member*
Neal Doyle, *Manager*
Gene Girouad, *Manager*
Joseph Wilson, *Manager*
▲ **EMP:** 70
SQ FT: 60,000
SALES: 23.7MM **Privately Held**
WEB: www.compoundingsolutions.net
SIC: 3087 Custom Compounding-Purchased Resins

(G-6310)
NEOKRAFT SIGNS INC
647 Pleasant St (04240-3914)
P.O. Box 336 (04243-0336)
PHONE....................207 782-9654
Peter Murphy, *President*
Phil Bolduc, *Vice Pres*
Paul Lessard, *Vice Pres*
Mike Mathieu, *VP Sales*
Clay Bublak, *Sales Staff*
EMP: 35 **EST:** 1947
SALES (est): 4.7MM **Privately Held**
WEB: www.neokraft.com
SIC: 3993 Mfg Signs/Advertising Specialties

(G-6311)
NEW ENGLAND OUTERWEAR
550 Lisbon St (04240-6580)
PHONE....................207 240-3069
EMP: 6
SALES (est): 100.9K **Privately Held**
SIC: 2499 Mfg Wood Products

(G-6312)
OBRIEN CONSOLIDATED INDS
680 Lisbon St Ste 1 (04240-6509)
P.O. Box 139 (04243-0139)
PHONE....................207 783-8543
Susan D Lagueux, *President*
Annette Dallaire, *Treasurer*
Sonia Parisi, *Office Mgr*
EMP: 11 **EST:** 1964
SQ FT: 22,000
SALES (est): 2.1MM **Privately Held**
WEB: www.maine-metals.org
SIC: 3541 3544 3599 Manufactures The Arch Punch-A Metal Cutting Tool Cutting Dies Machine Shop Custom Built Machinery

(G-6313)
ONESOURCE PRINTING
170 Summer St (04240-7532)
P.O. Box 560, Auburn (04212-0560)
PHONE....................207 784-1538
EMP: 6
SALES (est): 600K **Privately Held**
SIC: 2752 Lithographic Commercial Printing

(G-6314)
PANTHEON GUITARS LLC
Also Called: Bourgeois Guitars
41 Canal St (04240-7764)
PHONE....................207 755-0003
Patrick Theimer, *Principal*
Bonni Lloyd, *Sales Staff*
EMP: 10
SQ FT: 7,000
SALES (est): 1.4MM **Privately Held**
WEB: www.pantheonguitars.com
SIC: 3931 5099 Mfg Musical Instruments Whol Durable Goods

(G-6315)
PEDRO OHARAS
134 Main St Ste 2 (04240-8006)
PHONE....................207 783-6200
Pedro Oharas, *Owner*
EMP: 4
SALES (est): 408K **Privately Held**
SIC: 3421 Mfg Cutlery

(G-6316)
PENMOR LITHOGRAPHERS INC
8 Lexington St (04240-3500)
P.O. Box 2003 (04241-2003)
PHONE....................207 784-1341
Joseph Fillion, *CEO*
Paul Fillion, *President*
Glen Fillion, *Vice Pres*
Wayne Fillion, *Vice Pres*
Karen Nicole, *Treasurer*
EMP: 50 **EST:** 1969
SQ FT: 42,000
SALES: 7.6MM **Privately Held**
WEB: www.penmor.com
SIC: 2752 2789 Lithographic Commercial Printing Bookbinding/Related Work

(G-6317)
PUBLIC SCALES
32 Lexington St (04240-3510)
PHONE....................207 784-9466
Robert Blanchette, *President*
EMP: 10
SALES (est): 502.1K **Privately Held**
SIC: 3596 5046 Mfg Scales/Balances-Nonlaboratory Whol Commercial Equipment

(G-6318)
RANCOURT & CO SHOECRAFTERS INC
Also Called: Rancourt & Co.
9 Bridge St (04240-7505)
P.O. Box 9739, Portland (04104-5039)
PHONE....................207 782-1577
Michael Rancourt, *President*
Kyle Rancourt, *Vice Pres*
▲ **EMP:** 55
SQ FT: 25,000
SALES (est): 7.3MM **Privately Held**
SIC: 3143 Mfg Men's Footwear

(G-6319)
ROOPERS REDEMPTION & BEV CTR
Also Called: Roopers Main St
694 Main St (04240-5801)
PHONE....................207 782-1482
Deb Whittier, *Manager*
EMP: 10 **Privately Held**
SIC: 2086 5141 Mfg Bottled/Canned Soft Drinks Whol General Groceries
PA: Roopers Redemption & Beverage Center
794 Sabattus St
Lewiston ME 04240
-

(G-6320)
SCANMIX INC
36 Hogan Rd (04240-4015)
PHONE....................207 782-1885
Kirk Lundstrom, *President*
EMP: 4
SALES (est): 328.9K **Privately Held**
WEB: www.safeshower.com
SIC: 3273 Mfg Ready-Mixed Concrete

(G-6321)
SCOTIA COMPANY
358 Lincoln St (04240-6551)
PHONE....................207 782-3824
Paul R Libbey, *President*
Peter Libbey, *Director*
Robert Libbey, *Director*
EMP: 3
SQ FT: 70,000
SALES (est): 200K **Privately Held**
WEB: www.stitchbond.com
SIC: 2297 Mfg Non-Woven Fabrics

(G-6322)
SENIOR OPERATIONS LLC
29 Lexington St (04240-3511)
PHONE....................207 784-2338
EMP: 100
SALES (corp-wide): 1.4B **Privately Held**
SIC: 3441 3822 8711 Structural Metal Fabrication Mfg Environmental Controls Engineering Services
HQ: Senior Operations Llc
300 E Devon Ave
Bartlett IL 60103
630 372-3500

(G-6323)
SEPTITECH INC
69 Holland St (04240-7515)
PHONE..................................207 333-6940
Peter Cinchatte, *President*
Don Rousseau, *Senior VP*
▲ **EMP**: 15 **EST**: 1997
SQ FT: 9,000
SALES (est): 2.4MM
SALES (corp-wide): 6.7MM **Privately Held**
WEB: www.septitech.com
SIC: **3589** Manufactures Service Industry Machineries
PA: Bio-Microbics, Inc.
16002 W 110th St
Lenexa KS 66219
913 422-0707

(G-6324)
SML INC
777 Main St (04240-5803)
PHONE..................................207 784-2961
Daksha Bharadwaj, *General Mgr*
Jerry Dew, *General Mgr*
Kristie Graham, *General Mgr*
Sarah Julius, *Principal*
Doreen Jordan, *Accounts Exec*
▲ **EMP**: 25
SALES (est): 4.7MM **Privately Held**
SIC: **2241** Narrow Fabric Mills, Nsk

(G-6325)
TIM KAT INC
Also Called: Interstate Battery Southern ME
4 Gendron Dr Unit 5 (04240-1044)
PHONE..................................207 784-9675
Barry Doyle, *President*
EMP: 5
SALES (est): 373.2K **Privately Held**
SIC: **3691** Mfg Storage Batteries

(G-6326)
TRI-STAR MOLDING
555 Lincoln St (04240-6159)
PHONE..................................207 783-5820
Steve Roy, *Owner*
EMP: 5
SALES (est): 529.7K **Privately Held**
SIC: **3089** Mfg Plastic Products

(G-6327)
WAHLCOMETROFLEX INC
Also Called: Senior Flexonics Pthwy
29 Lexington St (04240-3533)
PHONE..................................207 784-2338
John Powell, *President*
Roger Poulin, *Principal*
John W Bader, *COO*
Scott F Hall, *Prdtn Mgr*
Roger H Poulin, *Opers Staff*
◆ **EMP**: 300 **EST**: 2000
SQ FT: 73,000
SALES (est): 62.4MM
SALES (corp-wide): 1.4B **Privately Held**
WEB: www.wahlcometroflex.com
SIC: **3441** 3822 8711 Structural Metal Fabrication Mfg Environmental Controls Engineering Services
HQ: Senior Operations Llc
300 E Devon Ave
Bartlett IL 60103
630 372-3500

(G-6328)
YVONS VALVOLINE EXPRESS CARE
698 Main St (04240-5801)
PHONE..................................207 777-3600
Heidi Gephtert, *Principal*
EMP: 5
SALES (est): 551K **Privately Held**
SIC: **3589** 7549 Mfg Service Industry Machinery Automotive Services

Lexington Twp
Somerset County

(G-6329)
MAINE MADE STUFFCOM
1687 Long Falls Dam Rd (04961-5004)
PHONE..................................207 628-3160
Deborah Mitchell, *Principal*
EMP: 3
SALES (est): 150.5K **Privately Held**
SIC: **3999** Mfg Misc Products

Liberty
Waldo County

(G-6330)
JWD PREMIUM PRODUCTS
27 W Main St (04949-3400)
P.O. Box 88 (04949-0088)
PHONE..................................617 429-8867
Susan Dieffenbacher, *Principal*
EMP: 3 **EST**: 2017
SALES (est): 174.8K **Privately Held**
SIC: **3944** Mfg Games/Toys

(G-6331)
LIBERTY GRAPHICS INC
Main St (04949)
P.O. Box 5 (04949-0005)
PHONE..................................207 589-4596
Tom Opper, *President*
Jeff Lord, *Sales Mgr*
EMP: 21
SQ FT: 12,000
SALES (est): 2.3MM **Privately Held**
WEB: www.naturetshirts.com
SIC: **2759** 2396 Commercial Printing Mfg Auto/Apparel Trimming

Limerick
York County

(G-6332)
BOSAL FOAM AND FIBER (PA)
Also Called: Bosal Foam Products
171 Washington St (04048-3545)
P.O. Box 489 (04048-0489)
PHONE..................................207 793-2245
Robert J Harrisburg, *President*
▼ **EMP**: 25 **EST**: 2001
SQ FT: 163,000
SALES (est): 4.2MM **Privately Held**
SIC: **3069** 5131 6512 5199 Mfg Fabrcatd Rubber Prdt Whol Piece Goods/Notions Nonresdentl Bldg Operatr Whol Nondurable Goods Mfg Plstc Material/Resin

(G-6333)
CAMERON INTERNATIONAL CORP
Cameron Flow Control Division
14 Business Park Rd (04048-3557)
PHONE..................................207 793-2289
Mike Harmon, *Principal*
EMP: 11 **Publicly Held**
SIC: **1389** Oil/Gas Field Services
HQ: Cameron International Corporation
4646 W Sam Houston Pkwy N
Houston TX 77041

(G-6334)
F R CARROLL INC
25 Doles Ridge Rd (04048-3400)
P.O. Box 9 (04048-0009)
PHONE..................................207 793-8615
Francis R Carroll, *President*
Barbara A Carroll, *Treasurer*
EMP: 33
SQ FT: 2,500
SALES (est): 6.1MM **Privately Held**
SIC: **3273** 1442 1771 2951 Mfg Ready-Mixed Concrete Construction Sand/Gravel Concrete Contractor Mfg Asphalt Mixtr/Blocks

(G-6335)
L M C LIGHT IRON INC
151 Range E Rd (04048-4220)
P.O. Box 521 (04048-0521)
PHONE..................................207 793-9957
Steve Hamilton, *President*
EMP: 10 **EST**: 1996
SQ FT: 6,000
SALES: 2.2MM **Privately Held**
SIC: **3441** 2431 Structural Metal Fabrication Mfg Millwork

(G-6336)
LIMERICK DOUGH BOY
8 Maple St (04048)
PHONE..................................207 793-4145
Micah Blanchette, *Owner*
Bob Blanchette, *Partner*
Eileen Blanchette, *Co-Owner*
EMP: 5
SALES: 170K **Privately Held**
SIC: **2051** Mfg Bread/Related Products

(G-6337)
LIMERICK MACHINE COMPANY INC
81 Central Ave (04048-3204)
P.O. Box 534 (04048-0534)
PHONE..................................207 793-2288
Thomas C West, *Principal*
Stephen Oliver, *Sales Mgr*
EMP: 39 **EST**: 2000
SQ FT: 13,000
SALES (est): 8.1MM **Privately Held**
WEB: www.limerickmachine.com
SIC: **3599** Mfg Industrial Machinery

(G-6338)
WEDGEROCK
34 Business Park Rd (04048-3557)
PHONE..................................207 793-2289
Thomas West, *President*
Keith Pierrotti, *General Mgr*
EMP: 6
SQ FT: 8,000
SALES (est): 359.6K **Privately Held**
SIC: **3593** Mfg Fluid Power Cylinders

Limestone
Aroostook County

(G-6339)
BLVD GRAPHIX
22 Main St (04750-1327)
PHONE..................................207 325-2583
Joe Lapierre, *Owner*
Becky Blodget, *Sales Associate*
EMP: 3
SALES (est): 273.4K **Privately Held**
SIC: **2254** Knit Underwear Mill

(G-6340)
GRAPHIC UTILITIES INCORPORATED
191 Development Dr (04750-6114)
PHONE..................................207 370-9178
Jacob Leby, *President*
Andrea Swanberg, *General Mgr*
Nancy Leby, *Vice Pres*
▲ **EMP**: 11
SALES (est): 2.5MM **Privately Held**
WEB: www.graphicutilities.com
SIC: **2893** Mfg Printing Ink

(G-6341)
HOMETOWN FUEL DBA HOMETO
3 Van Buren Rd (04750-1343)
PHONE..................................207 325-4411
Randy Brooker, *Principal*
EMP: 4
SALES (est): 385.2K **Privately Held**
SIC: **2869** Mfg Industrial Organic Chemicals

(G-6342)
LORING INDUSTRIES LLC
14 Colorado Rd (04750-6025)
PHONE..................................207 328-7005
Carl Flora, *Director*
EMP: 3
SALES (est): 106.7K **Privately Held**
SIC: **3711** Mfg Motor Vehicle/Car Bodies

(G-6343)
PATTISON SIGN GROUP (NE) INC
125 Kansas Rd Ste 100 (04750-6035)
P.O. Box 136, Madawaska (04756-0136)
PHONE..................................514 856-7756
EMP: 800 **EST**: 2003
SQ FT: 35,000
SALES (est): 38.4MM **Privately Held**
SIC: **3993** Mfg Signs/Advertising Specialties

(G-6344)
STAINLESS FDSRVICE EQP MFG INC
Also Called: SFE Mfg
14 Connecticut Rd (04750-6160)
PHONE..................................207 227-7747
Doug Morrell, *President*
William Busse, *Clerk*
EMP: 14
SALES: 1.7MM **Privately Held**
WEB: www.stainlessfoodservice.com
SIC: **2542** Mfg Partitions/Fixtures Non-Wood

(G-6345)
TROMBLEY INDUSTRIES INC
849 Access Hwy (04750-6311)
PHONE..................................207 328-4503
Geraldine Trombley, *President*
EMP: 4 **EST**: 1965
SQ FT: 750
SALES (est): 593.7K **Privately Held**
SIC: **2951** 3281 3273 3272 Mfg Of Asphalt Readi-Mixed Concrete Cut Stone And Stone Products

Limington
York County

(G-6346)
ARCHER MACHINE
Also Called: Metal Works
482 Sokokis Ave (04049)
P.O. Box 536 (04049-0536)
PHONE..................................207 637-3396
Michael Hanes, *President*
EMP: 6
SQ FT: 8,500
SALES (est): 930.5K **Privately Held**
SIC: **3599** Machine Shop Jobbing & Oem Work

(G-6347)
CHIP COMPONENT ELECTRONX
Also Called: CC Electronx
13 Airport Dr (04049-3550)
P.O. Box 483 (04049-0483)
PHONE..................................207 510-7608
Mahmoud Kanj, *President*
John Verzi, *COO*
EMP: 5
SQ FT: 7,500
SALES: 480K **Privately Held**
SIC: **3679** Mfg Electronic Components

(G-6348)
ROBERT W CARR & SONS INC
83 Millturn Rd (04049-3138)
PHONE..................................207 637-2885
Robert Carr, *President*
Lucianna Carr, *Vice Pres*
Richard Steeves, *Clerk*
EMP: 6
SALES (est): 540K **Privately Held**
SIC: **2411** Logging

(G-6349)
SSW INC
Also Called: Sebago Signworks
206 Ossipee Trl (04049-3504)
P.O. Box 891, Raymond (04071-0891)
PHONE..................................207 793-4440
Devin Fahie, *President*
EMP: 5
SQ FT: 3,000
SALES: 500K **Privately Held**
SIC: **3993** Mfg Signs/Advertising Specialties

(G-6350)
TOWNSEND CABINET MAKERS INC
Also Called: Stuart Townsend Carr
1 Malloy Mountain Rd (04049-4043)
PHONE..................................207 793-7086
Paul Townsend, *President*
Brenda Townsend, *Admin Sec*
EMP: 3
SQ FT: 5,000

SALES: 140K **Privately Held**
WEB: www.townsendcabinetmakers.com
SIC: 2511 Mfg Hardwood Furniture

(G-6351)
TRICO MILLWORKS INC
300 Hardscrabble Rd (04049-3011)
P.O. Box 69 (04049-0069)
PHONE..................................207 637-2711
Dave Baker, *President*
Gordon Leach, *Vice Pres*
EMP: 24
SQ FT: 15,000
SALES: 5MM **Privately Held**
WEB: www.tricomillwork.com
SIC: 2434 Mfg Wood Kitchen Cabinets

Lincoln
Penobscot County

(G-6352)
EVAD IMAGES
48 Main St (04457-1437)
PHONE..................................207 794-2930
David Mandravelis, *Owner*
EMP: 3
SALES (est): 170.9K **Privately Held**
SIC: 3861 Mfg Photographic Equipment/Supplies

(G-6353)
FOREST CHESTER PRODUCTS INC
Rr 116 (04457)
P.O. Box 189 (04457-0189)
PHONE..................................207 794-2303
William T Gardner, *President*
EMP: 30
SQ FT: 12,000
SALES: 2.8MM **Privately Held**
SIC: 2411 2421 Logging Sawmill/Planing Mill

(G-6354)
J C LOGGING INC
350 Transalpine Rd (04457-4237)
PHONE..................................207 794-4349
Jeff Harriman, *Principal*
EMP: 3
SALES (est): 156.8K **Privately Held**
SIC: 2411 Logging

(G-6355)
JOHNSTON DANDY COMPANY (PA)
Also Called: E.F. Cook Company
148 Main St (04457-1523)
P.O. Box 670 (04457-0670)
PHONE..................................207 794-6571
Robert A Johnston, *President*
Daniel J Johnston, *President*
Kyle Johnston, *Treasurer*
◆ **EMP:** 40 **EST:** 1955
SQ FT: 30,000
SALES (est): 10.4MM **Privately Held**
WEB: www.johnstondandy.com
SIC: 3554 Mfg Paper Industrial Machinery

(G-6356)
JORDAN MILLWORKS INC
Also Called: Casper's Janitorial Service
Rr 3 Box 1882 (04457)
PHONE..................................207 794-6178
Robert Jordan, *President*
Joseph Jordan, *Vice Pres*
Benjamin Jordan, *Admin Sec*
EMP: 3
SALES (est): 230K **Privately Held**
SIC: 2411 2431 Lumber & Wood Harvesting

(G-6357)
LINCOLN NEWS
Also Called: Gateway Press
78 W Broadway (04457-1312)
P.O. Box 35 (04457-0035)
PHONE..................................207 794-6532
Kevin Tenggren, *Owner*
EMP: 15
SQ FT: 1,000
SALES (est): 680K **Privately Held**
SIC: 2711 Newspapers-Publishing/Printing

(G-6358)
LMJ ENTERPRISES LLC (PA)
Also Called: Pine State Premium Shavings
445 Main St (04457-4701)
P.O. Box 219 (04457-0219)
PHONE..................................207 794-3489
Lee Haskell,
EMP: 5
SALES (est): 899.6K **Privately Held**
SIC: 2421 Sawmill/Planing Mill

(G-6359)
RAMSAYS WELDING & MACHINE INC
289 Enfield Rd (04457)
P.O. Box 298 (04457-0298)
PHONE..................................207 794-8839
Jeffrey L Fogg, *President*
Cynthia A Fogg, *Vice Pres*
EMP: 16 **EST:** 1966
SQ FT: 12,000
SALES (est): 2.7MM **Privately Held**
SIC: 3599 3441 7692 Mfg Industrial Machinery Structural Metal Fabrication Welding Repair

(G-6360)
THOMPSON TRUCKING INC
725 Enfield Rd (04457-4143)
P.O. Box 206 (04457-0206)
PHONE..................................207 794-6101
Mary Keegan, *President*
George Keegan, *Vice Pres*
EMP: 33
SQ FT: 2,500
SALES (est): 3MM **Privately Held**
SIC: 2411 4212 Logging Contractor & Trucking Of Timber

Lincolnville
Waldo County

(G-6361)
CELLAR DOOR WINERY (PA)
367 Youngtown Rd (04849-5427)
PHONE..................................207 763-4478
John Clapp, *Owner*
Stephanie Clapp, *Co-Owner*
McKenzie Brown, *Wholesale*
Emily Qualey, *Marketing Staff*
Wyatt Philbrook, *Manager*
EMP: 7
SALES (est): 330K **Privately Held**
WEB: www.mainewine.com
SIC: 2084 5182 Mfg Wines/Brandy/Spirits Whol Wine/Distilled Beverages

(G-6362)
JIM BROWN
Also Called: Windsor Chairmakers
2596 Atlantic Hwy (04849-5358)
P.O. Box 120 (04849-0120)
PHONE..................................207 789-5188
Jim Brown, *Owner*
Evelyn Collins, *Executive*
EMP: 12
SALES: 1MM **Privately Held**
WEB: www.windsorchair.com
SIC: 2511 Mfg Wood Household Furniture

Linneus
Aroostook County

(G-6363)
SWH INC
186 Drews Mills Rd (04730-4513)
PHONE..................................207 538-6666
Michael Lane, *President*
EMP: 6
SALES: 950K **Privately Held**
SIC: 2411 Logging

Lisbon
Androscoggin County

(G-6364)
MEMOIR NETWORK
Also Called: Turning Memories Into Memois
95 Gould Rd (04252-9760)
PHONE..................................207 353-5454
Denis G Le Doux, *Owner*
EMP: 3
SALES (est): 146.6K **Privately Held**
WEB: www.turningmemories.com
SIC: 2731 Books-Publishing/Printing

(G-6365)
STILETTO CUPCAKES
21 Donna Dr (04250-6240)
PHONE..................................207 212-9788
Alycia Beaulieu, *Principal*
EMP: 4
SALES (est): 207.8K **Privately Held**
SIC: 2051 Mfg Bread/Related Products

Lisbon Falls
Androscoggin County

(G-6366)
ADEPT SCREEN PRTG & GRAPHICS
644 Lisbon St (04252-1226)
PHONE..................................207 353-6094
Dave Wallace, *Partner*
Lawrence Gardella, *Partner*
Margaret Wallace, *Partner*
EMP: 6
SQ FT: 1,500
SALES: 365K **Privately Held**
SIC: 2759 Commercial Printing

(G-6367)
BLUE OX MALTHOUSE LLC
41 Capital Ave (04252-1102)
PHONE..................................207 649-0018
Steve Culver, *CFO*
EMP: 5
SALES (est): 187.7K **Privately Held**
SIC: 2083 Mfg Malt

(G-6368)
BOLDUC BROTHERS LOG & SHIPG
397 Ridge Rd (04252-6124)
PHONE..................................207 353-5990
Patrick R Bolduc, *Admin Sec*
EMP: 4
SALES (est): 306.1K **Privately Held**
SIC: 2411 Logging

(G-6369)
FIRST CHOICE PRINTING INC
60 Capital Ave (04252-1102)
PHONE..................................207 353-8006
Steven A Samson, *President*
EMP: 7
SQ FT: 2,500
SALES (est): 1.1MM **Privately Held**
SIC: 2752 7334 Lithographic Commercial Printing Photocopying Services

(G-6370)
JAMES H CARVILLE
134 Bowdoinham Rd (04252-6107)
PHONE..................................207 353-2625
James H Carville, *Principal*
EMP: 3
SALES (est): 242.2K **Privately Held**
SIC: 2411 Logging

(G-6371)
MAINE TOOL & MACHINE LLC
27 Canal St (04252)
P.O. Box 129 (04252-0129)
PHONE..................................207 725-0038
Clifton D Wilson,
EMP: 9
SQ FT: 17,000
SALES: 200K **Privately Held**
SIC: 3599 Mfg Industrial Machinery

(G-6372)
S3 DIGITAL PUBLISHING INC
60a Capital Ave (04252-1102)
PHONE..................................207 351-8006
Stephen Bonney, *President*
EMP: 3 **EST:** 2002
SQ FT: 2,000
SALES (est): 191.8K **Privately Held**
SIC: 2741 Misc Publishing

Livermore
Androscoggin County

(G-6373)
CASTONGUAY MEATS INC
252 Gibbs Mill Rd (04253-3415)
PHONE..................................207 897-4989
Donald Castonguay, *President*
Francis Castonguay, *Vice Pres*
EMP: 3
SALES: 110K **Privately Held**
SIC: 2011 Meat Packing Plant

(G-6374)
DARREL L TIBBETTS
Also Called: Tibbetts Logging and Trucking
115 Hathaway Hill Rd (04253-3201)
PHONE..................................207 897-4932
Darrell L Tibbetts, *Owner*
EMP: 3
SALES (est): 257.2K **Privately Held**
SIC: 2411 4212 Logging & Trucking Firm

(G-6375)
JOHNNY H CASTONGUAY
140 Shackley Hill Rd (04253-3703)
PHONE..................................207 897-5945
Johnny Castonguay, *Principal*
EMP: 6
SALES (est): 450.6K **Privately Held**
SIC: 2411 Logging

(G-6376)
R S PIDACKS INC
1801 Federal Rd (04253-4242)
PHONE..................................207 897-4622
Robert Pidacks, *President*
▼ **EMP:** 6
SQ FT: 2,000
SALES (est): 1.5MM **Privately Held**
SIC: 3532 Rock Crushing And Screening

(G-6377)
T&R FLAGG LOG SONS & DAUGHTERS
Also Called: Tr Flag Logging
68 Lake Rd (04253-3627)
PHONE..................................207 897-5212
Russell Flagg, *President*
EMP: 6
SALES (est): 570K **Privately Held**
SIC: 2411 Logging

Livermore Falls
Androscoggin County

(G-6378)
ISAACSON LUMBER CO INC
133 Park St (04254-1412)
P.O. Box L (04254)
PHONE..................................207 897-2115
Donald Isaacson, *President*
EMP: 3
SALES (est): 119.9K **Privately Held**
SIC: 2448 Wood Pallets And Skids, Nsk

(G-6379)
MASON PALLET INC
233 Strickland Loop Rd (04254-4744)
PHONE..................................207 897-6270
Charleen Mason, *Principal*
EMP: 3
SALES (est): 297.9K **Privately Held**
SIC: 2448 Mfg Wood Pallets/Skids

(G-6380)
PALLETONE OF MAINE INC
231 Park St (04254-4127)
P.O. Box L (04254-0711)
PHONE..................................207 897-5711

▲ = Import ▼=Export
◆ =Import/Export

Howe Q Wallace, *Ch of Bd*
James Isaacson, *Vice Pres*
Keith M Reinstetle, *Vice Pres*
Casey A Fletcher, *CFO*
Christopher Begin, *Manager*
▲ **EMP:** 115 **EST:** 1946
SQ FT: 50,000
SALES (est): 15.2MM
SALES (corp-wide): 422.1MM **Privately Held**
WEB: www.palex.com
SIC: 2448 2421 Mfg Wood Pallets/Skids Sawmill/Planing Mill
PA: Palletone, Inc
6001 Foxtrot Ave
Bartow FL 33830
800 771-1147

(G-6381)
PINE TREE ORTHOPEDIC LAB INC
175 Park St (04254-4125)
PHONE..................................207 897-5558
Bruce L Macdonald, *President*
▲ **EMP:** 15
SQ FT: 10,000
SALES (est): 2.3MM **Privately Held**
SIC: 3842 5661 Mfg Surgical Appliances/Supplies Ret Shoes

(G-6382)
TM AND TM INC
Also Called: Tm & Tm
49 Gilbert St (04254-4238)
PHONE..................................207 897-3442
Anthony Maxwell, *President*
Teri Maxwell, *Vice Pres*
EMP: 16
SALES (est): 660K **Privately Held**
SIC: 2051 Mfg Bread/Related Products

Long Island
Cumberland County

(G-6383)
JOHNSONS BOATYARD INC
88 Island Ave (04050-3510)
PHONE..................................207 766-3319
Steve Johnson, *President*
Lyn Johnson, *Vice Pres*
EMP: 3
SALES (est): 237.3K **Privately Held**
SIC: 3732 Boatbuilding/Repairing

Lovell
Oxford County

(G-6384)
LOVELL LUMBER CO INC
3 Mill Rd (04051)
P.O. Box 106 (04051-0106)
PHONE..................................207 925-6455
Helen A Woodbrey, *Ch of Bd*
Mark Woodbrey, *President*
EMP: 22
SQ FT: 1,200
SALES (est): 3.5MM **Privately Held**
WEB: www.lovelllumber.com
SIC: 2426 2421 Hardwood Dimension/Floor Mill Sawmill/Planing Mill

Lowell
Penobscot County

(G-6385)
FOGG LUMBERING INC
153 Tannery Rd (04493-3509)
P.O. Box 132, Enfield (04493-0132)
PHONE..................................207 732-4087
Barry Fogg, *President*
Eugene Fogg, *Vice Pres*
Althea Fogg, *Treasurer*
EMP: 4
SALES (est): 403.5K **Privately Held**
SIC: 2411 Logging Contractors

Lubec
Washington County

(G-6386)
LAND & SEA FUEL
417 S Lubec Rd (04652-3626)
PHONE..................................207 733-0005
EMP: 3
SALES (est): 184.1K **Privately Held**
SIC: 2869 Mfg Industrial Organic Chemicals

Ludlow
Aroostook County

(G-6387)
MAINE CEDAR SPECIALTY PRODUCTS
1938 Ludlow Rd (04730-7841)
PHONE..................................207 532-4034
Gary Brewer, *President*
Andy Brewer, *Vice Pres*
EMP: 7
SQ FT: 10,000
SALES (est): 984.8K **Privately Held**
SIC: 2421 Sawmill/Planing Mill

Lyman
York County

(G-6388)
COBRA POWDER COATING
29 Stagecoach Rd (04002-6262)
PHONE..................................207 391-3060
EMP: 3
SALES (est): 243.9K **Privately Held**
SIC: 3471 Plating/Polishing Service

(G-6389)
ECB MOTOR COMPANY INC
Also Called: Nutron Motor Company
1520 Alfred Rd (04002-7708)
PHONE..................................508 717-5441
Ellen Brady, *CEO*
EMP: 6 **Privately Held**
SIC: 3594 5084 Mfg Fluid Power Pumps/Motors Whol Industrial Equipment
PA: Ecb Motor Company Inc
56 Summersea Rd
Mashpee MA 02649
-

(G-6390)
J AND L SAND
221 S Waterboro Rd (04002)
PHONE..................................207 499-2545
Jeffery McDonald, *Owner*
Lesley Leighton, *Owner*
EMP: 7
SALES (est): 262.7K **Privately Held**
SIC: 1442 Construction Sand/Gravel

(G-6391)
MIKE GUILLEMETTE & SONS
Also Called: Cabinet Works
136 Howitt Rd (04002-6224)
PHONE..................................207 324-6221
Mike Guillemette, *Owner*
EMP: 3
SALES: 150K **Privately Held**
SIC: 2434 Mfg Wood Kitchen Cabinets And Furniture

Machias
Washington County

(G-6392)
MAINE WILD BLUEBERRY COMPANY (DH)
78 Elm St (04654)
P.O. Box 100, Old Town (04468-0100)
PHONE..................................207 255-8364
John Bragg, *President*
Ragner Kamp, *President*
Geoff Baldwin, *Treasurer*
EMP: 100
SQ FT: 120,000
SALES (est): 9.5MM
SALES (corp-wide): 3.3MM **Privately Held**
SIC: 2037 2033 Mfg Fruits Quick Frozen & Cold Pack & Mfg Fruits Packaged In Cans Jars Etc
HQ: Oxford Frozen Foods Limited
4881 Main St
Oxford NS B0M 1
902 447-2320

(G-6393)
MAINE WILD BLUEBERRY COMPANY
50 Elm St (04654-1415)
PHONE..................................207 255-8364
Regner Kemps, *Manager*
EMP: 55
SALES (corp-wide): 3.3MM **Privately Held**
SIC: 2037 2034 2033 Mfg Frozen Fruits/Vegetables Mfg Dehydrated Fruits/Vegetables Mfg Canned Fruits/Vegetables
HQ: Maine Wild Blueberry Company Inc
78 Elm St
Machias ME 04654
207 255-8364

(G-6394)
RSV MANAGEMENT
9 Valley View Rd (04654)
P.O. Box 840 (04654-0840)
PHONE..................................207 255-8608
Ed Tellon, *Owner*
Barbara Denbow, *Principal*
EMP: 5
SALES (est): 247.7K **Privately Held**
SIC: 2392 8741 Mfg Household Furnishings Management Services

(G-6395)
SHANNON DRILLING
684 Route 1 (04654)
P.O. Box 870 (04654-0870)
PHONE..................................207 255-6149
Christopher Getchell, *Owner*
EMP: 4
SALES (est): 401.5K **Privately Held**
SIC: 3533 Mfg Oil/Gas Field Machinery

(G-6396)
TWO OLD BROADS
41 Broadway (04654-1105)
P.O. Box 357 (04654-0357)
PHONE..................................207 255-6561
Daniel L Lacasse, *Principal*
Jackie Mills, *Administration*
EMP: 5
SALES (est): 351.8K **Privately Held**
SIC: 2711 7313 Newspapers-Publishing/Printing Advertising Representative

Machiasport
Washington County

(G-6397)
BRUCE C SMITH LOGGING
45 Smith Ln (04655-3146)
PHONE..................................207 255-3259
Bruce C Smith, *Owner*
EMP: 3
SALES (est): 283K **Privately Held**
SIC: 2411 Logging

(G-6398)
MAINE COAST NORDIC
133 Smalls Point Rd (04655-3231)
PHONE..................................207 255-6714
Glen Cooke, *President*
EMP: 10 **EST:** 1987
SALES (est): 563.9K **Privately Held**
SIC: 2092 Mfg Fresh/Frozen Packaged Fish

Macwahoc Plt
Penobscot County

(G-6399)
HANINGTON BROS INC
488 Us Hwy 2 (04451-4019)
PHONE..................................207 765-2681
Stephen Hanington, *President*
EMP: 33
SQ FT: 10,000
SALES: 9MM **Privately Held**
WEB: www.haningtonbros.com
SIC: 2411 Logging

Madawaska
Aroostook County

(G-6400)
MADTOWN LOGGING LLC
185 Lavoie Ave (04756-1315)
PHONE..................................207 728-6260
Susan Violette, *Principal*
EMP: 3
SALES (est): 217.9K **Privately Held**
SIC: 2411 Logging

(G-6401)
ROUSSEL LOGGING INC
386 11th Ave (04756-3009)
P.O. Box 197 (04756-0197)
PHONE..................................207 728-3250
EMP: 3
SALES (est): 309.2K **Privately Held**
SIC: 2411 Logging

(G-6402)
TWIN RIVERS PAPER COMPANY CORP
82 Bridge Ave (04756-1229)
PHONE..................................207 523-2350
Timothy Lowe, *CEO*
John Fuller, *COO*
John Reichert, *COO*
Jean-Pierre Grenon, *Vice Pres*
Gary Curtis, *Plant Mgr*
EMP: 667
SALES (est): 164.5MM **Privately Held**
SIC: 2621 Paper Mill

(G-6403)
TWIN RIVERS PAPER COMPANY LLC (PA)
82 Bridge Ave (04756-1229)
PHONE..................................207 728-3321
Ken Winterhalter, *CEO*
Steve Collard, *Vice Pres*
Michelle Morneault, *Production*
Linda Daigle, *Purch Mgr*
Stacey Bouchard, *Purchasing*
◆ **EMP:** 40
SALES (est): 320.7MM **Privately Held**
SIC: 2621 Paper Mill

Madison
Somerset County

(G-6404)
BURGER-ROY INC
Also Called: Agway
66 Main St (04950-1223)
PHONE..................................207 696-3978
Brent Burger, *President*
EMP: 51
SQ FT: 600
SALES: 6.9MM **Privately Held**
WEB: www.burger-roy.com
SIC: 2511 5261 Mfg Wood Household Furniture Ret Nursery/Garden Supplies

(G-6405)
LAKEWOOD LOGGING INC
132 Lakewood Rd (04950-3012)
PHONE..................................207 431-4052
Travis W Stratton, *Principal*
EMP: 3 **EST:** 2012
SALES (est): 185.4K **Privately Held**
SIC: 2411 Logging

GEOGRAPHIC

(G-6406)
MAINE CEDAR HOT TUBS INC
Wesserunsett Rd (04950)
P.O. Box 689, Skowhegan (04976-0689)
PHONE..................................207 474-0953
Steven Meisner, *President*
Stephen Meisner, *Treasurer*
EMP: 6
SQ FT: 5,000
SALES (est): 750K **Privately Held**
SIC: 3999 Mfg Cedar Hot Tubs

(G-6407)
TR DILLON LOGGING INC
144 Main St (04950-1523)
P.O. Box 296, Anson (04911-0296)
PHONE..................................207 696-8137
Scott Dillon, *Principal*
EMP: 13
SALES (est): 1.9MM **Privately Held**
SIC: 2411 Logging

Manchester
Kennebec County

(G-6408)
COMPOSIMOLD
903 Western Ave (04351-3533)
PHONE..................................888 281-2674
EMP: 3
SALES (est): 233.7K **Privately Held**
SIC: 3089 Mfg Plastic Products

(G-6409)
D R DESIGNS INC
980 Western Ave (04351-3406)
PHONE..................................207 622-3303
Rachel Bernier, *CEO*
EMP: 8
SALES: 450K **Privately Held**
SIC: 2395 2759 5999 Pleating/Stitching Services Commercial Printing Ret Misc Merchandise

(G-6410)
J S WHOLESALE FUELS
867 Western Ave (04351-3532)
PHONE..................................207 622-4332
John Babb Jr, *Owner*
EMP: 5
SALES (est): 334.8K **Privately Held**
SIC: 2869 Mfg Industrial Organic Chemicals

Mapleton
Aroostook County

(G-6411)
FLAGSTONE INC
235 Griffin Ridge Rd (04757-4405)
PHONE..................................207 227-5883
Victor Winslow, *Owner*
EMP: 3
SALES (est): 153.9K **Privately Held**
SIC: 3281 Mfg Cut Stone/Products

(G-6412)
G J LOGGING
1561 State Rd (04757-4006)
PHONE..................................207 764-3826
Garth Johnston, *Owner*
EMP: 3
SALES (est): 23.6K **Privately Held**
SIC: 2411 Logging

(G-6413)
JMK LOGGING LLC
555 Pulcifur Rd (04757-4310)
PHONE..................................207 227-2964
EMP: 6
SALES (est): 463.5K **Privately Held**
SIC: 2411 Logging

Mars Hill
Aroostook County

(G-6414)
HANTS WHITE LLC
24 E Ridge Rd (04758-3422)
P.O. Box 185 (04758-0185)
PHONE..................................207 429-9786
Dean Lawrence,
Martha Lawrence,
EMP: 4
SALES (est): 210.4K **Privately Held**
WEB: www.hantswhite.com
SIC: 3069 Manufacturing And Sales Foot Corrector

Masardis
Aroostook County

(G-6415)
DAAQUAM LUMBER MAINE INC (HQ)
1203 Aroostook Scenic Hwy (04732)
P.O. Box 749, Ashland (04732-0749)
PHONE..................................207 435-6401
Patrick Labonte, *Director*
▲ **EMP:** 132 **EST:** 1979
SQ FT: 50,000
SALES (est): 17.2MM
SALES (corp-wide): 118.3MM **Privately Held**
SIC: 2421 Sawmill/Planing Mill
PA: Groupe Lebel Inc
54 Rue Amyot
Riviere-Du-Loup QC G5R 3
877 567-5910

Mattawamkeag
Penobscot County

(G-6416)
WAYNE PETERS PHILL
24 Medway Rd (04459-3128)
PHONE..................................207 736-4191
Wayne Peters, *Principal*
EMP: 4
SALES (est): 500.5K **Privately Held**
SIC: 2411 Logging

Mechanic Falls
Androscoggin County

(G-6417)
AUBURN MANUFACTURING INC
5125 Walker Rd (04256)
P.O. Box 220 (04256-0220)
PHONE..................................207 345-8271
Kathie Leonard, *President*
EMP: 50
SALES (corp-wide): 14.8MM **Privately Held**
WEB: www.auburnmfg.com
SIC: 2262 Mfg High Temperature Textiles
PA: Auburn Manufacturing Incorporated
34 Walker Rd
Mechanic Falls ME 04256
207 345-8271

(G-6418)
AUBURN MANUFACTURING INC (PA)
34 Walker Rd (04256-5340)
P.O. Box 220 (04256-0220)
PHONE..................................207 345-8271
Kathie M Leonard, *President*
▲ **EMP:** 30 **EST:** 1979
SQ FT: 60,000
SALES (est): 14.8MM **Privately Held**
WEB: www.auburnmfg.com
SIC: 2262 2298 2295 2241 Manmade Fabric Fnshg Plt Mfg Cordage/Twine Mfg Coated Fabrics Narrow Fabric Mill Manmad Brdwv Fabric Mill

(G-6419)
DOWNEAST MACHINE & ENGRG INC
Also Called: Deme
26 Maple St (04256-6113)
PHONE..................................207 345-8111
Keith Beaule, *President*
Steve Hussey, *Vice Pres*
Michael Hamlyn, *Treasurer*
EMP: 17
SQ FT: 25,000
SALES (est): 5.2MM **Privately Held**
SIC: 3553 5084 Mfg Woodworking Machinery Whol Industrial Equipment

(G-6420)
ILLINOIS TOOL WORKS INC
Electro Static Technology
31 Winterbrook Rd (04256-5724)
PHONE..................................207 998-5140
William OH, *General Mgr*
EMP: 45
SALES (corp-wide): 14.7B **Publicly Held**
SIC: 3629 3829 3625 Mfg Electrical Industrial Apparatus Mfg Measuring/Controlling Devices Mfg Relays/Industrial Controls
PA: Illinois Tool Works Inc.
155 Harlem Ave
Glenview IL 60025
847 724-7500

(G-6421)
MAINE WOOD TREATERS INC
58 Walker Rd (04256-5340)
PHONE..................................207 345-8411
Harold Bumby, *President*
EMP: 30
SQ FT: 33,710
SALES (est): 8.5MM **Privately Held**
SIC: 2491 Wood Preserving

Medford
Piscataquis County

(G-6422)
DEWITT MACHINE & FABRICATION
1152 Medford Center Rd (04463-6208)
PHONE..................................207 732-3530
Keith Dewitt, *President*
EMP: 7
SQ FT: 80,000
SALES: 300K **Privately Held**
SIC: 3599 Mfg Industrial Machinery

Medway
Penobscot County

(G-6423)
DAYS AUTO BODY INC
Also Called: Day's Welding
16 Main Rd (04460-3133)
P.O. Box 396 (04460-0396)
PHONE..................................207 746-5310
Richard Day, *President*
EMP: 9
SALES (est): 570K **Privately Held**
SIC: 7692 7539 1542 1711 Welding Repair & Machine Shop & General Contractor

(G-6424)
ELLEN MCLAUGHLIN
Rr 157 (04460)
P.O. Box 637 (04460-0637)
PHONE..................................207 746-3398
Jay McLaughlin, *Owner*
Ellen McLaughlin, *Principal*
EMP: 20
SALES (est): 1.4MM **Privately Held**
WEB: www.ellenmclaughlin.com
SIC: 2411 Logging

(G-6425)
H ARTHUR YORK LOGGING INC (PA)
157 Main Rd (04460-3131)
P.O. Box 89 (04460-0089)
PHONE..................................207 746-5883
Howard Arthur York, *President*
Wakine Tameous, *Treasurer*
EMP: 25
SALES (est): 2.1MM **Privately Held**
SIC: 2411 Logging Contractor

(G-6426)
H ARTHUR YORK LOGGING INC
163 Turnpike Rd (04460-3240)
PHONE..................................207 746-5912
Arthur York, *Principal*
EMP: 8
SALES (corp-wide): 2.1MM **Privately Held**
SIC: 2411 Logging
PA: H Arthur York Logging Inc
157 Main Rd
Medway ME 04460
207 746-5883

(G-6427)
SCOTTS COMPANY LLC
100 Nicatou Industrial Ln (04460-3022)
P.O. Box 90 (04460-0090)
PHONE..................................207 746-9033
Derek Maxwell, *Branch Mgr*
EMP: 15
SALES (corp-wide): 3.1B **Publicly Held**
WEB: www.scottscompany.com
SIC: 2873 Mfg Nitrogenous Fertilizers
HQ: The Scotts Company Llc
14111 Scottslawn Rd
Marysville OH 43040
937 644-0011

Mexico
Oxford County

(G-6428)
NICOLS BROTHERS LOGGING INC
197 Poplar Hill Rd (04257-3108)
P.O. Box 12 (04257-0012)
PHONE..................................207 364-8685
James Nicols, *President*
James Nicols Jr, *President*
Billy Joe Nicols, *Vice Pres*
EMP: 12
SALES (est): 1.5MM **Privately Held**
SIC: 2411 Logging

(G-6429)
RICH LOGGING
62 Richards Ave (04257-1829)
PHONE..................................207 357-7863
Anthony M Rich, *Principal*
EMP: 3 **EST:** 2010
SALES (est): 182.1K **Privately Held**
SIC: 2411 Logging

(G-6430)
WAUGHS MOUNTAINVIEW ELEC
246 Roxbury Rd (04257-1116)
P.O. Box 97, Rumford (04276-0097)
PHONE..................................207 545-2421
Bruce Waugh, *Principal*
EMP: 10
SQ FT: 6,000
SALES (est): 1.6MM **Privately Held**
SIC: 3699 Mfg Electrical Equipment/Supplies

Milbridge
Washington County

(G-6431)
CHERRY POINT PRODUCTS INC
54 Wyman Rd (04658-3608)
PHONE..................................207 546-0930
Drusilla Ray, *President*
Lawrence Ray, *Vice Pres*
EMP: 70
SALES: 3MM **Privately Held**
SIC: 2091 2099 Mfg Canned/Cured Fish/Seafood Mfg Food Preparations

(G-6432)
FREDERICK WIENINGER MONUMENTS
Also Called: Fred Wieninger & Son
178 Main St (04658-3514)
P.O. Box 182 (04658-0182)
PHONE..................................207 546-2356
Frederick Weininger, *Owner*
EMP: 3
SALES: 125K **Privately Held**
SIC: 3272 5999 1799 Mfg Concrete Products Ret Misc Merchandise Trade Contractor

(G-6433)
JASPER WYMAN & SON (PA)
280 Main St (04658)
PHONE..................................207 546-3800
Elizabeth Doudoumopoulos, *Ch of Bd*
Edward Flanagan, *President*
Frederick Robinson, *Research*
Margaret Norton, *Info Tech Mgr*
◆ **EMP:** 5 **EST:** 1874
SQ FT: 3,000
SALES (est): 18.8MM **Privately Held**
SIC: 2037 2033 Mfg Frozen Fruits/Vegetables Mfg Canned Fruits/Vegetables

(G-6434)
JASPER WYMAN & SON
7 Wyman Rd (04658-3600)
P.O. Box 100 (04658-0100)
PHONE..................................207 546-2311
Robert Mancini, *Vice Pres*
Shannon Fickett, *QA Dir*
Tom Gardner, *Manager*
Tom Hugill, *IT/INT Sup*
EMP: 6
SALES (corp-wide): 18.8MM **Privately Held**
SIC: 2033 2037 Mfg Canned Fruits/Vegetables Mfg Frozen Fruits/Vegetables
PA: Jasper Wyman & Son
280 Main St
Milbridge ME 04658
207 546-3800

(G-6435)
L RAY PACKING COMPANY
27 Wyman Rd (04658-3600)
PHONE..................................207 546-2355
Ivan H Ray, *President*
Arletta R Tucker, *Treasurer*
EMP: 7
SQ FT: 12,000
SALES (est): 796K **Privately Held**
SIC: 2091 Mfg Canned/Cured Fish/Seafood

Milford
Penobscot County

(G-6436)
MILFORD FUEL
240 Main Rd (04461-3242)
PHONE..................................207 827-2701
Francis Carlow, *Principal*
EMP: 3
SALES (est): 202K **Privately Held**
SIC: 2869 Mfg Industrial Organic Chemicals

(G-6437)
PENOBSCOT SAND GRAV STONE LLC
Also Called: Harriman Pit
392 Main Rd (04461-3246)
PHONE..................................207 827-2829
Theda Honnell, *Principal*
EMP: 3
SALES (est): 170.5K **Privately Held**
SIC: 1442 Construction Sand/Gravel

Millinocket
Penobscot County

(G-6438)
BEAR SWAMP POWER COMPANY LLC
1024 Central St (04462-2111)
PHONE..................................207 723-4341
Jerome Montpetit, *Director*
EMP: 14
SALES: 1,000K **Privately Held**
SIC: 3621 Motors And Generators, Nsk

(G-6439)
BEN JORDAN LOGGING LLC
21 Granite St (04462-1804)
PHONE..................................207 694-2011
Ben Jordan, *Principal*
EMP: 3
SALES (est): 248.1K **Privately Held**
SIC: 2411 Logging

(G-6440)
BROOKFIELD POWER NENG LLC
1024 Central St (04462-2111)
PHONE..................................207 723-4341
Brian Stetson, *Manager*
EMP: 5
SALES (est): 840K **Privately Held**
SIC: 3612 Mfg Transformers

(G-6441)
KATAHDIN REGIONAL DEV CORP
217 Penobscot Ave (04462-1430)
P.O. Box 1122 (04462-1122)
PHONE..................................207 447-6913
EMP: 3
SALES (est): 120.9K **Privately Held**
SIC: 2711 Newspapers-Publishing/Printing

(G-6442)
MAINE HERITAGE TIMBER LLC
Also Called: Timberchic
450 Golden Rd (04462)
P.O. Box 778 (04462-0778)
PHONE..................................207 723-9200
Thomas Shafer, *Mng Member*
EMP: 20
SQ FT: 10,000
SALES (est): 2.5MM **Privately Held**
SIC: 2499 Mfg Wood Products

(G-6443)
MILLINCKET FABRICATION MCH INC (PA)
432 Katahdin Ave (04462-1624)
PHONE..................................207 723-9733
Fred Lewis, *President*
Jeanine Farrington, *Buyer*
Richard Currier,
EMP: 21 **EST:** 1909
SQ FT: 40,000
SALES (est): 5.4MM **Privately Held**
SIC: 3312 3599 3321 3443 Blast Furnace-Steel Work Mfg Industrial Machinery Gray/Ductile Iron Fndry Mfg Fabricated Plate Wrk

(G-6444)
PELLETIER MANUFACTURING INC
400 Golden Rd (04462)
P.O. Box 859 (04462-0859)
PHONE..................................207 723-6500
Jeffrey Pelletier, *Mng Member*
EMP: 12
SQ FT: 25,000
SALES: 1MM **Privately Held**
SIC: 3715 Mfg Truck Trailers

Milo
Piscataquis County

(G-6445)
DICKS BAKING
351 Pleasant River Rd (04463-1804)
PHONE..................................207 284-3779
Richard Labree, *Owner*
EMP: 3
SALES: 55K **Privately Held**
SIC: 2051 3547 Mfg Bread/Related Products Mfg Rolling Mill Machinery

(G-6446)
JSI STORE FIXTURES INC (PA)
140 Park St (04463-1740)
P.O. Box 38 (04463-0038)
PHONE..................................207 943-5203
Terry Awalt, *CEO*
Mark Awalt, *Exec VP*
Paula St Laurent, *Controller*
▲ **EMP:** 190
SQ FT: 75,000
SALES (est): 85.8MM **Privately Held**
WEB: www.jsistorefixtures.com
SIC: 2541 2499 5046 2542 Mfg Wood Partitions/Fixt Mfg Wood Products Whol Commercial Equip Mfg Nonwd Partition/Fixt

(G-6447)
MILO CHIP LLC
29 High St (04463-1350)
PHONE..................................207 943-2682
Stanley Reed, *Principal*
EMP: 5
SALES (est): 390K **Privately Held**
SIC: 2676 Mfg Sanitary Paper Products

(G-6448)
STANCHFIELD FARMS
73 Medford Rd (04463-1515)
PHONE..................................207 943-2133
Wilma J Stanchfield, *Owner*
EMP: 3 **EST:** 1997
SALES: 125K **Privately Held**
WEB: www.stanchfieldfarms.com
SIC: 2035 Specialty Foods

Monmouth
Kennebec County

(G-6449)
MAINE HERITAGE WEAVERS
904 Main St (04259-7017)
P.O. Box 149 (04259-0149)
PHONE..................................207 933-2605
Linda Cloutier, *President*
Katie Cloutier, *Manager*
EMP: 18
SALES (est): 1.2MM **Privately Held**
SIC: 2211 Cotton Broadwoven Fabric Mill

(G-6450)
MID STATE SHEET METAL & WLDG
119 Packard Rd (04259-7410)
PHONE..................................207 933-5603
Dick Desrosiers, *Owner*
EMP: 3 **EST:** 1999
SQ FT: 3,000
SALES (est): 274.7K **Privately Held**
SIC: 3441 Structural Metal Fabrication

(G-6451)
STEVENS ELECTRIC PUMP SERVICE
18 Berry Rd (04259-7001)
P.O. Box 238 (04259-0238)
PHONE..................................207 933-2143
Timothy Stevens, *President*
Sandra Stevens, *Treasurer*
Cindy Stevens, *Admin Sec*
EMP: 9 **EST:** 2001
SALES: 100K **Privately Held**
SIC: 3561 Mfg Pumps/Pumping Equipment

Monson
Piscataquis County

(G-6452)
SHELDON SLATE PRODUCTS CO INC
38 Farm Quarry Rd (04464-7035)
P.O. Box 245 (04464-0245)
PHONE..................................207 997-3615
John Tatko, *Principal*
EMP: 12
SALES (est): 1.2MM **Privately Held**
SIC: 3281 Mfg Cut Stone/Products

Moose River
Somerset County

(G-6453)
MOOSE RIVER LUMBER COMPANY INC
25 Talpey Rd (04945-4016)
P.O. Box 454, Jackman (04945-0454)
PHONE..................................207 668-4426
Charles Lumbert, *President*
Jeff Defjardins, *Vice Pres*
Steve Banahan, *Sales Executive*
EMP: 75
SQ FT: 11,000
SALES: 34.6MM **Privately Held**
WEB: www.mooseriverlumber.com
SIC: 2421 Sawmill/Planing Mill

Morrill
Waldo County

(G-6454)
INNOVASEA SYSTEMS INC
52 S Main St (04952-5104)
PHONE..................................207 322-3219
David Kelly, *CEO*
EMP: 7
SALES (corp-wide): 10MM **Privately Held**
SIC: 3523 Mfg Farm Machinery/Equipment
PA: Innovasea Systems, Inc.
266 Summer St Fl 2
Boston MA 02210
207 322-3219

(G-6455)
METAPHOR BRONZE TILEWORKS LLC
245 S Main St (04952-5200)
P.O. Box 176, Belfast (04915-0176)
PHONE..................................207 342-2597
Jay Gibson,
EMP: 4
SALES (est): 497.4K **Privately Held**
SIC: 3449 Mfg Misc Structural Metalwork

(G-6456)
OCEAN FARM TECHNOLOGIES INC
52 S Main St (04952-5104)
PHONE..................................207 322-4322
EMP: 9
SALES (est): 820K **Privately Held**
WEB: www.oceanfarmtech.com
SIC: 3523 Mfg Equipment

Mount Desert
Hancock County

(G-6457)
TRACY JOSEPH WOODWORKS
Rr 102 Box 447 (04660)
PHONE..................................207 244-0004
Joseph Tracy, *Owner*
EMP: 3
SALES (est): 186.5K **Privately Held**
SIC: 2511 Wood Household Furniture, Nsk

Mount Vernon
Kennebec County

(G-6458)
EDGAR CLARK & SONS PALLET INC
Also Called: Clark Pallet
1495 Pond Rd (04352-3511)
P.O. Box 218, Readfield (04355-0218)
PHONE..................................207 685-3888
Donald Clark, *President*
Mandi Clark, *Vice Pres*

GEOGRAPHIC

EMP: 3
SALES: 500K **Privately Held**
SIC: 2448 Mfg Wood Pallets/Skids

(G-6459)
JC MILLWORK INC
191 Cottle Hill Rd (04352-3741)
PHONE..................................207 293-4204
James S Clough, *President*
Jessie Clough, *Vice Pres*
EMP: 4
SQ FT: 10,000
SALES (est): 605K **Privately Held**
SIC: 2431 Commercial Cabinets & Arch Woodwork

Naples
Cumberland County

(G-6460)
GERRISH GLOBAL INDUSTRIES LLC
90 Pleasant View Dr (04055-3449)
P.O. Box 1154 (04055-1154)
PHONE..................................207 595-2150
EMP: 3 **EST:** 2012
SALES (est): 200.7K **Privately Held**
SIC: 3999 Mfg Misc Products

(G-6461)
GREAT NORTHERN DOCKS INC (PA)
1114 Roosevelt Trl (04055-3137)
P.O. Box 1615 (04055-1615)
PHONE..................................207 693-3770
Sam Merriam, *President*
Fremont Merriam, *Shareholder*
EMP: 9
SQ FT: 9,500
SALES: 1.8MM **Privately Held**
WEB: www.greatnortherndocks.com
SIC: 3448 Mfg Prefabricated Metal Buildings

New Canada
Aroostook County

(G-6462)
CB LOGGING
194 Fox Rd (04743-3027)
PHONE..................................207 231-4952
Cole Bernier, *Principal*
EMP: 6
SALES (est): 481.9K **Privately Held**
SIC: 2411 Logging

(G-6463)
ROBERT DAIGLE & SONS INC
603 New Canada Rd (04743-3007)
PHONE..................................207 834-3676
Robert Daigle, *Owner*
EMP: 6 **EST:** 2001
SALES (est): 663.8K **Privately Held**
SIC: 2411 Logging

New Gloucester
Cumberland County

(G-6464)
BELANGER WELDING & FABRICATION
118 Sabbathday Rd (04260-2654)
PHONE..................................207 657-5558
Norman Belanger, *President*
Ruth Belanger, *Treasurer*
EMP: 5
SQ FT: 7,000
SALES (est): 601.8K **Privately Held**
SIC: 3441 Welding Repair

(G-6465)
CAD MANAGEMENT RESOURCES INC
Also Called: Cadmanage
60 Pineland Dr Ste 107 (04260-5124)
PHONE..................................207 221-2911
Clinton Champman, *President*
Stephen Crandall, *Treasurer*
Steve Crandall, *Treasurer*
Loretta Mattor, *Analyst*
EMP: 6
SQ FT: 1,580
SALES (est): 517K **Privately Held**
WEB: www.cadmanage.com
SIC: 3571 8748 Mfg Electronic Computers Business Consulting Services

(G-6466)
GREENSTONE PRECAST
1 Oz Dr (04260-2677)
PHONE..................................207 926-5704
Jim Duhamel, *CEO*
EMP: 3
SALES (est): 336.4K **Privately Held**
SIC: 3272 Mfg Concrete Products

(G-6467)
HOTHAM & SONS LUMBER INC
Town Farm Rd (04260)
PHONE..................................207 926-4231
William Hotham, *Owner*
EMP: 3
SALES (est): 260.8K **Privately Held**
SIC: 2421 Custom Sawmill

(G-6468)
JF HUTCHINSON CO
Also Called: Jim's Metal Fabrication
616b Lewiston Rd (04260-4003)
P.O. Box 175 (04260-0175)
PHONE..................................207 926-3676
James Hutchinson, *President*
EMP: 10
SALES: 850K **Privately Held**
SIC: 3441 Mfg Misc Fabricated Metal Products

(G-6469)
MCCANN FABRICATION
1027 Lewiston Rd (04260-3412)
P.O. Box 169 (04260-0169)
PHONE..................................207 926-4118
Dick McCann, *President*
EMP: 30
SQ FT: 22,000
SALES (est): 7.1MM **Privately Held**
WEB: www.mccannfabrication.com
SIC: 3441 Structural Metal Fabrication

(G-6470)
PINE LAND FARM CHEESE FACTORY
92 Creamery Ln (04260-4460)
PHONE..................................207 688-6400
EMP: 9
SALES (est): 52.5K **Privately Held**
SIC: 2022 Mfg Cheese

(G-6471)
QUARTER POINT WOODWORKING LLC (PA)
483 Intervale Rd (04260-3647)
PHONE..................................207 926-1032
Bob Small, *Principal*
EMP: 3 **EST:** 2013
SALES (est): 456.5K **Privately Held**
SIC: 2431 Mfg Millwork

(G-6472)
SUN DIAGNOSTICS LLC
60 Pinelnd Dr Auburn Hl (04260)
PHONE..................................207 926-1125
Kwok Yeung, *CEO*
John Contois, *President*
EMP: 8
SALES (est): 1MM **Privately Held**
SIC: 2835 Mfg Diagnostic Substances

(G-6473)
THERMAL FAB INC
405 Tobey Rd (04260-3049)
PHONE..................................207 926-5212
Jeffrey Hunnwell, *President*
Marie Hunnwell, *Treasurer*
EMP: 5
SALES: 400K **Privately Held**
SIC: 3441 Structural Metal Fabrication

New Portland
Somerset County

(G-6474)
JUSTIN JORDAN
Also Called: Jr Fabrication
92 River Rd (04961)
PHONE..................................207 628-4123
Justin Jordan, *Owner*
EMP: 3
SALES (est): 270.3K **Privately Held**
SIC: 3599 Mfg Industrial Machinery

(G-6475)
USACCESS INC
57 Lemon Stream Rd (04961-3800)
PHONE..................................207 541-9421
Kevin B Pomerleau, *President*
Teresa Pomerleau, *Vice Pres*
EMP: 3
SALES (est): 347.5K **Privately Held**
SIC: 2421 Sawmill/Planing Mill

New Sharon
Franklin County

(G-6476)
IMELDAS FABRICS & DESIGNS
5 Starks Rd (04955-3314)
PHONE..................................207 778-0665
Janet Kennedy, *Principal*
EMP: 5 **EST:** 2007
SALES (est): 476.7K **Privately Held**
SIC: 2321 2331 2369 5137 Mfg Men/Boys Furnishings Mfg Women/Misses Blouses Mfg Girl/Child Outerwear Whol Women/Child Clothng

(G-6477)
INTERROTECH
57 Main St (04955-3401)
P.O. Box 128, Farmington (04938-0128)
PHONE..................................207 778-4907
Gary Sweatt, *Owner*
EMP: 5
SALES: 200K **Privately Held**
SIC: 3449 Mfg Misc Structural Metalwork

(G-6478)
LIVING ACRES LLC
251 Weeks Mills Rd (04955-3125)
PHONE..................................207 778-2390
Tony Ramsey, *Mng Member*
EMP: 4
SALES (est): 224.5K **Privately Held**
WEB: www.livingacres.com
SIC: 2873 Mfg Nitrogenous Fertilizers

(G-6479)
YORK HILL FARM
257 York Hill Rd (04955-3732)
PHONE..................................207 778-9741
John F Duncan, *Partner*
Penny Duncan, *Partner*
EMP: 5
SQ FT: 3,000
SALES: 75K **Privately Held**
SIC: 2022 Mfg Goat Milk Cheese

Newburgh
Penobscot County

(G-6480)
REGINOLD D RICKER
3222 Western Ave (04444-4762)
PHONE..................................207 234-4811
Reginold D Ricker, *Principal*
EMP: 3
SALES (est): 196.7K **Privately Held**
SIC: 2411 Logging

(G-6481)
WHITCOMBS FOREST HARVESTING
440 Chapman Rd (04444-5159)
PHONE..................................207 234-2351
Lawrence W Whitcomb, *President*
Terrance L Whitcomb, *Vice Pres*
Lois Whitcomb, *Treasurer*
EMP: 4
SALES (est): 387.5K **Privately Held**
SIC: 2411 Logging

Newcastle
Lincoln County

(G-6482)
EXACT DISPENSING SYSTEMS
1130 Route 1 (04553-3956)
PHONE..................................207 563-2299
Chris Conary, *Principal*
EMP: 7
SALES (est): 1.1MM **Privately Held**
SIC: 2891 Mfg Adhesives/Sealants

(G-6483)
LINCOLN COUNTY PUBLISHING CO
Also Called: Lincoln County News
116 Mills Rd (04553-3408)
P.O. Box 36, Damariscotta (04543-0036)
PHONE..................................207 563-3171
Christopher Roberts, *President*
EMP: 30
SALES (est): 2.6MM **Privately Held**
WEB: www.mainelincolncountynews.com
SIC: 2752 2711 Lithographic Commercial Printing Newspapers-Publishing/Printing

(G-6484)
MAINE INDUSTRIAL P & R CORP
21 Teague St (04553)
P.O. Box 381 (04553-0381)
PHONE..................................207 563-5532
Henry G Lee, *President*
Katherine C Lee, *Treasurer*
EMP: 7
SALES (est): 1.5MM **Privately Held**
WEB: www.miprcorp.com
SIC: 3069 Mfg Fabricated Rubber Products

Newport
Penobscot County

(G-6485)
NEWPORT INDUS FABRICATION INC
445 Elm St (04953-3311)
P.O. Box D (04953-0423)
PHONE..................................207 368-4344
Daniel Gerry, *President*
Bud Neale, *Purchasing*
Adam Guiggey, *QC Mgr*
Ryan Gerry, *Engineer*
Ray Lawrence, *Manager*
EMP: 37 **EST:** 1997
SQ FT: 31,000
SALES (est): 12.1MM **Privately Held**
WEB: www.nif-inc.com
SIC: 3441 Structural Metal Fabrication

(G-6486)
ROLLING THUNDER PRESS INC
Also Called: Rolling Thunder Express
134a Main St (04953-3105)
P.O. Box 480 (04953-0480)
PHONE..................................207 368-2028
Sylvia Angel, *President*
EMP: 9
SALES (est): 465.2K **Privately Held**
SIC: 2711 Newspapers-Publishing/Printing

(G-6487)
TW CLARK PULP & LOGGING LLC
Also Called: Clark's
607 Elm St (04953-3403)
PHONE..................................207 368-4766
Andrea Clark, *Owner*
EMP: 6 **EST:** 2013
SALES (est): 601.8K **Privately Held**
SIC: 2411 Logging

(G-6488)
VIC FIRTH COMPANY
77 High St (04953-3028)
PHONE..................................207 368-4358
Vic Firth, *Principal*
Brittni Reed, *Accountant*
EMP: 5
SALES (corp-wide): 8.1MM **Privately Held**
SIC: 2426 Hardwood Dimension/Floor Mill
PA: Vic Firth Company
22 Longwater Dr
Norwell MA 02061
617 364-6869

(G-6489)
VIC FIRTH MANUFACTURING INC
Also Called: Vic Firth Gourmet
77 High St (04953-3028)
PHONE..................................207 368-4358
Vic Firth, *CEO*
Mark Davenport, *Purch Mgr*
Merle E Wood, *CFO*
Tracy K Firth, *Treasurer*
▲ **EMP:** 115
SALES (est): 15.4MM **Privately Held**
WEB: www.vicfirthgourmet.com
SIC: 2426 Hardwood Dimension And Flooring Mills,Nsk

Newry
Oxford County

(G-6490)
ENVIRONMENTAL ENERGY & FINANCE
20 Walters Way (04261)
PHONE..................................978 807-0027
Richard Stone, *Principal*
EMP: 12
SALES: 950K **Privately Held**
SIC: 3569 Mfg General Industrial Machinery

(G-6491)
LESLIE W ROBERTSON
Also Called: Robertson Frm Log Land Claring
494 Bear River Rd (04261-3834)
PHONE..................................207 824-2764
Leslie Robertson, *Principal*
EMP: 3 **EST:** 2010
SALES (est): 203K **Privately Held**
SIC: 2411 Logging

Nobleboro
Lincoln County

(G-6492)
COASTAL WOODWORKING INC
Also Called: Coastal Woodworks & Display
16 Sand Hill Dr (04555-9051)
P.O. Box 137 (04555-0137)
PHONE..................................207 563-1072
Charles Agnew, *President*
EMP: 20
SQ FT: 13,000
SALES (est): 2.2MM **Privately Held**
WEB: www.coastalwoodworks.com
SIC: 2499 2431 Mfg Wood Products Mfg Millwork

(G-6493)
NS DESIGN
134 Back Meadow Rd (04555-9200)
PHONE..................................207 563-7705
Ned Steinberger, *Owner*
Neds Steinberger, *Owner*
▲ **EMP:** 6
SALES (est): 414.2K **Privately Held**
SIC: 3931 Mfg Musical Instruments

Norridgewock
Somerset County

(G-6494)
ALLAGASH GUIDE INC
292 River Rd (04957-3432)
PHONE..................................207 634-3748
Blaine Miller, *President*
Blaine R Miller, *Master*
EMP: 3
SALES (est): 189.3K **Privately Held**
WEB: www.allagashguide.com
SIC: 2741 Misc Publishing

(G-6495)
BERRY LOGGING/R A BERRY & SONS
24 Maple St (04957-3434)
PHONE..................................207 634-4808
Ed Berry, *Principal*
EMP: 3
SALES (est): 236.8K **Privately Held**
SIC: 2411 Logging

(G-6496)
CROOKED FACE CREAMERY LLC
552 River Rd (04957-3424)
P.O. Box 1134, Skowhegan (04976-7834)
PHONE..................................207 858-5096
Amy Rowbottom,
EMP: 4 **EST:** 2012
SALES (est): 201.4K **Privately Held**
SIC: 2022 Mfg Cheese

(G-6497)
JACKMAN EQUIPMENT
Also Called: Canadian Chains
617 Skowhegan Rd (04957-3334)
P.O. Box 861, Farmington (04938-0861)
PHONE..................................207 858-0690
Lyn Turner, *Manager*
EMP: 3
SALES (est): 352K
SALES (corp-wide): 1.7MM **Privately Held**
SIC: 3462 Mfg Iron/Steel Forgings
PA: Jackman Equipment
Rr 201
Jackman ME 04945
207 668-4177

(G-6498)
MAINELY MAPLE LLC
165 Burrill Hill Rd (04957-3323)
PHONE..................................207 634-3073
EMP: 3 **EST:** 2011
SALES (est): 70K **Privately Held**
SIC: 2099 Mfg Food Preparations

(G-6499)
NEW BALANCE ATHLETICS INC
20 Depot St (04957-3952)
PHONE..................................207 634-3033
Jeff Williams, *Manager*
EMP: 340
SALES (corp-wide): 3.2B **Privately Held**
SIC: 3149 3144 3143 3021 Mfg Footwear-Ex Rubber Mfg Women's Footwear Mfg Men's Footwear Mfg Rubber/Plstc Ftwear
HQ: New Balance Athletics, Inc.
100 Guest St Fl 5
Boston MA 02135
617 783-4000

North Anson
Somerset County

(G-6500)
COUSINEAU WOOD PRODUCTS ME LLC
3 Valley Rd (04958-7208)
P.O. Box 58 (04958-0058)
PHONE..................................207 635-4445
Curt Richmond, *General Mgr*
Randal Cousineau,
Brody Cousineau,
EMP: 17
SALES (est): 3.9MM **Privately Held**
WEB: www.cousineaus.com
SIC: 2421 Sawmill/Planing Mill

(G-6501)
FROST CEDAR PRODUCTS INC
Fahi Pond Rd (04958)
PHONE..................................207 566-5912
R Frank Frost, *President*
Debra S Frost, *Corp Secy*
EMP: 8
SALES (est): 1MM **Privately Held**
SIC: 2499 Mfg Cedar Rails Post & Cedar Fencing

(G-6502)
GLENN S VILES & SONS INC
Elm St (04958)
P.O. Box 135 (04958-0135)
PHONE..................................207 635-2493
Glenn S Viles, *President*
EMP: 5
SALES (est): 430K **Privately Held**
SIC: 2411 Logging

(G-6503)
KANGAS INC
51 New Portland Rd (04958)
P.O. Box 616 (04958-0616)
PHONE..................................207 635-3745
Pete Kangas, *President*
Erik Kangas, *COO*
EMP: 8
SQ FT: 1,200
SALES (est): 744K **Privately Held**
SIC: 2499 Mfg Wood Products

(G-6504)
MATTINGLY PRODUCTS COMPANY
25 Folon Rd (04958)
P.O. Box 105 (04958-0105)
PHONE..................................207 635-2719
Philip Mattingly, *President*
EMP: 31
SALES (est): 3.5MM **Privately Held**
SIC: 3273 3272 2951 Mfg Ready-Mixed Concrete Mfg Concrete Products Mfg Asphalt Mixtures/Blocks

North Berwick
York County

(G-6505)
CARPE DIEM COFFEE ROASTING CO
150 Wells St (03906-6745)
P.O. Box 547 (03906-0547)
PHONE..................................207 676-2233
Jane McLaughlin, *President*
Augusta Vonwellshiem, *Vice Pres*
EMP: 6
SQ FT: 1,600
SALES (est): 551.2K **Privately Held**
WEB: www.carpediemcoffee.com
SIC: 2095 5149 Mfg Roasted Coffee Whol Groceries

(G-6506)
HUSSEY CORPORATION (PA)
Also Called: Hussey Seating Co
38 Dyer St Ext (03906-6763)
PHONE..................................207 676-2271
Tim Hussey, *President*
Shannon Benedix, *Partner*
Thomas Hussey, *Partner*
Garri Marill, *Vice Pres*
Todd M Pierce, *Vice Pres*
◆ **EMP:** 196
SQ FT: 12,000
SALES (est): 67.2MM **Privately Held**
SIC: 2531 Mfg Public Building Furniture

(G-6507)
HUSSEY SEATING COMPANY
38 Dyer St Ext (03906-6763)
PHONE..................................207 676-2271
Timothy B Hussey, *President*
Todd Pierce, *Vice Pres*
Gary Merrill, *CFO*
Jack Rogers, *VP Sales*
◆ **EMP:** 260 **EST:** 1835
SQ FT: 200,000
SALES (est): 26.4MM
SALES (corp-wide): 67.2MM **Privately Held**
WEB: www.husseyseating.com
SIC: 2531 Mfg Public Building Furn
PA: Hussey Corporation
38 Dyer St Ext
North Berwick ME 03906
207 676-2271

(G-6508)
J B J MACHINE COMPANY INC
12 Elm St (03906-6725)
P.O. Box 640 (03906-0640)
PHONE..................................207 676-3380
John Doiron, *President*
EMP: 7
SALES (est): 1.1MM **Privately Held**
SIC: 3599 Mfg Industrial Machinery

(G-6509)
MCWILLIAMS INC
Also Called: Eastcoast Bio
211 Wells St Ste 1 (03906-6706)
P.O. Box 489 (03906-0489)
PHONE..................................207 676-7639
Clark L McDermith, *President*
Sharolyn W McDermith, *Vice Pres*
EMP: 6
SQ FT: 6,000
SALES (est): 1.1MM **Privately Held**
WEB: www.eastcoastbio.com
SIC: 2836 5122 Mfg Biological Products Whol Drugs/Sundries

(G-6510)
PRATT & WHITNEY ENGINE SVCS
Also Called: United Technologies Corp
113 Wells St (03906-6751)
PHONE..................................207 676-4100
Peter Borgel, *General Mgr*
Todd Lapierre, *Design Engr*
Bob Pfeiffenberger, *Info Tech Mgr*
David Cote, *Technical Staff*
EMP: 450
SALES (corp-wide): 66.5B **Publicly Held**
SIC: 3724 Mfg Aircraft Engines/Parts
HQ: Pratt & Whitney Engine Services, Inc.
1525 Midway Park Rd
Bridgeport WV 26330
304 842-5421

North Haven
Knox County

(G-6511)
J O BROWN & SON INC
Also Called: Brown Shop
1 Main St (04853)
P.O. Box 525 (04853-0525)
PHONE..................................207 867-4621
Foy Brown, *President*
Karen Cooper, *Treasurer*
EMP: 7 **EST:** 1888
SQ FT: 3,600
SALES (est): 792.5K **Privately Held**
SIC: 3732 5551 4493 7538 Boatbuilding/Repairing Ret Boats Marina Operation General Auto Repair

North Monmouth
Kennebec County

(G-6512)
TEX-TECH INDUSTRIES INC
105 N Main St (04265-6222)
PHONE..................................207 933-4404
Ciaran Lynch, *Ch of Bd*
Stephen Bero, *IT/INT Sup*
Eoin Lynch, *Director*
Pat Baril, *Clerk*
EMP: 140
SALES (corp-wide): 62.9MM **Privately Held**
SIC: 2221 Manmade Broadwoven Fabric Mill
PA: Tex-Tech Industries, Inc.
1 City Ctr Ste 11
Portland ME 04101
207 756-8606

GEOGRAPHIC

North Sullivan
Hancock County

(G-6513)
JEROME MARTIN PAUL
Also Called: No 7 Sand & Gravel
12 Martin Rd (04664-3715)
PHONE..................................207 422-3965
Paul J Martin, *Principal*
EMP: 3
SALES (est): 167.1K **Privately Held**
SIC: 1442 Construction Sand/Gravel

(G-6514)
LUNAFORM LLC
66 Cedar Ln (04664)
P.O. Box 189 (04664-0189)
PHONE..................................207 422-3306
Phid Lawless,
Dan Farrenkopf,
EMP: 8
SQ FT: 6,160
SALES (est): 550K **Privately Held**
WEB: www.lunaform.com
SIC: 3272 Mfg Garden Pottery

North Turner
Androscoggin County

(G-6515)
K L MASON & SONS INC
Rr 4 (04266)
P.O. Box 655 (04266-0655)
PHONE..................................207 224-7628
EMP: 3 **EST:** 2001
SALES (est): 230K **Privately Held**
SIC: 2421 Sawmill/Planing Mill

North Yarmouth
Cumberland County

(G-6516)
DANNY BOY FISHERIES INC
628 New Gloucester Rd (04097-6738)
PHONE..................................207 829-6622
Brian Pearce, *President*
EMP: 4
SQ FT: 2,000
SALES (est): 253.6K **Privately Held**
SIC: 2092 Mfg Fresh/Frozen Packaged Fish

(G-6517)
MAINE CLEANERS SUPPLY INC
Also Called: O'Neil Company, The
143 Cumberland Rd (04097-6557)
PHONE..................................207 657-3166
Raymond Giandrea, *President*
Heather Giandrea, *Principal*
EMP: 5 **EST:** 2013
SALES (est): 413.9K **Privately Held**
SIC: 2842 2676 2673 5087 Mfg Polish/Sanitation Gd Mfg Sanitary Paper Prdts Mfg Plstc/Coat Paper Bag Whol Svc Estblshmt Equip Mfg Misc Fab Wire Prdts

(G-6518)
MAINE POST & BEAM LLC
1274 North Rd (04097-6706)
P.O. Box 913, Yarmouth (04096-1913)
PHONE..................................207 751-6793
Brett Hellstedt, *Principal*
EMP: 4 **EST:** 2013
SALES (est): 280K **Privately Held**
SIC: 2421 Sawmill/Planing Mill

(G-6519)
STEAM TURBINE SERVICES
34 Fieldstone Dr (04097-6746)
PHONE..................................207 272-8664
EMP: 3
SALES (est): 118.7K **Privately Held**
SIC: 3511 Mfg Turbines/Generator Sets

Northport
Waldo County

(G-6520)
ATLANTIC BLANKET COMPANY INC
Also Called: Swans Island
231 Atlantic Hwy (04849-3004)
PHONE..................................207 338-9691
William Laurita, *President*
Scott McCormac, *General Mgr*
Claudia Wilcox, *Admin Asst*
EMP: 23
SALES (est): 2.3MM **Privately Held**
SIC: 2231 Mfg And Sell Blankets & Yarns

Norway
Oxford County

(G-6521)
ADVERTISER-DEMOCRAT
220 Main St Ste 1 (04268-5959)
P.O. Box 269 (04268-0269)
PHONE..................................207 743-7011
Howard A James, *President*
Jackie Roberge, *Principal*
EMP: 8
SALES (est): 218.7K
SALES (corp-wide): 2.2MM **Privately Held**
WEB: www.advertiserdemocrat.com
SIC: 2711 Newspaper Publishing
PA: James Newspapers, Inc
1 Pikes Hl
Norway ME 04268
207 743-7011

(G-6522)
INNOVTIVE MCHNING SLUTIONS INC
15 Ayer Dr (04268-4336)
PHONE..................................207 515-2033
David Moxcey, *President*
Seth Madore, *Vice Pres*
EMP: 5
SQ FT: 832
SALES: 300K **Privately Held**
SIC: 3599 Mfg Industrial Machinery

(G-6523)
JAMES NEWSPAPERS INC (PA)
Also Called: The Rumford Falls Times
1 Pikes Hl (04268-4350)
PHONE..................................207 743-7011
Howard A James, *President*
EMP: 36 **EST:** 1976
SQ FT: 7,000
SALES (est): 2.2MM **Privately Held**
WEB: www.finestsigns.com
SIC: 2711 Newspapers-Publishing/Printing & Mfg Signs & Website Hosting/Development & Digital Imaging

(G-6524)
NORTHEAST TOOL & DIE CO INC
16 Aldrich Ave (04268-5711)
P.O. Box 28 (04268-0028)
PHONE..................................207 743-7273
Arthur Lowe, *President*
Eric Adams, *Vice Pres*
Bruce Rood, *Admin Sec*
EMP: 6
SQ FT: 6,000
SALES (est): 915.3K **Privately Held**
WEB: www.northeasttool.com
SIC: 3544 3469 Mfg Dies/Tools/Jigs/Fixtures Mfg Metal Stampings

(G-6525)
SRODS LLC
30 Fair St (04268-5626)
PHONE..................................207 743-6194
Steve Rodrick, *Mng Member*
EMP: 12
SALES (est): 750K **Privately Held**
SIC: 2099 Mfg Food Preparations

(G-6526)
T R & H INC
186 Ashton Rd (04268-4853)
PHONE..................................207 743-8981
Bruce Skinner, *President*
Robert L Richardson, *President*
George W Tibbets, *Treasurer*
Elizabeth R Tibbetts, *Admin Sec*
EMP: 3 **EST:** 1965
SQ FT: 2,500
SALES: 130.4K **Privately Held**
SIC: 3599 Machine Shop

Oakfield
Aroostook County

(G-6527)
KATAHDIN FOREST PRODUCTS CO (PA)
Also Called: Katahdin Cedar Log Homes
205 Smyrna Rd (04763)
P.O. Box 145 (04763-0145)
PHONE..................................800 845-4533
David Gordon, *President*
Paul Dwyer, *Exec VP*
Barry Ivey, *Vice Pres*
Kevin Locke, *Human Res Dir*
EMP: 57
SALES (est): 12.7MM **Privately Held**
WEB: www.katahdincedarloghomes.com
SIC: 2452 2499 Mfg Prefabricated Wood Buildings Mfg Wood Products

Oakland
Kennebec County

(G-6528)
A W CHAFFEE (PA)
164 Belgrade Rd (04963-4537)
P.O. Box 69 (04963-0069)
PHONE..................................207 465-3234
Albert W Chafee, *President*
Shirley Chaffee, *Admin Sec*
EMP: 5
SQ FT: 936
SALES (est): 3.3MM **Privately Held**
SIC: 2421 5099 Mfg & Whol Wood Chips

(G-6529)
B & B EMBROIDERY INC
82 Libby Hill Rd (04963-4855)
PHONE..................................207 465-2846
Bob Kittredge, *CEO*
EMP: 5
SALES (est): 438.9K **Privately Held**
SIC: 2395 Pleating/Stitching Services

(G-6530)
CENTRAL MAINE CRANE INC
523 Belgrade Rd (04963-4402)
PHONE..................................207 465-2229
Byron Wrigley, *President*
EMP: 3
SALES: 300K **Privately Held**
SIC: 3536 Mfg Hoists/Cranes/Monorails

(G-6531)
CENTRAL MAINE CRATE INC
34 Clairmont Ave (04963-5319)
PHONE..................................207 873-5880
Dan Leclair, *President*
EMP: 5
SALES (est): 724.2K **Privately Held**
SIC: 2449 Mfg Wood Pallets/Skids

(G-6532)
DODLIN HILL STONE COMPANY LLC
49 Allagash Dr (04963-5026)
PHONE..................................207 465-6463
Joe Bixby, *Owner*
EMP: 3
SALES: 300K **Privately Held**
SIC: 1499 Nonmetallic Mineral Mining

(G-6533)
FLOYD BAKER METAL FABRICATION
Also Called: Central Maine Fabrication
263 Belgrade Rd (04963-4532)
PHONE..................................207 465-9346
Floyd Baker, *President*
Gayle Baker, *Vice Pres*
EMP: 4
SALES: 250K **Privately Held**
SIC: 3441 Structural Metal Fabrication

(G-6534)
MACHINING INNOVATIONS INC
279 Summer St (04963-4518)
PHONE..................................207 465-2500
Curtis Fisher, *President*
EMP: 9
SALES (est): 1.2MM **Privately Held**
SIC: 3599 3511 3524 Mfg Industrial Machinery Mfg Turbine/Genratr Sets Mfg Lawn/Garden Equip

(G-6535)
TITAN CHAIN & WELDING
15 Sportsmans Trl (04963-4337)
PHONE..................................207 465-4144
EMP: 7
SALES (est): 82.1K **Privately Held**
SIC: 7692 Welding Repair

(G-6536)
WRABACON INC
150 Old Waterville Rd (04963-5358)
P.O. Box 7 (04963-0007)
PHONE..................................207 465-2068
Robert Bartlett, *President*
Bob Bartlett Jr, *Vice Pres*
EMP: 16
SQ FT: 16,000
SALES (est): 4.6MM **Privately Held**
WEB: www.wrabacon.com
SIC: 3565 3569 Mfg Packaging Machinery Mfg General Industrial Machinery

Ogunquit
York County

(G-6537)
HARBOR CANDY SHOP INC
248 Main St (03907-3203)
P.O. Box 2064 (03907-2064)
PHONE..................................207 646-8078
E Sotiropoulos-Foss, *President*
Eugenie Sotiropoulos, *President*
Eugenie Sotiropoulos-Foss, *President*
EMP: 20
SALES: 2MM **Privately Held**
WEB: www.harborcandy.com
SIC: 2064 5441 5947 2066 Mfg Candy/Confectionery Ret Candy/Confectionery Ret Gifts/Novelties Mfg Chocolate/Cocoa Prdt

Old Town
Penobscot County

(G-6538)
GEORGIA-PACIFIC LLC
1 Portland St (04468-2007)
P.O. Box 547 (04468-0547)
PHONE..................................207 827-7711
Karen Dickinson, *Manager*
EMP: 450
SALES (corp-wide): 40.6B **Privately Held**
WEB: www.gp.com
SIC: 2621 Paper Mill
HQ: Georgia-Pacific Llc
133 Peachtree St Nw
Atlanta GA 30303
404 652-4000

(G-6539)
GOSSAMER PRESS
259 Main St Ste 1 (04468-1530)
PHONE..................................207 827-9881
David Larsen, *Owner*
EMP: 8

SALES (est): 748.3K **Privately Held**
WEB: www.gossamerpress.com
SIC: 2759 7334 Commercial Printing Photocopying Services

(G-6540)
GRAPHIX DESIGN
489 Kirkland Rd (04468-5805)
PHONE..................................207 827-4412
Tony A Sullivan, *President*
Sarah Zmihbowski, *Vice Pres*
EMP: 3
SALES: 250K **Privately Held**
SIC: 3993 Mfg Signs/Advertising Specialties

(G-6541)
JOHNSON OTDOORS WATERCRAFT INC (HQ)
Also Called: Old Town Canoe
125 Gilman Falls Ave B (04468-1325)
PHONE..................................207 827-5513
Helen P Johnson-Leipold, *CEO*
Tim Magoon, *COO*
Del McAlpine, *Vice Pres*
Steven Lacroix, *Safety Mgr*
Lana Phillips, *Human Res Mgr*
◆ **EMP:** 43
SQ FT: 186,000
SALES (est): 25.4MM
SALES (corp-wide): 562.4MM **Publicly Held**
WEB: www.oldtowncanoe.com
SIC: 3732 Boatbuilding/Repairing
PA: Johnson Outdoors Inc.
555 Main St
Racine WI 53403
262 631-6600

(G-6542)
KELLY LUMBER SALES INC
101 Brunswick St (04468-1409)
P.O. Box 288, Ashland (04732-0288)
PHONE..................................207 435-4950
Mike Kelly, *President*
Timothy Kelly, *Vice Pres*
Terry Kelly, *Opers Mgr*
▲ **EMP:** 14
SQ FT: 120,000
SALES: 3MM **Privately Held**
SIC: 2426 5031 Hardwood Dimension/Floor Mill Whol Lumber/Plywood/Millwork

(G-6543)
LABREES INC
Also Called: Labree's Bakery
169 Gilman Falls Ave (04468-1325)
P.O. Box 555 (04468-0555)
PHONE..................................207 827-6121
Bernie Labree, *President*
Bernard Labree, *President*
Jay Macdonald, *Opers Mgr*
Azalea Allen, *Purchasing*
David L Dorr, *CFO*
▲ **EMP:** 300 **EST:** 1948
SALES: 65.5MM **Privately Held**
WEB: www.labrees.com
SIC: 2051 Mfg Bread/Related Products

(G-6544)
MADDEN TIMBERLANDS INC
92 Beechwood Ave (04468-9749)
PHONE..................................207 827-0112
Scott M Madden, *President*
Karen Madden, *Treasurer*
EMP: 28
SALES (est): 3.9MM **Privately Held**
WEB: www.maddentimberlands.com
SIC: 2411 Logging

(G-6545)
ND OTM LLC
24 Portland St (04468-2024)
P.O. Box 546 (04468-0546)
PHONE..................................207 401-2879
Ken Liu, *CEO*
Craig Kreschner, *Site Mgr*
Brian Burcham, *Controller*
EMP: 120
SALES (est): 6.4MM **Privately Held**
SIC: 2611 Pulp Mill
HQ: Nd Paper Inc.
1901 S Meyers Rd Ste 600
Oakbrook Terrace IL 60181
513 200-0908

(G-6546)
PENOBSCOT TIMES INC
282 Main St (04468-1529)
PHONE..................................207 827-4451
William Kirkland, *President*
Lynn Higgins, *Publisher*
EMP: 5 **EST:** 1891
SQ FT: 5,000
SALES (est): 250K **Privately Held**
WEB: www.thepenobscottimes.com
SIC: 2711 Newspaper Publishing

(G-6547)
SOLIFOR TIMBERLANDS INC
1141 Main St (04468-2022)
PHONE..................................207 827-7195
Kenny Fergusson, *Principal*
EMP: 3
SQ FT: 3,500
SALES (est): 115.3K **Privately Held**
SIC: 2411 Logging

Oquossoc
Franklin County

(G-6548)
WALTS MACHINE SHOP
560 Rumford Rd (04964-3021)
P.O. Box 201 (04964-0201)
PHONE..................................207 864-5083
Walter House, *Owner*
Michael House, *Co-Owner*
Russell House, *Co-Owner*
EMP: 3
SALES: 90K **Privately Held**
SIC: 7692 Welding Repair

Orland
Hancock County

(G-6549)
G M ALLEN & SON INC
267 Front Ridge Rd (04472)
PHONE..................................207 469-7060
Wayne Allen, *President*
Kermit Allen, *Treasurer*
Annie Allen, *Manager*
Ruth Allen-Gray, *Admin Sec*
EMP: 7 **EST:** 1912
SALES (est): 695.9K **Privately Held**
WEB: www.gmallenwildblueberries.com
SIC: 2037 Mfg Frozen Fruit Specializing In Blueberries

(G-6550)
SELF DEFENSE INNOVATIONS INC
767 Acadia Hwy (04472-3916)
PHONE..................................207 991-1641
Travis Allen, *Principal*
EMP: 3
SALES (est): 178.9K **Privately Held**
SIC: 3812 Mfg Search/Navigation Equipment

(G-6551)
TWO ISLANDS CORPORATION
Also Called: Dunlap Weavers
583 Acadia Hwy (04472-3909)
P.O. Box 36 (04472-0036)
PHONE..................................207 469-3600
Susan Dunlap, *President*
EMP: 3 **EST:** 1973
SQ FT: 2,500
SALES: 300K **Privately Held**
SIC: 2339 Mfg Woolen Textiles

Orono
Penobscot County

(G-6552)
BYER MANUFACTURING COMPANY
Also Called: Byer of Maine
74 Mill St (04473-4040)
P.O. Box 100 (04473-0100)
PHONE..................................207 866-2171
James P Shields, *President*
Gerry Couture, *VP Sales*
Dan Hall, *Manager*
▲ **EMP:** 20
SQ FT: 30,000
SALES (est): 3.2MM **Privately Held**
WEB: www.byerofmaine.com
SIC: 3161 2511 2394 2393 Mfg Luggage Mfg Wood Household Furn Mfg Canvas/Related Prdts Mfg Textile Bags

(G-6553)
COURSESTORM INC
148 Main St (04473-3873)
PHONE..................................207 866-0328
Brian Rahill, *CEO*
EMP: 4
SALES (est): 98.3K **Privately Held**
SIC: 7372 7389 Prepackaged Software Services Business Services At Non-Commercial Site

(G-6554)
FLEXOR ENERGY COMPANY
99 Bennoch Rd (04473-3617)
PHONE..................................207 866-3527
David Labrecque, *Owner*
EMP: 4
SALES (est): 190K **Privately Held**
SIC: 3511 Mfg Turbines/Generator Sets

(G-6555)
LOBSTER RX
Also Called: Lobster Unlimited
99 Forest Ave (04473-3653)
P.O. Box 423, Brewer (04412-0423)
PHONE..................................207 949-2028
Catherine Billings, *Partner*
Robert Bayer, *Partner*
Stewart Hardison, *Partner*
EMP: 4
SALES (est): 170K **Privately Held**
SIC: 2836 Biological Products, Except Diagnostic

(G-6556)
NATIONAL POETRY FOUNDATION
5752 Neville Hall (04469-5752)
PHONE..................................207 581-3814
Burton Hatlen, *Director*
EMP: 3
SALES (est): 120K **Privately Held**
WEB: www.nationalpoetryfoundation.com
SIC: 2741 Misc Publishing

(G-6557)
ORONO HOUSE OF PIZZA
154 Park St (04473-4600)
PHONE..................................207 866-5505
Thomas Shanos, *Owner*
EMP: 5 **EST:** 2013
SALES (est): 256.6K **Privately Held**
SIC: 2038 5812 Mfg Frozen Specialties Eating Place

(G-6558)
S P HOLT CORPORATION
Also Called: Shaw & Tenney
20 Water St (04473-4069)
P.O. Box 213 (04473-0213)
PHONE..................................207 866-4867
Steven Holt, *President*
Nancy Forster-Holt, *Vice Pres*
Sam Martinelli, *Production*
EMP: 9 **EST:** 1858
SQ FT: 8,000
SALES (est): 1.3MM **Privately Held**
WEB: www.shawandtenney.com
SIC: 2499 Mfg Wood Products

(G-6559)
UNIVERSITY OF MAINE SYSTEM
Also Called: Wood Science/Technology
5755 Nutting Hall (04469-5755)
PHONE..................................207 581-2843
Doug Gardener, *Manager*
EMP: 10
SALES (corp-wide): 469.8MM **Privately Held**
WEB: www.umf.maine.edu
SIC: 2491 8221 Wood Preserving College/University
PA: University Of Maine System
5703 Alumni Hall Ste 101
Orono ME 04469
207 973-3300

(G-6560)
UNIVERSITY OF MAINE SYSTEM
Also Called: Main Campus Newspaper, The
5748 Memorial Un (04469-5748)
PHONE..................................207 581-1273
Kristine Saunders, *Principal*
EMP: 70
SALES (corp-wide): 469.8MM **Privately Held**
WEB: www.umf.maine.edu
SIC: 2711 8221 Newspapers-Publishing/Printing College/University
PA: University Of Maine System
5703 Alumni Hall Ste 101
Orono ME 04469
207 973-3300

Owls Head
Knox County

(G-6561)
AMERICAN LIGHTHOUSE FOUNDATION
186 Lighthouse Rd (04854)
P.O. Box 565, Rockland (04841-0565)
PHONE..................................207 594-4174
Jeremy D'Entremont, *Ch of Bd*
Christopher Glass, *President*
Marty Welt, *Corp Secy*
Brad Coupe, *Vice Pres*
Alen Ellse, *Treasurer*
EMP: 5
SQ FT: 100
SALES: 883.3K **Privately Held**
SIC: 3731 8412 Shipbuilding/Repairing Museum/Art Gallery

Oxford
Oxford County

(G-6562)
ARCAST INC
5 Park Rd (04270-3580)
PHONE..................................207 539-9638
EMP: 3
SALES (est): 267.4K **Privately Held**
SIC: 3567 Mfg Industrial Furnaces/Ovens

(G-6563)
ARCAST INC
264 Main St (04270-3134)
PHONE..................................207 539-9638
Rayland O'Neal, *President*
Sasha Long, *Officer*
▼ **EMP:** 9
SALES: 675K **Privately Held**
SIC: 3559 Mfg Misc Industry Machinery

(G-6564)
C J CRANAM INC
Also Called: Valley View Orchard Pies
15 Madison Ave (04270-3579)
P.O. Box 467 (04270-0467)
PHONE..................................207 739-1016
Cynthia Johnston, *President*
Lisa Dunham, *Vice Pres*
EMP: 25
SALES (est): 1.8MM **Privately Held**
SIC: 2051 2053 Mfg Bread/Related Products Mfg Frozen Bakery Products

(G-6565)
DAY BROS
25 Dat Rd (04270)
PHONE..................................207 743-0508
Kelby Day, *Partner*
Sewell Day, *Partner*
EMP: 3
SALES: 100K **Privately Held**
SIC: 2411 Logging Contractors

(G-6566)
GROVER GUNDRILLING LLC
59 Industrial Dr (04270-3536)
PHONE..................................207 743-7051

Garth Grover, *President*
Suzanne Grover, *President*
Rupert Grover, *Chairman*
Karen Vasil Busch, *Director*
Jessicca Grover, *Shareholder*
▲ **EMP:** 41
SQ FT: 24,000
SALES (est): 7.9MM **Privately Held**
WEB: www.grovergundrilling.com
SIC: 3599 Mfg Industrial Machinery

(G-6567)
JACKSON CALDWELL
Also Called: Breezy Hill
266 Hebron Rd (04270-2516)
PHONE..................................207 539-2325
Caldwell Jackson, *Owner*
EMP: 7
SQ FT: 5,500
SALES: 100K **Privately Held**
SIC: 2511 2512 5021 Mfg Wood Household Furniture Mfg Upholstered Household Furniture Whol Furniture

(G-6568)
JACKSON SGRHUSE VGTABLE STANDS
50 Hebron Rd (04270-2514)
PHONE..................................207 539-4613
Roger Jackson, *Owner*
EMP: 3
SALES: 11K **Privately Held**
WEB: www.meglink.net
SIC: 2099 Mfg Food Preparations

(G-6569)
M G A CAST STONE INC
7 Oxford Homes Ln (04270-3585)
P.O. Box 207 (04270-0207)
PHONE..................................207 926-5993
Greg Hamann, *Owner*
Tom Hamann, *Owner*
David Swasey, *CFO*
Chris Stearns, *Regl Sales Mgr*
EMP: 26
SALES (est): 5.4MM **Privately Held**
SIC: 3272 Mfg Concrete Products

(G-6570)
OXFORD TIMBER INC
60 E Oxford Rd (04270-2925)
PHONE..................................207 539-9656
Michael Record, *President*
Jean L Record, *Corp Secy*
Merle Record, *Vice Pres*
▲ **EMP:** 14
SQ FT: 800
SALES (est): 2.4MM **Privately Held**
SIC: 2421 5031 2491 Sawmill/Planing Mill Whol Lumber/Plywood/Millwork Wood Preserving

(G-6571)
RICHARD A TIBBETTS
73 Longview Dr (04270-4032)
PHONE..................................207 539-5073
Richard A Tibbetts, *Owner*
EMP: 3
SALES (est): 215.4K **Privately Held**
SIC: 2411 1741 Logging Masonry/Stone Contractor

(G-6572)
ROBINSON MANUFACTURING CO (PA)
283 King St (04270)
PHONE..................................207 539-4481
Joseph Robinson II, *Chairman*
Stewart Winslow, *Supervisor*
EMP: 13
SQ FT: 125,000
SALES (est): 1MM **Privately Held**
WEB: www.oxfordmillendstore.com
SIC: 2231 Mfg Wool Upholstery Fabrics & Flannels Wool Mohair Or Similar Fibers

(G-6573)
SCHIAVI HOMES LLC
754 Main St (04270-3561)
PHONE..................................207 539-9600
Dan Edwards, *Sales Staff*
Scott Stone,
EMP: 23 **EST:** 1996
SALES (est): 3.2MM **Privately Held**
WEB: www.schiavihomes.com
SIC: 2452 1521 Mfg Prefabricated Wood Buildings Single-Family House Construction

Parsonsfield
York County

(G-6574)
DANIEL L DUNNELLS LOGGING INC
58 Maplecrest Rd (04047-6628)
PHONE..................................207 793-2901
Daniel L Dunnells, *President*
EMP: 5 **EST:** 1968
SALES (est): 542.8K **Privately Held**
SIC: 2411 4212 Mfg Wood Chips Produced In The Field & Lumber & Timber Trucking

(G-6575)
HUMPHREY MH & SONS INC
92 Mudgett Rd (04047-6149)
P.O. Box 101 (04047-0101)
PHONE..................................207 625-4965
Michael Humphrey, *Owner*
Richard Humphrey, *Manager*
EMP: 10
SALES (est): 830K **Privately Held**
SIC: 2411 Logging

(G-6576)
M B EASTMAN LOGGING INC
146 North Rd (04047-6009)
PHONE..................................207 625-8020
Jennifer E Thomas, *Principal*
EMP: 4
SALES (est): 18.5K **Privately Held**
SIC: 2411 4212 Logging Local Trucking Operator

(G-6577)
TREE ENTERPRISES
Also Called: Wiseguide, The
1697 North Rd (04047-6429)
PHONE..................................207 233-6479
Debra Swasey, *Advt Staff*
Dee Battista, *Director*
EMP: 6
SQ FT: 1,000
SALES (est): 270K **Privately Held**
SIC: 2711 Newspapers-Publishing/Printing

Patten
Penobscot County

(G-6578)
KANTAHDIN WELDING
Also Called: Katahdin Welding
79 Potato Row (04765-3023)
PHONE..................................207 528-2924
Steve Crouse, *Owner*
EMP: 4
SALES: 120K **Privately Held**
WEB: www.mainecanoeracks.com
SIC: 3441 Structural Metal Fabrication

Pemaquid
Lincoln County

(G-6579)
CARPENTERS BOAT SHOP INC
440 Old County Rd (04558-4005)
PHONE..................................207 677-2614
EMP: 3
SALES: 453.5K **Privately Held**
WEB: www.carpentersboatshop.org
SIC: 3732 Boat Building And Repair

Pembroke
Washington County

(G-6580)
GULF OF MAINE INC
736 Leighton Point Rd (04666)
PHONE..................................207 726-4620
Timothy F Sheehan, *President*
▼ **EMP:** 6
SALES: 600K **Privately Held**
WEB: www.gulfofme.com
SIC: 2836 Mfg Biological Products

Penobscot
Hancock County

(G-6581)
DOWNEAST BOATS & COMPOSITES
The New Rd Rr 175 (04476)
P.O. Box 9 (04476-0009)
PHONE..................................207 326-9400
John Hutchins, *Owner*
EMP: 4
SQ FT: 4,800
SALES: 700K **Privately Held**
WEB: www.deboats.com
SIC: 3732 5551 Boatbuilding/Repairing Ret Boats

Perham
Aroostook County

(G-6582)
TOUGH END LOGGING CORP
320 High Meadow Rd (04766-4408)
P.O. Box 130, Caribou (04736-0130)
PHONE..................................207 455-8016
Roger Connolly, *President*
EMP: 4 **EST:** 1985
SALES: 1MM **Privately Held**
SIC: 2411 Logging Business

Peru
Oxford County

(G-6583)
ANDREW IRISH LOGGING
1264 Auburn Rd (04290)
P.O. Box 184 (04290-0184)
PHONE..................................207 562-8839
Andrew Irish, *Owner*
EMP: 15
SALES (est): 1.4MM **Privately Held**
SIC: 2411 Logging

(G-6584)
C B BOATWORKS INC
146 Tower Rd (04290-3432)
PHONE..................................207 562-8849
Gene F Foss, *General Mgr*
Dennis Newton, *Principal*
Lyle Butts, *Vice Pres*
Mimi Butts, *Treasurer*
EMP: 5
SQ FT: 33,000
SALES (est): 607.9K **Privately Held**
WEB: www.cbboatworks.com
SIC: 3732 Boatbuilding/Repairing

(G-6585)
DIMENSION LUMBER
85 Jug Hill Rd (04290)
PHONE..................................207 897-9973
Ceylon Putnam, *Owner*
Linda Putnam, *Co-Owner*
EMP: 8
SQ FT: 4,000
SALES: 500K **Privately Held**
SIC: 2421 Sawmill/Planing Mill

Phillips
Franklin County

(G-6586)
REGAN S PINGREE
989 Park St (04966)
PHONE..................................207 639-5706
Regan S Pingree, *Owner*
EMP: 10
SALES: 500K **Privately Held**
SIC: 2411 Logging

(G-6587)
WHEELER HILL LOGGING INC
37 Wheeler Hill Rd (04966-4028)
PHONE..................................207 639-2391
Todd Hargreaves, *Principal*
EMP: 3
SALES (est): 98.8K **Privately Held**
SIC: 2411 Logging

Pittsfield
Somerset County

(G-6588)
CIANBRO FBRCATION COATING CORP
335 Hunnewell Ave (04967-3511)
P.O. Box 1000 (04967-1000)
PHONE..................................207 487-3311
Peter G Vigue, *Ch of Bd*
Peter A Vigue, *President*
Christopher Howard, *Counsel*
Jack A Klimp, *Vice Pres*
Kyle K Holmstrom, *CFO*
EMP: 147
SALES: 23.4MM
SALES (corp-wide): 704.2MM **Privately Held**
WEB: www.cianbro.com
SIC: 3441 3479 Structural Metal Fabrication Coating/Engraving Service
PA: The Cianbro Companies
1 Hunnewell Ave
Pittsfield ME 04967
207 487-3311

(G-6589)
CM ALMY & SON INC
133 Ruth St (04967-4113)
P.O. Box 148 (04967-0148)
PHONE..................................207 487-3232
Michael Fendler, *Vice Pres*
Sandy Larrabee, *Engineer*
Barbara Hamilton, *Admin Mgr*
EMP: 105
SALES (corp-wide): 33.8MM **Privately Held**
WEB: www.almy.com
SIC: 2389 Mfg Apparel/Accessories
PA: C.M. Almy & Son, Inc.
28 Kaysal Ct Ste 1
Armonk NY 10504
914 864-9120

(G-6590)
FINYL VINYL
71 Crawford Rd (04967-5744)
PHONE..................................207 487-2753
Larry Morton, *Partner*
Jason Morton, *Partner*
EMP: 3
SALES (est): 240K **Privately Held**
SIC: 3993 Mfg Signs/Advertising Specialties

(G-6591)
SONOCO PRODUCTS COMPANY
101 Industrial Dr (04967-1433)
P.O. Box 486 (04967-0486)
PHONE..................................207 487-3206
Michael D Armitage, *Manager*
EMP: 30
SQ FT: 50,000
SALES (corp-wide): 5.3B **Publicly Held**
WEB: www.sonoco.com
SIC: 2631 2655 Paperboard Mill Mfg Fiber Cans/Drums

PA: Sonoco Products Company
1 N 2nd St
Hartsville SC 29550
843 383-7000

Pittston
Kennebec County

(G-6592)
DOOM FOREST DISTILLERY LLC
29 Chadwick Ln (04345-5764)
PHONE.................................207 462-1990
EMP: 3 **EST:** 2017
SALES (est): 147.2K **Privately Held**
SIC: 2085 Mfg Distilled/Blended Liquor

(G-6593)
WILLIAM B SPARROW JR
Also Called: Sparrow, Jacob
414 Whitefield Rd (04345-6612)
PHONE.................................207 582-5731
William Sparrow Jr, *Owner*
EMP: 3
SALES (est): 309.6K **Privately Held**
SIC: 2411 7389 Logging Business Services At Non-Commercial Site

Poland
Androscoggin County

(G-6594)
MAINE CONTAINER LLC
115 Poland Spring Dr (04274-5327)
PHONE.................................603 888-1315
EMP: 23
SALES (est): 2.3MM **Privately Held**
SIC: 3085 Whol Industrial/Service Paper
PA: Carr Management, Inc.
1 Tara Blvd Ste 303
Nashua NH 03062

(G-6595)
OLDCASTLE LAWN & GARDEN INC
481 Spring Water Rd (04274-5314)
P.O. Box 527, Poland Spring (04274-0527)
PHONE.................................207 998-5580
Richard Morrison, *Branch Mgr*
EMP: 42
SALES (corp-wide): 29.7B **Privately Held**
SIC: 3524 Mfg Lawn/Garden Equipment
HQ: Oldcastle Lawn & Garden, Inc.
3 Glenlake Pkwy 12
Atlanta GA 30328

(G-6596)
PROTECH DIGITAL SERVICES LLC
189 Tripp Lake Rd (04274-7118)
P.O. Box 7448, North Port FL (34290-0448)
PHONE.................................207 899-9237
Thomas P Peters II, *Mng Member*
EMP: 3 **EST:** 2011
SALES (est): 256.3K **Privately Held**
SIC: 3577 5044 Mfg Computer Peripheral Equipment Whol Office Equipment

(G-6597)
SAFE APPROACH INC
206 Mechanic Falls Rd (04274-6555)
PHONE.................................207 345-9900
Roger Dargie, *President*
David Kozlowsky, *General Mgr*
▲ **EMP:** 18
SQ FT: 12,760
SALES: 4MM **Privately Held**
WEB: www.safeapproach.com
SIC: 3199 Mfg Safety Equipment

Portage
Aroostook County

(G-6598)
MAINE WOODS COMPANY LLC
Also Called: Maine Wood Flooring
92 Fish Lake Rd (04768-8814)
PHONE.................................207 435-4393
Scott Ferland, *General Mgr*
EMP: 5 **EST:** 2017
SALES (est): 386.6K **Privately Held**
SIC: 2421 Sawmill/Planing Mill

(G-6599)
PORTAGE LKERS SNWMBILE CLB INC
22b School St (04768)
P.O. Box 149 (04768-0149)
PHONE.................................207 415-0506
Jennifer Curran, *President*
Susan Rogers, *Treasurer*
EMP: 15
SALES (est): 1.3MM **Privately Held**
SIC: 3531 Groom Snowmobile Trails

Porter
Oxford County

(G-6600)
CHESTER H CHAPMAN
Also Called: General Ftting Heat Trnsf Pdts
374 Spec Pond Rd (04068-3229)
PHONE.................................207 625-3349
Chester H Chapman, *Owner*
EMP: 3
SALES: 220K **Privately Held**
WEB: www.chester.ac.uk
SIC: 3443 3599 Mfg Fabricated Plate Work Mfg Industrial Machinery

(G-6601)
CHIPPING & LOGGING
37 Cross Rd (04068-3340)
P.O. Box 24 (04068-0024)
PHONE.................................207 625-4056
Laurence Taylor Jr, *President*
Dennis Scott, *Vice Pres*
Gary Taylor, *Vice Pres*
EMP: 8
SALES (est): 570K **Privately Held**
WEB: www.chippingaway.com
SIC: 2411 Logging

(G-6602)
DWIGHT R MILLS INC
271 Federal Rd (04068)
P.O. Box 718, Kezar Falls (04047-0718)
PHONE.................................207 625-3965
Dwight R Mills, *President*
Debbie Lajoie, *Office Mgr*
EMP: 5 **EST:** 1950
SALES: 400K **Privately Held**
SIC: 1442 Gravel Mining

(G-6603)
L E TAYLOR AND SONS INC
37 Cross Rd (04068-3340)
P.O. Box 24 (04068-0024)
PHONE.................................207 625-4056
Lawrence Taylor Jr, *President*
Brenda Taylor, *Treasurer*
Malcolm W Philbrook Jr, *Clerk*
EMP: 8
SALES (est): 997.7K **Privately Held**
SIC: 2411 Logging

(G-6604)
ROBERT W LIBBY
Also Called: Robert W Libby and Sons
483 Old Meetinghouse Rd (04068-3206)
PHONE.................................207 625-8285
Robert W Libby, *Owner*
EMP: 9
SALES (est): 946.6K **Privately Held**
SIC: 2411 2421 1629 Logging Sawmill/Planing Mill Heavy Construction

(G-6605)
VULCAN ELECTRIC COMPANY (PA)
28 Endfield St (04068-3502)
PHONE.................................207 625-3231
Michael Quick, *Ch of Bd*
Fred Conroy, *Vice Pres*
Paul Wieszeck, *Vice Pres*
EMP: 95
SQ FT: 40,000
SALES (est): 19.4MM **Privately Held**
SIC: 3567 Mfg Industrial Furnaces/Ovens

(G-6606)
VULCAN FLEX CIRCUIT CORP
28 Endfield St (04068-3502)
PHONE.................................603 883-1500
Michael Quick, *CEO*
Normand Sirois, *President*
Stanley Haupt, *Vice Pres*
William Benger, *CFO*
EMP: 70
SQ FT: 45,000
SALES (est): 7.1MM
SALES (corp-wide): 19.4MM **Privately Held**
WEB: www.vulcanelectric.com
SIC: 3674 Mfg Semiconductors/Related Devices
PA: Vulcan Electric Company
28 Endfield St
Porter ME 04068
207 625-3231

(G-6607)
WILLIAM A DAY JR & SONS INC
28 Wild Turkey Ln (04068-3663)
PHONE.................................207 625-8181
Brent Day, *President*
Brian Day, *Owner*
Scott Day, *Vice Pres*
EMP: 45
SALES (est): 2.6MM **Privately Held**
SIC: 2411 Logging

Portland
Cumberland County

(G-6608)
A-PO-G INC
Also Called: Coveside Conservation Products
23 Evergreen Dr (04103-1067)
P.O. Box 985, South Casco (04077-0985)
PHONE.................................207 774-7606
EMP: 9
SQ FT: 5,000
SALES: 500K **Privately Held**
WEB: www.coveside.com
SIC: 2499 Mfg Wooden Bird Houses

(G-6609)
ADVANCE ELECTRONIC CONCEPTS
26 Evergreen Dr Ste A (04103-1080)
PHONE.................................207 797-9825
Daniel Gagnon, *President*
Allen Cyr, *Vice Pres*
EMP: 4
SQ FT: 3,000
SALES (est): 500K **Privately Held**
WEB: www.aeconcepts.biz
SIC: 3679 Electronic Design And Assemby Services

(G-6610)
ADVANCEPIERRE FOODS INC
54 Saint John St (04102-3018)
PHONE.................................207 541-2800
EMP: 25
SALES (corp-wide): 42.4B **Publicly Held**
SIC: 2015 Mfg Food Preparations
HQ: Advancepierre Foods, Inc.
9990 Prnceton Glendale Rd
West Chester OH 45246
513 874-8741

(G-6611)
ALLAGASH BREWING COMPANY
50 Industrial Way (04103-1270)
PHONE.................................207 878-5385
George R Tod Jr, *President*
Sean Diffley, *Plant Engr*
Craig Frey, *CFO*
Shari Wise, *Finance Mgr*
Celine Frueh, *Human Res Dir*
▲ **EMP:** 82
SQ FT: 4,000
SALES (est): 18.9MM **Privately Held**
WEB: www.allagash.com
SIC: 2082 Mfg Malt Beverages

(G-6612)
ATLANTIC SPORTSWEAR INC
Also Called: Atlantic Cotton Company
36 Waldron Way (04103-5944)
PHONE.................................207 797-5028
John Fay, *President*
Dave St Germain, *Administration*
EMP: 23
SQ FT: 7,500
SALES (est): 3.7MM **Privately Held**
WEB: www.atlanticsportswear.com
SIC: 2759 2396 Commercial Printing Mfg Auto/Apparel Trimming

(G-6613)
ATLANTIC STANDARD MOLDING INC
380 Warren Ave Apt 2 (04103-1192)
PHONE.................................207 797-0727
James P Blanchard, *President*
EMP: 15
SQ FT: 10,750
SALES (est): 2.2MM **Privately Held**
SIC: 3944 Mfg Plastic Products

(G-6614)
AUDIO FILE PUBLICATIONS INC
Also Called: Audiofile Magazine
37 Silver St (04101-4132)
P.O. Box 109 (04112-0109)
PHONE.................................207 774-7563
Robin Whitten, *President*
EMP: 5
SQ FT: 2,000
SALES (est): 541.1K **Privately Held**
WEB: www.audiobookreferenceguide.com
SIC: 2721 7389 Periodicals-Publishing/Printing Business Services

(G-6615)
B AND R MODERN HAND TOOL INC
54 E Kidder St (04103-5014)
PHONE.................................207 773-6706
Richard Doyle, *President*
EMP: 5
SALES (est): 268.2K **Privately Held**
SIC: 2599 7389 Mfg Furniture/Fixtures Business Services

(G-6616)
B&G FOODS INC
Also Called: Burnham & Morrill
1 Beanpot Cir (04103-5304)
PHONE.................................207 772-8341
John Manoush, *Principal*
Mickey Morrill, *Mfg Staff*
EMP: 160
SALES (corp-wide): 1.7B **Publicly Held**
WEB: www.bgfoods.com
SIC: 2033 2087 2051 Mfg Canned Fruits/Vegetables Mfg Flavor Extracts/Syrup Mfg Bread/Related Products
PA: B&G Foods, Inc.
4 Gatehall Dr Ste 110
Parsippany NJ 07054
973 401-6500

(G-6617)
BALL AND CHAIN FORGE
56 Warren Ave Ste 106 (04103-1174)
PHONE.................................207 878-2217
Robert Menard, *Owner*
EMP: 3 **EST:** 1998
SALES: 120K **Privately Held**
SIC: 3462 Mfg Iron/Steel Forgings

(G-6618)
BANGOR MILLWORK & SUPPLY INC
460 Riverside St (04103-1069)
PHONE.................................207 878-8548
Mark Cameron, *Manager*
EMP: 12

GEOGRAPHIC

SALES (corp-wide): 5.6MM **Privately Held**
WEB: www.bangorwholesalelaminates.com
SIC: 2541 Mfg Wood Partitions/Fixtures
PA: Bangor Millwork & Supply, Inc.
355 Target Cir
Bangor ME 04401
207 947-6019

(G-6619)
BARBER FOODS (DH)
56 Milliken St (04103-1530)
P.O. Box 4821 (04112-4821)
PHONE..................................207 482-5500
David Barber, *President*
Vicki Mann, *CFO*
Bruce Codgeshell, *Treasurer*
EMP: 50
SQ FT: 16,000
SALES (est): 80.8MM
SALES (corp-wide): 42.4B **Publicly Held**
WEB: www.barberfoods.com
SIC: 2015 Poultry Processing
HQ: Advancepierre Foods, Inc.
9990 Prnceton Glendale Rd
West Chester OH 45246
513 874-8741

(G-6620)
BARBER FOODS
70 Saint John St (04102-3018)
P.O. Box 4821 (04112-4821)
PHONE..................................207 772-1934
EMP: 21
SALES (corp-wide): 42.4B **Publicly Held**
WEB: www.barberfoods.com
SIC: 2015 2038 Poultry Processing Mfg Frozen Specialties
HQ: Barber Foods
56 Milliken St
Portland ME 04103
207 482-5500

(G-6621)
BBI ENZYMES USA LTD
1037 Forest Ave (04103-3396)
PHONE..................................608 709-5270
EMP: 3
SALES (est): 81.8K **Privately Held**
SIC: 2869 Mfg Industrial Organic Chemicals

(G-6622)
BIO RAD LAB
1045 Riverside St (04103-1065)
PHONE..................................207 615-0571
Gary Goodrich, *Principal*
EMP: 5
SALES (est): 645.8K **Privately Held**
SIC: 3826 Mfg Analytical Instruments

(G-6623)
BIOPROCESSING INC
1045 Riverside St (04103-1065)
PHONE..................................207 457-0025
Gary Goodrich, *President*
Katherine Daigle, *COO*
EMP: 16
SQ FT: 10,000
SALES (est): 1.4MM **Privately Held**
WEB: www.bioprocessinginc.com
SIC: 2835 Mfg Diagnostic Substances

(G-6624)
BLETHEN MAINE NEWSPAPERS INC
390 Congress St (04101-3514)
P.O. Box 1460 (04104-5009)
PHONE..................................207 791-6650
Charles Cochrane, *CEO*
EMP: 8
SALES (est): 309.6K **Privately Held**
SIC: 2711 Newspapers-Publishing/Printing

(G-6625)
BLUE SKY INC
Also Called: GA Gear
987 Riverside St (04103-1070)
PHONE..................................207 772-0073
Jon R Chamoff, *President*
Sara Mack, *Training Spec*
▼ **EMP:** 8
SALES (est): 1MM **Privately Held**
SIC: 2759 Commercial Printing

(G-6626)
BRICKELL BRANDS LLC
Also Called: Brickell Men's Products
101 Mcalister Farm Rd (04103-5915)
PHONE..................................877 598-0060
Joshua Meyer, *Mng Member*
Matthew Bolduc,
EMP: 22
SALES: 15MM **Privately Held**
SIC: 2844 Beauty Shop

(G-6627)
BRISTOL SEAFOOD LLC
5 Portland Fish Pier (04101-4620)
P.O. Box 486 (04112-0486)
PHONE..................................207 761-4251
Darrell Pardy, *President*
Bristol Seafood, *Chairman*
Jennifer Cyr, *CFO*
EMP: 80
SQ FT: 30,000
SALES (est): 8.1MM **Privately Held**
SIC: 2092 5146 Mfg Fresh/Frozen Packaged Fish Whol Fish/Seafood
PA: Bristol Seafood Holdings Inc.
5 Portland Fish Pier
Portland ME 04101
-

(G-6628)
BUBBLE MNEIA DSSERT NOODLE BAR
15 Temple St (04101-4011)
PHONE..................................207 773-9559
Nancy Chen, *Owner*
EMP: 3
SALES (est): 115.9K **Privately Held**
SIC: 2098 Mfg Macaroni/Spaghetti

(G-6629)
BUNZL MAINE
150 Read St (04103-3445)
PHONE..................................207 772-9825
EMP: 4
SALES (est): 376.5K **Privately Held**
SIC: 2599 Mfg Furniture/Fixtures

(G-6630)
CAPRICORN PRODUCTS LLC
12 Rice St Ste 2 (04103-1497)
PHONE..................................207 321-0014
Jane Havey, *President*
John Manchester, *Purch Mgr*
Berni Reeves, *QC Mgr*
Anatoly Andreyko, *Research*
Dwight Havey, *Finance Dir*
▼ **EMP:** 21
SQ FT: 11,000
SALES (est): 3.5MM **Privately Held**
SIC: 2835 6719 Mfg Diagnostic Substances Holding Company
PA: Capricorn Products, Inc.
12 Rice St Ste 2
Portland ME 04103
-

(G-6631)
CARLISLE CONSTRUCTION MTLS LLC
Also Called: Hunter Panels
15 Franklin St (04101-4169)
PHONE..................................888 746-1114
EMP: 250
SALES (corp-wide): 4.4B **Publicly Held**
SIC: 3086 Mfg Plastic Foam Products
HQ: Carlisle Construction Materials, Llc
1285 Ritner Hwy
Carlisle PA 17013
-

(G-6632)
CASCO BAY BUTTER COMPANY LLC
146 Maine Ave (04103-3831)
PHONE..................................207 712-9148
EMP: 9
SALES (est): 975.3K **Privately Held**
SIC: 2021 5143 Mfg Creamery Butter Whol Dairy Products

(G-6633)
CASCO BAY DIESEL LLC
429 Warren Ave Unit 5 (04103-1294)
PHONE..................................207 878-9377
George Robert Chamberlin,
Cathy Chamberlin,
EMP: 4
SQ FT: 4,265
SALES (est): 609.4K **Privately Held**
SIC: 3519 Diesel Engine Repair

(G-6634)
CASCO BAY SBSTNCE ABUSE RSRCES
Also Called: Health Pro
205 Ocean Ave (04103-5712)
PHONE..................................207 773-7993
James Weaver, *Owner*
EMP: 15
SALES (est): 1.2MM **Privately Held**
SIC: 2721 Periodicals-Publishing/Printing

(G-6635)
CERTIFY INC (PA)
20 York St Ste 201 (04101-4694)
PHONE..................................207 773-6100
Robert Neveu, *President*
Mic Harris, *Business Mgr*
Kenny Eon, *Vice Pres*
Claire Milligan, *Vice Pres*
Katherine Edenbach, *CFO*
EMP: 40
SALES (est): 16.3MM **Privately Held**
SIC: 7372 Prepackaged Software Services

(G-6636)
CHECKSFORLESSCOM
200 Riverside Indus Pkwy (04103-1414)
PHONE..................................800 245-5775
Chris Lefevre, *President*
EMP: 4
SALES (est): 428.4K **Privately Held**
SIC: 2752 Lithographic Commercial Printing

(G-6637)
CHIMANI INC
148 Middle St Ste 1d (04101-4191)
P.O. Box 1072, Yarmouth (04096-2072)
PHONE..................................207 221-0266
Kerry Gallivan, *CEO*
Thomas Tash, *Marketing Mgr*
EMP: 6
SALES (est): 363.6K **Privately Held**
SIC: 7372 Prepackaged Software

(G-6638)
CLARIOS
Also Called: Johnson Controls
477 Congress St Fl 6 (04101-3427)
PHONE..................................603 222-2400
EMP: 4 **Privately Held**
SIC: 2531 Mfg Public Building Furniture
HQ: Johnson Controls Inc
5757 N Green Bay Ave
Milwaukee WI 53209
414 524-1200

(G-6639)
CLEARH2O
34 Danforth St (04101-4502)
PHONE..................................207 221-0039
Jay Palmer, *General Mgr*
Linda Pollock, *Principal*
EMP: 18
SALES (est): 3.5MM **Privately Held**
WEB: www.clearh2o.com
SIC: 2834 Mfg Pharmaceutical Preparations

(G-6640)
COAST MAINE ORGANIC PDTS INC (PA)
Also Called: Coast of Maine, Inc.
145 Newbury St Fl 3 (04101-4263)
PHONE..................................207 879-0002
Carlos Quijano, *President*
Nathaniel Henshaw, *Corp Secy*
Jean Quijano, *Vice Pres*
Felicia Newman, *QC Mgr*
Sue Lavallee, *Manager*
EMP: 13
SQ FT: 750
SALES: 7MM **Privately Held**
WEB: www.coastofmaine.com
SIC: 2879 Mfg Agricultural Chemicals

(G-6641)
COMNAV ENGINEERING INC
430 Riverside St (04103-1035)
PHONE..................................207 221-8524
Martin Geesaman, *President*
Bethany Burrill, *Business Mgr*
Kirk Riley, *Vice Pres*
EMP: 37
SALES (est): 7MM **Privately Held**
WEB: www.comnav-eng.com
SIC: 3569 5065 8711 Mfg General Industrial Machinery Whol Electronic Parts/Equipment Engineering Services

(G-6642)
CONSOLIDATED CONTAINER CO LLC
Also Called: Maine Plastics
364 Forest Ave (04101-2035)
PHONE..................................207 772-7468
Debbie Holvin, *Manager*
EMP: 15
SALES (corp-wide): 14B **Publicly Held**
WEB: www.ccllc.com
SIC: 3089 Mfg Plastic Products
HQ: Consolidated Container Company, Llc
2500 Windy Ridge Pkwy Se # 1400
Atlanta GA 30339
678 742-4600

(G-6643)
CONTROLLED CHAOS
116 Free St (04101-3925)
PHONE..................................802 274-5321
EMP: 3
SALES (est): 185.3K **Privately Held**
SIC: 3471 Plating/Polishing Service

(G-6644)
CREMARK INC
Also Called: Discover Maine Magazine
10 Exchange St Ste 208 (04101-5043)
PHONE..................................207 874-7720
Jim Burch, *President*
EMP: 5
SALES (est): 390K **Privately Held**
WEB: www.cremark.com
SIC: 2721 Magazine Publishing Company

(G-6645)
CURRY PRINTING & COPY CENTER
10 City Ctr (04101-4006)
PHONE..................................207 772-5897
John Mina, *President*
Jim Hatch, *General Mgr*
Evelyn Mina, *Treasurer*
Cindy Mina, *Exec Dir*
EMP: 13
SQ FT: 7,000
SALES (est): 2.1MM **Privately Held**
WEB: www.curryprinting.biz
SIC: 2752 7334 Offset Printing & Copying

(G-6646)
CYBERCOPY INC
Also Called: B Copy
1006 Forest Ave Ste 1 (04103-3343)
PHONE..................................207 775-2679
Brad Burns, *President*
Thomas Black, *President*
Brian McGinley, *General Mgr*
EMP: 9 **EST:** 1999
SQ FT: 4,500
SALES (est): 1MM **Privately Held**
SIC: 2752 Photo Printing

(G-6647)
DALE RAND PRINTING INC
508 Riverside St Ste A (04103-1277)
PHONE..................................207 773-8198
Dale Rand, *President*
Mike Rand, *Director*
EMP: 8
SALES (est): 1.4MM **Privately Held**
SIC: 2752 Commercial Offset Printing

(G-6648)
DAUNIS
Also Called: Daunis Fine Jewelry
616 Congress St Ste 2 (04101-3374)
P.O. Box 5066 (04101-0766)
PHONE..................................207 773-6011
Patricia Daunis Dunning, *President*
William Dunning, *Vice Pres*

John F Loyd Jr, *Clerk*
EMP: 10 **EST:** 1974
SQ FT: 2,300
SALES (est): 1.1MM **Privately Held**
WEB: www.daunis.com
SIC: 3911 5944 Mfg Precious Metal Jewelry Ret Jewelry

(G-6649)
DAVIC INC
Also Called: Bayside Print Services
417 Congress St (04101-3505)
PHONE..................................207 774-0093
David White, *President*
EMP: 11
SQ FT: 1,616
SALES (est): 1.7MM **Privately Held**
SIC: 2752 2791 2789 Lithographic Commercial Printing Typesetting Services Bookbinding/Related Work

(G-6650)
DESIGNTEX GROUP INC
Portland Color
14 Industrial Way (04103-1042)
PHONE..................................207 774-2689
Andrew Graham, *Branch Mgr*
EMP: 25
SALES (corp-wide): 3.4B **Publicly Held**
SIC: 2759 7336 Commercial Printing Commercial Art/Graphic Design
HQ: The Design Tex Group Inc
200 Hudson St Fl 9
New York NY 10013
212 886-8100

(G-6651)
DESK TOP GRAPHICS INC
Also Called: Spire Express
477 Congress St Ste 2b (04101-3455)
PHONE..................................207 828-0041
David Macelhiney, *Manager*
EMP: 3
SALES (corp-wide): 72.7MM **Privately Held**
SIC: 2796 Commercial Art/Graphic Design
HQ: Desk Top Graphics Inc
1 1st Ave
Peabody MA 01960
617 832-1927

(G-6652)
DIGITRY COMPANY INC (PA)
449 Forest Ave Ste 210 (04101-2008)
PHONE..................................207 774-0300
Richard Tenney, *President*
Ronald Shapiro, *Vice Pres*
Mary F Dunn, *Treasurer*
Mary Dunn, *Treasurer*
Yvette Tenney, *Admin Sec*
EMP: 6
SALES: 150K **Privately Held**
WEB: www.digitry.com
SIC: 3823 Mfg Industrial Temperature Controls & Monitors

(G-6653)
DOWNEAST NETWORKING SERVICES
98 Chestnut St (04101-2429)
P.O. Box 1264, Windham (04062-1264)
PHONE..................................772 485-4304
Timothy Bryan, *Principal*
EMP: 4 **EST:** 2008
SALES (est): 249.2K **Privately Held**
SIC: 2741 Misc Publishing

(G-6654)
DR PEPPER BOTTLING CO PORTLAND
250 Canco Rd (04103-4221)
PHONE..................................207 773-4258
Marcus Day, *Principal*
EMP: 3
SALES (est): 161.4K **Privately Held**
SIC: 2086 Mfg Bottled/Canned Soft Drinks

(G-6655)
DRAGON PRODUCTS COMPANY INC
960 Ocean Ave (04103-4703)
PHONE..................................207 879-2328
Terry Zeysey, *Branch Mgr*
EMP: 15 **Privately Held**
SIC: 3273 Mfg Ready Mix Concrete
HQ: Dragon Products Company, Llc
57 Atlantic Pl
South Portland ME 04106
207 774-6355

(G-6656)
E I PRINTING CO
200 Riverside Indus Pkwy (04103-1414)
PHONE..................................207 797-4838
Christopher Lefevere, *Manager*
EMP: 15
SALES (est): 2.7MM **Privately Held**
SIC: 2752 Lithographic Commercial Printing

(G-6657)
EAST SHORE PRODUCTION
Also Called: Studio Print
48 Free St Ste 302 (04101-3873)
PHONE..................................207 775-5353
Steven Register, *Owner*
EMP: 3
SALES (est): 261.6K **Privately Held**
SIC: 2759 Commercial Printing

(G-6658)
EASTMAN INDUSTRIES (PA)
70 Ingersol Dr (04103-1093)
PHONE..................................207 878-5353
Nicholas M Nikazmerad, *President*
▲ **EMP:** 20
SQ FT: 40,000
SALES (est): 2.8MM **Privately Held**
WEB: www.hovermower.com
SIC: 3524 Mfg Lawn/Garden Equipment

(G-6659)
ECO-KIDS LLC
273 Presumpscot St Ste 4 (04103-5226)
PHONE..................................207 899-2752
Cammie Weeks, *CEO*
Edward Weeks, *President*
EMP: 3
SQ FT: 3,000
SALES (est): 143.1K **Privately Held**
SIC: 3952 Mfg Lead Pencils/Art Goods

(G-6660)
EIMSKIP USA INC
468 Commercial St (04101-4637)
PHONE..................................207 221-5268
EMP: 8
SALES (est): 265K **Privately Held**
SIC: 3799 4783 Mfg Transportation Equipment Packing/Crating Service

(G-6661)
ENVIROLOGIX INC
500 Riverside Indus Pkwy (04103-1486)
PHONE..................................207 797-0300
John N Markin, *President*
Dan Myhaver, *Business Mgr*
Dean T Layton, *Vice Pres*
Dean Layton, *Vice Pres*
Breck O Parker, *Vice Pres*
EMP: 100
SQ FT: 26,000
SALES (est): 25.9MM **Privately Held**
WEB: www.envirologix.com
SIC: 3826 Mfg Analytical Instruments

(G-6662)
FETCH INC
195 Commercial St (04101-4717)
PHONE..................................207 773-5450
Kathy Palmer, *President*
Katherine Palmer, *President*
EMP: 6 **EST:** 2000
SQ FT: 1,800
SALES (est): 550.1K **Privately Held**
SIC: 3999 Sells Goods For Personal Or Household Consumption

(G-6663)
FORTUNE INC (PA)
256 Read St (04103-3446)
PHONE..................................207 878-5760
Richard Fortune III, *President*
Rchard Fortune IV, *Vice Pres*
Mary Fortune, *Treasurer*
William Howison, *Clerk*
EMP: 15 **EST:** 1946
SQ FT: 14,000
SALES (est): 1.1MM **Privately Held**
WEB: www.fortunecanvas.com
SIC: 2394 Mfg Canvas Products Interiors & Sails From Purchased Materials

(G-6664)
GATEWAY MASTERING STUDIOS INC
428 Cumberland Ave (04101-2823)
PHONE..................................207 828-9400
Robert Ludwig, *President*
EMP: 12
SALES (est): 1.5MM **Privately Held**
WEB: www.gatewaymastering.com
SIC: 3652 Mfg Prerecorded Records/Tapes

(G-6665)
GBO INC
340 Presumpscot St (04103-5235)
PHONE..................................207 772-0302
James Freeman, *President*
Danny Barter, *Office Mgr*
EMP: 5
SALES (est): 524.4K **Privately Held**
SIC: 3632 Mfg Home Refrigerators/Freezers

(G-6666)
GORGEOUS GELATO LLC
434 Fore St (04101-4028)
PHONE..................................207 699-4309
Donato Giovine, *Mng Member*
Mariagrazia Zanardi, *Mng Member*
▲ **EMP:** 9
SQ FT: 1,400
SALES (est): 655.3K **Privately Held**
SIC: 2024 Mfg Ice Cream/Frozen Desert

(G-6667)
GUN F X TACTICAL DEVELOPMENT (PA)
28 Stroudwater Rd Unit 10 (04102)
PHONE..................................207 797-8200
Forest Hatcher, *President*
Tracy Hatcher, *Vice Pres*
EMP: 5
SALES (est): 511.7K **Privately Held**
WEB: www.gunfx.com
SIC: 3483 Mfg Land Mines

(G-6668)
HANGER PRSTHETCS & ORTHO INC
959 Brighton Ave (04102-1020)
PHONE..................................207 773-4963
Wade Bonneson,
EMP: 9
SALES (corp-wide): 1B **Publicly Held**
SIC: 3842 Mfg Surgical Appliances/Supplies
HQ: Hanger Prosthetics & Orthotics, Inc.
10910 Domain Dr Ste 300
Austin TX 78758
512 777-3800

(G-6669)
HARMONS CLAM CAKES
165 Read St (04103-3438)
P.O. Box 1113, Kennebunkport (04046-1113)
PHONE..................................207 967-4100
Steve Liautaud, *President*
EMP: 4
SQ FT: 3,000
SALES: 500K **Privately Held**
WEB: www.harmonsclamcakes.com
SIC: 2092 Mfg Fresh/Frozen Packaged Fish

(G-6670)
HEALTHY HOMEWORKS
17 Kellogg St (04101-4303)
PHONE..................................207 415-4245
Amy Smith, *President*
Allie Smith, *Director*
EMP: 3
SQ FT: 1,500
SALES (est): 120.3K **Privately Held**
SIC: 2511 Mfg Wood Household Furniture

(G-6671)
HISTORIC MAP WORKS
3 Cottage Rd (04106)
PHONE..................................207 756-5215
Belinda Carpenter, *Principal*
EMP: 3
SALES (est): 582.6K **Privately Held**
SIC: 3469 Mfg Metal Stampings

(G-6672)
HP HOOD LLC
349 Park Ave (04102-2798)
PHONE..................................207 774-9861
Scott Blake, *Opers-Prdtn-Mfg*
EMP: 100
SALES (corp-wide): 2.2B **Privately Held**
WEB: www.hphood.com
SIC: 2024 2026 Mfg Ice Cream/Frozen Desert Mfg Fluid Milk
PA: Hp Hood Llc
6 Kimball Ln Ste 400
Lynnfield MA 01940
617 887-8441

(G-6673)
IMMUCELL CORPORATION (PA)
56 Evergreen Dr (04103-5907)
PHONE..................................207 878-2770
David S Tomsche, *Ch of Bd*
Michael F Brigham, *President*
Joseph H Crabb, *Vice Pres*
Elizabeth L Williams, *Vice Pres*
Micheal Brigham, *Treasurer*
▲ **EMP:** 47 **EST:** 1982
SQ FT: 35,000
SALES: 10.9MM **Publicly Held**
WEB: www.immucell.com
SIC: 2835 Mfg Veterinary Diagnostic Substances

(G-6674)
INLAND TECHNOLOGIES
140 Jetport Blvd (04102-1900)
PHONE..................................207 761-6951
EMP: 4
SALES (est): 427.4K **Privately Held**
SIC: 2869 Mfg Industrial Organic Chemicals

(G-6675)
J S RITTER JEWELERS SUPPLY LLC
50 Cove St (04101-2422)
PHONE..................................207 712-4744
EMP: 5
SQ FT: 4,500
SALES (est): 378.8K **Privately Held**
WEB: www.jsritter.com
SIC: 3915 Jewelers Materials And Lapidary Work

(G-6676)
J WESTON WALCH PUBLISHER
Also Called: Walch Publishing
40 Walch Dr (04103-1328)
PHONE..................................207 772-2846
Peter S Walch, *Ch of Bd*
Carolyn Slayman, *Vice Ch Bd*
Al Noyes, *President*
Charles Thomas, *Vice Pres*
EMP: 40 **EST:** 1927
SQ FT: 26,000
SALES (est): 6.5MM **Privately Held**
WEB: www.walch.com
SIC: 2731 2732 2759 Books-Publishing/Printing Book Printing Commercial Printing

(G-6677)
KERRY INC
Also Called: X Cafe
40 Quarry Rd Ste 200 (04103-3460)
PHONE 207 775-7060
Bryan Garrison, *Manager*
EMP: 27 **Privately Held**
SIC: 2095 Mfg Roasted Coffee
HQ: Kerry Inc.
3400 Millington Rd
Beloit WI 53511
608 363-1200

(G-6678)
LAMTEC INC
2301 Congress St (04102-1907)
P.O. Box 3889 (04104-3889)
PHONE..................................207 774-6560
Michael Caron, *President*
EMP: 3
SQ FT: 12,000
SALES (est): 377.9K **Privately Held**
SIC: 2679 Mfg Converted Paper Products

(G-6679)
LEAVITT & PARRIS INC
256 Read St (04103-3446)
PHONE..................................207 797-0100
John Hutchins, *President*
Lucretia Hutchins, *Vice Pres*
Shauna Moore, *Human Res Mgr*
Nancy York, *Manager*
EMP: 15 **EST:** 1919
SQ FT: 27,000
SALES: 2.2MM **Privately Held**
WEB: www.leavittandparris.com
SIC: 2394 7359 7699 Mfg Canvas/Related Products Equipment Rental/Leasing Repair Services

(G-6680)
LTS INC
37 Danforth St (04101-4501)
PHONE..................................207 774-1104
Linda Tobey, *President*
K C Hughes, *Vice Pres*
EMP: 21
SQ FT: 7,500
SALES (est): 3MM **Privately Held**
WEB: www.ltsmaine.com
SIC: 2759 Commercial Printing

(G-6681)
MAINE ARTFL LIMB ORTHOTICS CO
Also Called: Maine Artfl Limb & Orthotics
959 Brighton Ave Rear (04102-1041)
PHONE..................................207 773-4963
Marc N Karn, *President*
Wade Bonneson, *COO*
EMP: 10
SQ FT: 6,500
SALES (est): 869.9K **Privately Held**
WEB: www.maineartificiallimb.com
SIC: 3842 5999 Mfg & Ret Artificial Limbs

(G-6682)
MAINE BIO-FUEL INC
Also Called: Maine Standard Biofuels
51 Ingersol Dr (04103-1093)
PHONE..................................207 878-3001
James Kaltsas, *Owner*
Chris Geele, *Vice Pres*
Alex Pine, *Director*
Richard Bradsky, *Admin Sec*
EMP: 11
SQ FT: 2,000
SALES (est): 2.6MM **Privately Held**
SIC: 2869 2911 Mfg Industrial Organic Chemicals Petroleum Refiner

(G-6683)
MAINE BIOTECHNOLOGY SVCS INC
1037r Forest Ave (04103-3395)
PHONE..................................207 797-5454
Joseph Chandler, *President*
Michael Sullivan, *Prdtn Mgr*
Carla Dube, *QA Dir*
Jennifer Ackerman, *QC Mgr*
Carrie Cloutier, *Sales Dir*
▼ **EMP:** 32
SQ FT: 12,000
SALES (est): 4.3MM **Privately Held**
WEB: www.mainebiotechnology.com
SIC: 2835 2834 Mfg Diagnostic Substances Mfg Pharmaceutical Preparations

(G-6684)
MAINE COAST MARKETING
160 Presumpscot St Ste 1 (04103-5200)
PHONE..................................207 781-9801
Toll Free:..866 -
Peggy Ingram, *Owner*
EMP: 4
SALES (est): 251.2K **Privately Held**
WEB: www.mainecoastmarketing.com
SIC: 2395 Pleating/Stitching Services

(G-6685)
MAINE CRAFT DISTILLING LLC
123 Washington Ave (04101-2618)
PHONE..................................207 798-2528
Luke Davidson, *Owner*
Thomas John Dupree, *Partner*
EMP: 8
SQ FT: 2,800
SALES: 120K **Privately Held**
SIC: 2084 Mfg Wines/Brandy/Spirits

(G-6686)
MAINE FIBER COMPANY LLC
465 Congress St Ste 701 (04101-3574)
PHONE..................................207 699-4550
Dwight Allison III, *CEO*
EMP: 9
SALES (est): 907.3K
SALES (corp-wide): 124.1MM **Privately Held**
SIC: 3357 Nonferrous Wiredrawing/Insulating
PA: Firstlight Fiber, Inc.
41 State St Ste 37
Albany NY 12207
518 598-0900

(G-6687)
MAINE MICRO FURNACE INC
1368 Riverside St (04103)
PHONE..................................207 329-9207
Norman S Reef, *President*
EMP: 7
SALES (est): 55.3K **Privately Held**
SIC: 3448 Mfg Prefabricated Metal Buildings

(G-6688)
MAINE NWSPPERS IN EDUCATN FUND
390 Congress St (04101-3514)
PHONE..................................207 791-6650
EMP: 3
SALES (est): 118.4K **Privately Held**
SIC: 2711 Newspapers-Publishing/Printing

(G-6689)
MAINE PARTS & MACHINE INC
68 Waldron Way (04103-5944)
PHONE..................................207 797-0024
William W Kelton, *President*
Deborah P Kelton, *Treasurer*
▲ **EMP:** 23
SQ FT: 15,000
SALES (est): 4.3MM **Privately Held**
WEB: www.maineparts.com
SIC: 3599 Mfg Industrial Machinery

(G-6690)
MAINE SURFERS UNION
15 Free St (04101-3907)
PHONE..................................207 771-7873
Charlie Fox, *President*
EMP: 4 **EST:** 2013
SALES (est): 379.6K **Privately Held**
SIC: 3949 Mfg Sporting/Athletic Goods

(G-6691)
MAINTENANCE TECH INC
Also Called: Vehicle Wash Systems
235 Riverside Indus Pkwy (04103-1413)
PHONE..................................207 797-7233
Michael J Snow, *President*
EMP: 5
SQ FT: 5,000
SALES (est): 944.6K **Privately Held**
SIC: 3589 Mfg Service Industry Machinery

(G-6692)
MATHEMTICS PROBLEM SOLVING LLC
Also Called: J. Weston Walch, Publisher
40 Walch Dr (04103-1328)
PHONE..................................207 772-2846
EMP: 6
SALES (est): 276K **Privately Held**
SIC: 2731 7372 8299 Books-Publishing/Printing Prepackaged Software Services School/Educational Services

(G-6693)
MATHEWS BAKERY INC
Also Called: Botto's Bakery
550 Washington Ave (04103-5120)
PHONE..................................207 773-9647
Robert Mathews, *President*
Everett Mathews, *Vice Pres*
Stevens Mathews, *Treasurer*
Margaret Mathews, *Admin Sec*
EMP: 24
SQ FT: 3,600
SALES (est): 3.4MM **Privately Held**
SIC: 2051 Mfgs Bread & Rolls

(G-6694)
MONAHAN ASSOCIATES
2 Cotton St 200 (04101-3905)
PHONE..................................207 771-0900
Eileen Monahan, *Owner*
EMP: 3
SALES: 400K **Privately Held**
WEB: www.monahanassoc.com
SIC: 2819 6211 Mfg Industrial Inorganic Chemicals Security Broker/Dealer

(G-6695)
MPX
2301 Congress St (04102-1907)
PHONE..................................207 774-6116
Ryan Jackson, *CEO*
Brian Wood, *President*
Robert Willis, *Owner*
Thomas Donhauser, *Vice Pres*
Jacob Roberson, *Vice Pres*
EMP: 48
SALES (est): 9MM **Privately Held**
SIC: 2752 Lithographic Commercial Printing

(G-6696)
MTM OLDCO INC (PA)
Also Called: Maine Sunday Telegram
1 City Ctr Fl 5 (04101-4070)
PHONE..................................207 791-6650
Charles Cochrane, *CEO*
EMP: 465
SALES (est): 105.8MM **Privately Held**
WEB: www.seattletimes.nwsource.com
SIC: 2711 Newspapers-Publishing/Printing

(G-6697)
NANCY LAWRENCE
Also Called: Portmanteau
3 Wharf St (04101-4136)
PHONE..................................207 774-7276
Nancy Lawrence, *Owner*
EMP: 3
SQ FT: 816
SALES (est): 198.8K **Privately Held**
SIC: 2393 5999 3171 3161 Mfg Textile Bags Ret Misc Merchandise Mfg Womens Handbag/Purse Mfg Luggage Mfg Canvas/Related Prdts

(G-6698)
NAVIGATOR PUBLISHING LLC
Also Called: Ocean Navigator
30 Danforth St Ste 307 (04101-4574)
P.O. Box 569 (04112-0569)
PHONE..................................207 822-4350
Queeney Tim, *COO*
Virginia Howe, *Opers Staff*
Arthur Auger, *Advt Staff*
Casey Conley, *Assoc Editor*
Tim Benson, *Info Tech Mgr*
EMP: 22
SQ FT: 5,000
SALES (est): 2.2MM **Privately Held**
WEB: www.navigatorpublishing.com
SIC: 2721 5551 Periodicals-Publishing/Printing Ret Boats

(G-6699)
NEARPEER INC
63 Federal St (04101-4222)
PHONE..................................207 615-0414
Dustin Manocha, *CEO*
EMP: 8
SALES (est): 196K **Privately Held**
SIC: 7372 Prepackaged Software Services

(G-6700)
NEW ENGLAND BUSINESS MEDIA LLC
Also Called: Mainebiz
48 Free St Ste 109 (04101-3874)
PHONE..................................207 761-8379
Donna Brassard, *Publisher*
Peter Van Allen, *Editor*
Stephanie Meagher, *Research*
Alison Nason, *Marketing Staff*
Catherine Tanous, *Marketing Staff*
EMP: 13
SALES (corp-wide): 2.4MM **Privately Held**
WEB: www.mainebiz.biz
SIC: 2711 Newspapers-Publishing/Printing
PA: New England Business Media, Llc
172 Shrewsbury St Ste 1
Worcester MA 01604
508 755-8004

(G-6701)
NEW ENGLAND DISTILLING CO
26 Evergreen Dr (04103-1080)
PHONE..................................207 878-9759
Ned Wight, *Owner*
EMP: 3 **EST:** 2011
SALES (est): 276.5K **Privately Held**
SIC: 2085 5182 Mfg Distilled/Blended Liquor Whol Wine/Distilled Beverages

(G-6702)
NICHOLS PORTLAND LLC (PA)
2400 Congress St (04102-1949)
PHONE..................................207 774-6121
Thomas K Houck, *President*
EMP: 346
SQ FT: 200,000
SALES (est): 94.4MM **Privately Held**
SIC: 3714 8711 Mfg Motor Vehicle Parts/Accessories Engineering Services

(G-6703)
NILSEN CANVAS PRODUCTS
212 Warren Ave (04103-1150)
PHONE..................................207 797-4863
David C Nilsen, *Owner*
EMP: 6
SQ FT: 3,000
SALES: 350K **Privately Held**
SIC: 2394 Mfg Canvas/Related Products

(G-6704)
NORTH ATLANTIC INC
2 Portland Fish (04101)
P.O. Box 682 (04104-0682)
PHONE..................................207 774-6025
Gerald Knecht, *President*
Chris Bowker, *Sales Staff*
Greg Lavoie, *Director*
◆ **EMP:** 8
SQ FT: 1,500
SALES: 12MM **Privately Held**
WEB: www.northatlantic.com
SIC: 2092 5146 Mfg Fresh/Frozen Packaged Fish Whol Fish/Seafood

(G-6705)
OMNI PRESS INC
141 Preble St (04101-2440)
PHONE..................................207 780-6664
Michael Flanders, *President*
▲ **EMP:** 4
SALES (est): 270K **Privately Held**
SIC: 2759 Commercial Offset Printing

(G-6706)
ONE EYE OPEN BREWING CO LLC
55 Pitt St Apt 2 (04103-4831)
PHONE..................................207 536-4176
EMP: 4 **EST:** 2016
SALES (est): 119.8K **Privately Held**
SIC: 2082 Mfg Malt Beverages

(G-6707)
PEPSI-COLA METRO BTLG CO INC
Also Called: Pepsico
250 Canco Rd (04103-4221)
PHONE..................................207 773-4258
Marcus Day, *Branch Mgr*
EMP: 142
SALES (corp-wide): 64.6B **Publicly Held**
WEB: www.pbg.com
SIC: 2086 Carb Sft Drnkbtlcn
HQ: Pepsi-Cola Metropolitan Bottling Company, Inc.
1111 Westchester Ave
White Plains NY 10604
914 767-6000

(G-6708)
PIPING SPECIALTIES INC
Also Called: PSI Controls
36 Rainmaker Dr (04103-1291)
PHONE..................................207 878-3955
Mike Alt, *Manager*
EMP: 10

SALES (corp-wide): 11.7MM **Privately Held**
WEB: www.pipingspecialties.com
SIC: 2891 Mfg Process Control Instruments
PA: Piping Specialties, Inc.
250 North St Ste B10
Danvers MA 01923
978 774-1300

(G-6709)
PITNEY BOWES INC
970 Baxter Blvd Ste 203 (04103-5344)
PHONE..................................207 773-2345
Thomas Clarke, *Manager*
EMP: 20
SALES (corp-wide): 3.5B **Publicly Held**
SIC: 3579 7359 Mfg Office Machines Equipment Rental/Leasing
PA: Pitney Bowes Inc.
3001 Summer St Ste 3
Stamford CT 06905
203 356-5000

(G-6710)
PLASMINE TECHNOLOGY INC
33 Bishop St (04103-2614)
PHONE..................................207 797-5009
Steve Violette, *President*
EMP: 7 **Privately Held**
WEB: www.plasmine.com
SIC: 2819 Mfg Industrial Inorganic Chemicals
HQ: Plasmine Technology, Inc
3298 Summit Blvd Ste 35
Pensacola FL 32503
850 438-8550

(G-6711)
PORTLAND MONTHLY INC
Also Called: Portland Magazine
722 Congress St (04102-3306)
PHONE..................................207 775-4339
Collin Sargent, *President*
Nancy Sargent, *Vice Pres*
EMP: 8
SQ FT: 3,400
SALES (est): 1.1MM **Privately Held**
WEB: www.portlandmonthly.com
SIC: 2721 Periodicals-Publishing/Printing

(G-6712)
PORTLAND PUDGY INC
48 Tyng St (04102-3951)
PHONE..................................207 761-2428
David Hulbert, *President*
Deborah Paley, *Admin Sec*
EMP: 4
SALES (est): 393.7K **Privately Held**
WEB: www.portlandpudgy.com
SIC: 3732 Boatbuilding/Repairing

(G-6713)
PORTLAND STONE WORKS INC
Also Called: Portland Stoneworks
50 Allen Ave (04103-3742)
PHONE..................................207 878-6832
Paul G White, *President*
Richard Gadboif, *Clerk*
EMP: 11
SALES (est): 1MM **Privately Held**
WEB: www.portlandstoneworks.com
SIC: 2541 Mfg Granite Counter Tops

(G-6714)
POWERFUL ME
10 Beacon St (04103-4012)
P.O. Box 737 (04104-0737)
PHONE..................................207 370-8830
Danielle Wozniak, *Partner*
Christine Fiore, *Partner*
Allison Morrill, *Partner*
Melissa Neff, *Partner*
EMP: 4
SALES (est): 177.5K **Privately Held**
SIC: 7372 Prepackaged Software Services

(G-6715)
PRECISION DIRECT INC
Also Called: Filerx.com
200 Riverside Indus Pkwy (04103-1414)
PHONE..................................207 321-3677
Chris Lefevre, *President*
Carl Lefevre, *Principal*
John Lefevre, *Principal*
Cindy Wilson, *Principal*
EMP: 4
SQ FT: 22,000
SALES (est): 1.1MM **Privately Held**
WEB: www.filerx.com
SIC: 2759 Medical Related Filing And Printed Supplies

(G-6716)
PRINTGRAPHICS OF MAINE INC
Also Called: Gemforms
116 Riverside Indtl Pkwy (04103-1431)
PHONE..................................207 347-5700
Royal Macdonald, *President*
Royal Mac Donald, *President*
Chris Breen, *Vice Pres*
EMP: 5
SQ FT: 1,000
SALES: 1MM **Privately Held**
SIC: 2759 5112 Commercial Printing Whol Stationery/Office Supplies

(G-6717)
PROTEIN HOLDINGS INC (PA)
10 Moulton St Ste 5 (04101-5039)
PHONE..................................207 771-0965
Whit Gallagher, *CEO*
Stephan Lanfer, *Ch of Bd*
Frank Ruch, *President*
Andrew Pease, *Exec VP*
Scott W Andrews, *CFO*
▲ **EMP:** 15
SALES (est): 105.2MM **Privately Held**
SIC: 2026 2024 Mfg And Distributes Milk Juice And Ice Cream

(G-6718)
PYRAMID CHECKS & PRINTING
208 Riverside Indus Pkwy (04103-1414)
PHONE..................................207 878-9832
Carl J Lefevre, *President*
Christopher J Lefevre, *Vice Pres*
Mary Michals, *Accounting Mgr*
John Tower, *Info Tech Mgr*
Beth Shorey, *Representative*
EMP: 80
SQ FT: 20,000
SALES (est): 13MM **Privately Held**
WEB: www.pyramidchecks-printing.com
SIC: 2752 Lithographic Commercial Printing

(G-6719)
R2B INC
94 Abby Ln (04103-2271)
PHONE..................................207 797-0019
Richard L Beard, *President*
EMP: 10 **EST:** 2007
SALES: 500K **Privately Held**
SIC: 3423 5023 8742 Mfg Hand/Edge Tools Whol Homefurnishings Management Consulting Services

(G-6720)
RAMBLERS WAY FARM INC
75 Market St Ste 101 (04101-5031)
PHONE..................................207 699-4600
EMP: 8 **Privately Held**
SIC: 2231 Wool Broadwoven Fabric Mill
PA: Rambler's Way Farm, Inc.
2 Storer St Ste 207
Kennebunk ME

(G-6721)
REGINASPICES
47 Edgeworth Ave (04103-2411)
PHONE..................................207 632-5544
EMP: 3
SALES (est): 176K **Privately Held**
SIC: 2099 Mfg Food Preparations

(G-6722)
ROBERT MITCHELL CO INC (DH)
Also Called: Douglas Bros Div
423 Riverside Indus Pkwy (04103-1485)
PHONE..................................207 797-6771
William Mackeil, *General Mgr*
EMP: 20
SQ FT: 24,000
SALES: 10MM
SALES (corp-wide): 729.6MM **Privately Held**
SIC: 3441 Structural Metal Fabrication
HQ: Robert Mitchell Inc
350 Boul Decarie
Saint-Laurent QC
514 747-2471

(G-6723)
ROCKSTEP SOLUTIONS INC
48 Free St Ste 200 (04101-3872)
PHONE..................................844 800-7625
Charles Donnelly, *CEO*
Abigail Ames,
Carrie Leduc,
EMP: 4
SALES (est): 299.9K **Privately Held**
SIC: 7372 7389 Application Computer Software

(G-6724)
SEA BAGS LLC (PA)
25 Custom House Wharf (04101-4708)
PHONE..................................207 780-0744
Elizabeth Shissler, *President*
Sokunthy Yean, *Vice Pres*
Hilary Campbell, *Production*
Amber Henault, *Finance Mgr*
Amy Gaynor, *Sales Mgr*
▼ **EMP:** 24
SALES (est): 1.7MM **Privately Held**
WEB: www.seabags.com
SIC: 2299 5632 Manufacture Textile Goods Retail Accessories/Specialties

(G-6725)
SHED HAPPENS INC (PA)
Also Called: H2ohh
509 Warren Ave (04103-1005)
PHONE..................................207 892-3636
Michael Doherty, *President*
Dennis Doherty, *Vice Pres*
Tracy Doherty, *Treasurer*
EMP: 7
SALES (est): 1.1MM **Privately Held**
WEB: www.shedhappens.com
SIC: 2511 Mfg Wood Household Furniture

(G-6726)
SHIPYARD BREWING LTD LBLTY CO
86 Newbury St (04101-4274)
PHONE..................................207 761-0807
Erick Christensen, *Safety Mgr*
Joe Rank, *Production*
Irena Black, *Buyer*
Lindsey Murray, *Sales Staff*
Jason S Donati, *Sales Associate*
◆ **EMP:** 35
SALES (est): 11.8MM **Privately Held**
WEB: www.shipyard.com
SIC: 2082 Drinking Place
PA: Ashleigh, Inc
8 Western Ave Ste 6
Kennebunk ME 04043

(G-6727)
SIGN CONCEPTS
342 Warren Ave (04103-1183)
PHONE..................................207 699-2920
Steve Emma, *Vice Pres*
EMP: 12 **EST:** 2010
SALES (est): 1.4MM **Privately Held**
SIC: 3993 Mfg Signs/Advertising Specialties

(G-6728)
SIGN DESIGN INC
306 Warren Ave Ste 3 (04103-1191)
P.O. Box 207 (04112-0207)
PHONE..................................207 856-2600
Roger Flannery, *President*
EMP: 12 **EST:** 1990
SALES (est): 1.3MM **Privately Held**
SIC: 3993 Mfg Signs/Advertising Specialties

(G-6729)
SIGN SYSTEMS OF MAINE INC
Also Called: Ion Design Group
22 Free St Ste 303 (04101-3916)
PHONE..................................207 775-7110
Robert Verrier, *President*
Rob Verrier, *Principal*
Sarah Verrier, *Treasurer*
EMP: 4
SQ FT: 2,000
SALES (est): 238.1K **Privately Held**
WEB: www.iondesigngroup.com
SIC: 3993 7373 Mfg Signs/Advertising Specialties Ret Misc Merchandise

(G-6730)
SNUG
223 Congress St Ste 1 (04101-3657)
PHONE..................................207 772-6839
Margaret Lyons, *Owner*
EMP: 4 **EST:** 2007
SALES (est): 157.3K **Privately Held**
SIC: 2879 Mfg Agricultural Chemicals

(G-6731)
SOCK SHACK
564 Congress St (04101-3311)
PHONE..................................207 805-1348
Lori Dorr, *Principal*
EMP: 6 **EST:** 2016
SALES (est): 107.4K **Privately Held**
SIC: 2252 Mfg Hosiery

(G-6732)
SOLIDPHASE INC
44 Caddie Ln (04103-1298)
PHONE..................................207 797-0211
Stuart Miller, *President*
David Perry, *Vice Pres*
Pamela Zallerfarrington, *Treasurer*
EMP: 6
SALES (est): 510K **Privately Held**
SIC: 2836 2835 Mfg Biological Products Mfg Diagnostic Substances

(G-6733)
SONIC BLUE AEROSPACE INC
80 Exchange St Ste 36 (04101-5035)
PHONE..................................207 776-2471
Richard H Lugg, *President*
James Belanger, *Admin Sec*
EMP: 8
SALES (est): 590.9K **Privately Held**
SIC: 3721 Aircraft Manufacturing

(G-6734)
SUBX INC
Also Called: Quantrix
428 Fore St Unit 4 (04101-5108)
PHONE..................................207 775-0808
Peter M Murray, *President*
EMP: 5
SQ FT: 1,770
SALES (est): 514.8K **Privately Held**
WEB: www.subx.com
SIC: 7372 Prepackaged Software Services

(G-6735)
SUNRISE GUIDE LLC
503 Woodford St (04103-2439)
P.O. Box 163, Westbrook (04098-0163)
PHONE..................................207 221-3450
Heather Chandler, *President*
EMP: 10
SALES (est): 525.6K **Privately Held**
SIC: 2711 Newspapers-Publishing/Printing

(G-6736)
T R SIGN DESIGN INC
306 Warren Ave Ste 3 (04103-1191)
PHONE..................................207 856-2600
Roger Flannery, *President*
Tim Flannery, *President*
EMP: 12
SQ FT: 30,000
SALES (est): 1MM **Privately Held**
SIC: 3993 Mfg Signs & Advertising Specialties

(G-6737)
TAPROOT
49 Fox St (04101-2500)
PHONE..................................802 472-1617
Veronica Medwid, *Principal*
EMP: 3
SALES (est): 196.3K **Privately Held**
SIC: 2721 Periodicals-Publishing/Printing

(G-6738)
TEX-TECH INDUSTRIES INC (PA)
Also Called: Tex Tech Industries
1 City Ctr Ste 11 (04101-6412)
PHONE..................................207 756-8606
Ciaran Lynch, *President*

GEOGRAPHIC

Stephen Judge, *Exec VP*
Scott Janco, *Mfg Staff*
Moe Maheux, *Mfg Staff*
John Stankiewicz, *CFO*
▲ **EMP:** 185
SQ FT: 3,000
SALES (est): 62.9MM **Privately Held**
SIC: 2221 Manmade Broadwoven Fabric Mill

(G-6739)
TIDESTONE SOLUTIONS
30 Milk St Ste 3 (04101-5117)
PHONE..................................207 761-2133
Richard Tobey Scott, *President*
Lindsay Walsh, *Principal*
Sandra A Wyman, *Vice Pres*
Morgan Papi, *Opers Staff*
EMP: 5
SALES (est): 525.3K **Privately Held**
WEB: www.gilchristscott.com
SIC: 7372 Computer Related Services

(G-6740)
TIMKEN MOTOR & CRANE SVCS LLC
Also Called: Stultz Electric
190 Riverside St Unit 4a (04103-1073)
PHONE..................................207 699-2501
EMP: 15
SALES (corp-wide): 3.5B **Publicly Held**
SIC: 7694 7699 Armature Rewinding Repair Services
HQ: Timken Motor & Crane Services, Llc
4850 Moline St
Denver CO 80239
303 623-8658

(G-6741)
TORREFACTION TECH USA LLC
2 Market St Ste 500 (04101-5118)
P.O. Box 17536 (04112-8536)
PHONE..................................207 775-2464
Drew Swenson, *Partner*
EMP: 4
SALES: 100K **Privately Held**
SIC: 3559 Mfg Misc Industry Machinery

(G-6742)
TORTILLERIA PACHANGA
1 Industrial Way (04103-1072)
PHONE..................................207 797-9700
Lynne Rowe, *Principal*
EMP: 5
SALES (est): 243.9K **Privately Held**
SIC: 2099 Mfg Food Preparations

(G-6743)
TRUELINE PUBLISHING LLC
561 Congress St (04101-3308)
PHONE..................................207 510-4099
Haj Carr, *President*
EMP: 40 **EST:** 2010
SALES: 5.9MM **Privately Held**
SIC: 2721 Periodicals-Publishing/Printing

(G-6744)
VERVAIN MILL
35 Buttonwood Ln (04102-1629)
PHONE..................................207 774-5744
Wendy Taylor, *Principal*
EMP: 3
SALES (est): 167.5K **Privately Held**
SIC: 2099 Mfg Food Preparations

(G-6745)
WILD OCEAN AQUACULTURE LLC
Also Called: Bangs Island Mussels
72 Commercial St 15 (04101-4749)
PHONE..................................207 458-6288
Michael Dowd, *Vice Pres*
Cindy Koehler, *Vice Pres*
Mike Myers, *Vice Pres*
Matthew Moretti,
EMP: 7 **EST:** 2010
SALES (est): 502.1K **Privately Held**
SIC: 2091 Mfg Canned/Cured Fish/Seafood

(G-6746)
WRITING COMPANY
2 Portland Fish Pier # 213 (04101-4699)
PHONE..................................207 370-8078
Clint Willis, *President*
Frank Smith, *Principal*
Michaela Cavallaro, *Vice Pres*
Taylor Smith, *Vice Pres*
EMP: 5
SALES (est): 464.1K **Privately Held**
SIC: 2741 Misc Publishing

(G-6747)
XPRESS OF MAINE (PA)
Also Called: Xpress Copy Services
17 Westfield St Ste A (04102-2790)
P.O. Box 7524 (04112-7524)
PHONE..................................207 775-2444
Philip M Rhinelander, *President*
EMP: 9
SALES (est): 1.7MM **Privately Held**
WEB: www.xcopy.com
SIC: 2789 2759 7374 7334 Photocopying Service Bookbinding/Related Work Commercial Printing Data Processing/Prep

Pownal
Cumberland County

(G-6748)
BRADBURY MTN METALWORKS LLC
56 Minot Rd (04069-6201)
PHONE..................................207 688-5009
Nicholas Cote,
EMP: 3
SALES (est): 204.6K **Privately Held**
SIC: 3446 Mfg Architectural Metalwork

(G-6749)
JESSICAS DISCOUNT FUEL
247 Allen Rd (04069-6013)
PHONE..................................207 310-1966
Mike Brady, *Principal*
EMP: 3
SALES (est): 208.5K **Privately Held**
SIC: 2869 Mfg Industrial Organic Chemicals

(G-6750)
PONDERA PHARMACEUTICALS INC
Also Called: Pondera Nutraceuticals
209 Chadsey Rd (04069-6054)
PHONE..................................207 688-4494
William Crain, *President*
EMP: 4
SALES: 300K **Privately Held**
SIC: 2834 Mfg Pharmaceutical Preparations

Presque Isle
Aroostook County

(G-6751)
A & D PRINT SHOP
Also Called: Swap Buy Sell Guide
540 Main St (04769-2449)
P.O. Box 219, Washburn (04786-0219)
PHONE..................................207 764-2662
Andrew Turner, *Owner*
Donna Turner, *Co-Owner*
EMP: 6
SALES: 220K **Privately Held**
WEB: www.swapbuysellguide.com
SIC: 2741 Misc Publishing

(G-6752)
ALLENS ENVIRONMENTAL SVCS INC
Also Called: Allen's Drain Cleaning Service
27 Washburn Rd (04769)
P.O. Box 109 (04769-0109)
PHONE..................................207 764-9336
EMP: 3
SALES (est): 81.8K **Privately Held**
SIC: 2842 Mfg Polish/Sanitation Goods

(G-6753)
AROOSTACAST INC
217 Parsons Rd (04769-5116)
PHONE..................................207 764-0077
Timothy Wilcox, *President*
Tim Wilcox, *President*
EMP: 10
SQ FT: 12,000
SALES: 700K **Privately Held**
SIC: 3272 Mfg Concrete Products

(G-6754)
AROOSTOOK TRUSSES INC
655 Missile St (04769-2083)
P.O. Box 548 (04769-0548)
PHONE..................................207 768-5817
Gary Nelson, *President*
Harris Nickerson, *Vice Pres*
EMP: 20
SQ FT: 12,000
SALES (est): 3.5MM **Privately Held**
WEB: www.aroostooktrusses.com
SIC: 2439 Mfg Structural Wood Members

(G-6755)
CAM MFG INC
1215 Airport Dr (04769-2051)
PHONE..................................207 764-4199
Marc C Brown, *President*
Mark E Jones, *Treasurer*
Mark Jones, *Treasurer*
EMP: 7
SQ FT: 6,000
SALES (est): 750K **Privately Held**
SIC: 3599 Machine Shop Jobbing And Repair

(G-6756)
COCA-COLA BOTTLING COMPANY
1005 Airport Dr (04769-2098)
PHONE..................................207 764-4481
Wesley Elmer, *Manager*
EMP: 30 **Privately Held**
SIC: 2086 Carb Sft Drnkbtlcn
HQ: Coca-Cola Beverages Northeast, Inc.
1 Executive Park Dr # 330
Bedford NH 03110
603 627-7871

(G-6757)
COLUMBIA FOREST PRODUCTS INC
Also Called: Veneer Division
395 Missile St (04769-2084)
P.O. Box 848 (04769-0848)
PHONE..................................207 760-3800
Mark Kelly, *Branch Mgr*
EMP: 250
SALES (corp-wide): 778.2MM **Privately Held**
WEB: www.columbiaveneer.com
SIC: 2435 2426 Mfg Hardwood Veneer/Plywood Hardwood Dimension/Floor Mill
PA: Columbia Forest Products, Inc.
7900 Mccloud Rd Ste 200
Greensboro NC 27409
336 605-0429

(G-6758)
HAROLD HAINES INC
Also Called: Haines Manufacturing Co
243 Main St (04769-2858)
PHONE..................................207 762-1411
Fredrick Haines, *President*
Harold F Haines Jr, *Vice Pres*
Jacqueline Haines, *Treasurer*
EMP: 14
SQ FT: 25,000
SALES (est): 2.9MM **Privately Held**
SIC: 3523 Mfg Potato Grading Equipment

(G-6759)
HIPERFAX INC
470 State St (04769-5030)
PHONE..................................207 764-4319
EMP: 3 **EST:** 1994
SQ FT: 5,000
SALES: 500K **Privately Held**
SIC: 3089 Manufactures Rec Vehicle Accessories

(G-6760)
LOCKWOOD MFG INC
135 Parsons St (04769-2130)
PHONE..................................207 764-4196
Chuck Crary, *President*
EMP: 12
SALES (est): 1MM **Privately Held**
SIC: 3999 Mfg Misc Products

(G-6761)
M & M SHEET METAL & WELDING
32 Industrial St (04769-2536)
PHONE..................................207 764-6443
Robert Morin, *President*
Pat McCormick, *Treasurer*
EMP: 4
SQ FT: 4,000
SALES: 200K **Privately Held**
SIC: 7692 Welding Repair

(G-6762)
MIKES AND SONS
87 State St (04769-2320)
PHONE..................................207 762-6310
Jonathan Nadeau, *Owner*
EMP: 3
SQ FT: 1,000
SALES: 300K **Privately Held**
SIC: 3568 Mfg Power Transmission Equipment

(G-6763)
NORTHEAST PACKAGING CO (PA)
Also Called: Nepco
875 Skyway St (04769-2063)
P.O. Box 328 (04769-0328)
PHONE..................................207 764-6271
Robert Umphrey, *President*
Jesse Harris, *Prdtn Mgr*
Dale Shannon, *Maintence Staff*
▲ **EMP:** 45
SQ FT: 60,000
SALES (est): 7.8MM **Privately Held**
SIC: 2673 2674 Mfg Bags-Plastic/Coated Paper Mfg Bags-Uncoated Paper

(G-6764)
NORTHEAST PUBLISHING COMPANY (HQ)
Also Called: Aroostook Republican
260 Missile St (04769-2069)
P.O. Box 510 (04769-0510)
PHONE..................................207 764-4471
Richard J Warren, *President*
EMP: 60 **EST:** 1965
SQ FT: 48,000
SALES (est): 8.3MM
SALES (corp-wide): 74MM **Privately Held**
SIC: 2711 Newspapers-Publishing/Printing
PA: Bangor Publishing Company
1 Merchants Plz
Bangor ME 04401
207 990-8000

(G-6765)
NORTHEAST PUBLISHING COMPANY
Also Called: Print Works
260 Missile St (04769-2069)
P.O. Box 510 (04769-0510)
PHONE..................................207 764-4471
Pam Lynch, *Business Mgr*
EMP: 10
SALES (corp-wide): 74MM **Privately Held**
SIC: 2759 Commercial Printing
HQ: Northeast Publishing Company Inc
260 Missile St
Presque Isle ME 04769
207 764-4471

(G-6766)
NORTHEAST PUBLISHING COMPANY
Also Called: Starherald Newspaper Pubg
40 North St Ste 2 (04769-2269)
P.O. Box 510 (04769-0510)
PHONE..................................207 768-5431
Jim Berry, *Manager*
EMP: 6
SALES (corp-wide): 74MM **Privately Held**
SIC: 2711 Newspapers-Publishing/Printing
HQ: Northeast Publishing Company Inc
260 Missile St
Presque Isle ME 04769
207 764-4471

▲ = Import ▼=Export
◆ =Import/Export

(G-6767)
NORTHERN PRINTERS INC
30 Dudley St (04769-2614)
PHONE....................207 769-1231
Eugene Wright, *President*
EMP: 3
SALES (est): 240K **Privately Held**
SIC: 2752 Lithographic Commercial Printing

(G-6768)
P C NORTHERN PROSTHETICS
117 Academy St (04769-3000)
PHONE....................207 768-5348
Cory Lalante, *President*
Dan Macfarline, *Software Dev*
Patti Lento, *Receptionist*
EMP: 8
SALES (est): 1MM **Privately Held**
SIC: 3842 Mfg Surgical Appliances/Supplies

(G-6769)
PEPSI COLA BOTTLING AROOSTOOK
Also Called: Pepsico
52 Industrial St Ste 1 (04769-2598)
PHONE....................207 760-3000
J Gregory Freeman, *President*
Anne M Freeman, *Treasurer*
Tom Augustine, *Manager*
Kent McKay, *Manager*
Katherine Freeman, *Clerk*
EMP: 26 **EST:** 1946
SQ FT: 35,000
SALES: 5MM **Privately Held**
SIC: 2086 Carb Sft Drnkbtlcn

(G-6770)
TROMBLEY REDI-MIX INC (PA)
221 Parsons Rd (04769-5116)
PHONE....................207 551-3770
Craig Trombley, *President*
EMP: 5
SALES (est): 621.1K **Privately Held**
SIC: 3273 Mfg Ready-Mixed Concrete

Prospect Harbor
Hancock County

(G-6771)
RICHARD FISHER
Also Called: U S Bells
56 W Bay Rd (04669-5023)
P.O. Box 73 (04669-0073)
PHONE....................207 963-7184
Richard Fisher, *Owner*
EMP: 3
SQ FT: 4,000
SALES: 334.8K **Privately Held**
WEB: www.usbells.com
SIC: 3999 5999 3931 3429 Mfg Misc Products Ret Misc Merchandise Mfg Musical Instruments Mfg Hardware

Rangeley
Franklin County

(G-6772)
J & S LOGGING
3039 Main St (04970-4205)
P.O. Box 565 (04970-0565)
PHONE....................207 864-5617
David Haley, *President*
Scott Millbury, *Vice Pres*
EMP: 5
SQ FT: 4,000
SALES (est): 400K **Privately Held**
SIC: 2411 Logging Contractor

Raymond
Cumberland County

(G-6773)
GUTTER WHOLESALERS INC
Also Called: Gutter People, The
145 Webbs Mills Rd 93-1 (04071-6323)
P.O. Box 1954, Windham (04062-1954)
PHONE....................207 655-7407
Scott Lamson, *President*
Tammy Lamson, *Vice Pres*
EMP: 6
SALES: 325K **Privately Held**
SIC: 3444 1761 Mfg & Installs Aluminum Gutters

(G-6774)
SPX CORPORATION
Also Called: Radiodetection
22 Tower Rd (04071-6440)
P.O. Box 949 (04071-0949)
PHONE....................207 655-8100
Andre Skalina, *President*
Garrett Van Atta, *Manager*
EMP: 200
SQ FT: 7,500
SALES (corp-wide): 1.5B **Publicly Held**
WEB: www.spx.com
SIC: 3663 Mfg Radio/Tv Communication Equipment
PA: Spx Corporation
13320a Balntyn Corp Pl
Charlotte NC 28277
980 474-3700

(G-6775)
SPX CORPORATION
Radiodetection
28 Tower Rd (04071-6440)
PHONE....................207 655-8525
Zenya Brackett, *Branch Mgr*
EMP: 40
SALES (corp-wide): 1.5B **Publicly Held**
WEB: www.radiodetection.com
SIC: 3661 Mfg Telephone/Telegraph Apparatus
PA: Spx Corporation
13320a Balntyn Corp Pl
Charlotte NC 28277
980 474-3700

Readfield
Kennebec County

(G-6776)
EDGAR CLARK & SON INC
Rr 41 (04355)
P.O. Box 218 (04355-0218)
PHONE....................207 685-4568
Don Clark, *Owner*
EMP: 4
SALES (est): 400K **Privately Held**
SIC: 3429 Mfg Hardware

(G-6777)
GERARD POULIN & SONS LOGGING
115 Poulin Dr (04355-3540)
PHONE....................207 246-3537
Larry Poulin, *Principal*
EMP: 11 **EST:** 2009
SALES (est): 1.2MM **Privately Held**
SIC: 2411 Logging

(G-6778)
SAUNDERS MFG CO INC (PA)
Also Called: Saunders Manufacturing & Mktg
65 Nickerson Hill Rd (04355-3924)
PHONE....................207 685-9860
John Rosmarin, *President*
Donn Harriman, *CFO*
David Lipman, *Clerk*
▲ **EMP:** 65 **EST:** 1946
SQ FT: 40,000
SALES (est): 13.5MM **Privately Held**
WEB: www.saunders-usa.com
SIC: 3499 Mfg Misc Fabricated Metal Products

Reed Plt
Aroostook County

(G-6779)
HANINGTON TIMBERLANDS
95 Main St (04497-6000)
P.O. Box 90, Wytopitlock (04497-0090)
PHONE....................207 456-7003
Scott Hanington, *President*
Lorie Hanington, *Vice Pres*
EMP: 15
SALES (est): 1.3MM **Privately Held**
SIC: 2411 Logging

(G-6780)
WILLARD S HANINGTON & SON INC
1619 Military Rd (04497-6024)
P.O. Box 70, Wytopitlock (04497-0070)
PHONE....................207 456-7511
Willard Hanington Jr, *President*
Willard S Hanington, *Vice Pres*
EMP: 28
SQ FT: 336
SALES (est): 2.9MM **Privately Held**
SIC: 2411 Logging

Richmond
Sagadahoc County

(G-6781)
CALLAWAY GOLF BALL OPRTONS INC
County Rd (04357)
PHONE....................207 737-4324
Betty Bartos, *Human Resources*
EMP: 145
SALES (corp-wide): 1.2B **Publicly Held**
WEB: www.topflite.com
SIC: 3149 Mfg Footwear-Except Rubber
HQ: Callaway Golf Ball Operations, Inc.
425 Meadow St
Chicopee MA 01013
413 536-1200

(G-6782)
HODGDON YACHTS INC
150 Main St Ste 12 (04357-1156)
PHONE....................207 737-2802
EMP: 3
SALES (corp-wide): 25.2MM **Privately Held**
SIC: 3732 Boatbuilding/Repairing
PA: Hodgdon Yachts, Inc.
14 School St
East Boothbay ME 04544
207 737-2802

(G-6783)
SHUCKS MAINE LOBSTER LLC
150 Main St Ste 4 (04357-1156)
PHONE....................207 737-4800
Charlie Langston, *COO*
Caitlin Hathaway, *VP Mktg*
Suellen Hathaway, *Office Mgr*
John Hathaway,
Sueellen Hathaway,
EMP: 15 **EST:** 2005
SQ FT: 60,000
SALES (est): 2.2MM **Privately Held**
SIC: 2092 Whol Fish/Seafood

Rockland
Knox County

(G-6784)
BABTECH INC
Also Called: Beth Bowley
410 Main St (04841-3364)
PHONE....................207 594-7106
Beth Bowley, *Chairman*
▲ **EMP:** 3
SQ FT: 4,200
SALES (est): 335.6K **Privately Held**
WEB: www.babtech.com
SIC: 2253 Knit Outerwear Mill

(G-6785)
BIXBY & CO LLC
1 Sea Street Pl (04841-3412)
PHONE....................207 691-1778
Donna McAleer, *Mng Member*
Kate McAleer,
EMP: 8
SQ FT: 3,000
SALES: 460K **Privately Held**
SIC: 2066 2064 Mfg Chocolate/Cocoa Products Mfg Candy/Confectionery Whol Confectionery

(G-6786)
CAMDEN HERALD
91 Camden St Ste 403 (04841-2421)
P.O. Box 248, Camden (04843-0248)
PHONE....................207 236-8511
William Mebane, *President*
William Atkinson, *Principal*
EMP: 7
SALES (est): 363.5K
SALES (corp-wide): 9.6MM **Privately Held**
WEB: www.jobsformaine.com
SIC: 2711 Newspapers-Publishing/Printing
PA: Village Netmedia, Inc.
91 Camden St Ste 403
Rockland ME 04841
207 594-4401

(G-6787)
CAMDEN PRINTING INC
12 Moran Dr Ste F (04841-2165)
PHONE....................207 236-4112
George Tripp III, *President*
Catherine S Tripp, *Treasurer*
Stanley Karod,
EMP: 3 **EST:** 1970
SALES (est): 631.5K **Privately Held**
WEB: www.camdenprinting.com
SIC: 2752 Offset Printing

(G-6788)
CEDARWORKS OF MAINE INC
Also Called: Cedarworks Playsets
12 Merrill Dr (04841)
PHONE....................207 596-0771
Donald Protheroe, *Branch Mgr*
EMP: 25
SALES (corp-wide): 6.9MM **Privately Held**
WEB: www.cedarworks.com
SIC: 3949 Mfg Sporting/Athletic Goods
PA: Cedarworks Of Maine Inc
799 Commercial St
Rockport ME 04856
207 596-1010

(G-6789)
CHILD SAFETY SOLUTIONS INC
Also Called: I'M Safe Productions
75 Mechanic St (04841-3513)
P.O. Box 1403 (04841-1403)
PHONE....................207 226-3870
Wendy Gordon, *President*
David Gordon, *Vice Pres*
EMP: 3
SQ FT: 1,000
SALES (est): 433.3K **Privately Held**
WEB: www.imsafe.com
SIC: 2731 Books-Publishing/Printing

(G-6790)
DOUGLAS DYNAMICS LLC
Also Called: Fisher Engineering Division
50 Gordon Dr (04841-2139)
P.O. Box 529 (04841-0529)
PHONE....................207 701-4200
Raymond S Littlefield, *Principal*
Charles Carerros, *Analyst*
EMP: 225 **Publicly Held**
WEB: www.fishersnowplows.com
SIC: 3711 3531 3524 Mfg Motor Vehicle/Car Bodies Mfg Construction Machinery Mfg Lawn/Garden Equipment
HQ: Douglas Dynamics, L.L.C.
7777 N 73rd St
Milwaukee WI 53223
414 354-2310

(G-6791)
ELECTROTECH INC
344 Park St (04841-5303)
P.O. Box 1038 (04841-1038)
PHONE....................207 596-0556

Thomas Levasseur, *President*
Shawn Levasseur, *Vice Pres*
Beryl Levasseur, *Treasurer*
EMP: 16
SQ FT: 15,000
SALES (est): 3MM **Privately Held**
WEB: www.electrotech-inc.com
SIC: 3699 Mfg Electrical Equipment/Supplies

(G-6792)
FERRAIOLO CONSTRUCTION INC
279 Main St Ste 1 (04841-3368)
PHONE..................................207 582-6162
EMP: 30
SALES (corp-wide): 7.2MM **Privately Held**
SIC: 3272 Mfg Concrete Products
PA: Ferraiolo Construction, Inc.
28 Gordon Dr
Rockland ME 04841
207 594-9840

(G-6793)
FISHER LLC (PA)
50 Gordon Dr (04841-2168)
PHONE..................................207 701-4200
Darren Gillo, *President*
Andre Leblond, *Project Engr*
Steve Marsh, *Regl Sales Mgr*
EMP: 12
SALES (est): 2.2MM **Privately Held**
SIC: 2851 Mfg Paints/Allied Products

(G-6794)
FISHER ENGINEERING
50 Gordon Dr (04841-2168)
PHONE..................................207 701-4200
Jim Janik, *President*
Rob Somerville, *Safety Dir*
Bruce Knapp, *Buyer*
Ryan Fossett, *Engineer*
Andy Clement, *Controller*
▼ **EMP:** 250 **EST:** 1984
SALES (est): 58.2MM **Publicly Held**
SIC: 3585 Mfg Refrigeration/Heating Equipment
HQ: Douglas Dynamics, L.L.C.
7777 N 73rd St
Milwaukee WI 53223
414 354-2310

(G-6795)
FMC CORPORATION
Also Called: F M C Marine Colloid Division
341 Park St (04841-5302)
P.O. Box 308 (04841-0308)
PHONE..................................207 594-3200
Jeff Boutaugh, *Marketing Staff*
Kiran O'Dwyer, *Branch Mgr*
Rod Mason, *Maintence Staff*
Shawn Thissell, *Maintence Staff*
EMP: 200
SALES (corp-wide): 4.7B **Publicly Held**
WEB: www.fmc.com
SIC: 2869 3295 2899 2087 Mfg Industl Organic Chem Mfg Minerals-Earth/Treat Mfg Chemical Preparation Mfg Flavor Extracts
PA: Fmc Corporation
2929 Walnut St
Philadelphia PA 19104
215 299-6000

(G-6796)
FREE PRESS INC
8 N Main St Ste 101 (04841-3154)
PHONE..................................207 594-4408
Reade Brower, *President*
Charles Reade, *Human Resources*
EMP: 20
SQ FT: 6,000
SALES: 560K **Privately Held**
WEB: www.freepressonline.com
SIC: 2711 Newspapers-Publishing/Printing

(G-6797)
GS INC
12 Moran Dr Ste A1 (04841-2164)
PHONE..................................207 593-7730
Renee Philbrook, *Treasurer*
EMP: 7
SALES: 99.6K **Privately Held**
SIC: 3433 4832 Mfg Heating Equipment-Nonelectric Radio Broadcast Station

(G-6798)
IMAGINEERING INC
Also Called: Weatherend Estate Furniture
6 Gordon Dr (04841-2137)
PHONE..................................207 596-6483
Gil Harper, *President*
EMP: 41
SALES: 3.5MM **Privately Held**
WEB: www.weatherend.com
SIC: 2511 Mfg Wood Household Furniture

(G-6799)
INFORMTION CONSULTING SVCS INC
2a Gordon Dr (04841-2137)
PHONE..................................207 596-7783
Reade Brower, *Manager*
EMP: 50 **Privately Held**
WEB: www.traderonline.com
SIC: 2721 Periodicals-Publishing/Printing
HQ: Information Consulting Services, Inc.
120 Tillson Ave Ste 205
Rockland ME 04841
207 596-0641

(G-6800)
JOHANSONS BOATWORKS
11 Farwell Dr (04841-6313)
PHONE..................................207 596-7060
Peter Johanson, *Partner*
Mary Johanson, *Partner*
EMP: 10
SALES (est): 1.2MM **Privately Held**
WEB: www.jboatworks.com
SIC: 3732 Boatbuilding/Repairing

(G-6801)
KENNISTON MACHINES
Also Called: Kennison Machine Company
30 Moran Dr (04841-2147)
PHONE..................................207 594-7810
Toby W Kenniston, *Owner*
EMP: 4
SALES (est): 484K **Privately Held**
SIC: 3599 Mfg Industrial Machinery

(G-6802)
LONZA ROCKLAND INC
191 Thomaston St (04841-2130)
PHONE..................................207 594-3400
Stephan Borgas, *CEO*
Mary Riley, *Business Mgr*
Hugh White, *Research*
Rebekah Woodworth, *Manager*
EMP: 65
SQ FT: 40,000
SALES (est): 21.1MM
SALES (corp-wide): 5.6B **Privately Held**
WEB: www.lonza.com
SIC: 2836 Mfg Biological Products
HQ: Lonza America Inc.
412 Mount Kemble Ave 200s
Morristown NJ 07960
201 316-9200

(G-6803)
MARINE HYDRAULIC ENGRG CO (PA)
Also Called: Hydro-Slave
17 Gordon Dr (04841-2197)
PHONE..................................207 594-9525
Robert Crowe, *President*
Wayne R Crandall, *Clerk*
▲ **EMP:** 8 **EST:** 1961
SQ FT: 9,200
SALES (est): 1.5MM **Privately Held**
SIC: 3531 Whol Industrial Equipment

(G-6804)
MARKETING WORLDWIDE CORP (PA)
423 Main St 3 (04841-3383)
PHONE..................................631 444-8090
Charles Pinkerton, *CEO*
Michael Winzkowski, *Ch of Bd*
EMP: 5
SQ FT: 3,000
SALES: 790.2K **Publicly Held**
SIC: 3714 7532 Mfg Motor Vehicle Parts/Accessories Auto Body Repair/Painting

(G-6805)
MCDONALD DUVALL DESIGN INC
10 Farwell Dr (04841-6321)
P.O. Box 297, West Rockport (04865-0297)
PHONE..................................207 596-7940
Charles Duvall, *President*
Patricia J McDonald, *Vice Pres*
EMP: 5
SQ FT: 3,000
SALES (est): 603.8K **Privately Held**
SIC: 2394 Mfg Canvas/Related Products

(G-6806)
NORTH END COMPOSITES LLC
Also Called: Back Cove Yachts
23 Merrill Dr (04841-2142)
P.O. Box 548 (04841-0548)
PHONE..................................207 594-8427
Christopher Evans, *President*
Jason Constantine, *President*
Keith Warren, *Engineer*
Adam Carlson, *Design Engr*
Nancy Basselet, *Treasurer*
EMP: 163
SQ FT: 15,000
SALES (est): 24.2MM **Privately Held**
WEB: www.necomposites.com
SIC: 3732 Boatbuilding/Repairing

(G-6807)
OLIVE FIORE OILS & VINEGARS
503 Main St (04841-3336)
PHONE..................................207 596-0276
EMP: 3
SALES (est): 207.8K **Privately Held**
SIC: 2079 Mfg Edible Fats/Oils

(G-6808)
POPE SAILS AND RIGGING INC
237 Park St (04841-2127)
PHONE..................................207 596-7293
Doug Pope, *President*
Beth Pope, *Vice Pres*
EMP: 3
SALES: 350K **Privately Held**
WEB: www.popesails.com
SIC: 2394 Mfg Canvas/Related Products

(G-6809)
ROCKLAND MARINE CORPORATION
79 Mechanic St (04841-3513)
P.O. Box 309 (04841-0309)
PHONE..................................207 594-7860
Perry Holmes, *President*
Shirley Landin, *Manager*
EMP: 50
SALES (est): 10.1MM **Privately Held**
SIC: 3731 Shipbuilding/Repairing

(G-6810)
STEEL-PRO INC
Also Called: Steel Pro Services
771 Main St (04841-3427)
P.O. Box 449 (04841-0449)
PHONE..................................207 596-0061
Steve Ladd, *President*
Chris Beebe, *Chairman*
Craig Wells, *COO*
Jeanne Rimm, *CFO*
Norene Jones, *Office Mgr*
EMP: 45 **EST:** 1978
SQ FT: 21,000
SALES (est): 13.6MM **Privately Held**
WEB: www.steelprousa.com
SIC: 3443 3441 Mfg Fabricated Plate Wrk Structural Metal Fabrctn

(G-6811)
STUART MARINE CORP INC
38 Gordon Dr (04841-2139)
P.O. Box 469 (04841-0469)
PHONE..................................207 594-5515
David C Whittier, *President*
Peter Warren, *Clerk*
EMP: 6
SALES (est): 734.7K **Privately Held**
WEB: www.stuartmarine.net
SIC: 3732 Manufactures & Repais Fiberglass Boats

(G-6812)
TREMS INC
Also Called: Brio Promotions
19 Merrill Dr (04841-2142)
P.O. Box 667 (04841-0667)
PHONE..................................207 596-6989
Jeffrey Thibodeau, *President*
Marli Thibodeau, *Vice Pres*
EMP: 9 **EST:** 2015
SALES: 800K **Privately Held**
SIC: 2759 Commercial Printing

(G-6813)
VILLAGE NETMEDIA INC (PA)
Also Called: Courier Publications
91 Camden St Ste 403 (04841-2421)
P.O. Box 249 (04841-0249)
PHONE..................................207 594-4401
Diane Norton,
EMP: 30
SQ FT: 30,400
SALES (est): 9.6MM **Privately Held**
WEB: www.jobsformaine.com
SIC: 2711 Publishes & Prints Newspapers

(G-6814)
VILLAGE NETMEDIA INC
Also Called: Villagesoup
91 Camden St Ste 403 (04841-2421)
P.O. Box 249 (04841-0249)
PHONE..................................207 594-4401
Richard Anderson, *President*
Ron Belyea, *Principal*
EMP: 31
SALES (est): 1.8MM **Privately Held**
SIC: 2711 Newspapers-Publishing/Printing

(G-6815)
WILD FIBERS MAGAZINE
20 Elm St (04841-2868)
P.O. Box 1752 (04841-1752)
PHONE..................................207 594-9455
Hugh Nesbit, *Principal*
EMP: 5
SALES (est): 488.3K **Privately Held**
SIC: 2721 Periodicals-Publishing/Printing

(G-6816)
YORK MARINE INC
11 Gordon Dr (04841-2138)
PHONE..................................207 596-7400
Toll Free:..888 -
Michael York, *President*
Paul Le Compte, *General Mgr*
Susan McIntyre, *Finance Mgr*
Mike York, *Manager*
EMP: 6
SQ FT: 7,000
SALES (est): 719.1K **Privately Held**
WEB: www.yorkmarineinc.com
SIC: 3732 Boatbuilding And Repairing

Rockport
Knox County

(G-6817)
CEDARWORKS OF MAINE INC (PA)
Also Called: Cedarworks Playsets
799 Commercial St (04856-4204)
P.O. Box 990 (04856-0990)
PHONE..................................207 596-1010
Barrett Brown, *President*
Duncan Brown, *Chairman*
Mark Breton, *VP Finance*
Mark Odonell, *Marketing Staff*
Corey Fougner, *CIO*
EMP: 25
SQ FT: 2,500
SALES (est): 6.9MM **Privately Held**
WEB: www.cedarworks.com
SIC: 2511 Mfg Wood Household Furniture

(G-6818)
D E ENTERPRISE INC
Also Called: Fly Rod & Reel
680 Commercial St (04856-4201)
P.O. Box 679, Camden (04843-0679)
PHONE..................................207 594-9544
Robert Fernald, *President*
Brian Kevin, *Chief*
James E Butler, *Vice Pres*
Lawrence B Hollins, *Sales Dir*

▲ = Import ▼=Export
◆ =Import/Export

Linda Wood, *Advt Staff*
▲ **EMP:** 75 **EST:** 1954
SQ FT: 25,000
SALES (est): 7.4MM **Privately Held**
WEB: www.flyrodreel.com
SIC: 2721 2731 7389 Periodicals-Publishing/Printing Books-Publishing/Printing Business Services

(G-6819)
DANICA DESIGN INC (PA)
Also Called: Danica Candle Works
569 West St (04856-5308)
P.O. Box 206, West Rockport (04865-0206)
PHONE..................................207 236-3060
Erik Laustsen, *President*
Cindy Laustsen, *Vice Pres*
Cynthia Laustsen, *Vice Pres*
EMP: 6
SQ FT: 4,000
SALES (est): 1.7MM **Privately Held**
WEB: www.danicadesign.com
SIC: 3999 Mfg Candles

(G-6820)
DOWN EAST ENTERPRISE INC
680 Commercial St (04856-4201)
P.O. Box 679, Camden (04843-0679)
PHONE..................................207 594-9544
Robert Fernald, *President*
Brian Kevin, *Editor*
Sarah Stebbins, *Editor*
Kathleen Fleury, *Chief*
Jim Butler, *Vice Pres*
▲ **EMP:** 48
SALES: 1,000K **Privately Held**
SIC: 2721 Periodicals-Publishing/Printing

(G-6821)
E S BOHNDELL & CO INC
Also Called: Bohndell Sails
198 Commercial St (04856-5903)
P.O. Box 628 (04856-0628)
PHONE..................................207 236-3549
Robert M Chace, *President*
Charles Babb, *Vice Pres*
EMP: 6 **EST:** 1930
SQ FT: 6,000
SALES (est): 300K **Privately Held**
SIC: 2394 Mfg Sails

(G-6822)
GLOVER COMPANY INC
Also Called: Rockport Steel
17 Rockville St (04856-4409)
P.O. Box 1049 (04856-1049)
PHONE..................................207 236-8644
William Glover, *President*
Diana Glover, *Vice Pres*
▼ **EMP:** 12
SALES (est): 1.3MM **Privately Held**
WEB: www.glovercompany.com
SIC: 3441 Structural Metal Fabrication

(G-6823)
HARTLAND INC
61 Hope St (04856-6314)
P.O. Box 554 (04856-0554)
PHONE..................................207 785-4350
John Hart, *Owner*
EMP: 4
SALES (est): 534.1K **Privately Held**
SIC: 2411 Logging

(G-6824)
MICHAEL GOOD DESIGNS INC
325 Commercial St (04856-4403)
P.O. Box 788 (04856-0788)
PHONE..................................207 236-9619
Karen Jordan Good, *President*
Michael Good, *Treasurer*
EMP: 13
SQ FT: 4,000
SALES (est): 1.5MM **Privately Held**
WEB: www.michaelgood.com
SIC: 3911 3545 Mfg Jewelry Apparel Precious Metals

(G-6825)
REDDEN PUBLISHING CO LLC
160 Mistic Ave (04856-5730)
PHONE..................................207 236-0767
Dan Redden, *Owner*
EMP: 8
SALES (est): 457.6K **Privately Held**
SIC: 2754 Publishing Magazine

(G-6826)
ROCKPORT MARINE INC
1 Main St (04856-5960)
P.O. Box 203 (04856-0203)
PHONE..................................207 236-9651
Taylor M Allen, *President*
▼ **EMP:** 50 **EST:** 1962
SQ FT: 12,000
SALES (est): 8.6MM **Privately Held**
WEB: www.rockportmarine.com
SIC: 3732 Boatbuilding/Repairing

(G-6827)
WOODSOUND STUDIO
Also Called: Pinkham's Guitar
1103 Commercial St (04856-3843)
PHONE..................................207 596-7407
Ronald Pinkham, *Owner*
EMP: 3
SQ FT: 1,600
SALES (est): 279.2K **Privately Held**
SIC: 3931 5736 Mfg Musical Instruments Ret Musical Instruments

Rome
Kennebec County

(G-6828)
MACLEAY INTERACTIVE DESIGN INC
Also Called: Trailspace
17 Richardson Rd (04963-3164)
P.O. Box 499, Belgrade Lakes (04918-0499)
PHONE..................................207 495-2208
David Macleay, *President*
Alicia Macleay, *Treasurer*
Robert Marden, *Clerk*
EMP: 3 **EST:** 2000
SALES (est): 201.9K **Privately Held**
SIC: 2741 7389 Internet Publishing And Broadcasting Business Serv Non-Commercial Site

Round Pond
Lincoln County

(G-6829)
DANA ROBES BOAT BUILDERS
75 Southern Point Rd (04564-3703)
PHONE..................................207 529-2433
Dana Robes, *Partner*
Martha Robes, *Partner*
EMP: 7
SALES (est): 471.9K **Privately Held**
SIC: 3732 Boatbuilding/Repairing

(G-6830)
MASTERS MACHINE COMPANY INC
500 Lower Round Pond Rd (04564)
P.O. Box 16 (04564-0016)
PHONE..................................207 529-5191
Richard Masters, *President*
George Master Jr, *Vice Pres*
Steven Masters, *Plant Mgr*
▲ **EMP:** 114 **EST:** 1957
SQ FT: 120,000
SALES (est): 28.3MM **Privately Held**
WEB: www.mastersmachine.com
SIC: 3599 Mfg Industrial Machinery

(G-6831)
NORTH COUNTRY WIND BELLS INC
544 State Route 32 (04564-3728)
PHONE..................................207 677-2224
James L Davidson, *President*
May B Davidson, *Treasurer*
Constance Southwick, *Shareholder*
Timothy Southwick, *Shareholder*
EMP: 12 **EST:** 1950
SALES (est): 1.7MM **Privately Held**
WEB: www.northcountrybells.com
SIC: 3599 Mfg Industrial Machinery

(G-6832)
PADEBCO CUSTOM BOATS INC
Anchor Inn Rd (04564)
P.O. Box 197 (04564-0197)
PHONE..................................207 529-5106
S Bruce Cunningham, *President*
Paul Cunningham, *Treasurer*
Debra Cunningham, *Admin Sec*
EMP: 7
SQ FT: 4,000
SALES (est): 1.2MM **Privately Held**
WEB: www.padebco.com
SIC: 3732 4213 Boatbuilding/Repairing Trucking Operator-Nonlocal

Rumford
Oxford County

(G-6833)
CLINTON G BRADBURY INC
Also Called: Bradbury Enterprises
1180 Route 2 Ste 5 (04276-3644)
PHONE..................................207 562-8014
Clinton Bradbury, *President*
EMP: 9
SALES (est): 961K **Privately Held**
SIC: 2411 Logging

(G-6834)
GAMMON MILAM
286 Andover Rd (04276-4009)
PHONE..................................207 364-2889
Milam Gammon, *Owner*
Maureen Gammon, *Co-Owner*
EMP: 3
SALES (est): 180K **Privately Held**
SIC: 2411 Logging

(G-6835)
HOPE ASSOCIATION (PA)
85 Lincoln Ave (04276-1844)
PHONE..................................207 364-4561
Joseph Sirois, *Director*
EMP: 95
SALES: 3.8MM **Privately Held**
SIC: 3999 8322 Mfg Misc Products Individual/Family Services

(G-6836)
JAMES NEWSPAPERS INC
Also Called: Rumford Falls Times
69 Congress St (04276-2015)
PHONE..................................207 364-7893
Bruce Farrin, *Manager*
EMP: 7
SALES (corp-wide): 2.2MM **Privately Held**
WEB: www.finestsigns.com
SIC: 2759 Newspaper
PA: James Newspapers, Inc
1 Pikes Hl
Norway ME 04268
207 743-7011

(G-6837)
LEWISTON DAILY SUN
Also Called: Sun Journal Newspaper
69 Congress St (04276-2015)
PHONE..................................207 364-8728
Nancy Theriault, *Manager*
EMP: 5
SALES (corp-wide): 12.9MM **Privately Held**
WEB: www.sunjournal.com
SIC: 2711 Newspapers-Publishing/Printing
PA: Daily Lewiston Sun
104 Park St
Lewiston ME 04240
207 784-3555

(G-6838)
ND PAPER INC
Also Called: Nine Dragons Paper - Rumford
35 Hartford St (04276-2045)
PHONE..................................207 364-4521
Randy Chicoine, *Plant Mgr*
EMP: 3 **Privately Held**
SIC: 2611 Pulp Mill
HQ: Nd Paper Inc.
1901 S Meyers Rd Ste 600
Oakbrook Terrace IL 60181
513 200-0908

(G-6839)
ND PAPER LLC
35 Hartford St (04276-2045)
PHONE..................................207 364-4521
Ken Liu, *CEO*
EMP: 650 **Privately Held**
SIC: 2621 Paper Mill
HQ: Nd Paper Llc
1901 S Meyers Rd Ste 600
Oakbrook Terrace IL 60181
937 528-3870

(G-6840)
NICOLS BROTHERS INC
29 Industrial Park Rd (04276-3436)
PHONE..................................207 364-7032
James Nicols, *Principal*
Carlene Nicols, *Office Mgr*
EMP: 25
SALES (est): 1.5MM **Privately Held**
SIC: 2411 Logging

(G-6841)
NORTHWEST PRECISION INC
37 Canal St (04276-2001)
PHONE..................................207 364-7597
Jon Cantin, *President*
▲ **EMP:** 4
SQ FT: 2,600
SALES: 478.6K **Privately Held**
WEB: www.northwestprecision.com
SIC: 3599 Machine Shop

(G-6842)
PREMIUM LOG YARDS INC (PA)
Also Called: Maine Made Furniture
1180 Route 2 Ste 5 (04276-3644)
P.O. Box 562, Dixfield (04224-0562)
PHONE..................................207 364-7500
Clinton G Bradbury, *President*
Cary Bradbury, *Vice Pres*
Sandra Jones, *Bookkeeper*
EMP: 10
SQ FT: 8,000
SALES (est): 1.6MM **Privately Held**
SIC: 2411 2511 Logging Mfg Wood Household Furniture

Saco
York County

(G-6843)
BIODESIGN INTERNATIONAL INC
60 Industrial Park Rd (04072-1840)
PHONE..................................207 283-6500
Gerard Blain, *Treasurer*
Sheila Lathrop, *Manager*
EMP: 25
SQ FT: 10,000
SALES (est): 2.8MM
SALES (corp-wide): 201MM **Publicly Held**
WEB: www.biodesign.com
SIC: 2833 8731 2834 Mfg Medicinal/Botanical Products Commercial Physical Research Mfg Pharmaceutical Preparations
PA: Meridian Bioscience, Inc.
3471 River Hills Dr
Cincinnati OH 45244
513 271-3700

(G-6844)
BLACKBEAR SIGNWORKS INC
19 Industrial Park Rd (04072-1804)
PHONE..................................207 286-8004
Robert Laveault, *President*
Michael Thomes, *Vice Pres*
EMP: 5
SALES (est): 466K **Privately Held**
SIC: 3993 Mfg Signs/Advertising Specialties

(G-6845)
COASTAL INDUSTRIAL DISTRS
Also Called: Cid Performance Tool
6 Willey Rd (04072-1881)
PHONE..................................207 286-3319
John Lowery, *President*
Robert Richard, *Sales Engr*
David Garrett, *Sales Staff*
Kathy Lowery, *Manager*

GEOGRAPHIC

EMP: 14
SQ FT: 12,000
SALES (est): 2.8MM **Privately Held**
WEB: www.cidtools.com
SIC: 3541 Mfg Machine Tools-Cutting

(G-6846)
DER-TEX CORPORATION
Also Called: Frelonic
1 Lehner Rd (04072-1837)
PHONE..................................207 284-5931
Michael E Lunder, *President*
Cheryl Lunder, *Director*
▲ **EMP:** 45 **EST:** 1943
SQ FT: 100,000
SALES (est): 9.1MM **Privately Held**
WEB: www.dertexcorp.com
SIC: 3086 Mfg Plastic Foam Products

(G-6847)
GENERAL DYNAMICS-OTS INC
291 North St (04072-1809)
PHONE..................................207 283-3611
Christopher Fisher, *Engineer*
Dan Welch, *Engineer*
Gary Laperriere, *Info Tech Mgr*
Ron Cain, *Programmer Anys*
EMP: 41
SALES (corp-wide): 36.1B **Publicly Held**
WEB: www.gdatp.com
SIC: 3728 3812 Mfg Aircraft Parts/Equipment Mfg Search/Navigation Equipment
HQ: General Dynamics Ots (California), Inc.
11399 16th Ct N Ste 200
Saint Petersburg FL 33716
727 578-8100

(G-6848)
GRENIER FUELS LLC
184 Lewis Ave (04072-2919)
P.O. Box 266 (04072-0266)
PHONE..................................207 602-1400
Ronald Grenier, *Mng Member*
EMP: 6
SALES (est): 815K **Privately Held**
SIC: 2869 Mfg Industrial Organic Chemicals

(G-6849)
INTELLIGENT CONTROLS INC (HQ)
Also Called: Incon
34 Spring Hill Rd (04072-8607)
P.O. Box 638 (04072-0638)
PHONE..................................207 571-1123
Scott Trumbull, *President*
Greg Sengstack, *President*
▲ **EMP:** 29
SQ FT: 13,000
SALES (est): 2.7MM
SALES (corp-wide): 1.3B **Publicly Held**
WEB: www.incon.com
SIC: 3829 Mfg Measuring/Controlling Devices
PA: Franklin Electric Co., Inc.
9255 Coverdale Rd
Fort Wayne IN 46809
260 824-2900

(G-6850)
JOHNS MANVILLE CORPORATION
Also Called: N R G Barriers
15 Lund Rd (04072-1806)
P.O. Box 5108, Denver CO (80217-5108)
PHONE..................................207 283-8000
Michael Edwards, *Manager*
EMP: 50
SALES (corp-wide): 225.3B **Publicly Held**
WEB: www.jm.com
SIC: 3086 Mfg Insulation
HQ: Johns Manville Corporation
717 17th St Ste 800
Denver CO 80202
303 978-2000

(G-6851)
LUNDER MANUFACTURING INC
44 Spring Hill Rd (04072-9651)
PHONE..................................207 284-5961
Todd Gillis, *President*
Andrew Bisbing, *Sales Staff*
▲ **EMP:** 35
SQ FT: 55,000
SALES (est): 5.4MM **Privately Held**
SIC: 3131 Mfg Footwear Cut Stock

(G-6852)
MAINE MLCLAR QULTY CONTRLS INC
Also Called: Mmqci
23 Mill Brook Rd (04072-9806)
PHONE..................................207 885-1072
Joan Gordon, *President*
Sarah Tierney, *President*
Clark Rundell PHD, *Vice Pres*
Theresa Daigle, *Accountant*
EMP: 22
SQ FT: 6,200
SALES (est): 3.4MM **Privately Held**
WEB: www.mmqci.com
SIC: 3821 Mfg Lab Apparatus/Furniture

(G-6853)
MAINE SEAFOOD VENTURES LLC
1016 Portland Rd (04072-4000)
PHONE..................................207 303-0165
Kevin Burnsteel, *QC Mgr*
John Ready,
Brendam Ready,
EMP: 9
SALES (est): 986.5K **Privately Held**
SIC: 2092 Mfg Fresh/Frozen Packaged Fish

(G-6854)
O E M CONCEPTS (HQ)
60 Industrial Park Rd (04072-1840)
PHONE..................................207 283-6500
Susan Gibney, *Principal*
Sheila Lathrop, *Principal*
EMP: 7
SQ FT: 4,200
SALES (est): 3.6MM
SALES (corp-wide): 201MM **Publicly Held**
SIC: 2835 5122 Mfg Diagnostic Substances Whol Drugs/Sundries
PA: Meridian Bioscience, Inc.
3471 River Hills Dr
Cincinnati OH 45244
513 271-3700

(G-6855)
POND COVE MILLWORK INC
22 Mill Brook Rd (04072-9806)
PHONE..................................207 773-6819
Peter Flaherty, *President*
Tracy Chadbourne, *Vice Pres*
Kelley Gilbert, *Human Res Dir*
EMP: 40 **EST:** 1963
SQ FT: 31,000
SALES (est): 7.2MM **Privately Held**
WEB: www.pondcovemillwork.com
SIC: 2431 Mfg Millwork

(G-6856)
QUICK PRINT COLOR CENTER
Also Called: The Quick Print Color Center
74 Industrial Park Rd # 102 (04072-1840)
PHONE..................................207 282-6480
George W Wandell, *Owner*
EMP: 5
SQ FT: 2,000
SALES: 380K **Privately Held**
SIC: 2752 7334 2759 2791 Lithographic Coml Print Photocopying Service Commercial Printing Typesetting Services Bookbinding/Related Work

(G-6857)
SACO MANUFACTURING & WDWKG
39 Lincoln St (04072-3229)
PHONE..................................207 284-6613
Anthony Jendrek, *Owner*
Leslie Nicoll, *Vice Pres*
EMP: 6
SQ FT: 7,500
SALES (est): 673.4K **Privately Held**
WEB: www.sacomfg.com
SIC: 2499 8712 5099 5211 Mfg Wood Products Architectural Services Whol Durable Goods Ret Lumber/Building Mtrl

(G-6858)
SIGNARAMA SACO
872 Portland Rd (04072-9672)
PHONE..................................207 494-8085
EMP: 3
SALES (est): 277K **Privately Held**
SIC: 3993 Mfg Signs/Advertising Specialties

(G-6859)
TAYLOR BRYSON INC
199 New County Rd (04072-9714)
PHONE..................................207 838-0961
Deborah Landry, *Principal*
Darrin Landry, *Consultant*
EMP: 3
SALES (est): 254.2K **Privately Held**
SIC: 2741 Misc Publishing

(G-6860)
TRANSPARENT AUDIO INC
47 Industrial Park Rd (04072-1804)
PHONE..................................207 284-1100
Karen J Sumner, *President*
Charlton S Smith, *Vice Pres*
Evan Coffey, *Opers Mgr*
Charles M Sumner, *Treasurer*
Sarah Razak, *Accounting Mgr*
▲ **EMP:** 40
SALES (est): 8.6MM **Privately Held**
WEB: www.transparentcable.com
SIC: 3651 3357 Mfg Home Audio/Video Equipment Nonferrous Wiredrawing/Insulating

(G-6861)
URETHANE SOLUTIONS LLC
52 Spring Hill Rd (04072-9651)
PHONE..................................207 284-5400
John Hill III, *Owner*
Allan Guzi,
EMP: 3
SALES (est): 458.1K **Privately Held**
SIC: 2851 Mfg Paints/Allied Products

(G-6862)
XURON CORP
62 Industrial Park Rd (04072-1865)
PHONE..................................207 283-1401
Dennis Shores, *President*
Robert Dube, *Vice Pres*
▲ **EMP:** 40
SQ FT: 8,600
SALES (est): 6.8MM **Privately Held**
WEB: www.xuron.com
SIC: 3423 3545 Mfg Hand/Edge Tools Mfg Machine Tool Accessories

(G-6863)
YALE CORDAGE INC
77 Industrial Park Rd (04072-1804)
PHONE..................................207 282-3396
Thomas L Yale, *President*
Charleton Ames, *Principal*
Richard Hildebrand, *Vice Pres*
Edward M Schumacher, *Vice Pres*
Don Carpenter, *Traffic Mgr*
▲ **EMP:** 55
SQ FT: 40,000
SALES (est): 11MM **Privately Held**
WEB: www.yalecordage.com
SIC: 2298 Mfg Cordage/Twine

(G-6864)
ZAJAC LLC
92 Industrial Park Rd (04072-1840)
PHONE..................................207 286-9100
Laura Zajac, *President*
Mathew Reichl, *General Mgr*
Matt Reichl, *General Mgr*
EMP: 35
SQ FT: 14,000
SALES (est): 15.3MM **Privately Held**
WEB: www.zajac.com
SIC: 3565 8743 8711 Mfg Packaging Machinery Public Relations Services Engineering Services

Saint Albans
Somerset County

(G-6865)
SEBASTICOOK LUMBER LLC
446 Hartland Rd (04971)
P.O. Box 51 (04971-0051)
PHONE..................................207 660-1360
EMP: 9 **EST:** 2016
SALES (est): 1.1MM **Privately Held**
SIC: 2421 Sawmill/Planing Mill

Saint Francis
Aroostook County

(G-6866)
BP LOGGING
562 Main St (04774-3114)
PHONE..................................207 398-4457
Buddy Pelletier, *Principal*
EMP: 3 **EST:** 2010
SALES (est): 293.7K **Privately Held**
SIC: 2411 Logging

(G-6867)
NORTH SHORE LOGGING INC
1005 Main St (04774-3201)
PHONE..................................207 398-4173
EMP: 6
SALES (est): 476.6K **Privately Held**
SIC: 2411 Logging

(G-6868)
R B LOGGING INC
1327 Main St (04774-3205)
PHONE..................................207 398-3176
Patty A Martin, *Principal*
EMP: 3 **EST:** 2010
SALES (est): 204.5K **Privately Held**
SIC: 2411 Logging

Saint George
Knox County

(G-6869)
HIGHLINER ROPE CO LLC
Also Called: Hy-Liner Rope Co
71 Seal Harbor Rd (04860)
P.O. Box 170, Thomaston (04861-0170)
PHONE..................................207 372-6300
Craig Rackliff,
Glen Perini,
▼ **EMP:** 5
SALES (est): 841.8K **Privately Held**
WEB: www.highlineaccess.com
SIC: 2298 Mfg Cordage/Twine

Sanford
York County

(G-6870)
ADVANCED BUILDING PRODUCTS INC
95 Cyro Dr (04073-2551)
P.O. Box 98, Springvale (04083-0098)
PHONE..................................207 490-2306
Richard Lolley, *President*
Kenneth Roy, *President*
Ken Roy, *Exec VP*
Jason Roy, *Vice Pres*
Ryan Hajj, *Plant Mgr*
▲ **EMP:** 16
SQ FT: 30,000
SALES (est): 5MM **Privately Held**
WEB: www.advancedflashing.com
SIC: 3351 3083 Copper Rolling/Drawing Mfg Laminated Plastic Plate/Sheet

(G-6871)
BAKER COMPANY INC (PA)
Also Called: Baker Company, The
175 Gate House Rd (04073-2482)
PHONE..................................207 324-8773
Dennis Eagleson, *Ch of Bd*
David C Eagleson, *President*

▲ = Import ▼=Export
◆ =Import/Export

Scott Semle, *Vice Pres*
◆ **EMP:** 144 **EST:** 1949
SQ FT: 140,000
SALES (est): 28.1MM **Privately Held**
WEB: www.bakerco.com
SIC: 3821 3644 5047 Mfg Lab Apparatus/Furniture Mfg Nonconductive Wiring Devices Whol Medical/Hospital Equipment

(G-6872)
COLONIAL GREEN PRODUCTS LLC
Airport Plaza Mall 1725 5 Airport Plaza Mall (04073)
PHONE..................................207 614-6660
Rick Trottir, *Manager*
EMP: 3 **Privately Held**
SIC: 3296 Mfg Mineral Wool
PA: Colonial Green Products, Llc
1032 Nh Route 119 Unit 6
Rindge NH 03461
-

(G-6873)
CYRO INDUSTRY
1796 Main St (04073-2458)
PHONE..................................207 324-6000
Ralph Stevens, *Principal*
Drew R Scott, *Corp Comm Staff*
Shawn Marsh, *Maintence Staff*
EMP: 9
SALES (est): 926.6K **Privately Held**
SIC: 2821 Mfg Plastic Materials/Resins

(G-6874)
EKTO MANUFACTURING CORP
83 Eagle Dr (04073-5814)
P.O. Box 449 (04073-0449)
PHONE..................................207 324-4427
Karl F Epper, *President*
Willy Faessler, *COO*
Jacqueline Epper, *Vice Pres*
Karen Littlefield, *Treasurer*
▼ **EMP:** 30
SQ FT: 50,000
SALES (est): 5.4MM **Privately Held**
WEB: www.ekto.com
SIC: 3448 3444 Mfg Prefabricated Metal Buildings Mfg Sheet Metalwork

(G-6875)
EXPANDED RUBBER PRODUCTS INC (PA)
41 Industrial Ave (04073-5820)
P.O. Box 1070 (04073-1070)
PHONE..................................207 324-8226
Barbara G Ney, *President*
J Clayton Ney Jr, *Vice Pres*
Robert Ney, *Vice Pres*
Yvonne M Ney, *Admin Sec*
EMP: 34
SQ FT: 42,000
SALES (est): 4.5MM **Privately Held**
WEB: www.expandedrubberproducts.com
SIC: 3069 Mfg Fabricated Rubber Products

(G-6876)
FLEMISH MASTER WEAVERS INC
96 Gate House Rd (04073-2484)
PHONE..................................207 324-6600
Johan Moulin, *President*
Michael Litner, *Principal*
Ellen Ross, *COO*
▲ **EMP:** 33
SQ FT: 150,000
SALES (est): 21.6MM
SALES (corp-wide): 184.7MM **Privately Held**
SIC: 2273 Mfg Carpets/Rugs
PA: Natco Products Corporation
155 Brookside Ave
West Warwick RI 02893
401 828-0300

(G-6877)
GETCHELL BROS INC
1913 Main St (04073-4407)
PHONE..................................207 490-0809
Bob Morse, *CEO*
EMP: 20
SALES (corp-wide): 12.8MM **Privately Held**
SIC: 2097 5143 5142 5999 Mfg Ice Whol Dairy Products Whol Packaged Frzn Goods Ret Misc Merchandise
PA: Getchell Bros. Inc.
1 Union St
Brewer ME
-

(G-6878)
JR ROBERT AUSTIN
Also Called: Austin Machine & Fabrication
56 Jagger Mill Rd (04073-2414)
PHONE..................................207 490-1500
Toll Free:..877 -
Robert Austin Jr, *Owner*
EMP: 3
SQ FT: 6,144
SALES (est): 203.6K **Privately Held**
SIC: 3599 3441 Mfg Industrial Machinery Structural Metal Fabrication

(G-6879)
LEGU TOOL AND MOLD LLC
32 Smada Dr (04073-5825)
PHONE..................................207 850-1450
Randal Lagueux, *President*
EMP: 4
SALES: 250K **Privately Held**
SIC: 2869 Mfg Industrial Organic Chemicals

(G-6880)
LITTLE GOTTAGE BAKING
32 Guillemette St (04073-2031)
PHONE..................................207 432-2930
Claire Genest, *Principal*
EMP: 4
SALES (est): 162.9K **Privately Held**
SIC: 2051 Mfg Bread/Related Products

(G-6881)
MAINE MANUFACTURING LLC
Also Called: Gvs North America
63 Community Dr (04073-5809)
PHONE..................................207 324-1754
Bill Emhiser, *President*
Craig Cunningham, *Chief Engr*
Pierre Dizier, *Business Dir*
▲ **EMP:** 97
SALES (est): 28.9MM **Privately Held**
SIC: 3089 Mfg Plastic Products
HQ: Gvs Spa
Via Roma 50
Zola Predosa BO 40069
051 617-6311

(G-6882)
MARJA CORPORATION
Also Called: Electronic Assembly Service
14 Dale St (04073-3108)
P.O. Box 431 (04073-0431)
PHONE..................................207 324-2994
Anna Grondin, *President*
Robert Frechette Jr, *Vice Pres*
EMP: 12
SQ FT: 6,000
SALES (est): 2MM **Privately Held**
WEB: www.marja.com
SIC: 3672 Mfg Printed Circuit Boards

(G-6883)
MICHAEL V MORIN
Also Called: Mikini Embroidery
1298 Main St B (04073-3631)
PHONE..................................207 459-1200
Michael V Morin, *Owner*
EMP: 4
SALES (est): 172.4K **Privately Held**
SIC: 2395 Pleating/Stitching Services

(G-6884)
NORTH COUNTRY TRACTOR INC
Also Called: John Deere Authorized Dealer
8 Shaws Ridge Rd (04073-6210)
PHONE..................................207 324-5646
Tom Swan, *Branch Mgr*
Robert Gonyou, *Branch Mgr*
EMP: 10
SALES (est): 1.1MM **Privately Held**
SIC: 3537 5082 Mfg Industrial Trucks/Tractors Whol Construction/Mining Equipment
PA: North Country Tractor, Inc.
149 Sheep Davis Rd
Pembroke NH 03275
-

(G-6885)
OIZERO9 INC
Also Called: Province Automation
31 Smada Dr (04073-5824)
P.O. Box 690 (04073-0690)
PHONE..................................207 324-3582
Dan Richer, *President*
Patty Nolette, *General Mgr*
EMP: 13
SQ FT: 16,000
SALES (est): 2.4MM **Privately Held**
WEB: www.provinceauto.com
SIC: 3569 3599 5084 8711 Mfg General Indstl Mach Mfg Industrial Machinery Whol Industrial Equip Engineering Services Mfg Packaging Machinery

(G-6886)
R PEPIN & SONS INC
59 Shaw Rd (04073-6201)
P.O. Box 729 (04073-0729)
PHONE..................................207 324-6125
David Pepin, *President*
Rudy Pepin, *Vice Pres*
EMP: 25
SQ FT: 4,000
SALES (est): 4.2MM **Privately Held**
SIC: 3273 5032 Mfg Ready-Mixed Concrete Whol Brick/Stone Material

(G-6887)
R&V INDUSTRIES INC
Also Called: Shape Global Technologies
90 Community Dr (04073-5810)
PHONE..................................207 324-5200
Vincent Boragine, *President*
Richard Courcy, *Vice Pres*
EMP: 75 **EST:** 2001
SQ FT: 44,000
SALES (est): 9.3MM **Privately Held**
WEB: www.shapenet.com
SIC: 3089 Mfg Plastic Products

(G-6888)
RENAISSANCE GREETING CARDS INC
10 Renaissance Way (04073-3636)
PHONE..................................207 324-4153
Dan Stevers, *President*
EMP: 110
SQ FT: 35,000
SALES (est): 12.4MM **Privately Held**
WEB: www.ftdi.com
SIC: 2771 5947 Mfg Greeting Cards Ret Gifts/Novelties

(G-6889)
RH ROSENFIELD CO
Also Called: Edison Press
2066 Main St (04073-4444)
PHONE..................................207 324-1798
Robert H Rosenfield, *President*
Susan Rosenfield, *Vice Pres*
Ronald Bourque, *Clerk*
EMP: 30
SQ FT: 4,000
SALES (est): 3.7MM **Privately Held**
WEB: www.edisonpress.com
SIC: 2752 2711 Lithographic Commercial Printing Newspapers-Publishing/Printing

(G-6890)
RICHARD GENEST INC
Also Called: Genest Precast
238 Country Club Rd (04073-5225)
PHONE..................................207 324-7215
Richard Genest, *President*
Rita Genest, *Vice Pres*
EMP: 13
SQ FT: 13,000
SALES (est): 1.1MM **Privately Held**
WEB: www.genestprecast.com
SIC: 3272 Mfg Concrete Products

(G-6891)
ROEHM AMERICA LLC
Also Called: Sanford Manufacturing Facility
1796 Main St (04073-2458)
PHONE..................................207 324-6000
Richard Healy, *Manager*
EMP: 250
SALES (corp-wide): 195.2MM **Privately Held**
SIC: 2821 Mfg Plastic Materials/Resins
PA: Roehm America Llc
299 Jefferson Rd
Parsippany NJ 07054
973 929-8000

(G-6892)
RUBB INC
Also Called: Rubb Building Systems
1 Rubb Ln (04073-2231)
P.O. Box 711 (04073-0711)
PHONE..................................207 324-2877
David Nickerson, *President*
Christian Unger, *General Mgr*
Joseph Hyatt, *Vice Pres*
Mike Bouthot, *Purch Mgr*
Lynn Durost, *Human Resources*
▲ **EMP:** 55
SALES (est): 22MM **Privately Held**
WEB: www.rubb.com
SIC: 3448 Mfg Prefabricated Metal Buildings

(G-6893)
TAKE 2 DOUGH PRODUCTIONS INC
79 Emery St Ste B (04073-3177)
PHONE..................................207 490-6502
David Tully, *President*
EMP: 13
SALES: 1.5MM **Privately Held**
SIC: 2038 7812 Mfg Frozen Pizza Motion Picture & Video Production

(G-6894)
TOMS OF MAINE INC
27 Community Dr (04073-5809)
PHONE..................................207 985-2944
EMP: 150
SALES (corp-wide): 15.4B **Publicly Held**
SIC: 2844 Mfg Toilet Preparations
HQ: Tom's Of Maine, Inc.
2 Storer St Ste 302
Kennebunk ME 04043
207 985-2944

(G-6895)
U S FELT COMPANY INC
61 Industrial Ave (04073-5820)
PHONE..................................207 324-0063
Vincent Boragine, *President*
EMP: 42
SALES (est): 6.2MM **Privately Held**
SIC: 2231 5199 Wool Broadwoven Fabric Mill Whol Nondurable Goods

(G-6896)
W S BESSETT INC
1923 Main St (04073-4407)
PHONE..................................207 324-9232
Harold E Waitt, *President*
Michael Waitt, *Vice Pres*
Gerry Waitt, *Treasurer*
EMP: 12 **EST:** 1925
SQ FT: 9,600
SALES (est): 1.8MM **Privately Held**
WEB: www.wsbessett.com
SIC: 3639 3599 5722 Mfg Sewing Machine Parts Machine Shop & Ret Sewing Machines

(G-6897)
YANKEE HARDWOODS LLC
Lincoln St (04073)
PHONE..................................207 459-7779
Richard A Barnaby,
EMP: 6
SALES (est): 524K **Privately Held**
SIC: 2411 Logging

(G-6898)
YORK MANUFACTURING INC
43 Community Dr (04073-5809)
PHONE..................................207 324-1300
Geoffrey G Magnuson, *CEO*
Craig Wetmore, *President*
EMP: 12 **EST:** 1935
SQ FT: 21,000
SALES (est): 2.8MM **Privately Held**
WEB: www.yorkmfg.com
SIC: 3351 3083 Copper Rolling/Drawing Mfg Laminated Plastic Plate/Sheet

GEOGRAPHIC

Sangerville
Piscataquis County

(G-6899)
ERNEST R PALMER LUMBER CO INC
30 N Dexter Rd (04479)
P.O. Box 128 (04479-0128)
PHONE..................................207 876-2725
John Armstrong, *President*
David E Armstrong, *Treasurer*
EMP: 8
SALES: 750K **Privately Held**
SIC: 2426 5211 Hardwood Dimension Mill

(G-6900)
NUMBERALL STAMP & TOOL CO
1 High St (04479)
P.O. Box 187 (04479-0187)
PHONE..................................207 876-3541
Herman Bayerdorffer, *President*
Cynthia Bayerdorffer, *Treasurer*
EMP: 19 **EST:** 1930
SQ FT: 18,000
SALES (est): 3.5MM **Privately Held**
WEB: www.numberall.com
SIC: 3469 Mfg Metal Stampings

Scarborough
Cumberland County

(G-6901)
ABBOTT DGNSTICS SCRBOROUGH INC (DH)
Also Called: Alere Scarborough, Inc.
10 Southgate Rd (04074-8303)
PHONE..................................207 730-5750
Roger Piasio, *CEO*
Dean Miller, *Vice Pres*
Myron Hamer, *Treasurer*
Michael High, *Admin Sec*
▲ **EMP:** 82
SQ FT: 70,000
SALES (est): 15.8MM
SALES (corp-wide): 30.5B **Publicly Held**
WEB: www.binax.com
SIC: 3841 3829 2835 Mfg Surgical/Med Instr Mfg Measure/Control Dvcs Mfg Diagnostic Substance
HQ: Alere Inc.
51 Sawyer Rd Ste 200
Waltham MA 02453
781 647-3900

(G-6902)
ADJACENT BAKERY LLC
5 Lincoln Ave (04074-9783)
PHONE..................................207 252-6722
Jason Melanson, *President*
Mike White, *Vice Pres*
EMP: 4
SALES (est): 208.2K **Privately Held**
SIC: 3556 Mfg Food Products Machinery

(G-6903)
ALERE INC
10 Southgate Rd (04074-8303)
PHONE..................................207 730-5714
EMP: 4
SALES (est): 157.9K **Privately Held**
SIC: 2835 Mfg Diagnostic Substances

(G-6904)
AMERICAN HEALTHCARE
6 Lincoln Ave (04074-7706)
PHONE..................................888 567-7733
Jeff Lord, *President*
EMP: 11 **EST:** 1998
SALES (est): 1.6MM **Privately Held**
WEB: www.americanhealthcareinc.com
SIC: 3826 Manufacturer Oxygen Regulators

(G-6905)
ATLANTIC WOOD & CABINET WORKS
Also Called: Cook & Cook Cabinetry
94 Broadturn Rd (04074-9725)
P.O. Box 1657 (04070-1657)
PHONE..................................207 885-0767
Richard T Cook, *President*
Cheryl Cook, *Admin Sec*
EMP: 14
SQ FT: 6,000
SALES: 500K **Privately Held**
WEB: www.cookandcookcabinetry.com
SIC: 2434 Mfg Wood Kitchen Cabinets

(G-6906)
AUSTIN MERRILL
Also Called: Catch Kings, The
162 Pleasant Hill Rd (04074-8721)
PHONE..................................207 219-0593
Austin Merrill, *Owner*
EMP: 5
SQ FT: 2,500
SALES: 60K **Privately Held**
SIC: 3949 Mfg Sporting/Athletic Goods

(G-6907)
BARKER STEEL LLC
51 Us Route 1 Ste H (04074-7134)
PHONE..................................207 883-3444
Gene Matthews, *Manager*
EMP: 7
SALES (corp-wide): 25B **Publicly Held**
WEB: www.barker.com
SIC: 3449 5051 Mfg Misc Structural Metalwork Metals Service Center
HQ: Barker Steel Llc
55 Sumner St Ste 1
Milford MA 01757
800 363-3953

(G-6908)
BARRINGER INDUSTRIES LLC
2 Washington Ave (04074-8310)
PHONE..................................207 730-7125
John Barringer, *Principal*
EMP: 3
SALES (est): 211.6K **Privately Held**
SIC: 3999 Mfg Misc Products

(G-6909)
BAYLEY QUALITY SEAFOOD INC
21 Snow Canning Rd (04074-5001)
PHONE..................................207 883-4581
Stanley Bayley, *President*
EMP: 6
SQ FT: 4,000
SALES (est): 696K **Privately Held**
SIC: 2092 5146 Mfg Fresh/Frozen Packaged Fish Whol Fish/Seafood

(G-6910)
BCR TECHNOLOGY CENTER
83 Mussey Rd (04074-8919)
PHONE..................................207 885-9700
Bradford White, *Principal*
EMP: 3
SALES (est): 223.7K **Privately Held**
SIC: 3643 Mfg Conductive Wiring Devices

(G-6911)
BIMBO BAKERIES USA INC
3 Lincoln Ave (04074-9783)
PHONE..................................207 883-5252
EMP: 6 **Privately Held**
SIC: 2051 Mfg Bread/Related Products
HQ: Bimbo Bakeries Usa, Inc
255 Business Center Dr # 200
Horsham PA 19044
215 347-5500

(G-6912)
BLACK COVE CABINETRY
137 Pleasant Hill Rd (04074-9309)
PHONE..................................207 883-8901
Bill Livendosky, *Owner*
Bill Levandowski, *Owner*
EMP: 12
SALES (est): 592.1K **Privately Held**
WEB: www.blackcove.com
SIC: 2434 Mfg Wood Kitchen Cabinets

(G-6913)
BROWN FOX PRINTING INC (PA)
253 Us Route 1 (04074-9525)
P.O. Box 897 (04070-0897)
PHONE..................................207 883-9525
Russell Burleigh, *President*
EMP: 5
SQ FT: 1,000
SALES: 480K **Privately Held**
WEB: www.brownfoxprinting.com
SIC: 2752 Lithographic Commercial Printing

(G-6914)
CMYK PRINT SERVICES
49 Woodspell Rd (04074-8223)
PHONE..................................207 228-3838
Chris Kelley, *Principal*
EMP: 3
SALES (est): 324.7K **Privately Held**
SIC: 2752 Lithographic Commercial Printing

(G-6915)
CONTECH ENGNERED SOLUTIONS LLC
71 Us Route 1 Ste F (04074-7174)
PHONE..................................207 885-9830
Jennifer Knowles, *Engineer*
EMP: 26 **Privately Held**
SIC: 3084 3317 3441 3443 Mfg Plastic Pipe Mfg Steel Pipe/Tubes Structural Metal Fabrctn Mfg Fabricated Plate Wrk Mfg Sheet Metalwork
HQ: Contech Engineered Solutions Llc
9025 Centre Pointe Dr # 400
West Chester OH 45069
513 645-7000

(G-6916)
DERMALOGIX PARTNERS INC
672 Us Route 1 (04074-9745)
PHONE..................................207 883-4103
James Kerr, *President*
George Kerr, *President*
EMP: 25
SALES (est): 4.3MM **Privately Held**
WEB: www.itchyskin.net
SIC: 2834 Mfg Pharmaceutical Preparations

(G-6917)
FLUID IMAGING TECHNOLOGIES INC
200 Enterprise Dr (04074-7636)
PHONE..................................207 289-3200
Kent Peterson, *CEO*
Christian K Sieracki, *President*
Ali Naqui, *COO*
EMP: 20
SALES (est): 5.4MM **Privately Held**
WEB: www.fluidimaging.com
SIC: 3826 Mfg Analytical Instruments

(G-6918)
GAUSS CORPORATION
Also Called: Electrodyne Systems
1 Gibson Rd (04074-8333)
P.O. Box 877, Sapulpa OK (74067-0877)
PHONE..................................207 883-4121
EMP: 15
SALES: 750K **Privately Held**
WEB: www.electrodyne.com
SIC: 3694 Engine Electrical Equipment, Nsk

(G-6919)
GLIDDEN SIGNS INC
Also Called: Burr Signs
40a Manson Libby Rd (04074)
PHONE..................................207 396-6111
Jess Glidden, *President*
EMP: 12 **EST:** 2016
SALES: 1.5MM **Privately Held**
SIC: 3993 Mfg Signs/Advertising Specialties

(G-6920)
GLOBAL BIOTECHNOLOGIES INC
19 Rigby Rd (04074-9310)
PHONE..................................800 755-8420
Robert Bogosian, *President*
EMP: 6
SQ FT: 4,000
SALES (est): 1.1MM **Privately Held**
WEB: www.globalbio.com
SIC: 2834 2842 2833 Mfg Pharmaceutical Preps Mfg Polish/Sanitation Gd Mfg Medicinal/Botanicals

(G-6921)
GLOBECO MAINE LLC
19 Fowler Farm Rd (04074-7558)
PHONE..................................207 809-2671
Philip Pastore,
EMP: 3
SALES (est): 238.4K **Privately Held**
SIC: 2299 7389 Mfg Textile Goods Business Services At Non-Commercial Site

(G-6922)
GM SPECIALTIES INC
Also Called: CM Labs
1 Commercial Rd (04074-9868)
P.O. Box 8002, Portland (04104-8002)
PHONE..................................207 883-8300
Eugene B Mc Gurl, *President*
EMP: 3
SQ FT: 5,000
SALES (est): 529.7K **Privately Held**
SIC: 2842 Mfg Polish/Sanitation Goods

(G-6923)
H P FAIRFIELD LLC
65 Pleasant Hill Rd (04074-9306)
P.O. Box 188, Skowhegan (04976-0188)
PHONE..................................207 885-4895
Bob Nason, *Comp Spec*
Dave Dirbby,
EMP: 3
SALES (est): 358.9K **Privately Held**
SIC: 2851 Mfg Paints/Allied Products

(G-6924)
HOLY DONUT
398 Us Route 1 (04074-9772)
PHONE..................................207 303-0137
EMP: 8
SALES (corp-wide): 1.5MM **Privately Held**
SIC: 2051 Mfg Bread/Related Products
PA: The Holy Donut
194 Park Ave
Portland ME 04102
207 874-7774

(G-6925)
HOWARD P FAIRFIELD LLC
65 Pleasant Hill Rd (04074-9306)
P.O. Box 188, Skowhegan (04976-0188)
PHONE..................................207 885-4895
Mike Knox, *Principal*
Jeanine Libby, *Human Res Mgr*
EMP: 3 **EST:** 2010
SALES (est): 289.2K **Privately Held**
SIC: 2851 Mfg Paints/Allied Products

(G-6926)
IFCO SYSTEMS US LLC
7 Washington Ave (04074-9782)
PHONE..................................207 883-0244
Bob Lessard, *Branch Mgr*
EMP: 47 **Privately Held**
SIC: 2448 Mfg Wood Pallets/Skids
HQ: Ifco Systems Us, Llc
3030 N Rocky Point Dr W # 300
Tampa FL 33607

(G-6927)
ITLLBE LLC
Also Called: It'll Be Pizza
5 Lincoln Ave (04074-9783)
PHONE..................................207 730-7301
Nathaniel Getchell,
EMP: 8
SALES (est): 2.1MM **Privately Held**
SIC: 2041 Mfg Flour/Grain Mill Prooducts

(G-6928)
JAMES A MCBRADY INC
29 Parkway Dr (04074-7155)
P.O. Box 8239, Portland (04104-8239)
PHONE..................................207 883-4176
James McBrady Jr, *President*
Helen McBrady, *Vice Pres*
Robert Hills, *Manager*
EMP: 20 **EST:** 1954
SQ FT: 50,000
SALES (est): 4.8MM **Privately Held**
SIC: 3441 1791 Structural Metal Fabrication Structural Steel Erection

▲ = Import ▼=Export
◆ =Import/Export

(G-6929)
KENNEBEC MARINE COMPANY
162 Spurwink Rd (04074-9445)
PHONE..................................207 773-0392
James A Falt, *President*
Louise Falt, *Treasurer*
EMP: 4
SQ FT: 6,000
SALES: 250K **Privately Held**
SIC: 3531 3599 5088 Mfg Winches For Commercial Fishing Machine Shop And Whol Marine Supplies

(G-6930)
KRITZER INDUSTRIES INC
Also Called: Kady International
30 Parkway Dr (04074-7155)
P.O. Box 847 (04070-0847)
PHONE..................................207 883-4141
Robert Kritzer, *Vice Pres*
Todd Kritzer, *Vice Pres*
Kammy Marcotte, *Vice Pres*
Alan Earnhart, *Purchasing*
Dathan Bouchard, *Technician*
EMP: 14
SQ FT: 15,000
SALES (est): 2.6MM **Privately Held**
WEB: www.kadyinternational.com
SIC: 3699 Mfg Electrical Equipment/Supplies

(G-6931)
LEN LIBBYS INC
Also Called: Len Libby Candy Shops
419 Us Route 1 (04074-9705)
P.O. Box 657 (04070-0657)
PHONE..................................207 883-4897
Maureen Hemond, *President*
EMP: 20
SQ FT: 5,000
SALES (est): 2.7MM **Privately Held**
WEB: www.lenlibby.com
SIC: 2064 5441 Mfg & Ret Confectionery Products

(G-6932)
MAINE RADIO
68 Mussey Rd (04074-8921)
P.O. Box 7264 (04070-7264)
PHONE..................................207 883-2929
Richard A Barker, *President*
EMP: 10
SQ FT: 4,000
SALES: 1.4MM **Privately Held**
WEB: www.maineradios.com
SIC: 3663 4812 Mfg Radio/Tv Communication Equipment Radiotelephone Communication

(G-6933)
MAINE TOOLROOM INC
8 Washington Ave (04074-8311)
PHONE..................................207 883-2455
Bill Morrison, *President*
Leo McGarvan, *Manager*
EMP: 4
SALES (est): 496.2K **Privately Held**
SIC: 3469 Mfg Metal Stampings

(G-6934)
NEW ENGLAND BLDG SOLUTIONS LLC
9 Winding Way (04074-8659)
PHONE..................................603 323-0012
▼ **EMP:** 3 **EST:** 2007
SQ FT: 1,000
SALES (est): 290K **Privately Held**
SIC: 2452 Mfg Prefabricated Wood Buildings

(G-6935)
NORTH AMERICAN SUPAFLU SYSTEMS
15 Holly St Ste 201b (04074-8867)
P.O. Box 2350 (04070-2350)
PHONE..................................207 883-1155
Frederick E Howes, *President*
EMP: 10
SQ FT: 4,000
SALES (est): 1MM **Privately Held**
SIC: 3259 5039 1741 Mfg Structural Clay Products Whol Construction Materials Masonry/Stone Contractor

(G-6936)
PURE PUP LOVE INC
20 Cloverleaf Ln (04074-8440)
PHONE..................................207 588-8111
Carrie Caporino, *CEO*
Joshua Caporino, *President*
EMP: 3
SALES (est): 121.6K **Privately Held**
SIC: 2047 Mfg Dog/Cat Food

(G-6937)
RICH TECHNOLOGY INTERNATIONAL
28 Pond View Dr (04074-9316)
PHONE..................................207 883-7424
Stewart Kramer, *President*
EMP: 3
SALES (est): 319.7K **Privately Held**
SIC: 3599 Mfg Industrial Machinery

(G-6938)
RTS PACKAGING LLC
16 Washington Ave (04074-8311)
PHONE..................................207 883-8921
David Bodreau, *Branch Mgr*
EMP: 80
SALES (corp-wide): 18.2B **Publicly Held**
WEB: www.rtspackaging.com
SIC: 2653 2657 2631 Mfg Corrugated/Fiber Box Mfg Folding Paperbrd Box Paperboard Mill
HQ: Rts Packaging, Llc
504 Thrasher St
Norcross GA 30071
800 558-6984

(G-6939)
SCOREBUILDERS
6 Woodgate Rd (04074-8722)
P.O. Box 7242 (04070-7242)
PHONE..................................207 885-0304
Scott Giles, *President*
Therese C Giles, *Vice Pres*
EMP: 3
SALES (est): 260K **Privately Held**
WEB: www.ptexams.com
SIC: 2741 Misc Publishing

(G-6940)
SMITH & ASSOC
581 Us Route 1 (04074-9709)
PHONE..................................866 299-6487
EMP: 4
SALES (est): 274K **Privately Held**
SIC: 2096 8742 Mfg Potato Chips/Snacks Management Consulting Services

(G-6941)
SUNRISE HOME INC
324 Gorham Rd (04074-9637)
PHONE..................................207 839-8801
Toll Free:..866 -
Ken Beasley, *President*
EMP: 4
SALES: 400K **Privately Held**
SIC: 2431 Mfg Millwork

(G-6942)
WHITCRAFT SCRBOROUGH/TEMPE LLC
28 Pond View Dr (04074-9316)
PHONE..................................763 780-0060
Patrick J Gruetzmacher, *Branch Mgr*
EMP: 139
SALES (corp-wide): 115MM **Privately Held**
SIC: 3728 Mfg Aircraft Parts/Equipment
HQ: Whitcraft Scarborough/Tempe Llc
76 County Rd
Eastford CT 06242
860 974-0786

(G-6943)
ZEKES SHEET METAL
2 Washington Ave (04074-8310)
P.O. Box 814, Biddeford (04005-0814)
PHONE..................................207 883-3877
Marshal Parol, *President*
EMP: 5
SALES (est): 755.6K **Privately Held**
SIC: 3444 Mfg Sheet Metalwork

Searsmont
Waldo County

(G-6944)
COX MACHINE
39 Belfast Augusta Rd W (04973-3744)
PHONE..................................207 342-2267
EMP: 3
SALES: 120K **Privately Held**
SIC: 3599 Mfg Industrial Machinery

(G-6945)
ROBBINS LUMBER INC
53 Ghent Rd (04973)
PHONE..................................207 342-5221
James A Robbins, *President*
Alden J Robbins, *Vice Pres*
EMP: 125 **EST:** 1881
SQ FT: 2,400
SALES (est): 20.8MM **Privately Held**
SIC: 2421 2611 Sawmill/Planing Mill Pulp Mill

(G-6946)
THOMAS ENTERPRISES INC
72 Lime Kiln Rd (04973)
P.O. Box 6 (04973-0006)
PHONE..................................207 342-5001
Wayne Thomas, *President*
EMP: 6
SALES (est): 866.2K **Privately Held**
SIC: 3541 Mfg Of Small Parts Machining

Searsport
Waldo County

(G-6947)
BLUEJACKET INC
Also Called: Laughing Whale
160 E Main St (04974-3311)
PHONE..................................207 548-9970
Robert Hammer, *President*
EMP: 10
SQ FT: 5,500
SALES (est): 940K **Privately Held**
WEB: www.bluejacketinc.com
SIC: 3944 5945 5092 Mfg Ret And Whls Ship Model Kits

(G-6948)
BOSTON OCULAR PROSTHETICS INC
133 Mortland Rd (04974-3337)
P.O. Box 245 (04974-0245)
PHONE..................................800 824-2492
Kaylee Dougherty, *President*
EMP: 5
SALES (est): 278.2K **Privately Held**
SIC: 3842 Mfg Surgical Appliances/Supplies

(G-6949)
DAKINS MINIATURES INC (PA)
Also Called: M & R Builders
21 Prospect St (04974-3528)
PHONE..................................207 548-6084
Roy C Dakin, *President*
Marie Dakin, *Treasurer*
Lee Ann Marshall, *Office Mgr*
Peter Mason, *Clerk*
EMP: 4
SQ FT: 1,920
SALES: 70K **Privately Held**
SIC: 3999 5947 Mfg Misc Products Ret Gifts/Novelties

(G-6950)
DALEGIP AMERICA INC
34 Kidder Point Rd (04974-3111)
PHONE..................................207 323-1880
Hector Rivadeneyra Diaz, *President*
▲ **EMP:** 20
SALES (est): 2MM **Privately Held**
SIC: 2816 Mfg Inorganic Pigments

(G-6951)
GAC CHEMICAL CORPORATION (PA)
34 Kidder Point Rd (04974-3111)
PHONE..................................207 548-2525
James A Poure, *Ch of Bd*
David Colter, *President*
Barbara Haase, *Exec VP*
David Baillargeon, *Maint Spvr*
Peter Goodwin, *Production*
◆ **EMP:** 55
SALES (est): 19.6MM **Privately Held**
SIC: 2819 2873 5169 5084 Mfg Indstl Inorgan Chem Mfg Nitrogenous Fertlizr Whol Chemicals/Products Whol Industrial Equip

(G-6952)
GENERAL ALUM NEW ENGLAND CORP
Also Called: Gac Chemical
34 Kidder Point Rd (04974-3111)
PHONE..................................207 548-2525
David Colter, *CEO*
David M Colter, *President*
James A Poure, *Chairman*
Barbara S Haase, *Vice Pres*
▼ **EMP:** 60 **EST:** 1978
SQ FT: 3,000
SALES (est): 10.3MM **Privately Held**
WEB: www.gacchemical.com
SIC: 2819 Mfg Aluminum Sulfate
PA: Gac Chemical Corporation
34 Kidder Point Rd
Searsport ME 04974

(G-6953)
OTIS ENTERPRISES MARINE CORP
85 Prospect St (04974-3589)
PHONE..................................207 548-6362
Keith Otis, *President*
Terry L Otis, *Clerk*
EMP: 4
SQ FT: 4,080
SALES (est): 391.9K **Privately Held**
SIC: 3732 Builds & Repairs Fiberglass Commercial & Pleasure Boats

Sebago
Cumberland County

(G-6954)
REPOSE FIRE LOGS LLC
1301 Bridgton Rd (04029-3206)
PHONE..................................207 595-8035
Brian Grady, *Principal*
EMP: 3
SALES (est): 227.2K **Privately Held**
SIC: 2421 Sawmill/Planing Mill

Sebec
Piscataquis County

(G-6955)
BEN SAVAGE LOGGING INC
30 North Rd (04481-3009)
PHONE..................................207 735-6699
Ben Savage, *Principal*
EMP: 3
SALES (est): 273.3K **Privately Held**
SIC: 2411 Logging

(G-6956)
BRIAN D MURPHY
Also Called: J I L Software
24 Frandy Ln (04481-3332)
PHONE..................................207 564-2737
EMP: 3
SALES (est): 140K **Privately Held**
SIC: 7372 Prepackaged Software Services

(G-6957)
JACOB BURDIN LOGGING
115 Downs Rd (04481-3125)
PHONE..................................207 564-3384
EMP: 3
SALES (est): 119.6K **Privately Held**
SIC: 2411 Logging

Shapleigh
York County

(G-6958)
NORMAN WHITE INC
Also Called: White's Logging & Chipping
28 Grant Rd (04076-4137)
PHONE..................................207 636-1636
David White, *President*
Sandy White, *Treasurer*
EMP: 7
SALES: 1MM **Privately Held**
WEB: www.normanwhite.com
SIC: 2411 Logging

(G-6959)
RISING REVOLUTION STUDIO LLC
118 Granny Kent Pond Rd (04076-3227)
PHONE..................................207 636-7136
Karyn Doiron,
EMP: 3
SALES (est): 305.9K **Privately Held**
SIC: 3993 Mfg Signs/Advertising Specialties

Sherman Mills
Aroostook County

(G-6960)
CHARLES LANE INC
Also Called: Charles Lane Trucking
55 Ester Rd (04776)
P.O. Box 67, Sherman (04776-0067)
PHONE..................................207 365-4606
Charles Lane, *President*
EMP: 6
SALES: 1.2MM **Privately Held**
WEB: www.charleslane.com
SIC: 2411 Logging

Sidney
Kennebec County

(G-6961)
ALAN STEVENS
240 Philbrick Rd (04330-2644)
PHONE..................................207 547-3840
Alan Stevens, *Owner*
EMP: 4
SALES: 500K **Privately Held**
SIC: 2411 Logging

(G-6962)
J & M LOGGING INC
35 Harold Dr (04330-2012)
PHONE..................................207 622-6353
James Hasco, *President*
EMP: 14 **EST:** 1983
SALES (est): 1.8MM **Privately Held**
SIC: 2411 Logging

(G-6963)
NEVELLS PALLET INC
97 Pond Rd (04330-2208)
PHONE..................................207 547-4605
Tony Cummings, *President*
EMP: 6
SALES: 500K **Privately Held**
SIC: 2448 Mfg Wood Pallets/Skids

(G-6964)
R N HASKINS PRINTING INC
1795 Pond Rd (04330-1932)
P.O. Box 97, Oakland (04963-0097)
PHONE..................................207 465-2155
Richard Haskins, *President*
Barbara Haskins, *Vice Pres*
EMP: 10
SQ FT: 10,000
SALES (est): 1.2MM **Privately Held**
WEB: www.haskinsprinting.com
SIC: 2752 Commercial Offset Printing

(G-6965)
TREES LTD A PARTNR CONSISTING
2506 Middle Rd (04330-2840)
PHONE..................................207 547-3168
Donny Cole, *President*
EMP: 7
SALES (est): 839.5K **Privately Held**
SIC: 2411 Logging

(G-6966)
WILLIAM SMITH ENTERPRISES INC
5 Thistle Ln (04330-2342)
P.O. Box 127, Coopers Mills (04341-0127)
PHONE..................................207 549-3103
John Ryzewic, *President*
Julie Guimond, *Controller*
EMP: 3
SQ FT: 20,000
SALES: 4MM **Privately Held**
WEB: www.ehrinv.com
SIC: 3444 3443 3441 Mfg Sheet Metalwork Mfg Fabricated Plate Wrk Structural Metal Fabrctn
PA: Ehr Investments Inc
189 Admirals Way S
Ponte Vedra FL 32082
904 285-3250

Skowhegan
Somerset County

(G-6967)
ALLAGASH MAPLE PRODUCTS INC
279 Back Rd (04976-5027)
P.O. Box 581, Jackman (04945-0581)
PHONE..................................207 431-1481
Jermey Steeves, *Admin Sec*
EMP: 3
SALES (est): 147.4K **Privately Held**
SIC: 2099 Mfg Food Preparations

(G-6968)
AMBROSE G MCCARTHY JR
Also Called: CAM Logging
228 North Ave (04976-2144)
PHONE..................................207 474-8837
Ambrose G McCarthy, *Owner*
EMP: 34
SQ FT: 5,400
SALES (est): 2MM **Privately Held**
WEB: www.mccarthyenterprises.com
SIC: 2411 7389 5499 5199 Logging Bottle Return And Retail Soft Drinks Whol Christmas Wreaths Real Estate Agency And Operator Of Residential Buildings

(G-6969)
BELANGER SHEET METAL INC
689 Malbons Mills Rd (04976-4132)
PHONE..................................207 474-8990
David Belanger, *President*
EMP: 5
SQ FT: 1,200
SALES: 252K **Privately Held**
SIC: 3444 Mfg Sheet Metalwork

(G-6970)
BROMAR
Also Called: Skowhegan Press
17 Parlin St (04976-2142)
PHONE..................................207 474-3784
Jeremy Martinez, *President*
Brandon Fenton, *Production*
Todd Denno, *CIO*
EMP: 7
SQ FT: 4,800
SALES (est): 1.2MM **Privately Held**
WEB: www.skowpress.com
SIC: 2752 Lithographic Commercial Printing

(G-6971)
CARRIER CHIPPING INC
100 Carrier Ln (04976)
PHONE..................................207 858-4277
Suzanne Carrier, *President*
EMP: 15
SALES (est): 153.7K **Privately Held**
SIC: 2421 Chipper Mill

(G-6972)
DIRIGO STITCHING INC
40 Dane Ave (04976-2048)
P.O. Box 447 (04976-0447)
PHONE..................................207 474-8421
Peter Schultz, *President*
Caesar J Schiraldi, *Vice Pres*
Herbert E Paradis, *Treasurer*
EMP: 40
SQ FT: 53,000
SALES (est): 4MM **Privately Held**
SIC: 2391 2392 Mfg Curtains/Draperies Mfg Household Furnishings

(G-6973)
E M K INC
Also Called: Eaton Mountain Ski Area
89 Lambert Rd (04976-4448)
PHONE..................................207 474-2666
Eugene Kent, *President*
Mary Kent, *Vice Pres*
EMP: 12
SALES (est): 1.1MM **Privately Held**
WEB: www.emk.com
SIC: 3799 5813 5812 Mfg Transportation Equipment Drinking Place Eating Place

(G-6974)
GENPLEX INC
7 Industrial Park Rd # 1 (04976-4016)
PHONE..................................207 474-3500
Duane Colford, *President*
EMP: 7
SQ FT: 10,000
SALES (est): 1.5MM **Privately Held**
WEB: www.genplex.com
SIC: 3089 Mfg Plastic Products

(G-6975)
GIFFORDS DAIRY INC
Also Called: Gifford's Famous Ice Cream
25 Hathaway St (04976-1436)
PHONE..................................207 474-9821
Roger Gifford, *President*
Clement Teresa, *Vice Pres*
Carl Smith, *Safety Mgr*
John Gifford, *Treasurer*
Darcy Dow, *Finance*
EMP: 25
SALES: 1.6MM **Privately Held**
WEB: www.giffordsicecream.com
SIC: 2024 Eating Place

(G-6976)
HOWARD P FAIRFIELD LLC (DH)
Also Called: Skowhegan Machine
9 Green St (04976-1159)
P.O. Box 188 (04976-0188)
PHONE..................................207 474-9836
Ron Woodbrey, *Exec VP*
Dan Matchett, *Sales Staff*
Torrey Sheafe, *Marketing Mgr*
Howard E Sevey, *Mng Member*
Kerri Everett,
EMP: 45
SQ FT: 74,000
SALES (est): 6MM
SALES (corp-wide): 1B **Publicly Held**
WEB: www.hpfairfield.com
SIC: 3531 3991 Mfg Construction Machinery Mfg Brooms/Brushes
HQ: Alamo Group (Usa) Inc.
1627 E Walnut St
Seguin TX 78155
830 379-1480

(G-6977)
IMERYS USA INC
1329 Waterville Rd (04976-4908)
PHONE..................................207 238-9267
Mike Blevins, *Branch Mgr*
EMP: 222
SALES (corp-wide): 2.9MM **Privately Held**
SIC: 1455 Kaolin/Ball Clay Mining
HQ: Imerys Usa, Inc.
100 Mansell Ct E Ste 300
Roswell GA 30076
770 645-3300

(G-6978)
J & M MACHINING INC
313 North Ave (04976-4021)
PHONE..................................207 474-7300
Mark Hunter, *President*
Danny Slaney, *Vice Pres*
EMP: 13
SQ FT: 10,000
SALES (est): 2.3MM **Privately Held**
WEB: www.jmmach.com
SIC: 3599 7389 Mfg Industrial Machinery Business Services

(G-6979)
JACKMAN LUMBER INC
Also Called: Somerset Log Yard
318 Varney Rd (04976-4925)
P.O. Box 972 (04976-0972)
PHONE..................................207 858-0321
Mark Robinson, *Manager*
EMP: 3
SALES (est): 276.6K
SALES (corp-wide): 3MM **Privately Held**
SIC: 2411 Logging
PA: Jackman Lumber Inc
548 Main St
Jackman ME 04945
207 668-4407

(G-6980)
MAINE MEAL LLC
4 Madison Ave Fl 2 (04976-1220)
PHONE..................................207 779-4185
Mark Lacasse, *President*
Kelly Lacasse, *Vice Pres*
EMP: 5
SQ FT: 1,000
SALES: 35K **Privately Held**
SIC: 2038 Mfg Frozen Specialties

(G-6981)
MAINE STITCHING SPC LLC
Also Called: Maine Innkeepers Association
40 Dane Ave (04976-2048)
PHONE..................................207 812-5207
Julie Swain, *General Mgr*
William Swain, *Mng Member*
EMP: 12
SQ FT: 45,000
SALES: 500K **Privately Held**
SIC: 3552 5714 Mfg Textile Machinery Ret Draperies/Upholstery

(G-6982)
MARS MEDICAL PRODUCTS LLC
184 Norridgewock Ave (04976-4207)
PHONE..................................207 385-3278
Krishna Bhatta, *CEO*
EMP: 4
SALES (est): 158.1K **Privately Held**
SIC: 3841 Mfg Surgical/Medical Instruments

(G-6983)
NEW BALANCE ATHLETICS INC
Also Called: Showhegan New Balance
10 Walnut St (04976-1513)
PHONE..................................207 474-2042
Sheldon Kilkenny, *Manager*
EMP: 360
SALES (corp-wide): 3.2B **Privately Held**
SIC: 3149 3021 Mfg Footwear-Except Rubber Mfg Rubber/Plastic Footwear
HQ: New Balance Athletics, Inc.
100 Guest St Fl 5
Boston MA 02135
617 783-4000

(G-6984)
NORTHEAST DORAN INC
N Ave Industrial Park (04976)
P.O. Box 1042 (04976-1042)
PHONE..................................207 474-2000
Donald Williams, *President*
EMP: 8
SQ FT: 3,000
SALES (est): 1.2MM **Privately Held**
WEB: www.northeastdoran.com
SIC: 3599 Machine Shop

(G-6985)
SAPPI NORTH AMERICA INC
98 North Ave (04976-1942)
PHONE..................................207 858-4201
Bruce Hanson, *Vice Pres*
Dee Baum, *Director*
EMP: 8
SALES (corp-wide): 785.7K **Privately Held**
SIC: 2621 Paper Mill

HQ: Sappi North America, Inc.
255 State St Fl 4
Boston MA 02109
617 423-7300

(G-6986)
SAPPI NORTH AMERICA INC
Also Called: Sappi Fine Paper North America
1329 Waterville Rd (04976-4999)
PHONE..................................207 238-3000
Tony Ouellette, *Managing Dir*
Sherwood Swain, *Area Mgr*
Skip Pratt, *Safety Mgr*
John Leblanc, *Opers Staff*
Jonathan Shoulta, *Engineer*
EMP: 725
SALES (corp-wide): 785.7K **Privately Held**
SIC: 2679 2674 2672 2621 Mfg Converted Paper Prdt Mfg Bags-Uncoated Paper Mfg Coat/Laminated Paper Paper Mill
HQ: Sappi North America, Inc.
255 State St Fl 4
Boston MA 02109
617 423-7300

(G-6987)
STRAWBERRY HILL FARMS LLC
279 Back Rd (04976-5027)
PHONE..................................207 474-5262
Jeremy C Steeves,
Eva M Steeves,
John H Steeves,
EMP: 3
SALES (est): 287.6K **Privately Held**
WEB: www.puremaple.com
SIC: 2099 Mfg Food Preparations

(G-6988)
YORKS SIGNS
Also Called: York's Sign Shop
127 Waterville Rd (04976-1534)
P.O. Box 870 (04976-0870)
PHONE..................................207 474-9331
Gary York, *Owner*
EMP: 3
SALES: 110K **Privately Held**
WEB: www.yorksigns.com
SIC: 3993 Manufacturing Of Commercial Signs Excluding Electric Signs

Smithfield
Somerset County

(G-6989)
MAINELY METROLOGY INC
921 Smithfield Rd (04978-3501)
PHONE..................................207 362-5520
David Joy, *President*
Gerald Joy, *Vice Pres*
EMP: 3
SALES: 250K **Privately Held**
SIC: 3825 Calibration Of Grant Surface Palce And Resurfacing

(G-6990)
PAUL H WARREN FOREST PRODUCTS
195 Warren Hill Rd (04978-3522)
PHONE..................................207 362-3681
Paul Warren, *Owner*
Joan Warren, *Co-Owner*
EMP: 4
SALES: 210K **Privately Held**
SIC: 2411 Logging

Smyrna Mills
Aroostook County

(G-6991)
ESCHDALE LAWN & GRDN PDTS LLC
881 Smyrna Center Rd (04780-5217)
PHONE..................................207 757-7268
Zack Copp,
Daniel Esch,
EMP: 4
SQ FT: 2,400
SALES (est): 210K **Privately Held**
SIC: 3524 Mfg Lawn/Garden Equipment

(G-6992)
HERBERT L HARDY AND SON INC
1454 Dyerbrook (04780)
P.O. Box 164 (04780-0164)
PHONE..................................207 757-8550
Herbert L Hardy, *President*
Kerry Hardy, *Vice Pres*
Florence Hardy, *Treasurer*
EMP: 7 **EST:** 1957
SALES: 250K **Privately Held**
SIC: 2411 Logging

(G-6993)
K B LOGGING INC
Also Called: KB Logging
3276 Us Route 2 (04780-5013)
P.O. Box 189 (04780-0189)
PHONE..................................207 757-8818
Kevin Brannen, *President*
Kristy Brannen, *Corp Secy*
EMP: 10
SALES: 800K **Privately Held**
SIC: 2411 2426 2421 Logging Hardwood Dimension/Floor Mill Sawmill/Planing Mill

(G-6994)
NORTHEASTERN RUSTIC FURNI
2761 Us Route 2 (04780-5109)
PHONE..................................207 757-8300
Paul Schesph, *Partner*
EMP: 4 **EST:** 2013
SALES: 680K **Privately Held**
SIC: 2519 5712 Mfg Household Furniture Ret Furniture

(G-6995)
SPRING BREAK MAPLE & HONEY
3276 Us Route 2 (04780)
PHONE..................................207 757-7373
Kristi Brannen, *Owner*
EMP: 3
SALES: 15K **Privately Held**
SIC: 2099 Mfg Food Preparations

(G-6996)
STURDIBUILT STORAGE BLDGS LLC
2587 Us Route 2 (04780-5106)
PHONE..................................207 757-7877
Jason Johnson, *Mng Member*
Tom Johnson,
EMP: 4
SALES (est): 394.9K **Privately Held**
SIC: 3448 Manufacturer Of Pre Fabricated Buildings Retailer Of Pre Fabricated Buildings

Solon
Somerset County

(G-6997)
DIFFERENT DRUMMER
211 Eaton Hill Rd (04979-3329)
PHONE..................................207 643-2572
Frank Ridley, *Owner*
EMP: 3 **EST:** 1973
SALES: 92K **Privately Held**
WEB: www.mainetoys.com
SIC: 3944 5092 Mfg & Whol Toys & Hobby Goods

Somerville
Lincoln County

(G-6998)
CALEB CHURCHILL
Also Called: Churchill Wallstone & Gravel
5 Hisler Mt Rd (04348-3162)
PHONE..................................207 215-7949
Caleb A Churchill, *Principal*
EMP: 3 **EST:** 2012
SALES (est): 144K **Privately Held**
SIC: 1442 Construction Sand/Gravel

(G-6999)
PLANTES LOBSTER ESCAPE VENTS
3628 Turner Ridge Rd (04348-3007)
PHONE..................................207 549-7204
Eric Dedoes, *President*
EMP: 3
SALES (est): 193.9K **Privately Held**
WEB: www.plante.com
SIC: 3949 Ret Sporting Goods/Bicycles

Sorrento
Hancock County

(G-7000)
POWER GRIPPS USA INC
41 Pomola Ave (04677-3126)
PHONE..................................207 422-2051
Heather Parker, *President*
Michael Parker, *Vice Pres*
Willa Parker, *Purch Mgr*
EMP: 6
SALES (est): 655.7K **Privately Held**
WEB: www.versagripps.com
SIC: 3949 Mfg Sporting/Athletic Goods

South Berwick
York County

(G-7001)
CHRISTY MACHINE COMPANY
270 Oldfields Rd (03908-1756)
PHONE..................................207 748-1092
Jay Wilkie, *Owner*
Christina Wilkie, *Owner*
EMP: 3 **EST:** 1977
SALES (est): 210K **Privately Held**
WEB: www.sifters.com
SIC: 3599 Machine Shop

(G-7002)
F A WILNAUER WOODWORK INC
Also Called: F A Wildnauer Woodwork
28 Witchtrot Rd (03908-2170)
PHONE..................................207 384-4824
Fred Wildnauer, *President*
EMP: 4
SQ FT: 3,000
SALES: 600K **Privately Held**
WEB: www.fawildnauerwoodwork.com
SIC: 2541 2431 5712 Mfg Wood Partitions/Fixtures Mfg Millwork Ret Furniture

(G-7003)
OLIVE WILDROSE OIL
24 Great Hill Rd (03908-2015)
PHONE..................................603 767-0597
EMP: 3
SALES (est): 116.6K **Privately Held**
SIC: 2079 Edible Fats And Oils

(G-7004)
SIGNS BY MO
Railroad Avenue Ext (03908)
P.O. Box 231 (03908-0231)
PHONE..................................207 384-2363
Maurice Roberge, *Owner*
EMP: 3
SALES (est): 188.3K **Privately Held**
SIC: 3993 Mfg Signs/Advertising Specialties

South Bristol
Lincoln County

(G-7005)
JOHNS BAY BOAT CO
90 Poorhouse Cove Rd (04568-4249)
P.O. Box 58 (04568-0058)
PHONE..................................207 644-8261
Pete Kass, *Owner*
EMP: 3
SALES (est): 209K **Privately Held**
SIC: 3732 Boatbuilding/Repairing

South China
Kennebec County

(G-7006)
OUELLETTE SAND & GRAVEL INC
80 Southern Oaks Dr (04358)
P.O. Box 303 (04358-0303)
PHONE..................................207 445-4131
Daniel Ouellette, *President*
EMP: 3
SALES: 300K **Privately Held**
SIC: 2899 1442 Mfg Chemical Preparations Construction Sand/Gravel

(G-7007)
TOWN LINE
16 Jones Brook Xing (04358-5246)
P.O. Box 89 (04358-0089)
PHONE..................................207 445-2234
William Harry, *Exec Dir*
EMP: 4
SALES: 110K **Privately Held**
SIC: 2711 Newspapers-Publishing/Printing

South Harpswell
Cumberland County

(G-7008)
SETH HETHERINGTON
Also Called: Mobile Marine Canvas Co
66 Allen Point Rd (04079-3055)
P.O. Box 403, Harpswell (04079-0403)
PHONE..................................207 833-5400
Seth Hetherington, *Owner*
EMP: 4 **EST:** 1994
SALES: 319K **Privately Held**
WEB: www.mobilecanvas.com
SIC: 2394 3441 Mfg Canvas/Related Products Structural Metal Fabrication

South Paris
Oxford County

(G-7009)
A & W PAVING & SEALCOATING
501 Elm Rd (04281)
P.O. Box 585, Norway (04268-0585)
PHONE..................................207 743-6615
John Allen, *President*
Kurt Wilson, *Vice Pres*
EMP: 7
SALES (est): 1MM **Privately Held**
SIC: 2951 Highway/Street Construction

(G-7010)
FRANKE ASSOCIATES INC
2 Industry Dr (04281-6445)
PHONE..................................207 743-6654
Donald Franke, *President*
Carol A Franke, *Vice Pres*
EMP: 6
SQ FT: 7,500
SALES: 520K **Privately Held**
SIC: 3441 Mfg Metal Fabrication Including Expansion Joints & Dampers

(G-7011)
HAROLD C MOORE II
Also Called: T C M Trucking & Logging
604 Ryerson Hill Rd (04281-6207)
PHONE..................................207 595-5683
Harold Craig Moore II, *Principal*
EMP: 3
SALES (est): 136.5K **Privately Held**
SIC: 2411 Logging

(G-7012)
KBS BUILDING SYSTEMS INC
41 Main St (04281-1403)
PHONE..................................207 739-2222
Robert Farnham, *President*
EMP: 6
SALES (est): 575.2K **Privately Held**
SIC: 2452 Mfg Prefabricated Wood Buildings

GEOGRAPHIC

(G-7013)
MAINE MACHINE PRODUCTS COMPANY
79 Prospect Ave (04281-1108)
P.O. Box 260 (04281-0260)
PHONE..................................207 743-6344
David Macmahon, *President*
Robert Crepeau, *Opers Staff*
Paul Colby, *Production*
Dennis Martin, *Engineer*
Patrick McGowan, *Controller*
▲ **EMP:** 130 **EST:** 1956
SQ FT: 75,000
SALES (est): 30.3MM **Privately Held**
WEB: www.mmpco.com
SIC: 3599 Mfg Industrial Machinery
PA: Gennx360 Capital Partners, L.P.
590 Madison Ave Fl 27
New York NY 10022

(G-7014)
MODULAR FUN I INC
Also Called: Kbs Homes
300 Park St (04281-6417)
P.O. Box 220 (04281-0220)
PHONE..................................207 739-2400
Dan Koch, *Principal*
EMP: 203
SALES (est): 47.4MM **Privately Held**
SIC: 2452 Mfg Prefabricated Wood Buildings

(G-7015)
PARK STREET PRESS INC
8 High St (04281-1325)
P.O. Box 63 (04281-0063)
PHONE..................................207 743-7702
EMP: 5
SALES: 291K **Privately Held**
SIC: 2759 2752 Commercial Printing, Nec

(G-7016)
PERFECT STITCH EMROIDERY INC
19 James Rd (04281)
P.O. Box 137 (04281-0137)
PHONE..................................207 743-2830
Eben Hobbs, *President*
EMP: 4
SALES (est): 298.3K **Privately Held**
WEB: www.perfectstitchemb.com
SIC: 2395 Pleating/Stitching Services

South Portland
Cumberland County

(G-7017)
C-O BELLA ROUGE AT BELISSINO
472 Ocean St (04106-6639)
PHONE..................................207 318-5214
Anna Stasiv, *Owner*
EMP: 3
SALES (est): 107.6K **Privately Held**
SIC: 3089 Mfg Plastic Products

(G-7018)
CAPE TECHNOLOGIES LLC
120 Thadeus St Ste 2 (04106-6245)
PHONE..................................207 741-2995
Robert Harrison, *President*
Michael Slevin, *Principal*
EMP: 3
SQ FT: 3,000
SALES: 500K **Privately Held**
WEB: www.cape-tech.com
SIC: 2835 Mfg Diagnostic Substances

(G-7019)
CASCO BAY STEEL STRUCTURES INC
1 Wallace Ave (04106-6176)
PHONE..................................207 780-6722
Brian Tate, *President*
Wendy Tate, *Vice Pres*
Jason Trask, *Plant Supt*
Philip Hoilien, *Project Mgr*
Jeff Oemig, *Prdtn Mgr*
EMP: 10 **EST:** 1997
SALES: 48MM **Privately Held**
WEB: www.cascobaysteel.com
SIC: 3441 Structural Metal Fabrication

(G-7020)
COCA-COLA BOTTLING COMPANY
316 Western Ave (04106-1701)
PHONE..................................207 773-5505
Alton Hartt, *Branch Mgr*
EMP: 125 **Privately Held**
SIC: 2086 Carb Sft Drnkbtlcn
HQ: Coca-Cola Beverages Northeast, Inc.
1 Executive Park Dr # 330
Bedford NH 03110
603 627-7871

(G-7021)
DAVID SAUNDERS INC
Also Called: Saunders Electronics
192 Gannett Dr (04106-6938)
PHONE..................................207 228-1888
David Saunders, *President*
Jean Saunders, *Vice Pres*
EMP: 25
SQ FT: 9,000
SALES (est): 6.8MM **Privately Held**
WEB: www.saunderselectronics.com
SIC: 3845 3672 3823 8731 Mfg Electromedical Equip Mfg Printed Circuit Brds Mfg Process Cntrl Instr Coml Physical Research

(G-7022)
DRAGON PRODUCTS COMPANY LLC (DH)
57 Atlantic Pl (04106-2316)
PHONE..................................207 774-6355
Terrence L Veysey, *President*
John Slagle, *Human Resources*
◆ **EMP:** 25
SALES (est): 51MM **Privately Held**
SIC: 3273 3241 3281 3274 Mfg Ready-Mixed Concrete Mfg Hydraulic Cement Mfg Cut Stone/Products Mfg Lime Products

(G-7023)
FAIRCHILD ENERGY LLC
82 Running Hill Rd (04106-3218)
PHONE..................................207 775-8100
Mark S Thompson, *CEO*
EMP: 7
SALES (est): 1.9MM
SALES (corp-wide): 5.8B **Publicly Held**
SIC: 3674 Mfg Semiconductors/Devices
HQ: Fairchild Semiconductor International, Inc.
1272 Borregas Ave
Sunnyvale CA 94089
408 822-2000

(G-7024)
FAIRCHILD SEMICONDUCTOR CORP (DH)
82 Running Hill Rd (04106-3293)
PHONE..................................207 775-8100
Kevin B London, *President*
Vijay Ullal, *Principal*
Mark Thompson, *Chairman*
Justin Chiang, *Exec VP*
Robin G Goodwin, *Exec VP*
▲ **EMP:** 400 **EST:** 1997
SQ FT: 129,000
SALES (est): 934.4MM
SALES (corp-wide): 5.8B **Publicly Held**
SIC: 3674 Mfg Semiconductors/Related Devices
HQ: Fairchild Semiconductor International, Inc.
1272 Borregas Ave
Sunnyvale CA 94089
408 822-2000

(G-7025)
FAIRCHILD SEMICONDUCTOR CORP
333 Western Ave (04106-0022)
PHONE..................................207 775-8100
Steve Fesh, *Engineer*
Travis Haskell, *Engineer*
Robin Sawyer, *Controller*
Dan Peck, *Regl Sales Mgr*
Izak Bencuya, *Branch Mgr*
EMP: 250
SALES (corp-wide): 5.8B **Publicly Held**
SIC: 3674 Mfg Semiconductors/Related Devices
HQ: Fairchild Semiconductor Corporation
82 Running Hill Rd
South Portland ME 04106
207 775-8100

(G-7026)
FAIRCHILD SEMICONDUCTOR W CORP
82 Running Hill Rd (04106-3293)
PHONE..................................207 775-8100
Sam Lee, *CEO*
EMP: 4 **EST:** 2014
SALES (est): 239.6K
SALES (corp-wide): 5.8B **Publicly Held**
SIC: 3674 Mfg Semiconductors/Related Devices
HQ: Fairchild Semiconductor International, Inc.
1272 Borregas Ave
Sunnyvale CA 94089
408 822-2000

(G-7027)
FORECASTER PUBLISHING INC
295 Gannett Dr (04106-6910)
P.O. Box 66797, Falmouth (04105-6797)
PHONE..................................207 781-3661
David Costello, *President*
Karen Wood, *Publisher*
Marian McCue, *Principal*
MO Mehlsak, *Editor*
Suzanne Piecuch, *Prdtn Mgr*
EMP: 15
SALES (est): 726.4K **Privately Held**
WEB: www.theforecaster.net
SIC: 2711 Newspapers-Publishing/Printing

(G-7028)
GRANITE MOUNTAIN INDS LLC
Also Called: Rapid Assault Tools
174 Cash St 7 (04106-6228)
PHONE..................................978 369-0014
Gordon Steltzer, *Purch Agent*
Johanne Steltzer,
EMP: 5
SQ FT: 1,000
SALES (est): 593.7K **Privately Held**
SIC: 3728 7389 Mfg Military Parts/Equipment

(G-7029)
GRIPWET INC
55 Devereaux Cir (04106-1812)
P.O. Box 2292 (04116-2292)
PHONE..................................207 239-0486
EMP: 4
SALES (est): 263.8K **Privately Held**
SIC: 2891 Mfg Adhesives/Sealants

(G-7030)
IMERYS KAOLIN INC
27 Main St (04106-2617)
PHONE..................................207 741-2118
Mark Reynolds, *Manager*
EMP: 3
SALES (corp-wide): 2.9MM **Privately Held**
SIC: 1455 Kaolin Mining
HQ: Imerys Kaolin, Inc.
774 Georgia Kaolin Rd
Dry Branch GA 31020

(G-7031)
KOCH INDUSTRIES INC
5 Central Ave (04106-2636)
PHONE..................................207 767-2161
Charles L Hutchins, *Branch Mgr*
EMP: 14
SALES (corp-wide): 40.6B **Privately Held**
WEB: www.kochind.com
SIC: 2911 Petroleum Refiner
PA: Koch Industries, Inc.
4111 E 37th St N
Wichita KS 67220
316 828-5500

(G-7032)
MAINE SOFT DRINK ASSOCIATION
Also Called: Coca-Cola
316 Western Ave (04106-1720)
PHONE..................................207 773-5505
Oakley Jones, *Manager*
EMP: 70
SALES (est): 6MM **Privately Held**
SIC: 2086 Carb Sft Drnkbtlcn

(G-7033)
MRC GLOBAL (US) INC
169 Front St Bldg 9 (04106-1509)
PHONE..................................207 767-3861
Mark Duca, *Manager*
EMP: 11 **Publicly Held**
SIC: 1311 Whol Industrial Supplies
HQ: Mrc Global (Us) Inc.
1301 Mckinney St Ste 2300
Houston TX 77010
877 294-7574

(G-7034)
NANDU PRESS
53 Goudy St (04106-4939)
PHONE..................................207 767-3144
EMP: 3
SALES (est): 101.8K **Privately Held**
SIC: 2711 Newspapers-Publishing/Printing

(G-7035)
OUT SWEET TOOTH CUPCAKES
18 Romano Rd (04106-6305)
PHONE..................................207 272-4363
Valorie Jordan, *Principal*
EMP: 4
SALES (est): 183.6K **Privately Held**
SIC: 2051 Mfg Bread/Related Products

(G-7036)
PARTNERS PRINTING INC
800 Main St Ste 1 (04106-6050)
PHONE..................................207 773-0439
David Ducharme, *President*
Joan M Ducharme, *Treasurer*
Sarah Trask, *Cust Mgr*
EMP: 8
SQ FT: 2,000
SALES (est): 1.3MM **Privately Held**
WEB: www.kwikkopyme.com
SIC: 2752 Lithographic Commercial Printing

(G-7037)
PORT PRINTING SOLUTIONS INC
525 Main St Ste A (04106-5463)
P.O. Box 6209, Cape Elizabeth (04107-0009)
PHONE..................................207 741-5200
Michael Concannon, *President*
Stephanie Concannon, *Office Mgr*
Holly Peterson, *Manager*
EMP: 4
SQ FT: 800
SALES (est): 659.9K **Privately Held**
WEB: www.portgraphics.net
SIC: 2752 Lithographic Commercial Printing

(G-7038)
RAVE BROTHERS LLC
Also Called: Rave X
443b Western Ave (04106-1705)
PHONE..................................207 773-7727
Dave Colberg,
Ralph Gallagher,
EMP: 5
SALES (est): 560K **Privately Held**
SIC: 3751 Mfg Motorcycles/Bicycles

(G-7039)
SAPPI NORTH AMERICA INC
Also Called: Sappi Fine Paper North America
179 John Roberts Rd (04106-6990)
PHONE..................................207 854-7000
Jeff Wright, *Branch Mgr*
Alan Rubin, *Administration*
EMP: 64
SALES (corp-wide): 785.7K **Privately Held**
SIC: 2679 2674 2672 2621 Mfg Converted Paper Prdt Mfg Bags-Uncoated Paper Mfg Coat/Laminated Paper Paper Mill
HQ: Sappi North America, Inc.
255 State St Fl 4
Boston MA 02109
617 423-7300

(G-7040)
SELLERS PUBLISHING INC
Also Called: Ronnie Sellers Productions
161 John Roberts Rd Ste 1 (04106-3280)
PHONE..................................207 772-6833
Ronnie Sellers, *President*
Peter Doby, *Sales Mgr*
Scott Lovejoy, *Sales Mgr*
Debbie Marquis, *Cust Mgr*
Lisa Reitan, *Sales Staff*
◆ **EMP:** 29
SQ FT: 3,000
SALES (est): 4MM **Privately Held**
WEB: www.rsvp.com
SIC: 2741 5942 Misc Publishing Ret Books

(G-7041)
SUPERMEDIA LLC
600 Sthborough Dr Ste 100 (04106)
PHONE..................................207 828-6100
Chris Caswell, *Branch Mgr*
EMP: 254
SALES (corp-wide): 1.6B **Privately Held**
SIC: 2741 Business Services
HQ: Supermedia Llc
2200 W Airfield Dr
Dfw Airport TX 75261
972 453-7000

(G-7042)
TUFF PARTS INC
33 Haskell Ave (04106-4113)
P.O. Box 2419 (04116-2419)
PHONE..................................207 767-1063
Brian Ha Nion, *President*
EMP: 4
SQ FT: 5,000
SALES (est): 396.6K **Privately Held**
SIC: 3469 Mfg Machine Parts Stamped Or Pressed Metal

(G-7043)
TWIN RIVERS PAPER COMPANY LLC
707 Sable Oaks Dr Ste 100 (04106-6926)
PHONE..................................207 523-2350
EMP: 59 **Privately Held**
SIC: 2621 Paper Mill
PA: Twin Rivers Paper Company Llc
82 Bridge Ave
Madawaska ME 04756

(G-7044)
WATERFRONT GRAPHICS & PRTG LLC
104 Ocean St (04106-2832)
P.O. Box 2105 (04116-2105)
PHONE..................................207 799-3519
James Brown, *Mng Member*
EMP: 8
SQ FT: 3,500
SALES: 500K **Privately Held**
SIC: 2752 2759 Lithographic Commercial Printing Commercial Printing

South Thomaston
Knox County

(G-7045)
CLARK ISLAND BOAT WORKS
4 Rein Rd (04858)
PHONE..................................207 594-4112
Dan Mac Caffray, *Owner*
Dan Maccaffry, *Owner*
EMP: 6
SALES: 1.2MM **Privately Held**
SIC: 3732 3089 2499 Boatbuilding/Repairing Mfg Plastic Products Mfg Wood Products

Southwest Harbor
Hancock County

(G-7046)
ELLIS BOAT CO INC
265 Seawall Rd (04679-4043)
PHONE..................................207 244-9221
Donald R Ellis, *President*
EMP: 12 **EST:** 1948
SQ FT: 6,472
SALES (est): 1.1MM **Privately Held**
WEB: www.ellisboat.com
SIC: 3732 4493 Boat Building Repairing And Boat Storage Incidental Repair

(G-7047)
G C MANAGEMENT CORP (PA)
Also Called: Mount Desert Spring Water
78 Seal Cove Rd (04679-4628)
P.O. Box 166 (04679-0166)
PHONE..................................207 244-5363
Richard Evangelista, *President*
EMP: 6
SQ FT: 6,500
SALES (est): 933.7K **Privately Held**
WEB: www.acadiacabins.com
SIC: 2086 8744 4214 5149 Mfg Soft Drinks Facilities Support Svcs Local Truck-With Storage Whol Groceries

(G-7048)
LITTLE NOTCH BAKERY
11 Apple Ln (04679-4424)
P.O. Box 1295 (04679-1295)
PHONE..................................207 244-4043
Arthur Jacobs, *Owner*
EMP: 5
SALES (est): 296.4K **Privately Held**
SIC: 2051 Mfg Bread/Related Products

(G-7049)
MALCOLM L PETTEGROW INC
135 Seal Cove Rd (04679-4653)
P.O. Box 1160 (04679-1160)
PHONE..................................207 244-3514
EMP: 15
SQ FT: 12,480
SALES (est): 2.2MM **Privately Held**
WEB: www.pettegrowboats.com
SIC: 3732 Boat Building

(G-7050)
SALTY DOG GALLERY
322 Main St (04679-4243)
PHONE..................................207 244-5918
Joan Steele, *President*
EMP: 5
SALES (est): 231K **Privately Held**
SIC: 2711 Newspapers-Publishing/Printing

(G-7051)
T HENRI INC
Also Called: Maine Point
1 Apple Ln (04679-4424)
P.O. Box 1569 (04679-1569)
PHONE..................................207 244-7787
Patti Moore-Tinker, *President*
▲ **EMP:** 4
SQ FT: 1,200
SALES: 325.1K **Privately Held**
SIC: 3429 2395 Mfg Blanets & Covers Pleating/Stitching Services

(G-7052)
TALARIA COMPANY LLC
Also Called: Hinckley Yacht Services
130 Shore Rd (04679-4056)
PHONE..................................207 244-5572
Ruth Brunetti,
▲ **EMP:** 150 **EST:** 1999
SQ FT: 43,560
SALES (est): 10.6MM **Privately Held**
SIC: 3732 Boatbuilding/Repairing

Springvale
York County

(G-7053)
JAGGER BROTHERS
Also Called: Jagger Spun Division
5 Water St (04083-1329)
P.O. Box 188 (04083-0188)
PHONE..................................207 324-5622
David M Jagger, *President*
Linda Bishop, *Plant Mgr*
Scott Grey, *Manager*
Margaret Bullens, *Admin Sec*
▲ **EMP:** 45 **EST:** 1898
SQ FT: 60,000
SALES (est): 9MM **Privately Held**
WEB: www.jaggeryarn.com
SIC: 2281 Yarn Spinning Mill

(G-7054)
NEW ENGLAND WOODWORKS
10 Coleco Ln (04083-1203)
PHONE..................................207 324-6343
Lewis Libby, *Owner*
EMP: 4
SALES (est): 587.3K **Privately Held**
SIC: 2431 Mfg Millwork

(G-7055)
NOON FAMILY SHEEP FARM
Sunset Rd (04083)
PHONE..................................207 324-3733
Jean Noon, *Principal*
EMP: 6
SALES (est): 602.1K **Privately Held**
SIC: 2013 Mfg Prepared Meats

(G-7056)
WORSTED SPINNING NENG LLC
5 Water St (04083-1329)
PHONE..................................207 324-5622
Greg Fall, *Mng Member*
EMP: 9
SALES: 1MM **Privately Held**
SIC: 2281 Yarn Spinning Mill

Spruce Head
Knox County

(G-7057)
ROPE CO LLC
39 Deer Run Rd (04859-4412)
P.O. Box 130, Warren (04864-0130)
PHONE..................................207 838-4358
EMP: 5
SALES (est): 382.3K **Privately Held**
SIC: 2298 Mfg Cordage/Twine

St John Plt
Aroostook County

(G-7058)
IRVING WOODLANDS LLC (HQ)
1798 St John Rd (04743-4022)
P.O. Box 240, Fort Kent (04743-0240)
PHONE..................................207 834-5767
Kevin Michaud, *Office Mgr*
James K Irving, *Mng Member*
▲ **EMP:** 40
SQ FT: 15,000
SALES (est): 29MM
SALES (corp-wide): 2.8B **Privately Held**
SIC: 2421 Sawmill/Planing Mill
PA: Irving, J. D. Limited
300 Union St Suite 5
Saint John NB
506 632-7777

(G-7059)
T ROY INC
2356 St John Rd (04743-4028)
PHONE..................................207 834-6385
Roy Thibodeau, *President*
Lynn Thibodeau, *Admin Sec*
EMP: 4
SALES: 100K **Privately Held**
SIC: 2411 Logging

Standish
Cumberland County

(G-7060)
BOB WALKER INC
365 Northeast Rd (04084-6425)
PHONE..................................207 642-2083
Bob Walker, *President*
Brenda Walker, *Treasurer*
EMP: 10
SALES (est): 1.2MM **Privately Held**
SIC: 3444 1731 Mfg Sheet Metalwork Electrical Contractor

(G-7061)
CELLBLOCK FCS LLC
234 Northeast Rd Ste 5 (04084-6945)
PHONE..................................603 276-5785
Dylan Vandemark, *Vice Pres*
Matthew Vandemark,
EMP: 10
SALES (est): 293.5K **Privately Held**
SIC: 3999 Mfg Misc Products

(G-7062)
LA CREME CHOCOLAT INC
110 Standish Neck Rd (04084-5430)
PHONE..................................443 841-2458
EMP: 3
SALES (est): 147K **Privately Held**
SIC: 2066 Mfg Chocolate/Cocoa Products

(G-7063)
NEW ENGLAND CASTINGS LLC
234 Northeast Rd Ste 2 (04084-6945)
PHONE..................................207 642-3029
Walter Butler, *President*
Debra Butler, *Executive*
EMP: 23
SQ FT: 6,000
SALES (est): 5MM **Privately Held**
WEB: www.newenglandcastings.com
SIC: 3324 Mfg Investment Castings

(G-7064)
WIRELESS CONSTRUCTION INC
40 Blake Rd (04084-6415)
PHONE..................................207 642-5751
Michael Sullivan, *President*
Stanley Brown, *Vice Pres*
Sheldon Jones, *Project Mgr*
Jason Roberts, *Safety Mgr*
Matthew Langevin, *Purchasing*
EMP: 40
SALES (est): 6.1MM **Privately Held**
SIC: 1389 1629 Oil/Gas Field Services Heavy Construction

Stetson
Penobscot County

(G-7065)
LEIGHTONS CUSTOM MACHINING
Exeter Rd (04488)
P.O. Box 87 (04488-0087)
PHONE..................................207 296-2601
Charles Leighton, *Owner*
EMP: 5
SALES (est): 342.7K **Privately Held**
SIC: 3599 Mfg Industrial Machinery

(G-7066)
SIGN SERVICES INC
512 Wolfboro Rd (04488-3124)
PHONE..................................207 296-2400
Samuel Hands, *President*
Ellen Hands, *Treasurer*
EMP: 12
SQ FT: 3,200
SALES (est): 1.4MM **Privately Held**
SIC: 3993 1799 Mfg Signs/Advertising Specialties Trade Contractor

Steuben
Washington County

(G-7067)
H & H MARINE INC
932 Us Route 1 Ste 1 (04680-2942)
PHONE..................................207 546-7477
Eric Moores, *President*
Anne Ray, *Corp Secy*
Bruce Grindle, *Vice Pres*
EMP: 16
SQ FT: 20,000
SALES: 2MM **Privately Held**
SIC: 3732 Mfg Fishing Boats

Stockton Springs
Waldo County

(G-7068)
AMERICAN SOLARTECHNICS LLC
24 Us Rt 1 (04981-4333)
P.O. Box 882, Searsport (04974-0882)
PHONE..................................207 548-1122
Thomas Gocze, *President*
Maria Gocze, *President*
EMP: 3
SALES (est): 431.5K **Privately Held**
SIC: 3433 Mfg Heating Equipment-Non-electric

Stonington
Hancock County

(G-7069)
BILLINGS DIESEL & MARINE SVC
Moose Island Rd (04681)
P.O. Box 67 (04681-0067)
PHONE..................................207 367-2328
Harlan R Billings, *President*
Ryan Stickel, *Principal*
Suzette Griindle, *Vice Pres*
Stella Billings, *Treasurer*
Greg Diesel, *Manager*
EMP: 50 **EST:** 1954
SALES (est): 8.7MM **Privately Held**
SIC: 3732 Boat Building & Repair

(G-7070)
PENOBSCOT BAY PRESS INC (PA)
Also Called: Island Ad-Vantages
138 Main St (04681)
P.O. Box 36 (04681-0036)
PHONE..................................207 367-2200
R Nathaniel Barrows, *President*
Katie Frasier, *Treasurer*
EMP: 19
SALES (est): 1.6MM **Privately Held**
SIC: 2711 2759 2731 Newspaper Publishing

Strong
Franklin County

(G-7071)
GLORIA J GORDON LOGGING
74 Norton Hill Rd (04983-3333)
P.O. Box 88 (04983-0088)
PHONE..................................207 684-4462
Gloria J Gordon, *Owner*
EMP: 4
SALES: 500K **Privately Held**
SIC: 2411 Logging

(G-7072)
LIGNETICS OF MAINE
30 Norton Hill Rd (04983-3325)
PHONE..................................207 684-3457
EMP: 9
SALES (est): 1.5MM **Privately Held**
SIC: 2499 Mfg Wood Products

(G-7073)
MAINELY TREES INC
26 S Main St (04983-3319)
P.O. Box 260 (04983-0260)
PHONE..................................207 684-3301
Karen Phorndike, *President*
EMP: 3
SALES (est): 594.6K **Privately Held**
SIC: 2411 Logging

(G-7074)
WESTERN MAINE WELDING & PIPING
513 Pond Rd (04983-3509)
PHONE..................................207 652-2327
Joseph Haynes, *Owner*
EMP: 3
SALES (est): 140K **Privately Held**
SIC: 7692 Welding Repair

Sunset
Hancock County

(G-7075)
ISLAND APPROACHES INC
Also Called: Maine Camp Outfitters
300 Sunset Rd (04683-3800)
P.O. Box 67 (04683-0067)
PHONE..................................207 348-2459
Andrew Fuller, *CEO*
EMP: 12
SALES (est): 1.2MM **Privately Held**
WEB: www.embroiderymaine.com
SIC: 2759 5961 Commercial Printing Ret Mail-Order House

Surry
Hancock County

(G-7076)
ESPOSITOS WLDG & FABRICATION
159 Blue Hill Rd (04684-3229)
PHONE..................................207 667-2442
Corey Esposito, *Owner*
EMP: 3
SALES (est): 200K **Privately Held**
SIC: 7692 Welding Repair

(G-7077)
WESMAC CUSTOM BOATS INC (PA)
158 Blue Hill Rd (04684-3237)
P.O. Box 56 (04684-0056)
PHONE..................................207 667-4822
Stephen Wessel, *President*
Dan Hitchcock, *CFO*
EMP: 15
SQ FT: 10,000
SALES (est): 3.2MM **Privately Held**
WEB: www.wesmac.com
SIC: 3732 5551 Boatbuilding/Repairing Ret Boats

(G-7078)
WESMAC CUSTOM BOATS INC
Also Called: Wesmac Customs Bulds
Rr 172 (04684)
PHONE..................................207 667-4822
Stephen T Wessel, *President*
EMP: 4
SALES (est): 351.8K **Privately Held**
WEB: www.wesmac.com
SIC: 3732 Boatbuilding/Repairing
PA: Wesmac Custom Boats Inc
158 Blue Hill Rd
Surry ME 04684

Temple
Franklin County

(G-7079)
HELLGREN LOGGING LLC
156 Ernies Way (04984-3625)
PHONE..................................207 778-0401
EMP: 3
SALES (est): 250.8K **Privately Held**
SIC: 2411 Logging

(G-7080)
STRONG WOOD PRODUCTS INC
156 Cummings Hill Rd (04984-3403)
PHONE..................................207 778-4063
John A Distefano, *President*
Alfred Destephano, *Vice Pres*
Mike Destephano, *Vice Pres*
Charles Abbott, *Admin Sec*
EMP: 12
SQ FT: 45,000
SALES: 813K **Privately Held**
SIC: 2499 Mfg Wooden Toothpicks & Applicator Dowels

Thomaston
Knox County

(G-7081)
BEST FELTS INC
17 Dexter St Ext (04861-3214)
P.O. Box 266 (04861-0266)
PHONE..................................207 596-0566
John G Rosseel, *President*
Sherly Hocking, *Admin Sec*
EMP: 10
SQ FT: 2,500
SALES: 1.6MM **Privately Held**
SIC: 2299 Mfg Felt Goods

(G-7082)
CHEMROCK CORPORATION
94 Buttermilk Ln (04861-3204)
P.O. Box 177 (04861-0177)
PHONE..................................207 594-8225
Warren Dorr, *Opers-Prdtn-Mfg*
EMP: 8 **Privately Held**
SIC: 3677 3295 Mfg Electronic Coils/Transformers Mfg Minerals-Ground/Treated
HQ: Chemrock Corporation
225 E City Ave
Bala Cynwyd PA 19004
610 667-6640

(G-7083)
DRAGON PRODUCTS COMPANY LLC
107 New County Rd (04861)
PHONE..................................207 594-5555
Terry Veysey, *Branch Mgr*
EMP: 110 **Privately Held**
SIC: 3273 3241 1442 1422 Mfg Ready-Mixed Concrete Mfg Hydraulic Cement Construction Sand/Gravel Crushed/Broken Limestone
HQ: Dragon Products Company, Llc
57 Atlantic Pl
South Portland ME 04106
207 774-6355

(G-7084)
EPIFANES NORTH AMERICA INC
70 Water St (04861-3741)
PHONE..................................207 354-0804
Thomas Theobaldes, *President*
◆ **EMP:** 6
SALES (est): 480K **Privately Held**
WEB: www.epifanes.com
SIC: 3479 Coating Service

(G-7085)
LYMAN MORSE BOATBUILDING INC (PA)
84 Knox St (04861-3714)
PHONE..................................207 354-6904
Drew Lyman, *President*
JB Turner, *Vice Pres*
Peter Beal, *Safety Mgr*
Heidi Lyman, *Treasurer*
Scott Layton, *Broker*
EMP: 84
SQ FT: 90,000
SALES (est): 20.1MM **Privately Held**
WEB: www.lymanmorse.com
SIC: 3732 Boatbuilding/Repairing

(G-7086)
LYMAN MORSE BOATBUILDING INC
19 Elltee Cir (04861-3218)
PHONE..................................207 354-6904
Derw Lyman, *Branch Mgr*
EMP: 80
SALES (corp-wide): 20.1MM **Privately Held**
WEB: www.lymanmorse.com
SIC: 3732 Boatbuilding/Repairing
PA: Lyman Morse Boatbuilding, Inc.
84 Knox St
Thomaston ME 04861
207 354-6904

(G-7087)
MAINE AUTHORS PUBLISHING
12 High St (04861-3437)
PHONE..................................207 594-0090
Jane Karker, *Principal*
EMP: 3
SALES (est): 91.5K **Privately Held**
SIC: 2741 Misc Publishing

(G-7088)
SEASTREET GRAPHICS
Also Called: Sea Street Graphics
161 Main St (04861-3807)
PHONE..................................207 594-1915
EMP: 3
SQ FT: 5,000
SALES (est): 371K **Privately Held**
WEB: www.seastreetgraphics.com
SIC: 2759 Commercial Printing, Nec

(G-7089)
TILBURY HOUSE PUBLISHERS
12 Star St (04861-3803)
PHONE..................................800 582-1899
Tristram Colburn, *Principal*
EMP: 6
SALES (est): 279.4K **Privately Held**
SIC: 2731 Books-Publishing/Printing

Topsham
Sagadahoc County

(G-7090)
KESTREL TOOLING COMPANY
40 Rymat Rd (04086-5804)
P.O. Box 6157, Falmouth (04105-6157)
PHONE..................................207 721-0609
EMP: 6
SALES: 850K **Privately Held**
SIC: 3543 Mfg Industrial Patterns

(G-7091)
MORNING STAR MARBLE & GRAN INC
Also Called: Morningstar Stone & Tile
47 Park Dr (04086-1737)
PHONE..................................207 725-7309
John N Whatley, *President*
Nick Whatley, *President*
Laura Whatley, *Vice Pres*
Bob Ferro, *Mktg Dir*
▲ **EMP:** 19
SALES (est): 2.6MM **Privately Held**
WEB: www.morningstarmarble.com
SIC: 3281 1743 5032 Mfg Cut Stone/Products Tile/Marble Contractor Whol Brick/Stone Material

(G-7092)
PICKENS WOODWORKING
141 Tedford Rd (04086-1852)
PHONE..................................207 725-8955
Jeff Pickens, *Owner*
EMP: 3
SALES: 179K **Privately Held**
SIC: 2431 Mfg Millwork

(G-7093)
PICTURE FRAME INC
Also Called: Picture Framer
81 Main St (04086-1262)
PHONE..................................207 729-7765
John Noyes, *President*
EMP: 3
SALES (est): 281.7K **Privately Held**
WEB: www.thepictureframermaine.com
SIC: 2499 7699 5999 Mfg Wood Products Repair Services Ret Misc Merchandise

(G-7094)
SANDELIN FOUNDATION INC
82 Old Augusta Rd (04086-1141)
P.O. Box 224 (04086-0224)
PHONE..................................207 725-7004
Harold D Sandelin, *President*
Barbara J Sandelin, *Vice Pres*
EMP: 10
SQ FT: 7,000
SALES (est): 1.8MM **Privately Held**
SIC: 3272 1771 Mfg Concrete Products Concrete Contractor

(G-7095)
TOPSHAM WOODWORKING LLC
3 Rex Rd (04086)
P.O. Box 487 (04086-0487)
PHONE..................................207 751-1032
Ronald Utecht,
EMP: 3
SQ FT: 7,348
SALES (est): 303.7K **Privately Held**
SIC: 2431 2434 Mfg Millwork Mfg Wood Kitchen Cabinet

Trenton
Hancock County

(G-7096)
AD M HOLDINGS LLC
Also Called: Tempshield
23 Industrial Way (04605-6028)
P.O. Box 199, Mount Desert (04660-0199)
PHONE..................................207 667-9696
Andrew Gilman,
EMP: 14
SALES (est): 415.5K **Privately Held**
SIC: 2326 Mfg Men's/Boy's Work Clothing

(G-7097)
DOWNEAST FISHING GEAR INC
12 Bar Harbor Rd (04605-5800)
P.O. Box 1283, Ellsworth (04605-1283)
PHONE..................................207 667-3131
Alicin Holmquist, *Manager*
▲ **EMP:** 20
SQ FT: 5,000
SALES (est): 3.6MM **Privately Held**
SIC: 3496 5941 5091 Mfg Misc Fabricated Wire Products Ret Sporting Goods/Bicycles Whol Sporting/Recreational Goods

(G-7098)
GALLERY LEATHER CO INC
27 Industrial Way (04605-6028)
PHONE..................................207 667-9474
Geoffrey Lafond, *President*
▲ **EMP:** 35
SQ FT: 20,000
SALES (est): 5MM **Privately Held**
WEB: www.galleryleathercompany.com
SIC: 3199 Mfg Leather Goods

(G-7099)
JOHN SEAVEY ACADIA FUEL
711 Bar Harbor Rd (04605-5926)
PHONE..................................207 664-6050
John A Seavey, *Principal*
EMP: 4
SALES (est): 343.3K **Privately Held**
SIC: 2869 Mfg Industrial Organic Chemicals

(G-7100)
METAL MAGIC INC
979 Bar Harbor Rd (04605-6015)
PHONE..................................207 667-8519
Edward Libitzki, *President*
Cheryl Libitzki, *Corp Secy*
EMP: 6
SQ FT: 2,900
SALES (est): 843.6K **Privately Held**
WEB: www.metalmagicinc.com
SIC: 3441 1799 1721 Metal Painting Sandblasting

(G-7101)
RAINWISE INC
18 River Field Rd (04605-5902)
PHONE..................................800 762-5723
Bunny Emerson, *President*
Lonnie White, *Vice Pres*
EMP: 20
SALES: 2MM **Privately Held**
WEB: www.rainwise.com
SIC: 3829 Mfg Measuring/Controlling Devices

(G-7102)
TALARIA COMPANY LLC
Also Called: Hinckley Company, The
40 Industrial Way (04605-6029)
PHONE..................................207 667-1891
Paul Fredrick, *Manager*
EMP: 250
SALES (corp-wide): 209.7MM **Privately Held**
SIC: 3732 Builds Boats
PA: The Talaria Company Llc
1 Lil Hrbr Landing Prt
Portsmouth RI 02871
401 683-7100

(G-7103)
TROY WINGER
22 Old Brewer Farm Rd (04605-6536)
PHONE..................................207 667-1815
Troy Winger, *Owner*
EMP: 3
SALES (est): 257K **Privately Held**
SIC: 7692 Welding Repair

(G-7104)
WOODSHOP CUPOLAS INC
Also Called: Woodshop At Acdia Weathervanes
749 Bar Harbor Rd (04605-5915)
PHONE..................................207 667-6331
Philip Alley, *President*
EMP: 3
SALES: 168K **Privately Held**
SIC: 2499 5999 Manufacters And Retails Wooden Cupolas And Metal Weather Vanes

Turner
Androscoggin County

(G-7105)
BEAR POND DUMPSTER LLC
250 Bear Pond Rd (04282-3510)
PHONE..................................207 224-0337
Stephen Jones, *Principal*
EMP: 4
SALES (est): 329.2K **Privately Held**
SIC: 3443 Mfg Fabricated Plate Work

(G-7106)
CLARK METAL FABRICATION INC
1463 Auburn Rd (04282-3617)
P.O. Box 399 (04282-0399)
PHONE..................................207 330-6322
William W Clark Jr, *President*
EMP: 8
SALES (est): 150K **Privately Held**
SIC: 3441 3446 Structural Metal Fabrication Mfg Architectural Metalwork

(G-7107)
GARY GREEN TRUCKING LOGGING
517 General Turner Hl Rd (04282-3706)
PHONE..................................207 225-3433
Gary Green, *Principal*
EMP: 6
SALES (est): 480.5K **Privately Held**
SIC: 2411 Logging

(G-7108)
IRISH INC (PA)
625 Plains Rd (04282-3313)
PHONE..................................207 224-7605
Kevin Irish, *President*
James E Irish Jr, *Treasurer*
Charles Abbott, *Clerk*
▲ **EMP:** 4
SALES (est): 530.3K **Privately Held**
WEB: www.irish.com
SIC: 3714 5013 Manufacture Import & Distribute Snowmobile Parts

(G-7109)
MOOSE CREEK HOME CENTER INC
2319 Auburn Rd (04282-3416)
PHONE..................................207 224-7497
Dana Turner, *President*
Wendy Collet, *General Mgr*
EMP: 5
SQ FT: 20,000
SALES: 900K **Privately Held**
SIC: 2452 5211 5199 5031 Prefabricated Wood Buildings

(G-7110)
TRI STAR SHEET METAL COMPANY
1817 Auburn Rd (04282-3408)
P.O. Box 400 (04282-0400)
PHONE..................................207 225-2043
Janet Perron, *President*
Dana Perron, *Vice Pres*
EMP: 10
SQ FT: 25,000
SALES (est): 1.5MM **Privately Held**
SIC: 3444 Sheet Metal Fabrication & Installation

(G-7111)
TURNER PUBLISHING INC
5 Fern St (04282-4028)
P.O. Box 214 (04282-0214)
PHONE..................................207 225-2076
Steve Cornelio, *President*
Jodi Cornelio, *CFO*
EMP: 14
SALES (est): 1MM **Privately Held**
SIC: 2711 7331 Newspapers-Publishing/Printing Direct Mail Advertising Services

(G-7112)
TWO RIVERS PET PRODUCTS INC
Also Called: Pussums Cat Company
469 N Parish Rd (04282-3217)
PHONE..................................207 225-3965
Susan Shaw, *CEO*
Eben Shaw, *CFO*
EMP: 21
SQ FT: 1,500
SALES: 202.4K **Privately Held**
SIC: 3999 2392 5999 Mfg Misc Products Mfg Household Furnishings Ret Misc Merchandise

Union
Knox County

(G-7113)
GEORGE BAGGETT
158 Feyler Rd (04862-5257)
PHONE..................................207 785-5442
George Baggett, *Principal*
EMP: 3
SALES (est): 169.9K **Privately Held**
SIC: 3823 Mfg Process Control Instruments

(G-7114)
LUCE DIRT EXCAVATION
2879 N Union Rd (04862-6024)
PHONE..................................207 785-3478
Peter Luce, *Owner*
EMP: 6
SALES (est): 460.1K **Privately Held**
SIC: 2411 Excavation Contractor

Unity
Waldo County

(G-7115)
ENVIREM ORGANICS LTD
39 Cornshop Rd (04988-4126)
P.O. Box 402 (04988-0402)
PHONE..................................207 948-4500
Robert Kiely, *President*
EMP: 5 **EST:** 2016
SALES (est): 622K **Privately Held**
SIC: 2875 Mfg Fertilizers-Mix Only

(G-7116)
JIMS SALAD CO
557 Albion Rd (04988-3210)
P.O. Box 528 (04988-0528)
PHONE..................................207 948-2613
Ralph Nason, *Owner*
EMP: 3 **EST:** 2008
SALES (est): 185K **Privately Held**
SIC: 2099 Mfg Food Preparations

(G-7117)
NORTH COUNTRY PRESS
126 Main St (04988-3734)
P.O. Box 546 (04988-0546)
PHONE..................................207 948-2208
Mary Kenney, *President*
Patricia Newell, *President*
EMP: 3
SALES (est): 165.2K **Privately Held**
SIC: 2731 Books-Publishing/Printing

(G-7118)
R & N INC
557 Albion Rd (04988-3210)
P.O. Box 180 (04988-0180)
PHONE..................................207 948-2613
Ralph Nason, *President*
Nancy Nason, *Treasurer*
EMP: 8
SQ FT: 9,000
SALES: 500K **Privately Held**
SIC: 2099 5149 Whol & Processes Salads

(G-7119)
WIN-PRESSOR LLC
336 Stagecoach Rd (04988-4117)
PHONE..................................207 948-4800
Ervin Hochstetler, *Principal*
EMP: 3
SALES (est): 210.3K **Privately Held**
SIC: 3442 Mfg Metal Doors/Sash/Trim

Van Buren
Aroostook County

(G-7120)
G R LOGGING INC
107 Jefferson St (04785-1173)
PHONE..................................207 868-2692
Gabriel Rioux, *President*
EMP: 5
SALES (est): 686K **Privately Held**
SIC: 2411 Trucking

(G-7121)
LA VALLEY WOOD INC
101 Industrial Dr (04785)
PHONE..................................207 316-6263
Kenneth Dionne, *CEO*
Jason Dionne, *Manager*
EMP: 10
SALES: 1,000K **Privately Held**
SIC: 2499 Wood Products, Nec, Nsk

(G-7122)
LEVESQUE FARM PALLETS
182 Marquis Rd (04785-1715)
PHONE..................................207 868-3905
R Levesque, *Principal*
EMP: 4
SALES (est): 369.9K **Privately Held**
SIC: 2448 Mfg Wood Pallets/Skids

(G-7123)
R H FOSTER INC
83 Main St (04785-1028)
PHONE..................................207 868-2983
EMP: 4 **EST:** 2010
SALES (est): 288.9K **Privately Held**
SIC: 2869 Mfg Industrial Organic Chemicals

Vassalboro
Kennebec County

(G-7124)
BAKER COMMODITIES INC
1607 Riverside Dr (04989-4110)
PHONE..................................207 622-3505
Herbey Le Braton, *Manager*
EMP: 6
SALES (corp-wide): 153.6MM **Privately Held**
WEB: www.bakercommodities.com
SIC: 2077 Mfg Animal/Marine Fat/Oil
PA: Baker Commodities, Inc.
4020 Bandini Blvd
Vernon CA 90058
323 268-2801

(G-7125)
PAUL E WENTWORTH
Also Called: Pe Wentworth
1000 Cross Hill Rd (04989-3744)
PHONE..................................207 923-3547
EMP: 4 **EST:** 1988
SALES (est): 450K **Privately Held**
SIC: 2911 4785 3537 7699 Petroleum Refining Motor Frght Fixed Fclty Mfg Indstl Truck/Tractor Repair Services

Veazie
Penobscot County

(G-7126)
COLLABRIC
1017 School St (04401-6983)
PHONE..................................207 945-5095
Mark Sampson, *President*
EMP: 11
SALES (est): 1.2MM **Privately Held**
WEB: www.fabriccraftsman.com
SIC: 2394 Mfg Canvas/Related Products

(G-7127)
INITIAL THIS INC
25 Silver Rdg (04401-7086)
PHONE..................................207 992-7176
John McDonald, *President*
EMP: 4 **EST:** 2014
SALES (est): 355.2K **Privately Held**
SIC: 3999 Mfg Misc Products

Vinalhaven
Knox County

(G-7128)
ISLAND LOBSTER SUPPLY
E Main St (04863)
P.O. Box 334 (04863-0334)
PHONE..................................207 863-4807
Wallen Lazaro, *President*
EMP: 5
SALES (est): 489.1K **Privately Held**
SIC: 3429 Mfg Hardware

Waldoboro
Lincoln County

(G-7129)
ADVANCED INDUS SOLUTIONS INC
Also Called: Custom Cordage LLC
151 One Pie Rd (04572-5927)
P.O. Box 1387 (04572-1387)
PHONE..................................207 832-0569
Maurice Maheux, *CEO*
EMP: 23 **Privately Held**
SIC: 2298 5085 Cordage And Twine, Nsk
PA: Advanced Industrial Solutions, Inc.
36 Anthony Ave
Augusta ME 04330
-

(G-7130)
ALLIED ENDEAVERS INC
Also Called: Allied Tool & Fastener
760 Atlantic Hwy (04572-6015)
P.O. Box 641 (04572-0641)
PHONE..................................207 832-0511
Raymond C Faria, *President*
Lois M Faria, *Treasurer*
EMP: 3
SQ FT: 2,800
SALES (est): 410.3K **Privately Held**
SIC: 3965 3544 Mfg Fasteners/Buttons/Pins Mfg Dies/Tools/Jigs/Fixtures

(G-7131)
ATLANTIC LABORATORIES INC
Also Called: North American Kelp
41 Cross St (04572-5634)
PHONE..................................207 832-5376
Robert Morse Jr, *President*
EMP: 8
SQ FT: 12,000
SALES (est): 1.7MM **Privately Held**
WEB: www.noamkelp.com
SIC: 2874 Mfg Phosphatic Fertilizers

(G-7132)
DAVID BIRD LLC
151 One Pie Rd (04572-5927)
P.O. Box 1387 (04572-1387)
PHONE..................................207 832-0569
Kevin Race,
David Bird,
▲ **EMP:** 12
SQ FT: 13,550
SALES (est): 1.7MM **Privately Held**
WEB: www.customcordage.com
SIC: 2298 Mfg Cordage/Twine

(G-7133)
KWS INC
110 One Pie Rd (04572-5925)
P.O. Box 1313 (04572-1313)
PHONE..................................207 832-5095
Kimberley Sweetser, *President*
Seth Sweetser, *Director*
EMP: 7
SQ FT: 8,000
SALES (est): 813.1K **Privately Held**
WEB: www.kws.net
SIC: 2299 Mfg Textile Goods

(G-7134)
MAINE ANTIQUE DIGEST INC
911 Main St (04572-6042)
P.O. Box 1429 (04572-1429)
PHONE..................................207 832-7534
Mr Samuel Pennington, *President*
Clayton Pennington, *Editor*
Kate Pennington, *Editor*
Sally Pennington, *Treasurer*
Jane Gleason, *Accounting Mgr*
EMP: 23
SQ FT: 6,500
SALES (est): 1.9MM **Privately Held**
WEB: www.fundschools.com
SIC: 2721 5932 2711 Periodicals-Publishing/Printing Ret Used Merchandise Newspapers-Publishing/Printing

(G-7135)
MORSES SAUERKRAUT
3856 Washington Rd (04572-5502)
PHONE..................................207 832-5569
Cody Lamontagne, *Owner*
EMP: 12
SALES (est): 1.3MM **Privately Held**
WEB: www.morsessauerkraut.com
SIC: 2035 Mfg Pickles/Sauces/Dressing

(G-7136)
OCEAN ORGANICS CORP
141 One Pie Rd (04572-5927)
P.O. Box 1448 (04572-1448)
PHONE..................................207 832-4305
William Middleton, *President*
Douglas Middleton, *Vice Pres*
Veronica Sanitate, *Vice Pres*
George Seaver, *Vice Pres*
Mike Roberts, *Sales Staff*
▲ **EMP:** 20
SQ FT: 25,000
SALES (est): 4.4MM **Privately Held**
SIC: 2873 Whol Farm Supplies

(G-7137)
ULTRON LLC
Also Called: Varitrade
948 Back Cove Rd (04572-6348)
PHONE..................................207 832-4502
Dave Rawstron,
Ming Rawstron,
EMP: 5
SALES: 200K **Privately Held**
SIC: 2911 Export & Import Of Petroleum Coke

Wallagrass
Aroostook County

(G-7138)
DUCAS LOGGING INC
6 Dumond Rd (04781-3018)
PHONE..................................207 834-5506
Robert Ducas, *President*
Linda Ducas, *Corp Secy*
EMP: 3
SALES (est): 281.5K **Privately Held**
SIC: 2411 Logging

(G-7139)
HIGHLAND LOGGING INC
39 Station Rd (04781-3241)
PHONE..................................207 436-1113
EMP: 3
SALES (est): 144.7K **Privately Held**
SIC: 2411 Logging

Walpole
Lincoln County

(G-7140)
FARRINS BOAT SHOP
19 Sproul Rd (04573-3114)
PHONE..................................207 563-5510
Bruce Farrin, *Owner*
EMP: 4
SALES (est): 363.9K **Privately Held**
SIC: 3732 Boat Building & Refinishing

(G-7141)
FLOWERS BOAT WORKS INC
21 Ridge Rd (04573-3319)
PHONE..................................207 563-7404
David Flower, *President*
Candy Flower, *Treasurer*
EMP: 7
SQ FT: 7,000
SALES: 1MM **Privately Held**
WEB: www.flowersboatworks.com
SIC: 3732 Boatbuilding/Repairing

Warren
Knox County

(G-7142)
KNOX MACHINE CO INC
936 Eastern Rd (04864-4573)
P.O. Box 68 (04864-0068)
PHONE..................................207 273-2296
Richard B Maxcy, *President*
Charles D Maxcy, *Treasurer*
EMP: 60
SQ FT: 28,500
SALES (est): 10.5MM **Privately Held**
WEB: www.knoxmachine.com
SIC: 3599 Mfg Industrial Machinery

(G-7143)
LELAND BOGGS II
Also Called: Boggs Mobile Homes
715 Camden Rd (04864-4211)
P.O. Box 177 (04864-0177)
PHONE..................................207 273-2610
Leland Boggs II, *Partner*
Valerie Boggs, *Partner*
EMP: 8 **EST:** 1958
SQ FT: 2,400
SALES (est): 1.2MM **Privately Held**
WEB: www.boggshomes.com
SIC: 2452 6531 Mfg Modular Homes Real Estate Agent/Manager

(G-7144)
LIE-NIELSEN TOOLWORKS INC
264 Stirling Rd (04864-4384)
P.O. Box 9 (04864-0009)
PHONE..................................800 327-2520
Thomas Lie-Nielsen, *President*
Carolyn Herron, *CFO*
▲ **EMP:** 90
SQ FT: 15,000
SALES (est): 16.2MM **Privately Held**
WEB: www.lie-nielsen.com
SIC: 3425 3423 3999 Mfg Saw Blades/Handsaws Mfg Hand/Edge Tools Mfg Misc Products

(G-7145)
MYSTIC WOODWORKS
199 Camden Rd (04864-4207)
P.O. Box 39 (04864-0039)
PHONE..................................207 273-3937
Raymond J Doubleday, *Partner*
Jamie Doubleday, *Partner*
EMP: 4
SQ FT: 9,000
SALES (est): 364.1K **Privately Held**
WEB: www.mysticwoodworks.com
SIC: 2511 5719 Mfg & Ret Kitchen Accessories

(G-7146)
ON THE ROAD INC
2243 Camden Rd (04864-4113)
P.O. Box 271 (04864-0271)
PHONE..................................207 273-3780
Toll Free:..888 -
Matt McConnell, *President*
Peter C Armstrong, *President*
Lauren S Armstrong, *Treasurer*
Stephen A Little, *Clerk*
EMP: 20
SQ FT: 7,800
SALES (est): 4MM **Privately Held**
WEB: www.on-the-road.net
SIC: 3715 5599 4213 Mfg Truck Trailers Ret Misc Vehicles Trucking Operator-Nonlocal

Washburn
Aroostook County

(G-7147)
THOMPSON TIMBER HARVESTING
46 Cross Rd (04786-3451)
PHONE..................................207 227-6290
Kenneth Thompson, *President*
EMP: 3
SALES (est): 98.8K **Privately Held**
SIC: 2411 Logging

Washington
Knox County

(G-7148)
BENCH DOGS
747 Waldoboro Rd (04574-3016)
PHONE..................................207 845-2084
Weber Robert, *President*
EMP: 4
SQ FT: 7,000
SALES (est): 500K **Privately Held**
SIC: 2434 Mfg Wood Kitchen Cabinets

(G-7149)
C T L LAND MANAGEMENT INC
142 Hopkins Rd (04574-3234)
PHONE..................................207 845-2841
Gavin McLain, *President*
EMP: 5
SALES (est): 649.6K **Privately Held**
SIC: 2411 Logging

Waterboro
York County

(G-7150)
ARCHITECTURAL SKYLIGHT CO INC
Also Called: E-Skylight.com
661 Main St (04087-3002)
PHONE..................................207 247-6747
Adrian Ayotte, *President*
Francis O'Neill, *Vice Pres*
EMP: 55
SQ FT: 43,000
SALES (est): 9.3MM **Privately Held**
WEB: www.archsky.com
SIC: 3444 Mfg Sheet Metalwork

(G-7151)
BROOKS WELDING & MACHINING INC
897 West Rd (04087-3506)
PHONE..................................207 247-4141
David Brooks, *President*
EMP: 3
SALES (est): 122.8K **Privately Held**
SIC: 7692 Mfg Industrial Machinery

(G-7152)
TK MACHINING INC
Also Called: T K Machining
4 Dyer Ln (04087-3052)
P.O. Box 556 (04087-0556)
PHONE..................................207 247-3114
Robert J Dewitt, *President*
EMP: 11
SALES (est): 2MM **Privately Held**
SIC: 3599 Mfg Industrial Machinery

Waterville
Kennebec County

(G-7153)
CENTRAL MAINE MORNING SENTINEL
31 Front St (04901-6626)
PHONE..................................207 873-3341
James Shaffer, *President*
John Christie, *President*
EMP: 7
SALES (est): 367.7K **Privately Held**
SIC: 2711 Newspapers-Publishing/Printing

(G-7154)
CENTRAL MAINE ONLINE
800 W River Rd (04901-4434)
PHONE..................................207 872-2985
Phil Crandlemire, *Owner*
EMP: 3
SALES (est): 139.3K **Privately Held**
SIC: 2711 Newspapers-Publishing/Printing

(G-7155)
F3 MFG INC
977 W River Rd Unit 3 (04901-4486)
PHONE..................................207 692-7178
Julian Margitza, *Purch Mgr*
EMP: 10
SALES (est): 730.2K **Privately Held**
SIC: 3713 Mfg Truck/Bus Bodies

(G-7156)
HANGER PROSTHETICS & ORTHOTICS
325 Kennedy Memorial Dr (04901-4517)
PHONE..................................207 872-8779
Scott Ebert, *Manager*
EMP: 11
SQ FT: 3,100
SALES (est): 1.7MM **Privately Held**
SIC: 3842 Mfg Surgical Appliances/Supplies

(G-7157)
HUHTAMAKI INC
242 College Ave (04901-6226)
PHONE..................................207 873-3351
Michael J Deroche, *Principal*
Gary Gustafson, *Electrical Engi*
Vivienne Saayman, *Finance*
David Bouchard, *Administration*
EMP: 300
SALES (corp-wide): 3.4B **Privately Held**
SIC: 2621 Paper Mill
HQ: Huhtamaki, Inc.
9201 Packaging Dr
De Soto KS 66018
913 583-3025

(G-7158)
MAINE CRISP COMPANY LLC (PA)
10 Railroad Sq (04901-6133)
PHONE..................................207 213-9296
Karen Getz, *Mng Member*
EMP: 3
SALES (est): 423.4K **Privately Held**
SIC: 2052 Mfg Cookies/Crackers

Wells
York County

(G-7159)
ALL KINDS OF SIGNS LLC
676 Post Rd Ste 1 (04090-4144)
P.O. Box 4214, Peabody MA (01961-4214)
PHONE..................................978 531-7100
Gary Everbeck, *Mng Member*
Bonnie Everbeck, *Mng Member*
EMP: 5
SALES: 300K **Privately Held**
SIC: 3993 Mfg Signs/Advertising Specialties

(G-7160)
CYNTHIA CARROLL PALLIAN
Also Called: Pallian & Company
2049 Post Rd (04090-4717)
P.O. Box 1704 (04090-1704)
PHONE..................................207 646-1600
Cynthia C Pallian, *Owner*
EMP: 7
SALES (est): 700K **Privately Held**
SIC: 3499 Mfg Misc Fabricated Metal Products

(G-7161)
D & J FUELS LLC
287 Perry Oliver Rd (04090-6946)
P.O. Box 176, North Berwick (03906-0176)
PHONE..................................207 646-5561
Mary Hodgkins, *Principal*
EMP: 5
SALES (est): 428.2K **Privately Held**
SIC: 2869 Mfg Industrial Organic Chemicals

(G-7162)
ELEMENTAL ENERGIES
27 N Berwick Rd (04090-6807)
PHONE..................................207 641-5070
EMP: 3 **EST:** 2015
SALES (est): 197.7K **Privately Held**
SIC: 2819 Industrial Inorganic Chemicals, Nec

(G-7163)
JUSTLEATHERCOM
1284 N Berwick Rd (04090)
P.O. Box 1163 (04090-1163)
PHONE..................................207 641-8313
Dan Littlefield, *Partner*
Gary Hilton, *Partner*
Dwight Hubbard, *Partner*
EMP: 3 **EST:** 1998
SALES (est): 242K **Privately Held**
WEB: www.leather-hides.com
SIC: 3199 Mfg Leather Goods

(G-7164)
ROBINSON-GREAVES MARINE PNTG
26 Whippoorwill Trl (04090-6735)
PHONE..................................207 313-6132
James Robinson, *President*
Gregory Greaves, *Vice Pres*
EMP: 4
SALES (est): 296.3K **Privately Held**
SIC: 3731 Shipbuilding/Repairing

(G-7165)
SHORELINE PUBLICATIONS
Also Called: Weekly Sentinel, The
952 Post Rd Unit 10 (04090-4142)
PHONE..................................207 646-8448
Carol Brennan, *President*
Kevin Cox, *Accounts Mgr*
EMP: 12
SQ FT: 1,000
SALES (est): 763.9K **Privately Held**
WEB: www.theweeklysentinel.com
SIC: 2759 2711 Commercial Printing Newspapers-Publishing/Printing

(G-7166)
TALL OAK PRINTING LLC
1237 Tatnic Rd (04090-7519)
PHONE..................................207 251-4138
Garry P Markoff, *Mng Member*
EMP: 6
SALES (est): 711.7K **Privately Held**
SIC: 2752 Lithographic Commercial Printing

(G-7167)
VELUX AMERICA LLC
Also Called: Wasco Products
85 Spencer Dr Unit A (04090-9317)
PHONE..................................207 216-4500
Jeff Frank, *Manager*
EMP: 95
SQ FT: 56,000
SALES (corp-wide): 1.2MM **Privately Held**
SIC: 3441 Structural Metal Fabrication
HQ: Velux America Llc
450 Old Brickyard Rd
Greenwood SC 29649
864 941-4700

(G-7168)
VILLAGE CANDLE INC
Also Called: Camden Designs
90 Spencer Dr (04090-5548)
PHONE..................................207 251-4800
◆ **EMP:** 110
SQ FT: 88,000
SALES (est): 22MM **Privately Held**
WEB: www.villagecandle.com
SIC: 3999 Mfg Misc Products

West Bath
Sagadahoc County

(G-7169)
FOURNIER STEEL FABRICATION
341 State Rd (04530-6239)
PHONE..................................207 443-6404
Paul Fournier, *President*
EMP: 5
SQ FT: 4,500
SALES (est): 683.5K **Privately Held**
SIC: 3441 Welding Repair

West Enfield
Penobscot County

(G-7170)
EDWARD BERNARD INC
Main St (04493)
P.O. Box 114 (04493-0114)
PHONE..................................207 732-3987
EMP: 15 **EST:** 1957
SALES (est): 780K **Privately Held**
SIC: 2411 Logging

(G-7171)
NORTHWOODS PUBLICATIONS LLC
Also Called: Northwoods Sporting Journal
57 Old County Rd N (04493)
P.O. Box 195 (04493-0195)
PHONE..................................207 732-4880
Jim Thorne, *Sales Staff*
Victor Morin, *Mng Member*
EMP: 16 **EST:** 1993
SALES: 500K **Privately Held**
WEB: www.sportingjournal.com
SIC: 2711 Newspapers-Publishing/Printing

West Gardiner
Kennebec County

(G-7172)
HICKEY LOGGING
16 West Rd (04345-3641)
PHONE..................................207 724-3648
Gary Hickey, *Partner*
Wayne Hickey, *Partner*
William Hickey, *Partner*
EMP: 3
SALES (est): 253.3K **Privately Held**
SIC: 2411 Logging

(G-7173)
WEST GARDINER BEEF INC
10 Gilley Dr (04345-3525)
PHONE..................................207 724-3378
Todd Pierce, *President*
Sharon Gilley, *Corp Secy*
EMP: 3
SALES (est): 252.2K **Privately Held**
SIC: 2011 Meat Packing Plant

West Kennebunk
York County

(G-7174)
WILLIAM ARTHUR INC
Also Called: Ten Bamboo Studio
7 Alewive Park Rd (04094)
PHONE..................................413 684-2600
Stephen P Defalco, *CEO*
Hank Beresin, *Vice Pres*
Lisa Blinn, *Vice Pres*
Dorothy Leavitt, *Vice Pres*
Beth Madore, *CFO*
▲ **EMP:** 150 **EST:** 1949
SQ FT: 30,000
SALES (est): 15.1MM
SALES (corp-wide): 11B **Privately Held**
WEB: www.williamarthur.com
SIC: 2771 2678 Mfg Greeting Cards Mfg Stationery Products
PA: Hallmark Cards, Incorporated
2501 Mcgee St
Kansas City MO 64108
816 274-5111

West Minot
Androscoggin County

(G-7175)
WEST MINOT MILLWORK INC
296 W Minot Rd (04288)
P.O. Box 98 (04288-0098)
PHONE..................................207 966-3200
David Clark, *President*
Richard Clark, *Treasurer*
EMP: 6
SALES (est): 1.2MM **Privately Held**
SIC: 2434 2431 Millwork Shop Mfg Bathroom And Kitchen Cabinets

West Paris
Oxford County

(G-7176)
MAINE BALSAM FIR PRODCTS
Also Called: Maine Balsam Fir Products
16 Morse Hill Rd (04289-5317)
P.O. Box 9 (04289-0009)
PHONE..................................207 674-5090
Wendy Newmeyer, *President*
Jack Newmeyer, *Treasurer*
EMP: 10
SQ FT: 5,000
SALES: 300K **Privately Held**
WEB: www.mainebalsam.com
SIC: 2299 2392 Mfg Textile Goods Mfg Household Furnishings

(G-7177)
PRICE COMPANIES INC
Also Called: Midwest Price Companies
23 Bethel Rd (04289-5226)
PHONE..................................207 674-3663
Bruce Perkins, *Manager*
Ashley Hawkins, *Admin Mgr*
EMP: 50
SALES (corp-wide): 101.5MM **Privately Held**
SIC: 2421 Mfg Chips
PA: The Price Companies Inc
218 Midway Rte
Monticello AR 71655
870 367-9751

West Rockport
Knox County

(G-7178)
BRASS FOUNDRY
531 Park St (04865)
P.O. Box 7 (04865-0007)
PHONE..................................207 236-3200
Richard Remsen, *Owner*
EMP: 4

GEOGRAPHIC

SALES (est): 331.1K **Privately Held**
WEB: www.remsen.com
SIC: 3559 3231 3441 Mfg Misc Industry Machinery Mfg Products-Purchased Glass Structural Metal Fabrication

West Southport
Lincoln County

(G-7179)
MALONEY MARINE RIGGING INC
Ebeneck Rd Bth Bay Rgnbt (04576)
P.O. Box 364, Southport (04576-0364)
PHONE..................................207 633-6788
James W Maloney Jr, *President*
EMP: 3
SQ FT: 1,000
SALES: 300K **Privately Held**
SIC: 3731 5088 Shipbuilding/Repairing Whol Transportation Equipment

Westbrook
Cumberland County

(G-7180)
ARTEL INC
25 Bradley Dr (04092-2013)
PHONE..................................207 854-0860
Richard Curtis, *Ch of Bd*
Jim Kenny, *Prdtn Mgr*
Denise Nest, *Production*
Doreen Rumery, *QC Mgr*
Wendy Vaccaro, *Technical Mgr*
EMP: 38
SALES (est): 9.1MM **Privately Held**
WEB: www.artel-usa.com
SIC: 3845 3679 3826 Mfg Electromedical Equipment Mfg Electronic Components Mfg Analytical Instruments

(G-7181)
BAILEY SIGN INC
9 Thomas Dr (04092-3826)
PHONE..................................207 774-2843
Bruce W Bailey, *President*
Ralph Hutchenson, *Vice Pres*
Deanna Emery, *Sales Staff*
EMP: 25
SALES (est): 3.1MM **Privately Held**
WEB: www.baileysign.com
SIC: 2399 1799 3993 Mfg Fabrctd Textile Pdts Special Trade Contractor Mfg Signs/Ad Specialties

(G-7182)
BRACKETT MACHINE INC
355 Saco St (04092-2003)
P.O. Box 7 (04098-0007)
PHONE..................................207 854-9789
Herbert Howard, *President*
Betty Howard, *Treasurer*
EMP: 20 **EST:** 1982
SALES (est): 3.9MM **Privately Held**
SIC: 3599 Mfg Industrial Machinery

(G-7183)
BRIDGE EDUCATION
90 E Bridge St (04092-3109)
PHONE..................................207 321-1111
Andrew King, *President*
EMP: 3
SALES (est): 294.7K **Privately Held**
SIC: 7372 Prepackaged Software Services

(G-7184)
CML SERVICES INC
Also Called: SERVPRO of Portland
35 Bradley Dr Stop 1 (04092-2026)
PHONE..................................207 772-5032
Randall Fess, *President*
EMP: 3
SALES (est): 220K **Privately Held**
SIC: 2842 Mfg Polish/Sanitation Goods

(G-7185)
CROWN EQUIPMENT CORPORATION
Also Called: Crown Lift Trucks
82 Scott Dr (04092-1927)
PHONE..................................207 773-5890
Toll Free:..888 -
Steve Green, *Branch Mgr*
EMP: 22
SALES (corp-wide): 4.2B **Privately Held**
SIC: 3537 Mfg Industrial Trucks/Tractors Whol Industrial Equipment
PA: Crown Equipment Corporation
44 S Washington St
New Bremen OH 45869
419 629-2311

(G-7186)
D & G MACHINE PRODUCTS INC
50 Eisenhower Dr (04092-2009)
PHONE..................................207 854-1500
Duane Gushee, *President*
Charles Tarling III, *President*
Steven Sullivan, *Vice Pres*
Matt Burr, *Prdtn Mgr*
Hope Parker, *Purch Agent*
◆ **EMP:** 100
SQ FT: 90,000
SALES (est): 20.9MM **Privately Held**
WEB: www.dgmachine.com
SIC: 3599 Mfg Industrial Machinery

(G-7187)
DENNY MIKES CUE STUFF INC (PA)
55 Bradley Dr Ste A (04092-2080)
P.O. Box 256, York (03909-0256)
PHONE..................................207 591-5084
Dennis Sherman, *CEO*
▲ **EMP:** 6
SALES (est): 818.5K **Privately Held**
SIC: 2033 Mfg Canned Fruits/Vegetables

(G-7188)
EOS DESIGN LLC (PA)
Also Called: Air Head Composting Toilet
775 Main St S481 (04092-3438)
PHONE..................................740 392-3642
Geoffrey G Trott,
EMP: 7
SQ FT: 5,000
SALES (est): 626.5K **Privately Held**
SIC: 3432 Mfg Plumbing Fixture Fittings

(G-7189)
FULL COURT PRESS
855 Main St Ste 2 (04092-3069)
PHONE..................................207 464-0002
Gerald Sands, *President*
Edward Symbol, *Vice Pres*
EMP: 12 **EST:** 1998
SQ FT: 9,000
SALES (est): 1.5MM **Privately Held**
SIC: 2759 Lithographic Commercial Printing

(G-7190)
IDEXX DISTRIBUTION INC
1 Idexx Dr (04092-2040)
PHONE..................................207 556-0637
Jonathan Ayers, *President*
EMP: 80
SALES: 1MM
SALES (corp-wide): 2.2B **Publicly Held**
WEB: www.idexx.com
SIC: 3841 3826 3829 2835 Mfg Surgical/Med Instr Mfg Analytical Instr Mfg Measure/Control Dvcs Mfg Diagnostic Substance
PA: Idexx Laboratories, Inc.
1 Idexx Dr
Westbrook ME 04092
207 556-0300

(G-7191)
IDEXX LABORATORIES INC (PA)
1 Idexx Dr (04092-2041)
PHONE..................................207 556-0300
Jonathan W Ayers, *Ch of Bd*
Tonya Bowie, *Opers Staff*
Pete Marietta, *Research*
Thomas Bannen, *Auditor*
Ellen Arrigoni, *Finance*
▲ **EMP:** 710
SQ FT: 647,000
SALES: 2.2B **Publicly Held**
WEB: www.idexx.com
SIC: 3826 2834 5047 Mfg Analytical Instruments & Pharmaceutical Preparations

(G-7192)
KELLEY BROS NEW ENGLAND LLC
4 Delta Dr Ste 3 (04092-4743)
PHONE..................................207 517-4100
Ken McNamara, *Manager*
EMP: 4
SALES (corp-wide): 43.1MM **Privately Held**
SIC: 2431 Mfg Millwork
HQ: Kelley Bros. Of New England, Llc
17 Hampshire Dr Ste 20
Hudson NH 03051
603 881-5559

(G-7193)
LANCO ASSEMBLY SYSTEMS INC (PA)
Also Called: Lanco Integrated
12 Thomas Dr (04092-3824)
PHONE..................................207 773-2060
Edward Karabec, *President*
Tim Neale, *Vice Pres*
Philip Arena, *Project Mgr*
Eliot Pitney, *Project Mgr*
Isaac Allen, *Engineer*
▲ **EMP:** 75
SQ FT: 50,000
SALES: 72MM **Privately Held**
WEB: www.lanco.net
SIC: 3559 Mfg Misc Industry Machinery

(G-7194)
LAURA MARR PRODUCTIONS LLC
155 Warren Ave Ste C (04092-4435)
PHONE..................................207 856-9700
George Libby, *Vice Pres*
Beth Payson,
EMP: 6
SALES (est): 664.7K **Privately Held**
SIC: 2752 7812 Lithographic Commercial Printing Motion Picture/Video Production

(G-7195)
MATHESON TRI-GAS INC
75 Scott Dr (04092-1918)
PHONE..................................207 775-0515
EMP: 18
SALES (corp-wide): 34.9B **Privately Held**
SIC: 2813 Mfg Industrial Gases
HQ: Matheson Tri-Gas, Inc.
150 Allen Rd Ste 302
Basking Ridge NJ 07920
908 991-9200

(G-7196)
MESSER TRUCK EQUIPMENT (PA)
Also Called: Messer Petroleum Equipment
170 Warren Ave (04092-4439)
PHONE..................................207 854-9751
Jeffrey Messer, *President*
EMP: 22 **EST:** 1899
SQ FT: 34,000
SALES (est): 6.9MM **Privately Held**
SIC: 3711 3713 Mfg Motor Vehicle Bodies Mfg Truck/Bus Bodies

(G-7197)
MONTECITO ROADHOUSE INC
1102 Bridgton Rd (04092-2504)
PHONE..................................207 856-6811
Scott Rehart, *President*
EMP: 5 **EST:** 2007
SQ FT: 6,000
SALES: 500K **Privately Held**
SIC: 2099 Mfg Food Preparations

(G-7198)
MOORE-CLARK USA INC
Also Called: Bio-Oregon
15 Saunders Way Ste 500e (04092-4835)
PHONE..................................207 591-7077
Ron Gowan, *CEO*
EMP: 14 **Privately Held**
SIC: 3999 Mfg Misc Products
HQ: Moore-Clark U.S.A., Inc.
1140 Industrial Way
Longview WA 98632
360 425-6715

(G-7199)
NORTH ATL CSTM FABRICATION INC
3 Eisenhower Dr (04092-2002)
P.O. Box 520, Gorham (04038-0520)
PHONE..................................207 839-8410
Kevin Strout, *General Mgr*
EMP: 5 **EST:** 2014
SALES (est): 349.3K **Privately Held**
SIC: 3441 Structural Metal Fabrication

(G-7200)
NORTHEAST TIME TRAK SYSTEMS
79 Bradley Dr Ste A (04092-2081)
PHONE..................................207 774-2336
Richard B Smith, *Principal*
EMP: 3
SALES (est): 313.1K **Privately Held**
SIC: 3559 Mfg Misc Industry Machinery

(G-7201)
PIERCE POINT LASER
170 Forest St (04092-4201)
P.O. Box 859, Oxford (04270-0859)
PHONE..................................207 854-0133
EMP: 3
SALES (est): 322.6K **Privately Held**
SIC: 2499 Mfg Wood Products

(G-7202)
PIKA ENERGY INC
35 Bradley Dr Stop 1 (04092-2039)
PHONE..................................207 887-9105
Benjamin Polito, *President*
Bill Hetzel, *COO*
Joshua Kaufman, *CTO*
EMP: 10
SALES (est): 2MM **Publicly Held**
SIC: 3511 Manufacture Turbines/Generator Sets
PA: Generac Holdings Inc.
S45w29290 Hwy 59
Waukesha WI 53189

(G-7203)
PLANET VENTURES INC (PA)
85 Bradley Dr (04092-2013)
PHONE..................................207 761-1515
Colleen McCrasken, *CEO*
Alex Fisher, *COO*
Sean Callahan, *Director*
▲ **EMP:** 23
SQ FT: 3,000
SALES (est): 972.2K **Privately Held**
WEB: www.planetdog.com
SIC: 3999 Mfg Misc Products

(G-7204)
PRESUMPSCOT WATER POWER CO
89 Cumberland St (04092-3592)
PHONE..................................207 856-4000
Sarah Manchester, *Principal*
EMP: 4
SALES (est): 6MM
SALES (corp-wide): 785.7K **Privately Held**
SIC: 2621 Paper Mill
HQ: Sappi North America, Inc.
255 State St Fl 4
Boston MA 02109
617 423-7300

(G-7205)
SAPPI NORTH AMERICA INC
89 Cumberland St (04092-3592)
P.O. Box 5000 (04098-5000)
PHONE..................................207 856-4000
Mike Standel, *Managing Dir*
Michael Haws, *Vice Pres*
Allan Labonty, *Engineer*
Mark Philbrick, *Engineer*
Qi Wang, *Technology*
EMP: 350
SALES (corp-wide): 785.7K **Privately Held**
SIC: 2621 Paper Mill
HQ: Sappi North America, Inc.
255 State St Fl 4
Boston MA 02109
617 423-7300

(G-7206)
SCHLOTTERBECK & FOSS LLC (PA)
3 Ledgeview Dr (04092-3939)
PHONE.................................207 772-4666
Paul C Dioli, *President*
Nicole Thurston, *Vice Pres*
Michael Wallace, *CFO*
Daniel Guimond, *Accounting Mgr*
Tracy Benz, *VP Sales*
EMP: 34
SQ FT: 30,000
SALES (est): 8.9MM **Privately Held**
WEB: www.schlotterbeck-foss.com
SIC: 2035 2099 2087 Manufactures Pickles/Sauces And Food Preparations

(G-7207)
SIGCO LLC
600 County Rd (04092-1932)
PHONE.................................207 775-2676
EMP: 40
SALES (corp-wide): 29.7B **Privately Held**
SIC: 3231 3446 Mfg Products-Purchased Glass Mfg Architectural Metalwork
HQ: Sigco, Llc
48 Spiller Dr
Westbrook ME 04092
207 775-2676

(G-7208)
SIGCO LLC (DH)
48 Spiller Dr (04092-2099)
PHONE.................................207 775-2676
Dave McElhenny, *CEO*
Edward J Kelleher, *Clerk*
▲ **EMP:** 200
SQ FT: 55,000
SALES: 55MM
SALES (corp-wide): 29.7B **Privately Held**
WEB: www.sigcoinc.com
SIC: 3446 3231 Manufacturer Of Architectural Metalwork Mfg Products-Purchased Glass
HQ: Oldcastle Buildingenvelope, Inc.
5005 Lndn B Jnsn Fwy 10
Dallas TX 75244
214 273-3400

(G-7209)
SILVEX INCORPORATED
45 Thomas Dr (04092-3833)
PHONE.................................207 761-0392
Richard Atkinson, *CEO*
Philip Ridley, *President*
Dan Atkinson, *Vice Pres*
Ronald Cormier, *CFO*
Beverly Atkinson, *Treasurer*
EMP: 78
SQ FT: 40,000
SALES (est): 10MM **Privately Held**
WEB: www.silvexinc.com
SIC: 3471 Plating/Polishing Service

(G-7210)
THOMPSON & ANDERSON INC
53 Seavey St (04092-4393)
PHONE.................................207 854-2905
Andrew Anderson, *President*
EMP: 4 **EST:** 1968
SQ FT: 4,000
SALES (est): 601.9K **Privately Held**
SIC: 3444 Mfg Sheet Metal Work

(G-7211)
TRANE US INC
860 Spring St 1 (04092-3820)
PHONE.................................207 773-0637
Jack Borgschulte, *Branch Mgr*
Caron Caiazzo, *Administration*
EMP: 31 **Privately Held**
SIC: 3585 Mfg Refrigeration/Heating Equipment
HQ: Trane U.S. Inc.
3600 Pammel Creek Rd
La Crosse WI 54601
608 787-2000

(G-7212)
VALENTINE & COMPANY INC
90 Bridge St Ste 206 (04092-2948)
PHONE.................................207 774-4769
EMP: 7
SALES: 1.2MM **Privately Held**
WEB: www.academiccatalog.com
SIC: 2741 Misc Publishing

(G-7213)
VIROSTAT INC
8 Spiller Dr (04092-2077)
P.O. Box 8522, Portland (04104-8522)
PHONE.................................207 856-6620
Douglas McAllister, *President*
EMP: 4
SQ FT: 3,500
SALES (est): 517K **Privately Held**
WEB: www.virostat-inc.com
SIC: 2835 Commercial Physical Research

(G-7214)
WILBERT SWANS VAULT CO
674 Bridgton Rd (04092-3702)
PHONE.................................207 854-5324
Stephen Swan, *President*
Susan Swan, *Vice Pres*
Frank Frye, *Admin Sec*
EMP: 20 **EST:** 1947
SQ FT: 3,000
SALES (est): 2.4MM **Privately Held**
SIC: 3272 5211 Mfg Burial Vaults & Ret Concrete & Cinder Block

(G-7215)
XTREME SCREEN & SPORTSWEAR LLC
937 Main St (04092-2825)
PHONE.................................207 857-9200
EMP: 3
SALES (est): 310.3K **Privately Held**
SIC: 2759 Commercial Printing

Westport Island
Lincoln County

(G-7216)
DANAS BOAT SHOP
214 N End Rd (04578-3024)
PHONE.................................207 882-7205
Dana Faulkham, *President*
EMP: 3
SALES (est): 295.4K **Privately Held**
SIC: 3732 Boatbuilding/Repairing

Whitefield
Lincoln County

(G-7217)
MAINE PURSUIT LLC
Also Called: Maine Pursuits
279 E River Rd (04353-3514)
PHONE.................................207 549-7972
Marylou Smith, *Mng Member*
EMP: 3
SALES (est): 220.9K **Privately Held**
SIC: 2499 3399 Mfg Wood Products Mfg Primary Metal Products

(G-7218)
SPECIALTY PRODUCTS COMPANY
208 Rockland Rd (04353-3157)
PHONE.................................207 549-7232
Michel Cuthbertson, *President*
Paula Cuthbertson, *Manager*
EMP: 19
SQ FT: 10,000
SALES: 500K **Privately Held**
WEB: spcproducts.com
SIC: 3599 Mfg Industrial Machinery

(G-7219)
WENSTROM METALWORKS
268 N Howe Rd (04353-3026)
PHONE.................................207 215-0651
EMP: 3
SALES (est): 90.5K **Privately Held**
SIC: 1099 Metal Ore Mining

(G-7220)
WHITEFIELD DRY KILN INC
45 Mills Rd (04353-3100)
P.O. Box 200 (04353-0200)
PHONE.................................207 549-5470
Timothy Chase, *President*
EMP: 4
SALES (est): 280K **Privately Held**
SIC: 2421 Sawmill/Planing Mill

Whiting
Washington County

(G-7221)
LOOKS GOURMET FOOD CO INC (HQ)
Also Called: Bar Harbor Foods
1112 Cutler Rd (04691-3436)
PHONE.................................207 259-3341
Michael Cote, *President*
Mike Sansing, *General Mgr*
EMP: 20 **EST:** 2005
SQ FT: 10,000
SALES (est): 2.9MM
SALES (corp-wide): 114.7MM **Privately Held**
WEB: www.looksgourmetfood.com
SIC: 2091 5146 Mfg Canned/Cured Fish/Seafood Whol Fish/Seafood
PA: Sea Watch International, Ltd.
8978 Glebe Park Dr
Easton MD 21601
410 822-7501

Whitneyville
Washington County

(G-7222)
WHITNEY ORIGINALS INC
600 Us Route 1 (04654)
P.O. Box 157, Machias (04654-0157)
PHONE.................................207 255-3392
David Whitney, *President*
Dale Whitney, *Vice Pres*
Daniel McKay, *Clerk*
▲ **EMP:** 80
SQ FT: 21,000
SALES (est): 8.1MM **Privately Held**
WEB: www.whitneywreath.com
SIC: 3999 Mfg Christmas Wreaths & Handmade Products

Williamsburg Twp
Piscataquis County

(G-7223)
PAUL N FOULKES INC
801 Barnard Rd (04414-4102)
PHONE.................................207 965-9481
Paul N Foulkes, *President*
EMP: 3
SALES: 576K **Privately Held**
SIC: 2411 Logging

Wilton
Franklin County

(G-7224)
ATLANTIC HARDCHROME LTD
128 Weld Rd Ste 4 (04294-4401)
PHONE.................................207 645-4300
Rondo Pirri, *Manager*
EMP: 34
SALES (est): 2.1MM **Privately Held**
SIC: 2816 Mfg Inorganic Pigments

(G-7225)
CARRIER WLDG & FABRICATION LLC
469 Depot St (04294-6608)
P.O. Box 11, Rome GA (30162-0011)
PHONE.................................207 645-3100
Andrew Goodwin, *Mng Member*
Nathan Carrier, *Mng Member*
EMP: 4
SALES (est): 76K **Privately Held**
SIC: 2899 Mfg Chemical Preparations

(G-7226)
MINUTEMAN METAL LLC
469 Depot St (04294-6608)
P.O. Box 207, Oxford (04270-0207)
PHONE.................................207 217-8908
Evan Coleman, *Principal*
Dan Fletcher, *Principal*
EMP: 8
SALES (est): 619.6K **Privately Held**
SIC: 3499 Mfg Misc Fabricated Metal Products

(G-7227)
NICHOLS CUSTOM WELDING INC
Also Called: Nichols Development
128 Weld Rd Ste 2 (04294-4401)
PHONE.................................207 645-3101
Gill Reed, *President*
Robert Nichols, *Vice Pres*
Richard Johnson, *Treasurer*
Mark Berry, *Admin Sec*
EMP: 45
SALES: 1.1MM **Privately Held**
SIC: 7692 Welding Repair

Windham
Cumberland County

(G-7228)
ALARIS USA LLC
33r Main St Ste 1 (04062-4474)
PHONE.................................207 517-5304
Peter Farnum, *Mng Member*
EMP: 17
SALES (est): 652.2K **Privately Held**
SIC: 3663 Mfg Radio/Tv Communication Equipment

(G-7229)
ARMANNI USA INC
39 Enterprise Dr (04062-5697)
PHONE.................................207 893-0557
Chris Van Haasteren, *Principal*
▲ **EMP:** 3
SALES (est): 295.4K **Privately Held**
SIC: 3534 Mfg Elevators/Escalators

(G-7230)
BIOTECH SOURCE INC (PA)
12 Studio Dr (04062-4559)
PHONE.................................207 894-5690
William McDonald, *President*
Ryan McDonald, *Opers Staff*
EMP: 3
SALES (est): 363.6K **Privately Held**
SIC: 2834 Mfg Pharmaceutical Preparations

(G-7231)
CN BROWN COMPANY
Also Called: Red Shield Heating Oil
357 Roosevelt Trl (04062-5356)
PHONE.................................207 892-5955
Jen McKay, *Office Mgr*
EMP: 4
SALES (corp-wide): 181.1MM **Privately Held**
WEB: www.cnbrown.com
SIC: 2911 Petroleum Refiner
PA: C.N. Brown Company
1 C N Brown Way
South Paris ME 04281
207 743-9212

(G-7232)
ERIN MURPHY
824 Roosevelt Trl (04062-5370)
PHONE.................................928 525-2056
Erin Murphy, *Principal*
EMP: 3
SALES (est): 211.7K **Privately Held**
SIC: 2759 Commercial Printing

(G-7233)
FINETONE HEARING INSTRUMENTS
2 Plaza Dr (04062-5927)
PHONE.................................207 893-2922
Ed Gauthier, *Owner*
EMP: 3
SALES (est): 170K **Privately Held**
SIC: 3842 Ret Misc Merchandise

(G-7234)
FLUE GAS SOLUTIONS INC
19 Commons Ave (04062-5836)
PHONE.................................207 893-1510
Bruce Harlow, *President*

EMP: 8
SQ FT: 160,000
SALES: 2MM Privately Held
SIC: 3494 Mfg Valves/Pipe Fittings

(G-7235)
GENEST LANDSCAPE MASONRY
45 Enterprise Dr (04062-5697)
PHONE....207 892-3778
Dale Plante, *Manager*
Raymond Petrarca,
EMP: 6
SALES (est): 465K Privately Held
SIC: 3524 5082 Mfg Lawn/Garden Equipment Whol Construction/Mining Equipment

(G-7236)
HERITAGE LANTERNS
85 Sandbar Rd (04062-5522)
PHONE....207 893-1134
EMP: 12
SQ FT: 5,000
SALES (est): 1.6MM Privately Held
WEB: www.heritagelanterns.com
SIC: 3648 Mfg Hand-Crafted Lighting Fixtures Specializing In Lanterns

(G-7237)
IBCONTROLS
Also Called: Intelligent Building Controls
3 Pope Rd (04062-2309)
PHONE....207 893-0080
James Evers, *President*
EMP: 35
SQ FT: 8,000
SALES (est): 3.5MM Privately Held
WEB: www.ibcontrols.com
SIC: 3829 7373 Mfg Measuring/Controlling Devices Computer Systems Design

(G-7238)
K & D MILLWORKS INC
Also Called: K & D Distributing
7 Danielle Dr (04062-6933)
PHONE....207 892-5188
Dennis Dyer, *President*
Kelly C Dyer, *Vice Pres*
EMP: 22
SALES (est): 3.7MM Privately Held
SIC: 2541 5031 Mfg Wood Partitions/Fixtures Whol Lumber/Plywood/Millwork

(G-7239)
KENT NUTRITION GROUP INC
43 Main St (04062-4220)
PHONE....207 892-9411
Dana Woodsome, *Owner*
Scott Nashawatey, *Manager*
EMP: 6
SALES (corp-wide): 449.1MM Privately Held
WEB: www.blueseal.com
SIC: 2048 Mfg Prepared Feeds
HQ: Kent Nutrition Group, Inc.
1600 Oregon St
Muscatine IA 52761
866 647-1212

(G-7240)
LIGHTHOUSE IMAGING LLC
765 Roosevelt Trl (04062-5341)
PHONE....207 893-8233
Eric Z Gray, *Opers Staff*
Les Gardner, *QC Mgr*
Tom McDonald, *Engineer*
Benjamin Roy, *Engineer*
Dennis C Leiner, *CTO*
EMP: 5 EST: 1996
SQ FT: 3,000
SALES (est): 1.5MM Privately Held
WEB: www.lighthouseoptics.com
SIC: 3827 Mfg Optical Instruments/Lenses

(G-7241)
MAINE CONVEYOR INC
5 Maynard Rogers Rd (04062-5283)
PHONE....207 854-5661
Robert Oliver, *Branch Mgr*
EMP: 6
SALES (corp-wide): 1.9MM Privately Held
SIC: 7692 Welding Repair
PA: Maine Conveyor, Inc
259 New Portland Rd
Gorham ME 04038
207 854-5661

(G-7242)
MORRISON MILLWORK AND STR FIXS
270 Roosevelt Trl (04062-4353)
PHONE....207 892-9418
Roland Morrison, *President*
Jacquelin Morrison, *Treasurer*
EMP: 6
SALES (est): 604.4K Privately Held
SIC: 2431 Mfg Millwork

(G-7243)
MWAVE INDUSTRIES LLC
33r Main St Ste 1 (04062-4474)
PHONE....207 892-0011
Mike Cahill, *President*
Peter V Anania,
▲ EMP: 4
SALES: 711.6K Privately Held
WEB: www.mwavellc.com
SIC: 3663 Mfg Radio/Tv Communication Equipment

(G-7244)
NEWBERRY ENTERPRISE
Also Called: Rj Newbury
18 Swett Rd (04062-4239)
PHONE....207 892-8596
Robert J Newberry, *Partner*
Robert Newberry, *Partner*
Teresa Newberry, *Partner*
EMP: 4
SALES (est): 388.9K Privately Held
SIC: 3451 Mfg Screw Machine Products

(G-7245)
QUARTER POINT WOODWORKING LLC
7b Commons Ave (04062-5293)
PHONE....207 892-7022
EMP: 3
SALES (corp-wide): 456.5K Privately Held
SIC: 2431 Mfg Millwork
PA: Quarter Point Woodworking Llc
483 Intervale Rd
New Gloucester ME 04260
207 926-1032

(G-7246)
RBW INC
Also Called: Design Fab
113 Nash Rd (04062-4500)
PHONE....207 786-2446
Dennis E Worster, *President*
EMP: 15
SALES (est): 1.1MM Privately Held
WEB: www.designfabinc.com
SIC: 3441 Structural Metal Fabrication

(G-7247)
REVISION HEAT LLC
266 Gray Rd (04062-4250)
PHONE....207 221-5677
Lee Landry, *Principal*
▲ EMP: 13
SALES (est): 2MM Privately Held
SIC: 1311 Crude Petroleum/Natural Gas Production

(G-7248)
ROBERT BABB & SONS
28 Lotts Dr (04062-4887)
PHONE....207 892-9692
Robert Babb, *Owner*
EMP: 3 EST: 1962
SALES (est): 180.6K Privately Held
SIC: 2411 Logging

(G-7249)
ROBERT TIMMONS JR
Also Called: Timmons Machine & Fabricating
22 Commons Ave 8 (04062-5294)
PHONE....207 892-3366
Robert Timmons, *President*
Peggy Timmons, *Admin Sec*
EMP: 3
SALES: 210K Privately Held
WEB: www.teamsterslocal340.org
SIC: 3599 Machine Fabrication And Job Shop Work

(G-7250)
SEA LAND ENERGY MAINE INC
6 Brookhaven Dr (04062-5247)
PHONE....207 892-3284
Ryan G Debrosse, *Principal*
EMP: 3 EST: 1934
SALES (est): 361.7K Privately Held
SIC: 1321 Natural Gas Liquids Production

(G-7251)
SEBAGO CONVERTED PRODUCTS INC
15 Enterprise Dr (04062-5697)
PHONE....207 892-0576
Chris Van Haasteren, *President*
EMP: 4 EST: 1999
SQ FT: 1,200
SALES: 300K Privately Held
SIC: 3599 Mfg Industrial Machinery

(G-7252)
SIGN GUY INC
103 Tandberg Trl (04062-5202)
PHONE....207 892-5851
Jim Foley, *Principal*
EMP: 3 EST: 2007
SQ FT: 1,000
SALES (est): 153K Privately Held
SIC: 3993 Mfg Signs/Advertising Specialties

(G-7253)
SOUTHERN MAINE INDUSTRIES CORP
68 Outlet Cove Rd (04062-5536)
PHONE....207 856-7391
Cheryl A V Bolduc, *President*
EMP: 30
SQ FT: 22,000
SALES (est): 3.6MM Privately Held
SIC: 3471 Electroplating Of Metals Or Formed Products & Anodizing (Plating) Of Metals Or Formed Products

(G-7254)
SPECIAL DIVERSIFIED OPP INC
Also Called: Strategic Bio Solutions
52 Anderson Rd (04062-4010)
PHONE....207 856-6151
Colleen Crandel, *Principal*
Dr Thomas Judd, *Sales Staff*
Jeff Thompson, *Pediatrics*
EMP: 40
SALES (corp-wide): 365.7MM Publicly Held
WEB: www.sdix.com
SIC: 2836 3841 Mfg Biological Products Mfg Surgical/Medical Instruments
PA: Standard Diversified Inc.
155 Mineola Blvd
Mineola NY 11501
302 248-1100

(G-7255)
SUNRISE PRINTING & GRAPHICS
89 Tandberg Trl (04062-5201)
PHONE....207 892-3534
Richard Rivard, *President*
EMP: 6
SALES (est): 420K Privately Held
SIC: 2752 2759 Lithographic Commercial Printing Commercial Printing

(G-7256)
TENA GROUP LLC
2 Plaza Dr (04062-5927)
PHONE....207 893-2920
Edouard A Gauthier, *Principal*
EMP: 3
SALES (est): 266.7K Privately Held
SIC: 3842 Mfg Surgical Appliances/Supplies

(G-7257)
TIME4PRINTING INC
588 Roosevelt Trl (04062-4904)
PHONE....207 838-1496
Kelly Mank, *Owner*
EMP: 3
SALES (est): 211.1K Privately Held
SIC: 2752 Lithographic Commercial Printing

(G-7258)
TUBE HOLLOWS INTERNATIONAL
Also Called: Confluent Maine
39 Enterprise Dr Ste 2 (04062-5697)
PHONE....844 721-8823
Dean Schauer, *President*
EMP: 45
SQ FT: 50,000
SALES (est): 8.4MM Privately Held
SIC: 3599 Mfg Industrial Machinery
PA: Confluent Medical Technologies, Inc.
47533 Westinghouse Dr
Fremont CA 94539

(G-7259)
WARDWELL PIPING INC
Also Called: Ata Piping
194 Roosevelt Trl (04062-3396)
PHONE....207 892-0034
Nathan Wardwell, *President*
Andrea Wardwell, *Office Mgr*
EMP: 15
SQ FT: 6,000
SALES: 1.5MM Privately Held
SIC: 3498 1711 Mfg Fabricated Pipe & Pipe Fittings & Process Piping Contractor

(G-7260)
WINDHAM MILLWORK INC
Also Called: UNI-SIM
4 Architectural Dr (04062-5483)
P.O. Box 1358 (04062-1358)
PHONE....207 892-3238
Bruce Pulkkinen Sr, *CEO*
Bruce Pulkkinen Jr, *President*
Michael McNally, *CFO*
EMP: 95 EST: 1958
SQ FT: 42,000
SALES: 8.6MM Privately Held
WEB: www.windhammillwork.com
SIC: 2431 Mfg Millwork

(G-7261)
WINDHAM WEAPONRY INC
999 Roosevelt Trl Ste 22 (04062-5651)
P.O. Box 1900 (04062-1900)
PHONE....207 893-2223
Richard Dyke, *CEO*
Yung Edwards, *Vice Pres*
Allen Faraday, *Vice Pres*
Eric Jacobs, *Senior Buyer*
Kimberly Burnham, *CFO*
EMP: 65
SQ FT: 16,000
SALES: 40MM Privately Held
SIC: 3484 Mfg Small Arms

Windsor
Kennebec County

(G-7262)
AIR CONTROL INDUSTRIES INC
76 Augusta Rockland Rd (04363-3625)
PHONE....207 445-2518
Mark A Scribner, *President*
▲ EMP: 3
SALES (est): 516.3K Privately Held
SIC: 3564 Mfg Blowers/Fans

(G-7263)
COUSINS SAWMILL
Rr 105 (04363)
P.O. Box 98 (04363-0098)
PHONE....207 445-2467
EMP: 4 EST: 1976
SALES (est): 558.4K Privately Held
SIC: 2421 Sawmill/Lumber Mill

Winn
Penobscot County

(G-7264)
HERBERT C HAYNES INC (PA)
Also Called: H C Haynes
40 Route 168 (04495)
P.O. Box 96 (04495-0096)
PHONE..................................207 736-3412
Herbert C Haynes, *President*
Virginia Haynes, *Treasurer*
Ginger Haynes Maxwell, *Admin Sec*
EMP: 35 **EST:** 1930
SQ FT: 1,200
SALES (est): 4.6MM **Privately Held**
SIC: 2411 Mfg Pulpwood & Wood Chips & Logging Contractor

Winslow
Kennebec County

(G-7265)
ALBION MANUFACTURING
133 Halifax St (04901-7655)
P.O. Box 39, Albion (04910-0039)
PHONE..................................207 873-5633
Mike Cothran, *President*
EMP: 7
SALES (est): 964.3K **Privately Held**
WEB: www.albion-manufacturing.com
SIC: 3599 Mfg Industrial Machinery

(G-7266)
ALCOM LLC (PA)
Also Called: Machine Trailers
6 Millennium Dr (04901-0777)
PHONE..................................207 861-9800
Tratper Clark, *President*
Galen Brackett, *Purch Agent*
Josh Roberts, *CFO*
Courtney Rustemeyer, *Controller*
Heather Hutchinson, *Human Res Mgr*
▼ **EMP:** 20
SALES (est): 19.9MM **Privately Held**
SIC: 3715 Mfg Truck Trailers

(G-7267)
BABAC INC
166 China Rd (04901-0615)
PHONE..................................207 872-0889
John Wallingford, *President*
Donald B Kingsbury, *Vice Pres*
▲ **EMP:** 10
SQ FT: 3,000
SALES (est): 1.6MM **Privately Held**
WEB: www.babactirechains.com
SIC: 3842 Mfg Traction Devices

(G-7268)
BISHOP CROWN CO
404 Nowell Rd (04901-0046)
PHONE..................................207 873-2350
Tina McCaslin, *Owner*
Jeff McCaslin, *Co-Owner*
EMP: 4 **EST:** 1990
SALES: 50K **Privately Held**
SIC: 3993 Mfg Signs/Advertising Specialties

(G-7269)
HYDRAULIC SOLUTIONS OF NE
709 China Rd (04901-0316)
PHONE..................................207 859-9955
Craig Robbins, *Owner*
EMP: 3
SALES (est): 263.2K **Privately Held**
SIC: 3593 Mfg Fluid Power Cylinders

(G-7270)
LOHMANN ANIMAL HEALTH INTL INC
Also Called: Biologics Production
375 China Rd (04901-0632)
PHONE..................................207 873-3989
David Zacek, *CEO*
Frank Sterner, *President*
Crystal Olsen, *Corp Secy*
Dianna Rafue, *Vice Pres*
▲ **EMP:** 112
SQ FT: 30,000
SALES (est): 28.6MM
SALES (corp-wide): 24.5B **Publicly Held**
SIC: 2836 Mfg Biological Products
HQ: Lohmann Animal Health Gmbh
Heinz-Lohmann-Str. 4
Cuxhaven 27472
472 174-70

(G-7271)
MID STATE MACHINE PRODUCTS (PA)
83 Verti Dr (04901-0727)
PHONE..................................207 873-6136
Duane Pekar, *President*
Kevin Nelson, *Vice Pres*
▲ **EMP:** 160 **EST:** 1967
SQ FT: 85,000
SALES (est): 47.9MM **Privately Held**
WEB: www.mid-statemachine.com
SIC: 3599 3545 Mfg Industrial Machinery Mfg Machine Tool Accessories

(G-7272)
NORTHEAST LABORATORY SVCS INC (PA)
227 China Rd (04901-0629)
P.O. Box 788, Waterville (04903-0788)
PHONE..................................207 873-7711
Rodney E Mears, *President*
Melissa Higgins, *Vice Pres*
Jeremy Boutin, *Materials Mgr*
Francis Reed, *Info Tech Mgr*
Rhonda Cain, *Director*
EMP: 67 **EST:** 1972
SQ FT: 26,000
SALES: 8.1MM **Privately Held**
WEB: www.nelabservices.com
SIC: 2836 8734 Mfg Biological Products Testing Laboratory

(G-7273)
ORION ROPEWORKS INC (PA)
953 Benton Ave (04901-2618)
PHONE..................................207 877-2224
Matthew Gagnon, *President*
▲ **EMP:** 26
SALES (est): 9.1MM **Privately Held**
SIC: 2298 Mfg Cordage/Twine

(G-7274)
ORION ROPEWORKS LLC
953 Benton Ave (04901-2618)
PHONE..................................207 877-2224
Patty Taylor, *Human Res Dir*
Mark Walters, *Sales Mgr*
Matthew Gagnon,
▲ **EMP:** 55
SQ FT: 144,000
SALES (est): 6.5MM **Privately Held**
WEB: www.orionropeworks.com
SIC: 3552 Mfg Rope
PA: Orion Ropeworks, Inc.
953 Benton Ave
Winslow ME 04901

Winterport
Waldo County

(G-7275)
A&M SAND & GRAVEL LLC
180 Coles Corner Rd (04496-3625)
P.O. Box 662 (04496-0662)
PHONE..................................207 223-4189
Tami Thibodeau, *Principal*
EMP: 4
SALES (est): 501.1K **Privately Held**
SIC: 1442 Construction Sand/Gravel

(G-7276)
BERNARD GINN AND SONS INC
54 Perkins Rd (04496-4609)
PHONE..................................207 234-2187
Bernard Ginn, *President*
EMP: 4
SALES (est): 568K **Privately Held**
SIC: 2411 Logging

(G-7277)
DEREK WHITE
Also Called: Whico
15 Memorial Dr (04496-3447)
PHONE..................................207 223-5746
Derek A White, *Owner*
EMP: 5
SALES (est): 242.2K **Privately Held**
WEB: www.derekwhite.com
SIC: 7692 General Maintenance Welding & Repair

(G-7278)
WINTERPORT WINERY INC
Also Called: Penobscot Bay Brewery
279 S Main St (04496-3000)
P.O. Box 405 (04496-0405)
PHONE..................................207 223-4500
Michael T Anderson, *President*
Joan Anderson, *Vice Pres*
EMP: 5
SALES (est): 506.6K **Privately Held**
WEB: www.winterportwinery.com
SIC: 2084 Mfg Wines/Brandy/Spirits

Winthrop
Kennebec County

(G-7279)
ALTERNATIVE MANUFACTURING INC
Also Called: A M I
30 Summer St Ste B (04364-1253)
PHONE..................................207 377-9377
Greg Boyd, *CEO*
Kim Vandermeulen, *Ch of Bd*
Steve Martin, *Vice Pres*
Scot Story, *Vice Pres*
Matt Brown, *Engineer*
EMP: 85
SQ FT: 70,000
SALES (est): 19.6MM **Privately Held**
SIC: 3672 Mfg Printed Circuit Boards

(G-7280)
DAVID MICHAUD
Also Called: Michaud Machine Company
61 Birch St (04364-1301)
PHONE..................................207 377-8037
David Michaud, *Owner*
EMP: 3
SALES (est): 165.1K **Privately Held**
WEB: www.davidmichaud.net
SIC: 3423 3082 3451 Mfg Hand/Edge Tools Mfg Plastic Profile Shapes Mfg Screw Machine Products

(G-7281)
NATIONAL FILTER MEDIA CORP
40 Winada Dr (04364-3882)
PHONE..................................207 377-2626
EMP: 10
SALES (corp-wide): 922.9MM **Privately Held**
SIC: 3569 Mfg General Industrial Machinery
HQ: The National Filter Media Corporation
691 N 400 W
Salt Lake City UT 84103
801 363-6736

(G-7282)
NATIONAL FILTER MEDIA CORP
12 Winada Dr (04364-3882)
PHONE..................................207 377-2626
James Corgan, *Branch Mgr*
EMP: 52
SALES (corp-wide): 922.9MM **Privately Held**
SIC: 3569 Mfg General Industrial Machinery
HQ: The National Filter Media Corporation
691 N 400 W
Salt Lake City UT 84103
801 363-6736

(G-7283)
VALMET INC
Also Called: Metso Fabric
30 Summer St Ste G (04364-1253)
P.O. Box 485 (04364-0485)
PHONE..................................207 377-6909
Greg Stewart, *Branch Mgr*
EMP: 18
SALES (corp-wide): 3.6B **Privately Held**
SIC: 3541 Manufacturer Of Replacement Parts
HQ: Valmet, Inc.
2425 Commerce Ave Ste 100
Duluth GA 30096
770 263-7863

Wiscasset
Lincoln County

(G-7284)
COUNTY OF LINCOLN
Lincoln County Recycling
54 Huntoon Hill Rd (04578-4233)
PHONE..................................207 882-5276
Tim Richardson, *Supervisor*
EMP: 5 **Privately Held**
SIC: 2611 Pulp Mill
PA: County Of Lincoln
32 High St 1
Wiscasset ME 04578
207 882-0100

(G-7285)
MACHINERY SERVICE CO INC
166 W Alna Rd (04578-4092)
PHONE..................................207 882-6788
Kenneth R Boudin Jr, *President*
EMP: 9
SQ FT: 11,900
SALES (est): 1.5MM **Privately Held**
SIC: 3553 7699 3599 Mfg Woodworking Machinery Repair Services Mfg Industrial Machinery

(G-7286)
PEREGRINE TURBINE TECH LLC
29 S Point Dr (04578-3260)
PHONE..................................207 687-8333
David Stapp, *CEO*
Robert Brooks, *COO*
Ed Polewarczyk, *Executive*
EMP: 10
SALES (est): 3.1MM **Privately Held**
SIC: 3511 Mfg Turbines/Generator Sets

(G-7287)
RYNEL INC (DH)
11 Twin Rivers Dr (04578-4943)
PHONE..................................207 882-0200
James Detert, *President*
Mark Dignum, *Director*
◆ **EMP:** 70
SQ FT: 19,000
SALES (est): 18.7MM
SALES (corp-wide): 5.4B **Privately Held**
WEB: www.rynel.com
SIC: 3086 2821 Mfg Plastic Foam Products Mfg Plastic Materials/Resins
HQ: Molnlycke Health Care Ab
Gamlestadsvagen 3c
Goteborg 415 1
317 223-000

Woodland
Aroostook County

(G-7288)
MCBREAIRTY RANSFORD
Also Called: Quality Paving
163 Brown Rd (04736-5726)
P.O. Box 236, Caribou (04736-0236)
PHONE..................................207 498-3182
Ransford McBreairty, *Owner*
EMP: 3
SALES (est): 398K **Privately Held**
SIC: 2951 Mfg Asphalt Mixtures/Blocks

Woolwich
Sagadahoc County

(G-7289)
EATON TRAP CO INC
12 Birchwood Rd (04579-4842)
PHONE..................................207 443-3617
Martin R Eaton Jr, *President*
EMP: 5
SALES: 400K **Privately Held**
SIC: 3496 5088 Mfg And Wholesale Lobster Traps And Marine Supplies

GEOGRAPHIC

(G-7290)
MAINE DOCK & DREDGE LLC
107 George Wright Rd (04579-4553)
PHONE..................................207 660-5577
Christine Lockyer,
Robert Lockyer,
Keith McPherson,
EMP: 3
SALES (est): 769.5K **Privately Held**
SIC: 3531 Mfg Construction Machinery

(G-7291)
WOOLWICH ICE CREAM INC
35 Main St (04579-4533)
P.O. Box 354 (04579-0354)
PHONE..................................207 442-8830
Richard Ranta, *President*
EMP: 6
SALES (est): 527.9K **Privately Held**
SIC: 2024 Mfg Ice Cream/Frozen Desert

Yarmouth
Cumberland County

(G-7292)
BANNER SOURCE
387b E Elm St (04096-7510)
PHONE..................................207 846-0915
Leslie Gillert, *Partner*
John Gillert, *Partner*
EMP: 3
SALES (est): 170K **Privately Held**
SIC: 3993 5999 Wholesale And Retail Signs And Advertising Specialties

(G-7293)
CSG INC
Also Called: Yarmouth Printing & Graphics
247 Portland St Ste 5 (04096-8130)
PHONE..................................207 846-9567
Clarence S Gerberick, *President*
Marleene Gerberick, *Treasurer*
EMP: 4
SQ FT: 3,000
SALES (est): 270K **Privately Held**
WEB: www.yarmprint.com
SIC: 2759 Commercial Printing

(G-7294)
GARMIN INTERNATIONAL INC
2 Delorme Dr Ste 2 # 2 (04096-6968)
PHONE..................................800 561-5105
EMP: 135
SALES (corp-wide): 261.7K **Privately Held**
SIC: 2741 2731 7371 Misc Publishing Book-Publishing/Printing Computer Programming Svc
HQ: Garmin International, Inc.
1200 E 151st St
Olathe KS 66062

(G-7295)
HOLY TERRA PRODUCTS INC
Also Called: Anti-Pest-O
253 Royall Point Rd (04096-5762)
PHONE..................................207 846-4170
John Isacke, *President*
Neil Cambridge, *Vice Pres*
Mike St Clair, *Vice Pres*
James White, *Vice Pres*
EMP: 4
SQ FT: 3,800
SALES: 1,000K **Privately Held**
SIC: 2879 Manufacturer Of Biopesticide

(G-7296)
HONEYWELL INTERNATIONAL INC
10 Princess Rd (04096)
PHONE..................................207 846-3350
EMP: 673
SALES (corp-wide): 41.8B **Publicly Held**
SIC: 3724 Mfg Aircraft Engines/Parts
PA: Honeywell International Inc.
300 S Tryon St
Charlotte NC 28202
973 455-2000

(G-7297)
INREACH INC
2 Delorme Dr (04096-7002)
PHONE..................................207 846-7104
Lisa Brauch, *Principal*
EMP: 3
SALES (est): 133.9K **Privately Held**
SIC: 3812 Mfg Search/Navigation Equipment

(G-7298)
MAD GABS INC
25 Yarmouth Crossing Dr (04096-6740)
P.O. Box 426, Westbrook (04098-0426)
PHONE..................................207 854-1679
Gabrielle Melchionda, *President*
EMP: 8
SALES (est): 1.3MM **Privately Held**
WEB: www.madgabs.com
SIC: 2834 Mfg Lip Hand & Body Balm

(G-7299)
QUALITY CONTAINERS OF NENG
247 Portland St Ste 2 (04096-8130)
PHONE..................................207 846-5420
Gregory H Leonard, *President*
Kevin Burns, *Treasurer*
EMP: 8
SQ FT: 7,000
SALES (est): 1.5MM **Privately Held**
WEB: www.qualitycontainersne.com
SIC: 3085 5085 Mfg Plastic Bottles Whol Industrial Supplies

(G-7300)
SMA INC
Also Called: Notes, The
33 Yarmouth Crossing Dr (04096-6740)
P.O. Box 905 (04096-1905)
PHONE..................................207 846-4112
Andrew Labrie, *President*
Andy Labrie, *Treasurer*
EMP: 12
SALES (est): 660K **Privately Held**
WEB: www.thenotes.org
SIC: 2711 2741 Publishes Newspaper

(G-7301)
TYLER TECHNOLOGIES INC
Also Called: Munis
1 Tyler Dr (04096-6828)
PHONE..................................207 781-2260
Joan Glass, *Finance*
Christine Lyden, *Marketing Staff*
Lisa Chaisson, *Manager*
John Hill, *Manager*
Judy Rollins, *Manager*
EMP: 250
SALES (corp-wide): 935.2MM **Publicly Held**
WEB: www.tylertechnologies.com
SIC: 7372 Prepackaged Software Services
PA: Tyler Technologies, Inc.
5101 Tennyson Pkwy
Plano TX 75024
972 713-3700

(G-7302)
TYLER TECHNOLOGIES INC
Munis Division
1 Tyler Dr (04096-6828)
PHONE..................................207 781-4606
EMP: 500
SALES (corp-wide): 935.2MM **Publicly Held**
SIC: 7372 7378 7371 Prepackaged Software Services Custom Computer Programing Computer Maintenance/Repair
PA: Tyler Technologies, Inc.
5101 Tennyson Pkwy
Plano TX 75024
972 713-3700

(G-7303)
UNITED PUBLICATIONS INC
Also Called: Golf Course News
106 Lafayette St (04096-6125)
P.O. Box 995 (04096-1995)
PHONE..................................207 846-0600
Brook Taliaferro, *President*
Elizabeth Beaulieu, *Editor*
Paul Ragusa, *Editor*
Brad Durost, *Regl Sales Mgr*
Heather Kelly, *Marketing Mgr*
EMP: 30
SQ FT: 10,000
SALES (est): 4.8MM **Privately Held**
WEB: www.unitedpublications.com
SIC: 2721 Magazine Publisher Not Printed On Site

(G-7304)
YANKEE MARINA INC
Also Called: Yankee Marina and Billiards
142 Lafayette St (04096-6123)
P.O. Box 548 (04096-0548)
PHONE..................................207 846-9120
Deborah Delp, *President*
Curt Mildrum, *General Mgr*
Suzanne Stevens, *Treasurer*
EMP: 25 **EST:** 1968
SQ FT: 30,000
SALES (est): 4.3MM **Privately Held**
WEB: www.yankeemarina.com
SIC: 3731 4493 Shipbuilding/Repairing Marina Operation Shipbuilding/Repairing

York
York County

(G-7305)
ATLANTIC LASER CLINIC
433 Us Route 1 Ste 209 (03909-1647)
P.O. Box 1 (03909-0001)
PHONE..................................207 854-8200
Bob Adams, *Principal*
EMP: 3
SALES (est): 199.8K **Privately Held**
SIC: 3841 Mfg Surgical/Medical Instruments

(G-7306)
CHRIS DAVIS STONEWARE POTTERY
Also Called: Pottery Shop, The
81 Seabury Rd (03909-5151)
P.O. Box 2261, Ogunquit (03907-2261)
PHONE..................................207 363-7561
Chris Davis, *Owner*
EMP: 3
SALES (est): 182.1K **Privately Held**
WEB: www.perkinscovepottery.com
SIC: 3269 Mfg Pottery Products

(G-7307)
GRAIN SURFBOARDS
73 Webber Rd (03909-6349)
PHONE..................................207 457-5313
Mike Lavecchia, *Executive*
◆ **EMP:** 4
SALES (est): 350.8K **Privately Held**
SIC: 3949 Mfg Sporting/Athletic Goods

(G-7308)
HAWK MOTORS INC
1100 Us Route 1 (03909-5822)
PHONE..................................207 363-4716
John Hawk, *Owner*
EMP: 3
SALES (est): 355.9K **Privately Held**
WEB: www.hawkmotors.com
SIC: 3369 Non-Ferrous Foundries

(G-7309)
INFINITE IMAGING INC
470 Us Route 1 Ste 1 (03909-1656)
PHONE..................................207 363-4402
Cathy Clark, *Branch Mgr*
EMP: 21 **Privately Held**
SIC: 2752 Lithographic Commercial Printing
PA: Infinite Imaging, Inc
933 Islington St
Portsmouth NH 03801

(G-7310)
LYNNE BAILEY
Also Called: Graphiti Screenprinting Signs
180 Woodbridge Rd Unit 9 (03909-1462)
PHONE..................................207 363-7999
Lynne Bailey, *Principal*
EMP: 3
SQ FT: 2,000
SALES: 187.7K **Privately Held**
SIC: 2396 3993 7336 Mfg Auto/Apparel Trimming Mfg Signs/Advertising Specialties Commercial Art/Graphic Design

(G-7311)
MACOMBER LOOMS
130 Beech Ridge Rd (03909-5393)
P.O. Box 186 (03909-0186)
PHONE..................................207 363-2808
Frederick H Hart II, *Partner*
Linda L Hart, *Partner*
EMP: 6
SQ FT: 6,300
SALES (est): 480K **Privately Held**
SIC: 3552 Mfg Hand Looms

(G-7312)
MAINE WOOD & DESIGN LLC
55 Witchtrot Rd (03909-5348)
P.O. Box 113 (03909-0113)
PHONE..................................207 363-5270
John Steffens, *Hum Res Coord*
Patrick Dennis, *Manager*
Joseph Bumen,
EMP: 17
SQ FT: 30,000
SALES (est): 2.4MM **Privately Held**
SIC: 2542 Mfg Partitions/Fixtures-Nonwood

(G-7313)
MILLWORK CITY INTERNET SVCS
3 Parsons Ln (03909-5159)
PHONE..................................207 370-5020
EMP: 3
SALES (est): 208.9K **Privately Held**
SIC: 2491 Wood Preserving

(G-7314)
OFFSHORE MARINE OUTFITTERS
15 Hannaford Dr (03909-1667)
PHONE..................................207 363-8862
Matt Nagy, *Principal*
EMP: 3
SALES (est): 170.4K **Privately Held**
SIC: 2048 Mfg Prepared Feeds

(G-7315)
OLD YORK QUARRY INC
285 Bell Marsh Rd (03909)
P.O. Box 772, Moultonborough NH (03254-0772)
PHONE..................................603 772-6061
Michael Delsesto, *President*
Lawrence Willey, *Vice Pres*
EMP: 4
SQ FT: 4,000
SALES: 1MM **Privately Held**
SIC: 1411 Dimension Stone Quarry

(G-7316)
STONEWALL KITCHEN LLC (PA)
2 Stonewall Ln (03909-1665)
PHONE..................................207 351-2713
John Stiker, *CEO*
Lori King, *COO*
Tyler Pratt, *Controller*
Sharon Decato, *Human Res Dir*
Aaron Hickey, *Regl Sales Mgr*
◆ **EMP:** 120
SQ FT: 12,000
SALES (est): 122.2MM **Privately Held**
WEB: www.stonewallkitchen.com
SIC: 2033 2035 2032 5149 Mfg Canned Fruits/Vegtbl Mfg Pickles/Sauces Mfg Canned Specialties Whol Groceries

(G-7317)
STRATOSPHERE INC
611 Us Route 1 (03909-1695)
P.O. Box 65 (03909-0065)
PHONE..................................207 351-8011
▲ **EMP:** 57 **EST:** 2014
SALES (est): 4.6MM **Privately Held**
SIC: 3495 Mfg Wire Springs

(G-7318)
YOC
21 Railroad Ave (03909-6535)
PHONE..................................207 363-9322
Oliver Borrmann, *Vice Chairman*
EMP: 3
SALES (est): 176.2K **Privately Held**
SIC: 2869 Mfg Industrial Organic Chemicals

MASSACHUSETTS

▲ = Import ▼=Export
◆ =Import/Export

Abington
Plymouth County

(G-7319)
ADVANCED AIR SYSTEMS INC
43 Highland Rd Ste J (02351-3014)
PHONE..................................781 878-5733
Edward J Cardinal, *President*
EMP: 10
SALES (est): 670K **Privately Held**
SIC: 3444 Mfg Sheet Metalwork

(G-7320)
AROYAN INC
Also Called: Aroyan Alum Strefronts Windows
1423 Bedford St Ste 1 (02351-3107)
PHONE..................................781 421-3107
Robert Arroyan, *President*
Edward J Aroyan, *President*
EMP: 3
SQ FT: 3,000
SALES (est): 503K **Privately Held**
SIC: 3442 5031 Mfg Metal Doors/Sash/Trim Whol Lumber/Plywood/Millwork

(G-7321)
BELL RUBBER
477 Washington St (02351-2417)
PHONE..................................781 400-7262
Eric J Beltramini, *Owner*
EMP: 5
SALES (est): 334.4K **Privately Held**
SIC: 3625 Mfg Relays/Industrial Controls

(G-7322)
DILLON LABORATORIES INC
Also Called: Dillon Dental Laboratories
4 Thicket St (02351-1027)
PHONE..................................781 871-2333
William H Dillon III, *President*
EMP: 15
SQ FT: 14,000
SALES (est): 1.2MM **Privately Held**
SIC: 3843 8072 Mfg Dental Supplies

(G-7323)
DIXON BROS MILLWORK INC
200 Wales St (02351-5804)
PHONE..................................781 261-9962
Andrew Dixon, *President*
EMP: 8
SQ FT: 7,000
SALES (est): 752.6K **Privately Held**
SIC: 2431 2434 Mfg Millwork Mfg Wood Kitchen Cabinets

(G-7324)
ENVIRONMENTAL IMPROVEMENTS (PA)
545 N Quincy St (02351-1013)
PHONE..................................781 857-2375
Charles F Donahue, *President*
Daniel Gallagher,
EMP: 4
SALES (est): 434.1K **Privately Held**
SIC: 2421 3272 3441 Mfg Outdoor Wood Concrete And Steel Products

(G-7325)
J G PERFORMANCE INC
43 Highland Rd (02351-3014)
PHONE..................................781 871-1404
John Brown, *President*
Jarrod O Guimares, *Treasurer*
Gregory Giamelis, *Admin Sec*
EMP: 3 **EST:** 2011
SALES (est): 410.5K **Privately Held**
SIC: 2992 5531 7549 Mfg Lubricating Oils/Greases Ret Auto/Home Supplies Automotive Services

(G-7326)
KOL-TAR INC
Also Called: Black Shield Driveway Sealer
699 Adams St (02351-1324)
P.O. Box 115 (02351-0115)
PHONE..................................781 871-0883
Bridgette Cashman, *President*
EMP: 6
SQ FT: 8,200
SALES: 1.2MM **Privately Held**
WEB: www.koltar.skyrock.com
SIC: 2951 2952 Mfg Tar Driveway Sealer

(G-7327)
LENNOX ROOFING INC
23 Belcher St (02351-1380)
PHONE..................................508 328-5780
Robert Lennox, *Principal*
EMP: 3
SALES (est): 87.9K **Privately Held**
SIC: 3585 Roofing/Siding Contractor

(G-7328)
PRECAST SPECIALTIES CORP
999 Adams St (02351-1058)
P.O. Box 86 (02351-0086)
PHONE..................................781 878-7220
Robert Bouchard, *President*
Guy Bouchard, *Admin Sec*
EMP: 30
SALES (est): 6.5MM **Privately Held**
WEB: www.precastspecialtiescorp.com
SIC: 3272 Mfg Concrete Products

(G-7329)
S T WHITE CONCRETE FORMS
12 Central St (02351-1833)
P.O. Box 59 (02351-0059)
PHONE..................................781 982-9116
Steve White, *Owner*
EMP: 3
SALES (est): 266.2K **Privately Held**
WEB: www.stwhiteco.com
SIC: 3444 Mfg Sheet Metalwork

(G-7330)
SCHUERCH CORPORATION
Also Called: Schuremed
452 Randolph St (02351-1170)
PHONE..................................781 982-7000
Peter Schuerch, *President*
EMP: 18
SQ FT: 20,000
SALES (est): 3.5MM **Privately Held**
SIC: 3841 Mfg Surgical/Medical Instruments

(G-7331)
SCOTIA BOAT BUILDERS
624 Bedford St (02351-1930)
PHONE..................................781 871-2120
John Carr, *Partner*
Edward Hirt, *Partner*
EMP: 4
SQ FT: 2,132
SALES (est): 286.5K **Privately Held**
SIC: 3732 Boatbuilding/Repairing

(G-7332)
XYZ SHEET METAL INC
281 Washington St (02351-2415)
P.O. Box 391, Rockland (02370-0391)
PHONE..................................781 878-1419
EMP: 15
SQ FT: 7,700
SALES (est): 2.8MM **Privately Held**
WEB: www.xyzsheetmetal.com
SIC: 3444 Mfg Sheet Metalwork

Acton
Middlesex County

(G-7333)
ABISEE INC
30 Sudbury Rd Ste 1b (01720-5954)
P.O. Box 140, Sudbury (01776-0140)
PHONE..................................978 637-2900
Leon Reznik, *President*
Helen Reznik, *COO*
▲ **EMP:** 15
SQ FT: 5,000
SALES (est): 3.2MM **Privately Held**
SIC: 3699 Mfg Electrical Equipment/Supplies

(G-7334)
ACTON RESEARCH CORPORATION
15 Discovery Way (01720-4482)
PHONE..................................941 556-2601
Donald Templenan, *President*
Michael Case, *Opers Mgr*
Rosette Lenon, *Finance*
EMP: 25
SQ FT: 32,500
SALES (est): 9.1MM
SALES (corp-wide): 5.1B **Publicly Held**
WEB: www.actonresearch.com
SIC: 3827 3826 3648 3231 Manufactures Optical Instr/Lens Analytical Instr Lighting Equipment Prdt-Purchased Glass Adhesives/Sealants
PA: Roper Technologies, Inc.
6901 Prof Pkwy E Ste 200
Sarasota FL 34240
941 556-2601

(G-7335)
ACTON WOODWORKS INC
2 School St (01720-3605)
PHONE..................................978 263-0222
Glenn Berger, *President*
EMP: 7
SQ FT: 4,400
SALES: 1MM **Privately Held**
WEB: www.actonwoodworks.com
SIC: 2511 5712 1542 1521 Mfg Wood Household Furniture Ret Furniture Residential Construction

(G-7336)
ADRA RAND
23 Hartland Way (01720-5858)
PHONE..................................978 274-2652
James Rand, *Principal*
EMP: 3
SALES (est): 187.7K **Privately Held**
SIC: 3131 Mfg Footwear Cut Stock

(G-7337)
ALL METAL FABRICATORS INC
82 Hayward Rd (01720-3006)
P.O. Box 954 (01720-0954)
PHONE..................................978 263-3904
Donald E Robertson, *President*
Bradford P Robertson, *Vice Pres*
EMP: 12
SQ FT: 12,000
SALES (est): 1.9MM **Privately Held**
SIC: 3443 3444 Mfg Fabricated Plate Work Mfg Sheet Metalwork

(G-7338)
ALLEN MEDICAL SYSTEMS INC (DH)
100 Discovery Way Ste 100 # 100 (01720-4483)
PHONE..................................978 263-7727
Robert J Tennison, *President*
Jason Krieser, *Vice Pres*
Mark Cole, *Exec Dir*
Michael Nordling, *Exec Dir*
Pete Richardson, *Exec Dir*
▲ **EMP:** 10
SALES (est): 11.5MM
SALES (corp-wide): 2.9B **Publicly Held**
SIC: 3841 Mfg Surgical/Medical Instruments
HQ: Hill-Rom, Inc.
1069 State Route 46 E
Batesville IN 47006
812 934-7777

(G-7339)
ALPHA INSTRUMENTS INC
468 Great Rd Ste 3 (01720-4187)
PHONE..................................978 264-2966
Da Ke LI, *President*
EMP: 3
SALES (est): 268.2K **Privately Held**
SIC: 3585 Mfg Refrigeration/Heating Equipment

(G-7340)
AMATECH CORPORATION (DH)
Also Called: Amatech International
100 Discovery Way (01720-4481)
PHONE..................................978 263-5401
Kip P Van Steenburg, *President*
John J Greisch, *President*
Jason Krieser, *Vice Pres*
EMP: 25
SQ FT: 40,000
SALES (est): 11.5MM
SALES (corp-wide): 2.9B **Publicly Held**
SIC: 3842 Mfg Surgical Appliances/Supplies
HQ: Allen Medical Systems, Inc.
100 Discovery Way Ste 100 # 100
Acton MA 01720
978 263-7727

(G-7341)
APPS ASSOCIATES LLC
40 Nagog Park Ste 105 (01720-3425)
PHONE..................................978 399-0230
Sridhar Bogelli, *CEO*
Ben Pastro, *President*
Ajay Kapur, *Vice Pres*
Kundan Kumar, *Technical Mgr*
Preeti Lobo, *Cust Mgr*
EMP: 201
SQ FT: 5,200
SALES: 64MM **Privately Held**
WEB: www.appsassociates.com
SIC: 7372 Custom Computer Programing

(G-7342)
ASSOCIATED ENVMTL SYSTEMS INC (PA)
Also Called: Associated Envmtl Systems
8 Post Office Sq (01720-3966)
PHONE..................................978 772-0022
Beran Peter, *President*
Steve Munroe, *COO*
John O'Rourke, *Vice Pres*
Aaron Robinson, *Vice Pres*
Michelle Coffey, *Opers Staff*
EMP: 130
SQ FT: 200,000
SALES (est): 11.2MM **Privately Held**
WEB: www.associatedonline.com
SIC: 3829 Mfg Measuring/Controlling Devices

(G-7343)
ASTER ENTERPRISES INC
6 Eastern Rd (01720-5801)
PHONE..................................978 264-0499
Suzanne R Holsinger, *President*
Christopher Holssinger, *CFO*
Ronald F Holsinger, *Treasurer*
▲ **EMP:** 4
SQ FT: 3,500
SALES (est): 552.8K **Privately Held**
WEB: www.asterenterprises.com
SIC: 3499 Mfg Magnetic Devices

(G-7344)
BIDIRECTIONAL DISPLAY INC
8 Monument Pl (01720-4195)
PHONE..................................617 599-8282
Hsuanyeh Chang, *Principal*
Anping Liu, *Treasurer*
EMP: 3
SALES (est): 156.7K **Privately Held**
SIC: 3674 5043 3577 Mfg Semiconductors/Related Devices Whol Photo Equipment/Supplies Mfg Computer Peripheral Equipment

(G-7345)
BLUEJAY DIAGNOSTICS INC
360 Msschstts Ave Ste 203 (01720)
PHONE..................................978 631-0152
Svetlana Dey, *CEO*
Douglas C Wurth, *Ch of Bd*
Indranil Dey, *President*
Neil Dey, *COO*
Jeffrey Aidt, *Director*
EMP: 3
SALES (est): 145.8K **Privately Held**
SIC: 2835 Mfg Diagnostic Substances

(G-7346)
BONAMI SOFTWARE CORPORATION
34 Hammond St (01720-3205)
PHONE..................................978 264-6641
Allen Morris, *President*
Keith Gutfreund, *Principal*
Nick McCann, *Manager*
Daniel Calkin, *Software Engr*
EMP: 3
SALES (est): 158.1K **Privately Held**
SIC: 7372 Custom Computer Programing

(G-7347)
CHECK POINT SOFTWARE TECH INC
179 Great Rd Ste 111a (01720-5740)
PHONE..................................978 635-0300

GEOGRAPHIC

Helen Edwards, *Branch Mgr*
David Klusacek, *Director*
EMP: 3
SALES (corp-wide): 551.2MM **Privately Held**
WEB: www.checkpoint.com
SIC: 7372 Prepackaged Software Services
HQ: Check Point Software Technologies, Inc.
959 Skyway Rd Ste 300
San Carlos CA 94070

(G-7348)
COMPASS COMPANY
13 Gioconda Ave (01720-4330)
P.O. Box 2344 (01720-6344)
PHONE..................................978 635-0303
Bonnie Breslin, *Owner*
▲ **EMP:** 3
SALES: 500K **Privately Held**
WEB: www.thecompasscompany.com
SIC: 3499 5947 Mfg Misc Fabricated Metal Products Ret Gifts/Novelties

(G-7349)
DAVID L ELLIS COMPANY INC (PA)
Also Called: Patriot Manufacturing
310 Old High St (01720-5923)
P.O. Box 592 (01720-0592)
PHONE..................................978 897-1795
Richard A Ellis, *President*
Robert Ellis, *Finance Other*
EMP: 5
SQ FT: 4,000
SALES (est): 1.7MM **Privately Held**
WEB: www.hardness-testblocks.com
SIC: 3829 Mfg Hardness Testing Equipment

(G-7350)
DMH SOFTWARE
143 Butternut Holw (01718-1004)
P.O. Box 2714 (01720-6714)
PHONE..................................978 263-0526
Yigal Hochberg, *Owner*
EMP: 5
SALES (est): 269.1K **Privately Held**
SIC: 7372 Prepackaged Software Services

(G-7351)
EASTMAN WIND INSTRUMENTS INC
68 Nonset Path (01720-3418)
PHONE..................................800 789-2216
Qian Ni, *President*
EMP: 15
SALES (est): 1.3MM **Privately Held**
SIC: 3931 Mfg Musical Instruments

(G-7352)
ECOCHLOR INC
22 Silver Hill Rd (01720-4228)
PHONE..................................978 263-5478
Charles W Miller, *CEO*
Thomas Perlich, *President*
Marty Toyen, *Treasurer*
EMP: 6
SALES (est): 570.1K **Privately Held**
SIC: 3531 Mfg Construction Machinery

(G-7353)
ENOS ENGINEERING LLC
914 Main St (01720-5808)
PHONE..................................978 654-6522
Allen Tseng,
John Fitzgerald,
EMP: 7
SALES: 3MM **Privately Held**
SIC: 3599 3827 Mfg Industrial Machinery Mfg Optical Instruments/Lenses

(G-7354)
EO VISTA LLC
42 Nagog Park Ste 200 (01720-3445)
PHONE..................................978 635-8080
Steven Wein, *Principal*
EMP: 18
SALES (est): 1.6MM **Privately Held**
SIC: 3827 Mfg Optical Instruments/Lenses

(G-7355)
FARMER BROWN SERVICE INC
54 Knox Trl Bldg 2m (01720-5950)
P.O. Box 1388, Concord (01742-1388)
PHONE..................................978 897-7550
Scott Brown, *President*
EMP: 3
SALES (est): 419.9K **Privately Held**
SIC: 3559 Mfg Misc Industry Machinery

(G-7356)
FLUIDFORM INC
42 Nagog Park Ste 110 (01720-3445)
PHONE..................................978 287-4698
Michael Graffeo, *CEO*
Adam Feinberg, *Principal*
Alexander Lenz, *Manager*
EMP: 8
SALES (est): 365.4K **Privately Held**
SIC: 2759 Commercial Printing

(G-7357)
FULCRUM9 SYSTEMS INC
5 Jay Ln (01720-5754)
PHONE..................................978 549-3868
John Crossin, *President*
Kathy Breda, *Treasurer*
▼ **EMP:** 6
SALES (est): 419.5K **Privately Held**
SIC: 3825 System Testing Solutions/Design Circut Boards

(G-7358)
GEORGE HOWELL COFFEE CO LLC
Also Called: Terroir Coffee
312 School St (01720-5414)
PHONE..................................978 635-9033
Janet Hoshino, *Sales Staff*
Jerry O'Hare, *Sales Staff*
George H Howell, *Mng Member*
EMP: 15
SQ FT: 5,500
SALES (est): 2.1MM **Privately Held**
WEB: www.terroircoffee.com
SIC: 2095 5149 Mfg Roasted Coffee Whol Groceries

(G-7359)
HAARTZ CORPORATION (PA)
Also Called: Haartz Auto Fabric
87 Hayward Rd (01720-3000)
PHONE..................................978 264-2600
John Fox, *President*
Tucker Dewing, *Plant Mgr*
Rod Goguen, *Facilities Mgr*
Donna Macleod, *Buyer*
Andy Nicoletti, *Purchasing*
◆ **EMP:** 314 **EST:** 1922
SQ FT: 265,000
SALES (est): 112MM **Privately Held**
WEB: www.haartz.com
SIC: 2295 3069 Mfg Coated Fabrics Mfg Fabricated Rubber Products

(G-7360)
HIRSCH RETAIL STORE INC
Also Called: Great Wine, The
52 Eaton Dr (01719)
PHONE..................................978 621-4634
Robert Hirsch, *President*
EMP: 7
SALES: 1MM **Privately Held**
SIC: 2084 Mfg Wines/Brandy/Spirits

(G-7361)
HONEYWELL DATA INSTRUMENTS INC
100 Discovery Way (01720-4483)
PHONE..................................978 264-9550
Edward M Colbert, *Ch of Bd*
Peter R Russo, *President*
Herman Erichsen, *Vice Pres*
Mark Hatch, *Vice Pres*
Daniel R Weber, *Vice Pres*
▼ **EMP:** 340 **EST:** 1966
SQ FT: 80,000
SALES: 54.1MM **Privately Held**
SIC: 3825 3823 3842 Mfg Electrical Measuring Instruments Mfg Process Control Instruments

(G-7362)
HYDRODOT INC
3 Post Office Sq Ste K (01720-3956)
PHONE..................................978 399-0206
Kathleen M Principe, *President*
John P McPeck, *Treasurer*
Sheila A Hill, *Director*
William Principe, *Admin Sec*
EMP: 6
SALES (est): 596.8K **Privately Held**
SIC: 3845 Mfg Electromedical Equipment

(G-7363)
INFOTREE INC
30 Nagog Park Ste 210 (01720-3439)
PHONE..................................978 263-8558
Isen Yang, *President*
Mr Ifen Yang, *Founder*
Tanni Kuo, *Vice Pres*
EMP: 6
SALES (est): 727.2K **Privately Held**
WEB: www.shrubbery.net
SIC: 7372 Custom Computer Programing

(G-7364)
INK ETCETERA CORPORATION
165 Great Rd (01720-5712)
PHONE..................................978 263-1555
Paula Rotondo, *CEO*
Joe Rotondo, *President*
EMP: 3
SALES (est): 425.6K **Privately Held**
SIC: 2752 Lithographic Commercial Printing

(G-7365)
INSULET CORPORATION (PA)
100 Nagog Park (01720-3428)
PHONE..................................978 600-7000
Shacey Petrovic, *President*
Aiman Abdel-Malek, *Exec VP*
Charles Alpuche, *Exec VP*
David Colleran, *Senior VP*
Michael Spears, *Senior VP*
▲ **EMP:** 277
SALES: 563.8MM **Publicly Held**
WEB: www.insulet.com
SIC: 3841 Mfg Surgical & Medical Instruments

(G-7366)
INTECH INC
Also Called: Acra-Cut
979 Main St (01720-5898)
PHONE..................................978 263-2210
John W Baker, *President*
EMP: 30
SQ FT: 22,000
SALES (est): 4.6MM **Privately Held**
SIC: 3599 3541 3841 Mfg Industrial Machinery Mfg Machine Tools-Cutting Mfg Surgical/Medical Instruments

(G-7367)
JR HIGGINS ASSOCIATES LLC
898 Main St (01720-5865)
PHONE..................................978 266-1200
John R Higgins, *Mng Member*
EMP: 20
SQ FT: 20,000
SALES (est): 3.7MM **Privately Held**
WEB: www.jrhiggins.com
SIC: 3599 3993 Mfg Industrial Machinery Mfg Signs/Advertising Specialties

(G-7368)
LEO S CAVELIER INC
14 Wetherbee St (01720-5526)
P.O. Box 2135 (01720-6135)
PHONE..................................978 369-2770
Jean Shaw, *President*
Steven Cavelier, *Vice Pres*
EMP: 6
SQ FT: 5,000
SALES: 1MM **Privately Held**
SIC: 7692 Welding Repair

(G-7369)
LIQUID METRONICS INCORPORATED
Also Called: L M I
8 Post Office Sq Ste 1 (01720-3966)
PHONE..................................978 263-9800
Jean-Claude Pharmont, *President*
Thomas Rogan, *Treasurer*
Michael Monts, *Admin Sec*
▲ **EMP:** 140 **EST:** 1984
SQ FT: 72,000
SALES (est): 18.9MM
SALES (corp-wide): 381.9MM **Privately Held**
WEB: www.lmipumps.com
SIC: 3586 3823 Mfg Measuring/Dispensing Pumps Mfg Process Control Instruments
HQ: Milton Roy, Llc
201 Ivyland Rd
Ivyland PA 18974
215 441-0800

(G-7370)
LYFESHOT LLC
360 Massachusetts Ave # 103 (01720-3750)
PHONE..................................978 451-4662
Michael Aronson, *Mng Member*
Sarah Aronson,
EMP: 3
SALES (est): 160.8K **Privately Held**
SIC: 3651 5946 Mfg Home Audio/Video Equipment Ret Cameras/Photography Supplies

(G-7371)
MACKINNON PRINTING CO INC
6 Ledgerock Way Unit 7 (01720-4161)
P.O. Box 2035 (01720-6035)
PHONE..................................978 263-8435
John Mackinnon, *President*
Theresa Mac Kinnon, *Admin Sec*
EMP: 4
SQ FT: 2,800
SALES (est): 576.1K **Privately Held**
WEB: www.mackinnon-printing.com
SIC: 2752 Lithographic Commercial Printing

(G-7372)
MAGNETIC SCIENCES INC
367 Arlington St (01720-2217)
PHONE..................................978 266-9355
Paul Elliot, *President*
Dolores Elliot, *Owner*
Esther Kim, *Sales Staff*
EMP: 4
SALES: 226.2K **Privately Held**
WEB: www.magneticsciences.com
SIC: 3829 3679 3812 5961 Mfg Measure/Control Dvcs Mfg Elec Components Mfg Search/Navgatn Equip Electronic Shopping

(G-7373)
MAXON CORPORATION
75 Discovery Way (01720-4482)
PHONE..................................978 795-1285
Albert Welz, *Branch Mgr*
EMP: 4
SALES (corp-wide): 41.8B **Publicly Held**
WEB: www.maxoncorp.com
SIC: 3433 3494 Mfg Industrial Gas And Oil Burners And Fuel Shutoff Valves
HQ: Maxon Corporation
201 E 18th St
Muncie IN 47302
765 284-3304

(G-7374)
MEDICAL ASTHTICS ASSOC NENG PC
274 Great Rd Ste 2a (01720-4825)
PHONE..................................978 263-5376
Gert Walter, *President*
Stephanie Liatsis, *Treasurer*
EMP: 5
SALES: 400K **Privately Held**
WEB: www.medicalaestheticsne.com
SIC: 2834 7991 Mfg Pharmaceutical Preparations Physical Fitness Facilities

(G-7375)
NOVOTECH INC
916 Main St (01720-5808)
PHONE..................................978 929-9458
Michael Hulen, *President*
Stephen McNeill, *CFO*
EMP: 27
SQ FT: 7,000
SALES (est): 7MM **Privately Held**
WEB: www.novotech.net
SIC: 3827 Mfg Optical Instruments/Lenses

▲ = Import ▼=Export
◆ =Import/Export

(G-7376)
OP USA INC
6 Ledgerock Way Unit 4 (01720-4161)
PHONE..................................978 658-5135
G Giacopone, *General Mgr*
Grazia Giacopone, *General Mgr*
EMP: 3
SQ FT: 1,600
SALES: 1.5MM
SALES (corp-wide): 426.3K **Privately Held**
SIC: 3569 3549 3492 Mfg General Industrial Machinery Mfg Metalworking Machinery Mfg Fluid Power Valves/Fittings
HQ: Op Srl
Via Del Serpente 97
Brescia BS 25131
030 358-0401

(G-7377)
PERILLON SOFTWARE INC
33 Nagog Park Ste 205 (01720-3427)
PHONE..................................978 263-0412
John Niemoller, *CEO*
James Jensen, *President*
Julie Comeau, *CFO*
EMP: 5
SALES (est): 1.3MM
SALES (corp-wide): 632.5K **Privately Held**
WEB: www.perillon.com
SIC: 7372 Prepackaged Software Services
HQ: Lisam Systems
Boulevard De La Sennette 42a
Ecaussinnes 7190
674 900-03

(G-7378)
REX LUMBER COMPANY (PA)
840 Main St (01720-5804)
P.O. Box 2860 (01720-6860)
PHONE..................................800 343-0567
Benjamin Forester, *President*
A Ledyard Smith Jr, *COO*
William Clark, *CFO*
Cheryl Milroy, *Human Res Mgr*
Tom Dupont, *Sales Staff*
◆ **EMP:** 100 **EST:** 1946
SQ FT: 10,584
SALES (est): 57.3MM **Privately Held**
WEB: www.rexlumber.com
SIC: 2421 2431 Sawmill/Planing Mill Mfg Millwork

(G-7379)
RIVET DIRECT INC
54 Knox Trl Unit 2h1 (01720-5950)
PHONE..................................866 474-8387
EMP: 4
SALES (est): 317.9K **Privately Held**
SIC: 3452 Mfg Bolts/Screws/Rivets

(G-7380)
ROBB CURTCO MEDIA LLC
1 Acton Pl Ste 203 (01720-3951)
PHONE..................................978 264-7500
Linc Jackson, *COO*
EMP: 36
SALES (corp-wide): 17.6MM **Privately Held**
WEB: www.curtco.com
SIC: 2721 Periodicals-Publishing/Printing
PA: Curtco Robb Media Llc
29160 Heathercliff Rd # 1
Malibu CA 90265
310 589-7700

(G-7381)
ROPER SCIENTIFIC INC
Also Called: Princeton Instruments
15 Discovery Way (01720-4482)
PHONE..................................978 268-0337
Joseph McMahon, *Prdtn Mgr*
Keith Dowling, *Production*
Alex Tsalyuk, *Engineer*
Gene Yazback, *Engineer*
Maxim Rothenberg, *Finance*
EMP: 28
SALES (corp-wide): 5.1B **Publicly Held**
SIC: 3827 Mfg Optical Instruments/Lenses
HQ: Roper Scientific, Inc.
3660 Quakerbridge Rd
Trenton NJ 08619
941 556-2601

(G-7382)
SABR ENTERPRISES LLC
6 Eastern Rd (01720-5801)
PHONE..................................978 264-0499
Jennifer Smith, *Controller*
Robert J Mercurio, *Mng Member*
EMP: 4 **EST:** 2011
SQ FT: 12,000
SALES: 250K **Privately Held**
SIC: 3499 Mfg Misc Fabricated Metal Products

(G-7383)
SANOVA BIOSCIENCE INC
42 Nagog Park (01720-3445)
PHONE..................................978 429-8079
Xingfu Feng, *President*
Lihua Xie, *Vice Pres*
Bing Liu, *Treasurer*
Dale Devore, *Director*
Veronica Zhu, *Director*
EMP: 6 **EST:** 2014
SALES (est): 976.9K **Privately Held**
SIC: 2834 Mfg Pharmaceutical Preparations

(G-7384)
SB DEVELOPMENT CORP
Also Called: Minuteman Pre-Hung Door Co
17 Craig Rd (01720-5404)
PHONE..................................978 263-2744
John Brislouf, *President*
EMP: 9
SQ FT: 11,000
SALES: 940K **Privately Held**
SIC: 2431 Mfg Millwork

(G-7385)
SEACHANGE INTERNATIONAL INC (PA)
50 Nagog Park (01720-3409)
PHONE..................................978 897-0100
William Francis Markey III, *Ch of Bd*
David McEvoy, *Senior VP*
Peter Gibbons, *Vice Pres*
Peter Faubert, *CFO*
Yossi Aloni, *Ch Credit Ofcr*
▲ **EMP:** 188
SQ FT: 124,128
SALES: 62.4MM **Publicly Held**
WEB: www.schange.com
SIC: 3663 7822 7371 Mfg And Video Distribution & Software Development

(G-7386)
SEMITECH SOLUTIONS INC
43 Nagog Park Ste 115 (01720-3426)
PHONE..................................978 589-3850
Raymond Begin, *President*
Cheryl Latwas, *Office Mgr*
EMP: 6
SALES (est): 2.7MM **Privately Held**
SIC: 3674 Mfg Semiconductors/Related Devices

(G-7387)
SORRISO TECHNOLOGIES INC
Also Called: Block Island Software
40 Nagog Park Ste 110 (01720-3425)
PHONE..................................978 635-3900
John A Kowalonek, *President*
George Finn, *Vice Pres*
Yvette Oanh Nguyen, *Vice Pres*
Joshua Gentry, *Treasurer*
Juan Turruellas, *Admin Sec*
EMP: 27
SALES (est): 2.5MM **Privately Held**
SIC: 7372 Prepackaged Software Services

(G-7388)
SPERO DEVICES INC
125 Nagog Park Ste 220 (01720-3451)
PHONE..................................978 849-8000
Jai Gupta, *Vice Pres*
Abbie Mathew, *Vice Pres*
EMP: 3
SALES (est): 230.8K **Privately Held**
SIC: 3674 Mfg Semiconductors/Related Devices

(G-7389)
T H GROGAN & ASSOCIATES INC
12 Woodchester Dr (01720-2058)
PHONE..................................978 266-9548
EMP: 10
SALES (est): 1.3MM **Privately Held**
WEB: www.thgrogan.com
SIC: 3699 Mfg Electrical Equipment/Supplies

(G-7390)
TERARECON INC
42 Nagog Park Ste 202 (01720-3445)
PHONE..................................978 274-0461
Mike Knupp, *Manager*
EMP: 55
SALES (corp-wide): 50.4MM **Privately Held**
WEB: www.terarecon.com
SIC: 3577 Mfg Computer Peripheral Equipment
PA: Terarecon, Inc.
4000 E 3rd Ave Ste 200
Foster City CA 94404
650 372-1100

(G-7391)
TRIPLE SEAT SOFTWARE LLC
6 Ashwood Rd (01720-4402)
PHONE..................................978 635-0615
Jonathan Morse, *Principal*
EMP: 3
SALES (est): 140.8K **Privately Held**
SIC: 7372 Prepackaged Software Services

(G-7392)
TWIN COAST METROLOGY INC
6 Eastern Rd (01720-5801)
PHONE..................................508 517-4508
Jonathan Rafferty, *Technician*
EMP: 3 **EST:** 2017
SALES (est): 194.2K **Privately Held**
SIC: 3827 Mfg Optical Instruments/Lenses

(G-7393)
WILLIAM S HAYNES CO INC
68 Nonset Path (01720-3418)
PHONE..................................978 268-0600
Gerardo Discepolo, *President*
EMP: 3
SALES (est): 341.8K **Privately Held**
SIC: 3931 Mfg Musical Instruments

(G-7394)
WINTRISS CONTROLS GROUP LLC
100 Discovery Way Ste 110 (01720-4483)
PHONE..................................978 268-2700
Maya Parekh, *Buyer*
Barry Erlandson, *Engineer*
Dick Labelle, *Sales Mgr*
Tom Coperine, *Regl Sales Mgr*
Mark Hatch, *Mng Member*
▲ **EMP:** 31
SQ FT: 15,000
SALES (est): 12MM **Privately Held**
SIC: 3823 Mfg Process Control Instruments

(G-7395)
ZHANG FENGLING
Also Called: Sigwa Company
20 Main St (01720-3575)
PHONE..................................978 289-8606
Fengling Zhang, *Owner*
EMP: 3 **EST:** 2014
SALES (est): 133.3K **Privately Held**
SIC: 3845 Mfg Electromedical Equipment

Acushnet
Bristol County

(G-7396)
508TEES SCREENPRINTING
211 Middle Rd (02743-2017)
PHONE..................................508 717-3835
Debbie Macaroco, *Principal*
EMP: 3 **EST:** 2018
SALES (est): 117.2K **Privately Held**
SIC: 2759 Commercial Printing

(G-7397)
ACUSHNET COMPANY
Titleist
4 Slocum St (02743-2714)
PHONE..................................508 979-2000
Mary L Bohn, *President*
Richard Westgate, *Engineer*
Eric Bartsch, *Branch Mgr*
James Linhares, *Director*
EMP: 40 **Publicly Held**
WEB: www.titleist.com
SIC: 3949 Mfg Sporting/Athletic Goods
HQ: Acushnet Company
333 Bridge St
Fairhaven MA 02719
508 979-2000

(G-7398)
ACUSHNET MFG HOM
168 Lake St (02743-1310)
PHONE..................................508 763-2074
Richard Ellis, *Principal*
EMP: 3
SALES (est): 9.9K **Privately Held**
SIC: 3999 Mfg Misc Products

(G-7399)
ARMADILLO NOISE VIBRATION LLC
1 Titleist Dr (02743-2764)
PHONE..................................774 992-7156
Rob Haley, *Mng Member*
Jonathan Shaw, *Mng Member*
EMP: 6
SALES: 1.9MM **Privately Held**
SIC: 3542 5084 Mfg Machine Tools-Forming Whol Industrial Equipment

(G-7400)
CENTURY FOOD SERVICE INC
107 S Main St (02743-2838)
PHONE..................................508 995-3221
Michael A Goulart, *President*
Jeffrey M Goulart, *Treasurer*
EMP: 10
SALES (est): 1.3MM **Privately Held**
WEB: www.centuryhouse.biz
SIC: 3581 Mfg Vending Machines

(G-7401)
DESIGNER STAINED GLASS
4 Perkins Ln (02743-1014)
PHONE..................................508 763-3255
Philip Reynolds, *Owner*
Madeline Reynolds, *Co-Owner*
EMP: 4
SALES: 20K **Privately Held**
SIC: 3231 7699 5231 Mfg Products-Purchased Glass Repair Services Ret Paint/Glass/Wallpaper

(G-7402)
J & R PLASTICS
226 Nyes Ln (02743-1985)
PHONE..................................508 995-0893
Joseph Amarello Jr, *President*
Randy Amarello, *Vice Pres*
Jerry Melanson, *Prdtn Mgr*
EMP: 6 **EST:** 1998
SQ FT: 2,500
SALES (est): 795.6K **Privately Held**
WEB: www.jrplastics.net
SIC: 3599 Mfg Plastic Products

(G-7403)
L & S INDUSTRIES INC
72 S Main St (02743-2837)
PHONE..................................508 998-7900
Daniel McNutt, *Manager*
EMP: 25
SALES (corp-wide): 3.4MM **Privately Held**
SIC: 3273 Mfg Ready-Mixed Concrete
PA: L & S Industries, Inc.
32 Lambeth St
New Bedford MA 02745
508 995-4654

(G-7404)
LEO COONS JR
Also Called: Leo's Machine & Welding
1091 Main St (02743-1129)
PHONE..................................508 995-3300
Leo Coons Jr, *Owner*
EMP: 4
SQ FT: 4,200
SALES: 125K **Privately Held**
SIC: 3599 7699 3541 Mfg Industrial Machinery Repair Services Mfg Machine Tool-Cutting

(G-7405)
PJ KEATING COMPANY
72 S Main St (02743-2837)
P.O. Box 30114 (02743-0114)
PHONE..................................508 992-3542
Jack Freeman, *Manager*
EMP: 9
SALES (corp-wide): 29.7B **Privately Held**
SIC: 3531 Mfg Construction Machinery
HQ: P.J. Keating Company
998 Reservoir Rd
Lunenburg MA 01462
978 582-5200

(G-7406)
SEAFOOD HUT AND CREAMERY
2 S Main St (02743-2822)
PHONE..................................508 993-9355
Manuel A Correia, *Principal*
EMP: 5
SALES (est): 329.8K **Privately Held**
SIC: 2021 Mfg Creamery Butter

(G-7407)
WHALING CITY GRAPHICS INC
352 Main St (02743-5211)
PHONE..................................508 998-3511
Frank Joseph, *President*
Joseph Donnelly, *Vice Pres*
EMP: 5
SQ FT: 5,000
SALES (est): 506K **Privately Held**
WEB: www.wcgraphics.com
SIC: 2759 Commercial Printing

Adams
Berkshire County

(G-7408)
ADAMS REDEMPTION CENTER
56 Commercial St Ste 2 (01220-2095)
P.O. Box 700, Lanesborough (01237-0700)
PHONE..................................413 743-7691
Micheal Diaglo, *Owner*
EMP: 4
SQ FT: 6,000
SALES (est): 100K **Privately Held**
SIC: 2086 Mfg Bottled/Canned Soft Drinks

(G-7409)
ADAMS SPECIALTY & PRINTING CO
14 Pine St Ste 1 (01220-1457)
P.O. Box 66 (01220-0066)
PHONE..................................413 743-9101
Eugene Michalenko, *Partner*
Janice Hayer, *Partner*
Joseph Shaw, *Partner*
EMP: 6 **EST:** 1950
SQ FT: 2,500
SALES (est): 789.1K **Privately Held**
SIC: 2752 Lithographic Commercial Printing

(G-7410)
B&B MICRO MANUFACTURING INC
121 Union St Ste N1 Adams (01220)
PHONE..................................413 281-9431
Mitchell Bresett, *President*
Christopher St Cyr, *Treasurer*
Jason Koperniak, *Admin Sec*
EMP: 27 **EST:** 2017
SALES (est): 1.9MM **Privately Held**
SIC: 2541 5012 Mfg Wood Partitions/Fixtures Whol Autos/Motor Vehicles

(G-7411)
GREYLOCK SAND & GRAVEL LLC
5 Mill St (01220-1552)
PHONE..................................413 441-4967
Norman Dellaghelfa Jr, *Principal*
EMP: 4
SALES (est): 221.3K **Privately Held**
SIC: 1442 Construction Sand/Gravel

(G-7412)
H & R MACHINE CO INC
101 Alger St (01220-9738)
P.O. Box 6 (01220-0006)
PHONE..................................413 743-5610
Robert P Herrmann, *President*
Raymond Gingras, *Vice Pres*
EMP: 3
SQ FT: 2,500
SALES: 160K **Privately Held**
SIC: 3599 Machine Shop

(G-7413)
HOLLAND COMPANY INC
Also Called: PCA Systems
153 Howland Ave (01220-1199)
PHONE..................................413 743-1292
Thom Holland, *President*
Daniel J Holland, *Chairman*
▲ **EMP:** 35
SQ FT: 75,000
SALES (est): 12.1MM **Privately Held**
WEB: www.hollandcompany.com
SIC: 2899 2819 Mfg Chemical Preparations Mfg Industrial Inorganic Chemicals

(G-7414)
RAINBOW SHACK
85 Summer St Ste 3 (01220-9102)
PHONE..................................413 743-4031
EMP: 3
SALES (est): 203.9K **Privately Held**
SIC: 2024 Ice Cream And Frozen Desserts, Nsk

Agawam
Hampden County

(G-7415)
325 SILVER STREET INC
Also Called: O-A
325 Silver St (01001-2919)
P.O. Box 250 (01001-0250)
PHONE..................................413 789-1800
Philip A Vecchiarelli, *President*
Tim McCarthy, *General Mgr*
EMP: 30
SQ FT: 37,000
SALES (est): 5.7MM **Privately Held**
WEB: www.oainc.com
SIC: 3599 3728 3724 3769 Mfg Industrial Machinery Mfg Aircraft Parts/Equip Mfg Aircraft Engine/Part Mfg Space Vehicle Equip

(G-7416)
ACE PRECISION INC
1123 Suffield St (01001-3816)
P.O. Box 309 (01001-0309)
PHONE..................................413 789-7536
Christopher Gibson, *QC Mgr*
Antoine S Elias, *Treasurer*
Geraldine A Elias, *Admin Sec*
EMP: 18
SQ FT: 12,000
SALES (est): 3.6MM **Privately Held**
SIC: 3599 Mfg Industrial Machinery

(G-7417)
AEROSPACE SUPPORT INC
44 Russo Cir (01001-1542)
PHONE..................................413 789-3103
Christopher Unghire, *Vice Pres*
Charlene Mastrilia, *Vice Pres*
EMP: 4
SQ FT: 6,500
SALES (est): 466.4K **Privately Held**
WEB: www.aerospacesuppt.com
SIC: 3471 Plating/Polishing Service

(G-7418)
AGAWAM NOVELTY COMPANY INC
Also Called: Diaper To Go
354 Rowley St (01001-1626)
PHONE..................................413 536-0471
Walter Pieciak Jr, *President*
EMP: 7
SQ FT: 30,000
SALES (est): 957.8K **Privately Held**
SIC: 2396 2759 2675 7299 Mfg Auto/Apparel Trim Commercial Printing Mfg Die-Cut Paper/Board Misc Personal Service Mfg Household Furnishing

(G-7419)
AJ PRECISION INC
25 Century St (01001-2001)
P.O. Box 1225, Westfield (01086-1225)
PHONE..................................413 568-9099
Wade Austin, *President*
Wallace B Austin Jr, *Vice Pres*
EMP: 6
SALES (est): 1.1MM **Privately Held**
SIC: 3599 Mfg Industrial Machinery

(G-7420)
ATLAS FOUNDERS INC
90 Industrial Ln (01001-3133)
P.O. Box 303 (01001-0303)
PHONE..................................413 786-4210
Fax: 413 786-1357
EMP: 14 **EST:** 1956
SQ FT: 20,000
SALES (est): 2.2MM **Privately Held**
WEB: www.atlasfounders.com
SIC: 3363 3364 Mfg Aluminum Die-Castings Mfg Nonferrous Die-Castings

(G-7421)
BAY STATE ELEVATOR COMPANY INC (PA)
275 Silver St (01001-2982)
P.O. Box 910 (01001-0910)
PHONE..................................413 786-7000
Harold F Potts Jr, *President*
Roger T Duval, *Vice Pres*
James H Horth Jr, *Vice Pres*
James H Horth III, *Vice Pres*
Patricia Yamin, *Opers Staff*
EMP: 20 **EST:** 1909
SQ FT: 14,000
SALES (est): 15.1MM **Privately Held**
SIC: 3534 7699 1796 3842 Mfg Elevators/Escalators Repair Services Bldg Equip Installation Mfg Surgical Appliances

(G-7422)
BELT TECHNOLOGIES INC (PA)
11 Bowles Rd (01001-3812)
PHONE..................................413 786-9922
Alan Wosky, *President*
Brian Stefano, *Treasurer*
◆ **EMP:** 38
SQ FT: 22,000
SALES (est): 7.6MM **Privately Held**
WEB: www.belttechnologies.com
SIC: 3568 3535 Mfg Power Transmission Equipment Mfg Conveyors/Equipment

(G-7423)
BEN FRANKLIN DESIGN MFG CO INC
Also Called: Ben Franklin Manufacturing
938 Suffield St (01001-2930)
P.O. Box 502 (01001-0502)
PHONE..................................413 786-4220
Edward Leyden, *President*
EMP: 15
SQ FT: 12,000
SALES: 1.9MM **Privately Held**
WEB: www.benfranklindesign.com
SIC: 3625 3545 Mfg Computer Numerical Control Mfg Precision C&C Machining

(G-7424)
BLOCK JEWELERS INC
299 Walnut St Ste 1 (01001-1468)
PHONE..................................413 789-2940
Gary Block, *President*
Ellen Block, *Principal*
EMP: 5
SQ FT: 6,000
SALES: 700K **Privately Held**
SIC: 3911 5944 Mfg Precious Metal Jewelry Ret Jewelry

(G-7425)
BRIDGEPORT NAT BINDERY INC
662 Silver St (01001-2987)
P.O. Box 289 (01001-0289)
PHONE..................................413 789-1981
James M Larsen, *President*
Bruce F Jacobsen, *Exec VP*
▲ **EMP:** 90
SQ FT: 54,000
SALES (est): 20.4MM **Privately Held**
WEB: www.bnbindery.com
SIC: 2789 Bookbinding/Related Work

(G-7426)
CARANDO GOURMET FOODS CORP (PA)
Also Called: Carando Gourmet Frozen Foods
175 Main St (01001-1870)
PHONE..................................413 737-0183
Michael Carando, *Owner*
Miguel Velez, *Plant Mgr*
Jen Dufour, *Purch Mgr*
Kathleen Carando, *Marketing Staff*
Dino Carando, *Director*
EMP: 30
SQ FT: 15,000
SALES (est): 11.6MM **Privately Held**
SIC: 2013 Mfg Prepared Meats

(G-7427)
DFF CORP
59 Gen Creighto (01001)
P.O. Box 285 (01001-0285)
PHONE..................................413 786-8880
Ernest E Denby, *President*
Michael Getto, *Engineer*
Brian Hersey, *Engineer*
Jim Fish, *Marketing Mgr*
Jeanne Mano, *Manager*
▲ **EMP:** 129
SQ FT: 303,000
SALES: 75MM **Privately Held**
WEB: www.dffcorp.com
SIC: 3824 3545 Mfg Fluid Meter/Counting Devices Mfg Machine Tool Accessories

(G-7428)
DRT AEROSPACE LLC
325 Silver St (01001-2919)
PHONE..................................413 789-1800
Gary Van Gundy, *CEO*
EMP: 40 **Privately Held**
SIC: 3728 Mfg Aircraft Parts/Equipment
HQ: Drt Aerospace, Llc
8694 Rite Track Way
West Chester OH 45069
937 298-7391

(G-7429)
G & L TOOL CORP
952 Suffield St (01001-2930)
P.O. Box 428 (01001-0428)
PHONE..................................413 786-2535
Judith Asselin, *President*
Dave Smith, *Prdtn Mgr*
Doug Rose, *Purchasing*
Leopardi Ray, *Technology*
EMP: 15
SQ FT: 10,000
SALES (est): 2.3MM **Privately Held**
WEB: www.gltool.com
SIC: 3599 Mfg Industrial Machinery

(G-7430)
HAMPDEN FENCE SUPPLY INC
80 Industrial Ln (01001-3634)
P.O. Box 452 (01001-0452)
PHONE..................................413 786-4390
James Crawford, *CEO*
Rudika Ward-Horner, *President*
Lloyd Paro, *Plant Engr*
EMP: 10
SQ FT: 22,400
SALES (est): 2MM **Privately Held**
SIC: 3499 3315 Mfg Misc Fabricated Metal Products Mfg Steel Wire/Related Products

(G-7431)
HP HOOD LLC
233 Main St (01001-1851)
PHONE..................................413 786-2178
Brian Rigali, *Maint Spvr*
Mike Farino, *Branch Mgr*
Alan Distassio, *Director*
Bob Hale, *Maintence Staff*
EMP: 175
SQ FT: 50,000
SALES (corp-wide): 2.2B **Privately Held**
WEB: www.hphood.com
SIC: 2026 2033 Mfg Fluid Milk Mfg Canned Fruits/Vegetables
PA: Hp Hood Llc
6 Kimball Ln Ste 400
Lynnfield MA 01940
617 887-8441

▲ = Import ▼=Export
◆ =Import/Export

(G-7432)
INTERSTATE DESIGN COMPANY INC
84 Gold St (01001-2978)
PHONE..................................413 786-7730
Keith Stone, *President*
EMP: 14
SQ FT: 10,000
SALES (est): 1.1MM **Privately Held**
SIC: 3544 8711 Mfg Dies/Tools/Jigs/Fixtures Engineering Services

(G-7433)
INTERSTATE MANUFACTURING CO
84 Gold St (01001-2978)
PHONE..................................413 789-8674
Keith J Stone, *President*
EMP: 9
SQ FT: 6,000
SALES: 900K **Privately Held**
WEB: www.interstatecorps.com
SIC: 3544 Mfg Dies/Tools/Jigs/Fixtures

(G-7434)
J-K TOOL CO INC
41 Russo Cir (01001-1542)
PHONE..................................413 789-0613
Joseph Kowal, *President*
Christopher J Kowal, *Admin Sec*
EMP: 20
SQ FT: 5,000
SALES (est): 3.4MM **Privately Held**
WEB: www.j-ktool.com
SIC: 3544 Mfg Dies/Tools/Jigs/Fixtures

(G-7435)
JET INDUSTRIES INC
307 Silver St (01001-2919)
P.O. Box 345 (01001-0345)
PHONE..................................413 786-2010
Michael Turrini, *President*
John Turrini, *Corp Secy*
EMP: 50
SQ FT: 22,000
SALES: 15MM **Privately Held**
SIC: 3724 3511 3728 Mfg Aircraft Engines/Parts Mfg Turbines/Generator Sets Mfg Aircraft Parts/Equipment

(G-7436)
JRK PRECISION MACHINE
25 Century St (01001-2001)
PHONE..................................413 789-7200
EMP: 3
SALES (est): 375.7K **Privately Held**
SIC: 3599 Mfg Industrial Machinery

(G-7437)
LITRON LLC
207 Bowles Rd (01001-2964)
PHONE..................................413 789-0700
William Hubbard, *President*
EMP: 66 **EST:** 1997
SQ FT: 23,000
SALES (est): 10.5MM
SALES (corp-wide): 67.1MM **Privately Held**
WEB: www.litron.com
SIC: 3699 Mfg Electrical Equipment/Supplies
PA: Hermetic Solutions Group Inc.
4000 State Route 66 # 310
Tinton Falls NJ 07753
732 722-8780

(G-7438)
LUDLOW TOOL
68 Moylan Ln (01001-4606)
PHONE..................................413 786-6360
Jason Lucas, *Owner*
EMP: 12
SALES (est): 1.4MM **Privately Held**
SIC: 3423 Mfg Hand/Edge Tools

(G-7439)
LUDLOW TOOL CO
46 Moylan Ln (01001-4606)
PHONE..................................413 786-6415
Jason Lucas, *Owner*
EMP: 8
SQ FT: 12,800
SALES (est): 1.1MM **Privately Held**
SIC: 3312 Blast Furnace-Steel Works

(G-7440)
MILLENNIUM PRESS INC
570 Silver St (01001-2924)
PHONE..................................413 821-0028
James E Sullivan, *President*
Kelly Sullivan, *Vice Pres*
Chris Dube, *Manager*
EMP: 21
SQ FT: 11,500
SALES (est): 3.8MM **Privately Held**
WEB: www.millenniumpress.com
SIC: 2752 Lithographic Commercial Printing

(G-7441)
MOREN SIGNS INC
101 Ramah Cir S (01001-1560)
PHONE..................................413 786-0349
Gary Moren, *President*
Colleen Moren, *Corp Secy*
EMP: 4
SQ FT: 3,000
SALES (est): 402.9K **Privately Held**
SIC: 3993 Mfg Signs/Advertising Specialties

(G-7442)
OERLIKON BLZERS CATING USA INC
30 General (01001)
PHONE..................................413 786-9380
Paul Olore, *Manager*
EMP: 50
SALES (corp-wide): 2.6B **Privately Held**
WEB: www.balzers.com
SIC: 3369 Mfg Coat-Titanium Nitrite-Machine Cutting Tools
HQ: Oerlikon Balzers Coating Usa Inc.
1700 E Golf Rd Ste 200
Schaumburg IL 60173
847 619-5541

(G-7443)
OMG INC (DH)
153 Bowles Rd (01001-2908)
PHONE..................................413 789-0252
Hubert T McGovern, *President*
Bob Sullivan, *Regional Mgr*
James F McCabe Jr, *Senior VP*
Michael T Held, *Vice Pres*
Tom Wagner, *Vice Pres*
▲ **EMP:** 280
SQ FT: 58,000
SALES: 42.7MM
SALES (corp-wide): 1.5B **Publicly Held**
WEB: www.olyfast.com
SIC: 3452 3444 2952 3531 Mfg Construction Mach Mfg Bolts/Screws/Rivets Mfg Sheet Metalwork Mfg Asphalt Felt/Coating Mfg Construction Mach
HQ: Handy & Harman
C/O Steel Partners
New York NY 10022
212 520-2300

(G-7444)
OMG INC
95 Bowles Rd (01001-2925)
PHONE..................................413 786-0516
EMP: 155
SQ FT: 24,228
SALES (corp-wide): 1.5B **Publicly Held**
WEB: www.olyfast.com
SIC: 3531 Mfg Construction Machinery
HQ: Omg, Inc.
153 Bowles Rd
Agawam MA 01001
413 789-0252

(G-7445)
PARTS TOOL AND DIE INC
344 Shoemaker Ln (01001-3618)
PHONE..................................413 821-9718
Deborah L Elias, *President*
Aziz Elias, *Treasurer*
EMP: 25
SQ FT: 12,000
SALES (est): 6.8MM **Privately Held**
WEB: www.ptdinc.net
SIC: 3728 3324 3365 3369 Mfg Aircraft Parts/Equip Steel Investment Foundry Aluminum Foundry Nonferrous Metal Foundry Mfg Search/Navgatn Equip

(G-7446)
PLATING SUPPLIES INTL INC
71 Ramah Cir N (01001-1515)
P.O. Box 363 (01001-0363)
PHONE..................................413 786-2020
Normand G Boutin, *President*
Joyce Boutin, *Treasurer*
Erin M Boutin, *Clerk*
EMP: 6
SQ FT: 6,000
SALES (est): 1MM **Privately Held**
WEB: www.platingsupplies.com
SIC: 3569 Mfg General Industrial Machinery

(G-7447)
PRECISE TURNING AND MFG
28 Ramah Cir N (01001-1516)
P.O. Box 428, Westfield (01086-0428)
PHONE..................................413 562-0052
Gary Siedlik, *President*
EMP: 5
SALES (est): 923.1K **Privately Held**
SIC: 3599 Job Machine Shop

(G-7448)
PROS CHOICE INC
Also Called: Lil' Dogs
700 Silver St (01001-2907)
PHONE..................................413 583-3435
Andrew S Boyea Jr, *President*
Glen J Jusczyk, *President*
Pam Boyea, *Director*
EMP: 12
SQ FT: 11,000
SALES: 1.7MM **Privately Held**
WEB: www.lildogs.com
SIC: 2759 Letterpress Printing

(G-7449)
R K SOLUTIONS INC
81 Ramah Cir S Ste 1 (01001-1568)
PHONE..................................413 351-1401
Keith David, *President*
EMP: 5
SALES (est): 609.1K **Privately Held**
SIC: 3444 Mfg Sheet Metalwork

(G-7450)
SANTO C DE SPIRT MARBLE & GRAN
2 S Bridge Dr (01001-2015)
PHONE..................................413 786-7073
Philip S Schoville, *President*
Laura De Spirt, *Corp Secy*
Alicia Horning, *Vice Pres*
EMP: 7
SQ FT: 12,000
SALES (est): 1MM **Privately Held**
SIC: 3281 5999 Mfg Cut Stone/Products Ret Misc Merchandise

(G-7451)
SOUND SEAL HOLDINGS INC (HQ)
50 Hp Almgren Dr (01001-2971)
PHONE..................................413 789-1770
Joe Lupone, *CEO*
EMP: 6
SALES (est): 48.4MM **Privately Held**
SIC: 3229 Manufactures Pressed/Blown Glass

(G-7452)
SSB MANUFACTURING COMPANY
320 Bowles Rd (01001-2968)
PHONE..................................413 789-4410
Geri McCarthy, *Manager*
EMP: 165 **Privately Held**
WEB: www.simmonscompany.com
SIC: 2515 Mfg Mattresses Box Springs
HQ: Ssb Manufacturing Company
1 Concourse Pkwy Ste 800
Atlanta GA 30328
770 512-7700

(G-7453)
SUDDEKOR LLC (DH)
240 Bowles Rd (01001-2963)
PHONE..................................413 821-9000
Michel Ross, *Vice Pres*
Jay Oleksak, *Opers Staff*
Anthony Costa, *Production*
Michael Gilmore, *Production*
Ida Neylon, *Purchasing*
◆ **EMP:** 37
SQ FT: 65,000
SALES (est): 12MM
SALES (corp-wide): 775.1MM **Privately Held**
SIC: 2672 Manufacturing Coated/Laminated Paper
HQ: Surteco North America, Inc.
1175 Harrelson Blvd
Myrtle Beach SC 29577
843 848-3000

(G-7454)
SUN GRO HOLDINGS INC
770 Silver St (01001-2907)
PHONE..................................413 786-4343
Ken Blsbury, *President*
EMP: 800
SALES (est): 79.1MM **Privately Held**
SIC: 2875 5191 Mfg Fertilizers-Mix Only Whol Farm Supplies
HQ: Sun Gro Horticulture Canada Ltd
52130 Range Rd
Seba Beach AB T0E 2
780 797-3019

(G-7455)
SUN GRO HORTICULTURE DIST INC
Also Called: Sun Gro Horticulture Proc
770 Silver St (01001-2907)
PHONE..................................800 732-8667
Daniel Byarley, *General Mgr*
EMP: 30 **Privately Held**
WEB: www.sungro.com
SIC: 1499 2875 Nonmetallic Mineral Mining Mfg Fertilizers-Mix Only
PA: Sun Gro Horticulture Distribution Inc.
770 Silver St
Agawam MA 01001

(G-7456)
WEB DIE CUTTERS ETC INC
265 Main St (01001-1822)
PHONE..................................413 552-3100
Donald Cossette, *President*
▲ **EMP:** 15
SALES (est): 1.7MM **Privately Held**
SIC: 3053 Mfg Specializing In Paper Converting Off Webb

(G-7457)
WYZ MACHINE CO INC
95 Industrial Ln (01001-3635)
P.O. Box 404 (01001-0404)
PHONE..................................413 786-6816
Stephen J Wyzga, *President*
EMP: 10 **EST:** 1978
SQ FT: 2,400
SALES (est): 1.3MM **Privately Held**
SIC: 3599 Mfg Industrial Machinery

Allston
Suffolk County

(G-7458)
3D DIAGNOSTIX INC
Also Called: 3ddx
24 Denby Rd 211 (02134-1606)
PHONE..................................617 820-5279
Khaled Galal Elsaid, *President*
Alex Freeman, *Marketing Mgr*
Kenneth Filipponi, *Manager*
EMP: 4 **EST:** 2005
SALES (est): 510K **Privately Held**
SIC: 3843 Mfg Dental Equipment/Supplies

(G-7459)
73 75 MAGAZINE STREET LLC
1125 Commonwealth Ave (02134-3201)
PHONE..................................617 787-1913
Russell L Peterson, *Principal*
EMP: 3
SALES (est): 167K **Privately Held**
SIC: 2721 Periodicals-Publishing/Printing

(G-7460)
BOUNCE IMAGING INC
114 Western Ave Ste 1 (02134-1016)
PHONE..................................716 310-8281
Francisco Aguilar, *CEO*

GEOGRAPHIC

David Young, *Principal*
Aaron Kent, *CFO*
EMP: 10 **EST:** 2012
SALES (est): 680K **Privately Held**
SIC: 3812 Mfg Search/Navigation Equipment

(G-7461)
CALYX CONTAINERS LLC
500 Lincoln St Ste 2 (02134-1557)
PHONE..................................617 249-6870
Simon Knobel, *President*
EMP: 20
SALES (est): 1.6MM **Privately Held**
SIC: 3221 Mfg Glass Containers

(G-7462)
CORNER WASHERS INC
223 Harvard Ave (02134-4644)
PHONE..................................617 370-0350
Dennis C Woods, *Principal*
EMP: 4 **EST:** 2009
SALES (est): 252.1K **Privately Held**
SIC: 3452 Mfg Bolts/Screws/Rivets

(G-7463)
DAY ZERO DIAGNOSTICS INC
127 Western Ave (02134-1008)
PHONE..................................857 770-1125
Jong Lee, *CEO*
EMP: 3
SALES (est): 154.9K **Privately Held**
SIC: 3826 7389 Mfg Analytical Instruments

(G-7464)
EDITSHARE LLC
119 Braintree St Ste 173 (02134-1628)
PHONE..................................617 782-0479
Paul Hayes, *Business Mgr*
Rich Dangelo, *Sales Dir*
Jeff Barnes, *Sales Staff*
Andrew Liebman,
EMP: 5
SALES (est): 75.6K **Privately Held**
SIC: 3861 Mfg Photographic Equipment/Supplies

(G-7465)
ELEMENT BRAINERD LLC
65 Brainerd Rd (02134-4509)
PHONE..................................617 487-8114
EMP: 3
SALES (est): 242.9K **Privately Held**
SIC: 2819 Industrial Inorganic Chemicals, Nec

(G-7466)
GENZYME CORPORATION
114 Western Ave (02134-1015)
PHONE..................................617 252-7500
Nancy Kelly, *Marketing Staff*
EMP: 93 **Privately Held**
SIC: 2834 Mfg Pharmaceutical Preparations
HQ: Genzyme Corporation
50 Binney St
Cambridge MA 02142
617 252-7500

(G-7467)
HEALERSOURCE
50 Gordon St Ste 2 (02134-5007)
PHONE..................................212 464-7748
Daniel Levin, *Owner*
EMP: 3
SALES: 2.5K **Privately Held**
SIC: 7372 7389 Prepackaged Software

(G-7468)
KS MANUFACTURING INC
9 Sawyer Ter (02134-1803)
PHONE..................................508 427-5727
Tao Dang, *President*
Victor Medeiros, *Vice Pres*
▲ **EMP:** 88
SQ FT: 3,500
SALES: 1.5MM **Privately Held**
WEB: www.ksmfginc.com
SIC: 3841 Mfg Surgical/Medical Instruments

(G-7469)
MAUNA KEA TECHNOLOGIES INC
24 Denby Rd Ste 140 (02134-1606)
PHONE..................................617 657-1550
Chris Tihansky, *President*
Mauna Kea, *Officer*
EMP: 9
SALES (est): 2.5MM
SALES (corp-wide): 9.2MM **Privately Held**
SIC: 3841 Mfg Surgical/Medical Instruments
PA: Mauna Kea Technologies
9 Rue D Enghien
Paris 10e Arrondissement 75010
148 241-168

(G-7470)
MIXX FROZEN YOGURT INC (PA)
66 Brighton Ave (02134-2101)
PHONE..................................617 782-6499
Jimmy Nguyen, *President*
EMP: 15
SQ FT: 1,200
SALES (est): 1.1MM **Privately Held**
SIC: 2024 Mfg Ice Cream/Frozen Desert

(G-7471)
MSP DIGITAL MARKETING
117 Western Ave (02134)
PHONE..................................617 868-5778
Jay Kasaras, *Prdtn Mgr*
Missy Winn, *Accounts Mgr*
EMP: 4 **Privately Held**
WEB: www.tecdocdigital.com
SIC: 2741 Miscellaneous Publishing Services
HQ: Msp Digital Marketing Of Massachusetts, Inc.
399 River Rd
Hudson MA 01749
978 567-6000

(G-7472)
NIX INC
114 Western Ave (02134-1015)
PHONE..................................617 458-9407
Meridith Unger, *CEO*
EMP: 6
SALES (est): 262.2K **Privately Held**
SIC: 3841 3829 Mfg Surgical/Medical Instruments Mfg Measuring/Controlling Devices

(G-7473)
PIKE POWDER COATING LLC
318 Lincoln St (02134-1421)
PHONE..................................617 779-7311
Robert C Spearin Jr, *Principal*
EMP: 4
SALES (est): 396.7K **Privately Held**
SIC: 3479 Coating/Engraving Service

(G-7474)
SALK COMPANY INC
119 Braintree St Ste 701 (02134-1610)
PHONE..................................617 782-4030
Gilbert Salk, *Ch of Bd*
Lawrence H Salk, *President*
Michael Goshko, *Clerk*
EMP: 35 **EST:** 1935
SQ FT: 24,000
SALES (est): 5MM **Privately Held**
WEB: www.salkinc.com
SIC: 3842 2326 Mfg Surgical Appliances/Supplies Mfg Men's/Boy's Work Clothing

(G-7475)
SCHOLASTIC CORPORATION
1200 Soldiers Field Rd # 1 (02134-1021)
PHONE..................................617 924-3846
Richard Robinson, *Branch Mgr*
EMP: 9
SALES (corp-wide): 1.6B **Publicly Held**
SIC: 2741 Misc Publishing
PA: Scholastic Corporation
557 Broadway Lbby 1
New York NY 10012
212 343-6100

Amesbury
Essex County

(G-7476)
AAA ATM SERVICES
25 1st St (01913-2007)
PHONE..................................603 841-5615
Karl Julian, *Owner*
EMP: 3
SALES: 89K **Privately Held**
SIC: 3578 Mfg Calculating Equipment

(G-7477)
AMESBURY FOUNDRY CO
56 Mill St (01913-2900)
PHONE..................................978 388-0830
Claude Gonthier, *Owner*
EMP: 4 **EST:** 1960
SQ FT: 10,000
SALES: 250K **Privately Held**
SIC: 3365 3366 Aluminum Foundry Copper Foundry

(G-7478)
APPLIED GRAPHICS INC
61 S Hunt Rd (01913-4417)
PHONE..................................978 241-5300
Barbara Burnim, *President*
John Lecours, *Project Mgr*
Kay Burnim, *Human Res Mgr*
Darlene Cornin, *Manager*
▲ **EMP:** 47 **EST:** 1975
SQ FT: 33,200
SALES (est): 5.4MM **Privately Held**
WEB: www.appliedgraphics.com
SIC: 3479 2759 Coating/Engraving Service Commercial Printing

(G-7479)
BARTLEY MACHINE & MFG CO INC
35 Water St (01913-2914)
P.O. Box 677 (01913-0677)
PHONE..................................978 388-0085
Richard Bartley Jr, *President*
Sharon Carme, *Principal*
▲ **EMP:** 50 **EST:** 1938
SQ FT: 39,000
SALES (est): 8MM **Privately Held**
WEB: www.bartleym.com
SIC: 3599 Mfg Industrial Machinery

(G-7480)
BLACKBURN ENERGY INC
11 Chestnut St (01913-3024)
PHONE..................................800 342-9194
Andrew J Amigo, *CEO*
Peter Russo, *President*
▼ **EMP:** 5
SALES: 1MM **Privately Held**
SIC: 3694 Mfg Engine Electrical Equipment

(G-7481)
CELGENE CORPORATION
100 Macy St Unit F174 (01913-4315)
PHONE..................................857 225-2309
EMP: 3
SALES (corp-wide): 22.5B **Publicly Held**
SIC: 2834 Mfg Pharmaceutical Preparations
HQ: Celgene Corporation
86 Morris Ave
Summit NJ 07901
908 673-9000

(G-7482)
CODY BREWING COMPANY
36 Main St Ste 4 (01913-2847)
PHONE..................................978 387-4329
Sean W Cody, *Principal*
EMP: 5
SALES (est): 253.8K **Privately Held**
SIC: 2082 Mfg Malt Beverages

(G-7483)
DALTON MANUFACTURING COMPANY
6 Clark St (01913-2521)
P.O. Box 3 (01913-0001)
PHONE..................................978 388-2227
Howard G Dalton, *President*
EMP: 15
SQ FT: 3,600
SALES (est): 2.4MM **Privately Held**
WEB: www.daltonco.com
SIC: 3599 Mfg Industrial Machinery

(G-7484)
DEMARS
3 Essex St (01913-1503)
PHONE..................................978 388-2349
James Demars, *Principal*
EMP: 3
SALES (est): 250.6K **Privately Held**
SIC: 3728 Mfg Aircraft Parts/Equipment

(G-7485)
FLEXAUST INC
10 Industrial Way Ste 2 (01913-3222)
PHONE..................................978 388-1005
Dan Doumani, *Branch Mgr*
EMP: 6
SALES (corp-wide): 216.4MM **Privately Held**
SIC: 3052 Mfg Rubber/Plastic Hose/Belting
HQ: Flexaust Inc
1510 Armstrong Rd
Warsaw IN 46580

(G-7486)
GEORGE DAWE
Also Called: New England Wood Systems
23 Noel St (01913-3630)
P.O. Box 191 (01913-0004)
PHONE..................................978 388-5565
George Dawe, *Owner*
EMP: 5
SQ FT: 5,000
SALES (est): 688.5K **Privately Held**
SIC: 2431 Mfg Millwork

(G-7487)
GOOD TASTE LLC
Also Called: Old Newbury Crafters
36 Main St Ste 2 (01913-2847)
P.O. Box 196 (01913-0004)
PHONE..................................978 388-4026
Peter Dooney, *Mng Member*
EMP: 6
SQ FT: 15,000
SALES (est): 714.3K **Privately Held**
WEB: www.silvercrafters.com
SIC: 3914 Mfg Silverware

(G-7488)
GREENE LYON GROUP INC
18 S Hunt Rd Unit 6 (01913-4404)
PHONE..................................617 290-2276
Dale R Johnson, *President*
John Walshe, *Vice Pres*
Svitlana Grigorenko, *CTO*
EMP: 3
SQ FT: 3,000
SALES: 10MM **Privately Held**
SIC: 3341 Secondary Nonferrous Metal Producer

(G-7489)
HAWKES & HUBERDEAU WOODWORKING
23 Noel St Ste 5 (01913-3628)
PHONE..................................978 388-7747
Nathan Hawkes, *President*
EMP: 7
SALES (est): 500K **Privately Held**
SIC: 2431 Carpentry Contractor

(G-7490)
HGI INCORPORATED
10 Industrial Way (01913-3229)
PHONE..................................978 388-2808
EMP: 7
SALES (est): 887.9K **Privately Held**
SIC: 2819 Mfg Industrial Inorganic Chemicals

(G-7491)
INDEPENDENT PRODUCT SERVICE (PA)
Also Called: Ips
55 Congress St Apt 174 (01913-1955)
PHONE..................................978 352-8887
George Andreadakis, *President*
EMP: 3
SQ FT: 5,600

SALES (est): 314.2K Privately Held
SIC: 3843 Mfg Dental Equipment/Supplies

(G-7492)
INERT CORPORATION
1 Industrial Way (01913-3223)
PHONE..................978 462-4415
Daniel Clay, *President*
Peter Clay, *Chairman*
Charlie Walsh, *Sales Mgr*
Deborah Johnson, *Office Mgr*
Damian Mulligan, *Manager*
▲ EMP: 20
SQ FT: 20,400
SALES: 10MM Privately Held
WEB: www.gloveboxes.com
SIC: 3821 7699 5047 5999 Mfg Lab Apparatus/Furn Repair Services Whol Med/Hospital Equip Ret Misc Merchandise

(G-7493)
LEGACY MACHINE & MFG LLC
43 Clinton St (01913-1234)
PHONE..................978 388-0956
Louis Bartley, *Principal*
EMP: 3
SALES (est): 108.4K Privately Held
SIC: 3599 Mfg Industrial Machinery

(G-7494)
MERRIMAC TOOL COMPANY INC (PA)
91 High St (01913-1440)
PHONE..................978 388-7159
Alan Porter, *President*
▲ EMP: 17
SQ FT: 8,000
SALES (est): 3MM Privately Held
WEB: www.merrimactool.com
SIC: 3599 Machine Shop

(G-7495)
MERRIMAC VLY ALUM BRASS FNDRY
56 Mill St (01913-2900)
PHONE..................978 388-0830
Claude Gonghier, *Owner*
EMP: 4
SALES (est): 260.4K Privately Held
SIC: 3369 Nonferrous Metal Foundry

(G-7496)
MUNTERS CORPORATION
Munters Corp Cargo Care Div
79 Monroe St (01913-3204)
P.O. Box 640 (01913-0640)
PHONE..................978 241-1100
Michael McDonald, *President*
Gail Cassin, *Info Tech Mgr*
EMP: 22
SALES (corp-wide): 749.8MM Privately Held
WEB: www.muntersamerica.com
SIC: 3585 Mfg Refrigeration/Heating Equipment
HQ: Munters Corporation
79 Monroe St
Amesbury MA 01913

(G-7497)
MUNTERS CORPORATION
Also Called: Munters Zeol
79 Monroe St (01913-3204)
PHONE..................978 388-2666
Derrick Drohan, *Manager*
EMP: 10
SALES (corp-wide): 749.8MM Privately Held
WEB: www.muntersamerica.com
SIC: 3585 Mfg Refrigeration/Heating Equipment
HQ: Munters Corporation
79 Monroe St
Amesbury MA 01913

(G-7498)
MUNTERS CORPORATION (DH)
Also Called: Air Treatment Division
79 Monroe St (01913-3204)
PHONE..................978 241-1100
Maj Britt Hallmark, *President*
Camille Camasso, *General Mgr*
Erik Reese, *Regional Mgr*
Kevin Young, *Vice Pres*
Chris Higgins, *Plant Mgr*
▲ EMP: 150
SQ FT: 125,000
SALES (est): 177.9MM
SALES (corp-wide): 749.8MM Privately Held
WEB: www.moisturecontrolservice.com
SIC: 3585 3822 3569 3564 Mfg Refrig/Heat Equip Mfg Environmntl Controls Mfg General Indstl Mach Mfg Blowers/Fans
HQ: Munters Ab
Isafjordsgatan 1
Kista 164 4
862 663-00

(G-7499)
MUNTERS MOISTURE CONTROL SVCS
79 Monroe St (01913-3204)
PHONE..................978 388-4900
Mike Fiebig, *President*
EMP: 3
SALES (est): 343.9K Privately Held
SIC: 2879 Mfg Agricultural Chemicals

(G-7500)
MUNTERS USA INC
Also Called: Munters Cargocaire
79 Monroe St (01913-3204)
PHONE..................978 241-1100
Lennart Lindquist, *President*
William Cain, *Research*
Mario Ranieri, *Engineer*
Mike Herwald, *Regl Sales Mgr*
Cheryl Hughes, *Regl Sales Mgr*
▲ EMP: 700
SALES (est): 82.6MM
SALES (corp-wide): 749.8MM Privately Held
SIC: 3585 Mfg Refrigeration/Heating Equipment
HQ: Munters Ab
Isafjordsgatan 1
Kista 164 4
862 663-00

(G-7501)
NEWBURY PORT MERITOWN SOCIETY
Also Called: Lowell's Boat Shop
459 Main St (01913-4207)
PHONE..................978 834-0050
Malcolm J Odell, *President*
Marjorie R Odell, *Treasurer*
Mark Summers, *Director*
Susan O Hand, *Clerk*
EMP: 3 EST: 1793
SQ FT: 17,000
SALES (est): 230K Privately Held
SIC: 3732 5231 5551 Boatbuilding/Repairing Ret Paint/Glass/Wallpaper Ret Boats

(G-7502)
PARADIGM SPORTS INC
12 Oakland St 5 (01913-3014)
PHONE..................978 687-6687
Eivind Lange, *President*
▲ EMP: 6
SALES (est): 515.2K Privately Held
WEB: www.clubrunnergolf.com
SIC: 3949 Mfg Sporting/Athletic Goods

(G-7503)
QUARTER PRODUCTIONS
3 Hillside Ave (01913-2213)
PHONE..................774 217-8073
EMP: 3
SALES (est): 187.3K Privately Held
SIC: 3131 Footwear Cut Stock

(G-7504)
RAYCO INC
125 Cedar St (01913-1823)
PHONE..................978 388-1039
Raymond Laplant, *President*
EMP: 3
SALES (est): 283.2K Privately Held
SIC: 3441 Structural Metal Fabrication

(G-7505)
RE KIMBALL & CO INC
73 Merrimac St (01913-4097)
PHONE..................978 388-1826
Joy Kimball, *President*
EMP: 7 EST: 1956
SQ FT: 10,000
SALES: 750K Privately Held
SIC: 2033 2035 Mfg Preserves & Relishes Fruit And Vegetable

(G-7506)
SACAR ENTERPRISES LLC
12 Oakland St Ste 220 (01913-3014)
PHONE..................978 834-6494
Sarah Sturtezant, *CEO*
EMP: 4
SALES (est): 158.1K Privately Held
SIC: 2096 Mfg Potato Chips/Snacks

(G-7507)
SHEA CONCRETE PRODUCTS INC (PA)
87 Haverhill Rd (01913-3916)
PHONE..................978 658-2645
Ed Shea, *President*
Judi Shea, *Vice Pres*
Kathleen Shea, *Office Mgr*
Brenda S Stratis, *Admin Sec*
EMP: 50
SALES: 25.4MM Privately Held
WEB: www.sheaconcrete.com
SIC: 3272 Mfg Concrete Products

(G-7508)
SHEA CONCRETE PRODUCTS INC
Also Called: E F Shea Neng Con Pdts I
87 Haverhill Rd (01913-3916)
P.O. Box 807 (01913-0018)
PHONE..................978 388-1509
Gregory Stratis, *Branch Mgr*
EMP: 45
SALES (corp-wide): 25.4MM Privately Held
WEB: www.sheaconcrete.com
SIC: 3272 5211 Mfg Concrete Products Ret Lumber/Building Mtrl
PA: Shea Concrete Products, Inc.
87 Haverhill Rd
Amesbury MA 01913
978 658-2645

(G-7509)
SPECIALTY MANUFACTURING INC
Also Called: SMI Podwer Coating
40 Water St (01913-2915)
PHONE..................978 388-1601
James Bartley, *President*
EMP: 20
SALES (est): 3.2MM Privately Held
WEB: www.smipowder.com
SIC: 3599 2759 2396 Mfg Industrial Machinery Commercial Printing Mfg Auto/Apparel Trimming

(G-7510)
VALIANT INDUSTRIES INC
12 Merrill Ave (01913-2220)
P.O. Box 540 (01913-0012)
PHONE..................978 388-3792
Charles Little, *President*
Eric Danis, *Vice Pres*
▲ EMP: 20
SQ FT: 26,000
SALES (est): 3.6MM Privately Held
SIC: 2431 2541 Mfg Millwork Mfg Wood Partitions/Fixtures

Amherst
Hampshire County

(G-7511)
AMHERST BREWING CO INC
36 N Pleasant St (01002)
PHONE..................413 253-4400
John Korpita, *President*
Mark Parent, *Vice Pres*
Jake Bishop, *Treasurer*
EMP: 45
SQ FT: 6,000
SALES (est): 5.9MM Privately Held
WEB: www.amherstbrewing.com
SIC: 2082 5812 5813 Mfg Malt Beverages Eating Place Drinking Place

(G-7512)
AMHERST COLLEGE PUBLIC AFFAIRS
306 Converse Hl (01002)
PHONE..................413 542-2321
Stacey Schmeidel, *Director*
EMP: 12
SALES (est): 510.6K Privately Held
SIC: 2711 Newspapers-Publishing/Printing

(G-7513)
AMHERST MACHINE CO
16 Cowls Rd (01002-1014)
P.O. Box 9507 (01059-9507)
PHONE..................413 549-4551
James Bernotas, *Owner*
EMP: 11
SQ FT: 3,200
SALES: 750K Privately Held
WEB: www.amherstmachine.com
SIC: 3541 3544 Mfg Machine Tools-Cutting Mfg Dies/Tools/Jigs/Fixtures

(G-7514)
COW TOWN PRODUCTIONS INC
233 N Pleasant St (01002-1737)
PHONE..................413 259-1350
Bill Rowhan, *Owner*
EMP: 7
SALES (est): 485.2K Privately Held
WEB: www.cowtownproductions.com
SIC: 7372 Prepackaged Software Services

(G-7515)
G B ENTERPRISES
82 Spring St (01002-2332)
PHONE..................413 210-4658
Gary Beaudry, *Owner*
Susan Beaudry, *Business Mgr*
EMP: 3
SQ FT: 4,000
SALES: 350K Privately Held
SIC: 2759 2752 Commercial Printing Lithographic Commercial Printing

(G-7516)
JOURNAL COMPUTING IN HIGHER
127 Sunset Ave (01002-2019)
PHONE..................413 549-5150
Carol McKnight, *Owner*
EMP: 3
SALES (est): 99.4K Privately Held
SIC: 2711 2721 Newspapers-Publishing/Printing Periodicals-Publishing/Printing

(G-7517)
LIFESTYLE HQ LLC
Also Called: Lhq Bicycle Components
158 High Point Dr (01002-1259)
PHONE..................310 741-8489
Andrew J Rufe,
EMP: 3
SALES (est): 180K Privately Held
SIC: 3751 Mfg Motorcycles/Bicycles

(G-7518)
MASSACHUSETTS REVIEW INC
Also Called: MASSACHUSETTS REVIEW, THE
211 Hicks Way (01003-9371)
PHONE..................413 545-2689
Jim Hicks, *President*
Neal Abraham, *Principal*
Nigel Alderman, *Principal*
Lisa Brooks, *Principal*
Frank Couvares, *Principal*
EMP: 20
SALES: 134.6K Privately Held
SIC: 2721 Periodicals-Publishing/Printing

(G-7519)
MILLIMETER WAVE SYSTEMS LLC
9 Research Dr Ste 8 (01002-2775)
PHONE..................413 345-6467
Michael Marcus, *General Mgr*
Brenda Mangels, *Mng Member*
EMP: 4 EST: 2016
SALES: 400K Privately Held
SIC: 3829 Mfg Measuring/Controlling Devices

(G-7520)
NEXTCHAR LLC
99 Pulpit Hill Rd (01002-1031)
PHONE..................................877 582-1825
Keegan Pyle, *President*
Stephan Rogers, *President*
Tom Horton, *Principal*
EMP: 3 **EST:** 2015
SALES (est): 178.7K **Privately Held**
SIC: 3624 Carbon And Graphite Products

(G-7521)
PEDIPRESS INC
301 Spencer Dr (01002-3366)
PHONE..................................413 549-3918
Thomas F Plaut, *President*
Johanna Plaut, *General Mgr*
EMP: 4
SALES: 250K **Privately Held**
WEB: www.pedipress.com
SIC: 2731 Books-Publishing/Printing

(G-7522)
PROSENSING INC
107 Sunderland Rd (01002-1098)
PHONE..................................413 549-4402
James B Mead, *President*
Sandy Breiner, *Purchasing*
Craig Addis, *Engineer*
Geoff Lee, *Engineer*
Andrew Pazmany, *CFO*
▼ **EMP:** 15
SQ FT: 5,500
SALES (est): 3.3MM **Privately Held**
WEB: www.prosensing.com
SIC: 3812 Mfg Search/Navigation Equipment

(G-7523)
QTEROS LLC
99 Pulpit Hill Rd (01002-1031)
PHONE..................................413 531-6884
Judy Giordan, *Vice Pres*
EMP: 3
SALES (est): 176.8K **Privately Held**
SIC: 2835 Mfg Diagnostic Substances

(G-7524)
SAXSLAB US INC
7 Pomeroy Ln Ste 3 (01002-2971)
PHONE..................................413 237-4309
Karsten Joensen, *President*
Soren Skou, *Director*
EMP: 3
SALES (est): 525.1K **Privately Held**
SIC: 3844 Mfg X-Ray Apparatus/Tubes

(G-7525)
SEVEN MIST LLC
1040 N Pleasant St (01002-1374)
PHONE..................................413 210-7255
Yu Lei,
EMP: 3
SALES (est): 121.7K **Privately Held**
SIC: 3052 Mfg Rubber/Plastic Hose/Belting

(G-7526)
SHERWOOD TRUNKS
85 Mount Holyoke Dr (01002-2921)
PHONE..................................413 687-3167
Kaye Dougan, *Principal*
EMP: 3
SALES (est): 359.1K **Privately Held**
SIC: 3161 Mfg Luggage

(G-7527)
THERMO FISHER SCIENTIFIC INC
710 N Pleasant St (01003-9305)
PHONE..................................413 577-2600
Dennis Glick, *Principal*
EMP: 307
SALES (corp-wide): 24.3B **Publicly Held**
SIC: 3826 Mfg Analytical Instruments And Laboratory Products And Services
PA: Thermo Fisher Scientific Inc.
168 3rd Ave
Waltham MA 02451
781 622-1000

(G-7528)
UNIVERSITY MASSACHUSETTS INC
University Massachusetts Press
671 N Pleasant St (01003-9301)
PHONE..................................413 545-2217
Brice Wilcox, *Director*
EMP: 15
SALES (corp-wide): 2.4B **Privately Held**
WEB: www.umassp.edu
SIC: 2741 8221 Misc Publishing College/University
PA: University Of Massachusetts
1 Beacon St
Boston MA 02108
617 287-7000

(G-7529)
UNIVERSITY MASSACHUSETTS INC
Also Called: Umass Extention Book Store
40 Campus Center Way (01003-9244)
PHONE..................................413 545-2682
Nathaniel Schildbach, *General Mgr*
Augusta Mfuko, *Treasurer*
EMP: 3
SALES (corp-wide): 2.4B **Privately Held**
WEB: www.umassp.edu
SIC: 2711 8221 Newspapers-Publishing/Printing College/University
PA: University Of Massachusetts
1 Beacon St
Boston MA 02108
617 287-7000

(G-7530)
UNIVERSITY OF MASSACHUSETTS
Also Called: Massachusetts Daily Collegian
113 Campus Ctr (01003)
PHONE..................................413 545-3500
Maureen Majerowski, *Manager*
EMP: 82
SALES (corp-wide): 2.4B **Privately Held**
WEB: www.umassp.edu
SIC: 2711 2741 Newspapers-Publishing/Printing Misc Publishing
PA: University Of Massachusetts
1 Beacon St
Boston MA 02108
617 287-7000

(G-7531)
UNIVERSITY OF MASSACHUSETTS
Also Called: Printing Services
151 Whitmore University F Flr 1 (01003)
PHONE..................................413 545-2718
Betty Norton, *Manager*
EMP: 13
SALES (corp-wide): 2.4B **Privately Held**
WEB: www.umassp.edu
SIC: 2759 8221 Commercial Printing College/University
PA: University Of Massachusetts
1 Beacon St
Boston MA 02108
617 287-7000

Andover
Essex County

(G-7532)
ACEINNA INC
1 Tech Dr Ste 325 (01810-2452)
PHONE..................................978 965-3200
Yang Zhao, *CEO*
Patricia Niu, *CFO*
Mike Horton, *CTO*
Melissa Locastro, *Admin Sec*
EMP: 20
SQ FT: 8,799
SALES (est): 2.5MM **Privately Held**
SIC: 3674 Mfg Semiconductors/Related Devices

(G-7533)
AERTEC
11 Bartlet St (01810-3655)
P.O. Box 488, North Andover (01845-0488)
PHONE..................................978 475-6385
EMP: 4
SALES (est): 406.4K **Privately Held**
SIC: 3589 Mfg Service Industry Machinery

(G-7534)
AGILENT TECHNOLOGIES INC
40 Shattuck Rd Ste 201 (01810-2455)
PHONE..................................978 794-3664
Carl Witonsky, *Branch Mgr*
EMP: 3275
SALES (corp-wide): 5.1B **Publicly Held**
SIC: 3825 Mfr Electronic
PA: Agilent Technologies, Inc.
5301 Stevens Creek Blvd
Santa Clara CA 95051
408 345-8886

(G-7535)
AGRI-MARK INC (PA)
Also Called: Cabot Creamery
40 Shattuck Rd Ste 301 (01810-2456)
PHONE..................................978 552-5500
Paul P Johnston, *President*
Mike Barnes, *Principal*
Ed Townley, *COO*
Dr Richard Stammer, *Exec VP*
Margaret H Bertolino, *Senior VP*
◆ **EMP:** 64
SQ FT: 28,000
SALES (est): 382MM **Privately Held**
WEB: www.agrimark.net
SIC: 2026 2022 Mfg Fluid Milk Mfg Cheese

(G-7536)
ALFRED J CAVALLARO INC
470 S Main St (01810-6121)
PHONE..................................978 475-2466
Alfred J Cavallaro, *President*
Mary Cavallaro, *Corp Secy*
EMP: 3
SALES (est): 210K **Privately Held**
SIC: 2499 5032 5261 5083 Mfg Wood Products Whol Brick/Stone Matrls Ret Nursery/Garden Supp Whol Farm/Garden Mach Lawn/Garden Services

(G-7537)
AMASA TECHNOLOGIES INC
1 Harmony Ln (01810-4420)
PHONE..................................617 899-8223
Sabba Shah, *General Mgr*
Khalid Shah, *Director*
EMP: 4
SALES (est): 247.7K **Privately Held**
SIC: 2835 Diagnostic Substances, Nsk

(G-7538)
AURORA WIND PROJECT LLC
100 Brdgestone Sq Ste 300 (01810)
PHONE..................................978 409-9712
Steve Hickey,
EMP: 25
SALES (est): 899.6K **Privately Held**
SIC: 3621 Mfg Motors/Generators

(G-7539)
BECTON DICKINSON AND COMPANY
200 Bulfinch Dr Ste 1 (01810-1140)
PHONE..................................978 901-7319
Lyn Jackson, *Branch Mgr*
EMP: 100
SALES (corp-wide): 15.9B **Publicly Held**
SIC: 3841 Mfg Surgical/Medical Instruments
PA: Becton, Dickinson And Company
1 Becton Dr
Franklin Lakes NJ 07417
201 847-6800

(G-7540)
BEYONDTRUST SOFTWARE INC
Also Called: Lumigent Technologies
200 Brickstone Sq Ste G03 (01810-1439)
PHONE..................................978 206-3700
Robert Sommers, *Ch of Bd*
EMP: 15
SALES (corp-wide): 57.1MM **Privately Held**
SIC: 7372 5734 Prepackaged Software Services Ret Computers/Software
PA: Beyondtrust Software, Inc.
5090 N 40th St Ste 400
Phoenix AZ 85018
623 455-6499

(G-7541)
BLUBOX SECURITY INC
9 Bartlet St Ste 334 (01810-3655)
PHONE..................................508 414-3517
Sean Dyer, *President*
Simon Goldshmid, *Vice Pres*
Patrick J Barry, *Treasurer*
EMP: 6
SALES (est): 110.1K **Privately Held**
SIC: 7372 Prepackaged Software Services Prepackaged Software Services

(G-7542)
BODYCOTE IMT INC (DH)
Also Called: Bodycote Hot Isostatic Prsg
155 River St (01810-5923)
PHONE..................................978 470-0876
Jody Turin, *President*
Stephanie Edgar, *Corp Secy*
Yale Curtis, *Vice Pres*
David Landless, *Vice Pres*
Edmond J Tenerini, *Vice Pres*
▲ **EMP:** 57
SQ FT: 63,000
SALES (est): 23MM
SALES (corp-wide): 960MM **Privately Held**
WEB: www.bodycote.com
SIC: 3398 3269 Metal Heat Treating Mfg Pottery Products
HQ: Bodycote Usa, Inc.
12700 Park Central Dr # 700
Dallas TX 75251
214 904-2420

(G-7543)
BROADCOM CORPORATION
200 Brickstone Sq Ste 401 (01810-1429)
PHONE..................................978 719-1300
Doug Grearson, *President*
Al Cooper, *Software Engr*
Darren Elkerton, *Software Engr*
Sylvain Lauzon, *Software Engr*
David Partridge, *Software Engr*
EMP: 97
SALES (corp-wide): 22.6B **Publicly Held**
SIC: 3674 Mfg Semiconductors/Related Devices
HQ: Broadcom Corporation
1320 Ridder Park Dr
San Jose CA 95131

(G-7544)
CASA SYSTEMS INC (PA)
100 Old River Rd Ste 100 # 100 (01810-1030)
PHONE..................................978 688-6706
Jerry Guo, *Ch of Bd*
Joanne Torla, *Business Mgr*
Lucy Xie, *Senior VP*
Scott Bruckner, *Vice Pres*
Chuck Crannell, *Engineer*
▲ **EMP:** 153
SQ FT: 122,000
SALES: 297.1MM **Publicly Held**
WEB: www.casa-systems.com
SIC: 3663 Mfg Radio/Tv Communication Equipment

(G-7545)
DRAEGER MEDICAL SYSTEMS INC
6 Tech Dr (01810-2434)
PHONE..................................800 437-2437
Stefan Drager, *Ch of Bd*
Dennis Hering, *Opers Staff*
Bill Nicholson, *Opers Staff*
Candice Mackeen, *Buyer*
Kristen Kane, *Engineer*
▲ **EMP:** 140
SQ FT: 80,000
SALES (est): 38.2MM
SALES (corp-wide): 177.9K **Privately Held**
SIC: 3841 Mfg Surgical/Medical Instruments
HQ: Draeger, Inc.
3135 Quarry Rd
Telford PA 18969
215 721-5400

(G-7546)
EIKON CORPORATION
300 Brickstone Sq Ste 201 (01810-1497)
PHONE..................................978 662-5200

▲ = Import ▼=Export
◆ =Import/Export

Jeffrey Warming, *CEO*
Robert Postle, *Vice Pres*
Peter Rothschild, *Vice Pres*
EMP: 5
SQ FT: 400
SALES (est): 216K **Privately Held**
SIC: 3699 Electrical Equipment And Supplies, Nec

(G-7547)
ESMAIL RIYAZ
3 Cloverfield Dr (01810-2417)
PHONE..................................978 689-3837
Riyaz Esmail, *President*
EMP: 5
SALES (est): 641.8K **Privately Held**
SIC: 3679 5065 Mfg Electronic Components Whol Electronic Parts/Equipment

(G-7548)
FIBERLOCK TECHNOLOGIES INC
150 Dascomb Rd (01810-5873)
PHONE..................................978 623-9987
Joseph E Connor, *President*
Scott Deleo, *Vice Pres*
Meghan Parisi, *Opers Mgr*
John Alvarez, *Regl Sales Mgr*
EMP: 10
SQ FT: 3,000
SALES (est): 2.2MM
SALES (corp-wide): 145.8MM **Privately Held**
WEB: www.calprocorp.com
SIC: 3826 2819 Mfg Analytical Instruments Mfg Industrial Inorganic Chemicals
HQ: Icp Construction, Inc.
150 Dascomb Rd
Andover MA 01810
978 623-9980

(G-7549)
FISHMAN TRANSDUCERS INC
3 Riverside Dr Ste 1 (01810-1141)
PHONE..................................978 988-9199
Lawrence Fishman, *President*
Gary Lopez, *Business Mgr*
Bob Valyou, *Business Mgr*
Rob Ketch, *Vice Pres*
Mike Hoffer, *Purch Mgr*
▲ **EMP:** 64
SALES (est): 25MM **Privately Held**
WEB: www.fishman.com
SIC: 3825 3931 3651 Mfg Electrical Measuring Instruments Mfg Musical Instruments Mfg Home Audio/Video Equipment

(G-7550)
GENLYTE GROUP INCORPORATED
Also Called: Glyt
3000 Minuteman Rd (01810-1032)
PHONE..................................781 418-7900
Larry K Powers, *President*
Hans Van Wijngaarde, *Business Mgr*
Zia Eftekhar, *Vice Pres*
William G Ferko, *CFO*
Raymond L Zaccagnini, *Administration*
◆ **EMP:** 5000
SQ FT: 230,573
SALES (est): 228.8MM
SALES (corp-wide): 7B **Privately Held**
WEB: www.genlyte.com
SIC: 3646 3645 3648 Mfg Commercial Lighting Fixtures Mfg Residential Lighting Fixtures Mfg Lighting Equipment
PA: Signify N.V.
High Tech Campus 48
Eindhoven

(G-7551)
GENLYTE THOMAS GROUP LLC
Also Called: GENLYTE THOMAS GROUP LLC
200 Minuteman Rd Ste 205 (01810-1046)
PHONE..................................978 659-3732
Michael Manning, *Legal Staff*
EMP: 159
SALES (corp-wide): 7B **Privately Held**
SIC: 3645 3648 3646 Mfg Residentl Light Fixt
HQ: Genlyte Thomas Group Llc
200 Franklin Square Dr
Somerset NJ 08873

(G-7552)
GILLETTE COMPANY
30 Burtt Rd (01810-5989)
PHONE..................................781 662-9600
Patrick Ladd, *Plant Mgr*
EMP: 650
SALES (corp-wide): 67.6B **Publicly Held**
WEB: www.gillette.com
SIC: 3421 2844 3951 2899 Mfg Cutlery
HQ: The Gillette Company
1 Gillette Park
Boston MA 02127
617 421-7000

(G-7553)
GREATHEART INC
Also Called: Real Estate Guide
89 N Main St Ste 3 (01810-3581)
P.O. Box 999 (01810-0017)
PHONE..................................978 475-8732
Robert Finlayson, *President*
Muriel Finlayson, *Vice Pres*
Richard Finlayson, *Clerk*
EMP: 3
SQ FT: 1,500
SALES (est): 195K **Privately Held**
SIC: 2741 6531 Misc Publishing Real Estate Agent/Manager

(G-7554)
GWB CORPORATION
Also Called: Venture Publishing
9 Bartlet St Ste 55 (01810-3655)
PHONE..................................508 896-9486
Helen Best, *President*
George Best, *Executive*
▲ **EMP:** 4
SQ FT: 2,000
SALES: 500K **Privately Held**
WEB: www.vent-pub.com
SIC: 2731 Books-Publishing/Printing

(G-7555)
HARRIS ENVMTL SYSTEMS INC
11 Connector Rd (01810-5926)
PHONE..................................978 470-8600
Yury Zlobinsky, *CEO*
Alexander Murray, *President*
Richard Haley, *Engineer*
Chris Wentworth, *CFO*
EMP: 90 **EST:** 1940
SQ FT: 42,000
SALES (est): 21.9MM **Privately Held**
WEB: www.harrisenv.com
SIC: 3585 Mfg Refrig/Heat Equip

(G-7556)
ICP CONSTRUCTION INC (HQ)
150 Dascomb Rd (01810-5873)
PHONE..................................978 623-9980
Peter Longo, *CEO*
Zain Mahmood, *President*
Joseph Deangelis, *Exec VP*
Mark Longo, *Exec VP*
David G Lohr, *Senior VP*
◆ **EMP:** 115
SQ FT: 168,000
SALES (est): 73.7MM
SALES (corp-wide): 145.8MM **Privately Held**
WEB: www.calprocorp.com
SIC: 2851 Mfg Paints/Allied Products
PA: Innovative Chemical Products Group, Llc
150 Dascomb Rd
Andover MA 01810
978 623-9980

(G-7557)
ICP CONSTRUCTION INC
Plexipave Sport Surfacing
150 Dascomb Rd (01810-5873)
PHONE..................................508 829-0035
Zain Mahmoob, *President*
EMP: 4
SALES (corp-wide): 145.8MM **Privately Held**
SIC: 2273 Mfg Carpets/Rugs
HQ: Icp Construction, Inc.
150 Dascomb Rd
Andover MA 01810
978 623-9980

(G-7558)
INNOVATIVE CHEM PDTS GROUP LLC (PA)
Also Called: ICP Group
150 Dascomb Rd (01810-5873)
PHONE..................................978 623-9980
Doug Mattscheck, *President*
Jim Qian, *Vice Pres*
EMP: 31
SALES (est): 145.8MM **Privately Held**
SIC: 2891 8742 Manufacturing And Marketing Of Coatings And Adhesives

(G-7559)
JGP ENTERPRISES INC
Also Called: Biopharm Engineered Systems
200 Bulfinch Dr Ste 160 (01810-1149)
PHONE..................................978 691-2737
Paul A Brouillette, *President*
EMP: 20
SALES (est): 5.3MM **Privately Held**
WEB: www.bpesys.com
SIC: 3559 Mfg Misc Industry Machinery

(G-7560)
JULIE INDUSTRIES INC (PA)
Also Called: Staticsmart Flooring
2 Dundee Park Dr Ste 302a (01810-3725)
P.O. Box 153, North Reading (01864-0153)
PHONE..................................978 276-0820
Jerry M Giuliano, *President*
Ann Neely, *Credit Mgr*
▼ **EMP:** 8
SALES (est): 1.4MM **Privately Held**
WEB: www.julieind.com
SIC: 2273 Mfg Carpets/Rugs

(G-7561)
KEYSIGHT TECHNOLOGIES INC
40 Shattuck Rd (01810-2459)
PHONE..................................800 829-4444
EMP: 3
SALES (est): 138.7K **Privately Held**
SIC: 3825 Instruments To Measure Electricity

(G-7562)
KINGSLIDE USA INC
16 Haverhill St (01810-3002)
PHONE..................................978 475-0120
C T Lin, *President*
Willis Chen, *Treasurer*
T M Lin, *Shareholder*
Jean Chen, *Clerk*
EMP: 6
SQ FT: 900
SALES (est): 405.4K **Privately Held**
SIC: 3429 Mfg Hardware

(G-7563)
KPM TECHNOLOGIES INC
77 Main St (01810-3845)
PHONE..................................617 721-8770
Chris Riffe, *Vice Pres*
EMP: 6 **EST:** 2011
SALES (est): 286.1K **Privately Held**
SIC: 7372 Prepackaged Software Services

(G-7564)
LANDMARK FINISH INC
12 Dundee Park Dr (01810-3743)
PHONE..................................978 470-2040
Stewart Junge, *President*
EMP: 6
SALES (est): 665.5K **Privately Held**
SIC: 2434 Mfg Wood Kitchen Cabinets

(G-7565)
LATTIX INC
8 Harper Cir (01810-2300)
PHONE..................................978 474-4332
Neeraj Sangal, *President*
EMP: 6
SALES (corp-wide): 1.2MM **Privately Held**
WEB: www.lattix.com
SIC: 7372 Prepackaged Software Services
PA: Lattix, Inc.
352 Park St Ste 203w
North Reading MA 01864
978 664-5050

(G-7566)
LZJ HOLDINGS INC
3 Dundee Park Dr Ste B06 (01810-3723)
PHONE..................................978 409-1091
Laura Beohner, *President*
EMP: 4
SALES (est): 125.1K **Privately Held**
SIC: 3999 Mfg Misc Products

(G-7567)
MALCOM CO-LEISTER ✪
25 Abbot St (01810-4003)
PHONE..................................781 875-3121
EMP: 8 **EST:** 2019
SALES (est): 88.7K **Privately Held**
SIC: 7692 Welding Repair

(G-7568)
MATERIALS DEVELOPMENT CORP
10 Lowell Junction Rd (01810-5906)
PHONE..................................781 391-0400
Paul Doherty, *President*
Christopher E Cataldo, *Principal*
Mackenzie Martin, *QC Mgr*
Chris Cataldo, *CFO*
Craig Fallon, *Sales Executive*
EMP: 17
SQ FT: 25,000
SALES (est): 4.2MM
SALES (corp-wide): 4.4MM **Privately Held**
WEB: www.materialsdevelopment.com
SIC: 3398 3724 Metal Heat Treating Mfg Aircraft Engines/Parts
PA: Consolidated Investors Corporation
10 Lowell Junction Rd
Andover MA 01810
781 391-0400

(G-7569)
MEMSIC INC (HQ)
1 Tech Dr Ste 325 (01810-2452)
PHONE..................................978 738-0900
Yang Zhao PHD, *President*
Paul M Zavracky PHD, *President*
Patricia Niu, *CFO*
▲ **EMP:** 3 **EST:** 1999
SALES (est): 907.2K **Privately Held**
WEB: www.memsic.com
SIC: 3674 Mfg Semiconductors/Related Devices

(G-7570)
MERCURY SYSTEMS INC (PA)
50 Minuteman Rd (01810-1008)
PHONE..................................978 256-1300
Vincent Vitto, *Ch of Bd*
Mark Aslett, *President*
Didier M C Thibaud, *COO*
Christopher C Cambria, *Exec VP*
Christopher Cambria, *Exec VP*
▼ **EMP:** 211
SQ FT: 145,262
SALES: 654.7MM **Publicly Held**
WEB: www.mc.com
SIC: 3672 7372 Mfg Computer Systems & Software

(G-7571)
MINDGRAPH MEDICAL INC
11 Pipers Gln (01810-2334)
PHONE..................................508 904-2563
Navin Dewagan, *CEO*
EMP: 3
SALES (est): 205.2K **Privately Held**
SIC: 3841 Mfg Surgical/Medical Instruments

(G-7572)
MIOE INC
300 Brickstone Sq (01810-1492)
PHONE..................................978 494-9460
Geoff Taylor, *President*
EMP: 3
SALES (est): 125.7K **Privately Held**
SIC: 3679 Mfg Electronic Components

(G-7573)
MITTON MILLWORKS
53 Gould Rd (01810-5210)
PHONE..................................978 475-7761
EMP: 4
SALES (est): 310K **Privately Held**
SIC: 2431 Mfg Millwork

(G-7574)
MKS INSTRUMENTS INC (PA)
Also Called: M K S
2 Tech Dr Ste 201 (01810-2489)
PHONE....................................978 645-5500
Gerald G Colella, *CEO*
John Tc Lee, *President*
James A Schreiner, *COO*
Renee Donlan, *Counsel*
John R Abrams, *Senior VP*
◆ **EMP:** 350 **EST:** 1961
SQ FT: 158,000
SALES: 2B **Publicly Held**
WEB: www.mksinst.com
SIC: 3823 3491 3494 Mfg Instrument & Control Systems Power & Reactive Gas Products & Vacuum Products

(G-7575)
MKS INSTRUMENTS INC
6 Shattuck Rd (01810-2449)
PHONE....................................978 645-5500
John Hanzelka, *Engineer*
Philip Maiorana, *Engineer*
Jim Patrikis, *Engineer*
Kalin Jafferji, *Controller*
Kathleen F Burke, *Manager*
EMP: 20
SALES (corp-wide): 2B **Publicly Held**
WEB: www.mksinst.com
SIC: 3823 3491 3494 Mfg Process Control Instruments Mfg Industrial Valves Mfg Valves/Pipe Fittings
PA: Mks Instruments, Inc.
2 Tech Dr Ste 201
Andover MA 01810
978 645-5500

(G-7576)
MKS INSTRUMENTS INC
6 Shattuck Rd (01810-2449)
PHONE....................................978 738-3721
EMP: 20
SALES (corp-wide): 780.8MM **Publicly Held**
SIC: 3823 Mfg Process Control Instruments
PA: Mks Instruments, Inc.
2 Tech Dr Ste 201
Andover MA 01810
978 645-5500

(G-7577)
NORTHEAST DOCUMENT CONSERVATIO
100 Brickstone Sq Ste 401 (01810-1428)
PHONE....................................978 470-1010
Michael Comeau, *Ch of Bd*
Rob Maier, *Treasurer*
William Veillette, *Exec Dir*
Daria D'Arienzo, *Admin Sec*
EMP: 40
SQ FT: 20,000
SALES: 4.6MM **Privately Held**
WEB: www.rap-arcc.org
SIC: 2789 7334 2631 Bookbinding/Related Work Photocopying Services Paperboard Mill

(G-7578)
NORTHROP GRUMMAN SYSTEMS CORP
Also Called: Northrop Grumman Info Systems
100 Brickstone Sq Ste G03 (01810-1441)
PHONE....................................978 247-7812
EMP: 6 **Publicly Held**
SIC: 3812 Mfg Search/Navigation Equipment
HQ: Northrop Grumman Systems Corporation
2980 Fairview Park Dr
Falls Church VA 22042
703 280-2900

(G-7579)
NSIGHT INC
Also Called: Cohesion
300 Brickstone Sq Ste 201 (01810-1497)
PHONE....................................781 273-6300
John Owens, *President*
John Larson, *President*
Tess Kastning, *Exec VP*
EMP: 35
SQ FT: 5,400
SALES (est): 3.9MM **Privately Held**
WEB: www.nsightworks.com
SIC: 2731 7338 7363 8748 Book-Publishing/Printing Secy/Court Reporting Svc Help Supply Service Business Consulting Svcs

(G-7580)
PAKPRO INC
11 W Knoll Rd (01810-5015)
PHONE....................................978 474-5018
Susan Wang, *President*
Morris Wang, *Vice Pres*
Gillian Wang, *Sales Mgr*
▲ **EMP:** 4
SALES (est): 652.6K **Privately Held**
SIC: 2673 5113 Manufactures Bags-Plastic & Coated Paper Wholesales Industrial & Service Paper

(G-7581)
PFIZER INC
1 Burtt Rd (01810-5901)
PHONE....................................978 247-1000
Peter Mayhew, *Safety Mgr*
Andrew Duffty, *Maint Spvr*
Joseph Manning, *Mfg Staff*
Isabelle Ricard, *QC Mgr*
Boris Gorovits, *Research*
EMP: 146
SALES (corp-wide): 53.6B **Publicly Held**
SIC: 2834 Mfg Pharmaceutical Preparations
PA: Pfizer Inc.
235 E 42nd St Rm 107
New York NY 10017
212 733-2323

(G-7582)
PHILIPS HOLDING USA INC (HQ)
Also Called: Philips Consumer Lifestyle
3000 Minuteman Rd Ste 109 (01810-1032)
PHONE....................................978 687-1501
Brent Shafer, *CEO*
Hitesh Bhagat, *Production*
Nolan Billy, *Manager*
Wick Thijssen, *Manager*
◆ **EMP:** 209
SQ FT: 100,000
SALES (est): 7.6B
SALES (corp-wide): 20.1B **Privately Held**
SIC: 3674 5045 5047 3641 Mfg Semiconductors/Dvcs Whol Computer/Peripheral Whol Med/Hospital Equip
PA: Koninklijke Philips N.V.
High Tech Campus 5
Eindhoven 5656
402 791-111

(G-7583)
PHILIPS MEDICAL SYSTEMS HSG (PA)
3000 Minuteman Rd (01810-1032)
PHONE....................................978 687-1501
Jorod Klesterkei, *President*
Ron Wirahadiraksa, *CFO*
◆ **EMP:** 36
SALES (est): 221.3MM **Privately Held**
SIC: 3675 3676 Mfg Electronic Capacitors Mfg Electronic Resistors

(G-7584)
PITMAN AN AGFA COMPANY
160 Dascomb Rd (01810-0044)
PHONE....................................800 526-5441
EMP: 4 **EST:** 2012
SALES (est): 452.8K **Privately Held**
SIC: 3825 Instruments To Measure Electricity

(G-7585)
POLARTEC LLC (PA)
300 Brickstone Sq Ste 401 (01810-1497)
PHONE....................................978 659-5109
Gary Smith, *CEO*
Steven Stott, *Division Mgr*
Doug Kelliher, *Vice Pres*
Kyrie Rivera, *Purch Mgr*
Julie Riddle, *Buyer*
◆ **EMP:** 600
SQ FT: 60,000
SALES (est): 230.1MM **Privately Held**
WEB: www.maldenmills.com
SIC: 2299 Mfg Textile Goods

(G-7586)
POLYCOM INC
600 Federal St Ste 1 (01810-1065)
PHONE....................................978 292-5000
John Lisien, *Opers Mgr*
Jeff Askew, *Engineer*
Rommel Childress, *Engineer*
Jay Parikh, *Engineer*
Matthew Pierce, *Engineer*
EMP: 20
SALES (corp-wide): 1.6B **Publicly Held**
WEB: www.polycom.com
SIC: 3651 Mfg Home Audio/Video Equipment
HQ: Polycom, Inc.
345 Encinal St
Santa Cruz CA 95060
831 426-5858

(G-7587)
POWERSURE FUEL RCNDTIONING LLC
17 Alden Rd (01810-4914)
PHONE....................................978 886-2476
Mark Kappeler, *Owner*
EMP: 3 **EST:** 2011
SALES (est): 184.5K **Privately Held**
SIC: 2869 Mfg Industrial Organic Chemicals

(G-7588)
PXT PAYMENTS INC
300 Brickstone Sq Ste 201 (01810-1497)
PHONE....................................978 247-7164
EMP: 9
SQ FT: 2,000
SALES (est): 1MM **Privately Held**
SIC: 7372 Prepackaged Software Services

(G-7589)
QPHARMETRA LLC (PA)
9 Nollet Dr (01810-6313)
PHONE....................................978 655-1943
Kevin Dykstra, *President*
Nicolaas Hendrik Prins, *Manager*
EMP: 11
SALES (est): 1.6MM **Privately Held**
SIC: 2834 Mfg Pharmaceutical Preparations

(G-7590)
QUALCOMM INCORPORATED
100 Burtt Rd Ste 123 (01810-5920)
PHONE....................................858 587-1121
EMP: 350
SALES (corp-wide): 24.2B **Publicly Held**
SIC: 3674 Advanced Communication Systems And Equipment
PA: Qualcomm Incorporated
5775 Morehouse Dr
San Diego CA 92121
858 587-1121

(G-7591)
RAID INC
200 Brickstone Sq Ste 302 (01810-1429)
PHONE....................................978 683-6444
Marc Dizoglio, *President*
Jeff Martineau, *Purch Mgr*
Jad Ramey, *Regl Sales Mgr*
Mariana Haven, *Marketing Staff*
Kimberly Jolicoeur, *Admin Asst*
EMP: 21
SQ FT: 30,000
SALES (est): 13.6MM **Privately Held**
WEB: www.raidinc.com
SIC: 3572 Mfg Computer Storage Devices

(G-7592)
RAPISCAN SYSTEMS INC
23 Frontage Rd (01810-5424)
PHONE....................................866 430-1913
Pak Chin, *President*
Eric Luiz, *Treasurer*
Josh Greenberg, *Admin Sec*
EMP: 3 **EST:** 2017
SALES (est): 494.1K **Privately Held**
SIC: 3577 Mfg Computer Peripheral Equipment

(G-7593)
RAYSOLUTION LLC
43 Linwood St (01810-2747)
PHONE....................................765 714-0645
Chih-Hsiang Ho, *CEO*
EMP: 3
SALES (est): 152.1K **Privately Held**
SIC: 3674 Mfg Semiconductors/Related Devices

(G-7594)
RAYTHEON COMPANY
350 Lowell St (01810-4495)
PHONE....................................978 470-5000
EMP: 132
SALES (corp-wide): 27B **Publicly Held**
SIC: 3812 Mfg Search/Navigation Equipment
PA: Raytheon Company
870 Winter St
Waltham MA 02451
781 522-3000

(G-7595)
RAYTHEON COMPANY
362 Lowell St (01810-4491)
PHONE....................................781 522-3000
Richard Guzzardi, *President*
Stephen Lewis, *Plant Mgr*
Julia A Villineau, *Buyer*
Patrick Welch, *Purchasing*
Bill Hubner, *QC Mgr*
EMP: 99
SALES (corp-wide): 27B **Publicly Held**
SIC: 3812 Mfg Search/Navigation Equipment
PA: Raytheon Company
870 Winter St
Waltham MA 02451
781 522-3000

(G-7596)
RAYTHEON COMPANY
350 Lowell St (01810-4495)
PHONE....................................978 470-6922
Richard Guzzardi, *Manager*
EMP: 100
SALES (corp-wide): 27B **Publicly Held**
SIC: 3812 Mfg Search/Navigation Equipment
PA: Raytheon Company
870 Winter St
Waltham MA 02451
781 522-3000

(G-7597)
RAYTHEON ITALY LIAISON COMPANY
358 Lowell St (01810-4490)
PHONE....................................978 684-5300
James W Carter, *Principal*
Donna McCullough, *Principal*
EMP: 99
SALES: 2MM
SALES (corp-wide): 27B **Publicly Held**
SIC: 3812 Mfg Search/Navigation Equipment
PA: Raytheon Company
870 Winter St
Waltham MA 02451
781 522-3000

(G-7598)
REID GRAPHICS INC
7 Connector Rd (01810-5922)
P.O. Box 4247 (01810-0814)
PHONE....................................978 474-1930
Stephen R Dunlevy, *President*
Christopher Wright, *Production*
Helen Thirkell, *Human Res Dir*
Kathy Zibolis, *Natl Sales Mgr*
EMP: 59
SQ FT: 35,000
SALES (est): 9.5MM **Privately Held**
WEB: www.reidgraphics.com
SIC: 2759 3479 3993 2752 Commercial Printing Coating/Engraving Svcs Mfg Signs/Ad Specialties Lithographic Coml Print

(G-7599)
RICKENBACKER RESOURCES INC
77 Main St (01810-3845)
PHONE....................................978 475-4520
Maureen Rickenbacker, *President*
Denis Raimo, *CFO*
EMP: 5
SQ FT: 1,100

SALES (est): 744.6K Privately Held
WEB: www.rickenbackerconsulting.com
SIC: 2752 Lithographic Commercial Printing

(G-7600)
RMS MEDIA GROUP INC
300 Brickstone Sq Ste 904 (01810-1451)
P.O. Box 788, West Newbury (01985-2788)
PHONE..................................978 623-8020
Richard Sedler, *President*
EMP: 20
SALES (est): 3.7MM Privately Held
WEB: www.rmsmediagroup.com
SIC: 2721 7311 Periodicals-Publishing/Printing Advertising Agency

(G-7601)
ROCKSTAR NEW ENGLAND INC
3 Dundee Park Dr Ste 102 (01810-3723)
PHONE..................................978 409-6272
Ann Davis, *Principal*
EMP: 40 EST: 1999
SALES (est): 2.8MM Publicly Held
WEB: www.maddocsoftware.com
SIC: 7372 7371 Prepackaged Software Services Custom Computer Programing
HQ: Rockstar Games, Inc.
622 Broadway Fl 4
New York NY 10012
212 334-6633

(G-7602)
SCHNEIDER AUTOMATION INC
Also Called: Engineering
800 Federal St (01810-1067)
PHONE..................................978 975-9600
Chip Sheerin, *Principal*
Frank Prendergast, *Business Mgr*
Bruce Boardman, *Opers Staff*
John Zanco, *Opers Staff*
Nitin Dhayagude, *Engineer*
EMP: 80
SALES (corp-wide): 177.9K Privately Held
WEB: www.schneiderautomation.com
SIC: 3699 Mfg Electrical Equipment/Supplies
HQ: Schneider Automation Inc.
800 Federal St
Andover MA 01810
978 794-0800

(G-7603)
SEVENTY NINE N MAIN ST PRTG
Also Called: Minuteman Press
79 N Main St (01810-3510)
PHONE..................................978 475-4945
Tom Heffernan, *President*
EMP: 9
SALES (est): 1.3MM Privately Held
WEB: www.mmpand.com
SIC: 2752 Comm Prtg Litho

(G-7604)
SHAWSHEEN RUBBER CO INC
Also Called: Arrowhead Athletics
220 Andover St (01810-5695)
P.O. Box 4296 (01810-0814)
PHONE..................................978 470-1760
Denis J Kelley, *President*
Walter P Nugent, *Corp Secy*
▲ EMP: 52 EST: 1939
SQ FT: 60,000
SALES (est): 14.7MM Privately Held
WEB: www.shawsheencc.com
SIC: 2672 Mfg Coated/Laminated Paper

(G-7605)
SIFOS TECHNOLOGIES INC
1 Tech Dr Ste 100 (01810-2487)
PHONE..................................978 975-2100
David Lucia, *President*
Kendrick Bennett, *Shareholder*
John Cafarella, *Shareholder*
Peter Johnson, *Shareholder*
EMP: 6
SQ FT: 3,500
SALES (est): 1.2MM Privately Held
WEB: www.sifos.com
SIC: 3825 Mfg Electrical Measuring Instruments

(G-7606)
SKYWORKS SOLUTIONS INC
300 Federal St 100 (01810-1038)
PHONE..................................978 327-6850
William Vaillancourt, *Branch Mgr*
EMP: 195
SALES (corp-wide): 3.3B Publicly Held
SIC: 3674 Mfg Semiconductors/Related Devices
PA: Skyworks Solutions, Inc.
20 Sylvan Rd
Woburn MA 01801
781 376-3000

(G-7607)
SLOAN VALVE COMPANY
19 Connector Rd Ste 4 (01810-5933)
PHONE..................................617 796-9001
Marc Larosee, *Project Mgr*
Xiao MO, *Engineer*
Amy Parsons, *Manager*
EMP: 117
SALES (corp-wide): 199.1MM Privately Held
SIC: 3494 Mfg Valves/Pipe Fittings
PA: Sloan Valve Company
10500 Seymour Ave
Franklin Park IL 60131
847 671-4300

(G-7608)
SMITH & NEPHEW INC
150 Minuteman Rd (01810-1031)
PHONE..................................978 749-1000
Michael Carra, *Business Mgr*
Reed McGoldrick, *Vice Pres*
Ingeborg Oie, *Vice Pres*
Erik Wallace, *Vice Pres*
Masanori Kitoh, *Opers Staff*
EMP: 50
SALES (corp-wide): 4.9B Privately Held
WEB: www.smith-nephew.com/us
SIC: 3841 Mfg Surgical/Medical Instruments
HQ: Smith & Nephew, Inc.
7135 Goodlett Farms Pkwy
Cordova TN 38016
901 396-2121

(G-7609)
SMITH & NEPHEW ENDOSCOPY INC
150 Minuteman Rd (01810-1031)
PHONE..................................978 749-1000
Olivier Bohuon, *CEO*
Charles Federico, *President*
Mark Faucett, *President*
Sir John Buchanan, *Chairman*
Matt Griffith, *Mfg Mgr*
▲ EMP: 62 EST: 1964
SALES (est): 17.4MM
SALES (corp-wide): 4.9B Privately Held
SIC: 3841 3845 Mfg Surgical/Medical Instruments Mfg Electromedical Equipment
HQ: Smith & Nephew, Inc.
7135 Goodlett Farms Pkwy
Cordova TN 38016
901 396-2121

(G-7610)
SMITHS DETECTION LLC
23 Frontage Rd (01810-5424)
PHONE..................................510 449-4197
Cameron J Ritchie, *Vice Pres*
Mike Patterson, *Chief Engr*
Karim Ghodbane, *Branch Mgr*
Raymond Lockley, *Manager*
Pricelle Valdecanas, *Senior Mgr*
EMP: 200
SALES (corp-wide): 3.1B Privately Held
SIC: 3812 Mfg Search/Navigation Equipment
HQ: Smiths Detection, Llc
7151 Gateway Blvd
Newark CA 94560
510 739-2400

(G-7611)
SSQUARE DETECT MEDICAL DEVICES
108 Colonial Dr (01810-7359)
PHONE..................................978 202-5707
Govind Srinivasan, *CEO*
EMP: 4
SALES (est): 169.4K Privately Held
SIC: 3845 Mfg Electromedical Equipment

(G-7612)
STRAUMANN USA LLC (HQ)
60 Minuteman Rd (01810-1008)
PHONE..................................978 747-2500
Thomas Dressendrfer, *Principal*
Andreas L Meier, *Principal*
Beat Spalinger, *Principal*
Craig Kierst, *Vice Pres*
Bill Kukucka, *Vice Pres*
EMP: 200
SQ FT: 20,000
SALES (est): 48.7MM
SALES (corp-wide): 1.3B Privately Held
WEB: www.straumannusa.com
SIC: 3843 Mfg Dental Equipment/Supplies
PA: Straumann Holding Ag
Peter Merian-Weg 12
Basel BS 4002
619 651-111

(G-7613)
TAC INC (DH)
1 High St (01810-3527)
PHONE..................................978 470-0555
Arne Frank, *CEO*
◆ EMP: 200
SQ FT: 95,000
SALES (est): 122.6MM
SALES (corp-wide): 177.9K Privately Held
WEB: www.andovercontrols.com
SIC: 3822 Mfg Environmental Controls
HQ: Schneider Electric Buildings Americas, Inc.
1650 W Crosby Rd
Carrollton TX 75006
972 323-1111

(G-7614)
TRANSMEDICS INC (PA)
200 Minuteman Rd Ste 302 (01810-1046)
PHONE..................................978 552-0443
Waleed Hassanein, *President*
John Sullivan, *Vice Pres*
Dominic Micale, *CFO*
Jeffrey E Young, *Treasurer*
Ahmed Elbetanony, *Program Mgr*
EMP: 134
SQ FT: 32,000
SALES (est): 27.3MM Publicly Held
WEB: www.transmedics.com
SIC: 3845 Mfg Electromedical Equipment

(G-7615)
TRANSMEDICS GROUP INC
200 Minuteman Rd (01810-1047)
PHONE..................................978 552-0900
James R Tobin, *Ch of Bd*
Waleed Hassanein, *President*
John Carey, *Vice Pres*
Miriam Provost, *Vice Pres*
Jacqueline Sneve, *Vice Pres*
EMP: 92
SQ FT: 54,000
SALES (est): 3.3MM
SALES (corp-wide): 27.3MM Publicly Held
SIC: 3845 Electromedical And Electrotherapeutic Apparatus
PA: Transmedics, Inc.
200 Minuteman Rd Ste 302
Andover MA 01810
978 552-0443

(G-7616)
VICOR CORPORATION (PA)
25 Frontage Rd (01810-5499)
PHONE..................................978 470-2900
Patrizio Vinciarelli, *Ch of Bd*
Claudio Tuozzolo, *President*
Sean Crilly, *Vice Pres*
Philip D Davies, *Vice Pres*
Lynn Gagnon, *Vice Pres*
EMP: 277 EST: 1981
SQ FT: 90,000
SALES: 291.2MM Publicly Held
WEB: www.vicoreurope.com
SIC: 3679 3613 Mfg Electronic Components Switchgear & Switchboards

(G-7617)
VICOR CORPORATION
400 Federal St (01810-1092)
PHONE..................................978 470-2900
Patrizio Vinciarelli, *President*
EMP: 16
SALES (corp-wide): 291.2MM Publicly Held
WEB: www.vicoreurope.com
SIC: 3629 Mfg Power Conversion Sevices & Power System Components
PA: Vicor Corporation
25 Frontage Rd
Andover MA 01810
978 470-2900

(G-7618)
WATER ANALYTICS INC
100 School St (01810-3924)
PHONE..................................978 749-9949
Mark Spencer, *President*
Sue Hunter, *Finance*
Michelle Cormier, *Office Mgr*
▼ EMP: 10
SQ FT: 8,200
SALES: 900K Privately Held
SIC: 3823 Mfg Water Quality Monitoring & Control Systems

(G-7619)
WYETH PHARMACEUTICALS LLC
Also Called: Wyeth Biopharma Division
1 Burtt Rd (01810-5901)
PHONE..................................978 475-9214
Michelle Barrows, *Manager*
Kenn Coviello, *Technician*
Mat Martins, *Associate*
EMP: 450
SALES (corp-wide): 53.6B Publicly Held
SIC: 2834 Mfg Pharmaceutical Preparations
HQ: Wyeth Pharmaceuticals Llc
500 Arcola Rd
Collegeville PA 19426
484 865-5000

Aquinnah
Dukes County

(G-7620)
HUMMINGBIRD PRODUCTIONS
Also Called: Front Door Records
4 Pilot S Ldg (02535)
P.O. Box 426, Chilmark (02535-0426)
PHONE..................................508 645-3030
Katherine Taylor, *Owner*
EMP: 4
SALES (est): 218.9K Privately Held
WEB: www.katetaylor.com
SIC: 3911 Mfg Precious Metal Jewelry

Arlington
Middlesex County

(G-7621)
A TO Z FOODS INC
797 Massachusetts Ave (02476-4732)
PHONE..................................781 413-0221
Wagih Morcos, *Principal*
EMP: 3
SALES (est): 132.6K Privately Held
SIC: 2099 Mfg Food Preparations

(G-7622)
ACTUALITY SYSTEMS INC
1337 Massachusetts Ave (02476-4101)
PHONE..................................617 325-9230
Michael Goldstein, *President*
Gregg Favalora, *Vice Pres*
Robert Ryan, *Vice Pres*
▲ EMP: 9
SQ FT: 10,000
SALES (est): 766.3K Privately Held
WEB: www.actuality-systems.com
SIC: 3575 7372 Mfg Computer Terminals Prepackaged Software Services

GEOGRAPHIC

(G-7623)
ARLINGTON SWIFTY PRINTING INC
1386 Massachusetts Ave (02476-4102)
PHONE.................................781 646-8700
Charles Pappas, *President*
Nancy Pappas, *Treasurer*
EMP: 5
SALES (est): 659.8K **Privately Held**
WEB: www.arlingtonswifty.com
SIC: 2752 7389 Lithographic Commercial Printing Business Services

(G-7624)
EASY LOCATE LLC
32 Addison St (02476-8108)
PHONE.................................617 216-3654
John Bell, *Manager*
Mark Pitts,
EMP: 6
SALES (est): 353.7K **Privately Held**
SIC: 3663 Radio And T.V. Communications Equipment, Nsk

(G-7625)
ERGOSUTURE INC
196 Jason St (02476-8024)
PHONE.................................339 234-6289
Claude Nogard, *CEO*
Claude Nogaard, *Principal*
Carlos Gonzalez-Stawinski, *Bd of Directors*
Eric Halioua, *Bd of Directors*
EMP: 3
SALES (est): 209.9K **Privately Held**
SIC: 3845 Mfg Electromedical Equipment

(G-7626)
FORCED EXPOSURE INC
60 Lowell St (02476-4160)
PHONE.................................781 321-0320
James F Johnson, *President*
Dan Schnebly, *Vice Pres*
▲ **EMP:** 20
SQ FT: 40,000
SALES (est): 3.7MM **Privately Held**
WEB: www.forcedexposure.com
SIC: 2721 5099 5961 Periodical-Publish/Print Whol Durable Goods Ret Mail-Order House

(G-7627)
FORGE BAKING COMPANY INC
12 Elder Ter (02474-2701)
PHONE.................................617 764-5365
Jennifer A Park, *Principal*
EMP: 4
SALES (est): 171.6K **Privately Held**
SIC: 2051 Mfg Bread/Related Products

(G-7628)
GEMINI GAMES
197 Forest St (02474-8922)
PHONE.................................781 643-6965
Florenzo Di Donato, *Owner*
EMP: 3
SALES (est): 136.3K **Privately Held**
SIC: 3944 Mfg Games/Toys

(G-7629)
MASSINVESTOR INCORPORATED
Also Called: Vc News Daily
10 Farmer Rd (02476-6022)
PHONE.................................617 620-4606
Michael Stern, *President*
Paul Stern, *Director*
EMP: 5
SALES: 110K **Privately Held**
SIC: 2741 Misc Publishing

(G-7630)
MINUTEMAN SOFTWARE ASSOCIATES
63 Foster St (02474-6813)
PHONE.................................781 643-4918
John Davies, *President*
Barbara Davies, *Vice Pres*
Brenda Hill, *Treasurer*
EMP: 4
SQ FT: 1,200
SALES (est): 286.2K **Privately Held**
SIC: 7372 7373 Prepackaged Software Services Computer Systems Design

(G-7631)
MIRAK BUILDING TRUST
1125 Massachusetts Ave (02476-4316)
P.O. Box 268 (02476-0003)
PHONE.................................781 643-8000
Robert Mirak, *Trustee*
Charles Mirak, *Trustee*
Edward Mirak, *Trustee*
Muriel Mirak, *Trustee*
EMP: 5
SQ FT: 20,000
SALES: 767.2K **Privately Held**
WEB: www.mirak.com
SIC: 3711 Mfg Motor Vehicle/Car Bodies

(G-7632)
PELLION TECHNOLOGIES INC
1337 Massachusetts Ave (02476-4101)
PHONE.................................617 547-3191
Dave Eaglesham, *CEO*
Natasha George, *Engineer*
EMP: 20
SALES (est): 3.9MM **Privately Held**
SIC: 3694 8731 Mfg Engine Electrical Equipment Commercial Physical Research

(G-7633)
PERKINELMER INC
32 Glen Ave (02474-1234)
PHONE.................................617 350-9440
Rick Green, *Engineer*
Christopher Wright, *Manager*
EMP: 3
SALES (corp-wide): 2.7B **Publicly Held**
WEB: www.perkinelmer.com
SIC: 3826 Mfg Analytical Instruments
PA: Perkinelmer, Inc.
940 Winter St
Waltham MA 02451
781 663-6900

(G-7634)
PICTURE FRAME PRODUCTS INC
34 Hamilton Rd Apt 301 (02474-8285)
PHONE.................................781 648-7719
Robert Jolkovski, *President*
EMP: 3
SQ FT: 1,500
SALES (est): 330K **Privately Held**
SIC: 3565 3545 Mfg Shrink Wrapping Equipment Double Mitered Saws And Vices

(G-7635)
REVERE PHARMACEUTICALS INC
36 Orvis Rd (02474-8548)
PHONE.................................781 718-9033
Ian Silverman, *President*
EMP: 3 **EST:** 2016
SALES (est): 81.8K **Privately Held**
SIC: 2834 Mfg Pharmaceutical Preparations

(G-7636)
RUSSELL GROUP
56 College Ave (02474-1054)
PHONE.................................781 648-0302
Thomas J Russell, *Partner*
Walter E Russell, *Partner*
EMP: 8
SALES (est): 150K **Privately Held**
SIC: 2741 Publishes Local Phone Directories

(G-7637)
SEA SCIENCES INC
40 Massachusetts Ave (02474-8621)
PHONE.................................781 643-1600
Christian Casagrande, *President*
Dirk Casagrande, *Vice Pres*
EMP: 4
SALES (est): 558.7K **Privately Held**
WEB: www.seasciences.com
SIC: 3531 7371 Mfg Oceanographic Instrumentation Custom Computer Programing

(G-7638)
SHEWSTONE PUBLISHING LLC
165 Scituate St (02476-7727)
P.O. Box 410271, Cambridge (02141-0003)
PHONE.................................781 648-1251
EMP: 3
SALES (est): 69.2K **Privately Held**
SIC: 2711 Newspapers-Publishing/Printing

(G-7639)
SHORT PATH DISTILLERY INC
59 Magnolia St (02474-8725)
PHONE.................................857 417-2396
Jackson Hewlett, *Principal*
EMP: 5
SALES (est): 322.8K **Privately Held**
SIC: 2085 Mfg Distilled/Blended Liquor

(G-7640)
SOMERSETS USA LLC
30 Academy St (02476-6436)
PHONE.................................617 803-6833
Jessica Mason,
James Forrer,
EMP: 3
SALES (est): 320.1K **Privately Held**
SIC: 2844 Mfg Toilet Preparations

(G-7641)
TETRAGENETICS INC
91 Mystic St (02474-1129)
PHONE.................................617 500-7471
Douglas Kahn, *CEO*
John Reilly, *Vice Pres*
Kevin O'Brien, *CFO*
EMP: 10
SQ FT: 5,400
SALES: 2MM **Privately Held**
WEB: www.tetragenetics.com
SIC: 2836 Mfg Biological Products

(G-7642)
ZIPWALL LLC (PA)
37 Broadway Ste 2 (02474-5552)
PHONE.................................781 648-8808
Jeffrey Whitmore,
Doreen Bouvier, *Analyst*
Peter Micheli, *Analyst*
▲ **EMP:** 4
SALES (est): 790.9K **Privately Held**
SIC: 3599 Mfg Industrial Machinery

Ashburnham
Worcester County

(G-7643)
ABCROSBY & COMPANY INC
20 S Maple Ave (01430-1639)
PHONE.................................978 827-6064
Andrew B Crosby, *President*
Andy Crosby, *Manager*
EMP: 8
SQ FT: 22,000
SALES (est): 1.3MM **Privately Held**
WEB: www.maplewoodfurn.com
SIC: 2511 Mfg Wooden Household Furniture

(G-7644)
FLO CHEMICAL CORP
Also Called: Flow Chemicals
20 Puffer St (01430-1267)
PHONE.................................978 827-5101
Paul N Freeman,
EMP: 7
SALES (est): 948.1K **Privately Held**
SIC: 2833 Mfg Medicinal/Botanical Products

(G-7645)
SUSAN M REXFORD TITLE EXAMINER
6 Hillandale Rd (01430-1213)
PHONE.................................978 827-3015
Susan M Rexford, *Principal*
EMP: 4
SALES (est): 199K **Privately Held**
SIC: 2711 Newspapers-Publishing/Printing

Ashby
Middlesex County

(G-7646)
COUNTRY BED SHOP INC
328 Richardson Rd (01431-2005)
PHONE.................................978 386-7550
Alan Pease, *President*
EMP: 3
SQ FT: 2,000
SALES (est): 249.3K **Privately Held**
WEB: www.countrybed.com
SIC: 2511 5712 Mfg And Retail Furniture

(G-7647)
MINI-BROACH MACHINE CO INC
1266 Main St (01431-2311)
PHONE.................................978 386-7959
Steven Ingerson, *President*
EMP: 4 **EST:** 1974
SALES (est): 643.5K **Privately Held**
SIC: 3541 Mfg Mini-Broach Machines

(G-7648)
SELECT LOGGING
81 West Rd (01431-2240)
PHONE.................................978 386-6861
Robert Saari, *Principal*
EMP: 6 **EST:** 2010
SALES (est): 453.6K **Privately Held**
SIC: 2411 Logging

Ashfield
Franklin County

(G-7649)
ED BRANSON
Also Called: Ed Branson Glass
634 Bellus Rd (01330)
PHONE.................................413 625-2933
Edward Branson, *Owner*
EMP: 5
SQ FT: 3,872
SALES: 220K **Privately Held**
SIC: 3229 Mfg Pressed/Blown Glass

(G-7650)
ERATECH INC
Also Called: World Satellite Media
225 Smith Rd (01330-9503)
P.O. Box 292 (01330-0292)
PHONE.................................413 628-3219
John Angleman, *President*
EMP: 10
SALES (est): 442.6K **Privately Held**
WEB: www.eratech.net
SIC: 3993 Mfg Signs/Advertising Specialties

(G-7651)
GRAYTRON INC
888 Baptist Corner Rd (01330)
P.O. Box 51 (01330-0051)
PHONE.................................413 625-2456
Alden Gray, *President*
Audrey Gray, *Vice Pres*
EMP: 5
SQ FT: 5,000
SALES: 1MM **Privately Held**
SIC: 3679 Mfg Electronic Components

(G-7652)
JOBSMART INC
1157 Bug Hill Rd (01330-9795)
PHONE.................................724 272-3448
Deborah Keareney, *President*
EMP: 16
SALES: 1,000K **Privately Held**
SIC: 7372 8748 Employee Management Software

(G-7653)
JUST SOAP
1079 Hawley Rd (01330-9626)
PHONE.................................413 625-6990
Frederick Breeden, *Owner*
EMP: 3
SALES (est): 240.5K **Privately Held**
SIC: 2841 Mfg Soap/Other Detergents

(G-7654)
ROBERTS BROTHERS LUMBER CO
1450 Spruce Corner Rd (01330-9747)
PHONE..................................413 628-3333
Leonard Roberts, *President*
Joan Roberts, *Clerk*
EMP: 22
SQ FT: 20,000
SALES: 2MM **Privately Held**
SIC: 2421 2426 2411 Sawmill/Planing Mill Hardwood Dimension/Floor Mill Logging

Ashland
Middlesex County

(G-7655)
AGGREGATE INDS - NORTHEAST REG
71 Spring St (01721-2123)
PHONE..................................508 881-1430
Fred Cowen, *Principal*
Chris Hudson, *Director*
EMP: 20
SALES (corp-wide): 4.5B **Privately Held**
SIC: 1442 5211 2951 Construction Sand/Gravel Ret Lumber/Building Mtrl Mfg Asphalt Mixtr/Blocks
HQ: Aggregate Industries - Northeast Region, Inc
1715 Brdwy
Saugus MA 01906
781 941-7200

(G-7656)
B & K ENTERPRISES INC
Also Called: B&K Enterprises
223 Main St (01721-2171)
P.O. Box 3 (01721-0003)
PHONE..................................508 881-1168
Mary D Berry, *President*
Robert Berry, *Treasurer*
EMP: 3
SQ FT: 20,000
SALES (est): 408.2K **Privately Held**
SIC: 2675 Mfg Die-Cut Paper/Paperboard

(G-7657)
DIVINE STONEWORKS LLC
60 Pleasant St (01721-3127)
PHONE..................................774 221-6006
Michelle Campos Coelho, *Mng Member*
John C Dudley,
Davidson Pascoal Neto,
EMP: 8
SALES (est): 122K **Privately Held**
SIC: 3281 Mfg Cut Stone/Products

(G-7658)
DYNEX/RIVETT INC
54 Nickerson Rd (01721-1912)
PHONE..................................508 881-5110
Chuck Meserve, *Manager*
EMP: 9
SQ FT: 15,000
SALES (corp-wide): 15.2MM **Privately Held**
WEB: www.dynexhydraulics.com
SIC: 3714 Whol Industrial Equipment
PA: Dynex/Rivett Inc.
770 Capitol Dr
Pewaukee WI 53072
262 691-0300

(G-7659)
FORTERRA PIPE & PRECAST LLC
Fenwal Div
400 Main St (01721-2150)
PHONE..................................508 881-2000
William F Johnston, *Branch Mgr*
EMP: 1200
SQ FT: 500,000
SALES (corp-wide): 1.4B **Publicly Held**
SIC: 3272 Mfg Concrete Products
HQ: Forterra Pipe & Precast, Llc
511 E John Carpenter Fwy
Irving TX 75062
469 458-7973

(G-7660)
FREEDOM DIGITAL PRINTING LLC
200 Butterfield Dr Ste A2 (01721-2060)
PHONE..................................508 881-6940
Jim Giammarinaro,
Niel Henderson,
EMP: 10 **EST:** 2001
SALES (est): 1.3MM **Privately Held**
WEB: www.freedomdigitalprinting.com
SIC: 2752 Lithographic Commercial Printing

(G-7661)
HOT PLATES COMPANY
83 Nickerson Rd Ste 1e (01721-2064)
PHONE..................................508 429-1445
Robert Uriano, *Owner*
EMP: 4
SQ FT: 2,500
SALES: 250K **Privately Held**
SIC: 2796 5051 2759 Platemaking Services Metals Service Center Commercial Printing

(G-7662)
J C ENTERPRISES INC
Also Called: Sir Speedy
300 Eliot St Ste 12 (01721-2380)
PHONE..................................508 881-7228
Andrew Carini, *President*
EMP: 5
SQ FT: 2,000
SALES (est): 619.6K **Privately Held**
SIC: 2752 2796 2791 2789 Lithographic Coml Print Platemaking Services Typesetting Services Bookbinding/Related Work

(G-7663)
KIDDE-FENWAL INC (HQ)
Also Called: Kidde Fire System
400 Main St (01721-2150)
PHONE..................................508 881-2000
Michael C Burcham, *President*
John Vernon, *Principal*
Steven Hamel, *Buyer*
Edwin Moy, *QC Mgr*
Giovanni Digiallonardo, *Engineer*
◆ **EMP:** 600
SQ FT: 220,000
SALES (est): 205.9MM
SALES (corp-wide): 66.5B **Publicly Held**
SIC: 3669 3823 3825 3822 Mfg Communications Equip Mfg Process Cntrl Instr Mfg Elec Measuring Instr Mfg Environmntl Controls Mfg Conductive Wire Dvcs
PA: United Technologies Corporation
10 Farm Springs Rd
Farmington CT 06032
860 728-7000

(G-7664)
LENTROS ENGINEERING INC
280 Eliot St (01721-2392)
PHONE..................................508 881-1160
Peter G Lentros, *President*
Richard Payne, *Purch Agent*
John Huband, *Engineer*
James Towne, *Manager*
Kimberley A Lentros, *Admin Sec*
▲ **EMP:** 43
SQ FT: 28,000
SALES: 67MM **Privately Held**
WEB: www.lentros.com
SIC: 3599 Mfg Industrial Machinery

(G-7665)
NYACOL NANO TECHNOLOGIES INC
211 Megunko Rd (01721-1426)
P.O. Box 349 (01721-0349)
PHONE..................................508 881-2220
Robert Nehring, *President*
Steven Chamberland, *Research*
Audrey Colson, *Treasurer*
Jennifer George, *Office Mgr*
◆ **EMP:** 29
SQ FT: 35,000
SALES (est): 8.7MM **Privately Held**
WEB: www.nyacol.com
SIC: 2819 Mfg Industrial Inorganic Chemicals

(G-7666)
O A BOTH CORPORATION
Also Called: Schlenk Metallic Pigments
40 Nickerson Rd (01721-1912)
PHONE..................................508 881-4100
Thomas Schaller, *President*
Debra Morey, *Principal*
EMP: 4
SQ FT: 20,000
SALES (est): 681.4K
SALES (corp-wide): 177MM **Privately Held**
SIC: 2816 Mfg Inorganic Pigments
PA: Carl Schlenk Ag
Barnsdorfer Hauptstr. 5
Roth 91154
917 180-80

(G-7667)
RAYMOND SPINAZZOLA
Also Called: R & S Welding
13 Forest Ave (01721-1160)
PHONE..................................508 881-3089
EMP: 4
SQ FT: 2,400
SALES (est): 148.2K **Privately Held**
SIC: 7692 7538 Welding Repair General Auto Repair

(G-7668)
RF VENUE INC
72 Nickerson Rd (01721-1912)
PHONE..................................800 795-0817
Christopher Regan, *President*
Robert J Crowley, *Treasurer*
EMP: 7
SQ FT: 25,000
SALES (est): 1.2MM **Privately Held**
SIC: 3651 Mfg Home Audio/Video Equipment

(G-7669)
SCREWTRON ENGINEERING INC
32 Stone Ave (01721-2121)
PHONE..................................508 881-1370
Carl Castelli, *President*
Paul Castelli, *Vice Pres*
EMP: 3 **EST:** 1963
SQ FT: 3,600
SALES (est): 392.2K **Privately Held**
SIC: 3451 Mfg Screw Machine Products

(G-7670)
STAT PRODUCTS INC
200 Butterfield Dr Ste D (01721-2060)
PHONE..................................508 881-8022
David Franco, *President*
John Franco, *Vice Pres*
Jason Firth, *Prdtn Mgr*
EMP: 23 **EST:** 1962
SQ FT: 10,000
SALES (est): 3.5MM **Privately Held**
WEB: www.statproducts.com
SIC: 2761 2754 Mfg Manifold Business Forms Gravure Commercial Printing

(G-7671)
TEKNI-PLEX INC
150 Homer Ave (01721-1770)
PHONE..................................508 881-2440
Kerry Turner, *Manager*
EMP: 19
SALES (corp-wide): 1.1B **Privately Held**
SIC: 3081 2759 2672 Mfg Unsupported Plastic Film/Sheet Commercial Printing Mfg Coated/Laminated Paper
PA: Tekni-Plex, Inc.
460 E Swedesford Rd # 3000
Wayne PA 19087
484 690-1520

Ashley Falls
Berkshire County

(G-7672)
BONDED CONCRETE INC
Also Called: Century Concrete
49 Clayton Rd (01222-9713)
P.O. Box 297 (01222-0297)
PHONE..................................413 229-2075
Greg Marlow, *Manager*
EMP: 6
SALES (corp-wide): 10.8MM **Privately Held**
WEB: www.bondedconcrete.com
SIC: 3273 Mfg Ready-Mixed Concrete
PA: Bonded Concrete, Inc.
303 Watervliet Shaker Rd
Watervliet NY 12189
518 273-5800

(G-7673)
EURO PRECISION INC
125 Sheffield Business Pa (01222-9759)
PHONE..................................413 229-0004
Peter Leslie Fleming, *President*
EMP: 3
SALES (est): 341.3K **Privately Held**
SIC: 3599 Mfg Industrial Machinery

(G-7674)
GINGRAS LUMBER INC
77 Clayton Rd (01222-9713)
P.O. Box 232 (01222-0232)
PHONE..................................413 229-2182
David Rood, *President*
Robert Beham, *Vice Pres*
EMP: 9
SALES (est): 1MM **Privately Held**
SIC: 2421 Custom Sawmill

(G-7675)
VISUAL DEPARTURES LTD
48 Sheffield Business Par (01222-9758)
PHONE..................................413 229-2272
Allen Green, *President*
EMP: 6 **EST:** 2014
SALES (est): 579.2K **Privately Held**
SIC: 3861 Mfg Photographic Equipment/Supplies

Assonet
Bristol County

(G-7676)
ASHLAND LLC
238 S Main St (02702-1657)
PHONE..................................508 235-7164
Fred Hanna, *General Mgr*
Fran Minnock, *Engineer*
EMP: 35
SALES (corp-wide): 2.4B **Publicly Held**
SIC: 2899 Whol Chemicals/Products
HQ: Ashland Llc
50 E Rivercenter Blvd # 1600
Covington KY 41011
859 815-3333

(G-7677)
ASSONET INDUSTRIES INC
17 Mill St (02702-1134)
P.O. Box 408 (02702-0408)
PHONE..................................508 644-5001
Robert Korkolonis, *President*
EMP: 6 **EST:** 1953
SQ FT: 26,500
SALES: 530K **Privately Held**
SIC: 2499 Mfg Wood Products

(G-7678)
BRIGHTMAN CORP
Also Called: Brightman Lumber Co
181 S Main St (02702-1648)
PHONE..................................508 644-2620
John Brightman Jr, *President*
Edward Brightman, *Vice Pres*
John Brightman III, *Vice Pres*
Nancy Brightman, *Treasurer*
EMP: 20
SQ FT: 2,000
SALES (est): 1.9MM **Privately Held**
WEB: www.brightmanlumber.com
SIC: 2411 5211 Logging Ret Lumber/Building Materials

(G-7679)
FAR INDUSTRIES INC
11 Ridge Hill Rd (02702-1667)
P.O. Box 574 (02702-0899)
PHONE..................................508 644-3122
Joseph A Ferrazza, *President*
Albano P Robens, *Vice Pres*
David Ferrazza, *Accountant*
▲ **EMP:** 12
SQ FT: 12,000

SALES (est): 2MM Privately Held
SIC: 3442 3469 3444 Mfg Metal Doors/Sash/Trim Mfg Metal Stampings Mfg Sheet Metalwork

(G-7680)
FRAIN & ASSOCIATES INC
8 Chester St (02702-1220)
PHONE 508 644-3424
EMP: 5
SALES: 1.5MM Privately Held
SIC: 3672 Printed Circuit Boards

(G-7681)
ISP FREETOWN FINE CHEM INC
238 S Main St (02702-1657)
PHONE 508 672-0634
John E Panichella, *President*
Scott A Gregg, *Vice Pres*
Steven E Post, *Vice Pres*
J Kevin Willis, *Vice Pres*
Lynn P Freeman, *Treasurer*
▲ EMP: 75
SALES (est): 11.3MM Privately Held
SIC: 2869 2821 2911 2843 Mfg Industl Organic Chem Mfg Plstc Material/Resin Petroleum Refining Mfg Surface Active Agent
HQ: Isp Chemicals Llc
455 N Main St
Calvert City KY 42029
270 395-4165

(G-7682)
JOSEPH NACHADO
Also Called: Supreme Painting Company
5 Berkley Ave (02702-1357)
PHONE 508 644-3404
Joseph Nachado, *Principal*
EMP: 3
SALES (est): 130K Privately Held
SIC: 3479 7213 Coating/Engraving Service Linen Supply Services

(G-7683)
KLA SYSTEMS INC
31 Mill St (02702-1123)
P.O. Box 940 (02702-0896)
PHONE 508 359-7361
Mark E Neville, *President*
Fred Siino, *Vice Pres*
Sandra Matrone Mack, *Admin Sec*
◆ EMP: 8 EST: 2001
SQ FT: 3,000
SALES (est): 1.8MM Privately Held
WEB: www.klasystems.com
SIC: 3589 Mfg Service Industry Machinery

Athol
Worcester County

(G-7684)
ATHOL PRESS INC
Also Called: Athol Daily News
225 Exchange St (01331-1843)
P.O. Box 1000 (01331-5000)
PHONE 978 249-3535
Richard J Chase Jr, *President*
Stephen F Chase, *Treasurer*
Lisa Arnot, *Office Mgr*
Edward G Chase, *Shareholder*
EMP: 45
SQ FT: 16,500
SALES (est): 3.1MM Privately Held
WEB: www.atholdailynews.com
SIC: 2711 Newspapers-Publishing/Printing

(G-7685)
CAMBIUM CORP
339 Main St (01331-2233)
PHONE 978 249-7557
David Kazanowski, *President*
Colleen Kazanowski, *Treasurer*
EMP: 15
SQ FT: 60,000
SALES (est): 2.1MM Privately Held
SIC: 3995 Whol Service Establishment Equipment

(G-7686)
E W SYKES GENERAL CONTRACTORS
5567 S Athol Rd (01331)
P.O. Box 178 (01331-0178)
PHONE 978 249-7655
E William Sykes, *President*
Clinton Sykes, *Vice Pres*
Klint Sykes, *Vice Pres*
Cathi Sykes, *Treasurer*
EMP: 11
SALES: 2.1MM Privately Held
SIC: 3281 1794 Sand & Stone Quarry/Excavation Contractor

(G-7687)
HIGHLAND PRESS OF ATHOL INC
59 Marble St (01331-1803)
PHONE 978 249-6588
Edward Chase, *President*
EMP: 4 EST: 1925
SQ FT: 10,000
SALES (est): 483.3K Privately Held
SIC: 2759 Lithographic Commercial Printing

(G-7688)
KEO MILLING CUTTERS LLC
273 Main St (01331-2237)
PHONE 800 523-5233
Eli Crotzer, *President*
EMP: 386
SALES (est): 6.6MM
SALES (corp-wide): 724.3MM Privately Held
SIC: 3545 Mfg Machine Tool Accessories
HQ: Arch Global Precision Llc
2600 S Telg Rd Ste 180
Bloomfield Hills MI 48302
734 266-6900

(G-7689)
LS STARRETT COMPANY (PA)
121 Crescent St (01331-1915)
PHONE 978 249-3551
Douglas A Starrett, *President*
Mike Chessock, *Division Mgr*
T J Fleck, *General Mgr*
David J Whitham, *General Mgr*
Mike Baczewski, *Vice Pres*
▲ EMP: 1000
SQ FT: 535,000
SALES: 228MM Publicly Held
WEB: www.starrett.com
SIC: 3545 3423 3999 3425 Mfg Hand Measuring Tools Precision Instruments & Other Products

(G-7690)
LS STARRETT COMPANY
Also Called: Repair Dept
121 Crescent St (01331-1915)
PHONE 978 249-3551
Diane McDonald, *Manager*
EMP: 7
SALES (corp-wide): 228MM Publicly Held
WEB: www.starrett.com
SIC: 3545 Mfg Machine Tool Accessories
PA: The L S Starrett Company
121 Crescent St
Athol MA 01331
978 249-3551

(G-7691)
NIAGARA CUTTER ATHOL INC
273 Main St (01331-2237)
PHONE 978 249-2788
Sherwood L Bollier, *President*
William C Szabo, *Treasurer*
Gene May, *Manager*
William Sebring, *Technology*
EMP: 35
SALES (est): 4.9MM
SALES (corp-wide): 63.3MM Privately Held
WEB: www.niagaracutter.com
SIC: 3545 3542 Mfg Machine Tool Accessories Mfg Machine Tools-Forming
PA: Nc Industries, Inc.
150 S 5th St
Reynoldsville PA 15851
248 528-5200

(G-7692)
PEXCO LLC
764 S Athol Rd (01331-9812)
PHONE 978 249-5343
EMP: 126
SALES (corp-wide): 7.9B Privately Held
SIC: 3089 Mfg Plastic Products
HQ: Pexco Llc
6470 E Johns Rssng 430
Johns Creek GA 30097
770 777-8540

(G-7693)
PRODUCTION TOOL & GRINDING
273 Main St (01331-2237)
P.O. Box 440, Orange (01364-0440)
PHONE 978 544-8206
Michael Miller, *President*
Rolland F Rochon, *Vice Pres*
▲ EMP: 11
SQ FT: 8,000
SALES: 1.9MM Privately Held
SIC: 3541 Mfg Machine Tools-Cutting

(G-7694)
SPECTRUM PLASTICS GROUP
764 S Athol Rd (01331-9812)
PHONE 978 249-5343
EMP: 4
SALES (est): 403.8K Privately Held
SIC: 3089 Mfg Plastic Products

Attleboro
Bristol County

(G-7695)
3-D WELDING INC
5 Howard Ireland Dr (02703-4600)
PHONE 508 222-2500
Kevin Donahue, *President*
Greg Donahue, *Vice Pres*
EMP: 15
SALES (est): 2.2MM Privately Held
SIC: 3441 Structural Metal Fabrication

(G-7696)
A MURPHY JAMES & SON INC
Also Called: Murphy, JAS A & Son
1879 County St (02703-8105)
P.O. Box 3006 (02703-0908)
PHONE 508 761-5060
James A Murphy III, *President*
Carolyn Tousignant, *Treasurer*
Bruce Machado, *Manager*
▲ EMP: 25 EST: 1963
SQ FT: 14,500
SALES (est): 2.7MM Privately Held
WEB: www.jambeads.com
SIC: 3915 Whol Jewelry/Precious Stones

(G-7697)
A YOUNG CASTING
35 County St (02703-2126)
P.O. Box 540 (02703-0009)
PHONE 508 222-8188
Nancy Young, *Owner*
EMP: 15
SALES (est): 773.9K Privately Held
SIC: 3324 Investment Castings

(G-7698)
AB GROUP INC
40 John Williams St (02703-3707)
PHONE 508 222-1404
Jason Arenburg, *President*
▲ EMP: 11
SALES (est): 930K Privately Held
SIC: 3961 3911 Mfg Costume Jewelry

(G-7699)
ABBOTT-ACTION INC (PA)
Also Called: Action Container
3 Venus Way (02703-8149)
P.O. Box 2306, Pawtucket RI (02861-0306)
PHONE 401 722-2100
John S Abbott, *President*
Sam Abbott, *VP Opers*
Gail G Conca, *CFO*
Tom Barnes, *Sales Staff*
Marcia Pray, *Marketing Mgr*
EMP: 40
SQ FT: 50,000
SALES (est): 18.5MM Privately Held
SIC: 2653 Mfg Corrugated/Solid Fiber Boxes

(G-7700)
ACS AUXILIARIES GROUP INC
Also Called: Economizer USA
300 Turner St (02703-7713)
PHONE 508 399-3018
Thomas Breslin, *Owner*
EMP: 5
SALES (corp-wide): 1.4B Privately Held
SIC: 3999 Mfg Misc Products
HQ: Acs Auxiliaries Group, Inc.
2900 S 160th St
New Berlin WI 53151

(G-7701)
ADT/DIVERSITY INC
50 Perry Ave (02703-2418)
PHONE 508 222-9601
Enzo Lucciola, *President*
EMP: 8
SQ FT: 5,000
SALES: 500K Privately Held
WEB: www.advanceddie.com
SIC: 3544 Mfg Dies/Tools/Jigs/Fixtures

(G-7702)
AGRICLTRAL RESOURCES MASS DEPT
38 Forest St (02703-2451)
PHONE 774 331-2818
Wayne Andrews, *Manager*
EMP: 6 Privately Held
SIC: 2621 Paper Mill
HQ: Massachusetts Department Of Agricultural Resources
251 Causeway St Ste 500
Boston MA 02114

(G-7703)
ALVITI CREATIONS INC
67 Mechanic St Unit 4 (02703-2036)
PHONE 508 222-4030
EMP: 8
SALES: 500K Privately Held
WEB: www.alviti.com
SIC: 3914 Mfg Ecclesiastical Goods

(G-7704)
AMIC INC
60 Walton St (02703-1408)
PHONE 508 222-5300
Richard Barry, *President*
EMP: 3
SALES (est): 219.2K Privately Held
SIC: 3599 7692 Mfg Industrial Machinery Welding Repair

(G-7705)
ANGIES WORK ROOM INC
466 Washington St Ste 1 (02703-5952)
PHONE 508 761-5636
Earl Hallal Sr, *President*
Nancy Hallal, *Clerk*
EMP: 10
SQ FT: 8,000
SALES (est): 500K Privately Held
SIC: 2391 Mfg Curtains/Draperies

(G-7706)
APPLIED PRECISION TECHNOLOGY
Also Called: Liberty Plastics Company
81 West St (02703-1618)
PHONE 508 226-8700
Peter Desimone, *President*
Donald Jeppe, *VP Mfg*
EMP: 15
SQ FT: 70,000
SALES (est): 1.6MM Privately Held
WEB: www.apt-liberty.com
SIC: 3599 Mfg Industrial Machinery

(G-7707)
ATTLEBORO PANCAKES INC
Also Called: IHOP
383 Washington St (02703-5916)
PHONE 508 399-8189
Richard Sandnes, *President*
Mark Justice, *Treasurer*
EMP: 4

▲ = Import ▼=Export
◆ =Import/Export

SALES (est): 203.9K Privately Held
SIC: 2064 Mfg Candy/Confectionery

(G-7708)
ATTLEBORO SAND & GRAVEL CORP
125 Tiffany St (02703-6349)
P.O. Box 2189, Plainville (02762-0296)
PHONE....508 222-2870
Gerard C Lorusso, *President*
EMP: 7
SALES (est): 783K Privately Held
SIC: 3273 Construction Sand/Gravel

(G-7709)
ATTLEBORO SCHOLARSHIP CO
89 N Main St (02703-2292)
PHONE....508 226-4414
Charles Oliver, *Owner*
EMP: 3
SALES: 656.6K Privately Held
SIC: 3721 Mfg Aircraft

(G-7710)
AUTOMATED FINISHING CO INC
90 County St (02703-2120)
PHONE....508 222-6262
Roy Lambert, *President*
Justin Lambert, *Plant Mgr*
EMP: 42
SQ FT: 30,000
SALES (est): 4MM Privately Held
WEB: www.automatedfinishing.net
SIC: 3479 3471 Computer Engraving And Metal Finishing

(G-7711)
AXIOM WIRE AND CABLE
20 Townsend Rd Ste C (02703-4679)
PHONE....508 498-8899
Patrick Tiberio, *Owner*
EMP: 6
SALES: 1.7MM Privately Held
SIC: 3496 Mfg Misc Fabricated Wire Products

(G-7712)
BARRY INDUSTRIES INC
60 Walton St (02703-1408)
PHONE....508 226-3350
Richard L Barry, *President*
EMP: 75
SQ FT: 30,000
SALES (est): 14.5MM Privately Held
WEB: www.barryind.com
SIC: 3625 3672 Mfg Relays/Industrial Controls Mfg Printed Circuit Boards

(G-7713)
BOSTON FABRICATIONS
39 Franklin R Mckay Rd (02703-4625)
P.O. Box 8, Norwood (02062-0008)
PHONE....781 762-9185
Allen Brauneis, *President*
EMP: 10
SQ FT: 5,500
SALES (est): 988K Privately Held
WEB: www.bostonfab.com
SIC: 2541 Mfg Wood Partitions/Fixtures

(G-7714)
BRISTOL PLACE INC
555 Pleasant St Ste 201 (02703-2440)
PHONE....508 226-2300
EMP: 8
SALES (est): 1.2MM Privately Held
SIC: 2621 Paper Mills

(G-7715)
BRUCE DIAMOND CORPORATION
Also Called: D&S Engineered Products
1231 County St (02703-6101)
PHONE....508 222-3755
Stephen V Puleston, *President*
Robert B Puleston, *Principal*
Scott Obrien, *Vice Pres*
Sherly Cordero, *Purch Agent*
Joan Mc Kenna, *Controller*
EMP: 40 EST: 1955
SQ FT: 68,000
SALES: 9.9MM Privately Held
WEB: www.brucediamond.com
SIC: 3545 Mfg Machine Tool Accessories

(G-7716)
CASTECHNOLOGIES INC
40 Townsend Rd (02703-4628)
P.O. Box 478 (02703-0008)
PHONE....508 222-2915
James W Tenglin, *President*
Roger F Tenglin, *Vice Pres*
Malcolm C Tenglin, *Treasurer*
Kennith Tenglin, *Marketing Staff*
EMP: 19
SQ FT: 5,600
SALES (est): 3.4MM Privately Held
SIC: 3369 Nonferrous Metal Foundry

(G-7717)
CENDRES+METAUX USA INC
93 Tyler St (02703-5815)
PHONE....508 316-0962
Marc Diserens, *President*
▲ EMP: 3
SALES (est): 270K Privately Held
SIC: 3843 Mfg Dental Equipment/Supplies

(G-7718)
CHARDAN LTD
453 S Main St Ste 1 (02703-6440)
PHONE....508 992-0854
Charles E Katsanos, *President*
EMP: 4
SQ FT: 20,000
SALES (est): 397.9K Privately Held
SIC: 3061 Mfg Of Calendered Rubber Products

(G-7719)
CHARLES THOMAE & SON INC
15 Maynard St (02703-3005)
PHONE....508 222-0785
Charles F Thomae, *President*
Diane Thomae, *Treasurer*
EMP: 20 EST: 1920
SQ FT: 5,000
SALES (est): 2.6MM Privately Held
WEB: www.chasthomae.com
SIC: 3911 5944 3965 3961 Mfg Precious Mtl Jewelry Ret Jewelry Mfg Fastener/Button/Pins Mfg Costume Jewelry Mfg Games/Toys

(G-7720)
CITIWORKS CORP
20 Rutledge Dr (02703-7835)
PHONE....508 761-7400
John A Chatfield, *President*
EMP: 18 EST: 1885
SQ FT: 14,000
SALES (est): 4.2MM Privately Held
WEB: www.citiworks.com
SIC: 3496 8742 5063 1731 Mfg Misc Fab Wire Prdts Mgmt Consulting Svcs Whol Electrical Equip Electrical Contractor Special Trade Contractor

(G-7721)
CMT MATERIALS INC
Also Called: Engineered Syntactic Systems
107 Frank Mossberg Dr (02703-4615)
PHONE....508 226-3901
Anthony Colageo, *President*
Kathleen Boivin, *Engineer*
Michael Vidal, *Engineer*
Mark Donovan, *Accounting Mgr*
Conor Carlin, *Sales Staff*
▲ EMP: 19 EST: 1998
SQ FT: 20,000
SALES (est): 4.5MM Privately Held
WEB: www.cmtmaterials.com
SIC: 3089 Mfg Plastic Products

(G-7722)
COLONIAL LITHOGRAPH INC
129 Bank St Ste 5 (02703-1763)
P.O. Box 449 (02703-0008)
PHONE....508 222-1832
Charles Guillette, *President*
David H Redding, *Vice Pres*
Catherine La Salandra, *VP Finance*
EMP: 10
SQ FT: 7,200
SALES (est): 1.2MM Privately Held
SIC: 2752 Lithographic Commercial Printing

(G-7723)
COMPOSITE MODULES
Also Called: CMI
61 Union St (02703-2936)
PHONE....508 226-6969
Robert M Jones, *President*
David Charest, *Treasurer*
▲ EMP: 70
SQ FT: 100,000
SALES (est): 12.7MM Privately Held
WEB: www.cmodules.com
SIC: 3674 3441 Mfg Semiconductors/Related Devices Structural Metal Fabrication

(G-7724)
COMTRAN CABLE LLC
330 Turner St (02703-7714)
PHONE....508 399-7004
Dimitri Maistrellis, *President*
David A Allegrezza, *Treasurer*
Robert W Webb, *Admin Sec*
▲ EMP: 130
SQ FT: 150,000
SALES (est): 59.4MM
SALES (corp-wide): 225.3B Publicly Held
WEB: www.comtrancorp.com
SIC: 3356 Nonferrous Rolling/Drawing
HQ: Marmon Holdings, Inc.
181 W Madison St Ste 2600
Chicago IL 60602
312 372-9500

(G-7725)
CRAFT INC
1929 County St (02703-8107)
P.O. Box 3049 (02703-0912)
PHONE....508 761-7917
Eric J Roy, *President*
Raymond G Roy, *Shareholder*
◆ EMP: 36 EST: 1950
SQ FT: 67,000
SALES (est): 8.5MM Privately Held
WEB: www.craft-inc.com
SIC: 3429 3469 Mfg Hardware Mfg Metal Stampings

(G-7726)
DAL-TRAC OIL COMPANY
143 Fisher St (02703-4810)
PHONE....508 222-3935
Michael Santos, *Principal*
EMP: 3 EST: 2007
SALES (est): 412.5K Privately Held
SIC: 2911 Petroleum Refiner

(G-7727)
DORANCO INC
81 West St (02703-1618)
PHONE....508 236-0290
David J Doran, *CEO*
Joseph E Doran Jr, *Vice Pres*
Samuel M Andrews, *CFO*
▲ EMP: 6 EST: 1976
SQ FT: 36,000
SALES (est): 1.1MM Privately Held
WEB: www.doranco.net
SIC: 3613 3993 3651 3444 Mfg Switchgear/Boards Mfg Signs/Ad Specialties Mfg Home Audio/Video Eqp Mfg Sheet Metalwork

(G-7728)
DORIE ENTERPRISES INC
Also Called: New England Counter Top
470 Colvin St (02703-8052)
P.O. Box F, Pawtucket RI (02861-0606)
PHONE....508 761-7588
James H Maziarz, *President*
EMP: 4
SQ FT: 5,000
SALES (est): 350K Privately Held
SIC: 2541 Mfg Wood Partitions/Fixtures

(G-7729)
DUANE SMITH
139 Glendale Rd (02703-2603)
PHONE....508 222-9541
EMP: 3 EST: 2000
SALES (est): 130K Privately Held
SIC: 3949 Mfg Sporting/Athletic Goods

(G-7730)
E A DION INC
33 Franklin R Mckay Rd (02703-4625)
P.O. Box 2098 (02703-0035)
PHONE....800 445-1007
Edward A Dion Jr, *President*
Melissa Carvalho, *Vice Pres*
Dennis W Dion, *Vice Pres*
Dennis Dion, *Vice Pres*
Paul Prendergast, *Vice Pres*
▲ EMP: 105 EST: 1968
SQ FT: 30,000
SALES (est): 18MM Privately Held
WEB: www.eadion.com
SIC: 3911 3993 Mfg Precious Metal Jewelry Mfg Signs/Advertising Specialties

(G-7731)
EF LEACH & COMPANY
Also Called: General Findings
8 N Main St Ste 500 (02703-2273)
P.O. Box 358 (02703-0006)
PHONE....508 643-3309
Edwin F Leach II, *President*
Joe Sisto, *COO*
Richard St Pierre, *CFO*
▲ EMP: 425 EST: 1899
SQ FT: 100,000
SALES (est): 61.9MM Privately Held
SIC: 3356 3911 3915 3951 Nonferrous Rollng/Drawng

(G-7732)
EMS ENGNRED MTLS SOLUTIONS LLC (DH)
39 Perry Ave (02703-2417)
PHONE....508 342-2100
Paul Duffy, *COO*
Kevin Folan, *CFO*
▲ EMP: 200 EST: 2007
SALES (est): 104.6MM
SALES (corp-wide): 352.7MM Privately Held
WEB: www.emsclad.com
SIC: 3351 Copper Rolling/Drawing
HQ: Wickeder Westfalenstahl Gmbh
Hauptstr. 6
Wickede (Ruhr) 58739
237 791-701

(G-7733)
ENGINRED SYNTACTIC SYSTEMS LLC
107 Frank Mossberg Dr (02703-4615)
PHONE....508 226-3907
Thomas J Murray, *Mng Member*
Anthony J Colageo,
Noel J Tessier,
▲ EMP: 8
SALES (est): 699.8K Privately Held
SIC: 2821 Mfg Plastic Materials/Resins

(G-7734)
FETERIA TOOL & FINDINGS
1285 County St (02703-6103)
PHONE....508 222-7788
John Feteria, *Owner*
EMP: 9
SQ FT: 50,000
SALES (est): 894.1K Privately Held
SIC: 3423 7389 Mfg Jewelry Tools Assemble Electrical Products And Packages Jewelry

(G-7735)
FILTREX CORP
150 Bank St (02703-1743)
PHONE....508 226-7711
Sohail Zaiter, *President*
▲ EMP: 3
SQ FT: 10,000
SALES: 3.5MM Privately Held
WEB: www.filtrexsystems.com
SIC: 3569 Mfg Filters

(G-7736)
FINE EDGE TOOL COMPANY INC
13 Maynard St (02703-3005)
PHONE....508 222-7511
Messias C Vasconcelos, *President*
EMP: 8
SQ FT: 6,000

GEOGRAPHIC

SALES (est): 1MM **Privately Held**
SIC: 3423 3469 Mfg Hand/Edge Tools Mfg Metal Stampings

(G-7737)
FIREBALL HEAT TREATING CO INC
34 John Williams St (02703-3707)
PHONE..................................508 222-2617
Thomas Thomson, *President*
Jim Thomson, *Systems Mgr*
EMP: 8
SQ FT: 5,000
SALES (est): 1.3MM **Privately Held**
WEB: www.fireballheattreating.com
SIC: 3398 Metal Heat Treating

(G-7738)
FORTIFIBER CORPORATION
55 Starkey Ave (02703-1813)
P.O. Box 959 (02703-0959)
PHONE..................................508 222-3500
Stephanie Abdallah, *Purchasing*
Steve Fisk, *Branch Mgr*
EMP: 50
SQ FT: 20,000 **Privately Held**
WEB: www.fortifiber.com
SIC: 2671 2672 2621 Mfg Packaging Paper/Film Mfg Coated/Laminated Paper Paper Mill
HQ: Fortifiber, Llc
300 Industrial Dr
Fernley NV 89408
800 773-4777

(G-7739)
GARNER LEACH INC
23 Frank Mossberg Dr (02703-4623)
P.O. Box 2967 (02703-0967)
PHONE..................................508 226-5660
James P Brown, *Manager*
EMP: 50
SQ FT: 3,000
SALES (corp-wide): 225.3B **Publicly Held**
SIC: 3356 Nonferrous Rolling/Drawing Mfg Dental Equipment/Supplies
HQ: Leachgarner, Inc.
49 Pearl St
Attleboro MA 02703
508 222-7400

(G-7740)
GENERAL METAL FINISHING LLC
Also Called: Pep General Metal Finishing
42 Frank Mossberg Dr (02703-4697)
PHONE..................................508 222-9683
Stephen Chatfield, *President*
EMP: 98 **EST:** 1974
SQ FT: 30,000
SALES (est): 12.3MM
SALES (corp-wide): 770.6MM **Publicly Held**
WEB: www.genmetal.com
SIC: 3471 Plating/Polishing Service
HQ: Precision Engineered Products Llc
110 Frank Mossberg Dr
Attleboro MA 02703
508 226-5600

(G-7741)
GJM MANUFACTURING INC
453 S Main St (02703-6437)
P.O. Box 1074 (02703-0018)
PHONE..................................508 222-9322
Gary Mc Kearney, *President*
Kim McKearney, *Office Mgr*
EMP: 5
SQ FT: 6,500
SALES: 400K **Privately Held**
SIC: 3469 Mfg Metal Stampings

(G-7742)
GLOBAL ENTERPRISES INC
Also Called: Global Transfer
699 Washington St (02703-6946)
P.O. Box 3074 (02703-0915)
PHONE..................................508 399-8270
Stanley Golenia, *President*
Krystyna Golenia, *Agent*
EMP: 6
SALES (est): 452.5K **Privately Held**
SIC: 2741 Misc Publishing

(G-7743)
GUYOT BROTHERS COMPANY INC
20 John Williams St (02703-3707)
P.O. Box 2378 (02703-0040)
PHONE..................................508 222-2000
Stephen Guyot, *President*
Andrea Twombly, *Vice Pres*
Marshall A Guyot, *Treasurer*
Marsha Leary, *Admin Sec*
EMP: 17 **EST:** 1904
SQ FT: 26,000
SALES (est): 1.9MM **Privately Held**
WEB: www.guyotbrothers.com
SIC: 3915 Mfg Jewelers' Materials

(G-7744)
HALLMARK HEALY GROUP INC (DH)
Also Called: Leach Garner-A Brkshire Hathaw
49 Pearl St (02703-3940)
PHONE..................................508 222-9234
Howard Kilguss, *President*
EMP: 190 **EST:** 1965
SQ FT: 30,000
SALES (est): 26.9MM
SALES (corp-wide): 225.3B **Publicly Held**
WEB: www.hallmarksweet.com
SIC: 3915 5944 3911 Mfg Jewelers' Materials Ret Jewelry Mfg Precious Metal Jewelry
HQ: Leachgarner, Inc.
49 Pearl St
Attleboro MA 02703
508 222-7400

(G-7745)
HALLMARK SWEET/EKRU INC
49 Pearl St (02703-3940)
PHONE..................................508 226-9600
Richard Powers, *President*
Austin Carr, *CFO*
▲ **EMP:** 200
SALES (est): 26MM
SALES (corp-wide): 225.3B **Publicly Held**
SIC: 3339 Primary Nonferrous Metal Producer
HQ: Hallmark Healy Group, Inc
49 Pearl St
Attleboro MA 02703
508 222-9234

(G-7746)
HI-TECH INC
50 Perry Ave (02703-2418)
PHONE..................................401 454-4086
John B Lavin, *President*
Judy Lavin, *Vice Pres*
EMP: 12
SQ FT: 10,000
SALES (est): 1.9MM **Privately Held**
WEB: www.hitech-stamping.com
SIC: 3469 3714 Mfg Metal Stampings Mfg Motor Vehicle Parts/Accessories

(G-7747)
HILLMAN ENTERPRISES (PA)
24 Angeline St (02703)
PHONE..................................508 761-6967
Russell Hillman, *Owner*
EMP: 3
SQ FT: 5,000
SALES (est): 314.2K **Privately Held**
WEB: www.hillman.com
SIC: 3312 1791 1796 Blast Furnace-Steel Works Structural Steel Erection Building Equipment Installation

(G-7748)
HY-TEMP INC
34 John Williams St (02703-3707)
PHONE..................................508 222-6626
Bruce Sargeant, *President*
Bruce Sargent, *President*
Jane Sargeant, *Vice Pres*
EMP: 14
SQ FT: 2,500
SALES: 100.5K **Privately Held**
SIC: 3398 Metal Heat Treating

(G-7749)
INDUSTRIAL PRODUCTION SUPPLIES
19 Franklin St (02703-2701)
P.O. Box 1328 (02703-0023)
PHONE..................................508 226-1776
EMP: 14
SALES (est): 1.1MM **Privately Held**
SIC: 3089 Mfg Plastic Products

(G-7750)
INTERPLEX ENGINEERED PDTS INC (DH)
54 Venus Way (02703-8126)
PHONE..................................508 399-6810
Jack Seidler, *CEO*
Bob Hudson, *President*
Ronald Labow, *Chairman*
Paul Dickson, *Vice Pres*
Keith Maranto, *Engineer*
▲ **EMP:** 67
SQ FT: 125,000
SALES (est): 23.2MM **Privately Held**
SIC: 3471 Plating/Polishing Service
HQ: Interplex Industries, Inc.
231 Ferris Ave
Rumford RI 02916
718 961-6212

(G-7751)
INTERPLEX ETCH LOGIC LLC
54 Venus Way (02703-8126)
PHONE..................................508 399-6810
Mark Bowden, *General Mgr*
Rick Fay, *Engineer*
Timothy Diaz, *Technician*
Steven Feinstein,
EMP: 35
SALES: 6MM **Privately Held**
SIC: 3469 Mfg Metal Stampings

(G-7752)
INVERNESS CORPORATION (DH)
49 Pearl St (02703-3940)
PHONE..................................774 203-1130
William Mead, *President*
◆ **EMP:** 23
SQ FT: 30,000
SALES (est): 4.4MM
SALES (corp-wide): 225.3B **Publicly Held**
WEB: www.invernesscorp.com
SIC: 3999 Mfg Misc Products

(G-7753)
JAB INDUSTRIES INC
185 Washington St (02703-5550)
PHONE..................................401 447-9668
Carla M Bouthillette, *Principal*
EMP: 3 **EST:** 2012
SALES (est): 185.5K **Privately Held**
SIC: 3999 Mfg Misc Products

(G-7754)
JACK HODGDON
Also Called: Moore Co
67 Mechanic St Unit 3 (02703-2036)
PHONE..................................508 223-9990
Jack Hodgdon, *Owner*
EMP: 6
SQ FT: 1,400
SALES: 500K **Privately Held**
SIC: 3911 3479 Mfg Precious Metal Jewelry Coating/Engraving Service

(G-7755)
JOHN E LEPPER INC
10 Tappan Ave (02703-3126)
PHONE..................................508 222-6723
Robert W Lepper, *President*
John A Lepper, *Vice Pres*
EMP: 6 **EST:** 1954
SQ FT: 4,000
SALES (est): 470K **Privately Held**
WEB: www.jelepper.com
SIC: 3911 Mfg Pewter & Brass Jewelry

(G-7756)
KITA USA INC
64 Water St (02703-2056)
PHONE..................................774 331-2265
Tomohiko Kita, *Director*
EMP: 5
SQ FT: 7,000
SALES (est): 87.1K
SALES (corp-wide): 451.7MM **Publicly Held**
SIC: 3674 Mfg Semiconductors/Related Devices
PA: Cohu, Inc.
12367 Crosthwaite Cir
Poway CA 92064
858 848-8100

(G-7757)
KNOBBY KRAFTERS INC
129 Bank St Ste 5 (02703-1763)
P.O. Box 300 (02703-0005)
PHONE..................................508 222-7272
Nicholas W Nerney, *President*
Dexter P Nerney, *Treasurer*
▲ **EMP:** 40 **EST:** 1924
SALES (est): 4.5MM **Privately Held**
WEB: www.knobbyline.com
SIC: 3089 Plastic Injection Molding

(G-7758)
LARSON TOOL & STAMPING COMPANY
90 Olive St (02703-3802)
PHONE..................................508 222-0897
Charles Cederberg, *President*
William E Larson, *CFO*
Daniel G Larson, *Admin Sec*
▲ **EMP:** 70
SQ FT: 90,000
SALES (est): 26.1MM **Privately Held**
WEB: www.larsontool.com
SIC: 3469 3443 Mfg Metal Stampings Mfg Fabricated Plate Work

(G-7759)
LENN ARTS INC
65 Newcomb St (02703-1403)
PHONE..................................508 223-3400
Alfred G Germoni, *President*
Albert C Gemme Jr, *Vice Pres*
EMP: 24
SQ FT: 6,000
SALES (est): 3.3MM **Privately Held**
WEB: www.lennarts.com
SIC: 3911 3961 Mfg Precious Metal Jewelry Mfg Emblematic Jewelry

(G-7760)
M S COMPANY
61 School St (02703-3931)
P.O. Box 298 (02703-0005)
PHONE..................................508 222-1700
Kurt R Schweinshaut, *President*
Mark Schweinshaut, *Vice Pres*
Carl M Schweinshaut, *Treasurer*
Aimee Breindel, *Accounting Mgr*
David Cappuccino, *VP Sales*
▲ **EMP:** 75 **EST:** 1913
SQ FT: 45,000
SALES (est): 12.2MM **Privately Held**
WEB: www.mscompany.net
SIC: 3911 3915 Mfg Precious Metal Jewelry Mfg Jewelers' Materials

(G-7761)
MANTROSE-HAEUSER CO INC
113 Olive St (02703-3801)
PHONE..................................203 454-1800
Donald Young, *Principal*
Bin Zhong, *Research*
EMP: 75
SALES (corp-wide): 5.5B **Publicly Held**
WEB: www.mantrose.com
SIC: 2851 Mfg Paints/Allied Products
HQ: Mantrose-Haeuser Co., Inc.
100 Nyala Farms Rd
Westport CT 06880

(G-7762)
MARCOTT DESIGNS
48 Eddy St Ste 2 (02703-2406)
PHONE..................................508 226-2680
Marc Rempelakis, *Partner*
EMP: 4
SQ FT: 2,400
SALES (est): 493.4K **Privately Held**
SIC: 2396 2759 2395 Mfg Auto/Apparel Trimming Commercial Printing Pleating/Stitching Services

(G-7763)
MARLEY HALL INC
453 S Main St Ste 4 (02703-6440)
PHONE..................................508 226-2666
Kim McKirney, *Co-Owner*
EMP: 4
SALES (est): 280K **Privately Held**
SIC: 3911 Mfg Precious Metal Jewelry

(G-7764)
MARTELLS METAL WORKS
76 Dewey Ave (02703-1507)
PHONE..................................508 226-0136
George F Martell, *President*
George Martell, *President*
EMP: 3
SALES (est): 350.5K **Privately Held**
SIC: 3312 Blast Furnace-Steel Works

(G-7765)
MATRIX METAL PRODUCTS INC
53 County St (02703-2127)
P.O. Box 2173 (02703-0037)
PHONE..................................508 226-2374
Robert H Hanson Jr, *President*
Robert H Hanson, *Corp Secy*
EMP: 12
SQ FT: 4,000
SALES (est): 2.2MM **Privately Held**
WEB: www.matrixmetals.com
SIC: 3469 Mfg Metal Stampings

(G-7766)
MCVAN INC
35 Frank Mossberg Dr (02703-4623)
PHONE..................................508 431-2400
Frederick Adler, *President*
Angela McAdams, *General Mgr*
Craig Adler, *Vice Pres*
Brian Jacobson, *Plant Mgr*
Maureen Pinney, *Cust Mgr*
▲ **EMP:** 22 **EST:** 1946
SQ FT: 12,000
SALES (est): 5.5MM **Privately Held**
WEB: www.mcvaninc.com
SIC: 3911 5049 Mfg Precious Metal Jewelry Whol Professional Equipment

(G-7767)
MESSER LLC
525 Pleasant St (02703-2421)
PHONE..................................508 236-0222
Albert Brooks, *Branch Mgr*
EMP: 22
SALES (corp-wide): 1.4B **Privately Held**
SIC: 2813 Mfg Industrial Gases
HQ: Messer Llc
200 Somerset Corp Blvd # 7000
Bridgewater NJ 08807
908 464-8100

(G-7768)
MINI-SYSTEMS INC
Also Called: Thin Film Division
45 Frank Mossberg Dr (02703-4623)
PHONE..................................508 695-0203
Robert Lamar, *Vice Pres*
EMP: 70
SALES (est): 8.3MM
SALES (corp-wide): 14MM **Privately Held**
WEB: www.mini-systemsinc.com
SIC: 3676 Mfg Thin Film Electronic Resistors
PA: Mini-Systems, Inc.
20 David Rd
North Attleboro MA 02760
508 695-1420

(G-7769)
MORSE SAND & GRAVEL CORP
125 Tiffany St (02703-6349)
PHONE..................................508 809-4644
Leo Barry, *President*
EMP: 35
SQ FT: 1,000
SALES (est): 3.9MM **Privately Held**
WEB: www.morsesg.com
SIC: 3273 5211 Mfg Ready-Mixed Concrete Ret Lumber/Building Materials

(G-7770)
MR IDEA INC
Also Called: Storm Duds Raingear
100 Frank Mossberg Dr (02703-4632)
PHONE..................................508 222-0155
Gary Libman, *President*
▲ **EMP:** 30
SQ FT: 20,000
SALES: 7MM **Privately Held**
WEB: www.stormduds.com
SIC: 3911 5023 2385 Mfg Waterproof Outerwear Mfg Precious Mtl Jewelry Whol Homefurnishings

(G-7771)
NEPTUNE INC
39 Slater St (02703-5427)
PHONE..................................508 222-8313
Frank Torngren, *President*
Sherry Torngren, *Vice Pres*
EMP: 3 **EST:** 1977
SALES: 20K **Privately Held**
WEB: www.alliancemerc.com
SIC: 3949 Mfg Sporting/Athletic Goods

(G-7772)
NEW AGE EMS INC
527 Pleasant St (02703-2463)
PHONE..................................508 226-6090
EMP: 30
SALES (est): 1.2MM **Privately Held**
SIC: 3672 Mfg Printed Circuit Boards

(G-7773)
NORKING COMPANY INC
53 County St (02703-2127)
P.O. Box 446 (02703-0008)
PHONE..................................508 222-3100
Robert H Hanson, *President*
Chris Hanson, *Sales Mgr*
EMP: 22
SQ FT: 8,000
SALES (est): 3.8MM **Privately Held**
WEB: www.norkingco.com
SIC: 3469 3398 Mfg Metal Stampings Structural Metal Fabrication Metal Heat Treating

(G-7774)
NORTH ATTLEBORO JEWELRY CO
112 Bank St (02703-1738)
PHONE..................................508 222-4660
William Romero Jr, *President*
Lynn Allard, *Cust Mgr*
▲ **EMP:** 9
SQ FT: 10,000
SALES (est): 1.4MM **Privately Held**
SIC: 3911 3961 Mfg Precious Metal Jewelry Mfg Costume Jewelry

(G-7775)
PEEL PEOPLE LLC
140 N Main St Unit 4a (02703-2243)
PHONE..................................773 255-9886
EMP: 4
SALES (est): 130.4K **Privately Held**
SIC: 2754 Gravure Commercial Printing

(G-7776)
PEP INDUSTRIES LLC
110 Frank Mossberg Dr (02703-4632)
PHONE..................................508 226-5600
Alan Huffenus, *CEO*
John Manci, *Principal*
EMP: 1053
SALES (est): 71.6MM **Privately Held**
SIC: 3089 3351 3469 3471 Mfg Plastic Products Copper Rolling/Drawing Metal Stampings Plating/Polishing Svcs Conductive Wire Dvcs

(G-7777)
PLASTIC CRAFT NOVELTY CO INC
Also Called: P Craft Jewelry
12 Dunham St Apt A (02703-2946)
PHONE..................................508 222-1486
Peter Manickas III, *President*
EMP: 45 **EST:** 1931
SQ FT: 35,000
SALES (est): 5.6MM **Privately Held**
WEB: www.pcraftjewelry.com
SIC: 3961 5944 Mfg Costume Jewelry Ret Jewelry

(G-7778)
PLEASANT PRINTING CO
163 Pleasant St Ste 5 (02703-2472)
PHONE..................................508 222-3366
Lorraine Nye, *Owner*
Jeff Nye, *Executive*
EMP: 11
SQ FT: 2,900
SALES (est): 1.2MM **Privately Held**
WEB: www.pleasantprinting.com
SIC: 2752 Offset Printing

(G-7779)
POLYFIBER LLC
55 Starkey Ave (02703-1813)
PHONE..................................508 222-3500
Blair Holland, *General Mgr*
Andrew Dickens, *Principal*
Bill Griffith, *Principal*
Michael Johnson, *Principal*
Dave Lindblade, *Principal*
▲ **EMP:** 22
SALES (est): 6.6MM
SALES (corp-wide): 26.9MM **Privately Held**
SIC: 2671 Mfg Packaging Paper/Film
PA: Holland Manufacturing Company, Inc.
15 Main St
Succasunna NJ 07876
973 584-8141

(G-7780)
PORTELA SONI MEDICAL LLC
57 Totten Rd (02703-6392)
PHONE..................................508 818-2727
Francisco Portela, *CEO*
Amit Soni, *COO*
Kenneth Kim, *Vice Pres*
David Berger, *General Counsel*
EMP: 8
SALES (est): 322.9K **Privately Held**
SIC: 3841 7389 Mfg Surgical/Medical Instruments Business Serv Non-Commercial Site

(G-7781)
POWER EQUIPMENT CO INC (PA)
Also Called: Superior Power Systems
7 Franklin R Mckay Rd (02703-4692)
PHONE..................................508 226-3410
Paul Toher, *President*
EMP: 27
SQ FT: 15,000
SALES (est): 2.4MM **Privately Held**
WEB: www.powerequipmentco.com
SIC: 3621 Mfg Motors/Generators

(G-7782)
PRECISION ENGINEERED PDTS LLC (DH)
Also Called: P E P
110 Frank Mossberg Dr (02703-4632)
PHONE..................................508 226-5600
John Manzi, *President*
Tom Murray, *Finance Dir*
Cheryl Palmer, *Admin Sec*
EMP: 9
SQ FT: 12,000
SALES (est): 351.4MM
SALES (corp-wide): 770.6MM **Publicly Held**
WEB: www.pep-corp.com
SIC: 3643 3469 3841 3471 Mfg Conductive Wire Dvcs Mfg Metal Stampings Mfg Surgical/Med Instr Plating/Polishing Svcs Mfg Plastic Products
HQ: Precision Engineered Products Holdings, Inc.
42 Frank Mossberg Dr
Attleboro MA 02703
508 226-5600

(G-7783)
R H CHENEY INC
25 Townsend Rd (02703-4627)
P.O. Box 536 (02703-0009)
PHONE..................................508 222-7300
Stuart Neily, *CEO*
Brian Neily, *President*
◆ **EMP:** 10 **EST:** 1955
SQ FT: 10,500
SALES (est): 1.1MM **Privately Held**
WEB: www.rhcheney.com
SIC: 3469 Mfg Metal Stampings

(G-7784)
R L BARRY INC
60 Walton St (02703-1408)
PHONE..................................508 226-3350
Richard L Barry, *President*
James Soares, *Vice Pres*
EMP: 10
SALES (est): 691.9K **Privately Held**
WEB: www.amic.com
SIC: 3599 3471 Machine Shop & Plating Of Formed Products

(G-7785)
REEVES COINC
51 Newcomb St (02703-1420)
P.O. Box 509 (02703-0009)
PHONE..................................508 222-2877
Thomas Reeves, *President*
M Cronin, *Clerk*
EMP: 25 **EST:** 1947
SQ FT: 17,000
SALES (est): 3.9MM **Privately Held**
WEB: www.reevesnamepins.com
SIC: 3089 3993 3965 3452 Mfg Plastic Products Mfg Signs/Ad Specialties Mfg Fastener/Button/Pins Mfg Bolts/Screws/Rivets

(G-7786)
RHODE ISLAND MKTG & PRTG INC
Also Called: AlphaGraphics
41 Deerfield Rd Unit 11 (02703-7871)
PHONE..................................401 351-4000
Brian Decamp, *President*
EMP: 7
SALES (est): 593.8K **Privately Held**
SIC: 2752 Comm Prtg Litho

(G-7787)
RICHLINE GROUP INC
49 Pearl St (02703-3940)
PHONE..................................774 203-1199
EMP: 198
SALES (corp-wide): 225.3B **Publicly Held**
SIC: 3911 Mfg Precious Metal Jewelry
HQ: Richline Group, Inc.
1385 Broadway Fl 14
New York NY 10018

(G-7788)
RIKA DENSHI AMERICA INC
112 Frank Mossberg Dr (02703-4632)
PHONE..................................508 226-2080
Yasuko Toda, *President*
Steve Amadio, *QC Dir*
Keith Waterman, *Sales Staff*
Mark Sprague, *Manager*
EMP: 20
SQ FT: 18,000
SALES (est): 4.7MM **Privately Held**
WEB: www.testprobe.com
SIC: 3825 Mfg Electrical Measuring Instruments

(G-7789)
ROBBINS COMPANY
Also Called: Engage2excel
400 Oneil Blvd (02703-5147)
P.O. Box 2966 (02703-0966)
PHONE..................................508 222-2900
G Brett Tharpe, *President*
Joel Kepley, *CFO*
Neal Cao, *CIO*
Cameron Tartt, *Director*
▲ **EMP:** 216 **EST:** 1892
SQ FT: 100,000
SALES (est): 5.7MM **Privately Held**
WEB: www.therobbinsco.com
SIC: 3911 Mfg Precious Metal Jewelry
PA: Engage2excel, Inc.
149 Crawford Rd
Statesville NC 28625

(G-7790)
RONALD PRATT COMPANY INC
50 Perry Ave (02703-2418)
PHONE..................................508 222-9601
Michael Reil, *President*
EMP: 25 **EST:** 2013
SALES (est): 3MM **Privately Held**
SIC: 3915 Mfg Jewelers' Materials

GEOGRAPHIC

(G-7791)
RUSTOLEUM ATTLEBORO PLANT
113 Olive St (02703-3801)
PHONE..................................508 222-3710
Mike Jurist, *Principal*
◆ **EMP:** 4
SALES (est): 527.1K **Privately Held**
SIC: 2851 Mfg Paints/Allied Products

(G-7792)
SENSATA TECHNOLOGIES INC (HQ)
529 Pleasant St (02703-2421)
PHONE..................................508 236-3800
Martha Sullivan, *President*
Steven Beringhause, *Exec VP*
Allisha Elliott, *Senior VP*
Harry Fox, *Vice Pres*
Kate Raposa, *Opers Spvr*
◆ **EMP:** 800
SQ FT: 22,000
SALES: 3.3B
SALES (corp-wide): 3.5B **Privately Held**
WEB: www.sensata.com
SIC: 3679 Mfg Electronic Components

(G-7793)
SENSATA TECHNOLOGIES IND INC (DH)
529 Pleasant St (02703-2421)
PHONE..................................508 236-3800
Steven Dow, *President*
James Butler, *CFO*
Chris Reading, *Technology*
EMP: 6
SALES (est): 237.7MM
SALES (corp-wide): 3.5B **Privately Held**
SIC: 3676 3625 Mfg Electronic Resistors Mfg Relays/Industrial Controls
HQ: Sensata Technologies, Inc.
529 Pleasant St
Attleboro MA 02703
508 236-3800

(G-7794)
SENSATA TECHNOLOGIES MASS INC (DH)
529 Pleasant St (02703-2421)
P.O. Box 2964 (02703-0964)
PHONE..................................508 236-3800
Thomas Wroe, *Ch of Bd*
Fatima Silva, *Admin Sec*
▲ **EMP:** 60
SALES (est): 15.9MM
SALES (corp-wide): 3.5B **Privately Held**
SIC: 3679 Mfg Electronic Components
HQ: Sensata Technologies, Inc.
529 Pleasant St
Attleboro MA 02703
508 236-3800

(G-7795)
STERGIS ALUMINUM PRODUCTS CORP
Also Called: Stergis/Alliance
79 Walton St (02703-1418)
PHONE..................................508 455-0661
Augustus J Stergis, *President*
Michael Murphy, *Vice Pres*
Kathleen Courtney, *Treasurer*
John N Altomare, *Admin Sec*
EMP: 48 **EST:** 1962
SQ FT: 48,000
SALES (est): 12.2MM **Privately Held**
WEB: www.stergis.com
SIC: 3442 3089 Mfg Metal Doors/Sash/Trim Mfg Plastic Products

(G-7796)
STERNGOLD DENTAL LLC
Also Called: A P M Sterngold
23 Frank Mossberg Dr (02703-4653)
PHONE..................................508 226-5660
Gordon Craig, *CEO*
Ryan Mansfield, *Vice Pres*
Christopher Franklin, *CFO*
Laura Greige, *Accounts Mgr*
David Skalrski, *Mng Member*
▲ **EMP:** 25
SQ FT: 30,000
SALES (est): 4.7MM **Privately Held**
SIC: 3843 Mfg Dental Equipment/Supplies

(G-7797)
SUPERIOR DIE & STAMPING INC
96 County St (02703-2120)
PHONE..................................774 203-3674
Stephen Quaglia, *President*
Fred Capriccio, *Owner*
EMP: 9
SQ FT: 3,000
SALES (est): 961.8K **Privately Held**
SIC: 3544 Mfg Of Tools & Dies

(G-7798)
SUPERIOR POWER SYSTEMS
7 Franklin R Mckay Rd (02703-4625)
PHONE..................................508 226-3400
Paul Toher, *President*
EMP: 4
SALES (est): 242.6K **Privately Held**
WEB: www.superiorpowersys.com
SIC: 3621 Mfg Motors/Generators

(G-7799)
SWEET METAL FINISHING INC
Also Called: SMP DBA A BAND FOR BROTHERS
28 John Williams St (02703-3707)
P.O. Box 400 (02703-0007)
PHONE..................................508 226-4359
Scott Sweet, *President*
EMP: 22
SQ FT: 7,500
SALES (est): 341.8K **Privately Held**
SIC: 3961 3911 3471 Mfg Costume Jewelry Mfg Precious Metal Jewelry Plating/Polishing Service

(G-7800)
TDR CO INC
503 Tiffany St (02703-4647)
PHONE..................................508 226-1221
David Nelson, *President*
EMP: 3
SALES (est): 292.6K **Privately Held**
SIC: 3599 Mfg Industrial Machinery

(G-7801)
TECHNCAL HRDFCING MCHINING INC
Also Called: T H M
35 Extension St (02703-4642)
PHONE..................................508 223-2900
Paul Egasti, *President*
Dennis Bray, *Materials Mgr*
John McEntee, *Admin Sec*
EMP: 15
SQ FT: 18,000
SALES (est): 2.2MM **Privately Held**
WEB: www.thmonline.com
SIC: 3599 3469 Mfg Industrial Machinery Mfg Metal Stampings

(G-7802)
TEXAS INSTRUMENTS INCORPORATED
529 Pleasant St (02703-2421)
P.O. Box 2964 (02703-0964)
PHONE..................................508 236-3800
Martha Sullivan, *Vice Pres*
Tom Connors, *Manager*
EMP: 32
SALES (corp-wide): 15.7B **Publicly Held**
WEB: www.ti.com
SIC: 3679 3678 3674 3643 Mfg Elec Components Mfg Elec Connectors Mfg Semiconductors/Dvcs Mfg Conductive Wire Dvcs Mfg Relay/Indstl Control
PA: Texas Instruments Incorporated
12500 Ti Blvd
Dallas TX 75243
214 479-3773

(G-7803)
THEME MERCHANDISE INC
53 County St (02703-2127)
P.O. Box 976 (02703-0017)
PHONE..................................508 226-4717
Robert Ebert, *President*
EMP: 4
SQ FT: 3,000
SALES (est): 460.6K **Privately Held**
SIC: 3911 Mfg Precious Metal Jewelry

(G-7804)
UNITED COMMUNICATIONS CORP
Sun Chronicle, The
34 S Main St (02703-2920)
P.O. Box 600 (02703-0600)
PHONE..................................508 222-7000
Rusty D'Arconte, *President*
Lynda Vallatini, *Adv Dir*
Oreste D'Arconte, *Branch Mgr*
Nancy Devonis, *Executive*
EMP: 215
SALES (corp-wide): 86.8MM **Privately Held**
WEB: www.kenoshanews.com
SIC: 2711 Newspapers-Publishing/Printing
PA: United Communications Corporation
5800 7th Ave
Kenosha WI 53140
262 657-1000

(G-7805)
V-TRON ELECTRONICS CORP
10 Venus Way (02703-8126)
PHONE..................................508 761-9100
Doug Gobin, *President*
Wayne Brockmann, *Engineer*
Neil Vincent, *Engineer*
James Czarn, *CFO*
Jim Czarn, *Controller*
▼ **EMP:** 100
SQ FT: 43,000
SALES (est): 30.1MM **Privately Held**
WEB: www.v-tron.com
SIC: 3357 3679 Nonferrous Wiredrawing/Insulating Mfg Electronic Components

(G-7806)
W D C HOLDINGS INC
Also Called: Whiting & Davis Safety
200 John J Dietsch Blvd (02703)
P.O. Box 1270, Attleboro Falls (02763-0270)
PHONE..................................508 699-4412
Curtis R Smith, *President*
John H Boyles, *CFO*
Lelia Teixeira, *Sales Mgr*
EMP: 100 **EST:** 1876
SQ FT: 50,000
SALES (est): 10.7MM **Privately Held**
WEB: www.whitinganddavis.com
SIC: 3842 3496 3171 2326 Mfg Surgical Appliances Mfg Misc Fab Wire Prdts Mfg Womens Handbag/Purse Mfg Men/Boy Work Clothng

(G-7807)
W E RICHARDS CO INC
Also Called: A B Group
40 John Williams St (02703-3707)
P.O. Box 546 (02703-0010)
PHONE..................................508 226-1036
Robert Arenburg, *President*
Jason Arenburg, *President*
EMP: 12
SQ FT: 6,400
SALES (est): 1.2MM **Privately Held**
WEB: www.abgroup.com
SIC: 3911 Mfg Precious Metal Jewelry

(G-7808)
WABASH TECHNOLOGIES INC (DH)
529 Pleasant St (02703-2421)
PHONE..................................260 355-4100
Stephen Dow, *President*
Casey Kroll, *Senior VP*
Tom Martin, *Vice Pres*
Lawrence Denbo, *CFO*
James Butler, *Admin Sec*
▲ **EMP:** 90
SQ FT: 100,000
SALES (est): 237.7MM
SALES (corp-wide): 3.5B **Privately Held**
WEB: www.wabashtech.com
SIC: 3625 3676 Mfg Relays/Industrial Controls Mfg Electronic Resistors

(G-7809)
WEST PARK STAMPING CO INC
84 Lord St (02703-7705)
PHONE..................................508 399-7488
Douglas Platt, *President*
Kenneth Jackson, *Vice Pres*
EMP: 6
SQ FT: 4,000
SALES (est): 462.9K **Privately Held**
SIC: 2759 Embossing On Paper

Attleboro Falls
Bristol County

(G-7810)
ADVANCED ELECTRONIC DESIGN INC
Also Called: Patrol
344 John L Dietsch Blvd (02763-1072)
PHONE..................................508 699-0249
David Swithers, *President*
John St Pierre, *Buyer*
Jack Loughran, *Regl Sales Mgr*
EMP: 15 **EST:** 1995
SQ FT: 1,600
SALES (est): 3.8MM **Privately Held**
SIC: 3571 8748 Mfg Electronic Computers Business Consulting Services

(G-7811)
BUDGETCARD INC
171 Commonwealth Ave (02763-1178)
PHONE..................................508 695-8762
Christopher Roche, *President*
Patricia Dugan, *Vice Pres*
Mike Roche, *Prdtn Mgr*
Christopher J Roche, *Treasurer*
Paul J Roche, *Admin Sec*
▲ **EMP:** 14
SQ FT: 8,000
SALES: 6MM **Privately Held**
WEB: www.budgetcard.com
SIC: 3089 Mfg Plastic Products

(G-7812)
DELTRAN INC
65 John L Dietsch Blvd A (02763-1087)
PHONE..................................508 699-7506
Francis P Defino, *President*
Pete Fredette, *Production*
EMP: 20
SALES (est): 3.7MM **Privately Held**
SIC: 3469 Mfg Metal Stampings

(G-7813)
FISK INDUSTRIES INC
100 John L Dietsch Blvd A (02763-1063)
P.O. Box 1228 (02763-0228)
PHONE..................................508 695-3661
Richard Fisk, *President*
Ira Adler, *Vice Pres*
Jeanne Fisk, *Vice Pres*
EMP: 6
SQ FT: 5,000
SALES: 475K **Privately Held**
WEB: www.fiskind.com
SIC: 3915 3452 3451 Mfg Jewelers' Materials Mfg Bolts/Screws/Rivets Mfg Screw Machine Products

(G-7814)
J T INMAN CO INC
31 Larsen Way (02763-1068)
PHONE..................................508 226-0080
John L Reynolds, *President*
Kathryn Thorpe, *Manager*
EMP: 25 **EST:** 1971
SQ FT: 10,000
SALES (est): 3MM **Privately Held**
WEB: www.jtinman.com
SIC: 3911 3339 3914 Mfg Precious Metal Jewelry Primary Nonferrous Metal Producer Mfg Silverware/Plated Ware

(G-7815)
METFAB ENGINEERING INC
332 John L Dietsch Blvd (02763-1078)
PHONE..................................508 695-1007
Edward Urquhart, *President*
Nancy J Berndt, *CFO*
EMP: 50 **EST:** 1971
SQ FT: 48,000
SALES (est): 11.1MM **Privately Held**
WEB: www.metfabeng.com
SIC: 3444 Structural Metal Fabrication

(G-7816)
OUELLETTE INDUSTRIES INC
100 John L Dietsch Blvd B (02763-1063)
P.O. Box 2780 (02763-0897)
PHONE..................................508 695-0964
Ronald Boccanfuso, *President*
Christine Boccanfuso, *Co-Owner*
EMP: 7
SALES (est): 660.8K **Privately Held**
WEB: www.ouelletteindustries.com
SIC: 2399 3471 Mfg Fabricated Textile Products Plating/Polishing Service

(G-7817)
SOUSA BROS & DEMAYO INC
Also Called: Sousa & Demayo
266 John L Dietsch Blvd (02763-1077)
PHONE..................................508 695-6800
Louis R Sousa, *President*
Sandra J Gagne, *Treasurer*
EMP: 48 **EST:** 1961
SQ FT: 26,800
SALES (est): 11.1MM **Privately Held**
WEB: www.sousademayo.com
SIC: 3441 Structural Metal Fabrication

(G-7818)
VH BLACKINTON & CO INC
221 John L Dietsch Blvd (02763-1031)
P.O. Box 1300 (02763-0300)
PHONE..................................508 699-4436
Peter A Roque, *President*
Mario A Roque, *Vice Pres*
David Elliott, *Regl Sales Mgr*
Tammy Urenco, *Sales Staff*
Louise J Farrands, *Director*
EMP: 200 **EST:** 1852
SQ FT: 52,000
SALES (est): 24.3MM **Privately Held**
SIC: 2399 3499 Mfg Fabricated Textile Products Mfg Misc Fabricated Metal Products

(G-7819)
WHITING & DAVIS LLC
171 Commonwealth Ave # 2 (02763-1178)
PHONE..................................508 699-4412
Darrin Cutler,
Melissa Cutler,
EMP: 23
SALES (est): 2.9MM **Privately Held**
SIC: 3911 Mfg Precious Metal Jewelry

Auburn
Worcester County

(G-7820)
28 KITCHEN CABINET LLC
28 Coolidge St (01501-2914)
PHONE..................................774 321-6099
Tran Diep, *Manager*
EMP: 3
SALES (est): 118.1K **Privately Held**
SIC: 2434 Mfg Wood Kitchen Cabinets

(G-7821)
ACCELERATED MEDIA TECH INC
19 Technology Dr (01501-3210)
PHONE..................................508 459-0300
Thomas P Jennings, *President*
Rick Collette, *Vice Pres*
Peter Deary, *Vice Pres*
Dudley Freeman, *Vice Pres*
EMP: 50
SALES (est): 2.2MM **Privately Held**
SIC: 3663 Mfg Radio/Tv Communication Equipment

(G-7822)
AEARO TECHNOLOGIES LLC
48 Sword St Ste 101 (01501-2162)
PHONE..................................317 692-6645
Barbar Brodeur, *Manager*
EMP: 500
SALES (corp-wide): 32.7B **Publicly Held**
WEB: www.aearo.com
SIC: 3851 3842 Mfg Ophthalmic Goods Mfg Surgical Appliances/Supplies
HQ: Aearo Technologies Llc
5457 W 79th St
Indianapolis IN 46268
317 692-6666

(G-7823)
AIMTEK INC (PA)
Also Called: Aimco
201 Washington St (01501-3224)
PHONE..................................508 832-5035
Amar Kapur, *President*
Jay Kapur, *General Mgr*
Ani Kapur, *Vice Pres*
EMP: 21
SQ FT: 20,000
SALES (est): 10.6MM **Privately Held**
SIC: 3351 Copper Rolling/Drawing

(G-7824)
ALLIED MACHINED PRODUCTS CORP
4 Westec Dr (01501-3041)
P.O. Box 70569, Worcester (01607-0569)
PHONE..................................508 756-4290
Ann Marie Weber, *President*
Joseph L Wetton, *Vice Pres*
▲ **EMP:** 85 **EST:** 1945
SQ FT: 49,500
SALES (est): 16.3MM **Privately Held**
WEB: www.alliedmp.com
SIC: 3599 Mfg Industrial Machinery

(G-7825)
AMERICAN PRTG & ENVELOPE INC
211 Southbridge St (01501-2548)
P.O. Box 347 (01501-0347)
PHONE..................................508 832-6100
Anthony Penny, *President*
David Penny, *Vice Pres*
Francis T Penny, *Treasurer*
Peter Bianca, *Manager*
EMP: 25
SQ FT: 15,400
SALES (est): 3.3MM **Privately Held**
SIC: 2752 2791 2789 2677 Lithographic Coml Print Typesetting Services Book-binding/Related Work Mfg Envelopes

(G-7826)
ARCADE INDUSTRIES INC
Also Called: Arcade Snacks & Dried Fruits
205 Southbridge St (01501-2548)
P.O. Box 375 (01501-0375)
PHONE..................................508 832-6300
Ann Ethier, *Principal*
EMP: 18
SQ FT: 1,880
SALES (est): 4.1MM **Privately Held**
WEB: www.arcadesnacks.com
SIC: 2068 2034 Mfg Salted/Roasted Nuts/Seeds Mfg Dehydrated Fruits/Vegetables

(G-7827)
ASSA ABLOY ENTRANCE SYS US INC
Also Called: Besam Entrance Solutions
1 A St 2b (01501-2101)
PHONE..................................508 368-2600
Fred Pizzi, *Branch Mgr*
EMP: 20
SALES (corp-wide): 8.8B **Privately Held**
SIC: 3699 3442 Mfg Electrical Equipment/Supplies Mfg Metal Doors/Sash/Trim
HQ: Assa Abloy Entrance Systems Us Inc.
1900 Airport Rd
Monroe NC 28110
704 290-5520

(G-7828)
ATLAS DISTRIBUTING INC
44 Southbridge St (01501-2582)
P.O. Box 420 (01501-0420)
PHONE..................................508 791-6221
Ronald J Salois Jr, *President*
John Sadowsky, *Chairman*
John Lepore, *Treasurer*
▲ **EMP:** 160 **EST:** 1933
SQ FT: 130,000
SALES (est): 49.3MM **Privately Held**
WEB: www.atlasdistributing.com
SIC: 2082 Mfg Malt Beverages

(G-7829)
BAY STATE SURFACE TECHNOLOGIES
201 Washington St (01501-3224)
PHONE..................................508 832-5035
Amar Kapur, *President*
Ani Kapur, *Vice Pres*
EMP: 10
SALES: 1,000K
SALES (corp-wide): 10.6MM **Privately Held**
SIC: 3399 Thermal Spray Coating Mtls Equipment
PA: Aimtek, Inc.
201 Washington St
Auburn MA 01501
508 832-5035

(G-7830)
BRISCON ELECTRIC MFG CORP
93 Bancroft St (01501-2467)
P.O. Box 145 (01501-0145)
PHONE..................................508 832-3481
William D Rogers Jr, *President*
EMP: 11 **EST:** 1949
SQ FT: 14,000
SALES (est): 2.1MM **Privately Held**
WEB: www.brisconelectric.com
SIC: 3496 3965 Mfg Misc Fabricated Wire Products Mfg Fasteners/Buttons/Pins

(G-7831)
CMSR SERVICES LLC
Also Called: Central Math
482 Southbridge St Ste 3 (01501-2468)
PHONE..................................774 210-2513
Sean Patrick Noonan, *Principal*
EMP: 4
SQ FT: 200
SALES: 850K **Privately Held**
SIC: 3448 Prefabricated Metal Buildings

(G-7832)
COMMUNITY NEWSPAPER COMPANY
Also Called: C P Media
475 Washington St (01501-3234)
PHONE..................................508 721-5600
George Roy, *Owner*
EMP: 70
SALES (est): 2.3MM **Privately Held**
SIC: 2711 Newspapers-Publishing/Printing

(G-7833)
ENDOWMENTSOLUTIONS LLC
8 Booth Rd (01501-3324)
PHONE..................................617 308-7231
Michael Jarvis, *Principal*
EMP: 7
SALES (est): 251.9K **Privately Held**
SIC: 7372 Prepackaged Software Services

(G-7834)
FIELD PROTECTION AGENCY LLC
38 Silver St (01501-1224)
PHONE..................................508 832-0395
Raffaella Degruola, *Office Mgr*
Michael Zorena, *Mng Member*
EMP: 6
SALES (est): 483.4K **Privately Held**
SIC: 3949 Mfg Sporting/Athletic Goods

(G-7835)
FREE-FLOW PACKAGING INTL INC
Also Called: F T International
4 Saint Mark St (01501-3237)
PHONE..................................508 832-5369
Thomas Ruby, *Manager*
EMP: 24
SALES (corp-wide): 3.8B **Privately Held**
WEB: www.fpintl.com
SIC: 2671 Mfg Packaging Paper/Film
HQ: Free-Flow Packaging International, Inc.
1650 Lake Cook Rd Ste 400
Deerfield IL 60015
650 261-5300

(G-7836)
GEORGE GUERTIN TROPHY INC
Also Called: Guertin's Awards Plus
32 Auburn St (01501-2429)
PHONE..................................508 832-4001
A Robert Zannotti, *President*
Anthony Zannotti, *General Mgr*
EMP: 6 **EST:** 1993
SQ FT: 7,000
SALES (est): 651.4K **Privately Held**
SIC: 3914 3499 3299 3999 Mfg Trophies Plaques And Advertising Specialties

(G-7837)
HENRY J MONTVILLE
Also Called: Framer's Gallery, The
567 Southbridge St Ste 15 (01501-2269)
PHONE..................................508 832-6111
Henry J Montville, *Owner*
EMP: 4
SALES (est): 225.2K **Privately Held**
SIC: 3952 Mfg Lead Pencils/Art Goods

(G-7838)
HILLTOP WOOD CRAFTS
126 Pakachoag St (01501-3128)
PHONE..................................508 754-3915
Greg Gadboys, *Owner*
EMP: 4
SALES (est): 233.3K **Privately Held**
SIC: 2517 Mfg Wood Tv/Radio Cabinets

(G-7839)
J T GARDNER INC
Also Called: Curry Printing & Copy Center
567 Southbridge St Ste 14 (01501-2269)
PHONE..................................508 832-2036
Fax: 508 832-3923
EMP: 6
SQ FT: 2,200
SALES (corp-wide): 4.5MM **Privately Held**
SIC: 2752 Offset Printing Service
PA: J. T. Gardner, Inc.
190 Turnpike Rd
Westborough MA 01581
508 366-4060

(G-7840)
KADANT INC
AES
35 Sword St (01501-2146)
P.O. Box 7010, Queensbury NY (12801-7010)
PHONE..................................508 791-8171
Royal Gauvin, *Vice Pres*
George Grniet, *Engineer*
Jeffery Bachand, *Manager*
Bill Giguere, *Info Tech Mgr*
Joanne Stoner, *Executive Asst*
EMP: 130
SALES (corp-wide): 633.7MM **Publicly Held**
WEB: www.kadantaes.com
SIC: 3554 5084 Mfg Paper Industrial Machinery Whol Industrial Equipment
PA: Kadant Inc.
1 Technology Park Dr # 210
Westford MA 01886
978 776-2000

(G-7841)
KADANT INC
Webb Systems
35 Sword St (01501-2146)
P.O. Box 269 (01501-0269)
PHONE..................................508 791-8171
Jose Garcia, *President*
EMP: 150
SALES (corp-wide): 633.7MM **Publicly Held**
WEB: www.kadantaes.com
SIC: 3554 Mfg Paper Industrial Machinery
PA: Kadant Inc.
1 Technology Park Dr # 210
Westford MA 01886
978 776-2000

(G-7842)
MARVIC INC
Also Called: Brady-Built Sunrooms
160 Southbridge St (01501-2583)
PHONE..................................508 798-2600
Toll Free:..................................877 -
Mario Gabrielli, *CEO*
Marco Gabrielli, *President*
Robert Wironen, *Treasurer*
EMP: 35
SQ FT: 28,564
SALES (est): 5.6MM **Privately Held**
WEB: www.bradyrooms.com
SIC: 2452 Mfg Prefabricated Wood Buildings

GEOGRAPHIC

(G-7843)
MILES PRESS INC
14 Sword St Ste 5 (01501-2171)
PHONE..........508 752-6430
Peter Martinson, *President*
Nancy Martinson, *Treasurer*
EMP: 10
SQ FT: 7,500
SALES: 1.8MM **Privately Held**
WEB: www.milespress.us
SIC: 2752 2789 Lithographic Commercial Printing Bookbinding/Related Work

(G-7844)
MISTRAS GROUP INC
Also Called: Mistras Services
2 Millbury St (01501-3204)
PHONE..........508 832-5500
Dave Orlossky, *Manager*
EMP: 25 **Publicly Held**
SIC: 3829 Engineering Services
PA: Mistras Group, Inc.
195 Clarksville Rd Ste 2
Princeton Junction NJ 08550
-

(G-7845)
NORMAN ELLIS
Also Called: Vantage Printing
14 Sword St Ste 5 (01501-2171)
PHONE..........508 853-5833
Norman Ellis, *Owner*
EMP: 4
SQ FT: 1,500
SALES: 400K **Privately Held**
SIC: 2759 Commercial Printing Company

(G-7846)
NV CANDLES LLC
3 Jacobson Dr Ste 2 (01501-3047)
PHONE..........774 234-6895
Nicholas Robert Schifferle, *Principal*
Nicholas Schifferle, *Principal*
EMP: 6
SALES (est): 263.8K **Privately Held**
SIC: 3999 Mfg Misc Products

(G-7847)
PCC SPECIALTY PRODUCTS INC
Reed-Rico Division
28 Sword St (01501-2128)
PHONE..........508 753-6530
Lindsey Garner, *Principal*
EMP: 60
SQ FT: 100,000
SALES (corp-wide): 225.3B **Publicly Held**
WEB: www.pccspd.com
SIC: 3544 3542 3545 3541 Mfg Dies/Tools/Jigs/Fixt Mfg Machine Tool-Forming Mfg Machine Tool Access Mfg Machine Tool-Cutting
HQ: Pcc Specialty Products, Inc.
4650 Sw Mcdam Ave Ste 300
Portland OR 97239
503 417-4800

(G-7848)
PRAXAIR DISTRIBUTION INC
273 Washington St (01501-3251)
PHONE..........203 837-2000
Perry Leros, *General Mgr*
EMP: 41 **Privately Held**
SIC: 2813 Mfg Industrial Gases
HQ: Praxair Distribution, Inc.
10 Riverview Dr
Danbury CT 06810
203 837-2000

(G-7849)
SHEPPARD ENVELOPE COMPANY INC
133 Southbridge St (01501-2503)
P.O. Box 358 (01501-0358)
PHONE..........508 791-5588
J Lincoln Spaulding, *Ch of Bd*
L Brook Spaulding, *President*
Jane Andrews, *Design Engr*
Don Blair, *Sales Mgr*
Robin Spaulding, *Office Mgr*
EMP: 20 **EST:** 1921
SALES (est): 4.4MM **Privately Held**
WEB: www.sheppardenvelope.com
SIC: 2677 Mfg Envelopes

(G-7850)
SRC PUBLISHING INC
23 Midstate Dr Ste 114 (01501-1857)
PHONE..........508 749-3212
Dennis Hofmaier, *President*
EMP: 4
SALES (est): 232.2K **Privately Held**
SIC: 2741 Misc Publishing

(G-7851)
VISIMARK INC
Also Called: Kay Gee Sign and Graphics
200 Southbridge St (01501-2504)
PHONE..........508 832-3471
EMP: 10 **EST:** 1929
SQ FT: 13,000
SALES: 850K **Privately Held**
WEB: www.jantom.com
SIC: 3993 7532 1799 Mfg Electric Signs And Truck Lettering

(G-7852)
WACHUSETT MOLDING LLC
3 Cutting Ave (01501-2515)
PHONE..........508 459-0477
Gerald Finkle, *Principal*
EMP: 3 **EST:** 2008
SALES (est): 204.4K **Privately Held**
SIC: 3089 Mfg Plastic Products

(G-7853)
WORCESTER ENVELOPE COMPANY
22 Millbury St (01501-3200)
P.O. Box 406 (01501-0406)
PHONE..........508 832-5394
Eldon D Pond III, *President*
E Dexter Pond Jr, *Chairman*
Derek P Waterhouse, *Vice Pres*
David Nadeau, *Treasurer*
Richard P Waterhouse, *Admin Sec*
EMP: 155 **EST:** 1893
SQ FT: 180,000
SALES (est): 62.4MM **Privately Held**
WEB: www.worcesterenvelope.com
SIC: 2677 Mfg Envelopes

(G-7854)
WS ANDERSON ASSOCIATES INC
303 Washington St 313 (01501-3245)
PHONE..........508 832-5550
Ricard J Shea, *President*
EMP: 34
SQ FT: 44,000
SALES (est): 4.6MM **Privately Held**
SIC: 3599 Mfg Industrial Machinery

Auburndale
Middlesex County

(G-7855)
ALSERES PHARMACEUTICALS INC
275 Grove St Ste 2-400 (02466-2273)
PHONE..........508 497-2360
Peter G Savas, *Ch of Bd*
Steven I Engel, *Senior VP*
Noel Cusack, *Development*
Kenneth L Rice Jr, *CFO*
EMP: 3
SQ FT: 200
SALES (est): 473.7K **Privately Held**
WEB: www.bostonlifesciences.com
SIC: 2834 Mfg Pharmaceutical Preparations

(G-7856)
APEAK INC
63 Albert Rd (02466-1302)
PHONE..........617 964-1709
Stefan Vasile, *President*
EMP: 4 **EST:** 2001
SQ FT: 700
SALES: 345K **Privately Held**
WEB: www.apeakinc.com
SIC: 3674 Mfg Semiconductors/Related Devices

(G-7857)
BOOSTERCOM
275 Grove St Ste 1-305 (02466-2272)
PHONE..........855 631-6850
EMP: 3
SALES (est): 176K **Privately Held**
SIC: 2759 Commercial Printing

(G-7858)
CLEMENTIA PHARMACEUTICALS USA
275 Grove St Ste 2-400 (02466-2273)
PHONE..........857 226-5588
EMP: 3
SALES (est): 90K **Privately Held**
SIC: 2834 Mfg Pharmaceutical Preparations

(G-7859)
CONNANCE INC
275 Grove St Ste 1-100 (02466-2276)
PHONE..........781 577-5000
Stephen Farber, *CEO*
Steve Levin, *President*
Nicole Nye, *Vice Pres*
Michael Puffe, *Vice Pres*
Isabel Talentino, *Project Mgr*
EMP: 6
SALES (est): 1.3MM **Privately Held**
SIC: 7372 Prepackaged Software Srvcs

(G-7860)
ELEMENTAL SCENTS LLC
24 Hancock St (02466-2309)
PHONE..........617 504-2559
Roberta Gringorten, *Principal*
EMP: 3
SALES (est): 186.8K **Privately Held**
SIC: 2844 Mfg Toilet Preparations

(G-7861)
FAUX DESIGNS
72 Rowe St (02466-1535)
PHONE..........617 965-0142
Stacy Landua, *Owner*
EMP: 10
SALES (est): 757.5K **Privately Held**
SIC: 2759 Commercial Printing

(G-7862)
GINER ELX INC
89 Rumford Ave (02466-1311)
PHONE..........781 392-0300
Andrew Belt, *CEO*
Theresa Scavone, *Controller*
EMP: 15 **EST:** 2017
SQ FT: 7,900
SALES (est): 1.1MM **Privately Held**
SIC: 3699 1731 Mfg Electrical Equipment/Supplies Electrical Contractor

(G-7863)
GINER LIFE SCIENCES INC
Also Called: Ginerlabs
89 Rumford Ave (02466-1311)
PHONE..........781 529-0576
Andrew R Belt, *President*
Theresa Scavone, *Corp Secy*
EMP: 3
SALES (est): 141.3K **Privately Held**
SIC: 2869 Mfg Industrial Organic Chemicals

(G-7864)
LOWER LIMB TECHNOLOGY
130 Rumford Ave (02466-1365)
PHONE..........617 916-1650
EMP: 3 **EST:** 2013
SALES (est): 181.1K **Privately Held**
SIC: 3842 Mfg Surgical Appliances/Supplies

(G-7865)
NEUFORM PHARMACEUTICALS
450 Lexington St Ste 101 (02466-1921)
PHONE..........617 559-9822
Changfu Cheng, *Principal*
EMP: 5
SALES (est): 261.3K **Privately Held**
SIC: 2834 Whol Drugs/Sundries

(G-7866)
NEWTRON INC
132 Charles St Ste 201 (02466-1743)
PHONE..........617 969-1100
James A Arcuri, *President*
Jeffrey T Arcuri, *Vice Pres*
Joseph Arcuri, *Shareholder*
▼ **EMP:** 6
SQ FT: 20,000
SALES (est): 1.1MM **Privately Held**
WEB: www.newtron.com
SIC: 3541 Mfg Machine Tools-Cutting

(G-7867)
PEAR TREE PHARMACEUTICALS INC
275 Grove St Ste 2-400 (02466-2273)
PHONE..........617 500-3871
EMP: 4
SQ FT: 2,000
SALES (est): 310K **Privately Held**
SIC: 2834 Mfg And Dev Pharmaceutical Preparations

(G-7868)
SAPERION INC
275 Grove St Ste 2-400 (02466-2273)
PHONE..........781 899-1228
Andreas Cunze, *Principal*
EMP: 200
SALES (est): 6MM **Privately Held**
SIC: 7372 Prepackaged Software Services

(G-7869)
SIDNEY HUTTER GLASS & LIGHT
225 Riverview Ave Ste B5 (02466-1379)
PHONE..........617 630-1929
Sidney Hutter, *President*
EMP: 3 **EST:** 1985
SALES: 250K **Privately Held**
WEB: www.sidneyhutter.com
SIC: 3231 Mfg Products-Purchased Glass

(G-7870)
SPEEDWAY LLC
Also Called: Dunkin' Donuts
2370 Commonwealth Ave (02466-1719)
PHONE..........617 244-4601
Arturo Villos, *General Mgr*
EMP: 5 **Publicly Held**
SIC: 1311 5461 Crude Petroleum/Natural Gas Production Retail Bakery
HQ: Speedway Llc
500 Speedway Dr
Enon OH 45323
937 864-3000

(G-7871)
TELEVEH INC
132 Charles St Ste 201 (02466-1743)
PHONE..........857 400-1938
Xinye LI, *Principal*
EMP: 10
SALES (est): 295.2K **Privately Held**
SIC: 7372 Prepackaged Software Services

(G-7872)
UNIPOINT TECHNOLOGIES
275 Grove St (02466-2272)
PHONE..........617 952-4244
Gary Nard, *Principal*
Gary Norden, *Vice Pres*
EMP: 5
SALES (est): 400.5K **Privately Held**
SIC: 7372 Prepackaged Software Services

(G-7873)
WILLIGENT CORPORATION
Also Called: Willigent Technologies
275 Grove St Ste 2-400 (02466-2273)
PHONE..........617 663-5707
EMP: 9
SALES (est): 720K **Privately Held**
WEB: www.willigent.com
SIC: 3559 Physical Intrusion Detection Systems

Avon
Norfolk County

(G-7874)
ACCUROUNDS INC
15 Doherty Ave (02322-1186)
PHONE..........508 587-3500
Michael Tamasi, *CEO*
Mike McCormick, *Engineer*

Diane Ferrera, *Human Res Mgr*
Amanda Lewis, *Sales Staff*
Pat Mann, *Sales Staff*
EMP: 70 **EST:** 2010
SALES (est): 12.3MM **Privately Held**
SIC: 3599 Mfg Industrial Machinery

(G-7875)
ALLIANCE SHEET METAL
21 Ledin Dr (02322-1196)
PHONE..................................508 587-0314
Robert J Johnson, *Principal*
EMP: 8
SALES (est): 632.6K **Privately Held**
SIC: 3499 Mfg Misc Fabricated Metal Products

(G-7876)
ARCHITECTURAL GLAZING SYSTEMS
40 Murphy Dr (02322-1147)
PHONE..................................508 588-4845
Joseph Belanger, *President*
Brian Long, *Vice Pres*
Patricia Belanger, *Treasurer*
EMP: 22
SALES (est): 3.1MM **Privately Held**
SIC: 3442 Mfg Metal Doors/Sash/Trim

(G-7877)
AVON CABINET COMPANY
501 W Main St (02322-1711)
PHONE..................................508 587-9122
Eugene Anderson, *Owner*
EMP: 3 **EST:** 1979
SQ FT: 4,000
SALES: 400K **Privately Held**
SIC: 2434 5211 Mfg Wood Kitchen Cabinets Ret Lumber/Building Materials

(G-7878)
AVON CSTM EMB & SCREENPRINTING
Also Called: Avon Custom EMB & Screen Prtg
4 Brentwood Ave (02322-1602)
PHONE..................................781 341-4663
Carol Merlo, *President*
EMP: 11
SALES: 1.2MM **Privately Held**
SIC: 2395 2759 Embroidery & Screen Printing

(G-7879)
BE PETERSON INC
40 Murphy Dr Ste 2 (02322-1147)
PHONE..................................508 436-7900
Terry Moore, *President*
Jeff Visser, *Prdtn Mgr*
Jerry Leone, *Purchasing*
Sean Knowles, *Engrg Dir*
Mitch Johnson, *Engineer*
EMP: 80
SQ FT: 88,000
SALES (est): 22MM **Privately Held**
WEB: www.bepeterson.com
SIC: 3443 Structural Metal Fabrication

(G-7880)
BOSTON BRACE INTERNATIONAL INC (PA)
Also Called: Nopco
20 Ledin Dr Ste 1 (02322-1156)
PHONE..................................508 588-6060
Thomas Morrissey, *CEO*
James H Wynne, *Principal*
Joyce Lee, *Vice Pres*
Robin Meek, *Vice Pres*
James Miller, *Vice Pres*
EMP: 50
SQ FT: 25,000
SALES (est): 21.4MM **Privately Held**
WEB: www.bostonbrace.com
SIC: 3842 Mfg Surgical Appliances/Supplies

(G-7881)
BOSTON CENTERLESS INC
Also Called: Accurounds
15 Doherty Ave (02322-1163)
PHONE..................................508 587-3500
Michael Tamasi, *Branch Mgr*
EMP: 35
SQ FT: 26,300
SALES (corp-wide): 21.5MM **Privately Held**
WEB: www.bostoncenterless.com
SIC: 3599 3451 Mfg Industrial Machinery Mfg Screw Machine Products
PA: Boston Centerless, Inc.
11 Presidential Way
Woburn MA 01801
781 994-5000

(G-7882)
CHRIS MARTIN (PA)
Also Called: Shooters Pizza & Pub
36 E Main St (02322-1458)
PHONE..................................508 580-0069
Chris Martin, *Owner*
EMP: 4
SALES (est): 560.5K **Privately Held**
SIC: 3812 5813 Mfg Search/Navigation Equipment Drinking Place

(G-7883)
CJ SHAUGHNESSY CRANE SVC INC
520 Bodwell Street Ext (02322-1014)
PHONE..................................781 924-1168
Mr C J Shaughnessy, *Principal*
EMP: 3
SALES (est): 545.7K **Privately Held**
SIC: 2851 Mfg Paints/Allied Products

(G-7884)
CUMING MICROWAVE CORPORATION (HQ)
264 Bodwell St (02322-1119)
PHONE..................................508 521-6700
John W Cuming, *President*
Michael Caputo, *Vice Pres*
Michael Heafey, *Info Tech Mgr*
▲ **EMP:** 70
SALES (est): 29MM
SALES (corp-wide): 15.3B **Publicly Held**
SIC: 3679 Manufacturing Electronic Components
PA: Ppg Industries, Inc.
1 Ppg Pl
Pittsburgh PA 15272
412 434-3131

(G-7885)
DBI WOODWORKS INC
491 W Main St Ste 1 (02322-1660)
PHONE..................................781 739-2060
Alan F Shapiro, *President*
EMP: 7
SALES (est): 706.5K **Privately Held**
SIC: 2431 Mfg Millwork

(G-7886)
DESIGN COMMUNICATIONS LTD (PA)
85 Bodwell St (02322-1190)
PHONE..................................617 542-9620
Craig H Kutner, *CEO*
Mark Andreasson, *President*
Russell Brown, *Project Mgr*
James Hannon, *Project Mgr*
Sterling Cole, *Facilities Mgr*
▼ **EMP:** 65
SQ FT: 72,792
SALES (est): 30.7MM **Privately Held**
WEB: www.dclboston.com
SIC: 3993 Mfg Signs/Advertising Specialties

(G-7887)
INTEGRATED WEB FINISHING SYST
Also Called: I-Web
175 Bodwell St (02322-1122)
PHONE..................................508 580-5809
Robert Williams, *President*
Matt Williams, *Project Engr*
EMP: 26
SALES (est): 5.9MM **Privately Held**
WEB: www.iwebus.com
SIC: 3555 Mfg Printing Trades Machinery

(G-7888)
JACOBS PRECISION CORP
21 Ledin Dr Ste B (02322-1196)
PHONE..................................508 588-2121
Ralph S Jacobs, *President*
Marsha Jacobs, *Clerk*
EMP: 6 **EST:** 1959
SQ FT: 8,000
SALES (est): 793.6K **Privately Held**
WEB: www.jacobsprecision.com
SIC: 3451 3843 3841 Mfg Screw Machine Products & Dental & Medical Instruments

(G-7889)
JET GRAPHICS LLC
175 Bodwell St Ste 1 (02322-1122)
PHONE..................................508 580-5809
Robert Williams, *President*
EMP: 20
SQ FT: 2,000
SALES: 7.5MM **Privately Held**
SIC: 3555 Mfg Printing Trades Machinery

(G-7890)
NATIONAL STORE FRONTS CO INC
10 Tracy Dr (02322-1198)
PHONE..................................508 584-8880
Stacy Yeomans, *President*
EMP: 50
SALES (est): 5.3MM **Privately Held**
SIC: 3442 Mfg Store Fronts

(G-7891)
NEW ENGLAND WELDING INC
145 Bodwell St (02322-1179)
PHONE..................................508 580-2024
Ken McIntire, *President*
EMP: 16
SALES (est): 3.4MM **Privately Held**
WEB: www.newelding.com
SIC: 3441 Structural Metal Fabrication

(G-7892)
PORTAL INC
10 Tracy Dr (02322-1137)
PHONE..................................800 966-3030
Erik Naisuler, *Treasurer*
Pablo Alcaraz, *Director*
▲ **EMP:** 50
SQ FT: 50,000
SALES (est): 8.7MM **Privately Held**
WEB: www.portal-national.com
SIC: 3442 Mfg Metal Door/Sash/Trim

(G-7893)
R & B SPLICER SYSTEMS INC
145 Bodwell St (02322-1179)
PHONE..................................508 580-3500
Ernest D Rowe, *President*
Steven Pelletier, *Engineer*
EMP: 8
SALES (est): 1MM **Privately Held**
SIC: 3861 Mfg Photographic Equipment/Supplies

(G-7894)
RANFAC CORP
30 Doherty Ave Ste A (02322-1174)
P.O. Box 635 (02322-0635)
PHONE..................................508 588-4400
Robert M Adler, *President*
Jessica Adler, *Opers Mgr*
Tim Marmion, *Controller*
Dave Depatie, *Manager*
Eric Kreuz, *Manager*
EMP: 75
SQ FT: 40,000
SALES (est): 13MM **Privately Held**
WEB: www.ranfac.com
SIC: 3841 8011 3842 Mfg Surgical/Medical Instruments Medical Doctor's Office Mfg Surgical Appliances/Supplies

(G-7895)
SCRATCH ART COMPANY INC (PA)
11 Robbie Rd Ste A (02322-1100)
P.O. Box 590, Westport CT (06881-0590)
PHONE..................................508 583-8085
Nathan Polsky, *President*
Harvey Schwartz, *Vice Pres*
Janet Polsky, *Treasurer*
▲ **EMP:** 15
SQ FT: 25,000
SALES (est): 1.3MM **Privately Held**
SIC: 3952 Mfg Lead Pencils/Art Goods

(G-7896)
SELECTECH INC
33 Wales Ave Ste F (02322-1012)
PHONE..................................508 583-3200
Thomas Ricciardelli, *President*
Michael King, *Vice Pres*
John Crowe, *Shareholder*
Charles R Dwyer, *Shareholder*
SRP Voting Trust, *Shareholder*
▲ **EMP:** 6
SQ FT: 4,500
SALES: 2MM **Privately Held**
SIC: 3089 Mfg Plastic Products

(G-7897)
STAR KITCHEN CABINETS INC
75 Stockwell Dr Ste H (02322-1170)
PHONE..................................508 510-3123
Xiaoqing Wu, *Principal*
▲ **EMP:** 4
SALES (est): 263.6K **Privately Held**
SIC: 2434 Mfg Wood Kitchen Cabinets

(G-7898)
TAYLOR COMMUNICATIONS INC
81 Uraco Way (02322-1140)
PHONE..................................508 584-0102
Chuck Rozie, *Manager*
EMP: 13
SALES (corp-wide): 2.8B **Privately Held**
WEB: www.stdreg.com
SIC: 2761 2759 2752 Mfg Manifold Business Forms Commercial Printing Lithographic Commercial Printing
HQ: Taylor Communications, Inc.
1725 Roe Crest Dr
North Mankato MN 56003
866 541-0937

(G-7899)
TYCO FIRE PRODUCTS LP
Also Called: Tyco Fire Protection Products
27 Doherty Ave (02322-1124)
PHONE..................................508 583-8447
Derek Gimler, *Manager*
EMP: 8 **Privately Held**
SIC: 3569 Mfg General Industrial Machinery
HQ: Tyco Fire Products Lp
1400 Pennbrook Pkwy
Lansdale PA 19446
215 362-0700

(G-7900)
UNITED CURTAIN CO INC (PA)
91 Wales Ave Ste 1 (02322-1090)
PHONE..................................508 588-4100
Joseph N Resha Jr, *President*
Thomas M Resha, *Vice Pres*
▲ **EMP:** 15 **EST:** 1939
SQ FT: 15,000
SALES (est): 2.4MM **Privately Held**
SIC: 2391 Mfg Curtains/Draperies

(G-7901)
WEISS SHEET METAL INC
105 Bodwell St (02322-1112)
PHONE..................................508 583-8300
Wayne Delano, *President*
Brian Delano, *Treasurer*
EMP: 20 **EST:** 1965
SQ FT: 26,000
SALES: 3.3MM **Privately Held**
WEB: www.weiss-sheetmetal.com
SIC: 3444 Mfg Sheet Metalwork

(G-7902)
WESTERBEKE CORPORATION
41 Ledin Dr Avon Indus Pa Avon Industrial Park (02322)
PHONE..................................508 823-7677
John Westerbeke, *Branch Mgr*
EMP: 30
SALES (corp-wide): 11.4MM **Privately Held**
SIC: 3519 Mfg Internal Combustion Engines
PA: Westerbeke Corporation
150 John Hancock Rd
Taunton MA 02780
508 977-4273

(G-7903)
WROBEL ENGINEERING CO INC
154 Bodwell St Ste A (02322-1160)
PHONE..................................508 586-8338
Elizabeth Wrobel, *President*
Edward Wrobel, *Corp Secy*
Michael Long, *Opers Staff*
Maria Anderson, *Purch Mgr*

GEOGRAPHIC

Bill Sullivan, *Engineer*
EMP: 100
SQ FT: 60,000
SALES (est): 20.7MM **Privately Held**
WEB: www.wrobeleng.com
SIC: 3444 Mfg Sheet Metalwork

(G-7904)
XTRALIS INC
175 Bodwell St Ste 2 (02322-1122)
PHONE..................................800 229-4434
Michael D Flink, *President*
Paul Harris, *Director*
EMP: 36
SALES (est): 8.5MM **Privately Held**
WEB: www.vesda.com
SIC: 3669 Mfg Communications Equipment
HQ: Xtralis (Uk) Limited
Peoplebuilding Estate, Maylands Avenue
Hemel Hempstead HERTS HP2 4
144 224-2330

Ayer
Middlesex County

(G-7905)
ADVANCED ELECTRONIC TECHNOLOGY
12 Shirley St (01432-1208)
PHONE..................................978 846-6487
Giap Tran, *President*
EMP: 5
SALES (est): 150.7K **Privately Held**
SIC: 3999 Mfg Misc Products

(G-7906)
AJINOMOTO CAMBROOKE INC (DH)
Also Called: Cambrooke Therapeutics, Inc.
4 Copeland Dr (01432-1751)
PHONE..................................508 782-2300
Howard Lossing, *CEO*
Cambrooke Global, *Partner*
▲ **EMP:** 50
SQ FT: 65,000
SALES: 10.5MM **Privately Held**
WEB: www.cambrookefoods.com
SIC: 2023 Manufactures Dry/Evaporated Dairy Products
HQ: Ajinomoto Health & Nutrition North America, Inc.
1300 N Arlington Hts
Itasca IL 60143
630 931-6800

(G-7907)
AMERICAN SUPERCONDUCTOR CORP (PA)
Also Called: Amsc
114 E Main St (01432-1832)
PHONE..................................978 842-3000
Daniel P McGahn, *Ch of Bd*
James Maguire, *Exec VP*
John W Kosiba Jr, *CFO*
Arthur House, *Director*
▲ **EMP:** 233
SQ FT: 88,000
SALES: 56.2MM **Publicly Held**
WEB: www.amsc.com
SIC: 3674 3621 Mfg Semiconductors/Related Devices Motors/Generators

(G-7908)
ANCOM CUSTOM CABINETS
22 Bryan Way (01432-1575)
PHONE..................................978 456-7780
Andrew Kalafatis, *Executive*
EMP: 4
SALES (est): 320K **Privately Held**
WEB: www.ancomcabinets.com
SIC: 2434 Mfg Wood Kitchen Cabinets

(G-7909)
ANDREW ROLDEN PC
39 Main St (01432-1378)
PHONE..................................978 391-4655
Andrew Olden, *Principal*
EMP: 4 **EST:** 2010
SALES (est): 421.8K **Privately Held**
SIC: 3089 Mfg Plastic Products

(G-7910)
ANDREWS HOLDINGS INC
2 New England Way (01432-1514)
PHONE..................................978 772-4444
J Raymond Andrews, *President*
Richard Osterberg, *Clerk*
EMP: 15 **EST:** 1951
SQ FT: 20,000
SALES (est): 1.6MM **Privately Held**
WEB: www.silpro.com
SIC: 3241 Mfg Hydraulic Cement

(G-7911)
ARDENT MILLS LLC
Also Called: Cargill
35 Nemco Way (01432-1539)
PHONE..................................978 772-6337
Joe Kochan, *Manager*
EMP: 30
SALES (corp-wide): 473.4MM **Privately Held**
WEB: www.cargill.com
SIC: 2041 Mfg Flour/Grain Mill Products
PA: Ardent Mills, Llc
1875 Lawrence St Ste 1400
Denver CO 80202
800 851-9618

(G-7912)
AVS INCORPORATED
Also Called: Advanced Vacuum Systems
60 Fitchburg Rd (01432-1049)
PHONE..................................978 772-0710
Steven Levesque, *President*
Charles Creeden, *Vice Pres*
Bill Parker, *Purch Agent*
Stan Rzonca, *QC Mgr*
Donny Goyette, *Engineer*
◆ **EMP:** 100
SQ FT: 34,000
SALES (est): 25.6MM **Privately Held**
WEB: www.avsinc.com
SIC: 3567 Mfg Industrial Furnaces/Ovens

(G-7913)
CAPACITEC INC (PA)
87 Fitchburg Rd (01432-1003)
P.O. Box 819 (01432-0819)
PHONE..................................978 772-6033
Robert L Foster, *President*
Hai Trinh, *Engineer*
Joan M Foster, *Treasurer*
Joan Foster, *Treasurer*
Jeff Peduzzi, *Sales Dir*
EMP: 15
SQ FT: 12,000
SALES (est): 2.1MM **Privately Held**
WEB: www.capacitec.com
SIC: 3829 Mfg Measuring/Controlling Devices

(G-7914)
CATANIA-SPAGNA CORPORATION
Also Called: Catania Oils
3 Nemco Way (01432-1539)
P.O. Box 847315, Boston (02284-7315)
PHONE..................................978 772-7900
Anthony Basile, *CEO*
Joseph Basile, *President*
Stephen Basile, *Exec VP*
Robert Basile, *Director*
William Reilly, *Director*
◆ **EMP:** 45
SQ FT: 75,000
SALES (est): 37.6MM **Privately Held**
WEB: www.cataniausa.com
SIC: 2079 Mfg Edible Fats/Oils

(G-7915)
CERIC FABRICATION CO INC
Also Called: Ceric Fab Systems
70 Nemco Way (01432-1537)
PHONE..................................978 772-9034
Seth Wesson, *President*
Ed Arventos, *Vice Pres*
Seth K Wesson Jr, *Vice Pres*
Carol Wesson, *Director*
Eric J Wesson, *Director*
EMP: 50
SQ FT: 25,000
SALES (est): 10.7MM **Privately Held**
WEB: www.cericfab.com
SIC: 3444 Mfg Sheet Metalwork

(G-7916)
CREATIVE MATERIALS INC
Also Called: CMI
12 Willow Rd (01432-5513)
PHONE..................................978 391-4700
Silvio Morano, *President*
Matthew Ganslaw, *Vice Pres*
Janet K Morano, *Vice Pres*
Jon Knotts, *Engineer*
Brian Violette, *Engineer*
EMP: 14
SQ FT: 26,000
SALES (est): 4.2MM **Privately Held**
WEB: www.creativematerials.com
SIC: 2899 8731 2891 Mfg Chemical Preparation Coml Physical Research Mfg Adhesives/Sealants

(G-7917)
ECKEL INDUSTRIES INC (PA)
Also Called: Eckoustic Division
100 Groton Shirley Rd (01432-1047)
PHONE..................................978 772-0840
Alex Eckel, *President*
John Flood, *Vice Pres*
Jeff Morris, *Vice Pres*
Joseph Tunnera, *Treasurer*
Joseph Tunnerg, *Treasurer*
▲ **EMP:** 12 **EST:** 1952
SQ FT: 38,000
SALES: 9.6MM **Privately Held**
WEB: www.eckelacoustic.com
SIC: 3296 3446 3444 Mfg Mineral Wool Mfg Architectural Metalwork Mfg Sheet Metalwork

(G-7918)
ELLIOTT AUTO SUPPLY CO INC
Also Called: Splash Products
95 Fitchburg Rd (01432-1073)
PHONE..................................978 772-9882
Cheryl Engel, *Manager*
EMP: 4
SALES (corp-wide): 726.1MM **Privately Held**
SIC: 2842 Whol Auto Parts/Supplies
PA: Elliott Auto Supply Co., Inc.
1380 Corporate Center Cur
Eagan MN 55121
651 454-4100

(G-7919)
EPIC ENTERPRISES INC
11 Copeland Dr (01432-1767)
PHONE..................................978 772-2340
T Tenney, *President*
Robert H Rauh Jr, *President*
Robert Rauh, *Treasurer*
Donald Sorrie, *Treasurer*
David R Coffman, *Director*
EMP: 85
SQ FT: 500,000
SALES (est): 34.3MM
SALES (corp-wide): 64.6B **Publicly Held**
WEB: www.epicenterprises.com
SIC: 2086 Mfg Bottled/Canned Soft Drinks
PA: Pepsico, Inc.
700 Anderson Hill Rd
Purchase NY 10577
914 253-2000

(G-7920)
G H ALLEN ASSOCIATES INC
179 W Main St (01432-1259)
P.O. Box 501 (01432-0501)
PHONE..................................978 772-4010
George H Allen, *President*
David Allen, *Treasurer*
EMP: 5
SQ FT: 3,000
SALES: 525K **Privately Held**
SIC: 3999 Mfg Artificial Flower Supplies

(G-7921)
GRADY RESEARCH INC
323 W Main St Ste 1 (01432-1240)
PHONE..................................978 772-3303
John Grady, *Owner*
▲ **EMP:** 5
SALES (est): 742K **Privately Held**
WEB: www.gradyresearch.com
SIC: 3844 Mfg X-Ray Apparatus/Tubes

(G-7922)
J & S BUSINESS PRODUCTS INC
17 Main St Ste 5 (01432-1383)
PHONE..................................877 425-4049
Jose Banchs, *President*
EMP: 8
SALES (est): 852.1K **Privately Held**
SIC: 2759 Commercial Printing

(G-7923)
L3 ESSCO INC
90 Nemco Way (01432-1541)
PHONE..................................978 568-5100
Thomas J Casale, *President*
◆ **EMP:** 84 **EST:** 1961
SQ FT: 30,000
SALES (est): 27.2MM
SALES (corp-wide): 6.8B **Publicly Held**
WEB: www.esscoradomes.com
SIC: 3711 3663 Mfg Motor Vehicle/Car Bodies Mfg Radio/Tv Communication Equipment
HQ: L3 Technologies, Inc.
600 3rd Ave Fl 34
New York NY 10016
212 697-1111

(G-7924)
L3 TECHNOLOGIES INC
L-3 Maritime Systems
90 Nemco Way (01432-1541)
PHONE..................................978 462-2400
Don Roussinos, *Manager*
EMP: 11
SALES (corp-wide): 6.8B **Publicly Held**
SIC: 3812 Mfg Search/Navigation Equipment
HQ: L3 Technologies, Inc.
600 3rd Ave Fl 34
New York NY 10016
212 697-1111

(G-7925)
L3 TECHNOLOGIES INC
Also Called: L3 Henschel
90 Nemco Way (01432-1541)
PHONE..................................978 784-1999
EMP: 115
SALES (corp-wide): 6.8B **Publicly Held**
WEB: www.henschel.com
SIC: 3669 Mfg Radio/Tv Communication Equipment
HQ: L3 Technologies, Inc.
600 3rd Ave Fl 34
New York NY 10016
212 697-1111

(G-7926)
MICRON PLASTICS INC
30 Faulkner St (01432-1612)
PHONE..................................978 772-6900
Harold E Braselman, *President*
EMP: 17
SQ FT: 27,000
SALES (est): 2.3MM **Privately Held**
WEB: www.micron-plastics.com
SIC: 3081 Mfg Unsupported Plastic Film/Sheet

(G-7927)
NASOYA FOODS INC
1 New England Way (01432-1514)
PHONE..................................978 772-6880
Robert Jones, *President*
Nicole Lee, *Payroll Mgr*
Winston Lo, *Director*
Annemarie Abdell, *Executive*
EMP: 57
SALES (est): 18MM **Privately Held**
WEB: www.nasoya.com
SIC: 2099 5149 Mfg Food Preparations Whol Groceries
HQ: Vitasoy Usa Inc.
57 Russell St
Woburn MA 01801
781 430-8988

(G-7928)
NASOYA FOODS USA LLC
1 New England Way (01432-1514)
PHONE..................................978 772-6880
Ross Gatta, *President*
Thomas Perry, *COO*
EMP: 160 **EST:** 2016
SQ FT: 140,000

SALES: 60MM Privately Held
SIC: 2099 Mfg Food Preparations
HQ: Pulmuone Foods Usa, Inc.
2315 Moore Ave
Fullerton CA 92833

(G-7929)
NEWEDGE SIGNAL SOLUTIONS LLC
323 W Main St Ste 1 (01432-1240)
PHONE....978 425-5400
David J McIntosh, *President*
Phil Gelder, *Engineer*
EMP: 7
SALES: 1.1MM Privately Held
SIC: 3663 Mfg Radio/Tv Communication Equipment

(G-7930)
NORTHEAST HOT-FILL CO-OP INC
25 Copeland Dr (01432-1790)
PHONE....978 772-2338
Michael Matney, *Principal*
EMP: 45
SQ FT: 321,000
SALES (est): 7.8MM Privately Held
SIC: 2086 Mfg Bottled/Canned Soft Drinks

(G-7931)
NORTON LAND CLEARING AND LOG
5 Robbins Rd (01432-1772)
PHONE....978 391-4029
EMP: 3
SALES (est): 131.6K Privately Held
SIC: 2411 Logging

(G-7932)
ORION INDUSTRIES INCORPORATED
1 Orion Park Dr (01432-1582)
PHONE....978 772-0020
Francis J Widmayer, *President*
Michael J Widmayer, *President*
Stuart Husmer, *Vice Pres*
Sean Osullivan, *QC Mgr*
Kathryn Waller, *CFO*
EMP: 33
SQ FT: 17,000
SALES: 7MM Privately Held
SIC: 3679 Mfg Electronic Components

(G-7933)
PEPSI BOTTLING GROUP INC
Also Called: Pepsico
11 Copeland Dr (01432-1790)
PHONE....978 772-2340
Craig E Weatherup, *President*
EMP: 7
SALES (est): 813.5K Privately Held
SIC: 2086 Carb Sft Drnkbtlcn

(G-7934)
PLASTIC ASSEMBLY CORPORATION
Also Called: Blinky Products
1 Sculley Rd Unit A (01432-1238)
P.O. Box 632 (01432-0632)
PHONE....978 772-4725
Regis M Magnus, *President*
▲ EMP: 15
SQ FT: 2,500
SALES (est): 1.3MM Privately Held
WEB: www.blinkyproducts.com
SIC: 3089 Mfg Plastic Products

(G-7935)
R MURPHY COMPANY INC
13 Groton Harvard Rd (01432-1846)
P.O. Box 376 (01432-0376)
PHONE....978 772-3481
EMP: 16
SQ FT: 10,000
SALES (est): 3.1MM Privately Held
WEB: www.rmurphyknives.com
SIC: 3421 3423 Mfg Cutlery Mfg Hand/Edge Tools

(G-7936)
SEALED AIR CORP
100 Westford Rd (01432-1534)
PHONE....508 521-5694
Kate Hughes, *Principal*
EMP: 4
SALES (est): 109.8K Privately Held
SIC: 2671 Mfg Packaging Paper/Film

(G-7937)
SHANKLIN CORPORATION (HQ)
Also Called: Shrink Equipment
100 Westford Rd (01432-1552)
PHONE....978 487-2204
Lawrence J Pillote, *President*
Jonathan B Baker, *President*
Kenneth Chrisman, *Vice Pres*
Sean E Dempsey, *Admin Sec*
Sarah W Shanklin, *Admin Sec*
◆ EMP: 129
SQ FT: 170,000
SALES (est): 19.2MM
SALES (corp-wide): 4.7B Publicly Held
WEB: www.shanklincorp.com
SIC: 3565 Mfg Packaging Machinery
PA: Sealed Air Corporation
2415 Cascade Pointe Blvd
Charlotte NC 28208
980 221-3235

(G-7938)
SHANKLIN RESEARCH CORPORATION
100 Westford Rd (01432-1534)
PHONE....978 772-2090
Norman D Shanklin, *President*
EMP: 7 EST: 1961
SQ FT: 2,000
SALES (est): 904.5K Privately Held
WEB: www.shanklin.com
SIC: 3549 Mfg Metalworking Machinery

(G-7939)
SILPRO LLC (PA)
2 New England Way (01432-1548)
PHONE....978 772-4444
Brooks C Patterson, *Principal*
Joe Sanfratello, *Regional Mgr*
John Driscoll, *Production*
◆ EMP: 25
SALES (est): 4MM Privately Held
SIC: 3423 Mfg Hand/Edge Tools

(G-7940)
SUPERCONDUCTIVITY INC (HQ)
Also Called: Integrated Electronics
114 E Main St (01432-1832)
PHONE....608 831-5773
Greg Yurek, *President*
Alan Savoie, *Maintence Staff*
▲ EMP: 89
SALES (est): 11MM
SALES (corp-wide): 56.2MM Publicly Held
WEB: www.superconductivity.com
SIC: 3629 Mfg Electrical Industrial Apparatus
PA: American Superconductor Corporation
114 E Main St
Ayer MA 01432
978 842-3000

(G-7941)
TULCO INC
9 Bishop Rd (01432-1117)
PHONE....978 772-4412
William Fletcher, *President*
EMP: 5
SQ FT: 14,000
SALES (est): 471.9K Privately Held
WEB: www.tulcocorp.com
SIC: 2891 Mfg Amorphous Silica

(G-7942)
WAITECO MACHINE INC
18 Saratoga Blvd (01434-5217)
PHONE....978 772-5535
Paulette M Barros, *President*
William F Waite, *Vice Pres*
EMP: 3 EST: 2010
SALES (est): 612.3K Privately Held
SIC: 3543 Mfg Industrial Machinery

Baldwinville
Worcester County

(G-7943)
DEAN PAIGE WELDING INC
377 State Rd (01436-1125)
P.O. Box 11 (01436-0011)
PHONE....978 939-8187
Dean C Paige, *President*
Timothy Paige, *Clerk*
EMP: 5
SALES (est): 463.3K Privately Held
SIC: 3441 1711 1799 Metal Fabrication Mechanical Contractor & Welding Contractor

(G-7944)
JULIMA CHEESE INC
212 Freight Shed Rd (01436)
PHONE....978 939-8800
Paulo Souza, *President*
Karla Souza, *Vice Pres*
EMP: 5
SALES (est): 235.9K Privately Held
SIC: 2022 Mfg Cheese

(G-7945)
SEAMAN PAPER COMPANY MASS INC
51 Main St (01436-1158)
PHONE....978 939-5356
John Tew, *Prdtn Mgr*
Frank Hogan, *Branch Mgr*
Francesco Pagliani, *Executive*
EMP: 100
SALES (corp-wide): 44.6MM Privately Held
WEB: www.satinwrap.com
SIC: 2621 Paper Mill
PA: Seaman Paper Company Of Massachusetts, Inc.
35 Wilkins Rd
Gardner MA 01440
978 632-1513

Barnstable
Barnstable County

(G-7946)
APPETITES
2905 Main St (02630-1017)
PHONE....508 362-3623
Lisa Gage, *Owner*
EMP: 3 EST: 2008
SALES (est): 236K Privately Held
SIC: 2834 Mfg Pharmaceutical Preparations

(G-7947)
CAPE COD BEER INC
1336 Phinneys Ln (02630)
PHONE....508 790-4200
Todd Marcus, *President*
EMP: 19
SQ FT: 7,360
SALES (est): 3.1MM Privately Held
SIC: 2082 Mfg Malt Beverages

(G-7948)
HOWARD BOATS LLC
Beale Way (02630)
P.O. Box 125 (02630-0125)
PHONE....508 362-6859
Peter Eastman, *Mng Member*
Peter C Eastman,
EMP: 3 EST: 1938
SQ FT: 22,000
SALES (est): 391.6K Privately Held
SIC: 3732 Boatbuilding/Repairing

Barre
Worcester County

(G-7949)
BOLGER PRODUCTS
28 Summer St (01005-9549)
P.O. Box 74 (01005-0074)
PHONE....978 355-2226
Joe Bolger, *Owner*
EMP: 4
SQ FT: 908
SALES (est): 310.5K Privately Held
SIC: 3499 Mfg Misc Fabricated Metal Products

(G-7950)
CHAS G ALLEN REALTY LLC
25 Williamsville Rd (01005-9502)
PHONE....978 355-2911
Bert Allen, *Purch Agent*
Charles R Sargent, *Treasurer*
David E Krupp, *Director*
Bob Stebbins, *Officer*
Gary A Boudreau, *Admin Sec*
▲ EMP: 55
SQ FT: 90,000
SALES (est): 10.8MM Privately Held
WEB: www.chasgallen.com
SIC: 3541 3599 7699 3291 Mfg Machine Tool-Cutting Mfg Industrial Machinery

(G-7951)
TIM ROBINSON LOGGING
199 Wauwinet Rd (01005-9156)
P.O. Box 58 (01005-0058)
PHONE....978 355-4287
EMP: 12
SALES (est): 690K Privately Held
SIC: 2411 Logging

(G-7952)
TURLEY PUBLICATIONS INC
Also Called: Barre Gazette
5 Exchange St Fl 1 (01005-8702)
P.O. Box 448 (01005-0448)
PHONE....978 355-4000
Patrick Turley, *Owner*
Tim Mara, *Adv Mgr*
EMP: 6
SALES (corp-wide): 54.3MM Privately Held
WEB: www.turley.com
SIC: 2711 Newspapers-Publishing/Printing
PA: Turley Publications, Inc.
24 Water St
Palmer MA 01069
800 824-6548

Bass River
Barnstable County

(G-7953)
ARNOLD BAKERIES
17 Oyster Cove Rd (02664-2320)
PHONE....508 398-6588
David Dawson, *Principal*
EMP: 3
SALES (est): 153.9K Privately Held
SIC: 2051 Mfg Bread/Related Products

Becket
Berkshire County

(G-7954)
RONALD F BIRRELL
78 Parsons Way (01223-3279)
PHONE....413 219-6729
Ronald F Birrell, *Principal*
EMP: 4
SALES (est): 236.4K Privately Held
SIC: 2431 Mfg Millwork

Bedford
Middlesex County

(G-7955)
1366 TECHNOLOGIES INC
68 Preston Ct (01730)
PHONE....781 861-1611
Frank Van Mierlo, *President*
▲ EMP: 18
SALES (est): 4.9MM Privately Held
WEB: www.1366tech.com
SIC: 3674 Mfg Semiconductors/Related Devices

(G-7956)
ACCOUNTTECH
54 Middlesex Tpke Ste B2 (01730-1417)
PHONE.....................................781 276-1555
Mark Blagden, *Owner*
Tori Mueck, *Opers Mgr*
EMP: 4
SALES (est): 419.4K **Privately Held**
WEB: www.accounttech.com
SIC: 7372 Prepackaged Software Services

(G-7957)
ANIKA THERAPEUTICS INC (PA)
32 Wiggins Ave (01730-2315)
PHONE.....................................781 457-9000
Joseph Darling, *President*
Dana M Alexander, *COO*
Dana Alexander, *COO*
James Loerop, *Exec VP*
Steven Cyr, *Vice Pres*
▲ **EMP:** 107
SQ FT: 134,000
SALES: 105.5MM **Publicly Held**
WEB: www.anikatherapeutics.com
SIC: 3841 Mfg Surgical/Medical Instruments

(G-7958)
APPLIED BIOSYSTEMS LLC
Also Called: Applied Bosystems Part Lf Tech
2 Preston Ct (01730-2334)
PHONE.....................................781 271-0045
Tony White, *Branch Mgr*
EMP: 13
SALES (corp-wide): 24.3B **Publicly Held**
SIC: 3826 Mfg Analytical Instruments
HQ: Applied Biosystems, Llc
5791 Van Allen Way
Carlsbad CA 92008
-

(G-7959)
ARISTA FLUTES LLC
10 Railroad Ave (01730-2112)
PHONE.....................................781 275-8821
Juan Arista, *Mng Member*
EMP: 7
SALES (est): 717.3K **Privately Held**
WEB: www.aristaflutes.com
SIC: 3931 Mfg Musical Instruments

(G-7960)
AVETA BIOMICS INC
110 Great Rd Ste 302 (01730-2729)
PHONE.....................................339 927-5994
Parag Mehta, *CEO*
Sharmila Mudgal, *President*
Lynda Orsula, *Accountant*
EMP: 5 **EST:** 2014
SALES (est): 543.6K **Privately Held**
SIC: 2834 Mfg Pharmaceutical Preparations

(G-7961)
AVVIO NETWORKS INC
11 Donovan Dr (01730-1152)
PHONE.....................................781 271-0002
EMP: 9
SQ FT: 3,000
SALES: 5MM **Privately Held**
WEB: www.avvionetworks.com
SIC: 3661 Mfg Telephone/Telegraph Apparatus

(G-7962)
AWARE INC (PA)
40 Middlesex Tpke (01730-1432)
PHONE.....................................781 276-4000
Brent P Johnstone, *Ch of Bd*
Robert A Eckel, *President*
Kevin T Russell, *President*
David Benini, *Vice Pres*
Isaac Osesina, *Research*
▲ **EMP:** 56
SQ FT: 72,000
SALES: 16.1MM **Publicly Held**
SIC: 7372 3674 Prepackaged Software Services Mfg Semiconductors/Related Devices

(G-7963)
BLUELINE NDT LLC
Also Called: Nightsea
34 Dunelm Rd (01730-1362)
PHONE.....................................781 791-9511
Charles Mazel, *President*
EMP: 3
SQ FT: 1,100
SALES (est): 50K **Privately Held**
SIC: 3829 Mfg Measuring/Controlling Devices

(G-7964)
BOSTON SCIENTIFIC CORPORATION
140 Hanscom Dr (01730-2630)
PHONE.....................................781 259-2501
EMP: 4
SALES (corp-wide): 9.8B **Publicly Held**
SIC: 3841 Mfg Surgical/Medical Instruments
PA: Boston Scientific Corporation
300 Boston Scientific Way
Marlborough MA 01752
508 683-4000

(G-7965)
BRAND & OPPENHEIMER CO INC
Also Called: Cutting Edge Texstyles
4 Preston Ct Ste 200 (01730-2356)
PHONE.....................................781 271-0000
Valerie Chambers, *Sales Executive*
EMP: 20 **Privately Held**
SIC: 2261 2396 2221 2211 Cotton Finishing Plant Mfg Auto/Apparel Trim Manmad Brdwv Fabric Mill Cotton Brdwv Fabric Mill
PA: Brand & Oppenheimer Co., Inc.
208 Clock Tower Sq
Portsmouth RI 02871
-

(G-7966)
CASENET LLC
36 Crosby Dr (01730-1425)
PHONE.....................................781 357-2700
Kevin Brown,
EMP: 90
SQ FT: 20,000
SALES (est): 15.2MM **Publicly Held**
SIC: 7372 Prepackaged Software Services
PA: Centene Corporation
7700 Forsyth Blvd Ste 800
Saint Louis MO 63105
-

(G-7967)
CURA SOFTWARE SOLUTIONS CO
34 Crosby Dr (01730-1449)
PHONE.....................................781 325-7158
J Ramachandran, *CEO*
Vijay Sashti, *Managing Dir*
Bala Reddy, *Chairman*
Howard Zev, *Exec VP*
Merlin Knott, *Vice Pres*
EMP: 10
SQ FT: 4,200
SALES (est): 636.8K
SALES (corp-wide): 3.7MM **Privately Held**
SIC: 7372 Prepackaged Software Services
PA: Cura Risk Management Software (Pty) Ltd
13 Scott St
Johannesburg GP 2090
114 837-640

(G-7968)
CYTONOME/ST LLC
9 Oak Park Dr (01730-1413)
PHONE.....................................617 330-5030
John C Sharpe, *CEO*
Chris Negus, *Vice Pres*
Michael Morkos, *Research*
Etienne Dano, *Engineer*
Jacki Johnson, *Info Tech Mgr*
EMP: 15
SQ FT: 18,000
SALES (est): 4MM **Privately Held**
SIC: 3841 Mfg Surgical/Medical Instruments

(G-7969)
DALE ENGINEERING & SON INC
3 Alfred Cir (01730-2318)
PHONE.....................................781 541-6055
Christopher Hawkes, *President*
Hollis Dale Hawkes, *Vice Pres*
EMP: 15
SQ FT: 10,000
SALES (est): 1.5MM **Privately Held**
SIC: 3599 8711 Machine Shop Doing Jobbing & Repair Engineering Services

(G-7970)
DATAWATCH CORPORATION (HQ)
4 Crosby Dr (01730-1402)
PHONE.....................................978 441-2200
Michael A Morrison, *President*
Ken Tacelli, *COO*
James Eliason, *CFO*
Colin Mahony, *Bd of Directors*
Randall Seidl, *Bd of Directors*
EMP: 92
SQ FT: 20,360
SALES: 41.6MM
SALES (corp-wide): 396.3MM **Publicly Held**
WEB: www.datawatch.com
SIC: 7372 Business Software And Services
PA: Altair Engineering Inc.
1820 E Big Beaver Rd
Troy MI 48083
248 614-2400

(G-7971)
DMI NUTRACEUTICALS INC
Also Called: Clarex
1 Oak Park Dr Ste 2 (01730-1421)
PHONE.....................................617 999-7219
Eugene Chan, *President*
Ira Helfand, *Vice Pres*
EMP: 4
SALES (est): 317.2K **Privately Held**
SIC: 2023 Dry, Condensed, Evaporated Products

(G-7972)
EM4 INC (DH)
Also Called: Gooch & Housego Boston
7 Oak Park Dr (01730-1413)
PHONE.....................................781 275-7501
Mark Webster, *CEO*
Andy Boteler, *CEO*
Rick Sharp, *President*
Tony Radojevic, *Vice Pres*
Nancy Lykus, *QC Mgr*
EMP: 30
SQ FT: 29,300
SALES (est): 16MM
SALES (corp-wide): 163.5MM **Privately Held**
WEB: www.em4inc.com
SIC: 3661 Mfg Telephone/Telegraph Apparatus
HQ: Gooch & Housego (Florida) Llc
676 Alpha Dr
Cleveland OH 44143
321 242-7818

(G-7973)
EMD MILLIPORE CORPORATION
75 Wiggins Ave (01730-2337)
PHONE.....................................781 533-6000
Mike Titus, *Exec VP*
Meghan Higson, *Research*
EMP: 180
SALES (corp-wide): 16.4B **Privately Held**
WEB: www.millipore.com
SIC: 3826 Mfg Analysis & Purification Products
HQ: Emd Millipore Corporation
400 Summit Dr
Burlington MA 01803
781 533-6000

(G-7974)
EMD MILLIPORE CORPORATION
80 Ashby Rd (01730-2200)
PHONE.....................................781 533-6000
Martin Madaus, *President*
EMP: 200
SALES (corp-wide): 16.4B **Privately Held**
WEB: www.millipore.com
SIC: 3826 Mfg Analytical Instruments
HQ: Emd Millipore Corporation
400 Summit Dr
Burlington MA 01803
781 533-6000

(G-7975)
ENTEGRIS INC
9 Crosby Dr (01730-1401)
PHONE.....................................978 436-6575
EMP: 22
SALES (corp-wide): 1.5B **Publicly Held**
SIC: 3089 Mfg Plastic Products
PA: Entegris, Inc.
129 Concord Rd
Billerica MA 01821
978 436-6500

(G-7976)
EXCEL TECHNOLOGY INC (HQ)
125 Middlesex Tpke (01730-1409)
PHONE.....................................781 266-5700
Antoine Dominic, *CEO*
Peter Chang, *Vice Pres*
Deborah A Mulryan, *Vice Pres*
Alice H Varisano, *CFO*
EMP: 75
SQ FT: 65,000
SALES (est): 83MM **Publicly Held**
WEB: www.exceltechinc.com
SIC: 3699 3827 Mfg Electrical Equipment/Supplies Mfg Optical Instruments/Lenses

(G-7977)
FRACTAL ANTENNA SYSTEMS INC
213 Burlington Rd Ste 105 (01730-1468)
PHONE.....................................781 290-5308
Barry Unger, *Ch of Bd*
Valerie Smith, *Opers Mgr*
Phil Salkind, *Manager*
Nathan L Cohen, *CTO*
Mary L Shelman, *Director*
EMP: 10
SQ FT: 4,500
SALES (est): 1.7MM **Privately Held**
WEB: www.fractenna.com
SIC: 3663 Mfg Radio/Tv Communication Equipment

(G-7978)
FUJIFILM NORTH AMERICA CORP
Also Called: Fuji Film Microdisk USA
45 Crosby Dr (01730-1401)
PHONE.....................................781 271-4400
Lawrence Chiarella, *Vice Pres*
Scott Bartfield, *Vice Pres*
Peter Gray, *Vice Pres*
Todd Zimmerman, *Vice Pres*
Fred Maddage, *Software Engr*
EMP: 190 **Privately Held**
SIC: 3861 Mfg Photographic Equipment/Supplies
HQ: Fujifilm North America Corporation
200 Summit Lake Dr Fl 2
Valhalla NY 10595
914 789-8100

(G-7979)
FUJIFILM RCRDING MEDIA USA INC (DH)
Also Called: Fujifilm Microdisks U.S.a
45 Crosby Dr (01730-1401)
PHONE.....................................781 271-4400
Norio Shibata, *President*
Hironobu Taketomi, *Vice Pres*
Regan Nayve, *Engineer*
Suguru Enomoto, *Treasurer*
Laura Burke, *Manager*
◆ **EMP:** 77
SQ FT: 135,000
SALES (est): 54.2MM **Privately Held**
WEB: www.fujibedford.com
SIC: 3577 Mfg Computer Peripheral Equipment
HQ: Fujifilm Holdings America Corporation
200 Summit Lake Dr Fl 2
Valhalla NY 10595
914 789-8100

(G-7980)
HOLOGIC FOREIGN SALES CORP
35 Crosby Dr (01730-1401)
PHONE.....................................781 999-7300
William Roberts, *Principal*
Meg Eckenroad, *Vice Pres*
Maria Lattanzio-Rihan, *Project Mgr*
Joseph Ellis, *Engineer*
Catherine Gonzalez, *Engineer*
EMP: 870

SALES (est): 34.2MM
SALES (corp-wide): 3.3B **Publicly Held**
WEB: www.hologic.com
SIC: 3844 Mfg X-Ray Apparatus/Tubes
PA: Hologic, Inc.
250 Campus Dr
Marlborough MA 01752
508 263-2900

(G-7981)
HUBER + SHNER PLATIS PHOTONICS
213 Burlington Rd Ste 123 (01730-1468)
PHONE..................................781 275-5080
Gerald Wesel, *President*
Nick Parsons, *President*
Jeffery Farmer, *Vice Pres*
Jim Miller, *Vice Pres*
Martin Stephenson, *CFO*
EMP: 10 **EST:** 1998
SALES (est): 1.2MM
SALES (corp-wide): 898.3MM **Privately Held**
WEB: www.polatis.com
SIC: 3674 Mfg Semiconductors/Related Devices
HQ: Huber+Suhner Polatis, Inc.
213 Burlington Rd Ste 123
Bedford MA
781 275-5080

(G-7982)
INSTRUMENTATION LABORATORY CO (DH)
180 Hartwell Rd (01730-2443)
PHONE..................................781 861-0710
Ramon E Benet, *President*
Jose Luis Martin, *Vice Pres*
Jose Martin, *Vice Pres*
Steven Trotta, *Vice Pres*
Albert Capobianco, *Materials Dir*
▲ **EMP:** 700
SALES (est): 357.7MM
SALES (corp-wide): 111.5MM **Privately Held**
WEB: www.ilww.com
SIC: 3841 2819 8731 2835 Mfg Surgical/Med Instr Mfg Indstl Inorgan Chem Coml Physical Research Mfg Diagnostic Substance
HQ: Instrumentation Laboratory Spa
Viale Monza 338
Milano MI 20128
022 522-1

(G-7983)
INTERNTONAL TOTALIZING SYSTEMS (PA)
Also Called: I T S
10 Paul Revere Rd (01730-1640)
PHONE..................................978 521-8867
Peter Lillios, *President*
Thomas Warner, *Vice Pres*
David Otten, *Clerk*
▲ **EMP:** 26
SQ FT: 52,600
SALES: 1MM **Privately Held**
SIC: 3661 3581 Researches Designs & Mfg Electronic Public Telephones

(G-7984)
INTERTICKETCOM INC (PA)
2 Glenridge Dr (01730-2035)
PHONE..................................781 275-5724
Endre Jobbagy, *Owner*
EMP: 5
SALES (est): 3.4MM **Privately Held**
SIC: 2759 Commercial Printing

(G-7985)
IROBOT CORPORATION (PA)
Also Called: ENDEAVOR ROBOTICS
8 Crosby Dr (01730-1402)
PHONE..................................781 430-3000
Colin M Angle, *Ch of Bd*
Christian Cerda, *COO*
Alison Dean, *CFO*
▲ **EMP:** 277
SQ FT: 209,000
SALES: 1B **Publicly Held**
WEB: www.irobot.com
SIC: 3569 3731 Mfg Robots

(G-7986)
KADANT FIBERGEN INC (HQ)
8 Alfred Cir (01730-2340)
PHONE..................................781 275-3600
William A Rainville, *Ch of Bd*
Jonathan W Painter, *President*
Theo Melas-Kyriazi, *CFO*
EMP: 10
SALES (est): 5.7MM
SALES (corp-wide): 633.7MM **Publicly Held**
SIC: 3823 Holding Company Mfr Control Instruments
PA: Kadant Inc.
1 Technology Park Dr # 210
Westford MA 01886
978 776-2000

(G-7987)
L3HARRIS TECHNOLOGIES INC
Also Called: Govt Comm Sys.
175 Middlesex Tpke Ste 2 (01730-1459)
PHONE..................................781 538-4148
Jan Goldberg, *Manager*
EMP: 53
SALES (corp-wide): 6.8B **Publicly Held**
SIC: 3812 Mfg Search/Navigation Equipment
PA: L3harris Technologies, Inc.
1025 W Nasa Blvd
Melbourne FL 32919
321 727-9100

(G-7988)
LANTIQ BROADBAND HOLDCO INC
40 Middlesex Tpke (01730-1404)
PHONE..................................781 687-0400
John Knoll, *President*
EMP: 3 **EST:** 2010
SALES (est): 143.6K
SALES (corp-wide): 177.9K **Privately Held**
SIC: 7372 Prepackaged Software Services
HQ: Lantiq Beteiligungs-Gmbh & Co. Kg
Lilienthalstr. 15
Neubiberg

(G-7989)
MEGAPULSE INCORPORATED
23 Crosby Dr (01730-1423)
PHONE..................................781 538-5299
Paul Johannessen, *CEO*
Eric Johannessen, *President*
Robert Rines, *Admin Sec*
EMP: 50
SQ FT: 40,000
SALES (est): 6.8MM **Privately Held**
WEB: www.megapulse.com
SIC: 3812 3663 Mfg Search/Navigation Equipment Mfg Radio/Tv Communication Equipment

(G-7990)
MELT COGNITION
7 Alfred Cir (01730-2318)
PHONE..................................781 275-6400
Robert Desaro, *Principal*
EMP: 3
SALES (est): 187.3K **Privately Held**
SIC: 2611 Pulp Mill

(G-7991)
MERCK GROUP
80 Ashby Rd (01730-2200)
PHONE..................................781 858-3284
Diane Macdonald, *Info Tech Dir*
Petra Holst, *Executive Asst*
EMP: 4
SALES (est): 361.3K **Privately Held**
SIC: 2834 Mfg Pharmaceutical Preparations

(G-7992)
MLS SHEET METAL LLC
39 Crosby Dr (01730-1401)
PHONE..................................781 275-2265
EMP: 16
SQ FT: 5,500
SALES (est): 4MM **Privately Held**
SIC: 3444 Sheet Metalwork, Nsk

(G-7993)
N2 BIOMEDICAL LLC
1 Patriots Park (01730-2343)
PHONE..................................781 275-6001
Randall Sword, *President*
Eric Tobin, *Vice Pres*
Brian Drake, *Foreman/Supr*
Tim Egge, *Manager*
Little Mark, *Bd of Directors*
EMP: 26
SALES: 3.6MM **Privately Held**
SIC: 3479 Coating/Engraving Service

(G-7994)
NINEPOINT MEDICAL INC
12 Oak Park Dr Ste 2 (01730-1443)
PHONE..................................617 250-7190
Eman Namati, *President*
Mark Levin, *President*
Christopher Von Jako, *President*
Heather Reed, *Vice Pres*
Sofiya Pethania, *Mfg Staff*
EMP: 6
SALES (est): 1.6MM **Privately Held**
SIC: 3841 Mfg Surgical/Medical Instruments

(G-7995)
NOVANTA CORPORATION (HQ)
Also Called: Cambridge Technology
125 Middlesex Tpke (01730-1409)
PHONE..................................781 266-5700
Matthijs Glastra, *CEO*
Peter Chang, *Vice Pres*
Ron Honig, *Vice Pres*
Chris Riello, *Vice Pres*
Brian Young, *Vice Pres*
▲ **EMP:** 277 **EST:** 1989
SQ FT: 147,000
SALES (est): 410.9MM **Publicly Held**
WEB: www.gsig.com
SIC: 3699 Mfg Electrical Equipment/Supplies

(G-7996)
NOVANTA INC (PA)
125 Middlesex Tpke (01730-1409)
PHONE..................................781 266-5700
Matthijs Glastra, *CEO*
Stephen W Bershad, *Ch of Bd*
Robert Buckley, *CFO*
Michael Zhao, *Sales Engr*
Brian Young, *Officer*
EMP: 204
SQ FT: 147,000
SALES: 614.3MM **Publicly Held**
SIC: 3699 3845 Mfg Precision Motion Controls Laser Systems & Components

(G-7997)
OCULAR THERAPEUTIX INC (PA)
24 Crosby Dr (01730-1402)
PHONE..................................781 357-4000
Amarpreet Sawhney, *Ch of Bd*
Antony C Mattessich, *President*
Patricia Kitchen, *COO*
Eric Ankerud, *Exec VP*
Daniel Bollag, *Senior VP*
EMP: 43
SQ FT: 91,000
SALES: 1.9MM **Publicly Held**
SIC: 2834 Pharmaceutical Preparations

(G-7998)
OFFICERS WIVES CLUB
Also Called: Minuteman Thrift Shop
11 Barksdale St Bldg 1614 (01731-1700)
PHONE..................................781 274-8079
EMP: 6
SALES (est): 374.2K **Privately Held**
SIC: 2752 Lithographic Commercial Printing

(G-7999)
PEARSON EDUCATION INC
22 Crosby Dr (01730-1429)
PHONE..................................781 687-8800
EMP: 4
SALES (corp-wide): 5.4B **Privately Held**
WEB: www.phgenit.com
SIC: 2731 Books-Publishing/Printing
HQ: Pearson Education, Inc.
221 River St
Hoboken NJ 07030
201 236-7000

(G-8000)
PERMA INCORPORATED
Also Called: Industrial Floor Finishes, Div
605 Springs Rd (01730-1195)
PHONE..................................978 667-5161
Peter H Stevens, *President*
Dorothy Stevens, *Shareholder*
EMP: 16 **EST:** 1950
SQ FT: 12,400
SALES (est): 4MM **Privately Held**
WEB: www.chemicallabs.com
SIC: 2842 2851 Mfg Polish/Sanitation Goods Mfg Paints/Allied Products

(G-8001)
PING ELECTRONICS INC
240 Hartwell Rd (01730-2444)
P.O. Box 38 (01730)
PHONE..................................781 275-4731
Joe Cheng, *President*
Ping Cheng, *Vice Pres*
EMP: 7
SQ FT: 2,000
SALES (est): 440K **Privately Held**
SIC: 3672 Mnfr Printed Circuit Boards

(G-8002)
PROCESS DYNAMICS INC
209 Burlington Rd (01730-1422)
PHONE..................................781 271-0944
Mitchell Hayes, *President*
EMP: 3
SALES (est): 164.4K **Privately Held**
SIC: 7372 Prepackaged Software Services

(G-8003)
PROGRESS SOFTWARE CORPORATION (PA)
14 Oak Park Dr (01730-1485)
PHONE..................................781 280-4000
John R Egan, *Ch of Bd*
Yogesh Gupta, *President*
Yogesh K Gupta, *President*
John Ainsworth, *Senior VP*
Gary Quinn, *Senior VP*
EMP: 410
SQ FT: 258,000
SALES: 397.1MM **Publicly Held**
SIC: 7372 7371 Prepackaged Software & Custom Computer Programing Services

(G-8004)
PROXIMIE INC
143 Great Rd (01730-2743)
PHONE..................................617 391-6824
Talal Ali Ahmad, *Principal*
Nadine Haran, *COO*
EMP: 4
SQ FT: 1,000
SALES (est): 144K **Privately Held**
SIC: 7372 Prepackaged Software Services

(G-8005)
RAYTHEON LGSTICS SPPORT TRNING (HQ)
180 Hartwell Rd (01730-2443)
PHONE..................................310 647-9438
William H Swanson, *President*
John Steeves, *Executive*
EMP: 13
SALES (est): 45.9MM
SALES (corp-wide): 27B **Publicly Held**
SIC: 3761 Mfg Guided Missiles/Space Vehicles
PA: Raytheon Company
870 Winter St
Waltham MA 02451
781 522-3000

(G-8006)
RHEALTH CORPORATION
1 Oak Park Dr Ste 2 (01730-1421)
PHONE..................................617 913-7630
Eugene Chan, *CEO*
EMP: 22
SALES (est): 785K **Privately Held**
SIC: 3841 Mfg Surgical/Medical Instruments

(G-8007)
RSA SECURITY LLC (DH)
174 Middlesex Tpke (01730-1445)
P.O. Box 696009, San Antonio TX (78269-6009)
PHONE..................................781 515-5000

GEOGRAPHIC

Joseph M Tucci, *CEO*
Howard D Elias, *President*
Rohit Ghai, *President*
Rick Hedeman, *Partner*
John Tattan, *Partner*
▲ **EMP:** 750
SQ FT: 328,000
SALES (est): 924.9MM
SALES (corp-wide): 90.6B **Publicly Held**
WEB: www.RSA.com
SIC: 3577 7372 7373 Mfg Computer Peripheral Equipment Prepackaged Software Services Computer Systems Design
HQ: Emc Corporation
176 South St
Hopkinton MA 01748
508 435-1000

(G-8008)
SPERRY PRODUCT INNOVATION INC
12 Deangelo Dr (01730-2204)
PHONE..................................781 271-1400
Laurence Sperry, *President*
Dana Calumby, *Controller*
Mario Divasta, *Office Mgr*
▲ **EMP:** 11
SQ FT: 6,500
SALES (est): 3.1MM **Privately Held**
WEB: www.sperryinc.com
SIC: 3565 Mfg Packaging Machinery

(G-8009)
SPIRE SOLAR INC
1 Patriots Park (01730-2343)
P.O. Box 9, Nutting Lake (01865-0009)
PHONE..................................781 275-6000
Roger Little, *CEO*
Phil Jesoraldo, *Cust Mgr*
EMP: 200
SALES (est): 6.7MM
SALES (corp-wide): 16MM **Publicly Held**
SIC: 3433 5074 8731 Mfg Heating Equipment-Nonelectric Whol Plumbing Equipment/Supplies Commercial Physical Research
PA: Spire Corporation
25 Linnell Cir
Billerica MA 01821
978 584-3958

(G-8010)
SUDBURY SYSTEMS INC
Also Called: Rtas Systems
200 Great Rd Ste 211 (01730-2799)
P.O. Box 428 (01730-0428)
PHONE..................................800 876-8888
Gerald T Delaney, *CEO*
EMP: 20
SQ FT: 7,920
SALES (est): 3.9MM **Privately Held**
WEB: www.rtas.com
SIC: 3579 3572 Mfg Office Machines Mfg Computer Storage Devices

(G-8011)
SULLIVAN JW
244 South Rd (01730-2308)
P.O. Box 422 (01730-0422)
PHONE..................................781 275-5818
Joe Sullivan, *Principal*
EMP: 3
SALES (est): 231.4K **Privately Held**
SIC: 3463 Mfg Nonferrous Forgings

(G-8012)
SUNOPTA INGREDIENTS INC
25 Wiggins Ave (01730-2323)
PHONE..................................781 276-5100
Scott Gordon, *President*
Paul Franzman, *President*
George Klesaris, *Vice Pres*
EMP: 6
SALES (est): 1.8MM **Privately Held**
SIC: 2099 Mfg Food Preparations

(G-8013)
SYMPHONY TALENT LLC
209 Burlington Rd (01730-1422)
PHONE..................................781 275-2716
Lisa Bordinat, *Branch Mgr*
EMP: 15
SALES (corp-wide): 50MM **Privately Held**
SIC: 7372 7361 Prepackaged Software Services/Employment Service
PA: Symphony Talent, Llc
19 W 34th St Fl 10
New York NY 10001
212 999-9000

(G-8014)
TERADYNE INC
Also Called: Integra Test Division
9 Crosby Dr (01730-1401)
PHONE..................................617 482-2700
Marc Levine, *Branch Mgr*
EMP: 140
SALES (corp-wide): 2.1B **Publicly Held**
WEB: www.teradyne.com
SIC: 3825 8711 8731 Mfg Electrical Measuring Instruments Engineering Services Commercial Physical Research
PA: Teradyne, Inc.
600 Riverpark Dr
North Reading MA 01864
978 370-2700

(G-8015)
THERMACELL CORPORATION
26 Crosby Dr (01730-1462)
PHONE..................................816 510-9428
Adam Goess, *Marketing Mgr*
Douglas Kaczor, *Manager*
Jerry O'Leary, *CTO*
Heather Ryba, *Director*
EMP: 10
SALES (est): 1.6MM **Privately Held**
SIC: 3691 Mfg Storage Batteries

(G-8016)
THERMACELL REPELLENTS INC
26 Crosby Dr (01730-1462)
PHONE..................................781 541-6900
Stephen S Hill, *CEO*
Steve Hill, *President*
Charles Laughlin, *COO*
Chuck Laughlin, *COO*
Thomas Paganetti, *CFO*
▲ **EMP:** 25
SALES (est): 4.6MM **Privately Held**
WEB: www.schawbelcorporation.com
SIC: 2879 Mfg Agricultural Chemicals

(G-8017)
THERMO FISHER SCIENTIFIC INC
35 Wiggins Ave (01730-2314)
PHONE..................................781 280-5600
EMP: 130
SALES (corp-wide): 24.3B **Publicly Held**
SIC: 3826 Mfg Analytical Instruments
PA: Thermo Fisher Scientific Inc.
168 3rd Ave
Waltham MA 02451
781 622-1000

(G-8018)
VALORA TECHNOLOGIES INC
101 Great Rd (01730-2715)
PHONE..................................781 229-2265
Sandra E Serkes, *President*
Aaron Goodisman, *COO*
Cynthia Robinson, *Sr Project Mgr*
Laura Machado, *Manager*
Elise Tatosian, *Manager*
EMP: 20
SALES (est): 2.2MM **Privately Held**
WEB: www.valoratech.com
SIC: 7372 7378 5734 Prepackaged Software Services Computer Maintenance/Repair Ret Computers/Software

(G-8019)
VIZIENT INC
209 Burlington Rd Ste 111 (01730-1435)
PHONE..................................781 271-0980
Robert Cohen, *Branch Mgr*
EMP: 10
SALES (corp-wide): 969.1MM **Privately Held**
SIC: 7372 Prepackaged Software Services
PA: Vizient, Inc.
290 E John Carpenter Fwy # 1500
Irving TX 75062
972 830-0000

(G-8020)
WERFEN USA LLC
180 Hartwell Rd (01730-2443)
PHONE..................................781 861-0710
Ramon Benet, *President*
Brian Durkin, *Vice Pres*
Javier Gomez,
James Clayton, *Admin Sec*
EMP: 250
SALES (est): 20.7MM **Privately Held**
SIC: 2835 Mfg Diagnostic Substances

Belchertown
Hampshire County

(G-8021)
ARROW MACHINE LLC
151 N Washington St (01007-9337)
P.O. Box 902 (01007-0902)
PHONE..................................413 323-7280
Gail Pettengill, *Mng Member*
EMP: 5 **EST:** 1979
SALES (est): 617.4K **Privately Held**
SIC: 3599 Machine Job Shop

(G-8022)
BASSETTE PRINTERS LLC
326 Barton Ave (01007-9277)
PHONE..................................413 781-7140
Kevin M Kervick,
Bernard Spirito,
Bob Tannen,
▲ **EMP:** 65
SQ FT: 48,000
SALES (est): 10.4MM **Privately Held**
WEB: www.bassette.com
SIC: 2752 Lithographic Commercial Printing

(G-8023)
DANALEVI CORP
Also Called: Danalevi Powerboats
732 Daniel Shays Hwy (01007-9384)
PHONE..................................413 626-8120
Ross Hartman, *CEO*
Angelique Boulanger, *VP Mktg*
Michael Connor, *Shareholder*
▲ **EMP:** 4
SALES (est): 260K **Privately Held**
SIC: 3732 Mfg Fiberglass Boats

(G-8024)
GREAT THREADS
6 Berkshire Ave (01007-8901)
P.O. Box 849 (01007-0849)
PHONE..................................413 323-9402
Gary Ewing, *Partner*
Debra Ewing, *Partner*
EMP: 6
SQ FT: 1,400
SALES: 200K **Privately Held**
WEB: www.dancing-threads.com
SIC: 2395 Pleating/Stitching Services

(G-8025)
MACGREGOR BAY CORPORATION
Also Called: National Fiber
50 Depot St (01007-9619)
P.O. Box 1349 (01007-1349)
PHONE..................................413 283-8747
Christopher Hoch, *President*
Mary W Hoch, *Admin Sec*
EMP: 32
SQ FT: 14,000
SALES (est): 9.1MM **Privately Held**
SIC: 2821 Mfg Plastic Materials/Resins

(G-8026)
NORTHEAST TREATERS INC (PA)
201 Springfield Rd (01007-9039)
P.O. Box 802 (01007-0802)
PHONE..................................413 323-7811
David A Reed, *President*
Douglas C Elder, *Director*
Charles Geiger, *Director*
Henry G Page Jr, *Director*
David Sutherland, *Director*
EMP: 25
SQ FT: 6,100
SALES (est): 17MM **Privately Held**
WEB: www.netreaters.com
SIC: 2491 Wood Preserving

Bellingham
Norfolk County

(G-8027)
ACCUDYNE MACHINE TOOL INC
Also Called: A-D Scientific
128 Mendon St (02019-1549)
PHONE..................................508 966-3110
Denis F Plante, *President*
Maria Plante, *Clerk*
EMP: 3
SQ FT: 4,000
SALES (est): 430.2K **Privately Held**
SIC: 3599 3559 3484 2531 Mfg Industrial Machinery Mfg Misc Industry Mach Mfg Small Arms Mfg Public Building Furn

(G-8028)
ALGONQUIN INDUSTRIES INC (PA)
139 Farm St (02019-1266)
P.O. Box 176 (02019-0176)
PHONE..................................508 966-4600
Kazmier J Kasper, *President*
Eddie Frietas, *Vice Pres*
Kris Pela, *Production*
Monique Carpentier, *Human Resources*
Edward Freitas, *VP Sales*
EMP: 67 **EST:** 1974
SQ FT: 45,000
SALES: 12.1MM **Privately Held**
WEB: www.algonquinind.com
SIC: 3599 Mfg Industrial Machinery

(G-8029)
ALLEN WOODWORKING LLC
200 Center St (02019-1804)
PHONE..................................617 306-6479
Daniel Allen Ritts, *Principal*
EMP: 4
SALES (est): 287.7K **Privately Held**
SIC: 2431 Mfg Millwork

(G-8030)
ANTRON ENGINEERING & MCH CO
170 Mechanic St (02019-3106)
PHONE..................................508 966-2803
Anthony F Denietolis, *President*
Lynnne McManus, *Purchasing*
Doug Birman, *Engineer*
John Kauker IV, *Treasurer*
Allen Massie, *Director*
EMP: 85
SQ FT: 30,000
SALES (est): 20.4MM **Privately Held**
WEB: www.antroneng.com
SIC: 3599 Mfg Industrial Machinery

(G-8031)
B & L MANUFACTURING INC
8 Williams Way (02019-1527)
PHONE..................................508 966-3066
Lawrence Lowther, *President*
EMP: 14
SQ FT: 6,000
SALES: 1MM **Privately Held**
SIC: 3915 Mfg Jewelers' Materials

(G-8032)
BOSTON PIEZO-OPTICS INC
38b Maple St (02019-3011)
P.O. Box 80, Medway (02053-0080)
PHONE..................................508 966-4988
G Normand Benoit, *President*
Steve Wickstrom, *Vice Pres*
EMP: 12
SQ FT: 10,000
SALES: 1.1MM **Privately Held**
WEB: www.bostonpiezooptics.com
SIC: 3826 3827 5049 Custom Mfg Of Optical Components & Ultrasonic Crystals/Whol Professional Equipment

(G-8033)
CHOCORUA VALLEY LUMBER COMPANY
1210 Pulaski Blvd (02019-2127)
PHONE..................................508 883-6878

▲ = Import ▼=Export
◆ =Import/Export

Lloyd E Rhodes, *President*
Daniel Rhodes, *Vice Pres*
Barbara Rhodes, *Admin Sec*
Steve Goldman, *Clerk*
EMP: 18
SQ FT: 9,600
SALES (est): 1.7MM **Privately Held**
SIC: 2421 Sawmill

(G-8034)
CHOICE FOODS
770 S Main St Rm Main (02019-1848)
PHONE.................................508 332-2442
Kevin A Kelly, *Principal*
EMP: 3
SALES (est): 312.9K **Privately Held**
SIC: 2099 Mfg Food Preparations

(G-8035)
COUNTERWERKS INC
200 Center St (02019-1804)
PHONE.................................508 553-9600
Charles C Abate Jr, *President*
EMP: 3
SALES (est): 239.2K **Privately Held**
SIC: 2331 Mfg Women's/Misses' Blouses

(G-8036)
CYCLE-TEC
74 Mendon St (02019-1537)
PHONE.................................508 966-0066
EMP: 5
SALES (est): 725.3K **Privately Held**
SIC: 3354 Mfg Aluminum Extruded Products

(G-8037)
DEADWOOD PALLETS
93 Salisbury St (02019-2720)
PHONE.................................774 214-8628
Heather Girard, *Principal*
EMP: 5
SALES (est): 293.6K **Privately Held**
SIC: 2448 Mfg Wood Pallets/Skids

(G-8038)
EMC CORPORATION
Also Called: Dell EMC
7 Maddie Way (02019-3109)
PHONE.................................508 613-2022
EMP: 3
SALES (corp-wide): 90.6B **Publicly Held**
SIC: 3572 Mfg Computer Storage Devices
HQ: Emc Corporation
176 South St
Hopkinton MA 01748
508 435-1000

(G-8039)
GRAYCER SCREW PRODUCTS CO INC
113 Depot St (02019-1460)
P.O. Box 677 (02019-0677)
PHONE.................................508 966-1810
James J Cerutti, *President*
◆ **EMP:** 31 **EST:** 1955
SQ FT: 15,000
SALES: 4.5MM **Privately Held**
WEB: www.graycer.com
SIC: 3599 Mfg Industrial Machinery

(G-8040)
HI-TECH METALS INC
Also Called: Hitech Metals
139 Farm St (02019-1266)
P.O. Box 176 (02019-0176)
PHONE.................................508 966-0332
Kazmier J Kasper, *President*
Kazmier Kasper, *President*
Mary Mc Govern, *General Mgr*
Joseph Kasper, *Vice Pres*
EMP: 60
SQ FT: 45,000
SALES: 6.7MM **Privately Held**
WEB: www.hitechmetals.com
SIC: 3444 Mfg Sheet Metalwork

(G-8041)
HPM LLC
52 Fox Run Rd (02019-2905)
PHONE.................................508 958-5565
Ken Otzel,
Chris Sequirea,
EMP: 3
SQ FT: 2,700
SALES: 12MM **Privately Held**
SIC: 3542 Mfg Machine Tools-Forming

(G-8042)
IDEAL ENGINEERING CO INC
105 Depot St (02019-1460)
P.O. Box 402 (02019-0402)
PHONE.................................508 966-2324
EMP: 5 **EST:** 1967
SQ FT: 4,000
SALES: 700K **Privately Held**
SIC: 3599 Industrial Machinery, Nec, Nsk

(G-8043)
L3HARRIS TECHNOLOGIES INC
5 Sand Castle Ln (02019-3103)
PHONE.................................508 966-9500
EMP: 60
SALES (corp-wide): 6.8B **Publicly Held**
SIC: 3812 Mfg Rf Communications
PA: L3harris Technologies, Inc.
1025 W Nasa Blvd
Melbourne FL 32919
321 727-9100

(G-8044)
MANNING WAY CPITL PARTNERS LLC
Also Called: Consolidated Coating Company
5 Williams Way (02019-1527)
PHONE.................................508 966-4800
Jeffrey Rudman, *President*
Robert Bartlett, *Prdtn Mgr*
Malai Piccinin, *Facilities Mgr*
Tammy Tavares, *Manager*
EMP: 25 **EST:** 1979
SQ FT: 31,000
SALES (est): 4.8MM **Privately Held**
WEB: www.consolidatedcoating.com
SIC: 3479 Metal Coating And Allied Services, Nsk

(G-8045)
MARCHAND MACHINE WORKS INC
435 Wrentham Rd (02019-2652)
PHONE.................................508 883-4040
Gerald Marchand, *President*
Joan Marchand, *Manager*
EMP: 3 **EST:** 1948
SQ FT: 15,000
SALES (est): 270K **Privately Held**
WEB: www.mmwiembroidery.com
SIC: 3599 Job Machine Shop

(G-8046)
MARKS WELLS & PUMPS INC
55 Maple St (02019-3012)
PHONE.................................508 528-1741
W Wyllie, *Principal*
EMP: 4
SALES (est): 292.3K **Privately Held**
SIC: 1381 Oil/Gas Well Drilling

(G-8047)
MARS INCORPORATED
444 Hartford Ave (02019-1249)
PHONE.................................508 966-0022
EMP: 6
SALES (corp-wide): 32.1B **Privately Held**
SIC: 2047 Mfg Dog/Cat Food
PA: Mars, Incorporated
6885 Elm St
Mc Lean VA 22101
703 821-4900

(G-8048)
MASSACHUSETTS BEV ALIANCE LLC
190 Mechanic St (02019-3161)
PHONE.................................617 701-6238
William G Burke,
Mark Placek,
Frank B Sousa III,
Richard Tatelman,
EMP: 11
SALES (est): 667.9K **Privately Held**
SIC: 2082 Mfg Malt Beverages

(G-8049)
MEDICAL CMPNENT SPCIALISTS INC
42 Williams Way (02019-1527)
PHONE.................................508 966-0992
Jim Moore, *Owner*
Linda Rubin, *Office Mgr*
EMP: 20
SQ FT: 3,874
SALES (est): 3.4MM **Privately Held**
SIC: 3599 Coating/Engraving Service

(G-8050)
MESSER LLC
Also Called: Boc Gases
92a Depot St (02019-1439)
PHONE.................................508 966-3148
Joe Marchetti, *Manager*
EMP: 15
SALES (corp-wide): 1.4B **Privately Held**
SIC: 2813 Mfg Industrial Gases
HQ: Messer Llc
200 Somerset Corp Blvd # 7000
Bridgewater NJ 08807
908 464-8100

(G-8051)
MRC GLOBAL (US) INC
47 S Maple St (02019-1627)
PHONE.................................508 966-3205
EMP: 29 **Publicly Held**
SIC: 1311 Whol Industrial Supplies
HQ: Mrc Global (Us) Inc.
1301 Mckinney St Ste 2300
Houston TX 77010
877 294-7574

(G-8052)
MUNRO WOODWORKING
315 Farm St (02019-1126)
PHONE.................................508 966-2654
Richard Munro, *Owner*
EMP: 3
SQ FT: 4,200
SALES (est): 230K **Privately Held**
SIC: 2434 2431 Mfg Wood Kitchen Cabinets Mfg Millwork

(G-8053)
NEFAB PACKAGING NORTH EAST LLC
23 Williams Way (02019-1527)
PHONE.................................800 258-4692
Moises Diaz, *Mfg Spvr*
Mike Pectorelli, *Manager*
EMP: 13
SALES (est): 493.4K
SALES (corp-wide): 470.8MM **Privately Held**
SIC: 2448 2449 2441 Mfg Wood Pallets/Skids Mfg Wood Containers Mfg Wood Boxes/Shooks
HQ: Nefab Packaging, Inc.
204 Airline Dr Ste 100
Coppell TX 75019
469 444-5264

(G-8054)
OLIMPIA INDUSTRIES INCORPORATE
175 North St (02019-1756)
PHONE.................................508 966-3392
James McGrath, *Owner*
EMP: 3
SALES (est): 297.9K **Privately Held**
SIC: 3999 Mfg Misc Products

(G-8055)
ONCE UPON A KILN
15 N Main St Ste C8 (02019-1592)
PHONE.................................508 657-1739
EMP: 3
SALES (est): 267.9K **Privately Held**
SIC: 3559 Mfg Misc Industry Machinery

(G-8056)
PAUL YOUNG PRECAST COMPANY
81 Depot St (02019-1437)
PHONE.................................508 966-4333
Paul Young, *Principal*
EMP: 3
SALES (est): 248.2K **Privately Held**
SIC: 3272 Mfg Concrete Products

(G-8057)
POPULAR PRECAST PRODUCTS
26 N Main St (02019-1570)
PHONE.................................508 966-4622
Jerry Lemire, *Partner*
Mike Griffith, *Partner*
EMP: 5
SQ FT: 18,000
SALES: 2MM **Privately Held**
SIC: 3272 Mfg Concrete Products

(G-8058)
SCANDIA KITCHENS INC
38 Maple St (02019-3011)
P.O. Box 456 (02019-0456)
PHONE.................................508 966-0300
David Dorrer, *President*
Linda Dorrer, *Admin Sec*
EMP: 20
SQ FT: 22,000
SALES (est): 2.6MM **Privately Held**
WEB: www.scandiakitchens.com
SIC: 2434 Mfg Wood Kitchen Cabinets

(G-8059)
SON CO INC
Also Called: Son-Co Printing & Copying
15 N Main St (02019-1548)
P.O. Box 304 (02019-0304)
PHONE.................................508 966-2970
Richard Sergi, *President*
EMP: 5
SQ FT: 3,500
SALES: 380K **Privately Held**
SIC: 2752 Lithographic Commercial Printing

(G-8060)
THEATRE STRICKEN APPAREL LLC
246 Theresa Rd (02019-1396)
PHONE.................................978 325-2335
Matthew Perkins,
EMP: 4
SALES (est): 202.4K **Privately Held**
SIC: 2396 2326 5611 5699 Mfg Auto/Apparel Trim Mfg Men/Boy Work Clothng Ret Men's/Boy's Clothing Ret Misc Apparel/Access Direct Retail Sales

(G-8061)
VAN WAL MACHINE INC
97 Depot St (02019-1437)
P.O. Box 800 (02019-0800)
PHONE.................................508 966-0733
John Van Der Wal, *President*
Eric Van Der Wal, *Principal*
Johann Van Der Wal, *Principal*
Leo Van Der Wal, *Principal*
Karin Van Der Wal, *Clerk*
EMP: 18 **EST:** 1972
SQ FT: 10,000
SALES (est): 3.3MM **Privately Held**
WEB: www.vanwalmachine.com
SIC: 3545 Mfg Precision Machined Parts

(G-8062)
VARNEY BROS SAND & GRAVEL INC
Also Called: Varney Bros Concrete
79 Hartford Ave (02019-1026)
P.O. Box 94 (02019-0094)
PHONE.................................508 966-1313
Linda Varney, *President*
EMP: 35
SQ FT: 1,800
SALES (est): 5.2MM **Privately Held**
SIC: 3273 1442 Mfg Ready-Mixed Concrete Construction Sand/Gravel

(G-8063)
W G MACHINE WORKS INC
140 Suffolk St Ste 140 # 140 (02019-2352)
PHONE.................................508 883-4903
William J Gallant, *President*
EMP: 4
SQ FT: 3,000
SALES (est): 413.4K **Privately Held**
SIC: 3599 Mfg Industrial Machinery

(G-8064)
WRENTHAM TOOL GROUP LLC
155 Farm St (02019-1105)
PHONE.................................508 966-2332
James Ehrhardt,
EMP: 60
SQ FT: 18,000
SALES (est): 10MM **Privately Held**
WEB: www.wrenthamtool.com
SIC: 3423 Mfg Hand/Edge Tools

Belmont
Middlesex County

(G-8065)
AVIATION EDGE LLC
43 Lantern Rd (02478-1706)
PHONE..................................781 405-3246
Dimitris Bertsimas, *Partner*
Michael Frankovich, *Partner*
Amedeo Odoni, *Partner*
Nikolas Pyrgiotis, *Partner*
EMP: 4
SALES (est): 270.3K **Privately Held**
SIC: 7372 Prepackaged Software Services

(G-8066)
BELMONT PRINTING COMPANY
46 Brighton St (02478-4172)
PHONE..................................617 484-0833
Stanley D Garfield, *Owner*
EMP: 40 **EST:** 1965
SQ FT: 8,000
SALES (est): 3.7MM **Privately Held**
WEB: www.belmontprinting.com
SIC: 2752 2796 2759 2791 Lithographic Coml Print Commercial Printing Platemaking Services Typesetting Services Bookbinding/Related Work

(G-8067)
CAMBRIDGE ELECTRONICS INC
15 Amherst Rd (02478-2102)
PHONE..................................617 710-7013
Tomas Palacios, *Director*
EMP: 3
SALES (est): 245.8K **Privately Held**
SIC: 3674 Mfg Semiconductors/Related Devices

(G-8068)
CATALYST MEDICAL LLC
23 Oak St (02478-3006)
PHONE..................................857 928-8817
Gregory Sorensen, *Principal*
Peter Caravan, *Principal*
EMP: 3
SALES (est): 215.8K **Privately Held**
SIC: 2835 Mfg Diagnostic Substances

(G-8069)
CELENO COMMUNICATIONS
464 Common St Ste 279 (02478-2704)
PHONE..................................617 500-3683
Gil Rosenzweig, *Vice Pres*
Meir Shiri, *Engineer*
Naiyer Imam, *Manager*
EMP: 4
SALES (corp-wide): 6.2MM **Privately Held**
SIC: 3674 Mfg Semiconductors/Related Devices
PA: Celeno Communications (Israel) Ltd
26 Zarchin Alexander
Raanana 43662
974 546-46

(G-8070)
COLLAGEN MEDICAL LLC
23 Oak St (02478-3006)
PHONE..................................857 928-8817
Gregory Sorensen, *Principal*
Peter Caravan, *Principal*
EMP: 3
SALES (est): 349.4K **Privately Held**
SIC: 2834 Mfg Pharmaceutical Preparations

(G-8071)
CUSTOM LEARNING DESIGNS INC
375 Concord Ave Ste 101 (02478-3045)
PHONE..................................617 489-1702
Donna M Kilcoyne, *President*
Laura Ferraro, *Sales Executive*
Joan Hudak, *Sr Project Mgr*
Paul Lizotte, *Sr Project Mgr*
EMP: 75 **EST:** 1979
SQ FT: 23,025
SALES (est): 8.6MM **Privately Held**
WEB: www.cldinc.com
SIC: 3999 Mfg Misc Products

(G-8072)
DESIGN JEWELRY
Also Called: G V S Jewelers
6 Apollo Rd (02478)
PHONE..................................617 489-0764
Veladimir Arustamyan, *Owner*
EMP: 3
SQ FT: 850
SALES (est): 450K **Privately Held**
SIC: 3911 Mfg Precious Metal Jewelry

(G-8073)
FELDHAUS CONSULTING LLC
110 Crestview Rd (02478-2109)
PHONE..................................603 276-0508
EMP: 3
SALES (est): 104.8K **Privately Held**
SIC: 2075 Soybean Oil Mills, Nsk

(G-8074)
FIREFLY GLOBAL
556 Trapelo Rd (02478-1427)
PHONE..................................781 835-6548
Tina Ahern, *Manager*
EMP: 3
SALES (est): 104.8K **Privately Held**
SIC: 3841 Surgical And Medical Instruments

(G-8075)
HORIZON INTERNATIONAL INC
385 Concord Ave Ste 104 (02478-3037)
PHONE..................................617 489-6666
Ram Ghanta, *Principal*
Ram Ghata, *Sales Mgr*
EMP: 3
SALES (est): 265.2K **Privately Held**
SIC: 7372 Prepackaged Software Services

(G-8076)
IQ MEDICAL DEVICES LLC
50 Summit Rd (02478-1058)
PHONE..................................617 484-3188
Donald McKay MD,
EMP: 10
SALES (est): 571.8K **Privately Held**
SIC: 3841 Medical Device Developer

(G-8077)
LONGRUN LLC
Also Called: Extra Origin Foods
464 Common St U207 (02478-2704)
PHONE..................................617 758-8674
Richard Tieken,
EMP: 4
SQ FT: 1,000
SALES (est): 154.6K **Privately Held**
SIC: 2099 Mfg Food Preparations

(G-8078)
NEWTON LABORATORIES INC
10 Meadows Ln (02478-1153)
PHONE..................................617 484-7003
Charles W Von Rosenberg Jr, *President*
Stephen Fulghum, *Vice Pres*
EMP: 4
SALES (est): 310K **Privately Held**
SIC: 3841 Mfg Of Surgical And Medical Apparatus

(G-8079)
PURECOAT INTERNATIONAL LLC
30 Brighton St (02478-4172)
PHONE..................................561 844-0100
Thomas Mahoney, *Branch Mgr*
EMP: 44
SALES (corp-wide): 6.9MM **Privately Held**
SIC: 3313 3559 Mfg Electrometallurgical Prdts-Ex Steel Mfg Misc Industry Machinery
PA: Purecoat International, Llc
3301 Elec Way Ste B
West Palm Beach FL 33407
561 844-0100

(G-8080)
PURECOAT NORTH LLC
39 Hittinger St (02478-4039)
P.O. Box 107 (02478-0902)
PHONE..................................617 489-2750
Thomas Mahoney, *General Mgr*
Marshall Menachem, *Sales Executive*
Stephen Aldred, *Manager*
George S Bognar,
John Aldred, *Maintence Staff*
▼ **EMP:** 55
SQ FT: 40,000
SALES (est): 7.3MM **Privately Held**
WEB: www.purecoatnorth.com
SIC: 3471 Plating/Polishing Service

(G-8081)
SMART SOFTWARE INC
4 Hill Rd Ste 2 (02478-4351)
PHONE..................................617 489-2743
Nelson Hartunian, *Ch of Bd*
Greg Hartunian, *President*
Thomas R Willemain, *Senior VP*
Kate Afonso, *Vice Pres*
Jeffrey Scott, *VP Bus Dvlpt*
EMP: 22
SQ FT: 4,200
SALES (est): 2.6MM **Privately Held**
WEB: www.smartcorp.com
SIC: 7372 Prepackaged Software Services

(G-8082)
WELLMAN ENGINEERING INC
35 Louise Rd (02478-3922)
PHONE..................................617 484-8338
Mark Boland, *President*
Adam Boland, *Shareholder*
Peter G Mac Laren, *Clerk*
EMP: 5
SQ FT: 8,000
SALES (est): 458.3K **Privately Held**
SIC: 3545 Mfg Cutting Tools For Machine Tools

(G-8083)
WESTPORT GROUP LTD
29 Oliver Rd (02478-4620)
PHONE..................................617 489-6581
EMP: 4 **EST:** 1983
SALES (est): 360K **Privately Held**
SIC: 7372 Prepackaged Software Services

Berkley
Bristol County

(G-8084)
COMMON CROSSING INC
11 N Main St (02779-1312)
PHONE..................................508 822-8225
Elizabeth Jackson, *Principal*
EMP: 7
SALES (est): 455.7K **Privately Held**
SIC: 2082 Mfg Malt Beverages

(G-8085)
CORRUGATED STITCHER SERVICE
88 Jerome St (02779-1007)
PHONE..................................508 823-2844
Charles Laplante, *Principal*
EMP: 3
SALES (est): 263K **Privately Held**
SIC: 2653 Mfg Corrugated/Solid Fiber Boxes

(G-8086)
EVERGREEN ENTERPRISES INC
23 Howland Rd (02779-1919)
PHONE..................................508 823-2377
Louise A Walsh, *President*
EMP: 4
SQ FT: 1,000
SALES (est): 224K **Privately Held**
SIC: 2253 5611 5632 5999 Knit Outerwear Mill Ret Men's/Boy's Clothing Ret Women's Accessories/Specialties Ret Misc Merchandise

(G-8087)
J AND R PRE CAST INC
16 County St (02779-1206)
PHONE..................................508 822-3311
Robert Katon, *President*
Robert Katon Jr, *Vice Pres*
Judith Katon, *Treasurer*
EMP: 12
SQ FT: 4,000
SALES (est): 1.9MM **Privately Held**
WEB: www.jrprecast.com
SIC: 3272 Mfg Precast Cement Products

(G-8088)
NUANCE COMMUNICATIONS INC
151 Bryant St (02779-2106)
PHONE..................................508 821-5954
Steve Leary, *General Mgr*
EMP: 5 **Publicly Held**
WEB: www.nuance.com
SIC: 7372 Mfg Photographic Equipment/Supplies
PA: Nuance Communications, Inc.
1 Wayside Rd
Burlington MA 01803

(G-8089)
TAUNTON ALUMINUM FOUNDRY INC
632 Berkley St (02779-1306)
PHONE..................................508 822-4141
Fernando Freire, *President*
Anna Freire, *Clerk*
EMP: 6
SQ FT: 24,000
SALES (est): 827.1K **Privately Held**
SIC: 3365 3366 Aluminum Foundry Copper Foundry

Berlin
Worcester County

(G-8090)
A1 PALLETS INC
163 River Rd W (01503-1648)
P.O. Box 1263, Middletown Springs VT (05757-1263)
PHONE..................................978 838-2720
EMP: 7
SALES (est): 864.5K **Privately Held**
SIC: 2448 Mfg Wood Pallets/Skids

(G-8091)
MASSACHUSETTS BROKEN STONE CO (PA)
Also Called: Holden Trap Rock Company
332 Sawyerhill Rd (01503-1206)
P.O. Box 276 (01503-0276)
PHONE..................................978 838-9999
Andrew Forest, *President*
Richard Harrison, *Treasurer*
EMP: 7 **EST:** 1908
SQ FT: 5,000
SALES (est): 3.4MM **Privately Held**
SIC: 2951 1429 Mfg Asphalt Mixtures/Blocks Crushed/Broken Stone

(G-8092)
ORGANOMATION ASSOCIATES INC
266 River Rd W (01503-1699)
PHONE..................................978 838-7300
Andrew R McNiven, *President*
David Oliva, *Office Mgr*
Kristen Aubin, *Technician*
EMP: 16 **EST:** 1959
SQ FT: 5,500
SALES: 2MM **Privately Held**
WEB: www.organomation.com
SIC: 3826 Whol Professional Equipment

Bernardston
Franklin County

(G-8093)
FARM TABLE AT KRINGLE CANDLE
219 South St (01337-9452)
PHONE..................................413 648-5200
Brent Menke, *Principal*
EMP: 3
SALES (est): 113.8K **Privately Held**
SIC: 3999 Mfg Misc Products

▲ = Import ▼=Export
◆ =Import/Export

Beverly
Essex County

(G-8094)
7AC TECHNOLOGIES INC
100 Cummings Ctr Ste 265g (01915-6143)
PHONE....................................781 574-1348
Peter Vandermeulen, *CEO*
Jed Swan, *CEO*
Roberto Ramirez, *Principal*
Mitchell Tyson, *Principal*
Stephen Young, *Principal*
EMP: 15
SALES (est): 3.7MM **Privately Held**
SIC: 3822 3585 3564 Mfg Environmental Controls Mfg Refrigeration/Heating Equipment Mfg Blowers/Fans

(G-8095)
ACERA INC
100 Cummings Ctr Ste 439c (01915-6132)
PHONE....................................978 998-4281
Thomas V Root, *President*
Michael Epstein, *Corp Secy*
EMP: 3
SALES (est): 357K **Privately Held**
SIC: 3641 Mfg Electric Lamps

(G-8096)
AERO MANUFACTURING CORP
100 Sam Fonzo Dr Ste 1 (01915-1059)
PHONE....................................978 720-1000
Salvatore Fonzo, *President*
David Fonzo, *President*
Michael Godzik, *CFO*
Michael Murphy, *Manager*
Greg Potcner, *Technology*
EMP: 80 **EST:** 1962
SQ FT: 30,000
SALES (est): 20.2MM **Privately Held**
WEB: www.aeromanufacturing.com
SIC: 3444 3469 7692 Mfg Sheet Metalwork Mfg Metal Stampings Welding Repair

(G-8097)
AKSTON BIOSCIENCES CORPORATION
100 Cummings Ctr Ste 454c (01915-6513)
PHONE....................................978 969-3381
Todd Zion, *CEO*
Thomas Lancaster, *Treasurer*
James Herriman, *Admin Sec*
EMP: 4
SQ FT: 2,000
SALES (est): 588.8K **Privately Held**
SIC: 2834 Druggists' Preparations (Pharmaceuticals)

(G-8098)
AMERICAN & SCHOEN MACHINERY CO
100 Cummings Ctr Ste 140a (01915-6135)
PHONE....................................978 524-0168
Edmund Skoniecki Jr, *President*
Jerry Hughes, *Vice Pres*
Georg Nikel, *Treasurer*
Juergen Schneider, *Director*
Debra Turner, *Admin Sec*
▲ **EMP:** 25
SQ FT: 28,000
SALES: 5.8MM **Privately Held**
WEB: www.asm-schoen.com
SIC: 3559 Mfg Misc Industry Machinery
HQ: Schoen + Sandt Machinery Gmbh
Lemberger Str. 82
Pirmasens 66955
633 171-3100

(G-8099)
AMPHENOL PCD INC (HQ)
72 Cherry Hill Dr Ste 2 (01915-1045)
PHONE....................................978 921-1531
Adam Norwitt, *CEO*
Mark Kichar, *Business Mgr*
Thomas Schaefer, *Business Mgr*
Plinio Perez, *Counsel*
Edward G Jepsen, *Vice Pres*
▲ **EMP:** 75
SQ FT: 22,000
SALES (est): 60.3MM
SALES (corp-wide): 8.2B **Publicly Held**
SIC: 3625 Whol Electronic Parts/Equipment
PA: Amphenol Corporation
358 Hall Ave
Wallingford CT 06492
203 265-8900

(G-8100)
ANEXIS LLC
115 Valley St (01915-2223)
PHONE....................................978 921-6293
EMP: 5
SALES (est): 370K **Privately Held**
SIC: 2833 7389 Mfg Medicinal/Botanical Products Business Services At Non-Commercial Site

(G-8101)
ARCHERDX INC
123 Brimbal Ave (01915-1869)
PHONE....................................978 232-3570
Jason Myers, *CEO*
EMP: 87 **EST:** 2014
SQ FT: 5,000
SALES: 20MM **Privately Held**
SIC: 2282 Throwing/Winding Mill

(G-8102)
ARMSTRONG MACHINE CO INC
117 Elliott St Ste 3 (01915-3252)
PHONE....................................978 232-9466
Raymond Armstrong, *President*
EMP: 15
SQ FT: 14,000
SALES (est): 1.3MM **Privately Held**
WEB: www.armstrongmachine.com
SIC: 3569 3555 Mfg General Industrial Machinery Mfg Printing Trades Machinery

(G-8103)
AUBURN FILTERSENSE LLC
800 Cummings Ctr Ste 355w (01915-6174)
PHONE....................................978 777-2460
Vahid Mirsaiidi, *Engineer*
Ronald Dechene,
EMP: 30
SALES (est): 186.4K
SALES (corp-wide): 374.1MM **Privately Held**
SIC: 3829 Mfg Measuring/Controlling Devices
PA: Nederman Holding Ab
Sydhamnsgatan 2
Helsingborg 252 2
424 952-687

(G-8104)
AUBURN INTERNATIONAL INC
800 Cummings Ctr Ste 355w (01915-6174)
PHONE....................................978 777-2460
Ronald L Dechene, *President*
D Tyler Drolet, *Controller*
▼ **EMP:** 10
SQ FT: 23,000
SALES (est): 1.9MM **Privately Held**
SIC: 3823 Mfg Electronic Devices Measuring Flow Of Solids

(G-8105)
AUBURN SYSTEMS LLC
800 Cummings Ctr Ste 355w (01915-6174)
P.O. Box 2008, Danvers (01923-5008)
PHONE....................................978 777-2460
Ronald L Dechene, *President*
Justin Dechene, *Exec VP*
Earl Parker, *Vice Pres*
EMP: 7
SQ FT: 10,000
SALES (est): 1.8MM **Privately Held**
WEB: www.auburnsys.com
SIC: 3823 5084 Mfg Process Control Instruments Whol Industrial Equipment

(G-8106)
AXCELIS TECHNOLOGIES INC (PA)
108 Cherry Hill Dr (01915-1066)
PHONE....................................978 787-4000
Richard J Faubert, *Ch of Bd*
Mary G Puma, *President*
Lynnette C Fallon, *Exec VP*
Douglas A Lawson, *Exec VP*
Russell J Low, *Exec VP*
▲ **EMP:** 249
SQ FT: 417,000
SALES: 442.5MM **Publicly Held**
SIC: 3559 3829 Mfg Semiconductor Machinery & Ion Implantation Systems

(G-8107)
BASS PRECISION PRODUCTS
62 Bridge St (01915-2932)
P.O. Box 3204 (01915-0896)
PHONE....................................978 922-3608
John Dennesen, *Owner*
EMP: 3
SQ FT: 3,000
SALES: 130K **Privately Held**
WEB: www.soundprecision.com
SIC: 3599 Machine Shop

(G-8108)
BEVERLY CITIZEN
48 Dunham Rd (01915-1844)
PHONE....................................978 927-2777
Charles Goodrich, *Principal*
EMP: 3
SALES (est): 132.5K **Privately Held**
SIC: 2711 Newspapers-Publishing/Printing

(G-8109)
BEVERLY QIAGEN INC
100 Cummings Ctr Ste 407j (01915-6101)
PHONE....................................978 927-7027
Chris Benoit, *President*
Michael Nolan, *President*
George Von Oertezn, *General Mgr*
Jack Percoskie, *CFO*
▼ **EMP:** 65
SALES: 20MM
SALES (corp-wide): 1.5B **Privately Held**
SIC: 2836 Mfg Biological Products
PA: Qiagen N.V.
Hulsterweg 82
Venlo 5912
773 556-600

(G-8110)
BEVERLY SHADE SHOPPE
81 Bridge St Ste C (01915-2957)
PHONE....................................978 922-0374
Anthony Conte, *President*
Anthony V Conte Jr, *Owner*
EMP: 3 **EST:** 1929
SQ FT: 1,000
SALES (est): 323.7K **Privately Held**
SIC: 2591 5719 5714 Mfg Window Shades Retails Venetian Blinds Vertical Blinds And Ready Made Curtains

(G-8111)
BIOHELIX CORPORATION
500 Cummings Ctr Ste 5550 (01915-6517)
PHONE....................................978 927-5056
Huimin Kong PHD, *President*
EMP: 13
SQ FT: 15,000
SALES (est): 2.8MM
SALES (corp-wide): 522.2MM **Publicly Held**
WEB: www.biohelix.com
SIC: 2836 Manufacturing Biological Products
PA: Quidel Corporation
9975 Summers Ridge Rd
San Diego CA 92121
858 552-1100

(G-8112)
BLUEFIN BIOMEDICINE INC
32 Tozer Rd (01915-5510)
PHONE....................................978 712-8105
John Zicaro, *General Mgr*
Scott Lonning, *Research*
EMP: 25
SALES (est): 2.6MM **Privately Held**
SIC: 2834 Mfg Pharmaceutical Preparations

(G-8113)
BRUCE BARROWCLOUGH
Also Called: Micronics
140 Elliott St Bldg A (01915-3220)
PHONE....................................978 524-0022
Bruce Barrowclough, *Owner*
EMP: 6
SQ FT: 1,600
SALES (est): 300K **Privately Held**
SIC: 3469 Mfg Metal Stampings

(G-8114)
CELLANYX DIAGNOSTICS LLC
100 Cummings Ctr Ste 451d (01915-6115)
PHONE....................................571 212-9991
Guy Fish, *CEO*
Mani Foroohar, *Corp Secy*
Delaney Berger, *Vice Pres*
Michael Manak, *Vice Pres*
Jonathan Varsanik, *Vice Pres*
EMP: 9 **EST:** 2013
SQ FT: 500
SALES (est): 1.1MM **Privately Held**
SIC: 2835 5047 Mfg Diagnostic Substances Whol Medical/Hospital Equipment

(G-8115)
CENTERLINE MACHINE COMPANY INC
60 Park St (01915-4217)
PHONE....................................978 524-8842
John Henry Shairs, *President*
EMP: 15
SQ FT: 6,000
SALES (est): 1MM **Privately Held**
WEB: www.ctrlne.com
SIC: 3873 7539 Mfg Watches/Clocks/Parts Automotive Repair

(G-8116)
CHROMATRA LLC
100 Cummings Ctr Ste 231g (01915-6158)
PHONE....................................978 473-7005
Alan Burt, *CEO*
Paul Stump, *President*
EMP: 4
SALES (est): 398.4K **Privately Held**
SIC: 3827 Mfg Optical Instruments/Lenses

(G-8117)
CLC BIO LLC (PA)
100 Cummings Ctr Ste 407j (01915-6101)
PHONE....................................617 945-0178
Richard Lussier, *Managing Dir*
William Porter, *Managing Dir*
Peder Nielsen, *Software Dev*
Jan Lomholdt,
Anika Joecker,
EMP: 12
SALES (est): 1.8MM **Privately Held**
SIC: 7372 7371 Prepackaged Software Services Custom Computer Programing

(G-8118)
CLINT SALES & MANUFACTURING
117 Elliott St Ste 2 (01915-3252)
P.O. Box 314 (01915-0006)
PHONE....................................978 927-3010
Courtney Modugno, *President*
EMP: 4 **EST:** 1964
SQ FT: 6,500
SALES: 300K **Privately Held**
WEB: www.clintsales.com
SIC: 2891 2842 Mfg Adhesives/Sealants Mfg Polish/Sanitation Goods

(G-8119)
COMMUNICATIONS & PWR INDS LLC
CPI
150 Sohier Rd (01915-5536)
PHONE....................................978 922-6000
Don Coleman, *General Mgr*
EMP: 300
SALES (corp-wide): 411.3MM **Privately Held**
WEB: www.cpii.com
SIC: 3671 Mfg Electron Tubes
HQ: Communications & Power Industries Llc
811 Hansen Way
Palo Alto CA 94304

(G-8120)
CONTRACT ENGINEERING INC
128 Park St Ste B5 (01915-3274)
PHONE....................................978 921-0501
James Robichau, *President*
John Galvi, *Vice Pres*
EMP: 20
SALES: 3MM **Privately Held**
WEB: www.contractengineering.com
SIC: 3599 Mfg Industrial Machinery

GEOGRAPHIC

(G-8121)
CORNELL ORTHOTICS PROSTHETICS (PA)
100 Cummings Ctr Ste 207h (01915-6104)
PHONE..................................978 922-2866
Keith Cornell, *President*
Ken Cornell, *Vice Pres*
Jennifer Percy, *Officer*
EMP: 11
SALES (est): 1.6MM **Privately Held**
SIC: 3842 Mfg Orthopedic Braces & Artificial Limbs

(G-8122)
CYTOCURE LLC
100 Cummings Ctr Ste 430c (01915-6122)
PHONE..................................978 232-1243
Fax: 978 232-1243
EMP: 6
SQ FT: 2,000
SALES (est): 570K **Privately Held**
SIC: 2836 Mfg Biological Products

(G-8123)
DAILY PRINTING INC
25 West St (01915-2225)
P.O. Box 5254 (01915-0515)
PHONE..................................978 927-4630
Gerald Difazio, *President*
EMP: 4
SALES (est): 567.3K **Privately Held**
WEB: www.dailyprinting.biz
SIC: 2752 Lithographic Commercial Printing

(G-8124)
DANVERS INDUSTRIAL PACKG CORP
39 Tozer Rd (01915-5513)
PHONE..................................978 777-0020
Leo Chester Thibeault Jr, *CEO*
Jeffrey Denoncour, *President*
EMP: 49
SQ FT: 85,300
SALES (est): 12.4MM **Privately Held**
SIC: 3086 2631 5199 Mfg Plastic Foam Products Paperboard Mill Whol Nondurable Goods

(G-8125)
DELTA ELECTRONICS MFG CORP
416 Cabot St (01915-3152)
P.O. Box 53 (01915-0053)
PHONE..................................978 927-1060
Diane J Delaney, *President*
Edward J Skurski, *Vice Pres*
Robert Dreesen, *Engineer*
Andrew Krauss, *Design Engr*
Linda Stewart, *Asst Controller*
▲ **EMP:** 115
SQ FT: 65,000
SALES (est): 28.4MM **Privately Held**
WEB: www.deltarf.com
SIC: 3678 3679 Mfg Electronic Connectors Mfg Electronic Components

(G-8126)
DESIGNFLOW WRAPS INC
Also Called: Design Flow Wraps
51 Park St (01915-4229)
PHONE..................................978 729-5415
Jeffrey Gregorio, *CEO*
Lindsay Gregorio, *Treasurer*
EMP: 3
SALES (est): 210K **Privately Held**
SIC: 3993 Mfg Signs/Advertising Specialties

(G-8127)
DJM PRECISION MACHINING
200 Rantoul St Rear (01915-4207)
PHONE..................................978 922-0407
Fax: 978 921-9180
EMP: 6
SQ FT: 3,500
SALES (est): 320K **Privately Held**
SIC: 3599 Machine Shop

(G-8128)
ENON COPY INC (PA)
Also Called: Minuteman Press
409 Cabot St Ste 4 (01915-3177)
PHONE..................................978 927-8757
Joseph Bubriski, *President*
Judith H Bubriski, *Vice Pres*
EMP: 16 **EST:** 1982
SQ FT: 5,000
SALES (est): 2.3MM **Privately Held**
SIC: 2752 Comm Prtg Litho

(G-8129)
EXCELIMMUNE INC
376 Hale St Rm 329 (01915-2096)
PHONE..................................617 262-8055
EMP: 4
SALES (corp-wide): 739.3K **Privately Held**
SIC: 2836 Mfg Biological Products
PA: Excelimmune, Inc.
1776 Massachusetts Ave
Lexington MA 02420
781 262-8055

(G-8130)
FAIR WINDS PRESS AND QUIVER
100 Cummings Ctr Ste 406l (01915-6101)
PHONE..................................978 282-9590
Ken Fund, *Owner*
Russ McGill, *CFO*
William Keister, *Administration*
EMP: 3
SALES (est): 78.4K **Privately Held**
SIC: 2731 Books-Publishing/Printing

(G-8131)
FLOW CONTROL LLC
Also Called: Flojet
100 Cummings Ctr (01915-6115)
PHONE..................................978 281-0440
Robert Wolpert, *President*
Gretchen McClain, *Vice Pres*
John Sullivan, *Vice Pres*
Eric Weago, *Controller*
◆ **EMP:** 50
SALES (est): 8.5MM **Publicly Held**
WEB: www.ittind.com
SIC: 3561 Mfg Pumps/Pumping Equipment
PA: Xylem Inc.
1 International Dr
Rye Brook NY 10573

(G-8132)
FOUR LGGERS DOGGIE DAYCARE LLC
950 Cummings Ctr Ste 101x (01915-6507)
PHONE..................................978 922-4182
Elizabeth Bucco, *Principal*
EMP: 3
SALES (est): 197.2K **Privately Held**
SIC: 3999 Mfg Misc Products

(G-8133)
FOURTH STREET PRESS INC
3 Ellis Sq (01915-4500)
PHONE..................................978 232-9251
George Hatch, *Principal*
EMP: 4 **EST:** 2009
SALES (est): 268.1K **Privately Held**
SIC: 2741 Misc Publishing

(G-8134)
GATEHOUSE MEDIA MASS I INC
Also Called: Beverly Citizen
72 Cherry Hill Dr (01915-1030)
PHONE..................................781 233-2040
Peter Chianca, *Branch Mgr*
EMP: 20
SALES (corp-wide): 1.5B **Publicly Held**
SIC: 2711 Newspapers-Publishing/Printing
HQ: Gatehouse Media Massachusetts I, Inc.
48 Dunham Rd
Beverly MA 01915
585 598-0030

(G-8135)
GATEHOUSE MEDIA MASS I INC (HQ)
Also Called: Community Newspaper
48 Dunham Rd (01915-1844)
PHONE..................................585 598-0030
Sandra Britto, *Sales Staff*
Summer Moore, *Manager*
Garrett J Cummings,
EMP: 1200
SALES (est): 112.3MM
SALES (corp-wide): 1.5B **Publicly Held**
SIC: 2711 Newspapers-Publishing/Printing
PA: Gannett Co., Inc.
7950 Jones Branch Dr
Mc Lean VA 22102
703 854-6000

(G-8136)
GATEHOUSE MEDIA MASS I INC
Also Called: Swampscott Reporter
48 Dunham Rd (01915-1844)
PHONE..................................781 639-4800
Lynn Sears, *Principal*
EMP: 5
SALES (corp-wide): 1.5B **Publicly Held**
SIC: 2711 Newspapers-Publishing/Printing
HQ: Gatehouse Media Massachusetts I, Inc.
48 Dunham Rd
Beverly MA 01915
585 598-0030

(G-8137)
GLYCOZYM USA INC
100 Cummings Ctr Ste 430j (01915-6122)
PHONE..................................425 985-2556
Thayer White, *President*
EMP: 7
SALES (est): 560K **Privately Held**
SIC: 2835 Mfg Diagnostic Substances

(G-8138)
HAMILTON THORNE INC (PA)
100 Cummings Ctr Ste 465e (01915-6143)
PHONE..................................978 921-2050
David Wolf, *CEO*
Meg Spencer, *Ch of Bd*
Keith F Edwards, *Senior VP*
Thomas Kenny, *Engineer*
Derek Maxwell, *Engineer*
▼ **EMP:** 30
SQ FT: 6,000
SALES (est): 5.1MM **Privately Held**
WEB: www.hamiltonthorne.com
SIC: 3829 3841 Mfg Measuring/Controlling Devices Mfg Surgical/Medical Instruments

(G-8139)
HEALTHQUARTERS INC
900 Cummings Ctr (01915-6198)
PHONE..................................978 922-4490
Gabrielle C Ross, *Exec Dir*
EMP: 4
SALES (est): 345.4K
SALES (corp-wide): 2.8MM **Privately Held**
SIC: 3131 Mfg Footwear Cut Stock
PA: Healthquarters, Inc.
100 Cummings Ctr Ste 220b
Beverly MA 01915
978 927-9824

(G-8140)
IMPOLIT ENVMTL CTRL CORP
Also Called: Filtersense
800 Cummings Ctr Ste 355w (01915-6174)
PHONE..................................978 927-4619
J Matthew Andrews, *President*
EMP: 24
SQ FT: 10,000
SALES (est): 5.2MM **Privately Held**
WEB: www.filtersense.com
SIC: 3823 3564 Mfg Process Control Instruments Mfg Blowers/Fans

(G-8141)
INNOVATION PHARMACEUTICALS INC (PA)
100 Cummings Ctr Ste 151b (01915-6117)
PHONE..................................978 921-4125
Leo Ehrlich, *CEO*
Jane Harness, *Senior VP*
Arthur P Bertolino, *Chief Mktg Ofcr*
Zorik Spektor, *Director*
EMP: 4
SALES (est): 926.7K **Publicly Held**
SIC: 2834 Pharmaceutical Preparations

(G-8142)
IXYS INTGRTED CIRCUITS DIV LLC
78 Cherry Hill Dr (01915-1065)
PHONE..................................978 524-6700
Nathan Zommer, *President*
Mark Heisig, *General Mgr*
Fred Day, *Prdtn Mgr*
Lana Keltgen, *Buyer*
Beverly Dean, *QC Mgr*
◆ **EMP:** 100
SQ FT: 83,000
SALES (est): 24.9MM
SALES (corp-wide): 1.7B **Publicly Held**
WEB: www.clare.com
SIC: 3674 Mfg Semiconductors/Related Devices
HQ: Ixys, Llc
1590 Buckeye Dr
Milpitas CA 95035
408 457-9000

(G-8143)
JACKIESTEES
238 Rantoul St (01915-4211)
PHONE..................................617 799-8404
Jackie Moldau, *Principal*
EMP: 3
SALES (est): 193.5K **Privately Held**
SIC: 2759 Commercial Printing

(G-8144)
JULES A GOURDEAU INC
94 Corning St (01915-3837)
P.O. Box 3 (01915-0001)
PHONE..................................978 922-0102
David Kampersal, *President*
EMP: 8 **EST:** 1945
SQ FT: 7,500
SALES (est): 956.8K **Privately Held**
SIC: 2541 Mfg Wood Cabinets

(G-8145)
KBIOSCIENCE LLC
100 Cummings Ctr Ste 420h (01915-6244)
PHONE..................................978 232-9430
Graham Love, *Chairman*
EMP: 3 **EST:** 2008
SALES (est): 220K **Privately Held**
SIC: 2836 Mfg Biological Products

(G-8146)
KWIK KOPY PRINTING
100 Cummings Ctr Ste 210d (01915-6104)
PHONE..................................978 232-3552
Santo Parisi, *Partner*
Ellen Parisi, *Partner*
EMP: 5
SQ FT: 2,000
SALES (est): 394.9K **Privately Held**
SIC: 2759 Thermography

(G-8147)
LAUNCHWORKS LLC
Also Called: Launchworks Manufacturing Lab
123 Brimbal Ave (01915-1869)
PHONE..................................978 338-3045
Maurice Barakat, *Mng Member*
Ken Fioretti, *Info Tech Dir*
EMP: 35
SALES (est): 8.8MM
SALES (corp-wide): 33.9MM **Privately Held**
SIC: 2836 Mfg Biological Products
PA: Tcp Reliable Inc.
551 Raritan Center Pkwy
Edison NJ 08837
848 229-2466

(G-8148)
LIBERTY PUBLISHING INC
100 Cummings Ctr (01915-6115)
PHONE..................................978 777-8200
M Jeffrey Rosen, *President*
Kimberly Aulson, *General Mgr*
EMP: 30
SQ FT: 6,500
SALES (est): 2.8MM **Privately Held**
WEB: www.libertyink.com
SIC: 2741 2721 7319 Misc Publishing Periodicals-Publishing/Printing Advertising Services

(G-8149)
MACHINE TECHNOLOGY INC
148 Sohier Rd (01915-5536)
PHONE..................................978 927-1900
Danial Shatford, *President*
Patricia M Shatford, *President*
Keith Shatford, *Vice Pres*
EMP: 15
SQ FT: 6,500

SALES (est): 2.3MM Privately Held
SIC: 3599 Machine Shop

(G-8150)
MELROSE FREE PRESS INC
48 Dunham Rd (01915-1844)
PHONE..................................781 665-4000
Frank E Schueler Jr, *President*
Marlene Swipzer, *Manager*
Dorothy Schueler, *Clerk*
EMP: 52
SALES (est): 1.3MM Privately Held
SIC: 2711 Newspapers-Publishing/Printing

(G-8151)
MEMOIRS UNLIMITED INC
Also Called: Commonwealth Editions
266 Cabot St Ste 2 (01915-3368)
PHONE..................................978 985-3206
Webster Bull, *President*
Kathleen M Bull, *Vice Pres*
Gary Larrabee, *VP Mktg*
▲ EMP: 7
SALES (est): 660.9K Privately Held
WEB: www.commonwealtheditions.com
SIC: 2731 Books-Publishing/Printing

(G-8152)
MEYERS GLUTEN FREE BAKING LLC
1025 Hale St (01915-2238)
PHONE..................................978 381-9629
Michael C Williams, *Principal*
EMP: 6
SALES (est): 460.8K Privately Held
SIC: 2051 Mfg Bread/Related Products

(G-8153)
MICROLINE SURGICAL INC (HQ)
Also Called: MSI
50 Dunham Rd Ste 1500 (01915-1882)
PHONE..................................978 922-9810
Dr Jean Luc Boulnois, *Ch of Bd*
Sharad H Joshi, *President*
Jose Falcao, *CFO*
Joel Spielman, *Manager*
▼ EMP: 143
SQ FT: 75,000
SALES (est): 33.2MM Privately Held
WEB: www.microlineinc.com
SIC: 3841 Mfg Surgical/Medical Instruments

(G-8154)
MICROSEMI CORPORATION
163 Cabot St (01915-5906)
PHONE..................................978 232-0040
Stephen Ouellette, *Principal*
EMP: 5
SALES (corp-wide): 5.3B Publicly Held
WEB: www.microsemicorp.com
SIC: 3674 Mfg Semiconductors/Related Devices
HQ: Microsemi Corporation
1 Enterprise
Aliso Viejo CA 92656
949 380-6100

(G-8155)
MICROSEMI FREQUENCY TIME CORP
34 Tozer Rd (01915-5510)
PHONE..................................978 232-0040
Larry Zanca, *Engineer*
Matthew Stanczyk, *Electrical Engi*
Paul Bya, *Branch Mgr*
EMP: 100
SALES (corp-wide): 5.3B Publicly Held
WEB: www.symmetricom.com
SIC: 3825 7371 Mfg Electrical Measuring Instruments Custom Computer Programing
HQ: Microsemi Frequency And Time Corporation
3870 N 1st St
San Jose CA 95134

(G-8156)
MOJO COLD BREWED COFFEE INC
30 Henderson Rd St Lot (01915-1024)
PHONE..................................617 877-2997
Annie Brainard, *Principal*
Laura Apgar, *COO*
Todd Brainard, *CFO*
EMP: 6
SALES (est): 534.7K Privately Held
SIC: 2095 Mfg Roasted Coffee

(G-8157)
MRP TRADING INNOVATIONS LLC
85 Sam Fonzo Dr (01915-1069)
PHONE..................................978 762-3900
Mark Landgren,
Peter Cranston,
▲ EMP: 10
SQ FT: 1,200
SALES: 2MM Privately Held
SIC: 2087 Mfg Flavor Extracts/Syrup

(G-8158)
MY PRINT AND COPY LLC
100 Cummings Ctr Ste 210d (01915-6104)
PHONE..................................978 232-3552
Richard E McElroy, *Mng Member*
Kevin Hogan, *Graphic Designe*
Adam M Chase,
EMP: 7
SALES (est): 897.9K Privately Held
SIC: 2752 Lithographic Commercial Printing

(G-8159)
NAUGLER MOLD & ENGINEERING
60 Dunham Rd (01915-1844)
P.O. Box 545, Moody ME (04054-0545)
PHONE..................................978 922-5634
EMP: 12
SQ FT: 4,600
SALES (est): 1.5MM Privately Held
WEB: www.nauglermold.com
SIC: 3089 Mfg Plastic Products

(G-8160)
NOVA ANALYTICS CORPORATION
100 Cummings Ctr Ste 535n (01915-6231)
PHONE..................................781 897-1208
Jim Barbookles, *Branch Mgr*
EMP: 5 Publicly Held
SIC: 3541 Mfg Machine Tools-Cutting
HQ: Nova Analytics Corporation
11390 Amalgam Way
Gold River CA 95670
866 664-6682

(G-8161)
O E M HEALTH INFORMATION INC
Also Called: O E M Press
8 West St (01915-2226)
P.O. Box 5518 (01915-0519)
PHONE..................................978 921-7300
Curtis R Vouwie, *President*
Catherine Vouwie, *Vice Pres*
Alexis Rautio, *Director*
EMP: 3
SQ FT: 1,000
SALES (est): 286.8K Privately Held
WEB: www.oempress.com
SIC: 2741 2731 5192 Newsletter & Book Publishing & Whol Distributor Of Books

(G-8162)
OAK BARREL IMPORTS LLC
421r Essex St (01915-1334)
PHONE..................................617 286-2524
Frank Dinoia, *General Ptnr*
Umberto Eramo, *General Ptnr*
Nick Horsley, *VP Pub Rel*
▲ EMP: 8
SALES (est): 453.7K Privately Held
SIC: 2084 Mfg Wines/Brandy/Spirits

(G-8163)
OSRAM SYLVANIA INC
71 Cherry Hill Dr (01915-1068)
PHONE..................................978 750-1529
John Fairbanks, *Branch Mgr*
EMP: 125
SALES (corp-wide): 3.8B Privately Held
WEB: www.sylvania.com
SIC: 3641 Mfg Electric Lamps
HQ: Osram Sylvania Inc
200 Ballardvale St # 305
Wilmington MA 01887
978 570-3000

(G-8164)
PARLEE CYCLES INC
69 Federal St (01915-5708)
PHONE..................................978 998-4880
Bob Parlee, *President*
Jared Porter, *Opers Mgr*
Bill Douglas, *QC Mgr*
Brian Burke, *Supervisor*
EMP: 8
SALES (est): 910K Privately Held
WEB: www.parleecycles.com
SIC: 3751 Mfg Motorcycles/Bicycles

(G-8165)
PIP ITSA INC
Also Called: PIP Printing
13 Holly Ln (01915-1572)
PHONE..................................978 927-5717
Robert G Freeman, *President*
Phyllis I Freeman, *Treasurer*
EMP: 4 EST: 1977
SQ FT: 1,500
SALES (est): 458K Privately Held
SIC: 2752 2791 2789 2759 Lithographic Coml Print Typesetting Services Bookbinding/Related Work Commercial Printing

(G-8166)
QUARTO PUBG GROUP USA INC
100 Cummings Ctr Ste 265g (01915-6143)
PHONE..................................978 282-9590
Ken Fund, *President*
EMP: 30
SALES (corp-wide): 149.2MM Privately Held
SIC: 2731 Misc Publishing
HQ: Quarto Publishing Group Usa Inc.
401 2nd Ave N Ste 310
Minneapolis MN 55401
612 344-8100

(G-8167)
QUAYSIDE PUBLISHING GROUP
Also Called: Rockport Publishing
100 Cummings Ctr Ste 406l (01915-6101)
PHONE..................................978 282-9590
Ken Fund, *President*
Peter Read, *Chairman*
Kevin Hamric, *Vice Pres*
Mary D Aarons, *Director*
▲ EMP: 8
SALES (est): 509.3K
SALES (corp-wide): 149.2MM Privately Held
SIC: 2731 2741 Books-Publishing/Printing Misc Publishing
HQ: Quarto Group Inc
276 5th Ave Rm 205
New York NY 10001
212 779-0700

(G-8168)
QUIDEL CORPORATION
500 Cummings Ctr # 55500 (01915-6142)
PHONE..................................866 800-5458
EMP: 3
SALES (corp-wide): 522.2MM Publicly Held
SIC: 2835 Mfg Diagnostics Substances
PA: Quidel Corporation
9975 Summers Ridge Rd
San Diego CA 92121
858 552-1100

(G-8169)
R H M GROUP INC
Also Called: PELLETIER AWNING DBA
51 Park St (01915-4229)
PHONE..................................978 745-4710
EMP: 7
SQ FT: 3,000
SALES: 364K Privately Held
WEB: www.rhmgroup.com
SIC: 2394 Mfg Custom Awnings Canopies Comercial & Residential

(G-8170)
R HUETER CO
416 Cabot St (01915-3152)
PHONE..................................978 927-3482
Raymond Hueter, *Mng Member*
EMP: 4
SQ FT: 2,100
SALES (est): 1MM Privately Held
SIC: 3451 Mfg Of Swiss Screw Machine Parts

(G-8171)
ROBERTS MACHINE SHOP INC
117 Elliott St Ste 7 (01915-3252)
P.O. Box 84 (01915-0002)
PHONE..................................978 927-6111
Paul Sidilou, *President*
Peter Sidilou, *Vice Pres*
EMP: 7 EST: 1974
SQ FT: 3,800
SALES (est): 1MM Privately Held
SIC: 3599 Machine Shop Jobbing & Repair

(G-8172)
ROCKPORT CUSTOM PUBLISHING LLC
100 Cummings Ctr Ste 207p (01915-6104)
PHONE..................................978 522-4316
Thomas E Tetreault, *Manager*
Thomas Tetreault,
▲ EMP: 4
SALES (est): 350.3K Privately Held
WEB: www.rockportpubs.com
SIC: 2741 Publisher Of Magazines

(G-8173)
RUGGLES-KLINGEMANN MFG CO (PA)
Also Called: The Ruggles-Klingemann Company
78 Water St (01915-5291)
PHONE..................................978 232-8300
Anthony Kline, *CEO*
Lawrence Kline, *President*
Mike Thibault, *Purchasing*
Max Cipriani, *Engineer*
Eric Englehardt, *Engineer*
EMP: 13 EST: 1897
SQ FT: 40,000
SALES (est): 2.5MM Privately Held
WEB: www.r-kmfg.com
SIC: 3491 Mfg Industrial Valves

(G-8174)
SAUGUS ADVERTISER
72 Cherry Hill Dr (01915-1030)
PHONE..................................781 233-2040
Elizabeth Christiansen, *Manager*
EMP: 3
SALES (est): 115.4K Privately Held
SIC: 2711 Newspapers-Publishing/Printing

(G-8175)
SEABORN MANAGEMENT INC
Also Called: Seaborn Networks
600 Cummings Ctr Fl 2 (01915-6194)
PHONE..................................978 377-8366
EMP: 17
SQ FT: 8,000
SALES (est): 634.5K
SALES (corp-wide): 3.7MM Privately Held
SIC: 3661 4822 Mfg Telephone/Telegraph Apparatus Telegraph Communications
PA: Seaborn Networks Holdings, Llc
600 Cummings Ctr Fl 2
Beverly MA 01915
978 471-3171

(G-8176)
SEABORN NETWORKS HOLDINGS LLC (PA)
600 Cummings Ctr Fl 2 (01915-6194)
PHONE..................................978 471-3171
Larry Schwartz, *CEO*
Andy Bax, *COO*
Paul Cannon, *Vice Pres*
Dan Taylor, *Vice Pres*
Roger Kuebel, *CFO*
◆ EMP: 18
SQ FT: 2,000
SALES (est): 3.8MM Privately Held
SIC: 3661 Mfg Telephone/Telegraph Apparatus

(G-8177)
SENSITECH INC (DH)
800 Cummings Ctr Ste 258x (01915-6197)
PHONE..................................978 927-7033
Mike Hurton, *President*
Andrea M Quercia, *Principal*
Tom Chase, *Vice Pres*

GEOGRAPHIC

Michael Hurton, *Vice Pres*
Richard Bukulu, *Engineer*
◆ **EMP:** 70
SQ FT: 30,000
SALES (est): 105MM
SALES (corp-wide): 66.5B **Publicly Held**
SIC: 3826 3823 3822 Mfg Analytical Instruments Mfg Process Control Instruments Mfg Environmental Controls
HQ: Carrier Corporation
13995 Pasteur Blvd
Palm Beach Gardens FL 33418
800 379-6484

(G-8178)
SIONYX LLC (PA)
100 Cummings Ctr 303b (01915-6115)
PHONE..................................978 922-0684
Stephen Saylor, *CEO*
Chris Vineis, *Vice Pres*
Pam Alman, *Office Mgr*
EMP: 13
SQ FT: 11,000
SALES (est): 3MM **Privately Held**
SIC: 3674 Mfg Semiconductors/Related Devices

(G-8179)
SPORTS INSIGHTS INC
100 Cummings Ctr Ste 226q (01915-6126)
PHONE..................................877 838-2853
Daniel Fabrizio, *Principal*
EMP: 5
SALES (est): 665.5K **Privately Held**
SIC: 2836 Mfg Biological Products

(G-8180)
STANDLEY BROTHERS MCH CO INC
96 Park St (01915-4312)
P.O. Box 85 (01915-0002)
PHONE..................................978 927-0278
John G Standley Jr, *President*
Carl W Standley, *Vice Pres*
John Zanoli, *Sales Dir*
David C Standley, *Shareholder*
EMP: 20 **EST:** 1956
SQ FT: 15,500
SALES (est): 2.9MM **Privately Held**
WEB: www.standleybros.com
SIC: 3599 Mfg Industrial Machinery

(G-8181)
STARBOARD EXCHANGE INC
14 Exeter Rd (01915-1604)
PHONE..................................978 810-5577
Graham Boardman, *CEO*
Shahav Afsharian, *President*
EMP: 6
SALES: 2MM **Privately Held**
SIC: 3679 Mfg Electronic Components

(G-8182)
STEELFISH MEDIA LLC
619 Hale St 4 (01915-2116)
PHONE..................................312 730-8016
Mike Kelly,
EMP: 5 **EST:** 2011
SALES (est): 283.6K **Privately Held**
SIC: 2721 Periodicals-Publishing/Printing

(G-8183)
SUMO STEEL CORP
6 Dearborn Ave (01915-3408)
PHONE..................................978 927-4950
Michael Regan, *President*
EMP: 5
SALES (est): 452.6K **Privately Held**
SIC: 3315 Mfg Steel Wire/Related Products

(G-8184)
SUN RAY BAKERY
Also Called: Sunray Bakery
240 Rantoul St (01915-4267)
P.O. Box 56 (01915-0001)
PHONE..................................978 922-1941
Mark Musumeci, *Owner*
EMP: 3
SQ FT: 800
SALES (est): 178.8K **Privately Held**
SIC: 2051 Mfg Bread/Related Products

(G-8185)
SUTURE CONCEPTS INC
100 Cummings Ctr Ste 414g (01915-6111)
PHONE..................................978 969-0070
Christopher Runnells, *CEO*
Dana Coulter, *Director*
Edward Fuerst, *Director*
EMP: 4 **EST:** 2015
SALES (est): 258.2K **Privately Held**
SIC: 3841 Mfg Surgical/Medical Instruments

(G-8186)
TAUTEN INC
100 Cummings Ctr Ste 215f (01915-6123)
PHONE..................................978 961-3272
EMP: 3
SALES (est): 116.6K **Privately Held**
SIC: 2298 Mfg Cordage/Twine

(G-8187)
TC DESIGN WORKS INC
94 Hart St (01915-2125)
PHONE..................................978 768-0034
Ronald Daley, *President*
EMP: 3
SALES: 120K **Privately Held**
SIC: 3069 5999 Mfg Fabricated Rubber Products Ret Misc Merchandise

(G-8188)
TEN WEST TRUNK SHOWS
10 West St (01915-2226)
PHONE..................................508 755-7547
EMP: 3 **EST:** 2010
SALES (est): 17.3K **Privately Held**
SIC: 3161 Mfg Luggage

(G-8189)
TERRAVERDAE BIOWORKS INC
100 Cummings Ctr Ste 235c (01915-6126)
PHONE..................................978 712-0220
William Bardosh, *CEO*
EMP: 5
SQ FT: 500
SALES (est): 432K **Privately Held**
SIC: 2899 Mfg Diagnostic Apparatus

(G-8190)
THEOLOGICAL THREADS INC
Also Called: Gordons of Beverly
48 Park St (01915-4217)
P.O. Box 115 (01915-0002)
PHONE..................................978 927-7031
George Gordon, *President*
Juanita Gordon, *Vice Pres*
EMP: 6
SQ FT: 6,000
SALES (est): 700K **Privately Held**
SIC: 2389 6513 5949 Mfg Religious Vestments & Operators Of Apartment Buildings

(G-8191)
THORNE DIAGNOSTICS INC
100 Cummings Ctr Ste 465e (01915-6143)
PHONE..................................978 299-1727
Harry McCoy, *President*
Thomas Beals, *Director*
EMP: 3
SQ FT: 1,200
SALES (est): 204.1K **Privately Held**
SIC: 2835 Mfg Diagnostic Substances

(G-8192)
TK&K SERVICES LLC
Also Called: Environmental Division
719 Hale St Ste 3 (01915-2199)
PHONE..................................770 844-8710
EMP: 106 **Privately Held**
SIC: 2869 8711 Mfg Industrial Organic Chemicals Engineering Services
PA: Tk&K Services, L.L.C.
5665 Atlanta Hwy Ste 103
Alpharetta GA
-

(G-8193)
UNITED SIGN CO INC
33 Tozer Rd Ste 3 (01915-5500)
P.O. Box 3106 (01915-0898)
PHONE..................................978 927-9346
Ed Juralewicz, *President*
EMP: 3
SALES (est): 355.2K **Privately Held**
SIC: 3993 Mfg Signs/Advertising Specialties

(G-8194)
VAMPFANGS / 321FX STUDIOS LLC
100 Cummings Ctr Ste 245g (01915-6541)
PHONE..................................781 799-5048
Scott Smiledge, *Manager*
EMP: 3
SALES (est): 510.4K **Privately Held**
SIC: 2389 Mfg Apparel/Accessories

(G-8195)
VIBRATION & SHOCK TECH LLC
13 Arbella Dr (01915-1401)
PHONE..................................781 281-0721
Darryl Huttunen, *Mng Member*
▼ **EMP:** 7
SALES (est): 933.7K **Privately Held**
SIC: 3599 Mfg Industrial Machinery

(G-8196)
WATERS TECHNOLOGIES CORP
100 Cummings Ctr Ste 407n (01915-6101)
PHONE..................................978 927-7468
Lance Nicolaysen, *Principal*
Lance Nicholas, *Vice Pres*
Viki Brooks, *Manager*
EMP: 10 **Publicly Held**
SIC: 3826 Mfg Analytical Instruments
HQ: Waters Technologies Corporation,
34 Maple St
Milford MA 01757
508 478-2000

(G-8197)
WILKSCRAFT INC
Also Called: Wilkscraft Creative Printing
59 Park St (01915-4253)
P.O. Box 632, Somerville (02143-0008)
PHONE..................................978 922-1855
EMP: 15 **EST:** 1947
SQ FT: 7,000
SALES (est): 1.1MM **Privately Held**
SIC: 2752 Offset Printing Including Color Lithography

(G-8198)
WORLDWIDE INFORMATION INC
100 Cummings Ctr Ste 235m (01915-6126)
PHONE..................................888 273-3260
James Fields, *President*
EMP: 5
SALES (est): 620K **Privately Held**
SIC: 7372 7375 Provides Investigative Search Software

(G-8199)
XENICS USA INC
600 Cummings Ctr Ste 166y (01915-6148)
PHONE..................................978 969-1706
Luc Debrouckere, *CEO*
Stefany Eck, *Engineer*
EMP: 3
SALES (est): 364.9K
SALES (corp-wide): 10.7MM **Privately Held**
SIC: 3861 Mfg Photographic Equipment/Supplies
PA: Xenics
Ambachtenlaan 44
Leuven 3001
164 054-10

(G-8200)
XYLEM INC
100 Cummings Ctr Ste 535n (01915-6231)
PHONE..................................978 778-1010
Gretchen McClain, *Branch Mgr*
▲ **EMP:** 21 **Publicly Held**
SIC: 3821 Mfg Lab Apparatus/Furniture
PA: Xylem Inc.
1 International Dr
Rye Brook NY 10573
-

(G-8201)
ZERIOUS ELECTRONIC PUBG CORP
Also Called: CD Works
93 Park St Ste 1 (01915-4311)
PHONE..................................978 922-4990
Jeffrey B Starfield, *President*
EMP: 4
SQ FT: 3,000
SALES (est): 509.4K **Privately Held**
WEB: www.dvdworks.com
SIC: 3572 7379 Cd & Dvd Duplication Replication And Authoring

Billerica
Middlesex County

(G-8202)
ABACO SYSTEMS TECHNOLOGY CORP
900 Technology Park Dr # 200
(01821-4167)
PHONE..................................256 382-8115
Alan Dillbero, *Ch of Bd*
Bernie Anger, *President*
George Hearn, *Exec VP*
Christopher Lever, *Vice Pres*
David Tetley, *Engineer*
EMP: 23
SQ FT: 30,000
SALES (est): 4.6MM
SALES (corp-wide): 302.4MM **Privately Held**
WEB: www.radstone.co.uk
SIC: 3571 Mfg Electronic Computers
HQ: Abaco Systems Limited
Tove Valley Business Park
Towcester NORTHANTS NN12
-

(G-8203)
ABLE SOFTWARE CORP
655 Boston Rd Ste 1b (01821-5338)
PHONE..................................978 667-2400
Yecheng Wu, *Branch Mgr*
EMP: 4
SALES (est): 219.8K **Privately Held**
SIC: 7372 Prepackaged Software Services
PA: Able Software Corp
5 Appletree Ln
Lexington MA 02420
-

(G-8204)
ABSOLUTE SHEET METAL
559 Boston Rd (01821-3713)
PHONE..................................978 667-0236
Mary Barry, *Owner*
EMP: 20
SALES (est): 2.1MM **Privately Held**
SIC: 3444 Mfg Sheet Metalwork

(G-8205)
AETRUIM INCORPORATED
4 Federal St (01821-3569)
PHONE..................................651 773-4200
Joe Levesque, *President*
Tim Foley, *Principal*
Dean Hedstrom, *Vice Pres*
EMP: 50
SQ FT: 61,500
SALES (est): 6.5MM
SALES (corp-wide): 104.1MM **Publicly Held**
WEB: www.aetrium.com
SIC: 3825 3674 7389 Mfg & Distributes Environmental Conditioning Chambers & Provides Board Assembly & Burn-In Testing Services
HQ: Atrm Holdings, Inc.
5215 Gershwin Ave N
Oakdale MN 55128
651 704-1800

(G-8206)
AGILYNX INC
4 Rodeo Cir (01821-1241)
PHONE..................................617 314-6463
Robert Bianchi, *President*
EMP: 5
SQ FT: 150
SALES (est): 814.4K **Privately Held**
WEB: www.agilynx.com
SIC: 3812 Mfg Search/Navigation Equipment

(G-8207)
AIRGAS USA LLC
1 Plank St (01821-5726)
PHONE..................................978 439-1344
Thomas Fyrer, *Vice Pres*
Josh Santerre, *Manager*
EMP: 30
SALES (corp-wide): 121.9MM **Privately Held**
SIC: 2813 5169 5085 Mfg Industrial Gases Whol Chemicals/Products Whol Industrial Supplies
HQ: Airgas Usa, Llc
259 N Radnor Chester Rd
Radnor PA 19087
610 687-5253

(G-8208)
AMNIS CORPORATION
290 Concord Rd (01821-3405)
PHONE..................................206 374-7000
EMP: 3
SALES (est): 219.3K **Privately Held**
SIC: 3826 Mfg Analytical Instruments

(G-8209)
AMPHENOL ADVANCED SENSORS
900 Middlesex Tpke (01821-3929)
PHONE..................................978 294-8300
Robert Cerpovicz, *Design Engr*
EMP: 3
SALES (est): 257.7K **Privately Held**
SIC: 3823 Mfg Process Control Instruments

(G-8210)
AOTCO METAL FINISHING INC
11 Suburban Park Dr (01821-3997)
PHONE..................................781 275-0880
Elliot E Wilke, *President*
Frank Oliveira, *Supervisor*
EMP: 40
SQ FT: 26,000
SALES (est): 5.5MM **Privately Held**
WEB: www.aotco.com
SIC: 3471 Plating/Polishing Service

(G-8211)
APPLIED NNSTRCTRED SLTIONS LLC
157 Concord Rd (01821-4600)
PHONE..................................978 670-6959
Yakov Kutsovsky, *President*
William Krents, *Bus Dvlpt Dir*
EMP: 20
SALES: 350K
SALES (corp-wide): 3.3B **Publicly Held**
SIC: 3624 3081 3084 Mfg Carbon/Graphite Products Mfg Unsupported Plastic Film/Sheet Mfg Plastic Pipe
PA: Cabot Corporation
2 Seaport Ln Ste 1300
Boston MA 02210
617 345-0100

(G-8212)
APPLIED SCIENCE GROUP INC
Also Called: Applied Science Laboratories
900 Middlesex Tpke 5-5 (01821-3929)
PHONE..................................781 275-4000
Valerie Sinclair, *President*
Joshua Borah, *President*
Robert Sinclair, *President*
Mark Crowley, *COO*
EMP: 25
SQ FT: 12,000
SALES (est): 4.8MM **Privately Held**
WEB: www.a-s-l.com
SIC: 3827 8748 Mfg Optical Instruments/Lenses Business Consulting Services

(G-8213)
APRIL TWENTY ONE CORPORATION
Also Called: Swing Center Factory Outlet
749 Boston Rd (01821-5933)
PHONE..................................978 667-8472
Salvatore C Turco Jr, *President*
EMP: 7
SQ FT: 12,000
SALES (est): 847.6K **Privately Held**
WEB: www.theswingsenter.com
SIC: 2499 5941 Mfg Wood Products Ret Sporting Goods/Bicycles

(G-8214)
ASM NEXX INC
900 Middlesex Tpke (01821-3929)
PHONE..................................978 436-4600
Thomas Walsh, *President*
Kurt Williams, *General Mgr*
▲ **EMP:** 38 **EST:** 2001
SQ FT: 15,000
SALES (est): 10.5MM **Privately Held**
WEB: www.nexxsystems.com
SIC: 3674 Mfg Semiconductors/Related Devices
HQ: Asm Pacific Technology Limited
16/F & 18-20/F Gateway Ts
Tsing Yi Island NT

(G-8215)
ATI FLOWFORM PRODUCTS LLC
12 Suburban Park Dr (01821-3903)
PHONE..................................978 667-0202
Christine Donovan, *Finance*
Mathew Fonte, *Mng Member*
Venanzioro Fonte,
▲ **EMP:** 45
SQ FT: 43,500
SALES (est): 10.5MM **Publicly Held**
WEB: www.flowform.com
SIC: 3542 Mfg Machine Tools-Forming
HQ: Tdy Industries, Llc
1000 Six Ppg Pl
Pittsburgh PA 15222
412 394-2800

(G-8216)
AVAYA INC
600 Technology Park Dr # 1 (01821-4154)
PHONE..................................908 953-6000
Christie Blake, *Principal*
Michael Houle, *Info Tech Dir*
EMP: 111 **Publicly Held**
SIC: 3661 Telephone And Telegraph Apparatus
HQ: Avaya Inc.
4655 Great America Pkwy
Santa Clara CA 95054
908 953-6000

(G-8217)
AXSUN TECHNOLOGIES INC
1 Fortune Dr (01821-3923)
PHONE..................................978 262-0049
Jonathan Hartmann, *CEO*
Peter Whitney, *Vice Pres*
Chris Baldwin, *CFO*
Lloyd Dube, *Technician*
▲ **EMP:** 90 **EST:** 1999
SQ FT: 65,000
SALES (est): 22.1MM
SALES (corp-wide): 1.2B **Privately Held**
WEB: www.axsun.com
SIC: 3827 Manufacturing Of Optical Engines
HQ: Excelitas Technologies Corp.
200 West St
Waltham MA 02451

(G-8218)
BELMONT INSTRUMENT LLC (PA)
Also Called: Belmont Medical Technologies
780 Boston Rd Ste 3 (01821-5939)
PHONE..................................978 663-0212
Brian Ellacott, *CEO*
Jeffrey Forward, *CFO*
EMP: 35 **EST:** 1999
SQ FT: 15,200
SALES (est): 8.3MM **Privately Held**
WEB: www.belmontinstrument.com
SIC: 3845 3841 Mfg Electromedical Equipment Mfg Surgical/Medical Instruments

(G-8219)
BIOVIEW
44 Manning Rd Ste 4 (01821-3931)
PHONE..................................978 670-4741
Emmanuel Gill, *Ch of Bd*
Opher Shapira, *President*
Yuval Harrari, *Vice Pres*
Allen Schwevel, *Vice Pres*
EMP: 9
SALES: 4.5MM **Privately Held**
SIC: 3845 Mfg Electromedical Equipment

(G-8220)
BRISTOL-MYERS SQUIBB COMPANY
331 Trebble Cove Rd (01821)
PHONE..................................978 667-9532
Cory Zwerling, *Manager*
EMP: 40
SALES (corp-wide): 22.5B **Publicly Held**
WEB: www.bms.com
SIC: 2834 Mfg Pharmaceutical Preparations
PA: Bristol-Myers Squibb Company
430 E 29th St Fl 14
New York NY 10016
212 546-4000

(G-8221)
BRUKER AXS INC
40 Manning Rd (01821-3915)
PHONE..................................978 663-3660
EMP: 12
SALES (corp-wide): 1.9B **Publicly Held**
SIC: 3826 Mfg Analytical Instruments
HQ: Bruker Axs Inc.
5465 E Cheryl Pkwy
Fitchburg WI 53711
800 234-9729

(G-8222)
BRUKER BIOSPIN MRI INC
15 Fortune Dr (01821-3958)
PHONE..................................978 667-9580
Joerg Laukien, *President*
Frank H Laukien, *General Mgr*
Richard Hoffman, *Engineer*
Barbara Burgess, *Treasurer*
▲ **EMP:** 10
SQ FT: 1,000
SALES: 30.4MM
SALES (corp-wide): 1.9B **Publicly Held**
WEB: www.bruker-biospin.com
SIC: 3826 Mfg Analytical Instruments
PA: Bruker Corporation
40 Manning Rd
Billerica MA 01821
978 663-3660

(G-8223)
BRUKER CORPORATION (PA)
40 Manning Rd (01821-3915)
PHONE..................................978 663-3660
Frank H Laukien, *Ch of Bd*
Juergen Srega, *President*
Mark R Munch, *Exec VP*
Jay Chiarelli, *Vice Pres*
Robert Walcott, *Vice Pres*
▲ **EMP:** 224
SALES: 1.9B **Publicly Held**
WEB: www.bruker.com
SIC: 3826 3844 Mfg Analytical Instruments & X-Ray Apparatus

(G-8224)
BRUKER DALTONICS INC
15 Fortune Dr (01821-3958)
PHONE..................................978 663-2548
Gail Johnson, *Marketing Staff*
Norbert Schuehler, *Branch Mgr*
EMP: 6
SALES (corp-wide): 1.9B **Publicly Held**
WEB: www.brukerdaltonics.com
SIC: 3826 5049 Mfg Analytical Instruments Whol Professional Equipment
HQ: Bruker Scientific Llc
40 Manning Rd
Billerica MA 01821

(G-8225)
BRUKER DETECTION CORPORATION
40 Manning Rd (01821-3915)
PHONE..................................978 663-3660
William Knight, *President*
EMP: 13
SALES (est): 1.9MM
SALES (corp-wide): 1.9B **Publicly Held**
WEB: www.bruker-biosciences.com
SIC: 2819 Mfg Industrial Inorganic Chemicals
PA: Bruker Corporation
40 Manning Rd
Billerica MA 01821
978 663-3660

(G-8226)
BRUKER ENRGY SUPERCON TECH INC (HQ)
15 Fortune Dr (01821-3958)
PHONE..................................978 901-7550
Burkhard Prause, *CEO*
David Lyons, *Engineer*
Thomas Rosa, *CFO*
Tony W Keller, *Director*
EMP: 7
SALES (est): 17.9MM
SALES (corp-wide): 1.9B **Publicly Held**
SIC: 3826 Mfg Analytical Instruments
PA: Bruker Corporation
40 Manning Rd
Billerica MA 01821
978 663-3660

(G-8227)
BRUKER OPTICS INC (HQ)
40 Manning Rd (01821-3915)
PHONE..................................978 901-1528
Dirk Laukien, *President*
Dan Klevisha, *Vice Pres*
Arno Simon, *Vice Pres*
Terry Ellis, *Prdtn Mgr*
Barbara Burgess, *Treasurer*
▲ **EMP:** 50
SQ FT: 20,000
SALES (est): 56.3MM
SALES (corp-wide): 1.9B **Publicly Held**
WEB: www.brukeroptics.com
SIC: 3826 5049 Mfg Analytical Instruments Whol Professional Equipment
PA: Bruker Corporation
40 Manning Rd
Billerica MA 01821
978 663-3660

(G-8228)
BRUKER SCIENTIFIC LLC (HQ)
40 Manning Rd (01821-3915)
P.O. Box 83228, Woburn (01813-3228)
PHONE..................................978 667-9580
Frank Laukien, *CEO*
Frank Thibodeau, *Vice Pres*
Mary Roane, *Opers Staff*
Scott Baldwin, *Senior Buyer*
Michael Fey, *Research*
▲ **EMP:** 110
SQ FT: 90,000
SALES (est): 118.5MM
SALES (corp-wide): 1.9B **Publicly Held**
WEB: www.brukerdaltonics.com
SIC: 3826 5049 Mfg Analytical Instruments Whol Professional Equipment
PA: Bruker Corporation
40 Manning Rd
Billerica MA 01821
978 663-3660

(G-8229)
C-R MACHINE CO INC (PA)
13 Alexander Rd Ste 10 (01821-5000)
PHONE..................................978 663-3989
Gary Rigoli, *President*
Sean Osborne, *Technology*
Julie Rigoli, *Admin Sec*
John Comeau, *Maintence Staff*
EMP: 60 **EST:** 1974
SQ FT: 10,000
SALES (est): 13.2MM **Privately Held**
WEB: www.crmach.com
SIC: 3599 Mfg Industrial Machinery

(G-8230)
CABOT CORPORATION
157 Concord Rd (01821-4698)
P.O. Box 7001 (01821-7001)
PHONE..................................978 671-4000
Steven Varney, *Facilities Mgr*
Fred Rumpf, *Research*
Dave Murray, *Finance*
Benjamin Roberts, *Sales Staff*
Steve Reznek, *Manager*
EMP: 25
SALES (corp-wide): 3.3B **Publicly Held**
WEB: www.cabot-corp.com
SIC: 2895 2899 Mfg Carbon Black Mfg Chemical Preparations

GEOGRAPHIC

PA: Cabot Corporation
2 Seaport Ln Ste 1300
Boston MA 02210
617 345-0100

(G-8231)
CLEARMOTION INC (PA)
805 Middlesex Tpke (01821-3914)
PHONE..................................617 313-0822
Christian Steinmann, *CEO*
Phillip Lachman, *Business Mgr*
Zackary Anderson, *COO*
Ricardo Rodriguez, *Senior VP*
Omkar Athavale, *Engineer*
EMP: 15
SALES (est): 5.9MM **Privately Held**
SIC: 3714 Mfg Motor Vehicle Parts/Accessories

(G-8232)
CONFORMIS INC (PA)
600 Technology Park Dr # 3 (01821-4154)
PHONE..................................781 345-9001
Kenneth Fallon III, *Ch of Bd*
Mark A Augusti, *President*
Norman Eckley, *Regional Mgr*
Lisa Donnelly, *Senior VP*
Gary Maingot, *Senior VP*
EMP: 139
SQ FT: 45,000
SALES: 89.7MM **Publicly Held**
SIC: 3841 Joint Replacement Implants

(G-8233)
CONTRACT GLASS SERVICE INC
44 Dunham Rd (01821-5727)
P.O. Box 514, Woburn (01801-0514)
PHONE..................................978 262-1323
William Crawford, *President*
Mary Best, *Owner*
George Leonhardt, *Project Mgr*
George Best, *Opers Mgr*
Jim Runyan, *Prdtn Mgr*
EMP: 22
SQ FT: 16,000
SALES (est): 3.5MM **Privately Held**
SIC: 3211 1793 Mfg Insulated Glass

(G-8234)
COSMIC SOFTWARE INC
17 Bridge St Ste 101 (01821-1000)
PHONE..................................978 667-2556
Maurice Fathi, *President*
Mike Burns, *Clerk*
EMP: 12
SALES (est): 1.3MM **Privately Held**
WEB: www.cosmic-us.com
SIC: 7372 7371 Prepackaged Software Services Custom Computer Programing

(G-8235)
DAUGHTERS OF ST PAUL INC
Also Called: Saint Thecla Retreat House
77 Dudley Rd (01821-4132)
PHONE..................................617 522-2566
EMP: 4
SALES (corp-wide): 7MM **Privately Held**
SIC: 2731 Mfg Books Publishing And Printing
PA: Daughters Of St. Paul, Inc.
50 Saint Pauls Ave
Boston MA 02130
617 522-8911

(G-8236)
DETAIL WOODWORKING LTD
19 Linnell Cir (01821-3928)
PHONE..................................617 323-8100
Enrico Lecce, *Owner*
EMP: 6
SALES (est): 900K **Privately Held**
SIC: 2434 Mfg Wood Kitchen Cabinets

(G-8237)
DODGE COMPANY INC (PA)
9 Progress Rd (01821-5731)
PHONE..................................800 443-6343
Debrah Dodge, *President*
John Dodge, *President*
Kristie Dodge, *Vice Pres*
Patrick J Hurley, *Vice Pres*
Dennis Alphen, *Facilities Mgr*
◆ **EMP:** 4 **EST:** 1893
SALES (est): 3.2MM **Privately Held**
WEB: www.dodgeco.com
SIC: 2869 5087 Mfg Industrial Organic Chemicals Whol Service Establishment Equipment

(G-8238)
DRUCK LLC (HQ)
Also Called: Druck, Inc.
1100 Tech Park Dr Ste 300 (01821-4111)
PHONE..................................978 437-1000
Brian Palmer, *President*
Jessica Wenzell, *Vice Pres*
Kris McBride, *CFO*
◆ **EMP:** 101
SALES (est): 84.9MM
SALES (corp-wide): 121.6B **Publicly Held**
WEB: www.druck.com
SIC: 3829 3823 3824 3674 Mfg Measure/Control Dvcs Mfg Process Cntrl Instr Mfg Fluid Meters/Devices Mfg Semiconductors/Dvcs
PA: General Electric Company
5 Necco St
Boston MA 02210
617 443-3000

(G-8239)
DURRIDGE COMPANY INC
900 Technology Park Dr # 200 (01821-4167)
P.O. Box 54 (01821-0054)
PHONE..................................978 667-9556
Wendell Clough, *President*
Ronda Wang, *Vice Pres*
Adam Shrey, *VP Engrg*
Jesse Simko, *Software Dev*
Linda Albertelli, *Technician*
EMP: 10
SQ FT: 2,000
SALES: 1.6MM **Privately Held**
WEB: www.durridge.com
SIC: 3825 Mfg Electrical Measuring Instruments

(G-8240)
DYNISCO INSTRUMENTS LLC
Dj Instruments
37 Manning Rd Ste 2 (01821-3950)
PHONE..................................978 215-3401
Steve Debries, *Branch Mgr*
EMP: 60
SALES (corp-wide): 5.1B **Publicly Held**
SIC: 3829 Mfg Measuring/Controlling Devices
HQ: Dynisco Instruments Llc
38 Forge Pkwy
Franklin MA 02038
508 541-9400

(G-8241)
DYNISCO PARENT INC
37 Manning Rd Ste 2 (01821-3950)
PHONE..................................978 667-5301
Michael Testa, *Manager*
EMP: 20
SALES (corp-wide): 5.1B **Publicly Held**
SIC: 3823 3829 Mfg Process Control Instruments Mfg Measuring/Controlling Devices
HQ: Dynisco Parent Inc
38 Forge Pkwy
Franklin MA 02038

(G-8242)
E INK CORPORATION
1000 Technology Park Dr (01821-4165)
PHONE..................................617 499-6000
Felix Ho, *President*
Daniel P Button, *President*
Michael D McCreary, *Principal*
Rishik Jariwala, *Business Mgr*
David N Cole, *Counsel*
▲ **EMP:** 55
SQ FT: 45,000
SALES (est): 42MM **Privately Held**
WEB: www.eink.com
SIC: 2653 Mfg Corrugated/Solid Fiber Boxes
PA: E Ink Holdings Inc.
No. 3, Lixing 1st Rd., Kexuegongyeyuan District,
Hsinchu City 30078

(G-8243)
EMD MILLIPORE CORPORATION
290 Concord Rd 2 (01821-3405)
PHONE..................................978 715-4321
Vivek Joshi, *Principal*
Paul Clark, *Business Mgr*
James Hoberg, *Business Mgr*
Lucas Hank, *Vice Pres*
Ross R Rosenau, *Vice Pres*
EMP: 317
SALES (corp-wide): 16.4B **Privately Held**
SIC: 3826 Mfg Analytical Instruments
HQ: Emd Millipore Corporation
400 Summit Dr
Burlington MA 01803
781 533-6000

(G-8244)
EMD SERONO INC
290 Concord Rd (01821-3405)
PHONE..................................781 982-9000
Michael Gordon, *Exec VP*
Ellen Costello, *Human Res Dir*
Shinji Okitsu, *Research Analys*
EMP: 3
SALES (corp-wide): 16.4B **Privately Held**
SIC: 2834 Pharmaceutical Preparations
HQ: Emd Serono, Inc.
1 Technology Pl
Rockland MA 02370
781 982-9000

(G-8245)
EMD SERONO BIOTECH CENTER INC
45a Middlesex Tpke (01821-3936)
PHONE..................................978 294-1100
Stephen Arkinstall, *President*
EMP: 54
SALES (corp-wide): 16.4B **Privately Held**
SIC: 2834 Mfg Pharmaceutical Preparations
HQ: Emd Serono Biotech Center, Inc.
1 Technology Pl
Rockland MA 02370
800 283-8088

(G-8246)
ENTEGRIS INC (PA)
129 Concord Rd (01821-4600)
PHONE..................................978 436-6500
Paul L H Olson, *Ch of Bd*
Bertrand Loy, *President*
Todd Edlund, *COO*
Bruce W Beckman, *Senior VP*
Gregory B Graves, *CFO*
◆ **EMP:** 1050
SQ FT: 175,000
SALES: 1.5B **Publicly Held**
WEB: www.entegris.com
SIC: 3089 3081 3674 Mfg Semiconductor Equipment And Materials

(G-8247)
ENTEGRIS INC
Also Called: Mykrolis
129 Concord Rd Bldg 2 (01821-4600)
PHONE..................................978 436-6500
N A BR, *Manager*
EMP: 17
SQ FT: 175,000
SALES (corp-wide): 1.5B **Publicly Held**
WEB: www.entegris.com
SIC: 3823 Mfr Of Industrial Process Measurement Equipment
PA: Entegris, Inc.
129 Concord Rd
Billerica MA 01821
978 436-6500

(G-8248)
EPOXY TECHNOLOGY INC (PA)
Also Called: Epo-Tek
14 Fortune Dr (01821-3972)
PHONE..................................978 667-3805
Andrew R Horne, *President*
Donna Sullivan, *Mfg Dir*
Keri Nunes, *Production*
Brian Betty, *Sales Mgr*
EMP: 50 **EST:** 1966
SQ FT: 40,000
SALES (est): 9.1MM **Privately Held**
WEB: www.epotek.com
SIC: 2891 2834 2869 Manufacture Adhesives/Sealants Pharmaceutical Preparations & Industrial Organic Chemicals

(G-8249)
GE INFRASTRUCTURE SENSING LLC (DH)
Also Called: GE Sensing & Inspection Tech
1100 Technology Park Dr # 100 (01821-4111)
P.O. Box 370049, Boston (02241-0001)
PHONE..................................978 437-1000
Kristopher McBride, *President*
Sheila Van Kuren, *General Mgr*
Barbara A Cameron, *Vice Pres*
Stephen Rehn, *Mfg Staff*
Yufeng Huang, *Engineer*
◆ **EMP:** 600 **EST:** 1960
SQ FT: 300,000
SALES: 277.9MM
SALES (corp-wide): 121.6B **Publicly Held**
WEB: www.panametrics.com
SIC: 3823 5084 3699 3674 Mfg Process Cntrl Instr Whol Industrial Equip Mfg Elec Mach/Equip/Supp Mfg Semiconductors/Dvcs Mfg Radio/Tv Comm Equip
HQ: Ge Energy Management Services, Llc
4200 Wildwood Pkwy
Atlanta GA 30339
678 844-6000

(G-8250)
GE PANAMETRICS INC
1100 Tech Park Dr Ste 100 (01821-4111)
PHONE..................................978 670-6454
EMP: 4 **EST:** 2011
SALES (est): 396.7K **Privately Held**
SIC: 3823 Mfg Process Control Instruments

(G-8251)
GENBAND US LLC
3 Federal St (01821-3500)
PHONE..................................972 521-5800
Dennis Racca, *VP Engrg*
EMP: 9
SALES (corp-wide): 618.5MM **Publicly Held**
SIC: 3661 Mfg Telephone/Telegraph Apparatus
HQ: Genband Us Llc
2801 Network Blvd Ste 300
Frisco TX 75034
972 521-5800

(G-8252)
GSR GLOBAL CORPORATION
700 Technology Park Dr # 210 (01821-4134)
PHONE..................................781 687-9191
Neel A Jhaveri, *President*
A A Jhaveri, *Treasurer*
K J Jhaveri, *Admin Sec*
▲ **EMP:** 5
SQ FT: 2,500
SALES (est): 1MM **Privately Held**
WEB: www.gsrusa.com
SIC: 3661 Mfg Telephone/Telegraph Apparatus

(G-8253)
GXT GREEN INC
505 Middlesex Tpke # 11 (01821-3578)
PHONE..................................978 735-4367
Manas Chatterjee, *CEO*
Stephen Beach, *Sales Dir*
EMP: 25
SQ FT: 10,000
SALES (est): 1.3MM **Privately Held**
SIC: 2821 Mfg Plastic Materials/Resins

(G-8254)
HOCKEY12COM
12 Beaumont Ave (01821-5913)
PHONE..................................781 910-2877
Stephen Sheridan, *Principal*
EMP: 3 **EST:** 2010
SALES (est): 212.3K **Privately Held**
SIC: 2836 Mfg Biological Products

(G-8255)
IDEMIA AMERICA CORP (DH)
Also Called: Oberthur Technologies
296 Concord Rd Ste 300 (01821-3487)
PHONE..................................978 215-2400
Martin Ferenczi, *President*
Steve Masters, *Engineer*
Ahmed Mohammad, *Marketing Mgr*

William Hoskins, *Manager*
Paul Daniels, *Consultant*
▲ **EMP:** 300
SALES (est): 658.2MM
SALES (corp-wide): 3.5B **Privately Held**
WEB: www.oberthurcs.com
SIC: 3089 7382 3953 3578 Mfg Plastic Products Security System Svcs Mfg Marking Devices Mfg Calculating Equip

(G-8256)
IMABIOTECH CORP
44 Manning Rd (01821-3935)
PHONE..................................978 362-1825
Jonathan Stauber, *CEO*
EMP: 6
SALES (est): 700.7K **Privately Held**
SIC: 2834 Mfg Pharmaceutical Preparations

(G-8257)
INNOVIVE LLC
129 Concord Rd (01821-4600)
PHONE..................................617 500-1691
William Zebuhr, *Principal*
EMP: 8
SALES (corp-wide): 11.3MM **Privately Held**
SIC: 3496 Mfg Misc Fabricated Wire Products
PA: Innovive, Llc
10019 Waples Ct
San Diego CA 92121
858 309-6620

(G-8258)
INTERSENSE INCORPORATED
700 Technology Park Dr # 102 (01821-4153)
PHONE..................................781 541-6330
Thomas C Browne, *President*
William Kea, *CFO*
EMP: 23
SQ FT: 13,000
SALES (est): 3.2MM
SALES (corp-wide): 143.3MM **Privately Held**
WEB: www.isense.com
SIC: 3643 Manufactures Conductive Wiring Devices
PA: Gentex Corporation
324 Main St
Simpson PA 18407
570 282-3550

(G-8259)
JEIO TECH INC
19 Alexander Rd Ste 7 (01821-5094)
PHONE..................................781 376-0700
Sangyong Kim, *CEO*
Hyunjoo Shin, *President*
◆ **EMP:** 9
SALES: 2MM **Privately Held**
SIC: 3821 5049 5084 Mfg Lab Apparatus/Furniture Whol Professional Equipment Whol Industrial Equipment
PA: Jeio Tech Co., Ltd.
153 Techno 2-Ro, Yuseong-Gu
Daejeon 34025

(G-8260)
K V A ELECTRONICS
Also Called: Kva Electronics
77 Alexander Rd Ste 1 (01821-5065)
PHONE..................................978 262-2264
EMP: 6
SALES (est): 330K **Privately Held**
SIC: 3679 Mfg Electronic Printed Circuits

(G-8261)
KODIAK INDUSTRIES LLC
17 Ciccone Way (01821-2309)
PHONE..................................617 839-1298
Brett Robillard, *Principal*
EMP: 3
SALES (est): 150K **Privately Held**
SIC: 3999 Mfg Misc Products

(G-8262)
LAB MEDICAL MANUFACTURING INC
28 Cook St (01821-6060)
PHONE..................................978 663-2475
Leon W Bester, *President*
EMP: 80
SQ FT: 29,200
SALES: 16.7MM **Privately Held**
SIC: 3841 Mfg Surgical/Medical Instruments

(G-8263)
LUTRONIC USA
19 Fortune Dr (01821-3923)
PHONE..................................888 588-7644
EMP: 4
SALES (est): 389.3K **Privately Held**
SIC: 2834 Mfg Pharmaceutical Preparations

(G-8264)
MARKFORGED INC
4 Suburban Park Dr (01821-3904)
PHONE..................................617 666-1935
EMP: 20
SALES (corp-wide): 3.6MM **Privately Held**
SIC: 3599 Mfg Industrial Machinery
PA: Markforged, Inc.
480 Pleasant St
Watertown MA 02472
866 496-1805

(G-8265)
METTLER-TOLEDO PROCESS ANALYTI
Also Called: Mettler-Toledo Ingold, Inc.
900 Middlesex Tpke 8-1 (01821-3929)
PHONE..................................781 301-8800
James L Bryant, *President*
Lanora Medwar, *General Mgr*
Anthony Bevilacqua, *Research*
Vivian Feng, *Engineer*
Richard Kunicki, *Engineer*
EMP: 100
SQ FT: 41,500
SALES (est): 19.2MM
SALES (corp-wide): 2.9B **Publicly Held**
SIC: 3699 3845 3822 Mfg Electrical Equipment/Supplies Mfg Electromedical Equipment Mfg Environmental Controls
HQ: Mettler-Toledo, Llc
1900 Polaris Pkwy Fl 6
Columbus OH 43240
614 438-4511

(G-8266)
METTLER-TOLEDO THORNTON INC
900 Middlesex Tpke 8-1 (01821-3943)
PHONE..................................978 262-0210
James L Bryant, *President*
Charles O Staples, *President*
Mary Finnegan, *Treasurer*
Richard Brouillette, *Director*
Peter Mosgrove, *Director*
EMP: 75 **EST:** 1964
SQ FT: 41,500
SALES (est): 20.8MM
SALES (corp-wide): 2.9B **Publicly Held**
WEB: www.thorntoninc.com
SIC: 3823 5084 3812 3613 Mfg Process Cntrl Instr Whol Industrial Equip Mfg Search/Navgatn Equip Mfg Switchgear/Boards
HQ: Mettler-Toledo, Llc
1900 Polaris Pkwy Fl 6
Columbus OH 43240
614 438-4511

(G-8267)
NEW ENGLAND WHEELS INC (PA)
33 Manning Rd (01821-3925)
PHONE..................................978 663-9724
Paul Larose, *President*
John Larose, *Manager*
EMP: 45
SQ FT: 62,500
SALES (est): 7.4MM **Privately Held**
WEB: www.newenglandwheels.com
SIC: 3713 Mfg Truck/Bus Bodies

(G-8268)
NOVA BIOMEDICAL CORPORATION
39 Manning Rd (01821-3925)
PHONE..................................781 894-0800
EMP: 11
SALES (corp-wide): 309.9MM **Privately Held**
SIC: 2833 Mfg Medicinal/Botanical Products
PA: Nova Biomedical Corporation
200 Prospect St
Waltham MA 02453
781 894-0800

(G-8269)
NUVERA FUEL CELLS LLC
129 Concord Rd Bldg 1 (01821-4600)
PHONE..................................617 245-7500
Byron Hollis, *Mfg Mgr*
Ralph Grimse, *Opers Staff*
Jonathan Armstrong, *QC Mgr*
Stuart Blaine, *Engineer*
Thomas Deng, *Engineer*
▲ **EMP:** 100 **EST:** 1997
SALES (est): 57.6MM
SALES (corp-wide): 3.1B **Publicly Held**
WEB: www.nuvera.com
SIC: 1382 Oil/Gas Exploration Services
PA: Hyster-Yale Materials Handling, Inc.
5875 Landerbrook Dr # 300
Cleveland OH 44124
440 449-9600

(G-8270)
ORBOTECH INC
Also Called: Orbograph USA
44 Manning Rd Ste 1 (01821-3990)
PHONE..................................978 667-6037
Margaret Duncan, *Exec VP*
Stewart Levine, *Vice Pres*
Tim McPherson, *Vice Pres*
Carlos Prado, *Engineer*
Ravi Pathman, *Project Engr*
EMP: 12
SALES (corp-wide): 4.5B **Publicly Held**
SIC: 7372 Prepackaged Software Services
HQ: Orbotech, Inc.
44 Manning Rd Ste 1
Billerica MA 01821
978 667-6037

(G-8271)
ORPRO VISION LLC
44 Manning Rd Ste 4 (01821-3931)
PHONE..................................617 676-1101
Arnon Tuval,
EMP: 7
SALES (est): 925.7K **Privately Held**
SIC: 3827 Mfg Optical Instruments/Lenses

(G-8272)
PAREXEL INTERNATIONAL LLC
2 Federal St (01821-3559)
PHONE..................................978 313-3435
Regina Sohn, *Branch Mgr*
EMP: 15
SALES (corp-wide): 2.4B **Privately Held**
SIC: 2834 Mfg Pharmaceutical Preparations
HQ: Parexel International, Llc
8 Federal St
Billerica MA 01821

(G-8273)
PHARMALUCENCE INC (HQ)
29 Dunham Rd (01821-5729)
PHONE..................................781 275-7120
Glenn Alto, *President*
Bob Campbell, *President*
Paula Woodworth, *President*
Edward Connolly, *COO*
Patti Cummings, *Vice Pres*
◆ **EMP:** 73
SQ FT: 70,250
SALES: 19.6MM
SALES (corp-wide): 1.3B **Privately Held**
SIC: 2834 Manufacturing Pharmaceutical Preparations
PA: Sun Pharmaceutical Industries Limited
Sun House, Plot No. 201 B/1, Western Express Highway,
Mumbai MH 40006
224 324-4324

(G-8274)
PHILIPS ADVANCED METROLOGY SYS
47 Manning Rd (01821-3925)
PHONE..................................508 647-8400
David A Dripchak, *President*
Dr Christopher Jl Moore, *President*
Joseph Innamorati, *Senior VP*
Mark Heber, *Director*
EMP: 5
SALES (est): 493.6K **Privately Held**
SIC: 3674 Mfg Semiconductors/Related Devices

(G-8275)
PHOTONIC SYSTEMS INC
900 Middlesex Tpke 5-2 (01821-3929)
PHONE..................................978 670-4990
Charles Cox III, *CEO*
Edward Ackerman, *Vice Pres*
Carol Cox, *Vice Pres*
Douglas Dillon, *Vice Pres*
Joelle Prince, *Vice Pres*
EMP: 10 **EST:** 1999
SQ FT: 5,697
SALES (est): 1.3MM **Privately Held**
WEB: www.photonicsinc.com
SIC: 2298 Mfg Cordage/Twine

(G-8276)
PRECISION DYNAMICS CORPORATION
Also Called: Temtec
3 Federal St Ste 300 (01821-3500)
PHONE..................................800 528-8005
Jenny Kuo, *Buyer*
Jason Campbell, *QC Mgr*
James Gross, *Branch Mgr*
EMP: 100
SALES (corp-wide): 1.1B **Publicly Held**
SIC: 3089 3861 3699 Mfg Plastic Products Mfg Photographic Equipment/Supplies Mfg Electrical Equipment/Supplies
HQ: Precision Dynamics Corporation
25124 Sprngfeld Ct Ste 20
Valencia CA 91355
818 897-1111

(G-8277)
PRINTING & GRAPHIC SERVICES
505 Middlesex Tpke Unit 8 (01821-3579)
PHONE..................................978 667-6950
Neelam Wali, *Owner*
EMP: 3
SQ FT: 1,000
SALES (est): 210K **Privately Held**
SIC: 2752 7336 Offset Printing And Graphic Arts And Related Design

(G-8278)
PRODUCTION BASICS INC
31 Dunham Rd Ste 3 (01821-5701)
PHONE..................................617 926-8100
Adam Wisnia, *President*
Rob Desmarais, *Natl Sales Mgr*
Erica Rice, *Mktg Dir*
Ryan Southard, *Marketing Staff*
◆ **EMP:** 20
SQ FT: 40,000
SALES (est): 3.6MM **Privately Held**
WEB: www.pbasics.com
SIC: 2522 3499 2531 Mfg Office Furniture-Nonwood Mfg Misc Fabricated Metal Products Mfg Public Building Furniture

(G-8279)
PSJL CORPORATION (PA)
780 Boston Rd Ste 4 (01821-5939)
PHONE..................................978 313-2500
Peter Schofield, *President*
Jeffrey Lang, *Corp Secy*
▲ **EMP:** 60
SQ FT: 31,000
SALES (est): 67.5MM **Privately Held**
WEB: www.atronix.com
SIC: 3577 3599 5065 Mfg Computer Peripheral Equipment Mfg Industrial Machinery Whol Electronic Parts/Equipment

(G-8280)
QUALITY ENGINEERING ASSOC INC
Also Called: Q E A
755 Middlesex Tpke Ste 3 (01821-3949)
PHONE..................................978 528-2034
Ming-Kai TSE, *President*
Ananna TSE, *Treasurer*
Karen Mathiasen, *Clerk*
EMP: 15
SQ FT: 9,000

GEOGRAPHIC

SALES (est): 3MM **Privately Held**
WEB: www.qea.com
SIC: 3829 8711 Mfg Measuring/Controlling Devices Engineering Services

(G-8281)
QUANTERIX CORPORATION (PA)
900 Middlesex Tpke 1-1 (01821-3944)
PHONE....................................617 301-9400
E Kevin Hrusovsky, *Ch of Bd*
Jeff Pieri, *Business Mgr*
David C Duffy, *Senior VP*
Dawn R Mattoon, *Senior VP*
Mark T Roskey, *Senior VP*
EMP: 126
SALES: 37.6MM **Publicly Held**
SIC: 3845 Electromedical Apparatus

(G-8282)
RALPH TRAYNHAM
Also Called: Minuteman Press
258 Salem Rd Ste 10 (01821-2151)
PHONE....................................978 667-0977
Ralph Traynham, *Owner*
EMP: 4
SALES (est): 284.3K **Privately Held**
SIC: 2752 Comm Prtg Litho

(G-8283)
RAYTHEON ARABIAN SYSTEMS CO
880 Technology Park Dr (01821-4164)
PHONE....................................978 858-4547
Thomas Kennedy, *CEO*
EMP: 3 **EST:** 2007
SALES (est): 144K
SALES (corp-wide): 27B **Publicly Held**
SIC: 3679 Mfg Electronic Components
PA: Raytheon Company
870 Winter St
Waltham MA 02451
781 522-3000

(G-8284)
RAYTHEON EUROPEAN MGT SYSTEMS
880 Technology Park Dr (01821-4164)
PHONE....................................978 858-4547
Thomas Kennedy, *CEO*
EMP: 3
SALES (est): 104.4K
SALES (corp-wide): 27B **Publicly Held**
SIC: 3679 Mfg Electronic Components
PA: Raytheon Company
870 Winter St
Waltham MA 02451
781 522-3000

(G-8285)
RAYTHEON INTL SUPPORT CO
880 Technology Park Dr (01821-4164)
PHONE....................................978 858-4547
Thomas Kennedy, *CEO*
EMP: 4
SALES (est): 145K
SALES (corp-wide): 27B **Publicly Held**
SIC: 3679 Mfg Electronic Components
PA: Raytheon Company
870 Winter St
Waltham MA 02451
781 522-3000

(G-8286)
RAYTHEON KOREAN SUPPORT CO
880 Technology Park Dr (01821-4164)
PHONE....................................978 858-4547
EMP: 18
SALES (corp-wide): 27B **Publicly Held**
SIC: 3679 Mfg Electronic Components
HQ: Raytheon Korean Support Company
880 Technology Park Dr # 2
Billerica MA 01821
339 645-6111

(G-8287)
RAYTHEON MIDDLE E SYSTEMS CO
880 Technology Park Dr (01821-4164)
PHONE....................................978 858-4547
Thomas Kennedy, *CEO*
EMP: 3
SALES (est): 102.2K
SALES (corp-wide): 27B **Publicly Held**
SIC: 3679 Mfg Electronic Components
PA: Raytheon Company
870 Winter St
Waltham MA 02451
781 522-3000

(G-8288)
RAYTHEON RADAR LTD
880 Technology Park Dr (01821-4164)
PHONE....................................978 858-4547
Thomas Kennedy, *CEO*
EMP: 3
SALES (est): 103.8K
SALES (corp-wide): 27B **Publicly Held**
SIC: 3679 Mfg Electronic Components
PA: Raytheon Company
870 Winter St
Waltham MA 02451
781 522-3000

(G-8289)
RAYTHEON SUTHEAST ASIA SYSTEMS (HQ)
880 Technology Park Dr (01821-4164)
P.O. Box 2030, Andover (01810-0036)
PHONE....................................978 470-5000
William Swanson, *CEO*
Suzanne Creegan, *Project Mgr*
Paul Lessard, *Opers Mgr*
Jeffrey Heinrichs, *Safety Mgr*
Billy Guan, *Engineer*
▲ **EMP:** 32
SALES (est): 5.7MM
SALES (corp-wide): 27B **Publicly Held**
SIC: 3812 3663 3674 1629 Mfg Search/Navgatn Equip Mfg Radio/Tv Comm Equip
PA: Raytheon Company
870 Winter St
Waltham MA 02451
781 522-3000

(G-8290)
RAYTHEON TCHNICAL ADM SVCS LTD
880 Technology Park Dr (01821-4164)
PHONE....................................978 858-4547
Thomas Kennedy, *CEO*
EMP: 4
SALES (est): 119.8K
SALES (corp-wide): 27B **Publicly Held**
SIC: 3679 Mfg Electronic Components
PA: Raytheon Company
870 Winter St
Waltham MA 02451
781 522-3000

(G-8291)
RESONANCE RESEARCH INC
Also Called: R R I
31 Dunham Rd Ste 1 (01821-5701)
PHONE....................................978 671-0811
Piotr M Starewicz, *President*
Stana Mihajlovic, *Corp Secy*
Jane Punchard, *Corp Secy*
David F Hillenbrand, *Vice Pres*
Robert L Mackeen, *Vice Pres*
EMP: 20
SQ FT: 10,000
SALES (est): 4.5MM **Privately Held**
WEB: www.rricorp.com
SIC: 3826 Mfg Analytical Instruments

(G-8292)
RUBIL ASSOCIATES INC
Also Called: Spectro-Film
34 Dunham Rd (01821-5727)
PHONE....................................978 670-7192
Ruth Constant, *President*
William White, *Vice Pres*
EMP: 17 **EST:** 1969
SQ FT: 6,100
SALES (est): 1MM **Privately Held**
SIC: 3827 Manufactures Optical Filters

(G-8293)
SHAW WELDING COMPANY INC
7 Innis Dr (01821-2604)
P.O. Box 435 (01821-0435)
PHONE....................................978 667-0197
Richard Shaw, *CEO*
Courtney Powderly, *Office Admin*
EMP: 11
SQ FT: 3,500
SALES (est): 1.6MM **Privately Held**
SIC: 7692 Welding Repair

(G-8294)
SIMFER PRECISION MACHINE CO
42 Manning Rd (01821-3915)
PHONE....................................978 667-1138
Enzo Ferrara, *Partner*
Pompeo Simeone, *Partner*
EMP: 7
SQ FT: 7,500
SALES (est): 1.1MM **Privately Held**
SIC: 3599 Machine Shop

(G-8295)
SIRIUS ANALYTICAL INC
10 Cook St Ste 6 (01821-6000)
PHONE....................................978 338-5790
Brett Hughes, *President*
Fiona Watts, *Corp Secy*
EMP: 6
SALES (est): 723.7K **Privately Held**
SIC: 3826 Mfg Analytical Instruments

(G-8296)
SL MONTEVIDEO TECHNOLOGY INC
6 Enterprise Rd (01821-5735)
PHONE....................................978 667-5100
Jeff Smith, *Branch Mgr*
EMP: 40
SALES (corp-wide): 1.5B **Publicly Held**
WEB: www.cmccontrols.com
SIC: 3625 Manufacturing Relays/Industrial Controls
HQ: Sl Montevideo Technology, Inc.
8201 109th St 500
Pleasant Prairie WI 53158
320 269-5583

(G-8297)
SPIRE CORPORATION (PA)
25 Linnell Cir (01821-3928)
P.O. Box 9, Bedford (01730-0009)
PHONE....................................978 584-3958
Rodger W Lafavre, *President*
Robert S Lieberman, *CFO*
▲ **EMP:** 431
SQ FT: 144,230
SALES (est): 16MM **Publicly Held**
SIC: 3674 Mfg Semiconductors/Related Devices

(G-8298)
SST COMPONENTS INC (PA)
Also Called: Vpt Components
780 Boston Rd Ste 1 (01821-5939)
PHONE....................................978 670-7300
Joseph Benedetto, *CEO*
Alfred Patane, *President*
John Bishop, *VP Opers*
Tracey Hynes, *Human Res Mgr*
Joanne Dauteuil, *Manager*
EMP: 22
SQ FT: 30,000
SALES (est): 3.7MM **Privately Held**
SIC: 3674 7389 Mfg Semiconductors/Related Devices Business Services

(G-8299)
TANYX MEASUREMENTS INC
505 Middlesex Tpke Unit 9 (01821-3578)
PHONE....................................978 671-0183
Robert Kieser, *President*
Jerry Schulze, *Treasurer*
EMP: 30
SALES (est): 3.5MM **Privately Held**
SIC: 3694 7389 Mfg Engine Electrical Equipment Business Services

(G-8300)
TARK INC
35 Dunham Rd Ste 7 (01821-5711)
PHONE....................................978 663-8074
Al Robins, *Manager*
EMP: 16
SALES (corp-wide): 10.1MM **Privately Held**
WEB: www.tarkinc.com
SIC: 3561 Mfg Pumps/Pumping Equipment
PA: Tark, Inc.
420 Congress Park Dr
Dayton OH 45459
937 434-6766

(G-8301)
TECNAU INC (DH)
4 Suburban Park Dr (01821-3904)
PHONE....................................978 608-0356
William Carroll, *CEO*
Jeff Kewin, *President*
▲ **EMP:** 30
SQ FT: 20,000
SALES (est): 40MM **Privately Held**
WEB: www.roll-systems.com
SIC: 3554 Mfg Paper Industrial Machinery
HQ: Tecnau Ab
Langgatan 21
Ljungby 341 3
372 256-00

(G-8302)
TEL EPION INC
900 Middlesex Tpke 6-1 (01821-3929)
PHONE....................................978 436-2300
Louis Steen, *CEO*
EMP: 50
SQ FT: 11,000
SALES (est): 11.3MM **Privately Held**
WEB: www.epion.com
SIC: 3674 3081 5012 3699 Mfg Semiconductors/Dvcs Mfg Unsupport Plstc Film Whol Auto/Motor Vehicles Mfg Elec Mach/Equip/Supp Mfg Optical Instr/Lens
HQ: Tokyo Electron U.S. Holdings, Inc.
2400 Grove Blvd
Austin TX 78741
512 424-1000

(G-8303)
TELEDYNE DGITAL IMAGING US INC (HQ)
700 Technology Park Dr # 2 (01821-4153)
PHONE....................................978 670-2000
Brian Doody, *CEO*
Steve Geraghty, *Vice Pres*
Laura Farnham, *Opers Staff*
Evelyn Mountain, *Purchasing*
Brad Finney, *VP Sales*
EMP: 31
SQ FT: 46,000
SALES (est): 3.5MM
SALES (corp-wide): 2.9B **Publicly Held**
WEB: www.goipd.com
SIC: 3577 8734 8711 Mfg Computer Peripheral Equipment Testing Laboratory Engineering Services
PA: Teledyne Technologies Inc
1049 Camino Dos Rios
Thousand Oaks CA 91360
805 373-4545

(G-8304)
THERMO FISHER SCIENTIFIC INC
9 Andover Rd (01821-1915)
PHONE....................................978 667-4016
Jerry Welch, *Branch Mgr*
EMP: 22
SALES (corp-wide): 24.3B **Publicly Held**
SIC: 3826 Mfg Analytical Instruments
PA: Thermo Fisher Scientific Inc.
168 3rd Ave
Waltham MA 02451
781 622-1000

(G-8305)
THERMO SCIENTIFIC PORTABLE ANA
Also Called: Corporation Niton
900 Middlesex Tpke 8-1 (01821-3929)
PHONE....................................978 670-7460
EMP: 180
SALES (corp-wide): 16.8B **Publicly Held**
SIC: 3825 Mfg Electrical Measuring Instruments
HQ: Thermo Scientific Portable Analytical Instruments Inc.
2 Radcliff Rd
Tewksbury MA 01876
978 657-5555

(G-8306)
THOMAS HIGGINS
66 Shawsheen Rd (01821-5702)
P.O. Box 8472, Salem (01971-8472)
PHONE....................................978 930-0573
Tom Higgins, *Principal*
EMP: 3

SALES (est): 192.5K **Privately Held**
SIC: 3596 Mfg Scales/Balances-Nonlaboratory

(G-8307)
TREMCO PRODUCTS INC
Also Called: Tremco Police Products
34 Sullivan Rd Unit 17 (01821)
PHONE..................................781 275-7692
Theodore Tremblay, *President*
Mark Tremblay, *President*
Gary Tremblay, *Vice Pres*
Matt Tremblay, *Admin Sec*
EMP: 6
SALES: 1MM **Privately Held**
WEB: www.tremcopoliceproducts.com
SIC: 3714 8111 Mfg Motor Vehicle Parts/Accessories Legal Services Office

(G-8308)
VOLCANO CORPORATION
1 Fortune Dr (01821-3923)
PHONE..................................978 439-3560
EMP: 5
SALES (est): 373.7K **Privately Held**
SIC: 3845 Mfg Electromedical Equipment

(G-8309)
WHIFFLETREE CNTRY STR GIFT SP
Also Called: Whiffle Tree Candle
101 Andover Rd (01821-1932)
PHONE..................................978 663-6346
Stephen Blinn, *President*
Susan Blinn, *Vice Pres*
EMP: 8
SQ FT: 6,800
SALES (est): 874.4K **Privately Held**
WEB: www.whiffletreecandles.com
SIC: 3999 5947 Mfg Misc Products Ret Gifts/Novelties

(G-8310)
WILEVCO INC
10 Fortune Dr (01821-3996)
PHONE..................................978 667-0400
Leverett P Flint, *President*
David Marrotta, *Vice Pres*
John A Whitmore, *Vice Pres*
Putnam P Flint, *Treasurer*
Neal Hunt, *Treasurer*
▲ **EMP:** 11 **EST:** 1961
SQ FT: 16,400
SALES (est): 2.5MM **Privately Held**
WEB: www.wilevco.com
SIC: 3556 7359 2045 Mfg & Lease Mixers Applicators And Coating Equipment For The Food Industry

Blackstone
Worcester County

(G-8311)
EAST COAST FILTER CORP
61 Main St Ste 3 (01504-2215)
PHONE..................................508 883-7744
Kevin Zagrodny, *President*
Glenn Clancy, *Vice Pres*
Brian Roberts, *Vice Pres*
EMP: 5
SALES (est): 369.3K **Privately Held**
WEB: www.eastcoastfilter.com
SIC: 3569 Mfg General Industrial Machinery

(G-8312)
F W DERBYSHIRE INC
38 Main St (01504-2205)
PHONE..................................508 883-2385
Douglas Smith, *President*
Stuart Smith, *Treasurer*
Derick Smith, *Admin Sec*
EMP: 4
SQ FT: 4,000
SALES (est): 594.4K **Privately Held**
WEB: www.fwderbyshireinc.com
SIC: 3541 Mfg Machine Tools-Cutting

(G-8313)
P & R MACHINES
22 David Dr (01504-2005)
PHONE..................................508 883-8727
Ronald La Salle, *Owner*
EMP: 5
SALES (est): 387.8K **Privately Held**
SIC: 3599 Mfg Industrial Machinery

(G-8314)
POPUTEES CO
278 Lincoln St (01504-1206)
PHONE..................................401 497-6512
EMP: 3
SALES (est): 124K **Privately Held**
SIC: 2759 Commercial Printing

(G-8315)
ROLAND LE GARE
Also Called: R & R Machine
25 Rhode Island Ave (01504-1875)
PHONE..................................508 883-2869
Roland Le Gare, *Owner*
EMP: 4
SALES: 200K **Privately Held**
SIC: 3599 Mfg Industrial Machinery

Bolton
Worcester County

(G-8316)
149 MEDICAL INC
1173 Main St (01740-1208)
PHONE..................................617 410-8123
Antoniu Fantana, *President*
William Shaw, *Admin Sec*
EMP: 5
SALES (est): 198.4K **Privately Held**
SIC: 3845 3841 Mfg Electromedical Equipment Mfg Surgical/Medical Instruments

(G-8317)
BOLTON PRINTING CO
553 Wattaquadock Hill Rd (01740-1234)
P.O. Box 96 (01740-0096)
PHONE..................................978 365-4844
Betty Dedecko, *President*
John Dedecko, *Vice Pres*
EMP: 3 **EST:** 1953
SQ FT: 3,600
SALES (est): 335.9K **Privately Held**
SIC: 2752 Offset & Conversion Printing

(G-8318)
BROOMFIELD LABORATORIES INC
164 Still River Rd (01740-1073)
P.O. Box 157 (01740-0157)
PHONE..................................978 779-6600
Thomas L Broomfield, *President*
Andrew Broomfield, *Vice Pres*
Alan Tuttle, *Purchasing*
Bruce Crosby, *Engineer*
Bill Wolfe, *Electrical Engi*
EMP: 41 **EST:** 1958
SQ FT: 60,000
SALES (est): 8.4MM **Privately Held**
WEB: www.broomfieldusa.com
SIC: 3549 Mfg Metalworking Machinery

(G-8319)
HEADWALL PHOTONICS INC
580 Main St (01740-1368)
PHONE..................................978 353-4100
David Bannon, *CEO*
James Gennari, *CFO*
EMP: 60 **EST:** 1976
SQ FT: 6,250
SALES (est): 11.2MM **Privately Held**
WEB: www.headwallphotonics.com
SIC: 3827 Mfg Optical Instruments/Lenses

(G-8320)
HORIZON SALES
56 Powder Hill Rd (01740-1083)
PHONE..................................978 779-0487
EMP: 3 **EST:** 2001
SALES (est): 140K **Privately Held**
SIC: 2621 Paper Mill

(G-8321)
NASHOBA VALLEY SPIRITS LIMITED
Also Called: Nashoba Valley Winery
100 Wattaquadock Hill Rd (01740-1238)
PHONE..................................978 779-5521
Richard A Pelletier, *President*
Cindy Pelletier, *Vice Pres*
EMP: 50
SQ FT: 10,000
SALES (est): 7.2MM **Privately Held**
WEB: www.nashobawinery.com
SIC: 2084 5431 Mfg Wine

(G-8322)
NEMONIX ENGINEERING INC
580 Main St Ste 5 (01740-1369)
PHONE..................................508 393-7700
Duane P Harris, *CEO*
Daniel Bumbarger, *President*
EMP: 4
SALES (est): 609K **Privately Held**
WEB: www.nemonixengineering.com
SIC: 3577 7373 7371 Mfg Computer Peripheral Equipment Computer Systems Design Custom Computer Programing

(G-8323)
ROBERTS MACHINE AND ENGRG
42 Flanagan Rd (01740-1028)
PHONE..................................978 779-5039
Dana Roberts, *Owner*
EMP: 3
SALES: 125K **Privately Held**
WEB: www.robertsmachine.com
SIC: 3599 Mfg Industrial Machinery

(G-8324)
VMS SOFTWARE INC
580 Main St Ste 7 (01740-1369)
PHONE..................................978 451-0110
Duane P Harris, *CEO*
Eddie Orcutt, *Vice Pres*
Susan Skonetski, *Vice Pres*
Clair Grant, *Research*
John Reagan, *Engineer*
EMP: 4
SALES (est): 232.8K **Privately Held**
SIC: 7372 7371 Prepackaged Software Services Custom Computer Programing

Bondsville
Hampden County

(G-8325)
SOURCE TWO INC
7 Third St (01009)
P.O. Box 1025 (01009-1025)
PHONE..................................413 289-1251
Michael W Shields Jr, *CEO*
Linda Sheilds, *Treasurer*
◆ **EMP:** 6
SQ FT: 5,000
SALES (est): 948.6K **Privately Held**
WEB: www.sourcetwo.com
SIC: 3861 Engineering Services

Boston
Suffolk County

(G-8326)
1 BEYOND INC
Also Called: A1 Beyond Video Services
529 Main St Ste 109 (02129-1112)
PHONE..................................617 591-2200
Terry Cullen, *President*
Marion Dancy, *COO*
Rony Sebok, *Vice Pres*
Cara Shannon, *Marketing Staff*
EMP: 15
SALES (est): 3.3MM **Privately Held**
WEB: www.1beyond.com
SIC: 3861 Mfg Photographic Equipment/Supplies

(G-8327)
21ST CENTURY FOODS INC
Also Called: Twenty First Century Foods
30 Germania St Ste 2 (02130-2312)
PHONE..................................617 522-7595
Rudy Canale, *President*
Sookdei Canale, *Vice Pres*
EMP: 3
SQ FT: 2,000
SALES: 250K **Privately Held**
WEB: www.newstream.com
SIC: 2099 2084 Mfg Food Preparations Mfg Wines/Brandy/Spirits

(G-8328)
3DERM SYSTEMS INC
101 Huntington Ave # 1300 (02199-7603)
PHONE..................................617 237-6041
Elliot Swart, *Principal*
Barbara Kohler, *COO*
EMP: 6 **EST:** 2012
SALES (est): 461.7K **Privately Held**
SIC: 7372 3861 Prepackaged Software Services Mfg Photographic Equipment/Supplies

(G-8329)
3DFORTIFY INC
28 Damrell St Ste B4 (02127-3077)
PHONE..................................978 399-4075
Joshua Martin, *President*
Karlo Delos Reyes, *Corp Secy*
EMP: 7
SALES (est): 1MM **Privately Held**
SIC: 3089 Mfg Plastic Products

(G-8330)
861 CORP
Also Called: Al's Doughnuts
226 W Broadway (02127-1020)
PHONE..................................617 268-8855
Al Carney, *President*
EMP: 6
SQ FT: 5,000
SALES (est): 537.5K **Privately Held**
SIC: 2082 5182 Mfg Malt Beverages Whol Wine/Distilled Beverages

(G-8331)
A & P WOODWORKING INC
136 Bennington St (02128-1707)
PHONE..................................617 569-4664
Pietro Di Placido, *President*
EMP: 4
SQ FT: 500
SALES (est): 497.5K **Privately Held**
WEB: www.apwoodworking.com
SIC: 2431 Mfg Millwork

(G-8332)
A LOT BAKERY PRODUCTS INC
Also Called: Red-E-Mix
255 Maverick St (02128-3126)
PHONE..................................617 561-1122
Alfred L Amendola Sr, *President*
EMP: 6 **EST:** 1946
SQ FT: 3,200
SALES (est): 660.5K **Privately Held**
SIC: 2099 5149 5499 Mfg Bread Crumbs Whol & Ret Spices

(G-8333)
A&S BREWING COLLABORATIVE LLC
1 Design Center Pl # 850 (02210-2313)
PHONE..................................617 368-5000
Stacey Steinmetz, *Branch Mgr*
EMP: 3 **Publicly Held**
SIC: 2082 Mfg Malt Beverages
HQ: A&S Brewing Collaborative Llc
209 Battery St Ste 100
Burlington VT
617 368-5165

(G-8334)
ABB ENTERPRISE SOFTWARE INC
2 Oliver St (02109-4901)
PHONE..................................617 574-1130
Arun Nayar, *Branch Mgr*
EMP: 3
SALES (corp-wide): 36.7B **Privately Held**
SIC: 3674 Mfg Semiconductors/Related Devices
HQ: Abb Inc.
305 Gregson Dr
Cary NC 27511

(G-8335)
ABCORP NA INC
225 Rivermoor St Ste 225 # 225 (02132-4905)
PHONE..................................617 325-9600

Bill Brown, *CEO*
Rola Hamandi, *Senior VP*
Erik Mitterhofer, *Senior VP*
Michelle Lehouck, *Vice Pres*
Lawrence Plackman, *VP Finance*
▲ **EMP:** 300
SQ FT: 120,000
SALES (est): 99.2MM
SALES (corp-wide): 292.8MM **Privately Held**
WEB: www.arthurblank.com
SIC: 3081 5199 Mfg Unsupported Plastic Film/Sheet Whol Nondurable Goods
PA: American Banknote Corporation
1055 Washington Blvd Fl 6
Stamford CT 06901
203 941-4090

(G-8336)
ACCU-TIME SYSTEMS INC
175 Federal St Ste 1225 (02110-2221)
PHONE....860 870-5000
EMP: 3 **Privately Held**
SIC: 3579 3873 Mfg Office Machines Mfg Watches/Clocks/Parts
HQ: Accu-Time Systems, Inc.
420 Somers Rd
Ellington CT 06029
-

(G-8337)
ACQUIA INC (PA)
53 State St Ste 1101 (02109-2300)
PHONE....888 922-7842
Michael Sullivan, *CEO*
Clare Madden, *CEO*
Amy Hughes, *Partner*
Ahmed Koshok, *Business Mgr*
Stephen Reny, *COO*
EMP: 146 **EST:** 2007
SALES (est): 51.6MM **Privately Held**
SIC: 7372 Prepackaged Software Services

(G-8338)
ACS DIVISION BIOCHEMICAL TECH
42 Chauncy St Ste 10a (02111-2308)
PHONE....617 216-6144
David Roush, *Chairman*
EMP: 15
SALES (est): 666.2K **Privately Held**
SIC: 2836 Mfg Biological Products

(G-8339)
ACTNANO INC (PA)
100 Morrissey Blvd (02125-3300)
PHONE....857 333-8631
S Taymur Ahmad, *President*
James Sheridan Jr, *COO*
Bruce Acton, *Vice Pres*
Justin Kleingartner, *CTO*
William Brewer, *General Counsel*
EMP: 11
SQ FT: 2,000
SALES (est): 1.9MM **Privately Held**
SIC: 3479 Coating/Engraving Service

(G-8340)
AD PLUS INC
631 Tremont St Apt 2 (02118-1256)
PHONE....617 859-3128
Michel Mercure, *President*
EMP: 3
SQ FT: 1,200
SALES (est): 210K **Privately Held**
SIC: 2759 Printing

(G-8341)
ADVANCED CAREER TECH INC (PA)
1 International Pl 19 (02110-2602)
PHONE....508 620-5904
Andree I Fontaine Ms, *CEO*
Edward Little, *Principal*
David Lowe, *Chairman*
EMP: 30
SQ FT: 8,000
SALES (est): 8.3MM **Privately Held**
SIC: 7372 5112 8243 Data Processing School Prepackaged Software Svc Whol Stationery/Offc Sup

(G-8342)
ADVANTAGE DATA INC (PA)
1 Federal St Fl 25 (02110-2048)
P.O. Box 961210 (02196-1210)
PHONE....212 227-8870
Rene Robert, *President*
Gina Robert, *COO*
Bill Petrunik, *Vice Pres*
Srimal Sourav, *Vice Pres*
Mark McKenna, *Opers Staff*
EMP: 28
SALES (est): 4.3MM **Privately Held**
WEB: www.advantagedata.com
SIC: 7372 Software Services

(G-8343)
AGENCYPORT SOFTWARE CORP (HQ)
22 Boston Wharf Rd 10 (02210-1838)
PHONE....866 539-6623
Michael Jackowski, *President*
Allan Egbert, *President*
Judy Kauffman, *President*
Yogesh Sapre, *President*
Matt Foster, *CFO*
EMP: 60 **EST:** 2000
SALES (est): 16MM
SALES (corp-wide): 21MM **Privately Held**
WEB: www.agencyport.com
SIC: 7372 Prepackaged Software Services
PA: Duck Creek Technologies Llc
22 Boston Wharf Rd Fl 10
Boston MA 02210
857 239-5709

(G-8344)
AGILE DEVICES INC
28 Damrell St Ste 101 (02127-2775)
PHONE....617 416-5495
Benjamin Merewitz, *Principal*
Yuyin Chen, *Principal*
Vyas Ramanan, *Principal*
Suresh Reddy, *Principal*
Leo Tsai, *Principal*
EMP: 5
SALES (est): 376K **Privately Held**
SIC: 3841 Mfg Surgical/Medical Instruments

(G-8345)
AIRWORKS SOLUTIONS INC
180 Canal St Ste 303 (02114-1804)
PHONE....857 990-1060
David Morczinek, *CEO*
Adam Kersnowski, *COO*
EMP: 13
SQ FT: 900
SALES (est): 612.4K **Privately Held**
SIC: 7372 Prepackaged Software Services Business Services

(G-8346)
AISLEBUYER LLLC
321 Summer St Fl 8 (02210-1725)
PHONE....617 606-7062
Andrew Paradise,
EMP: 15
SALES (est): 819.4K
SALES (corp-wide): 6.7B **Publicly Held**
SIC: 7372 Prepackaged Software Services
PA: Intuit Inc.
2700 Coast Ave
Mountain View CA 94043
650 944-6000

(G-8347)
AKCEA THERAPEUTICS INC (HQ)
22 Boston Wharf Rd Fl 9 (02210-3032)
PHONE....617 207-0202
Damien McDevitt, *CEO*
Maura Bullock, *Vice Pres*
Kathleen Gallagher, *Vice Pres*
Joshua Patterson, *Vice Pres*
Philip Piscitelli, *Opers Staff*
EMP: 100
SQ FT: 30,175
SALES: 64.8MM
SALES (corp-wide): 599.6MM **Publicly Held**
SIC: 2834 8731 Pharmaceutical Preparations Biological Research
PA: Ionis Pharmaceuticals, Inc.
2855 Gazelle Ct
Carlsbad CA 92010
760 931-9200

(G-8348)
AKUMO SOFTWARE INC
35 Channel Ctr St # 405 (02210-3412)
PHONE....617 466-9818
Suresh Madhu, *President*
EMP: 10
SALES: 200K **Privately Held**
SIC: 7372 Prepackaged Software Services

(G-8349)
ALAN W LEAVITT COMPANY
Also Called: Leavitt Jewelers
333 Washington St Ste 328 (02108-5175)
PHONE....617 338-9335
Alan W Leavitt, *Owner*
EMP: 6
SQ FT: 686
SALES: 295K **Privately Held**
SIC: 3911 Mfg Precious Metal Jewelry

(G-8350)
ALBERTO VASALLO JR
Also Called: Caribe Communications
175 Wm F Mcclellan Hwy (02128-1185)
PHONE....617 522-5060
Alberto Vasallo Jr, *Owner*
Mximo Torres, *Editor*
EMP: 15
SALES (est): 694.9K **Privately Held**
WEB: www.elmundoboston.com
SIC: 2711 Newspapers-Publishing/Printing

(G-8351)
ALBIREO PHARMA INC
10 Post Office Sq 500s (02109-4624)
PHONE....857 415-4774
EMP: 6 **EST:** 2003
SALES (est): 446K **Privately Held**
SIC: 2834 Mfg Pharmaceutical Preparations

(G-8352)
ALBIREO PHARMA INC (PA)
10 Post Office Sq Ste 502 (02109-4603)
PHONE....857 254-5555
David Chiswell, *Ch of Bd*
Ronald H W Cooper, *President*
Simon N R Harford, *CFO*
Simon Harford, *CFO*
Patrick T Horn, *Chief Mktg Ofcr*
EMP: 22
SQ FT: 5,116
SALES: 12.7MM **Publicly Held**
WEB: www.biodelinc.com
SIC: 2834 Mfg Pharmaceutical Preparations

(G-8353)
ALEXION PHARMACEUTICALS INC (PA)
121 Seaport Blvd (02210-2050)
PHONE....475 230-2596
Ludwig N Hantson, *CEO*
David R Brennan, *Ch of Bd*
Ellen Chiniara, *Exec VP*
John Orloff, *Exec VP*
Aradhana Sarin, *CFO*
EMP: 186
SQ FT: 150,000
SALES: 4.1B **Publicly Held**
WEB: www.alexionpharm.com
SIC: 2834 8733 Pharmaceutical Preparations & Medical Research

(G-8354)
ALEXIS BITTAR LLC
130 Newbury St (02116-2904)
PHONE....617 236-0505
Guy Sommerhalder, *Principal*
EMP: 4
SALES (est): 219.8K **Privately Held**
SIC: 3911 5944 Mfg Precious Metal Jewelry Ret Jewelry

(G-8355)
ALIGNABLE INC
205 Portland St Ste 500 (02114-1708)
PHONE....978 376-5852
Eric Groves, *President*
Venkat Krishnamurthy, *COO*
Caitlin Kullberg, *Manager*
EMP: 10
SALES (est): 573.2K **Privately Held**
SIC: 7372 Prepackaged Software Services

(G-8356)
ALIVIA CAPITAL LLC
Also Called: Alivia Technology
100 Cambridge St Ste 1400 (02114-2545)
PHONE....781 569-5212
Paul McLaughlin, *Branch Mgr*
EMP: 6 **Privately Held**
SIC: 7372 Prepackaged Software Services
PA: Alivia Capital, Llc
400 Tradecenter Ste 5900
Woburn MA 01801
-

(G-8357)
ALKALOL COMPANY
580 Harrison Ave Ste 400 (02118-2639)
PHONE....617 304-3668
James P Whitters III, *CEO*
James P Whitters IV, *Vice Pres*
EMP: 3
SQ FT: 250
SALES (est): 300K **Privately Held**
WEB: www.alkalolcompany.com
SIC: 2834 Mfg Pharmaceutical Preparations

(G-8358)
AMCS GROUP INC
179 Lincoln St Lbby (02111-2410)
P.O. Box 98, Oxford PA (19363-0098)
PHONE....610 932-4006
Jimmy Martin, *CEO*
Kevin Yake, *Vice Pres*
EMP: 23 **Privately Held**
SIC: 7372 Prepackaged Software Services
PA: Amcs Nominees Limited
Fanningstown
Limerick
-

(G-8359)
AMERICAN CRAFT BREWERY LLC (DH)
1 Design Center Pl # 850 (02210-2313)
PHONE....617 368-5000
William F Urich, *CFO*
Kathleen H Wade, *Admin Sec*
EMP: 4
SALES (est): 40.2MM **Publicly Held**
SIC: 2082 Mfg Malt Beverages
HQ: Boston Beer Corporation
1 Design Center Pl # 850
Boston MA 02210
617 368-5000

(G-8360)
AMERICAN CRANE AND HOIST CORP
Also Called: Bellamy-Robie
1234 Washington St (02118-2109)
PHONE....617 482-8383
Arthur Leon, *President*
Robert C Carmichael, *Vice Pres*
Karen Chan, *Director*
James Leon, *Admin Sec*
▲ **EMP:** 112
SQ FT: 80,000
SALES (est): 28.4MM **Privately Held**
WEB: www.ac-h.com
SIC: 3536 3531 Mfg Hoist/Crane/Monorail Mfg Construction Mach

(G-8361)
AMERICAN MTEOROLOGICAL SOC INC (PA)
Also Called: AMS
45 Beacon St (02108-3693)
PHONE....617 227-2425
Josh Cingranelli, *Vice Pres*
David Cook, *Vice Pres*
Charles Paxton, *Vice Pres*
David Rahn, *Vice Pres*
Joseph Roy, *Vice Pres*
EMP: 52
SQ FT: 14,000
SALES: 16.7MM **Privately Held**
SIC: 2721 8621 Periodicals-Publishing/Printing Professional Organization

(G-8362)
AMERICAN NUT & CHOCOLATE INC
121 Newmarket Sq (02118-2603)
PHONE.....617 427-1510
Robert Novac, *President*
EMP: 3 **EST:** 1930
SQ FT: 16,000
SALES (est): 330K **Privately Held**
SIC: 2068 2034 Mfg Nuts & Dried Fruit

(G-8363)
AMERICAN WELL CORPORATION
Also Called: Amwell
75 State St Fl 26 (02109-1827)
PHONE.....617 204-3500
Roy Schoenberg, *CEO*
Danielle Russella, *President*
Ido Schoenberg, *Chairman*
Mike Earley, *Vice Pres*
Jon Freshman, *Vice Pres*
EMP: 300
SQ FT: 25,000
SALES (est): 47.5MM **Privately Held**
WEB: www.americanwell.com
SIC: 7372 5045 Prepackaged Software Services Whol Computers/Peripherals

(G-8364)
AMEX INC
256 Marginal St Ste 3 (02128-2800)
PHONE.....617 569-5630
John Flanagan, *President*
Paul Flanagan, *Vice Pres*
Valerie Fitzpatrick, *Human Resources*
EMP: 30
SQ FT: 2,500
SALES (est): 4.6MM **Privately Held**
SIC: 3479 Coating/Engraving Service

(G-8365)
AMPLITUDE LASER INC
50 Milk St Fl 16 (02109-5002)
PHONE.....617 401-2195
Eric Mottay, *President*
EMP: 3
SALES (est): 493K **Privately Held**
SIC: 3827 Mfg Optical Instruments/Lenses

(G-8366)
ANDREW T JOHNSON COMPANY INC (PA)
Also Called: Wales Copy Center
15 Tremont Pl (02108-4096)
PHONE.....617 742-1610
Robert Leslie, *President*
Warren K Leslie, *President*
Helene Gerstein, *Treasurer*
EMP: 27 **EST:** 1938
SQ FT: 15,000
SALES (est): 3.7MM **Privately Held**
WEB: www.andrewtjohnson.com
SIC: 2791 2789 2752 7334 Typesetting Services Bookbinding/Related Work Lithographic Coml Print Photocopying Service

(G-8367)
ANTEC (USA) LLC
Also Called: Antec Scientific USA
1 Boston Pl Fl 26 (02108-4407)
PHONE.....888 572-0012
Jean-Pierre Chervet,
Donna Marie Tarabbio, *Administration*
Martin Eysberg,
Nico Reinhoud,
EMP: 9
SALES: 350K **Privately Held**
SIC: 3826 Mfg Analytical Instruments

(G-8368)
APIFIA INC (PA)
Also Called: Mavrck
200 State St Mrktplace Ct (02109)
PHONE.....585 506-2787
Lyle Stevens, *President*
Ryan Donohue, *Senior Mgr*
Sean Naegeli, *Admin Sec*
EMP: 25
SALES (est): 3.8MM **Privately Held**
SIC: 3993 7372 Mfg Signs/Advertising Specialties Prepackaged Software Services

(G-8369)
APPNETA INC (PA)
285 Summer St Fl 4 (02210-1518)
PHONE.....781 235-2470
Matt Stevens, *CEO*
Jim Melvin, *CEO*
Jack Sweeney, *Ch of Bd*
Mark Riendeau, *Senior VP*
Michael Hustler, *Vice Pres*
EMP: 21
SALES (est): 20.6MM **Privately Held**
SIC: 7372 Custom Computer Programing

(G-8370)
APREA (US) INC
Also Called: Aprea Therapeutics
535 Boylston St (02116-3720)
PHONE.....857 239-9072
Christian S Schade, *President*
Scott M Rocklage, *Chairman*
Johan Christenson, *Director*
Jonathan Hepple, *Director*
Guido Magni, *Director*
EMP: 4
SALES (est): 323.2K **Privately Held**
SIC: 2834 Mfg Pharmaceutical Preparations

(G-8371)
APREA THERAPEUTICS INC
535 Boylston St (02116-3720)
PHONE.....617 463-9385
Scott M Rocklage, *Ch of Bd*
Christian S Schade, *President*
Lars Abrahmsen, *Senior VP*
Gregory A Korbel, *Vice Pres*
Scott M Coiante, *CFO*
EMP: 14
SQ FT: 2,295
SALES (est): 732.7K **Privately Held**
SIC: 2834 Pharmaceutical Preparations

(G-8372)
ARATANA THERAPEUTICS INC
200 Clarendon St Fl 54 (02116-5021)
PHONE.....617 425-9226
EMP: 5
SALES (corp-wide): 3B **Publicly Held**
SIC: 2834 Mfg Pharmaceutical Preparations
HQ: Aratana Therapeutics, Inc.
11400 Tomahawk Creek Pkwy # 340
Leawood KS 66211
913 353-1000

(G-8373)
ARCHER ROOSE INC
Also Called: Archer Roose Wine
21 Drydock Ave (02210-2384)
PHONE.....646 283-4152
Marian Leitner,
David Waldman,
◆ **EMP:** 4 **EST:** 2014
SALES (est): 450K **Privately Held**
SIC: 2084 Mfg Wines/Brandy/Spirits

(G-8374)
ARCHITECTURAL ILLUSIONS
300 Summer St Apt 11 (02210-1113)
PHONE.....617 338-8118
Benjamin Cheung, *Owner*
EMP: 4
SQ FT: 1,332
SALES (est): 280.1K **Privately Held**
SIC: 3999 Mfg Misc Products

(G-8375)
ARION JRNL OF HMNTIES CLASSICS
621 Commonwealth Ave Fl 4 (02215-1605)
PHONE.....617 353-6480
Herb Golder, *Publisher*
Nicholas Poburko, *Manager*
Herbert Golder, *Exec Dir*
EMP: 3
SALES: 26.8K **Privately Held**
SIC: 2711 Newspapers-Publishing/Printing

(G-8376)
ART NEW ENGLAND MAGAZINE
560 Harrison Ave (02118-2436)
PHONE.....617 259-1040
EMP: 9
SQ FT: 1,100
SALES (est): 590K **Privately Held**
WEB: www.artnewengland.com
SIC: 2721 7389 Magazine Publisher & Lecture Bureau For Visual Arts

(G-8377)
ASKCODY INC
745 Atlantic Ave Ste 100 (02111-2735)
PHONE.....617 455-2075
Steffen Moerch, *President*
EMP: 4
SALES (est): 91.3K
SALES (corp-wide): 680.2K **Privately Held**
SIC: 7372 Prepackaged Software Services
PA: Askcody Aps
Gasvarksvej 30d
Aalborg
981 310-98

(G-8378)
ATC INFORMATION INC
85 E India Row Apt 16c (02110-3397)
PHONE.....617 723-7030
EMP: 3
SALES: 100K **Privately Held**
SIC: 2721 Periodicals-Publishing/Printing

(G-8379)
ATC PONDEROSA B-I LLC
116 Huntington Ave (02116-5749)
PHONE.....617 375-7500
James Taiclet, *CEO*
Jacob Mucha, *Manager*
EMP: 3
SALES (est): 106.3K **Publicly Held**
SIC: 3663 Mfg Radio/Tv Communication Equipment
PA: American Tower Corporation
116 Huntington Ave # 1100
Boston MA 02116

(G-8380)
ATC PONDEROSA K LLC
116 Huntington Ave (02116-5749)
PHONE.....617 375-7500
James Tacilet, *CEO*
James Mucha, *Manager*
EMP: 3
SALES (est): 128.9K **Publicly Held**
SIC: 3663 Mfg Radio/Tv Communication Equipment
PA: American Tower Corporation
116 Huntington Ave # 1100
Boston MA 02116

(G-8381)
ATIIM INC
399 Boylston St Fl 6 (02116-3325)
PHONE.....800 735-4071
Kyle Silberbauer, *CEO*
EMP: 10
SALES (est): 877K
SALES (corp-wide): 177.9MM **Privately Held**
SIC: 7372 Prepackaged Software Services
PA: Workfront, Inc.
3301 N Thanksgiving Way
Lehi UT 84043
801 373-3266

(G-8382)
ATLANTIC POWER GP INC
200 Clarendon St Ste 2502 (02116-5096)
PHONE.....617 977-2400
EMP: 3
SALES (est): 121.3K **Privately Held**
SIC: 3621 Mfg Motors/Generators

(G-8383)
ATLAS DEVICES LLC
56 Roland St Ste 114 (02129-1233)
PHONE.....617 415-1657
Eric Vandyke, *Engineer*
Siri Belton, *Design Engr*
Loretta Gaudet, *Controller*
Steve Stegich, *Sales Staff*
Bryan Schmid, *Mng Member*
EMP: 5
SALES (est): 1.4MM **Privately Held**
SIC: 3674 7372 7389 Mfg Semiconductors/Related Devices Prepackaged Software Services

(G-8384)
ATLAS GLOBAL LTG SOLUTIONS INC (PA)
338 Commercial St (02109-1110)
PHONE.....617 304-3264
Anthony D' Amore, *President*
Howard Sterling, *Vice Pres*
◆ **EMP:** 5
SQ FT: 2,500
SALES (est): 1.1MM **Privately Held**
SIC: 3229 Mfg Pressed/Blown Glass

(G-8385)
ATTIVIO INC
100 Summer St Ste 3150 (02110-2106)
PHONE.....857 226-5040
Stephen Baker, *CEO*
Peter Lee, *Ch of Bd*
Alan Cooke, *CFO*
Will Johnson, *CTO*
EMP: 100
SQ FT: 5,600
SALES: 17MM **Privately Held**
WEB: www.attivio.com
SIC: 7372 Prepackaged Software Services

GEOGRAPHIC

(G-8386)
AU SOLEIL
711 Boylston St Ste 5 (02116-2616)
PHONE.....617 535-6040
Frank McClelland, *Owner*
EMP: 3
SALES (est): 144.7K **Privately Held**
SIC: 2032 Mfg Canned Specialties

(G-8387)
B N M PRINTING & PROMOTION
Also Called: Proforma Printing & Promotion
71 Commercial St Ste 304 (02109-1320)
PHONE.....617 464-1120
Barry Resnick, *President*
Bill Resnick, *President*
Mark Resnick, *President*
Coleen Resnick, *Treasurer*
Jane McMorrow, *Admin Sec*
EMP: 5
SALES (est): 930.2K **Privately Held**
SIC: 2752 Lithographic Commercial Printing

(G-8388)
BAKERY TO GO INC
Also Called: East Meets West
314 Shawmut Ave (02118-2190)
PHONE.....617 482-1015
Scott Popkowski, *President*
EMP: 8
SQ FT: 1,000
SALES (est): 520K **Privately Held**
SIC: 2051 5812 Mfg Bread/Related Products Eating Place

(G-8389)
BALANCETEK
19 Joy St (02114-4143)
PHONE.....617 320-4340
Conrad Wall III, *Principal*
EMP: 3
SALES (est): 140.5K **Privately Held**
SIC: 3845 Mfg Electromedical Equipment

(G-8390)
BAMBOO ROSE LLC
98 N Washington St (02114-1918)
PHONE.....857 284-4360
Susan Welch, *CEO*
EMP: 6 **Privately Held**
SIC: 7372 Prepackaged Software Services
PA: Bamboo Rose Llc
17 Rogers St
Gloucester MA 01930

(G-8391)
BANCWARE INC (DH)
100 High St Fl 19 (02110-2321)
PHONE.....617 542-2800
Terence Faherty, *CEO*
Terence F Faherty, *CEO*
EMP: 65
SALES (est): 4.6MM
SALES (corp-wide): 8.4B **Publicly Held**
WEB: www.bancware.com
SIC: 7372 Prepackaged Software Services

HQ: Fis Data Systems Inc.
200 Campus Dr
Collegeville PA 19426
484 582-2000

(G-8392)
BARMAKIAN BROTHERS LTD PARTNR
333 Washington St Ste 701 (02108-5191)
PHONE..................................617 227-3724
ARA Barmakian, *Partner*
Adam Barmakian, *Partner*
Diran Barmakian, *Partner*
Vahan Barmakian, *Partner*
Julie Poirier, *Sales Associate*
EMP: 50 **EST:** 1910
SQ FT: 15,000
SALES (est): 8.5MM **Privately Held**
WEB: www.barmakian.com
SIC: 3911 5944 Mfg Precious Metal Jewelry Ret Jewelry

(G-8393)
BAY STATE PARTITION & FIX CO
37 Antwerp St (02135-1312)
PHONE..................................617 782-1113
Charlie Romneos, *CEO*
Charles Romneos, *President*
EMP: 4
SQ FT: 12,000
SALES (est): 487.3K **Privately Held**
SIC: 2431 Mfg Millwork

(G-8394)
BB WALPOLE LIQUIDATION NH INC
220 Clarendon St (02116-3709)
PHONE..................................617 303-0113
EMP: 6
SALES (est): 525.8K **Privately Held**
SIC: 2064 Mfg Candy/Confectionery
PA: Bb Walpole Liquidation Nh, Inc.
47 Main St Unit 1
Walpole NH 03608

(G-8395)
BEACON HILL CHOCOLATES
91 Charles St Ste 1 (02114-4642)
PHONE..................................617 725-1900
Paula Noia-Barth, *Principal*
EMP: 3
SALES: 640K **Privately Held**
WEB: www.beaconhillchocolates.com
SIC: 2066 Ret Candy/Confectionery

(G-8396)
BEAGLE LEARNING INC
281 Summer St Fl 2 (02210-1579)
PHONE..................................617 784-3817
Turner Bohlen, *CEO*
Linda Elkins-Tanton, *Co-Owner*
EMP: 5 **EST:** 2016
SALES (est): 204.3K **Privately Held**
SIC: 7372 7389 Prepackaged Software Services Business Serv Non-Commercial Site

(G-8397)
BEANSTOX INC
60 State St Ste 700 (02109-1894)
PHONE..................................617 878-2102
Louise Anne Poirier, *Treasurer*
EMP: 3
SALES: 300K **Privately Held**
SIC: 7372 Prepackaged Software Services

(G-8398)
BEDFORD FREEMAN & WORTH
75 Arlington St Fl 8 (02116-3974)
PHONE..................................617 426-7440
Charles Christensen, *Manager*
EMP: 100
SALES (corp-wide): 1.6B **Privately Held**
WEB: www.bfwpub.com
SIC: 2731 Books-Publishing/Printing
HQ: Bedford, Freeman & Worth Publishing Group, Llc
1 New York Plz Ste 4500
New York NY 10004
212 576-9400

(G-8399)
BEHAVIORAL RESEARCH TOOLS
191 W Canton St (02116-5972)
P.O. Box 333, East Burke VT (05832-0333)
PHONE..................................802 578-4874
Conrad Hertz, *Principal*
EMP: 3
SALES (est): 174.8K **Privately Held**
SIC: 3826 Mfg Analytical Instruments

(G-8400)
BEL LEGACY CORPORATION
84 State St Fl 11 (02109-2202)
PHONE..................................508 923-5000
Louis A Di Corpo, *Ch of Bd*
David A Brookfield, *President*
Robert P Bishop, *Vice Pres*
Shawn Adams, *Purchasing*
Tracey Perkins, *Purchasing*
▼ **EMP:** 184 **EST:** 1947
SALES (est): 44.4MM **Privately Held**
WEB: www.brookfieldengineering.com
SIC: 3826 3823 Mfg Analytical Instruments Mfg Process Control Instruments

(G-8401)
BENTLEY MILLS INC
27 Drydock Ave Ste 7 (02210-2383)
PHONE..................................617 439-0405
Edmund Chang, *Branch Mgr*
EMP: 4
SALES (corp-wide): 222.2MM **Privately Held**
SIC: 2273 Mfg Carpets/Rugs
PA: Bentley Mills, Inc.
14641 Don Julian Rd
City Of Industry CA 91746
626 333-4585

(G-8402)
BERRY TWIST
200 Faneuil Hall Mkt Pl (02109)
PHONE..................................857 362-7455
Sergio Gonsalves, *Owner*
EMP: 7
SALES (est): 488.6K **Privately Held**
SIC: 2024 Mfg Ice Cream/Frozen Desert

(G-8403)
BETA BIONICS INC
8 Saint Marys St Ste 936 (02215-2421)
PHONE..................................949 293-2076
Edward Damiano, *CEO*
Edward Raskin, *Vice Pres*
EMP: 17
SQ FT: 3,000
SALES (est): 292.5K **Privately Held**
SIC: 3845 Mfg Electromedical Equipment

(G-8404)
BETHCARE INC
Also Called: Benevolent Tech For Hlth
110 Chauncy St (02111-1720)
P.O. Box 425871, Cambridge (02142-0016)
PHONE..................................617 997-1069
Ramin Abrishamian, *President*
EMP: 4
SQ FT: 1,000
SALES (est): 284.7K **Privately Held**
SIC: 3842 Mfg Surgical Appliances/Supplies

(G-8405)
BFI PRINT COMMUNICATIONS INC (PA)
Also Called: Fastforms
255 State St Fl 7 (02109-2618)
PHONE..................................781 447-1199
Donna Anderson, *President*
Arthur Graham Jr, *President*
EMP: 57
SALES (est): 7MM **Privately Held**
WEB: www.bfiprint.com
SIC: 2761 Mfg Manifold Business Forms

(G-8406)
BICON LLC (PA)
501 Arborway (02130-3663)
PHONE..................................617 524-4443
Barbara Moore, *Human Resources*
Vincent Morgan, *Mng Member*
▲ **EMP:** 45
SQ FT: 2,000
SALES (est): 10MM **Privately Held**
SIC: 3843 Mfg Dental Equipment/Supplies

(G-8407)
BIENA LLC
Also Called: Biena Foods
119 Braintree St Ste 409 (02134-1642)
P.O. Box 3031 (02241-3031)
PHONE..................................617 202-5210
Poorvi Patodia, *Mng Member*
Deanna Maheras, *Director*
Annette Rubin,
EMP: 3
SQ FT: 800
SALES (est): 644.1K **Privately Held**
SIC: 2041 5411 Mfg Flour/Grain Mill Prooducts Ret Groceries

(G-8408)
BIO DEFENSE CORPORATION
12 Channel St Ste 9 (02210-2323)
PHONE..................................617 778-1800
Michael Lu, *CEO*
Jennar Jirompini, *CEO*
EMP: 12
SALES (est): 1.3MM **Privately Held**
WEB: www.biodf.com
SIC: 3579 Mfg Office Machines

(G-8409)
BIO ENERGY INC
739 Washington St (02124-4411)
PHONE..................................617 822-1220
Joseph M Pizziferri, *President*
EMP: 3 **EST:** 2010
SALES (est): 184K **Privately Held**
SIC: 2869 Mfg Industrial Organic Chemicals

(G-8410)
BIOBRIGHT LLC (PA)
2 Park Plz Ste 605 (02116-3947)
PHONE..................................617 444-9007
Edward Chung, *Chief Mktg Ofcr*
Adam Marblestone,
Charles Fracchia,
EMP: 8
SALES (est): 1MM **Privately Held**
SIC: 7372 Prepackaged Software Services

(G-8411)
BIOMERIEUX INC
201 Wshington St Ste 4030 (02108)
PHONE..................................617 879-8000
EMP: 3
SALES (corp-wide): 7.5MM **Privately Held**
SIC: 3845 8071 3841 3826 Mfg Electromedical Equip Medical Laboratory Mfg Surgical/Med Instr Mfg Analytical Instr
HQ: Biomerieux, Inc.
100 Rodolphe St
Durham NC 27712
919 620-2000

(G-8412)
BLAKE PRESS INC
11 Beacon St Bsmt (02108-3015)
PHONE..................................617 742-8700
EMP: 5 **EST:** 1931
SQ FT: 3,000
SALES (est): 359.1K **Privately Held**
SIC: 2752 2759 Lithographic Commercial Printing Commercial Printing

(G-8413)
BLANCHE P FIELD LLC
1 Design Center Pl # 336 (02210-2313)
PHONE..................................617 423-0714
Wayne Garabee, *Vice Pres*
Steve Walk, *Finance*
Kevin Todd, *Consultant*
Stephen G Walk,
EMP: 35
SQ FT: 3,000
SALES (est): 3.5MM **Privately Held**
WEB: www.blanchefield.com
SIC: 3999 5023 7629 3645 Mfg Misc Products Whol Homefurnishings Electrical Repair Mfg Residentl Light Fixt

(G-8414)
BLITZ FOODS LLC
75 Park Plz Ste 3 (02116-3934)
PHONE..................................617 243-7446
Andre Wood, *Principal*
EMP: 3 **EST:** 2011
SALES (est): 220.6K **Privately Held**
SIC: 2099 Mfg Food Preparations

(G-8415)
BLUE ATLANTIC FABRICATORS LLC
256 Marginal St Ste 2 (02128-2800)
PHONE..................................617 874-8503
Deborah Driscoll, *Office Mgr*
Frederick L Nolan III,
EMP: 10
SALES (est): 523.3K **Privately Held**
SIC: 3441 Structural Metal Fabrication

(G-8416)
BLUECONIC INC
207 South St Ste 671 (02111-2723)
PHONE..................................888 440-2583
Bart Heilbron, *CEO*
Michele Szabocsik, *Vice Pres*
Kieran Hillery, *Accounts Exec*
Kevin Elliot, *Director*
Dana Fuller, *Executive*
EMP: 22 **EST:** 2014
SQ FT: 4,900
SALES: 2MM
SALES (corp-wide): 10.5MM **Privately Held**
SIC: 7372 Prepackaged Software Services
PA: Blueconic Holding, Inc.
179 Lincoln St Ste 501
Boston MA 02111
888 440-2583

(G-8417)
BLUEDAY INC
50 Federal St Fl 2 (02110-2509)
PHONE..................................978 461-4500
Graeme Grant, *CEO*
EMP: 4
SALES (est): 122.2K **Privately Held**
SIC: 7372 Prepackaged Software Services

(G-8418)
BOC GASES
60 State St (02109-1800)
PHONE..................................617 878-2090
Wayne Koch, *Vice Pres*
EMP: 3
SALES (est): 166.1K **Privately Held**
SIC: 2813 Mfg Industrial Gases

(G-8419)
BOMBARDIER SERVICES CORP
Also Called: Bombardier Mass Transit
2 Frontage Rd (02118-2803)
PHONE..................................617 464-0323
Phil Pronchuk, *Branch Mgr*
EMP: 3
SALES (corp-wide): 16.2B **Privately Held**
SIC: 3743 Mfg Railroad Equipment
HQ: Bombardier Services Corp
2400 Aviation Way
Bridgeport WV 26330
304 842-6300

(G-8420)
BONE BIOLOGICS CORPORATION (PA)
321 Columbus Ave Ste 3fl (02116-5168)
PHONE..................................732 661-2224
Stephen R La Neve, *President*
Jeffrey Frelick, *COO*
Catherine Doll, *CFO*
William J Treat, *CTO*
EMP: 6
SALES (est): 1MM **Privately Held**
SIC: 3826 Mfg Analytical Instruments

(G-8421)
BOSTON BAKING INC
101 Sprague St Ste 3 (02136-2174)
PHONE..................................617 364-6900
Julee Robey Boschetto, *President*
Kristen M Boschetto, *Admin Sec*
EMP: 28
SALES (est): 5.1MM **Privately Held**
SIC: 2051 Mfg Bread/Related Products

(G-8422)
BOSTON BEER COMPANY INC
30 Germania St Ste 1 (02130-2312)
PHONE..................................617 368-5080
David Grinnell, *Manager*

EMP: 10 **Publicly Held**
SIC: 2082 Mfg Malt Beverages
PA: The Boston Beer Company Inc
1 Design Center Pl # 850
Boston MA 02210

(G-8423)
BOSTON BEER COMPANY INC (PA)
1 Design Center Pl # 850 (02210-2300)
PHONE..................................617 368-5000
C James Koch, *Ch of Bd*
David A Burwick, *President*
George J Pastran, *President*
Samuel A Calagione III, *Founder*
Quincy B Troupe, *Senior VP*
◆ **EMP:** 277
SQ FT: 54,200
SALES: 995.6MM **Publicly Held**
SIC: 2082 Mfg Malt Beverages

(G-8424)
BOSTON BEER CORPORATION (DH)
1 Design Center Pl # 850 (02210-2300)
PHONE..................................617 368-5000
William F Urich, *CFO*
Kathleen H Wade, *Admin Sec*
EMP: 150
SALES (est): 194.7MM **Publicly Held**
SIC: 2082 Mfg Malt Beverages

(G-8425)
BOSTON BLACKSMITH INC
46 Business St (02136-2107)
P.O. Box 567, Foxboro (02035-0567)
PHONE..................................617 364-1499
EMP: 4 **EST:** 1967
SALES: 374.3K **Privately Held**
WEB: www.bostonblacksmith.com
SIC: 3446 Mfg Rod Iron Railings

(G-8426)
BOSTON BUSINESS JOURNAL INC
70 Franklin St Ste 800 (02110-1313)
PHONE..................................617 330-1000
Mike Olivieri, *President*
Gale Murray, *Natl Sales Mgr*
Dana Peterson, *Sales Staff*
Conrad Paquette, *Advt Staff*
Craig Douglas, *Assoc Editor*
EMP: 41
SQ FT: 9,500
SALES (est): 2.5MM
SALES (corp-wide): 1.3B **Privately Held**
SIC: 2711 Publish Weekly Business Newspaper
HQ: American City Business Journals, Inc.
120 W Morehead St Ste 400
Charlotte NC 28202
704 973-1000

(G-8427)
BOSTON BUSINESS PRINTING INC
115 Broad St Bsmt (02110-3061)
PHONE..................................617 482-7955
Sheryl Read, *President*
William Joseph, *Vice Pres*
▲ **EMP:** 10
SQ FT: 6,000
SALES: 3.5MM **Privately Held**
WEB: www.bbpinc.net
SIC: 2752 7334 Lithographic Commercial Printing Photocopying Services

(G-8428)
BOSTON CHIPYARD THE INC
257 Faneuil Hall Pl (02109)
PHONE..................................617 742-9537
Dana Joly, *General Mgr*
EMP: 15
SALES (est): 1.4MM
SALES (corp-wide): 1MM **Privately Held**
SIC: 2052 5461 5149 Mfg Cookies & Crackers Retail Bakery Whol Groceries
PA: Boston Chipyard, The Inc
100 W Chapman Ave
Orange CA 92866
714 547-0262

(G-8429)
BOSTON COMMERCE INC
119 Braintree St Ste 510 (02134-1640)
PHONE..................................617 782-8998
Richard Rogers, *President*
EMP: 6
SALES (est): 135.3K **Privately Held**
SIC: 7372 Prepackaged Software Services

(G-8430)
BOSTON FORGING & WELDING CORP
336 Border St (02128-2402)
PHONE..................................617 567-2300
Ronald Giovanni, *President*
EMP: 4
SQ FT: 12,000
SALES (est): 581.8K **Privately Held**
SIC: 7692 3446 3444 3441 Welding Repair Mfg Architectural Mtlwrk Mfg Sheet Metalwork Structural Metal Fabrctn

(G-8431)
BOSTON GLOBE LLC
53 State St Fl 23 (02109-2820)
PHONE..................................617 929-2684
Michael Sheehan, *CEO*
Stacey Myers, *Editor*
James Levy, *CFO*
Jennifer Putzbach, *Finance*
Heather Wedlake, *Finance*
EMP: 2200 **EST:** 2013
SALES (est): 176.4MM
SALES (corp-wide): 453.3MM **Privately Held**
SIC: 2711 Newspapers-Publishing/Printing
PA: Ne Media Group Inc.
1 Exchange Pl Ste 201
Boston MA 02109
617 929-2000

(G-8432)
BOSTON HEALTH ECONOMICS LLC
265 Franklin St Ste 1100 (02110-3116)
PHONE..................................781 290-0808
Joseph Menzin, *President*
Joe Branca, *CFO*
Jordan Menzin, *CTO*
EMP: 12
SALES: 3MM **Privately Held**
WEB: www.bhei.com
SIC: 7372 Prepackaged Software Services

(G-8433)
BOSTON LAMB & VEAL CO INC
155 Hampden St (02119-2822)
PHONE..................................617 442-3644
Dennis Breen, *CEO*
Les Oesterreich, *President*
Jeff Evanson, *CFO*
▲ **EMP:** 65
SQ FT: 25,000
SALES (est): 5.9MM **Privately Held**
WEB: www.superiorfarms.com
SIC: 2011 2013 Meat Packing Plant Mfg Prepared Meats
PA: Transhumance Holding Company, Inc.
2530 River Plaza Dr # 200
Sacramento CA 95833

(G-8434)
BOSTON LTIGATION SOLUTIONS LLC
100 Franklin St (02110-1537)
PHONE..................................617 933-9780
EMP: 16 **EST:** 2007
SALES (est): 1.8MM **Privately Held**
SIC: 2752 Lithographic Commercial Printing

(G-8435)
BOSTON NEIGHBORHOOD NEWS INC
Also Called: Boston Hatian Reporter
150 Munt Vrnon St Ste 120 (02125)
PHONE..................................617 436-1222
William Forry, *President*
Ed Forry, *Treasurer*
Jack Conboy, *Adv Mgr*
EMP: 8
SQ FT: 2,000
SALES (est): 552.8K **Privately Held**
SIC: 2711 Newspapers-Publishing/Printing

(G-8436)
BOSTON PAPER BOARD CORP
40 Roland St (02129-1222)
P.O. Box 290086 (02129-0202)
PHONE..................................617 666-1154
Mark Feinberg, *President*
▲ **EMP:** 25 **EST:** 1908
SQ FT: 75,000
SALES (est): 7MM **Privately Held**
SIC: 2621 Paper Mill

(G-8437)
BOSTON PLSTIC ORAL SRGERY FNDT
300 Longwood Ave (02115-5724)
PHONE..................................617 355-6058
Karl O D, *President*
Craig J Nesta, *Treasurer*
Charles A D, *Clerk*
EMP: 3
SALES: 20.5MM **Privately Held**
SIC: 3841 Mfg Surgical/Medical Instruments

(G-8438)
BOSTON PRETZEL BAKERY INC
284 Amory St Ste 2 (02130-2340)
P.O. Box 181074 (02118-0011)
PHONE..................................617 522-9494
Linda Demarco, *President*
Dana Marie Bauer, *Treasurer*
EMP: 12
SALES (est): 1.3MM **Privately Held**
WEB: www.bostonpretzel.com
SIC: 2064 Mfg Candy/Confectionery

(G-8439)
BOSTON SALADS AND PROVS INC
57 Food Mart Rd (02118-2801)
PHONE..................................617 307-6340
John A Zofchak, *CEO*
Tom Watson, *Vice Pres*
Lynn A Zofchak, *Treasurer*
EMP: 50
SQ FT: 9,000
SALES (est): 10.5MM **Privately Held**
SIC: 2099 Mfg Food Preparations

(G-8440)
BOSTON SAND & GRAVEL COMPANY (PA)
100 N Washington St Fl 2 (02114-1712)
P.O. Box 9187 (02114-9187)
PHONE..................................617 227-9000
Dean M Boylan Sr, *Ch of Bd*
Dean M Boylan Jr, *Corp Secy*
David B McNeil, *Senior VP*
Jeanne-Marie Boylan, *Vice Pres*
Joseph Gallagher, *Vice Pres*
EMP: 35 **EST:** 1914
SQ FT: 6,000
SALES (est): 121MM **Privately Held**
WEB: www.bostonsand.com
SIC: 3273 1442 Mfg Ready-Mixed Concrete Construction Sand/Gravel

(G-8441)
BOSTON SHIP REPAIR LLC
32a Drydock Ave (02210-2308)
PHONE..................................617 330-5045
Edward Snyder, *President*
Donna Connors, *President*
Bruce Zaniol, *CFO*
◆ **EMP:** 130
SQ FT: 17,000
SALES: 40MM **Privately Held**
SIC: 3731 Shipbuilding/Repairing
PA: Northeast Ship Repair, Inc.
32a Drydock Ave
Boston MA 02210

(G-8442)
BOSTON SMOKED FISH COMPANY LLC
Bays 16 20 Boston Fish Pe Ys St Ba (02210)
PHONE..................................617 819-5476
Matthew Baumann, *CEO*
Christopher A Avery,
Benjamin Baugh Baumann,
EMP: 7 **EST:** 2013
SQ FT: 9,000
SALES: 300K **Privately Held**
SIC: 2091 Mfg Canned/Cured Fish/Seafood

(G-8443)
BOXEVER US INC
34 Farnsworth St Fl 4 (02210-1257)
PHONE..................................617 599-2420
EMP: 30
SALES (est): 1.9MM **Privately Held**
SIC: 7372 Prepackaged Software Services

(G-8444)
BRIDGESAT INC
100 High St Fl 28 (02110-2321)
PHONE..................................617 419-1800
David Mitlyng, *Senior VP*
Matthew Thoms, *Director*
EMP: 3 **EST:** 2015
SALES (est): 146.7K **Privately Held**
SIC: 3669 Mfg Communications Equipment

(G-8445)
BRILL USA INC
Also Called: Brill Academic Publishers
2 Liberty Sq Fl 11 (02109-4890)
PHONE..................................617 263-2323
Michiel K Swormink, *Editor*
Steve Dane, *Vice Pres*
Sylvia Bonadio, *Sales Staff*
Rose Luongo, *Manager*
EMP: 10
SALES (est): 1.3MM
SALES (corp-wide): 242.1K **Privately Held**
WEB: www.brill.nl
SIC: 2731 Books-Publishing/Printing
HQ: Koninklijke Brill N.V.
Plantijnstraat 2
Leiden 2321
715 353-596

(G-8446)
BRILLACADEMIC PUBLISHERS INC
112 Water St Ste 400 (02109-4211)
PHONE..................................617 742-5277
Steve Dane, *Director*
EMP: 5
SALES (est): 247.9K **Privately Held**
SIC: 2731 Books-Publishing/Printing

(G-8447)
BROWNMED INC (PA)
Also Called: Brown Med
101 Federal St Fl 29 (02110-1873)
PHONE..................................857 317-3354
Ivan E Brown, *President*
Paul Katzfey, *Vice Pres*
Terry Kounkel, *Vice Pres*
Trista McCaffery, *Vice Pres*
Brian Miller, *Vice Pres*
▲ **EMP:** 50 **EST:** 1965
SQ FT: 30,000
SALES (est): 9.7MM **Privately Held**
WEB: www.brownmed.com
SIC: 3842 5047 Mfg Surgical Appliances/Supplies Whol Medical/Hospital Equipment

(G-8448)
BUDIPRODUCTS
404 Marlborough St (02115-1582)
PHONE..................................617 470-3086
Michael J McCarthy, *Principal*
EMP: 4
SALES: 850K **Privately Held**
SIC: 2051 Baked Goods

(G-8449)
BUILDIUM LLC
3 Center Plz Ste 400 (02108-2010)
PHONE..................................888 414-1988
Christopher Litster, *CEO*
Sridhar Raju, *QC Mgr*
Jack Hoffman, *Accounts Mgr*
Kegan Hoffman, *Accounts Mgr*
Michael Azzolino, *Sales Staff*
EMP: 9
SALES (est): 2.4MM **Privately Held**
WEB: www.buildium.com
SIC: 7372 Prepackaged Software Services

GEOGRAPHIC

(G-8450)
BULLHORN INC (PA)
100 Summer St Ste 1700 (02110-2105)
PHONE.................................617 478-9100
Arthur Papas, *CEO*
Ryan Murphy, *Exec VP*
Danielle Du Toit, *Senior VP*
Deb Hordon, *Vice Pres*
Mark Hounslow, *Vice Pres*
EMP: 121
SQ FT: 20,000
SALES (est): 60.9MM **Privately Held**
WEB: www.bullhorn.com
SIC: 7372 Prepackaged Software Services

(G-8451)
BUY BOXESCOM LLC
1 Boston Pl Ste 3400 (02108-4407)
PHONE.................................617 305-7865
Brian Kates, *Principal*
EMP: 4
SQ FT: 4,000
SALES (est): 237K **Privately Held**
SIC: 2653 Mfg Corrugated/Solid Fiber Boxes

(G-8452)
CABOT CORPORATION (PA)
2 Seaport Ln Ste 1300 (02210-2019)
PHONE.................................617 345-0100
Sue H Rataj, *Ch of Bd*
Sean D Keohane, *President*
Ariel Kuan, *President*
Walter Miller, *Superintendent*
David Tate, *Superintendent*
◆ **EMP:** 140 **EST:** 1882
SALES: 3.3B **Publicly Held**
WEB: www.cabot-corp.com
SIC: 2895 3081 3084 2819 Mfg Carbon Black Plastic Products Silica & Electronic Materials

(G-8453)
CABOT SPECIALTY CHEMICALS INC (HQ)
2 Seaport Ln Ste 1300 (02210-2058)
PHONE.................................617 345-0100
▲ **EMP:** 8
SALES: 150K
SALES (corp-wide): 3.3B **Publicly Held**
SIC: 2899 Mfg Chemical Preparations
PA: Cabot Corporation
2 Seaport Ln Ste 1300
Boston MA 02210
617 345-0100

(G-8454)
CAKEWALK BAKERS LLC
Also Called: Flour Bakery Cafe
12 Farnsworth St Fl 1 (02210-1224)
PHONE.................................617 903-4352
Mike Geldart, *General Mgr*
Jerry Bocchino, *Facilities Mgr*
Carro Oldham, *Manager*
Kirsten Dozier, *Asst Mgr*
Nour Elgharib, *Asst Mgr*
EMP: 4
SALES (est): 540.5K **Privately Held**
SIC: 2051 Mfg Bread/Related Products

(G-8455)
CALDWELL CMMNICATIONS ADVISORS
500 Harrison Ave Ste 3r (02118-2439)
PHONE.................................617 425-7318
EMP: 4 **EST:** 2004
SALES (est): 190K **Privately Held**
SIC: 2741 Misc Publishing

(G-8456)
CAMBRIDGE POLYMER GROUP INC
56 Roland St Ste 310 (02129-1223)
PHONE.................................617 629-4400
Stephen Spiegelberg, *President*
Gavin Braithwaite, *Vice Pres*
Adam Kozak, *Research*
EMP: 16
SQ FT: 14,500
SALES (est): 3.6MM **Privately Held**
WEB: www.campoly.com
SIC: 2821 8734 8731 Mfg Plstc Material/Resin Testing Laboratory Coml Physical Research

(G-8457)
CAMBRIDGE SEMANTICS INC
1 Beacon St Ste 3400 (02108-3116)
PHONE.................................617 245-0517
Chuck Pieper, *CEO*
Alok Prasad, *President*
Barry Zane, *President*
John O'Sullivan, *Vice Pres*
Frank Schwichtenberg, *Vice Pres*
EMP: 10
SALES (est): 1.7MM **Privately Held**
SIC: 7372 Prepackaged Software Services

(G-8458)
CARBONITE INC (PA)
2 Avenue De Lafayette # 6 (02111-1888)
PHONE.................................617 587-1100
Steve Munford, *CEO*
Megan Oliver, *Counsel*
Rob Beeler, *Senior VP*
Norman Guadagno, *Senior VP*
Paul Mellinger, *Senior VP*
EMP: 133
SQ FT: 52,588
SALES: 296.4MM **Privately Held**
WEB: www.gcassoc.com
SIC: 7372 7374 Prepackaged Software & Data Processing

(G-8459)
CARIBE CMMNCTIONS PUBLICATIONS
Also Called: El Mundo Newspapers
175 Wm F Mcclellan Hwy (02128-1185)
PHONE.................................617 522-5060
Alberto Vasallo Jr, *President*
EMP: 15
SALES (est): 841.7K **Privately Held**
SIC: 2711 Newspapers-Publishing/Printing

(G-8460)
CAROLE SOUSA JEWELRY
64 Cypress St Ste 1 (02132-5023)
PHONE.................................617 232-4087
Carole Sousa, *Owner*
EMP: 3
SALES (est): 100K **Privately Held**
WEB: www.sousajewelry.com
SIC: 3961 5632 Mfg Costume Jewelry Ret Women's Accessories/Specialties

(G-8461)
CELYAD INC
2 Seaport Ln (02210-2001)
PHONE.................................857 990-6900
Patrick Jeanmart, *President*
Graham Morrell, *Vice Pres*
Richard Mountfield, *Vice Pres*
EMP: 8
SALES (est): 411.4K **Privately Held**
SIC: 2834 Mfg Pharmaceutical Preparations

(G-8462)
CENGAGE LEARNING INC (PA)
Also Called: Course Technology
200 Pier 4 Blvd Ste 400 (02210-2457)
PHONE.................................617 289-7918
Michael Hansen, *President*
Gordon T Macomber, *President*
Ron Mobed, *President*
Michelle Eickmeyer, *Principal*
Adam Goodman, *Editor*
◆ **EMP:** 60
SALES (est): 1.2B **Privately Held**
WEB: www.thomsonlearning.com
SIC: 2731 Books-Publishing/Printing

(G-8463)
CENGAGE LRNG HOLDINGS II INC (PA)
20 Channel Ctr St (02210-3437)
PHONE.................................617 289-7700
Michael Hansen, *CEO*
William Rieders, *Exec VP*
Lindsay Stanley, *Vice Pres*
Dean D Durbin, *CFO*
Brian Mulligan, *Treasurer*
EMP: 50
SALES: 1.4B **Privately Held**
SIC: 2731 Books-Publishing/Printing

(G-8464)
CENTREXION THERAPEUTICS CORP
200 State St Ste 6 (02109-2696)
PHONE.................................617 837-6911
Jeffrey B Kindler, *CEO*
Sol J Barer, *Ch of Bd*
Isaac Blech, *Vice Ch Bd*
James N Campbell, *President*
B Nicholas Harvey, *CFO*
EMP: 14 **EST:** 2013
SQ FT: 11,486
SALES (est): 3.1MM **Privately Held**
SIC: 2834 Pharmaceutical Preparations

(G-8465)
CEREVANCE INC (PA)
1 Marina Park Dr Fl 14 (02210-1832)
PHONE.................................408 220-5722
Brad Margus, *CEO*
David H Margolin, *Senior VP*
Lee A Dawson, *Vice Pres*
Robert Middlebrook, *CFO*
EMP: 5
SALES (est): 534.5K **Privately Held**
SIC: 2834 Mfg Pharmaceutical Preparations

(G-8466)
CHANGS PUBLISHING COMPANY
216 Lincoln St (02111-2404)
PHONE.................................617 542-1230
Thomas Chang, *Owner*
EMP: 7
SALES (est): 270K **Privately Held**
SIC: 2711 Newspapers-Publishing/Printing

(G-8467)
CHANNEL FISH CO INC
370 E Eagle St (02128-2571)
PHONE.................................617 569-3200
Louis A Silvestro, *President*
Rosario Silvestro, *President*
Paula Monaco, *Administration*
◆ **EMP:** 65
SQ FT: 2,500
SALES (est): 12.9MM **Privately Held**
WEB: www.channelfishco.com
SIC: 2048 2092 2047 Mfg Prepared Feeds Mfg Fresh/Frozen Packaged Fish Mfg Dog/Cat Food

(G-8468)
CHAR SOFTWARE INC (PA)
Also Called: Localytics
2 Center Plz Fl 3 (02108-1909)
PHONE.................................617 418-4422
Jude McColgan, *CEO*
Adam Buggia, *Vice Pres*
Kristin Cronin, *Vice Pres*
Brian Preti, *Vice Pres*
Jon Wu, *Vice Pres*
EMP: 80
SALES (est): 12.8MM **Privately Held**
WEB: www.charsoftware.com
SIC: 7372 Custom Computer Programing

(G-8469)
CHINAMERICA FOOD MANUFACTURE
81 Tyler St A (02111-1848)
PHONE.................................617 426-1818
Way Fui Young, *President*
EMP: 10 **EST:** 1993
SALES (est): 753.1K **Privately Held**
SIC: 2038 2099 Mfg Frozen Specialties Mfg Food Preparations

(G-8470)
CHINESE SPAGHETTI FACTORY
73 Essex St (02111-2174)
PHONE.................................617 542-0224
John So, *Manager*
EMP: 3
SALES (est): 131.6K **Privately Held**
SIC: 2098 5812 Mfg Macaroni/Spaghetti Eating Place

(G-8471)
CHINESE SPAGHETTI FACTORY INC
83 Newmarket Sq (02118-2619)
PHONE.................................617 445-7714
Lai Fou Sou, *President*
Irene Sou, *Treasurer*
▲ **EMP:** 10
SQ FT: 2,000
SALES (est): 1.3MM **Privately Held**
SIC: 2098 Mfg Macaroni/Spaghetti

(G-8472)
CHMC OTLRYNGLGIC FUNDATION INC (PA)
Also Called: BOSTON'S CHILDREN HOSPITAL
300 Longwood Ave (02115-5724)
PHONE.................................617 355-8290
Howard Shane, *President*
Irene Abrams, *Vice Pres*
EMP: 15
SQ FT: 8,000
SALES: 32.9MM **Privately Held**
SIC: 3841 Mfg Surgical/Medical Instruments

(G-8473)
CHRISTIAN SCIENCE PUBG SOC (PA)
Also Called: Christian Science Monitor
210 Massachusetts Ave (02115-3012)
PHONE.................................617 450-2000
Kim Campbell, *Editor*
Mark Sappenfield, *Editor*
Suzanne Smedley, *Editor*
Margaret Campbell, *Trustee*
Karen Craft, *Trustee*
EMP: 280 **EST:** 1888
SALES: 49.1MM **Privately Held**
WEB: www.csmonitor.com
SIC: 2711 2721 4833 4832 Publishes A Newspaper & Magazines And Produces Domestic & International Shortwave Radio Programming

(G-8474)
CHRONOLOGICS LLC
3 Arlington St (02116-3408)
PHONE.................................617 686-6770
Frank Mondan,
Juliane Balliro Mondano,
EMP: 3
SALES (est): 71.1K **Privately Held**
SIC: 7372 Prepackaged Software Services

(G-8475)
CIMETRICS INC
180 Lincoln St Ste 3 (02111-2400)
PHONE.................................617 350-7550
James M Lee, *President*
Albert Putnam, *President*
Mary Ellen Cantabene, *COO*
John Biagiotti, *Engineer*
James F Butler, *CTO*
EMP: 60
SQ FT: 11,000
SALES: 5MM **Privately Held**
SIC: 3823 Mfg Process Control Instruments

(G-8476)
CLIENT SERVER ENGINEERING SVCS
177 Tremont St (02111-1020)
PHONE.................................617 338-7898
Joseph Quartararo, *President*
Jeffery A Evans, *COO*
EMP: 45
SQ FT: 2,500
SALES (est): 1.4MM **Privately Held**
SIC: 7372 Prepackaged Software Services

(G-8477)
CLIFLEX BELLOWS CORPORATION
45 W 3rd St (02127-1184)
PHONE.................................617 268-5774
EMP: 50 **EST:** 1962
SQ FT: 29,108
SALES (est): 4.9MM **Privately Held**
WEB: www.cliflex.com
SIC: 3599 3769 Mfg Industrial Machinery Mfg Space Vehicle Equipment

(G-8478)
CLP PB LLC
Also Called: Perseus Books Group
53 State St Ste 9 (02109-3106)
PHONE.................................617 252-5213
EMP: 196

SALES (corp-wide): 173.4MM **Privately Held**
SIC: 2731 Books-Publishing/Printing
PA: Clp Pb, Llc
1290 Ave Of The Amrcas
New York NY 10104
212 340-8100

(G-8479)
COCOMAMA FOODS INC
406 W 1st St (02127-1343)
PHONE....................978 621-2126
Sara Gragnolati, *Principal*
EMP: 4
SALES (est): 248.6K **Privately Held**
SIC: 2099 Mfg Food Preparations

(G-8480)
COLOR MEDIA GROUP LLC
4 Copley Pl Ste 120 (02116-6512)
PHONE....................617 620-0229
EMP: 11
SALES (est): 1MM **Privately Held**
SIC: 3993 5199 Signs And Advertising Specialties

(G-8481)
CONNELL LIMITED PARTNERSHIP (PA)
Also Called: Danly IEM
1 International Pl Fl 31 (02110-2602)
PHONE....................617 737-2700
Margot C Connell, *Partner*
Frank A Doyle, *Partner*
Catherine R Gallagher, *Partner*
Kurt Keady, *Partner*
◆ **EMP:** 15
SQ FT: 11,000
SALES: 500MM **Privately Held**
WEB: www.connell-lp.com
SIC: 3443 3444 3341 3544 Mfg Fabricated Plate Wrk Mfg Sheet Metalwork Secndry Nonfrs Mtl Prdcr Mfg Dies/Tools/Jigs/Fixt Holding Company

(G-8482)
CONTINENTAL MACHINE PDTS INC
400 Border St (02128-2402)
PHONE....................617 567-7396
Anna Todesca, *President*
Michael Todesca, *Treasurer*
EMP: 4 **EST:** 1950
SQ FT: 4,000
SALES: 200K **Privately Held**
SIC: 3599 Machine Shop

(G-8483)
CONVERGENT NETWORKS INC
500 Boylston St Fl 4 (02116-3740)
PHONE....................978 262-0231
Surya Panditi, *President*
Bing Yang, *Senior VP*
Dennis J Maddock, *Vice Pres*
John Collins, *Treasurer*
Robert Chow, *Admin Sec*
EMP: 70
SQ FT: 72,000
SALES (est): 8.3MM **Privately Held**
WEB: www.convergentnet.com
SIC: 3669 Mfg Telecommunications Network Equipment

(G-8484)
COREDGE NETWORKS INC
Also Called: Slt Logic
50 Commonwealth Ave # 504
(02116-3025)
PHONE....................617 267-5205
William Chu, *President*
EMP: 55
SALES (est): 4.8MM **Privately Held**
WEB: www.coredgenetworks.com
SIC: 3669 Mfg Communications Equipment

(G-8485)
COVERED SECURITY INC
170 Milk St Ste 2 (02109-3448)
PHONE....................781 218-9894
Chris Zannetos, *CEO*
Brian Milas, *CTO*
EMP: 7 **EST:** 2015
SALES (est): 73K **Privately Held**
SIC: 7372 Prepackaged Software Services

(G-8486)
CRAIN COMMUNICATIONS INC
77 Franklin St Lbby (02110-1519)
PHONE....................617 357-9090
Jeff Furman, *Manager*
EMP: 3
SALES (corp-wide): 225MM **Privately Held**
WEB: www.crainsnewyork.com
SIC: 2741 7311 Misc Publishing Advertising Agency
PA: Crain Communications, Inc.
1155 Gratiot Ave
Detroit MI 48207
313 446-6000

(G-8487)
CRANE & CO INC (HQ)
Also Called: Crane Currency
1 Beacon St Ste 1702 (02108-3106)
Rural Route 30, Dalton (01226)
PHONE....................617 648-3799
Annemarie C Watson, *President*
Shaun Driscoll, *Maint Spvr*
Hannah Delisle, *QC Mgr*
Chris Francis, *Engineer*
Douglas Prince, *CFO*
◆ **EMP:** 146
SQ FT: 700,000
SALES (est): 256.2MM
SALES (corp-wide): 3.3B **Publicly Held**
WEB: www.crane.com
SIC: 2621 Paper Mill
PA: Crane Co.
100 1st Stamford Pl # 300
Stamford CT 06902
203 363-7300

(G-8488)
CRANE CURRENCY US LLC
1 Beacon St Ste 1702 (02108-3106)
PHONE....................617 648-3710
Stephen Defalco, *CEO*
EMP: 3
SALES (est): 97.5K
SALES (corp-wide): 3.3B **Publicly Held**
SIC: 2759 Commercial Printing
PA: Crane Co.
100 1st Stamford Pl # 300
Stamford CT 06902
203 363-7300

(G-8489)
CREDO REFERENCE LIMITED
50 Milk St Fl 16 (02109-5002)
PHONE....................617 292-6100
Michael Sweet, *CEO*
Michael McFarland, *President*
John Dove, *Vice Pres*
Ian Singer, *Vice Pres*
EMP: 18
SALES (est): 2MM **Privately Held**
WEB: www.xrefer.com
SIC: 2731 Books-Publishing/Printing

(G-8490)
CUREVAC INC
34 Farnsworth St Ste 101 (02210-1239)
PHONE....................617 694-1537
EMP: 3
SALES (est): 314.4K **Privately Held**
SIC: 2836 Mfg Biological Products

(G-8491)
CURRENT LTG EMPLOYEECO LLC
745 Atlantic Ave (02111-2735)
PHONE....................216 266-2906
Maryrose Sylvester, *President*
John Irvine, *CFO*
Sok Cheng Soh, *Treasurer*
Janine Dascenzo, *Admin Sec*
EMP: 1100
SALES (est): 22.6MM
SALES (corp-wide): 240.3MM **Privately Held**
SIC: 3648 5063 Mfg Lighting Equipment Whol Electrical Equipment
PA: Current Lighting Holdco, Inc.
745 Atlantic Ave
Boston MA 02111
216 266-2906

(G-8492)
CURRICULUM ASSOCIATES LLC
12 Beacon St Ste 510 (02108-3764)
PHONE....................978 313-1331
Jim Finco, *Manager*
EMP: 5
SALES (corp-wide): 14MM **Privately Held**
SIC: 2731 Books-Publishing/Printing
PA: Curriculum Associates, Llc
153 Rangeway Rd
North Billerica MA 01862
978 667-8000

(G-8493)
CYBERTOOLS INC
Also Called: Cybertools For Libraries
75 Arlington St 500 (02116-3936)
PHONE....................978 772-9200
Mark V Roux, *Principal*
Lori A Roux, *Treasurer*
EMP: 5
SQ FT: 1,400
SALES: 1MM **Privately Held**
WEB: www.cytools.com
SIC: 3823 7371 Mfg Process Control Instruments Custom Computer Programing

(G-8494)
DA CAPO PRESS
53 State St Ste 9 (02109-3106)
PHONE....................617 252-5200
EMP: 25
SALES (est): 1.6MM
SALES (corp-wide): 186MM **Privately Held**
SIC: 2731 Books-Publishing/Printing
PA: Clp Pb, Llc
1290 Ave Of The Amrcas
New York NY 10104
212 340-8100

(G-8495)
DATADOG INC
33 Arch St (02110-1424)
PHONE....................866 329-4466
Olivier Promel, *CEO*
Aaron Radez, *Managing Prtnr*
EMP: 4
SALES (corp-wide): 198MM **Publicly Held**
SIC: 7372 Prepackaged Software Services
PA: Datadog, Inc.
620 8th Ave Fl 45
New York NY 10018
866 329-4466

(G-8496)
DAVID KING & CO INC
134 Beach St (02111-2817)
PHONE....................617 482-6950
David King, *President*
Murray Burwick, *CFO*
▲ **EMP:** 5
SQ FT: 4,000
SALES (est): 545.7K **Privately Held**
WEB: www.ussuitcase.com
SIC: 3161 5099 Mfg & Whol Leather Briefcases

(G-8497)
DAVID R GODINE PUBLISHER INC (PA)
15 Court Sq Ste 320 (02108-2536)
PHONE....................617 451-9600
David Godine, *President*
Sue Ramin, *Publisher*
▲ **EMP:** 8 **EST:** 1969
SQ FT: 2,500
SALES (est): 939.9K **Privately Held**
WEB: www.blacksparrowpress.com
SIC: 2731 Books-Publishing/Printing

(G-8498)
DELVE LABS INC
31 Saint James Ave (02116-4101)
PHONE....................617 820-9798
Gabriel Tremblay, *CEO*
EMP: 11 **EST:** 2017
SALES (est): 239.1K **Privately Held**
SIC: 7372 Prepackaged Software Services

(G-8499)
DENTOVATIONS INC
Also Called: Dentovations Company
100 Cambridge St Ste 104 (02114-2532)
PHONE....................617 737-1199
David Brown, *CEO*
▲ **EMP:** 12 **EST:** 2009
SALES: 10MM **Privately Held**
SIC: 2844 5047 Mfg Toilet Preparations Whol Medical/Hospital Equipment

(G-8500)
DENTOVATIONS INC
100 Franklin St (02110-1537)
PHONE....................617 737-1199
Adam Diasti, *President*
Damon Brown, *Vice Pres*
Terek Diasti, *Vice Pres*
Tim Diasti, *Vice Pres*
Graham Philp, *Vice Pres*
▲ **EMP:** 10
SQ FT: 1,000
SALES (est): 1.4MM **Privately Held**
WEB: www.dentovations.com
SIC: 3843 Mfg Dental Equipment/Supplies

(G-8501)
DEVENEY & WHITE INC
Also Called: Deveney & White Monuments
664 Gallivan Blvd (02124-5439)
PHONE....................617 288-3080
Gerard Deveney, *President*
EMP: 6 **EST:** 1900
SQ FT: 2,000
SALES (est): 694.4K **Privately Held**
WEB: www.deveneymonuments.com
SIC: 3281 5942 Mfg Cut Stone/Products Ret Books

(G-8502)
DIACRITECH INC
4 S Market St Fl 4 # 4 (02109)
PHONE....................617 236-7500
Madhusudhanan Rajamani, *President*
EMP: 18
SALES: 1.9MM **Privately Held**
WEB: www.laureltech.com
SIC: 2721 2731 2741 7371 Periodical-Publish/Print Book-Publishing/Printing Misc Publishing

(G-8503)
DIAMOND WINDOWS DOORS MFG INC
99 E Cottage St (02125-2622)
PHONE....................617 282-1688
Yu Liang Tseng, *President*
Erik Tseng, *Marketing Mgr*
▲ **EMP:** 30
SQ FT: 20,000
SALES (est): 9MM **Privately Held**
WEB: www.diamondwindows.com
SIC: 3089 3231 3442 Mfg Plastic Products Mfg Products-Purchased Glass Mfg Metal Doors/Sash/Trim

(G-8504)
DIG MEDIA GROUP INC
24 Spice St Ste 203 (02129-1312)
PHONE....................617 418-9075
John Loftus', *Principal*
EMP: 4
SALES (est): 239.8K **Privately Held**
SIC: 2711 Newspapers-Publishing/Printing

(G-8505)
DIGITAL LUMENS INCORPORATED
374 Congress St Ste 601 (02210-1807)
PHONE....................617 723-1200
Wolfram Unold, *CEO*
Sam Lafalce, *Partner*
Jon Scavone, *Business Mgr*
Brian Bernstein, *Vice Pres*
Steve Ronneberg, *Vice Pres*
▲ **EMP:** 50
SQ FT: 16,000
SALES: 40MM
SALES (corp-wide): 3.8B **Privately Held**
SIC: 3674 Mfg Semiconductors/Related Devices
HQ: Osram Sylvania Inc
200 Ballardvale St # 305
Wilmington MA 01887
978 570-3000

GEOGRAPHIC

(G-8506)
DIGITAL PARADIGMS INC
151 Tremont St Ste 110 (02111-1125)
PHONE....................................617 723-9400
Michael Moore, *President*
Cheryl L Moore, *Director*
Derreck M Ryan, *Admin Sec*
EMP: 4
SQ FT: 800
SALES (est): 333.5K **Privately Held**
SIC: 7372 Prepackaged Software Services

(G-8507)
DOLAN LLC
10 Milk St Ste 1000 (02108-4620)
PHONE....................................617 451-7300
Richard Gard, *Principal*
EMP: 3
SALES (corp-wide): 474.3MM **Privately Held**
SIC: 2711 Newspapers-Publishing/Printing
HQ: Dolan Llc
222 S 9th St Ste 2300
Minneapolis MN 55402

(G-8508)
DORCHESTER BEER HOLDINGS LLC
1250 Massachusetts Ave (02125-1608)
PHONE....................................617 869-7092
Travis Lee, *Principal*
EMP: 7 **EST:** 2015
SALES (est): 165.9K **Privately Held**
SIC: 2082 Mfg Malt Beverages

(G-8509)
DOWNEAST CIDER HOUSE LLC
256 Marginal St Ste 2 (02128-2800)
PHONE....................................857 301-8881
Tyler Mosher, *Principal*
Edward Valenta, *Opers Staff*
Ross Brockman,
EMP: 4
SALES (est): 213.4K **Privately Held**
SIC: 2082 2085 Mfg Malt Beverages Mfg Distilled/Blended Liquor

(G-8510)
DRIZLY INC
334 Boylston St Ste 301 (02116-3496)
PHONE....................................972 234-1033
Nicholas Rellas, *President*
Cory Rellas, *COO*
Michael Dilo, *Vice Pres*
Jacqueline P Flug, *Vice Pres*
Joe Grabmeier, *CFO*
EMP: 5
SALES: 500K **Privately Held**
SIC: 7372 7389 Prepackaged Software Services Business Services At Non-Commercial Site

(G-8511)
DUCK CREEK TECHNOLOGIES LLC (PA)
Also Called: Accenture Duck Creek
22 Boston Wharf Rd Fl 10 (02210-3032)
PHONE....................................857 239-5709
Michael A Jackowski, *CEO*
Andy Dey, *Chief*
Lauren Szurek, *Director*
EMP: 23 **EST:** 2015
SALES (est): 21MM **Privately Held**
SIC: 7372 Prepackaged Software Services

(G-8512)
DUCK CREEK TECHNOLOGIES LLC
Also Called: Yodil
22 Boston Wharf Rd Fl 10 (02210-3032)
PHONE....................................980 613-8044
Michael A Jackowski, *CEO*
EMP: 3
SALES (corp-wide): 21MM **Privately Held**
SIC: 7372 Custom Computer Programing
PA: Duck Creek Technologies Llc
22 Boston Wharf Rd Fl 10
Boston MA 02210
857 239-5709

(G-8513)
DYNASTY PRODUCTION
36 Tileston St (02113)
PHONE....................................617 361-5297
Cynthia Coker, *President*
EMP: 5
SALES (est): 407.8K **Privately Held**
WEB: www.dynasty-productions.com
SIC: 2389 Mfg Apparel/Accessories

(G-8514)
E D ABBOTT COMPANY INC
Also Called: Abbott Printers
179 Mass Ave (02115-3009)
PHONE....................................617 267-5550
Thomas F True Jr, *President*
Paul V True, *Vice Pres*
EMP: 10 **EST:** 1906
SQ FT: 4,000
SALES (est): 640K **Privately Held**
SIC: 2752 General Commercial Job Printing

(G-8515)
EAST BOSTON TIMES INC
Also Called: Independent Newspaper
40 Central Sq (02128-1911)
PHONE....................................617 567-9600
Steven Quigley, *President*
Colin Bohill, *Principal*
Debra De Gregorio, *Principal*
Terri Schryuman, *Principal*
Joshua Resneck, *Vice Pres*
EMP: 40
SQ FT: 1,500
SALES: 430K **Privately Held**
WEB: www.eastbostontimes.com
SIC: 2711 Newspapers-Publishing/Printing

(G-8516)
EAST WEST BOSTON LLC
12 Channel St Ste 301 (02210-2323)
PHONE....................................617 598-3000
Agnes Young, *Branch Mgr*
EMP: 90
SALES (corp-wide): 99.2MM **Privately Held**
SIC: 3679 3672 Mfg Electronic Components Mfg Printed Circuit Boards
HQ: East West Boston, Llc
4170 Ashford Dnwody Rd Ne
Brookhaven GA 30319
404 252-9441

(G-8517)
EASTERN CABINET SHOP INC
1450 Hyde Park Ave (02136-2622)
PHONE....................................617 361-7575
Joseph La Vita, *President*
Josephine La Vita, *Treasurer*
EMP: 5
SQ FT: 5,000
SALES (est): 495.5K **Privately Held**
SIC: 2434 Mfg Kitchen Cabinets

(G-8518)
EDIC BI WEEKLY
43 Hawkins St Ste 2 (02114-2918)
PHONE....................................617 918-5406
Clark John, *Principal*
EMP: 4
SALES (est): 285.4K **Privately Held**
SIC: 2711 Newspapers-Publishing/Printing

(G-8519)
EDWARD SPENCER
Also Called: Skylight Jewelers
44 School St Lbby A (02108-4224)
PHONE....................................617 426-0521
Edward Spencer, *Owner*
EMP: 4
SQ FT: 1,000
SALES: 500K **Privately Held**
SIC: 3915 5094 5944 3911 Mfg Jewelers' Materials Whol Jewelry/Precs Stone Ret Jewelry Mfg Precious Mtl Jewelry

(G-8520)
EGLEAN INC
Also Called: Eglean.com
35 Kingston St Apt 2 (02111-2223)
PHONE....................................617 229-5863
Ray Deck, *President*
EMP: 8
SALES (est): 472.5K **Privately Held**
WEB: www.eglean.com
SIC: 2741 Misc Publishing

(G-8521)
EL PAISSA BUTCHERSHOP
1010 Bennington St (02128-1138)
PHONE....................................617 567-0493
Jose Medina, *Principal*
EMP: 4
SALES (est): 319.7K **Privately Held**
SIC: 3421 Mfg Cutlery

(G-8522)
ELECTRA VEHICLES INC
22 Boston Wharf Rd Fl 7 (02210-3032)
PHONE....................................617 313-7848
Fabrizio Martini, *CEO*
Britany Straley, *Vice Pres*
EMP: 14
SALES (est): 1.1MM **Privately Held**
SIC: 7372 Prepackaged Software Services

(G-8523)
ELECTRO OPTICAL INDUSTRIES (PA)
50 Milk St Fl 16 (02109-5002)
PHONE....................................617 401-2196
Thierry Campos, *President*
EMP: 20 **EST:** 2008
SALES (est): 4.9MM **Privately Held**
SIC: 3827 Mfg Optical Instruments/Lenses

(G-8524)
ELECTROSONICS MEDICAL INC
2 Oliver St Ste 616 (02109-4946)
PHONE....................................216 357-3310
Trevor O Jones, *CEO*
Bob Purcell, *President*
EMP: 7 **EST:** 1998
SQ FT: 5,000
SALES: 5MM **Privately Held**
SIC: 3845 Mfg Electromedical Equipment

(G-8525)
ENDURANCE BREWING COMPANY LLC
72 Joy St Apt 18 (02114-4026)
PHONE....................................617 725-0256
EMP: 4
SALES (est): 147.3K **Privately Held**
SIC: 2082 Mfg Malt Beverages

(G-8526)
ENVVISUAL INC
56 Roland St (02129-1235)
PHONE....................................800 982-3221
Robert McIntosh, *President*
Sivan Leoni, *Chief Engr*
Thomas Moore, *Treasurer*
Brett Van Beever, *Director*
EMP: 6
SALES (est): 329.2K **Privately Held**
SIC: 7372 Prepackaged Software Services

(G-8527)
ERECRUIT HOLDINGS LLC
100 Summer St Ste 1700 (02110-2105)
PHONE....................................617 535-3720
David Perotti, *CEO*
Greg Stott, *CFO*
EMP: 60
SALES (est): 9.3MM
SALES (corp-wide): 60.9MM **Privately Held**
SIC: 7372 Prepackaged Software Services
PA: Bullhorn, Inc.
100 Summer St Ste 1700
Boston MA 02110
617 478-9100

(G-8528)
ETHNIC PUBLISHERS INC
Also Called: Post-Gazette Publishers
5 Prince St (02113-2443)
P.O. Box 135 (02133-0135)
PHONE....................................617 227-8929
Pamela Donnaruma, *President*
EMP: 5
SALES (est): 313.3K **Privately Held**
WEB: www.bostonpostgazette.com
SIC: 2711 Newspapers-Publishing/Printing

(G-8529)
EUROPEAN CUBICLES LLC
Also Called: Thrislington Cubicles
38 3rd Ave Ste 100w (02129-4503)
PHONE....................................617 681-6700
Majid Bonakdarpour, *Managing Dir*
EMP: 4
SALES (est): 464.9K **Privately Held**
SIC: 2844 Mfg Toilet Preparations

(G-8530)
EVERTEAM INC
745 Atlantic Ave (02111-2735)
PHONE....................................650 596-1800
Firas Raouf, *CEO*
Bechara Wakim, *President*
Dominique Lacheval, *Corp Secy*
EMP: 10
SALES (est): 432.3K **Privately Held**
SIC: 7372 Prepackaged Software Services

(G-8531)
EVERTRUE INC
290 Congress St Fl 7 (02210-1005)
PHONE....................................617 460-3371
Brent Grinna, *CEO*
Ken Keefer, *Senior VP*
Jessica Appelson, *Opers Staff*
Melissa Herman, *VP Finance*
Erik Rapp, *Sales Staff*
EMP: 22
SALES (est): 2.2MM **Privately Held**
SIC: 7372 Prepackaged Software Services

(G-8532)
EVERVEST CO
21 School St (02108-4319)
PHONE....................................585 697-4170
Michael Reynolds, *CEO*
Teasha Feldman-Fitzthum,
EMP: 4
SQ FT: 200
SALES (est): 106.7K **Privately Held**
SIC: 7372 Prepackaged Software Services

(G-8533)
EXARI GROUP INC (PA)
745 Boylston St (02116-2636)
PHONE....................................617 938-3777
William M Hewitt, *CEO*
Terence Lee, *President*
Scott Mars, *General Mgr*
Lindsay Chryssis, *Opers Mgr*
Joe Bradley, *CFO*
EMP: 8
SALES (est): 3.6MM **Privately Held**
SIC: 7372 Prepackaged Software Services

(G-8534)
EXARI SYSTEMS INC
745 Boylston St Ste 201 (02116-2614)
PHONE....................................617 938-3777
William Hewitt, *CEO*
Allison Cusano, *Vice Pres*
Gary Warzynski, *Vice Pres*
Lindsay Chryssis, *Finance*
Terence Lee, *VP Sales*
EMP: 20
SQ FT: 10,000
SALES (est): 11.2MM **Publicly Held**
SIC: 7372 Prepackaged Software Services
PA: Coupa Software Incorporated
1855 S Grant St
San Mateo CA 94402

(G-8535)
EZE CASTLE SOFTWARE INC (HQ)
12 Farnsworth St Fl 6 (02210-1282)
PHONE....................................617 316-1100
Pete Sinisgalli, *CEO*
Thomas P Gavin, *Principal*
Peter Cameron Hyzer, *Treasurer*
Heather A Sisler, *Admin Sec*
EMP: 125
SQ FT: 10,000
SALES (est): 29.6MM **Privately Held**
WEB: www.ezecastlesoftware.com
SIC: 7372 Prepackaged Software Services

(G-8536)
FA FINALE INC
24 Prime Park Way Ste 305 (02116)
PHONE....................................617 226-7888

Bernard Chiu, *Ch of Bd*
Ronald Izen, *Vice Ch Bd*
Mark Izen, *President*
Anthony J Natale Jr, *CFO*
▲ **EMP:** 53
SALES: 0
SALES (corp-wide): 6.8B **Publicly Held**
SIC: 3931 5099 Mfg Musical Instruments Whol Durable Goods
HQ: Jazwares, Llc
1067 Shotgun Rd
Sunrise FL 33326

(G-8537)
FARGO TA LLC
Also Called: Tivoli Audio
745 Atlantic Ave Fl 8 (02111-2735)
PHONE..................................617 345-0066
Lisa Kaufman, *CEO*
Stacey Kerek, *President*
Bob Brown,
Wayne Garrett,
James M Merberg,
▲ **EMP:** 30
SQ FT: 3,600
SALES (est): 4.4MM **Privately Held**
WEB: www.tivoliaudio.com
SIC: 3651 5731 Mfg Home Audio/Video Equipment Ret Radio/Tv/Electronics

(G-8538)
FASHIONS INC (PA)
Also Called: Fiandaca
535 Albany St Ste 2 (02118-2558)
PHONE..................................617 338-0163
Caroline Collings, *President*
▲ **EMP:** 8
SQ FT: 2,000
SALES (est): 915.3K **Privately Held**
WEB: www.fashions.net
SIC: 2339 Mfg Women's & Misses' Outerwear

(G-8539)
FASTCAP SYSTEMS CORPORATION
Also Called: Nanoramic
21 Drydock Ave Fl 8e (02210-2384)
PHONE..................................857 239-7500
Riccardo Signorelli, *CEO*
John Cooley, *President*
Christopher Deane, *Technical Mgr*
Jim Epstein, *Chief Engr*
John Hyde, *Engineer*
EMP: 17
SQ FT: 25,000
SALES (est): 2.6MM **Privately Held**
SIC: 3691 Mfg Storage Batteries

(G-8540)
FAVERCO INC
Also Called: Flying Colors
16 Aberdeen St (02215-3800)
PHONE..................................617 247-1440
Mark Favermann, *President*
Barbara Lewis, *Treasurer*
EMP: 8 **EST:** 1977
SQ FT: 5,000
SALES (est): 650K **Privately Held**
WEB: www.flyingcolors.net
SIC: 2399 8712 Mfg Fabricated Textile Products Architectural Services

(G-8541)
FEDERAL METAL FINISHING INC
18 Dorrance St (02129-1027)
P.O. Box 474, Stratham NH (03885-0474)
PHONE..................................617 242-3371
Fax: 617 242-4574
EMP: 32
SQ FT: 35,000
SALES (est): 3.7MM **Privately Held**
SIC: 3471 Plating/Polishing Service

(G-8542)
FENWAY CMMUNICATIONS GROUP INC
Also Called: Minuteman Press
870 Commonwealth Ave F (02215-1233)
PHONE..................................617 226-1900
Richard E Sands, *President*
Todd M Nugent, *Vice Pres*
EMP: 28
SQ FT: 4,050
SALES (est): 6.8MM **Privately Held**
WEB: www.mmpbrookline.com
SIC: 2752 Comm Prtg Litho

(G-8543)
FIGULO CORPORATION
22 Elkins St (02127-1620)
PHONE..................................617 269-0807
EMP: 3
SQ FT: 5,000
SALES (est): 177.2K **Publicly Held**
SIC: 3253 Manufactures Ceramic Wall And Floor Tiles
PA: 3d Systems Corporation
333 Three D Systems Cir
Rock Hill SC 29730

(G-8544)
FIL-TECH INC
190 Old Colony Ave Ste 1 (02127-2420)
PHONE..................................617 227-1133
Paul Becker, *President*
EMP: 3
SALES (est): 223.3K **Privately Held**
SIC: 3671 Electron Tubes, Nsk

(G-8545)
FILTECH INC
6 Pinckney St (02114-4800)
PHONE..................................617 227-1133
G Paul Becker, *President*
Paula L Becker, *Vice Pres*
Diana Becker, *Treasurer*
▲ **EMP:** 9
SALES (est): 1.1MM **Privately Held**
WEB: www.filtech.com
SIC: 3671 3625 Mfg & Distributors Of Vacuum Products Such As Tubes Fluids & Crystals Used By The Electronics Industry

(G-8546)
FINOMIAL CORPORATION
101 Arch St Ste 400 (02110-1103)
PHONE..................................646 820-7637
EMP: 5
SALES (corp-wide): 618.2K **Privately Held**
SIC: 7372 Prepackaged Software Services
PA: Finomial Corporation
30 Kelley St
Cambridge MA 02138
917 488-6050

(G-8547)
FIRST WIND HOLDINGS INC
179 Lincoln St Ste 500 (02111-2427)
PHONE..................................617 960-2888
EMP: 19
SALES (est): 2.9MM **Privately Held**
SIC: 3621 Mfg Motors/Generators

(G-8548)
FIS SYSTEMS INTERNATIONAL LLC
Also Called: Sungard
75 Federal St 101 (02110-1913)
PHONE..................................617 728-7722
Joseph Marcinkowski, *Technical Staff*
EMP: 5
SALES (corp-wide): 8.4B **Publicly Held**
SIC: 7372 Prepackaged Software Services
HQ: Fis Systems International Llc
200 Campus Dr
Collegeville PA 19426
484 582-2000

(G-8549)
FITBIT INC
1 Marina Park Dr Ste 1 # 1 (02210-1873)
PHONE..................................857 277-0594
Jonathan Blunt, *Engineer*
EMP: 8 **Publicly Held**
SIC: 3829 Mfg Measuring/Controlling Devices
PA: Fitbit, Inc.
199 Fremont St Fl 14
San Francisco CA 94105

(G-8550)
FITNOW INC
101 Tremont St Ste 900 (02108-5005)
PHONE..................................617 699-5585
Charles Teague, *CEO*
Joseph J Allaire, *President*
Kevin McCoy, *Vice Pres*
Patrick Rills, *Software Engr*
EMP: 50
SQ FT: 1,000
SALES (est): 3.6MM **Privately Held**
SIC: 3949 Mfg Sporting/Athletic Goods

(G-8551)
FRAIVILLIG TECHNOLOGIES CO
145 Pinckney St Apt 401 (02114-3230)
PHONE..................................512 784-5698
Jim Fraivillig, *President*
Jack Kleinert, *CFO*
EMP: 4
SQ FT: 2,200
SALES: 405.3K **Privately Held**
WEB: www.fraivillig.com
SIC: 2821 Mfg Power Semiconductor Magnetic Devises

(G-8552)
FRAMESHIFT LABS INC
129 Newbury St Ste 400 (02116-2928)
PHONE..................................617 319-1357
Alistair Ward, *Principal*
Gabor Marth,
Chase Miller,
EMP: 3 **EST:** 2015
SALES (est): 125.3K **Privately Held**
SIC: 7372 Prepackaged Software Services

(G-8553)
FREE FLOW POWER CORPORATION
239 Causeway St Ste 300 (02114-2130)
P.O. Box 9308 (02114-0043)
PHONE..................................978 283-2822
Daniel Irvin, *CEO*
Christopher Williams, *Bd of Directors*
EMP: 25
SALES (est): 3.5MM **Privately Held**
SIC: 3511 Developer Turbines/Generator Sets

(G-8554)
FREEMAN BEDFORD
Bedford/St. Martin's
75 Arlington St Ste 8000 (02116-3946)
PHONE..................................617 399-4000
Joan Fienberg, *President*
Heidi Hood, *Senior Editor*
EMP: 110
SALES (corp-wide): 1.6B **Privately Held**
SIC: 2731 Books-Publishing/Printing
HQ: Bedford, Freeman & Worth Publishing Group, Llc
1 New York Plz Ste 4500
New York NY 10004
212 576-9400

(G-8555)
GAZETTE PUBLICATIONS INC
7 Harris Ave (02130-2888)
P.O. Box 301119, Jamaica Plain (02130-0010)
PHONE..................................617 524-2626
Sandra Storey, *President*
EMP: 9
SALES (est): 332.3K **Privately Held**
WEB: www.missionhillgazette.com
SIC: 2711 Newspapers-Publishing/Printing

(G-8556)
GDM SOFTWARE LLC
225 Franklin St (02110-2804)
PHONE..................................617 416-6333
Daniel C Elfort, *CEO*
EMP: 4
SALES (est): 221.8K **Privately Held**
SIC: 7372 Prepackaged Software Services

(G-8557)
GE ENERGY PARTS INTL LLC (HQ)
41 Farnsworth St (02210-1236)
PHONE..................................617 443-3000
EMP: 4
SALES (est): 2.9MM
SALES (corp-wide): 121.6B **Publicly Held**
SIC: 3511 Mfg Turbines/Generator Sets
PA: General Electric Company
5 Necco St
Boston MA 02210
617 443-3000

(G-8558)
GENERAL ELECTRIC COMPANY (PA)
5 Necco St (02210)
PHONE..................................617 443-3000
H Lawrence Culp Jr, *Ch of Bd*
EMP: 550 **EST:** 1892
SALES: 121.6B **Publicly Held**
SIC: 3511 3845 3533 3631 Mfg Turbine/Genratr Sets

(G-8559)
GENZYME CORPORATION
Also Called: Genzyme Allston
500 Soldiers Field Rd (02134-1842)
PHONE..................................617 779-3100
Charles Clancy, *Opers Mgr*
Ann Faldetta, *Facilities Mgr*
Bill Messier, *Mfg Spvr*
Richard Gagnon, *Production*
Anthony Fontellio, *Purch Agent*
EMP: 150 **Privately Held**
WEB: www.genzyme.com
SIC: 2835 2834 Mfg Diagnostic Substances Mfg Pharmaceutical Preparations
HQ: Genzyme Corporation
50 Binney St
Cambridge MA 02142
617 252-7500

(G-8560)
GEORGES BANK LLC
310 Northern Ave Areac (02210-2316)
PHONE..................................617 423-3474
Mike Geraty, *Mng Member*
Max Harvey,
Mathew Henderson,
EMP: 15 **EST:** 2012
SALES (est): 1.3MM **Privately Held**
SIC: 2092 Mfg Fresh/Frozen Packaged Fish

(G-8561)
GILLETTE COMPANY (HQ)
1 Gillette Park (02127-1096)
PHONE..................................617 421-7000
Edward F Degraan, *President*
Mark M Leckie, *President*
Terry Overbey, *Vice Pres*
Gail Sullivan, *Treasurer*
Joseph Schena, *VP Finance*
◆ **EMP:** 550 **EST:** 1901
SQ FT: 278,000
SALES (est): 3.7B
SALES (corp-wide): 67.6B **Publicly Held**
WEB: www.gillette.com
SIC: 3421 3634 2844 3951 Mfg Cutlery Mfg Elec Housewares/Fans
PA: The Procter & Gamble Company
1 Procter And Gamble Plz
Cincinnati OH 45202
513 983-1100

(G-8562)
GILLETTE COMPANY
1 Gillette Park (02127-1096)
P.O. Box 999108 (02199)
PHONE..................................617 268-1363
EMP: 96
SALES (corp-wide): 67.6B **Publicly Held**
WEB: www.gillette.com
SIC: 2844 Mfg Toilet Preparations
HQ: The Gillette Company
1 Gillette Park
Boston MA 02127
617 421-7000

(G-8563)
GILLETTE DE MEXICO INC
800 Boylston St (02199-1900)
PHONE..................................617 421-7000
Edward Degaraan, *President*
Terry Overbey, *President*
EMP: 1500
SALES (est): 13.8MM
SALES (corp-wide): 67.6B **Publicly Held**
WEB: www.gillette.com
SIC: 3634 Mfg Electric Housewares/Fans

HQ: The Gillette Company
1 Gillette Park
Boston MA 02127
617 421-7000

(G-8564)
GINGHAM VENTURES LLC (PA)
6 Liberty Sq Ste 2151 (02109-5800)
PHONE..................................617 206-1197
Scott Dubois, *Principal*
EMP: 6
SALES (est): 915.3K **Privately Held**
SIC: 2211 Cotton Broadwoven Fabric Mill

(G-8565)
GINKGO BIOWORKS INC
27 Drydock Ave Ste 8 (02210-2383)
PHONE..................................814 422-5362
Jason Kelly, *CEO*
Marijn Dekkers, *Ch of Bd*
Reshma Shetty, *President*
Thomas Knight, *Chairman*
Kiki Barchey-Robinso, *Research*
EMP: 149
SALES (est): 6.3MM **Privately Held**
SIC: 2836 Mfg Biological Products

(G-8566)
GLENNS GARDENING & WOODWORKING
491 Arborway Apt 20 (02130-3658)
PHONE..................................617 548-7977
Glenn Inghram, *Principal*
EMP: 3
SALES (est): 253.9K **Privately Held**
SIC: 2431 Mfg Millwork

(G-8567)
GLOBAL FIRE PRODUCTS INC
745 Atlantic Ave Fl 8 (02111-2735)
PHONE..................................617 750-1125
Lawrence Genovesi, *CEO*
EMP: 6
SALES (est): 390.8K **Privately Held**
SIC: 3823 Mfg Process Control Instruments

(G-8568)
GLOBAL TOWER HOLDINGS LLC
116 Huntington Ave (02116-5749)
PHONE..................................617 375-7500
James Tacilet, *CEO*
James Mucha, *Manager*
EMP: 3
SALES (est): 108.8K **Publicly Held**
SIC: 3663 Mfg Radio/Tv Communication Equipment
PA: American Tower Corporation
116 Huntington Ave # 1100
Boston MA 02116

(G-8569)
GMO THRESHOLD LOGGING II LLC
40 Rowes Wharf Ste 600 (02110-3327)
PHONE..................................617 330-7500
EMP: 3
SALES (est): 182.4K **Privately Held**
SIC: 2411 Logging

(G-8570)
GMO THRESHOLD LOGGING LLC
40 Rowes Wharf Ste 600 (02110-3327)
PHONE..................................617 330-7500
EMP: 3
SALES (est): 176.6K **Privately Held**
SIC: 2411 Logging

(G-8571)
GMO THRSHOLD TMBER HLDINGS LLC
40 Rowes Wharf Ste 600 (02110-3327)
PHONE..................................617 330-7500
Eran Baruch, *Principal*
EMP: 3
SALES (est): 152.6K **Privately Held**
SIC: 2411 Logging

(G-8572)
GO2 MEDIA INC
10 High St Ste 1002 (02110-1686)
PHONE..................................617 457-7870
Dan Smith, *CEO*
EMP: 12
SALES (est): 1.2MM **Privately Held**
SIC: 3695 Mfg Magnetic/Optical Recording Media

(G-8573)
GOOD TERN PRESS INC
15 Channel Ctr St Apt 616 (02210-3426)
PHONE..................................508 277-5500
Samuel Bauer, *Principal*
EMP: 3
SALES (est): 47.7K **Privately Held**
SIC: 2741 Misc Publishing

(G-8574)
GOOSE VALLEY NATURAL FOODS LLC
100 City Hall Plz Ste 305 (02108-2105)
P.O. Box 130130 (02113-0003)
PHONE..................................617 914-0126
George P Denny III, *Mng Member*
Scott Almeida,
Barbara Mattaliano,
EMP: 5
SQ FT: 2,000
SALES (est): 88.5K **Privately Held**
SIC: 2099 Mfg Food Preparations

(G-8575)
GORDON INDUSTRIES INC (PA)
Also Called: Amramp
202 W 1st St (02127-1110)
PHONE..................................857 401-1114
Julian Gordon, *President*
Doug Pumarlo, *General Mgr*
David Wallentine, *Regional Mgr*
Bill Bowles, *Area Mgr*
Sheri Hutto, *Area Mgr*
EMP: 49
SQ FT: 15,000
SALES (est): 10.1MM **Privately Held**
WEB: www.amramp.com
SIC: 3448 6794 Mfg Prefabricated Metal Buildings Patent Owner/Lessor

(G-8576)
GRANDSTREAM NETWORKS INC (PA)
126 Brookline Ave Ste 3 (02215-3920)
PHONE..................................617 566-9300
David LI, *President*
Bill Zhang, *Vice Pres*
Richard Huang, *Engineer*
Dante Frontiera, *Hum Res Coord*
Vytas Lenkutis, *Sales Staff*
▲ **EMP:** 50
SALES (est): 10.9MM **Privately Held**
WEB: www.grandstream.com
SIC: 3577 Custom Computer Programing

(G-8577)
GRANDTEN DISTILLING LLC
383 Dorchester Ave # 130 (02127-2422)
PHONE..................................617 269-0497
Matthew Nuernberger, *Principal*
Nikhil Khanna, *Manager*
EMP: 8 **EST:** 2012
SALES (est): 1MM **Privately Held**
SIC: 3556 Mfg Food Products Machinery

(G-8578)
GREAT NORTHERN INDUSTRIES INC (PA)
266 Beacon St Ste 2 (02116-1287)
PHONE..................................617 262-4314
M Leonard Lewis, *President*
Anthony Lucivero, *Manager*
Alexis Evangelos, *Graphic Designe*
EMP: 200
SQ FT: 1,000
SALES (est): 10.1MM **Privately Held**
SIC: 3965 3089 2678 Mfg Stationery & Related Paper Products

(G-8579)
GREENER 3000 LLC
800 Boylston St Fl 16 (02199-7637)
PHONE..................................781 589-5777
Homayoun Amighi, *Treasurer*
EMP: 7
SALES: 150K **Privately Held**
SIC: 2911 1382 7389 Petroleum Refiner Oil/Gas Exploration Services Business Services At Non-Commercial Site

(G-8580)
GREENSIGHT AGRONOMICS INC
12 Channel St Ste 605 (02210-2333)
PHONE..................................617 633-4919
James Peverill, *CEO*
Joel Pedlikin, *COO*
Justin McClellan, *CFO*
EMP: 6 **EST:** 2015
SQ FT: 4,000
SALES (est): 372K **Privately Held**
SIC: 3721 3861 8711 8713 Mfg Aircraft Mfg Photo Equip/Supplies Engineering Services Surveying Services

(G-8581)
GREENWOOD PUBLISHING GROUP LLC (DH)
125 High St (02110-2704)
PHONE..................................617 351-5000
Lesa Scott, *President*
William Bayers, *Exec VP*
Michael Dolan, *Senior VP*
Tony Zubinski, *Opers Staff*
Eric Shuman, *CFO*
EMP: 49
SALES (est): 8.1MM
SALES (corp-wide): 1.3B **Publicly Held**
WEB: www.greenwood.com
SIC: 2731 Books-Publishing/Printing
HQ: Hmh Publishers Llc
125 High St
Boston MA 02110
617 351-5000

(G-8582)
GRENIER PRINT SHOP INC
3702 Washington St (02130-3701)
PHONE..................................617 522-2225
Jeanne Remondi, *President*
Jeffrey Remondi, *Treasurer*
Joseph F Remondi Sr, *Director*
Linda Remondi, *Admin Sec*
EMP: 4
SALES (est): 578.3K **Privately Held**
SIC: 2752 Lithographic Commercial Printing

(G-8583)
GROUPGLOBALNET CORP
768 Morton St (02126-1847)
P.O. Box 300446, Jamaica Plain (02130-0004)
PHONE..................................857 212-4012
Claretta Taylor Webb, *President*
EMP: 7
SALES: 1.6MM **Privately Held**
SIC: 2741 Mfg Miscellaneous Publishing

(G-8584)
GROWTH I M33 L P
888 Boylston St Ste 500 (02199-8192)
PHONE..................................617 877-0046
Brian Shortsleeve, *Managing Dir*
Mike Anello, *Managing Dir*
Gabe Ling, *Managing Dir*
EMP: 24
SALES (est): 1.2MM **Privately Held**
SIC: 3519 Mfg Internal Combustion Engines

(G-8585)
H E MOORE CORP
485 E 1st St (02127-1424)
PHONE..................................617 268-1262
Douglas Moore, *Owner*
EMP: 3
SQ FT: 5,194
SALES (corp-wide): 370K **Privately Held**
SIC: 3599 Mfg Industrial Machinery
PA: H E Moore Corp
45 Lakeshore Dr
Norfolk MA 02056
617 268-1262

(G-8586)
HACHETTE BOOK GROUP INC
3 Center Plz (02108-2003)
PHONE..................................617 227-0730
Judy Graham, *Branch Mgr*
James Pappas, *Software Engr*
Ryan Pugatch, *Exec Dir*
Torrey Oberfest, *Associate Dir*
David Haines, *Administration*
EMP: 75
SALES (corp-wide): 66.5MM **Privately Held**
SIC: 2731 Books-Publishing/Printing
HQ: Hachette Book Group, Inc.
1290 Ave Of The Americas
New York NY 10104
800 759-0190

(G-8587)
HACHETTE BOOK GROUP INC
Also Called: Da Capo Press
53 State St Ste 9 (02109-3106)
PHONE..................................617 227-0730
David Young, *Ch of Bd*
Stephen Mubarek, *Senior VP*
Jill Delucia, *Supervisor*
Joan Rohracker, *Director*
EMP: 7
SALES (corp-wide): 66.5MM **Privately Held**
SIC: 2731 Books-Publishing/Printing
HQ: Hachette Book Group, Inc.
1290 Ave Of The Americas
New York NY 10104
800 759-0190

(G-8588)
HARBUS NEWS CORPORATION
Harvard Busines Schl Bldg (02163)
PHONE..................................617 495-6528
Elizabeth Mc Fadden, *President*
Erika Murdocca, *Treasurer*
EMP: 3
SALES: 121K **Privately Held**
SIC: 2711 Newspaper Publication And Printing

(G-8589)
HARRY MILLER CO INC
Also Called: We Palmer Co
850 Albany St (02119-2545)
P.O. Box 191490 (02119-0029)
PHONE..................................617 427-2300
Fred Barkstale, *Controller*
Michael Frisch, *Program Mgr*
Rand Goddard, *Technology*
EMP: 50
SALES (corp-wide): 11.4MM **Privately Held**
WEB: www.harrymiller.com
SIC: 2394 Mfg Canvas/Related Products
PA: Harry Miller Co., Llc
19 Hampden St
Boston MA 02119
617 427-2300

(G-8590)
HARRY MILLER CO LLC (PA)
Also Called: American Canvas Co
19 Hampden St (02119-2911)
P.O. Box 191480, Roxbury (02119-0028)
PHONE..................................617 427-2300
Harry Miller, *President*
Scott Simons, *Vice Pres*
Suzanne Nadeski, *CFO*
Maureen Patten, *Credit Mgr*
Frederick W Barksdale, *Sales Engr*
▲ **EMP:** 40 **EST:** 1910
SQ FT: 40,000
SALES (est): 11.4MM **Privately Held**
WEB: www.harrymiller.com
SIC: 2394 Mfg Canvas/Related Products

(G-8591)
HAYSTACK ID
100 Franklin St (02110-1537)
PHONE..................................617 422-0075
EMP: 5
SALES (est): 552.5K **Privately Held**
SIC: 7372 Prepackaged Software Services

(G-8592)
HEALIGO INC
472 Jamaicaway (02130-2009)
PHONE..................................508 208-0461
Nicholas Fontana, *Principal*
David Lemoine, *Principal*
Jonathan McKenzie, *Principal*
Hollan Oliver, *Principal*
Lauren Ripley, *Admin Sec*
EMP: 5 **EST:** 2015

▲ = Import ▼=Export
◆ =Import/Export

SALES (est): 260.2K Privately Held
SIC: 7372 Prepackaged Software Services

(G-8593)
HEFRING LLC
280 Summer St (02210-1131)
PHONE..................................617 206-5750
EMP: 5
SQ FT: 800
SALES (est): 797.1K Privately Held
WEB: www.nortekusa.com
SIC: 3829 Mfg/Research Of Oceanographic Instruments

(G-8594)
HENRY N SAWYER CO INC
Also Called: Sawyer Printers
586 Rutherford Ave (02129-1310)
PHONE..................................617 242-4610
Fax: 617 242-3067
EMP: 18 EST: 1949
SQ FT: 11,000
SALES (est): 2.2MM Privately Held
WEB: www.sawyerprinters.com
SIC: 2752 Lithographic Commercial Printing

(G-8595)
HENRYS RAILINGS
1690 Hyde Park Ave (02136-2458)
PHONE..................................617 333-0535
Henry Hasenrichter, *Owner*
Henry Hasenritcher, *Owner*
EMP: 3
SALES (est): 298.2K Privately Held
SIC: 3312 Blast Furnace-Steel Works

(G-8596)
HERCULES PRESS
91 Spring St (02132-4315)
PHONE..................................617 323-1950
Michael Macrides, *Owner*
Shirley Woodward, *Graphic Designe*
EMP: 7
SQ FT: 2,700
SALES (est): 741.5K Privately Held
WEB: www.herculespress.com
SIC: 2759 7334 Commercial Printing Photocopying Services

(G-8597)
HEVC ADVANCE LLC
28 State St Ste 3202 (02109-1718)
PHONE..................................617 367-4802
James Digiorgio, *Vice Pres*
Paula Bournival, *Accounting Mgr*
EMP: 10
SALES (est): 1.3MM Privately Held
SIC: 3651 Mfg Home Audio/Video Equipment

(G-8598)
HM PUBLISHING CORP
222 Berkeley St (02116-3748)
PHONE..................................617 251-5000
Stephen Richards, *Exec VP*
Gerald Hughes, *Senior VP*
Paul Weaver, *Senior VP*
▲ EMP: 3546
SQ FT: 246,000
SALES (est): 102.4MM
SALES (corp-wide): 460.3MM Privately Held
SIC: 2731 Books-Publishing/Printing
PA: Houghton Mifflin Holdings Inc
125 High St Ste 900
Boston MA 02110
617 351-5000

(G-8599)
HMH PUBLISHERS LLC (DH)
Also Called: Houghton Mifflin Harcourt
125 High St (02110-2704)
PHONE..................................617 351-5000
Laura Blanton, *Editor*
Meredith Montgomery, *Vice Pres*
Bill Weiler, *Vice Pres*
John Winkler, *Vice Pres*
Beth Karwoski, *Project Mgr*
EMP: 7 EST: 2012
SALES (est): 8.3MM
SALES (corp-wide): 1.3B Publicly Held
SIC: 2731 Books-Publishing/Printing

(G-8600)
HMH SUPPLEMENTAL PUBLISHERS
Also Called: Harcourt Achieve
222 Berkeley St (02116-3748)
PHONE..................................407 345-2000
EMP: 9
SALES (est): 700K Privately Held
SIC: 2741 Misc Publishing

(G-8601)
HORN BOOK INC
Also Called: Horn Book Magazine
300 Fenway Ste P311 (02115-5820)
PHONE..................................617 278-0225
Thomas Todd, *President*
Jane Manthorne, *Vice Pres*
Roger Sutton, *Executive*
EMP: 12 EST: 1924
SALES (est): 1.3MM Privately Held
SIC: 2721 Publishes Magazines And Statistical Guides
PA: Media Source Inc.
123 William St Rm 802
New York NY 10038
646 380-0747

(G-8602)
HOUGHTON MIFFLIN LLC
222 Berkeley St Lbby 1 (02116-3733)
PHONE..................................617 351-5000
Noel Mier, *Partner*
Paul Griffin, *Vice Pres*
Ciara Smyth, *Vice Pres*
Steve Zukowski, *Vice Pres*
Beth Karwoski, *Project Mgr*
EMP: 35
SALES (est): 4.7MM Privately Held
SIC: 2731 Books-Publishing/Printing

(G-8603)
HOUGHTON MIFFLIN CO INTL INC
222 Berkeley St (02116-3748)
PHONE..................................617 351-5000
William Bayers, *Exec VP*
Michael Dolan, *Senior VP*
Eric Shuman, *CFO*
Joseph Flaherty, *Treasurer*
David Mills, *Asst Treas*
EMP: 4 EST: 1992
SALES (est): 242.8K
SALES (corp-wide): 1.3B Publicly Held
SIC: 2731 Books-Publishing/Printing
HQ: Houghton Mifflin Harcourt Publishing Company
125 High St Ste 900
Boston MA 02110
617 351-5000

(G-8604)
HOUGHTON MIFFLIN HARCOURT
125 High St Ste 900 (02110-2777)
PHONE..................................617 351-5000
Gordon Crovitz, *President*
Eric Shuman, *CFO*
Joseph Flaherty, *Treasurer*
William Bayers, *Admin Sec*
EMP: 12
SALES (est): 755.3K Privately Held
SIC: 2731 Books-Publishing/Printing

(G-8605)
HOUGHTON MIFFLIN HARCOURT (HQ)
125 High St Ste 900 (02110-2777)
PHONE..................................617 351-5000
Francie Alexander, *Ch Acad Ofcr*
William Bayers, *Exec VP*
Michael Dolan, *Senior VP*
Dan Cavalli, *Vice Pres*
Charlie Christina, *Vice Pres*
EMP: 11
SALES (est): 969.7MM
SALES (corp-wide): 1.3B Publicly Held
SIC: 2731 Books-Publishing/Printing
PA: Houghton Mifflin Harcourt Company
125 High St Ste 900
Boston MA 02110
617 351-5000

(G-8606)
HOUGHTON MIFFLIN HARCOURT CO (PA)
Also Called: Hmh
125 High St Ste 900 (02110-2777)
PHONE..................................617 351-5000
L Gordon Crovitz, *CEO*
Lawrence K Fish, *Ch of Bd*
Ellen Archer, *President*
David Dockterman, *Chief*
William F Bayers, *Exec VP*
▲ EMP: 277
SALES: 1.3B Publicly Held
SIC: 3999 2731 Mfg Education Aids Devices And Supplies Books Publishing

(G-8607)
HOUGHTON MIFFLIN HARCOURT PUBG (HQ)
Also Called: Houghton Mifflin Publishing
125 High St Ste 900 (02110-2777)
PHONE..................................617 351-5000
Gary Gentel, *President*
James G Nicholson, *President*
Lesa Scott, *President*
William Bayers, *Exec VP*
Tim Cannon, *Exec VP*
◆ EMP: 970
SQ FT: 246,000
SALES (est): 969.7MM
SALES (corp-wide): 1.3B Publicly Held
WEB: www.hmco.com
SIC: 2731 Books-Publishing/Printing
PA: Houghton Mifflin Harcourt Company
125 High St Ste 900
Boston MA 02110
617 351-5000

(G-8608)
HOUGHTON MIFFLIN HOLDINGS INC (PA)
125 High St Ste 900 (02110-2777)
PHONE..................................617 351-5000
Bill Weiler, *President*
Stephen Richards, *Exec VP*
Brook Colangelo, *Exec VP*
Kathy Busby, *Vice Pres*
◆ EMP: 4
SALES (est): 460.3MM Privately Held
SIC: 2731 Books-Publishing/Printing

(G-8609)
HUGHES RISKAPPS LLC
139a Charles St Pmb 382 (02114-3252)
PHONE..................................617 936-0301
Brian Drohan, *President*
Sherwood Hughes, *COO*
Kevin Hughes,
Bruce Lin,
EMP: 4
SQ FT: 24,000
SALES (est): 309.2K Privately Held
SIC: 7372 Prepackaged Software Services

(G-8610)
HUMAN CARE SYSTEMS INC (PA)
1 Faneuil Hall Sq (02109-1604)
PHONE..................................617 720-7838
Matthew P Hall, *President*
Thomas S Doyle, *Principal*
Courtney Saye, *COO*
Nancy Santilli, *Vice Pres*
Jared Silver, *Vice Pres*
EMP: 29
SALES (est): 11.7MM Privately Held
SIC: 7372 Prepackaged Software Services

(G-8611)
HUMANSCALE CORPORATION
179 South St Fl 1 (02111-2729)
PHONE..................................617 338-0077
Jenniffer Harris, *Branch Mgr*
EMP: 12
SALES (corp-wide): 156.4MM Privately Held
SIC: 3577 Manufacture Computer Equipment
PA: Humanscale Corporation
1114 Avenue Of The Americ
New York NY 10036
212 725-4749

(G-8612)
HYCU INC
109 State St (02109-2903)
PHONE..................................617 681-9100
Simon Taylor, *President*
Nathan Owen, *COO*
Beth Smith, *Project Mgr*
Terry Curtis Jr, *Treasurer*
Susan Fletcher, *Admin Sec*
EMP: 1276
SQ FT: 4,000
SALES: 333.9MM Privately Held
SIC: 7372 Prepackaged Software Services
HQ: Comtrade Group B.V.
Prins Bernhardplein 200
Amsterdam 1097
205 214-777

(G-8613)
IDG (HQ)
Also Called: International Data Group
1 Exeter Plz Fl 15 (02116)
PHONE..................................508 875-5000
Ted Bloom, *President*
Patrick Kenealy, *Managing Dir*
Jane Enos, *Vice Pres*
Jim Ghirardi, *Vice Pres*
Hanh Nghi, *Finance Dir*
EMP: 8
SALES (est): 1.9MM
SALES (corp-wide): 1.7B Privately Held
SIC: 2721 Periodicals
PA: International Data Group, Inc.
1 Exeter Plz Fl 15
Boston MA 02116
508 875-5000

(G-8614)
INCREDIBLE FOODS INC
Also Called: Wikifoods
75 Sprague St (02136-2021)
PHONE..................................617 491-6600
Kevin B Murphy, *President*
Jonathan Huot, *CFO*
Joseph J Speroni, *CTO*
David Edwards, *Director*
Terry Maguire, *Director*
EMP: 35 EST: 2012
SQ FT: 27,680
SALES (est): 411.4K
SALES (corp-wide): 7.6MM Privately Held
SIC: 2024 Mfg Ice Cream/Frozen Desert
PA: Quantum Designs, Llc
161 First St Ste 3
Cambridge MA 02142
617 491-6600

(G-8615)
INFORMATICS IN CONTEXT INC
1 Boston Pl Ste 2600 (02108-4420)
PHONE..................................650 200-5110
Vikarm Simha, *CEO*
Steven Sandy, *COO*
Janet Boudreau, *Officer*
EMP: 4
SALES (est): 287.9K Privately Held
SIC: 7372 Prepackaged Software Services

(G-8616)
INNOVATIVE CHEM PDTS GROUP LLC
Also Called: Ideapaint
1 Beacon St (02108-3107)
PHONE..................................800 393-5250
Doug Mattscheck, *CEO*
EMP: 18
SALES (corp-wide): 145.8MM Privately Held
SIC: 2851 Mfg Paints/Allied Products
PA: Innovative Chemical Products Group, Llc
150 Dascomb Rd
Andover MA 01810
978 623-9980

(G-8617)
INOZYME PHARMA INC (PA)
280 Summer St Fl 5 (02210-1131)
PHONE..................................857 330-4340
Axel Bolte, *President*
Gus Khursigara, *Vice Pres*
Catherine Nester, *Vice Pres*
Pedro Huertas, *Chief Mktg Ofcr*
EMP: 13

GEOGRAPHIC

SALES (est): 6.3MM **Privately Held**
SIC: 2834 Mfg Pharmaceutical Preparations

(G-8618)
INTERNATIONAL DATA GROUP INC (PA)
Also Called: Executrain
1 Exeter Plz Fl 15 (02116)
PHONE..................................508 875-5000
Mohamad Ali, *CEO*
Zhiqiang Lu, *Chairman*
Martin Canning, *Vice Pres*
Jeffrey Gallagher, *Vice Pres*
Bill Keyworth, *Vice Pres*
◆ **EMP:** 12
SQ FT: 15,000
SALES (est): 1.7B **Privately Held**
WEB: www.workscape.net
SIC: 2721 8732 7389 Periodicals-Publishing/Printing Commercial Nonphysical Research Business Services

(G-8619)
INVENSENSE INC (PA)
100 Summer St (02110-2106)
PHONE..................................857 268-4400
EMP: 11
SALES (est): 1.8MM **Privately Held**
SIC: 3823 Mfg Process Control Instruments

(G-8620)
INVERSANT INC
561 Boylston St (02116-3617)
PHONE..................................617 423-0331
Gene Miller, *COO*
Steve Desir, *Research*
Tracy Aguila, *Comms Mgr*
Robert Hildreth, *Exec Dir*
Robert J Hildreth, *Exec Dir*
EMP: 19
SALES: 1MM **Privately Held**
SIC: 2869 Mfg Industrial Organic Chemicals

(G-8621)
IRODY
30 Newbury St Ste 3 (02116-3239)
PHONE..................................781 262-0440
Eyal Bartfeld, *President*
EMP: 4
SALES (est): 235.9K **Privately Held**
WEB: www.irody.com
SIC: 7372 Prepackaged Software Services

(G-8622)
IRONWOOD PHARMACEUTICALS INC (PA)
100 Summer St Ste 2300 (02110-2156)
PHONE..................................617 621-7722
Mark Mallon, *CEO*
William Huyett, *COO*
Mark G Currie, *Senior VP*
Michael Hines, *Opers Mgr*
Gina Consylman, *CFO*
EMP: 244 **EST:** 1998
SQ FT: 223,000
SALES: 346.6MM **Publicly Held**
WEB: www.microbia.com
SIC: 2834 8731 Pharmaceutical Preparations Commercial Physical Research

(G-8623)
ITRICA CORP
125 High St Fl 2 (02110-2704)
PHONE..................................617 340-7777
Richard Palumbo, *President*
Dave Sampson, *CTO*
EMP: 8
SQ FT: 1,800
SALES (est): 910.2K **Privately Held**
SIC: 7372 Prepackaged Software Srvcs

(G-8624)
JAHRLING OCULAR PROSTHETICS (PA)
50 Staniford St Fl 8 (02114-2517)
PHONE..................................617 523-2280
Raymond Jahrling, *President*
EMP: 7 **EST:** 1953
SQ FT: 1,200
SALES (est): 855.2K **Privately Held**
SIC: 3842 Mfg Surgical Appliances/Supplies

(G-8625)
JAMAICA PLAIN PORCHFEST INC
50 Dunster Rd (02130-2704)
PHONE..................................617 320-6230
Bryan Tucker, *Principal*
EMP: 3
SALES (est): 103.3K **Privately Held**
SIC: 2711 Newspapers-Publishing/Printing

(G-8626)
JDA SOFTWARE GROUP INC
320 Congress St Ste 401 (02210-1231)
PHONE..................................857 305-8330
EMP: 4
SALES (corp-wide): 451.5MM **Privately Held**
SIC: 7372 Prepackaged Software Services
HQ: Jda Software Group, Inc.
15059 N Scottsdale Rd # 400
Scottsdale AZ 85254

(G-8627)
JEDOX INC
50 Milk St Fl 16 (02109-5002)
PHONE..................................617 514-7300
Douglas Levin, *Principal*
Diana Kuch, *Relations*
EMP: 5 **EST:** 2015
SALES (est): 471K **Privately Held**
SIC: 7372 Prepackaged Software Services

(G-8628)
JENZABAR INC (PA)
101 Huntington Ave # 2200 (02199-8087)
PHONE..................................617 492-9099
Robert Maginn Jr, *Ch of Bd*
Ling Chai, *President*
John Orahood, *Business Mgr*
Phil Orahood, *Business Mgr*
Sam Burgio, *Exec VP*
EMP: 100
SALES: 1.5MM **Privately Held**
SIC: 7372 Prepackaged Software Services

(G-8629)
JEWISH ADVOCATE PUBG CORP
Also Called: Jewish Times
15 School St Fl 2 (02108-4315)
PHONE..................................617 523-6232
Grand Rabbi Korff, *President*
Art Rosenberg, *Accounts Exec*
EMP: 13
SQ FT: 7,000
SALES (est): 803.8K **Privately Held**
SIC: 2711 6512 Newspapers-Publishing/Printing Nonresidential Building Operator

(G-8630)
JILL ROSENWALD CERAMIC DESIGN
369 Congress St Fl 2 (02210-1837)
PHONE..................................617 422-0787
Jill Rosenwald, *Owner*
EMP: 5
SQ FT: 6,000
SALES (est): 220K **Privately Held**
SIC: 3269 Make Ceramics

(G-8631)
JIMINNY INC
745 Atlantic Ave (02111-2735)
PHONE..................................917 940-5886
Thomas Lavery, *CEO*
James Graham, *CTO*
EMP: 5
SALES (est): 198K **Privately Held**
SIC: 7372 Prepackaged Software Services

(G-8632)
JOHN BROWN US LLC
1 South Sta Fl 3 (02110-2253)
PHONE..................................617 449-4354
Andrew Hirish, *CEO*
Emily Ross, *Vice Pres*
EMP: 10
SALES: 1MM **Privately Held**
SIC: 2759 Commercial Printing

(G-8633)
JOHN CARTER FIRE ESCAPE SVCS
70 G St (02127-2919)
PHONE..................................617 990-7387
John Carter, *Owner*
EMP: 3
SALES: 250K **Privately Held**
SIC: 3446 1799 Mfg Architectural Metalwork Trade Contractor

(G-8634)
JOHN LEWIS INC
352 Msschstts Ave Apt 515 (02115)
PHONE..................................617 266-6665
John Lewis, *President*
Louise Lewis, *President*
EMP: 5
SALES (est): 538.6K **Privately Held**
WEB: www.johnlewisinc.com
SIC: 3911 5944 Mfg & Ret Gold Jewelry

(G-8635)
JOHN P POW COMPANY INC
49 D St (02127-2401)
PHONE..................................617 269-6040
John F Pow, *President*
Thomas Finneran Jr, *Clerk*
EMP: 32 **EST:** 1935
SQ FT: 13,390
SALES (est): 5.5MM **Privately Held**
WEB: www.jppow.com
SIC: 2752 Lithographic Commercial Printing

(G-8636)
JOHNSON CONTROLS INC
33 Avenue Louis Pasteur (02115-5727)
PHONE..................................617 992-2073
EMP: 94 **Privately Held**
SIC: 2531 Mfg Automotive Seating
HQ: Johnson Controls Inc
5757 N Green Bay Ave
Milwaukee WI 53209
414 524-1200

(G-8637)
JOHNSONS FOOD PRODUCTS CORP
1 Mount Vernon St (02108)
PHONE..................................617 265-3400
Chris P Anton, *President*
Dieter Anton, *Vice Pres*
Peter Anton, *Vice Pres*
Helen Anton, *Treasurer*
John Anton, *Sales Mgr*
EMP: 14 **EST:** 1940
SQ FT: 15,000
SALES (est): 1.8MM **Privately Held**
SIC: 2026 Mfg Fluid Milk

(G-8638)
JORDAN BROS SEAFOOD CO INC
Also Called: Jordan Brothers Seafood
314 Northern Ave (02210-2316)
P.O. Box 101, Stoughton (02072-0101)
PHONE..................................508 583-9797
Thomas J Jordan III, *CEO*
Robert Jordan, *Treasurer*
EMP: 11
SALES (est): 129.8K **Privately Held**
SIC: 2092 5146 Mfg Fresh/Frozen Packaged Fish Whol Fish/Seafood

(G-8639)
JOURNAL INFECTIOUS DISEASES
225 Friend St (02114-1800)
PHONE..................................617 367-1848
Martin Hirsch, *Principal*
EMP: 4
SALES (est): 197.2K **Privately Held**
SIC: 2711 Newspapers-Publishing/Printing

(G-8640)
JOURNAL OF COMMERCE INC
88 Black Falcon Ave # 240 (02210-2425)
PHONE..................................617 439-7099
Matt Denapoli, *Opers Mgr*
Kara Mack, *CFO*
EMP: 3
SALES (est): 69.2K **Privately Held**
SIC: 2711 Newspapers-Publishing/Printing

(G-8641)
JOYN BIO LLC
27 Drydock Ave Ste 8 (02210-2383)
PHONE..................................978 549-3723
Mike Mille, *CEO*
Laurelin Wyntre, *Manager*
EMP: 20
SALES (est): 3.6MM **Privately Held**
SIC: 2836 Mfg Biological Products

(G-8642)
JRNI INC
179 Lincoln St (02111-2424)
PHONE..................................857 305-6477
John Federman, *CEO*
Glenn Shoosmith, *President*
Andy Watt, *CFO*
EMP: 4 **EST:** 2015
SALES (est): 196K **Privately Held**
SIC: 7372 Prepackaged Software Services

(G-8643)
JSI MEDICAL SYSTEMS CORP
1 Boston Pl Ste 2600 (02108-4420)
PHONE..................................917 472-5022
EMP: 3
SALES (est): 229.7K **Privately Held**
SIC: 3826 Mfg Analytical Instruments

(G-8644)
JUNIPER PHARMACEUTICALS INC (DH)
33 Arch St Ste 1000 (02110-1442)
PHONE..................................617 639-1500
Nikin Patel, *President*
Joel Dube, *Vice Pres*
Cristina Csimma, *Bd of Directors*
Mary Gray, *Bd of Directors*
Robert Harris, *Officer*
EMP: 31
SQ FT: 7,050
SALES: 49.9MM **Publicly Held**
WEB: www.columbialabs.com
SIC: 2834 Pharmaceutical Preparations

(G-8645)
JURIBA LIMITED
30 Newbury St (02116-3236)
PHONE..................................617 356-8681
Barry Angell, *Mng Member*
EMP: 30
SALES (est): 867.5K **Privately Held**
SIC: 7372 Prepackaged Software Services

(G-8646)
KAMROWSKI METAL REFINISHING
80 K St (02127-1613)
PHONE..................................508 877-0367
Richard Kamrowski, *Owner*
Deborah Kawrowski, *Co-Owner*
EMP: 7
SALES: 600K **Privately Held**
SIC: 3549 Mfg Metalworking Machinery

(G-8647)
KARUNA THERAPEUTICS INC
33 Arch St Ste 3110 (02110-1424)
PHONE..................................857 449-2244
Steven Paul, *Ch of Bd*
Andrew Miller, *COO*
Troy Ignelzi, *CFO*
Stephen Brannan, *Chief Mktg Ofcr*
EMP: 16
SQ FT: 7,000
SALES (est): 3MM **Privately Held**
SIC: 2834 Pharmaceutical Preparations

(G-8648)
KIDSBOOKS LLC
569 Boylston St Ste 200 (02116-3752)
PHONE..................................617 425-0300
Vic Cavallaro, *CEO*
Laura G Galvin, *Editor*
EMP: 9
SALES (corp-wide): 8.5MM **Privately Held**
SIC: 2731 Books-Publishing/Printing
PA: Kidsbooks Llc
3535 W Peterson Ave
Chicago IL 60659
773 509-0707

(G-8649)
KINETIC SYSTEMS INC
20 Arboretum Rd (02131-1102)
PHONE..................................617 522-8700
Alan D Gertel, *CEO*
Peter M Maris, *President*
Judith Solomon, *Treasurer*
◆ **EMP:** 45
SQ FT: 24,000
SALES (est): 9.9MM **Privately Held**
WEB: www.kineticsystems.com
SIC: 3829 3827 3821 3571 Mfg Measure/Control Dvcs Mfg Optical Instr/Lens Mfg Lab Apparatus/Furn Mfg Electronic Computers

(G-8650)
KINOTON AMERICA DISTRIBUTION
8 Goodenough St (02135-1903)
PHONE..................................617 562-0003
▲ **EMP:** 6
SALES: 3.6MM
SALES (corp-wide): 9.2MM **Privately Held**
WEB: www.kinotonamerica.com
SIC: 3861 Photographic Equipment/Supplies
PA: Boston Light & Sound, Incorporated
290 North Beacon St
Boston MA 02135
617 787-3131

(G-8651)
KITEWHEEL LLC
186 South St Ste 301 (02111-2701)
PHONE..................................617 447-2138
Lawrence Smith, *CEO*
Mark Smith, *President*
James Allum, *Partner*
Tim Claytor, *Vice Pres*
Sophie Slowe, *Vice Pres*
EMP: 25 **EST:** 2014
SQ FT: 5,000
SALES (est): 1.5MM **Privately Held**
SIC: 7372 Prepackaged Software Services

(G-8652)
KLEERMAIL LLC
30 Newbury St Ste 3 (02116-3239)
PHONE..................................888 273-3420
Brandon Beatty, *CFO*
EMP: 4
SQ FT: 1,200
SALES (est): 332.8K **Privately Held**
SIC: 7372 Prepackaged Software Services

(G-8653)
KNOLL INC
281 Summer St Fl 1 (02210-1536)
PHONE..................................617 695-0220
John Finken, *Regional Mgr*
Jennifer Roth, *Sales Staff*
Joseph Gierka, *Technical Staff*
Julia Leblanc, *Assistant*
EMP: 20
SQ FT: 2,000 **Publicly Held**
WEB: www.knoll.com
SIC: 2521 5021 5131 Mfg Wood Office Furniture Whol Furniture Whol Piece Goods/Notions
PA: Knoll, Inc.
1235 Water St
East Greenville PA 18041

(G-8654)
KOPLOW GAMES INC
369 Congress St Fl 5 (02210-1871)
P.O. Box 965, Hull (02045-0965)
PHONE..................................617 482-4011
James H Koplow, *President*
Lenny Kasanoff, *Opers Mgr*
Annmarie Gentile, *Sales Staff*
Gary Levine, *Sales Staff*
▲ **EMP:** 12
SQ FT: 7,000
SALES (est): 1.1MM **Privately Held**
WEB: www.koplowgames.com
SIC: 3944 Manufactures Dice Dice Cups & Board Games

(G-8655)
KRAVET INC
1 Design Center Pl # 300 (02210-2325)
PHONE..................................617 428-0370
EMP: 5
SALES (corp-wide): 197.2MM **Privately Held**
SIC: 2211 2221 2231 5131 Cotton Brdwv Fabric Mill Manmad Brdwv Fabric Mill Wool Brdwv Fabric Mill Whol Piece Goods/Notions
PA: Kravet Inc.
225 Cent Ave S
Bethpage NY 11714
516 293-2000

(G-8656)
KRUEGER INTERNATIONAL INC
109 Broad St (02110)
PHONE..................................617 542-4043
Paul Whalen, *Principal*
EMP: 7
SALES (corp-wide): 649.9MM **Privately Held**
SIC: 2522 Mfg Office Furniture-Nonwood
PA: Krueger International, Inc.
1330 Bellevue St
Green Bay WI 54302
920 468-8100

(G-8657)
KYON PHARMA INC
156 Porter St Apt 249 (02128-2137)
PHONE..................................617 567-2436
Phil Stears, *Principal*
EMP: 3
SALES (est): 346.7K **Privately Held**
SIC: 2834 Business Services At Non-Commercial Site

(G-8658)
LA SEMANA NEWSPAPER
Also Called: Cuenca Vision
903 Albany St (02119-2534)
P.O. Box 255258, Uphams Corner (02125-5258)
PHONE..................................617 427-6212
Pedro Cuenca, *Owner*
EMP: 3
SALES (est): 154.1K **Privately Held**
SIC: 2759 Commercial Printing

(G-8659)
LASH LAMOUR
129 Newbury St Fl 2 (02116-2928)
PHONE..................................617 247-1871
Cynthia Tsang, *Owner*
EMP: 3
SALES (est): 191.9K **Privately Held**
SIC: 3432 Beauty Shop

(G-8660)
LAWYERS WEEKLY LLC (PA)
40 Court St Fl 5 (02108-2202)
PHONE..................................617 451-7300
Jim Dolan, *President*
Scott J Pollei, *Treasurer*
EMP: 133
SALES (est): 6.8MM **Privately Held**
WEB: www.valawyersweekly.com
SIC: 2711 Operates As A Newspaper Publisher

(G-8661)
LEADING MARKET TECHNOLOGIES
58 Winter St Ste 5 (02108-4770)
PHONE..................................617 494-4747
Jay Kemp Smith, *CEO*
Austin Mao, *Marketing Staff*
Steven Clark, *CTO*
Rudy Parker, *Director*
Jason Smith, *Officer*
EMP: 32
SQ FT: 5,000
SALES (est): 3.1MM **Privately Held**
WEB: www.lmtech.com
SIC: 7372 Computer Software Development

(G-8662)
LEFTFIELD SOFTWARE
153 South St (02130-3884)
PHONE..................................617 524-3842
Conall McCabe, *Owner*
EMP: 5
SALES (est): 198.9K **Privately Held**
SIC: 7372 Prepackaged Software Services

(G-8663)
LEVR INC
260 Everett St Ste 2 (02128-2272)
PHONE..................................605 261-0083
Alonso Holmes, *Principal*
Ethan Sherr, *Director*
Patrick Walsh, *Director*
EMP: 3 **EST:** 2012
SALES (est): 122.9K **Privately Held**
SIC: 7372 Prepackaged Software

(G-8664)
LIBERTY MTALS MIN HOLDINGS LLC (PA)
175 Berkeley St (02116-5066)
PHONE..................................617 654-4374
A Alexander Fontanes, *Manager*
Elisa Gruber, *Analyst*
EMP: 5
SALES (est): 1.6MM **Privately Held**
SIC: 1081 Metal Mining Services

(G-8665)
LIFE FORCE BEVERAGES LLC
Also Called: Jubali
196 Quincy St (02121-1996)
PHONE..................................551 265-9482
Liam Madden, *President*
Theodore B Howell,
EMP: 5
SALES (est): 259.8K **Privately Held**
SIC: 2082 Mfg Malt Beverages

(G-8666)
LIGHTHOUSE WOODWORKS LLC
175 Wlliam F Mcclllan Hwy (02128-1185)
PHONE..................................781 223-4302
Daniel Noe, *Mng Member*
Lucas Jablonski,
EMP: 3
SALES (est): 114.3K **Privately Held**
SIC: 3429 Mfg Hardware

(G-8667)
LIGHTMATTER INC
61 Chatham St Fl 5 (02109)
PHONE..................................857 244-0460
Nicholas C Harris, *President*
Thomas Graham, *COO*
EMP: 23
SALES (est): 800.7K **Privately Held**
SIC: 3674 Mfg Semiconductors/Related Devices

(G-8668)
LISTEN INC
580 Harrison Ave Ste 3w (02118-2637)
PHONE..................................617 556-4104
Stephen F Temme, *President*
Nicholas Alston, *Mfg Spvr*
Kelly Pierce, *Opers Staff*
Pascal Brunet, *Research*
Daniel Knighten, *Engineer*
EMP: 15
SALES (est): 3.6MM **Privately Held**
SIC: 3826 Mfg Analytical Instruments

(G-8669)
LIVE CELL TECHNOLOGIES LLC
4 Longfellow Pl Apt 1805 (02114-2815)
PHONE..................................646 662-4157
Ramaswamy Krishnan PHD,
EMP: 3
SALES (est): 173K **Privately Held**
SIC: 3829 Mfg Measuring/Controlling Devices

(G-8670)
LOGAN STAMP WORKS INC
104 Meridian St 106 (02128-1972)
P.O. Box 521 (02128-0006)
PHONE..................................617 569-2121
Robert Vitale, *President*
Gary Vitale, *Vice Pres*
Tillie Vitale, *Treasurer*
Janice Vitale, *Clerk*
EMP: 7
SQ FT: 2,800
SALES (est): 793.9K **Privately Held**
WEB: www.loganstamp.com
SIC: 3953 Mfg Marking Devices

(G-8671)
LOGMEIN INC (PA)
320 Summer St Ste 100 (02210-1701)
PHONE..................................781 638-9050
William R Wagner, *President*
Michael J Donahue, *Senior VP*
Padmanabhan T Srinivasan, *Senior VP*
Mark F Strassman, *Senior VP*
Kevin Bardos, *Vice Pres*
▲ **EMP:** 120
SQ FT: 220,000
SALES: 1.2B **Publicly Held**
WEB: www.3amlabs.com
SIC: 7372 7379 Prepackaged Software And Consulting Services

(G-8672)
LOUIS W MIAN INC (PA)
547 Rutherford Ave (02129-1622)
PHONE..................................617 241-7900
Louis W Mian Jr, *President*
Bill Mian, *Owner*
Chanelle Romano, *Controller*
▲ **EMP:** 20
SQ FT: 4,423
SALES (est): 2.1MM **Privately Held**
WEB: www.louismian.com
SIC: 3281 5032 5211 1743 Mfg Cut Stone/Products Whol Brick/Stone Matrls Ret Lumber/Building Mtrl

(G-8673)
LUMENPULSE LIGHTING CORP
10 Post Office Sq Ste 900 (02109-4603)
PHONE..................................617 307-5700
Francois-Xavier Souvay, *President*
Ken Bruns, *Manager*
EMP: 25
SALES (est): 4.9MM
SALES (corp-wide): 36.3B **Privately Held**
SIC: 3646 Mfg Commercial Lighting Fixtures
HQ: Groupe Lumenpulse Inc
1220 Boul Marie-Victorin
Longueuil QC J4G 2
514 937-3003

(G-8674)
LUXCATH LLC
33 Arch St Fl 32 (02110-1424)
PHONE..................................617 419-1800
Terry Ransbury, *CTO*
Omar Amirana,
Christopher Silva,
EMP: 4 **EST:** 2012
SQ FT: 5,700
SALES (est): 422.8K **Privately Held**
SIC: 3845 Mfg Electromedical Equipment

(G-8675)
LUZY TECHNOLOGIES LLC
778 Boylston St Apt 6b (02199-7844)
PHONE..................................514 577-2295
Joaquin Leal Jimenez,
EMP: 30
SALES (est): 526.6K **Privately Held**
SIC: 7372 Prepackaged Software Services

(G-8676)
M1 PROJECT LLC
930 Commonwealth Ave (02215-1274)
PHONE..................................617 906-6032
James Murphy, *Mng Member*
EMP: 6
SALES (est): 74.5K **Privately Held**
SIC: 2511 Mfg Wood Household Furniture

(G-8677)
MACMILLAN PUBLISHING GROUP LLC
Bedford Books St Martins Press
75 Arlington St Fl 8 (02116-3936)
PHONE..................................646 307-5617
Joan Fineberg, *General Mgr*
Laura Arcari, *Editor*
Sophia Snyder, *Editor*
Ryan Sullivan, *Editor*
Victoria Anzalone, *Production*
EMP: 70
SQ FT: 3,000
SALES (corp-wide): 1.6B **Privately Held**
WEB: www.stmartins.com
SIC: 2731 Books-Publishing/Printing

GEOGRAPHIC

HQ: Macmillan Publishing Group, Llc
175 5th Ave
New York NY 10010
212 674-5145

(G-8678)
MACROMICRO LLC
20 Rowes Wharf Apt 409 (02110-3377)
PHONE..................................617 818-1291
Brad Peterson, *President*
EMP: 4 **EST:** 2011
SALES (est): 284.1K **Privately Held**
SIC: 7372 Prepackaged Software Services

(G-8679)
MAD RIVER DISTILLERS
321 Beacon St (02116-1102)
PHONE..................................617 262-1990
John Egan, *Principal*
EMP: 3
SALES (est): 147.2K **Privately Held**
SIC: 2085 Mfg Distilled/Blended Liquor

(G-8680)
MAMA ROSIES CO INC
10 Dorrance St (02129-1027)
PHONE..................................617 242-4300
Anthony Sardo, *President*
Charles Sardo, *Corp Secy*
Nicholas Sardo, *Treasurer*
EMP: 35 **EST:** 1976
SQ FT: 16,000
SALES (est): 7.1MM **Privately Held**
WEB: www.mamarosies.com
SIC: 2038 Mfg Frozen Specialties

(G-8681)
MARTINS NEWS SHOP
143 Hemenway St Apt 4 (02115-3741)
PHONE..................................617 267-1334
Paula Depina, *Principal*
EMP: 3 **EST:** 2008
SALES (est): 128.6K **Privately Held**
SIC: 2711 Newspapers-Publishing/Printing

(G-8682)
MASS BAY BREWING COMPANY INC (PA)
Also Called: Harpoon Brewery
306 Northern Ave (02210-2330)
PHONE..................................617 574-9551
Richard A Doyle, *CEO*
Daniel C Kenary, *President*
Warren Dibble, *CFO*
Mark Edwards, *Director*
▲ **EMP:** 125
SQ FT: 45,000
SALES (est): 35.4MM **Privately Held**
SIC: 2082 5921 Mfg Malt Beverages Ret Alcoholic Beverages

(G-8683)
MASSACHSTTS MED DVCS JURNL LLC
Also Called: Massdevice
8 Saint Marys St Ste 611 (02215-2421)
PHONE..................................617 358-5631
Brian Johnson,
EMP: 3
SALES: 150K **Privately Held**
SIC: 2711 Newspapers-Publishing/Printing

(G-8684)
MASSACHUSETTS CLEAN ENERGY CTR
Also Called: Masscec
63 Franklin St Fl 3 (02110-1301)
PHONE..................................617 315-9355
Stephen Pike, *CEO*
Joshua Kriesberg, *Project Mgr*
Jennifer R Daloisio, *CFO*
Susan Mlodozeniec, *Mktg Dir*
Ben Dodge, *Manager*
EMP: 41
SALES (est): 9MM **Privately Held**
SIC: 3822 Mfg Environmental Controls

(G-8685)
MASSACHUSETTS MEDICAL SOCIETY
Also Called: New England Journal Medicine
10 Shattuck St (02115-6030)
PHONE..................................617 734-9800
Mary Beth Hamel, *Editor*
John A Jarcho, *Editor*
Dan Longo, *Editor*
Jeff Drazen, *Manager*
Jeffrey Drazen, *Manager*
EMP: 50
SALES (corp-wide): 135.2MM **Privately Held**
SIC: 2721 8621 Periodicals-Publishing/Printing Professional Organization
PA: Massachusetts Medical Society Inc
860 Winter St
Waltham MA 02451
781 893-4610

(G-8686)
MASSACHUSETTS REPRO LTD
Also Called: Sir Speedy
1 Milk St Lbby Lbby (02109-5403)
P.O. Box 961406 (02196-1406)
PHONE..................................617 227-2237
Linda A Borash, *President*
Mark A Borash, *Treasurer*
EMP: 11
SQ FT: 5,000
SALES (est): 1.9MM **Privately Held**
SIC: 2752 2791 2789 Lithographic Commercial Printing Typesetting Services Bookbinding/Related Work

(G-8687)
MASSBIOLOGICS
460 Walk Hill St (02126-3120)
PHONE..................................617 474-3000
Michael F Collins, *Chancellor*
Bryant Fay, *Project Mgr*
Neal McNair, *Mfg Mgr*
Kyle Giroux, *Mfg Staff*
Stephen Greene, *Mfg Staff*
EMP: 200
SALES: 55.3MM
SALES (corp-wide): 2.4B **Privately Held**
SIC: 2836 8071 Mfg Biological Products Medical Laboratory
PA: University Of Massachusetts
1 Beacon St
Boston MA 02108
617 287-7000

(G-8688)
MATRIVAX RESEARCH & DEV CORP
650 Albany St Ste 117 (02118-2518)
PHONE..................................617 385-7640
Yichen Lu, *President*
EMP: 8
SQ FT: 1,200
SALES (est): 1.4MM **Privately Held**
SIC: 2834 Mfg Pharmaceutical Preparations

(G-8689)
MAVEL AMERICAS INC
121 Mount Vernon St (02108-1104)
PHONE..................................617 242-2204
Jeanne L Hilsinger, *President*
Kristi Gealy, *CFO*
EMP: 5
SALES (est): 1MM **Privately Held**
SIC: 3511 Mfg Turbines/Generator Sets

(G-8690)
MBM BUILDING SYSTEMS LTD
160 Federal St (02110-1700)
PHONE..................................617 478-3466
Damien Murtagh, *CEO*
EMP: 10
SALES: 200K **Privately Held**
SIC: 3999 7389 Mfg Misc Products Business Services

(G-8691)
MCKEARNEY ASSOCIATES INC (PA)
850 Summer St Ste 102 (02127-1569)
PHONE..................................617 269-7600
Donald Savoy, *Principal*
EMP: 7
SALES (est): 827.7K **Privately Held**
SIC: 2521 5021 Mfg Wood Office Furniture Whol Furniture

(G-8692)
MEDALLION GALLERY INC
350 Boylston St (02116-3805)
PHONE..................................617 236-8283
Amir H Shiranian, *President*
EMP: 3
SALES (est): 353.7K **Privately Held**
SIC: 2273 Mfg Carpets/Rugs

(G-8693)
MEDI - PRINT INC
Also Called: Printhouse, The
660 Huntin Ave (02115)
PHONE..................................617 566-7594
Gerry Ventola, *Branch Mgr*
EMP: 4
SALES (est): 294.5K
SALES (corp-wide): 4.2MM **Privately Held**
WEB: www.printhouse.com
SIC: 2752 2759 Lithographic Commercial Printing Commercial Printing
PA: Medi - Print Inc.
200 Maplewood St
Malden MA 02148
781 324-4455

(G-8694)
MEDICAL PUBLISHING ASSOC
55 Temple Pl (02111-1300)
PHONE..................................617 530-6222
Bob Cavilla, *Principal*
Peter Harrison, *Treasurer*
EMP: 3
SALES (est): 102.8K **Privately Held**
SIC: 2721 Periodicals-Publishing/Printing

(G-8695)
MENDIX INC
22 Boston Wharf Rd Fl 8 (02210-3032)
PHONE..................................857 263-8200
Derek Roos, *CEO*
Eric Erston, *Senior VP*
Derckjan Kruit, *Senior VP*
Donna Williams, *Senior VP*
Marcel Karssen, *CFO*
EMP: 120
SALES (est): 19.9MM
SALES (corp-wide): 96.9B **Privately Held**
SIC: 7372 Prepackaged Software Services
PA: Siemens Ag
Werner-Von-Siemens-Str. 1
Munchen 80333
896 360-0

(G-8696)
MERCK RESEARCH LABORATORIES
33 Avenue Louis Pasteur (02115-5727)
PHONE..................................617 992-2000
Christophe Winkelmann, *Owner*
EMP: 14 **EST:** 2016
SALES (est): 1.5MM **Privately Held**
SIC: 2834 Mfg Pharmaceutical Preparations

(G-8697)
MERCK SHARP & DOHME CORP
33 Avenue Louis Pasteur (02115-5727)
PHONE..................................617 992-2074
EMP: 3
SALES (est): 157K **Privately Held**
SIC: 2834 Mfg Pharmaceutical Preparations

(G-8698)
MERRILL CORPORATION
101 Federal St Ste 2102 (02110-1820)
PHONE..................................617 535-1500
Sean Othmer, *Manager*
Kathy Burke, *Director*
EMP: 40
SALES (corp-wide): 566.6MM **Privately Held**
WEB: www.merrillcorp.com
SIC: 2759 2752 Commercial Printing Lithographic Commercial Printing
PA: Merrill Corporation
1 Merrill Cir
Saint Paul MN 55108
651 646-4501

(G-8699)
METALSMITHS INC
15 Banton St (02124-2419)
PHONE..................................617 265-4040
Kevin Bronski, *President*
Cornelius O'Callaghan, *Vice Pres*
Ann Marie Bronski, *Treasurer*
EMP: 9
SQ FT: 14,000
SALES (est): 1.3MM **Privately Held**
WEB: www.metalsmiths.com
SIC: 3599 Mfg Industrial Machinery

(G-8700)
METASTAT INC (PA)
27 Drydock Ave Ste 2 (02210-2382)
PHONE..................................617 531-6500
Jerome B Zeldis, *Ch of Bd*
Douglas A Hamilton, *President*
Daniel H Schneiderman, *VP Finance*
Michael J Donovan, *Officer*
EMP: 6
SALES: 23.3K **Publicly Held**
SIC: 2834 Pharmaceutical Preparations

(G-8701)
METRO BOSTON LLC
234 Congress St Fl 4 (02110-2470)
PHONE..................................617 210-7905
Oskar Bjorner, *CFO*
Herman Miles, *Manager*
Robert Waterman, *Manager*
Mark Bonanni, *Account Dir*
EMP: 31
SALES (est): 2.1MM **Privately Held**
SIC: 2711 Newspapers-Publishing/Printing
HQ: Boston Sb Publishing Inc.
234 Congress St Fl 4
Boston MA 02110
617 210-7905

(G-8702)
METRO CORP
Also Called: Boston Magazine
300 Massachusetts Ave (02115-4544)
PHONE..................................617 262-9700
Rick Waechter, *CEO*
Kara Butterfield, *Editor*
Tessa Yannone, *Editor*
Grace Spinali, *Sales Staff*
EMP: 40 **Privately Held**
WEB: www.elegantwedding.com
SIC: 2721 Periodicals-Publishing/Printing
HQ: Metro Corp.
170 S Independence Mall
Philadelphia PA 19106
215 564-7700

(G-8703)
METSO USA INC (HQ)
133 Federal St Ste 302 (02110-1703)
PHONE..................................617 369-7850
Gabe White, *General Mgr*
Mike Phillips, *Senior VP*
Devin Cole, *Project Mgr*
Christopher Hampton, *Project Mgr*
John Hamilton, *Buyer*
◆ **EMP:** 4
SQ FT: 3,000
SALES (est): 722.3MM
SALES (corp-wide): 3.5B **Privately Held**
SIC: 3554 5084 Mfg Paper Industrial Machinery Whol Industrial Equipment
PA: Metso Oyj
Toolonlahdenkatu 2
Helsinki 00100
204 841-00

(G-8704)
MICHELE MERCALDO
Also Called: Mercaldo Studio
276 Shawmut Ave (02118-2125)
PHONE..................................617 350-7909
Michele Mercaldo, *Owner*
EMP: 3
SALES (est): 234.2K **Privately Held**
WEB: www.michelemercaldo.com
SIC: 3911 Ret Jewelry

(G-8705)
MIDDLESEX TRUCK & AUTO BDY INC
Also Called: Middlesex Truck & Coach
65 Gerard St (02119-2938)
PHONE..................................617 442-3000
Brian A Maloney, *President*
Sandra Maloney, *Clerk*
EMP: 42
SQ FT: 40,000
SALES: 6.9MM **Privately Held**
SIC: 3713 7532 5531 Mfg Truck/Bus Bodies Auto Body Repair/Paint Ret Auto/Home Supplies

▲ = Import ▼=Export
◆ =Import/Export

(G-8706)
MILK STREET PRESS INC
Also Called: Allegra Print & Imaging
8 Faneuil Hall Market Pl (02109-6114)
PHONE....................617 742-7900
Jonathan Hostage, *Vice Pres*
Jeffrey Hostage, *Treasurer*
Roseanne Dimino, *Accountant*
EMP: 17
SALES (est): 2.8MM **Privately Held**
SIC: 2752 8744 7334 Lithographic Commercial Printing Facilities Support Services Photocopying Services

(G-8707)
MILLENNIAL MEDIA INC
Also Called: Jumptap
155 Seaport Blvd Ste 800 (02210-2619)
PHONE....................617 301-4550
Paul Palmieri, *President*
EMP: 12
SALES (corp-wide): 130.8B **Publicly Held**
SIC: 7372 Prepackaged Software Services
HQ: Millennial Media, Inc.
2400 Boston St Ste 300
Baltimore MD 21224
410 522-8705

(G-8708)
MM REIF LTD
850 Albany St (02119-2545)
P.O. Box 191490 (02119-0029)
PHONE....................617 442-9500
Sydney Miller, *Ch of Bd*
Harry Miller, *President*
▲ **EMP:** 100
SALES (est): 8.4MM **Privately Held**
WEB: www.mmreif.com
SIC: 2394 2393 2241 Mfg Canvas/Related Products Mfg Textile Bags Narrow Fabric Mill

(G-8709)
MOLECULAR HEALTH INC
70 Fargo St Ste 902 (02210-2127)
PHONE....................832 482-3898
Lloyd Everson, *CEO*
Sven Riethmueller, *Senior VP*
Torsten Buergermeister, *Treasurer*
EMP: 22
SALES (est): 5.5MM **Privately Held**
SIC: 3822 Mfg Environmental Controls

(G-8710)
MOMEDX INC
285 Columbus Ave Unit 301 (02116-5293)
PHONE....................617 401-7780
Yuri Ostrovsky, *President*
EMP: 3
SALES (est): 195.7K **Privately Held**
SIC: 7372 Prepackaged Software Services

(G-8711)
MOQUIN AND DALEY PA
24 School St Ste 704 (02108-5113)
PHONE....................617 536-0606
Edmand Daley, *Partner*
EMP: 7
SQ FT: 1,666
SALES (corp-wide): 2.6MM **Privately Held**
WEB: www.moquindaley.com
SIC: 2711 Newspapers-Publishing/Printing
PA: Moquin And Daley Pa
212 Coolidge Ave
Manchester NH 03102
603 669-9400

(G-8712)
MORPHISEC INC
745 Atlantic Ave Ste 211 (02111-2735)
PHONE....................617 209-2552
Andrew Homer, *Vice Pres*
Yoav Tzruya, *Director*
EMP: 20
SALES (est): 57.7K **Privately Held**
SIC: 7372 Prepackaged Software Services
PA: Morphisec Information Security 2014 Ltd
77 Haenergia
Beer Sheva
885 637-31

(G-8713)
MOTIVE POWER
34 Farnsworth St (02210-1288)
PHONE....................857 350-3765
Paul Rosie, *Principal*
EMP: 3
SALES (est): 195.5K **Privately Held**
SIC: 3743 Mfg Railroad Equipment

(G-8714)
MOVIRI INC
211 Congress St Ste 400 (02110-2414)
PHONE....................857 233-5705
Sarah Towsley, *Human Res Mgr*
Andrea Gallo, *Technology*
EMP: 7
SALES (est): 587.5K
SALES (corp-wide): 25.5MM **Privately Held**
SIC: 7372 Prepackaged Software Services
PA: Moviri Spa
Via Simone Schiaffino 11
Milano MI 20158
024 951-7001

(G-8715)
MR DUMPSTER
145 Dorchester St Ste 292 (02127-2647)
PHONE....................781 233-3006
EMP: 3
SALES (est): 156.2K **Privately Held**
SIC: 3443 Mfg Fabricated Plate Work

(G-8716)
MULTEX AUTOMATION CORPORATION
263 Huntington Ave (02115-4506)
PHONE....................617 347-7278
Gary Multer, *President*
EMP: 6 **EST:** 1980
SQ FT: 2,500
SALES (est): 840.4K **Privately Held**
WEB: www.multexautomation.com
SIC: 3569 6531 Mfg Industrial Machinery Real Estate Agents & Brokers

(G-8717)
MUTUAL BEEF CO INC
Also Called: Victoria Brand
126 Newmarket Sq (02118-2603)
PHONE....................617 442-3238
Augustus D Martucci, *President*
Anthony E Martucci, *Director*
EMP: 15
SQ FT: 7,200
SALES (est): 2.2MM **Privately Held**
WEB: www.victoriabrand.com
SIC: 2011 Meat Packing Plant

(G-8718)
MYINVENIO US CORP
50 Milk St Fl 16 (02109-5002)
PHONE....................408 464-0565
Massimiliano Delsante, *CEO*
George Bennett, *Vice Pres*
EMP: 3
SALES (est): 71.1K **Privately Held**
SIC: 7372 Prepackaged Software Services

(G-8719)
MYSUNBUDDY INC
1 Center Plz Ste 320 (02108-1808)
PHONE....................404 219-2640
Kathryn Wright, *CEO*
Wilson Rickerson, *Vice Pres*
EMP: 4
SALES (est): 118.2K **Privately Held**
SIC: 7372 Prepackaged Software Services

(G-8720)
NATIONAL BRAILLE PRESS INC
88 Saint Stephen St (02115-4302)
PHONE....................617 425-2400
Brian A Macdonald, *President*
Paul Parravano, *Chairman*
Kimberley Ballard, *Vice Pres*
Jennifer Stewart, *Vice Pres*
Neal Rosen, *Treasurer*
EMP: 65
SQ FT: 14,000
SALES: 4.7MM **Privately Held**
WEB: www.nbp.org
SIC: 2721 2731 Periodicals-Publishing/Printing Books-Publishing/Printing

(G-8721)
NE MEDIA GROUP INC (PA)
Also Called: Boston Globe
1 Exchange Pl Ste 201 (02109-2132)
PHONE....................617 929-2000
Michael J Sheehan, *CEO*
Christopher Mayer, *President*
Kenneth Arichieri, *President*
R Anthony Benten, *Vice Pres*
Laurena L Emhoff, *Treasurer*
EMP: 100 **EST:** 1989
SQ FT: 669,000
SALES (est): 453.3MM **Privately Held**
WEB: www.bostonglobe.com
SIC: 2711 Newspapers-Publishing/Printing

(G-8722)
NEPTUNE GARMENT COMPANY
242 E Berkeley St Ste 3 (02118-2797)
PHONE....................617 482-3980
John Kindregan, *President*
EMP: 100 **EST:** 1922
SQ FT: 20,000
SALES: 4.8MM **Privately Held**
SIC: 2311 2385 Mfg Men's/Boy's Suits/Coats Mfg Waterproof Outerwear

(G-8723)
NETSUITE
268 Summer St Ste 400 (02210-1108)
PHONE....................877 638-7848
Ben Roberts, *Manager*
EMP: 7
SALES (est): 667.1K **Privately Held**
SIC: 7372 Prepackaged Software Services

(G-8724)
NEUROBO PHARMACEUTICALS INC (PA)
177 Huntington Ave # 1700 (02115-3165)
PHONE....................617 313-7331
Jeong Gu Kang, *President*
Nicola Shannon, *Vice Pres*
Mark Versavel, *Chief Mktg Ofcr*
EMP: 12 **EST:** 2008
SQ FT: 5,300
SALES (est): 2.1MM **Publicly Held**
SIC: 2834 Pharmaceutical Preparations

(G-8725)
NEUROBO THERAPEUTICS INC
177 Huntington Ave # 1700 (02115-3165)
PHONE....................617 313-7331
Jeong Gu Kang, *President*
Nicola Shannon, *Vice Pres*
Mark Versavel, *Chief Mktg Ofcr*
EMP: 13
SALES (est): 2.1MM **Publicly Held**
SIC: 2834 Pharmaceutical Preparations
PA: Neurobo Pharmaceuticals, Inc
177 Huntington Ave # 1700
Boston MA 02115
617 313-7331

(G-8726)
NEUROMOTION INC
Also Called: Neuromotion Labs
200 Portland St (02114-1722)
PHONE....................415 676-9326
Craig Lund, *CEO*
Trevor Stricker, *Vice Pres*
Jason Kahn, *Security Dir*
EMP: 12 **EST:** 2014
SALES: 50K **Privately Held**
SIC: 3944 7371 Mfg Games/Toys Custom Computer Programing

(G-8727)
NEW BALANCE ATHLETICS INC (HQ)
100 Guest St Fl 5 (02135-2088)
PHONE....................617 783-4000
Joe Preston, *President*
Barry Gutwillig, *President*
James S Davis, *Chairman*
Anne Davis, *Vice Chairman*
Sarah Harris, *Counsel*
◆ **EMP:** 400
SQ FT: 115,000
SALES (est): 722.6MM
SALES (corp-wide): 3.2B **Privately Held**
SIC: 3021 2321 2329 2339 Mfg Rubber/Plstc Ftwear Mfg Men/Boys Furnishings
PA: New Balance, Inc.
100 Guest St
Brighton MA 02135
617 783-4000

(G-8728)
NEW BEVERAGE PUBLICATIONS INC
Also Called: Massachusetts Beverage Bus
55 Clarendon St Ste 1 (02116-6067)
PHONE....................617 598-1900
Samuel Stone, *President*
Ben Stone, *Advt Staff*
Joyce Stone, *Clerk*
EMP: 7
SALES (est): 700K **Privately Held**
WEB: www.beveragebusiness.com
SIC: 2721 Magazine Publishing

(G-8729)
NEW BRAND SEBSATIANS LLC
100 Summer St (02110-2106)
PHONE....................617 624-7999
Eric Obeng, *Principal*
EMP: 4 **EST:** 2010
SALES (est): 221.3K **Privately Held**
SIC: 2051 Mfg Bread/Related Products

(G-8730)
NEW ENGLAND COMPOUNDING PHRM
Also Called: New England Compounding Center
100 High St Ste 2400 (02110-1767)
PHONE....................800 994-6322
Barry J Cadden, *President*
Carla Donigliaro, *Director*
EMP: 20 **EST:** 1998
SQ FT: 3,000
SALES (est): 4.3MM **Privately Held**
WEB: www.neccrx.com
SIC: 2834 Mfg Pharmaceutical Preparations

(G-8731)
NEW ENGLAND HOME
Also Called: New England Home Magazine
530 Harrison Ave Ste 302 (02118-2816)
P.O. Box 180464 (02118-0005)
PHONE....................617 938-3991
Kathy Bush-Dutton, *Publisher*
Roberta T Mancuso, *Publisher*
Kurt Coey, *Principal*
Debbie Hagan, *Editor*
Jill Korff, *Sales Mgr*
EMP: 3
SALES (est): 263.2K **Privately Held**
SIC: 2721 Periodicals-Publishing/Printing

(G-8732)
NEW ENGLAND SPT VENTURES LLC
4 Jersey St (02215-4148)
PHONE....................617 267-9440
John W Henry, *Owner*
EMP: 4
SALES (est): 421.7K **Privately Held**
SIC: 3949 Mfg Sporting/Athletic Goods

(G-8733)
NEW FRONTIER ADVISORS LLC (PA)
155 Federal St Ste 1000 (02110-1717)
PHONE....................617 482-1433
Matthew Pierce, *COO*
Abigail Gabrielse, *Vice Pres*
David Schubach, *Vice Pres*
Neha Sharma, *Vice Pres*
David Esch, *Research*
EMP: 3
SQ FT: 5,000
SALES: 1.8MM **Privately Held**
WEB: www.newfrontieradvisors.com
SIC: 7372 6282 Investment Advisory And Technology

(G-8734)
NEW GENERATION RESEARCH INC
Also Called: Turnaround Letter, The
88 Broad St Fl 2 (02110-3403)
PHONE....................617 573-9550
James Hammond, *CEO*
J Linzee Brown, *President*
Ben Schlafman, *Vice Pres*

GEOGRAPHIC

EMP: 10
SQ FT: 1,000
SALES (est): 1.4MM **Privately Held**
WEB: www.newgenerationresearch.com
SIC: 2721 6211 Periodicals-Publishing/Printing Security Broker/Dealer

(G-8735)
NEW VALENCE ROBOTICS CORP
Also Called: NV Bots
12 Channel St Ste 601 (02210-2333)
PHONE....................................857 529-6397
Alfonso Perez, *President*
Mateo Pea, *President*
Christopher Haid, *COO*
Mateo Pena Doll, *Vice Pres*
Edward Brady, *Finance Dir*
EMP: 8 **EST:** 2014
SALES (est): 1.1MM **Privately Held**
SIC: 2752 Lithographic Commercial Printing

(G-8736)
NEXTHINK INC
294 Washington St Ste 510 (02108-4612)
PHONE....................................617 576-2005
Pedro Bados, *President*
Vincent Bieri, *Admin Sec*
EMP: 25
SALES: 2MM
SALES (corp-wide): 35.5MM **Privately Held**
SIC: 7372 Prepackaged Software Services
PA: Nexthink Sa
Chemin Du Viaduc 1
Prilly VD 1008
215 665-440

(G-8737)
NICHOLAS BREALEY PUBG INC
Also Called: Nicholas Brealey North America
20 Park Plz Ste 610 (02116-4325)
PHONE....................................617 523-3801
Nicholas Brealey, *President*
Janet Crockett, *Principal*
EMP: 5
SQ FT: 1,000
SALES (est): 587.4K **Privately Held**
WEB: www.interculturalpress.com
SIC: 2731 Books-Publishing/Printing

(G-8738)
NINTH SENSE INC
8 Saint Marys St Ste 611 (02215-2421)
PHONE....................................617 835-4472
Raj Mohanty, *President*
EMP: 3
SALES (est): 159.6K **Privately Held**
SIC: 2835 Mfg Diagnostic Substances

(G-8739)
NORTEKUSA INC
21 Drydock Ave Ste 740e (02210-4508)
PHONE....................................617 205-5750
EMP: 8 **EST:** 2014
SALES (est): 1MM **Privately Held**
SIC: 3829 Mfg Measuring/Controlling Devices

(G-8740)
NORTH COAST SEA-FOODS CORP (PA)
5 Drydock Ave (02210-2303)
PHONE....................................617 345-4400
Norman A Stavis, *President*
James M Stavis, *Vice Pres*
Kathleen Moriarty, *Human Resources*
◆ **EMP:** 108
SQ FT: 100,000
SALES (est): 56.4MM **Privately Held**
SIC: 2092 5146 Mfg Fresh/Frozen Packaged Fish Whol Fish/Seafood

(G-8741)
NORTH END PRESS INC
5 Prince St (02113-2443)
PHONE....................................617 227-8929
Pamela Donnaruma, *President*
Donna Madiros, *Admin Sec*
EMP: 5
SALES (est): 426.3K **Privately Held**
SIC: 2752 Lithographic Commercial Printing

(G-8742)
NORTHAST RENEWABLE ENRGY GROUP
Also Called: Nereg
60 State St Ste 700 (02109-1894)
PHONE....................................617 878-2063
Richard Camarra, *Owner*
EMP: 8
SALES: 950K **Privately Held**
SIC: 3511 Mfg Turbines/Generator Sets

(G-8743)
NORTHEAST SHIP REPAIR INC (PA)
32a Drydock Ave (02210-2308)
PHONE....................................617 330-5045
Edward Snyder, *President*
Donna Connors, *Vice Pres*
Michelle Simpson, *Senior Buyer*
Bruce Zaniol, *CFO*
Ken Gentle, *Program Mgr*
EMP: 150
SQ FT: 32,580
SALES: 61MM **Privately Held**
SIC: 3731 Shipbuilding/Repairing

(G-8744)
NTT DATA INC
100 City Sq Ste 1 (02129-3730)
PHONE....................................617 241-9200
Dean Williams, *Exec VP*
Deborah Strayer, *Vice Pres*
Vijayakiran Kalavacharla, *Sr Project Mgr*
Barry Shurkey, *CIO*
EMP: 200 **Privately Held**
SIC: 7372 7379 7373 Prepackaged Software Services Computer Related Services Computer Systems Design
HQ: Ntt Data Inc.
7950 Legacy Dr Ste 900
Plano TX 75024
800 745-3263

(G-8745)
OLD IRONSIDES ENERGY LLC
10 Saint James Ave Ste 19 (02116-3533)
PHONE....................................617 366-2030
Gregory S Morzano, *Principal*
Sean P O'Neill, *Principal*
Daniel A Rioux, *Principal*
Edward Joullian, *Vice Pres*
David Delmore, *CFO*
EMP: 15
SALES (est): 2MM **Privately Held**
SIC: 1389 Oil/Gas Field Services

(G-8746)
OLDE BOSTONIAN
66 Von Hillern St (02125-1182)
PHONE....................................617 282-9300
David Greenwood, *Owner*
EMP: 9
SQ FT: 5,000
SALES: 120K **Privately Held**
SIC: 2431 Mfg Millwork

(G-8747)
ONAPSIS INC (PA)
60 State St Ste 1020 (02109-1842)
PHONE....................................617 603-9932
Mariano Nunez, *CEO*
Bob Darabant, *Vice Pres*
Darren Gaeta, *Vice Pres*
Lynn Nolitt, *Vice Pres*
Ezequiel Gresia, *Engineer*
EMP: 18 **EST:** 2012
SQ FT: 1,200
SALES (est): 5MM **Privately Held**
SIC: 7372 Prepackaged Software Services

(G-8748)
ONEBIN
19 Stanhope St Apt 1b (02116-5152)
PHONE....................................617 851-6402
Benjamin Levitt, *CEO*
Stephen Ajemian, *Director*
EMP: 3
SALES (est): 123.8K **Privately Held**
SIC: 3089 Mfg Plastic Products

(G-8749)
ONECLOUD LABS LLC
250 Summer St (02210-1151)
PHONE....................................781 437-7966
EMP: 16
SALES (est): 1.1MM **Privately Held**
SIC: 7372 Prepackaged Software Services

(G-8750)
ONEVIEW COMMERCE INC
70 Fargo St Ste 905 (02210-2127)
PHONE....................................617 292-0400
Stuart Mitchell, *CEO*
Maria Oha, *Partner*
Linda Palanza, *COO*
Chad Bratschi, *Sales Staff*
Giuseppe Bua, *Business Anlyst*
EMP: 15
SQ FT: 3,400
SALES: 6MM
SALES (corp-wide): 4.2MM **Privately Held**
SIC: 7372 7379 Prepackaged Software Services Computer Related Services
PA: Oneview Group Limited
201 Temple Chambers
London EC4Y
163 467-3172

(G-8751)
OPEN STUDIOS PRESS INC
Also Called: New American Paintings
450 Harrison Ave Ste 304 (02118-2502)
PHONE....................................617 778-5265
Steven Zevitas, *President*
Liz Morlock, *Editor*
Kayelani Ricks, *Opers Mgr*
Steven T Zevitas, *Production*
Alexandra Simpson, *Marketing Mgr*
▲ **EMP:** 3
SQ FT: 2,600
SALES: 1.5MM **Privately Held**
WEB: www.newamericanpaintings.com
SIC: 2721 Periodicals-Publishing/Printing

(G-8752)
OPEN TEXT INC
200 State St Fl 12 (02109-2605)
PHONE....................................617 378-3364
Paul J McFeeters, *CFO*
EMP: 3
SALES (corp-wide): 2.8B **Privately Held**
WEB: www.opentext.com
SIC: 7372 Prepackaged Software
HQ: Open Text Inc.
2950 S Delaware St
San Mateo CA 94403
650 645-3000

(G-8753)
OPENAIR INC
211 Congress St Fl 8 (02110-2410)
PHONE....................................617 351-0232
Morris J Panner, *CEO*
Tom Brennan, *CFO*
EMP: 60
SQ FT: 10,000
SALES (est): 3.8MM **Privately Held**
WEB: www.openair.com
SIC: 7372 Prepackaged Software Services

(G-8754)
OPENBRIDGE INC
119 Braintree St Ste 413 (02134-1697)
P.O. Box 990811 (02199-0811)
PHONE....................................857 234-1008
Thomas Spicer, *CEO*
Anna Shmelkova, *Marketing Staff*
EMP: 7
SQ FT: 1,500
SALES (est): 404.7K **Privately Held**
SIC: 7372 Prepackaged Software Services

(G-8755)
OPS-CORE INC
12 Channel St Ste 901b (02210-2323)
PHONE....................................617 670-3547
LP Frieder, *President*
David Garvey, *Director*
Heather M Acker, *Admin Sec*
▲ **EMP:** 13
SALES (est): 2.9MM **Privately Held**
WEB: www.ops-core.com
SIC: 3842 Mfg Surgical Appliances/Supplies

(G-8756)
OPSEC SECURITY INC
330 Congress St Fl 3 (02210-1216)
PHONE....................................617 226-3000
Jeffery Unger, *Branch Mgr*
Patrick Roach, *Director*
EMP: 17
SALES (corp-wide): 84.6MM **Privately Held**
SIC: 2671 3953 Mfg Packaging Paper/Film Mfg Marking Devices
HQ: Opsec Security, Inc.
1857 Colonial Village Ln
Lancaster PA 17601

(G-8757)
OPTIRTC INC
356 Boylston St Fl 2 (02116-3805)
PHONE....................................844 678-4782
David Rubinstein, *President*
Jon Dickinson, *Treasurer*
Danielle Fleming, *Office Mgr*
Darcy Parker, *Sr Software Eng*
EMP: 15
SALES (est): 1.2MM **Privately Held**
SIC: 7372 Prepackaged Software Services

(G-8758)
OREILLY MEDIA INC
2 Avenue De Lafayette # 6 (02111-1750)
PHONE....................................617 354-5800
Tim O Reilly, *Manager*
EMP: 250
SALES (corp-wide): 114.7MM **Privately Held**
WEB: www.oreilly.com
SIC: 2731 2741 Books-Publishing/Printing Misc Publishing
PA: O'reilly Media, Inc
1005 Gravenstein Hwy N
Sebastopol CA 95472
707 827-7000

(G-8759)
ORIGYN INC
780 Boylston St Apt 25k (02199-7825)
PHONE....................................781 888-8834
EMP: 3
SALES (est): 116.9K **Privately Held**
SIC: 2821 Mfg Plastic Materials/Resins

(G-8760)
ORSTED NORTH AMERICA INC
1 International Pl # 2610 (02110-2669)
PHONE....................................857 284-1430
Thomas Brostrm, *Director*
Martin Neubert, *Director*
Ole Kjems Srensen, *Director*
Ulrik Jarlov, *Admin Sec*
EMP: 4
SALES (est): 287.3K
SALES (corp-wide): 46.1MM **Privately Held**
SIC: 3511 Mfg Turbines/Generator Sets
HQ: Orsted A/S
Kraftvarksvej 53
Fredericia 7000
995 511-11

(G-8761)
OSCOMP SYSTEMS INC (PA)
337 Summer St 40 (02210-1702)
PHONE....................................617 418-4640
Pedro Santos, *President*
Jeremy Pitts, *Vice Pres*
◆ **EMP:** 4
SQ FT: 10,000
SALES (est): 711.6K **Privately Held**
SIC: 3563 Mfg Air/Gas Compressors

(G-8762)
OSSIPEE AGGREGATES CORPORATION (HQ)
100 N Washington St (02114-2128)
P.O. Box 9187 (02114-9187)
PHONE....................................617 227-9000
Dean Boylan, *President*
EMP: 3
SQ FT: 4,000
SALES (est): 5.6MM
SALES (corp-wide): 121MM **Privately Held**
SIC: 1442 Sand & Gravel Mining
PA: Boston Sand & Gravel Company Inc
100 N Washington St Fl 2
Boston MA 02114
617 227-9000

(G-8763)
OUTSYSTEMS INC
55 Thomson Pl (02210-1244)
PHONE..................................617 837-6840
Paulo Rosado, *Branch Mgr*
EMP: 15
SALES (corp-wide): 12.4MM **Privately Held**
SIC: 7372 Prepackaged Software Services
PA: Outsystems, Inc.
5901-C Peachtree Dunwoody
Atlanta GA 30328
404 719-5100

(G-8764)
PARAMETRIC TECHNOLOGY CORP
121 Seaport Blvd (02210-2050)
PHONE..................................781 370-5000
James E Heppelmann, *President*
Dave Rakestraw, *Engineer*
EMP: 8
SALES (est): 530.6K
SALES (corp-wide): 1.2B **Publicly Held**
SIC: 7372 Prepackaged Software Services
PA: Ptc Inc.
121 Seaport Blvd
Boston MA 02210
781 370-5000

(G-8765)
PARAMOUNT SOUTH BOSTON
667 E Broadway (02127-1503)
PHONE..................................617 269-9999
Joe Green, *Owner*
EMP: 7
SALES (est): 110.5K **Privately Held**
SIC: 2038 5812 Mfg Frozen Specialties Eating Place

(G-8766)
PARATEK PHARMACEUTICALS INC (PA)
75 Park Plz Ste 4 (02116-3934)
PHONE..................................617 807-6600
Evan Loh, *CEO*
Michael F Bigham, *Ch of Bd*
Randy Brenner, *Vice Pres*
Sarah Higgins, *Vice Pres*
Jeanne Jew, *Vice Pres*
EMP: 8
SQ FT: 12,000
SALES: 17.1MM **Publicly Held**
WEB: www.transcept.com
SIC: 2834 Pharmaceutical Preparations

(G-8767)
PATHAI INC
120 Brookline Ave (02215-3905)
PHONE..................................617 543-5250
Andrew Beck, *President*
EMP: 3
SALES (est): 138.6K **Privately Held**
SIC: 7372 7379 Prepackaged Software Services Computer Related Services

(G-8768)
PATHMAKER NEUROSYSTEMS INC
1 International Pl # 1400 (02110-2602)
PHONE..................................617 968-3006
Nader Yaghoubi, *CEO*
Jerry Jennings, *CTO*
EMP: 4
SALES (est): 291.4K **Privately Held**
SIC: 3845 Mfg Electromedical Equipment

(G-8769)
PATRIOT-NEWS CO
1 International Pl # 180 (02110-2600)
PHONE..................................617 345-0971
Andy Patel, *Branch Mgr*
EMP: 7
SALES (corp-wide): 55MM **Privately Held**
WEB: www.pennlive.com
SIC: 2711 Newspaper Printers & Publishers
PA: The Patriot-News Co
2020 Tech Pkwy Ste 300
Mechanicsburg PA 17050
717 255-8100

(G-8770)
PEARSON EDUCATION INC
Also Called: Pearson Eductl Measurement
501 Boylston St (02116-3798)
PHONE..................................617 848-6000
Kate Thibeault, *Safety Mgr*
Donald Kilburn, *Branch Mgr*
John Barrett, *Manager*
Pearl Weinstein, *Manager*
Nicholas Sweeny, *Producer*
EMP: 20
SALES (corp-wide): 5.4B **Privately Held**
WEB: www.phgenit.com
SIC: 2741 2731 Misc Publishing Books-Publishing/Printing
HQ: Pearson Education, Inc.
221 River St
Hoboken NJ 07030
201 236-7000

(G-8771)
PEARSON EDUCATION HOLDINGS INC
Prentice Hall
501 Boylston St Ste 900 (02116-3798)
PHONE..................................617 671-2000
Will Ethridge, *President*
William Henry Harrison, *Governor*
EMP: 99
SALES (corp-wide): 5.4B **Privately Held**
WEB: www.pearsoned.com
SIC: 2731 Books-Publishing/Printing
HQ: Pearson Education Holdings Inc.
330 Hudson St Fl 9
New York NY 10013
201 236-6716

(G-8772)
PEERGRADE INC (PA)
361 Newbury St Ste 412 (02115-2738)
PHONE..................................857 302-4023
David Kofoed Wind, *CEO*
Victor Wang, *Vice Pres*
EMP: 12
SALES (est): 664.2K **Privately Held**
SIC: 7372 Prepackaged Software Services

(G-8773)
PENINSULA SKINCARE LABS INC
7 Bulfinch Pl Ste 3 (02114-2929)
PHONE..................................650 339-4299
Belinda Nivaggioli, *President*
Lori Hoffman, *Vice Pres*
EMP: 3
SQ FT: 1,000
SALES (est): 272.6K **Privately Held**
SIC: 2844 Mfg Toilet Preparations

(G-8774)
PERFECT CURVE INC (PA)
137 South St Fl 3 (02111-2848)
PHONE..................................617 224-1600
Gregg Myles Levin, *President*
▲ **EMP:** 3
SQ FT: 3,500
SALES (est): 419.9K **Privately Held**
WEB: www.perfectcurve.com
SIC: 2339 2329 3949 Mfg Women's/Misses' Outerwear Mfg Men's/Boy's Clothing Mfg Sporting/Athletic Goods

(G-8775)
PERI FORMWORK SYSTEMS INC
11 Elkins St Ste 110 (02127-1628)
PHONE..................................857 524-5182
Chris Wells, *Sales Engr*
EMP: 3
SALES (corp-wide): 1.7B **Privately Held**
WEB: www.peri-usa.com
SIC: 3444 Mfg Sheet Metalwork
HQ: Peri Formwork Systems, Inc.
7135 Dorsey Run Rd
Elkridge MD 21075
410 712-7225

(G-8776)
PERKINELMER INC
549 Albany St (02118-2512)
PHONE..................................617 596-9909
Lorna Crocker, *Materials Mgr*
Sandra Thayer, *QA Dir*
Blas Cerda, *Engineer*
Richard Fischer, *Engineer*
Lisa Allen, *Manager*
EMP: 25
SALES (corp-wide): 2.7B **Publicly Held**
SIC: 3826 Mfg Analytical Instruments
PA: Perkinelmer, Inc.
940 Winter St
Waltham MA 02451
781 663-6900

(G-8777)
PHASE-N CORPORATION
Also Called: Phase N
256 Marginal St Ste 7 (02128-2800)
PHONE..................................617 737-0064
Steven B Woolfson, *President*
Samuel Pierce, *Engineer*
EMP: 4 **EST:** 2008
SALES (est): 710.6K **Privately Held**
SIC: 3841 Mfg Surgical/Medical Instruments

(G-8778)
PHILLIPS CANDY HOUSE INC
818 Wlliam T Mrrssey Blvd (02122-3404)
PHONE..................................617 282-2090
Phillip A Strazzula, *President*
Joseph Sammartino, *Clerk*
EMP: 23 **EST:** 1952
SQ FT: 5,000
SALES (est): 2.8MM
SALES (corp-wide): 13.7MM **Privately Held**
WEB: www.bostonbasket.com
SIC: 2064 5813 5812 2066 Mfg Candy/Confectionery Drinking Place Eating Place Mfg Chocolate/Cocoa Prdt
PA: Bay Colony Associates
818 Wlliam T Mrrssey Blvd
Boston MA 02122
617 287-9100

(G-8779)
PICTEX CORPORATION
1260 Boylston St (02215-4445)
PHONE..................................617 375-5801
Paul Lam, *Manager*
EMP: 3
SALES (est): 187.1K **Privately Held**
SIC: 2759 Commercial Printing

(G-8780)
PIONEER INSTNL SOLUTIONS
85 Devonshire St Fl 8 (02109-3574)
PHONE..................................617 723-2277
EMP: 3
SALES (est): 193.9K **Privately Held**
SIC: 2834 Mfg Pharmaceutical Preparations

(G-8781)
PLYNK CONNECT INC
19 Stanhope St Apt 2c (02116-5152)
PHONE..................................760 815-2955
Andrew Dimitruk, *CEO*
James Carlson, *Co-Owner*
EMP: 4
SALES (est): 200K **Privately Held**
SIC: 7372 Prepackaged Software Services

(G-8782)
PNDEROSA K ATC ACQUISITION INC
116 Huntington Ave (02116-5749)
PHONE..................................617 375-7500
James Tacilet, *CEO*
James Mucha, *Manager*
EMP: 3
SALES (est): 138.2K **Privately Held**
SIC: 3663 Mfg Radio/Tv Communication Equipment

(G-8783)
POINTILLIST INC
321 Summer St Fl 8 (02210-1725)
PHONE..................................617 752-2214
Ron Ruccico, *CEO*
EMP: 35
SALES (est): 594.5K **Privately Held**
SIC: 7372 Prepackaged Software Services

(G-8784)
POLKA DOG DESIGNS LLC (PA)
Also Called: Polka Dog Bakery
256 Shawmut Ave (02118-2125)
PHONE..................................617 338-5155
Deborah Gregg, *COO*
▲ **EMP:** 17
SALES (est): 1.6MM **Privately Held**
SIC: 2047 Mfg Dog/Cat Food

(G-8785)
POTOMAC ELECTRIC CORP
1 Westinghouse Plz A17 (02136-2075)
PHONE..................................617 364-0400
Leonard Chertov, *President*
Ellen Orengberg, *Corp Secy*
Leny Chertov, *Vice Pres*
Ellen Chertov, *Marketing Mgr*
▲ **EMP:** 20
SQ FT: 18,000
SALES: 2MM **Privately Held**
WEB: www.potomacelectric.com
SIC: 3625 Armature Rewinding

(G-8786)
POURER FEDORA LLC
35 Marlborough St (02116-2126)
PHONE..................................617 267-0333
Christopher Evans, *Principal*
EMP: 3
SALES (est): 214.3K **Privately Held**
SIC: 3089 Mfg Plastic Products

(G-8787)
POWER ADVOCATE INC
179 Lincoln St Ste 100 (02111-2425)
PHONE..................................415 615-0146
Ian Kalin, *Managing Dir*
EMP: 3
SALES (est): 172.2K **Publicly Held**
SIC: 7372 Prepackaged Software Services
HQ: Power Advocate, Inc.
179 Lincoln St
Boston MA 02111
857 453-5700

(G-8788)
POWEROPTIONS INC
Also Called: MASSHEFA
129 South St Fl 5 (02111-2837)
PHONE..................................617 737-8480
Cynthia Arcate, *President*
Meg Lusardi, *Vice Pres*
EMP: 7 **EST:** 1997
SALES: 3.3MM **Privately Held**
SIC: 1311 Crude Petroleum/Natural Gas Production

(G-8789)
PPG INDUSTRIES INC
272 Dorchester Ave (02127-2013)
PHONE..................................617 268-4111
Mark Edwards, *Branch Mgr*
EMP: 24
SALES (corp-wide): 15.3B **Publicly Held**
WEB: www.ppg.com
SIC: 2851 Mfg Paints/Allied Products
PA: Ppg Industries, Inc.
1 Ppg Pl
Pittsburgh PA 15272
412 434-3131

(G-8790)
PRECISION BIOPSY INC
100 High St Ste 2800 (02110-1761)
PHONE..................................720 859-3553
Amir Tehrani, *CEO*
Sarah Downing, *Engineer*
EMP: 5
SALES (est): 765.7K
SALES (corp-wide): 5.5MM **Privately Held**
SIC: 3841 Manufacture Surgical/Medical Instruments
PA: Allied Minds Plc
40 Dukes Place
London EC3A
203 727-1000

(G-8791)
PRESERVICA INC
50 Milk St Fl 16 (02109-5002)
PHONE..................................617 294-6676
Mike Thuman, *General Mgr*
Michael Thuman, *Principal*
Jonathan Tilbury, *Principal*
Frank Bruno, *Vice Pres*
Paul Allman, *CFO*
EMP: 20
SALES (est): 838.4K **Privately Held**
SIC: 7372 Prepackaged Software Services

(G-8792)
PRESIDENT FLLOWS HRVARD CLLEGE
Also Called: Harvard Business Review
60 Harvard Way (02163-1001)
PHONE..................................617 783-7888
Jason McNamara, *Vice Pres*
Gwen Gulick, *Marketing Staff*
Denise Clouse, *Branch Mgr*
Heidi Jarchow, *Manager*
Kevin Davis, *Technical Staff*
EMP: 4
SALES (corp-wide): 5.5B **Privately Held**
WEB: www.harvard.edu
SIC: 2711 5192 Newspapers-Publishing/Printing Whol Books/Newspapers
PA: President And Fellows Of Harvard College
1350 Massachusetts Ave
Cambridge MA 02138
617 496-4873

(G-8793)
PRESSED FOR TIME PRINTING INC
Also Called: Proprint
133 South St (02111-2802)
PHONE..................................617 267-4113
Joseph H Arthur, *President*
EMP: 4
SALES (est): 458.1K **Privately Held**
SIC: 2752 Lithographic Commercial Printing

(G-8794)
PRETTY INSTANT LLC
300 Summer St Apt 14b (02210-1113)
PHONE..................................888 551-6765
Christopher Thomas, *Principal*
Chris Cave, *COO*
Shef Reynolds, *Opers Staff*
Ben Collins, *Sales Staff*
EMP: 4
SALES (est): 305.9K **Privately Held**
SIC: 2752 Lithographic Commercial Printing

(G-8795)
PRFRRED LANCASTER PARTNERS LLC
200 Berkeley St (02116-5022)
P.O. Box 8880, Lancaster PA (17604-8880)
PHONE..................................717 299-0782
Joseph Handerhan, *Mng Member*
James Frantz, *Mng Member*
▲ **EMP:** 180
SQ FT: 260,000
SALES (est): 20.2MM **Privately Held**
WEB: www.lpllc.com
SIC: 3711 Mfg Motor Vehicle/Car Bodies

(G-8796)
PRINT ALL OF BOSTON INC
1279 Hyde Park Ave (02136-2703)
PHONE..................................617 361-7400
Kamalu L Macphilips, *Principal*
EMP: 4
SALES (est): 238.3K **Privately Held**
SIC: 2752 Lithographic Commercial Printing

(G-8797)
PROMISEC HOLDINGS LLC
1 Boston Pl Ste 2600 (02108-4420)
PHONE..................................781 453-1105
Daniel Ross, *CEO*
Pantelis Georgiadis, *Ch of Bd*
John Reilly, *CFO*
EMP: 5
SALES (est): 525.7K **Privately Held**
SIC: 7372 Prepackaged Software Services

(G-8798)
PROTEOSTASIS THERAPEUTICS INC
80 Guest St Ste 500 (02135-2071)
PHONE..................................617 225-0096
M James Barrett, *Ch of Bd*
Meenu Chhabra, *President*
Sheila Wilson, *COO*
Janet Smart, *Vice Pres*
Geoffrey Gilmartin, *Chief Mktg Ofcr*
EMP: 52
SQ FT: 30,000
SALES: 2.8MM **Privately Held**
SIC: 2834 Pharmaceutical Preparations

(G-8799)
PURETECH HEALTH LLC (PA)
Also Called: Bio Pharmaceutical
6 Tide St Ste 400 (02210-2658)
PHONE..................................617 482-2333
Stephen Muniz, *COO*
Jacob Stein, *Vice Pres*
Joep Muijrers, *CFO*
William Berry, *Controller*
Joseph Bolen, *Officer*
▲ **EMP:** 51
SQ FT: 4,712
SALES (est): 52.1MM **Privately Held**
WEB: www.puretechventures.com
SIC: 2836 Mfg Non Diagnostic Biological Products

(G-8800)
PURITAN FOOD CO INC
17 Food Mart Rd (02118-2801)
PHONE..................................617 269-5650
Mark J Wolff, *President*
EMP: 40
SQ FT: 9,000
SALES (est): 4.6MM **Privately Held**
SIC: 2015 Poultry Processing

(G-8801)
PURITAN ICE CREAM CO OF BOSTON
3895 Washington St (02131-1297)
PHONE..................................617 524-3580
Charles Rando Jr, *President*
Stephen Rando, *Treasurer*
Katherine Coats, *Clerk*
EMP: 9
SQ FT: 25,000
SALES (est): 520K **Privately Held**
SIC: 2024 Mfg Ice Cream/Frozen Desserts

(G-8802)
Q A S
125 Summer St Ste 1910 (02110-1615)
PHONE..................................617 345-3000
▲ **EMP:** 5 **EST:** 2008
SALES (est): 740K **Privately Held**
SIC: 2048 Mfg Prepared Feeds

(G-8803)
QUANTUM DISCOVERIES INC
53 State St Ste 500 (02109-3111)
PHONE..................................857 272-9998
Ilan Naor, *President*
EMP: 3 **EST:** 2017
SALES (est): 271.2K **Privately Held**
SIC: 1382 1021 Oil/Gas Exploration Services Copper Ore Mining

(G-8804)
QUARTER LLC
867 Boylston St (02116-2774)
PHONE..................................617 848-1249
EMP: 3
SALES (est): 75.6K **Privately Held**
SIC: 3131 Footwear Cut Stock

(G-8805)
QUINLAN PUBLISHING CO INC (PA)
Also Called: Quinlan Publishing Group
23 Drydock Ave Fl 2 (02210-2371)
PHONE..................................617 439-0076
E Michael Quinlan, *President*
Anne T Moran, *Treasurer*
EMP: 9
SQ FT: 16,000
SALES: 2.5MM **Privately Held**
WEB: www.quinlan.com
SIC: 2721 2731 2741 Periodicals-Publishing/Printing Books-Publishing/Printing Misc Publishing

(G-8806)
R R DONNELLEY & SONS COMPANY
Donnelley Financial
20 Custom House St # 650 (02110-3513)
PHONE..................................617 345-4300
Robert Smithson, *Principal*
EMP: 60
SALES (corp-wide): 6.8B **Publicly Held**
WEB: www.rrdonnelley.com
SIC: 2759 Commercial Printing
PA: R. R. Donnelley & Sons Company
35 W Wacker Dr
Chicago IL 60601
312 326-8000

(G-8807)
RACEMAKER PRESS
39 Church St (02116-5311)
PHONE..................................617 391-0911
Joseph S Freeman, *Principal*
▲ **EMP:** 4 **EST:** 2008
SALES (est): 292.5K **Privately Held**
SIC: 2741 Misc Publishing

(G-8808)
RADIUS PIPESYSTEMS CORP
465 Commonwealth Ave # 2 (02215-2220)
PHONE..................................857 263-7161
Dmitry Ostrovsky, *Treasurer*
EMP: 3
SALES (est): 179.7K **Privately Held**
SIC: 3089 Mfg Plastic Products

(G-8809)
RAND CORPORATION
20 Park Plz Ste 920 (02116-4316)
PHONE..................................617 338-2059
Kristin Sereyko, *Admin Asst*
EMP: 6
SALES (corp-wide): 295.7MM **Privately Held**
SIC: 3131 Mfg Footwear Cut Stock
PA: The Rand Corporation
1776 Main St
Santa Monica CA 90401
310 393-0411

(G-8810)
RAPID7 INC (PA)
120 Causeway St Ste 400 (02114-1314)
PHONE..................................617 247-1717
Corey E Thomas, *Ch of Bd*
Andrew Burton, *President*
Jillian Finch, *Partner*
Peter Kaes, *Senior VP*
Maureen Henderson, *Project Mgr*
EMP: 106
SQ FT: 75,000
SALES: 244MM **Publicly Held**
SIC: 7372 Prepackaged Software

(G-8811)
REACH DISTRIBUTION INC
Also Called: Kahla Porcelain USA
6 Tide St (02210-2658)
PHONE..................................617 542-6466
Curt Cartenter, *President*
▲ **EMP:** 5
SALES (est): 450K **Privately Held**
WEB: www.reachdistribution.com
SIC: 3634 Mfg Electric Housewares/Fans

(G-8812)
REAL DATA CORP
280 Summer St Fl 8 (02210-1131)
PHONE..................................603 669-3822
Irvin Tolles, *President*
EMP: 6
SQ FT: 1,500
SALES (est): 504.1K **Privately Held**
SIC: 2741 8111 Misc Publishing Legal Services Office

(G-8813)
REBISCAN INC
Also Called: Rebion
100 Cambridge St 14 (02114-2509)
PHONE..................................857 600-0982
Justin Shaka, *CEO*
David G Hunter, *Ch of Bd*
EMP: 11
SALES (est): 261.7K **Privately Held**
SIC: 3841 Mfg Surgical/Medical Instruments

(G-8814)
RED FRAMES INC (HQ)
Also Called: Apperian
285 Summer St Fl 2 (02210-1518)
PHONE..................................617 477-8740
Brian Day, *CFO*
Mark Lorion, *Chief Mktg Ofcr*
John Caldas, *Software Engr*
EMP: 10
SALES (est): 4.9MM
SALES (corp-wide): 24.8MM **Privately Held**
SIC: 7372 Prepackaged Software Services
PA: Arxan Technologies, Inc.
650 California St Fl 2750
San Francisco CA 94108
415 247-0900

(G-8815)
REDI2 TECHNOLOGIES INC
211 Congress St 200 (02110-2410)
PHONE..................................617 910-3282
Seth B Johnson, *CEO*
Thomas Huddleston, *Managing Dir*
Aubree Browning, *Marketing Staff*
EMP: 35
SALES (est): 4MM **Privately Held**
WEB: www.redi2.com
SIC: 7372 Prepackaged Software Services

(G-8816)
REEBOK INTERNATIONAL LTD (HQ)
25 Drydock Ave Ste 110 (02210-2636)
PHONE..................................781 401-5000
Mark King, *President*
Ulrich Becker, *Partner*
Suzanne Biszantz, *Partner*
David A Pace, *Partner*
Terry R Pillow, *Partner*
◆ **EMP:** 400
SQ FT: 13,272
SALES (est): 2.6B
SALES (corp-wide): 24.3B **Privately Held**
WEB: www.reebok.com
SIC: 3149 3143 3144 2329 Mfg Footwear-Ex Rubber Mfg Men's Footwear Mfg Women's Footwear Mfg Mens/Boys Clothing Mfg Women/Miss Outerwear
PA: Adidas Ag
Adi-DaBler-Str. 1
Herzogenaurach 91074
913 284-0

(G-8817)
REIFY HEALTH INC
745 Atlantic Ave (02111-2735)
PHONE..................................617 861-8261
Michael Lin, *Director*
EMP: 5
SALES (est): 253.9K **Privately Held**
SIC: 7372 Prepackaged Software Services

(G-8818)
RESTORBIO INC
500 Boylston St Ste 1300 (02116-3791)
PHONE..................................857 315-5521
Chen Schor, *President*
John J McCabe, *CFO*
Meredith Manning, *Ch Credit Ofcr*
Joan Mannick, *Chief Mktg Ofcr*
EMP: 21
SQ FT: 4,544
SALES (est): 2.1MM **Privately Held**
SIC: 2834 8731 Pharmaceutical Preparations And Commercial Physical Research

(G-8819)
RF BIOCIDICS INC
33 Arch St Fl 29 (02110-1424)
PHONE..................................617 419-1800
Marc Eichenberger, *CEO*
Chris Silva, *Ch of Bd*
EMP: 7
SQ FT: 2,000
SALES (est): 853.8K **Privately Held**
SIC: 3523 Mfg Agricultural Disinfection Equipment

(G-8820)
RHYTHM PHARMACEUTICALS INC
222 Berkeley St Ste 1200 (02116-3733)
PHONE..................................857 264-4280
David P Meeker, *Ch of Bd*
Keith M Gottesdiener, *President*
Hunter C Smith, *CFO*
Nithya Desikan, *Ch Credit Ofcr*
Simon Kelner, *VP Human Res*
EMP: 36
SQ FT: 6,830
SALES (est): 9.1MM **Privately Held**
SIC: 2834 Mfg Pharmaceutical Preparations

(G-8821)
RIFFR LLC
7 Faneuil Hall Market Pl # 4 (02109-6113)
PHONE....617 851-5989
Toufic Mobarak,
EMP: 5
SALES (est): 117.2K **Privately Held**
SIC: 7372 Prepackaged Software Services

(G-8822)
RJ PRINTING LLC
Also Called: Sir Speedy
98 N Washington St Ste B2 (02114-1913)
PHONE....617 523-7656
Joseph Rydzewski, *Mng Member*
EMP: 5
SALES (est): 570K **Privately Held**
SIC: 2752 Comm Prtg Litho

(G-8823)
ROAM DATA INC
Also Called: Ingenico Mobile Solutions
101 Federal St Ste 700 (02110-1852)
PHONE....888 589-5885
Jacques Gurin, *CEO*
Ward Hewins, *Vice Pres*
Kevin West, *VP Sales*
Tim Reidy, *Sales Staff*
Ketan Deshpande, *Marketing Staff*
EMP: 40
SALES (est): 8.3MM **Privately Held**
WEB: www.roamdata.com
SIC: 7372 Prepackaged Software Services
PA: Ingenico International India Private Limited
A-5,6,7 Amco Tower, 2nd Floor
Noida UP 20130

(G-8824)
ROBBINS BEEF CO INC
35 Food Mart Rd 37 (02118-2801)
PHONE....617 269-1826
Jeff Corin, *President*
EMP: 18
SQ FT: 6,000
SALES (est): 3.5MM **Privately Held**
SIC: 2011 Meat Packing Plant

(G-8825)
ROBERT WEISS ASSOCIATES INC
Also Called: Air Travel Journal
256 Marginal St Ste 2 (02128-2800)
PHONE....617 561-4000
Robert H Weiss, *President*
▲ **EMP:** 5
SALES (est): 280K **Privately Held**
SIC: 2711 Newspaper Publisher

(G-8826)
ROGERSON ORTHOPEDIC APPLS INC
483 Southampton St (02127-2798)
PHONE....617 268-1135
Peter Rogerson, *President*
John Rogerson, *Vice Pres*
Paula Doherty, *Admin Sec*
EMP: 10
SQ FT: 1,600
SALES: 1MM **Privately Held**
SIC: 3842 Mfg Orthopedic Appliances

(G-8827)
ROOTPATH GENOMICS INC
43 Charles St Ste 2 (02114-4640)
PHONE....501 258-0969
EMP: 3 **EST:** 2017
SALES (est): 259.9K **Privately Held**
SIC: 2835 Mfg Diagnostic Substances

(G-8828)
ROYAL LABEL CO INC
50 Park St Ste 3 (02122-3287)
PHONE....617 825-6050
Paul Clifford, *President*
Eileen Ezepik, *Treasurer*
EMP: 18
SQ FT: 20,000
SALES (est): 2.7MM **Privately Held**
WEB: www.royallabel.com
SIC: 2759 Commercial Printing

(G-8829)
RS NAZARIAN INC
Also Called: R S Nasarian
333 Washington St Ste 625 (02108-5172)
PHONE....617 723-3040
Sarkis Nazarian, *President*
Robert S Nazarian, *Principal*
EMP: 15
SQ FT: 500
SALES (est): 2.9MM **Privately Held**
WEB: www.rsnazarian.com
SIC: 3911 Mfg Precious Metal Jewelry

(G-8830)
S M LORUSSO & SONS INC
Also Called: West Roxbury Crushed Stone Div
10 Grove St (02132-4510)
PHONE....617 323-6380
Edward Sonia, *General Mgr*
EMP: 20
SALES (corp-wide): 29.4MM **Privately Held**
SIC: 1442 Construction Sand/Gravel
PA: S. M. Lorusso & Sons, Inc.
331 West St
Walpole MA 02081
508 668-2600

(G-8831)
SAFARI BOOKS ONLINE LLC
2 Avenue De Lafayette 6 (02111-1750)
PHONE....617 426-8600
Andrew Savikas, *President*
Jeanette Mayer, *Office Mgr*
EMP: 5
SALES (corp-wide): 7.4MM **Privately Held**
SIC: 2741 Internet Publishing And Broadcasting
PA: Safari Books Online, Llc
1003 Gravenstein Hwy N
Sebastopol CA 95472
707 827-7000

(G-8832)
SALARIUS PHARMACEUTICALS INC (PA)
800 Boylston St Fl 24 (02199-1900)
PHONE....617 874-1821
Christoph Westphal, *Ch of Bd*
William McVicar, *President*
Katharine Lindemann, *COO*
Elizabeth Woo, *Senior VP*
David Golod, *Vice Pres*
EMP: 30
SQ FT: 7,234
SALES: 838.1K **Publicly Held**
SIC: 2023 Dietary Supplements

(G-8833)
SALEM PREFERRED PARTNERS LLC (PA)
200 Berkeley St Fl 3 (02116-5030)
PHONE....540 389-3922
Joseph Handerhan,
EMP: 150
SQ FT: 140,000
SALES (est): 12.9MM **Privately Held**
SIC: 3519 Mfg Internal Combustion Engines

(G-8834)
SALESBRIEF INC
695 Atlantic Ave (02111-2623)
PHONE....203 216-0270
EMP: 3
SALES (est): 71.1K **Privately Held**
SIC: 7372 Prepackaged Software Services

(G-8835)
SALESFORCECOM INC
500 Boylston St Fl 19 (02116-3740)
PHONE....857 415-3510
Sal Caruso, *Engineer*
Anand Deb, *Manager*
Pat Regan, *Executive*
EMP: 6
SALES (corp-wide): 13.2B **Publicly Held**
SIC: 7372 Prepackaged Software Services
PA: Salesforce.Com, Inc.
415 Mission St Fl 3
San Francisco CA 94105
415 901-7000

(G-8836)
SALON MONET
176 Newbury St Ste 400 (02116-2872)
PHONE....617 425-0010
Sharon Martin, *Principal*
EMP: 3
SALES (est): 193.5K **Privately Held**
SIC: 3999 Mfg Misc Products

(G-8837)
SAMARC INC
Also Called: Coop's Microcreamery
28 Damrell St Ste B01 (02127-3066)
PHONE....617 924-3884
Marc L Cooper, *President*
Felice Mendell, *Admin Sec*
EMP: 5
SQ FT: 1,000
SALES (est): 292.8K **Privately Held**
WEB: www.samarc.org
SIC: 2064 2066 Mfg Candy/Confectionery Mfg Chocolate/Cocoa Products

(G-8838)
SARA CAMPBELL LTD (PA)
67 Kemble St Ste 4 (02119-2841)
PHONE....617 423-3134
Sara Campbell, *President*
Courtney Harris, *Store Mgr*
Nicole Conley, *Buyer*
Jessica Slavin, *Buyer*
Kenneth Maloney, *Treasurer*
▲ **EMP:** 19
SQ FT: 10,000
SALES (est): 4.5MM **Privately Held**
WEB: www.bundle-track.com
SIC: 2337 7389 Mfg Women's/Misses' Suits/Coats Business Services

(G-8839)
SCHNEIDER ELECTRIC USA INC (DH)
201 Wshington St Ste 2700 (02108)
PHONE....978 975-9600
Annette Clayton, *President*
Barry Mosbrucker, *President*
Kevin Sweeney, *President*
Marcel Hochet, *Managing Dir*
Jean P Cherighy, *Principal*
◆ **EMP:** 600
SALES (est): 5.9B
SALES (corp-wide): 177.9K **Privately Held**
WEB: www.squared.com
SIC: 3643 3612 3823 3625 Mfg Conductive Wire Dvcs Mfg Transformers Mfg Process Cntrl Instr

(G-8840)
SCIENTIFIC INSTRUMENT FACILITY
590 Commonwealth Ave # 255 (02215-2521)
PHONE....617 353-5056
Mike McKanna, *Director*
EMP: 10
SQ FT: 12,000
SALES (est): 597.5K **Privately Held**
SIC: 3599 Machine Shop Jobbing & Repair Mfg

(G-8841)
SEA MACHINES ROBOTICS INC (PA)
256 Marginal St Ste 14a (02128-2859)
PHONE....617 455-6266
Michael Johnson, *CEO*
Jim Daly, *COO*
Don Black, *VP Sls/Mktg*
EMP: 8
SALES (est): 1.1MM **Privately Held**
SIC: 3829 Mfg Measuring/Controlling Devices

(G-8842)
SEABOARD FLOUR LLC (PA)
6 Liberty Sq (02109-5800)
PHONE....917 928-6040
EMP: 4
SALES (est): 6.5B **Publicly Held**
SIC: 2041 Mfg Flour/Grain Mill Proroducts

(G-8843)
SELVITA INC
100 Cambridge St Ste 1400 (02114-2545)
PHONE....857 998-4075
Peter N Barnes-Brown, *Principal*
EMP: 4
SALES (est): 222.4K **Privately Held**
SIC: 2834 Mfg Pharmaceutical Preparations

(G-8844)
SENSOMOTORIC INSTRUMENTS INC
236 Lewis Wharf (02110-3927)
P.O. Box 4425, Salem (01970-6425)
PHONE....617 557-0010
EMP: 6
SQ FT: 300
SALES (est): 1MM
SALES (corp-wide): 6.8MM **Privately Held**
WEB: www.smiusa.com
SIC: 3845 3812 Mfg Electromedical Apparatus
PA: Smi Holding Gmbh
Warthestr. 21
Teltow 14513
332 839-5510

(G-8845)
SIGNS BY J INC
100 Tenean St (02122-3620)
PHONE....617 825-9855
Edmund P A Jagiello, *President*
Michael P Cohen, *Vice Pres*
EMP: 7
SQ FT: 9,000
SALES (est): 1.2MM **Privately Held**
WEB: www.signsbyj.com
SIC: 3993 2394 Mfg Signs/Advertising Specialties Mfg Canvas/Related Products

(G-8846)
SILEX MICROSYSTEMS INC
9 Hamilton Pl Ste 300 (02108-4715)
PHONE....617 834-7197
Gary Johnson, *President*
Peter Himes, *Vice Pres*
Roland Nilsson, *Treasurer*
Susanne Palo, *Admin Sec*
EMP: 10
SALES (est): 1.1MM **Privately Held**
SIC: 3674 Mfg Semiconductors/Related Devices

(G-8847)
SIMON PEARCE US INC
115 Newbury St Ste 1 (02116-2970)
PHONE....617 450-8388
Christine Deliveau, *Principal*
EMP: 8
SALES (corp-wide): 64.2MM **Privately Held**
WEB: www.simonpearce.com
SIC: 3229 Mfg Glass Furnishings
PA: Simon Pearce U.S., Inc.
109 Park Rd
Windsor VT 05089
802 674-6280

(G-8848)
SING TAO NEWSPAPERS NY LTD
128 Lincoln St Ste 106 (02111-2545)
PHONE....617 426-9642
Klysler Yen, *Manager*
EMP: 20 **Privately Held**
WEB: www.nysingtao.com
SIC: 2711 Newspapers-Publishing/Printing
PA: Sing Tao Newspapers New York Ltd.
188 Lafayette St
New York NY 10013

(G-8849)
SKELMET INC
21 Drydock Ave Ste 610 (02210-2384)
PHONE....617 396-0612
Rain Wang, *CEO*
EMP: 3 **EST:** 2015
SALES (est): 85.1K **Privately Held**
SIC: 3851 Mfg Ophthalmic Goods

GEOGRAPHIC

(G-8850)
SMARTER TRAVEL MEDIA LLC
Also Called: Smarter Living
226 Causeway St Ste 3 (02114-2283)
PHONE..................................617 886-5555
David Krauter, *Vice Pres*
Adam Holbrook, *Technical Mgr*
Mike Johnson, *Engineer*
Brett Milliken, *Accounting Mgr*
Colin Quigley, *Sales Mgr*
EMP: 130 **EST:** 1998
SALES (est): 13.7MM
SALES (corp-wide): 1.6B **Publicly Held**
WEB: www.smartermagazine.com
SIC: 2721 4724 Periodicals-Publishing/Printing Travel Agency
HQ: Tripadvisor, Inc.
400 1st Ave
Needham MA 02494
781 800-5000

(G-8851)
SOFTBANK ROBOTICS AMERICA INC
55 Thomson Pl (02210-1244)
PHONE..................................617 986-6700
Eric Stevenson, *President*
Valerie Jabot, *Exec VP*
Dai Sakata, *Exec VP*
Kenichi K Yoshida, *Exec VP*
Nicolas Boudot, *Vice Pres*
EMP: 30 **EST:** 2010
SALES (est): 6MM
SALES (corp-wide): 42.7MM **Privately Held**
SIC: 3535 5099 Mfg Conveyors/Equipment Whol Durable Goods
PA: Softbank Robotics Europe
Aldebaran Violet Softbank Robotics Eur
Paris 15e Arrondissement 75015
177 371-752

(G-8852)
SOLOS ENDOSCOPY INC
65 Sprague St (02136-2061)
PHONE..................................617 360-9700
Dom Gatto, *Ch of Bd*
Fred Schiemann, *Treasurer*
Amanda B Segersten, *Treasurer*
EMP: 8
SQ FT: 7,000
SALES: 1MM
SALES (corp-wide): 197.9K **Privately Held**
WEB: www.solosendoscopy.com
SIC: 3845 5049 7699 Manufactures Wholesales Retails And Repairs Medical Video Devices And Related Optical Products
PA: American Medical Group Llc
1698 Post Rd E
Westport CT 06880
203 292-8444

(G-8853)
SOLUTEK CORPORATION
94 Shirley St (02119-3029)
PHONE..................................617 445-5335
Marlowe Sigal, *President*
▲ **EMP:** 30 **EST:** 1946
SQ FT: 29,200
SALES (est): 5.1MM **Privately Held**
WEB: www.solutekcorporation.com
SIC: 3861 Mfg Photographic Equipment/Supplies

(G-8854)
SOLUTIONS ATLANTIC INC
75 State St Ste 100bston (02109-1827)
PHONE..................................617 423-2699
Mitchell Greess, *President*
Monteiro Anna, *VP Sls/Mktg*
▼ **EMP:** 6
SQ FT: 750
SALES (est): 770K **Privately Held**
WEB: www.solutions-atlantic.com
SIC: 7372 Ret Computers/Software

(G-8855)
SOUNDCURE INC
100 High St 28 (02110-2321)
PHONE..................................408 938-5745
William Perry, *CEO*
Chris Silva, *President*
EMP: 8 **EST:** 2010
SQ FT: 200
SALES (est): 707.7K **Privately Held**
SIC: 3845 Mfg Electromedical Equipment

(G-8856)
SOUTH BOSTON TODAY
396 W 4th St (02127-2622)
PHONE..................................617 268-4032
EMP: 5
SALES (est): 265.5K **Privately Held**
SIC: 2711 Newspapers-Publishing/Printing

(G-8857)
SPECTACLE EYE WARE INC
544 Tremont St (02116-6301)
PHONE..................................617 542-9600
Paul B Fox, *Principal*
EMP: 5
SALES (est): 499.2K **Privately Held**
SIC: 3851 Mfg Ophthalmic Goods

(G-8858)
SPIKE AEROSPACE INC
292 Newbury St (02115-2801)
PHONE..................................617 338-1400
Vik Kachoria, *CEO*
EMP: 15 **EST:** 2013
SQ FT: 5,000
SALES (est): 1.3MM **Privately Held**
SIC: 3721 3812 Mfg Aircraft Mfg Search/Navigation Equipment

(G-8859)
SPINELLI RAVIOLI MFG CO INC
Also Called: Spinelli Bky Ravioli Pastry Sp
282 Bennington St (02128-1447)
PHONE..................................617 567-1992
Rita Roberto, *President*
Louis Roberto, *Vice Pres*
EMP: 25
SQ FT: 7,000
SALES (est): 3.5MM **Privately Held**
WEB: www.spinellisfunction.com
SIC: 2098 2033 5812 2051 Manufacture Macaroni/Spaghetti Manufacture Canned Fruits/Vegetable Eating Place Manufactur Bread/Related Prdts Retail Bakery

(G-8860)
SPRINGBOARD RETAIL INC
361 Newbury St Ste 500 (02115-2738)
PHONE..................................888 347-2191
Gordon C Russell, *CEO*
Jay Stotz, *Principal*
Jennifer Raines-Loring, *Vice Pres*
Hannah Parker, *Finance*
Petra Geiger, *Marketing Mgr*
EMP: 50
SQ FT: 1,600
SALES (est): 508.8K **Privately Held**
SIC: 7372 Prepackaged Software Services

(G-8861)
STANDARD PUBLISHING CORP (PA)
10 High St Ste 1107 (02110-1657)
PHONE..................................617 457-0600
John Cross, *CEO*
John C Cross, *CEO*
Scott Flaherty, *Managing Prtnr*
Susanne Dillman, *Publisher*
Crockett Barbara, *Editor*
EMP: 10
SQ FT: 5,000
SALES: 50K **Privately Held**
WEB: www.standardpublishingcorp.com
SIC: 2721 Periodicals-Publishing/Printing

(G-8862)
STARRY INC
38 Chauncy St Ste 200 (02111-2301)
PHONE..................................617 861-8300
Chaitanya Kanojia, *President*
Anthony Ontiveros, *Senior VP*
Marc Emmons, *Vice Pres*
Brandy Sandborg, *Opers Mgr*
Ben Russell, *Engineer*
EMP: 15 **EST:** 2014
SALES (est): 661.2K **Privately Held**
SIC: 3669 Mfg Communications Equipment

(G-8863)
STARTING TREATMENT EFFCTVLY
554 Washington St (02124-6947)
PHONE..................................857 544-8051
Sharon D Campbell, *Principal*
EMP: 4 **EST:** 2013
SALES (est): 218K **Privately Held**
SIC: 2711 Newspapers-Publishing/Printing

(G-8864)
STATISTICAL SOLUTIONS LTD
1 International Pl (02110-2602)
PHONE..................................617 535-7677
Mary Byrne, *General Mgr*
Helen Murphy, *Sales Staff*
EMP: 15
SQ FT: 10,000
SALES (est): 1.1MM **Privately Held**
WEB: www.statsolusa.com
SIC: 7372 Prepackaged Software Services
PA: Statistical Solutions Limited
4000 Cork Airport Business Park
Cork T12 N

(G-8865)
STERLINGWEAR OF BOSTON INC (PA)
175 Wlliam F Mcclllan Hwy (02128-1185)
PHONE..................................617 567-2100
Frank G Fredella, *President*
Gina Fredella Tenaglia, *Treasurer*
▲ **EMP:** 53 **EST:** 1982
SALES (est): 56.3MM **Privately Held**
WEB: www.sterlingwear.com
SIC: 2337 2385 2311 Mfg Women/Miss Suit/Coat Mfg Waterproof Outerwear Mfg Mens/Boys Suit/Coats

(G-8866)
STERLINGWEAR OF BOSTON INC
175 William F Mcclellan H (02128-1185)
PHONE..................................617 567-6465
Megan Phase, *Branch Mgr*
EMP: 140
SALES (corp-wide): 56.3MM **Privately Held**
SIC: 2311 2337 2385 Mfg Men's/Boy's Suits/Coats Mfg Women's/Misses' Suits/Coats Mfg Waterproof Outerwear
PA: Sterlingwear Of Boston, Inc.
175 Wlliam F Mcclllan Hwy
Boston MA 02128
617 567-2100

(G-8867)
STILISTI
116 Newbury St Fl 2 (02116-2948)
PHONE..................................617 262-2234
Marrisa Morleno, *Owner*
EMP: 3
SALES (est): 213.2K **Privately Held**
SIC: 3999 7231 Mfg Misc Products Beauty Shop

(G-8868)
STREAK MEDIA LLC
109 Kingston St Fl 2 (02111-2134)
PHONE..................................617 242-9460
Michael Nardella, *President*
John C Rives,
Darren Ross,
EMP: 4 **EST:** 2014
SALES (est): 147K
SALES (corp-wide): 783.3K **Privately Held**
SIC: 2711 4813 Campus-Based Daily Online Newsletter
PA: Campus Entertainment Llc
109 Kingston St Fl 2r
Boston MA 02111
617 242-9460

(G-8869)
SUNDAY RIVER BREWING CO INC
Also Called: Moose's Tale Food & Ale
320 D St Unit 426 (02127-1283)
PHONE..................................207 824-4253
Grant L Wilson, *President*
EMP: 60
SQ FT: 10,000
SALES (est): 5.2MM **Privately Held**
WEB: www.stonecoast.com
SIC: 2082 5812 5921 5813 Mfg Malt Beverages Eating Place Ret Alcoholic Beverages Drinking Place

(G-8870)
SUNNY YOUNG LLC
150 Causeway St (02114-1301)
PHONE..................................917 667-0528
Jinmei Yang,
EMP: 38
SALES (est): 1.4MM **Privately Held**
SIC: 3577 Mfg Computer Peripheral Equipment

(G-8871)
SWAROVSKI NORTH AMERICA LTD
Also Called: Swarovski Gallery Store
800 Boylston St Spc 160 (02199-7083)
PHONE..................................617 578-0705
Daniela Natcheva, *Manager*
EMP: 5
SALES (corp-wide): 4.7B **Privately Held**
SIC: 3961 Mfg Costume Jewelry
HQ: Swarovski North America Limited
1 Kenney Dr
Cranston RI 02920
401 463-6400

(G-8872)
TAMALE SOFTWARE INC (DH)
201 South St Ste 3 (02111-2706)
PHONE..................................617 443-1033
Mark Grace, *CEO*
EMP: 5
SALES (est): 1.8MM
SALES (corp-wide): 3.4B **Publicly Held**
SIC: 7372 Prepackaged Software Services
HQ: Advent Software, Inc.
600 Townsend St Fl 5
San Francisco CA 94103
415 543-7696

(G-8873)
TANGO SEAPORT
200 Seaport Blvd (02210-2031)
PHONE..................................857 277-1191
Trevor Brown, *CFO*
EMP: 5 **EST:** 2011
SALES (est): 618.6K **Privately Held**
SIC: 2339 Mfg Women's/Misses' Outerwear

(G-8874)
TAPESTRY INC
S Market Building (02109)
PHONE..................................617 723-1777
EMP: 4
SALES (corp-wide): 6B **Publicly Held**
WEB: www.coach.com
SIC: 3171 Ret Luggage/Leather Goods
PA: Tapestry, Inc.
10 Hudson Yards
New York NY 10001
212 946-8400

(G-8875)
TEI BIOSCIENCES INC
7 Elkins St (02127-1601)
PHONE..................................617 268-1616
Peter Arduini, *CEO*
Glen Coleman, *CFO*
EMP: 49
SQ FT: 36,000
SALES (est): 8.3MM **Publicly Held**
WEB: www.teibio.com
SIC: 3841 Manufacturer Of Surgical And Medical Instruments
HQ: Integra Lifesciences Corporation
311 Enterprise Dr
Plainsboro NJ 08536
609 275-2700

(G-8876)
TEKSCAN INC
307 W 1st St Ste 1 (02127-1387)
PHONE..................................617 464-4500
Stephen V Jacobs, *President*
Mark Lowe, *Vice Pres*
Charles F Malacaria, *Vice Pres*
EMP: 61
SQ FT: 28,000

SALES (est): 13.8MM Privately Held
WEB: www.tekscan.com
SIC: 3843 Mfg Dental Equipment/Supplies

(G-8877)
TELETYPESETTING COMPANY INC
Also Called: Books On Disk
10 Post Office Sq 800s (02109-4629)
PHONE..................................617 542-6220
Edward Friedman, *President*
Marlene Winer, *Vice Pres*
EMP: 10
SALES (est): 1.1MM Privately Held
WEB: www.teletype.com
SIC: 7372 2791 Publisher Of Computer Software & A Photo Typesetting Service

(G-8878)
TEX APPS 1 LLC
38 Chauncy St (02111-2301)
PHONE..................................781 375-6975
John Bosch, *Principal*
Greg Gomer, *Mng Member*
EMP: 55
SALES (est): 848.5K Privately Held
SIC: 7372 Prepackaged Software Services

(G-8879)
TEXTILE BUFF & WHEEL CO INC
511 Medford St Ste 1 (02129-1495)
P.O. Box 290060 (02129-0201)
PHONE..................................617 241-8100
Andrew Wise, *President*
Karen Wise, *Clerk*
EMP: 38 EST: 1946
SQ FT: 59,000
SALES (est): 4.3MM Privately Held
SIC: 3291 Mfgpolishing And Buffing Wheels

(G-8880)
TEXTILE WASTE SUPPLY LLC
511 Medford St (02129-1495)
P.O. Box 290060 (02129-0201)
PHONE..................................617 241-8100
Jerold Wise, *Partner*
Andrew Wise,
EMP: 25
SQ FT: 50,000
SALES (est): 3.1MM Privately Held
WEB: www.textilebuff.com
SIC: 2211 Cotton Broadwoven Fabric Mill

(G-8881)
THERMOCERAMIX INC
241 A St Ste 300 (02210-1308)
PHONE..................................978 425-0404
Richard C Abbott, *President*
EMP: 4
SQ FT: 8,000
SALES (est): 403.4K Privately Held
WEB: www.thermoceramix.com
SIC: 3479 3585 Coating/Engraving Service Mfg Refrigeration/Heating Equipment

(G-8882)
THL-NORTEK INVESTORS LLC (PA)
100 Federal St Ste 3100 (02110-1847)
PHONE..................................617 227-1050
Joseph L Bower, *Mng Member*
Vernon R Alden,
Stanley A Feldberg,
Thomas Lee,
▲ EMP: 70
SALES (est): 334.7MM Privately Held
SIC: 3585 3444 3634 2431 Mfg Refrig/Heat Equip Mfg Sheet Metalwork Mfg Elec Housewares/Fans Mfg Millwork

(G-8883)
THOS MOSER CABINETMAKERS INC
19 Arlington St Ste 1 (02116-3422)
PHONE..................................617 224-1245
Christopher Emorad, *Manager*
EMP: 3
SALES (corp-wide): 19.4MM Privately Held
SIC: 2511 Mfg Wood Household Furniture
PA: Thos. Moser Cabinetmakers, Inc.
72 Wrights Lndg
Auburn ME 04210
207 753-9834

(G-8884)
THOUGHT INDUSTRIES INC
3 Post Office Sq Ste 400 (02109-3939)
PHONE..................................617 669-7725
R Douglas Murphy, *President*
Eric Haugh, *Sales Staff*
Stephen Newman, *Marketing Staff*
EMP: 6 EST: 2013
SALES: 253.2K Privately Held
SIC: 3999 5045 7389 Mfg Misc Products Whol Computers/Peripherals Business Services

(G-8885)
TIBCO SOFTWARE INC
Spotfire Division
281 Summer St Fl 3 (02210-1569)
PHONE..................................617 859-6800
Christopher Ahlberg, *Division Pres*
Thomas Been, *VP Mktg*
EMP: 55
SALES (corp-wide): 885.6MM Privately Held
WEB: www.tibco.com
SIC: 7372 Prepackaged Software Services
HQ: Tibco Software Inc.
3307 Hillview Ave
Palo Alto CA 94304

(G-8886)
TOAST INC (PA)
401 Park Dr Ste 801 (02215-3325)
PHONE..................................617 682-0225
Chris Comparato, *CEO*
Steve Fredette, *President*
Chase Cox, *District Mgr*
Josh Gottlieb, *District Mgr*
Joe Starzec, *Vice Pres*
EMP: 95 EST: 2011
SALES (est): 99MM Privately Held
SIC: 7372 Prepackaged Software Services

(G-8887)
TOOLSGROUP INC
75 Federal St Ste 920 (02110-1938)
PHONE..................................617 263-0080
Joseph Shamir, *CEO*
Eugenio Cornacchia, *Principal*
Ida Huang, *Opers Staff*
Debbie Frattaroli, *Controller*
Bob Bryant, *Sales Dir*
EMP: 26
SQ FT: 8,000
SALES: 11MM Privately Held
SIC: 7372 Prepackaged Software Services

(G-8888)
TOTO USA HOLDINGS INC
123 N Washington St (02114-2113)
PHONE..................................617 227-1321
Derrick Jarrodson, *Director*
EMP: 3 Privately Held
SIC: 3088 Mfg Plastic Plumbing Fixtures
HQ: Toto U.S.A. Holdings, Inc.
1155 Southern Rd
Morrow GA 30260

(G-8889)
TOUCANECT INC
14 Hancock St (02114-4159)
PHONE..................................617 437-1400
Shayne Gilbert, *President*
EMP: 3 EST: 2012
SALES (est): 127.3K Privately Held
SIC: 7372 Prepackaged Software Services

(G-8890)
TOUCH AHEAD SOFTWARE LLC
2 Liberty Sq Ste 700 (02109-4944)
PHONE..................................866 960-9301
Catherine Briggette, *Mktg Dir*
Timothy Lasonde, *CTO*
Nancy Keddy,
EMP: 12
SALES (est): 65.2K Privately Held
SIC: 7372 Prepackaged Software Services

(G-8891)
TRACKSMITH CORPORATION
285 Newbury St (02115-2809)
PHONE..................................781 235-0037
Matt Taylor, *CEO*
Megan Kiwada, *Opers Mgr*
Lee Glandorf, *Corp Comm Staff*
EMP: 10
SALES (est): 1.3MM Privately Held
SIC: 2329 2339 Mfg Men's/Boy's Clothing Mfg Women's/Misses' Outerwear

(G-8892)
TUCKERMAN STL FABRICATORS INC
256 Marginal St Ste 2 (02128-2800)
PHONE..................................617 569-8373
Joseph W Burm, *President*
EMP: 75
SQ FT: 50,000
SALES (est): 12.9MM Privately Held
SIC: 3441 Structural Metal Fabrication

(G-8893)
TUFIN SOFTWARE NORTH AMER INC
2 Oliver St (02109-4901)
PHONE..................................781 685-4940
Steve Moscarelli, *Vice Pres*
Bob Adams, *Regl Sales Mgr*
EMP: 18
SALES (est): 1.5MM Privately Held
SIC: 7372 Prepackaged Software Services

(G-8894)
UNERECTORS INC
82 Crescent Ave (02125-1291)
PHONE..................................617 436-8333
Steven Collins, *CEO*
EMP: 10 EST: 1972
SQ FT: 20,000
SALES (est): 1.2MM Privately Held
WEB: www.unerectors.com
SIC: 3479 8712 Construction Of Porcelain Enamel Panels And Does Architectural Engineering

(G-8895)
UNION MINIERE
Semiconductor Processing Co
12 Channel St Ste 702 (02210-2331)
PHONE..................................617 960-5900
Nicholas C Sink, *Branch Mgr*
EMP: 29
SALES (corp-wide): 3.6B Privately Held
SIC: 3674 Processes Semiconductor Materials
PA: Umicore
Rue Du Marais 31
Bruxelles 1000
222 771-11

(G-8896)
UNISITE LLC
116 Huntington Ave # 1750 (02116-5749)
PHONE..................................781 926-7135
James D Taiclet Jr, *Ch of Bd*
EMP: 4
SALES (est): 374K Publicly Held
SIC: 3663 Mfg Radio/Tv Communication Equipment
PA: American Tower Corporation
116 Huntington Ave # 1100
Boston MA 02116

(G-8897)
UNITARIAN UNIVERSALIST ASSN
Also Called: Beacon Press
41 Mount Vernon St (02108-1453)
PHONE..................................617 742-2110
Helen Hatwan, *Branch Mgr*
EMP: 20
SALES (corp-wide): 18.5MM Privately Held
WEB: www.ucevanston.org
SIC: 2731 Religious Organization
PA: Unitarian Universalist Association, Inc
24 Farnsworth St Fl 1
Boston MA 02210
617 742-2100

(G-8898)
UNITED FOODS INCORPORATED (PA)
Also Called: Sun Hing Noodle Co
170 Lincoln St (02111-2404)
PHONE..................................617 482-9879
Ngar Wong, *President*
EMP: 7
SALES (est): 1.3MM Privately Held
SIC: 2098 Mfg Macaroni/Spaghetti

(G-8899)
UNIVERSAL HARDWOOD FLOORING
85 Arlington St (02135-2152)
PHONE..................................617 783-2307
Nee Tran, *Manager*
EMP: 8
SALES (est): 534.7K Privately Held
SIC: 2426 Hardwood Dimension/Floor Mill

(G-8900)
UNO FOODS INC (DH)
100 Charles Park Rd (02132-4902)
PHONE..................................617 323-9200
George Herz, *Senior VP*
Louie Psallieas, *CFO*
EMP: 19
SQ FT: 10,000
SALES (est): 32.4MM Privately Held
WEB: www.unofoods.com
SIC: 2099 Mfg Food Preparations

(G-8901)
UNRULY STUDIOS INC
2 Avenue De Lafayette (02111-1750)
P.O. Box 121190 (02112-1190)
PHONE..................................857 327-5080
Bryanne Leeming, *CEO*
EMP: 6
SALES: 37K Privately Held
SIC: 3999 5092 5999 Mfg Misc Products Whol Toys/Hobby Goods Ret Misc Merchandise

(G-8902)
US BIOFUELS INC
225 Franklin St Ste 2320 (02110-2880)
PHONE..................................706 291-4829
Gene J Gebolys,
EMP: 14 EST: 2014
SALES (est): 5.6MM Privately Held
SIC: 2869 Mfg Industrial Organic Chemicals

(G-8903)
VARSTREET INC
66 Charles St (02114-4604)
PHONE..................................781 273-3979
Gopalan Shankar, *President*
Rahul Choudhary, *Accounts Mgr*
Shiv Agarwal, *Sales Staff*
Roshan Tayade, *Sales Staff*
EMP: 25
SALES (est): 1.5MM Privately Held
SIC: 7372 Application Computer Software

(G-8904)
VAULTIVE INC
470 Atlantic Ave Fl 12 (02210-2249)
PHONE..................................212 875-1210
Elad Yoran, *CEO*
Shelley Vereen, *Vice Pres*
Joska Jansen, *Engineer*
Avishay Shahar, *Engineer*
EMP: 35
SALES (est): 2.2MM Privately Held
SIC: 7372 Prepackaged Software Services

(G-8905)
VE INTERACTIVE LLC
580 Harrison Ave Ste 400 (02118-2639)
PHONE..................................857 284-7000
Donn Worby, *CFO*
Cristina Balan, *Office Mgr*
Stephen Polinsky Mr, *Mng Member*
Terri Mock, *Officer*
EMP: 3
SALES (est): 4.4MM Privately Held
SIC: 2721 8742 7311 7313 Periodical-Publish/Print Mgmt Consulting Svcs Advertising Agency Advertising Rep

(G-8906)
VEOLIA NA REGENERATION SRVCS (DH)
53 State St (02109-2820)
PHONE..................................312 552-2800
Gregg Macqueen, *President*
EMP: 8

GEOGRAPHIC

SALES (est): 18MM
SALES (corp-wide): 582.1MM **Privately Held**
SIC: 2819 Mfg Industrial Inorganic Chemicals

(G-8907)
VERMILION SOFTWARE
50 Congress St Ste 500 (02109-4005)
PHONE....617 279-0799
Ben McCormack, *President*
EMP: 4
SALES (est): 230K **Privately Held**
SIC: 7372 Prepackaged Software Services

(G-8908)
VERTEX PHARMACEUTICALS INC
1 Harbor St (02210-2359)
PHONE....617 201-4171
Tracy Bychowski, *Vice Pres*
EMP: 17
SALES (est): 4.4MM **Privately Held**
SIC: 2834 Mfg Pharmaceutical Preparations

(G-8909)
VERTEX PHARMACEUTICALS INC (PA)
50 Northern Ave (02210-1862)
PHONE....617 341-6100
Jeffrey M Leiden, *President*
David Altshuler, *Exec VP*
Paul Negulescu, *Vice Pres*
Koji Kubota, *Plant Mgr*
Rieko Arimoto, *Research*
◆ **EMP:** 320
SQ FT: 1,100,000
SALES: 3B **Publicly Held**
WEB: www.vrtx.com
SIC: 2834 8731 Pharmaceutical Preparation Biotechnological Research

(G-8910)
VESPER TECHNOLOGIES INC
77 Summer St Ste 801 (02110-1017)
PHONE....617 315-9144
Matthew Crowley, *CEO*
Julian Aschieri, *Vice Pres*
Craig Core, *Vice Pres*
Wang Sung, *Engineer*
Arthur Zhao, *Engineer*
EMP: 12
SALES (est): 3.5MM **Privately Held**
SIC: 3651 Mfg Home Audio/Video Equipment

(G-8911)
VILLAGE FORGE INC
51 Industrial Dr (02136-2355)
P.O. Box 55, Readville (02137-0055)
PHONE....617 361-2591
Christine M Killeen, *President*
EMP: 17 **EST:** 1952
SQ FT: 32,000
SALES (est): 4.6MM **Privately Held**
SIC: 3441 3446 Structural Metal Fabrication Mfg Architectural Metalwork

(G-8912)
VISIBLE MEASURES CORP (PA)
745 Atlantic Ave Fl 9 (02111-2735)
PHONE....617 482-0222
Brian Shin, *President*
Matt Cutler, *Vice Pres*
Rishi Dean, *Vice Pres*
Sarel Meirovich, *Vice Pres*
Ronald Tache, *Vice Pres*
EMP: 45
SQ FT: 5,000
SALES (est): 14.5MM **Privately Held**
SIC: 7372 Prepackaged Software Services

(G-8913)
VIVANTIO INC
200 Portland St Ste 500 (02114-1715)
PHONE....617 982-0390
Greg Rich, *President*
EMP: 35 **EST:** 2012
SALES (est): 508.4K **Privately Held**
SIC: 7372 Prepackaged Software Services
PA: Vivantio Limited
25-31 Boulevard
Weston-Super-Mare

(G-8914)
W C CANNIFF & SONS INC (PA)
531 Cummins Hwy (02131-3943)
PHONE....617 323-3690
Edward T Canniff Jr, *President*
William Canniff, *Principal*
Claire Sullivan, *Vice Pres*
EMP: 6
SQ FT: 200,000
SALES (est): 1.1MM **Privately Held**
WEB: www.canniffmonuments.com
SIC: 3281 Mfg Monuments Cut Stone

(G-8915)
WALTER DE GRUYTER INC
Also Called: Birkhauser
121 High St Fl 3 (02110-2475)
PHONE....857 284-7073
Carsten Tuhr, *CEO*
Lindsey Griffith, *General Mgr*
Joshua Gannon, *Editor*
Kerstin Maiazza, *Human Resources*
Jeffrey Pepper, *Director*
EMP: 8
SALES (est): 1MM **Privately Held**
SIC: 2731 Misc Publishing

(G-8916)
WASHINGTON ABC IMAGING INC
274 Summer St (02210-1106)
PHONE....857 753-4241
Medi Falsafi, *Principal*
EMP: 75
SALES (est): 7MM
SALES (corp-wide): 218.2MM **Privately Held**
SIC: 2759 Commercial Printing
PA: Abc Imaging Of Washington, Inc
5290 Shawnee Rd Ste 300
Alexandria VA 22312
202 429-8870

(G-8917)
WATERFRONT PRINTING COMPANY
12 Channel St Ste 7 (02210-2323)
PHONE....617 345-9711
Peter J Boginski, *President*
Virginia W Boginski, *Treasurer*
EMP: 14 **EST:** 1974
SQ FT: 12,000
SALES (est): 1.1MM **Privately Held**
SIC: 2752 Offset Printer

(G-8918)
WEALTH2KCOM INC
75 Arlington St Ste 5000 (02116-3987)
PHONE....781 989-5200
David Macchia, *President*
Paul H Lefevre, *General Mgr*
Michael J Filosa, *Vice Pres*
Brian Donahue, *Director*
EMP: 10 **EST:** 2000
SQ FT: 4,000
SALES (est): 817.7K **Privately Held**
WEB: www.wealth2k.com
SIC: 7372 Prepackaged Software Services

(G-8919)
WEBPORT GLOBAL LLC
2 Seaport Ln Fl 9 (02210-2179)
PHONE....617 385-5058
Carolyn Jepsen, *Mktg Dir*
Jim Krzywicki,
EMP: 5 **EST:** 2011
SALES (est): 356.4K **Privately Held**
SIC: 7372 Prepackaged Software Services

(G-8920)
WELLFLEET PHARMACEUTICALS INC
121 Mount Vernon St (02108-1104)
PHONE....617 767-6264
Dennis McCoy MD, *President*
EMP: 3
SALES (est): 181.3K **Privately Held**
SIC: 2834 Mfg Pharmaceutical Preparations

(G-8921)
WESCOR LTD
77 Avenue Louis Pasteur (02115-5727)
PHONE....617 731-3963
EMP: 6
SALES (corp-wide): 3.1MM **Privately Held**
SIC: 2431 Mfg Millwork
PA: Wescor, Ltd.
271 Main St Ste G01
Stoneham MA 02180
781 279-0490

(G-8922)
WEST END STROLLERS
1 Faneuil Hall Market Pl (02109-6117)
PHONE....617 720-6020
Johnny Bistany, *Owner*
EMP: 3
SALES (est): 293.9K **Privately Held**
SIC: 3944 Strollers

(G-8923)
WESTREX INTERNATIONAL INC
25 Denby Rd (02134-1605)
PHONE....617 254-1200
Domenic P Emello, *President*
▲ **EMP:** 18
SQ FT: 17,160
SALES (est): 2.5MM **Privately Held**
SIC: 2752 5045 7379 Lithographic Commercial Printing Whol Computers/Peripherals Computer Related Services

(G-8924)
WESTROCK - SOUTHERN CONT LLC
84 State St (02109-2202)
PHONE....978 772-5050
Steve Grossman, *Manager*
EMP: 15
SALES (corp-wide): 18.2B **Publicly Held**
SIC: 2679 2653 Mfg Converted Paper Products Mfg Corrugated/Solid Fiber Boxes
HQ: Westrock - Southern Container, Llc
1000 Abernathy Rd Ste 125
Atlanta GA 30328
770 448-2193

(G-8925)
WHERE INC
1 International Pl # 315 (02110-2602)
PHONE....617 502-3100
Walter A Doyle Jr, *CEO*
Craig Forman, *Ch of Bd*
Jerry King, *COO*
Naill Hawkins, *Vice Pres*
Mok OH, *Officer*
EMP: 52
SQ FT: 1,000
SALES (est): 6.5MM **Privately Held**
WEB: www.ulocate.com
SIC: 3812 Mfg Search/Navigation Equipment

(G-8926)
WHITEWOOD ENCRYTION
100 High St Fl 28 (02110-2321)
PHONE....617 419-1800
John Serafini, *General Mgr*
Shonda Ellerbe, *Administration*
EMP: 3 **EST:** 2014
SALES (est): 191.6K **Privately Held**
SIC: 3577 Mfg Computer Peripheral Equipment

(G-8927)
WHOOP INC
1325 Boylston St Ste 401 (02215-3900)
PHONE....617 670-1074
Will Ahmed, *CEO*
John Capodilupo, *Principal*
Aurelian Nicolae, *Principal*
Carlos Famadas, *CFO*
Jennifer Parlin, *Cust Mgr*
EMP: 15
SALES (est): 4MM **Privately Held**
SIC: 3829 Mfg Measuring/Controlling Devices

(G-8928)
WILLIAMS LEA BOSTON
260 Franklin St Ste 730 (02110-3112)
PHONE....617 371-2300
EMP: 3
SALES (est): 332K **Privately Held**
SIC: 3577 Mfg Computer Peripheral Equipment

(G-8929)
WILMINGTON COMPLIANCE WEEK
77 N Washington St (02114-1908)
PHONE....888 519-9200
Matt Kelly, *Editor*
Bill Coffin, *Chief*
Dave Lefort, *Chief*
Donna Rice, *Vice Pres*
Michelle Politano, *Regl Sales Mgr*
EMP: 22
SALES (est): 2.7MM **Privately Held**
SIC: 2721 Periodicals

(G-8930)
WIRED INFORMATICS LLC
265 Franklin St Ste 1702 (02110-3144)
PHONE....646 623-7459
Pei Jun Chen, *Principal*
EMP: 5
SALES (est): 264.2K **Privately Held**
SIC: 7372 Prepackaged Software Services

(G-8931)
WIREOVER CO
323 Commonwealth Ave (02115-1927)
PHONE....617 308-7993
Trent Ashburn, *CEO*
EMP: 3
SQ FT: 3,000
SALES (est): 190K **Privately Held**
SIC: 7372 Prepackaged Software Services

(G-8932)
WOOLRICH INC
299 Newbury St Ste 1 (02115-2883)
PHONE....857 263-7554
Lucy Snyder, *Branch Mgr*
EMP: 4 **Privately Held**
SIC: 2311 Mfg Men's/Boy's Suits/Coats
HQ: Woolrich, Inc.
2 Mill St
Woolrich PA 17779
570 769-6464

(G-8933)
WORDSTREAM INC
101 Huntington Ave Fl 7 (02199-7607)
PHONE....617 963-0555
Howard Kogan, *CEO*
Nicole Desisto, *Partner*
Kristen Yerardi, *Senior VP*
John Judge, *Vice Pres*
Mitchell Leiman, *Vice Pres*
EMP: 10
SALES (est): 1.8MM
SALES (corp-wide): 1.5B **Publicly Held**
SIC: 7372 Prepackaged Software Services
HQ: Gannett Media Corp.
7950 Jones Branch Dr
Mc Lean VA 22102
703 854-6000

(G-8934)
WORKDAY INC
33 Arch St Ste 2200 (02110-1451)
PHONE....617 936-1100
EMP: 9
SALES (corp-wide): 2.8B **Publicly Held**
SIC: 7372 Prepackaged Software Services
PA: Workday, Inc.
6110 Stoneridge Mall Rd
Pleasanton CA 94588
925 951-9000

(G-8935)
WORLD ASSET MANAGEMENT LLC
225 Franklin St Ste 2320 (02110-2880)
PHONE....617 889-7300
Gene Gebolys, *Mng Member*
EMP: 13
SQ FT: 8,000
SALES (est): 4.2MM **Privately Held**
SIC: 2869 Mfg Industrial Organic Chemicals

(G-8936)
WORLD ENERGY BIOX BIOFUELS LLC (PA)
225 Franklin St Ste 2320 (02110-2880)
PHONE....617 889-7300
Gene Gebolys,
EMP: 16

SALES (est): 47.3MM Privately Held
SIC: 2869 Mfg Industrial Organic Chemicals

(G-8937)
WORLD JOURNAL CHINESE DAILY
216 Lincoln St (02111-2404)
PHONE....................617 542-1230
Thomas Chan, *President*
EMP: 7
SALES (est): 467K Privately Held
SIC: 2711 Newspapers-Publishing/Printing

(G-8938)
XENOTHERAPEUTICS LLC
21 Drydock Ave Ste 610e (02210-4501)
PHONE....................617 750-1907
Paul Holzer, *CEO*
Jonathan Adkins, *COO*
EMP: 3 EST: 2015
SALES (est): 171.3K Privately Held
SIC: 3841 Mfg Surgical/Medical Instruments

(G-8939)
YUEN HO BAKERY INC
54 Beach St Ste 1 (02111-2086)
PHONE....................617 426-8320
Julie T L Lee, *Owner*
EMP: 9
SQ FT: 1,500
SALES (est): 585.9K Privately Held
SIC: 2051 Mfg Bread/Related Products

(G-8940)
ZACHARY SHUSTER HRMSWOTH AGNCY
545 Boylston St Ste 1103 (02116-3606)
PHONE....................617 262-2400
Todd Shuster, *Branch Mgr*
EMP: 8
SALES (est): 684.2K
SALES (corp-wide): 508.7K Privately Held
WEB: www.zshliterary.com
SIC: 2731 Books-Publishing/Printing
PA: Zachary Shuster Harmsworth Agency Llc
19 W 21st St Rm 501
New York NY 10010
212 765-6900

(G-8941)
ZAFGEN INC
13 Center Plz (02108)
PHONE....................617 622-4003
Jeffrey S Hatfield, *CEO*
Peter Barrett, *Ch of Bd*
Patricia L Allen, *CFO*
Patricia Allen, *CFO*
Karin Zeh, *Manager*
EMP: 38
SQ FT: 17,705
SALES (est): 8.4MM Privately Held
SIC: 2834 Pharmaceutical Preparations

(G-8942)
ZOIRAY TECHNOLOGIES INC
8 Saint Marys St Ste 611 (02215-2421)
PHONE....................617 358-6003
David Bergstein, *President*
EMP: 3
SALES: 500K Privately Held
WEB: www.zoiray.com
SIC: 3599 Manufacturer Of Scientific Equipment

(G-8943)
ZONE & CO SFTWR CONSULTING LLC
800 Boylston St Fl 16 (02199-7637)
PHONE....................617 307-7068
Derek Zanga, *Partner*
EMP: 5 EST: 2016
SALES (est): 171.6K Privately Held
SIC: 7372 Prepackaged Software Services

(G-8944)
ZOOM TELEPHONICS INC (PA)
99 High St Ste 2801 (02110-2374)
PHONE....................617 423-1072
Joe Wytanis, *President*
John Lauten, *Senior VP*
Deena Randall, *Vice Pres*
Jacquelyn Barry Hamilton, *CFO*
EMP: 33
SALES: 32.3MM Privately Held
WEB: www.hayesmicro.com
SIC: 3661 3577 Communication Equipment

Bourne
Barnstable County

(G-8945)
D 2 INCORPORATED
6 Otis Park Dr Ste 1 (02532-3931)
PHONE....................508 329-2046
Alan Fougere, *President*
EMP: 5
SQ FT: 3,000
SALES: 1MM Privately Held
SIC: 3823 Mfg Process Control Instruments

(G-8946)
HAMILTON FERRIS CO INC
Also Called: Ferris Power Products
3 Angelo Dr (02532-3923)
PHONE....................508 743-9901
Hamilton Y Ferris, *President*
▼ EMP: 5
SALES (est): 685.5K Privately Held
WEB: www.hamiltonferris.com
SIC: 3621 5063 Mfg Motors/Generators Whol Electrical Equipment

(G-8947)
MASS AUTOMATION CORPORATION
6 Colonel Dr Unit 1 (02532-3921)
PHONE....................508 759-0770
John R Fraser, *President*
Daniel R Macgregor, *Vice Pres*
Daniel Macgregor, *Vice Pres*
Julie Lefavor, *Office Mgr*
EMP: 9
SQ FT: 5,500
SALES: 2.5MM Privately Held
WEB: www.massautomation.com
SIC: 3599 Mfg Industrial Machinery

(G-8948)
ONSET COMPUTER CORPORATION
Also Called: Hobo
470 Macarthur Blvd (02532-3838)
P.O. Box 3450, Pocasset (02559-3450)
PHONE....................508 759-9500
Justin Testa, *President*
Ellen G Hocker, *Corp Secy*
Lon O Hocker, *Vice Pres*
Paul Goodrich, *Engineer*
Jim Towey, *Engineer*
◆ EMP: 120
SQ FT: 40,000
SALES (est): 31.6MM Privately Held
WEB: www.onsetcomp.com
SIC: 3823 3571 3674 3577 Mfg Process Cntrl Instr Mfg Electronic Computers Mfg Semiconductors/Dvcs Mfg Computer Peripherals

(G-8949)
SOUTHEASTERN MILLWORK CO INC
150 State Rd (02532)
PHONE....................508 888-6038
Charles S Cooper, *President*
Thomas P Dudgeon, *Treasurer*
EMP: 14
SQ FT: 17,000
SALES (est): 122.4K Privately Held
SIC: 2431 5211 Mfg Millwork Ret Lumber/Building Materials

(G-8950)
TOP NOTCH MILL WORK
245 County Rd (02532-4207)
PHONE....................508 432-4976
Thomas Spence, *Owner*
EMP: 3
SALES: 125K Privately Held
SIC: 2431 Mfg Millwork

Boxboro
Middlesex County

(G-8951)
ARCHITECTURAL ELEMENTS INC
972 Massachusetts Ave (01719-1416)
PHONE....................978 263-2482
Mark White, *President*
▲ EMP: 5
SQ FT: 4,000
SALES (est): 811.4K Privately Held
WEB: www.architecturalelements.com
SIC: 2431 Mfg Millwork

(G-8952)
FINE LINE WOODWORKING INC
972 Massachusetts Ave (01719-1416)
PHONE....................978 263-4322
Mark White, *President*
Kathleen Vorce, *Clerk*
EMP: 6
SQ FT: 3,200
SALES: 550K Privately Held
WEB: www.woodwork.com
SIC: 2511 1521 5211 5031 Mfg Household Furniture & Remodeling Contractor

(G-8953)
MASS LOGIC INC
648 Stow Rd (01719-2102)
PHONE....................978 635-1917
Scott W Spalding, *President*
EMP: 5
SALES (est): 295.7K Privately Held
WEB: www.masslogic.com
SIC: 3999 Mfg Misc Products

(G-8954)
SETRA SYSTEMS INC
159 Swanson Rd Ste 1 (01719-1304)
PHONE....................978 263-1400
David C Carr, *President*
Chuck Clarkson, *President*
Barbara Evans, *Vice Pres*
Robert S Lutz, *Vice Pres*
Sunil Barot, *Engineer*
▲ EMP: 10 EST: 1967
SQ FT: 102,000
SALES (est): 2.3MM
SALES (corp-wide): 6.4B Publicly Held
WEB: www.setra.com
SIC: 3829 3821 3824 3823 Mfg Measure/Control Dvcs Mfg Lab Apparatus/Furn Mfg Fluid Meters/Devices Mfg Process Cntrl Instr
PA: Fortive Corporation
6920 Seaway Blvd
Everett WA 98203
425 446-5000

(G-8955)
VALIDITY INC
1300 Mamaachsts Ave 205 (01719)
PHONE....................978 635-3400
EMP: 14
SALES (est): 970K Privately Held
SIC: 3999 Mfg Misc Products

Boxborough
Middlesex County

(G-8956)
ADVANCED MICRO DEVICES INC
90 Central St (01719-1250)
PHONE....................978 795-2500
Gordon Glover, *Branch Mgr*
Tony Jarvis, *Director*
EMP: 143
SALES (corp-wide): 6.4B Publicly Held
WEB: www.amd.com
SIC: 3674 Mfg Semiconductors/Related Devices
PA: Advanced Micro Devices, Inc.
2485 Augustine Dr Ms6184
Santa Clara CA 95054
408 749-4000

(G-8957)
APPLIED MATERIALS INC
80 Central St Ste 325 (01719-1249)
PHONE....................978 795-8000
Bg Lee, *Manager*
EMP: 48
SALES (corp-wide): 14.6B Publicly Held
WEB: www.appliedmaterials.com
SIC: 3674 Mfg Semiconductors/Related Devices
PA: Applied Materials, Inc.
3050 Bowers Ave
Santa Clara CA 95054
408 727-5555

(G-8958)
ARTHUR H GAEBEL INC
36 Sargent Rd (01719-1208)
PHONE....................978 263-4401
Gerald Gaebel, *President*
Sheila Martin, *Office Mgr*
◆ EMP: 4
SALES (est): 280K Privately Held
WEB: www.gaebel.com
SIC: 3423 5199 Mfg Hand/Edge Tools Whol Nondurable Goods

(G-8959)
ASSABET MACHINE CORP
1145 Massachusetts Ave (01719-1408)
P.O. Box 467, Hudson (01749-0467)
PHONE....................978 562-7992
Neal M Dougherty, *President*
Matt Dougherty, *General Mgr*
EMP: 20
SQ FT: 19,800
SALES (est): 3.7MM Privately Held
WEB: www.assabetmachine.com
SIC: 3599 Mfg Industrial Machinery

(G-8960)
CISCO SYSTEMS INC
1414 Massachusetts Ave (01719-2205)
PHONE....................408 526-4000
Jonathan M Moulton, *Principal*
Jacy Orms, *Business Mgr*
Jeff Winters, *Business Mgr*
Steve Denney, *Engineer*
Allen Gaynor, *Engineer*
EMP: 656
SALES (corp-wide): 51.9B Publicly Held
SIC: 3577 Mfg Computer Peripheral Equipment
PA: Cisco Systems, Inc.
170 W Tasman Dr
San Jose CA 95134
408 526-4000

(G-8961)
DOLAN-JENNER INDUSTRIES INC
159 Swanson Rd (01719-1316)
PHONE....................978 263-1400
Steven M Rales, *Ch of Bd*
Mike Balas, *President*
Charles G Clarkson, *General Mgr*
Mitchell P Rales, *Chairman*
▲ EMP: 47
SQ FT: 60,000
SALES (est): 5.1MM
SALES (corp-wide): 19.8B Publicly Held
WEB: www.dolan-jenner.com
SIC: 3823 3625 3648 3674 Mfg Process Cntrl Instr Mfg Relay/Indstl Control Mfg Lighting Equipment Mfg Semiconductors/Dvcs Mfg Electric Lamps
PA: Danaher Corporation
2200 Penn Ave Nw Ste 800w
Washington DC 20037
202 828-0850

(G-8962)
FIBERTECH NETWORKS LLC
80 Central St (01719-1245)
PHONE....................978 264-6000
Robert Shanahan, *CEO*
Eric Sandman, *CFO*
EMP: 3
SALES (est): 133.4K Privately Held
SIC: 3661 Telephone And Telegraph Apparatus

(G-8963)
G360LINK
85 Swanson Rd Ste 110 (01719-1300)
PHONE....................978 266-1500

GEOGRAPHIC

Bill Ren, *Principal*
EMP: 3 **EST:** 2013
SALES (est): 239.2K **Privately Held**
SIC: 7372 Prepackaged Software Services

(G-8964)
INVETECH INC
Also Called: Dover Motion
159 Swanson Rd (01719-1316)
PHONE..................................508 475-3400
Jeff Beal, *Engineer*
Zachary Haubert, *Engineer*
Colleen Van Order, *Human Resources*
Mark Wilson, *Manager*
EMP: 61 **Privately Held**
WEB: www.neat.com
SIC: 3823 3625 Mfg Process Control Instruments Relays/Industrial Controls
HQ: Invetech, Inc.
9980 Huennekens St # 140
San Diego CA 92121
858 768-3232

(G-8965)
LTS GROUP HOLDINGS LLC (HQ)
80 Central St Ste 240 (01719-1245)
PHONE..................................978 264-6001
Robert Shanahan, *CEO*
Eric Sandman, *CFO*
EMP: 19
SALES (est): 274.3MM
SALES (corp-wide): 5.4B **Publicly Held**
SIC: 3661 Mfg Telephone/Telegraph Apparatus
PA: Crown Castle International Corp.
1220 Augusta Dr Ste 600
Houston TX 77057
713 570-3000

(G-8966)
PHOTO DIAGNOSTIC SYSTEMS INC
85 Swanson Rd Ste 110 (01719-1300)
PHONE..................................978 266-0420
Olof Johnson, *President*
Bernard M Gordon, *Chairman*
Ross Brown, *COO*
Michael King, *Engineer*
Anthony Macadino, *Engineer*
EMP: 22
SALES: 5MM **Privately Held**
SIC: 3841 Mfg Surgical/Medical Instruments

(G-8967)
PONY SHACK CIDER COMPANY
188 Picnic St (01719-1105)
PHONE..................................781 367-4060
Nathan John McKinley, *Principal*
EMP: 4
SALES (est): 218.5K **Privately Held**
SIC: 2084 Mfg Wines/Brandy/Spirits

(G-8968)
QUALCOMM INCORPORATED
90 Central St Ste 1 (01719-1252)
PHONE..................................858 587-1121
EMP: 350
SALES (corp-wide): 24.2B **Publicly Held**
SIC: 3674 7372 6794 Mfg Semiconductors/Related Devices Prepackaged Software Services Patent Owner/Lessor
PA: Qualcomm Incorporated
5775 Morehouse Dr
San Diego CA 92121
858 587-1121

(G-8969)
RESIDENT ARTIST STUDIO LLC
438 Hill Rd (01719-1028)
PHONE..................................978 635-9162
Charles L Summers,
EMP: 4
SALES: 25K **Privately Held**
SIC: 3827 Mfg Optical Instruments/Lenses

(G-8970)
SYNQOR HOLDINGS LLC
155 Swanson Rd (01719-1316)
PHONE..................................978 849-0600
Martin Schlecht, *President*
Suzanne Carroll, *Admin Asst*
EMP: 99
SQ FT: 100,000
SALES (est): 2.9MM **Privately Held**
SIC: 3679 Mfg Electronic Components

(G-8971)
SYNQOR INC (PA)
155 Swanson Rd (01719-1316)
PHONE..................................978 849-0600
Martin F Schlecht, *Ch of Bd*
Rene Hemond, *Exec VP*
Buzz Hofmann, *Exec VP*
John Gucfa, *Materials Mgr*
Ralph Silva, *Facilities Mgr*
EMP: 225
SQ FT: 25,000
SALES (est): 51.7MM **Privately Held**
WEB: www.synqor.com
SIC: 3679 Mfg Electronic Components

(G-8972)
X SONIX
159 Swanson Rd (01719-1316)
PHONE..................................978 266-2106
EMP: 5
SALES (est): 914.1K
SALES (corp-wide): 19.8B **Publicly Held**
SIC: 3823 3829 Mfg Process Control Instruments Mfg Measuring/Controlling Devices
PA: Danaher Corporation
2200 Penn Ave Nw Ste 800w
Washington DC 20037
202 828-0850

Boxford
Essex County

(G-8973)
ALL AROUND ACTIVE CO
15 Chapman Rd (01921-2305)
PHONE..................................978 561-1033
Joseph Egan, *Principal*
EMP: 5
SALES (est): 286.9K **Privately Held**
SIC: 7372 Prepackaged Software Services

(G-8974)
CELLARIA BIOSCIENCES LLC
26 Bennett Rd (01921-2243)
PHONE..................................617 981-4208
David Deems, *General Mgr*
EMP: 9
SALES (est): 233.4K **Privately Held**
SIC: 2836 Mfg Biological Products

(G-8975)
CHARGE ANALYTICS LLC
34 Silvermine Rd (01921-1108)
PHONE..................................978 201-7952
Edward Cline,
EMP: 3
SALES (est): 125.7K **Privately Held**
SIC: 3674 Mfg Semiconductors/Related Devices

(G-8976)
DAHL GROUP
196 Middleton Rd (01921-2523)
PHONE..................................978 887-2598
Susan Dahl, *Owner*
EMP: 4
SALES (est): 340.9K **Privately Held**
WEB: www.thedahlgroup.com
SIC: 3993 8742 Mfg Signs/Advertising Specialties Management Consulting Services

(G-8977)
EZ RATER SYSTEMS INC
93 Killam Hill Rd (01921-2015)
P.O. Box 287, Georgetown (01833-0387)
PHONE..................................978 887-8322
Judith Ernsoy, *President*
EMP: 5
SALES: 430K **Privately Held**
SIC: 7372 Prepackaged Software Services

(G-8978)
SOULAS HOMEMADE SALSA LLC
21 Stonecleave Rd (01921-2209)
PHONE..................................978 314-7735
Sue Michael Brown, *Principal*
EMP: 3
SALES (est): 124.5K **Privately Held**
SIC: 2099 Mfg Food Preparations

Boylston
Worcester County

(G-8979)
DEN TECHNOLOGIES CORP
5 Compass Cir (01505-2049)
PHONE..................................401 263-7579
David Paley, *President*
EMP: 37
SALES (est): 1.6MM **Privately Held**
SIC: 3496 Miscellaneous Fabricated Wire Products

(G-8980)
HONEMATIC MACHINE CORPORATION
222 Shrewsbury St (01505-1404)
P.O. Box 1100 (01505-1800)
PHONE..................................508 869-2131
Joseph J Cusimano Jr, *President*
Gregory Cusimano, *Vice Pres*
Patricia A Cusimano, *Director*
▲ **EMP:** 25 **EST:** 1956
SQ FT: 28,000
SALES (est): 5MM **Privately Held**
WEB: www.honematic.com
SIC: 3599 Mfg Industrial Machinery

(G-8981)
JET COATING CO
240 Shrewsbury St (01505-1403)
P.O. Box 1109 (01505-1809)
PHONE..................................508 869-2158
John Tremblay, *Partner*
Edward Jasiewicz, *Partner*
EMP: 7
SQ FT: 8,000
SALES (est): 500K **Privately Held**
SIC: 3479 Coating/Engraving Service

(G-8982)
PEPSICO INC
311 Main St (01505-2016)
PHONE..................................508 869-1000
Craig Dumas, *Principal*
EMP: 3 **EST:** 2016
SALES (est): 135K **Privately Held**
SIC: 2086 Carb Sft Drnkbtlcn

(G-8983)
PHILLIPS PRECISION INC
240 Shrewsbury St (01505-1403)
P.O. Box 1094 (01505-1694)
PHONE..................................508 869-3344
Steven Phillips, *CEO*
Cathrine Phillips, *CFO*
EMP: 10
SQ FT: 9,000
SALES (est): 1.9MM **Privately Held**
SIC: 3599 Machine Shop

Braintree
Norfolk County

(G-8984)
7 WAVES INC
Also Called: Smartcatcher Mats
97 Thayer Rd (02184-4323)
PHONE..................................781 519-9389
Randolph Tam, *President*
▲ **EMP:** 5 **EST:** 2013
SALES (est): 483.6K **Privately Held**
SIC: 2392 7389 Mfg Household Furnishings Business Services At Non-Commercial Site

(G-8985)
AFRICA CHINA MINING CORP
420 Washington St Ste 302 (02184-4777)
PHONE..................................617 921-5500
Louis Slaughter, *President*
EMP: 3
SALES (est): 152.2K **Privately Held**
SIC: 1061 Ferroalloy Ore Mining

(G-8986)
ALTRA INDUSTRIAL MOTION CORP (PA)
300 Granite St Ste 201 (02184-3950)
PHONE..................................781 917-0600
Carl R Christenson, *Ch of Bd*
Glenn E Deegan, *Vice Pres*
Glenn Deegan, *Vice Pres*
Gerald P Ferris, *Vice Pres*
Craig Schuele, *Vice Pres*
EMP: 277
SQ FT: 126,141
SALES: 1.1B **Publicly Held**
SIC: 3568 5085 3542 3625 Mfg Power Transmission Equipment

(G-8987)
AMERICAN PROSTHETICS INC (PA)
197 Quincy Ave Ste 102 (02184-2348)
PHONE..................................617 328-0606
Jeff Goode, *President*
EMP: 5 **EST:** 1977
SQ FT: 3,600
SALES (est): 856.8K **Privately Held**
WEB: www.americanprosthetics.com
SIC: 3842 Mfg Artificial Limbs

(G-8988)
AXON COMMUNICATIONS INC
6 Brooks Dr (02184-3839)
PHONE..................................781 849-6700
Christopher S Mutkoski, *President*
EMP: 4
SALES (est): 393.4K **Privately Held**
SIC: 2741 Misc Publishing

(G-8989)
BAKER PETROLITE LLC
Also Called: Baker Petrolite S Suelnis
82 Winthrop Ave (02184-8008)
PHONE..................................781 849-9699
Susan Svelnis, *Manager*
EMP: 114
SALES (corp-wide): 22.8B **Publicly Held**
WEB: www.bakerpetrolite.com
SIC: 2899 Mfg Chemical Preparations
HQ: Baker Petrolite Llc
12645 W Airport Blvd
Sugar Land TX 77478
281 276-5400

(G-8990)
BH MEDIA INC (HQ)
Also Called: Boston Herald
100 Grossman Dr Ste 400 (02184-4957)
PHONE..................................617 426-3000
Patrick J Purcell, *President*
Jennifer Gallagher, *Vice Pres*
Jeff Magram, *CFO*
Jon Couture, *Officer*
EMP: 84 **EST:** 1984
SALES: 0
SALES (corp-wide): 4.2B **Privately Held**
WEB: www.bostonherald.com
SIC: 2711 2752 Newspapers-Publishing/Printing Lithographic Commercial Printing

(G-8991)
BRAINTREE FORUM & OBSERVER
91 Washington St (02184)
PHONE..................................781 843-2937
Cathy Conley, *Principal*
EMP: 3
SALES (est): 114.9K **Privately Held**
SIC: 2711 Newspapers-Publishing/Printing

(G-8992)
BRAINTREE PRINTING INC
230 Wood Rd (02184-2408)
PHONE..................................781 848-5300
Jose Tafur, *CEO*
Jerry Hogan, *President*
James Corliss, *Vice Pres*
EMP: 26
SQ FT: 10,000
SALES (est): 5.2MM **Privately Held**
SIC: 2752 Lithographic Commercial Printing

(G-8993)
BRAINTREE SCIENTIFIC INC
60 Columbian St W (02184-7367)
P.O. Box 850498 (02185-0498)
PHONE....................................781 348-0768
Kristin Hunt, *President*
Ruth Benvie, *Mktg Dir*
EMP: 6 **EST:** 1980
SALES (est): 1.2MM **Privately Held**
WEB: www.braintreesci.com
SIC: 3841 5047 Mfg Surgical/Medical Instruments Whol Medical/Hospital Equipment

(G-8994)
CITRA LABS LLC
55 Messina Dr Ste 4 (02184-6784)
PHONE....................................781 848-9386
Stuart Kleopfer,
EMP: 39
SALES (est): 8MM **Privately Held**
SIC: 2834 Mfg Pharmaceutical Preparations

(G-8995)
CONSOLDTED PRECISION PDTS CORP
205 Wood Rd (02184-2407)
PHONE....................................781 848-3333
William F Earley, *President*
EMP: 205
SALES (corp-wide): 6.4B **Privately Held**
SIC: 3324 3365 Steel Investment Foundry Aluminum Foundry
HQ: Consolidated Precision Products Corp.
1621 Euclid Ave Ste 1850
Cleveland OH 44115
216 453-4800

(G-8996)
CORDEN PHARMA INTL INC
639 Granite St Ste 408 (02184-5369)
PHONE....................................781 305-3332
EMP: 9
SALES (corp-wide): 6.1MM **Privately Held**
SIC: 2833 8748 2834 Mfg Medicinal/Botanical Products Business Consulting Services Mfg Pharmaceutical Preparations
HQ: Corden Pharma International Inc.
2144 Larry Jeffers Rd
Elgin SC 29045
303 442-1926

(G-8997)
CREATICS LLC
60 Columbian St (02184-7342)
PHONE....................................781 843-2202
Tom Kelly, *Principal*
Mark Cleveland, *Principal*
EMP: 10 **EST:** 2012
SALES (est): 471.1K **Privately Held**
SIC: 2835 Mfg Diagnostic Substances

(G-8998)
CYTOSOL LABORATORIES INC
55 Messina Dr Ste 4 (02184-6775)
PHONE....................................781 848-9386
William J Fileti, *CEO*
EMP: 12
SQ FT: 13,500
SALES (est): 1.3MM
SALES (corp-wide): 7.9B **Publicly Held**
SIC: 2834 Mfg Pharmaceutical Preparations
HQ: Biomet, Inc.
345 E Main St
Warsaw IN 46580
574 267-6639

(G-8999)
DAVIDS DRAPERY
264 Middle St (02184-4851)
PHONE....................................781 849-9499
Tracy Barber, *Owner*
EMP: 3
SALES (est): 124.6K **Privately Held**
SIC: 2391 Mfg Curtains/Draperies

(G-9000)
DESIGNER BOARD SPECIALTIES
Also Called: Bay State Blackboard
144 Lundquist Dr (02184-5222)
P.O. Box 167, Wollaston (02170-0002)
PHONE....................................781 794-9413
Sean Mahony, *President*
EMP: 4
SQ FT: 2,800
SALES (est): 470K **Privately Held**
SIC: 2493 Mfg Reconstituted Wood Products

(G-9001)
DIAUTE BROS
Also Called: Master Welders
475 Quincy Ave (02184-1334)
PHONE....................................781 848-0524
Richard Diaute Jr, *Partner*
Richard Diaute, *Vice Pres*
EMP: 3
SQ FT: 4,000
SALES (est): 376.8K **Privately Held**
SIC: 7692 Welding Repair

(G-9002)
EARTHWORKS GRANITE & MARBLE
89 Pearl St Ste 4 (02184-6539)
PHONE....................................781 356-3544
David Ferrini, *President*
Deana Ferrini, *CFO*
EMP: 4
SQ FT: 3,000
SALES (est): 484K **Privately Held**
SIC: 3281 Trade Contractor

(G-9003)
EDMUND CARR
230 Evergreen Ave (02184-7606)
PHONE....................................781 817-5616
Edmund Carr, *Principal*
EMP: 3 **EST:** 2010
SALES (est): 247.3K **Privately Held**
SIC: 3559 Mfg Misc Industry Machinery

(G-9004)
EMBROIDERY CLINIC LLC
53 Plain St Ste 2 (02184-7059)
PHONE....................................781 843-5293
Paul Richard Vannelli, *Mng Member*
Gerard P Adams,
EMP: 3
SALES (est): 177K **Privately Held**
SIC: 2395 Pleating/Stitching Services

(G-9005)
EMCO/FGS LLC
1 Rex Dr (02184-5226)
PHONE....................................617 389-0076
Jeff Johnson, *Exec VP*
Val Caufirld, *Department Mgr*
Ed Kole, *Manager*
Richard Jr Malacina,
John E Ball,
EMP: 56 **EST:** 1957
SQ FT: 35,000
SALES (est): 10.1MM **Privately Held**
SIC: 2752 Lithographic Commercial Printing

(G-9006)
ETEX CORPORATION
55 Messina Dr (02184-6783)
PHONE....................................617 577-7270
David A Nolan Jr, *President*
Jeffrey A Wellkamp, *Vice Pres*
Richard Kim, *CFO*
EMP: 50
SQ FT: 8,100
SALES (est): 7.6MM
SALES (corp-wide): 7.9B **Publicly Held**
WEB: www.etexcorp.com
SIC: 3841 Mfg Surgical/Medical Instruments
PA: Zimmer Biomet Holdings, Inc.
345 E Main St
Warsaw IN 46580
574 267-6131

(G-9007)
FINANCIAL GRAPHIC SERVICES INC
Also Called: Fgs
1 Rex Dr (02184-5226)
PHONE....................................617 389-0076
EMP: 11 **Privately Held**
SIC: 2759 Commercial Printing
PA: Financial Graphic Services, Inc.
2910 S 18th Ave
Broadview IL 60155

(G-9008)
FRITO-LAY NORTH AMERICA INC
100 Commerce Dr (02184-7144)
PHONE....................................781 348-1500
Sam Roundy, *Principal*
EMP: 15
SALES (corp-wide): 64.6B **Publicly Held**
WEB: www.fritolay.com
SIC: 2096 Whol Confectionery
HQ: Frito-Lay North America, Inc.
7701 Legacy Dr
Plano TX 75024

(G-9009)
GLAD PRODUCTS COMPANY
220 Forbes Rd (02184-2705)
PHONE....................................781 848-6272
EMP: 3
SALES (corp-wide): 5.5B **Publicly Held**
SIC: 3081 Mfg Unsupported Plastic Film/Sheet
HQ: The Glad Products Company
1221 Broadway Ste A
Oakland CA 94612
510 271-7000

(G-9010)
GLAXOSMITHKLINE LLC
100 Catherine Dr (02184-8003)
PHONE....................................617 828-9028
EMP: 26
SALES (corp-wide): 40.6B **Privately Held**
SIC: 2834 Mfg Pharmaceutical Preparations
HQ: Glaxosmithkline Llc
5 Crescent Dr
Philadelphia PA 19112
215 751-4000

(G-9011)
GODIVA CHOCOLATIER INC
250 Granite St Ste 168 (02184-2815)
PHONE....................................781 843-0466
Fax: 781 843-0466
EMP: 10 **Privately Held**
SIC: 2066 Mfg Chocolate/Cocoa Products
HQ: Godiva Chocolatier, Inc.
333 W 34th St Fl 6
New York NY 10001
212 984-5900

(G-9012)
GRAPHIC ARTS REPAIR
76 Bradley Road Ext (02184-4907)
PHONE....................................781 843-7954
Ronald W McLachlan, *Owner*
EMP: 4
SQ FT: 20,000
SALES: 150K **Privately Held**
SIC: 2732 General Printing And Bindery

(G-9013)
GROUP ARTIC INC
55 Messina Dr (02184-6783)
PHONE....................................781 848-2174
Ronald H Lewis, *President*
EMP: 25
SALES (est): 2MM **Privately Held**
SIC: 2834 Mfg Pharmaceutical Preparations

(G-9014)
GUESS INC
250 Granite St Ste B (02184-2834)
PHONE....................................781 843-3147
EMP: 25
SALES (corp-wide): 2.5B **Publicly Held**
SIC: 2325 Mfg Men's/Boys Trousers
PA: Guess , Inc.
1444 S Alameda St
Los Angeles CA 90021
213 765-3100

(G-9015)
HAEMONETICS ASIA INCORPORATED (HQ)
400 Wood Rd (02184-2486)
PHONE....................................781 848-7100
EMP: 9
SALES (est): 1.3MM
SALES (corp-wide): 967.5MM **Publicly Held**
SIC: 3841 3845 Mfg Surgical/Medical Instruments And Electromedical Equipments
PA: Haemonetics Corporation
400 Wood Rd
Braintree MA 02184
781 848-7100

(G-9016)
HAEMONETICS CORPORATION (PA)
400 Wood Rd (02184-2486)
PHONE....................................781 848-7100
Richard J Meelia, *Ch of Bd*
Christopher Simon, *President*
Stewart W Strong, *President*
Michelle L Basil, *Exec VP*
Said Bolorforosh, *Exec VP*
▲ **EMP:** 700
SQ FT: 224,000
SALES: 967.5MM **Publicly Held**
WEB: www.haemonetics.com
SIC: 3841 3845 Mfg Surgical/Medical Instruments And Electromedical Equipment

(G-9017)
HEALTHSTAR INC
62 Johnson Ln (02184-6702)
PHONE....................................781 428-3696
William J Grabowski, *President*
Dan Walsh, *Manager*
Leslie R Eliopoulos, *Admin Sec*
EMP: 25
SQ FT: 7,000
SALES (est): 5.5MM **Privately Held**
SIC: 3559 Mfg Misc Industry Machinery

(G-9018)
HUB PEN COMPANY INC (PA)
1525 Washington St Ste 1 (02184-7533)
PHONE....................................781 535-5500
Joseph A Fleming, *President*
Robert Mc Gaughey, *Vice Pres*
Jing Rong, *Vice Pres*
Steve McDonald, *Production*
Cindy Petrie, *Production*
▲ **EMP:** 54 **EST:** 1954
SALES: 29.2MM **Privately Held**
WEB: www.hubpen.com
SIC: 3951 Mfg Pens/Mechanical Pencils

(G-9019)
IGT GLOBAL SOLUTIONS CORP
Also Called: Gtech
60 Columbian St (02184-7342)
PHONE....................................781 849-5642
Patrick McHugh, *Branch Mgr*
EMP: 12
SALES (corp-wide): 4.8B **Privately Held**
WEB: www.gtech.com
SIC: 3575 Amusement/Recreation Services
HQ: Igt Global Solutions Corporation
10 Memorial Blvd
Providence RI 02903
401 392-1000

(G-9020)
INSPIRE HOPE FOUNDTN FOR UREA
95 Linda Rd (02184-7715)
PHONE....................................781 817-6664
John Dinon, *Director*
EMP: 3 **EST:** 2011
SALES (est): 287.7K **Privately Held**
SIC: 2873 Mfg Nitrogenous Fertilizers

GEOGRAPHIC

(G-9021)
JAMES CABLE LLC (PA)
Also Called: James Communications
15 Braintree Hill Park # 102 (02184-8722)
P.O. Box 536, Lebanon NJ (08833-0536)
PHONE....................................781 356-8701
Daniel Shoemaker, *Mng Member*
EMP: 50
SALES (est): 13.5MM **Privately Held**
SIC: 3315 Mfg Steel Wire/Related Products

(G-9022)
LENNYS SCREEN PRINTING
78 Quincy Ave (02184-4429)
PHONE....................................781 267-5977
Larry Collins, *Owner*
EMP: 3
SALES (est): 130K **Privately Held**
SIC: 2759 7389 Commercial Printing

(G-9023)
LIBERTY PACKAGING CO INC
Also Called: Liberty Intercept
22 Raleigh Rd (02184-4926)
PHONE....................................781 849-3355
Elaine Spitz, *President*
Joseph Spitz, *Treasurer*
EMP: 3
SALES: 1MM **Privately Held**
WEB: www.libertypackaging.com
SIC: 3086 5199 5999 Mfg Plastic Foam Products Whol Nondurable Goods Ret Misc Merchandise

(G-9024)
LOGAN INSTRUMENTS INC
101a French Ave (02184-6503)
P.O. Box 490951, Everett (02149-0016)
PHONE....................................617 394-0601
Charles Gambale, *President*
Jimmy Luong, *Manager*
EMP: 11
SALES: 600K **Privately Held**
SIC: 3841 8733 Mfg Surgical/Medical Instruments Noncommercial Research Organization

(G-9025)
MEANS PRE-CAST CO INC
151 Adams St (02184-1917)
PHONE....................................781 843-1909
Brian Ricciardi, *President*
Mark Ricciardi, *Treasurer*
EMP: 7
SQ FT: 3,000
SALES (est): 1.3MM **Privately Held**
WEB: www.meansprecast.com
SIC: 3272 Mfg Concrete Products

(G-9026)
MERRILL GRAPHICS INCORPORATED
35 Crescent Ave (02184-7050)
PHONE....................................781 843-0666
Jeffrey Hall, *President*
EMP: 4 **EST:** 1971
SQ FT: 2,500
SALES (est): 504.1K **Privately Held**
SIC: 2752 2791 Lithographic Commercial Printing Typesetting Services

(G-9027)
NORFOLK FACTORY DIRECT KITCHEN
265 Wood Rd (02184-2407)
PHONE....................................781 848-5333
Stew Rosen, *President*
Brian Silva, *Buyer*
Sue Warjas, *Manager*
EMP: 6
SQ FT: 1,200
SALES (est): 669.2K **Privately Held**
WEB: www.norfolkfactorydirect.com
SIC: 2434 Mfg Wood Kitchen Cabinets

(G-9028)
NORTHAST CAB CNTRTOP DSTRS INC
140 Campanelli Dr Ste 1 (02184-5240)
PHONE....................................617 296-2100
Stewart M Rosen, *President*
EMP: 5
SALES (est): 431.7K **Privately Held**
SIC: 2434 Mfg Wood Kitchen Cabinets

(G-9029)
ORTHOTIC AND PROSTHETIC CENTER
197 Quincy Ave Ste 102 (02184-2348)
PHONE....................................508 775-2570
James Tierney, *Mng Member*
EMP: 9
SALES (est): 1.1MM **Privately Held**
SIC: 3842 Mfg Surgical Appliances/Supplies

(G-9030)
PLANON CORPORATION
45 Braintree Hill Park # 400 (02184-8730)
PHONE....................................781 356-0999
Jim Nauen, *Principal*
Colby Tuttle, *Sales Dir*
Trish Frawley, *Sales Mgr*
Michelle Gaff, *Sales Staff*
Jay Shah, *Sales Staff*
EMP: 19
SALES (est): 3.1MM
SALES (corp-wide): 78.4MM **Privately Held**
WEB: www.planon-fm.com
SIC: 7372 Prepackaged Software Services
HQ: Planon Group B.V.
Wijchenseweg 8
Nijmegen 6537
246 413-135

(G-9031)
PRECAST VAULT CO INC (PA)
Also Called: Lee Burial Vaults
131 Adams St (02184-1917)
PHONE....................................508 252-4886
Brian Riccardi, *President*
Mark Riccardi, *Treasurer*
EMP: 5
SALES: 700K **Privately Held**
SIC: 3272 Mfg Concrete Products

(G-9032)
PROMOUNDS INC (PA)
Also Called: On Deck Sports
150 Wood Rd Ste 200 (02184-2510)
PHONE....................................508 580-6171
Joseph T Murphy, *President*
Laura Gilbert, *Executive*
▲ **EMP:** 42 **EST:** 2001
SQ FT: 36,970
SALES (est): 7MM **Privately Held**
WEB: www.ondecksports.com
SIC: 3949 Mfg Sporting/Athletic Goods

(G-9033)
PUMPING SYSTEMS INC
67 Water St (02184-8640)
PHONE....................................508 588-6868
Donald Deems, *President*
EMP: 7 **EST:** 1973
SALES (est): 1.9MM **Privately Held**
SIC: 3589 Mfg Service Industry Machinery

(G-9034)
RICHELIEU FOODS INC (DH)
222 Forbes Rd Ste 401 (02184-2717)
PHONE....................................781 786-6800
Tim O'Connor, *CEO*
David Meltzer, *Vice Pres*
Phil Paustian, *Surgery Dir*
Shwet Patel, *Admin Asst*
Angela Tuchalski, *Administration*
◆ **EMP:** 20
SQ FT: 7,500
SALES (est): 201.8MM
SALES (corp-wide): 851.2K **Privately Held**
WEB: www.richelieufoods.com
SIC: 2099 Mfg Food Preparations

(G-9035)
RIVER STREET METAL FINISHING
35 Johnson Ln (02184-6701)
PHONE....................................781 843-9351
Brian Reeves, *President*
Glen Reeves, *Foreman/Supr*
Pamela Reeves, *Treasurer*
EMP: 7
SQ FT: 7,500
SALES (est): 750K **Privately Held**
WEB: www.riverstreetmetalfinishing.com
SIC: 3471 Plating/Polishing Service

(G-9036)
SEPINUCK SIGN CO INC
130 Wood Rd (02184-2502)
PHONE....................................781 849-1181
Michael Supinuck, *President*
EMP: 5
SALES (est): 410K **Privately Held**
SIC: 3993 Mfg Signs/Advertising Specialties

(G-9037)
SKYRAY INSTRUMENT INC
6 Brooks Dr (02184-3839)
PHONE....................................617 202-3879
Haiming LI, *President*
EMP: 10
SALES: 500K **Privately Held**
SIC: 3826 Mfg Analytical Instruments

(G-9038)
SPEEDY SIGN-A-RAMA USA
130 Wood Rd (02184-2502)
PHONE....................................781 849-1181
Mike Sepinuck, *Owner*
EMP: 7
SALES (est): 549.3K **Privately Held**
SIC: 3993 1799 Mfg Signs/Advertising Specialties Trade Contractor

(G-9039)
SUPERIOR BINDERY INC
Also Called: Superior Packaging & Finishing
1 Federal Dr (02184-5238)
PHONE....................................781 303-0022
Donald Charlebois, *President*
Jim Stanley, *Sr Exec VP*
Robert Najarian, *CFO*
Brad Lopez, *Manager*
Jeffrey Heath, *Technology*
▲ **EMP:** 101
SQ FT: 16,000
SALES (est): 16.2MM **Privately Held**
WEB: www.superiorbindery.com
SIC: 2789 Bookbinding/Related Work

(G-9040)
SUPERMEDIA LLC
186 Forbes Rd (02184-2612)
PHONE....................................781 849-7670
Jeff Rodenbush, *Branch Mgr*
EMP: 254
SALES (corp-wide): 1.6B **Privately Held**
SIC: 2741 Communication Services
HQ: Supermedia Llc
2200 W Airfield Dr
Dfw Airport TX 75261
972 453-7000

(G-9041)
SYMMONS INDUSTRIES INC (PA)
31 Brooks Dr (02184-3804)
PHONE....................................781 848-2250
Timothy E O'Keefe, *CEO*
John W Graves, *President*
Mike Billingsley, *Business Mgr*
Dale Emerson, *Business Mgr*
Jessica Flint, *Business Mgr*
▲ **EMP:** 245 **EST:** 1939
SQ FT: 88,000
SALES (est): 43.3MM **Privately Held**
WEB: www.symmons.com
SIC: 3494 3432 Mfg Valves/Pipe Fittings Mfg Plumbing Fixture Fittings

(G-9042)
SYMMONS INDUSTRIES INC
11 Brooks Dr (02184-3809)
PHONE....................................781 664-5236
Jeffrey Reilly, *Branch Mgr*
EMP: 3
SALES (corp-wide): 43.3MM **Privately Held**
SIC: 3494 Mfg Valves/Pipe Fittings
PA: Symmons Industries, Inc.
31 Brooks Dr
Braintree MA 02184
781 848-2250

(G-9043)
TAYLOR COMMUNICATIONS INC
400 Washington St (02184-4729)
PHONE....................................781 843-0250
Chris Copley, *Branch Mgr*
EMP: 12
SALES (corp-wide): 2.8B **Privately Held**
WEB: www.stdreg.com
SIC: 2761 Mfg Manifold Business Forms
HQ: Taylor Communications, Inc.
1725 Roe Crest Dr
North Mankato MN 56003
866 541-0937

(G-9044)
TWIN CY UPHOLSTERING & MAT CO
476 Quincy Ave (02184-1346)
PHONE....................................781 843-1780
George J Dubois Jr, *CEO*
James Dubois, *Treasurer*
EMP: 10
SQ FT: 9,600
SALES: 600K **Privately Held**
SIC: 2512 5712 2515 Mfg & Ret Upholstered Living Room Furniture & Inner Spring Mattresses & Ret Reclining Chairs

(G-9045)
ULTRA ELEC OCEAN SYSTEMS INC
115 Bay State Dr (02184-5203)
PHONE....................................781 848-3400
William Terry, *President*
Rochelle Borden, *Exec VP*
Thomas P Bourgault, *Vice Pres*
Thomas Bourgault, *Vice Pres*
Dan Fischbach, *Vice Pres*
▲ **EMP:** 100
SQ FT: 50,000
SALES (est): 25.1MM
SALES (corp-wide): 1B **Privately Held**
WEB: www.ultra-os.com
SIC: 3446 Mfg Architectural Metalwork
HQ: Ultra Electronics Defense Inc.
4101 Smith School Rd
Austin TX 78744
512 327-6795

(G-9046)
VAUGHAN W C CO LTD INC
Also Called: W C Vaughn
55 Messina Dr (02184-6783)
P.O. Box 850914 (02185-0914)
PHONE....................................781 848-0308
Glenn Pratt, *President*
Geoff Muther, *Principal*
▲ **EMP:** 3
SALES (est): 287K **Privately Held**
SIC: 3429 Mfg Hardware

(G-9047)
VERA BRADLEY DESIGNS INC
250 Granite St Ste 131 (02184-2808)
PHONE....................................781 794-9860
Patty Curran, *Branch Mgr*
EMP: 4
SALES (corp-wide): 416.1MM **Publicly Held**
SIC: 3171 Ret Women's Accessories/Specialties
HQ: Vera Bradley Designs, Inc.
12420 Stonebridge Rd
Roanoke IN 46783
260 482-4673

(G-9048)
WARNER ELECTRIC
300 Granite St Ste 201 (02184-3950)
PHONE....................................781 917-0600
Rosa Mark, *CTO*
EMP: 8
SALES (est): 542.7K
SALES (corp-wide): 1.1B **Publicly Held**
SIC: 3568 5085 3542 3625 Mfg Power Transmission Equipment
PA: Altra Industrial Motion Corp.
300 Granite St Ste 201
Braintree MA 02184
781 917-0600

(G-9049)
WERNER PUBLISHING CORPORATION
Also Called: Golf Tips
25 Braintree Hill Park # 404 (02184-8702)
PHONE....................................310 820-1500
Dorothy L Werner, *Ch of Bd*
Steven D Werner, *President*
Lynne Werner, *Vice Pres*
EMP: 53

SALES (est): 16.6MM **Privately Held**
WEB: www.wernerpublishing.com
SIC: 2721 Periodicals-Publishing/Printing

(G-9050)
WHYTE ELECTRIC LLC
95 Shaw St (02184-4311)
PHONE....781 348-6239
Daniel E Whyte, *Principal*
EMP: 4
SALES (est): 146.9K **Privately Held**
SIC: 3699 1731 Mfg Electrical Equipment/Supplies Electrical Contractor

(G-9051)
WOLLASTON ALLOYS INC
205 Wood Rd (02184-2498)
PHONE....781 848-3333
William F Earley, *President*
Ali Ghavami, *COO*
David Andrew Adams, *Vice Pres*
David Andrew Moreland, *Vice Pres*
Ron Hamilton, *CFO*
▲ **EMP:** 180 **EST:** 1947
SALES (est): 50.4MM
SALES (corp-wide): 6.4B **Privately Held**
WEB: www.wollastonalloys.com
SIC: 3325 3369 Steel Foundry Nonferrous Metal Foundry
HQ: Consolidated Precision Products Corp.
1621 Euclid Ave Ste 1850
Cleveland OH 44115
216 453-4800

Brewster
Barnstable County

(G-9052)
BREWSTER ICE CO
Main St (02631)
P.O. Box 1816 (02631-7816)
PHONE....508 896-3593
Roland W Bassett, *Owner*
Roger Bassett, *Co-Owner*
EMP: 5
SALES (est): 300K **Privately Held**
WEB: www.planethockey.com
SIC: 2097 Mfg Ice

(G-9053)
GLINES RHODES INC
381 Satucket Rd (02631-2379)
PHONE....508 385-8828
E Crowell, *Principal*
EMP: 3
SALES (est): 222.6K **Privately Held**
SIC: 3369 Nonferrous Metal Foundry

(G-9054)
MUSSEL BOUND LLC
80 Joe Long Rd (02631-2074)
P.O. Box 749 (02631-0749)
PHONE....774 212-5488
Terry M Jones, *President*
Carla S Jones, *Admin Sec*
EMP: 8
SQ FT: 2,000
SALES: 100K **Privately Held**
SIC: 2891 Mfg Adhesives/Sealants

(G-9055)
PARACLETE PRESS INC (HQ)
36 Southern Eagle Cartway (02631-1558)
P.O. Box 1568, Orleans (02653-1568)
PHONE....508 255-4685
Robert J Edmonson, *President*
Sharon Pfeiffer, *Editor*
Dave Ortolani, *Buyer*
Cori Shannon, *Finance Mgr*
Phoenix Catlin, *Sales Staff*
▲ **EMP:** 40
SQ FT: 15,000
SALES (est): 7.2MM
SALES (corp-wide): 8.6MM **Privately Held**
WEB: www.paracletepress.com
SIC: 2731 Books-Publishing/Printing
PA: The Community Of Jesus Inc
5 Bay View Dr
Orleans MA 02653
508 255-1094

(G-9056)
PARACLETE PRESS INC
39 Eldridge Rd (02631-1552)
P.O. Box 1568, Orleans (02653-1568)
PHONE....508 255-4685
Robert Edmondson, *Branch Mgr*
EMP: 6
SALES (corp-wide): 8.6MM **Privately Held**
WEB: www.paracletepress.com
SIC: 2731 2721 7819 Book & Magazine Publishing Printing And Video Editing
HQ: Paraclete Press, Inc.
36 Southern Eagle Cartway
Brewster MA 02631
508 255-4685

(G-9057)
RIFE MLTPLWAVE OSCILLATORS LLC
2114 Main St (02631-1820)
PHONE....508 737-8468
James D Girard, *Principal*
EMP: 3
SALES (est): 150.5K **Privately Held**
SIC: 3679 Mfg Electronic Components

(G-9058)
SYDENSTRICKER GALLERIES INC (PA)
Also Called: Sydenstricker Glass
490 Main St (02631-1001)
PHONE....508 385-3272
Anthony Geradi, *President*
Angelo Geradi, *Treasurer*
EMP: 10
SQ FT: 5,000
SALES (est): 1MM **Privately Held**
WEB: www.sydenstricker.com
SIC: 3229 Mfg Pressed/Blown Glass

Bridgewater
Plymouth County

(G-9059)
A LUONGO & SONS INCORPORATED
160 Fireworks Cir (02324-3036)
P.O. Box 1051, Attleboro (02703-0018)
PHONE....508 226-0788
Frank Luongo, *President*
Tony Luongo, *Vice Pres*
Peter Luongo, *Treasurer*
EMP: 8
SQ FT: 15,000
SALES: 985K **Privately Held**
WEB: www.aluongo.com
SIC: 3544 3469 Mfg Dies/Tools/Jigs/Fixtures Mfg Metal Stampings

(G-9060)
ASHMONT WELDING COMPANY INC
10 Cranmore Dr (02324-2157)
P.O. Box 5 (02324-0005)
PHONE....508 279-1977
Jim Welch, *President*
EMP: 12
SALES (est): 2.1MM **Privately Held**
SIC: 7692 5084 Welding Repair Whol Industrial Equipment

(G-9061)
B R S INC
Also Called: Bridgewater Raynham Sand Stone
1453 Plymouth St (02324-2098)
P.O. Box 187 (02324-0187)
PHONE....508 697-5448
Daniel G Kirker, *President*
Joseph A Arruda, *Vice Pres*
EMP: 20
SALES (est): 2.1MM **Privately Held**
SIC: 3281 5032 1442 Mfg Cut Stone/Products Whol Brick/Stone Material Construction Sand/Gravel

(G-9062)
BAY STEEL CO INC
81 Bridge St (02324-1903)
PHONE....508 697-7083
EMP: 10
SALES (corp-wide): 984.8K **Privately Held**
SIC: 3449 Mfg Misc Structural Metalwork
PA: Bay Steel Co Inc
87 Lake St
Halifax MA 02338
781 294-8308

(G-9063)
BAYSTATE LIGHTNING PROTECTION
55 Three Rivers Dr (02324-1961)
PHONE....508 697-7727
James R Smith, *President*
EMP: 9
SALES (est): 1.5MM **Privately Held**
SIC: 3643 Mfg Conductive Wiring Devices

(G-9064)
BETA DYNE INC
110 Elm St Unit 12 (02324-1039)
PHONE....508 697-1993
Anastasios Simotoulos, *President*
Beth Merithew, *Administration*
EMP: 10
SQ FT: 2,000
SALES (est): 1.7MM **Privately Held**
WEB: www.beta-dyne.com
SIC: 3679 Parametric Amplifiers

(G-9065)
BRIDGEWATER PRTG COPY CTR LLC
100 Broad St (02324-1797)
PHONE....508 697-5227
Gregg Goudreau, *Mng Member*
EMP: 4
SALES (est): 441.5K **Privately Held**
SIC: 2752 Lithographic Commercial Printing

(G-9066)
CHASE CORP
26 Summer St (02325-1218)
PHONE....508 819-4200
Leslie Smith, *President*
Ken Stuart, *Prdtn Mgr*
Joseph Gedraitis, *Warehouse Mgr*
Teresa Atkins, *Production*
Daniel Libby, *Research*
EMP: 17
SALES (est): 2MM **Privately Held**
SIC: 2821 Mfg Plastic Materials/Resins

(G-9067)
CIM INDUSTRIES INC
26 Summer St (02325-1218)
PHONE....800 543-3458
Peter R Chase, *Principal*
EMP: 3
SALES (est): 111.9K
SALES (corp-wide): 281.3MM **Publicly Held**
SIC: 3999 Mfg Misc Products
PA: Chase Corporation
295 University Ave
Westwood MA 02090
781 332-0700

(G-9068)
CONTROL 7 INC
Also Called: C7
55 Scotland Blvd (02324-2302)
PHONE....508 697-3197
Mark W Jacoby, *President*
John Nelson, *Shareholder*
EMP: 20
SQ FT: 12,500
SALES: 8.7MM **Privately Held**
WEB: www.control7.com
SIC: 3613 Mfg Switchgear/Switchboards

(G-9069)
COTTA TRUCK EQUIPMENT
30 Bedford Park Ste 4 (02324-3046)
PHONE....508 269-1960
Carlos Cotta, *Owner*
EMP: 6
SALES (est): 503.2K **Privately Held**
SIC: 3713 Mfg Truck/Bus Bodies

(G-9070)
DAILY GRIND
23 Central Sq (02324-2508)
PHONE....508 279-9952
Sandra Araujo, *Principal*
EMP: 3
SALES (est): 184.3K **Privately Held**
SIC: 3599 Mfg Industrial Machinery

(G-9071)
DEPUY SYNTHES SALES INC
50 Scotland Blvd (02324-2303)
PHONE....508 880-8100
EMP: 15
SALES (corp-wide): 81.5B **Publicly Held**
SIC: 3841 Mfg Surgical/Medical Instruments
HQ: Depuy Synthes Sales Inc
325 Paramount Dr
Raynham MA 02767
508 880-8100

(G-9072)
EARTHS ELEMENTS INC
1070 Vernon St (02324-3545)
PHONE....508 697-2277
Kelly Souza, *Principal*
EMP: 4
SALES (est): 338.8K **Privately Held**
SIC: 3423 Mfg Hand/Edge Tools

(G-9073)
FIBERTEC INC
35 Scotland Blvd (02324-2302)
PHONE....508 697-5100
Joseph Aten, *President*
John Kidd, *Safety Mgr*
◆ **EMP:** 55
SQ FT: 52,500
SALES (est): 13.2MM **Privately Held**
WEB: www.fibertecinc.com
SIC: 3089 3231 Mfg Plastic Products Mfg Products-Purchased Glass

(G-9074)
GRAZIANO REDI-MIX INC
60 1st St (02324-1054)
PHONE....508 697-8350
John Graziano, *President*
Gene Graziano, *Vice Pres*
EMP: 25
SQ FT: 9,000
SALES (est): 4.6MM **Privately Held**
WEB: www.grazianoredimix.com
SIC: 3273 Mfg Ready-Mixed Concrete

(G-9075)
HARRYS MOLD & MACHINE INC
275 Elm St (02324-1007)
P.O. Box 500 (02324-0500)
PHONE....508 697-6432
Harry Jahnke, *President*
Susan L Jahnke, *Admin Sec*
EMP: 8
SALES (est): 1MM **Privately Held**
SIC: 3544 Mfg Industrial Machinery

(G-9076)
HENRY PERKINS COMPANY
180 Broad St (02324-1751)
P.O. Box 215 (02324-0215)
PHONE....508 697-6978
Tom Perkins, *President*
David Perkins Jr, *Vice Pres*
Peter Perkins, *Treasurer*
▼ **EMP:** 11 **EST:** 1848
SQ FT: 3,000
SALES (est): 2.2MM **Privately Held**
SIC: 3321 Gray/Ductile Iron Foundry

(G-9077)
INSULATION TECHNOLOGY INC
35 1st St (02324-1054)
P.O. Box 578 (02324-0578)
PHONE....508 697-6926
Robert Anderson, *President*
Marcia Anderson, *Vice Pres*
▲ **EMP:** 7
SQ FT: 20,000
SALES (est): 1.1MM **Privately Held**
WEB: www.insultech-eps.com
SIC: 3086 Mfg Plastic Foam Products

(G-9078)
JERRYS CUSTOM UPHOLSTERY
259 Plain St (02324-1923)
PHONE....508 697-2183
EMP: 3 **EST:** 2001

SALES (est): 140K **Privately Held**
SIC: 2512 Mfg Upholstered Household Furniture

(G-9079)
JP OBELISK INC
10 Duck Farm Ln (02324-1332)
PHONE..................................508 942-6248
Joseph P Fernald, *Principal*
EMP: 4
SALES (est): 522.5K **Privately Held**
SIC: 3531 Mfg Construction Machinery

(G-9080)
JP PLASTICS INC
45 1st St (02324-1054)
P.O. Box 579 (02324-0579)
PHONE..................................508 697-4202
John P Cheever, *President*
Nicole Cheever, *Vice Pres*
EMP: 8
SQ FT: 17,000
SALES: 1.9MM **Privately Held**
SIC: 3081 Mfg Unsupported Plastic Film/Sheet

(G-9081)
KEVIN LYMAN ROOFING CO
123 Green St (02324-3543)
PHONE..................................508 697-8244
Kevin Lyman, *Owner*
Brenda Lyman, *Co-Owner*
EMP: 6
SALES (est): 528.4K **Privately Held**
WEB: www.kevinlymanroofing.com
SIC: 3069 Mfg Fabricated Rubber Products

(G-9082)
LARKIN MOTORS LLC
25 Firwrks Cir Brdgewater Bridgewater (02324)
PHONE..................................508 807-1333
Jeff Ingargiola, *CEO*
EMP: 3
SQ FT: 5,000
SALES (est): 252.5K **Privately Held**
SIC: 7692 3011 3089 7549 Welding Repair Mfg Tires/Inner Tubes Mfg Plastic Products Automotive Services

(G-9083)
MEDICAL DEVICE BUS SVCS INC
Also Called: Depuy Orthopaedics
50 Scotland Blvd (02324-2303)
PHONE..................................508 828-6155
EMP: 5
SALES (corp-wide): 81.5B **Publicly Held**
SIC: 3842 Mfg Surgical Appliances/Supplies
HQ: Medical Device Business Services, Inc.
700 Orthopaedic Dr
Warsaw IN 46582

(G-9084)
MJ MACHINE INC
1 1st St 9 (02324-1054)
PHONE..................................508 697-5329
John R Hay, *President*
EMP: 5
SALES (est): 550K **Privately Held**
SIC: 3599 Mfg Industrial Machinery

(G-9085)
MODERN MARKING PRODUCTS INC
Also Called: Bridgewater Trophy
43 Central Sq (02324-2508)
P.O. Box 475 (02324-0475)
PHONE..................................508 697-6066
John Sylvia, *President*
EMP: 5 **EST:** 1981
SQ FT: 1,500
SALES (est): 664.4K **Privately Held**
WEB: www.bridgewatertrophy.com
SIC: 3479 5999 7389 Engraving & Etching Of Name Plates Rubber Stamps & Vinyl Lettering Services

(G-9086)
PAUL MCNAMARA
Also Called: P M Tile and Grout Care
110 Dundee Dr (02324-2208)
PHONE..................................508 245-5654
Paul S McNamara, *Owner*
EMP: 10
SALES (est): 508.9K **Privately Held**
WEB: www.paulmcnamara.com
SIC: 3471 Plating/Polishing Service

(G-9087)
SAWMILL BROOK FARM
140 Lyman Pl (02324-3037)
PHONE..................................508 697-7847
Stanley Kravitz, *Owner*
EMP: 4
SALES (est): 400K **Privately Held**
SIC: 2421 0181 Sawmill/Planing Mill Ornamental Nursery

(G-9088)
STILES & HART BRICK COMPANY
127 Cook St (02324-3307)
P.O. Box 367 (02324-0367)
PHONE..................................508 697-6928
Jean Andrews, *President*
James Kenn, *Vice Pres*
Francis Mansfield, *Vice Pres*
Kevin Barry, *VP Sales*
◆ **EMP:** 44
SQ FT: 2,500
SALES: 7.7MM **Privately Held**
WEB: www.stilesandhart.com
SIC: 3271 3229 2426 3251 Mfg Brick/Structrl Tile Mfg Concrete Block/Brick Mfg Pressed/Blown Glass Hdwd Dimension/Flr Mill

(G-9089)
TECHNICAL ENTERPRISES INC
Also Called: Tei
40 Country Club Dr (02324-2147)
PHONE..................................781 603-9402
Thomas C Trocki, *President*
Scott M Trocki, *General Mgr*
Lois J Trocki, *Treasurer*
EMP: 5
SQ FT: 5,000
SALES (est): 441.1K **Privately Held**
SIC: 3599 3469 8711 General Machine & Mfg Sheet Metal Fabrications & Mechanical Engineering Service

(G-9090)
TOP SHELF INSTALLATIONS
400 Walnut St (02324-2842)
PHONE..................................508 697-1550
Brian Killea, *Owner*
EMP: 6
SALES (est): 362K **Privately Held**
SIC: 2542 Mfg Partitions/Fixtures-Nonwood

(G-9091)
TWD INC
Also Called: Twd Surfaces
75 Hale St (02324-1708)
PHONE..................................508 279-2650
Raymond C St Gelais, *President*
EMP: 43
SQ FT: 30,000
SALES: 6.7MM **Privately Held**
SIC: 2541 Trade Contractor

Brighton
Suffolk County

(G-9092)
ALIP CORPORATION
60a Waverly St (02135-1210)
PHONE..................................857 234-6073
EMP: 5 **EST:** 2012
SALES (est): 243.5K **Privately Held**
SIC: 3845 Mfg Electromedical Equipment

(G-9093)
ALLSTON POWER LLC
84 Lincoln St (02135-1409)
PHONE..................................617 562-4054
Aileen Liu, *Principal*
EMP: 10 **EST:** 2012
SALES: 500K **Privately Held**
SIC: 3679 Mfg Electronic Components

(G-9094)
ARCHETYPE HARDWARE
124 Sutherland Rd Apt 9 (02135-7263)
PHONE..................................707 303-6003
EMP: 3
SALES (est): 139.7K **Privately Held**
SIC: 3841 Mfg Surgical/Medical Instruments

(G-9095)
ATHANS INC
Also Called: Athan's Bakery
407 Washington St (02135-2731)
PHONE..................................617 783-0313
Aris Athan, *Branch Mgr*
EMP: 13
SALES (corp-wide): 500K **Privately Held**
WEB: www.athansbakery.com
SIC: 2051 Bakery
PA: Athan's Inc
1621 Beacon St
Brookline MA 02446
617 734-7028

(G-9096)
BLINK NEUROTECH CORP
48 Englewood Ave 3 (02135-7810)
PHONE..................................917 767-6829
EMP: 5
SALES (est): 261.9K **Privately Held**
SIC: 3845 Mfg Electromedical Equipment

(G-9097)
DAILY STROLL LLC
2001 Commonwealth Ave (02135-5114)
PHONE..................................678 770-4531
Bryn Paige Ambrose, *Principal*
EMP: 4
SALES (est): 220.3K **Privately Held**
SIC: 2711 Newspapers-Publishing/Printing

(G-9098)
EZRA J LEBOFF CO INC
74 Lincoln St (02135-1409)
PHONE..................................617 783-4200
Alfred E Santosuosso, *President*
EMP: 5 **EST:** 1950
SQ FT: 5,200
SALES (est): 843.5K **Privately Held**
SIC: 3644 3089 2796 Mfg Nonconductive Wiring Devices Mfg Plastic Products Platemaking Services

(G-9099)
FUEL AMERICA
152 Chestnut Hill Ave (02135-4639)
PHONE..................................617 782-0999
Jeff Bonasia, *Principal*
EMP: 5
SALES (est): 670.2K **Privately Held**
SIC: 2869 Mfg Industrial Organic Chemicals

(G-9100)
HARVARD BUS SCHL PUBG CORP (HQ)
Also Called: Harvard Business Review
20 Guest St Ste 700 (02135-2063)
PHONE..................................617 783-7400
David Wan, *President*
Patrick McManus, *President*
Ann Cichon, *Managing Dir*
Raymond Carvey, *COO*
Sarah Cliffe, *Exec Officer*
▲ **EMP:** 173
SALES: 207.5MM
SALES (corp-wide): 5.5B **Privately Held**
SIC: 2721 2731 2741 Periodicals-Publishing/Printing Books-Publishing/Printing Misc Publishing
PA: President And Fellows Of Harvard College
1350 Massachusetts Ave
Cambridge MA 02138
617 496-4873

(G-9101)
HDM SYSTEMS CORPORATION
84 Lincoln St (02135-1409)
PHONE..................................617 562-4054
Aileen Liu, *President*
James Zeng, *Design Engr*
Anne Lam, *Accounting Dir*
Leeann Liu, *Executive*
CHI Fu Yeh, *Admin Sec*
▲ **EMP:** 14
SQ FT: 12,000
SALES (est): 1.7MM **Privately Held**
WEB: www.hdmsys.com
SIC: 3679 Mfg Electronic Components For Battery Base System

(G-9102)
NEW BALANCE LICENSING LLC
20 Guest St Fl 8 (02135-2040)
PHONE..................................800 343-4648
Anne M Davis, *Principal*
EMP: 3
SALES (est): 157.5K **Privately Held**
SIC: 3021 Mfg Rubber/Plastic Footwear

(G-9103)
PATRICIA SEYBOLD GROUP INC
208 Allston St Apt 3 (02135-7634)
PHONE..................................617 742-5200
Patricia Seybold, *President*
David Marshak, *Senior VP*
EMP: 13
SQ FT: 3,300
SALES (est): 730K **Privately Held**
WEB: www.psgroup.com
SIC: 2741 8742 8748 Misc Publishing Management Consulting Services Business Consulting Services

(G-9104)
PECO PALLET
34 Lake St Apt 2 (02135-3819)
PHONE..................................845 642-2780
EMP: 4
SALES (est): 218.9K **Privately Held**
SIC: 2448 Mfg Wood Pallets/Skids

(G-9105)
PRIDE INDIA INC (PA)
Also Called: Pride of India
329 Summit Ave Apt 7 (02135-7508)
PHONE..................................617 202-9659
Akshat Jain, *President*
Prateek Jain, *Vice Pres*
Ashish Jain, *Director*
Neelam Jain, *Director*
◆ **EMP:** 10
SQ FT: 8,000
SALES (est): 550K **Privately Held**
SIC: 2099 2844 Mfg Food Preparations Mfg Toilet Preparations

(G-9106)
SINGING RIVER PUBLICATIONS
172 Foster St (02135-3902)
PHONE..................................218 365-3498
Christine Moroni, *President*
EMP: 3
SALES (est): 160K **Privately Held**
WEB: www.singingriverpublications.com
SIC: 2731 2741 Books-Publishing/Printing Misc Publishing

(G-9107)
STUDIO OF ENGAGING LEARNING
167 Corey Rd Ste 209 (02135-8214)
PHONE..................................617 975-0268
Katherine Klimukhina, *Principal*
EMP: 3
SALES (est): 255.1K **Privately Held**
SIC: 3826 Mfg Analytical Instruments

(G-9108)
XL HYBRIDS INC (PA)
Also Called: Xl Fleet
145 Newton St (02135-1508)
PHONE..................................617 718-0329
Dimitri Kazarinoff, *CEO*
David Breault, *Business Mgr*
Clayton W Siegert, *COO*
Kristin Brief, *Senior VP*
Andrew Gregg, *Prdtn Mgr*
EMP: 50
SALES (est): 11.9MM **Privately Held**
SIC: 3714 Mfg Motor Vehicle Parts/Accessories

Brimfield
Hampden County

(G-9109)
BRIMFIELD PRECISION LLC
68 Mill Ln (01010-9749)
PHONE..................................413 245-7144
Donald J Spence, *CEO*
Medsource Technologies LLC,
EMP: 95 **EST:** 1965
SQ FT: 32,500
SALES (est): 8MM
SALES (corp-wide): 1.2B **Publicly Held**
SIC: 3841 3842 Mfg Surgical/Medical Instruments Mfg Surgical Appliances/Supplies
HQ: Medsource Technologies, Llc
100 Fordham Rd Ste 1
Wilmington MA 01887
978 570-6900

(G-9110)
MK FUEL INC
341 Sturbridge Rd (01010-9640)
PHONE..................................413 245-7507
Anwar Afrede, *President*
EMP: 6
SALES (est): 428.4K **Privately Held**
SIC: 2869 Mfg Industrial Organic Chemicals

(G-9111)
TOWN OF BRIMFIELD
Also Called: Brimfield Hwy Dept
34b Wales Rd (01010-9678)
PHONE..................................413 245-4103
Robert Hanna, *Principal*
EMP: 3 **Privately Held**
WEB: www.brimfieldfd.org
SIC: 3531 Mfg Construction Machinery
PA: Town Of Brimfield
23 Main St
Brimfield MA

Brockton
Plymouth County

(G-9112)
3 M N CORP
12 Perry Ave (02302-3630)
PHONE..................................508 586-4471
Michael Carpentieri, *Principal*
EMP: 5 **EST:** 2010
SALES (est): 352K **Privately Held**
SIC: 3412 Mfg Metal Barrels/Pails

(G-9113)
A & S TRANSPORT WHEELCHAIR SVC
40 Highland St (02301-3959)
PHONE..................................617 701-4407
EMP: 3 **EST:** 2013
SALES (est): 104.7K **Privately Held**
SIC: 3842 Mfg Surgical Appliances/Supplies

(G-9114)
ABLE PEST CONTROL SERVICE
610 N Main St Ste 2 (02301-2497)
PHONE..................................508 559-7987
Joe Giammatteo, *Partner*
Mike Polvere, *Partner*
EMP: 6
SALES (est): 982.6K **Privately Held**
WEB: www.ablepestcontrolservice.com
SIC: 2879 7342 Mfg Agricultural Chemicals Disinfecting/Pest Services

(G-9115)
ACUSHNET COMPANY
Also Called: Titalist and Footjoy Worldwide
144 Field St (02302-1608)
PHONE..................................508 979-2309
Robert C Boehm, *Exec VP*
EMP: 536 **Publicly Held**
SIC: 3949 Mfg Sporting/Athletic Goods
HQ: Acushnet Company
333 Bridge St
Fairhaven MA 02719
508 979-2000

(G-9116)
ACUSHNET COMPANY
Also Called: Titleist
144 Field St (02302-1608)
P.O. Box 965, Fairhaven (02719-0965)
PHONE..................................508 979-2343
Bob Daniels, *Vice Pres*
Fred Langevin, *Director*
EMP: 40 **Publicly Held**
WEB: www.titleist.com
SIC: 3949 Mfg Sporting/Athletic Goods
HQ: Acushnet Company
333 Bridge St
Fairhaven MA 02719
508 979-2000

(G-9117)
AGM INDUSTRIES INC
16 Jonathan Dr (02301-5549)
PHONE..................................508 587-3900
Tom Karjama, *CEO*
Kenneth Reale, *President*
Ernst Hatz, *Vice Pres*
Norma Searle, *Treasurer*
EMP: 30 **EST:** 1961
SQ FT: 30,000
SALES (est): 4.8MM **Privately Held**
WEB: www.agmind.com
SIC: 3548 Mfg Welding Apparatus

(G-9118)
AMPHENOL ALDEN PRODUCTS CO (HQ)
Also Called: Amphenol Alden
117 N Main St (02301-3908)
PHONE..................................508 427-7000
Elizabeth Alden, *Ch of Bd*
R Adam Norwitt, *President*
Dona Gentile, *Principal*
Martin H Loeffler, *Principal*
Mike Aneiros, *Business Mgr*
▲ **EMP:** 112 **EST:** 1929
SQ FT: 60,000
SALES (est): 24.4MM
SALES (corp-wide): 8.2B **Publicly Held**
WEB: www.aldenproducts.com
SIC: 3678 Mfg Electronic Connectors
PA: Amphenol Corporation
358 Hall Ave
Wallingford CT 06492
203 265-8900

(G-9119)
AMS GRINDING CO INC
959 W Chestnut St Ste 1 (02301-5559)
PHONE..................................508 588-2283
Antonio Sousa, *President*
Diane Sousa, *Treasurer*
Jose Romao, *Shareholder*
EMP: 7
SQ FT: 5,500
SALES: 900K **Privately Held**
SIC: 3599 Mfg Industrial Machinery

(G-9120)
ANTENNA ASSOCIATES INC
21 Burke Dr (02301-5504)
PHONE..................................508 583-3241
Ronald A Sandquist, *President*
Dana Sandquist, *Vice Pres*
Kimberly Brady, *Manager*
Radu Gafitanu, *Manager*
Dan Hamilton, *Manager*
EMP: 25
SQ FT: 20,000
SALES: 7.3MM **Privately Held**
WEB: www.antennaassociates.com
SIC: 3812 Mfg Search/Navigation Equipment

(G-9121)
ATRENNE CMPT SOLUTIONS LLC (DH)
10 Mupac Dr (02301-5548)
PHONE..................................508 588-6110
Chris Boutilier, *President*
Jim Tierney, *Vice Pres*
Mark Cosenza, *Plant Mgr*
Tom Heasley, *Engineer*
Rick White, *Controller*
EMP: 273 **EST:** 1946
SALES: 64MM
SALES (corp-wide): 23.7B **Privately Held**
WEB: www.cbttechnology.com
SIC: 3354 3469 3429 Mfg Aluminum Extruded Products Mfg Metal Stampings Mfg Hardware
HQ: Atrenne Integrated Solutions, Inc.
9210 Science Center Dr
New Hope MN 55428
763 533-3533

(G-9122)
ATRENNE CMPT SOLUTIONS LLC
11 Burke Dr (02301-5504)
PHONE..................................508 588-6110
EMP: 4
SALES (corp-wide): 23.7B **Privately Held**
SIC: 3354 Mfg Aluminum Extruded Products
HQ: Atrenne Computing Solutions, Llc
10 Mupac Dr
Brockton MA 02301
508 588-6110

(G-9123)
BABIN MACHINE INC
Also Called: Babin Machine Tool
14 Upland Rd (02301-2326)
PHONE..................................508 588-9189
Paul Bibinski, *President*
EMP: 5 **EST:** 1959
SQ FT: 4,000
SALES: 1.1MM **Privately Held**
WEB: www.babinmachine.com
SIC: 3541 3542 Machine Tool Rebuilding & Repair Retrofitting Sales

(G-9124)
BARBOUR CORPORATION (PA)
Also Called: Barbour Plastics
1001 N Montello St (02301-1640)
P.O. Box 2158 (02305-2158)
PHONE..................................508 583-8200
Richard K Hynes, *President*
Frederick Bowen, *CFO*
Rick Bowen, *CFO*
Bruce Pearson, *Admin Sec*
▲ **EMP:** 117 **EST:** 1892
SQ FT: 130,000
SALES (est): 24.6MM **Privately Held**
SIC: 3131 Mfg Footwear Cut Stock

(G-9125)
BARBOUR PLASTICS INC (HQ)
1001 N Montello St (02301-1640)
P.O. Box 2158 (02305-2158)
PHONE..................................508 583-8200
Richard K Hynes, *President*
Bruce Pearson, *Senior VP*
Frederick Bowen, *CFO*
▲ **EMP:** 50
SQ FT: 65,000
SALES (est): 7.4MM
SALES (corp-wide): 24.6MM **Privately Held**
WEB: www.barbourcorp.com
SIC: 3131 3111 3053 Mfg Footwear Cut Stock Leather Tanning/Finishing Mfg Gaskets/Packing/Sealing Devices
PA: Barbour Corporation
1001 N Montello St
Brockton MA 02301
508 583-8200

(G-9126)
CARLO GAVAZZI INCORPORATED
10 Mupac Dr (02301-5548)
PHONE..................................508 588-6110
Mads Lillelund, *CEO*
Paula Adams, *Program Mgr*
EMP: 5
SALES (est): 697.5K **Privately Held**
SIC: 3679 Mfg Electronic Components

(G-9127)
CC-TEKNOLOGIES INC
21 Marsden St Brockton (02302)
PHONE..................................508 444-8810
Marek Oles, *President*
EMP: 9
SALES (est): 1.3MM **Privately Held**
SIC: 3699 Mfg Electrical Equipment/Supplies

(G-9128)
CDI LLC A VALLEY FORGE CO
637 N Montello St (02301-2454)
PHONE..................................508 587-7000
Diana Dobin Kauppinen, *Mng Member*
Michael Dobin,
EMP: 120
SALES: 17MM
SALES (corp-wide): 326.1MM **Privately Held**
SIC: 2591 Mfg Drapery Hardware/Blinds
PA: Valley Forge Fabrics, Inc.
1650 W Mcnab Rd
Fort Lauderdale FL 33309
954 971-1776

(G-9129)
CDP MANUFACTURING LLC
15 Jonathan Dr Ste 6 (02301-5566)
PHONE..................................508 588-6400
Marcia Morris, *Controller*
Mark P Cutting, *Mng Member*
EMP: 10
SQ FT: 200,000
SALES: 1.5MM **Privately Held**
WEB: www.cdpmanufacturing.com
SIC: 3449 Mfg Misc Structural Metalwork

(G-9130)
CHATHAM PLASTIC VENTURES INC
Also Called: Chatco
1200 W Chestnut St (02301-5574)
PHONE..................................518 392-5761
Daniel Crellin, *President*
EMP: 30
SALES (est): 2.6MM **Privately Held**
WEB: www.chatco.com
SIC: 3089 Mfg Plastic Products

(G-9131)
CONCORD FOODS LLC
Also Called: Red-E-Made
10 Minuteman Way (02301-7508)
PHONE..................................508 580-1700
Robert Geoffrey Neville, *Chairman*
James Macdonald, *Vice Pres*
Jim Connolly, *Opers Staff*
John Hoffman, *Production*
Carolyn Roscoe, *Buyer*
◆ **EMP:** 218
SQ FT: 255,000
SALES (est): 89.1MM **Privately Held**
WEB: www.concordfoods.com
SIC: 2099 2045 Mfg Food Preparations Mfg Prepared Flour Mixes/Doughs

(G-9132)
CONTRACT DECOR INTL INC
637 N Montello St (02301-2454)
PHONE..................................508 587-7000
Laurence Handler, *President*
Jerry Scully, *Purch Mgr*
Jennifer Starck, *VP Sales*
◆ **EMP:** 100
SQ FT: 23,000
SALES (est): 20.7MM
SALES (corp-wide): 326.1MM **Privately Held**
WEB: www.contractdecor.com
SIC: 2211 Cotton Broadwoven Fabric Mill
PA: Valley Forge Fabrics, Inc.
1650 W Mcnab Rd
Fort Lauderdale FL 33309
954 971-1776

(G-9133)
COUNTER PRODUCTIONS INC
103 Liberty St (02301-5518)
P.O. Box 511, East Wareham (02538-0511)
PHONE..................................508 587-0416
Richard E Savage, *President*
Russell A Savage, *Treasurer*
EMP: 12
SQ FT: 10,000
SALES: 225K **Privately Held**
SIC: 2434 Mfg Counter Tops

(G-9134)
CREATIVE EXTRUSION & TECH INC
230 Elliot St (02302-2314)
PHONE..................................508 587-2290
John D Hopkins Jr, *President*
David Flynn, *Vice Pres*

GEOGRAPHIC

Melissa Hopkins, *Treasurer*
▲ **EMP:** 25
SQ FT: 57,000
SALES (est): 7.1MM **Privately Held**
WEB: www.rextrude.com
SIC: 3089 Mfg Plastic Products

(G-9135)
CROCETTI-OAKDALE PACKING INC
Also Called: South Shore Meats
12 Taylor Ave (02302-3622)
PHONE..................................508 941-0458
Paulo Crocetti, *Manager*
EMP: 26
SALES (corp-wide): 7.5MM **Privately Held**
SIC: 2013 Ret Meat/Fish
PA: Crocetti-Oakdale Packing, Inc.
378 Pleasant St
East Bridgewater MA 02333
508 587-0035

(G-9136)
DAVID A PAYNE
Also Called: Aag-All American Gasket
291 Howard St (02302-1021)
PHONE..................................508 588-7500
David A Payne, *Owner*
EMP: 3
SALES (est): 224K **Privately Held**
SIC: 3069 Mfg Fabricated Rubber Products

(G-9137)
DAWN AUGER
Also Called: Party Design
156 Grove St (02302-3517)
P.O. Box 364, Whitman (02382-0364)
PHONE..................................508 587-0363
Dawn Auger, *Owner*
EMP: 4
SQ FT: 6,000
SALES (est): 234.8K **Privately Held**
SIC: 2211 Mfg & Rent Table Linens

(G-9138)
DEFENSE INTEGRATION
15 W Elm Ter (02301-3628)
PHONE..................................617 515-2470
EMP: 3
SALES (est): 150.8K **Privately Held**
SIC: 3812 Mfg Search/Navigation Equipment

(G-9139)
DENTAL DREAMS LLC
698 Crescent St (02302-3360)
PHONE..................................508 583-2256
Troy T Kluck, *Branch Mgr*
EMP: 4
SALES (corp-wide): 3.5MM **Privately Held**
SIC: 3843 Dentist's Office
PA: Dental Dreams, Llc
350 N Clark St Ste 600
Chicago IL 60654
312 274-0308

(G-9140)
DRA-COR INDUSTRIES INC
65 N Main St (02301-3906)
PHONE..................................508 580-3770
Ralph Brancaccio, *President*
Vincent Brancaccio, *Vice Pres*
Faye Brenner, *Office Admin*
EMP: 25
SQ FT: 30,000
SALES (est): 3.9MM **Privately Held**
WEB: www.dra-cor.com
SIC: 2391 Mfg Curtains/Draperies

(G-9141)
EAST COAST INDUCTION INC
506 N Warren Ave (02301-2684)
P.O. Box 2039 (02305-2039)
PHONE..................................508 587-2800
Sheldon Nitenson, *President*
Alan Prodouz, *Vice Pres*
EMP: 11 **EST:** 1963
SQ FT: 75,000
SALES (est): 1.2MM **Privately Held**
WEB: www.eastcoastind.com
SIC: 3567 Mfg Industrial Furnaces/Ovens

(G-9142)
EJ USA INC
1125 Pearl St (02301-5406)
PHONE..................................508 586-3130
Walter Oleary, *Sales Mgr*
T L Gasse, *Manager*
EMP: 12 **Privately Held**
SIC: 3321 Gray/Ductile Iron Foundry
HQ: Ej Usa, Inc.
301 Spring St
East Jordan MI 49727
800 874-4100

(G-9143)
ELIE BAKING CORPORATION
Also Called: Near East Bakery
204 N Montello St (02301-3918)
PHONE..................................508 584-4890
Elie T Ata, *President*
Abe Ata, *Vice Pres*
Ibrahim T Ata, *Admin Sec*
EMP: 19
SALES (est): 4.8MM **Privately Held**
SIC: 2051 Mfg Bread/Related Products

(G-9144)
EVANS MACHINE CO INC
32 N Manchester St (02302-2354)
PHONE..................................508 584-8085
Daniel Evans Jr, *President*
Daniel Evans Sr, *Shareholder*
▲ **EMP:** 35 **EST:** 1970
SQ FT: 10,000
SALES (est): 7.3MM **Privately Held**
SIC: 3599 Mfg Industrial Machinery

(G-9145)
F B WASHBURN CANDY CORPORATION
Also Called: Sevignys
137 Perkins Ave (02302-3850)
P.O. Box 3277 (02304-3277)
PHONE..................................508 588-0820
Jim Gilson, *President*
Douglas Gilson, *Treasurer*
James Gilson, *Human Res Dir*
▲ **EMP:** 42 **EST:** 1856
SQ FT: 150,000
SALES (est): 9MM **Privately Held**
WEB: www.fbwashburncandy.com
SIC: 2064 Ret Candy/Confectionery

(G-9146)
FASPRINT INC (PA)
Also Called: Allegra Print & Imaging
195 Liberty St Ste 1 (02301-5555)
PHONE..................................508 588-9961
Tony Ward, *President*
EMP: 11 **EST:** 1971
SQ FT: 2,000
SALES (est): 2MM **Privately Held**
WEB: www.fasprint.com
SIC: 2752 7334 2791 Lithographic Commercial Printing Photocopying Services Typesetting Services

(G-9147)
G T R FINISHING CORPORATION
1 Jonathan Dr (02301-5549)
PHONE..................................508 588-3240
Raymond J Timmons, *CEO*
Corinne King, *President*
James Craig, *Vice Pres*
Richard G Barnard, *Treasurer*
Bill Klaila, *Admin Sec*
EMP: 21
SQ FT: 10,000
SALES: 1.3MM **Privately Held**
SIC: 3479 Industrial Finishing

(G-9148)
G T R MANUFACTURING CORP
1 Jonathan Dr (02301-5549)
PHONE..................................508 588-3240
James E Craig, *President*
Corinne King, *Vice Pres*
Daniel E Almeida, *Treasurer*
EMP: 63
SQ FT: 52,000
SALES: 13.6MM **Privately Held**
WEB: www.gtrmfg.com
SIC: 3444 Mfg Sheet Metalwork

(G-9149)
GEMINI SCREENPRINTING & EMB CO
Also Called: Gemini Screen Printing & EMB
959 W Chestnut St (02301-5559)
PHONE..................................508 586-8223
Steve Saltzman, *President*
Elsa Chau, *Vice Pres*
EMP: 6
SQ FT: 4,000
SALES: 500K **Privately Held**
WEB: www.geminicraftcreations.com
SIC: 3552 2395 2396 Mfg Textile Machinery Pleating/Stitching Services Mfg Auto/Apparel Trimming

(G-9150)
GEO KNIGHT & CO INC
52 Perkins St (02302-3540)
PHONE..................................508 588-0186
Chesterton S Knight, *President*
Aaron Knight, *Vice Pres*
▲ **EMP:** 32 **EST:** 1885
SQ FT: 46,000
SALES: 8MM **Privately Held**
WEB: www.heatpress.com
SIC: 3443 Mfg Fabricated Plate Work

(G-9151)
GILL METAL FAB INC
Also Called: Moduline
170 Oak Hill Way (02301-7124)
P.O. Box 339, West Bridgewater (02379-0339)
PHONE..................................508 580-4445
Paul Gill, *President*
EMP: 30
SQ FT: 18,000
SALES (est): 5.8MM **Privately Held**
WEB: www.gillmetal.com
SIC: 7692 3443 3599 2521 Welding Repair Mfg Fabricated Plate Wrk Mfg Industrial Machinery Mfg Wood Office Furn Structural Metal Fabrctn

(G-9152)
GOWELL CANDY SHOP INC
Also Called: Gowell's Home Made Candy
727 N Main St (02301-2411)
PHONE..................................508 583-2521
Richard E Gowell, *President*
M Evelyn Gowell, *Vice Pres*
EMP: 6 **EST:** 1959
SQ FT: 3,680
SALES (est): 800.5K **Privately Held**
SIC: 2066 5441 Mfg Chocolate/Cocoa Products Ret Candy/Confectionery

(G-9153)
GREENCORE OARS LLC
121 Liberty St (02301-5518)
PHONE..................................508 586-8418
Liam McClennon, *President*
Kevin Becker, *CFO*
◆ **EMP:** 100
SQ FT: 35,000
SALES (est): 12.7MM **Privately Held**
WEB: www.onarollsales.com
SIC: 2099 Mfg Food Preparations
HQ: Clover Us Holdings, Llc
3333 Finley Rd Ste 800
Downers Grove IL 60515
630 967-3600

(G-9154)
HILLTOP CANDIES
15 Jonathan Dr Ste 3 (02301-5566)
PHONE..................................508 583-0895
Paul Mazzeo, *Owner*
EMP: 3
SQ FT: 8,000
SALES (est): 392K **Privately Held**
SIC: 2064 Ret Candy/Confectionery

(G-9155)
INKSTONE INC
Also Called: Inkstone Printing
129 Liberty St (02301-5518)
PHONE..................................508 587-5200
Robert P Donahoe, *President*
Paul Cicone, *Shareholder*
EMP: 25
SQ FT: 18,000
SALES (est): 3.1MM **Privately Held**
WEB: www.inkstone.com
SIC: 2752 Lithographic Commercial Printing

(G-9156)
ITE LLC
Also Called: Industrial Trucks & Equipment
140 Manley St (02301-5509)
PHONE..................................508 313-5600
Gregory G Wiley,
EMP: 33
SQ FT: 16,000
SALES (est): 3.2MM **Privately Held**
SIC: 3537 Mfg Industrial Trucks/Tractors

(G-9157)
J & O CONSTRUCTION INC
4 Brian Dr (02301-4602)
PHONE..................................508 586-4900
Jose Rodriguez, *President*
Oscar M Rodriguez, *Treasurer*
Marianella Perry, *Asst Treas*
Melissa Rodriguez, *Admin Sec*
Maria Rodriguez, *Asst Sec*
EMP: 4
SALES: 300K **Privately Held**
SIC: 3271 1542 1721 1761 Mfg Concrete Block/Brick Nonresidential Cnstn Painting/Paper Hanging Roofing/Siding Contr Concrete Contractor

(G-9158)
JONES & VINING INCORPORATED (PA)
1115 W Chestnut St Ste 2 (02301-7501)
PHONE..................................508 232-7470
Mark A Krentzman, *Ch of Bd*
George Markley, *Vice Pres*
Patricia Moretti, *CFO*
Patrick O'Malley, *Controller*
Luka Odak, *Accounts Mgr*
▲ **EMP:** 21
SALES (est): 71.5MM **Privately Held**
WEB: www.jvmaine.com
SIC: 2499 3131 Mfg Wood Products Mfg Footwear Cut Stock

(G-9159)
KINGS DRAPERIES INC
17 Davis Ave (02301-6727)
PHONE..................................508 230-0055
Gary King, *President*
David P King, *President*
EMP: 6
SALES: 750K **Privately Held**
SIC: 2211 2591 Mfg Draperies Drapery Hardware Window Blinds And Shades

(G-9160)
KROHN-HITE CORPORATION
15 Jonathan Dr Ste 4 (02301-5566)
PHONE..................................508 580-1660
Richard M Haddad, *President*
Joseph Inglis, *Sales Mgr*
Jim Vincent, *CIO*
Joe Inglis, *Executive*
Darryl Hill, *Technician*
EMP: 18
SQ FT: 10,000
SALES (est): 3.4MM **Privately Held**
WEB: www.krohn-hite.com
SIC: 3826 3829 3825 Mfg Measure/Control Dvcs Mfg Elec Measuring Instr Mfg Analytical Instr

(G-9161)
LD PLASTICS INC
1130 Pearl St (02301-5409)
PHONE..................................508 584-7651
Charles Harlfinger, *President*
Kenneth B Smith, *Treasurer*
EMP: 30 **EST:** 1975
SQ FT: 28,800
SALES (est): 6.7MM **Privately Held**
WEB: www.ldplastics.net
SIC: 3089 Mfg Plastic Products

(G-9162)
LIBERTY PRINTING CO INC
99 Lawrence St (02302-3550)
P.O. Box 726 (02303-0726)
PHONE..................................508 586-6810
Diane Barbour, *President*
Matt Barbour, *General Mgr*
Chris Barbour, *Vice Pres*

▲ = Import ▼=Export
◆ =Import/Export

Joseph Barbour, *Vice Pres*
EMP: 8 **EST:** 1901
SQ FT: 5,000
SALES: 675K **Privately Held**
WEB: www.libertyprintinginc.com
SIC: 2752 2759 Lithographic Commercial Printing Commercial Printing

(G-9163)
LYNE LABORATORIES INC
Also Called: Pharmaceutical Resources
10 Burke Dr (02301-5505)
PHONE..................................508 583-8700
Stephen Tarallo, *President*
Top Linda, *Vice Pres*
Philip J Tarallo, *Treasurer*
Philip Tarallo, *Treasurer*
▲ **EMP:** 68 **EST:** 1964
SQ FT: 67,000
SALES (est): 25.8MM **Privately Held**
WEB: www.lyne.com
SIC: 2834 8731 Mfg Pharmaceutical Preparations Commercial Physical Research

(G-9164)
MAIR-MAC MACHINE COMPANY INC
86 N Montello St (02301-3916)
PHONE..................................508 895-9001
Mary A Macdonald, *President*
Ed Macdonald, *Vice Pres*
Edward Mac Donald, *Treasurer*
Karl Northon, *Sales Mgr*
EMP: 15
SQ FT: 9,000
SALES (est): 2.9MM **Privately Held**
WEB: www.mairmac.com
SIC: 3354 3443 3089 Mfg Aluminum Extruded Products Mfg Fabricated Plate Work Mfg Plastic Products

(G-9165)
MERIDIAN CUSTOM WOODWORKING IN
443 Summer St 1 (02302-4118)
PHONE..................................508 587-4400
Allen W Cayer, *President*
James P Bentley, *Principal*
EMP: 4
SALES (est): 629.4K **Privately Held**
SIC: 2431 Mfg Millwork

(G-9166)
MICRO WIRE PRODUCTS INC
120 N Main St (02301-3911)
P.O. Box 427, Holbrook (02343-0427)
PHONE..................................508 584-0200
Jeff Weafer, *President*
▲ **EMP:** 35 **EST:** 1952
SQ FT: 70,000
SALES (est): 6.8MM **Privately Held**
SIC: 3496 Mfg Misc Fabricated Wire Products

(G-9167)
MONTELLO HEEL MFG INC
Also Called: Colt Heel Div Montello Heel
13 Emerson Ave Ste 4 (02301-2455)
P.O. Box 2116 (02305-2116)
PHONE..................................508 586-0603
J Richard Pearson, *President*
▲ **EMP:** 50
SQ FT: 10,000
SALES (est): 7.2MM **Privately Held**
SIC: 3131 3172 Mfg Footwear Cut Stock Mfg Personal Leather Goods

(G-9168)
MOONLIGHT LTD
244 Liberty St Ste 11 (02301-5561)
PHONE..................................508 584-0094
Anthony Galante, *Owner*
EMP: 3
SALES (est): 301.5K **Privately Held**
SIC: 2759 Commercial Printing

(G-9169)
NEW HAMPSHIRE BORING INC
1215 W Chestnut St (02301-5578)
PHONE..................................508 584-8201
Gary Twombly, *Manager*
EMP: 12
SALES (est): 769.1K **Privately Held**
WEB: www.nhboring.com
SIC: 1241 Coal Mining Services

(G-9170)
PASTA BENE INC
1050 Pearl St Ste 1 (02301-5401)
PHONE..................................508 583-1515
Benjamin Alvanese, *President*
Joyce Alvanese, *Principal*
EMP: 10
SALES (est): 981.4K **Privately Held**
SIC: 2099 5149 Mfg & Whol Home-Made Pasta

(G-9171)
PILGRIM BADGE & LABEL CORP
Also Called: Pilgrim Plastics Products Co
1200 W Chestnut St (02301-5574)
P.O. Box 317 (02303-0317)
PHONE..................................508 436-6300
Mark Abraham, *President*
EMP: 85 **EST:** 1915
SQ FT: 40,000
SALES (est): 8.7MM **Privately Held**
WEB: www.pilgrimplastics.com
SIC: 3083 3993 3423 Mfg Laminated Plastic Plate/Sheet Mfg Signs/Advertising Specialties Mfg Hand/Edge Tools

(G-9172)
PRINT SYNERGY SOLUTIONS LLC
Also Called: Printsynergy Solutions
129 Liberty St (02301-5518)
PHONE..................................508 587-5200
Bob Oliveira, *Vice Pres*
Stanley Pypec, *Plant Mgr*
Gail Sesock, *Project Mgr*
Maureen Hogan, *Accounting Mgr*
Robert P Donahoe, *Mng Member*
EMP: 14 **EST:** 2011
SALES (est): 2.3MM **Privately Held**
SIC: 2752 Lithographic Commercial Printing

(G-9173)
SHARON VACUUM CO INC
69 Falmouth Ave (02301-3403)
PHONE..................................508 588-2323
Lawrence A Resnick, *President*
Patricia McMahon, *Treasurer*
EMP: 10
SQ FT: 6,000
SALES (est): 1.5MM **Privately Held**
WEB: www.sharonvacuum.com
SIC: 3443 Mfg High Vacuum Equipment & Components

(G-9174)
SIE COMPUTING SOLUTIONS INC
10 Mupac Dr (02301-5548)
PHONE..................................508 588-6110
Chris Boutilier, *President*
James Tierney, *Vice Pres*
Al Ghizzoni, *Buyer*
Ann Zenus, *Buyer*
Mark Sullivan, *CFO*
▲ **EMP:** 75
SQ FT: 55,000
SALES (est): 19.5MM
SALES (corp-wide): 177.9K **Privately Held**
WEB: www.gavazzi-computing.com
SIC: 3571 3679 Mfg Electronic Computers Mfg Electronic Components
HQ: System Industrie Electronic Holding Ag
Millennium Park 12
Lustenau 6890
557 789-900

(G-9175)
SIGN DESIGN INC
Also Called: Alumasign
170 Liberty St (02301-5522)
PHONE..................................508 580-0094
Whitney Ferrigno, *President*
Ron Ferrigno, *Vice Pres*
Steven Rabs, *Manager*
EMP: 70
SQ FT: 30,000
SALES (est): 12.4MM **Privately Held**
WEB: www.signdesigninc.com
SIC: 3993 Mfg Signs/Advertising Specialties

(G-9176)
SIGNS BY RUSS INC
244 Liberty St Ste 9a (02301-5561)
P.O. Box 393, South Easton (02375-0393)
PHONE..................................508 580-2221
Denise N Baker, *President*
Russell D Baker, *Treasurer*
EMP: 5
SQ FT: 7,500
SALES (est): 502.1K **Privately Held**
WEB: www.gwcollier.com
SIC: 3993 Mfg Signs

(G-9177)
SPENCE & CO LTD
76 Campanelli Indus Dr (02301-1809)
PHONE..................................508 427-5577
Charles Alan Spence, *President*
◆ **EMP:** 45
SQ FT: 20,000
SALES (est): 8.1MM
SALES (corp-wide): 18.6MM **Privately Held**
WEB: www.spenceltd.com
SIC: 2091 2092 Mfg Canned/Cured Fish/Seafood Mfg Fresh/Frozen Packaged Fish
PA: Acme Smoked Fish Corp.
30 Gem St 56
Brooklyn NY 11222
954 942-5598

(G-9178)
SPILLDAM ENVIRONMENTAL INC
89 N Montello St (02301-3938)
P.O. Box 960 (02303-0960)
PHONE..................................508 583-7850
Timothy Prevost, *President*
Patti S Prevost, *Admin Sec*
▼ **EMP:** 12
SQ FT: 40,000
SALES (est): 2.8MM **Privately Held**
WEB: www.spilldam.com
SIC: 3589 4959 Mfg Service Industry Machinery Sanitary Services

(G-9179)
STRANGE PLANET PRINTING
1041 Pearl St (02301-5400)
PHONE..................................508 857-1816
Alexa Noe, *Treasurer*
EMP: 4
SALES (est): 284.8K **Privately Held**
SIC: 2752 Lithographic Commercial Printing

(G-9180)
SUPERIOR BAKING CO INC
176 N Warren Ave (02301-3431)
PHONE..................................508 586-6601
Michael Debenedictis, *President*
Robert De Benedictis, *Treasurer*
Joseph Ferrini Jr, *Admin Sec*
EMP: 50
SQ FT: 15,000
SALES (est): 7.1MM **Privately Held**
SIC: 2051 5461 Mfg & Ret Italian Bread Products

(G-9181)
TAMBOO BISTRO
252 Main St (02301-5321)
PHONE..................................508 584-8585
Chrispin Charlot, *Owner*
EMP: 6
SALES (est): 484.8K **Privately Held**
SIC: 2253 5812 Knit Outerwear Mill Eating Place

(G-9182)
THERAPEDIC OF NEW ENGLAND LLC
135 Spark St (02302-1620)
PHONE..................................508 559-9944
Mark R Corvese,
EMP: 7
SALES (est): 168.7K **Privately Held**
SIC: 2392 2515 Mfg Household Furnishings Mfg Mattresses/Bedsprings

(G-9183)
THERESE ROSE MANUFACTURING
Also Called: Rose Therese Caps & Gown Co
59 Pleasant St 69 (02301-3921)
P.O. Box 186, Stoughton (02072-0186)
PHONE..................................508 586-5812
Mike Mc Gillivray, *President*
Terry Gillivray, *Vice Pres*
Mark Mc Gillivray, *Treasurer*
▲ **EMP:** 5
SQ FT: 5,000
SALES (est): 735.2K **Privately Held**
WEB: www.rosetherese.com
SIC: 2339 5699 2353 Mfg Women's/Misses' Outerwear Ret Misc Apparel/Accessories Mfg Hats/Caps/Millinery

(G-9184)
TRIPLE P PACKG & PPR PDTS INC
20 Burke Dr (02301-5505)
PHONE..................................508 588-0444
Richard M Shaughnessy, *President*
Greg O'Connell, *Vice Pres*
Gregory M O'Connell, *Vice Pres*
Gregory Oconnell, *Treasurer*
Margie Verissimo, *Manager*
EMP: 53 **EST:** 1963
SQ FT: 66,000
SALES: 12MM **Privately Held**
WEB: www.ppppack.com
SIC: 2653 Whol Nondurable Goods

(G-9185)
UNO FOODS INC
180 Spark St (02302-1621)
PHONE..................................508 580-1561
EMP: 24 **Privately Held**
SIC: 2038 Mfg Frozen Specialties
HQ: Uno Foods Inc.
100 Charles Park Rd
Boston MA 02132
617 323-9200

(G-9186)
US CUTTING CHAIN MFG CO INC
95 Spark St (02302-1706)
P.O. Box 437 (02303-0437)
PHONE..................................508 588-0322
Richard Le Duc Jr, *President*
EMP: 5
SQ FT: 10,000
SALES: 500K **Privately Held**
SIC: 3545 5084 Mfg Machine Tool Accessories Whol Industrial Equipment

(G-9187)
VALCO PRECISION MACHINE INC
800 W Chestnut St (02301-5513)
P.O. Box 3369 (02304-3369)
PHONE..................................508 559-9009
John M Mascheri, *President*
Peter Lanoue, *Vice Pres*
EMP: 6
SALES (est): 973.9K **Privately Held**
SIC: 3599 8711 Mfg Industrial Machinery Engineering Services

(G-9188)
YSNC FUEL INC
64 N Montello St (02301-3915)
PHONE..................................508 436-2716
Yaniv Sostiel, *Principal*
EMP: 5
SALES (est): 495.3K **Privately Held**
SIC: 2869 Mfg Industrial Organic Chemicals

Brookfield
Worcester County

(G-9189)
CUSTOM PALLETS INC
2 Mill St (01506-1534)
P.O. Box 41 (01506-0041)
PHONE..................................508 867-2411
Adam Norton, *President*
Terry Anderson, *Admin Sec*
EMP: 5 **EST:** 1974

GEOGRAPHIC

SQ FT: 40,000
SALES: 800K **Privately Held**
SIC: 2448 Mfg Wood Pallets/Skids

(G-9190)
PRO TECH MACHINE INC
200 Fiskdale Rd (01506-1747)
PHONE..................................508 867-7994
James Booth, *President*
EMP: 5
SALES (est): 487.8K **Privately Held**
WEB: www.protechmachine.com
SIC: 3599 Mfg Industrial Machinery

(G-9191)
ROBERTS ENTERPRISES INC
32 W Main St (01506-1513)
P.O. Box 281 (01506-0281)
PHONE..................................508 867-7640
Robert Pawlowski, *President*
Rosemarie Pawlowski, *Vice Pres*
EMP: 15
SQ FT: 2,000
SALES (est): 2.5MM **Privately Held**
SIC: 3444 Mfg Sheet Metalwork

(G-9192)
SOCKS FOR SIBERIA INC
122 Long Hill Rd (01506-1740)
P.O. Box 426 (01506-0426)
PHONE..................................774 200-1617
Wallace L Connor Jr, *Principal*
EMP: 4
SALES: 10.6K **Privately Held**
SIC: 2252 Mfg Hosiery

(G-9193)
SPENCER METAL FINISHING INC (PA)
55 Mill St (01506-1516)
PHONE..................................508 885-6477
George S Beer Sr, *President*
George Beer Sr, *President*
Brian Beer, *Vice Pres*
David Beer, *Vice Pres*
John Vasil, *Vice Pres*
EMP: 13
SALES (est): 1.8MM **Privately Held**
WEB: www.spencermetalfinishing.com
SIC: 3479 3471 Coating/Engraving Service Plating/Polishing Service

Brookline
Norfolk County

(G-9194)
ASPECT INC
Also Called: Zephyr Press
50 Kenwood St (02446-2413)
PHONE..................................617 713-2813
James Kates, *President*
Leora Zeitlin, *Vice Pres*
EMP: 3
SALES: 75.5K **Privately Held**
SIC: 2731 Books-Publishing/Printing

(G-9195)
BLACKBOARD INC
Also Called: Beep On Beacon
1187 Beacon St (02446-5441)
PHONE..................................617 713-5471
EMP: 3
SALES (corp-wide): 2.6MM **Privately Held**
SIC: 7372 Prepackaged Software Services
HQ: Blackboard Inc.
1111 19th St Nw
Washington DC 20036
202 463-4860

(G-9196)
BOGARIS CORPORATION
29 Sargent Beechwood (02445-7519)
PHONE..................................617 505-6696
Rodrigo Charlo Molina, *President*
EMP: 3
SALES (est): 156.7K **Privately Held**
SIC: 2079 Mfg Edible Fats/Oils

(G-9197)
BORDERLINES FOUNDATION
Also Called: Academic Studies Press
1577 Beacon St (02446-4602)
PHONE..................................617 365-9438
Igor Nemirovsky, *President*
Kira Nemirovsky, *Prdtn Mgr*
EMP: 4
SALES: 119.9K **Privately Held**
SIC: 2731 Books-Publishing/Printing

(G-9198)
BRUMBERG PUBLICATIONS INC
124 Harvard St Ste 9 (02446-6439)
PHONE..................................617 734-1979
Bruce Brumberg, *President*
EMP: 15
SQ FT: 800
SALES (est): 1.1MM **Privately Held**
WEB: www.factorytour.com
SIC: 2721 Misc Publishing

(G-9199)
DAILY CATCH
441 Harvard St (02446-2411)
PHONE..................................617 734-2700
Paul Freddura, *Owner*
EMP: 3
SALES (est): 195.5K **Privately Held**
SIC: 2711 Newspapers-Publishing/Printing

(G-9200)
DAILY GENERAL COUNSEL PLLC
12 Stedman St (02446-6024)
PHONE..................................617 721-4342
Jan A Glassman, *Principal*
EMP: 4
SALES (est): 173.4K **Privately Held**
SIC: 2711 Newspapers-Publishing/Printing

(G-9201)
GONE TROPPO INC (PA)
Also Called: Emack & Bolio's
108 Codman Rd (02445-7555)
P.O. Box 470703, Brookline Village (02447-0703)
PHONE..................................617 739-7995
Robert Rook, *CEO*
◆ **EMP:** 4
SQ FT: 700
SALES (est): 503.3K **Privately Held**
WEB: www.emackandbolios.com
SIC: 2024 5149 Mfg Ice Cream/Frozen Dessert

(G-9202)
HERB CHAMBERS BROOKLINE INC
308 Boylston St (02445-7603)
PHONE..................................617 278-3920
Herbert G Chambers, *President*
EMP: 105 **EST:** 2014
SALES (est): 871.9K
SALES (corp-wide): 541.7MM **Privately Held**
SIC: 3443 Mfg Fabricated Plate Work
PA: Herb Chambers I-93, Inc.
259 Mcgrath Hwy
Somerville MA 02143
617 666-4100

(G-9203)
HOLY CROSS ORTHODOX PRESS
Also Called: Holy Cross Book Store
50 Goddard Ave (02445-7415)
PHONE..................................800 245-0599
Michael Vaporis, *Principal*
N Michael Vaporis, *Principal*
EMP: 6
SQ FT: 1,800
SALES (est): 472.3K **Privately Held**
WEB: www.holycrossbookstore.com
SIC: 2731 Books-Publishing/Printing

(G-9204)
IONIC PHARMACEUTICALS LLC
189 Tappan St (02445-5819)
PHONE..................................978 509-4980
Mark Grinstaff, *Mng Member*
EMP: 3
SALES (est): 208.2K **Privately Held**
SIC: 2833 Mfg Medicinal/Botanical Products

(G-9205)
J MAGAZINE INC
338 Saint Paul St Apt 6 (02446-3611)
PHONE..................................617 515-1822
Masahiko Takinami, *President*
EMP: 4
SALES (est): 280K **Privately Held**
WEB: www.jmag.com
SIC: 2721 Periodicals-Publishing/Printing

(G-9206)
JANE DIAGNOSTICS INC
201 Freeman St Apt A7 (02446-6806)
PHONE..................................617 651-2295
Natalia Rodriguez, *CEO*
Mario Cabodi, *Principal*
Catherine Klapperich, *Admin Sec*
EMP: 4
SALES (est): 208.5K **Privately Held**
SIC: 2835 Mfg Diagnostic Substances

(G-9207)
JUST PUBLICATIONS INC
Also Called: Just Rentals
8 Alton Pl Ste 2 (02446-6448)
PHONE..................................617 739-5878
Matthew Newman, *President*
EMP: 8
SQ FT: 1,500
SALES (est): 880.4K **Privately Held**
SIC: 2721 6531 Periodicals-Publishing/Printing Real Estate Agent/Manager

(G-9208)
MACRAIGOR SYSTEMS LLC (PA)
Also Called: Macraigor Systems,
227 Cypress St Ste 1 (02445-7799)
P.O. Box 471008, Brookline Village (02447-1008)
PHONE..................................617 264-4459
Craig Haller, *Managing Prtnr*
Craig A Haller, *Managing Prtnr*
Kate Smith, *Sales Mgr*
EMP: 4
SQ FT: 1,000
SALES (est): 396.5K **Privately Held**
WEB: www.ocdemon.com
SIC: 3577 7371 5045 Mfg Computer Peripherals Computer Programming Svc Whol Computer/Peripheral Whol Computer/Peripheral

(G-9209)
MINDSTORM TECHNOLOGIES INC
2 Saint Paul St Apt 405 (02446-6599)
PHONE..................................781 642-1700
Jerry Polucci, *President*
Nick Handley, *Comp Lab Dir*
EMP: 5
SALES (est): 305.3K **Privately Held**
WEB: www.mindstorm.net
SIC: 7372 Prepackaged Software Services

(G-9210)
MYOLEX INC
1309 Beacon St Ste 300 (02446-5252)
PHONE..................................888 382-8656
Jerry Panos, *CEO*
EMP: 6
SALES (est): 879K **Privately Held**
SIC: 3845 Development Of Medical Sensors

(G-9211)
MYSTOCKPLANCOM INC
Also Called: Mystockoptions.com
124 Harvard St Ste 9 (02446-6439)
PHONE..................................617 734-1979
Bruce Brumberg, *President*
Karen Axelrod, *Manager*
Steven O'Donnell, *Technology*
EMP: 10
SALES (est): 757.1K **Privately Held**
WEB: www.mystockoptions.com
SIC: 2741 Misc Publishing

(G-9212)
NANO-ICE LLC
20 Chapel St Apt C611 (02446-7403)
PHONE..................................617 512-8811
Sam White, *Mng Member*
EMP: 3
SALES: 300K **Privately Held**
SIC: 3961 Mfg Costume Jewelry

(G-9213)
ODWALLA INC
102 Longwood Ave (02446-6696)
PHONE..................................336 877-1634
John Sunderman, *Branch Mgr*
EMP: 39
SALES (corp-wide): 31.8B **Publicly Held**
SIC: 2033 Mfg Canned Fruits/Vegetables
HQ: Odwalla, Inc.
1 Coca Cola Plz Nw
Atlanta GA 30313
479 721-6260

(G-9214)
PAGODA GROUP LLC
Also Called: Cityscapes Books
1038 Beacon St Apt 304 (02446-4024)
PHONE..................................617 833-3137
Stephen Hung,
Steven Hung,
EMP: 5
SQ FT: 2,000
SALES (est): 411.2K **Privately Held**
SIC: 2731 Engaged In Publishing Or Publishing And Printing Of Books

(G-9215)
PISON TECHNOLOGY INC
258 Harvard St Ste 312 (02446-2904)
PHONE..................................540 394-0998
Dexter Ang, *CEO*
EMP: 8
SALES (est): 490.7K **Privately Held**
SIC: 3577 Mfg Computer Peripheral Equipment

(G-9216)
PURE COLD PRESS
326 Harvard St (02446-2917)
PHONE..................................617 487-8948
EMP: 4
SALES (est): 66.5K **Privately Held**
SIC: 2741 Misc Publishing

(G-9217)
QUICKDOC INC
1415 Beacon St Ste 119 (02446-4811)
PHONE..................................617 738-1800
Edwyn Daley Griffin, *President*
John Roberge, *Corp Secy*
Thomas Griffin, *Director*
EMP: 5
SQ FT: 600
SALES: 150K **Privately Held**
SIC: 7372 Prepackaged Software Services

(G-9218)
RADIO ACT CORPORATION
101 Winthrop Rd (02445-4589)
PHONE..................................617 731-6542
Arkady Pittel, *CEO*
EMP: 7
SALES (est): 567.6K **Privately Held**
SIC: 3674 Radiation Protection

(G-9219)
SCHOOL YOURSELF INC
45 Longwood Ave Apt 510 (02446-5217)
PHONE..................................516 729-7478
Zachary Wissner-Gross, *CEO*
John Lee, *Chief Engr*
Kenny Peng, *Director*
Vivek Venkatachalam, *Director*
EMP: 4
SALES (est): 192.9K **Privately Held**
SIC: 2731 7372 Books-Publishing/Printing Prepackaged Software Services

(G-9220)
SUMMER INK INC
258 Harvard St (02446-2904)
PHONE..................................617 714-0263
Richard Schaye, *President*
EMP: 3 **EST:** 2010
SALES (est): 132.9K **Privately Held**
SIC: 2711 Newspapers-Publishing/Printing

(G-9221)
SURGIBOX INC
8 Juniper St Apt 18 (02445-7121)
PHONE..................................617 982-3908
Mike Teodorescu, *CEO*
Debbie Teodorescu, *President*

Stephen Okajima, *Chief Engr*
Daniel Brown, *CFO*
Robert Smalley, *Director*
EMP: 3 **EST:** 2017
SALES (est): 135.1K **Privately Held**
SIC: 3841 7389 Commercial Physical Research

(G-9222)
T LEX INC
105 Babcock St (02446-5912)
PHONE..................................617 731-8606
Lee Glickenhaus, *President*
EMP: 3
SALES (est): 248.5K **Privately Held**
WEB: www.tlex.com
SIC: 7372 8111 Prepackaged Software Services Legal Services Office

(G-9223)
TRUSTEES OF BOSTON UNIVERSITY
Also Called: Bostonia Magazine
10 Lenox St Fl 3 (02446-4042)
PHONE..................................617 353-3081
Michael Shavelson, *Director*
EMP: 13
SALES (corp-wide): 2.1B **Privately Held**
WEB: www.bu.edu
SIC: 2721 8221 Periodicals-Publishing/Printing College/University
PA: Trustees Of Boston University
1 Silber Way
Boston MA 02215
617 353-9550

(G-9224)
UPPERMARK LLC
147 Coolidge St (02446-5807)
PHONE..................................413 303-9653
EMP: 4
SALES (est): 210K **Privately Held**
SIC: 3999 Mfg Study Materials

(G-9225)
YOWAY LLC
1376 Beacon St (02446-2807)
PHONE..................................617 505-5158
EMP: 7
SALES (corp-wide): 699.3K **Privately Held**
SIC: 2026 Mfg Fluid Milk
PA: Yoway Llc
395 Park Ave Ste 2
Worcester MA 01610
508 459-0611

(G-9226)
ZENNA NOODLE BAR
1374 Beacon St (02446-2807)
PHONE..................................781 883-8624
Tien Trong, *Principal*
EMP: 8
SALES (est): 564.2K **Privately Held**
SIC: 2098 Mfg Macaroni/Spaghetti

Burlington
Middlesex County

(G-9227)
128 TECHNOLOGY INC (PA)
200 Summit Dr (01803-5264)
PHONE..................................781 203-8400
Andrew Ory, *CEO*
Christina Mendonca, *Principal*
Patrick J Melampy, *COO*
Mike Clement, *Vice Pres*
Kevin Klett, *Vice Pres*
EMP: 24
SQ FT: 25,000
SALES (est): 13MM **Privately Held**
SIC: 7372 Prepackaged Software Services

(G-9228)
ACRONIS NORTH AMERICA INC
1 Van De Graaff Dr # 301 (01803-5188)
PHONE..................................781 782-9100
Michael Inbar, *CFO*
EMP: 10
SALES (est): 221.8K **Privately Held**
SIC: 7372 Prepackaged Software Services

(G-9229)
ADVANSTAR COMMUNICATIONS INC
70 Blanchard Rd Ste 301 (01803-5100)
PHONE..................................339 298-4200
Lauren Moras, *Business Mgr*
Kathy Coffey, *Branch Mgr*
EMP: 26
SALES (corp-wide): 1.3B **Privately Held**
SIC: 2721 Periodicals-Publishing/Printing
HQ: Advanstar Communications Inc.
2501 Colorado Ave Ste 280
Santa Monica CA 90404
310 357-7500

(G-9230)
AEROVIRONMENT INC
141 S Bedford St Ste 250 (01803-5291)
PHONE..................................805 520-8350
Tom Vaneck, *Branch Mgr*
EMP: 20
SALES (corp-wide): 314.2MM **Publicly Held**
SIC: 3721 Mfg Aircraft
PA: Aerovironment, Inc.
900 Innovators Way
Simi Valley CA 93065
805 581-2187

(G-9231)
ALLOCATION SOLUTIONS LLC
1 Wall St Fl 6 (01803-4757)
PHONE..................................339 234-5695
EMP: 5
SALES (est): 400K **Privately Held**
SIC: 7372 Prepackaged Software Services

(G-9232)
ALLSCRPTS HLTHCARE SLTIONS INC
1 Burlington Woods Dr # 3 (01803-4535)
PHONE..................................800 720-7351
Paul Reilly, *Principal*
Carolyn Gaudette, *Engineer*
Peter Cafferty, *Program Mgr*
EMP: 983
SALES (corp-wide): 1.7B **Publicly Held**
SIC: 7372 Prepackaged Software
PA: Allscripts Healthcare Solutions, Inc.
222 Merchandise Mart Plz
Chicago IL 60654
800 334-8534

(G-9233)
AMRI BURLINGTON INC (DH)
Also Called: Amri Global
99 S Bedford St (01803-5179)
PHONE..................................781 270-7900
Thomas E D'Ambra, *CEO*
William Marth, *President*
Bruce J Sargent, *Senior VP*
Michael M Nolan, *Vice Pres*
Brian D Russell, *Vice Pres*
EMP: 30
SALES (est): 6.2MM
SALES (corp-wide): 137.4MM **Privately Held**
WEB: www.hyaluron.net
SIC: 2834 Mfg Pharmaceutical Preparations

(G-9234)
ARQULE INC (PA)
1 Wall St Ste 7 (01803-4757)
PHONE..................................781 994-0300
Paolo Pucci, *CEO*
Patrick J Zenner, *Ch of Bd*
Peter S Lawrence, *President*
Shirish Hirani, *Senior VP*
Marc Schegerin, *CFO*
▲ **EMP:** 32
SQ FT: 15,000
SALES: 25.7MM **Privately Held**
WEB: www.arqule.com
SIC: 2834 8731 Pharmaceutical Preparations Biotechnical Research & Development

(G-9235)
AVID TECHNOLOGY INC (PA)
75 Network Dr (01803-2756)
PHONE..................................978 640-6789
Peter Westley, *Ch of Bd*
Jeff Rosica, *President*
Jason A Duva, *Exec VP*
Tom Cordiner, *Senior VP*
Dana Ruzicka, *Senior VP*
▲ **EMP:** 950
SQ FT: 124,000
SALES: 413.2MM **Publicly Held**
WEB: www.avid.com
SIC: 3861 7372 Mfg Digital Editing Systems & Prepackaged Software

(G-9236)
AVID TECHNOLOGY INC
65 Network Dr (01803-2767)
PHONE..................................978 640-3063
John Bottari, *Branch Mgr*
EMP: 214
SALES (corp-wide): 413.2MM **Publicly Held**
WEB: www.avid.com
SIC: 3861 Mfg Photographic Equipment/Supplies
PA: Avid Technology, Inc.
75 Network Dr
Burlington MA 01803
978 640-6789

(G-9237)
AZARA HEALTHCARE LLC
70 Blanchard Rd Ste 401 (01803-5100)
PHONE..................................781 365-2208
Jeff Brandes, *CEO*
Gregory Augustine, *COO*
Paul Doucette, *Engineer*
Marie Cody, *Accountant*
John Leonard, *Technical Staff*
EMP: 3
SALES (est): 353.7K **Privately Held**
SIC: 7372 Prepackaged Software Services

(G-9238)
BAE SYSTEMS INFO & ELEC SYS
600 District Ave (01803-5046)
PHONE..................................781 273-3388
Stephen Eng, *Software Engr*
Michael Cusack, *Administration*
EMP: 100
SALES (corp-wide): 22.1B **Privately Held**
SIC: 3812 Mfg Search/Navigation Equipment
HQ: Bae Systems Information And Electronic Systems Integration Inc.
65 Spit Brook Rd
Nashua NH 03060
603 885-4321

(G-9239)
BAY STATE SCALE & SYSTEMS INC
Also Called: Bay State Scale Co
7 Ray Ave (01803-4720)
PHONE..................................781 993-9035
Harry Spatz, *President*
Gail Spatz, *Admin Sec*
EMP: 5
SQ FT: 5,500
SALES: 900K **Privately Held**
SIC: 3596 8734 3545 Mfg Scale/Balance-Nonlab Testing Laboratory Mfg Machine Tool Access

(G-9240)
BOSTON ARTIFICIAL LIMB CO
44 Middlesex Tpke (01803-4986)
PHONE..................................781 272-3132
William L Rogers, *President*
Stephen Leo, *Vice Pres*
Howard Mooney, *Treasurer*
EMP: 4 **EST:** 1905
SALES: 800K **Privately Held**
WEB: www.asqboston.org
SIC: 3842 Mfg Surgical Appliances/Supplies

(G-9241)
BOSTON BRACE INTERNATIONAL
Also Called: Nopco of Burlington
50 Mall Rd Ste G10 (01803-4508)
PHONE..................................781 270-3650
David Decosmo, *Director*
EMP: 9 **Privately Held**
WEB: www.bostonbrace.com
SIC: 3842 Mfg Surgical Appliances/Supplies
PA: Boston Brace International, Inc.
20 Ledin Dr Ste 1
Avon MA 02322

(G-9242)
BURLINGTON FOUNDRY CO INC
13 Adams St (01803-4916)
P.O. Box 362, Tilton NH (03276-0362)
PHONE..................................781 272-1182
Kenneth Marvin, *President*
Kurt Marvin, *Corp Secy*
EMP: 6 **EST:** 1957
SQ FT: 4,000
SALES (est): 764.1K **Privately Held**
WEB: www.burlingtonfoundry.com
SIC: 3365 Aluminum Foundry

(G-9243)
CAMBRIDGE INTERVENTIONAL LLC
78 Cambridge St (01803-4137)
PHONE..................................978 793-2674
Briana Morey, *Principal*
EMP: 3
SALES (est): 138.6K **Privately Held**
SIC: 3841 Mfg Surgical/Medical Instruments

(G-9244)
CASSINI USA INC
1 Wall St Fl 6 (01803-4757)
PHONE..................................781 487-7000
Jeroen Cammeraat, *Principal*
EMP: 6
SALES (est): 337.7K **Privately Held**
SIC: 3826 Mfg Analytical Instruments

(G-9245)
CASSIOPAE US INC
1 Van De Graaff Dr # 102 (01803-5188)
PHONE..................................435 647-9940
EMP: 4 **EST:** 2006
SALES (est): 255.9K
SALES (corp-wide): 1.7B **Privately Held**
SIC: 7372 Prepackaged Software Services
HQ: Sopra Banking Software
Petite Avenue
Annecy 74940
450 333-030

(G-9246)
CERENCE INC (PA)
15 Wayside Rd (01803-4620)
PHONE..................................781 565-5507
Sanjay Dhawan, *CEO*
Leanne Fitzgerald, *Vice Pres*
Mark Gallenberger, *CFO*
EMP: 100
SALES (est): 1.3MM **Publicly Held**
SIC: 7372 Prepackaged Software Services

(G-9247)
CERTEON INC
5 Wall St Fl 5 # 5 (01803-4771)
PHONE..................................781 425-5099
Massood Zarrabian, *Ch of Bd*
Denise Moore, *Vice Pres*
Jeffrey Black, *Treasurer*
Christopher Chandler, *Regl Sales Mgr*
Mark M Nakamura, *Project Leader*
EMP: 30
SQ FT: 10,000
SALES (est): 3MM **Privately Held**
WEB: www.certeon.com
SIC: 7372 Prepackaged Software Services

(G-9248)
CHERRYBROOK KITCHEN LLC
Also Called: Charles Rosenberg
20 Mall Rd Ste 410 (01803-4129)
P.O. Box 8301, Worcester (01614-8301)
PHONE..................................781 272-0400
Chip Rosenberg, *Mng Member*
Patsy Rosenberg,
EMP: 7
SQ FT: 3,000
SALES (est): 804.5K **Privately Held**
WEB: www.cherrybrookkitchen.com
SIC: 2099 Mfg Food Preparations

(G-9249)
CIMCON SOFTWARES INC (PA)
200 Summit Dr Ste 500s (01803-5264)
PHONE..................................978 692-9868
Anil Agrawal, *CEO*

Sanjay Agrawal, *President*
EMP: 80
SQ FT: 10,000
SALES (est): 22.5MM **Privately Held**
WEB: www.cimcon.com
SIC: 7372 Custom Computer Programing

(G-9250)
CIRCOR INTERNATIONAL INC (PA)
30 Corporate Dr Ste 200 (01803-4252)
P.O. Box 146699, Boston (02114-0019)
PHONE....................................781 270-1200
Scott A Buckhout, *President*
Jennifer Allen, *Senior VP*
David Mullen, *Vice Pres*
Teresa Sodkomkum, *Export Mgr*
Lee Goolsby, *Production*
EMP: 277
SALES: 1.1B **Publicly Held**
WEB: www.circor.com
SIC: 3491 Mfg Industrial Valves

(G-9251)
CLINICAL INSTRUMENTS INTL
63 2nd Ave (01803-4413)
PHONE....................................781 221-2266
Jerome Priest, *President*
Rudra Tamm, *Treasurer*
EMP: 12 **EST:** 1989
SQ FT: 3,000
SALES (est): 1.4MM **Privately Held**
WEB: www.clinicalinstrument.com
SIC: 3841 Mfg Surgical/Medical Instruments

(G-9252)
COMPUTR IMPRNTBLE LBL SYSTMS
Also Called: Manufacturing
1500 District Ave (01803-5069)
PHONE....................................877 512-8763
Oliver Stockton, *Managing Dir*
Ross Woodward, *Principal*
Matt Parker, *Accounts Mgr*
Graham Tunks, *Manager*
EMP: 10
SALES (est): 1.4MM **Privately Held**
SIC: 2672 Mfg Coated/Laminated Paper

(G-9253)
DATACON INC
60 Blanchard Rd (01803-5180)
PHONE....................................781 273-5800
John A Marshall, *President*
EMP: 50
SQ FT: 50,000
SALES: 16MM **Privately Held**
WEB: www.data-con.com
SIC: 3679 Mfg Electronic Components

(G-9254)
DESKTOP METAL INC (PA)
63 3rd Ave (01803-4430)
PHONE....................................978 224-1244
Ric Fulop, *CEO*
Rick Chin, *Vice Pres*
Tuan Tranpham, *Vice Pres*
Thomas Nogueira, *Mfg Staff*
Derek Cheng, *Engineer*
EMP: 140
SQ FT: 10,000
SALES (est): 10.9MM **Privately Held**
SIC: 3541 Mfg Machine Tools-Cutting

(G-9255)
DH INDUSTRIES USA INC
67 S Bedford St Ste 400w (01803-5177)
PHONE....................................781 229-5814
Ronald Den Heijer, *President*
EMP: 4
SQ FT: 400
SALES: 2.2MM **Privately Held**
SIC: 3559 Mfg Misc Industry Machinery

(G-9256)
DIGITAL ALLOYS INCORPORATED
37 North Ave (01803-3305)
PHONE....................................617 557-3432
Duncan McCallum, *President*
Ben Hollander, *Research*
Carl Calabria, *CTO*
EMP: 14
SALES (est): 2.5MM **Privately Held**
SIC: 3441 Structural Metal Fabrication

(G-9257)
DIGITAL IMMUNITY LLC
60 Mall Rd Ste 309 (01803-4549)
PHONE....................................508 630-0321
John Murgo, *CEO*
EMP: 8
SALES (est): 284.6K **Privately Held**
SIC: 7372 Prepackaged Software Services

(G-9258)
DIMENSIONAL INSIGHT INC (PA)
60 Mall Rd Ste 210 (01803-4548)
PHONE....................................781 229-9111
Frederick A Powers, *President*
Nancy Berkowitz, *Vice Pres*
Stan Zanarotti, *Vice Pres*
David Tiertant, *Manager*
EMP: 40
SQ FT: 7,500
SALES (est): 18.2MM **Privately Held**
WEB: www.dimins.com
SIC: 7372 Prepackaged Software Services

(G-9259)
DYNAMICOPS INC
1 Wall St Fl 2 (01803-4773)
PHONE....................................781 221-2136
Pei MA, *President*
EMP: 4
SALES (est): 206.6K **Privately Held**
SIC: 7372 Prepackaged Software

(G-9260)
EASY ACCESS DISTRIBUTION INC
141 Middlesex Tpke Ste 4 (01803-4424)
PHONE....................................781 893-3999
Cindy Cazano, *President*
Charles Papachristos, *Treasurer*
Stephen Presti Giacomo, *Admin Sec*
EMP: 6
SALES (est): 1.5MM **Privately Held**
WEB: www.easyaccessdistribution.com
SIC: 3613 Mfg Switchgear/Switchboards

(G-9261)
EGYPTIAN COTTON TSHIRTS LLC
11 Makechnie Rd (01803-1831)
P.O. Box 138 (01803-0138)
PHONE....................................781 272-7922
Sally Seaver,
EMP: 3 **EST:** 2007
SALES: 123K **Privately Held**
SIC: 2253 7389 Knit Outerwear Mill

(G-9262)
EMD MILLIPORE CORPORATION (DH)
Also Called: Milliporesigma
400 Summit Dr (01803-5258)
PHONE....................................781 533-6000
Udit Batra, *President*
Jean-Paul Mangeolle, *President*
Kevin Sanborn, *President*
Hideo Takahashi, *President*
Klaus Bischoff, *Exec VP*
◆ **EMP:** 1000 **EST:** 1954
SALES (est): 3.2B
SALES (corp-wide): 16.4B **Privately Held**
WEB: www.millipore.com
SIC: 3559 3999 1541 Mfg Misc Industry Machinery Mfg Misc Products Industrial Building Construction

(G-9263)
EMD MILLIPORE CORPORATION
400 Summit Dr (01803-5258)
PHONE....................................800 854-3417
James Hoberg, *Business Mgr*
Timothy Boyle, *Production*
Jeff Hudson, *Production*
Jagat Adhiya, *Research*
Monica Bennett, *Research*
EMP: 317
SALES (corp-wide): 16.4B **Privately Held**
SIC: 3826 Mfg Analytical Instr
HQ: Emd Millipore Corporation
400 Summit Dr
Burlington MA 01803
781 533-6000

(G-9264)
EMD MILLIPORE CORPORATION
400 Summit Dr (01803-5258)
PHONE....................................978 715-4321
Francis J Lunger, *President*
Jagruti Desai, *QC Mgr*
Sonal Patel, *Research*
Joseph Almasian, *Engineer*
Robert P Castro, *Engineer*
EMP: 100
SALES (corp-wide): 16.4B **Privately Held**
WEB: www.millipore.com
SIC: 3826 Mfg Analysis And Purification Products
HQ: Emd Millipore Corporation
400 Summit Dr
Burlington MA 01803
781 533-6000

(G-9265)
EMD SERONO INC
Also Called: EMD Pharmaceuticals
400 Summit Dr Fl 4 (01803-5258)
PHONE....................................978 715-1804
EMP: 3
SALES (corp-wide): 16.4B **Privately Held**
SIC: 2834 Pharmaceutical Preparations
HQ: Emd Serono, Inc.
1 Technology Pl
Rockland MA 02370
781 982-9000

(G-9266)
EMERGING CPD TRTMNT TECHNGY
Also Called: Ect2
70 Blanchard Rd Ste 204 (01803-5100)
PHONE....................................617 886-7400
Steven Woodard, *President*
Andrew G Bishop, *Treasurer*
William R Fisher, *Director*
Lawrence P Smith, *Director*
Patricia E McKee, *Admin Sec*
EMP: 6
SQ FT: 10,000
SALES (est): 723.4K
SALES (corp-wide): 155.1MM **Privately Held**
SIC: 3589 Mfg Service Industry Machinery
PA: Haley & Aldrich, Inc.
70 Blanchard Rd Ste 204
Burlington MA 01803
617 886-7400

(G-9267)
ENCITE LLC
1 North Ave Ste E (01803-3313)
PHONE....................................781 750-8241
Stephen Marsh, *Managing Prtnr*
EMP: 6
SALES (est): 677K **Privately Held**
SIC: 3674 Mfg Semiconductors/Related Devices

(G-9268)
ENDURNCE INTL GROUP HLDNGS INC (PA)
10 Corporate Dr Ste 300 (01803-4200)
PHONE....................................781 852-3200
Hari Ravichandran, *CEO*
James C Neary, *Ch of Bd*
Manish Dalal, *Managing Dir*
Marc Montagner, *COO*
Candice Macias, *VP Opers*
EMP: 67 **EST:** 1997
SQ FT: 77,000
SALES: 1.1B **Publicly Held**
SIC: 7372 Prepackaged Software

(G-9269)
EQUITRAC CORPORATION
1 Wayside Rd (01803-4609)
PHONE....................................781 565-5000
EMP: 3
SALES (est): 153.8K **Publicly Held**
SIC: 7372 Prepackaged Software Services
PA: Nuance Communications, Inc.
1 Wayside Rd
Burlington MA 01803

(G-9270)
EUSA PHARMA (US) LLC
15 Wayside Rd Ste 2 (01803-4622)
PHONE....................................617 584-8012
Melissa Lovequist,
EMP: 12
SALES (est): 553.1K **Privately Held**
SIC: 2834 Mfg Pharmaceutical Preparations

(G-9271)
EVERBRIDGE INC (PA)
25 Corporate Dr Ste 400 (01803-4245)
PHONE....................................818 230-9700
Jaime Ellertson, *Ch of Bd*
Robert Hughes, *President*
Vick Vaishnavi, *General Mgr*
Daniel Hekier, *Counsel*
James Totton, *Exec VP*
EMP: 147
SQ FT: 45,000
SALES: 147MM **Publicly Held**
WEB: www.everbridge.com
SIC: 7372 4899 Prepackaged Software Communication Services

(G-9272)
EXA CORPORATION (DH)
55 Network Dr (01803-2765)
PHONE....................................781 564-0200
John J Shields III, *Ch of Bd*
Stephen A Remondi, *President*
Doug Hatfield, *Managing Dir*
Hudong Chen, *Senior VP*
Richard F Gilbody, *CFO*
EMP: 86
SQ FT: 44,000
SALES: 72.5MM
SALES (corp-wide): 1.7B **Privately Held**
WEB: www.exa.com
SIC: 7372 7373 Prepackaged Software Services Computer Systems Design
HQ: Dassault Systemes Simulia Corp.
1301 Atwood Ave Ste 101w
Johnston RI 02919
401 531-5000

(G-9273)
EXATEL VISUAL SYSTEMS INC
111 S Bedford St Ste 201 (01803-5145)
PHONE....................................781 221-7400
Eli Warsawski, *President*
Gary Learner, *Vice Pres*
EMP: 11
SALES (est): 1.3MM **Privately Held**
WEB: www.exatel-vs.com
SIC: 3699 Electrical Equipment And Supplies, Nec

(G-9274)
FIS FINANCIAL SYSTEMS LLC
Also Called: Sungard
3 Van De Graaff Dr Ste 2 (01803-5131)
PHONE....................................952 935-3300
Roy Nicholas, *Architect*
Jerery Murphy, *Manager*
EMP: 5
SALES (corp-wide): 8.4B **Publicly Held**
SIC: 7372 7371 Prepackaged Software Services Custom Computer Programing
HQ: Fis Financial Systems Llc
601 Riverside Ave
Jacksonville FL 32204
904 438-6000

(G-9275)
FLEXION THERAPEUTICS INC (PA)
10 Mall Rd Ste 301 (01803-4131)
PHONE....................................781 305-7777
Michael D Clayman, *President*
Mark Levin, *Senior VP*
Carolyn Scimemi, *Vice Pres*
Dan Thornton, *Vice Pres*
Kerry Wentworth, *Vice Pres*
EMP: 48
SQ FT: 22,000
SALES: 22.5MM **Publicly Held**
SIC: 2834 Pharmaceutical Preparations

(G-9276)
FUNDTECH CORPORATION
2400 District Ave Ste 150 (01803-5238)
PHONE....................................781 993-9100
Fax: 781 203-9205
EMP: 30
SALES (corp-wide): 132.4MM **Privately Held**
SIC: 7372 Prepackaged Software Services

PA: Fundtech Corporation
30 Montgomery St Ste 501
Jersey City NJ 07302
201 324-0203

(G-9277)
G5 SCIENTIFIC LLC
10 Fred St (01803-4546)
PHONE....781 272-7877
Arthur A Giordano,
Ning Yang,
EMP: 5
SALES (est): 430K **Privately Held**
SIC: 3663 Mfg Radio/Tv Communication Equipment

(G-9278)
GALAXIE LABS INC
18 A St (01803-3418)
PHONE....781 272-3750
Peter Tocci, *President*
Kristine Tocci, *Vice Pres*
EMP: 7 **EST:** 1962
SQ FT: 13,000
SALES (est): 990.9K **Privately Held**
WEB: www.galaxielabs.com
SIC: 3599 Machine Shop

(G-9279)
GENLYTE THOMAS GROUP LLC
Also Called: Philips Lighting
3 Burlington Woods Dr # 100 (01803-4514)
PHONE....781 418-7900
EMP: 126
SALES (corp-wide): 7B **Privately Held**
SIC: 3646 3645 3648 Mfg Commercial Lighting Fixtures Mfg Residential Lighting Fixtures Mfg Lighting Equipment
HQ: Genlyte Thomas Group Llc
200 Franklin Square Dr
Somerset NJ 08873

(G-9280)
GUARDION INC
151 S Bedford St 7 (01803-5228)
PHONE....603 769-7265
Daniel Esposito, *CEO*
Yung Joon Jung, *Shareholder*
Swastik Kar, *Shareholder*
EMP: 3
SALES (est): 138.3K **Privately Held**
SIC: 3674 Mfg Semiconductors/Related Devices

(G-9281)
HCI CLEANING PRODUCTS LLC
2 Burlington Woods Dr (01803-4515)
PHONE....508 864-5510
Sandy Posa, *CEO*
Trip Flavin, *COO*
Mark Kost, *CFO*
EMP: 5
SQ FT: 800
SALES: 1.8MM **Privately Held**
SIC: 3999 Mfg Misc Products

(G-9282)
HEALTHEDGE SOFTWARE INC (PA)
30 Corporate Dr Ste 150 (01803-4257)
PHONE....781 285-1300
Rob Gillette, *President*
Rob Armstrong, *President*
Robert Levy, *President*
Steve Sharp, *COO*
Matt Hughes, *CFO*
EMP: 97
SALES (est): 32MM **Privately Held**
SIC: 7372 Prepackaged Software Services

(G-9283)
HYPOXYPROBE INC
121 Middlesex Tpke Ste 2 (01803-4990)
PHONE....781 272-6888
Tina Lee, *CEO*
EMP: 6
SALES: 250K **Privately Held**
SIC: 2835 Mfg Diagnostic Substances

(G-9284)
I-OPTICS CORP
1 Wall St Fl 6 (01803-4757)
PHONE....508 366-1600
Jeroen Cammeraat, *CEO*
Thomas Van Elzakker, *COO*
Erik Valks, *Exec VP*
Stephen Morris, *Vice Pres*
Joris Vogels, *Vice Pres*
EMP: 3
SALES (est): 258.6K **Privately Held**
SIC: 3827 Mfg Optical Instruments/Lenses

(G-9285)
INFOGIX INC
Also Called: Data3sixty
15 New England Exec Park (01803-5202)
PHONE....617 826-6020
EMP: 6
SALES (corp-wide): 64.6MM **Privately Held**
SIC: 7372 Prepackaged Software Services
PA: Infogix, Inc.
1240 E Diehl Rd Ste 400
Naperville IL 60563
630 505-1800

(G-9286)
IRVING CONSUMER PRODUCTS INC
Also Called: Scottis Brand US
25 Burlington Mall Rd # 608 (01803-4156)
PHONE....781 273-3222
EMP: 10
SALES (corp-wide): 2.8B **Privately Held**
SIC: 2621 Paper Mill
HQ: Irving Consumer Products, Inc.
1 Eddy St
Fort Edward NY 12828

(G-9287)
IRVING TISSUE CORPORATION
25 Burlington Mall Rd (01803-4156)
PHONE....781 273-3222
Robert K Irving, *Branch Mgr*
EMP: 3
SALES (corp-wide): 2.8B **Privately Held**
SIC: 2676 Mfg Sanitary Paper Products
HQ: Irving Consumer Products Limited
100 Prom Midland
Dieppe NB E1A 6
506 858-7777

(G-9288)
ISUBSCRIBED INC
15 Network Dr Fl 3 (01803-2766)
PHONE....844 378-4646
Ryan Toohil, *COO*
Hari Ravichandran, *Exec Dir*
Blake Cunneen, *Director*
Trevor Oelschig, *Director*
Albert Sokol, *Director*
EMP: 20
SALES: 1MM **Privately Held**
SIC: 7372 Prepackaged Software Services

(G-9289)
JONES & BARTLETT LEARNING LLC (PA)
5 Wall St Fl 3 (01803-4700)
P.O. Box 417289, Boston (02241-7289)
PHONE....978 443-5000
Gregory Sabasky, *CEO*
James Walsh, *President*
James Homer, *COO*
David Cella, *Vice Pres*
Ty Field, *Vice Pres*
▲ **EMP:** 150
SQ FT: 25,000
SALES (est): 49.9MM **Privately Held**
WEB: www.jbpub.com
SIC: 2731 Books-Publishing/Printing

(G-9290)
JOTAS CORPORATION
Also Called: Minuteman Press
158 Cambridge St Ste 158 # 158 (01803-2920)
PHONE....781 273-1155
Stephen Bentas, *President*
EMP: 3
SQ FT: 2,400
SALES: 420K **Privately Held**
SIC: 2752 Comm Prtg Litho

(G-9291)
KASALIS INC
11 North Ave (01803-3305)
PHONE....781 273-6200
Justin Roe, *President*
Richard By, *Principal*
Mark Kozak, *Engineer*
Aaron Israelski, *Director*
EMP: 27 **EST:** 2011
SALES (est): 6.5MM
SALES (corp-wide): 25.2B **Publicly Held**
SIC: 3612 Mfg Transformers
PA: Jabil Inc.
10560 Dr Mrtn Lther King
Saint Petersburg FL 33716
727 577-9749

(G-9292)
KEURIG DR PEPPER INC (PA)
53 South Ave (01803-4903)
PHONE....781 418-7000
Robert Gamgort, *Ch of Bd*
Rodger L Collins, *President*
Brian Loucks, *President*
Alexsandra Chirco, *Production*
Julio Martinez, *Engineer*
◆ **EMP:** 100
SALES: 7.4B **Publicly Held**
SIC: 2086 2087 5149 Mfg Beverages

(G-9293)
KEURIG GREEN MOUNTAIN INC
Also Called: Green Mountain Coffee Roasters
53 South Ave (01803-4903)
PHONE....781 246-3466
Richard Sweeney, *President*
Jack Bonanno, *Vice Pres*
Janet Osterlind, *Vice Pres*
Jennifer Bailey, *Engineer*
Marius Caramiciu, *Engineer*
EMP: 57 **Publicly Held**
SIC: 2086 Mfg Bottled/Canned Soft Drinks
HQ: Keurig Green Mountain, Inc.
33 Coffee Ln
Waterbury VT 05676
802 244-5621

(G-9294)
KEYSTONE DENTAL INC (PA)
154 Middlesex Tpke Ste 2 (01803-4469)
PHONE....781 328-3300
Michael A Kehoe, *President*
Michael Gibbs, *Vice Pres*
Connie Lu, *Production*
Arthur Simental, *QC Mgr*
Michael Nealon, *CFO*
EMP: 99
SALES (est): 19.6MM **Privately Held**
SIC: 3843 Mfg Dental Equipment/Supplies

(G-9295)
L3 TECHNOLOGIES INC
Also Called: L-3 Advanced Systems Divisions
1 Wall St Ste 7 (01803-4757)
PHONE....781 270-2100
Edward R Abate, *Manager*
EMP: 208
SALES (corp-wide): 6.8B **Publicly Held**
SIC: 3663 3669 3679 3812 Mfg Radio/Tv Comm Equip Mfg Communications Equip Mfg Elec Components Mfg Search/Navgatn Equip Mfg Space Vehicle Equip
HQ: L3 Technologies, Inc.
600 3rd Ave Fl 34
New York NY 10016
212 697-1111

(G-9296)
LATTICE SEMICONDUCTOR CORP
Also Called: Lattice Semi-Conductor
67 S Bedford St Ste 400w (01803-5177)
PHONE....781 229-5819
Al Siemer, *President*
EMP: 5
SALES (corp-wide): 398.8MM **Publicly Held**
WEB: www.latticesemi.com
SIC: 3674 Mfg Semiconductors/Related Devices
PA: Lattice Semiconductor Corp
5555 Ne Moore Ct
Hillsboro OR 97124
503 268-8000

(G-9297)
LEMAITRE VASCULAR INC (PA)
63 2nd Ave (01803-4413)
PHONE....781 221-2266
George W Lemaitre, *Ch of Bd*
David B Roberts, *President*
Laurie A Churchill, *Senior VP*
Andrew Hodgkinson, *Senior VP*
Trent G Kamke, *Senior VP*
EMP: 223
SQ FT: 27,098
SALES: 105.5MM **Publicly Held**
WEB: www.lemaitre.com
SIC: 3841 5047 Mfg & Selling Surgical/Medical Instruments

(G-9298)
LOCKHEED MARTIN CORP - BOSTON
Also Called: Lockheed Martin - RMS
35 Corporate Dr Ste 250 (01803-4244)
PHONE....781 565-1100
Wayne Civinskas, *Manager*
Charles Turbe, *Manager*
Joanne Ouillette, *Director*
EMP: 20 **Publicly Held**
WEB: www.lockheedmartin.com
SIC: 3812 Mfg Search/Navigation Equipment
PA: Lockheed Martin Corporation
6801 Rockledge Dr
Bethesda MD 20817

(G-9299)
MAGNITUDE SOFTWARE INC
2400 District Ave Ste 320 (01803-5239)
PHONE....781 202-3200
EMP: 5
SALES (corp-wide): 48.7MM **Privately Held**
SIC: 7372 Prepackaged Software Services
PA: Magnitude Software, Inc.
515 Congress Ave Ste 1510
Austin TX 78701
866 466-3849

(G-9300)
MAKSCIENTIFIC LLC
151 S Bedford St 104 (01803-5228)
P.O. Box 3 (01803-0003)
PHONE....781 365-0958
Caroline Clayton,
Alexandros Makriyannis,
EMP: 4
SALES (est): 376.4K **Privately Held**
WEB: www.makscientific.com
SIC: 2834 Mfg Pharmaceutical Preparations

(G-9301)
MEMENTO INC
55 Network Dr (01803-2765)
PHONE....781 221-3030
John E Omalley, *CEO*
Mike Braatz, *Vice Pres*
James Glover, *Vice Pres*
Maria Loughlin, *Vice Pres*
Paul Whitelam, *Vice Pres*
EMP: 70
SQ FT: 18,000
SALES (est): 5.7MM **Privately Held**
WEB: www.mementosecurity.com
SIC: 7372 Prepackaged Software Services

(G-9302)
META SOFTWARE CORPORATION (PA)
15 New England Exec Park (01803-5202)
PHONE....781 238-0293
Robert Seltzer, *President*
Robert Shapiro, *Chairman*
Peter G Johannsen, *Asst Clerk*
EMP: 15
SQ FT: 10,656
SALES (est): 1.2MM **Privately Held**
WEB: www.metasoftware.com
SIC: 7372 7371 Prepackaged Software Services Custom Computer Programing

(G-9303)
MICROSOFT CORPORATION
5 Wayside Rd (01803-4609)
PHONE....781 487-6400
EMP: 3
SALES (corp-wide): 125.8B **Publicly Held**
SIC: 7372 Prepackaged Software Services
PA: Microsoft Corporation
1 Microsoft Way
Redmond WA 98052
425 882-8080

GEOGRAPHIC

(G-9304)
MURPHY SOFTWARE INC
3 Fairfax St (01803-2830)
PHONE..................................781 710-8419
Kenneth Murphy, *President*
EMP: 3
SALES (est): 135.3K **Privately Held**
WEB: www.murphysoftware.net
SIC: 7372 Prepackaged Software Services

(G-9305)
NEDAP INC
Also Called: Nedap Retail North America
25 Corporate Dr Ste 101 (01803-4238)
PHONE..................................844 876-3327
Martin Bomers, *President*
Hugo Kruijssen, *Vice Pres*
EMP: 14
SALES (est): 1.1MM
SALES (corp-wide): 212.2MM **Privately Held**
SIC: 3648 Mfg Lighting Equipment
PA: Nedap N.V.
Parallelweg 2
Groenlo 7141
544 471-111

(G-9306)
NETBRAIN TECHNOLOGIES INC (PA)
15 Network Dr Ste 2 (01803-2766)
PHONE..................................781 221-7199
Lingping Gao, *CEO*
Paul Charchaflian, *Vice Pres*
Emily Liang, *Vice Pres*
Eric Wang, *Vice Pres*
David Bentley, *Opers Staff*
EMP: 160
SQ FT: 13,864
SALES (est): 35.8MM **Privately Held**
SIC: 7372 Prepackaged Software Services

(G-9307)
NETZSCH INSTRUMENTS N AMER LLC (DH)
129 Middlesex Tpke (01803-4404)
PHONE..................................781 272-5353
Melinda Tucker, *Buyer*
Paul Staudinger, *Purchasing*
Robert Levins, *Engineer*
Peter Vichos, *Sales Mgr*
Stewart Rissley, *Sales Staff*
EMP: 22
SQ FT: 15,000
SALES (est): 4.4MM
SALES (corp-wide): 628.6MM **Privately Held**
WEB: www.micromet.com
SIC: 3823 8734 Mfg Process Control Instruments Testing Laboratory
HQ: Netzsch - Geratebau Gesellschaft Mit Beschrankter Haftung
Wittelsbacherstr. 42
Selb
928 788-10

(G-9308)
NETZSCH USA HOLDINGS INC (PA)
37 North Ave (01803-3305)
PHONE..................................781 272-5353
Thomas Streubel, *President*
Dr Otto Max Schaefer, *Managing Dir*
Mark Drazen, *Treasurer*
EMP: 9
SALES (est): 21MM **Privately Held**
SIC: 3561 Mfg Pumps/Pumping Equipment

(G-9309)
NGAC LLC
Also Called: Nextgen Adhesive
25 B St (01803-3401)
P.O. Box 535, Lexington (02420-0005)
PHONE..................................781 258-0008
Amy Nelson, *Vice Pres*
Brian Flaherty,
EMP: 20
SALES (est): 136K **Privately Held**
SIC: 2891 Mfg Adhesives/Sealants

(G-9310)
NIKE INC
25 Corporate Dr Ste 360 (01803-4245)
PHONE..................................781 564-9929
EMP: 15
SALES (corp-wide): 32.3B **Publicly Held**
SIC: 3021 Mfg Rubber/Plastic Footwear
PA: Nike, Inc.
1 Sw Bowerman Dr
Beaverton OR 97005
503 671-6453

(G-9311)
NORTHBRIDGE COMPANIES
15 3rd Ave Ste 1 (01803-4410)
PHONE..................................781 272-2424
James Coughlin, *CEO*
Wendy Nowokunski, *President*
Mel Horan, *Vice Pres*
Kristin Gowdy, *Portfolio Mgr*
Kris Hoarty, *Executive Asst*
EMP: 18
SALES (est): 2.6MM **Privately Held**
SIC: 3443 Mfg Fabricated Plate Work

(G-9312)
NUANCE COMMUNICATIONS INC (PA)
1 Wayside Rd (01803-4609)
PHONE..................................781 565-5000
Mark Benjamin, *CEO*
Sanjay Dhawan, *CEO*
Lloyd Carney, *Ch of Bd*
Paul A Ricci, *Ch of Bd*
Earl Simmons, *Regional Mgr*
▲ **EMP:** 550
SALES: 1.8B **Publicly Held**
WEB: www.nuance.com
SIC: 7372 Prepackaged Software Services

(G-9313)
ORACLE AMERICA INC
10 Van De Graaff Dr (01803-6815)
PHONE..................................781 744-0000
James Marceau, *Exec VP*
James Carey, *Software Dev*
David Greenfield, *Software Dev*
Riggs Roger, *Director*
EMP: 11
SALES (corp-wide): 39.5B **Publicly Held**
SIC: 7372 Prepackaged Software Services
HQ: Oracle America, Inc.
500 Oracle Pkwy
Redwood City CA 94065
650 506-7000

(G-9314)
ORACLE CORPORATION
10 Van De Graaff Dr Ste 1 (01803-6816)
PHONE..................................781 744-0000
Lisa Schreiber, *Vice Pres*
Kevin Hopke, *Project Mgr*
Carrie Lauterbach, *Purch Mgr*
WEI Yin, *Purch Mgr*
Chris Kuwada, *QA Dir*
EMP: 191
SALES (corp-wide): 39.5B **Publicly Held**
WEB: www.oracle.com
SIC: 7372 Prepackaged Software Services
PA: Oracle Corporation
500 Oracle Pkwy
Redwood City CA 94065
650 506-7000

(G-9315)
OSHKOSH CORPORATION
6 Wayside Rd (01803-4607)
PHONE..................................800 392-9921
Jessica Rosenow, *Principal*
EMP: 115
SALES (corp-wide): 8.3B **Publicly Held**
SIC: 3711 Mfg Heavy-Duty Specialized Trucks
PA: Oshkosh Corporation
1917 Four Wheel Dr
Oshkosh WI 54902
920 502-3000

(G-9316)
PALOMAR MEDICAL PRODUCTS LLC
Also Called: Palomar Medical Products, Inc.
15 Network Dr (01803-2766)
PHONE..................................781 993-2300
Joseph Caruso, *President*
Paul Weiner, *Treasurer*
Patricia Davis, *Admin Sec*
EMP: 119
SQ FT: 25,000
SALES (est): 11.3MM
SALES (corp-wide): 3.3B **Publicly Held**
WEB: www.palomarmedical.com
SIC: 3842 3845 Mfg Surgical Appliances/Supplies Mfg Electromedical Equipment
HQ: Palomar Medical Technologies, Llc
15 Network Dr
Burlington MA 01803
781 993-2330

(G-9317)
PALOMAR MEDICAL TECH LLC (DH)
15 Network Dr (01803-2766)
PHONE..................................781 993-2330
Michael Davin, *CEO*
Joseph Caruso, *President*
Timothy Baker, *COO*
Jim Barrett, *Engineer*
Patrick Fitzgerald, *Engineer*
▲ **EMP:** 32 **EST:** 2013
SALES (est): 22.2MM
SALES (corp-wide): 3.3B **Publicly Held**
SIC: 3841 3845 Lasers And Other Light-Based Products For Medical And Cosmetic Procedures

(G-9318)
PANDA SECURITY
Also Called: Panda Software
77 S Bedford St Ste 350 (01803-5130)
PHONE..................................407 215-3020
Diego Navarrete, *CEO*
Mikel Urizabarrena, *President*
Santiago Mayoralas, *CFO*
EMP: 40 **EST:** 1997
SQ FT: 7,000
SALES (est): 3.8MM **Privately Held**
SIC: 7372 Prepackaged Software Services

(G-9319)
PHOTRONIX INC
35 Sandy Brook Rd (01803-3933)
PHONE..................................781 221-0442
Phil Lamarre, *President*
EMP: 4
SALES: 375K **Privately Held**
SIC: 3674 Mfg Semiconductors/Related Devices

(G-9320)
PITCHERVILLE SAND AND GRAVEL
40 Mall Rd (01803-4519)
PHONE..................................781 365-1721
EMP: 3 **EST:** 2011
SALES (est): 130K **Privately Held**
SIC: 1442 Construction Sand/Gravel

(G-9321)
PRECISION DYNAMICS CORPORATION
Also Called: Jam Plastics
85 Terrace Hall Ave (01803-3410)
PHONE..................................888 202-3684
James Gross, *Manager*
EMP: 69
SALES (corp-wide): 1.1B **Publicly Held**
WEB: www.identicard.com
SIC: 3089 3861 3699 Mfg Plastic Products Mfg Photographic Equipment/Supplies Mfg Electrical Equipment/Supplies
HQ: Precision Dynamics Corporation
25124 Sprngfeld Ct Ste 20
Valencia CA 91355
818 897-1111

(G-9322)
PRIMEARRAY SYSTEMS INC
1500 District Ave (01803-5069)
PHONE..................................978 455-9488
Sean Campbell, *President*
EMP: 4
SQ FT: 2,500
SALES (est): 654.4K **Privately Held**
WEB: www.primearray.com
SIC: 3572 Mfg Cdrom Towers

(G-9323)
PROFITECT INC (HQ)
Also Called: Profit Ect
200 Summit Dr Ste 405 (01803-5289)
PHONE..................................781 290-0009
Guy Yehiav, *CEO*
Tal Harel, *Business Mgr*
Amanda Duguay, *CFO*
Colin McComb, *Sales Staff*
EMP: 13
SALES (est): 723.5K
SALES (corp-wide): 4.2B **Publicly Held**
SIC: 7372 Prepackaged Software Services
PA: Zebra Technologies Corporation
3 Overlook Pt
Lincolnshire IL 60069
847 634-6700

(G-9324)
PURE ENERGY CORPORATION (PA)
Also Called: Pure Energy of America
101 Middlesex Tpke Ste 6 (01803-4914)
PHONE..................................201 843-8100
Irshad Ahmed, *President*
Stephen J Morris, *Chairman*
EMP: 10
SQ FT: 1,200
SALES: 1MM **Privately Held**
SIC: 2869 Mfg Industrial Organic Chemicals

(G-9325)
QSA GLOBAL INC (HQ)
30 North Ave Ste 3 (01803-3327)
PHONE..................................781 272-2000
Larry Swift, *President*
Curt Auznne, *General Mgr*
Jeanne Greenland, *General Mgr*
Tom McCollem, *Business Mgr*
Ted Beagen, *Buyer*
◆ **EMP:** 70
SQ FT: 40,000
SALES (est): 19.8MM
SALES (corp-wide): 14.7B **Publicly Held**
SIC: 3844 2835 2819 Mfg X-Ray Apparatus/Tubes Mfg Diagnostic Substances Mfg Industrial Inorganic Chemicals
PA: Illinois Tool Works Inc.
155 Harlem Ave
Glenview IL 60025
847 724-7500

(G-9326)
QSR INTERNATIONAL AMERICAS INC
35 Corporate Dr Ste 140 (01803-4203)
PHONE..................................617 607-5112
John Owens, *CEO*
John Woolcott, *President*
Kerri McInnis, *Info Tech Mgr*
◆ **EMP:** 8
SALES (est): 1.2MM **Privately Held**
SIC: 3695 Mfg Magnetic/Optical Recording Media

(G-9327)
QSTREAM INC (PA)
3 Burlington Woods Dr # 303 (01803-4514)
PHONE..................................781 222-2020
Richard Lanchantin, *CEO*
Duncan Lennox, *Ch of Bd*
Jeff Borkowski, *Vice Pres*
Jim Bowley, *Vice Pres*
Gary Greenberger, *Vice Pres*
EMP: 5
SALES (est): 1.6MM **Privately Held**
SIC: 7372 Prepackaged Software Services

(G-9328)
RACHAD FUEL INC
161 Bedford St (01803-2737)
PHONE..................................781 273-0292
Nizar Abdallah, *President*
EMP: 5 **EST:** 2011
SALES (est): 570.2K **Privately Held**
SIC: 2869 Mfg Industrial Organic Chemicals

(G-9329)
REDSHIFT BIOANALYTICS INC
131 Middlesex Tpke Ste 1 (01803-4431)
PHONE..................................781 345-7300
Julien Bradley, *CEO*
Charles Marshall, *COO*
EMP: 5
SQ FT: 7,500
SALES (est): 970.4K **Privately Held**
SIC: 3829 Mfg Measuring/Controlling Devices

(G-9330)
RMI TITANIUM COMPANY LLC
Also Called: Arconic Ttnium Engineered Pdts
8 A St (01803-3405)
PHONE....................................781 272-5967
Susan Abkowitz, *Branch Mgr*
EMP: 11
SALES (corp-wide): 14B **Publicly Held**
SIC: 3399 3356 1741 3533 Mfg Primary Metal Prdts Nonferrous Rollng/Drawng Masonry/Stone Contractor Oil/Gas Field Mach
HQ: Rmi Titanium Company, Llc
1000 Warren Ave
Niles OH 44446
330 652-9952

(G-9331)
SABA SOFTWARE INC
25 Burlington Mall Rd (01803-4156)
PHONE....................................781 238-6730
Fax: 781 238-6747
EMP: 6
SALES (corp-wide): 116.6MM **Publicly Held**
SIC: 7372 Software Development
PA: Saba Software, Inc.
2400 Bridge Pkwy
Redwood City CA 94568
650 581-2500

(G-9332)
SALLY SEAVER
Also Called: Active Cutting Fluids
11 Makechnie Rd (01803-1831)
PHONE....................................833 322-8483
Sally Seaver, *Owner*
EMP: 3
SALES (est): 134.6K **Privately Held**
SIC: 2992 7389 Mfg Lubricating Oils/Greases Business Serv Non-Commercial Site

(G-9333)
SANTHERA PHARMACEUTICALS USA
25 Corporate Dr (01803-4240)
PHONE....................................781 552-5145
EMP: 3
SALES (est): 130.5K **Privately Held**
SIC: 2834 Mfg Pharmaceutical Preparations

(G-9334)
SAP AMERICA INC
15 Wayside Rd (01803-4620)
PHONE....................................781 852-3000
Peter Barker, *Principal*
EMP: 22
SALES (corp-wide): 27.4B **Privately Held**
WEB: www.sybase.com
SIC: 3577 Custom Computer Programing
HQ: Sap America, Inc.
3999 West Chester Pike
Newtown Square PA 19073
610 661-1000

(G-9335)
SCPHARMACEUTICALS INC
2400 District Ave Ste 310 (01803-5239)
PHONE....................................617 517-0730
Jack A Khattar, *Ch of Bd*
John H Tucker, *President*
Rachael Nokes, *Senior VP*
Jay Rheingold, *Vice Pres*
Barbara Cornelius, *Research*
EMP: 23
SQ FT: 13,066
SALES (est): 4.4MM **Privately Held**
SIC: 2834 Pharmaceutical Preparations

(G-9336)
SEKISUI DIAGNOSTICS LLC (DH)
1 Wall St Ste 301 (01803-4775)
PHONE....................................781 652-7800
Mitsuhisa Manabe, *CEO*
Bob Schruender, *President*
Ann Hou, *Research*
Rosemary Petrone, *Program Mgr*
▲ **EMP:** 122
SALES (est): 143.4MM **Privately Held**
SIC: 3841 Mfg Surgical/Medical Instruments
HQ: Sekisui America Corporation
333 Meadowlands Pkwy
Secaucus NJ 07094
201 423-7960

(G-9337)
SIGNIFY NORTH AMERICA CORP
Philips Lighting
3 Burlington Woods Dr # 4 (01803-4532)
PHONE....................................617 423-9999
Erik Bouts, *President*
EMP: 280
SQ FT: 200,000
SALES (corp-wide): 7B **Privately Held**
WEB: www.usa.philips.com
SIC: 3646 Mfg Commercial Lighting Fixtures
HQ: Signify North America Corporation
200 Franklin Square Dr
Somerset NJ 08873
732 563-3000

(G-9338)
SIMILARWEB INC
100 Summit Dr (01803-5197)
PHONE....................................800 540-1086
Donna Dror, *Branch Mgr*
EMP: 12
SALES (corp-wide): 3MM **Privately Held**
SIC: 7372 Prepackaged Software Services
HQ: Similarweb, Inc.
35 E 21st St Fl 9
New York NY 10010
347 685-5422

(G-9339)
SQ INNOVATION INC
20 Mall Rd Ste 220 (01803-4127)
PHONE....................................617 500-0121
Pieter Muntendam, *President*
EMP: 7
SQ FT: 3,500
SALES (est): 304.1K **Privately Held**
SIC: 2834 Mfg Pharmaceutical Preparations

(G-9340)
SS&C TECHNOLOGIES INC
3 Burlington Woods Dr (01803-4532)
PHONE....................................781 654-6498
EMP: 5
SALES (corp-wide): 3.4B **Publicly Held**
SIC: 7372 Prepackaged Software Services
HQ: Ss&C Technologies, Inc.
80 Lamberton Rd
Windsor CT 06095
860 298-4500

(G-9341)
STREETSCAN INC
151 S Bedford St Ste 2 (01803-5228)
PHONE....................................617 399-8236
Ralf Birken, *CEO*
Yubo Zhao, *Research*
Jessica Solimini, *Office Mgr*
EMP: 20
SQ FT: 2,000
SALES (est): 346K **Privately Held**
SIC: 7372 7389 Prepackaged Software Services Business Services

(G-9342)
STRESCON OF NEW ENGLAND
25 Mall Rd Ste 104 (01803-4166)
PHONE....................................781 221-2153
Gerald Grassby, *Sales Staff*
EMP: 7
SALES (corp-wide): 106.1MM **Privately Held**
WEB: www.strescon.com
SIC: 3272 Mfg Concrete Products
HQ: Strescon Limited
400 Chesley Dr Suite 3
Saint John NB E2K 5
506 633-8877

(G-9343)
TEESMILE INC
15 New England Exec Park (01803-5202)
PHONE....................................781 325-8587
Paula Dore, *Marketing Mgr*
EMP: 3
SALES (est): 124.3K **Privately Held**
SIC: 2759 Commercial Printing

(G-9344)
TERATECH CORPORATION
Also Called: Terason Ultrasound
77 Terrace Hall Ave (01803)
PHONE....................................781 270-4143
Alice Chiang, *President*
Jeffrey Sirek, *General Mgr*
Jody Graziano, *Vice Pres*
Jim Lucas, *Vice Pres*
Willy Wong, *Vice Pres*
▲ **EMP:** 50
SQ FT: 20,000
SALES (est): 9.9MM **Privately Held**
WEB: www.terason.com
SIC: 3845 Mfg Electromedical Equipment

(G-9345)
THORATEC CORPORATION
168 Middlesex Tpke (01803-4403)
PHONE....................................781 272-0139
EMP: 147
SALES (corp-wide): 30.5B **Publicly Held**
SIC: 3845 Mfg Electromedical Equipment
HQ: Thoratec Llc
6035 Stoneridge Dr
Pleasanton CA 94588
925 847-8600

(G-9346)
THORATEC CORPORATION
23 4th Ave Ste 2 (01803-3326)
PHONE....................................781 272-0139
Matt Wagers, *Engineer*
Ted Naughton, *Branch Mgr*
EMP: 100
SALES (corp-wide): 30.5B **Publicly Held**
WEB: www.thoratec.com
SIC: 3845 3826 Engineering And Marketing Office
HQ: Thoratec Llc
6035 Stoneridge Dr
Pleasanton CA 94588
925 847-8600

(G-9347)
TOMOPHASE CORPORATION
1 North Ave Ste A (01803-3313)
PHONE....................................781 229-5700
Peter Norris, *CEO*
Ralph S Johnston, *President*
Xiao-LI LI, *Treasurer*
Jeff Stoler, *Admin Sec*
EMP: 4
SQ FT: 5,000
SALES (est): 624.2K **Privately Held**
WEB: www.tomophase.com
SIC: 3845 Mfg Electromedical Equipment

(G-9348)
TOSHIBA INTERNATIONAL CORP
2400 District Ave Ste 130 (01803-5242)
PHONE....................................781 273-9000
Noriyuki Takizawa, *Branch Mgr*
EMP: 5 **Privately Held**
SIC: 3621 Mfg Motors/Generators
HQ: Toshiba International Corporation
13131 W Little York Rd
Houston TX 77041
800 231-1412

(G-9349)
TOWN OF BURLINGTON
62 Winter St (01803)
PHONE....................................781 270-1680
Bill Keene, *Branch Mgr*
EMP: 3 **Privately Held**
SIC: 2899 Mfg Chemical Preparations
PA: Burlington, Town Of (Inc)
29 Center St
Burlington MA 01803
781 270-1600

(G-9350)
UNIT4 BUSINESS SOFTWARE INC (DH)
3 Burlington Woods Dr # 201 (01803-4514)
PHONE....................................877 704-5974
Lars Noreng, *President*
Christophe Haugen, *Exec VP*
Matt Hinchliffe, *Accounts Exec*
Sascha Alber, *Manager*
Emma Keates, *Manager*
EMP: 10 **EST:** 2000
SALES (est): 8.3MM
SALES (corp-wide): 2.6MM **Privately Held**
SIC: 7372 Prepackaged Software Services
HQ: Unit4 N.V.
Papendorpseweg 100
Utrecht 3528
184 444-444

(G-9351)
VANS INC
75 Middlesex Tpke # 1303 (01803-5310)
PHONE....................................781 229-7700
Hildegard Throop, *Branch Mgr*
EMP: 5
SALES (corp-wide): 13.8B **Publicly Held**
SIC: 3021 Ret Shoes
HQ: Vans, Inc.
1588 S Coast Dr
Costa Mesa CA 92626
855 909-8267

(G-9352)
VERSATILE PRINTING
18 Lisa St (01803-1108)
P.O. Box 49 (01803-0125)
PHONE....................................781 221-2112
Roger Bell, *President*
EMP: 3
SQ FT: 3,000
SALES (est): 280K **Privately Held**
WEB: www.versatileprint.com
SIC: 2752 Offset Printing

(G-9353)
VIKEN DETECTION CORPORATION
21 North Ave (01803-3305)
PHONE....................................617 467-5526
Henry Grodzins, *President*
Jeff Warming, *CFO*
EMP: 22
SALES (est): 4.5MM **Privately Held**
SIC: 3826 Mfg Analytical Instruments

(G-9354)
VIRTUAL SOFTWARE SYSTEMS INC
1500 District Ave (01803-5069)
PHONE....................................774 270-1207
John Conway, *CEO*
Frederick Smith, *CFO*
Richard Fiorentino, *Treasurer*
Thomas Wetmore, *Admin Sec*
EMP: 7
SALES (est): 208.1K **Privately Held**
SIC: 7372 Prepackaged Software Services

(G-9355)
VOLICON INC
99 S Bedford St Ste 209 (01803-5153)
PHONE....................................781 221-7400
Eli Warsawski, *President*
Ishai Gandelsman, *CFO*
EMP: 60
SALES (est): 8.9MM
SALES (corp-wide): 130.8B **Publicly Held**
WEB: www.volicon.com
SIC: 3651 Manufacture Home Audio/Video Equipment
HQ: Verizon Digital Media Services Inc.
13031 W Jefferson Blvd # 900
Los Angeles CA 90094

(G-9356)
WEBB-MASON INC
50 Mall Rd Ste 207 (01803-4508)
PHONE....................................781 272-5530
Scott Davis, *Vice Pres*
EMP: 3
SALES (corp-wide): 113.5MM **Privately Held**
WEB: www.webbmason.com
SIC: 2752 Lithographic Commercial Printing
PA: Webb-Mason, Inc.
10830 Gilroy Rd
Hunt Valley MD 21031
410 785-1111

(G-9357)
ZAPPIX INC
25 Mall Rd (01803-4156)
PHONE....................................781 214-8124

GEOGRAPHIC

Yossi Abraham, *President*
Gal Steinberg, *Vice Pres*
Ryan McColgan, *Sales Dir*
Sally Cooper, *Marketing Mgr*
Ajay Bhandari, *CTO*
EMP: 12
SQ FT: 3,000
SALES (est): 599.4K **Privately Held**
SIC: 7372 Prepackaged Software Services

(G-9358)
ZORAN CORPORATION
Also Called: Imaging Division
1 Wall St Ste 10 (01803-4733)
PHONE..................................408 523-6500
Rosemary Grande, *Branch Mgr*
EMP: 150
SALES (corp-wide): 24.2B **Publicly Held**
WEB: www.zoran.com
SIC: 7372 Prepackaged Software Services
HQ: Zoran Corporation
1060 Rincon Cir
San Jose CA 95131
972 673-1600

Buzzards Bay
Barnstable County

(G-9359)
CONFERENCE MEDAL & TROPHY CO
530 Macarthur Blvd (02532-3839)
P.O. Box 3137, Pocasset (02559-3137)
PHONE..................................508 563-3600
Kevin Healy, *President*
Michael Healy, *Vice Pres*
Lillian Healy, *Treasurer*
EMP: 14 **EST:** 1951
SQ FT: 8,000
SALES (est): 2.1MM **Privately Held**
SIC: 3499 3914 Mfg Plaques Medals & Trophies

(G-9360)
CREATIVE STONE SYSTEMS INC
Also Called: Breakthrough Coatings
169 Clay Pond Rd Ste 1 (02532-8303)
PHONE..................................866 608-7625
Jason Larosa, *President*
EMP: 10
SALES (est): 1.6MM **Privately Held**
SIC: 2865 2851 Mfg Paints/Allied Prdts Mfg Cyclic Crudes/Intrmd

(G-9361)
MV3 LLC
Also Called: Freeaire Refrigeration
11 Mizzen Ln (02532-3313)
PHONE..................................617 658-4420
John Desimone,
David Mac Isaac,
C Kenneth Strachan,
EMP: 7
SALES (est): 458.5K **Privately Held**
SIC: 3822 5078 Mfg Environmental Controls Whol Refrigeration Equipment/Supplies

Byfield
Essex County

(G-9362)
DIEMAT INC
19 Central St Ste 9 (01922-1233)
PHONE..................................978 499-0900
Raymond Deitz, *President*
Maciej Patelka, *Engineer*
Brian Haley, *Technology*
Terry Hartman, *Admin Sec*
Marie Roy, *Administration*
EMP: 10
SQ FT: 1,876
SALES (est): 2.1MM **Privately Held**
WEB: www.diemat.com
SIC: 2891 Mfg Adhesives/Sealants
HQ: Namics Corporation
3993, Nigorikawa, Kita-Ku
Niigata NIG 950-3

(G-9363)
DITECH
144 Elm St (01922-2818)
P.O. Box 320 (01922-0320)
PHONE..................................978 463-0665
Walter Harmer, *Owner*
EMP: 3
SALES: 500K **Privately Held**
SIC: 3544 Mfg Dies/Tools/Jigs/Fixtures

(G-9364)
R H SPENCER COMPANY
141 Main St (01922-1102)
P.O. Box 264 (01922-0264)
PHONE..................................978 463-0433
Shawn Spencer, *Owner*
EMP: 4 **EST:** 1965
SALES (est): 303K **Privately Held**
SIC: 3599 Mfg Industrial Machinery

(G-9365)
STARENSIER INC (PA)
Also Called: Cosmo
12 Kent Way Ste 201 (01922-1244)
P.O. Box 737 (01922-0737)
PHONE..................................978 462-7311
Richard Van Dernoot, *Ch of Bd*
Joshua Van Dernoot, *President*
Nicole Van Dernoot, *Manager*
▲ **EMP:** 10
SQ FT: 4,630
SALES (est): 2MM **Privately Held**
WEB: www.starensier.com
SIC: 2261 2262 2295 Cotton Finishing Plant Manmade Fiber & Silk Finishing Plant Mfg Coated Fabrics

Cambridge
Middlesex County

(G-9366)
24M TECHNOLOGIES INC
130 Brookline St Ste 200 (02139-4505)
PHONE..................................617 553-1012
Richard Feldt, *President*
Jeff Disko, *Research*
Yet-Ming Chiang, *Treasurer*
Fergus Ryan, *Controller*
Caren Devetto, *Office Mgr*
▲ **EMP:** 6
SQ FT: 10,000
SALES (est): 2.1MM **Privately Held**
SIC: 3691 Mfg Storage Batteries

(G-9367)
3DM INC
Also Called: 3d-Matrix
245 1st St (02142-1200)
P.O. Box 425025 (02142-0001)
PHONE..................................617 875-6204
Keiji Nagano, *President*
Alex Rich MD, *Chairman*
Conor M Joyce, *Project Mgr*
Karl Gilbert, *Technician*
EMP: 8
SALES (est): 1.1MM **Privately Held**
SIC: 2836 Mfg Biological Products

(G-9368)
AASTROM BIOSCIENCES INC
64 Sidney St (02139-4170)
PHONE..................................617 761-8642
EMP: 5
SALES (est): 422.1K **Privately Held**
SIC: 2834 Mfg Pharmaceutical Preparations

(G-9369)
ABBVIE INC
200 Sidney St (02139-4218)
PHONE..................................617 335-7640
EMP: 3
SALES (corp-wide): 32.7B **Publicly Held**
SIC: 2834 Mfg Pharmaceutical Preparations
PA: Abbvie Inc.
1 N Waukegan Rd
North Chicago IL 60064
847 932-7900

(G-9370)
ACCELERON PHARMA INC (PA)
128 Sidney St (02139-4239)
PHONE..................................617 649-9200
Francois Nader, *Ch of Bd*
EMP: 139
SQ FT: 99,000
SALES: 13.9MM **Publicly Held**
WEB: www.acceleronpharma.com
SIC: 2836 2834 Biological Products And Pharmaceutical Preparations

(G-9371)
ACENNA DATA INC
Also Called: Mimir Insights
10 Harvey St (02140-1830)
P.O. Box 400507 (02140-0006)
PHONE..................................443 878-9292
EMP: 6 **EST:** 2016
SALES (est): 180.1K **Privately Held**
SIC: 7372 Prepackaged Software

(G-9372)
ACUSPHERE INC
38 Sidney St (02139-4169)
PHONE..................................617 577-8800
Sherri C Oberg, *President*
EMP: 3
SALES (est): 158.8K **Publicly Held**
WEB: www.acusphere.com
SIC: 2834 Mfg Pharmaceutical Preparations
PA: Acusphere, Inc.
99 Hayden Ave Ste 1
Lexington MA 02421

(G-9373)
ADAPTIVE SURFACE TECH INC
Also Called: AST
85 Bolton St Ste 122 (02140-3367)
PHONE..................................617 360-7080
Daniel Behr, *CEO*
Joseph Lomakin, *Research*
Reena Paink, *Research*
Grant Tremelling, *Engineer*
EMP: 7 **EST:** 2014
SQ FT: 1,000
SALES: 500K **Privately Held**
SIC: 2899 Mfg Chemical Preparations

(G-9374)
ADVANCED DIAMOND SOLUTIONS INC
12 Inman St Apt 15 (02139-2413)
PHONE..................................617 291-3497
James Sung, *President*
Barnas Monteith, *Vice Pres*
Mike Sung, *Vice Pres*
EMP: 3
SALES (est): 290K **Privately Held**
WEB: www.advanceddiamond.com
SIC: 3624 Mfg Carbon/Graphite Products

(G-9375)
AEGERION PHARMACEUTICALS INC (HQ)
245 1st St Ste 18 (02142-1292)
PHONE..................................877 764-3131
Joe Wiley, *CEO*
John Orloff, *Exec VP*
Michael Eging, *Vice Pres*
Clinton Gilliam, *Vice Pres*
Roger Louis, *Vice Pres*
EMP: 12
SQ FT: 62,271
SALES (est): 215.9MM **Privately Held**
WEB: www.aegerionpharmaceuticals.com
SIC: 2834 Mfg Pharmaceutical Preparations

(G-9376)
AFFINITY PROJECT INC
3 Concord Ave (02138-3627)
PHONE..................................202 841-4011
Ron Suskind, *CEO*
Joan Nevins, *CFO*
EMP: 5
SALES (est): 300.6K **Privately Held**
SIC: 7372 Prepackaged Software Services

(G-9377)
AGIOS PHARMACEUTICALS INC (PA)
88 Sidney St (02139-4137)
PHONE..................................617 649-8600
John M Maraganore, *Ch of Bd*
David P Schenkein, *President*
Orlando Oliveira, *Senior VP*
Michael Giorgetti, *Vice Pres*
Michael Landine, *Vice Pres*
EMP: 124
SQ FT: 146,030
SALES: 94.3MM **Publicly Held**
SIC: 2834 8731 Pharmaceutical Preparations Biotechnical Research

(G-9378)
AKAMAI TECHNOLOGIES INC (PA)
145 Broadway (02142-1058)
PHONE..................................617 444-3000
F Thomson Leighton, *CEO*
Adam Karon, *Senior VP*
Bill Wheaton, *Security Dir*
▲ **EMP:** 500 **EST:** 1998
SQ FT: 480,000
SALES: 2.7B **Publicly Held**
WEB: www.akamai.com
SIC: 7372 7374 Prepackaged Software Services Data Processing/Preparation

(G-9379)
AKEBIA THERAPEUTICS INC (PA)
245 1st St Ste 1400 (02142-1292)
PHONE..................................617 871-2098
Muneer Satter, *Ch of Bd*
John P Butler, *President*
Brad Maroni, *Senior VP*
Nicole R Hadas, *Vice Pres*
Jason A Amello, *CFO*
EMP: 58
SQ FT: 39,411
SALES: 207.7MM **Publicly Held**
SIC: 2834 2836 8731 Pharmaceutical Preparations

(G-9380)
AKRIVIS TECHNOLOGIES LLC
1 Broadway Fl 14 (02142-1187)
PHONE..................................617 233-4097
Joel A Berniac,
EMP: 3
SALES (est): 444.8K **Privately Held**
SIC: 2835 Mfg Diagnostic Substances

(G-9381)
ALINEA PHARMACEUTICALS INC
101 Main St Ste 182 (02142-1532)
PHONE..................................617 500-7867
Robert Mashal, *President*
Andrew Nichols, *Vice Pres*
EMP: 3
SALES: 150K **Privately Held**
WEB: www.alineapharma.com
SIC: 2834 Mfg Pharmaceutical Preparations

(G-9382)
ALNARA PHARMACEUTICALS INC
840 Memorial Dr (02139-3789)
PHONE..................................617 349-3690
Alexey Margolin PHD, *President*
EMP: 10
SALES (est): 959K
SALES (corp-wide): 24.5B **Publicly Held**
SIC: 2834 Mfg Pharmaceutical Preparations
PA: Eli Lilly And Company
Lilly Corporate Ctr
Indianapolis IN 46285
317 276-2000

(G-9383)
ALNYLAM PHARMACEUTICALS INC
Also Called: Alnylam Alewife Mfg Fcilty
665 Concord Ave (02138-1047)
PHONE..................................617 551-8200
Mark Johnson, *Manager*
EMP: 15

▲ = Import ▼=Export ◆ =Import/Export

SALES (corp-wide): 74.9MM **Publicly Held**
SIC: 2834 Mfg Pharmaceutical Preparations
PA: Alnylam Pharmaceuticals, Inc.
300 3rd St Ste 3
Cambridge MA 02142
617 551-8200

(G-9384)
ALNYLAM PHARMACEUTICALS INC (PA)
300 3rd St Ste 3 (02142-1106)
PHONE....617 551-8200
John M Maraganore, *CEO*
Michael W Bonney, *Ch of Bd*
Barry E Greene, *President*
Yvonne L Greenstreet, *COO*
Kelley Boucher, *Senior VP*
EMP: 215
SQ FT: 129,000
SALES: 74.9MM **Publicly Held**
WEB: www.alnylam.com
SIC: 2834 8731 Pharmaceutical Preparations And Biotechnical Research

(G-9385)
ALNYLAM US INC
300 3rd St Ste 3 (02142-1106)
PHONE....617 551-8200
John A Maraganore, *President*
Michael E Placke, *Senior VP*
John Kyranos, *Vice Pres*
Christine Lindenboom, *Vice Pres*
Don Foster, *Research*
EMP: 25
SALES (est): 5.7MM
SALES (corp-wide): 74.9MM **Publicly Held**
WEB: www.alnylam.com
SIC: 2834 Mfg Pharmaceutical Preparations
PA: Alnylam Pharmaceuticals, Inc.
300 3rd St Ste 3
Cambridge MA 02142
617 551-8200

(G-9386)
AMALGAMATED TITANIUM INTL CORP
94 Hampshire St Apt C (02139-1761)
PHONE....617 395-7700
David Lamoureux, *CEO*
Gregory White, *Senior VP*
EMP: 11 **EST:** 2012
SALES (est): 850K **Privately Held**
SIC: 3949 7389 Mfg Sporting/Athletic Goods

(G-9387)
AMERICAN ACADEMY ARTS SCIENCES
Daedalus Journal
136 Irving St (02138-1996)
PHONE....617 491-2600
James Miller, *Manager*
EMP: 3
SALES (corp-wide): 9.2MM **Privately Held**
SIC: 2721 Periodicals-Publishing/Printing
PA: American Academy Of Arts & Sciences
136 Irving St
Cambridge MA 02138
617 441-6100

(G-9388)
AMGEN INC
360 Binney St (02142-1011)
PHONE....617 444-5000
John Dunlop, *Vice Pres*
Aine Hanly, *Vice Pres*
Virginia Berry, *Research*
Doris Glykys, *Engineer*
Alexander Macgrogan, *Engineer*
EMP: 40
SALES (corp-wide): 23.7B **Publicly Held**
WEB: www.amgen.com
SIC: 2836 Mfg Pharmaceutical Preparations
PA: Amgen Inc.
1 Amgen Center Dr
Thousand Oaks CA 91320
805 447-1000

(G-9389)
AMS QI INC
1 Broadway Fl 14 (02142-1187)
PHONE....617 797-4709
Naftaly Menn, *CEO*
Noan Josethy, *Shareholder*
Joseph Krimerman, *Shareholder*
EMP: 5
SALES: 51.9K **Privately Held**
SIC: 3674 3827 Mfg Semiconductors/Related Devices Mfg Optical Instruments/Lenses

(G-9390)
ANTI-PHISHING WKG GROUP INC
38 Rice St Ste 200 (02140-1817)
PHONE....404 434-7282
David Jevans, *President*
Nicholas W Bradford, *Director*
EMP: 4
SALES: 606.8K **Privately Held**
SIC: 2731 Books-Publishing/Printing

(G-9391)
ARCHITEXA INC
1035 Cambridge St Ste 1 (02141-1154)
PHONE....617 500-7391
Vineet Sinha, *CEO*
Abhishek Rakshit, *Software Engr*
EMP: 5
SALES: 410K **Privately Held**
SIC: 7372 Prepackaged Software Services

(G-9392)
ARIAD PHARMACEUTICALS INC
40 Landsdowne St (02139-4234)
PHONE....617 494-0400
Harvey J Berger, *Ch of Bd*
Alexander J Denner, *Ch of Bd*
Timothy P Clackson, *President*
Paris Panayiotopoulos, *President*
Maria Cantor, *Vice Pres*
EMP: 459
SQ FT: 100,000
SALES: 118.8MM **Privately Held**
WEB: www.ariad.com
SIC: 2836 8731 Manufacturer Of Biological Products And Commercial Physical Research
PA: Takeda Pharmaceutical Company Limited
2-1-1, Nihombashihoncho
Chuo-Ku TKY 103-0

(G-9393)
ASCEND ROBOTICS LLC
245 First St Ste 18 (02142-1292)
PHONE....978 451-0170
David Askey, *Mng Member*
EMP: 18
SALES: 17.7MM **Privately Held**
SIC: 3535 Mfg Conveyors/Equipment

(G-9394)
ASHAMETRICS INC
1035 Cambridge St Ste 8 (02141-1154)
PHONE....617 694-1428
EMP: 3
SALES: 150K **Privately Held**
SIC: 3845 Electromedical Equipment

(G-9395)
ASIMOV INC
700 Main St (02139-3543)
PHONE....425 750-4182
Alec Nielsen, *CEO*
EMP: 25
SALES (est): 1.6MM **Privately Held**
SIC: 2835 Mfg Diagnostic Substances

(G-9396)
ASPMD
38 8th St Apt 5 (02141-1525)
PHONE....617 864-6844
Chris Kreis, *President*
EMP: 5
SALES (est): 493.2K **Privately Held**
SIC: 7372 Application Service Provider For Physcians

(G-9397)
AURORA FLIGHT SCIENCES CORP
150 Cambridgepark Dr Fl 4 (02140-2370)
PHONE....617 500-4800
Tom Vaneck, *Manager*
EMP: 12
SALES (corp-wide): 101.1B **Publicly Held**
SIC: 3721 Mfg Aircraft
HQ: Aurora Flight Sciences Corp
9950 Wakeman Dr
Manassas VA 20110
703 369-3633

(G-9398)
AVEO PHARMACEUTICALS INC
12 Emily St (02139-4507)
PHONE....617 299-5000
EMP: 10
SALES (corp-wide): 19MM **Publicly Held**
SIC: 2834 Pharmaceutical Preparations
PA: Aveo Pharmaceuticals, Inc.
1 Broadway Fl 14
Cambridge MA 02142
617 588-1960

(G-9399)
AVEO PHARMACEUTICALS INC (PA)
1 Broadway Fl 14 (02142-1187)
PHONE....617 588-1960
Michael P Bailey, *President*
Nikhil Mehta, *Senior VP*
Karuna Rubin, *Senior VP*
Matthew Dallas, *CFO*
Michael N Needle, *Chief Mktg Ofcr*
EMP: 17
SQ FT: 3,000
SALES: 5.4MM **Publicly Held**
WEB: www.aveopharma.com
SIC: 2834 Pharmaceutical Preparations

(G-9400)
AVEO SECURITIES CORPORATION
1 Broadway Fl 14 (02142-1187)
PHONE....617 588-1960
Michael P Bailey, *President*
EMP: 5
SALES (est): 152.2K
SALES (corp-wide): 5.4MM **Publicly Held**
SIC: 2834 Mfg Pharmaceutical Preparations
PA: Aveo Pharmaceuticals, Inc.
1 Broadway Fl 14
Cambridge MA 02142
617 588-1960

(G-9401)
AVROBIO INC (PA)
1 Kendall Sq Ste B2001 (02139-1593)
PHONE....617 914-8420
Bruce Booth, *Ch of Bd*
Geoff Mackay, *President*
Katina Dorton, *CFO*
Nerissa Kreher, *Chief Mktg Ofcr*
Lisamarie Fahy, *Exec Dir*
EMP: 36
SQ FT: 11,218
SALES (est): 7.3MM **Publicly Held**
SIC: 2834 Pharmaceutical Preparations

(G-9402)
BARRETT TECHNOLOGY INC
139 Main St (02142-1530)
PHONE....617 252-9000
William T Townsend, *Principal*
EMP: 3 **EST:** 2011
SALES (est): 399.5K **Privately Held**
SIC: 3535 Mfg Conveyors/Equipment

(G-9403)
BASHO TECHNOLOGIES INC (PA)
485 Msschsetts Ave Ste 1a (02139)
PHONE....617 714-1700
Adam Wray, *CEO*
Earl Galleher, *Ch of Bd*
Donald J Rippert, *President*
Peter Coppola, *Vice Pres*
Marisa Linardos, *Vice Pres*
EMP: 20
SQ FT: 10,000
SALES (est): 2.3MM **Privately Held**
WEB: www.basho.com
SIC: 7372 Prepackaged Software Services

(G-9404)
BASIS TECHNOLOGY CORPORATION
101 Main St Ste 1400 (02142-1527)
PHONE....617 386-2000
Carl W Hoffman, *Chairman*
EMP: 3 **Privately Held**
SIC: 7372 Prepackaged Software Services
PA: Basis Technology Corporation
1 Alewife Ctr Ste 400
Cambridge MA 02140

(G-9405)
BAXALTA US INC
650 Kendall Dr (02142)
PHONE....312 656-8021
Michael Shires, *Vice Pres*
Carter Clanton, *Marketing Staff*
EMP: 10
SALES (corp-wide): 15.1B **Privately Held**
SIC: 2834 Mfg Pharmaceutical Preparations
HQ: Baxalta Us Inc.
1200 Lakeside Dr
Bannockburn IL 60015
224 948-2000

(G-9406)
BB WALPOLE LIQUIDATION NH INC
52d Brattle St (02138-3731)
PHONE....617 491-4340
Larry Burdick, *Owner*
EMP: 22
SALES (est): 1.6MM **Privately Held**
SIC: 2066 5441 Mfg Chocolate/Cocoa Products Ret Candy/Confectionery
PA: Bb Walpole Liquidation Nh, Inc.
47 Main St Unit 1
Walpole NH 03608

(G-9407)
BEIGENE USA INC (HQ)
55 Cambrdge Pkwy Ste 700w (02142)
PHONE....781 801-1887
John Oyler, *CEO*
Ji Li, *Exec VP*
Dan Maller, *Vice Pres*
Jane Huang, *Chief Mktg Ofcr*
Amy Peterson, *Chief Mktg Ofcr*
EMP: 6
SALES (est): 2.1MM **Privately Held**
SIC: 2834 5122 8731 Mfg Pharmaceutical Preparations Whol Drugs/Sundries Commercial Physical Research

(G-9408)
BIOANALYTIX INC
Also Called: Accelerating Biologics
790 Memorial Dr (02139-4648)
PHONE....857 829-3200
Kirtland Poss, *President*
John Ziolkowski, *CFO*
EMP: 6 **EST:** 2013
SALES (est): 965.2K **Privately Held**
SIC: 2836 Mfg Biological Products

(G-9409)
BIOGEN INC (PA)
225 Binney St (02142-1031)
P.O. Box 425025 (02142-0001)
PHONE....617 679-2000
Michel Vounatsos, *CEO*
◆ **EMP:** 348
SQ FT: 800,000
SALES: 13.4B **Publicly Held**
WEB: www.idecpharm.com
SIC: 2834 2836 8731 Pharmaceutical Preparations Biological Products & Research

(G-9410)
BIOGEN MA INC (HQ)
225 Binney St (02142-1031)
PHONE....617 679-2000
George A Scangos, *CEO*
Susan H Alexander, *Exec VP*
John G Cox, *Exec VP*
Kenneth Dipietro, *Exec VP*
Steven H Holtzman, *Exec VP*

▲ **EMP:** 180
SQ FT: 150,000
SALES (est): 190.7MM
SALES (corp-wide): 13.4B **Publicly Held**
WEB: www.biogen.com
SIC: 2836 8731 Mfg Biological Products Commercial Physical Research
PA: Biogen Inc.
225 Binney St
Cambridge MA 02142
617 679-2000

(G-9411)
BIONX MEDICAL TECHNOLOGIES INC
Also Called: Biom
27 Moulton St (02138-1118)
PHONE....................................781 761-1545
Charles Carignan, *CEO*
Geoff Pardo, *Ch of Bd*
Mark Chiappetta, *Senior VP*
David Reissfelder, *CFO*
EMP: 51
SQ FT: 1,900
SALES (est): 8.3MM
SALES (corp-wide): 1.1B **Privately Held**
WEB: www.iwalkpro.com
SIC: 3842 Mfg Surgical Appliances/Supplies
HQ: Ottobock Se & Co. Kgaa
Max-Nader-Str. 15
Duderstadt 37115
552 784-80

(G-9412)
BLUEPRINT MEDICINES CORP (PA)
45 Sidney St (02139-4133)
PHONE....................................617 374-7580
Daniel S Lynch, *Ch of Bd*
Jeffrey W Albers, *President*
Christopher K Murray, *Senior VP*
Helen Ho, *Vice Pres*
Christopher Turner, *Vice Pres*
EMP: 120
SQ FT: 99,833
SALES: 44.5MM **Publicly Held**
SIC: 2834 Pharmaceutical Preparations

(G-9413)
BOC GASSES AT MIT
77 Massachusetts Ave 22 (02139-4301)
PHONE....................................617 374-9992
John Jordan, *Principal*
EMP: 3
SALES (est): 374.5K **Privately Held**
SIC: 2813 Mfg Industrial Gases

(G-9414)
BONAPP
14 Story St (02138-4955)
PHONE....................................917 488-5202
Laurent Adamowicz, *President*
EMP: 4
SALES (est): 164.6K **Privately Held**
SIC: 7372 Prepackaged Software Services

(G-9415)
BOSTON BIOCHEM INC
840 Memorial Dr Ste 3 (02139-3771)
PHONE....................................617 241-7072
Francesco Melandri, *President*
EMP: 8
SALES (est): 1.2MM
SALES (corp-wide): 714MM **Publicly Held**
WEB: www.bostonbiochem.com
SIC: 2836 Mfg Biological Products
HQ: Research And Diagnostic Systems, Inc.
614 Mckinley Pl Ne
Minneapolis MN 55413
612 379-2956

(G-9416)
BOSTON BIOMEDICAL PHARMA INC
640 Memorial Dr (02139-4853)
PHONE....................................617 674-6800
EMP: 6
SALES (est): 821.9K
SALES (corp-wide): 20.5B **Privately Held**
SIC: 2834 Mfg Pharmaceutical Preparations
HQ: Dainippon Sumitomo Pharma America Holdings Inc.
1 Bridge Plz N Ste 510
Fort Lee NJ 07024

(G-9417)
BOSTON CHINESE NEWS INC
1105 Mass Ave Apt 3e (02138-5221)
PHONE....................................617 354-4154
EMP: 4
SALES (est): 180K **Privately Held**
SIC: 2711 Newspapers-Publishing/Printing

(G-9418)
BOSTON CRITIC INC
Also Called: BOSTON REVIEW
30 Wadsworth St (02142-1320)
P.O. Box 425786 (02142-0015)
PHONE....................................617 324-1360
Joshua Cohen, *President*
Katherine Ablutz, *Principal*
EMP: 4
SALES: 788.9K **Privately Held**
SIC: 2721 Periodicals-Publishing/Printing

(G-9419)
BOSTON MICROFLUIDICS INC
125 Cambridgepark Dr # 101 (02140-2393)
PHONE....................................857 239-9665
Brandon T Johnson, *CEO*
Sarah Kalil, *COO*
Bill Frezza, *Vice Pres*
EMP: 20
SALES (est): 966.9K **Privately Held**
SIC: 3845 Whol Medical/Hospital Equipment

(G-9420)
BOSTON ONCOLOGY LLC
245 First St Ste 1800 (02142-1292)
PHONE....................................857 209-5052
Abdullah Baaj, *Mng Member*
EMP: 5
SALES (est): 450.8K **Privately Held**
SIC: 2834 Mfg Pharmaceutical Preparations

(G-9421)
BOTIFY CORPORATION
185 Alewife Brook Pkwy (02138-1100)
PHONE....................................617 576-2005
Adrien Menard, *President*
EMP: 8 **EST:** 2015
SALES (est): 247.7K
SALES (corp-wide): 247.3K **Privately Held**
SIC: 7372 Prepackaged Software Services
PA: Botify
15 Rue De Laborde
Paris 8e Arrondissement 75002
183 629-078

(G-9422)
BRING UP INC
618 Cambridge St (02141-1123)
PHONE....................................617 803-4248
Eduardo Varela, *CEO*
EMP: 5
SALES (est): 117.2K **Privately Held**
SIC: 7372 7389 Prepackaged Software Services Business Serv Non-Commercial Site

(G-9423)
BRISTOL MYERS SQUIBB
100 Binney St (02142-1096)
PHONE....................................781 209-2309
EMP: 3
SALES (est): 290.6K **Privately Held**
SIC: 2621 Mfg Pharmaceutical Preparations

(G-9424)
C5BIO
69 Chestnut St (02139-4835)
PHONE....................................617 955-4626
Deepak Dugar, *Principal*
EMP: 3
SALES (est): 114.6K **Privately Held**
SIC: 2869 Mfg Industrial Organic Chemicals

(G-9425)
CAMBRIDGE BRANDS MFG INC
810 Main St (02139-3588)
PHONE....................................617 491-2500
Ellen R Gordon, *President*
Paula Yetman, *Opers Mgr*
EMP: 200
SALES (corp-wide): 518.9MM **Publicly Held**
SIC: 2064 2066 Mfg Candy/Confectionery Mfg Chocolate/Cocoa Products
HQ: Cambridge Brands Manufacturing, Inc.
7401 S Cicero Ave
Chicago IL 60629

(G-9426)
CAMBRIDGE BREWING CO INC
1 Kendall Sq Ste B1102 (02139-1592)
PHONE....................................617 494-1994
Phillip C Bannatyne, *President*
EMP: 45
SQ FT: 4,000
SALES (est): 5.5MM **Privately Held**
WEB: www.cambrew.com
SIC: 2082 5812 Brewery & Restaurant

(G-9427)
CAMBRIDGE PRINTING CO INC
47 7th St (02141-2144)
PHONE....................................617 547-0270
Anthony Miano, *President*
Joseph Maranto, *Vice Pres*
EMP: 4
SQ FT: 1,500
SALES (est): 629.9K **Privately Held**
SIC: 2752 2759 Offset & Letterpress Printing

(G-9428)
CARDURION PHARMACEUTICALS INC
350 Mssachusetts Ave Fl 3 Flr 3 (02139)
PHONE....................................617 863-8088
Daniel Bloomfield, *CEO*
Michael Mendelsohn, *Chairman*
Rebecca Frey, *COO*
EMP: 4
SALES (est): 190.1K **Privately Held**
SIC: 2834 Mfg Pharmaceutical Preparations

(G-9429)
CASMA THERAPEUTICS INC
400 Technology Sq Ste 201 (02139-3583)
PHONE....................................857 777-4248
Frank Gentile, *COO*
Daniel Ory, *Senior VP*
Jeffrey Saunders, *Senior VP*
Caren Block, *Vice Pres*
EMP: 18
SALES (est): 4.7MM **Privately Held**
SIC: 2834 Mfg Pharmaceutical Preparations

(G-9430)
CATABASIS PHARMACEUTICALS INC
1 Kendall Sq Ste B14202 (02139-1573)
PHONE....................................617 349-1971
Jill C Milne, *President*
Deirdre A Cunnane, *Senior VP*
Ted Hibben, *Senior VP*
Leslie Cowen, *Research*
Andrew A Komjathy, *CFO*
EMP: 37
SQ FT: 19,000
SALES: 500K **Privately Held**
SIC: 2834 Pharmaceutical Preparations

(G-9431)
CEDILLA THERAPEUTICS INC
38 Sidney St Ste 200 (02139-4169)
PHONE....................................617 581-9333
Alexandra Glucksmann, *President*
Delphine Collin, *Vice Pres*
Colleen Desimone, *Finance*
EMP: 10
SALES (est): 1.6MM **Privately Held**
SIC: 2834 Mfg Pharmaceutical Preparations

(G-9432)
CELGENE AVILOMICS RESEARCH INC
200 Cambridgepark Dr (02140-2307)
PHONE....................................857 706-1311
EMP: 11
SALES (est): 2MM **Privately Held**
SIC: 2834 Mfg Pharmaceutical Preparations

(G-9433)
CELL PRESS INC
50 Hampshire St (02139-1548)
PHONE....................................617 397-2800
Lynne Herndon, *CEO*
▲ **EMP:** 60
SALES (est): 4.2MM
SALES (corp-wide): 9.8B **Privately Held**
WEB: www.cell.com
SIC: 2721 Periodicals-Publishing/Printing
HQ: Elsevier Inc.
230 Park Ave Fl 8
New York NY 10169
212 989-5800

(G-9434)
CELLAY LLC
100 Inman St Ste 207 (02139-1295)
PHONE....................................617 995-1307
Edward O'Lear,
EMP: 10
SALES (est): 1MM **Privately Held**
SIC: 2835 Mfg Diagnostic Substances

(G-9435)
CERENOVA INC
11 Douglas St (02139-3403)
PHONE....................................715 212-2595
Christian Wentz, *President*
EMP: 3
SALES (est): 161.6K **Privately Held**
SIC: 3845 Mfg Electromedical Equipment

(G-9436)
CHANG SHING TOFU INC
37 Rogers St (02142-1511)
PHONE....................................617 868-8878
Albert Dao, *President*
Kathy Huynh, *Treasurer*
▲ **EMP:** 7
SQ FT: 16,679
SALES (est): 880K **Privately Held**
SIC: 2099 Mfg Food Preparations

(G-9437)
CHANGE WATER LABS INC
413 Broadway (02138-4278)
PHONE....................................917 292-5160
Diana Yousef, *CEO*
EMP: 4 **EST:** 2015
SALES: 2MM **Privately Held**
SIC: 3589 Mfg Service Industry Machinery

(G-9438)
CIRCLET PRESS INC
1770 Mass Ave Ste 278 (02140-2808)
PHONE....................................617 864-0663
Cecilia Tan, *President*
Jonathan Coburn, *Corp Secy*
EMP: 3
SALES: 45K **Privately Held**
WEB: www.circlet.com
SIC: 2731 5942 Books-Publishing/Printing Ret Books

(G-9439)
COLUCID PHARMACEUTICALS INC
222 3rd St Ste 1320 (02142-1188)
P.O. Box 14401, Durham NC (27709-4401)
PHONE....................................857 285-6495
Thomas P Mathers, *CEO*
Matthew D Dallas, *CFO*
EMP: 7
SQ FT: 2,455
SALES (est): 1MM
SALES (corp-wide): 24.5B **Publicly Held**
SIC: 2834 Manufactures Pharmaceutical Preparations
PA: Eli Lilly And Company
Lilly Corporate Ctr
Indianapolis IN 46285
317 276-2000

(G-9440)
CONSTELLATION DIAGNOSTICS INC
700 Main St (02139-3543)
PHONE..................................617 233-4554
Christian Bailey, *Principal*
Anna Gannon, *Principal*
EMP: 5 **EST:** 2014
SALES (est): 270K **Privately Held**
SIC: 7372 Prepackaged Software Services

(G-9441)
CONSTLLTION PHRMACEUTICALS INC
215 1st St Ste 200 (02142-1293)
PHONE..................................617 714-0555
Mark A Goldsmith, *Ch of Bd*
Jigar Raythatha, *President*
John McGrath, *Research*
Emma Reeve, *CFO*
Adrian Senderowicz, *Chief Mktg Ofcr*
EMP: 64
SQ FT: 36,309
SALES (est): 19.5MM **Privately Held**
SIC: 2834 Pharmaceutical Preparations

(G-9442)
CONTEXT LABS INC
222 3rd St Ste 2242 (02142-1122)
PHONE..................................617 902-0932
EMP: 20 **EST:** 2012
SQ FT: 2,500
SALES (est): 13.5MM
SALES (corp-wide): 155.2K **Privately Held**
SIC: 3825 Mfg Electrical Measuring Instruments
HQ: Context Labs B.V.
Herengracht 25 A
Amsterdam

(G-9443)
CORDENPHARMA
500 Kendall St (02142-1108)
PHONE..................................617 401-2828
Karen Praisner, *President*
EMP: 3
SALES (est): 186.2K **Privately Held**
SIC: 2834 Mfg Pharmaceutical Preparations

(G-9444)
CREW BY TRUE ROWING INC
243 Bent St Apt 5 (02141-2092)
PHONE..................................617 398-7480
Chris Paul, *CTO*
Bruce Smith,
EMP: 9
SALES (est): 204.2K **Privately Held**
SIC: 7372 Prepackaged Software Services

(G-9445)
CRIMSONBIKES LLC
1001 Mass Ave Ste 1 (02138-5327)
PHONE..................................617 958-1727
Charles James,
EMP: 25
SALES (est): 1.3MM **Privately Held**
SIC: 3751 Mfg Motorcycles/Bicycles

(G-9446)
CUE BIOPHARMA INC (PA)
21 Erie St Ste 1 (02139-4223)
PHONE..................................617 949-2680
Barry Simon, *Ch of Bd*
Daniel R Passeri, *President*
Anish Suri, *President*
Colin G Sandercock, *Senior VP*
Kerri-Ann Millar, *VP Finance*
EMP: 27
SQ FT: 19,800
SALES: 1.1MM **Publicly Held**
SIC: 2834 Mfg Pharmaceutical Preparations

(G-9447)
CYCLERION THERAPEUTICS INC (PA)
301 Binney St (02142-1071)
PHONE..................................857 327-8778
Peter M Hecht, *CEO*
Mark G Currie, *President*
William Huyett, *CFO*
EMP: 8
SQ FT: 114,000
SALES (est): 22.7MM **Publicly Held**
SIC: 2834 Pharmaceutical Preparations

(G-9448)
DAEDALUS SOFTWARE INC
215 First St Ste 7 (02142-1213)
P.O. Box 425857 (02142-0016)
PHONE..................................617 851-5157
Azita Sharif, *CEO*
Imran Zahid, *Sr Software Eng*
Scott Stockholm, *Director*
EMP: 25
SQ FT: 4,000
SALES (est): 2MM **Privately Held**
WEB: www.daedalussoftware.com
SIC: 7372 Prepackaged Software Services

(G-9449)
DAKTARI DIAGNOSTICS INC
85 Bolton St Ste 229 (02140-3370)
PHONE..................................617 336-3299
Donald B Hawthorne, *President*
Gorman Matt, *Admin Asst*
EMP: 13
SALES (est): 3.3MM **Privately Held**
SIC: 2835 Mfg Diagnostic Substances

(G-9450)
DANCE PAWS LLC
82 Normandy Ave (02138-1017)
PHONE..................................617 945-3044
Elizabeth Feigenbaum, *Risk Mgmt Dir*
EMP: 3
SALES (est): 303K **Privately Held**
SIC: 3021 Mfg And Ret Dancer Foot Protection

(G-9451)
DARK MATTER CHOCOLATE LLC
407 Washington St (02139-2720)
PHONE..................................303 718-3835
Paul Weaver,
EMP: 4
SALES: 100K **Privately Held**
SIC: 2066 Mfg Chocolate/Cocoa Products

(G-9452)
DEMIURGE GAME DEVELOPMENT LLC
130 Prospect St (02139-1844)
PHONE..................................617 354-7772
Albert Reed, *Partner*
William Reed, *Partner*
Albert J Reed, *Principal*
EMP: 25 **EST:** 2011
SALES (est): 847.1K **Privately Held**
SIC: 7372 Prepackaged Software Services

(G-9453)
DESTRAIL
45 Museum St Apt D (02138-1921)
PHONE..................................818 687-7037
Daniel Wallman, *Director*
EMP: 3
SALES (est): 86.5K **Privately Held**
SIC: 2741 Misc Publishing

(G-9454)
DIVLAN INC
Also Called: Seratis
69 Harvey St Apt 1 (02140-1703)
PHONE..................................347 338-8843
EMP: 3
SQ FT: 100
SALES (est): 180K **Privately Held**
SIC: 7372 Prepackaged Software Services

(G-9455)
DJD ENTERPRISES LLC
330 Columbia St (02141-1310)
PHONE..................................617 803-6875
David D Chaves,
EMP: 3
SALES (est): 81.8K **Privately Held**
SIC: 2834 Mfg Pharmaceutical Preparations

(G-9456)
DOORBELL INC
Also Called: Doorbell.me
10 Holyoke Pl 277 (02138-5006)
PHONE..................................516 375-5507
Benjamin Pleat, *CEO*
Steven Petteruti, *Chief Engr*
EMP: 3
SALES (est): 71.1K **Privately Held**
SIC: 7372 Prepackaged Software Services

(G-9457)
DROPWISE TECHNOLOGIES CORP
1035 Cambridge St Ste 15b (02141-1154)
PHONE..................................617 945-5180
Adam Paxson, *CEO*
EMP: 3
SALES (est): 480.2K **Privately Held**
SIC: 2899 Mfg Chemical Preparations

(G-9458)
EDITAS MEDICINE INC
11 Hurley St (02141-2110)
PHONE..................................617 401-9000
James C Mullen, *Ch of Bd*
Cynthia Collins, *President*
Alexandra Glucksmann, *COO*
Harry Gill, *Senior VP*
Richard A Morgan, *Senior VP*
EMP: 89
SQ FT: 59,783
SALES: 31.9MM **Privately Held**
SIC: 2836 Biological Products

(G-9459)
EIP PHARMA INC
210 Broadway Ste 201 (02139-1959)
PHONE..................................617 945-9146
John Alam, *Principal*
Kevin Sarney, *Vice Pres*
Noel Donnelly, *CFO*
EMP: 7
SALES (est): 451.8K **Privately Held**
SIC: 2834 Mfg Pharmaceutical Preparations

(G-9460)
EISAI INC
35 Cambridgepark Dr # 200 (02140-2325)
PHONE..................................978 837-4616
Frank Fang, *Vice Pres*
Zhihong Chen, *Research*
Heather Percy, *Sales Mgr*
Frank Aiesi, *Branch Mgr*
Kathleen Ranney, *Branch Mgr*
EMP: 21 **Privately Held**
SIC: 2834 Mfg Pharmaceutical Preparations
HQ: Eisai Inc.
100 Tice Blvd
Woodcliff Lake NJ 07677
201 692-1100

(G-9461)
ELAN PHARMA
300 Technology Sq Ste 3 (02139-3520)
PHONE..................................415 885-6780
Pamela Kong, *Analyst*
EMP: 8
SALES (est): 995.9K **Privately Held**
SIC: 2834 Mfg Pharmaceutical Preparations
PA: Perrigo Company Public Limited Company
Treasury Building
Dublin 2

(G-9462)
ELI LILLY AND COMPANY
450 Kendall St Fl 3 (02142-1227)
PHONE..................................317 209-6287
EMP: 3
SALES (est): 192.6K **Privately Held**
SIC: 2834 Mfg Pharmaceutical Preparations

(G-9463)
ELICIO THERAPEUTICS INC
1 Kendall Sq Bldg 1400w (02139-1562)
PHONE..................................617 945-2077
Robert Connelly, *CEO*
Julian Adams, *Ch of Bd*
Christopher Haqq, *Exec VP*
Charles Chase, *Vice Pres*
Peter Demuth, *Vice Pres*
EMP: 4
SALES (est): 483.7K **Privately Held**
SIC: 2836 Mfg Biological Products

(G-9464)
ELSEVIER INC
50 Hampshire St Fl 5 (02139-1548)
PHONE..................................781 663-5200
Leah Berry, *Human Resources*
EMP: 90
SALES (corp-wide): 9.8B **Privately Held**
WEB: www.elsevierfoundation.org
SIC: 2741 Misc Publishing
HQ: Elsevier Inc.
230 Park Ave Fl 8
New York NY 10169
212 989-5800

(G-9465)
EMRI SYSTEMS LLP
41 Kinnaird St (02139-3267)
PHONE..................................617 417-9798
Hernan Millan, *Partner*
Giorgio Bonmassar, *Partner*
Ping Chen, *Manager*
EMP: 4
SALES: 1MM **Privately Held**
SIC: 3845 7389 Mfg Electromedical Equipment Business Serv Non-Commercial Site

(G-9466)
ENCHANTED WORLD BOXES INC
445 Concord Ave (02138-1216)
PHONE..................................617 492-6941
Teresa Witkowska, *President*
Krzysztof Kowalski, *Treasurer*
▲ **EMP:** 4
SALES (est): 596.3K **Privately Held**
WEB: www.enchantedboxes.com
SIC: 3553 Whol Nondurable Goods

(G-9467)
EOS IMAGING INC
185 Alewife Brook Pkwy # 205
(02138-1104)
PHONE..................................678 564-5400
Gisela Bryant, *Opers Mgr*
EMP: 12
SQ FT: 200 **Privately Held**
WEB: www.biospacelab.com
SIC: 3841 Mfg Surgical/Medical Instruments
PA: Eos Imaging
10 Rue Mercoeur
Paris 11e Arrondissement 75011

(G-9468)
EOS PHOTONICS INC
30 Spinelli Pl Ste A (02138-1070)
PHONE..................................617 945-9137
Mark Witinski, *President*
Federico Capasso, *Chairman*
Laurent Diehl, *Vice Pres*
Christian Pfluegl, *Vice Pres*
EMP: 6
SALES (est): 1.2MM **Privately Held**
SIC: 3674 Mfg Semiconductors/Related Devices

(G-9469)
EPIZYME INC
400 Technology Sq Ste 4 (02139-3584)
PHONE..................................617 229-5872
David M Mott, *Ch of Bd*
Robert B Bazemore Jr, *President*
John Larus, *Vice Pres*
Kelli Armstrong, *Research*
Berent Lundeen, *Research*
EMP: 131
SQ FT: 43,066
SALES: 21.7MM **Privately Held**
SIC: 2834 8731 Pharmaceutical Preparations Commercial Physical Research

(G-9470)
EPOCH TIMES BOSTON-CHINESE
32 Oxford St (02138-1960)
P.O. Box 381426 (02238-1426)
PHONE..................................617 968-8019
Timothy Pl, *Principal*
EMP: 4 **EST:** 2010
SALES (est): 146K **Privately Held**
SIC: 2711 Newspapers-Publishing/Printing

GEOGRAPHIC

(G-9471)
ERA7 BIOINFORMATICS INC
Cic 14th Flr 1 Broadway (02142)
PHONE....................................617 576-2005
Eduardo Pareja, *President*
EMP: 3
SALES (est): 71.1K **Privately Held**
SIC: 7372 Prepackaged Software Services

(G-9472)
ERYTECH PHARMA INC
1 Main St Ste 300 (02142-1531)
PHONE....................................360 320-3325
Gil Beyen, *CEO*
Eric Soyer, *COO*
EMP: 6
SALES (est): 108.9K
SALES (corp-wide): 1.5MM **Privately Held**
SIC: 2834 Mfg Pharmaceutical Preparations
PA: Erytech Pharma
Batiment Adenine
Lyon 69008
478 744-438

(G-9473)
ETA DEVICES INC
245 First St (02142-1200)
PHONE....................................617 577-8300
Mattias Astrom, *CEO*
Gene Tkachenko, *Exec VP*
Joel Dawson, *CTO*
EMP: 20
SQ FT: 2,000
SALES (est): 1.4MM
SALES (corp-wide): 25B **Privately Held**
SIC: 3674 Manufactures Semiconductors/Related Devices
PA: Nokia Oyj
Karakaari 7
Espoo 02610
104 488-000

(G-9474)
EUSTIS ENTERPRISES INC
Also Called: Eustis Chair
431 Huron Ave (02138-2103)
PHONE....................................978 827-3103
Frederic George Eustis, *President*
EMP: 3
SQ FT: 30,000
SALES (est): 489.1K **Privately Held**
WEB: www.eustischair.com
SIC: 2511 5712 Mfg Wood Household Furniture Ret Furniture

(G-9475)
EXACT CHANGE
5 Brewster St (02138-2203)
PHONE....................................617 492-5405
Damon Krukowski, *Owner*
Deborah Krukowski, *Owner*
EMP: 3
SALES (est): 149.4K **Privately Held**
WEB: www.exactchange.com
SIC: 2731 5942 Books-Publishing/Printing Ret Books

(G-9476)
EXECUTIVE FORCE PROTECTION LLC
245 1st St Ste 1800 (02142-1292)
PHONE....................................617 470-9230
EMP: 11
SALES (est): 760K **Privately Held**
SIC: 3482 1541 8299 7376 Mfg Small Arms Ammo Industrial Bldg Cnstn School/Educational Svcs Computer Facility Mgmt Detective/Armor Car Svcs

(G-9477)
EYENETRA INC
2 James Way (02141-1434)
PHONE....................................973 229-3341
David Schafran, *President*
Vitor Pamplona, *Chief Engr*
Ramesh Raskar, *Bd of Directors*
EMP: 5 **EST:** 2011
SALES (est): 332.4K **Privately Held**
SIC: 3841 Mfg Surgical/Medical Instruments

(G-9478)
FINOMIAL CORPORATION (PA)
30 Kelley St (02138-1314)
PHONE....................................917 488-6050
Meredith Moss, *Principal*
EMP: 3
SALES (est): 618.2K **Privately Held**
SIC: 7372 Prepackaged Software Services

(G-9479)
FLEXCAR
25 1st St Ste 11 (02141-1826)
PHONE....................................617 995-4231
Steve Case, *President*
EMP: 3
SALES (est): 252.4K **Privately Held**
SIC: 3711 Mfg Motor Vehicle/Car Bodies

(G-9480)
FOG PHARMACEUTICALS INC
100 Acorn Park Dr Fl 6 (02140-2303)
PHONE....................................617 945-9510
Gregory Verdine, *President*
Milenko Cicmil, *Vice Pres*
Michael Hale, *Vice Pres*
Diana Chai, *Associate Dir*
EMP: 5
SALES (est): 294.9K **Privately Held**
SIC: 2834 Mfg Pharmaceutical Preparations

(G-9481)
FOG PHARMACEUTICALS INC
245 1st St (02142-1200)
PHONE....................................781 929-9187
EMP: 4 **EST:** 2016
SALES (est): 329.7K **Privately Held**
SIC: 2834 Mfg Pharmaceutical Preparations

(G-9482)
FULCRUM THERAPEUTICS INC
26 Landsdowne St Ste 525 (02139-4249)
PHONE....................................617 651-8851
Robert J Gould, *President*
Bryan Stuart, *COO*
Diego Cadavid, *Senior VP*
Angela Cacace, *Vice Pres*
Peter G Thomson, *Vice Pres*
EMP: 62 **EST:** 2015
SQ FT: 28,731
SALES (est): 16.2MM **Privately Held**
SIC: 2834 Pharmaceutical Preparations

(G-9483)
FULCRUM THRPTICS SCRITIES CORP
26 Landsdowne St Ste 525 (02139-4249)
PHONE....................................617 651-8851
Robert J Gould, *President*
EMP: 4
SALES (est): 396.6K **Privately Held**
SIC: 2833 Mfg Medicinal/Botanical Products

(G-9484)
FURNISHED QUARTERS LLC
303 3rd St (02142-1156)
PHONE....................................212 367-9400
EMP: 64
SALES (corp-wide): 13MM **Privately Held**
SIC: 3131 Mfg Footwear Cut Stock
PA: Furnished Quarters, Llc
158 W 27th St Fl 7
New York NY 10001
212 367-9400

(G-9485)
GB AND SMITH INC
90 Sherman St (02140-3264)
PHONE....................................617 319-3563
Sebastien Goiffon, *CEO*
Bruno Masek, *Vice Pres*
EMP: 6
SQ FT: 1,000
SALES: 1.5MM
SALES (corp-wide): 2.4MM **Privately Held**
SIC: 7372 Prepackaged Software Services
HQ: Gb And Smith
7 Rue Nationale
Lille 59800

(G-9486)
GCP APPLIED TECHNOLOGIES INC (PA)
62 Whittemore Ave (02140-1623)
PHONE....................................617 876-1400
Gregory E Poling, *CEO*
William Dickens, *District Mgr*
Jeff Slaughter, *District Mgr*
Greg Laugeni, *Business Mgr*
Susan Dalton, *Vice Pres*
EMP: 277 **EST:** 2015
SALES: 1.1B **Publicly Held**
SIC: 2819 2899 Mfg Chemicals & Allied Products

(G-9487)
GENERATIVE LABS INC
70 Pacific St (02139-4204)
PHONE....................................434 326-8061
Guolong Wang, *CEO*
EMP: 12
SALES: 3K **Privately Held**
SIC: 7372 Prepackaged Software Services

(G-9488)
GENOCEA BIOSCIENCES INC
100 Acorn Park Dr Fl 5 (02140-2303)
PHONE....................................617 876-8191
Kenneth Bate, *Ch of Bd*
William Clark, *President*
Pamela Carroll, *Senior VP*
Derek Meisner, *Senior VP*
Narinder Singh, *Senior VP*
EMP: 61
SQ FT: 34,200
SALES (est): 609.5K **Privately Held**
WEB: www.genocea.com
SIC: 2836 2834 Biological Products & Pharmaceutical Preparation

(G-9489)
GENZYME CORPORATION (DH)
Also Called: Genzyme Therapeutics Division
50 Binney St (02142-1512)
PHONE....................................617 252-7500
Christopher A Viehbacher, *CEO*
Paul Beninger, *Vice Pres*
Gerald F Cox, *Vice Pres*
Michael Halpin, *Vice Pres*
Jim Magner, *Vice Pres*
▲ **EMP:** 600
SQ FT: 267,278
SALES (est): 3.4B **Privately Held**
WEB: www.genzyme.com
SIC: 2835 2834 8071 3842 Mfg Diagnostic Substance Mfg Pharmaceutical Preps Medical Laboratory Mfg Surgical Appliances
HQ: Sanofi Us Services Inc.
55 Corporate Dr
Bridgewater NJ 08807
336 407-4994

(G-9490)
GENZYME CORPORATION
Also Called: Genzyme Biosurgery
55 Cambridge Pkwy Ste 19 (02142-1234)
PHONE....................................508 271-2919
Laura Emig, *Research*
Ana Reinherz, *Research*
Robert Pelletier, *Manager*
EMP: 93 **Privately Held**
SIC: 2835 2834 Mfg Diagnostic Substances Mfg Surgical/Medical Instruments
HQ: Genzyme Corporation
50 Binney St
Cambridge MA 02142
617 252-7500

(G-9491)
GENZYME CORPORATION
1 Kendall Sq (02139-1562)
PHONE....................................508 872-8400
Patty Ahern, *Vice Pres*
Peter Cook, *Branch Mgr*
Vincent Lawler, *Director*
Andy Siegel, *Director*
Vaneza Nazario, *Associate Dir*
EMP: 216 **Privately Held**
WEB: www.genzyme.com
SIC: 2834 Mfg Pharmaceutical Preparations
HQ: Genzyme Corporation
50 Binney St
Cambridge MA 02142
617 252-7500

(G-9492)
GENZYME CORPORATION
1 Kendall Sq Ste 113 (02139-1562)
PHONE....................................617 252-7500
Frank Ollington, *President*
Lou Cicchese, *Project Mgr*
Christopher Lombardi, *Mfg Staff*
Eric Desmond, *Engineer*
George Dias, *Technology*
EMP: 216 **Privately Held**
SIC: 2834 Mfg Pharmaceutical Preparations
HQ: Genzyme Corporation
50 Binney St
Cambridge MA 02142
617 252-7500

(G-9493)
GENZYME CORPORATION
Genzyme Tissue Repair Division
500 St Kendall (02142)
PHONE....................................617 494-8484
David Meaker, *Vice Pres*
Henk Schuring, *Vice Pres*
James Assini, *Information Mgr*
EMP: 300 **Privately Held**
WEB: www.genzyme.com
SIC: 2834 Mfg Pharmaceutical Preparations
HQ: Genzyme Corporation
50 Binney St
Cambridge MA 02142
617 252-7500

(G-9494)
GENZYME SECURITIES CORPORATION
50 Binney St (02142-1512)
PHONE....................................617 252-7500
Joanne M Vasily Cioffi, *Asst Sec*
EMP: 3
SQ FT: 267,278
SALES (est): 170.3K **Privately Held**
SIC: 2834 Mfg Pharmaceutical Preparations

(G-9495)
GLOBAL LIGHT CO LLC
328 Harvard St Apt 3 (02139-2038)
PHONE....................................617 620-2084
Paul Morris, *Principal*
EMP: 3
SALES (est): 219.5K **Privately Held**
SIC: 3645 Mfg Residential Lighting Fixtures

(G-9496)
GLOGOOD INC
27 Gray Gdns E (02138-1401)
P.O. Box 380536 (02238-0536)
PHONE....................................617 491-3500
Fred Good, *President*
Cecile Pham, *Vice Pres*
EMP: 5
SQ FT: 900
SALES: 620K **Privately Held**
SIC: 7372 Prepackaged Software Services

(G-9497)
GRAPHENEA INC
1 Broadway Fl 14 (02142-1187)
PHONE....................................415 568-6243
Jesus De La Fuente, *CEO*
Tom Fedolak, *Business Mgr*
EMP: 15
SALES (est): 1MM
SALES (corp-wide): 257.2K **Privately Held**
SIC: 3674 Mfg Semiconductors/Related Devices
HQ: Graphenea Sa
Paseo De Mikeletegi (Pq. Tecnologico De Miramon) 83
Donostia/San Sebastian 20009
943 359-937

(G-9498)
GVD CORPORATION (PA)
45 Spinelli Pl (02138-1046)
PHONE....................................617 661-0060
Hilton Pryce Lewis, *President*
Karen Gleason, *Corp Secy*
Charles Popkin, *CFO*
EMP: 15

SALES (est): 2.4MM Privately Held
WEB: www.gvdcorp.com
SIC: 3479 Coating/Engraving Service

(G-9499)
HACKETT PUBLISHING COMPANY
847 Massachusetts Ave (02139-3001)
P.O. Box 390007 (02139-0001)
PHONE..............................617 497-6303
James Hullett, *Manager*
EMP: 12
SQ FT: 4,694
SALES (corp-wide): 6.8MM Privately Held
WEB: www.hackettpublishing.com
SIC: 2731 Books-Publishing/Printing
PA: Hackett Publishing Company Inc
3333 Massachusetts Ave
Indianapolis IN 46218
317 635-9250

(G-9500)
HARBOUR BIOMED
1 Broadway Fl 14 (02142-1187)
PHONE..............................617 682-3679
Jingsong Wang, *CEO*
EMP: 15
SALES (est): 666.2K Privately Held
SIC: 2834 Mfg Pharmaceutical Preparations

(G-9501)
HARTWELL ASSCOIATES
24 Thorndike St (02141-1882)
PHONE..............................617 686-7571
Stephen Hartwell, *Principal*
EMP: 3 EST: 2010
SALES (est): 172.8K Privately Held
SIC: 3081 Mfg Unsupported Plastic Film/Sheet

(G-9502)
HARVARD CRIMSON INC
14 Plympton St (02138-6606)
PHONE..............................617 576-6600
Peter Zhu, *President*
EMP: 3
SQ FT: 2,000
SALES: 283.9K Privately Held
WEB: www.thecrimson.com
SIC: 2711 2721 Newspapers-Publishing/Printing Periodicals-Publishing/Printing

(G-9503)
HARVARD LAMPOON INC
44 Bow St (02138-5108)
PHONE..............................617 495-7801
Elmer Green, *President*
Donovan Keene, *Adv Mgr*
EMP: 35
SQ FT: 15,000
SALES: 142.9K Privately Held
SIC: 2721 Magazine Publishing

(G-9504)
HARVARD MAGAZINE INC
7 Ware St (02138-4037)
PHONE..............................617 495-5746
Irina Kuksin, *President*
John Rosenberg, *Editor*
Virginia V Aisner, *Asst Director*
Robert C Stowe, *Asst Director*
EMP: 20
SQ FT: 9,000
SALES: 4.3MM Privately Held
WEB: www.harvardmagazine.com
SIC: 2721 Magazine Publishing

(G-9505)
HARVARD SCIENTIFIC CORPORATION
799 Concord Ave (02138-1048)
P.O. Box 391651 (02139-0030)
PHONE..............................617 876-5033
Jacob Dahan, *President*
EMP: 12
SQ FT: 1,000
SALES (est): 1.3MM Privately Held
SIC: 3679 Develops & Mfg Waveguides

(G-9506)
HEAD PRONE INC
777 Concord Ave Ste 103 (02138-1053)
PHONE..............................617 864-0780
Margaret Nichols, *CEO*
Byron Hartunian, *President*
EMP: 4
SALES: 50K Privately Held
WEB: www.headprone.com
SIC: 3842 5999 Surgical Appliances And Supplies

(G-9507)
HUBENGAGE INC
1035 Cambridge St Ste 1 (02141-1154)
PHONE..............................877 704-6662
Tushneem Dharmagadda, *CEO*
Erick Michael Crowell, *Principal*
EMP: 3 EST: 2010
SALES (est): 50.7K Privately Held
SIC: 7372 Prepackaged Software Services

(G-9508)
HUBSPOT INC (PA)
25 1st St Ste 200 (02141-1814)
PHONE..............................888 482-7768
Brian Halligan, *Ch of Bd*
J D Sherman, *President*
Sam Belt, *Partner*
Isaac Moche, *Partner*
Christian Mongillo, *Business Mgr*
EMP: 550 EST: 2005
SQ FT: 280,000
SALES: 512.9MM Publicly Held
SIC: 7372 Prepackaged Software

(G-9509)
HYPERION CATALYSIS INTL INC (PA)
38 Smith Pl (02138-1008)
PHONE..............................617 354-9678
Samuel Wohlstadter, *President*
Nadine H Wohlstadter, *President*
Jason Kupperschmidt, *General Mgr*
Bob Hoch, *Vice Pres*
John Walker, *Prdtn Mgr*
▲ EMP: 48
SQ FT: 50,000
SALES (est): 8.5MM Privately Held
WEB: www.hyperioncatalysis.com
SIC: 3624 Mfg Carbon/Graphite Products

(G-9510)
IDENIX PHARMACEUTICALS INC (HQ)
320 Bent St (02141-2005)
PHONE..............................617 995-9800
Ronald C Renaud Jr, *President*
Jacques Dumas, *Exec VP*
Douglas Mayers, *Exec VP*
Maureen W Myers PH D, *Senior VP*
EMP: 37
SQ FT: 46,418
SALES (est): 9.1MM
SALES (corp-wide): 42.2B Publicly Held
WEB: www.idenix.com
SIC: 2834 Mfg Pharmaceutical Preparations
PA: Merck & Co., Inc.
2000 Galloping Hill Rd
Kenilworth NJ 07033
908 740-4000

(G-9511)
IDENIX PHARMACEUTICALS INC
60 Hampshire St (02139-1524)
PHONE..............................617 876-5883
EMP: 90
SALES (corp-wide): 40.1B Publicly Held
SIC: 2834 Pharmacuetical Manufacturer
HQ: Idenix Pharmaceuticals, Inc.
320 Bent St
Cambridge MA 02141
617 995-9800

(G-9512)
IGGYS BREAD LTD (PA)
Also Called: Iggy's Bread of The World
130 Fawcett St (02138-1112)
PHONE..............................617 491-7600
Klaus Nygaard, *President*
Igor Ivanovic, *Treasurer*
▲ EMP: 75
SQ FT: 30,000
SALES (est): 13.4MM Privately Held
WEB: www.iggysbread.com
SIC: 2051 5461 Mfg Bread/Related Products Retail Bakery

(G-9513)
IL PHARMA INC
1 Broadway Fl 14 (02142-1187)
PHONE..............................617 355-6910
EMP: 6
SALES (est): 640.9K
SALES (corp-wide): 305.3K Privately Held
SIC: 2834 Mfg Pharmaceutical Preparations
PA: Medrx Co.,Ltd.
431-7, Nishiyama
Higashikagawa KGA
879 233-071

(G-9514)
INFINITE FOREST INC
172 Charles St Ste B (02141-2118)
PHONE..............................617 299-1382
Pawan Gupta, *CEO*
EMP: 11
SALES (est): 239.1K Privately Held
SIC: 7372 Prepackaged Software Services

(G-9515)
INFINITY PHARMACEUTICALS INC (PA)
1100 Massachusetts Ave # 4 (02138-5241)
PHONE..............................617 453-1000
Adelene Q Perkins, *Ch of Bd*
William C Bertrand Jr, *Exec VP*
Sujay Kango, *Exec VP*
Claudio Dansky Ullmann, *Senior VP*
Melissa Hackel, *Vice Pres*
EMP: 69
SQ FT: 61,000
SALES: 22.1MM Publicly Held
WEB: www.cyera.com
SIC: 2834 8731 Pharmaceutical Preparations And Commercial Physical Research

(G-9516)
INK INC PUBLISHING SERVICE
280 Green St Fl 2 (02139-3312)
PHONE..............................617 576-6740
Rob Madrick, *President*
Giovanna Salerno, *Editor*
EMP: 5
SALES (est): 263K Privately Held
WEB: www.inkincpub.com
SIC: 2741 Misc Publishing

(G-9517)
INTELLIA THERAPEUTICS INC (PA)
40 Erie St (02139-4254)
PHONE..............................857 285-6200
Perry Karsen, *Ch of Bd*
Nessan Bermingham, *President*
John M Leonard, *Exec VP*
Jose E Rivera, *Exec VP*
Laura Sepp-Lorenzino, *Exec VP*
EMP: 96
SQ FT: 65,000
SALES: 30.4MM Publicly Held
SIC: 2836 Biological Products

(G-9518)
INVIVO THRPUTICS HOLDINGS CORP
1 Kendall Sq Ste B14402 (02139-1675)
PHONE..............................617 863-5500
Richard M Toselli, *President*
Richard Christopher, *CFO*
EMP: 6
SQ FT: 5,104
SALES (est): 2.4MM Privately Held
SIC: 3841 Mfg Surgical And Medical Instruments

(G-9519)
IPSEN BIOSCIENCE INC
1 Kendall Sq Ste B7401 (02139-1599)
PHONE..............................617 679-8500
John Kehoe, *Vice Pres*
EMP: 21
SALES (corp-wide): 177.9K Privately Held
SIC: 2834 Mfg Pharmaceutical Preparations
HQ: Ipsen Bioscience, Inc.
650 E Kendall St
Cambridge MA 02142
617 679-8500

(G-9520)
IZOTOPE INC (PA)
60 Hampshire St (02139-1548)
PHONE..............................617 577-7799
Mark S Ethier, *President*
Scott Simon, *General Mgr*
Emily Ferola, *QA Dir*
Caleb Hoffman, *Engineer*
Nicholas Lapenn, *Engineer*
EMP: 69
SALES (est): 18.7MM Privately Held
SIC: 7372 Prepackaged Software Services

(G-9521)
JOHN KARL DIETRICH & ASSOC
Also Called: Classic Copy & Printing
26 Central Sq (02139-3311)
PHONE..............................617 868-4140
John Dietrich, *President*
Anne Shuhler, *Vice Pres*
EMP: 15
SQ FT: 1,600
SALES (est): 860K Privately Held
SIC: 2791 2759 7334 Typesetting Services Commercial Printing Photocopying Services

(G-9522)
JOUNCE THERAPEUTICS INC (PA)
780 Memorial Dr (02139-4613)
PHONE..............................857 259-3840
Richard Murray, *President*
Anna L Barry, *Senior VP*
Ted Harding, *Vice Pres*
Steve Sazinsky, *Research*
Masie Wong, *Research*
EMP: 55
SQ FT: 51,000
SALES: 65.2MM Publicly Held
SIC: 2836 8731 Biological Products Commercial Physical Research

(G-9523)
KADMON CORPORATION LLC
55 Cambrdge Pkwy Ste 300e (02142)
PHONE..............................724 778-6125
EMP: 4
SALES (est): 103.4K Privately Held
SIC: 2834 Mfg Pharmaceutical Preparations
PA: Kadmon Corporation, Llc
450 E 29th St Fl 5
New York NY 10016

(G-9524)
KALVISTA PHARMACEUTICALS INC (PA)
55 Cambrdge Pkwy Ste 901e (02142)
PHONE..............................857 999-0075
T Andrew Crockett, *CEO*
Martin Edwards, *Ch of Bd*
Nicholas Crockett, *General Mgr*
Andreas Maetzel, *Senior VP*
Benjamin L Palleiko, *CFO*
EMP: 14
SQ FT: 2,700
SALES: 16.1MM Publicly Held
WEB: www.carbylan.com
SIC: 2834 8071 Pharmaceutical Preparations

(G-9525)
KENDALL PRODUCTIONS
26 Cpl Mcternan St 2 (02139)
PHONE..............................617 661-0402
Maureen McNamara, *Owner*
EMP: 3
SALES: 80K Privately Held
SIC: 2515 Mfg Mattresses/Bedsprings

(G-9526)
KERYX BIOPHARMACEUTICALS INC (HQ)
245 1st St (02142-1200)
PHONE..............................617 871-2098
Jodie P Morrison, *CEO*
Nicole R Hadas, *President*
Christine Carberry, *COO*

GEOGRAPHIC

Scott A Holmes, *CFO*
Michael Ala, *Sales Staff*
EMP: 88
SQ FT: 27,300
SALES: 60.6MM **Publicly Held**
WEB: www.keryx.com
SIC: 2834 Pharmaceutical Preparations

(G-9527)
KINTAI THERAPEUTICS INC
26 Landsdowne St Ste 4 (02139-4216)
PHONE..................................617 409-7395
David Berry, *President*
Charles Carelli, *Treasurer*
Ken Mace, *Admin Sec*
EMP: 22
SALES (est): 6.3MM **Privately Held**
SIC: 2834 Mfg Pharmaceutical Preparations Specializing In Precision Enteric Medicines

(G-9528)
KSPLICE INC
1 Main St Ste 7f (02142-1599)
PHONE..................................765 577-5423
Jeff Arnold, *President*
EMP: 9
SALES (est): 551.8K
SALES (corp-wide): 39.5B **Publicly Held**
SIC: 7372 Prepackaged Software Services
PA: Oracle Corporation
500 Oracle Pkwy
Redwood City CA 94065
650 506-7000

(G-9529)
KT ASSOCS INC
19 Cottage St (02139-3903)
PHONE..................................617 547-3737
John King, *President*
EMP: 3 **EST:** 1998
SALES (est): 175.3K **Privately Held**
SIC: 3826 Mfg Analytical Instruments

(G-9530)
LAMBIENT TECHNOLOGIES LLC
649 Msschusetts Ave Ste 4 (02139)
PHONE..................................857 242-3963
Lee Huan, *Vice Pres*
Huan Lee, *Mng Member*
Stephen W Pomeroy, *Mng Member*
EMP: 8
SALES: 500K **Privately Held**
SIC: 3559 Mfg Misc Industry Machinery

(G-9531)
LAMPLIGHTER BREWING CO LLC
284 Broadway (02139-1808)
PHONE..................................207 650-3325
Cayla Marvil,
Andrew Jones,
Cayla E Marvil,
EMP: 3 **EST:** 2014
SQ FT: 10,003
SALES (est): 237K **Privately Held**
SIC: 2082 Mfg Malt Beverages

(G-9532)
LAVEEM INC
255 Main St Ste 6 (02142-1066)
PHONE..................................617 286-6517
Varun Chirravuri, *CEO*
EMP: 5
SQ FT: 75
SALES (est): 330K **Privately Held**
SIC: 7372 Prepackaged Software Services

(G-9533)
LEAP THERAPEUTICS INC (PA)
47 Thorndike St Ste B1-1 (02141-1799)
PHONE..................................617 714-0360
Christopher K Mirabelli, *Ch of Bd*
Augustine Lawlor, *COO*
Doug Onsi, *CFO*
EMP: 25 **EST:** 2011
SQ FT: 7,667
SALES (est): 5.6MM **Publicly Held**
SIC: 2834 Pharmaceutical Preparations

(G-9534)
LETS GO INC
67 Mount Auburn St (02138-4961)
PHONE..................................617 495-9659
Anne Chisholm, *General Mgr*
EMP: 1000
SQ FT: 5,000
SALES (est): 2.1MM **Privately Held**
WEB: www.letsgo.com
SIC: 2741 Publisher Of Travel Guide
PA: Harvard Student Agencies Inc
67 Mount Auburn St
Cambridge MA 02138
617 495-3030

(G-9535)
LIBRING TECHNOLOGIES INC
1 Broadway Fl 14 (02142-1187)
PHONE..................................617 553-1015
Marcelo Ballestiero, *President*
EMP: 3
SALES (est): 97.7K
SALES (corp-wide): 177.3K **Privately Held**
SIC: 7372 Prepackaged Software Services
HQ: Annie App Inc
23 Geary St Ste 3
San Francisco CA 94108
844 277-2664

(G-9536)
LIFECANVAS TECHNOLOGIES INC
1035 Cambridge St Ste 9 (02141-1154)
PHONE..................................404 274-1953
Rhie-Young Chung, *Principal*
EMP: 4
SALES (est): 415.7K **Privately Held**
SIC: 2211 Cotton Broadwoven Fabric Mill

(G-9537)
LIPOMED INC
150 Cambridgepark Dr # 705 (02140-2300)
PHONE..................................617 577-7222
Mario Pasquier, *Vice Pres*
Shawn Magsig, *Sales Mgr*
EMP: 3 **EST:** 1997
SALES (est): 469.8K **Privately Held**
WEB: www.lipomed.com
SIC: 2834 Mfg Pharmaceutical Preparations

(G-9538)
LIQUIGLIDE INC
75 Sidney St Fl 5 (02139-4134)
PHONE..................................617 901-0700
Jonathan David Smith, *President*
Ali Nejat, *Engineer*
Brian Jordan, *Technical Staff*
Kripa Varanasi, *Advisor*
EMP: 32 **EST:** 2012
SQ FT: 4,000
SALES (est): 5.7MM **Privately Held**
SIC: 2869 3721 Mfg Industrial Organic Chemicals Mfg Aircraft

(G-9539)
LIVING POWER SYSTEMS INC
16 Divinity Ave 3085 (02138-2020)
PHONE..................................617 496-8328
Peter Girguis, *CEO*
EMP: 4
SALES (est): 294.3K **Privately Held**
SIC: 3699 Mfg Electrical Equipment/Supplies

(G-9540)
LOGICBIO THERAPEUTICS INC
99 Erie St Ste 1 (02139-4560)
PHONE..................................617 230-0399
Frederic Chereau, *President*
Kenneth Huttner, *Senior VP*
Matthias Jaffe, *CFO*
Dean Falb, *Security Dir*
EMP: 23
SQ FT: 11,800
SALES (est): 5.9MM **Privately Held**
SIC: 2836 Biological Products

(G-9541)
M & C PRESS INC
Also Called: Kendall Press
1 Main St Ste 105 (02142-1531)
PHONE..................................617 354-2584
Mark D Lemley, *President*
Cheryl A Lemley, *Senior VP*
EMP: 12
SQ FT: 3,500
SALES (est): 2.3MM **Privately Held**
WEB: www.kendall-press.com
SIC: 2752 Lithographic Commercial Printing

(G-9542)
M SQUARED LASERS INC
1 Broadway Fl 14 (02142-1187)
PHONE..................................408 667-0553
Dr Graeme Malcolm, *CEO*
EMP: 4
SALES (est): 296.3K **Privately Held**
SIC: 2759 Commercial Printing

(G-9543)
MAGENTA THERAPEUTICS INC
100 Technology Sq (02139-3585)
PHONE..................................857 242-0170
Michael W Bonney, *Ch of Bd*
Jason Gardner, *President*
Jason Ryan, *COO*
Jan Pinkas, *Senior VP*
John C Davis Jr, *Chief Mktg Ofcr*
EMP: 62 **EST:** 2015
SQ FT: 69,000
SALES (est): 18.3MM **Privately Held**
SIC: 2834 Pharmaceutical Preparations

(G-9544)
MAKEMESUSTAINABLE INC
91 Kinnaird St Ste 2 (02139-2913)
PHONE..................................617 821-1375
Benjamin N S Brown, *President*
David Delcourt, *COO*
EMP: 3
SALES (est): 108.5K **Privately Held**
SIC: 7372 Prepackaged Software Svcs
PA: Noveda Technologies, Inc
3434 Us Highway 22 # 110
Branchburg NJ 08876

(G-9545)
MASSACHUSETTS INSTITUTE TECH
Also Called: Tech, The
84 Masschstts Ave Ste 483 (02139)
PHONE..................................617 253-1541
Michael McGraw-Herdeg, *Chairman*
EMP: 50
SQ FT: 300
SALES (corp-wide): 3.9B **Privately Held**
SIC: 2711 2741 Newspapers-Publishing/Printing Misc Publishing
PA: Massachusetts Institute Of Technology
77 Massachusetts Ave
Cambridge MA 02139
617 253-1000

(G-9546)
MASSACHUSETTS INSTITUTE TECH
Also Called: Mit Press, The
1 Rogers St (02142-1209)
PHONE..................................617 253-5646
Ellen Faran, *Director*
EMP: 100
SALES (corp-wide): 3.9B **Privately Held**
SIC: 2721 8221 Periodicals-Publishing/Printing College/University
PA: Massachusetts Institute Of Technology
77 Massachusetts Ave
Cambridge MA 02139
617 253-1000

(G-9547)
MASSACHUSETTS INSTITUTE TECH
Also Called: Mit
400 Main St (02142-1017)
PHONE..................................617 253-1000
Benjamin Freed, *General Mgr*
Kenneth Williams, *Officer*
Lindsey Fieldman, *Asst Director*
EMP: 100
SALES (corp-wide): 3.9B **Privately Held**
SIC: 2731 2721 Books-Publishing/Printing Periodicals-Publishing/Printing
PA: Massachusetts Institute Of Technology
77 Massachusetts Ave
Cambridge MA 02139
617 253-1000

(G-9548)
MASSACHUSETTS INSTITUTE TECH
Also Called: Sloan MGT Review
77 Mass Ave Ste E60 (02139-4307)
PHONE..................................617 253-7183
Stephen Alter, *Principal*
EMP: 9
SALES (corp-wide): 3.9B **Privately Held**
SIC: 2711 8221 Newspapers-Publishing/Printing College/University
PA: Massachusetts Institute Of Technology
77 Massachusetts Ave
Cambridge MA 02139
617 253-1000

(G-9549)
MASSACHUSETTS MTLS TECH LLC
810 Memorial Dr Ste 105 (02139-4662)
PHONE..................................617 502-5636
Simon Bellemare, *President*
Richard Howe, *Vice Pres*
Steven Palkovic, *Manager*
EMP: 4
SALES (corp-wide): 594.2K **Privately Held**
SIC: 3829 7389 Mfg Measuring/Controlling Devices Business Services
PA: Massachusetts Materials Technologies Llc
12 Gowell Ln
Weston MA 02493
617 500-8325

(G-9550)
MEDISIGHT CORPORATION
38 Spring St (02141-1717)
PHONE..................................415 205-2764
Thomas Anderson, *President*
Jeon Woong Kang,
Peter So,
EMP: 3
SALES (est): 117.4K **Privately Held**
SIC: 3841 7389 Mfg Surgical/Medical Instruments Business Serv Non-Commercial Site

(G-9551)
MERRIMACK PHARMACEUTICALS INC
1 Broadway Fl 14 (02142-1187)
PHONE..................................617 441-1000
Gary Crocker, *Ch of Bd*
Gary L Crocker, *Ch of Bd*
Deborah Waldie, *Partner*
Bruce Belanger, *Vice Pres*
Khalid Mamlouk, *Vice Pres*
EMP: 72
SQ FT: 112,300
SALES (est): 69MM **Privately Held**
WEB: www.merrimackpharma.com
SIC: 2834 Mfg Pharmaceutical Preparations

(G-9552)
MERSANA THERAPEUTICS INC (PA)
840 Memorial Dr Ste 4 (02139-3860)
PHONE..................................617 498-0020
David Mott, *Ch of Bd*
Anna Protopapas, *President*
Brian Deschuytner, *Senior VP*
Michael Kaufman, *Senior VP*
Ashish Mandelia, *Vice Pres*
EMP: 76
SQ FT: 34,000
SALES: 10.5MM **Publicly Held**
WEB: www.mersana.com
SIC: 2834 8731 Pharmaceutical Preparations Commercial Physical Research

(G-9553)
MICRO FOCUS SOFTWARE INC
Also Called: Novell
150 Cambridgepark Dr # 800 (02140-2305)
PHONE..................................617 613-2000
Angelo Papanastasiou, *Engineer*
Bob Reynolds, *Engineer*
Steve Williams, *Engineer*
Katey McMahon, *Branch Mgr*
Mike Friesenegger, *Technical Staff*
EMP: 314
SALES (corp-wide): 1B **Privately Held**
WEB: www.novell.com
SIC: 7372 Prepackaged Software Services
PA: Micro Focus Software Inc.
1800 Novell Pl
Provo UT 84606
801 861-7000

(G-9554)
MICROSOFT CORPORATION
255 Main St Ste 401 (02142-1036)
PHONE....................................781 398-4600
Trent Collie, *Partner*
Sadie Van Buren, *Partner*
Bob Vernaglia, *Accounts Exec*
Richard Hall, *Sales Staff*
Ali Forelli, *Program Mgr*
EMP: 20
SALES (corp-wide): 125.8B **Publicly Held**
SIC: 7372 Prepackaged Software Services
PA: Microsoft Corporation
1 Microsoft Way
Redmond WA 98052
425 882-8080

(G-9555)
MICROSOFT CORPORATION
1 Memorial Dr Ste 1 # 1 (02142-1346)
PHONE....................................857 453-6000
Henry Cohn, *Branch Mgr*
Priya Ravichandran, *Manager*
EMP: 101
SALES (corp-wide): 125.8B **Publicly Held**
SIC: 7372 Prepackaged Software Services
PA: Microsoft Corporation
1 Microsoft Way
Redmond WA 98052
425 882-8080

(G-9556)
MILLENNIUM PHARMACEUTICALS INC
1 Kendall Sq Bldg 200 (02139-1562)
PHONE....................................617 679-7000
Mark J Levin, *Ch of Bd*
Diane Beck, *Vice Pres*
Varun Kumar, *Mng Member*
EMP: 200 **Privately Held**
WEB: www.mlnm.com
SIC: 2834 Mfg Pharmaceutical Preparations
HQ: Millennium Pharmaceuticals, Inc.
1 Takeda Pkwy
Deerfield IL 60015
-

(G-9557)
MILLENNIUM PHARMACEUTICALS INC
Takeda Oncology
40 Landsdowne St (02139-4234)
PHONE....................................617 679-7000
Melody Brown, *Project Mgr*
Robin Gibbs, *Project Mgr*
John Matusiak, *Project Mgr*
John Matusuak, *Project Mgr*
Jeannette Potts, *Project Mgr*
EMP: 99 **Privately Held**
SIC: 2834 Mfg Pharmaceutical Preparations
HQ: Millennium Pharmaceuticals, Inc.
1 Takeda Pkwy
Deerfield IL 60015
-

(G-9558)
MILLENNIUM PHARMACEUTICALS INC
45 Sidney St (02139-4133)
PHONE....................................617 679-7000
Mark J Levin, *Ch of Bd*
Jeannette Potts, *President*
EMP: 200 **Privately Held**
WEB: www.mlnm.com
SIC: 2834 Mfg Pharmaceutical Preparations
HQ: Millennium Pharmaceuticals, Inc.
1 Takeda Pkwy
Deerfield IL 60015

(G-9559)
MILLENNIUM PHARMACEUTICALS INC
35 Landsdowne St (02139-4232)
PHONE....................................617 679-7000
Veronique Kugener, *Vice Pres*
Mike Johnson, *Research*
Mihaela Plesescu, *Research*
George Mulligan, *Branch Mgr*
Nenad Grubor, *Associate Dir*
EMP: 16 **Privately Held**
WEB: www.mlnm.com
SIC: 2834 8731 Biopharmaceuticals
HQ: Millennium Pharmaceuticals, Inc.
1 Takeda Pkwy
Deerfield IL 60015
-

(G-9560)
MILLENNIUM PHARMACEUTICALS INC
640 Memorial Dr Ste 3w (02139-4853)
PHONE....................................617 679-7000
Ray Roane, *Manager*
Subhani Shaik, *Database Admin*
EMP: 250 **Privately Held**
WEB: www.mlnm.com
SIC: 2834 Mfg Pharmaceutical Preparations
HQ: Millennium Pharmaceuticals, Inc.
1 Takeda Pkwy
Deerfield IL 60015
-

(G-9561)
MINA CUSTOM PRINT
766a Cambridge St (02141-1401)
PHONE....................................617 520-4797
Mina Becho, *Principal*
EMP: 4 **EST:** 2015
SALES (est): 111.6K **Privately Held**
SIC: 2752 Lithographic Commercial Printing

(G-9562)
MOBILEPRO CORPORATION
25 Mount Auburn St (02138-6028)
PHONE....................................480 398-0909
Christopher Lopez, *President*
EMP: 5
SALES (est): 238.4K **Privately Held**
SIC: 7372 Prepackaged Software Services

(G-9563)
MOBILESUITES INC
35 Brookline St Apt 5 (02139-4123)
PHONE....................................302 593-3055
Dennis Meng, *CEO*
EMP: 3
SALES (est): 160.9K **Privately Held**
SIC: 7372 7389 Prepackaged Software Services

(G-9564)
MODERNA INC (PA)
200 Technology Sq (02139-3578)
PHONE....................................617 714-6500
Noubar B Afeyan, *Ch of Bd*
Stephen Hoge, *President*
John Mendlein, *President*
EMP: 30
SQ FT: 190,712
SALES: 135MM **Publicly Held**
SIC: 2836 2834 Mfg Biological Products Except Diagnostics Pharmaceutical Preparations

(G-9565)
MODERNA LLC (HQ)
Also Called: Moderna Therapeutics
200 Tech Sq (02139)
PHONE....................................617 714-6500
Stephen Kelsey, *President*
Lorence Kim, *CFO*
EMP: 9
SALES (est): 23.2MM
SALES (corp-wide): 135MM **Publicly Held**
SIC: 2833 2834 2835 2836 Mfg Medicinal/Botanicals Mfg Pharmaceutical Preps Mfg Diagnostic Substance Mfg Biological Products Mfg Surgical/Med Instr
PA: Moderna, Inc.
200 Technology Sq
Cambridge MA 02139
617 714-6500

(G-9566)
MODERNA THERAPEUTICS INC
200 Technology Sq (02139-3578)
PHONE....................................617 714-6500
EMP: 24
SALES (est): 5.3MM **Privately Held**
SIC: 2834 Mfg Pharmaceutical Preparations

(G-9567)
MODKIT LLC
254 Garden St (02138-1233)
P.O. Box 390654 (02139-0008)
PHONE....................................617 838-1784
Edward Baafi,
EMP: 3
SALES (est): 180.1K **Privately Held**
SIC: 7372 Prepackaged Software Services

(G-9568)
MOHAWK SHADE & BLIND CO INC
2098 Massachusetts Ave (02140-2012)
PHONE....................................617 868-6000
Edward Kelley, *President*
EMP: 5
SQ FT: 3,000
SALES (est): 509.4K **Privately Held**
SIC: 2591 2391 Mfg Drapery Hardware/Blinds Mfg Curtains/Draperies

(G-9569)
MOMENTA PHARMACEUTICALS INC (PA)
301 Binney St (02142-1071)
PHONE....................................617 491-9700
James R Sulat, *Ch of Bd*
Craig A Wheeler, *President*
Carolyn Huntenburg, *Vice Pres*
Jennifer Smith, *Vice Pres*
Kristina Storey, *Vice Pres*
EMP: 279
SQ FT: 78,500
SALES: 75.5MM **Publicly Held**
WEB: www.mimeon.com
SIC: 2834 Pharmaceutical Preparations

(G-9570)
MONSANTO COMPANY
245 1st St Ste 2 (02142-1292)
PHONE....................................617 551-7200
Sarge Francolini, *Facilities Mgr*
William McCusker, *Technician*
EMP: 62
SALES (corp-wide): 43.9B **Privately Held**
SIC: 2879 Mfg Agricultural Chemicals
HQ: Monsanto Company
800 N Lindbergh Blvd
Saint Louis MO 63167
314 694-1000

(G-9571)
MTOZ BIOLABS INC
210 Broadway 201 (02139-1959)
PHONE....................................617 401-8103
Alex Cheung, *CEO*
EMP: 50
SALES (est): 1.7MM **Privately Held**
SIC: 3826 Mfg Analytical Instruments

(G-9572)
MYJOVE CORPORATION
1 Alewife Ctr Ste 200 (02140-2323)
PHONE....................................617 945-9051
Moshe Pritsker, *CEO*
Nick Blanchette, *Editor*
Ryan Dalley, *Editor*
Jacqueline Kern, *Editor*
Quintin Marcelino, *Editor*
EMP: 55
SQ FT: 9,000
SALES (est): 6.1MM **Privately Held**
SIC: 2741 Misc Publishing

(G-9573)
MYOMO INC
1 Broadway Fl 14 (02142-1187)
PHONE....................................617 996-9058
Paul R Gudonis, *Ch of Bd*
David A Henry, *CFO*
Micah J Mitchell, *Ch Credit Ofcr*
Thomas Crowley, *Bd of Directors*
Thomas Kirk, *Bd of Directors*
EMP: 46
SQ FT: 1,562
SALES: 2.4MM **Privately Held**
SIC: 3842 Orthopedic Equipment

(G-9574)
NANOBIOSYM INC
245 1st St Ste 18 (02142-1292)
PHONE....................................781 391-7979
Anita Goel MD, *CEO*
EMP: 23
SALES (est): 5.1MM **Privately Held**
SIC: 2835 Mfg Diagnostic Substances

(G-9575)
NAVITOR PHARMACEUTICALS INC
1030 Massachusetts Ave (02138-5388)
PHONE....................................857 285-4300
Thomas E Hughes, *CEO*
James Randall Owen, *Chief Mktg Ofcr*
Andreas Machl, *Director*
EMP: 11
SALES (est): 1.4MM **Privately Held**
SIC: 2834 Mfg Pharmaceutical Preparations

(G-9576)
NETTWERK MUSIC GROUP LLC
15 Richdale Ave (02140-2600)
PHONE....................................617 497-8200
Dalton Sim, *Branch Mgr*
EMP: 8 **Privately Held**
SIC: 2782 Mfg Blankbooks/Binders
HQ: Nettwerk Music Group Llc
1545 Wilcox Ave Ste 103
Los Angeles CA 90028
323 301-4200

(G-9577)
NEURASENSE INC
2016 Mass Ave Apt 23 (02140-2127)
PHONE....................................618 917-4686
Daniel Morden, *CEO*
EMP: 3
SALES (est): 145.4K **Privately Held**
SIC: 3845 7389 Mfg Electromedical Equipment Business Serv Non-Commercial Site

(G-9578)
NEURO PHAGE PHRMACEUTICALS INC
222 3rd St (02142-1102)
PHONE....................................617 941-7004
Jonathan Solomon, *CEO*
John F Dee, *Ch of Bd*
Franz Hefti, *President*
Hampus Hillerstrom, *Exec VP*
Roxanne Bales, *Vice Pres*
EMP: 14
SALES (est): 2.3MM **Privately Held**
SIC: 2834 Mfg Pharmaceutical Preparations

(G-9579)
NEUROELECTRICS CORPORATION
210 Broadway Ste 2 (02139-1958)
PHONE....................................617 390-6447
Ana Maiques, *CEO*
Giulio Ruffini, *President*
Albert Estevez, *Technical Mgr*
Laura Vall, *Technical Mgr*
EMP: 6
SALES (est): 353.1K
SALES (corp-wide): 355.8K **Privately Held**
SIC: 3845 Mfg Electromedical Equipment
HQ: Starlab Barcelona Sl
Avenida Tibidabo, 47 - Bis
Barcelona 08035
932 540-366

(G-9580)
NEW ENGLAND COUNTRY FOODS LLC
1 Broadway Ste 12 (02142-1189)
PHONE....................................617 682-3650
▲ **EMP:** 6 **EST:** 2010
SALES (est): 741.4K **Privately Held**
SIC: 2032 Mfg Canned Specialties

(G-9581)
NEW ENGLAND TECHNOLOGY GROUP
1 Davenport St Ste 1 # 1 (02140-1415)
PHONE....................................617 864-5551
Steven K Gregory, *President*
EMP: 10 **EST:** 1981
SALES (est): 1.5MM **Privately Held**
WEB: www.netgworld.com
SIC: 3577 Mfg Interactive Video-Graphic Systems

(G-9582)
NIHON KHDEN INNOVATION CTR INC
237 Putnam Ave (02139-3807)
PHONE..................................617 318-5904
Steve Weisner, *President*
Naoki Kobayashi, *Corp Secy*
EMP: 6
SQ FT: 8,000
SALES: 1.4MM **Privately Held**
SIC: 3845 Mfg Electromedical Equipment
PA: Nihon Kohden Corporation
1-31-4, Nishiochiai
Shinjuku-Ku TKY 161-0

(G-9583)
NIMBUS LAKSHMI INC
130 Prospect St Ste 301 (02139-1844)
PHONE..................................857 999-2009
Jeb Keiper, *President*
Annie Chen, *President*
Abbas Kazimi, *Vice Pres*
Holly Whittemore, *CFO*
Peter Tummino, *Security Dir*
EMP: 7
SALES (est): 472.4K **Privately Held**
SIC: 2834 Mfg Pharmaceutical Preparations

(G-9584)
NORTONLIFELOCK INC
Also Called: Symantec
2 Canal Park Ste 5 (02141-2232)
PHONE..................................781 530-2200
Greg Gotta, *Manager*
EMP: 100
SALES (corp-wide): 4.7B **Publicly Held**
WEB: www.symantec.com
SIC: 7372 Prepackaged Software Services
PA: Nortonlifelock Inc.
60 E Rio Salado Pkwy # 1
Tempe AZ 85281
650 527-8000

(G-9585)
NOTCH INC
501 Massachusetts Ave (02139-4018)
PHONE..................................203 258-9141
Shahriar Khushrushahi, *Officer*
EMP: 3
SALES (est): 285K **Privately Held**
SIC: 3663 Mfg Radio/Tv Comm Equip

(G-9586)
NOVARTIS CORPORATION
22 Windsor St (02139)
PHONE..................................617 871-3594
Daniel Karavakis, *Branch Mgr*
EMP: 9
SALES (corp-wide): 51.9B **Privately Held**
SIC: 2834 Mfg Pharmaceutical Preparations
HQ: Novartis Corporation
1 S Ridgedale Ave Ste 1 # 1
East Hanover NJ 07936
212 307-1122

(G-9587)
NOVARTIS CORPORATION
400 Technology Sq Ste 7 (02139-3584)
PHONE..................................617 871-8000
Tanisha Hall, *Principal*
Evan Beckman, *Vice Pres*
Akash Jain, *Research*
Ilya Preygel, *Prgrmr*
EMP: 5
SALES (corp-wide): 51.9B **Privately Held**
WEB: www.novartis.com
SIC: 2834 Mfg Pharmaceutical Preparations
HQ: Novartis Corporation
1 S Ridgedale Ave Ste 1 # 1
East Hanover NJ 07936
212 307-1122

(G-9588)
NOVARTIS CORPORATION
500 Technology Sq (02139-3521)
PHONE..................................617 871-8000
Jo A Dzink Fox, *Branch Mgr*
Andrea Knight, *Associate Dir*
EMP: 56
SALES (corp-wide): 51.9B **Privately Held**
WEB: www.novartis.com
SIC: 2834 Mfg Pharmaceutical Preparations
HQ: Novartis Corporation
1 S Ridgedale Ave Ste 1 # 1
East Hanover NJ 07936
212 307-1122

(G-9589)
NOVARTIS INST FOR BIOMEDICAL R
100 Technology Sq (02139-3585)
PHONE..................................617 871-7523
EMP: 26
SALES (corp-wide): 51.9B **Privately Held**
SIC: 2834 Mfg Pharmaceutical Preparations
HQ: Novartis Institutes For Biomedical Research, Inc.
250 Massachusetts Ave
Cambridge MA 02139
617 871-8000

(G-9590)
NOVARTIS INST FOR BIOMEDICAL R (HQ)
Also Called: Nibr
250 Massachusetts Ave (02139-4229)
PHONE..................................617 871-8000
Mark Fishman, *President*
Laurence Reid, *Vice Pres*
Aaron Bickel, *Project Mgr*
Michelle Andruk, *Opers Staff*
Michael Boisclair, *Opers Staff*
▲ **EMP:** 24
SQ FT: 1,500
SALES (est): 9.2MM
SALES (corp-wide): 51.9B **Privately Held**
WEB: www.novartis.com
SIC: 2834 Mfg Pharmaceutical Preparations
PA: Novartis Ag
Lichtstrasse 35
Basel BS 4056
613 241-111

(G-9591)
NOVARTIS VCCNES DAGNOSTICS INC
350 Massachusetts Ave (02139-4182)
PHONE..................................617 871-7000
Joerg Reinhardt, *CEO*
Samit Hirawat, *Exec VP*
Rob Kowalski, *Exec VP*
Stuart Bailey, *Vice Pres*
Jorge Carreras, *Vice Pres*
EMP: 4455
SALES (corp-wide): 40.6B **Privately Held**
SIC: 2834 Mfg Pharmaceutical Preparations
HQ: Novartis Vaccines And Diagnostics, Inc.
475 Green Oaks Pkwy
Holly Springs NC 27540
617 871-7000

(G-9592)
NOVARTIS VCCNES DAGNOSTICS INC
350 Massachusetts Ave (02139-4182)
PHONE..................................617 871-7000
EMP: 51
SALES (corp-wide): 36B **Privately Held**
SIC: 2834 Mfg Pharmaceutical Preparations
HQ: Novartis Vaccines And Diagnostics, Inc.
350 Massachusetts Ave
Cambridge MA 27540
617 871-7000

(G-9593)
NOVELION THERAPEUTICS INC
1 Main St 800 (02142-1531)
PHONE..................................877 764-3131
Mary Szela, *CEO*
EMP: 12
SALES (corp-wide): 130.4MM **Privately Held**
SIC: 2834 Pharmeceutical Preparation
PA: Novelion Therapeutics Inc
510 West Georgia St Suite 1800
Vancouver BC V6B 0
877 764-3131

(G-9594)
NOVOGY INC
85 Bolton St Ste 124 (02140-3368)
PHONE..................................617 674-5800
Colin South, *CEO*
Ginja Tavares Da Silva, *Vice Pres*
John Niles, *Vice Pres*
Hannah Blitzblau, *Research*
Maureen Hamilton, *Research*
EMP: 15
SALES (est): 2.6MM **Privately Held**
SIC: 2869 Mfg Industrial Organic Chemicals

(G-9595)
NUCLEAD INCORPORATED
100 Pacific St (02139-4562)
P.O. Box 390668 (02139-0008)
PHONE..................................508 583-2699
Harold Feinberg, *President*
EMP: 9
SQ FT: 5,000
SALES: 1MM **Privately Held**
SIC: 3842 Mfg Radiation & X-Ray Shielding Products

(G-9596)
OBSIDIAN THERAPEUTICS INC
1030 Mass Ave Ste 400 (02138-5390)
PHONE..................................339 364-6721
Paul K Wotton, *CEO*
Karen Brown, *Owner*
Ryan Daws, *CFO*
Erin Boyer, *VP Human Res*
Sharon Morani, *Executive Asst*
EMP: 9
SALES (est): 1.2MM **Privately Held**
SIC: 3845 Mfg Electromedical Equipment

(G-9597)
OKCHEM INC
47 3rd St Ste 3 (02141-1265)
PHONE..................................978 992-1811
EMP: 5 **EST:** 2014
SALES (est): 383.9K **Privately Held**
SIC: 2816 Mfg Inorganic Pigments

(G-9598)
ON THE BEAT INC
Also Called: American Police Beat
43 Thorndike St Ste 2-4 (02141-1762)
PHONE..................................617 491-8878
EMP: 8
SQ FT: 1,000
SALES (est): 497K **Privately Held**
WEB: www.apbweb.com
SIC: 2711 Newspapers-Publishing/Printing

(G-9599)
ONSHAPE INC
1 Alewife Ctr Ste 130 (02140-2323)
PHONE..................................844 667-4273
Jon Hirschtick, *CEO*
Todd Lloyd, *President*
Dave Corcoran, *Vice Pres*
Dan Shore, *CFO*
EMP: 14
SALES (est): 2.1MM
SALES (corp-wide): 1.2B **Publicly Held**
SIC: 7372 Prepackaged Software Services
PA: Ptc Inc.
121 Seaport Blvd
Boston MA 02210
781 370-5000

(G-9600)
OPENEYE SCIENTIFIC SFTWR INC
222 Third St Ste 3120 (02142-1265)
PHONE..................................617 374-8844
Joseph Corkery, *Branch Mgr*
EMP: 5
SALES (corp-wide): 4.9MM **Privately Held**
WEB: www.eyesopen.com
SIC: 7372 Prepackaged Software Services
PA: Openeye Scientific Software, Inc.
9 Bisbee Ct Ste D
Santa Fe NM 87508
505 473-7385

(G-9601)
OPTEON CORPORATION
119 Mount Auburn St (02138-5748)
PHONE..................................617 520-6658
Eric Hopkins, *President*
EMP: 5
SALES (est): 488.4K **Privately Held**
WEB: www.opteontech.com
SIC: 3599 Mfg Industrial Machinery

(G-9602)
ORACLE CORPORATION
101 Main St Ste 1 (02142-1519)
PHONE..................................617 497-7713
William Crevan, *Owner*
Ellen Lapriore, *Vice Pres*
Mike Gravel, *Technology*
Louis Virgadula, *Technology*
Paul Scott, *Information Mgr*
EMP: 302
SALES (corp-wide): 39.5B **Publicly Held**
SIC: 7372 Prepackaged Software Services
PA: Oracle Corporation
500 Oracle Pkwy
Redwood City CA 94065
650 506-7000

(G-9603)
ORACLE OTC SUBSIDIARY LLC
Also Called: Atg
1 Main St Ste 7 (02142-1599)
PHONE..................................617 386-1000
Robert D Burke, *President*
Lawrence Joseph Ellison, *President*
Mike Lande, *President*
Lou Frio, *Vice Pres*
EMP: 545
SQ FT: 59,000
SALES (est): 54MM
SALES (corp-wide): 39.5B **Publicly Held**
WEB: www.atg.com
SIC: 7372 Prepackaged Software Services
PA: Oracle Corporation
500 Oracle Pkwy
Redwood City CA 94065
650 506-7000

(G-9604)
PADLOCK THERAPEUTICS INC
200 Cambridge Park Dr (02140)
P.O. Box 4000, Princeton NJ (08543-4000)
PHONE..................................978 381-9601
Michael Gilman, *CEO*
Rajesh Devraj, *Security Dir*
EMP: 8 **EST:** 2014
SALES (est): 1MM
SALES (corp-wide): 22.5B **Publicly Held**
SIC: 2834 Mfg Pharmaceutical Preparations
PA: Bristol-Myers Squibb Company
430 E 29th St Fl 14
New York NY 10016
212 546-4000

(G-9605)
PANTHER THERAPEUTICS INC
700 Main St (02139-3543)
PHONE..................................857 413-1698
Laura Indolfi, *President*
Elazer Edelman, *Vice Pres*
David Ting, *Vice Pres*
EMP: 3
SALES (est): 159.7K **Privately Held**
SIC: 3842 Mfg Surgical Appliances/Supplies

(G-9606)
PAPERPILE LLC
28 Glenwood Ave Apt 2 (02139-4787)
PHONE..................................617 682-9250
Stefan Washietl, *CEO*
EMP: 5
SALES: 200K **Privately Held**
SIC: 7372 7389 Custom Computer Programing Business Serv Non-Commercial Site

(G-9607)
PATHFINDER CELL THERAPY INC
12 Bow St (02138-5104)
PHONE..................................617 245-0289
Joerg Gruber, *Ch of Bd*
Richard L Franklin, *President*
John Benson, *CFO*
EMP: 3
SQ FT: 700
SALES (est): 95.6K **Privately Held**
WEB: www.synthemed.com
SIC: 2834 Pharmaceutical Preparation

▲ = Import ▼=Export
◆ =Import/Export

(G-9608)
PENDAR TECHNOLOGIES LLC (PA)
30 Spinelli Pl (02138-1070)
PHONE..................................617 588-2128
Gokhan Ulu, *Opers Staff*
Seamus Fogarty, *CFO*
Daryoosh Vakhshoori, *Mng Member*
EMP: 4
SALES (est): 1.1MM **Privately Held**
SIC: 3845 Mfg Electromedical Equipment

(G-9609)
PERKINELMER INC
245 1st St (02142-1200)
PHONE..................................617 577-7744
EMP: 3
SALES (corp-wide): 2.2B **Publicly Held**
SIC: 3826 Mfg Analytical Instruments
PA: Perkinelmer, Inc.
940 Winter St
Waltham MA 02451
781 663-6900

(G-9610)
PHARMATE INC
1555 Mass Ave Ste B (02138-2934)
PHONE..................................617 800-5804
Petit Pierre, *CEO*
Ali Jafary, *COO*
Katherine Clarke, *CFO*
EMP: 3
SALES (est): 163.9K **Privately Held**
SIC: 2834 8699 Mfg Pharmaceutical Preparations Membership Organization

(G-9611)
PINKBERRY
1380 Massachusetts Ave (02138-3822)
PHONE..................................617 547-0573
EMP: 4
SALES (est): 242.2K **Privately Held**
SIC: 2026 Mfg Fluid Milk

(G-9612)
PLENOPTIKA INC (PA)
955 Msschstts Ave Box 339 (02139)
PHONE..................................617 862-2203
Shivang Dave, *CEO*
EMP: 5 **EST:** 2014
SALES (est): 450.1K **Privately Held**
SIC: 3841 Mfg Surgical/Medical Instruments

(G-9613)
POSTDOC VENTURES LLC
1668 Massachusetts Ave (02138-1838)
PHONE..................................617 492-3555
Matthew Alan Wallace, *Principal*
EMP: 4
SALES (est): 295.3K **Privately Held**
SIC: 2026 Mfg Fluid Milk

(G-9614)
POWER STEERING SOFTWARE
15 Mount Auburn St (02138-6030)
PHONE..................................617 520-2100
David Boghoian, *President*
EMP: 3
SALES (est): 166.4K **Privately Held**
SIC: 7372 Prepackaged Software Services

(G-9615)
PRESIDENT FLLOWS HRVARD CLLEGE
Also Called: Harvard Observatory Model Shop
60 Garden St (02138-1516)
PHONE..................................617 495-2020
Rick Bruni, *Engineer*
Laura Conway, *Human Res Mgr*
Tom Regan, *Technology*
Lawrence Knowells, *Director*
Branden Allen, *Professor*
EMP: 3
SALES (corp-wide): 5.5B **Privately Held**
WEB: www.harvard.edu
SIC: 3541 8221 Mfg Machine Tools-Cutting College/University
PA: President And Fellows Of Harvard College
1350 Massachusetts Ave
Cambridge MA 02138
617 496-4873

(G-9616)
PRESIDENT FLLOWS HRVARD CLLEGE
Also Called: Harvard University Press
79 Garden St (02138-1423)
PHONE..................................617 495-9897
William P Sisler, *Director*
EMP: 100
SQ FT: 25,335
SALES (corp-wide): 5.5B **Privately Held**
WEB: www.harvard.edu
SIC: 2741 2731 Misc Publishing Books-Publishing/Printing
PA: President And Fellows Of Harvard College
1350 Massachusetts Ave
Cambridge MA 02138
617 496-4873

(G-9617)
PRESIDENT FLLOWS HRVARD CLLEGE
Also Called: President Fllows Hrvard Cllege
16 Divinity Ave Rm B061 (02138-2020)
PHONE..................................617 495-4043
William Lane, *Director*
EMP: 215
SALES (corp-wide): 5.5B **Privately Held**
WEB: www.harvard.edu
SIC: 3826 8221 Mfg Analytical Instruments College/University
PA: President And Fellows Of Harvard College
1350 Massachusetts Ave
Cambridge MA 02138
617 496-4873

(G-9618)
PREVENTLY INC
30 Cambridgepark Dr 412 (02140-2340)
PHONE..................................617 981-0920
Laurence Girard, *President*
EMP: 4
SALES (est): 174.2K **Privately Held**
SIC: 7372 7389 Prepackaged Software Services Business Services At Non-Commercial Site

(G-9619)
PTC THERAPEUTICS GT INC
245 First St Ste 1800 (02142-1292)
PHONE..................................781 799-9179
Mark Pykett, *CEO*
Christopher J Silber, *Officer*
EMP: 7 **EST:** 2013
SALES (est): 561.7K
SALES (corp-wide): 264.7MM **Publicly Held**
SIC: 2834 Manufacturer Of Pharmaceutical Preparations
PA: Ptc Therapeutics, Inc.
100 Corporate Ct
South Plainfield NJ 07080
908 222-7000

(G-9620)
QUALITY INCENSE
316 Rindge Ave Unit 6 (02140-3148)
PHONE..................................339 224-0655
Nazir Jinwala, *Owner*
EMP: 4
SALES (est): 365.3K **Privately Held**
SIC: 2899 Mfg Chemical Preparations

(G-9621)
QUANTUM DESIGNS LLC (PA)
161 First St Ste 3 (02142-1211)
PHONE..................................617 491-6600
Kevin Murphy, *CEO*
EMP: 6 **EST:** 2016
SALES (est): 7.6MM **Privately Held**
SIC: 2834 Mfg Pharmaceutical Preparations

(G-9622)
QUANTUM SIMULATION TECH INC
Also Called: Qsimulate
625 Massachusetts Ave (02139-3357)
PHONE..................................847 626-5535
Toru Shiozaki, *CEO*
Garnet Chan, *Principal*
Guanhua Chen, *Principal*
EMP: 3
SALES (est): 71.1K **Privately Held**
SIC: 7372 Prepackaged Software Services

(G-9623)
QUICKBASE INC (PA)
150 Cambridgepark Dr # 500 (02140-2370)
PHONE..................................855 725-2293
Rick Willett, *Ch of Bd*
Steve Percoco, *Vice Pres*
Adam Hoover, *Engineer*
David Phillips, *Sales Dir*
Joshua Keane, *Accounts Mgr*
EMP: 101 **EST:** 2016
SQ FT: 75,000
SALES: 88MM **Privately Held**
SIC: 7372 Prepackaged Software Services

(G-9624)
RA PHARMACEUTICALS INC
87 Cambridgepark Dr (02140-2311)
PHONE..................................617 401-4060
Douglas A Treco, *President*
David C Lubner, *CFO*
John C King, *Ch Credit Ofcr*
Ramin Farzaneh-Far, *Chief Mktg Ofcr*
Christian Phillips, *Director*
EMP: 40
SQ FT: 27,000
SALES: 2.5MM **Privately Held**
SIC: 2834 Pharmaceutical Preparations

(G-9625)
RAW DIAMOND INC
10 Kirkland Pl (02138-2034)
PHONE..................................857 222-5601
Cynthia Breazeal, *CEO*
EMP: 3
SALES (est): 154.7K **Privately Held**
SIC: 7372 Prepackaged Software Services

(G-9626)
RAYSECUR INC (PA)
125 Cambridgepark Dr # 301 (02140-2329)
PHONE..................................844 729-7328
Eric Giroux, *CEO*
Nancy Elkas, *Principal*
Alex Sappok, *Principal*
EMP: 6
SQ FT: 1,000
SALES: 5MM **Privately Held**
SIC: 3699 Mfg Electrical Equipment/Supplies

(G-9627)
READY 4
285 3rd St Unit 221 (02142-1117)
PHONE..................................857 233-5455
EMP: 6
SALES (est): 497.4K **Privately Held**
SIC: 3273 Mfg Ready-Mixed Concrete

(G-9628)
REJJEE INC
7 Newport Rd Apt 8 (02140-1524)
PHONE..................................617 283-5057
Gary O'Neil, *CEO*
Kenneth H Smith, *Admin Sec*
EMP: 5 **EST:** 2014
SALES (est): 256.2K **Privately Held**
SIC: 7372 Application Software

(G-9629)
RELX INC
Reed Business Information
50 Hampshire St 5 (02139-1548)
PHONE..................................781 663-5200
Susan Patel, *General Mgr*
EMP: 70
SALES (corp-wide): 9.8B **Privately Held**
WEB: www.lexis-nexis.com
SIC: 2741 Publisher
HQ: Relx Inc.
230 Park Ave Ste 700
New York NY 10169
212 309-8100

(G-9630)
RESEARCH APPLICATIONS AND
Also Called: Bioraft
222 3rd St Ste 234 (02142-1102)
PHONE..................................800 939-7238
Nathan Watson, *CEO*
Jeff Mohan, *Finance Dir*
Rachel Jordan, *Manager*
Jeremy Devoid, *Software Dev*
Charlie Wong, *Director*
EMP: 5
SALES (est): 200K **Privately Held**
SIC: 7372 7371 Prepackaged Software Services Custom Computer Programing

(G-9631)
RESERVOIR GENOMICS INC
38 Tremont St Apt 1 (02139-1287)
PHONE..................................412 304-5063
Peter Kerpedjiev, *President*
EMP: 3 **EST:** 2017
SALES (est): 162K **Privately Held**
SIC: 2835 Mfg Diagnostic Substances

(G-9632)
RHENOVIA INCORPORATED
185 Alewife Brook Pkwy (02138-1100)
PHONE..................................310 382-4079
Serge Bischoff, *CEO*
Christine Bouteiller Vidal, *Project Mgr*
Jean-Marie Bouteiller, *Opers Staff*
Michel Baudry, *Admin Sec*
EMP: 4 **EST:** 2012
SALES: 280K **Privately Held**
SIC: 2834 Mfg Pharmaceutical Preparations

(G-9633)
RHYTHM RHYME RESULTS LLC
155 Brookline St Apt 8 (02139-4548)
PHONE..................................617 674-7524
Isaiah A Jackson, *Principal*
Helen Jackson, *Administration*
EMP: 5
SALES: 100K **Privately Held**
SIC: 3571 Mfg Electronic Computers

(G-9634)
RIPTIDE SYNTHETICS INC
108 Amory St Apt 1 (02139-1277)
PHONE..................................617 945-8832
David Shrier, *CEO*
EMP: 3
SALES (est): 123.2K **Privately Held**
SIC: 2834 Mfg Pharmaceutical Preparations

(G-9635)
RIVERBED TECHNOLOGY INC
125 Cambridgepark Dr # 302 (02140-2393)
PHONE..................................617 250-5300
Paul Brady, *Principal*
Joe Kane, *Engineer*
Charles Kaplan, *CTO*
Laura Hutchinson, *Technology*
Brendan Dunn, *Software Engr*
EMP: 3 **Privately Held**
SIC: 3577 Mfg Computer Peripheral Equipment
PA: Riverbed Technology, Inc.
680 Folsom St Ste 500
San Francisco CA 94107

(G-9636)
ROBERT BENTLEY INC
Also Called: Bentley Publishers
1734 Massachusetts Ave (02138-1804)
PHONE..................................617 547-4170
Michael Bentley, *CEO*
Maurice Iglesias, *Vice Pres*
Pamela Greene, *Accountant*
Stefan Gaa, *Mktg Dir*
Janet Barnes, *Director*
▲ **EMP:** 50 **EST:** 1950
SQ FT: 10,000
SALES (est): 4.4MM **Privately Held**
WEB: www.bentleypublishers.com
SIC: 2731 5192 Publishing & Printing Whol Books

(G-9637)
ROBERT H THOMS
15 Meacham Rd (02140-1213)
P.O. Box 400984 (02140-0010)
PHONE..................................617 876-0662
Robert Thoms, *Owner*
EMP: 3 **EST:** 2015
SALES (est): 89.2K **Privately Held**
SIC: 2329 Mfg Men's/Boy's Clothing

(G-9638)
ROOTPATH GENOMICS
325 Vassar St Ste 2a (02139-4818)
PHONE..................................857 209-1060

GEOGRAPHIC

Xi Chen, *Principal*
EMP: 4
SALES (est): 346K **Privately Held**
SIC: 2835 Mfg Diagnostic Substances

(G-9639)
ROUNDTOWN INC
45 Prospect St (02139-2402)
PHONE..................................415 425-6891
Adam Dingle, *CEO*
Steven Shwartz, *Principal*
EMP: 8
SQ FT: 300
SALES (est): 460K **Privately Held**
SIC: 2741 Internet Publishing And Broadcasting

(G-9640)
SAGE THERAPEUTICS INC (PA)
215 1st St (02142-1213)
PHONE..................................617 299-8380
Kevin P Starr, *Ch of Bd*
Jeffrey M Jonas, *President*
Anne Marie Cook, *Senior VP*
Ryan Arnold, *Vice Pres*
Joe McGrath, *Vice Pres*
EMP: 100
SQ FT: 58,442
SALES: 90.2MM **Publicly Held**
SIC: 2834 Pharmaceutical Preparations

(G-9641)
SAND 9 INC
Also Called: Www.sand9.com
1 Kendall Sq Ste B2305 (02139-1594)
P.O. Box 119, Bolton (01740-0119)
PHONE..................................617 358-0957
Vincent Graziani, *CEO*
Paul Hallee, *Corp Secy*
Alex Erhart, *Vice Pres*
◆ **EMP:** 30
SQ FT: 1,300
SALES (est): 4.1MM **Privately Held**
WEB: www.sand9.com
SIC: 3674 Mfg Semiconductors/Related Devices

(G-9642)
SANGSTAT MEDICAL LLC
500 Kendall St (02142-1108)
PHONE..................................510 789-4300
Richard D Murdock, *President*
Adrian Arima, *Senior VP*
Stephen G Dance, *CFO*
EMP: 299
SQ FT: 44,000
SALES (est): 18.8MM **Privately Held**
WEB: www.sangstat.com
SIC: 2834 2835 3841 Mfg Pharmaceutical Preparations Mfg Diagnostic Substances Mfg Surgical/Medical Instruments
HQ: Genzyme Corporation
50 Binney St
Cambridge MA 02142
617 252-7500

(G-9643)
SANOFI US SERVICES INC
500 Kendall St Ste 500 # 500 (02142-1108)
PHONE..................................617 562-4555
June Strupczewski, *Manager*
Alison Derosa, *Director*
Mary Belmore, *Associate Dir*
EMP: 23 **Privately Held**
WEB: www.aventispharma-us.com
SIC: 2834 Mfg Pharmaceutical Preparations
HQ: Sanofi Us Services Inc.
55 Corporate Dr
Bridgewater NJ 08807
336 407-4994

(G-9644)
SAREPTA THERAPEUTICS INC (PA)
215 1st St Ste 415 (02142-1213)
PHONE..................................617 274-4000
M Kathleen Behrens, *Ch of Bd*
Douglas S Ingram, *President*
David Tyronne Howton Jr, *Senior VP*
Diane Berry, *Vice Pres*
Bo Cumbo, *Vice Pres*
EMP: 255
SQ FT: 88,459
SALES: 301MM **Publicly Held**
WEB: www.avibio.com
SIC: 2834 Pharmaceutical Preparations

(G-9645)
SCHLUMBERGER TECHNOLOGY CORP
Also Called: Schlumberger-Doll Research
1 Hampshire St Ste 1 # 1 (02139-1579)
PHONE..................................617 768-2000
Phillipe Lacour-Gayet, *Engrg Dir*
EMP: 130 **Publicly Held**
SIC: 1389 1382 Oil/Gas Field Services Oil/Gas Exploration Services
HQ: Schlumberger Technology Corp
300 Schlumberger Dr
Sugar Land TX 77478
281 285-8500

(G-9646)
SCHOLAR ROCK HOLDING CORP (PA)
620 Memorial Dr Fl 2 (02139-4815)
PHONE..................................857 259-3860
David Hallal, *Ch of Bd*
Nagesh K Mahanthappa, *President*
Rhonda M Chicko, *CFO*
Yung H Chyung, *Chief Mktg Ofcr*
Alan J Buckler, *Security Dir*
EMP: 6
SQ FT: 21,000
SALES (est): 6.3MM **Publicly Held**
SIC: 2834 2836 Pharmaceutical Preparations Biological Products

(G-9647)
SCHOOL SPECIALTY INC
Also Called: Educators Publishing Service
625 Mount Auburn St Ste 4 (02138-4555)
PHONE..................................617 547-6706
Rick Holden, *President*
EMP: 80
SALES (corp-wide): 673.4MM **Publicly Held**
WEB: www.delta-edu.com
SIC: 2731 2741 Books-Publishing/Printing Misc Publishing
PA: School Specialty, Inc.
W6316 Design Dr
Greenville WI 54942
920 734-5712

(G-9648)
SEVENOAKS BIOSYSTEMS
1 Mifflin Pl Ste 320 (02138-4907)
PHONE..................................617 299-0404
EMP: 3 **EST:** 2014
SALES (est): 214.3K **Privately Held**
SIC: 3841 Surgical And Medical Instruments

(G-9649)
SHIRE HUMN GNTIC THERAPIES INC
Also Called: Shire Pharmaceuticals
125 Binney St (02142-1123)
PHONE..................................617 349-0200
Howard Mayer, *Vice Pres*
EMP: 4
SALES (corp-wide): 15.1B **Privately Held**
SIC: 2834 Mfg Pharmaceutical Preparations
HQ: Shire Human Genetic Therapies, Inc.
300 Shire Way
Lexington MA 02421
617 349-0200

(G-9650)
SHIRE PHARMACEUTICALS LLC
650 E Kendall St (02142-4201)
PHONE..................................617 588-8800
Shalayne Lighty, *COO*
Jason Booth, *Branch Mgr*
EMP: 5
SALES (corp-wide): 15.1B **Privately Held**
SIC: 2834 Mfg Pharmaceutical Preparations
HQ: Shire Pharmaceuticals Llc
300 Shire Way
Lexington MA 02421
617 349-0200

(G-9651)
SIGILON THERAPEUTICS INC
100 Binney St Ste 600 (02142-1096)
PHONE..................................617 336-7540
Rogerio Vivaldi, *CEO*
Olivia G Kelly, *Vice Pres*
Glenn Reicin, *CFO*
David Aubuchon, *VP Finance*
Vanya Sagar, *VP Human Res*
EMP: 25
SQ FT: 13,568
SALES (est): 439K **Privately Held**
SIC: 2834 Mfg Pharmaceutical Preparations

(G-9652)
SKY PUBLISHING CORPORATION
Also Called: Sky & Telescope
90 Sherman St Ste D (02140-3264)
PHONE..................................617 864-7360
Joel Toner, *President*
Peter Tyson, *Chief*
Alan Macroberts, *Purch Mgr*
EMP: 30
SALES (est): 2.7MM **Privately Held**
SIC: 2741 Misc Publishing

(G-9653)
SKYBUILDERSDOTCOM INC
Also Called: Skybuilders.com
77 Huron Ave (02138-6707)
PHONE..................................617 876-5678
Robert Doyle, *President*
Holly Doyle, *Vice Pres*
EMP: 3
SALES: 100K **Privately Held**
SIC: 7372 7371 Prepackaged Software Services Custom Computer Programing

(G-9654)
SOLEMMA LLC
2 Reed Street Ct (02140-2417)
PHONE..................................415 238-2231
Jeff Niemasz, *Vice Pres*
Christoph F Reinhart,
John Alstan Jakubiec,
Kera Lagios,
Jeffrey Niemasz,
EMP: 5 **EST:** 2011
SALES (est): 224.2K **Privately Held**
SIC: 7372 Prepackaged Software Services

(G-9655)
SOLID BIOSCIENCES INC (PA)
141 Portland St Fl Gr (02139-1937)
PHONE..................................617 337-4680
Andrey Zarur, *Ch of Bd*
Ilan Ganot, *President*
Alvaro Amorrortu, *COO*
Jennifer Ziolkowski, *CFO*
Jorge A Quiroz, *Chief Mktg Ofcr*
EMP: 57
SQ FT: 16,000
SALES (est): 27.2MM **Publicly Held**
SIC: 2836 8731 Mfg Biological Products Commercial Physical Research

(G-9656)
SOMERVILLE QUICK PRINT INC
Also Called: Porter Square Press
1722 Massachusetts Ave A (02138-1804)
PHONE..................................617 492-5343
William Ashman, *President*
EMP: 6 **EST:** 1981
SQ FT: 1,500
SALES (est): 552.6K **Privately Held**
SIC: 2752 7334 Lithographic Commercial Printing Photocopying Services

(G-9657)
SONY DADC
545 Concord Ave Ste 102 (02138-1173)
PHONE..................................617 714-5776
EMP: 6
SALES (est): 511K **Privately Held**
SIC: 3695 Mfg Magnetic/Optical Recording Media

(G-9658)
SPERO THERAPEUTICS INC (PA)
675 Msschusetts Ave Fl 14 Flr 14 (02139)
PHONE..................................857 242-1600
Ankit Mahadevia, *President*
Cristina Larkin, *COO*
Joel Sendek, *CFO*
Steve Garbacz, *VP Finance*
Brenda Duane, *Human Res Mgr*
EMP: 28
SQ FT: 15,600
SALES: 3.9MM **Publicly Held**
SIC: 2834 Pharmaceutical Preparations

(G-9659)
SPIROLL INTERNATIONAL CORP
190 Hamilton St (02139-3924)
PHONE..................................617 876-8141
Raymond Ahlberg, *President*
Catherine Wood, *Vice Pres*
Agnes Winnie Hillard, *Manager*
John Martin, *Admin Sec*
EMP: 6
SQ FT: 11,500
SALES (est): 1.1MM **Privately Held**
WEB: www.spiroll.com
SIC: 3829 Mfg Drafting Instruments & Machines

(G-9660)
STALLRGENES GREER HOLDINGS INC
55 Cambridge Pkwy (02142-1234)
PHONE..................................617 588-4900
Richard Russell, *President*
Anthony Palombo, *Treasurer*
EMP: 25
SQ FT: 5,500
SALES (est): 1.2MM **Privately Held**
SIC: 2834 Mfg Pharmaceutical Preparations

(G-9661)
STANDARD MOLECULAR INC
1 Broadway Fl 14 (02142-1187)
PHONE..................................617 401-3318
Nathaniel Weiss, *CEO*
EMP: 4 **EST:** 2016
SALES (est): 144K **Privately Held**
SIC: 7372 Prepackaged Software Services

(G-9662)
SUMMIT THERAPEUTICS INC
1 Broadway Fl 14 (02142-1187)
PHONE..................................617 225-4455
Glyn Edwards, *CEO*
Erik Ostrowski, *CFO*
David Roblin, *Chief Mktg Ofcr*
EMP: 9 **EST:** 2014
SALES (est): 375K **Privately Held**
SIC: 2834 Mfg Pharmaceutical Preparations

(G-9663)
SUNBORNE ENERGY TECHNOLOGIES
Also Called: Sunborne Energy Holding
20 University Rd Ste 450 (02138-5815)
PHONE..................................617 234-7000
James Abraham, *President*
Anil Nayar, *CFO*
Yogi Goswami, *Director*
Hemant Taneja, *Director*
EMP: 3
SALES (est): 250.9K **Privately Held**
SIC: 3433 Nonclassified Establishment

(G-9664)
SUNU INC
245 Main St Fl 2 (02142-1064)
PHONE..................................617 980-9807
Marco Trujillo, *CEO*
Fernando Albertorio, *COO*
EMP: 4
SALES (est): 172.8K **Privately Held**
SIC: 3663 Mfg Radio/Tv Communication Equipment

(G-9665)
SUPERIOR NUT COMPANY INC
225 Monsignor Obrien Hwy (02141-1249)
P.O. Box 410086 (02141-0001)
PHONE..................................800 251-6060
Harry N Hintlian, *President*
Joanne Carrejo, *General Mgr*
John Rocktashel, *Regl Sales Mgr*
Justin H Hintlian, *Director*
Lauren Hintlian, *Director*
◆ **EMP:** 40 **EST:** 1933
SQ FT: 80,000

SALES (est): 11.5MM **Privately Held**
WEB: www.superior.com
SIC: 2068 2099 Mfg Salted/Roasted Nuts/Seeds Mfg Food Preparations

(G-9666)
SUPERPEDESTRIAN INC
84 Hamilton St (02139-4680)
PHONE..................................617 945-1892
Assaf Biderman, *President*
Gil Arbel, *COO*
Ryan Schneider, *Project Mgr*
Martin Pitwood, *Research*
Eric Barber, *Engineer*
EMP: 3
SALES (est): 803.9K **Privately Held**
SIC: 3621 3751 7371 7373 Mfg Motors/Generators Mfg Motorcycles/Bicycles Computer Programming Svc Computer Systems Design

(G-9667)
SUSE LLC
Also Called: Suse Linux
10 Canal Park Ste 200 (02141-2250)
PHONE..................................617 613-2000
EMP: 20
SALES (corp-wide): 17.7MM **Privately Held**
SIC: 7372 Prepackaged Software Services
PA: Suse Llc
1800 Novell Pl
Provo UT 84606
206 217-7500

(G-9668)
SUSE LLC
150 Cambridgepark Dr # 10 (02140-2370)
PHONE..................................617 613-2111
EMP: 10
SALES (corp-wide): 17.7MM **Privately Held**
SIC: 7372 Prepackaged Software Services
PA: Suse Llc
1800 Novell Pl
Provo UT 84606
206 217-7500

(G-9669)
SUSPECT TECHNOLOGIES INC
618 Cambridge St (02141-1123)
PHONE..................................843 318-8278
Jacob Sniff, *CEO*
Matthew Sniff, *Product Mgr*
EMP: 6
SALES (est): 163.7K **Privately Held**
SIC: 7372 Prepackaged Software Services

(G-9670)
SYNCHRGNIX INFO STRATEGIES INC
238 Main St Ste 317 (02142-1016)
PHONE..................................302 892-4800
Trish Moroz, *Branch Mgr*
EMP: 6 **Privately Held**
SIC: 2721 8999 8742 Periodicals-Publishing/Printing Services-Misc Management Consulting Services
HQ: Synchrogenix Information Strategies, Llc
2 Righter Pkwy Ste 205
Wilmington DE 19803
302 892-4800

(G-9671)
SYNLOGIC INC (PA)
301 Binney St Ste 3 (02142-1071)
PHONE..................................617 401-9975
Peter Barrett, *Ch of Bd*
Aoife Brennan, *President*
Gregg Beloff, *CFO*
EMP: 50
SALES: 2.5MM **Publicly Held**
SIC: 2834 8731 Pharmaceutical Preparations Biological Research

(G-9672)
SYROS PHARMACEUTICALS INC (PA)
35 Cambridgepark Dr Fl 4 (02140-2325)
PHONE..................................617 744-1340
Nancy Simonian, *President*
Kyle D Kuvalanka, *COO*
Lisa Roberts, *Opers Mgr*
Joseph J Ferra, *CFO*
David A Roth, *Chief Mktg Ofcr*
EMP: 51
SQ FT: 21,488
SALES: 2MM **Publicly Held**
SIC: 2834 Pharmaceutical Preparations

(G-9673)
TAKEDA BUILDING 35 5
35 Landsdowne St (02139-4232)
PHONE..................................617 444-4352
EMP: 6
SALES (est): 515.1K **Privately Held**
SIC: 2834 Mfg Pharmaceutical Preparations

(G-9674)
TAKEDA PHARMACEUTICALS
300 Massachusetts Ave (02139-4130)
PHONE..................................617 441-6930
Rob Marshall, *Regl Sales Mgr*
Jasdeep Nanra, *Associate Dir*
Leslie Burke, *Executive Asst*
EMP: 10 **EST:** 2017
SALES (est): 1.4MM **Privately Held**
SIC: 2834 Mfg Pharmaceutical Preparations

(G-9675)
TAKEDA PHARMACEUTICALS USA INC
40 Landsdowne St (02139-4234)
PHONE..................................617 444-1348
Trent Carrier, *President*
Tom Rotte, *Regional Mgr*
Brenda Emerzian, *Research*
Stephen Hitchcock, *Research*
James Maguire, *Engineer*
EMP: 31 **Privately Held**
SIC: 2834 Mfg Pharmaceutical Preparations
HQ: Takeda Pharmaceuticals U.S.A., Inc.
95 Hayden Ave
Lexington MA 02421
617 349-0200

(G-9676)
TAKEDA VACCINES INC
40 Landsdowne St (02139-4234)
PHONE..................................970 672-4918
Patrick Green, *Principal*
EMP: 4 **Privately Held**
SIC: 2836 Mfg Pharmaceutical Preparations
HQ: Takeda Vaccines, Inc.
75 Sidney St
Cambridge MA 02139

(G-9677)
TECHNOLOGY REVIEW INC
Also Called: MIT
1 Main St Ste 7 (02142-1599)
P.O. Box 9169 (02139-9169)
PHONE..................................617 475-8000
R Bruce Journey, *President*
Jason Pontin, *Principal*
Bruce Rhodes, *Vice Pres*
James Labelle, *Accountant*
Matthew Beyette, *Sales Staff*
EMP: 40
SALES: 13.1MM
SALES (corp-wide): 3.9B **Privately Held**
WEB: www.technologyreview.com
SIC: 2721 Periodicals-Publishing/Printing
PA: Massachusetts Institute Of Technology
77 Massachusetts Ave
Cambridge MA 02139
617 253-1000

(G-9678)
TEGOS TECHNOLOGY INC
81 Pemberton St (02140-1912)
PHONE..................................617 571-5077
Joshua Kanner, *CEO*
EMP: 3
SALES (est): 159.6K **Privately Held**
SIC: 7372 Prepackaged Software

(G-9679)
TELEFLEX INCORPORATED
1 Kendall Sq 14101 (02139-1562)
PHONE..................................617 577-2200
Victoria Wagner, *Research*
Gwen Watanabe, *Branch Mgr*
EMP: 100
SALES (corp-wide): 2.4B **Publicly Held**
SIC: 3841 Mfg Medical And Surgical Equipments
PA: Teleflex Incorporated
550 E Swedesford Rd # 400
Wayne PA 19087
610 225-6800

(G-9680)
TEVA PHARMACEUTICALS
700 Technology Sq (02139-3557)
PHONE..................................617 252-6586
EMP: 5 **EST:** 2013
SALES (est): 464.9K **Privately Held**
SIC: 2834 Mfg Pharmaceutical Preparations

(G-9681)
THROMBOLYTIC SCIENCE LLC
Also Called: Thrombolytic Science Intl
763d Concord Ave (02138-1290)
PHONE..................................617 661-1107
Alexis Wallace, *Mng Member*
Victor Gurewich,
Jian Ning Liu,
Paolo Sarmientos,
EMP: 4
SALES (est): 363.9K **Privately Held**
SIC: 2834 Mfg Pharmaceutical Preparations

(G-9682)
TOLERX INC
300 Technology Sq Ste 4 (02139-3520)
PHONE..................................617 354-8100
Douglas J Ringler, *CEO*
Elizabeth Czerepak, *Director*
Wayne T Hockmeyer, *Director*
Stephen Hoffman, *Director*
John Littlechild, *Director*
EMP: 55
SQ FT: 37,000
SALES (est): 6MM **Privately Held**
WEB: www.tolerrx.com
SIC: 2834 Mfg Pharmaceutical Preparations

(G-9683)
TRANSLATIONAL SCIENCES CORP
Also Called: TSC
1 Mifflin Pl Ste 400 (02138-4946)
PHONE..................................617 331-4014
Howard Pinsky, *Principal*
EMP: 5
SALES (est): 212.2K **Privately Held**
SIC: 3845 Mfg Electromedical Equipment

(G-9684)
TYPESAFE INC
1 Brattle Sq (02138-3723)
PHONE..................................617 622-2200
Martin Odersky, *Ch of Bd*
EMP: 20
SALES (est): 741.8K **Privately Held**
SIC: 7372 Prepackaged Software Services

(G-9685)
ULTRAGENYX PHARMACEUTICAL INC
840 Memorial Dr (02139-3789)
PHONE..................................617 949-4010
Deb Geraghty, *Vice Pres*
Sam Wadsworth, *Officer*
EMP: 4 **Publicly Held**
SIC: 2834 Mfg Pharmaceutical Preparations
PA: Ultragenyx Pharmaceutical Inc.
60 Leveroni Ct
Novato CA 94949

(G-9686)
UNIVERSITY WINE SHOP INC
1737 Massachusetts Ave (02138-1805)
PHONE..................................617 547-4258
Paul Deruzzo, *President*
Michael Tye, *President*
EMP: 5
SQ FT: 1,500
SALES (est): 542.9K **Privately Held**
SIC: 2084 5921 Mfg Wines/Brandy/Spirits Ret Alcoholic Beverages

(G-9687)
UNUM THERAPEUTICS INC
200 Cmbrdge Pk Dr Ste 310 (02140)
PHONE..................................617 945-5576
Charles Wilson, *President*
Geoffrey Hodge, *Senior VP*
Michael O'Meara, *Vice Pres*
Jessica Sachs, *Chief Mktg Ofcr*
Michael Vasconcelles, *Chief Mktg Ofcr*
EMP: 56
SQ FT: 33,500
SALES: 9.7MM **Privately Held**
SIC: 2834 Pharmaceutical Preparations

(G-9688)
VARIATION BTECHNOLOGIES US INC
222 3rd St Ste 2241 (02142-1259)
PHONE..................................617 830-3031
Jeff Baxter, *President*
Egidio Nascimento, *CFO*
Nancy Bouveret, *Chief Mktg Ofcr*
EMP: 35
SALES (est): 213.2K
SALES (corp-wide): 395.9K **Privately Held**
SIC: 2836 Manufacturing Biological Products
PA: Vbi Vaccines (Delaware) Inc.
222 3rd St Ste 2241
Cambridge MA 02142
617 830-3031

(G-9689)
VBI VACCINES
222 3rd St Ste 2242 (02142-1122)
PHONE..................................617 714-3451
EMP: 3
SALES: 0 **Privately Held**
SIC: 2836 Mfg Biological Products

(G-9690)
VBI VACCINES INC
222 3rd St Ste 2241 (02142-1259)
PHONE..................................617 830-3031
Steven Gillis, *Ch of Bd*
Jeff R Baxter, *President*
Jeff Baxter, *Principal*
Vlad Popovic, *Vice Pres*
Christopher McNulty, *CFO*
EMP: 5
SQ FT: 2,359
SALES: 3.3MM **Privately Held**
SIC: 2836 Vaccines

(G-9691)
VELEX CORPORATION
Also Called: Gorilla Gym
215 Western Ave (02139-3750)
PHONE..................................617 440-4948
Peter Velikin, *President*
Kiril Alexandrov, *Director*
▲ **EMP:** 3
SALES: 750K **Privately Held**
SIC: 3949 Mfg Sporting/Athletic Goods

(G-9692)
VERICEL CORPORATION
64 Sidney St (02139-4170)
PHONE..................................857 600-8191
Tim McKeen, *Manager*
EMP: 4 **Publicly Held**
SIC: 2836 Bioloical Products
PA: Vericel Corporation
64 Sidney St
Cambridge MA 02139

(G-9693)
VERICEL CORPORATION (PA)
64 Sidney St (02139-4170)
P.O. Box 376, Ann Arbor MI (48106-0376)
PHONE..................................800 556-0311
Robert L Zerbe, *Ch of Bd*
Dominick C Colangelo, *President*
Michael Halpin, *COO*
Sean C Flynn, *Vice Pres*
Gerard Michel, *CFO*
EMP: 119
SQ FT: 57,000
SALES: 90.8MM **Publicly Held**
WEB: www.aastrom.com
SIC: 2836 Biological Products

(G-9694)
VERIFY LLC
Also Called: Ready Slump
62 Whittemore Ave (02140-1623)
PHONE..................................513 285-7258
Joe Sostaric, *Mng Member*
Kenneth Feldmann,
Ron Strich,
EMP: 18
SALES (est): 2.6MM
SALES (corp-wide): 1.9B **Publicly Held**
WEB: www.readyslump.com
SIC: 3823 3824 3829 Mfg Process Control Instruments Mfg Fluid Meter/Counting Devices Mfg Measuring/Controlling Devices
PA: W. R. Grace & Co.
7500 Grace Dr
Columbia MD 21044
410 531-4000

(G-9695)
VERITAS MEDICINE INC
11 Cambridge Ctr (02142-1400)
PHONE..................................617 234-1500
Joseph Avellone, *CEO*
EMP: 17
SQ FT: 5,000
SALES (est): 1.4MM **Privately Held**
SIC: 2741 Misc Publishing

(G-9696)
VERTICA SYSTEMS LLC
150 Cambridgepark Dr (02140-2370)
PHONE..................................617 386-4400
Chris Selland, *President*
Teri Bolduc, *General Mgr*
Stephen Crossman, *Engineer*
Majid Seghatoleslami, *Engineer*
Hochan Won, *Engineer*
EMP: 120
SALES (est): 11.3MM **Privately Held**
WEB: www.vertica.com
SIC: 7372 Prepackaged Software Services
HQ: Micro Focus (Us), Inc.
700 King Farm Blvd # 125
Rockville MD 20850
301 838-5000

(G-9697)
VIRGINIA STAINLESS DIV
20 Water St (02141)
PHONE..................................508 823-1747
EMP: 5
SALES (est): 21.9K **Privately Held**
SIC: 3498 Mfg Fabricated Pipe/Fittings

(G-9698)
VOYAGER THERAPEUTICS INC (PA)
75 Sidney St Fl 4 (02139-4134)
PHONE..................................857 259-5340
Mark Levin, *Ch of Bd*
Steven M Paul, *President*
Matthew P Ottmer, *COO*
Allison Dorval, *CFO*
Bernard Ravina, *Chief Mktg Ofcr*
EMP: 83
SQ FT: 47,493
SALES: 7.6MM **Publicly Held**
SIC: 2836 8731 Biological Products Commercial Physical Research

(G-9699)
WAVEGUIDE CORPORATION
85 Bolton St Ste 153 (02140-3366)
P.O. Box 607, New Town (02456-0607)
PHONE..................................617 892-9700
Nelson K Stacks, *CEO*
Peter Rock, *Principal*
Marcus Semones, *Principal*
EMP: 7
SQ FT: 300
SALES (est): 706.1K **Privately Held**
SIC: 3826 Mfg Analytical Instruments

(G-9700)
WEATHER BUILD INC
486 Green St (02139-3203)
PHONE..................................617 460-5556
Adam Omansky, *CEO*
Jonathan Rosen, *Officer*
EMP: 3 **EST:** 2015
SQ FT: 6,000
SALES (est): 82.7K **Privately Held**
SIC: 7372 Prepackaged Software Services

(G-9701)
WILEX INC
100 Acorn Park Dr Fl 6 (02140-2303)
PHONE..................................617 492-3900
EMP: 10
SALES (est): 1MM **Privately Held**
SIC: 2834 Mfg Pharmaceutical Preparations

(G-9702)
WISCASSET MUSIC PUBLISHING CO
10 Mason St (02138-3417)
PHONE..................................617 492-5720
Betsy Davis, *Owner*
EMP: 3
SALES (est): 130K **Privately Held**
WEB: www.wiscassetmusicpublishing.com
SIC: 2741 Misc Publishing

(G-9703)
WORK PLAY SLEEP INC
Also Called: Tap Lab, The
222 3rd St Ste 4000 (02142-1266)
P.O. Box 425028 (02142-0001)
PHONE..................................617 902-0827
David Bisceglia, *CEO*
Ralph Shao, *COO*
EMP: 5
SQ FT: 10,500
SALES (est): 369.3K **Privately Held**
SIC: 7372 Prepackaged Software Services

(G-9704)
WORK TECHNOLOGY CORPORATION (PA)
1 Mercer Cir (02138-4833)
PHONE..................................617 625-5888
E Jackson Hall, *President*
John Travis, *Sales Associate*
EMP: 23
SQ FT: 2,000
SALES (est): 2.6MM **Privately Held**
WEB: www.worktechnology.com
SIC: 7372 Prepackaged Software Services

(G-9705)
WORLDWIDE INNVTIVE HLTHCARE IN
Also Called: Wicare
217 Thorndike St Apt 207 (02141-1505)
P.O. Box 425584 (02142-0011)
PHONE..................................646 694-2273
Danielle Zurovcik, *CEO*
EMP: 3
SALES (est): 205.1K **Privately Held**
SIC: 3841 Mfg Surgical/Medical Instruments

(G-9706)
X4 PHARMACEUTICALS INC (PA)
955 Mssachusetts Ave Fl 4 Flr 4 (02139)
PHONE..................................857 529-8300
Paula Ragan, *President*
Darlene Noci, *Vice Pres*
Renato Skerlj, *Vice Pres*
Thomas Feinberg, *Opers Staff*
Adam S Mostafa, *CFO*
EMP: 15
SALES: 3.5MM **Publicly Held**
SIC: 2836 8731 Biological Products Commercial Physical Research

(G-9707)
XAM ONLINE INC (PA)
25 1st St (02141-1802)
PHONE..................................781 662-9268
Sharon A Wynne, *President*
EMP: 8
SQ FT: 2,100
SALES (est): 799.8K **Privately Held**
WEB: www.xamonline.com
SIC: 2731 Books-Publishing/Printing

(G-9708)
YBLANK
766 Cambridge St (02141-1401)
PHONE..................................857 544-9991
Bzumina Becho, *President*
EMP: 3
SALES (est): 228.6K **Privately Held**
SIC: 2759 Commercial Printing

(G-9709)
YUMA THERAPEUTICS CORPORAITON
10 Linnaean St (02138-1613)
PHONE..................................617 953-4618
Yukari Perrella, *President*
Martin Williams, *Principal*
EMP: 3
SALES (est): 373.4K **Privately Held**
SIC: 2833 Mfg Medicinal/Botanical Products

Canton
Norfolk County

(G-9710)
ABBOTT-ACTION INC
10 Campanelli Cir (02021-2481)
PHONE..................................781 702-5710
Brian French, *Vice Pres*
EMP: 22
SALES (corp-wide): 18.5MM **Privately Held**
SIC: 2449 4783 Mfg Wood Containers Packing/Crating Service
PA: Abbott-Action, Inc.
3 Venus Way
Attleboro MA 02703
401 722-2100

(G-9711)
ADVANCED CONTROL SYSTEMS CORP
Also Called: Telescada
222 Bolivar St (02021-3199)
PHONE..................................781 829-9228
Charles Marshall, *President*
EMP: 6
SQ FT: 10,000
SALES (est): 1.2MM **Privately Held**
WEB: www.acsmotion.com
SIC: 3625 3823 8731 Mfg Relays/Industrial Controls Mfg Process Control Instruments Commercial Physical Research

(G-9712)
AMERICAN WATER SYSTEMS LLC
9 Pequot Way (02021-2305)
PHONE..................................781 830-9722
Michael Lombardi,
EMP: 90
SALES (est): 11.1MM **Privately Held**
WEB: www.americanwatersystems.com
SIC: 3589 5999 7699 Mfg Service Industry Machinery Ret Misc Merchandise Repair Services

(G-9713)
AMERICANBIO INC
20 Dan Rd (02021-2809)
PHONE..................................508 655-4336
Wayne Gagnon, *CEO*
Vincent Cooney, *President*
David Cooney, *Vice Pres*
Heidi Fleshman, *Vice Pres*
EMP: 20 **EST:** 1977
SQ FT: 6,000
SALES (est): 5.4MM **Privately Held**
WEB: www.americanbio.com
SIC: 2819 Mfg Industrial Inorganic Chemicals

(G-9714)
APA LLC
4 Campanelli Cir (02021-2481)
PHONE..................................781 986-5900
Alexander Alfieri, *Principal*
EMP: 50
SALES (est): 620.1K **Privately Held**
SIC: 3564 Mfg Blowers/Fans

(G-9715)
ARMSTRONG PHARMACEUTICALS INC
25 John Rd (02021-2816)
PHONE..................................617 323-7404
John Robinson, *Manager*
EMP: 29
SALES (corp-wide): 294.6MM **Publicly Held**
WEB: www.armstrong-pharma.com
SIC: 2834 Mfg Pharmaceutical Preparations
HQ: Armstrong Pharmaceuticals, Inc.
423 Lagrange St
West Roxbury MA 02132
617 323-7404

(G-9716)
ARTCO OFFSET INC
340 Turnpike St Ste 1-3b (02021-2700)
PHONE..................................781 830-7900
Daniel L Bauman, *President*
EMP: 62
SQ FT: 47,000
SALES (est): 12.4MM **Privately Held**
WEB: www.artco.biz
SIC: 2752 Lithographic Commercial Printing

(G-9717)
ASD LIGHTING CORP
120 Shawmut Rd (02021-1430)
PHONE..................................781 739-3977
Michael V Mashkovtsev, *President*
Mikhail V Mashkovtcev, *President*
Igor Kozhemiakin, *Owner*
John Benatti, *Sales Staff*
Marc Reingold, *Exec Dir*
▲ **EMP:** 15
SALES (est): 3.1MM **Privately Held**
SIC: 3646 Mfg Commercial Lighting Fixtures

(G-9718)
BOYAJIAN INC
144 Will Dr (02021-3704)
PHONE..................................781 828-9966
John S Boyajian, *President*
Zovig Boyajian, *General Mgr*
▲ **EMP:** 12
SALES (est): 2.4MM **Privately Held**
WEB: www.boyajianinc.com
SIC: 2099 5149 5499 Mfg Food Preparations Whol Groceries Ret Misc Foods

(G-9719)
CA J&L ENTERPRISES INC
15 Marshall St (02021)
P.O. Box 304, Randolph (02368-0304)
PHONE..................................781 963-6666
Jeffrey S Lepes, *President*
Elayne M Lepes, *Admin Sec*
▲ **EMP:** 30 **EST:** 1948
SQ FT: 53,000
SALES (est): 9.8MM **Privately Held**
WEB: www.marshallpapertube.com
SIC: 2655 Mfg Fiber Cans/Drums

(G-9720)
CAMIO CUSTOM CABINETRY INC
130 Jackson St Ste 2 (02021-2094)
PHONE..................................781 562-1573
Chris Constantino, *President*
Rob Gray, *General Mgr*
Michael J Shea, *Vice Pres*
EMP: 11
SQ FT: 11,000
SALES (est): 1.6MM **Privately Held**
SIC: 2434 Mfg Wood Kitchen Cabinets

(G-9721)
CANTON CITIZEN INC
866 Washington St Ste 1 (02021-2588)
P.O. Box 291 (02021-0291)
PHONE..................................781 821-4418
Beth Ericson, *President*
EMP: 13
SALES (est): 851.1K **Privately Held**
SIC: 2711 Newspapers-Publishing/Printing

(G-9722)
COPLEY CONTROLS CORPORATION (DH)
20 Dan Rd (02021-2809)
PHONE..................................781 828-8090
Matthew Lorber, *President*
Carl Delillo, *Engineer*
Bob Ferguson, *Engineer*
Dustin Gorman, *Engineer*
Todd Horton, *Engineer*
▲ **EMP:** 276
SQ FT: 104,000

SALES (est): 32.2MM
SALES (corp-wide): 396.1MM Privately Held
WEB: www.copleycontrols.com
SIC: 3679 3663 Mfg Electronic Components Mfg Radio/Tv Communication Equipment
HQ: Analogic Corporation
8 Centennial Dr
Peabody MA 01960
978 326-4000

(G-9723)
COUNTERRA LLC
399 Neponset St Ste 202 (02021-1959)
PHONE....781 821-2100
Shaun Weston, *Manager*
EMP: 10
SQ FT: 2,500
SALES (est): 832.3K Privately Held
SIC: 2434 3281 Mfg Wood Kitchen Cabinets Mfg Cut Stone/Products

(G-9724)
DENTAL KALEIDOSCOPE MAGAZINE
2184 Washington St (02021-1145)
PHONE....781 821-8898
Konstantin Ronkin, *Principal*
EMP: 3 EST: 2007
SALES (est): 166.4K Privately Held
SIC: 2721 Dentist's Office

(G-9725)
DESCO INDUSTRIES INC
1 Colgate Way (02021-1558)
PHONE....781 821-8370
Fernando Amorim, *Opers Mgr*
Darryl Allen, *Manager*
EMP: 40
SALES (corp-wide): 66.3MM Privately Held
WEB: www.desco.com
SIC: 3629 Mfg Static Control Products
PA: Desco Industries, Inc.
3651 Walnut Ave
Chino CA 91710
909 627-8178

(G-9726)
DESCO INDUSTRIES INC
Also Called: E S D Systems
1 Colgate Way (02021-1558)
PHONE....781 821-8370
EMP: 20
SALES (corp-wide): 32.2MM Privately Held
SIC: 3629 2521 2522 2851 Mfg Elctrcl Ind Apprts Mfg Wd Offc Frntr Mfg Offc Frntr-Nonwd Mfg Pnts/Alld Prd Mfg Elc Msrng Instr Mfg Plstc Fm Prdts
PA: Desco Industries, Inc.
3651 Walnut Ave
Chino CA 91710
909 627-8178

(G-9727)
DIREX SYSTEMS CORP
956 Turnpike St (02021-2807)
PHONE....339 502-6013
Gabriel Henkin, *CEO*
EMP: 7
SQ FT: 6,000
SALES (est): 1.3MM Privately Held
SIC: 3841 Mfg Surgical/Medical Instruments
HQ: Direx Systems Gmbh
Blumenstr. 10
Wiesbaden 65189
611 361-90

(G-9728)
DRAPER KNITTING COMPANY INC
28 Draper Ln Ste 1 (02021-1598)
PHONE....781 828-0029
Kristin Draper, *President*
Scott Draper, *Vice Pres*
▲ EMP: 40
SQ FT: 130,000
SALES: 4.3MM
SALES (corp-wide): 11.2MM Privately Held
WEB: www.draperknitting.com
SIC: 2297 2257 Mfg Nonwoven Fabrics Weft Knit Fabric Mill
PA: Draper Brothers Company
1105 N Market St Ste 1300
Wilmington DE
302 777-4726

(G-9729)
DYNASOL INDUSTRIES INC
330 Pine St (02021-3366)
PHONE....781 821-8888
Jacob Fleshel, *President*
▲ EMP: 15
SQ FT: 25,000
SALES (est): 2.5MM Privately Held
SIC: 2842 2841 Mfg Polish/Sanitation Goods Mfg Soap/Other Detergents

(G-9730)
EMCO ENGINEERING INC
118 Will Dr (02021-3704)
PHONE....508 314-8305
Salim Shalhoub, *President*
Wael Salim Shalhoub, *Treasurer*
Elie Salim Shalhoub, *Admin Sec*
▼ EMP: 6 EST: 1973
SQ FT: 30,000
SALES (est): 1.4MM Privately Held
SIC: 3589 Mfg Service Industry Machinery

(G-9731)
EMERGENT BIODEFENSE OPS
50 Shawmut Rd (02021-1409)
PHONE....718 302-3000
Lori Feier, *Principal*
EMP: 3 EST: 2017
SALES (est): 452.2K Privately Held
SIC: 3812 Mfg Search/Navigation Equipment

(G-9732)
FASTECH INC
18 Washington St Ste 33 (02021-4004)
PHONE....781 964-3010
▲ EMP: 28
SQ FT: 30,000
SALES: 8.3MM Privately Held
SIC: 2342 Mfg Bras/Girdles

(G-9733)
FRESENIUS KABI COMPOUNDING LLC
20 Dan Rd (02021-2809)
PHONE....224 358-1150
Andrew Basso, *Mng Member*
EMP: 35 EST: 2017
SALES (est): 2.1MM
SALES (corp-wide): 37.1B Privately Held
SIC: 2834 Mfg Pharmaceutical Preparations
HQ: Fresenius Kabi Pharmaceuticals Holding, Llc
3 Corporate Dr
Lake Zurich IL 60047
847 550-2300

(G-9734)
FRY COMPANY J M
Also Called: THE FRY COMPANY J. M.
480 Neponset St Ste 11b (02021-1936)
PHONE....781 575-1520
Jim Jordan, *Principal*
EMP: 6
SALES (corp-wide): 23.4MM Privately Held
WEB: www.jmfryinks.com
SIC: 2893 Mfg Printing Ink
PA: The J M Fry Company
4329 Eubank Rd
Henrico VA 23231
804 236-8100

(G-9735)
HARBAR LLC
320 Turnpike St (02021-2703)
PHONE....781 828-0848
Jose E Sanchez, *President*
Luis Tueme, *VP Opers*
Imelda Gutierrez, *Safety Mgr*
Alex Gonzalez, *Warehouse Mgr*
Elizabeth Becker, *Research*
▲ EMP: 170
SQ FT: 39,000
SALES (est): 28.4MM Privately Held
WEB: www.harbar.com
SIC: 2099 5461 Mfg Food Preparations Retail Bakery

(G-9736)
HARRISON SPECIALTY CO INC (PA)
15 University Rd Ste A (02021-1434)
P.O. Box 190 (02021-0190)
PHONE....781 828-8180
George P Bates, *President*
Stephen Bates, *General Mgr*
Louis A Sgarzi, *Vice Pres*
▲ EMP: 49 EST: 1961
SQ FT: 90,000
SALES (est): 7.2MM Privately Held
WEB: www.harrisonspecialty.com
SIC: 2844 Mfg Toilet Preparations

(G-9737)
HARRISON SPECIALTY CO INC
15 University Rd Ste A (02021-1434)
P.O. Box 8 (02021-0008)
PHONE....781 828-8180
Russell Fontaine, *Manager*
EMP: 25
SALES (corp-wide): 7.2MM Privately Held
WEB: www.harrisonspecialty.com
SIC: 2844 Mfg Toilet Preparations
PA: Harrison Specialty Co., Inc.
15 University Rd Ste A
Canton MA 02021
781 828-8180

(G-9738)
HEALTHY LIFE SNACK INC
905 Turnpike St Ste D2 (02021-2833)
PHONE....781 575-6744
Royce Williams, *Principal*
EMP: 8
SALES (est): 1.1MM Privately Held
WEB: www.healthylifefoods.com
SIC: 2671 Mfg Packaging Paper/Film

(G-9739)
HOMELAND FUELS COMPANY LLC
40 Shawmut Rd Ste 200 (02021-1409)
PHONE....781 737-1892
Charles Dornbush, *CEO*
Victor Gatto, *President*
Gregory L Benik, *Exec VP*
EMP: 10
SALES (est): 692.6K Privately Held
SIC: 2869 2992 2911 Mfg Industrial Organic Chemicals Mfg Lubricating Oils/Greases Petroleum Refiner

(G-9740)
HONEYWELL INTERNATIONAL INC
65 Shawmut Rd Unit 5 (02021-1461)
PHONE....781 298-2700
David Cote, *Branch Mgr*
EMP: 657
SALES (corp-wide): 41.8B Publicly Held
SIC: 3724 Mfg Aerospace Products/Systems
PA: Honeywell International Inc.
300 S Tryon St
Charlotte NC 28202
973 455-2000

(G-9741)
IDEAL INSTRUMENT CO INC
863 Washington St (02021-2513)
PHONE....781 828-0881
Renato J Perfetti, *President*
Christopher Perfetti, *Vice Pres*
John Perfetti, *Treasurer*
EMP: 11 EST: 1951
SQ FT: 7,000
SALES: 1.5MM Privately Held
WEB: www.idealinstrument.com
SIC: 3599 Mfg Industrial Machinery

(G-9742)
IDEC
60 Shawmut Rd Ste 5 (02021-1410)
PHONE....617 527-7878
EMP: 5
SALES (est): 468.2K Privately Held
SIC: 3993 Mfg Signs/Advertising Specialties

(G-9743)
IET SOLUTIONS LLC (DH)
25 Dan Rd (02021-2817)
PHONE....818 838-0606
Corry S Homg, *President*
Paul G Kincaid, *Exec VP*
EMP: 35
SQ FT: 7,000
SALES (est): 4.3MM
SALES (corp-wide): 508.4MM Privately Held
WEB: www.ietsol.com
SIC: 7372 7371 Prepackaged Software Services Custom Computer Programing
HQ: Unicom Systems Inc.
15535 San Fernando
Mission Hills CA 91345
818 838-0606

(G-9744)
INTEGER HOLDINGS CORPORATION
Electrochem Industries Div
670 Paramount Dr (02021)
PHONE....781 830-5800
Nicholas D'Amore, *Engineer*
George Murray, *Manager*
EMP: 130
SALES (corp-wide): 1.2B Publicly Held
WEB: www.greatbatch.com
SIC: 3845 3692 3691 Mfg Electromedical Equip Mfg Primary Batteries Mfg Storage Batteries
PA: Integer Holdings Corporation
5830 Gran Pkwy Ste 1150
Plano TX 75024
214 618-5243

(G-9745)
INTERPOLYMER CORPORATION (DH)
200 Dan Rd (02021-2843)
PHONE....781 828-7120
Norwin W Wolff, *President*
Patti Converse, *Corp Secy*
Judy Bragg, *Purchasing*
William Stamoulis, *QC Mgr*
Nancy White, *Research*
▼ EMP: 25 EST: 1963
SQ FT: 41,000
SALES (est): 14.9MM
SALES (corp-wide): 669.6MM Privately Held
WEB: www.interpolymer.com
SIC: 2821 Mfg Plastic Materials/Resins
HQ: Zschimmer & Schwarz Gmbh
Max-Schwarz-Str. 3-5
Lahnstein
262 112-0

(G-9746)
J F KESSLER INC
Also Called: Kessler Machine Works
283 Neponset St (02021-2970)
PHONE....781 828-0134
Joseph F Kessler III, *President*
EMP: 5
SQ FT: 8,500
SALES (est): 450K Privately Held
SIC: 3599 Machine Shop

(G-9747)
J R V SMITA COMPANY LLC
Also Called: Minuteman Press
566 Washington St (02021-3000)
PHONE....781 828-6490
Vikram S Shah,
Smita Shah,
EMP: 3
SQ FT: 1,500
SALES: 130K Privately Held
SIC: 2752 Comm Prtg Litho

(G-9748)
JEWELRY SOLUTIONS LLC
Also Called: J R S
448 Turnpike St Ste 2 (02021)
PHONE....781 821-6100
Louis Karten,
Carolyn Karten,
EMP: 8
SQ FT: 1,500
SALES (est): 751.4K Privately Held
SIC: 3911 Mfg Precious Metal Jewelry

GEOGRAPHIC

(G-9749)
KEATING COMMUNICATION GROUP
Also Called: Ke Printing & Graphics
956 Turnpike St (02021-2877)
PHONE....................................781 828-9030
Sharon Keating, *President*
Michael Keating, *Vice Pres*
EMP: 7
SQ FT: 6,500
SALES (est): 1MM **Privately Held**
WEB: www.keprint.com
SIC: 2752 3993 2791 2789 Lithographic Coml Print Mfg Signs/Ad Specialties Typesetting Services Bookbinding/Related Work

(G-9750)
KEURIG DR PEPPER INC
250 Royall St (02021-1011)
PHONE....................................781 575-4033
EMP: 94 **Publicly Held**
SIC: 2086 Mfg Bottled/Canned Soft Drinks
PA: Keurig Dr Pepper Inc.
53 South Ave
Burlington MA 01803

(G-9751)
KING GT INC
480 Neponset St Ste 4a (02021-1936)
P.O. Box 417, West Bridgewater (02379-0417)
PHONE....................................781 562-1554
Rashid Azeem, *President*
EMP: 4 **EST:** 2015
SALES (est): 188.7K **Privately Held**
SIC: 3999 Mfg Misc Products

(G-9752)
LENIS INC
Also Called: Leni's Textiles
480 Neponset St Ste 4a (02021-1936)
PHONE....................................781 401-3273
Leni Joyce, *President*
Mark Albion, *Treasurer*
EMP: 8
SQ FT: 4,400
SALES: 1MM **Privately Held**
SIC: 2299 Mfg Textile Goods

(G-9753)
M8TRIX TECH LLC
Also Called: M8trix Technology
45 Dan Rd (02021-2852)
PHONE....................................617 925-7030
John Pisarczyk, *Mng Member*
EMP: 6
SALES (est): 243.4K **Privately Held**
SIC: 3577 7379 Mfg Computer Peripheral Equipment Computer Related Services

(G-9754)
MAGCAP ENGINEERING LLC
100 Energy Dr (02021-2897)
PHONE....................................781 821-2300
Stella Karavas, *Vice Pres*
Ethel Poulos,
EMP: 15
SQ FT: 32,000
SALES (est): 1.1MM **Privately Held**
SIC: 3677 3825 3812 3663 Mfg Elec Coil & Transformers Mfg Elec Measuring Instr Mfg Search & Navigation Equip Mfg Radio & Tv Comm Equip

(G-9755)
MAJESTIC MARBLE & GRANITE INC
253 Revere St (02021-2920)
PHONE....................................781 830-1020
Reza Alemi, *President*
EMP: 8
SQ FT: 10,000
SALES (est): 959.7K **Privately Held**
WEB: www.majesticfabrication.com
SIC: 3281 Mfg Cut Stone/Products

(G-9756)
MASSMICRO LLC
50 Energy Dr (02021-2863)
PHONE....................................781 828-6110
EMP: 12
SALES (est): 1.1MM **Privately Held**
SIC: 3769 3679 3823 Space Vehicle Equipment, Nec, Nsk

(G-9757)
MASSMICROELECTRONICS LLC
50 Energy Dr Ste 202 (02021-2863)
P.O. Box 231311, Great Neck NY (11023-0311)
PHONE....................................781 828-6110
EMP: 12
SQ FT: 8,000
SALES (est): 1.6MM
SALES (corp-wide): 53.5MM **Privately Held**
SIC: 3679 Mfg Electronic Components
PA: Imrex, Llc
55 Sandy Hill Rd
Oyster Bay NY 11771
516 479-3675

(G-9758)
MURRAY BISCUIT COMPANY LLC
Also Called: Famous Amos of Boston
55 North St (02021-3354)
PHONE....................................781 760-0220
Dan Morgan, *Manager*
EMP: 9
SALES (corp-wide): 13.5B **Publicly Held**
WEB: www.littlebrownie.com
SIC: 2052 2051 Bakery
HQ: Murray Biscuit Company, L.L.C.
1550 Marvin Griffin Rd
Augusta GA 30906
706 798-8600

(G-9759)
NATIONAL RESOURCE MGT INC (PA)
Also Called: N R M
480 Neponset St Ste 2a (02021-1935)
PHONE....................................781 828-8877
Emre Schveighoffer, *President*
Bernhard Berner, *President*
Emre J Schveighoffer, *President*
Carol Tobian, *Business Mgr*
James Staley, *COO*
EMP: 25
SQ FT: 9,000
SALES: 17MM **Privately Held**
WEB: www.nrminc.com
SIC: 3823 8711 8748 Mfg Process Control Instruments Engineering Services Business Consulting Services

(G-9760)
NATIONAL WATER MAIN CLG CO
25 Marshall St (02021-2479)
PHONE....................................617 361-5533
Fax: 617 361-5501
EMP: 26
SALES (corp-wide): 149.3MM **Privately Held**
SIC: 3589 Mfg Service Industry Machinery
HQ: National Water Main Cleaning Co Inc
1806 Newark Tpke
Kearny NJ 07032
973 483-3200

(G-9761)
NECI LLC
530 Turnpike St (02021-2761)
PHONE....................................781 828-4883
Steve McCoy, *Mng Member*
Paul Bittrich,
EMP: 50
SQ FT: 1,000
SALES (est): 15.7MM **Privately Held**
SIC: 2675 2679 Mfg Die-Cut Paper/Paperboard Mfg Converted Paper Products

(G-9762)
NEW ENGLAND SCENIC LLC
8 Carver Cir (02021-2456)
PHONE....................................781 562-1792
Jared Coffin, *Mng Member*
EMP: 3 **EST:** 2016
SALES: 150K **Privately Held**
SIC: 2531 Mfg Public Building Furniture

(G-9763)
NEW ENGLAND WHLCHAIR ATHC ASSN
3 Randolph St (02021-2351)
PHONE....................................781 830-8751
Dale Wise, *Principal*
EMP: 3
SALES (est): 228.5K **Privately Held**
SIC: 3842 Mfg Surgical Appliances/Supplies

(G-9764)
ORGANOGENESIS INC (HQ)
85 Dan Rd (02021-2810)
PHONE....................................781 575-0775
Gary S Gillheeney Sr, *CEO*
Patrick Bilbo, *COO*
Howard Walthall, *Exec VP*
Zorina Pitkin, *Vice Pres*
Richard Shaw, *Vice Pres*
▲ **EMP:** 277
SALES (est): 199.3MM
SALES (corp-wide): 193.4MM **Publicly Held**
WEB: www.organogenesis.com
SIC: 2836 Manufacture Non-Diagnostic Biological Products
PA: Organogenesis Holdings Inc.
85 Dan Rd
Canton MA 02021
781 575-0775

(G-9765)
PAYNE ENGRG FABRICATION CO INC
28 Draper Ln Ste 3 (02021-1694)
P.O. Box 520 (02021-0520)
PHONE....................................781 828-9046
Harry F Payne, *President*
Beverly Butterworth, *Treasurer*
Katherine Payne, *Clerk*
EMP: 32
SQ FT: 13,500
SALES (est): 5.8MM **Privately Held**
SIC: 3499 3444 3441 3599 Mfg Misc Fab Metal Prdts Mfg Sheet Metalwork Structural Metal Fabrctn Mfg Industrial Machinery

(G-9766)
PEARLCO OF BOSTON INC
Also Called: Saratoga Salad Dressing
5 Whitman Rd (02021-2707)
PHONE....................................781 821-1010
Judith Pearlstein, *President*
EMP: 20
SQ FT: 25,000
SALES (est): 3.8MM **Privately Held**
SIC: 2035 Mfg Pickles/Sauces/Dressing

(G-9767)
PHOENIX ELECTRIC CORP
40 Hudson Rd (02021-1407)
P.O. Box 53, Boston (02137-0053)
PHONE....................................781 821-0200
Christine T Clark, *Ch of Bd*
Thomas P Clark, *President*
Paul Clark, *Principal*
Stephen G Simo, *Vice Pres*
Philip Smith, *Vice Pres*
▲ **EMP:** 50
SQ FT: 25,000
SALES (est): 12.4MM **Privately Held**
WEB: www.phoenixelectric-usa.com
SIC: 3629 5063 3823 3676 Mfg Elec Indstl Equip Whol Electrical Equip Mfg Process Cntrl Instr Mfg Electronic Resistors Mfg Conductive Wire Dvcs

(G-9768)
PLYMOUTH RUBBER COMPANY LLC
104 Revere St (02021-2964)
PHONE....................................781 828-0220
Maurice Hamilburg, *Principal*
Ricardo Valeiras, *CFO*
Jan Zemlicka, *Sales Mgr*
Andy Rice, *Sales Staff*
▲ **EMP:** 22 **EST:** 2009
SALES (est): 3.1MM **Privately Held**
SIC: 3069 Mfg Fabricated Rubber Products

(G-9769)
PLYMOUTH RUBBER EUROPA SA
960 Turnpike St Ste 2a (02021-2851)
PHONE....................................781 828-0220
Christine George, *Manager*
EMP: 16
SALES (corp-wide): 211.1K **Privately Held**
SIC: 3069 Mfg Fabricated Rubber Products
HQ: Plymouth Rubber Europa Sa
Carretera Salceda (Km 1,500)
O Porrino 36400
986 344-148

(G-9770)
PODGURSKI WLDG & HVY EQP REPR
8 Springdale Ave Ste 2 (02021-3281)
PHONE....................................781 830-9901
Christopher Podgurski, *Principal*
EMP: 6
SALES (corp-wide): 323.6K **Privately Held**
SIC: 7692 Welding Repair
PA: Podgurski Welding And Heavy Equipment Repair
607 East St
Bridgewater MA 02324
781 830-9901

(G-9771)
PRECIOUS METALS RECLAIMING SVC (PA)
Also Called: Research Lab Supply Co
253 Revere St B (02021-2920)
PHONE....................................781 326-3442
Allan Nyborn, *President*
Larry Nyborn Jr, *Vice Pres*
EMP: 5 **EST:** 1931
SALES (est): 1.2MM **Privately Held**
SIC: 3341 5094 5944 Processes Metal Scrap

(G-9772)
PRESCIENTPHARMA LLC
Also Called: Prescient Pharma
580 Washington St (02021-3000)
PHONE....................................617 955-0490
Pavel Idelevich, *Mng Member*
Kenneth Reed,
EMP: 3
SQ FT: 1,200
SALES: 3K **Privately Held**
SIC: 2023 Mfg Dry/Evaporated Dairy Products

(G-9773)
PRODRIVE TECHNOLOGIES INC
15 University Rd Ste A (02021-1434)
PHONE....................................617 475-1617
Pieter Janssen, *CEO*
EMP: 9
SALES (est): 453.2K **Privately Held**
SIC: 3672 Mfg Printed Circuit Boards

(G-9774)
RESEARCH CMPT CONSULTING SVCS (PA)
Also Called: Research Cmpt Cnsulting Servic
960 Turnpike St (02021-2824)
PHONE....................................781 821-1221
Kayode I Bright, *President*
Daniel N Carney, *Vice Pres*
EMP: 8
SQ FT: 2,500
SALES: 1.2MM **Privately Held**
WEB: www.rccsinc.com
SIC: 7372 7374 7375 7376 Computer Network Engineering

(G-9775)
SARNAFIL SERVICES INC
100 Dan Rd (02021-2898)
PHONE....................................781 828-5400
Brian J Whelan, *CEO*
Stanley Graveline, *VP Admin*
Stan Graveline, *Vice Pres*
Gary Dadekian, *CFO*
Don Piccolo, *Controller*
EMP: 140
SQ FT: 60,000

SALES: 29MM
SALES (corp-wide): 427.8MM Privately Held
WEB: www.sarnafilus.com
SIC: 2952 1761 Mfg Asphalt Felts/Coatings Roofing/Siding Contractor
HQ: Sika Corporation
201 Polito Ave
Lyndhurst NJ 07071
201 933-8800

(G-9776)
SCHLAGE LOCK COMPANY LLC
Kryptonite
437 Turnpike St (02021-2758)
PHONE..................................781 828-6655
EMP: 30 Privately Held
SIC: 3429 5091 Mfg Bicycle And Motorcycle Locks
HQ: Schlage Lock Company Llc
11819 N Penn St
Carmel IN 46032
317 810-3700

(G-9777)
SEA STREET TECHNOLOGIES INC
779 Washington St Ste 2c (02021-3022)
PHONE..................................617 600-5150
Harley Stowell, *CEO*
Jeff Boone, *President*
Stephen J Ivanoski, *CFO*
EMP: 50 EST: 2012
SALES (est): 520.8K Privately Held
SIC: 7372 Prepackaged Software Services

(G-9778)
SHERMAN PRINTING CO INC
1020 Turnpike St Ste 11 (02021-2814)
PHONE..................................781 828-8855
Peter W Sherman, *President*
Mike Shields, *Vice Pres*
Peter Grinham, *Plant Mgr*
Scott Frasu, *Manager*
Jay Nemoda, *Manager*
EMP: 25
SQ FT: 12,000
SALES (est): 5.2MM Privately Held
WEB: www.shermanprinting.com
SIC: 2752 2791 2789 Lithographic Commercial Printing Typesetting Services Bookbinding/Related Work

(G-9779)
SIEMENS INDUSTRY INC
Also Called: M.A.C. Systems
40 Shawmut Rd Ste 100 (02021-1409)
PHONE..................................781 364-1000
Catherine McMenimon, *Chairman*
EMP: 65
SALES (corp-wide): 96.9B Privately Held
WEB: www.sibt.com
SIC: 3699 Mfg Electrical Equipment/Supplies
HQ: Siemens Industry, Inc.
1000 Deerfield Pkwy
Buffalo Grove IL 60089
847 215-1000

(G-9780)
SIKA SARNAFIL INC (HQ)
100 Dan Rd (02021-2842)
PHONE..................................781 828-5400
Brian J Whelan, *CEO*
Ernst Baertschi, *Ch of Bd*
Stanley P Graveline, *Vice Pres*
Derreck Mabasa, *Opers Staff*
Steven Masterson, *Buyer*
◆ EMP: 120
SQ FT: 185,000
SALES (est): 120.5MM
SALES (corp-wide): 427.8MM Privately Held
WEB: www.sarnafilus.com
SIC: 2295 3081 5033 5211 Mfg Coated Fabrics Mfg Unsupport Plstc Film Whol Roof/Siding/Insultn Ret Lumber/Building Mtrl
PA: Sika Ag
Zugerstrasse 50
Baar ZG 6341
584 366-800

(G-9781)
SIKA SARNAFIL INC
Also Called: Sarna Div
225 Dan Rd (02021-2845)
PHONE..................................800 451-2502
Kevin Hamblett, *Manager*
EMP: 6
SALES (corp-wide): 427.8MM Privately Held
WEB: www.sarnafilus.com
SIC: 2952 Mfg Roofing Materials
HQ: Sika Sarnafil Inc.
100 Dan Rd
Canton MA 02021
781 828-5400

(G-9782)
SOLEO HEALTH INC
5 Shawmut Rd Ste 103 (02021-1408)
PHONE..................................781 298-3427
EMP: 4 Privately Held
SIC: 2834 5912 Mfg Pharmaceutical Preparations Ret Drugs/Sundries
HQ: Soleo Health Inc.
950 Calcon Hook Rd Ste 19
Sharon Hill PA 19079
888 244-2340

(G-9783)
SOUTHEAST RAILING CO INC
901 Turnpike St Unit A (02021-2861)
PHONE..................................781 828-7088
Robert De Voe, *Owner*
EMP: 10
SQ FT: 5,000
SALES (est): 1.4MM Privately Held
SIC: 3446 1799 Mfg Architectural Metalwork Trade Contractor

(G-9784)
SPECTROWAX CORPORATION (PA)
Also Called: Safeworld International
330 Pine St (02021-3366)
PHONE..................................617 543-0400
Arnold Rosenberg, *President*
Arnold H Rosenberg, *President*
EMP: 60 EST: 1967
SQ FT: 18,000
SALES (est): 4.8MM Privately Held
WEB: www.spectrowax.com
SIC: 2841 2842 Mfg Soap/Other Detergents Mfg Polish/Sanitation Goods

(G-9785)
SPECTRUM LITHO INC
112 Will Dr (02021-3704)
PHONE..................................781 575-0700
Mark H Zimmerman, *President*
EMP: 6
SALES (est): 1MM Privately Held
SIC: 2752 Lithographic Commercial Printing

(G-9786)
SPECTRUM PRESS INC
112 Will Dr (02021-3704)
PHONE..................................781 828-5050
Daniel K Crowley, *Principal*
EMP: 4
SALES (est): 219.1K Privately Held
SIC: 2741 Misc Publishing

(G-9787)
STONERIDGE INC
Pollak Engineered Pdts Group
300 Dan Rd (02021-2848)
PHONE..................................781 830-0340
Mike Seely, *Branch Mgr*
EMP: 400
SALES (corp-wide): 866.2MM Publicly Held
WEB: www.stoneridge.com
SIC: 3714 3699 Mfg Motor Vehicle Parts/Accessories Mfg Electrical Equipment/Supplies
PA: Stoneridge, Inc.
39675 Mackenzie Dr # 400
Novi MI 48377
248 489-9300

(G-9788)
SUBURBAN SHOPPER INC
780 Washington St (02021-3009)
P.O. Box 328 (02021-0328)
PHONE..................................781 821-2590
Marjory Binder, *President*
EMP: 5
SQ FT: 900
SALES (est): 410K Privately Held
SIC: 2721 Periodicals-Publishing/Printing

(G-9789)
TDL INC
Also Called: T D L
550 Turnpike St (02021-2725)
P.O. Box 266 (02021-0266)
PHONE..................................781 828-3366
Tobe Deutschmann Jr, *President*
John J Ahearn, *Vice Pres*
Ruth Darcy, *Admin Sec*
EMP: 20 EST: 1959
SQ FT: 12,000
SALES (est): 2.6MM Privately Held
WEB: www.tdl.com
SIC: 3675 5065 Mfg Electronic Components

(G-9790)
TRI TOWN DISCOUNT LIQUORS
100 Washington St Ste A (02021-4017)
PHONE..................................781 828-8393
Michael Chen, *Principal*
EMP: 4 EST: 2007
SALES (est): 323K Privately Held
SIC: 2082 Mfg Malt Beverages

(G-9791)
UNICOM ENGINEERING INC (HQ)
Also Called: Nei
25 Dan Rd (02021-2817)
PHONE..................................781 332-1000
Corry Hong, *President*
Timothy Dalton, *Vice Pres*
Richard Graber, *Vice Pres*
William O'Connell, *Vice Pres*
Tom Paquette, *Vice Pres*
▲ EMP: 264
SQ FT: 52,000
SALES: 275MM
SALES (corp-wide): 508.4MM Privately Held
WEB: www.networkengines.com
SIC: 3572 7372 Mfg Computer Storage Devices Prepackaged Software Services
PA: Unicom Global, Inc.
15535 San Fernando Mssion
Mission Hills CA 91345
818 838-0606

(G-9792)
VANITY WORLD INC
Also Called: Absolute Marble & Granite
348 Turnpike St Ste 1 (02021-2708)
PHONE..................................508 668-1800
George Dolabany, *President*
EMP: 3
SQ FT: 12,000
SALES (est): 184.7K Privately Held
SIC: 3281 2434 Mfg Cut Stone/Products Mfg Wood Kitchen Cabinets

(G-9793)
VBRICK SYSTEMS INC
1743 Washington St (02021-1668)
PHONE..................................203 265-0044
Jim Glick, *Manager*
EMP: 3
SALES (corp-wide): 33.5MM Privately Held
WEB: www.vbrick.com
SIC: 3661 Mfg Telephone/Telegraph Apparatus
PA: Vbrick Systems, Inc.
127 Wshington Ave Fl 3w Flr 3
North Haven CT 06473
866 827-4251

(G-9794)
VOLTREE POWER INC
34 Mohawk Rd (02021-1236)
P.O. Box 477 (02021-0477)
PHONE..................................781 858-4939
Stella J Karavas, *CEO*
Chris Lagadinos, *CTO*
EMP: 4
SALES (est): 441.3K Privately Held
WEB: www.voltreepower.com
SIC: 3669 0851 3679 3944 Mfg Communications Equip Forestry Services Mfg Elec Components Mfg Games/Toys

(G-9795)
WESTWOOD SYSTEMS INC
Also Called: Newman Associates
80 Hudson Rd Ste 200 (02021-1416)
PHONE..................................781 821-1117
Henry Newman III, *President*
Tom Gover, *Purch Mgr*
Jamison Mrozewicz, *Engineer*
EMP: 10
SALES (est): 1.3MM Privately Held
SIC: 3441 Steel Fabricaiton

(G-9796)
WOODCRAFT DESIGNERS BLDRS LLC
45 North St (02021-3338)
PHONE..................................508 584-4200
Chris Laverdiere, *Inv Control Mgr*
Maciek Butkiewicz, *Manager*
Lukasz Wasiak, *Manager*
EMP: 6
SALES (est): 1.2MM Privately Held
SIC: 2431 Mfg Millwork

GEOGRAPHIC

Carlisle
Middlesex County

(G-9797)
CARLISLE COMMUNICATIONS INC
Also Called: CARLISLE MOSQUITO
662a Bedford Rd (01741-1859)
PHONE..................................978 369-7921
Susan Emmons, *General Mgr*
Leonard Johnson, *Treasurer*
EMP: 4
SALES: 215.8K Privately Held
WEB: www.carlislemosquito.org
SIC: 2711 Newspapers-Publishing/Printing

(G-9798)
HALF-TIME VENTURES INC
103 Meadowbrook Rd (01741-1115)
PHONE..................................978 369-2907
EMP: 3 EST: 2007
SQ FT: 1,000
SALES: 120K Privately Held
SIC: 3365 Aluminum Foundry

(G-9799)
PHOTONIC SYSTEMS INC
100 Wildwood Dr (01741-1411)
PHONE..................................978 369-0729
Carol Cox, *Senior Partner*
EMP: 4 EST: 2014
SALES (est): 297.8K Privately Held
SIC: 3661 Mfg Telephone/Telegraph Apparatus

(G-9800)
WEE FOREST FOLK INC
887 Bedford Rd (01741-1811)
PHONE..................................978 369-0286
William R Peterson, *President*
Richard E Peterson, *Treasurer*
Annette Peterson, *Admin Sec*
EMP: 25
SALES (est): 2.3MM Privately Held
SIC: 3299 Mfg Ceramic Mice

(G-9801)
YANKEE GLASS BLOWER INC
117 Robbins Dr (01741-1719)
PHONE..................................978 369-7545
Patrick De Florio, *President*
William J De Florio, *Vice Pres*
EMP: 5
SALES: 225K Privately Held
WEB: www.yankeeglassblower.com
SIC: 3229 3221 Mfg Industrial & Scientific Glassware & Containers

Carver
Plymouth County

(G-9802)
BRIAN LEOPOLD
Also Called: Global Coding Solutions
53 Myles Standish Dr (02330-1632)
PHONE....................................508 465-0345
Brian Leopold, *President*
EMP: 3
SALES: 1MM **Privately Held**
SIC: 2893 8742 Mfg Printing Ink Management Consulting Services

(G-9803)
DECAS CRANBERRY CO INC (PA)
4 Old Forge Way Ste 1 (02330-1765)
PHONE....................................508 866-8506
Cynthia Parola, *President*
Charles Dillon, *COO*
John Decas, *Treasurer*
Ellen Lakey, *Controller*
Norman Beauregard, *Accounts Mgr*
◆ **EMP:** 3
SQ FT: 10,000
SALES (est): 8MM **Privately Held**
WEB: www.decascranberry.com
SIC: 2033 Mfg Canned Fruits/Vegetables

(G-9804)
DECAS CRANBERRY PRODUCTS INC
4 Old Forge Way Ste 1 (02330-1765)
PHONE....................................508 866-8506
Charles B Dillon, *President*
Norman R Beauregard, *Treasurer*
Gregory Decas, *Director*
John Decas, *Director*
Cynthia Parola, *Director*
▼ **EMP:** 50
SALES (est): 11.5MM **Privately Held**
WEB: www.decascranberry.com
SIC: 2034 0171 8611 Mfg Dehydrated Fruits/Vegetables Berry Crop Farm Business Association

(G-9805)
NEWPORT JERKY COMPANY
116 Meadow St (02330-1523)
PHONE....................................347 913-6882
EMP: 3
SALES (est): 168.5K **Privately Held**
SIC: 2013 Mfg Prepared Meats

(G-9806)
PLYMOUTH GRATING LAB INC
5 Commerce Way (02330-1080)
PHONE....................................508 465-2274
Douglas Smith, *President*
Eileen Smith, *Corp Secy*
Mark Imus, *Mktg Dir*
▼ **EMP:** 15
SQ FT: 7,500
SALES (est): 3.4MM **Privately Held**
WEB: www.plymouthgrating.com
SIC: 3827 Mfg Optical Instruments/Lenses

(G-9807)
SANDY POINT BOAT WORKS LLC
57 Cranberry Rd (02330-1606)
P.O. Box 687 (02330-0687)
PHONE....................................508 878-8057
John K Battersby, *Principal*
EMP: 3
SALES (est): 294.1K **Privately Held**
SIC: 3732 Boatbuilding/Repairing

(G-9808)
SUBURBAN NEWS DEALERS LLC
19 Shaw St (02330-1183)
PHONE....................................508 962-9807
Anthony James Bossi Jr, *Principal*
EMP: 3
SALES (est): 171.1K **Privately Held**
SIC: 2711 Newspapers-Publishing/Printing

(G-9809)
TLI GROUP LTD
35 Kennedy Dr (02330-1623)
PHONE....................................508 866-9825
William Coviello, *President*
EMP: 10
SQ FT: 2,000
SALES: 5MM **Privately Held**
WEB: www.tligroup.com
SIC: 2899 Mfg Fire Extinguisher Charges

Cataumet
Barnstable County

(G-9810)
CAPE COD SAILMAKERS INC
Also Called: Squeteague Sailmakers
4b Long Hill Rd (02534)
PHONE....................................508 563-3080
Marc Daniels, *President*
EMP: 4
SQ FT: 2,200
SALES (est): 426K **Privately Held**
WEB: www.squeteaguesailmakers.com
SIC: 3731 5551 2394 Shipbuilding/Repairing Ret Boats Mfg Canvas/Related Products

(G-9811)
CLASSIC WOODWORKS INC
1231 Rte 28a (02534)
P.O. Box 767 (02534-0767)
PHONE....................................508 563-9922
Douglas Abbe, *President*
Ralph Restino, *Treasurer*
EMP: 3 **EST:** 1997
SALES (est): 98K **Privately Held**
SIC: 2434 Mfg Wood Kitchen Cabinets

(G-9812)
DEEP SEA SYSTEMS INTL INC
Also Called: Dssi
1130 Rte 28a (02534)
PHONE....................................508 540-6732
Chris Nicholsen, *President*
▲ **EMP:** 9
SQ FT: 8,800
SALES (est): 870K **Privately Held**
WEB: www.deepseasystems.com
SIC: 3861 7335 3731 Mfg Photographic Equipment/Supplies Commercial Photography Shipbuilding/Repairing

Centerville
Barnstable County

(G-9813)
BARNSTABLE BAT INC
40 Pleasant Pines Ave (02632-1423)
PHONE....................................508 362-8046
Thomas Bednark, *Owner*
Christine Bednark, *Co-Owner*
EMP: 3
SQ FT: 1,800
SALES (est): 203K **Privately Held**
WEB: www.baseballbat.net
SIC: 3949 Mfg Sporting/Athletic Goods

(G-9814)
EMBROIDER-ISM LLC
10 Hillside Dr (02632-1702)
PHONE....................................508 375-6461
Yolanda Johnson, *Owner*
EMP: 3
SALES (est): 173.7K **Privately Held**
SIC: 2395 Pleating/Stitching Services

(G-9815)
FEIN THINGS
1656 Falmouth Rd (02632-2948)
PHONE....................................508 778-5200
Susan Fein, *Owner*
EMP: 6
SALES (est): 885.8K **Privately Held**
SIC: 2771 Mfg Greeting Cards

(G-9816)
IMPACT PROTECTION SYSTEMS INC
41 Wilton Dr (02632-2942)
PHONE....................................508 737-8850
Brian O Covell, *President*
Brian Covell, *President*
EMP: 3
SALES (est): 236K **Privately Held**
SIC: 3446 Mfg Architectural Metalwork

(G-9817)
MINUTEMAN PRESS
1694 Falmouth Rd (02632-2933)
PHONE....................................508 775-9890
Judy Herring, *President*
EMP: 4
SALES (est): 135.1K **Privately Held**
SIC: 2752 Comm Prtg Litho

(G-9818)
MUSICAL PLAYGROUND
142 Willow Run Dr (02632-2419)
PHONE....................................508 778-6679
Adam Wannie, *Principal*
EMP: 3
SALES (est): 199.7K **Privately Held**
SIC: 3679 Mfg Electronic Components

Charlemont
Franklin County

(G-9819)
CHICOPEE WELDING & TOOL INC
94 W Hawley Rd (01339-9618)
PHONE....................................413 598-8215
Wayne G Lemoine, *President*
Donna Lemoine, *Vice Pres*
EMP: 10
SALES (est): 1.4MM **Privately Held**
WEB: www.chicwelding.com
SIC: 3444 7692 5085 Mfg Sheet Metalwork Welding Repair Whol Industrial Supplies

(G-9820)
LEPRECHAUN SHEEPSKIN COMPANY
464 Tea St (01339)
P.O. Box 302 (01339-0302)
PHONE....................................413 339-4355
H Thomas Hayward, *Owner*
EMP: 4
SALES: 200K **Privately Held**
WEB: www.lsheepskin.com
SIC: 2386 Manufactures Sheepskin Coats Hats And Garments

(G-9821)
NEWJEN CORP
488 Tea St (01339-9775)
PHONE....................................413 543-4888
William Jennings, *CEO*
EMP: 3
SALES: 250K **Privately Held**
SIC: 3599 Mfg Industrial Machinery

(G-9822)
PAUL R HICKS
1255 Route 2 E (01339-3904)
PHONE....................................413 625-2623
Paul Hicks, *Principal*
EMP: 3
SALES (est): 198.4K **Privately Held**
SIC: 2411 Logging

Charlestown
Suffolk County

(G-9823)
ACME BOOKBINDING COMPANY INC
92 Cambridge St (02129-1231)
PHONE....................................617 242-1100
Angelo Parisi, *President*
Paul Parisi, *President*
Antoinette Parisi, *Principal*
John Parisi, *Director*
EMP: 100 **EST:** 1959
SALES (est): 12.2MM
SALES (corp-wide): 28MM **Privately Held**
WEB: www.acmebook.com
SIC: 2789 Bookbinding/Related Work
PA: Hf Group, Llc
8844 Mayfield Rd
Chesterland OH 44026
440 729-2445

(G-9824)
ATW ELECTRONICS INC
24 Spice St Ste 2 (02129-1312)
PHONE....................................617 304-3579
Jeffrey Spinks, *CEO*
Russ Leblanc, *General Mgr*
EMP: 13
SQ FT: 1,400
SALES (est): 1.7MM **Privately Held**
SIC: 3677 Mfg Electronic Transformers

(G-9825)
BOSTON BOATWORKS LLC
333 Terminal St (02129-3901)
PHONE....................................617 561-9111
Stephen King, *Purch Dir*
Jon Clermont, *Cust Mgr*
Scott Rs Smith, *Mng Member*
Val Ferreira, *Master*
Mark Lindsay,
◆ **EMP:** 40
SALES (est): 11MM **Privately Held**
WEB: www.bostonboatworks.com
SIC: 3732 Boatbuilding/Repairing

(G-9826)
BOSTON SAND & GRAVEL COMPANY
40 Bunker Hill Indus Park (02129)
PHONE....................................617 242-5540
Jomarie Bolen, *President*
EMP: 102
SALES (corp-wide): 121MM **Privately Held**
SIC: 3273 Mfg Ready-Mixed Concrete
PA: Boston Sand & Gravel Company Inc
100 N Washington St Fl 2
Boston MA 02114
617 227-9000

(G-9827)
BOUNCEPAD NORTH AMERICA INC
50 Termi St Unit 710bldg (02129)
PHONE....................................617 804-0110
Tobi Schneidler, *President*
EMP: 10
SALES (est): 1.6MM **Privately Held**
SIC: 2678 Mfg Stationery Products

(G-9828)
BROWN PUBLISHING NETWORK INC (PA)
10 City Sq Ste 3 (02129-3740)
PHONE....................................781 547-7600
Marie L Brown, *President*
Mark S Brown, *CFO*
EMP: 30
SQ FT: 12,000
SALES: 7.2MM **Privately Held**
WEB: www.brownpubnet.com
SIC: 2741 2731 Misc Publishing Books-Publishing/Printing

(G-9829)
CHARLESTOWN BRIDGE
87 Warren St (02129-3615)
PHONE....................................617 241-8500
Karen Taylor, *Principal*
Dan Murphy, *Editor*
EMP: 4
SALES (est): 211.6K **Privately Held**
SIC: 2711 Newspapers-Publishing/Printing

(G-9830)
CONFER HEALTH INC
56 Roland St Ste 208 (02129-1223)
PHONE....................................617 433-8810
Mounir Ahmad Koussa, *President*
Joshua John Forman, *Treasurer*
Zhi-Yang Tsun, *Admin Sec*
EMP: 8
SALES (est): 712.7K **Privately Held**
SIC: 2835 Mfg Diagnostic Substances

▲ = Import ▼=Export
◆ =Import/Export

(G-9831)
DIVERSIFIED INDUSTRIAL SUP LLC
100 Terminal St (02129-1980)
PHONE.....800 244-3647
Dave Gorman, *Manager*
Richard Callahan, *Manager*
EMP: 10
SALES (est): 1.3MM **Privately Held**
SIC: 3052 Mfg Rubber/Plastic Hose/Belting

(G-9832)
ECOVENT CORP
24 Cambridge St Ste 6 (02129-1307)
P.O. Box 729, Bolton (01740-0729)
PHONE.....620 983-6863
Dipul Patel, *CEO*
EMP: 10
SALES (est): 1.5MM **Privately Held**
SIC: 3634 Mfg Electric Housewares/Fans

(G-9833)
ELECTRONIC PUBLISHING SERVICES
529 Main St (02129-1125)
PHONE.....508 544-1254
Gary F Florindo, *CEO*
EMP: 3
SALES (est): 101.5K **Privately Held**
SIC: 2741 Misc Publishing

(G-9834)
EMBR LABS INC
24 Roland St 102 (02129-1249)
PHONE.....413 218-0629
Matthew Smith, *CEO*
David Cohen-Tanugi, *Director*
Samuel Shames, *Director*
EMP: 3
SALES (est): 269.5K **Privately Held**
SIC: 3679 Mfg Electronic Components

(G-9835)
GLOBAL RES INNOVATION TECH INC
Also Called: Grit
56 Roland St Ste 102b (02129-1243)
PHONE.....617 383-4748
Natasha Scolnik, *President*
EMP: 4 **EST:** 2015
SALES (est): 218.5K **Privately Held**
SIC: 3842 Mfg Surgical Appliances/Supplies

(G-9836)
HF GROUP LLC
Also Called: Acme Bookbinding Company
92 Cambridge St (02129-1231)
PHONE.....617 242-1100
Paul A Parisi,
EMP: 6 **EST:** 2015
SALES (est): 566.7K **Privately Held**
SIC: 2789 Bookbinding/Related Work

(G-9837)
HYDRATION LABS INCORPORATED
Also Called: Bevi
529 Main St Ste 311 (02129-1119)
PHONE.....617 333-8191
Sean Grundy, *CEO*
Elizabeth Becton, *President*
James Koller, *Opers Staff*
Joel Leiby, *Opers Staff*
Sean McElduff, *CFO*
EMP: 6 **EST:** 2014
SALES (est): 1.6MM **Privately Held**
SIC: 3565 Mfg Packaging Machinery

(G-9838)
JOINERY SHOP INC
92 Arlington Ave (02129-1031)
PHONE.....617 242-4718
Patrick Brady, *President*
James Brady, *Treasurer*
EMP: 7
SQ FT: 7,000
SALES (est): 1MM **Privately Held**
WEB: www.thejoineryshop.com
SIC: 2431 Mfg Millwork

(G-9839)
NAVARRETE FOODS INC
50 Terminal St (02129-1973)
PHONE.....508 735-7319
Edwin Navarrete, *President*
EMP: 4
SALES: 380.5K **Privately Held**
SIC: 2099 Mfg Food Preparations

(G-9840)
NEWTON SCIENTIFIC INC
529 Main St Ste 600 (02129-1106)
PHONE.....617 354-9469
Ruth Shefer, *CEO*
Robert Klinkowstein, *Treasurer*
EMP: 20
SQ FT: 10,000
SALES (est): 2.6MM **Privately Held**
WEB: www.newtonscientificinc.com
SIC: 3841 Mfg Surgical/Medical Instruments

(G-9841)
POMEROY & CO INC
18 Spice St Ste 1 (02129-1395)
PHONE.....617 241-0234
Gregory E Pomeroy, *President*
Aidan Lindh, *Project Mgr*
Barry Mann, *Project Mgr*
Harty Dan, *Engineer*
Jennifer Mello, *Engineer*
EMP: 35
SALES (est): 8.1MM **Privately Held**
WEB: www.pomeroyco.com
SIC: 2431 Mfg Millwork

(G-9842)
R F MC MANUS COMPANY INC
7 Sherman St (02129-1024)
PHONE.....617 241-8081
Ray McManus, *President*
Bill Kenney, *Senior Engr*
EMP: 13
SALES (est): 1.1MM **Privately Held**
SIC: 2434 Mfg Wood Products

(G-9843)
SANTHERA PHRMCEUTICALS USA INC
40 Warren St Fl 3 (02129-3608)
PHONE.....617 886-5161
Klaus Schollmeier, *President*
Stephan Haefelfinger, *VP Finance*
Anne Atkins, *Director*
EMP: 6
SALES (est): 764.2K **Privately Held**
SIC: 2834 Mfg Pharmaceutical Preparations

(G-9844)
SMUDGE INK INCORPORATED
50 Terminal St Ste 21 (02129-1973)
PHONE.....617 242-8228
Katherine Saliba, *President*
Deb Bastien, *Vice Pres*
EMP: 8
SALES (est): 865.3K **Privately Held**
SIC: 2759 7334 Commercial Printing Photocopying Services

(G-9845)
ZIOPHARM ONCOLOGY INC
1 1st Ave (02129-4552)
PHONE.....617 259-1970
Jonathan Lewis PHD, *CEO*
David Connolly, *Vice Pres*
EMP: 7
SALES (corp-wide): 146K **Publicly Held**
SIC: 2834 Mfg Pharmaceutical Preparations
PA: Ziopharm Oncology, Inc.
1 1st Ave Ste 34
Boston MA 02129
617 259-1970

Charlton
Worcester County

(G-9846)
ALL GRANITE & MARBLE INC II
379 Worcester Rd (01507-1503)
PHONE.....508 434-0611
Altramiro Abranches, *President*
Alecxandro Santos, *Vice Pres*
▲ **EMP:** 8
SALES (est): 1MM **Privately Held**
SIC: 3281 Mfg Cut Stone/Products

(G-9847)
CRONIN CABINET MARINE LLP
164 Sturbridge Rd Ste 20 (01507-5324)
PHONE.....508 248-7026
John D Cronin Sr, *Partner*
Caroline Cronin, *Partner*
Cindy Cronin, *Partner*
Jeffery Cronin, *Partner*
John D Cronin Jr, *Partner*
EMP: 8
SQ FT: 6,000
SALES: 450K **Privately Held**
WEB: www.cronincabinets.com
SIC: 2434 Mfg Wood Kitchen Cabinets

(G-9848)
DADS
417 Worcester Rd (01507-1505)
PHONE.....508 248-9774
Donald Daigle, *Owner*
EMP: 6
SALES (est): 359.5K **Privately Held**
SIC: 2024 5812 Mfg Ice Cream/Frozen Desert Eating Place

(G-9849)
DNS INC
Also Called: Business Printer, The
123 Hammond Hill Rd (01507-1564)
PHONE.....508 248-5901
EMP: 12
SQ FT: 9,000
SALES (est): 1.4MM **Privately Held**
WEB: www.dnsprint.com
SIC: 2752 Lithographic Commercial Printing

(G-9850)
GHM INDUSTRIES INC (PA)
Also Called: Gessner Company
100 Sturbridge Rd Unit A (01507-5380)
PHONE.....508 248-3941
Paul Jankovic, *President*
Al Papesy, *Vice Pres*
Adam Caisse, *Design Engr*
Marty Kloss, *Sales Staff*
Shawn Bickford, *Info Tech Dir*
▲ **EMP:** 15
SALES (est): 2.7MM **Privately Held**
WEB: www.gessner.net
SIC: 3531 Mfg Construction Machinery

(G-9851)
INCOM INC
Also Called: Manfucturer
294 Southbridge Rd (01507-5238)
PHONE.....508 909-2200
Anthony M Detarando, *Ch of Bd*
Michael Detarando, *President*
Michael A Detarando, *Principal*
David Reno, *Mfg Mgr*
Michael Lefebvre, *Purch Mgr*
▲ **EMP:** 150
SQ FT: 52,000
SALES (est): 33.7MM **Privately Held**
WEB: www.incomusa.com
SIC: 3827 Mfg Optical Instruments/Lenses

(G-9852)
KARL STORZ ENDOVISION INC
91 Carpenter Hill Rd (01507-5274)
PHONE.....508 248-9011
Gary Macker, *President*
Sybill Storz, *Owner*
Raymond Celmer, *Research*
Michael Laforest, *Research*
Emmanuel Asante, *Engineer*
EMP: 400
SQ FT: 85,000
SALES (est): 113.4MM
SALES (corp-wide): 1.9B **Privately Held**
SIC: 3841 Mfg Surgical/Medical Instruments
PA: Karl Storz Se & Co. Kg
Dr.-Karl-Storz-Str. 34
Tuttlingen 78532
746 170-80

(G-9853)
L & P PAPER INC
267 Southbridge Rd (01507-5241)
P.O. Box 96, Southbridge (01550-0096)
PHONE.....508 248-3265
Martin Gubb, *President*
Ronald Camarra, *Director*
Margaret M Desantis, *Director*
EMP: 60
SALES (est): 20.4MM **Privately Held**
SIC: 2621 Paper Mill

(G-9854)
MTD MICRO MOLDING INC
15 Trolley Crossing Rd (01507-1351)
PHONE.....508 248-0111
Richard J Tully, *CEO*
Dennis Tully, *Admin Sec*
EMP: 34 **EST:** 1970
SQ FT: 16,500
SALES (est): 3.8MM **Privately Held**
WEB: www.miniaturetool.com
SIC: 3089 Mfg Plastic Products

(G-9855)
RAN WOODWORKING
160 Center Depot Rd (01507-1214)
PHONE.....508 248-4818
Robert Nolette, *Principal*
Terri Nolette, *Director*
EMP: 3
SALES: 750K **Privately Held**
SIC: 2431 Mfg Millwork

(G-9856)
RER MACHINE CO
15 H Putnam Rd (01507-1221)
P.O. Box 560 (01507-0560)
PHONE.....508 248-3029
Robert Ricrad, *Owner*
EMP: 5
SALES: 100K **Privately Held**
SIC: 3599 Mfg Industrial Machinery

Chartley
Bristol County

(G-9857)
RELIABLE ELECTRO PLATING INC
Also Called: Reliable Plating
304 W Main St (02712)
P.O. Box 91 (02712-0091)
PHONE.....508 222-0620
Dale Broadbent, *President*
Karen Broadbent, *Vice Pres*
EMP: 7 **EST:** 1932
SQ FT: 6,500
SALES (est): 1MM **Privately Held**
SIC: 3471 Electroplating Of Metals

(G-9858)
T J HOLMES CO INC
Also Called: Holmspray
301 W Main St (02712)
P.O. Box 368 (02712-0368)
PHONE.....508 222-1723
Roy F Schlenker, *President*
Joan Schlenker, *Vice Pres*
EMP: 20 **EST:** 1870
SQ FT: 65,000
SALES (est): 1.6MM **Privately Held**
SIC: 3999 3231 Mfg Misc Products Mfg Products-Purchased Glass

Chatham
Barnstable County

(G-9859)
GUSTARE OILS & VINEGARS (PA)
461 Main St (02633-2460)
PHONE.....508 945-4505
Catherine Ferraresi, *Principal*
EMP: 3
SALES (est): 373.1K **Privately Held**
SIC: 2099 Ret Misc Foods

GEOGRAPHIC

(G-9860)
HYORA PUBLICATIONS INC
Also Called: Cape Cod Chronicle
60 Munson Meeting Way C (02633-1992)
PHONE..................................508 430-2700
Henry C Hyora, *President*
Karen Hyora, *Treasurer*
EMP: 19
SALES (est): 1.1MM **Privately Held**
WEB: www.capecodchronicle.com
SIC: 2711 Newspapers-Publishing/Printing

(G-9861)
NIXIE SPARKLING WATER LLC
149 Cross St (02633-2278)
PHONE..................................617 784-8671
Nicole Dawes, *Mng Member*
Peter Dawes,
EMP: 9 **EST:** 2018
SALES: 8MM **Privately Held**
SIC: 2086 Mfg Bottled/Canned Soft Drinks

(G-9862)
PEASE BOAT WORKS & MARINE RLWY
43 Eliphamets Ln (02633-2406)
PHONE..................................508 945-7800
John Pease, *President*
EMP: 5
SQ FT: 50,000
SALES (est): 553.1K **Privately Held**
WEB: www.peaseboatworks.com
SIC: 3732 Boatbuilding/Repairing

(G-9863)
PVH CORP
Also Called: Van Heusen
1238 Main St (02633-1861)
PHONE..................................508 945-4063
Kay Janulewicz, *Branch Mgr*
EMP: 7
SALES (corp-wide): 9.6B **Publicly Held**
WEB: www.pvh.com
SIC: 2321 Mfg Men's/Boy's Furnishings
PA: Pvh Corp.
200 Madison Ave Bsmt 1
New York NY 10016
212 381-3500

Chelmsford
Middlesex County

(G-9864)
3D EDUCATIONAL SERVICES INC
Also Called: 3des
321 Billerica Rd Ste 1 (01824-4100)
PHONE..................................978 364-2728
Dayananda Vellal, *President*
Richard Thall, *Principal*
EMP: 3
SALES: 20K **Privately Held**
SIC: 3999 Mfg Misc Products

(G-9865)
3M COMPANY
279 Billerica Rd (01824-4180)
PHONE..................................978 256-3911
Brian Nilsson, *Branch Mgr*
EMP: 118
SQ FT: 65,000
SALES (corp-wide): 32.7B **Publicly Held**
WEB: www.mmm.com
SIC: 3629 3317 3083 Mfg Electrical Industrial Apparatus Mfg Steel Pipe/Tubes Mfg Laminated Plastic Plate/Sheet
PA: 3m Company
3m Center
Saint Paul MN 55144
651 733-1110

(G-9866)
ACCUTRONICS INC
10 Elizabeth Dr Ste 3 (01824-4145)
PHONE..................................978 250-9144
Luis M Pedroso, *President*
Maria Silva, *Treasurer*
Michael Panagopoulos, *Director*
Paul Pedroso, *Director*
Luis Pedroso, *Executive*
EMP: 50
SQ FT: 31,000
SALES (est): 14.2MM **Privately Held**
SIC: 3699 Mfg Electrical Equipment/Supplies

(G-9867)
ADVA OPTICAL NETWORKING NORTH
Also Called: Mrv Communications
300 Apollo Dr (01824-3629)
PHONE..................................978 674-6800
EMP: 150
SALES (corp-wide): 556.7MM **Privately Held**
SIC: 3661 Mfg Telephone/Telegraph Apparatus
HQ: Adva Optical Networking North America, Inc.
5755 Peachtree Indus Blvd
Norcross GA 30092

(G-9868)
ALARMSAFE INC
6 Omni Way (01824-4141)
PHONE..................................978 658-6717
Phil Stevens, *President*
Philip Stevens, *President*
Luann Kessler, *Purch Mgr*
EMP: 30 **EST:** 1979
SALES (est): 4.4MM **Privately Held**
WEB: www.alarmsaf.com
SIC: 3669 Mfg Communications Equipment

(G-9869)
ALLIED SEALANT INC
10 Jean Ave Ste 16 (01824-1740)
PHONE..................................978 254-7117
Robert Joyce, *Principal*
EMP: 5 **EST:** 2009
SALES (est): 426.4K **Privately Held**
SIC: 2891 Mfg Adhesives/Sealants

(G-9870)
AMAL FUEL INC
5 Drum Hill Rd (01824-1503)
PHONE..................................978 934-9704
EMP: 4
SALES (est): 309.4K **Privately Held**
SIC: 2869 Mfg Industrial Organic Chemicals

(G-9871)
ARROW INTERNATIONAL INC
Also Called: Teleflex Medical
16 Elizabeth Dr (01824-4112)
PHONE..................................978 250-5100
Jim Athans, *Sales Staff*
Mike Harpin, *Manager*
EMP: 100
SALES (corp-wide): 2.4B **Publicly Held**
WEB: www.arrowintl.com
SIC: 3841 Mfg Surgical/Medical Instruments
HQ: Arrow International, Inc.
550 E Swedesford Rd # 400
Wayne PA 19087
610 225-6800

(G-9872)
ARROW INTERVENTIONAL INC
Also Called: Teleflex
16 Elizabeth Dr (01824-4112)
PHONE..................................919 433-4948
William Schaal, *Regl Sales Mgr*
Travis Coleman, *Sales Staff*
EMP: 31
SALES (est): 5MM
SALES (corp-wide): 2.4B **Publicly Held**
SIC: 3841 3842 Mfg Surgical/Medical Instruments Mfg Surgical Appliances/Supplies
PA: Teleflex Incorporated
550 E Swedesford Rd # 400
Wayne PA 19087
610 225-6800

(G-9873)
ASPECT SOFTWARE INC
300 Apollo Dr Ste 1 (01824-3630)
PHONE..................................978 250-7900
Bob Stent, *Chief*
Jeff Magenau, *Counsel*
Guido Dekoning, *Vice Pres*
Spencer Demetros, *Vice Pres*
Bruce Hallowell, *Vice Pres*
EMP: 50
SALES (corp-wide): 303.2MM **Privately Held**
SIC: 7372 Custom Computer Programing
HQ: Aspect Software, Inc.
2325 E Camelback Rd # 700
Phoenix AZ 85016
978 250-7900

(G-9874)
ASSEMBLY GUIDANCE SYSTEMS INC
Also Called: Aligned Vision
27 Industrial Ave Unit 4 (01824-3618)
PHONE..................................978 244-1166
Scott W Blake, *President*
Robert G Coyne, *Treasurer*
Miriam Kadansky, *Software Engr*
Stephen Silbert, *Administration*
▼ **EMP:** 19
SQ FT: 90,000
SALES (est): 4.1MM **Privately Held**
WEB: www.assemblyguide.com
SIC: 3823 Mfg Process Control Instruments

(G-9875)
ASSURANCE TECHNOLOGY CORP
303 Littleton Rd (01824-3311)
PHONE..................................978 250-8060
Cosmo Di Ciaccio, *Vice Pres*
Steven Brassard, *Branch Mgr*
EMP: 70
SALES (corp-wide): 88.7MM **Privately Held**
WEB: www.assurtech.com
SIC: 3629 3663 Mfg Electrical Industrial Apparatus Mfg Radio/Tv Communication Equipment
PA: Assurance Technology Corp
84 South St
Carlisle MA 01741
978 369-8848

(G-9876)
AURIGA MEASUREMENT SYSTEMS
2 Executive Dr (01824-2565)
PHONE..................................978 452-7700
EMP: 20
SALES (corp-wide): 3.5MM **Privately Held**
SIC: 3663 Mfg Radio/Tv Communication Equipment
PA: Auriga Measurement Systems Limited Liability Company
302 Willow Brook Dr
Wayland MA 01778
978 452-7700

(G-9877)
BOSTON MACHINE INC
10 Tracy Rd (01824-4110)
PHONE..................................978 458-7722
Han Y Moon, *President*
EMP: 5
SALES (est): 656.7K **Privately Held**
WEB: www.bostonmachine.net
SIC: 3599 Mfg Industrial Machinery

(G-9878)
BROADCAST PIX INC
27 Industrial Ave Unit 5 (01824-3618)
PHONE..................................978 600-1100
Kenneth Swanton, *President*
Edgar Whittaker, *Chairman*
Jack Swanton, *Vice Pres*
Russell Whittaker, *Vice Pres*
Bob Carsley, *Senior Engr*
EMP: 30
SQ FT: 13,000
SALES: 3.8MM **Privately Held**
WEB: www.broadcastpix.com
SIC: 3861 Mfg Photographic Equipment/Supplies

(G-9879)
BROOKS AUTOMATION INC
12 Elizabeth Dr (01824-4147)
PHONE..................................978 262-2795
Robert Anastasi, *Exec VP*
Michael Violette, *Engineer*
EMP: 450
SALES (corp-wide): 780.8MM **Publicly Held**
SIC: 3563 3561 3559 Mfg Air/Gas Compressors Mfg Pumps/Pumping Equip Mfg Cryogenic Machinery Industrial
PA: Brooks Automation, Inc.
15 Elizabeth Dr
Chelmsford MA 01824
978 262-2400

(G-9880)
BROOKS AUTOMATION INC (PA)
15 Elizabeth Dr (01824-4111)
PHONE..................................978 262-2400
Joseph R Martin, *Ch of Bd*
Stephen S Schwartz, *President*
David C Gray, *Senior VP*
Jason W Joseph, *Senior VP*
William T Montone, *Senior VP*
▲ **EMP:** 277
SQ FT: 298,000
SALES: 780.8MM **Publicly Held**
SIC: 3559 3563 3823 7699 Mfg And Servicing Of Semiconductor Devices

(G-9881)
BROOKS PRECISION MACHINING
4 Kidder Rd (01824-3382)
PHONE..................................978 256-7477
Charles Brooks, *President*
Denise M Brooks, *Vice Pres*
EMP: 10
SQ FT: 6,000
SALES (est): 1.7MM **Privately Held**
WEB: www.brooks-machine.com
SIC: 3599 Mfg Industrial Machinery

(G-9882)
BULL DATA SYSTEMS INC (DH)
285 Billerica Rd Ste 200 (01824-4174)
PHONE..................................978 294-6000
Gervais Pellissier, *President*
Richard Griesbach, *Corp Secy*
Eves Blanc, *CFO*
Doug Parisek, *Software Dev*
EMP: 3
SQ FT: 12,000
SALES (est): 103.9MM
SALES (corp-wide): 161.4MM **Privately Held**
WEB: www.bull.com
SIC: 3571 3577 7378 Mfg Electronic Computers Mfg Computer Peripheral Equipment Computer Maintenance/Repair
HQ: Bull
Avenue Jean Jaures
Les Clayes-Sous-Bois 78340
130 807-000

(G-9883)
BULL HN INFO SYSTEMS INC
285 Billerica Rd Ste 200 (01824-4174)
PHONE..................................978 256-1033
EMP: 4
SALES (corp-wide): 145MM **Privately Held**
SIC: 3571 3577 7378 7373 Mfg Sales & Maintenance Of Computers & Related Equipment Systems Integration/Software Services
HQ: Bull Hn Information Systems Inc.
285 Billerica Rd Ste 200
Chelmsford MA 01824
978 294-6000

(G-9884)
C R BARD INC
Also Called: C R Bard Ep
1 Executive Dr Ste 303 (01824-2564)
PHONE..................................978 441-6202
Andy Chiavetta, *Branch Mgr*
EMP: 446
SALES (corp-wide): 15.9B **Publicly Held**
SIC: 3841 Mfg Surgical/Medical Instruments
HQ: C. R. Bard, Inc.
1 Becton Dr
Franklin Lakes NJ 07417
908 277-8000

(G-9885)
CADENCE DESIGN SYSTEMS INC
270 Billerica Rd (01824-4179)
PHONE..................................978 262-6404
EMP: 90
SQ FT: 82,000
SALES (corp-wide): 1.9B **Publicly Held**
SIC: 7372 Prepackaged Software Services
PA: Cadence Design Systems, Inc.
2655 Seely Ave Bldg 5
San Jose CA 95134
408 943-1234

(G-9886)
CASTLE COMPLEMENTS PRINTING CO
74 Bridge St (01824-2604)
PHONE..................................978 250-9122
Mathew Richards, *Principal*
EMP: 4
SALES (est): 424.7K **Privately Held**
SIC: 2752 Lithographic Commercial Printing

(G-9887)
CHRISTPHRS EMRGNCY EQPTMNT &
Also Called: Christopher's Towing
76 Riverneck Rd (01824-2942)
PHONE..................................978 265-8363
Sherry Ferreira, *President*
EMP: 4
SALES (est): 200K **Privately Held**
SIC: 3711 Mfg Motor Vehicle/Car Bodies

(G-9888)
CORIANT AMERICA INC (HQ)
220 Mill Rd (01824-4127)
PHONE..................................978 250-2900
Pat Dipietro, *CEO*
John Valentine, *CEO*
Bob Leggett, *Ch of Bd*
Herbert Merz, *President*
Ken Craft, *Exec VP*
EMP: 158
SALES (est): 25MM **Privately Held**
SIC: 3661 Mfg Telephone/Telegraph Apparatus

(G-9889)
CREATIVE EXCHANGE INC
3 Brook St (01824-3111)
P.O. Box 428 (01824-0428)
PHONE..................................978 863-9955
Debra Monroe, *President*
EMP: 4 **EST:** 1995
SQ FT: 1,200
SALES (est): 1.7MM **Privately Held**
WEB: www.cexiinc.com
SIC: 3672 Mfg Printed Circuit Boards

(G-9890)
CUNNINGHAM MACHINE CO INC
35 Hunt Rd (01824-2601)
PHONE..................................978 256-7541
Wayne Cunningham, *President*
Susan Cunningham, *Corp Secy*
EMP: 7
SQ FT: 4,000
SALES (est): 1MM **Privately Held**
SIC: 3599 3469 Mfg Industrial Machinery Mfg Metal Stampings

(G-9891)
CUSTOM MMIC DESIGN SVCS INC
300 Apollo Dr (01824-3629)
PHONE..................................978 467-4290
Paul Blount, *President*
David Folding, *Vice Pres*
Tom Rosa, *CFO*
Kathy Hazen, *Admin Asst*
EMP: 27
SQ FT: 8,000
SALES (est): 1.6MM **Privately Held**
WEB: www.custommmic.com
SIC: 3674 Mfg Semiconductors/Related Devices

(G-9892)
DEMS FUEL INC
87 Littleton Rd (01824-2623)
P.O. Box 4068 (01824-0768)
PHONE..................................978 660-0018
EMP: 3
SALES (est): 220.5K **Privately Held**
SIC: 2869 Mfg Industrial Organic Chemicals

(G-9893)
DSA PRINTING & PUBLISHING INC
14 Alpha Rd (01824-4102)
PHONE..................................978 256-3900
James Sullivan, *President*
Kevin Sullivan, *Treasurer*
EMP: 5
SQ FT: 3,000
SALES: 800K **Privately Held**
WEB: www.dsaprint.com
SIC: 2759 2752 Commercial Printing Lithographic Commercial Printing

(G-9894)
EAGLE FIRE SAFETY INC
56 Bridge St (01824-2604)
PHONE..................................978 256-3777
Michael Hazel, *President*
Kathryn Hazel, *Exec VP*
EMP: 5
SALES (est): 530K **Privately Held**
WEB: www.eaglefiresafety.com
SIC: 2899 5099 Mfg Chemical Preparations Whol Durable Goods

(G-9895)
EAST COAST SILKS INC
Also Called: East Coast Florist & Silks
55 Drum Hill Rd (01824-1503)
PHONE..................................978 970-5510
James Palavras, *President*
EMP: 3
SALES (est): 310.7K **Privately Held**
SIC: 3999 Ret Florist

(G-9896)
EDWARDS VACUUM LLC
12 Elizabeth Dr (01824-4147)
PHONE..................................978 262-7565
EMP: 3
SALES (corp-wide): 10B **Privately Held**
SIC: 3563 Mfg Air/Gas Compressors
HQ: Edwards Vacuum Llc
6400 Inducon Corporate Dr
Sanborn NY 14132
800 848-9800

(G-9897)
EUGENE F DELFINO COMPANY INC
72 Amble Rd (01824-1959)
P.O. Box 309 (01824-0309)
PHONE..................................978 221-6496
Lisa Delfino-Mc Laird, *President*
Lisa Delfino-Mclaird, *President*
Andrew P McLaird, *Vice Pres*
EMP: 3
SALES: 3.5MM **Privately Held**
SIC: 3444 Mfg Sheet Metalwork

(G-9898)
FEDEX OFFICE & PRINT SVCS INC
61 Drum Hill Rd (01824-1503)
PHONE..................................978 275-0574
EMP: 4
SALES (corp-wide): 69.6B **Publicly Held**
WEB: www.fedex.com
SIC: 2759 5099 7334 Commercial Printing Whol Durable Goods Photocopying Services
HQ: Fedex Office And Print Services, Inc.
7900 Legacy Dr
Plano TX 75024
800 463-3339

(G-9899)
FLIR UNMNNED GRUND SYSTEMS INC (DH)
19 Alpha Rd Ste 101 (01824-4124)
PHONE..................................978 769-9333
Sean Bielat, *CEO*
Tom Frost, *President*
Peter Manos, *Owner*
Abreu Maximo, *Purchasing*
Annan Mozeika, *Engineer*
EMP: 83 **EST:** 2016
SQ FT: 20,000
SALES (est): 26.8MM
SALES (corp-wide): 1.7B **Publicly Held**
SIC: 3549 Mfg Metalworking Machinery
HQ: Endeavor Robotic Holdings, Inc.
19 Alpha Rd Ste 101
Chelmsford MA 01824
978 769-9333

(G-9900)
FOUR IN ONE LLC
12 Alpha Rd (01824-4102)
PHONE..................................978 250-0751
EMP: 80
SALES (est): 13.5MM **Privately Held**
SIC: 2035 Pickles, Sauces, And Salad Dressings

(G-9901)
G4S TECHNOLOGY SOFTWARE
1 Executive Dr (01824-2563)
PHONE..................................781 457-0700
Noel Keith Whitelock, *President*
EMP: 100
SALES (est): 14.1MM **Privately Held**
SIC: 3577 7371 Mfg Computer Peripheral Equipment Custom Computer Programing
HQ: G4s Technology Holdings (Usa) Inc.
1395 University Blvd
Jupiter FL 33458

(G-9902)
GATEHOUSE MEDIA MASS I INC
Also Called: Community Newspaper
15 Fletcher St (01824-2743)
PHONE..................................978 256-7196
Mack O'Neil, *President*
EMP: 50
SALES (corp-wide): 1.5B **Publicly Held**
SIC: 2711 Newspapers-Publishing/Printing
HQ: Gatehouse Media Massachusetts I, Inc.
48 Dunham Rd
Beverly MA 01915
585 598-0030

(G-9903)
HARDY DORIC INC
22 Progress Ave (01824-3607)
PHONE..................................978 250-1113
Gerald Hardy, *President*
Jeffrey Hardy, *Vice Pres*
Robert Hardy, *Vice Pres*
Sheila M Hardy, *Admin Sec*
EMP: 7 **EST:** 1930
SQ FT: 10,000
SALES (est): 1.2MM **Privately Held**
SIC: 3272 Manufactures Burial Vaults

(G-9904)
HIGH TECH MACHINISTS INC
177 Riverneck Rd (01824-2926)
PHONE..................................978 256-1600
Robert K Moores Jr, *President*
▲ **EMP:** 45
SQ FT: 25,000
SALES (est): 7.1MM **Privately Held**
WEB: www.hightechmachinists.com
SIC: 3599 Mfg Industrial Machinery

(G-9905)
HITTITE MICROWAVE LLC (HQ)
2 Elizabeth Dr (01824-4112)
PHONE..................................978 250-3343
Rick D Hess, *President*
Susan J Dicecco, *Vice Pres*
William D Hannabach, *Vice Pres*
Larry W Ward, *Vice Pres*
William W Boecke, *CFO*
EMP: 133
SQ FT: 103,000
SALES (est): 161.9MM
SALES (corp-wide): 5.9B **Publicly Held**
WEB: www.hittite.com
SIC: 3674 Mfg Semiconductors/Related Devices
PA: Analog Devices, Inc.
1 Technology Way
Norwood MA 02062
781 329-4700

(G-9906)
IMPRESS SYSTEMS INC
7 Stuart Rd (01824-4107)
PHONE..................................978 441-2022
Stephen Aroneo, *President*
EMP: 4
SALES (est): 598.9K **Privately Held**
SIC: 2752 Lithographic Commercial Printing

(G-9907)
JAY ENGINEERING CORP
35 Hunt Rd Ste B (01824-2601)
P.O. Box 125 (01824-0125)
PHONE..................................978 250-0115
EMP: 13
SQ FT: 12,000
SALES (est): 1.3MM **Privately Held**
SIC: 3444 Mfg Sheet Metalwork

(G-9908)
KEWILL INC (DH)
1 Executive Dr Ste 201 (01824-2564)
PHONE..................................978 482-2500
Doug Braun, *CEO*
Joy Burkholder Meier, *Exec VP*
Greg Carter, *Senior VP*
Matt Gaywood, *Senior VP*
Sin Hopwood, *Senior VP*
EMP: 68
SQ FT: 37,000
SALES (est): 49.8MM
SALES (corp-wide): 153.5MM **Privately Held**
SIC: 7372 7371 7373 Prepackaged Software Services Custom Computer Programing Computer Systems Design
HQ: Blujay Solutions Ltd
1st Floor 4m Building Malaga Avenue
Manchester M90 3
161 905-4600

(G-9909)
KLYPPER INC
12 Brush Hill Rd (01824-3825)
PHONE..................................978 987-8548
EMP: 4
SALES (est): 167.3K **Privately Held**
SIC: 7372 7389 Prepackaged Software Services Business Services At Non-Commercial Site

(G-9910)
KONECRANES INC
Also Called: Crane Pro Services
25 Industrial Ave Ste 1 (01824-3617)
PHONE..................................978 256-5525
Greg Davis, *Branch Mgr*
Laurie Melisse-Pina, *Manager*
EMP: 12
SALES (corp-wide): 3.5B **Privately Held**
WEB: www.kciusa.com
SIC: 3536 Mfg Hoists/Cranes/Monorails
HQ: Konecranes, Inc.
4401 Gateway Blvd
Springfield OH 45502

(G-9911)
L3HARRIS TECHNOLOGIES INC
Also Called: M/A Com
150 Apollo Dr (01824-3696)
P.O. Box 376 (01824-0376)
PHONE..................................978 905-3500
Charles Dougherty, *President*
John Mahon, *Mfg Staff*
Tim Fox, *Engineer*
Paul Gehlert, *Engineer*
Chris McLean, *Engineer*
EMP: 441
SALES (corp-wide): 6.8B **Publicly Held**
SIC: 3663 Mfg Radio/Tv Communication Equipment
PA: L3harris Technologies, Inc.
1025 W Nasa Blvd
Melbourne FL 32919
321 727-9100

(G-9912)
LARCHMONT ENGINEERING INC
11 Billerica Rd (01824-3010)
PHONE..................................978 250-1177
EMP: 4
SALES (corp-wide): 1.8MM **Privately Held**
SIC: 3585 3949 Mfg Snowmaking Equipment

GEOGRAPHIC

PA: Larchmont Engineering, Inc.
12 Revere St
Lexington MA 02420
978 250-1260

(G-9913)
LOCKHEED MARTIN CORPORATION
16 Maple Rd (01824-3737)
PHONE..................................978 256-4113
Joel Naidus, *President*
Michael Koziel, *Managing Dir*
Gary Bellerose, *Facilities Mgr*
Paul Aldrich, *Engineer*
John Kennedy, *Engineer*
EMP: 150 **Publicly Held**
WEB: www.lockheedmartin.com
SIC: 3812 Mfg Search/Navigation Equipment
PA: Lockheed Martin Corporation
6801 Rockledge Dr
Bethesda MD 20817
-

(G-9914)
LOCKHEED MARTIN CORPORATION
Also Called: Lockheed Martin Mis Fire Ctrl
16 Maple Rd (01824-3737)
PHONE..................................978 256-4113
EMP: 1261 **Publicly Held**
WEB: www.lockheedmartin.com
SIC: 3812 Mfg Aeronautical Systems
PA: Lockheed Martin Corporation
6801 Rockledge Dr
Bethesda MD 20817
-

(G-9915)
MAGELLAN DIAGNOSTICS INC (HQ)
Also Called: Dionex
22 Alpha Rd (01824-4123)
PHONE..................................978 250-7000
Walter Di Giusto, *President*
Wayne Matson, *Vice Pres*
James P Whelan, *Vice Pres*
John Ranalli, *Sales Staff*
Herbert H Hooper, *Director*
▲ **EMP:** 84
SALES (est): 9.9MM
SALES (corp-wide): 24.3B **Publicly Held**
SIC: 3826 2819 8071 3825 Mfg Analytical Instr Mfg Indstl Inorgan Chem Medical Laboratory Mfg Elec Measuring Instr
PA: Thermo Fisher Scientific Inc.
168 3rd Ave
Waltham MA 02451
781 622-1000

(G-9916)
MELLANOX TECHNOLOGIES INC
100 Apollo Dr Ste 302 (01824-3605)
PHONE..................................978 439-5400
Marc Sultzbaugh, *Vice Pres*
Sal Onorato, *Regl Sales Mgr*
EMP: 9
SALES (corp-wide): 313.1MM **Privately Held**
SIC: 3674 Mfg Semiconductors/Related Devices
HQ: Mellanox Technologies, Inc.
350 Oakmead Pkwy
Sunnyvale CA 94085
408 970-3400

(G-9917)
MINUTEMAN LABORATORIES INC
7a Stuart Rd (01824-4107)
PHONE..................................978 263-2632
Jerome Nihen, *President*
John Gilmore, *Vice Pres*
EMP: 17
SQ FT: 20,000
SALES (est): 1MM **Privately Held**
SIC: 3826 Mfg Spectrometers

(G-9918)
ON-SITE ANALYSIS INC (DH)
1 Executive Dr Ste 101 (01824-2564)
PHONE..................................561 775-5756
William C Willis, *President*
Rose Lynch, *Controller*
EMP: 7
SQ FT: 1,862
SALES (est): 3.6MM
SALES (corp-wide): 4.8B **Publicly Held**
WEB: www.globaltechnovations.com
SIC: 3826 Manufacturing Analytical Instruments
HQ: Spectro Scientific, Inc.
1 Executive Dr Ste 101
Chelmsford MA 01824
978 486-0123

(G-9919)
OSAAP AMERICA LLC
10 Kidder Rd (01824-3375)
PHONE..................................877 652-7227
James B Chase, *President*
EMP: 4
SALES (est): 529.2K **Privately Held**
SIC: 3086 Mfg Plastic Foam Products

(G-9920)
PACKAGING CORPORATION AMERICA
Also Called: Pca/Chelmsford 310
33 Glen Ave (01824-2857)
PHONE..................................978 256-4586
Gary Downs, *Manager*
EMP: 25
SQ FT: 40,000
SALES (corp-wide): 7B **Publicly Held**
WEB: www.packagingcorp.com
SIC: 2653 Mfg Corrugated/Solid Fiber Boxes
PA: Packaging Corporation Of America
1 N Field Ct
Lake Forest IL 60045
847 482-3000

(G-9921)
PARISI ASSOCIATES LLC
6 Omni Way (01824-4141)
PHONE..................................978 667-8700
John M Caputo, *President*
EMP: 19 **EST:** 1967
SQ FT: 9,410
SALES (est): 3.4MM **Privately Held**
WEB: www.parisiassociatesinc.com
SIC: 3679 Mfg Electronic Circuits

(G-9922)
PARTNERSHIP RESOURCES
139 Billerica Rd Ste 1 (01824-3634)
PHONE..................................978 256-0499
Philip Capodanno, *Principal*
Kerin Putnam, *Manager*
EMP: 6
SALES (est): 772.6K **Privately Held**
SIC: 2752 Lithographic Commercial Printing

(G-9923)
QORVO INC
2 Executive Dr (01824-2565)
PHONE..................................978 770-2158
EMP: 6
SALES (corp-wide): 3B **Publicly Held**
SIC: 3825 Mfg Semiconductors/Related Devices
PA: Qorvo, Inc.
7628 Thorndike Rd
Greensboro NC 27409
336 664-1233

(G-9924)
QUICK PRINT LTD INC
Also Called: Qpl
27 Industrial Ave Unit 4a (01824-3618)
PHONE..................................978 256-1822
Maxine C Derby, *President*
Peter Derby, *Vice Pres*
Karen O'Blenes,
EMP: 7
SQ FT: 2,800
SALES (est): 1MM **Privately Held**
WEB: www.qplimage.com
SIC: 2752 3993 Lithographic Commercial Printing Mfg Signs/Advertising Specialties

(G-9925)
RAYTHEON COMPANY
49 Amble Rd (01824-1931)
PHONE..................................978 256-6054
Sharon Broughton, *Branch Mgr*
EMP: 170
SALES (corp-wide): 27B **Publicly Held**
SIC: 3812 Mfg Search/Nav Equip
PA: Raytheon Company
870 Winter St
Waltham MA 02451
781 522-3000

(G-9926)
RED MILL GRAPHICS INCORPORATED
14 Alpha Rd (01824-4102)
PHONE..................................978 251-4081
Bernie E Gilet, *President*
Jim Gilet, *Vice Pres*
Janice Correale, *Admin Sec*
EMP: 15
SQ FT: 1,000
SALES (est): 1.8MM **Privately Held**
WEB: www.redmillgraphics.com
SIC: 2759 7331 Commercial Printing Direct Mail Advertising Services

(G-9927)
REVIVEFLOW INC
119 Drum Hill Rd Ste 272 (01824-1505)
PHONE..................................978 621-9466
Raymond Riddick, *President*
EMP: 5
SALES (est): 290.4K **Privately Held**
SIC: 3845 Medical Device Development

(G-9928)
ROCKWELL AUTOMATION INC
2 Executive Dr (01824-2565)
PHONE..................................978 441-9500
Elik Fooks, *Vice Pres*
Brad Chasan, *Opers Mgr*
Dennis Mackey, *Engineer*
Phil Schiavo, *Engineer*
James Dogul, *Project Engr*
EMP: 130 **Publicly Held**
SIC: 3625 Mfg Relays/Industrial Controls
PA: Rockwell Automation, Inc.
1201 S 2nd St
Milwaukee WI 53204
-

(G-9929)
S & H ENGINEERING INC
248 Mill Rd Ste 4 (01824-4148)
PHONE..................................978 256-7231
Stephen Smith, *President*
William Palermo, *General Mgr*
Bill Palermo, *Production*
Steve Smith, *Info Tech Mgr*
EMP: 25
SQ FT: 30,000
SALES (est): 3.5MM **Privately Held**
SIC: 3549 Mfg Metalworking Machinery

(G-9930)
SCHLEIFRING NORTH AMERICA LLC
Also Called: Schleiefring
222 Mill Rd (01824-4127)
PHONE..................................978 677-2500
James Piper,
▲ **EMP:** 12
SQ FT: 7,000
SALES: 6.9MM
SALES (corp-wide): 1.6B **Privately Held**
WEB: www.schleifring.com
SIC: 3824 Mfg Fluid Meter/Counting Devices
HQ: Schleifring Gmbh
Am Hardtanger 10
Furstenfeldbruck 82256
814 140-30

(G-9931)
SCHOEFFEL INTERNATIONAL CORP
Also Called: McPherson
7a Stuart Rd (01824-4107)
PHONE..................................978 256-4512
Chris Schoeffel, *CEO*
Dietmar Schoeffel, *Corp Secy*
▼ **EMP:** 24
SQ FT: 23,000
SALES (est): 5.9MM **Privately Held**
WEB: www.mcphersoninc.com
SIC: 3826 3829 Mfg Analytical Instruments Mfg Measuring/Controlling Devices

(G-9932)
SILICON TRANSISTOR CORPORATION
27 Katrina Rd (01824)
PHONE..................................978 256-3321
Stephen Apostolides, *President*
Robert Cauldwell, *Treasurer*
Borick B Frusztajer, *Shareholder*
EMP: 60
SQ FT: 40,000
SALES (est): 4.6MM **Privately Held**
SIC: 3674 Mfg Silicon Transistors & Modules

(G-9933)
SKY COMPUTERS INC
27 Industrial Ave Unit 1 (01824-3618)
PHONE..................................978 250-2420
Henry Shean, *President*
Bob Hoenig, *General Mgr*
Gary St Laurent, *Purch Agent*
Barry Jackson, *Director*
EMP: 15
SQ FT: 10,000
SALES (est): 3.1MM **Privately Held**
WEB: www.skycomputers.com
SIC: 3577 Mfg Computer Peripheral Equipment

(G-9934)
SUNS INTERNATIONAL LLC
127 Riverneck Rd (01824-2951)
PHONE..................................978 349-2329
Fan Ye, *Mng Member*
Christine Ni,
▲ **EMP:** 9
SQ FT: 3,000
SALES (est): 740.4K
SALES (corp-wide): 564.9K **Privately Held**
WEB: www.sunsinternational.com
SIC: 3625 Mfg Relays/Industrial Controls
PA: Shanghai Suns Electric Co., Ltd.
Block 1, Floor 11, East Tower Of Hi-Tech Wor, No.668, Beijing Ea
Shanghai 20000
139 173-6372

(G-9935)
TECH RIDGE INC
190 Hunt Rd (01824-3722)
P.O. Box 4001 (01824-0601)
PHONE..................................978 256-5741
Stephen Comeau, *President*
Gary Comeau, *Vice Pres*
EMP: 20
SQ FT: 11,000
SALES (est): 3.2MM **Privately Held**
SIC: 3544 3599 Mfg Dies/Tools/Jigs/Fixtures Mfg Industrial Machinery

(G-9936)
THERMO FISHER SCIENTIFIC INC
22 Alpha Rd (01824-4123)
PHONE..................................978 250-7000
Patrcia McDermott, *Manager*
Karen Sun, *Manager*
Ann Osgood, *Senior Mgr*
Russ Bennett, *Analyst*
EMP: 16
SALES (corp-wide): 24.3B **Publicly Held**
SIC: 3826 Mfg Analytical Instruments
PA: Thermo Fisher Scientific Inc.
168 3rd Ave
Waltham MA 02451
781 622-1000

(G-9937)
THERMO ORION INC (HQ)
22 Alpha Rd (01824-4123)
PHONE..................................800 225-1480
Marc N Casper, *CEO*
Seth Hoogasian, *President*
James Barbookles, *President*
Alan J Malus, *President*
Mark P Stevenson, *Exec VP*
▲ **EMP:** 50
SALES (est): 37.4MM
SALES (corp-wide): 24.3B **Publicly Held**
SIC: 3823 3826 3825 3561 Mfg Process Cntrl Instr Mfg Analytical Instr Mfg Elec Measuring Instr Mfg Pumps/Pumping Equip

▲ = Import ▼=Export
◆ =Import/Export

PA: Thermo Fisher Scientific Inc.
168 3rd Ave
Waltham MA 02451
781 622-1000

(G-9938)
V J ELECTRONIX INC
19 Alpha Rd (01824-4124)
PHONE..................................631 589-8800
Vijay Alreja, *President*
Kamla Alreja, *Treasurer*
Satya Korlipara, *Admin Sec*
▲ **EMP:** 45
SQ FT: 30,000
SALES (est): 7.1MM **Privately Held**
WEB: www.vjt.com
SIC: 3844 Mfg X-Ray Apparatus/Tubes

(G-9939)
VACUUM PLUS MANUFACTURING INC
80 Turnpike Rd (01824-3526)
PHONE..................................978 441-3100
David J Rioux, *President*
William P McGrath, *Vice Pres*
EMP: 17
SALES (est): 3MM **Privately Held**
SIC: 3674 Mfg Semiconductors/Related Devices

(G-9940)
WADDINGTON GROUP INC
6 Stuart Rd (01824-4108)
PHONE..................................201 610-6728
Bradford Turner, *Principal*
EMP: 13
SALES (est): 2.4MM **Privately Held**
SIC: 3089 Mfg Plastic Products

(G-9941)
WADDINGTON NORTH AMERICA INC
Also Called: Wna
6 Stuart Rd (01824-4108)
PHONE..................................978 256-6551
Dave Brouillette, *Prdtn Mgr*
Maryann Bissett, *Buyer*
Malcolm Harris, *Technical Mgr*
Laura Boitnott, *Sales Staff*
Jody Beal, *Analyst*
EMP: 182
SALES (corp-wide): 2.9B **Privately Held**
SIC: 3089 3086 3263 Mfg Plastic Products Mfg Plastic Foam Prdts
HQ: Waddington North America, Inc.
50 E Rivercenter Blvd # 650
Covington KY 41011

(G-9942)
ZOLL MEDICAL CORPORATION (HQ)
269 Mill Rd (01824-4105)
PHONE..................................978 421-9655
Richard A Packer, *CEO*
Marshal W Linder, *President*
James Palazzolo, *President*
Jonathan A Rennert, *President*
Ward M Hamilton, *Senior VP*
▲ **EMP:** 1180 **EST:** 1980
SQ FT: 221,000
SALES (est): 573.2MM **Privately Held**
WEB: www.zoll.com
SIC: 3845 7372 Mfg Electromedical Equipment Prepackaged Software Services

Chelsea
Suffolk County

(G-9943)
ADI PRINT SOLUTIONS INC
Also Called: American Digital Imaging
22 Willow St 4 (02150-3506)
PHONE..................................508 230-7024
Michael Fresolone, *President*
Lisa Peterson, *Manager*
Shawn Fresolone, *Assistant*
▲ **EMP:** 5
SALES (est): 525.9K **Privately Held**
WEB: www.adiprint.com
SIC: 2759 Commercial Printing

(G-9944)
AMERICAN BOLT & NUT CO INC
124 Carter St 38 (02150-1519)
P.O. Box 6119 (02150-0009)
PHONE..................................617 884-3331
Ralph A Carbone, *President*
Catherine McCue, *Director*
Priscilla Carbone, *Clerk*
EMP: 8 **EST:** 1931
SQ FT: 8,000
SALES (est): 1.9MM **Privately Held**
WEB: www.americanboltandnut.com
SIC: 3452 Mfr Bolts & Nuts

(G-9945)
BILTRITE CORPORATION
Also Called: Biltrite Manufacturing Plant
31 Highland St (02150-3549)
P.O. Box 9045, Waltham (02454)
PHONE..................................617 884-3124
Gary Winkleman, *Branch Mgr*
EMP: 40
SALES (est): 8.5MM
SALES (corp-wide): 13MM **Privately Held**
WEB: www.biltrite.com
SIC: 3021 3069 Rubber And Vinyl Matting
PA: The Biltrite Corporation
1350 Belmont St Ste 112
Brockton MA 02301
781 647-1700

(G-9946)
BM UNDERCAR WAREHOUSE
115 Carter St (02150-1537)
PHONE..................................516 736-0476
Alexander Morales, *President*
EMP: 6 **EST:** 2017
SALES (est): 269.2K **Privately Held**
SIC: 3714 Mfg Motor Vehicle Parts/Accessories

(G-9947)
CATALYST/SPRING I LTD PARTNER
Also Called: Hardware Products Company
191 Williams St (02150-3805)
PHONE..................................617 884-9410
Ted White, *Partner*
Juan Garcia, *Engineer*
Laurent Porter, *Accountant*
Jessica Gonzalez, *Sales Staff*
EMP: 29
SQ FT: 33,000
SALES (est): 5.6MM **Privately Held**
WEB: www.hardwareproducts.com
SIC: 3495 Mfg Wire Springs

(G-9948)
CHELSEA CLOCK LLC
101 2nd St (02150-1828)
P.O. Box 1082, West Chatham (02669-1082)
PHONE..................................617 884-0250
Anastasios Parafestas, *Principal*
Barbara Censullo, *Sales Staff*
Patrick Capozzi, *Marketing Staff*
John Kirby Nicholas, *Mng Member*
Lisa Polidoro, *Info Tech Dir*
▲ **EMP:** 35
SQ FT: 27,000
SALES (est): 6.1MM **Privately Held**
WEB: www.chelseaclock.com
SIC: 3873 Mfg Watches/Clocks/Parts

(G-9949)
CIVITAS THERAPEUTICS INC
Also Called: Acorda Therapeutics
190 Everett Ave (02150-1817)
PHONE..................................617 884-3004
Glenn Batchelder, *President*
Kyle Lavigne, *Research*
Peter Courossi, *CFO*
James Wright, *Treasurer*
Rick Batycky, *Admin Sec*
EMP: 93
SALES (est): 72.9MM **Publicly Held**
SIC: 2834 Manufacturer Of Pharmaceutical Preparations
PA: Acorda Therapeutics, Inc.
420 Saw Mill River Rd
Ardsley NY 10502

(G-9950)
COOPER INTERCONNECT INC
222 Williams St (02150-3820)
PHONE..................................617 389-7080
Preston Shultz, *CEO*
EMP: 80 **Privately Held**
SIC: 3679 3643 3812 3672 Mfg Elec Components Mfg Conductive Wire Dvcs Mfg Search/Navgatn Equip Mfg Printed Circuit Brds Nonfrs Wiredrwng/Insltng
HQ: Cooper Interconnect, Inc.
750 W Ventura Blvd
Camarillo CA 93010
805 484-0543

(G-9951)
COPRICO INC
40 Washington Ave (02150-3947)
PHONE..................................617 889-0520
Joanne Tarason, *President*
EMP: 6 **EST:** 1988
SQ FT: 2,000
SALES: 950K **Privately Held**
SIC: 2752 7334 2791 2789 Lithographic Coml Print Photocopying Service Typesetting Services Bookbinding/Related Work

(G-9952)
DAVIN MACHINING AND WELDING CO
1 Winnisimmet St Ste 1 # 1 (02150-2650)
P.O. Box 6462 (02150-0013)
PHONE..................................617 884-8933
Vincent Demore, *President*
Dawn Demore, *Treasurer*
EMP: 7
SQ FT: 7,500
SALES (est): 899.5K **Privately Held**
WEB: www.davinmachining.com
SIC: 3599 Mfg Industrial Machinery

(G-9953)
E Z TELECOM
227 Broadway (02150-2740)
PHONE..................................617 466-0826
Edward Bautista, *Owner*
EMP: 3
SALES (est): 260.7K **Privately Held**
SIC: 3663 Retails Beepers

(G-9954)
ICE TREAT INC
170 Everett Ave Unit 3 (02150-1813)
PHONE..................................617 889-0300
Patricia Shelton, *Owner*
EMP: 3
SALES (est): 153.4K **Privately Held**
SIC: 2024 Mfg Ice Cream/Frozen Desert

(G-9955)
J B SASH & DOOR COMPANY INC
280 2nd St (02150-1710)
PHONE..................................617 884-8940
Richard Bertolami, *President*
Ugo Bertolami, *President*
Eleanor Dall, *Accounting Mgr*
Jim Carney, *Sales Staff*
Steve Chiasson, *Sales Staff*
EMP: 32 **EST:** 1940
SALES (est): 5.6MM **Privately Held**
WEB: www.jbsash.com
SIC: 2431 5211 Mfg Millwork Ret Lumber/Building Mtrl

(G-9956)
JEFF SCHIFF
Also Called: Schiff Architectual Detail
120 Eastern Ave Ste 205 (02150-3354)
PHONE..................................617 887-0202
Jeff Schiff, *Owner*
EMP: 4
SALES (est): 750K **Privately Held**
SIC: 3441 5932 3446 Structural Metal Fabrication Ret Used Merchandise Mfg Architectural Metalwork

(G-9957)
KAYEM FOODS INC (PA)
75 Arlington St (02150-2365)
PHONE..................................781 933-3115
Ralph O Smith, *President*
Peter Monkiewicz, *Vice Pres*
Stephan Monkiewicz, *Treasurer*
Sean Corrinet, *Manager*
Michael Monkiewicz, *Admin Sec*
▲ **EMP:** 375 **EST:** 1909
SQ FT: 160,000
SALES (est): 117.2MM **Privately Held**
WEB: www.kayem.com
SIC: 2011 2013 Meat Packing Plant Mfg Prepared Meats

(G-9958)
L & L NOODLE INC
22 Willow St (02150-3506)
PHONE..................................617 889-6888
Kok Lau Kin, *Principal*
EMP: 4
SALES (est): 256.8K **Privately Held**
SIC: 2098 Mfg Macaroni/Spaghetti

(G-9959)
LAMCO CHEMICAL COMPANY INC
212 Arlington St (02150-2313)
PHONE..................................617 884-8470
James Lamm, *President*
EMP: 3
SQ FT: 15,000
SALES (est): 443.5K **Privately Held**
SIC: 2842 Mfg Cleaners & Floor Waxes

(G-9960)
LARIAT BIOSCIENCES INC
39 John St (02150-2124)
PHONE..................................603 244-9657
Jonathan William Larson, *Principal*
EMP: 3 **EST:** 2010
SALES (est): 283.1K **Privately Held**
SIC: 2836 Mfg Biological Products

(G-9961)
NOODLE LAB LLC
417 Crescent Ave Apt 3 (02150-4207)
PHONE..................................617 717-4370
Audrey Yap, *Principal*
EMP: 4
SALES (est): 110.5K **Privately Held**
SIC: 2098 Mfg Macaroni/Spaghetti

(G-9962)
OUTLAST UNIFORM CORPORATION
6 Hancock St (02150-1210)
PHONE..................................617 889-0510
Nicholas Theodoridis, *President*
EMP: 3
SQ FT: 2,000
SALES: 95K **Privately Held**
WEB: www.outlastuniform.com
SIC: 2326 Mfg Men's/Boy's Work Clothing

(G-9963)
P&N JEWELRY INC
312 Broadway (02150-2808)
PHONE..................................617 889-3200
Nelly Bequarano, *Owner*
EMP: 4
SALES (est): 93.2K **Privately Held**
SIC: 3911 Mfg Precious Metal Jewelry

(G-9964)
PILLSBURY COMPANY LLC
100 Justin Dr Ste 2 (02150-4032)
PHONE..................................617 884-9800
Jerry Murphy, *Branch Mgr*
Anthony Rodriguez, *Administration*
EMP: 55
SALES (corp-wide): 16.8B **Publicly Held**
WEB: www.pillsbury.com
SIC: 2041 Mfg Flour/Grain Mill Prooducts
HQ: The Pillsbury Company Llc
1 General Mills Blvd
Minneapolis MN 55426

(G-9965)
RUBBER RIGHT ROLLERS INC
120 Eastern Ave Ste 3 (02150-3354)
PHONE..................................617 466-1447
Lorraine Ottaviano, *Principal*
EMP: 10 **EST:** 2014
SALES (est): 1.3MM **Privately Held**
SIC: 3069 Mfg Fabricated Rubber Products

(G-9966)
SCHIFF ARCHITECTURAL DETAIL LLC
120 Eastern Ave (02150-3354)
PHONE....................................617 846-6437
Jeff Schiff, *Mktg Dir*
Sandra Joneck, *Executive*
EMP: 3
SALES: 1MM **Privately Held**
WEB: www.schiffarchitectural.com
SIC: 3441 Structural Metal Fabrication

(G-9967)
SINCERE SPECIALTY FABRICATION
214 Arlington St (02150-2313)
PHONE....................................781 974-9580
Daniel Kendall, *Mng Member*
EMP: 3 **EST:** 2015
SQ FT: 3,200
SALES: 500K **Privately Held**
SIC: 2514 2511 3299 3366 Mfg Metal Household Furn Mfg Wood Household Furn Mfg Nonmtlc Mineral Prdt Copper Foundry

(G-9968)
SPRING AIR OHIO LLC
124 2nd St (02150-1833)
PHONE....................................617 884-0041
Michael Brown, *Mng Member*
EMP: 21
SALES (est): 1.4MM **Privately Held**
SIC: 2515 Mfg Mattresses & Box Springs

(G-9969)
STANDARD BOX COMPANY INC
1 Boatswains Way (02150-4017)
PHONE....................................617 884-2345
EMP: 4
SALES (est): 412.2K **Privately Held**
SIC: 2657 Mfg Folding Paperboard Boxes

(G-9970)
STEELE CANVAS BASKET CORP
201 Williams St (02150-3805)
P.O. Box 6267 (02150-0995)
PHONE....................................800 541-8929
John Lordan, *President*
Sylvia M Lordan, *Vice Pres*
Geffken Paul, *Vice Pres*
Michelle Freeman, *Sales Staff*
Lordan John, *Director*
▲ **EMP:** 36 **EST:** 1921
SQ FT: 24,000
SALES (est): 5.9MM **Privately Held**
WEB: www.steele-canvas.com
SIC: 2393 3799 3537 2394 Mfg Textile Bags Mfg Transportation Equip Mfg Indstl Truck/Tractor Mfg Canvas/Related Prdts Manmad Brdwv Fabric Mill

(G-9971)
STILL WATER DESIGN INC
1 Winnisimmet St Ste 1 # 1 (02150-2650)
PHONE....................................617 308-5820
Julius R Pereli, *President*
EMP: 5
SQ FT: 5,700
SALES: 135K **Privately Held**
WEB: www.stillwaterdesign.com
SIC: 3732 Boat Building And Repairing

(G-9972)
SUMMIT PRESS INC (PA)
63 6th St (02150-2442)
PHONE....................................617 889-3991
Lenore Delvecchio, *President*
Steven Canter, *Opers Mgr*
Domenic Paolo, *Prdtn Mgr*
Wayne Gardner, *VP Sales*
Bob Chiulli, *Cust Mgr*
EMP: 11 **EST:** 1961
SQ FT: 5,000
SALES (est): 3.1MM **Privately Held**
WEB: www.summitpress.com
SIC: 2752 Lithographic Commercial Printing

(G-9973)
TOWN & COUNTRY FINE JWLY GROUP
Also Called: Feature Ring Co
25 Union St (02150-1214)
PHONE....................................617 345-4771
C William Carey, *Ch of Bd*
EMP: 700
SALES (est): 25.7MM **Privately Held**
SIC: 3911 5094 Mfg Fine Jewelry & Whol Diamonds

(G-9974)
WALTHAM FUEL
295 Eastern Ave (02150-3344)
PHONE....................................617 364-2890
Vincent Tuzzo, *Principal*
EMP: 4
SALES (est): 214.4K **Privately Held**
SIC: 2869 Mfg Industrial Organic Chemicals

(G-9975)
WILLIAMSON NENG ELC MTR SVC
25 Griffin Way (02150-3377)
PHONE....................................617 884-9200
John McCall, *Principal*
EMP: 7
SALES (est): 1.3MM **Privately Held**
SIC: 3629 Whol Electrical Equipment

Cherry Valley
Worcester County

(G-9976)
RALPH SEAVER
Also Called: Cherry Valley Welding
51 Redfield Rd (01611-3106)
P.O. Box 478, Leicester (01524-0478)
PHONE....................................508 892-9486
Ralph Seaver, *Owner*
EMP: 3
SALES (est): 140K **Privately Held**
SIC: 7692 3444 Welding Repair Mfg Sheet Metalwork

(G-9977)
SKYLINE PRODUCTIONS
130 Sargent St (01611-3102)
PHONE....................................508 326-4982
Robert Daigneault, *Owner*
EMP: 5
SQ FT: 800
SALES: 100K **Privately Held**
SIC: 2752 Lithographic Commercial Printing

(G-9978)
VALLEY PRINTING COMPANY
31 Redfield Rd (01611-3106)
PHONE....................................508 892-9818
Donald Manseau, *Owner*
EMP: 3
SALES: 200K **Privately Held**
SIC: 2752 Lithographic Commercial Printing

Cheshire
Berkshire County

(G-9979)
LOVALLO METALSPINNING
915 N State Rd (01225-9621)
P.O. Box 753 (01225-0753)
PHONE....................................413 743-3947
Peter Lovallo, *Owner*
EMP: 3 **EST:** 1995
SQ FT: 2,000
SALES: 200K **Privately Held**
SIC: 3469 Mfg Metal Stampings

Chester
Hampden County

(G-9980)
BANNISH LUMBER INC
632 Route 20 (01011-9652)
P.O. Box 338 (01011-0338)
PHONE....................................413 354-2279
Harold M Bannish, *President*
Aaron Bannish, *Vice Pres*
Matthew Bannish, *Vice Pres*
Marlene Bannish, *Asst Treas*
EMP: 16
SQ FT: 12,300
SALES (est): 2.1MM **Privately Held**
WEB: www.bannishlumber.com
SIC: 2421 2426 Sawmill/Planing Mill Hardwood Dimension/Floor Mill

Chestnut Hill
Middlesex County

(G-9981)
ADHEREAN INC
219 Crafts Rd (02467-1421)
PHONE....................................617 652-0304
Josiah Seale, *Principal*
Angela Kilby, *Principal*
EMP: 4
SALES (est): 248.7K **Privately Held**
SIC: 3845 Mfg Electromedical Equipment

(G-9982)
BEWELL BODY SCAN
25 Boylston St Ste LI07 (02467-1710)
PHONE....................................617 754-0300
Jane Corey, *Principal*
EMP: 4
SALES (est): 244.5K **Privately Held**
WEB: www.bewellbodyscan.com
SIC: 3845 Mfg Electromedical Equipment

(G-9983)
BULCAST LLC
55 Crosby Rd (02467-1172)
PHONE....................................617 901-6836
Vadmier Zlatez,
EMP: 4
SALES: 400K **Privately Held**
WEB: www.bulcast.com
SIC: 3365 3363 Aluminum Foundry Mfg Aluminum Die-Castings

(G-9984)
CHARBERT INC
Also Called: Charbert Fabrics
830 Boylston St Ste 209 (02467-2502)
PHONE....................................401 364-7751
Bill Maher, *Principal*
▲ **EMP:** 150
SALES (est): 11.9MM **Privately Held**
SIC: 2258 Lace/Warp Knit Fabric Mill

(G-9985)
CYTOVERA INC
10 Hammond Pond Pkwy # 102 (02467-2149)
P.O. Box 2441, Woburn (01888-0841)
PHONE....................................617 682-8981
L Richard Huang, *President*
EMP: 3
SALES (est): 302.2K **Privately Held**
SIC: 3841 Mfg Surgical/Medical Instruments

(G-9986)
DI AN ENTERPRISES INC
Also Called: Concession Master
85 Wallis Rd (02467-3174)
PHONE....................................617 469-0819
EMP: 12
SQ FT: 9,000
SALES (est): 1.2MM **Privately Held**
SIC: 3577 7378 Mfg & Services Turnkey Computer Systems

(G-9987)
MER+GE
217 Reservoir Rd (02467-1426)
PHONE....................................512 665-2266
Victoria Jones, *Principal*
EMP: 3 **EST:** 2014
SALES (est): 152K **Privately Held**
SIC: 3724 Mfg Aircraft Engines/Parts

(G-9988)
MOM CENTRAL
440 Beacon St (02467-1105)
PHONE....................................617 332-6819
Stacy Debroff, *President*
EMP: 4 **EST:** 1997
SALES (est): 217.9K **Privately Held**
SIC: 2741 Misc Publishing

(G-9989)
NEMEREVER VINEYARDS LLC
535 Hammond St (02467-1703)
PHONE....................................617 320-6994
Virginia Nemerever, *Principal*
EMP: 4
SALES (est): 189.9K **Privately Held**
SIC: 2084 Mfg Wines/Brandy/Spirits

(G-9990)
PLANE FANTASY
30 Rangeley Rd (02467-3018)
PHONE....................................617 734-4950
Glorie Vokonas, *Owner*
EMP: 4
SALES (est): 155.8K **Privately Held**
SIC: 3721 Mfg Aircraft

(G-9991)
PRINT BUYERS INTERNATIONAL LLC
118 Arlington Rd (02467-2617)
PHONE....................................617 730-5951
EMP: 4 **EST:** 2008
SALES (est): 281.4K **Privately Held**
SIC: 2752 Lithographic Commercial Printing

(G-9992)
PSYTON SOFTWARE
50 Vine St (02467-3052)
PHONE....................................617 308-5058
David Goldblatt, *Owner*
EMP: 3
SALES: 300K **Privately Held**
WEB: www.psyton.com
SIC: 7372 Prepackaged Software Services

(G-9993)
TRUSTEES OF BOSTON COLLEGE
Also Called: Center For Work and Family
22 Stone Ave (02467-3953)
PHONE....................................617 552-2844
Brad Harrington, *Exec Dir*
EMP: 10
SALES (corp-wide): 835.6MM **Privately Held**
WEB: www.bc.edu
SIC: 2741 8221 Misc Publishing College/University
PA: Trustees Of Boston College
140 Commonwealth Ave
Chestnut Hill MA 02467
617 552-8000

(G-9994)
VAN BENTEN JOSEPH FURN MAKERS
823 Boylston St (02467-1458)
PHONE....................................617 738-6575
Joseph Van Benten, *Owner*
EMP: 5
SQ FT: 2,400
SALES: 500K **Privately Held**
WEB: www.vanbenten.com
SIC: 2511 Mfg Wood Household Furniture

Chicopee
Hampden County

(G-9995)
A1 SCREW MACHINE PRODUCTS INC
717 Fuller Rd (01020-3755)
P.O. Box 569 (01021-0569)
PHONE....................................413 594-8939
Steven Fido, *President*

Jack Fido, *Treasurer*
EMP: 16
SQ FT: 13,000
SALES (est): 2.3MM **Privately Held**
SIC: 3599 3452 Mfg Industrial Machinery Mfg Bolts/Screws/Rivets

(G-9996)
ADVANCED AEROSTRUCTURES INC (PA)
340 Mckinstry Ave Ste 300 (01013-1849)
PHONE..................................413 315-9284
Victor Archakov, *President*
EMP: 5 **EST:** 2009
SALES: 500K **Privately Held**
SIC: 3728 Mfg Aircraft Parts/Equipment

(G-9997)
AEROSPACE ADHSIVE BONDING TECH
340 Mckinstry Ave Ste 300 (01013-1849)
PHONE..................................413 315-9349
EMP: 3
SALES (est): 123.2K **Privately Held**
SIC: 2891 Mfg Adhesives/Sealants

(G-9998)
AGILENT TECHNOLOGIES INC
300 Griffith Rd (01022-2126)
PHONE..................................413 593-2900
EMP: 10
SALES (corp-wide): 5.1B **Publicly Held**
SIC: 3825 Mfg Electrical Measuring Instruments
PA: Agilent Technologies, Inc.
5301 Stevens Creek Blvd
Santa Clara CA 95051
408 345-8886

(G-9999)
BAXTER SAND & GRAVEL INC
652 Prospect St (01020-3048)
PHONE..................................413 536-3370
Leo E Ouellette, *President*
Lorainne Ouellette, *Admin Sec*
EMP: 30 **EST:** 1967
SQ FT: 300
SALES (est): 1.3MM **Privately Held**
WEB: www.baxtersandgravel.com
SIC: 1442 5211 Construction Sand/Gravel Ret Lumber/Building Materials

(G-10000)
BBU INC
21 Taxiway Dr (01022-1085)
PHONE..................................413 593-2700
EMP: 22 **Privately Held**
SIC: 2051 Mfg Bread/Related Products
HQ: Bbu, Inc.
255 Business Center Dr # 200
Horsham PA 19044

(G-10001)
BERNARDINOS BAKERY INC (PA)
105 Exchange St (01013-1211)
P.O. Box 180 (01014-0180)
PHONE..................................413 592-1944
Fernando A Goncalves, *President*
Manuel A Silva, *Treasurer*
Carlos Albert, *Sales Mgr*
Alfred Cunha, *Maintence Staff*
EMP: 58
SQ FT: 20,000
SALES: 4.8MM **Privately Held**
SIC: 2051 Mfg Bread/Related Products

(G-10002)
BTD PRECISION INC
75 Marion St (01013-2569)
P.O. Box 387 (01014-0387)
PHONE..................................413 594-2783
Wayne M Beaulieu, *President*
EMP: 12 **EST:** 1966
SQ FT: 7,000
SALES (est): 1.8MM **Privately Held**
WEB: www.btdprecision.com
SIC: 3544 Mfg Dies/Tools/Jigs/Fixtures

(G-10003)
BURKE MEDICAL EQUIPMENT INC
516 Montgomery St (01020-1469)
PHONE..................................413 592-5464
Francis Burke, *President*
Marcia Burke, *Vice Pres*
EMP: 23
SQ FT: 15,000
SALES (est): 2.1MM **Privately Held**
WEB: www.burkemedical.com
SIC: 3842 5999 Mfg Surgical Appliances/Supplies Ret Misc Merchandise

(G-10004)
C & C LAMINATION
34 Pajak St (01013-1318)
PHONE..................................413 594-6910
Corol Cataldo, *President*
EMP: 3
SALES (est): 178.2K **Privately Held**
SIC: 3089 Mfg Plastic Products

(G-10005)
CALLAWAY GOLF COMPANY
425 Meadow St (01013-2201)
PHONE..................................413 536-1200
Steve Conley, *Sales Dir*
David A Laverty, *Branch Mgr*
Michael Nevlida, *Technology*
Chris Bascom, *Technician*
EMP: 33
SALES (corp-wide): 1.2B **Publicly Held**
WEB: www.callawaygolf.com
SIC: 3949 Mfg Sporting/Athletic Goods
PA: Callaway Golf Company
2180 Rutherford Rd
Carlsbad CA 92008
760 931-1771

(G-10006)
CARAUSTAR INDUSTRIES INC
70 Better Way (01022-2118)
PHONE..................................413 593-9700
Wayne Kelch, *Manager*
EMP: 80
SALES (corp-wide): 4.6B **Publicly Held**
WEB: www.newarkpaperboardproducts.com
SIC: 2655 Mfg Fiber Cans/Drums
HQ: Caraustar Industries, Inc.
5000 Austell Powder Sprin
Austell GA 30106
770 948-3101

(G-10007)
CHICOPEE FOUNDATIONS INC (PA)
652 Prospect St (01020-3048)
PHONE..................................413 536-3370
Leo E Ouelette, *President*
Norman Magnanti, *Vice Pres*
Leo Ouelette, *Vice Pres*
Cindy Bacor, *Accountant*
Lorraine G Ouelette, *Clerk*
EMP: 25
SALES (est): 5MM **Privately Held**
WEB: www.chicopeeconcrete.com
SIC: 3273 Mfg Ready-Mixed Concrete

(G-10008)
CHICOPEE FOUNDATIONS INC
Also Called: Dispatch Plant
158 New Lombard Rd (01020-4859)
PHONE..................................413 594-4700
Leo Ouette, *Manager*
EMP: 23
SALES (corp-wide): 5MM **Privately Held**
WEB: www.chicopeeconcrete.com
SIC: 3273 1521 Mfg Ready-Mixed Concrete Single-Family House Construction
PA: Chicopee Foundations, Inc.
652 Prospect St
Chicopee MA 01020
413 536-3370

(G-10009)
CHICOPEE PROVISION COMPANY INC
19 Sitarz Ave (01013-1342)
P.O. Box 7 (01014-0007)
PHONE..................................413 594-4765
Tina Vezina, *President*
Gary Bernatowicz, *Vice Pres*
Thomas Bardon, *Treasurer*
Thomas J Bardon, *Manager*
Carolyn Donnelly, *Admin Sec*
EMP: 32 **EST:** 1920
SQ FT: 25,500
SALES: 3.5MM **Privately Held**
WEB: www.bluesealkielbasa.com
SIC: 2013 5147 2011 Mfg Prepared Meats Whol Meats/Products Meat Packing Plant

(G-10010)
CHICOPEE REGISTER NEWSPAPER
333 Front St Ste 5 (01013-2798)
PHONE..................................413 592-3599
Patrick Turley, *President*
EMP: 4
SALES (est): 144.8K **Privately Held**
SIC: 2711 Newspapers-Publishing/Printing

(G-10011)
CHICOPEE TRIBUNE
582 Britton St (01020-4229)
PHONE..................................413 552-3775
Michael Corzay, *Principal*
EMP: 3
SALES (est): 98.1K **Privately Held**
SIC: 2711 Newspapers-Publishing/Printing

(G-10012)
CHUCKS SIGN CO
658 Fuller Rd (01020-3711)
PHONE..................................413 592-3710
Chuck Martin, *Owner*
EMP: 3
SALES (est): 240.3K **Privately Held**
WEB: www.chuckssign.com
SIC: 3993 Mfg Signs/Advertising Specialties

(G-10013)
CITY OF CHICOPEE
Also Called: Water Treatment Plant
1356 Burnett Rd (01020-4613)
PHONE..................................413 594-1870
Allen Ryccek, *Superintendent*
EMP: 3 **Privately Held**
WEB: www.chicopeema.gov
SIC: 3823 Mfg Process Control Instruments
PA: City Of Chicopee
274 Front St
Chicopee MA 01013
413 594-1490

(G-10014)
CLARK & SONS SEAMLESS GUTTER
48 Woodcrest Ct (01020-2041)
PHONE..................................413 732-3934
Allen Clark, *Owner*
EMP: 3
SALES (est): 252.1K **Privately Held**
SIC: 3444 1761 Mfg Sheet Metalwork Roofing/Siding Contractor

(G-10015)
COMMONWEALTH PACKAGING CORP
1146 Sheridan St (01022-2101)
P.O. Box 329 (01021-0329)
PHONE..................................413 593-1482
Joseph V Gosselin Jr, *President*
EMP: 55
SQ FT: 90,000
SALES (est): 11MM **Privately Held**
WEB: www.cartons.com
SIC: 2653 Mfg Corrugated/Solid Fiber Boxes

(G-10016)
CONVERGENT - PHOTONICS LLC
Also Called: Prima Electro North Amer LLC
711 E Main St (01020-3606)
PHONE..................................413 598-5200
Terry L Vanderwert, *President*
Francesco Sgandurra, *Vice Pres*
Federico Ziliani, *Vice Pres*
Vittorio Rubbiani, *Export Mgr*
Lasante Linda, *Buyer*
▲ **EMP:** 67
SQ FT: 88,000
SALES (est): 15.3MM
SALES (corp-wide): 249.2MM **Privately Held**
WEB: www.prima-na.com
SIC: 3699 Mfg Electrical Equipment/Supplies
HQ: Prima Electro Spa
Strada Carignano 48/2
Moncalieri TO 10024
011 989-9804

(G-10017)
DIAMOND WATER SYSTEMS INC
863 Montgomery St (01013-3823)
PHONE..................................413 536-8186
William Dalton, *President*
EMP: 21
SQ FT: 105,000
SALES: 2.5MM **Privately Held**
WEB: www.diamondwater.com
SIC: 3589 5113 Mfg Service Industry Machinery Whol Industrial/Service Paper

(G-10018)
DIECUTTING TOOLING SVCS INC (PA)
680 Meadow St (01013-1824)
P.O. Box 7, South Hadley (01075-0007)
PHONE..................................413 331-3500
Mark K Lambert, *President*
EMP: 10
SALES (est): 1.7MM **Privately Held**
SIC: 3544 Mfg Dies/Tools/Jigs/Fixtures

(G-10019)
DIELECTRICS INC (HQ)
300 Burnett Rd (01020-4636)
PHONE..................................413 594-8111
R Jeffrey Bailly, *President*
Ronald J Lataille, *Corp Secy*
Bart Rietkerk, *Vice Pres*
Bob Merrill, *Purch Mgr*
Robin White, *Purch Mgr*
▲ **EMP:** 23 **EST:** 1954
SQ FT: 140,000
SALES (est): 47.7MM
SALES (corp-wide): 190.4MM **Publicly Held**
WEB: www.dielectrics.com
SIC: 3081 Manufacture Unsupported Plastic Film/Sheet
PA: Ufp Technologies, Inc.
100 Hale St
Newburyport MA 01950
978 352-2200

(G-10020)
DOW JONES & COMPANY INC
200 Burnett Rd (01020-4615)
P.O. Box 7007 (01021-7007)
PHONE..................................413 598-4000
Qi Yuan, *Engineer*
Margo Connolly, *Mktg Coord*
Adriana Hurtado, *Marketing Staff*
Ann Charest, *Supervisor*
Mark Neeley, *Info Tech Mgr*
EMP: 46
SQ FT: 62,000
SALES (corp-wide): 10B **Publicly Held**
SIC: 2711 2721 Newspapers-Publishing/Printing Periodicals-Publishing/Printing
HQ: Dow Jones & Company, Inc.
1211 Avenue Of The Americ
New York NY 10036
609 627-2999

(G-10021)
DOW JONES & COMPANY INC
84 2nd Ave (01020-4607)
PHONE..................................212 416-3858
Rica Woyan, *Asst Director*
EMP: 46
SALES (corp-wide): 10B **Publicly Held**
SIC: 2711 Newspapers-Publishing/Printing
HQ: Dow Jones & Company, Inc.
1211 Avenue Of The Americ
New York NY 10036
609 627-2999

(G-10022)
EASTERN ETCHING AND MFG CO
35 Lower Grape St Bldg 1 (01013-2674)
PHONE..................................413 594-6601
Joseph Lavallee, *CEO*
John A Lavallee, *Vice Pres*
Joseph Lavallee Jr, *Vice Pres*
Jay Wallace, *Vice Pres*
Michael Cocco, *Opers Mgr*

EMP: 49
SQ FT: 100,000
SALES (est): 6.3MM **Privately Held**
SIC: 3479 3993 2752 2759 Coating/Engraving Svcs Mfg Signs/Ad Specialties Lithographic Coml Print Commercial Printing Mfg Unsupport Plstc Film

(G-10023)
ELECTRONIC DISTRIBUTION CORP
698 Chicopee St (01013-2709)
PHONE.................................413 536-3400
Michael Roth, *President*
EMP: 4
SQ FT: 900
SALES (est): 209.5K **Privately Held**
WEB: www.edtmag.com
SIC: 2791 Computerized Typesetting

(G-10024)
ETHOSENERGY TC INC
1310 Sheridan St (01022-2102)
PHONE.................................413 593-0500
Barry Bradley, *Branch Mgr*
EMP: 104
SALES (corp-wide): 10B **Privately Held**
SIC: 3511 Mfg Turbines/Generator Sets
HQ: Ethosenergy Tc, Inc.
2140 Westover Rd
Chicopee MA 01022
802 257-2721

(G-10025)
ETHOSENERGY TC INC (DH)
2140 Westover Rd (01022-1046)
PHONE.................................802 257-2721
Neil Sigmund, *President*
Mark Jones, *Vice Pres*
Bryan Joyce, *Vice Pres*
Neil Frey, *Plant Mgr*
Brian Atkinson, *Project Mgr*
◆ **EMP:** 130
SQ FT: 15,300
SALES (est): 42.5MM
SALES (corp-wide): 10B **Privately Held**
WEB: www.turbocare.com
SIC: 3511 3612 4789 Mfg Turbines/Generator Sets Mfg Transformers Transportation Services

(G-10026)
FLEMING INDUSTRIES INC
Also Called: Iron Duck Division
102 1st Ave (01020-4621)
PHONE.................................413 593-3300
A Michael Fleming, *CEO*
Michael J Fleming, *President*
Shela Fleming, *Vice Pres*
▲ **EMP:** 75
SALES (est): 7.3MM **Privately Held**
WEB: www.ironduck.com
SIC: 2393 3842 2396 Mfg Textile Bags Mfg Surgical Appliances/Supplies Mfg Auto/Apparel Trimming

(G-10027)
GARAN ENTERPRISES INC
Also Called: Millies Pierogi
129 Broadway St (01020-2693)
PHONE.................................413 594-4991
Anna Lopuk, *President*
Anna Kerigan, *Vice Pres*
EMP: 15
SQ FT: 100,000
SALES (est): 1.8MM **Privately Held**
WEB: www.milliespierogi.com
SIC: 2032 Mfg Canned Specialties

(G-10028)
GUARDAIR CORPORATION
47 Veterans Dr (01022-1062)
PHONE.................................413 594-4400
Thomas C Tremblay, *President*
Darcy Slingerland, *Cust Mgr*
Stuart Champiny, *Technology*
Hardy Hamann, *Director*
Philip C Hanson, *Director*
▲ **EMP:** 40 **EST:** 1943
SQ FT: 6,500
SALES (est): 9.9MM **Privately Held**
WEB: www.guardaircorp.com
SIC: 3546 3492 3052 3563 Mfg Power-driven Handtool Mfg Fluid Power Valves Mfg Rubr/Plstc Hose/Belt Mfg Air/Gas Compressors

(G-10029)
HOPPE TECHNOLOGIES INC
107 First Ave (01020-4620)
PHONE.................................413 592-9213
Eric D Hagopian, *President*
Ann Pagebarrett, *Purch Mgr*
Douglas M Hagopian, *Treasurer*
Sonja Hutchins, *Human Res Mgr*
Steve Delude, *Marketing Staff*
▲ **EMP:** 75 **EST:** 1941
SQ FT: 40,000
SALES (est): 18.7MM **Privately Held**
WEB: www.hoppetool.com
SIC: 3544 3545 Mfg Dies/Tools/Jigs/Fixtures Mfg Machine Tool Accessories
HQ: Trimaster/Htech Holding, Llc
590 Madison Ave Fl 27
New York NY 10022
212 257-6772

(G-10030)
IDEAL KITCHENS OF PALMER (PA)
838 Grattan St (01020-1271)
PHONE.................................413 532-2253
Steven Wenninger, *Owner*
EMP: 8
SQ FT: 1,000
SALES (est): 902.9K **Privately Held**
SIC: 2434 Mfg Wood Kitchen Cabinets

(G-10031)
IMAGING SOLUTIONS & MORE
324 Shawinigan Dr (01020-3735)
PHONE.................................413 331-4100
Sean R Diver, *Principal*
EMP: 3
SALES (est): 339.9K **Privately Held**
SIC: 3577 5112 3575 Mfg Computer Peripherals Whol Stationery/Offc Sup Mfg Computer Terminals

(G-10032)
INDUSTRIAL STL BOILER SVCS INC
939 Chicopee St Ste 2 (01013-2893)
PHONE.................................413 532-7788
William E O'Neil, *President*
Bill O'Neil, *Principal*
Alex Korobkov, *Opers Mgr*
Gayle Rae, *Treasurer*
Wendy Hocog, *Clerk*
▲ **EMP:** 23
SQ FT: 26,000
SALES: 4.1MM **Privately Held**
WEB: www.isbservices.com
SIC: 3443 3531 3441 7699 Mfg Fabricated Plate Wrk Mfg Construction Mach Structural Metal Fabrctn Repair Services

(G-10033)
INTERNATIONAL METAL PDTS INC
Also Called: I M P
1165 Montgomery St (01013-3924)
PHONE.................................413 532-2411
Michael Dupuis, *President*
Christine Hills, *Purchasing*
Mark Bergeron, *Engineer*
Gerald Burke, *Treasurer*
▲ **EMP:** 41
SQ FT: 60,000
SALES (est): 8.5MM **Privately Held**
WEB: www.imp-co.org
SIC: 3469 3496 Mfg Metal Stampings Mfg Misc Fabricated Wire Products

(G-10034)
J P PRECISION MACHINE CO
Also Called: JP Precision Machine Co
90 Exchange St (01013-1244)
PHONE.................................413 592-8191
Jan Piskorowski, *Owner*
EMP: 5
SALES (est): 505K **Privately Held**
SIC: 3599 Mfg Industrial Machinery

(G-10035)
JAIN AMERICA FOODS INC
Also Called: Nucedar Mills
1000 Sheridan St (01022-1031)
PHONE.................................413 593-8883
Bruce Worchington, *Manager*
EMP: 21 **Privately Held**
SIC: 2431 Mfg Millwork
HQ: Jain America Foods, Inc.
1819 Walcutt Rd Ste 1
Columbus OH 43228

(G-10036)
KAD MACHINE INC
Also Called: K A D Machine & Tool
28 Holgate Ave (01020-4018)
PHONE.................................413 538-8684
Douglas A Abbey, *President*
EMP: 9
SQ FT: 5,000
SALES (est): 814.6K **Privately Held**
SIC: 3599 Machine Shop

(G-10037)
LAMB KNITTING MACHINE CORP
66 New Lombard Rd (01020-4899)
PHONE.................................413 592-2501
William Giokas, *President*
Andrew Giokas, *Vice Pres*
Amy Lonczak, *Engineer*
Besse F Giokas, *Asst Treas*
EMP: 7 **EST:** 1931
SQ FT: 12,000
SALES (est): 1.4MM **Privately Held**
WEB: www.lambkmc.com
SIC: 3552 Mfg Knitting & Braiding Machines

(G-10038)
LEONI WIRE INC
301 Griffith Rd (01022-2129)
PHONE.................................413 593-6618
Andreas Zinner, *President*
Jean-Marc Vico, *General Mgr*
Reed Lisa, *Business Mgr*
Dieter Fuenfer, *Opers Mgr*
Angelica Gallardo, *Buyer*
▲ **EMP:** 92
SQ FT: 162,000
SALES (est): 28MM
SALES (corp-wide): 5.6B **Privately Held**
WEB: www.leoniwire.com
SIC: 3351 3315 Copper Rolling/Drawing Mfg Steel Wire/Related Products
HQ: Leoni Wiring Systems, Inc.
3100 N Campbell Ave # 101
Tucson AZ 85719

(G-10039)
MAGNAT-FAIRVIEW LLC
1102 Sheridan St (01022-1043)
PHONE.................................413 593-5742
Glenn Geddis, *General Mgr*
June Griswold, *Purch Mgr*
Alan Labroad, *Engineer*
Sean Parnell, *Engineer*
Lou Bargatti, *Design Engr*
EMP: 15 **EST:** 2017
SQ FT: 65,000
SALES: 8MM
SALES (corp-wide): 2.9B **Privately Held**
SIC: 3599 3554 Mfg Industrial Machinery Mfg Paper Industrial Machinery
HQ: Maxcess Americas, Inc.
222 W Memorial Rd
Oklahoma City OK 73114
405 755-1600

(G-10040)
MASCAROS WOODCRAFT CO INC (PA)
101 Front St (01013-1220)
P.O. Box 404 (01014-0404)
PHONE.................................413 594-4255
Robert F Mascaro, *President*
Barbara Henderson, *Manager*
Jeffrey B Sagalyn, *Admin Sec*
EMP: 3 **EST:** 1970
SQ FT: 4,000
SALES (est): 456.5K **Privately Held**
SIC: 2434 Mfg Wood Kitchen Cabinets

(G-10041)
MASSASOIT/TACKBAND INC
118 Dulong Cir (01022-1153)
PHONE.................................413 593-6731
Samuel J Rickless, *President*
Marsha Rickless, *Admin Sec*
▲ **EMP:** 20
SQ FT: 18,000
SALES (est): 2.3MM **Privately Held**
SIC: 2241 Narrow Fabric Mill

(G-10042)
MECHANICAL DRV COMPONENTS INC
317 Meadow St Ste 6a (01013-2250)
PHONE.................................413 535-2000
Joseph Giffune, *President*
Chris Aldrich, *Vice Pres*
EMP: 6
SQ FT: 5,500
SALES (est): 707.6K **Privately Held**
WEB: www.mechdrive.com
SIC: 3599 Mfg Industrial Machinery

(G-10043)
MEDTRONIC INC
2 Ludlow Park Dr (01022-1318)
PHONE.................................413 593-6400
EMP: 10 **Privately Held**
SIC: 3841 Mfg Surgical/Medical Instruments
HQ: Medtronic, Inc.
710 Medtronic Pkwy
Minneapolis MN 55432
763 514-4000

(G-10044)
MERCHANTS METALS LLC
390 Burnett Rd (01020-4602)
PHONE.................................413 562-9981
Wayne Theriaque, *Manager*
Thomas Plasse, *Manager*
EMP: 18
SQ FT: 45,000
SALES (corp-wide): 2.9B **Privately Held**
SIC: 3496 Mfg Misc Fabricated Wire Products
HQ: Merchants Metals Llc
211 Perimeter Center Pkwy
Atlanta GA 30346
770 741-0306

(G-10045)
METAL MEN
280 Ludlow Rd (01020)
PHONE.................................413 533-0513
Walter Rose, *Owner*
EMP: 10
SALES (est): 1.2MM **Privately Held**
SIC: 3444 Mfg Sheet Metalwork

(G-10046)
MICROTEK INC
2070 Westover Rd (01022-1079)
PHONE.................................413 593-1025
Maria Goncalves, *President*
Diane Lavoie, *Vice Pres*
Patricia Behan, *Treasurer*
Rosemary Tarantino, *Treasurer*
Anne Paradis, *Exec Dir*
EMP: 120
SQ FT: 24,000
SALES (est): 1.3MM **Privately Held**
WEB: www.microtek-cables.com
SIC: 3679 3613 Mfg Electronic Components Mfg Switchgear/Switchboards

(G-10047)
MOSHER COMPANY INC
15 Exchange St (01013-1294)
P.O. Box 177 (01014-0177)
PHONE.................................413 598-8341
Jeffrey Templeton, *President*
EMP: 10
SQ FT: 25,000
SALES (est): 2.4MM **Privately Held**
WEB: www.mocomfg.com
SIC: 3291 Mfg Abrasive Products

(G-10048)
NATIONAL SEATING MOBILITY INC
150 Padgette St Ste F (01022-1333)
PHONE.................................413 420-0054
Francis Burke, *Branch Mgr*
EMP: 9 **Privately Held**
SIC: 3842 Ret Misc Merchandise
PA: National Seating & Mobility, Inc.
320 Premier Ct S Ste 220
Franklin TN 37067

(G-10049)
NATIONAL VINYL LLC
7 Coburn St (01013-3809)
PHONE..................................413 420-0548
Scott Channell, *General Mgr*
Rob McMahon, *Purchasing*
Ben Surner, *Mng Member*
EMP: 50
SQ FT: 100,000
SALES: 6MM **Privately Held**
SIC: 3089 Mfg Plastic Products

(G-10050)
PIONEER PACKAGING INC (PA)
220 Padgette St (01022-1316)
PHONE..................................413 378-6930
Jeffrey G Shinners, *President*
Jill Camossi, *Treasurer*
Mike Crane, *Manager*
Tony Wesolowski, *Manager*
Louise Laflamme, *Admin Sec*
EMP: 55 **EST:** 1946
SQ FT: 92,775
SALES (est): 8MM **Privately Held**
WEB: www.pioneerpackaginginc.com
SIC: 2671 2657 3089 Mfg Folding Paperboard Boxes Mfg Plastic Products Mfg Packaging Paper/Film

(G-10051)
POLY PLATING INC
2096 Westover Rd (01022-1055)
PHONE..................................413 593-5477
Edwin Ondrick Jr, *President*
Chris Ondrick, *Vice Pres*
Carol Ondrick, *Treasurer*
EMP: 13 **EST:** 1976
SQ FT: 15,000
SALES (est): 1.5MM **Privately Held**
WEB: www.poly-ond.com
SIC: 3471 Electroplating

(G-10052)
POREX CLEANROOM PRODUCTS INC
Also Called: Essentra Porous Technologies
2255 Westover Rd (01022-1060)
PHONE..................................800 628-8606
Jon Peacock, *CEO*
Tim McArthy, *Vice Pres*
John Udelhofen, *Vice Pres*
◆ **EMP:** 85 **EST:** 1906
SQ FT: 70,000
SALES: 30MM
SALES (corp-wide): 206.3MM **Privately Held**
WEB: www.johnrlyman.com
SIC: 2842 Mfg Polish/Sanitation Goods
PA: Filtration Group Corporation
600 W 22nd St Ste 300
Oak Brook IL 60523
512 593-7999

(G-10053)
PRIMA NORTH AMERICA INC
711 E Main St (01020-3606)
PHONE..................................413 598-5200
Musse Awale, *Principal*
James Morrison, *Principal*
Chih Hao Wang, *Principal*
Maurizio Gattiglio, *Chairman*
Imtiaz Majid, *Vice Pres*
EMP: 5
SALES (est): 435.6K
SALES (corp-wide): 249.2MM **Privately Held**
SIC: 3444 Mfg Sheet Metalwork
PA: Prima Industrie Spa
Via Alessandro Antonelli 32
Collegno TO 10093
011 410-31

(G-10054)
PYNCHON PRESS CO INC
873 Grattan St (01020-1217)
PHONE..................................413 315-8798
Anita Labrie, *President*
Anita La Brie, *President*
EMP: 6 **EST:** 1964
SQ FT: 7,000
SALES (est): 630K **Privately Held**
SIC: 2752 Offset Printing

(G-10055)
R DUCHARME INC
451 Mckinstry Ave (01020-1101)
PHONE..................................413 534-4516
Dean E Ducharme, *President*
EMP: 8
SQ FT: 11,000
SALES (est): 1MM **Privately Held**
SIC: 3271 Mfg Concrete Block/Brick

(G-10056)
R M MACHINE LLC
32 Dulong Cir (01022-1153)
PHONE..................................413 331-0576
Robert Scribner,
EMP: 5 **EST:** 2010
SALES (est): 494.1K **Privately Held**
SIC: 3599 Mfg Industrial Machinery

(G-10057)
REPRO CRAFT INC
354 Montcalm St (01020-4073)
PHONE..................................413 533-4937
Gary Bourque, *President*
EMP: 5 **EST:** 1965
SQ FT: 5,500
SALES (est): 673.3K **Privately Held**
SIC: 2262 Mfg Printing Screens

(G-10058)
REPUBLIC IRON WORKS INC
40 Champion Dr (01020-2833)
PHONE..................................413 594-8819
Gary Visconti, *President*
EMP: 7
SQ FT: 15,000
SALES: 1MM **Privately Held**
SIC: 3441 Structural Metal/Steel Fabrication

(G-10059)
ROGERS GENERAL MACHINING INC
181 Ludlow Rd (01020-4477)
PHONE..................................413 532-4673
Steve Guyott, *President*
Kenneth Guyott, *Vice Pres*
EMP: 10
SQ FT: 8,000
SALES: 850K **Privately Held**
SIC: 3599 Machine Shop

(G-10060)
SIGN TECHNIQUES INC
361 Chicopee St (01013-1746)
PHONE..................................413 594-8240
Zenon Lemanski, *President*
Jane Lemanski, *Treasurer*
EMP: 12
SQ FT: 3,150
SALES (est): 1.8MM **Privately Held**
SIC: 3993 Mfg Signs

(G-10061)
SOLENIS LLC
Also Called: Hercules Pulp and Paper Div
1111 Grattan St (01013-5213)
PHONE..................................413 536-6426
Terry Shepherd, *Accountant*
William D Langhans, *Manager*
Thomas Bernard, *Senior Mgr*
Adrian Bernard, *Commercial*
EMP: 45
SALES (corp-wide): 767.2MM **Privately Held**
WEB: www.herc.com
SIC: 2899 Mfg Chemical Preparations
HQ: Solenis Llc
2475 Pinnacle Dr
Wilmington DE 19803
866 337-1533

(G-10062)
STANDEX INTERNATIONAL CORP
Also Called: Mullen Testers
939 Chicopee St Ste 3 (01013-2893)
PHONE..................................413 536-1311
Pat Saczawa, *Branch Mgr*
EMP: 3
SALES (corp-wide): 791.5MM **Publicly Held**
SIC: 3825 Mfg Electrical Measuring Instruments
PA: Standex International Corporation
11 Keewaydin Dr Ste 300
Salem NH 03079
603 893-9701

(G-10063)
TECHFLEX ENTERPRISES INC
717 Fuller Rd (01020-3755)
P.O. Box 441, Ludlow (01056-0441)
PHONE..................................413 592-2800
Mike Venancio, *President*
EMP: 6
SQ FT: 9,000
SALES: 1MM **Privately Held**
WEB: www.techflexhose.com
SIC: 3052 Mfg Rubber/Plastic Hose/Belting

(G-10064)
TED ONDRICK COMPANY LLC (PA)
58 Industry Rd (01020-3715)
PHONE..................................413 592-2565
Theodore J Ondrick,
EMP: 12
SQ FT: 1,500
SALES (est): 3.1MM **Privately Held**
WEB: www.tedondrickco.com
SIC: 2951 1741 1611 4953 Mfg Asphalt Mixtr/Blocks Masonry/Stone Contractor Highway/Street Cnstn Refuse Systems

(G-10065)
TUNSTALL CORPORATION (PA)
118 Exchange St (01013-1243)
P.O. Box 434, Springfield (01101-0434)
PHONE..................................413 594-8695
Timothy P Tunstall, *President*
Laura Maspo, *COO*
Ryan Tunstall, *Admin Sec*
▲ **EMP:** 35
SQ FT: 15,000
SALES (est): 6MM **Privately Held**
WEB: www.maconcontrols.com
SIC: 3433 Mfg Heating Equipment-Non-electric

(G-10066)
UNECO MANUFACTURING INC
330 Fuller Rd (01020-3724)
PHONE..................................413 594-2700
Al Fontana, *President*
Walter K Twarowski, *Vice Pres*
Walter Twarowski, *Vice Pres*
EMP: 30
SQ FT: 17,000
SALES (est): 2MM **Privately Held**
WEB: www.unecomfg.com
SIC: 3469 3544 Mfg Metal Stampings Mfg Dies/Tools/Jigs/Fixtures

(G-10067)
US TSUBAKI AUTOMOTIVE LLC (DH)
106 Lonczak St (01022-1305)
PHONE..................................413 593-1100
Tadasu Suzuki, *President*
Jay Mastalerz, *QC Mgr*
Paul Drewniak, *Engineer*
Derek Dumouchel, *Engineer*
Richard Paxson, *Engineer*
▲ **EMP:** 200
SALES (est): 51MM **Privately Held**
SIC: 3462 3568 3496 Manufactures Iron And Steel Forgings Mechanical Power Transmission Equipment And Fabricated Wire Products
HQ: U.S. Tsubaki Holdings, Inc.
301 E Marquardt Dr
Wheeling IL 60090
847 459-9500

(G-10068)
WALL STREET JOURNAL
84 2nd Ave (01020-4625)
PHONE..................................800 369-5663
Richard Zannino, *Principal*
EMP: 9
SALES (est): 315.7K **Privately Held**
SIC: 2711 Newspapers-Publishing/Printing

(G-10069)
WESTFIELD READY-MIX INC
652 Prospect St (01020-3048)
PHONE..................................413 594-4700
Lee Ouellette, *President*
EMP: 20
SALES (est): 1.7MM **Privately Held**
SIC: 3273 Mfg Ready-Mixed Concrete

(G-10070)
ZB CERAMIC
61 Taylor St (01020-2730)
PHONE..................................413 512-0879
Zbigniew Borkowski, *Principal*
EMP: 3
SALES (est): 225.2K **Privately Held**
SIC: 3269 Mfg Pottery Products

(G-10071)
ZERO DISCHARGE
2096 Westover Rd (01022-1079)
PHONE..................................413 593-5470
Edwin Ondrick, *CEO*
EMP: 3
SALES (est): 309.9K **Privately Held**
WEB: www.zerodt.com
SIC: 3589 Mfg Service Industry Machinery

Chilmark
Dukes County

(G-10072)
CHILMARK CHOCOLATES INC
583 State Rd (02535-1679)
P.O. Box 649 (02535-0649)
PHONE..................................508 645-3013
Allison G Burger, *President*
Mary Beth Grady, *Clerk*
EMP: 17
SALES (est): 1.3MM **Privately Held**
SIC: 2066 Ret Candy/Confectionery

Clarksburg
Berkshire County

(G-10073)
M & G METAL INC
161 River Rd (01247-2147)
P.O. Box 76, North Adams (01247-0076)
PHONE..................................413 664-4057
Debra Blanchard, *President*
EMP: 4
SQ FT: 20,000
SALES: 250K **Privately Held**
SIC: 3679 Mfg Electronic Circuits

(G-10074)
PERIOD LIGHTING FIXTURES INC
167 River Rd (01247-2147)
PHONE..................................413 664-7141
Chris Berta, *Treasurer*
EMP: 10
SQ FT: 6,000
SALES: 638K **Privately Held**
WEB: www.periodlighting.com
SIC: 3645 5961 5063 3648 Mfg Residentl Light Fixt Ret Mail-Order House Whol Electrical Equip Mfg Lighting Equipment Mfg Architectural Mtlwrk

(G-10075)
R I BAKER CO INC (PA)
Also Called: Ribco Supply Co
163 River Rd (01247-2147)
P.O. Box 895, North Adams (01247-0895)
PHONE..................................413 663-3791
Thomas Pelczynski, *President*
Maynard A Hodgdon, *Director*
EMP: 30 **EST:** 1968
SQ FT: 20,000
SALES (est): 6.4MM **Privately Held**
WEB: www.bakerengineering.com
SIC: 3599 1711 5074 3441 Mfg Industrial Machinery Plumbing/Heat/Ac Contr Whol Plumbing Equip/Supp

(G-10076)
TIM MEIKLEJOHN LOGGING
499 East Rd (01247-2191)
PHONE..................................413 652-1223
Bill Meiklejohn, *Principal*
EMP: 3
SALES (est): 221.8K **Privately Held**
SIC: 2411 Logging

Clinton
Worcester County

(G-10077)
CENTRAL MASS POWDR COATING INC
32 Greeley St (01510-1902)
PHONE..................................978 365-1700
Jefferson Gould, *President*
Megan Magorian, *Plant Mgr*
EMP: 9
SQ FT: 10,000
SALES (est): 970.4K **Privately Held**
WEB: www.centralmasspowdercoating.com
SIC: 3479 Coating/Engraving Service

(G-10078)
CPI RADANT TECH DIV INC
100 Adams St (01510-1546)
PHONE..................................978 562-3866
Frank Turczyn, *CFO*
EMP: 15
SALES (corp-wide): 411.3MM **Privately Held**
SIC: 3663 Mfg Radio/Tv Communication Equipment
HQ: Cpi Radant Technologies Division Inc.
255 Hudson Rd
Stow MA 01775
978 562-3866

(G-10079)
DMAR ENVIRONMENTAL LLC
184 Stone St Ste 1 (01510-1631)
PHONE..................................508 331-1884
Gary Salter, *Managing Prtnr*
EMP: 4
SALES (est): 275.8K **Privately Held**
SIC: 2842 Mfg Polish/Sanitation Goods

(G-10080)
DUNN & CO INC
75 Green St Ste 1 (01510-3017)
PHONE..................................978 368-8505
Dave Dunn, *Principal*
Paul Cherubini, *CFO*
▼ **EMP:** 125 **EST:** 1976
SQ FT: 250,000
SALES (est): 21.7MM **Privately Held**
WEB: www.booktrauma.com
SIC: 2732 Book Printing

(G-10081)
IMAGING DATA CORPORATION
67 Plain St (01510-1623)
P.O. Box 88 (01510-0088)
PHONE..................................978 365-9353
David Baird, *President*
EMP: 5
SQ FT: 2,400
SALES (est): 831.9K **Privately Held**
WEB: www.imagingdata.com
SIC: 3577 2759 Mfg Computer Peripheral Equipment Commercial Printing

(G-10082)
KEITH INDUSTRIAL GROUP INC
104 Sterling St Ste 5 (01510-1900)
PHONE..................................978 365-5555
Scott Keith, *Principal*
EMP: 3 **EST:** 2016
SALES (est): 48K **Privately Held**
SIC: 3999 Mfg Misc Products

(G-10083)
LEGACY PUBLISHING GROUP INC
75 Green St Ste 1 (01510-3017)
P.O. Box 299 (01510-0299)
PHONE..................................800 322-3866
Carlos Llanso, *CEO*
Cathleen Llanso, *President*
Mary Pat Heelan, *Vice Pres*
Pamela Cross, *Treasurer*
Judy Nieves, *Comptroller*
▲ **EMP:** 20
SQ FT: 20,000
SALES (est): 4MM **Privately Held**
WEB: www.legacypublishinggroup.com
SIC: 2741 Misc Publishing

(G-10084)
N P MEDICAL INC
101 Union St (01510-2908)
PHONE..................................978 365-9721
Courtney Ryan, *President*
Sergio Cadavid, *Treasurer*
John Macinnes, *Treasurer*
Tim Bachelder, *IT/INT Sup*
David Beamer, *Admin Sec*
◆ **EMP:** 32
SQ FT: 2,000
SALES (est): 8MM
SALES (corp-wide): 25.2B **Publicly Held**
WEB: www.npmedical.com
SIC: 3089 Mfg Plastic Products
HQ: Nypro Inc.
101 Union St
Clinton MA 01510
978 365-8100

(G-10085)
NYPRO FINPACK CLINTON
25 School St (01510-3419)
PHONE..................................978 368-6021
Courtney Ryan, *President*
Bruce Marchioni, *Vice Pres*
Erich Stein, *Engineer*
Sergio Cadavid, *Treasurer*
Ed Philbin, *Info Tech Dir*
EMP: 15
SQ FT: 26,000
SALES (est): 1.5MM **Privately Held**
SIC: 2834 Mfg Pharmaceutical Preparations

(G-10086)
NYPRO INC (HQ)
Also Called: Clinton Nypro
101 Union St (01510-2935)
PHONE..................................978 365-8100
Mary Venuti, *CEO*
Courtney Ryan, *President*
Gregory G Adams, *President*
Bryan Check, *Plant Mgr*
Erik Bedding, *Project Mgr*
◆ **EMP:** 1000
SQ FT: 500,000
SALES (est): 4.7B
SALES (corp-wide): 25.2B **Publicly Held**
WEB: www.nypro.com
SIC: 3089 3559 7389 8711 Mfg Plastic Products Mfg Misc Industry Mach Business Services Engineering Services
PA: Jabil Inc.
10560 Dr Mrtn Lther King
Saint Petersburg FL 33716
727 577-9749

(G-10087)
NYPROMOLD INC (PA)
144 Pleasant St (01510-3416)
PHONE..................................978 365-4547
William Muldoon, *President*
Chris Stefaniak, *Engineer*
John Casali, *Treasurer*
Chris Bussiere, *Program Mgr*
Tom Casali MBA, *Program Mgr*
▲ **EMP:** 100
SQ FT: 9,000
SALES (est): 28.2MM **Privately Held**
WEB: www.nypromold.com
SIC: 3544 Mfg Dies/Tools/Jigs/Fixtures

(G-10088)
PEAKS TARPS
89 Parker St Ste 5 (01510-1544)
PHONE..................................978 365-5555
Scott Keith, *President*
EMP: 3
SALES (est): 252.1K **Privately Held**
SIC: 2394 Mfg Canvas/Related Products

(G-10089)
PHILLIPS-MEDISIZE LLC
1 Union St (01510-2916)
PHONE..................................978 365-1262
Daniel Daly, *Project Engr*
Robert Reeder, *Program Mgr*
Amal Sen, *Program Mgr*
EMP: 3
SALES (corp-wide): 40.6B **Privately Held**
SIC: 3089 Mfg Plastic Products
HQ: Pantheon Topco, Inc.
7 Long Lake Dr
Phillips WI 54555
715 386-4320

(G-10090)
POLY-MARK CORP
99 Parker St (01510-1530)
PHONE..................................978 368-1300
Paul E Cremonini, *President*
EMP: 3 **EST:** 2010
SALES (est): 175.9K **Privately Held**
SIC: 2821 Mfg Plastic Materials/Resins

(G-10091)
QEP CO INC
179 Brook St (01510-1503)
PHONE..................................978 368-8991
Joseph Kelly, *CEO*
EMP: 7
SALES (corp-wide): 334.6MM **Publicly Held**
SIC: 3089 Mfg Plastic Products
PA: Q.E.P. Co., Inc.
1001 Brkn Snd Pkwy Nw A
Boca Raton FL 33487
561 994-5550

(G-10092)
R T CLARK MANUFACTURING INC
104 Sterling St Bldg C (01510-1900)
PHONE..................................800 921-4330
EMP: 3
SALES (est): 164.9K **Privately Held**
SIC: 3999 Mfg Misc Products

(G-10093)
STERLING PRECISION INC
90 Parker St (01510-1531)
PHONE..................................978 365-4999
Robert Heckman, *President*
Richard Lazazzero, *Corp Secy*
EMP: 15
SQ FT: 10,000
SALES (est): 3MM **Privately Held**
SIC: 3599 Mfg Industrial Machinery

(G-10094)
TYCA CORPORATION (PA)
470 Main St (01510-2422)
PHONE..................................978 612-0002
Franklin V Hardy, *President*
Mary Ann Castillo, *Exec VP*
▲ **EMP:** 34
SQ FT: 26,000
SALES (est): 2.9MM **Privately Held**
WEB: www.tyca.com
SIC: 2326 3089 2329 2339 Mfg Men/Boy Work Clothng Mfg Plastic Products Mfg Mens/Boys Clothing Mfg Women/Miss Outerwear

(G-10095)
WORTHEN INDUSTRIES INC
Also Called: Nylco
530 Main St (01510-2412)
PHONE..................................978 365-6345
Troy Medeiros, *Plant Mgr*
Troy Medearos, *Branch Mgr*
EMP: 40
SQ FT: 45,000
SALES (corp-wide): 66.2MM **Privately Held**
SIC: 3069 3089 Mfg Fabricated Rubber Products Mfg Plastic Products
HQ: Worthen Industries, Inc.
3 E Spit Brook Rd
Nashua NH 03060
603 888-5443

Cohasset
Norfolk County

(G-10096)
COHASSET SPORTS COMPLEX
34 Crocker Ln (02025-1553)
PHONE..................................781 383-0278
Rob Schwandt, *Principal*
Fouad Alzaibak, *Principal*
Guy Reynolds, *Principal*
Frank Teixeira, *Principal*
EMP: 4
SALES (est): 258.7K **Privately Held**
SIC: 3949 Mfg Sporting/Athletic Goods

(G-10097)
DAILY JUICE PRESS LLC
132 Chief Justice Cushing (02025-1259)
PHONE..................................781 261-6099
John Peraino, *Principal*
EMP: 4 **EST:** 2014
SALES (est): 66.5K **Privately Held**
SIC: 2741 Misc Publishing

(G-10098)
EVERYBODY WATER LLC
35 Elm Ct (02025-1832)
PHONE..................................855 374-6539
Megan Hayes,
Kimberly Reilly,
EMP: 6
SALES: 300K **Privately Held**
SIC: 2086 Mfg Bottled Water

(G-10099)
HARPOON PRODUCTIONS
445 Beechwood St Ste 1 (02025-1528)
P.O. Box 85 (02025-0085)
PHONE..................................781 383-0500
Richard Silvia, *Owner*
EMP: 5
SALES: 200K **Privately Held**
SIC: 3089 Mfg Automotive Highway Safety Devices

(G-10100)
HASSAN WOODCARVING & SIGN CO
799 Chief Jstice Cshing (02025-2141)
PHONE..................................781 383-6075
David Hassan, *Owner*
EMP: 6 **EST:** 1971
SQ FT: 600
SALES: 400K **Privately Held**
WEB: www.hassansign.com
SIC: 3993 7389 Mfg Signs/Advertising Specialties Business Services

(G-10101)
OBRIEN PUBLICATIONS INC
Also Called: Paper Age
20 Schofield Rd (02025-1922)
PHONE..................................781 378-2126
John F O'Brien, *President*
Michael O'Brien, *Treasurer*
EMP: 3
SALES (est): 229.4K **Privately Held**
WEB: www.paperage.com
SIC: 2741 Publishing Company

(G-10102)
TINYTOWN GAZETTE (PA)
Also Called: A Day Trip Com
172 S Main St (02025-2009)
PHONE..................................781 383-9115
Tanna Kaasperowicz, *Owner*
EMP: 3
SALES: 70K **Privately Held**
WEB: www.tinytowngazette.com
SIC: 2711 Newspapers-Publishing/Printing

(G-10103)
US FLAG MANUFACTURING INC
166 King St Ste 5 (02025-1392)
PHONE..................................781 383-6607
Wallace St John, *President*
EMP: 6
SALES: 900K **Privately Held**
WEB: www.usflagmfg.com
SIC: 2399 Mfg Fabricated Textile Products

Colrain
Franklin County

(G-10104)
BARNHARDT MANUFACTURING CO
247 Main Rd (01340-9746)
PHONE..................................413 624-3471
Katie Scranton, *Purchasing*
Maria Soderberg, *Human Res Mgr*
Albert Sheridan, *Branch Mgr*
Juanita Bousquet, *Manager*
Gary James, *Director*
EMP: 45

▲ = Import ▼=Export
◆ =Import/Export

SALES (corp-wide): 268.7MM Privately Held
WEB: www.barnhardt.net
SIC: 3842 Mfg Surgical Appliances/Supplies
PA: Barnhardt Manufacturing Company
1100 Hawthorne Ln
Charlotte NC 28205
704 376-0380

(G-10105)
SLOWINSKI WOOD PRODUCTS
13 Bennett Galipo Dr (01340-9760)
PHONE....413 624-3415
Mathew Slowinski, Owner
▲ EMP: 5
SALES (est): 486.9K Privately Held
SIC: 2448 Mfg Wood Pallets/Skids

(G-10106)
WEST COUNTY WINERY
248 Greenfield Rd (01340-9637)
P.O. Box 29 (01340-0029)
PHONE....413 624-3481
Judith Maloney, Owner
EMP: 3
SALES: 75K Privately Held
WEB: www.westcountycider.com
SIC: 2084 Mfg Wines/Brandy/Spirits

Concord
Middlesex County

(G-10107)
ADONEH LLC
428 Lowell Rd (01742-1713)
PHONE....978 618-0389
David Barash,
EMP: 3
SALES (est): 175.8K Privately Held
SIC: 3841 Mfg Surgical/Medical Instruments

(G-10108)
ALOPEXX PHARMACEUTICALS LLC
100 Main St Ste 110 (01742-2528)
PHONE....617 945-2510
Daniel R Vlock, Principal
EMP: 10
SALES (est): 1MM Privately Held
SIC: 2834 Mfg Pharmaceutical Preparations

(G-10109)
ANDOR TECHNOLOGY INC
300 Baker Ave Ste 150 (01742-2124)
PHONE....978 405-1116
Brian Dutko, President
EMP: 36
SALES (est): 1.7MM Privately Held
SIC: 3826 Mfg Analytical Instruments

(G-10110)
ANDOR TECHNOLOGY LTD
300 Baker Ave Ste 150 (01742-2124)
PHONE....860 290-9211
Christopher Calling, Branch Mgr
Susan Karen Johnson -Brett, Admin Sec
EMP: 22
SALES (corp-wide): 429.1MM Privately Held
WEB: www.andor.com
SIC: 3851 Mfg Scientific Intstruments
HQ: Andor Technology Ltd.
300 Baker Ave Ste 150
Concord MA 01742
860 290-9211

(G-10111)
ANSYS INC
150 Baker Avenue Ext # 100 (01742-2199)
PHONE....781 229-8900
Daniel Dvorscak, Engineer
EMP: 6
SALES (corp-wide): 1.2B Publicly Held
SIC: 7372 Prepackaged Software Services
PA: Ansys, Inc.
2600 Ansys Dr
Canonsburg PA 15317
884 462-6797

(G-10112)
APRIORI TECHNOLOGIES INC (PA)
300 Baker Ave Ste 170 (01742-2148)
PHONE....978 371-2006
Stephanie A Feraday, President
Arnie Greenfield, Chairman
Mark West, COO
Scott Carlyle, Vice Pres
Julie Driscoll, Vice Pres
EMP: 55
SQ FT: 15,000
SALES (est): 15.7MM Privately Held
SIC: 7372 Prepackaged Software Services

(G-10113)
ARTINIAN GARABET CORPORATION
39 Main St (01742-2560)
PHONE....978 371-7110
Garabet Artinian, President
EMP: 12
SQ FT: 800
SALES (est): 1MM Privately Held
SIC: 3911 5094 5944 Mfg Whol & Ret Jewelry

(G-10114)
ATLANTIS TECHNOLOGY CORP
1620 Sudbury Rd Ste 1 (01742-5800)
PHONE....978 341-0999
Thomas Biggins, CEO
Ron Ayers, Marketing Staff
Forrest Grant, Software Dev
EMP: 7
SALES: 1MM Privately Held
WEB: www.atlantistech.com
SIC: 7372 Prepackaged Software

(G-10115)
AUSTIN PRINT
23 Allen Farm Ln (01742-2202)
PHONE....978 369-8591
Michael Edward Austin, Owner
EMP: 3
SALES (est): 50K Privately Held
WEB: www.austinprinters.com
SIC: 2752 Lithographic Commercial Printing

(G-10116)
BLUECATBIO MA INC
58 Elsinore St (01742-2316)
PHONE....978 405-2533
Frank Feist, President
EMP: 7
SALES (est): 300K Privately Held
SIC: 3821 5963 8711 Mfg Lab Apparatus/Furniture Direct Retail Sales Engineering Services

(G-10117)
BOEING COMPANY
49 Edgewood Rd (01742-3905)
PHONE....978 369-9522
Patricia Boeing, Branch Mgr
EMP: 895
SALES (corp-wide): 101.1B Publicly Held
SIC: 3721 Mfg Aircraft
PA: The Boeing Company
100 N Riverside Plz
Chicago IL 60606
312 544-2000

(G-10118)
BUDGET PRINTING CONCORD LLC
97 Thoreau St (01742-2443)
PHONE....978 369-4630
Diane B Smigel, Corp Secy
Richard F Krug Jr,
EMP: 4
SQ FT: 1,300
SALES (est): 481.9K Privately Held
SIC: 2752 7334 Lithographic Commercial Printing Photocopying Services

(G-10119)
BUZZWORTHY BAKING LLC
454 Harrington Ave (01742-4034)
PHONE....978 254-5910
Alison S Millerick, Principal
EMP: 4
SALES (est): 152.5K Privately Held
SIC: 2051 Mfg Bread/Related Products

(G-10120)
CALLENSTITCH LLC
52 Domino Dr (01742-2817)
PHONE....978 369-9080
Dicksie Callen, Sales Mgr
Lisa Aideuis, Director
Andrew Callen,
EMP: 40
SQ FT: 10,000
SALES (est): 2.9MM Privately Held
WEB: www.corporatecasuals.com
SIC: 3999 2395 Mfg Misc Products Pleating/Stitching Services

(G-10121)
COGNOPTIX INC
100 Main St Ste 110 (01742-2528)
PHONE....978 263-0005
Paul D Hartung, Ch of Bd
EMP: 4
SALES (est): 444.2K Privately Held
SIC: 3841 Mfg Surgical/Medical Instruments

(G-10122)
COMPOSITE ENGINEERING INC
Also Called: Van Dusen Racing Boats
277 Baker Ave (01742-2115)
PHONE....978 371-3132
Edward S Van Dusen, President
Edward V Dusen, Manager
EMP: 8
SQ FT: 19,000
SALES: 850K Privately Held
WEB: www.vandusenracingboats.com
SIC: 3296 3732 Mfg Racing Shells Carbon Fiber Sailboat Masts & Fiberglass Parts

(G-10123)
CONCORD TEACAKES ETCETERA INC
59 Commonwealth Ave (01742-3003)
PHONE....978 369-7644
Gery Armsdy, Manager
EMP: 14
SALES (est): 1.4MM
SALES (corp-wide): 3.1MM Privately Held
SIC: 2051 2052 5461 Mfg Bread/Related Prdts Mfg Cookies/Crackers Retail Bakery
PA: Concord Teacakes Etcetera, Inc.
30 Domino Dr Ste 1
Concord MA 01742
978 369-2409

(G-10124)
CONCORD TEACAKES ETCETERA INC (PA)
30 Domino Dr Ste 1 (01742-2802)
P.O. Box 1427 (01742-1427)
PHONE....978 369-2409
Judy Fersch, President
Peter Mahler, Vice Pres
EMP: 27
SQ FT: 5,300
SALES (est): 3.1MM Privately Held
WEB: www.concordteacakes.com
SIC: 2051 Mfg Bread/Related Products

(G-10125)
CRISTCOT INC
9 Damonmill Sq Ste 4a (01742-2873)
PHONE....978 212-6380
Jennifer Davagian Ensign, CEO
Mark Ensign, Vice Pres
EMP: 5
SALES (est): 713.7K Privately Held
SIC: 3841 Mfg Surgical/Medical Instruments

(G-10126)
CRISTCOT LLC
9 Damonmill Sq Ste 4a (01742-2873)
PHONE....978 212-6380
Jennifer J Davagian, President
Mark A Parent, CFO
Mark C Ensign, Security Dir
EMP: 4
SALES (est): 261.8K Privately Held
SIC: 2834 Mfg Pharmaceutical Preparations

(G-10127)
DBMAESTRO INC
300 Baker Ave Ste 300 # 300 (01742-2124)
PHONE....508 641-6108
David Rosi, Exec VP
EMP: 5
SALES (est): 128.9K Privately Held
SIC: 7372 Prepackaged Software Services

(G-10128)
DMR PRINT INC (PA)
Also Called: Ambit Creative Group
13 Dover St (01742-5712)
PHONE....617 876-3688
David M Reed, President
Pam Reed, Corp Secy
Peter Reed, Vice Pres
Jarrett Brimmer, Project Mgr
Wes Narron, Manager
EMP: 35
SALES (est): 4.1MM Privately Held
WEB: www.mmpcambridge.com
SIC: 2752 2789 2791 Lithographic Commercial Printing Bookbinding/Related Work Typesetting Services

(G-10129)
DONCAR INC
Also Called: Action Unlimited Newspaper
100 Domino Dr 1 (01742-2817)
PHONE....978 371-2442
Carol Margraf, President
Janice Vonfettweis, Sales Associate
Phil Green, Supervisor
EMP: 25 EST: 1970
SALES (est): 1.6MM Privately Held
SIC: 2711 Newspapers-Publishing/Printing

(G-10130)
GATEHOUSE MEDIA LLC
Also Called: Arlington Advocate
150 Baker Avenue Ext # 101 (01742-2126)
PHONE....978 263-4736
Barbara Bliss, Principal
EMP: 3
SALES (corp-wide): 1.5B Publicly Held
SIC: 2711 Newspapers-Publishing/Printing
HQ: Gatehouse Media, Llc
175 Sullys Trl Fl 3
Pittsford NY 14534
585 598-0030

(G-10131)
GATEHOUSE MEDIA MASS I INC
Also Called: Billerica Minute-Man
150 Baker Avenue Ext # 101 (01742-2126)
P.O. Box 9191 (01742-9191)
PHONE....978 667-2156
Anne Marie Magerman, Manager
EMP: 75
SQ FT: 2,147
SALES (corp-wide): 1.5B Publicly Held
SIC: 2711 Newspapers-Publishing/Printing
HQ: Gatehouse Media Massachusetts I, Inc.
48 Dunham Rd
Beverly MA 01915
585 598-0030

(G-10132)
GOOD2GETHER
23 Anson Rd (01742-5704)
PHONE....978 371-3172
Mr Jesse Moran, President
EMP: 3
SALES (est): 207.1K Privately Held
SIC: 7372 Prepackaged Software Services

(G-10133)
GRAINPRO INC (PA)
200 Baker Ave Ste 309 (01742-2182)
PHONE....978 371-7118
Philippe Villers, President
Tom De Bruin, Vice Pres
Marvin Tala, Research
Nicole Burkel, Finance Mgr
Sharon Novales, Human Res Mgr
▲ EMP: 4
SALES: 5.5MM Privately Held
WEB: www.grainpro.com
SIC: 3089 Mfg Plastic Products

GEOGRAPHIC

(G-10134)
HYDROGEN ENERGY CALIFORNIA LLC
30 Monument Sq Ste 235 (01742-1869)
PHONE..................................978 287-9529
James Croyle, *CEO*
Mark Lerdal, *President*
Julie Millar, *Vice Pres*
EMP: 20
SALES (est): 2MM
SALES (corp-wide): 4.7MM **Privately Held**
SIC: 2813 Manufacturing Of Industrial Gases
PA: S C S Energy Llc
30 Monument Sq Ste 235
Concord MA 01742
978 287-0281

(G-10135)
I2BIOMED INC
365 Garfield Rd (01742-4906)
PHONE..................................857 259-4410
John Shumway, *CEO*
EMP: 4
SALES (est): 156.7K **Privately Held**
SIC: 2841 Mfg Soap/Other Detergents

(G-10136)
INRIVER TANK & BOAT INC
152 Commonwealth Ave # 21
(01742-2990)
PHONE..................................978 287-9534
Julius Pereli, *President*
Kendreen Green, *Vice Pres*
▲ **EMP:** 8
SALES (est): 990K **Privately Held**
SIC: 3732 Boatbuilding/Repairing

(G-10137)
LANCASTER TIMES INC
Also Called: Community Newspaper Company
150 Baker Avenue Ext # 101 (01742-2126)
PHONE..................................978 368-3393
Kirrk Davis, *Principal*
EMP: 5
SQ FT: 2,400
SALES (est): 244.5K **Privately Held**
SIC: 2711 Newspapers-Publishing/Printing

(G-10138)
LEXIA LEARNING SYSTEMS LLC
300 Baker Ave Ste 320 (01742-2131)
PHONE..................................800 435-3942
Robert Lemire, *Ch of Bd*
Nick Kaider, *President*
Mathew Bacon, *Vice Pres*
Nancy Johnson, *Vice Pres*
Ben Vincent, *Production*
EMP: 37
SQ FT: 6,500
SALES (est): 6.8MM **Publicly Held**
WEB: www.lexialearning.com
SIC: 7372 Prepackaged Software Services
HQ: Rosetta Stone Ltd.
135 W Market St
Harrisonburg VA 22801

(G-10139)
LUXURIANCE BIOPHARMA INC
8 N Branch Rd (01742-3808)
PHONE..................................617 817-6679
Hongxiang Lu, *Principal*
EMP: 4
SALES (est): 232.2K **Privately Held**
SIC: 2834 Business Services At Non-Commercial Site

(G-10140)
MEDICAL CMPRESSION SYSTEMS INC
2352 Main St Ste 102 (01742-3896)
P.O. Box 1608 (01742-6608)
PHONE..................................800 377-5804
Gerry Feldman, *CEO*
Sagi Peled, *COO*
Avital Perelstein, *CFO*
Sean D Murphy, *Surgery Dir*
EMP: 3
SALES (est): 593.2K
SALES (corp-wide): 7.9B **Publicly Held**
SIC: 3841 Mfg Surgical/Medical Instruments
PA: Zimmer Biomet Holdings, Inc.
345 E Main St
Warsaw IN 46580
574 267-6131

(G-10141)
MINUTEMAN PRINTING CORP
Also Called: Minuteman Press
20 Beharrell St Ste 1 (01742-2987)
P.O. Box 1026 (01742-1026)
PHONE..................................978 369-2808
Robert P Steinman, *President*
James D Steinman, *Vice Pres*
Maureen Steinman, *Admin Sec*
F David Edes, *Clerk*
EMP: 10 **EST:** 1916
SQ FT: 20,000
SALES (est): 1.1MM **Privately Held**
SIC: 2752 2789 Lithographic Commercial Printing Bookbinding/Related Work

(G-10142)
MONUMENT STREET ENTPS LLC
51 Ministerial Dr (01742-4015)
PHONE..................................781 820-1888
Peter M Atwood Jr, *Principal*
EMP: 3
SALES (est): 218.9K **Privately Held**
SIC: 3272 Mfg Concrete Products

(G-10143)
MUNICIPAL MARKET ANALYTICS INC (PA)
75 Main St Fl 2 (01742-2503)
PHONE..................................978 287-0014
Thomas DOE, *President*
EMP: 10
SQ FT: 400
SALES (est): 770K **Privately Held**
SIC: 2721 Periodicals-Publishing/Printing

(G-10144)
NATIONAL CON TNKS / FRGUARD JV
82 Tarbell Spring Rd (01742-4023)
PHONE..................................978 505-5533
Robert Barbarisi, *Vice Pres*
Thomas Macelhaney, *Vice Pres*
EMP: 10
SALES: 1MM **Privately Held**
SIC: 3272 Construction Of Water Tanks

(G-10145)
NATIONAL GRAPE COOP ASSN INC
555 Virginia Rd (01742-2770)
PHONE..................................978 371-1000
Dianna Hammer, *Branch Mgr*
EMP: 8
SALES (corp-wide): 608.4MM **Privately Held**
SIC: 2033 Mfg Canned Fruits/Vegetables
PA: National Grape Co-Operative Association, Inc.
80 State St
Westfield NY 14787
716 326-5200

(G-10146)
NEW ENGLAND OLIVE OIL COMPANY
191 Sudbury Rd (01742-3467)
PHONE..................................978 610-6776
Samantha English, *Owner*
EMP: 3
SALES (est): 237.9K **Privately Held**
SIC: 2079 Mfg Edible Fats/Oils

(G-10147)
NORTH ATLANTIC PUBG SYSTEMS
66 Commonwealth Ave Ste 5 (01742-2974)
PHONE..................................978 371-8989
Peter J Baumgartner, *President*
Pierre Leveille, *Shareholder*
EMP: 5
SQ FT: 1,500
SALES (est): 370.4K **Privately Held**
WEB: www.napsys.com
SIC: 7372 Prepackaged Software Services

(G-10148)
OMNIPROBE INC
300 Baker Ave Ste 150 (01742-2124)
PHONE..................................214 572-6800
Gonzalo Amador, *President*
Chris Fraser, *Treasurer*
Ian Berkshire, *Director*
EMP: 23
SQ FT: 18,000
SALES (est): 5.1MM
SALES (corp-wide): 429.1MM **Privately Held**
WEB: www.omniprobe.com
SIC: 3826 Mfg Analytical Instruments
PA: Oxford Instruments Plc
Tubney Woods
Abingdon OXON OX13
186 539-3200

(G-10149)
OXFORD INSTRS MSREMENT SYSTEMS
Also Called: Oxford Instruments America
300 Baker Ave Ste 150 (01742-2124)
PHONE..................................978 369-9933
Scott Reiman, *President*
Christopher S Fraser, *Treasurer*
James Pollock, *Admin Sec*
EMP: 99
SQ FT: 120,000
SALES (est): 13.6MM
SALES (corp-wide): 429.1MM **Privately Held**
WEB: www.msys.oxinst.com
SIC: 3829 Mfg Measuring/Controlling Devices
PA: Oxford Instruments Plc
Tubney Woods
Abingdon OXON OX13
186 539-3200

(G-10150)
PHOTOGRAPHIC CORP NEW ENGLAND
Also Called: P G of New England
177 Old Bedford Rd Fl 2 (01742-2707)
P.O. Box 581 (01742-0581)
PHONE..................................978 369-3002
Daniel X Coffey, *President*
Mary Ellen Groden Coffey, *Treasurer*
EMP: 4
SALES (est): 298.7K **Privately Held**
SIC: 2752 Mfg Lithographic Calendars & Greeting Cards & Posters

(G-10151)
POTTING SHED INC
43 Bradford St Ste 3 (01742-2972)
PHONE..................................617 899-6290
Richard M Starr, *President*
EMP: 6 **EST:** 1977
SQ FT: 28,000
SALES (est): 481.6K **Privately Held**
WEB: www.harelooms.com
SIC: 3269 5719 Mfg & Ret Handcrafted Pottery

(G-10152)
PRYSM INC
45 Winthrop St Ste D (01742-2088)
PHONE..................................408 586-1100
Sreeni Garlapati, *Vice Pres*
Michael McMahon, *Engineer*
Monica Vought, *Branch Mgr*
EMP: 40 **Privately Held**
SIC: 3999 Mfg Misc Products
PA: Prysm, Inc.
180 Baytech Dr Ste 200
San Jose CA 95134

(G-10153)
QUALCOMM INCORPORATED
30 Monument Sq Ste 235 (01742-1869)
PHONE..................................978 318-0650
William Dill, *Engineer*
Jianming Zhu, *Engineer*
Karen Stahl, *Branch Mgr*
EMP: 100
SALES (corp-wide): 24.2B **Publicly Held**
WEB: www.qualcomm.com
SIC: 3663 Mfg Advanced Communications Systems
PA: Qualcomm Incorporated
5775 Morehouse Dr
San Diego CA 92121
858 587-1121

(G-10154)
QUICKPOINT CORPORATION
23b Bradford St (01742-2901)
PHONE..................................978 371-3267
Allen Aronie, *President*
Joel Aronie, *Treasurer*
▲ **EMP:** 4
SALES (est): 432.7K **Privately Held**
WEB: www.quikpoint.com
SIC: 3423 Mfg Hand/Edge Tools

(G-10155)
RECALL SERVICES HEALTHWATCH
389 Lindsay Pond Rd (01742-5217)
PHONE..................................978 369-7253
David Zarchan, *CEO*
EMP: 3
SALES (est): 266.7K **Privately Held**
SIC: 3625 Mfg Relays/Industrial Controls

(G-10156)
RENESAS ELECTRONICS AMER INC
Also Called: Intersil Design Center
300 Baker Ave Ste 300 # 300
(01742-2124)
PHONE..................................978 805-6900
Maher Matta, *Manager*
EMP: 600 **Privately Held**
SIC: 3674 Mfg Semiconductors/Related Devices
HQ: Renesas Electronics America Inc.
1001 Murphy Ranch Rd
Milpitas CA 95035
408 432-8888

(G-10157)
SMASHFLY TECHNOLOGIES INC (HQ)
9 Damonmill Sq Ste 3a (01742-2842)
PHONE..................................978 369-3932
Thom Kenney, *CEO*
Jon Finnimore, *Vice Pres*
Marisa Linardos, *CFO*
Russ Mikowski, *Risk Mgmt Dir*
EMP: 10
SALES (est): 8.2MM
SALES (corp-wide): 50MM **Privately Held**
SIC: 7372 Prepackaged Software Services
PA: Symphony Talent, Llc
19 W 34th St Fl 10
New York NY 10001
212 999-9000

(G-10158)
TECHNICAL COMMUNICATIONS CORP (PA)
100 Domino Dr (01742-2817)
PHONE..................................978 287-5100
Carl H Guild Jr, *Ch of Bd*
Michael P Malone, *CFO*
Bogdan Antonescu, *Manager*
EMP: 25 **EST:** 1960
SALES: 7MM **Publicly Held**
WEB: www.tccsecure.com
SIC: 3663 Mfg Encryption Equipment

(G-10159)
VIBRAM CORPORATION (HQ)
Also Called: Vibram USA Inc.
9 Damonmill Sq Fl 2 (01742-2858)
PHONE..................................978 318-0000
Michael Gionfriddo, *CEO*
Richard Riegel, *Ch of Bd*
Fabrizio Gamberini, *President*
Bill Ells, *Vice Pres*
Chris Favreau, *Vice Pres*
▲ **EMP:** 45
SALES (est): 48.1MM
SALES (corp-wide): 160.3MM **Privately Held**
SIC: 3069 3131 5661 Mfg Fabricated Rubber Products Mfg Footwear Cut Stock Ret Shoes
PA: Vibram Spa
Via Cristoforo Colombo 5
Albizzate VA 21041
033 199-9700

(G-10160)
WELCH FOODS INC A COOPERATIVE (HQ)
Also Called: Welch's
575 Virginia Rd (01742-2761)
PHONE..........................978 371-1000
Trevor Bynum, *President*
Carey Haubenschild, *Business Mgr*
David Moore, *Business Mgr*
Matt Aufman, *VP Legal*
Delisle Flynn, *Vice Pres*
◆ **EMP:** 275
SQ FT: 60,000
SALES (est): 306.9MM
SALES (corp-wide): 608.4MM **Privately Held**
WEB: www.welchs.com
SIC: 2033 2037 Mfg Canned Fruits/Vegtbl
PA: National Grape Co-Operative Association, Inc.
80 State St
Westfield NY 14787
716 326-5200

(G-10161)
WELCH FOODS INC A COOPERATIVE
300 Baker Ave Ste 101 (01742-2131)
PHONE..........................978 371-3762
William Hewins, *Branch Mgr*
EMP: 139
SALES (corp-wide): 608.4MM **Privately Held**
SIC: 2033 Mfg Canned Fruits/Vegetables
HQ: Welch Foods Inc., A Cooperative
575 Virginia Rd
Concord MA 01742
978 371-1000

(G-10162)
WILLIAM CROSBY
Also Called: Crosby Designs
53 Bradford St (01742-2901)
PHONE..........................978 371-1111
William Crosby, *Owner*
EMP: 3
SALES (est): 229.4K **Privately Held**
WEB: www.crosbydesigninc.com
SIC: 2499 3993 Mfg Wood Products Mfg Signs/Advertising Specialties

(G-10163)
WILLIAMSON CORPORATION
70 Domino Dr (01742-2893)
PHONE..........................978 369-9607
William R Barron Sr, *President*
William Barron Jr, *Vice Pres*
Thomas Huff, *Sales Staff*
Henson Troy, *Manager*
EMP: 20 **EST:** 1954
SQ FT: 7,500
SALES (est): 5.6MM **Privately Held**
WEB: www.williamsonir.com
SIC: 3826 3823 Mfg Analytical Instruments Mfg Process Control Instruments

Conway
Franklin County

(G-10164)
OESCO INC
Also Called: Orchard Equipment & Supply Co
8 Ashfield Rd (01341-9786)
P.O. Box 540 (01341-0540)
PHONE..........................413 369-4335
Russell A French, *President*
Lynn Olynik, *Accounting Mgr*
▲ **EMP:** 24 **EST:** 1954
SQ FT: 20,000
SALES: 4.5MM **Privately Held**
WEB: www.oescoinc.com
SIC: 3556 5999 5083 3523 Mfg Food Prdts Mach Ret Misc Merchandise Whol Farm/Garden Mach Mfg Farm Machinery/Equip

(G-10165)
POPLAR HILL MACHINE INC
2077 Roaring Brook Rd (01341-9767)
PHONE..........................413 369-4252
Michael J Kurkulonis, *President*
John Hill, *Manager*
EMP: 11
SALES (est): 2.6MM **Privately Held**
SIC: 3599 Mfg Industrial Machinery

(G-10166)
SANGER EQUIPMENT AND MFG
Wilder Hill Rd (01341)
P.O. Box 201, Shelburne Falls (01370-0201)
PHONE..........................413 625-8304
Peter R Sanger, *President*
▲ **EMP:** 6
SALES (est): 656.9K **Privately Held**
WEB: www.sanger.net
SIC: 1442 5084 Construction Sand/Gravel Whol Industrial Equipment

(G-10167)
SOUTH RIVER MISO CO INC
888 Shelburne Falls Rd (01341-9661)
PHONE..........................413 369-4057
Christian Elwell, *President*
Margaret Gaella Elwell, *Treasurer*
EMP: 3
SALES (est): 276.9K **Privately Held**
WEB: www.southrivermiso.com
SIC: 2075 Soybean Oil Mill

Cotuit
Barnstable County

(G-10168)
BIOPHARMA OF CAPE COD INC
656 Putnam Ave (02635-2813)
PHONE..........................508 428-5823
Carlos A Castro, *Principal*
EMP: 4
SALES (est): 290.5K **Privately Held**
SIC: 2834 Business Services At Non-Commercial Site

(G-10169)
COTUIT WORKS
50 Shell Ln (02635-3330)
PHONE..........................508 428-3971
Allen Davies, *CEO*
EMP: 3
SALES: 150K **Privately Held**
SIC: 3559 3999 Mfg Misc Industry Machinery Mfg Misc Products

(G-10170)
LUJEAN PRINTING CO INC
4507 Falmouth Rd (02635-2652)
P.O. Box 571, Osterville (02655-0571)
PHONE..........................508 428-8700
Michael Lally, *President*
EMP: 11
SQ FT: 7,500
SALES (est): 1.5MM **Privately Held**
WEB: www.lujeanprintingcompany.com
SIC: 2752 2711 2759 Lithographic Commercial Printing Newspapers-Publishing/Printing Commercial Printing

(G-10171)
PARTS PER MILLION INC
904 Main St (02635-3236)
PHONE..........................508 479-5438
Deran Campbell Hanesian, *Principal*
EMP: 4
SALES (est): 450.8K **Privately Held**
SIC: 3589 Mfg Service Industry Machinery

Cummaquid
Barnstable County

(G-10172)
RICHARD PG MILLWORK CO INC
4022 Main St (02637)
PHONE..........................508 776-2433
Paul G Richard, *President*
Nancy Richard, *Admin Sec*
EMP: 6
SALES (est): 549.1K **Privately Held**
SIC: 2431 Mfg Millwork

Cummington
Hampshire County

(G-10173)
OLD CREAMERY GROCERY STORE
445 Berkshire Trl (01026-9610)
PHONE..........................413 634-5560
Ammy Pulley, *Partner*
Alice Cozzolino, *Partner*
EMP: 8
SALES (est): 590K **Privately Held**
SIC: 2043 5921 5541 5411 Ret Groceries Mfg Cereal Breakfast Fds Ret Alcoholic Beverages Gasoline Service Station Ret Groceries

Dalton
Berkshire County

(G-10174)
BERKSHIRE BRIDGE & IRON CO INC
140 E Housatonic St (01226-1928)
P.O. Box 254 (01227-0254)
PHONE..........................413 684-3182
Dennis Fusini, *President*
Pete Fusini, *Vice Pres*
Carlo Fusini, *Shareholder*
EMP: 15 **EST:** 1965
SQ FT: 20,000
SALES (est): 3.8MM **Privately Held**
SIC: 3441 Structural Metal Fabrication

(G-10175)
COUNTY CONCRETE CORP (PA)
290 Hubbard Ave (01226)
P.O. Box 1306, Pittsfield (01202-1306)
PHONE..........................413 499-3359
Joseph Kroboth, *President*
EMP: 28 **EST:** 1973
SQ FT: 5,000
SALES (est): 3.2MM **Privately Held**
SIC: 3272 Mfg Concrete Products

(G-10176)
CRANE & CO INC
30 South St (01226-1797)
PHONE..........................413 684-2600
Sandy Streeter, *Administration*
Mike Baumgartner, *Maintence Staff*
EMP: 7
SALES (corp-wide): 3.3B **Publicly Held**
SIC: 2621 Paper Mill
HQ: Crane & Co., Inc.
1 Beacon St Ste 1702
Boston MA 02108
617 648-3799

(G-10177)
CRANE & CO INC
Also Called: Weston Papers
800 Main St (01226)
PHONE..........................413 684-2600
Steve Defalco, *CEO*
EMP: 200
SALES (corp-wide): 3.3B **Publicly Held**
WEB: www.crane.com
SIC: 2621 Paper Mill
HQ: Crane & Co., Inc.
1 Beacon St Ste 1702
Boston MA 02108
617 648-3799

(G-10178)
HOLIDAY FARM INC
Holiday Cottage Rd (01226)
PHONE..........................413 684-0444
Dicken Crane, *President*
Carrie Crane, *Treasurer*
Mary Crane, *Treasurer*
Tim Crane, *Admin Sec*
EMP: 3
SALES (est): 200K **Privately Held**
WEB: www.holidayfarmresort.com
SIC: 2099 0139 Mfg Food Preparations Field Crop Farm

(G-10179)
KROFTA TECHNOLOGIES LLC (DH)
401 South St (01226-1758)
PHONE..........................413 236-5634
Harish Kumar Khanna, *President*
Mp Jain, *President*
EMP: 3
SALES (est): 485.8K
SALES (corp-wide): 62.5MM **Privately Held**
SIC: 3589 Mfg Service Industry Machinery
HQ: Waterleau Inc.
50 Square Dr Ste 200
Victor NY 14564
585 421-3500

(G-10180)
NEENAH TECHNICAL MATERIALS INC (HQ)
Ashuelot Park Ii 448 Hbbr (01226)
PHONE..........................678 518-3343
Dennis G Lockyer, *President*
Douglas S Prince, *Treasurer*
James W Hackett Jr, *Admin Sec*
▲ **EMP:** 18
SALES (est): 6.1MM
SALES (corp-wide): 1B **Publicly Held**
SIC: 2621 5943 2752 Paper Mill Ret Stationery Lithographic Commercial Printing
PA: Neenah, Inc.
3460 Preston Ridge Rd # 150
Alpharetta GA 30005
678 566-6500

(G-10181)
PIERCE MACHINE CO INC (PA)
74 E Housatonic St (01226-1961)
P.O. Box 251 (01227-0251)
PHONE..........................413 684-0056
Mark Busch, *President*
J Robert Busch, *Chairman*
EMP: 25 **EST:** 1920
SQ FT: 13,000
SALES (est): 3.1MM **Privately Held**
WEB: www.piercemachine.com
SIC: 3599 Mfg Industrial Machinery

(G-10182)
RBD ELECTRONICS INC (PA)
63 Flansburg Ave (01226-1410)
PHONE..........................413 442-1111
Ronald Sanders, *President*
Ron Sanders, *Principal*
EMP: 10
SQ FT: 27,000
SALES (est): 2.3MM **Privately Held**
WEB: www.rbdelectronics.com
SIC: 3672 5065 Mfg Printed Circuit Boards Whol Electronic Parts/Equipment

(G-10183)
SAFARILAND LLC
401 South St (01226-1758)
PHONE..........................413 684-3104
Dawn Milesi, *Principal*
EMP: 59
SALES (corp-wide): 1B **Privately Held**
WEB: www.protecharmored.com
SIC: 3842 3199 Mfg Body Armour/Gun Holsters
HQ: Safariland, Llc
13386 International Pkwy
Jacksonville FL 32218
904 741-5400

(G-10184)
SEW WHAT EMBROIDERY
Also Called: Berkshire Spt & Sew What EMB
385 Main St Ste 1 (01226-1631)
PHONE..........................413 684-0672
Maryann Ogden, *Owner*
EMP: 3
SQ FT: 1,200
SALES: 150K **Privately Held**
SIC: 2395 3993 5611 5621 Embroidery Services Manufactures Advertising Specialties Retails And Wholesales Active Wear And Bags

(G-10185)
SILVER BEAR DISTILLERY LLC
63 Flansburg Ave (01226-1410)
PHONE..........................413 242-4892
B O Peter Sternerup, *Principal*

GEOGRAPHIC

EMP: 4
SALES (est): 213.5K **Privately Held**
SIC: 2085 Mfg Distilled/Blended Liquor

(G-10186)
SINICON PLASTICS INC
455 Housatonic St (01226-1836)
P.O. Box 204 (01227-0204)
PHONE..................................413 684-5290
David K Allen, *President*
EMP: 29
SQ FT: 35,000
SALES (est): 7.9MM **Privately Held**
WEB: www.sinicon.com
SIC: 3089 Mfg Plastic Products

(G-10187)
STUDLEY PRESS INC
151 E Housatonic St (01226-1929)
P.O. Box 214 (01227-0214)
PHONE..................................413 684-0441
Charles Gillett, *President*
Suzanne Salinetti, *Vice Pres*
EMP: 30
SQ FT: 20,000
SALES (est): 4.4MM **Privately Held**
WEB: www.thestudleypress.com
SIC: 2752 Lithographic Commercial Printing

Danvers
Essex County

(G-10188)
A A PLASTIC & MET FABRICATORS
250 North St Ste A2 (01923-1206)
PHONE..................................978 777-0367
Dana Foy, *President*
EMP: 5 **EST:** 1973
SALES (est): 750K **Privately Held**
SIC: 3089 Mfg Plastic Products

(G-10189)
ABIOMED INC (PA)
22 Cherry Hill Dr (01923-2599)
PHONE..................................978 646-1400
Michael R Minogue, *Ch of Bd*
David M Weber, *COO*
David Weber, *COO*
Andrew J Greenfield, *Vice Pres*
Michael G Howley, *Vice Pres*
EMP: 277 **EST:** 1981
SQ FT: 163,560
SALES: 769.4MM **Publicly Held**
WEB: www.abiomed.com
SIC: 3845 Mfg Electromedical Equipment

(G-10190)
ABIOMED CARDIOVASCULAR INC
22 Cherry Hill Dr (01923-2599)
PHONE..................................978 777-5410
Charles B Haaser, *Director*
EMP: 55
SQ FT: 24,000
SALES (est): 4.5MM
SALES (corp-wide): 769.4MM **Publicly Held**
WEB: www.abiomed.com
SIC: 3845 Mfg Electronic Cardiac Support Systems
PA: Abiomed, Inc.
22 Cherry Hill Dr
Danvers MA 01923
978 646-1400

(G-10191)
ABIOMED R&D INC
22 Cherry Hill Dr (01923-2599)
PHONE..................................978 646-1400
David M Lederman, *President*
John P Thero, *Treasurer*
EMP: 6
SQ FT: 80,000
SALES (est): 514.5K
SALES (corp-wide): 769.4MM **Publicly Held**
WEB: www.abiomed.com
SIC: 3841 Mfg Surgical/Medical Instruments
PA: Abiomed, Inc.
22 Cherry Hill Dr
Danvers MA 01923
978 646-1400

(G-10192)
ACCUTECH MACHINE INC
370 Andover St (01923-1350)
PHONE..................................978 922-7271
EMP: 15
SALES (est): 1.9MM **Privately Held**
SIC: 3541 Mfg Industrial Machinery

(G-10193)
ADVANCED ENGINEERING CORP
45 Prince St (01923-1437)
PHONE..................................978 777-7147
Richard F Varney Jr, *President*
Mike Malo, *Manager*
EMP: 12
SALES (est): 1.9MM **Privately Held**
SIC: 3599 Mfg Industrial Machinery

(G-10194)
ANDY COLLAZZO
15 Mill St (01923-3367)
PHONE..................................978 539-8962
Andy Collazzo, *Principal*
EMP: 3
SALES (est): 250K **Privately Held**
SIC: 3519 Mfg Internal Combustion Engines

(G-10195)
ARCHIMEDIA SOLUTIONS GROUP LLC (PA)
11 Sylvan St Ste 5 (01923-2748)
PHONE..................................978 774-5400
John Gerraughty, *Director*
Steven Volpe, *Director*
Mark Dipasquale,
Jane Simmons,
EMP: 9
SQ FT: 1,000
SALES (est): 1.3MM **Privately Held**
SIC: 2759 Commercial Printing

(G-10196)
ARCK ENTERPRISES INC
100 High St (01923-3114)
PHONE..................................978 777-9166
Sanjay Patel, *Owner*
EMP: 5 **EST:** 2001
SALES (est): 559.1K **Privately Held**
SIC: 3578 Mfg Calculating Equipment

(G-10197)
AURORA HEALTHCARE US CORP
8 Electronics Ave Ste 1 (01923-1081)
PHONE..................................978 204-5240
Steven James, *CFO*
EMP: 10
SQ FT: 8,000
SALES (est): 456.3K **Privately Held**
SIC: 3845 Mfg Electromedical Equipment

(G-10198)
AURORA IMAGING TECHNOLOGY INC (PA)
8 Electronics Ave Ste 1 (01923-1081)
PHONE..................................877 975-7530
Gordon M Olsen, *Ch of Bd*
Steven J James, *CFO*
▼ **EMP:** 50 **EST:** 1999
SQ FT: 63,179
SALES (est): 13.1MM **Privately Held**
WEB: www.auroramri.com
SIC: 3841 Mfg Surgical/Medical Instruments

(G-10199)
AUTO INDUSTRIAL MACHINE INC
3 Electronics Ave Ste 2 (01923-1099)
PHONE..................................978 777-3772
Robert Pratt, *President*
EMP: 14
SQ FT: 13,500
SALES: 1.5MM **Privately Held**
SIC: 3599 Mfg Industrial Machinery

(G-10200)
BABCOCK POWER CAPITAL CORP (HQ)
222 Rosewood Dr Fl 3 (01923-4502)
PHONE..................................978 646-3300
Michael D Leclair, *CEO*
William J Ferguson Jr, *Vice Pres*
Earl Mason, *Vice Pres*
James Nelligan, *Vice Pres*
Anthony A Brandano, *CFO*
EMP: 11
SALES (est): 142.8MM
SALES (corp-wide): 509MM **Privately Held**
SIC: 3443 Mfg Fabricated Plate Work
PA: Babcock Power Inc.
6 Kimball Ln Ste 210
Lynnfield MA 01940
978 646-3300

(G-10201)
BACKER HOTWATT INC
16a Electronics Ave (01923-1011)
PHONE..................................978 777-0000
Jamie Holley, *President*
EMP: 4
SALES (est): 491.5K
SALES (corp-wide): 2.3B **Privately Held**
SIC: 3585 Mfg Refrigeration/Heating Equipment
PA: Nibe Industrier Ab
Jarnvagsgatan 40
Markaryd 285 3
433 730-00

(G-10202)
BERRY GLOBAL FILMS LLC
199 Rosewood Dr Ste 240 (01923-4523)
PHONE..................................978 532-2000
EMP: 135 **Publicly Held**
SIC: 3081 Mfg Unsupported Plastic Film/Sheet
HQ: Berry Global Films, Llc
95 Chestnut Ridge Rd
Montvale NJ 07645
201 641-6600

(G-10203)
BISCO ENVIRONMENTAL INC
55 Ferncroft Rd Ste 110 (01923-4001)
PHONE..................................508 738-5100
Rich Abrams, *President*
James T Donelan, *Treasurer*
Thomas W Gorman, *Admin Sec*
EMP: 22
SALES (est): 6.9MM **Privately Held**
SIC: 3559 Mfg Misc Industry Machinery

(G-10204)
BURNELL CONTROLS INC
Also Called: Honeywell Authorized Dealer
153 Andover St Ste 202 (01923-1477)
PHONE..................................978 646-9992
Thomas Burnell, *President*
Allen Burnell, *Vice Pres*
Michael D Cristofom, *Vice Pres*
Tim Wareham, *Sales Mgr*
Casey Smolla, *Sales Engr*
EMP: 5
SQ FT: 3,500
SALES (est): 1.1MM **Privately Held**
WEB: www.burnellcontrols.com
SIC: 3822 Manufactures Automatic Temperature Control Devices

(G-10205)
BURR INDUSTRIES INC
495 Newbury St (01923-1078)
PHONE..................................978 774-2527
Paul Cavanagh, *President*
EMP: 8 **EST:** 1964
SQ FT: 7,200
SALES (est): 957.9K **Privately Held**
SIC: 3599 Machine Shop

(G-10206)
COTTER BROTHERS CORPORATION
8 Southside Rd (01923-1409)
PHONE..................................978 777-5001
Randy Cotter, *Principal*
Timothy Cotter, *Vice Pres*
Robert Roufail, *Project Mgr*
Bartholomew P Molloy, *Admin Sec*
▼ **EMP:** 43
SQ FT: 25,000
SALES (est): 16MM **Privately Held**
WEB: www.cotterbrothers.com
SIC: 3559 Mfg Misc Industry Machinery

(G-10207)
COTTER CORPORATION
8 Southside Rd (01923-1409)
PHONE..................................978 774-6777
Louis J Giuliano, *CEO*
EMP: 50 **EST:** 1979
SQ FT: 25,000
SALES (est): 7.8MM
SALES (corp-wide): 2.7B **Publicly Held**
WEB: www.ittind.com
SIC: 3443 Mfg Fabricated Plate Work
HQ: Itt Llc
1133 Westchester Ave N-100
White Plains NY 10604
914 641-2000

(G-10208)
CREATIVE CELEBRATIONS
46 Longbow Rd (01923-1639)
PHONE..................................978 774-7737
Ruth Helmen, *Owner*
EMP: 10
SALES (est): 677.2K **Privately Held**
SIC: 2621 Paper Mill

(G-10209)
CUNNINGHAM ENGINEERING INC
9 Electronics Ave (01923-1008)
PHONE..................................978 774-4169
Thomas Cunningham, *President*
Katherine Cunningham, *Treasurer*
EMP: 17
SQ FT: 10,000
SALES: 2MM **Privately Held**
WEB: www.cunninghamengineering.com
SIC: 3599 Machine Shop

(G-10210)
D V DIE CUTTING INC
45 Prince St (01923-1474)
PHONE..................................978 777-0300
Richard F Varney, *President*
EMP: 28
SQ FT: 14,000
SALES (est): 4.9MM **Privately Held**
WEB: www.transformplastics.com
SIC: 3053 3544 Mfg Gaskets/Packing/Sealing Devices Mfg Dies/Tools/Jigs/Fixtures

(G-10211)
DANVERS ENGINEERING CO INC
88 Holten St Ste 3 (01923-1968)
PHONE..................................978 774-7501
Betty Pelletier, *President*
Richard Pelletier, *Vice Pres*
Michael Pelletier, *Treasurer*
EMP: 5
SQ FT: 5,000
SALES: 300K **Privately Held**
SIC: 3599 7692 3441 Mfg Industrial Machinery Welding Repair Structural Metal Fabrication

(G-10212)
DANVERS HERALD
152 Sylvan St (01923-3558)
PHONE..................................978 774-0505
Cathryn O'Hare, *Publisher*
EMP: 4
SALES (est): 147.5K **Privately Held**
SIC: 2711 Newspapers-Publishing/Printing

(G-10213)
DILUIGIS INC
41 Popes Ln (01923-1410)
PHONE..................................978 750-9900
Louis J Diluigi Jr, *President*
Michael Delande, *Purch Agent*
Kevin Larocque, *Buyer*
Rick Clark, *Engineer*
Kristi Cunningham, *Marketing Mgr*
EMP: 100
SQ FT: 18,000
SALES (est): 21.1MM **Privately Held**
WEB: www.diluigisausage.com
SIC: 2013 Mfg Prepared Meats

(G-10214)
DOWNS SAILS
57 N Putnam St (01923-2081)
PHONE....................978 750-8140
Roy Downs, *Owner*
EMP: 3
SALES (est): 220.7K **Privately Held**
WEB: www.downssails.com
SIC: 2394 Mfg Canvas/Related Products

(G-10215)
EMD MILLIPORE CORPORATION
17 Cherry Hill Dr (01923-2565)
PHONE....................978 762-5100
Louis Bonhomme, *Research*
James Groves, *Branch Mgr*
David Sturrock, *Info Tech Mgr*
EMP: 30
SALES (corp-wide): 16.4B **Privately Held**
WEB: www.millipore.com
SIC: 3826 Mfg Analytical Instruments
HQ: Emd Millipore Corporation
400 Summit Dr
Burlington MA 01803
781 533-6000

(G-10216)
ENJET AERO DANVERS LLC (HQ)
13 Mill St (01923-3310)
PHONE....................978 777-1980
Bruce Breckenridge, *CEO*
Kayla Walker, *Business Mgr*
Mark Doherty, *Vice Pres*
Duffy Comeau, *Purchasing*
Christopher Ferraro, *CFO*
EMP: 32 **EST:** 1998
SALES (est): 4MM
SALES (corp-wide): 42.7MM **Privately Held**
WEB: www.jetenginetech.com
SIC: 3724 Mfg Industrial Machinery
PA: Enjet Aero, Llc
9401 Indian Creek Pkwy
Overland Park KS 66210
913 717-7396

(G-10217)
FIRE DEFENSES NEW ENGLAND LLC
Also Called: Allstate Fire Equipment
44 Garden St Ste 1 (01923-1451)
P.O. Box 1025, Lynnfield (01940-3025)
PHONE....................978 304-1506
Renee Cooper, *Human Resources*
Ronald Cooper,
EMP: 16
SQ FT: 7,500
SALES (est): 418.9K **Privately Held**
SIC: 3999 7389 Mfg Misc Products Business Services

(G-10218)
FRIEND BOX COMPANY INC
90 High St (01923-3196)
P.O. Box 275 (01923-0475)
PHONE....................978 774-0240
Charles J Fox, *President*
Rich Lombardo, *QC Dir*
EMP: 55
SQ FT: 40,100
SALES (est): 13MM **Privately Held**
SIC: 2653 2652 Mfg Corrugated/Solid Fiber Boxes Mfg Setup Paperboard Boxes

(G-10219)
GRUENEWALD MFG CO INC
250 North St Ste A10 (01923-1206)
PHONE....................978 777-0200
Thomas Muldoon, *President*
Rickey Schwed, *Sales Staff*
▼ **EMP:** 10
SQ FT: 40,000
SALES (est): 1.2MM **Privately Held**
WEB: www.whipcream.com
SIC: 3556 Mfg Food Products Machinery

(G-10220)
GT ADVANCED TECHNOLOGIES
1 Industrial Dr Unit 1 # 1 (01923-1039)
PHONE....................508 954-8249
Ted Smick, *Principal*
EMP: 99
SALES (est): 9.7MM **Privately Held**
SIC: 3559 Mfg Misc Industry Machinery

(G-10221)
HANNAH ENGINEERING INC
150 Maple St (01923-2099)
P.O. Box 2033 (01923-5033)
PHONE....................978 777-5892
Richard Barker Jr, *President*
Craig Davarich, *Purch Agent*
Edward Cormier, *Technology*
EMP: 22
SQ FT: 10,000
SALES (est): 1.7MM **Privately Held**
WEB: www.hannaheng.com
SIC: 3599 Machine Shop

(G-10222)
HILLSIDE ENGINEERING INC
10r Rainbow Ter Ste A (01923-3779)
PHONE....................978 762-6640
Charles Cummings, *President*
▼ **EMP:** 9
SALES: 1.5MM **Privately Held**
SIC: 3599 Mfg Industrial Machinery

(G-10223)
HONEYWELL INTERNATIONAL INC
199 Rosewood Dr Ste 300 (01923-1388)
PHONE....................978 774-3007
John Penman, *President*
Kevin McDonough, *Branch Mgr*
EMP: 60
SALES (corp-wide): 41.8B **Publicly Held**
SIC: 3822 8711 Mfg Environmental Controls Engineering Services
PA: Honeywell International Inc.
300 S Tryon St
Charlotte NC 28202
973 455-2000

(G-10224)
HOWARD FOODS INC (PA)
5 Ray St (01923-3531)
P.O. Box 2072 (01923-5072)
PHONE....................978 774-6207
Charles M Waite, *President*
Robert Romsavich, *Treasurer*
Barbara W Waite, *Admin Sec*
EMP: 4
SQ FT: 500
SALES (est): 888.2K **Privately Held**
SIC: 2033 2035 Mfg Canned Fruits/Vegetables Mfg Pickles/Sauces/Dressing

(G-10225)
ILLINOIS TOOL WORKS INC
ITW Polymers Adhesives NA
30 Endicott St (01923-3712)
PHONE....................978 777-1100
Chris Stevens, *Vice Pres*
EMP: 50
SALES (corp-wide): 14.7B **Publicly Held**
SIC: 2891 Mfg Adhesives/Sealants
PA: Illinois Tool Works Inc.
155 Harlem Ave
Glenview IL 60025
847 724-7500

(G-10226)
ISOLUX LLC
100 Ferncroft Rd Ste 110 (01923-4035)
PHONE....................978 774-9136
Paul Beech, *Branch Mgr*
EMP: 3
SALES (corp-wide): 820.9K **Privately Held**
WEB: www.isoluxllc.com
SIC: 3841 Mfg Surgical & Medical Instruments
PA: Isolux Llc
1045 Collier Center Way # 7
Naples FL 34110
239 514-7475

(G-10227)
ITW DEVCON INC
30 Endicott St (01923-3712)
PHONE....................978 777-1100
Chow Yee Chu, *Controller*
▲ **EMP:** 43
SALES (est): 9MM **Privately Held**
SIC: 2891 Mfg Adhesives/Sealants

(G-10228)
JAKES MINT CHEW LLC
10r Rainbow Ter Ste H (01923-3779)
PHONE....................978 304-0528
Adam Benezra, *Mng Member*
Paul Sweeney,
EMP: 5 **EST:** 2011
SALES (est): 493.2K **Privately Held**
SIC: 2899 Mfg Chemical Preparations

(G-10229)
KERNCO INC
28 Harbor St (01923-3391)
P.O. Box 378 (01923-0678)
PHONE....................978 777-1956
EMP: 15 **EST:** 1978
SQ FT: 10,000
SALES (est): 1.4MM **Privately Held**
WEB: www.kernco.com
SIC: 3679 Mfg Electronic Components

(G-10230)
LABEL HAUS INC
3 Southside Rd Ste B (01923-1695)
PHONE....................978 777-1773
John McNally, *President*
EMP: 9
SQ FT: 9,000
SALES: 1.5MM **Privately Held**
WEB: www.labelhausinc.com
SIC: 2759 Mfg Labels

(G-10231)
LEE ELECTRIC INC
128 Maple St (01923-2061)
PHONE....................978 777-0070
Robert S Lee, *Ch of Bd*
William E Lee, *President*
Samuel Sayward, *Exec VP*
Robert F Cummings, *Treasurer*
▼ **EMP:** 120 **EST:** 1952
SQ FT: 70,000
SALES (est): 26.1MM **Privately Held**
SIC: 3822 Mfg Environmental Controls

(G-10232)
LEICA BIOSYSTEMS
38 Cherry Hill Dr (01923-2575)
PHONE....................978 471-0625
Richard Sidlowski, *Accounting Mgr*
David Pugliano, *Sales Staff*
EMP: 17 **EST:** 2015
SALES (est): 1MM **Privately Held**
SIC: 3826 Mfg Analytical Instruments

(G-10233)
LINESIDER COMMUNICATIONS INC
Also Called: Linesider Technologies
55 Ferncroft Rd Ste 120 (01923-4001)
PHONE....................617 671-0000
Harley Stowell, *CEO*
Matt Collins, *COO*
Harrison Flynn, *VP Bus Dvlpt*
Steve Ivanoski, *CFO*
EMP: 40
SALES (est): 2.3MM **Privately Held**
WEB: www.linesider.net
SIC: 7372 Software Services

(G-10234)
M & H ENGINEERING CO INC
183 Newbury St Ste 1 (01923-1090)
PHONE....................978 777-1222
Richard Haley, *President*
Andrew J Martens, *Vice Pres*
Michael A Martens, *Vice Pres*
Timothy H Martens, *Vice Pres*
Timothy Martens, *Vice Pres*
EMP: 40 **EST:** 1966
SQ FT: 20,000
SALES (est): 9.3MM **Privately Held**
WEB: www.mheng.com
SIC: 3599 3544 Manufactures Industrial Machinery/Dies/Tools/Jigs & Fixtures

(G-10235)
MAXAM TIRE NORTH AMERICA INC
300 Rosewood Dr Ste 102 (01923-1389)
PHONE....................844 629-2662
Troy Kline, *CEO*
Ian Thomas, *Director*
Radek Costa Sarnicki, *Admin Sec*
▲ **EMP:** 4
SALES (est): 167.3K **Privately Held**
SIC: 3011 Mfg Tires/Inner Tubes

(G-10236)
MCNEILLY EMS EDUCATORS INC
125 Liberty St Ste 102 (01923-3325)
P.O. Box 7, Manchester (01944-0007)
PHONE....................978 375-7373
Steven Volpe, *Director*
David Mondi, *Instructor*
Brian Oneill, *Instructor*
James Weston, *Instructor*
EMP: 9
SALES (est): 570K **Privately Held**
SIC: 3999 Mfg Misc Products

(G-10237)
MEDDATA GROUP LLC
300 Rosewood Dr Ste 250 (01923-4509)
PHONE....................978 887-0039
Melissa Chang, *Principal*
EMP: 10
SALES (est): 851.5K **Privately Held**
SIC: 7372 Prepackaged Software Services

(G-10238)
MEDTRNIC INTRVNTNAL VSCLAR INC
37a Cherry Hill Dr (01923-2565)
PHONE....................978 777-0042
Sean Salmon, *President*
Philip Albert, *Vice Pres*
Karan Jhaveri, *QC Mgr*
Jessica Sacks, *Research*
Linda Harty, *Treasurer*
▲ **EMP:** 750
SQ FT: 40,000
SALES (est): 89.5MM **Privately Held**
WEB: www.medtronic.com
SIC: 3841 Mfg Surgical/Medical Instruments
HQ: Medtronic, Inc.
710 Medtronic Pkwy
Minneapolis MN 55432
763 514-4000

(G-10239)
MEDTRONIC INC
35 Cherry Hill Dr (01923-4393)
PHONE....................978 739-3080
Thomas Nowak, *Manager*
EMP: 16 **Privately Held**
SIC: 3845 3842 3841 Mfg Medical Equipment/Supplies
HQ: Medtronic, Inc.
710 Medtronic Pkwy
Minneapolis MN 55432
763 514-4000

(G-10240)
MEDTRONIC INC
37 Cherry Hill Dr (01923-2565)
PHONE....................978 777-0042
Thomas Hudson, *Info Tech Mgr*
Yem Sin, *Administration*
EMP: 16 **Privately Held**
SIC: 3845 3842 3841 Mfg Medical Equipment/Supplies
HQ: Medtronic, Inc.
710 Medtronic Pkwy
Minneapolis MN 55432
763 514-4000

(G-10241)
MG2 TECHNOLOGIES LLC
41 Sherwood Ave (01923-2322)
PHONE....................978 739-1068
Miguel Galvez, *Partner*
EMP: 4
SALES (est): 331.8K **Privately Held**
SIC: 3646 7389 Mfg Commercial Lighting Fixtures

(G-10242)
NEUROLOGICA CORP
14 Electronics Ave (01923-1011)
PHONE....................978 564-8500
Philip Sullivan, *CEO*
Kwang Chae Park, *President*
Moon Hyung Lyu, *Treasurer*
▲ **EMP:** 180
SQ FT: 80,000

SALES (est): 47.1MM **Privately Held**
WEB: www.neurologica.com
SIC: 3841 Mfg Surgical/Medical Instruments
HQ: Samsung Electronics America, Inc.
85 Challenger Rd Fl 7
Ridgefield Park NJ 07660
201 229-4000

(G-10243)
NEUTRON THERAPEUTICS INC
1 Industrial Dr Ste 1 # 1 (01923-1039)
PHONE..................................978 326-8999
Theodore Smick, *CEO*
EMP: 23 **EST:** 2016
SQ FT: 33,000
SALES (est): 1.4MM **Privately Held**
SIC: 3845 Mfg Electromedical Equipment

(G-10244)
OLD SALT BOX PUBLISHING & DIST
20 Locust St (01923-2272)
PHONE..................................978 750-8090
EMP: 4
SQ FT: 500
SALES: 200K **Privately Held**
SIC: 2731 Publish Books

(G-10245)
ORBIT PLASTICS CORP
45 Prince St (01923-1437)
PHONE..................................978 465-5300
Thomas Feid, *President*
Frederick Jackson, *Treasurer*
EMP: 22 **EST:** 1971
SALES (est): 3.3MM **Privately Held**
WEB: www.orbitplastics.com
SIC: 3089 Mfg Plastic Products

(G-10246)
OV LOOP INC
240 Newbury St (01923-1067)
PHONE..................................781 640-2234
William Graylin, *President*
Karen Harris, *Controller*
EMP: 25
SQ FT: 5,000
SALES: 52K **Privately Held**
SIC: 3699 Mfg Electrical Equipment/Supplies

(G-10247)
QUICK MANUFACTURING CO
4 Electronics Ave (01923-1043)
PHONE..................................978 750-4202
Thomas Manolakos, *President*
John Manolakos, *Vice Pres*
EMP: 8
SQ FT: 6,000
SALES (est): 865.2K **Privately Held**
WEB: www.quickmanufacturing.com
SIC: 3599 Mfg Industrial Machinery

(G-10248)
QUINN MANUFACTURING INC
149 Village Post Rd (01923-2680)
PHONE..................................978 524-0310
Sean J Quinn, *President*
Peter J Walton, *Treasurer*
EMP: 4
SQ FT: 3,200
SALES (est): 607K **Privately Held**
SIC: 3469 Mfg Metal Stampings

(G-10249)
R WALTERS FOODS
Also Called: Meninno Brothers Gourmet Foods
144 Pine St (01923-2630)
PHONE..................................978 646-8950
Rick Walters, *Mng Member*
EMP: 53
SQ FT: 13,000
SALES: 11MM **Privately Held**
SIC: 2032 Mfg Canned Specialties

(G-10250)
REGIONAL INDUSTRIES INC
301 Newbury St 332 (01923-1092)
PHONE..................................978 750-8787
Robert Pratt, *President*
Robert K Pratt, *President*
Monica H Pratt, *Admin Sec*
EMP: 50
SQ FT: 100,000
SALES (est): 7.2MM **Privately Held**
SIC: 3599 Mfg Industrial Machinery

(G-10251)
REHEAT CO INC
10 School St (01923-2916)
PHONE..................................978 777-4441
Paul Meinerth, *President*
EMP: 10
SQ FT: 5,000
SALES (est): 1.7MM **Privately Held**
WEB: www.reheat.com
SIC: 3567 5074 Mfg Industrial Furnaces/Ovens Whol Plumbing Equipment/Supplies

(G-10252)
REIFENHAUSER INCORPORATED
27 Garden St Ste B (01923-1686)
PHONE..................................847 669-9972
Richard B Dexter Jr, *General Mgr*
John Wise, *General Mgr*
Florian Bachmair, *Marketing Staff*
EMP: 9
SQ FT: 19,132
SALES (est): 1.3MM
SALES (corp-wide): 549.1MM **Privately Held**
WEB: www.reifenhauserinc.com
SIC: 3559 Sales Service & Spare Parts Distribution Of Plastic Extrusion Equipment
HQ: Reifenhauser Gmbh & Co. Kg Maschinenfabrik
Spicher Str. 46
Troisdorf 53844
224 123-5100

(G-10253)
ROWLEY BIOCHEMICAL INSTITUTE
10 Electronics Ave (01923-1011)
PHONE..................................978 739-4883
Nancy Hecht, *President*
EMP: 5
SALES (est): 869.1K **Privately Held**
WEB: www.rowleybio.com
SIC: 2836 2865 Mfg Chemical Reagents Dyes Stains & Powders

(G-10254)
SANTORELLA PUBLICATION LTD (PA)
24 Water St (01923-3728)
PHONE..................................978 750-0566
Tony Santorella, *President*
Denise Gendron, *Editor*
▲ **EMP:** 4
SALES (est): 320.5K **Privately Held**
SIC: 2741 Misc Publishing

(G-10255)
SHAWMUT ADVERTISING INC (PA)
33 Cherry Hill Dr (01923-2594)
PHONE..................................978 762-7500
Dominick C Peluso, *President*
Michael Peluso, *Vice Pres*
Tony Delucia, *Production*
Daniel M Peluso, *CFO*
Tricia Zampitella, *Comptroller*
EMP: 40 **EST:** 1951
SQ FT: 25,000
SALES (est): 10.3MM **Privately Held**
WEB: www.shawmutprinting.com
SIC: 2752 3823 7331 5199 Lithographic Coml Print Mfg Process Cntrl Instr Direct Mail Ad Svcs Whol Nondurable Goods

(G-10256)
SHAWMUT PRINTING
33 Cherry Hill Dr Ste 1 (01923-2579)
PHONE..................................978 762-7500
Dom Peluso, *Principal*
Stacy Peluso, *VP Bus Dvlpt*
Tricia Zampitella, *Comptroller*
Bob McCaughey, *Accounts Exec*
Charles Valeri, *Accounts Exec*
▲ **EMP:** 11
SALES (est): 29.1K **Privately Held**
SIC: 2752 Lithographic Commercial Printing

(G-10257)
SIGN-A-RAMA
75 High St (01923-3105)
PHONE..................................978 774-0936
Keith Linares, *Owner*
EMP: 4
SQ FT: 1,000
SALES (est): 270.3K **Privately Held**
WEB: www.northshoresignarama.com
SIC: 3993 Signsadv Specs

(G-10258)
STEVEN TEDESCO
Also Called: North Shore Marble & Granite
100 Newbury St Ste A (01923-1042)
PHONE..................................978 777-4070
Steve Tedesco, *Principal*
▲ **EMP:** 8
SQ FT: 10,000
SALES (est): 624.3K **Privately Held**
WEB: www.nsmarbleandgranite.com
SIC: 3281 Mfg Cut Stone/Products

(G-10259)
T D F METAL FINISHING CO INC
9 Electronics Ave (01923-1008)
P.O. Box 8026, Lynn (01904-0026)
PHONE..................................978 223-4292
Thomas D Ferrairo, *President*
Slav Kozhebrodskiy, *Manager*
EMP: 12
SQ FT: 5,800
SALES (est): 1.5MM **Privately Held**
WEB: www.tdfmetalfinishing.com
SIC: 3471 Plating/Polishing Service

(G-10260)
T-SHIRTS N JEANS INC
Also Called: Expertees
3 Southside Rd 2 (01923-1695)
PHONE..................................781 279-4220
Michael Sarmanian, *President*
Donna Sarmanian, *Treasurer*
EMP: 3 **EST:** 1977
SQ FT: 1,900
SALES (est): 351K **Privately Held**
SIC: 2262 Manmade Fiber & Silk Finishing Plant

(G-10261)
TDF METAL FINISHING CO INC
6 Electronics Ave (01923-1008)
PHONE..................................978 223-4292
Thomas D Ferrairo, *President*
EMP: 4
SALES (est): 255.3K **Privately Held**
SIC: 3471 Plating/Polishing Service

(G-10262)
THERMO FISHER SCIENTIFIC INC
99 Rosewood Dr Ste 220 (01923-1300)
PHONE..................................978 223-1540
EMP: 4
SALES (corp-wide): 24.3B **Publicly Held**
SIC: 3826 Mfg Analytical Instruments
PA: Thermo Fisher Scientific Inc.
168 3rd Ave
Waltham MA 02451
781 622-1000

(G-10263)
THERMO WAVE TECHNOLOGIES LLC
12 Garden St (01923-1431)
PHONE..................................800 733-9615
Ralph Faia, *CEO*
Bruce Secovich, *Principal*
▼ **EMP:** 8
SQ FT: 6,000
SALES: 2MM **Privately Held**
SIC: 3589 Mfg Service Industry Machinery

(G-10264)
TRANS FORM PLASTICS CORP
45 Prince St (01923-1437)
PHONE..................................978 777-1440
P P Varney, *President*
Tom Holloran, *President*
EMP: 25
SQ FT: 14,000
SALES (est): 3.9MM **Privately Held**
SIC: 3089 Mfg Plastic Products

(G-10265)
TRANSENE COMPANY INC
10 Electronics Ave (01923-1011)
PHONE..................................978 777-7860
Christopher Christuk, *President*
Martin E Hecht, *President*
▲ **EMP:** 11
SQ FT: 16,000
SALES (est): 3.1MM **Privately Held**
WEB: www.transene.com
SIC: 2819 3674 3644 2899 Mfg Indstl Inorgan Chem Mfg Semiconductors/Dvcs Mfg Nonconductv Wire Dvc Mfg Chemical Preparation Mfg Adhesives/Sealants

(G-10266)
TRI TOWN TRANSCRIPT
152 Sylvan St (01923-3558)
PHONE..................................978 887-4146
EMP: 3 **EST:** 2010
SALES (est): 117.3K **Privately Held**
SIC: 2711 Newspapers-Publishing/Printing

(G-10267)
TRIPLE S MACHINE INC
19 Warren St (01923-3011)
PHONE..................................978 774-0354
Sam Sayward III, *President*
EMP: 5
SQ FT: 6,000
SALES: 700K **Privately Held**
WEB: www.triplesmachine.com
SIC: 3599 Mfg Industrial Machinery

(G-10268)
TWIN CREEKS TECHNOLOGIES INC
1 Industrial Dr Unit 1 # 1 (01923-1039)
PHONE..................................978 777-0846
Srinivasan Sivaram, *Branch Mgr*
EMP: 22 **Privately Held**
SIC: 3674 Mfg Semiconductors/Related Devices
PA: Twin Creeks Technologies, Inc.
3930 N 1st St Ste 10
San Jose CA 95134

(G-10269)
U S MADE CO INC
76 Newbury St (01923-1034)
PHONE..................................978 777-8383
Anthony Bernardo, *President*
Maria Bernardo, *Treasurer*
▲ **EMP:** 32
SQ FT: 10,000
SALES (est): 3.1MM **Privately Held**
SIC: 2386 Manufactures Leather Garments

(G-10270)
UNION ETCHANTS INTERNATIONAL
10 Electronics Ave (01923-1011)
P.O. Box 506, Woburn (01801-0506)
PHONE..................................978 777-7860
Robert E Union, *President*
EMP: 4
SQ FT: 12,000
SALES (est): 426.9K **Privately Held**
SIC: 2819 8748 Mfg Specialty Chemicals For Micro-Electronics & Opto-Electronics & Provides Consulting Services

(G-10271)
VEGAN PUBLISHERS LLC
6 Moore Cir (01923-3800)
PHONE..................................857 364-4344
Casey Taft, *Principal*
▲ **EMP:** 3
SALES (est): 125.4K **Privately Held**
SIC: 2741 Misc Publishing

(G-10272)
WAFER LLC
54 Cherry Hill Dr (01923-2575)
P.O. Box 86, Hanover NH (03755-0086)
PHONE..................................978 304-3821
Ryan Gardner,
EMP: 7
SQ FT: 70,000
SALES (est): 94.4K **Privately Held**
SIC: 3629 Mfg Electrical Industrial Apparatus

▲ = Import ▼=Export
◆ =Import/Export

(G-10273)
WELLUMINA HEALTH INC
300 Rosewood Dr Ste 107 (01923-1389)
PHONE....................................978 777-1854
Niraj Agarwal, *CEO*
George Adam, *President*
EMP: 4 **EST:** 2014
SALES (est): 247.8K **Privately Held**
SIC: 3826 Analytical Instruments, Nsk

(G-10274)
WINNING MOVES INC
Also Called: Winning Moves Games
75 Sylvan St Ste C104 (01923-5609)
PHONE....................................978 777-7464
Phil E Orbanes, *Ch of Bd*
Philip C Orbanes, *President*
Mark Parsons, *Senior VP*
Mike Meyers, *Vice Pres*
Laura Pecci, *Vice Pres*
▲ **EMP:** 13
SQ FT: 8,000
SALES (est): 8.8MM **Privately Held**
WEB: www.winning-moves.com
SIC: 3944 Mfg Games/Toys

Dartmouth
Bristol County

(G-10275)
HERITAGE WHARF COMPANY LLC
218 Elm St (02748-3420)
PHONE....................................508 990-1011
David J Nolan Jr, *Principal*
EMP: 3
SALES (est): 269.4K **Privately Held**
SIC: 3732 Boatbuilding/Repairing

(G-10276)
SENSING SYSTEMS CORPORATION
7 Commerce Way (02747)
P.O. Box 50180, New Bedford (02745-0006)
PHONE....................................508 992-0872
Ricardo Bermudez, *President*
EMP: 10
SQ FT: 9,500
SALES (est): 1.5MM **Privately Held**
WEB: www.sensing-systems.com
SIC: 3586 1389 Mfg Measuring/Dispensing Pumps Oil/Gas Field Services

(G-10277)
SIGNATURE SIGNS
634 State Rd Unit F (02747-1818)
PHONE....................................508 993-8511
EMP: 4
SALES (est): 277.5K **Privately Held**
SIC: 3993 Mfg Signs/Advertising Specialties

(G-10278)
TROPICAL SMOOTHIE OF BRISTOL
14 Eliza Ln (02747-2395)
PHONE....................................508 636-1424
Gilbert M Desousa, *President*
Ana Desousa, *Admin Sec*
EMP: 3 **EST:** 2007
SALES (est): 311.8K **Privately Held**
SIC: 2621 Paper Mill

Dedham
Norfolk County

(G-10279)
ALL SEASONAL FUEL INC
1079 East St (02026-6300)
PHONE....................................781 329-7800
Paul V Casto, *Principal*
EMP: 6 **EST:** 2008
SALES (est): 566.5K **Privately Held**
SIC: 2869 Mfg Industrial Organic Chemicals

(G-10280)
ATLANTIC PWR ENRGY SVCS US LLC
3 Allied Dr Ste 155 (02026-6101)
PHONE....................................617 977-2400
EMP: 3
SALES (est): 112.7K **Publicly Held**
SIC: 3621 Mfg Motors/Generators
PA: Atlantic Power Corporation
3 Allied Dr Ste 220
Dedham MA 02026

(G-10281)
BENJAMIN MARTIN CORP
115 Commerce Way (02026-2994)
P.O. Box 4218 (02027-4218)
PHONE....................................781 326-8311
Benjamin Seltzer, *President*
Martin Seltzer, *Treasurer*
Jerry Kummins, *Natl Sales Mgr*
▲ **EMP:** 19
SQ FT: 10,000
SALES (est): 3.4MM **Privately Held**
SIC: 3499 Mfg Picture Frames

(G-10282)
CELERITY SOLUTIONS INC (PA)
Also Called: Slingshot Software
990 Washington St Ste 304 (02026-6717)
PHONE....................................781 329-1900
Paul Carr, *President*
EMP: 8
SQ FT: 5,000
SALES (est): 1.5MM **Privately Held**
SIC: 7372 Prepackaged Software Services

(G-10283)
CLARK HAMMERBEAM CORPORATION
886 Washington St (02026-6010)
P.O. Box 381 (02027-0381)
PHONE....................................781 461-1946
Jim Bardolph, *President*
Maria Reichenhall, *Treasurer*
EMP: 24 **EST:** 1998
SALES (est): 2MM **Privately Held**
SIC: 2295 Mfg Coated Fabrics

(G-10284)
CRANE MDSG SYSTEMS INC
Also Called: Streamware
990 Washington St Ste 205 (02026-6717)
PHONE....................................781 501-5800
Fabrice Tummino, *Engineer*
Rich Horrigan, *Director*
EMP: 10
SALES (corp-wide): 3.3B **Publicly Held**
SIC: 3589 Mfg Service Industry Machinery
HQ: Crane Merchandising Systems. Inc.
2043 Wdlnd Pkwy Ste 102
Saint Louis MO 63146
314 298-3500

(G-10285)
CUMMINS NORTHEAST LLC
100 Allied Dr (02026-6146)
PHONE....................................781 329-1750
David Letts, *Manager*
EMP: 4
SALES (corp-wide): 23.7B **Publicly Held**
WEB: www.cummins.com
SIC: 3519 Mfg Internal Combustion Engines
HQ: Cummins Northeast, Llc
30 Braintree Hill Park # 101
Braintree MA 02184

(G-10286)
DAVIS ENTERPRISES INC
Also Called: Minuteman Press
51 Legacy Blvd (02026-2639)
PHONE....................................781 461-8444
Brian Davis, *President*
Anita Davis, *Vice Pres*
EMP: 4
SQ FT: 2,100
SALES: 450K **Privately Held**
WEB: www.minutemanpressdedham.com
SIC: 2752 Comm Prtg Litho

(G-10287)
DEDHAM RECYCLED GRAVEL INC
Also Called: Fed
1039 East St (02026-6363)
PHONE....................................781 329-1044
Joseph Federico Jr, *President*
Al Morteo, *Vice Pres*
EMP: 10
SQ FT: 6,600
SALES: 870K **Privately Held**
SIC: 1442 Construction Sand/Gravel

(G-10288)
DIVERSIFIED BIOTECH INC
65 Commerce Way (02026-2953)
PHONE....................................781 326-6709
Mark L Fins, *President*
Michael Smith, *Purch Agent*
▲ **EMP:** 10
SQ FT: 10,000
SALES (est): 1.8MM **Privately Held**
WEB: www.divbio.com
SIC: 2836 Mfg Biological Products

(G-10289)
FABLEVISION LEARNING LLC
368 Washington St Ste 207 (02026-1868)
P.O. Box 1242 (02027-1242)
PHONE....................................781 320-3225
Becky Conners, *President*
Andrea Calvin, *Vice Pres*
Andrew Reynolds, *CFO*
Peter Reynolds, *Mng Member*
EMP: 11 **EST:** 2007
SQ FT: 1,500
SALES (est): 1.1MM **Privately Held**
SIC: 7372 Prepackaged Software Services

(G-10290)
FONZY INC
190 Milton St (02026-2902)
PHONE....................................857 342-3143
Roberto Jorge, *President*
EMP: 5
SQ FT: 8,300
SALES (est): 156K **Privately Held**
SIC: 7372 Prepackaged Software Services

(G-10291)
GENERAL DYNAMICS MISSION
150 Rustcraft Rd (02026-4534)
PHONE....................................781 410-9635
Christopher Marzilli, *President*
EMP: 340
SALES (corp-wide): 36.1B **Publicly Held**
SIC: 3571 Mfg Electronic Computers
HQ: General Dynamics Mission Systems, Inc.
12450 Fair Lakes Cir # 200
Fairfax VA 22033
703 263-2800

(G-10292)
IMD SOFT INC (DH)
980-990 Wash St Ste 115 (02026)
PHONE....................................781 449-5567
Shahar Sery, *COO*
Eran David, *CTO*
EMP: 26
SALES (est): 9.9MM
SALES (corp-wide): 3B **Privately Held**
WEB: www.imd-soft.com
SIC: 7372 Prepackaged Software Services
HQ: N. Harris Computer Corporation
1 Antares Dr Suite 400
Nepean ON K2E 8
613 226-5511

(G-10293)
INSTITUTE FOR SCIAL CLTRAL CMM
Also Called: Z Magazine
47 Barrows St (02026-3025)
PHONE....................................508 548-9063
Michael Albert, *President*
Lydia Sargent, *Corp Secy*
EMP: 3
SALES: 498.3K **Privately Held**
SIC: 2721 Magazine Publisher

(G-10294)
J P LICKS HOMEMADE ICE CREAM
704 Legacy Pl (02026-6837)
PHONE....................................781 329-9100
Vince Petryk, *Branch Mgr*
EMP: 4
SALES (corp-wide): 1MM **Privately Held**
SIC: 2024 Eating Place
PA: J P Lick's Homemade Ice Cream Company Inc
659 Centre St
Boston MA 02130
617 524-2020

(G-10295)
JAMES DEVANEY FUEL CO
111 River St (02026-2910)
PHONE....................................781 326-7608
Geoff Mc Carthy, *Manager*
EMP: 4
SALES (est): 427.4K **Privately Held**
SIC: 2869 Mfg Industrial Organic Chemicals

(G-10296)
ROSARIO CABINETS INC
49 Lower East St Ste 2 (02026-2082)
PHONE....................................781 329-0639
Rosario Papparazzo, *President*
Josephine Papparazzo, *Treasurer*
▲ **EMP:** 8
SQ FT: 30,000
SALES (est): 1.4MM **Privately Held**
WEB: www.rosariocabinets.com
SIC: 2434 Mfg Wood Kitchen Cabinets

(G-10297)
SAP PROFESSIONAL JOURNAL (PA)
Also Called: View, The
20 Carematrix Dr (02026-6149)
PHONE....................................781 407-0360
David Penzias, *President*
Bonnie Penzias, *Treasurer*
Uwe Krger, *Manager*
Dieter Krieger, *Manager*
EMP: 60
SALES (est): 3.8MM **Privately Held**
WEB: www.sappro.com
SIC: 2741 Misc Publishing

(G-10298)
SKG ASSOCIATES INC
59 Mcdonald St (02026-3914)
PHONE....................................781 878-7250
Donald C Brayshaw, *President*
Mark Brayshaw, *Vice Pres*
Norman Goldberg, *Clerk*
EMP: 7 **EST:** 1966
SALES: 200K **Privately Held**
SIC: 3469 3544 Mfg Metal Stampings Mfg Dies/Tools/Jigs/Fixtures

(G-10299)
VANTAGE REPORTING INC
Also Called: Vantage Software
3 Allied Dr Ste 303 (02026-6148)
PHONE....................................212 750-2256
Gregory J Woolf, *President*
EMP: 26
SQ FT: 2,500
SALES (est): 1.7MM **Privately Held**
SIC: 7372 Prepackaged Software Services

(G-10300)
VILLA MACHINE ASSOCIATES INC
61 Mcdonald St (02026-3914)
PHONE....................................781 326-5969
Louis R Villa, *President*
EMP: 13 **EST:** 1965
SQ FT: 8,000
SALES (est): 2.3MM **Privately Held**
SIC: 3599 7692 Jobbing & Repair Machine Shop

(G-10301)
WELLESLEY INFORMATION SVCS LLC (HQ)
Also Called: Sap Press
20 Carematrix Dr (02026-6149)
PHONE....................................781 407-0360
Jamie Bedard, *President*
Rizal Ahmed, *Exec VP*

GEOGRAPHIC

Sean Edwards, *Exec VP*
Holly Lee, *Exec VP*
Yolanda Maggi, *Exec VP*
EMP: 99
SQ FT: 70,000
SALES (est): 26.7MM
SALES (corp-wide): 8.3MM **Privately Held**
SIC: 2731 Books-Publishing/Printing
PA: Jaz'd Advisors Investment Co., Llc
20 Carematrix Dr
Dedham MA 02026
781 407-0360

(G-10302)
WETECH
44 Trenton Rd (02026-5318)
PHONE.................................781 320-8646
EMP: 4 **EST:** 2007
SALES (est): 200K **Privately Held**
SIC: 3589 Mfg Service Industry Machinery

Deerfield
Franklin County

(G-10303)
R MOODY MACHINE & FABRICATION
667 River Rd (01342-9757)
PHONE.................................413 773-3329
Richard Moody, *Owner*
EMP: 5
SQ FT: 8,000
SALES: 600K **Privately Held**
SIC: 3441 7692 Welding Repair Structural Metal Fabrication

(G-10304)
TREW CORP
901 River Rd (01342-9753)
P.O. Box 395, Sunderland (01375-0395)
PHONE.................................413 773-9798
Mike Smead, *Manager*
EMP: 13
SALES (corp-wide): 1.2MM **Privately Held**
SIC: 2951 Mfg Asphalt Mixtures/Blocks
PA: Trew Corp
Amherst Rd
Sunderland MA 01375
413 665-4051

Dennis
Barnstable County

(G-10305)
AGGREGATE INDS - NORTHEAST REG
230 Great Western Rd (02638)
PHONE.................................508 398-8865
Barry Powers, *Manager*
EMP: 5
SALES (corp-wide): 4.5B **Privately Held**
SIC: 3273 Mfg Ready-Mixed Concrete
HQ: Aggregate Industries - Northeast Region, Inc
1715 Brdwy
Saugus MA 01906
781 941-7200

(G-10306)
CAPE COD POLISH COMPANY INC
Also Called: Cape Cod Metal Polsg Cloths
348 Hokum Rock Rd (02638)
P.O. Box 2039 (02638-5039)
PHONE.................................508 385-5099
William Block, *President*
EMP: 8
SQ FT: 5,000
SALES: 1MM **Privately Held**
WEB: www.capecodpolish.com
SIC: 2842 Mfg Metal Polish Cloths

(G-10307)
EAGLE VISION INC
1017 Main St (02638)
P.O. Box 1243 (02638-6243)
PHONE.................................508 385-2283
Donald J Weagle, *Principal*
EMP: 3 **EST:** 2010
SALES (est): 198.2K **Privately Held**
SIC: 3841 Mfg Surgical/Medical Instruments

(G-10308)
OLSEN MARINE
Also Called: Fisher Sails
357 Hokum Rock Rd (02638)
P.O. Box 1481, East Dennis (02641-1481)
PHONE.................................508 385-2180
Thomas Olsen, *Owner*
EMP: 5
SALES (est): 377.4K **Privately Held**
WEB: www.olsenmarine.com
SIC: 2394 Mfg Canvas/Related Products

(G-10309)
PRUE FOUNDRY INC
52 Paddocks Path (02638-2003)
P.O. Box 412 (02638-0412)
PHONE.................................508 385-3011
Paul F Prue, *President*
Grandval Prue, *Treasurer*
EMP: 3 **EST:** 1949
SQ FT: 2,400
SALES (est): 250K **Privately Held**
SIC: 3365 Aluminum Foundry

(G-10310)
SALLYHARROLD INC
Also Called: Shi Printing
49 Corporation Rd (02638-1418)
PHONE.................................508 258-0253
William H Silverstein, *President*
EMP: 3
SALES (est): 170.8K **Privately Held**
SIC: 2759 Commercial Printing

(G-10311)
SCARGO STONEWARE POTTERY
30 Doctor Lords Rd (02638-1607)
P.O. Box 956 (02638-0956)
PHONE.................................508 385-3894
Harry W Holl, *Owner*
Tina Holl, *Co-Owner*
EMP: 8 **EST:** 1952
SALES (est): 552.8K **Privately Held**
WEB: www.scargopottery.com
SIC: 3269 5719 Mfg Pottery Products Ret Misc Homefurnishings

Dennis Port
Barnstable County

(G-10312)
DRIVE-O-RAMA INC
Drive O Rama Inc (02639)
P.O. Box 95 (02639-0095)
PHONE.................................508 394-0028
Michael Baroni, *President*
Philip J Baroni, *Chairman*
Derrick Sanford, *Manager*
EMP: 70
SQ FT: 47,700
SALES (est): 6.6MM **Privately Held**
SIC: 2511 5021 5712 Mfg Wood Household Furniture Whol Furniture Ret Furniture

(G-10313)
FRITZ GLASS
36 Upper County Rd (02639-1119)
PHONE.................................508 394-0441
Fritz Lauenstein, *Principal*
EMP: 3
SALES (est): 167.3K **Privately Held**
SIC: 3229 Mfg Pressed/Blown Glass

(G-10314)
SIGN COMPANY
343 Main St (02639-1309)
P.O. Box 501 (02639-0501)
PHONE.................................508 760-5400
Jim Sullivan, *Owner*
EMP: 45
SALES (est): 2.6MM **Privately Held**
SIC: 3993 Mfg Signs/Advertising Specialties

(G-10315)
STAGE STOP CANDY LTD INC
411 Main St (02639-1308)
PHONE.................................508 394-1791
Donna M Hebert, *President*
Raymond L Hebert, *Clerk*
EMP: 8
SQ FT: 6,100
SALES (est): 350K **Privately Held**
WEB: www.stagestopcandy.com
SIC: 2064 5441 5145 Mfg Ret & Whol Candy

Devens
Middlesex County

(G-10316)
ADAPTIVE OPTICS ASSOCIATES INC
Also Called: Aoa Xinetics
115 Jackson Rd (01434-4408)
PHONE.................................978 757-9600
Jeffrey Yorsz, *President*
EMP: 12 **Publicly Held**
SIC: 3827 Mfg Optical Instruments/Lenses
HQ: Adaptive Optics Associates, Inc.
115 Jackson Rd
Devens MA 01434
978 757-9600

(G-10317)
ADAPTIVE OPTICS ASSOCIATES INC (DH)
Also Called: Aoa Xinetics
115 Jackson Rd (01434-4408)
PHONE.................................978 757-9600
Richard Close, *Ch of Bd*
Prabu Natarajan, *President*
Jeffrey Yorsz, *President*
Lewis Paragona, *General Mgr*
Carlos Caicedo, *Engineer*
EMP: 100
SQ FT: 60,000
SALES (est): 28.1MM **Publicly Held**
WEB: www.aoainc.com
SIC: 3827 3695 3861 3577 Mfg Optical Instr/Lens Mfg Magnetic Disks/Tapes Mfg Photo Equip/Supplies Mfg Computer Peripherals
HQ: Northrop Grumman Systems Corporation
2980 Fairview Park Dr
Falls Church VA 22042
703 280-2900

(G-10318)
ADAPTIVE OPTICS ASSOCIATES INC
Also Called: Aoa Xinetics
53 Jackson Rd (01434-4026)
PHONE.................................978 391-0000
Mark Ealey, *Manager*
EMP: 20 **Publicly Held**
WEB: www.xinetics.com
SIC: 3827 Mfg Optical Instruments/Lenses
HQ: Adaptive Optics Associates, Inc.
115 Jackson Rd
Devens MA 01434
978 757-9600

(G-10319)
BIONOSTICS INC
Also Called: Rna Medical Division
7 Jackson Rd (01434-4026)
PHONE.................................978 772-7070
Micheal Thomas, *CEO*
Matthew Rice, *Principal*
Randy Beard, *Vice Pres*
Nancy Barck, *QA Dir*
Steve Hjelm, *Engineer*
▲ **EMP:** 90
SQ FT: 45,000
SALES (est): 34.1MM
SALES (corp-wide): 714MM **Publicly Held**
WEB: www.bionostics.com
SIC: 2835 Mfg Diagnostic Substances
HQ: Research And Diagnostic Systems, Inc.
614 Mckinley Pl Ne
Minneapolis MN 55413
612 379-2956

(G-10320)
FOSTER-MILLER INC
Also Called: Qinetiq North America
116 Queenstown St (01434-5608)
PHONE.................................781 684-4000
Jeffrey Yorsz, *President*
EMP: 90
SALES (est): 1.7MM **Privately Held**
SIC: 2323 3423 3569 3812 Mfg Mens/Boys Neckwear Mfg Hand/Edge Tools Mfg General Indstl Mach Mfg Search/Navgatn Equip Mfg Measure/Control Dvcs

(G-10321)
JOHNSON MATTHEY PHRM MTLS INC (DH)
Also Called: Pharm Eco Laboratories
25 Patton Rd (01434-3803)
PHONE.................................978 784-5000
John B Fowler, *President*
John Sheldrick, *Principal*
Edward H Ravert Jr, *Vice Pres*
Steven Collier, *Research*
Michael Markey, *Research*
▲ **EMP:** 135 **EST:** 1972
SQ FT: 160,000
SALES (est): 22.6MM
SALES (corp-wide): 13.8B **Privately Held**
WEB: www.jmpharmaservices.com
SIC: 2834 8731 Mfg Pharmaceutical Preparations Commercial Physical Research
HQ: Johnson Matthey Inc.
435 Devon Park Dr Ste 600
Wayne PA 19087
610 971-3000

(G-10322)
LADDAWN INC (HQ)
155 Jackson Rd (01434-5614)
PHONE.................................800 446-3639
Katie Card, *Partner*
Caila Fuller, *Partner*
Juan Pena, *Partner*
Tim Theriault, *Partner*
Owen Richardson, *Vice Pres*
▲ **EMP:** 100
SQ FT: 110,000
SALES (est): 143.8MM **Publicly Held**
WEB: www.laddawn.com
SIC: 2673 3081 Manufactures Bags-Plastic/Coated Paper And Unsupported Plastic Film/Sheet

(G-10323)
MAGNEMOTION INC
139 Barnum Rd (01434-3509)
PHONE.................................978 757-9100
Todd Webber, *CEO*
Eric Wildi, *President*
Michael Hannon, *Corp Secy*
EMP: 72
SQ FT: 43,000
SALES: 25MM **Publicly Held**
SIC: 3535 Manufactures Conveyors/Equipment
PA: Rockwell Automation, Inc.
1201 S 2nd St
Milwaukee WI 53204

(G-10324)
MAXANT INDUSTRIES INC
58 Barnum Rd (01434-3508)
P.O. Box 454, Ayer (01432-0454)
PHONE.................................978 772-0576
Valerie Delker, *President*
William T Maxant, *Treasurer*
EMP: 10
SQ FT: 16,000
SALES (est): 2.2MM **Privately Held**
WEB: www.maxantindustries.com
SIC: 3556 3559 Mfg Honey Processing Equipment

(G-10325)
MEDIANEWS GROUP INC
78 Barnum Rd (01434-3508)
P.O. Box 362, Ayer (01432-0362)
PHONE.................................978 772-0777
Becky Pellerin, *Office Mgr*
EMP: 70
SALES (corp-wide): 4.2B **Privately Held**
SIC: 2759 Commercial Printing

HQ: Medianews Group, Inc.
101 W Colfax Ave Ste 1100
Denver CO 80202

(G-10326)
NEW ENGLAND SHEETS LLC (PA)
36 Saratoga Blvd (01434-5217)
PHONE..................................978 487-2500
Philip Barrett, *Plant Mgr*
Fred Hamilton, *Mng Member*
EMP: 19
SALES (est): 8.9MM **Privately Held**
SIC: 3444 Mfg Sheet Metalwork

(G-10327)
NORTHROP GRUMMAN CORPORATION
115 Jackson Rd (01434-4408)
PHONE..................................978 772-0352
Terry Bruno, *Branch Mgr*
EMP: 3 **Publicly Held**
SIC: 3812 Mfg Search/Navigation Equipment
PA: Northrop Grumman Corporation
2980 Fairview Park Dr
Falls Church VA 22042

(G-10328)
NYPRO INC
112 Barnum Rd (01434-3506)
PHONE..................................978 784-2006
Brent Bethel, *CEO*
EMP: 7
SALES (corp-wide): 25.2B **Publicly Held**
SIC: 3089 Mfg Plasti Products
HQ: Nypro Inc.
101 Union St
Clinton MA 01510
978 365-8100

(G-10329)
PARKER-HANNIFIN CORPORATION
Also Called: Gas Turbine Fuel Systems Div
14 Robbins Pond Rd (01434-5613)
PHONE..................................978 784-1200
Edward Harley, *Project Engr*
Roger Janson, *Design Engr*
Venlenanne Cooazzo, *Branch Mgr*
Robert Eglitis, *Executive Asst*
EMP: 123
SALES (corp-wide): 14.3B **Publicly Held**
WEB: www.parker.com
SIC: 3728 3724 Mfg Aircraft Parts/Equipment Mfg Aircraft Engines/Parts
PA: Parker-Hannifin Corporation
6035 Parkland Blvd
Cleveland OH 44124
216 896-3000

(G-10330)
POLYCARBON INDUSTRIES INC
Also Called: PCI Synthesis
88 Jackson Rd (01434-4407)
PHONE..................................978 772-2111
Gail Perkins, *CEO*
EMP: 9
SALES (corp-wide): 7.5MM **Privately Held**
SIC: 2834 Mfg Pharmaceutical Preparations
HQ: Polycarbon Industries, Inc.
9 Opportunity Way
Newburyport MA 01950

(G-10331)
QUIET LOGISTICS
66 Saratoga Blvd (01434-5218)
PHONE..................................978 391-4439
Darby French, *CFO*
▲ **EMP:** 14
SALES (est): 4.9MM **Privately Held**
SIC: 3549 Mfg Metalworking Machinery

(G-10332)
ROFIN-BAASEL INC (DH)
68 Barnum Rd (01434-3508)
PHONE..................................978 635-9100
Lou Molnar, *President*
Armin Renneisen, *Managing Dir*
Cindy Denis, *Treasurer*
Ken Beyler, *Regl Sales Mgr*
Bruce Dickinson, *Sales Staff*
▲ **EMP:** 30
SQ FT: 14,500
SALES (est): 10.7MM
SALES (corp-wide): 183.7K **Privately Held**
SIC: 3699 3953 Mfg Electrical Equipment/Supplies Mfg Marking Devices
HQ: Coherent Munich Gmbh & Co. Kg
Zeppelinstr. 10
Gilching 82205
810 539-650

(G-10333)
SMC LTD
18 Independence Dr (01434-5294)
P.O. Box 460, Sterling (01564-0460)
PHONE..................................978 422-6800
Chetan N Patel, *President*
EMP: 80
SQ FT: 32,000
SALES (est): 24.7MM
SALES (corp-wide): 593MM **Privately Held**
WEB: www.cyclesincorporated.com
SIC: 3089 Mfg Plastic Products
PA: Scientific Molding Corporation, Ltd.
330 Smc Dr
Somerset WI 54025
715 247-3500

(G-10334)
TM ELECTRONICS INC
68 Barnum Rd (01434-3508)
PHONE..................................978 772-0970
Doug Lindemann, *President*
EMP: 15 **EST:** 1961
SQ FT: 12,750
SALES (est): 5.1MM **Privately Held**
WEB: www.tmelectronics.com
SIC: 3829 Mfg Measuring/Controlling Devices

Dighton
Bristol County

(G-10335)
ARMIN INNOVATIVE PRODUCTS INC
Also Called: Metalgrommets.com
1424 Somerset Ave (02715-1238)
P.O. Box 26 (02715-0026)
PHONE..................................508 822-4629
Kenneth Raifman, *President*
▲ **EMP:** 39
SQ FT: 43,000
SALES (est): 12.2MM **Privately Held**
WEB: www.rnrplastics.com
SIC: 2673 Mfg Bags-Plastic/Coated Paper

(G-10336)
BLACK EARTH TECHNOLOGIES INC
2575 County St (02715-1606)
PHONE..................................508 397-1335
Roger Teixeira, *Principal*
EMP: 6 **EST:** 2008
SALES (est): 659.1K **Privately Held**
SIC: 3674 Mfg Semiconductors/Related Devices

(G-10337)
LINS PROPANE TRUCKS CORP
2281 Cedar St (02715-1009)
PHONE..................................508 669-6665
Andrew Johnson, *President*
Chris Day, *Business Mgr*
Timothy Johnson, *Director*
▼ **EMP:** 18
SQ FT: 8,000
SALES: 7.2MM **Privately Held**
WEB: www.linspropanetrucks.com
SIC: 3715 Mfg Truck Trailers

(G-10338)
QUINTAL BURIAL VAULTS
3425 Sharps Lot Rd (02715-1417)
PHONE..................................508 669-5717
Joseph Quintal, *Owner*
EMP: 10
SALES (est): 980K **Privately Held**
SIC: 3281 3272 5087 4226 Mfg Cut Stone/Products Mfg Concrete Products Whol Svc Estblshmt Equip Special Warehse/Storage

Dorchester
Suffolk County

(G-10339)
2 DOGS TREATS LLC
171 Neponset Ave (02122-3343)
PHONE..................................617 286-4844
Buttra Christian Sann, *Mng Member*
Michael Patrick Merfeld,
Richard Sann,
EMP: 3 **EST:** 2013
SALES: 170K **Privately Held**
SIC: 2047 Mfg Dog/Cat Food

(G-10340)
BOSTON IRISH REPORTER
Also Called: Dorchester Reporter
150 Munt Vrnon St Ste 120 (02125)
PHONE..................................617 436-1222
Ed Forry, *President*
Thomas Mulvoy, *Editor*
Jennifer Smith, *Editor*
Thomas F Mulvoy Jr, *Assoc Editor*
EMP: 10
SALES (est): 560.8K **Privately Held**
WEB: www.bostonirish.com
SIC: 2711 Newspapers-Publishing/Printing

(G-10341)
BOSTON WINERY LLC
26 Ericsson St (02122-3602)
PHONE..................................617 265-9463
Ralph Bruno, *President*
EMP: 5
SQ FT: 10,000
SALES (est): 189.6K **Privately Held**
SIC: 2084 Mfg Wines/Brandy/Spirits

(G-10342)
FIRST ELECTRONICS CORPORATION
71 Von Hillern St Ste 1 (02125-1193)
PHONE..................................617 288-2430
William L Tregoning, *President*
Hung Ngo, *Engineer*
Charlie Zaidan, *Engineer*
Judy Reid, *Human Res Mgr*
Alex Durso, *Sales Dir*
EMP: 88
SQ FT: 50,000
SALES (est): 20.4MM **Privately Held**
WEB: www.feccables.com
SIC: 3679 3643 Mfg Electronic Components Mfg Conductive Wiring Devices

(G-10343)
HOT STEPZ MAGAZINE
42 Edson St (02124-4304)
PHONE..................................617 959-6403
Neeca L Wilder, *Owner*
EMP: 3
SALES (est): 123.5K **Privately Held**
WEB: www.hotstepzmagazine.com
SIC: 2721 Periodicals-Publishing/Printing

(G-10344)
IMPRINT BOSTON INC
620 Blue Hill Ave (02121-3212)
PHONE..................................857 251-9383
Charles Seagraves, *Principal*
Roger Libert, *Principal*
EMP: 3
SQ FT: 675
SALES: 26K **Privately Held**
SIC: 2752 Lithographic Commercial Printing

(G-10345)
KAPSON PRINTING SERVICE INC
10 Winter St (02122-3024)
PHONE..................................617 265-2543
EMP: 7
SALES: 140K **Privately Held**
SIC: 2752 Lithographic Commercial Printing

(G-10346)
L S HARDWOOD FLOOR
14 Arcadia St (02122-2140)
PHONE..................................617 288-0339
Dong Huynh, *Owner*
EMP: 5
SALES (est): 353.6K **Privately Held**
SIC: 2426 1752 Hardwood Dimension/Floor Mill Floor Laying Contractor

(G-10347)
MULTIFAB PLASTICS INC
Also Called: Multi-Fab Plastics
889 Dorchester Ave (02125-1253)
PHONE..................................617 287-1411
Fax: 617 287-0299
EMP: 14
SALES (est): 2MM **Privately Held**
WEB: www.multifab.com
SIC: 3089 Mfg Plastics Hardware And Building Products

(G-10348)
ROSSCOMMON QUILTS INC
15 Fairfax St (02124-5113)
PHONE..................................617 436-5848
Ann Walsh, *Owner*
Jack Cunningham, *Principal*
EMP: 5
SALES (est): 236.6K **Privately Held**
WEB: www.rosscommon.com
SIC: 2711 2221 Newspapers-Publishing/Printing Manmade Broadwoven Fabric Mill

(G-10349)
VIETAZ INC
Also Called: Caring Pharmacy 2
2288 Dorchester Ave (02124-5622)
PHONE..................................617 322-1933
Christine Phan, *President*
EMP: 5
SALES (est): 654.6K **Privately Held**
SIC: 2834 Mfg Pharmaceutical Preparations

Dover
Norfolk County

(G-10350)
DOUBLE DIAMOND SUGAR HOUSE
21 Edgewater Dr (02030-2123)
PHONE..................................508 479-4950
Kris Ochs, *Principal*
EMP: 3
SALES (est): 173.9K **Privately Held**
SIC: 2099 Mfg Food Preparations

(G-10351)
NEW ENGLAND WHEELCHAIR SPT INC
20 Haven St (02030-2128)
PHONE..................................508 785-0393
Joseph Sullivan, *Principal*
EMP: 3
SALES: 9.7K **Privately Held**
SIC: 3842 Mfg Surgical Appliances/Supplies

(G-10352)
ONLINE MODERATION INC
11 Woodland Rd (02030-2557)
PHONE..................................617 686-7737
Mark Somol, *CEO*
EMP: 5
SALES (est): 209.5K **Privately Held**
SIC: 2741 Internet Publishing And Broadcasting

(G-10353)
WILLIAM CONNELL LLC
2 Mill St (02030-2240)
PHONE..................................508 785-1292
William V Connell, *Principal*
William Connell, *Principal*
EMP: 4 **EST:** 2011
SALES (est): 285.1K **Privately Held**
SIC: 3442 Mfg Metal Doors/Sash/Trim

GEOGRAPHIC

Dracut
Middlesex County

(G-10354)
BIOSOLVE COMPANY
24 Victory Ln (01826-4643)
PHONE....781 482-7900
James B Edgerly, *Managing Dir*
Karl D Loos,
EMP: 4
SALES: 3MM **Privately Held**
SIC: 2899 Mfg Chemical Preparations

(G-10355)
BROX INDUSTRIES INC (PA)
1471 Methuen St (01826-5499)
PHONE....978 454-9105
Stephen M Brox, *President*
Michael Bucuzzo, *Superintendent*
Greg McKensy, *VP Opers*
Vic Goulet, *Safety Dir*
Dave Roma, *Sales Mgr*
EMP: 60 **EST:** 1982
SQ FT: 3,000
SALES (est): 233MM **Privately Held**
WEB: www.broxindustries.com
SIC: 1442 1499 1611 1629 Construction Sand/Gravel Nonmetellic Mineral Mng Highway/Street Cnstn Heavy Construction

(G-10356)
DAKOTA SYSTEMS INC
1057 Broadway Rd (01826-2807)
PHONE....978 275-0600
John M Thomas, *President*
Ann Thomas, *Treasurer*
EMP: 90
SQ FT: 25,500
SALES: 33MM **Privately Held**
WEB: www.dakotasystems.com
SIC: 3312 Blast Furnace-Steel Works

(G-10357)
DAVES SHEET METAL INC
13 Chuck Dr Bldg 5 (01826)
P.O. Box 218 (01826-0218)
PHONE....978 454-3144
Bob Talbot, *President*
EMP: 8
SALES (est): 1.5MM **Privately Held**
SIC: 3444 Mfg Sheet Metalwork

(G-10358)
DE MARI PASTA DIES USA INC
48 Chuck Dr (01826-2613)
PHONE....978 454-4099
Mauricio Demari, *President*
Giovanni Cannata, *Vice Pres*
Gabriella Cannata, *Director*
▲ **EMP:** 8
SALES (est): 1.4MM **Privately Held**
WEB: www.demaripastadies.com
SIC: 3544 Sells Dies & Inserts

(G-10359)
DRACUT KITCHEN & BATH
18 Chuck Dr (01826-2613)
PHONE....978 453-3869
Charlie Thellen, *Partner*
Peter Szurley, *Partner*
Dick Poremba, *Manager*
EMP: 5
SALES (est): 466.3K **Privately Held**
SIC: 2434 Mfg Wood Kitchen Cabinets

(G-10360)
ECONOMOU PLUMBING & HEATING
49 Settlers Way (01826-3135)
PHONE....978 957-6953
James Economou, *Owner*
EMP: 3
SALES (est): 243.6K **Privately Held**
SIC: 3494 Mfg Valves/Pipe Fittings

(G-10361)
JM SOFTWARE INC
32 Elene St (01826)
PHONE....978 957-9105
John Maniatakos, *President*
EMP: 3
SALES: 150K **Privately Held**
WEB: www.jmsoftware.com
SIC: 7372 7371 Prepackaged Software Services Custom Computer Programing

(G-10362)
M & A PLASTICS INC
95 Jones Ave (01826-1501)
PHONE....978 319-9930
Michael J Poirier, *President*
EMP: 3
SALES (est): 170.6K **Privately Held**
SIC: 3089 Mfg Plastic Products

(G-10363)
MAJILITE CORPORATION
1530 Broadway Rd (01826-2830)
PHONE....978 441-6800
Bruce Eben Pindyck, *CEO*
Michael Willwerth, *President*
Al Pinto, *Opers Mgr*
John Silva, *Production*
Bell Aaron, *Engineer*
◆ **EMP:** 75 **EST:** 1979
SQ FT: 150,000
SALES (est): 13.3MM
SALES (corp-wide): 379.3MM **Privately Held**
WEB: www.nytek-usa.com
SIC: 2295 2261 Mfg Coated Fabrics Cotton Finishing Plant
PA: Meridian Industries, Inc.
735 N Water St Ste 630
Milwaukee WI 53202
414 224-0610

(G-10364)
MAJILITE MANUFACTURING INC
1530 Broadway Rd (01826-2830)
PHONE....978 441-6800
Michael Willewerth, *President*
Douglas C Miller, *Treasurer*
Douglas J Arnold, *Admin Sec*
Joseph B Tyson, *Admin Sec*
EMP: 66
SQ FT: 100,000
SALES: 23MM
SALES (corp-wide): 379.3MM **Privately Held**
WEB: www.meridiancompanies.com
SIC: 2262 Manmade Fiber & Silk Finishing Plant
PA: Meridian Industries, Inc.
735 N Water St Ste 630
Milwaukee WI 53202
414 224-0610

(G-10365)
MICROWAVE COMPONENTS INC
1794 Bridge St Ste 21r (01826-2688)
PHONE....978 453-6016
Preston G Smith, *President*
Robin Nazarian, *Vice Pres*
EMP: 18
SQ FT: 5,000
SALES (est): 2.5MM **Privately Held**
SIC: 3677 Mfg Electronic Coils/Transformers

(G-10366)
MILL CITY IRON FABRICATORS
479 Textile Ave (01826-4424)
PHONE....978 957-6833
Jean R Soucy, *President*
EMP: 19
SQ FT: 10,000
SALES (est): 4MM **Privately Held**
WEB: www.millcityiron.com
SIC: 3449 3441 Mfg Misc Structural Metalwork Structural Metal Fabrication

(G-10367)
PORTLAND STONE WARE CO INC (PA)
50 Mcgrath Rd (01826-2840)
P.O. Box 670 (01826-0670)
PHONE....978 459-7272
Donna Morgan, *President*
Mary Beeley, *Vice Pres*
Dave Foreman, *Purchasing*
Vicki Zimmerschied, *Purchasing*
Rich Carageane, *Sales Staff*
▲ **EMP:** 35 **EST:** 1847
SQ FT: 41,000
SALES (est): 4.4MM **Privately Held**
SIC: 3272 5051 5032 Mfg Concrete Products Metals Service Center Whol Brick/Stone Material

(G-10368)
SYNTHETIC LABS INC
24 Victory Ln (01826-4643)
PHONE....978 957-2919
Edward Hosmer, *President*
David Miller, *Treasurer*
Suzanne Hosmer, *Clerk*
EMP: 18 **EST:** 1963
SQ FT: 15,000
SALES (est): 5.3MM **Privately Held**
WEB: www.syntecpro.com
SIC: 2841 Mfg Soap/Other Detergents

(G-10369)
THERMOKINETICS
25 Tobey Rd U55 (01826-4916)
PHONE....978 459-6073
George Angnstpls, *Principal*
EMP: 11
SALES (est): 515.7K **Privately Held**
SIC: 3714 Mfg Motor Vehicle Parts/Accessories

(G-10370)
VINTAGE MILLWORK CORPORATION
19 School St (01826-4684)
PHONE....978 957-1400
Raymond Bullock, *President*
Joseph Cusano, *Vice Pres*
EMP: 7
SALES (est): 1.2MM **Privately Held**
WEB: www.vintagemillworkcorp.com
SIC: 2431 Mfg Millwork

(G-10371)
WASIK ASSOCIATES INC
29 Diana Ln (01826-1500)
PHONE....978 454-9787
Peter T Wasik Jr, *President*
Kathy Ricciardi, *Purchasing*
EMP: 17
SQ FT: 14,000
SALES (est): 3.2MM **Privately Held**
WEB: www.wasik.com
SIC: 3679 7629 Mfg Electronic Components Electrical Repair

Dudley
Worcester County

(G-10372)
AMERICANSUB
Also Called: ASAP
137 Schofield Ave (01571-6074)
P.O. Box 417, Webster (01570-0417)
PHONE....508 949-2320
Douglas Sherblom, *President*
EMP: 20
SQ FT: 7,000
SALES (est): 3.8MM **Privately Held**
SIC: 3679 1731 3677 Mfg Electronic Components Electrical Contractor Mfg Electronic Coils/Transformers

(G-10373)
BONIFACE TOOL & DIE INC
181 Southbridge Rd (01571-6925)
PHONE....508 764-3248
Peter Didonato, *President*
David Di Donato, *General Mgr*
David Didonato, *General Mgr*
Angelo Didonato, *Vice Pres*
▲ **EMP:** 30
SQ FT: 33,000
SALES (est): 6.1MM **Privately Held**
WEB: www.bonifacetool.com
SIC: 3544 3599 3728 Mfg Aircraft Parts/Equip Mfg Dies/Tools/Jigs/Fixt Mfg Industrial Machinery

(G-10374)
ESSILOR INDUSTRIES CORP
183 W Main St (01571-3814)
PHONE....787 848-4130
Francois Deterre, *General Mgr*
Sobeida Irizarry, *Vice Pres*
Brad Gunn, *Train & Dev Mgr*
◆ **EMP:** 230
SQ FT: 100,000
SALES (est): 21.9MM
SALES (corp-wide): 1.4MM **Privately Held**
WEB: www.essilorgroupe.com
SIC: 3851 Mfg Ophthalmic Goods
PA: Essilorluxottica
147 Rue De Paris
Charenton-Le-Pont 94220
149 774-224

(G-10375)
GENTEX OPTICS INC
183 W Main St (01571-3835)
P.O. Box 307 (01571-0307)
PHONE....508 713-5267
Ed Chamberland, *Manager*
EMP: 417
SALES (corp-wide): 1.4MM **Privately Held**
WEB: www.gentexoptics.com
SIC: 3827 5049 3851 Mfg Optical Instruments/Lenses Whol Professional Equipment Mfg Ophthalmic Goods
HQ: Gentex Optics, Inc.
183 W Main St
Dudley MA 01571
570 282-8531

(G-10376)
GENTEX OPTICS INC (DH)
183 W Main St (01571-3835)
PHONE....570 282-8531
L P Frieder, *CEO*
Eric Javellaud, *CEO*
Gerard Malledant, *President*
Helene Greuzard, *Vice Pres*
Heather M Acker, *CFO*
▲ **EMP:** 200
SQ FT: 98,000
SALES (est): 95.3MM
SALES (corp-wide): 1.4MM **Privately Held**
WEB: www.gentexoptics.com
SIC: 3851 3842 Mfg Ophthalmic Goods Mfg Surgical Appliances/Supplies
HQ: Essilor Of America, Inc.
13555 N Stemmons Fwy
Dallas TX 75234
214 496-4000

(G-10377)
I F ENGINEERING CORP
3 Foshay Rd (01571)
P.O. Box 1 (01571-0001)
PHONE....860 935-0280
Lee C Foshay, *President*
Joe Schroder, *QA Dir*
Michael Darche, *Engineer*
Lois A Foshay, *Admin Sec*
EMP: 27
SQ FT: 7,500
SALES (est): 5.9MM **Privately Held**
SIC: 3669 Mfg Communications Equipment

(G-10378)
JOHN F WIELOCK
Also Called: Wielock Farms
27 Mill Rd (01571-6308)
PHONE....508 943-5366
John Wielock, *Owner*
EMP: 4
SQ FT: 8,000
SALES (est): 240K **Privately Held**
SIC: 3089 4213 Mfg Custom Molded Plastic Containers/Trucking Operator-Nonlocal

(G-10379)
KERRIN GRAPHICS & PRINTING
42 W Dudley Rd (01571-6915)
P.O. Box 970, Southbridge (01550-0970)
PHONE....508 765-1339
Jean Daoust, *President*
EMP: 5
SQ FT: 8,500
SALES (est): 679.9K **Privately Held**
WEB: www.kerringraphics.com
SIC: 2752 Lithographic Commercial Printing

(G-10380)
MACE ADHESIVES COATINGS CO INC
38 Roberts Rd (01571-6817)
P.O. Box 37 (01571-0037)
PHONE....................................508 943-9052
James F Gilloran, *President*
Joseph A Compagnone, *Chairman*
▲ **EMP:** 20
SQ FT: 12,500
SALES (est): 3.3MM **Privately Held**
SIC: 2891 Mfg Adhesives/Sealants

(G-10381)
METALOGIC INDUSTRIES LLC
115 Schofield Ave (01571)
PHONE....................................508 461-6787
Thomas Kokosinski, *Mng Member*
EMP: 12
SALES (est): 2.7MM **Privately Held**
SIC: 3679 Mfg Electronic Components

(G-10382)
MYRIAD FIBER IMAGING TECH INC
56 Southbridge Rd (01571-6923)
PHONE....................................508 949-3000
John Gauvin, *President*
Cheryl Gauvin, *Vice Pres*
Tyler Gauvin, *Vice Pres*
EMP: 15
SQ FT: 3,500
SALES (est): 2MM **Privately Held**
WEB: www.myriadfiber.com
SIC: 3845 3229 Mfg Electromedical Equipment Mfg Pressed/Blown Glass

(G-10383)
RYSZARD A KOKOSINSKI
Also Called: Kokos Machine Co
75 Oxford Ave (01571-5603)
PHONE....................................508 943-2700
Ryszard A Kokosinski, *Owner*
Ursala Kokosinski, *Co-Owner*
EMP: 20
SQ FT: 20,000
SALES (est): 2.4MM **Privately Held**
WEB: www.kokosmachine.com
SIC: 3599 Mfg Industrial Machinery

(G-10384)
SHIELD PACKAGING CO INC
50 Oxford Rd (01571)
PHONE....................................508 949-0900
Bruce Simpson, *Manager*
Ryan Simpson, *Maintence Staff*
EMP: 100
SALES (corp-wide): 28MM **Privately Held**
WEB: www.shieldpackaging.com
SIC: 2813 5169 3087 2879 Mfg Industrial Gases Whol Chemicals/Products Custm Cmpnd Prchsd Resin Mfg Agricultural Chemcl Mfg Polish/Sanitation Gd
PA: Shield Packaging Co., Inc.
99 University Rd
Canton MA 02021

(G-10385)
SOUTHBRIDGE TOOL & MFG INC
181 Southbridge Rd (01571-6925)
PHONE....................................508 764-6819
Peter Didonato, *President*
Angelo Didonato, *Treasurer*
EMP: 30
SQ FT: 24,000
SALES (est): 6.1MM **Privately Held**
SIC: 3599 Mfg Dies/Tools/Jigs/Fixtures

(G-10386)
STARCHEM INC
Also Called: Webco
420 W Main St (01571-5936)
PHONE....................................508 943-2337
Mark Pulifiaco, *President*
EMP: 8 **Privately Held**
SIC: 2841 Manufacturer Of Cleaning Supplies
PA: Starchem Inc
85 Beaver Rd
Ware MA 01082

(G-10387)
STEVENS LINEN ASSOCIATES INC
137 Schofield Ave Ste 5 (01571-6074)
PHONE....................................508 943-0813
Gregory C Kline, *President*
Carl W Copeland, *Principal*
▲ **EMP:** 100 **EST:** 1846
SQ FT: 142,000
SALES (est): 9.9MM **Privately Held**
WEB: www.stevenslinen.com
SIC: 2392 2211 2259 2262 Mfg Household Furnishing Cotton Brdwv Fabric Mill Knitting Mill

(G-10388)
UNIVERSAL TAG INC
36 Hall Rd (01571-5964)
P.O. Box 1518 (01571-1518)
PHONE....................................508 949-2411
Paul J Mandeville, *President*
A Robert Mandeville, *Treasurer*
Jeanne L Mandeville, *Admin Sec*
EMP: 28 **EST:** 1927
SQ FT: 28,000
SALES: 3.9MM **Privately Held**
WEB: www.universaltag.com
SIC: 2679 2752 Mfg Converted Paper Products Lithographic Commercial Printing

Dunstable
Middlesex County

(G-10389)
D CLEMENT INC
130 Pond St (01827-2307)
PHONE....................................978 649-3263
Dennis Clement, *President*
Tammy Clement, *Admin Sec*
EMP: 6
SALES (est): 828.7K **Privately Held**
SIC: 3441 Structural Metal Fabrication

(G-10390)
MSR UTILITY
209 Pleasant St (01827-1717)
PHONE....................................978 649-0002
Matthew Raymond, *Owner*
EMP: 9
SALES (est): 682.6K **Privately Held**
SIC: 1389 Oil/Gas Field Services

(G-10391)
SILVER BAY SOFTWARE LLC
100 Adams St (01827-1638)
PHONE....................................800 364-2889
Robert Durst, *Manager*
Kevin Hunter, *Manager*
EMP: 3
SALES (est): 197.7K **Privately Held**
SIC: 7372 Prepackaged Software Services

Duxbury
Plymouth County

(G-10392)
AV MEDICAL TECHNOLOGIES INC
20 Ryans Ln (02332-3550)
PHONE....................................612 200-0118
Limor Sandach, *CEO*
John Rappe, *COO*
EMP: 3 **EST:** 2015
SALES (est): 129.1K **Privately Held**
SIC: 3841 Surgical And Medical Instruments

(G-10393)
BLUEMOON OYSTER CO LCC
10 Wendell Pond Rd (02332-4338)
PHONE....................................781 585-6000
Joseph M Grady Jr, *Principal*
EMP: 3 **EST:** 2010
SALES (est): 203.5K **Privately Held**
SIC: 2092 Mfg Fresh/Frozen Packaged Fish

(G-10394)
BRITE-STRIKE TECHNOLOGIES INC
Also Called: Brite Strike Tctcal Illmntion
1145 Franklin St Duxbury (02332)
PHONE....................................781 585-3525
Glenn Bushee, *President*
Sarah Bushe, *Vice Pres*
Todd Bailey, *Training Dir*
EMP: 12
SQ FT: 14,000
SALES (est): 2MM **Privately Held**
SIC: 3648 Mfg Lighting Equipment

(G-10395)
C E D CORP
791 Keene St (02332-2905)
P.O. Box 2115 (02331-2115)
PHONE....................................781 834-9312
Shawn R Moniri, *President*
EMP: 5 **EST:** 1995
SALES (est): 909.8K **Privately Held**
WEB: www.cedcorp.com
SIC: 3589 5074 Mfg And Wholesales Industrial Water Purification Equipment

(G-10396)
DUXBURY CLIPPER INC
11 S Station St (02332-4534)
P.O. Box 1656 (02331-1656)
PHONE....................................781 934-2811
David Cutler, *President*
Joshua Cutler, *Principal*
David S Cutler, *Clerk*
EMP: 15
SQ FT: 1,000
SALES (est): 884.1K **Privately Held**
WEB: www.duxburyclipper.com
SIC: 2711 Newspapers-Publishing/Printing

(G-10397)
GEAR2SUCCEED LLC
81 Marshall St (02332-5125)
P.O. Box 1157 (02331-1157)
PHONE....................................781 733-0559
Robert Daniels, *CEO*
EMP: 4
SALES: 30K **Privately Held**
SIC: 3961 Mfg Costume Jewelry

(G-10398)
GRIFFIN PUBLISHING CO INC
Also Called: Griffin Report Food Marketing
21 Chestnut St (02332-4419)
P.O. Box 2826 (02331-2826)
PHONE....................................781 829-4700
Kevin B Griffin, *President*
EMP: 10
SQ FT: 3,500
SALES (est): 1.4MM **Privately Held**
WEB: www.griffinreport.com
SIC: 2721 Trade Journals

(G-10399)
INSITE SIGN LLC
Also Called: Signs On Site
40 Tremont St Ste 50 (02332-5316)
PHONE....................................781 934-5664
Lawrence Bray, *Partner*
Jessica Erickson, *Vice Pres*
EMP: 3
SALES (est): 228.1K **Privately Held**
SIC: 3993 Mfg Signs/Advertising Specialties

(G-10400)
MERCURY LEARNING AND INFO LLC
455 Washington St (02331)
PHONE....................................781 934-0500
David Pallai, *Mng Member*
EMP: 3
SALES (corp-wide): 1MM **Privately Held**
SIC: 2741 Misc Publishing
PA: Mercury Learning And Information Llc
22883 Quicksilver Dr
Dulles VA 20166
800 232-0223

(G-10401)
RESILIENCE THERAPEUTICS INC
536 Bay Rd (02332-5220)
PHONE....................................617 780-2375
Dr Emer Leahy, *CEO*
Retsina Meyer, *Principal*
Jeff Sabados, *Principal*
EMP: 5 **EST:** 2014
SQ FT: 500
SALES (est): 447.1K **Privately Held**
SIC: 2833 Mfg Medicinal/Botanical Products

(G-10402)
SYNCHRONEURON INC
130 Tobey Garden St (02332-4945)
PHONE....................................617 538-5688
William D Kerns, *CEO*
Marc R Cote, *CFO*
Kei-Lai Fong, *CFO*
Gerald Chan, *Director*
Isaac Cheng, *Director*
EMP: 6
SALES (est): 590.4K **Privately Held**
SIC: 3559 Mfg Misc Industry Machinery

(G-10403)
TAKEDA PHARMACEUTICALS USA INC
38 Deerpath Trl N (02332-2942)
PHONE....................................781 837-1528
Scott Craig, *Principal*
EMP: 3 **Privately Held**
SIC: 2834 Mfg Pharmaceutical Preparations
HQ: Takeda Pharmaceuticals U.S.A., Inc.
95 Hayden Ave
Lexington MA 02421
617 349-0200

(G-10404)
W2W PARTNERS LLC
Also Called: Organic Project The
65 Acorn Street Duxbury (02332)
PHONE....................................781 424-7824
Thyme Sullivan, *Mng Member*
Denielle Finkelstein, *Mng Member*
EMP: 4
SALES (est): 357.7K **Privately Held**
SIC: 2676 Mfg Sanitary Paper Products

East Bridgewater
Plymouth County

(G-10405)
ALCIDES D FORTES D/B/A CUSTOM
225 Elm St (02333-1419)
PHONE....................................508 378-7815
Alcides D Fortes, *Principal*
EMP: 4
SALES (est): 236.3K **Privately Held**
SIC: 2434 Mfg Wood Kitchen Cabinets

(G-10406)
ALLOY CASTINGS CO INC
151 W Union St (02333-1745)
P.O. Box 473 (02333-0473)
PHONE....................................508 378-2541
Franklin J Santilli, *President*
EMP: 11 **EST:** 1948
SQ FT: 90,000
SALES (est): 1.3MM **Privately Held**
WEB: www.alloycastings.com
SIC: 3366 Copper Foundry

(G-10407)
BARANOWSKI WOODWORKING CO INC
14 Washington St (02333-1219)
PHONE....................................508 690-1515
Michael Baranowski, *President*
EMP: 3
SQ FT: 10,000
SALES (est): 393.1K **Privately Held**
WEB: www.baranowskiwoodworking.com
SIC: 2431 2541 Mfg Wood Doors & Cabinet Doors

(G-10408)
CENTCO ARCHITECTURAL METALS
523 Spring St (02333-1802)
PHONE....................................508 456-1888
Larry Dale, *President*
EMP: 10
SQ FT: 10,000

GEOGRAPHIC

SALES (est): 1.4MM **Privately Held**
WEB: www.centcometals.com
SIC: 3442 Mfg Metal Doors/Sash/Trim

(G-10409)
CHRISTEYNS LAUNDRY TECH LLC
100 Laurel St Ste 120 (02333-1847)
PHONE..................................617 203-2169
Jef Wittouck, *COO*
Paul Bostoen,
EMP: 15
SALES (est): 2.7MM **Privately Held**
SIC: 2841 Mfg Soap/Other Detergents

(G-10410)
CROCETTI-OAKDALE PACKING INC (PA)
Also Called: South Shore Meats
378 Pleasant St (02333-1349)
PHONE..................................508 587-0035
Carl F Crocetti, *President*
Joan A Hurkett, *Admin Sec*
EMP: 50
SQ FT: 15,000
SALES (est): 7.5MM **Privately Held**
SIC: 2013 2011 Mfg Prepared Meats Meat Packing Plant

(G-10411)
D W CLARK INC (PA)
692 N Bedford St (02333-1126)
P.O. Box 448 (02333-0448)
PHONE..................................508 378-4014
Jeffrey Burek, *President*
Mary Burek, *Vice Pres*
John Galvin, *Sales Staff*
Brian White, *Technology*
Mary Ann Burek, *Admin Sec*
EMP: 30 **EST:** 1902
SQ FT: 12,000
SALES (est): 5.1MM **Privately Held**
WEB: www.dwclark.com
SIC: 3325 3369 3366 Steel Foundry Non-ferrous Metal Foundry Copper Foundry

(G-10412)
DESIGNERS METALCRAFT
530 Spring St (02333-1834)
PHONE..................................508 378-0404
Glen Mueller, *Owner*
Alan Rink, *Foreman/Supr*
EMP: 5 **EST:** 1955
SQ FT: 5,000
SALES (est): 951.8K **Privately Held**
SIC: 3679 Mfg Industrial Machinery

(G-10413)
FTC ENTERPRISE INC
170 W Union St (02333-1746)
PHONE..................................508 378-2799
Fred Climo III, *President*
Patrick Climo, *Vice Pres*
EMP: 10 **EST:** 1988
SALES: 1.5MM **Privately Held**
SIC: 2299 Mfg

(G-10414)
JET MACHINED PRODUCTS LLC
221 Highland St (02333-1409)
P.O. Box 577 (02333-0577)
PHONE..................................508 378-3200
David Slutz,
Michael Hullinger,
Peter Kershaw,
Edward P Schatz,
Michael R Trota,
EMP: 14
SQ FT: 10,000
SALES (est): 2.6MM **Privately Held**
SIC: 3599 Mfg Industrial Machinery

(G-10415)
KITCHENS R US INC
Also Called: Kitchens By US
494 N Bedford St (02333-1150)
PHONE..................................508 378-7474
Russell Mills, *President*
EMP: 4
SQ FT: 2,000
SALES (est): 422.1K **Privately Held**
WEB: www.kitchensbyus.com
SIC: 2434 Mfg Wood Kitchen Cabinets

(G-10416)
L T TECHNOLOGIES
612 Plymouth St Ste 12 (02333-2057)
PHONE..................................508 456-0315
Thomas Belmont, *President*
EMP: 7 **EST:** 2010
SALES (est): 618.5K **Privately Held**
SIC: 3589 Mfg Service Industry Machinery

(G-10417)
MCSTOWE ENGINEERING & MET PDTS
Also Called: McStowe Engrg & Met Pdts Co
548 Spring St (02333-1896)
PHONE..................................508 378-7400
Paul Mc Stowe Jr, *President*
Evelyn E Mc Stowe, *Vice Pres*
Linda Mc Stowe, *Vice Pres*
EMP: 12 **EST:** 1962
SQ FT: 16,000
SALES (est): 1.7MM **Privately Held**
SIC: 3644 3429 3613 Mfg Electrical Equipment

(G-10418)
MUELLER CORPORATION
530 Spring St (02333-1834)
PHONE..................................508 456-4500
Mark D Svizzero, *President*
Bob Bishop, *COO*
Glenn Mueller, *Vice Pres*
Dorene Austin, *QC Mgr*
Kathleen Anderson, *Controller*
▲ **EMP:** 160 **EST:** 1955
SQ FT: 20,000
SALES (est): 19.8MM **Privately Held**
WEB: www.muellercorp.com
SIC: 3471 Plating/Polishing Service

(G-10419)
R&R SWEEPING SERVICES INC
6 Winterfield Dr (02333-1087)
PHONE..................................508 586-5705
Marci Ryan, *President*
EMP: 3
SALES: 80K **Privately Held**
SIC: 3991 Mfg Brooms/Brushes

(G-10420)
SPARTA KEFALAS ORGANICS LLC
361 Central St (02333-2021)
PHONE..................................978 810-5300
Rebecca H Dawson, *Principal*
EMP: 3
SALES (est): 174.6K **Privately Held**
SIC: 3674 Mfg Semiconductors/Related Devices

(G-10421)
THORNDIKE CORPORATION
680 N Bedford St Ste 1 (02333-1292)
P.O. Box 533 (02333-0533)
PHONE..................................508 378-9797
James O Thorndike III, *President*
Mary Ellen Thorndike, *Treasurer*
EMP: 12
SQ FT: 3,500
SALES (est): 2MM **Privately Held**
WEB: www.thorndikecorp.com
SIC: 3679 Mfg Electronic Components

(G-10422)
WARE RITE DISTRIBUTORS INC
40 Industrial Dr (02333-1680)
PHONE..................................508 690-2145
Roger Ware, *President*
Matthew St Amand, *General Mgr*
Dan Skinner, *Administration*
▲ **EMP:** 100
SQ FT: 40,000
SALES (est): 23.9MM **Privately Held**
SIC: 2821 2541 Mfg Plastic Materials/Resins Mfg Wood Partitions/Fixtures

East Brookfield
Worcester County

(G-10423)
SPARROW ENGINEERING
108 North St (01515-1612)
PHONE..................................508 867-3984
Jay McKinney, *President*
EMP: 4
SALES: 500K **Privately Held**
SIC: 3089 Mfg Plastic Products

East Douglas
Worcester County

(G-10424)
ANTIQUE HOMES MAGAZINE
73 Wallis St (01516-2234)
PHONE..................................508 476-7271
John Petraglia, *Principal*
EMP: 4
SALES (est): 201.2K **Privately Held**
SIC: 2711 Newspapers-Publishing/Printing

(G-10425)
CLASSIC ENVELOPE INC
120 Gilboa St Unit 1 (01516-2275)
PHONE..................................508 731-6747
Rick Nieuwendyk, *General Mgr*
Peter Decaro, *Vice Pres*
EMP: 70
SALES (est): 25.2MM
SALES (corp-wide): 147.4MM **Privately Held**
WEB: www.classicenvelopeinc.com
SIC: 2677 2759 2752 Manufacture Envelopes Commercial Printing Lithographic Commercial Printing
PA: Supremex Inc
7213 Rue Cordner
Lasalle QC H8N 2
514 595-0555

(G-10426)
DEREK CICCONE
334 Se Main St (01516-2725)
PHONE..................................508 476-2105
Derek Ciccone, *Principal*
EMP: 5 **EST:** 2014
SALES (est): 256.6K **Privately Held**
SIC: 3272 Mfg Concrete Products

(G-10427)
J T MACHINE CO INC
Also Called: Jt Machine Shop
175 Davis St (01516-2313)
P.O. Box 297 (01516-0297)
PHONE..................................508 476-1508
Ronald Deschene, *President*
Kevin Decshene, *VP Mfg*
Diane Deschene, *Office Mgr*
EMP: 20
SQ FT: 15,000
SALES (est): 3.5MM **Privately Held**
SIC: 3541 3599 Mfg Machine Tools-Cutting Mfg Industrial Machinery

(G-10428)
LASER LIGHTNING LLC (PA)
174 Davis St (01516-2310)
PHONE..................................508 476-0138
Arleen Kennedy, *Mng Member*
EMP: 7
SALES (est): 570.3K **Privately Held**
WEB: www.laserprinterexperts.com
SIC: 3861 5734 Mfg Photographic Equipment/Supplies Ret Computers/Software

(G-10429)
M & M PRINTING RUSH SERVICE
20 Yew St (01516-2412)
P.O. Box 166 (01516-0166)
PHONE..................................508 476-4495
Gary Morrelee, *Owner*
EMP: 4
SALES (est): 330.6K **Privately Held**
SIC: 2752 Lithographic Commercial Printing

(G-10430)
NASON MACHINE COMPANY
26 Cobblestone Ln (01516-2377)
PHONE..................................508 865-3545
Don Nason, *Owner*
EMP: 3
SALES: 38K **Privately Held**
SIC: 3599 Mfg Industrial Machinery

(G-10431)
OLEARY WELDING CORP
124 Davis St (01516-2310)
P.O. Box 1039 (01516-1039)
PHONE..................................508 476-9793
Ed Oleary, *President*
Karen O Leary, *Vice Pres*
EMP: 6
SQ FT: 6,000
SALES (est): 762.1K **Privately Held**
SIC: 7692 Welding Repair

East Falmouth
Barnstable County

(G-10432)
A1A STEEL LLC
120 Bernard E Saint Jean (02536-4445)
PHONE..................................774 763-2503
Peter Murphy, *Owner*
Jose Franco, *Principal*
EMP: 3
SALES (est): 668.8K **Privately Held**
WEB: www.a1asteel.com
SIC: 3317 5085 5087 Mfg Steel Pipe/Tubes Whol Industrial Supplies Whol Svc Estblshmt Equip

(G-10433)
ACCURATE COMPOSITES LLC
Also Called: Accurate Plastics
33 Technology Park Dr (02536-4442)
PHONE..................................508 457-9097
John R Egan Jr,
EMP: 60
SALES (est): 3.1MM **Privately Held**
SIC: 3999 Mfg Misc Products

(G-10434)
ACCURATE PLASTICS INC
33 Technology Park Dr (02536-4442)
PHONE..................................508 457-9097
Joseph Roy, *Manager*
EMP: 25
SALES (corp-wide): 10.9MM **Privately Held**
WEB: www.acculam.com
SIC: 2821 Mfg Plastic Materials
PA: Accurate Plastics, Inc.
18 Morris Pl
Yonkers NY 10705
914 476-0700

(G-10435)
ASSOCIATES OF CAPE COD INC (PA)
Also Called: ACC
124 Bernard E Saint Jean (02536-4445)
PHONE..................................508 540-3444
A J Meuse, *President*
Debbie Fraser, *General Mgr*
Alison Skinner, *COO*
Eric Johnson, *Vice Pres*
Robert Leonard, *Materials Mgr*
▲ **EMP:** 70
SQ FT: 80,000
SALES (est): 22.6MM **Privately Held**
WEB: www.acciusa.com
SIC: 2835 Mfg Diagnostic Substances

(G-10436)
ATLANTIC MBL & GRAN GROUP INC
59 Technology Park Dr (02536-4442)
PHONE..................................508 540-9770
Danffsney P Goncalves, *President*
Sandoval Pereira, *Director*
EMP: 7
SALES (est): 214.5K **Privately Held**
SIC: 3281 1743 Mfg Cut Stone/Products Tile/Marble Contractor

(G-10437)
CAPE BIORESEARCH INC
7 Smilin Jack Ln (02536-8511)
PHONE..................................413 658-5426
Richard K Brown, *President*
Richard Brown, *President*
EMP: 3 **EST:** 2016
SALES (est): 151.8K **Privately Held**
SIC: 3826 Mfg Analytical Instruments

(G-10438)
CAPE COD WINERY
681 Sandwich Rd (02536-4747)
P.O. Box 401 (02536-0401)
PHONE..................................508 457-5592
Kristina Lazzari, *President*
EMP: 10
SALES (est): 517.9K **Privately Held**
WEB: www.capecodwinery.com
SIC: 2084 Mfg Wines/Brandy/Spirits

(G-10439)
CLOS DE LA TECH
3 Judy Ann Dr (02536-6130)
PHONE..................................508 648-2505
Thurman J Rodgers, *President*
EMP: 4 **EST:** 2010
SALES (est): 98.4K **Privately Held**
SIC: 2084 Mfg Wines/Brandy/Spirits

(G-10440)
CUNNIFF CORP (PA)
Also Called: Falmouth Sheet Metal
36 Round Pond Dr (02536-4737)
PHONE..................................508 540-6232
Charles V Cuniff Jr, *President*
Tamra Cunniff, *Manager*
EMP: 6 **EST:** 2000
SQ FT: 5,000
SALES (est): 729.9K **Privately Held**
SIC: 3444 3585 3433 Mfg Sheet Metalwork Mfg Refrigeration/Heating Equipment Mfg Heating Equipment-Nonelectric

(G-10441)
E PAINT COMPANY
Also Called: Epaint Company
25 Research Rd (02536-4440)
PHONE..................................508 540-4412
Myles Walsh IV, *President*
Jake Goodwin, *Representative*
▼ **EMP:** 10
SQ FT: 7,500
SALES (est): 1.5MM **Privately Held**
WEB: www.epaint.com
SIC: 2851 8748 Mfg Paints/Allied Products Business Consulting Services

(G-10442)
FALMOUTH PRODUCTS INC
530 Thomas B Landers Rd (02536-4454)
P.O. Box 541, Falmouth (02541-0541)
PHONE..................................508 548-6686
Charles Cleary, *President*
James M Cleary, *Vice Pres*
M L Cleary, *Treasurer*
▼ **EMP:** 9
SQ FT: 1,600
SALES (est): 1.4MM **Privately Held**
WEB: www.falmouthproducts.com
SIC: 3822 Business Consulting Services

(G-10443)
FALMOUTH READY MIX INC
475 Thomas B Landers Rd (02536-4406)
PHONE..................................508 548-6100
Robert A Moniz, *President*
Catherine A Moniz, *Treasurer*
EMP: 12
SALES (est): 1.4MM **Privately Held**
WEB: www.falmouthreadymix.com
SIC: 3273 Mfg Ready-Mixed Concrete

(G-10444)
FUCCILLO READY MIX INC
548 Thomas B Landers Rd (02536-4414)
PHONE..................................508 540-2821
Valerie Fuccillo, *President*
David P Fuccillo, *Vice Pres*
EMP: 10
SALES (est): 1.1MM **Privately Held**
SIC: 3273 Mfg Ready-Mixed Concrete

(G-10445)
MCLANE RESEARCH LABS INC (PA)
121 Bernard E Saint Jean (02536-4444)
PHONE..................................508 495-4000
Susumu Honjo, *President*
Jon Magal, *General Mgr*
Michael Mathewson, *General Mgr*
Harry J Honan, *Corp Secy*
Yuki Honjo, *COO*
▲ **EMP:** 7
SALES (est): 1.4MM **Privately Held**
WEB: www.mclanelabs.com
SIC: 3699 8731 Mfg Electrical Equipment/Supplies Commercial Physical Research

(G-10446)
PELAGIC ELECTRONICS
174 Lake Shore Dr (02536-4792)
PHONE..................................508 540-1200
Clyde L Tyndale, *President*
Timothy Parker, *Partner*
Elizabeth Tyndale, *Partner*
EMP: 3
SALES (est): 399.3K **Privately Held**
SIC: 3826 5049 Mfg Analytical Instruments Whol Professional Equipment

(G-10447)
RAJESSA LLC
Also Called: Richards Design
117 Bernard E Saint Jean (02536-4444)
PHONE..................................508 540-4420
Hindy Richards, *Mng Member*
EMP: 11 **EST:** 2009
SALES (est): 667.1K **Privately Held**
SIC: 3545 Mfg Machine Tool Accessories

(G-10448)
RICHARDS DESIGN INC
117 Bernard E Saint Jean (02536-4444)
PHONE..................................508 540-4420
Robert Richards, *President*
EMP: 5
SQ FT: 6,000
SALES (est): 770K **Privately Held**
SIC: 3599 Mfg Industrial Machinery

(G-10449)
SOPHIC ALLIANCE INC
99 Meadow Neck Rd (02536-7711)
P.O. Box 968 (02536-0968)
PHONE..................................508 495-3801
Patrick Blake, *President*
EMP: 5
SALES (est): 243.6K **Privately Held**
SIC: 7372 7371 7373 8748 Publisher's Computer Software Custom Computer Programmng Srvcs Computer Integrated Systms Dsgn Systems Engineering Consultan

(G-10450)
THEODORE WOLF INC
Also Called: Cataumet Sawmills
494 Thomas B Landers Rd (02536-4415)
PHONE..................................508 457-0667
Theodore Wolf, *President*
Thomas D Adams, *Treasurer*
EMP: 9
SQ FT: 9,000
SALES (est): 1.2MM **Privately Held**
WEB: www.cataumetsawmill.com
SIC: 2421 5211 5031 Sawmill/Planing Mill Ret Lumber/Building Materials

(G-10451)
WALPOLE WOODWORKERS INC
958 E Falmouth Hwy (02536-6228)
P.O. Box 28 (02536-0028)
PHONE..................................508 540-0300
Richard Kolbert, *Branch Mgr*
EMP: 15
SALES (corp-wide): 83.9MM **Privately Held**
WEB: www.walpolewoodworkers.com
SIC: 2499 5211 5712 2452 Mfg Wood Products Ret Lumber/Building Mtrl Ret Furniture Mfg Prefabrcatd Wd Bldgs Mfg Prefab Metal Bldgs
PA: Walpole Outdoors Llc
100 Rver Ridge Dr Ste 302
Norwood MA 02062
508 668-2800

East Freetown
Bristol County

(G-10452)
HOWLAND TOOL & MACHINE LTD
159 Chace Rd (02717-1009)
P.O. Box 469, Assonet (02702-0469)
PHONE..................................508 763-8472
Bruce W Wilbur, *President*
EMP: 6
SQ FT: 9,080
SALES (est): 499.1K **Privately Held**
WEB: www.htmplastic.com
SIC: 3089 Mfg Plastic Injection Molding Forms

(G-10453)
J E SCHELL WELDING
253 Bullock Rd (02717-1418)
PHONE..................................508 763-4658
James Schell, *Partner*
Donald R Schell, *Partner*
EMP: 4
SALES: 180K **Privately Held**
SIC: 7692 Welding Repair

(G-10454)
LIZOTTE WELDING
Also Called: Lizotte's Machine & Welding
12 Carpenter Ln (02717-1414)
PHONE..................................508 763-8784
Richard Lizotte, *Owner*
EMP: 3
SALES (est): 265.7K **Privately Held**
SIC: 7692 1799 Welding Repair Trade Contractor

(G-10455)
LPS ENTERPRISES INC
128 Braley Rd Bldg A3 (02717-1147)
P.O. Box 67 (02717-0067)
PHONE..................................508 763-3830
Anthony Little, *President*
Linda Veronneau, *President*
Tony Lisa, *General Mgr*
EMP: 26 **EST:** 1989
SQ FT: 6,000
SALES (est): 7.2MM **Privately Held**
WEB: www.calllps.com
SIC: 3524 7349 Mfg Lawn/Garden Equipment Building Maintenance Services

(G-10456)
PACHECO GEAR INC
24 Middleboro Rd (02717-1725)
PHONE..................................508 763-5709
Christopher Pacheco, *Director*
EMP: 5
SALES (est): 389.6K **Privately Held**
SIC: 2393 Mfg Textile Bags

(G-10457)
PREFERRED CONCRETE CORP
66 Braley Rd (02717-1100)
P.O. Box 539 (02717-0539)
PHONE..................................508 763-5500
Amelia McNutt, *President*
Antonio Sousa, *Vice Pres*
EMP: 17
SALES (est): 2.7MM **Privately Held**
WEB: www.preferredconcrete.com
SIC: 3273 Mfg Ready-Mixed Concrete

(G-10458)
REFRESCO BEVERAGES US INC
65 Chace Rd (02717-1128)
PHONE..................................508 763-3515
EMP: 3
SALES (corp-wide): 3.2B **Privately Held**
SIC: 2086 Mfg Bottled/Canned Soft Drinks
HQ: Refresco Beverages Us Inc.
8112 Woodland Center Blvd
Tampa FL 33614
813 313-1800

(G-10459)
ROCHE ENGINEERING LLC
4 Marks Ln (02717-1063)
PHONE..................................508 287-1964
Noreen Winderlick, *Principal*
David Roche,
Gerald Roche,
Robin Roche,
EMP: 4
SALES (est): 218K **Privately Held**
SIC: 3812 Search And Navigation Equipment, Nsk

(G-10460)
STILLWATER FASTENERS LLC
25 Gurney Rd (02717-1107)
P.O. Box 300 (02717-0300)
PHONE..................................508 763-8044
Lea A Mola,
▲ **EMP:** 35
SALES (est): 4.8MM **Privately Held**
SIC: 3452 Mfg Bolts/Screws/Rivets

(G-10461)
TOWN BOOKBINDERY INC
154 County Rd (02717-1219)
P.O. Box 91 (02717-0091)
PHONE..................................508 763-2713
Raymond De Costa, *President*
EMP: 50
SQ FT: 2,800
SALES (est): 4MM **Privately Held**
WEB: www.townbookbindery.com
SIC: 2789 Bookbinding/Related Work

(G-10462)
VERTEX TOOL & DIE CO
11 Quanapoag Rd (02717-1503)
P.O. Box 86 (02717-0086)
PHONE..................................508 763-4749
Wayne B Cunningham, *Owner*
Wayne Cunningham, *Owner*
EMP: 4 **EST:** 1967
SQ FT: 2,000
SALES (est): 352.8K **Privately Held**
SIC: 3599 Mfg Industrial Machinery

(G-10463)
WEST WEARHAM PINE
10 Long Pond Rd (02717-1239)
P.O. Box 581 (02717-0581)
PHONE..................................508 763-4108
Paul S Darling, *Owner*
EMP: 3
SALES (est): 136.3K **Privately Held**
SIC: 2421 Sawmill/Planing Mill

East Longmeadow
Hampden County

(G-10464)
ALTERNATE MODE INC
Also Called: K A T
30 Westwood Ave (01028-2119)
PHONE..................................413 594-5190
Mario J Deciutiis, *President*
Connie Decutis, *Vice Pres*
Connie R Deciutiis, *Treasurer*
Connie Deciutiis, *Treasurer*
Danielle Cook, *Admin Sec*
▲ **EMP:** 6
SQ FT: 10,000
SALES (est): 801.4K **Privately Held**
WEB: www.alternatemode.com
SIC: 3931 5736 Mfg Musical Instruments Ret Musical Instruments

(G-10465)
ALVIN JOHNSON
Also Called: Eba
26 Maple Ct (01028-2737)
P.O. Box 108 (01028-0108)
PHONE..................................413 525-6334
Alvin Johnson, *Owner*
EMP: 8
SQ FT: 2,800
SALES: 1MM **Privately Held**
SIC: 3496 3443 3599 7692 Mfg Misc Fab Wire Prdts Mfg Fabricated Plate Wrk Mfg Industrial Machinery Welding Repair Mfg Tire Cord/Fabrics

GEOGRAPHIC

(G-10466)
AMERICAN SAW & MFG COMPANY INC
Also Called: Lenox
301 Chestnut St (01028-2823)
PHONE....................................413 525-3961
Stephen Davis, *President*
Joe Desantis, *Engineer*
Peter Mustis, *Senior Engr*
Cara Bogacz, *Finance*
Don Quinn, *Sales Staff*
◆ **EMP:** 74
SALES (est): 17.1MM
SALES (corp-wide): 8.6B **Publicly Held**
SIC: 3545 Mfg Machine Tool Accessories
PA: Newell Brands Inc.
6655 Pachtree Dunwoody Rd
Atlanta GA 30328
770 418-7000

(G-10467)
ARCLIN SURFACES - E LONGMEADOW
82 Deer Park Dr (01028-3196)
PHONE....................................678 781-5341
Shelia Waters, *CEO*
▲ **EMP:** 11 **EST:** 1993
SALES (est): 2.1MM **Privately Held**
SIC: 2672 Mfg Coated/Laminated Paper

(G-10468)
BLACK & DECKER (US) INC
301 Chestnut St (01028-2742)
PHONE....................................413 526-5150
Jeffrey Ansell, *Principal*
EMP: 5
SALES (corp-wide): 13.9B **Publicly Held**
SIC: 3546 Power-Driven Handtools, Nsk
HQ: Black & Decker (U.S.) Inc.
1000 Stanley Dr
New Britain CT 06053
860 225-5111

(G-10469)
CARTAMUNDI EAST LONGMEADOW LLC
443 Shaker Rd (01028-3124)
PHONE....................................413 526-2000
Jeffrey Lombard, *CEO*
Joseph Francisco, *Facilities Mgr*
Joshua Desjarlais, *Project Engr*
Eric Defilipi, *CFO*
Lisa Denver, *Manager*
▼ **EMP:** 400
SQ FT: 1,200,000
SALES (est): 146.4MM
SALES (corp-wide): 177.9K **Privately Held**
SIC: 3944 3999 Mfg Games/Toys Mfg Misc Products
PA: Cartamundi
Visbeekstraat 22
Turnhout
144 202-01

(G-10470)
CREATIVE SERVICES
788 Somers Rd (01028-2930)
PHONE....................................413 525-4993
Donald Coombs, *Principal*
EMP: 4
SALES (est): 355.8K **Privately Held**
SIC: 3714 Mfg Motor Vehicle Parts/Accessories

(G-10471)
DAVRIEL JEWELERS INC
Also Called: Davriel Promotions
37 Harkness Ave (01028-1042)
P.O. Box 590 (01028-0590)
PHONE....................................413 525-4975
Joseph Hershon, *President*
EMP: 3
SQ FT: 800
SALES: 900K **Privately Held**
SIC: 3915 7631 5944 7389 Mfg Jewelers' Materials Watch/Clock/Jewelry Repair Ret Jewelry

(G-10472)
DESIGNING HEALTH INC
302 Benton Dr (01028-3208)
PHONE....................................661 257-1705
Robert M Collett, *CEO*
Bernard Collett, *CEO*
Nate Armstrong, *Vice Pres*
▲ **EMP:** 27
SQ FT: 9,000
SALES (est): 5.9MM **Privately Held**
WEB: www.designinghealth.com
SIC: 2833 5961 2048 5499 Mfg Medicinal/Botanicals Ret Mail-Order House Mfg Prepared Feeds Ret Misc Foods

(G-10473)
DIEBOLT & COMPANY
341 Shaker Rd (01028-3125)
P.O. Box 744, Old Lyme CT (06371-0744)
PHONE....................................860 434-2222
Mark Diebolt, *CEO*
EMP: 15
SQ FT: 30,000 **Privately Held**
SIC: 3491 Mfg Industrial Valves
PA: Diebolt & Company
18 Riverview Dr
Old Lyme CT 06371

(G-10474)
DUC-PAC CORPORATION
21 Baldwin St (01028-2231)
PHONE....................................413 525-3302
Carl F Fisher, *President*
Greg Merchant, *General Mgr*
Douglas Fisher, *Vice Pres*
Rudolph J Fisher, *Treasurer*
EMP: 35 **EST:** 1955
SQ FT: 15,000
SALES (est): 6.7MM **Privately Held**
WEB: www.ducatipacifica.com
SIC: 3444 3585 3567 Mfg Sheet Metalwork Mfg Refrigeration/Heating Equipment Mfg Industrial Furnaces/Ovens

(G-10475)
EXCEL DRYER INC
357 Chestnut St (01028-2742)
P.O. Box 365 (01028-0365)
PHONE....................................413 525-4531
Denis Gagnon, *President*
Bruce Bohmer, *Vice Pres*
Bill Gagnon, *Vice Pres*
Denis G Gagnon Jr, *Vice Pres*
William Gagnon, *Vice Pres*
▲ **EMP:** 50
SQ FT: 35,000
SALES (est): 15.1MM **Privately Held**
WEB: www.exceldryer.com
SIC: 3699 Mfg Electrical Equipment/Supplies

(G-10476)
GENSCOPE INC
18 Deer Park Dr (01028-3196)
P.O. Box 386 (01028-0386)
PHONE....................................413 526-0802
David A Reeves, *President*
EMP: 10
SQ FT: 5,000
SALES: 2MM **Privately Held**
WEB: www.genesysinstruments.com
SIC: 3827 Mfg Optical Instruments/Lenses

(G-10477)
GROUP FOUR TRANSDUCERS INC (PA)
22 Deer Park Dr (01028-3196)
PHONE....................................413 525-2705
Steve Torres, *President*
▲ **EMP:** 13
SQ FT: 5,000
SALES: 5.1MM **Privately Held**
WEB: www.group-4.com
SIC: 3825 Mfg Transducers For The Scale And Weight Industry

(G-10478)
HAMPDEN ENGINEERING CORP
99 Shaker Rd (01028-2762)
P.O. Box 563 (01028-0563)
PHONE....................................413 525-3981
John M Flynn, *President*
John D Flynn, *Vice Pres*
Michael J Flynn, *Vice Pres*
Sheila R Flynn, *Treasurer*
Kim Dixon, *Human Res Mgr*
▲ **EMP:** 85 **EST:** 1954
SQ FT: 50,000
SALES (est): 24.2MM **Privately Held**
WEB: www.hampden.com
SIC: 3825 Mfg Electrical Measuring Instruments

(G-10479)
INDUSTRIAL ETCHING INC
Also Called: Northeast Screen Graphics
21 Fisher Ave (01028-1707)
P.O. Box 304 (01028-0304)
PHONE....................................413 525-4110
Dan Major, *President*
Paul Major, *Shareholder*
Tom Isham, *Graphic Designe*
EMP: 13 **EST:** 1958
SQ FT: 17,500
SALES (est): 2.4MM **Privately Held**
WEB: www.industrialetching.com
SIC: 2759 3479 Commercial Printing Coating/Engraving Service

(G-10480)
IRWIN INDUSTRIAL TOOL COMPANY
Also Called: Lenox Division
301 Chestnut St (01028-2742)
PHONE....................................413 525-3961
Paul Drumheller, *Branch Mgr*
EMP: 800
SALES (corp-wide): 13.9B **Publicly Held**
SIC: 3423 Mfg Hand/Edge Tools
HQ: Irwin Industrial Tool Company
8935 N Pointe Exec Pk Dr
Huntersville NC 28078
704 987-4555

(G-10481)
JOMA DIAMOND TOOL COMPANY
46 Baldwin St Ste A (01028-2232)
P.O. Box 68 (01028-0068)
PHONE....................................413 525-0760
John Basiliere, *Partner*
P D Crane, *Partner*
Brian Hembdt, *Manager*
EMP: 10
SQ FT: 2,000
SALES: 500K **Privately Held**
WEB: www.jomatool.com
SIC: 3545 5085 Mfg Machine Tool Accessories Whol Industrial Supplies

(G-10482)
LETS YO YOGURT
436 N Main St (01028-1850)
PHONE....................................413 525-4002
EMP: 3
SALES (est): 139.6K **Privately Held**
SIC: 2026 Mfg Fluid Milk

(G-10483)
MACKENZIE VAULT INC
165 Benton Dr (01028-3214)
P.O. Box 264 (01028-0264)
PHONE....................................413 525-8827
Neil G McKenzie, *President*
Brad Austin, *Mfg Staff*
Jeremy Pietrowski, *Director*
EMP: 13
SQ FT: 5,000
SALES (est): 1.2MM **Privately Held**
WEB: www.mackenzievault.com
SIC: 3281 Mfg Marble Cast Stone Urns

(G-10484)
NEWELL BRANDS INC
Also Called: Lenox
301 Chestnut St (01028-2742)
PHONE....................................413 526-5150
Shawn Shea, *Opers Mgr*
John Guzzo, *Opers Staff*
Daniel Rhodes, *Technical Staff*
Bill Wilder, *Director*
Dave Robinson, *Director*
EMP: 500
SALES (corp-wide): 8.6B **Publicly Held**
SIC: 3089 Mfg Plastic Products
PA: Newell Brands Inc.
6655 Pachtree Dunwoody Rd
Atlanta GA 30328
770 418-7000

(G-10485)
PELICAN PRODUCTS INC
60 Shaker Rd Ste 14 (01028-2760)
PHONE....................................413 525-3990
Jim Rooney, *Branch Mgr*
EMP: 3
SALES (corp-wide): 208.2MM **Privately Held**
SIC: 3161 Mfg Luggage
PA: Pelican Products, Inc.
23215 Early Ave
Torrance CA 90505
310 326-4700

(G-10486)
PMS PRINTING INC (PA)
175 Benton Dr Ste 100 (01028-3216)
PHONE....................................860 563-1676
James Stemnerman, *President*
Mark Maid, *Vice Pres*
EMP: 3
SQ FT: 1,200
SALES (est): 280.3K **Privately Held**
SIC: 2752 Lithographic Commercial Printing

(G-10487)
POSTAL INSTANT PRESS (PA)
Also Called: PIP Printing
175 Benton Dr Ste 100 (01028-3216)
PHONE....................................413 525-4044
Robert Pelzek, *President*
Michael Tarby, *Vice Pres*
Claudia Pelzek, *Treasurer*
Vicki Tarby, *Clerk*
EMP: 5
SQ FT: 2,000
SALES (est): 1.9MM **Privately Held**
SIC: 2752 7334 2791 Lithographic Commercial Printing Photocopying Services Typesetting Services

(G-10488)
PRECISION FEEDING SYSTEMS INC
45 Deer Park Dr (01028-3198)
P.O. Box 630, Hampden (01036-0630)
PHONE....................................413 525-9200
Raymond C Legary, *President*
Caroline Bayne, *Manager*
EMP: 8
SQ FT: 5,000
SALES (est): 1.3MM **Privately Held**
SIC: 3569 Mfg Vibratory Feeding Equipment

(G-10489)
PROCESS SOLUTIONS INC
198 Benton Dr (01028-3204)
PHONE....................................413 525-5870
Carlton Nappin, *President*
▼ **EMP:** 7
SALES (est): 790K **Privately Held**
SIC: 3861 Chemical Mixing Company

(G-10490)
QUAD/GRAPHICS INC
Springfield Division
245 Benton Dr (01028-3221)
P.O. Box 328 (01028-0328)
PHONE....................................413 525-8552
Len Fitzmaurice, *Branch Mgr*
EMP: 130
SALES (corp-wide): 4.1B **Publicly Held**
WEB: www.vertisinc.com
SIC: 2759 7331 2752 Commercial Printing Direct Mail Advertising Services Lithographic Commercial Printing
PA: Quad/Graphics Inc.
N61w23044 Harrys Way
Sussex WI 53089
414 566-6000

(G-10491)
REMINDER PUBLICATIONS
Also Called: The Childsplay
280 N Main St Ste 1 (01028-1865)
PHONE....................................413 525-3947
Dan Buendo, *Publisher*
Barbara Perry, *Vice Pres*
Noreen Brennan, *Purch Agent*
Martine Iampetro, *Human Res Dir*
Nancy Banning, *Executive*
EMP: 35
SQ FT: 4,500
SALES (est): 3.1MM **Privately Held**
WEB: www.reminderpublications.com
SIC: 2711 2791 2741 Newspapers-Publishing/Printing Typesetting Services Misc Publishing

(G-10492)
SHAFIIS INC (PA)
Also Called: Copycat Print Shop
50 Industrial Dr (01028-3102)
P.O. Box 215 (01028-0215)
PHONE....................................413 224-2100
Jennifer R Shafii, *CEO*
Reza M Shafii, *President*
Larry Adams, *Vice Pres*
Chris Malloy, *Production*
Dan Allie, *Sales Staff*
▲ **EMP:** 25
SQ FT: 20,000
SALES: 12.4MM **Privately Held**
WEB: www.tigerpress.com
SIC: 2752 7334 Lithographic Commercial Printing Photocopying Services

(G-10493)
SPRINGFIELD SPRING CORPORATION (PA)
311 Shaker Rd (01028-3125)
P.O. Box 505 (01028-0505)
PHONE....................................413 525-6837
Norman L Rodriques, *President*
Tina Malley, *Vice Pres*
Bob Ferriter, *Prdtn Mgr*
Ryan Nadeau, *Opers Staff*
Nate Gaudet, *Accounting Mgr*
EMP: 42
SQ FT: 15,000
SALES (est): 9.2MM **Privately Held**
WEB: www.springfieldspring.com
SIC: 3469 3495 Mfg Metal Stampings Mfg Wire Springs

(G-10494)
STREAMLINE PLASTICS CO INC
35 Industrial Dr (01028-3162)
PHONE....................................718 401-4000
Joseph Bartner, *President*
Stewart Bartner, *Vice Pres*
EMP: 35 **EST:** 1939
SALES (est): 7.3MM **Privately Held**
SIC: 3089 Mfg Plastic Products (Custom Extrusion Profiles Custom Injection Molding)

(G-10495)
SUDDEKOR LLC
82 Deer Park Dr (01028-3196)
PHONE....................................413 525-4070
Andrei Scottsman,
▲ **EMP:** 30
SALES (est): 6.5MM **Privately Held**
SIC: 2671 Mfg Packaging Paper/Film

(G-10496)
TAYLOR RENTAL CENTER
Also Called: Taylor Rentl Ctr E Longmeadows
200 Shaker Rd (01028)
PHONE....................................413 525-2576
Pierre Chapdelaine, *President*
EMP: 4
SALES (est): 521.1K **Privately Held**
SIC: 3694 7539 Mfg Engine Electrical Equipment Automotive Repair

(G-10497)
TECHNI-PRODUCTS INC
126 Industrial Dr (01028-3102)
P.O. Box 215 (01028-0215)
PHONE....................................413 525-6321
Margery Morehardt, *President*
Bruce Morehardt, *Vice Pres*
Robert C Morehardt Jr, *Vice Pres*
EMP: 35
SQ FT: 33,000
SALES: 4.5MM **Privately Held**
WEB: www.techni-products.com
SIC: 3599 3444 Mfg Industrial Machinery Mfg Sheet Metalwork

(G-10498)
TONER PLASTICS INC
35 Industrial Dr (01028-3162)
PHONE....................................413 789-1300
Steven L Graham, *President*
Jeffrey Walters, *President*
Jean M Graham, *Clerk*
▲ **EMP:** 35
SQ FT: 120,000
SALES (est): 9.3MM **Privately Held**
WEB: www.tonerplastics.com
SIC: 3089 Mfg Plastic Products

(G-10499)
TRE OLIVE LLC
180 Shaker Rd (01028-2733)
P.O. Box 139 (01028-0139)
PHONE....................................617 680-0096
Alexandro Falvo,
Peppino Maruca,
EMP: 5
SALES (est): 340K **Privately Held**
SIC: 2079 Mfg Edible Fats/Oils

(G-10500)
U S FLUIDS INC
198 Benton Dr 202 (01028-3204)
PHONE....................................413 525-0660
Carlton Mappin, *President*
Richard Daniel Tufo, *Treasurer*
EMP: 6
SQ FT: 35,000
SALES: 3MM **Privately Held**
SIC: 2833 Mfg Medicinal/Botanical Products

(G-10501)
VOLO AERO MRO INC
140 Industrial Dr (01028-3102)
P.O. Box 955 (01028-0955)
PHONE....................................413 525-7211
Andrew Walmsley, *President*
EMP: 7
SQ FT: 3,500
SALES (est): 732K **Privately Held**
WEB: www.citationinc.com
SIC: 3599 Machine Shop/Jig Grinding

(G-10502)
VULCAN INDUSTRIES INC
16 Deer Park Dr (01028-3196)
P.O. Box 714 (01028-0714)
PHONE....................................413 525-8846
Jan Liao, *President*
Joe Reale, *Vice Pres*
▲ **EMP:** 7
SALES (est): 803.3K **Privately Held**
SIC: 3562 Mfg Ball/Roller Bearings

(G-10503)
W F YOUNG INCORPORATED (PA)
302 Benton Dr (01028-3210)
PHONE....................................800 628-9653
Tyler F Young, *President*
Adam D Raczkowski, *President*
Jim Baldyga, *Opers Staff*
Jean Young, *Treasurer*
Cindy Hamlin, *Accounting Mgr*
◆ **EMP:** 25 **EST:** 1892
SALES (est): 5.2MM **Privately Held**
WEB: www.absorbine.com
SIC: 2834 Mfg Pharmaceutical Preparations

East Otis
Berkshire County

(G-10504)
WILLIAMS STONE CO INC
1158 Lee Westfield Rd (01029-4538)
P.O. Box 278 (01029-0278)
PHONE....................................413 269-4544
Edwin C Williams, *President*
Charlotte I Williams, *Treasurer*
Jon Ertl, *Sales Staff*
Ron Mack, *Maintence Staff*
EMP: 40
SQ FT: 50,000
SALES (est): 6.4MM **Privately Held**
WEB: www.williamsstone.com
SIC: 3281 1411 3272 Mfg Cut Stone/Products Dimension Stone Quarry Mfg Concrete Products

East Sandwich
Barnstable County

(G-10505)
CAPE COLON HYDROTHERAPY
74 Mill Rd (02537-1649)
PHONE....................................508 833-9855
Pamela McDermott, *Principal*
EMP: 4 **EST:** 2010
SALES (est): 211.3K **Privately Held**
SIC: 3845 Mfg Electromedical Equipment

(G-10506)
CRANE COMPOSITION INC
23 Ploughed Neck Rd (02537-1048)
P.O. Box 208, Sagamore Beach (02562-0208)
PHONE....................................774 338-5183
Thomas Lewis, *President*
Theodore D Dunn, *Vice Pres*
EMP: 9
SALES (est): 650K **Privately Held**
SIC: 2791 Typesetting Services

(G-10507)
PAUL WHITE WOODCARVING
295 Route 6a (02537-1308)
P.O. Box 323, Cotuit (02635-0323)
PHONE....................................508 888-1394
Paul J White, *Owner*
Paul Schrader, *Owner*
EMP: 4
SALES: 180K **Privately Held**
WEB: www.paulwhitewoodcarving.com
SIC: 2499 Mfg Wood Products

(G-10508)
RELCOR INC
10 Jacobs Meadow Rd (02537-1080)
PHONE....................................561 844-8335
Lazzaro Fattori, *CEO*
Armando Diaz, *President*
◆ **EMP:** 5
SQ FT: 2,500
SALES: 200K **Privately Held**
WEB: www.relcor.com
SIC: 3429 Mfg Hardware

East Taunton
Bristol County

(G-10509)
ADVANCED TRIMWRIGHT INC
103 Old Colony Ave Unit 8 (02718-1141)
P.O. Box 278 (02718-0278)
PHONE....................................508 822-7745
▲ **EMP:** 26
SQ FT: 45,000
SALES (est): 3.6MM **Privately Held**
SIC: 2431 Mfg Millwork

(G-10510)
ARK-LES CONNECTORS CORPORATION
350 Revolutionary Dr (02718-1368)
PHONE....................................781 297-6324
EMP: 10
SALES (est): 1.5MM **Privately Held**
SIC: 3643 Mfg Conductive Wiring Devices

(G-10511)
BROUILLETTE HVAC & SHTMTL INC
13 Stevens St (02718-1026)
PHONE....................................508 822-4800
Donald Provencher, *President*
Carlton A Caron, *Asst Sec*
EMP: 8 **EST:** 2010
SALES (est): 1.7MM **Privately Held**
SIC: 3444 Mfg Sheet Metalwork

(G-10512)
EMAGINE
73 Stevens St 1e (02718)
PHONE....................................508 692-9522
Bill Gadless, *Owner*
Kathryn Morris, *Project Mgr*
Anne Barbetto, *Office Mgr*
Daniel McVay, *Web Dvlpr*
EMP: 5
SALES (est): 489.6K **Privately Held**
SIC: 7372 Prepackaged Software Services

(G-10513)
G AND JW ELDING INC ✪
468 Wren St (02718-5143)
PHONE....................................774 565-0223
EMP: 8 **EST:** 2019
SALES (est): 88.7K **Privately Held**
SIC: 7692 Welding Repair

(G-10514)
J W FISHERS MFG INC
1953 County St (02718-1322)
PHONE....................................508 822-7330
Karen Fisher, *President*
Brian Fisher, *COO*
EMP: 11
SALES (est): 1.1MM **Privately Held**
WEB: www.jwfishers.com
SIC: 3812 Mfg Search/Navigation Equipment

(G-10515)
KENNETRON INC
103 Old Colony Ave Unit 3 (02718-1141)
P.O. Box 218 (02718-0218)
PHONE....................................508 828-9363
Kenny Dang, *President*
Vaugan Enokian, *Vice Pres*
David Hogan, *Treasurer*
EMP: 6
SALES (est): 500K **Privately Held**
WEB: www.kennetron.com
SIC: 3679 Mfg Electronic Components

(G-10516)
NORWELL MFG CO INC
82 Stevens St (02718-1398)
PHONE....................................508 822-2831
Alan Indursky, *President*
Ruth Parr, *Vice Pres*
▲ **EMP:** 42 **EST:** 1947
SQ FT: 72,000
SALES (est): 8.5MM **Privately Held**
WEB: www.norwellinc.com
SIC: 3645 Mfg Residential Lighting Fixtures

(G-10517)
PANCON CORPORATION (PA)
350 Revolutionary Dr (02718-1368)
PHONE....................................781 297-6000
Mike Kirkman, *CEO*
Jason Fricks, *Materials Mgr*
Ernie Abdon, *Engineer*
Tim Mullin, *Controller*
Ronald Levine, *Admin Sec*
▲ **EMP:** 98
SALES (est): 38.1MM **Privately Held**
SIC: 3613 Mfg Switchgear/Switchboards

(G-10518)
STRAFELLO PRECAST INC
250 Cape Hwy Ste 12 (02718-1552)
PHONE....................................774 501-2628
EMP: 13
SALES (corp-wide): 1.1MM **Privately Held**
SIC: 3272 Mfg Concrete Products
PA: Strafello Precast Inc
601 Pleasant St
Stoughton MA

East Templeton
Worcester County

(G-10519)
KAYJAY FOODS INC
119 Patriots Rd (01438)
PHONE....................................978 833-0728
Thomas G O Brien, *Principal*
EMP: 3 **EST:** 2010
SALES (est): 178K **Privately Held**
SIC: 2099 Mfg Food Preparations

(G-10520)
RAGGED HILL INCORPORATED
Also Called: Graves Concrete
147 Gardner Rd (01438)
P.O. Box 680 (01438-0680)
PHONE....................................978 939-5712
John Fletcher, *President*
James Fletcher, *Treasurer*
Tom Dow, *Manager*
Lynn McAvene, *Clerk*
EMP: 29 **EST:** 1997
SALES: 12MM **Privately Held**
SIC: 3273 Mfg Ready-Mixed Concrete

(G-10521)
TRELLIS STRUCTURES INC
25 N Main St (01438)
PHONE..................................888 285-4624
David Valcovic, *President*
Patricia Cornell, *Partner*
EMP: 14
SQ FT: 2,500
SALES: 843K **Privately Held**
SIC: 2431 Mfg Exterior And Ornamental Woodwork & Trim & Trellises

East Walpole
Norfolk County

(G-10522)
COMMERCIAL GEAR SPROCKET INC
618 Washington St (02032-1300)
PHONE..................................508 668-1073
Thomas Shaw, *President*
Harold Boden, *President*
Margaret A Shaw, *Clerk*
EMP: 13 **EST:** 1946
SQ FT: 7,500
SALES: 1MM **Privately Held**
WEB: www.commercialgear.com
SIC: 3566 Mfg Speed Changers/Drives

(G-10523)
GSK INNOVATIONS
17 Woodland Rd (02032-1212)
PHONE..................................508 566-5212
Kerry Leppo, *Branch Mgr*
EMP: 6
SALES (corp-wide): 40.6B **Privately Held**
WEB: www.gskinnovations.com
SIC: 2834 Mfg Pharmaceutical Preparations
HQ: Glaxosmithkline Finance Plc
G S K House
Brentford MIDDX TW8 9
208 047-5000

(G-10524)
HOLLINGSWORTH & VOSE COMPANY (PA)
112 Washington St (02032-1098)
PHONE..................................508 850-2000
Val Hollingsworth, *President*
Jean Francois, *Vice Pres*
David Von Loesecke, *Vice Pres*
John S Madej, *CFO*
Michael Byrne, *Credit Mgr*
◆ **EMP:** 250 **EST:** 1728
SQ FT: 125,000
SALES (est): 726MM **Privately Held**
WEB: www.hovo.com
SIC: 2621 3053 2297 2499 Paper Mill Mfg Gasket/Packing/Seals Mfg Nonwoven Fabrics Mfg Wood Products

(G-10525)
INNOVATIVE DEVELOPMENT INC
153 Washington St Ste 9 (02032-1163)
PHONE..................................508 668-9080
Marc Freedgood, *President*
EMP: 3
SALES (est): 279.3K **Privately Held**
WEB: www.innovative-development.net
SIC: 3944 Mfg Games/Toys

(G-10526)
MASS COATING CORP
Also Called: McC
7 Endean Dr (02032-1041)
P.O. Box 193 (02032-0193)
PHONE..................................347 325-0001
Jay Song, *President*
EMP: 9
SALES (est): 1.3MM **Privately Held**
SIC: 3479 Coating/Engraving Service

(G-10527)
PAUL PARRINO
25 Coney St (02032-1246)
PHONE..................................508 668-2936
Paul Parrino, *Principal*
EMP: 3
SALES (est): 184K **Privately Held**
SIC: 3572 Mfg Computer Storage Devices

(G-10528)
PEGGY LAWTON KITCHENS INC
255 Washington St (02032-1199)
P.O. Box 33 (02032-0033)
PHONE..................................508 668-1215
William Wolf, *President*
EMP: 25 **EST:** 1949
SQ FT: 30,000
SALES (est): 2.7MM **Privately Held**
SIC: 2052 Mfg Cookies/Crackers/Brownies

(G-10529)
PRIMROSE MEDICAL INC
286 Union St (02032-1037)
PHONE..................................508 660-8688
Fletcher T Longley, *President*
Tom Kottelles, *Manager*
▲ **EMP:** 10
SQ FT: 4,000
SALES: 600K **Privately Held**
SIC: 3841 Mfg Surgical/Medical Instruments

East Wareham
Plymouth County

(G-10530)
FIRESLATE 2 INC
3065 Cranberry Hwy A24 (02538-1325)
P.O. Box 431, Buzzards Bay (02532-0431)
PHONE..................................508 273-0047
Thomas B Worthen, *President*
EMP: 12
SQ FT: 9,000
SALES (est): 1.2MM **Privately Held**
WEB: www.fireslate.com
SIC: 3272 Mfg/Converts Man-Made Concrete Panels To Stove Boards Fireplace Surrounds & Solar Floors

(G-10531)
KENT PEARCE
Also Called: Kent's Welding & Radiator Svc
3039 Cranberry Hwy (02538-1357)
P.O. Box 175 (02538-0175)
PHONE..................................508 295-3791
Kent Pearce, *Owner*
EMP: 4
SQ FT: 1,440
SALES (est): 357.5K **Privately Held**
SIC: 7692 3548 7539 5013 Welding Repair Mfg Welding Apparatus Automotive Repair Whol Auto Parts/Supplies Mfg Sheet Metalwork

East Weymouth
Norfolk County

(G-10532)
A & M WELDING FABRICATION INC
276 Libbey Indus Pkwy 2 (02189-3102)
PHONE..................................781 335-9548
Joseph A Mortland II, *President*
Geraldine Mortland, *Treasurer*
▲ **EMP:** 5
SQ FT: 15,000
SALES (est): 546K **Privately Held**
SIC: 7692 3444 Welding Repair Mfg Sheet Metalwork

(G-10533)
AGGREGATE INDUSTRIES - MWR INC
611 Pleasant St (02189-3201)
PHONE..................................781 337-2304
Alan Shabet, *Branch Mgr*
EMP: 21
SALES (corp-wide): 4.5B **Privately Held**
SIC: 3273 Mfg Ready-Mixed Concrete
HQ: Aggregate Industries - Mwr, Inc.
2815 Dodd Rd
Eagan MN 55121
651 683-0600

(G-10534)
ALMONT COMPANY INC
Also Called: Boxerbrand
293 Libbey Indstrl Pkwy (02189-3112)
PHONE..................................617 269-8244
David E Salk, *President*
◆ **EMP:** 25
SALES (est): 3.5MM **Privately Held**
WEB: www.boxerbrand.com
SIC: 2392 Mfg Household Furnishings

(G-10535)
AMERICAN METALCRAFT CO
55 Woodrock Rd Ste 12 (02189-2343)
PHONE..................................781 331-8588
Bryan Anderson, *President*
EMP: 3
SALES (est): 508.1K **Privately Held**
SIC: 3441 5031 Structural Metal Fabrication Whol Lumber/Plywood/Millwork

(G-10536)
ART FOR A CAUSE LLC
Also Called: Art For Literacy
224 Libbey Indus Pkwy (02189-3102)
PHONE..................................248 645-3966
EMP: 45
SQ FT: 5,984
SALES: 3MM **Privately Held**
WEB: www.artforacause.com
SIC: 3423 Mfg Hand/Edge Tools

(G-10537)
BATES BROS SEAM FACE GRAN CO
611 Pleasant St (02189-3201)
PHONE..................................781 337-1150
James Bristol, *CEO*
Mary Bristol, *Corp Secy*
EMP: 13
SQ FT: 15,000
SALES (est): 1.3MM **Privately Held**
WEB: www.batesbrothers.com
SIC: 3281 Mfg Cut Stone/Products

(G-10538)
BRADY ENTERPRISES INC (PA)
167 Moore Rd (02189-2332)
P.O. Box 890099 (02189-0002)
PHONE..................................781 682-6280
John J Brady, *Ch of Bd*
Kevin Maguire, *President*
Charles Leduc, *Research*
Mary A Gudolawicz, *CFO*
▲ **EMP:** 80
SQ FT: 160,000
SALES (est): 21.1MM **Privately Held**
WEB: www.brady-ent.com
SIC: 2099 2087 2842 Mfg Food Preparations Mfg Flavor Extracts Mfg Polish/Sanitation Gd

(G-10539)
BUCKEYE INTERNATIONAL INC
Also Called: Buckeye Cleaning Center
65 Mathewson Dr Ste Q (02189-2347)
PHONE..................................617 827-2137
Dan Coney, *Manager*
EMP: 4
SALES (corp-wide): 111MM **Privately Held**
WEB: www.buckeyeinternational.com
SIC: 2842 2841 Mfg Polish/Sanitation Goods Mfg Soap/Other Detergents
PA: Buckeye International, Inc.
2700 Wagner Pl
Maryland Heights MO 63043
314 291-1900

(G-10540)
CUTLASS MARINE INC
Also Called: CMI
55 Woodrock Rd Ste 8 (02189-2343)
PHONE..................................781 740-1260
Fred Caldwell, *President*
Joe Munsch, *President*
EMP: 4
SQ FT: 3,600
SALES: 500K **Privately Held**
SIC: 3732 3353 3312 Boatbuilding/Repairing

(G-10541)
DRESCO BELTING CO INC
122 East St (02189-2198)
PHONE..................................781 335-1350
Robert Dresser Jr, *Shareholder*
James G Dresser, *Shareholder*
Norman K Dresser, *Shareholder*
EMP: 8 **EST:** 1929
SQ FT: 1,500
SALES (est): 1.2MM **Privately Held**
WEB: www.drescobelt.com
SIC: 3052 Fabricates Rubber Belting

(G-10542)
FRANCER INDUSTRIES INC
44 Wharf St (02189-2251)
P.O. Box 890124 (02189-0003)
PHONE..................................781 337-2882
Sidney H Francer, *President*
Gary Francer, *Principal*
Stephen M Francer, *Treasurer*
EMP: 20
SQ FT: 100,000
SALES (est): 3.4MM **Privately Held**
SIC: 3444 5074 Mfg Sheet Metalwork Whol Plumbing Equipment/Supplies

(G-10543)
KENNEDY SHEET METAL INC
1319 Pleasant St (02189-2797)
PHONE..................................781 331-7764
James B Kennedy Sr, *President*
Don Macneill, *Manager*
EMP: 25
SQ FT: 9,000
SALES (est): 1.7MM **Privately Held**
SIC: 3444 1711 Mfg Sheet Metalwork Plumbing/Heating/Air Cond Contractor

(G-10544)
KINGSTON WIND INDEPENDENCE LLC
649 Broad St (02189-2041)
PHONE..................................781 871-8200
Bradford S Cleaves, *Mng Member*
Duncan S Peterson, *Mng Member*
Kially M Ruiz,
EMP: 3
SALES: 500K **Privately Held**
SIC: 3511 Mfg Turbines/Generator Sets

(G-10545)
L D G CORPORATION
Also Called: Unique Woodworking
143 Moore Rd (02189-2332)
PHONE..................................781 337-7155
Gary Medeiros, *President*
EMP: 7
SQ FT: 5,000
SALES (est): 1.1MM **Privately Held**
SIC: 2522 Mfg Office Furniture-Nonwood

(G-10546)
S M LORUSSO & SONS INC
Also Called: Lorusso-Bristol Stone
611 Pleasant St (02189-3201)
P.O. Box 890144, Weymouth (02189-0003)
PHONE..................................781 337-6770
Bob Bedard, *Manager*
EMP: 24
SQ FT: 1,991
SALES (corp-wide): 29.4MM **Privately Held**
SIC: 3281 Crushed/Broken Limestone
PA: S. M. Lorusso & Sons, Inc.
331 West St
Walpole MA 02081
508 668-2600

(G-10547)
ZIGGY WOODWORKING
60 Charles St (02189-1841)
PHONE..................................781 335-5218
EMP: 4
SALES (est): 332.1K **Privately Held**
SIC: 2431 Mfg Millwork

Eastham
Barnstable County

(G-10548)
CAPE COD DOG
3 Main St Unit 1 (02642-2169)
PHONE..................................508 255-4206
Katrina Boucher, *Owner*
EMP: 3
SALES (est): 110K **Privately Held**
SIC: 3999 Mfg Misc Products

(G-10549)
HOLE IN ONE
Also Called: Hole In One Donut Shop
4295 Us 6 (02642)
P.O. Box 854, North Eastham (02651-0854)
PHONE..................................508 255-5359
Gaetano Bazzano, *Partner*
Cindy Bazzano, *Principal*
EMP: 40
SQ FT: 5,933
SALES (est): 4.3MM **Privately Held**
SIC: 2051 5461 5812 Mfg Bread/Related Products Retail Bakery Eating Place

(G-10550)
LOWER CAPE SAND AND GRAVEL INC
2740 Nauset Rd (02642-1720)
P.O. Box 766, North Eastham (02651-0766)
PHONE..................................508 255-2839
Nathan Nickerson, *Owner*
EMP: 3
SALES (est): 287.2K **Privately Held**
SIC: 1442 Construction Sand/Gravel

Easthampton
Hampshire County

(G-10551)
ABBY PRINTING CO INC
Also Called: Abbey Printing
58 Oneil St (01027-1104)
PHONE..................................413 536-5269
Mark Goodwin, *CEO*
Paula Goodwin, *Vice Pres*
Kathleen V McCabe, *Director*
EMP: 4
SQ FT: 1,700
SALES (est): 440K **Privately Held**
SIC: 2759 2752 2791 Commercial Printing Lithographic Commercial Printing Typesetting Services

(G-10552)
ADHESIVE APPLICATIONS INC
45 Ferry St (01027-1203)
PHONE..................................413 527-7120
Lyn Doran, *Technical Staff*
EMP: 3
SALES (est): 143.6K **Privately Held**
SIC: 2891 Mfg Adhesives/Sealants

(G-10553)
ADHESIVE APPLICATIONS INC
Also Called: Stik-II Products
41 Oneil St (01027-1103)
P.O. Box 71 (01027-0071)
PHONE..................................413 527-7120
Michael Schaefer, *President*
Gary Litman, *President*
Wayne Tangel, *President*
Chandresh Thakur, *Engineer*
Jennifer Gazda, *Sales Staff*
◆ **EMP:** 45
SQ FT: 40,000
SALES (est): 17.9MM **Privately Held**
SIC: 2891 Mfg Adhesives/Sealants

(G-10554)
ADHESIVE TAPES INTL INC
41 Oneil St (01027-1103)
PHONE..................................203 792-8279
Dieter Woll, *President*
Fred Macaluso, *Treasurer*
◆ **EMP:** 8
SALES (est): 1.3MM **Privately Held**
WEB: www.atitapes.com
SIC: 3842 Mfg Surgical Appliances/Supplies

(G-10555)
BERRY GLOBAL INC
44 Oneil St (01027-1146)
PHONE..................................812 424-2904
Steve Rafter, *Branch Mgr*
EMP: 228 **Publicly Held**
SIC: 3089 Mfg Plastic Products
HQ: Berry Global, Inc.
101 Oakley St
Evansville IN 47710
812 424-2904

(G-10556)
BERRY PLASTICS CORP
122 Pleasant St (01027-1358)
P.O. Box 567 (01027-0567)
PHONE..................................413 529-2183
Braun Wilson, *Manager*
▲ **EMP:** 12 **EST:** 2009
SALES (est): 1.6MM **Privately Held**
SIC: 3089 Mfg Plastic Products

(G-10557)
BERRY PLASTICS CORPORATION
44 Oneil St (01027-1146)
P.O. Box 567 (01027-0567)
PHONE..................................413 527-1250
Michael Gutowski, *Plant Mgr*
EMP: 5
SALES (est): 422.7K **Privately Held**
SIC: 3089 Mfg Plastic Products

(G-10558)
DAILY HAMPSHIRE GAZETTE
72 Main St (01027-2049)
PHONE..................................413 527-4000
Louis Groccia, *President*
EMP: 3
SALES (est): 109.4K **Privately Held**
SIC: 2711 Newspapers-Publishing/Printing

(G-10559)
DANS MACHINE
14a Nashawannuck St (01027-2432)
PHONE..................................413 529-9635
Dan Krug, *Owner*
EMP: 5
SALES (est): 239.4K **Privately Held**
SIC: 3499 Mfg Misc Fabricated Metal Products

(G-10560)
DZI
150 Pleasant St Ste 320 (01027-1547)
PHONE..................................413 527-4500
Mac Coy, *Principal*
▲ **EMP:** 11
SALES (est): 1.6MM **Privately Held**
SIC: 3621 Mfg Motors/Generators

(G-10561)
EASTHAMPTON MACHINE & TOOL INC
72 Parsons St (01027-1550)
PHONE..................................413 527-8770
Christopher Heon, *President*
EMP: 9
SQ FT: 5,000
SALES: 542.5K **Privately Held**
SIC: 3599 Mfg Industrial Machinery

(G-10562)
EASTHAMPTON PRECISION MFG INC
16 Arthur St (01027-1202)
PHONE..................................413 527-1650
Jeremy Segal, *President*
EMP: 8 **EST:** 1989
SQ FT: 12,200
SALES (est): 1.5MM **Privately Held**
SIC: 3599 Mfg Industrial Machinery

(G-10563)
ERICH HUSEMOLLER IMPORT & EXPO
116 Pleasant St Ste 229 (01027-2753)
PHONE..................................413 585-9855
Erich Husemoller, *President*
Alison Sinkler, *Vice Pres*
▲ **EMP:** 5
SQ FT: 600
SALES: 1.5MM **Privately Held**
SIC: 2284 5198 Thread Mill Whol Paints/Varnishes

(G-10564)
GAZETTE PRINTING CO INC
58 Oneil St (01027-1157)
PHONE..................................413 527-7700
Mark Goodwyn, *President*
EMP: 14 **EST:** 1874
SQ FT: 8,500
SALES (est): 2.2MM **Privately Held**
WEB: www.gazetteprintingcompany.com
SIC: 2752 2759 Offset Printing

(G-10565)
INFLIGHT CORPORATION
1 Cottage St Ste 5-19 (01027-1672)
PHONE..................................413 203-2056
James La Brash, *Managing Dir*
John Bonin, *Principal*
EMP: 6
SALES (est): 495.2K **Privately Held**
SIC: 7372 Prepackaged Software Services

(G-10566)
JANNA UGONE & ASSOCIATES INC
1 Cottage St Unit 6 (01027-1773)
PHONE..................................413 527-5530
Janna Ugone, *President*
Brad Albert, *Sales Staff*
Deborah Symanski, *Manager*
EMP: 18
SQ FT: 2,200
SALES (est): 3MM **Privately Held**
SIC: 3645 3646 Mfg Residential And Commercial Lighting Fixtures Custom And Standard

(G-10567)
MICHAEL BRISEBOIS
Also Called: Mountainbase Mold & Mfg
6 Industrial Pkwy (01027-1164)
PHONE..................................413 527-9590
Michael P Brisebois, *Owner*
EMP: 12
SQ FT: 3,000
SALES (est): 1.6MM **Privately Held**
SIC: 3545 Tool & Die Shop

(G-10568)
NATIONAL NONWOVENS INC (PA)
110 Pleasant St (01027-1342)
P.O. Box 150 (01027-0150)
PHONE..................................413 527-3445
Anthony J Centofanti, *Ch of Bd*
William Spencer, *Vice Pres*
Paul Viveiros, *Vice Pres*
Robert Oliveira, *Controller*
Sandra Daigle, *Marketing Staff*
◆ **EMP:** 75
SQ FT: 115,000
SALES (est): 36.3MM **Privately Held**
WEB: www.nationalnonwovens.com
SIC: 2231 2297 Wool Broadwoven Fabric Mill Mfg Nonwoven Fabrics

(G-10569)
NATIONAL NONWOVENS INC
Also Called: Wool Felt Division
27 Mechanic St (01027-1561)
PHONE..................................413 527-3445
Ken Piazzo, *Branch Mgr*
EMP: 35
SALES (corp-wide): 36.3MM **Privately Held**
WEB: www.nationalnonwovens.com
SIC: 2299 Mfg Felt Products
PA: National Nonwovens Inc.
110 Pleasant St
Easthampton MA 01027
413 527-3445

(G-10570)
NATIONAL NONWOVENS INC
180 Pleasant St (01027-1287)
PHONE..................................413 527-3445
Anthony J Centofanti, *Manager*
EMP: 35
SALES (corp-wide): 36.3MM **Privately Held**
WEB: www.nationalnonwovens.com
SIC: 2231 2297 Mfg Wool Felts & Non-Woven Fabrics
PA: National Nonwovens Inc.
110 Pleasant St
Easthampton MA 01027
413 527-3445

(G-10571)
NORTHAMPTON MACHINE CO INC
Also Called: Baystate Machine Co.
16 Industrial Pkwy (01027-1164)
PHONE..................................413 529-2530
Frank Basile, *President*
Vincent Basile, *VP Opers*
EMP: 21 **EST:** 1975
SQ FT: 10,800
SALES (est): 3.8MM **Privately Held**
SIC: 3599 Mfg Industrial Machinery

(G-10572)
OCTOBER COMPANY INC (PA)
Also Called: Chemetal Division
51 Ferry St (01027-1235)
P.O. Box 71 (01027-0071)
PHONE..................................413 527-9380
H Michael Schaefer, *President*
Paul St Georges, *Engineer*
Greg Squire, *Info Tech Mgr*
James Thompson, *Executive*
David J Podolski, *Admin Sec*
▲ **EMP:** 159 **EST:** 1959
SQ FT: 150,000
SALES (est): 20MM **Privately Held**
WEB: www.octobercompany.com
SIC: 3499 2599 Mfg Misc Fabricated Metal Products Mfg Furniture/Fixtures

(G-10573)
OCTOBER COMPANY INC
Also Called: Chemetal Division
39 Oneil St (01027-1103)
PHONE..................................413 529-0718
Leo Forrest, *Natl Sales Mgr*
Dottie Patterson, *Office Mgr*
H Michael Schaefer-Chm, *Manager*
Joe Wozniak, *Administration*
Steve Perrier,
EMP: 40
SQ FT: 45,000
SALES (corp-wide): 20MM **Privately Held**
WEB: www.chemetalco.com
SIC: 3499 3083 Mfg Misc Fabricated Metal Products Mfg Laminated Plastic Plate/Sheet
PA: The October Company Inc
51 Ferry St
Easthampton MA 01027
413 527-9380

(G-10574)
OVERLOOK INDUSTRIES INC
193 Northampton St Ste 2 (01027-1074)
P.O. Box 869 (01027-0869)
PHONE..................................413 527-4344
John Morin, *President*
EMP: 15
SQ FT: 10,000
SALES: 500K **Privately Held**
WEB: www.overlookindustries.com
SIC: 3559 Mfg Of Pharmaceutical And Cosmetic Equip

(G-10575)
PHILIPP MANUFACTURING CO INC
19 Ward Ave (01027-2214)
PHONE..................................413 527-4444
Herman R Tauscher, *President*
Elwood W Beebe, *Clerk*
EMP: 85 **EST:** 1875
SQ FT: 50,000
SALES (est): 12.5MM **Privately Held**
SIC: 3442 Mfg Metal Doors

(G-10576)
PRAXIS BOOKBINDING
Also Called: Praxis Bindery
1 Cottage St Unit 18 (01027-1667)
PHONE..................................413 527-7275
Peter Geraty, *Owner*
EMP: 3
SALES: 90K **Privately Held**
WEB: www.praxisbindery.com
SIC: 2789 Bookbinding Services

(G-10577)
ROCK VALLEY TOOL LLC
54 Oneil St (01027-1169)
PHONE..................................413 527-2350
Elizabeth Paquette, *President*
Jason Paquette,
EMP: 34
SQ FT: 20,000
SALES (est): 6.6MM **Privately Held**
WEB: www.rockvalleytool.com
SIC: 3599 Mfg Industrial Machinery

(G-10578)
SET AMERICAS INC
180 Pleasant St Ste 207 (01027-1356)
PHONE..................................413 203-6130
Christopher Bakker, *CEO*
Burt Snover, *CTO*
EMP: 7
SALES: 1MM **Privately Held**
SIC: 3823 Mfg Process Control Instruments

(G-10579)
SMAALL BEER PRESS
150 Pleasant St Ste 306 (01027-1264)
PHONE..................................413 203-1636
Kelly Link, *Principal*
EMP: 4
SALES (est): 266.4K **Privately Held**
SIC: 2741 Misc Publishing

(G-10580)
STONE SOUP CONCRETE
122 Pleasant St Ste B (01027-1359)
PHONE..................................413 203-5600
Michael Paulsen, *Partner*
Michael Kramody, *Partner*
EMP: 7 **EST:** 2001
SALES: 250K **Privately Held**
WEB: www.stonesoupconcrete.com
SIC: 3272 Mfg Concrete Products Mfg Concrete Products

(G-10581)
TECH180 CORP
Also Called: Tech180 System
180 Pleasant St Ste 211 (01027-1356)
PHONE..................................413 203-6123
Christopher Bakker, *CEO*
Roy Walker, *Principal*
Burt Snober, *Principal*
Sarah Robinson, *Administration*
EMP: 10
SALES: 500K **Privately Held**
SIC: 3825 5049 5999 Mfg Electrical Measuring Instruments Whol Professional Equipment Ret Misc Merchandise

(G-10582)
VAN PELT CAPITAL PRECISION INC
69 Ferry St Ste 10 (01027-1286)
PHONE..................................413 527-1204
Gerald J Van Pelt, *President*
EMP: 10
SQ FT: 1,200
SALES: 1.2MM **Privately Held**
SIC: 3724 Mfg Aircraft Engines/Parts

(G-10583)
YANKEE HILL MACHINE CO INC
412 Main St (01027-1918)
PHONE..................................413 584-1400
James J Graham, *President*
Bonita Graham, *Treasurer*
Sherry Barcomb, *Info Tech Mgr*
Paul Tetreault, *Info Tech Mgr*
EMP: 85
SQ FT: 38,000
SALES (est): 14.8MM **Privately Held**
WEB: www.yhm.net
SIC: 3451 Mfg Screw Machine Products

Easton
Bristol County

(G-10584)
LECAM MACHINE INC
7 Renker Dr (02356)
P.O. Box 297, South Easton (02375-0297)
PHONE..................................508 588-2300
Lee Camarra, *President*
Michael Cammara, *Vice Pres*
EMP: 3
SALES: 500K **Privately Held**
SIC: 3599 Mfg Industrial Machinery

Edgartown
Dukes County

(G-10585)
INNOVATIVE PUBLISHING CO LLC
91 Litchfield Rd (02539-4317)
P.O. Box 980 (02539-0980)
PHONE..................................267 266-8876
Rick Biros, *Mng Member*
Beth Biros,
EMP: 10
SALES: 1.4MM **Privately Held**
SIC: 2741 8742 7389 Misc Publishing Management Consulting Services Business Serv Non-Commercial Site

(G-10586)
MEDDEVICE CONCEPTS LLC
Also Called: Statvideo
34 Fuller St (02539)
PHONE..................................617 834-7420
James Rueter, *Officer*
Albert S Kyle,
EMP: 4
SALES: 50K **Privately Held**
WEB: www.med-device.com
SIC: 3699 Mfg Information Technology Equipment/Supplies

(G-10587)
MICROTRONIC INC
5 Peases Point Rd (02539)
P.O. Box 3359 (02539-3359)
PHONE..................................508 627-8951
Reiner Fenske, *President*
EMP: 25
SALES (est): 335.1K **Privately Held**
SIC: 3674 Mfg Semiconductors/Related Devices

(G-10588)
VINEYARD GAZETTE LLC (PA)
34 S Summer St (02539-8104)
P.O. Box 66 (02539-0066)
PHONE..................................508 627-4311
Jane Seagraee, *Principal*
Nicole Mercier, *Assistant*
EMP: 35 **EST:** 1846
SQ FT: 15,000
SALES (est): 2.7MM **Privately Held**
WEB: www.mvgazette.com
SIC: 2711 2731 Newspapers-Publishing/Printing Books-Publishing/Printing

Erving
Franklin County

(G-10589)
ERVING INDUSTRIES INC (PA)
Also Called: Erving Paper Mills
97 E Main St (01344-9717)
PHONE..................................413 422-2700
Charles B Housen, *Ch of Bd*
Morris Housen, *President*
William Wescott, *CFO*
Marjorie G Housen, *Director*
Jennifer Johnson, *Lab Dir*
◆ **EMP:** 130
SQ FT: 250,000
SALES (est): 39.8MM **Privately Held**
WEB: www.ervingpaper.com
SIC: 2621 2676 Paper Mill Mfg Sanitary Paper Products

(G-10590)
ERVING PAPER MILLS INC
97 E Main St (01344-9717)
PHONE..................................413 422-2700
Charles B Housen, *Ch of Bd*
Morris Housen, *President*
Denis L Emmett, *CFO*
▼ **EMP:** 125
SQ FT: 300,000
SALES (est): 16MM
SALES (corp-wide): 39.8MM **Privately Held**
WEB: www.ervingpaper.com
SIC: 2621 Paper Mill
PA: Erving Industries, Inc.
97 E Main St
Erving MA 01344
413 422-2700

Essex
Essex County

(G-10591)
ATLANTIC INDUSTRIAL MODELS LLC
7 Essex Park Rd (01929-1125)
PHONE..................................978 768-7686
Joseph Fassa,
EMP: 22
SQ FT: 5,000
SALES (est): 3.5MM **Privately Held**
WEB: www.atlanticind.com
SIC: 3999 3443 Mfg Industrial Models & Metal Parts

(G-10592)
COLLINS MANUFACTURING INC
239 Western Ave (01929-1102)
PHONE..................................978 768-2553
Robert J Collins, *President*
Kevin T Collins, *Regional Mgr*
Ben Swann, *Opers Mgr*
Terry Boone, *Purch Mgr*
Eleanor A Collins, *Treasurer*
EMP: 13
SQ FT: 11,000
SALES (est): 2MM **Privately Held**
SIC: 3599 Machine Shop Mfg Precision Machined Parts

(G-10593)
GLASS DIMENSION INC
197 Western Ave (01929-1115)
P.O. Box 220 (01929-0004)
PHONE..................................978 768-7984
David R Perkins, *President*
Darrell Perkins, *CFO*
Maureen Perkins, *Treasurer*
Perkins David, *Senior Mgr*
▼ **EMP:** 25
SQ FT: 30,000
SALES (est): 2.2MM **Privately Held**
WEB: www.glassdimensions.com
SIC: 3229 5947 3231 Mfg Pressed/Blown Glass Ret Gifts/Novelties Mfg Products-Purchased Glass

(G-10594)
JETO ENGINEERING INC
191 Western Ave (01929-1115)
PHONE..................................978 768-6472
Thomas M Weinburg, *President*
▲ **EMP:** 11
SQ FT: 1,600
SALES (est): 1.7MM **Privately Held**
WEB: www.jetoeng.com
SIC: 3599 Mfg Industrial Machinery

(G-10595)
MARBLEHEAD ENGINEERING
7 Essex Park Rd (01929-1125)
PHONE..................................978 432-1386
David Gardner, *Owner*
EMP: 11
SQ FT: 4,800
SALES: 1.2MM **Privately Held**
WEB: www.dpglawyer.com
SIC: 3449 8711 7692 3444 Mfg Misc Structural Mtl Engineering Services Welding Repair Mfg Sheet Metalwork

(G-10596)
MEZZANINE SAFETI GATES INC
Also Called: Roly Safeti-Gate
174 Western Ave (01929-1110)
PHONE..................................978 768-3000
James M Conway, *President*
Aaron Conway, *Vice Pres*
EMP: 7
SQ FT: 4,500
SALES (est): 1.1MM **Privately Held**
WEB: www.mezzaninesafetygates.com
SIC: 3446 5084 Mfg Mezzanine Safety Gates

(G-10597)
RICHARDS DEAN CUSTOM WDWKG
17 Winthrop St (01929-1203)
PHONE..................................978 768-7104
Dean Richards, *President*
Patrica Richards, *Treasurer*
EMP: 4
SALES (est): 432K **Privately Held**
SIC: 2434 Mfg Woodworking Machinery

(G-10598)
WE DREAM IN COLUR LLC
31 Forest Ave (01929-1430)
PHONE..................................978 768-0168
EMP: 6
SALES (est): 376.6K **Privately Held**
SIC: 3911 5094 5961 Mfg /Whol/Ret Jewelery

Everett
Middlesex County

(G-10599)
ACROSS USA INC
91 Summer St 1 (02149-3746)
PHONE..................................617 678-0350
Julyana C Macedo, *Principal*
EMP: 4 **EST:** 2013
SALES (est): 334.3K **Privately Held**
SIC: 3624 Mfg Carbon/Graphite Products

(G-10600)
ACS GROUP INC
27 Carter St (02149-2501)
PHONE..................................617 381-0822
Mucio M Aquino, *Principal*
EMP: 12 **EST:** 2008
SALES (est): 1.7MM **Privately Held**
SIC: 3621 Mfg Motors/Generators

(G-10601)
ADVOCATE NEWSPAPERS (PA)
573 Broadway (02149-3712)
P.O. Box 490407 (02149-0006)
PHONE..................................617 387-2200
James Mitchell, *President*
EMP: 5
SALES (est): 520.9K **Privately Held**
SIC: 2711 Newspapers-Publishing/Printing

(G-10602)
ALVIN PRODUCTS INC
85 Paris St (02149-4411)
PHONE..................................978 975-4580
Dennis Aikman, *President*
EMP: 5
SALES (est): 664.7K **Privately Held**
WEB: www.alvinproducts.com
SIC: 2992 Mfg Lubricating Oils/Greases

(G-10603)
AVACEA
102 Edith St (02149-1749)
PHONE..................................617 294-0261
Candrew Macdonald, *Owner*
EMP: 3
SALES: 100K **Privately Held**
WEB: www.avacea.com
SIC: 3669 Mfg Communications Equipment

(G-10604)
BAY STATE GALVANIZING INC
128 Spring St 132 (02149-4505)
PHONE..................................617 389-0671
Gary Dubinsky, *President*
Feth Dubinsky, *Vice Pres*
Seth Dubinsky, *Vice Pres*
EMP: 15
SQ FT: 28,000
SALES (est): 2.1MM **Privately Held**
WEB: www.baystategalvanizing.com
SIC: 3479 3471 2899 Coating/Engraving Service Plating/Polishing Service Mfg Chemical Preparations

(G-10605)
BYD CORP
Also Called: By Design Screen Printing
167 Bow St Ste 2 (02149-3339)
PHONE..................................617 394-0799
Joseph Curreri, *President*

▲ = Import ▼=Export
◆ =Import/Export

EMP: 3
SQ FT: 5,000
SALES (est): 236.6K **Privately Held**
WEB: www.bydesignscreenprinting.com
SIC: 2759 Commercial Printing

(G-10606)
CLIVES JAMS LLC
32 Freeman Ave (02149-5205)
PHONE..................................617 294-9766
Michelle Audrey Cronin, *Principal*
EMP: 3 **EST:** 2017
SALES (est): 125.8K **Privately Held**
SIC: 2033 Mfg Canned Fruits/Vegetables

(G-10607)
COLEMAN MANUFACTURING CO INC
48 Waters Ave (02149-2099)
PHONE..................................617 389-0380
Richard W Coleman, *President*
EMP: 6
SQ FT: 20,000
SALES (est): 550K **Privately Held**
SIC: 3297 5169 Mfg Nonclay Refractories Whol Chemicals/Products

(G-10608)
COLONIAL MARBLE CO INC
25 Garvey St (02149-4499)
PHONE..................................617 389-1130
Stephen B Fichera, *CEO*
EMP: 7
SQ FT: 120
SALES (est): 963.8K **Privately Held**
SIC: 2493 1743 Mfg Reconstd Wood Prdts Tile/Marble Contractor

(G-10609)
DAMPNEY COMPANY INC
85 Paris St (02149-4411)
PHONE..................................617 389-2805
Raymond K Pavlik, *President*
Peter Barrett, *Vice Pres*
Harvey Kacamburas, *Plant Mgr*
Tim Eggers, *Sales Staff*
EMP: 25 **EST:** 1917
SQ FT: 43,000
SALES (est): 9.8MM **Privately Held**
WEB: www.dampney.com
SIC: 2851 Mfg Paints/Allied Products

(G-10610)
DUNCAN GALVANIZING CORPORATION
69 Norman St Ste 2 (02149-1946)
PHONE..................................617 389-8440
Richard L Brooks, *Ch of Bd*
Abby Brooks, *President*
Dan Bever, *CFO*
EMP: 56 **EST:** 1912
SQ FT: 62,000
SALES (est): 9MM **Privately Held**
WEB: www.duncangalvanizing.com
SIC: 3479 Coating/Engraving Service

(G-10611)
FRUIT BASKET WORLD DIVISION
210 Beacham St (02149-5505)
P.O. Box 6178, Chelsea (02150-0010)
PHONE..................................617 389-8989
EMP: 20
SALES (est): 1.4MM **Privately Held**
SIC: 2448 Mfg Wood Pallets/Skids

(G-10612)
GREEN SUMMER
Also Called: Glenwood Press
308 Main St (02149-5724)
PHONE..................................617 387-0120
Summer Green, *Owner*
EMP: 3 **EST:** 1940
SQ FT: 450
SALES (est): 190K **Privately Held**
SIC: 2759 2752 Commercial Printing Lithographic Commercial Printing

(G-10613)
HI-TECH PLATING INC
69 Norman St Ste 2 (02149-1946)
PHONE..................................617 389-3400
Richard L Brooks, *President*
Dan Bever, *Vice Pres*
Barry C Brooks, *Treasurer*
EMP: 15
SQ FT: 15,000
SALES (est): 1.2MM **Privately Held**
SIC: 3471 Plating/Polishing Service

(G-10614)
L & M MACHINE INC
115 Tremont St (02149-1132)
PHONE..................................617 294-0378
Ann H Moran, *President*
Richard C Moran, *Admin Sec*
EMP: 20 **EST:** 1957
SQ FT: 15,000
SALES (est): 2.2MM **Privately Held**
WEB: www.lmmachine.net
SIC: 3599 Mfg Industrial Machinery

(G-10615)
LEADER PUBLISHING CO INC
Also Called: News Gazette
28 Church St (02149-2719)
PHONE..................................617 387-4570
Joseph Curnane Jr, *President*
Elizabeth Curnnane, *Treasurer*
EMP: 5 **EST:** 1940
SALES (est): 282.9K **Privately Held**
SIC: 2711 Newspaper Publisher

(G-10616)
LEAVITT CORPORATION (HQ)
Also Called: Teddie Peanut Butter
100 Santilli Hwy (02149-1938)
PHONE..................................617 389-2600
Mark Hintlian, *President*
Frank Ciampa, *President*
James Hintlian Jr, *Treasurer*
Michael Spivey, *Admin Sec*
◆ **EMP:** 102 **EST:** 1925
SQ FT: 100,000
SALES (est): 17.4MM
SALES (corp-wide): 252.1K **Privately Held**
WEB: www.teddie.com
SIC: 2099 2068 Mfg Food Preparations Mfg Salted/Roasted Nuts/Seeds
PA: Shaghalians Incorporated
100 Santilli Hwy
Everett MA 02149
617 389-2600

(G-10617)
LILLYS GASTRONOMIA ITALIAN
Also Called: Lilly's Fresh Pasta
208 Main St (02149-5736)
PHONE..................................617 387-9666
Pasqualina D'Alelio, *President*
Antonio D'Alelio, *Vice Pres*
▲ **EMP:** 11
SQ FT: 3,000
SALES: 4MM **Privately Held**
SIC: 2099 Mfg Food Preparations

(G-10618)
LIMA FREDY
Also Called: Boston Iron Works
69 Norman St Ste 17 (02149-1946)
PHONE..................................781 599-3055
Fredy Lima, *Owner*
Daniel Dennis, *Principal*
EMP: 10 **EST:** 2009
SALES (est): 989.6K **Privately Held**
SIC: 7692 Welding Repair

(G-10619)
LOGAN GRATE INC
42 Lynde St (02149-3232)
PHONE..................................617 569-5280
Vincenzio Grimaldi, *President*
EMP: 5
SQ FT: 6,000
SALES (est): 672.2K **Privately Held**
SIC: 3442 Mfg Of Steel Doors

(G-10620)
M & M GARMENT MANUFACTURING
167 Bow St Ste 2 (02149-3339)
PHONE..................................617 389-7787
Kim M Phung, *President*
EMP: 11
SALES (est): 665.6K **Privately Held**
SIC: 2339 2329 Mfg Apparel/Accessories

(G-10621)
MARIOS OIL CORP
22 Forest Ave (02149-2622)
P.O. Box 490216 (02149-0009)
PHONE..................................617 202-8259
Mario Martinez, *President*
EMP: 9
SQ FT: 11,000
SALES (est): 550.8K **Privately Held**
SIC: 3433 Mfg Heating Equipment-Non-electric

(G-10622)
MKL STONE LLC
100 Ashland St (02149-3301)
PHONE..................................781 844-9811
Matthew Kent Luther,
EMP: 3
SALES (est): 72.6K **Privately Held**
SIC: 1499 3281 5032 Nonmetallic Mineral Mining Mfg Cut Stone/Products Whol Brick/Stone Material

(G-10623)
NINOS IRONWORKS
57 Kelvin St (02149-1830)
PHONE..................................617 389-6603
Anthony Dellanno, *Owner*
EMP: 3
SALES (est): 255K **Privately Held**
WEB: www.ninosironworks.com
SIC: 3446 Mfg Architectural Metalwork

(G-10624)
PASHI INC
167 Bow St Ste 3 (02149-3339)
PHONE..................................617 304-2742
Elise Pashigian, *President*
▲ **EMP:** 5
SQ FT: 7,000
SALES (est): 572.2K **Privately Held**
WEB: www.pashi.net
SIC: 2339 Mfg Women's/Misses' Outerwear

(G-10625)
PEELFLY INC
Also Called: Peel, LLC
25 Charlton St Apt 425 (02149-2471)
PHONE..................................860 608-3819
Brian M Sullivan, *CEO*
EMP: 3 **EST:** 2015
SALES (est): 71.1K **Privately Held**
SIC: 7372 8732 Prepackaged Software Services Commercial Nonphysical Research

(G-10626)
RELIABLE FABRICS INC
Also Called: House of Kobrin
29 Henderson St (02149-2610)
PHONE..................................617 387-5321
Charles Schultz, *President*
Lily Schultz, *CIO*
EMP: 25 **EST:** 1928
SQ FT: 15,000
SALES (est): 2.3MM **Privately Held**
WEB: www.reliablefabrics.com
SIC: 2391 5714 5719 Mfg Custom Draperies Ret Custom Draperies Window Furnishings Bedding & Linens

(G-10627)
RICHIES KING SLUSH MFG CO INC
Also Called: Richie's Classic Italian Ice
3 Garvey St (02149-4403)
PHONE..................................800 287-5874
Richard Cardillo, *President*
Pamela Cardillo, *Vice Pres*
Frati Thomas, *Vice Pres*
Michael McPherson, *Manager*
EMP: 15
SQ FT: 15,000
SALES (est): 3.3MM **Privately Held**
WEB: www.richiesslush.com
SIC: 2024 Mfg Ice Cream/Frozen Desert

(G-10628)
ROLAND TEINER COMPANY INC
134 Tremont St (02149-1135)
PHONE..................................617 387-7800
Fax: 617 381-9270
EMP: 15 **EST:** 1946
SQ FT: 20,000
SALES: 629.5K **Privately Held**
SIC: 3469 3444 3599 7692 Mfg Metal Stampings Mfg Sheet Metalwork Mfg Industrial Machinery Welding Repair

(G-10629)
RUBBERRIGHT ROLLERS INC
101 Tileston St (02149-1928)
PHONE..................................617 387-6060
Stephen Ottaviano, *President*
EMP: 7
SQ FT: 5,000
SALES (est): 145.4K **Privately Held**
WEB: www.rubberright.com
SIC: 3069 Mfg Fabricated Rubber Products

(G-10630)
SALS CLOTHING & FABRIC RESTOR
15 Henderson St (02149-2610)
PHONE..................................617 387-6726
Sal Barresi, *President*
EMP: 30
SALES (est): 2MM **Privately Held**
SIC: 3842 Mfg Surgical Appliances/Supplies

(G-10631)
SHORT PATH DISTILLERY INC
71 Kelvin St (02149-1923)
PHONE..................................617 830-7954
Jackson Hewlett, *Principal*
Danielle Mendiola, *Sales Staff*
EMP: 6 **EST:** 2015
SALES (est): 367.2K **Privately Held**
SIC: 2085 Mfg Distilled/Blended Liquor

(G-10632)
STATE-LINE GRAPHICS INC
6 Victoria St Ste 109 (02149-3533)
P.O. Box 490587 (02149-0010)
PHONE..................................617 389-1200
Arthur F Berardino, *President*
Stephen T Berardino, *Vice Pres*
EMP: 12
SQ FT: 15,000
SALES (est): 1.8MM **Privately Held**
WEB: www.statelinegraphics.com
SIC: 2752 4226 5112 Lithographic Commercial Printing Special Warehouse/Storage Whol Stationery/Office Supplies

(G-10633)
UNIVERSAL SCREENING STUDIO INC
175 Ferry St (02149-5634)
PHONE..................................617 387-1832
Robert Noe, *President*
EMP: 8
SQ FT: 10,000
SALES (est): 140K **Privately Held**
WEB: www.universalscreeningstudio.com
SIC: 2396 7336 2395 Mfg Auto/Apparel Trimming Commercial Art/Graphic Design Pleating/Stitching Services

(G-10634)
WORLD STONE
142 Hancock St (02149-1331)
PHONE..................................617 293-4373
John Neto, *Principal*
EMP: 3 **EST:** 2004
SALES (est): 114.1K **Privately Held**
SIC: 1411 Dimension Stone Quarry

Fairhaven
Bristol County

(G-10635)
ACUSHNET COMPANY (DH)
333 Bridge St (02719-4900)
P.O. Box 965 (02719-0965)
PHONE..................................508 979-2000
David Maher, *CEO*
Walter R Uihlein, *CEO*
Joanne Deneault, *General Mgr*
Rick Papreck, *General Mgr*
Gerald Bellis, *Exec VP*
◆ **EMP:** 1445
SQ FT: 760,000

GEOGRAPHIC

SALES (est): 1.3B **Publicly Held**
WEB: www.titleist.com
SIC: 3949 3149 2381 Mfg Sport/Athletic Goods Mfg Footwear-Ex Rubber
HQ: Acushnet Holdings Corp.
333 Bridge St
Fairhaven MA 02719
800 225-8500

(G-10636)
ACUSHNET HOLDINGS CORP (HQ)
333 Bridge St (02719-4905)
PHONE....................800 225-8500
David Maher, *President*
Mary Lou Bohn, *President*
John Duke Jr, *President*
Christopher Lindner, *President*
Steven Pelisek, *President*
EMP: 23
SQ FT: 222,720
SALES: 1.6B **Publicly Held**
SIC: 3949 Mfg Golf Equipment

(G-10637)
ACUSHNET INTERNATIONAL INC (DH)
333 Bridge St (02719-4905)
P.O. Box 965 (02719-0965)
PHONE....................508 979-2000
Peg Nicholson, *CIO*
EMP: 200
SQ FT: 760,000
SALES (est): 46.1MM **Publicly Held**
SIC: 3431 Mfg Metal Sanitary Ware
HQ: Acushnet Holdings Corp.
333 Bridge St
Fairhaven MA 02719
800 225-8500

(G-10638)
BRAHMIN LEATHER WORKS LLC
77 Alden Rd (02719-4618)
PHONE....................509 994-4000
William R Martin,
EMP: 3
SALES (est): 85.1K
SALES (corp-wide): 6.8B **Publicly Held**
SIC: 3161 3171 3172 Mfg Luggage Mfg Womens Handbag/Purse
PA: Markel Corporation
4521 Highwoods Pkwy
Glen Allen VA 23060
804 747-0136

(G-10639)
BROWNELL BOAT TRAILERS INC
129 Alden Rd (02719-4738)
PHONE....................508 996-3110
Robert Gardner, *Principal*
EMP: 6
SQ FT: 1,200
SALES (est): 235.4K **Privately Held**
SIC: 3799 Mfg Transportation Equipment

(G-10640)
BROWNELL TRAILERS LLC
129 Alden Rd (02719-4738)
PHONE....................508 996-3110
John Medeiros,
James P Hayes,
EMP: 11
SALES (est): 2.1MM **Privately Held**
SIC: 3799 Ret Misc Vehicles

(G-10641)
CANVASMITH
31 Fort St (02719-2728)
PHONE....................207 379-2121
Jody Smith, *Owner*
EMP: 3
SALES (est): 155.1K **Privately Held**
SIC: 2394 5091 Mfg Canvas/Related Products Whol Sporting/Recreational Goods

(G-10642)
MIAMI HEAT DISCOUNT FUEL
391 Main St (02719-3435)
PHONE....................508 991-2875
EMP: 3
SALES (est): 198.4K **Privately Held**
SIC: 2869 Mfg Industrial Organic Chemicals

(G-10643)
MONAGHAN PRINTING COMPANY
59 Alden Rd (02719-4639)
PHONE....................508 991-8087
Julia Monaghan, *President*
EMP: 13
SALES (est): 1.7MM **Privately Held**
SIC: 2752 Commercial Printers Specializing In Two Color Commercial Printing And Offset Printing

(G-10644)
NEW BEDFORD THREAD CO INC
10 Howland Rd (02719-3453)
P.O. Box 7072, New Bedford (02742-7072)
PHONE....................508 996-8584
George L Unhoch Jr, *President*
▲ **EMP:** 35 **EST:** 1953
SQ FT: 14,000
SALES (est): 5.1MM **Privately Held**
WEB: www.newbedfordthread.com
SIC: 2284 Thread Mill

(G-10645)
PHARMAHEALTH SPECIALTY/LON
132 Alden Rd (02719-4721)
PHONE....................508 998-8000
EMP: 12
SALES (est): 1.9MM **Privately Held**
SIC: 2834 Mfg Pharmaceutical Preparations

(G-10646)
RJD WOODWORKING LLC
92 Long Rd (02719-4206)
PHONE....................508 984-4315
Richard J Desrosiers, *Principal*
EMP: 4
SALES (est): 22.5K **Privately Held**
SIC: 2431 Mfg Millwork

(G-10647)
S K MACHINE CO INC
83 Harding Rd (02719-4519)
PHONE....................508 993-6387
Stephen King, *President*
Nora L King, *Corp Secy*
EMP: 9
SQ FT: 3,800
SALES (est): 610K **Privately Held**
SIC: 3599 Mfg Industrial Machinery

Fall River
Bristol County

(G-10648)
A BISMARK COMPANY
Also Called: White Dog Press
5 Probber Ln Ste 1 (02720-1342)
PHONE....................508 675-2002
Donald Paquette, *President*
Diana Paquette, *Admin Sec*
EMP: 7
SQ FT: 24,000
SALES: 900K **Privately Held**
WEB: www.whitedogpress.com
SIC: 2741 Misc Publishing

(G-10649)
A L ELLIS INC
113 Griffin St Ste 1 (02724-2773)
PHONE....................508 672-4799
Mike Ellis, *President*
Eva D Ellis, *Corp Secy*
Brad Biancuzzo, *Vice Pres*
Alan Paverman, *Sales Mgr*
Robert Fontaine, *Director*
▲ **EMP:** 73
SQ FT: 10,000
SALES (est): 15.6MM **Privately Held**
WEB: www.elliscurtain.com
SIC: 2391 Mfg Curtains/Draperies

(G-10650)
ACCURATE SERVICES INC
951 Broadway Ste 4 (02724-2769)
P.O. Box 6129 (02724-0697)
PHONE....................508 674-5773
Frank Teixeira, *President*
Suzanne Teixeira, *Vice Pres*
EMP: 25
SALES (est): 5.4MM **Privately Held**
SIC: 2674 5137 5136 2369 Mfg Bags-Uncoated Paper Whol Women/Child Clothng Whol Mens/Boys Clothing Mfg Girl/Child Outerwear Mfg Women/Miss Outerwear

(G-10651)
ALCO TECHNOLOGY
560 Ray St (02720-7208)
PHONE....................508 678-7449
Jean Alves, *President*
EMP: 3
SALES (est): 219.5K **Privately Held**
SIC: 3639 Mfg Household Appliances

(G-10652)
ALDEN ACOREANA REALTY TRUST (PA)
Also Called: Acorean Manufacturing
210 Alden St (02723-1805)
PHONE....................508 678-2098
Antonio Nunes, *Partner*
Marcel Aguire, *Partner*
Maria Nunes, *Partner*
EMP: 7 **EST:** 1968
SQ FT: 5,000
SALES (est): 601.3K **Privately Held**
SIC: 2013 5411 Mfg Prepared Meats Ret Groceries

(G-10653)
ALLERGAN SALES LLC
927 Currant Rd (02720-4712)
PHONE....................508 324-1481
EMP: 7 **Privately Held**
SIC: 2834 Mfg Pharmaceutical Preparations
HQ: Allergan Sales, Llc
2525 Dupont Dr
Irvine CA 92612
862 261-7000

(G-10654)
ALVES BAKING CO
19 Norfolk St (02720-1259)
PHONE....................508 673-8003
Joaquim F Alves, *Principal*
EMP: 4
SALES (est): 201.7K **Privately Held**
SIC: 2051 Mfg Bread/Related Products

(G-10655)
AMERAMESH TECHNOLOGIES INC
218 Shove St (02724-2018)
PHONE....................508 324-9977
EMP: 3 **EST:** 2004
SQ FT: 7,800
SALES (est): 250K **Privately Held**
SIC: 2821 Mfg Plastic Materials/Resins

(G-10656)
AMERICAN DRYER CORPORATION
88 Currant Rd (02720-4781)
PHONE....................508 678-9000
Christopher Fitzgerald, *President*
Michael Davidson, *CFO*
◆ **EMP:** 230 **EST:** 1965
SQ FT: 300,000
SALES (est): 52.4MM
SALES (corp-wide): 21B **Publicly Held**
WEB: www.amdry.com
SIC: 3582 Mfg Commercial Laundry Equipment
PA: Whirlpool Corporation
2000 N M 63
Benton Harbor MI 49022
269 923-5000

(G-10657)
AMERICAN POWER SOURCE INC (PA)
Also Called: American Players
15 Shaw St (02724-1423)
PHONE....................508 672-8847
Roxanne Ferreiro, *President*
EMP: 225
SQ FT: 2,000
SALES (est): 19.5MM **Privately Held**
WEB: www.american-player.com
SIC: 2325 2331 Mfg Men's/Boy's Trousers Mfg Women's/Misses' Blouses

(G-10658)
ANCHOR
887 Highland Ave (02720-3820)
PHONE....................508 675-7151
George Coleman, *President*
EMP: 6
SALES (est): 382.6K **Privately Held**
WEB: www.anchornews.org
SIC: 2711 Newspapers-Publishing/Printing

(G-10659)
ANDERSEN CORPORATION
16 Currant Rd (02720-4726)
PHONE....................508 235-0300
Bob Gates, *Branch Mgr*
EMP: 8
SALES (corp-wide): 2.8B **Privately Held**
SIC: 2431 Mfg Millwork
PA: Andersen Corporation
100 4th Ave N
Bayport MN 55003
651 264-5150

(G-10660)
APPLIED WATER MANAGEMENT INC
21 Father Devalles Blvd # 1 (02723-1519)
PHONE....................508 675-5755
Jeff Marshall, *Branch Mgr*
EMP: 3
SALES (corp-wide): 30MM **Privately Held**
SIC: 3589 Mfg Service Industry Machinery
HQ: Applied Water Management Inc.
2 Clerico Ln Ste 210
Hillsborough NJ 08844

(G-10661)
AQUABOTIX TECHNOLOGY CORP
21 Father Devalles Blvd # 8 (02723-1519)
P.O. Box 255, Jamestown RI (02835-0255)
PHONE....................508 676-1000
David Batista, *CEO*
Derek Daly, *COO*
Durval Tavares, *Chief Engr*
Debra A Tavares, *Admin Sec*
EMP: 20 **EST:** 2011
SALES (est): 4MM **Privately Held**
SIC: 3651 Mfg Home Audio/Video Equipment

(G-10662)
ARCHITECTURAL STAR LTG LLC
21 Father Devalles Blvd # 12 (02723-1519)
PHONE....................508 678-1900
Jason Cyr,
EMP: 13
SALES (est): 2.5MM **Privately Held**
SIC: 3646 Mfg Commercial Lighting Fixtures

(G-10663)
ASHWORTH BROS INC (PA)
222 Milliken Blvd Ste 7 (02721-1623)
PHONE....................508 674-4693
George Boyce, *Vice Ch Bd*
Vincent L Moretti, *President*
Robert Ashworth III, *Principal*
Joseph M Lackner, *Vice Pres*
Paul Steinhoff, *Opers Staff*
▼ **EMP:** 5 **EST:** 1894
SALES (est): 65.8MM **Privately Held**
WEB: www.ashworth.com
SIC: 3535 Mfg Conveyors/Equipment

(G-10664)
ASHWORTH INTERNATIONAL INC
222 Milliken Blvd Ste 7 (02721-1623)
PHONE....................508 674-4693
Sara Dieters, *Branch Mgr*
Robert Ashworth III, *Director*
EMP: 4

▲ = Import ▼=Export
◆ =Import/Export

SALES (est): 301.8K **Privately Held**
SIC: 3086 Mfg Plastic Foam Products

(G-10665)
ATLANTIC LIGHTING INC
231 Commerce Dr (02720-4761)
PHONE..........508 678-5411
Gabe Estrela, *President*
Radu Gafitanu, *Engineer*
Manny Vieira, *Engineer*
Chris Lajoie, *Natl Sales Mgr*
Eduarda Estrela, *Admin Sec*
◆ **EMP:** 29
SQ FT: 18,000
SALES (est): 8.2MM **Privately Held**
SIC: 3646 3645 Mfg Commercial Lighting Fixtures Mfg Residential Lighting Fixtures

(G-10666)
BAKER SIGN WORKS INC
75 Ferry St Ste 5 (02721-1111)
PHONE..........508 674-6600
Linda Baker, *President*
EMP: 10 **EST:** 2008
SALES (est): 1MM **Privately Held**
SIC: 3993 Mfg Signs/Advertising Specialties

(G-10667)
BEES KNEES ZIPPER WAX LLC
11 Courtney St Apt 11 # 11 (02720-6741)
PHONE..........203 521-5727
Linda M Mendonca, *Principal*
EMP: 6
SALES (est): 152.4K **Privately Held**
SIC: 3965 Mfg Fasteners/Buttons/Pins

(G-10668)
BISZKO CONTRACTING CORP
20 Development St (02721-3246)
PHONE..........508 679-0518
Alan Biszko, *President*
EMP: 43
SALES (est): 5.5MM **Privately Held**
SIC: 1389 Oil/Gas Field Services

(G-10669)
BLOUNT FINE FOODS CORP (PA)
630 Currant Rd (02720-4713)
PHONE..........774 888-1300
Ted Blount, *President*
Nelson Blount II, *President*
Jonathan Arena, *Vice Pres*
William Bigelow, *Vice Pres*
Peter Hopkins, *Prdtn Mgr*
▲ **EMP:** 175
SQ FT: 65,000
SALES (est): 80.7MM **Privately Held**
WEB: www.blountseafood.com
SIC: 2092 2038 Mfg Fresh/Frozen Packaged Fish Mfg Frozen Specialties

(G-10670)
BOLGER & OHEARN INC
47 Slade St (02724-1347)
P.O. Box 250 (02724-0250)
PHONE..........508 676-1518
Shaun O'Hearn, *President*
Kelly O'Hearn, *Vice Pres*
◆ **EMP:** 25
SQ FT: 2,500
SALES (est): 7MM **Privately Held**
SIC: 2899 Mfg Chemical Preparations

(G-10671)
BOTELHO WOOD WORKING
21 Reuben St (02723-1620)
PHONE..........774 240-7235
Roberto Botelho, *President*
EMP: 3
SALES (est): 234.2K **Privately Held**
SIC: 2431 Mfg Millwork

(G-10672)
BRENDAN C KINNANE INC
Also Called: Troy City Woodworking
394 Kilburn St (02724-2214)
P.O. Box 279 (02724-0279)
PHONE..........508 679-8479
Brendan C Kinnane, *President*
EMP: 5
SALES (est): 410K **Privately Held**
SIC: 2431 Mfg Millwork

(G-10673)
C H YATES RUBBER CORP
222 Sykes Rd (02720-4728)
PHONE..........508 674-3378
Carlton H Yates, *President*
Dale Yates-Berg, *Exec VP*
Dale Berg, *Vice Pres*
Bob Yates, *Vice Pres*
Edwin Yates, *Vice Pres*
▲ **EMP:** 5
SQ FT: 75,000
SALES (est): 1.3MM **Privately Held**
SIC: 3069 Mfg Fabricated Rubber Products

(G-10674)
CIRCULATION
207 Pocasset St (02721-1532)
PHONE..........508 676-2526
John Rose, *Director*
Norman O Sinclair, *Director*
EMP: 4
SALES (est): 143.2K **Privately Held**
WEB: www.circulation.com
SIC: 2711 Newspapers-Publishing/Printing

(G-10675)
CLEAN PRODUCTS LLC
537 Quequechan St (02721-4004)
PHONE..........508 676-9355
Edward Layne,
Alan Perlman,
Marc Perlman,
EMP: 6 **EST:** 2015
SALES: 9.7MM **Privately Held**
SIC: 3089 Mfg Plastic Products

(G-10676)
CM BEDDING GROUP INC
451 Quarry St (02723-1007)
PHONE..........508 673-1001
David C Nguyen, *President*
EMP: 14
SALES: 2.7MM **Privately Held**
SIC: 2211 Cotton Broadwoven Fabric Mill

(G-10677)
COMMONWEALTH LIQUIDS LLC
537 Quequechan St (02721-4004)
PHONE..........508 676-9355
EMP: 3 **EST:** 2017
SALES (est): 294.5K **Privately Held**
SIC: 2841 Mfg Soap/Other Detergents

(G-10678)
COMMONWLTH SOAP TOILETRIES INC (PA)
Also Called: CST
537 Quequechan St (02721-4004)
PHONE..........508 676-9355
Julie Bergeron, *General Mgr*
Edward N Layne, *Principal*
Bob Durand, *Vice Pres*
Roland Byam, *Accountant*
Louise Goulet, *Human Res Mgr*
▲ **EMP:** 75
SQ FT: 280,000
SALES: 19MM **Privately Held**
WEB: www.cstsoap.com
SIC: 2844 2841 Mfg Toilet Preparations Mfg Soap/Other Detergents

(G-10679)
CONGRUITY 360 LLC
456 Bedford St (02720-4802)
PHONE..........508 689-9516
Sean Brady,
EMP: 51
SALES (corp-wide): 6MM **Privately Held**
SIC: 2752 7336 Lithographic Commercial Printing Commercial Art/Graphic Design
PA: Congruity 360, Llc
93 Longwater Cir Ste 201
Norwell MA 02061
781 829-0140

(G-10680)
CORPORATE IMAGE APPAREL INC
Also Called: CIA Ink
596 Airport Rd (02720-4735)
PHONE..........508 676-3099
Mark N Dumont, *President*
Gilbert Lloyd, *Vice Pres*
▲ **EMP:** 28
SQ FT: 10,000
SALES (est): 2.6MM **Privately Held**
WEB: www.ciainc.com
SIC: 2395 2759 Pleating/Stitching Services Commercial Printing

(G-10681)
CURTAIN MANUFACTURERS PLUS
113 Griffin St (02724-2773)
PHONE..........508 675-8680
Ken Chace, *CEO*
EMP: 50
SALES (est): 3.5MM **Privately Held**
SIC: 2391 Mfg Curtains/Draperies

(G-10682)
DHM THREAD CORPORATION
Also Called: Consolidated Thread Mills
192 Anawan St Ste 301 (02721-1557)
P.O. Box 1107 (02722-1107)
PHONE..........508 672-0032
Donald Ashton, *President*
Consolidated Mills, *Administration*
EMP: 17 **EST:** 1933
SQ FT: 30,000
SALES (est): 2.1MM **Privately Held**
WEB: www.consolidatedthreadmills.com
SIC: 2284 2298 Thread Mill Mfg Cordage/Twine

(G-10683)
DIOCESAN PRESS INC
887 Highland Ave (02720-3820)
P.O. Box 7 (02722-0007)
PHONE..........508 675-3857
George Coleman, *Owner*
EMP: 6
SALES (est): 279K **Privately Held**
WEB: www.diosanjoaquin.org
SIC: 2711 Newspapers-Publishing/Printing

(G-10684)
E-I-E-I-O INCORPORATED
502 Bedford St (02720-4855)
PHONE..........508 324-9311
Karen Golden, *President*
Stephen Oronte, *Vice Pres*
Clifford Bail, *Treasurer*
EMP: 9
SQ FT: 10,000
SALES: 1.4MM **Privately Held**
SIC: 2369 Mfg Girl/Youth Outerwear

(G-10685)
EASTERN ICE COMPANY INC
281 Commerce Dr (02720-4761)
PHONE..........508 672-1800
C Joseph Rossi, *President*
Joseph Rossi, *President*
Robert F Clooney, *Vice Pres*
Chad J Rossi, *Vice Pres*
Craig M Rossi, *Vice Pres*
EMP: 22
SQ FT: 8,000
SALES (est): 4.5MM **Privately Held**
SIC: 2097 5999 Mfg Ice Ret Misc Merchandise

(G-10686)
ECIN INDUSTRIES INC
Also Called: Harvey Bigelow Designs
1 Ace St Unit 2 (02720-1355)
PHONE..........508 675-6920
Patricia Macmillen, *President*
EMP: 31
SQ FT: 53,000
SALES (est): 3.8MM **Privately Held**
WEB: www.ecinindustries.com
SIC: 2515 5712 Mfg Mattresses/Bedsprings Ret Furniture

(G-10687)
ELBE-CESCO INC
Also Called: L B Products
649 Alden St (02723-1826)
P.O. Box 3160 (02722-3160)
PHONE..........508 676-8531
Elliot Comenitz, *President*
EMP: 60
SQ FT: 184,000
SALES (est): 7.3MM
SALES (corp-wide): 7.5MM **Privately Held**
WEB: www.lbproducts.com
SIC: 2675 2782 2759 Mfg Die-Cut Paper/Board Mfg Blankbooks/Binders Commercial Printing
PA: Union Bookbinding Company Inc
649 Alden St
Fall River MA 02723
508 676-8580

(G-10688)
EMCO SERVICES INC
37 Slade St (02724-1347)
PHONE..........508 674-5504
Edward J Mc Namara, *President*
Arthur Nikoro, *Director*
EMP: 9
SALES (est): 440K **Privately Held**
SIC: 2261 2899 Cotton Finishing Plant Mfg Chemical Preparations

(G-10689)
ENTERPRISE PUBLISHING CO LLC
Also Called: Enterprise, The
10 Purchase St (02720-3100)
PHONE..........585 598-0030
EMP: 881
SQ FT: 65,000
SALES (est): 55MM
SALES (corp-wide): 1.5B **Publicly Held**
WEB: www.enterprisenews.com
SIC: 2711 Newspapers-Publishing/Printing
PA: Gannett Co., Inc.
7950 Jones Branch Dr
Mc Lean VA 22102
703 854-6000

(G-10690)
EPHESIAN ARMS INC
112 Tripp St (02724-2424)
PHONE..........508 674-7030
EMP: 6 **EST:** 2013
SQ FT: 4,300
SALES: 25K **Privately Held**
SIC: 3545 Mfg Machine Tool Accessories

(G-10691)
ERGONOMIC PRODUCTS INC
198 Airport Rd (02720-4770)
PHONE..........508 636-2263
David J Ahearn, *CEO*
Jennifer Ahearn, *Admin Sec*
EMP: 23
SALES (est): 3.6MM **Privately Held**
SIC: 3843 Mfg Dental Equipment/Supplies

(G-10692)
EXEMPLAR LABORATORIES LLC
Also Called: Xemplar Pharmaceuticals
200 Riggenbach Rd (02720-4737)
PHONE..........508 676-6726
Richard C Armstrong,
Charles Eck,
▲ **EMP:** 5
SALES (est): 556.8K **Privately Held**
SIC: 2834 Mfg Pharmaceutical Preparations

(G-10693)
EXEMPLAR PHARMA LLC
Also Called: Exemplar Pharmaceuticals
927 Currant Rd (02720-4712)
PHONE..........508 676-6726
Charles R Eck, *President*
Abdul Zahir, *Vice Pres*
EMP: 9
SQ FT: 10,000
SALES (est): 1.2MM **Privately Held**
WEB: www.xemplarpharm.com
SIC: 2834 Pharmaceutical Preparations
HQ: Allergan, Inc.
5 Giralda Farms
Madison NJ 07940
862 261-7000

(G-10694)
FALL RIVER APPAREL INC
1 Ace St Unit 3 (02720-1355)
PHONE..........508 677-1975
Mary Cordeiro, *Owner*
EMP: 7

SALES (est): 407.5K Privately Held
SIC: 2392 2391 2393 2335 Mfg Household Furnishing Mfg Curtains/Drapery Mfg Textile Bags Mfg Women/Misses Dresses

(G-10695)
FALL RIVER BOILER & WELDING CO
Also Called: Fabco Engineering
994 Jefferson St Ste 2 (02721-4823)
P.O. Box 4237 (02723-0413)
PHONE..................................508 677-4479
Raymond A Guay, *President*
Gene N Guay, *Treasurer*
EMP: 6
SQ FT: 25,000
SALES (est): 640K Privately Held
SIC: 3443 3441 Mfg Stainless Steel Tanks & Fabricated Structural Metal Products

(G-10696)
FALL RIVER MFG CO INC
540 Currant Rd (02720-4711)
PHONE..................................508 675-1125
Timothy J Csanadi, *President*
John Conte, *Vice Pres*
David Monti, *Vice Pres*
EMP: 72
SALES (est): 14.2MM Privately Held
SIC: 3452 3316 Mfg Bolts/Screws/Rivets Mfg Cold-Rolled Steel Shapes

(G-10697)
FALL RIVER MODERN PRINTING CO
Also Called: Quick Copy
798 Plymouth Ave (02721-1946)
PHONE..................................508 673-9421
Raymond Schenck, *President*
Donald R Schenck, *Vice Pres*
Richard R Schenck, *Vice Pres*
Rita Schenck, *Treasurer*
EMP: 11 EST: 1948
SQ FT: 2,000
SALES (est): 1.5MM Privately Held
SIC: 2752 2759 Lithographic Commercial Printing

(G-10698)
FALL RIVER READY-MIX CON LLC
245 Tripp St (02724-2434)
P.O. Box 57 (02724-0057)
PHONE..................................508 675-7540
EMP: 4 EST: 2016
SALES (est): 124.7K Privately Held
SIC: 3273 1611 Central-Mixed Concrete

(G-10699)
FALL RIVER TOOL & DIE CO INC
994 Jefferson St Ste 2 (02721-4823)
P.O. Box 4070 (02723-0400)
PHONE..................................508 674-4621
Joseph Fontaine, *President*
Ronald Fontaine, *Vice Pres*
David Fontaine, *Clerk*
EMP: 14 EST: 1947
SQ FT: 25,000
SALES: 1MM Privately Held
SIC: 3364 3544 3089 Mfg Nonferrous Die Castings & Dies And Plastic Injection Molding

(G-10700)
FIELDSTON CLOTHES INC (HQ)
Also Called: Izzi Clothes
40 County St (02723-2104)
PHONE..................................508 646-2900
Isadore Friedman, *Ch of Bd*
Mark Friedman, *President*
Paul Friedman, *Vice Pres*
▲ EMP: 4 EST: 1945
SALES (est): 7.3MM
SALES (corp-wide): 8MM Privately Held
SIC: 2329 2339 Mfg Men's/Boy's Clothing Mfg Women's/Misses' Outerwear
PA: S. Rothschild & Co., Inc.
1407 Broadway Fl 10
New York NY 10018
212 354-8550

(G-10701)
GATEHOUSE MEDIA LLC
Also Called: Herald News, The
207 Pocasset St (02721-1532)
PHONE..................................508 676-8211
Sean Burke, *Branch Mgr*
Mike Niland, *Director*
EMP: 150
SALES (corp-wide): 1.5B Publicly Held
WEB: www.gatehousemedia.com
SIC: 2711 2741 Newspapers-Publishing/Printing Misc Publishing
HQ: Gatehouse Media, Llc
175 Sullys Trl Fl 3
Pittsford NY 14534
585 598-0030

(G-10702)
GENERAL AIRMOTIVE PWR PDTS LLC
994 Jefferson St Ste 10 (02721-4823)
PHONE..................................508 674-6400
Roger Steger,
EMP: 5
SALES (est): 632K Privately Held
SIC: 3357 3728 3663 Nonferrous Wiredrawing/Insulating Mfg Aircraft Parts/Equipment Mfg Radio/Tv Communication Equipment

(G-10703)
GINSCO INC
1572 President Ave (02720-7148)
PHONE..................................508 677-4767
Steven Cohen, *Owner*
EMP: 14
SALES (est): 1MM
SALES (corp-wide): 3.6MM Privately Held
SIC: 2051 Mfg Bread/Related Products
PA: Ginsco Inc
1706 President Ave
Fall River MA 02720
508 677-4767

(G-10704)
GINSCO INC (PA)
Also Called: New York Bagel Co
1706 President Ave (02720-7115)
PHONE..................................508 677-4767
Steve Ginsberg, *President*
Steve Cohen, *Vice Pres*
EMP: 14
SQ FT: 2,000
SALES (est): 3.6MM Privately Held
SIC: 2051 5461 5812 Mfg Whol & Ret Of Bagels Delicatessen & Caterer

(G-10705)
GOLD MEDAL BAKERY INC (PA)
21 Penn St (02724-1276)
P.O. Box I (02724-0391)
PHONE..................................508 674-5766
Roland S Lecomte, *President*
Brian R Lecomte, *Corp Secy*
Roland Lecompte, *Vice Pres*
William Rocha, *Vice Pres*
Wayne Vaillancourt, *Opers Dir*
EMP: 450
SQ FT: 410,000
SALES (est): 114.4MM Privately Held
WEB: www.goldmedalbakery.com
SIC: 2051 Mfg Bread/Related Products

(G-10706)
GRAPHIX PLUS INC
52 Queen St (02724-1422)
P.O. Box 6180 (02724-0697)
PHONE..................................508 677-2122
Christopher Gagnon, *President*
Roger Lachapelle, *Vice Pres*
EMP: 12
SQ FT: 6,000
SALES (est): 2MM Privately Held
SIC: 2752 Lithographic Commercial Printing

(G-10707)
GRIFFIN MANUFACTURING CO INC
502 Bedford St (02720-4855)
P.O. Box 1671 (02722-1671)
PHONE..................................508 677-0048
Gene Laudon, *President*
Olivia Perry, *Admin Sec*
▲ EMP: 200
SQ FT: 60,000
SALES (est): 21.2MM Privately Held
SIC: 2329 2339 Mfg Men's/Boy's Clothing Mfg Women's/Misses' Outerwear

(G-10708)
GS RUBBER INDUSTRIES LLC
104 Anawan St Ste 2 (02721-1521)
PHONE..................................508 672-0742
Joseph Sarlo, *Owner*
Christine Mongeon, *Principal*
EMP: 10
SQ FT: 35,000
SALES (est): 1.2MM Privately Held
WEB: www.gsrubbermfg.com
SIC: 3069 Mfg Fabricated Rubber Products

(G-10709)
H & S TOOL AND ENGINEERING INC
777 Airport Rd (02720-4724)
PHONE..................................508 672-6509
Karl D Hetzler, *President*
Peter Martin, *Buyer*
Lou Almeida, *Supervisor*
EMP: 25
SQ FT: 25,000
SALES (est): 3.9MM Privately Held
SIC: 3599 Mfg Industrial Machinery

(G-10710)
HAGUE TEXTILES INC (PA)
168 Stevens St (02721-5112)
P.O. Box 4206 (02723-0413)
PHONE..................................508 678-7556
Timothy R Couto, *President*
EMP: 3
SALES (est): 1.2MM Privately Held
SIC: 3199 Mfg Leather Goods

(G-10711)
HAGUE TEXTILES INC
168 Stevens St (02721-5112)
P.O. Box 4026 (02723-0401)
PHONE..................................508 678-7556
William Hague, *Branch Mgr*
EMP: 49 Privately Held
SIC: 3172 3199 Mfg Leather Goods
PA: Hague Textiles, Inc.
168 Stevens St
Fall River MA 02721

(G-10712)
HANCOCK MARINE INC
300 River St (02720-1621)
P.O. Box 9341 (02720-0006)
PHONE..................................508 678-0301
Arthur V Hancock, *President*
EMP: 3 EST: 1935
SQ FT: 5,000
SALES (est): 508.7K Privately Held
SIC: 3315 3429 3531 Mfg Steel Wire/Related Products Mfg Hardware Mfg Construction Machinery

(G-10713)
HEVEATEX CORPORATION
106 Ferry St Ste 1 (02721-1113)
P.O. Box 2573 (02722-2573)
PHONE..................................508 675-0181
Paul Valentine, *President*
Grafton Corbett, *Clerk*
◆ EMP: 17
SQ FT: 30,000
SALES (est): 1.9MM
SALES (corp-wide): 44.4MM Privately Held
WEB: www.heveatex.com
SIC: 3069 2822 Mfg Fabricated Rubber Products Mfg Synthetic Rubber
PA: Tillotson Corporation
1539 Fall River Ave Ste 1
Seekonk MA 02771
781 402-1731

(G-10714)
HIGSON INC
Also Called: Higson Seafood
917 S Main St (02724-2923)
PHONE..................................508 678-4970
Brad W Higson, *President*
Chris Higson, *Vice Pres*
EMP: 3
SALES (est): 300K Privately Held
SIC: 2092 Mfg Fresh/Frozen Packaged Fish

(G-10715)
IQF CUSTOM PACKING LLC
140 Waldron Rd (02720-4723)
PHONE..................................508 646-0400
EMP: 5
SALES (est): 383.6K Privately Held
SIC: 2091 Mfg Canned/Cured Fish/Seafood

(G-10716)
JEM PRECISION TECHNOLOGIES
Also Called: Jem Precision Technology
1567 N Main St Ste 1 (02720-2978)
PHONE..................................508 672-0666
Eduardo Melo, *President*
EMP: 5
SQ FT: 2,800
SALES (est): 645.9K Privately Held
SIC: 3599 Machine Shop Jobbing And Repair

(G-10717)
JOURNAL REGISTER COMPANY
O Jornal
207 Pocasset St (02721-1532)
PHONE..................................508 678-3844
Ric Oliveria, *Manager*
EMP: 12
SALES (corp-wide): 693.9MM Privately Held
WEB: www.journalregister.com
SIC: 2711 Newspapers-Publishing/Printing
PA: Journal Register Company
5 Hanover Sq Fl 25
New York NY 10004

(G-10718)
JS INTERNATIONAL INC
Also Called: Jsi Quality Cabinetry
485 Commerce Dr (02720-4706)
PHONE..................................508 675-4722
Jiam Shen, *President*
▼ EMP: 49
SQ FT: 125,000
SALES (est): 9.7MM Privately Held
WEB: www.jsicabinetry.com
SIC: 2599 2434 Mfg Furniture/Fixtures Mfg Wood Kitchen Cabinets

(G-10719)
KELLSPORT INDUSTRIES INC
22 Boomer St (02720-2714)
PHONE..................................508 646-0855
Robert Smith, *President*
▲ EMP: 35
SALES (est): 3.2MM Privately Held
SIC: 2329 2339 Mfg Men's/Boy's Clothing Mfg Women's/Misses' Outerwear

(G-10720)
KEVINS WOODWORKS LLC
221 London St (02723-5418)
PHONE..................................508 989-8692
Kevin Pereira, *Principal*
EMP: 3 EST: 2012
SALES (est): 318.1K Privately Held
SIC: 2431 Mfg Millwork

(G-10721)
KLEAR-VU CORPORATION (PA)
600 Airport Rd (02720-4735)
PHONE..................................508 674-5723
Robert W Cooper, *CEO*
Jacob Mintz, *Principal*
Denise Smith, *Admin Sec*
▲ EMP: 100
SQ FT: 100,000
SALES (est): 12MM Privately Held
WEB: www.klearvu.com
SIC: 2392 Mfg Household Furnishings

(G-10722)
LAVOIE INDUSTRIES LLC
969 Charles St (02724-4202)
PHONE..................................508 542-1062
Paul Lavoie, *Principal*
EMP: 8 EST: 2008
SALES (est): 816.1K Privately Held
SIC: 3999 Mfg Misc Products

(G-10723)
LINCOLN PRESS CO INC
Also Called: Jiffy Print Copy Center
407 Pleasant St (02721-3030)
P.O. Box 904 (02722-0904)
PHONE..................................508 673-3241
Paul Senra, *President*
Alan Hutchinson, *Shareholder*
EMP: 20
SQ FT: 14,000
SALES (est): 2.7MM **Privately Held**
WEB: www.geoknight.com
SIC: 2759 2752 3953 Commercial Printing Lithographic Commercial Printing Mfg Marking Devices

(G-10724)
MALLARD PRINTING INC
657 Quarry St Ste 9 (02723-1021)
PHONE..................................508 675-5733
Robert Lunquest, *President*
Mario Rodriguez, *Principal*
Jeffrey Marques, *Vice Pres*
Patti Sowersby, *Bookkeeper*
Kathy Pendergast, *Sales Staff*
EMP: 18
SQ FT: 5,000
SALES (est): 3.5MM **Privately Held**
WEB: www.mallardprinting.com
SIC: 2752 Lithographic Commercial Printing

(G-10725)
MAP PRINTING INC
54 Mcdonald St (02720-2822)
PHONE..................................508 676-5177
Manuel Silva, *President*
EMP: 3
SQ FT: 2,400
SALES (est): 340K **Privately Held**
SIC: 2752 Commercial Printing

(G-10726)
MAPLEWOOD MACHINE CO INC
271 Anthony St (02721-3307)
PHONE..................................508 673-6710
Edward Viveiros, *President*
Donna Viveiros, *Treasurer*
EMP: 10
SALES: 800K **Privately Held**
WEB: www.maplewoodmachine.com
SIC: 3599 Mfg Industrial Machinery

(G-10727)
MARIOS WELDING
185 Welcome St (02721-3113)
PHONE..................................508 646-1038
Mario Silva, *Owner*
EMP: 3
SALES (est): 160K **Privately Held**
SIC: 3446 1799 Mfg Architectural Metalwork Trade Contractor

(G-10728)
MATOUK TEXTILE WORKS INC
925 Airport Rd (02720-4724)
PHONE..................................508 997-3444
George Matouk Sr, *President*
Carly Schaeder, *Mktg Coord*
Sasha Maule, *Marketing Staff*
Frankie Phillips, *Manager*
Colleen Daniels, *Director*
EMP: 50
SALES (est): 4MM **Privately Held**
SIC: 2395 Apparel And Other Textile Products

(G-10729)
MELLOS NORTH END MFG CO INC
63 N Court St (02720-2701)
PHONE..................................508 673-2320
Eldwado Rego, *President*
Daniel Rego, *Plant Mgr*
◆ **EMP:** 3
SQ FT: 3,000
SALES (est): 352K **Privately Held**
SIC: 2013 5411 Mfg Prepared Meats Ret Groceries

(G-10730)
MERCHANT MACHINE INC
50 Merchant St (02723-1110)
PHONE..................................508 672-1991
Robert Corey, *President*
Bruce Willette, *Vice Pres*
EMP: 6 **EST:** 1999
SALES: 700K **Privately Held**
SIC: 3599 Mfg Industrial Machinery

(G-10731)
MERIDA LLC
1 Currant Rd Ste 1 # 1 (02720-4741)
PHONE..................................508 675-6572
Bob Segal, *Branch Mgr*
EMP: 35
SALES (corp-wide): 4.6MM **Privately Held**
SIC: 2273 Mfg Carpets/Rugs
PA: Merida, Llc
1 Design Center Pl # 330
Boston MA 02210
800 345-2200

(G-10732)
MICRO MAGNETICS INC
617 Airport Rd (02720-4722)
P.O. Box 9366 (02720-0007)
PHONE..................................508 672-4489
Gang Xiao, *Chairman*
Matthew Carter, *VP Mfg*
▲ **EMP:** 10
SQ FT: 7,000
SALES: 1.1MM **Privately Held**
WEB: www.micromagnetics.com
SIC: 3674 8731 Develops & Mfrs Magnetic Sensors & Applications

(G-10733)
MILLSTONE MED OUTSOURCING LLC (PA)
580 Commerce Dr (02720-4759)
PHONE..................................508 679-8384
Karl Neuberger, *CEO*
Kelly Lucenti, *President*
Richard Worthen, *Exec VP*
James Dwyer, *Vice Pres*
Victoria Hughes, *Vice Pres*
▲ **EMP:** 130
SQ FT: 26,230
SALES (est): 22.3MM **Privately Held**
WEB: www.millstonemedical.com
SIC: 2671 2631 Mfg Packaging Paper/Film Paperboard Mill

(G-10734)
MINUTEMAN PRESS
435 Columbia St (02721-1545)
PHONE..................................508 673-1407
Joseph Plant, *Owner*
EMP: 3
SQ FT: 1,000
SALES (est): 283.7K **Privately Held**
SIC: 2752 Comm Prtg Litho

(G-10735)
MIRANDA BROTHERS INC
Also Called: Micheals Provision
317 Lindsey St (02720-1132)
PHONE..................................508 672-0982
Ronnie Miranda, *President*
Joe Miranda, *Vice Pres*
EMP: 9
SALES: 3.5MM **Privately Held**
SIC: 2013 Mfg Prepared Meats

(G-10736)
MIW CORP
1205 Bay St (02724-1203)
PHONE..................................508 672-4029
George Malatos, *President*
EMP: 25
SQ FT: 18,000
SALES (est): 3.9MM **Privately Held**
SIC: 3411 Mfg Metal

(G-10737)
NEW ENGLAND ELECTROPOLISHING
Also Called: N E E
220 Shove St (02724-2018)
P.O. Box 845 (02722-0845)
PHONE..................................508 672-6616
Alvin Almedia, *President*
Luke Almeida, *Business Mgr*
EMP: 25
SALES (est): 2.5MM **Privately Held**
WEB: www.neelectropolishing.com
SIC: 3471 Plating/Polishing Service

(G-10738)
NEW ENGLAND FLEECE COMPANY
147 Plymouth Ave (02721-4303)
PHONE..................................508 678-5550
Peter Moubayed, *President*
Jonathan Dow, *Vice Pres*
▲ **EMP:** 4
SQ FT: 15,000
SALES (est): 576.2K **Privately Held**
WEB: www.nefleece.com
SIC: 2231 5131 Mfg Fleece Products And Broker Of Fabrics

(G-10739)
NEW ENGLAND SHIRT CO LLC
657 Quarry St 33 (02723-1020)
PHONE..................................508 672-2223
Robert T Kidder,
▲ **EMP:** 6
SALES (est): 1MM **Privately Held**
SIC: 2253 Knit Outerwear Mill

(G-10740)
NORTHEAST EQUIPMENT INC
Also Called: Delta Mechanical Seals
44 Probber Ln (02720-1308)
PHONE..................................508 324-0083
Carl C Bjornson, *President*
EMP: 28
SALES (est): 4.4MM **Privately Held**
WEB: www.delta-seals.com
SIC: 3561 3053 Mfg Pumps/Pumping Equipment Mfg Gaskets/Packing/Sealing Devices

(G-10741)
NORTHEAST KNITTING MILLS INC (PA)
69 Alden St (02723-1787)
PHONE..................................508 678-7553
Gary Reitzas, *President*
Max Blum, *President*
Jay Elias, *Treasurer*
Lois Reitzas, *Clerk*
EMP: 21
SQ FT: 150,000
SALES (est): 4.2MM **Privately Held**
WEB: www.neknitting.com
SIC: 2253 5949 2339 Knit Outerwear Mill Ret Sewing Supplies/Fabrics Mfg Women's/Misses' Outerwear

(G-10742)
O C M INC
Also Called: Oriental Chow Mein Co
42 8th St (02720-3014)
PHONE..................................508 675-7711
Frederick Wong, *President*
Nelson Wong, *Vice Pres*
Alfred Wong, *Treasurer*
EMP: 12 **EST:** 1937
SQ FT: 2,600
SALES (est): 1.2MM **Privately Held**
SIC: 2098 Mfg Food Preparations

(G-10743)
OPALALA INC
994 Jefferson St Ste 10 (02721-4823)
PHONE..................................508 646-0950
Ron E Stager, *President*
Lydia Sotomayer, *Technology*
Kim Tavares, *Admin Sec*
▲ **EMP:** 19
SQ FT: 10,000
SALES (est): 3.1MM **Privately Held**
WEB: www.andersonairmotive.com
SIC: 3728 3643 Mfg Aircraft Parts/Equipment Mfg Conductive Wiring Devices

(G-10744)
PARAMOUNT TOOL LLC
473 Pleasant St (02721-3026)
PHONE..................................508 672-0844
David Gardikis Sr,
Jacqueline Gardikis,
▲ **EMP:** 25
SQ FT: 25,000
SALES (est): 4.7MM **Privately Held**
SIC: 3469 3599 Mfg Metal Stampings Mfg Industrial Machinery

(G-10745)
PASCALE INDUSTRIES INC
Ey Technologies
939 Currant Rd (02720-4712)
PHONE..................................508 673-3307
Raymond Pascale, *General Mgr*
EMP: 45 **Privately Held**
SIC: 2295 Mfg Coated Fabrics
PA: Pascale Industries, Inc.
1301 Ridgway Rd
Pine Bluff AR 71603

(G-10746)
PDK WORLDWIDE ENTPS INC (PA)
Also Called: Pdk Worldwide
10 N Main St Ste 3g (02720-2130)
PHONE..................................508 676-2155
Paul Zheng, *President*
▲ **EMP:** 20
SQ FT: 50,000
SALES (est): 1.9MM **Privately Held**
WEB: www.pdkworldwide.com
SIC: 2392 Mfg Household Furnishings

(G-10747)
POTTERS PRINTING INC
Also Called: Cambridge Offsett Printing
822 Eastern Ave (02723-2804)
PHONE..................................617 547-3161
Kris Sousa, *Principal*
Greg Potter, *Programmer Anys*
EMP: 9
SQ FT: 8,000
SALES: 1MM **Privately Held**
WEB: www.cambridgeoffset.com
SIC: 2752 Lithographic Commercial Printing

(G-10748)
PRECISION SPORTSWEAR INC
54 Front St Unit 3 (02721-4399)
PHONE..................................508 674-3034
Neal Venancio, *President*
Nelson Ferreira, *Manager*
EMP: 27
SALES (est): 2.2MM **Privately Held**
WEB: www.precspts.com
SIC: 2369 2329 Mfg Girl/Youth Outerwear Mfg Men's/Boy's Clothing

(G-10749)
PURSUIT TOBOGGAN LLC
75 Ferry St Ste 5 (02721-1111)
PHONE..................................508 567-0550
Christopher J Biafore Esq, *Principal*
EMP: 4
SALES (est): 321.3K **Privately Held**
SIC: 3949 Mfg Sporting/Athletic Goods

(G-10750)
R & M PRECISION MACHINE
130 Moorland St (02724-1113)
P.O. Box 6192 (02724-0600)
PHONE..................................508 678-2488
Micheal Langton, *Owner*
EMP: 5
SQ FT: 2,400
SALES (est): 457K **Privately Held**
SIC: 3599 7692 Mfg Industrial Machinery Welding Repair

(G-10751)
RAILINGS UNLIMITED
20 Weybosset St (02723-1626)
PHONE..................................508 679-5678
Robert Joseph, *Owner*
EMP: 3 **EST:** 1972
SQ FT: 2,000
SALES (est): 200K **Privately Held**
SIC: 3446 3444 Mfg Architectural Metalwork Mfg Sheet Metalwork

(G-10752)
RAMSBOTTOM PRINTING INC
Also Called: RPI Printing
135 Waldron Rd (02720-4723)
PHONE..................................508 730-2220
P Scott Ramsbottom, *President*
Bud Moran, *Regl Sales Mgr*
Jack Eaken, *VP Mktg*
Celeste Dufault, *Marketing Staff*
EMP: 52
SQ FT: 12,000

SALES (est): 14.6MM **Privately Held**
WEB: www.rpiprinting.com
SIC: 2752 2791 Lithographic Commercial Printing Typesettig Services

(G-10753)
RAW SEA FOODS INC
481 Currant Rd (02720-4712)
PHONE..................................508 673-0111
Jason Hutchens, *President*
Scott Hutchens, *Vice Pres*
Rob Farias, *VP Opers*
Eric Cruz, *Prdtn Mgr*
Brian Maccini, *Purch Dir*
▲ **EMP:** 175
SQ FT: 80,000
SALES (est): 47.2MM **Privately Held**
WEB: www.rawseafoods.com
SIC: 2092 Mfg Fresh/Frozen Packaged Fish

(G-10754)
RECTORSEAL
1244 Davol St (02720-1108)
PHONE..................................508 673-7561
◆ **EMP:** 6
SALES (est): 1MM **Privately Held**
SIC: 3561 Mfg Pumps/Pumping Equipment

(G-10755)
RECTORSEAL CORPORATION
1244 Davol St (02720-1108)
PHONE..................................508 673-7561
K Ortler, *Principal*
EMP: 8
SALES (corp-wide): 350.1MM **Publicly Held**
WEB: www.metacaulk.com
SIC: 2891 2899 2842 Mfg Adhesives/Sealants Mfg Chemical Preparations Mfg Polish/Sanitation Goods
HQ: Rectorseal, Llc
2601 Spenwick Dr
Houston TX 77055
713 263-8001

(G-10756)
REFLEK CORP
240 Crawford St (02724-2302)
PHONE..................................508 603-6807
EMP: 4
SALES (est): 459.6K **Privately Held**
SIC: 3648 Mfg Lighting Equipment

(G-10757)
REX CUT PRODUCTS INCORPORATED
960 Airport Rd (02720-4799)
PHONE..................................508 678-1985
Claude M Gelinas, *President*
Robert J Gauvin, *CFO*
▲ **EMP:** 56
SQ FT: 84,000
SALES (est): 9.6MM **Privately Held**
WEB: www.rexcut.com
SIC: 3291 Mfg Abrasive Products

(G-10758)
RICKS SHEET METAL INC
82 Lea Ln (02721-2385)
PHONE..................................774 488-9576
Eric Christopher Nadich, *President*
EMP: 8
SALES (est): 1MM **Privately Held**
SIC: 3444 Mfg Sheet Metalwork

(G-10759)
RIVER FALLS MANUFACTURING CO
40 County St (02723-2104)
PHONE..................................508 646-2900
Isidore Friedman, *Ch of Bd*
Mark Friedman, *President*
Paul Friedman, *Vice Pres*
William Fuchs, *Treasurer*
EMP: 96
SALES (est): 6.1MM
SALES (corp-wide): 8MM **Privately Held**
SIC: 2253 Contract Mfr Girls Outerwear
HQ: Fieldston Clothes, Inc
40 County St
Fall River MA 02723
508 646-2900

(G-10760)
ROBBINS MANUFACTURING CO INC
1200 Airport Rd (02720-4736)
P.O. Box 704 (02722-0704)
PHONE..................................508 675-2555
Barry Robbins, *President*
EMP: 50 **EST:** 1970
SQ FT: 90,000
SALES (est): 8.6MM **Privately Held**
SIC: 3452 Mfg Bolts/Screws/Rivets

(G-10761)
SIGNIFY NORTH AMERICA CORP
Also Called: Lightolier
631 Airport Rd (02720-4722)
PHONE..................................508 679-8131
Mary Donelan, *Branch Mgr*
EMP: 286
SALES (corp-wide): 7B **Privately Held**
SIC: 3646 Mfg Commercial Lighting Fixtures
HQ: Signify North America Corporation
200 Franklin Square Dr
Somerset NJ 08873
732 563-3000

(G-10762)
SPECTRUM LIGHTING INC
994 Jefferson St Ste 5 (02721-4823)
PHONE..................................508 678-2303
Christopher Roenlin, *President*
Robert Thomas, *President*
Julie Romano, *Purch Mgr*
Horatio Furtado, *Engineer*
Ray Furtado, *Design Engr*
▲ **EMP:** 100
SALES (est): 42.6MM **Privately Held**
WEB: www.speclight.com
SIC: 3646 Mfg Commercial Lighting Fixtures

(G-10763)
STEGER POWER CONNECTION INC
Also Called: Anderson Airmotive Products Co
994 Jefferson St Ste 10 (02721-4823)
PHONE..................................508 646-0950
Matthew Steger, *President*
EMP: 19
SQ FT: 15,000
SALES (est): 715.5K **Privately Held**
SIC: 3728 3643 Mfg Aircraft Parts/Equipment Mfg Conductive Wiring Devices

(G-10764)
STIRRINGS LLC
Also Called: Stirrings Better Cocktails
1 West St Unit 2 (02720-1336)
PHONE..................................508 324-9800
William H Creelman,
Theodore S Borek,
Robert K Burke,
Gillean Maclean,
Paul B Nardone,
EMP: 40
SALES (est): 3.2MM
SALES (corp-wide): 16.3B **Privately Held**
SIC: 2085 2087 Mfg Distilled/Blended Liquor Mfg Flavor Extracts/Syrup
HQ: Diageo North America Inc.
801 Main Ave
Norwalk CT 06851
203 229-2100

(G-10765)
SUPERIOR MANUFACTURING CORP
1 Ace St Unit 12 (02720-1355)
P.O. Box 5207 (02723-0406)
PHONE..................................508 677-0100
Kenneth A Soares, *President*
Joseph Travers, *President*
M McDermott, *Vice Pres*
▲ **EMP:** 3
SQ FT: 50,000
SALES (est): 477.4K **Privately Held**
SIC: 3639 5084 5722 1799 Sewing Manufacturer

(G-10766)
SWAN DYEING AND PRINTING CORP
Also Called: Swan Fabrics
372 Stevens St (02721-4934)
PHONE..................................508 674-4611
Michael A Rodriguez, *President*
▲ **EMP:** 95
SALES (est): 11.8MM **Privately Held**
SIC: 2396 Mfg Auto/Apparel Trimming

(G-10767)
SWAN FINISHING COMPANY INC (PA)
372 Stevens St (02721-4999)
PHONE..................................508 674-4611
Pat Guerriero, *President*
Michael Rodrigues, *Vice Pres*
Ralph A Guerriero Jr, *Treasurer*
▲ **EMP:** 229
SQ FT: 200,000
SALES (est): 19.9MM **Privately Held**
SIC: 2231 2261 2262 Wool Broadwoven Fabric Mill Cotton Finishing Plant Manmade Fiber & Silk Finishing Plant

(G-10768)
SWIMEX INC
390 Airport Rd Ste 3 (02720-4707)
PHONE..................................508 646-1600
Mark Pearson, *President*
Suzanne Vaughan, *President*
Mark Fyrer, *Engineer*
Alexander Powers, *Engineer*
Karen Dias, *Controller*
▼ **EMP:** 50
SQ FT: 22,500
SALES (est): 7.7MM **Privately Held**
SIC: 3949 Mfg Sporting/Athletic Goods

(G-10769)
TACO INC
583 Bedford St (02720-4807)
PHONE..................................508 675-7300
Robert E Lee, *Vice Pres*
Brian Powers, *Manager*
EMP: 100
SQ FT: 65,000
SALES (corp-wide): 162.6MM **Privately Held**
WEB: www.taco-hvac.com
SIC: 3433 3561 3494 3443 Mfg Heat Equip-Nonelec Mfg Pumps/Pumping Equip Mfg Valves/Pipe Fittings Mfg Fabricated Plate Wrk Structural Metal Fabrctn
PA: Taco, Inc.
1160 Cranston St
Cranston RI 02920
401 942-8000

(G-10770)
TECH-ETCH INC
100 Riggenbach Rd (02720-4708)
PHONE..................................508 675-5757
Karen Bitterman, *Principal*
Kevin Fenney, *Principal*
Jorgen Mortenson, *Branch Mgr*
Raymond Brodeur, *CTO*
Allan Steele, *Executive*
EMP: 90
SALES (corp-wide): 112.4MM **Privately Held**
WEB: www.techetch.com
SIC: 3357 3469 3444 Nonferrous Wiredrawing/Insulating Mfg Metal Stampings Mfg Sheet Metalwork
PA: Tech-Etch, Inc.
45 Aldrin Rd
Plymouth MA 02360
508 747-0300

(G-10771)
TEKNIKOR AUTOMTN & CONTRLS INC
Also Called: E C S
595 Airport Rd (02720-4702)
PHONE..................................508 679-9474
Ken Potvin, *President*
EMP: 16
SALES (est): 3.6MM **Privately Held**
WEB: www.ecsinco.com
SIC: 3625 3613 3823 Mfg Relays/Industrial Controls Mfg Switchgear/Switchboards Mfg Process Control Instruments

(G-10772)
TEUFELBERGER FIBER ROPE CORP
848 Airport Rd (02720-4735)
PHONE..................................508 678-8200
Christopher T Lavin, *President*
John Tedder, *Vice Pres*
Tom Dacosta, *Production*
Lisa Cardoza, *Purch Mgr*
Matt Hrivnak, *QC Mgr*
◆ **EMP:** 189
SQ FT: 150,000
SALES (est): 32.9MM **Privately Held**
SIC: 2298 Mfg Cordage/Twine

(G-10773)
TUFTANE EXTRUSION TECH INC
Also Called: Tuftane Eti
96 Wordell St (02721-4311)
PHONE..................................978 921-8200
Duncan Skinner, *President*
Sun Sasongko, *Vice Pres*
EMP: 10
SQ FT: 13,000
SALES (est): 2.5MM **Privately Held**
WEB: www.tuftaneeti.com
SIC: 3089 Mfg Plastic Products

(G-10774)
TWEAVE LLC
1450 Brayton Ave (02721-5235)
PHONE..................................508 285-6701
Laura Pickering, *Vice Pres*
George G Gehring Jr, *Mng Member*
EMP: 50
SALES (est): 8.4MM
SALES (corp-wide): 64MM **Privately Held**
SIC: 2241 Narrow Fabric Mill
PA: Gehring Tricot Corporation
68 Ransom St
Dolgeville NY 13329
315 429-8551

(G-10775)
UNION BOOKBINDING COMPANY INC (PA)
Also Called: Union Group , The
649 Alden St (02723-1826)
P.O. Box 3160 (02722-3160)
PHONE..................................508 676-8580
Elliot Comenitz, *President*
Bruce Comenitz, *Vice Pres*
Lynne Medeiros, *Controller*
▲ **EMP:** 35 **EST:** 1927
SQ FT: 184,000
SALES (est): 7.5MM **Privately Held**
SIC: 2782 2675 2759 3161 Mfg Blankbooks/Binders Mfg Die-Cut Paper/Board Commercial Printing Mfg Luggage

(G-10776)
UNION BOOKBINDING II LLC
Also Called: Union Group, The
649 Alden St (02723-1826)
P.O. Box 3160 (02722-3160)
PHONE..................................508 676-8580
Bruce Comenitz,
Jay Comenitz,
Lynne Medeiros,
EMP: 25 **EST:** 2010
SALES (est): 1.4MM **Privately Held**
SIC: 2782 Mfg Blankbooks/Binders

(G-10777)
US BEDDING INC
451 Quarry St (02723-1007)
PHONE..................................508 678-6988
David Wayne, *President*
▲ **EMP:** 18
SALES (est): 2.7MM **Privately Held**
SIC: 2515 2221 5712 Manmad Brdwv Fabric Mill Ret Furniture

(G-10778)
VANSON LEATHERS INC
951 Broadway Ste 1 (02724-2769)
PHONE..................................508 678-2000
Michael Van Der Sleesen, *President*
◆ **EMP:** 56
SALES (est): 6.6MM **Privately Held**
WEB: www.vansonleathers.com
SIC: 2386 Mfg Leather Clothing

(G-10779)
VETERANS AFFAIRS US DEPT
144 Winthrop St (02721-2542)
PHONE....................................774 240-6764
EMP: 3 **Publicly Held**
SIC: 2621 Paper Mill
HQ: United States Dept Of Veterans Affairs
810 Vermont Ave Nw
Washington DC 20420
800 827-1000

(G-10780)
VITAL WOOD PRODUCTS INC
218 Shove St (02724-2068)
P.O. Box 86, Westport (02790-0086)
PHONE....................................508 673-7976
Patricia Vital, *President*
EMP: 15
SQ FT: 22,000
SALES (est): 1.5MM **Privately Held**
SIC: 2515 Mfg Mattresses/Bedsprings

(G-10781)
W R H INDUSTRIES LTD
957 Airport Rd (02720-4724)
PHONE....................................508 674-2444
Warren R Hartwell, *President*
Nancy Hartwell, *Sales Staff*
Ward Hartwell, *Sales Staff*
▲ **EMP:** 6
SQ FT: 14,200
SALES (est): 1MM **Privately Held**
SIC: 3089 Injection Molding Of Plastics

(G-10782)
WALTER A FURMAN CO INC
180 Liberty St (02724-1433)
PHONE....................................508 674-7751
Carl Furman, *President*
Walter A Furman, *Treasurer*
▲ **EMP:** 75 **EST:** 1954
SQ FT: 35,000
SALES (est): 5.5MM **Privately Held**
SIC: 2431 Mfg Millwork

(G-10783)
WHOLE EARTH HAT CO INC
Also Called: Korber Hats
394 Kilburn St (02724-2214)
P.O. Box 336 (02724-0336)
PHONE....................................508 672-7033
Richard Silverstein, *President*
Tricia Field, *Controller*
Trisha Field, *Finance Dir*
Jason Korber, *Manager*
EMP: 18
SALES (est): 1.5MM **Privately Held**
WEB: www.korberhats.com
SIC: 2353 Mfg Hats

(G-10784)
WOODSMITHS INC
168 Stevens St Ste 2c (02721-5112)
PHONE....................................508 548-8343
Marilyn Hatt, *President*
EMP: 6
SQ FT: 7,200
SALES (est): 990K **Privately Held**
SIC: 2431 5211 5031 Mfg Millwork Ret Lumber/Building Materials Whol Lumber/Plywood/Millwork

(G-10785)
XILECTRIC INC
151 Martine St Rm 125 (02723-1514)
PHONE....................................617 312-5678
Steven Weiss, *President*
EMP: 4
SALES (est): 327.7K **Privately Held**
SIC: 3691 7389 Mfg Storage Batteries

(G-10786)
XL ADHESIVES NORTH LLC
63 Water St (02721-1559)
P.O. Box 2682 (02722-2682)
PHONE....................................508 675-0528
Christopher Horton Jr, *Manager*
▲ **EMP:** 6
SALES (est): 1.2MM
SALES (corp-wide): 250.3MM **Privately Held**
SIC: 2891 Mfg Adhesives/Sealants
PA: Textile Rubber And Chemical Company, Inc.
1300-1350 Tiarco Dr Sw
Dalton GA 30721
706 277-1300

Falmouth
Barnstable County

(G-10787)
BEN & BILLS CHOCOLATE EMPORIUM
209 Main St (02540-2749)
PHONE....................................508 548-7878
Jeannette Michaud, *Manager*
EMP: 10
SALES (corp-wide): 1.3MM **Privately Held**
SIC: 2064 5441 Mfg Candy/Confectionery Ret Candy/Confectionery
PA: Ben & Bill's Chocolate Emporium, Inc.
143 Main St
Northampton MA 01060
413 584-5695

(G-10788)
COOPER ELDRED BOAT BUILDERS
267 Sippewissett Rd (02540-1881)
PHONE....................................508 540-7130
Douglas Cooper, *Principal*
EMP: 3
SALES (est): 182.1K **Privately Held**
SIC: 3732 Boatbuilding/Repairing

(G-10789)
ENTERPRISE PUBLICATIONS (PA)
Also Called: Falmouth Enterprise
50 Depot Ave (02540-2349)
PHONE....................................508 548-4700
Bill Hough, *President*
John Hough, *Sales Dir*
Julien Courbon, *Advt Staff*
EMP: 35 **EST:** 1929
SQ FT: 7,100
SALES (est): 5.5MM **Privately Held**
WEB: www.capenews.net
SIC: 2711 2721 Newspapers-Publishing/Printing Periodicals-Publishing/Printing

(G-10790)
HEYOKA SOLUTIONS LLC
19 Howes Ln (02540-2890)
PHONE....................................866 389-8578
Kate Raymer, *Principal*
EMP: 3
SALES (est): 313.4K **Privately Held**
SIC: 2421 Sawmill/Planing Mill

(G-10791)
HOGY LURE COMPANY LLC
15 Simpson Ln (02540-2230)
P.O. Box 570 (02541-0570)
PHONE....................................617 699-5157
Michael Hogan, *Principal*
▲ **EMP:** 4
SALES (est): 327.3K **Privately Held**
SIC: 3949 Mfg Sporting/Athletic Goods

(G-10792)
HOMELAND SECURITY WIRELESS INC
Also Called: Fibercape Internet Services
5 Robinson Rd (02540-3840)
PHONE....................................508 299-1404
Peter K Butler, *President*
EMP: 5
SALES: 350K **Privately Held**
WEB: www.hlswireless.com
SIC: 3663 Mfg Radio/Tv Communication Equipment

(G-10793)
INUKSHUKBIO INTERACTIVE INC
104 Woods Hole Rd (02540-1646)
PHONE....................................612 916-6606
Christophe Echeverri, *CEO*
Robert Elde, *Principal*
EMP: 3 **EST:** 2015
SALES (est): 158K **Privately Held**
SIC: 7372 Prepackaged Software Services

(G-10794)
KIWI SIGNS & MAR GRAPHICS LLC
56 Scranton Ave (02540-3587)
PHONE....................................732 930-4121
Matthew Anderson, *Principal*
EMP: 3
SALES (est): 253.4K **Privately Held**
SIC: 3993 Mfg Signs/Advertising Specialties

(G-10795)
LISA JO RUDY
21 Ridgeview Dr (02540-2158)
PHONE....................................508 540-7293
EMP: 3 **EST:** 2012
SALES (est): 145.2K **Privately Held**
SIC: 2711 Newspapers-Publishing/Printing

(G-10796)
MCKNIGHT MANAGEMENT CO INC (PA)
505 Palmer Ave (02540-2954)
PHONE....................................508 540-5051
Robert McKnight, *President*
Martin Miller, *Vice Pres*
EMP: 8
SQ FT: 6,000
SALES (est): 1.3MM **Privately Held**
SIC: 2721 Periodicals-Publishing/Printing

(G-10797)
SEAK INC (PA)
316 Gifford St Unit 2 (02540-2962)
P.O. Box 729 (02541-0729)
PHONE....................................508 548-7023
Steven Babitsky, *President*
James Mangraviti, *Vice Pres*
EMP: 5
SQ FT: 1,500
SALES (est): 488.5K **Privately Held**
WEB: www.seak.com
SIC: 2721 8111 Periodicals-Publishing/Printing Legal Services Office

Feeding Hills
Hampden County

(G-10798)
GE STEAM POWER INC
853 S West St (01030-1074)
PHONE....................................860 688-1911
Tim Curran, *President*
EMP: 3
SALES (corp-wide): 121.6B **Publicly Held**
SIC: 3463 Mfg Nonferrous Forgings
HQ: Ge Steam Power, Inc.
175 Addison Rd
Windsor CT 06095
866 257-8664

(G-10799)
HANDYAID CO
106 S Westfield St (01030-2768)
P.O. Box 337 (01030-0337)
PHONE....................................413 786-9865
EMP: 4
SALES (est): 201.9K **Privately Held**
SIC: 3089 Mfg Plastic Products

(G-10800)
HP HOOD LLC
86 Oak Ln (01030-1430)
PHONE....................................413 789-8194
EMP: 300
SALES (corp-wide): 2.2B **Privately Held**
SIC: 2026 Mfg Fluid Milk
PA: Hp Hood Llc
6 Kimball Ln Ste 400
Lynnfield MA 01940
617 887-8441

(G-10801)
MICHAEL VINCENT
Also Called: Vincent Enterprises
20 Liquori Dr (01030-1628)
P.O. Box 506 (01030-0506)
PHONE....................................413 786-4911
Michael Vincent, *Owner*
▼ **EMP:** 3
SALES (est): 122.3K **Privately Held**
SIC: 3911 5094 Mfg Precious Metal Jewelry Whol Jewelry/Precious Stones

(G-10802)
NORGAARD MACHINE INC
370 Garden St (01030-2508)
P.O. Box 249 (01030-0249)
PHONE....................................413 789-1291
Gerald Norgaard, *President*
EMP: 8 **EST:** 1975
SQ FT: 10,000
SALES (est): 1.1MM **Privately Held**
SIC: 3599 Machine Shop Jobbing & Repair

(G-10803)
PARROT THE & BIRD EMPORIUM
360 N Westfield St Ste 12 (01030-1223)
PHONE....................................413 569-5555
Janet L Berube, *President*
EMP: 3
SALES (est): 378.8K **Privately Held**
SIC: 2211 Ret Misc Merchandise

(G-10804)
TURLEY PUBLICATIONS INC
14 Southwick St (01030-2024)
PHONE....................................413 786-7747
Sarah Tsitso, *Principal*
EMP: 11
SALES (corp-wide): 54.3MM **Privately Held**
SIC: 2741 Misc Publishing
PA: Turley Publications, Inc.
24 Water St
Palmer MA 01069
800 824-6548

(G-10805)
WANIEWSKI FARMS INC
409 S Westfield St (01030-2721)
PHONE....................................413 786-1182
Matthew Waniewski, *President*
EMP: 11
SQ FT: 3,000
SALES (est): 1.1MM **Privately Held**
SIC: 2013 Mfg Prepared Meats

Fiskdale
Worcester County

(G-10806)
G&F MEDICAL INC
709 Main St (01518-1304)
PHONE....................................978 560-2622
John J Argitis, *CEO*
Nirav Patel, *COO*
David W Argitis, *Vice Pres*
Nancy Quintanilla, *Purchasing*
Dipan Shah, *Engineer*
▲ **EMP:** 22
SQ FT: 14,500
SALES (est): 5.5MM **Privately Held**
SIC: 3089 Mfg Plastic Products

(G-10807)
G&F PRECISION MOLDING INC (PA)
709 Main St (01518-1304)
PHONE....................................508 347-9132
John G Argitis, *President*
John J Argitis, *President*
Andrew Dow, *President*
John Argitis, *Vice Pres*
Edward Bizier, *VP Mfg*
▲ **EMP:** 99 **EST:** 1962
SQ FT: 61,000
SALES (est): 16MM **Privately Held**
SIC: 3089 3544 Mfg Plastic Products Mfg Dies/Tools/Jigs/Fixtures

(G-10808)
PIONEER BREWING COMPANY LLC
195 Arnold Rd (01518-1010)
PHONE....................................508 347-7500
Timothy P Daley, *Principal*
EMP: 6
SALES (est): 383.4K **Privately Held**
SIC: 2082 Mfg Malt Beverages

GEOGRAPHIC

Fitchburg
Worcester County

(G-10809)
ADVANCED PRINT TECHNOLOGY INC
Also Called: APT
76 Laurel St (01420-7710)
PHONE..................................978 342-0093
Alvah M Reida, *President*
Judith E Reida, *Corp Secy*
EMP: 7
SQ FT: 4,800
SALES: 550K **Privately Held**
WEB: www.aptshirts.com
SIC: 2396 5136 5137 Screen Printing On Fabric Articles And Whol Screen Printed Articles

(G-10810)
AVERY DENNISON CORPORATION
Also Called: Avery Dennison Fastener Div
224 Industrial Rd (01420-4634)
PHONE..................................978 353-2100
Gary Buchholz, *Branch Mgr*
EMP: 220
SQ FT: 40,000
SALES (corp-wide): 7.1B **Publicly Held**
WEB: www.avery.com
SIC: 2672 Mfg Coated/Laminated Paper
PA: Avery Dennison Corporation
207 N Goode Ave
Glendale CA 91203
626 304-2000

(G-10811)
BIRCH POINT PAPER PRODUCTS INC
Also Called: Tk Cups-Sorg's
750 Crawford St (01420-6814)
PHONE..................................978 422-1447
Karen J Laufer, *President*
James Fedewa, *Sales Staff*
Gilbert Benghiat, *Admin Sec*
EMP: 45
SALES (est): 5.9MM **Privately Held**
SIC: 2621 5113 Paper Mill Whol Industrial/Service Paper

(G-10812)
BLAZING SIGNWORKS INC
57 Sarah Ln (01420-6744)
PHONE..................................800 672-4887
Kathleen Lemoine, *CEO*
Norm Lemoine, *President*
EMP: 4
SALES (est): 320.2K **Privately Held**
SIC: 3993 Mfg Signs/Advertising Specialties

(G-10813)
BOUTWELL OWENS & CO INC (PA)
251 Authority Dr (01420-6044)
PHONE..................................978 343-3067
Ward W Mc Laughlin, *President*
Ward McLaughlin, *President*
William Hodges, *Vice Pres*
Ellen Murphy, *Materials Mgr*
Jessica Elliot, *Purch Agent*
▲ **EMP:** 140 **EST:** 1887
SQ FT: 80,000
SALES (est): 44.6MM **Privately Held**
SIC: 2752 2759 2671 2657 Lithographic Coml Print Commercial Printing Mfg Packaging Paper/Film Mfg Folding Paperbrd Box

(G-10814)
BRENMAR MOLDING INC
1361 Rindge Rd (01420-1323)
PHONE..................................978 343-3198
Mark Puputti, *President*
Brenda Boucher-Puputti, *Admin Sec*
EMP: 3
SQ FT: 5,000
SALES (est): 390K **Privately Held**
WEB: www.brenmar.com
SIC: 3089 3544 3599 Injection Molding Of Finished Plastics Products & Mfg Industrial Molds & Machine Shop

(G-10815)
C V TOOL COMPANY INC
12 Baltic Ln Ste 1 (01420-2800)
PHONE..................................978 353-7901
Ken Mattson, *Manager*
EMP: 19
SALES (corp-wide): 10MM **Privately Held**
WEB: www.cvtool.com
SIC: 3599 Mfg Industrial Machinery
PA: C. V. Tool Company, Inc.
44 Robert Porter Rd
Southington CT 06489
978 353-7901

(G-10816)
CADO MANUFACTURING INC
1 Princeton Rd Ste 2 (01420-4638)
PHONE..................................978 343-2989
Claude Chapdelaine, *President*
EMP: 10
SQ FT: 16,000
SALES (est): 1.7MM **Privately Held**
SIC: 3089 Mfg Plastic Products

(G-10817)
CADO PRODUCTS INC
Also Called: Union Products
1b Princeton Rd (01420-4609)
PHONE..................................978 343-2989
Bruce Zarozny, *President*
Claude Chapdelaine, *Vice Pres*
EMP: 30
SQ FT: 70,000
SALES: 4.2MM **Privately Held**
WEB: www.cadocompany.com
SIC: 3544 Mfg Dies/Tools/Jigs/Fixtures

(G-10818)
CANO CORPORATION (PA)
225 Industrial Rd (01420-4635)
PHONE..................................978 342-0953
Anna Kapstad, *Ch of Bd*
Jan Kapstad, *President*
Bjorn Kapstad, *Vice Pres*
EMP: 41
SQ FT: 64,000
SALES: 6.7MM **Privately Held**
WEB: www.canocorp.com
SIC: 2522 2521 2541 2542 Mfg Nonwood Office Furn Mfg Wood Office Furn Mfg Wood Partitions/Fixt Mfg Nonwd Partition/Fixt

(G-10819)
CARAUSTAR INDUSTRIES INC
Also Called: Newark America
100 Newark Ave (01420-4637)
PHONE..................................978 665-2632
Michael Berger, *Facilities Mgr*
Dana Pelletier, *Branch Mgr*
Richard Johnson, *Technology*
EMP: 75
SALES (corp-wide): 4.6B **Publicly Held**
WEB: www.newarkgroup.com
SIC: 2631 Paperboard Mill
HQ: Caraustar Industries, Inc.
5000 Austell Powder Sprin
Austell GA 30106
770 948-3101

(G-10820)
CONVERSATION CONCEPTS LLC
339 Broad St Ste 2 (01420-3052)
PHONE..................................978 342-1414
Joyce Sinnott, *Controller*
Scott Flynn,
▲ **EMP:** 12
SQ FT: 20,000
SALES (est): 1.2MM **Privately Held**
WEB: www.conversationconcepts.com
SIC: 3269 3961 Mfg Pottery Products Mfg Costume Jewelry

(G-10821)
CORRUGATED PACKAGING INC
215 Cleghorn (01420)
PHONE..................................978 342-6076
Lynn Thornton, *President*
Alexander Urquhart, *Treasurer*
EMP: 15
SQ FT: 35,000
SALES (est): 2.3MM **Privately Held**
SIC: 2653 Mfg Corrugated/Solid Fiber Boxes

(G-10822)
CRISTY CORPORATION
260 Authority Dr (01420-6097)
PHONE..................................978 343-4330
Donald A Cristy, *President*
EMP: 12 **EST:** 1943
SQ FT: 25,000
SALES (est): 2.2MM **Privately Held**
SIC: 2899 Mfg Chemical Preparations

(G-10823)
DRS POWER TECHNOLOGY INC
166 Boulder Dr Ste 201 (01420-3168)
PHONE..................................978 343-9719
Roger Sexauer, *President*
Terence J Murphy, *Vice Pres*
Jason Rinsky, *Vice Pres*
John Haven, *Engineer*
Bryan Zogg, *Engineer*
▲ **EMP:** 120
SQ FT: 100,000
SALES (est): 48.5MM
SALES (corp-wide): 8.9B **Privately Held**
SIC: 3679 Mfg Electronic Components
HQ: Drs Naval Power Systems, Inc
4265 N 30th St
Milwaukee WI 53216
414 875-4314

(G-10824)
E & D MANUFACTURING
1006 Ashburnham St (01420-2736)
PHONE..................................978 345-0183
Donald A Palo, *Partner*
Eric A Palo, *Partner*
EMP: 4
SQ FT: 1,000
SALES: 175K **Privately Held**
SIC: 3599 Mfg Industrial Machinery

(G-10825)
FITCHBURG PATTERN AND MODEL CO
21 Myrtle Ave (01420-7818)
PHONE..................................978 342-0770
Peter J Belli, *President*
EMP: 4 **EST:** 1921
SQ FT: 6,500
SALES (est): 200K **Privately Held**
SIC: 3543 Mfg Industrial Patterns

(G-10826)
FLANGE INC
21 Myrtle Ave (01420-7818)
PHONE..................................978 343-9200
John Belli, *President*
Peter Belli, *Admin Sec*
EMP: 3
SQ FT: 4,700
SALES (est): 237.6K **Privately Held**
SIC: 3463 Mfg Pool Flanges

(G-10827)
FOAMTECH LLC
1 Nursery Ln (01420-3043)
PHONE..................................978 343-4022
Bradley K Rousseau,
EMP: 17
SALES (est): 3.8MM **Privately Held**
SIC: 2295 Mfg Coated Fabrics

(G-10828)
HARRIS TOOL & DIE COMPANY INC
655 Westminster St (01420-4615)
PHONE..................................978 479-1842
Warren A Landry, *President*
Malcolm G Krapf, *Vice Pres*
Kenneth P Krapf, *Treasurer*
Ruth Krapf, *Manager*
Mary Krapf, *Administration*
EMP: 3
SQ FT: 10,000
SALES (est): 210K **Privately Held**
SIC: 7692 3544 Cracked Casting Repair Service & A Mfg Of Plastics Working Machinery

(G-10829)
HEADWALL PHOTONICS INC (PA)
601 River St (01420-2975)
PHONE..................................978 353-4040
David Bannon, *CEO*
Donald Battistoni, *VP Sls/Mktg*
EMP: 13
SALES (est): 3MM **Privately Held**
SIC: 3826 Mfg Analytical Instruments

(G-10830)
KELLEY WOOD PRODUCTS INC
85 River St (01420-3093)
PHONE..................................978 345-7531
S Michael Kelley, *President*
John Kelley, *Treasurer*
Florence I Kelley, *Clerk*
EMP: 18
SQ FT: 17,000
SALES (est): 2.8MM **Privately Held**
SIC: 2448 2441 Mfg Wood Pallets/Skids Mfg Wood Boxes/Shook

(G-10831)
M R RESOURCES INC
160 Authority Dr (01420-6045)
PHONE..................................978 696-3060
Jonathan O Webb, *President*
Shellie Hammond, *Production*
Robert Crosby, *Treasurer*
EMP: 33
SQ FT: 22,000
SALES (est): 5.5MM **Privately Held**
WEB: www.mrr.com
SIC: 3826 5049 5047 3845 Mfg Analytical Instr Whol Professional Equip

(G-10832)
MA MFG LLC
Also Called: Peak Manufacturing
325 Authority Dr (01420-6049)
PHONE..................................978 400-9991
Gerald Scutt, *Sales Staff*
Karl Koch,
EMP: 20
SALES (est): 2.2MM **Privately Held**
SIC: 3599 Mfg Industrial Machinery

(G-10833)
MAR-LEE COMPANIES INC
Also Called: Mar Lee Companies Tech Ctrs
190 Authority Dr (01420-6045)
PHONE..................................978 343-9600
Al Gravelle, *Manager*
EMP: 8
SALES (corp-wide): 7.3MM **Privately Held**
WEB: www.mar-leecompanies.com
SIC: 3089 Mfg Plastic Products
HQ: Mar-Lee Companies, Inc.
180 Authority Dr
Fitchburg MA 01420
978 343-9600

(G-10834)
MAR-LEE COMPANIES INC
180 Authority Dr (01420-6045)
PHONE..................................978 348-1291
Mark Gravelle, *Manager*
EMP: 80
SALES (corp-wide): 7.3MM **Privately Held**
WEB: www.mar-leecompanies.com
SIC: 3544 Mfg Dies/Tools/Jigs/Fixtures
HQ: Mar-Lee Companies, Inc.
180 Authority Dr
Fitchburg MA 01420
978 343-9600

(G-10835)
MEDIANEWS GROUP INC
Also Called: Sentinel and Enterprise
808 Main St (01420-5388)
P.O. Box 730 (01420-0007)
PHONE..................................978 343-6911
Richard Barker, *Manager*
Sherrie P Gentry, *Director*
EMP: 77
SALES (corp-wide): 4.2B **Privately Held**
SIC: 2711 2752 Newspapers-Publishing/Printing Lithographic Commercial Printing
HQ: Medianews Group, Inc.
101 W Colfax Ave Ste 1100
Denver CO 80202

(G-10836)
MERIT MACHINE MANUFACTURING
25 Willow St (01420-7824)
PHONE..................................978 342-7677

▲ = Import ▼=Export
◆ =Import/Export

Ross Barber, *President*
Roger Barber, *Vice Pres*
June A Barber, *Admin Sec*
EMP: 14
SQ FT: 12,000
SALES (est): 1.9MM **Privately Held**
SIC: 3599 3541 Mfg Industrial Machinery Mfg Machine Tools-Cutting

(G-10837)
MICRON PRODUCTS INC
25 Sawyer Passway (01420-5702)
PHONE..................................978 345-5000
James E Rouse, *President*
Salvatore Emma Jr, *President*
Mark Laviolette, *Vice Pres*
David Garrison, *CFO*
Derek T Welch, *Treasurer*
▲ **EMP:** 105
SQ FT: 116,000
SALES (est): 21.6MM
SALES (corp-wide): 19.5MM **Publicly Held**
SIC: 3544 Mfg Dies/Tools/Jigs/Fixtures
PA: Micron Solutions, Inc.
25 Sawyer Passway
Fitchburg MA 01420
978 345-5000

(G-10838)
MICRON SOLUTIONS INC (PA)
25 Sawyer Passway (01420-5769)
PHONE..................................978 345-5000
Andrei Soran, *Ch of Bd*
Salvatore Emma Jr, *President*
Derek T Welch, *CFO*
Marco Benedetti, *Director*
Rodd Friedman, *Director*
EMP: 3
SQ FT: 116,000
SALES: 19.5MM **Publicly Held**
SIC: 3845 Mfg Electromedical Equipment

(G-10839)
MINUTEMAN PRESS
386 Summer St (01420-5956)
PHONE..................................978 345-0818
Ann Carlson, *Owner*
EMP: 5
SALES (est): 519.3K **Privately Held**
SIC: 2752 2759 2796 2791 Lithographic Coml Print Commercial Printing Platemaking Services Typesetting Services Bookbinding/Related Work

(G-10840)
MODERNE RUG INC
Also Called: Modern Rug & Awning Co
123 Airport Rd (01420-8142)
PHONE..................................978 343-3210
David Guillette, *President*
EMP: 3
SQ FT: 5,400
SALES: 250K **Privately Held**
SIC: 2394 5713 7217 Mfg Canvas Awnings

(G-10841)
MODU FORM INC (PA)
172 Industrial Rd (01420-4639)
PHONE..................................978 345-7942
William L Weissman, *President*
Thomas C Hurd, *Vice Pres*
Josh Weissman, *Vice Pres*
▼ **EMP:** 80 **EST:** 1976
SQ FT: 100,000
SALES (est): 21.2MM **Privately Held**
WEB: www.librarybureau.com
SIC: 2511 2521 2522 2531 Mfg Wood Household Furn Mfg Wood Office Furn

(G-10842)
MODU FORM INC
Library Bureau
172 Industrial Rd (01420-4639)
PHONE..................................978 345-7942
William Weissman, *President*
EMP: 6
SALES (est): 422.1K
SALES (corp-wide): 21.2MM **Privately Held**
WEB: www.librarybureau.com
SIC: 2522 2521 2531 Mfg Nonwood Office Furn
PA: Form Modu Inc
172 Industrial Rd
Fitchburg MA 01420
978 345-7942

(G-10843)
NEW ENGLAND KEYBOARD INC
Also Called: N E K
1 Princeton Rd Ste 1 # 1 (01420-4638)
PHONE..................................978 345-8332
David P Myers, *President*
Frank Accordino, *Opers Mgr*
Bill Ouellette, *Purch Agent*
Peter Laier, *Engineer*
Cory Bridge, *Design Engr*
▲ **EMP:** 50
SQ FT: 16,000
SALES (est): 10.5MM **Privately Held**
WEB: www.newenglandkeyboard.com
SIC: 3575 Mfg Computer Terminals

(G-10844)
NEW ENGLAND WIRECLOTH CO LLC
123 Kelly Ave (01420-4530)
PHONE..................................978 343-4998
Daniel Whitney,
EMP: 9 **EST:** 1999
SALES (est): 1.8MM **Privately Held**
SIC: 3496 Mfg Misc Fabricated Wire Products

(G-10845)
OMNOVA SOLUTIONS INC
83 Authority Dr (01420-6087)
PHONE..................................978 342-5831
Andrew Polana, *Production*
Sarah Degnan, *Buyer*
Dan Slint, *Manager*
EMP: 28
SQ FT: 23,556
SALES (corp-wide): 769.8MM **Publicly Held**
WEB: www.omnova.com
SIC: 2819 2821 Mfg Industrial Inorganic Chemicals Mfg Plastic Materials/Resins
PA: Omnova Solutions Inc.
25435 Harvard Rd
Beachwood OH 44122
216 682-7000

(G-10846)
OPCO LABORATORY INC
704 River St (01420-2913)
PHONE..................................978 345-2522
David Maldari, *President*
Saverio Maldari, *Chairman*
Arlene Nevin, *Office Mgr*
Deb Charsky, *Administration*
EMP: 20
SQ FT: 10,000
SALES (est): 3.9MM **Privately Held**
WEB: www.opcolab.com
SIC: 3827 Mfg Optical Instruments/Lenses

(G-10847)
P J ALBERT INC
199 Upham St (01420-4594)
P.O. Box 2165 (01420-0013)
PHONE..................................978 345-7828
Jacqueline M Albert, *President*
William Wheeler, *Vice Pres*
Philip J Albert, *Treasurer*
EMP: 42
SQ FT: 2,800
SALES (est): 6MM **Privately Held**
WEB: www.pjalbert.com
SIC: 3295 1611 1771 Mfg Minerals-Ground/Treated Highway/Street Construction Concrete Contractor

(G-10848)
PALLETS RECREATED
169 Clarendon St (01420-4005)
PHONE..................................978 345-5936
Patrick Martin, *Principal*
EMP: 3
SALES (est): 131.9K **Privately Held**
SIC: 2448 Mfg Wood Pallets/Skids

(G-10849)
PORTANCE CORP
Also Called: Peak Manufacturing
325 Authority Dr (01420-6049)
PHONE..................................978 400-9991
Peter Mendes, *Principal*
EMP: 18
SALES (est): 894.6K **Privately Held**
SIC: 3599 Mfg Industrial Machinery

(G-10850)
PROSTHETIC DESIGN INC
1141 South St Ste 2 (01420-7038)
PHONE..................................978 345-2588
Rene Cormier, *President*
Jill Cormier, *Vice Pres*
EMP: 3
SALES (est): 348.8K **Privately Held**
SIC: 3843 Dental Laboratory

(G-10851)
ROCHELEAU TOOL AND DIE CO INC
Also Called: Rocheleau Blow Molding Systems
117 Indl Rd (01420)
PHONE..................................978 345-1723
Steven Roland Rocheleau, *President*
Daniel Rocheleau, *Vice Pres*
Jeffrey Rocheleau, *Vice Pres*
Alex Rocheleau, *Facilities Mgr*
Lisa Ann Rocheleau, *Treasurer*
◆ **EMP:** 57
SQ FT: 32,000
SALES: 14.2MM **Privately Held**
WEB: www.rocheleautool.com
SIC: 3559 Mfg Industrial Machinery

(G-10852)
SHEPARD & PARKER INC
18 Lincoln St (01420-3599)
PHONE..................................978 343-3907
James Parker, *President*
EMP: 3
SQ FT: 6,000
SALES (est): 653.1K **Privately Held**
SIC: 7694 5063 Electric Motor Repair

(G-10853)
SIMONDS INDUSTRIES INTL
135 Intervale Rd (01420-6519)
P.O. Box 500 (01420-0005)
PHONE..................................978 424-0100
Ray Martino, *President*
▲ **EMP:** 30
SALES (est): 5.3MM **Privately Held**
SIC: 3545 Mfg Machine Tool Accessories

(G-10854)
SIMONDS INTERNATIONAL LLC
139 Intervale Rd (01420)
PHONE..................................978 424-0327
EMP: 4
SALES (corp-wide): 181.3MM **Privately Held**
SIC: 3553 Mfg Woodworking Machinery
HQ: Simonds International L.L.C.
135 Intervale Rd
Fitchburg MA 01420
978 424-0100

(G-10855)
SIMONDS INTERNATIONAL LLC (HQ)
135 Intervale Rd (01420-6519)
P.O. Box 600 (01420-0054)
PHONE..................................978 424-0100
Raymond J Martino, *President*
Henry J Botticello, *CFO*
David P Witman, *Admin Sec*
◆ **EMP:** 300
SQ FT: 400,000
SALES (est): 198.2MM
SALES (corp-wide): 181.3MM **Privately Held**
WEB: www.simondsinternational.com
SIC: 3553 Mfg Woodworking Machinery
PA: Wood Fiber Holdings, Inc.
139 Intervale Rd
Fitchburg MA 01420
419 832-2918

(G-10856)
SIMONDS SAW LLC (PA)
Also Called: Simon Holding
135 Intervale Rd (01420-6519)
P.O. Box 500 (01420-0005)
PHONE..................................978 424-0100
Raymond Martino, *President*
Philip Cochran, *Finance Dir*
▲ **EMP:** 23
SALES: 40MM **Privately Held**
SIC: 3545 Mfg Machine Tool Accessories

(G-10857)
STEEL-FAB INC
430 Crawford St (01420-6892)
P.O. Box 2145 (01420-0013)
PHONE..................................978 345-1112
Mark W Freeman, *President*
Louis Bartolini, *Vice Pres*
Bernard M Freeman, *Treasurer*
Shelly Cloecchi, *Admin Sec*
Sanford L Crane, *Admin Sec*
EMP: 40
SQ FT: 43,000
SALES: 6MM **Privately Held**
WEB: www.steel-fab-inc.com
SIC: 3443 3441 Mfg Fabricated Plate Work Structural Metal Fabrication

(G-10858)
U S SYNTHETICS CORP
158 Airport Rd (01420-8112)
PHONE..................................978 345-0176
Andrew Pavlin, *President*
James Pavlin, *Shareholder*
EMP: 7 **EST:** 1964
SQ FT: 26,000
SALES: 3.5MM **Privately Held**
SIC: 2865 Mfg Color Concentrates/Dyes & Pigments

(G-10859)
UNIVERSAL MACHINE & DESIGN
323 Princeton Rd (01420-4879)
PHONE..................................978 343-4688
Jess Ouellette, *Owner*
▲ **EMP:** 8
SALES (est): 765.2K **Privately Held**
SIC: 3599 Mfg Industrial Machinery

(G-10860)
UTZ QUALITY FOODS INC
759 Water St (01420-6479)
PHONE..................................978 342-6038
Edward Krysiak, *Manager*
EMP: 50
SALES (corp-wide): 640.7MM **Privately Held**
SIC: 2096 Manufactures Potato Chips Or Snacks
PA: Utz Quality Foods, Llc
900 High St
Hanover PA 17331
800 367-7629

(G-10861)
VINYL TECHNOLOGIES INC
Also Called: Vytek
195 Industrial Rd (01420-4654)
PHONE..................................978 342-9800
Dirk Burrowes, *President*
▲ **EMP:** 35
SQ FT: 40,000
SALES: 6MM **Privately Held**
WEB: www.vy-tek.com
SIC: 3599 Mfg Industrial Machinery

(G-10862)
WESTMINSTER MILLWORK CORP
310 Broad St (01420-3030)
P.O. Box 696, Westminster (01473-0696)
PHONE..................................978 665-9200
Ronald Bujold, *President*
EMP: 15
SQ FT: 12,000
SALES (est): 2MM **Privately Held**
SIC: 2431 1751 Mfg Millwork Carpentry Contractor

(G-10863)
WHITNEY & SON INC
95 Kelly Ave (01420-4520)
PHONE..................................978 343-6353
Daniel M Whitney, *CEO*
Charlie Jones, *President*
Doug Baker, *Principal*
Jim Hanscom, *Principal*
Jason Whitney, *Principal*
▲ **EMP:** 21
SQ FT: 8,000

GEOGRAPHIC

SALES (est): 14.5MM Privately Held
WEB: www.whitneyandson.com
SIC: 3559 5084 7359 3496 Mfg Misc Industry Mach Whol Industrial Equip Equipment Rental/Leasing Mfg Misc Fab Wire Prdts

Florence
Hampshire County

(G-10864)
BI-QEM INC
238 Nonotuck St (01062-2671)
PHONE 413 584-2472
EMP: 8 EST: 1983
SALES (est): 1.3MM Privately Held
SIC: 2821 Mfg Plastic Materials/Resins

(G-10865)
CHEMIPLASTICA INC
238 Nonotuck St (01062-2671)
PHONE 413 584-2472
Gabriel Munck, *President*
Claudio Colombo, *Principal*
Scott Chisholm, *Treasurer*
Linda Haskell, *Treasurer*
Jeanne Mazuch, *Admin Sec*
◆ EMP: 25
SQ FT: 200,000
SALES (est): 6.6MM
SALES (corp-wide): 115.8MM Privately Held
WEB: www.thermosets.com
SIC: 2821 Mfg Plastic Materials/Resins
HQ: Biqem Spa
Via Dante Alighieri 60
Carbonate CO 22070
033 183-6511

(G-10866)
FLORENCE CASKET COMPANY
16 Bardwell St (01062-1306)
PHONE 413 584-4244
Russell W Christenson, *President*
Priscilla Christenson, *Treasurer*
Ethel Christenson Beach, *Asst Treas*
EMP: 55
SQ FT: 60,000
SALES (est): 7.2MM Privately Held
WEB: www.florencecasket.com
SIC: 3995 Manufacturer Of Caskets

(G-10867)
FREE PRESS
40 Main St Ste 301 (01062-3100)
P.O. Box 60238 (01062-0238)
PHONE 413 585-1533
Robert McChesney, *President*
EMP: 35
SALES: 5.6MM Privately Held
SIC: 2711 Newspapers-Publishing/Printing

(G-10868)
RAREDON RESOURCES INC
Also Called: Tom Raredon Metal Work
30 N Maple St Ste 2 (01062-1360)
PHONE 413 586-0941
Tom Raredon, *President*
EMP: 12
SALES (est): 1.6MM Privately Held
SIC: 2514 Mfg Metal Household Furniture

(G-10869)
SUNDIAL WIRE LLC
296 Nonotuck St (01062-2657)
PHONE 413 582-6909
James V Kent, *Mng Member*
Hilary Zaloom,
EMP: 3 EST: 2010
SALES (est): 485.2K Privately Held
SIC: 3315 Mfg Steel Wire/Related Products

(G-10870)
W G FRY CORP
28 Sylvan Ln (01062-9616)
PHONE 413 747-2551
Saul Kuhr, *President*
EMP: 35
SQ FT: 50,000
SALES (est): 7.1MM Privately Held
WEB: www.fry-kamket.com
SIC: 2679 5112 2782 2789 Mfg Converted Paper Prdt Whol Stationery/Offc Sup Mfg Blankbooks/Binders Bookbinding/Related Work

Florida
Berkshire County

(G-10871)
J CROSIER MOLD POLISHING
133 Mohawk Trl (01247-9646)
PHONE 413 663-6262
Jeffrey Crosier, *Owner*
EMP: 3
SALES: 320K Privately Held
SIC: 3471 Plating/Polishing Service

Forestdale
Barnstable County

(G-10872)
PRIMA PRODUCTS
2 Spruce Tree Ln (02644-1644)
PHONE 508 553-8875
EMP: 3 EST: 2015
SALES (est): 130.4K Privately Held
SIC: 2796 Platemaking Services

Foxboro
Norfolk County

(G-10873)
ACCUTECH PACKAGING INC
157 Green St (02035-2868)
PHONE 508 543-3800
Richard J Madigan Jr, *President*
Tim Wood, *Business Mgr*
Patrick L Madigan, *Vice Pres*
Adam Claflin, *Plant Mgr*
Jim Parr, *Production*
▲ EMP: 71
SQ FT: 72,000
SALES (est): 27.2MM Privately Held
WEB: www.accutechpkg.com
SIC: 3089 3544 3565 2674 Mfg Plastic Products Mfg Dies/Tools/Jigs/Fixt Mfg Packaging Machinery Mfg Bags-Uncoated Paper

(G-10874)
ACE ARCHERS INC
131 Morse St (02035-5220)
P.O. Box 174, Foxborough (02035-0174)
PHONE 508 697-5647
Fax: 508 718-2015
EMP: 4
SALES (est): 374.7K Privately Held
SIC: 3949 Mfg Sporting/Athletic Goods

(G-10875)
ACTION ORGAN SERVICE
77 Lakeview Rd (02035-1749)
P.O. Box 366 (02035-0366)
PHONE 508 543-2161
Ron Polk, *Owner*
EMP: 3
SALES (est): 229.4K Privately Held
SIC: 3931 Electronic Organ & Keyboard Service

(G-10876)
AUTO-CHLOR SYSTEM NY CY INC
140 Washington St Ste 1 (02035-1379)
PHONE 508 543-6767
Tony Pecci, *COO*
EMP: 31
SALES (corp-wide): 3MM Privately Held
SIC: 3589 Mfg Service Industry Machinery
PA: Auto-Chlor System Of New York City, Inc.
450 Ferguson Dr
Mountain View CA 94043
650 967-3085

(G-10877)
BL HEALTHCARE INC
100 Foxboro Blvd Ste 230 (02035-2878)
PHONE 508 543-4150
John Poole, *CEO*
Michael Mathur, *President*
Gurkeerat Sidhu, *Software Engr*
EMP: 5
SALES: 350K Privately Held
SIC: 3841 5047 Mfg Surgical/Medical Instruments Whol Medical/Hospital Equipment

(G-10878)
CHAUVIN ARNOUX INC
Also Called: Aemc Instruments
200 Foxboro Blvd Ste 300 (02035-2872)
PHONE 508 698-2115
Melissa Montgomery, *Purchasing*
John Olobri, *Exec Dir*
EMP: 15
SALES (est): 2.2MM
SALES (corp-wide): 11.5MM Privately Held
WEB: www.chauvinarnoux.com
SIC: 3829 Mfg Testing Equipment
PA: Chauvin Arnoux, Inc.
15 Faraday Dr
Dover NH 03820
603 749-6434

(G-10879)
CHRISTOPHER-GORDON PUBLISHING
3 Bailey St (02035-2836)
PHONE 781 762-5577
EMP: 10
SALES (est): 1.1MM Privately Held
WEB: www.christopher-gordon.com
SIC: 2731 Book & Journal Publishing

(G-10880)
CONOPCO INC
Also Called: Auto Chlor Systems Co
140 Washington St Ste 1 (02035-1379)
PHONE 508 543-6767
Richard Goldstein, *President*
EMP: 10
SALES (corp-wide): 56.5B Privately Held
SIC: 2844 Mfg Toilet Preparations
HQ: Conopco, Inc.
700 Sylvan Ave
Englewood Cliffs NJ 07632
201 894-7760

(G-10881)
DOREL JUVENILE GROUP INC
Also Called: Safety 1st
25 Forbes Blvd Unit 4 (02035-2873)
PHONE 800 544-1108
Vincent D Alleva, *Branch Mgr*
EMP: 97
SALES (corp-wide): 2.6B Privately Held
WEB: www.coscoproducts.com
SIC: 3089 3069 3429 3699 Mfg Plastic Products Mfg Fabrcatd Rubber Prdt Mfg Hardware
HQ: Dorel Juvenile Group, Inc.
2525 State St
Columbus IN 47201
800 457-5276

(G-10882)
EPIRUS BIOPHARMACEUTICALS INC (PA)
124 Washington St Ste 101 (02035-1368)
PHONE 617 600-3497
Mark H N Corrigan, *Ch of Bd*
Amit Munshi, *President*
Robert Ticktin, *Senior VP*
Michael Wyand, *Senior VP*
Scott A Holmes, *CFO*
EMP: 22
SQ FT: 8,000
SALES (est): 2.4MM Publicly Held
WEB: www.combinatorx.com
SIC: 2834 Mfg Pharmaceutical Preparations

(G-10883)
GALLIVAN COMPANY INC
71 Elm St Ste 9 (02035-2519)
PHONE 508 543-5233
Tim Gallivan, *President*
EMP: 3
SQ FT: 3,009
SALES (est): 361.9K Privately Held
SIC: 2531 Mfg Public Building Furniture

(G-10884)
GNR USA INSTRUMENTS LLC
6 Nason Ln (02035-5202)
PHONE 508 698-3816
Vitaly Dumanis,
Elena Dumanis,
EMP: 3
SALES (est): 392K Privately Held
SIC: 3826 Mfg Analytical Instruments

(G-10885)
GPX INTERNATIONAL TIRE CORP (PA)
124 Washington St Ste 101 (02035-1368)
PHONE 781 321-3910
Robert Sherkin, *Ch of Bd*
Craig A Steinke, *President*
Bryan Ganz, *President*
Jeffrey Lucas, *Treasurer*
◆ EMP: 31
SQ FT: 250,000
SALES (est): 108.4MM Privately Held
WEB: www.galaxytire.com
SIC: 3011 Mfg Tires/Inner Tubes

(G-10886)
HY9 CORPORATION
124 Washington St Ste 101 (02035-1368)
PHONE 508 698-1040
Donald S Bradshaw Jr, *CEO*
Gary Clarke, *President*
Walter Juda, *Chairman*
Ann H Oppenheimer, *Corp Secy*
Todd Bombard, *Vice Pres*
EMP: 7
SALES (est): 971.1K Privately Held
SIC: 3621 Mfg Motors/Generators

(G-10887)
INDUSTRIAL DEFENDER INC
225 Foxboro Blvd (02035-3062)
PHONE 508 718-6777
James Crowey, *CEO*
Phil Dunbar, *CTO*
EMP: 68
SALES: 30MM Privately Held
SIC: 7372 Prepackaged Software Services

(G-10888)
INTELLIGENT MEDICAL DVCS INC
Also Called: Imdx
124 Washington St Ste 101 (02035-1368)
PHONE 617 871-6401
EMP: 9
SQ FT: 7,601
SALES: 1MM Privately Held
WEB: www.intelligentmd.com
SIC: 3829 Mfg Measuring/Controlling Devices

(G-10889)
INVENSYS SYSTEMS ARGENTINA
38 Neponset Ave (02035-2037)
PHONE 508 543-8750
George Spencer, *President*
EMP: 23
SALES (est): 3.8MM
SALES (corp-wide): 177.9K Privately Held
SIC: 3823 8711 8741 Mfg Process Control Instruments Engineering Services Management Services
HQ: Invensys Limited
2nd Floor 80 Victoria Street
London
870 608-8608

(G-10890)
KRAFT GROUP LLC (PA)
1 Patriot Pl (02035-1374)
PHONE 508 384-4230
Jonathan A Kraft, *President*
Robert Kraft, *Chairman*
Jennifer Ferron, *Vice Pres*
Michael Quattromani, *CFO*
Kara Gallagher, *Accountant*
EMP: 103

▲ = Import ▼=Export
◆ =Import/Export

SALES (est): 1.1B **Privately Held**
SIC: 2653 Mfg Corrugated/Solid Fiber Boxes

(G-10891)
L3 TECHNOLOGIES INC
Also Called: L3 Open Water Power
124 Washington St Ste 101 (02035-1368)
PHONE..................................617 895-6841
EMP: 5
SALES (corp-wide): 6.8B **Publicly Held**
SIC: 3691 Mfg Storage Batteries
HQ: L3 Technologies, Inc.
600 3rd Ave Fl 34
New York NY 10016
212 697-1111

(G-10892)
MODERN WOODWORKS CO
131 Morse St Ste 4 (02035-5200)
P.O. Box 608 (02035-0608)
PHONE..................................508 543-9830
Ed Ransom, *Owner*
EMP: 3
SQ FT: 7,000
SALES (est): 298.1K **Privately Held**
SIC: 2434 2521 Mfg Wood Kitchen Cabinets Mfg Wood Office Furniture

(G-10893)
N12 TECHNOLOGIES INC
124 Washington St Ste 101 (02035-1368)
PHONE..................................857 259-6622
Bradley Berkson, *President*
Trip Flavin, *Chairman*
Chris Holt, *Engineer*
EMP: 7
SALES (est): 1.5MM **Privately Held**
SIC: 3624 Mfg Carbon/Graphite Products

(G-10894)
NEW-INDY CNTINERBOARD HOLD LLC (HQ)
5100 Jurupa St (02035)
PHONE..................................508 384-4230
Richard Hartman, *CEO*
Robert K Kraft,
▲ **EMP:** 105
SALES (est): 61MM
SALES (corp-wide): 257.8MM **Privately Held**
SIC: 2631 Paperboard Mill
PA: New-Indy Jv Corp.
3500 Porsche Way Ste 150
Ontario CA 91764
909 296-3400

(G-10895)
OASYS WATER INC
124 Washington St Ste 101 (02035-1368)
PHONE..................................617 963-0450
James Matheson, *President*
Aaron Mandell, *Principal*
Bob Muscat, *Principal*
Edward Freedman, *Corp Secy*
Patrick Cheng Song, *Vice Pres*
▲ **EMP:** 39
SALES (est): 10.1MM **Privately Held**
SIC: 3559 Mfg Misc Industry Machinery

(G-10896)
OWNCLOUD INC
124 Washington St Ste 101 (02035-1368)
PHONE..................................617 515-3664
Markus Rex, *CEO*
Victor Dubiniuk, *Partner*
Matthew Richards, *Vice Pres*
Daniel Curtis, *CFO*
Pasquale Tripodi, *Software Engr*
EMP: 35 **EST:** 2011
SALES (est): 3MM **Privately Held**
SIC: 7372 Prepackaged Software Services

(G-10897)
PEPSICO
2 Hampshire St Ste 104 (02035-2997)
PHONE..................................508 216-1681
Robert Froman, *Principal*
EMP: 5
SALES (est): 368.7K **Privately Held**
SIC: 2086 Carb Sft Drnkbtlcn

(G-10898)
POLAR FUEL INC
95 Washington St (02035-1370)
PHONE..................................508 543-5200
Paul Saegh, *Principal*
EMP: 3
SALES (est): 204.2K **Privately Held**
SIC: 2869 Mfg Industrial Organic Chemicals

(G-10899)
REA-CRAFT PRESS INCORPORATED
10 Wall St (02035-2914)
P.O. Box 398 (02035-0398)
PHONE..................................508 543-8710
Tom Shannon, *President*
Maureen Madden, *Vice Pres*
EMP: 16 **EST:** 1937
SQ FT: 13,000
SALES (est): 2MM **Privately Held**
WEB: www.reacraft.com
SIC: 2752 Commercial Offset Printing

(G-10900)
SAFETY & GLOVES INC
100 Foxborough Blvd # 240 (02035-2878)
PHONE..................................800 221-0570
EMP: 3
SALES (est): 167.8K **Privately Held**
SIC: 3842 Mfg Surgical Appliances/Supplies

(G-10901)
SCHNEIDER ELC SYSTEMS USA INC
38 Neponset Ave (02035-2037)
PHONE..................................508 543-8750
Al Luggier, *General Mgr*
EMP: 10
SALES (corp-wide): 177.9K **Privately Held**
WEB: www.foxboro.com
SIC: 3823 8711 8741 Mfg Process Control Instruments Engineering Services Management Services
HQ: Schneider Electric Systems Usa, Inc.
38 Neponset Ave
Foxboro MA 02035
508 543-8750

(G-10902)
SCHNEIDER ELC SYSTEMS USA INC
70 Mechanic St (02035-2040)
PHONE..................................508 543-8750
Guy Grumbles, *Vice Pres*
Dan Carrie, *Manager*
EMP: 10
SALES (corp-wide): 177.9K **Privately Held**
WEB: www.foxboro.com
SIC: 3823 8711 Mfg Process Control Instruments Engineering Services
HQ: Schneider Electric Systems Usa, Inc.
38 Neponset Ave
Foxboro MA 02035
508 543-8750

(G-10903)
SCHNEIDER ELECTRIC USA INC
15 Pond Ave (02035-2006)
PHONE..................................508 549-3385
Joe Masciovecchio, *Sr Software Eng*
EMP: 5
SALES (corp-wide): 177.9K **Privately Held**
SIC: 3643 3612 3823 3625 Mfg Conductive Wire Dvcs Mfg Transformers Mfg Process Cntrl Instr
HQ: Schneider Electric Usa, Inc.
201 Wshington St Ste 2700
Boston MA 02108
978 975-9600

(G-10904)
SENTRY COMPANY
62 Main St (02035-1899)
PHONE..................................508 543-5391
Bristol B Crocker, *Ch of Bd*
Thomas P Crocker, *President*
Janet Vigor, *Admin Sec*
EMP: 9 **EST:** 1921
SQ FT: 40,000
SALES: 696.6K **Privately Held**
WEB: www.sentryfurnaces.com
SIC: 3567 Mfg Industrial Electric Heat Treating Furnaces & Accessories

(G-10905)
SIEBE INC (DH)
33 Commercial St B51-2c (02035-5309)
PHONE..................................508 549-6768
Nigel Rudd, *Chairman*
EMP: 5
SALES (est): 778.8K
SALES (corp-wide): 177.9K **Privately Held**
SIC: 3822 Mfg Enviromental Controls
HQ: Schneider Electric Systems Usa Inc
10900 Equity Dr
Houston TX 77041
713 329-1600

(G-10906)
TELTRON ENGINEERING INC
131 Morse St Ste 9 (02035-5200)
PHONE..................................508 543-6600
Ernest Whitaker, *President*
Carol Downey, *Office Admin*
EMP: 15
SQ FT: 25,000
SALES (est): 3.3MM **Privately Held**
WEB: www.teltron-engineering.com
SIC: 3444 Mfg Sheet Metalwork

(G-10907)
UNLIMITED FUEL HEATING INC
11 Maple Pl (02035-2964)
PHONE..................................508 543-1043
Agustina Henriquez, *CEO*
EMP: 3 **EST:** 2010
SALES (est): 279.9K **Privately Held**
SIC: 2869 Mfg Industrial Organic Chemicals

(G-10908)
VIAMET PHRMCTCALS HOLDINGS LLC
124 Washington St Ste 101 (02035-1368)
PHONE..................................919 467-8539
Robert A Ingram, *Ch of Bd*
Robert J Schotzinger, *President*
Richard D Katz, *CFO*
Oren J Cohen, *Officer*
Volker Herrmann, *Officer*
EMP: 32
SALES: 679K **Privately Held**
SIC: 2834 Mfg Pharmaceutical Preparations

(G-10909)
WOODFORMS INC
131 Morse St Ste 10 (02035-5200)
P.O. Box 69 (02035-0069)
PHONE..................................508 543-9417
Robert O'Hare, *President*
EMP: 7
SQ FT: 11,000
SALES (est): 502.1K **Privately Held**
WEB: www.woodforms.net
SIC: 2511 Mfg Wooden Bedroom Furniture

Foxborough
Norfolk County

(G-10910)
ACE ARCHERS INC
131 Morse St (02035-5220)
P.O. Box 174 (02035-0174)
PHONE..................................774 215-5292
Thomas Herrington, *President*
EMP: 4
SQ FT: 7,000
SALES (est): 149.5K **Privately Held**
SIC: 3949 Mfg Sporting/Athletic Goods

(G-10911)
BANDERA ACQUISITION LLC (DH)
2 Hampshire St (02035-2896)
PHONE..................................480 553-6400
EMP: 120
SALES (est): 23.6MM
SALES (corp-wide): 368.7MM **Privately Held**
SIC: 3069 3089 Manufactures Fabricated Rubber Products Plastic Products

(G-10912)
CAMBRIDGE HEART INC (PA)
124 Washington St (02035-1368)
PHONE..................................978 654-7600
Ali Haghighi-Mood, *President*
Vincenzo Licausi, *CFO*
EMP: 31
SALES: 2.2MM **Privately Held**
WEB: www.cambridgeheart.com
SIC: 3841 3845 Mfg Diagnostic & Electromedical Equipment

(G-10913)
RED OAK SOURCING LLC
2 Hampshire St Ste 200 (02035-2950)
PHONE..................................401 742-0701
Craig Heneghan, *President*
EMP: 60
SQ FT: 20,605
SALES (est): 19.7MM
SALES (corp-wide): 194.5B **Publicly Held**
SIC: 2834 Mfg Pharmaceutical Preparations
PA: Cvs Health Corporation
1 Cvs Dr
Woonsocket RI 02895
401 765-1500

GEOGRAPHIC

Framingham
Middlesex County

(G-10914)
AB SCIEX LLC
500 Old Connecticut Path B (01701-4574)
PHONE..................................508 383-7300
Frank McFaden, *Branch Mgr*
EMP: 5
SALES (corp-wide): 19.8B **Publicly Held**
SIC: 3826 Mfg Analytical Instruments
HQ: Ab Sciex Llc
1201 Radio Rd
Redwood City CA 94065

(G-10915)
AB SCIEX SALES LP
500 Old Connecticut Path B (01701-4574)
PHONE..................................508 383-7700
Matthew Christiansen, *District Mgr*
David Roblin, *COO*
Daniel Burkhoff, *Vice Pres*
Austin Byrd, *Vice Pres*
Fraser McLeod, *Vice Pres*
EMP: 67
SALES (est): 14.3MM **Privately Held**
SIC: 3826 Mfg Analytical Instruments

(G-10916)
ACE TORWEL INC (HQ)
38 Simpson Dr (01701-4076)
P.O. Box 1739, Willmar MN (56201-1739)
PHONE..................................888 878-0898
Carl McKenzie, *President*
James M Ruff, *Principal*
EMP: 11
SALES (est): 989.6K
SALES (corp-wide): 4.1MM **Privately Held**
SIC: 3531 Salt And Sand Spreaders
PA: Ace Group, Llc
3761 Highway 12 E
Willmar MN 56201
320 235-5536

(G-10917)
ADAPTIVE INSIGHTS INC
50 Speen St Ste 300 (01701-1802)
PHONE..................................508 532-4947
Charlie Hill, *Manager*
EMP: 5
SALES (corp-wide): 2.8B **Publicly Held**
SIC: 7372 Prepackaged Software Services
HQ: Adaptive Insights Llc , A Workday Company
2300 Geng Rd Ste 100
Palo Alto CA 94303
650 528-7500

(G-10918)
ADVANTAGE MEDIA & MARKETING
225 Arlington St Ste D (01702-8773)
PHONE....................508 875-0011
Michael Herman, *President*
EMP: 3
SALES: 400K **Privately Held**
SIC: 2752 Off-Set Printing

(G-10919)
ALZHEON INC
111 Speen St Ste 306 (01701-2090)
PHONE....................508 861-7709
Jean-Pierre Garnier, *Ch of Bd*
Neil Flanzraich, *Vice Ch Bd*
Martin Tolar, *President*
Petr Kocis, *Vice Pres*
Aidan C Power, *Vice Pres*
EMP: 6
SQ FT: 3,317
SALES (est): 1.4MM **Privately Held**
SIC: 2834 Pharmaceutical Preparations

(G-10920)
AMERICAN LIGHTING FIXTURE CORP
Also Called: Wilshire Manufacturing Co.
58 Flanagan Dr (01701-3745)
PHONE....................508 824-1970
William Segill, *President*
Mark Segill, *Vice Pres*
Robert Segill, *Treasurer*
Paul Segill, *Admin Sec*
◆ **EMP**: 180
SQ FT: 150,000
SALES (est): 27.1MM **Privately Held**
WEB: www.wilshiremfg.com
SIC: 3646 Mfg Commercial Lighting Fixtures

(G-10921)
APPLAUSE LLC
100 Pennsylvania Ave # 500 (01701-8869)
PHONE....................508 665-6910
Doron Reuveni, *CEO*
Sanji Alwis, *President*
Tom Bonos, *Senior VP*
Rob Mason, *Senior VP*
John Montgomery, *Senior VP*
EMP: 51
SALES (est): 7MM **Privately Held**
SIC: 7372 Business Consulting Services

(G-10922)
APPLIED BIOSYSTEMS LLC
1455 Concord St Ste 8 (01701-7773)
PHONE....................508 877-1307
EMP: 4
SALES (corp-wide): 24.3B **Publicly Held**
SIC: 3826 Mfg Analytical Instruments
HQ: Applied Biosystems, Llc
5791 Van Allen Way
Carlsbad CA 92008

(G-10923)
AVERY DENNISON CORPORATION
175 Crossing Blvd Ste 510 (01702-4476)
PHONE....................508 988-8200
Logan David, *Vice Pres*
Bill Cooper, *Manager*
EMP: 115
SALES (corp-wide): 7.1B **Publicly Held**
SIC: 2672 Mfg Coated/Laminated Paper
PA: Avery Dennison Corporation
207 N Goode Ave
Glendale CA 91203
626 304-2000

(G-10924)
B C AMES INCORPORATED
1644 Concord St (01701-3531)
PHONE....................781 893-0095
Francis Gardner, *President*
Susan Gardner, *Office Mgr*
EMP: 9
SQ FT: 10,000
SALES (est): 880K **Privately Held**
WEB: www.bcames.com
SIC: 3825 3823 Mfg Electrical Measuring Instruments Mfg Process Control Instruments

(G-10925)
BARAMUNDI SOFTWARE USA INC
550 Cochituate Rd Ste 25 (01701-4683)
PHONE....................508 861-7561
Christian Burghart, *Admin Sec*
Luke Gyure, *Administration*
EMP: 3 **EST**: 2016
SALES (est): 78.2K
SALES (corp-wide): 477.9MM **Privately Held**
SIC: 7372 Prepackaged Software Services
HQ: Baramundi Software Ag
Beim Glaspalast 1
Augsburg 86153
821 567-080

(G-10926)
BEACON APPLICATION SVCS CORP (PA)
40 Speen St Ste 305 (01701-1898)
PHONE....................508 663-4433
Daniel P Maude, *President*
EMP: 35
SALES (est): 8.2MM **Privately Held**
SIC: 7372 8742 5045 Prepackaged Software Services Management Consulting Services Whol Computers/Peripherals

(G-10927)
BERG LLC (PA)
500 Old Connecticut Path # 3
(01701-4574)
PHONE....................617 588-0083
Niven R Narain, *Principal*
EMP: 63
SALES (est): 19MM **Privately Held**
SIC: 2834 Mfg Pharmaceutical Preparations

(G-10928)
BOSE CORPORATION (PA)
100 The Mountain Rd (01701-8863)
PHONE....................508 879-7330
Phil Hess, *President*
Robert Maresca, *Chairman*
Colette Burke, *Vice Pres*
Bryan K Fontaine, *Vice Pres*
Mike Spina, *Project Mgr*
◆ **EMP**: 2000
SQ FT: 900,000
SALES (est): 2.5B **Privately Held**
WEB: www.bose.com
SIC: 3651 5731 Mfg Home Audio/Video Equipment Ret Radio/Tv/Electronics

(G-10929)
BOSE CORPORATION
145 Pennsylvania Ave (01701-8866)
PHONE....................508 766-1265
Jeff Duclos, *Opers Mgr*
Peter Raymond, *Engineer*
Douglas Schow, *Engineer*
Joseph Tesini, *Cust Mgr*
James Kostinden, *Branch Mgr*
EMP: 20
SALES (corp-wide): 2.5B **Privately Held**
SIC: 3825 3651 Mfg Electrical Measuring Instruments Mfg Home Audio/Video Equipment
PA: Bose Corporation
100 The Mountain Rd
Framingham MA 01701
508 879-7330

(G-10930)
BRIDGE 12 TECHNOLOGIES INC
37 Loring Dr (01702-8768)
PHONE....................617 674-2766
Louis Tarricone, *President*
Dennis Gautreau, *Engineer*
Darpan Gokharu, *Treasurer*
Valerie Del Padre, *Info Tech Mgr*
EMP: 6
SALES (est): 500K **Privately Held**
SIC: 3671 Mfg Electron Tubes

(G-10931)
CAUSEWAY GRAPHICS
27 Cochituate Rd (01701-7914)
PHONE....................508 309-6592
Anne Curll, *Principal*
EMP: 3
SALES (est): 189K **Privately Held**
SIC: 2759 Commercial Printing

(G-10932)
CCL LABEL INC (HQ)
Also Called: Syntel
161 Worcester Rd Ste 603 (01701-5315)
PHONE....................508 872-4511
Geoffrey T Martin, *President*
Lalitha Vaidyanathan, *Senior VP*
Mark A McClendon, *Vice Pres*
Sean P Washchuk, *CFO*
Timothy Duffy, *VP Sales*
◆ **EMP**: 85
SALES (est): 613.3MM
SALES (corp-wide): 3.9B **Privately Held**
SIC: 2759 3411 2671 Commercial Printing Mfg Metal Cans Mfg Packaging Paper/Film
PA: Ccl Industries Inc
111 Gordon Baker Rd Suite 801
Toronto ON M2H 3
800 563-2464

(G-10933)
CHOCOLATE THERAPY
60 Worcester Rd Ste 10 (01702-5312)
PHONE....................508 875-1571
Pamela Griffith, *President*
EMP: 10
SALES (est): 725K **Privately Held**
SIC: 2066 5441 Mfg Chocolate/Cocoa Products Ret Candy/Confectionery

(G-10934)
CIRCLE TWELVE INC
945 Concord St (01701-4613)
PHONE....................508 620-5360
Adam Bogue, *President*
EMP: 6
SALES (est): 436.5K **Privately Held**
SIC: 3577 Mfg Computer Peripheral Equipment

(G-10935)
COMMUNITY NEWSPAPER
Also Called: Mansfield News
5 Cohannat St (01701)
PHONE....................508 339-8977
Kirk Davis, *CEO*
EMP: 6
SALES (est): 354.3K **Privately Held**
SIC: 2711 Newspapers-Publishing/Printing

(G-10936)
CONCRETEBENCHMOLDS LLC
75 Angelica Dr (01701-3646)
PHONE....................800 242-1809
Cara Merusi, *Owner*
EMP: 3 **EST**: 2012
SALES (est): 203.4K **Privately Held**
SIC: 3272 Mfg Concrete Products

(G-10937)
CROSSED GENRES
204 Arthur St (01702-8183)
PHONE....................617 335-2101
EMP: 3
SALES (est): 115K **Privately Held**
SIC: 2741 Misc Publishing

(G-10938)
CXO MEDIA INC (DH)
492 Old Connecticut Path # 200
(01701-4580)
P.O. Box 9208 (01701-9208)
PHONE....................508 766-5696
Abbie Lundberg, *Senior VP*
Mathew Smith, *CFO*
Edward B Bloom, *Treasurer*
Kristin Darby, *Officer*
EMP: 138
SQ FT: 30,000
SALES (est): 12.4MM
SALES (corp-wide): 1.7B **Privately Held**
SIC: 2791 2721 Typesetting Services Periodicals-Publishing/Printing
HQ: Idg Communications, Inc.
5 Speen St
Framingham MA 01701
508 872-8200

(G-10939)
D CEDRONE INC
7 Hiram Rd (01701-2607)
PHONE....................508 405-4260
Dino Cedrone, *Principal*
EMP: 3 **EST**: 2009
SALES (est): 288.2K **Privately Held**
SIC: 3721 Mfg Aircraft

(G-10940)
DAVID GILBERT
Also Called: D C M Services
10 Olympic St (01701-4528)
PHONE....................508 879-1507
David Gilbert, *Owner*
EMP: 8
SQ FT: 10,000
SALES (est): 440K **Privately Held**
WEB: www.davidgilbert.com
SIC: 3599 7692 Mfg Industrial Machinery Welding Repair

(G-10941)
DEERFIELD CORPORATION
Also Called: Deerfield Optics
6 Doyle Cir (01701-2824)
PHONE....................508 877-0143
EMP: 6
SALES: 1.3MM **Privately Held**
SIC: 3841 5063 Mfg Optical Instruments & Whol Electrical Construction Materials

(G-10942)
DUGGAN ASSOCIATES INC
Also Called: Sir Speedy
375 Worcester Rd (01701-5307)
PHONE....................508 879-3277
David Riley, *President*
EMP: 3 **EST**: 1972
SQ FT: 1,500
SALES (est): 457.1K **Privately Held**
SIC: 2752 Comm Prtg Litho

(G-10943)
E H PUBLISHING INC (PA)
Also Called: Electronic House
111 Speen St Ste 200 (01701-2090)
P.O. Box 989 (01701-0989)
PHONE....................508 663-1500
Kenneth D Moyes, *Principal*
Steve Martini, *COO*
Manuela Rosengard, *Prdtn Dir*
Amy Brennan, *Production*
Steve McCoy, *Natl Sales Mgr*
EMP: 47
SQ FT: 8,000
SALES (est): 8.3MM **Privately Held**
WEB: www.ehpub.com
SIC: 2741 Misc Publishing

(G-10944)
EAST COAST PLASTICS INC
763 Waverley St Ste 3 (01702-8564)
PHONE....................508 429-8080
Michael Bagge, *President*
EMP: 7 **EST**: 1947
SQ FT: 6,500
SALES: 509K **Privately Held**
WEB: www.eastcoastplastics.com
SIC: 3479 Plastic & Dip Coating

(G-10945)
ELBONAIS INCORPORATED
Also Called: AlphaGraphics
1451 Concord St Ste 1 (01701-7782)
PHONE....................508 626-2318
Harold Noble Jr, *President*
EMP: 8
SQ FT: 2,200
SALES (est): 119K **Privately Held**
SIC: 2752 2791 2789 2759 Lithographic Coml Print Typesetting Services Bookbinding/Related Work Commercial Printing

(G-10946)
FRAMINGHAM ENGRAVING CO
Also Called: Neew England Badge
20 Nadine Rd (01701-7603)
PHONE....................508 877-7867
Nicholas Martin, *Owner*
EMP: 4
SALES (est): 167.2K **Privately Held**
SIC: 3479 5999 Coating/Engraving Service Ret Misc Merchandise

(G-10947)
FRAMINGHAM SOURCE
124 Fay Rd (01702-6867)
PHONE....................508 315-7176
Susan Petroni, *Principal*
EMP: 3 **EST**: 2016

▲ = Import ▼=Export
◆ =Import/Export

SALES (est): 144.9K Privately Held
SIC: 2711 Newspapers-Publishing/Printing

(G-10948)
GATEHOUSE MEDIA MASS I INC
Also Called: Framingham Tab
33 New York Ave (01701-8857)
PHONE....................508 626-4412
Richard Lodge, *Principal*
Sheehan Gayle, *Director*
EMP: 108
SALES (corp-wide): 1.5B Publicly Held
SIC: 2711 Newspapers-Publishing/Printing
HQ: Gatehouse Media Massachusetts I, Inc.
48 Dunham Rd
Beverly MA 01915
585 598-0030

(G-10949)
GEMS PUBLISHING USA INC
12 Walnut St (01702-7515)
PHONE....................508 872-0066
Tom Orent, *President*
EMP: 5
SALES (est): 412.2K Privately Held
WEB: www.1000gems.com
SIC: 2741 Misc Publishing

(G-10950)
GENZYME CORPORATION
31 New York Ave (01701-8834)
PHONE....................508 271-3631
Ron Keefe, *Manager*
Seng Cheng, *Director*
EMP: 5 Privately Held
WEB: www.genzyme.com
SIC: 2835 Mfg Pharmaceutical Preparations
HQ: Genzyme Corporation
50 Binney St
Cambridge MA 02142
617 252-7500

(G-10951)
GENZYME CORPORATION
200 Crossing Blvd (01702-4486)
PHONE....................508 271-2642
Oxana Beskrovnaya, *Vice Pres*
Cindy Maclean, *Project Mgr*
Jan Stepanik, *Mfg Spvr*
Marc Fieischman, *Engineer*
John Sicurella, *Engineer*
EMP: 122 Privately Held
SIC: 2834 Mfg Pharmaceutical Preparations
HQ: Genzyme Corporation
50 Binney St
Cambridge MA 02142
617 252-7500

(G-10952)
GENZYME CORPORATION
78 New York Ave (01701-8859)
PHONE....................617 252-7500
Charles Thyne, *Vice Pres*
Walter Eaton, *Mfg Spvr*
Michelle Busch, *Research*
Frances Egan, *Case Mgr*
Tracie Atkins, *Manager*
EMP: 93 Privately Held
SIC: 2834 Mfg Pharmaceutical Preparations
HQ: Genzyme Corporation
50 Binney St
Cambridge MA 02142
617 252-7500

(G-10953)
GENZYME CORPORATION
80 New York Ave (01701-8859)
PHONE....................508 370-9690
Jorge Colado, *Principal*
EMP: 20 Privately Held
WEB: www.genzyme.com
SIC: 2834 Mfg Pharmaceutical Preparations
HQ: Genzyme Corporation
50 Binney St
Cambridge MA 02142
617 252-7500

(G-10954)
GENZYME CORPORATION
Also Called: Sanofi Genzyme
1 The Mountain Rd (01701-8858)
PHONE....................508 872-8400
Sarah Nsereko, *Research*
Paul Grasso, *CFO*
Scott Schaefer, *Branch Mgr*
Ki S Lee, *Program Mgr*
Cynthia Laird, *Info Tech Dir*
EMP: 84 Privately Held
SIC: 2834 Mfg Pharmaceutical Preparations
HQ: Genzyme Corporation
50 Binney St
Cambridge MA 02142
617 252-7500

(G-10955)
GENZYME CORPORATION
51 New York Ave (01701-8861)
PHONE....................508 872-8400
Marshall John, *Manager*
Christine Demaria, *Associate Dir*
EMP: 216 Privately Held
SIC: 2834 Mfg Pharmaceutical Preparations
HQ: Genzyme Corporation
50 Binney St
Cambridge MA 02142
617 252-7500

(G-10956)
GENZYME CORPORATION
45 New York Ave (01701-8861)
PHONE....................508 872-8400
Kuber Sampath, *Branch Mgr*
Robert Donaldson, *Director*
EMP: 216 Privately Held
SIC: 2834 Mfg Pharmaceutical Preparations
HQ: Genzyme Corporation
50 Binney St
Cambridge MA 02142
617 252-7500

(G-10957)
GENZYME CORPORATION
74 New York Ave (01701-8859)
PHONE....................508 872-8400
Joanne Ward, *Mfg Staff*
Scott G Bobbitt, *Branch Mgr*
Denise Woodcock, *Manager*
Matthew Offenbacher, *Supervisor*
EMP: 216 Privately Held
SIC: 2834 Mfg Pharmaceutical Preparations
HQ: Genzyme Corporation
50 Binney St
Cambridge MA 02142
617 252-7500

(G-10958)
GENZYME CORPORATION
68 New York Ave (01701-8859)
PHONE....................508 872-8400
Douglas Kennedy, *Mfg Staff*
Jonathan Pickell, *Mfg Staff*
Allison Cacciatore, *Branch Mgr*
EMP: 216 Privately Held
SIC: 2834 Mfg Pharmaceutical Preparations
HQ: Genzyme Corporation
50 Binney St
Cambridge MA 02142
617 252-7500

(G-10959)
GERARD FARMS INC
447 Water St (01701-7610)
PHONE....................781 858-1013
Michael Gerard, *President*
EMP: 5 EST: 1930
SQ FT: 4,000
SALES (est): 359K Privately Held
WEB: www.gerardfarm.com
SIC: 2015 5812 Poultry Processing Eating Place

(G-10960)
GLENWOOD KITCHENS USA
1291 Worcester Rd Ste 3 (01701-5353)
PHONE....................508 875-1180
Doug McLeod, *Principal*
EMP: 4 EST: 2008
SALES (est): 293.4K Privately Held
SIC: 2434 Mfg Wood Kitchen Cabinets

(G-10961)
GREENTREE MARKETING INC
Also Called: Norco
10 Central St (01701-4163)
P.O. Box 3500 (01705-3500)
PHONE....................508 877-2581
Lee Jensen, *President*
EMP: 10
SQ FT: 10,000
SALES (est): 1.4MM Privately Held
SIC: 2752 Lithographic Commercial Printing

(G-10962)
HEARTWARE INTERNATIONAL INC (DH)
500 Old Connecticut Path (01701-4574)
PHONE....................508 739-0950
Douglas Godshall, *President*
Larry Knopf, *Senior VP*
Peter F McAree, *CFO*
Jeffrey Larose, *Officer*
Katrin Leadley MD, *Officer*
EMP: 21
SQ FT: 74,000
SALES: 276.8MM Privately Held
SIC: 3841 Manufactures Surgical/Medical Instruments
HQ: Medtronic, Inc.
710 Medtronic Pkwy
Minneapolis MN 55432
763 514-4000

(G-10963)
HOPKINTON CRIER
33 New York Ave (01701-8857)
PHONE....................508 626-3939
Greg Rush, *Principal*
Nicole Simmons, *Technology*
EMP: 3
SALES (est): 125.3K Privately Held
SIC: 2711 Newspapers-Publishing/Printing

(G-10964)
I-PASS PATIENT SAFETY INST INC
Also Called: I-Pass Institute
161 Worcester Rd Ste 402 (01701-5300)
PHONE....................617 932-7926
William Floyd, *CEO*
Christopher Landrigan, *Principal*
Timothy O'Shea, *Principal*
Theodore Sectish, *Principal*
Nancy Spector, *Principal*
EMP: 4 EST: 2017
SALES (est): 108.2K Privately Held
SIC: 7372 Prepackaged Software Services

(G-10965)
IDG COMMUNICATIONS INC (HQ)
5 Speen St (01701-4674)
P.O. Box 1912 (01701-0112)
PHONE....................508 872-8200
Matthew Yorke, *CEO*
Kumaran Ramanathan, *President*
Charles Lee, *President*
Bob Melk, *President*
York Von Heimburg, *President*
EMP: 150
SQ FT: 5,000
SALES (est): 168.8MM
SALES (corp-wide): 1.7B Privately Held
WEB: www.idglist.com
SIC: 2721 2731 Periodicals-Publishing/Printing Books-Publishing/Printing
PA: International Data Group, Inc.
1 Exeter Plz Fl 15
Boston MA 02116
508 875-5000

(G-10966)
IDG COMMUNICATIONS INC
Also Called: Idg Brokerage Services
492 Old Connecticut Path (01701-4584)
P.O. Box 9151 (01701-9151)
PHONE....................508 766-5300
Andrew Sambrook, *General Mgr*
EMP: 12
SALES (corp-wide): 1.7B Privately Held
WEB: www.idglist.com
SIC: 2721 Periodicals-Publishing/Printing
HQ: Idg Communications, Inc.
5 Speen St
Framingham MA 01701
508 872-8200

(G-10967)
IDG CORPORATE SERVICES GROUP
5 Speen St Ste 5 # 5 (01701-4674)
P.O. Box 3 (01704-0003)
PHONE....................508 875-5000
Deb Goldstein, *President*
EMP: 11
SALES (est): 654.1K
SALES (corp-wide): 1.7B Privately Held
WEB: www.idglist.com
SIC: 2721 8732 Periodicals-Publishing/Printing Commercial Nonphysical Research
HQ: Idg Communications, Inc.
5 Speen St
Framingham MA 01701
508 872-8200

(G-10968)
IDG PAPER SERVICES
492 Old Connecticut Path # 410 (01701-4584)
PHONE....................508 875-5000
Patricia Sims, *Principal*
EMP: 25
SALES (est): 594.8K
SALES (corp-wide): 1.7B Privately Held
WEB: www.workscape.net
SIC: 2741 2731 Misc Publishing Books-Publishing/Printing
PA: International Data Group, Inc.
1 Exeter Plz Fl 15
Boston MA 02116
508 875-5000

(G-10969)
INTACT MEDICAL CORPORATION
550 Cochituate Rd Ste 25 (01701-4683)
PHONE....................508 655-7820
EMP: 20 EST: 2000
SQ FT: 1,500
SALES (est): 3.9MM Privately Held
SIC: 3841 Mfg Surgical/Medical Instruments

(G-10970)
INTERNATIONAL DATA GROUP INC
Also Called: Idg List Services
3 Speen St Ste 300 (01701-4664)
PHONE....................508 766-5632
Nevena Conic, *Regional Mgr*
Karen Timons, *Opers Mgr*
Nina Turner, *Research*
Dan Vesset, *Research*
John Villali, *Research*
EMP: 20
SALES (corp-wide): 1.7B Privately Held
WEB: www.workscape.net
SIC: 2721 Periodicals-Publishing/Printing
PA: International Data Group, Inc.
1 Exeter Plz Fl 15
Boston MA 02116
508 875-5000

(G-10971)
INTERNATIONAL DATA GROUP INC
5 Speen St Ste 1 (01701-4665)
PHONE....................508 935-4719
Fax: 508 935-4288
EMP: 16
SALES (corp-wide): 3.5B Privately Held
SIC: 2721 Publishers
PA: International Data Group, Inc.
1 Exeter Plz Fl 15
Boston MA 02116
617 423-9030

(G-10972)
JMD MANUFACTURING INC
59 Fountain St Ste 5 (01702-6269)
PHONE....................508 620-6563
Sushil Bhatia, *President*
Mishi Jaggi, *Manager*

EMP: 5
SQ FT: 2,800
SALES (est): 200K **Privately Held**
SIC: 2671 Mfg Marking & Coding Machines & Supplies

(G-10973)
JNJ INC
Also Called: Alltype Signs & Graphics
505 Worcester Rd (01701-5302)
PHONE..................................508 620-0202
John Grocer, *President*
EMP: 5
SQ FT: 1,200
SALES (est): 399.9K **Privately Held**
WEB: www.alltype.com
SIC: 3993 Mfg Signs/Advertising Specialties

(G-10974)
JOHN HARVARDS BREWHOUSE LLC
Also Called: John Harvard's Brew House
1 Worcester Rd (01701-5359)
PHONE..................................508 875-2337
Grenville Buyford, *CEO*
Bob Vernava, *General Mgr*
EMP: 100 **Privately Held**
SIC: 2082 5812 Manufactures Beer/Steak & Seafood Restaurant
PA: John Harvard's Brewhouse, Llc
1 Federal St
Boston MA

(G-10975)
KAMROWSKI REFINISHING CO INC
Also Called: Kamrowski Metal Refinishing
12 Bradford Rd (01701-7617)
PHONE..................................508 877-0367
Richard Kamrowski, *President*
Deborah Kamrowski, *Treasurer*
EMP: 10
SALES: 500K **Privately Held**
SIC: 3446 Mfg Architectural Metalwork

(G-10976)
LIFE TECHNOLOGIES CORPORATION
Applied Biosystems Group
500 Old Connecticut Path # 10
(01701-4574)
PHONE..................................508 383-7700
Kevin Tillis, *Manager*
EMP: 13
SALES (corp-wide): 24.3B **Publicly Held**
SIC: 3826 Mfg Surgical/Medical Instruments
HQ: Life Technologies Corporation
5781 Van Allen Way
Carlsbad CA 92008
760 603-7200

(G-10977)
LIFELINE SYSTEMS COMPANY (DH)
Also Called: Philips Lifeline
111 Lawrence St (01702-8171)
PHONE..................................508 988-1000
Kimberly O'Laughlin, *President*
Gerard Van Spaendonck, *President*
Richard M Reich, *Senior VP*
Donald G Strange, *Senior VP*
Paul Cavanaugh, *Vice Pres*
▲ **EMP:** 544
SQ FT: 84,000
SALES (est): 231.2MM
SALES (corp-wide): 20.1B **Privately Held**
SIC: 3669 Mfg Communications Equipment

(G-10978)
LIFELINE SYSTEMS COMPANY
Also Called: Lifeline Systems Securities
111 Lawrence St (01702-8171)
PHONE..................................508 988-3000
Michael Cannon, *Branch Mgr*
EMP: 150
SALES (corp-wide): 20.1B **Privately Held**
SIC: 3669 Security Broker/Dealer
HQ: Lifeline Systems Company
111 Lawrence St
Framingham MA 01702
508 988-1000

(G-10979)
M E BAKER COMPANY (PA)
945 Concord St (01701-4613)
PHONE..................................508 620-5304
Stephen H Roiter, *President*
M E Baker, *Partner*
Roger H Love, *Exec VP*
EMP: 16 **EST:** 1940
SQ FT: 27,000
SALES (est): 5.4MM **Privately Held**
SIC: 3559 3589 5084 5085 Mfg Misc Industry Mach Mfg Svc Industry Mach Whol Industrial Equip Whol Industrial Supplies

(G-10980)
MAGIC PRINTING INC
945 Concord St (01701-4613)
PHONE..................................413 363-1711
Richard Wechter, *President*
Emily Wechter, *Vice Pres*
Joseph Wechter, *Vice Pres*
EMP: 3 **EST:** 2006
SALES (est): 300.8K **Privately Held**
WEB: www.magicvinylprinting.com
SIC: 3993 Mfg Signs/Advertising Specialties

(G-10981)
MASONRY & MORE INC
34 Benson Ave (01702-6858)
PHONE..................................508 740-8537
EMP: 3
SALES (est): 106.4K **Privately Held**
SIC: 2024 Mfg Ice Cream/Frozen Desert

(G-10982)
MEDICAL ARTS PRESS INC
500 Staples Dr 30352v (01702-4478)
PHONE..................................508 253-5000
Lawrence Morse, *Principal*
EMP: 8
SALES (est): 522.9K **Privately Held**
SIC: 2741 Ret Stationery

(G-10983)
MEDITECH
550 Cochituate Rd (01701-4654)
PHONE..................................781 821-3000
Pmp Coughlin, *Assoc VP*
EMP: 5 **EST:** 2013
SALES (est): 388.3K **Privately Held**
SIC: 7372 Prepackaged Software Services

(G-10984)
MEDTRONIC
500 Old Connecticut Path # 3
(01701-4574)
PHONE..................................508 739-0950
Lawrence Knopf, *Vice Pres*
Mark Strong, *Vice Pres*
Jim Yearick, *Vice Pres*
Kimberlee Krou, *Engineer*
Alexis Perez, *Engineer*
EMP: 5 **Privately Held**
WEB: www.heartwareinc.com
SIC: 3845 Mfg Electromedical Equipment
HQ: Medtronic
14400 Nw 60th Ave
Miami Lakes FL 33014
305 818-4100

(G-10985)
MIDDLESEX NEWS
33 New York Ave (01701-8880)
PHONE..................................508 626-3800
Chuck Goodrick, *Principal*
EMP: 3
SALES (est): 183K **Privately Held**
SIC: 2711 Newspapers-Publishing/Printing

(G-10986)
NETWORK WORLD INC
492 Old Connecticut Path # 311
(01701-4583)
PHONE..................................800 622-1108
Evilee Ebb, *CEO*
Cheryl Crivello, *Opers Staff*
Sue Yanovitch, *VP Mktg*
EMP: 132
SALES (est): 10MM
SALES (corp-wide): 1.7B **Privately Held**
WEB: www.networkworldpartners.com
SIC: 2721 8742 Periodicals-Publishing/Printing Management Consulting Services
PA: International Data Group, Inc.
1 Exeter Plz Fl 15
Boston MA 02116
508 875-5000

(G-10987)
NEW ENGLAND SAND & GRAVEL CO
Corner Danforth & Birch (01701)
P.O. Box 3248 (01705-3248)
PHONE..................................508 877-2460
Frank Generazio Jr, *President*
Richard Generazio, *Treasurer*
EMP: 12 **EST:** 1939
SQ FT: 750
SALES (est): 819K **Privately Held**
SIC: 1442 Sand & Gravel Pit

(G-10988)
NEWMAN ENTERPRISES INC
Also Called: Sign-A-Rama
280 Worcester Rd Ste 118 (01702-5356)
PHONE..................................508 875-7446
Jeffrey H Newman, *President*
EMP: 6 **EST:** 2002
SQ FT: 3,000
SALES: 680K **Privately Held**
SIC: 3993 Signsadv Specs

(G-10989)
OPUS TELECOM INC
119 Herbert St (01702-8774)
PHONE..................................508 875-4444
Jay L Gainsboro, *President*
Roseann Rinaldo, *Manager*
Edward Stumpf, *Software Dev*
Barbara Gainsboro, *Clerk*
EMP: 35
SQ FT: 8,000
SALES: 9MM **Privately Held**
SIC: 3661 Designs & Mfg Custom Micro-Process Based Telecommunications Equipment

(G-10990)
ORIENTAL RESEARCH PARTNERS
61 Tripp St (01702-8771)
PHONE..................................781 642-1216
Philip Clendenning, *Owner*
EMP: 4
SALES (est): 131.9K **Privately Held**
SIC: 2731 Books-Publishing/Printing

(G-10991)
OVERTONE STUDIO INC
492 Old Connecticut Path # 102
(01701-4583)
PHONE..................................774 290-2900
Nick Burt, *General Mgr*
EMP: 8
SALES (est): 196K **Privately Held**
SIC: 7372 Prepackaged Software Services

(G-10992)
PACON CORPORATION
79 Main St Ste 202 (01702-2945)
PHONE..................................508 370-0780
Andrew P Thomspon, *Principal*
EMP: 20
SALES (corp-wide): 14.2MM **Privately Held**
WEB: www.paconcorporation.com
SIC: 2672 Mfg Coated/Laminated Paper
PA: Pacon Corporation
145 Park Rd
Putnam CT 06260
860 315-9030

(G-10993)
PHILIPS HLTHCARE INFRMTICS INC
Phillips Lifeline Systems
111 Lawrence St (01702-8156)
PHONE..................................508 988-1000
EMP: 16
SALES (corp-wide): 20.1B **Privately Held**
SIC: 3669 Whol Medical/Hospital Equipment
HQ: Philips Healthcare Informatics, Inc.
4430 Rosewood Dr Ste 200
Pleasanton CA 94588
650 293-2300

(G-10994)
PHOENIX TRADING CO INC (PA)
92 Blandin Ave Ste J (01702-7072)
PHONE..................................617 794-8368
Marc Cohen, *President*
EMP: 4
SQ FT: 18,000
SALES (est): 415.3K **Privately Held**
SIC: 2221 Manmade Broadwoven Fabric Mill

(G-10995)
PIP FOUNDATION INC
Also Called: S M O C
7 Bishop St (01702-8323)
PHONE..................................508 757-0103
Bruce Hulme, *President*
EMP: 40
SALES: 203.2K
SALES (corp-wide): 83.8MM **Privately Held**
SIC: 2752 Lithographic Commercial Printing
PA: South Middlesex Opportunity Council, Inc.
7 Bishop St
Framingham MA 01702
508 620-2300

(G-10996)
PP MANUFACTURING CORPORATION
Also Called: Ppm
175 Crossing Blvd Ste 200 (01702-4472)
PHONE..................................508 766-2700
Pierre Pages, *President*
Michel Garaudet, *Treasurer*
Florence Bambuck, *Admin Sec*
▼ **EMP:** 19
SQ FT: 21,000
SALES (est): 4.3MM
SALES (corp-wide): 295.5MM **Privately Held**
WEB: www.virbac.fr
SIC: 2834 Mfg Pharmaceutical Preparations
PA: Virbac
Lid
Carros 06510
492 087-100

(G-10997)
QUESTEX BRAZIL LLC
3 Speen St Ste 300 (01701-4664)
PHONE..................................617 219-8300
Andrea Hutchinson, *Buyer*
EMP: 4
SALES (est): 195.2K **Privately Held**
SIC: 2721 Periodicals-Publishing/Printing

(G-10998)
RACK ATTACK USA LLP
745 Worcester Rd (01701-5204)
PHONE..................................508 665-4361
Charlie Carp, *General Mgr*
Graeme Paterson, *Regional Mgr*
EMP: 9
SALES (est): 950K **Privately Held**
SIC: 2542 Mfg Partitions/Fixtures-Nonwood

(G-10999)
RAYTHEON COMPANY
6 Huron Dr (01701-3038)
PHONE..................................508 877-5231
Jerome Hanfling, *Engineer*
EMP: 195
SALES (corp-wide): 27B **Publicly Held**
SIC: 3812 Mfg Search/Navigation Equipment
PA: Raytheon Company
870 Winter St
Waltham MA 02451
781 522-3000

(G-11000)
REVO BIOLOGICS INC (DH)
175 Crossing Blvd (01702-4475)
PHONE..................................508 620-9700
William Heiden, *President*
Yann Echelard, *President*
Harry M Meade PHD, *Senior VP*
Richard A Scotland, *Senior VP*
Daniel S Woloshen, *Senior VP*
EMP: 83
SQ FT: 106,793

SALES (est): 20.4MM
SALES (corp-wide): 4.2MM Privately Held
WEB: www.gtc-bio.com
SIC: 2836 6794 Mfg Biological Products Patent Owner/Lessor
HQ: Lfb-Biotechnologies
Zone Artisanale De Courtaboeuf
Les Ulis 91940
169 827-010

(G-11001)
SANOFI GENZYME
1 The Mountain Rd (01701-8803)
PHONE....508 871-5871
Pray Jessica, *Financial Analy*
Beth Carey, *Finance*
Nancy Peterson, *Manager*
Douglas Robertson, *Telecomm Mgr*
Vikas Dua, *Director*
EMP: 25
SALES (est): 10.2MM Privately Held
SIC: 2834 Pharmaceutical Preparations

(G-11002)
SCHEDULING SYSTEMS INC
85 Speen St Ste 300 (01701-1902)
PHONE....508 620-0390
John Pararas, *President*
Ahmet Buharali, *Vice Pres*
EMP: 8
SQ FT: 6,000
SALES (est): 958.8K Privately Held
WEB: www.schedsys.com
SIC: 7372 Prepackaged Software Services

(G-11003)
SCORPIAN PRINTING
72 Nicholas Rd Apt 23 (01701-3459)
PHONE....617 319-6114
EMP: 30
SALES (est): 412.6K Privately Held
SIC: 2752 Lithographic Commercial Printing

(G-11004)
SHADE ADAMS & SCREEN CO
Also Called: Adam Shade and Screen
182 Central St (01701-4118)
PHONE....617 244-2188
Daniel J Gentile Jr, *Owner*
EMP: 3 EST: 1944
SALES (est): 240K Privately Held
WEB: www.adamsshadeandscreen.com
SIC: 2591 Mfg Drapery Hardware/Blinds

(G-11005)
SHREWSBURY CHRONICLE
33 New York Ave (01701-8857)
PHONE....508 842-8787
Glenda Hazard, *Publisher*
EMP: 3
SALES (est): 128.7K Privately Held
SIC: 2711 Newspapers-Publishing/Printing

(G-11006)
SOLACE THERAPEUTICS INC
135 Newbury St Ste 1 (01701-4590)
PHONE....508 283-1200
John Kilcoyne, *President*
Scott Blood, *Vice Pres*
Nicole Shugrue, *Vice Pres*
Kristie Jensen, *Research*
Sandy Beccia, *Office Mgr*
EMP: 6
SALES (est): 1.1MM Privately Held
WEB: www.solacetx.com
SIC: 3845 5999 Mfg Electromedical Equipment Ret Misc Merchandise

(G-11007)
THERMO FISHER SCIENTIFIC INC
1455 Concord St (01701-7773)
PHONE....978 735-3091
EMP: 4
SALES (corp-wide): 24.3B Publicly Held
SIC: 3826 Mfg Analytical Instruments
PA: Thermo Fisher Scientific Inc.
168 3rd Ave
Waltham MA 02451
781 622-1000

(G-11008)
TOKAY SOFTWARE INCORPORATED
237 Belknap Rd (01701-4714)
P.O. Box 1429, Boynton Beach FL (33425-1429)
PHONE....508 788-0896
Jim Mc Coy, *President*
EMP: 10
SQ FT: 1,000
SALES (est): 1MM Privately Held
SIC: 7372 Prepackaged Software Services

(G-11009)
UTC FIRE SEC AMERICAS CORP INC
Also Called: Sentrol Lifesafety
945 Concord St Ste 220 (01701-4613)
PHONE....508 620-4773
Charles Darsch, *Sales/Mktg Mgr*
EMP: 3
SALES (corp-wide): 66.5B Publicly Held
SIC: 3669 Mfg Communications Equipment
HQ: Utc Fire & Security Americas Corporation, Inc.
8985 Town Center Pkwy
Lakewood Ranch FL 34202

(G-11010)
VELOXINT CORPORATION
125 Newbury St Ste 200 (01701-4592)
PHONE....774 777-3369
Alan Lund, *CEO*
John Gaspervich, *Exec VP*
Judson Marte, *Vice Pres*
Derek Sharron, *Vice Pres*
Troy Holland, *Research*
EMP: 30
SALES (est): 153K
SALES (corp-wide): 3.3MM Privately Held
SIC: 3499 7389 Mfg Misc Fabricated Metal Products Business Serv Non-Commercial Site
PA: Braidy Industries, Inc.
1544 Winchester Ave # 300
Ashland KY 41101
606 420-4645

(G-11011)
VIACOMCBS INC
10 California Ave (01701-8802)
PHONE....508 620-3342
Ken Olsen, *Branch Mgr*
EMP: 30
SALES (corp-wide): 25.9B Publicly Held
SIC: 3613 Mfg Switchgear/Switchboards
HQ: Viacomcbs Inc.
1515 Broadway
New York NY 10036
212 258-6000

(G-11012)
VIVOX INC (DH)
40 Speen St Ste 305 (01701-1898)
PHONE....508 650-3571
Robert A Seaver, *CEO*
Evan Stamoulis, *Opers Staff*
Kevin Hendricks, *Software Engr*
Dave Verrati, *Director*
Mark Rosedale, *Administration*
EMP: 22
SALES (est): 3.7MM
SALES (corp-wide): 418.9K Privately Held
SIC: 3669 Manufactures Communications Equipment
HQ: Unity Software Inc.
30 3rd St
San Francisco CA 94103
415 848-2533

(G-11013)
WALPOLE TIMES INC
1 Speen St Ste 200 (01701-4644)
P.O. Box 388, Walpole (02081-0388)
PHONE....508 668-0243
Kay Macdonald, *President*
Kay Mac Donald, *President*
EMP: 12
SALES (est): 681.5K Privately Held
WEB: www.walpoletimes.com
SIC: 2711 Newspapers-Publishing/Printing

(G-11014)
WEB CONVERTING INC
160 Fountain St (01702-6213)
PHONE....508 879-4442
Fax: 508 879-8833
EMP: 5
SALES (est): 369.6K Privately Held
SIC: 3089 Plastics Products, Nec, Nsk

(G-11015)
WESTWOOD PRESS
33 New York Ave (01701-8857)
PHONE....781 433-8354
Shawn Burke, *President*
EMP: 50
SALES (est): 1.5MM Privately Held
SIC: 2741 Misc Publishing

(G-11016)
WORKSCAPE
500 Old Connecticut Path (01701-4574)
PHONE....508 861-5500
Tim Clifford, *CEO*
EMP: 5
SALES (est): 475.8K Privately Held
SIC: 7372 Prepackaged Software Services

(G-11017)
XENETIC BIOSCIENCES INC
40 Speen St Ste 102 (01701-1898)
PHONE....781 778-7720
Jeffrey Eisenberg, *CEO*
James Parslow, *CFO*
Timothy Cote, *Director*
Firdaus Dastoor, *Director*
Peter Weinstein, *General Counsel*
EMP: 4
SQ FT: 1,700
SALES: 7.5MM
SALES (corp-wide): 4.4MM Publicly Held
SIC: 2834 Pharmaceutical Preparation
PA: Farmsintez, Pao
D. Stantsiya Kapitolovo 134 Litera 1
S. Kuzmolovski 18866
812 329-8089

(G-11018)
ZENITH DIE CUTTING INC
2 Watson Pl Bldg 3 (01701-4109)
PHONE....508 877-8811
Jack Poirier, *President*
Paul Poirier, *Treasurer*
EMP: 3
SALES (est): 359.2K Privately Held
SIC: 2675 Die Cutting For Printing

Franklin
Norfolk County

(G-11019)
A D & G ENTERPRISES INC
23 Forge Pkwy 1 (02038)
PHONE....508 528-0232
Roland A Giles Sr, *President*
EMP: 3
SALES: 150K Privately Held
SIC: 3599 Machine Shop

(G-11020)
AIRLOC CORPORATION
5 Fisher St (02038-2114)
PHONE....508 528-0022
Robert Kucher, *CEO*
EMP: 7 EST: 2007
SALES (est): 3.2MM
SALES (corp-wide): 5.3MM Privately Held
SIC: 3625 Mfg Relays/Industrial Controls
PA: Airloc Ag
Industriestrasse 2
Oetwil Am See ZH 8618
449 297-700

(G-11021)
ALLEGRA NETWORK LLC
317 Union St (02038-2435)
PHONE....508 528-5339
Deborah Reed, *Branch Mgr*
EMP: 4
SALES (corp-wide): 44.2MM Privately Held
SIC: 2752 Lithographic Commercial Printing
HQ: Allegra Network Llc
47585 Galleon Dr
Plymouth MI 48170
248 596-8600

(G-11022)
ALPHA GRAINGER MFG INC
20 Discovery Way (02038-2555)
PHONE....508 520-4005
Jacob Grainger, *President*
Gary Grainger, *Vice Pres*
Ed Godin, *Engineer*
Ray Harper, *Engineer*
Barbara Grainger, *Treasurer*
▲ EMP: 118
SQ FT: 90,000
SALES (est): 26.9MM Privately Held
WEB: www.agmi.com
SIC: 3451 Mfg Screw Machine Products

(G-11023)
AMERICAN EARTH ANCHORS INC
20 Grove St Ste 6 (02038-3242)
PHONE....508 520-8511
Cy Henry, *President*
◆ EMP: 5
SQ FT: 3,200
SALES (est): 657.7K Privately Held
SIC: 3462 Mfg Iron/Steel Forgings

(G-11024)
AR METALLIZING LTD
24 Forge Pkwy (02038-3134)
PHONE....508 541-7700
Paul Van Emmerick, *President*
◆ EMP: 100
SALES (est): 71.5MM Privately Held
SIC: 2672 Mfg Coated/Laminated Paper
HQ: Ar Metallizing
Woudstraat 8
Genk 3600
898 480-00

(G-11025)
BELLINGHAM METAL WORKS LLC
101 Jefferson Rd (02038-3388)
PHONE....617 519-5958
Robert L Stow, *Mng Member*
EMP: 8
SQ FT: 2,400
SALES (est): 1.7MM Privately Held
SIC: 3441 7699 Structural Metal Fabrication Repair Services

(G-11026)
BERRY GLOBAL INC
25 Forge Pkwy (02038-3135)
PHONE....508 918-1715
Dart Jennifer, *Human Resources*
Brendan Fenn, *Regl Sales Mgr*
Jeff Hill, *Sales Staff*
EMP: 127 Publicly Held
SIC: 3089 Mfg Plastic Products
HQ: Berry Global, Inc.
101 Oakley St
Evansville IN 47710
812 424-2904

(G-11027)
CASTALDO PRODUCTS MFG CO INC
Also Called: F E Knight
120 Constitution Blvd (02038-2569)
PHONE....508 520-1666
Michael Knight, *President*
▼ EMP: 7
SQ FT: 10,000
SALES (est): 1MM
SALES (corp-wide): 2.5MM Privately Held
WEB: www.castaldo.com
SIC: 3559 Mfg Misc Industry Machinery
PA: F.E. Knight, Inc.
120 Constitution Blvd
Franklin MA 02038
508 520-1666

(G-11028)
COHESIVE TECHNOLOGIES INC (HQ)
Also Called: Cohesive Biotechnologies
101 Constitution Blvd F (02038-2587)
PHONE....508 528-7989

GEOGRAPHIC

Peter H Glick, *President*
Hubert Quinn, *Officer*
▲ **EMP:** 27
SQ FT: 10,000
SALES (est): 2MM
SALES (corp-wide): 24.3B **Publicly Held**
SIC: 3826 Mfg Material Used For The Purification & Separation Of Biopharmaceuticals
PA: Thermo Fisher Scientific Inc.
168 3rd Ave
Waltham MA 02451
781 622-1000

(G-11029)
COLD CHAIN TECHNOLOGIES INC
Also Called: Massachusetts Thermal Tstg Lab
135 Constitution Blvd (02038-2584)
PHONE..................................508 429-1395
Larry Gordon, *Branch Mgr*
EMP: 70
SALES (corp-wide): 46MM **Privately Held**
SIC: 3841 Mfg Surgical/Med Instr
PA: Cold Chain Technologies, Inc.
135 Constitution Blvd
Franklin MA 02038
508 429-1395

(G-11030)
COLD CHAIN TECHNOLOGIES INC (PA)
135 Constitution Blvd (02038-2584)
PHONE..................................508 429-1395
Lawrence Gordon, *President*
Stephen Kolb, *Business Mgr*
Ivona Koppel, *Business Mgr*
Bob Bohne, *Vice Pres*
Anthony Rizzo, *Vice Pres*
◆ **EMP:** 75
SQ FT: 96,000
SALES (est): 46MM **Privately Held**
WEB: www.coldchaintech.com
SIC: 3841 3412 2899 2821 Mfg Surgical/Med Instr Mfg Metal Barrels/Pails Mfg Chemical Preparation Mfg Plstc Material/Resin

(G-11031)
CONSOLIDATED CONTAINER CO LLC
Franklin Plastics
1253 W Central St (02038-3109)
PHONE..................................508 520-8800
Ed Baggie, *Manager*
EMP: 300
SALES (corp-wide): 14B **Publicly Held**
WEB: www.ccllc.com
SIC: 3089 Mfg Plastic Products
HQ: Consolidated Container Company, Llc
2500 Windy Ridge Pkwy Se # 1400
Atlanta GA 30339
678 742-4600

(G-11032)
CORE CONCEPTS INC
305 Union St Ste 7 (02038-2480)
PHONE..................................508 528-0070
Stephen C Dunn, *President*
Jeanne B Fox, *Admin Sec*
EMP: 25 **EST:** 1998
SQ FT: 25,000
SALES (est): 7.3MM **Privately Held**
WEB: www.coreconceptsinc.com
SIC: 2631 1541 Paperboard Mill Industrial Building Construction

(G-11033)
COVALNCE SPCALTY ADHESIVES LLC
25 Forge Pkwy (02038-3135)
PHONE..................................812 424-2904
Mike E Hill, *Branch Mgr*
EMP: 110 **Publicly Held**
SIC: 3089 Mfg Plastic Products
HQ: Covalence Specialty Adhesives Llc
101 Oakley St
Evansville IN 47710

(G-11034)
CUSTOM KTCHENS BY CHMPAGNE INC
170 Grove St (02038-3171)
PHONE..................................508 528-7919
Roland A Champagne, *President*
Patricia Champagne, *Treasurer*
EMP: 25
SQ FT: 15,000
SALES (est): 2.7MM **Privately Held**
SIC: 2541 2517 2511 2434 Mfg Wood Partitions/Fixt Mfg Wd Tv/Radio Cabinets Mfg Wood Household Furn Mfg Wood Kitchen Cabinet

(G-11035)
DALE MEDICAL PRODUCTS INC (PA)
40 Kenwood Cir Ste 7 (02038-3298)
P.O. Box 1556, Plainville (02762-0556)
PHONE..................................508 695-9316
John C Brezack, *President*
John Vandegrift, *Exec VP*
Wayne Hall, *VP Opers*
Glen Campbell, *Purch Mgr*
Tom Elder, *Purch Mgr*
◆ **EMP:** 110 **EST:** 1961
SQ FT: 17,000
SALES (est): 22.2MM **Privately Held**
WEB: www.dalemed.com
SIC: 3841 Whol Medical/Hospital Equipment

(G-11036)
DANGELO BURIAL VAULTS
30 Raymond St (02038-1829)
PHONE..................................508 528-0385
Nancy Spencer, *Principal*
EMP: 3 **EST:** 2010
SALES (est): 214.1K **Privately Held**
SIC: 3272 Mfg Concrete Products

(G-11037)
DYNISCO INSTRUMENTS LLC (HQ)
Also Called: Dj Instruments
38 Forge Pkwy (02038-3134)
PHONE..................................508 541-9400
Brian D Jellison, *CEO*
Ron Conrad, *Opers Dir*
Catherine Lindquist, *Corp Comm Staff*
Marc Malefatto, *IT/INT Sup*
◆ **EMP:** 130
SQ FT: 62,500
SALES (est): 82.9MM
SALES (corp-wide): 5.1B **Publicly Held**
WEB: www.dynisco.com
SIC: 3829 5084 3825 3823 Mfg Measure/Control Dvcs Whol Industrial Equip Mfg Elec Measuring Instr Mfg Process Cntrl Instr Mfg Relay/Indstl Control
PA: Roper Technologies, Inc.
6901 Prof Pkwy E Ste 200
Sarasota FL 34240
941 556-2601

(G-11038)
DYNISCO LLC (HQ)
Also Called: Dj Instruments
38 Forge Pkwy (02038-3134)
PHONE..................................508 541-3195
John Biagioni, *President*
Gradivel Rodriguez, *Production*
Ye Tian, *Engineer*
Glen Devane, *Controller*
EMP: 65
SALES (est): 15.2MM
SALES (corp-wide): 5.1B **Publicly Held**
SIC: 3829 Mfg Measuring/Controlling Devices
PA: Roper Technologies, Inc.
6901 Prof Pkwy E Ste 200
Sarasota FL 34240
941 556-2601

(G-11039)
EATON CORPORATION
165 Grove St Ste 10 (02038-3195)
PHONE..................................508 520-2444
Kevin Finnerty, *Manager*
EMP: 37 **Privately Held**
WEB: www.eaton.com
SIC: 3613 Mfg Switchgear/Switchboards
HQ: Eaton Corporation
1000 Eaton Blvd
Cleveland OH 44122
440 523-5000

(G-11040)
ELEMENTS EAST LLC
44 Main St (02038-1917)
PHONE..................................508 528-1902
EMP: 3
SALES (est): 196.4K **Privately Held**
SIC: 2819 Mfg Industrial Inorganic Chemicals

(G-11041)
EMC CORPORATION
50 Constitution Blvd (02038-2531)
P.O. Box 9103, Hopkinton (01748-9103)
PHONE..................................508 435-1000
Cynthia Svensson, *President*
Drew Codner, *Partner*
Marcelle Esposito, *Partner*
Sarah Griffin, *Partner*
Srinivasa Meka, *Partner*
EMP: 65
SALES (corp-wide): 90.6B **Publicly Held**
WEB: www.emc.com
SIC: 3572 Mfg Computer Storage Devices Prepackaged Software Services
HQ: Emc Corporation
176 South St
Hopkinton MA 01748
508 435-1000

(G-11042)
EMC CORPORATION
Also Called: Vce
109 Constitution Blvd # 2 (02038-2584)
PHONE..................................508 528-2546
EMP: 65
SALES (corp-wide): 78.6B **Publicly Held**
SIC: 3572 Mfg Computer Storage Devices
HQ: Emc Corporation
176 South St
Hopkinton MA 01748
508 435-1000

(G-11043)
EMC CORPORATION
111 Constitution Blvd (02038-2584)
PHONE..................................866 438-3622
Eric Gallerani, *Branch Mgr*
Beth Kelly, *Manager*
EMP: 65
SALES (corp-wide): 90.6B **Publicly Held**
SIC: 3572 Mfg Computer Storage Devices
HQ: Emc Corporation
176 South St
Hopkinton MA 01748
508 435-1000

(G-11044)
EMC CORPORATION
55 Constitution Blvd (02038-2545)
PHONE..................................800 275-8777
Jamie Pasquarello, *Partner*
Nathaniel Fagundo, *Engineer*
Dan Brown, *Sales Staff*
Ryan Howard, *Sales Staff*
William Stout, *Sales Associate*
EMP: 65
SALES (corp-wide): 90.6B **Publicly Held**
SIC: 3572 Mfg Computer Storage Devices
HQ: Emc Corporation
176 South St
Hopkinton MA 01748
508 435-1000

(G-11045)
FE KNIGHT INC (PA)
Also Called: Castaldo Proudcts
120 Constitution Blvd (02038-2572)
PHONE..................................508 520-1666
Michael Knight, *President*
Rona Knight, *Vice Pres*
EMP: 7
SQ FT: 10,000
SALES (est): 2.5MM **Privately Held**
WEB: www.castaldo.com
SIC: 3915 Mfg Jewelry Castings

(G-11046)
FORM CENTERLESS GRINDING INC
1 Kenwood Cir (02038-3201)
PHONE..................................508 520-0900
Alan Rose, *Ch of Bd*
Leo Blair, *Treasurer*
▲ **EMP:** 10
SQ FT: 28,000
SALES (est): 3MM **Privately Held**
SIC: 3599 Machine Shop

(G-11047)
FRANKLIN PAINT COMPANY INC
259 Cottage St (02038-3006)
PHONE..................................800 486-0304
Lawrence H Boise, *President*
Stephen S Schultz, *Exec VP*
Marissa Coffey, *Purchasing*
Paul Merritt, *Sales Staff*
Greg Chapin, *Director*
▲ **EMP:** 26 **EST:** 1947
SQ FT: 45,000
SALES (est): 8.5MM **Privately Held**
WEB: www.franklinpaint.com
SIC: 2851 Mfg Paints/Allied Products

(G-11048)
FRANKLIN SHEET METAL WORKS INC
231 Cottage St (02038-3006)
P.O. Box 368 (02038-0368)
PHONE..................................508 528-3600
Fred C Baglioni, *President*
Peter C Baglioni, *Treasurer*
EMP: 9
SQ FT: 12,000
SALES: 500K **Privately Held**
SIC: 3444 Mfg Sheet Metalwork

(G-11049)
GARELICK FARMS LLC (DH)
1199 W Central St Ste 1 (02038-3160)
PHONE..................................508 528-9000
Brian J Willey, *Mng Member*
Tom Davis,
Rachel A Gonzalez,
Steve Lincoln,
Cynthia Pike,
▲ **EMP:** 600 **EST:** 1902
SQ FT: 35,000
SALES (est): 405.4MM **Publicly Held**
WEB: www.overthemoonmilk.com
SIC: 2026 Mfg Fluid Milk
HQ: Dean East, Llc
2900 Bristol Hwy
Johnson City TN 37601
423 283-5700

(G-11050)
GARELICK FARMS LLC
1199 W Central St (02038-3160)
PHONE..................................508 528-9000
Phil Drexler, *Branch Mgr*
EMP: 110 **Publicly Held**
SIC: 2026 Mfg Fluid Milk
HQ: Garelick Farms, Llc
1199 W Central St Ste 1
Franklin MA 02038
508 528-9000

(G-11051)
HAMILTON STORAGE TECH INC (DH)
3 Forge Pkwy (02038-3135)
PHONE..................................508 544-7000
Steve T Hamilton, *President*
David Slocum, *Mfg Spvr*
Theresa Woods, *Purch Mgr*
Dan Billington, *Engineer*
Edmund Closson, *Engineer*
▲ **EMP:** 50 **EST:** 1982
SQ FT: 15,000
SALES (est): 14.5MM
SALES (corp-wide): 192.1MM **Privately Held**
WEB: www.biophileinc.com
SIC: 3823 Mfg Process Control Instruments
HQ: Hamilton Company
4970 Energy Way
Reno NV 89502
775 858-3000

(G-11052)
HAMILTON STORAGE TECH INC
Biophile
3 Forge Pkwy (02038-3135)
PHONE..................................508 544-7000

Matthew Hamilton, *President*
Robert Rovingdull, *Manager*
EMP: 9
SALES (corp-wide): 192.1MM **Privately Held**
WEB: www.biophileinc.com
SIC: 3821 Mfg Automated Low-Temperature Sample Storage & Retrieval Systems
HQ: Hamilton Storage Technologies, Inc.
3 Forge Pkwy
Franklin MA 02038
508 544-7000

(G-11053)
HOWESTEMCO INC
50 Earls Way (02038-1268)
PHONE..................................508 528-6500
Christopher R Maloof, *President*
Chris Maloof, *President*
Robert J Maloof, *Treasurer*
▲ **EMP:** 93
SQ FT: 80,000
SALES (est): 4MM **Privately Held**
SIC: 3599 Mfg Industrial Machinery

(G-11054)
IDEALAB INC
305 Union St Ste 10 (02038-2480)
P.O. Box 427 (02038-0427)
PHONE..................................508 528-9260
James Pritchard, *President*
EMP: 14
SQ FT: 6,000
SALES (est): 1.2MM
SALES (corp-wide): 152.9MM **Privately Held**
WEB: www.idealab.us
SIC: 3827 Mfg Optical Instruments/Lenses
PA: Idealab Holdings, L.L.C.
130 W Union St
Pasadena CA 91103
626 585-6900

(G-11055)
IMPERIAL BAG AND PAPER
111 Constitution Blvd (02038-2584)
PHONE..................................508 541-7220
EMP: 5
SALES (est): 225.1K **Privately Held**
SIC: 2621 Whol Industrial/Service Paper

(G-11056)
JACO INC
140 Constitution Blvd (02038-2544)
PHONE..................................508 553-1000
Alfred Rossini, *CEO*
Noreen Rossini, *President*
Len Halio, *President*
Donald Lamoureux, *Mfg Spvr*
Kim Burgess, *Purch Mgr*
EMP: 112
SQ FT: 94,000
SALES (est): 24.6MM **Privately Held**
WEB: www.jacoinc.com
SIC: 3499 Mfg Misc Fabricated Metal Products

(G-11057)
JEM ELECTRONICS INC
23 National Dr (02038-0259)
PHONE..................................508 520-3105
John S McDonald, *President*
Heather Pimental, *General Mgr*
Jami Reeve, *Accounts Mgr*
Jason Frasca, *Sales Staff*
Gopi Patel, *Manager*
▲ **EMP:** 125
SQ FT: 32,000
SALES (est): 22.8MM **Privately Held**
WEB: www.jemelectronics.com
SIC: 3671 Mfg Electron Tubes

(G-11058)
JNJ INDUSTRIES INC
290 Beaver St (02038-3022)
PHONE..................................508 553-0529
John J Volpe, *President*
Gail Howe, *Treasurer*
▲ **EMP:** 22
SQ FT: 89,000
SALES (est): 5.1MM **Privately Held**
WEB: www.jnj-industries.com
SIC: 3672 3555 Mfg Printed Circuit Boards Mfg Printing Trades Machinery

(G-11059)
K & C INDUSTRIES INC
3 Kenwood Cir (02038-3201)
PHONE..................................508 520-4600
Jeffrey B Klaus, *President*
Daniel J Congdon, *Treasurer*
EMP: 18
SQ FT: 12,000
SALES (est): 3.1MM **Privately Held**
SIC: 3089 Mfg Plastic Products

(G-11060)
KEEBLER COMPANY
17 Forge Pkwy (02038-3135)
PHONE..................................508 520-7223
Steve O'Sullivan, *Manager*
EMP: 75
SQ FT: 50,000
SALES (corp-wide): 13.5B **Publicly Held**
WEB: www.keebler.com
SIC: 2052 Mfg Cookies/Crackers
HQ: Keebler Company
1 Kellogg Sq
Battle Creek MI 49017
269 961-2000

(G-11061)
KENSOL-FRANKLIN INC
842 Union St Ste 1 (02038-2599)
PHONE..................................508 528-2000
Arthur Standre, *President*
EMP: 8
SALES (est): 594.1K **Privately Held**
SIC: 3599 Mfg Industrial Machinery

(G-11062)
KIMBERLY-CLARK CORPORATION
38 Pawn St Ste 108 (02038)
PHONE..................................508 520-1355
Gerald Gibbs, *Principal*
EMP: 8
SALES (corp-wide): 18.4B **Publicly Held**
WEB: www.kimberly-clark.com
SIC: 2621 2676 Paper Mill Mfg Sanitary Paper Products
PA: Kimberly-Clark Corporation
351 Phelps Dr
Irving TX 75038
972 281-1200

(G-11063)
LANDRY ENTERPRISES INC
41 Summer St (02038-1788)
PHONE..................................508 528-9122
Louis Landry, *President*
EMP: 5
SALES (est): 461.8K **Privately Held**
SIC: 3492 Mfg Fluid Power Valves/Fittings

(G-11064)
MGB US INC
157 Grove St Ste 30 (02038-3193)
PHONE..................................774 415-0060
Veronique Roda, *President*
EMP: 10
SQ FT: 15,000
SALES (est): 488.1K **Privately Held**
SIC: 3451 Mfg Screw Machine Products

(G-11065)
MICROSORB TECHNOLOGIES INC
8 Independence Way # 124 (02038-7316)
P.O. Box 455, Norfolk (02056-0455)
PHONE..................................401 767-2269
EMP: 9
SALES (est): 700K **Privately Held**
WEB: www.microsorbtech.com
SIC: 3679 Mfg Microwave Absorbers

(G-11066)
MIDSTATE MOLD & ENGINEERING
20 Liberty Way Ste D (02038-2577)
PHONE..................................508 520-0011
Steven Devine, *Principal*
EMP: 14
SALES (est): 2.3MM **Privately Held**
SIC: 3089 Mfg Plastic Products

(G-11067)
MINARIK CORPORATION
38 Forge Pkwy Ste 150 (02038-3134)
PHONE..................................781 329-2700
John Reilley, *Vice Pres*
Seth McEttrick, *Engineer*
Scott Frater, *Senior Engr*
Tim Anderson, *VP Mktg*
Garcia Caroline, *Mktg Coord*
EMP: 3 **EST:** 2016
SALES (est): 215.2K **Privately Held**
SIC: 3679 Mfg Electronic Components

(G-11068)
MOSELEY CORPORATION
31 Hayward St Ste A2 (02038-2166)
PHONE..................................508 520-4004
Thomas C Moseley Jr, *President*
Christine Milloff, *Managing Prtnr*
EMP: 40
SQ FT: 50,000
SALES (est): 3.2MM **Privately Held**
WEB: www.moseleycorp.com
SIC: 3799 8748 3444 3441 Mfg Transportation Equip Business Consulting Svcs Mfg Sheet Metalwork Structural Metal Fabrctn

(G-11069)
NEW ENGLAND CM INC
31 Hayward St Ste H (02038-2166)
PHONE..................................508 541-1307
Steven Leacu, *President*
EMP: 5
SQ FT: 2,000
SALES (est): 677.9K **Privately Held**
SIC: 3679 Mfg Electronic Components

(G-11070)
NEWPORT CORPORATION
Newport Franklin
8 Forge Pkwy Ste 2 (02038-3138)
PHONE..................................508 553-5035
Robert Bulis, *Principal*
Mike Carta, *Branch Mgr*
Paul Tran, *Technician*
EMP: 100
SALES (corp-wide): 2B **Publicly Held**
WEB: www.corion.com
SIC: 3827 Mfg Optical Coponents
HQ: Newport Corporation
1791 Deere Ave
Irvine CA 92606
949 863-3144

(G-11071)
PLANSEE USA LLC (DH)
115 Constitution Blvd (02038-2584)
P.O. Box 13288, Newark NJ (07101-3288)
PHONE..................................508 553-3800
Anders Hallbro, *CEO*
Lee Paula, *Accounting Mgr*
▲ **EMP:** 87
SQ FT: 60,000
SALES (est): 58.7MM
SALES (corp-wide): 242.1K **Privately Held**
WEB: www.stc-ma.com
SIC: 3499 Mfg Misc Fabricated Metal Products
HQ: Pse Holding Corp.
115 Constitution Blvd
Franklin MA 02038
508 553-3800

(G-11072)
PRECISION ENGINEERED PDTS LLC
Howestemco
50 Earls Way (02038-1268)
PHONE..................................508 528-6500
EMP: 8
SALES (corp-wide): 770.6MM **Publicly Held**
SIC: 3599 Mfg Industrial Machinery
HQ: Precision Engineered Products Llc
110 Frank Mossberg Dr
Attleboro MA 02703
508 226-5600

(G-11073)
PRECISION MACHINISTS CO INC
9 Forge Pkwy (02038-3150)
PHONE..................................508 528-2325
Janice Underwood, *Purchasing*
Joe Kajano, *Branch Mgr*
EMP: 12
SALES (corp-wide): 5.1MM **Privately Held**
SIC: 3599 Mfg Industrial Machinery
PA: Precision Machinists Company Inc.
299 Littleton Rd
Chelmsford MA
978 256-4592

(G-11074)
PRINCETON SECURITY TECH INC (HQ)
27 Forge Pkwy (02038-3135)
PHONE..................................609 924-7310
EMP: 5
SALES: 4.1MM
SALES (corp-wide): 16.9B **Publicly Held**
SIC: 3829 3812 3844 Mfg Measuring & Controlling Devices Search & Navigation Equipment X-Ray Apparatus
PA: Thermo Fisher Scientific Inc.
168 3rd Ave
Waltham MA 02451
781 622-1000

(G-11075)
PRINCTON GAMMA-TECH INSTRS INC
Also Called: P G T
27 Forge Pkwy (02038-3135)
PHONE..................................609 924-7310
Juhani Taskinen, *CEO*
EMP: 11
SQ FT: 26,000
SALES (est): 1MM
SALES (corp-wide): 24.3B **Publicly Held**
WEB: www.pgt.com
SIC: 3829 3812 3844 5049 Mfg Measure/Control Dvcs Mfg Search/Navgatn Equip Mfg X-Ray Apparatus/Tube Whol Professional Equip
PA: Thermo Fisher Scientific Inc.
168 3rd Ave
Waltham MA 02451
781 622-1000

(G-11076)
RPH ENTERPRISES INC
50 Earls Way (02038-1268)
PHONE..................................508 238-3351
Russell P Holmes, *President*
Peter J Randall, *Vice Pres*
EMP: 55 **EST:** 1979
SQ FT: 15,000
SALES (est): 8.1MM **Privately Held**
WEB: www.holmed.net
SIC: 3841 3842 Mfg Surgical/Medical Instruments Mfg Surgical Appliances/Supplies

(G-11077)
RYPOS INC (PA)
40 Kenwood Cir Ste 8 (02038-3298)
PHONE..................................508 429-4552
Klaus J Peter, *President*
Peter C Bransfield, *Chairman*
John Brennan, *Vice Pres*
Tony Knox, *Warehouse Mgr*
Jim Brown, *Mfg Staff*
▲ **EMP:** 35
SQ FT: 25,000
SALES (est): 8.7MM **Privately Held**
SIC: 3569 Mfg General Industrial Machinery

(G-11078)
SCHALLER CORPORATION
857 Union St (02038-2583)
PHONE..................................508 655-9171
Robert M Schaller, *President*
EMP: 4
SALES (est): 562.6K **Privately Held**
WEB: www.schallercorp.com
SIC: 3089 Plastics Injection Molding

(G-11079)
SIBCO LLC
837 Upper Union St C14 (02038-5005)
PHONE..................................508 520-2040
Antonius Joseph Schless,
EMP: 8
SALES (est): 1MM **Privately Held**
SIC: 3728 Mfg Aircraft Parts/Equipment

(G-11080)
SIGNS BY CAM INC
837 Upper Union St C18 (02038-5005)
PHONE..................................508 528-0766
Camilo A Afonso, *Principal*
EMP: 3

GEOGRAPHIC

SALES (est): 350.3K **Privately Held**
SIC: 3993 Mfg Signs/Advertising Specialties

(G-11081)
SLUGGO-OX CORPORATION
Also Called: Www.sluggo-Ox.com
430 Franklin Village Dr (02038-4007)
PHONE..................................508 726-8221
Fred L Foster, *CEO*
EMP: 3
SALES (est): 282.8K **Privately Held**
WEB: www.sluggo-ox.com
SIC: 3699 Manufacture Distribute And Sell Electrical Products And Accesssories And Electrician Products And Accessories And Engage In Any

(G-11082)
STEEL CONNECTIONS INC
101 Jefferson Rd (02038-3388)
PHONE..................................508 958-5129
Robert L Snow Jr, *Principal*
EMP: 8
SALES (est): 1.3MM **Privately Held**
SIC: 3441 Structural Metal Fabrication

(G-11083)
SYMPTLLGNCE MED INFRMATICS LLC
73 Stone Ridge Rd (02038-3144)
PHONE..................................617 755-0576
Jeff Schwartz,
Jerry Blaivas,
Harvey Brown,
Stuart Smyth,
EMP: 4
SALES (est): 175.9K **Privately Held**
SIC: 3841 7389 Mfg Surgical/Medical Instruments Business Serv Non-Commercial Site

(G-11084)
TEGRA MEDICAL LLC (HQ)
9 Forge Pkwy (02038-3150)
PHONE..................................508 541-4200
J Mark King, *CEO*
Sean Mikus, *General Mgr*
Walter Gacek, *Vice Pres*
Steve Cassidy, *Engineer*
Gabriel Lozano, *Engineer*
EMP: 200
SQ FT: 81,000
SALES (est): 99.3MM
SALES (corp-wide): 1.7B **Privately Held**
WEB: www.tegramedical.com
SIC: 3841 Mfg Surgical/Medical Instruments
PA: Sfs Group Ag
Rosenbergsaustrasse 8
Heerbrugg SG 9435
717 275-151

(G-11085)
TERRACON CORPORATION
1376 W Central St Ste 130 (02038-7100)
PHONE..................................508 429-9950
Robert N Jewett, *President*
Tom Dillen, *Traffic Mgr*
Kathleen Wentworth, *Controller*
Rob Jewett,
EMP: 15
SQ FT: 12,000
SALES (est): 3.4MM **Privately Held**
WEB: www.terracontanks.com
SIC: 3089 Mfg Plastic & Fiberglass Tanks Whol Plastics Materials & Basic Shapes

(G-11086)
THERMO ENVMTL INSTRS LLC (HQ)
27 Forge Pkwy (02038-3135)
PHONE..................................508 520-0430
Seth H Hoogasian, *President*
Brian Fisher, *CFO*
Anthony H Smith, *Treasurer*
Sandra Lambert, *Admin Sec*
▲ **EMP:** 145
SQ FT: 30,000
SALES (est): 25.7MM
SALES (corp-wide): 24.3B **Publicly Held**
SIC: 3826 3845 3829 3823 Mfg Analytical Instr Mfg Electromedical Equip Mfg Measure/Control Dvcs Mfg Process Cntrl Instr
PA: Thermo Fisher Scientific Inc.
168 3rd Ave
Waltham MA 02451
781 622-1000

(G-11087)
THERMO FISHER SCIENTIFIC INC
27 Forge Pkwy (02038-3135)
PHONE..................................508 520-0430
Sried Jeffery, *General Mgr*
EMP: 14
SALES (corp-wide): 24.3B **Publicly Held**
WEB: www.thermo.com
SIC: 3826 Mfg Analytical Instruments
PA: Thermo Fisher Scientific Inc.
168 3rd Ave
Waltham MA 02451
781 622-1000

(G-11088)
THERMO OPTEK CORPORATION
27 Forge Pkwy (02038-3135)
PHONE..................................508 553-5100
Fax: 508 553-5110
EMP: 1150
SALES (est): 75.7MM
SALES (corp-wide): 16.9B **Publicly Held**
SIC: 3823 Mfg Process Control Instruments
PA: Thermo Fisher Scientific Inc.
168 3rd Ave
Waltham MA 02451
781 622-1000

(G-11089)
THERMO PROCESS INSTRUMENTS LP
Also Called: Thermo Electron
27 Forge Pkwy (02038-3135)
PHONE..................................508 553-6913
Andrew Walder, *Partner*
Kevin Smith, *General Mgr*
Kuehl John, *Area Mgr*
Mary Connell, *Vice Pres*
Keith Baker, *Engineer*
◆ **EMP:** 190
SALES (est): 28MM
SALES (corp-wide): 24.3B **Publicly Held**
WEB: www.thermo.com
SIC: 3823 3829 Mfg Process Control Instruments Mfg Measuring/Controlling Devices
PA: Thermo Fisher Scientific Inc.
168 3rd Ave
Waltham MA 02451
781 622-1000

(G-11090)
THERMO VISION CORP (HQ)
8 Forge Pkwy Ste 4 (02038-3138)
PHONE..................................508 520-0083
Kristin Stotz Langdon, *President*
EMP: 11
SALES (est): 10.9MM
SALES (corp-wide): 24.3B **Publicly Held**
SIC: 3827 Mfg Application Specific & Electro Optical Products
PA: Thermo Fisher Scientific Inc.
168 3rd Ave
Waltham MA 02451
781 622-1000

(G-11091)
THOMSON NATIONAL PRESS COMPANY (PA)
Also Called: Thompson Press
842 Union St Ste 1 (02038-2599)
PHONE..................................508 528-2000
Arthur F St Andre Jr, *President*
EMP: 4 **EST:** 1923
SQ FT: 16,000
SALES (est): 687.2K **Privately Held**
SIC: 3554 3544 3542 3469 Mfg Paper Indstl Mach Mfg Dies/Tools/Jigs/Fixt Mfg Machine Tool-Forming Mfg Metal Stampings

(G-11092)
TITANIUM ADVISORS
9 Summer St Unit 303 (02038-1493)
PHONE..................................508 528-3120
Kevin Nulton, *Principal*
EMP: 5
SALES (est): 486.6K **Privately Held**
SIC: 3356 Nonferrous Rolling/Drawing

(G-11093)
TOMKINS CORPORATION
117 Dean Ave (02038-1758)
PHONE..................................508 528-2000
EMP: 30
SQ FT: 36,000
SALES (est): 3.6MM **Privately Held**
WEB: www.thethomsongroup.com
SIC: 3625 Mfg Electrical And Mechanical Assemblies

(G-11094)
TYCO ADHESIVES
25 Forge Pkwy (02038-3135)
PHONE..................................508 918-1600
Edward Breen, *Principal*
EMP: 4 **EST:** 2011
SALES (est): 291.2K **Privately Held**
SIC: 2891 Mfg Adhesives/Sealants

(G-11095)
VOLPE TOOL & DIE INCORPORATED
290 Beaver St (02038-3022)
PHONE..................................508 528-8103
John J Volpe III, *President*
EMP: 6 **EST:** 1969
SQ FT: 10,000
SALES (est): 2MM **Privately Held**
SIC: 3544 Mfg Dies/Tools/Jigs/Fixtures

(G-11096)
WAJA ASSOCIATES INC
38 Forge Pkwy (02038-3134)
PHONE..................................508 543-6050
Don Adams, *President*
EMP: 12
SQ FT: 6,000
SALES (est): 2.7MM **Privately Held**
WEB: www.waja.net
SIC: 3625 8721 Mfg Relays/Industrial Controls

(G-11097)
WATERS TECHNOLOGIES CORP
210 Grove St (02038-3119)
PHONE..................................508 482-4807
Kathleen Wright, *Manager*
EMP: 25
SQ FT: 56,000 **Publicly Held**
SIC: 3826 Mfg Analytical Instruments
HQ: Waters Technologies Corporation,
34 Maple St
Milford MA 01757
508 478-2000

(G-11098)
WINCHESTER INTERCONNECT CORP
101 Constitution Blvd (02038-2587)
PHONE..................................978 717-2543
John Davies, *VP Sales*
Jerome Farnan, *Branch Mgr*
EMP: 12
SALES (corp-wide): 16.6B **Privately Held**
SIC: 3496 3678 Mfg Misc Fabricated Wire Products Mfg Electronic Connectors
HQ: Winchester Interconnect Corporation
68 Water St
Norwalk CT 06854

(G-11099)
XPRESSION PRINTS
31 Hayward St Ste I1 (02038-2166)
PHONE..................................401 413-6930
Dale A Allen, *Principal*
EMP: 5
SALES (est): 492.1K **Privately Held**
SIC: 2752 Lithographic Commercial Printing

(G-11100)
XTHERA CORPORATION
Also Called: Theracycle
31 Hayward St Ste B1 (02038-2166)
PHONE..................................508 528-3100
Peter Blumenthal, *President*
David St German, *Vice Pres*
Rich Blumenthal, *VP Bus Dvlpt*
Richard Blumenthal, *Manager*
Corey Nogueira, *Manager*
▲ **EMP:** 7 **EST:** 1932
SALES (est): 3.3MM **Privately Held**
WEB: www.exercycle.com
SIC: 3949 Mfg Sporting/Athletic Goods

(G-11101)
ZYGO CORPORATION
13 Main St (02038-1946)
PHONE..................................508 541-1268
EMP: 21
SALES (corp-wide): 3.8B **Publicly Held**
SIC: 3827 Mfg Optical Instruments/Lenses
HQ: Zygo Corporation
21 Laurel Brook Rd
Middlefield CT 06455
860 347-8506

Gardner
Worcester County

(G-11102)
ADOLF JANDRIS & SONS INC
202 High St (01440-3632)
PHONE..................................978 632-0089
Dana Morse, *President*
Rodney T Moore, *Vice Pres*
EMP: 37 **EST:** 1920
SQ FT: 125,000
SALES (est): 7.2MM **Privately Held**
SIC: 3271 Mfg Concrete Block/Brick

(G-11103)
AMERICAN SCREW & BARRELS INC
60 Linus Allain Ave (01440-2478)
PHONE..................................978 630-1300
Alfonzo Toro, *President*
Maria Toro, *Bookkeeper*
▲ **EMP:** 12
SQ FT: 6,000
SALES: 1.3MM **Privately Held**
WEB: www.americanscrew-barrel.com
SIC: 3599 Mfg Industrial Machinery

(G-11104)
BLUE BARN INC
708 Whitney St (01440-3442)
PHONE..................................617 894-6987
Jason Hoynash, *President*
EMP: 12 **EST:** 2011
SALES (est): 1.5MM **Privately Held**
SIC: 2541 Mfg Wood Partitions/Fixtures

(G-11105)
BRATTLEWORKS COMPANY INC
134 Chelsea St (01440-3392)
P.O. Box 380536, Cambridge (02238-0536)
PHONE..................................978 410-5078
Ivica Indruh, *President*
Craig Stuber, *President*
EMP: 5
SQ FT: 10,000
SALES: 300K **Privately Held**
SIC: 2499 2449 Mfg Wood Products Mfg Wood Containers

(G-11106)
BRIGGS LUMBER PRODUCTS
104 E Broadway (01440-3387)
PHONE..................................978 630-4207
EMP: 5
SALES (corp-wide): 1MM **Privately Held**
SIC: 2448 Mfg Wood Pallets
PA: Briggs Lumber Products
336 E County Rd
Rutland MA 01543
508 886-2054

(G-11107)
CDL PRINT MAIL LLC
205 School St Ste 102 (01440-2781)
P.O. Box 1149 (01440-6149)
PHONE..................................978 410-5148
Cindy Barnes,
David Barnes,
Pamela Leblanc,
EMP: 6 **EST:** 2010
SALES (est): 646.3K **Privately Held**
SIC: 2752 Lithographic Commercial Printing

(G-11108)
CHAIR CITY MEATS INC
766 W Broadway (01440-2882)
P.O. Box 1051 (01440-6051)
PHONE..................................978 630-1050
Joshua Paddock, *President*
Bonnie Paddock, *Treasurer*
Peter Paddock,
EMP: 14
SALES (est): 7.5MM **Privately Held**
SIC: 2013 5421 Mfg Prepared Meats Ret Meat

(G-11109)
CONTI PRECISION TOOL CO INC
104 E Broadway (01440-3387)
PHONE..................................978 632-6224
Bruce Conti, *President*
EMP: 6
SQ FT: 3,500
SALES (est): 677.8K **Privately Held**
SIC: 3599 Mfg Industrial Machinery

(G-11110)
CRS STEAM INC
35 Chatham St (01440-3629)
PHONE..................................978 630-2308
Thomas Leblanc, *President*
Steve Dzurik, *Vice Pres*
EMP: 3
SQ FT: 1,500
SALES (est): 250K **Privately Held**
SIC: 3491 Mfg Continuous Flow Steam Traps

(G-11111)
DATA GUIDE CABLE CORPORATION
Also Called: D G C
232 Sherman St (01440-3000)
PHONE..................................978 632-0900
Donald R Irving, *President*
Donald Benoit, *Purch Mgr*
Bill Dinardo, *Engineer*
Jim Ayers, *VP Bus Dvlpt*
Robert Beardsley, *Treasurer*
▲ **EMP:** 93
SQ FT: 45,500
SALES (est): 21.3MM **Privately Held**
WEB: www.dataguidecable.com
SIC: 3643 3357 3351 Mfg Conductive Wiring Devices Nonferrous Wiredrawing/Insulating Copper Rolling/Drawing

(G-11112)
DENNECREPE CORPORATION
70 Fredette St (01440-3722)
PHONE..................................978 630-8669
George D Jones III, *President*
Joseph Lichwell, *Treasurer*
James B Jones, *Admin Sec*
EMP: 83
SALES (est): 15.8MM
SALES (corp-wide): 44.6MM **Privately Held**
WEB: www.satinwrap.com
SIC: 2679 2621 Mfg Converted Paper Products Paper Mill
PA: Seaman Paper Company Of Massachusetts, Inc.
35 Wilkins Rd
Gardner MA 01440
978 632-1513

(G-11113)
E F INC
88 Suffolk Ln (01440-1760)
PHONE..................................978 630-3800
Michael E Lenihan, *President*
Michael T Pappas, *Treasurer*
EMP: 10
SQ FT: 27,000
SALES (est): 1.6MM **Privately Held**
WEB: www.feswiss.com
SIC: 3451 3089 Mfg Screw Machine Products Mfg Plastic Products

(G-11114)
GARDNER NEWS INCORPORATED
309 Central St (01440-3839)
P.O. Box 340 (01440-0340)
PHONE..................................978 632-8000
Alberta Bell, *President*
EMP: 46 **EST:** 1869
SALES (est): 1.2MM
SALES (corp-wide): 1.5B **Publicly Held**
WEB: www.thegardnernews.com
SIC: 2711 Newspapers-Publishing/Printing
HQ: Gatehouse Media, Llc
175 Sullys Trl Fl 3
Pittsford NY 14534
585 598-0030

(G-11115)
GARDNER TOOL & STAMPING CO
13 Travers St (01440-3397)
PHONE..................................978 632-0823
Jerry Bouchard, *President*
Elaine Bouchard, *Vice Pres*
EMP: 5
SQ FT: 20,000
SALES: 500K **Privately Held**
SIC: 3599 3469 Mfg Industrial Machinery Mfg Metal Stampings

(G-11116)
GARLOCK PRTG & CONVERTING CORP
77 Industrial Rowe (01440-2831)
PHONE..................................978 630-1028
Lisa Field, *Asst Controller*
Pete Bugarlock, *Manager*
EMP: 175
SALES (corp-wide): 73.5MM **Privately Held**
SIC: 2759 2679 Commercial Printing & Converts Their Own Printed Paper Products
PA: Garlock Printing And Converting Corp.
164 Fredette St
Gardner MA 01440
978 630-1028

(G-11117)
GARLOCK PRTG & CONVERTING CORP (PA)
164 Fredette St (01440-3722)
PHONE..................................978 630-1028
Peter Garlock, *President*
Nicholas Schaffer, *President*
Kevin King, *COO*
Tom Brehm, *Exec VP*
Thomas Oconnor, *Vice Pres*
◆ **EMP:** 75
SQ FT: 69,000
SALES (est): 73.5MM **Privately Held**
SIC: 2759 2679 3554 Commercial Printing Mfg Converted Paper Prdt Mfg Paper Indstl Mach

(G-11118)
GO GREEN MFG INC
232 Chapel St (01440-1708)
PHONE..................................978 928-4333
David Iacaboni, *Principal*
EMP: 3
SALES (est): 277.6K **Privately Held**
SIC: 3999 Mfg Misc Products

(G-11119)
MACK PROTOTYPE INC
424 Main St (01440-3019)
PHONE..................................978 632-3700
Ric Perry, *President*
Fran Preseault, *Program Mgr*
Ivan Dignan, *Manager*
Steve Fidrych, *Director*
Debbie Lyon, *Director*
EMP: 30
SQ FT: 75,000
SALES (est): 5.3MM
SALES (corp-wide): 432.8MM **Privately Held**
WEB: www.mackprototype.com
SIC: 3089 3544 3369 Mfg Plastic Products Mfg Dies/Tools/Jigs/Fixtures Nonferrous Metal Foundry
PA: Mack Group, Inc.
608 Warm Brook Rd
Arlington VT 05250
802 375-2511

(G-11120)
MORSE ELECTRIC MOTORS CO INC
380 E Broadway (01440-3390)
PHONE..................................978 632-3733
Mark A Morse, *President*
Elssie Morse, *Principal*
EMP: 4 **EST:** 1980
SQ FT: 1,800
SALES (est): 619.8K **Privately Held**
SIC: 7694 5063 Services & Whol Electric Motors

(G-11121)
NEW ENGLAND PEPTIDE INC
65 Zub Ln (01440-1767)
PHONE..................................978 630-0020
Samuel Massoni, *CEO*
Charles Fricault, *Shareholder*
EMP: 30
SALES (est): 7.9MM **Privately Held**
SIC: 2834 Whol Chemicals/Products

(G-11122)
NEW ENGLAND WOODEN WARE CORP (PA)
205 School St Ste 201 (01440-2781)
PHONE..................................978 632-3600
David Urquhart, *President*
Dave Erkhart, *COO*
Mark S Salisbury, *Vice Pres*
Alexander Urquhart, *CFO*
Michelle Varieur, *Controller*
▲ **EMP:** 30
SQ FT: 173,000
SALES: 35.5MM **Privately Held**
WEB: www.newoodenware.com
SIC: 3993 2653 Mfg Signs/Advertising Specialties Mfg Corrugated/Solid Fiber Boxes

(G-11123)
PRECISION OPTICS CORP INC (PA)
Also Called: Poc
22 E Broadway (01440-7311)
PHONE..................................978 630-1800
Peter H Woodward, *Ch of Bd*
Joseph N Forkey, *President*
Jonathan Everett, *VP Engrg*
Daniel Habhegger, *CFO*
Donald A Major, *CFO*
EMP: 30
SALES: 6.8MM **Publicly Held**
WEB: www.poci.com
SIC: 3827 3845 Mfg Optical Instr/Lens Mfg Electromedical Equip

(G-11124)
RALPH CURCIO CO INC
Also Called: Chair City Wayside
372 E Brdway Bldg 372to # 372 (01440)
P.O. Box 114 (01440-0114)
PHONE..................................978 632-1120
Leonard R Curcio, *President*
Marie Curcio, *Treasurer*
EMP: 4
SQ FT: 20,000
SALES: 100K **Privately Held**
WEB: www.chaircitywayside.com
SIC: 2511 5712 5719 Mfr Chairs & Ret Furniture

(G-11125)
ROYAL FURNITURE MFG CO INC
1 S Main St (01440-3343)
PHONE..................................978 632-1301
Mel Ostroff, *President*
Steven K Ostroff, *Vice Pres*
Richard A Ostroff, *Treasurer*
EMP: 3 **EST:** 1934
SQ FT: 75,000
SALES: 400K **Privately Held**
SIC: 2511 Mfg Wood Household Furniture

(G-11126)
SEAMAN PAPER COMPANY MASS INC (PA)
35 Wilkins Rd (01440-2833)
P.O. Box 21, Baldwinville (01436-0021)
PHONE..................................978 632-1513
George D Jones III, *President*
Patrick Beatty, *Vice Pres*
Lee Chauvette, *Safety Mgr*
Keith Sanborn, *Engineer*
Joseph F Lichwell, *Treasurer*
◆ **EMP:** 25 **EST:** 1954
SQ FT: 550,000
SALES (est): 44.6MM **Privately Held**
WEB: www.satinwrap.com
SIC: 2621 Paper Mill

(G-11127)
SEAMAN PAPER WAREHOUSE
21 Industrial Rowe (01440-2831)
PHONE..................................978 632-5524
James B Jones, *CEO*
George D Jones III, *Treasurer*
EMP: 25
SQ FT: 50,000
SALES (est): 3.6MM **Privately Held**
SIC: 2679 Mfg Converted Paper Products

(G-11128)
SPECIALTY WHOLESALE SUP CORP
101 Linus Allain Ave (01440-2483)
PHONE..................................978 632-1472
Jim Le Blanc, *Manager*
EMP: 40
SALES (corp-wide): 23.2MM **Privately Held**
SIC: 2431 5031 Mfg Millwork Whol Lumber/Plywood/Millwork
HQ: Specialty Wholesale Supply Corp.
160 Massachusetts Ave
Lunenburg MA
978 343-7422

(G-11129)
STANDARD CHAIR GARDNER INC
1 S Main St (01440-3343)
PHONE..................................978 632-1301
Steven K Ostroff, *President*
Jimmy Roy, *Plant Mgr*
▼ **EMP:** 55 **EST:** 1957
SQ FT: 75,000
SALES (est): 6.5MM **Privately Held**
WEB: www.standardchair.com
SIC: 2511 Mfg Wood Household Furniture

(G-11130)
SUPERIOR KITCHEN DESIGNS INC
166 Mill St (01440-3292)
P.O. Box 398 (01440-0398)
PHONE..................................978 632-5072
Rheale McCaie, *President*
Emery J McCaie, *Vice Pres*
Sylvia Le Blanc, *Executive*
Laura Morgan, *Admin Asst*
EMP: 31
SQ FT: 15,952
SALES: 2MM **Privately Held**
WEB: www.superiorkitchens.net
SIC: 2434 2517 Mfg Wood Kitchen Cabinets Mfg Wood Tv/Radio Cabinets

(G-11131)
TRAVERS PRINTING INC
32 Mission St (01440-2196)
P.O. Box 279 (01440-0279)
PHONE..................................978 632-0530
Ellen Courtemanche, *President*
EMP: 20 **EST:** 1983
SQ FT: 24,000
SALES (est): 3.4MM **Privately Held**
WEB: www.traversprinting.com
SIC: 2752 Lithographic Commercial Printing

(G-11132)
URQUHART FAMILY LLC
205 School St Ste 203 (01440-2781)
PHONE..................................978 632-3600
David L Urquhart, *Principal*
EMP: 3 **EST:** 2008
SALES (est): 551.3K **Privately Held**
SIC: 3699 Mfg Electrical Equipment/Supplies

(G-11133)
WHITE DOG PRINTING INC
35 Parker St (01440-3806)
PHONE..................................978 630-1091
John A Deveau, *President*
EMP: 3
SALES (est): 330.6K **Privately Held**
SIC: 2759 Lithographic Commercial Printing

GEOGRAPHIC

Georgetown
Essex County

(G-11134)
17 CHESTNUT INC
Also Called: American Power Service
97 Tenney St Unit 1 (01833-2200)
PHONE..................................800 897-3117
Walter Kelsey, *President*
EMP: 9
SQ FT: 7,500
SALES (est): 740K **Privately Held**
WEB: www.babbittrepair.com
SIC: 3599 Machine Shop-Jobbing & Repair

(G-11135)
A I C INC (PA)
Also Called: Cai Inks
7 Martel Way (01833-2224)
PHONE..................................978 352-4510
Vincent Sartorelli, *Principal*
▲ **EMP:** 20
SALES (est): 8.2MM **Privately Held**
SIC: 2851 2893 Mfg Paints/Allied Products Mfg Printing Ink

(G-11136)
ARM CENTERLESS GRINDING
36 Jackman St Unit 14 (01833-1200)
PHONE..................................978 352-2410
Karl Jones, *Owner*
EMP: 3
SALES (est): 261.7K **Privately Held**
SIC: 3599 Mfg Industrial Machinery

(G-11137)
BLACK DIAMOND MFG & ENGRG INC
8 Searle St (01833-1705)
PHONE..................................978 352-6716
Carline Denley, *Owner*
▲ **EMP:** 10
SALES (est): 668.2K **Privately Held**
SIC: 3089 Mfg Plastic Products

(G-11138)
BOB BERGERON
Also Called: Costal
132 Tenney St (01833-1823)
PHONE..................................978 352-7615
Bob Bergeron, *Owner*
EMP: 6
SALES (est): 327.6K **Privately Held**
SIC: 3471 Plating/Polishing Service

(G-11139)
CAMBRIDGEPORT AIR SYSTEMS INC
4 Carleton Dr (01833-2501)
PHONE..................................978 465-8481
John S Desmond, *President*
David Smith, *President*
Steve Petro, *Vice Pres*
David Larocque, *Engineer*
Gerard E Dumont, *Treasurer*
EMP: 125
SALES (est): 41.6MM
SALES (corp-wide): 72.8MM **Privately Held**
WEB: www.curbadapter.com
SIC: 3444 3585 Mfg Sheet Metalwork Mfg Refrigeration/Heating Equipment
PA: Cox Engineering Company
35 Industrial Dr
Canton MA 02021
781 302-3300

(G-11140)
COATINGS ADHESIVES INKS
7 Martel Way (01833-2224)
PHONE..................................978 352-7273
Vincent Sartorelli, *Owner*
EMP: 25
SALES (est): 2.6MM **Privately Held**
SIC: 2891 2893 2759 Mfg Adhesives/Sealants Mfg Printing Ink Commercial Printing

(G-11141)
ESSEX COLUMN CORP
95 Tenney St Ste 1 (01833-2259)
P.O. Box 309 (01833-0409)
PHONE..................................978 352-7670
John F Rayner, *President*
EMP: 10
SQ FT: 15,500
SALES (est): 1.5MM **Privately Held**
SIC: 3272 Mfg Columns

(G-11142)
GEOMETRIC ENGINEERING CO
97 Tenney St Unit 7 (01833-2200)
PHONE..................................978 352-4651
Robert Smith, *Owner*
EMP: 6
SQ FT: 3,200
SALES: 450K **Privately Held**
SIC: 3599 Jobbing Or Repair Machine Shop

(G-11143)
GUNCANCO LTD
Also Called: Manufcturers Mart Publications
117 W Main St (01833-1526)
P.O. Box 310 (01833-0410)
PHONE..................................978 352-3320
Philip Cannon, *President*
Ilse Cannon, *Vice Pres*
Philip Cannon Jr, *Vice Pres*
Richard Cannon, *Manager*
EMP: 4
SQ FT: 1,500
SALES: 500K **Privately Held**
SIC: 2721 Magazine Publishing Not Printed On Site

(G-11144)
L W BILLS CO
Also Called: Alarm Engineering
79 Park St (01833-2024)
P.O. Box 7 (01833-0007)
PHONE..................................978 352-6660
Harold C Roeder, *President*
Karen Hopkins, *Engineer*
Jim Marshall, *Manager*
EMP: 24
SQ FT: 2,000
SALES (est): 3.7MM **Privately Held**
WEB: www.lwbills.com
SIC: 3669 Mfg Municipal Fire Alarms

(G-11145)
M J INDUSTRIES INC
4 Carleton Dr (01833-2501)
P.O. Box 259 (01833-0359)
PHONE..................................978 352-6190
▲ **EMP:** 25
SALES (est): 4.1MM **Privately Held**
SIC: 2514 Mfg Metal Household Furniture

(G-11146)
METAL TRONICS INC
Also Called: MTI
400 E Main St (01833-2512)
PHONE..................................978 659-6960
Peter B Orthwein, *President*
▲ **EMP:** 47
SQ FT: 20,000
SALES (est): 9.9MM
SALES (corp-wide): 42.8MM **Privately Held**
WEB: www.metaltronics.com
SIC: 3444 Mfg Sheet Metalwork
PA: Nsa Industries, Llc
210 Pierce Rd
Saint Johnsbury VT 05819
802 748-5007

(G-11147)
NOACK ORGAN COMPANY INC
36 W Main St (01833-2087)
PHONE..................................978 352-6266
Fritz Noack, *President*
▲ **EMP:** 6 **EST:** 1960
SQ FT: 2,000
SALES (est): 730.5K **Privately Held**
SIC: 3931 Mfg Pipe Organs

(G-11148)
PARALLEL SYSTEMS CORP
118 Tenney St (01833-1823)
PHONE..................................978 352-7100
Paul Schmitt, *President*
Gordon Lassar, *COO*
EMP: 11
SQ FT: 3,800
SALES (est): 1.3MM **Privately Held**
SIC: 3577 3821 Mfg Computer Peripheral Equipment Mfg Lab Apparatus/Furniture

(G-11149)
QUARTER LINE DRSSGE UNLMTED
79 Jewett St Rear (01833-1243)
PHONE..................................978 476-6554
EMP: 3
SALES (est): 250.1K **Privately Held**
SIC: 3131 Footwear Cut Stock

(G-11150)
ROLAND GATCHELL
119 Thurlow St (01833-1132)
PHONE..................................978 352-6132
Roland Gatchell, *Owner*
EMP: 4
SALES (est): 389K **Privately Held**
SIC: 3444 Mfg Sheet Metalwork

(G-11151)
TRUE TECHNOLOGY
2c Moulton St (01833-1942)
PHONE..................................978 352-8701
Daniel Thomeczek, *Owner*
EMP: 4
SALES: 500K **Privately Held**
SIC: 3599 Mfg Industrial Machinery

(G-11152)
UNIWELD INC
36 Jackman St Unit 7 (01833-1200)
PHONE..................................978 352-8008
Patrick McHardy, *President*
EMP: 5
SALES (est): 831.3K **Privately Held**
SIC: 3441 Structural Metal Fabrication

Gilbertville
Worcester County

(G-11153)
CAPRALOGICS INC
235 Czesky Rd (01031-9826)
PHONE..................................413 477-6866
Stan White, *President*
Bente Freeman, *Manager*
Sonya Reed, *Manager*
EMP: 6
SALES (est): 1.1MM **Privately Held**
WEB: www.capralogics.com
SIC: 2836 Mfg Biological Products

(G-11154)
HARDWICK LAMINATORS INC
268 Main St (01031-9604)
P.O. Box 37 (01031-0037)
PHONE..................................413 477-6600
Robert T Salem, *President*
David S Salem, *Corp Secy*
Ernest L Salem, *Treasurer*
Richard Salem, *Administration*
EMP: 8 **EST:** 1966
SQ FT: 12,000
SALES (est): 660K **Privately Held**
SIC: 2295 Laminator Of Fabrics

(G-11155)
SHAWN ROBERTS WOODWORKING
830 Lower Rd (01031-9843)
PHONE..................................413 477-0060
Shawn Roberts, *Owner*
EMP: 7
SALES (est): 646.3K **Privately Held**
SIC: 2431 Mfg Millwork

Gill
Franklin County

(G-11156)
GREEN BURIAL MASSACHUSETTS
270 Mountain Rd (01354-9724)
PHONE..................................413 863-4634
Joan Pillsbury, *Treasurer*
EMP: 3
SALES (est): 146.3K **Privately Held**
SIC: 3272 Mfg Concrete Products

(G-11157)
PETERMANS BOARDS AND BOWLS INC
61 French King Hwy (01354-9718)
P.O. Box 776, Turners Falls (01376-0776)
PHONE..................................413 863-2116
Spencer L Peterman, *Principal*
EMP: 26
SALES (est): 2.3MM **Privately Held**
SIC: 2499 5023 5719 Mfg Wood Products Whol Homefurnishings Ret Misc Homefurnishings

Gloucester
Essex County

(G-11158)
ACME MERCHANDISE AND AP INC
Also Called: Acme Apparel
46 Blackburn Ctr Ste 47 (01930-2271)
P.O. Box 820 (01931-0820)
PHONE..................................978 282-4800
Elaine Butter, *President*
Alejandro Laverde, *Managing Prtnr*
Michael Butter, *Treasurer*
Dan Smith, *Sales Mgr*
Chad Lok, *Manager*
◆ **EMP:** 27
SQ FT: 9,000
SALES (est): 3.4MM **Privately Held**
WEB: www.acmeapparel.com
SIC: 2321 2331 Mfg Men's/Boy's Furnishings Mfg Women's/Misses' Blouses

(G-11159)
ANCHOR-SEAL INC
54 Great Republic Dr (01930-2277)
PHONE..................................978 515-6004
Peter E Spinney, *President*
Marjorie Spinney, *Treasurer*
EMP: 9
SQ FT: 12,500
SALES (est): 3.2MM **Privately Held**
WEB: www.anchorseal.com
SIC: 2891 Mfg Adhesives/Sealants

(G-11160)
APPLIED MATERIALS
80 Blackburn Ctr (01930-2273)
PHONE..................................978 282-2917
Alissa Herrick, *Admin Asst*
▲ **EMP:** 4
SALES (est): 722K **Privately Held**
SIC: 3674 Mfg Semiconductors/Related Devices

(G-11161)
ATLAS MACHINE TOOL INC
18 Sargent St Ste 1 (01930-2876)
PHONE..................................508 284-3542
Irene Frontiero, *President*
EMP: 4 **EST:** 2014
SALES (est): 370.5K **Privately Held**
SIC: 3559 Mfg Misc Industry Mach

(G-11162)
ATOLL-BIO USA INC
468 Washington St (01930-1792)
PHONE..................................978 281-4595
Udo Vetter, *Ch of Bd*
Martin Reuter, *Managing Dir*
Lynn Sutherland, *Principal*
EMP: 13 **EST:** 2014
SQ FT: 1,500
SALES (est): 945.6K **Privately Held**
SIC: 2821 Mfg Plastic Materials/Resins

(G-11163)
AXIAM INC (PA)
58 Blackburn Ctr (01930-2271)
PHONE..................................978 281-3550
Donald W Lohin, *Ch of Bd*
Bob Lee, *President*
Bill Priest, *Vice Pres*
Robert Parsons, *VP Engrg*
Kevin Corbett, *Controller*
EMP: 8
SQ FT: 7,000

▲ = Import ▼=Export
◆ =Import/Export

SALES (est): 2.9MM Privately Held
WEB: www.axiam.com
SIC: 3825 Mfg Electronic Automated High Accuracy Metrology Equipment

(G-11164)
BAMBOO ROSE LLC (PA)
Also Called: Bamboo Rose Software
17 Rogers St (01930-5038)
PHONE....978 281-3723
Susan Welch, *CEO*
Tim O'Brien, *CFO*
Kate Munro, *VP Mktg*
EMP: 3
SALES (est): 6.4MM Privately Held
SIC: 7372 Prepackaged Software Services

(G-11165)
BENCO PRECISION MACHINING INC
10 Pond Rd (01930-1833)
PHONE....978 281-2055
Ronald Benjamin, *President*
Carla Benjamin, *Treasurer*
EMP: 6
SQ FT: 2,000
SALES (est): 850.8K Privately Held
SIC: 3599 Mfg Industrial Machinery

(G-11166)
BLACK EARTH COMPOST LLC
2 Hillside Rd (01930-4248)
PHONE....262 227-1067
Andrew Brousseau, *Opers Staff*
Conor Solberg Miller, *Mng Member*
Justin Sandler,
EMP: 11 EST: 2013
SALES (est): 1.8MM Privately Held
SIC: 2875 Mfg Fertilizers-Mix Only

(G-11167)
BOMCO INC
125 Gloucester Ave (01930-2294)
PHONE....978 283-9000
Michael A McCarthy, *President*
Paul Hubbert, *Vice Pres*
Walter Black, *Safety Dir*
Maynard Tucker, *Plant Mgr*
Jonathan Fried, *Mfg Staff*
EMP: 108 EST: 1958
SQ FT: 46,000
SALES (est): 25MM Privately Held
WEB: www.bomco.com
SIC: 3444 Mfg Sheet Metalwork

(G-11168)
C B FISK INC
21 Kondelin Rd (01930-5108)
PHONE....978 283-1909
Virginia Lee Fisk, *Ch of Bd*
Steven Dieck, *President*
David Pike, *Vice Pres*
Andrew Gingery, *Project Mgr*
▲ EMP: 30
SQ FT: 20,000
SALES (est): 3.3MM Privately Held
WEB: www.cbfisk.com
SIC: 3931 Mfg Musical Instruments

(G-11169)
CAPE ANN BREWING COMPANY INC
11 Rogers St (01930-5014)
PHONE....978 281-4782
Michael Goldberg, *President*
Dylan L'Abbe-Lindquist, *General Mgr*
Jeremy Goldberg, *Admin Sec*
EMP: 12
SQ FT: 5,000
SALES (est): 1.8MM Privately Held
WEB: www.capeannbrewing.com
SIC: 2082 Mfg Malt Beverages

(G-11170)
CAPE ANN OLIVE OIL COMPANY
57 Main St (01930-5752)
PHONE....978 281-1061
Patricia Gates, *Owner*
EMP: 4
SALES (est): 288.5K Privately Held
SIC: 2079 5719 5149 5169 Mfg Edible Fats/Oils Ret Misc Homefurnishings Whol Groceries Whol Chemicals/Products

(G-11171)
CAPE COD POLISH COMPANY INC
27 Kondelin Rd (01930-5162)
PHONE....800 682-4246
Jared E Block, *President*
EMP: 4
SALES (est): 373.3K Privately Held
SIC: 2842 Mfg Polish/Sanitation Goods

(G-11172)
CAPE POND ICE COMPANY (PA)
Also Called: Bresna Hand Ice
104 Commercial St (01930-5042)
P.O. Box 440 (01931-0440)
PHONE....978 283-0174
Richard C Memhard, *Ch of Bd*
R Scott Memhard, *President*
Robert Despres, *Vice Pres*
Laura M Fleming, *Clerk*
EMP: 20
SQ FT: 37,000
SALES (est): 1.5MM Privately Held
WEB: www.capepondice.com
SIC: 2097 Mfg Ice

(G-11173)
CHISHOLM AND HUNT PRINTERS INC
14 Whittemore St (01930-2553)
PHONE....978 283-0318
David Hunt, *President*
EMP: 5
SQ FT: 5,000
SALES (est): 621.8K Privately Held
WEB: www.chisholmhunt.com
SIC: 2752 Lithographic Commercial Printing

(G-11174)
CLASSIC ENGINEERING LLC
19 Kettle Cove Ln Unit 2 (01930-5167)
PHONE....978 526-9003
Steven J Crane,
EMP: 5
SQ FT: 5,400
SALES: 600K Privately Held
SIC: 3549 Mfg Metalworking Machinery

(G-11175)
COVE WOODWORKING INC
5 Hesperus Ave (01930-4021)
PHONE....978 704-9773
Dennis Whiitemore, *President*
EMP: 5
SQ FT: 9,000
SALES (est): 534.1K Privately Held
WEB: www.covewoodworking.com
SIC: 2599 2511 Mfg Wooden Restaurant Tables And Custom Furniture

(G-11176)
CUSTOM SEASONINGS INC
12 Heritage Way (01930-2216)
PHONE....978 762-6300
Mark D Dellafera, *President*
EMP: 23
SQ FT: 35,000
SALES (est): 5.3MM Privately Held
SIC: 2099 Mfg Food Preparations

(G-11177)
DIFFERENTIAL PIPETTING INC
11 Dory Rd (01930-2236)
P.O. Box 543, Newburyport (01950-0643)
PHONE....978 515-3392
Don Schwartz, *Principal*
EMP: 3
SALES (est): 191.7K Privately Held
SIC: 3841 Mfg Surgical/Medical Instruments

(G-11178)
DITUSA CORPORATION
19 Shepherd St (01930-5501)
PHONE....978 335-5259
Miguel Peralta Cobo, *President*
Alvaro Macerias, *Sales Staff*
EMP: 45 EST: 2013
SALES (est): 265.6K
SALES (corp-wide): 144.2K Privately Held
SIC: 2091 Mfg Canned/Cured Fish/Seafood
HQ: Discefa Sl.
Calle Marconi (Pol Industrial Espiritu), 131 -132
Cambre 15660
981 649-252

(G-11179)
EAGLE-TRIBUNE PUBLISHING CO
Also Called: Gloucester Daily Times
36 Whittemore St (01930-2553)
PHONE....978 282-0077
Ray Lamont, *Publisher*
Marybeth Callahan, *Manager*
EMP: 25 Privately Held
WEB: www.clintonnc.com
SIC: 2711 Newspapers-Publishing/Printing
HQ: Eagle-Tribune Publishing Company
100 Turnpike St
North Andover MA 01845
978 946-2000

(G-11180)
EASTERN COPY FAX INC
Also Called: Eastern Copy-Fax
42 Blackburn Ctr (01930-2271)
P.O. Box 220 (01931-0220)
PHONE....978 768-3808
Anthony T Loiacano, *President*
EMP: 4
SALES (est): 646.9K Privately Held
WEB: www.easterncopyfax.com
SIC: 3861 7699 Mfg Photographic Equipment/Supplies Repair Services

(G-11181)
FELICIA OIL CO INC
78 Commercial St (01930-5025)
PHONE....978 283-3808
Grace Nicastro, *President*
John B Nicastro, *Vice Pres*
EMP: 6
SQ FT: 1,000
SALES (est): 510K Privately Held
SIC: 2869 Mfg Industrial Organic Chemicals

(G-11182)
FLAVRZ BEVERAGE CORPORATION
33 Commercial St Ste 3 (01930-5040)
PHONE....978 879-4567
Karen Bartz, *President*
EMP: 5 EST: 2008
SALES (est): 341K Privately Held
SIC: 2086 Mfg Bottled/Canned Soft Drinks

(G-11183)
FOOTSOX INC
16 Whittemore St (01930-2553)
PHONE....800 338-0833
Arthur F De Santis, *President*
Barbara Scoppa, *General Mgr*
Josephine De Santis, *Clerk*
EMP: 5
SQ FT: 3,000
SALES: 2MM Privately Held
SIC: 2251 Mfg Women's Hosiery

(G-11184)
FREUDENBERG MEDICAL LLC
Also Called: Freudenberg Nok
92 Blackburn Ctr (01930-2273)
PHONE....978 281-2023
Edward Callahan, *Vice Pres*
EMP: 28
SALES (corp-wide): 10.5B Privately Held
SIC: 3842 Mfg Surgical Appliances/Supplies
HQ: Freudenberg Medical, Llc
1110 Mark Ave
Carpinteria CA 93013
805 684-3304

(G-11185)
GAP PROMOTIONS LLC
1 Washington St (01930-5733)
PHONE....978 281-0335
Heather Macdonald, *Partner*
Kim Parker, *Project Mgr*
Gayle A Piraino, *Mng Member*
Justin Burkinshaw, *Manager*
Kim Olson, *Director*
▲ EMP: 14
SALES (est): 2.7MM Privately Held
SIC: 3993 7389 Mfg Signs/Advertising Specialties Business Services

(G-11186)
GLOUCESTER ENGINEERING CO INC (DH)
Also Called: G E C
11 Dory Rd (01930-2236)
PHONE....978 281-1800
Rick Tattersfield, *CEO*
Carl Johnson, *President*
Bill Schmidt, *CFO*
◆ EMP: 100 EST: 1961
SQ FT: 165,000
SALES (est): 37.9MM Privately Held
WEB: www.gloucesterengineering.com
SIC: 3559 Manufacturing Miscellaneous Industry Machinery

(G-11187)
GLOUCESTER ENGINEERING CO INC
18 Sargent St (01930-2875)
PHONE....978 515-7008
Bob Snider, *Manager*
EMP: 5 Privately Held
SIC: 3559 Mfg Plastics Working Machinery
HQ: Gloucester Engineering Co., Inc.
11 Dory Rd
Gloucester MA 01930
978 281-1800

(G-11188)
GLOUCESTER GRAPHICS INC (PA)
19 Pond Rd (01930-1834)
PHONE....978 281-4500
P Sean Gibney, *President*
Norma Gibney, *Treasurer*
Charlene Prescott, *Manager*
Amber Gibney, *Admin Sec*
EMP: 14 EST: 1981
SQ FT: 26,000
SALES (est): 1.4MM Privately Held
WEB: www.gloucester-graphics.com
SIC: 2759 3993 5199 2262 Commercial Printing Mfg Signs/Ad Specialties Whol Nondurable Goods Manmade Fabric Fnshg Plt Mfg Auto/Apparel Trim

(G-11189)
GORTONS INC (DH)
Also Called: Gortons
128 Rogers St (01930-5005)
P.O. Box 361 (01931-0361)
PHONE....978 283-3000
Judson Reis, *President*
◆ EMP: 300
SALES (est): 186.9MM Privately Held
WEB: www.gortons.com
SIC: 2092 2091 Mfg Fresh/Frozen Packaged Fish Mfg Canned/Cured Fish/Seafood
HQ: Nippon Suisan (U.S.A.), Inc.
15400 Ne 90th St Ste 100
Redmond WA 98052
425 869-1703

(G-11190)
GP AGGREGATE CORP
19 Pond Rd (01930-1834)
PHONE....978 283-5318
Paul M Butman Jr, *Principal*
EMP: 7
SALES (est): 950.2K Privately Held
SIC: 3273 Mfg Ready-Mixed Concrete

(G-11191)
GUSTAFSON MACHINE
44 Whittemore St Ste 5 (01930-2581)
PHONE....978 281-2012
Keith Gustafson, *Owner*
EMP: 3
SQ FT: 2,000
SALES (est): 300K Privately Held
SIC: 3599 Machine Shop

(G-11192)
HARBOR WELDING
5 Marsh St (01930-4823)
PHONE....978 281-5771
EMP: 7 EST: 2017
SALES (est): 103.1K Privately Held
SIC: 7692 Welding Repair

(G-11193)
J & L WELDING & MACHINE CO
Also Called: J&L
19 Arthur St 25 (01930-2736)
PHONE..................................978 283-3388
Jeffery Amero, *President*
EMP: 25
SQ FT: 11,000
SALES (est): 3.6MM **Privately Held**
SIC: 7692 3599 Welding Repair Mfg Industrial Machinery

(G-11194)
KATHERINE MCALOON
Also Called: Kate's Canvas Works
32 Lexington Ave (01930)
PHONE..................................978 525-2223
Kate McAloon, *Owner*
EMP: 3
SALES (est): 221.2K **Privately Held**
SIC: 2394 Canvas Rltd Prdcts

(G-11195)
KENYON COMPOSITES
321 Western Ave (01930-4068)
PHONE..................................617 803-3198
Paul Kenyon,
EMP: 3
SALES (est): 109.9K **Privately Held**
SIC: 1389 Oil/Gas Field Services

(G-11196)
KLEIN DESIGN INC
99 Sadler St (01930-2998)
PHONE..................................978 281-5276
Gerhart P Klein, *President*
Brigitte I Klein, *Treasurer*
EMP: 4
SQ FT: 6,000
SALES: 200K **Privately Held**
WEB: www.kleindesign.com
SIC: 2511 Mfg Wood Household Furniture

(G-11197)
NICHOLS CANDIES INC
1 Crafts Rd (01930-2135)
PHONE..................................978 283-9850
Barbara Nichols, *President*
EMP: 13 **EST:** 1954
SQ FT: 21,500
SALES (est): 2MM **Privately Held**
SIC: 2064 5441 Mfg Candy/Confectionery Ret Candy/Confectionery

(G-11198)
OCEAN CREST SEAFOOD INC
88 Commercial St (01930-5025)
PHONE..................................978 281-0232
Leonard Parco, *President*
Tom Molloy, *Opers Mgr*
EMP: 15
SQ FT: 10,000
SALES (est): 1.1MM **Privately Held**
SIC: 2092 Processes Fish Products

(G-11199)
OCEAN CREST SEAFOODS INC (PA)
88 Commercial St (01930-5025)
P.O. Box 1183 (01931-1183)
PHONE..................................978 281-0232
Leonard Parco, *President*
Maria Churchill, *Treasurer*
Rosalie Vitale, *Treasurer*
John Turner, *Marketing Staff*
Edward E Mc Collum Jr, *Shareholder*
▲ **EMP:** 30
SQ FT: 100,000
SALES (est): 3.6MM **Privately Held**
WEB: www.neptunesharvest.com
SIC: 2873 5146 2092 2875 Mfg Nitrogenous Fertlizr Whol Fish/Seafoods Mfg Fresh/Frozen Fish Mfg Fertilizer

(G-11200)
P M S MANUFACTURED PDTS INC
Also Called: PMS Mfg
10 Sadler St (01930-2918)
PHONE..................................978 281-2600
Richard Perruzzi, *President*
Dayne Perruzzi, *Vice Pres*
EMP: 11 **EST:** 1960
SQ FT: 10,000
SALES (est): 1.8MM **Privately Held**
WEB: www.pmsmetal.com
SIC: 3444 3469 Mfg Sheet Metalwork Mfg Metal Stampings

(G-11201)
PARA RESEARCH INC
Also Called: Champlain Software
85 Eastern Ave Ste G106 (01930-1889)
PHONE..................................978 282-1100
Tonia N Molinski, *President*
EMP: 11
SQ FT: 1,000
SALES (est): 1.2MM **Privately Held**
WEB: www.pararesearch.com
SIC: 7372 7371 Prepackaged Software Services Custom Computer Programing

(G-11202)
PEARCE PROCESSING SYSTEMS
8 Kettle Cove Ln (01930-5107)
P.O. Box 386, Beverly (01915-0007)
PHONE..................................978 283-3800
Charles Morse, *President*
EMP: 3
SQ FT: 8,000
SALES (est): 300K **Privately Held**
WEB: www.pearcepsi.com
SIC: 3556 7699 Mfg Food Processing Equipment

(G-11203)
POLARIS SHEET METAL INC
18 Sargent St Ste 1 (01930-2876)
PHONE..................................978 281-5644
William P Goveny, *President*
Gordon Goveny, *Vice Pres*
EMP: 5
SQ FT: 9,500
SALES (est): 856.4K **Privately Held**
SIC: 3444 Mfg Sheet Metalwork

(G-11204)
PRESSROOM INCORPORATED
32 River Rd (01930-1352)
PHONE..................................978 283-5562
David C McAveeney, *President*
EMP: 20
SQ FT: 6,700
SALES (est): 2.8MM **Privately Held**
SIC: 2752 Lithographic Commercial Printing

(G-11205)
PROTEUS INDUSTRIES INC
33 Commercial St Ste 4 (01930-5040)
PHONE..................................978 281-9545
William R Fielding, *CEO*
Stephen Kelleher, *President*
Douglas Hall III, *Treasurer*
◆ **EMP:** 7
SQ FT: 5,000
SALES (est): 1.2MM **Privately Held**
SIC: 2824 Mfg Organic Fiber-Noncellulosic

(G-11206)
RAYMOND AGLER
16 Pleasant St (01930-5910)
PHONE..................................978 281-5048
Raymond Agler, *Principal*
EMP: 3
SALES (est): 216.2K **Privately Held**
SIC: 2851 Mfg Paints/Allied Products

(G-11207)
RENBRANDT INC
32 Blackburn Ctr (01930-2270)
PHONE..................................617 445-8910
G Stewart Renner, *CEO*
Raymond Renner, *President*
EMP: 11 **EST:** 1951
SQ FT: 4,500
SALES (est): 950K **Privately Held**
WEB: www.renbrandt.com
SIC: 3568 Mfg Power Transmission Equipment

(G-11208)
RYAN & WOOD DISTILLERY
15 Great Republic Dr # 2 (01930-2343)
PHONE..................................978 281-2282
Robert Ryan, *President*
EMP: 3
SALES (est): 270.3K **Privately Held**
SIC: 2085 Mfg Distilled/Blended Liquor

(G-11209)
SANDY BAY MACHINE INC
11 Dory Rd 2 (01930-2236)
PHONE..................................978 546-1331
MO Shahin, *President*
EMP: 38
SALES (est): 6.8MM
SALES (corp-wide): 66.5B **Publicly Held**
WEB: www.sandybaymachine.net
SIC: 3661 7629 Mfg Telephone/Telegraph Apparatus Electrical Repair
HQ: Tsi Group, Inc.
94 Tide Mill Rd
Hampton NH 03842

(G-11210)
SOITEC USA INC (HQ)
2 Blackburn Ctr (01930-2201)
PHONE..................................978 531-2222
Andre Auberton-Herve, *CEO*
Andrew Wittkower, *President*
Paul Boudre, *COO*
Christophe Vicat, *Buyer*
EMP: 12
SQ FT: 1,000
SALES (est): 1.6MM
SALES (corp-wide): 506.4MM **Privately Held**
WEB: www.soitecusa.com
SIC: 3674 5063 Mfg Semiconductors/Related Devices Whol Electrical Equipment
PA: Soitec
Parc Techno Des Fontaines
Bernin 38190
476 927-500

(G-11211)
SONOLITE PLASTICS CORPORATION
10 Fernwood Lake Ave (01930-3331)
PHONE..................................978 281-0662
Peter J Lawrence, *President*
Jonathan B Lawrence, *Treasurer*
Ronald J Yoder, *Financial Exec*
▲ **EMP:** 18 **EST:** 1963
SQ FT: 22,000
SALES: 2.6MM **Privately Held**
WEB: www.sonoliteplastics.com
SIC: 3089 3542 Mfg Plastic Products Mfg Machine Tools-Forming

(G-11212)
STRONG GROUP INC (PA)
Also Called: Strong Leather Co
39 Grove St (01930-2669)
P.O. Box 1195 (01931-1195)
PHONE..................................978 281-3300
David A Cutter, *President*
Richard Cutter, *Vice Pres*
Steve Kaity, *Vice Pres*
Brian Cutter, *Purch Mgr*
Richard Lindner, *CFO*
▲ **EMP:** 31
SQ FT: 53,000
SALES (est): 3.3MM **Privately Held**
WEB: www.strongbadgecase.com
SIC: 3993 5199 3172 3199 Mfg Signs/Ad Specialties Whol Nondurable Goods Mfg Personal Leather Gds

(G-11213)
SUNDANCE SCREENPRINTS
14a Whittemore St (01930-2553)
PHONE..................................978 281-6006
Kevin Flaherty, *Partner*
Judy Flaherty, *Partner*
Stephen Wallack, *Principal*
EMP: 6
SQ FT: 6,000
SALES: 350K **Privately Held**
SIC: 2396 Apparel Related Products

(G-11214)
SURFARI INC
210 Main St (01930-6003)
PHONE..................................978 704-9051
C S Del Rosario, *President*
EMP: 10
SALES (est): 932.4K **Privately Held**
SIC: 3949 Mfg Sporting/Athletic Goods

(G-11215)
TEKKWARE INC
Also Called: Harvest Yeast
11 Dory Rd (01930-2236)
PHONE..................................603 380-4257
EMP: 5
SALES (est): 256.8K **Privately Held**
SIC: 2099 Mfg Food Preparations

(G-11216)
VACUUM TECHNOLOGY INC
15 Great Republic Dr (01930-2343)
PHONE..................................510 333-6562
Yuling Cai, *President*
▲ **EMP:** 7
SQ FT: 2,700
SALES (est): 1.2MM **Privately Held**
SIC: 3564 3821 3826 Mfg Blowers/Fans Mfg Lab Apparatus/Furn Mfg Analytical Instr

(G-11217)
VITEC INDUSTRIES INC
1 Blackburn Ctr (01930-2296)
PHONE..................................978 282-7700
Gary Kerr, *President*
Dominic Favaloro, *Vice Pres*
EMP: 8
SQ FT: 800
SALES (est): 650K **Privately Held**
SIC: 3577 Mfg Computer Peripheral Equipment

(G-11218)
VSEA INC
35 Dory Rd (01930-2236)
PHONE..................................978 282-2000
Kevin Twan, *General Mgr*
Louis Chance, *Engineer*
Thomas Baker, *Controller*
Mitch Mahoney, *Info Tech Dir*
Cindy Lucido, *Technology*
▲ **EMP:** 32
SALES (est): 7.1MM **Privately Held**
SIC: 3674 Mfg Semiconductors/Related Devices

(G-11219)
WINCHESTER FISHING INC
54 Cherry St (01930-1830)
PHONE..................................978 282-0679
Richard Winchester, *President*
EMP: 5
SALES: 150K **Privately Held**
SIC: 3949 5941 5231 Mfg & Ret Of Lobster Traps Fishing Equipment & Paint

(G-11220)
XP POWER LLC
Also Called: Xp Comdel
11 Kondelin Rd (01930-5108)
PHONE..................................978 282-0620
Scott Johnson, *Branch Mgr*
EMP: 59 **Privately Held**
SIC: 3674 8711 Engineering Services Mfg Semiconductors/Related Devices
HQ: Xp Power Llc
990 Benecia Ave
Sunnyvale CA 94085
408 732-7777

(G-11221)
ZEUS PACKING INC
27 Harbor Loop 29 (01930-5052)
PHONE..................................978 281-6900
Kristian Kristensen, *CEO*
▼ **EMP:** 25
SQ FT: 20,000
SALES: 6.9MM **Privately Held**
SIC: 2092 Mfg Fresh/Frozen Packaged Fish

Goshen
Hampshire County

(G-11222)
ACCUFAB IRON WORKS INC
82 S Main St (01032-9614)
P.O. Box 328 (01032-0328)
PHONE..................................413 268-7133
Jeffrey Slesinski, *President*
Russel Laroche, *Treasurer*
EMP: 10

▲ = Import ▼=Export
◆ =Import/Export

SQ FT: 5,700
SALES (est): 1.7MM Privately Held
SIC: 3441 Fabricated Miscellaneous Iron And Structural Metal

Grafton
Worcester County

(G-11223)
MEDCON BIOLAB TECHNOLOGIES INC
50 Brigham Hill Rd (01519-1136)
P.O. Box 196 (01519-0196)
PHONE....508 839-4203
Virgil F Pichierri, *President*
Damian Pichierri, *Exec VP*
Robert Borgatti, *Vice Pres*
John McCloud, *Vice Pres*
Laura Pichierri, *Clerk*
EMP: 7
SQ FT: 3,200
SALES (est): 161.3K Privately Held
WEB: www.ilexpaste.com
SIC: 3841 Mfg Surgical/Medical Instruments

(G-11224)
QUANTEK INSTRUMENTS
183 Magill Dr (01519-1327)
PHONE....508 839-0108
Richard Syrjala, *President*
EMP: 5
SQ FT: 10,000
SALES (est): 905.2K Privately Held
WEB: www.quantekinstruments.com
SIC: 3829 Mfg Measuring/Controlling Devices

(G-11225)
VAN-GO GRAPHICS
94 Fitzpatrick Rd (01519-1095)
PHONE....508 865-7300
Robert Vanasse, *President*
Donna Duggan, *Purch Mgr*
Michael Goulet, *Treasurer*
EMP: 15
SALES (est): 1.8MM Privately Held
WEB: www.vangographics.com
SIC: 2759 2752 Commercial Printing Lithographic Commercial Printing

(G-11226)
WHITE KNIGHT STUDIO
70 North St (01519-1255)
PHONE....781 799-0569
Jay R Snyder, *Owner*
EMP: 4
SALES (est): 213.5K Privately Held
SIC: 2741 Misc Publishing

Granby
Hampshire County

(G-11227)
C & G MACHINE TOOL CO INC
180 W State St (01033-9463)
PHONE....413 467-9556
Omer Gingras Jr, *President*
Shirley Gingras, *Admin Sec*
EMP: 17
SQ FT: 4,000
SALES (est): 2.7MM Privately Held
SIC: 3599 Mfg Industrial Machinery

(G-11228)
INTER-ALL CORPORATION
25 W State St (01033-9467)
PHONE....413 467-7181
Gino E Maggi Jr, *President*
EMP: 20
SQ FT: 17,000
SALES (est): 1.7MM Privately Held
SIC: 2395 2397 Pleating/Stitching Services Mfg Schiffli Embroideries

(G-11229)
LEGION FLYING CLUB INC
70 Kendall St (01033-9510)
PHONE....413 467-7844
Chuster Danek, *President*
Joe Trega, *Vice Pres*
Dan Darcy, *Treasurer*
EMP: 4 EST: 1961
SALES: 220K Privately Held
SIC: 3721 Mfg Aircraft

Granville
Hampden County

(G-11230)
HILLTOWN PORK INC
243 Sodom St (01034-9478)
PHONE....413 357-6661
Edwin A Beckwith, *Branch Mgr*
EMP: 15
SALES (corp-wide): 1.6MM Privately Held
SIC: 2013 Mfg Prepared Meats
PA: Hilltown Pork Inc
12948 State Route 22
Canaan NY 12029
518 781-4050

(G-11231)
WACKERBARTH BOX MFG CO
Also Called: Wackerbarth Box Shop
383 Granby Rd (01034-9483)
P.O. Box 257 (01034-0257)
PHONE....413 357-8816
James F Wackerbarth, *President*
Nancy Petersen, *Treasurer*
EMP: 11 EST: 1924
SQ FT: 10,000
SALES (est): 2MM Privately Held
SIC: 2448 Mfg Wood Pallets

Great Barrington
Berkshire County

(G-11232)
ANTHROPOSOPHIC PRESS INC
610 Main St (01230-2010)
P.O. Box 799 (01230-0799)
PHONE....212 414-2275
Gene Gollogly, *CEO*
Christopher Bamford, *Principal*
EMP: 14
SALES: 1.2MM Privately Held
SIC: 2741 Misc Publishing

(G-11233)
BERKSHIRE CORPORATION (HQ)
21 River St (01230-1330)
PHONE....413 528-2602
Whitmore Kelley, *President*
Christen Cilona, *Business Mgr*
George Bacigalupo, *Exec VP*
Richard M Marotta, *Exec VP*
Robert J Gutmann, *Treasurer*
◆ EMP: 30
SQ FT: 30,000
SALES (est): 18.6MM Privately Held
WEB: www.berkshire.com
SIC: 2269 2392 Finishing Plant Mfg Household Furnishings

(G-11234)
BERKSHIRE MOUNTAIN DISTLRS INC
1640 Home Rd (01230-9331)
P.O. Box 922 (01230-0922)
PHONE....413 229-0219
Christopher Parsons Weld, *President*
EMP: 6
SALES (est): 774.4K Privately Held
SIC: 2085 Mfg Distilled/Blended Liquor

(G-11235)
BERKSHIRE PUBLISHING GROUP LLC
Also Called: Berkshire Reference Works
122 Castle St (01230)
PHONE....413 528-0206
Karen Christensen,
EMP: 10
SALES (est): 931.4K Privately Held
SIC: 2731 Books-Publishing/Printing

(G-11236)
CHAMBERLAIN GROUP LLC
934 Main St (01230-2013)
PHONE....413 528-7744
Jessica Larkin, *General Mgr*
Eric Chamberlain,
EMP: 10
SQ FT: 2,500
SALES: 850K Privately Held
WEB: www.thecgroup.com
SIC: 3842 Mfg Surgical Appliances/Supplies

(G-11237)
CONNTEXT LABELS
5 Butternut Ln Ste 2 (01230-9509)
PHONE....413 528-3303
Howard Fox, *Partner*
James Barnes, *Manager*
EMP: 7
SALES (est): 364.6K Privately Held
WEB: www.conntext.com
SIC: 2269 Finishing Plant

(G-11238)
GREAT BARRINGTON AUTO SUP INC
Also Called: NAPA Auto Parts
227 Stockbridge Rd (01230-2212)
PHONE....413 528-0838
Anthony S Lioy, *President*
Susan S Lioy, *Admin Sec*
EMP: 9
SALES (est): 143.1K Privately Held
SIC: 3465 Mfg Automotive Stampings

(G-11239)
GUARDUCCI STAINED GL STUDIOS
64 Stoney Brook Rd (01230-1272)
PHONE....413 528-6287
David Guarducci, *Owner*
EMP: 4
SALES: 350K Privately Held
SIC: 3231 Ret Paint/Glass/Wallpaper

(G-11240)
KWIK PRINT INC
35 Bridge St (01230-1310)
PHONE....413 528-2885
John Raifstanger Jr, *President*
Cheryl Raifstanger, *Treasurer*
EMP: 14
SQ FT: 2,100
SALES (est): 2.2MM Privately Held
SIC: 2752 Offset Printing

(G-11241)
LIMESTONE COMMUNICATIONS (PA)
Also Called: Berkshire Record
21 Elm St (01230-1516)
P.O. Box 868 (01230-0868)
PHONE....413 528-5380
Anthony Prisendorf, *President*
Alexis Prisebdorf, *Vice Pres*
Donna Prisendorf, *Vice Pres*
Justin Prisendorf, *Vice Pres*
EMP: 35
SQ FT: 6,000
SALES (est): 1.4MM Privately Held
WEB: www.berkshirerecord.com
SIC: 2711 Newspapers-Publishing/Printing

(G-11242)
MYRIN INSTITUTE INC
Also Called: Orion Society, The
187 Main St (01230-1602)
PHONE....413 528-4422
Marion Gilliam, *President*
Emerson Blake, *Principal*
▲ EMP: 14
SALES: 974.7K Privately Held
WEB: www.myrin.org
SIC: 2721 Periodicals-Publishing/Printing

(G-11243)
NORTH RIVER PRESS PUBG CORP
27 Rosseter St Ste 1 (01230-1522)
P.O. Box 567 (01230-0567)
PHONE....413 528-0034
Laurence Gadd, *President*
Amy Gallagher, *Vice Pres*
EMP: 15
SQ FT: 600
SALES (est): 1.2MM Privately Held
WEB: www.northriverpress.com
SIC: 2731 8742 Printing And Publishing Engineering And Management Services

(G-11244)
OLDE VILLAGE MONOGRAMMING INC
2 Stillwell St Ste 1 (01230-1753)
PHONE....413 528-3904
Helen Eline, *President*
EMP: 3
SQ FT: 1,700
SALES: 200K Privately Held
SIC: 2395 3552 Pleating/Stitching Services Mfg Textile Machinery

(G-11245)
SCHOOLSUITE LLC
301 State Rd (01230-1439)
PHONE....800 671-1905
Jeff Pzynski,
Hilary Mueller,
EMP: 4
SALES: 1MM Privately Held
SIC: 7372 Prepackaged Software Services

(G-11246)
SOUTHERN BERKSHIRE SHOPPERS GU
141 West Ave (01230-1811)
P.O. Box 89 (01230-0089)
PHONE....413 528-0095
Eunice Raifstanger, *President*
Robin Hare, *Treasurer*
John Raifstanger Jr, *Clerk*
EMP: 11
SQ FT: 2,200
SALES (est): 1.1MM Privately Held
WEB: www.shoppersguide-inc.com
SIC: 2741 6531 2796 2791 Misc Publishing Real Estate Agent/Mgr Platemaking Services Typesetting Services

(G-11247)
SPROUTMAN PUBLICATIONS
Also Called: Sproutman and Co
20 W Sheffield Rd (01230-1933)
P.O. Box 1100 (01230-6100)
PHONE....413 528-5200
Steve Meyerowitz, *Owner*
EMP: 3
SALES (est): 312.5K Privately Held
SIC: 2731 Books-Publishing/Printing

(G-11248)
THE ORION SOCIETY INC
Also Called: ORION MAGAZINE
187 Main St Ste 1 (01230-1623)
PHONE....413 528-4422
Marion Gilliam, *President*
Karen Gagne, *Business Mgr*
Chris Nye, *Bd of Directors*
EMP: 13
SALES: 1.1MM Privately Held
SIC: 2721 Periodicals-Publishing And Printing

(G-11249)
WAINWRIGHT USA LLC
Also Called: Panthera
964 S Main St Ste 5 (01230-2118)
PHONE....413 717-4211
Michael Wainwright,
EMP: 3
SALES (est): 70.4K Privately Held
SIC: 3262 Mfg Vitreous China Tableware

Greenfield
Franklin County

(G-11250)
ARGOTEC LLC (HQ)
53 Silvio O Conte Dr (01301-1382)
PHONE....413 772-2564
Jeffrey Kramer, *CEO*
Michel Fievez, *Exec VP*
Daniel Lister, *Exec VP*
Allison Aden, *CFO*
Joshua McComb, *Technical Staff*
◆ EMP: 102
SQ FT: 55,000

GEOGRAPHIC

SALES (est): 65MM Publicly Held
WEB: www.argotec.com
SIC: 3081 2821 Mfg Unsupported Plastic Film/Sheet Mfg Plastic Materials/Resins

(G-11251)
ASSOCTION FOR GRVSTONE STUDIES
278 Main St Ste 209 (01301-3230)
PHONE....413 772-0836
Tom Malloy, *President*
Robert Young, *Vice Pres*
Penelope Davis, *Administration*
EMP: 13
SALES: 105.8K Privately Held
SIC: 2741 Publish Journals For Restoration Of Graveyards

(G-11252)
BETE FOG NOZZLE INC (PA)
50 Greenfield St (01301-1378)
PHONE....413 772-0846
Matthew Bete, *Ch of Bd*
Tom Bass, *President*
Tom Fitch, *President*
Thomas Bassett, *Vice Pres*
Doug Dziadzio, *VP Mfg*
◆ EMP: 130
SQ FT: 54,000
SALES (est): 33.8MM Privately Held
WEB: www.bete.com
SIC: 3499 Mfg Misc Fabricated Metal Products

(G-11253)
CHAUNCEY WINGS SONS INC
78 Pierce St (01301-1720)
P.O. Box 420, Marion (02738-0007)
PHONE....413 772-6611
Donald Wing, *President*
Paul Sevrens, *Vice Pres*
EMP: 3
SQ FT: 7,000
SALES (est): 370.6K Privately Held
WEB: www.chauncey-wing.com
SIC: 3579 Mfg Label Applicators

(G-11254)
CNS OUTDOOR TECHNOLOGIES LLC
627 Barton Rd (01301-1011)
PHONE....413 475-3840
Albert N Orsmond,
EMP: 13
SALES (est): 477.7K Privately Held
SIC: 2421 Sawmill/Planing Mill

(G-11255)
COCA-COLA REFRESHMENTS USA INC
180 Silvio O Conte Dr (01301-1356)
PHONE....413 772-2617
John O'Neil, *Branch Mgr*
EMP: 113
SALES (corp-wide): 31.8B Publicly Held
WEB: www.cokecce.com
SIC: 2086 5149 Mfg Bottled/Canned Soft Drinks Whol Groceries
HQ: Coca-Cola Refreshments Usa, Inc.
2500 Windy Ridge Pkwy Se
Atlanta GA 30339
770 989-3000

(G-11256)
COLD RIVER MINING INC
246 Silver St (01301-1400)
PHONE....413 219-3315
Gary R Alger, *Principal*
▲ EMP: 3
SALES (est): 315.4K Privately Held
SIC: 2673 Mfg Bags-Plastic/Coated Paper

(G-11257)
COMPANY OF COCA-COLA BOTTLING
180 Silvio O Conte Dr (01301-1356)
PHONE....413 448-8296
Randy Markland, *Manager*
EMP: 35 Privately Held
WEB: www.coke.com
SIC: 2086 Carb Sft Drnkbtlcn
HQ: Coca-Cola Bottling Company Of Southeastern New England, Inc.
150 Waterford Parkway S
Waterford CT 06385
860 443-2816

(G-11258)
COMPOUND MANUFACTURING LLC
43 Warner St (01301-1823)
PHONE....413 773-8909
Matthew Gifford, *Principal*
Neal Gifford, *Engineer*
EMP: 3
SALES (est): 192.2K Privately Held
SIC: 3999 Mfg Misc Products

(G-11259)
DECKER MACHINE WORKS INC
201 Munson St (01301-9605)
P.O. Box 1001, Ashfield (01330-1001)
PHONE....413 628-3300
Scott A Decker, *President*
Noah Decker, *General Mgr*
EMP: 20
SQ FT: 10,000
SALES (est): 2.1MM Privately Held
WEB: www.deckermachineworks.com
SIC: 3599 Mfg Industrial Machinery

(G-11260)
EWING CONTROLS INC
321 Deerfield St (01301-3412)
PHONE....413 774-7500
Tim James, *President*
Tom Ewing, *Vice Pres*
John Schuster, *Project Engr*
Terri Lauricella, *Accountant*
EMP: 10 EST: 2001
SQ FT: 1,000
SALES (est): 2MM Privately Held
WEB: www.ewingcontrols.com
SIC: 3625 Mfg Relays/Industrial Controls

(G-11261)
FRANKLIN COUNTY FABRICATORS
Also Called: Franklin Country Fabricators
144 Adams Rd (01301-1310)
PHONE....413 774-3518
John W Campbell, *President*
James H Wenzel, *Treasurer*
EMP: 5
SQ FT: 6,000
SALES (est): 709.5K Privately Held
SIC: 3443 1799 7389 Welding Fabricator & Crane Rigging Service

(G-11262)
GREENFIELD SILVER INC (PA)
Also Called: Lunt Silversmiths
298 Federal St (01301-1971)
PHONE....413 774-2774
Denham C Lunt Jr, *Ch of Bd*
James H Lunt, *President*
▲ EMP: 100
SQ FT: 62,000
SALES (est): 8.5MM Privately Held
WEB: www.luntsilver.com
SIC: 3914 3421 3423 Mfg Silver/Plated Ware

(G-11263)
GSOUTFITTING
58 Summer St (01301-1463)
PHONE....413 773-0247
EMP: 3
SALES (est): 200K Privately Held
SIC: 2421 Sawmill/Planing Mill

(G-11264)
JH SMITH CO INC (PA)
330 Chapman St (01301-1799)
PHONE....413 772-0191
Kenneth Wayne Sittig, *President*
Jeane B Smith, *Chairman*
Sherrell J Smith, *Vice Pres*
Victoria Sittig, *Treasurer*
▲ EMP: 16
SQ FT: 30,000
SALES (est): 2.6MM Privately Held
WEB: www.jhsmithcompany.com
SIC: 3499 5099 3423 3421 Mfg Misc Fab Metal Prdts Whol Durable Goods Mfg Hand/Edge Tools Mfg Cutlery Mfg Semivtrs China Tblwr

(G-11265)
KATALYST KOMBUCHA LLC
324 Wells St (01301-1636)
PHONE....413 773-9700
Jeffrey Canter, *Manager*
EMP: 6
SALES (est): 220K Privately Held
SIC: 2086 Mfg Bottled/Canned Soft Drinks

(G-11266)
KATZ EYE OPTICS
14 Greenway Ln (01301-1857)
PHONE....413 743-2523
Rachael Katz, *Owner*
◆ EMP: 4
SALES (est): 230K Privately Held
SIC: 3861 Mfg Photographic Equipment/Supplies

(G-11267)
KENNAMETAL INC
34 Sanderson St (01301-2715)
PHONE....802 626-3331
Kerri Vassar, *QC Mgr*
Jeff Cox, *Engineer*
David Perez, *Engineer*
James Whittier, *Engineer*
Mike Kinsman, *Sales & Mktg St*
EMP: 262
SALES (corp-wide): 2.3B Publicly Held
WEB: www.kennametal.com
SIC: 3545 Mfg Machine Tool Accessories
PA: Kennametal Inc.
525 William Penn Pl # 33
Pittsburgh PA 15219
412 248-8000

(G-11268)
LEON M FISKE COMPANY INC
Also Called: Forest Products Associates
75 Oak Hill Rd (01301-9728)
PHONE....413 772-6833
Leon M Fiske Jr, *CEO*
Susan Fiske, *President*
EMP: 3
SALES (est): 489.4K Privately Held
WEB: www.forestproductsassociates.com
SIC: 2421 5211 Kiln Drying & Ret Lumber

(G-11269)
MARTINS FARM RECYCLING
341 Plain Rd (01301-9780)
PHONE....413 774-5631
Robert Martin, *Owner*
EMP: 5
SALES (est): 505.8K Privately Held
WEB: www.martinsfarmrecycling.com
SIC: 2875 Mfg Fertilizers-Mix Only

(G-11270)
NEWSPAPERS OF MASSACHUSETTS
Also Called: The Recorder
14 Hope St (01301-3308)
P.O. Box 1367 (01302-1367)
PHONE....978 544-2118
Kay Derenson, *President*
Natasha Kulisanski, *Sales Staff*
Samuel Nelson, *Administration*
EMP: 412
SALES (est): 16.5MM
SALES (corp-wide): 80.7MM Privately Held
WEB: www.recorder.com
SIC: 2711 2791 2752 Newspapers-Publishing/Printing Typesetting Services Lithographic Commercial Printing
PA: Newspapers Of New England, Inc.
1 Monitor Dr
Concord NH 03301
603 224-5301

(G-11271)
NORTHEAST BIODIESEL LLC
179 Silvio O Conte Dr (01301-1356)
P.O. Box 688 (01302-0688)
PHONE....413 772-8891
Lynn Benander,
EMP: 4
SQ FT: 6,600
SALES (est): 92.4K
SALES (corp-wide): 628.5K Privately Held
WEB: www.northeastbiodiesel.com
SIC: 2869 Mfg Industrial Organic Chemicals
PA: Co-Op Power, Inc.
296 Nonotuck St Ste 4
Florence MA 01062
413 772-8898

(G-11272)
PIONEER VLY MILK MKTG COOP INC
Also Called: Our Family Farms Massachusetts
324 Wells St (01301-1636)
P.O. Box 167 (01302-0167)
PHONE....413 772-2332
Faith Williams, *President*
Angie Facey, *Vice Pres*
Deborah Barton-Duprey, *Treasurer*
Karen Gould, *Admin Sec*
EMP: 5
SQ FT: 200
SALES: 950K Privately Held
SIC: 2026 8742 Processing And Marketing Of Dairy Products

(G-11273)
REAL PICKLES COPERATIVE INC
311 Wells St (01301-1639)
PHONE....413 774-2600
Annie Winkler, *Principal*
Brendan Flannelly-King, *Principal*
Addie Rose Holland, *Principal*
Kristin Howard, *Principal*
Tamara McKerchie, *Principal*
EMP: 22 EST: 2014
SALES (est): 1MM Privately Held
SIC: 2035 Mfg Pickles/Sauces/Dressing

(G-11274)
SAW MILL SITE FARM
324 Wells St (01301-1636)
PHONE....413 665-3005
Terry Grinnan, *Owner*
EMP: 3
SALES (est): 155K Privately Held
SIC: 2044 Rice Milling

(G-11275)
SILVER SCREEN DESIGN INC
324 Wells St Ste 3 (01301-1636)
PHONE....413 773-1692
Cheryl Termo, *President*
EMP: 14
SQ FT: 14,000
SALES: 1.9MM Privately Held
WEB: www.silverscreendesign.com
SIC: 2261 2759 7336 3993 Finishing Plant Screen Printing Graphic Arts & Related Design Mfg Signs & Advertising Automotive & Apparel Trimmings

(G-11276)
SMALL CORP
19 Butternut St (01301-1379)
PHONE....413 772-0889
Van Wood, *President*
Frank Degnen, *Business Mgr*
Wendy Sawyer, *Sales Executive*
Sarah Elmer,
EMP: 3
SALES (est): 363.5K Privately Held
SIC: 3999 Mfg Misc Products

(G-11277)
SNOWS NICE CREAM CO INC
Also Called: Bart's Homemade
80 School St (01301-4207)
PHONE....413 774-7438
Barbara Fingold, *President*
Gary Schaefer, *Treasurer*
EMP: 4 EST: 1925
SQ FT: 8,000
SALES: 980K Privately Held
WEB: www.bartshomemade.com
SIC: 2024 Eating Place

(G-11278)
SWM
53 Silvio O Conte Dr (01301-1382)
PHONE....413 772-2564
EMP: 14
SALES (est): 7.2MM Privately Held
SIC: 2821 Mfg Plastic Materials/Resins

(G-11279)
SWM INTERNATIONAL
49 Greenfield St (01301-1378)
PHONE..................................413 774-3772
Richard A Barnes, *Principal*
EMP: 8 **Publicly Held**
SIC: 3081 2821 Mfg Unsupported Plastic Film/Sheet Mfg Plastic Materials/Resins
HQ: Argotec, Llc
53 Silvio O Conte Dr
Greenfield MA 01301
413 772-2564

(G-11280)
THIN FILM IMAGING TECHNOLOGIES
Also Called: Tfi Technologies
11 Blanker Ln (01301-1111)
PHONE..................................413 774-6692
Michael T Krawczyk, *President*
EMP: 10
SALES (est): 1.4MM **Privately Held**
WEB: www.tfitech.com
SIC: 3827 Mfg Optical Instrument Filters

(G-11281)
THOMAS & THOMAS RODMAKERS
627 Barton Rd Ste 1 (01301-1001)
PHONE..................................413 475-3840
Tom Dorsey, *Manager*
▲ **EMP:** 23
SALES (est): 2.6MM **Privately Held**
WEB: www.thomasandthomas.com
SIC: 3949 5091 5941 Mfg Sporting/Athletic Goods Whol Sporting/Recreational Goods Ret Sporting Goods/Bicycles

(G-11282)
VALLEY STEEL STAMP INC
Also Called: Vss
15 Greenfield St (01301-1378)
PHONE..................................413 773-8200
Steven Capshaw, *President*
Robert Gritzner, *Prdtn Mgr*
Marc Eckstrom, *Sales Staff*
Mike Towne, *Maintence Staff*
EMP: 35 **EST:** 1971
SQ FT: 22,000
SALES (est): 11.1MM **Privately Held**
WEB: www.valleysteelstamp.com
SIC: 3953 5088 Mfg Marking Devices Whol Transportation Equipment

(G-11283)
WELLS TOOL COMPANY
106 Hope St (01301-3569)
P.O. Box 1531 (01302-1531)
PHONE..................................413 773-3465
Phillip Duda, *President*
Sandra Duda, *Vice Pres*
EMP: 11 **EST:** 1928
SALES (est): 1.8MM **Privately Held**
SIC: 3545 Mfg Machine Tool Taps

(G-11284)
WOOD & WOOD INC
19 Butternut St (01301-1379)
PHONE..................................413 772-0889
Van V Wood, *President*
Molly L Wood, *Treasurer*
Wendy Sawyer, *Sales Mgr*
▼ **EMP:** 30
SQ FT: 36,000
SALES (est): 4MM **Privately Held**
WEB: www.smallcorp.com
SIC: 2542 2499 Mfg Partitions/Fixtures-Nonwood Mfg Wood Products

Groton
Middlesex County

(G-11285)
CASTLEWOOD SURGICAL
20 Whiley Rd (01450-2206)
PHONE..................................978 448-3628
EMP: 3
SALES (est): 220K **Privately Held**
SIC: 3841 Mfg Surgical/Medical Instruments

(G-11286)
CHEMTRAC SYSTEMS
5 Lakeside Dr (01450-2029)
PHONE..................................978 448-0061
Joseph Zimmerman, *Marketing Staff*
EMP: 3 **EST:** 2017
SALES (est): 184.9K **Privately Held**
SIC: 3823 Mfg Process Control Instruments

(G-11287)
COLONIAL LANDSCAPE CORP
Also Called: Colonial Stone Yard
66 North St (01450-1424)
PHONE..................................978 448-3329
Toll Free:..................................888 -
Gerald Croteau, *President*
EMP: 3
SQ FT: 10,000
SALES (est): 327.2K **Privately Held**
WEB: www.colonialstoneyard.com
SIC: 3281 1741 5211 5032 Mfg Ret & Whol Stone Products & Stone & Masonry Construction Contractor

(G-11288)
EBSNET INC
Also Called: On Time Software
274e Main St (01450-1236)
P.O. Box 819 (01450-0819)
PHONE..................................978 448-9000
Sarah Richardson, *President*
Tom Vanoudenaren, *Vice Pres*
Tom V Oudenaren, *CTO*
EMP: 8
SQ FT: 1,500
SALES (est): 847.6K **Privately Held**
WEB: www.ebsnetinc.com
SIC: 7372 Prepackaged Software Services

(G-11289)
GROTON HERALD INC
161 Main St (01450-1237)
P.O. Box 610 (01450-0610)
PHONE..................................978 448-6061
Deborah Johnson, *President*
EMP: 5
SQ FT: 1,000
SALES (est): 290.8K **Privately Held**
WEB: www.grotonherald.com
SIC: 2711 Newspapers Publishing

(G-11290)
GROTON PALLET INCORPORATED
183 Kemp St (01450-1123)
PHONE..................................978 448-5651
James G Downes Jr, *President*
EMP: 4 **EST:** 2001
SALES (est): 250K **Privately Held**
SIC: 2448 Mfg Wood Pallets/Skids

(G-11291)
NEW ENGLAND BUSINESS SVC INC (HQ)
Also Called: Nebs
500 Main St (01471-0001)
PHONE..................................978 448-6111
Richard H Rhoads, *President*
Paul F Robinson, *Corp Secy*
Barbara Baklund, *Vice Pres*
Ellen Mc Gowan, *Human Res Mgr*
Norman Mc Coy, *Director*
▼ **EMP:** 75 **EST:** 1952
SQ FT: 126,000
SALES (est): 441.8MM
SALES (corp-wide): 2B **Publicly Held**
WEB: www.nebs.com
SIC: 2771 5045 2653 3089 Mfg Greeting Cards Whol Computer/Peripheral Mfg Corrugated/Fiber Box
PA: Deluxe Corporation
3680 Victoria St N
Shoreview MN 55126
651 483-7111

(G-11292)
OLD FASHION MILK PAINT CO INC
Also Called: Oldfashioned Milk Paint Co
436 Main St (01450-1232)
P.O. Box 222 (01450-0222)
PHONE..................................978 448-6336
Ann S Thibeau, *President*
EMP: 5
SALES (est): 1MM **Privately Held**
SIC: 2851 Mfg Paints/Allied Products

(G-11293)
OPTEK SYSTEMS INC
97 Long Hill Rd (01450-1239)
PHONE..................................978 448-9376
Andrew Webb, *Principal*
EMP: 3 **EST:** 2011
SALES (est): 242.3K **Privately Held**
SIC: 3674 Mfg Semiconductors/Related Devices

(G-11294)
PHARMA INTERFACE ANALYSIS LLC
101 Castle Dr (01450-1291)
PHONE..................................978 448-6137
James Castner, *Principal*
EMP: 3 **EST:** 2012
SALES (est): 197.7K **Privately Held**
SIC: 2834 Mfg Pharmaceutical Preparations

(G-11295)
TEAM-AT-WORK
20 Whiley Rd Ste 101 (01450-2206)
PHONE..................................978 448-8562
EMP: 4 **EST:** 2002
SALES (est): 240K **Privately Held**
SIC: 3841 Medical Engineering

(G-11296)
TRIAD DESIGNS
35 Crosswinds Dr (01450-1129)
PHONE..................................978 952-0136
Patrick Greene, *Principal*
EMP: 3
SALES (est): 334.9K **Privately Held**
SIC: 2759 5099 Commercial Printing Whol Durable Goods

(G-11297)
YOGA FOR DAILY LIVING
104 Mill St (01450-1220)
PHONE..................................978 448-3751
Barbara Rich, *Principal*
EMP: 3 **EST:** 2011
SALES (est): 125.1K **Privately Held**
SIC: 2711 Newspapers-Publishing/Printing

Groveland
Essex County

(G-11298)
A W CHESTERTON COMPANY (PA)
860 Salem St (01834-1563)
P.O. Box 3351, Boston (02241-3351)
PHONE..................................781 438-7000
Richard Hoyle, *CEO*
Brian O'Donnell, *President*
Andrew Chesterton, *Owner*
David Rummel, *General Mgr*
Stan Toal, *Area Mgr*
▲ **EMP:** 45 **EST:** 1884
SQ FT: 65,000
SALES (est): 311.2MM **Privately Held**
WEB: www.chesterton.com
SIC: 3053 2851 2992 2891 Mfg Gasket/Packing/Seals Mfg Paints/Allied Prdts Mfg Lubrictng Oil/Grease Mfg Adhesives/Sealants Whol Chemicals/Products

(G-11299)
A W CHESTERTON COMPANY
860 Salem St (01834-1563)
P.O. Box 189 (01834-0189)
PHONE..................................781 438-7000
Greg Plakias, *Branch Mgr*
George Fennelley, *Technology*
EMP: 400
SALES (corp-wide): 311.2MM **Privately Held**
WEB: www.chesterton.com
SIC: 2819 3561 3053 2992 Mfg Indstl Inorgan Chem Mfg Pumps/Pumping Equip Mfg Gasket/Packing/Seals Mfg Lubrictng Oil/Grease Mfg Chemical Preparation
PA: A. W. Chesterton Company
860 Salem St
Groveland MA 01834
781 438-7000

(G-11300)
HIGHTECHSPEED LLC
8 Federal Way Ste 4 (01834-1567)
PHONE..................................978 600-8222
Michael Brunton, *Mng Member*
EMP: 3
SALES (est): 121.3K **Privately Held**
SIC: 3647 Mfg Vehicle Lighting Equipment

(G-11301)
ITAL-TECH MACHINED PDTS LLC
3 Federal Way (01834-1564)
PHONE..................................978 373-6773
David Slutz, *Mng Member*
EMP: 16
SQ FT: 12,000
SALES: 2.2MM **Privately Held**
SIC: 3599 Mfg Industrial Machinery

(G-11302)
MILLENNIUM PLASTICS INC
154 Center St (01834-1524)
PHONE..................................978 372-4822
Steve Fitzgerald, *President*
EMP: 10
SQ FT: 6,800
SALES (est): 1.7MM **Privately Held**
SIC: 3089 5162 Plastic Fabrication Shop

(G-11303)
PARK BIO SERVICES LLC
154 Center St (01834-1524)
PHONE..................................978 794-8500
Frank Razzaboni,
▼ **EMP:** 5 **EST:** 1997
SQ FT: 7,200
SALES (est): 987.8K **Privately Held**
WEB: www.parkbio.com
SIC: 3826 3841 Mfg Scientific Instruments & Surgical Instruments

(G-11304)
UNION MACHINE COMPANY LYNN INC (PA)
6 Federal Way (01834-1564)
PHONE..................................978 521-5100
Eric Harper, *President*
Laura Wright, *Vice Pres*
John Castino, *Purchasing*
Zachary Nowicki, *Engineer*
Robin Trickett, *CFO*
EMP: 45 **EST:** 1954
SQ FT: 25,000
SALES: 5.9MM **Privately Held**
WEB: www.unionmachine.com
SIC: 3599 7692 3728 3724 Mfg Industrial Machinery Welding Repair Mfg Aircraft Parts/Equip Mfg Aircraft Engine/Part

Hadley
Hampshire County

(G-11305)
ARCHITECTURAL TIMBER MLLWK INC
49 Mount Warner Rd (01035-9674)
P.O. Box 719 (01035-0719)
PHONE..................................413 586-3045
Thomas N Harris, *President*
EMP: 19
SQ FT: 7,500
SALES (est): 3MM **Privately Held**
WEB: www.atimber.com
SIC: 2452 5031 5039 2439 Mfg Prefabrcatd Wd Bldgs Whol Lumber/Plywd/Millwk Whol Cnstn Materials Mfg Structural Wd Member Mfg Millwork

(G-11306)
HADLEY PROPELLER INC
28 Stockwell Rd (01035-9644)
PHONE..................................413 585-0500
Andre Laflamme, *President*
Anna Laflamme, *Treasurer*
EMP: 3
SALES (est): 381.9K **Privately Held**
SIC: 3599 5551 Propeller Services & Machine Shop

GEOGRAPHIC

(G-11307)
HOLLROCK ENGINEERING INC
294 Russell St (01035-9539)
P.O. Box 378 (01035-0378)
PHONE....413 586-2256
J Richard Hollrock, *President*
Richard H Hollrock Sr, *Vice Pres*
▲ **EMP:** 13
SQ FT: 3,000
SALES (est): 1.5MM **Privately Held**
SIC: 3949 5091 7999 Mfg & Distribute Golf Equipment And Golf Driving Range

(G-11308)
INTELLIGENT PLATFORMS LLC
4 Bay Rd Ste 105 (01035-9569)
PHONE....413 586-7884
Maryrose Sylvester, *Manager*
EMP: 3
SALES (corp-wide): 18.3B **Publicly Held**
SIC: 3625 Mfg Relays/Industrial Controls
HQ: Intelligent Platforms, Llc
2500 Austin Dr
Charlottesville VA 22911

(G-11309)
LOCAL TORTILLA LLC
113 Bay Rd (01035-9720)
P.O. Box 230 (01035-0230)
PHONE....413 387-7140
Jorge Sosa, *Principal*
EMP: 3
SALES (est): 226.3K **Privately Held**
SIC: 2099 Mfg Food Preparations

(G-11310)
MAPLE VALLEY CREAMERY
102 Mill Valley Rd (01035-9577)
PHONE....413 588-4881
Laurie Cuevas, *Principal*
EMP: 5
SALES (est): 356.9K **Privately Held**
SIC: 2021 Mfg Creamery Butter

(G-11311)
MOUNT WARNER VINEYARDS LLC
85 Mount Warner Rd (01035-9699)
PHONE....413 531-4046
Gary Kamen, *Principal*
EMP: 7
SALES (est): 567.4K **Privately Held**
SIC: 2084 Mfg Wines/Brandy/Spirits

(G-11312)
ZEN ART & DESIGN INC
119 Rocky Hill Rd (01035-9598)
PHONE....800 215-6010
Will Carswell, *President*
EMP: 14
SQ FT: 2,750
SALES (est): 983.8K **Privately Held**
SIC: 3944 Mfg Games/Toys

Halifax
Plymouth County

(G-11313)
ADVANCED BATTERY SYSTEMS INC
274 Plymouth St (02338-1434)
PHONE....508 378-2284
Brian Kmito, *President*
◆ **EMP:** 6
SALES (est): 846.3K **Privately Held**
WEB: www.batteryprice.com
SIC: 3691 Ret Auto/Home Supplies

(G-11314)
BANKS WHITE POLIARIS CO INC
500 Industrial Dr (02338-1254)
PHONE....781 293-3033
Katherine Malone, *President*
EMP: 4 **EST:** 1943
SQ FT: 13,500
SALES: 200K **Privately Held**
SIC: 3599 Machine Job Shop

(G-11315)
BAY STEEL CO INC (PA)
87 Lake St (02338-1138)
PHONE....781 294-8308
Christopher Davies, *President*
EMP: 5
SQ FT: 4,000
SALES (est): 984.8K **Privately Held**
SIC: 3441 3449 Structural Metal Fabrication Mfg Misc Structural Metalwork

(G-11316)
CHAPINS WOOD PRODUCTS INC (PA)
6 Delia Way (02338-1187)
P.O. Box 49 (02338-0049)
PHONE....781 294-0758
Michael Chapin, *President*
Karen Chapin, *Treasurer*
EMP: 4
SQ FT: 900
SALES (est): 713.4K **Privately Held**
WEB: www.chapinswoodproducts.com
SIC: 2452 Retail Sale Of Shedsgazebosplaysets

(G-11317)
DAVID LEFORT
Also Called: Lefort Fine Furniture
13 Arrowhead Path (02338-1647)
PHONE....781 826-9033
David Lefort, *President*
EMP: 20
SQ FT: 12,000
SALES: 750K **Privately Held**
SIC: 2511 2512 Mfg Wood Household Furniture

(G-11318)
FIBERGLASS BUILDING PDTS INC
546a Plymouth St (02338)
P.O. Box 139 (02338-0139)
PHONE....847 650-3045
Edward Mayo, *President*
EMP: 7
SALES (est): 143.2K **Privately Held**
SIC: 3089 5031 Mfg Plastic Products Whol Lumber/Plywd/Millwk

Hampden
Hampden County

(G-11319)
AMS GLASS BEAD CABINETS
267 Allen St (01036-9740)
PHONE....413 566-0037
John Zanetti, *Owner*
EMP: 20
SALES (est): 1MM **Privately Held**
SIC: 3231 3429 Mfg Products-Purchased Glass Mfg Hardware

(G-11320)
CUSTOM WOODS DESIGNS M MARION
76 Bennett Rd (01036-9653)
PHONE....413 566-8230
Michael J Marion, *Owner*
EMP: 4
SALES: 600K **Privately Held**
WEB: www.cuwood.com
SIC: 2511 5712 Mfg Wood Household Furniture Ret Furniture

(G-11321)
LACUCINA EXPRESS
9 Allen St (01036-9789)
PHONE....413 566-8015
Geri Cimmino, *Principal*
EMP: 3
SALES (est): 255.7K **Privately Held**
SIC: 3421 Mfg Cutlery

(G-11322)
NEW ENGLAND TIME SOLUTIONS INC
112 E Longmeadow Rd Fl 2 (01036-9672)
P.O. Box 12, East Longmeadow (01028-0012)
PHONE....888 222-3396
Karl Cook Bailey, *President*
EMP: 5 **EST:** 2011
SQ FT: 1,000
SALES (est): 374.3K **Privately Held**
SIC: 7372 Prepackaged Software Services

(G-11323)
PHARMA COMPLIANCE GROUP LLC
24 Glendale View Dr (01036-9517)
PHONE....508 377-4561
Matthew Murphy, *President*
EMP: 4
SQ FT: 500
SALES (est): 355.2K **Privately Held**
SIC: 2834 Mfg Pharmaceutical Preparations

Hancock
Berkshire County

(G-11324)
BBMC INC
1 N Main St (01237-9782)
PHONE....413 443-3333
Blair Anthony, *President*
EMP: 17
SQ FT: 15,000
SALES (est): 1.2MM **Privately Held**
SIC: 3086 Mfg Plastic Foam Products

(G-11325)
LANSEN MOLD CO INC
1 Main St (01237-9201)
P.O. Box 1481, Lanesborough (01237-1481)
PHONE....413 443-5328
Neil C Kristensen Jr, *President*
Karen Rosier, *Corp Secy*
EMP: 10
SQ FT: 24,400
SALES (est): 2.8MM **Privately Held**
WEB: www.lansenmold.com
SIC: 3089 3544 Mfg Plastic Products Mfg Dies/Tools/Jigs/Fixtures

Hanover
Plymouth County

(G-11326)
AMERICAN CUSTOM DISPLAYS
348 Circuit St Ste 3 (02339-2143)
P.O. Box 464 (02339-0464)
PHONE....781 829-0585
Catherine Franzini, *President*
EMP: 7
SALES: 600K **Privately Held**
WEB: www.americancustomdisplays.com
SIC: 2541 Mfg Wood Partitions/Fixtures

(G-11327)
ATOM MARKETING INC (PA)
127 American Elm Ave (02339-1243)
PHONE....781 982-9930
Edward Radovich, *President*
Susan Radovich, *Admin Sec*
EMP: 3
SALES (est): 1.2MM **Privately Held**
WEB: www.plasticendplugs.com
SIC: 3089 Mfg Plastic Products

(G-11328)
BMI SURPLUS INC
149 King St (02339-2407)
PHONE....781 871-8868
Robert Brams, *Owner*
EMP: 5
SALES (est): 835.7K **Privately Held**
SIC: 3829 Mfg Measuring/Controlling Devices

(G-11329)
BOND PRINTING COMPANY INC
104 Plain St (02339-2170)
P.O. Box 43 (02339-0043)
PHONE....781 871-3990
Jonathan Bond, *President*
Joyanne Bond, *Treasurer*
Robert Norris, *Clerk*
EMP: 6
SQ FT: 4,000
SALES (est): 912.1K **Privately Held**
WEB: www.bondprinting.com
SIC: 2752 Lithographic Commercial Printing

(G-11330)
BOSTON GARAGE
145 Webster St Ste D (02339-1228)
PHONE....339 788-9580
Benjamin A Bennett, *Principal*
Michael Kenney, *Principal*
EMP: 10
SALES (est): 1.1MM **Privately Held**
SIC: 3429 7359 Mfg Hardware Equipment Rental/Leasing

(G-11331)
BRYANT SHEET METAL & CNSTR
301 Winter St Ste 3 (02339-2581)
PHONE....781 826-4113
Russell Bryant Jr, *CEO*
Rita Bryant, *Treasurer*
EMP: 3
SQ FT: 3,974
SALES (est): 763K **Privately Held**
SIC: 3444 Mfg Sheet Metalwork

(G-11332)
CAMBRIDGE SOUNDWORKS INC
1422 Washington St (02339-1647)
PHONE....781 829-8818
EMP: 3
SALES (corp-wide): 191.7MM **Privately Held**
SIC: 3651 5731 Mfg Home Audio/Video Equipment Ret Radio/Tv/Electronics
HQ: Cambridge Soundworks, Inc.
1519 Cimarron Plz
Stillwater OK 74075
405 742-6704

(G-11333)
CRI-TECH INC
85 Winter St (02339-2553)
PHONE....781 826-5600
Shigeru Ushijima, *President*
Mitsuru Kishine, *Vice Pres*
Lisa Strassman, *Treasurer*
Robert Berg, *Admin Sec*
▲ **EMP:** 28
SQ FT: 6,600
SALES (est): 8.6MM **Privately Held**
WEB: www.critech.com
SIC: 3069 Mfg Fabricated Rubber Products
HQ: Daikin America, Inc.
20 Olympic Dr
Orangeburg NY 10962

(G-11334)
CUSTOM MACHINE & TOOL CO INC
301 Winter St Ste 2 (02339-2581)
P.O. Box 298 (02339-0298)
PHONE....781 924-1003
Robert Bennett, *President*
Marc Sematones, *Info Tech Mgr*
EMP: 12
SQ FT: 10,000
SALES (est): 256.9K **Privately Held**
WEB: www.cmtco.com
SIC: 3566 3568 Mfg Speed Changers/Drives Mfg Power Transmission Equipment

(G-11335)
DESIGNER SINKS & FAUCETS
74 Maplewood Dr (02339-1927)
PHONE....781 924-1768
Sherry McCafferty, *Owner*
Sherry Mc Cafferty, *Owner*
EMP: 4
SALES (est): 315K **Privately Held**
SIC: 3431 Mfg Metal Sanitary Ware

(G-11336)
ELDRED WHEELER COMPANY
199 Winter St Ste 3 (02339-2597)
PHONE....781 924-5067
Eldred Wheeler, *Owner*
EMP: 9 **EST:** 2010
SALES (est): 1.1MM **Privately Held**
SIC: 3532 Mfg Mining Machinery

(G-11337)
EYESAVER INTERNATIONAL INC
Also Called: E S I
348 Circuit St Ste 2 (02339-2143)
PHONE..................................781 829-0808
Steven George, *President*
Matthew B Smillie, *Vice Pres*
Tom Larson, *Prdtn Mgr*
Cindy Kain, *Purch Mgr*
Marie Gagliard, *Financial Exec*
▲ **EMP:** 70
SQ FT: 50,000
SALES (est): 11.1MM **Privately Held**
WEB: www.eyesaverinternational.com
SIC: 3599 Mfg Industrial Machinery

(G-11338)
GAVA GROUP INC
691 Main St (02339-1575)
PHONE..................................781 878-9889
Chris Giovanucci, *President*
Turk Giovanucci, *Vice Pres*
EMP: 3
SALES: 160K **Privately Held**
SIC: 2389 Mfg Apparel/Accessories

(G-11339)
GEM GRAVURE CO INC (PA)
112 School St (02339-2400)
P.O. Box 1158 (02339-1003)
PHONE..................................781 878-0456
David J Gemelli, *President*
Paul Gemelli, *Exec VP*
Jean Patton, *QC Mgr*
Richard Chamberland, *Engineer*
Kevin Gilbert, *Engineer*
◆ **EMP:** 80 **EST:** 1952
SQ FT: 30,000
SALES (est): 21.6MM **Privately Held**
WEB: www.gemgravure.com
SIC: 3555 2893 Mfg Printing Trades Machinery Mfg Printing Ink

(G-11340)
GRAPHIC DEVELOPMENTS INC
70 Mayflower Dr (02339-2007)
P.O. Box 1415 (02339-1010)
PHONE..................................781 878-2222
Robert Damon, *President*
George E Davis, *President*
Jay Leach, *Prdtn Mgr*
Helen Printers, *Supervisor*
EMP: 44 **EST:** 1973
SQ FT: 13,500
SALES (est): 7.5MM **Privately Held**
WEB: www.graphicdevelopments.com
SIC: 2752 Lithographic Commercial Printing

(G-11341)
HAITI PROJECTS INC
335 Water St (02339-2831)
PHONE..................................978 969-1064
Adlumia Gannett, *Ch of Bd*
Martha Fox, *Vice Ch Bd*
Lucy Levenson, *President*
Susan Baldwin, *Treasurer*
EMP: 103
SALES: 1.1MM **Privately Held**
SIC: 2395 Pleating/Stitching Services

(G-11342)
INTESET TECHNOLOGIES LLC
Also Called: Inteset Systems
51 Mill St Ste 21 (02339-1641)
PHONE..................................781 826-1560
James A Lloyd, *Mng Member*
EMP: 3
SALES (est): 129.1K **Privately Held**
SIC: 3577 5045 Mfg Computer Peripheral Equipment Whol Computers/Peripherals

(G-11343)
J & R GRAPHICS INC
155 Webster St Ste L (02339-1229)
PHONE..................................781 871-7577
Richard J Fougere, *President*
Janet Fougere, *Vice Pres*
Mark McGuire, *Manager*
EMP: 11
SQ FT: 8,000
SALES (est): 1.2MM **Privately Held**
SIC: 2752 Lithographic Commercial Printing

(G-11344)
JACK KNIGHT CO
Also Called: Knight, Jack Sign Co
972 Washington St Ste 2 (02339-1689)
PHONE..................................781 340-1500
Jack Knight, *Owner*
EMP: 3
SQ FT: 2,000
SALES (est): 211.3K **Privately Held**
SIC: 3993 Mfg Signs/Advertising Specialties

(G-11345)
LOHNES PALLET
Also Called: Lohnes' Pallet Co
72 B St (02339)
PHONE..................................781 878-6801
Robert Lohnes, *Owner*
EMP: 3
SQ FT: 1,000
SALES: 1MM **Privately Held**
SIC: 2448 Mfg Wood Pallets

(G-11346)
LUBRITE LLC
Also Called: Lubrite Technologies
145 Webster St Ste J (02339-1228)
PHONE..................................781 871-1420
Chester Dabkowski, *Principal*
EMP: 6
SALES (corp-wide): 14.3MM **Privately Held**
SIC: 3569 Mfg General Industrial Machinery
HQ: Lubrite, L.L.C.
18649 Brake Shoe Rd
Meadville PA 16335
814 337-4234

(G-11347)
MICROTRAINING ASSOC INC
141 Walnut St (02339-1220)
PHONE..................................781 982-8984
Allen Ivey, *President*
EMP: 4
SALES (est): 183.5K **Privately Held**
SIC: 2731 2741 Books-Publishing/Printing Misc Publishing

(G-11348)
MONDELEZ GLOBAL LLC
188 Ledgewood Dr (02339-3319)
PHONE..................................781 878-0103
Patrick Beringer, *Branch Mgr*
EMP: 3 **Publicly Held**
SIC: 2022 Mfg Packaged Food Products
HQ: Mondelez Global Llc
3 N Pkwy Ste 300
Deerfield IL 60015
847 943-4000

(G-11349)
NORRIS ENTERPRISES INC
Also Called: Norris Litho
605 Main St (02339-1574)
PHONE..................................781 982-8158
Donald Norris, *President*
Doris Norris, *Clerk*
EMP: 3 **EST:** 1980
SQ FT: 3,000
SALES (est): 248.9K **Privately Held**
SIC: 2741 Desktop Publishing

(G-11350)
RUSTIC MARLIN DESIGNS LLC
389 Columbia Rd Ste 40 (02339-2499)
PHONE..................................508 376-1004
Maureen Burns, *Manager*
Brian Oneil,
Melanie Oneil,
EMP: 32
SQ FT: 50,000
SALES: 1MM **Privately Held**
SIC: 3993 Mfg Signs/Advertising Specialties

(G-11351)
SOUTH SHORE DENTAL LABS
Also Called: Swanson Moore Dental Mfg
159 Plymouth Rd (02339-2643)
PHONE..................................781 924-5382
Dennis Moore, *President*
EMP: 4
SQ FT: 800
SALES: 300K **Privately Held**
SIC: 3843 Mfg Dental Equipment/Supplies

(G-11352)
SRC MEDICAL INC
263 Winter St (02339-2557)
PHONE..................................781 826-9100
Roy Clifton Tinkham, *President*
Jeff Tinkham, *General Mgr*
Lisa Lynne Raasch, *Corp Secy*
Leslie Carey, *Purch Mgr*
Maria Barbosa, *Technology*
EMP: 98
SQ FT: 40,000
SALES (est): 9.3MM **Privately Held**
WEB: www.srcmedical.com
SIC: 3089 3069 Mfg Plastic Products Mfg Fabrcatd Rubber Prdt

(G-11353)
STANDARD RUBBER PRODUCTS INC
Also Called: S & D Rubber Co Div
64 B St (02339-1885)
P.O. Box 1157 (02339-1003)
PHONE..................................781 878-2626
Patricia Davis, *President*
Joseph Davis, *Vice Pres*
EMP: 40 **EST:** 1958
SQ FT: 95,000
SALES (est): 8.4MM **Privately Held**
SIC: 2891 3069 Mfg Adhesives/Sealants Mfg Fabricated Rubber Products

(G-11354)
STOUGHTON STEEL COMPANY INC
347 Circuit St (02339-2036)
PHONE..................................781 826-6496
Andry Lagsdin, *President*
Andris Lagsdin, *Vice Pres*
Eric Lagsdin, *Vice Pres*
Dolores Lagsdin, *Treasurer*
Joy Hurley, *Admin Asst*
▼ **EMP:** 30 **EST:** 1976
SQ FT: 21,000
SALES (est): 8.2MM **Privately Held**
WEB: www.stoughtonsteel.com
SIC: 3531 3441 Mfg Construction Machinery Structural Metal Fabrication

(G-11355)
STURTEVANT INC (PA)
Also Called: Sturtevant Mill Company
348 Circuit St Ste 1 (02339-2143)
PHONE..................................781 829-6501
William S English, *Ch of Bd*
W Sturtevant English Jr, *Corp Secy*
Wayne Doherty, *Sls & Mktg Exec*
Edna English, *Treasurer*
Erin Barr, *Controller*
◆ **EMP:** 34 **EST:** 1883
SQ FT: 33,000
SALES: 8MM **Privately Held**
WEB: www.sturtevantinc.com
SIC: 3559 Mfg Misc Industry Machinery

(G-11356)
TRIANGLE ENGINEERING INC
6 Industrial Way (02339-2425)
PHONE..................................781 878-1500
Robert N Coulstring Jr, *President*
Robert Coulstring III, *COO*
Jason Coulstring, *Foreman/Supr*
Rob Coulstring, *Engineer*
Matthew Coulstring, *Treasurer*
EMP: 15 **EST:** 1960
SQ FT: 20,000
SALES (est): 5MM **Privately Held**
WEB: www.trieng.com
SIC: 3443 3829 3498 8711 Mfg Fabricated Plate Wrk Mfg Measure/Control Dvcs Mfg Fabrctd Pipe/Fitting Engineering Services

(G-11357)
TRUEX MACHINE CO INC
25 Pond St (02339-1607)
PHONE..................................781 826-6875
Ruth G Flood, *President*
Stephen Flood, *Vice Pres*
EMP: 9 **EST:** 1977
SQ FT: 6,000
SALES (est): 1.2MM **Privately Held**
WEB: www.truexmachine.com
SIC: 3599 Mfg Industrial Machinery

(G-11358)
US BRONZE FOUNDRY & MCH INC
Also Called: Lubrite Technology
145 Webster St Ste J (02339-1228)
PHONE..................................781 871-1420
Chet Dabkowski, *Branch Mgr*
EMP: 5
SALES (corp-wide): 14.3MM **Privately Held**
SIC: 3568 Mfg Power Transmission Equipment
PA: U.S. Bronze Foundry And Machine, Inc.
18649 Brake Shoe Rd
Meadville PA 16335
814 337-4234

Hanson
Plymouth County

(G-11359)
A A A SHEET METAL INC
23 Winslow Dr (02341-2125)
PHONE..................................781 523-1227
Brian O'Connor, *President*
EMP: 3
SQ FT: 2,000
SALES (est): 300K **Privately Held**
SIC: 3444 Mfg Roof/Siding

(G-11360)
A PERSONAL TOUCH INC (PA)
23 Commercial Waye Ste E (02341-1554)
P.O. Box 147, Whitman (02382-0147)
PHONE..................................781 447-0467
Richard May, *President*
Norine May, *Clerk*
EMP: 6
SQ FT: 11,000
SALES (est): 1.8MM **Privately Held**
WEB: www.personaltouchinc.com
SIC: 2331 2337 2339 Mfg Women/Misses Blouses Mfg Women/Miss Suit/Coat Mfg Women/Miss Outerwear

(G-11361)
BRENNAN MACHINE CO INC
820 Monponsett St (02341-2005)
PHONE..................................781 293-3997
Andrew J Brennan Jr, *President*
EMP: 20
SQ FT: 3,200
SALES (est): 2.7MM **Privately Held**
WEB: www.brennanmachine.com
SIC: 3599 Mfg Industrial Machinery

(G-11362)
EASTERN MACHINE & DESIGN CORP
1062 Main St (02341-1521)
P.O. Box 120 (02341-0120)
PHONE..................................781 293-6391
Raymond Holman, *President*
James Holman, *Vice Pres*
Rob Ralph, *Prgrmr*
Raymond A Holman, *MIS Staff*
Diane E Holman, *Admin Sec*
EMP: 16 **EST:** 1964
SQ FT: 14,530
SALES (est): 2.2MM **Privately Held**
WEB: www.emadcorp.com
SIC: 3599 Machine Shop

(G-11363)
HANSON WHITMAN EXPRESS
1000 Main St (02341-1560)
PHONE..................................781 293-0420
EMP: 3
SALES (est): 123.6K **Privately Held**
SIC: 2711 Newspapers-Publishing/Printing

(G-11364)
JBNJ FOODS INCORPORATED
48 Phillips St (02341-1520)
PHONE..................................781 293-0912
Brian Guilmet, *Principal*
EMP: 3
SALES (est): 153.8K **Privately Held**
SIC: 2099 Mfg Food Preparations

(G-11365)
JMC ASSET HOLDINGS INC
162 Industrial Blvd Ste 7 (02341-1538)
PHONE..................................781 447-9264
John McGrail, *President*
▲ **EMP:** 8
SQ FT: 3,200
SALES (est): 800K **Privately Held**
WEB: www.jacksmachine.com
SIC: 3599 Mfg Industrial Machinery

(G-11366)
MENTON MACHINE CO INC
1299 Main St (02341-1534)
PHONE..................................781 293-8394
John Parks, *President*
EMP: 7
SQ FT: 9,488
SALES (est): 816.8K **Privately Held**
WEB: www.mentonmachine.com
SIC: 3599 Mfg Industrial Machinery

(G-11367)
NORTHEAST BUILDING SUPPLY LLC
91 Franklin St (02341-1806)
PHONE..................................781 294-0400
James Paskell,
Marianne Paskell,
EMP: 5
SALES (est): 205.5K **Privately Held**
SIC: 3272 Mfg Concrete Products

(G-11368)
S & R TOOL & DIE INC
24 Commercial Waye (02341-1527)
PHONE..................................781 447-8446
Steven Russo, *President*
EMP: 10
SQ FT: 6,000
SALES (est): 1.5MM **Privately Held**
SIC: 3599 Mfg Industrial Machinery

(G-11369)
TUBE CHASSIS DESIGNZ
1484 Main St (02341-1504)
PHONE..................................781 293-5005
John Sandahl, *Owner*
Kristin Sandahl, *Principal*
EMP: 3
SALES (est): 331.9K **Privately Held**
WEB: www.tubechassisdesignz.com
SIC: 3711 Mfg Motor Vehicle/Car Bodies

(G-11370)
WEBSTER PRINTING COMPANY INC (PA)
1069 W Washington St (02341-1536)
PHONE..................................781 447-5484
Ernest W Foster, *President*
Julia Realini, *COO*
Jason Boissel, *Exec VP*
Lisa Jewett, *Accountant*
Rick Macdonald, *Accounts Exec*
EMP: 38 **EST:** 1957
SQ FT: 18,600
SALES (est): 8.4MM **Privately Held**
WEB: www.websterprinting.com
SIC: 2752 Lithographic Commercial Printing

Hardwick
Hampshire County

(G-11371)
AMERICAN DISPOSABLES INC
2705 Greenwich Rd (01082-9395)
P.O. Box 800, Ware (01082-0800)
PHONE..................................413 967-6201
Louis J Despres Jr, *President*
Steve Schwartz,
▲ **EMP:** 20
SQ FT: 55,000
SALES (est): 4MM **Privately Held**
WEB: www.americandisposables.com
SIC: 2676 Mfg Sanitary Paper Products

(G-11372)
HARDWICKVMEYARD & WINERY
3305 Greenwich Rd (01082-9322)
PHONE..................................413 967-7763
John J Samek, *Manager*
EMP: 4
SALES (est): 307.3K **Privately Held**
SIC: 2084 Mfg Wines/Brandy/Spirits

Hardwick
Worcester County

(G-11373)
CERSOSIMO LUMBER COMPANY INC
18 Shunpike Rd (01037)
P.O. Box 544 (01037-0544)
PHONE..................................413 477-6258
EMP: 17
SALES (corp-wide): 46.8MM **Privately Held**
WEB: www.cersosimolumber.com
SIC: 2421 Drying Lumber
PA: Cersosimo Lumber Company, Inc.
1103 Vernon St
Brattleboro VT 05301
802 254-4508

(G-11374)
J DANA DESIGN INC
232 Lucas Rd (01037-7700)
PHONE..................................413 477-6844
Jeffrey U Dana Sr, *President*
Justin Dana, *Vice Pres*
Lynn Dana, *Treasurer*
Jeffrey Dana Jr, *Admin Sec*
EMP: 4
SQ FT: 400
SALES: 800K **Privately Held**
SIC: 2434 5021 Mfg Wood Kitchen Cabinets Whol Furniture

Harvard
Worcester County

(G-11375)
ELDERSAFE TECHNOLOGIES INC
127 Poor Farm Rd (01451-1240)
PHONE..................................617 852-3018
EMP: 14
SALES (corp-wide): 40K **Privately Held**
SIC: 3845 Mfg Electromedical Equipment
PA: Eldersafe Technologies, Inc.
16192 Coastal Hwy
Lewes DE 19958
617 852-3018

(G-11376)
HARVARD DOUBLE REEDS
69 S Shaker Rd (01451-1207)
PHONE..................................978 772-1898
John Ferrillo, *Owner*
EMP: 4
SALES (est): 172.1K **Privately Held**
SIC: 3999 Mfg Of Oboe Reed Equipment

(G-11377)
HARVARD PRESS
5 Littleton Rd (01451-1428)
PHONE..................................978 456-3700
Adam Horowitz, *Manager*
EMP: 4
SALES (est): 186.6K **Privately Held**
SIC: 2711 Newspapers-Publishing/Printing

(G-11378)
HARVARD PRODUCTS INC
Also Called: Harvard Machinery
325 Ayer Rd Ste A105 (01451-1151)
P.O. Box 338 (01451-0338)
PHONE..................................978 772-0309
Bryce B Larrabee Jr, *President*
EMP: 10
SQ FT: 15,000
SALES (est): 1.6MM **Privately Held**
WEB: www.harvardmachinery.com
SIC: 3599 5084 Mfg Custom Machinery & Wholesales New & Used Machine Tools

(G-11379)
HXI LLC
Also Called: Hxi Millimeter Wave Products
12 Lancaster County Rd # 1 (01451-1152)
PHONE..................................978 772-7774
Thampy Kurian, *CEO*
Earle Stewart, *Business Mgr*
EMP: 19
SQ FT: 16,400
SALES (est): 3.1MM **Privately Held**
WEB: www.rec-usa.com
SIC: 3812 3679 3663 Mfg Search/Navgatn Equip Mfg Elec Components Mfg Radio/Tv Comm Equip
PA: Renaissance Electronics & Communications, Llc
12 Lancaster County Rd
Harvard MA 01451

(G-11380)
IMAGE STREAM MEDICAL LLC
20 White Ln (01451-1246)
PHONE..................................978 456-9087
Eddie Mitchell, *CEO*
Eugene Antonie, *President*
Peter Reazi, *Vice Pres*
Elizabeth Dowd,
EMP: 5
SALES: 180K **Privately Held**
WEB: www.imagestreammedical.com
SIC: 3841 Mfg Digital Imaging Medical Devices

(G-11381)
KINEMETRICS INC
325 Ayer Rd Ste A118 (01451-1151)
PHONE..................................978 772-4774
EMP: 7
SALES (corp-wide): 423.9MM **Privately Held**
SIC: 3829 8711 Mfg Measure/Control Dvcs Engineering Services
HQ: Kinemetrics, Inc.
222 Vista Ave
Pasadena CA 91107
626 795-2220

(G-11382)
MP OPTICAL COMMUNICATIONS INC (PA)
283 Littleton Rd (01451-1236)
PHONE..................................978 456-7728
Veronica Yu, *CEO*
Martha Lin, *Director*
EMP: 4
SALES: 500K **Privately Held**
SIC: 3229 7389 Mfg Pressed/Blown Glass

(G-11383)
RENAISSNCE ELEC CMMNCTIONS LLC (PA)
12 Lancaster County Rd (01451-1152)
PHONE..................................978 772-7774
Anuj Srivastava, *President*
▲ **EMP:** 39
SQ FT: 15,000
SALES (est): 8.7MM **Privately Held**
WEB: www.rec-usa.com
SIC: 3663 Mfg Radio/Tv Communication Equipment

(G-11384)
RENNAISSANCE ELECTRONIC CORP
12 Lancaster County Rd (01451-1152)
PHONE..................................978 772-7774
Tom Kurian, *President*
▲ **EMP:** 40
SALES: 8MM **Privately Held**
SIC: 3663 Mfg Radio/Tv Communication Equipment

(G-11385)
WILD APPLES INC
38 Eldridge Rd (01451-1903)
PHONE..................................978 456-9616
Susan Richmond, *Administration*
EMP: 6
SALES: 38.5K **Privately Held**
SIC: 2731 Books-Publishing/Printing

Harwich
Barnstable County

(G-11386)
ACME-SHOREY PRECAST CO INC (PA)
Also Called: Shorey Precast Division
36 Great Western Rd (02645-2314)
P.O. Box 1539 (02645-6539)
PHONE..................................508 432-0530
John D Our, *President*
Christopher W Our, *Vice Pres*
Joan A Our, *Treasurer*
EMP: 10 **EST:** 1974
SQ FT: 1,600
SALES (est): 3.8MM **Privately Held**
SIC: 3272 5084 Mfg Concrete Products Whol Industrial Equipment

(G-11387)
ALLMAC SIGNS
10 Captain Scott Rd (02645-1242)
PHONE..................................508 430-4174
Gary McMahon, *Owner*
EMP: 5
SQ FT: 4,000
SALES (est): 200K **Privately Held**
WEB: www.allmacsigns.com
SIC: 3993 Mfg Signs/Advertising Specialties

(G-11388)
ARCOR EPOXY INC
117 Queen Anne Rd (02645-2406)
P.O. Box 273, South Dennis (02660-0273)
PHONE..................................508 385-5598
Ken Fowler, *President*
EMP: 12
SALES (est): 2.3MM **Privately Held**
SIC: 2891 Mfg Adhesives/Sealants

(G-11389)
BIG ROCK OYSTER COMPANY INC
501 Depot St (02645-2309)
PHONE..................................774 408-7951
Aaron Brochu, *Principal*
EMP: 9
SALES (est): 1.2MM **Privately Held**
SIC: 3089 Mfg Plastic Products

(G-11390)
CAPE STROBE EMERGENCY LIGHTING
10 Captains Ln (02645-3139)
PHONE..................................508 776-0911
Norman M Clarke Jr, *Owner*
EMP: 4
SALES: 150K **Privately Held**
SIC: 3647 Mfg Vehicle Lighting Equipment

(G-11391)
COASTAL IMAGE INC
Also Called: Cape Cod
129 Queen Anne Rd (02645-2406)
PHONE..................................508 430-7870
David M Condon, *President*
Ingrid Condon, *Vice Pres*
EMP: 6
SALES: 350K **Privately Held**
SIC: 2395 Pleating/Stitching Services

(G-11392)
COATINGS AND COVERINGS
4 Jilfrey Way (02645-1965)
PHONE..................................774 237-0882
Craig Bardsley, *Principal*
EMP: 3 **EST:** 2010
SALES (est): 165.8K **Privately Held**
SIC: 3479 Coating/Engraving Service

(G-11393)
GENERAL ELECTRIC COMPANY
6 Mcelway Rd (02645-2445)
PHONE..................................617 444-8777
EMP: 158
SALES (corp-wide): 121.6B **Publicly Held**
SIC: 3569 Mfg General Industrial Machinery

▲ = Import ▼=Export
◆ =Import/Export

PA: General Electric Company
5 Necco St
Boston MA 02210
617 443-3000

(G-11394)
JR CHEMICAL COATINGS LLC
139 Queen Anne Rd (02645-2406)
PHONE..................................508 896-3383
John Redihan, *Branch Mgr*
EMP: 7
SALES (corp-wide): 848.3K **Privately Held**
SIC: 3479 Coating/Engraving Service
PA: Jr Chemical Coatings Llc
400 Tubman Rd
Brewster MA

(G-11395)
KARLS BOAT SHOP INC
50 Great Western Rd (02645-2314)
PHONE..................................508 432-4488
Karl Anderson, *President*
▲ **EMP:** 12
SQ FT: 3,072
SALES (est): 1.5MM **Privately Held**
WEB: www.karlsboatshop.com
SIC: 3732 5551 Boatbuilding/Repairing Ret Boats

(G-11396)
NOVOLAC EPOXY TECHNOLOGIES INC (PA)
172 Queen Anne Rd (02645)
P.O. Box 990 (02645-0990)
PHONE..................................508 385-5598
Jordan Fowler, *President*
EMP: 4
SALES (est): 577.5K **Privately Held**
SIC: 2821 2851 7371 Mfg Plastic Materials/Resins Mfg Paints/Allied Products Custom Computer Programing

(G-11397)
ROMA STONE
181 Queen Anne Rd (02645-2405)
PHONE..................................508 430-1200
Christopher Wickstrom, *Principal*
EMP: 6
SALES (est): 424.9K **Privately Held**
SIC: 3281 Mfg Cut Stone/Products

Harwich Port
Barnstable County

(G-11398)
CAPE COD WIND WTHER INDICATORS
Also Called: Cape Cod Flag Poles, Division
Allan Harbor Marine (02646)
P.O. Box 454 (02646-0454)
PHONE..................................508 432-9475
David M Davis, *Partner*
EMP: 3
SQ FT: 2,000
SALES (est): 341K **Privately Held**
WEB: www.capewind.org
SIC: 3829 3873 3825 3823 Mfg Measure/Control Dvcs Mfg Watches/Clocks/Parts Mfg Elec Measuring Instr Mfg Process Cntrl Instr

(G-11399)
CAREY BROTHERS INC
12 Hiawatha Rd (02646-2110)
PHONE..................................508 222-7234
EMP: 35 **EST:** 1924
SALES (est): 2MM **Privately Held**
SIC: 3479 Coating/Engraving Service

Hatfield
Hampshire County

(G-11400)
FUEL MAGAZINE
38 Elm St Apt 7 (01038-9797)
PHONE..................................413 247-5579
Tamra Geryk, *Principal*
EMP: 4 **EST:** 2007
SALES (est): 301.1K **Privately Held**
SIC: 2869 Mfg Industrial Organic Chemicals

(G-11401)
INTER-EGO SYSTEMS INC (PA)
Also Called: Pinnacle Loud Speakers
131 Main St Ste 1 (01038-9786)
PHONE..................................516 576-9052
Marc Rothenberg, *Ch of Bd*
Richard Rothenberg, *President*
Michael Rothenberg, *Vice Pres*
▲ **EMP:** 12
SQ FT: 10,000
SALES (est): 1.3MM **Privately Held**
WEB: www.pinnaclespeakers.com
SIC: 3651 Mfg Home Audio/Video Equipment

Haverhill
Essex County

(G-11402)
3M COMPANY
55 Foundation Ave Ste 100 (01835-7291)
PHONE..................................978 659-9000
Mark Smolinsky, *Manager*
EMP: 500
SALES (corp-wide): 32.7B **Publicly Held**
SIC: 2679 Mfg Converted Paper Products
PA: 3m Company
3m Center
Saint Paul MN 55144
651 733-1110

(G-11403)
3M COMPANY
55 Ward Hill Ave (01835-6930)
PHONE..................................978 420-0001
Todd Kingsbury, *Owner*
EMP: 9
SALES (corp-wide): 32.7B **Publicly Held**
SIC: 3291 2842 2891 3841 Mfg Abrasive Products Mfg Polish/Sanitation Gd Mfg Adhesives/Sealants Mfg Surgical/Med Instr Mfg Surgical Appliances
PA: 3m Company
3m Center
Saint Paul MN 55144
651 733-1110

(G-11404)
APEM INC (HQ)
63 Neck Rd (01835-8025)
PHONE..................................978 372-1602
Peter Brouilette, *CEO*
Tara Cronin-Rodgers, *Purch Mgr*
Laurel Pittera, *CFO*
Marc Enjalbert, *Admin Sec*
◆ **EMP:** 30
SQ FT: 13,000
SALES: 38MM **Privately Held**
SIC: 3577 3679 Mfg Computer Peripheral Equipment Mfg Electronic Components

(G-11405)
ARDEO SYSTEMS INC
17 Parkridge Rd Ste 2 (01835-8511)
PHONE..................................978 373-4680
Mark Finocchario, *President*
EMP: 8
SQ FT: 4,000
SALES (est): 1MM **Privately Held**
SIC: 3674 Mfg Semiconductors/Related Devices

(G-11406)
ATC SCREW MACHINE INC
419 River St (01832-5114)
PHONE..................................781 939-0725
John J Triggs, *President*
Paul Kierce, *Treasurer*
Petrina Triggs, *Clerk*
EMP: 15
SQ FT: 5,500
SALES: 1.5MM **Privately Held**
SIC: 3451 Mfg Screw Machine Products

(G-11407)
BARIL CORPORATION
50 Ward Hill Ave (01835-6929)
PHONE..................................978 373-7910
Dan Baril, *CEO*
Neil Muchin, *Vice Pres*
Kevin Ouellette, *Opers Staff*
Chris Duddy, *Engineer*
John Weymouth, *Engineer*
▲ **EMP:** 33
SQ FT: 25,000
SALES (est): 10.5MM **Privately Held**
WEB: www.barildie.com
SIC: 3841 Mfg Surgical/Medical Instruments

(G-11408)
BAY STATE ESPRESSO
35 Walnut St (01830-5605)
PHONE..................................978 686-5049
Andrea Tondo, *Owner*
▲ **EMP:** 6 **EST:** 2009
SALES (est): 820.1K **Privately Held**
SIC: 3589 Mfg Service Industry Machinery

(G-11409)
BOSTON STEEL & MFG CO
89 Newark St (01832-1348)
PHONE..................................781 324-3000
David L Burke, *President*
Ronald J Burke, *Admin Sec*
EMP: 50 **EST:** 1915
SQ FT: 36,000
SALES (est): 8.3MM **Privately Held**
WEB: www.bostonsteel.com
SIC: 3443 3714 Mfg Fabricated Plate Work Mfg Motor Vehicle Parts/Accessories

(G-11410)
BRADFORD FINSHG POWDR COAT INC
2 S Grove St (01835-7518)
PHONE..................................978 469-9965
Michael Pushee, *President*
EMP: 9
SALES (est): 855.2K **Privately Held**
SIC: 3471 7389 Plating/Polishing Service Business Services

(G-11411)
BURGETT BROTHERS INCORPORATED
Also Called: Mason & Hamlin
35 Duncan St (01830-4801)
PHONE..................................978 374-8888
Kirk A Burgett, *President*
Gary Burgett, *Treasurer*
▲ **EMP:** 50 **EST:** 1996
SALES (est): 7.5MM **Privately Held**
WEB: www.masonhamlin.com
SIC: 3931 Mfg Musical Instruments

(G-11412)
CABOT COACH BUILDERS INC (PA)
Also Called: Royale Limousines
99 Newark St (01832-1348)
PHONE..................................978 374-4530
Cabot B Smith, *President*
Richard Portors, *Vice Pres*
Macgregor Smith, *Admin Sec*
◆ **EMP:** 50
SQ FT: 30,000
SALES (est): 10MM **Privately Held**
WEB: www.royalelimo.com
SIC: 3711 Mfg Motor Vehicle/Car Bodies

(G-11413)
CABOT CORPORATION
50 Rogers Rd Ste 1 (01835-8038)
PHONE..................................978 556-8400
Dirk Sykes, *Manager*
EMP: 112
SALES (corp-wide): 3.3B **Publicly Held**
WEB: www.cabot-corp.com
SIC: 2895 3081 3084 2819 Mfg Carbon Black Plastic Products Silica And Electronic Materials
PA: Cabot Corporation
2 Seaport Ln Ste 1300
Boston MA 02210
617 345-0100

(G-11414)
CENTERS OF NEW ENGLAND MRC
1 Park Way (01830-6278)
PHONE..................................978 241-8232
EMP: 3
SALES (est): 162.6K **Privately Held**
SIC: 3845 Mfg Electromedical Equipment

(G-11415)
CENTRAL PRINTING & SUPPLY
21 Bradley Ave (01832-3402)
PHONE..................................781 322-1220
EMP: 4
SALES (est): 397.2K **Privately Held**
SIC: 2752 Lithographic Commercial Printing

(G-11416)
CHAUCER ACCESSORIES INC
Also Called: Chaucer Leather
143 Essex St Ste 3 (01832-5732)
PHONE..................................978 373-1566
Tom Bates, *President*
Patricia Goodrich, *Vice Pres*
▲ **EMP:** 15
SQ FT: 15,000
SALES (est): 1.6MM **Privately Held**
SIC: 2387 2389 Mfg Men's & Boys' Leather Belts & Suspenders

(G-11417)
CIRCUIT TECHNOLOGY CENTER INC
Also Called: Circuitmedic
22 Parkridge Rd (01835-7278)
PHONE..................................978 374-5000
Jeffrey S Ferry, *President*
Peter Vigneau, *General Mgr*
Joanne M Ferry, *Corp Secy*
Jose Irizarry, *Purch Agent*
Andy Price, *Sales Mgr*
◆ **EMP:** 27
SQ FT: 13,000
SALES (est): 4.7MM **Privately Held**
WEB: www.circuittechctr.com
SIC: 3672 Mfg Printed Circuit Boards

(G-11418)
COASTAL INDUSTRIES INC
77 Newark St (01832-1399)
PHONE..................................978 373-1543
William J Cunningham Sr, *President*
EMP: 25
SQ FT: 47,500
SALES (est): 7.4MM **Privately Held**
WEB: www.coastalindustries.net
SIC: 3442 Mfg Metal Doors/Sash/Trim

(G-11419)
CONVECTRONICS INC
111 Neck Rd (01835-8027)
PHONE..................................978 374-7714
Philip G Aberizk Jr, *President*
Bryce Budrow, *Engineer*
Leslie Woodfall, *Marketing Staff*
John Kuhne, *Manager*
EMP: 16
SQ FT: 20,000
SALES (est): 2.3MM **Privately Held**
WEB: www.convectronics.com
SIC: 3829 3634 Mfg Measuring/Controlling Devices Mfg Electric Housewares/Fans

(G-11420)
CTR ENTERPRISES
60 Railroad St Ste 1 (01835-7563)
PHONE..................................978 794-2093
Rick Morgano, *President*
EMP: 8
SQ FT: 9,700
SALES (est): 772.9K **Privately Held**
SIC: 3444 Sheet Metal Specialties

(G-11421)
D B S INDUSTRIES INC
Also Called: Diversified Business Systems
144 Hilldale Ave (01832-3830)
P.O. Box 110 (01831-1111)
PHONE..................................978 373-4748
EMP: 52 **EST:** 1969
SQ FT: 55,000
SALES (est): 9.7MM **Privately Held**
WEB: www.dbsforms.com
SIC: 2752 2741 2754 2791 Lithographic Coml Print Misc Publishing Gravure Coml Printing Typesetting Services Mfg Converted Paper Prdt

GEOGRAPHIC

(G-11422)
DAMARK WOODCRAFT INC
115 Hale St (01830-3991)
PHONE..................................978 373-6670
Mark Brady, *President*
David Brady, *Vice Pres*
EMP: 3
SQ FT: 10,000
SALES (est): 324K **Privately Held**
SIC: 2511 Trade Contractor Mfg Non-Upholstered Household Furniture

(G-11423)
DAN-RAY MACHINE CO INC
93 Essex St (01832-5527)
P.O. Box 1447 (01831-1947)
PHONE..................................978 374-7611
Daniel Germaine, *President*
Dianna Germaine, *Principal*
Christine Germaine-Snow, *Manager*
EMP: 4
SQ FT: 3,000
SALES: 300K **Privately Held**
SIC: 3639 Mfg Industrial Sewing Attachments

(G-11424)
DELA INCORPORATED (PA)
Also Called: Dela Lamimnation Solutions
175 Ward Hill Ave Ste 1 (01835-6943)
P.O. Box 8235 (01835-0735)
PHONE..................................978 372-7783
Charles J Abrams, *President*
Julian R Diaz, *Purch Mgr*
Kathleen Marth, *Controller*
Arlene Patao, *Accountant*
Isela Castro, *Technology*
▲ **EMP:** 35
SQ FT: 52,400
SALES (est): 5.6MM **Privately Held**
WEB: www.delaquality.com
SIC: 2295 3089 Mfg Coated Fabrics Mfg Plastic Products

(G-11425)
DL TECHNOLOGY LLC
216 River St (01832-5211)
PHONE..................................978 374-6451
Donna Lee Fugere, *Principal*
Corey Fugere, *VP Sales*
Jeffrey Paul Fugere, *Mng Member*
Richard E Massero Jr,
EMP: 12
SQ FT: 6,500
SALES (est): 2.6MM **Privately Held**
SIC: 3679 Mfg Electronic Components

(G-11426)
DUSOBOX CO INC
233 Neck Rd (01835-8029)
PHONE..................................978 372-7192
Richard J Kelley Sr, *President*
EMP: 20
SQ FT: 34,000
SALES (est): 2.5MM **Privately Held**
SIC: 2657 5113 Mfg Folding Paperboard Boxes Whol Industrial/Service Paper

(G-11427)
DUSTIN W CIAMPA
Also Called: Cnc Mill Specs
65 Avco Rd Unit M (01835-8502)
PHONE..................................603 571-4325
Dustin Ciampa, *Owner*
EMP: 4 **EST:** 2014
SQ FT: 3,000
SALES (est): 180.8K **Privately Held**
SIC: 3443 Mfg Fabricated Plate Work

(G-11428)
DYNAWAVE CABLE INCORPORATED
135 Ward Hill Ave (01835-8508)
P.O. Box 8189 (01835-0689)
PHONE..................................978 469-9448
Robert McLaughlin, *CEO*
EMP: 6
SQ FT: 2,618
SALES (est): 648.7K **Privately Held**
SIC: 3679 3357 Mfg Electronic Components Nonferrous Wiredrawing/Insulating

(G-11429)
DYNAWAVE INCORPORATED
135 Ward Hill Ave Ste 3 (01835-8509)
P.O. Box 8224 (01835-0724)
PHONE..................................978 469-0555
Christopher Lewis, *President*
Bob Thiele, *Vice Pres*
Rick Cote, *Materials Mgr*
Stan Hardin, *VP Engrg*
Don Cook, *Engineer*
EMP: 60
SQ FT: 45,000
SALES (est): 10.4MM **Privately Held**
WEB: www.dynawave.com
SIC: 3679 3643 Mfg Electronic Components Mfg Conductive Wiring Devices

(G-11430)
EAGLE-TRIBUNE PUBLISHING CO
Also Called: Haverhill Gazette
181 Merrimack St (01830-6129)
PHONE..................................978 374-0321
EMP: 20 **Privately Held**
WEB: www.eagletribune.com
SIC: 2711 7313 Newspapers-Publishing/Printing Advertising Representative
HQ: Eagle-Tribune Publishing Company
100 Turnpike St
North Andover MA 01845
978 946-2000

(G-11431)
ELITE ADHESIVES LLC
61 Standish Rd (01832-2959)
PHONE..................................978 852-8269
Richard Restivo, *Principal*
EMP: 4
SALES (est): 270.4K **Privately Held**
SIC: 2891 Mfg Adhesives/Sealants

(G-11432)
ENGINERED PRESSURE SYSTEMS INC
Also Called: E P S I
165 Ferry Rd (01835-8017)
PHONE..................................978 469-8280
Gary Nelson, *Vice Pres*
Ken Morse, *Sales Mgr*
Harry Kling, *Director*
◆ **EMP:** 12
SQ FT: 7,000
SALES (est): 2.9MM
SALES (corp-wide): 13.5MM **Privately Held**
WEB: www.epsi-highpressure.com
SIC: 3462 Mfg Iron/Steel Forgings
PA: Engineered Pressure Systems International
Walgoedstraat 19
Temse 9140
371 124-64

(G-11433)
FDM ADHESIVES LLC
5 Lavantie St (01830-1644)
PHONE..................................978 423-3553
Michele J Cloyd, *Principal*
EMP: 3
SALES (est): 143K **Privately Held**
SIC: 2891 Mfg Adhesives/Sealants

(G-11434)
FIREJUDGE WORLDWIDE INC
21 Westland Ter (01830-4124)
PHONE..................................978 604-0009
Mark J Lewis, *President*
Eric Grover, *Treasurer*
Ruby M Lewis, *Admin Sec*
EMP: 3
SALES: 675K **Privately Held**
SIC: 3949 7389 Mfg Sporting/Athletic Goods

(G-11435)
FRAME MY TVCOM LLC
419 River St (01832-5114)
PHONE..................................978 912-7200
Kevin Hancock, *Mng Member*
Rashid Beg,
EMP: 6
SALES (est): 752.8K **Privately Held**
SIC: 2517 Mfg Wooden Television Frames

(G-11436)
FREEBIRD SEMICONDUCTOR CORP
17 Parkridge Rd Ste 5e (01835-8511)
PHONE..................................617 955-7152
Simon Wainwright, *President*
James Larrauri, *Treasurer*
Dan Sable, *Director*
Maxime Zafrani, *Admin Sec*
EMP: 3
SQ FT: 2,331
SALES (est): 245K **Privately Held**
SIC: 3674 Mfg Semiconductors/Related Devices

(G-11437)
GARE INCORPORATED
165 Rosemont St (01832-1340)
P.O. Box 1686 (01831-2386)
PHONE..................................978 373-9131
Thomas L Alaimo Sr, *Ch of Bd*
David Alaimo, *President*
Gerald Murphy, *Vice Pres*
Scott Feener, *Warehouse Mgr*
Tom Alaimo, *CFO*
◆ **EMP:** 50
SQ FT: 103,000
SALES (est): 8.6MM **Privately Held**
WEB: www.gare.com
SIC: 3269 3544 2851 2821 Mfg Pottery Products Mfg Dies/Tools/Jigs/Fixt Mfg Paints/Allied Prdts Mfg Plstc Material/Resin

(G-11438)
GARELICK FARMS LLC
10 Creek Brook Dr (01832-1548)
PHONE..................................781 599-1300
William Dodge, *Branch Mgr*
Jess Van Durme, *Clerk*
EMP: 10 **Publicly Held**
WEB: www.overthemoonmilk.com
SIC: 2026 Mfg Fluid Milk
HQ: Garelick Farms, Llc
1199 W Central St Ste 1
Franklin MA 02038
508 528-9000

(G-11439)
GOLDEN FLEECE MFG GROUP LLC (HQ)
Also Called: Southwick
25 Computer Dr (01832-1236)
PHONE..................................978 686-3833
Claudio Del Vecchio, *President*
John Martynec, *Vice Pres*
Edward J Ponto, *CFO*
▲ **EMP:** 470
SALES (est): 148.2MM **Privately Held**
SIC: 2329 Mfg Men's/Boy's Clothing

(G-11440)
HANS KISSLE COMPANY LLC
9 Haverhill St (01830)
PHONE..................................978 556-4500
Mike Allegra, *Business Mgr*
Alexandra Brown, *Business Mgr*
Chris Gelinas, *Plant Mgr*
Edgar Bonilla, *Production*
Bob Pobiedzinski, *Production*
EMP: 140
SQ FT: 110,000
SALES (est): 35.3MM **Privately Held**
WEB: www.hanskissle.com
SIC: 2099 Mfg Food Preparations
PA: Mitsui & Co., Ltd.
1-1-3, Marunouchi
Chiyoda-Ku TKY 100-0

(G-11441)
HIGH SPEED ROUTING LLC
42 Newark St (01832-1342)
PHONE..................................603 527-8027
Mark Bailey, *Principal*
EMP: 7
SALES (est): 847K **Privately Held**
SIC: 3083 Mfg Laminated Plastic Plate/Sheet

(G-11442)
IMI INC
140 Hilldale Ave (01832-3830)
PHONE..................................978 373-9190
Peter Bigelow, *President*
EMP: 30 **EST:** 1971
SQ FT: 33,000
SALES (est): 5.5MM **Privately Held**
WEB: www.imipcb.com
SIC: 3672 Mfg Printed Circuit Boards

(G-11443)
JOSEPHS GOURMET PASTA COMPANY
262 Primrose St (01830-3930)
PHONE..................................978 521-1718
David Zwartendijk, *CEO*
John Birch, *CFO*
Ian B Mactaggart, *Admin Sec*
▼ **EMP:** 300
SALES (est): 62.9MM
SALES (corp-wide): 153.5MM **Privately Held**
SIC: 2099 Mfg Food Preparations
HQ: Jgps Holdings, Llc
8 Sound Shore Dr Ste 265
Greenwich CT 06830
203 622-1790

(G-11444)
JTL FALCON TITLE EXAMINER
105 Hyatt Ave (01835-8264)
PHONE..................................978 377-0223
EMP: 4
SALES (est): 82.2K **Privately Held**
SIC: 2711 Newspapers-Publishing/Printing

(G-11445)
KERRIGAN PAPER PRODUCTS INC
293 Neck Rd (01835)
P.O. Box 510 (01831-1310)
PHONE..................................978 374-4797
William Law, *President*
L William Law, *Clerk*
EMP: 7
SQ FT: 15,000
SALES (est): 1MM **Privately Held**
SIC: 2653 Mfg Boxes Corrugated Made From Purchased Materials

(G-11446)
L3 SECRITY DTCTION SYSTEMS INC
179-181 Ferry Rd (01835)
PHONE..................................781 939-3800
Mark Bush, *Branch Mgr*
EMP: 10
SALES (corp-wide): 6.8B **Publicly Held**
SIC: 3663 Mfg Radio/Tv Communication Equipment
HQ: L3 Security & Detection Systems, Inc.
1 Radcliff Rd
Tewksbury MA 01876
781 939-5627

(G-11447)
LAWRENCE CRANKSHAFT INC
500 Groveland St (01830-6721)
PHONE..................................978 372-0504
James Driscoll, *Owner*
EMP: 3 **EST:** 2011
SALES (est): 257.9K **Privately Held**
SIC: 3599 Mfg Industrial Machinery

(G-11448)
LEISURE MANUFACTURING
Also Called: Northeast Sample Co
42 Phoenix Row (01832)
P.O. Box 630 (01831-1380)
PHONE..................................978 373-3831
Ernest Dodier, *Owner*
EMP: 15
SQ FT: 12,000
SALES (est): 1.2MM **Privately Held**
SIC: 3131 Mfg Footwear Cut Stock

(G-11449)
LIGHTSPEED MFG CO LLC
63 Neck Rd (01835-8025)
PHONE..................................978 521-7676
Robert Falso, *Opers Staff*
Richard Breault,
EMP: 15
SALES (est): 2.5MM **Privately Held**
WEB: www.lightspeedmfg.com
SIC: 3699 Mfg Electrical Equipment/Supplies

(G-11450)
LUMINA POWER INC
26 Ward Hill Ave (01835-6929)
PHONE......978 241-8260
Tung Huynh, *President*
John Diaco, *Engineer*
EMP: 42
SALES (est): 8.1MM **Publicly Held**
WEB: www.luminapower.com
SIC: 3699 Mfg Electrical Equipment/Supplies
PA: Heico Corporation
3000 Taft St
Hollywood FL 33021

(G-11451)
LYNX SYSTEM DEVELOPERS INC
179 Ward Hill Ave (01835-6973)
PHONE......978 556-9780
Douglas J De Angelis, *President*
Matthew Gouette, *Prdtn Mgr*
Stacey Lewis, *Technology*
EMP: 20
SALES (est): 4.8MM **Privately Held**
WEB: www.finishlynx.com
SIC: 3625 Mfg Relays/Industrial Controls

(G-11452)
MAGELLAN AROSPC HAVERHILL INC
Also Called: Middleton Aerospace
20 Computer Dr (01832-3625)
PHONE......978 774-6000
James S Butyniec, *President*
Elena Milantoni, *Treasurer*
Daniel Chaisson, *Director*
John Marcello, *Director*
John Dekker, *Admin Sec*
▲ **EMP:** 120
SALES (est): 19.9MM
SALES (corp-wide): 730.6MM **Privately Held**
WEB: www.midaero.com
SIC: 3724 Mfg Aircraft Engines/Parts
HQ: Magellan Aerospace Usa, Inc.
20 Computer Dr
Haverhill MA 01832
978 774-6000

(G-11453)
MERRIMAC SPOOL AND REEL CO INC
203 Essex St (01832-5595)
PHONE......978 372-7777
Joseph J Alosky, *President*
Beverly Graham, *Exec VP*
EMP: 35 **EST:** 1951
SQ FT: 18,500
SALES (est): 7.4MM **Privately Held**
WEB: www.spool.com
SIC: 2655 2675 Mfg Fiber Cans/Drums Mfg Die-Cut Paper/Paperboard

(G-11454)
MORGAN SCIENTIFIC INC (PA)
151 Essex St Ste 8 (01832-5733)
PHONE......978 521-4440
Patrick F Morgan, *President*
Christina Morgan, *Human Res Mgr*
EMP: 12
SQ FT: 12,000
SALES: 3.5MM **Privately Held**
WEB: www.morgansci.com
SIC: 7372 5045 3841 Whol Medical/Hospital Equipment Prepackaged Software Services Whol Computers/Peripherals

(G-11455)
NEWCASTLE SYSTEMS INC
73 Ward Hill Ave (01835-6930)
PHONE......781 935-3450
John O'Kelly, *President*
EMP: 20
SQ FT: 6,000
SALES (est): 6.4MM **Privately Held**
WEB: www.newcastlesys.com
SIC: 3577 Mfg Computer Peripheral Equipment

(G-11456)
OLYMPIC ENGINEERING SERVICE
65 Avco Rd Unit C (01835-8502)
PHONE......978 373-2789
Robert Demers, *President*
George Demers, *Vice Pres*
Joanne Demers, *Treasurer*
Boissonneault Denise, *Manager*
Robert Matthews, *Manager*
EMP: 9
SQ FT: 2,800
SALES (est): 910K **Privately Held**
SIC: 3599 Machine Shop

(G-11457)
PARKER-HANNIFIN CORPORATION
Also Called: Filtration & Separation Div
242 Neck Rd (01835-8034)
PHONE......978 858-0505
Jerry Durand, *Safety Mgr*
Scott Feeman, *Branch Mgr*
Jeff Slaski, *Manager*
EMP: 123
SALES (corp-wide): 14.3B **Publicly Held**
WEB: www.parker.com
SIC: 3569 3564 Mfg General Industrial Machinery Mfg Blowers/Fans
PA: Parker-Hannifin Corporation
6035 Parkland Blvd
Cleveland OH 44124
216 896-3000

(G-11458)
PEDROS INC
147 Essex St (01832-5528)
P.O. Box 320635, West Roxbury (02132-0011)
PHONE......978 657-7101
Christopher Zigmont, *CEO*
Jay Seiter, *Research*
Jim Hale, *Sales Mgr*
Jim Hill, *Accounts Mgr*
EMP: 5
SALES (est): 506.8K **Privately Held**
SIC: 3545 Mfg Machine Tool Accessories

(G-11459)
PLASTIC DISTRS FABRICATORS INC
419 River St (01832-5114)
PHONE......978 374-0300
Mark Abare, *President*
Bob Decelle, *General Mgr*
Robert Decelle, *General Mgr*
Kevin Munger, *Purch Mgr*
James E Abare, *Treasurer*
EMP: 40 **EST:** 1974
SQ FT: 36,000
SALES (est): 8.2MM **Privately Held**
WEB: www.pdf1.com
SIC: 3089 Mfg Plastic Products

(G-11460)
PRESSURE TECHNIQUES INTL CORP
114 Hale St (01830-3976)
PHONE......978 686-2211
Peter Rubenstein, *President*
EMP: 5
SQ FT: 9,000
SALES (est): 512.7K **Privately Held**
SIC: 3523 5169 Mfg Farm Machinery/Equipment Whol Chemicals/Products

(G-11461)
PRINTPRO SILKSCREEN & EMB
233 Neck Rd (01835-8029)
PHONE......978 556-1695
Derek Coughlin, *Owner*
EMP: 15 **EST:** 1995
SQ FT: 35,000
SALES (est): 1.2MM **Privately Held**
SIC: 2759 Commercial Printing

(G-11462)
PROTECT & HEAL CHILDREN MASS
57 5th Ave (01830-3964)
PHONE......978 374-8304
Eva Montibello, *Principal*
EMP: 3
SALES (est): 96.3K **Privately Held**
SIC: 7372 Prepackaged Software Services

(G-11463)
PWH CORPORATION
55 Ward Hill Ave (01835-6930)
PHONE......978 373-9111
Richard D Welch, *President*
EMP: 29
SQ FT: 60,000
SALES (est): 2MM **Privately Held**
WEB: www.powell-nonwovens.net
SIC: 2297 2221 Mfg Nonwoven Fabrics Manmade Broadwoven Fabric Mill

(G-11464)
QUALITY CARTON CONVERTING LLC
175 Ward Hill Ave Ste 4 (01835-6943)
PHONE......978 556-5008
David Hatch, *President*
Sheri Curry, *Cust Mgr*
Audrey Hatch,
EMP: 15
SQ FT: 15,000
SALES (est): 5.1MM **Privately Held**
SIC: 2631 Paperboard Mill

(G-11465)
QUALITY DIE CUTTING INC (PA)
506 River St (01832-5159)
PHONE......978 374-8027
Ray Ayers, *President*
Jerry Isabelle, *President*
EMP: 14
SQ FT: 7,200
SALES (est): 2.1MM **Privately Held**
SIC: 3423 3544 Mfg Hand/Edge Tools Mfg Dies/Tools/Jigs/Fixtures

(G-11466)
R W HATFIELD COMPANY INC (PA)
Also Called: Pro-Line
10 Avco Rd Ste 1 (01835-6997)
PHONE......978 521-2600
Robert W Hatfield Jr, *President*
Robert Simmons, *Vice Pres*
EMP: 46
SQ FT: 12,500
SALES (est): 9.1MM **Privately Held**
WEB: www.1proline.com
SIC: 2599 Mfg Office Furniture-Nonwood

(G-11467)
REBARS & MESH INC
111 Avco Rd (01835-6956)
PHONE......978 374-2244
Kathryn Grady, *President*
Katie R Roche, *General Mgr*
John T Grady, *Treasurer*
William J Barron, *Admin Sec*
▲ **EMP:** 20
SQ FT: 30,000
SALES (est): 9.1MM **Privately Held**
WEB: www.rebarsandmesh.com
SIC: 3449 5211 5051 Mfg Misc Structural Mtl Ret Lumber/Building Mtrl Metals Service Center

(G-11468)
REGCO CORPORATION
Also Called: Regenie's All Natural Snacks
46 Rogers Rd (01835-6957)
PHONE......978 521-4370
Regina A Ragonese, *Principal*
EMP: 30
SQ FT: 30,000
SALES (est): 5.9MM **Privately Held**
WEB: www.regenies.com
SIC: 2096 Mfg Potato Chips/Snacks

(G-11469)
RUNTAL NORTH AMERICA INC
Also Called: Sterling Hydraulics
187 Neck Rd (01835-8027)
P.O. Box 8278 (01835-0778)
PHONE......800 526-2621
Hans Peter Zehneder, *Chairman*
Rick Arrajj, *Sales Staff*
John Wiberg, *Sales Staff*
Katrin Grant, *Office Mgr*
Cynthia Wright, *Technology*
▲ **EMP:** 45
SQ FT: 53,000
SALES (est): 12.3MM
SALES (corp-wide): 667.4MM **Privately Held**
WEB: www.runtalnorthamerica.com
SIC: 3567 1711 3433 Mfg Indstl Furnace/Ovens Plumbing/Heat/Ac Contr Mfg Heat Equip-Nonelec
PA: Zehnder Group Ag
Moortalstrasse 1
GrAnichen AG
628 551-500

(G-11470)
S & F MACHINE CO INC
1405 River St (01832-3599)
PHONE......978 374-1552
Peter Strozza, *President*
EMP: 10
SQ FT: 10,000
SALES: 500K **Privately Held**
SIC: 3599 Job Machine Shop

(G-11471)
SEICA INC (PA)
110 Avco Rd (01835-6955)
PHONE......603 890-6002
Antonio Grassino, *President*
▼ **EMP:** 9
SQ FT: 2,500
SALES (est): 2.3MM **Privately Held**
WEB: www.seica.com
SIC: 3699 Mfg Electrical Equipment/Supplies

(G-11472)
SOUTHWICK CLOTHING LLC (HQ)
25 Computer Dr (01832-1236)
PHONE......800 634-5312
Robert Nelson, *CFO*
Robert Bayer,
▲ **EMP:** 179 **EST:** 1999
SQ FT: 240,000
SALES (est): 24.4MM **Privately Held**
WEB: www.southwickclothing.com
SIC: 2311 2325 Mfg Men's/Boy's Suits/Coats Mfg Men's/Boy's Trousers

(G-11473)
SPECIALIZED PLATING INC
Also Called: S P I
15 Ward Hill Ave (01835-6998)
PHONE......978 373-8030
Paul Kelly, *President*
Brad Kelly, *CFO*
EMP: 20
SQ FT: 15,000
SALES (est): 2.4MM **Privately Held**
WEB: www.specializedplating.com
SIC: 3471 Plating/Polishing Service

(G-11474)
SPECTRAL EVOLUTION INC
26 Parkridge Rd Ste 1a (01835-8515)
PHONE......978 687-1833
Dennis Witz, *CEO*
Matthew Nagelschmidt, *Engineer*
Joseph Mayr, *Marketing Mgr*
Bob Gampert, *Software Engr*
EMP: 7
SALES (est): 1.3MM **Privately Held**
SIC: 3826 Mfg Analytical Instruments

(G-11475)
SPRUCE ENVIRONMENTAL TECH INC (PA)
Also Called: Radonaway
3 Saber Way (01835-0000)
P.O. Box 8244 (01835-0744)
PHONE......978 521-0901
Alan Zucchino, *President*
David Kapturowski, *Vice Pres*
Howie Zidel, *Treasurer*
Julie Meeks, *Sales Staff*
Linda Crowe, *Marketing Staff*
▲ **EMP:** 55
SQ FT: 26,000
SALES (est): 11.7MM **Privately Held**
WEB: www.radonaway.com
SIC: 3634 3564 Mfg Electric Housewares/Fans Mfg Blowers/Fans

(G-11476)
SRI HERMETICS INC
43 Magnavista Dr (01830-2286)
PHONE......508 321-1023

GEOGRAPHIC

EMP: 3 EST: 2016
SALES (est): 177.8K **Privately Held**
SIC: 3679 Mfg Electronic Components

(G-11477)
TREMCAR USA
89 Newark St (01832-1348)
PHONE..................................978 556-5330
David Burke, *Principal*
Denny Radlein, *Project Mgr*
Paul Bacik, *Manager*
Ross Longson, *Manager*
EMP: 11
SALES (est): 1.6MM **Privately Held**
SIC: 3711 Mfg Motor Vehicle/Car Bodies

(G-11478)
TRONICA CIRCUITS INC
26 Parkridge Rd (01835-8514)
PHONE..................................978 372-7224
Kuldip Bains, *President*
EMP: 4
SQ FT: 4,000
SALES (est): 312.6K **Privately Held**
SIC: 3672 Mfg Printed Circuit Boards

(G-11479)
TRU CHOCOLATE INC
610 Kenoza St (01830-2331)
PHONE..................................855 878-2462
John Cappadona, *President*
EMP: 7 **EST:** 2017
SALES: 1MM **Privately Held**
SIC: 2066 Mfg Chocolate/Cocoa Products

(G-11480)
UFP TECHNOLOGIES INC
175 Ward Hill Ave (01835-6960)
PHONE..................................978 352-2200
Richard Lesavoy, *Branch Mgr*
Richard Woodward, *Maintence Staff*
EMP: 10
SALES (corp-wide): 190.4MM **Publicly Held**
WEB: www.ufpt.com
SIC: 3086 Mfg Plastic Foam Products
PA: Ufp Technologies, Inc.
100 Hale St
Newburyport MA 01950
978 352-2200

(G-11481)
ULTRASONIC SYSTEMS INC
135 Ward Hill Ave (01835-8508)
PHONE..................................978 521-0095
Drew Erickson, *CEO*
Stuart Erickson, *President*
EMP: 25
SQ FT: 20,000
SALES (est): 5.7MM **Privately Held**
WEB: www.ultrasonicsystems.com
SIC: 3559 Mfg Misc Industry Machinery

(G-11482)
UNITED TECHNICAL COATING INC
Also Called: UTC
115 Hale St Ste 1 (01830-3997)
PHONE..................................978 521-2779
Fax: 978 521-4264
EMP: 9
SALES (est): 620K **Privately Held**
SIC: 3479 Industrial Spray Painting Shop

(G-11483)
UPTITE COMPANY INC
1001 Hilldale Ave (01832-1352)
PHONE..................................978 377-0451
Joseph G Beshara Jr, *CEO*
Beverly Bergeron, *President*
Cheryl Beshara Mquillian, *Treasurer*
EMP: 7
SQ FT: 5,000
SALES (est): 52.5K **Privately Held**
SIC: 2834 Mfg Veterinary Pharmaceutical Medicine

(G-11484)
W B MACHINE INC
40 Middlesex St (01835-7403)
PHONE..................................978 372-5396
David A Wyman, *President*
Christopher Blake, *Treasurer*
EMP: 3
SALES: 500K **Privately Held**
SIC: 3599 Mfg Industrial Machinery

(G-11485)
WBC EXTRUSION PRODUCTS INC (HQ)
60 Fondi Rd (01832-1302)
P.O. Box 700, Atkinson NH (03811-0700)
PHONE..................................978 469-0668
Christian Ganser, *President*
Bill Stein, *Vice Pres*
Wolf Jachimowicz, *Treasurer*
Ernest W Steen, *Admin Sec*
▲ **EMP:** 27
SQ FT: 45,000
SALES (est): 3.4MM
SALES (corp-wide): 8.1MM **Privately Held**
WEB: www.wbcextrusion.com
SIC: 3081 Mfg Unsupported Plastic Film/Sheet
PA: Gelpac Inc
400 Rue Henri-Bourassa
Marieville QC J3M 1
450 460-4466

(G-11486)
WHITMAN PRODUCTS COMPANY INC
96 Powder House Ave (01830-6557)
PHONE..................................978 975-0502
John Rupp, *President*
EMP: 20 **EST:** 1967
SALES: 4MM **Privately Held**
WEB: www.whitmanproducts.com
SIC: 3672 Mfg Printed Circuit Boards

Haydenville
Hampshire County

(G-11487)
PAULS SUGAR HOUSE
16 Depot Rd (01039-9716)
PHONE..................................413 268-3544
Paul Zononi, *Owner*
EMP: 3
SALES: 90K **Privately Held**
SIC: 2099 Mfg Food Preparations

Heath
Franklin County

(G-11488)
BROOK HEATH STUDIO
24 W Main St (01346-9701)
P.O. Box 34 (01346-0034)
PHONE..................................413 337-5736
Robert Dane, *Owner*
EMP: 3
SALES (est): 130K **Privately Held**
SIC: 3229 Mfg Pressed/Blown Glass

Hingham
Plymouth County

(G-11489)
AGRI-MARK INC
Also Called: Cabot Creamery
50 Derby St Ste 100 (02043-3740)
PHONE..................................781 740-0090
EMP: 7
SALES (corp-wide): 235MM **Privately Held**
SIC: 2022 5143 5451 Mfg Cheese Whol Dairy Products Ret Dairy Products
PA: Agri-Mark, Inc.
100 Milk St Ste 5
Methuen MA 01810
978 689-4442

(G-11490)
ALL AMERICAN DELEADING INC
136 Nokomis Rd (02043-1136)
PHONE..................................781 953-1673
Robert Madden, *President*
EMP: 3
SALES: 250K **Privately Held**
SIC: 1481 Nonmetallic Mineral Services

(G-11491)
APPLIED TISSUE TECH LLC
99 Derby St Ste 200 (02043-4216)
PHONE..................................781 366-3848
Michael Broomhead, *CEO*
EMP: 7
SALES (est): 630.8K **Privately Held**
SIC: 3841 Mfg Surgical/Medical Instruments

(G-11492)
ARMSTRONG MOLD CORPORATION
28 South St Ste 1 (02043-2538)
PHONE..................................781 749-3207
EMP: 3
SALES (corp-wide): 19.8MM **Privately Held**
SIC: 3089 Mfg Plastic Products
PA: Armstrong Mold Corporation
6910 Manlius Center Rd
East Syracuse NY 13057
315 437-1517

(G-11493)
BEANTOWN BEDDING LLC
137 Main St (02043-2506)
PHONE..................................781 608-9915
Kirsten Lambert, *Principal*
Kristi Shreenan, *Opers Mgr*
EMP: 12 **EST:** 2012
SALES (est): 1.2MM **Privately Held**
SIC: 2392 Mfg Household Furnishings

(G-11494)
BRADFORD DISTILLERY LLC
3 Pond Park Rd Ste 4 (02043-4331)
PHONE..................................781 385-7145
EMP: 8
SALES (corp-wide): 699.3K **Privately Held**
SIC: 2085 Mfg Distilled/Blended Liquor
PA: Bradford Distillery, Llc
604 First Parish Rd
Scituate MA 02066
781 378-2491

(G-11495)
BRAYTON WILSON COLE CORP
70 Sharp St (02043-4312)
PHONE..................................781 803-6624
David Roffo, *President*
Beverly Roffo, *Admin Sec*
EMP: 7 **EST:** 1924
SQ FT: 20,000
SALES: 1.2MM **Privately Held**
WEB: www.bwcboston.com
SIC: 3446 3441 Mfg Architectural Metalwork Structural Metal Fabrication

(G-11496)
COLONIAL VILLAGE REFINISHING
Also Called: Faneuil Kitchen Cabinet
165 Beal St (02043-1501)
PHONE..................................781 740-8844
Andrew Bargende, *President*
Peter Bargende, *Treasurer*
Patty Bargende, *Office Mgr*
Alex Bargende, *Manager*
EMP: 5
SALES (est): 430K **Privately Held**
SIC: 2434 7641 Mfg Wood Kitchen Cabinets Reupholstery/Furniture Repair

(G-11497)
CONCEPT CHEMICALS INC
9 Eldridge Ct (02043-2203)
PHONE..................................781 740-0711
EMP: 11
SQ FT: 18,000
SALES: 1.2MM **Privately Held**
WEB: www.conceptchemicals.com
SIC: 2819 2844 2842 Mfg Chemicals Hair Care Products Skin Care Products & Germicidal Disinfectant Products

(G-11498)
EAST COAST PRINTING INC
2 Keith Way Ste 5 (02043-4246)
PHONE..................................781 331-5635
Lou Silva, *President*
Tony Fontes, *Treasurer*
EMP: 8
SQ FT: 2,000
SALES (est): 1.7MM **Privately Held**
WEB: www.copyconnect.com
SIC: 2752 Lithographic Commercial Printing

(G-11499)
HEAT EXCHANGER PRODUCTS CORP
Also Called: Hepco
55 Industrial Park Rd (02043-4306)
PHONE..................................781 749-0220
Robert Bell, *Vice Pres*
Timothy Hennigan, *Director*
EMP: 3
SALES (est): 369K **Privately Held**
SIC: 3443 Mfg Fabricated Plate Work

(G-11500)
KEYLIUM INC
47 Lafayette Ave (02043-2430)
PHONE..................................781 385-9178
Charles Goldman, *Principal*
EMP: 3 **EST:** 2012
SALES (est): 172.2K **Privately Held**
SIC: 7372 Prepackaged Software

(G-11501)
MASSA PRODUCTS CORPORATION
280 Lincoln St (02043-1796)
PHONE..................................781 749-3120
Donald P Massa, *President*
Richard M Carpenter, *Exec VP*
Richard Carpenter, *Exec VP*
Edward G Casey, *CFO*
Robert Wadja, *Marketing Staff*
▲ **EMP:** 65
SALES (est): 13.7MM **Privately Held**
WEB: www.massa.com
SIC: 3679 3812 3625 Mfg Electronic Components Mfg Search/Navigation Equipment Mfg Relays/Industrial Controls

(G-11502)
MEDIAVUE SYSTEMS INC
35 Pond Park Rd Ste 14 (02043-4366)
PHONE..................................781 926-0676
David L Degiorgi, *President*
Richard Berman, *Opers Mgr*
David Nguyen, *Mfg Staff*
Eric Schneiderhan, *Production*
Brian Kane, *Engineer*
EMP: 25
SALES: 1.7MM **Privately Held**
SIC: 3993 7373 Mfg Signs/Advertising Specialties Computer Systems Design

(G-11503)
MEMBRANE STRUCTURE SOLUTIONS
71 Summer St (02043-1963)
PHONE..................................908 520-0112
Waldemar Ptaszek, *President*
EMP: 25
SQ FT: 4,000
SALES (est): 3MM **Privately Held**
WEB: www.membranesolutions.com
SIC: 3448 Mfg Prefabricated Metal Buildings

(G-11504)
MENCHIES FROZEN YOGURT
15 Shipyard Dr Ste 1e (02043-1662)
PHONE..................................781 740-1245
Weimin Zhao, *Owner*
EMP: 10
SALES: 400K **Privately Held**
SIC: 2656 Mfg Sanitary Food Containers

(G-11505)
MICROBOT MEDICAL INC (PA)
25 Recreation Park Dr # 108 (02043-4256)
PHONE..................................781 875-3605
Harel Gadot, *Ch of Bd*
David Ben Naim, *CFO*
EMP: 9
SALES (est): 6.7MM **Publicly Held**
WEB: www.stemcellsinc.com
SIC: 2836 2834 8731 Biopharmaceutical Products & Biotechnical Research

▲ = Import ▼=Export
◆ =Import/Export

(G-11506)
MONAHAN PRODUCTS LLC
Also Called: Uppababy
60 Sharp St Ste 3 (02043-4334)
PHONE..................................781 413-3000
Joanne Apothloz, *Vice Pres*
Carl Sukeforth, *Project Mgr*
Maureen Fisher, *Opers Staff*
Alyssa Wilson, *Opers Staff*
Madison Paulsen, *Accountant*
◆ **EMP:** 50
SALES (est): 9.5MM **Privately Held**
SIC: 3944 Mfg Games/Toys

(G-11507)
NEW ENGLAND GEN-CONNECT LLC
Also Called: Genconnex
35 Pond Park Rd Ste 11 (02043-4366)
PHONE..................................617 571-6884
Gary A Mook, *Principal*
Gary Mook,
EMP: 4
SALES (est): 340K **Privately Held**
SIC: 3569 3621 Mfg General Industrial Machinery Mfg Motors/Generators

(G-11508)
NORTHEAST EQUIPMENT DESIGN INC
150 Recreation Park Dr # 6 (02043-4251)
PHONE..................................781 740-0007
John Kennedy, *President*
EMP: 45
SQ FT: 15,000
SALES (est): 9.4MM **Privately Held**
WEB: www.ned-automation.com
SIC: 3535 Mfg Automation Machinery

(G-11509)
RUSSELECTRIC INC (DH)
99 Industrial Park Rd (02043-4387)
PHONE..................................781 749-6000
Dorian Alexandrescu, *President*
James Mandeville Jr, *Vice Pres*
EMP: 236
SQ FT: 110,000
SALES (est): 106MM
SALES (corp-wide): 96.9B **Privately Held**
WEB: www.russelectric.com
SIC: 3613 Mfg Switchgear/Switchboards
HQ: Siemens Corporation
300 New Jersey Ave Nw # 10
Washington DC 20001
202 434-4800

(G-11510)
SCOUT OUT LLC
18 Shipyard Dr Ste 2a-50 (02043-1670)
PHONE..................................970 476-0209
Thomas Speer, *CEO*
Brad Cohen, *Chairman*
Tim Delay, *COO*
EMP: 5
SALES (est): 128.9K **Privately Held**
SIC: 7372 Prepackaged Software Services

(G-11511)
SLESAR BROS BREWING CO INC
18 Shipyard Dr (02043-1670)
PHONE..................................781 749-2337
EMP: 40 **Privately Held**
SIC: 2082 Mfg Malt Beverages
PA: Slesar Bros. Brewing Company, Inc.
110 Canal St
Boston MA

(G-11512)
SUBMARINE RESEARCH LABS
Also Called: Systems Limited
Porters Cove Is (02043)
PHONE..................................781 749-0900
Donald S Willy, *President*
Linda H Willy, *Treasurer*
Brian G Willy, *Clerk*
EMP: 8 **EST:** 1960
SALES (est): 790K **Privately Held**
SIC: 3663 3429 Mfg Radio/Tv Communication Equipment Mfg Hardware

(G-11513)
VACUUM TECHNOLOGY ASSOCIATES
Also Called: Dynavac
110 Industrial Park Rd (02043-4369)
PHONE..................................781 740-8600
Thomas P Foley, *President*
Joel Smolka, *COO*
Peter H Kehew, *Treasurer*
Catherine Casey, *Office Admin*
EMP: 99
SQ FT: 22,000
SALES (est): 30.6MM **Privately Held**
WEB: www.dynavac.com
SIC: 3563 Mfg Air/Gas Compressors

(G-11514)
VENUS WAFERS INC
100 Research Rd (02043-4345)
PHONE..................................781 740-1002
Luke E Barmakian, *President*
Robert Pollara, *Plant Engr*
Rich Housman, *CFO*
Jill Barmakian, *Treasurer*
Patricia Maxwell, *Assistant*
▲ **EMP:** 26 **EST:** 1933
SQ FT: 56,500
SALES (est): 6MM **Privately Held**
WEB: www.venuswafers.com
SIC: 2052 Mfg Cookies/Crackers

(G-11515)
VULCAN COMPANY INC (PA)
Also Called: Vulcan Tool Mfg
51 Sharp St (02043-4311)
P.O. Box 36 (02018-0036)
PHONE..................................781 337-5970
Alexander G Clark, *President*
William P Kennedy, *Treasurer*
◆ **EMP:** 55 **EST:** 1890
SQ FT: 50,000
SALES (est): 12.9MM **Privately Held**
WEB: www.vulcantools.com
SIC: 3546 3545 3531 Mfg Power-Driven Handtools Mfg Machine Tool Accessories Mfg Construction Machinery

(G-11516)
WESTON CORPORATION
Also Called: Weston Communications
45 Industrial Park Rd (02043-4306)
PHONE..................................781 749-0936
Alden Weston Sr, *President*
Alden Weston Jr, *Vice Pres*
Jack Weston, *Vice Pres*
John Weston, *Vice Pres*
Blanche Weston, *Clerk*
EMP: 15
SQ FT: 7,200
SALES (est): 2.1MM **Privately Held**
WEB: www.westoncommunications.com
SIC: 2791 7336 7334 Typesetting Services Coml Art/Graphic Design Photocopying Service

(G-11517)
WESTWOOD MILLS CORP
55 Sharp St Ste 6 (02043-4353)
PHONE..................................781 335-4466
Douglas Laughlin, *President*
▲ **EMP:** 12
SALES (est): 99.9K **Privately Held**
SIC: 3469 Mfg Metal Stampings

(G-11518)
WINGBRACE LLC
6 Evergreen Ln (02043-1014)
PHONE..................................617 480-8737
Peter Schnorr, *CEO*
David Perme, *Principal*
EMP: 4
SALES (est): 295.1K **Privately Held**
SIC: 3721 7389 Mfg Aircraft Business Services At Non-Commercial Site

(G-11519)
XTREME SEAL LLC
67 Sharp St (02043-4349)
PHONE..................................508 933-1894
Bruno Xavier, *Principal*
EMP: 3
SALES (est): 145.3K **Privately Held**
SIC: 3053 Gaskets; Packing And Sealing Devices

Hinsdale
Berkshire County

(G-11520)
GENERAL DYNAMICS CORPORATION
34 E Windsor Rd Rm 2563 (01235-9275)
PHONE..................................413 494-3137
EMP: 44
SALES (corp-wide): 36.1B **Publicly Held**
SIC: 3731 Shipbuilding/Repairing
PA: General Dynamics Corporation
11011 Sunset Hills Rd
Reston VA 20190
703 876-3000

Holbrook
Norfolk County

(G-11521)
AVON CUSTOM MIXING SVCS INC
55 High St (02343-2005)
P.O. Box 187, Cohasset (02025-0187)
PHONE..................................781 767-0511
Mark Chase, *President*
Timothy Nestor, *Vice Pres*
EMP: 22
SQ FT: 200,000
SALES (est): 3.8MM **Privately Held**
SIC: 3069 Mfg Fabricated Rubber Products

(G-11522)
BOSTON STEEL FABRICATORS INC
610 South St (02343-1300)
P.O. Box 310 (02343-0310)
PHONE..................................781 767-1540
Barry Brown, *President*
Dan Brown, *Vice Pres*
Stephen Brown, *Treasurer*
EMP: 9 **EST:** 1956
SQ FT: 22,000
SALES: 5.6MM **Privately Held**
SIC: 3441 3446 Structural Metal Fabrication Mfg Architectural Metalwork

(G-11523)
DELTA MAGNETICS AND CONTROLS
275 Centre St Ste 16 (02343-1079)
PHONE..................................781 963-2544
Ioannis Demestihas, *President*
Paul Fitopoulos, *Vice Pres*
John D Katsaros, *Treasurer*
John Katsaros, *Treasurer*
EMP: 16
SQ FT: 17,000
SALES: 1.5MM **Privately Held**
SIC: 3625 Mfg Relays/Industrial Controls

(G-11524)
DRAPER METAL FABRICATION INC
260 Centre St Unit A (02343-1074)
PHONE..................................781 961-3146
Diane Giblin, *President*
John Giblin, *Vice Pres*
EMP: 8
SQ FT: 10,000
SALES: 1.2MM **Privately Held**
WEB: www.draperelevator.com
SIC: 3534 Mfg Elevators/Escalators

(G-11525)
GRAPHIC FLLFILLMENT FINSHG INC
145 Union St Ste 3 (02343-1463)
PHONE..................................781 727-8845
EMP: 8
SQ FT: 25,000
SALES (est): 1MM **Privately Held**
SIC: 2789 Bookbinding And Related Work

(G-11526)
I G MARSTON COMPANY
Also Called: Igm
8 Mear Rd (02343-1339)
P.O. Box 432 (02343-0432)
PHONE..................................781 767-2894
Evelyn Piercy, *President*
Sarah Piercy, *Treasurer*
John Demarco, *Sales Staff*
EMP: 15 **EST:** 1844
SQ FT: 10,000
SALES (est): 2.5MM **Privately Held**
WEB: www.igmarston.com
SIC: 3089 3053 Mfg Plastic Products Mfg Gaskets/Packing/Sealing Devices

(G-11527)
JANNEL MANUFACTURING INC
5 Mear Rd (02343-1329)
PHONE..................................781 767-0666
Yves Nahmias, *President*
Eva Da Rosa, *Purch Dir*
Pyarlai Nanji, *Treasurer*
Bentley Steve, *Technician*
◆ **EMP:** 35
SQ FT: 60,000
SALES (est): 7MM
SALES (corp-wide): 38.9MM **Privately Held**
WEB: www.jannel.com
SIC: 2677 2673 Mfg Envelopes Mfg Bags-Plastic/Coated Paper
PA: Belle-Pak Packaging Inc
7465 Birchmount Rd
Markham ON L3R 5
905 475-5151

(G-11528)
LANDMARK WINDOW FASHIONS INC
5 Mear Rd Ste 4 (02343-1329)
P.O. Box 350 (02343-0350)
PHONE..................................781 767-3535
Harlan Bliss, *President*
William J Buckley, *VP Sales*
Judith H Bliss, *Admin Sec*
EMP: 27
SQ FT: 12,000
SALES (est): 4.7MM **Privately Held**
SIC: 2591 Mfg Drapery Hardware/Blinds

(G-11529)
LANE PRINTING CO INC
Also Called: Lane PRInting& Advertising
210 S Franklin St (02343-1461)
PHONE..................................781 767-4450
Francis P Lane Jr, *President*
Carolyn P Lane, *Treasurer*
EMP: 14
SQ FT: 5,500
SALES (est): 3.1MM **Privately Held**
WEB: www.laneprint.com
SIC: 2752 3993 7312 7336 Lithographic Coml Print Mfg Signs/Ad Specialties Outdoor Advertising Svcs Coml Art/Graphic Design

(G-11530)
MARONEY ASSOCIATES INC
Also Called: Printing Unlimited
63 Plymouth St (02343-1510)
PHONE..................................781 767-3970
Vincent Maroney, *President*
Mary Lou Maroney, *Admin Sec*
EMP: 5
SALES: 1MM **Privately Held**
SIC: 2752 Lithographic Commercial Printing

(G-11531)
MICA-TRON PRODUCTS CORP
275 Centre St Ste 13 (02343-1079)
PHONE..................................781 767-2163
Paul J Tassinari, *President*
Flora Tassinari, *Treasurer*
EMP: 7
SQ FT: 6,000
SALES: 1.5MM **Privately Held**
WEB: www.mica-tron.com
SIC: 3599 Mfg Industrial Machinery

(G-11532)
NADCO INTERNATIONAL INC
Also Called: Model Engineering
604 South St (02343-1300)
PHONE..................................781 767-1797

Charles F Nadler Jr, *President*
EMP: 9 **EST:** 1958
SQ FT: 16,000
SALES (est): 1.5MM **Privately Held**
WEB: www.model-eng.com
SIC: 3599 Mfg Industrial Machinery

(G-11533)
NEW CAN COMPANY INC (HQ)
1 Mear Rd (02343-1338)
P.O. Box 421 (02343-0421)
PHONE..................................781 767-1650
Ted Bustany, *CEO*
Thomas Houston, *President*
Ann Bilodeau, *CFO*
Cathy Tangstrom, *Accounting Mgr*
Laufey V Bustany, *Admin Sec*
EMP: 30
SQ FT: 115,000
SALES (est): 8.3MM
SALES (corp-wide): 8.4MM **Privately Held**
WEB: www.newcan.com
SIC: 3469 Mfg Metal Stampings
PA: New Can Holdings, Inc.
1 Mear Rd
Holbrook MA 02343
781 767-1650

(G-11534)
NEW CAN HOLDINGS INC (PA)
Also Called: New Can Company
1 Mear Rd (02343-1338)
P.O. Box 421 (02343-0421)
PHONE..................................781 767-1650
Ted Bustany, *CEO*
EMP: 8 **EST:** 1993
SQ FT: 114,000
SALES (est): 8.4MM **Privately Held**
SIC: 3317 Mfg Steel Pipe/Tubes

(G-11535)
OLDCASTLE APG NORTHEAST INC
Also Called: Oldcastle North Atlantic
46 Spring St (02343-2019)
PHONE..................................781 506-9473
Steve Getto, *Branch Mgr*
EMP: 55
SQ FT: 106,000
SALES (corp-wide): 29.7B **Privately Held**
SIC: 3271 3272 Mfg Concrete Block/Brick
HQ: Oldcastle Apg Northeast, Inc.
13555 Wellington Cntr Cir
Gainesville VA 20155
703 365-7070

(G-11536)
PROCOAT PRODUCTS INC
260 Centre St Ste 1 (02343-1074)
PHONE..................................781 767-2270
Kenneth Woolf, *Ch of Bd*
Lisa Ploss, *President*
Tammy Rothwell, *Opers Staff*
Anita Woolf, *Treasurer*
Ken Woolf, *IT/INT Sup*
EMP: 6
SQ FT: 3,900
SALES (est): 1.1MM **Privately Held**
WEB: www.procoat.com
SIC: 2851 1742 Mfg Paints/Allied Products Drywall/Insulating Contractor

(G-11537)
QUALITY AIR METALS INC
283 Centre St Ste B (02343-1075)
PHONE..................................781 986-9967
Thomas Gunning, *President*
EMP: 50
SALES (est): 12.6MM **Privately Held**
SIC: 3444 Mfg Sheet Metalwork

(G-11538)
SOUTH SHORE WOOD PELLETS INC
279 Centre St Ste 2 (02343-1072)
PHONE..................................781 986-7797
Lynn Lewis, *President*
EMP: 6
SALES (est): 698.9K **Privately Held**
SIC: 2426 Hardwood Dimension/Floor Mill

(G-11539)
SPECTOR METAL PRODUCTS CO INC
608 South St (02343-1300)
PHONE..................................781 767-5600
Morris Spector, *President*
Brian Spector, *Vice Pres*
Steven Spector, *Vice Pres*
EMP: 11 **EST:** 1952
SQ FT: 24,000
SALES (est): 2.2MM **Privately Held**
SIC: 3441 Mfg Prefabricated Metal Bridge & Highway Structures

(G-11540)
VATER PERCUSSION INC
270 Centre St Unit D (02343-1073)
PHONE..................................781 767-1877
Ronald Vater, *President*
Allan Vater, *Vice Pres*
▲ **EMP:** 30
SQ FT: 7,200
SALES (est): 5.5MM **Privately Held**
WEB: www.vater.com
SIC: 3931 Mfg Musical Instruments

Holden
Worcester County

(G-11541)
ALEXIS FOODS INC (PA)
160 Reservoir St Ste 4 (01520-1271)
PHONE..................................508 829-9111
Vasso Drosos, *Principal*
EMP: 3
SALES (est): 456.5K **Privately Held**
SIC: 2099 Mfg Food Preparations

(G-11542)
CAMELOT TOOLS LLC
800 Main St (01520-1838)
PHONE..................................508 981-7443
Antonio E Cacela, *Mng Member*
Lauren C Cacela,
Joaquim F Silva,
EMP: 3
SALES (est): 300K **Privately Held**
SIC: 3423 Mfg Hand/Edge Tools

(G-11543)
CLARIANT PLAS COATINGS USA LLC
Reedspectrum Division
85 Industrial Dr (01520-1848)
PHONE..................................508 829-6321
Cecilia Loke, *General Mgr*
Phil Strassle, *Mng Member*
Baur Ruediger, *Info Tech Mgr*
EMP: 99
SQ FT: 63,320
SALES (corp-wide): 6.7B **Privately Held**
WEB: www.myclariant.com
SIC: 3087 2816 Custom Compounding-Purchased Resins Mfg Inorganic Pigments
HQ: Clariant Plastics & Coatings Usa Llc
4000 Monroe Rd
Charlotte NC 28205
704 331-7000

(G-11544)
HOLDEN WINE & SPIRITS INC
140 Reservoir St (01520-1204)
P.O. Box 68 (01520-0068)
PHONE..................................508 829-6632
EMP: 7
SQ FT: 3,000
SALES (est): 600K **Privately Held**
SIC: 2084 Mfg Wines/Brandy/Spirits

(G-11545)
INCASE INC
118 Salisbury St (01520-1416)
PHONE..................................508 478-6500
Walter Frick, *President*
Frank Zanghi, *Exec VP*
▲ **EMP:** 8
SALES (est): 1.4MM **Privately Held**
WEB: www.incaseinc.com
SIC: 3089 Mfg Plastic Products

(G-11546)
INNER-TITE CORP
110 Industrial Dr (01520-1893)
PHONE..................................508 829-6361
George W Davis, *President*
Bill Johnson, *Engineer*
Bonnie Williams, *Finance Spvr*
Jose Cubria, *Sales Staff*
John C Mahaney, *Manager*
◆ **EMP:** 85 **EST:** 1917
SQ FT: 100,000
SALES (est): 19.4MM **Privately Held**
WEB: www.inner-tite.com
SIC: 3699 3429 Mfg Electrical Equipment/Supplies Mfg Hardware

(G-11547)
MASSACHUSETTS BROKEN STONE CO
Also Called: Holden Trap Rock Co
2077 N Main St (01520)
P.O. Box 31 (01520-0031)
PHONE..................................508 829-5353
Andrew Forrest, *Vice Pres*
EMP: 12
SALES (corp-wide): 3.4MM **Privately Held**
SIC: 2951 Mfg Asphalt Mixtures/Blocks
PA: Massachusetts Broken Stone Company
332 Sawyerhill Rd
Berlin MA 01503
978 838-9999

(G-11548)
MOLLY MERCHANDISING UNLIMITED
907 Main St (01520-1804)
PHONE..................................508 829-2544
EMP: 5
SALES (est): 280K **Privately Held**
SIC: 3429 Mfg Architectural Woodworking Goods

(G-11549)
PEPSI-COLA BTLG OF WRCSTER INC (PA)
Also Called: Pepsico
90 Industrial Dr (01520-1898)
PHONE..................................508 829-6551
Robert W Rauh, *President*
William T Rauh, *Vice Pres*
Anil Kapoor, *Purchasing*
Michael Berg, *QC Mgr*
Richard Rauh, *Treasurer*
EMP: 85 **EST:** 1936
SQ FT: 60,000
SALES (est): 16.5MM **Privately Held**
WEB: www.pepsiworcester.com
SIC: 2086 Carb Sft Drnkbtlcn

(G-11550)
PRISMIC PHARMACEUTICALS INC
650 South Rd (01520-1042)
PHONE..................................971 506-6415
Peter Moriarty, *CEO*
Zachary Dutton, *President*
EMP: 7
SALES (est): 279.1K
SALES (corp-wide): 67K **Privately Held**
SIC: 2834 Mfg Pharmaceutical Preparations
PA: Fsd Pharma Inc
520 William St
Toronto ON K9A 3
416 854-8884

(G-11551)
WORCESTER INDUS RBR SUP CO INC
172 Doyle Rd (01520-2016)
P.O. Box 60119, Worcester (01606-0119)
PHONE..................................508 853-2332
Stephen J Gaskin, *President*
EMP: 4 **EST:** 1955
SQ FT: 2,000
SALES (est): 750K **Privately Held**
SIC: 3053 5085 Mfg Gasket/Packing/Seals Whol Industrial Supplies

(G-11552)
WORCESTER SUN LLC
20 Cook St (01520-2408)
PHONE..................................774 364-0553
Mark A Henderson, *Principal*
EMP: 3
SALES (est): 121.7K **Privately Held**
SIC: 2711 Newspapers-Publishing/Printing

Holland
Hampden County

(G-11553)
HERRICK EVERETT WELDING & MCH
Also Called: Herrick's Welding and Machine
51 E Brimfield Rd (01521-3101)
PHONE..................................413 245-7533
Everret Herrick, *Owner*
EMP: 3
SALES: 210K **Privately Held**
SIC: 7692 Welding Repair

Holliston
Middlesex County

(G-11554)
A B T MACHINE CO
1649 Washington St Ste 1 (01746-2220)
PHONE..................................508 429-4355
Thomas Hodgdon, *Partner*
William Niethe, *Partner*
EMP: 3
SQ FT: 6,000
SALES: 270K **Privately Held**
SIC: 3599 Automotive Machine Shop

(G-11555)
ABBESS INSTRS & SYSTEMS INC
75 October Hill Rd (01746-1344)
P.O. Box 498, Ashland (01721-0498)
PHONE..................................508 429-0002
Geoffrey Zeamer, *President*
Michelle Zeamer, *Vice Pres*
Matthew Garland, *Engineer*
EMP: 15
SQ FT: 4,000
SALES (est): 4MM **Privately Held**
WEB: www.abbess.com
SIC: 3829 Mfg Measuring/Controlling Devices

(G-11556)
ADVANCED METAL SYSTEMS CORP
34 Pope Rd Bldg 5 (01746-2218)
P.O. Box 6757 (01746-6757)
PHONE..................................508 429-0480
David Cohen, *President*
EMP: 7 **Privately Held**
SIC: 3444 Mfg & Installs Metal Panel Systems
PA: Advanced Metal Systems Corp
34 Pope Rd
Holliston MA 01746

(G-11557)
AUTOGEN INC
84 October Hill Rd Ste 5 (01746-1371)
PHONE..................................508 429-5965
Robert J Sullivan, *CEO*
Michael Messier, *President*
Sandi Pandiscio, *Finance Mgr*
Rob Osborn, *Sales Staff*
Jill Podzka, *Mktg Coord*
▲ **EMP:** 25 **EST:** 1998
SQ FT: 3,500
SALES (est): 5.9MM **Privately Held**
WEB: www.autogen.com
SIC: 3826 Mfg Analytical Instruments

(G-11558)
BAGGE INC
Also Called: East Coast Perfection Coating
150 Kuniholm Dr Ste 4 (01746-1398)
PHONE..................................508 429-8080
Michael Bagge, *President*
EMP: 8

SQ FT: 7,000
SALES (est): 437.3K **Privately Held**
SIC: 2821 Mfg Plastic Materials/Resins

(G-11559)
BIG 3 PRECISION PRODUCTS INC
140 Lowland St (01746-2031)
PHONE..................................508 429-4774
Allen Scheidt, *President*
EMP: 19 **Privately Held**
SIC: 3544 Mfg Dies & Tools
HQ: Big 3 Precision Products, Inc.
2923 S Wabash Ave
Centralia IL 62801
618 533-3251

(G-11560)
BIOCHROM US INC
84 October Hill Rd Ste 10 (01746-1371)
PHONE..................................508 893-8999
James Green, *CEO*
Susan Luscinski, *Treasurer*
Robert Gagnon, *Director*
▲ **EMP:** 4
SALES (est): 537K **Publicly Held**
SIC: 3826 Mfg Analytical Instruments
PA: Harvard Bioscience, Inc.
84 October Hill Rd Ste 10
Holliston MA 01746

(G-11561)
BIOSTAGE INC
84 October Hill Rd Ste 11 (01746-1371)
PHONE..................................774 233-7300
James J McGorry, *CEO*
Jason Jing Chen, *Ch of Bd*
Hong Yu, *President*
Thomas McNaughton, *CFO*
Saverio Lafrancesca, *Chief Mktg Ofcr*
EMP: 28 **EST:** 2007
SQ FT: 17,000
SALES (est): 145.2K **Privately Held**
SIC: 3841 Mfg Surgical/Medical Instruments

(G-11562)
CADWELL PRODUCTS COMPANY INC
Also Called: Cadwell Company
3 Kuniholm Dr (01746-1376)
PHONE..................................508 429-3100
Mindy Murray, *President*
Michael Todisco, *Vice Pres*
Jim Murray, *Treasurer*
EMP: 14
SQ FT: 7,000
SALES (est): 1.3MM **Privately Held**
WEB: www.cadwellsign.com
SIC: 3993 Mfg Signs/Advertising Specialties

(G-11563)
CENTURY-TY WOOD MFG INC
79 Lowland St (01746-2030)
PHONE..................................508 429-4011
Faith K Tiberio, *President*
Maurice N St Germain, *Vice Pres*
Susan Payne, *Sales Staff*
Patricia St Germain, *Asst Mgr*
Joan M Currier, *Admin Sec*
EMP: 70 **EST:** 1947
SQ FT: 35,000
SALES (est): 12.2MM **Privately Held**
WEB: www.century-tywood.com
SIC: 3452 3469 2392 Mfg Bolts/Screws/Rivets Mfg Metal Stampings Mfg Household Furnishings

(G-11564)
CONVANTA HOLLISTON
115 Washington St (01746-1345)
PHONE..................................508 429-9750
EMP: 4
SALES (est): 413.5K **Privately Held**
SIC: 2673 Mfg Bags-Plastic/Coated Paper

(G-11565)
CORMIERS SELF DEFENSE ACA
72 Morton St (01746-1552)
P.O. Box 5810 (01746-5810)
PHONE..................................508 596-7326
EMP: 3
SALES (est): 169.6K **Privately Held**
SIC: 3812 Mfg Search/Navigation Equipment

(G-11566)
DAHLSTROM & COMPANY INC
50 October Hill Rd (01746-1308)
PHONE..................................508 429-3367
Harry Dahlstrom, *President*
Gail Dahlstrom, *Vice Pres*
EMP: 5
SQ FT: 8,000
SALES (est): 701.4K **Privately Held**
WEB: www.dahlstromco.com
SIC: 2731 Books-Publishing/Printing

(G-11567)
DIAMOND DIAGNOSTICS INC (PA)
Also Called: Diamond Diagnostics -USA
333 Fiske St (01746-2048)
PHONE..................................508 429-0450
Steven Kovacs, *President*
Denise Boucher, *Business Mgr*
Peter Kovacs, *Vice Pres*
Agnes Kovacs, *Treasurer*
Mary Archambault, *Human Resources*
◆ **EMP:** 75
SQ FT: 38,000
SALES (est): 12.7MM **Privately Held**
WEB: www.diamonddiagnostics.com
SIC: 3841 5047 Mfg Surgical/Medical Instruments Whol Medical/Hospital Equipment

(G-11568)
DIGILAB GENOMIC SOLUTIONS INC
84 October Hill Rd Ste 7 (01746-1371)
PHONE..................................508 893-3130
David Giddings, *President*
Joseph Griffin, *Vice Pres*
EMP: 56
SALES (est): 4.7MM **Privately Held**
SIC: 3841 Mfg Surgical/Medical Instruments

(G-11569)
EMBEDDED NOW INC
13 Water St Ste 2 (01746-2375)
PHONE..................................508 246-8196
Jeffrey Moore, *President*
Eric Marthisen, *Vice Pres*
EMP: 3
SQ FT: 1,300
SALES: 195K **Privately Held**
SIC: 3571 Mfg Electronic Computers

(G-11570)
ESCO TECHNOLOGIES INC
Also Called: Esco Tool
75 October Hill Rd (01746-1344)
PHONE..................................508 429-4441
Matthew Brennan, *President*
James Moruzzi, *Vice Pres*
Craig Winterseld, *Vice Pres*
Ben Moruzzi, *Sales Staff*
▲ **EMP:** 35 **EST:** 1935
SQ FT: 18,000
SALES (est): 6.5MM **Privately Held**
SIC: 3545 5085 Mfg Machine Tool Accessories Whol Industrial Supplies

(G-11571)
FLEXHEAD INDUSTRIES INC
56 Lowland St (01746-2029)
PHONE..................................508 893-9596
John P Williamson, *President*
Charles M Cohrs, *Treasurer*
Daniel S Kelly, *Admin Sec*
▲ **EMP:** 15
SALES (est): 3.9MM **Privately Held**
SIC: 3569 Manufactures General Industrial Machinery
HQ: Anvil International, Llc
2 Holland Way
Exeter NH 03833
603 418-2800

(G-11572)
GENOMIC SOLUTIONS INC
84 October Hill Rd Ste 7 (01746-1371)
PHONE..................................734 975-4800
EMP: 30
SQ FT: 14,500
SALES (est): 4.1MM **Publicly Held**
WEB: www.genomicsolutions.com
SIC: 3826 Mfg Analytical Instruments
PA: Harvard Bioscience, Inc.
84 October Hill Rd Ste 10
Holliston MA 01746

(G-11573)
GF MACHINING SOLUTIONS LLC
150 Hopping Brook Rd (01746-1455)
PHONE..................................508 474-1100
Gordon McLean, *Branch Mgr*
EMP: 6
SALES (corp-wide): 4.7B **Privately Held**
SIC: 3599 Mfg Industrial Machinery
HQ: Gf Machining Solutions Llc
560 Bond St
Lincolnshire IL 60069
847 913-5300

(G-11574)
H G COCKRILL CORP
349 Fiske St (01746-2048)
PHONE..................................508 429-2005
Huston G Cockrill, *President*
EMP: 7
SQ FT: 1,200
SALES (est): 605K **Privately Held**
SIC: 3599 Mfg Industrial Machinery

(G-11575)
HARVARD BIOSCIENCE INC (PA)
84 October Hill Rd Ste 10 (01746-1371)
PHONE..................................508 893-8999
Earl R Lewis, *Ch of Bd*
James Green, *President*
Yash Singh, *Exec VP*
Frank Aubuchon, *Vice Pres*
John Christensen, *Vice Pres*
EMP: 122
SQ FT: 83,123
SALES: 120.7MM **Publicly Held**
WEB: www.harvardbioscience.com
SIC: 3821 3826 Mfg Laboratory Apparatus/Analytical Instruments

(G-11576)
HEKA INSTRUMENTS INCORPORATED
84 October Hill Rd Ste 10 (01746-1371)
PHONE..................................516 882-1155
Peter Schulze, *President*
Hugh Macpherson, *Treasurer*
EMP: 3
SQ FT: 3,800
SALES (est): 389.1K
SALES (corp-wide): 2.6MM **Privately Held**
SIC: 2836 Mfg Biological Products Except Diagnostic
PA: Heka Electronics Incorporated
643 Highway 14
Chester NS B0J 1
902 624-0606

(G-11577)
HIGHLAND LABS INC
163 Woodland St (01746-1821)
PHONE..................................508 429-2918
Peter Lewis, *Owner*
EMP: 25
SQ FT: 21,600
SALES (est): 2.3MM **Privately Held**
WEB: www.highlandlabs.com
SIC: 3999 3559 3841 3596 Mfg Misc Products Mfg Misc Industry Mach Mfg Surgical/Med Instr Mfg Scale/Balance-Nonlab Mfg Paints/Allied Prdts

(G-11578)
HOLLIS INDUSTRIES INC
1485 Washington St (01746-2216)
P.O. Box 6227 (01746-6227)
PHONE..................................508 429-4328
Paul A Champney, *Owner*
Arthur G Champney, *Treasurer*
Lillian Champney, *Clerk*
EMP: 20 **EST:** 1957
SQ FT: 10,000
SALES: 1MM **Privately Held**
SIC: 3599 Job Machine Shop

(G-11579)
IWAKI AMERICA INCORPORATED (HQ)
5 Boynton Rd (01746-1460)
PHONE..................................508 429-1440
John P Miersma, *President*
Mark Pantazes, *President*
Robert J Dziekiewicz Jr, *Corp Secy*
Dan Costigan, *Buyer*
Shigeru Fujinaka, *Director*
▲ **EMP:** 60
SQ FT: 53,000
SALES (est): 13.2MM **Privately Held**
WEB: www.walchem.com
SIC: 3561 5084 3823 3625 Mfg Pumps/Pumping Equip Whol Industrial Equip Mfg Process Cntrl Instr Mfg Relay/Indstl Control

(G-11580)
IWAKI PUMPS INC (DH)
5 Boynton Rd (01746-1460)
PHONE..................................508 429-1440
Richard Jewett, *Ch of Bd*
Ronald Yates, *President*
▲ **EMP:** 20
SQ FT: 30,000
SALES (est): 7.9MM **Privately Held**
WEB: www.iwakiwalchem.com
SIC: 3561 7699 3674 Mfg Pumps/Pumping Equipment Repair Services Mfg Semiconductors/Related Devices
HQ: Iwaki America Incorporated
5 Boynton Rd
Holliston MA 01746
508 429-1440

(G-11581)
JF2 LLC
215 Hopping Brook Rd (01746-1456)
PHONE..................................508 429-1022
John Sallona, *Owner*
EMP: 74
SALES (corp-wide): 59.2MM **Privately Held**
SIC: 3448 Mfg Prefabricated Metal Buildings
PA: Jf2, Llc
617 Water St
Gardiner ME 04345
207 588-3300

(G-11582)
LIBERATING TECHNOLOGIES INC
Also Called: L T I
325 Hopping Brook Rd A (01746-1456)
PHONE..................................508 893-6363
William Hanson, *President*
Todd Farrell, *Engineer*
Thane Hunt, *Engineer*
Jennifer Johansson, *Engineer*
▲ **EMP:** 8
SQ FT: 4,500
SALES (est): 1.5MM **Privately Held**
WEB: www.liberatingtech.com
SIC: 3842 Mfg Surgical Appliances/Supplies

(G-11583)
MBF PRINTING
118 Washington St (01746-1373)
PHONE..................................774 233-0337
EMP: 4 **EST:** 2015
SALES (est): 111.6K **Privately Held**
SIC: 2752 Lithographic Commercial Printing

(G-11584)
MD CHEMICALS LLC
120 Jeffrey Ave Ste 2 (01746-1786)
PHONE..................................508 314-9664
Mark Willis, *Mng Member*
EMP: 3 **EST:** 2012
SALES (est): 248.7K **Privately Held**
SIC: 2899 Mfg Chemical Preparations

(G-11585)
MIANO PRINTING SERVICES INC
Also Called: MPS
330 Woodland St (01746-1824)
PHONE..................................617 935-2830
Stephen M Miano, *President*
EMP: 12

SALES (est): 1.3MM **Privately Held**
SIC: 2752 Lithographic Commercial Printing

(G-11586)
MILLER H C WOOD WORKING INC
93 Bartzak Dr (01746-1374)
PHONE..................................508 429-4220
Bob De Marre, *President*
EMP: 8 **EST:** 1931
SQ FT: 10,000
SALES (est): 911.9K **Privately Held**
SIC: 2431 2434 Mfg Millwork Mfg Wood Kitchen Cabinet

(G-11587)
MLC SERVICES LLC
35 Jeffrey Ave (01746-2027)
PHONE..................................781 366-1132
Brett Webster, *CEO*
EMP: 6 **EST:** 2015
SALES (est): 276.6K **Privately Held**
SIC: 3663 Mfg Radio/Tv Communication Equipment

(G-11588)
NANMAC CORP
1657 Washington St Unit B (01746-2289)
P.O. Box 6640 (01746-6640)
PHONE..................................508 872-4811
Daniel Nanigian, *President*
Michael Pike, *Mfg Staff*
Judi Briggs, *Technical Staff*
Kim Nanigian, *Admin Sec*
Sally Mom,
EMP: 31
SALES (est): 7.2MM **Privately Held**
WEB: www.nanmac.com
SIC: 3829 3822 Mfg Measuring/Controlling Devices Mfg Environmental Controls

(G-11589)
NEW ENGLAND ABRASIVES
35 Louis St (01746-1549)
PHONE..................................508 893-9540
R Keith Brown, *Principal*
▲ **EMP:** 3
SALES (est): 170K **Privately Held**
SIC: 3291 Mfg Abrasive Products

(G-11590)
NEW ENGLAND EMULSIONS CORP
201 Lowland St (01746-2032)
P.O. Box 5821 (01746-5821)
PHONE..................................508 429-5550
David E Johnson, *President*
Richmond Mann, *Asst Mgr*
EMP: 5
SQ FT: 3,500
SALES (est): 985.5K
SALES (corp-wide): 202.2MM **Privately Held**
WEB: www.allstatesasphalt.com
SIC: 2951 Mfg Asphalt Emulsions
PA: All States Asphalt, Inc.
325 Amherst Rd
Sunderland MA 01375
413 665-7021

(G-11591)
NORTHEASTERN PUBLISHING CO
112 Central St (01746-2130)
PHONE..................................508 429-5588
EMP: 3
SALES (est): 202.5K **Privately Held**
WEB: www.northeasternpub.com
SIC: 2741 Publishes Phone Books

(G-11592)
OLIGO FACTORY INC
70 Bartzak Dr 1 (01746-1375)
PHONE..................................508 275-3561
Rick Neves, *President*
Michael Richmond, *Opers Staff*
EMP: 6
SALES: 580K **Privately Held**
WEB: www.oligofactory.com
SIC: 3821 Mfg Lab Apparatus/Furniture

(G-11593)
OX PAPER TUBE AND CORE INC
89 October Hill Rd (01746-1378)
PHONE..................................508 879-1141
Edward Santiago, *Manager*
EMP: 17 **Privately Held**
SIC: 2655 Mfg Fiber Cans/Drums
PA: Ox Paper Tube And Core, Inc.
600 W Elm Ave
Hanover PA 17331

(G-11594)
PAGELL CORPORATION
74 Lowland St (01746-2029)
PHONE..................................508 429-2998
Brett Kane, *President*
▲ **EMP:** 45 **EST:** 1961
SQ FT: 72,000
SALES (est): 8MM **Privately Held**
WEB: www.pagell.com
SIC: 2621 Paper Mill

(G-11595)
PATRIOT WORLDWIDE INC
Also Called: Nanmac
1657 Washington St Ste 3 (01746-2288)
PHONE..................................800 786-4669
Robert Harrington, *President*
EMP: 5
SALES (est): 469.1K **Privately Held**
SIC: 3823 Mfg Process Control Instruments

(G-11596)
PEGASUS INC
39 Locust St (01746-1377)
P.O. Box 6160 (01746-6160)
PHONE..................................508 429-2461
Christopher Best, *President*
Peter Best, *Treasurer*
Corine Arnold, *Clerk*
EMP: 8
SQ FT: 5,600
SALES (est): 1.1MM **Privately Held**
SIC: 3599 Job Machine Shop

(G-11597)
PRI FINANCIAL PUBLISHING
Also Called: Moneyletters
479 Washington St (01746-1828)
P.O. Box 6020 (01746-6020)
PHONE..................................508 429-5949
Bruce Hardy, *President*
Brian Kelley, *Principal*
Walter Frank, *Manager*
EMP: 3
SALES (est): 300K **Privately Held**
SIC: 2741 Misc Publishing

(G-11598)
RECOGNITION CENTER INC
326 Woodland St (01746-1824)
PHONE..................................508 429-5881
Cliff Reeves, *President*
Diane Reeves, *Treasurer*
EMP: 4
SQ FT: 2,400
SALES (est): 266.2K **Privately Held**
WEB: www.recognitioncenter.com
SIC: 3993 Mfg Signs/Advertising Specialties

(G-11599)
ROAR INDUSTRIES INC
120 Jeffrey Ave Ste 1 (01746-1786)
PHONE..................................508 429-5952
Guile Wood Jr, *President*
EMP: 10
SQ FT: 10,000
SALES: 1.8MM **Privately Held**
SIC: 3444 7692 Mfg Sheet Metalwork Welding Repair

(G-11600)
SANTA ROSA LEAD PRODUCTS LLC
70 Bartzak Dr (01746-1375)
PHONE..................................508 893-6021
EMP: 15
SALES (corp-wide): 3.5MM **Privately Held**
SIC: 3531 Mfg Construction Machinery
PA: Santa Rosa Lead Products, Llc
33 S University St
Healdsburg CA 95448
800 916-5323

(G-11601)
SE SHIRES INC
260 Hopping Brook Rd (01746-1455)
PHONE..................................508 634-6805
Stephen Shires, *President*
Samantha Glazier, *Sales Staff*
Tom Otto, *Manager*
Susan Chandler, *Director*
Dale Shires, *Shareholder*
▲ **EMP:** 34
SQ FT: 12,000
SALES (est): 5.5MM **Privately Held**
WEB: www.seshires.com
SIC: 3931 Mfg Musical Instruments

(G-11602)
SILVER LEAF BOOKS LLC
13 Temi Rd (01746-1219)
P.O. Box 6460 (01746-6460)
PHONE..................................781 799-6609
Clifford B Bowyer,
Marilyn Bowyer,
EMP: 20
SALES (est): 1.4MM **Privately Held**
SIC: 2731 Books-Publishing/Printing

(G-11603)
SPORTS POWER DRIVE INC
539 Fiske St (01746-2025)
PHONE..................................774 233-0175
Debra Miller, *Principal*
EMP: 4
SALES (est): 222.1K **Privately Held**
SIC: 3949 Mfg Sporting/Athletic Goods

(G-11604)
STANLEY INDUSTRIAL & AUTO LLC
Also Called: Lista International
106 Lowland St (01746-2031)
PHONE..................................508 429-1350
Donald Brown, *President*
Jonathan Daby, *Buyer*
Noah Pelon, *Engineer*
EMP: 458
SALES (corp-wide): 13.9B **Publicly Held**
SIC: 2599 Mfg Furniture/Fixtures
HQ: Stanley Industrial & Automotive, Llc
505 N Cleveland Ave
Westerville OH 43082
614 755-7000

(G-11605)
STANLEY VIDMAR
Also Called: Storage and Workplace Systems
106 Lowland St (01746-2031)
PHONE..................................610 797-6600
EMP: 5
SALES (corp-wide): 13.9B **Publicly Held**
SIC: 2542 Mfg Partitions/Fixtures-Nonwood
HQ: Stanley Vidmar
11 Grammes Rd
Allentown PA 18103

(G-11606)
STARBURST PRTG & GRAPHICS INC
300 Hopping Brook Rd (01746-3405)
PHONE..................................508 893-0900
Paul Nunez Jr, *President*
EMP: 18
SQ FT: 13,000
SALES (est): 3MM **Privately Held**
WEB: www.starburstprinting.com
SIC: 2752 Lithographic Commercial Printing

(G-11607)
STEVENSON LEARNING SKILLS INC
220 Marked Tree Rd (01746-1678)
P.O. Box 6397 (01746-6397)
PHONE..................................774 233-0457
William Stevenson, *President*
EMP: 4
SQ FT: 3,200
SALES: 150K **Privately Held**
WEB: www.stevensonlearning.com
SIC: 2731 8748 Books-Publishing/Printing Business Consulting Services

(G-11608)
TBS TECHNOLOGIES LLC
68 Briarcliff Ln (01746-1040)
PHONE..................................508 429-3111
John E Sullivan, *CEO*
Thomas Dee, *Principal*
Mort Rosenberg, *Principal*
EMP: 4
SALES (est): 306.7K **Privately Held**
SIC: 2842 Mfg Polish/Sanitation Goods

(G-11609)
TOTAL RECOIL MAGNETICS INC
Also Called: Blue Hill Transformer
84 October Hill Rd Ste 6a (01746-1371)
PHONE..................................508 429-9600
Dick Clarke, *President*
John Trischitta, *Treasurer*
EMP: 16
SQ FT: 6,000
SALES (est): 3.7MM **Privately Held**
WEB: www.dahlstromandcompany.com
SIC: 3612 Mfg Transformers

(G-11610)
UNION BIOMETRICA INC (PA)
84 October Hill Rd Ste 12 (01746-1371)
PHONE..................................508 893-3115
David Strack, *President*
Christopher Bogan, *COO*
Lori Wilcox, *Vice Pres*
Tom Mullins, *Engineer*
Mullins Tom, *Engineer*
EMP: 20
SQ FT: 20,000
SALES (est): 2.6MM **Privately Held**
WEB: www.unionbio.com
SIC: 3826 Mfg Analytical Instruments

(G-11611)
UNIVERSAL WILDE INC
201 Summer St (01746-2258)
P.O. Box 9110, Norwood (02062-9110)
PHONE..................................508 429-5515
Evelyn Edmonds, *President*
Ted Kulpinski, *VP Opers*
Monroe Jackson, *Accounts Mgr*
Sony Raghavan, *Programmer Anys*
Jill McNeilly, *Prgrmr*
EMP: 147 **Privately Held**
SIC: 2752 Lithographic Commercial Printing
PA: Universal Wilde, Inc.
26 Dartmouth St Ste 1
Westwood MA 02090

(G-11612)
VISION CONSULTING GROUP INC
104 Fairview St (01746-3503)
PHONE..................................508 314-5378
Robert Giachetti, *President*
Mark Dawson, *Treasurer*
EMP: 10
SALES: 2MM **Privately Held**
SIC: 7372 Prepackaged Software Services

(G-11613)
WARD PROCESS INC
Also Called: American Acoustical Products
311 Hopping Brook Rd (01746-1456)
PHONE..................................508 429-1165
Russell S Moody, *President*
Ken Owens, *COO*
Emanuele Bianchini, *Engineer*
Kathleen Loughlin, *Manager*
Dennis Young, *Manager*
▲ **EMP:** 55
SQ FT: 80,000
SALES: 14.1MM **Privately Held**
WEB: www.aapusa.com
SIC: 3081 3296 3229 3086 Mfg Unsupport Plstc Film Mfg Mineral Wool Mfg Pressed/Blown Glass Mfg Plastic Foam Prdts

(G-11614)
WINFIELD WOODWORKING INC
1278 Washington St (01746-2213)
PHONE..................................508 429-4320

EMP: 8
SQ FT: 2,400
SALES (est): 500K Privately Held
SIC: 2434 Mfg Wood Kitchen Cabinets

Holyoke
Hampden County

(G-11615)
A-T SURGICAL MFG CO INC
115 Clemente St (01040-5644)
PHONE..................................413 532-4551
Eugene P Kirejczyk, *President*
Cynthia F Kirejczyk, *Vice Pres*
EMP: 38
SQ FT: 10,000
SALES (est): 4.2MM Privately Held
WEB: www.atsurgical.com
SIC: 3842 Mfg Surgical And Industrial Safety Supports

(G-11616)
APPLIED LIGHT MANUFACTURING
48 Commercial St (01040-4704)
PHONE..................................413 552-3600
EMP: 10
SALES (est): 1.2MM Privately Held
SIC: 3449 Mfg Misc Structural Metalwork

(G-11617)
BARCLAY FURNITURE ASSOCIATES
532 Main St Ste 6 (01040-5598)
PHONE..................................413 536-8084
Michael Hynek, *President*
Ronald Hynek, *Treasurer*
EMP: 8
SQ FT: 16,000
SALES (est): 1.1MM Privately Held
SIC: 2512 Mfg Upholstered Household Furniture Specializing In Couches And Chairs

(G-11618)
BAY STATE PLATING INC
18 N Bridge St (01040-5827)
P.O. Box 187 (01041-0187)
PHONE..................................413 533-6927
Timothy Roberts, *President*
EMP: 9
SQ FT: 18,000
SALES (est): 1.1MM Privately Held
SIC: 3559 3471 Mfg Misc Industry Machinery Plating/Polishing Service

(G-11619)
BLENDCO SYSTEMS LLC
C.A.R. Products
630 Beaulieu St (01040-5439)
PHONE..................................800 537-7797
Robert Goldenberg, *Manager*
EMP: 25 Privately Held
SIC: 2841 5013 5087 3714 Mfg Soap/Other Detergent Whol Auto Parts/Supplies Whol Svc Estblshmt Equip Mfg Motor Vehicle Parts Mfg Polish/Sanitation Gd
HQ: Blendco Systems, Llc
1 Pearl Buck Ct
Bristol PA 19007
215 785-3147

(G-11620)
CITY MACHINE CORPORATION
155 N Canal St (01040-6246)
PHONE..................................413 538-9766
Allan Lukasik, *President*
Charles P Burns III, *Vice Pres*
Ovila Pimpare Jr, *Vice Pres*
Patricia Hamel, *Treasurer*
EMP: 21
SQ FT: 12,200
SALES (est): 3.4MM Privately Held
SIC: 3599 Machine Shop

(G-11621)
D & S PLATING CO INC
102 Cabot St Ste 6 (01040-6074)
PHONE..................................413 533-7771
Steve M Dupuis, *President*
Debbie Dupuis, *Treasurer*
EMP: 17
SQ FT: 6,000
SALES (est): 1.8MM Privately Held
SIC: 3471 Plating/Polishing Service

(G-11622)
DUPONT PACKAGING INC
68 Winter St 4b (01040-6409)
PHONE..................................413 552-0048
William Dupont, *President*
Marie Helene-Forest, *Treasurer*
EMP: 10 EST: 1969
SALES: 600K Privately Held
WEB: www.dupontpkg.net
SIC: 3089 Mfg Plastic Products

(G-11623)
E S SPORTS CORPORATION
47 Jackson St (01040-5512)
P.O. Box 771 (01041-0771)
PHONE..................................413 534-5634
Eric Suher, *President*
Frank Suher, *Vice Pres*
Kate Labombard, *Accounts Exec*
Burton S Resnic, *Clerk*
▲ EMP: 70
SQ FT: 120,000
SALES (est): 7.7MM Privately Held
WEB: www.essports.com
SIC: 2396 2395 Mfg Auto/Apparel Trimming Pleating/Stitching Services

(G-11624)
EDARON INC (PA)
100 Appleton St (01040-6402)
PHONE..................................413 533-7159
Louis Moretti, *President*
Edmund Babski, *Treasurer*
Alice Shevlin, *Controller*
▲ EMP: 147
SQ FT: 225,000
SALES (est): 23MM Privately Held
WEB: www.edaron.com
SIC: 3944 Mfg Games/Toys

(G-11625)
EUREKA LAB BOOK INC
Also Called: Eureka Blank Book Co
110 Winter St (01040-6411)
P.O. Box 150 (01041-0150)
PHONE..................................413 534-5671
EMP: 10
SQ FT: 65,000
SALES (est): 4MM Privately Held
WEB: www.eurekalabbook.com
SIC: 2678 2782 Mfg Stationery Products Mfg Blankbooks/Binders

(G-11626)
EXPRESSIVE DESIGN GROUP INC
49 Garfield St (01040-5407)
PHONE..................................413 315-6296
Robert P Milos, *President*
Steve Kenniston, *Vice Pres*
John D Conforti, *Treasurer*
Alan Pearlman, *Admin Sec*
◆ EMP: 45
SALES (est): 5.9MM Privately Held
SIC: 2771 2679 5112 5113 Mfg Greeting Cards Mfg Converted Paper Prdt Whol Stationery/Offc Sup Whol Indstl/Svc Paper

(G-11627)
GENERAL MACHINE INC
56 Jackson St Ste 1 (01040-5583)
PHONE..................................413 533-5744
Kenneth H Lubold, *President*
EMP: 7 EST: 1975
SQ FT: 5,500
SALES: 450K Privately Held
SIC: 3599 Mfg Industrial Machinery

(G-11628)
GREGORY MANUFACTURING INC
Also Called: G M I
102 Cabot St Ste 2 (01040-6074)
PHONE..................................413 536-5432
William J Gregory, *President*
John W Gregory, *Treasurer*
▲ EMP: 70
SQ FT: 50,000
SALES (est): 12.3MM Privately Held
SIC: 3841 3089 3081 Mfg Surgical/Medical Instruments Mfg Plastic Products Mfg Unsupported Plastic Film/Sheet

(G-11629)
HADLEY PRINTING COMPANY INC
58 N Canal St (01040-5880)
PHONE..................................413 536-8517
Christopher Desrosiers, *President*
Greg Desrosiers, *Vice Pres*
Chris Desrosiers, *Treasurer*
Marc Desrosiers, *Treasurer*
Claudette Pelletier, *Sales Staff*
EMP: 30 EST: 1944
SQ FT: 30,000
SALES (est): 4.6MM Privately Held
WEB: www.hadleyprinting.com
SIC: 2752 2759 Lithographic Commercial Printing Commercial Printing

(G-11630)
HAMPDEN PAPERS INC (PA)
100 Water St (01040-6298)
PHONE..................................413 536-1000
Robert K Fowler, *CEO*
Richard J Wells, *President*
John W Phelps, *Vice Pres*
Michael E Archambeault, *VP Mfg*
Robert H Adams, *VP Sales*
▲ EMP: 93 EST: 1880
SQ FT: 350,000
SALES (est): 27.1MM Privately Held
WEB: www.hampdenpapers.com
SIC: 2671 2672 2631 Mfg Packaging Paper/Film Mfg Coated/Laminated Paper Paperboard Mill

(G-11631)
HAZEN PAPER COMPANY (PA)
240 S Water St (01040-5979)
P.O. Box 189 (01041-0189)
PHONE..................................413 538-8204
John H Hazen, *President*
Jeff Hopkins, *Export Mgr*
Al Zuffoletti, *QC Mgr*
Robert M Sylvester, *CFO*
Judith Getto, *Cust Mgr*
▲ EMP: 195 EST: 1925
SQ FT: 200,000
SALES (est): 79.1MM Privately Held
WEB: www.hazen.com
SIC: 2672 3497 Mfg Coated/Laminated Paper Mfg Metal Foil/Leaf

(G-11632)
HITCHCOCK PRESS INC
8 Hanover St (01040-5412)
P.O. Box 803 (01041-0803)
PHONE..................................413 538-8811
J Guy Gaulin, *President*
Michelle Robert, *General Mgr*
Deanna Gaulin, *Vice Pres*
Geraldine Gaulin, *Vice Pres*
EMP: 12 EST: 1897
SQ FT: 11,000
SALES (est): 1.5MM Privately Held
WEB: www.hitchcockpress.com
SIC: 2752 2759 Offset Printing

(G-11633)
HOLYOKE MACHINE COMPANY (PA)
514 Main St (01040-5585)
P.O. Box 988 (01041-0988)
PHONE..................................413 534-5612
James Sagalyn, *President*
Raphael Sagalyn, *Director*
▲ EMP: 40 EST: 1863
SQ FT: 48,000
SALES (est): 6.5MM Privately Held
SIC: 3554 3552 3599 Mfg Paper Industrial Machinery Mfg Textile Machinery Mfg Industrial Machinery

(G-11634)
INTERNATIONAL LASER SYSTEMS
Also Called: I L S
362 Race St (01040-5613)
PHONE..................................413 533-4372
Ed Sordillo, *President*
EMP: 7
SALES (est): 713.5K Privately Held
WEB: www.myils.com
SIC: 2759 Commercial Printing

(G-11635)
JOHNSTON DANDY COMPANY
Spencer, H M Division
78 N Canal St (01040-5829)
P.O. Box 1430 (01041-1430)
PHONE..................................413 315-4596
Paul Fay, *General Mgr*
Sarah Cooke, *Office Mgr*
Megan Kelly, *Office Mgr*
EMP: 12
SALES (corp-wide): 10.4MM Privately Held
WEB: www.johnstondandy.com
SIC: 3554 3496 2679 5084 Mfg Paper Indstl Mach Mfg Misc Fab Wire Prdts Mfg Converted Paper Prdt Whol Industrial Equip
PA: Johnston Dandy Company
148 Main St
Lincoln ME 04457
207 794-6571

(G-11636)
MANSIR PRINTING LLC
24 Shawmut Ave (01040-2324)
P.O. Box 471 (01041-0471)
PHONE..................................413 536-4250
Todd Collier, *Partner*
Debbie Bara, *Office Mgr*
Douglas Riel,
EMP: 19
SQ FT: 52,000
SALES (est): 5.6MM Privately Held
SIC: 2752 Lithographic Commercial Printing

(G-11637)
MARCUS COMPANY INC
Also Called: Marcus Printing Co
750 Main St (01040-5391)
PHONE..................................413 534-3303
Ben Marcus, *CEO*
Susan Goldsmith, *President*
Tierney Salvini, *COO*
EMP: 42 EST: 1930
SQ FT: 30,500
SALES (est): 6.3MM Privately Held
WEB: www.marcusprinting.com
SIC: 2752 7334 2791 2789 Lithographic Coml Print Photocopying Service Typesetting Services Bookbinding/Related Work

(G-11638)
MAROX CORPORATION
373 Whitney Ave (01040-2855)
PHONE..................................413 536-1300
Manfred Rosenkranz, *CEO*
Barry H Rosenkranz, *President*
Paul Daris, *Vice Pres*
Dale Bojanowski, *Opers Staff*
Michael Coratti, *QC Mgr*
EMP: 11
SQ FT: 48,000
SALES (est): 8.2MM
SALES (corp-wide): 9.8MM Privately Held
WEB: www.marox.com
SIC: 3599 Mfg Industrial Machinery
PA: Sussex Wire, Inc.
4 Danforth Dr
Easton PA 18045
610 250-7750

(G-11639)
MERIDIAN INDUSTRIAL GROUP LLC
529 S East St (01040-6005)
PHONE..................................413 538-9880
Steven Grande,
EMP: 22
SALES: 4MM Privately Held
SIC: 3599 Mfg Industrial Machinery

(G-11640)
MR GUTTER INC
740 High St Ste 2 (01040-4762)
PHONE..................................413 536-7451
Toll Free:..................................877 -
Gary Rehbein, *Owner*
Maureen Rehbein, *Co-Owner*
EMP: 5

GEOGRAPHIC

SQ FT: 16,500
SALES (est): 682.3K **Privately Held**
SIC: 3444 1761 Mfg Sheet Metalwork Roofing/Siding Contractor

(G-11641)
MRS MITCHELLS KITCHEN INC
514 Westfield Rd (01040-1633)
PHONE..................................413 322-8816
John Mitchell, *President*
EMP: 3
SALES (est): 251.4K **Privately Held**
SIC: 3634 Mfg Electric Housewares/Fans

(G-11642)
MT TOM GENERATING COMPANY LLC
200 Easthampton Rd (01040)
PHONE..................................413 536-9586
EMP: 99
SALES (est): 4.9MM
SALES (corp-wide): 5.4B **Publicly Held**
SIC: 3621 Manufactures Motors/Generators
HQ: Vistra Intermediate Company Llc
601 Travis St Ste 1400
Houston TX 77002
713 507-6400

(G-11643)
NEW ENGLAND ETCHING CO INC
23 Spring St (01040-5794)
PHONE..................................413 532-9482
Walter Foerster Jr, *President*
▼ **EMP:** 27 **EST:** 1931
SQ FT: 32,500
SALES: 2MM **Privately Held**
WEB: www.neetching.com
SIC: 3479 Coating/Engraving Service

(G-11644)
NEW ENGLAND ULTIMATE FINISHING
709 Main St (01040-5337)
PHONE..................................413 532-7777
Robert A Beaupre, *President*
Dale Darosa, *Vice Pres*
▲ **EMP:** 32
SQ FT: 30,000
SALES (est): 8.8MM **Privately Held**
WEB: www.nefinishing.com
SIC: 2675 2672 Mfg Die-Cut Paper/Paperboard Mfg Coated/Laminated Paper

(G-11645)
NTP/REPUBLIC CLEAR THRU CORP
Also Called: N T P Republic
475 Canal St (01040-6426)
P.O. Box 2448 (01041-2448)
PHONE..................................413 493-6800
James J Macarthy, *President*
James J McCarthy, *President*
Joseph Feigen, *Treasurer*
▲ **EMP:** 22
SQ FT: 45,000
SALES (est): 597.9K
SALES (corp-wide): 2.7MM **Privately Held**
WEB: www.walterdrake.com
SIC: 3089 Mfg Plastic Products
PA: Walter Drake Inc
85 Sargeant St
Holyoke MA 01040
413 536-5463

(G-11646)
OLD SAN JUAN BAKERY INC
408 High St (01040-4961)
PHONE..................................413 534-5555
Alicia Rosario, *President*
Oscar Rosario, *Treasurer*
EMP: 10
SALES (est): 974.8K **Privately Held**
SIC: 2051 Mfg Bread/Related Products

(G-11647)
ORTHOTICS WEST INC
49 Liberty St (01040-2009)
PHONE..................................413 736-3000
Jim Reed, *President*
EMP: 6
SALES (est): 927.4K **Privately Held**
WEB: www.orthoticswest.com
SIC: 3842 Mfg Surgical Appliances/Supplies

(G-11648)
PACKAGE MACHINERY COMPANY INC
80 Commercial St (01040-4704)
P.O. Box 407, West Springfield (01090-0407)
PHONE..................................413 315-3801
Katherine E Putnam, *President*
Paul E Striebel, *Vice Pres*
EMP: 8
SQ FT: 22,000
SALES (est): 1.6MM **Privately Held**
WEB: www.packagemachinery.com
SIC: 3565 Mfg Packaging Machinery

(G-11649)
R R LEDUC CORP
100 Bobala Rd (01040-9657)
PHONE..................................413 536-4329
Robert R Leduc, *President*
Eric Leduc, *Vice Pres*
Kerry Leduc, *Vice Pres*
Kurt Leduc, *Vice Pres*
Carrie Le Duc, *Manager*
EMP: 48
SQ FT: 61,000
SALES (est): 11.2MM **Privately Held**
WEB: www.rrleduc.com
SIC: 3444 Mfg Sheet Metalwork

(G-11650)
RED HAWK FIRE & SECURITY LLC
9 Sullivan Rd (01040-2841)
PHONE..................................413 568-4709
Jennifer Jersey, *Principal*
EMP: 7
SALES (corp-wide): 4.5B **Publicly Held**
SIC: 3999 Mfg Misc Products
HQ: Red Hawk Fire & Security, Llc
5100 Town Center Cir # 350
Boca Raton FL 33486
877 387-0188

(G-11651)
RELIANCE ELECTRIC SERVICE
573 S Canal St (01040-5591)
PHONE..................................413 533-3557
Paul Snopek, *President*
EMP: 7
SQ FT: 6,000
SALES (est): 730K **Privately Held**
SIC: 7694 5999 Electric Motor Repair

(G-11652)
RIVERVIEW MACHINE COMPANY INC
102 Cabot St Ste 1 (01040-6074)
PHONE..................................413 533-5366
Dennis C Carboneau, *President*
Joan Simard, *Clerk*
EMP: 11 **EST:** 1965
SQ FT: 30,000
SALES (est): 910K **Privately Held**
SIC: 3599 General Machine Shop

(G-11653)
RUSSELL BRANDS LLC
Spalding Division
489 Whitney Ave Ste 301 (01040-2711)
PHONE..................................413 735-1400
Larry Dismukes, *CFO*
EMP: 6
SALES (corp-wide): 225.3B **Publicly Held**
WEB: www.russellcorp.com
SIC: 2253 Knit Outerwear Mill
HQ: Russell Brands, Llc
1 Fruit Of The Loom Dr
Bowling Green KY 42103
270 781-6400

(G-11654)
RUWAC INC
54 Winter St (01040-6409)
PHONE..................................413 532-4030
Wolfgang Schloesser, *President*
Ray Ehrhardt, *Sales Mgr*
Paul Disanza, *Regl Sales Mgr*
▲ **EMP:** 19
SQ FT: 20,000
SALES (est): 5.2MM **Privately Held**
WEB: www.ruwac.com
SIC: 3563 Mfg Air/Gas Compressors

(G-11655)
S & S COMPUTER IMAGING INC
252 Open Square Way # 415 (01040-5879)
PHONE..................................413 536-0117
Stanley S Sikorski, *President*
EMP: 5
SQ FT: 1,500
SALES (est): 605.3K **Privately Held**
WEB: www.sscomputerimaging.com
SIC: 2759 2386 Commercial Printing Mfg Leather Clothing

(G-11656)
SEALED AIR CORPORATION
Packaging Products Div
2030 Homestead Ave Lowr (01040-9765)
PHONE..................................413 534-0231
Mark Moran, *Project Mgr*
Dan McGonigle, *Branch Mgr*
Matt Bleakley, *Exec Dir*
EMP: 100
SALES (corp-wide): 4.7B **Publicly Held**
WEB: www.sealedair.com
SIC: 3086 5199 2671 Mfg Plastic Foam Products Whol Nondurable Goods Mfg Packaging Paper/Film
PA: Sealed Air Corporation
2415 Cascade Pointe Blvd
Charlotte NC 28208
980 221-3235

(G-11657)
SIGNATURE ENGRV SYSTEMS INC
120 Whiting Farms Rd (01040-2832)
PHONE..................................413 533-7500
Christopher A Parent, *President*
Michael Zanga, *Engineer*
Eric Parent, *Treasurer*
James Richmond, *Admin Sec*
▲ **EMP:** 40
SQ FT: 60,000
SALES: 1.2MM **Privately Held**
WEB: www.signature-engravers.com
SIC: 3555 Mfg Printing Trades Machinery

(G-11658)
SONOCO PRODUCTS COMPANY
200 S Water St (01040-5979)
PHONE..................................413 536-4546
Dave Schultz, *Plant Mgr*
Angela Hamm, *Purch Agent*
James Shackett, *Project Engr*
David Perez, *Human Res Mgr*
Cheryl Smith, *Hum Res Coord*
EMP: 65
SALES (corp-wide): 5.3B **Publicly Held**
WEB: www.sonoco.com
SIC: 2631 2621 Paperboard Mill Paper Mill
PA: Sonoco Products Company
1 N 2nd St
Hartsville SC 29550
843 383-7000

(G-11659)
SONOCO PRODUCTS COMPANY
111 Mosher St (01040-6305)
PHONE..................................413 493-1298
Jeff Tomaszewski, *General Mgr*
Brian Hunt, *Principal*
EMP: 50
SALES (corp-wide): 5.3B **Publicly Held**
WEB: www.sonoco.com
SIC: 2631 2655 Paperboard Mill Mfg Fiber Cans/Drums
PA: Sonoco Products Company
1 N 2nd St
Hartsville SC 29550
843 383-7000

(G-11660)
SPRINGDALE MACHINE & GEAR CO
21 Temple St (01040-3423)
P.O. Box 829 (01041-0829)
PHONE..................................413 536-2976
Glenn Carboneau, *President*
Phyllis Carboneau, *Treasurer*
Lynn McKinnon, *Clerk*
EMP: 5 **EST:** 1946
SQ FT: 10,000
SALES: 1MM **Privately Held**
WEB: www.springdalemachine.com
SIC: 3599 Mfg Industrial Machinery

(G-11661)
STIEBEL ELTRON INC
242 Suffolk St (01040-5462)
PHONE..................................413 535-1734
Frank Stiebel, *President*
▼ **EMP:** 6
SQ FT: 3,000
SALES (est): 664.9K
SALES (corp-wide): 611.3MM **Privately Held**
SIC: 3423 3433 Mfg Hand/Edge Tools Mfg Heating Equipment-Nonelectric
HQ: Stiebel Eltron Gmbh & Co. Kg
Dr.-Stiebel-Str. 33
Holzminden 37603
553 170-2702

(G-11662)
UNI-PAC INC
Also Called: UNI Pac
150 Middle Water St (01040-5588)
PHONE..................................413 534-5284
George N Leclair, *President*
George N Le Clair, *President*
Mary Leclair, *Purch Mgr*
John Leclair, *Human Res Dir*
▲ **EMP:** 60 **EST:** 1937
SQ FT: 78,000
SALES (est): 12.5MM **Privately Held**
WEB: www.uni-pac.com
SIC: 2652 2657 Mfg Setup Paperboard Boxes Mfg Folding Paperboard Boxes

(G-11663)
UNITED INNOVATIONS INC
120 Whiting Farms Rd # 2 (01040-2812)
PHONE..................................413 533-7500
Christopher A Parent, *President*
James Richmond, *Admin Sec*
EMP: 10
SQ FT: 50,000
SALES: 2MM **Privately Held**
SIC: 3829 Mfg Measuring/Controlling Devices

(G-11664)
UNIVERSAL PLASTICS CORPORATION (PA)
Also Called: Universal Bath Systems
75 Whiting Farms Rd (01040-2831)
PHONE..................................413 592-4791
Joseph Peters, *CEO*
Jay Kumar, *President*
Sunil Kumar, *Principal*
Paul Flebotte, *Prdtn Mgr*
Don Moreau, *QC Mgr*
EMP: 85
SQ FT: 65,000
SALES (est): 21.3MM **Privately Held**
WEB: www.universalplastics.com
SIC: 3089 Mfg Plastic Products

(G-11665)
US TSUBAKI POWER TRANSM LLC
821 Main St (01040-5449)
PHONE..................................413 536-1576
Charles Monty, *General Mgr*
Denise Forgue, *Buyer*
Gary Bomar, *Engineer*
Robert Hogan, *Engineer*
James Shannon, *Engineer*
EMP: 250
SQ FT: 210,000 **Privately Held**
SIC: 3568 Mfg Power Transmission Equipment
HQ: U.S. Tsubaki Power Transmission Llc
301 E Marquardt Dr
Wheeling IL 60090
847 459-9500

(G-11666)
WALTER DRAKE INC (PA)
85 Sargeant St (01040-5632)
P.O. Box 691 (01041-0691)
PHONE..................................413 536-5463
James J Mc Carthy, *President*
Joseph M Feigen, *Vice Pres*
EMP: 7 **EST:** 1959
SQ FT: 70,000

▲ = Import ▼=Export
◆ =Import/Export

SALES (est): 2.7MM **Privately Held**
WEB: www.walterdrake.com
SIC: 3089 3081 2671 Mfg Plastic Products Mfg Unsupported Plastic Film/Sheet Mfg Packaging Paper/Film

(G-11667)
WESTSIDE FINISHING CO INC
15 Samosett St (01040-6112)
PHONE..................................413 533-4909
Brian Bell, *President*
Jeanne L Bell, *Vice Pres*
EMP: 40 **EST:** 1965
SQ FT: 20,000
SALES (est): 5.5MM **Privately Held**
WEB: www.wsfinish.com
SIC: 3479 Coating/Engraving Service

Hopedale
Worcester County

(G-11668)
ABS PALLET
72 Laurelwood Dr (01747-1953)
PHONE..................................508 246-1041
Thomas Abbruzzese, *Owner*
EMP: 3
SALES (est): 158.4K **Privately Held**
WEB: www.abspallet.com
SIC: 2448 Pallet And Crate Manufacture And Management

(G-11669)
AEREO INC
2 Rosenfeld Dr Ste F (01747-2114)
PHONE..................................617 861-8287
Chaitanya Kanojia, *President*
Ramon Rivera, *Corp Secy*
Amish Jani, *Director*
EMP: 35
SALES (est): 10.9MM **Privately Held**
WEB: www.bamboom.com
SIC: 3577 Mfg Computer Peripheral Equipment

(G-11670)
COLCORD MACHINE CO INC
2 Rosenfeld Dr Ste G (01747-2114)
PHONE..................................508 634-8840
Robert Colcord, *President*
Robert L Colcord, *President*
EMP: 14
SQ FT: 4,000
SALES (est): 1.6MM **Privately Held**
SIC: 3599 Machine Shop

(G-11671)
EXPOSE SIGNS & GRAPHICS INC
13 Airport Rd (01747-1547)
PHONE..................................508 381-0941
Andrew Clark, *President*
Marjorie McCurley, *Office Mgr*
EMP: 4
SALES: 390K **Privately Held**
SIC: 3993 Mfg Signs/Advertising Specialties

(G-11672)
FORT HILL SIGN PRODUCTS INC
13 Airport Rd (01747-1547)
PHONE..................................781 321-4320
Paula Dolan, *Clerk*
EMP: 9 **EST:** 1908
SQ FT: 3,500
SALES (est): 963.8K **Privately Held**
WEB: www.forthillsigns.com
SIC: 3479 3089 3083 3544 Engravers Of Brass Steel & Plastics Mfg Of Plastic Letters Vinyl Signs & Gold Leaf Applicating Equipment

(G-11673)
GREEN MOUNTAIN CHOCOLATE CO (PA)
1 Rosenfeld Dr (01747-2110)
PHONE..................................508 473-9060
William Campbell, *President*
Lisa Campbell, *Treasurer*
▲ **EMP:** 6
SQ FT: 8,000
SALES: 2.5MM **Privately Held**
WEB: www.greenmountainchocolate.com
SIC: 2066 5947 Mfg Chocolate/Cocoa Prdt Ret Gifts/Novelties

(G-11674)
JENA PIEZOSYSTEM INC
2 Rosenfeld Dr Ste B (01747-2114)
PHONE..................................508 634-6688
James Litynski, *President*
Peter Viglas, *Sales Engr*
▲ **EMP:** 3
SQ FT: 2,000
SALES (est): 270K **Privately Held**
WEB: www.piezojena.com
SIC: 3625 Whol Fiber Switches And Positioning Equipment

(G-11675)
L&E FLOORCOVERING
10 Mellen St (01747-1526)
PHONE..................................508 473-0723
Lucien Bejnoche, *Partner*
Ed Feijl, *Partner*
EMP: 3
SALES (est): 229.9K **Privately Held**
SIC: 3069 Mfg Fabricated Rubber Products

(G-11676)
LARAD EQUIPMENT CORP
18 Menfi Way (01747-1542)
PHONE..................................508 473-2700
Robert Bernstein, *President*
EMP: 5
SQ FT: 2,400
SALES: 350K **Privately Held**
WEB: www.larad.com
SIC: 3494 Mfg Valves/Pipe Fittings

(G-11677)
M C MACHINE CO INC
98 Mill St (01747-2002)
P.O. Box 9 (01747-0009)
PHONE..................................508 473-3642
Michael Cogliandro Jr, *President*
EMP: 6
SQ FT: 15,000
SALES (est): 809.6K **Privately Held**
SIC: 3599 3965 Machine Shop & Mfg Fasteners

(G-11678)
MILFORD MANUFACTURING SVCS LLC
4 Business Way (01747-1540)
PHONE..................................508 478-8544
Jason Price, *Mng Member*
Edward R Price,
▲ **EMP:** 100
SQ FT: 110,000
SALES (est): 14.1MM **Privately Held**
WEB: www.milfordmfg.com
SIC: 3672 7373 3577 3357 Mfg Printed Circuit Brds Computer Systems Design Mfg Computer Peripherals Nonfrs Wiredrwng/Insltng

(G-11679)
PBD PRODUCTIONS LLC
3b Landing Ln (01747-1531)
PHONE..................................508 482-9300
Rene Paradis, *Mng Member*
EMP: 10
SALES: 1.2MM **Privately Held**
SIC: 3446 2541 Mfg Architectural Mtlwrk Mfg Wood Partitions/Fixt

(G-11680)
PROTOTYPE SERVICES INC
17 Airport Rd (01747-1547)
PHONE..................................508 478-8887
Linda J Morrell, *President*
Linda Morrell, *Owner*
Hasmukh Doshi, *Principal*
EMP: 3
SQ FT: 4,000
SALES (est): 235.4K **Privately Held**
WEB: www.prototypeservices.com
SIC: 3599 Mfg Industrial Machinery

(G-11681)
REC MANUFACTURING CORP
50 Mellen St (01747-1522)
P.O. Box 5959, Holliston (01746-5959)
PHONE..................................508 634-7999
Robert E Chick Jr, *President*
Stephen M Chick, *President*
▼ **EMP:** 20 **EST:** 1943
SQ FT: 50,000
SALES (est): 4.8MM **Privately Held**
WEB: www.recmfg.com
SIC: 3089 Mfg Plastic Products

(G-11682)
ROSENFELD CONCRETE CORP (HQ)
75 Plain St (01747-2100)
P.O. Box 9187, Boston (02114-9187)
PHONE..................................508 473-7200
Jeanne-M Boylan, *President*
EMP: 45
SQ FT: 2,400
SALES (est): 3.5MM
SALES (corp-wide): 121MM **Privately Held**
SIC: 3273 1442 Mfg Ready-Mixed Concrete Construction Sand/Gravel
PA: Boston Sand & Gravel Company Inc
100 N Washington St Fl 2
Boston MA 02114
617 227-9000

(G-11683)
SPECTROS INSTRUMENTS INC
17d Airport Rd (01747-1547)
PHONE..................................508 478-1648
Dennis J Glennon, *President*
Marlene Dunia, *Office Mgr*
EMP: 3
SALES (est): 357.5K **Privately Held**
SIC: 3826 Mfg Analytical Instruments

(G-11684)
SUDBURY GRANITE & MARBLE INC (PA)
12 Rosenfeld Dr (01747-2111)
PHONE..................................508 478-3976
Mohamad C Hachicho, *President*
Ademilde Melquiades Dos Reis, *President*
▲ **EMP:** 20
SALES (est): 7.8MM **Privately Held**
WEB: www.sudbury-granite.com
SIC: 1411 5032 Dimension Stone Quarry Whol Brick/Stone Material

Hopkinton
Middlesex County

(G-11685)
A ARENA & SONS INC
159 Ash St (01748-1903)
PHONE..................................508 435-3673
Paul Arena, *President*
Joseph Arena, *Vice Pres*
Robert Arena, *Vice Pres*
Marie Arena, *Treasurer*
Joanne Arena, *Clerk*
EMP: 6 **EST:** 1956
SQ FT: 6,250
SALES (est): 522.5K **Privately Held**
SIC: 2011 Meat Packers

(G-11686)
ABB INSTALLATION PRODUCTS INC
Aster Products
86 South St (01748-2213)
PHONE..................................508 435-0101
EMP: 102
SALES (corp-wide): 34.3B **Privately Held**
SIC: 3357 Mfg Fiber Optic Couplers
HQ: Abb Installation Products Inc.
860 Ridge Lake Blvd
Memphis TN 38120
901 252-5000

(G-11687)
ACBEL (USA) POLYTECH INC
227 South St (01748-2208)
PHONE..................................508 625-1768
Jesse Wang, *Manager*
EMP: 7 **Privately Held**
SIC: 3572 3571 Mfg Computer Storage Devices Mfg Electronic Computers
HQ: Acbel (Usa) Polytech, Inc.
251 Dominion Dr Ste 111
Morrisville NC 27560
919 388-4316

(G-11688)
AIR PRODUCTS AND CHEMICALS INC
52 Wilson St (01748-1200)
PHONE..................................508 435-3428
Michael Tetreault, *Opers-Prdtn-Mfg*
EMP: 20
SALES (corp-wide): 8.9B **Publicly Held**
WEB: www.airproducts.com
SIC: 2813 Whol Chemicals/Products
PA: Air Products And Chemicals, Inc.
7201 Hamilton Blvd
Allentown PA 18195
610 481-4911

(G-11689)
ALAKAI TECHNOLOGIES CORP
22 Piazza Ln (01748-1045)
PHONE..................................774 248-4964
Brian D Morrison, *President*
EMP: 5
SALES (est): 519.3K **Privately Held**
SIC: 3812 Mfg Search/Navigation Equipment

(G-11690)
ARTERIOCYTE MED SYSTEMS INC
45 South St (01748-2237)
PHONE..................................508 497-9350
Donald J Brown, *Manager*
EMP: 10
SALES (corp-wide): 4.7MM **Privately Held**
SIC: 3841 Mfg Surgical/Medical Instruments
HQ: Arteriocyte Medical Systems, Inc.
45 South St Ste 3c
Hopkinton MA 01748

(G-11691)
ARTERIOCYTE MED SYSTEMS INC (HQ)
Also Called: Isto Biologics
45 South St Ste 3c (01748-2237)
PHONE..................................866 660-2674
Donald Brown, *CEO*
John Mitchell, *COO*
EMP: 25
SQ FT: 8,000
SALES (est): 4.7MM **Privately Held**
SIC: 3845 Mfg Electromedical Equipment
PA: Isto Technologies Ii, Llc
45 South St Ste C
Hopkinton MA 01748
888 705-4786

(G-11692)
ATK SPACE SYSTEMS INC
65 South St Ste 105 (01748-2234)
PHONE..................................508 497-9457
EMP: 7
SQ FT: 15,000 **Publicly Held**
SIC: 3812 Mfg Search/Navigation Equipment
HQ: Atk Space Systems Inc.
11310 Frederick Ave
Beltsville MD 20705
301 595-5500

(G-11693)
BENCO DENTAL
63 South St Ste 194 (01748-2229)
PHONE..................................508 435-3000
Chuck Cohen, *President*
EMP: 30
SALES (est): 2.9MM **Privately Held**
SIC: 3843 Whol Medical/Hospital Equipment

(G-11694)
CALIPER LIFE SCIENCES INC (DH)
68 Elm St (01748-1668)
PHONE..................................203 954-9442
E Kevin Hrusovsky, *President*
Bruce J Bal, *Senior VP*
Paula J Cassidy, *Senior VP*
Stephen E Creager, *Senior VP*
Joseph H Griffith IV, *Vice Pres*
▲ **EMP:** 200
SQ FT: 137,000

SALES (est): 99.8MM
SALES (corp-wide): 2.7B **Publicly Held**
WEB: www.caliperls.com
SIC: 3826 Mfg Analytical Instruments

(G-11695)
CAMBRDGE RES INSTRMNTATION INC
Also Called: C R I
68 Elm St (01748-1602)
PHONE..................................781 935-9099
George Abe, *President*
Peter Miller, *Vice Pres*
Theodore I Les, *CFO*
EMP: 35
SALES (est): 5.3MM
SALES (corp-wide): 2.7B **Publicly Held**
WEB: www.cri-inc.com
SIC: 3827 8733 8731 Mfg Optical Instruments/Lenses Noncommercial Research Organization Commercial Physical Research
HQ: Caliper Life Sciences, Inc.
68 Elm St
Hopkinton MA 01748

(G-11696)
CIELO THERAPEUTICS INC
1 Meadowland Dr (01748-1570)
PHONE..................................617 649-2005
EMP: 5
SALES (est): 373.2K **Privately Held**
SIC: 2834 Mfg Pharmaceutical Preparations

(G-11697)
CONTROL TECHNOLOGY CORPORATION (PA)
Also Called: C T C
25 South St (01748-2217)
PHONE..................................508 435-9596
Thomas Schermerhorn, *President*
F Steven Crater, *Vice Pres*
Tim Leavitt, *Engineer*
Kenneth Crater, *Treasurer*
Lenore Tracey, *Director*
EMP: 25
SQ FT: 15,000
SALES (est): 3MM **Privately Held**
WEB: www.control.com
SIC: 3625 Mfg Relays/Industrial Controls

(G-11698)
CRI RUBBER LLC (HQ)
Also Called: C R I
5 Ridge Rd (01748-1147)
PHONE..................................508 657-8488
Leya Thomas,
Prijoei K Abraham,
EMP: 3
SALES (est): 550K
SALES (corp-wide): 955.7K **Privately Held**
SIC: 3011 Mfg Tires/Inner Tubes
PA: Cochin Rubbers International Llc
241 Francis Ave
Mansfield MA 02048
877 289-0364

(G-11699)
CTS VALPEY CORPORATION (HQ)
75 South St (01748-2204)
PHONE..................................508 435-6831
Michael J Ferrantino Jr, *President*
Walt Oliwa, *Senior VP*
Lee Ann Gibree, *Materials Mgr*
Michael J Kroll, *CFO*
Matthew Perry, *Info Tech Mgr*
EMP: 49
SQ FT: 32,000
SALES (est): 8MM
SALES (corp-wide): 470.4MM **Publicly Held**
WEB: www.valpeyfisher.com
SIC: 3825 3829 Mfg Electrical Measuring Instruments Mfg Measuring/Controlling Devices
PA: Cts Corporation
4925 Indiana Ave
Lisle IL 60532
630 577-8800

(G-11700)
DIGILAB INC
105 South St (01748-2206)
PHONE..................................508 305-2410
Joe Griffin, *President*
EMP: 54
SALES (est): 8.8MM **Privately Held**
SIC: 3821 Mfg Lab Apparatus/Furniture

(G-11701)
ECKERT ZIEGLER RADIOPHARMA INC (PA)
63 South St Ste 110 (01748-2229)
PHONE..................................508 497-0060
Dr Andre Hess, *President*
Rainer Schiller, *Treasurer*
Amanda North, *Manager*
Andrea Hawerkamp, *Director*
Dr Roger Knopp, *Director*
EMP: 8 **EST:** 2009
SALES (est): 1.2MM **Privately Held**
SIC: 3821 Mfg Lab Apparatus/Furniture

(G-11702)
ELI LILLY AND COMPANY
Also Called: Elanco Animal Health
3 Maria Ln (01748-2422)
PHONE..................................508 435-8326
EMP: 13
SALES (corp-wide): 24.5B **Publicly Held**
WEB: www.lilly.com
SIC: 2834 Mfg Pharmaceutical Preparations
PA: Eli Lilly And Company
Lilly Corporate Ctr
Indianapolis IN 46285
317 276-2000

(G-11703)
EM &M BUILDERS LLC
59 Oakhurst Rd (01748-2721)
PHONE..................................508 497-3446
Derek A Desrochers, *Manager*
EMP: 3
SALES (est): 172.9K **Privately Held**
SIC: 3572 Mfg Computer Storage Devices

(G-11704)
EMC CORPORATION
228 South St (01748-2233)
PHONE..................................508 249-5883
Tim Hay, *Accounts Mgr*
Kevin Gray, *Marketing Mgr*
James Donovan, *Consultant*
EMP: 100
SALES (corp-wide): 90.6B **Publicly Held**
SIC: 3572 Mfg Computer Storage Devices
HQ: Emc Corporation
176 South St
Hopkinton MA 01748
508 435-1000

(G-11705)
EMC CORPORATION
171 South St (01748-2222)
PHONE..................................508 346-2900
Scott Hoag, *Vice Pres*
Rich Cole, *Engineer*
Brian Millette, *Engineer*
Helene Winn, *Program Mgr*
Geoffrey Reid, *Software Engr*
EMP: 50
SALES (corp-wide): 90.6B **Publicly Held**
WEB: www.emc.com
SIC: 3572 Mfg Computer Storage Devices
HQ: Emc Corporation
176 South St
Hopkinton MA 01748
508 435-1000

(G-11706)
EMC CORPORATION (HQ)
Also Called: Dell EMC
176 South St (01748-2230)
PHONE..................................508 435-1000
David I Goulden, *President*
Richard Cheung, *Partner*
Scott Crossman, *Partner*
Russ Greene, *Partner*
David Treadwell, *Division Mgr*
▼ **EMP:** 500
SQ FT: 1,681,000
SALES (est): 30.5B
SALES (corp-wide): 90.6B **Publicly Held**
WEB: www.emc.com
SIC: 3572 7372 7371 3577 Mfg Computer Storage Dvc Prepackaged Software Svc Computer Programming Svc Mfg Computer Peripherals
PA: Dell Technologies Inc.
1 Dell Way
Round Rock TX 78682
800 289-3355

(G-11707)
EMC CORPORATION
117 South St (01748-2206)
PHONE..................................508 435-0369
EMP: 10
SALES (corp-wide): 90.6B **Publicly Held**
SIC: 3572 Mfg Computer Storage Devices
HQ: Emc Corporation
176 South St
Hopkinton MA 01748
508 435-1000

(G-11708)
EMC CORPORATION
80 South St (01748-2205)
PHONE..................................800 445-2588
EMP: 10
SALES (corp-wide): 90.6B **Publicly Held**
SIC: 3572 Mfg Computer Storage Devices
HQ: Emc Corporation
176 South St
Hopkinton MA 01748
508 435-1000

(G-11709)
EMC GLOBAL HOLDINGS COMPANY
176 South St (01748-2230)
PHONE..................................508 544-2852
Tyler Wise Johnson II, *Trustee*
EMP: 4 **EST:** 2002
SALES (est): 410.6K
SALES (corp-wide): 90.6B **Publicly Held**
SIC: 3572 Mfg Computer Storage Devices
PA: Dell Technologies Inc.
1 Dell Way
Round Rock TX 78682
800 289-3355

(G-11710)
EMC INTERNATIONAL HOLDINGS INC (DH)
Also Called: Emc2
176 South St (01748-2230)
P.O. Box 9103 (01748-9103)
PHONE..................................508 435-1000
Joseph Tucci, *President*
W Paul Fitzgerald, *Vice Pres*
Rich Colbert, *Director*
Paul T Dacier, *Director*
Daniel Roche, *Director*
EMP: 3
SQ FT: 205,000
SALES: 20B
SALES (corp-wide): 90.6B **Publicly Held**
SIC: 3572 3577 Mfg Computer Storage Devices Mfg Computer Peripheral Equipment
HQ: Emc Corporation
176 South St
Hopkinton MA 01748
508 435-1000

(G-11711)
EMC INVESTMENT CORPORATION
176 South St (01748-2230)
PHONE..................................508 435-1000
EMP: 3 **EST:** 2017
SALES (est): 187.7K
SALES (corp-wide): 90.6B **Publicly Held**
SIC: 3572 Mfg Computer Storage Devices
PA: Dell Technologies Inc.
1 Dell Way
Round Rock TX 78682
800 289-3355

(G-11712)
EVERETT CUSTOM WOODWORKING
32 W Main St (01748-1620)
PHONE..................................508 435-7675
Dwight Everett, *Principal*
EMP: 3
SALES (est): 215.1K **Privately Held**
SIC: 2431 Mfg Millwork

(G-11713)
FISHMAN CORPORATION
192 South St (01748-2209)
PHONE..................................508 435-2115
Scott W Beebe, *President*
Virginia Beebe, *Shareholder*
▲ **EMP:** 17 **EST:** 1958
SQ FT: 12,000
SALES (est): 5.2MM **Privately Held**
WEB: www.fishmancorp.com
SIC: 3586 Mfg Measuring/Dispensing Pumps

(G-11714)
FLIMP MEDIA
2 Hayden Rowe St Ste 2 # 2 (01748-1946)
PHONE..................................508 435-5220
Wane Wall, *Partner*
Chip Arndt, *Exec VP*
Heidi Thompson, *Marketing Staff*
Armin Kaspar, *Web Dvlpr*
Jeff Fritts, *Creative Dir*
EMP: 25
SALES (est): 2.1MM **Privately Held**
SIC: 7372 Prepackaged Software Services

(G-11715)
FOSTER CARROLL INC
2 Chestnut St (01748-2506)
PHONE..................................508 497-0068
Michael J Carroll, *President*
EMP: 4
SALES (est): 394.5K **Privately Held**
SIC: 2752 Lithographic Commercial Printing

(G-11716)
GLIXX LABORATORIES INC
63 South St Ste 130 (01748-2229)
PHONE..................................781 333-5348
Jun Xian, *President*
Fushuang Liu, *Director*
EMP: 9 **EST:** 2014
SALES (est): 950.2K **Privately Held**
SIC: 2869 Testing Laboratory

(G-11717)
GM MERC INC
158 W Main St (01748-2148)
PHONE..................................508 878-1305
Torben Pedersen, *President*
EMP: 3
SALES: 1MM **Privately Held**
WEB: www.gmcope.com
SIC: 3812 Mfg Search/Navigation Equipment

(G-11718)
HUTCHINSON AROSPC & INDUST INC (DH)
82 South St (01748-2205)
PHONE..................................508 417-7000
Julie Holland, *CEO*
Robert Anderson, *CEO*
Kevin Underwood, *Materials Mgr*
Thomas David, *Engineer*
Shano Cristilli, *Treasurer*
▲ **EMP:** 262 **EST:** 1943
SALES (est): 94MM
SALES (corp-wide): 8.1B **Publicly Held**
WEB: www.barrycontrols.com
SIC: 3714 3061 3724 Mfg Motor Vehicle Parts/Accessories Mfg Mechanical Rubber Goods Mfg Aircraft Engines/Parts
HQ: Hutchinson Corporation
460 Fuller Ave Ne
Grand Rapids MI 49503
616 459-4541

(G-11719)
HUTCHINSON AROSPC & INDUST INC
Also Called: Barry Controls
82 South St (01748-2205)
PHONE..................................508 417-7000
Cedric Duclos, *CEO*
Tom Foley, *General Mgr*
Paul Stupinski, *Vice Pres*
Donovan Deal, *Project Mgr*
Mike Hamilton, *Engineer*
EMP: 200

SALES (corp-wide): 8.1B **Publicly Held**
WEB: www.barrycontrols.com
SIC: 3545 Mfg Machine Tool Accessories
HQ: Hutchinson Aerospace & Industry, Inc.
82 South St
Hopkinton MA 01748
508 417-7000

(G-11720)
HUTCHINSON AROSPC & INDUST INC
Vlier
82 South St (01748-2205)
PHONE....................................508 417-7000
Tom Foley, *General Mgr*
EMP: 30
SALES (corp-wide): 8.1B **Publicly Held**
WEB: www.barrycontrols.com
SIC: 3699 Mfg Electrical Equipment/Supplies
HQ: Hutchinson Aerospace & Industry, Inc.
82 South St
Hopkinton MA 01748
508 417-7000

(G-11721)
ILLINOIS TOOL WORKS INC
ITW Electronics Assembly Eqp
35 Parkwood Dr Ste 10 (01748-1727)
PHONE....................................508 520-0083
Isaiah Smith, *Sales Engr*
Tammy McCrohan, *Branch Mgr*
EMP: 50
SALES (corp-wide): 14.7B **Publicly Held**
SIC: 3565 3569 Mfg Packaging Machinery Mfg General Industrial Machinery
PA: Illinois Tool Works Inc.
155 Harlem Ave
Glenview IL 60025
847 724-7500

(G-11722)
INSENSE MEDICAL LLC
4 Wyman Ln (01748-1944)
PHONE....................................518 316-4759
Kimberly Southern, *CEO*
EMP: 3
SALES (est): 201.3K **Privately Held**
SIC: 3829 Mfg Measuring/Controlling Devices

(G-11723)
ISILON SYSTEMS LLC
176 South St (01748-2209)
PHONE....................................206 315-7500
Christopher Boyd, *Regional Mgr*
Todd Haller, *Area Mgr*
Raj Takher, *Accounting Mgr*
Steve Orlick, *Manager*
Brandon Ward, *Manager*
EMP: 4
SALES (corp-wide): 90.6B **Publicly Held**
SIC: 3674 Semiconductors And Related Devices, Nsk
HQ: Isilon Systems Llc
505 1st Ave S
Seattle WA 98104
206 315-7500

(G-11724)
KAMEL PERIPHERALS INC (PA)
88a Elm St Ste 7 (01748-1675)
PHONE....................................508 435-7771
Michael Le Vangie, *President*
▲ **EMP:** 29
SQ FT: 10,000
SALES (est): 2.1MM **Privately Held**
WEB: www.kamel-peripherals.com
SIC: 3577 Mfg Computer Peripheral Pdts

(G-11725)
KENNETH CROSBY CO INC
103 South St (01748-2206)
PHONE....................................508 497-0048
Susan Costa, *Principal*
EMP: 10 **EST:** 2015
SALES (est): 253.3K **Privately Held**
SIC: 3625 Mfg Relays/Industrial Controls

(G-11726)
LABTECH INC (PA)
114 South St (01748-2214)
PHONE....................................508 435-5500
Ke Hu, *President*
Marcus Guerrero, *Sales Mgr*
Xiaowei Jiao, *Manager*
▲ **EMP:** 5 **EST:** 2011
SALES (est): 4.6MM **Privately Held**
SIC: 3821 Mfg Lab Apparatus/Furniture

(G-11727)
MEDTRNIC SOFAMOR DANEK USA INC
239 South St Ste 2 (01748-2250)
PHONE....................................508 497-0792
Mike Mantegia, *Branch Mgr*
EMP: 5 **Privately Held**
WEB: www.mysinustools.com
SIC: 3841 Mfg Surgical/Medical Instruments
HQ: Medtronic Sofamor Danek Usa, Inc.
1800 Pyramid Pl
Memphis TN 38132
901 396-3133

(G-11728)
MILLIBAR INC
122 South St Rear (01748-2209)
PHONE....................................508 488-9870
Brian C Ferri, *Principal*
Brian Ferri, *Director*
▲ **EMP:** 10 **EST:** 2012
SALES (est): 1MM **Privately Held**
SIC: 3563 Mfg Air/Gas Compressors

(G-11729)
MINUTEMAN GOVERNANCE INC
43 Forest Ln (01748-3201)
PHONE....................................508 837-3004
John Moynihan, *Principal*
EMP: 4
SALES (est): 278.2K **Privately Held**
SIC: 2752 Lithographic Commercial Printing

(G-11730)
NORTHEAST LENS CORP
118 South St (01748-2209)
PHONE....................................617 964-6797
EMP: 37
SQ FT: 4,000
SALES (est): 4.5MM **Privately Held**
SIC: 3851 Mfg Eyeglasses

(G-11731)
PERKINELMER INC
68 Elm St Bldg 2 (01748-1602)
PHONE....................................508 435-9500
Sunand Banerji, *Engineer*
Rick Anselmo, *Technology*
EMP: 13
SALES (corp-wide): 2.7B **Publicly Held**
SIC: 3826 Mfg Analytical Instruments
PA: Perkinelmer, Inc.
940 Winter St
Waltham MA 02451
781 663-6900

(G-11732)
PHOSPHOREX INCORPORATED
106 South St (01748-2207)
PHONE....................................508 435-9100
Bin Wu, *Director*
EMP: 10
SQ FT: 5,000
SALES (est): 2MM **Privately Held**
SIC: 2834 Mfg Pharmaceutical Preparations

(G-11733)
PRECISION DIGITAL CORPORATION
233 South St (01748-2208)
PHONE....................................508 655-7300
Jeffrey L Peters, *President*
Scott Ewen, *Vice Pres*
Alan Williams, *Vice Pres*
Orod Bavar, *Engineer*
Jose Umana, *Engineer*
▲ **EMP:** 37
SQ FT: 9,000
SALES (est): 9.8MM **Privately Held**
WEB: www.predig.com
SIC: 3823 Mfg Process Control Instruments

(G-11734)
PRINT WORKS INC
25 South St Ste 2b (01748-2217)
PHONE....................................508 589-4626
Jack O'Leary, *President*
EMP: 8
SQ FT: 6,000
SALES (est): 831.3K **Privately Held**
WEB: www.theprintworks.net
SIC: 2752 Lithographic Commercial Printing

(G-11735)
SIGN SYSTEM SOLUTIONS LLC
7 Sadie Ln (01748-2582)
PHONE....................................508 497-6340
Richard J Cameron, *Principal*
EMP: 14
SALES (est): 1.2MM **Privately Held**
SIC: 3993 Mfg Signs/Advertising Specialties

(G-11736)
SOLECT ENERGY DEVELOPMENT LLC
45 South St (01748-2237)
PHONE....................................508 250-8358
Rick Mayhem, *Branch Mgr*
EMP: 3
SALES (est): 125.7K **Privately Held**
SIC: 3674 Mfg Semiconductors/Related Devices

(G-11737)
SOLECT ENERGY DEVELOPMENT LLC
89 Hayden Rowe St Ste E (01748-2507)
PHONE....................................508 598-3511
Kenneth Driscoll, *CEO*
Alex Keally, *Senior VP*
John Mosher, *Vice Pres*
Matt Shortsleeve, *Vice Pres*
Michael Whatmough, *Controller*
EMP: 13
SALES (est): 3.6MM **Privately Held**
SIC: 3674 Mfg Semiconductors/Related Devices

(G-11738)
SPRING BNK PHARMACEUTICALS INC (PA)
35 Parkwood Dr Ste 210 (01748-1729)
PHONE....................................508 473-5993
Martin Driscoll, *Ch of Bd*
Atif Abbas, *Vice Pres*
Kevin Leach, *Vice Pres*
Dillon Cleary, *Research*
Nezam H Afdhal, *Chief Mktg Ofcr*
EMP: 20
SQ FT: 12,200
SALES: 352K **Publicly Held**
SIC: 2834 Pharmaceutical Preparations

(G-11739)
STRYKER CORPORATION
Also Called: Stryker Biotech
35 South St Ste C (01748-2218)
PHONE....................................508 416-5200
Anthony Anastasi, *Accounts Mgr*
Brian Colborne, *Sales Staff*
Matthew Roland, *Sales Staff*
Dave Ranker, *Branch Mgr*
Christopher Hicks, *Manager*
EMP: 312
SALES (corp-wide): 13.6B **Publicly Held**
SIC: 3841 Mfg Surgical/Medical Instruments
PA: Stryker Corporation
2825 Airview Blvd
Portage MI 49002
269 389-4934

(G-11740)
TEST EVOLUTION CORPORATION
102 South St (01748-2207)
PHONE....................................508 377-5757
Lev Alperovich, *President*
Al Czamara, *President*
Bob Smith, *Engineer*
Rich Proto, *Design Engr*
EMP: 6 **EST:** 2007
SALES (est): 740K **Privately Held**
SIC: 3823 Mfg Process Control Instruments

(G-11741)
TTE LABORATORIES INC
Also Called: Tte Lab Services
77 Main St (01748-3118)
PHONE....................................800 242-6022
Benjamin Leverone, *CEO*
Brian Silven, *Vice Pres*
Jen Leverone, *Human Res Mgr*
Jim Macrae, *Sales Staff*
Aubrey Carr, *Director*
EMP: 18
SQ FT: 3,000
SALES (est): 4.5MM **Privately Held**
WEB: www.pipettes.com
SIC: 3823 Mfg Process Control Instruments

Housatonic
Berkshire County

(G-11742)
HOUSATONIC WELDING COMPANY
57 Van Dusenfled Rd (01236)
P.O. Box 596 (01236-0596)
PHONE....................................413 274-6631
Richard A Bailly, *Owner*
EMP: 3
SALES (est): 279.8K **Privately Held**
SIC: 7692 Welding Repair

Hubbardston
Worcester County

(G-11743)
CUSTOM WOODWORKING LLC
12 Old Westminster Rd (01452-1423)
PHONE....................................978 928-3366
Bryan Sasseville, *President*
EMP: 4
SALES (est): 369.1K **Privately Held**
SIC: 2431 Mfg Millwork

(G-11744)
HUBB EQUIPMENT INC
31 Old Boston Tpke (01452-1109)
PHONE....................................978 928-4258
Brian Handy, *President*
Wayne Handy, *Treasurer*
EMP: 5
SALES: 200K **Privately Held**
SIC: 7692 Welding Repair

(G-11745)
JACK DILLING
122 Worcester Rd (01452-1143)
PHONE....................................978 928-4002
Jack Dilling, *Owner*
EMP: 3
SALES (est): 247.1K **Privately Held**
SIC: 3599 Mfg Industrial Machinery

(G-11746)
STABILIZING TECHNOLOGIES LLC
45 Williamsville Rd (01452-1314)
PHONE....................................978 928-4142
EMP: 3
SALES (est): 157K **Privately Held**
SIC: 2869 Mfg Industrial Organic Chemicals

(G-11747)
WIDE ANGLE MARKETING INC
27d Old Colony Rd (01452-1127)
PHONE....................................978 928-5400
Kraig Kaijala, *President*
EMP: 20
SALES (est): 2.8MM **Privately Held**
SIC: 2431 Mfg Millwork

Hudson
Middlesex County

(G-11748)
2L INC
4 Kane Industrial Dr (01749-2906)
P.O. Box 105 (01749-0105)
PHONE..................................978 567-8867
Lance Nelson, *President*
EMP: 10
SALES (est): 1.7MM **Privately Held**
WEB: www.2linc.com
SIC: 3441 3555 Structural Metal Fabrication Mfg Printing Trades Machinery

(G-11749)
AC GENERAL INC
Also Called: Corporation
10 Technology Dr 316 (01749-2791)
PHONE..................................978 568-8229
Sandy Bouchard, *President*
EMP: 5
SALES (est): 346K **Privately Held**
SIC: 3625 Whol Electronic Parts/Equipment

(G-11750)
ACCUMET ENGINEERING CORP
518 Main St (01749-2966)
PHONE..................................978 568-8311
Adrian E Schrauwen, *President*
EMP: 28
SQ FT: 6,400
SALES (est): 5MM **Privately Held**
WEB: www.accumet.com
SIC: 3264 3471 7389 Mfg Porcelain Electrical Suppplies Plating/Polishing Service Business Services

(G-11751)
ADAPTIVE WRELESS SOLUTIONS LLC
577 Main St (01749-3096)
PHONE..................................978 875-6000
Bruce Thompson, *CEO*
Philip Hunt, *President*
EMP: 16
SALES (est): 3.1MM
SALES (corp-wide): 177.9K **Privately Held**
SIC: 3829 Mfg Measuring/Controlling Devices
HQ: Schneider Electric Systems Usa, Inc.
38 Neponset Ave
Foxboro MA 02035
508 543-8750

(G-11752)
ADVANCED CAM MANUFACTURING LLC
526 Main St (01749-2909)
PHONE..................................978 562-2825
Stephen Woodworth, *Manager*
EMP: 3
SALES (est): 245.8K **Privately Held**
SIC: 3999 Mfg Misc Products

(G-11753)
AIS GROUP HOLDINGS LLC (PA)
Also Called: A I S
4 Robert Rd (01749-1013)
PHONE..................................978 562-7500
Bruce Platzman, *CEO*
Arthur Maxwell, *Chairman*
Steve Savage, *COO*
Bryan Poist, *CFO*
◆ **EMP:** 3
SALES (est): 56.4MM **Privately Held**
SIC: 2522 Mfg Office Furniture-Nonwood

(G-11754)
ALTERNATE FINISHING INC
15 Kane Industrial Dr (01749-2905)
PHONE..................................978 567-9205
David Buswell, *President*
Robert Peterson, *Vice Pres*
Marie Mungillo, *Treasurer*
EMP: 7
SQ FT: 10,000
SALES (est): 879.1K **Privately Held**
WEB: www.alternatefinishing.com
SIC: 3471 Plating/Polishing Service

(G-11755)
ANVER CORPORATION
36 Parmenter Rd (01749-3214)
PHONE..................................978 568-0221
Franck M Vernooy, *President*
Anton J Vernooy, *Chairman*
Stephen Zaino, *Vice Pres*
Nathan Rossi, *Info Tech Mgr*
Aliette Vernooy, *Admin Sec*
▲ **EMP:** 62 **EST:** 1968
SQ FT: 54,000
SALES (est): 13.3MM **Privately Held**
WEB: www.anver.com
SIC: 3599 5084 3563 Mfg Industrial Machinery Whol Industrial Equipment Mfg Air/Gas Compressors

(G-11756)
ARROW MOCCASIN COMPANY
120 Central St Ste 2 (01749-1352)
P.O. Box 699 (01749-0699)
PHONE..................................978 562-7870
EMP: 8
SQ FT: 4,000
SALES (est): 586.5K **Privately Held**
WEB: www.arrowmoc.com
SIC: 3149 5661 Mfg & Ret Leather Moccasins

(G-11757)
ARTCRAFT BRAID CO LLC
11 Bonazzoli Ave (01749-2849)
PHONE..................................401 831-9077
Manuel Shaves, *Mng Member*
Eva Shaves,
▼ **EMP:** 20 **EST:** 1945
SQ FT: 50,000
SALES (est): 1.7MM **Privately Held**
SIC: 2298 Mfg Cordage/Twine

(G-11758)
AUCIELLO IRON WORKS INC (PA)
560 Main St Ste 6 (01749-2969)
PHONE..................................978 568-8382
Michael A Auciello, *President*
Ralph J Auciello, *Director*
Anthony R Auciello, *Admin Sec*
EMP: 25 **EST:** 1932
SQ FT: 17,000
SALES (est): 5.8MM **Privately Held**
WEB: www.aiw-inc.com
SIC: 3444 3441 Mfg Sheet Metalwork Structural Metal Fabrication

(G-11759)
BLANK INDUSTRIES INC
17 Brent Dr (01749-2903)
PHONE..................................855 887-3123
Andrew Blank, *CEO*
EMP: 10 **EST:** 2016
SALES (est): 1.2MM **Privately Held**
SIC: 2499 2899 5169 Mfg Wood Products Mfg Chemical Preparations Whol Chemicals/Products

(G-11760)
BORG DESIGN INC
19 Brent Dr (01749-2903)
PHONE..................................978 562-1559
Karl S Borg, *President*
K Andrew Borg, *Exec VP*
Brandon Borg, *Vice Pres*
Andrew Borg, *Engineer*
Tania Borg, *Marketing Staff*
EMP: 15
SQ FT: 22,000
SALES: 2.5MM **Privately Held**
WEB: www.borgdesign.com
SIC: 3599 Mfg Industrial Machinery

(G-11761)
BUTLER HOME PRODUCTS LLC (DH)
Also Called: Cleaner Home Living
2 Cabot Rd Ste 1 (01749-2942)
PHONE..................................508 597-8000
Robert Michelson, *CEO*
Harris Footer, *President*
Tim Young, *General Mgr*
Alan Weed, *Principal*
Mike Ortale, *Vice Pres*
▲ **EMP:** 10
SALES: 194.7MM
SALES (corp-wide): 337.5MM **Privately Held**
WEB: www.mrcleantools.com
SIC: 3991 2392 Mfg Brooms/Brushes Mfg Household Furnishings
HQ: Bradshaw International, Inc.
9409 Buffalo Ave
Rancho Cucamonga CA 91730
909 476-3884

(G-11762)
CENTERLINE TECHNOLOGIES LLC
577 Main St Ste 270 (01749-3056)
PHONE..................................978 568-1330
Hugh Muffloetto, *CEO*
Sandy Osbaldeston, *Office Mgr*
EMP: 13
SQ FT: 6,500
SALES (est): 2.1MM **Privately Held**
WEB: www.centerlinetech-usa.com
SIC: 3599 Mfg Industrial Machinery

(G-11763)
CLARK SOLUTIONS
10 Brent Dr (01749-2904)
PHONE..................................978 568-3400
▲ **EMP:** 12
SALES (est): 1.2MM **Privately Held**
SIC: 3561 3491 Mfg Pumps/Pumping Equipment Mfg Industrial Valves & Instrumentation

(G-11764)
CONNEXUS MANUFACTURING LLC
312 Main St (01749-1777)
PHONE..................................978 568-1831
Robert McKay,
Ann McKay,
EMP: 4
SQ FT: 4,000
SALES: 1MM **Privately Held**
SIC: 3824 Electromechanical Contract Assembly

(G-11765)
CONSOLDTED UTLITIES CORPORAION
503 River Rd (01749-2626)
PHONE..................................978 562-3500
EMP: 4 **EST:** 2014
SALES (est): 148K **Privately Held**
SIC: 1389 Oil And Gas Field Services, Nec, Nsk

(G-11766)
CONTRONAUTICS INCORPORATED
31 Wilkins St (01749-1801)
PHONE..................................978 568-8883
John Siwko, *President*
Eric Siwko, *Vice Pres*
Robert Siwko, *Project Mgr*
Dolores Siwko, *Treasurer*
Robert Siwco, *Manager*
EMP: 9
SQ FT: 14,500
SALES (est): 995.5K **Privately Held**
WEB: www.contronautics.com
SIC: 3822 3625 Mfg Environmental Controls Mfg Relays/Industrial Controls

(G-11767)
D & R PRODUCTS CO INC
455 River Rd (01749-2626)
P.O. Box 718 (01749-0718)
PHONE..................................978 562-4137
Cece Z Newman, *Ch of Bd*
Richard B Newman, *President*
Fran Hartigan, *Engineer*
Dave Hemsworth, *Engineer*
Christopher Maccready, *Project Engr*
EMP: 50
SQ FT: 26,500
SALES (est): 13MM **Privately Held**
WEB: www.drproducts.com
SIC: 3545 Mfg Machine Tool Accessories

(G-11768)
DIVERSIFIED MACHINING INC
9 Bonazzoli Ave Ste 24 (01749-2857)
PHONE..................................978 562-2213
Chester Macdonald, *President*
Robert Mitchell, *Treasurer*
EMP: 3
SQ FT: 1,250
SALES: 300K **Privately Held**
SIC: 3599 Mfg Industrial Machinery

(G-11769)
EDGETECH INSTRUMENTS INC
399 River Rd (01749)
PHONE..................................508 263-5900
Himanshu Patel, *President*
Stephanie Wild, *Corp Secy*
John Allcott, *COO*
Vicki Wilson, *Manager*
EMP: 15
SQ FT: 2,000
SALES (est): 3MM **Privately Held**
SIC: 3823 Mfg Process Control Instruments

(G-11770)
ELECTRO-MECHANICAL TECH CO
34 Tower St (01749-1721)
PHONE..................................978 562-7898
Peter E Mongeau, *President*
George E Danis, *Treasurer*
EMP: 6
SALES (est): 1MM **Privately Held**
SIC: 3669 Mfg Communications Equipment

(G-11771)
ENERGY RELEASE LLC
14 Brent Dr (01749-2904)
PHONE..................................978 466-9700
EMP: 4
SALES (est): 339.6K **Privately Held**
SIC: 3465 Mfg Automotive Stampings

(G-11772)
ENTWISTLE COMPANY (HQ)
6 Bigelow St (01749-2697)
PHONE..................................508 481-4000
Herbert I Corkin, *Ch of Bd*
Dennis Cummings, *Plant Mgr*
Joe Sousa, *Mfg Staff*
Mark Ryan, *Production*
Mark Cohen, *Purchasing*
▲ **EMP:** 120 **EST:** 1951
SQ FT: 134,000
SALES (est): 30.3MM
SALES (corp-wide): 40MM **Privately Held**
WEB: www.entwistleco.com
SIC: 3489 3599 3812 3537 Mfg Ordnance/Accessories Mfg Industrial Machinery Mfg Search/Navgatn Equip
PA: The Entwistle Trust
6 Bigelow St
Hudson MA 01749
508 481-4000

(G-11773)
FABCO MFG INC
Also Called: F M I
14 Bonazzoli Ave (01749-2850)
P.O. Box 340 (01749-0340)
PHONE..................................978 568-8519
Vincent S Natale, *President*
EMP: 35
SQ FT: 10,000
SALES (est): 7.2MM **Privately Held**
WEB: www.fabcomfg.com
SIC: 3444 Mfg Sheet Metalwork

(G-11774)
FLINTEC INC
18 Kane Industrial Dr (01749-2906)
PHONE..................................978 562-4548
Jeff Robidoux, *Principal*
Harry Lockery, *Chairman*
▲ **EMP:** 30
SQ FT: 13,000
SALES (est): 6.6MM
SALES (corp-wide): 1.7B **Privately Held**
WEB: www.flintec.net
SIC: 3679 8731 3825 Mfg Electronic Components Commercial Physical Research Mfg Electrical Measuring Instruments
HQ: Flintec Group Ab
Badhusgatan 12
Vasteras
211 201-55

(G-11775)
GRAND IMAGE INC
560 Main St Ste 3 (01749-2919)
PHONE.................................888 973-2622
Eli Luria, *President*
Javier Berdecio, *General Mgr*
Leah Luria, *Vice Pres*
Tamir Luria, *Office Mgr*
Jon Gabis, *Executive*
▲ **EMP:** 31
SQ FT: 20,000
SALES: 4.2MM **Privately Held**
WEB: www.grandimageinc.com
SIC: 3993 Mfg Signs/Advertising Specialties

(G-11776)
HUDSON POLY BAG INC
578 Main St (01749-3099)
PHONE.................................978 562-7566
William J Renwick, *President*
Richard D Renwick, *Vice Pres*
▼ **EMP:** 14 **EST:** 1965
SQ FT: 17,120
SALES (est): 3.9MM **Privately Held**
WEB: www.hudsonpoly.com
SIC: 3081 3949 Mfg Unsupported Plastic Film/Sheet Mfg Sporting/Athletic Goods

(G-11777)
INTEL MASSACHUSETTS INC
75 Reed Rd (01749-2895)
PHONE.................................978 553-4000
Arvind Sodhani, *President*
Linda Westphal, *Project Mgr*
Mark While, *Project Mgr*
Rakesh Koul, *Engineer*
Jon Krause, *Engineer*
▲ **EMP:** 900 **EST:** 1997
SALES (est): 117.7MM
SALES (corp-wide): 70.8B **Publicly Held**
WEB: www.scic.intel.com
SIC: 3674 Mfg Semiconductors/Related Devices
PA: Intel Corporation
2200 Mission College Blvd
Santa Clara CA 95054
408 765-8080

(G-11778)
INTEL NETWORK SYSTEMS INC (HQ)
77 Reed Rd (01749-2809)
PHONE.................................978 553-4000
Jeffrey Dawkins, *General Mgr*
Dale Myers, *Principal*
Craig Barrett, *Chairman*
Karl Brace, *Engineer*
Vicky Duerk, *Engineer*
EMP: 160
SQ FT: 117,139
SALES (est): 62.7MM
SALES (corp-wide): 70.8B **Publicly Held**
SIC: 3577 7373 Mfg Computer Peripheral Equipment Computer Systems Design
PA: Intel Corporation
2200 Mission College Blvd
Santa Clara CA 95054
408 765-8080

(G-11779)
INTELLITECH INTERNATIONAL INC
43 Broad St Ste B404 (01749-2557)
PHONE.................................978 212-7200
Joseph Tamker, *President*
▲ **EMP:** 10
SQ FT: 6,600
SALES (est): 1.6MM **Privately Held**
WEB: www.intellitech-intl.com
SIC: 3577 Mfg Computer Peripheral Equipment

(G-11780)
J W MACHINING INC
17 Bonazzoli Ave (01749-2850)
PHONE.................................978 562-5611
Charles Bourgeois, *President*
Darlene Bourgeois, *Corp Secy*
EMP: 11
SQ FT: 10,000
SALES (est): 1.5MM **Privately Held**
SIC: 3599 Machine Shop

(G-11781)
KATAHDIN INDUSTRIES INC (PA)
51 Parmenter Rd (01749-3213)
PHONE.................................781 329-1420
Tim Cabot, *President*
EMP: 45
SQ FT: 30,000
SALES (est): 17.7MM **Privately Held**
WEB: www.duralectra.com
SIC: 2851 3471 2899 Mfg Paints/Allied Products Plating/Polishing Service Mfg Chemical Preparations

(G-11782)
KONNEXT INC
7 Kane Industrial Dr # 2 (01749-2920)
PHONE.................................978 567-0800
EMP: 7
SQ FT: 6,000
SALES (est): 1.1MM **Privately Held**
WEB: www.konnextinc.com
SIC: 3643 Mfg Conductive Wiring Devices

(G-11783)
KOROLATH OF NEW ENGLAND INC
498 River Rd (01749-2621)
PHONE.................................978 562-7366
Arsenio Sousa, *General Mgr*
William J Cosgrove, *Vice Pres*
EMP: 13
SQ FT: 9,000
SALES (corp-wide): 16.5MM **Privately Held**
WEB: www.korolath.com
SIC: 3089 Mfg Plastic Products
HQ: Korolath Of New England, Inc.
310 Salem St
Woburn MA 01801
781 933-6004

(G-11784)
LAPOINTE HUDSON BROACH CO INC
11 Brent Dr (01749-2903)
PHONE.................................978 562-7943
Gary Ezor, *President*
▼ **EMP:** 33
SQ FT: 18,040
SALES (est): 5.1MM **Privately Held**
SIC: 3545 Mfg Machine Tool Accessories

(G-11785)
LEDGEROCK WELDING AND FABG
6 Loring St (01749-2341)
PHONE.................................978 562-6500
Robert Caras, *Owner*
EMP: 3
SQ FT: 5,000
SALES: 300K **Privately Held**
WEB: www.ledgerockfab.com
SIC: 7692 Welding Repair

(G-11786)
LINCOLN TOOL & MACHINE CORP
43 Parmenter Rd (01749-3213)
P.O. Box 443 (01749-0443)
PHONE.................................508 485-2940
Scott Ferrechia, *Vice Pres*
EMP: 30
SQ FT: 34,000
SALES: 5.3MM **Privately Held**
WEB: www.lincolntool.com
SIC: 3599 Mfg Industrial Machinery

(G-11787)
LLOYDS WOODWORKING INC
86 River St (01749-2010)
P.O. Box 281 (01749-0281)
PHONE.................................978 562-9007
Lloyd P Dubois, *President*
Doris E Dubois, *Treasurer*
EMP: 8
SALES (est): 1MM **Privately Held**
SIC: 2431 Mfg Millwork

(G-11788)
MACH MACHINE INC
569 Main St (01749-3035)
PHONE.................................978 274-5700
Daniel Olsen, *President*
EMP: 11
SQ FT: 2,500
SALES (est): 726.7K **Privately Held**
SIC: 3599 Mfg Industrial Machinery

(G-11789)
MACHINING FOR ELECTRONICS INC
4 Bigelow St (01749-2638)
P.O. Box 149 (01749-0149)
PHONE.................................978 562-7554
Metrophane Zayka, *President*
Nicholas Zayka, *Admin Sec*
EMP: 7
SQ FT: 10,000
SALES (est): 812.8K **Privately Held**
WEB: www.machiningforelectronics.com
SIC: 3599 Machine Shop

(G-11790)
MAGNOS INCORPORATED
9 Robert Rd (01749-1012)
PHONE.................................978 562-1173
Hugh Frederick, *President*
Jan Leibert, *Shareholder*
Diane Frederick, *Clerk*
EMP: 3
SQ FT: 2,000
SALES (est): 480.6K **Privately Held**
WEB: www.magnos.com
SIC: 3825 Mfg Electronic Equipment

(G-11791)
MEDUSA BREWING COMPANY INC
111 Main St (01749-2210)
PHONE.................................978 310-1933
Keith Antul, *President*
Thomas Sutter, *Treasurer*
Keith Sullivan, *Director*
EMP: 3 **EST:** 2013
SQ FT: 5,000
SALES (est): 309K **Privately Held**
SIC: 2082 Mfg Malt Beverages

(G-11792)
METAL HOUSINGS ENCLOSURES
34 Tower St (01749-1721)
PHONE.................................978 567-3324
EMP: 3
SALES (est): 178.1K **Privately Held**
SIC: 3399 Mfg Primary Metal Products

(G-11793)
MIDDLESEX RESEARCH MFG CO INC
27 Apsley St (01749-1594)
P.O. Box 444 (01749-0444)
PHONE.................................978 562-3697
Douglas Russell, *CEO*
Sara Coldwell, *Admin Sec*
▲ **EMP:** 20 **EST:** 1945
SQ FT: 100,000
SALES (est): 4.1MM **Privately Held**
WEB: www.mbcoct.com
SIC: 2295 2891 2261 Mfg Coated Fabrics Mfg Adhesives/Sealants Cotton Finishing Plant

(G-11794)
MINUTEMAN SEAMLESS GUTTERS
Also Called: Minuteman Leaseguard
2 Kane Industrial Dr (01749-2906)
PHONE.................................978 562-1744
Mike Deldon, *President*
EMP: 15
SQ FT: 4,000
SALES (est): 2.5MM
SALES (corp-wide): 45MM **Privately Held**
SIC: 3444 1761 Mfg & Installs Seamless Metal Gutters
HQ: Leafguard By Beldon, Inc.
5039 West Ave
San Antonio TX 78213
210 775-6722

(G-11795)
NETCO EXTRUDED PLASTICS INC
Also Called: New England Tape Co
30 Tower St (01749-1721)
PHONE.................................978 562-3485
Knut Schmiedeknecht, *President*
Francis W Murphy, *Admin Sec*
EMP: 20 **EST:** 1937
SQ FT: 48,000
SALES (est): 3.2MM
SALES (corp-wide): 769.8K **Privately Held**
WEB: www.netcoplastics.com
SIC: 3089 Mfg Plastic Products
HQ: Regumed Regulative Medizintechnik Gmbh
Robert-Koch-Str. 1a
Planegg 82152
898 546-101

(G-11796)
OCONNELL LOGGING LLC
27 Zina Rd (01749-1803)
PHONE.................................978 568-9740
EMP: 3
SALES (est): 200K **Privately Held**
SIC: 2411 Logging

(G-11797)
OK ENGINEERING INC
14 Main St Ste 10 (01749-2178)
P.O. Box 788 (01749-0788)
PHONE.................................978 562-1010
James T O'Keefe, *President*
Dan O' Keefe, *Treasurer*
EMP: 7
SALES (est): 834.1K **Privately Held**
SIC: 3559 Mfg Misc Industry Machinery

(G-11798)
ON LINE CONTROLS INC
9a Kane Industrial Dr (01749-2905)
PHONE.................................978 562-5353
Kay Dewolfe, *President*
EMP: 4 **EST:** 1980
SQ FT: 5,000
SALES: 671.3K **Privately Held**
WEB: www.onlinecontrols.com
SIC: 3829 Mfg Measuring/Controlling Devices

(G-11799)
OYO SPORTSTOYS INC
108 Forest Ave (01749-2974)
PHONE.................................978 264-2000
Thomas K Skripps, *President*
Laura Carolan, *Buyer*
Crystal Doane, *Accountant*
Sharon Stoddard, *Office Mgr*
Timothy Notaro, *Graphic Designe*
▲ **EMP:** 75
SALES (est): 6.6MM **Privately Held**
SIC: 3942 3944 Mfg Dolls/Stuffed Toys Mfg Games/Toys

(G-11800)
PATRIOT COATINGS INC
17 Kane Industrial Dr # 2 (01749-2921)
PHONE.................................978 567-9006
Roy Rector, *Officer*
EMP: 7
SALES (est): 1.1MM **Privately Held**
SIC: 3499 Mfg Misc Fabricated Metal Products

(G-11801)
PATTEN MACHINE INC
299 Central St (01749-1334)
PHONE.................................978 562-9847
Wayne E Cavanagh, *CEO*
EMP: 11
SQ FT: 5,000
SALES (est): 1.3MM **Privately Held**
SIC: 3599 3069 Metal Machine Shop

(G-11802)
PLASTIC MOLDING MFG INC (PA)
34 Tower St (01749-1721)
PHONE.................................978 567-1000
George E Danis, *Principal*
Dave Jones, *VP Opers*
Jon Gaylord, *Prdtn Mgr*
Don Marut, *Maintence Staff*

GEOGRAPHIC

EMP: 53
SQ FT: 50,000
SALES (est): 17.2MM **Privately Held**
SIC: 3089 Mfg Plastic Products

(G-11803)
POLYTEC INC
1 Cabot Rd Ste 102 (01749-2792)
PHONE..................................508 417-1040
Josephine Kamei, *President*
EMP: 16
SALES (corp-wide): 86.7MM **Privately Held**
SIC: 3699 5063 Mfg Electrical Equipment/Supplies Whol Electrical Equipment
HQ: Polytec, Inc.
16400 Bake Pkwy Ste 200
Irvine CA 92618
949 943-3033

(G-11804)
POLYTECH FILTRATION SYSTEMS
100 Forest Ave (01749-2826)
PHONE..................................978 562-7700
Erik J Andresen, *President*
▲ **EMP:** 10
SALES (est): 1.9MM **Privately Held**
WEB: www.polytech-filtration.com
SIC: 3569 5084 Mfg General Industrial Machinery Whol Industrial Equipment

(G-11805)
PRECISION COATING CO INC (HQ)
51 Parmenter Rd (01749-3213)
PHONE..................................781 329-1420
Robert A Deangelis, *President*
Ernest K Anderson Jr, *Vice Pres*
Mike Sung, *Vice Pres*
EMP: 51 **EST:** 1956
SALES (est): 10.7MM
SALES (corp-wide): 17.7MM **Privately Held**
WEB: www.duralectra.com
SIC: 3479 5131 Coating/Engraving Service Whol Piece Goods/Notions
PA: Katahdin Industries, Inc.
51 Parmenter Rd
Hudson MA 01749
781 329-1420

(G-11806)
PRECISION COATING CO INC
Also Called: Boyd Coatings
51 Parmenter Rd (01749-3213)
PHONE..................................978 562-7561
Walter Romero, *Prdtn Mgr*
Richard Buxton, *Engineer*
Peter Lin, *Engineer*
Haniel Olivera, *Engineer*
Renata Santos, *Engineer*
EMP: 50
SALES (corp-wide): 17.7MM **Privately Held**
SIC: 3479 Coating/Engraving Service
HQ: Precision Coating Co, Inc.
51 Parmenter Rd
Hudson MA 01749
781 329-1420

(G-11807)
PRECISION INDUSTRIAL METALS
1 Brent Dr (01749-2903)
PHONE..................................978 562-1800
Kathy Gorman, *President*
EMP: 4
SALES (est): 315.1K **Privately Held**
SIC: 3444 Mfg Sheet Metalwork

(G-11808)
PROTEK POWER NORTH AMERICA INC
43 Broad St Ste B206 (01749-2565)
PHONE..................................978 567-9615
Bruce Chen, *President*
Linda Cormolli, *Admin Sec*
▲ **EMP:** 3
SQ FT: 4,000
SALES (est): 304.2K **Privately Held**
SIC: 3679 Mfg Electronic Components

(G-11809)
PROVERIS SCIENTIFIC CORP
2 Cabot Rd Ste 5 (01749-2942)
PHONE..................................508 460-8822
Dino J Farina, *CEO*
Raymond Leveille, *President*
John Grega, *Electrical Engi*
Leveille Chip, *CFO*
Deborah Jones, *Sales Staff*
EMP: 28
SQ FT: 7,300
SALES (est): 7MM **Privately Held**
SIC: 3826 Mfg Analytical Instruments

(G-11810)
R G M METALS INC
5 Parmenter Rd (01749-3213)
PHONE..................................978 562-9773
Richard G Mercadante, *President*
George Eckard, *Project Mgr*
Jim Kissner, *Engineer*
Karen Mercadante, *Treasurer*
EMP: 7
SALES: 750K **Privately Held**
SIC: 3444 Mfg Sheet Metalwork

(G-11811)
RES-TECH CORPORATION (HQ)
Also Called: Restech Plastic Molding
34 Tower St (01749-1721)
PHONE..................................978 567-1000
George Danis, *President*
Ken Wheeler, *Engineer*
▲ **EMP:** 48
SQ FT: 20,000
SALES (est): 17.2MM **Privately Held**
SIC: 3089 2821 Mfg Plastic Products Mfg Plastic Materials/Resins

(G-11812)
RESTECH PLASTIC MOLDING LLC (DH)
Also Called: Plastic Moulding Manufacturing
34 Tower St (01749-1721)
PHONE..................................978 567-1000
George Danis, *CEO*
EMP: 15
SALES (est): 12MM **Privately Held**
SIC: 3089 Mfg Plastic Products
HQ: Res-Tech Corporation
34 Tower St
Hudson MA 01749
978 567-1000

(G-11813)
ROMAX INC
14 Barretts Rd (01749-2883)
PHONE..................................502 327-8555
EMP: 3 **EST:** 1994
SALES: 500K **Privately Held**
WEB: www.romaxinc.com
SIC: 3552 5084 Mfg Textile Machinery Whol Industrial Equipment

(G-11814)
SALIGA MACHINE CO INC
10 Bonazzoli Ave (01749-2862)
PHONE..................................978 562-7959
Michael P Saliga, *President*
Donald F Saliga, *Chairman*
Patrick Saliga, *Treasurer*
Mary Ellen Sherman, *Office Mgr*
Mary-Ellen Sherman, *Office Mgr*
EMP: 40
SQ FT: 10,000
SALES (est): 7.5MM **Privately Held**
SIC: 3599 Mfg Industrial Machinery

(G-11815)
SEYMOUR ASSOCIATES INC
43 Parmenter Rd (01749-3213)
P.O. Box 115 (01749-0115)
PHONE..................................978 562-1373
Richard M Seymour, *President*
EMP: 5
SQ FT: 1,000
SALES: 700K **Privately Held**
SIC: 3549 3082 Mfg Metalworking Machinery Mfg Plastic Profile Shapes

(G-11816)
SHARP TOOL CO INC
7 Bonazzoli Ave (01749-2849)
PHONE..................................978 568-9292
Paul J Morette, *President*
Mike Morette, *Sales Associate*
▲ **EMP:** 28
SQ FT: 12,000
SALES (est): 6.5MM **Privately Held**
WEB: www.sharptool.com
SIC: 2819 7699 Mfg Industrial Inorganic Chemicals Repair Services

(G-11817)
SMITHS INTRCNNECT AMERICAS INC
16 Brent Dr (01749-2904)
PHONE..................................978 568-0451
Dom Matos, *President*
EMP: 135
SALES (corp-wide): 3.1B **Privately Held**
SIC: 3679 Mfg Electronic Components
HQ: Smiths Interconnect Americas, Inc.
5101 Richland Ave
Kansas City KS 66106
913 342-5544

(G-11818)
SP MACHINE INC
Also Called: Tessier Machine Company
526 Main St (01749-2909)
PHONE..................................978 562-2019
Stephen Woodworth, *President*
EMP: 20 **EST:** 1979
SQ FT: 5,000
SALES (est): 3.5MM **Privately Held**
SIC: 3469 3599 Mfg Metal Stampings Mfg Industrial Machinery

(G-11819)
SPECIALIZED PLASTICS INC
567 Main St (01749-3035)
PHONE..................................978 562-9314
Beverly Simmons, *President*
Glenn Simmons, *Vice Pres*
EMP: 22
SQ FT: 24,000
SALES (est): 5.2MM **Privately Held**
WEB: www.specializedplasticsinc.com
SIC: 3081 Mfg Unsupported Plastic Film/Sheet

(G-11820)
STOKES WOODWORKING CO INC (PA)
Also Called: Albert K Stokes
12 Bonazzoli Ave (01749-2849)
PHONE..................................508 481-0414
Albert K Stokes, *President*
EMP: 9
SALES (est): 300K **Privately Held**
SIC: 2431 2434 Mfg Millwork Mfg Wood Kitchen Cabinets

(G-11821)
TELEMED SYSTEMS INC
8 Kane Industrial Dr (01749-2906)
PHONE..................................978 567-9033
Michael Carrol, *President*
Nathaniel Beale, *Principal*
George Briley, *QC Mgr*
Gilbert Wilcox, *Treasurer*
Maria Moura, *Technology*
EMP: 25
SALES (est): 3.4MM **Privately Held**
WEB: www.telemedsystems.com
SIC: 3841 3845 Mfg Surgical/Medical Instruments Mfg Electromedical Equipment

(G-11822)
THERMAL PRINTING SOLUTIONS
80 Priest St (01749-1743)
PHONE..................................978 562-1329
Dale A Scovil Jr, *Principal*
Dale Scovil, *Bd of Directors*
EMP: 6
SALES (est): 575.1K **Privately Held**
SIC: 2752 Lithographic Commercial Printing

(G-11823)
THERMALOGIC CORPORATION
22 Kane Industrial Dr (01749-2922)
PHONE..................................800 343-4492
John Du Bois PHD, *Ch of Bd*
Louis Grein, *President*
Joe Grein, *General Mgr*
Domenic Mancini, *Executive*
EMP: 26 **EST:** 1971
SQ FT: 22,000
SALES (est): 5.4MM **Privately Held**
WEB: www.thlogic.com
SIC: 3829 Mfg Measuring/Controlling Devices

(G-11824)
UNITED STRETCH DESIGN CORP
Also Called: Artcraft
11 Bonazzoli Ave (01749-2849)
PHONE..................................978 562-7781
Manuel P Chaves, *President*
Eva Chaves, *Treasurer*
▲ **EMP:** 40
SQ FT: 50,000
SALES: 3MM **Privately Held**
WEB: www.usdcorp.com
SIC: 2241 Narrow Fabric Mill

(G-11825)
USPACK INC
14 Brent Dr (01749-2904)
PHONE..................................978 562-8522
Svet Lana, *President*
Svetlana Aptekman, *President*
EMP: 40
SALES (est): 10MM **Privately Held**
SIC: 3559 Mfg Misc Industry Machinery

(G-11826)
WILL KIRKPATRICKS DECOY SHOP
124 Forest Ave (01749-2840)
PHONE..................................978 562-7841
Will E Kirkpatrick, *President*
Anne Kirkpatrick, *Vice Pres*
EMP: 10
SALES: 100K **Privately Held**
WEB: www.kirkpatrickdecoys.com
SIC: 3949 Mfg Sporting/Athletic Goods

(G-11827)
XPONENT GLOBAL INC
Also Called: Netco Extruded Plastics
30 Tower St (01749-1721)
PHONE..................................978 562-3485
Christopher Sullivan, *President*
EMP: 23
SALES (est): 912K **Privately Held**
SIC: 3089 Mfg Plastic Products

Hull
Plymouth County

(G-11828)
MARGIES SWEET SURRENDER
179 Nantasket Rd (02045-2650)
PHONE..................................781 925-2271
William McClory, *Principal*
EMP: 5
SALES (est): 323.1K **Privately Held**
SIC: 2051 Mfg Bread/Related Products

(G-11829)
NEON GOOSE
34 Brookline Ave (02045-2274)
PHONE..................................781 925-5118
John Burke, *Principal*
EMP: 3
SALES (est): 123.2K **Privately Held**
SIC: 2813 Mfg Industrial Gases

(G-11830)
S & S PUBLICATIONS INC
Also Called: Hull Times, The
41 Highland Ave (02045-1133)
P.O. Box 477 (02045-0477)
PHONE..................................781 925-9266
Susan Ovans, *President*
Roger Jackson, *Vice Pres*
EMP: 5
SALES (est): 321.5K **Privately Held**
SIC: 2741 2711 Misc Publishing Newspapers-Publishing/Printing

(G-11831)
TOWNIE FROZEN DESSERTS LLC
46 G St (02045-1825)
PHONE..................................781 925-6095
Robin A Flint,

Stephen Gore,
EMP: 3
SALES (est): 132.8K **Privately Held**
SIC: 3999 Mfg Misc Products

Hyannis
Barnstable County

(G-11832)
ABCO TOOL & DIE INC
11 Thornton Dr (02601-1814)
P.O. Box 458 (02601-0458)
PHONE..................................508 771-3225
David B Bourque, *President*
Brian Veroneau, *Executive*
EMP: 25
SQ FT: 11,000
SALES (est): 4.2MM **Privately Held**
WEB: www.abcomolds.com
SIC: 3544 Mfg Dies/Tools/Jigs/Fixtures

(G-11833)
ADVANCED ORTHOPEDIC SERVICES (PA)
680 Falmouth Rd (02601-2318)
PHONE..................................508 771-5050
Erdvills Janulaitis, *President*
EMP: 5
SALES (est): 483.5K **Privately Held**
SIC: 3842 Mfg Surgical Appliances/Supplies

(G-11834)
ADVANCED ORTHOPEDIC SVCS INC
680 Falmouth Rd (02601-2318)
PHONE..................................508 771-5050
Erdvilis Janulaitis, *President*
Ausra Janulaitis, *Manager*
EMP: 3
SALES (est): 180K **Privately Held**
SIC: 3842 Mfg Surgical Appliances/Supplies

(G-11835)
BARNSTABLE PATRIOT NEWSPPR INC
4 Ocean Ave (02601)
P.O. Box 1208 (02601-1208)
PHONE..................................508 771-1427
Rob Senott, *Publisher*
EMP: 17
SQ FT: 3,000
SALES (est): 984.2K **Privately Held**
SIC: 2711 Newspapers-Publishing/Printing

(G-11836)
CAPE COD DRMATS OF DISTINCTION
Also Called: Cape Cod Door Mats
105 Ferndoc St Ste E1 (02601-2065)
PHONE..................................508 790-0070
Dawn Stahl, *President*
EMP: 30
SALES (est): 2.7MM **Privately Held**
WEB: www.capecoddoormats.com
SIC: 3069 2273 Mfg Fabricated Rubber Products Mfg Carpets/Rugs

(G-11837)
CLASSIC KITCHEN DESIGN INC
Also Called: Classic Kitchens & Interiors
127 Airport Rd (02601-1856)
PHONE..................................508 775-3075
Peter Polhemus, *President*
Richard Stonge, *CFO*
Leonard H Savery, *Treasurer*
EMP: 12
SALES (est): 1.1MM **Privately Held**
WEB: www.ckdcapecod.com
SIC: 2434 Mfg Wood Kitchen Cabinets

(G-11838)
CUSTOM COATINGS
104 Enterprise Rd (02601-2215)
PHONE..................................508 771-8830
Chris Vangelder, *Principal*
EMP: 4
SALES (est): 292.3K **Privately Held**
SIC: 3479 Coating/Engraving Service

(G-11839)
DAILY PAPER
644 W Main St (02601-3423)
PHONE..................................508 790-8800
Aaron Webb, *Principal*
EMP: 8 **EST:** 2007
SALES (est): 594.6K **Privately Held**
SIC: 2711 Newspapers-Publishing/Printing

(G-11840)
EASTWIND COMMUNICATIONS INC
75 Perseverance Way (02601-1816)
PHONE..................................508 862-8600
Anthony Agostinelli, *President*
Joseph Norton, *Admin Sec*
EMP: 16
SALES (est): 2.3MM **Privately Held**
SIC: 3674 Mfg Semiconductors/Related Devices

(G-11841)
FRAME CENTER OF NORWOOD INC (PA)
460 Bearses Way (02601-2763)
P.O. Box 5055, Vineyard Haven (02568-0947)
PHONE..................................781 762-2535
Wayne D Petty, *President*
EMP: 6
SQ FT: 5,000
SALES (est): 555.9K **Privately Held**
SIC: 2499 5999 Mfg & Ret Wood Picture Frames

(G-11842)
GATCO INC
Also Called: Folio Associates
297 North St Ste 212 (02601-5133)
PHONE..................................508 815-4910
Paul Rooker, *President*
EMP: 12
SALES: 1MM **Privately Held**
WEB: www.foliomed.com
SIC: 2741 Publishing Company

(G-11843)
INSTANT OFFSET PRESS INC
Also Called: Sunderland Printing
115 Enterprise Rd (02601-2212)
PHONE..................................508 790-1100
Marc Sunderland, *President*
Priscilla Sunderland, *Clerk*
EMP: 10
SQ FT: 6,000
SALES (est): 960K **Privately Held**
SIC: 2752 2759 Lithographic Commercial Printing Commercial Printing

(G-11844)
INTUIT INC
Also Called: Intuit- Eclispe
75 Perseverance Way Ste 3 (02601-1816)
PHONE..................................508 862-1050
EMP: 128
SALES (corp-wide): 4.5B **Publicly Held**
SIC: 7372 Prepackaged Software Services
PA: Intuit Inc.
2700 Coast Ave
Mountain View CA 94043
650 944-6000

(G-11845)
LIGHTHOUSE PUBLICATIONS (PA)
350 Kidds Hill Rd (02601-1884)
PHONE..................................508 534-9291
Russell Piersons, *Director*
EMP: 6 **EST:** 2010
SALES (est): 380.1K **Privately Held**
SIC: 2741 Misc Publishing

(G-11846)
LOCAL JUICE INC
539 South St (02601-5406)
PHONE..................................508 813-9282
Jen Villa, *President*
Nicole Cormier, *Director*
EMP: 4 **EST:** 2014
SALES (est): 175.9K **Privately Held**
SIC: 2037 Mfg Frozen Fruits/Vegetables

(G-11847)
LOCAL MEDIA GROUP INC
Cape Cod Times
319 Main St (02601-4037)
PHONE..................................508 775-1200
Sean Driscoll, *Editor*
Scott Freeman, *Facilities Mgr*
Sheri Theroux, *Opers Staff*
Mark Bergeron, *Production*
Leslie Terry, *Persnl Mgr*
EMP: 275
SALES (corp-wide): 1.5B **Publicly Held**
WEB: www.ottaway.com
SIC: 2711 Newspapers- Publishing/Printing
HQ: Local Media Group, Inc.
40 Mulberry St
Middletown NY 10940
845 341-1100

(G-11848)
LUND PRECISION PRODUCTS INC
175 Bay Shore Rd (02601-4708)
PHONE..................................617 413-0236
John Schwanbeck, *President*
Stephen Cote, *Exec VP*
EMP: 5
SALES: 15MM **Privately Held**
SIC: 3423 6719 Holding Company

(G-11849)
MEDICAL INSTRUMENT TECHNOLOGY
110 Breeds Hill Rd Ste 9 (02601-1864)
PHONE..................................508 775-8682
Thomas F Barone, *President*
Mary Barone, *Treasurer*
Eileen S Marks, *Clerk*
EMP: 6
SQ FT: 1,000
SALES: 300K **Privately Held**
SIC: 3841 Whol Medical/Hospital Equipment

(G-11850)
MINUTEMAN PRESS
223 Barnstable Rd (02601-2929)
PHONE..................................508 778-0220
Judy Herring, *Principal*
EMP: 6
SALES (est): 355.1K **Privately Held**
SIC: 2752 Comm Prtg Litho

(G-11851)
OCCLUSION PROSTHETICS
17 School St (02601-3117)
PHONE..................................508 827-4377
EMP: 3
SALES (est): 187.5K **Privately Held**
SIC: 3842 Mfg Surgical Appliances/Supplies

(G-11852)
OTTAWAY NEWSPAPERS
319 Main St (02601-4037)
PHONE..................................508 775-1200
Patrick Purcell, *Principal*
Gary York, *Controller*
William Zurilla, *Controller*
Ken Ketterling, *CPA*
Karen Andreas, *Branch Mgr*
EMP: 6 **EST:** 2010
SALES (est): 307K **Privately Held**
SIC: 2711 Newspapers-Publishing/Printing

(G-11853)
PAIN DAVIGNON II INC
15 Hinckley Rd Unit C (02601-1948)
PHONE..................................508 771-9771
Toma Stamenkovic, *President*
Mario Mariani, *General Mgr*
Branislav Stamenkovich, *Vice Pres*
EMP: 30
SQ FT: 8,000
SALES (est): 5.7MM **Privately Held**
WEB: www.paindavignon.com
SIC: 2051 Mfg Bread/Related Products

(G-11854)
PRECISION PASTA DIES INC
198 Compass Cir (02601-2741)
PHONE..................................978 866-7720
Jamie Cabral, *President*
Jaime L Cabral, *Principal*
EMP: 3
SALES (est): 204.1K **Privately Held**
SIC: 2099 Mfg Food Preparations

(G-11855)
RICCIARDI MARBLE AND GRANITE
174 Airport Rd (02601-1804)
PHONE..................................508 790-2734
Brian Ricciardi, *Owner*
▲ **EMP:** 9
SALES (est): 1.1MM **Privately Held**
SIC: 3281 Mfg Cut Stone/Products

(G-11856)
RM EDUCATION INC (HQ)
Also Called: Rm Educational Software,
310 Barnstable Rd Ste 101 (02601-2902)
PHONE..................................508 862-0700
Kevin J Pawsey, *President*
Craig Lewendon, *Finance Dir*
Hayley Champion, *Human Resources*
Simon Carter, *Marketing Staff*
Jayne Davies, *Director*
EMP: 35
SALES (est): 5.2MM
SALES (corp-wide): 291.9MM **Privately Held**
SIC: 7372 5999 Prepackaged Software Services Ret Misc Merchandise
PA: Rm Plc
142b Park Drive
Abingdon OXON OX14
123 585-4800

(G-11857)
SAVANT SYSTEMS LLC (PA)
45 Perseverance Way (02601-1812)
PHONE..................................508 683-2500
Robert Madonna, *CEO*
Kevin Huppert, *Sales Engr*
▲ **EMP:** 90
SALES (est): 64.8MM **Privately Held**
WEB: www.886ventures.com
SIC: 3651 Mfg Home Audio/Video Equipment

(G-11858)
SNYDERS-LANCE INC
Also Called: Cape Cod Potato Chips
100 Breeds Hill Rd (02601-1860)
PHONE..................................508 771-1872
Paul Murphy, *Accounts Mgr*
EMP: 9
SALES (corp-wide): 8.1B **Publicly Held**
SIC: 2052 Mfg Cookies/Crackers
HQ: Snyder's-Lance, Inc.
13515 Balntyn Corp Pl
Charlotte NC 28277
704 554-1421

(G-11859)
THREADHEAD INC
Also Called: Advanced Embroidery
38 Plant Rd (02601-1916)
PHONE..................................508 778-6516
Damon E Collins, *President*
EMP: 14
SALES (est): 1.4MM **Privately Held**
WEB: www.advancedembroidery.biz
SIC: 2395 Pleating/Stitching Services

(G-11860)
TOBY LEARY FINE WDWKG INC
135 Barnstable Rd Ste A (02601-2928)
PHONE..................................508 957-2281
Tober Leary, *President*
EMP: 12
SQ FT: 12,000
SALES (est): 637.5K **Privately Held**
SIC: 2431 Mfg Millwork

(G-11861)
VIOLA ASSOCIATES INC
110 Rosary Ln Ste A (02601-2076)
PHONE..................................508 771-3457
John T Viola Jr, *President*
EMP: 17
SALES (est): 2.4MM **Privately Held**
SIC: 3432 Mfg Plumbing Fixture Fittings

Hyde Park
Suffolk County

(G-11862)
B&J SHEET METAL
232 Turtle Pond Pkwy (02136-1222)
PHONE..................................617 590-2295
Robert Gentile, *Principal*
EMP: 8
SALES (est): 797.3K **Privately Held**
SIC: 3444 Mfg Sheet Metalwork

(G-11863)
BOSTON BAGEL INC
101 Sprague St Ste 3 (02136-2385)
PHONE..................................617 364-6900
Bob Boschetto, *President*
EMP: 22
SQ FT: 18,000
SALES (est): 3.6MM **Privately Held**
SIC: 2051 Mfg Bread/Related Products

(G-11864)
BULLETIN NEWSPAPERS INC
Also Called: Hyde Park Bulletin Newspaper
695 Truman Hwy Ste 99 (02136-3552)
PHONE..................................617 361-1406
EMP: 3 **Privately Held**
WEB: www.bulletinnewspapers.com
SIC: 2711 Newspapers-Publishing/Printing
PA: The Bulletin Newspapers Inc
695 Truman Hwy Ste 99
Hyde Park MA 02136

(G-11865)
BULLETIN NEWSPAPERS INC (PA)
Also Called: Hyde Park Bulletin
695 Truman Hwy Ste 99 (02136-3552)
PHONE..................................617 361-8400
Paul Di Monica, *President*
Carolyn Sax, *Senior Partner*
Dennis Cawley, *Vice Pres*
EMP: 15
SQ FT: 1,100
SALES: 1MM **Privately Held**
WEB: www.bulletinnewspapers.com
SIC: 2711 Newspapers-Publishing/Printing

(G-11866)
FEENEY FENCE INC
Also Called: Feeney's Welding and Fence Co.
120 Business St Ste 5 (02136-1612)
PHONE..................................617 364-1407
Edward J Feeney Jr, *President*
Steven V Furbush, *Vice Pres*
EMP: 8
SQ FT: 2,000
SALES: 400K **Privately Held**
WEB: www.feeney.tcvmedia.com
SIC: 7692 1799 Welding Anf Fence Contractor

(G-11867)
GEBELEIN GROUP INC
Also Called: Orleans Packing & Dist Co
1715 Hyde Park Ave (02136-2457)
PHONE..................................617 361-6611
George Gebelein, *President*
◆ **EMP:** 13 **EST:** 1947
SQ FT: 10,000
SALES (est): 2.2MM **Privately Held**
WEB: www.orleanspacking.com
SIC: 2033 Mfg Canned Fruits/Vegetables

(G-11868)
GLOBAL PRINTS INC
65 Sprague St Ste 25 (02136-2098)
PHONE..................................800 578-4278
Paul Kennedy, *President*
▲ **EMP:** 4
SQ FT: 9,000
SALES (est): 482.7K **Privately Held**
WEB: www.globalprints.com
SIC: 2741 Misc Publishing

(G-11869)
HYDE PARK CONCRETE INC
8 B St (02136-2606)
PHONE..................................617 364-5485
Anthony Musto, *President*
Mario Musto, *Vice Pres*
EMP: 4
SQ FT: 10,000
SALES (est): 488K **Privately Held**
SIC: 3273 Mfg Ready-Mixed Concrete

(G-11870)
INFINITE COMPOST
44 Myopia Rd (02136-1522)
PHONE..................................617 922-6419
George Zahka, *Principal*
EMP: 3
SALES (est): 221.4K **Privately Held**
SIC: 2875 Mfg Fertilizers-Mix Only

(G-11871)
K K WELDING INC
107 Providence St (02136-1855)
P.O. Box 170447, Boston (02117-0427)
PHONE..................................617 361-1780
James A Delaney, *President*
Denny Kenneally, *President*
EMP: 6
SALES (est): 520.4K **Privately Held**
SIC: 7692 Structural Metal Fabrication

(G-11872)
KEVIN CRADOCK WOODWORKING INC
119 Business St (02136-1640)
PHONE..................................617 524-2405
Kevin P Cradock, *President*
EMP: 4
SALES (est): 684.3K **Privately Held**
SIC: 2431 Mfg Millwork

(G-11873)
LARKIN IRON WORKS INC
9 B St (02136-2605)
PHONE..................................617 333-9710
Steven Larkin, *President*
Andrea Larkin, *Controller*
EMP: 9
SQ FT: 5,500
SALES (est): 960K **Privately Held**
SIC: 3446 Mfg Architectural Metalwork

(G-11874)
MCCREA CAPITAL ADVISORS INC
Also Called: McCrea's Candies
202 Neponset Valley Pkwy (02136-2410)
PHONE..................................617 276-3388
Jason McCrea, *President*
Catherine Michmerhuizen, *Principal*
Kate Michmerhuizen, *Marketing Staff*
EMP: 7
SALES: 1MM **Privately Held**
SIC: 2064 Mfg Candy/Confectionery

(G-11875)
MINUTEMAN PRESS
1279 Hyde Park Ave (02136-2703)
PHONE..................................617 361-7400
Kamalu L Macphilips, *Principal*
EMP: 4 **EST:** 2008
SALES (est): 380.9K **Privately Held**
SIC: 2752 Comm Prtg Litho

(G-11876)
MODERN SHOE COMPANY LLC
101 Sprague St Ste 1 (02136-2172)
PHONE..................................617 333-7470
Kimberly Bradley,
Richard Brandt,
Roger Monks,
James Sabitus,
▲ **EMP:** 11
SQ FT: 14,000
SALES (est): 1.9MM **Privately Held**
WEB: www.modernshoe.net
SIC: 3144 5139 Mfg Women's Footwear Whol Footwear

(G-11877)
R R DONNELLEY & SONS COMPANY
65 Sprague St (02136-2061)
PHONE..................................617 360-2000
John Sheehan, *Branch Mgr*
EMP: 389
SALES (corp-wide): 6.8B **Publicly Held**
SIC: 2752 Commercial Printing
PA: R. R. Donnelley & Sons Company
35 W Wacker Dr
Chicago IL 60601
312 326-8000

(G-11878)
SAMS DRAPERY WORKROOM INC
Also Called: Sam's & Son
63 Sprague St Ste 2-3 (02136-2000)
PHONE..................................617 364-9440
Howard Bernstein, *President*
Roberta Bernstein, *Treasurer*
EMP: 12 **EST:** 1971
SQ FT: 5,000
SALES: 540K **Privately Held**
SIC: 2391 Mfg Curtains/Draperies

(G-11879)
SMH FINE FOODS INC
Also Called: Hurley's Boston Soda Breads
139 Milton Ave (02136-4035)
PHONE..................................617 364-1772
Sean Hurley, *President*
EMP: 3
SQ FT: 500
SALES (est): 240K **Privately Held**
SIC: 2051 Mfg Bread/Related Products

(G-11880)
SORENSON SEWING INC
Also Called: Mooradian Cover Company
65 Sprague St (02136-2061)
PHONE..................................617 333-6955
Peter Hoffman, *President*
▼ **EMP:** 6
SQ FT: 4,900
SALES (est): 633.1K **Privately Held**
SIC: 2393 Mfg Instrument Bags

(G-11881)
TED BEST
Also Called: Best Quality Printing
1205 Hyde Park Ave (02136-2837)
PHONE..................................617 361-7258
Ted Best, *Owner*
EMP: 4
SALES (est): 217.1K **Privately Held**
SIC: 2759 2791 2789 2752 Commercial Printing Typesetting Services Bookbinding/Related Work Lithographic Coml Print

Indian Orchard
Hampden County

(G-11882)
42 DESIGN FAB STUDIO INC
34 Front St (01151-1176)
P.O. Box 51942 (01151-5942)
PHONE..................................413 203-4948
Todd Harris, *President*
EMP: 7
SALES (est): 120.7K **Privately Held**
SIC: 2599 Mfg Furniture/Fixtures

(G-11883)
A & D TOOL CO
34 Front St Ste 5 (01151-1148)
P.O. Box 51081 (01151-5081)
PHONE..................................413 543-3166
Felix Dynak, *Owner*
EMP: 3 **EST:** 1998
SQ FT: 2,500
SALES (est): 351.2K **Privately Held**
SIC: 3559 3599 Mfg Misc Industry Machinery Mfg Industrial Machinery

(G-11884)
AL GAGS
34 Front St (01151-1176)
PHONE..................................413 285-8023
EMP: 3 **EST:** 2017
SALES (est): 115.7K **Privately Held**
SIC: 3949 Sporting And Athletic Goods Nec

(G-11885)
BUTLER METAL FABRICATORS INC
91 Pinevale St (01151-1562)
PHONE..................................413 306-5762
Lisa Brodeur-Mcgan, *Principal*
EMP: 8
SALES (est): 125.7K **Privately Held**
SIC: 3441 Structural Metal Fabrication

(G-11886)
FIORE MACHINE INC
140 Michon St (01151-1931)
P.O. Box 51972 (01151-5972)
PHONE..................................413 543-5767
Angelo R Fiore, *President*
David Fiore, *Vice Pres*
Angelina R Fiore, *Treasurer*
EMP: 6
SQ FT: 4,800
SALES (est): 693.6K **Privately Held**
SIC: 3544 Mfr Precision Parts For Tool & Die Shops

(G-11887)
HEATBATH CORPORATION (HQ)
107 Front St (01151-1124)
P.O. Box 51048 (01151-5048)
PHONE..................................413 452-2000
Ernest Walen, *President*
Tom Walen, *Chief Mktg Ofcr*
▲ **EMP:** 30 **EST:** 1939
SQ FT: 5,000
SALES (est): 17.6MM **Privately Held**
SIC: 3398 Metal Heat Treating

(G-11888)
JESKO TOOL & KNIFE
34 Front St (01151-1176)
PHONE..................................413 543-1520
EMP: 4
SALES (est): 377.6K **Privately Held**
SIC: 3599 Mfg Industrial Machinery

(G-11889)
M R D DESIGN & MANUFACTURING
1294 Worcester St Rear (01151-1647)
P.O. Box 51112 (01151-5112)
PHONE..................................413 543-2012
Randall Chaves, *President*
Darren Chaves, *Shareholder*
Angela Prenofil, *Admin Sec*
EMP: 6
SQ FT: 4,000
SALES (est): 699.8K **Privately Held**
SIC: 3599 Mfg Industrial Machinery

(G-11890)
NIXON COMPANY INC
161 Main St (01151-1193)
P.O. Box 51977 (01151-5977)
PHONE..................................413 543-3701
Jonathan Boz Beckian, *President*
Deborah Raptopoulos, *Vice Pres*
Janice Palukian, *Treasurer*
EMP: 50 **EST:** 1935
SQ FT: 15,000
SALES (est): 5.2MM **Privately Held**
WEB: www.nixonawards.com
SIC: 3999 2399 3965 2395 Mfg Misc Products Mfg Fabrctd Textile Pdts Mfg Fastener/Button/Pins Pleating/Stitching Svcs Mfg Nonmtlc Mineral Prdt

(G-11891)
NORTHEAST METAL CO
1022 Berkshire Ave (01151-1367)
P.O. Box 51754 (01151-5754)
PHONE..................................413 568-1981
Adrienne Rider, *President*
Wilson H Rider, *Treasurer*
David Sanborn, *Clerk*
EMP: 5
SALES (est): 519.9K **Privately Held**
SIC: 3452 Mfg Bolts/Screws/Rivets

(G-11892)
ORCHARD TOOL DIE INC
34 Front St Ste 29 (01151-1148)
PHONE..................................413 433-1233
Alan P Drew, *Principal*
EMP: 3
SALES (est): 424.9K **Privately Held**
SIC: 3544 Mfg Dies/Tools/Jigs/Fixtures

(G-11893)
PELLYS SPORTS
152 Main St (01151-1131)
PHONE..................................413 301-0889
Calvin Babbie, *Owner*
EMP: 3

▲ = Import ▼=Export
◆ =Import/Export

SALES (est): 220.5K **Privately Held**
SIC: 2339 Mfg Women's/Misses' Outerwear

(G-11894)
PRESENT ARMS INC
34 Front St Ste 326 (01151-1176)
P.O. Box 51478 (01151-5478)
PHONE..................................413 575-4656
Mark Jenkinson, *President*
EMP: 4
SALES: 160K **Privately Held**
SIC: 3589 3484 2542 Mfg Service Industry Machinery Mfg Small Arms Mfg Partitions/Fixtures-Nonwood

(G-11895)
SPECIALTY PACKAGING INC
34 Front St Ste 38 (01151-1148)
P.O. Box 51398 (01151-5398)
PHONE..................................413 543-1814
Joseph C Tolpa, *President*
John Tolpa, *Treasurer*
Themis J Tsoumas, *Clerk*
◆ **EMP:** 8
SQ FT: 7,300
SALES (est): 1.2MM **Privately Held**
SIC: 2652 3161 Mfg Setup Paperboard Boxes Mfg Luggage

(G-11896)
SPRINGFIELD PALLET INC
1819 Page Blvd (01151-1326)
PHONE..................................413 593-0044
Scott Smith, *Manager*
EMP: 6 **EST:** 2011
SALES (est): 553K **Privately Held**
SIC: 2448 Mfg Wood Pallets/Skids

(G-11897)
STUART SPORTS SPECIALTIES INC
Also Called: Al's Goldfish Lure Co
34 Front St Ste 6 (01151-1148)
P.O. Box 51013 (01151-5013)
PHONE..................................413 543-1524
John Occhialini, *President*
Mike Lee, *Assoc VP*
▲ **EMP:** 5 **EST:** 1954
SQ FT: 14,000
SALES: 300K **Privately Held**
WEB: www.alsgoldfish.com
SIC: 3949 Mfg Fishing Lures

(G-11898)
TRUSS ENGINEERING CORPORATION
181 Goodwin St (01151-2112)
P.O. Box 51027 (01151-5027)
PHONE..................................413 543-1298
W Paul Griswold, *President*
Joseph Henley, *Corp Secy*
EMP: 45 **EST:** 1961
SQ FT: 33,200
SALES (est): 6.7MM **Privately Held**
WEB: www.trussec.com
SIC: 2439 Mfg Structural Wood Members

Ipswich
Essex County

(G-11899)
1634 MEADERY
3 Short St (01938-1970)
PHONE..................................508 517-4058
Daniel Clapp, *Principal*
EMP: 4
SALES (est): 285.5K **Privately Held**
SIC: 2084 Mfg Wines/Brandy/Spirits

(G-11900)
ADIDAS PRINTING INC
20 Mulholland Dr (01938-2823)
PHONE..................................978 851-6337
John H Bolles, *President*
Fred Curl, *Vice Pres*
EMP: 10
SQ FT: 9,000
SALES (est): 1.1MM **Privately Held**
WEB: www.adidasprinting.com
SIC: 2752 Commercial Printing Service

(G-11901)
ALL STAR FABRICATION INC
8 Hood Farm Rd (01938-1073)
PHONE..................................978 887-7617
EMP: 3 **EST:** 1989
SALES (est): 210K **Privately Held**
SIC: 3441 Fabricated Structural Metal

(G-11902)
ARTS IPSWICH
134 Town Farm Rd (01938-1367)
PHONE..................................978 356-5335
Art Rousseau, *Owner*
EMP: 5
SALES (est): 489.6K **Privately Held**
SIC: 3599 Mfg Industrial Machinery

(G-11903)
ATLANTIC ATM LLC
383 Linebrook Rd (01938-1090)
PHONE..................................978 356-4051
George Kitsakos, *Director*
Joseph Mello Jr,
EMP: 4
SALES (est): 476.7K **Privately Held**
SIC: 3578 Mfg Calculating Equipment

(G-11904)
AVENGER INC
Also Called: Avenger Filter Force
53 Mitchell Rd (01938-1257)
PHONE..................................978 356-7311
Russell Morris, *President*
John Naves, *Vice Pres*
Patricia Kavanagh, *Treasurer*
EMP: 10
SQ FT: 4,800
SALES (est): 1.1MM **Privately Held**
WEB: www.filterforce.com
SIC: 3569 Mfg Filter Elements

(G-11905)
BEVERLY PALLET COMPANY INC
51 Mitchell Rd (01938-1218)
P.O. Box 187 (01938-0187)
PHONE..................................978 356-1121
Edward Gauthier, *President*
EMP: 5
SQ FT: 6,000
SALES (est): 641.2K **Privately Held**
SIC: 2448 Mfg Wood Pallets/Skids

(G-11906)
BODYCOTE THERMAL PROC INC
11 Old Right Rd Ste C (01938-1191)
PHONE..................................978 356-3818
Mike Sakelakos, *Branch Mgr*
EMP: 40
SALES (corp-wide): 960MM **Privately Held**
SIC: 3398 Metal Heat Treating
HQ: Bodycote Thermal Processing, Inc.
12700 Park Central Dr # 700
Dallas TX 75251
214 904-2420

(G-11907)
C & C FABRICATING INC
24 Hayward St Ste A (01938-2035)
P.O. Box 542 (01938-0542)
PHONE..................................978 356-9980
Craig Marquis, *President*
Roland Mower, *Vice Pres*
EMP: 11
SQ FT: 3,700
SALES (est): 1.9MM **Privately Held**
SIC: 3599 Mfg Industrial Machinery

(G-11908)
C NEWSPAPER INC
55 Market St Ste 208 (01938-2262)
PHONE..................................978 412-1800
Patrick Purcell, *President*
EMP: 3
SALES (est): 100.9K **Privately Held**
SIC: 2711 Newspapers-Publishing/Printing

(G-11909)
CAPE ANN SIGN CO INC
Also Called: Cape Ann Sign & Screen
43 S Main St (01938-2321)
PHONE..................................978 356-0960
Gary Jernegan, *President*
EMP: 5
SQ FT: 2,400
SALES (est): 637.6K **Privately Held**
SIC: 3993 Mfg Signs/Advertising Specialties

(G-11910)
CASE TECHNOLOGY INC
26 Hayward St (01938-2012)
PHONE..................................978 356-6011
Barry P Cristoforo, *President*
Brian Cristoforo, *Treasurer*
EMP: 8
SQ FT: 15,000
SALES (est): 1.3MM **Privately Held**
WEB: www.casetechnology.com
SIC: 3161 Mfg Luggage

(G-11911)
CASTLE MACHINE CO
Also Called: Castle Machine Company
59 Old Right Rd (01938-1119)
PHONE..................................978 356-2151
David Morin, *Owner*
EMP: 4
SALES: 300K **Privately Held**
SIC: 3599 Mfg Industrial Machinery

(G-11912)
CENTER MANUFACTURING CORP
17 Hayward St Ste 2 (01938-2041)
PHONE..................................978 356-8420
Rolando Bisentini, *President*
Rolando V Visentini, *Manager*
EMP: 3
SQ FT: 1,500
SALES: 180K **Privately Held**
SIC: 3599 Mfg Industrial Machinery

(G-11913)
COMPANYSTUFFCOM INC
45 S Main St (01938-2321)
PHONE..................................978 282-1525
Steve Lindland, *President*
EMP: 3 **EST:** 2001
SALES (est): 267.9K **Privately Held**
WEB: www.companystuff.com
SIC: 2329 Mfg Men's/Boy's Clothing

(G-11914)
D J FABRICATORS INC
94 Turnpike Rd (01938-1047)
PHONE..................................978 356-0228
David C Theriault, *President*
EMP: 18
SQ FT: 24,000
SALES (est): 3.5MM **Privately Held**
WEB: www.djfab.com
SIC: 3444 Mfg Sheet Metalwork

(G-11915)
DALTON ELECTRIC HEATING CO INC
28 Hayward St (01938-2096)
PHONE..................................978 356-9844
Thomas A Shields, *CEO*
Elliott Whitney, *President*
Tara Fowler, *Technology*
Seth Bartlett, *Director*
EMP: 41 **EST:** 1926
SQ FT: 17,000
SALES (est): 8.8MM **Privately Held**
WEB: www.daltonelectric.com
SIC: 3567 Mfg Industrial Furnaces/Ovens

(G-11916)
EASTERN PRECISION MACHINING CO (PA)
25 Plains Rd (01938-1039)
PHONE..................................978 356-2372
Jeremiah Surette, *Partner*
Kevin Surette, *Partner*
EMP: 3
SALES (est): 369.6K **Privately Held**
SIC: 3599 Machine Shop

(G-11917)
EBSCO PUBLISHING INC (HQ)
Also Called: Ebscohost
10 Estes St (01938-2106)
PHONE..................................978 356-6500
Timothy R Collins, *President*
Tina Grantham, *Publisher*
Thomas Smith, *Publisher*
Brian Alper, *Chief*
Karl Baumann, *Regional Mgr*
EMP: 828
SQ FT: 275,000
SALES (est): 203.6MM
SALES (corp-wide): 2.8B **Privately Held**
SIC: 2741 7375 2731 2721 Misc Publishing Information Retrieval Sv Book-Publishing/Printing Periodical-Publish/Print
PA: Ebsco Industries, Inc.
5724 Highway 280 E
Birmingham AL 35242
205 991-6600

(G-11918)
ESSEX BAY ENGINEERING INC
19 Mitchell Rd (01938-1292)
PHONE..................................978 412-9600
John Burroughs, *CEO*
Julia Burroughs, *President*
Chris Burroughs, *Principal*
Ed Enos, *Engineer*
Linda Matook, *Treasurer*
EMP: 5
SQ FT: 24,000
SALES (est): 22.3MM **Privately Held**
SIC: 3599 Mfg Industrial Machinery

(G-11919)
FIRST FABRICATORS CO INC
27 Turnpike Rd (01938-1048)
PHONE..................................978 356-2901
Greg Mc Carthy, *President*
Ronald Mc Carthy, *Treasurer*
EMP: 5
SALES (est): 900K **Privately Held**
SIC: 3441 Structural Metal Fabrication

(G-11920)
FR FLOW CTRL VLVES US BDCO INC (PA)
Also Called: Trillium Valves USA
29 Old Right Rd (01938-1119)
PHONE..................................978 744-5690
Mark Claffey, *President*
Allen Fisher, *Engineer*
Laura Schelkle, *Human Resources*
◆ **EMP:** 100 **EST:** 1986
SALES (est): 21.1MM **Privately Held**
WEB: www.weirvalve.com
SIC: 3491 Mfg Industrial Valves

(G-11921)
FRONT RUN ORGANX INC
17 Hayward St Ste 3 (01938-2041)
PHONE..................................978 356-7133
EMP: 4
SQ FT: 1,000
SALES (est): 300K **Privately Held**
SIC: 2834 8742 Mfg Pharmaceutical Preparations Management Consulting Services

(G-11922)
IPSWICH CABINETRY INC
4 Poplar St (01938-2320)
PHONE..................................978 356-1123
Mark Welling, *President*
EMP: 4
SALES (est): 396K **Privately Held**
SIC: 2434 Mfg Wood Kitchen Cabinets

(G-11923)
IPSWICH CHRONICLE
2 Washington St (01938-1810)
PHONE..................................978 356-5141
Richard Chella, *Principal*
EMP: 3
SALES (est): 131.9K **Privately Held**
SIC: 2711 Newspapers-Publishing/Printing

(G-11924)
JAQUITH CAIBIDE CORP
31 Turnpike Rd (01938-1048)
PHONE..................................978 356-7770
David J Swain, *President*
Kendall Evans, *Principal*
EMP: 8 **EST:** 1977
SQ FT: 3,000
SALES (est): 1MM **Privately Held**
SIC: 3544 Mfg Special Dies & Punches

(G-11925)
JNC REBUILDERS INC
Also Called: Hub Automotive Rebuilders
91 Turnpike Rd Ste 5 (01938-1077)
PHONE..........978 356-2996
Joseph Carabello, *President*
EMP: 3
SQ FT: 2,000
SALES (est): 300K **Privately Held**
SIC: 3694 3714 3625 Mfg Engine Electrical Equipment Mfg Motor Vehicle Parts/Accessories Mfg Relays/Industrial Controls

(G-11926)
KC PRECISION MACHINING LLC
23 Old Right Rd Unit 1 (01938-1164)
PHONE..........978 356-8900
Bill Casey, *President*
Scott Melin, *General Mgr*
Mark Baldwin, *Plant Mgr*
Pam Casey, *Treasurer*
William Casey, *CTO*
EMP: 22
SQ FT: 20,000
SALES (est): 4MM **Privately Held**
WEB: www.kcprecision.com
SIC: 3599 Mfg Industrial Machinery

(G-11927)
KODIAK MACHINING CO INC
20 Hayward St (01938-2044)
P.O. Box 595 (01938-0595)
PHONE..........978 356-9876
Arthur R Gaudet Jr, *President*
EMP: 17
SQ FT: 5,000
SALES (est): 2.9MM **Privately Held**
SIC: 3599 Mfg Industrial Machinery

(G-11928)
LARSDALE INC (PA)
Also Called: Gilbert Manufacturing Co
4 S Main St Ste 7 (01938-2345)
PHONE..........978 356-9995
Daniel Larson Jr, *President*
▲ **EMP:** 68
SQ FT: 2,200
SALES (est): 4.8MM **Privately Held**
SIC: 3315 2221 Mfg Electronic Wire Components

(G-11929)
LITTLE ENTERPRISES INC
31 Locust Rd (01938-1252)
PHONE..........978 356-7422
Scott Little, *President*
Steven Lavely, *Vice Pres*
EMP: 72
SQ FT: 40,000
SALES (est): 12.7MM **Privately Held**
SIC: 3599 Mfg Industrial Machinery

(G-11930)
MERCURY BREWING & DIST CO
Also Called: Ipswich Brewery
2 Brewery Pl (01938-1196)
PHONE..........978 356-3329
Rob Martin, *President*
Mary Gormley, *Marketing Mgr*
EMP: 15 **EST:** 1998
SALES (est): 1.4MM **Privately Held**
SIC: 2082 Mfg Malt Beverages

(G-11931)
MICRO-MECH INC
33 Turnpike Rd (01938-1048)
P.O. Box 229 (01938-0229)
PHONE..........978 356-2966
Takehiko Hayashi, *President*
John E Beaucher, *Vice Pres*
Gail Devine, *Plant Mgr*
Seiji Minoura, *Treasurer*
▲ **EMP:** 48 **EST:** 1976
SALES (est): 7.7MM **Privately Held**
WEB: www.micro-mech.com
SIC: 3295 Mfg Minerals-Ground/Treated
HQ: Ibiden U.S.A. Corporation
3900 Freedom Cir Ste 130
Santa Clara CA 95054

(G-11932)
NORTH EAST INDUS COATINGS INC
9 Old Right Rd Unit C (01938-1119)
PHONE..........978 356-1200
Glenn Harlow, *President*
EMP: 7
SALES (est): 791K **Privately Held**
SIC: 3479 Coating/Engraving Service

(G-11933)
OLIVER WELDING & FABRICATING
30 Avery St (01938-1211)
PHONE..........978 356-4488
Richard Oliver, *President*
▲ **EMP:** 9
SQ FT: 5,000
SALES: 1.3MM **Privately Held**
WEB: www.oliverwelding.com
SIC: 7692 1761 3599 Welding Repair Roofing/Siding Contractor Mfg Industrial Machinery

(G-11934)
PHOENIX VINTNERS LLC
Also Called: Traveling Vineyard
127 High St (01938-1238)
PHONE..........877 340-9869
Rick Libby, *President*
EMP: 12
SQ FT: 50,000
SALES: 2MM **Privately Held**
SIC: 2084 Mfg Wines/Brandy/Spirits

(G-11935)
PRIVATEER INTERNATIONAL LLC
28 Mitchell Rd (01938-1217)
PHONE..........978 356-0477
Andrew Cabot, *President*
Bob McCoy, *Sales Staff*
▲ **EMP:** 11 **EST:** 2010
SALES (est): 1.4MM **Privately Held**
SIC: 2085 Mfg Distilled/Blended Liquor

(G-11936)
SAN-TRON INC (PA)
4 Turnpike Rd (01938-1024)
PHONE..........978 356-1585
Ronald C Sanders, *President*
Kenneth Wayne Sanders, *Vice Pres*
Ron Sanders, *Vice Pres*
Carl Sanders, *VP Sls/Mktg*
Carl H Sanders, *Treasurer*
▲ **EMP:** 75 **EST:** 1955
SQ FT: 30,000
SALES (est): 15MM **Privately Held**
WEB: www.santron.com
SIC: 3678 3451 3643 Mfg Electronic Connectors Mfg Screw Machine Products Mfg Conductive Wiring Devices

(G-11937)
TARGET MACHINE INC
36 Mitchell Rd Unit C (01938-1217)
PHONE..........978 356-7373
Gary M Prendergast, *President*
EMP: 5
SALES: 500K **Privately Held**
WEB: www.targetmachine.com
SIC: 3599 Machine Shop

(G-11938)
WE LOVE CONSTRUCTION
1 Arrowhead Trl (01938-2413)
PHONE..........978 239-1308
EMP: 3
SALES (est): 172.7K **Privately Held**
WEB: www.weloveconstruction.com
SIC: 1442 Construction Sand/Gravel

(G-11939)
XYBOL INTERLYNKS INC
89 Turnpike Rd Ste 204 (01938-1085)
PHONE..........978 356-0750
Mark A Gauthier, *President*
Barry Mitchell, *Vice Pres*
EMP: 10
SALES (est): 1.1MM **Privately Held**
SIC: 3678 Mfg Electronic Connectors

Jamaica Plain
Suffolk County

(G-11940)
BITOME INC
18 Park Ln (02130-2906)
PHONE..........207 812-8099
Herbert Ryan, *CEO*
Trevor Kemp, *COO*
Jens Hoefflin, *Chief Engr*
EMP: 3
SALES (est): 140.9K **Privately Held**
SIC: 3826 3845 3841 Mfg Analytical Instr Mfg Electromedical Equip Mfg Surgical/Med Instr

(G-11941)
BOSTON FAMILY BOAT BUILDING
133 Paul Gore St (02130-1814)
PHONE..........617 522-5366
John Rowse, *Principal*
EMP: 3
SALES (est): 263.7K **Privately Held**
SIC: 3732 Boatbuilding/Repairing

(G-11942)
COOLCOMPOSITES INC
25 Chilcott Pl Ste 1 (02130-4512)
PHONE..........510 717-9125
Andres Potes, *Director*
Alan Ransil, *Bd of Directors*
Wenhao Sun, *Bd of Directors*
Josh Wolff, *Bd of Directors*
EMP: 5
SALES (est): 428.6K **Privately Held**
SIC: 3644 Mfg Nonconductive Wiring Devices

(G-11943)
DUNFEY PUBLISHING COMPANY INC
Also Called: Boston Red Sox Yearbook
39 Eliot St (02130-2751)
PHONE..........617 522-3267
Richard Dunfey, *President*
EMP: 3
SALES (est): 360.9K **Privately Held**
SIC: 2721 Publishing Of Magazines

(G-11944)
JASON SANTELLI ENTERPRISES LLC
Also Called: Jackson Square Laundromat
274 Centre St (02130-1638)
PHONE..........617 942-2205
Jason Santelli,
EMP: 6
SALES (est): 557.8K **Privately Held**
SIC: 3582 Commercial Laundry Equipment

(G-11945)
KENYON WOODWORKING INC
179 Boylston St (02130-4544)
PHONE..........617 524-6883
Dave Kenyon, *President*
Jim Kenyon, *Admin Sec*
EMP: 12
SQ FT: 10,000
SALES (est): 1.9MM **Privately Held**
WEB: www.kenyonwoodworking.com
SIC: 2431 2541 Mfg Millwork Mfg Wood Partitions/Fixtures

(G-11946)
MEDSIX INC
101 S Huntington Ave (02130-4768)
PHONE..........617 935-2716
Nikin Tharan, *CEO*
EMP: 6
SALES (est): 230.9K **Privately Held**
SIC: 3841 3842 Mfg Surgical/Medical Instruments Mfg Surgical Appliances/Supplies

(G-11947)
PALOMA PHARMACEUTICALS INC
37 Neillian Cres (02130-2416)
PHONE..........617 407-6314
David Sherris, *President*
EMP: 16
SALES (est): 1.8MM **Publicly Held**
WEB: www.sherrispharma.com
SIC: 2834 Mfg Pharmaceutical Preparations
PA: Diffusion Pharmaceuticals Inc.
1317 Carlton Ave Ste 400
Charlottesville VA 22902

(G-11948)
RAND GRANTWRITING
49 Orchardhill Rd (02130-3724)
PHONE..........617 524-5367
Randy Meyers, *Principal*
EMP: 3
SALES (est): 199K **Privately Held**
SIC: 3131 Mfg Footwear Cut Stock

(G-11949)
RED SUN PRESS INC
94 Green St (02130-2298)
PHONE..........617 524-6822
Ricardo Huembes, *President*
Eric Johnson, *Treasurer*
Tia Phillips, *Director*
Paul Normandia, *Administration*
EMP: 11
SQ FT: 10,000
SALES (est): 1.6MM **Privately Held**
WEB: www.redsunpress.com
SIC: 2752 2621 2732 2791 Lithographic Coml Print Paper Mill Book Printing

(G-11950)
STONYBROOK FINE ARTS LLC
24 Porter St (02130-2326)
PHONE..........617 799-3644
Morris Norvin, *Manager*
EMP: 3
SALES (est): 395.1K **Privately Held**
WEB: www.stonybrookfinearts.com
SIC: 3446 Mfg Architectural Metalwork

(G-11951)
WELD RITE
Also Called: Armor Roll
3371 Washington St (02130-2617)
PHONE..........617 524-9747
Walter Craven, *Owner*
EMP: 9 **EST:** 1970
SQ FT: 10,000
SALES (est): 1MM **Privately Held**
WEB: www.armorroll.com
SIC: 3446 7692 3444 Mfg Architectural Mtlwrk Welding Repair Mfg Sheet Metalwork

Jefferson
Worcester County

(G-11952)
BAY STATE SPRING CORP
1864 Main St (01522-1145)
PHONE..........508 829-5702
Paul Laroche, *President*
John J Laroche, *Treasurer*
EMP: 3 **EST:** 1962
SQ FT: 3,500
SALES: 310K **Privately Held**
SIC: 3495 3493 Mfg Wire Springs Mfg Steel Springs-Nonwire

(G-11953)
FIELD PENDLETON
1951 Main St (01522-1123)
PHONE..........508 829-2470
Bob Field, *Owner*
EMP: 3
SALES (est): 140K **Privately Held**
SIC: 2511 Mfg Wood Household Furniture

(G-11954)
LEADING EDGE ATTACHMENTS INC (PA)
Also Called: L E A
72 Heather Cir (01522-1419)
P.O. Box 178 (01522-0178)
PHONE..........508 829-4855
Lee A Horton, *President*
Michael Carney, *Director*
Timothy McGee, *Director*
▼ **EMP:** 3

▲ = Import ▼=Export
◆ =Import/Export

SALES (est): 496.6K Privately Held
WEB: www.leattach.com
SIC: 3531 Mfg Construction Machinery

Kingston
Plymouth County

(G-11955)
CATON CONNECTOR CORP
26 Wapping Rd Ste 1 (02364-1333)
PHONE....781 585-4315
Daniel Galambos, *President*
Tom Ross, *Exec VP*
Chuck Saba, *Vice Pres*
Donald Enos, *Engineer*
▲ EMP: 32
SQ FT: 50,000
SALES (est): 8.9MM Privately Held
WEB: www.caton.com
SIC: 3357 3643 Nonferrous Wiredrawing/Insulating Mfg Conductive Wiring Devices

(G-11956)
CRAFT BEER GUILD DISTRG VT LLC (PA)
Also Called: Craft Beer Guild of Vermont
35 Elder Ave (02364-1503)
PHONE....781 585-5165
Conor Giard, *Mng Member*
EMP: 20
SALES (est): 2.2MM Privately Held
SIC: 2082 5963 Mfg Malt Beverages Direct Retail Sales

(G-11957)
GLIDECAM INDUSTRIES INC
23 Joseph St (02364-1122)
PHONE....781 585-7900
Martin Stevens, *President*
David Stevens, *Treasurer*
EMP: 10
SQ FT: 10,000
SALES (est): 910K Privately Held
WEB: www.glidecam.com
SIC: 3861 Mfg Photographic Equipment/Supplies

(G-11958)
JLP MACHINE AND WELDING LLC
10 Winter St (02364-1115)
PHONE....781 585-1744
Jim Libby, *Mng Member*
EMP: 8
SQ FT: 6,800
SALES (est): 711.4K Privately Held
SIC: 3841 Mfg Surgical/Medical Instruments

(G-11959)
KINGSTON ALUMINUM FOUNDRY INC
7 Pembroke St (02364-1108)
PHONE....781 585-6631
Robert Barbieri Jr, *President*
Phil Rondo, *Office Mgr*
EMP: 7
SQ FT: 2,500
SALES (est): 622.4K Privately Held
SIC: 3363 3364 3365 Mfg Aluminum Die-Castings Mfg Nonferrous Die-Castings Aluminum Foundry

(G-11960)
KINGSTON BLOCK CO INC
72 Main St (02364-3028)
PHONE....781 585-6400
John Iannucci, *President*
Camille Iannucci, *Clerk*
EMP: 6 EST: 1948
SQ FT: 14,500
SALES (est): 920.8K Privately Held
SIC: 3272 3271 Mfg Cement Blocks & Septic Tanks

(G-11961)
KINGSTON MANUFACTURING CO INC
3 Pleasant St (02364-2108)
PHONE....781 585-4476
Joseph T Adamcewicz, *President*
Jadwiga E Adamcewicz, *Treasurer*
EMP: 7 EST: 1977
SQ FT: 1,000
SALES (est): 905.3K Privately Held
SIC: 3599 Machine Shop

(G-11962)
OMEGA OLIVE OIL INC
47 Newcombs Mill Rd (02364-1372)
PHONE....781 585-3179
Felicia Pakalnis, *President*
EMP: 3 EST: 2011
SALES (est): 174.3K Privately Held
SIC: 2079 Mfg Edible Fats/Oils

(G-11963)
ROGERS CORPORATION
63 Smiths Ln (02364-3008)
PHONE....508 746-3311
EMP: 5
SALES (corp-wide): 879MM Publicly Held
SIC: 2891 Mfg Plastic Materials And Resins
PA: Rogers Corporation
2225 W Chandler Blvd
Chandler AZ 85224
480 917-6000

(G-11964)
SOUTHEASTERN SAND AND GRAV INC
27 Pine Hill Rd (02364-1883)
PHONE....781 413-6884
Peter J Opachinski, *Principal*
EMP: 3
SALES (est): 224.6K Privately Held
SIC: 1442 Construction Sand/Gravel

(G-11965)
TITUS & BEAN GRAPHICS INC
Also Called: Sign-A-Rama
62 Main St Ste 107 (02364-3046)
PHONE....781 585-1355
Harold Titus, *President*
Brenda Titus, *Vice Pres*
EMP: 12
SQ FT: 3,000
SALES (est): 1.7MM Privately Held
SIC: 3993 3953 2752 Mfg Signs/Advertising Specialties Mfg Marking Devices Lithographic Commercial Printing

(G-11966)
WE PRINT TODAY LLC
66 Summer St (02364-1469)
PHONE....781 585-6021
Scott Eddy, *Bookkeeper*
David Struski,
EMP: 11
SQ FT: 8,000
SALES: 1.5MM Privately Held
SIC: 2752 2789 7334 Mfg Offset Printing Binding Repair Books Magazines Pamphlets & Photocopying Duplicating Srvcs

(G-11967)
WEB HOME PHOENIX FABRICATION
106 Wapping Rd (02364-1304)
P.O. Box 303 (02364-0303)
PHONE....781 424-8076
Eric Gray, *Principal*
EMP: 3
SALES (est): 306.9K Privately Held
SIC: 3842 Mfg Surgical Appliances/Supplies

(G-11968)
WORLDWIDE ANTENNA SYSTEMS LLC
Also Called: Wwas
42 Elm St Ste 3 (02364-1943)
PHONE....781 275-1147
Shane O'Neil,
EMP: 4 EST: 2012
SALES (est): 225.7K Privately Held
SIC: 3663 Mfg Radio/Tv Communication Equipment

Lakeville
Plymouth County

(G-11969)
A B METAL FABRICATORS
155 Millenium Cir (02347-1248)
PHONE....508 947-5577
Kieth Beadling, *Principal*
EMP: 4 EST: 2010
SALES (est): 427.6K Privately Held
SIC: 3499 Mfg Misc Fabricated Metal Products

(G-11970)
ABRA-CADABRA PROMOTIONAL AP
Also Called: Abra-Cadabra EMB & Screen Prtg
155 Millenium Cir Ste 101 (02347-1248)
PHONE....508 821-2002
Robert Preston, *Owner*
EMP: 4
SALES: 300K Privately Held
SIC: 2395 Pleating/Stitching Services

(G-11971)
ACCUDYNAMICS LLC
240 Kenneth Welch Dr (02347-1348)
PHONE....508 946-4545
George Ballou III, *President*
Steve D Sowell, *Corp Secy*
EMP: 55
SQ FT: 45,000
SALES (est): 10.5MM
SALES (corp-wide): 1.5B Privately Held
WEB: www.accudynamics.com
SIC: 3599 Mfg Industrial Machinery
PA: Halma Public Limited Company
Misbourne Court
Amersham BUCKS HP7 0
149 472-1111

(G-11972)
ACCURATE TOOL & MACHINE INC
155 Millenium Cir Ste 105 (02347-1248)
PHONE....508 946-3414
Paul Souza, *President*
EMP: 7
SALES (est): 847K Privately Held
SIC: 3599 Machine Shop

(G-11973)
BAY STATE ASSOCIATES INC
Also Called: Bay State Specialty Co
101 Charles Eldridge Rd (02347-1376)
P.O. Box 392, Middleboro (02346-0392)
PHONE....508 947-6700
Mike Moore, *President*
Richard V Keyo, *Treasurer*
Richard Keyo, *Human Res Dir*
Michael Moore, *Sales Mgr*
Josette Bosse, *Program Mgr*
▲ EMP: 35 EST: 1955
SQ FT: 36,000
SALES (est): 4.2MM Privately Held
WEB: www.baystateline.com
SIC: 3993 Mfg Signs/Advertising Specialties

(G-11974)
C & C SCALE CO INC
17 Hybrid Dr (02347-1252)
PHONE....508 947-0001
Paul Cinelli, *President*
EMP: 3
SALES: 900K Privately Held
SIC: 3596 Mfg Scales/Balances-Nonlaboratory

(G-11975)
COUNTRY PRESS INC
1 Commercial Dr (02347-1661)
P.O. Box 489, Middleboro (02346-0489)
PHONE....508 947-4485
Micheal Pintel, *President*
EMP: 10 EST: 1967
SQ FT: 15,000
SALES: 700K Privately Held
WEB: www.countrypressinc.com
SIC: 2752 Lithographic Commercial Printing

(G-11976)
HOME KORE MFG CO MASS INC
210 Kenneth Welch Dr (02347-1348)
P.O. Box 747, Stoughton (02072-0747)
PHONE....508 947-0000
William V Brophy, *President*
Mary Lou Brophy, *Treasurer*
Vincent A Murray Jr, *Admin Sec*
EMP: 4
SQ FT: 5,000
SALES (est): 680K Privately Held
SIC: 2452 Mfg Prefabricated Wood Buildings

(G-11977)
OCEAN SPRAY INTL SVCS INC (HQ)
1 Ocean Spray Dr (02347-1339)
PHONE....508 946-1000
Kenneth Romanzi, *President*
Grant Forrest, *Opers Spvr*
Richard A Lees, *Treasurer*
Richard A Stamm, *Admin Sec*
Anny Pacheco, *Admin Asst*
◆ EMP: 32
SALES (est): 69.6MM
SALES (corp-wide): 1.6B Privately Held
SIC: 2034 2033 2037 Mfg Dehydrated Fruits/Vegetables Mfg Canned Fruits/Vegetables Mfg Frozen Fruits/Vegetables
PA: Ocean Spray Cranberries, Inc.
1 Ocean Spray Dr
Middleboro MA 02349
508 946-1000

(G-11978)
SPACE BUILDING CORP
8 Harding St Ste 107 (02347-1230)
P.O. Box 283, East Taunton (02718-0283)
PHONE....508 947-7277
Robert Di Croce Jr, *President*
Carolyn Di Croce, *Treasurer*
EMP: 40 EST: 1951
SQ FT: 300,000
SALES (est): 6MM Privately Held
WEB: www.spacebldgs.com
SIC: 3448 1541 1542 1522 Mfg Prefab Metal Bldgs Industrial Bldg Cnstn Nonresidential Cnstn Residential Construction

(G-11979)
TODRIN INDUSTRIES INC
305 Kenneth Welch Dr (02347-1373)
PHONE....508 946-3600
Richard Nichols, *President*
Todd Nichols, *Vice Pres*
EMP: 15
SQ FT: 7,500
SALES (est): 4.2MM Privately Held
SIC: 3444 Mfg Sheet Metalwork

(G-11980)
UNDER PRESSURE LLC
1 Apple House Rd (02347-1836)
PHONE....508 641-0421
Mary E Zakarian, *Principal*
EMP: 6 EST: 2008
SALES (est): 400K Privately Held
SIC: 3589 Mfg Service Industry Machinery

Lancaster
Worcester County

(G-11981)
BUILT-RITE TOOL AND DIE INC
Reliance Engineering
851 Sterling Rd (01523-2915)
PHONE....978 365-3867
Craig Bovaird, *Branch Mgr*
EMP: 12
SALES (corp-wide): 13MM Privately Held
SIC: 3544 Custom Plastic Molding And Moldmaking
PA: Built-Rite Tool And Die, Inc.
807 Sterling Rd
Lancaster MA 01523
978 368-7250

GEOGRAPHIC

(G-11982)
BUILT-RITE TOOL AND DIE INC (PA)
Also Called: Reliance Engineering Division
807 Sterling Rd (01523-2915)
PHONE..................................978 368-7250
Craig Bovaird, *President*
Joy Bounville, *Executive*
EMP: 45
SQ FT: 10,000
SALES (est): 13MM **Privately Held**
SIC: 3089 Mfg Plastic Products

(G-11983)
GOVERNOR SUPPLY CO
Also Called: GSC
22 Hunter Ln (01523-3041)
P.O. Box 111 (01523-0111)
PHONE..................................978 870-6888
Gregg O'Donnell, *Managing Prtnr*
Douglas O'Donnell, *Partner*
EMP: 7
SQ FT: 1,000
SALES (est): 800K **Privately Held**
SIC: 3089 Mfg Plastic Products

(G-11984)
HORN CORPORATION (PA)
580 Fort Pond Rd (01523-3224)
PHONE..................................800 832-7020
Peter Hamilton, *CEO*
David Gomer, *Vice Pres*
Michael Gill, *CFO*
Edward Gerard Jager, *Admin Sec*
EMP: 50
SQ FT: 100,000
SALES (est): 8.2MM **Privately Held**
WEB: www.horncorp.com
SIC: 2653 5113 3086 7389 Mfg Corrugated/Fiber Box Whol Indstl/Svc Paper Mfg Plastic Foam Prdts Business Services

(G-11985)
STAINLESS STEEL COATINGS INC
Also Called: Steel-It
835 Sterling Rd (01523-2915)
PHONE..................................978 365-9828
Ivan M Faigen, *CEO*
Michael Faigen, *President*
▲ **EMP:** 11
SQ FT: 10,000
SALES (est): 3.1MM **Privately Held**
WEB: www.steel-it.com
SIC: 2851 Mfg Paints/Allied Products

(G-11986)
STERLING MANUFACTURING CO INC
640 Sterling St (01523-1852)
PHONE..................................978 368-8733
John Gravelle, *CEO*
Stanley Bowker, *President*
Michael Gravelle, *Marketing Staff*
▲ **EMP:** 35
SQ FT: 35,000
SALES: 9.7MM **Privately Held**
WEB: www.sterlingmfg.net
SIC: 3089 Mfg Plastic Products

Lanesborough
Berkshire County

(G-11987)
INJECTED SOLUTIONS INC
840 Cheshire Rd (01237-9775)
PHONE..................................413 499-5800
Henry Kirchner, *CEO*
Joseph A Kirchner, *President*
Susan Kirchner, *Treasurer*
▲ **EMP:** 13
SQ FT: 22,000
SALES: 3MM **Privately Held**
WEB: www.injectedsolutions.com
SIC: 3089 Mfg Plastic Products

Lawrence
Essex County

(G-11988)
99DEGREES CUSTOM INC
15 Union St Ste 205 (01840-1879)
PHONE..................................978 655-3362
Brenna N Schneider, *President*
▲ **EMP:** 6 **EST:** 2013
SALES (est): 331.4K **Privately Held**
SIC: 3999 Mfg Misc Products

(G-11989)
ACE METAL FINISHING INC
125 Glenn St (01843-1036)
PHONE..................................978 683-2082
Sharon Coskren, *President*
James Coskren, *Vice Pres*
EMP: 43 **EST:** 2008
SQ FT: 5,000
SALES (est): 3.3MM **Privately Held**
SIC: 3471 Plating/Polishing Service

(G-11990)
AEROSPACE SEMICONDUCTOR INC
Also Called: Sanchez Associates
439 S Union St Unit 2105 (01843-2800)
PHONE..................................978 688-1299
Adrian Pyke, *President*
EMP: 15
SQ FT: 4,357
SALES (est): 2.1MM **Privately Held**
SIC: 3674 3672 Mfg Semiconductors/Related Devices Mfg Printed Circuit Boards

(G-11991)
AIT MANUFACTURING LLC
678 Andover St (01843-1076)
PHONE..................................978 655-7257
April Messer, *Principal*
EMP: 3 **EST:** 2015
SALES (est): 63.9K **Privately Held**
SIC: 3999 Mfg Misc Products

(G-11992)
AMERICAN ADHESIVE COATINGS LLC (PA)
Also Called: Aacc
12 Osgood St (01843-1828)
P.O. Box 1708 (01842-3708)
PHONE..................................978 688-7400
Ea Krug, *President*
Gerald Villa, *Vice Pres*
Jerry Villa, *Vice Pres*
▲ **EMP:** 27
SQ FT: 15,000
SALES (est): 4.1MM **Privately Held**
WEB: www.aacc-hotmelts.com
SIC: 2891 Mfg Adhesives/Sealants

(G-11993)
ANDOVER MEDICAL DEV GROUP
51 S Canal St Unit 2 (01843-1500)
PHONE..................................978 685-0838
Thomas Prezkop, *President*
Susan Bowser, *Project Mgr*
EMP: 4
SQ FT: 2,600
SALES (est): 398.7K **Privately Held**
SIC: 3599 8711 Engineering Services Mfg Industrial Machinery

(G-11994)
ANDOVER ORGAN COMPANY INC
560 Broadway (01841-2446)
P.O. Box 36, Methuen (01844-0036)
PHONE..................................978 686-9600
Donald H Olson, *President*
Ben Mague, *Treasurer*
Benjamin Mague, *Treasurer*
Matthew Bellocchio, *Bd of Directors*
Lisa Lucius, *Admin Asst*
EMP: 15 **EST:** 1948
SQ FT: 12,000
SALES (est): 2.1MM **Privately Held**
WEB: www.andoverorgan.com
SIC: 3931 7699 Mfg & Services Pipe Organs

(G-11995)
ASAHI/AMERICA INC (HQ)
655 Andover St (01843-1032)
P.O. Box 1108 (01842-2108)
PHONE..................................781 321-5409
Daniel Anderson, *CEO*
Hidetoshi Hashimoto, *Ch of Bd*
Harry Aiba, *President*
Robert Marsiglia, *Business Mgr*
Rick Siberine, *Business Mgr*
◆ **EMP:** 105
SQ FT: 94,000
SALES (est): 17.8MM **Privately Held**
WEB: www.asahi-america.com
SIC: 3084 3089 3491 3625 Mfg Plastic Pipe Mfg Plastic Products Mfg Industrial Valves Mfg Relay/Indstl Control

(G-11996)
ASAHI/AMERICA INC
655 Andover St (01843-1032)
PHONE..................................800 343-3618
Hal Hashimoto, *CEO*
EMP: 7 **Privately Held**
SIC: 3084 Whol Industrial Equipment
HQ: Asahi/America, Inc.
655 Andover St
Lawrence MA 01843
781 321-5409

(G-11997)
B G PECK COMPANY INC
Also Called: Peck Precision Fabrication
50 Shepard St (01843-1024)
PHONE..................................978 686-4181
Stephen Greer, *Ch of Bd*
David Greer, *Treasurer*
EMP: 25
SQ FT: 52,000
SALES (est): 5.3MM **Privately Held**
WEB: www.bgpeck.com
SIC: 3053 3469 Mfg Gaskets/Packing/Sealing Devices Mfg Metal Stampings

(G-11998)
BAGEL BOY INC
485 S Union St (01843-2811)
PHONE..................................978 682-8646
Chaouki M Bouchrouche, *President*
Wally Khoury, *Purch Mgr*
John Boghos, *Treasurer*
Chuck Bouchrouche, *Manager*
▲ **EMP:** 80
SQ FT: 30,000
SALES (est): 20.4MM **Privately Held**
SIC: 2051 Mfg Bread/Related Products

(G-11999)
BUSINESS CARDS OVERNIGHT INC
Also Called: Wholesale Printing Specialists
15 Union St Ste 19 (01840-1866)
PHONE..................................978 974-9271
Linda Hannan, *CEO*
Kenneth Hannan, *CFO*
EMP: 6
SQ FT: 3,500
SALES: 720K **Privately Held**
SIC: 2759 2791 2789 2752 Commercial Printing Typesetting Services Bookbinding Commercial Printing

(G-12000)
C Q P BAKERY
19 Blanchard St (01843-1413)
PHONE..................................978 557-5626
Fernando Cafua, *Partner*
Frank Pino, *Partner*
Mike Quinn, *Partner*
EMP: 49 **EST:** 2000
SQ FT: 11,000
SALES (est): 1MM **Privately Held**
SIC: 2051 Mfg Bread/Related Products

(G-12001)
CAMBRIDGE BRICKHOUSE INC
60 Island St Ste 2 (01840-1835)
PHONE..................................978 725-8001
Yanitzia Canetti, *President*
▲ **EMP:** 9
SALES (est): 857.1K **Privately Held**
WEB: www.cambridgebh.com
SIC: 2741 Internet Publishing And Broadcasting

(G-12002)
CAPE POND ICE COMPANY
48 Winthrop Ave (01843-2817)
PHONE..................................978 688-2300
Joe Bresnahan Jr, *Owner*
EMP: 4
SALES (corp-wide): 1.5MM **Privately Held**
SIC: 2097 Mfg Ice
PA: Cape Pond Ice Company
104 Commercial St
Gloucester MA 01930
978 283-0174

(G-12003)
CARDINAL SHOE CORPORATION
468 N Canal St Ste 3 (01840-1211)
PHONE..................................978 686-9706
Richard A Bass, *President*
Andrew Bass, *Vice Pres*
Allan Ornsteen, *Vice Pres*
▲ **EMP:** 25 **EST:** 1962
SQ FT: 160,000
SALES (est): 3.4MM **Privately Held**
SIC: 3144 4225 Mfg Women's Footwear General Warehouse/Storage

(G-12004)
CENTRAL VACUUM CLEANERS
Also Called: C V C
250 Canal St (01840-1642)
PHONE..................................978 682-5295
EMP: 8
SALES (corp-wide): 2.5MM **Privately Held**
SIC: 3589 3444 3635 Mfg Service Industry Machinery Mfg Sheet Metalwork Mfg Home Vacuum Cleaners
PA: Central Vacuum Cleaners
476 Lowell St Ste 1
Methuen MA 01844
978 682-5294

(G-12005)
CHARM SCIENCES INC (PA)
659 Andover St (01843-1032)
PHONE..................................978 687-9200
Stanley E Charm, *President*
Kevin Macmillan, *COO*
Rick Skiffington, *Vice Pres*
Mark Tess, *Vice Pres*
Shirley Z Charm, *Treasurer*
◆ **EMP:** 150 **EST:** 1978
SQ FT: 90,000
SALES (est): 47.3MM **Privately Held**
WEB: www.charm.com
SIC: 2899 Mfg Chemical Preparations

(G-12006)
CHEMCO CORPORATION
46 Stafford St (01841-2422)
PHONE..................................978 687-9000
Paul Lewis, *President*
Kim Brown, *Controller*
◆ **EMP:** 22
SALES (est): 3.8MM **Privately Held**
WEB: www.chemco.net
SIC: 2842 Manufactures Chemicals & Allied Products

(G-12007)
CIL ELECTROPLATING INC (PA)
Also Called: Ace Metal Finishing
125 Glenn St (01843-1036)
PHONE..................................978 683-2082
James Coskren, *CEO*
Melissa Mc Kallagat, *Office Mgr*
EMP: 140
SALES (est): 14.2MM **Privately Held**
WEB: www.adtecelectroplating.com
SIC: 3471 Plating/Polishing Service

(G-12008)
CIL ELECTROPLATING INC
9 Mill St (01840-1635)
PHONE..................................978 683-2082
Eric Sideri Jr, *Manager*
EMP: 85
SALES (corp-wide): 14.2MM **Privately Held**
WEB: www.adtecelectroplating.com
SIC: 3471 Electroplating Of Metals

PA: C.I.L. Electroplating, Inc.
125 Glenn St
Lawrence MA 01843
978 683-2082

(G-12009)
CIL INC
400 Canal St (01840-1221)
PHONE..................................978 685-8300
James Coskren, *President*
Mike Venable, *General Mgr*
John Hoegen, *Sales Mgr*
David Oneil, *Info Tech Dir*
EMP: 80
SQ FT: 15,000
SALES: 3MM **Privately Held**
WEB: www.cilinc.com
SIC: 3471 3479 Plating/Polishing Service Coating/Engraving Service

(G-12010)
CLIVUS MULTRUM INC
15 Union St Ste 412 (01840-1867)
PHONE..................................978 725-5591
Abby A Rockefeller, *President*
Richard Cataldo, *Treasurer*
▼ **EMP:** 8
SQ FT: 15,000
SALES (est): 920K **Privately Held**
WEB: www.clivus.com
SIC: 3261 Mfg Plumbing Fixtures And Toilet Fixtures Vitreous China

(G-12011)
CLIVUS NEW ENGLAND INC
60 Island St Ste 8 (01840-1835)
P.O. Box 127, North Andover (01845-0127)
PHONE..................................978 794-9400
William F Wall, *President*
Joseph Ducharme, *General Mgr*
Janette Wall, *Vice Pres*
▲ **EMP:** 5
SALES (est): 593.4K **Privately Held**
WEB: www.clivusne.com
SIC: 3261 1711 Mfg Vitreous Plumbing Fixtures Plumbing/Heating/Air Cond Contractor

(G-12012)
COLUMBIA ASC INC
165 S Broadway Ste 167 (01843-1426)
PHONE..................................978 683-2205
Marilyn Reilly Cochran, *President*
Salvatore Messina, *Vice Pres*
EMP: 12 **EST:** 1935
SQ FT: 8,000
SALES: 1.4MM **Privately Held**
SIC: 3544 2394 7641 3444 Mfg Dies/Tools/Jigs/Fixt Mfg Canvas/Related Prdts Reupholstery/Furn Repair Mfg Sheet Metalwork Mfg Machine Tool Access

(G-12013)
CORK TECHNOLOGIES LLC
29 S Canal St Ste 204 (01843-1403)
PHONE..................................978 687-9500
Bruce Macomber, *Mng Member*
Michael Macomber,
EMP: 8
SALES (est): 1MM **Privately Held**
SIC: 2499 Mfg Wood Products

(G-12014)
D CRONINS WELDING SERVICE
70 State St (01843-2637)
PHONE..................................978 664-4488
David J Cronin, *President*
EMP: 6
SQ FT: 14,000
SALES (est): 1.3MM **Privately Held**
SIC: 7692 3446 1799 1791 Welding Repair Mfg Architectural Mtlwrk Special Trade Contractor Structural Steel Erectn Industrial Bldg Cnstn

(G-12015)
DAVIS PRECISION MFG LLC
250 Canal St Ste 27 (01840-1642)
PHONE..................................978 794-0042
Shawn William Davis, *Principal*
EMP: 3 **EST:** 2009
SALES (est): 231.7K **Privately Held**
SIC: 3999 Mfg Misc Products

(G-12016)
DEFENSE SUPPORT SOLUTIONS LLC
60 Island St Ste 2 (01840-1835)
PHONE..................................978 989-9460
Randall Kaminsky,
EMP: 3
SALES (est): 160K **Privately Held**
SIC: 3812 Mfg Search/Navigation Equipment

(G-12017)
DIAMOND IRONWORKS INC
109 Blanchard St (01843-1415)
PHONE..................................978 794-4640
Steven Doherty, *President*
EMP: 34
SALES: 19MM **Privately Held**
WEB: www.diamondironworks.com
SIC: 3441 Structural Metal Fabrication

(G-12018)
DIKE CORPORATION (PA)
1 Broadway Ste 1b (01840-1082)
PHONE..................................978 208-7046
John H Dike Jr, *President*
EMP: 3
SALES (est): 480.7K **Privately Held**
SIC: 3594 3613 Mfg Hydraulic Systems & Control Panels

(G-12019)
EAGLE WOODWORKING INC
678 Andover St Ste 1 (01843-1077)
PHONE..................................978 681-6194
Christian Kreilkamp, *President*
EMP: 10
SQ FT: 15,000
SALES (est): 1.4MM **Privately Held**
SIC: 2499 2541 Mfg Custom Drawers & Cabinets

(G-12020)
EASTERN PACKAGING INC
283 Lowell St (01840-1097)
PHONE..................................978 685-7723
Erik P Curtis, *President*
Loreen D Curtis, *Corp Secy*
Henry Pires, *Opers Mgr*
Robert Faulkner, *Controller*
EMP: 60
SQ FT: 85,000
SALES (est): 12.2MM **Privately Held**
WEB: www.easternpackaginginc.com
SIC: 2821 2673 Mfg Plastic Materials/Resins Mfg Bags-Plastic/Coated Paper

(G-12021)
EBANO WOODWORKS INC
616 Essex St Ste 1 (01841-4373)
PHONE..................................978 879-7206
EMP: 4
SALES (est): 354.9K **Privately Held**
SIC: 2431 Mfg Millwork

(G-12022)
EMERSON PROCESS MANAGEMENT
Also Called: Rpp
12 Ballard Way (01843-1044)
PHONE..................................978 689-2800
Bill McCarron, *Manager*
EMP: 200
SALES (corp-wide): 18.3B **Publicly Held**
SIC: 3823 Mfg Process Control Instruments
HQ: Emerson Process Management Power & Water Solutions, Inc.
200 Beta Dr
Pittsburgh PA 15238
412 963-4000

(G-12023)
FIVE STAR PLATING LLC
7a Broadway (01840-1002)
PHONE..................................978 655-4081
Pedro Inoa, *Vice Pres*
Fausto Garcia, *Mng Member*
EMP: 30
SQ FT: 20,000
SALES: 1.8MM **Privately Held**
SIC: 3471 Plating/Polishing Service
PA: Inoa Y Torres, Accesorios Y Suministros De Informatica, C. Por A.
Ave Nunez De Caceres
Santo Domingo

(G-12024)
FLAMETECH STEELS INC
600 Essex St (01841-4320)
PHONE..................................978 686-9518
Samuel F Facella, *President*
EMP: 7
SQ FT: 150,000
SALES (est): 648.1K **Privately Held**
SIC: 3441 Structural Metal Fabrication

(G-12025)
FLOWSERVE US INC
Also Called: Lawrence Pumps
280 Merrimack St (01843-1779)
PHONE..................................978 682-5248
Samuel Barrett, *Branch Mgr*
EMP: 110
SALES (corp-wide): 3.8B **Publicly Held**
SIC: 3561 Manufacturer Of Pumps/Pumping Equipment Manufacture Of Engineered Centrifugal Pumps For Petroleum Refining
HQ: Flowserve Us Inc.
5215 N Oconnor Blvd Ste Connor
Irving TX 75039
972 443-6500

(G-12026)
FROZEN CUPS LLC
265 Merrimack St Ste 6 (01843-1700)
PHONE..................................978 918-1872
Vinh Le, *Principal*
EMP: 3
SALES (est): 189K **Privately Held**
SIC: 2026 Mfg Fluid Milk

(G-12027)
GAYNOR MINDEN INC
468 Canal St (01840)
PHONE..................................212 929-0087
Eliza Minden, *Branch Mgr*
EMP: 3 **Privately Held**
SIC: 3131 Mfg Footwear Cut Stock
PA: Gaynor Minden Inc.
140 W 16th St Apt 1re
New York NY 10011

(G-12028)
GLOBAL CONNECTOR TECH LTD
354 Merrimack St Ste 260 (01843-1757)
PHONE..................................978 208-1618
Louis Guerra, *Principal*
Shelley Smith, *Regl Sales Mgr*
EMP: 10
SALES (est): 1.3MM **Privately Held**
SIC: 3661 Mfg Telephone/Telegraph Apparatus

(G-12029)
H & S MACHINE COMPANY INC
35 Marston St (01841-2312)
P.O. Box 897 (01842-1797)
PHONE..................................978 686-2321
George D Younker, *President*
Gary Schwardenberg, *Vice Pres*
EMP: 10 **EST:** 1948
SQ FT: 11,500
SALES: 1.1MM **Privately Held**
SIC: 3599 Mfg Industrial Machinery

(G-12030)
HARVARD FOLDING BOX CO INC
Also Called: Ideal Box Company
15 Union St Ste 555 (01840-1823)
PHONE..................................978 683-2802
David Simkins, *CEO*
Leon J Simkins, *President*
Barbara Camera, *Treasurer*
Karen Llera, *Admin Sec*
◆ **EMP:** 3 **EST:** 1951
SQ FT: 130,000
SALES (est): 19.7MM **Privately Held**
SIC: 2657 Mfg Folding Paperboard Boxes

(G-12031)
HAWK MEASUREMENT AMERICA LLC (PA)
90 Glenn St Ste 100b (01843-1022)
PHONE..................................978 304-3000
Les Richards, *CEO*
John W Evans Jr, *President*
EMP: 4
SQ FT: 5,100
SALES (est): 748.7K **Privately Held**
WEB: www.krohne.com
SIC: 3829 Mfg Measuring/Controlling Devices

(G-12032)
HD MERRIMACK
60 Island St Ste 4 (01840-1835)
PHONE..................................978 681-9969
Harlyene Goss, *Owner*
EMP: 3
SQ FT: 450
SALES: 48K **Privately Held**
WEB: www.hdmerrimack.com
SIC: 2678 Mfg Stationery Products

(G-12033)
HELFRICH BROS BOILER WORKS INC
39 Merrimack St (01843-1436)
PHONE..................................978 975-2464
Vincent Helfrich, *President*
Joseph Helfrich, *Treasurer*
Mitchell Charles, *Senior Mgr*
Jack Grimmer, *Director*
▲ **EMP:** 35 **EST:** 1948
SQ FT: 21,000
SALES (est): 16.2MM **Privately Held**
WEB: www.hbbwinc.com
SIC: 3443 1711 1541 3444 Mfg Fabricated Plate Wrk Plumbing/Heat/Ac Contr Industrial Bldg Cnstn Mfg Sheet Metalwork

(G-12034)
HELFRICH CONSTRUCTION SVCS LLC
39 Merrimack St (01843-1436)
PHONE..................................978 683-7244
Ken Nydam, *CFO*
EMP: 25
SQ FT: 2,000
SALES (est): 1MM **Privately Held**
SIC: 3443 Mfg Fabricated Plate Work

(G-12035)
HIGH-SPEED PROCESS PRTG CORP
Also Called: Graphic Litho
130 Shepard St (01843-1026)
PHONE..................................978 683-2766
Ralph E Wilbur, *President*
Mike Devine, *General Mgr*
Kari Wilbur, *Treasurer*
Randi Collins, *Controller*
EMP: 12
SQ FT: 28,000
SALES: 1.5MM **Privately Held**
WEB: www.graphiclitho.com
SIC: 2752 Lithographic Commercial Printing

(G-12036)
HOOKE LABORATORIES INC
439 S Union St (01843-2837)
PHONE..................................617 475-5114
Suzana Marusic, *President*
David Lindbergh, *Exec VP*
Tim Delp, *Sr Project Mgr*
Amy Claus, *Admin Asst*
EMP: 99
SALES (est): 14.4MM **Privately Held**
SIC: 2836 Mfg Biological Products

(G-12037)
IDEAL BOX COMPANY
15 Union St Ste 455 (01840-1866)
PHONE..................................978 683-2802
David Simkins, *President*
Michael Simkins, *Principal*
Barbara Camera, *Corp Secy*
Anthony Battaglia, *CFO*
Patricia Vanlandingham, *Marketing Staff*
▼ **EMP:** 8
SQ FT: 7,000

GEOGRAPHIC

SALES: 16.2MM **Privately Held**
SIC: 2653 Mfg Corrugated/Solid Fiber Boxes

(G-12038)
INFINITY TAPES LLC
300 Canal St Ste 7 (01840-1420)
P.O. Box 385 (01842-0785)
PHONE..................................978 686-0632
Craig L Allard,
◆ **EMP:** 42
SQ FT: 65,000
SALES (est): 13.1MM **Privately Held**
WEB: www.shepcompany.com
SIC: 2672 Mfg Coated/Laminated Paper

(G-12039)
INTER-CONNECTION TECH INC
250 Canal St (01840-1642)
PHONE..................................978 975-7510
Benny Shamash, *CEO*
EMP: 13
SALES (est): 1.2MM **Privately Held**
SIC: 3357 Nonferrous Wiredrawing/Insulating

(G-12040)
JAYBIRD & MAIS INC
360 Merrimack St Ste 20 (01843-1749)
PHONE..................................978 686-8659
Scott M Garfield, *President*
Norman Mais, *Treasurer*
Lorraine Lane, *Bookkeeper*
Jerold Garfield, *Director*
Stephanie Garfield, *Admin Sec*
◆ **EMP:** 35
SQ FT: 33,000
SALES (est): 8.6MM **Privately Held**
WEB: www.jaybird.com
SIC: 2672 Mfg Coated/Laminated Paper

(G-12041)
JOE BATSON
Also Called: Alo Systems
530 Essex St (01840-1242)
PHONE..................................978 689-0072
Joe Batson, *Owner*
EMP: 5
SALES (est): 188K **Privately Held**
SIC: 2499 1751 2434 Mfg Wood Products Carpentry Contractor Mfg Wood Kitchen Cabinets

(G-12042)
KEY POLYMER CORPORATION
17 Shepard St (01843-1023)
PHONE..................................978 683-9411
Robert A Baker, *President*
Eddy Pena, *Prdtn Mgr*
Al Commito, *Mfg Staff*
Ryan Batchelder, *Engineer*
Randy Vandeventer, *Controller*
▲ **EMP:** 47 **EST:** 1959
SQ FT: 165,000
SALES (est): 20.7MM **Privately Held**
WEB: www.keypolymer.com
SIC: 2899 Mfg Chemical Preparations

(G-12043)
KEY POLYMER HOLDINGS LLC
17 Shepard St (01843-1023)
PHONE..................................978 683-9411
Mark Kaluzny, *CFO*
William Newman, *Mng Member*
EMP: 50
SALES (est): 3.7MM **Privately Held**
SIC: 2891 Mfg Adhesives/Sealants

(G-12044)
LANFORD MANUFACTURING CORP
43 Merrimack St (01843-1463)
PHONE..................................978 557-0240
Mark McCrill, *President*
EMP: 20
SQ FT: 11,000
SALES (est): 3MM **Privately Held**
WEB: www.lmc—inc.com
SIC: 3599 Mfg Industrial Machinery

(G-12045)
LAPLUME & SONS PRINTING INC
1 Farley St (01843-2614)
PHONE..................................978 683-1009
Ronald Laplume, *President*
Ronald La Plume, *President*
Raymond La Plume, *Treasurer*
Jimmy La Plume, *Shareholder*
EMP: 25
SQ FT: 20,000
SALES (est): 3.1MM **Privately Held**
SIC: 2791 2789 2759 2752 Typesetting Services Bookbinding/Related Work Commercial Printing Lithographic Coml Print Gravure Coml Printing

(G-12046)
LAWRENCE FUEL INC
233 Winthrop Ave (01843-3822)
PHONE..................................978 984-5255
Joseph M Topor, *Principal*
EMP: 5
SALES (est): 564.9K **Privately Held**
SIC: 2869 Mfg Industrial Organic Chemicals

(G-12047)
LAWRENCE TEXTILE INC
1 Logan St (01841-1925)
PHONE..................................978 689-4355
John Benigno, *President*
▲ **EMP:** 5
SQ FT: 50,000
SALES (est): 421.7K **Privately Held**
SIC: 2261 Finishing Of Fabrics

(G-12048)
LINTON WELDING & FABRICATION
4 Home St (01841-1301)
PHONE..................................978 681-7736
Mark Linton, *Owner*
EMP: 3
SALES (est): 63.9K **Privately Held**
SIC: 7692 Welding Repair

(G-12049)
M R P GROUP INC (DE)
49 Blanchard St Ste 405 (01843-1443)
PHONE..................................978 687-7979
Matthew Carnezale, *President*
Matt Carnevale, *Treasurer*
EMP: 6
SALES (est): 418.8K
SALES (corp-wide): 9.6MM **Privately Held**
SIC: 3841 8742 Mfg Surgical/Medical Instruments Management Consulting Services
PA: Escalon Medical Corp.
435 Devon Park Dr Ste 100
Wayne PA 19087
610 688-6830

(G-12050)
MDS NXSTAGE CORPORATION (DH)
350 Merrimack St (01843-1748)
PHONE..................................866 697-8243
Jeffrey H Burbank, *President*
Jeff Rains, *Vice Pres*
Michael Williams, *Engineer*
Matthew W Towse, *Treasurer*
◆ **EMP:** 30
SQ FT: 11,500
SALES (est): 6MM
SALES (corp-wide): 18.3B **Privately Held**
WEB: www.medisystems.com
SIC: 3841 Mfg Surgical/Medical Instruments
HQ: Nxstage Medical, Inc.
350 Merrimack St
Lawrence MA 01843
978 687-4700

(G-12051)
MERRIMACK VALLEY WATER ASSN
Also Called: Pure One Systems
15 Union St Ste 800 (01840-1823)
PHONE..................................978 975-1800
Carl M Sutera, *President*
EMP: 6
SALES (est): 1.5MM **Privately Held**
SIC: 3589 5074 Mfg Service Industry Machinery Whol Plumbing Equipment/Supplies

(G-12052)
MICROSEMI CORP-MASSACHUSETTS
6 Lake St Ste 1 (01841-3032)
PHONE..................................978 794-1666
EMP: 3
SALES (corp-wide): 1.6B **Publicly Held**
SIC: 3674 Mfg Semiconductors/Related Devices
HQ: Microsemi Corp.- Massachusetts
1 Enterprise
Aliso Viejo CA 92656
978 794-1666

(G-12053)
MICROSEMI CORP-MASSACHUSETTS
Also Called: Microsemi-Lawrence
6 Lake St Ste 1 (01841-3032)
PHONE..................................978 620-2600
EMP: 400
SALES (corp-wide): 5.3B **Publicly Held**
WEB: www.microsemi.com
SIC: 3674 Mfg Semiconductors/Related Devices
HQ: Microsemi Corp.- Massachusetts
1 Enterprise
Aliso Viejo CA 92656
978 794-1666

(G-12054)
MICROSEMI CORP-COLORADO
6 Lake St Ste 1 (01841-3032)
PHONE..................................480 941-6300
EMP: 99
SQ FT: 115,000
SALES (est): 11MM
SALES (corp-wide): 1.6B **Publicly Held**
SIC: 3674 Mfg Semiconductors/Related Devices
PA: Microsemi Corporation
1 Enterprise
Aliso Viejo CA 92656
949 380-6100

(G-12055)
MICROSEMI CORPORATION
Also Called: Microsemi-Cdi
6 Lake St Ste 1 (01841-3032)
PHONE..................................781 665-1071
Thomas J Kachel, *General Mgr*
Chris Barnes, *Engineer*
Mark McNamara, *Manager*
Charlie Amico, *Supervisor*
Ed Lawrence, *Supervisor*
EMP: 74
SALES (corp-wide): 5.3B **Publicly Held**
SIC: 3674 Mfg Semiconductor Diodes
HQ: Microsemi Corporation
1 Enterprise
Aliso Viejo CA 92656
949 380-6100

(G-12056)
MICROSEMI NES INC
6 Lake St (01841-3032)
PHONE..................................978 794-1666
George Yencho, *President*
Kare Karlsen, *Vice Pres*
Douglas Milne, *Clerk*
EMP: 165
SQ FT: 38,500
SALES (est): 11.5MM
SALES (corp-wide): 5.3B **Publicly Held**
SIC: 3674 Mfg Semiconductors/Related Devices
HQ: Microsemi Corporation
1 Enterprise
Aliso Viejo CA 92656
949 380-6100

(G-12057)
MIDDLE EAST BAKERY INC (PA)
Also Called: Joseph's Online Bakery
30 International Way (01843-1064)
PHONE..................................978 688-2221
Joseph Boghos, *Principal*
▲ **EMP:** 85
SQ FT: 25,000
SALES (est): 15.9MM **Privately Held**
SIC: 2051 Retail Bakery

(G-12058)
MKS INSTRUMENTS INC
17 Ballard Way (01843-1045)
PHONE..................................978 975-2350
Onni Wirtanem, *Personnel*
EMP: 110
SALES (corp-wide): 2B **Publicly Held**
WEB: www.mksinst.com
SIC: 3829 3825 3823 Mfg Measuring/Controlling Devices Mfg Electrical Measuring Instruments Mfg Process Control Instruments
PA: Mks Instruments, Inc.
2 Tech Dr Ste 201
Andover MA 01810
978 645-5500

(G-12059)
MOBILE SPECIALTIES
610 S Union St (01843-3742)
PHONE..................................978 416-0107
Warren Gallagher, *Owner*
EMP: 4
SALES (est): 421K **Privately Held**
SIC: 3694 Mfg Engine Electrical Equipment

(G-12060)
MULTIGRAINS INC
Also Called: Multigrains Bakery
117 Water St (01841-4720)
PHONE..................................978 691-6100
Joseph A Faro, *President*
Rosa Munoz, *Human Res Dir*
Laura Flenniken, *Sales Staff*
Darren Tiero, *Manager*
Luz Hernandez, *Receptionist*
▲ **EMP:** 205 **EST:** 1966
SQ FT: 139,000
SALES (est): 42.3MM **Privately Held**
SIC: 2051 Whol Groceries

(G-12061)
N-TEK INC
22 Ballard Rd (01843-1046)
PHONE..................................978 687-4010
Paul K Mello, *President*
Richard Mulloy, *Treasurer*
EMP: 5
SQ FT: 3,200
SALES (est): 606.2K **Privately Held**
SIC: 3471 Machine Job Shop Specializing In Assembly & Coating

(G-12062)
NATIONAL FIBER TECHNOLOGY LLC
15 Union St Ste 320 (01840-1823)
PHONE..................................978 686-2964
Kim Clark, *Mng Member*
Fred Fehrmann,
EMP: 5
SQ FT: 17,000
SALES (est): 562.7K **Privately Held**
WEB: www.nftech.com
SIC: 3999 Mfg Custom Hair Wigs And Fur Fabrics

(G-12063)
NEW BALANCE ATHLETICS INC
5 S Union St (01843-1699)
PHONE..................................978 685-8400
Toll Free:..877 -
John Wilson, *Exec VP*
Jim Mattison, *Admin Asst*
EMP: 490
SQ FT: 140,000
SALES (corp-wide): 3.2B **Privately Held**
SIC: 3149 8731 3021 Mfg Footwear-Except Rubber Commercial Physical Research Mfg Rubber/Plastic Footwear
HQ: New Balance Athletics, Inc.
100 Guest St Fl 5
Boston MA 02135
617 783-4000

(G-12064)
NEW ENGLAND PRTZEL POPCORN INC
15 Bay State Rd (01841-4701)
PHONE..................................978 687-0342
Warren J Sideri Jr, *President*
EMP: 7
SQ FT: 13,000

▲ = Import ▼=Export
◆ =Import/Export

SALES (est): 1MM **Privately Held**
WEB: www.nepretzel.com
SIC: 2052 2096 2099 Mfg Cookies/Crackers Mfg Potato Chips/Snacks Mfg Food Preparations

(G-12065)
NEXCELOM BIOSCIENCE LLC
360 Merrimack St Ste 47 (01843-1740)
PHONE..................................978 327-5340
Scott McMenemy, *Business Mgr*
Bruce Zheng, *QC Mgr*
Tim Smith, *Technical Mgr*
Leo Chan, *Research*
Suzanne Shahin, *Research*
EMP: 23
SQ FT: 2,000
SALES (est): 6.2MM **Privately Held**
WEB: www.nexcelom.com
SIC: 3821 Mfg Lab Apparatus/Furniture

(G-12066)
NORTH AMERICAN CHEMICAL CO
Also Called: Cork Technologies
19 S Canal St Ste 2 (01843-1412)
PHONE..................................978 687-9500
Lance Macomber, *President*
Bruce Macomber, *Treasurer*
EMP: 9 **EST:** 1939
SQ FT: 85,000
SALES: 1.4MM **Privately Held**
SIC: 3131 Mfg Of Composition Cork Compounds & Products

(G-12067)
NXSTAGE MEDICAL INC (DH)
350 Merrimack St (01843-1748)
PHONE..................................978 687-4700
William Valle, *CEO*
Dan Pommer, *Area Mgr*
James Brugger, *Vice Pres*
Lisa Curtis, *Vice Pres*
Judith Taylor, *Vice Pres*
EMP: 267
SQ FT: 141,000
SALES: 393.9MM
SALES (corp-wide): 18.3B **Privately Held**
WEB: www.nxstage.com
SIC: 3845 Mfg Electromedical Equipment

(G-12068)
ONYX SPECTRUM TECHNOLOGY
Shearwater Em
15 Union St Ste 525 (01840-1823)
PHONE..................................978 686-7000
Larry Garneau, *Branch Mgr*
EMP: 3
SALES (corp-wide): 886.8K **Privately Held**
SIC: 3559 Mfg Misc Industry Machinery
PA: Onyx Spectrum Technology
78 Fisher Ave 2
Boston MA 02120
617 407-2826

(G-12069)
OPTIMUM SPORTSWEAR INC
34 Groton St Fl 1 (01843-2616)
PHONE..................................978 689-2290
Joseph Comeau, *President*
EMP: 7
SQ FT: 10,000
SALES: 1.3MM **Privately Held**
WEB: www.optimumsportswear.com
SIC: 2759 5949 Commercial Printing Ret Sewing Supplies/Fabrics

(G-12070)
OVERTONE LABS INC
Also Called: Tune-Bot
60 Island St Ste 1 (01840-1835)
PHONE..................................978 682-1257
David Ribner, *President*
Simon Ribner, *Manager*
▲ **EMP:** 3 **EST:** 2014
SALES: 800K **Privately Held**
SIC: 3161 Mfg Luggage

(G-12071)
PLANET SMALL COMMUNICATIONS
15 Union St Ste 5 (01840-1823)
PHONE..................................978 794-2201
Joseph Buschini, *President*
Lloyd Herendeen, *Treasurer*
EMP: 8
SQ FT: 1,600
SALES (est): 896.1K **Privately Held**
WEB: www.smplanet.com
SIC: 2731 7372 Books-Publishing/Printing Prepackaged Software Services

(G-12072)
PORT ELECTRONICS CORPORATION
60 Island St Ste 306 (01840-1835)
PHONE..................................800 253-8510
Denise Jones, *President*
Louise Elliott, *Exec VP*
Bob Wentworth, *Vice Pres*
EMP: 10
SQ FT: 740
SALES: 99.8MM **Privately Held**
SIC: 3679 Mfg Electronic Components

(G-12073)
S A N INC (PA)
Also Called: Omni Digital Printers
92 S Broadway (01843-1411)
PHONE..................................978 686-3875
Kishor Shah, *President*
Bharat Shah, *Treasurer*
Maya Shah, *Manager*
Alex Garcia, *Exec Dir*
EMP: 8
SQ FT: 5,000
SALES: 500K **Privately Held**
SIC: 2752 2791 2789 7334 Lithographic Coml Print Typesetting Services Bookbinding/Related Work Photocopying Service

(G-12074)
SILVER SWEET PRODUCTS CO
Also Called: Silver Sweet Candies Co
522 Essex St (01840-1242)
PHONE..................................978 688-0474
Samuel Silverstein, *Owner*
EMP: 8
SQ FT: 9,000
SALES (est): 403.9K **Privately Held**
SIC: 2064 Mfg Candy

(G-12075)
SMITH & NEPHEW INC
100 Glenn St (01843-1022)
PHONE..................................978 208-0680
EMP: 8
SALES (corp-wide): 4.9B **Privately Held**
SIC: 3842 Mfg Surgical Appliances/Supplies
HQ: Smith & Nephew, Inc.
7135 Goodlett Farms Pkwy
Cordova TN 38016
901 396-2121

(G-12076)
SOLECTRIA RENEWABLES LLC
Also Called: Yaskawa - Solectria Solar
360 Merrimack St Ste 9 (01843-1764)
PHONE..................................978 683-9700
Michael S Knapek, *CEO*
Mark Bernicky, *Vice Pres*
Eric Every, *Engineer*
Emily Hwang, *Engineer*
Aegir Jonsson, *Engineer*
◆ **EMP:** 130
SALES (est): 40.7MM **Privately Held**
WEB: www.solren.com
SIC: 3629 8748 Mfg Electrical Industrial Apparatus Business Consulting Services
HQ: Yaskawa America, Inc.
2121 Norman Dr
Waukegan IL 60085
847 887-7000

(G-12077)
TECHPRINT INC
137 Marston St (01841-2201)
PHONE..................................978 975-1245
Paul J Durant, *President*
Lissa Reynolds, *General Mgr*
Sally Wallett, *Purch Agent*
Gina Galizia, *Purchasing*
Ken Donovan, *Engineer*
▲ **EMP:** 75 **EST:** 1974
SQ FT: 35,000
SALES (est): 17.8MM **Privately Held**
WEB: www.techprintinc.com
SIC: 2759 2752 Commercial Printing Lithographic Commercial Printing

(G-12078)
TRIPOLI BAKERY INC
106 Common St Ste 6 (01840-1633)
PHONE..................................978 682-7754
Rosario Zappella, *President*
Angelo Zappella, *Treasurer*
Steven Zappella, *Clerk*
EMP: 50
SALES (est): 5.3MM **Privately Held**
WEB: www.tripolibakery.com
SIC: 2051 5461 Mfg Bread/Related Prdts Retail Bakery

(G-12079)
ULS OF NEW ENGLAND LLC
65 Manchester St (01841-3018)
PHONE..................................978 683-7390
John Butchard, *Manager*
EMP: 99 **Privately Held**
SIC: 2842 Mfg Polish/Sanitation Goods
PA: Uls Of New England, Llc
55 5th St E Ste 960
Saint Paul MN 55101

(G-12080)
UNITED GLASS TO METAL SEALING
15 Union St Ste G30 (01840-1823)
PHONE..................................978 327-5880
Richard Darwin, *President*
EMP: 15
SQ FT: 6,000
SALES (est): 2.1MM **Privately Held**
SIC: 3599 1799 Machining Sealing Glass To Metal

(G-12081)
VAPCO INC
360 Merrimack St Ste 23 (01843-1750)
PHONE..................................978 975-0302
Thomas Macneil, *President*
EMP: 3
SQ FT: 10,000
SALES (est): 456.5K **Privately Held**
WEB: www.vapco.com
SIC: 2834 Manufacturing Animal Health Care Products

(G-12082)
VOGEL PRINTING COMPANY INC
300 Canal St (01840-1420)
P.O. Box 127 (01842-0227)
PHONE..................................978 682-6828
Nicholas Vogel, *President*
▲ **EMP:** 6
SQ FT: 5,000
SALES (est): 675K **Privately Held**
SIC: 2752 Lithographic Commercial Printing

(G-12083)
WHITTEMORE COMPANY INC
30 Glenn St (01843-1020)
P.O. Box 3099, Andover (01810-0802)
PHONE..................................978 681-8833
Jeffrey Sheehy, *President*
Kathleen Sheehy, *Shareholder*
◆ **EMP:** 20 **EST:** 1948
SQ FT: 28,000
SALES (est): 3.6MM **Privately Held**
WEB: www.whittemoreco.com
SIC: 3295 Mfg Minerals Ground/Treated

(G-12084)
WISH DESIGNS INC (PA)
15 Union St Ste 209 (01840-1823)
PHONE..................................978 566-1232
E Caltabiano-Schneider, *President*
Fred Schneider, *Vice Pres*
EMP: 10
SALES (est): 1.2MM **Privately Held**
WEB: www.wishdesigns.com
SIC: 2759 7389 Sign Designer

(G-12085)
WOOD MILL LLC
250 Merrimack St (01843-1716)
PHONE..................................978 683-2901
Robert D Ansin, *Principal*
EMP: 6
SALES (est): 348.8K **Privately Held**
SIC: 2491 Wood Preserving

(G-12086)
ZOLIN TECHNOLOGIES INC
300 Canal St Bldg 12nd (01840-1420)
PHONE..................................978 794-4300
Thomas Devlin, *President*
EMP: 11
SALES (est): 1.2MM **Privately Held**
WEB: www.zolintechnologies.com
SIC: 3672 Coating Circuit Boards

Lee
Berkshire County

(G-12087)
ANDRUS POWER SOLUTIONS INC
Also Called: APS
690 Pleasant St (01238-9323)
PHONE..................................413 243-0043
Dan Andrus, *President*
EMP: 10 **EST:** 2003
SQ FT: 2,000
SALES: 1.7MM **Privately Held**
WEB: www.andruspowersolutions.com
SIC: 3621 1731 Mfg Motors/Generators Electrical Contractor

(G-12088)
BERKSHIRE STERILE MFG INC
480 Pleasant St (01238-9265)
PHONE..................................413 243-0330
Shawn Kinney, *President*
Debbie Smith, *Vice Pres*
P Devin Wigington, *Vice Pres*
Jeremy Griffin, *VP Engrg*
Paul Souza, *CFO*
EMP: 17 **EST:** 2014
SALES (est): 2.2MM **Privately Held**
SIC: 2834 Mfg Pharmaceutical Preparations

(G-12089)
BIASIN ENTERPRISES INC
515 Marble St (01238-9330)
PHONE..................................413 243-0885
EMP: 3
SQ FT: 2,400
SALES (est): 190K **Privately Held**
SIC: 3446 3312 7692 Mfg Architectural Metalwork Blast Furnace-Steel Works Welding Repair

(G-12090)
BONSAL AMERICAN INC
110 Marble St (01238-9514)
P.O. Box 710 (01238-0710)
PHONE..................................413 243-0053
Jeff Jager, *Branch Mgr*
EMP: 35
SALES (corp-wide): 29.7B **Privately Held**
WEB: www.bonsalamerican.com
SIC: 3281 3272 3274 Mfg Cut Stone/Products Mfg Concrete Products Mfg Lime Products
HQ: Bonsal American, Inc.
625 Griffith Rd Ste 100
Charlotte NC 28217
704 525-1621

(G-12091)
CSL BUILDING GROUP LLC (PA)
Also Called: Prozone
10 Park Pl (01238-1618)
P.O. Box 9456, Schenectady NY (12309-0456)
PHONE..................................616 669-6692
Craig Lynch,
EMP: 3 **EST:** 2016
SALES (est): 768.4K **Privately Held**
SIC: 2541 Mfg Wood Partitions/Fixtures

(G-12092)
FOX MODULAR HOMES INC
225 Housatonic St (01238-1329)
PHONE..................................413 243-1950
Louis Digrigoli, *President*
Dave Brown, *Vice Pres*
EMP: 12
SQ FT: 1,200

SALES (est): 1.2MM **Privately Held**
SIC: 2452 6552 Modular Construction And Private Development Operator

(G-12093)
NIKE INC
530 Prime Outlets Blvd (01238-8505)
PHONE..................................413 243-1861
Kelly Sears, *Branch Mgr*
EMP: 25
SALES (corp-wide): 39.1B **Publicly Held**
SIC: 3021 Mfg Rubber/Plastic Footwear
PA: Nike, Inc.
1 Sw Bowerman Dr
Beaverton OR 97005
503 671-6453

(G-12094)
ORACEUTICAL LLC
815 Pleasant St (01238-9325)
PHONE..................................413 243-6634
Eric Montgomery, *Mng Member*
▲ **EMP:** 23
SQ FT: 42,000
SALES (est): 4.8MM **Privately Held**
SIC: 2844 Mfg Toilet Preparations

(G-12095)
PROTECTIVE ARMORED SYSTEMS INC
Also Called: P A S
100 Valley St (01238)
PHONE..................................413 637-1060
Philip Martino, *President*
EMP: 22
SQ FT: 27,000
SALES (est): 3.4MM **Privately Held**
WEB: www.pasarmored.com
SIC: 3211 3231 Mfg Flat Glass Mfg Products-Purchased Glass

(G-12096)
TAPESTRY INC
Also Called: Coach Leatherware
100 Premium Outlets Blvd (01238-8501)
PHONE..................................413 243-4897
Debra Bailey, *Site Mgr*
Kathleen Pease, *Branch Mgr*
EMP: 10
SALES (corp-wide): 6B **Publicly Held**
WEB: www.coach.com
SIC: 3199 Ret Luggage/Leather Goods
PA: Tapestry, Inc.
10 Hudson Yards
New York NY 10001
212 946-8400

Leeds
Hampshire County

(G-12097)
AXIO INC
Also Called: Melon
77 Grove Ave (01053-9740)
PHONE..................................413 552-8355
Arye Barnehama, *CEO*
EMP: 4
SALES (est): 264.9K **Privately Held**
SIC: 3845 Mfg Electromedical Equipment

(G-12098)
CUSTOM METAL FABRICATION
40 Audubon Rd (01053-9726)
P.O. Box 555 (01053-0555)
PHONE..................................413 584-8200
Mark Day, *Owner*
▲ **EMP:** 4
SALES (est): 690.2K **Privately Held**
SIC: 2295 Mfg Coated Fabrics

Lenox
Berkshire County

(G-12099)
16SUR20 MANAGEMENT LLC
Also Called: Seize Sur Vingt
30 Kemble St (01240-2813)
P.O. Box 2280 (01240-5280)
PHONE..................................413 637-5061
James Jurney, *President*
Gwendolyn Jurney, *President*
EMP: 15
SQ FT: 2,000
SALES (est): 1.6MM **Privately Held**
SIC: 2329 2321 2325 Mfg Men's/Boy's Clothing Mfg Men's/Boy's Furnishings Mfg Men's/Boy's Trousers
PA: Groupe 16sur20, Llc
198 Bowery
New York NY 10012

(G-12100)
GL&V USA INC
GL&v Lenox
175 Crystal St (01240)
P.O. Box 846 (01240-0846)
PHONE..................................413 637-2424
Bob Short, *Engineer*
D Digennaro, *Human Res Mgr*
Daivd V Sepavich, *Sales Staff*
Laurent Verreault, *Branch Mgr*
EMP: 220
SALES (corp-wide): 110MM **Privately Held**
WEB: www.glv.com
SIC: 3554 Mfg Paper Industrial Machinery
HQ: Gl&V Usa Inc.
1 Cellu Dr Ste 200
Nashua NH 03063
603 882-2711

(G-12101)
INNOVATIVE TOOLING COMPANY INC
Also Called: I T C
180 Pittsfield Rd (01240-2131)
PHONE..................................413 637-1031
Karl Dastoli, *President*
Bill Pigott, *Vice Pres*
William J Pigott, *Treasurer*
EMP: 10
SQ FT: 7,500
SALES (est): 1.4MM **Privately Held**
WEB: www.innovativetool.net
SIC: 3544 3089 3599 Mfg Dies/Tools/Jigs/Fixtures Mfg Plastic Products Mfg Industrial Machinery

(G-12102)
N & M PRO SOLUTIONS INC
Also Called: Medicredits
212 East St (01240)
PHONE..................................413 822-1009
Matthew D Noyes, *President*
EMP: 3
SALES: 100K **Privately Held**
SIC: 7372 Prepackaged Software Services

(G-12103)
SAM KASTEN HANDWEAVER LLC
55 Pittsfield Rd Ste 12a (01240-2122)
P.O. Box 861 (01240-0861)
PHONE..................................413 637-8900
Sam Kasten,
Faye Morgan-Amidon,
▲ **EMP:** 4
SQ FT: 6,000
SALES: 1.5MM **Privately Held**
WEB: www.samkasten.com
SIC: 2391 2221 2273 2241 Mfg Curtains/Drapery Manmad Brdwv Fabric Mill Mfg Carpets/Rugs Narrow Fabric Mill

Lenox Dale
Berkshire County

(G-12104)
PATRIOT ARMORED SYSTEMS LLC
140 Crystal St (01242)
P.O. Box 400 (01242-0400)
PHONE..................................413 637-1060
Thomas J Briggs, *President*
Ralph Tassone, *CFO*
EMP: 35
SALES (est): 9.2MM **Privately Held**
SIC: 3231 Mfg Products-Purchased Glass

Leominster
Worcester County

(G-12105)
AARON INDUSTRIES CORP
20 Mohawk Dr Ste 1 (01453-3393)
P.O. Box 607 (01453-0607)
PHONE..................................978 534-6135
Robert G Tocci, *President*
Mike Carota, *Vice Pres*
Robert M Tocci, *Vice Pres*
Patty Blanchard, *Office Mgr*
▲ **EMP:** 30
SQ FT: 20,000
SALES (est): 13.9MM **Privately Held**
WEB: www.aaroninc.com
SIC: 2821 Mfg Plastic Materials/Resins

(G-12106)
ACCUCON INC
12 Mount Pleasant Ave # 100 (01453-5887)
PHONE..................................978 840-0337
John J White, *President*
Forrest E Hawes Jr, *Vice Pres*
EMP: 9
SQ FT: 3,500
SALES (est): 1.5MM **Privately Held**
WEB: www.accuconlabels.com
SIC: 2752 2672 Lithographic Commercial Printing Mfg Coated/Laminated Paper

(G-12107)
ADVANCED PROTOTYPES & MOLDING
Also Called: A P M
21 Howe St (01453-3801)
PHONE..................................978 534-0584
Craig W Powell, *President*
Erin Powell, *Admin Sec*
EMP: 8
SQ FT: 5,000
SALES (est): 916K **Privately Held**
SIC: 3089 3544 Mfg Plastic Products Mfg Dies/Tools/Jigs/Fixtures

(G-12108)
AFFORDABLE INTR SYSTEMS INC (DH)
Also Called: A I S
25 Tucker Dr (01453-6502)
PHONE..................................978 562-7500
Ben Maxwell, *President*
David Morales, *President*
Courtney Pirosko, *Vice Pres*
Stephen Boris, *Project Mgr*
Keith Leblanc, *Engineer*
◆ **EMP:** 100
SQ FT: 100,000
SALES (est): 56.4MM **Privately Held**
SIC: 2522 Mfg Office Furniture-Nonwood

(G-12109)
AHLSTROM-MUNKSJO PAPER INC
100 Erdman Way Ste S-101 (01453-1804)
PHONE..................................978 342-1080
Jan Alston, *CEO*
Andrew J Rice, *President*
Kim Henriksson, *Exec VP*
Anne Krun, *Sales Mgr*
Kenneth Schroeder, *Sales Mgr*
◆ **EMP:** 10
SQ FT: 1,200
SALES (est): 2.6MM
SALES (corp-wide): 2.7B **Privately Held**
WEB: www.us.munksjo.com
SIC: 2621 Paper Mill
HQ: Ahlstrom-Munksjo Germany Holding Gmbh
Nordlicher Stadtgraben 4
Aalen 73430
736 150-60

(G-12110)
AIS HOLDINGS CORP (DH)
25 Tucker Dr Ste 1 (01453-6502)
PHONE..................................978 562-7500
Bruce Platzman, *CEO*
Arthur Maxwell, *President*
▲ **EMP:** 9
SQ FT: 100,000
SALES (est): 56.4MM **Privately Held**
SIC: 2522 Mfg Office Furniture-Nonwood

(G-12111)
ALBRIGHT TECHNOLOGIES INC
30 Patriots Cir (01453-5967)
PHONE..................................978 466-5870
Robert Witt, *President*
Julie Kibbe, *Manager*
EMP: 15
SALES (est): 3.2MM **Privately Held**
WEB: www.albright1.com
SIC: 3089 Mfg Plastic Products

(G-12112)
ALLIED RESIN TECHNOLOGIES LLC
Also Called: Garden By Artech
25 Litchfield St (01453-4251)
PHONE..................................978 401-2267
Daniele La Posta,
Edward O Mazzaferro,
EMP: 6
SALES (est): 699.8K **Privately Held**
SIC: 2295 Mfg Coated Fabrics

(G-12113)
AMERICAN MARKETING & SALES
Also Called: Innovative Designs
20 Mohawk Dr (01453-3393)
P.O. Box 768 (01453-0768)
PHONE..................................978 514-8929
Leonard Tocci, *President*
EMP: 6
SQ FT: 52,000
SALES (est): 1.1MM **Privately Held**
SIC: 3089 Mfg Plastic Products

(G-12114)
AMERICAN MOLDING CORPORATION
35 Tisdale Ave (01453-4001)
PHONE..................................978 534-0009
Wayne J Richard, *President*
Brian J Richard, *Treasurer*
Brian Richard, *Treasurer*
Francis Richard, *Clerk*
EMP: 3
SQ FT: 20,000
SALES (est): 505.5K **Privately Held**
SIC: 3089 Molding Primary Plastics & Plastics Processing

(G-12115)
AZELIS AMERICAS LLC
Monson
154 Pioneer Dr (01453-3474)
PHONE..................................212 915-8178
Holly Daley, *Manager*
EMP: 6
SALES (corp-wide): 9.1MM **Privately Held**
SIC: 3569 Mfg General Industrial Machinery
HQ: Azelis Americas, Llc
262 Harbor Dr Fl 1
Stamford CT 06902
203 274-8691

(G-12116)
BANNER MOLD & DIE CO INC
251 Florence St (01453-4499)
PHONE..................................978 534-6558
James M De Felice, *President*
Ralph De Felice, *Vice Pres*
EMP: 40
SQ FT: 46,000
SALES: 3MM **Privately Held**
SIC: 3544 Mfg Industrial Injection Molds & Dies For Plastics Working Machinery

(G-12117)
BELDEN INC
Alpha Wire
128 Tolman Ave (01453-1926)
PHONE..................................978 537-8911
Joseph Brown, *Manager*
EMP: 45
SALES (corp-wide): 2.5B **Publicly Held**
WEB: www.belden.com
SIC: 3315 3357 Mfg Steel Wire/Related Products Nonferrous Wiredrawing/Insulating

PA: Belden Inc.
1 N Brentwood Blvd Fl 15
Saint Louis MO 63105
314 854-8000

(G-12118)
BEVOVATIONS LLC (PA)
Also Called: New England Apple Products Co
320 Industrial Rd (01453-1684)
PHONE..................................978 227-5469
Steven D Rowse, *Mng Member*
EMP: 13
SALES (est): 2MM **Privately Held**
SIC: 2037 Mfg Frozen Fruits/Vegetables

(G-12119)
BRIDEAU SHTMTL & FABRICATION
29 Phillips St (01453-4023)
PHONE..................................978 537-3372
David E Brideau, *President*
EMP: 12 **EST:** 1966
SQ FT: 11,000
SALES (est): 1.5MM **Privately Held**
SIC: 3444 1711 Mfg Sheet Metalwork Plumbing/Heating/Air Cond Contractor

(G-12120)
BUILT-RITE TOOL AND DIE INC
Also Called: Reliance Engineering
11 Jytek Rd (01453-5986)
PHONE..................................978 751-8432
EMP: 12
SALES (est): 689.1K
SALES (corp-wide): 13MM **Privately Held**
SIC: 3544 Mfg Dies/Tools/Jigs/Fixtures
PA: Built-Rite Tool And Die, Inc.
807 Sterling Rd
Lancaster MA 01523
978 368-7250

(G-12121)
BWAY CORPORATION
196 Industrial Rd (01453-1640)
PHONE..................................978 537-4911
Tina Boyer, *Human Res Mgr*
Elton Francis, *Branch Mgr*
Mauro Dominguez, *Technical Staff*
EMP: 12
SALES (corp-wide): 1.2B **Privately Held**
SIC: 3089 Mfg Plastic Products
HQ: Bway Corporation
375 Northridge Rd Ste 600
Atlanta GA 30350

(G-12122)
BWI OF MA LLC
248 Industrial Rd (01453-1642)
PHONE..................................978 534-4065
John Cortese, *Principal*
EMP: 4
SALES (est): 402.6K **Privately Held**
SIC: 2431 Mfg Millwork

(G-12123)
CAMCO MANUFACTURING INC
165 Pioneer Dr (01453-3475)
PHONE..................................978 537-6777
Randy Catalucci, *Manager*
EMP: 14
SALES (corp-wide): 118.7MM **Privately Held**
SIC: 2899 3085 Mfg Chemical Preparations Mfg Plastic Bottles
PA: Camco Manufacturing, Inc.
121 Landmark Dr
Greensboro NC 27409
336 668-7661

(G-12124)
CARBON COMPOSITES INC
Also Called: C C I
12 Jytek Rd (01453-5966)
PHONE..................................978 840-0707
Ben Evans, *President*
Michelle Leger, *Office Mgr*
◆ **EMP:** 10
SQ FT: 15,000
SALES (est): 2.3MM **Privately Held**
WEB: www.carboncompositesinc.com
SIC: 3624 Mfg Carbon/Graphite Products

(G-12125)
CARDINAL COMB & BRUSH MFG CORP
Also Called: Cardinal Comb Mfg
106 Carter St Ste 3 (01453-7303)
PHONE..................................978 537-6330
Anthony J Mazzaferro, *President*
Aldo J Mazzaferro Sr, *Treasurer*
Anna R Mazzaferro, *Clerk*
EMP: 40
SQ FT: 54,600
SALES (est): 2MM **Privately Held**
WEB: www.cardinalcomb.com
SIC: 3991 3089 Mfg Brooms/Brushes Mfg Plastic Products

(G-12126)
CASTLE PLASTICS INC
11 Francis St (01453-4911)
PHONE..................................978 534-6220
Joseph Serafini Jr, *President*
EMP: 8 **EST:** 1940
SQ FT: 10,000
SALES (est): 1.3MM **Privately Held**
WEB: www.castleplastics.com
SIC: 3089 Mfg Plastic Products

(G-12127)
CRH AMERICAS INC
Also Called: Old Materials New England
14 Monument Sq Ste 302 (01453-5766)
PHONE..................................978 840-1176
John Keating, *President*
EMP: 6
SALES (corp-wide): 29.7B **Privately Held**
SIC: 3273 Mfg Ready-Mixed Concrete
HQ: Crh Americas, Inc.
900 Ashwood Pkwy Ste 600
Atlanta GA 30338
770 804-3363

(G-12128)
CRISCI TOOL AND DIE INC
Also Called: Acro-Matic Plastics
32 Jungle Rd Ste 1 (01453-5995)
PHONE..................................978 537-4102
Peter Crisci, *President*
Lora Grimley, *Purch Agent*
Vincent Crisci, *Treasurer*
▲ **EMP:** 48 **EST:** 1964
SQ FT: 110,000
SALES: 8MM **Privately Held**
WEB: www.acromaticplastics.com
SIC: 3089 3544 Mfg Plastic Products Mfg Dies/Tools/Jigs/Fixtures

(G-12129)
CUSTOM SPORTS SLEEVES LLC
49 Royal Oaks Way (01453-2077)
PHONE..................................508 344-9749
Anne F Josephs, *Principal*
EMP: 5
SALES (est): 354.4K **Privately Held**
SIC: 2329 Mfg Men's/Boy's Clothing

(G-12130)
CUTTING EDGE CARBIDE TECH INC
36 School St (01453-3324)
PHONE..................................888 210-9670
William C S Weir, *President*
David P Bodanza, *Treasurer*
EMP: 3
SALES (est): 81.8K **Privately Held**
SIC: 2819 3545 Mfg Industrial Inorganic Chemicals Mfg Machine Tool Accessories

(G-12131)
DAHLICIOUS HOLDINGS LLC
320 Hamilton St Ste 3 (01453-2385)
PHONE..................................978 401-2103
Jaidesh Sethi, *Mng Member*
Ajeet Burns,
Tom Burns,
EMP: 14
SQ FT: 35,000
SALES: 6.5MM **Privately Held**
SIC: 2026 5141 Mfg Fluid Milk Whol General Groceries

(G-12132)
DAHLICIOUS LLC
320 Hamilton St Ste 3 (01453-2385)
PHONE..................................505 200-0396
Tom Burns,
Ajeet Burns,
Dharm Khalsa,
JD Sethi,
EMP: 40
SALES (est): 2.5MM **Privately Held**
SIC: 2026 Mfg Fluid Milk

(G-12133)
DIXIE CONSUMER PRODUCTS LLC
149 Hamilton St (01453-2342)
PHONE..................................978 537-4701
EMP: 8
SALES (corp-wide): 40.6B **Privately Held**
SIC: 2656 Mfg Sanitary Food Containers
HQ: Dixie Consumer Products Llc
133 Peachtree St Ne # 1
Atlanta GA 30303

(G-12134)
E T DUVAL & SON INC
386 Main St (01453-2937)
P.O. Box 419 (01453-0419)
PHONE..................................978 537-7596
Jeffrey Duval, *President*
Francis L Duval, *Principal*
Rebecca Duval, *Train & Dev Mgr*
EMP: 8
SQ FT: 3,200
SALES (est): 1.5MM **Privately Held**
SIC: 3441 3444 3541 Structural Metal Fabrication Mfg Sheet Metalwork Mfg Machine Tools-Cutting

(G-12135)
ETHOSENERGY TC INC
9 Leominster Connector # 301 (01453-3791)
PHONE..................................978 353-3089
Robert Beck, *Manager*
EMP: 12
SALES (corp-wide): 10B **Privately Held**
WEB: www.turbocare.com
SIC: 3511 Mfg Turbine Blades
HQ: Ethosenergy Tc, Inc.
2140 Westover Rd
Chicopee MA 01022
802 257-2721

(G-12136)
F & D PLASTICS INC (PA)
Also Called: Fd Plastics
23 Jytek Dr (01453-5984)
PHONE..................................978 668-5140
Roger Rosbury, *CEO*
Darren J Rosbury, *Exec VP*
Chuck Walkovich, *CFO*
David Leboeuf, *Manager*
Jean Rosbury, *Admin Sec*
▲ **EMP:** 40
SQ FT: 23,000
SALES (est): 8.2MM **Privately Held**
WEB: www.fdplastics.com
SIC: 3089 2851 2816 Mfg Plastic Products Mfg Paints/Allied Products Mfg Inorganic Pigments

(G-12137)
F & M TOOL & DIE CO INC
25 Jytek Rd (01453-5934)
PHONE..................................978 537-0290
Michael F Gasbarro, *President*
EMP: 20 **EST:** 1974
SQ FT: 11,000
SALES (est): 3.1MM **Privately Held**
SIC: 3544 Mfg Dies/Tools/Jigs/Fixtures

(G-12138)
F & M TOOL & PLASTICS INC
Also Called: Smartware Products
175 Pioneer Dr (01453-3475)
PHONE..................................978 840-1897
Mark Gasbarro, *President*
Mary McKenzie, *Manager*
▲ **EMP:** 93
SQ FT: 35,000
SALES (est): 66.4MM **Privately Held**
WEB: www.fmtool.com
SIC: 3089 Mfg Plastic Products

(G-12139)
FIRST PLASTICS CORP
Also Called: F P
22 Jytek Rd (01453-5966)
PHONE..................................978 537-0367
Edward Mazzaferro, *President*
Aldo J Mazzaferro, *Treasurer*
Anna R Mazzaferro, *Clerk*
▲ **EMP:** 10
SQ FT: 33,000
SALES (est): 2.7MM **Privately Held**
WEB: www.firstplastics.com
SIC: 3089 Mfg Plastic Products

(G-12140)
FORESTER MOULDING & LUMBER
152 Hamilton St Ste A (01453-2399)
P.O. Box 1526, Littleton (01460-4526)
PHONE..................................978 840-3100
William Mischel, *President*
EMP: 18
SQ FT: 15,000
SALES (est): 2.5MM **Privately Held**
WEB: www.forestermoulding.com
SIC: 2431 Mfg Millwork

(G-12141)
FOSTA-TEK OPTICS INC (PA)
320 Hamilton St Ste 1 (01453-2371)
PHONE..................................978 534-6511
John Morrison Jr, *President*
James R Leblanc, *Senior VP*
Jim Leblane, *Vice Pres*
Jim Peloquin, *Facilities Mgr*
Karen Olivari, *CFO*
EMP: 98
SQ FT: 113,000
SALES (est): 22.2MM **Privately Held**
WEB: www.fostatek.com
SIC: 3851 3842 Mfg Ophthalmic Goods Mfg Surgical Appliances/Supplies

(G-12142)
G F L INDUSTRIES
29 June St (01453-4317)
PHONE..................................978 728-4800
EMP: 3 **EST:** 2015
SALES (est): 189.8K **Privately Held**
SIC: 3999 Mfg Misc Products

(G-12143)
GDJR MACHINING INCORPORATED
Also Called: Action Precision Machining
823 Lancaster St (01453-4503)
PHONE..................................978 365-3568
George Mongeau, *President*
EMP: 3 **EST:** 2011
SALES: 400K **Privately Held**
SIC: 3599 Mfg Industrial Machinery

(G-12144)
GEORGIA-PACIFIC LLC
149 Hamilton St (01453-2342)
PHONE..................................978 537-4701
Steve Lambrose, *Engr R&D*
Samantha Wood, *Human Res Mgr*
EMP: 249
SALES (corp-wide): 40.6B **Privately Held**
WEB: www.gp.com
SIC: 2297 3086 3861 2631 Mfg Nonwoven Fabrics Mfg Plastic Foam Prdts Mfg Photo Equip/Supplies Paperboard Mill
HQ: Georgia-Pacific Llc
133 Peachtree St Nw
Atlanta GA 30303
404 652-4000

(G-12145)
GFORCE GRAFIX CORPORATION
12 Mount Pleasant Ave (01453-5887)
PHONE..................................978 840-4401
Emilie Gerber, *Principal*
EMP: 3 **EST:** 2010
SALES (est): 290.8K **Privately Held**
SIC: 3577 Mfg Computer Peripheral Equipment

(G-12146)
GIROUARD TOOL & DIE INC
218 Viscoloid Ave (01453-4372)
PHONE..................................978 534-4147
Francis J Girouard Jr, *President*

Dave Girouard, *Vice Pres*
EMP: 5
SQ FT: 3,500
SALES (est): 695.7K **Privately Held**
WEB: www.girouardtool.com
SIC: 3544 3089 Mfg Plastic Injection Molds & Injection Molding Of Plastics

(G-12147)
GIROUARD TOOL CORP
218 Viscoloid Ave (01453-4372)
PHONE..................................978 534-4147
Robert Julius, *President*
Lori Julius, *Vice Pres*
EMP: 8 **EST:** 2002
SALES (est): 1.3MM **Privately Held**
SIC: 2869 Mfg Industrial Organic Chemicals

(G-12148)
GROVE PRODUCTS INC
17 Marguerite Ave Ste 1 (01453-4202)
P.O. Box 240 (01453-0240)
PHONE..................................978 534-5188
David Braune, *President*
Simon Braune, *Vice Pres*
▼ **EMP:** 11 **EST:** 1966
SQ FT: 8,000
SALES (est): 2.3MM **Privately Held**
WEB: www.groveproductsinc.com
SIC: 3089 Mfg Plastic Products

(G-12149)
HANGER PROSTHETICS & ORTHOTICS
Also Called: Hanger Clinic
100 Erdman Way Ste S-100 (01453-1804)
PHONE..................................978 466-7400
Rig Taylor, *President*
Dennis Fitzpatrick, *VP Opers*
Steven Sasnoff, *Manager*
EMP: 4
SALES (est): 396.2K **Privately Held**
SIC: 3842 Ret Misc Merchandise

(G-12150)
HANGER PRSTHETCS & ORTHO INC
100 Erdman Way Ste S-100 (01453-1804)
PHONE..................................978 466-7400
Harvey Sosnofoff, *Manager*
EMP: 4
SALES (corp-wide): 1B **Publicly Held**
SIC: 3842 Whol Artifical Limbs
HQ: Hanger Prosthetics & Orthotics, Inc.
10910 Domain Dr Ste 300
Austin TX 78758
512 777-3800

(G-12151)
HEAT TRACE PRODUCTS LLC
233 Florence St (01453-4409)
PHONE..................................978 534-2810
Wayne Canty,
EMP: 20
SQ FT: 30,000
SALES (est): 6.6MM **Privately Held**
WEB: www.heattraceproducts.com
SIC: 3315 Mfg Steel Wire/Related Products

(G-12152)
HOME PDTS INTL - N AMER INC
Also Called: Tamor Plastics
106 Carter St (01453-7323)
PHONE..................................978 534-6536
Kenneth Flatery, *Manager*
EMP: 206
SALES (corp-wide): 551.5MM **Privately Held**
SIC: 3089 Mfg Plastic Products
HQ: Home Products International - North America, Inc.
4501 W 47th St
Chicago IL 60632
773 890-1010

(G-12153)
HUDSON COLOR CONCENTRATES LLC
Also Called: Chroma Color
50 Francis St (01453-4911)
PHONE..................................978 537-3538
Howard Demonte, *President*
EMP: 67
SALES (est): 803K
SALES (corp-wide): 24.7MM **Privately Held**
SIC: 2816 Mfg Inorganic Pigments
PA: Chroma Color Corporation
3900 W Dayton St
Mchenry IL 60050
877 385-8777

(G-12154)
IMANOVA PACKAGING
7 New Lancaster Rd (01453-5224)
PHONE..................................978 537-8534
Dave Fischer, *Principal*
Berry Collins, *CFO*
Paula Moisan, *Executive*
Harvey Stewart, *Executive*
EMP: 100
SALES (est): 8MM **Privately Held**
WEB: www.imanova.com
SIC: 3086 Mfg Plastic Foam Products

(G-12155)
INNOVATIVE MOLD SOLUTIONS INC
Also Called: I M S
42 Jungle Rd (01453-5208)
PHONE..................................978 840-1503
Paul Boudreau, *President*
Debbie Martinez, *Accountant*
Richard Cella, *Admin Sec*
▲ **EMP:** 50 **EST:** 1996
SQ FT: 6,000
SALES (est): 12.4MM **Privately Held**
WEB: www.innovativemold.com
SIC: 3089 Mfg Plastic Products

(G-12156)
JAM PLASTICS INC
22 Tucker Dr (01453-6500)
PHONE..................................978 537-2570
J D Mazzaferro Sr, *President*
Joseph Mazzaferro, *President*
Joseph D Mazzaferro Sr, *President*
Joseph D Mazzaferro Jr, *Vice Pres*
Matthew Mazzaferro, *Vice Pres*
▲ **EMP:** 22
SQ FT: 32,500
SALES: 2.9MM **Privately Held**
WEB: www.jam-plastics.com
SIC: 3089 2752 1799 Mfg Plastic Products Lithographic Commercial Printing Trade Contractor

(G-12157)
JUMBO PLASTICS INC
218 Willard St (01453-5051)
P.O. Box 1447 (01453-8447)
PHONE..................................978 537-7835
Joe Ashey, *President*
James Defelice, *Treasurer*
EMP: 10
SQ FT: 40,000
SALES (est): 1MM **Privately Held**
SIC: 3089 Mfg Plastic Products

(G-12158)
K AND C PLASTICS INC
18 Crawford St (01453-2326)
P.O. Box 781 (01453-0781)
PHONE..................................978 537-0605
Kirt D Wilbur, *President*
Carol Wilbur, *Financial Exec*
▲ **EMP:** 50
SQ FT: 24,000
SALES (est): 7.3MM **Privately Held**
SIC: 3089 Mfg Plastic Products

(G-12159)
KREST PRODUCTS CORP
707 Lancaster St (01453-4545)
P.O. Box 176 (01453-0176)
PHONE..................................978 537-1244
Richard Di Marzio, *President*
Dean Dimarzio, *Vice Pres*
Pat Di Marzio, *Treasurer*
Esther Di Marzio, *Clerk*
EMP: 25
SQ FT: 17,000
SALES (est): 3.4MM **Privately Held**
WEB: www.krestcombs.com
SIC: 3089 Mfg Plastic Combs

(G-12160)
LEAKTITE CORPORATION (PA)
40 Francis St (01453-4911)
PHONE..................................978 537-8000
Rodney G Sparrow, *President*
Tobey Marchal, *VP Human Res*
Jon Hoden, *Manager*
▲ **EMP:** 86
SQ FT: 100,000
SALES (est): 19MM **Privately Held**
WEB: www.leaktite.com
SIC: 3089 3411 Mfg Plastic Products Mfg Metal Cans

(G-12161)
LEOMINSTER CHAMPION
285 Central St Ste 202b (01453-6144)
PHONE..................................978 534-6006
Modestino Tropeano, *Treasurer*
EMP: 4
SALES (est): 173.6K **Privately Held**
SIC: 2711 Newspapers-Publishing/Printing

(G-12162)
LEOMINSTER ICE COMPANY INC
Also Called: Leominster Ice & Oil Co
5 Chestnut St (01453-3999)
PHONE..................................978 537-5322
Royal F Turner Jr, *President*
George E Douglas, *Treasurer*
Stephen Douglas, *Clerk*
EMP: 7
SQ FT: 2,500
SALES (est): 813.9K **Privately Held**
SIC: 2097 5999 Mfg Ice Ret Misc Merchandise

(G-12163)
LOLLI COMPANY INC
Also Called: Delta Molding
637 Lancaster St (01453-4543)
P.O. Box 747 (01453-0747)
PHONE..................................978 537-8343
Eric Yantz, *President*
EMP: 20 **EST:** 1968
SQ FT: 20,000
SALES (est): 2.6MM **Privately Held**
SIC: 3544 Mfg Dies/Tools/Jigs/Fixtures

(G-12164)
M & K INDUSTRIES INC
Also Called: Subcon Technology
177 Florence St (01453-4782)
PHONE..................................978 514-9850
Bimal Patel, *President*
Jayshri Patel, *Treasurer*
▲ **EMP:** 25
SQ FT: 1,500
SALES: 5.2MM **Privately Held**
SIC: 3823 Mfg Process Control Instruments

(G-12165)
MAUSER PACKG SOLUTIONS HOLDG
25 Tucker Dr (01453-6502)
PHONE..................................978 728-5000
John Clementi, *Branch Mgr*
EMP: 180
SALES (corp-wide): 1.2B **Privately Held**
SIC: 3089 Mfg Plastic Products
HQ: Mauser Packaging Solutions Holding Company
8607 Roberts Dr Ste 250
Atlanta GA 30350
770 645-4800

(G-12166)
MEXICHEM SPCALTY COMPOUNDS INC (HQ)
170 Pioneer Dr (01453-3474)
PHONE..................................978 537-8071
Enrique Ramirez, *President*
William Temkin, *President*
Mike Funderburg, *CFO*
◆ **EMP:** 205 **EST:** 1992
SQ FT: 130,000
SALES (est): 79MM **Privately Held**
WEB: www.alphagary.com
SIC: 3087 2899 Custom Compounding-Purchased Resins Mfg Chemical Preparations

(G-12167)
MICRO MACHINE & ELECTRONICS
283 Whitney St (01453-3222)
PHONE..................................978 466-9350
John A Heroux, *President*
EMP: 6
SQ FT: 4,000
SALES (est): 1MM **Privately Held**
SIC: 3599 Machine & Electronic Job Shop

(G-12168)
MODERN DISPERSIONS INC (PA)
78 Maguerite Ave (01453)
PHONE..................................978 534-3370
Janos Kozma, *President*
Michael Belcher, *Opers Staff*
Paul Lafrennie, *Production*
Gabor Kozma, *Purch Mgr*
Fran Boutell, *QC Mgr*
◆ **EMP:** 70 **EST:** 1967
SQ FT: 105,000
SALES (est): 22.9MM **Privately Held**
WEB: www.moderndispersions.com
SIC: 2821 Mfg Plastic Materials/Resins

(G-12169)
MONTACHSETT TCCI BURIAL VAULTS
Also Called: Montachsett Tcci Burial Vaults
38 Castle St (01453-4206)
P.O. Box 916 (01453-0916)
PHONE..................................978 537-6190
Scott Penniman, *Owner*
EMP: 3
SQ FT: 2,000
SALES (est): 180K **Privately Held**
SIC: 3272 Mfg Burial Vaults

(G-12170)
NEW ENGLAND FAB MTLS INC
Also Called: Nefm
101 Crawford St (01453-2327)
PHONE..................................978 466-7823
Michael J Boyer, *President*
Sally A Boyer, *Treasurer*
EMP: 25
SQ FT: 17,000
SALES (est): 4.8MM **Privately Held**
WEB: www.nefm.com
SIC: 3444 Mfg Sheet Metalwork

(G-12171)
NEW ENGLAND WIRE PRODUCTS INC (PA)
9 Mohawk Dr (01453-3321)
P.O. Box 276, Weston (02493-0002)
PHONE..................................800 254-9473
Charles Peters Jr, *President*
Karen Peters, *Treasurer*
Jim Shaw, *Controller*
Zachary Berlo, *Accountant*
Holly Rice, *Human Res Dir*
EMP: 152
SQ FT: 96,000
SALES (est): 33.6MM **Privately Held**
WEB: www.displayracks.com
SIC: 3496 3993 2542 Mfg Misc Fabricated Wire Products Mfg Signs/Advertising Specialties Mfg Partitions/Fixtures-Nonwood

(G-12172)
NORTH/WIN LTD
Also Called: South Win
272 Nashua St (01453-3304)
PHONE..................................978 537-5518
William Dubose, *Managing Prtnr*
Blaine Dubose, *Partner*
EMP: 5
SALES (est): 875.1K **Privately Held**
SIC: 3089 Mfg Plastic Products

(G-12173)
NORTHERN PRODUCTS INC
645 Lancaster St (01453-4543)
PHONE..................................978 840-3383
Edward T Rockwell, *President*
Donald Erb, *Admin Sec*
▲ **EMP:** 10
SQ FT: 25,000
SALES (est): 1.8MM **Privately Held**
SIC: 3089 Mfg Plastic Products

(G-12174)
NOVA PACKAGING SYSTEMS INC
Also Called: Imanova
7 New Lancaster Rd (01453-5224)
PHONE....................................978 537-8534
Marco Grassilli, *President*
Dana Blanchard, *Info Tech Mgr*
John Ruggieri, *Officer*
Stewart Harvey, *Admin Sec*
▲ **EMP:** 80 **EST:** 2004
SQ FT: 150,000
SALES (est): 13.9MM **Privately Held**
WEB: www.novapackagingsystems.com
SIC: 3565 Mfg Packaging Machinery
HQ: I.M.A. Industria Macchine Automatiche Spa
Via Bruno Tosarelli 182/184
Castenaso BO 40055
051 651-4111

(G-12175)
OPTOMISTIC PRODUCTS INC
61 N Main St (01453-5507)
P.O. Box 751, South Freeport ME (04078-0751)
PHONE....................................207 865-9181
Frank Langely, *President*
EMP: 10 **EST:** 1991
SALES (est): 463.9K **Privately Held**
WEB: www.optomisticproducts.com
SIC: 3674 Mfg Semiconductors/Related Devices

(G-12176)
PLASTICAN INC
196 Industrial Rd (01453-1662)
PHONE....................................978 728-5000
John R Clementi, *President*
Kenneth M Roessler, *President*
Jeffrey O Connell, *Senior VP*
Eva M Kalawski, *Vice Pres*
Mary Ann Sigler, *Vice Pres*
▲ **EMP:** 550 **EST:** 1970
SQ FT: 360,000
SALES (est): 1MM
SALES (corp-wide): 1.2B **Privately Held**
WEB: www.plastican.com
SIC: 3089 5719 Mfg Plastic Products Ret Misc Homefurnishings
HQ: Mauser Packaging Solutions Holding Company
8607 Roberts Dr Ste 250
Atlanta GA 30350
770 645-4800

(G-12177)
PROCESS COOLING SYSTEMS INC
213 Nashua St (01453-3301)
PHONE....................................978 537-1996
Theodore Rudy, *President*
Mark Roy, *Safety Mgr*
Tony Gallo, *Engineer*
David Doucet, *Treasurer*
Brian White, *Manager*
EMP: 43
SQ FT: 10,000
SALES (est): 14.9MM **Privately Held**
WEB: www.processcooling.net
SIC: 3585 1711 Mfg Refrigeration/Heating Equipment Plumbing/Heating/Air Cond Contractor

(G-12178)
PT PLUS AT WHITNEY FIELD
31 Cinema Blvd (01453-3290)
PHONE....................................978 534-5922
Liz Kelley, *Principal*
EMP: 3
SALES (est): 317.9K **Privately Held**
SIC: 3577 Mfg Computer Peripheral Equipment

(G-12179)
QG PRINTING CORP
27 Nashua St (01453-3311)
PHONE....................................978 534-8351
Mike Agnew, *Branch Mgr*
EMP: 200
SALES (corp-wide): 4.1B **Publicly Held**
SIC: 2752 Lithographic Commercial Printing
HQ: Qg Printing Corp.
N61w23044 Harrys Way
Sussex WI 53089

(G-12180)
QUAD/GRAPHICS INC
Also Called: Quadgraphics
27 Nashua St (01453-3311)
PHONE....................................860 741-0150
Steve Viens, *Vice Pres*
EMP: 512
SALES (corp-wide): 4.1B **Publicly Held**
SIC: 2752 Lithographic Commercial Printing
PA: Quad/Graphics Inc.
N61w23044 Harrys Way
Sussex WI 53089
414 566-6000

(G-12181)
REED & PRINCE MFG CORP
272 Nashua St (01453-3304)
PHONE....................................978 466-6903
James W Richardson, *President*
Jane B Richardson, *Admin Sec*
▲ **EMP:** 28
SQ FT: 45,000
SALES (est): 5.4MM **Privately Held**
SIC: 3452 Mfg Bolts/Screws/Rivets

(G-12182)
RESOURCE COLORS LLC
517 Lancaster St (01453-7515)
PHONE....................................978 537-3700
Jack O Donnell, *Mng Member*
EMP: 17
SALES (est): 3.9MM **Privately Held**
SIC: 2821 Mfg Plastic Materials/Resins

(G-12183)
ROEHR TOOL CORP
52 Old Willard Rd Unit 1 (01453-5269)
PHONE....................................978 562-4488
Paul Catalanotti, *President*
EMP: 12
SQ FT: 10,000
SALES (est): 2.3MM
SALES (corp-wide): 37.4MM **Privately Held**
WEB: www.roehrtool.com
SIC: 3543 Mfg Foundry Cores
PA: Progressive Components International Corporation
235 Industrial Dr
Wauconda IL 60084
847 487-1000

(G-12184)
ROGERS PRINTING CO INC
136 Pond St Ste 1 (01453-3599)
PHONE....................................978 537-9791
Bruce Lynch, *President*
Mary Rogers, *Admin Sec*
EMP: 40 **EST:** 1955
SQ FT: 2,500
SALES (est): 4.1MM **Privately Held**
WEB: www.rogersprinting.com
SIC: 2752 2796 2791 2789 Lithographic Coml Print Platemaking Services Typesetting Services Bookbinding/Related Work

(G-12185)
RUGG MANUFACTURING COMPANY INC
554 Willard St (01453-5923)
PHONE....................................413 773-5471
Elizabeth Rugg Grybko, *President*
Stanley Mellas, *Exec VP*
Jonathan Daen, *Director*
▲ **EMP:** 11 **EST:** 1842
SQ FT: 40,000
SALES (est): 3.1MM **Privately Held**
WEB: www.rugg.com
SIC: 3531 3423 Mfg Construction Machinery Mfg Hand/Edge Tools

(G-12186)
SANI TANK INC
60 Lanides Ln (01453-2336)
P.O. Box 96 (01453-0096)
PHONE....................................978 537-9784
Carl Di Massa, *President*
EMP: 4 **EST:** 1960
SQ FT: 6,000
SALES (est): 599.4K **Privately Held**
SIC: 3272 Mfg Concrete Septic Tanks

(G-12187)
SOIL EXPLORATION CORP (PA)
148 Pioneer Dr (01453-3474)
PHONE....................................978 840-0391
Marilou Bonetti, *President*
EMP: 8
SQ FT: 11,000
SALES (est): 2.2MM **Privately Held**
WEB: www.soilexcorp.com
SIC: 1481 1381 Soil Test Boring & Installation Of Monitor Wells

(G-12188)
SPECTRO COATING CORP
Claremont Flock, Div of
107 Scott Dr (01453-3320)
PHONE....................................978 534-6191
Rajesh Shah, *Branch Mgr*
EMP: 26
SALES (corp-wide): 12MM **Privately Held**
SIC: 2299 Mfg Textile Goods
PA: Spectro Coating Corp.
101 Scott Dr
Leominster MA 01453
978 534-1800

(G-12189)
SPECTRO COATING CORP (PA)
101 Scott Dr (01453-3320)
PHONE....................................978 534-1800
Hemendra Shah, *President*
Hemendra K Shah, *President*
Barbara Valley, *Controller*
Rajesh H Shah, *Admin Sec*
▲ **EMP:** 59
SQ FT: 102,000
SALES (est): 11.9MM **Privately Held**
WEB: www.spectrocoating.com
SIC: 2299 Mfg Textile Goods

(G-12190)
STYLETECH COMPANY
28 Jytek Rd (01453-5966)
PHONE....................................978 537-0711
▲ **EMP:** 3 **EST:** 2009
SALES (est): 338K **Privately Held**
SIC: 2821 Mfg Plastic Materials/Resins

(G-12191)
SWISS ACE MANUFACTURING INC
36 School St (01453-3324)
PHONE....................................978 860-3199
EMP: 3
SALES (est): 182.9K **Privately Held**
SIC: 3999 Mfg Misc Products

(G-12192)
TAYLOR MADE CABINETS LLC
139 Central St (01453-6146)
PHONE....................................978 840-0100
Thomas Bump, *Principal*
Robert Taylor, *COO*
Angela Taylor, *Treasurer*
EMP: 4
SALES (est): 328.3K **Privately Held**
SIC: 2434 Mfg Wood Kitchen Cabinets

(G-12193)
TEKNOR APEX ELASTOMERS INC
31 Fuller St (01453-4225)
PHONE....................................978 466-5344
Jonathan D Fain, *President*
James E Morrison, *Treasurer*
Richard Leonard, *Manager*
Edward T Massoud, *Admin Sec*
Ann Bergeron, *Admin Asst*
◆ **EMP:** 67
SQ FT: 1,500
SALES (est): 15.4MM
SALES (corp-wide): 845.9MM **Privately Held**
SIC: 2295 Mfg Coated Fabrics
PA: Teknor Apex Company
505 Central Ave
Pawtucket RI 02861
401 725-8000

(G-12194)
THOMAS B FULLEN
Also Called: Printworks
225 Viscoloid Ave Ste 1 (01453-4388)
PHONE....................................978 534-5255
Thomas B Fullen, *Owner*
EMP: 4
SQ FT: 5,500
SALES (est): 445.5K **Privately Held**
WEB: www.printworksnet.com
SIC: 2752 2759 Commercial Printing Web Design Web Site Hosting

(G-12195)
TIM GRATUSKI
Also Called: Add-A-Sign
136 Pond St (01453-3552)
PHONE....................................978 466-9000
Tim Grautski, *Owner*
EMP: 4
SQ FT: 2,700
SALES: 500K **Privately Held**
WEB: www.addasign.com
SIC: 3993 2394 Mfg Signs/Advertising Specialties Mfg Canvas/Related Products

(G-12196)
UNITED COMB & NOVELTY CORP (PA)
Also Called: United Plastics
33 Patriots Cir (01453-5967)
P.O. Box 358 (01453-0358)
PHONE....................................978 537-2096
Edward W Zephir Jr, *President*
Ed Zephier, *Partner*
◆ **EMP:** 60
SQ FT: 175,000
SALES (est): 33.4MM **Privately Held**
SIC: 3089 Mfg Plastic Products

(G-12197)
USPACK INC
Also Called: Energy Release
300 Whitney St (01453-3209)
PHONE....................................978 466-9700
Bob Waalkes, *CEO*
Alexander Aptekman, *President*
Dan Byrne, *Risk Mgmt Dir*
EMP: 35
SQ FT: 12,000
SALES (est): 10.5MM **Privately Held**
SIC: 3559 Mfg Misc Industry Machinery

Leverett
Franklin County

(G-12198)
MUDPIE POTTERS
13 Montague Rd (01054-9725)
PHONE....................................413 548-3939
Donna Gates, *Director*
EMP: 31 **EST:** 1991
SALES: 20.1K **Privately Held**
SIC: 3269 Mfg Pottery Products

Lexington
Middlesex County

(G-12199)
3M COMPANY
10 Maguire Rd Ste 310 (02421-3110)
PHONE....................................651 733-1110
Eric Paley, *Branch Mgr*
EMP: 324
SALES (corp-wide): 32.7B **Publicly Held**
SIC: 3841 Mfg Surgical/Medical Instruments
PA: 3m Company
3m Center
Saint Paul MN 55144
651 733-1110

(G-12200)
ABLE SOFTWARE CORP (PA)
5 Appletree Ln (02420-2406)
PHONE....................................781 862-2804
Yecheng Wu, *President*
Sarah Yang, *Vice Pres*
EMP: 10

GEOGRAPHIC

SALES (est): 924.7K **Privately Held**
WEB: www.ablesw.com
SIC: 7372 7371 Prepackaged Software Services Custom Computer Programing

(G-12201)
ACUSPHERE INC (PA)
99 Hayden Ave Ste 1 (02421-7965)
PHONE..................................617 648-8800
Mark Leuchtenberger, *President*
Mark Keegan, *Principal*
Lawrence A Gyenes, *CFO*
William I Ramage, *Officer*
EMP: 58
SQ FT: 47,500
SALES (est): 9MM **Publicly Held**
WEB: www.acusphere.com
SIC: 2834 Mfg Pharmaceutical Preparations

(G-12202)
ADOLOR CORPORATION
65 Hayden Ave (02421-7994)
PHONE..................................781 860-8660
Michael R Dougherty, *President*
John M Limongelli, *Senior VP*
George R Maurer, *Senior VP*
Michael D Adelman, *Vice Pres*
Richard M Mangano, *Vice Pres*
EMP: 75
SQ FT: 80,000
SALES (est): 7.2MM
SALES (corp-wide): 42.2B **Publicly Held**
WEB: www.adolor.com
SIC: 2834 Manufactures Pharmaceutical Preparations
HQ: Cubist Pharmaceuticals Llc
2000 Galloping Hill Rd
Kenilworth NJ 07033
-

(G-12203)
AGENTUS THERAPEUTICS INC (HQ)
3 Forbes Rd (02421-7305)
PHONE..................................701 674-4400
Bruno Lucidi, *CEO*
EMP: 4
SALES (est): 225.9K
SALES (corp-wide): 36.7MM **Publicly Held**
SIC: 2834 Mfg Pharmaceutical Preparations
PA: Agenus Inc.
3 Forbes Rd
Lexington MA 02421
781 674-4400

(G-12204)
AGENUS INC (PA)
3 Forbes Rd (02421-7305)
PHONE..................................781 674-4400
Garo H Armen, *Ch of Bd*
Jennifer Buell, *COO*
Alfred Dadson, *Vice Pres*
Evan Kearns, *Vice Pres*
Christine Klaskin, *Vice Pres*
EMP: 188
SQ FT: 82,000
SALES: 36.7MM **Publicly Held**
WEB: www.antigenics.com
SIC: 2836 8731 Mfg Biological Products Biotechnology Research

(G-12205)
AGILENT TECHNOLOGIES INC
Vacuum Products Division
121 Hartwell Ave (02421-3125)
PHONE..................................781 861-7200
John Ehmann, *General Mgr*
Fred Campbell, *Principal*
James Almeida, *Project Mgr*
EMP: 163
SALES (corp-wide): 5.1B **Publicly Held**
WEB: www.varianinc.com
SIC: 3825 Mfg Electrical Measuring Instruments
PA: Agilent Technologies, Inc.
5301 Stevens Creek Blvd
Santa Clara CA 95051
408 345-8886

(G-12206)
ALDEYRA THERAPEUTICS INC (PA)
131 Hartwell Ave Ste 320 (02421-3105)
PHONE..................................781 761-4904
C Boyd Clarke, *Ch of Bd*
Todd C Brady, *President*
Stephen G Machatha, *Senior VP*
David McMullin, *CFO*
Joshua Reed, *CFO*
EMP: 8
SQ FT: 3,700
SALES (est): 1.1MM **Publicly Held**
SIC: 2834 Pharmaceutical Preparations

(G-12207)
ARINC INCORPORATED
Also Called: ARINC Research
175 Bedford St Ste 12 (02420-4481)
PHONE..................................781 863-0711
John Orr, *Manager*
Charles Russell, *Systems Analyst*
EMP: 60
SALES (corp-wide): 66.5B **Publicly Held**
WEB: www.arinc.com
SIC: 3669 8711 Operates Air/Ground Communications Systems & Global Data Networks & Provides Engineering Services
HQ: Arinc Incorporated
2551 Riva Rd
Annapolis MD 21401
410 266-4000

(G-12208)
BAE SYSTEMS INFO & ELEC SYS
2 Forbes Rd (02421-7306)
PHONE..................................603 885-4321
Lyman Blair, *Mfg Mgr*
Brian Murphy, *Purch Mgr*
Scott Carpenter, *Engineer*
Robert Cunningham, *Engineer*
Joseph W Henderson, *Engineer*
EMP: 284
SALES (corp-wide): 22.1B **Privately Held**
WEB: www.iesi.na.baesystems.com
SIC: 3827 3679 3823 3674 Mfg Optical Instr/Lens Mfg Elec Components Mfg Process Cntrl Instr Mfg Semiconductors/Dvcs
HQ: Bae Systems Information And Electronic Systems Integration Inc.
65 Spit Brook Rd
Nashua NH 03060
603 885-4321

(G-12209)
BURLINGTON UNION
9 Myrna Rd (02420-1809)
PHONE..................................781 229-0918
Dave Smith, *Principal*
EMP: 3
SALES (est): 138.4K **Privately Held**
SIC: 2711 Newspapers-Publishing/Printing

(G-12210)
BUTTERGIRL BAKING CO
12 Moon Hill Rd (02421-6113)
PHONE..................................857 891-6625
John D Roberts, *Principal*
EMP: 4 **EST:** 2012
SALES (est): 174.7K **Privately Held**
SIC: 2051 Mfg Bread/Related Products

(G-12211)
CENTRA SOFTWARE INC (DH)
430 Bedford St Ste 220 (02420-1527)
PHONE..................................781 861-7000
Richard D Cramer, *Senior VP*
Martin V Deise, *Senior VP*
John J Walsh Jr, *Senior VP*
Michelle M Caggiano, *CFO*
EMP: 92
SQ FT: 49,000
SALES (est): 15MM
SALES (corp-wide): 45.6MM **Privately Held**
SIC: 7372 Prepackaged Software Services
HQ: Saba Software, Inc.
4120 Dublin Blvd Ste 200
Dublin CA 94568
877 722-2101

(G-12212)
COLONIAL TIMES PUBLISHING
805 Massachusetts Ave (02420-3918)
PHONE..................................781 274-9997
Jim Shaw, *Owner*
MA Lexington, *Minister*
EMP: 10
SALES: 400K **Privately Held**
SIC: 2711 Newspapers-Publishing/Printing

(G-12213)
CONCERT PHARMACEUTICALS INC (PA)
65 Hayden Ave Ste 3000n (02421-7994)
PHONE..................................781 860-0045
Richard H Aldrich, *Ch of Bd*
Roger D Tung, *President*
Nancy Stuart, *COO*
Marc Becker, *CFO*
Jeffrey A Munsie,
EMP: 71
SQ FT: 55,500
SALES: 10.5MM **Publicly Held**
SIC: 2834 Pharmaceutical Preparations

(G-12214)
COPIOUS IMAGING LLC
83 Hartwell Ave (02421-3116)
PHONE..................................617 921-0485
Curtis Colonero, *Chief Engr*
Justin Baker, *Engineer*
Joe Bari, *Engineer*
Chris Bowen, *Engineer*
Chris David, *Engineer*
EMP: 14
SALES: 2.7MM **Privately Held**
SIC: 3826 Mfg Analytical Instruments

(G-12215)
CSA MEDICAL INC
Also Called: Crymed Technologies
91 Hartwell Ave Ste 1 (02421-3130)
PHONE..................................443 921-8053
William H Floyd, *CEO*
Stephen Mascioli, *Vice Pres*
Bruce Xayvethy, *Research*
Patrick McMahon, *Engineer*
Steven E Schaefer, *CFO*
EMP: 55
SQ FT: 2,000
SALES (est): 9MM **Privately Held**
WEB: www.csamedical.com
SIC: 3845 Mfg Electromedical Equipment

(G-12216)
CUBIST PHARMACEUTICALS LLC
65 Hayden Ave (02421-7994)
PHONE..................................781 860-8660
Joel Joiner, *Business Mgr*
Robert Perez, *COO*
Pam Sears, *Vice Pres*
Jorge Ramos, *Mfg Staff*
Florizel Anderson, *Research*
EMP: 100
SALES (corp-wide): 42.2B **Publicly Held**
WEB: www.cubist.com
SIC: 2834 Mfg Pharmaceutical Preparations
HQ: Cubist Pharmaceuticals Llc
2000 Galloping Hill Rd
Kenilworth NJ 07033
-

(G-12217)
CURIS INC (PA)
4 Maguire Rd (02421-3112)
PHONE..................................617 503-6500
James R McNab Jr, *Ch of Bd*
Mani Mohindru, *Senior VP*
David Tuck, *Senior VP*
Reinhard Von Roemeling, *Senior VP*
Christine Guertin, *Vice Pres*
EMP: 20
SQ FT: 24,529
SALES: 10.4MM **Publicly Held**
WEB: www.curis.com
SIC: 2836 Biological Products

(G-12218)
DEERWALK INC (PA)
430 Bedford St Ste 175 (02420-1548)
PHONE..................................781 325-1775
Jeff Gasser, *President*
Dave Hansen, *President*
Rudra Pandey, *President*
John Cassella, *Exec VP*
Tim Huke, *Senior VP*
EMP: 335
SALES (est): 9.4MM **Privately Held**
SIC: 7372 7378 Prepackaged Software Services Computer Maintenance/Repair

(G-12219)
DICERNA PHARMACEUTICALS INC
33 Hayden Ave (02421-7972)
PHONE..................................617 621-8097
J Kevin Buchi, *Ch of Bd*
Douglas M Fambrough III, *President*
James B Weissman, *COO*
Bob D Brown, *Exec VP*
Regina Detore Paglia, *Senior VP*
EMP: 44 **EST:** 2006
SALES: 6.1MM **Privately Held**
SIC: 2834 2836 8731 Pharmaceutical Preparations Biological Research

(G-12220)
DIVYA MARIGOWDA
Also Called: Gsoft
39 Woodpark Cir (02421-7207)
PHONE..................................781 863-5189
Marigowda Divya, *Owner*
Elaine Y Ning, *Research*
EMP: 6
SALES (est): 305.9K **Privately Held**
SIC: 3577 7371 Mfg Computer Peripheral Equipment Custom Computer Programing

(G-12221)
DYAX CORP
300 Shire Way (02421-2101)
PHONE..................................617 349-0200
Micahel Garry, *President*
Siobhan Fitzgerald, *Sales Staff*
Anna Yurkovetsky, *Advt Staff*
Brian Linder, *Senior Mgr*
Kelly Duncan, *Director*
EMP: 124
SQ FT: 120,000
SALES (est): 73.5MM **Privately Held**
WEB: www.dyax.com
SIC: 2834 8731 Mfg Pharmaceutical Preparations Commercial Physical Research
HQ: Shire Pharmaceuticals International Unlimited Company
Plaza, Blocks 2 And 3
Dublin D02 Y
-

(G-12222)
ELECTRON SOLUTIONS INC
1 Briggs Rd (02421-6305)
PHONE..................................781 674-2440
Daniel L Goodman, *President*
EMP: 10
SALES (est): 820K **Privately Held**
SIC: 3761 8731 Mfg Guided Missiles/Space Vehicles Commercial Physical Research

(G-12223)
EXARCA PHARMACEUTICALS LLC
20 Meriam St (02420-3640)
PHONE..................................617 620-2776
David Dove, *President*
Yoav Golan, *Director*
Abraham Sonenshein, *Director*
EMP: 3 **EST:** 2015
SALES (est): 240.2K **Privately Held**
SIC: 2834 Mfg Pharmaceutical Preparations

(G-12224)
EXCELIMMUNE INC (PA)
1776 Massachusetts Ave (02420-5340)
P.O. Box 729, Bolton (01740-0729)
PHONE..................................781 262-8055
Elizabeth Reczek, *CEO*
Karoly Nikolich, *Ch of Bd*
Quinton Zondervan, *Principal*
Jason Walsh, *CFO*
Mark De Souza, *Bd of Directors*
EMP: 7
SQ FT: 800
SALES (est): 598.8K **Privately Held**
WEB: www.excelimmune.com
SIC: 2836 Mfg Biological Products

(G-12225)
GASWORLD PUBLISHING LLC
Also Called: Cryogas International
5 Militia Dr Ste 16 (02421-4706)
PHONE..................................781 862-0624
EMP: 7
SALES (est): 469.5K **Privately Held**
SIC: 2721 Periodicals
PA: Gasworld.Com Limited
Spectrum, Underground House
Truro

(G-12226)
GATEHOUSE MEDIA LLC
9 Meriam St (02420-5300)
PHONE..................................781 275-7204
Bryan Mahony, *Branch Mgr*
EMP: 3
SALES (corp-wide): 1.5B **Publicly Held**
SIC: 2752 Lithographic Commercial Printing
HQ: Gatehouse Media, Llc
175 Sullys Trl Fl 3
Pittsford NY 14534
585 598-0030

(G-12227)
GATEHOUSE MEDIA MASS I INC
Also Called: Lexington Minuteman
9 Meriam St Ste 11 (02420-5312)
PHONE..................................781 861-9110
Bryan Mahony, *Branch Mgr*
EMP: 7
SALES (corp-wide): 1.5B **Publicly Held**
SIC: 2711 Newspapers-Publishing/Printing
HQ: Gatehouse Media Massachusetts I, Inc.
48 Dunham Rd
Beverly MA 01915
585 598-0030

(G-12228)
GENERAL STEEL PRODUCTS CO INC
16 Russell Rd (02420-2709)
PHONE..................................617 387-5400
George Meltz, *President*
Christine Glucker, *Office Mgr*
EMP: 10
SALES (est): 1.6MM **Privately Held**
WEB: www.gentexscaffolds.com
SIC: 3441 Structural Metal Fabrication

(G-12229)
HIGHTECH AMERICAN INDUS LABS
Also Called: Hai Labs
320 Massachusetts Ave (02420-4010)
PHONE..................................781 862-9884
Vivian Xue, *President*
▲ **EMP:** 20
SALES (est): 2.5MM **Privately Held**
WEB: www.hailabs.com
SIC: 3841 Mfg Surgical/Medical Instruments

(G-12230)
HYALEX ORTHOPAEDICS INC
99 Hayden Ave Ste 360 (02421-7966)
PHONE..................................347 871-5850
Mira Sahney, *Principal*
EMP: 5
SALES (est): 277K **Privately Held**
SIC: 3841 Mfg Surgical/Medical Instruments

(G-12231)
IDG WOIT MODEM
30 Edgewood Rd (02420-3539)
PHONE..................................781 861-6541
Steven Woit, *Principal*
EMP: 3
SALES (est): 221.2K **Privately Held**
SIC: 3661 Mfg Telephone/Telegraph Apparatus

(G-12232)
INTELON OPTICS INC
91 Hartwell Ave Ste 301 (02421-3137)
PHONE..................................310 980-3087
Jang Lawrence Yoo, *CEO*
Huong Wu, *Principal*
EMP: 4
SALES (est): 231.7K **Privately Held**
SIC: 3841 7389 Mfg Surgical/Medical Instruments

(G-12233)
JOURNAL OF INTERDISCPLINARY
14 Barberry Rd (02421-8026)
PHONE..................................781 862-4089
Robert I Rotberg, *President*
EMP: 5
SALES: 88.4K **Privately Held**
SIC: 2711 Newspapers-Publishing/Printing

(G-12234)
KALEIDO BIOSCIENCES INC (PA)
65 Hayden Ave (02421-7994)
PHONE..................................617 674-9000
Michael Bonney, *Ch of Bd*
Alison Lawton, *President*
Joshua Brumm, *COO*
Wendy Arnold, *Senior VP*
Michael Bruce, *Senior VP*
EMP: 75
SQ FT: 53,000
SALES (est): 21.9MM **Publicly Held**
SIC: 2836 8731 Mfg Biological Products Commercial Physical Research

(G-12235)
KATAHDIN HILL CO
29 Marrett St (02421-7314)
PHONE..................................781 862-7566
Ken Brady, *Owner*
EMP: 3 **EST:** 2001
SALES (est): 188.9K **Privately Held**
SIC: 3299 Mfg Nonmetallic Mineral Products

(G-12236)
KINIKSA PHARMACEUTICALS CORP
100 Hayden Ave Ste 1 (02421-7974)
PHONE..................................781 431-9100
Theresa Boni, *Vice Pres*
Christopher Heberlig, *Treasurer*
Jennifer Mason, *Office Mgr*
EMP: 8
SALES (est): 619.6K **Privately Held**
SIC: 2836 Mfg Pharmaceutical Preparations

(G-12237)
LEXINGTON GRAPHICS
Also Called: Sir Speedy
76 Bedford St Ste 6 (02420-4640)
PHONE..................................781 863-9510
Ilhami Cinkilic, *Owner*
Turan Cinkilic, *Treasurer*
EMP: 12
SALES: 1MM **Privately Held**
WEB: www.lexingtongraphics.net
SIC: 2752 Comm Prtg Litho

(G-12238)
LEXINGTON PRESS INC
15 Meriam St (02420-5308)
P.O. Box 51 (02420-0001)
PHONE..................................781 862-8900
Robert Sacco, *President*
EMP: 5
SQ FT: 10,000
SALES (est): 750.7K **Privately Held**
WEB: www.lexingtonpress.com
SIC: 2752 2732 7331 7374 Offset Printing Book Printing Mailing Service And Desktop Publishing

(G-12239)
LOCKHEED MARTIN CORPORATION
2 Forbes Rd (02421-7306)
PHONE..................................781 862-6222
Terry Trent, *Principal*
Norman Jones, *Principal*
James A Thurber, *Manager*
EMP: 9 **Publicly Held**
WEB: www.lockheedmartin.com
SIC: 3812 Mfg Search/Navigation Equipment
PA: Lockheed Martin Corporation
6801 Rockledge Dr
Bethesda MD 20817

(G-12240)
LONGRAY INC
14 Taft Ave (02421-4119)
PHONE..................................781 862-5137
Albert Wai-Kit Chan, *President*
Mengqi Xia, *Principal*
EMP: 3
SALES (est): 163.6K **Privately Held**
SIC: 2834 8733 Mfg Pharmaceutical Preparations Noncommercial Research Organization

(G-12241)
MASSACHUSETTS CHESS ASSN (PA)
Also Called: Maca
234 Manor Ter (02420-2339)
PHONE..................................781 862-3799
Harvey Reed, *President*
Steven Frymer, *Director*
EMP: 4
SALES (est): 215.9K **Privately Held**
SIC: 3944 Mfg Games/Toys

(G-12242)
MC10 INC
10 Maguire Rd Bldg 31fl (02421-3110)
PHONE..................................617 234-4448
Carmichael Roberts, *Ch of Bd*
Scott Pomerantz, *President*
Paul Klingenstein, *Principal*
Don Fuchs, *Vice Pres*
Sanjay Gupta, *Vice Pres*
◆ **EMP:** 30
SQ FT: 5,000
SALES (est): 6.9MM **Privately Held**
SIC: 3699 Mfg Electrical Equipment/Supplies

(G-12243)
MERCK SHARP & DOHME CORP
65 Hayden Ave (02421-7994)
PHONE..................................781 860-8660
Greg Wells, *Business Anlyst*
Sharron Rose, *Branch Mgr*
EMP: 150
SALES (corp-wide): 42.2B **Publicly Held**
SIC: 2834 Mfg Pharmaceutical Preparations
HQ: Merck Sharp & Dohme Corp.
2000 Galloping Hill Rd
Kenilworth NJ 07033
908 740-4000

(G-12244)
MILLENNIAL NET INC
24 Hartwell Ave Ste 2 (02421-3139)
PHONE..................................978 569-1921
Sheng Liu, *CEO*
▲ **EMP:** 30 **EST:** 2000
SQ FT: 15,000
SALES (est): 5.2MM **Privately Held**
WEB: www.millennial.net
SIC: 3663 Mfg Radio/Tv Communication Equipment

(G-12245)
MU NET INC
442 Marrett Rd Ste 9 (02421-7749)
PHONE..................................781 861-8644
Vincent Moeyersoms, *President*
▲ **EMP:** 12
SALES (est): 2.8MM **Privately Held**
WEB: www.munet.com
SIC: 3825 Mfg Electrical Measuring Instruments

(G-12246)
NANO BEAM TECHNOLOGIES
5 Tricorne Rd (02421-5705)
PHONE..................................617 548-9495
Vitali Vinokour, *Principal*
Justin Delva, *Principal*
EMP: 3
SALES (est): 192.8K **Privately Held**
SIC: 3827 Mfg Optical Instruments/Lenses

(G-12247)
NEOVII BIOTECH NA INC
430 Bedford St Ste 195 (02420-1523)
PHONE..................................781 966-3830
Andy Pate, *COO*
Anne Rice, *Vice Pres*
Tory Scoggins, *Opers Staff*
Martin Devine, *Finance*
Melissa Bourke, *Supervisor*
EMP: 12
SALES (est): 1.8MM
SALES (corp-wide): 1.4MM **Privately Held**
SIC: 2834 5812 Mfg Pharmaceutical Preparations Eating Place
HQ: Neovii Biotech Gmbh
Am Haag 6+
Grafelfing 82166
898 988-880

(G-12248)
NET VANTAGE POINT INC
149 E Emerson Rd (02420-2132)
PHONE..................................781 860-9158
David Evanson, *Owner*
EMP: 3
SALES (est): 219.4K **Privately Held**
WEB: www.netvantagepoint.com
SIC: 3555 Mfg Printing Trades Machinery

(G-12249)
NEW ENGLAND IMMUNOLOGY ASSOC
Also Called: N E I A
217 Concord Ave (02421-8205)
PHONE..................................781 863-5774
EMP: 5
SQ FT: 1,500
SALES: 500K **Privately Held**
SIC: 2835 2836 Mfg Diagnostic Substances Mfg Biological Products

(G-12250)
NEWPRINT OFFSET INC
405 Waltham St (02421-7934)
PHONE..................................781 891-6002
Anthony Soave, *President*
EMP: 14
SALES (est): 1.9MM **Privately Held**
WEB: www.newprintinc.com
SIC: 2752 Lithographic Commercial Printing

(G-12251)
OASIS PHARMACEUTICALS LLC
64 Fifer Ln (02420-1226)
PHONE..................................781 752-6094
Lidija Covic,
EMP: 3
SALES (est): 240.1K **Privately Held**
SIC: 2834 Mfg Pharmaceutical Preparations

(G-12252)
PACE MEDICAL INC
2643 Massachusetts Ave (02421-6721)
PHONE..................................781 862-4242
Ralph E Hanson, *Ch of Bd*
Steven E Hanson, *President*
Drusilla F Hays, *Vice Pres*
EMP: 12
SQ FT: 2,600
SALES (est): 1.2MM **Privately Held**
WEB: www.pacemedicalinc.com
SIC: 3845 Mfg Electromedical Equipment

(G-12253)
PARTNER THERAPEUTICS INC (PA)
19 Muzzey St Ste 105 (02421-5211)
PHONE..................................781 727-4259
Robert Mulroy, *CEO*
Colleen Mockbee, *Officer*
EMP: 5
SALES (est): 1.4MM **Privately Held**
SIC: 2834 Mfg Pharmaceutical Preparations

(G-12254)
PRESS GANEY
70 Westview St Ste 6 (02421-3131)
PHONE..................................800 232-8032
Richard Siegrist, *President*
EMP: 4
SALES (est): 165.1K **Privately Held**
SIC: 2741 Misc Publishing

(G-12255)
PROMEDIOR INC
81 Hartwell Ave Ste 105 (02421-3127)
P.O. Box 456, Devault PA (19432-0456)
PHONE..................................781 538-4200

GEOGRAPHIC

Suzanne L Bruhn, *President*
Mark Lupher, *Senior VP*
Elizabeth G Trehu, *Chief Mktg Ofcr*
Brian Frye, *Manager*
Lara Voytko, *Manager*
EMP: 13
SALES (est): 2.7MM **Privately Held**
WEB: www.promedior.com
SIC: 2834 Mfg Pharmaceutical Preparations

(G-12256)
PULMATRIX INC (PA)
99 Hayden Ave Ste 390 (02421-7966)
PHONE..................................781 357-2333
Ted Raad, *CEO*
Mark Iwicki, *Ch of Bd*
William E Duke Jr, *CFO*
James Roach, *Chief Mktg Ofcr*
Lorenzo Phillips, *Associate Dir*
EMP: 22
SQ FT: 21,810
SALES: 153K **Publicly Held**
SIC: 2834 Mfg Pharmaceutical Preparations

(G-12257)
PULMATRIX OPERATING CO INC
99 Hayden Ave Ste 390 (02421-7966)
PHONE..................................781 357-2333
John P Hanrahan, *Chief Mktg Ofcr*
EMP: 6
SQ FT: 8,000
SALES (est): 1.2MM
SALES (corp-wide): 153K **Publicly Held**
WEB: www.pulmatrix.com
SIC: 2834 Manufacturing Pharmaceutical Preparations
PA: Pulmatrix, Inc.
99 Hayden Ave Ste 390
Lexington MA 02421
781 357-2333

(G-12258)
RAYTHEON COMPANY
420 Bedford St Ste 120 (02420-1567)
PHONE..................................781 862-6800
Lee Hughes, *Manager*
EMP: 3
SALES (corp-wide): 27B **Publicly Held**
SIC: 3812 8732 Mfg Search/Navigation Equipment Commercial Nonphysical Research
PA: Raytheon Company
870 Winter St
Waltham MA 02451
781 522-3000

(G-12259)
REALTIME DX INC
Also Called: Vxe
106 N Hancock St (02420-3417)
P.O. Box 2874, Woburn (01888-1574)
PHONE..................................508 479-9818
Leslie G Fritzemeier, *CEO*
EMP: 3
SALES (est): 172.9K **Privately Held**
SIC: 3674 Mfg Semiconductors/Related Devices

(G-12260)
SA PHOTONICS INC
450 Bedford St (02420-1535)
PHONE..................................781 861-1430
EMP: 3
SALES (est): 193.3K **Privately Held**
SIC: 3674 Mfg Semiconductors/Related Devices

(G-12261)
SAFE HYDROGEN LLC
30 York St (02420-2009)
PHONE..................................781 861-7016
Andrew McClaine, *Mng Member*
Sigmar Tullman, *Mng Member*
EMP: 3
SALES: 450K **Privately Held**
WEB: www.safehydrogen.com
SIC: 2813 Hydrogen Producer

(G-12262)
SAFE HYDROGEN LLC
4 Bates Rd (02421-6402)
PHONE..................................781 861-7252
Andrew McClanine,
Ken Brown,
Sig Tullmann,
EMP: 3
SALES: 800K **Privately Held**
SIC: 2813 Mfg Industrial Gases

(G-12263)
SEAHORSE BIOSCIENCE INC (HQ)
Also Called: Seahorse Labware
121 Hartwell Ave (02421-3125)
PHONE..................................978 671-1600
Jay Teich, *President*
Al Bukys, *Vice Pres*
Steven Chomicz, *Vice Pres*
Mike Tanner, *Vice Pres*
Jeff Templer, *CFO*
EMP: 27
SQ FT: 5,000
SALES (est): 11.7MM
SALES (corp-wide): 5.1B **Publicly Held**
SIC: 3825 Mfg Electrical Measuring Instruments
PA: Agilent Technologies, Inc.
5301 Stevens Creek Blvd
Santa Clara CA 95051
408 345-8886

(G-12264)
SENSORMATIC ELECTRONICS LLC
70 Westview St Ste 1 (02421-3131)
PHONE..................................781 466-6660
Paul Piccolomini, *Branch Mgr*
EMP: 200 **Privately Held**
WEB: www.sensormatic.com
SIC: 3812 Mfg Electronic Detection Devices
HQ: Sensormatic Electronics, Llc
6600 Congress Ave
Boca Raton FL 33487
561 912-6000

(G-12265)
SENTIEN BIOTECHNOLOGIES INC
99 Hayden Ave Ste 200 (02421-7966)
PHONE..................................781 361-9031
Brian Miller, *President*
Biju Parekkadan, *Owner*
Johannes Fruehauf, *Principal*
Rich Ganz, *Principal*
Martin Heidecker, *Principal*
EMP: 4
SALES (est): 866.4K **Privately Held**
SIC: 2834 Mfg Pharmaceutical Preparations

(G-12266)
SHEMIN NURSERIES INC
Also Called: Shemin Landscape Supply Co
1265 Massachusetts Ave (02420-3825)
PHONE 781 861-1111
Pat Grego, *Branch Mgr*
EMP: 11
SALES (corp-wide): 2.1B **Publicly Held**
SIC: 3531 5193 Mfg Construction Machinery Whol Flowers/Florist Supplies
HQ: Shemin Nurseries, Inc.
42 Old Ridgebury Rd Ste 3
Danbury CT 06810

(G-12267)
SHIRE INC (HQ)
300 Shire Way (02421-2101)
PHONE..................................781 482-9222
John Miller, *President*
Jen Bailey, *Business Mgr*
Mariette Boerstoel, *Vice Pres*
Wolfram Nothaft, *Vice Pres*
Gooding Ann, *Opers Dir*
EMP: 177
SALES (est): 216.2MM
SALES (corp-wide): 15.1B **Privately Held**
SIC: 2834 Mfg Pharmaceutical Preparations
PA: Shire Plc
1 Kingdom Street
London W2 6B
125 689-4003

(G-12268)
SHIRE HUMN GNTIC THERAPIES INC (HQ)
Also Called: Shire Pharmaceuticals
300 Shire Way (02421-2101)
PHONE..................................617 349-0200
Dr Flemming Ornskov, *CEO*
Bill Ciambrone, *President*
Mark Labrecque, *Business Mgr*
David Pendergast, *Exec VP*
Wayne Eppinger, *Vice Pres*
EMP: 169
SALES (est): 126.8MM
SALES (corp-wide): 15.1B **Privately Held**
SIC: 2834 Mfg Pharmaceutical Preparations
PA: Shire Plc
1 Kingdom Street
London W2 6B
125 689-4003

(G-12269)
SHIRE HUMN GNTIC THERAPIES INC
300 Patriot Way (02421)
PHONE..................................617 349-0200
Flemming Ornskov, *Branch Mgr*
EMP: 4
SALES (corp-wide): 15.1B **Privately Held**
SIC: 2834 Mfg Pharmaceutical Preparations
HQ: Shire Human Genetic Therapies, Inc.
300 Shire Way
Lexington MA 02421
617 349-0200

(G-12270)
SHIRE INC (HQ)
125 Spring St (02421-7801)
PHONE..................................781 274-1248
Calias Perry, *Principal*
Tom Burns, *Opers Mgr*
Vikas Dhingra, *Research*
Eric Park, *Research*
EMP: 29
SALES (est): 8.1MM
SALES (corp-wide): 15.1B **Privately Held**
SIC: 2834 Mfg Pharmaceutical Preparations
PA: Shire Plc
1 Kingdom Street
London W2 6B
125 689-4003

(G-12271)
SHIRE PHARMACEUTICALS LLC
45 Hayden Ave (02421-7956)
PHONE..................................617 349-0200
EMP: 5
SALES (est): 332.8K **Privately Held**
SIC: 2834 Mfg Pharmaceutical Preparations

(G-12272)
SHIRE US INC (DH)
Also Called: Shire Pharmaceuticals
300 Shire Way (02421-2101)
PHONE..................................781 482-9222
Flemming Ornskov, *CEO*
Thomas Dittrich, *CFO*
Thomas Harvey, *Admin Mgr*
Kevin Dekofski, *Network Enginr*
Hugh McLaughlin, *Admin Sec*
▲ **EMP:** 560
SALES (est): 341MM
SALES (corp-wide): 15.1B **Privately Held**
WEB: www.shirepharmaceuticals.com
SIC: 2834 Mfg Pharmaceutical Preparations

(G-12273)
SHIRE VIROPHARMA INCORPORATED (DH)
300 Shire Way (02421-2101)
PHONE..................................610 458-7300
Vincent J Milano, *CEO*
Daniel B Soland, *COO*
J Peter Wolf, *Vice Pres*
Charles A Rowland, *CFO*
Caroline West, *Ch Credit Ofcr*
▲ **EMP:** 43
SQ FT: 78,264
SALES (est): 52.3MM **Privately Held**
WEB: www.viropharma.com
SIC: 2834 Mfg Pharmaceutical Preparations

(G-12274)
SHIRE-NPS PHARMACEUTICALS INC (DH)
300 Shire Way (02421-2101)
PHONE..................................617 349-0200
Flemming Ornskov MD, *CEO*
Paul Firuta, *President*
John Miller, *President*
Nancy Bryan, *Vice Pres*
Jason Baranski, *Admin Sec*
EMP: 5000
SALES (est): 140.5MM **Privately Held**
WEB: www.npsp.com
SIC: 2834 Mfg Pharmaceutical Preparations

(G-12275)
SMARTSTRIPE SOFTWARE CORP
21 Carriage Dr (02420-1141)
PHONE..................................781 861-1812
Sheldon Lowenthal, *Principal*
EMP: 5 **EST:** 2001
SALES (est): 320K **Privately Held**
SIC: 7372 Prepackaged Software Services

(G-12276)
T2 BIOSYSTEMS INC (PA)
101 Hartwell Ave (02421-3125)
PHONE..................................781 761-4646
John Sperzel, *President*
John McDonough, *Chairman*
Alec Barclay, *Senior VP*
Michael Gibbs, *Vice Pres*
John M Sprague, *CFO*
EMP: 115
SQ FT: 31,000
SALES: 10.5MM **Publicly Held**
SIC: 3841 2835 Mfg Surgical/Medical Instruments & Diagnostic Substances

(G-12277)
TAKEDA PHARMACEUTICALS USA INC (HQ)
95 Hayden Ave (02421-7942)
PHONE..................................617 349-0200
Ramona Sequeira, *President*
Mary-Jo Dempson, *President*
Perry Bongiani, *District Mgr*
Julia Jackson, *Counsel*
Ken Greisman, *Senior VP*
▲ **EMP:** 558 **EST:** 1998
SALES (est): 1.1B **Privately Held**
SIC: 2834 Mfg Pharmaceutical Preparations

(G-12278)
TARIS BIOMEDICAL LLC
113 Hartwell Ave (02421-3138)
PHONE..................................781 676-7750
Tony Kingsley, *President*
Julie Coughlan, *Business Mgr*
Joseph Higgins, *Vice Pres*
Mark Lewis, *Vice Pres*
David Flanagan, *Project Mgr*
EMP: 20
SQ FT: 19,802
SALES (est): 4.8MM
SALES (corp-wide): 81.5B **Publicly Held**
SIC: 2834 Mfg Pharmaceutical Preparations
PA: Johnson & Johnson
1 Johnson And Johnson Plz
New Brunswick NJ 08933
732 524-0400

(G-12279)
TOMMY HILFIGER FOOTWEAR INC
191 Spring St Fl 4 (02421-8045)
PHONE..................................617 824-6000
EMP: 45
SQ FT: 20,000
SALES (est): 2.1MM
SALES (corp-wide): 2.2B **Publicly Held**
WEB: www.strideritecorp.com
SIC: 3149 Footwear, Except Rubber, Nec, Nsk

HQ: The Stride Rite Corporation
500 Totten Pond Rd Ste 1
Waltham MA 02451
617 824-6000

(G-12280)
UNIMACTS GLOBAL LLC (PA)
2 Sedge Rd (02420-1830)
PHONE....................................410 415-6070
Matthew Arnold, *CEO*
Alan Hays, *COO*
George Olshavsky, *Opers Staff*
Jack Percoskie, *CFO*
Vikas Sharma, *Manager*
▲ **EMP:** 25
SQ FT: 5,000
SALES (est): 5MM **Privately Held**
WEB: www.unimacts.com
SIC: 3599 Mfg Industrial Machinery

(G-12281)
VANU INC
81 Hartwell Ave Ste 4 (02421-3127)
PHONE....................................617 864-1711
Vanu Bose, *President*
Tony Matias, *Mfg Staff*
EMP: 52
SQ FT: 75,000
SALES (est): 9.7MM **Privately Held**
WEB: www.vanu.com
SIC: 7372 Prepackaged Software Services

(G-12282)
VIROPHARMA BIOLOGICS INC
300 Shire Way (02421-2101)
PHONE....................................610 458-7300
Daniel Soland, *President*
James Nash, *Vice Pres*
Robert Pietrusko, *Vice Pres*
Richard Morris, *Treasurer*
EMP: 6
SQ FT: 78,000
SALES (est): 467.6K **Privately Held**
SIC: 2834 Mfg Pharmaceutical Preparations
HQ: Shire Viropharma Incorporated
300 Shire Way
Lexington MA 02421

(G-12283)
W R GRACE & CO
Grace Performance Chemicals
91 Hartwell Ave Ste 2 (02421-3130)
PHONE....................................617 876-1400
Richard Williams, *Vice Pres*
EMP: 479
SQ FT: 151,000
SALES (corp-wide): 1.9B **Publicly Held**
SIC: 2819 2833 Mfg Industrial Inorganic Chemicals Mfg Medicinal/Botanical Products
PA: W. R. Grace & Co.
7500 Grace Dr
Columbia MD 21044
410 531-4000

(G-12284)
WALTER SCOTT
Also Called: Scott's Vanilla
16 S Rindge Ave (02420-3056)
PHONE....................................781 862-4893
Walter Scott, *Owner*
EMP: 4
SALES: 125K **Privately Held**
SIC: 2087 2099 Mfg Flavor Extracts/Syrup Mfg Food Preparations

Lincoln
Middlesex County

(G-12285)
ADVENT MEDICAL PRODUCTS INC
Also Called: Concord Medical Products
55 Beaver Pond Rd (01773-3308)
PHONE....................................781 272-2813
Randall Fincke, *President*
EMP: 50 **EST:** 2010
SALES (est): 5.6MM **Privately Held**
SIC: 3069 Mfg Fabricated Rubber Products

(G-12286)
LAMA YESHE WISDOM ARCHIVE INC
6 Goose Pond Rd (01773-2506)
P.O. Box 636 (01773-0636)
PHONE....................................781 259-4466
Nicholas Ribush, *CEO*
Jennifer Barlow, *Office Mgr*
EMP: 15
SALES: 669.2K **Privately Held**
WEB: www.lamayeshe.com
SIC: 2731 Books-Publishing/Printing

(G-12287)
LINCOLN LEARNING SOLUTIONS LLC
23 Birchwood Ln (01773-4907)
PHONE....................................781 259-9696
Jean Welsh, *Mng Member*
Robert Reinert,
EMP: 3
SALES: 700K **Privately Held**
WEB: www.lincolnlearning.com
SIC: 7372 7389 Prepackaged Software Services Business Services At Non-Commercial Site

(G-12288)
N A RAILRUNNER INC
55 Old Bedford Rd Ste 106 (01773-1125)
PHONE....................................781 860-7245
Charles T Foskett, *President*
Christian Gielke, *Project Mgr*
Gelu Ciuica, *Engineer*
EMP: 5
SQ FT: 2,617
SALES (est): 1MM **Privately Held**
WEB: www.railrunner.com
SIC: 3743 Mfg Railroad Equipment

(G-12289)
SIMPLY MEDIA INC
Also Called: Black Tooth Games Brand
59 S Great Rd (01773-4701)
P.O. Box 481 (01773-0481)
PHONE....................................781 259-8029
EMP: 21
SQ FT: 1,000
SALES (est): 1.5MM **Privately Held**
WEB: www.deaverbrown.com
SIC: 2741 Multi-Media Publisher

Littleton
Middlesex County

(G-12290)
ALEXIS FOODS INC
173 Goldsmith St (01460-1942)
PHONE....................................978 952-6777
Vasso Drosos, *Branch Mgr*
EMP: 3
SALES (corp-wide): 456.5K **Privately Held**
SIC: 2099 Mfg Food Preparations
PA: Alexis Foods, Inc.
160 Reservoir St Ste 4
Holden MA 01520
508 829-9111

(G-12291)
ALPHA TECH PET INC
Also Called: Lexington Cat Clinic
25 Porter Rd Ste 210 (01460-1434)
PHONE....................................978 486-3690
Shawn Scitz, *President*
EMP: 10
SQ FT: 5,676
SALES: 1.4MM **Privately Held**
WEB: www.alphatechpet.com
SIC: 3999 8742 5199 0742 Mfg Misc Products Mgmt Consulting Svcs Whol Nondurable Goods Veterinary Services

(G-12292)
APPLEWOOD CONTROLS INC
37 Ayer Rd (01460-1033)
P.O. Box 37 (01460-0037)
PHONE....................................978 486-9220
Ronald Ricci, *President*
Steve Caruso, *Engineer*
Deborah Ricci, *Treasurer*
EMP: 5
SQ FT: 3,200
SALES (est): 1MM **Privately Held**
WEB: www.applewoodcontrols.com
SIC: 3823 Mfg Industrial Controls

(G-12293)
ARRADIANCE LLC
11a Beaver Brook Rd (01460-6232)
PHONE....................................508 202-0593
Thomas Clay, *Ch of Bd*
Michael Trotter, *Mng Member*
David Beaulieu,
Jeff Plante,
EMP: 10
SALES (est): 1.7MM **Privately Held**
WEB: www.arradiance.com
SIC: 3674 Mfg Semiconductors/Related Devices

(G-12294)
ATLANTIC RUBBER COMPANY INC
37 Ayer Rd Ste 6 (01460-1034)
P.O. Box 2295 (01460-3295)
PHONE....................................800 882-3666
William L Carey, *President*
Darlene Dowdy, *Vice Pres*
Ralph K Lowey, *Admin Sec*
▲ **EMP:** 11
SQ FT: 10,000
SALES: 3MM **Privately Held**
WEB: www.atlanticrubber.com
SIC: 3053 Mfg Gaskets/Packing/Sealing Devices

(G-12295)
BURK TECHNOLOGY INC
7 Beaver Brook Rd (01460-6232)
PHONE....................................978 486-0086
Peter Burk, *President*
EMP: 24
SQ FT: 7,600
SALES (est): 4.6MM **Privately Held**
WEB: www.burk.com
SIC: 3663 Mfg Radio/Tv Communication Equipment

(G-12296)
CLOAK & DAGGER CREATIONS
61 Gilson Rd (01460-1300)
PHONE....................................978 486-4414
Dina Flockhart, *Owner*
EMP: 5
SALES (est): 209.3K **Privately Held**
WEB: www.cloakmaker.com
SIC: 2339 5699 Mfg Women's/Misses' Outerwear Ret Misc Apparel/Accessories

(G-12297)
CONTROL RESOURCES INC
Also Called: Smartfan
11 Beaver Brook Rd (01460-6232)
PHONE....................................978 486-4160
James W Kundert, *President*
Warren R Kundert, *Chairman*
EMP: 26
SQ FT: 10,000
SALES (est): 5.6MM **Privately Held**
WEB: www.controlres.com
SIC: 3625 3822 3829 3674 Mfg Relay/Indstl Control Mfg Environmntl Controls Mfg Measure/Control Dvcs Mfg Semiconductors/Dvcs Mfg Speed Changer/Drives

(G-12298)
CURRICULUM ASSOCIATES LLC
1 Distribution Center Cir # 200
(01460-6250)
PHONE....................................978 313-1276
Sandy Batista, *Manager*
EMP: 47
SALES (corp-wide): 14MM **Privately Held**
SIC: 2731 Books-Publishing/Printing
PA: Curriculum Associates, Llc
153 Rangeway Rd
North Billerica MA 01862
978 667-8000

(G-12299)
DAKIN ROAD INVESTMENTS INC
Also Called: P&L Machine
162 Ayer Rd (01460-1103)
PHONE....................................978 443-4020
Joe D Croman, *President*
Eleanor Ting, *Treasurer*
EMP: 17
SALES (est): 1.4MM **Privately Held**
SIC: 3469 Mfg Metal Stampings

(G-12300)
DIAMOND ANTENNA MICROWAVE CORP
59 Porter Rd (01460-1479)
PHONE....................................978 486-0039
Jeffrey T Gilling, *CEO*
Michael Montemagno, *Vice Pres*
EMP: 63
SQ FT: 20,000
SALES (est): 12.8MM **Privately Held**
WEB: www.diamondantenna.com
SIC: 3663 Mfg Radio/Tv Communication Equipment

(G-12301)
DIAMOND RF LLC
59 Porter Rd (01460-1479)
PHONE....................................978 486-0039
Jeffery Gilling, *Mng Member*
EMP: 5
SALES: 1MM **Privately Held**
SIC: 3679 Mfg Electronic Components

(G-12302)
DIAMOND-ROLTRAN LLC
59 Porter Rd Ste 2 (01460-1479)
PHONE....................................978 486-0039
Jeffrey Gilling,
EMP: 11
SALES: 950K **Privately Held**
SIC: 3699 Mfg Electrical Equipment/Supplies

(G-12303)
DIVERSITY STUDIO INC
Instant Imaging
160 Ayer Rd 14 (01460-1146)
PHONE....................................978 250-5553
Michael Cote, *Manager*
EMP: 3
SALES (est): 184.6K
SALES (corp-wide): 2.7MM **Privately Held**
SIC: 2759 Commercial Printing
PA: Diversity Studio, Inc.
671 Great Rd Ste 2
Littleton MA 01460
978 250-5553

(G-12304)
ELMA & SANA LLC
550 Newtown Rd Ste 800 (01460-2130)
PHONE....................................617 529-4532
Elmahfoud Achtam,
▲ **EMP:** 3
SQ FT: 1,200
SALES: 350K **Privately Held**
SIC: 2844 Mfg Toilet Preparations

(G-12305)
FIBA TECHNOLOGIES INC (PA)
53 Ayer Rd (01460-1007)
PHONE....................................508 887-7100
Jack Finn, *CEO*
Frank Finn, *Principal*
John F Finn, *Principal*
Bob Morrison, *COO*
Frank H Finn Jr, *Vice Pres*
◆ **EMP:** 240
SQ FT: 45,000
SALES: 54.5MM **Privately Held**
WEB: www.fibatech.com
SIC: 3443 Mfg Fabricated Plate Work

(G-12306)
FOREST ECONOMIC ADVISORS LLC
Also Called: Fea
298 Great Rd (01460-1996)
PHONE....................................978 496-6336
Brendan K Lowney, *Principal*
Paul F Jannke, *Principal*
Rocky Goodnow, *Vice Pres*

GEOGRAPHIC

Gregory H Lewis, *Vice Pres*
EMP: 6
SALES (est): 560.2K **Privately Held**
SIC: 2491 Wood Preserving

(G-12307)
HP INC
550 King St (01460-6245)
PHONE..................................650 857-1501
Ted McKie, *Principal*
Marc Johnson, *Sales Staff*
EMP: 900
SALES (corp-wide): 58.7B **Publicly Held**
SIC: 3571 Mfg Electronic Computers
PA: Hp, Inc.
1501 Page Mill Rd
Palo Alto CA 94304
650 857-1501

(G-12308)
HP INC
153 Taylor St (01460-1407)
PHONE..................................800 222-5547
Frank Lanza, *Sales Staff*
Sue Regan, *Business Anlyst*
EMP: 52
SALES (corp-wide): 58.7B **Publicly Held**
WEB: www.3com.com
SIC: 3571 Mfg Electronic Computers
PA: Hp, Inc.
1501 Page Mill Rd
Palo Alto CA 94304
650 857-1501

(G-12309)
IMAGE STREAM MEDICAL INC
1 Monarch Dr Ste 102 (01460-1440)
PHONE..................................978 486-8494
Eddie Mitchell, *President*
Todd Brigance, *Business Mgr*
Patrick Egan, *Vice Pres*
Roberta Mills, *Project Mgr*
Steve Refnes, *Project Mgr*
EMP: 90
SQ FT: 32,693
SALES (est): 23.2MM **Privately Held**
SIC: 3669 3841 5047 Mfg Surgical/Med Instr Whol Med/Hospital Equip Mfg Communications Equip

(G-12310)
JOSEPH A OWEN JR
56 Wychwood Hts (01460-1114)
P.O. Box 686 (01460-2686)
PHONE..................................978 486-3318
Joseph A Owen Jr, *Principal*
Joseph Owen, *Principal*
EMP: 3
SALES (est): 335.2K **Privately Held**
SIC: 2353 Mfg Hats/Caps/Millinery

(G-12311)
JOWA USA INC
59 Porter Rd (01460-1479)
PHONE..................................978 486-9800
Per Ola Hogdahl, *President*
David McCarthy, *General Mgr*
Berndt Bittner, *Vice Pres*
Ned Crosby, *Chief Engr*
Jan Seehuusen, *Treasurer*
▲ **EMP:** 21 **EST:** 1965
SQ FT: 20,000
SALES (est): 5MM
SALES (corp-wide): 13.4MM **Privately Held**
WEB: www.metritape.com
SIC: 3823 Mfg Process Control Instruments
HQ: Jowa Ab
Tulebovagen 104
Kallered 428 3
317 265-400

(G-12312)
KENEXA BRASSRING INC
550 King St (01460-6245)
PHONE..................................781 530-5000
Ben Kingsbury, *President*
Deborah Besemer, *Executive*
Gary Cormier,
Stephen Turner,
Jan Wahby,
EMP: 250
SQ FT: 65,000
SALES (est): 11.4MM
SALES (corp-wide): 79.5B **Publicly Held**
SIC: 7372 7379 Prepackaged Software Services Computer Related Services
HQ: Kenexa Corporation
650 E Swedesford Rd # 200
Wayne PA 19087
877 971-9171

(G-12313)
MSI TRANSDUCERS CORP
543 Great Rd (01460-1208)
PHONE..................................978 486-0404
Matthew Boucher, *President*
Stephen Boucher, *Treasurer*
Barbara Dee, *Manager*
EMP: 15 **EST:** 2016
SALES (est): 737.1K
SALES (corp-wide): 47.8MM **Privately Held**
SIC: 3812 Mfg Search/Navigation Equipment
PA: Airmar Technology Corp.
35 Meadowbrook Dr
Milford NH 03055
603 673-9570

(G-12314)
OAK GALLERY INC (PA)
Also Called: Fine Woodcrafters
160 Ayer Rd Unit 5 (01460-1146)
PHONE..................................978 486-9846
Vahe J Kouyoumdjian, *President*
EMP: 5
SQ FT: 10,000
SALES (est): 485.9K **Privately Held**
SIC: 2426 5712 Manufactures Hardwood Furniture & Retails Household Furniture

(G-12315)
OLDCASTLE INFRASTRUCTURE INC
265 Foster St (01460-2005)
PHONE..................................978 486-9600
EMP: 48
SALES (corp-wide): 29.7B **Privately Held**
SIC: 3272 Mfg Concrete Products
HQ: Oldcastle Infrastructure, Inc.
7000 Cntl Prkaway Ste 800
Atlanta GA 30328
470 602-2000

(G-12316)
OPTOMETRICS CORPORATION
521 Great Rd Ste 1 (01460-1208)
PHONE..................................978 772-1700
Gary J Bishop, *Exec VP*
Jonathan Carver, *Engineer*
Joe Sommers, *Engineer*
David Ventola, *Engineer*
Laura S Lunardo, *CFO*
▲ **EMP:** 50 **EST:** 1972
SQ FT: 10,000
SALES (est): 8.9MM
SALES (corp-wide): 43.7MM **Privately Held**
WEB: www.optometrics.com
SIC: 3827 Mfg Optical Instruments/Lenses
PA: Dynasil Corporation Of America
313 Washington St Ste 403
Newton MA 02458
617 668-6855

(G-12317)
PAGE SAME PUBLISHING INC
Also Called: In Compliance Magazine
531 King St Ste 5 (01460-1279)
PHONE..................................978 486-4684
Lorie Nichols, *President*
Sharon Smith, *Treasurer*
Ashleigh O'Connor, *Marketing Staff*
Erin Feeney, *Admin Sec*
EMP: 4
SALES: 750K **Privately Held**
SIC: 2721 Periodicals-Publishing/Printing

(G-12318)
PHILADELPHIA SIGN CO
50 Porter Rd (01460-1414)
PHONE..................................978 486-0137
Patrick Polazzo, *COO*
Kevin O Conner, *Manager*
EMP: 15
SALES (corp-wide): 83.2MM **Privately Held**
WEB: www.philadelphiasign.com
SIC: 3993 Mfg Signs/Advertising Specialties
PA: Philadelphia Sign Co.
707 W Spring Garden St
Palmyra NJ 08065
856 829-1460

(G-12319)
POLYONE CORPORATION
Also Called: Plastic Distributing
305 Foster St Ste 103 (01460-2021)
PHONE..................................978 772-0764
Tom Konop, *Manager*
EMP: 35 **Publicly Held**
WEB: www.polyone.com
SIC: 2821 Mfg Plastic Materials/Resins
PA: Polyone Corporation
33587 Walker Rd
Avon Lake OH 44012

(G-12320)
PROGRAMMED TEST SOURCES INC
Also Called: Pts
9 Beaver Brook Rd (01460-6232)
P.O. Box 517 (01460-0517)
PHONE..................................978 486-3008
Michael G Lohrer, *President*
George H Lohrer, *Chairman*
Michael Auger, *Vice Pres*
Michael Lohrer, *Plant Mgr*
Ilse Lohrer, *Treasurer*
EMP: 10
SALES (est): 1.8MM **Privately Held**
WEB: www.programmedtest.com
SIC: 3825 Mfg Electrical Measuring Instruments

(G-12321)
QBIT SEMICONDUCTOR LTD
1 Monarch Dr Ste 203 (01460-1440)
PHONE..................................351 205-0005
EMP: 3 **EST:** 2017
SALES (est): 189.7K **Privately Held**
SIC: 3674 Mfg Semiconductors/Related Devices

(G-12322)
ROBERT J MORAN INC
410 Great Rd (01460-1200)
P.O. Box 592 (01460-0592)
PHONE..................................978 486-4718
Robert J Moran Sr, *President*
Abbie Moran, *Executive Asst*
EMP: 9
SQ FT: 7,000
SALES (est): 987.1K **Privately Held**
SIC: 3599 Machine Shop

(G-12323)
SAJAWI CORPORATION
Also Called: ETM Manufacturing
24 Porter Rd (01460-1414)
PHONE..................................978 486-9050
Douglas Alan Scheffel, *CEO*
Elizabeth Scheffel, *President*
EMP: 25
SQ FT: 6,000
SALES: 2.5MM **Privately Held**
SIC: 3441 Structural Metal Fabrication

(G-12324)
TAPESTRY PRESS LTD
19 Nashoba Rd (01460-2210)
PHONE..................................978 486-0200
Michael Miskin, *President*
Elizabeth Miskin, *Vice Pres*
EMP: 3
SALES (est): 234.4K **Privately Held**
SIC: 2731 Books-Publishing/Printing

(G-12325)
VERYFINE PRODUCTS INC (DH)
20 Harvard Rd (01460-1015)
PHONE..................................978 486-0812
James A Rowse Sr, *Ch of Bd*
William Cyr, *President*
Samuel B Rowse, *President*
Steven Rowse, *Vice Pres*
Tim Voelkerding, *Treasurer*
EMP: 100 **EST:** 1865
SQ FT: 52,000
SALES (est): 39.8MM
SALES (corp-wide): 1.2B **Privately Held**
WEB: www.veryfine.com
SIC: 2086 Mfg Bottled/Canned Soft Drinks
HQ: Sunny Delight Beverage Co
10300 Alliance Rd Ste 500
Blue Ash OH 45242
513 483-3300

(G-12326)
VISIONQUEST HOLDINGS LLC
305 Foster St Ste 204 (01460-2021)
PHONE..................................978 776-9518
Elizabeth Kent, *VP Mktg*
Thomas G D, *Medical Dir*
EMP: 10
SQ FT: 6,000
SALES: 350K **Privately Held**
SIC: 3841 Mfg Surgical/Medical Instruments

(G-12327)
VIVAPRODUCTS INC
521 Great Rd (01460-1208)
PHONE..................................978 952-6868
Denis Hunt, *President*
Jen Allen, *General Mgr*
Bob Tutunjian, *General Mgr*
Nancy Hunt, *Treasurer*
EMP: 12
SALES (est): 2.3MM **Privately Held**
WEB: www.vivascience-us.com
SIC: 3569 Whol Medical/Hospital Equipment

(G-12328)
WINCHESTER SYSTEMS INC (PA)
305 Foster St (01460-2021)
PHONE..................................781 265-0200
Joel Leider, *CEO*
Jerry Namery, *President*
EMP: 25 **EST:** 1982
SQ FT: 15,000
SALES: 5.5MM **Privately Held**
SIC: 3572 3577 Mfg Computer Storage Devices Mfg Computer Peripheral Equipment

(G-12329)
XPHOTONICS LLC
32 Surrey Rd (01460-2258)
PHONE..................................978 952-2568
EMP: 5
SALES (est): 547.9K **Privately Held**
SIC: 3661 Mfg Telephone/Telegraph Apparatus

(G-12330)
ZEEVEE INC
295 Foster St Ste 2 (01460-2022)
PHONE..................................978 467-1395
Robert Michaels, *President*
Paul Levy, *Principal*
Andrew Marcuvitz, *Principal*
Dan Bettencourt, *Vice Pres*
Bob McHaels, *Vice Pres*
EMP: 36
SQ FT: 13,325
SALES (est): 3.5MM **Privately Held**
SIC: 3663 Mfg Radio/Tv Communication Equipment

Longmeadow
Hampden County

(G-12331)
BOMBICH SOFTWARE INC
63 Greenacre Ave (01106-1905)
P.O. Box 60753 (01116-0753)
PHONE..................................413 935-2300
Michael Bombich, *Ch of Bd*
Sarah Bombich, *COO*
EMP: 4 **EST:** 2012
SALES (est): 272.2K **Privately Held**
SIC: 7372 Prepackaged Software Services

(G-12332)
DOUGLAS DK COMPANY INCORPORATE
299 Bliss Rd (01106-1535)
PHONE..................................413 567-8572
DK Douglas, *President*

Patricia Douglas, *Clerk*
EMP: 5
SALES (est): 515.8K **Privately Held**
WEB: www.wetwrap.com
SIC: 2253 Mfg Aquatic Apparel

(G-12333)
EXTRAFRESH LLC
25 Andover Rd (01106-2913)
PHONE..................................413 567-8995
Joel B Kaufman, *President*
Frank Lenge, *Vice Pres*
EMP: 3
SALES (est): 258.2K **Privately Held**
WEB: www.extrafresh.com
SIC: 2673 Mfg Bags-Plastic/Coated Paper

(G-12334)
INTELLIGENT SIGNAGE INC
28 Greenmeadow Dr (01106-2306)
PHONE..................................413 567-8399
EMP: 3 **Privately Held**
WEB: www.intelligentsignage.net
SIC: 3993 Mfg Signs/Advertising Specialties
PA: Intelligent Signage Inc
4006 Coleridge Rd
Wilmington DE 19802

(G-12335)
LONGMEADOW PACKAGE STORE INC
400 Longmeadow St (01106-1315)
PHONE..................................413 567-3201
Fred Burritt, *President*
John Burritt, *Vice Pres*
Mary Burritt, *Treasurer*
EMP: 3
SALES (est): 258K **Privately Held**
SIC: 2084 5921 Mfg Wines/Brandy/Spirits Ret Alcoholic Beverages

(G-12336)
MAPLE ROAD SERVICE STATION
773 Maple Rd (01106-3127)
PHONE..................................413 567-6233
Abed Al-Hafid Zoghol, *President*
EMP: 5
SQ FT: 1,924
SALES (est): 527.6K **Privately Held**
SIC: 1389 Oil/Gas Field Services

(G-12337)
MERCOLINO BAKERY
287 Frank Smith Rd (01106-2921)
PHONE..................................413 733-9595
Peter Buoniconti, *Owner*
Joanne Buoniconti, *Principal*
EMP: 5
SQ FT: 2,500
SALES (est): 334.1K **Privately Held**
SIC: 2051 Mfg Bread/Related Products

(G-12338)
WARM WATER SALES GROUP
24 Knollwood Dr Ste 78 (01106-2714)
PHONE..................................413 567-0750
EMP: 3
SALES (est): 163.4K **Privately Held**
SIC: 3433 Mfg Heating Equipment-Nonelectric

Lowell
Middlesex County

(G-12339)
ADVANCED MATERIALS PROCESSING
Also Called: AMP Corp
225 Stedman St Ste 14 (01851-2784)
PHONE..................................978 251-3060
Harry Karimy, *President*
EMP: 3
SQ FT: 1,700
SALES (est): 315.9K **Privately Held**
WEB: www.ampcoatings.com
SIC: 3443 Mfg Fabricated Plate Work

(G-12340)
ADVANCED WOODWORKING TECHNOLOG
258 W Manchester St (01852-4438)
PHONE..................................978 937-1400
Maria T Marlowe, *Manager*
EMP: 5
SALES (est): 447.5K **Privately Held**
SIC: 2431 Mfg Millwork

(G-12341)
AEROFLEX / METELICS INC
100 Chelmsford St (01851-2620)
PHONE..................................603 641-3800
EMP: 6 **Publicly Held**
SIC: 3674 Manufactures Semiconductors/Related Devices
HQ: Aeroflex / Metelics, Inc.
100 Chelmsford St
Lowell MA 01851
408 737-8181

(G-12342)
AIR-MART HEATING & COOLING LLC
225 Stedman St Ste 13 (01851-2784)
PHONE..................................603 821-1416
Richard Martir, *Opers Mgr*
EMP: 8
SALES: 1MM **Privately Held**
WEB: www.airmart.org
SIC: 3585 Mfg Refrigeration/Heating Equipment

(G-12343)
AMERICRAFT CARTON INC
164 Meadowcroft St (01852-5399)
P.O. Box 270 (01853-0270)
PHONE..................................978 459-9328
Christine Tamblingson, *General Mgr*
Steve Chartier, *Purch Mgr*
Jim Klecak, *Engineer*
Melinda Darocha, *Human Res Mgr*
Kim Houston, *Office Mgr*
EMP: 165
SALES (corp-wide): 174.7MM **Privately Held**
WEB: www.americraft.com
SIC: 2657 Mfg Folding Paperboard Boxes
PA: Americraft Carton, Inc.
7400 State Line Rd # 206
Prairie Village KS 66208
913 387-3700

(G-12344)
APPLIED NANOFEMTO TECH LLC
240 Varnum Ave Apt 12 (01854-2522)
PHONE..................................978 761-4293
Jing Chen, *Branch Mgr*
EMP: 3
SALES (corp-wide): 498.1K **Privately Held**
SIC: 3674 Mfg Semiconductors/Related Devices
PA: Applied Nanofemto Technologies Llc
181 Stedman St Ste 2
Lowell MA 01851
978 794-5518

(G-12345)
ARLIN MFG CO INC
239 Industrial Ave E (01852-5113)
P.O. Box 222 (01853-0222)
PHONE..................................978 454-9165
John R Mitchell, *Ch of Bd*
John R Mitchell Jr, *President*
Paul R Mitchell, *Corp Secy*
Steve Mitchell, *Vice Pres*
Paul McLaughlin, *Accounts Exec*
▲ **EMP:** 15 **EST:** 1954
SQ FT: 4,500
SALES (est): 4.4MM **Privately Held**
WEB: www.arlinmfg.com
SIC: 3081 Mfg Unsupported Plastic Film/Sheet

(G-12346)
ARRIS TECHNOLOGY INC
900 Chelmsford St (01851-8100)
PHONE..................................978 614-2900
EMP: 11
SALES (est): 1.3MM **Privately Held**
SIC: 3663 Mfg Radio/Tv Communication Equipment

(G-12347)
AVCARB LLC
Also Called: Avcarb Material Solutions
2 Indl Ave (01851)
PHONE..................................978 452-8961
Charles Harris, *Vice Pres*
Don Connors, *VP Opers*
Cheryl Dexter, *Senior Buyer*
Mark Tambling, *Engineer*
Andrea Benoit, *Accountant*
▲ **EMP:** 64
SQ FT: 30,000
SALES: 24.4MM **Privately Held**
SIC: 3955 2221 Mfg Carbon Paper/Ink Ribbons Manmade Broadwoven Fabric Mill

(G-12348)
AXIS TECHNOLOGIES INC
39 Wilbur St Ste 2 (01851-5221)
PHONE..................................978 275-9908
Dennis W Gibson, *President*
Dawn Sheehan, *CFO*
Michael Vapolski, *VP Sales*
EMP: 42
SALES: 5MM **Privately Held**
WEB: www.axistechnologiesinc.com
SIC: 3599 Prototype Machine Shop

(G-12349)
AYAN ELECTRIC INC
225 Stedman St Ste 7 (01851-2784)
PHONE..................................978 256-6306
Edward Ayan, *President*
Denise Ayan, *Shareholder*
EMP: 4
SQ FT: 2,000
SALES (est): 410K **Privately Held**
WEB: www.ayan.com
SIC: 3613 Mfg Control Panels

(G-12350)
BASSETT & CASSIDY INC
Also Called: Minuteman Press
1527 Middlesex St (01851-1271)
PHONE..................................978 452-9595
Mark Cassidy, *President*
Christopher Bassett, *Vice Pres*
EMP: 7
SQ FT: 2,400
SALES (est): 849.1K **Privately Held**
SIC: 2752 Lithographic Commercial Printing

(G-12351)
BATIAN PEAK COFFEE
Also Called: Kenya Coffee and Tea Import
10 Hurd St (01852-2206)
PHONE..................................978 663-2305
Peter Kagunye, *Owner*
Phillip Gatua, *Manager*
▲ **EMP:** 6
SQ FT: 4,000
SALES: 10K **Privately Held**
WEB: www.batianpeakcoffee.com
SIC: 2095 Kenyan Coffee Import Export Roasting And Packaging

(G-12352)
BATTALION CO INC (PA)
Also Called: Ymittos Candle Mfg Co
325 Chelmsford St (01851-4429)
P.O. Box 1748 (01853-1748)
PHONE..................................978 453-2824
Mark Vanderberg, *President*
Michael Kaplan, *Vice Pres*
EMP: 5
SQ FT: 15,000
SALES (est): 885.5K **Privately Held**
SIC: 3999 Mfg Misc Products

(G-12353)
BERTRAM & LEITHNER INC
210 Stedman St (01851-5206)
PHONE..................................978 459-7474
Ted Bertram, *President*
Paul Leithner, *Vice Pres*
EMP: 4
SALES (est): 484K **Privately Held**
SIC: 3531 Mfg Construction Machinery

(G-12354)
BRADFORD COATINGS INC
Also Called: Bradford Coatings, LLC
75 Rogers St (01852-3617)
PHONE..................................978 459-4100
Jay Kumar, *CEO*
Stephen Olsen, *President*
John Filer, *Vice Pres*
Deborah Bunch, *Opers Staff*
Dan Petullo, *QA Dir*
▲ **EMP:** 75
SALES (est): 22.8MM **Privately Held**
WEB: www.bradfordind.com
SIC: 2295 Mfg Coated Fabrics
PA: Wembly Enterprises Llc
931 Briarwoods Rd
Franklin Lakes NJ

(G-12355)
BRADY BUSINESS FORMS INC
171 Lincoln St Ste 1 (01852-6021)
P.O. Box 667, Tyngsboro (01879-0667)
PHONE..................................978 458-2585
Mark Brady, *President*
Lou Ann Brady, *Vice Pres*
EMP: 8
SQ FT: 10,000
SALES (est): 1MM **Privately Held**
SIC: 2759 5112 2752 Prints & Whol Business Forms & Offset Printing

(G-12356)
BROADSTONE INDUSTRIES
195 Circuit Ave (01852-5587)
PHONE..................................978 691-2790
Vincent Broadstone, *Owner*
EMP: 4
SQ FT: 7,500
SALES (est): 421.2K **Privately Held**
SIC: 3089 3585 Mfg Of Metal And Plastic Products

(G-12357)
BRUCE LUONG DBA PURE FROYO
108 Merrimack St (01852-1718)
PHONE..................................978 996-7800
EMP: 5 **EST:** 2012
SALES (est): 305.7K **Privately Held**
SIC: 2024 Mfg Ice Cream/Frozen Desert

(G-12358)
CHAPMAN FUEL
210 Cross St (01854-3320)
PHONE..................................978 452-9656
Debrah Chapman, *Owner*
EMP: 3
SALES (est): 174.8K **Privately Held**
SIC: 2869 Mfg Industrial Organic Chemicals

(G-12359)
COATING SYSTEMS INC
90 Phoenix Ave (01852-4981)
PHONE..................................978 937-3712
Arthur C Sacco, *President*
Linda J Sacco, *Vice Pres*
EMP: 54
SQ FT: 20,000
SALES (est): 7.3MM **Privately Held**
WEB: www.coatingsystemsgroup.com
SIC: 3471 Plating/Polishing Service

(G-12360)
COCA-COLA BOTTLING COMPANY
160 Industrial Ave E (01852-5152)
PHONE..................................978 459-9378
Jeff Polak, *General Mgr*
EMP: 70 **Privately Held**
SIC: 2086 Carb Sft Drnkbtlcn
HQ: Coca-Cola Beverages Northeast, Inc.
1 Executive Park Dr # 330
Bedford NH 03110
603 627-7871

(G-12361)
COELHO FUEL INC
493 Princeton Blvd (01851-2204)
PHONE..................................978 458-8252
Francisco Coelho, *President*
EMP: 3
SALES (est): 381K **Privately Held**
SIC: 2869 Mfg Industrial Organic Chemicals

(G-12362)
CORTRON INC
59 Technology Dr (01851-2851)
PHONE..................................978 975-5445
Eric Friedrichs, *President*
Jon Koeller, *Project Mgr*
Herman L Kabakoff, *Treasurer*
EMP: 48
SQ FT: 28,000
SALES (est): 12MM **Privately Held**
WEB: www.cortroninc.com
SIC: **3575** 3699 3577 Mfg Computer Terminals Mfg Electrical Equipment/Supplies Mfg Computer Peripheral Equipment

(G-12363)
CRISTEK INTERCONNECTS INC
663 Lawrence St (01852-3535)
PHONE..................................978 735-2161
Kelly Boulard, *Branch Mgr*
EMP: 8
SALES (corp-wide): 26.7MM **Privately Held**
SIC: **3678** Mfg Electronic Connectors
PA: Cristek Interconnects, Inc.
5395 E Hunter Ave
Anaheim CA 92807
714 696-5200

(G-12364)
CSP INC (PA)
Also Called: Cspi
175 Cabot St Ste 210 (01854-3635)
PHONE..................................978 954-5038
C Shelton James, *Ch of Bd*
Victor Dellovo, *President*
Mike Newbanks, *Vice Pres*
Gary W Levine, *CFO*
Michael Newbanks,
EMP: 63
SQ FT: 13,515
SALES: 79MM **Publicly Held**
WEB: www.cspi.com
SIC: **3577** 7372 7373 Mfg Computer Processors Software & Hardware Packages Information Technology Services

(G-12365)
D S GRAPHICS INC (PA)
120 Stedman St (01851-2797)
PHONE..................................978 970-1359
Jeffrey F Pallis, *President*
James J Pallis, *CFO*
Bob Daley, *Manager*
Kevin Perron, *Manager*
Justin R Pallis, *Admin Sec*
▲ **EMP:** 160 **EST:** 1974
SQ FT: 140,000
SALES (est): 51MM **Privately Held**
WEB: www.dsgraphics.com
SIC: **2752** 2791 2789 Lithographic Commercial Printing Typesetting Services Bookbinding/Related Work

(G-12366)
DCB WELDING AND FABRICATION
143 Meadowcroft St (01852)
PHONE..................................978 587-3883
Christine Bartholomew, *President*
EMP: 3
SALES: 174K **Privately Held**
SIC: **3446** 1791 1799 7692 Mfg Architectural Mtlwrk Structural Steel Erectn Special Trade Contractor Welding Repair

(G-12367)
DIAGNOSYS LLC (PA)
55 Technology Dr Ste 1 (01851-5203)
PHONE..................................978 458-1600
Bruce Doran, *Mng Member*
Richard Robson,
▲ **EMP:** 23
SALES (est): 2.9MM **Privately Held**
WEB: www.diagnosysuk.com
SIC: **2836** 3845 3841 Mfg Biological Products Mfg Electromedical Equipment Mfg Surgical/Medical Instruments

(G-12368)
DISPATCH NEWS
Also Called: Lowell Sun
491 Dutton St (01854-4289)
PHONE..................................978 458-7100
Dean Singleton, *President*
EMP: 8 **EST:** 2010
SALES (est): 419.8K **Privately Held**
SIC: **2711** Newspapers-Publishing/Printing

(G-12369)
EPROPELLED INC (PA)
116 John St Ste 205 (01852-1124)
PHONE..................................978 703-1350
Nick Grewal, *CEO*
EMP: 5 **EST:** 2018
SQ FT: 12,000
SALES (est): 2.6MM **Privately Held**
SIC: **3621** 5063 Mfg Motors/Generators Whol Electrical Equipment

(G-12370)
EVOQUA WATER TECHNOLOGIES LLC
10 Technology Dr (01851-2728)
PHONE..................................978 934-9349
Richard Pond, *Engineer*
Francis Ferrara, *Branch Mgr*
EMP: 200
SQ FT: 1,000
SALES (corp-wide): 1.4B **Publicly Held**
SIC: **3589** Mfg Svc Industry Mach
HQ: Evoqua Water Technologies Llc
210 6th Ave Ste 3300
Pittsburgh PA 15222
724 772-0044

(G-12371)
FLUIGENT INC
600 Suffolk St Ste M2d2 (01854-3643)
PHONE..................................978 934-5283
Robert P Pelletier, *President*
EMP: 3
SALES (est): 181.5K **Privately Held**
SIC: **3625** Mfg Relays/Industrial Controls

(G-12372)
G3 INCORPORATED (PA)
Also Called: Photo Etch Technology
71 Willie St (01854-4125)
PHONE..................................978 805-5001
Lisa Guidi, *President*
Dan Latessa, *Vice Pres*
EMP: 30
SALES (est): 3.7MM **Privately Held**
SIC: **2631** 3953 3672 Paperboard Mill Mfg Marking Devices Mfg Printed Circuit Boards

(G-12373)
GENERAL WOODWORKING INC (PA)
Also Called: Phoenix Workstation Division
105 Pevey St (01851-1357)
PHONE..................................978 458-6625
John Thompson, *President*
Dan Thompson, *Vice Pres*
Michael Thompson, *Vice Pres*
Judith A Thompson, *Treasurer*
Sara A Axon, *Admin Sec*
EMP: 10
SALES (est): 8.1MM **Privately Held**
WEB: www.genwood.com
SIC: **2599** 3083 2541 2431 Mfg Furniture/Fixtures Mfg Lamnatd Plstc Plates Mfg Wood Partitions/Fixt Mfg Millwork

(G-12374)
GENERAL WOODWORKING INC
Also Called: Phoenix Workstations
299 Western Ave (01851-1414)
PHONE..................................978 251-4070
EMP: 40
SALES (corp-wide): 8.1MM **Privately Held**
WEB: www.genwood.com
SIC: **2599** Machine Shop
PA: General Woodworking, Inc.
105 Pevey St
Lowell MA 01851
978 458-6625

(G-12375)
GILBRIDE ENTERPRISES LLC
Also Called: George's Textile
360 Merrimack St (01852-5906)
PHONE..................................978 452-0878
Linda J Gilbride, *Mng Member*
EMP: 3
SALES: 200K **Privately Held**
SIC: **2299** Mfg Textile Goods

(G-12376)
GLOBAL MATERIALS INC
Also Called: Specialty Materials
1449 Middlesex St (01851-1111)
PHONE..................................978 322-1900
Monica Rommel, *CEO*
Monte Treasure, *President*
▲ **EMP:** 36
SQ FT: 54,000
SALES (est): 15.7MM **Privately Held**
WEB: www.specmaterials.com
SIC: **2823** Mfg Cellulosic Manmade Fibers

(G-12377)
GN AUDIO USA INC (DH)
Also Called: Gn Netcom, Inc.
900 Chelmsford St (01851-8100)
PHONE..................................800 826-4656
Toon Bouten, *CEO*
Peter Fox, *President*
Hanf Hendric Lund, *Principal*
Dean G Kacos, *CFO*
Anna Johnson, *Treasurer*
▲ **EMP:** 350
SQ FT: 57,000
SALES (est): 66.6MM
SALES (corp-wide): 1.5B **Privately Held**
WEB: www.gnnetcom-usa.com
SIC: **3661** Mfg Telephone/Telegraph Apparatus
HQ: Gn Audio A/S
Lautrupbjerg 7
Ballerup 2750
457 500-00

(G-12378)
GREENER GROUP LLC
123 Bolt St (01852-5376)
PHONE..................................978 441-3900
Darlene McSorley,
Dorothy McSorley, *Admin Asst*
Jeremy L McSorley,
EMP: 80
SQ FT: 3,000
SALES: 13MM **Privately Held**
SIC: **3271** Mfg Concrete Block/Brick

(G-12379)
HEALTH HELM INC
110 Canal St Fl 4 (01852-4574)
PHONE..................................508 951-2156
Pamela McNamara, *CEO*
EMP: 6
SALES (est): 368K **Privately Held**
SIC: **7372** Prepackaged Software Services

(G-12380)
HORSEPOWER TECHNOLOGIES INC
175 Cabot St Ste 500 (01854-3640)
PHONE..................................844 514-6773
Mouli Ramani, *President*
EMP: 50 **EST:** 2017
SALES: 25MM **Privately Held**
SIC: **3841** Mfg Surgical/Medical Instruments

(G-12381)
IDEAL TAPE CO INC
Also Called: Ideal Tape Co-A Div Amercn Bil
1400 Middlesex St (01851-1296)
PHONE..................................978 458-6833
Michel Merkx, *General Mgr*
John Poulton, *Vice Pres*
Diane Stewart, *Research*
Jennifer Coleman, *Controller*
Joe Mariani, *Info Tech Dir*
◆ **EMP:** 70
SQ FT: 50,000
SALES (est): 24.9MM
SALES (corp-wide): 63.6MM **Publicly Held**
WEB: www.ambilt.com
SIC: **2672** 2671 Mfg Coated/Laminated Paper Mfg Packaging Paper/Film
PA: American Biltrite Inc.
57 River St Ste 302
Wellesley MA 02481
781 237-6655

(G-12382)
IDEAS INC
160 Tanner St (01852-4473)
PHONE..................................978 453-6864
Charles Mc Namara Jr, *President*
Patrick Mc Namara, *Admin Sec*
EMP: 9 **EST:** 1969
SQ FT: 25,000
SALES (est): 1.4MM **Privately Held**
SIC: **3444** Mfg Sheet Metalwork

(G-12383)
INTERSTATE CONT LOWELL LLC (DH)
Also Called: Ds Smith Packaging
240 Industrial Ave E (01852-5114)
PHONE..................................978 458-4555
Henry Faria, *Plant Mgr*
Antoine Frem,
Charles A Feghali,
Dave Mc Quade,
Doug Russell,
◆ **EMP:** 94 **EST:** 1997
SQ FT: 175,000
SALES (est): 21.8MM
SALES (corp-wide): 8.1B **Privately Held**
SIC: **2653** Mfg Corrugated/Solid Fiber Boxes
HQ: Interstate Resources, Inc.
3475 Piedmont Rd Ne # 1525
Atlanta GA 30305
703 243-3355

(G-12384)
INTOUCH LABELS AND PACKG INC
181 Industrial Ave E (01852-5131)
PHONE..................................800 370-2693
Lauren Hayes, *President*
Lou Berceli, *Sales Staff*
EMP: 3
SALES (est): 377.3K **Privately Held**
SIC: **2759** Commercial Printing

(G-12385)
J G MACLELLAN CON CO INC (PA)
180 Phoenix Ave (01852-4931)
PHONE..................................978 458-1223
John G Maclellan III, *President*
Paul Curry, *Credit Staff*
Jennifer Benton, *Sales Staff*
David Osgood, *Sales Staff*
Matt Benincasa, *Manager*
EMP: 60 **EST:** 1965
SQ FT: 1,200
SALES (est): 20.9MM **Privately Held**
SIC: **3273** 1442 Mfg Ready-Mixed Concrete Construction Sand/Gravel

(G-12386)
JOAN FABRICS LLC
134 Middle St Ste 300 (01852-1878)
PHONE..................................978 454-3777
EMP: 4
SALES: 437.3K **Privately Held**
SIC: **2299** Mfg Textile Goods

(G-12387)
KENCO PRINTING
24b Rockingham St (01852-4821)
PHONE..................................781 391-9500
Glen Kendall, *Owner*
EMP: 4
SALES: 200K **Privately Held**
WEB: www.kencoprinting.com
SIC: **2752** Commercial Printing

(G-12388)
KHMERPOST USA LLC
45 Merrimack St (01852-1729)
PHONE..................................978 677-7163
Soben Pin, *Principal*
EMP: 5 **EST:** 2013
SALES (est): 320.5K **Privately Held**
SIC: **2711** Newspapers-Publishing/Printing

(G-12389)
KING FISHER CO INC
81 Old Ferry Rd (01854-1907)
PHONE..................................978 596-0214
Frank Carideo, *CEO*
Mario Bulhoes, *Vice Pres*
EMP: 25
SQ FT: 25,000
SALES (est): 6.3MM **Privately Held**
WEB: www.kfco.com
SIC: **3669** 3569 2899 7371 Mfg Communications Equip Mfg General Indstl Mach Mfg Chemical Preparation Computer Programming Svc

▲ = Import ▼=Export
◆ =Import/Export

(G-12390)
KING PRINTING COMPANY INC
181 Industrial Ave E (01852-5147)
PHONE..................................978 458-2345
Aditya Chinai, *President*
Martin Aalsma, *Vice Pres*
Tom Campbell, *Vice Pres*
Tom Plain, *Vice Pres*
Siddharth Chinai, *Treasurer*
▼ **EMP:** 80
SALES (est): 24.5MM **Privately Held**
WEB: www.kingprinting.com
SIC: 2752 Lithographic Commercial Printing

(G-12391)
KRONOS ACQUISITION CORPORATION (HQ)
900 Chelmsford St # 312 (01851-8100)
PHONE..................................978 250-9800
Aron J AIN, *CEO*
Mark S AIN, *Chairman*
Mark Julien, *CFO*
EMP: 5
SALES (est): 1B
SALES (corp-wide): 1B **Privately Held**
SIC: 7372 7373 6726 Prepackaged Software Services Computer Systems Design Closed-End Investment Office
PA: Kronos Parent Corporation
900 Chelmsford St # 312
Lowell MA 01851
978 250-9800

(G-12392)
KRONOS INCORPORATED (DH)
900 Chelmsford St # 312 (01851-8312)
PHONE..................................978 250-9800
Mark S AIN, *Ch of Bd*
Patricia Dyble, *Principal*
Steven Mersch, *Principal*
John Morrison, *Principal*
Kevin Clark, *Business Mgr*
◆ **EMP:** 164 **EST:** 1977
SQ FT: 400,000
SALES (est): 1B **Privately Held**
WEB: www.kronos.com
SIC: 7372 7373 Prepackaged Software Services Computer Systems Design

(G-12393)
KRONOS INTERNATIONAL MGT LLC
900 Chelmsford St # 312 (01851-8100)
PHONE..................................978 250-9800
Alyce Moore, *Manager*
EMP: 3
SALES (est): 134.2K
SALES (corp-wide): 1B **Privately Held**
SIC: 7372 Prepackaged Software Services
HQ: Kronos Incorporated
900 Chelmsford St # 312
Lowell MA 01851
978 250-9800

(G-12394)
KRONOS PARENT CORPORATION (PA)
900 Chelmsford St # 312 (01851-8100)
PHONE..................................978 250-9800
Aron J AIN, *President*
Alyce Moore, *Vice Pres*
Nicole Fieser, *Project Mgr*
Jacqueline Jay, *Project Mgr*
Danielle Thomas, *Project Mgr*
EMP: 3
SALES (est): 1B **Privately Held**
SIC: 7372 7373 Prepackaged Software Services Computer Systems Design

(G-12395)
KRONOS SOLUTIONS INC (DH)
900 Chelmsford St # 312 (01851-8312)
PHONE..................................978 805-9971
Aron J AIN, *CEO*
Deirdre Aubuchon, *COO*
Peter George, *Senior VP*
Mark Julien, *CFO*
EMP: 5
SQ FT: 20,000
SALES (est): 4.9MM
SALES (corp-wide): 1B **Privately Held**
WEB: www.deploy.com
SIC: 7372 Prepackaged Software Services
HQ: Kronos Incorporated
900 Chelmsford St # 312
Lowell MA 01851
978 250-9800

(G-12396)
LITTLE DELIGHTS BAKERY
132 Merrimack St (01852)
PHONE..................................978 455-0040
Many Pho, *Owner*
EMP: 4
SQ FT: 1,100
SALES (est): 284.4K **Privately Held**
SIC: 2051 Mfg Bread/Related Products

(G-12397)
LOCKHEED MARTIN SERVICES LLC
175 Cabot St Ste 415 (01854-3633)
PHONE..................................978 275-9730
EMP: 20 **Publicly Held**
SIC: 3812 Mfg Search/Navigation Equipment
HQ: Lockheed Martin Services, Llc
700 N Frederick Ave
Gaithersburg MD 20879
-

(G-12398)
LOWELL DIGISONDE INTL LLC
175 Cabot St Ste 200 (01854-3635)
PHONE..................................978 735-4752
Bodo W Reinisch, *Principal*
Jason Grochmal, *Prdtn Mgr*
Ryan Hamel, *Engineer*
Igor Lisysyan, *Electrical Engi*
EMP: 5
SALES (est): 950K **Privately Held**
SIC: 3812 Mfg Search/Navigation Equipment

(G-12399)
LOWELL SUN PUBLISHING COMPANY (DH)
491 Dutton St Ste 2 (01854-4294)
PHONE..................................978 459-1300
Charles St Amand, *Publisher*
Mack O Neal, *Principal*
John Habbe, *CFO*
Paula Hammond, *Advt Staff*
Carmen Azevedo, *Consultant*
EMP: 24 **EST:** 1878
SQ FT: 55,000
SALES (est): 21.4MM
SALES (corp-wide): 4.2B **Privately Held**
WEB: www.lowellsun.com
SIC: 2711 Newspapers-Publishing/Printing

(G-12400)
MACOM METELICS LLC
Also Called: M/A-Com
100 Chelmsford St (01851-2694)
PHONE..................................978 656-2500
Brian Sailor, *CFO*
EMP: 55 **EST:** 1978
SQ FT: 20,000
SALES: 22MM **Publicly Held**
WEB: www.aeroflex-metelics.com
SIC: 3674 Mfg Semiconductors/Related Devices
PA: Macom Technology Solutions Holdings, Inc.
100 Chelmsford St
Lowell MA 01851
-

(G-12401)
MACOM TECH SLTONS HOLDINGS INC (PA)
100 Chelmsford St (01851-2694)
PHONE..................................978 656-2500
John Ocampo, *Ch of Bd*
Stephen Daly, *President*
Ron Karfelt, *General Mgr*
Alex Behfar, *Senior VP*
Robert Dennehy, *Senior VP*
EMP: 121
SQ FT: 157,600
SALES: 499.7MM **Publicly Held**
SIC: 3674 Mfg Semiconductors & Related Devices

(G-12402)
MACOM TECHNOLOGY SOLUTIONS INC
121 Hale St (01851-3311)
PHONE..................................978 656-2500
EMP: 3 **Publicly Held**
SIC: 3663 3679 Mfg Radio/Tv Communication Equipment Mfg Electronic Components
HQ: Macom Technology Solutions Inc.
100 Chelmsford St
Lowell MA 01851
-

(G-12403)
MACOM TECHNOLOGY SOLUTIONS INC (HQ)
Also Called: M/A-Com
100 Chelmsford St (01851-2694)
PHONE..................................978 656-2500
John Croteau, *President*
Karen Hanlon, *General Mgr*
Vivek Rajgarhia, *General Mgr*
James Rame, *Principal*
Stefano Dagostino, *Vice Pres*
EMP: 355
SALES (est): 166.2MM **Publicly Held**
SIC: 3663 3679 Manufacturing Radio/Tv Communication Equipment

(G-12404)
MAXIMUS
11 Mill St Ste 2 (01852-3588)
PHONE..................................978 728-8000
EMP: 4
SALES (est): 155.4K **Privately Held**
SIC: 2752 Lithographic Commercial Printing

(G-12405)
MC GARVIN ENGINEERING CO
35 Maple St Ste 1 (01852-4561)
PHONE..................................978 454-2741
Bob Skinner, *President*
EMP: 10 **EST:** 1969
SQ FT: 10,000
SALES (est): 1.2MM **Privately Held**
WEB: www.mcgarvin.com
SIC: 3444 Mfg Sheet Metalwork

(G-12406)
MCF ELECTRONIC SERVICES INC
39 1st St (01850-2501)
PHONE..................................603 718-2256
Lucinda Mailloux, *Principal*
EMP: 6
SALES (est): 64.4K **Privately Held**
SIC: 3999 Mfg Misc Products

(G-12407)
MEDICAMETRIX INC
600 Suffolk St (01854-3643)
PHONE..................................617 694-1713
EMP: 5
SALES (est): 548.6K **Privately Held**
WEB: www.medicametrix.com
SIC: 3845 Mfg Medical Devices

(G-12408)
METELICS CORP
100 Chelmsford St (01851-2620)
PHONE..................................408 737-8197
Randy Cavanaugh, *CFO*
EMP: 106
SALES (est): 11.1MM **Privately Held**
WEB: www.metelics.com
SIC: 3674 Mfg Semiconductors/Related Devices

(G-12409)
MICROSEMI CORP-MASSACHUSETTS
Also Called: Microsemi-Lowell
75 Technology Dr (01851-2729)
PHONE..................................978 442-5600
John A Caruso, *Vice Pres*
EMP: 76
SALES (corp-wide): 5.3B **Publicly Held**
WEB: www.microsemi.com
SIC: 3674 Mfg Semiconductor Components
HQ: Microsemi Corp.- Massachusetts
1 Enterprise
Aliso Viejo CA 92656
978 794-1666

(G-12410)
MICROSEMI CORPORATION
75 Technology Dr (01851-2729)
PHONE..................................978 442-5637
Peter Bergeron, *Engineer*
Dean Morgan, *Branch Mgr*
Leon Gross, *Director*
EMP: 100
SALES (corp-wide): 5.3B **Publicly Held**
SIC: 3674 Mfg Semiconductors/Related Devices
HQ: Microsemi Corporation
1 Enterprise
Aliso Viejo CA 92656
949 380-6100

(G-12411)
MICROSENSE LLC (HQ)
205 Industrial Ave E (01852-5113)
PHONE..................................978 843-7670
James A Pelusi, *CEO*
Tom McNabb, *President*
Jacques Fauque, *Vice Pres*
Erik Samwel, *Info Tech Mgr*
Robert C Abbe, *Exec Dir*
EMP: 34
SALES (est): 6.2MM
SALES (corp-wide): 4.5B **Publicly Held**
SIC: 3829 Mfg Measuring/Controlling Devices
PA: Kla Corporation
1 Technology Dr
Milpitas CA 95035
408 875-3000

(G-12412)
MILLENNIUM PLATING COMPANY INC
75 Phoenix Ave (01852-4987)
PHONE..................................978 454-0526
Stephen Rohrbacher, *President*
Ruth Rohrbacher, *Vice Pres*
Gregg Maclean, *Shareholder*
Richard Wallace, *Shareholder*
EMP: 6
SQ FT: 10,000
SALES: 1MM **Privately Held**
WEB: www.magplate.com
SIC: 3471 Plating & Polishing Services

(G-12413)
MOR-WIRE & CABLE INC
50 Newhall St Ste 1 (01852-4166)
P.O. Box 1782 (01853-1782)
PHONE..................................978 453-1782
Michael Morin, *President*
Gale Vochum, *Treasurer*
EMP: 10
SQ FT: 16,000
SALES (est): 1.8MM **Privately Held**
SIC: 3357 Nonferrous Wiredrawing/Insulating

(G-12414)
NORTH EAST FORM ENGINEERING
44 Stedman St Ste 9 (01851-2734)
PHONE..................................978 454-5290
Margaret J Randall, *President*
EMP: 4
SQ FT: 2,500
SALES: 500K **Privately Held**
SIC: 3545 Mfg Industrial Machinery

(G-12415)
OFFBEET COMPOSTING LLC
90 Bolt St (01852-5316)
PHONE..................................603 568-2756
Kesiah K Bascom, *Principal*
EMP: 3
SALES (est): 237.5K **Privately Held**
SIC: 2875 Mfg Fertilizers-Mix Only

(G-12416)
ONLINE MARKETING SOLUTIONS
128 Warren St (01852-2284)
PHONE..................................978 937-2363
Peter Campbell, *COO*
Tj Caveney, *Exec VP*

Keith Caveney, *Manager*
Lisa Guy, *Administration*
EMP: 15
SQ FT: 3,000
SALES (est): 1.3MM **Privately Held**
WEB: www.o-ms.com
SIC: 7372 Prepackaged Software Services

(G-12417)
ORIGO AUTOMATION INC
175 Cabot St Ste 100 (01854-3635)
PHONE.....877 943-5677
Jeffrey Bruce, *CEO*
Matthew Sweetland, *Principal*
EMP: 3 **EST:** 2016
SQ FT: 100
SALES (est): 128K **Privately Held**
SIC: 3825 7371 8742 Mfg Electrical Measuring Instruments Custom Computer Programing Management Consulting Services

(G-12418)
OWL STAMP COMPANY INC
Also Called: Owlstamp Visual Solutions
142 Middle St (01852-6241)
PHONE.....978 452-4541
Peter Bergeron, *President*
EMP: 8
SQ FT: 3,000
SALES (est): 1.3MM **Privately Held**
SIC: 2752 7389 3993 7331 Mfg Marking Devices Lithographic Coml Print Business Services Mfg Signs/Ad Specialties

(G-12419)
PDI INTERNATIONAL INC
1100 Gorham St (01852-5019)
P.O. Box 1311 (01853-1311)
PHONE.....978 446-0840
Babu Deb, *President*
▲ **EMP:** 5
SALES (est): 503.5K **Privately Held**
SIC: 3495 Mfg Wire Springs

(G-12420)
PEROXYGEN SYSTEMS INC
116 John St Ste 315 (01852-1124)
PHONE.....248 835-9026
Ming Qi, *CEO*
Alan Pezeshki, *Treasurer*
Gustavo Bottan, *Director*
EMP: 5 **EST:** 2014
SALES (est): 942K **Privately Held**
SIC: 2819 Mfg Industrial Inorganic Chemicals

(G-12421)
PHOTO TOOL ENGINEERING INC
Also Called: Pohto Etch Tech
71 Willie St (01854-4125)
PHONE.....978 805-5000
Arthur Guidi, *President*
Lisa Guidi, *Treasurer*
Roberta Guidi, *Clerk*
EMP: 45
SALES (est): 5.5MM **Privately Held**
SIC: 3672 Mfg Printed Circuit Boards

(G-12422)
PLENUS GROUP INC
Also Called: Pgi
101 Phoenix Ave (01852-4930)
PHONE.....978 970-3832
Joseph Jolly III, *President*
Stephen Post, *CFO*
Jamie Crane, *Sales Mgr*
Rocky Anzalone, *Sales Executive*
John Berube, *Manager*
EMP: 50
SQ FT: 13,000
SALES (est): 10.5MM **Privately Held**
WEB: www.plenus-group.com
SIC: 2038 2035 Mfg Frozen Specialties Mfg Pickles/Sauces/Dressing

(G-12423)
POLNOX CORPORATION
225 Stedman St Ste 23 (01851-2792)
PHONE.....978 735-4438
Ashok Cholli, *President*
▲ **EMP:** 3
SALES (est): 366.2K **Privately Held**
SIC: 2869 Mfg Antioxidants

(G-12424)
PRECISE INDUSTRIES INC
639 Lakeview Ave (01850-1827)
PHONE.....978 453-8490
Charles Dehney, *President*
Sal Lopez, *Manager*
EMP: 27
SALES (est): 5.2MM **Privately Held**
SIC: 3444 Sheet Metal Contractor

(G-12425)
RAPID MICRO BIOSYSTEMS INC (PA)
1001 Pawtucket Blvd 280 (01854-1040)
PHONE.....978 349-3200
Robert Spignesi, *CEO*
Phil Stewart, *Vice Pres*
Scott White, *Vice Pres*
Erick Langlois, *Buyer*
Stephen Furlong, *CFO*
▲ **EMP:** 95
SQ FT: 40,000
SALES (est): 20.4MM **Privately Held**
WEB: www.rapidmicrobio.com
SIC: 3559 Mfg Misc Industry Machinery

(G-12426)
REBOOT MEDICAL INC
110 Canal St Fl 4 (01852-4574)
PHONE.....818 621-6554
Madalyn Berns, *Principal*
Joseph Lomakin, *Principal*
Jeffrey Maynard, *Principal*
EMP: 3 **EST:** 2016
SALES (est): 230.3K **Privately Held**
SIC: 3841 Commercial Physical Research Mfg Surgical/Medical Instruments

(G-12427)
RGC MILLWORK INCORPORATED
175a Old Canal Dr (01851-2736)
PHONE.....978 275-9529
Richard P Garofano, *President*
EMP: 8
SALES (est): 1.2MM **Privately Held**
SIC: 2431 2434 Mfg Millwork Mfg Wood Kitchen Cabinets

(G-12428)
ROCHE BROS BARREL & DRUM CO
161 Phoenix Ave (01852-4998)
PHONE.....978 454-9135
Michael Roche, *President*
Charles Roche, *Treasurer*
EMP: 28 **EST:** 1920
SALES (est): 4.9MM **Privately Held**
SIC: 3412 Mfg Metal Shipping Barrels & Drums

(G-12429)
ROCHE MANUFACTURING INC
161 Phoenix Ave (01852-4930)
PHONE.....978 454-9135
Michael Roche, *President*
Charles Roche, *Treasurer*
EMP: 10
SALES: 2.5MM **Privately Held**
SIC: 3412 Mfg Metal Shipping Barrels & Drums

(G-12430)
RUCKUS WIRELESS INC
Also Called: General Instrs Wrline Networks
900 Chelmsford St (01851-8100)
PHONE.....978 614-2900
EMP: 69 **Privately Held**
SIC: 3661 Mfg Telephone/Telegraph Apparatus
HQ: Ruckus Wireless, Inc.
350 W Java Dr
Sunnyvale CA 94089
650 265-4200

(G-12431)
SCANNELL BOILER WORKS INC
50 Tanner St Ste 1 (01852-4406)
PHONE.....978 454-5629
Dennis Scannell, *President*
John Scannell Jr, *General Mgr*
George Scannell, *Vice Pres*
Phillip L Scannell Jr, *Treasurer*
EMP: 19 **EST:** 1867
SQ FT: 28,000
SALES (est): 1.9MM **Privately Held**
SIC: 3443 3441 Mfg Fabricated Plate Work Structural Metal Fabrication

(G-12432)
SEGUE MANUFACTURING SVCS LLC
70 Industrial Ave E (01852-5110)
PHONE.....978 970-1200
Peter Frasso, *CEO*
Chris Brothers, *Vice Pres*
Brian Desmarais, *Vice Pres*
Stephanie Lin, *Vice Pres*
William Roderick, *Vice Pres*
▲ **EMP:** 100
SQ FT: 44,000
SALES (est): 32.1MM **Privately Held**
WEB: www.cabledesign.com
SIC: 3669 3643 3357 Mfg Communications Equipment Mfg Conductive Wiring Devices Nonferrous Wiredrawing/Insulating

(G-12433)
SOMERSET INDUSTRIES INC
137 Phoenix Ave (01852-4930)
PHONE.....978 667-3355
George Athanadiadis, *President*
Paul Athanadiadis, *General Mgr*
Paul Athanasiadis, *General Mgr*
Andrew D Voyatzakis, *Treasurer*
Andrew Voyatzakis, *Executive*
◆ **EMP:** 20
SQ FT: 20,000
SALES (est): 6.5MM **Privately Held**
WEB: www.smrset.com
SIC: 3556 Mfg Food Products Machinery

(G-12434)
STARFLEX INC
52 Meadowcroft St (01852-5023)
PHONE.....978 937-3889
Richard S Breslin, *President*
EMP: 12
SQ FT: 10,000
SALES (est): 1.8MM **Privately Held**
WEB: www.starflex.com
SIC: 3672 Mfg Printed Circuit Boards

(G-12435)
T & T ANODIZING INC
Also Called: T & T Anonizing & Indus Spray
35 Maple St (01852-4565)
PHONE.....978 454-9631
Joseph Teneriello, *President*
Mike Teneriello, *Vice Pres*
EMP: 20
SQ FT: 8,000
SALES (est): 1.8MM **Privately Held**
WEB: www.ttanodizing.com
SIC: 3471 Anodizing Metals

(G-12436)
T & T ANODIZING INCORPORATED
35 Maple St Ste 8 (01852-4561)
PHONE.....978 454-9631
Joe Teneriello, *President*
Mike Teneriello, *Vice Pres*
Peter Teneriello, *Treasurer*
Corene Teneriello, *Admin Sec*
EMP: 19 **EST:** 1981
SALES (est): 2.3MM **Privately Held**
SIC: 3471 Plating/Polishing Service

(G-12437)
TOTAL POWER INTERNATIONAL INC
418 Bridge St Ste 206 (01850-2400)
PHONE.....978 453-7272
Carl W Fryatt, *President*
Carl Fryatt, *President*
Anastasia Fryatt, *Admin Sec*
▲ **EMP:** 11
SQ FT: 10,000
SALES (est): 2.4MM **Privately Held**
WEB: www.total-power.com
SIC: 3613 Mfg Switchgear/Switchboards

(G-12438)
TRANS MAG CORP
250 Jackson St (01852-2167)
PHONE.....978 458-1487
Ashok Berajawala, *President*
EMP: 8
SQ FT: 8,000
SALES (est): 950K **Privately Held**
WEB: www.transmagcorp.com
SIC: 3612 Mfg Transformers

(G-12439)
TRILAP COMPANY INC
649 Lawrence St Ste 1 (01852-3584)
PHONE.....978 453-2205
Kenneth Velcourt, *President*
EMP: 6 **EST:** 1974
SQ FT: 6,500
SALES (est): 698.8K **Privately Held**
SIC: 3599 3545 Machine Shop

(G-12440)
TRIVAK INC
280 Howard St (01852-4485)
PHONE.....978 453-7123
Paul Novak, *President*
Richard Novak, *Treasurer*
EMP: 21
SQ FT: 12,625
SALES (est): 4.8MM **Privately Held**
SIC: 3599 7692 Mfg Industrial Machinery Welding Repair

(G-12441)
UMACO INC
60 Newhall St Rear (01852-4160)
PHONE.....978 453-8881
Carmine Martigenneti, *President*
EMP: 5 **EST:** 1994
SQ FT: 15,000
SALES (est): 834.3K **Privately Held**
WEB: www.umaco.com
SIC: 3272 Manufacturer Concrete/Masonry Products

(G-12442)
UNLIMITED MANUFACTURING SVC
20 Foot Of Crosby St (01852-4122)
P.O. Box 716 (01853-0716)
PHONE.....978 835-4915
Roselyn Parkhurst, *President*
James Parkhurst, *Vice Pres*
EMP: 5
SQ FT: 2,500
SALES: 300K **Privately Held**
SIC: 3469 Mfg Metal Stampings

(G-12443)
UNWRAPPED INC
95 Rock St Fl 1 (01854-4300)
PHONE.....978 441-0242
Stephen Katz, *President*
▲ **EMP:** 85
SQ FT: 16,000
SALES: 20.1MM **Privately Held**
WEB: www.unwrappedinc.com
SIC: 2393 2392 Mfg Textile Bags Mfg Household Furnishings

(G-12444)
VEONEER ROADSCAPE AUTO INC
Also Called: Veoneer Roadscape Lowell
1011 Pawtucket Blvd (01854-1040)
PHONE.....978 656-2500
EMP: 6
SALES (corp-wide): 2.2B **Publicly Held**
SIC: 3694 4225 Mfg Engine Electrical Equipment General Warehouse/Storage
HQ: Veoneer Roadscape Automotive, Inc.
1011 Pawtucket Blvd
Lowell MA 01854
978 656-2500

(G-12445)
VEONEER ROADSCAPE AUTO INC (DH)
1011 Pawtucket Blvd (01854-1040)
PHONE.....978 656-2500
Eric Swanson, *CEO*
Stefan Kroenung, *President*
Donghyun Thomas Hwang, *Senior VP*
Robert McMullan, *CFO*
EMP: 8 **EST:** 2008
SQ FT: 157,000
SALES (est): 2.3MM
SALES (corp-wide): 2.2B **Publicly Held**
SIC: 3694 Mfg Semiconductors/Related Devices

HQ: Veoneer Us, Inc.
26360 American Dr
Southfield MI 48034
248 223-8074

(G-12446)
VEONEER US INC
Also Called: Veoneer Lowell
1001 Pawtucket Blvd (01854-1040)
PHONE....978 674-6500
Glen Pedneault, *Info Tech Mgr*
EMP: 205
SALES (corp-wide): 2.2B **Publicly Held**
SIC: 3694 Mfg Engine Electrical Equipment
HQ: Veoneer Us, Inc.
26360 American Dr
Southfield MI 48034
248 223-8074

(G-12447)
VXI CORPORATION
900 Chelmsford St # 313 (01851-8313)
PHONE....603 742-2888
Michael W Ferguson, *President*
Tom Manero, *CFO*
▲ **EMP:** 50
SQ FT: 19,000
SALES (est): 11.3MM
SALES (corp-wide): 1.5B **Privately Held**
WEB: www.vxicorp.com
SIC: 3661 Mfg Telephone/Telegraph Apparatus
PA: Gn Store Nord A/S
Lautrupbjerg 7
Ballerup 2750
457 500-00

(G-12448)
WATERLAC COATING INC
142 Starr Ave (01852-2914)
PHONE....573 885-2506
Edmund Rosa, *President*
Phillip Burke, *General Mgr*
EMP: 7 **EST:** 1950
SQ FT: 7,000
SALES (est): 650K **Privately Held**
SIC: 2851 Mfg Paints/Allied Products

(G-12449)
WRISTIES INC
650 Suffolk St (01854-3642)
P.O. Box 8768 (01853-8768)
PHONE....978 937-9500
EMP: 3 **EST:** 1995
SALES (est): 230K **Privately Held**
WEB: www.wristies.com
SIC: 2385 2731 Mfg Waterproof Outerwear Books-Publishing/Printing

(G-12450)
YMITTOS CANDLE MFG CO
279 Dutton St (01852-1804)
P.O. Box 1748 (01853-1748)
PHONE....978 453-2824
Mark Vanderberg, *President*
Michael Kaplan, *Vice Pres*
EMP: 6
SQ FT: 15,000
SALES (est): 449.1K **Privately Held**
SIC: 3999 Mfg Candles
PA: Battalion Co Inc
325 Chelmsford St
Lowell MA 01851

(G-12451)
ZERO BALLA
67 Payne St (01851-1436)
PHONE....978 735-2015
Jose Nilton Nascimento, *Principal*
EMP: 4 **EST:** 2009
SALES (est): 389.4K **Privately Held**
SIC: 3699 Mfg Electrical Equipment/Supplies

Ludlow
Hampden County

(G-12452)
ADVANCED DRAINAGE SYSTEMS INC
58 Wyoming St (01056-1096)
PHONE....413 589-0515
John Stelmokas, *Sales Staff*
Dick Navin, *Manager*
EMP: 36
SALES (corp-wide): 1.3B **Publicly Held**
WEB: www.ads-pipe.com
SIC: 3084 Mfg Corrugated Plastic Tubing
PA: Advanced Drainage Systems, Inc.
4640 Trueman Blvd
Hilliard OH 43026
614 658-0050

(G-12453)
AMAZON FRUIT CORP
Also Called: Amazon Food Service
1158 East St (01056-1514)
PHONE....774 244-2820
Ricardo Contrucci, *President*
▲ **EMP:** 4
SALES: 800K **Privately Held**
SIC: 2013 5148 7389 Mfg Prepared Meats Whol Fruits/Vegetables

(G-12454)
AUBE PRECISION TOOL CO INC
54 Moody St (01056-1245)
PHONE....413 589-9048
Lucien A Aube, *President*
Phil Schuman, *Corp Secy*
Beverly Aube, *Vice Pres*
EMP: 7 **EST:** 1980
SQ FT: 2,500
SALES (est): 956.2K **Privately Held**
SIC: 3599 3546 General Machine Shop

(G-12455)
B & R MACHINE INC
305a Moody St Ste A (01056-1246)
PHONE....413 589-0246
Gerald A Renaud, *President*
EMP: 25
SQ FT: 8,500
SALES (est): 5.2MM **Privately Held**
SIC: 3599 Mfg Industrial Machinery

(G-12456)
BANAS SAND & GRAVEL CO INC
246 Fuller St (01056-1325)
PHONE....413 583-8321
John Banas Jr, *President*
James E Banas, *Clerk*
EMP: 14 **EST:** 1931
SQ FT: 8,000
SALES (est): 2.1MM **Privately Held**
SIC: 3273 Mfg Ready-Mix Concrete

(G-12457)
C M G PRECISION
45 State St (01056-3434)
PHONE....413 547-8124
Carlos Genovevo, *Owner*
EMP: 5
SQ FT: 1,500
SALES: 100K **Privately Held**
SIC: 3599 Mfg Industrial Machinery

(G-12458)
CHEMI-GRAPHIC INC
340 State St (01056-3439)
P.O. Box 410 (01056-0410)
PHONE....413 589-0151
Paul R Pohl, *President*
Jason Pohl, *Vice Pres*
Ginger Hicks, *Opers Mgr*
Joanne Moynihan, *Sales Mgr*
EMP: 50 **EST:** 1947
SQ FT: 30,000
SALES (est): 7.8MM **Privately Held**
WEB: www.chemigraphic.com
SIC: 3479 2796 Coating/Engraving Service Platemaking Services

(G-12459)
CO PRESS
Also Called: Co-Op Printing
388 Chapin St (01056-3728)
P.O. Box 787, East Longmeadow (01028-0787)
PHONE....413 525-6686
Russell George, *Principal*
EMP: 3
SALES (est): 399.4K **Privately Held**
SIC: 2752 Lithographic Commercial Printing

(G-12460)
COMMERCIAL MACHINE INC
305 Moody St Ste B (01056-1246)
PHONE....413 583-3670
Kevin J Sullivan, *President*
Kevin Sullivan, *General Mgr*
EMP: 6
SQ FT: 4,300
SALES (est): 878.2K **Privately Held**
SIC: 3599 Mfg Industrial Machinery

(G-12461)
CSW INC (PA)
45 Tyburski Rd (01056-1249)
PHONE....413 589-1311
Laura Wright, *President*
Dan Priest, *Opers Mgr*
Ed Begy, *Production*
Jane Dinnie, *Purch Mgr*
Mary Slusars, *Asst Controller*
▲ **EMP:** 150
SQ FT: 35,000
SALES: 16.6MM **Privately Held**
WEB: www.citystamp.com
SIC: 2796 3544 Platemaking Services Mfg Dies/Tools/Jigs/Fixtures

(G-12462)
DAVINCI ARMS LLC
100 State St Bldg 123-A (01056-3435)
PHONE....413 583-4327
Wayne Thresher, *President*
Joseph Salvador, *Research*
EMP: 3
SQ FT: 1,400
SALES (est): 125.7K **Privately Held**
SIC: 3484 Mfg Small Arms

(G-12463)
DURO-LAST INC
Also Called: Duro-Last Roofing Company
84 Westover Rd (01056-1200)
PHONE....413 631-0050
Glen Sullivan, *Plant Mgr*
EMP: 22
SALES (corp-wide): 207.6MM **Privately Held**
SIC: 2952 Mfg Asphalt Felts/Coatings
PA: Duro-Last, Inc.
525 E Morley Dr
Saginaw MI 48601
800 248-0280

(G-12464)
ELITE METAL FABRICATORS INC
100 State St Bldg 203 (01056-3435)
P.O. Box 372 (01056-0372)
PHONE....413 547-2588
Ricardo Salvador, *President*
EMP: 7
SALES: 600K **Privately Held**
SIC: 3469 Mfg Metal Stampings

(G-12465)
FALCON PRECISION MACHINE CO
97 Center St (01056-2741)
PHONE....413 583-2117
Dennis Brasile, *President*
▲ **EMP:** 6
SQ FT: 2,000
SALES (est): 801.7K **Privately Held**
WEB: www.cens.com
SIC: 3599 7692 Mfg Industrial Machinery Welding Repair

(G-12466)
HERON MACHINE & ENGRG INC
100 State St Bldg 217 (01056-3435)
P.O. Box 434 (01056-0434)
PHONE....413 547-6308
Christopher Lukomski, *President*
EMP: 3
SALES (est): 168.8K **Privately Held**
SIC: 3599 Mfg Industrial Machinery

(G-12467)
HOSETECH PLUS MORE INC
83 Carmelinas Cir (01056-3161)
P.O. Box 560 (01056-0560)
PHONE....413 385-0035
Antonio D Vital, *President*
EMP: 6
SALES (est): 1.2MM **Privately Held**
SIC: 3492 5211 Mfg Fluid Power Valves/Fittings Ret Lumber/Building Materials

(G-12468)
HUOT ENTERPRISES INC
Also Called: Castle Interiors
54 Moody St (01056-1245)
PHONE....413 589-7422
David Huot, *President*
EMP: 3
SQ FT: 3,000
SALES (est): 294K **Privately Held**
SIC: 2512 2391 Furniture Upholstery And Mfr Drapes And Window Treatments

(G-12469)
JAMES AUSTIN COMPANY
Also Called: Elite Division
203 West Ave (01056-2156)
PHONE....413 589-1600
Mark Chevrier, *Branch Mgr*
EMP: 49
SALES (corp-wide): 75.6MM **Privately Held**
WEB: www.jamesaustin.com
SIC: 2841 Mfg Soap/Other Detergents
PA: James Austin Company
115 Downieville Rd
Mars PA 16046
724 625-1535

(G-12470)
KLEEBERG SHEET METAL INC
65 Westover Rd (01056-1298)
PHONE....413 589-1854
Dan Bauer, *General Mgr*
Dan Kleeberg, *Principal*
Todd Davis, *Vice Pres*
Kevin Fitzsimonds, *Project Mgr*
Shawn Gagnon, *Project Mgr*
▲ **EMP:** 100
SQ FT: 93,000
SALES (est): 33.1MM **Privately Held**
WEB: www.kleeberg.com
SIC: 3444 1711 Mfg Sheet Metalwork Plumbing/Heating/Air Cond Contractor

(G-12471)
LEE TOOL CO INC
40 Ravenwood Dr (01056-3311)
P.O. Box 509 (01056-0509)
PHONE....413 583-8750
Victor Swist, *President*
EMP: 12
SQ FT: 8,700
SALES (est): 1.2MM **Privately Held**
WEB: www.leetool.com
SIC: 3545 3469 Mfg Precision Measuring & Cutting Tools And Parts

(G-12472)
LUDLOW PRINTING AND COPY CTR
44 Sewall St Ste 1 (01056-3402)
PHONE....413 583-5220
Richard Kelleher, *Partner*
Barbara Kelleher, *Partner*
EMP: 6
SQ FT: 3,600
SALES: 900K **Privately Held**
WEB: www.ludlowprinting.com
SIC: 2759 Printing Shop

(G-12473)
NEW ENGLAND PALLETS SKIDS INC
250 West St (01056-1248)
P.O. Box 342 (01056-0342)
PHONE....413 583-6628
Peter S Kawie, *President*
EMP: 15
SQ FT: 50,000

SALES (est): 4MM **Privately Held**
WEB: www.nepallets.com
SIC: 2448 Mfg Wood Pallets/Skids

(G-12474)
P A W INC
200 State St Bldg 102 (01056)
P.O. Box 375 (01056-0375)
PHONE..................................413 589-0399
Rose Proietti, *President*
EMP: 5 **EST:** 1997
SQ FT: 6,500
SALES (est): 719.4K **Privately Held**
SIC: 2431 Mfg Millwork

(G-12475)
PORTUAMERICA INC
60 Lehigh St (01056-3616)
P.O. Box 213 (01056-0213)
PHONE..................................413 589-0095
Fernando Silva, *President*
Georgina Silva, *Treasurer*
EMP: 5
SQ FT: 3,600
SALES (est): 802.3K **Privately Held**
SIC: 3569 3089 Mfg General Industrial Machinery Mfg Plastic Products

(G-12476)
ROMA MARBLE INC
15 Westover Rd (01056-1205)
P.O. Box 685, Wilbraham (01095-0685)
PHONE..................................413 583-5017
John A Ruell, *President*
James Steigmeyer, *Vice Pres*
▲ **EMP:** 35 **EST:** 1967
SQ FT: 22,600
SALES (est): 4.5MM **Privately Held**
WEB: www.romamarbleinc.com
SIC: 3088 Mfg Plastic Plumbing Fixtures

(G-12477)
RPM TECHNOLOGIES INC
100 State St (01056-3435)
PHONE..................................413 583-3385
▲ **EMP:** 6
SALES (est): 1.7MM **Privately Held**
SIC: 2679 3589 Mfg Converted Paper Products Mfg Service Industry Machinery
PA: Coldwater Group, Inc.
1396 Chattahoochee Ave Nw
Atlanta GA 30318

(G-12478)
VALMONT INC
656 Chapin St (01056-2351)
P.O. Box 421 (01056-0421)
PHONE..................................413 583-8351
M J Mack Jr, *Enginr/R&D Mgr*
EMP: 18
SQ FT: 8,000
SALES (corp-wide): 3.3MM **Privately Held**
SIC: 2342 Mfg Bras/Girdles
PA: Valmont, Inc.
1 W 34th St Rm 303
New York NY 10001
212 685-1653

(G-12479)
WEST SIDE METAL DOOR CORP
190 Moody St (01056-1230)
PHONE..................................413 589-0945
Dale Croteau, *Vice Pres*
EMP: 10
SQ FT: 32,000
SALES (est): 1.5MM **Privately Held**
SIC: 3442 Mfg Metal Doors/Sash/Trim

Lunenburg
Worcester County

(G-12480)
AGGREGATE INDUSTRIES
1000 Reservoir Rd (01462-1646)
PHONE..................................978 582-0261
Peter Maldonado, *Branch Mgr*
EMP: 20
SALES (corp-wide): 4.5B **Privately Held**
SIC: 3273 Mfg Ready-Mixed Concrete
HQ: Aggregate Industries - Mwr, Inc.
2815 Dodd Rd
Eagan MN 55121
651 683-0600

(G-12481)
ECOLOGICAL FIBERS INC (PA)
40 Pioneer Dr (01462-1699)
PHONE..................................978 537-0003
John Quill, *President*
Ronnie Hamilton, *Vice Pres*
Holly Rice, *Safety Mgr*
Jason McCarthy, *Purch Agent*
Jen Thomas, *Purch Agent*
◆ **EMP:** 159
SQ FT: 72,000
SALES (est): 66.6MM **Privately Held**
WEB: www.ecofibers.com
SIC: 2679 Mfg Converted Paper Products

(G-12482)
MS INDUSTRIES INC
450 Leominster Rd (01462-2010)
PHONE..................................978 582-1492
Jane Louise Ranley, *Principal*
EMP: 3
SALES (est): 206.9K **Privately Held**
SIC: 3999 Mfg Misc Products

(G-12483)
S&E SPECIALTY POLYMERS LLC
Also Called: Aurora Plastics
140 Leominster Shirley Rd # 100 (01462-1691)
PHONE..................................978 537-8261
Ilia Charlat, *Vice Pres*
Vincent Dotse, *Controller*
▲ **EMP:** 70
SQ FT: 60,000
SALES (est): 20.3MM **Privately Held**
WEB: www.sespoly.com
SIC: 2821 Mfg Plastic Materials/Resins
PA: Aurora Plastics, Llc
9280 Jefferson St
Streetsboro OH 44241

(G-12484)
TURN KEY LUMBER INC
305 Leominster Shirley Rd (01462-1645)
PHONE..................................978 798-1370
Juliano Fernandes, *President*
Doug Jeffers, *Sales Mgr*
Shane Decato, *Sr Project Mgr*
Chris Fox, *Manager*
EMP: 20
SQ FT: 12,500
SALES (est): 6.6MM **Privately Held**
SIC: 3272 5211 2421 Mfg Concrete Products Ret Lumber/Building Materials Sawmill/Planing Mill

(G-12485)
VECTOR 5 COLLABORATIVE LLC
198 Summer St (01462-2337)
PHONE..................................978 348-2997
John Davis, *Vice Pres*
Cheryl Leblanc, *Sales Staff*
Dawn Perkins,
John M Davis,
Dennis Healey,
EMP: 4
SALES (est): 664.8K **Privately Held**
SIC: 3999 Mfg Misc Products

(G-12486)
WAKEFIELD INVESTMENTS INC
Also Called: Keating Concrete
1000 Reservoir Rd (01462-1646)
PHONE..................................978 582-0261
David Schelzi, *President*
EMP: 60
SALES (corp-wide): 27.5MM **Privately Held**
SIC: 3273 1442 Mfg Ready-Mixed Concrete Construction Sand/Gravel
PA: Wakefield Investments, Inc.
50 Salem St B3
Lynnfield MA 01940
781 246-2572

Lynn
Essex County

(G-12487)
A & G MANUFACTURING CO INC
500 Lynnway (01905-3014)
PHONE..................................781 581-1892
Robert Lonigro, *President*
Anthony Lonigro, *Vice Pres*
Diana Lonigro, *Director*
▲ **EMP:** 5
SQ FT: 10,000
SALES (est): 1.1MM **Privately Held**
SIC: 3312 Manufacturer Of Structural Shapes

(G-12488)
ACCURATE GRAPHICS INC
26 Alley St (01902-4403)
PHONE..................................781 593-1630
Pappi Bolognese, *President*
Danielle Battaglia, *Manager*
EMP: 7
SALES (est): 899.3K **Privately Held**
SIC: 3993 Mfg Signs/Advertising Specialties

(G-12489)
AMERICAN POWER DEVICES INC
69 Bennett St Ste 1 (01905-3060)
PHONE..................................781 592-6090
Paul Flaherty, *President*
EMP: 30 **EST:** 1967
SALES (est): 4MM **Privately Held**
SIC: 3674 Mfg Semiconductors/Related Devices

(G-12490)
B & R METAL PRODUCTS INC
120 Broadway (01904-1863)
PHONE..................................781 593-0888
Richard Kelly, *President*
Barbara L Kelly, *Treasurer*
EMP: 4
SQ FT: 5,500
SALES (est): 464.4K **Privately Held**
SIC: 3469 Mfg Metal Stampings

(G-12491)
BARRY MANUFACTURING CO INC
15 Bubier St (01901-1704)
PHONE..................................781 598-1055
Richard W Rothbard, *President*
Jack Rothbard, *President*
Robert W Rothbard, *Treasurer*
Bernice Rothbard, *Admin Sec*
▲ **EMP:** 20
SQ FT: 8,600
SALES (est): 2.8MM **Privately Held**
SIC: 3149 Mfg Footwear-Except Rubber

(G-12492)
BENT WATER BREWING CO
180 Commercial St (01905-3054)
PHONE..................................781 780-9948
EMP: 4 **EST:** 2016
SALES (est): 75.4K **Privately Held**
SIC: 2082 Mfg Malt Beverages

(G-12493)
BREAKWATER FOODS LLC
82 Sanderson Ave (01902-1974)
P.O. Box 1565, Manchester (01944-0865)
PHONE..................................617 335-6475
Andrew Dunbar, *Principal*
EMP: 3
SALES (est): 183.4K **Privately Held**
SIC: 2099 Mfg Food Preparations

(G-12494)
BUZZAFRICOCOM
7 Chestnut St (01902-3003)
PHONE..................................617 903-0152
Anthony Acholonu, *Owner*
EMP: 5
SQ FT: 700
SALES (est): 170K **Privately Held**
SIC: 2741 7383 Misc Publishing News Syndicate

(G-12495)
C L HAUTHAWAY & SONS CORP
Also Called: Hauthane
638 Summer St (01905-2044)
PHONE..................................781 592-6444
John Zermani, *President*
Wayne Hess, *Purch Agent*
Leopoldo Johnson, *Treasurer*
James Bertorelli, *Controller*
Theodore J Johnson, *Director*
◆ **EMP:** 45
SQ FT: 60,000
SALES (est): 14.7MM
SALES (corp-wide): 10.3MM **Privately Held**
WEB: www.hauthaway.com
SIC: 2851 2891 Mfg Paints/Allied Products Mfg Adhesives/Sealants
PA: L H C Inc
638 Summer St
Lynn MA 01905
781 592-6444

(G-12496)
CASA ANTIGUA
129 Oxford St (01901-1117)
PHONE..................................781 584-8240
Sul Sanchez,
EMP: 3
SALES (est): 308.8K **Privately Held**
SIC: 3634 Mfg Electric Housewares/Fans

(G-12497)
CHEF CREATIONS LLC
330 Lynnway Ste 301 (01901-1713)
P.O. Box 2066, Winter Park FL (32790-2066)
PHONE..................................407 228-0069
Hal Valdes, *CEO*
Russell Barkett, *Corp Secy*
Barry Curran, *CFO*
EMP: 96
SALES (est): 14.7MM
SALES (corp-wide): 105MM **Privately Held**
SIC: 2099 Mfg Food Preparations
PA: Kettle Cuisine, Llc
330 Lynnway
Lynn MA 01901
617 409-1100

(G-12498)
CUIZINA FOODS COMPANY
330 Lynnway Ste 102 (01901-1713)
PHONE..................................425 486-7000
Ric Ferrera, *President*
Erik Bugge, *Corp Secy*
John Ferrera, *Vice Pres*
▲ **EMP:** 35
SALES (est): 6.4MM
SALES (corp-wide): 99.2MM **Privately Held**
SIC: 2099 Mfg Food Preparations
PA: Joshua Green Corporation
1425 4th Ave Ste 420
Seattle WA
206 622-0420

(G-12499)
DEMAKES ENTERPRISES INC (PA)
Also Called: Old Neighborhood Foods Div
37 Waterhill St (01905-2134)
PHONE..................................781 417-1100
Thomas L Demakes, *President*
John N Demakes, *Treasurer*
Carol Langlois, *Accounting Mgr*
◆ **EMP:** 220
SQ FT: 66,000
SALES (est): 49.6MM **Privately Held**
WEB: www.thinntrim.com
SIC: 2013 Mfg Prepared Meats

(G-12500)
DEMAKES ENTERPRISES INC
34 Riley Way (01905-3036)
PHONE..................................781 586-0212
EMP: 200
SALES (corp-wide): 49.6MM **Privately Held**
WEB: www.thinntrim.com
SIC: 2013 2011 Mfg Prepared Meats Meat Packing Plant

PA: Demakes Enterprises, Inc.
37 Waterhill St
Lynn MA 01905
781 417-1100

(G-12501)
DENNY S SWEET ONION RINGS
21 Neptune Blvd (01902-4472)
PHONE....781 598-5317
EMP: 5
SQ FT: 1,500
SALES (est): 330K **Privately Held**
SIC: 2096 Mfg Potato Chips/Snacks

(G-12502)
DESIGNS BY LAINIE
300 Lynn Shore Dr Apt 802 (01902-2930)
PHONE....781 592-2126
Lainie Levine, *Owner*
EMP: 3
SALES (est): 113.5K **Privately Held**
SIC: 2759 Design/Retail/Wholesales Note Paper

(G-12503)
DURKEE-MOWER INC
2 Empire St (01902-1815)
P.O. Box 470 (01903-0570)
PHONE....781 593-8007
Donald D Durkee, *President*
Paul Walker, *Vice Pres*
Jonathan Durkee, *Treasurer*
EMP: 24 **EST:** 1919
SQ FT: 33,000
SALES (est): 4.9MM **Privately Held**
WEB: www.marshmallowfluff.com
SIC: 2099 Mfg Food Preparations

(G-12504)
EAST COAST MARBLE & GRAN CORP
142 Lynnfield St (01904-2242)
PHONE....781 760-0207
James Maravelias, *President*
Bertha Maravelias, *Treasurer*
EMP: 4
SALES (est): 292.8K **Privately Held**
SIC: 3281 Mfg Cut Stone/Products

(G-12505)
EASTERN INDEX INC
154 Lynnway Unit 402 (01902-5103)
PHONE....781 581-1100
Foster McCafferty, *President*
Susan Loprete, *President*
EMP: 12
SQ FT: 10,500
SALES (est): 800K **Privately Held**
SIC: 2675 Mfr Die Cut Index Cards Made From Purchased Material

(G-12506)
ESSEX ENGINEERING INC
Also Called: Essex Engineering & Mfg Co
20 Day St (01905-3008)
P.O. Box 328 (01905-0628)
PHONE....781 595-2114
James S Munro Jr, *President*
Barbara Lopresti, *Info Tech Mgr*
Wendy B Munro, *Director*
Robert A Munro, *Admin Sec*
EMP: 50 **EST:** 1956
SQ FT: 16,000
SALES (est): 7.8MM **Privately Held**
WEB: www.essexengineering.com
SIC: 3599 3444 Mfg Industrial Machinery Mfg Sheet Metalwork

(G-12507)
FALMER
168 Broad St Fl 2 (01901-1627)
PHONE....781 593-0088
Fax: 781 598-0280
EMP: 3 **EST:** 2010
SALES (est): 180K **Privately Held**
SIC: 2891 Mfg Adhesives/Sealants

(G-12508)
FILTERED BY FOREST LLC
115 Nahant St Unit 1 (01902-3318)
PHONE....978 590-3203
Daniel Nathan,
EMP: 6
SALES: 500K **Privately Held**
SIC: 2087 Mfg Flavor Extracts/Syrup

(G-12509)
FLEETWOOD MULTI-MEDIA INC
Also Called: Fleetwood On Site Cnfrnce
20 Wheeler St Ste 202 (01902-4419)
PHONE....781 599-2400
Wayne Termenillo, *President*
Darleen Terminello, *President*
Steve Doherty, *Technology*
EMP: 12 **EST:** 1997
SALES: 7MM **Privately Held**
WEB: www.fltwood.com
SIC: 3652 Motion Picture/Video Production

(G-12510)
GE AVIATION
1000 Western Ave (01901)
PHONE....513 552-3272
John Burke, *Principal*
Paul Anastas, *Engineer*
Shawn Duffen, *Senior Engr*
Robert Cote, *Planning*
EMP: 21
SALES (est): 6.3MM **Privately Held**
SIC: 3724 Mfg Aircraft Engines/Parts

(G-12511)
GENERAL ELECTRIC COMPANY
1000 Western Ave (01905-2690)
PHONE....781 598-7303
Lee Dillon, *Opers Mgr*
Premal Desai, *Engineer*
Kathleen Hendricks, *Engineer*
Abraham Levatter, *Engineer*
David P Miller, *Engineer*
EMP: 68
SALES (corp-wide): 121.6B **Publicly Held**
SIC: 3724 3714 Mfg Aircraft Engines/Parts Mfg Motor Vehicle Parts/Accessories
PA: General Electric Company
5 Necco St
Boston MA 02210
617 443-3000

(G-12512)
GENERAL ELECTRIC COMPANY
1000 Western Ave (01910-0002)
PHONE....781 594-0100
William Hruves, *Manager*
EMP: 603
SALES (corp-wide): 121.6B **Publicly Held**
SIC: 3724 Mfg Aircraft Engines/Parts
PA: General Electric Company
5 Necco St
Boston MA 02210
617 443-3000

(G-12513)
GOOD WIVES INC
86 Sanderson Ave Ste 3 (01902-1965)
PHONE....781 596-0070
EMP: 3
SALES (est): 146K **Privately Held**
SIC: 2099 Mfg Food Preparations

(G-12514)
GOODBEV INC
7 Chestnut St (01902-3003)
PHONE....617 545-5240
Anthony Acholonu, *CEO*
EMP: 5
SALES (est): 213.4K **Privately Held**
SIC: 2086 Mfg Bottled/Canned Soft Drinks

(G-12515)
H O ZIMMAN INC
152 Lynnway (01902-3491)
PHONE....781 598-9230
Josh Zimman, *Owner*
Helen Zimman, *Treasurer*
Cheryl Lampert, *Director*
Adam Scharff, *Associate*
EMP: 15
SQ FT: 4,000
SALES (est): 2.2MM **Privately Held**
SIC: 2721 Publishes/Prints Periodical Books/Magazines

(G-12516)
HIGH GRADE SHADE & SCREEN CO
Also Called: High Grade Sales
41 Sutton St (01901-1016)
PHONE....781 592-5027
Fax: 781 284-3769
EMP: 10 **EST:** 1920
SQ FT: 11,000
SALES (est): 930K **Privately Held**
SIC: 2591 3442 3444 3448 Mfg Whol & Ret Of Aluminium Doors And Blades

(G-12517)
ITAL MARBLE CO INC
500 Lynnway (01905-3014)
PHONE....781 595-4859
Edward Lonigro, *President*
▼ **EMP:** 15
SQ FT: 3,000
SALES (est): 1.5MM **Privately Held**
WEB: www.italmarbleco.com
SIC: 3281 Mfg Cut Stone/Products

(G-12518)
JET TECH INC
52 Alley St (01902-4403)
PHONE....781 599-8685
Michael Bubar, *President*
Gary Sauve, *Vice Pres*
EMP: 18
SQ FT: 12,000
SALES (est): 2MM **Privately Held**
WEB: www.jet-tech.com
SIC: 3479 Coating/Engraving Service

(G-12519)
KETTLE CUISINE LLC (PA)
330 Lynnway (01901-1706)
P.O. Box 73, Windsor Locks CT (06096-0073)
PHONE....617 409-1100
Liam McClennon, *CEO*
Jeremy Kacuba, *COO*
Mike Illum, *Exec VP*
Nora McCarthy, *Exec VP*
Lorie Donnelly, *Senior VP*
▲ **EMP:** 250
SQ FT: 85,000
SALES: 105MM **Privately Held**
WEB: www.kettlecuisine.com
SIC: 2032 2035 Mfg Canned Specialties Mfg Pickles/Sauces Mfg Canned Specialties

(G-12520)
L H C INC (PA)
638 Summer St (01905-2044)
PHONE....781 592-6444
Leopoldo A Johnson, *President*
John Zermani, *Principal*
EMP: 47
SQ FT: 60,000
SALES (est): 10.3MM **Privately Held**
WEB: www.clh.com
SIC: 2891 2851 2821 Mfg Adhesives/Sealants Mfg Paints/Allied Products Mfg Plastic Materials/Resins

(G-12521)
LMI LIQUIDATION CORPORATION
15 Marion St (01905)
PHONE....781 593-2561
Charlie Garrard, *Partner*
Tim Wadlow, *Partner*
▲ **EMP:** 3
SALES (est): 373.8K **Privately Held**
SIC: 3297 3255 3585 Mfg Nonclay Refractories Mfg Clay Refractories Mfg Refrigeration/Heating Equipment

(G-12522)
LUNDYS COMPANY INC
34 Boston St (01904-2537)
PHONE....781 595-8639
Charles Lundrigan, *President*
Kristin Lee Larson, *Treasurer*
Carole Lundrigan, *Admin Sec*
EMP: 12
SQ FT: 27,000
SALES: 1.7MM **Privately Held**
SIC: 2591 1799 Mfg Drapery Hardware/Blinds Trade Contractor

(G-12523)
LYN-LAD GROUP LTD (PA)
20 Boston St (01904-2527)
P.O. Box 8096 (01904-0096)
PHONE....781 598-6010
Susan Kline, *Principal*
Alan Kline, *Director*
Roberta Kline, *Director*
▲ **EMP:** 15
SQ FT: 50,000
SALES (est): 56.1MM **Privately Held**
SIC: 2499 5082 5251 7359 Mfg Wood Products Whol Cnstn/Mining Mach Ret Hardware Equipment Rental/Leasing

(G-12524)
LYNN PRODUCTS CO
400 Boston St Ste 1 (01905-1699)
PHONE....781 593-2500
Daniel C Cullinane Jr, *President*
EMP: 50 **EST:** 1927
SALES (est): 7.7MM **Privately Held**
SIC: 3823 3255 3825 Mfg Process Control Instruments Mfg Clay Refractories Mfg Electrical Measuring Instruments

(G-12525)
MARKET SQUARE BEVERAGE CO INC
Also Called: Discount Liquors
3 Market Sq (01905-2420)
PHONE....781 593-2150
Pauline Stevens, *President*
Craig Stevens, *Manager*
EMP: 6
SALES (est): 471.7K **Privately Held**
SIC: 2086 Ret Alcoholic Beverages

(G-12526)
MEMBRANE-SWITCHESCOM
10 Ocean St (01902-2023)
P.O. Box 875, Marblehead (01945-0875)
PHONE....508 277-2892
John Nering, *Owner*
EMP: 3
SALES (est): 116.1K **Privately Held**
SIC: 3643 Mfg Conductive Wiring Devices

(G-12527)
NEW ENGLAND BRIDGE PRODUCTS
93 Brookline St (01902-1809)
PHONE....781 592-2444
John Conti, *President*
EMP: 8
SQ FT: 12,000
SALES (est): 1.2MM **Privately Held**
SIC: 3441 Structural Metal Fabrication

(G-12528)
NEW ENGLAND COUNTRY PIES LLC
161b Pleasant St (01901-1513)
PHONE....781 596-0176
Kent Issenberg, *Mng Member*
EMP: 10
SALES (est): 1.4MM **Privately Held**
SIC: 2053 Mfg Frozen Bakery Products

(G-12529)
NORTH SHORE COMPOST LLC
56 Sanderson Ave (01902-1937)
PHONE....781 581-3489
Matthew M Leahy, *Mng Member*
Matthew Leahy, *Mng Member*
EMP: 3
SALES (est): 328.3K **Privately Held**
SIC: 2875 Mfg Fertilizers-Mix Only

(G-12530)
NORTH SHORE STEEL CO INC (PA)
16 Oakville St (01905-2817)
P.O. Box 330 (01905 0630)
PHONE....781 598-1645
Subhash Kakkar, *President*
EMP: 27 **EST:** 1954
SQ FT: 40,000
SALES (est): 14.4MM **Privately Held**
SIC: 3441 Structural Metal Fabrication

(G-12531)
OLD NEIGHBORHOOD FOODS
37 Waterhill St (01905-2194)
PHONE....781 595-1557
Thomas Demakes, *CEO*
EMP: 8
SALES (est): 718.4K **Privately Held**
SIC: 2013 Mfg Prepared Meats

(G-12532)
ORACLE SYSTEMS CORPORATION
124 Ocean St (01902-2036)
PHONE....................781 744-0900
David Fison, *Branch Mgr*
EMP: 373
SALES (corp-wide): 39.5B **Publicly Held**
WEB: www.forcecapital.com
SIC: 7372 Prepackaged Software Services
HQ: Oracle Systems Corporation
500 Oracle Pkwy
Redwood City CA 94065
650 506-7000

(G-12533)
PLASTI-GRAPHICS INC
102 Central Ave (01901-1013)
PHONE....................781 599-7766
Daniel King, *President*
Judith Brennan, *Treasurer*
Mary Brennan, *Clerk*
EMP: 5
SQ FT: 6,000
SALES (est): 711.1K **Privately Held**
SIC: 3082 Manufactures Plastic Profile Shapes Including Molds

(G-12534)
PRISM PRODUCTS LLC
319 Lynnway Ste 303a (01901-1810)
PHONE....................781 581-1740
Lisa Fitzpatrick, *Mng Member*
EMP: 4
SQ FT: 1,800
SALES: 2MM **Privately Held**
SIC: 3545 Mfg Machine Tool Accessories

(G-12535)
PROFAB METAL PRODUCTS INC
Also Called: Pro-Fab Metal Products
541 Chestnut St (01904-2716)
PHONE....................781 599-8500
Edward Varjabedian, *President*
EMP: 20 **EST:** 1981
SQ FT: 12,000
SALES (est): 3.5MM **Privately Held**
SIC: 3444 Mfg Sheet Metalwork

(G-12536)
SAN FRANCISO MARKET
2 Lafayette Park (01902-2412)
PHONE....................781 780-3731
Francisco Lora, *Owner*
EMP: 3
SALES (est): 239.6K **Privately Held**
SIC: 3643 Mfg Conductive Wiring Devices

(G-12537)
SAVORY CREATIONS INTERNATIONAL
330 Lynnway Ste 401 (01901-1713)
PHONE....................650 638-1024
Doug Takizawa, *President*
Hidemasa Takizawa, *Principal*
▲ **EMP:** 17
SALES (est): 2.2MM **Privately Held**
WEB: www.savory-creations.com
SIC: 2048 Mfg Prepared Feeds

(G-12538)
SCHNEIDER ELECTRIC USA INC
24 Alison Way (01904-1442)
PHONE....................781 571-9677
EMP: 152
SALES (corp-wide): 177.9K **Privately Held**
SIC: 3613 Mfg Switchgear/Switchboards
HQ: Schneider Electric Usa, Inc.
201 Wshington St Ste 2700
Boston MA 02108
978 975-9600

(G-12539)
SIDEKIM LLC
82 Sanderson Ave Ste 112 (01902-1975)
PHONE....................781 595-3663
Peter E Mikedis, *CEO*
EMP: 43 **EST:** 2007
SALES (est): 7.9MM **Privately Held**
SIC: 2099 5812 5963 Mfg Food Preparations Eating Place Direct Retail Sales

(G-12540)
STACEYS SHADE SHOP INC (PA)
Also Called: Stacey's Window Fashions
20 Melvin Ave (01902-1214)
PHONE....................781 595-0097
Vincent Lozzi Jr, *President*
EMP: 3
SQ FT: 5,000
SALES (est): 451.4K **Privately Held**
WEB: www.staceyswindowfashions.com
SIC: 2591 2211 5719 5714 Mfg Drape Hardware/Blind Cotton Brdwv Fabric Mill

(G-12541)
STERLING MACHINE COMPANY INC
23 Farrar St (01901-1699)
PHONE....................781 593-3000
Scott M Livingston, *CEO*
Robert Struzziero, *President*
Joseph Ippolitto, *Vice Pres*
Eric Lee, *Facilities Mgr*
EMP: 34 **EST:** 1966
SQ FT: 15,000
SALES (est): 6.8MM
SALES (corp-wide): 22.3MM **Privately Held**
SIC: 3724 3599 3451 Mfg Aircraft Engines/Parts Mfg Industrial Machinery Mfg Screw Machine Products
PA: Horst Engineering & Manufacturing Co
36 Cedar St
East Hartford CT 06108
860 289-8209

(G-12542)
SYNTHETIC SURFACES INC
638 Summer St (01905-2044)
PHONE....................781 593-0860
James U Bertorelli, *Controller*
John Parks, *Manager*
EMP: 17
SALES (corp-wide): 2MM **Privately Held**
WEB: www.syntheticsurfacesinc.com
SIC: 2891 Mfg Adhesives/Sealants
PA: Synthetic Surfaces, Inc.
2450 Plainfield Ave
Scotch Plains NJ 07076
908 233-6803

(G-12543)
THERMO CRAFT ENGINEERING CORP
701 Western Ave (01905-2297)
PHONE....................781 599-4023
Ralph E Faia Jr, *President*
Ralph E Faia Sr, *President*
EMP: 40
SQ FT: 32,000
SALES (est): 10.3MM **Privately Held**
SIC: 3599 3444 7692 Mfg Industrial Machinery Mfg Sheet Metalwork Welding Repair

(G-12544)
TRADITIONAL BREADS INC
161 Pleasant St (01901-1513)
PHONE....................781 598-4451
Fitzroy Alexander, *President*
Harold Berk, *Treasurer*
EMP: 20
SQ FT: 6,000
SALES (est): 4.4MM **Privately Held**
WEB: www.traditionalbreads.com
SIC: 2051 Mfg Bread/Related Products

Lynnfield
Essex County

(G-12545)
BABCOCK POWER INC (PA)
6 Kimball Ln Ste 210 (01940-2684)
PHONE....................978 646-3300
Michael D Leclair, *President*
Glenn Craig, *Business Mgr*
William J Ferguson Jr, *Exec VP*
Edward Dean, *Vice Pres*
Xavier Dorai, *Vice Pres*
◆ **EMP:** 9
SALES: 509MM **Privately Held**
SIC: 3443 3569 3433 Mfg Fabricated Plate Wrk Mfg General Indstl Mach Mfg Heat Equip-Nonelec

(G-12546)
BLUE COW SOFTWARE INC
50 Salem St Ste 103a (01940-0030)
PHONE....................781 224-2583
Amy Nardone, *Principal*
EMP: 3
SALES (est): 438.7K **Privately Held**
SIC: 7372 Prepackaged Software Services

(G-12547)
CLARIOS
Also Called: Johnson Controls
39 Salem St (01940-2621)
PHONE....................781 213-3463
Mark Mc Caleaghan, *Manager*
EMP: 150 **Privately Held**
SIC: 3822 Mfg Environmental Controls
HQ: Johnson Controls Inc
5757 N Green Bay Ave
Milwaukee WI 53209
414 524-1200

(G-12548)
FIRE EMERGENCY MAINT CO LLC
29 Stillman Rd (01940-1704)
PHONE....................781 334-3100
Karen Burnham, *Mng Member*
Allan Burnham,
Mark Burnham,
EMP: 3
SALES (est): 298.8K **Privately Held**
SIC: 3711 Mfg Motor Vehicle/Car Bodies

(G-12549)
HP HOOD LLC (PA)
6 Kimball Ln Ste 400 (01940-2685)
PHONE....................617 887-8441
Andrea Fountain, *CEO*
John Powers, *Area Mgr*
Julie Biviano, *Business Mgr*
Danny Tyndell, *Vice Pres*
Andre Frey-Thomas, *Plant Mgr*
◆ **EMP:** 163
SALES: 2.2B **Privately Held**
WEB: www.hphood.com
SIC: 2024 2022 2026 Mfg Ice Cream/Frozen Desert Mfg Cheese Mfg Fluid Milk

(G-12550)
INTELLISENSE SOFTWARE CORP
220 Broadway Ste 102 (01940-2352)
PHONE....................781 933-8098
Yie He, *President*
Joe Johnson, *Business Mgr*
EMP: 20
SALES (est): 1.4MM **Privately Held**
WEB: www.intellisensesoftware.com
SIC: 3679 3695 Mfg Electronic Components Mfg Magnetic/Optical Recording Media

(G-12551)
KEENE BRADFORD ESQ PC
7 Kimball Ln (01940-2617)
PHONE....................781 246-4545
Bradford Keene, *Treasurer*
EMP: 3
SALES (est): 188.8K **Privately Held**
SIC: 3625 5063 5065 8111 Mfg Relay/Indstl Control Whol Electrical Equip Whol Electronic Parts Legal Services Office

(G-12552)
MACKENZIE COUTURE ACC INC
1 Friendship Ln (01940-1023)
P.O. Box 359 (01940-0359)
PHONE....................781 334-2805
Jean Tishler, *Principal*
EMP: 3
SALES (est): 225.6K **Privately Held**
SIC: 2399 2387 Mfg Fabricated Textile Products Mfg Apparel Belts

(G-12553)
NEW ENGLAND BRIDE INC
Also Called: New England Bride Magazine
29 Durham Dr (01940-1067)
PHONE....................781 334-6093
Thomas Parello, *President*
EMP: 10
SQ FT: 4,500
SALES: 1MM **Privately Held**
WEB: www.newenglandbride.com
SIC: 2721 Periodicals-Publishing/Printing

(G-12554)
PERLEY BURRILL FUEL
906 Lynnfield St (01940)
PHONE....................781 593-9292
Denise Quist, *Principal*
EMP: 5 **EST:** 2007
SALES (est): 439K **Privately Held**
SIC: 2869 Mfg Industrial Organic Chemicals

(G-12555)
PTC AS LLC
6 Kimball Ln (01940-2682)
PHONE....................339 440-5818
EMP: 6
SALES (est): 569.1K **Privately Held**
SIC: 2834 Manufactures Pharmaceutical Preparations

Malden
Middlesex County

(G-12556)
ACE-LON CORPORATION
960 Eastern Ave (02148-6090)
P.O. Box 642 (02148-0006)
PHONE....................781 322-7121
Harry T Gentile, *President*
EMP: 29
SQ FT: 40,000
SALES (est): 6.3MM **Privately Held**
WEB: www.ace-lon.com
SIC: 2673 Mfg Bags-Plastic/Coated Paper

(G-12557)
ALL SET PRESS LLC
988 Eastern Ave (02148-6033)
PHONE....................781 397-1993
Vance Ferratusco, *Principal*
EMP: 4
SALES (est): 270K **Privately Held**
SIC: 2741 Misc Publishing

(G-12558)
ANDERSON COMPONENTS CORP
61 Clinton St (02148-2604)
PHONE....................781 324-0350
John A Anderson Sr, *President*
▲ **EMP:** 18
SQ FT: 10,000
SALES (est): 2.7MM **Privately Held**
SIC: 3429 Mfg Metal Fasteners

(G-12559)
ARMATRON INTERNATIONAL INC (PA)
Also Called: Flowtron Outdoor Products Div
15 Highland Ave (02148-6603)
PHONE....................781 321-2300
Charles J Housman, *President*
Sal De Yoreo, *Vice Pres*
Edward L Housman, *Admin Sec*
▲ **EMP:** 60 **EST:** 1920
SQ FT: 84,000
SALES (est): 12.2MM **Privately Held**
WEB: www.echovision.net
SIC: 3714 3524 3699 Mfg Motor Vehicle Parts Mfg Lawn/Garden Equip Mfg Elec Mach/Equip/Supp

(G-12560)
AXIOMED SPINE CORPORATION (PA)
350 Main St Ste 31 (02148-5024)
PHONE....................978 232-3990
Patrick A McBrayer, *President*
James M Kuras, *COO*
Nancy Rubin, *CFO*
EMP: 15
SQ FT: 3,000
SALES (est): 1.3MM **Privately Held**
SIC: 3845 Mfg Electromedical Equipment

(G-12561)
B-C-D METAL PRODUCTS INC
205 Maplewood St (02148-5913)
P.O. Box 667 (02148-0006)
PHONE....................................781 397-9922
Karin Carlson, *President*
Jane Carlson, *Vice Pres*
Jane A Carlson, *Vice Pres*
Andrew Carlson, *Prdtn Mgr*
Anne Fields, *Admin Asst*
EMP: 30 **EST:** 1935
SQ FT: 13,000
SALES (est): 6.6MM **Privately Held**
WEB: www.bcdmetal.com
SIC: 3599 Mfg Industrial Machinery

(G-12562)
BBHS THERMAL SOLUTIONS CORP
18 Ellis St (02148-6808)
PHONE....................................781 718-2352
Frank Rosatone, *President*
EMP: 4
SALES (est): 366.4K **Privately Held**
SIC: 3822 Engineering Services

(G-12563)
CALIPER WOODWORKING CORP
49 Clinton St (02148-2604)
PHONE....................................781 322-9760
Kathleen M Keenan, *President*
EMP: 21
SQ FT: 12,000
SALES: 3.1MM **Privately Held**
SIC: 2431 2439 Mfg Millwork Mfg Structural Wood Members

(G-12564)
CB SPORTS INC
359 Washington St Ste C (02148-1395)
PHONE....................................781 322-0307
Charles J Bettano, *President*
EMP: 6
SQ FT: 4,200
SALES (est): 738.4K **Privately Held**
SIC: 2393 Mfg Textile Bags

(G-12565)
CHARLES RO MFG CO INC
Also Called: U S A Trains
662 Cross St Ste 1 (02148-4371)
P.O. Box 100 (02148-0993)
PHONE....................................781 322-6084
Ruth L Ro, *President*
Charles F Ro Sr, *Principal*
Charles F Ro Jr, *Treasurer*
▲ **EMP:** 6
SQ FT: 88,000
SALES (est): 789K **Privately Held**
WEB: www.usatrains.com
SIC: 3944 Mfg Games/Toys

(G-12566)
CRAFT INTERIORS
13 Irving St (02148-5005)
PHONE....................................781 321-8695
Burton D Golner, *Owner*
Rochelle Golner, *Co-Owner*
EMP: 3 **EST:** 1946
SALES: 120K **Privately Held**
SIC: 2391 2392 2591 7641 Mfg Curtains/Drapery Mfg Household Furnishing Mfg Drape Hardware/Blind Reupholstery/Furn Repair

(G-12567)
DEVINCENTIS PRESS INC
988 Eastern Ave (02148-6033)
PHONE....................................781 605-3796
Linsey A Devincentis, *President*
Rhonda E Devincentis, *Treasurer*
Joseph A Devincentis, *Admin Sec*
EMP: 15 **EST:** 2007
SALES (est): 2MM **Privately Held**
SIC: 2752 Lithographic Commercial Printing

(G-12568)
DISTRIBUTION & CONTROL PRODUCT
730 Eastern Ave (02148-5906)
PHONE....................................781 324-0070
Di Panfilo, *Owner*
EMP: 4
SALES (est): 129.4K **Privately Held**
SIC: 3699 Mfg Electrical Equipment/Supplies

(G-12569)
EASTERN MDDLSEX PRESS PBLCTONS (PA)
Also Called: Daily News-Mercury
277 Commercial St (02148-6708)
PHONE....................................781 321-8000
Daniel Hogan, *President*
EMP: 20
SQ FT: 19,000
SALES (est): 1.5MM **Privately Held**
SIC: 2711 Newspaper Publishers

(G-12570)
ENJET AERO MALDEN LLC
60 Winter St (02148-1426)
PHONE....................................781 321-0366
Bruce Breckenridge, *CEO*
Dana Munick, *President*
Kayla Walker, *Business Mgr*
Bruce Munick, *Vice Pres*
Christopher Ferraro, *CFO*
▼ **EMP:** 55 **EST:** 1957
SQ FT: 50,000
SALES: 15.8MM
SALES (corp-wide): 42.7MM **Privately Held**
WEB: www.metalspin.com
SIC: 3469 Mfg Metal Stampings
PA: Enjet Aero, Llc
9401 Indian Creek Pkwy
Overland Park KS 66210
913 717-7396

(G-12571)
EXCELLA GRAPHICS
300 Main St (02148-5011)
PHONE....................................781 763-7768
Ricardo Dlogene, *Partner*
Vonel Lamour, *Partner*
EMP: 3
SALES (est): 339.4K **Privately Held**
SIC: 2752 Lithographic Commercial Printing

(G-12572)
F M CALLAHAN AND SON INC
22 Sharon St (02148-5915)
PHONE....................................781 324-5101
Eric W Jacklin, *President*
Heather J Hennigar, *Corp Secy*
Robert L Hennigar, *Vice Pres*
Kevin Reynolds, *Manager*
George Abelli, *Technical Staff*
EMP: 60 **EST:** 1942
SALES: 11.2MM **Privately Held**
WEB: www.fmcallahan.com
SIC: 3471 5031 Plating/Polishing Service Whol Lumber/Plywood/Millwork

(G-12573)
G AND M WELDING
59 Waite St (02148-4455)
PHONE....................................781 480-4247
EMP: 7
SALES (est): 97.6K **Privately Held**
SIC: 7692 Welding Repair

(G-12574)
KABINET KORNER INC
Also Called: Windsor Architectural Wdwkg
212 Maplewood St (02148-5914)
PHONE....................................781 324-9600
Marshall Mazzarella, *CEO*
Michael Moscaritolo, *CFO*
EMP: 25
SQ FT: 25,000
SALES (est): 4.1MM **Privately Held**
WEB: www.windsorwoodworking.com
SIC: 2431 Mfg Millwork

(G-12575)
KPT COMPANY INC
14 Clarendon St (02148-7614)
PHONE....................................978 558-4009
Jian Ming Guan, *President*
▲ **EMP:** 5
SALES (est): 435.6K **Privately Held**
SIC: 2821 Mfg Plastic Materials/Resins

(G-12576)
L & J ENTERPRISES INC
67 Maplewood St (02148-4320)
PHONE....................................781 233-1966
Lori A Widener, *President*
EMP: 8
SALES (est): 998.9K **Privately Held**
SIC: 3441 Structural Metal Fabrication

(G-12577)
LION GOLD MINING LLC
110 Central Ave (02148-3470)
PHONE....................................617 785-2345
Francinei C Souza, *Principal*
EMP: 5 **EST:** 2012
SALES (est): 278.8K **Privately Held**
SIC: 1041 Gold Ore Mining

(G-12578)
LUV MANUFACTURING
513 Broadway (02148)
PHONE....................................857 277-3573
Barbara M Murphy,
EMP: 4
SALES (est): 125.1K **Privately Held**
SIC: 3999 Mfg Misc Products

(G-12579)
M & M LABEL CO INC
380 Pearl St (02148-6607)
PHONE....................................781 321-2737
Michael McCourt, *President*
Micheli Mary, *Manager*
▼ **EMP:** 9
SALES (est): 2.3MM **Privately Held**
SIC: 2672 Mfg Coated/Laminated Paper

(G-12580)
M & M SCALE COMPANY INC
Also Called: M&M Label Company
380 Pearl St (02148-6607)
PHONE....................................781 321-2737
Michael J Mc Court, *President*
John Martin, *Prdtn Mgr*
Linda Difiore, *Marketing Staff*
Micheli Mary, *Manager*
Tammy Barnes, *Assistant*
EMP: 18
SALES (est): 1.6MM **Privately Held**
WEB: www.mmlabel.com
SIC: 3596 7699 Manufacture Design Repair And Install Scales

(G-12581)
MALDEN CENTERLESS GRINDING CO
910 Eastern Ave (02148-6056)
PHONE....................................781 324-7991
Robert Jordan, *President*
Bob Jordan, *Executive*
EMP: 5
SQ FT: 4,000
SALES (est): 627.3K **Privately Held**
SIC: 3599 Mfg Industrial Machinery

(G-12582)
MEDI - PRINT INC (PA)
Also Called: Print House
200 Maplewood St (02148-5914)
PHONE....................................781 324-4455
Paul T Doucette, *President*
A Thomas Cyr, *Treasurer*
EMP: 22
SQ FT: 10,000
SALES (est): 4.2MM **Privately Held**
WEB: www.printhouse.com
SIC: 2752 Lithographic Commercial Printing

(G-12583)
MYSTIC PARKER PRINTING INC
66 Willow St (02148-5832)
PHONE....................................781 321-4948
Christopher J Towle, *Principal*
EMP: 6
SALES (est): 485.9K **Privately Held**
SIC: 2752 Lithographic Commercial Printing

(G-12584)
NANOFUSE BIOLOGICS LLC
Also Called: Medical Device & Biologics
350 Main St Fl 2 (02148-5089)
PHONE....................................978 232-3990
Kingsley R Chin, *CEO*
Jake Lubinski, *President*
EMP: 15
SALES (est): 687.7K **Privately Held**
SIC: 2834 5047 Mfg Pharmaceutical Preparations Whol Medical/Hospital Equipment

(G-12585)
P & K CUSTOM ACRYLICS INC
Also Called: Tek Scientific Division
40 Faulkner St (02148-4209)
PHONE....................................781 388-2601
Paul Wenzel, *President*
EMP: 5
SALES (est): 950.9K **Privately Held**
WEB: www.tekscientific.com
SIC: 2821 Mfg Plastic Materials/Resins

(G-12586)
PALMER MANUFACTURING CO LLC (DH)
Also Called: P M C
243 Medford St (02148-7383)
P.O. Box K (02148-0008)
PHONE....................................781 321-0480
Michael Cowell,
Tom Mitchell,
▲ **EMP:** 145 **EST:** 1965
SQ FT: 63,000
SALES (est): 53.9MM
SALES (corp-wide): 368.2MM **Privately Held**
WEB: www.palmermfgco.com
SIC: 3724 Mfg Aircraft Engines/Parts

(G-12587)
PARADIGM PRCISION HOLDINGS LLC
243 Medford St (02148-7301)
PHONE....................................781 321-0480
Mike Cowell, *Principal*
EMP: 13
SALES (corp-wide): 368.2MM **Privately Held**
SIC: 3462 Mfg Iron/Steel Forgings
HQ: Paradigm Precision Holdings, Llc
404 W Guadalupe Rd
Tempe AZ 85283

(G-12588)
PARKER PRESS INC
66 Willow St (02148-5832)
PHONE....................................781 321-4948
Stephen Vasquez, *President*
Charlene Vasquez, *Treasurer*
EMP: 3
SQ FT: 2,500
SALES (est): 360K **Privately Held**
WEB: www.parkerpress.com
SIC: 2752 Commercial Offset Printing

(G-12589)
PIANTEDOSI BAKING CO
240 Commercial St (02148-6709)
PHONE....................................781 321-3400
John Piantedosi, *Partner*
Family Trust of John Piantedos, *Partner*
EMP: 3
SQ FT: 65,000
SALES (est): 152K **Privately Held**
SIC: 2051 Mfg Bread/Related Products

(G-12590)
PIANTEDOSI BAKING CO INC (PA)
240 Commercial St (02148-6709)
PHONE....................................781 321-3400
Thomas L Piantedosi, *President*
Joseph A Piantedosi, *Director*
Robert J Piantedosi, *Director*
◆ **EMP:** 238
SQ FT: 65,000
SALES (est): 54.5MM **Privately Held**
WEB: www.piantedosi.com
SIC: 2051 5812 Mfg Bread/Related Products Eating Place

(G-12591)
PRECISION ASSEMBLIES
19 Shurtleff St (02148-6217)
PHONE....................................781 324-9054
Reginald Rodrick, *Owner*
EMP: 3

GEOGRAPHIC

SALES (est): 221K **Privately Held**
WEB: www.precisionassemblies.com
SIC: 3053 3599 Mfg Gaskets/Packing/Sealing Devices Mfg Industrial Machinery

(G-12592)
QUARTZITE PROCESSING INC
6 Holyoke St (02148-5608)
PHONE..................................781 322-3611
Brian Yanofsky, *President*
EMP: 10 **EST:** 1956
SQ FT: 5,000
SALES: 750K **Privately Held**
WEB: www.quartzite.net
SIC: 3679 Mfg Electronic Components

(G-12593)
REILY FOODS COMPANY
100 Charles St (02148-6704)
PHONE..................................504 524-6131
David Darragh, *President*
Donna Reese, *Purchasing*
EMP: 3
SALES (corp-wide): 358.5MM **Privately Held**
SIC: 2099 2095 Mfg Food Preparations Mfg Roasted Coffee
HQ: Reily Foods Company
400 Poydras St Fl 10
New Orleans LA 70130

(G-12594)
SAMTAN ENGINEERING CORP
127 Wyllis Ave (02148-7525)
PHONE..................................781 322-7880
Philip D Askenazy, *President*
Samuel Askenazy, *President*
George Laberis, *Vice Pres*
Richard B Askenazy, *Treasurer*
EMP: 30
SQ FT: 30,000
SALES (est): 5.3MM **Privately Held**
WEB: www.samtanengineering.com
SIC: 3599 3544 3469 Mfg Industrial Machinery Mfg Dies/Tools/Jigs/Fixtures Mfg Metal Stampings

(G-12595)
SENSEDRIVER TECHNOLOGIES LLC
350 Main St Ste 31 (02148-5024)
PHONE..................................978 232-3990
Kingsley Chin, *Principal*
EMP: 4
SQ FT: 300
SALES (est): 273.7K **Privately Held**
SIC: 3812 Mfg Search/Navigation Equipment

(G-12596)
SIGN ART INC
60 Sharon St (02148-5915)
PHONE..................................781 322-3785
Andy Layman, *President*
EMP: 13
SQ FT: 4,000
SALES (est): 2MM **Privately Held**
WEB: www.signartboston.com
SIC: 3993 Mfg Signs/Advertising Specialties

(G-12597)
SPADAFORA SLUSH CO
195 Pearl St (02148-6417)
PHONE..................................617 548-5870
William Spadafora Sr, *Owner*
EMP: 3
SQ FT: 1,500
SALES (est): 176.7K **Privately Held**
SIC: 2024 5143 5812 Manufacture And Wholesales Frozen Food And Retails Ice Cream

(G-12598)
SUNSETTER PRODUCTS LTD PARTNR
184 Charles St (02148-6714)
PHONE..................................781 321-9600
Jonathan Hershberg, *President*
Ido Eilam, *Partner*
Les Snader, *Partner*
Tim McCoy, *Plant Mgr*
Heidi Mc Coy, *Inv Control Mgr*
◆ **EMP:** 73
SQ FT: 68,000
SALES (est): 17.9MM
SALES (corp-wide): 3B **Privately Held**
WEB: www.sunsetter.com
SIC: 2394 3446 Manufacturing Canvas/Related Products And Architectural Metalwork
HQ: Springs Window Fashions, Llc
7549 Graber Rd
Middleton WI 53562
608 836-1011

(G-12599)
SUPER SPORT SCREEN PRINTING
910 Eastern Ave (02148-6056)
PHONE..................................781 397-8166
Mark Barletta, *Owner*
EMP: 5
SALES (est): 418.7K **Privately Held**
WEB: www.supersportusa.com
SIC: 2759 Commercial Printing

(G-12600)
VAN STRY DESIGN INC
420 Pearl St Ste 2 (02148-6697)
PHONE..................................781 388-9998
Kevin Van Stry, *CEO*
Jimmy King, *District Mgr*
Barrett Stowell, *Vice Pres*
Ying Chen, *Project Mgr*
Kevin Vanstry, *Sales Executive*
▲ **EMP:** 50
SQ FT: 20,000
SALES (est): 8.3MM **Privately Held**
WEB: www.vanstry.com
SIC: 2541 Mfg Wood Partitions/Fixtures

Manchester
Essex County

(G-12601)
A LYONS & COMPANY INC
40 Beach St Unit 105 (01944-1464)
PHONE..................................978 526-4244
Richard J Sullivan Jr, *President*
Rick Fine, *Vice Pres*
▲ **EMP:** 14
SQ FT: 2,200
SALES (est): 2.5MM **Privately Held**
WEB: www.alyons.com
SIC: 2211 Cotton Broadwoven Fabric Mill

(G-12602)
ALBION BEAMS INC
Also Called: Albion Systems
9 Spy Rock Hill Rd (01944-1514)
PHONE..................................978 526-4406
Nicholas R White, *President*
Alison L Anholt - White, *Vice Pres*
Brian B Terry, *Treasurer*
EMP: 4
SALES (est): 160K **Privately Held**
SIC: 3674 Mfg Semiconductors/Related Devices

(G-12603)
AMERICAN PRFMCE POLYMERS LLC
1 Beaver Dam Rd Ste 6 (01944-1298)
P.O. Box 412 (01944-0412)
PHONE..................................603 237-8001
Richard A Renehan,
EMP: 6
SALES (est): 274.7K
SALES (corp-wide): 1.8MM **Privately Held**
SIC: 2822 8711 Mfg Synthetic Rubber Engineering Services
PA: Renco Corporation
1 Beaver Dam Rd Ste 6
Manchester MA 01944
978 526-8494

(G-12604)
CRICKET PRESS INC
50 Summer St (01944-1518)
P.O. Box 357 (01944-0357)
PHONE..................................978 526-7131
Fax: 978 526-8193
EMP: 19 **EST:** 1915
SQ FT: 21,000
SALES (est): 1.4MM **Privately Held**
SIC: 2711 2752 Newspapers-Publishing/Printing Lithographic Commercial Printing

(G-12605)
HOLLAN PUBLISHING INC
4 Butler Ave (01944-1602)
PHONE..................................978 704-9342
Monica Sweeney, *Assoc Editor*
Allan Penn, *Officer*
EMP: 4 **EST:** 2016
SALES (est): 185.9K **Privately Held**
SIC: 2711 Newspapers-Publishing/Printing

(G-12606)
RENCO CORPORATION (PA)
Also Called: American Prfmce Polymers LLC
1 Beaver Dam Rd Ste 6 (01944-1298)
P.O. Box 412 (01944-0412)
PHONE..................................978 526-8494
Richard Renehan, *President*
Howard Genser, *COO*
Suesan Randlett, *Vice Pres*
◆ **EMP:** 5
SQ FT: 3,000
SALES: 1.8MM **Privately Held**
WEB: www.rencogloves.com
SIC: 3069 Mfg Fabricated Rubber Products

(G-12607)
STONYBROOK WATER COMPANY LLC
11 Beach St Unit 1 (01944-1548)
P.O. Box 321 (01944-0321)
PHONE..................................978 865-9899
Neidhardt Molly, *Regl Sales Mgr*
Timothy A Brown, *Mng Member*
EMP: 3 **EST:** 2009
SALES (est): 581.8K **Privately Held**
SIC: 3556 Mfg Food Products Machinery

(G-12608)
TOM WATERS GOLF SHOP
Also Called: Golf Shop The
153 School St (01944-1236)
PHONE..................................978 526-7311
Tom Waters, *Owner*
EMP: 7
SALES (est): 506.7K **Privately Held**
SIC: 3949 Mfg Sporting/Athletic Goods

(G-12609)
WINNING SOLUTIONS INC
66 Summer St Ste 2 (01944-1517)
PHONE..................................978 525-2813
Dana A Silva, *President*
Michael Doyle, *General Mgr*
▲ **EMP:** 4
SALES (est): 330K **Privately Held**
SIC: 3944 2511 Mfg Games/Toys Mfg Wood Household Furniture

Mansfield
Bristol County

(G-12610)
ACCUTECH PACKAGING INC
71 Hampden Rd (02048-1875)
PHONE..................................508 543-3800
EMP: 11 **EST:** 2015
SALES (est): 1.9MM **Privately Held**
SIC: 3089 Mfg Plastic Products

(G-12611)
ACORN MANUFACTURING CO INC
457 School St (02048-2011)
P.O. Box 31 (02048-0031)
PHONE..................................508 339-4500
Eric L Delong, *CEO*
Eva Castellano, *Bookkeeper*
Irene Deneault, *Sales Staff*
Venessa Delong, *Admin Sec*
◆ **EMP:** 37 **EST:** 1937
SQ FT: 34,000
SALES (est): 7.2MM **Privately Held**
WEB: www.acornmfg.com
SIC: 3429 3462 Mfg Hardware Mfg Iron/Steel Forgings

(G-12612)
ALLEGRA PRINT & IMAGING
1 Fowler St Ste 3 (02048-1261)
PHONE..................................508 339-3555
Tony Ward, *President*
EMP: 3
SALES (corp-wide): 2MM **Privately Held**
WEB: www.fasprint.com
SIC: 2752 Lithographic Commercial Printing
PA: Fasprint, Inc.
195 Liberty St Ste 1
Brockton MA 02301
508 588-9961

(G-12613)
AMERICAN PAPER RECYCLING CORP (PA)
87 Central St Bldg 1 (02048-1309)
PHONE..................................800 422-3220
Kenneth S Golden, *President*
Richard Kossack, *Senior VP*
Ron Smith, *Plant Mgr*
Duke Bates, *CFO*
Nancy Von Esh, *Director*
EMP: 25 **EST:** 1908
SQ FT: 2,000
SALES: 31.3MM **Privately Held**
WEB: www.aprcorp.com
SIC: 2611 5093 Pulp Mill Whol Scrap/Waste Material

(G-12614)
BAY STATE ENVELOPE INC (PA)
440 Chauncy St (02048-1133)
PHONE..................................508 337-8900
Diana W Skogseth, *CEO*
Diana Skogseth, *CEO*
Russell Frizzell, *President*
Dave Luongo, *President*
Eric Skogseth, *Exec VP*
EMP: 35
SQ FT: 24,000
SALES (est): 4.4MM **Privately Held**
SIC: 2759 Commercial Printing

(G-12615)
BEDROCK AUTOMTN PLATFORMS INC
171 Forbes Blvd Ste 1000 (02048-1172)
PHONE..................................781 821-0280
Robert Honor, *President*
EMP: 8 **EST:** 2013
SALES (est): 282.6K **Privately Held**
SIC: 3823 Mfg Process Control Instruments

(G-12616)
CANNAN FUELS
157 Pratt St (02048-1555)
PHONE..................................508 339-3317
Sameh Kanan, *President*
EMP: 8 **EST:** 2009
SALES (est): 1.1MM **Privately Held**
SIC: 2869 Mfg Industrial Organic Chemicals

(G-12617)
CHARLES A RICHARDSON INC
330 Otis St (02048-2056)
P.O. Box 29 (02048-0029)
PHONE..................................508 339-8600
Jeffrey Richardson, *President*
Jeffrey C Richardson, *President*
Edward A Richardson, *Vice Pres*
William A Richardson, *Vice Pres*
Todd R Richardson, *CFO*
▼ **EMP:** 11
SQ FT: 20,000
SALES (est): 1.4MM **Privately Held**
SIC: 3463 3469 Mfg Nonferrous Forgings Mfg Metal Stampings

(G-12618)
COCHIN RUBBERS INTL LLC (PA)
241 Francis Ave (02048-1548)
PHONE..................................877 289-0364
Joe Abraham, *Mng Member*
▲ **EMP:** 6
SALES (est): 955.7K **Privately Held**
SIC: 3011 Mfg Tires/Inner Tubes

▲ = Import ▼=Export
◆ =Import/Export

(G-12619)
CONTEMPORARY APPAREL INC
Also Called: Ferrara For Contemporary AP
127 N Main St (02048-3809)
P.O. Box 575 (02048-0575)
PHONE..................................508 339-3523
Anthony Ferrara, *President*
Rosemarie Ferrara, *Clerk*
EMP: 5
SQ FT: 21,000
SALES (est): 499.9K **Privately Held**
SIC: 2331 2387 Mfg Women's Blouses Shirts & Belts

(G-12620)
COVIDIEN FRANCE HOLDINGS INC
15 Hampshire St (02048-1113)
PHONE..................................508 261-8000
Matthew J Nicolella, *Principal*
EMP: 3
SALES (est): 147.8K
SALES (corp-wide): 2.6MM **Privately Held**
SIC: 3842 Mfg Surgical Appliances/Supplies
HQ: Covidien Limited
20 Lower Hatch Street
Dublin 2
-

(G-12621)
COVIDIEN LLC
15 Hampshire St (02048-1113)
PHONE..................................508 261-8000
EMP: 3
SALES (est): 101.1K **Privately Held**
SIC: 3842 Mfg Surgical Appliances/Supplies
PA: Medtronic Public Limited Company
20 Hatch Street
Dublin
-

(G-12622)
COVIDIEN LP (HQ)
15 Hampshire St (02048-1113)
PHONE..................................763 514-4000
Omar Ishrak, *Ch of Bd*
Jimmy Vickery, *Plant Mgr*
Cristina Messina, *Purch Mgr*
Ed Kalous, *VP Engrg*
Casey Ladtkow, *Research*
◆ **EMP:** 1000
SALES (est): 5.1B **Privately Held**
WEB: www.tycohealthcare.com
SIC: 3842 3841 3845 5122 Mfg Surgical Appliances Mfg Surgical/Med Instr Mfg Electromedical Equip

(G-12623)
COVIDIEN US HOLDINGS INC
15 Hampshire St (02048-1113)
PHONE..................................508 261-8000
EMP: 7
SALES (est): 111.4K **Privately Held**
SIC: 3842 Mfg Surgical Appliances/Supplies
PA: Medtronic Public Limited Company
20 Hatch Street
Dublin
-

(G-12624)
CROSBY VALVE & GAGE INTL INC
Also Called: Andersn Greenwd Crosby Valve
55 Cabot Blvd (02048-1137)
PHONE..................................508 384-3121
Greg Hyland, *President*
EMP: 80
SALES (est): 6.8MM
SALES (corp-wide): 18.3B **Publicly Held**
SIC: 3491 5085 Mfg Industrial Valves Whol Industrial Supplies
PA: Emerson Electric Co.
8000 West Florissant Ave
Saint Louis MO 63136
314 553-2000

(G-12625)
CUPCAKE TOWN
237 West St (02048-1206)
PHONE..................................774 284-4667
EMP: 4
SALES (est): 232.6K **Privately Held**
SIC: 2051 Mfg Bread/Related Products

(G-12626)
CUSA TECHNOLOGIES INC
Also Called: Serv
800 S Main St Ste 301 (02048-3144)
PHONE..................................508 339-7675
EMP: 30
SALES (est): 1.6MM **Privately Held**
SIC: 7372 Prepackaged Software Services

(G-12627)
DATEL INC
120 Forbes Blvd Ste 125 (02048-1274)
PHONE..................................508 964-5131
Antonio Khazen, *CEO*
David Piccirilli, *Purch Mgr*
Healan Coffin, *Controller*
Roy Cabral, *Marketing Mgr*
Rahul Sharma, *Marketing Staff*
EMP: 23
SALES: 4.5MM **Privately Held**
SIC: 3679 3568 Mfg Electronic Components Mfg Power Transmission Equipment

(G-12628)
DIAGEO NORTH AMERICA INC
800 S Main St (02048-3144)
PHONE..................................508 324-9800
Peter McDonough, *Branch Mgr*
EMP: 9
SALES (corp-wide): 16.3B **Privately Held**
SIC: 2087 Mfg Flavor Extracts/Syrup
HQ: Diageo North America Inc.
801 Main Ave
Norwalk CT 06851
203 229-2100

(G-12629)
DRISCOLLS RESTAURANT
Also Called: Devon's Place
535 S Main St (02048-3105)
PHONE..................................508 261-1574
Mike Di Mascio, *President*
EMP: 13
SALES: 325K **Privately Held**
SIC: 2812 5461 Mfg Alkalies/Chlorine Retail Bakery

(G-12630)
EMERSON AUTOMATION SOLUTIONS
Also Called: Navy Product Team
55 Cabot Blvd (02048-1137)
PHONE..................................508 594-4356
David Cubberley, *Manager*
EMP: 55
SALES (corp-wide): 18.3B **Publicly Held**
SIC: 3491 Mfg Industrial Valves
HQ: Emerson Automation Solutions Final Control Us Lp
10707 Clay Rd
Houston TX 77041
-

(G-12631)
EMERSON AUTOMATION SOLUTIONS
Also Called: Marine Product Team
55 Cabot Blvd (02048-1137)
PHONE..................................508 594-4410
David Smith, *General Mgr*
EMP: 55
SQ FT: 285,000
SALES (corp-wide): 18.3B **Publicly Held**
SIC: 3491 Mfg Industrial Valves
HQ: Emerson Automation Solutions Final Control Us Lp
10707 Clay Rd
Houston TX 77041
-

(G-12632)
EMERSON ELECTRIC CO
9 Oxford Rd (02048-1126)
PHONE..................................774 266-4136
EMP: 3
SALES (corp-wide): 18.3B **Publicly Held**
SIC: 3823 Mfg Process Control Instruments
PA: Emerson Electric Co.
8000 West Florissant Ave
Saint Louis MO 63136
314 553-2000

(G-12633)
FUTURE FOAM INC
47 Maple St (02048-1508)
PHONE..................................508 339-0354
Ryan Alwardt, *Manager*
EMP: 15
SALES (corp-wide): 376.3MM **Privately Held**
SIC: 3086 Mfg Plastic Foam Products
PA: Future Foam, Inc.
1610 Avenue N
Council Bluffs IA 51501
712 323-9122

(G-12634)
HARTMANN INCORPORATED
575 West St Ste 110 (02048-1160)
PHONE..................................508 851-1400
David A Herman, *President*
Jerome J Ciszewski, *Director*
Augustus Griffin, *Director*
Louis A Fantin, *Admin Sec*
EMP: 65
SALES (est): 3.5MM **Privately Held**
SIC: 3161 Mfg Luggage

(G-12635)
HL OPERATING LLC (DH)
Also Called: Hartmann
575 West St Ste 110 (02048-1160)
PHONE..................................508 851-1400
Frank Johnston,
◆ **EMP:** 40
SQ FT: 20,000
SALES (est): 10.7MM
SALES (corp-wide): 177.9K **Privately Held**
WEB: www.hartmann.com
SIC: 3161 3172 Mfg Luggage Mfg Personal Leather Goods
HQ: Samsonite Llc
575 West St Ste 110
Mansfield MA 02048
508 851-1400

(G-12636)
HUB FOLDING BOX COMPANY INC
Also Called: Plastic Technology Division
774 Norfolk St (02048-1826)
PHONE..................................508 339-0005
Alfred Dirico, *President*
John Dirico, *Partner*
Jeff Belinski, *Business Mgr*
Anthony H Dirico, *Vice Pres*
Mark A Dirico, *Vice Pres*
▲ **EMP:** 315 **EST:** 1921
SQ FT: 275,000
SALES (est): 124.6MM **Privately Held**
SIC: 2657 Mfg Folding Paperboard Boxes

(G-12637)
INTEGRA LIFESCIENCES PROD CORP
11 Cabot Blvd (02048-1137)
PHONE..................................781 971-5682
Peter J Arduini, *President*
Glenn G Coleman, *Vice Pres*
Jeff Mosebrook, *Vice Pres*
EMP: 3
SALES (est): 113.8K **Publicly Held**
SIC: 3841 Mfg Surgical/Medical Instruments
PA: Integra Lifesciences Holdings Corporation
311 Enterprise Dr
Plainsboro NJ 08536
-

(G-12638)
IRONMAN INC
150 Rumford Ave Apt 230 (02048-2166)
PHONE..................................989 386-8975
James Lloyd Hatch, *Principal*
EMP: 4
SALES (est): 532K **Privately Held**
SIC: 3441 Structural Metal Fabrication

(G-12639)
JORDI LABS LLC
200 Gilbert St (02048-2051)
PHONE..................................508 719-8543
Howard C Jordi, *President*
Pamela J Jordi, *Treasurer*
EMP: 22
SQ FT: 4,800
SALES (est): 7.1MM **Privately Held**
WEB: www.jordiflp.com
SIC: 2819 8734 Mfg Industrial Inorganic Chemicals Testing Laboratory

(G-12640)
KRAFT HEINZ FOODS COMPANY
Also Called: Kraft Foods
111 Forbes Blvd (02048-1124)
PHONE..................................508 763-3311
EMP: 100
SALES (corp-wide): 26.2B **Publicly Held**
WEB: www.kraftfoods.com
SIC: 2043 Mfg Canned Fruits/Vegetables
HQ: Kraft Heinz Foods Company
1 Ppg Pl Fl 34
Pittsburgh PA 15222
412 456-5700

(G-12641)
LACERTA GROUP INC
50 Suffolk Rd (02048-1816)
PHONE..................................508 339-3312
EMP: 7 **Privately Held**
SIC: 3089 3559 Mfg Plastic Products Mfg Misc Industry Machinery
PA: Lacerta Group, Inc.
360 Forbes Blvd
Mansfield MA 02048
-

(G-12642)
LACERTA GROUP INC (PA)
360 Forbes Blvd (02048-1806)
PHONE..................................508 339-3312
Ali Reza Lotfi, *President*
Denise L Lotfi, *Admin Sec*
▲ **EMP:** 90
SQ FT: 47,000
SALES (est): 10.8MM **Privately Held**
WEB: www.lacerta.com
SIC: 3089 3559 Mfg Plastic Products Mfg Misc Industry Machinery

(G-12643)
LUDLOW CORPORATION (DH)
Also Called: Ludlow Jute Company Limited
15 Hampshire St (02048-1113)
PHONE..................................508 261-8000
Matthew Harbaugh, *President*
John Kapples, *Vice Pres*
Kevin Dasilva, *Treasurer*
Matthew Nicolella, *Director*
▲ **EMP:** 5
SALES (est): 24.6MM **Privately Held**
SIC: 2834 Pharmaceuticals Biotechnology
HQ: Mallinckrodt Llc
675 Jmes S Mcdonnell Blvd
Hazelwood MO 63042
314 654-2000

(G-12644)
MANSFIELD MACHINERY CO INC
27 Rock St (02048-2362)
PHONE..................................508 339-7973
Robert Holt, *President*
Irene Erwin, *Vice Pres*
Robert Erwin, *Treasurer*
Pauline Holt, *Clerk*
EMP: 10
SQ FT: 2,000
SALES (est): 800K **Privately Held**
SIC: 3451 Mfg Screw Machine Products

(G-12645)
MEDTRONIC
15 Hampshire St (02048-1113)
PHONE..................................508 452-4203
Santina Wendling, *Principal*
Elaine SE Llmayer, *Principal*
Ben Huebener, *Regional Mgr*
Bob Fouts, *Engineer*
Joseph Liotta, *Sales Staff*
EMP: 11 **EST:** 2015
SALES (est): 288.6K **Privately Held**
SIC: 3841 Mfg Surgical/Medical Instruments

(G-12646)
MOCKINGBIRD STUDIOS INC
905 S Main St (02048-3149)
PHONE..................................508 339-6755
Mark Deluzio, *Principal*
EMP: 3

SALES (est): 202.6K Privately Held
SIC: 2515 Mfg Mattresses/Bedsprings

(G-12647)
MOTOROLA SOLUTIONS INC
20 Cabot Blvd M2280 (02048-1158)
PHONE..................................508 261-4502
Mandy O Lean, *Principal*
Leon Katcharian, *Principal*
EMP: 4
SALES (corp-wide): 7.3B Publicly Held
WEB: www.motorola.com
SIC: 3663 Mfg Communication Equipment
PA: Motorola Solutions, Inc.
500 W Monroe St Ste 4400
Chicago IL 60661
847 576-5000

(G-12648)
NAUSET ENGINEER EQUIPMENT
51 Fram Dr (02048-1695)
P.O. Box 78 (02048-0078)
PHONE..................................508 339-2662
Richard Shea, *Principal*
EMP: 5 EST: 2007
SALES (est): 622.8K Privately Held
SIC: 3564 5075 5084 Mfg Blowers/Fans Whol Heat/Air Cond Equipment/Supplies Whol Industrial Equipment

(G-12649)
NELLCOR PURITAN BENNETT LLC (DH)
Also Called: Covidien
15 Hampshire St (02048-1113)
PHONE..................................508 261-8000
Joseph Parks, *Supervisor*
James W Dennis,
▲ EMP: 300 EST: 1981
SQ FT: 141,000
SALES (est): 270.8MM Privately Held
WEB: www.nellcor.com
SIC: 3845 3841 Mfg Electromedical Equip Mfg Surgical/Med Instr
HQ: Covidien Lp
15 Hampshire St
Mansfield MA 02048
763 514-4000

(G-12650)
NORTHEAST DATA DESTRUCTION LLC
73 Plymouth St (02048-2034)
P.O. Box 74 (02048-0074)
PHONE..................................800 783-6766
Maria Reyes, *Principal*
EMP: 4
SALES (est): 417.5K Privately Held
SIC: 3559 Mfg Misc Industry Machinery

(G-12651)
PENTAIR VALVES & CONTRLS US LP
55 Cabot Blvd (02048-1137)
PHONE..................................508 594-4410
EMP: 110
SALES (corp-wide): 4.4B Publicly Held
SIC: 3491 Industrial Valves, Nsk
HQ: Pentair Valves & Controls Us Lp
10707 Clay Rd
Houston TX 77041
713 986-4665

(G-12652)
PROVEN PROCESS MED DVCS INC
110 Forbes Blvd (02048-1145)
PHONE..................................508 261-0800
Kenneth Fine, *President*
Paul Burke, *COO*
Chuck Aubin, *Vice Pres*
David Yavorski, *Vice Pres*
Julio Pereira, *Buyer*
EMP: 67
SQ FT: 43,000
SALES (est): 14.9MM Privately Held
WEB: www.provenprocess.com
SIC: 3845 Mfg Electromedical Equipment

(G-12653)
QC INDUSTRIES INC (PA)
Also Called: Qual-Craft
60 Maple St (02048-1876)
P.O. Box 36 (02048-0036)
PHONE..................................781 344-1000
Norman Katz, *Ch of Bd*
Robert P Berish, *President*
Ed Berzins, *Purch Agent*
Myrna Katz, *Shareholder*
▲ EMP: 90 EST: 1953
SQ FT: 55,000
SALES (est): 14.4MM Privately Held
WEB: www.qualcraft.com
SIC: 3429 3471 Mfg Hardware Plating/Polishing Service

(G-12654)
QUADRANT LLC
120 Forbes Blvd Ste A (02048-1150)
PHONE..................................508 594-2700
EMP: 45
SQ FT: 5,000
SALES (est): 1.5MM
SALES (corp-wide): 8.1MM Privately Held
SIC: 7372 Prepackaged Software
PA: Fresche Solutions Inc
995 Rue Wellington Bureau 200
Montreal QC H3C 1
514 747-7007

(G-12655)
RELIABLE TRUSS & COMPONENTS IN
71 Maple St (02048-1508)
PHONE..................................508 339-8020
Manuel M Pina, *President*
EMP: 7
SALES (est): 1.2MM Privately Held
SIC: 2439 Mfg Structural Wood Members

(G-12656)
ROSEMOUNT INC
9 Oxford Rd (02048-1126)
PHONE..................................508 261-2928
Gary Gregory, *Manager*
EMP: 7
SALES (corp-wide): 18.3B Publicly Held
WEB: www.rosemount.com
SIC: 3823 Mfg Process Control Instruments
HQ: Rosemount Inc.
8200 Market Blvd
Chanhassen MN 55317
952 906-8888

(G-12657)
SCOREBOARD ENTERPRISES INC
Also Called: Score Board Enterprises
274 Fruit St (02048-3117)
PHONE..................................508 339-8113
John C Hurley, *President*
EMP: 4
SQ FT: 7,000
SALES (est): 330K Privately Held
WEB: www.scoreboardenterprises.com
SIC: 3669 Manufacturing Communications Equipment

(G-12658)
SIGMA SYSTEMS CORP
41 Hampden Rd (02048-1807)
PHONE..................................781 688-2354
Robert Stewart, *President*
EMP: 40
SQ FT: 5,000
SALES (est): 4.1MM
SALES (corp-wide): 78.5MM Publicly Held
WEB: www.sigmasystems.com
SIC: 3822 Mfg Environmental Controls
PA: Intest Corporation
804 E Gate Dr Ste 200
Mount Laurel NJ 08054
856 505-8800

(G-12659)
SMITH & NEPHEW INC
Osteobiologics
130 Forbes Blvd (02048-1145)
PHONE..................................508 261-3600
Mike Ferragamo, *Vice Pres*
Peter Furfari, *Mfg Staff*
John Santos, *Senior Buyer*
Rick Graber, *Research*
Mark Housman, *Engineer*
EMP: 44
SALES (corp-wide): 4.9B Privately Held
WEB: www.smith-nephew.com/us
SIC: 3841 Whol Medical/Hospital Equipment
HQ: Smith & Nephew, Inc.
7135 Goodlett Farms Pkwy
Cordova TN 38016
901 396-2121

(G-12660)
SMITH & NEPHEW INC
130 Forbes Blvd (02048-1145)
PHONE..................................508 261-3600
Gabriele G Niederauer, *Manager*
EMP: 50
SALES (corp-wide): 4.9B Privately Held
WEB: www.smith-nephew.com/us
SIC: 3841 3845 Manufacturing Arthoscopic Surgical Wquipment And Medical Grade Video Cameras
HQ: Smith & Nephew, Inc.
7135 Goodlett Farms Pkwy
Cordova TN 38016
901 396-2121

(G-12661)
SPECS TII INC
20 Cabot Blvd Ste 300 (02048-1183)
PHONE..................................508 618-1292
Petrik Sharon, *Branch Mgr*
EMP: 4
SALES (corp-wide): 35.8MM Privately Held
SIC: 3826 Mfg Analytical Instruments
HQ: Specs Tii Inc.
411 Cleveland St 290
Clearwater FL 33755

(G-12662)
TELCO SYSTEMS INC (HQ)
Also Called: Telco Systems/Integrol Sytems
15 Berkshire Rd (02048-1135)
PHONE..................................508 339-1516
Itzik Weinstein, *CEO*
Reini Florin, *Vice Pres*
Hector Menjivar, *Vice Pres*
David Moses, *Vice Pres*
Moti Rosenshtock, *Vice Pres*
▲ EMP: 25
SQ FT: 28,000
SALES (est): 5MM
SALES (corp-wide): 34.3MM Privately Held
WEB: www.telco.com
SIC: 3674 Mfg Semiconductors/Related Devices
PA: Batm Advanced Communications Ltd.
4 Hacharash
Hod Hasharon 45240
986 625-25

(G-12663)
TELEFLEX MEDICAL INCORPORATED
375 Forbes Blvd (02048-1805)
PHONE..................................800 474-0178
Liam Kelly, *CEO*
EMP: 3
SALES (corp-wide): 2.4B Publicly Held
SIC: 3842 Mfg Surgical Appliances/Supplies
HQ: Teleflex Medical Incorporated
3015 Carrington Mill Blvd
Morrisville NC 27560
919 544-8000

(G-12664)
TEMPTRONIC CORPORATION (HQ)
Also Called: Intest Thermal Solutions
41 Hampden Rd (02048-1807)
PHONE..................................781 688-2300
James Pelrin, *President*
Thomas G Gerendas, *President*
Hugh T Regan Jr, *Vice Pres*
Johann Gomez, *Opers Staff*
Dona Butcher, *Engineer*
▲ EMP: 100 EST: 1999
SQ FT: 62,000
SALES (est): 25.9MM
SALES (corp-wide): 78.5MM Publicly Held
WEB: www.temptronic.com
SIC: 3823 Mfg Process Control Instruments
PA: Intest Corporation
804 E Gate Dr Ste 200
Mount Laurel NJ 08054
856 505-8800

(G-12665)
THERMONICS INC
41 Hampden Rd (02048-1807)
PHONE..................................408 542-5900
Jim Kufis, *President*
EMP: 7
SALES (est): 614.9K
SALES (corp-wide): 78.5MM Publicly Held
SIC: 3823 Mfg Process Control Instruments
PA: Intest Corporation
804 E Gate Dr Ste 200
Mount Laurel NJ 08054
856 505-8800

(G-12666)
TOUCH BIONICS
35 Hampden Rd (02048-1807)
PHONE..................................774 719-2199
Ian Stevens, *CEO*
EMP: 3
SALES (est): 174.6K Privately Held
SIC: 3842 Mfg Surgical Appliances/Supplies

(G-12667)
TYCO INTERNATIONAL MGT CO LLC
15 Hampshire St (02048-1113)
PHONE..................................508 261-6200
EMP: 5 Privately Held
SIC: 3999 1711 1731 3669 Mfg Misc Products Plumbing/Heat/Ac Contr Electrical Contractor
HQ: Tyco International Management Company, Llc
9 Roszel Rd Ste 2
Princeton NJ 08540
609 720-4200

(G-12668)
VICTAULIC COMPANY
145 Plymouth St Ste A (02048-2093)
PHONE..................................508 406-3220
Kevin Collins, *Branch Mgr*
EMP: 7
SALES (corp-wide): 769MM Privately Held
SIC: 3494 Mfg Valves/Pipe Fittings
PA: Victaulic Company
4901 Kesslersville Rd
Easton PA 18040
610 559-3300

(G-12669)
VIKING CORPORATION
60 Maple St Ste 3 (02048-1876)
PHONE..................................508 594-1800
EMP: 5 Privately Held
SIC: 3499 Mfg Misc Fabricated Metal Products
HQ: Viking Corporation
210 Industrial Park Dr
Hastings MI 49058
269 945-9501

(G-12670)
WBMX MIX 985 TWEETER CNTR
885 S Main St (02048-3148)
PHONE..................................508 339-1296
EMP: 3 EST: 2007
SALES (est): 172.3K Privately Held
SIC: 3273 Mfg Ready-Mixed Concrete

(G-12671)
WESTROCK CP LLC
47 Maple St (02048-1508)
PHONE..................................770 448-2193
Randy Tharacher, *Manager*
EMP: 147
SALES (corp-wide): 18.2B Publicly Held
WEB: www.smurfit-stone.com
SIC: 2653 2671 2652 2631 Mfg Corrugated/Fiber Box Mfg Packaging Paper/Film Mfg Setup Paperboard Box Paperboard Mill
HQ: Westrock Cp, Llc
1000 Abernathy Rd
Atlanta GA 30328

▲ = Import ▼=Export
◆ =Import/Export

(G-12672)
WESTROCK CP LLC
60 Maple St (02048-1876)
PHONE..................................508 337-0400
Alan M Schwartz, *General Mgr*
EMP: 50
SQ FT: 60,000
SALES (corp-wide): 18.2B **Publicly Held**
SIC: 2631 Paper Mill
HQ: Westrock Cp, Llc
1000 Abernathy Rd
Atlanta GA 30328

Marblehead
Essex County

(G-12673)
ALINE SYSTEMS INC
30 Doaks Ln (01945-3659)
PHONE..................................781 990-1462
Derek Carroll, *President*
EMP: 5
SALES (est): 664.8K **Privately Held**
SIC: 3089 Mfg Plastic Products

(G-12674)
ALPHA INNOVATION INC
86 Pleasant St (01945-3498)
P.O. Box 388 (01945-0388)
PHONE..................................978 744-1100
Bill Larkin, *President*
Lisa Gorman, *Opers Mgr*
EMP: 6
SALES (est): 1.1MM **Privately Held**
WEB: www.stopstatic.com
SIC: 3629 Mfg Electrical Industrial Apparatus

(G-12675)
BARNEY RABIN COMPANY INC
2 Foss Ter (01945-2509)
PHONE..................................781 639-0593
Paul Rabin, *President*
Kathy Rabin, *Admin Sec*
EMP: 15 **EST:** 1933
SQ FT: 5,460
SALES: 540K **Privately Held**
WEB: www.barneyrabinco.com
SIC: 2759 Commercial Printing

(G-12676)
BIGFOOT SEO STRATEGIES
27 Smith St Unit 1305 (01945-4552)
PHONE..................................617 448-4848
Paul Gregory,
EMP: 5
SALES: 1MM **Privately Held**
SIC: 2741 Internet Publishing And Broadcasting

(G-12677)
BLUE ANCHOR WOODWORKS INC
208 Beacon St (01945-1506)
PHONE..................................781 631-2390
Pike Noyes, *President*
EMP: 5
SALES (est): 669.3K **Privately Held**
SIC: 2431 Mfg Millwork

(G-12678)
BLUE MAGIC INC
60 Village St (01945-2215)
PHONE..................................781 639-8428
David Smith, *President*
EMP: 3
SALES (est): 258.3K **Privately Held**
SIC: 3714 Mfg Motor Vehicle Parts/Accessories

(G-12679)
COMMUNITY NEWSPAPER INC
122 Washington St (01945-3590)
PHONE..................................781 639-4800
Kris Olson, *Principal*
EMP: 4
SALES (est): 21.6K **Privately Held**
SIC: 2711 Newspapers-Publishing/Printing

(G-12680)
CW HOOD YACHTS INC
3 Beacon St Ste 4 (01945-2687)
P.O. Box 443 (01945-0443)
PHONE..................................781 631-0192
Chris Hood, *President*
Chris Stirling, *Vice Pres*
Kimberlee McDonald, *Office Admin*
▲ **EMP:** 11
SQ FT: 6,600
SALES (est): 1.7MM **Privately Held**
WEB: www.cwhoodyachts.com
SIC: 3732 Boatbuilding/Repairing

(G-12681)
ENCORE IMAGES INC
21 Lime St Ste 12 (01945-2585)
PHONE..................................781 631-4568
Laurel Mervis, *President*
Paul Mervis, *Director*
EMP: 14
SQ FT: 6,000
SALES (est): 2.4MM
SALES (corp-wide): 4MM **Privately Held**
WEB: www.encoreimages.com
SIC: 3577 7629 7699 5943 Mfg Computer Peripherals Electrical Repair Repair Services Ret Stationery
PA: Printer Pro Solutions Incorporated
174 Davis St
East Douglas MA 01516
508 476-9003

(G-12682)
FLEX O FOLD NORTH AMERICA INC
91 Front St (01945-3201)
PHONE..................................781 631-3190
Jack Skrydstrup, *Exec VP*
Keld Willberg, *Sales Mgr*
EMP: 10 **EST:** 2000
SALES (est): 797.1K **Privately Held**
WEB: www.flexofold.com
SIC: 3366 Copper Foundry

(G-12683)
FOSTERS PROMOTIONAL GOODS
16 Anderson St Ste 101 (01945-2488)
PHONE..................................781 631-3824
EMP: 10 **EST:** 1925
SQ FT: 9,000
SALES (est): 1.1MM **Privately Held**
WEB: www.fosterspromo.com
SIC: 2262 2395 Finishing Plants, Manmade

(G-12684)
GRID SOLUTIONS CORP
132 One Half Wash St (01945)
PHONE..................................781 718-4266
Mitchell Wondolowski, *CEO*
John Garrett, *Chairman*
John Chu, *Admin Sec*
EMP: 6
SALES (est): 322.8K **Privately Held**
SIC: 7372 Prepackaged Software Services

(G-12685)
HEADWATERS INC
Also Called: Sound Oasis Company
134 Pleasant St (01945-2364)
PHONE..................................781 715-6404
Troy G Anderson, *President*
Stephanie Anderson, *Opers Staff*
Rudy Vanderbelt, *Treasurer*
▲ **EMP:** 8
SQ FT: 750
SALES (est): 1.5MM **Privately Held**
WEB: www.filterstream.com
SIC: 3564 3651 3635 3634 Mfg Blowers/Fans Mfg Home Audio/Video Eqp Mfg Home Vacuum Cleaners Mfg Elec Housewares/Fans

(G-12686)
HOT TOOLS INC
24 Tioga Way (01945-1575)
PHONE..................................781 639-1000
Charles F Loutrel Jr, *President*
EMP: 12
SQ FT: 2,000
SALES (est): 1MM **Privately Held**
SIC: 3423 Mfg Woodburning Tools Used In Carving & Etching

(G-12687)
M M NEWMAN CORPORATION
24 Tioga Way (01945-1575)
P.O. Box 615 (01945-0615)
PHONE..................................781 631-7100
Charles F Loutrel Jr, *President*
EMP: 12 **EST:** 1957
SQ FT: 24,000
SALES (est): 2.3MM **Privately Held**
WEB: www.mmnewman.com
SIC: 3423 3083 Manufacture Hand/Edge Tools Manufacture Laminated Plastic Plate/Sheet

(G-12688)
MARBLEHEAD WEATHER GMTS LLC
Also Called: Proquip USA
100 Hoods Ln Ste U8 (01945-2574)
PHONE..................................781 639-1060
Peter Dalton, *CEO*
Edward M Kennedy, *VP Opers*
EMP: 8
SALES (est): 895.4K **Privately Held**
SIC: 2389 Mfg Apparel/Accessories

(G-12689)
OAKUM BAY SAIL CO
9 State St (01945-3592)
PHONE..................................781 631-8983
Dave Arthur, *Owner*
EMP: 6 **EST:** 1973
SQ FT: 8,000
SALES (est): 500K **Privately Held**
SIC: 2394 Mfg Canvas/Related Products

(G-12690)
PEPPERCORN FOOD SERVICE INC
91 Pitman Rd (01945-1441)
PHONE..................................781 639-6035
Emanual Argiros, *President*
Ellen Argiros, *Vice Pres*
Jim Bouley, *Vice Pres*
EMP: 40
SQ FT: 22,000
SALES: 6MM **Privately Held**
WEB: www.peppercornfoodservice.com
SIC: 2053 Mfg Frozen Bakery Products

(G-12691)
RAVEN CREATIVE INC
15a Sewall St (01945-3350)
PHONE..................................781 476-5529
Robin Taliesin, *President*
Mary Ann Murphy, *Vice Pres*
EMP: 4
SQ FT: 1,000
SALES (est): 357.5K **Privately Held**
WEB: www.raven2.com
SIC: 3993 Advertising/Graphic Design

(G-12692)
SCALLOP IMAGING LLC
18 Sewall St (01945-3322)
PHONE..................................617 849-6400
Olaf Krohg, *CEO*
EMP: 20
SALES (est): 3.3MM **Privately Held**
SIC: 3861 Mfg Photographic Equipment/Supplies

(G-12693)
SEVEN SWEETS INC
Also Called: Stowaway Sweets
154 Atlantic Ave (01945-3012)
PHONE..................................781 631-0303
Michael Canniffe, *President*
Allycia Canniffe, *Vice Pres*
EMP: 10
SQ FT: 3,000
SALES: 475K **Privately Held**
SIC: 2064 5441 Mfg And Ret Chocolate Candy

(G-12694)
SHORT COURSES
16 Preston Beach Rd (01945-1725)
PHONE..................................781 631-1178
Dennis Curtin, *Owner*
EMP: 3
SALES (est): 172.1K **Privately Held**
WEB: www.shortcourses.com
SIC: 2731 Books-Publishing/Printing

(G-12695)
STROUD INTERNATIONAL LTD
123 Pleasant St Ste 300 (01945-2381)
PHONE..................................781 631-8806
Nat Greene, *CEO*
Patrick Smith, *Sr Associate*
EMP: 5
SALES (est): 119.9K **Privately Held**
SIC: 1382 Oil/Gas Exploration Services

(G-12696)
WILD BLUE YONDER FOODS
65 Tedesco St (01945-1039)
PHONE..................................978 532-3400
Deborah Waugh, *Owner*
EMP: 4
SALES (est): 264.8K **Privately Held**
SIC: 2043 Mfg Cereal Breakfast Foods

Marion
Plymouth County

(G-12697)
HARDING SAILS INC
Also Called: Harding Sails Nb
732 Mill St (02738-2209)
PHONE..................................508 748-0334
Graham Quinn, *President*
EMP: 15 **EST:** 1965
SQ FT: 5,000
SALES: 1MM **Privately Held**
WEB: www.hardingsails.com
SIC: 2394 Mfg Sails/Marine Canvas Related Products

(G-12698)
IDEAL BIAS BINDING CORP
Also Called: Ideal Little Things
35 Bullivant Farm Rd (02738-1153)
PHONE..................................508 748-2712
Kenneth Kevelson, *CEO*
▲ **EMP:** 4 **EST:** 1936
SQ FT: 38,000
SALES (est): 227.9K **Privately Held**
SIC: 2385 2339 2326 2361 Mfg Waterproof Outerwear Mfg Women/Miss Outerwear Mfg Men/Boy Work Clothng Mfg Girls Dresses/Blouse

(G-12699)
LOCKHEED MARTIN SIPPICAN INC (HQ)
7 Barnabas Rd (02738-1421)
PHONE..................................508 748-3399
Latisha Rourke, *President*
Douglas J Dapprich, *Vice Pres*
Lawrence C Hall, *Vice Pres*
Thomas L Jarbeau, *Vice Pres*
James Langenheim, *Vice Pres*
▲ **EMP:** 310
SQ FT: 220,000
SALES (est): 87.6MM **Publicly Held**
WEB: www.sippican.com
SIC: 3812 3826 3499 3672 Mfg Search/Navgatn Equip Mfg Analytical Instr Mfg Misc Fab Metal Prdts Mfg Printed Circuit Brds Mfg Measure/Control Dvcs

(G-12700)
LOCKHEED MARTIN SIPPICAN INC
7 Barnabas Rd (02738-1421)
PHONE..................................774 553-6282
Michael Balboni, *Manager*
EMP: 40 **Publicly Held**
SIC: 3812 Mfg Search/Navigation Equipment
HQ: Lockheed Martin Sippican, Inc.
7 Barnabas Rd
Marion MA 02738
508 748-3399

(G-12701)
OVTENE INC
11 Sassamon Trl Ste 221 (02738-2121)
P.O. Box 482 (02738-0009)
PHONE..................................617 852-4828
Alberto Tomasini, *CEO*
Sal Giglia, *President*
▼ **EMP:** 40
SQ FT: 2,000

GEOGRAPHIC

SALES: 500K **Privately Held**
SIC: 2671 Mfg Packaging Paper/Film

(G-12702)
POLARIS CONTRACT MFG INC
15 Barnabas Rd (02738-1421)
PHONE..................................508 748-3399
Lisa B Callahan, *President*
Frank Lamir, *Admin Sec*
EMP: 400 **EST:** 2000
SALES (est): 84.4MM **Publicly Held**
WEB: www.sippican.com
SIC: 3812 Mfg Search/Navigation Equipment
HQ: Lockheed Martin Sippican, Inc.
7 Barnabas Rd
Marion MA 02738
508 748-3399

(G-12703)
SIPPI/GSM SUBMA ANTENN JOINT V
7 Barnabas Rd (02738-1421)
PHONE..................................774 553-6218
Derek King, *Buyer*
Joshua Borsari, *Engineer*
Phil Foster, *Software Engr*
Joseph Rappisi,
Thomas L Jarbeau,
▼ **EMP:** 3
SALES (est): 214.3K **Privately Held**
SIC: 3812 Mfg Search/Navigation Equipment

(G-12704)
SIPPICAN WEEK
163 Front St (02738-1526)
PHONE..................................774 553-5250
EMP: 3
SALES (est): 85.5K **Privately Held**
SIC: 2711 Newspapers-Publishing/Printing

(G-12705)
SPERRY SAILS INC
11 Marconi Ln (02738-1445)
P.O. Box 215 (02738-0004)
PHONE..................................508 748-2581
Matthew Sperry, *President*
Stephen C Sperry, *Treasurer*
Joan Wing, *Admin Sec*
◆ **EMP:** 9
SQ FT: 4,000
SALES (est): 1.5MM **Privately Held**
WEB: www.sperrytents.com
SIC: 3732 2394 Boatbuilding/Repairing Mfg Canvas/Related Products

(G-12706)
SPERRY TENTS INC
11 Marconi Ln (02738-1445)
P.O. Box 460, West Wareham (02576-0460)
PHONE..................................508 748-1792
Toll Free:..................................888 -
Tim Sperry, *Manager*
EMP: 3 **Privately Held**
SIC: 2394 Mfg Canvas/Related Products
PA: Sperry Tents Inc
28 Pattersons Brook Rd # 2
West Wareham MA 02576

(G-12707)
TELEDYNE LECROY INC
Teledyne Test Services
513 Mill St (02738-1549)
PHONE..................................508 748-0103
David Thrall, *General Mgr*
Chuck Sturtevant, *Controller*
Roger Masson, *Branch Mgr*
Eric Solla, *Prgrmr*
EMP: 30
SALES (corp-wide): 2.9B **Publicly Held**
WEB: www.teledyne.com
SIC: 3825 Mfg Electrical Measuring Instruments
HQ: Teledyne Lecroy, Inc.
700 Chestnut Ridge Rd
Chestnut Ridge NY 10977
845 425-2000

Marlborough
Middlesex County

(G-12708)
A2Z DENTAL LLC
5 Mount Royal Ave Ste 300 (01752-1900)
PHONE..................................844 442-5587
Daniel Elkin, *President*
EMP: 5 **EST:** 2016
SALES (est): 364.5K **Privately Held**
SIC: 3843 Mfg Dental Equipment/Supplies

(G-12709)
ACME UNITED CORPORATION
Also Called: Diamond Machining Technology
89 Hayes Memorial Dr (01752)
PHONE..................................508 481-5944
Walter C Johnsen, *Branch Mgr*
EMP: 3
SALES (corp-wide): 137.3MM **Publicly Held**
SIC: 3599 Mfg Industrial Machinery
PA: Acme United Corporation
55 Walls Dr Ste 201
Fairfield CT 06824
203 254-6060

(G-12710)
ADCOLE CORPORATION (HQ)
669 Forest St (01752-3067)
PHONE..................................508 485-9100
Peter Hunter, *Ch of Bd*
Jeff Walker, *President*
Stephen Corrado, *Vice Pres*
Cathy King, *Vice Pres*
Thomas K Macdonald, *Vice Pres*
◆ **EMP:** 111 **EST:** 1957
SQ FT: 43,000
SALES (est): 31.5MM
SALES (corp-wide): 33.6MM **Privately Held**
WEB: www.adcole.com
SIC: 3812 3823 Mfg Process Control Instruments Mfg Search/Navigation Equipment
PA: Maryland Adcole Aerospace Llc
2145 Priest Bridge Dr # 15
Crofton MD 21114
410 451-2505

(G-12711)
ALLEGRO MICROSYSTEMS LLC
100 Crowley Dr (01752-1289)
PHONE..................................508 853-5000
Richard Du, *Vice Pres*
Ravi Vig, *VP Mktg*
Ross Eisenbeis, *Marketing Staff*
EMP: 220 **Privately Held**
SIC: 3674 Mfg Semiconductors/Related Devices
HQ: Allegro Microsystems, Llc
955 Perimeter Rd
Manchester NH 03103
603 626-2300

(G-12712)
ANGIODYNAMICS INC
26 Forest St (01752-3068)
PHONE..................................508 658-7990
John Soto, *Owner*
EMP: 13
SALES (corp-wide): 270.6MM **Publicly Held**
SIC: 3841 Mfg Surgical/Medical Instruments
PA: Angiodynamics, Inc.
14 Plaza Dr
Latham NY 12110
518 795-1400

(G-12713)
ANJEN FINISHING
432 Northboro Road Centl (01752-1823)
PHONE..................................508 251-1532
K Scott Wyman, *Principal*
EMP: 8 **EST:** 2011
SALES (est): 809.1K **Privately Held**
SIC: 3479 Coating/Engraving Service

(G-12714)
APAHOUSER INC
40 Hayes Memorial Dr (01752-1830)
PHONE..................................508 786-0309
Glenn Prouty, *President*
EMP: 50
SQ FT: 35,000
SALES (est): 9.9MM **Privately Held**
WEB: www.apahouser.com
SIC: 3444 Mfg Sheet Metalwork

(G-12715)
APB ENTERPRISES INC
Also Called: Minuteman Press
160 Main St (01752-3865)
PHONE..................................508 481-0966
Arie Bregman, *President*
EMP: 4
SQ FT: 1,200
SALES: 375K **Privately Held**
WEB: www.mmanpress1.com
SIC: 2752 2791 2789 Lithographic Commercial Printing Typesetting Services Bookbinding/Related Work

(G-12716)
API ELECTRONICS INC
Also Called: API Technologies Corp
400 Nickerson Rd (01752-4717)
PHONE..................................508 485-6350
Jason Dezwirek, *CEO*
Thomas Mills, *President*
Phillip Dezwirek, *Vice Pres*
EMP: 50
SQ FT: 15,000
SALES (est): 5.1MM **Privately Held**
SIC: 3674 Mfg Semiconductors/Related Devices
PA: Api Technologies Corp.
400 Nickerson Rd Ste 1
Marlborough MA 01752

(G-12717)
API TECHNOLOGIES CORP (PA)
400 Nickerson Rd Ste 1 (01752-4690)
PHONE..................................855 294-3800
Terrence Hahn, *CEO*
Michael Schwarm, *Vice Pres*
Rogelio Olmos, *Engineer*
Eric F Seeton, *CFO*
EMP: 147
SALES (est): 497.9MM **Privately Held**
SIC: 3674 Mfg Semiconductors/Related Devices

(G-12718)
API TECHNOLOGIES CORPORATION
165 Cedar Hill St (01752-3035)
PHONE..................................508 485-0336
Walter Gordon, *Manager*
EMP: 60
SALES (corp-wide): 63.8MM **Privately Held**
WEB: www.spectrummicrowave.com
SIC: 3679 3674 Mfg Electronic Components Mfg Semiconductors/Related Devices
PA: Api Technologies Corporation
1900 W College Ave
State College PA 16801
814 272-2700

(G-12719)
API TECHNOLOGIES CORPORATION
400 Nickerson Rd Ste 1 (01752-4690)
PHONE..................................508 251-6400
Walt Gordon, *Branch Mgr*
EMP: 64
SALES (corp-wide): 63.8MM **Privately Held**
SIC: 3679 3812 Mfg Electronic Components Mfg Search/Navigation Equipment
PA: Api Technologies Corporation
1900 W College Ave
State College PA 16801
814 272-2700

(G-12720)
ASCO POWER TECHNOLOGIES LP
2 Maple St (01752-2905)
PHONE..................................508 624-0466
George Marrino, *Manager*
EMP: 5
SALES (corp-wide): 177.9K **Privately Held**
SIC: 3629 3663 3699 Mfg Electrical Industrial Apparatus Mfg Radio/Tv Communication Equipment Mfg Electrical Equipment/Supplies
HQ: Asco Power Technologies, L.P.
160 Park Ave
Florham Park NJ 07932

(G-12721)
ASPEN COMPRESSOR LLC
Also Called: Aspen Systems
24 Saint Martin Dr Ste 2 (01752-3060)
PHONE..................................508 281-5322
Lee P Kang, *President*
S Ronald Wysk, *VP Bus Dvlpt*
EMP: 23
SALES (corp-wide): 27MM **Privately Held**
SIC: 3585 Mfg Refrigeration/Heating Equipment
HQ: Aspen Compressor, Llc
825 Chappells Dairy Rd
Somerset KY 42503

(G-12722)
ASPEN PRODUCTS GROUP INC
184 Cedar Hill St (01752-3017)
PHONE..................................508 481-5058
Kang P Lee, *President*
Mark Fokema, *Vice Pres*
Larissa Stein, *Accounts Mgr*
EMP: 9
SQ FT: 14,000
SALES: 1.2MM **Privately Held**
WEB: www.aspensystems.com
SIC: 2899 Mfg Chemical Preparations

(G-12723)
ASSAYQUANT TECHNOLOGIES INC
260 Cedar Hill St (01752-3037)
PHONE..................................774 278-3302
Erik Schaefer, *President*
Barbara Imperiali, *Treasurer*
EMP: 3
SALES (est): 180.4K **Privately Held**
SIC: 2899 Mfg Chemical Preparations

(G-12724)
AUTOMATIC SPECIALTIES INC
422 Northboro Rd Central (01752-1895)
PHONE..................................508 481-2370
Joseph H Moineau, *President*
Beverly S Drohan, *Admin Sec*
EMP: 20
SQ FT: 29,000
SALES (est): 5MM **Privately Held**
WEB: www.auspin.com
SIC: 3496 3469 Mfg Misc Fabricated Wire Products Mfg Metal Stampings

(G-12725)
BARBARAS BAKERY INC (DH)
500 Nickerson Rd (01752-4695)
PHONE..................................800 343-0590
Stephen Van Tassel, *CEO*
Ken Wood, *President*
Lorraine Hood, *Vice Pres*
Dave Weber, *Vice Pres*
▲ **EMP:** 40
SQ FT: 50,000
SALES (est): 16.4MM
SALES (corp-wide): 401.7MM **Privately Held**
WEB: www.barbarasbakery.com
SIC: 2096 2052 2064 2043 Mfg Potato Chips/Snacks Mfg Cookies/Crackers Mfg Candy/Confectionery
HQ: Weetabix Limited
Weetabix Mills
Kettering NORTHANTS NN15
153 672-2181

(G-12726)
BIOLUCENT LLC
250 Campus Dr (01752-3020)
PHONE..................................508 263-2900
EMP: 3
SALES (est): 157K
SALES (corp-wide): 3.3B **Publicly Held**
SIC: 3845 3844 Mfg Electromedical Equipment Mfg X-Ray Apparatus/Tubes

▲ = Import ▼=Export
◆ =Import/Export

PA: Hologic, Inc.
250 Campus Dr
Marlborough MA 01752
508 263-2900

(G-12727)
BOSTON SCIENTIFIC CORPORATION (PA)
300 Boston Scientific Way (01752-1291)
PHONE....................................508 683-4000
Michael F Mahoney, *Ch of Bd*
Joseph M Fitzgerald, *President*
Jeff Mirviss, *President*
Jeffrey B Mirviss, *President*
Maulik Nanavaty, *President*
▲ **EMP:** 277
SALES: 9.8B **Publicly Held**
WEB: www.bsci.com
SIC: 3841 3842 3845 Mfg Medical Appliances & Equipment

(G-12728)
BOSTON SCIENTIFIC CORPORATION
100 Boston Scientific Way (01752-1234)
PHONE....................................508 382-0200
Reggie Hartwell, *Regional Mgr*
Frank Thoburn, *Project Mgr*
Ashley Talberg, *Buyer*
Tina King, *Purchasing*
Kristen Hastings, *QC Mgr*
EMP: 285
SALES (corp-wide): 9.8B **Publicly Held**
WEB: www.bsci.com
SIC: 3841 Mfg Surgical/Medical Instruments
PA: Boston Scientific Corporation
300 Boston Scientific Way
Marlborough MA 01752
508 683-4000

(G-12729)
BOSTON SCIENTIFIC INTL CORP
300 Boston Scientific Way (01752-1291)
PHONE....................................508 683-4000
EMP: 3 **EST:** 2017
SALES (est): 117.4K
SALES (corp-wide): 9.8B **Publicly Held**
SIC: 3841 Mfg Surgical/Medical Instruments
PA: Boston Scientific Corporation
300 Boston Scientific Way
Marlborough MA 01752
508 683-4000

(G-12730)
BTL INDUSTRIES INC
362 Elm St (01752-4553)
PHONE....................................866 285-1656
Marcel Besse, *President*
EMP: 150
SALES (est): 1.7MM
SALES (corp-wide): 8.7K **Privately Held**
SIC: 3841 Mfg Surgical/Medical Instruments
PA: Btl Medical Technologies S.R.O.
Evropska 423/178
Praha 6 - Vokovice
270 001-600

(G-12731)
BWT PHARMA & BIOTECH INC
417 South St Ste 5 (01752-3192)
PHONE....................................508 485-4291
Cay Mansson, *Principal*
Robert Vecchione, *Vice Pres*
EMP: 22
SQ FT: 10,500
SALES: 7.7MM
SALES (corp-wide): 355.8K **Privately Held**
SIC: 2834 Mfg Industrial Water Purification Systems
HQ: Bwt Pharma & Biotech Limited
Unit 2a
Ashbourne

(G-12732)
CABINET WAREHOUSE LLC (PA)
636 Boston Post Rd E (01752-3724)
PHONE....................................508 281-2077
Phillip Stcyr, *Principal*
▲ **EMP:** 3 **EST:** 2009
SALES (est): 280.3K **Privately Held**
SIC: 2434 Mfg Wood Kitchen Cabinets

(G-12733)
CAMIANT INC
200 Nickerson Rd Ste 200 # 200 (01752-4635)
PHONE....................................508 486-9996
Steve Slattery, *President*
Ed Delaney, *Vice Pres*
Susie Kim Riley, *CTO*
EMP: 65
SQ FT: 25,000
SALES (est): 10MM **Privately Held**
WEB: www.camiant.com
SIC: 3577 Mfg Computer Peripheral Equipment

(G-12734)
CANDELA CORPORATION (DH)
Also Called: Syneron Candela
251 Locke Dr (01752-7220)
PHONE....................................508 969-1837
Louis P Scafuri, *President*
Robert Ruck, *Exec VP*
Annemarie Silvia, *Mfg Staff*
Ety Hovav, *Purch Mgr*
Lou Amberg, *Engineer*
▲ **EMP:** 150 **EST:** 1970
SALES (est): 93.1MM **Privately Held**
WEB: www.candelalaser.com
SIC: 3845 Mfg Electromedical Equipment

(G-12735)
CARDIOFOCUS INC
500 Nicksn Rd Ste 500200 (01752)
PHONE....................................508 658-7200
Stephen Sagon, *CEO*
Burke T Barrett, *Vice Pres*
Jerry Melsky, *Vice Pres*
Mark Olsen, *Vice Pres*
Anjie Roldan, *Vice Pres*
EMP: 25 **EST:** 1999
SQ FT: 13,000
SALES (est): 6.6MM **Privately Held**
SIC: 3845 3841 Mfg Electromedical Equipment Mfg Surgical/Medical Instruments

(G-12736)
CAVIUM INC
600 Nickerson Rd (01752-4661)
PHONE....................................508 357-4111
Brian Amick, *Vice Pres*
Brian Folsom, *Engineer*
David King, *Engineer*
Curtis Miller, *Engineer*
Madhav Rajan, *Branch Mgr*
EMP: 18 **Privately Held**
WEB: www.cavium.com
SIC: 3674 Mfg Semiconductors/Related Devices
HQ: Cavium, Llc
5488 Marvell Ln
Santa Clara CA 95054

(G-12737)
CEQUR CORPORATION
734 Forest St Ste 100 (01752-3032)
PHONE....................................508 486-0010
James Peterson, *CEO*
Douglas Lawrence, *CEO*
Mike Hassman, *President*
Eric Milledge, *Chairman*
Mads Dall, *Exec VP*
EMP: 20
SQ FT: 12,500
SALES (est): 5.3MM
SALES (corp-wide): 698.7K **Privately Held**
SIC: 2833 Mfg Medicinals & Botanicals Products
PA: Cequr Sa
Ebenaustrasse 10
Horw LU 6048

(G-12738)
CMT FILTERS INC
Also Called: API Technologies
400 Nickerson Rd (01752-4717)
PHONE....................................508 258-6400
Randall Wilson, *President*
Michael Sexton, *Vice Pres*
EMP: 50
SALES (est): 6.3MM **Privately Held**
WEB: www.cmtfilters.com
SIC: 3679 Mfg Electronic Components
PA: Api Technologies Corp.
400 Nickerson Rd Ste 1
Marlborough MA 01752

(G-12739)
CONNORS DESIGN LTD
257 Simarano Dr Ste 105 (01752-3086)
PHONE....................................508 481-1930
Daniel Connors, *President*
Sandra Connors, *Vice Pres*
EMP: 7
SQ FT: 10,000
SALES (est): 460K **Privately Held**
WEB: www.fmdesign.com
SIC: 2511 Mfg Furniture

(G-12740)
CONSOLIDATED CONT HOLDINGS LLC
Also Called: Marlboro Plastics
1 Dangelo Dr (01752-3066)
PHONE....................................508 485-2109
Chuck Cassano, *Branch Mgr*
EMP: 15
SALES (corp-wide): 1.6B **Privately Held**
SIC: 3089 Mfg Plastic Containers
PA: Consolidated Container Holdings Llc
2500 Windy Ridge Pkwy Se
Atlanta GA 30339
678 742-4600

(G-12741)
CORERO NETWORK SECURITY INC
293 Boston Post Rd W # 310 (01752-4825)
PHONE....................................978 212-1500
Ashley Stephenson, *CEO*
Leah Callahan, *General Mgr*
Dave Larson, *COO*
Joe Branca, *Vice Pres*
Michael Connolly, *Vice Pres*
▲ **EMP:** 46
SALES (est): 14MM **Privately Held**
WEB: www.toplayer.com
SIC: 3577 Mfg Computer Peripheral Equipment

(G-12742)
COSMAN MEDICAL LLC
300 Boston Scientific Way (01752-1291)
PHONE....................................781 272-6561
Michael Alan Arnold, *President*
Eric R Cosman Sr, *Principal*
EMP: 88
SALES (est): 14.2MM
SALES (corp-wide): 9.8B **Publicly Held**
SIC: 3845 8011 Manufactures Electromedical Equipment Provides Neurosurgery Services
HQ: Boston Scientific Neuromodulation Corporation
25155 Rye Canyon Loop
Valencia CA 91355

(G-12743)
CREDIT CARD SUPPLIES CORP
Also Called: Sylvesters Sales
105 Bartlett St (01752-3025)
PHONE....................................508 485-4230
Patrick T Daley, *President*
Frederick M Daley III, *Treasurer*
Kelly A Barringer, *Admin Sec*
▲ **EMP:** 15
SQ FT: 10,000
SALES (est): 1.9MM **Privately Held**
WEB: www.laminationplates.com
SIC: 3443 Mfg Fabricated Plate Work

(G-12744)
CYTYC CORPORATION (HQ)
250 Campus Dr (01752-3020)
PHONE....................................508 263-2900
Patrick Sullivan, *Ch of Bd*
Robert A Cascella, *President*
Daniel J Levangie, *Exec VP*
A Meszner Eltrich, *Senior VP*
David P Harding, *Senior VP*
▲ **EMP:** 457
SQ FT: 97,000
SALES (est): 172MM
SALES (corp-wide): 3.3B **Publicly Held**
WEB: www.cytyc.com
SIC: 3841 Mfg Surgical/Medical Instruments
PA: Hologic, Inc.
250 Campus Dr
Marlborough MA 01752
508 263-2900

(G-12745)
CYTYC CORPORATION
445 Simarano Dr (01752-3073)
PHONE....................................508 303-4746
Angela Trabucco, *Administration*
EMP: 109
SALES (corp-wide): 3.3B **Publicly Held**
WEB: www.cytyc.com
SIC: 3841 Mfg Surgical/Medical Instruments
HQ: Cytyc Corporation
250 Campus Dr
Marlborough MA 01752
508 263-2900

(G-12746)
CYTYC SURGICAL PRODUCTS LLC
250 Campus Dr (01752-3020)
PHONE....................................508 263-2900
John Griffin, *President*
Patricia K Dolan, *Vice Pres*
Sarah Rana, *Vice Pres*
EMP: 58
SQ FT: 185,740
SALES: 930K
SALES (corp-wide): 3.3B **Publicly Held**
WEB: www.hologic.com
SIC: 3844 Mfg X-Ray Apparatus/Tubes
PA: Hologic, Inc.
250 Campus Dr
Marlborough MA 01752
508 263-2900

(G-12747)
DAV-TECH PLATING INC
40 Cedar Hill St (01752-3006)
P.O. Box 836 (01752-0836)
PHONE....................................508 485-8472
David C Mason Jr, *President*
Leanna Goine, *Principal*
Leeanna L Goyne, *Vice Pres*
Bob Redden, *Prdtn Mgr*
Tony D'Amato, *Engineer*
EMP: 50
SQ FT: 30,000
SALES (est): 7.1MM **Privately Held**
WEB: www.dav-techplatinginc.com
SIC: 3471 Plating/Polishing Service

(G-12748)
DMT EXPORT INC
85 Hayes Memorial Dr # 1 (01752-1892)
PHONE....................................508 481-5944
Christine Miller, *President*
EMP: 45
SALES (est): 3.1MM
SALES (corp-wide): 137.3MM **Publicly Held**
WEB: www.dmtsharp.com
SIC: 3545 Machine Tool Accessories
HQ: Vogel Capital, Inc.
85 Hayes Memorial Dr
Marlborough MA 01752
508 481-5944

(G-12749)
DOCUSERVE INC
72 Cedar Hill St Ste B (01752-3040)
PHONE....................................508 786-5820
Kevin C Flanigan, *President*
Sylvester Campagna, *Director*
Pam Foley, *Director*
EMP: 24
SQ FT: 16,000
SALES (est): 4.4MM **Privately Held**
WEB: www.docuserve.com
SIC: 2759 2752 Commercial Printing Lithographic Commercial Printing

(G-12750)
DOW CHEMICAL COMPANY
455 Forest St (01752-3001)
PHONE....................................508 229-7676
Joon Bae, *Marketing Staff*
Pierre Brondeau, *Branch Mgr*

EMP: 25
SALES (corp-wide): 61B **Publicly Held**
SIC: 2819 2821 Mfg Industrial Inorganic Chemicals Mfg Plastic Materials/Resins
HQ: The Dow Chemical Company
2211 H H Dow Way
Midland MI 48642
989 636-1000

(G-12751)
DUPLIFORM CASTING CO
158 Winter St (01752-4562)
PHONE....508 485-9333
George Pacific Jr, *Owner*
EMP: 6 **EST:** 1981
SALES: 400K **Privately Held**
SIC: 3369 Nonferrous Metal Foundry

(G-12752)
EGOH PACKAGING INC
Also Called: Designpak
175 Maple St (01752-3272)
PHONE....508 460-6683
Gary Hajduk, *President*
Mark Fields, *Vice Pres*
EMP: 30
SQ FT: 100,000
SALES (est): 3.9MM **Privately Held**
WEB: www.designpak.com
SIC: 2652 Mfg Setup Paperboard Boxes

(G-12753)
ERNEST JOHNSON
Also Called: Ernest Johnson Co
146 Phelps St (01752-2732)
P.O. Box 270 (01752-0270)
PHONE....508 259-6727
Ernest Johnson, *Owner*
EMP: 8
SALES: 500K **Privately Held**
SIC: 3441 2821 Mfg Rep

(G-12754)
EXPERTEK SYSTEMS INC
100 Locke Dr Ste 4 (01752-7235)
PHONE....508 624-0006
Kenneth P Mostello, *President*
Paul F Sorrento, *Vice Pres*
Michelle Maglaty, *CFO*
Tucker Mac Gregor, *Manager*
Richard Haskell, *Info Tech Dir*
EMP: 15
SQ FT: 6,000
SALES: 5MM **Privately Held**
WEB: www.expertek.com
SIC: 7372 7371 7379 Prepackaged Software Services Custom Computer Programing Computer Related Services

(G-12755)
FOR ASTELLAS INSTITUTE (HQ)
33 Locke Dr (01752-1167)
PHONE....508 756-1212
Paul Wotton, *President*
Paul K Wotton, *President*
Jeffrey Zeldman, *Publisher*
Edward Myles, *COO*
Kendal Rivard, *Safety Mgr*
EMP: 38
SQ FT: 30,000
SALES (est): 231.1K **Privately Held**
WEB: www.advancedcelltechnology.com
SIC: 2834 Manufactures Pharmaceutical Preparations

(G-12756)
FORTIMING CORPORATION
209 Main St (01752-3850)
PHONE....508 281-5980
James Wang, *Owner*
EMP: 5
SALES (est): 554.9K **Privately Held**
SIC: 3675 Mfg Quartz Crystals & Clock Oscillators For Electronic Application

(G-12757)
FRESENIUS USA INC
Also Called: National Medical Care-Npd
360 Cedar Hill St (01752-4175)
PHONE....508 460-1150
EMP: 40
SALES (corp-wide): 18.3B **Privately Held**
SIC: 2834 3841 3842 2836 Mfg Pharmaceutical Preps Mfg Surgical/Med Instr Mfg Surgical Appliances Mfg Biological Products
HQ: Fresenius Usa, Inc.
4040 Nelson Ave
Concord CA 94520
925 288-4218

(G-12758)
GATEHOUSE MEDIA MASS I INC
Also Called: Southborough Villager
40 Mechanic St (01752-4425)
PHONE....508 626-3859
Glenda Hazard, *Manager*
EMP: 12
SALES (corp-wide): 1.5B **Publicly Held**
SIC: 2711 Newspapers-Publishing/Printing
HQ: Gatehouse Media Massachusetts I, Inc.
48 Dunham Rd
Beverly MA 01915
585 598-0030

(G-12759)
GE HEALTHCARE INC (DH)
Also Called: GE Healthcare Life Sciences
100 Results Way (01752-3078)
P.O. Box 982357, El Paso TX (79998-2357)
PHONE....800 526-3593
Kieran Murphy, *President*
Mikel Blanchard, *Engineer*
Michael Hughes, *Engineer*
Jianhong Jin, *Engineer*
Ali Mihankhah, *Engineer*
▲ **EMP:** 340
SALES (est): 769.6MM
SALES (corp-wide): 121.6B **Publicly Held**
SIC: 2833 5122 Mfg Medicinal/Botanical Products Whol Drugs/Sundries
HQ: Ge Healthcare Limited
Pollards Wood
Chalfont St Giles BUCKS HP8 4
149 454-4000

(G-12760)
GEMINI SIGN COMPANY INC
128 S Bolton St (01752-2889)
PHONE....508 485-3343
Mark E Evangelous, *President*
Matthew Evangelous, *Vice Pres*
◆ **EMP:** 6
SQ FT: 3,500
SALES (est): 780.3K **Privately Held**
SIC: 3993 7389 Mfg Signs/Advertising Specialties Business Services

(G-12761)
GLOBAL LF SCNCES SLTONS USA LL
Also Called: GE Healthcare Life Sciences
170 Locke Dr (01752-7217)
PHONE....508 480-9235
Joseph M Hogan, *CEO*
Douglas Knight, *Project Mgr*
Joel Carrigan, *Engineer*
EMP: 100
SALES (corp-wide): 121.6B **Publicly Held**
SIC: 2836 Whol Drugs/Sundries
HQ: Global Life Sciences Solutions Usa Llc
100 Results Way
Marlborough MA 01752
800 526-3593

(G-12762)
GOTHAM INK OF NEW ENGLAND INC
Also Called: Gotham Ink In Color
255 E Main St (01752-2631)
PHONE....508 485-7911
Paul Freitas, *Branch Mgr*
EMP: 8
SALES (corp-wide): 151.6MM **Privately Held**
SIC: 2893 Mfg Printing Ink
HQ: Gotham Ink Of New England Inc
100 North St
Teterboro NJ 07608
201 478-5600

(G-12763)
GRANITE RELIABLE POWER LLC
200 Donald Lynch Blvd # 300 (01752-4816)
PHONE....508 251-7650
Scot Arthur,
EMP: 3
SALES (est): 297.9K **Privately Held**
SIC: 3825 Mfg Electrical Measuring Instruments

(G-12764)
GREENBRIER GAMES LLP
12 Bicknell St (01752-4102)
PHONE....978 618-8442
Jeff Gracia,
EMP: 9
SALES (est): 865.3K **Privately Held**
SIC: 3944 7389 Mfg Games/Toys Business Services At Non-Commercial Site

(G-12765)
GREGORY ENGINEERING CORP
Also Called: Sylvester Products Division
105 Bartlett St (01752-3025)
P.O. Box 22 (01752-0022)
PHONE....508 481-0480
Frederick Daley Jr, *President*
Frederick Daley III, *Treasurer*
EMP: 18
SQ FT: 10,000
SALES (est): 2.4MM **Privately Held**
SIC: 3443 Mfg Fabricated Plate Work

(G-12766)
GUIDANT CORPORATION
300 Boston Scientific Way (01752-1291)
PHONE....508 683-4000
Michael F Mahoney, *CEO*
Michael Mahoney, *CEO*
Paul Rotzien, *Database Admin*
EMP: 10800 **EST:** 1994
SALES (est): 228.8MM
SALES (corp-wide): 9.8B **Publicly Held**
SIC: 3841 Mfg Surgical/Medical Instruments
PA: Boston Scientific Corporation
300 Boston Scientific Way
Marlborough MA 01752
508 683-4000

(G-12767)
HELIXBIND INC
181 Cedar Hill St Ste 3 (01752-3057)
PHONE....508 460-1028
Alon Singer, *President*
EMP: 11
SALES (est): 154.9K **Privately Held**
SIC: 2836 8731 Mfg Biological Products Commercial Physical Research

(G-12768)
HOLLAND WOODWORKING INC
666 Brigham St (01752-3139)
PHONE....508 481-2990
Richard K Holland, *President*
EMP: 4
SQ FT: 8,000
SALES: 400K **Privately Held**
SIC: 2434 1799 Mfg & Installs Wood Kitchen Cabinets

(G-12769)
HOLOGIC INC
250 Campus Dr (01752-3020)
PHONE....508 263-2900
Mike Hoffa, *Vice Pres*
EMP: 195
SALES (corp-wide): 3.3B **Publicly Held**
SIC: 3844 3841 3845 Mfg X-Ray Apparatus/Tube Mfg Surgical/Med Instr Mfg Electromedical Equip
PA: Hologic, Inc.
250 Campus Dr
Marlborough MA 01752
508 263-2900

(G-12770)
HOLOGIC INC
445 Simarano Dr (01752-3073)
PHONE....508 263-2900
Donna Kempskie, *Branch Mgr*
EMP: 195
SALES (corp-wide): 3.3B **Publicly Held**
SIC: 3844 Mfg X-Ray Apparatus/Tubes
PA: Hologic, Inc.
250 Campus Dr
Marlborough MA 01752
508 263-2900

(G-12771)
HOLOGIC INC (PA)
250 Campus Dr (01752-3020)
PHONE....508 263-2900
Stephen P Macmillan, *Ch of Bd*
Allison P Bebo, *Senior VP*
Karleen M Oberton, *CFO*
Jack McCrorey, *Program Mgr*
John M Griffin, *General Counsel*
◆ **EMP:** 224
SQ FT: 216,000
SALES: 3.3B **Publicly Held**
WEB: www.hologic.com
SIC: 3845 3844 3841 Mfg Medical Diagnostic And Medical Imaging Equipment

(G-12772)
HOLOGRAPHIX LLC
140 Locke Dr Ste A (01752-7206)
PHONE....978 562-4474
David Rowe, *President*
David Millet, *Chairman*
Jason Volk, *Engineer*
Jesse Roy, *Program Mgr*
Donna Rowe, *Admin Sec*
EMP: 10
SQ FT: 8,300
SALES: 1.6MM **Privately Held**
WEB: www.holographix.com
SIC: 3827 Mfg Optical Instruments/Lenses

(G-12773)
HONLE UV AMERICA INC
261 Cedar Hill St Ste 5 (01752-3056)
PHONE....508 229-7774
James B McCusker, *President*
Nathan Ciara, *Engineer*
John Stout, *CFO*
John A Stout, *Treasurer*
Lynn Chevalier, *Marketing Mgr*
EMP: 7
SQ FT: 6,500
SALES (est): 5MM **Privately Held**
WEB: www.honleuv.com
SIC: 3826 Sale And Service Of Ultraviolet Drying Systems

(G-12774)
HOSHIZAKI AMERICA INC
360 Cedar Hill St (01752-4175)
PHONE....508 251-7060
EMP: 190 **Privately Held**
SIC: 3585 Mfg Refrigeration/Heating Equipment
HQ: Hoshizaki America, Inc.
618 Highway 74 S
Peachtree City GA 30269
770 487-2331

(G-12775)
HOTTINGER BLDWIN MSREMENTS INC (DH)
Also Called: H B M
19 Bartlett St (01752-3014)
PHONE....508 624-4500
Kevin Coffey, *President*
Mary T Hall, *Finance*
Mary Hall, *Admin Sec*
▲ **EMP:** 98
SQ FT: 45,000
SALES (est): 16.9MM
SALES (corp-wide): 2.1B **Privately Held**
WEB: www.hbm.com
SIC: 3679 7371 Mfg Electronic Components Custom Computer Programing
HQ: Spectris Inc.
117 Flanders Rd
Westborough MA 01581
508 768-6400

(G-12776)
INGERSOLL-RAND COMPANY
362 Elm St (01752-4553)
PHONE....508 573-1524
EMP: 9 **Privately Held**
SIC: 3131 Mfg Footwear Cut Stock
HQ: Ingersoll-Rand Company
800 Beaty St Ste B
Davidson NC 28036
704 655-4000

(G-12777)
INTEGRATED DYNAMIC METALS CORP
66 Brigham St Unit A (01752-3137)
PHONE....................................508 624-7271
Remi Doiron, *President*
Ray Richard, *Business Mgr*
Jim McNamara, *Vice Pres*
EMP: 12
SQ FT: 20,000
SALES (est): 2MM **Privately Held**
SIC: 3444 Mfg Sheet Metalwork

(G-12778)
IPG PHOTONICS CORPORATION
377 Simarano Dr Ste 302 (01752-3087)
PHONE....................................508 229-2130
EMP: 12
SALES (corp-wide): 1.4B **Publicly Held**
SIC: 3699 Mfg Electrical Equipment/Supplies
PA: Ipg Photonics Corporation
50 Old Webster Rd
Oxford MA 01540
508 373-1100

(G-12779)
IPG PHOTONICS CORPORATION
259 Cedar Hill St (01752-3004)
PHONE....................................508 506-2812
EMP: 13
SALES (corp-wide): 1.4B **Publicly Held**
SIC: 3699 Mfg Electrical Equipment/Supplies
PA: Ipg Photonics Corporation
50 Old Webster Rd
Oxford MA 01540
508 373-1100

(G-12780)
J&J MACHINE COMPANY INC
66b Brigham St (01752-3137)
P.O. Box 702 (01752-0702)
PHONE....................................508 481-8166
Devin Brown, *President*
Eric Johnson, *Production*
EMP: 10
SQ FT: 11,000
SALES (est): 1.8MM **Privately Held**
SIC: 3599 Mfg Industrial Machinery

(G-12781)
JORDAN ENTERPRISES INC
Also Called: Super Dup'r Instant Printing
40 Hudson St Ste B (01752-1266)
PHONE....................................508 481-2948
Robert J Jordan, *President*
Jennifer R Jordan, *Vice Pres*
Joanne Jordan, *Clerk*
EMP: 10 **EST:** 1970
SQ FT: 6,000
SALES (est): 1.3MM **Privately Held**
WEB: www.sdvisualimages.com
SIC: 2752 Lithographic Commercial Printing

(G-12782)
KENS FOODS INC (PA)
1 Dangelo Dr (01752-3066)
P.O. Box 849 (01752-0849)
PHONE....................................508 229-1100
Frank A Crowley III, *President*
Wes Little, *Regional Mgr*
Dan Pagel, *Regional Mgr*
Bob Merchant, *COO*
Brian L Crowley, *Vice Pres*
◆ **EMP:** 428 **EST:** 1958
SQ FT: 340,000
SALES (est): 295.2MM **Privately Held**
WEB: www.kensfoods.com
SIC: 2033 Mfg Canned Fruits/Vegetables

(G-12783)
KNM HOLDINGS LLC
Also Called: John Deere Authorized Dealer
410 Forest St Ste 3 (01752-4172)
PHONE....................................508 229-1400
Michael Kingsley,
Kenneth A Rapoport,
EMP: 8
SQ FT: 2,000
SALES (est): 2.2MM **Privately Held**
SIC: 3511 5082 Mfg Turbines/Generator Sets Whol Construction/Mining Equipment

(G-12784)
KTRON INC
90 Bartlett St (01752-3013)
PHONE....................................508 229-0919
Barry Kittredge, *President*
Jack Blease, *General Mgr*
Daren Kittredge, *Vice Pres*
EMP: 40
SQ FT: 35,500
SALES (est): 8.7MM **Privately Held**
WEB: www.ktron.net
SIC: 3549 Mfg Metalworking Machinery

(G-12785)
KUBOTEK USA INC
2 Mount Royal Ave Ste 500 (01752-1960)
PHONE....................................508 229-2020
Naotake Kakishita, *President*
Mark Parent, *COO*
Takeo Fujitani, *Senior VP*
Dr Paul Stallings, *Vice Pres*
John Reis, *Manager*
EMP: 39
SQ FT: 10,000
SALES (est): 6.4MM **Privately Held**
WEB: www.kubotekusa.com
SIC: 7372 7373 Prepackaged Software Services Computer Systems Design
PA: Kubotek Corporation
4-3-36, Nakanoshima, Kita-Ku
Osaka OSK 530-0

(G-12786)
LINDE GAS NORTH AMERICA LLC
Also Called: Lifegas
50 Dangelo Dr Ste 1 (01752-3097)
PHONE....................................508 229-8118
Don Bongarzone, *Branch Mgr*
EMP: 19 **Privately Held**
SIC: 2813 Mfg Nitrogen/ Oxygen
HQ: Linde Gas North America Llc
200 Smrst Corp Blvd # 7000
Bridgewater NJ 08807

(G-12787)
LINMEL ASSOCIATES INC
Also Called: Sir Speedy
160 Main St (01752-3865)
PHONE....................................508 481-6699
Steven Hitner, *President*
EMP: 10
SQ FT: 4,000
SALES: 1.2MM **Privately Held**
WEB: www.metrowestprinting.com
SIC: 2752 2796 2791 2789 Lithographic Coml Print Platemaking Services Typesetting Services Bookbinding/Related Work

(G-12788)
LOCKHEED MARTIN CORPORATION
5 Mount Royal Ave (01752-1981)
PHONE....................................508 460-0086
EMP: 435 **Publicly Held**
SIC: 3812 Mfg Search/Navigation Equipment
PA: Lockheed Martin Corporation
6801 Rockledge Dr
Bethesda MD 20817

(G-12789)
MAGNETIKA EAST LTD
34 Saint Martin Dr Ste 11 (01752-3021)
PHONE....................................508 485-7555
Basil Caloyeras, *Partner*
William Hubbell, *General Mgr*
Carol Gass, *Purch Mgr*
EMP: 13
SQ FT: 5,000
SALES: 2.2MM **Privately Held**
SIC: 3612 Mfg Transformers

(G-12790)
MARBOROUGH ENTERPRISE
40 Mechanic St (01752-4425)
PHONE....................................508 485-5200
Theresa Float, *Exec VP*
EMP: 3
SALES (est): 98.2K **Privately Held**
SIC: 2711 Newspapers-Publishing/Printing

(G-12791)
MARLBOROUGH FOUNDRY INC
555 Maple St (01752-3268)
PHONE....................................508 485-2848
Robert L Nye, *President*
Joyce L Nye-Taylor, *Vice Pres*
Joyce Nye, *CFO*
EMP: 21 **EST:** 1954
SQ FT: 44,000
SALES (est): 4.7MM **Privately Held**
WEB: www.marlboroughfoundry.com
SIC: 3365 Aluminum Foundry

(G-12792)
MASON INDUSTRIES INC
40 Cedar Hill St (01752-3006)
P.O. Box 836 (01752-0836)
PHONE....................................508 485-8494
David C Mason, *President*
Linda Mason, *Treasurer*
EMP: 4
SQ FT: 30,000
SALES (est): 373.1K **Privately Held**
SIC: 3559 Manufacturers Chemical Kilns

(G-12793)
MASSACHUSETTS CONTAINER CORP
300 Cedar Hill St (01752-3036)
PHONE....................................508 481-1100
Lawrence Perkins, *President*
Louis Cerruzi, *Vice Pres*
Harry Perkins, *Vice Pres*
▲ **EMP:** 114 **EST:** 1963
SALES (est): 23.2MM
SALES (corp-wide): 121.1MM **Privately Held**
WEB: www.massrestaurantassoc.org
SIC: 2653 Mfg Corrugated/Solid Fiber Boxes
PA: Connecticut Container Corp.
455 Sackett Point Rd
North Haven CT 06473
203 248-2161

(G-12794)
MICHAEL MONTEIRO
Also Called: Monteiro Machine Company
667 Farm Rd Ste 1 (01752-7903)
PHONE....................................508 481-1881
Michael Monteiro, *Owner*
EMP: 3
SQ FT: 6,000
SALES (est): 250K **Privately Held**
SIC: 3599 Mfg Industrial Machinery

(G-12795)
MORAIS MARIZETE
Also Called: Chiero Sabor Restaurant
416 Boston Post Rd E # 3 (01752-3605)
PHONE....................................508 460-8200
EMP: 4 **EST:** 2008
SALES (est): 140K **Privately Held**
SIC: 2051 Mfg Bread/Related Products

(G-12796)
MOTOROLA MOBILITY LLC
111 Locke Dr Ste 3 (01752-7236)
PHONE....................................847 523-5000
Kevin Sullivan, *Branch Mgr*
EMP: 58 **Privately Held**
WEB: www.motorola.com
SIC: 3663 Mfg Communication Equipment
HQ: Motorola Mobility Llc
222 Mdse Mart Plz # 1800
Chicago IL 60654

(G-12797)
NORDSON MED DESIGN & DEV INC (HQ)
Also Called: Vention Medical
261 Cedar Hill St Ste 1 (01752-3056)
PHONE....................................508 481-6233
Dan Croteau, *CEO*
Randy Beyreis, *President*
Alan Hershey, *President*
Katrina Boynton, *Engineer*
Steve Evans, *Design Engr*
EMP: 22
SQ FT: 14,000
SALES (est): 6.1MM
SALES (corp-wide): 2.2B **Publicly Held**
WEB: www.tdcmedical.com
SIC: 3841 Mfg Surgical/Medical Instruments
PA: Nordson Corporation
28601 Clemens Rd
Westlake OH 44145
440 892-1580

(G-12798)
NORTHEAST BUILDING PRODUCTS
362 Elm St (01752-4553)
PHONE....................................508 786-5600
John Consoletti, *Principal*
EMP: 3
SALES (est): 233.7K **Privately Held**
SIC: 2421 Sawmill/Planing Mill

(G-12799)
O/K MACHINERY CORPORATION
73 Bartlett St (01752-3071)
PHONE....................................508 303-8286
Owen Kellett, *President*
EMP: 40
SQ FT: 25,000
SALES: 2MM **Privately Held**
SIC: 3496 3565 Mfg Misc Fabricated Wire Products Mfg Packaging Machinery

(G-12800)
OK DURABLE PACKAGING INC
73 Bartlett St (01752-3071)
PHONE....................................508 303-8067
Adam Kwiek, *President*
EMP: 17
SALES (est): 2.3MM **Privately Held**
SIC: 2671 Mfg Misc Products

(G-12801)
OMTEC CORP
Also Called: Omtec Ball Transfers
181 Liberty St (01752-4333)
PHONE....................................508 481-3322
Susan Masciarelli, *President*
Camillo Masciarelli, *President*
Tina Turner, *Administration*
▲ **EMP:** 13
SQ FT: 8,000
SALES (est): 3.1MM **Privately Held**
WEB: www.omtec.com
SIC: 3535 5084 Mfg Conveyors/Equipment Whol Industrial Equipment

(G-12802)
ON-SITE ANALYSIS INC
Also Called: Luvetrak
72 Cedar Hill St (01752-3006)
PHONE....................................508 460-7778
EMP: 20
SALES (corp-wide): 54.1MM **Privately Held**
SIC: 1389 Oil/Gas Field Services
HQ: On-Site Analysis, Inc.
1 Executive Dr Ste 101
Chelmsford MA 01824
561 775-5756

(G-12803)
OPTOS INC
Also Called: Optos North America
500 Nickerson Rd Ste 201 (01752-4637)
PHONE....................................508 787-1400
Stephane Sallmard, *CEO*
Anne Cairns, *Vice Pres*
Bryan Farrell, *Vice Pres*
Stevens Mark, *Vice Pres*
Joe Phelan, *Vice Pres*
▲ **EMP:** 85
SQ FT: 3,800
SALES (est): 38MM **Privately Held**
WEB: www.optos.com
SIC: 3827 Mfg Optical Instruments/Lenses
HQ: Optos Public Limited Company
Queensferry House, Carnegie Business Campus
Inverkeithing KY11
138 384-3300

(G-12804)
OXFORD IMMUNOTEC INC (DH)
Also Called: Oxford Diagnostic Laboratories
700 Nickerson Rd Ste 200 (01752-4699)
PHONE....................................508 481-4648
Peter Wrighton Smith, *CEO*

GEOGRAPHIC

Richard Sandberg, *Ch of Bd*
Jeff R Schroeder, *President*
Simon Turner, *Corp Secy*
Stefan Linn, *COO*
EMP: 75 **EST:** 2008
SQ FT: 7,800
SALES (est): 19.9MM
SALES (corp-wide): 105.1MM **Privately Held**
SIC: 2835 Manufactures Diagnostic Substances
HQ: Oxford Immunotec Limited
94c Innovation Drive
Abingdon OXON OX14
123 544-2780

(G-12805)
OXFORD IMMUNOTEC USA INC
700 Nickerson Rd Ste 200 (01752-4699)
PHONE..................................833 682-6933
Peter Wrighton-Smith, *CEO*
Stefan Linn, *COO*
Richard Altieri, *CFO*
EMP: 90
SALES: 22MM **Privately Held**
SIC: 3841 Mfg Surgical/Medical Instruments

(G-12806)
PHARMA MODELS LLC
257 Simarano Dr (01752-3070)
PHONE..................................617 306-2281
EMP: 6 **EST:** 2013
SALES (est): 462K **Privately Held**
SIC: 2834 Mfg Pharmaceutical Preparations

(G-12807)
PHIO PHARMACEUTICALS CORP (PA)
Also Called: RXI
257 Simarano Dr Ste 101 (01752-3070)
PHONE..................................508 767-3681
Robert J Bitterman, *Ch of Bd*
Gerrit Dispersyn, *President*
Katherine Birdsall, *General Mgr*
James Cardia, *Research*
EMP: 15 **EST:** 2011
SQ FT: 7,581
SALES: 138K **Publicly Held**
SIC: 2834 Mfg Pharmaceutical Preparations

(G-12808)
POINTCARE TECHNOLOGIES INC
19 Brigham St Unit 9 (01752-3182)
PHONE..................................508 281-6925
▲ **EMP:** 20
SALES (est): 3.7MM **Privately Held**
WEB: www.pointcaretechnologies.net
SIC: 3841 Mfg Medical Diagnostic Apparatus

(G-12809)
POLY-CEL INC
53 Brigham St Unit 2 (01752-5128)
P.O. Box 41, Stow (01775-0041)
PHONE..................................508 229-8310
Denise Kelly, *President*
Mike Kelly, *Vice Pres*
EMP: 16
SALES (est): 2.8MM **Privately Held**
SIC: 3089 Mfg Plastic Products

(G-12810)
PROGRAM LLC
289 Elm St Ste 2 (01752-4591)
P.O. Box 1128, Sagamore Beach (02562-1128)
PHONE..................................781 281-0751
Eric Kapitulik,
Sam Cila, *Instructor*
EMP: 6
SALES (est): 282.8K **Privately Held**
SIC: 2836 Mfg Biological Products

(G-12811)
QUADTECH INC
734 Forest St Ste 500 (01752-3008)
PHONE..................................978 461-2100
Philip H Harris, *President*
EMP: 30
SQ FT: 25,000
SALES (est): 4.8MM **Privately Held**
WEB: www.quadtech.com
SIC: 3825 3829 Mfg Electrical Measuring Instruments Mfg Measuring/Controlling Devices
HQ: Baldwin Technology Company, Inc.
8040 Forsyth Blvd
Saint Louis MO 63105
314 726-2152

(G-12812)
RAYTHEON COMPANY
1001 Boston Post Rd E (01752-3770)
PHONE..................................978 440-1000
Brian Morrison, *Principal*
James Ebrookner, *Principal*
J T Galey, *QC Mgr*
Peter Boltruczyk, *Engineer*
Glen Flanigan, *Engineer*
EMP: 300
SQ FT: 30,000
SALES (corp-wide): 27B **Publicly Held**
SIC: 3812 Mfg Search/Navigation Equipment
PA: Raytheon Company
870 Winter St
Waltham MA 02451
781 522-3000

(G-12813)
RAYTHEON COMPANY
1001 Boston Post Rd E (01752-3770)
PHONE..................................310 647-9438
Jerry Powlen, *Vice Pres*
Laurie Logan, *Admin Asst*
EMP: 34
SQ FT: 1,000
SALES (corp-wide): 27B **Publicly Held**
SIC: 3812 3663 3761 Mfg Search/Navgatn Equip Mfg Radio/Tv Comm Equip Mfg Missiles/Space Vehcl
PA: Raytheon Company
870 Winter St
Waltham MA 02451
781 522-3000

(G-12814)
RAYTHEON COMPANY
1001 Boston Post Rd E (01752-3770)
PHONE..................................508 490-1000
Kerry Spangler, *Principal*
Pavan Reddy, *Engineer*
Tom Hirsh, *Electrical Engi*
Frank S Marchilena, *Branch Mgr*
Mark O'Brien, *Software Engr*
EMP: 200
SALES (corp-wide): 27B **Publicly Held**
SIC: 3812 7371 3728 Mfg Search/Navigation Equipment Custom Computer Programming Mfg Aircraft Parts/Equipment
PA: Raytheon Company
870 Winter St
Waltham MA 02451
781 522-3000

(G-12815)
REWALK ROBOTICS INC
200 Donald Lynch Blvd # 100 (01752-4816)
PHONE..................................508 251-1154
Larry J Jasinski, *Principal*
Kathryn Vaughn, *Business Mgr*
Jodi Gricci, *Vice Pres*
David Hexner, *Project Mgr*
Kevin Hershberger, *CFO*
EMP: 8
SALES (est): 1.4MM **Privately Held**
SIC: 3842 Mfg Surgical Appliances/Supplies

(G-12816)
RF1 HOLDING COMPANY (PA)
400 Nickerson Rd (01752-4717)
PHONE..................................855 294-3800
Robert Tavares, *President*
Eric F Seeton, *CFO*
EMP: 13
SALES (est): 401.4MM **Privately Held**
SIC: 3674 6719 Holding Company Manufactures Semiconductors/Related Devices

(G-12817)
RILEY POWER INC
26 Forest St Ste 300 (01752-3068)
PHONE..................................508 852-7100
Edward C Dean, *President*
Anthony A Brandano, *Exec VP*
William J Ferguson Jr, *Senior VP*
W Burke Allred, *Vice Pres*
Donna Anderson, *Vice Pres*
◆ **EMP:** 243 **EST:** 1913
SQ FT: 120,000
SALES: 142.8MM
SALES (corp-wide): 509MM **Privately Held**
SIC: 3569 3443 3433 1711 Mfg General Indstl Mach Mfg Fabricated Plate Wrk Mfg Heat Equip-Nonelec Plumbing/Heat/Ac Contr Mfg Blowers/Fans
HQ: Babcock Power Capital Corporation
222 Rosewood Dr Fl 3
Danvers MA 01923
978 646-3300

(G-12818)
ROCHE TOOL & DIE
170 Maple St (01752-3238)
PHONE..................................508 485-6460
James Roche, *President*
EMP: 6
SQ FT: 2,400
SALES (est): 615.2K **Privately Held**
SIC: 3544 3542 Mfg Dies/Tools/Jigs/Fixtures Mfg Machine Tools-Forming

(G-12819)
ROCKWELL AUTOMATION INC
100 Nickerson Rd Fl 1 (01752-4613)
PHONE..................................508 357-8400
Keith Nosbusch, *Manager*
EMP: 60 **Publicly Held**
SIC: 3625 Mfg Relays/Industrial Controls
PA: Rockwell Automation, Inc.
1201 S 2nd St
Milwaukee WI 53204

(G-12820)
ROHM HAAS ELECTRONIC MTLS LLC (DH)
455 Forest St (01752-3001)
PHONE..................................508 481-7950
Thomas Ermi, *Mng Member*
Terrence Brennan,
Rajiv Gupta,
Joe E Harlan,
Jerome A Peribere,
◆ **EMP:** 750
SALES (est): 257.2MM
SALES (corp-wide): 61B **Publicly Held**
SIC: 2819 2869 Mfg Industrial Inorganic Chemicals Mfg Industrial Organic Chemicals
HQ: The Dow Chemical Company
2211 H H Dow Way
Midland MI 48642
989 636-1000

(G-12821)
ROHM HAAS ELECTRONIC MTLS LLC
455 Forest St (01752-3001)
PHONE..................................978 689-1503
Joseph Reiser, *Branch Mgr*
EMP: 40
SALES (corp-wide): 61B **Publicly Held**
SIC: 2869 Mfg Metalorganics
HQ: Rohm And Haas Electronic Materials Llc
455 Forest St
Marlborough MA 01752
508 481-7950

(G-12822)
ROTATION DYNAMICS CORPORATION
Also Called: Rotadyne
33 Hayes Memorial Dr (01752-1831)
PHONE..................................508 481-0900
Dave Agbay, *Mktg Dir*
Matt Cavic, *Manager*
EMP: 12
SALES (corp-wide): 145.7MM **Privately Held**
SIC: 3555 2796 Mfg Printing Trades Machinery Platemaking Services
PA: Rotation Dynamics Corporation
1101 Windham Pkwy
Romeoville IL 60446
630 769-9255

(G-12823)
SAFETY-KLEEN SYSTEMS INC
50a Brigham St (01752-3137)
P.O. Box B (01752)
PHONE..................................508 481-3116
Nicholas Brickl, *Manager*
EMP: 12
SQ FT: 7,500
SALES (corp-wide): 3.3B **Publicly Held**
SIC: 3559 Mfg Misc Industry Machinery
HQ: Safety-Kleen Systems, Inc.
2600 N Central Expy # 400
Richardson TX 75080
972 265-2000

(G-12824)
SEPATON INC
Also Called: Hitachi Protection Platform
400 Nickerson Rd (01752-4717)
PHONE..................................508 490-7900
Michael R Thompson, *President*
Jerry Chueng, *Partner*
Bob Iacono, *COO*
John Tonnison, *Exec VP*
Paul McDermott, *CFO*
EMP: 87
SALES (est): 12.1MM **Privately Held**
WEB: www.sepaton.com
SIC: 3572 7371 Manufacturing Computer Storage Devices Custom Computer Programming
HQ: Hitachi Vantara Corporation
2535 Augustine Dr
Santa Clara CA 95054
408 970-1000

(G-12825)
SHEAUMANN LASER INC
45 Bartlett St (01752-4171)
PHONE..................................508 970-0600
Jim Hsieh, *CEO*
Frank C Hsieh, *President*
Gary Sousa, *COO*
Tim Shea, *Vice Pres*
Edward N Gadsby Jr, *Admin Sec*
EMP: 5
SALES (est): 1.3MM **Privately Held**
WEB: www.sheaumann.com
SIC: 3674 Whol Professional Equipment

(G-12826)
SIGNALFIRE TELEMETRY INC
140 Lock Dr (01752)
PHONE..................................978 212-2868
Scott Keller, *CEO*
Alfred Hamilton, *President*
▲ **EMP:** 3
SALES (est): 438.4K
SALES (corp-wide): 84.7MM **Privately Held**
SIC: 3823 Manufactures Process Control Instruments
PA: Tasi Holdings, Inc
10100 Progress Way
Harrison OH 45030
513 202-5182

(G-12827)
SPECTRA ANALYSIS INC (PA)
257 Simarano Dr Ste 106 (01752-3070)
PHONE..................................508 281-6232
George J Giansanti Jr, *President*
Cheryl McCarthy, *Controller*
EMP: 10
SALES (est): 1.2MM **Privately Held**
SIC: 3826 Mfg Analytical Instruments

(G-12828)
SPECTRA ANALYSIS INSTRS INC
Also Called: Dani Instruments, Inc.
257 Simarano Dr Ste 106 (01752-3070)
PHONE..................................508 281-6233
George Giansanti Jr, *CEO*
EMP: 10
SQ FT: 3,000
SALES (est): 1.4MM
SALES (corp-wide): 533.7K **Privately Held**
SIC: 3826 Manufacturer Of Solid Phase Ir Spectroscopy Detectors For Gas And Liquid Chromatography
HQ: Verola Srl
Viale Brianza 81
Cologno Monzese MI 20093
022 539-941

(G-12829)
SPIRE METERING TECHNOLOGY LLC
Also Called: Shenitech
249 Cedar Hill St (01752-4174)
PHONE..................................978 263-7100
Richard Centauro, *Sales Mgr*
Chang Shen, *Mng Member*
▲ **EMP:** 14
SALES (est): 2.8MM **Privately Held**
WEB: www.shenitech.com
SIC: 3829 Mfg Measuring/Controlling Devices

(G-12830)
STATIC SOLUTIONS INC (PA)
331 Boston Post Rd E # 12 (01752)
PHONE..................................508 480-0700
Leonard Cohen, *President*
Katrina Cohen, *Treasurer*
▲ **EMP:** 15
SALES (est): 1.8MM **Privately Held**
WEB: www.staticsolutions.com
SIC: 3822 3635 Mfg Environmental Controls Mfg Home Vacuum Cleaners

(G-12831)
SUNDANCE/NEWBRIDGE LLC (HQ)
33 Boston Post Rd W # 440 (01752-1867)
PHONE..................................800 343-8204
George Franzak Jr,
Paul Konowitch,
James Lyons,
EMP: 4
SALES (est): 20MM
SALES (corp-wide): 293.8MM **Privately Held**
SIC: 2731 5192 4832 Books-Publishing/Printing Whol Books/Newspapers Radio Broadcast Station
PA: The Rowman & Littlefield Publishing Group Inc
4501 Forbes Blvd Ste 200
Lanham MD 20706
301 459-3366

(G-12832)
SUNOVION PHARMACEUTICALS INC (DH)
Also Called: Sunovion Respiratory Dev
84 Waterford Dr (01752-7010)
PHONE..................................508 481-6700
Hiroshi Nomura, *CEO*
Charles McLeod, *Business Mgr*
Robert Gregorio, *Exec VP*
Antony Loebel, *Exec VP*
Matthew Dambrosio, *Senior VP*
▲ **EMP:** 2100
SQ FT: 192,600
SALES (est): 680MM **Privately Held**
WEB: www.sunovion.com
SIC: 2834 Mfg Pharmaceutical Preparations

(G-12833)
SUPERIOR PRINTING INK CO INC
255 E Main St (01752-2631)
PHONE..................................508 481-8250
Bryan Campbell, *Manager*
EMP: 28
SQ FT: 500
SALES (corp-wide): 151.6MM **Privately Held**
SIC: 2893 Mfg Printing Ink
PA: Superior Printing Ink Co Inc
100 North St
Teterboro NJ 07608
201 478-5600

(G-12834)
TARGET THERAPEUTICS INC (HQ)
300 Boston Scientific Way (01752-1291)
PHONE..................................508 683-4000
Peter M Nicholas, *Ch of Bd*
Michael Mahoney, *President*
Gary R Bang, *President*
Erik T Engelson, *Senior VP*
Abhi Acharya PHD, *Vice Pres*
EMP: 325
SQ FT: 76,000
SALES: 69.8MM
SALES (corp-wide): 9.8B **Publicly Held**
SIC: 3841 Mfg Surgical Instruments & Apparatus
PA: Boston Scientific Corporation
300 Boston Scientific Way
Marlborough MA 01752
508 683-4000

(G-12835)
TARPON BIOSYSTEMS INC
197 Boston Post Rd W M (01752)
PHONE..................................978 979-4222
Robert A Dishman, *CEO*
Ard A Tijsterman, *Principal*
Lynne Bartkowski Frick, *Vice Pres*
EMP: 7
SALES (est): 795.2K **Privately Held**
SIC: 2834 Mfg Pharmaceutical Preparations

(G-12836)
THIRD WAVE TECHNOLOGIES INC (HQ)
250 Campus Dr (01752-3020)
PHONE..................................608 273-8933
David A Thompson, *Ch of Bd*
Kevin T Conroy, *President*
Ivan D Trifunovich PHD, *Senior VP*
Cindy S Ahn, *Vice Pres*
Lander R Brown, *Vice Pres*
EMP: 37
SQ FT: 68,000
SALES (est): 20.9MM
SALES (corp-wide): 3.3B **Publicly Held**
SIC: 2835 Mfg Diagnostic Substances
PA: Hologic, Inc.
250 Campus Dr
Marlborough MA 01752
508 263-2900

(G-12837)
TOSHIBA AMERICA ELECTRONIC
290 Donald Lynch Blvd # 201 (01752-4705)
PHONE..................................508 481-0034
James R Walker, *Manager*
EMP: 4 **Privately Held**
SIC: 3679 Mfg Electronic Components
HQ: Toshiba America Electronic Components Inc
5231 California Ave
Irvine CA 92617
949 462-7700

(G-12838)
TRIMBLE INC
200 Nickerson Rd Ste 175 (01752-4672)
PHONE..................................508 381-5800
EMP: 8
SALES (corp-wide): 3.1B **Publicly Held**
SIC: 3812 3829 Mfg Search/Navigation Equipment Mfg Measuring/Controlling Devices
PA: Trimble Inc.
935 Stewart Dr
Sunnyvale CA 94085
408 481-8000

(G-12839)
TWENTYFRST CNTURY BCHMCALS INC
Also Called: 21st
260 Cedar Hill St (01752-3037)
PHONE..................................508 303-8222
Jordan Fishman, *President*
Eric Berg, *VP Opers*
Pamela Crowley, *Manager*
William Mello, *Director*
Andrew Doucette, *Technician*
EMP: 20
SQ FT: 8,000
SALES (est): 4.3MM **Privately Held**
SIC: 2836 Mfg Biochemical & Antibodies

(G-12840)
UNIVERSAL WINDOW AND DOOR LLC
303 Mechanic St (01752-4422)
PHONE..................................508 481-2850
Andrew Dudka, *VP Opers*
Robert Houde, *Controller*
Charlotte Broussard, *Mng Member*
▼ **EMP:** 90
SQ FT: 73,000
SALES (est): 12MM **Privately Held**
WEB: www.universalwindow.com
SIC: 3442 Mfg Metal Doors/Sash/Trim

(G-12841)
VALERITAS INC
293 Boston Post Rd W # 330 (01752-4615)
PHONE..................................774 239-2498
Jason Doyle, *Engineer*
Geoff Jenkins, *Branch Mgr*
EMP: 20 **Privately Held**
SIC: 3841 Mfg Surgical/Medical Instruments
PA: Valeritas, Inc.
750 Us Highway 202 # 600
Bridgewater NJ 08807

(G-12842)
VERAX BIOMEDICAL INCORPORATED
148 Bartlett St (01752-3016)
PHONE..................................508 755-7029
James Lousararian, *CEO*
Nancy A Hornbaker, *President*
Yli Vallejo, *Senior VP*
Elizabeth Krodel, *Vice Pres*
Joe Sanders, *Vice Pres*
▲ **EMP:** 19
SALES (est): 4.8MM **Privately Held**
WEB: www.veraxbiomedical.com
SIC: 3841 Mfg Surgical/Medical Instruments

(G-12843)
VETERAN SOFTWARE SOLUTIONS LLC
209 Vega Rd (01752-1680)
PHONE..................................508 330-4553
Patricia A Servaes, *Mng Member*
Patricia Servaes, *Mng Member*
EMP: 3
SALES (est): 108.1K **Privately Held**
SIC: 7372 Prepackaged Software Services

(G-12844)
VIASAT INC
300 Nickerson Rd Ste 100 (01752-4639)
PHONE..................................508 229-6500
Henry Debardeleben, *Manager*
Merwyn Dsouza, *Administration*
EMP: 16
SALES (corp-wide): 2B **Publicly Held**
WEB: www.viasat.com
SIC: 3663 Mfg Satellites
PA: Viasat, Inc.
6155 El Camino Real
Carlsbad CA 92009
760 476-2200

(G-12845)
VIKING INDUSTRIAL PRODUCTS
3 Brigham St (01752-3140)
P.O. Box 291 (01752-0291)
PHONE..................................508 481-4600
Aubrey Elms, *Owner*
Douglas Doyle, *Manager*
EMP: 25
SQ FT: 5,000
SALES (est): 2.8MM **Privately Held**
WEB: www.vikingindustrialproducts.com
SIC: 3621 3625 3651 Mfg Motors/Generators Mfg Relays/Industrial Controls Mfg Home Audio/Video Equipment

(G-12846)
VOGEL CAPITAL INC (HQ)
Also Called: Diamond Machining Technology
85 Hayes Memorial Dr (01752-1831)
PHONE..................................508 481-5944
Mark Brandon, *President*
Mark Bettke, *Plant Mgr*
Donald Gemma, *Manager*
Ramona Lachapelle, *Supervisor*
Fabricio Souza, *MIS Staff*
EMP: 27 **EST:** 1976
SQ FT: 28,000
SALES (est): 7.6MM
SALES (corp-wide): 137.3MM **Publicly Held**
WEB: www.dmtsharp.com
SIC: 3545 3291 Manufacturing Of Machine Tool Accessories Abrasive Products
PA: Acme United Corporation
55 Walls Dr Ste 201
Fairfield CT 06824
203 254-6060

(G-12847)
WAYLAND MILLWORK CORPORATION
344 Boston Post Rd E # 1 (01752-3655)
P.O. Box 377 (01752-0377)
PHONE..................................508 485-4172
Paul Ishkanian, *President*
Michael Pappas, *Clerk*
EMP: 12 **EST:** 1959
SQ FT: 12,000
SALES (est): 2.2MM **Privately Held**
WEB: www.waylandinteriorfinishing.com
SIC: 2431 Mfg Millwork

(G-12848)
WEB INDUSTRIES INC (PA)
700 Nickerson Rd Ste 250 (01752-4715)
PHONE..................................508 898-2988
Don Romine, *CEO*
Mark Pihl, *President*
Josh Chernin, *General Mgr*
Nathan Jones, *General Mgr*
Mark Richardson, *General Mgr*
▲ **EMP:** 7
SQ FT: 2,000
SALES (est): 117.8MM **Privately Held**
SIC: 2671 5162 3089 2269 Mfg Packaging Paper/Film Structural Metal Fabrctn Whol Plastic Mtrl/Shapes Finishing Plant Mfg Plastic Products

(G-12849)
WECARE ENVIRONMENTAL LLC
856 Boston Post Rd E (01752-3767)
PHONE..................................508 480-9922
C Wesley Gregory III, *Manager*
EMP: 7
SALES (est): 1.2MM **Privately Held**
SIC: 2875 Mfg Fertilizers-Mix Only

(G-12850)
WEIL MCLAIN
313 Boston Post Rd W # 125 (01752-4612)
PHONE..................................508 485-8050
David Walsh, *Manager*
EMP: 7
SALES (est): 946.3K **Privately Held**
SIC: 3443 Mfg Fabricated Plate Work

(G-12851)
WHEELCHAIR RECYCLER CUSTM & R
54 Linda Cir (01752-1632)
PHONE..................................978 760-4444
David Heim, *Principal*
EMP: 3
SALES (est): 264.5K **Privately Held**
SIC: 3842 Mfg Surgical Appliances/Supplies

(G-12852)
WORKSCAPE INC (HQ)
313 Boston Post Rd W # 210 (01752-4612)
PHONE..................................508 573-9000
Timothy T Clifford, *President*
Ed Hurley Wales, *Senior VP*
Nicolette M Brant, *Vice Pres*
Donald R Fitch Jr, *CFO*
William Bergen, *CIO*
EMP: 240
SALES (est): 38.3MM
SALES (corp-wide): 14.1B **Publicly Held**
WEB: www.workscape.com/
SIC: 7372 Prepackaged Software
PA: Automatic Data Processing, Inc.
1 Adp Blvd Ste 1 # 1
Roseland NJ 07068
973 974-5000

(G-12853)
WYEBOT INC
2 Mount Royal Ave Ste 310 (01752-1976)
PHONE..................................508 481-2603
EMP: 5
SALES (est): 560.5K **Privately Held**
SIC: 7372 Prepackaged Software Services

(G-12854)
XTALIC CORPORATION
260 Cedar Hill St Ste 4 (01752-3075)
PHONE..................................508 485-9730
George Thomas Clay, *CEO*
John Cahalen, *Vice Pres*
John Kinne, *Vice Pres*
Larry Masur, *Vice Pres*
Lisa Chan, *Research*
▲ **EMP:** 21
SALES (est): 3.7MM **Privately Held**
SIC: 3479 Coating/Engraving Service

(G-12855)
YKK (USA) INC
5 Mount Royal Ave Ste 3 (01752-1900)
PHONE..................................978 458-3200
Richard Spargo, *Branch Mgr*
EMP: 3
SQ FT: 9,000 **Privately Held**
SIC: 3965 Mfg Zippers
HQ: Ykk (U.S.A.), Inc.
1300 Cobb Industrial Dr
Marietta GA 30066
770 427-5521

Marshfield
Plymouth County

(G-12856)
BUREAU OF NATIONAL AFFAIRS INC
150 Fairways Edge Dr (02050-4937)
PHONE..................................781 843-9422
Thomas Caso, *Branch Mgr*
EMP: 17
SALES (corp-wide): 1.8B **Privately Held**
WEB: www.bna.com
SIC: 2711 Newspapers-Publishing/Printing
HQ: The Bureau Of National Affairs Inc
1801 S Bell St Ste Cn110
Arlington VA 22202
703 341-3000

(G-12857)
CHRISTHOPHER DINATALE
15 Bailey Ter (02050-2901)
PHONE..................................781 834-4248
Christopher P Dinatale, *Principal*
EMP: 3 **EST:** 2010
SALES (est): 204.7K **Privately Held**
SIC: 2091 Mfg Canned/Cured Fish/Seafood

(G-12858)
COMPLETE WELDING SERVICES
1235 Main St (02050-2029)
PHONE..................................781 837-9024
Michael Silvia, *Owner*
EMP: 3
SALES (est): 181.7K **Privately Held**
SIC: 7692 Welding Repair

(G-12859)
DISPATCH
1248 Ferry St (02050-1815)
PHONE..................................781 837-8700
EMP: 4
SALES (est): 213.1K **Privately Held**
SIC: 2711 Newspapers-Publishing/Printing

(G-12860)
ENGINEERED ASSEMBLY & SERVICES
210 King Phillips Pathe (02050-5717)
P.O. Box 1053 (02050-1053)
PHONE..................................781 834-9085
Raymond A Jones, *President*
EMP: 4
SQ FT: 400
SALES (est): 341.2K **Privately Held**
WEB: www.eng-assy.com
SIC: 3822 3585 Contract Manufacturing

(G-12861)
KIRWAN ENTERPRISE LLC
180 Enterprise Dr (02050-2110)
PHONE..................................781 834-9500
Michelle Covell, *Marketing Staff*
Scott Kirwan,
EMP: 3 **EST:** 1996
SQ FT: 50,000
SALES (est): 223.3K **Privately Held**
SIC: 3841 Mfg Surgical/Medical Instruments

(G-12862)
MARINER ABLNGTON EDITION
165 Enterprise Dr (02050-2132)
PHONE..................................781 878-4489
Greg Mathis, *Principal*
EMP: 3
SALES (est): 131.5K **Privately Held**
SIC: 2711 Newspapers-Publishing/Printing

(G-12863)
MBO ADVERTISING SERVICES
184 Standish St (02050-2651)
P.O. Box 1150 (02050-1150)
PHONE..................................781 837-5897
Vincent Gale, *Partner*
EMP: 5
SALES: 500K **Privately Held**
SIC: 2741 Newsletter

(G-12864)
NORFOLK CORPORATION
Also Called: Zrc Worldwide
145 Enterprise Dr (02050-2132)
PHONE..................................781 319-0400
Matthew R Steele, *President*
Steven P Collins, *Vice Pres*
◆ **EMP:** 15 **EST:** 1978
SQ FT: 31,000
SALES (est): 3.9MM **Privately Held**
WEB: www.speco.net
SIC: 2851 Mfg Air Curing Coatings

(G-12865)
PRECISION ELECTRONICS CORP
Also Called: Percision Electronics
427 Plain St (02050-2788)
PHONE..................................781 834-6677
Jon L Chandler, *President*
EMP: 10 **EST:** 1955
SQ FT: 7,500
SALES (est): 800K **Privately Held**
SIC: 3677 3621 3612 3548 Mfg Elec Coil/Transfrmrs Mfg Motors/Generators Mfg Transformers Mfg Welding Apparatus

(G-12866)
RAY SCITUATE PRECAST CON CORP
120 Clay Pit Rd (02050-2404)
P.O. Box 636 (02050-0636)
PHONE..................................781 837-1747
Richard W Hoffman, *President*
William E Hoffman, *Treasurer*
EMP: 40
SQ FT: 10,000
SALES (est): 7.9MM **Privately Held**
SIC: 3272 Mfg Concrete Products

(G-12867)
S & S MACHINE COMPANY INC
65 Commerce Way (02050-2755)
PHONE..................................781 319-9882
Robert M Smith, *President*
EMP: 5
SQ FT: 9,725
SALES: 825K **Privately Held**
SIC: 3599 Jobbing & Repair Machine Shop

(G-12868)
SOUTH SHORE SIGNS
846 Webster St Ste 3 (02050-3496)
PHONE..................................781 834-1120
John Valianti, *Owner*
EMP: 3
SALES (est): 168.9K **Privately Held**
SIC: 3993 Mfg Signs/Advertising Specialties

(G-12869)
SOUTHERN REDI-MIX CORPORATION
506 Plain St Ste 105 (02050-2745)
P.O. Box 961749, Boston (02196-1749)
PHONE..................................781 837-5353
EMP: 20
SQ FT: 1,000
SALES (est): 3.8MM **Privately Held**
SIC: 3273 Central-Mixed Concrete

(G-12870)
STYSIL ENTERPRISES LTD
Also Called: Creative Business
38 Indian Rd 200 (02050-1742)
PHONE..................................781 834-7279
EMP: 3
SALES (est): 210.4K **Privately Held**
WEB: www.creativebusiness.com
SIC: 2721 Periodicals-Publishing/Printing

Marstons Mills
Barnstable County

(G-12871)
B V T V INC
109 Carlson Ln (02648)
PHONE..................................508 737-7754
Robert J Vila, *President*
Jeanne Flynn, *Admin Asst*
EMP: 5
SALES (est): 300K **Privately Held**
WEB: www.bvtv.com
SIC: 2741 Misc Publishing

(G-12872)
CAPE COD BRAIDED RUG CO INC
Also Called: Jhb Enterprises
75 Olde Homestead Dr (02648-1752)
PHONE..................................508 432-3133
Thomas Benton, *President*
Nancy Benton, *Vice Pres*
EMP: 15
SQ FT: 3,400
SALES (est): 1.5MM **Privately Held**
WEB: www.capecodbraidedrug.com
SIC: 2273 5713 Mfg Carpets/Rugs Ret Floor Covering

(G-12873)
PERSISTOR INSTRUMENTS INC
153 Lovells Ln Ste A (02648-5710)
P.O. Box 1300 (02648-5300)
PHONE..................................508 420-1600
John Godley, *President*
Brian Kelley, *Admin Sec*
EMP: 4
SALES (est): 1MM **Privately Held**
WEB: www.periph.com
SIC: 3572 Mfg Single Board Computers

Mashpee
Barnstable County

(G-12874)
ALEPACK LLC
10 Alden Cir (02649-2148)
PHONE..................................508 274-5792
Charles Alexander Jr, *Mng Member*
Maria Alexander,
EMP: 6
SALES: 750K **Privately Held**
SIC: 3565 7389 Mfg Packaging Machinery Business Services At Non-Commercial Site

(G-12875)
BIGWOOD CORPORATION
57 Industrial Dr (02649-3405)
PHONE..................................508 477-2220
Jonathan L Bigwood, *President*
EMP: 8
SALES (est): 630K **Privately Held**
WEB: www.bigwoodcorp.com
SIC: 3599 Mfg Industrial Machinery

(G-12876)
BUMBOOSA LLC
25 Brewster Rd (02649-2923)
PHONE..................................508 539-1373
Sonja Sheasley, *President*
Bobby Pellant, *Vice Pres*
▲ **EMP:** 5
SALES (est): 788.5K **Privately Held**
SIC: 2676 2844 Mfg Sanitary Paper Products Mfg Toilet Preparations

(G-12877)
CAPE COD LIFE LLC
Also Called: Cape Cod Life Publications
13 Steeple St Ste 204 (02649)
P.O. Box 1439 (02649-1439)
PHONE..................................508 419-7381
Brian F Shortsleeve, *President*
Elizabeth Flynn, *Controller*
Miki Keil, *Admin Asst*
EMP: 15
SALES: 4MM **Privately Held**
SIC: 2721 7941 8742 Periodicals-Publishing/Printing Sports Club/Manager/Promoter Management Consulting Services

(G-12878)
CAPE COD MANUFACTURING
94 Industrial Dr Ste 1 (02649-3498)
P.O. Box 1804 (02649-1804)
PHONE..................................508 477-1188
David Doyle, *Owner*
EMP: 3
SALES (est): 170K **Privately Held**
SIC: 2387 Mfg Apparel Belts

(G-12879)
COASTAL N COUNTERS INC
92 Industrial Dr (02649-3404)
P.O. Box 2040 (02649-8040)
PHONE..................................508 539-3500
Mark Ducharme, *President*
Stacey Ducharme, *Clerk*
EMP: 11
SQ FT: 4,800
SALES: 1.2MM **Privately Held**
SIC: 2434 2514 5031 5211 Mft Whol & Ret Lumber & Building Materials

(G-12880)
CREATIVE KITCHEN & BATH INC
451 Nathan Ellis Hwy (02649-6002)
PHONE..................................508 477-3347
Deborah Dougherty, *Treasurer*
EMP: 4
SQ FT: 11,000
SALES (est): 650.3K **Privately Held**
SIC: 2434 Mfg Wood Kitchen Cabinets

(G-12881)
KERFOOT TECHNOLOGIES INC
766 Falmouth Rd Ste B12 (02649-3339)
PHONE..................................508 539-3002
William B Kerfoot, *President*
Patricia Kerfoot, *Treasurer*
EMP: 10
SQ FT: 3,000
SALES (est): 2MM **Privately Held**
WEB: www.kerfoottech.com
SIC: 3589 3594 3829 8748 Mfg Svc Industry Mach Mfg Fluid Power Pump/Mtr Mfg Measure/Control Dvcs Business Consulting Svcs

(G-12882)
PRINTSAKE INC
681 Falmouth Rd Ste C12 (02649-3327)
PHONE..................................508 419-7393
Mark Hattman, *Principal*
EMP: 4 **EST:** 2014
SALES (est): 341.7K **Privately Held**
SIC: 2752 Lithographic Commercial Printing

Mattapan
Suffolk County

(G-12883)
DISTINCT ELEMENT
52 Ormond St (02126-1508)
PHONE..................................617 322-3979
EMP: 5
SALES (est): 690.7K **Privately Held**
SIC: 2819 Industrial Inorganic Chemicals, Nec

(G-12884)
STUDIO 24 GRAPHIX & PRTG INC
1182 Blue Hill Ave (02126-1819)
PHONE..................................617 296-2058
Ansy Chevalier, *President*
EMP: 3

▲ = Import ▼=Export
◆ =Import/Export

SALES (est): 515K Privately Held
SIC: 2752 Lithographic Commercial Printing

Mattapoisett
Plymouth County

(G-12885)
BROWNELL BOAT STANDS INC
Also Called: Brownell Boatstands
5 Boat Rock Rd (02739-1325)
PHONE.....508 758-3671
Peter Hughes, *Vice Pres*
Peter T Kavanaugh, *Mng Member*
Nicole Quinones, *Administration*
▼ EMP: 12
SQ FT: 30,000
SALES (est): 3.3MM Privately Held
SIC: 3537 Mfg Industrial Trucks/Tractors

(G-12886)
DATA INDUSTRIAL CORPORATION
6 County Rd Ste 6 # 6 (02739-1585)
PHONE.....508 758-6390
Norman Bartlett, *General Mgr*
Kevin O'Brien, *Vice Pres*
EMP: 28
SQ FT: 23,000
SALES (est): 3.7MM
SALES (corp-wide): 433.7MM Publicly Held
WEB: www.dataindustrial.com
SIC: 3823 3824 Mfg Process Control Instruments Mfg Fluid Meter/Counting Devices
PA: Badger Meter, Inc.
4545 W Brown Deer Rd
Milwaukee WI 53223
414 355-0400

(G-12887)
JULIUS KOCH USA INC
15 Crooks Way (02739-1215)
PHONE.....508 995-9565
Lewis M Coco, *President*
Richard Gamache, *President*
Thomas P Kefor, *Vice Pres*
Michael J Sitarz, *Vice Pres*
Daniel Silva, *Warehouse Mgr*
▲ EMP: 75
SQ FT: 88,000
SALES: 7.5MM Privately Held
WEB: www.jkusa.com
SIC: 2298 2241 Mfg Cordage/Twine Narrow Fabric Mill

(G-12888)
MARK GAUVIN
Also Called: Mattapoisett Millworks
7 Noyes Ave (02739-2348)
PHONE.....508 758-2324
Mark Gauvin, *Owner*
EMP: 3
SQ FT: 1,600
SALES (est): 246.2K Privately Held
SIC: 2499 2431 Mfg Wood Products Mfg Millwork

(G-12889)
PEINERT BOATWORKS INC
46 Marion Rd (02739-1645)
P.O. Box 1029 (02739-0406)
PHONE.....508 758-3020
Paul Milde, *President*
Paul Pienart, *COO*
EMP: 3
SQ FT: 9,600
SALES (est): 180K Privately Held
WEB: www.sculling.com
SIC: 3732 Designs & Mfg Racing Rowboats

(G-12890)
SOUTHCOAST WOODWORKING INC
13 Industrial Dr Unit 3 (02739-1324)
PHONE.....508 758-3184
Bruce Dionne, *President*
EMP: 4
SALES: 300K Privately Held
SIC: 2431 Mfg Wood Kitchen Cabinets

(G-12891)
SPORTSSCARF LLC
Also Called: Soccerscarf.com
8 County Rd Ste 5 (02739-1586)
P.O. Box 1796 (02739-0446)
PHONE.....508 758-8176
Dara Midwood, *Sales Staff*
Carl Coelho,
Linda Coelho,
Jeffrey R Perry,
▲ EMP: 3
SQ FT: 2,000
SALES: 4MM Privately Held
SIC: 3949 5699 Mfg Sporting/Athletic Goods Ret Misc Apparel/Accessories

(G-12892)
WANDERER COMMUNICATIONS INC
55 County Rd (02739-1652)
P.O. Box 102 (02739-0102)
PHONE.....508 758-9055
Paul Lopes, *President*
▲ EMP: 4
SALES (est): 328.1K Privately Held
WEB: www.wanderer.com
SIC: 2711 Newspapers-Publishing/Printing

Maynard
Middlesex County

(G-12893)
40PARKLANE LLC
Also Called: Carolyn's Handmade
4 Apple Rdg Unit 3 (01754-2705)
PHONE.....978 369-2940
Hans Van Putten, *President*
Tracey A Van Putten, *Vice Pres*
Tracey Van Putten, *Vice Pres*
EMP: 14
SQ FT: 3,600
SALES (est): 1.6MM Privately Held
WEB: www.40parklane.com
SIC: 2068 Mfg Salted/Roasted Nuts/Seeds/Toffee/Chocolate Bark/Chutney/Sauces/Marinades

(G-12894)
ACACIA COMMUNICATIONS INC (PA)
3 Mill And Main Pl # 400 (01754-2656)
PHONE.....978 938-4896
Vincent T Roche, *Ch of Bd*
Murugesan Shanmugaraj, *President*
Eric L Fisher, *Vice Pres*
Mehrdad Givehchi, *Vice Pres*
Christian J Rasmussen, *Vice Pres*
EMP: 124 EST: 2009
SQ FT: 121,000
SALES: 339.8MM Publicly Held
SIC: 3674 8999 Semiconductors & Related Devices Communication Services

(G-12895)
AVANTGARDE MOLECULAR LLC
63 Great Rd Ste 107 (01754-2097)
PHONE.....617 549-2238
Violeta Stanojevic, *Principal*
EMP: 3 EST: 2009
SALES (est): 241.9K Privately Held
SIC: 2869 Mfg Industrial Organic Chemicals

(G-12896)
BELARC INC
2 Mill And Main Pl # 520 (01754-2672)
PHONE.....978 461-1100
Gary Newman, *President*
Sumin Tchen, *Chairman*
Richard Defuria, *Engineer*
Henri Cousseillant, *Comptroller*
Ken Shaw, *Sales Mgr*
EMP: 18 EST: 1995
SALES (est): 2.2MM Privately Held
WEB: www.belarc.com
SIC: 7372 Prepackaged Software Services

(G-12897)
CERAMICS GRINDING CO INC
12 Walnut St (01754-1628)
PHONE.....978 461-5935
Richard Lalli, *Treasurer*
EMP: 5 EST: 1962
SQ FT: 3,200
SALES (est): 763.5K Privately Held
WEB: www.ceramicsgrinding.com
SIC: 3264 Mfg Porcelain Electrical Insulators

(G-12898)
ECOCHLOR INC
14 Nason St Ste 309 (01754-2598)
PHONE.....978 298-1463
Charlie Miller, *CEO*
Peter J Bollier, *CFO*
Kathleen Hunt, *Office Mgr*
Connor Fray, *Technical Staff*
Katherine Weaver, *Technical Staff*
▲ EMP: 4
SALES (est): 722.7K Privately Held
SIC: 2899 3823 Mfg Chemical Preparations Mfg Process Control Instruments

(G-12899)
KABLES AND KONNECTOR SERVICES
13 Vernon St (01754-1215)
P.O. Box 353 (01754-0353)
PHONE.....978 897-4852
Ilene Kelly, *President*
John Kelly, *Vice Pres*
EMP: 5
SALES: 170K Privately Held
SIC: 3443 Mfg Fabricated Plate Work

(G-12900)
LONGWOOD SOFTWARE INC
Also Called: Tagteam.com
107 Main St (01754-2514)
PHONE.....978 897-2900
Scott Richardson, *President*
Gail Riep, *Finance Mgr*
Bill Good, *Sales Staff*
Charles Smith, *Director*
EMP: 12
SQ FT: 3,000
SALES (est): 970K Privately Held
WEB: www.longwoodsw.com
SIC: 7372 Prepackaged Software Services

(G-12901)
MACIEL JOHN
Also Called: Quick Removal Service
4 Rickey Dr (01754-1052)
PHONE.....978 897-5865
John Maciel, *Owner*
EMP: 4
SALES: 180K Privately Held
SIC: 3639 Mfg Household Appliances

(G-12902)
NORTHEAST MONITORING INC
Also Called: Northeast Fluid Technologies
141 Parker St Ste 101 (01754-2179)
PHONE.....978 461-3992
Mark Hubelbank, *President*
Scott Winick, *Sales Staff*
Linda Saengkheune, *Office Mgr*
Sherry Steele, *Office Mgr*
Stella Reis, *Technical Staff*
EMP: 6
SQ FT: 3,000
SALES: 2.5MM Privately Held
SIC: 3845 Mfg Electromedical Equipment

(G-12903)
PHOTONEX CORPORATION
200 Metrowest Tech Dr (01754)
PHONE.....978 723-2200
Kristin Rauschenbach, *President*
Phil Francisco, *Vice Pres*
Patrick J Scannell Jr, *CFO*
EMP: 173
SALES (est): 13.1MM Privately Held
SIC: 3661 Mfg Telephone/Telegraph Apparatus

(G-12904)
TEA FORTE INC
5 Mill Main Pl Ste 05211 (01754)
PHONE.....978 369-7777
Raymond Orner, *Admin Sec*
◆ EMP: 45
SALES (est): 6.8MM
SALES (corp-wide): 1.2MM Privately Held
WEB: www.teaforte.com
SIC: 2099 Mfg Food Preparations
HQ: Oak 1753 B.V.
Oosterdoksstraat 80
Amsterdam
205 581-753

(G-12905)
VERNE Q POWELL FLUTES INC
Also Called: Sonare Winds
1 Mill And Main Pl # 300 (01754-2653)
PHONE.....978 461-6111
Francois Kloc, *President*
Daniel Sharp, *Sales Staff*
◆ EMP: 60
SQ FT: 29,000
SALES: 7MM
SALES (corp-wide): 3.5MM Privately Held
WEB: www.sonarewinds.com
SIC: 3931 5099 Mfg Musical Instruments Whol Durable Goods
HQ: Buffet Crampon
5 Rue Maurice Berteaux
Mantes-La-Ville 78711
130 985-130

(G-12906)
WILDLIFE ACOUSTICS INC
3 Mill And Main Pl # 210 (01754-2656)
PHONE.....978 369-5225
Ian Agranat, *President*
Peter Mellor, *General Mgr*
Bill Chiarchiaro, *Engineer*
EMP: 5
SQ FT: 5,000
SALES: 4MM Privately Held
WEB: www.wildlifeacoustics.com
SIC: 3829 Mfg Measuring/Controlling Devices

(G-12907)
ZLINK INC
141 Parker St Ste 311 (01754-2180)
PHONE.....978 309-3628
Anupam Sachdev, *CEO*
EMP: 6
SQ FT: 2,318
SALES (est): 215.3K Privately Held
SIC: 2741 7374 7371 8712 Internet Pub & Broad Data Processing/Prep Computer Programming Svc Architectural Services Prepackaged Software Svc

Medfield
Norfolk County

(G-12908)
AC NAVIGATION LLC
16 Ledgetree Rd (02052-2129)
PHONE.....508 359-5903
Donato Cardarelli,
EMP: 4
SALES (est): 247.8K Privately Held
SIC: 3812 Mfg Search/Navigation Equipment

(G-12909)
ATLANTIC PRINTING CO INC
5 Causeway Ln (02052-2301)
PHONE.....781 449-2700
Barry A Feldman, *President*
Robert Feldman, *Vice Pres*
Stephen Feldman, *VP Sales*
EMP: 11
SQ FT: 10,000
SALES: 2.5MM Privately Held
WEB: www.atlanticprinting.com
SIC: 2721 2741 2731 2752 Prints Brochures Newsletters Annual Reports And Provides Typesetting & Graphic Design Services

(G-12910)
BALL SLIDES INC
102 Adams St (02052-1529)
PHONE.....508 359-4348
Janet Howie, *President*
EMP: 7
SQ FT: 4,000
SALES (est): 836.7K Privately Held
WEB: www.ballslides.com
SIC: 3599 Mfg Industrial Machinery

GEOGRAPHIC

(G-12911)
CAMBRIDGE FUND RAISING ASSOC
Also Called: Contributions
15 Brook St Ste 6 (02052-2058)
P.O. Box 338 (02052-0338)
PHONE....508 359-0019
Kathleen Brennan, *Partner*
Jerry Cianciolo, *Partner*
EMP: 3
SALES (est): 274.8K **Privately Held**
WEB: www.contributionsmagazine.com
SIC: 2721 Periodicals-Publishing/Printing

(G-12912)
CLEARWAY SOFTWARE CORP
266 Main St Ste 39 (02052-2099)
P.O. Box 589 (02052-0589)
PHONE....508 906-6333
Eugene J Rodgers Jr, *President*
EMP: 5
SALES (est): 299K **Privately Held**
SIC: 7372 Prepackaged Software Services

(G-12913)
ELECTRIC TIME COMPANY INC
97 West St (02052-1513)
P.O. Box 466 (02052-0466)
PHONE....508 359-4396
Thomas Erb, *President*
David Cournoyer, *Vice Pres*
Tyler Eisner, *Engineer*
Brandie Morris, *Mktg Dir*
Christina Castagna, *Info Tech Mgr*
▼ **EMP:** 30
SQ FT: 13,000
SALES (est): 5.3MM **Privately Held**
WEB: www.electrictime.com
SIC: 3873 Mfg Watches/Clocks/Parts

(G-12914)
ELITE SEM INC
266 Main St Ste 27 (02052-2099)
PHONE....508 955-0414
Carlos Cashman, *Branch Mgr*
EMP: 5
SALES (corp-wide): 10.8MM **Privately Held**
SIC: 3999 5199 Mfg Misc Products Whol Nondurable Goods
PA: Elite Sem Inc.
142 W 36th St Fl 11
New York NY 10018
646 350-2789

(G-12915)
NSM MARKETING INC
2 Newell Dr (02052-1538)
PHONE....508 359-5297
Richard G Dove, *President*
EMP: 6
SALES (est): 473.5K **Privately Held**
SIC: 3845 Mfg Electromedical Equipment

(G-12916)
PHARMASK INC
28 Bridge St (02052-1521)
PHONE....508 359-6700
EMP: 3
SALES (est): 230K **Privately Held**
SIC: 3821 Mfg Lab Apparatus/Furniture

(G-12917)
PRECISION SENSING DEVICES INC
93 West St Ste D (02052-1556)
PHONE....508 359-2833
Anthony J Intrieri, *President*
Mike Sellars, *Vice Pres*
EMP: 9
SQ FT: 1,200
SALES: 1MM **Privately Held**
SIC: 3674 Mfg Semiconductors/Related Devices

(G-12918)
QUINN CURTIS INC
18 Hearthstone Dr (02052-2105)
PHONE....508 359-6639
Richard Quinn, *President*
EMP: 4
SQ FT: 3,000
SALES (est): 282.8K **Privately Held**
WEB: www.quinn-curtis.com
SIC: 7372 5734 5045 Develops & Rets & Whols Computer Software

(G-12919)
SEA-LAND ENVMTL SVCS INC
18 N Meadows Rd Ste 1 (02052-2334)
PHONE....508 359-1085
Richard Waterhouse, *President*
EMP: 8
SQ FT: 800
SALES: 475K **Privately Held**
SIC: 1389 Environmental Tank Cleaning Title 5 Inspections

Medford
Middlesex County

(G-12920)
ACCENT BANNER LLC
17 Locust St (02155-5713)
PHONE....781 391-7300
Hannah Tran, *Prdtn Mgr*
Jim Bouchard, *Sales Staff*
Aice R Deitrich, *Mng Member*
EMP: 10
SQ FT: 800
SALES: 1MM **Privately Held**
WEB: www.accentbanner.com
SIC: 2399 5999 5131 Mfg Fabricated Textile Products Ret Misc Merchandise Whol Piece Goods/Notions

(G-12921)
ANTHONY MANUFACTURING CO INC
410 Riverside Ave (02155-4916)
PHONE....781 396-1400
Anthony Fabrizio, *President*
EMP: 10 **EST:** 1967
SQ FT: 10,000
SALES (est): 830K **Privately Held**
SIC: 2541 2434 Mfg Wooden Store Fixtures & Cabinets

(G-12922)
BIMBO BAKERIES USA INC
4110 Mystic Valley Pkwy (02155-6931)
PHONE....781 306-0221
EMP: 17 **Privately Held**
SIC: 2051 Mfg Bread/Related Products
HQ: Bimbo Bakeries Usa, Inc
255 Business Center Dr # 200
Horsham PA 19044
215 347-5500

(G-12923)
BOSTON RETAIL PRODUCTS INC (PA)
400 Riverside Ave (02155-4949)
PHONE....781 395-7417
Russell J Rubin, *President*
Susan L Ward, *Vice Pres*
Thomas Smith, *Plant Mgr*
Andy Lowen, *Opers Staff*
Vinni Paolini, *Engineer*
◆ **EMP:** 102
SQ FT: 117,000
SALES (est): 21.7MM **Privately Held**
WEB: www.bostonretail.com
SIC: 2542 3446 Mfg Partitions/Fixtures-Nonwood Mfg Architectural Metalwork

(G-12924)
BRICK KILN PLACE LLC
200 Boston Ave Ste 2530 (02155-4212)
P.O. Box 850330, Braintree (02185-0330)
PHONE....781 826-6027
EMP: 3
SALES (est): 184.2K **Privately Held**
SIC: 3559 Mfg Misc Industry Machinery

(G-12925)
CARR-DEE CORP
37 Linden St (02155-4929)
PHONE....781 391-4500
Arthur Desimone, *President*
Arthur De Simone, *President*
Henry De Simone, *Vice Pres*
EMP: 10 **EST:** 1951
SQ FT: 6,000
SALES: 1.1MM **Privately Held**
WEB: www.carrdeecorp.com
SIC: 1481 Nonmetallic Mineral Services

(G-12926)
CLARKS STEEL DRUM COMPANY
76 Wolcott St (02155-3423)
PHONE....781 396-1109
Martha Clark, *Ch of Bd*
Paul Clark, *President*
EMP: 4
SALES: 300K **Privately Held**
SIC: 3412 5085 Mfg Metal Barrels/Pails Whol Industrial Supplies

(G-12927)
COLLEGIATE UNIFORMS INC
Also Called: Collegiate House
970 Fellsway Ste 1 (02155-4114)
PHONE....781 219-4952
Gene Kaminski, *President*
Naum Kaminski, *Treasurer*
EMP: 6 **EST:** 1934
SQ FT: 4,500
SALES: 550K **Privately Held**
WEB: www.collegiatehouse.com
SIC: 2337 2339 5136 2329 Mfg Women/Miss Suit/Coat Mfg Women/Miss Outerwear Whol Mens/Boys Clothing Mfg Mens/Boys Clothing Whol Women/Child Clothng

(G-12928)
CYR SIGN & BANNER COMPANY
40 Canal St Ste 2 (02155-3677)
PHONE....781 395-7297
Raymond L Cyr, *President*
EMP: 4
SQ FT: 2,000
SALES (est): 477.5K **Privately Held**
WEB: www.cyrsign.com
SIC: 3993 2399 Mfg Signs/Advertising Specialties Mfg Fabricated Textile Products

(G-12929)
DAVID P DEVENEY MEMORIAL CO
Also Called: Deveney, David P Memorial Co
165 Mystic Ave (02155-4617)
PHONE....781 396-7772
David P Deveney, *Owner*
EMP: 3
SALES (est): 146.5K **Privately Held**
SIC: 3281 Ret Misc Merchandise

(G-12930)
DELTA ELC MTR REPR SLS & SVC
Also Called: Delta Elc Mtr Repr Sls & Serv
101 Hicks Ave (02155-6318)
PHONE....781 395-0551
Scott Prussman, *President*
EMP: 3
SQ FT: 3,000
SALES (est): 623.1K **Privately Held**
WEB: www.deltaelectricmotor.com
SIC: 7694 5999 5084 5063 Armature Rewinding Ret Misc Merchandise Whol Industrial Equip Whol Electrical Equip

(G-12931)
DIV CABOT ROAD LLC
1 Cabot Rd (02155-5117)
PHONE....781 396-3122
Scott D Spelfogel, *Principal*
EMP: 11
SALES (est): 1.6MM **Privately Held**
SIC: 2819 Mfg Industrial Inorganic Chemicals

(G-12932)
EASTERN TOOL CORPORATION
58 Swan St (02155-4644)
PHONE....781 395-1472
Joseph Fustolo, *President*
EMP: 10
SALES (est): 1.2MM **Privately Held**
SIC: 3599 Machine Shop Jobbing & Repair

(G-12933)
FABRIZIO CORPORATION
410 Riverside Ave (02155-4916)
PHONE....781 396-1400
Anthony Fabrizio Jr, *President*
Ryan Reid, *Manager*
EMP: 20
SQ FT: 18,000
SALES (est): 2.3MM **Privately Held**
SIC: 2511 Mfg Wood Household Furniture

(G-12934)
GHG ELECTRONIC SERVICES
49 Baxter St (02155-1036)
PHONE....781 391-1147
Richard J Guarini, *Owner*
EMP: 3
SALES (est): 275.1K **Privately Held**
WEB: www.ghgelectronics.com
SIC: 3825 Testing Of Electronic Components

(G-12935)
HOUSING DEVICES INC
407r Mystic Ave Ste 32b (02155-6329)
PHONE....781 395-5200
Thomas Richardson, *President*
EMP: 10
SQ FT: 6,000
SALES (est): 2MM **Privately Held**
WEB: www.housingdevices.com
SIC: 3669 Mfg Intercom Systems

(G-12936)
INKBIT LLC
200 Boston Ave Ste 1850 (02155-4257)
PHONE....617 433-8842
Davide Marini,
Javier Ramos,
EMP: 4
SALES: 282.6K **Privately Held**
SIC: 3555 Mfg Printing Trades Machinery

(G-12937)
IZON SCIENCE US LTD
196 Boston Ave Ste 3500 (02155-4262)
PHONE....617 945-5936
Johannes Van Der Voorn, *CEO*
Greg Bouwer, *Research*
Pragnesh Patel, *Sales Engr*
Anoop Pal, *Manager*
Josimar Sorto, *Office Admin*
EMP: 4
SALES (est): 288.6K
SALES (corp-wide): 484.6K **Privately Held**
SIC: 3826 Analytical Instruments, Nsk
PA: Izon Science Limited
Unit C - 8 Homersham Place
Christchurch
335 742-70

(G-12938)
LABTHINK INTERNATIONAL INC
200 Rivers Edge Dr Ste 1 (02155-5480)
PHONE....617 830-2190
Haimo Jiang, *President*
Craig Primiani, *President*
Yunzhong Jiang, *Director*
EMP: 12
SALES (est): 305.8K
SALES (corp-wide): 5.9MM **Privately Held**
SIC: 7372 Prepackaged Software Services
PA: Labthink Instruments Co., Ltd.
No.144, Wuyingshan Road, Tianqiao Dist.
Jinan 25003
531 850-6856

(G-12939)
MAPLE LEAF CPITL VENTURES CORP (PA)
322 Mystic Ave (02155-6317)
PHONE....781 569-6311
Graham Howard West, *President*
EMP: 9
SQ FT: 10,000
SALES (est): 1.1MM **Privately Held**
WEB: www.morganawning.com
SIC: 2394 Mfg Canvas/Related Products

(G-12940)
MARIAS FOOD PRODUCTS INC
Also Called: Maria's Ravioli
48 Suffolk St (02155-2333)
PHONE....781 396-4110
Richard D'Orsi Jr, *President*
Richard Dorsi, *President*
EMP: 3

▲ = Import ▼=Export
◆ =Import/Export

SQ FT: 3,000
SALES: 200K **Privately Held**
WEB: www.mariasravioli.com
SIC: 2038 2033 2013 Mfg Frozen Specialties Mfg Canned Fruits/Vegetables Mfg Prepared Meats

(G-12941)
MASS-FLEX RESEARCH INC
18 Canal St Ste 3 (02155-3684)
PHONE..................................781 391-3640
Matthew B Hobbs, *President*
Evelyn Pierce, *Clerk*
EMP: 15 **EST:** 1973
SQ FT: 7,500
SALES (est): 2.5MM **Privately Held**
SIC: 3568 Mfg Flexible Shafts Specializing In Monocoil Casings And Sheathings

(G-12942)
MASSACHUSETTS IMPORTING CO
255 Main St (02155-5629)
P.O. Box 560205, West Medford (02156-0205)
PHONE..................................781 395-1210
Richard Freda, *President*
Maria Freda, *Treasurer*
EMP: 3
SALES: 350K **Privately Held**
SIC: 2013 Mfg Prepared Meats

(G-12943)
MEDFORD TRANSCRIPT
57 High St (02155-3808)
PHONE..................................781 396-1982
Sara Knowles, *Manager*
EMP: 4 **EST:** 2000
SALES (est): 144.6K **Privately Held**
SIC: 2711 Newspaper

(G-12944)
NANOBIOSYM INC
200 Boston Ave Ste 4700 (02155-4242)
PHONE..................................781 391-7979
Anita Goel, *President*
Lisa Goel, *Opers Staff*
EMP: 11
SALES (est): 1.3MM **Privately Held**
SIC: 2835 Mfg Diagnostic Substances

(G-12945)
O & E HIGH-TECH CORPORATION
139 Washington St (02155-4702)
PHONE..................................617 497-1108
Jicheng Gu, *President*
EMP: 5
SALES: 950K **Privately Held**
SIC: 2992 Mfg Lubricating Oils/Greases

(G-12946)
RIVERSIDE SHEET METAL & CONTG
15 Reardon Rd 15 # 15 (02155-4624)
PHONE..................................781 396-0070
Raymond Magliozzi, *President*
Janet Magliozzi, *Treasurer*
EMP: 15
SQ FT: 10,000
SALES (est): 3.6MM **Privately Held**
SIC: 3444 Roofing/Siding Contractor

(G-12947)
SANTINI BROTHERS IR WORKS INC
28 Sycamore Ave (02155-4942)
PHONE..................................781 396-1450
Maria Torriani, *President*
John Santini, *Vice Pres*
Robyn Santini, *Treasurer*
Mt T Torriani, *Manager*
John A Santini, *Director*
EMP: 15 **EST:** 1971
SQ FT: 23,000
SALES: 2.8MM **Privately Held**
WEB: www.santinibros.com
SIC: 3446 3449 Mfg Architectural Metalwork Mfg Misc Structural Metalwork

(G-12948)
SENSARRAY INFRARED CORPORATION
150 George St (02155-5443)
PHONE..................................781 306-0338
David Smith, *President*
Karl Schlieff, *Vice Pres*
Paul F Murphy, *CTO*
EMP: 8
SQ FT: 7,800
SALES (est): 923.5K
SALES (corp-wide): 22.5MM **Privately Held**
WEB: www.sensarrayinfrared.com
SIC: 3812 Mfg Search/Navigation Equipment
PA: Agiltron, Inc.
15 Presidential Way
Woburn MA 01801
781 935-1200

(G-12949)
SYRATECH ACQUISITION CORP (HQ)
22 Blake St (02155-4922)
PHONE..................................781 539-0100
Jeffrey Siegel, *President*
Robert McNally, *Vice Pres*
Ronald Shiftan, *Vice Pres*
Gary Meek, *CFO*
Sara A Shindel, *Admin Sec*
◆ **EMP:** 200
SQ FT: 325,000
SALES (est): 33.6MM
SALES (corp-wide): 704.5MM **Publicly Held**
SIC: 3914 3999 Mfg Silver/Plated Ware Mfg Misc Products
PA: Lifetime Brands, Inc.
1000 Stewart Ave
Garden City NY 11530
516 683-6000

(G-12950)
TOWLE MANUFACTURING COMPANY (DH)
Also Called: Towle Silversmiths
22 Blake St (02155-4922)
PHONE..................................781 539-0100
Alan Kanter, *President*
Jeff Siegel, *President*
▲ **EMP:** 3
SALES (est): 529.2K
SALES (corp-wide): 704.5MM **Publicly Held**
SIC: 3914 Mfg & Distr Sterling Silver Flatware Hollowware & Plated Hollowware
HQ: Syratech Acquisition Corporation
22 Blake St
Medford MA 02155
781 539-0100

(G-12951)
TRUSTEES OF TUFTS COLLEGE
Also Called: Tufts Daily
520 Boston Ave (02155-5500)
PHONE..................................617 628-5000
John Di Biaggio, *President*
Marya Schnedeker, *Research*
EMP: 50
SALES (corp-wide): 914.4MM **Privately Held**
WEB: www.tecnet.org
SIC: 2711 8221 Newspapers-Publishing/Printing College/University
PA: Trustees Of Tufts College
169 Holland St Ste 318
Somerville MA 02144
617 628-5000

Medway
Norfolk County

(G-12952)
AD PRINT
96 Main St (02053-1801)
PHONE..................................508 533-7411
Michael Aoud, *Owner*
EMP: 3
SALES (est): 326.7K **Privately Held**
SIC: 2752 Lithographic Commercial Printing

(G-12953)
ADVANCED BURNER SOLUTIONS CORP
Also Called: Burner Booster, The
4 Overlook Dr (02053-1941)
PHONE..................................508 400-3289
Steve Hayes, *CEO*
Eric Lavoie, *Chief Engr*
EMP: 3 **EST:** 2015
SALES (est): 217.2K **Privately Held**
SIC: 3433 Mfg Heating Equipment-Nonelectric

(G-12954)
ADVANCED ID DETECTION LLC
23 Jayar Rd (02053-1735)
PHONE..................................617 544-8030
Brandon S Currul, *Principal*
Theodore Kuklinski, *Manager*
EMP: 8 **EST:** 2010
SALES (est): 1.1MM **Privately Held**
SIC: 3812 Mfg Search/Navigation Equipment

(G-12955)
ADVANCED SIGNING LLC
4 Industrial Park Rd (02053-1709)
PHONE..................................508 533-9000
Rick Dushman, *Vice Pres*
Michael Luccio, *Vice Pres*
Kevin Iacuzzi, *Production*
Jo Mc Conaghy, *Treasurer*
William Galligan, *Sales Staff*
EMP: 40
SQ FT: 17,000
SALES (est): 5.5MM **Privately Held**
WEB: www.advancedsigning.com
SIC: 3993 Mfg Signs/Advertising Specialties

(G-12956)
AZZ INC
51 Alder St (02053-2291)
PHONE..................................774 854-0700
Fitzgerald Patrick, *Electrical Engi*
Sean Noel, *Branch Mgr*
EMP: 50
SALES (corp-wide): 927MM **Publicly Held**
SIC: 3699 Mfg Electrical Equipment/Supplies
PA: Azz Inc.
3100 W 7th St Ste 500
Fort Worth TX 76107
817 810-0095

(G-12957)
BOSTON SPORTS JOURNAL LLC
Also Called: Bostonsportsjournal.com
4 Daniels Rd (02053-6103)
P.O. Box 160 (02053-0160)
PHONE..................................617 306-0166
Rita Bedard,
Greg Bedard,
EMP: 7 **Privately Held**
SIC: 2741 7389 Internet Publishing And Broadcasting Business Serv Non-Commercial Site

(G-12958)
CYBEX INTERNATIONAL INC
51 Alder St (02053-2291)
PHONE..................................508 533-4167
Luke Berry, *Regl Sales Mgr*
Robert Briggs, *Manager*
Paul M Juris, *Exec Dir*
EMP: 250
SALES (corp-wide): 5.1B **Publicly Held**
SIC: 3949 Mfg's Fitness Equipment
HQ: Cybex International, Inc.
1975 24th Ave Sw
Owatonna MN 55060
508 533-4300

(G-12959)
ENVIRONMENTAL SVCS GROUP INC
Also Called: Radon Environmental Monitoring
11 Awl St (02053-1674)
P.O. Box 158 (02053-0158)
PHONE..................................508 533-7683
Carolyn Allen, *President*
Howard Ziidel, *Treasurer*
Dave Katturswoski, *Director*
EMP: 20
SQ FT: 3,000
SALES (est): 3.1MM
SALES (corp-wide): 11.7MM **Privately Held**
WEB: www.radonaway.com
SIC: 3829 8748 Mfg Measuring/Controlling Devices Business Consulting Services
PA: Spruce Environmental Technologies, Inc.
3 Saber Way
Haverhill MA 01835
978 521-0901

(G-12960)
GENERAL DISPLAY INC
6 Industrial Park Rd (02053-1797)
P.O. Box 224 (02053-0224)
PHONE..................................508 533-6676
Arthur Mastrodicasa, *CEO*
Chris Mastrodicasa, *President*
Glenn Mastrodicasa, *Treasurer*
Phillip Delaney, *Director*
Lydia Mastro, *Administration*
▲ **EMP:** 100 **EST:** 1958
SQ FT: 85,000
SALES (est): 11.9MM **Privately Held**
WEB: www.generaldisplay.com
SIC: 3993 Mfg Signs/Advertising Specialties

(G-12961)
INNOVATIVE COATINGS INC
24 Jayar Rd (02053-1734)
PHONE..................................508 533-6101
George Maravelias, *President*
Robert Buckley, *Vice Pres*
Irene Maravelias, *Clerk*
EMP: 17
SQ FT: 30,000
SALES: 1.8MM **Privately Held**
WEB: www.innovativecoatings.com
SIC: 3479 Coating/Engraving Service

(G-12962)
ITG GROUP INC
Also Called: Ink N Thredz
4 Main St Ste H (02053-1752)
PHONE..................................508 645-4994
Harry G Schreffler, *Principal*
Joseph Cataldo, *Principal*
EMP: 4
SALES (est): 130.2K **Privately Held**
SIC: 2759 7389 5699 Commercial Printing Business Services Ret Misc Apparel/Accessories

(G-12963)
JOEL CASSIDY
Also Called: J C Custom Woodworking
54 Holliston St (02053-1423)
PHONE..................................508 533-5887
Joel Cassidy, *Owner*
EMP: 3
SQ FT: 3,000
SALES: 300K **Privately Held**
SIC: 2434 Mfg Wood Kitchen Cabinets

(G-12964)
JUNES PLACE
122 Main St (02053-1801)
PHONE..................................508 533-5037
Eric Kirby, *Owner*
EMP: 4
SALES (est): 193.9K **Privately Held**
SIC: 2051 Mfg Bread/Related Products

(G-12965)
LITTLE SHOP OF OLIVE OILS INC
23 Broken Tree Rd (02053-2447)
PHONE..................................508 533-5522
Michael Wilkinson, *Principal*
EMP: 3 **EST:** 2017
SALES (est): 158.9K **Privately Held**
SIC: 2079 Mfg Edible Fats/Oils

(G-12966)
MASS METALWORKS LLC
89 Main St Ste 104 (02053-1818)
PHONE..................................508 533-7500
Erik M Svensen, *Principal*
EMP: 4
SALES (est): 519.2K **Privately Held**
SIC: 3441 Structural Metal Fabrication

(G-12967)
MICRO FINANCIAL CMPT SYSTEMS
Also Called: Micro Financial Systems
89 Main St Ste 204 (02053-1818)
PHONE..................................508 533-1233
John J Anderson Jr, *President*
Lenny Udell, *Vice Pres*
EMP: 4
SQ FT: 1,000
SALES (est): 471.5K **Privately Held**
WEB: www.microfinancial.net
SIC: 7372 7373 Computer Systems Design Prepackaged Software Services

(G-12968)
NRT INC
Also Called: Our Town Publishing
74 Main St Unit 16 (02053-1822)
PHONE..................................508 533-4588
Charles Tashjiam, *CEO*
Nicole Renee Tashjian, *President*
EMP: 10
SALES (est): 571.6K **Privately Held**
SIC: 2741 2711 Misc Publishing Newspapers-Publishing/Printing

(G-12969)
PLASTIC MONOFIL CO LTD
Also Called: Green Mountain Knitting
8 Tulip Way (02053-6204)
PHONE..................................732 629-7701
William Wilson, *CEO*
▼ **EMP:** 10 **EST:** 1970
SQ FT: 20,000
SALES (est): 1.5MM **Privately Held**
SIC: 3089 Mfg Plastic Products

(G-12970)
SANDLER & SONS CO
2 Franklin St Ste 1 (02053-1676)
PHONE..................................508 533-8282
Frank Sandler, *President*
Carol Sandler, *Treasurer*
EMP: 3
SALES (est): 261.2K **Privately Held**
SIC: 3999 Mfg Misc Products

(G-12971)
TEXAS DIP MOLDING COATING INC (PA)
24 Jayar Rd (02053-1734)
PHONE..................................508 533-6101
Robert Buckley, *Principal*
EMP: 9
SALES (est): 943.5K **Privately Held**
SIC: 3089 Mfg Plastic Products

(G-12972)
VACCON COMPANY INC
9 Industrial Park Rd (02053-1732)
PHONE..................................508 359-7200
Ellen P Ferri, *President*
David Haynes, *Engineer*
Joan H Ferri, *Admin Sec*
▲ **EMP:** 20 **EST:** 1972
SQ FT: 9,600
SALES (est): 5.3MM
SALES (corp-wide): 2.5B **Privately Held**
WEB: www.vaccon.com
SIC: 3563 5084 3561 Manufactures Air/Gas Compressors Whosales Industrial Equipment Manufactures Pumps/Pumping Equipment
HQ: Bimba Manufacturing Company Inc
25150 S Governors Hwy
University Park IL 60484
708 534-8544

Melrose
Middlesex County

(G-12973)
AAA RADIATOR
163 Beech Ave (02176-4901)
PHONE..................................781 662-7203
Martin Dotl, *Owner*
EMP: 3
SALES (est): 170K **Privately Held**
SIC: 3433 Mfg Heating Equipment-Non-electric

(G-12974)
ACKTIFY INC
142 Franklin St (02176-1821)
PHONE..................................781 462-3942
David Ingemi, *Principal*
EMP: 5
SALES (est): 584.4K **Privately Held**
SIC: 7372 Prepackaged Software Services

(G-12975)
ATLEE DELAWARE INCORPORATED
9 Clinton Rd (02176-4406)
PHONE..................................978 681-1003
Gary Bergholtz, *President*
William Berkley, *Chairman*
EMP: 10
SQ FT: 22,500
SALES (est): 2.1MM **Privately Held**
WEB: www.atlee.com
SIC: 3643 3678 3496 Mfg Conductive Wire Dvcs Mfg Elec Connectors Mfg Misc Fab Wire Prdts

(G-12976)
CEEK ENTERPRISES INC
1 City Hall Plz (02176-3149)
PHONE..................................919 522-4837
Fahti Khosrowshahi Self, *Officer*
Darius Naigamwalla, *Officer*
EMP: 4 **EST:** 2015
SALES (est): 198.6K **Privately Held**
SIC: 3841 Mfg Surgical/Medical Instruments

(G-12977)
CERAMIC TO METAL SEALS INC
78 Stone Pl Ste 4 (02176)
PHONE..................................781 665-5002
Nancy Ingemi, *President*
EMP: 16
SQ FT: 7,500
SALES (est): 1.7MM **Privately Held**
WEB: www.ceramictometalseals.com
SIC: 3679 Mfg Electronic Components

(G-12978)
CHURCHILL CORPORATION
344 Franklin St (02176-1825)
P.O. Box 761038 (02176-0007)
PHONE..................................781 665-4700
Marshall W Schermerhorn, *President*
Warren Schermerhorn, *Vice Pres*
Rhoda H Schermerhorn, *Treasurer*
EMP: 25 **EST:** 1948
SQ FT: 8,000
SALES (est): 5.5MM **Privately Held**
WEB: www.atrbox.com
SIC: 3444 Mfg Sheet Metalwork

(G-12979)
CIPEM USA INC
44b Grove St Unit 78 (02176)
PHONE..................................347 642-1106
Marc L'Hoste, *Director*
EMP: 3
SQ FT: 400
SALES (est): 331.5K
SALES (corp-wide): 3MM **Privately Held**
SIC: 3629 3559 5065 Mfg Electrical Industrial Apparatus Mfg Misc Industry Machinery Whol Electronic Parts/Equipment
PA: Icape Holding
33 Avenue Du General Leclerc
Fontenay-Aux-Roses 92260
146 446-695

(G-12980)
CREST PRINTING CO INC
152 Vinton St (02176-2634)
PHONE..................................617 889-1171
Debra McGonagle, *President*
Debra Mc Gonagle, *President*
EMP: 5 **EST:** 1965
SQ FT: 2,300
SALES: 450K **Privately Held**
SIC: 2752 2759 Commercial Offset Printing

(G-12981)
DORN EQUIPMENT CORP
27 Upham St (02176-3505)
PHONE..................................781 662-9300
Matthew Flynn, *President*
Alice Flynn, *Treasurer*
Phylliss Wilson, *Shareholder*
EMP: 15 **EST:** 1939
SQ FT: 17,000
SALES (est): 2.6MM **Privately Held**
WEB: www.dornequipment.com
SIC: 2891 3643 Mfg Sealants And Electric Connectors & Plugs

(G-12982)
HILLSIDE PRESS
192 Green St (02176-1920)
PHONE..................................617 742-1922
James Micheli Jr, *Owner*
EMP: 3
SALES (est): 363.8K **Privately Held**
SIC: 2759 Commercial Printing

(G-12983)
JORNAL DOS SPORTS LLC
30 Oakland St 1 (02176-2608)
PHONE..................................857 888-9186
Alex Colombini, *President*
EMP: 3 **EST:** 2012
SALES (est): 140K **Privately Held**
SIC: 2711 Newspapers-Publishing/Printing

(G-12984)
KHOURY FUEL INC
386 Main St (02176-4623)
PHONE..................................781 251-0993
Richard Elkhoury, *Principal*
EMP: 6
SALES (est): 553.3K **Privately Held**
SIC: 2869 Mfg Industrial Organic Chemicals

(G-12985)
MICROWAVE VIDEO SYSTEMS LLC
165c Tremont St (02176-2247)
PHONE..................................781 665-6600
Warren Parece Jr,
EMP: 4
SALES (est): 379.7K **Privately Held**
SIC: 3663 Mfg Radio/Tv Communication Equipment

(G-12986)
OMNIMEDICS
33 Chipman Ave (02176-1202)
PHONE..................................617 527-4590
Andrew Biagioni, *Owner*
EMP: 4
SALES (est): 181.4K **Privately Held**
WEB: www.omnimedics.com
SIC: 3845 Mfg Electromedical Equipment

(G-12987)
PARECE JP COMPANY
165c Tremont St (02176-2247)
PHONE..................................781 662-8640
James Parece, *Owner*
EMP: 3
SALES: 500K **Privately Held**
SIC: 3663 Mfg Radio/Tv Communication Equipment

(G-12988)
PRINTING PLACE INC
26 Philip Cir (02176-5810)
PHONE..................................781 272-7209
EMP: 4
SQ FT: 3,000
SALES (est): 470K **Privately Held**
SIC: 2752 2791 2789 Lithographic Commercial Printing Typesetting Services Bookbinding/Related Work

(G-12989)
PRO AM ENTERPRISES INC
180 Tremont St (02176-2204)
PHONE..................................781 662-8888
Tom Hirschfeld, *President*
EMP: 4
SQ FT: 1,800
SALES (est): 299.4K **Privately Held**
SIC: 2395 2396 Custom Embroidery

(G-12990)
PROMAX SUPPLY LLC
142 Franklin St (02176-1821)
PHONE..................................781 620-1602
David R Ingemi,
EMP: 15 **EST:** 2007
SALES (est): 4.7MM **Privately Held**
SIC: 2741 Internet Publishing And Broadcasting

(G-12991)
ROWE CONTRACTING CO
90 Woodcrest Dr (02176-3416)
PHONE..................................781 620-0052
Warren C Rowe Jr, *President*
Warren C Rowe Sr, *Treasurer*
EMP: 8
SQ FT: 1,000
SALES (est): 470.4K **Privately Held**
SIC: 1481 6531 Nonmetallic Mineral Services Real Estate Agent/Manager

(G-12992)
SCHOFIELD CONCRETE FORMS INC
195 Warwick Rd (02176-2615)
PHONE..................................781 662-0796
Steven Schofield, *President*
EMP: 5
SALES (est): 509.3K **Privately Held**
SIC: 3272 Concrete Products

Mendon
Worcester County

(G-12993)
FIRE-1 MANUFACTURING INC
70 Millville Rd (01756-1269)
PHONE..................................508 478-8473
Stanley J Wojnowski Jr, *Principal*
EMP: 6
SALES (est): 375.6K **Privately Held**
SIC: 3999 Mfg Misc Products

(G-12994)
RAND BARTHEL TREASURER
50 Asylum St (01756-1229)
PHONE..................................508 473-3305
EMP: 3
SALES (est): 214.2K **Privately Held**
SIC: 3131 Mfg Footwear Cut Stock

(G-12995)
RRK WALKER INC
22 Park St (01756-1226)
PHONE..................................508 541-8100
Robert Walker, *Principal*
EMP: 3
SALES (est): 212.5K **Privately Held**
SIC: 3842 Mfg Surgical Appliances/Supplies

(G-12996)
TECHNICAL METAL FABRICATORS
134 Uxbridge Rd (01756-1217)
P.O. Box 317 (01756-0317)
PHONE..................................508 473-2223
Mike Candela, *President*
Joseph Candela, *Vice Pres*
Evelyn Candela, *Treasurer*
EMP: 14
SQ FT: 1,800
SALES (est): 1.4MM **Privately Held**
SIC: 3444 Mfg Sheet Metalwork

(G-12997)
VISUAL MAGNETICS LTD
1 Emerson St (01756-1273)
PHONE..................................508 381-2400
Dayton J Deetz, *President*
Sandra L Deetz, *Corp Secy*
Alan Roseman, *Human Res Dir*
Sue Auty, *Executive Asst*
▲ **EMP:** 30
SALES (est): 6.4MM **Privately Held**
SIC: 2672 Mfg Coated/Laminated Paper

(G-12998)
VISUAL MAGNETICS LTD PARTNR
1 Emerson St (01756-1273)
PHONE..................................508 381-2400
Joe Deetz, *Managing Prtnr*
EMP: 14
SALES (est): 2.4MM **Privately Held**
SIC: 2672 Mfg Coated/Laminated Paper

▲ = Import ▼=Export
◆ =Import/Export

Merrimac
Essex County

(G-12999)
ALPHA FIERCE LLC
2 Prospect Hill St (01860-1524)
PHONE..................................781 518-3311
Viviane Silveira,
EMP: 3 **EST:** 2017
SALES (est): 83.9K **Privately Held**
SIC: 3999 Mfg Misc Products

(G-13000)
ANGLO-SAXON FEDERATION OF AMER
Also Called: Destiny Publishers
43 Grove St (01860-1807)
P.O. Box 177 (01860-0177)
PHONE..................................978 346-9311
Henry D Lay Sr, *President*
Gerald Lay, *Vice Pres*
Priscilla M Fitgerald, *Treasurer*
Mildred Prime, *Asst Treas*
Shirley B Campbell, *Clerk*
EMP: 6
SALES: 102.6K **Privately Held**
SIC: 2731 Books-Publishing/Printing

(G-13001)
H I FIVE RENEWABLES
8 Church St (01860-1500)
PHONE..................................978 384-8032
Louise Hart, *Exec Dir*
EMP: 5
SALES (est): 217.3K **Privately Held**
SIC: 2869 Mfg Industrial Organic Chemicals

(G-13002)
JAMES F MULLEN CO INC
Also Called: J F M
51 E Main St (01860-2034)
PHONE..................................978 346-0045
Robert J Mullen, *President*
John P Mullen, *Corp Secy*
Nancy Tanzella, *Supervisor*
EMP: 60
SQ FT: 90,000
SALES (est): 10.2MM **Privately Held**
WEB: www.jfmullen.net
SIC: 3599 Mfg Industrial Machinery

(G-13003)
JAS F MULLEN CO INC
Also Called: Manufacturing
51 E Main St (01860-2034)
PHONE..................................978 346-0045
Robert J Mullen, *Principal*
EMP: 5
SALES (est): 484.8K **Privately Held**
SIC: 3469 Mfg Metal Stampings

(G-13004)
NORTHAST GREEN ENRGY GROUP INC
Also Called: Negeg
49 W Main St (01860-2211)
PHONE..................................978 478-8425
Thomas R Terrazzano, *CFO*
EMP: 3
SALES: 100K **Privately Held**
SIC: 3648 Mfg Lighting Equipment

(G-13005)
PARKER HANNIFIN CORPORA
13 Little Pond Rd (01860-2256)
PHONE..................................978 346-0578
EMP: 3 **EST:** 2017
SALES (est): 182.6K **Privately Held**
SIC: 3594 Mfg Fluid Power Pumps/Motors

(G-13006)
TECHNOLOGIES/TYPOGRAPHY
Also Called: Technologies 'n Typography
8 Church St (01860-1500)
PHONE..................................978 346-4867
Kevin Krugh, *Owner*
EMP: 3
SALES (est): 254.3K **Privately Held**
WEB: www.p-kive.com
SIC: 2791 2731 Typesetting Services Books-Publishing/Printing

Methuen
Essex County

(G-13007)
3M COMPANY
501 Griffin Brook Park Dr (01844-1870)
PHONE..................................978 659-9000
Lisa Pustis, *Branch Mgr*
EMP: 500
SALES (corp-wide): 32.7B **Publicly Held**
SIC: 2679 Display And Graphics
PA: 3m Company
3m Center
Saint Paul MN 55144
651 733-1110

(G-13008)
3M TOUCH SYSTEMS INC (HQ)
501 Griffin Brook Dr (01844-1870)
PHONE..................................978 659-9000
Makoto M Ishii, *President*
Dennis P Duerst, *Treasurer*
Terry Jones, *Business Dir*
Amy Sanders, *Admin Sec*
◆ **EMP:** 325 **EST:** 1983
SQ FT: 96,000
SALES (est): 123MM
SALES (corp-wide): 32.7B **Publicly Held**
WEB: www.dynapro.com
SIC: 3577 Mfg Computer Peripheral Equipment
PA: 3m Company
3m Center
Saint Paul MN 55144
651 733-1110

(G-13009)
3M TOUCH SYSTEMS INC
501 Griffin Brook Park Dr (01844-1870)
PHONE..................................978 659-9000
Lisa Pustis, *Manager*
EMP: 300
SALES (corp-wide): 32.7B **Publicly Held**
WEB: www.dynapro.com
SIC: 3577 Mfg Computer Peripheral Equipment
HQ: 3m Touch Systems, Inc.
501 Griffin Brook Dr
Methuen MA 01844
978 659-9000

(G-13010)
ACCORD SOFTWARE INC
42 Olympic Village Dr (01844-4159)
PHONE..................................978 687-2320
Arun Taylor, *President*
Divya Taylor, *Treasurer*
EMP: 5
SALES (est): 460K **Privately Held**
WEB: www.accord.com
SIC: 7372 Prepackaged Software Services

(G-13011)
AN ELECTRONIC INSTRUMENTATION
Also Called: R M Electronics
300 Griffin Brook Dr (01844-1821)
PHONE..................................978 208-4555
Bob Monaco, *Manager*
EMP: 80
SALES (corp-wide): 71MM **Privately Held**
WEB: www.suntroncorp.com
SIC: 3672 Contract Manufacturer Specializing In Circuit Board Assembly
PA: Electronic Instrumentation And Technology, Llc
309 Kellys Ford Plz Se
Leesburg VA 20175
703 478-0700

(G-13012)
BAY STATE ELECTRIC MOTOR CO
20 Aegean Dr Ste 6 (01844-1580)
PHONE..................................978 686-7089
Andrew Hammond, *President*
EMP: 3
SQ FT: 3,200
SALES (est): 482.9K **Privately Held**
SIC: 7694 5999 Repairs & Ret Electric Motors

(G-13013)
CENTRAL VACUUM CLEANERS (PA)
Also Called: C V C
476 Lowell St Ste 1 (01844-2284)
PHONE..................................978 682-5294
William De Pippo, *President*
Joyce N Thomas, *General Mgr*
Bill Depippo, *Vice Pres*
▲ **EMP:** 12
SQ FT: 17,250
SALES: 2.2MM **Privately Held**
WEB: www.galaxie-vac.com
SIC: 3589 3444 Mfg Service Industry Machinery Mfg Sheet Metalwork

(G-13014)
CIRCLE METAL FINISHING INC
55 Chase St Ste 3 (01844-3700)
PHONE..................................978 682-4297
John J Provasolia, *President*
EMP: 3
SQ FT: 2,500
SALES: 300K **Privately Held**
SIC: 3471 Plating/Polishing Service

(G-13015)
COLOR IMAGES INC
Also Called: American Speedy Printing
99 West St (01844-1319)
PHONE..................................978 688-4994
Steve Clark, *President*
Robert Reddish, *Vice Pres*
EMP: 4
SALES (est): 322.8K **Privately Held**
SIC: 2752 7334 2791 2789 Lithographic Coml Print Photocopying Service Typesetting Services Bookbinding/Related Work

(G-13016)
CR TECHNOLOGY INC
55 Chase St Ste 3 (01844-3700)
PHONE..................................978 681-5305
Gerald Kiley, *President*
EMP: 5
SALES (est): 844.4K **Privately Held**
SIC: 3544 Mfg Dies/Tools/Jigs/Fixtures

(G-13017)
D&P MEDIA FOR PRINT INC
46 Bridle Path Ln (01844-1570)
PHONE..................................978 685-2210
William Lescarbeau, *President*
EMP: 4
SALES (est): 207.3K **Privately Held**
SIC: 2752 Lithographic Commercial Printing

(G-13018)
DMJL CONSULTING LLC
145 Milk St (01844-4664)
PHONE..................................978 989-0790
John R Loconte, *Principal*
EMP: 19
SALES (est): 4.2MM **Privately Held**
SIC: 3273 Mfg Ready-Mixed Concrete

(G-13019)
ELECTRONIC ASSEMBLIES MFG INC
Also Called: Conductrf
126 Merrimack St (01844-6109)
PHONE..................................978 374-6840
Diane Pessinis, *President*
Denise Shaw, *Vice Pres*
Steve Pessinis, *Treasurer*
Dean Gammell, *Director*
EMP: 41
SQ FT: 10,000
SALES (est): 7MM **Privately Held**
WEB: www.eassymfg.com
SIC: 3679 Mfg Electronic Components

(G-13020)
EMBROIDERY LOFT
60 Pine St Ste F (01844-6832)
PHONE..................................978 681-1155
Ann Ford, *Owner*
EMP: 4
SALES (est): 323.3K **Privately Held**
WEB: www.embroideryloft.com
SIC: 2395 Pleating/Stitching Services

(G-13021)
ESSEX RULING & PRINTING CO
Also Called: Essex Printing
154 Haverhill St Ste 2 (01844-3400)
PHONE..................................978 682-2457
Edward Bonaccorsi, *President*
John Bonaccorsi, *Vice Pres*
Sandra Bonaccorsi, *Admin Sec*
EMP: 9 **EST:** 1941
SALES: 350K **Privately Held**
SIC: 2752 Lithographic Commercial Printing

(G-13022)
FOCUSED RESOLUTIONS INC
40 Arrowwood St (01844-1411)
PHONE..................................978 794-7981
Lawrence Barry, *President*
EMP: 3
SALES: 200K **Privately Held**
WEB: www.focusedresolutions.com
SIC: 3827 5049 Mfg Optical Instruments/Lenses Whol Professional Equipment

(G-13023)
FUJI MATS LLC
12 Cameron Way (01844-2697)
PHONE..................................205 419-5080
Jimmy Pedro, *President*
Thomas Tschida, *Associate*
EMP: 4
SALES (est): 417.9K **Privately Held**
SIC: 3949 Mfg Sporting/Athletic Goods

(G-13024)
GOOBY INDUSTRIES CORP
Also Called: Century Box
45 Chase St Ste 45 # 45 (01844-3771)
PHONE..................................978 689-0100
Joanna Kagan, *President*
Alvin Kagan, *Treasurer*
David Kagan, *Admin Sec*
Mark Kagan, *Admin Sec*
EMP: 125
SQ FT: 122,000
SALES (est): 32.3MM **Privately Held**
WEB: www.centurybox.com
SIC: 2657 Mfg Folding Paperboard Boxes

(G-13025)
H & H ENGINEERING CO INC
Also Called: Mechancal Engrg Met Fbrication
6 Pine St (01844-6818)
PHONE..................................978 682-0567
Joseph P Helfrich Jr, *President*
Mike Helfrich, *Vice Pres*
Richard A Helfrich, *Treasurer*
EMP: 12
SQ FT: 12,000
SALES: 1MM **Privately Held**
WEB: www.hhengineers.com
SIC: 3443 Mfg Fabricated Plate Work

(G-13026)
HANGER PRSTHETCS & ORTHO INC
100 Milk St Ste 120 (01844-4600)
PHONE..................................978 683-5509
John Dieli, *Manager*
EMP: 3
SALES (corp-wide): 1B **Publicly Held**
SIC: 3842 Mfg Surgical Appliances/Supplies
HQ: Hanger Prosthetics & Orthotics, Inc.
10910 Domain Dr Ste 300
Austin TX 78758
512 777-3800

(G-13027)
HARVEY SIGNS INC
30 Osgood St (01844-3030)
PHONE..................................978 794-2071
Don Harvey, *President*
Richard Harvey, *Vice Pres*
EMP: 4
SQ FT: 11,760
SALES (est): 416.2K **Privately Held**
WEB: www.harveysigns.com
SIC: 3993 Mfg Signs/Advertising Specialties

(G-13028)
JAMLAB ENTERPRISES
190 Haverhill St (01844-3462)
PHONE....................978 688-8750
John Sullivan, *Owner*
EMP: 4
SALES: 75K **Privately Held**
SIC: 3599 Mfg Industrial Machinery

(G-13029)
JOBART INC (PA)
Also Called: New England Outdoor Wood Pdts
37 1/2 Oakland Ave (01844-3741)
PHONE....................978 689-4414
Joseph Bartolotta Sr, *President*
Joseph Bartolotta Jr, *Vice Pres*
Kathleen Bartolotta, *Treasurer*
EMP: 15
SQ FT: 13,000
SALES (est): 3.5MM **Privately Held**
SIC: 2452 5712 Mfg Prefabricated Wood Buildings Ret Furniture

(G-13030)
KSARIA CORPORATION (PA)
300 Griffin Brook Dr (01844-1821)
PHONE....................866 457-2742
Sebastian J Sicari, *Ch of Bd*
Anthony Christopher, *President*
Paul Jortberg, *Vice Pres*
Dora Dos, *Buyer*
Michael A Dipoto, *CFO*
EMP: 80
SALES (est): 15.3MM **Privately Held**
WEB: www.ksaria.com
SIC: 3679 3678 Mfg Electronic Components Mfg Electronic Connectors

(G-13031)
KSARIA SERVICE CORPORATION
300 Griffin Brook Dr (01844-1821)
PHONE....................978 933-0000
Sebastian J Sicari, *CEO*
Michael Dipoto, *CFO*
EMP: 40
SALES (est): 1.4MM **Privately Held**
SIC: 3731 Shipbuilding/Repairing

(G-13032)
LABOMBARD MACHINE
55 Chase St (01844-3709)
PHONE....................978 688-7773
Raymond Cloutier, *Owner*
EMP: 6
SQ FT: 4,500
SALES: 350K **Privately Held**
SIC: 3451 Manufactures Screw Machine Products

(G-13033)
LOOP WEEKLY
238 Pleasant St (01844-7153)
PHONE....................978 683-8800
EMP: 3
SALES (est): 127.9K **Privately Held**
SIC: 2711 Newspapers-Publishing/Printing

(G-13034)
MASS CABINETS INC
99 Cross St (01844-1654)
PHONE....................978 738-0600
Mike Sarno, *President*
Bill Shay, *General Mgr*
Korin McDaniel, *Admin Sec*
EMP: 20
SQ FT: 20,000
SALES (est): 3.5MM **Privately Held**
SIC: 2434 Mfg Wood Kitchen Cabinets

(G-13035)
MERRIMACK ENGRAVING & MKG CO
55 Chase St (01844-3709)
P.O. Box 2054 (01844-1098)
PHONE....................978 683-5335
John Ness, *President*
Cynthia Ness, *President*
EMP: 4
SALES (est): 377.6K **Privately Held**
WEB: www.memco.net
SIC: 3993 Mfg Signs/Advertising Specialties

(G-13036)
METALCRAFTERS INC
104 Pleasant Valley St (01844-7204)
P.O. Box 729 (01844-0729)
PHONE....................978 683-7097
Andrew Tucker, *President*
Eric Morgan, *Project Mgr*
Jim Blouin, *Prdtn Mgr*
Jay Proctor, *Foreman/Supr*
Marla Collins, *Asst Treas*
▲ **EMP:** 50
SQ FT: 150,000
SALES (est): 14.1MM **Privately Held**
SIC: 3444 Mfg Sheet Metalwork

(G-13037)
MKS INSTRUMENTS INC
Also Called: Mks Astex Products
651 Lowell St (01844-1855)
PHONE....................978 682-3512
Mike Utegg, *Buyer*
Bruce Welsh, *Design Engr*
Paul Loomis, *Branch Mgr*
Gordon Jarvis, *Planning*
EMP: 75
SALES (corp-wide): 2B **Publicly Held**
SIC: 3823 Mfg Process Control Instruments
PA: Mks Instruments, Inc.
2 Tech Dr Ste 201
Andover MA 01810
978 645-5500

(G-13038)
NAFP INC
Also Called: New American Food Products
983 Riverside Dr (01844-6703)
PHONE....................978 682-1855
John Morrissey, *Ch of Bd*
Thomas M Reilly, *President*
Robin Birch, *Vice Pres*
▲ **EMP:** 60
SQ FT: 30,000
SALES (est): 11.8MM **Privately Held**
WEB: www.candybreak.com
SIC: 2064 Mfg Candy/Confectionery

(G-13039)
NEW ENGLAND DIE CUTTING INC
Also Called: Nedc Sealing Solutions
96 Milk St (01844-4620)
PHONE....................978 374-0789
Kimberly L Abare, *President*
David G Abare, *Vice Pres*
Garrett Abare, *Sales Staff*
Sue Graham, *Office Mgr*
EMP: 27 **EST:** 1982
SQ FT: 71,000
SALES: 5.6MM **Privately Held**
WEB: www.nedc.com
SIC: 3053 Mfg Gaskets/Packing/Sealing Devices

(G-13040)
NHV AMERICA INC
100 Griffin Brook Dr (01844-1867)
PHONE....................978 682-4900
Yaz Hoshi, *President*
▲ **EMP:** 16
SALES (est): 2.5MM **Privately Held**
SIC: 3699 Mfg Electrical Equipment/Supplies
HQ: Nhv Corporation
47, Takazecho, Umezu, Ukyo-Ku
Kyoto KYO 615-0

(G-13041)
PARLEX
145 Milk St (01844-4699)
PHONE....................978 946-2500
Christopher John Hasson, *Principal*
▲ **EMP:** 14
SALES (est): 2.1MM **Privately Held**
SIC: 3672 Mfg Printed Circuit Boards

(G-13042)
PLEASANT STREET DESIGNS INC
1 Aegean Dr (01844-1560)
PHONE....................978 682-3910
Sean Quinn, *President*
Sandra Grenier, *Vice Pres*
EMP: 5 **EST:** 2010
SALES (est): 465.8K **Privately Held**
SIC: 3499 Mfg Misc Fabricated Metal Products

(G-13043)
PRECISIVE LLC
651 Lowell St (01844-1855)
PHONE....................781 850-4469
Duane Sword, *CEO*
Vidi Saptari, *President*
EMP: 6
SALES (est): 1MM
SALES (corp-wide): 2B **Publicly Held**
SIC: 3674 Manufacturing Semiconductors/Related Devices
PA: Mks Instruments, Inc.
2 Tech Dr Ste 201
Andover MA 01810
978 645-5500

(G-13044)
PROXY MANUFACTURING INC
55 Chase St Ste 7 (01844-3700)
PHONE....................978 687-3138
Shawn Foy, *President*
Kathleen M Dugas, *CFO*
EMP: 30
SQ FT: 30,000
SALES (est): 8.5MM **Privately Held**
WEB: www.proxyinc.com
SIC: 3672 Mfg Printed Circuit Boards

(G-13045)
SUNSET ENGRAVERS
678 Lowell St (01844-1819)
PHONE....................978 687-1111
Phillip A Silverio, *Owner*
EMP: 3
SQ FT: 4,000
SALES (est): 125K **Privately Held**
WEB: www.sunsetengravers.com
SIC: 3479 3353 2396 Coating/Engraving Service Mfg Aluminum Sheet/Foil Mfg Auto/Apparel Trimming

(G-13046)
THERMATRON ENGINEERING INC
687 Lowell St (01844-1869)
PHONE....................978 687-8844
David P Savoy, *President*
Robert J Rabbitt, *Vice Pres*
John Urrata, *Engineer*
Bryan Rabbitt, *Design Engr*
Robert Rabbitt Jr, *Treasurer*
EMP: 50
SALES (est): 12.3MM **Privately Held**
WEB: www.thermatroneng.com
SIC: 3351 3317 3443 Copper Rolling/Drawing Mfg Steel Pipe/Tubes Mfg Fabricated Plate Work

(G-13047)
TRI-STAR MACHINE INC
55 Chase St Ste 1 (01844-3700)
PHONE....................978 683-2600
Keith Daykin, *President*
EMP: 5
SQ FT: 3,500
SALES (est): 615.3K **Privately Held**
SIC: 3599 Machine Shop

(G-13048)
WOOD PRODUCTS UNLIMITED INC
60 Hidden Rd (01844-1860)
P.O. Box 855, Wilmington (01887-0855)
PHONE....................978 687-7449
David Labrecque, *President*
Jim Wetterberg, *Clerk*
EMP: 3
SALES: 300K **Privately Held**
SIC: 2448 2631 2653 3089 Mfg Wood Pallets/Skids Paperboard Mill Mfg Corrugated/Fiber Box Mfg Plastic Products

(G-13049)
ZOLIKON INC
55 Chase St Ste 17 (01844-3700)
PHONE....................978 689-4789
Fax: 978 689-4813
EMP: 4
SQ FT: 5,000
SALES (est): 300K **Privately Held**
SIC: 3599 Mfg Industrial Machinery

Middleboro
Plymouth County

(G-13050)
ALDEN SHOE COMPANY INC
Also Called: Alden New England
1 Taunton St (02346-1426)
PHONE....................508 947-3926
Arthur S Tarlow, *President*
Arthur S Tarlow Jr, *President*
Robert J Clark, *Director*
Richard G Hajjar, *Admin Sec*
▲ **EMP:** 200 **EST:** 1884
SQ FT: 70,000
SALES (est): 28MM **Privately Held**
SIC: 3143 Mfg Men's Footwear

(G-13051)
AMETEK ARIZONA INSTRUMENT LLC
Also Called: Ametek Brookfield
11 Commerce Blvd (02346-1031)
PHONE....................508 946-6200
Mike Sampou, *Materials Mgr*
Melissa Kidd, *Branch Mgr*
EMP: 190
SALES (corp-wide): 4.8B **Publicly Held**
SIC: 3823 3824 3825 3621 Mfg Process Cntrl Instr
HQ: Ametek Arizona Instrument Llc
3375 N Delaware St
Chandler AZ 85225
602 470-1414

(G-13052)
ANDYS MACHINE INC
Also Called: AMI
23 Abbey Ln (02346-3230)
PHONE....................508 947-1192
Paul E Singley, *President*
Stacy Reidy, *Materials Mgr*
Charles Gillis, *Director*
Cheryl Mahoney, *Administration*
EMP: 30
SQ FT: 17,000
SALES (est): 4.8MM **Privately Held**
WEB: www.amimachining.com
SIC: 3599 Mfg Industrial Machinery

(G-13053)
AQUA SOLUTIONS INC
154 W Grove St Ste D (02346-1484)
PHONE....................508 947-5777
Christopher Shea, *President*
James Deluca, *Treasurer*
EMP: 4 **EST:** 2000
SALES (est): 931.2K **Privately Held**
SIC: 3823 Water Quality Systems

(G-13054)
ATLANTIC METALCRAFT CO
14 Cooney Ln (02346-3434)
PHONE....................781 447-9900
Kathleen Cooney, *President*
Thomas McGuinness, *General Mgr*
EMP: 3
SQ FT: 4,000
SALES: 375K **Privately Held**
WEB: www.atlanticmetalcraftco.com
SIC: 3823 Mfg Water Purification Equipment

(G-13055)
BIMBO BAKERIES USA INC
45 Leona Dr (02346-1404)
PHONE....................508 923-1023
EMP: 18 **Privately Held**
SIC: 2051 Mfg Bread/Related Products
HQ: Bimbo Bakeries Usa, Inc
255 Business Center Dr # 200
Horsham PA 19044
215 347-5500

(G-13056)
BOUCHER CON FOUNDATION SUPS
80 Cambridge St (02346-4013)
PHONE....................508 947-4279
Mike Boucher, *Principal*
EMP: 5
SALES (est): 514.3K **Privately Held**
SIC: 3273 Mfg Ready-Mixed Concrete

(G-13057)
BUTLER AUTOMATIC INC (PA)
41 Leona Dr (02346-1404)
PHONE..................................508 923-0544
David Johns II, *President*
Andrew Butler, *Corp Secy*
Mike Mucci, *Vice Pres*
Michael Mucci, *VP Engrg*
Paul Cleary, *CFO*
▲ **EMP:** 75 **EST:** 1956
SQ FT: 30,000
SALES: 11.3MM **Privately Held**
WEB: www.butlerautomatic.com
SIC: 3555 3565 3554 Mfg Printing Trades Machinery Mfg Packaging Machinery Mfg Paper Industrial Machinery

(G-13058)
BYRNE SAND & GRAVEL CO INC
210 Wood St (02346-2853)
PHONE..................................508 947-0724
Donald Gallant, *President*
William L Byrne, *President*
Don Gallant, *Vice Pres*
Susan Byrne, *Treasurer*
EMP: 16 **EST:** 1966
SALES: 3MM **Privately Held**
SIC: 3272 Mfg Concrete Products

(G-13059)
CONCENTRIC FABRICATION LLC
7 Coombs St (02346-2409)
PHONE..................................508 672-4098
Rob Lorenson, *Mng Member*
EMP: 10
SALES (est): 887K **Privately Held**
SIC: 3446 3312 Mfg Architectural Metalwork Blast Furnace-Steel Works

(G-13060)
CRANBERRY COUNTRY MACHINE & TL
15 Summer St (02346-1318)
PHONE..................................508 923-1107
Stephen McDermott, *Owner*
EMP: 3
SALES (est): 331.8K **Privately Held**
SIC: 3599 Mfg Industrial Machinery

(G-13061)
D & D PRECISION MACHINE CO INC
395 Plymouth St (02346-1624)
PHONE..................................508 946-8010
Joseph Vallatini, *Vice Pres*
EMP: 21
SALES (est): 3.8MM **Privately Held**
SIC: 3599 Mfg Industrial Machinery

(G-13062)
DI-MO MANUFACTURING INC
Also Called: Di MO Tool
35 Harding St (02346-1013)
PHONE..................................508 947-2200
Albert S Diaz, *President*
EMP: 9
SQ FT: 38,000
SALES (est): 1.6MM **Privately Held**
SIC: 3089 Mfg Plastic Products

(G-13063)
GORMAN MACHINE CORP
122 E Grove St (02346-2747)
P.O. Box 512 (02346-0512)
PHONE..................................508 923-9462
Kenneth P Gorman, *President*
Daniel Gorman, *Managing Prtnr*
Diane Sanford, *CFO*
▼ **EMP:** 20
SQ FT: 15,800
SALES (est): 3.5MM **Privately Held**
WEB: www.gormanmachine.com
SIC: 3549 5084 Mfg Metalworking Machinery Whol Industrial Equipment

(G-13064)
IDEX HEALTH & SCIENCE LLC
Also Called: Sapphire Engineering
16 Leona Dr (02346-1433)
PHONE..................................774 213-0200
Keith Besse, *Branch Mgr*
Liz Woolfrey, *Info Tech Mgr*
EMP: 120
SALES (corp-wide): 2.4B **Publicly Held**
SIC: 3821 7389 3231 3264 Mfg Lab Apparatus/Furn Business Services Mfg Prdt-Purchased Glass Mfg Porcelain Elc Supply Mfg Plumbing Fxtr Fittng
HQ: Idex Health & Science Llc
600 Park Ct
Rohnert Park CA 94928
707 588-2000

(G-13065)
LOUIS M GERSON CO INC (PA)
16 Commerce Blvd Ste D (02346-1085)
PHONE..................................508 947-4000
Ronald L Gerson, *Ch of Bd*
Ron Zayas, *Vice Pres*
Joe Mandile, *Plant Mgr*
Michael Silvia, *Production*
Harry Blaser, *Engineer*
◆ **EMP:** 25 **EST:** 1945
SQ FT: 22,500
SALES (est): 25.1MM **Privately Held**
WEB: www.gersonco.com
SIC: 3842 Mfg Surgical Appliances/Supplies

(G-13066)
LOUIS M GERSON CO INC
15 Sumner Ave (02346-1535)
PHONE..................................508 947-4000
Ronald L Gerson, *Branch Mgr*
EMP: 34
SALES (corp-wide): 25.1MM **Privately Held**
SIC: 3842 Mfg Surgical Appliances/Supplies
PA: Louis M. Gerson Co., Inc
16 Commerce Blvd Ste D
Middleboro MA 02346
508 947-4000

(G-13067)
MALDEN INTL DESIGNS INC
Also Called: Giovanni
19 Cowan Dr (02346-3700)
PHONE..................................508 946-2270
John Aucello, *President*
Cheryl Lesser, *Natl Sales Mgr*
Arlene Faria, *Sales Mgr*
Paul Pasternak, *Sales Mgr*
◆ **EMP:** 75 **EST:** 1948
SQ FT: 120,000
SALES (est): 12MM **Privately Held**
WEB: www.malden.com
SIC: 2499 3499 Mfg Wood Products Mfg Misc Fabricated Metal Products

(G-13068)
MASS ENGINEERING & TANK INC
29 Abbey Ln (02346-3230)
PHONE..................................508 947-8669
Carl Horstmann, *President*
EMP: 23
SQ FT: 58,000
SALES (est): 3.2MM **Privately Held**
WEB: www.masstec.com
SIC: 3412 3443 Mfg Metal Barrels/Pails Mfg Fabricated Plate Work

(G-13069)
MASS TANK SALES CORP
29 Abbey Ln (02346-3230)
PHONE..................................508 947-8826
Carl Horstmann, *President*
EMP: 25
SALES: 5MM **Privately Held**
WEB: www.masstank.com
SIC: 3443 Steel Fabrication

(G-13070)
MUELLER WATER PRODUCTS INC
48 Leona Dr Ste C (02346-5400)
PHONE..................................508 923-2870
Seyamak Keyghobad, *Branch Mgr*
Derek Sewall, *Analyst*
Laura Wilhelm, *Analyst*
EMP: 17
SALES (corp-wide): 968MM **Publicly Held**
SIC: 3491 Mfg Industrial Valves
PA: Mueller Water Products, Inc.
1200 Abernathy Rd # 1200
Atlanta GA 30328
770 206-4200

(G-13071)
OCEAN SPRAY (EUROPE) LTD
1 Ocean Spray Dr (02349-0001)
PHONE..................................508 946-1000
Pat Clark, *CEO*
Randy C Papadellis, *CEO*
Andre Chambers, *President*
Charlie Dulany, *Treasurer*
◆ **EMP:** 10
SALES (est): 1.4MM
SALES (corp-wide): 1.6B **Privately Held**
WEB: www.oceanspraycrantastics.com
SIC: 2033 Mfg Canned Fruits/Vegetables
PA: Ocean Spray Cranberries, Inc.
1 Ocean Spray Dr
Middleboro MA 02349
508 946-1000

(G-13072)
OCEAN SPRAY CRANBERRIES INC (PA)
1 Ocean Spray Dr (02349-0001)
PHONE..................................508 946-1000
Bobby J Chacko, *President*
◆ **EMP:** 475 **EST:** 1930
SQ FT: 165,000
SALES: 1.6B **Privately Held**
WEB: www.oceanspraycrantastics.com
SIC: 2033 2034 2037 Mfg Canned Fruits/Vegtbl Mfg Dhydrtd Fruit/Vegtbl

(G-13073)
OCEAN SPRAY CRANBERRIES INC
152 Bridge St (02346-1693)
PHONE..................................508 947-4940
Carl Ferrari, *Chief Engr*
Jim Ropeto, *Manager*
Joe Boileau, *Supervisor*
EMP: 110
SQ FT: 400,000
SALES (corp-wide): 1.6B **Privately Held**
WEB: www.oceanspraycrantastics.com
SIC: 2033 2037 Mfg Canned Fruits/Vegetables Mfg Frozen Fruits/Vegetables
PA: Ocean Spray Cranberries, Inc.
1 Ocean Spray Dr
Middleboro MA 02349
508 946-1000

(G-13074)
OCEAN SPRAY INTERNATIONAL INC (HQ)
1 Ocean Spray Dr (02349-0001)
PHONE..................................508 946-1000
Kenneth Romanzi, *President*
Daniel Crocker, *Counsel*
Joseph Harrington, *Counsel*
Laura Tobin, *Vice Pres*
David Denmark, *Opers Mgr*
◆ **EMP:** 99
SALES (est): 98.1MM
SALES (corp-wide): 1.6B **Privately Held**
SIC: 2033 2037 2034 Mfg Canned Fruits/Vegtbl Mfg Frozen Fruits/Vegtbl
PA: Ocean Spray Cranberries, Inc.
1 Ocean Spray Dr
Middleboro MA 02349
508 946-1000

(G-13075)
PAVESTONE LLC
18 Cowan Dr (02346-3703)
PHONE..................................508 947-6001
Greg Swider, *Plant Mgr*
Doug Scott, *Regl Sales Mgr*
Patricia Perez, *Office Mgr*
EMP: 100 **Privately Held**
WEB: www.pavestone.com
SIC: 3272 Mfg Concrete Products
HQ: Pavestone, Llc
5 Concourse Pkwy Ste 1900
Atlanta GA 30328
404 926-3167

(G-13076)
PROGRESS PALLET INC
98 W Grove St (02346-1418)
PHONE..................................508 923-1930
Paul Shaughnessy, *President*
EMP: 25
SQ FT: 30,000
SALES (est): 4.3MM **Privately Held**
SIC: 2448 Mfg Wood Pallets/Skids

(G-13077)
QUALITY ENVELOPE & PRINTING CO
22 Cambridge St Ste H (02346-2090)
PHONE..................................508 947-8878
Arthur McDaniels Jr, *President*
EMP: 7
SQ FT: 4,000
SALES (est): 956.3K **Privately Held**
SIC: 2752 2759 Offset And Envelope Printing Service

(G-13078)
TOTAL TEMP INC
Also Called: Total Temperature Control
22 Cambridge St Ste C (02346-2090)
PHONE..................................508 947-8628
Andy Xenakis, *President*
Jacquelyn Levangie, *Office Mgr*
Sonja Xenakis, *Admin Sec*
EMP: 3
SALES (est): 360K **Privately Held**
SIC: 3585 1711 Mfg Refrigeration/Heating Equipment Plumbing/Heating/Air Cond Contractor

(G-13079)
UNITED SHOE MACHINERY CORP
Also Called: United Global Supply
3 Abbey Ln Ste B (02346-3233)
PHONE..................................508 923-6001
Michael Taricano, *Branch Mgr*
EMP: 4
SALES (corp-wide): 3.4MM **Privately Held**
SIC: 3965 Mfg Fasteners/Buttons/Pins
PA: United Shoe Machinery Corporation
32 Stevens St
Haverhill MA 01830
978 374-0303

(G-13080)
USMDUMPSTERS
35 E Main St (02346-2405)
PHONE..................................774 218-2822
EMP: 3
SALES (est): 143.2K **Privately Held**
SIC: 3443 Mfg Fabricated Plate Work

(G-13081)
WARREN ENVIRONMENTAL INC (PA)
137 Pine St (02346-3732)
P.O. Box 1206, Carver (02330-5206)
PHONE..................................508 947-8539
Jane Warren, *President*
Philip Warren, *Marketing Mgr*
EMP: 8
SALES: 2.8MM **Privately Held**
SIC: 2851 Mfg Paints/Allied Products

(G-13082)
WOOD ST WOOD CO
Also Called: Peter Paquin Cranberries
225 Wood St (02346-2915)
PHONE..................................508 947-6886
Peter G Paquin, *Owner*
EMP: 6
SQ FT: 4,000
SALES: 500K **Privately Held**
SIC: 2421 0171 Sawmill & Cranberry Farm

Middleton
Essex County

(G-13083)
ARMSET LLC
2 De Bush Ave (01949-1678)
PHONE..................................978 774-0035
Levon Harutyunyan,
EMP: 3
SQ FT: 3,200
SALES: 300K **Privately Held**
SIC: 3545 Mfg Machine Tool Accessories

(G-13084)
AXENICS INC (PA)
161 S Main St (01949-2485)
PHONE..................................978 774-9393
Haywood K Schmidt, *President*

GEOGRAPHIC

Chris Coutis, *Vice Pres*
Cindy Whiteman, *CFO*
EMP: 26
SQ FT: 3,820
SALES (est): 3.9MM **Privately Held**
WEB: www.rentecorp.com
SIC: 3494 Mfg Valves/Pipe Fittings

(G-13085)
BOSTIK INC
211 Boston St (01949-2128)
PHONE..................................978 777-0100
Roger Sheldon, *Plant Mgr*
Nancy Baker, *Opers Staff*
Thomas Burch, *Production*
Steve Lima, *Technical Mgr*
Kurt Zintner, *Technical Mgr*
EMP: 200
SALES (corp-wide): 95.3MM **Privately Held**
WEB: www.bostik-us.com
SIC: 2891 Mfg Adhesives/Sealants
HQ: Bostik, Inc.
11320 W Wtertown Plank Rd
Wauwatosa WI 53226
414 774-2250

(G-13086)
BOURGEOIS MACHINE CO
Also Called: Burgess Machine
15 Bixby Ave (01949-2259)
P.O. Box 115 (01949-0115)
PHONE..................................978 774-6240
EMP: 3
SALES: 100K **Privately Held**
SIC: 3599 3451 Mfg Industrial Machinery Mfg Screw Machine Products

(G-13087)
CUSTOM STEEL FABRICATION CORP
26 Lonergan Rd (01949-2402)
PHONE..................................978 774-4555
Gary Dyke, *President*
EMP: 3
SALES: 800K **Privately Held**
SIC: 3441 Steel Fabrication

(G-13088)
EWM CORP (PA)
Also Called: E. C. Mitchell Co.
88 Boston St (01949-2158)
P.O. Box 607 (01949-0907)
PHONE..................................978 774-1191
Everett W Mitchell, *President*
Thomas J Bongiorno, *Admin Sec*
EMP: 5 **EST:** 1920
SQ FT: 11,000
SALES (est): 682.5K **Privately Held**
SIC: 3291 Mfg Abrasive Products

(G-13089)
INIRAM PRECISION MCH TL LLC
Also Called: Iniram Precision Machinery
333 N Main St (01949-1614)
PHONE..................................978 854-3037
Lucien Marini, *Mng Member*
EMP: 4
SQ FT: 5,500
SALES: 10MM **Privately Held**
SIC: 3541 Mfg Machine Tools-Cutting

(G-13090)
INTELLICUT INC
2 De Bush Ave Unit A8 (01949-1679)
PHONE..................................617 417-5236
Knarik Chavushyan, *President*
EMP: 3
SALES (est): 316.2K **Privately Held**
SIC: 3599 Mfg Industrial Machinery

(G-13091)
JLS TOOL & DIE INC
13 Eddington St (01949-1667)
P.O. Box 131 (01949-0231)
PHONE..................................978 304-3111
EMP: 3 **EST:** 2001
SALES (est): 260K **Privately Held**
SIC: 3544 Manufacturing Tools And Die

(G-13092)
JODYS QUICK PRINT
14 East St (01949-1504)
P.O. Box 1068 (01949-3068)
PHONE..................................978 777-6114
John Riddle, *Owner*
EMP: 4
SALES (est): 354.3K **Privately Held**
WEB: www.jodysquikprint.com
SIC: 2752 Offset Printing

(G-13093)
LAB FRNTURE INSTLLTONS SLS INC
11 River St Ste 2 (01949-2429)
PHONE..................................978 646-0600
Michael D Hall, *President*
Gordon R Hall, *Vice Pres*
Cathleen J Young, *Treasurer*
Darlene Hall, *Admin Sec*
EMP: 15
SQ FT: 12,250
SALES (est): 4.7MM **Privately Held**
WEB: www.lab-furniture.com
SIC: 3821 Mfg Lab Apparatus/Furniture

(G-13094)
LISHA & NIRALI FUEL LLC
223 Maple St (01949-2232)
PHONE..................................908 433-6504
Suresh Kumar Patel, *Principal*
EMP: 3
SALES (est): 232K **Privately Held**
SIC: 2869 Mfg Industrial Organic Chemicals

(G-13095)
MARJORIE ROYER INTERIORS INC
50 N Liberty St (01949-1009)
P.O. Box 795 (01949-2795)
PHONE..................................978 774-0533
▲ **EMP:** 6
SALES (est): 570K **Privately Held**
SIC: 2211 2591 1799 1721 Cotton Broadwoven Fabric Mill Mfg Drapery Hardware/Blinds Trade Contractor Painting/Paper Hanging

(G-13096)
MK SERVICES CORP
194 S Main St (01949-2451)
PHONE..................................978 777-2196
Robert Faia, *President*
Lee Quach, *Vice Pres*
Syed Ovais, *Prdtn Mgr*
EMP: 50
SQ FT: 30,000
SALES: 16MM **Privately Held**
SIC: 3545 Mfg Machine Tool Accessories

(G-13097)
NORTHERN GRAPHICS INC
Also Called: Velocity Print Solutions
161 S Main St Ste 210 (01949-2478)
PHONE..................................978 646-9925
EMP: 12
SQ FT: 7,000
SALES: 2.7MM
SALES (corp-wide): 34.3MM **Privately Held**
WEB: www.velocityprint.com
SIC: 2752 7334 2791 2789 Lithographic Coml Print Photocopying Service Typesetting Services Bookbinding/Related Work Commercial Printing
PA: Shipmates/Printmates Holding Corp.
705 Corporation Park # 2
Scotia NY 12302
518 370-1158

(G-13098)
POCAHONTAS SPRING WATER CO (PA)
42 School St (01949)
PHONE..................................978 774-2690
Donald Le Colst, *President*
Kenneth Le Colst, *Vice Pres*
Frank Le Colst Jr, *Treasurer*
EMP: 3
SQ FT: 500
SALES (est): 456.5K **Privately Held**
WEB: www.pocahontasspringwater.com
SIC: 2086 Mfg Spring Water

(G-13099)
RPT HOLDINGS LLC
30 Log Bridge Rd Bldg 200 (01949-2284)
PHONE..................................877 997-3674
David L Gershaw, *President*
▲ **EMP:** 21
SALES (est): 4.1MM **Privately Held**
SIC: 3646 Mfg Commercial Lighting Fixtures

(G-13100)
SALEM METAL INC
177 N Main St (01949-1656)
PHONE..................................978 774-2100
Jason M Vining, *President*
James E Vining, *Exec VP*
Robert McKenzie, *QC Mgr*
Robert Grandolfi, *Engineer*
Dennis Rocheford, *Manager*
EMP: 50 **EST:** 1941
SALES (est): 11.8MM **Privately Held**
WEB: www.salemmetal.com
SIC: 3444 Mfg Sheet Metalwork

(G-13101)
SHELPAK PLASTICS INC
339 N Main St (01949-1614)
PHONE..................................781 305-3937
Andrew Sakellarios, *Principal*
EMP: 8
SALES (est): 803.4K **Privately Held**
SIC: 3089 Mfg Plastic Products

(G-13102)
STARWIND SOFTWARE INC
35 Village Rd Ste 100 (01949-1238)
PHONE..................................617 449-7717
Zorian Rotenberg, *CEO*
Artem Berman, *COO*
Richard Pierro, *Sales Staff*
Katherine Sheehan, *Sales Staff*
Tatiana Gusarova, *Manager*
▼ **EMP:** 3
SALES (est): 401.8K **Privately Held**
SIC: 7372 Prepackaged Software Services

(G-13103)
T G G INC
3 Birch Rd (01949-2261)
P.O. Box 366 (01949-0666)
PHONE..................................978 777-5010
George King Jr, *President*
George E King Jr, *President*
Chris King, *General Mgr*
Diana Perovencher, *Safety Mgr*
Herc Perreira, *Safety Mgr*
EMP: 35
SQ FT: 20,000
SALES: 5MM **Privately Held**
WEB: www.gtgmach.com
SIC: 3599 Mfg Industrial Machinery

(G-13104)
TOOL TECHNOLOGY INC
Riverview Indl Pk 3 (01949)
PHONE..................................978 777-5006
Brian Noel, *President*
Robert Leblanc, *Executive*
Gregg Noel, *Admin Sec*
▼ **EMP:** 20
SQ FT: 18,000
SALES (est): 3MM **Privately Held**
WEB: www.tooltechinc.com
SIC: 3545 Mfg Machine Tool Accessories

(G-13105)
WAGNER LIFESCIENCE LLC
136 N Main St (01949-1652)
PHONE..................................978 539-8102
Scott Vanderwoude, *Mng Member*
EMP: 4
SALES (est): 598.6K **Privately Held**
SIC: 3825 8731 Mfg Electrical Measuring Instruments Commercial Physical Research

(G-13106)
WATSON BROTHERS INC
6 Birch Rd (01949-2261)
P.O. Box 803 (01949-2803)
PHONE..................................978 774-7677
David Watson, *President*
Michael Watson, *Treasurer*
EMP: 13
SALES (est): 1.9MM **Privately Held**
WEB: www.watson-brothers.com
SIC: 2434 2431 2499 Mfg Wood Kitchen Cabinets Mfg Millwork Mfg Wood Products

Milford
Worcester County

(G-13107)
ALLEGHENY RIVER GROUP INC
258 Main St Ste 305 (01757-2506)
PHONE..................................508 634-0181
Timothy Spino, *President*
▲ **EMP:** 25
SALES (est): 1.6MM **Privately Held**
SIC: 2514 Mfg Metal Household Furniture

(G-13108)
BENJAMIN MOORE & CO
49 Sumner St (01757-1656)
PHONE..................................508 473-8900
Marian Beauleiu, *Principal*
Tom Sheridan, *Principal*
Lisa Leary, *COO*
Bernie Hilton, *Mfg Mgr*
Dennis Swanson, *Branch Mgr*
EMP: 100
SALES (corp-wide): 225.3B **Publicly Held**
WEB: www.benjaminmoore.com
SIC: 2851 Mfg Paint
HQ: Benjamin Moore & Co.
101 Paragon Dr
Montvale NJ 07645
201 573-9600

(G-13109)
BIOVIA CORP
9 Industrial Rd Ste 4 (01757-3736)
PHONE..................................508 497-9911
Max Carnecchia, *CEO*
Michael Piraino, *CFO*
David Mersten, *Admin Sec*
EMP: 5
SALES (est): 187.6K
SALES (corp-wide): 1.7B **Privately Held**
SIC: 7372 Prepackaged Software Services
PA: Dassault Systemes
10 Rue Marcel Dassault
Velizy Villacoublay 78140
161 623-000

(G-13110)
COMARK LLC (PA)
440 Fortune Blvd (01757-1722)
PHONE..................................508 359-8161
Gregory Baletsa, *CEO*
Jeff Roberts, *President*
Tim McNamara, *Research*
Phil Beren, *Engineer*
Paul Fricault, *Engineer*
▲ **EMP:** 55
SQ FT: 25,000
SALES (est): 19.3MM **Privately Held**
WEB: www.comarkcorp.com
SIC: 3571 Mfg Electronic Computers

(G-13111)
CONCRETE & MORTAR PACKG LLC
12 S Free St (01757-3752)
PHONE..................................508 473-1799
Jeffrey Nanfeldt, *Mng Member*
EMP: 4
SALES (est): 696K **Privately Held**
SIC: 3273 Mfg Ready-Mixed Concrete

(G-13112)
DILLA ST CORP
130 Cedar St (01757-5117)
PHONE..................................508 478-3419
EMP: 3
SALES (est): 200K **Privately Held**
SIC: 3672 Mfg Printed Circuit Boards

(G-13113)
EASTON JOURNAL
159 Main St (01757-2610)
PHONE..................................508 230-7964
Donna Whitehead, *Manager*
EMP: 3
SALES (est): 125.8K **Privately Held**
SIC: 2711 Newspapers-Publishing/Printing

▲ = Import ▼=Export
◆ =Import/Export

(G-13114)
ECO2 OFFICE INC
Also Called: Minuteman Press
231 E Main St (01757-2821)
PHONE..................................508 478-8511
Norman Gariepy, *President*
EMP: 3
SALES (est): 115.1K **Privately Held**
SIC: 2752 Comm Prtg Litho

(G-13115)
ELENEL INDUSTRIES INC (PA)
Also Called: Photo Fab Engineering
500 Fortune Blvd (01757-1722)
PHONE..................................508 478-2025
William M Lehrer, *President*
Betsy Lehrer, *Clerk*
EMP: 42
SQ FT: 40,000
SALES: 5MM **Privately Held**
SIC: 3479 Coating/Engraving Service

(G-13116)
EMC CORPORATION
5 Technology Dr (01757-3681)
P.O. Box 9103, Hopkinton (01748-9103)
PHONE..................................508 634-2774
Michael Ruettgers, *Principal*
Craig Wagenhoffer, *Engineer*
Harold Waterman, *Technical Staff*
Peter Reynolds, *Sr Ntwrk Engine*
EMP: 340
SALES (corp-wide): 90.6B **Publicly Held**
WEB: www.emc.com
SIC: 3572 7373 Mfg Computer Storage Devices Computer Systems Design
HQ: Emc Corporation
176 South St
Hopkinton MA 01748
508 435-1000

(G-13117)
EXOTIC FOODS
53 Sumner St (01757-1656)
PHONE..................................508 422-9540
Paul Jaggi, *Principal*
EMP: 4
SALES (est): 570.4K **Privately Held**
SIC: 3421 Mfg Cutlery

(G-13118)
GATEHOUSE MEDIA MASS I INC
Also Called: Milford Daily News
197 Main St (01757-2635)
PHONE..................................508 634-7522
Liz Banks, *President*
EMP: 10
SALES (corp-wide): 1.5B **Publicly Held**
SIC: 2711 Newspapers-Publishing/Printing
HQ: Gatehouse Media Massachusetts I, Inc.
48 Dunham Rd
Beverly MA 01915
585 598-0030

(G-13119)
GLASS MOLDERS POTTERY PLA
42 Taft St (01757-2249)
PHONE..................................508 634-2932
Kevin Maher, *Principal*
EMP: 3
SALES: 61.4K **Privately Held**
SIC: 3089 Mfg Plastic Products

(G-13120)
J & D ASSOCIATES CORP
355 Purchase St (01757-3809)
PHONE..................................508 478-9770
Domingos Gomes, *Principal*
EMP: 4 **EST:** 2010
SALES (est): 352.9K **Privately Held**
SIC: 3272 Mfg Concrete Products

(G-13121)
JET PRESS
323 Main St (01757-2514)
PHONE..................................508 478-1814
Joe Tosches, *Owner*
EMP: 4
SALES (est): 307.2K **Privately Held**
WEB: www.jetpress.com
SIC: 2752 Lithographic Commercial Printing

(G-13122)
KPM ANALYTICS INC (PA)
113 Cedar St Ste 1 (01757-1192)
PHONE..................................774 462-6700
Brian Mitchell, *CEO*
Peter McGuire, *Vice Pres*
Bernadette Marcelo, *Treasurer*
Morgan Jones, *Director*
Chris McIntire, *Admin Sec*
EMP: 4
SALES (est): 410.7K **Privately Held**
SIC: 2041 Mfg Flour/Grain Mill Prooducts

(G-13123)
KPM ANALYTICS NORTH AMER CORP (PA)
113 Cedar St Ste 3 (01757-1192)
PHONE..................................508 473-9901
Robert J Winson, *President*
Timothy Carey, *Vice Pres*
Marty Peters, *Technical Mgr*
William P Hardin, *Director*
EMP: 40
SQ FT: 7,500
SALES (est): 4.7MM **Privately Held**
WEB: www.processsensors.com
SIC: 3823 Mfg Process Control Instruments

(G-13124)
LASER ENGINEERING
113 Cedar St Ste S5 (01757-1192)
PHONE..................................508 520-2500
John Casey, *Director*
◆ **EMP:** 5
SQ FT: 5,520
SALES (est): 578.6K **Privately Held**
SIC: 3841 Mfg Surgical/Medical Instruments
PA: Laser Engineering, Inc.
475 Metroplex Dr Ste 401
Nashville TN 37211

(G-13125)
MARTIN SPROCKET & GEAR INC
357 Fortune Blvd (01757-1723)
PHONE..................................508 634-3990
Shawn Surbey, *Manager*
Tom Collins, *Supervisor*
EMP: 9
SALES (corp-wide): 456MM **Privately Held**
SIC: 3566 3568 Mfg Speed Changers/Drives Mfg Power Transmission Equipment
PA: Martin Sprocket & Gear, Inc.
3100 Sprocket Dr
Arlington TX 76015
817 258-3000

(G-13126)
MIKE MURPHY
Also Called: Prosthetic and Orthotic Labs
2 S Main St (01757-3771)
PHONE..................................508 473-9943
Mike Murphy, *Partner*
William Lewis Jr, *Partner*
EMP: 7
SQ FT: 1,716
SALES (est): 424.1K **Privately Held**
SIC: 3842 Mfg Surgical Appliances/Supplies

(G-13127)
MILARA INC
49 Maple St (01757-3650)
PHONE..................................508 533-5322
Krassy Petkov, *CEO*
Jordan Naydenov, *President*
Eric Taylor, *Prdtn Mgr*
Chris Lo, *Engineer*
Will Angenent, *Finance*
▲ **EMP:** 68
SQ FT: 37,000
SALES (est): 15.2MM **Privately Held**
WEB: www.milara.net
SIC: 3549 3555 Mfg Metalworking Machinery Mfg Printing Trades Machinery

(G-13128)
MILFORD WOODWORKING COMPANY
294 West St (01757-1247)
PHONE..................................508 473-2335
Rudolph V Lioce Jr, *President*
Susan Lioce, *Clerk*
EMP: 11 **EST:** 1955
SALES: 967K **Privately Held**
SIC: 2434 Mfg Wood Kitchen Cabinets

(G-13129)
MORNSUN AMERICA LLC
13 Country Club Ln (01757)
PHONE..................................978 293-3923
Yin Xiangyang, *Principal*
EMP: 3
SALES (est): 204.7K **Privately Held**
SIC: 3679 Mfg Electronic Components

(G-13130)
MOSSMAN ASSOCIATES INC
9 Village Cir (01757-1379)
PHONE..................................508 488-6169
Donald Mossman, *President*
▲ **EMP:** 4
SQ FT: 2,500
SALES: 100K **Privately Held**
WEB: www.mossmanassociates.com
SIC: 3841 Mfg Surgical/Medical Instruments

(G-13131)
NITTO DENKO AVECIA INC (DH)
125 Fortune Blvd (01757-1746)
PHONE..................................508 532-2500
Detlef Rethage, *President*
Scott Brown, *President*
Seiji Fujioka, *President*
EMP: 227
SQ FT: 78,000
SALES (est): 30MM **Privately Held**
SIC: 2833 Mfg Medicinal/Botanical Products
HQ: Nitto Americas, Inc.
48500 Fremont Blvd
Fremont CA 94538
510 445-5400

(G-13132)
NORTHEAST STAMP & ENGRAVING
Also Called: Mug Factory, The
3 E Main St (01757-2701)
P.O. Box 721 (01757-0721)
PHONE..................................508 473-5818
Michael J Elliot, *President*
Michael Elliot, *Owner*
Roseanne Elliot, *Owner*
Roseanna M Elliot, *Treasurer*
EMP: 3
SQ FT: 3,600
SALES: 200K **Privately Held**
SIC: 3479 7389 3999 Coating/Engraving Service Business Services And Mfg Misc Products

(G-13133)
NOVA SPORTS USA INC
6 Industrial Rd Ste 2 (01757-3594)
PHONE..................................508 473-6540
Robert Righter, *President*
Dave Commito, *Opers Staff*
Bill Righter, *Treasurer*
Ruth M Righter, *Treasurer*
Laurie Swanfeldt, *Credit Staff*
◆ **EMP:** 11
SQ FT: 20,000
SALES (est): 3.3MM **Privately Held**
WEB: www.novasports.com
SIC: 2891 5941 Mfg Adhesives/Sealants Ret Sporting Goods/Bicycles

(G-13134)
NOYES SHEET METAL
66 Sumner St (01757-1660)
PHONE..................................508 482-9302
Stephen M Noyes, *Owner*
EMP: 10 **EST:** 2010
SALES (est): 1.4MM **Privately Held**
SIC: 3499 3444 Mfg Misc Fabricated Metal Products Mfg Sheet Metalwork

(G-13135)
OCEAN TUG & BARGE ENGRG CORP
258 Main St Ste 401 (01757-2528)
PHONE..................................508 473-0545
Robert Hill, *President*
EMP: 5 **EST:** 1995
SALES (est): 690.6K **Privately Held**
WEB: www.oceantugbarge.com
SIC: 3731 Boatbuilding/Repairing

(G-13136)
PEI REALTY TRUST
500 Fortune Blvd (01757-1722)
PHONE..................................508 478-2025
William M Lehrer, *President*
EMP: 43 **EST:** 2001
SALES (est): 2.6MM
SALES (corp-wide): 5MM **Privately Held**
WEB: www.photoetching.com
SIC: 3999 Mfg Misc Products
HQ: Photofabrication Engineering, Inc.
500 Fortune Blvd
Milford MA 01757
508 478-2025

(G-13137)
PHOTOFABRICATION ENGRG INC (HQ)
500 Fortune Blvd (01757-1722)
PHONE..................................508 478-2025
Charles Lehrer, *President*
Betsy M Lehrer, *Vice Pres*
▲ **EMP:** 43
SQ FT: 40,000
SALES (est): 6.7MM
SALES (corp-wide): 5MM **Privately Held**
WEB: www.photoetching.com
SIC: 3479 Mfg Industrial Machinery
PA: Elenel Industries Inc
500 Fortune Blvd
Milford MA 01757
508 478-2025

(G-13138)
PIN HSIAO & ASSOCIATES LLC
Also Called: Zen Bakery, MA
146a S Main St (01757-3254)
PHONE..................................206 818-0155
Pin Hsiano,
EMP: 60
SALES (corp-wide): 20MM **Privately Held**
SIC: 2051 Bakery
PA: Pin Hsiao & Associates L.L.C.
5501 West Valley Hwy E A101
Sumner WA 98390
425 637-3357

(G-13139)
PROJECT PLASMA HOLDINGS CORP (DH)
37 Birch St (01757-5501)
PHONE..................................508 244-6400
Charlie Mamrak, *CEO*
EMP: 5
SALES (est): 44.2MM **Privately Held**
SIC: 2836 Develop And Manufacture The Highest Quality Biologically-Based Products
HQ: Seracare Life Sciences Holdings, Llc
37 Birch St
Milford MA 01757
508 244-6400

(G-13140)
RENTSCHLER BIOPHARMA INC
27 Maple St (01757-3650)
PHONE..................................508 282-5800
Ralf Otto, *CEO*
Stefan Rampf, *CFO*
EMP: 5
SALES (est): 171K **Privately Held**
SIC: 2834 Mfg Pharmaceutical Preparations

(G-13141)
RGP CORP
Also Called: Minuteman Press
231 E Main St Ste C (01757-2821)
PHONE..................................508 478-8511
Roger Parsons, *President*
EMP: 4
SQ FT: 2,200
SALES (est): 536.3K **Privately Held**
SIC: 2752 7334 4822 2791 Lithographic Coml Print Photocopying Service Telegraph Communications Typesetting Services Commercial Printing

(G-13142)
ROCK BOTTOM STONE FACTORY OUTL
235 E Main St (01757-2836)
PHONE....................508 634-9300
EMP: 6
SALES (est): 320K **Privately Held**
SIC: 3469 Mfg Metal Stampings

(G-13143)
SERACARE LIFE SCIENCES INC (DH)
37 Birch St (01757-5501)
PHONE....................508 244-6400
Charles Mamrak, *CEO*
Paula Kiernan, *COO*
Bharathi Anekella, *Vice Pres*
Michael K Steele, *Vice Pres*
Elizabeth Smith, *Mfg Staff*
▲ **EMP:** 151
SQ FT: 60,000
SALES (est): 40.5MM **Privately Held**
WEB: www.seracare.com
SIC: 2835 Mfg Diagnostic Substances

(G-13144)
SIGNS PLUS
89 S Main St (01757-3251)
PHONE....................508 478-5077
Fred Boehm, *Owner*
EMP: 4
SALES (est): 324.3K **Privately Held**
WEB: www.signsplus.com
SIC: 3993 Mfg Signs/Advertising Specialties

(G-13145)
SUNRISE PROSTHETICS ORTHOTICS
2 S Main St (01757-3771)
PHONE....................508 473-9943
Karen Lynch, *President*
Kelly Jones, *Manager*
EMP: 5
SALES (est): 465.5K **Privately Held**
SIC: 3842 Mfg Surgical Appliances/Supplies
PA: Sunrise Prosthetics And Orthotics Inc
10 Harvard St
Worcester MA 01609

(G-13146)
TECHNOLOGIES 2010 INC
45 Pond St 2 (01757-3419)
P.O. Box 717 (01757-0717)
PHONE....................508 482-0164
Ross Bradley, *President*
EMP: 4
SQ FT: 2,000
SALES (est): 451K **Privately Held**
SIC: 7372 7379 4813 Whl Hardware/Software & Provides Computer Services Including Internet Services

(G-13147)
TEMPRON PRODUCTS CORP
21 Maple St (01757-3650)
PHONE....................508 473-5880
Harold D Schmidt, *President*
Edward A Schmidt, *Treasurer*
Carolyn Schmidt, *Clerk*
EMP: 6 **EST:** 1959
SQ FT: 3,000
SALES (est): 914.2K **Privately Held**
WEB: www.tempron.com
SIC: 3069 Mfg Fabricated Rubber Products

(G-13148)
THAT CORPORATION (PA)
45 Sumner St (01757-1656)
PHONE....................508 478-9200
Leslie B Tyler, *President*
Dave Woodland, *Materials Mgr*
Ben Macdonald, *Production*
Gregory Benulis, *Engineer*
Paul Travaline, *Treasurer*
EMP: 35
SQ FT: 10,000
SALES (est): 4.4MM **Privately Held**
SIC: 3679 3674 Mfg Electronic Components Mfg Semiconductors/Related Devices

(G-13149)
UNITY SCIENTIFIC LLC
113 Cedar St Ste S3 (01757-1192)
PHONE....................203 740-2999
Joseph Platano, *CEO*
Douglas J Evans,
EMP: 40
SQ FT: 2,000
SALES (est): 1MM **Privately Held**
SIC: 3821 Mfg Lab Apparatus/Furniture

(G-13150)
UVA LIDKOPING INC
4 Industrial Rd Ste 4 # 4 (01757-3589)
PHONE....................508 634-4301
Bradford Klar, *President*
Conny Nyberg, *Sales Staff*
EMP: 8
SALES (est): 1.2MM
SALES (corp-wide): 2B **Privately Held**
SIC: 3541 Mfg Machine Tools-Cutting
HQ: Uva LidkOping Ab
Fabriksgatan 2
Lidkoping 531 3
510 880-00

(G-13151)
VITA-CRETE INC
Also Called: B Vitalini
12 S Free St Ste 1 (01757-3752)
P.O. Box 279 (01757-0279)
PHONE....................508 473-1799
William J Vitalini, *President*
EMP: 3
SQ FT: 7,000
SALES: 312.4K **Privately Held**
SIC: 3273 Mfg Ready-Mixed Concrete

(G-13152)
WATERS CORPORATION
Also Called: Waters Corp USA
34 Maple St (01757-3696)
PHONE....................508 478-0208
EMP: 4 **Publicly Held**
SIC: 3826 Mfg Analytical Instruments
PA: Waters Corporation
34 Maple St
Milford MA 01757

(G-13153)
WATERS CORPORATION (PA)
34 Maple St (01757-3696)
PHONE....................508 478-2000
Christopher J O'Connell, *Ch of Bd*
Terrance P Kelly, *President*
Mark T Beaudouin, *Senior VP*
Robert G Carson, *Senior VP*
Michael C Harrington, *Senior VP*
▲ **EMP:** 249
SALES: 2.4B **Publicly Held**
SIC: 3826 3829 7371 7372 Mfg Liquid Chromatography Spectrometry Instruments & Develops & Supplies Software Based Products

(G-13154)
WATERS TECHNOLOGIES CORP (HQ)
34 Maple St (01757-3696)
P.O. Box Dept Ch 14373, Palatine IL (60055-0001)
PHONE....................508 478-2000
Christopher J O'Connell, *CEO*
John Lynch, *Treasurer*
Chuck Santoro, *Accountant*
William Flynn, *Sr Software Eng*
Mark Beaudouin, *Admin Sec*
▲ **EMP:** 1000
SQ FT: 500,000
SALES (est): 805.3MM **Publicly Held**
SIC: 3829 3826 Mfg Measuring/Controlling Devices Mfg Analytical Instruments

Millbury
Worcester County

(G-13155)
ALL IN ONE DUMPSTER SERVICE
4 John St (01527-4212)
PHONE....................508 735-8979
Edward Pageau, *Owner*
EMP: 3
SALES (est): 137K **Privately Held**
SIC: 3443 Mfg Fabricated Plate Work

(G-13156)
BARRDAY CORPORATION (HQ)
Also Called: Barrday Advanced Mtl Solutions
86 Providence St Bldg 3 (01527-3922)
PHONE....................508 581-2100
Tony Fiorenzi, *President*
▲ **EMP:** 78 **EST:** 1982
SQ FT: 55,000
SALES (est): 20.2MM
SALES (corp-wide): 18.3MM **Privately Held**
WEB: www.lewcott.com
SIC: 2655 2821 Mfg Fiber Can/Drums Mfg Plstc Material/Resin
PA: Barrday, Inc
260 Holiday Inn Dr
Cambridge ON N3C 4
519 621-3620

(G-13157)
BONSAL AMERICAN INC
18 Mccracken Rd (01527-1514)
PHONE....................508 791-6366
David Letourneau, *Manager*
EMP: 4
SALES (corp-wide): 29.7B **Privately Held**
WEB: www.bonsalamerican.com
SIC: 3272 Mfg Concrete Products
HQ: Bonsal American, Inc.
625 Griffith Rd Ste 100
Charlotte NC 28217
704 525-1621

(G-13158)
CENTRAL MA WATERJET INC
32 Grafton St (01527-3918)
PHONE....................508 769-4308
Stephen M Haglund, *Principal*
EMP: 7
SALES (est): 795.9K **Privately Held**
SIC: 3541 Mfg Machine Tools-Cutting

(G-13159)
CESYL MILLS INC
95 W Main St (01527-1936)
P.O. Box 133 (01527-0133)
PHONE....................508 865-6129
Mark Aronson, *President*
Louise Miller, *Treasurer*
◆ **EMP:** 65 **EST:** 1982
SQ FT: 80,000
SALES: 8MM **Privately Held**
SIC: 2211 Cotton Broadwoven Fabric Mill

(G-13160)
COUNTRY CANDLE CO INC (PA)
Also Called: Egan Church Supply
22 West St (01527-2676)
PHONE....................508 865-6061
Joan Laurence, *CEO*
Andrew Laurence, *President*
James F Laurence, *Admin Sec*
EMP: 34 **EST:** 1973
SQ FT: 4,000
SALES (est): 4.7MM **Privately Held**
WEB: www.countrycandle.com
SIC: 3999 5947 5999 Mfg Misc Products Ret Gifts/Novelties Ret Misc Merchandise

(G-13161)
CREATIVE SIGNWORKS
20 West St (01527-2622)
PHONE....................508 865-7330
Bob Rochon, *Owner*
EMP: 3 **EST:** 1993
SALES (est): 204.5K **Privately Held**
WEB: www.creativesignworks.com
SIC: 3993 Mfg Signs/Advertising Specialties

(G-13162)
DOSCO SHEET METAL AND MFG
6 Grafton St (01527-3918)
PHONE....................508 865-9998
David Sauer, *President*
EMP: 8
SQ FT: 7,200
SALES: 1MM **Privately Held**
SIC: 3444 Mfg Sheet Metalwork

(G-13163)
EM SCREEN SYSTEMS INC
45 River St Ste A (01527-2666)
PHONE....................508 865-9995
Richard Gurski, *President*
Joyce Gurski, *Treasurer*
Edward Pacocha, *Sales Mgr*
EMP: 4
SQ FT: 5,000
SALES (est): 447.5K **Privately Held**
WEB: www.emscreensystems.com
SIC: 2759 Screen Printing

(G-13164)
G & W FOUNDRY CORP
50 Howe Ave Ste G (01527-3264)
P.O. Box 68, Rehoboth (02769-0068)
PHONE....................508 581-8719
Richard Bruso, *President*
James Bruso, *Vice Pres*
EMP: 30
SQ FT: 60,000
SALES (est): 6.4MM **Privately Held**
WEB: www.gwfoundry.com
SIC: 3321 3322 Gray/Ductile Iron Foundry Malleable Iron Foundry

(G-13165)
GRANGER LYNCH CORP
Also Called: Northeast Sealcoat
18 Mccracken Rd Ste 1 (01527-1546)
P.O. Box 319 (01527-0319)
PHONE....................508 756-6244
Stephen P Lynch, *President*
William Cabral, *Treasurer*
EMP: 21 **EST:** 1981
SQ FT: 8,000
SALES (est): 3.8MM
SALES (corp-wide): 95.6MM **Privately Held**
SIC: 2951 2891 Mfg Asphalt Mixtures/Blocks Mfg Adhesives/Sealants
PA: J.H. Lynch & Sons, Inc.
50 Lynch Pl
Cumberland RI 02864
401 333-4300

(G-13166)
GREAT NECK SAW MFRS INC
Also Called: Buck Brothers
100 Riverlin St (01527-4140)
P.O. Box 192 (01527-0192)
PHONE....................508 865-4482
Gerald K Sortor, *General Mgr*
EMP: 30
SQ FT: 42,000
SALES (corp-wide): 288.1MM **Privately Held**
SIC: 3423 3545 3949 Mfg Hand/Edge Tools Mfg Machine Tool Accessories Mfg Sporting/Athletic Goods
PA: Great Neck Saw Manufacturers, Inc.
165 E 2nd St
Mineola NY 11501
516 746-5352

(G-13167)
I B A INC
Also Called: I B A Print Shop
19 River St (01527-2605)
PHONE....................508 865-2507
Douglas Sturgis, *Branch Mgr*
EMP: 6
SALES (corp-wide): 21MM **Privately Held**
WEB: www.ibainc.com
SIC: 2752 Lithographic Commercial Printing
PA: I B A, Inc.
27 Providence St
Millbury MA 01527
508 865-6911

(G-13168)
JEN MFG INC
3 Latti Farm Rd (01527-2132)
P.O. Box 20128, Worcester (01602-0128)
PHONE....................508 753-1076
Gerald Gendron, *President*
Jeffrey Gendron, *Vice Pres*
▲ **EMP:** 35 **EST:** 1956
SQ FT: 62,000
SALES (est): 5.2MM **Privately Held**
WEB: www.jenmfg.com
SIC: 3991 3952 Mfg Brooms/Brushes Mfg Lead Pencils/Art Goods

(G-13169)
MANUFACTURING SERVICE CORP
Also Called: Manufacturing Services
11 Waters St (01527-2619)
P.O. Box 453, Sutton (01590-0453)
PHONE....................................508 865-2550
Lan Goodwin, *President*
EMP: 3
SALES (est): 376.6K **Privately Held**
SIC: 3599 2821 5084 5162 Mfg Industrial Machinery Mfg Plstc Material/Resin Whol Industrial Equip Whol Plastic Mtrl/Shapes

(G-13170)
MERRICK SERVICES
368 Greenwood St (01527-1522)
PHONE....................................508 802-3751
Hal Merreick, *President*
EMP: 5
SALES: 367K **Privately Held**
SIC: 3674 5082 Mfg Semiconductors/Related Devices Whol Construction/Mining Equipment

(G-13171)
METAL SOLUTIONS LLC
1 Herricks Ln (01527-2516)
P.O. Box 314 (01527-0314)
PHONE....................................774 276-0096
Philip K Gosselin, *Principal*
EMP: 4
SALES (est): 405.2K **Privately Held**
SIC: 3444 3531 3993 3441 Mfg Sheet Metalwork Mfg Construction Mach Mfg Signs/Ad Specialties Structural Metal Fabrctn

(G-13172)
MINUTEMAN SPRING COMPANY INC
34 Howe Ave (01527-3211)
PHONE....................................508 299-6100
Guy C Roberge, *President*
Cheryl A Roberge, *Treasurer*
EMP: 4
SALES (est): 148.4K **Privately Held**
SIC: 3493 Mfg Steel Springs-Nonwire

(G-13173)
PRINTGUARD INC
1521 Grafton Rd (01527-4330)
PHONE....................................508 890-8822
Daniel J Rizika, *President*
▲ **EMP:** 12
SQ FT: 30,000
SALES: 1.5MM **Privately Held**
WEB: www.briteideasusa.com
SIC: 3231 Mfg Glass Products

(G-13174)
RANGER AUTOMATION SYSTEMS INC
9 Railroad Ave (01527-4122)
PHONE....................................508 842-6500
Fidel Ramos, *President*
Cliff Robson, *Manager*
EMP: 35
SQ FT: 29,500
SALES (est): 11.1MM **Privately Held**
WEB: www.rangerautomation.com
SIC: 3559 Mfg Misc Industry Machinery

(G-13175)
S & D SPINNING MILL INC
190 W Main St (01527-1416)
P.O. Box 186 (01527-0186)
PHONE....................................508 865-2267
David Dearnley, *President*
John Dearnley, *Vice Pres*
Jeffrey Dearnley, *Treasurer*
Thomas Dearnley, *Clerk*
EMP: 34 **EST:** 1952
SQ FT: 16,000
SALES (est): 1.4MM **Privately Held**
SIC: 2281 Commission Spinning Yarn Service

(G-13176)
STEELCRAFT INC
115 W Main St (01527-1914)
P.O. Box 111 (01527-0111)
PHONE....................................508 865-4445
Douglas Backman, *President*
▲ **EMP:** 36 **EST:** 1946
SQ FT: 75,000
SALES (est): 5.3MM **Privately Held**
WEB: www.steelcraft-inc.com
SIC: 3842 Mfg Surgical Appliances/Supplies

(G-13177)
STELLAR INDUSTRIES CORP
50 Howe Ave (01527-3264)
PHONE....................................508 865-1668
Ronald C Visser, *President*
Eric Brown, *Vice Pres*
Lisa Naumann, *QC Mgr*
Michele Maynard, *Manager*
Barbara Corley, *Admin Asst*
▲ **EMP:** 40
SALES (est): 8.5MM **Privately Held**
WEB: www.stellarind.com
SIC: 3674 3699 Mfg Semiconductors/Related Devices Mfg Electrical Equipment/Supplies

(G-13178)
UNITED SCREW MACHINE PRODUCTS
34 Howe Ave (01527-3211)
PHONE....................................508 865-7295
Thomas Brady, *President*
EMP: 5 **EST:** 1949
SQ FT: 12,000
SALES: 400K **Privately Held**
SIC: 3451 Mfg Screw Machine Products

(G-13179)
UNITED-COUNTY INDUSTRIES CORP
Also Called: County Heat Treat
32 Howe Ave (01527-3211)
P.O. Box 330 (01527-0330)
PHONE....................................508 865-5885
William J Nartowt, *President*
Chris Kania, *Plant Mgr*
Al Freeman, *Maint Spvr*
Barbara Ann Nartowt, *Treasurer*
Stephen S Dery, *Technical Staff*
EMP: 43
SQ FT: 33,000
SALES (est): 4.5MM **Privately Held**
WEB: www.countyheattreat.com
SIC: 3398 Metal Heat Treating

Millers Falls
Franklin County

(G-13180)
HONEY HILL FARM
98 W Mineral Rd (01349-1238)
PHONE....................................413 659-3141
Karen Rice, *Partner*
Jaime Barber, *Partner*
Josh Barber, *Partner*
Robert Rice, *Partner*
EMP: 4
SALES (est): 226K **Privately Held**
SIC: 2411 Burls, Wood

(G-13181)
RENOVATORS SUPPLY INC
Also Called: Rensup.com, Old Mill Marketing
Renovators Old Ml (01349)
PHONE....................................413 423-3300
Claude Jeanloz, *President*
▲ **EMP:** 25 **EST:** 1978
SQ FT: 300,000
SALES (est): 4.1MM **Privately Held**
WEB: www.rensup.com
SIC: 3429 3645 3646 3432 Mfg Hardware Mfg Residentl Light Fixt Mfg Coml Light Fixtures Mfg Plumbing Fxtr Fittng Ret Mail-Order House

Millis
Norfolk County

(G-13182)
AD HOC ENERGY LLC
1492r Main St (02054-1405)
P.O. Box 113, Norfolk (02056-0113)
PHONE....................................508 507-8005
Keith Daley, *Mng Member*
EMP: 3
SALES (est): 360.8K **Privately Held**
SIC: 3585 3621 Mfg Refrigeration/Heating Equipment Mfg Motors/Generators

(G-13183)
COLLT MFG INC
1375 Main St (02054-1450)
PHONE....................................508 376-2525
Liselotte Ward, *President*
Lisa Sellers, *Treasurer*
▲ **EMP:** 32
SQ FT: 45,000
SALES (est): 4.8MM **Privately Held**
WEB: www.collt.com
SIC: 3479 3469 Coating/Engraving Service Mfg Metal Stampings

(G-13184)
INTERACTIVE MEDIA CORP
Also Called: Kanguru Solutions
1360 Main St (02054-1402)
PHONE....................................508 376-4245
Donald L Brown, *President*
Nate Cote, *Exec VP*
Don Wright, *Marketing Mgr*
Ken Lee, *Manager*
Jose Figueroa, *Supervisor*
▲ **EMP:** 45
SQ FT: 15,000
SALES (est): 8.4MM **Privately Held**
WEB: www.kanguru.com
SIC: 3572 Mfg Computer Storage Devices

(G-13185)
KHALSA JOT
Also Called: Life Knives
368 Village St (02054-1799)
PHONE....................................508 376-6206
Jot Khalsa, *Owner*
EMP: 3
SQ FT: 1,000
SALES: 250K **Privately Held**
WEB: www.lifeknives.com
SIC: 3911 3421 Mfg Precious Metal Jewelry Mfg Cutlery

(G-13186)
RADIO FREQUENCY COMPANY INC
Also Called: Larose Rf Systems
150 Dover Rd (02054-1335)
P.O. Box 158 (02054-0158)
PHONE....................................508 376-9555
Melvyn H Harris, *Ch of Bd*
Thomas W James, *President*
Brian Maley, *Info Tech Mgr*
▲ **EMP:** 30 **EST:** 1946
SQ FT: 26,000
SALES (est): 8.8MM **Privately Held**
WEB: www.radiofrequency.com
SIC: 3567 Mfg Industrial Furnaces/Ovens

Millville
Worcester County

(G-13187)
PINE TREE CONCRETE PRODUCTS
151 Lincoln St (01529)
P.O. Box 603 (01529-0603)
PHONE....................................508 883-7072
John Lesperance, *President*
Michael Lesperance, *Treasurer*
EMP: 7
SQ FT: 6,000
SALES: 800K **Privately Held**
SIC: 3272 Mfg Concrete Products

(G-13188)
W AND D ENTERPRISE INC
159 Lincoln St (01529-1608)
P.O. Box 75, Blackstone (01504-0075)
PHONE....................................508 883-4811
David Laporte, *President*
EMP: 3
SQ FT: 2,486
SALES (est): 337.1K **Privately Held**
SIC: 3446 Mfg Architectural Metalwork

Milton
Norfolk County

(G-13189)
BABY BRIEFCASE LLC
51 Randolph Ave (02186-3404)
PHONE....................................617 696-7668
William J Doyle, *Principal*
▲ **EMP:** 3
SALES (est): 340.7K **Privately Held**
SIC: 3161 Mfg Luggage

(G-13190)
BELGIUMS CHOCOLATE SOURCE INC
Also Called: Nirvana Chocolates
480 Adams St Ste 202 (02186-4914)
PHONE....................................781 283-5787
Christophe Van Riet, *President*
▲ **EMP:** 4
SQ FT: 15,000
SALES (est): 487.4K **Privately Held**
WEB: www.belgiumsbestchocolates.com
SIC: 2064 Mfg Candy/Confectionery

(G-13191)
EYES ON EUROPE LLC
44 Fox Hill Ln (02186-3706)
PHONE....................................617 696-9311
Richard Hammel,
▲ **EMP:** 3
SALES (est): 283.9K **Privately Held**
SIC: 3851 Mfg Ophthalmic Goods

(G-13192)
G H BENT COMPANY
Also Called: Bent's Cookie Factory
7 Pleasant St (02186-4523)
PHONE....................................617 322-9287
Eugene Pierotti, *President*
James Pierotti, *Vice Pres*
EMP: 21 **EST:** 1801
SQ FT: 15,000
SALES: 650K **Privately Held**
WEB: www.hardtackcracker.com
SIC: 2052 5812 5461 2051 Mfg Cookies/Crackers Eating Place Retail Bakery

(G-13193)
KALION INC
92 Elm St (02186-3111)
PHONE....................................617 698-2113
Darcy Prather, *President*
EMP: 3
SALES (est): 304.4K **Privately Held**
SIC: 2869 Mfg Industrial Organic Chemicals

(G-13194)
KILLORAN CONTRACTING INC
5 Eager Rd (02186-5243)
PHONE....................................617 298-5248
EMP: 3
SALES (est): 270K **Privately Held**
SIC: 3423 Mfg Hand/Edge Tools

(G-13195)
MASSACHSETTS PROSECUTORS GUIDE
30 Hinckley Rd (02186-1624)
P.O. Box 1333, Dedham (02027-1333)
PHONE....................................617 696-6729
Richard G Stearns, *Partner*
EMP: 3
SALES (est): 116.8K **Privately Held**
SIC: 2731 Books-Publishing/Printing

(G-13196)
MILTON TIMES INC
3 Boulevard St Ste 5 (02186-5400)
P.O. Box 444 (02186-0004)
PHONE....................................617 696-7758
Patricia L Desmond, *President*
Susan Generous, *Accounts Exec*
June Desmond, *Director*
Timothy A Desmond, *Director*
Aldo Pinto, *Graphic Designe*
EMP: 4
SQ FT: 800
SALES (est): 294.3K **Privately Held**
SIC: 2711 Newspapers-Publishing/Printing

GEOGRAPHIC

(G-13197)
NEXUS PRINT GROUP INC
49 Westvale Rd (02186-4854)
PHONE..................................617 429-9666
Richard M Hutchinson, *Principal*
EMP: 4
SALES (est): 369.5K **Privately Held**
SIC: 2752 Lithographic Commercial Printing

(G-13198)
PIG ROCK SAUSAGES LLC
52 Dyer Ave (02186-1512)
PHONE..................................617 851-9422
Arthur Welch, *Mng Member*
EMP: 5 **EST:** 2014
SALES (est): 177.8K **Privately Held**
SIC: 2013 Mfg Prepared Meats

(G-13199)
PROFORMA PRINTING & PROMOTION
Also Called: B and M
33 Gaskins Rd (02186-2221)
PHONE..................................617 464-1120
William Resnick, *Owner*
EMP: 3
SALES (est): 257.1K **Privately Held**
SIC: 2759 Commercial Printing

(G-13200)
SEAMANS MEDIA INC
552 Adams St Ste 2 (02186-5627)
PHONE..................................617 773-9955
Eric W Seamans, *President*
EMP: 5
SALES: 200K **Privately Held**
SIC: 2721 Periodicals-Publishing/Printing

Monson
Hampden County

(G-13201)
ACE MOULDING CO INC
91 Bethany Rd (01057-9558)
P.O. Box 216 (01057-0216)
PHONE..................................413 267-4875
Alice Davey, *President*
Rick Dodd, *General Mgr*
Mark Davey, *Vice Pres*
EMP: 5 **EST:** 1961
SQ FT: 5,000
SALES: 500K **Privately Held**
SIC: 3089 Plastic Injection Molding

(G-13202)
ACOM PUBLISHING INC
Also Called: Indian News
97 Main St (01057-1320)
P.O. Box 115 (01057-0115)
PHONE..................................413 267-4999
Richard Baer, *President*
Tim Baer, *Vice Pres*
EMP: 3
SALES: 50K **Privately Held**
SIC: 2731 Books-Publishing/Printing

(G-13203)
CHRISTMAS STUDIO
Also Called: Studio 2
252 Main St (01057-1314)
P.O. Box 133 (01057-0133)
PHONE..................................413 267-3342
Lewis D Garland, *Owner*
EMP: 4
SALES (est): 280K **Privately Held**
SIC: 3999 5999 Mfg Misc Products Ret Misc Merchandise

(G-13204)
CNC SPECIALTIES INC
85 Bethany Rd (01057-9558)
P.O. Box 84 (01057-0084)
PHONE..................................413 267-5051
Robert Marouski, *President*
Michael Grimes, *Vice Pres*
Mary Clark, *Treasurer*
Rachell Casavant, *Manager*
EMP: 15
SQ FT: 12,000
SALES: 900K **Privately Held**
SIC: 3599 Mfg Industrial Machinery

(G-13205)
COLTON HOLLOW CANDLE COMPANY
Also Called: Echo Hill Orchards
101 Wilbraham Rd (01057-9659)
PHONE..................................413 267-3986
Richard Krupczak, *Partner*
Teresa Krupczak, *Partner*
EMP: 4
SQ FT: 20,000
SALES (est): 378K **Privately Held**
SIC: 3999 5999 5199 0175 Manufacture Retail And Wholesales Candles/Apple Orchard

(G-13206)
DOUBLE A PLASTICS CO INC
85 Bethany Rd (01057-9558)
P.O. Box 332 (01057-0332)
PHONE..................................413 267-4403
Clifford Farquhar, *President*
Todd St Germain, *VP Sales*
EMP: 6
SQ FT: 7,000
SALES (est): 839.8K **Privately Held**
SIC: 3089 Plastic Injection Molding

(G-13207)
GARY HULLIHEN
Also Called: Hullihen Machine
5 Beebe Rd (01057-9549)
PHONE..................................413 283-2383
Gary Hullihen, *Owner*
EMP: 3
SALES (est): 229.2K **Privately Held**
SIC: 3599 Mfg Industrial Machinery

(G-13208)
LAMINATING COATING TECH INC
Also Called: Lamcotec
152 Bethany Rd (01057-9538)
P.O. Box 279 (01057-0279)
PHONE..................................413 267-4808
Richard Anderson, *President*
Joe Obrien, *Safety Mgr*
Rick Malo, *Opers Staff*
Debbie Ogulnick, *Accounting Mgr*
Roman Lavrov, *Info Tech Mgr*
▲ **EMP:** 69
SQ FT: 56,000
SALES (est): 17.8MM
SALES (corp-wide): 71.6MM **Privately Held**
SIC: 2295 Manufactures Coated Fabrics
PA: Trelleborg Coated Systems Italy Spa
Strada Provinciale Per Tavazzano 140
Lodi Vecchio LO 26855
037 140-61

(G-13209)
METEOR GLOBL MFG SOLUTIONS INC
Also Called: Meteor Gms
87 Munn Rd (01057-9649)
PHONE..................................617 733-6506
Christopher Carlin, *President*
Mary Carlin, *Corp Secy*
EMP: 3
SALES (est): 139.9K **Privately Held**
SIC: 3364 3363 Mfg Nonfrs Die-Castings Mfg Aluminum Die-Casting

(G-13210)
QUEEN BEE VINEYARD INC
173 Moulton Hill Rd (01057-9692)
PHONE..................................413 267-9329
Roy Edward McGuill, *Principal*
EMP: 4
SALES (est): 106.9K **Privately Held**
SIC: 2084 Mfg Wines/Brandy/Spirits

(G-13211)
SAFE T CUT INC
97 Main St (01057-1320)
P.O. Box 466, Palmer (01069-0466)
PHONE..................................413 267-9984
Richard Baer Sr, *President*
EMP: 10
SQ FT: 5,000
SALES (est): 1.3MM **Privately Held**
WEB: www.safetcut.com
SIC: 3545 5251 5085 3423 Mfg Machine Tool Access Ret Hardware Whol Industrial Supplies Mfg Hand/Edge Tools

Montague
Franklin County

(G-13212)
OBORAIN
7 Ripley Rd (01351-9568)
PHONE..................................413 376-8854
EMP: 3
SALES (est): 253.2K **Privately Held**
SIC: 2499 Mfg Wood Products

Monterey
Berkshire County

(G-13213)
CRAWFORD CHANDLER AGENCY INC
642 Harmon Rd (01245)
P.O. Box 144, Great Barrington (01230-0144)
PHONE..................................413 528-3035
Chandler Crawford, *President*
EMP: 3
SALES (est): 225.6K **Privately Held**
SIC: 2731 Books-Publishing/Printing

Monument Beach
Barnstable County

(G-13214)
CANALSIDE PRINTING
443 Shore Rd (02553)
P.O. Box 950 (02553-0950)
PHONE..................................508 759-4141
James Dwyer, *Owner*
EMP: 4
SQ FT: 2,000
SALES (est): 340K **Privately Held**
SIC: 2752 7334 4822 Lithographic Commercial Printing Photocopying Services Telegraph Communications

Nahant
Essex County

(G-13215)
GOODE BRUSH COMPANY
89 Bass Point Rd (01908-1526)
PHONE..................................781 581-0280
Walter R Goode Jr, *Partner*
Robert Goode, *Partner*
Roy Goode, *Partner*
EMP: 3 **EST:** 1898
SQ FT: 450
SALES (est): 326.9K **Privately Held**
SIC: 3991 Mfg Brooms/Brushes

Nantucket
Nantucket County

(G-13216)
8 RACEWAY DRIVE LLC
8 Raceway Dr (02554-4366)
PHONE..................................508 325-0040
EMP: 3
SALES (est): 128K **Privately Held**
SIC: 3644 Mfg Nonconductive Wiring Devices

(G-13217)
ACK 60 MAIN LLC
58 Main St (02554-3711)
PHONE..................................508 228-1398
David R Cox, *Principal*
EMP: 3
SALES (est): 119.8K **Privately Held**
SIC: 2711 Newspapers-Publishing/Printing

(G-13218)
ACK SURF SCHOOL LLC
5 Amelia Dr (02554-6063)
PHONE..................................508 325-2589
Gaven Norton, *Principal*
EMP: 3
SALES (est): 98.7K **Privately Held**
SIC: 2711 Newspapers-Publishing/Printing

(G-13219)
ANDERSON PUBLISHING INC
27 Mill St (02554-3313)
P.O. Box 1018 (02554-1018)
PHONE..................................508 228-3866
Deborah M Anderson, *President*
EMP: 4 **EST:** 2001
SQ FT: 400
SALES (est): 446.6K **Privately Held**
WEB: www.nolutil.com
SIC: 2721 7374 Magazines Publisher And Wed Design

(G-13220)
AUDIO VIDEO DESIGNS
9 Windy Way (02554-2776)
PHONE..................................508 325-9989
Ryan Dobbins, *Manager*
EMP: 4
SALES (est): 300.8K **Privately Held**
SIC: 3679 Ret Misc Merchandise

(G-13221)
BERRY GLOBAL INC
8 Amelia Dr Ste 1 (02554-6064)
PHONE..................................508 325-0004
Stephen Mc Donough, *Manager*
EMP: 3 **Publicly Held**
WEB: www.6sens.com
SIC: 3089 Mfg Plastic Products
HQ: Berry Global, Inc.
101 Oakley St
Evansville IN 47710
812 424-2904

(G-13222)
CISCO BREWERS INC
5 Bartlett Farm Rd (02554-4341)
P.O. Box 2928 (02584-2928)
PHONE..................................508 325-5929
Jay Harman, *CEO*
▲ **EMP:** 37
SQ FT: 3,000
SALES (est): 557.3K **Privately Held**
WEB: www.ciscobrewers.com
SIC: 2082 Mfg Malt Beverages

(G-13223)
E W WINSHIP LTD INC
Also Called: Nantucket Looms
51 Main St (02554-3542)
P.O. Box 1510 (02554-1510)
PHONE..................................508 228-1908
Elizabeth Winship, *President*
Betty Browning, *Treasurer*
▲ **EMP:** 8
SQ FT: 2,000
SALES (est): 1.5MM **Privately Held**
WEB: www.nantucketlooms.com
SIC: 2221 5949 2241 2231 Ret Sewing Supplies/Fbrc Manmad Brdwv Fabric Mill Narrow Fabric Mill Wool Brdwv Fabric Mill Cotton Brdwv Fabric Mill

(G-13224)
GEORGE A VOLLANS
Also Called: Sconset Woodman
27 New St (02554-3905)
P.O. Box 11, Siasconset (02564-0011)
PHONE..................................508 257-6241
George A Vollans, *Owner*
EMP: 6
SALES (est): 339.8K **Privately Held**
SIC: 2411 1731 Logging Electrical Contractor

(G-13225)
GOT ICE LLC
Also Called: Nantucket Ice House
8 Miacomet Ave (02554-2722)
P.O. Box 2888 (02584-2888)
PHONE..................................508 228-1156
Brian Bridges,
EMP: 4
SQ FT: 800
SALES (est): 322.4K **Privately Held**
SIC: 2097 Mfg Ice

(G-13226)
INQUIRER AND MIRROR INC
1 Old South Rd (02554-2836)
P.O. Box 1198 (02554-1198)
PHONE..................................508 228-0001
Marianne Stanton, *President*
Garrett J Cummings,
EMP: 14 **EST:** 1821
SALES: 1MM
SALES (corp-wide): 1.5B **Publicly Held**
WEB: www.inquirermirror.com
SIC: 2711 Newspapers-Publishing/Printing
PA: Gannett Co., Inc.
7950 Jones Branch Dr
Mc Lean VA 22102
703 854-6000

(G-13227)
MOORE WOODWORKING INC
300 Polpis Rd (02554-2402)
PHONE..................................508 364-7338
Benjamin P Moore, *Principal*
EMP: 4
SALES (est): 316.9K **Privately Held**
SIC: 2431 Mfg Millwork

(G-13228)
NANTUCKET BAKE SHOP INC
17 1/2 Old South Rd Ste C (02554)
P.O. Box 539 (02554-0539)
PHONE..................................508 228-2797
Margarette Detmer, *President*
Eugene Detmer, *Vice Pres*
EMP: 4 **EST:** 1935
SQ FT: 1,500
SALES (est): 389.9K **Privately Held**
WEB: www.nantucketbakeshop.com
SIC: 2052 5461 2051 Mfg Cookies/Crackers Retail Bakery Mfg Bread/Related Prdts

(G-13229)
NANTUCKET GLASS & MIRROR INC
15 Sun Island Rd (02554-3111)
P.O. Box 3329 (02584-3329)
PHONE..................................508 228-3713
Lee Bradley, *President*
Derek S Tibbetts, *Vice Pres*
Mary Beth Bradley, *Treasurer*
EMP: 6
SQ FT: 1,600
SALES: 1.3MM **Privately Held**
SIC: 3211 Mfg Flat Glass

(G-13230)
POETS CORNER PRESS INC
16a Amelia Dr (02554-6064)
P.O. Box 2152 (02584-2152)
PHONE..................................508 228-1051
Peter Sylvia, *President*
Susan Sylvia, *Vice Pres*
EMP: 3 **EST:** 1964
SQ FT: 1,200
SALES (est): 488.9K **Privately Held**
SIC: 2752 Lithographic Commercial Printing

(G-13231)
TENNIS LOFT
12 Straight Wharf (02554-3767)
PHONE..................................508 228-9228
Tina Hoskins, *Owner*
EMP: 4
SALES (est): 387.6K **Privately Held**
SIC: 3949 Mfg Sporting/Athletic Goods

Natick
Middlesex County

(G-13232)
ALEX AND ANI LLC
1245 Worcester St (01760-1515)
PHONE..................................401 336-1397
EMP: 3 **Privately Held**
SIC: 3915 Mfg Jewelers' Materials
PA: Alex And Ani, Llc
2000 Chapel View Blvd # 360
Cranston RI 02920

(G-13233)
ALPS SPORTSWEAR MFG CO INC
5 Commonwealth Rd Ste 1a (01760-1526)
PHONE..................................978 685-5159
Marvin F Axelrod, *President*
▲ **EMP:** 20 **EST:** 1931
SQ FT: 50,000
SALES (est): 3MM **Privately Held**
WEB: www.alps-sportswear.com
SIC: 2253 Knit Outerwear Mill

(G-13234)
ANACONDA USA INC
154 E Central St (01760-3644)
P.O. Box 358, Bellingham (02019-0358)
PHONE..................................800 285-5721
▲ **EMP:** 10
SALES (est): 1.9MM **Privately Held**
SIC: 3535 Conveyors And Conveying Equipment, Nsk

(G-13235)
ANDREW ROBERTS INC
Also Called: An Rob
215 Oak St Ste 1 (01760-1324)
P.O. Box 3775 (01760-0030)
PHONE..................................508 653-6412
Andrew Keane, *President*
EMP: 6 **EST:** 1966
SQ FT: 1,500
SALES (est): 1.5MM **Privately Held**
WEB: www.andrewroberts.com
SIC: 2821 Mfg Plastic Materials/Resins

(G-13236)
BAUER ASSOCIATES INC
8 Tech Cir (01760-1029)
PHONE..................................508 310-0201
Paul Glenn, *President*
John Glenn, *Vice Pres*
Justine Gorodecki, *IT/INT Sup*
EMP: 3
SQ FT: 3,500
SALES (est): 619.4K **Privately Held**
WEB: www.bauerinc.com
SIC: 3827 8748 Mfg Optical Instruments/Lenses Business Consulting Services

(G-13237)
BEAVER MEDICAL LLC
10 Coleman Ct (01760-2018)
PHONE..................................617 935-3500
Joan Spiegel,
EMP: 4
SALES (est): 251.8K **Privately Held**
SIC: 3841 Mfg Surgical/Medical Instruments

(G-13238)
BLOOM BOSS LLC
251 W Central St (01760-3758)
PHONE..................................774 777-5208
Ethan Holmes, *President*
EMP: 7
SALES (est): 574.3K **Privately Held**
SIC: 3648 Mfg Lighting Equipment

(G-13239)
BOAOPHARMA INC
19 Erie Dr Ste 1 (01760-1338)
PHONE..................................508 315-8080
Yiming Yao, *President*
EMP: 3
SALES: 500K **Privately Held**
WEB: www.boaopharma.com
SIC: 2834 Mfg Pharmaceutical Preparations

(G-13240)
BOSTON WOOD ART
Also Called: Eaton Woodworking
5 Maple Ave (01760-4312)
PHONE..................................508 353-4129
David Eaton, *Owner*
EMP: 3
SALES (est): 140K **Privately Held**
WEB: www.eatonwoodworking.com
SIC: 3553 2499 Mfg Woodworking Machinery Mfg Wood Products

(G-13241)
BRIGHTEC INC
8 Pleasant St Fl 1c (01760-5622)
PHONE..................................508 647-9710
Patrick Planche, *Ch of Bd*
Stephney Smith, *Manager*
EMP: 3
SALES (est): 339.4K **Privately Held**
WEB: www.brightec.com
SIC: 3081 Mfg Unsupported Plastic Film/Sheet

(G-13242)
CAPESYM INC
Also Called: Cape Simulations
6 Huron Dr Ste 1 (01760-1325)
PHONE..................................508 653-7100
Shariar Motakef, *President*
John Fiala, *General Mgr*
EMP: 5
SQ FT: 3,200
SALES (est): 811.6K **Privately Held**
WEB: www.capesim.com
SIC: 3559 Equipment Simulation And Development

(G-13243)
CENTAGE CORPORATION
24 Superior Dr Ste 201 (01760-1684)
PHONE..................................800 366-5111
Ken Marshall, *Ch of Bd*
John Murdock, *President*
Scott Jennings, *Senior VP*
Chris Howard, *Vice Pres*
Piyush Jain, *Vice Pres*
EMP: 100
SQ FT: 8,000
SALES: 1MM **Privately Held**
WEB: www.centage.com
SIC: 7372 Prepackaged Software Services

(G-13244)
CERTAINTEED CORPORATION
22 Winter St (01760-1017)
PHONE..................................508 655-9731
William Northgraves, *Manager*
EMP: 3
SALES (corp-wide): 209.1MM **Privately Held**
WEB: www.certainteed.net
SIC: 3069 Mfg Fabricated Rubber Products
HQ: Certainteed Llc
20 Moores Rd
Malvern PA 19355
610 893-5000

(G-13245)
CHARLES SUPPER COMPANY INC
15 Tech Cir Ste 1 (01760-1026)
PHONE..................................508 655-4610
Lee Supper, *President*
Anne Supper, *Asst Treas*
Steven Nelles, *Executive*
EMP: 5 **EST:** 1941
SQ FT: 14,000
SALES (est): 390K **Privately Held**
WEB: www.charles-supper.com
SIC: 3821 Mfg Lab Apparatus/Furniture

(G-13246)
COGNEX CORPORATION (PA)
1 Vision Dr (01760-2077)
PHONE..................................508 650-3000
Robert J Willett, *President*
Sheila Dipalma, *Vice Pres*
Herb Lade, *VP Opers*
Dawn Daigneault, *Project Mgr*
Karen Winters, *Project Mgr*
▲ **EMP:** 400
SQ FT: 100,000
SALES: 806.3MM **Publicly Held**
WEB: www.cognex.com
SIC: 3823 Mfg Process Control Instruments

(G-13247)
COGNEX CORPORATION
801 Worcester St (01760-2099)
PHONE..................................508 650-3044
EMP: 6
SALES (corp-wide): 806.3MM **Publicly Held**
SIC: 3823 Mfg Process Control Instruments
PA: Cognex Corporation
1 Vision Dr
Natick MA 01760
508 650-3000

(G-13248)
COGNEX GERMANY INC
1 Vision Dr (01760-2083)
PHONE..................................508 650-3000
Robert Shimllan, *President*
Marty Flynn, *Project Mgr*
Zak Devries, *Engineer*
Mike Peyerk, *Engineer*
Jesse Toland, *Engineer*
EMP: 250
SALES (est): 13.2MM
SALES (corp-wide): 806.3MM **Publicly Held**
WEB: www.cognex.com
SIC: 3841 Holding Company
PA: Cognex Corporation
1 Vision Dr
Natick MA 01760
508 650-3000

(G-13249)
COGNEX INTERNATIONAL INC (HQ)
1 Vision Dr (01760-2083)
PHONE..................................508 650-3000
Robert Willett, *CEO*
Robert J Shillman, *Chairman*
Richard A Morin, *Exec VP*
Patrick A Alias, *Senior VP*
Theodor Krantz, *Vice Pres*
EMP: 10
SALES (est): 21.6MM
SALES (corp-wide): 806.3MM **Publicly Held**
WEB: www.cognex.com
SIC: 3823 Mfg Process Control Instruments
PA: Cognex Corporation
1 Vision Dr
Natick MA 01760
508 650-3000

(G-13250)
DEBCO MACHINE INC
85 North Ave (01760-3556)
PHONE..................................508 655-4469
Daniel E Collari, *President*
Mike Gingras, *General Mgr*
EMP: 10
SQ FT: 10,000
SALES (est): 990K **Privately Held**
SIC: 3599 Mfg Industrial Machinery

(G-13251)
DELSYS INC
23 Strathmore Rd Ste 1 (01760-2444)
P.O. Box 1167, Framingham (01701-1167)
PHONE..................................508 545-8200
Carlo J De Luca, *President*
Gianluca De Luca, *Vice Pres*
Michael Twardowski, *Research*
Kunal Jariwala, *Engineer*
Devi Bheemappa, *VP Mktg*
EMP: 10
SQ FT: 3,000
SALES (est): 2MM **Privately Held**
WEB: www.delsys.com
SIC: 3845 Mfg Electromedical Equipment

(G-13252)
DOGWATCH INC (PA)
10 Michigan Dr (01760-1342)
PHONE..................................508 650-0600
Frederick P King, *President*
Barbara Mason, *Controller*
Demie Lyons, *Marketing Staff*
Charlie King, *Manager*
▲ **EMP:** 17
SQ FT: 10,000
SALES (est): 3.7MM **Privately Held**
WEB: www.dogwatch.com
SIC: 3699 0752 1799 Mfg Electrical Equipment/Supplies Animal Services Trade Contractor

(G-13253)
EIDOLON CORPORATION
3 Erie Dr (01760-1312)
PHONE..................................781 400-0586
Victor J Doherty, *President*
Jane M Doherty, *Vice Pres*

GEOGRAPHIC

EMP: 4
SQ FT: 5,000
SALES (est): 449.9K **Privately Held**
WEB: www.slitlamp.com
SIC: 3827 Mfg Optical Instruments/Lenses

(G-13254)
ELASTIC CLOUD GATE LLC
93 E Central St Unit 5 (01760-3667)
PHONE....................................617 500-8284
Remek Hetman, *CEO*
EMP: 4
SALES (est): 282.8K **Privately Held**
SIC: 7372 Prepackaged Software Services

(G-13255)
EXCEL SIGN & DECORATION CORP
4 Eastleigh Ln (01760-4275)
PHONE....................................617 479-8552
Jian Gao, *President*
EMP: 4
SALES (est): 440.2K **Privately Held**
SIC: 3993 Mfg Signs/Advertising Specialties

(G-13256)
FUEL FOR FIRE INC
13 Tech Cir (01760-1023)
PHONE....................................508 975-4573
Rob Gilfeather, *President*
Mary Damkot, *CFO*
Mark Neville, *Sales Staff*
Krystle Orlando, *Marketing Staff*
Mark Zamcheck, *Prgrmr*
EMP: 11
SALES (est): 1.8MM **Privately Held**
SIC: 2099 Food Preparations, Nec, Nsk

(G-13257)
GENELEC INC
7 Tech Cir (01760-1023)
PHONE....................................508 652-0900
Ilpo Martikainen, *President*
Lisa Kaufmann, *Mktg Dir*
William Eggleston, *Mktg Dir*
▲ **EMP:** 11
SQ FT: 10,000
SALES (est): 1.7MM
SALES (corp-wide): 38MM **Privately Held**
WEB: www.genelec.com
SIC: 3651 7629 Mfg Home Audio/Video Equipment Electrical Repair
PA: Genelec Oy
Olvitie 5
Iisalmi 74100
178 388-1

(G-13258)
GENZYME CORPORATION
41 Everett St (01760-5571)
PHONE....................................617 768-9292
EMP: 127
SALES (corp-wide): 429.3MM **Privately Held**
SIC: 2835 Mfg Diagnostic Substance
HQ: Genzyme Corporation
500 Kendall St
Cambridge MA 02142
617 252-7500

(G-13259)
HARVARD CLINICAL TECH INC
22 Pleasant St (01760-5632)
PHONE....................................508 655-2000
Diane A Gargano, *President*
Paul Grindle, *Treasurer*
EMP: 20
SQ FT: 42,000
SALES (est): 2.2MM **Privately Held**
WEB: www.harvardclinical.com
SIC: 3841 3586 3561 Mfg Surgical/Medical Instruments Mfg Measuring/Dispensing Pumps Mfg Pumps/Pumping Equipment

(G-13260)
HEALTHCARE PUBLISHING INC
25 Washington Ave Ste 4 (01760-3461)
P.O. Box 430 (01760-0430)
PHONE....................................508 655-4489
Terry Boyle, *President*
Cindy Boyle, *Treasurer*
EMP: 5
SALES (est): 530.5K **Privately Held**
SIC: 2721 Periodicals-Publishing/Printing

(G-13261)
IMPRINT MARKETING
9 Wedgewood Rd (01760-1746)
PHONE....................................508 315-3433
William Mesrobian, *Owner*
EMP: 3
SALES (est): 180K **Privately Held**
SIC: 2752 Lithographic Commercial Printing

(G-13262)
INFUTRONIX LLC
177 Pine St (01760-1331)
PHONE....................................508 650-2007
Chaoyoung Lee, *President*
EMP: 3 **EST:** 2015
SQ FT: 500
SALES (est): 214.3K **Privately Held**
SIC: 3561 Mfg Pumps/Pumping Equipment

(G-13263)
KATHY CLARK
Also Called: Multiplicity
37 Oak Knoll Rd (01760-1103)
PHONE....................................508 655-3666
Kathy Clark, *Owner*
EMP: 3
SALES (est): 243.6K **Privately Held**
SIC: 2321 2335 2339 Mfg Men's/Boy's Furnishings Mfg Women's/Misses' Dresses Mfg Women's/Misses' Outerwear

(G-13264)
LITHOPTEK LLC
8 Tech Cir (01760-1029)
PHONE....................................408 533-5847
EMP: 6
SALES (corp-wide): 861.4K **Privately Held**
SIC: 3827 Mfg Optical Instruments/Lenses
PA: Lithoptek Llc
26 Ridge Rd
Summit NJ 07901
408 533-5847

(G-13265)
LOLAS ITALIAN HARVEST LLC
9 Main St (01760-4505)
PHONE....................................508 651-0524
David Alves,
EMP: 4
SALES (est): 230.2K **Privately Held**
SIC: 2032 5812 Mfg Canned Specialties Eating Place

(G-13266)
MATHWORKS INC
Also Called: Mathworks Lakeside Campus
1 Lakeside Campus Dr (01760-1687)
PHONE....................................508 647-7000
Bob Camuso, *Principal*
EMP: 4
SALES (corp-wide): 1B **Privately Held**
SIC: 7372 Prepackaged Software Services
PA: The Mathworks Inc
3 Apple Hill Dr
Natick MA 01760
508 647-7000

(G-13267)
METROPOLITAN CAB DISTRS CORP
Also Called: Metropolitan Cab & Countertops
10 Mercer Rd (01760-2415)
PHONE....................................508 651-8950
Diane Aucello, *Manager*
EMP: 5
SALES (corp-wide): 30.4MM **Privately Held**
SIC: 2434 2541 Mfg Wood Kitchen Cabinets Mfg Wood Partitions/Fixtures
PA: Metropolitan Cabinet Distributors Corp.
505 University Ave
Norwood MA 02062
781 949-8900

(G-13268)
MICROSOFT CORPORATION
1245 Worcester St # 3072 (01760-1515)
PHONE....................................508 545-2957
EMP: 5
SALES (corp-wide): 125.8B **Publicly Held**
SIC: 7372 Prepackaged Software Services
PA: Microsoft Corporation
1 Microsoft Way
Redmond WA 98052
425 882-8080

(G-13269)
MINUTEMAN IMPLANT CLUB INC
2 Westview Ter (01760-4753)
PHONE....................................413 549-4108
Gary Kilberg, *Principal*
EMP: 3
SALES: 61.7K **Privately Held**
SIC: 2752 Lithographic Commercial Printing

(G-13270)
MR PLOW
222 E Central St (01760-3630)
PHONE....................................508 207-8999
Ciro Sansossio, *Principal*
EMP: 3
SALES (est): 258K **Privately Held**
SIC: 2851 Mfg Paints/Allied Products

(G-13271)
PHILIPS NORTH AMERICA LLC
Also Called: E D A X International Division
12 Michigan Dr (01760-1339)
PHONE....................................508 647-1130
Alan Devenish, *Branch Mgr*
EMP: 150
SALES (corp-wide): 20.1B **Privately Held**
WEB: www.usa.philips.com
SIC: 3826 Mfg Analytical Instruments Specializing In E D S Instruments
HQ: Philips North America Llc
222 Jacobs St Fl 3
Cambridge MA 02141
978 659-3000

(G-13272)
PHOENIX DIAGNOSTICS INC
8 Tech Cir (01760-1029)
PHONE....................................508 655-8310
Ram Nunna, *President*
Rajiv Nunna, *Manager*
▲ **EMP:** 10
SQ FT: 12,000
SALES (est): 770K **Privately Held**
WEB: www.phoenixdiagnostics.com
SIC: 2835 Mfg Diagnostic Substances

(G-13273)
PRECEDING INC
Also Called: Precidiag
27 Strathmore Rd (01760-2442)
PHONE....................................617 953-6173
Jian Shao, *CEO*
Dong Kong, *Ch of Bd*
EMP: 5
SALES (est): 99K **Privately Held**
SIC: 2835 Mfg Diagnostic Substances

(G-13274)
PRECISION SYSTEMS INC
16 Tech Cir Ste 100 (01760-1038)
PHONE....................................508 655-7010
Charles A Bell, *President*
Ann C Bell, *Treasurer*
EMP: 25 **EST:** 1962
SQ FT: 33,000
SALES (est): 4.1MM **Privately Held**
SIC: 3841 3826 Mfg Medical Instruments & Laboratory Analytical Instruments

(G-13275)
PRINTING SERVICES INC
21 Tyler Ct (01760-2736)
PHONE....................................508 655-2535
John R Carr, *President*
EMP: 5
SALES (est): 380K **Privately Held**
SIC: 2752 Lithographic Commercial Printing

(G-13276)
R D WEBB CO INC
6 Huron Dr Ste 3a (01760-1325)
PHONE....................................508 650-0110
Richard Webb, *President*
Sebastian Kent, *General Mgr*
EMP: 3
SQ FT: 1,500
SALES: 500K **Privately Held**
SIC: 3821 Mfg Laboratory Heating Apparatus

(G-13277)
REGENOCELL THERAPEUTICS INC
16 David Dr (01760-3538)
PHONE....................................508 651-1598
James Frank Mongiardo, *Ch of Bd*
James Mongiardo, *Ch of Bd*
Joanna C Coogan, *Admin Sec*
▲ **EMP:** 9
SALES (est): 695.5K **Privately Held**
SIC: 2835 Mfg Diagnostic Substances

(G-13278)
SBH DIAGNOSTICS INC
2 Mercer Rd (01760-2415)
PHONE....................................508 545-0333
EMP: 8
SQ FT: 6,000
SALES (est): 996.2K **Privately Held**
SIC: 2835 Diagnostic Substances, Nsk

(G-13279)
SNOW ECONOMICS INC
Also Called: Hkd Snowmakers
15 Mercer Rd (01760-2414)
PHONE....................................508 655-3232
Charles N Santry, *President*
Charles Lavoie, *Vice Pres*
Jean-Philippe Lacasse, *Prdtn Mgr*
Scott Gunnell, *Sales Staff*
Sophie Allen, *Marketing Staff*
EMP: 7
SALES (est): 1.4MM **Privately Held**
SIC: 3585 Mfg Refrigeration/Heating Equipment

(G-13280)
SWAPONZ INC
190 N Main St Ste 1 (01760-2057)
PHONE....................................508 650-4456
Louis Kronfeld, *Vice Pres*
▲ **EMP:** 3
SALES: 1MM **Privately Held**
SIC: 3089 Mfg Misc Products

(G-13281)
TEXTCAFE
325 Speen St Apt 602 (01760-1566)
PHONE....................................508 654-8520
Martin Hensel, *Owner*
EMP: 4
SALES (est): 99.8K **Privately Held**
SIC: 2731 7379 7389 Books-Publishing/Printing Computer Related Services Business Serv Non-Commercial Site

(G-13282)
THINKLITE LLC
117 W Central St Ste 201 (01760-4383)
PHONE....................................617 500-6689
Dinesh Wadhwani, *CEO*
Jaclyn Noble, *Opers Staff*
Danny Wadgwani, *CFO*
Gaconnier Karen, *Accountant*
Andersen Michael, *CTO*
▲ **EMP:** 6
SQ FT: 1,300
SALES (est): 4MM **Privately Held**
SIC: 3629 Mfg Electrical Industrial Apparatus

(G-13283)
TRANSAMERICA PRINTING CORP
2 Appletree Ln (01760-1759)
PHONE....................................781 821-6166
Jon Rosenberg, *President*
EMP: 7
SALES: 977K **Privately Held**
SIC: 2752 Lithographic Commercial Printing

(G-13284)
VDC RESEARCH GROUP INC (PA)
679 Worcester St Ste 2 (01760-1845)
PHONE....................................508 653-9000
Mitchell Solomon, *CEO*
Lewis Solomon, *President*

▲ = Import ▼=Export
◆ =Import/Export

Chris Rommel, *Exec VP*
David Krebs, *Vice Pres*
Ellen Slaby, *Vice Pres*
EMP: 29
SQ FT: 6,500
SALES (est): 2.9MM **Privately Held**
WEB: www.vdcresearch.com
SIC: 2721 8742 Periodicals-Publishing/Printing Management Consulting Services

(G-13285)
VERIZON COMMUNICATIONS INC
Also Called: Nynex
1245 Worcester St (01760-1515)
PHONE....................508 647-4008
Kevin Dorcey, *Manager*
EMP: 10
SALES (corp-wide): 130.8B **Publicly Held**
WEB: www.verizon.com
SIC: 3575 3663 5731 Mfg Computer Terminals Mfg Radio/Tv Communication Equipment Ret Radio/Tv/Electronics
PA: Verizon Communications Inc.
1095 Ave Of The Americas
New York NY 10036
212 395-1000

(G-13286)
VF OUTDOOR INC
1245 Worcester St # 4016 (01760-1515)
PHONE....................508 651-7676
EMP: 16
SALES (corp-wide): 13.8B **Publicly Held**
SIC: 2329 Ret Family Clothing
HQ: Vf Outdoor, Llc
2701 Harbor Bay Pkwy
Alameda CA 94502
855 500-8639

(G-13287)
VIRTUAL COVE INC
6 Kelsey Rd (01760-3330)
PHONE....................781 354-0492
Robert Levy, *CEO*
EMP: 3
SALES (est): 78.2K **Privately Held**
SIC: 7372 7389 Prepackaged Software Services Business Serv Non-Commercial Site

(G-13288)
ZYNO MEDICAL LLC
177 Pine St (01760-1331)
PHONE....................508 650-2008
Chao Young Lee, *President*
Lowell Warner, *Vice Pres*
▲ **EMP:** 18 **EST:** 2007
SQ FT: 7,000
SALES (est): 4.3MM **Privately Held**
SIC: 3841 Mfg Surgical/Medical Instruments

Needham
Norfolk County

(G-13289)
ACCUFUND INC
400 Hillside Ave Ste 5 (02494-1226)
PHONE....................781 433-0233
Peter J Stam, *President*
Kimberly Rodriguez, *Sales Mgr*
Joe Sabella, *Sales Mgr*
Kristen Faiola, *Consultant*
Trudy Coit, *Sr Consultant*
EMP: 9
SQ FT: 1,500
SALES (est): 1.2MM **Privately Held**
WEB: www.accufund.com
SIC: 7372 Prepackaged Software Services

(G-13290)
ACTIFIO FEDERAL INC
105 Cabot St Ste 301e (02494-2801)
PHONE....................781 795-9182
John Meyers, *CEO*
EMP: 10
SQ FT: 100
SALES (est): 299.3K **Privately Held**
SIC: 7372 7389 Prepackaged Software Services

(G-13291)
ADAPTIVE NETWORKS INC
123 Highland Ave (02494-3005)
PHONE....................781 444-4170
Michael B Propp, *President*
David Propp, *Vice Pres*
EMP: 15
SQ FT: 3,000
SALES (est): 2.6MM **Privately Held**
WEB: www.adaptivenetworks.com
SIC: 3663 Mfg Radio/Tv Communication Equipment

(G-13292)
BEES MANUFACTURING LLC
40 Wildwood Dr (02492-2736)
PHONE....................781 400-1280
Louis J Quattrucci Jr, *Principal*
Mark Leskanic, *Mng Member*
EMP: 8 **EST:** 2003
SQ FT: 4,500
SALES (est): 763.4K **Privately Held**
SIC: 3599 Manufacture Machine And Other Job Shop Work

(G-13293)
BELTRONICS INC
124 Crescent Rd Ste 7 (02494-1442)
PHONE....................617 244-8696
Robert Bishop, *Ch of Bd*
Roger Stern, *Software Engr*
EMP: 12
SQ FT: 3,900
SALES (est): 1.8MM **Privately Held**
SIC: 3845 Mfg Electromedical Equipment

(G-13294)
BMC SOFTWARE INC
250 1st Ave Ste 205 (02494-2886)
PHONE....................781 810-4494
Bret Siakowski, *Manager*
EMP: 5
SALES (corp-wide): 1.5B **Privately Held**
WEB: www.coradiant.com
SIC: 7372 Prepackaged Software Services
HQ: Bmc Software, Inc.
2103 Citywest Blvd # 2100
Houston TX 77042
713 918-8800

(G-13295)
CANTON JOURNAL
254 2nd Ave (02494-2829)
PHONE....................781 828-0006
Jeff Adair, *Principal*
EMP: 3 **EST:** 2010
SALES (est): 120.7K **Privately Held**
SIC: 2711 Newspapers-Publishing/Printing

(G-13296)
CHIASMA INC
140 Kendrick St Bldg Ce (02494-2739)
PHONE....................617 928-5300
Raj Kannan, *CEO*
David Stack, *Ch of Bd*
Mark J Fitzpatrick, *President*
William Ludlam, *Senior VP*
Dana Gelbaum, *Vice Pres*
EMP: 16 **EST:** 2001
SALES (est): 3MM **Privately Held**
SIC: 2834 Pharmaceutical Preparations

(G-13297)
CLIO DESIGNS INCORPORATED
1000 Highland Ave Ste 2 (02494-1262)
PHONE....................781 449-9500
James Leventhal, *President*
Harvey Gordon, *CFO*
◆ **EMP:** 15
SQ FT: 3,000
SALES: 10MM **Privately Held**
SIC: 2834 Mfg Pharmaceutical Preparations

(G-13298)
CURRIER ENGINEERING
316 Hunnewell St (02494-1330)
PHONE....................781 449-7706
Walter Currier, *Owner*
EMP: 3
SQ FT: 3,000
SALES: 200K **Privately Held**
SIC: 3677 3679 Microwale Power Generators And Components

(G-13299)
EYEDEAL SCANNING LLC
124 Crescent Rd Ste 3b (02494-1458)
PHONE....................617 519-8696
Dr Robert Bishop, *President*
EMP: 3
SALES (est): 221.4K **Privately Held**
SIC: 3577 Mfg Computer Peripheral Equipment

(G-13300)
HEARING ARMOR LLC
378 Hillside Ave (02494-1230)
PHONE....................781 789-5017
Jason M Dunn, *Partner*
EMP: 10
SALES (est): 671.4K **Privately Held**
SIC: 3842 Mfg Surgical Appliances/Supplies

(G-13301)
INFOTRAK NATIONAL DATA SERVICE
67 Holmes St (02492-3646)
PHONE....................781 276-1711
EMP: 14
SALES: 2MM **Privately Held**
WEB: www.mtgeinfo.com
SIC: 2711 Newspapers-Publishing/Printing

(G-13302)
JOURNAL OF BONE JINT SRGERY IN
Also Called: Jbjs
20 Pickering St Ste 3 (02492-3145)
PHONE....................781 449-9780
Kent Anderson, *CEO*
Edward Hanley, *Ch of Bd*
James Beaty, *Trustee*
James Herndon, *Trustee*
Terry Light, *Trustee*
EMP: 34
SQ FT: 20,000
SALES: 9.6MM **Privately Held**
WEB: www.jbjs.org
SIC: 2721 Periodicals-Publishing/Printing

(G-13303)
KENEXA COMPENSATION INC (DH)
160 Gould St (02494-2313)
PHONE....................877 971-9171
Donald F Volk, *President*
Cooper Moo, *Partner*
Archie L Jones, *Vice Pres*
EMP: 30
SQ FT: 36,288
SALES (est): 33.9MM
SALES (corp-wide): 79.5B **Publicly Held**
WEB: www.salary.com
SIC: 7372 Prepackaged Software Services
HQ: Kenexa Corporation
650 E Swedesford Rd # 200
Wayne PA 19087
877 971-9171

(G-13304)
LYNWOOD LABORATORIES INC
Also Called: Shoofly
945 Great Plain Ave Ste 1 (02492-3004)
P.O. Box 920198 (02492-0002)
PHONE....................781 449-6776
Irving Kanin, *President*
Dennis Kanin, *Principal*
Doris Kanin, *Treasurer*
Paul Ledoux, *Manager*
EMP: 3
SQ FT: 1,500
SALES (est): 528.3K **Privately Held**
SIC: 2879 Mfg Household Insecticides & Repellents & Rodenticides

(G-13305)
N-VISION OPTICS LLC
220 Reservoir St Ste 26 (02494-3133)
PHONE....................781 505-8360
Max Rivkin, *COO*
Olga Rivkin, *CFO*
Matt Champney, *Sales Associate*
EMP: 5
SALES (est): 1MM **Privately Held**
WEB: www.nvisionoptics.com
SIC: 3827 Mfg Optical Instruments/Lenses

(G-13306)
NANO OPS INC
8 Elder Rd (02494-2415)
PHONE....................617 543-2921
Ahmed Busnaina, *CEO*
Krassimir Petkov, *COO*
EMP: 3
SALES (est): 110.4K **Privately Held**
SIC: 2759 Commercial Printing

(G-13307)
OBJECT MANAGEMENT GROUP INC
Also Called: INDUSTRIAL INTERNET CONSORTIUM
109 Highland Ave Ste 303 (02494-3021)
PHONE....................781 444-0404
Richard Soley, *Ch of Bd*
William Hoffman, *President*
Robert Freund, *COO*
Deron Jett, *Exec VP*
Victor Harrison, *Vice Pres*
▲ **EMP:** 28
SQ FT: 11,500
SALES: 8.8MM **Privately Held**
WEB: www.omg.org
SIC: 7372 Prepackaged Software Services

GEOGRAPHIC

(G-13308)
PLANT SNACKS LLC
60 Kendrick St Ste 200 (02494-2726)
P.O. Box 920514 (02492-0006)
PHONE....................617 480-6265
Angela Hockman, *CFO*
EMP: 3
SALES (est): 104.8K **Privately Held**
SIC: 2096 Mfg Potato Chips/Snacks

(G-13309)
PTC PARAMETRIC TECHNOLOGY
159 Laurel Dr (02492-3206)
PHONE....................781 370-5699
James E Heppelmann, *President*
EMP: 3 **EST:** 2010
SALES (est): 79.6K **Privately Held**
SIC: 7372 Prepackaged Software Services

(G-13310)
SHARKNINJA OPERATING LLC (HQ)
89 A St Ste 100 (02494-2806)
PHONE....................617 243-0235
David Aquino, *Exec VP*
Dan Bilger, *Exec VP*
Ron Difabio, *Vice Pres*
Jurjen Jacobs, *Vice Pres*
Ajay Kataria, *Vice Pres*
◆ **EMP:** 35
SALES (est): 53.5MM
SALES (corp-wide): 1.1B **Privately Held**
SIC: 3639 Mfg Household Appliances
PA: Joyoung Co., Ltd.
No.760, Yinhang St., Xiasha Sub-District, Jianggan Dist.
Hangzhou 31001
571 816-3909

(G-13311)
SIMPLE SYRUP GLASS STUDIO LLC
60 Otis St (02492-3422)
PHONE....................781 444-8275
Jonathan H Betsch, *Manager*
Emily Abbott, *Manager*
EMP: 3
SALES (est): 220K **Privately Held**
WEB: www.simplesyrup.com
SIC: 3229 Mfg Pressed/Blown Glass

(G-13312)
ST EQUIPMENT AND TECH LLC
101 Hampton Ave (02494-2628)
PHONE....................781 972-2300
Mike Allen,
James Bittner,
EMP: 4 **EST:** 2015
SALES (est): 143K **Privately Held**
SIC: 3569 Mfg General Industrial Machinery

(G-13313)
TECHTRADE INC
964 Great Plain Ave (02492)
PHONE....................781 724-7878

Francis C K Fung, *President*
◆ **EMP:** 10
SQ FT: 2,500
SALES: 2.8MM **Privately Held**
WEB: www.techtradeinc.com
SIC: 3672 Mfg Printed Circuit Boards

(G-13314)
THINKFLOOD INC
295 Reservoir St (02494-3100)
PHONE..................................617 299-2000
Matthew Eagar, *President*
Adam Shapiro, *COO*
▲ **EMP:** 8
SQ FT: 2,500
SALES: 1.2MM **Privately Held**
SIC: 3571 Mfg Electronic Computers

(G-13315)
TLS INTERNATIONAL LLC
76 Brewster Dr (02492-1130)
PHONE..................................781 449-4454
Stephen Goldberg,
Lois Goldberg,
▲ **EMP:** 4
SALES (est): 499K **Privately Held**
WEB: www.tlsinternational.com
SIC: 2261 Manufacturer's Headwear

(G-13316)
VERASTEM INC (PA)
117 Kendrick St Ste 500 (02494-2730)
PHONE..................................781 292-4200
Brian Stuglik, *CEO*
Daniel Paterson, *President*
Mahesh Padval, *Vice Pres*
Robert Gagnon, *CFO*
Joseph Lobacki, *Ch Credit Ofcr*
EMP: 60 **EST:** 2010
SQ FT: 27,810
SALES: 26.7MM **Publicly Held**
SIC: 2834 Pharmaceutical Preparations

(G-13317)
WHITNEY VGAS ARCHTECTURAL PDTS
56 Coulton Park (02492-3302)
PHONE..................................781 449-1351
Travis Veigas, *President*
EMP: 5
SALES (est): 573.7K **Privately Held**
WEB: www.whitneyveigas.com
SIC: 3993 Mfg Signs/Advertising Specialties

Needham Heights
Norfolk County

(G-13318)
BERGQUIST FAMILY ENTPS INC
Also Called: Guide & Directory
89 Central Ave (02494-2927)
P.O. Box 37, Newton Upper Falls (02464-0001)
PHONE..................................781 449-9196
Donna C Bergquist, *President*
EMP: 5 **EST:** 1952
SQ FT: 600
SALES (est): 450K **Privately Held**
WEB: www.britton2000.com
SIC: 2741 Misc Publishing

(G-13319)
BIG BELLY SOLAR INC
150 A St Ste 103 (02494-2824)
P.O. Box 920142, Needham (02492-0002)
PHONE..................................888 820-0300
Brian Phillips, *CEO*
Jackie Carrico, *Project Mgr*
Jeff Wakely, *CFO*
Jason-D A Vergados, *Manager*
Menice Kevin, *Technical Staff*
◆ **EMP:** 35
SQ FT: 1,000
SALES (est): 8.8MM **Privately Held**
WEB: www.seahorsepower.com
SIC: 3823 Mfg Process Control Instruments

(G-13320)
BOSTON SOFTWARE CORP
189 Reservoir St (02494-3130)
PHONE..................................781 449-8585
Tom O'Connor, *President*
Charles F Walsh, *Vice Pres*
Danny Blood, *Software Engr*
Stephen Palmucci, *Software Engr*
Andrew Wyllie, *Prgrmr*
EMP: 10
SALES (est): 1MM **Privately Held**
WEB: www.bostonsoftware.com
SIC: 7372 6411 Prepackaged And Custom Software Services For Insurance Insdustry

(G-13321)
BROOKLINE T A B
254 2nd Ave (02494-2829)
PHONE..................................617 566-3585
EMP: 3
SALES (est): 114.3K **Privately Held**
SIC: 2711 Newspapers-Publishing/Printing

(G-13322)
COMPANY OF COCA-COLA BOTTLING
9 B St (02494-2701)
P.O. Box 4108, Boston (02211-4108)
PHONE..................................781 449-4300
Gary Dumas, *Manager*
EMP: 60 **Privately Held**
WEB: www.coke.com
SIC: 2086 2087 Mfg Bottled/Canned Soft Drinks Mfg Flavor Extracts/Syrup
HQ: Coca-Cola Bottling Company Of Southeastern New England, Inc.
150 Waterford Parkway S
Waterford CT 06385
860 443-2816

(G-13323)
CONVERGENT DENTAL INC
140 Kendrick St Ste C110 (02494-2739)
PHONE..................................508 500-5656
Michael J Cataldo, *CEO*
Christopher Barron, *Vice Pres*
Wayne Craig, *Vice Pres*
Colby Ledbetter, *Vice Pres*
Charles Dresser, *Research*
EMP: 50
SALES (est): 12.1MM **Privately Held**
SIC: 3843 Mfg Dental Equipment/Supplies

(G-13324)
CROCKERGRAPHICS INC
80 Spring Rd (02494-1617)
PHONE..................................781 444-7020
Arthur Crocker, *President*
Roberta Crocker, *Treasurer*
EMP: 4
SALES: 200K **Privately Held**
WEB: www.crockergraphics.com
SIC: 2752 2791 Offset Printing & Typesetting

(G-13325)
CURAGEN CORPORATION (HQ)
119 4th Ave (02494-2725)
PHONE..................................908 200-7500
Anthony S Marucci, *CEO*
Thomas Davis, *Exec VP*
Tibor Keler, *Exec VP*
Avery W Catlin, *Senior VP*
Elizabeth Crowley, *Senior VP*
EMP: 11
SALES (est): 1MM
SALES (corp-wide): 9.5MM **Publicly Held**
WEB: www.curagen.com
SIC: 2834 Mfg Pharmaceutical Preparations
PA: Celldex Therapeutics, Inc.
53 Frontage Rd Ste 220
Hampton NJ 08827
908 200-7500

(G-13326)
D & L ASSOCIATES INC
Also Called: J T C Printing
679 Highland Ave Rear (02494-2221)
PHONE..................................781 400-5068
John Luz, *President*
David Roche, *Exec VP*
EMP: 7 **EST:** 1981
SQ FT: 5,120
SALES: 1MM **Privately Held**
SIC: 2752 2791 2789 Lithographic Commercial Printing Typesetting Services Bookbinding/Related Work

(G-13327)
DAILY NEWS TRIBUNE
254 2nd Ave Ste 1 (02494-2829)
PHONE..................................781 329-5008
Ellen Ishkanian, *Principal*
EMP: 4
SALES (est): 125.1K **Privately Held**
SIC: 2711 Newspapers-Publishing/Printing

(G-13328)
DG INTERNATIONAL HOLDINGS CORP
75 2nd Ave Ste 720 (02494-2826)
PHONE..................................781 577-2016
Tim Conley, *COO*
Michael Greiner, *CFO*
EMP: 5
SALES (est): 106.3K **Privately Held**
SIC: 3993 Mfg Signs/Advertising Specialties
HQ: Digital Generation, Inc.
75 2nd Ave Ste 720
Needham Heights MA 02494

(G-13329)
EAS HOLDINGS LLC (DH)
15 Crawford St (02494-2648)
PHONE..................................781 449-3056
Bruce Albelda,
Jonathon Bilzin,
Mark Zionts,
EMP: 3
SALES (est): 33.1MM
SALES (corp-wide): 449.4K **Privately Held**
WEB: www.excelswitching.com
SIC: 3661 3669 Mfg Telephone/Telegraph Apparatus Mfg Communications Equipment
HQ: Dialogic Corporation
9800 Cavendish 5e Etage
Saint-Laurent QC H4M 2
514 745-5500

(G-13330)
EURO-PRO HOLDCO LLC
89 A St 100 (02494-2806)
PHONE..................................617 243-0235
Mark Rosenzweig, *CEO*
Brian Lagarto, *Exec VP*
Dan Bilger, *Vice Pres*
Brian McGee, *Vice Pres*
Jason Thorne, *Vice Pres*
EMP: 100
SALES (est): 19.7MM **Privately Held**
SIC: 3639 6719 Mfg Household Appliances Holding Company

(G-13331)
FALLON FINE CABINETRY
171 Reservoir St (02494-3143)
PHONE..................................781 453-6988
Peter Fallon, *Owner*
EMP: 10
SALES (est): 470K **Privately Held**
SIC: 2434 Mfg Wood Kitchen Cabinets

(G-13332)
FAR REACH GRAPHICS INC
Also Called: Fastsigns
15 Kearney Rd (02494-2501)
PHONE..................................781 444-4889
Maria Schwede, *President*
EMP: 7
SQ FT: 2,000
SALES: 800K **Privately Held**
SIC: 3993 Signsadv Specs

(G-13333)
FLEXIBLE INFORMATION SYSTEMS
Also Called: Fis
62 Lynn Rd (02494-1754)
P.O. Box 813 (02494-0013)
PHONE..................................781 326-9977
Amir Kassiff, *Principal*
Ken Vogel, *Principal*
EMP: 3
SALES (est): 422.4K **Privately Held**
SIC: 3695 Mfr Of Commercial Software

(G-13334)
GENERAL DYNAMICS MISSION
89 A St (02494-2806)
PHONE..................................954 846-3000
Thomas Turner, *Branch Mgr*
Dave Tuttle, *Manager*
EMP: 760
SALES (corp-wide): 36.1B **Publicly Held**
SIC: 3669 Mfg Communications Equipment
HQ: General Dynamics Mission Systems, Inc.
12450 Fair Lakes Cir # 200
Fairfax VA 22033
703 263-2800

(G-13335)
KAMINARIO INC (PA)
75 2nd Ave Ste 620 (02494-2865)
PHONE..................................877 982-2555
Dani Golan, *CEO*
Steven Patterson, *Partner*
Jerry Swartz, *Partner*
Itay Shoshani, *COO*
Moshe Amir, *Vice Pres*
EMP: 48
SALES (est): 11.4MM **Privately Held**
SIC: 3572 Mfg Computer Storage Devices

(G-13336)
MENO PUBLISHING INC
Also Called: Meno Reunion Books
460 Hillside Ave Ste 6 (02494-1224)
PHONE..................................781 209-2665
Mark Harding, *CEO*
EMP: 4 **EST:** 2012
SQ FT: 1,000
SALES: 150K **Privately Held**
SIC: 2741 2731 Misc Publishing Books-Publishing/Printing

(G-13337)
MICROWAVE DEVELOPMENT LABS INC
Also Called: M D L
135 Crescent Rd (02494-1483)
P.O. Box 3294, Boston (02241-3294)
PHONE..................................781 292-6600
Gordon P Riblet, *President*
Bruce K Johnson, *Vice Pres*
James J Lynch, *Director*
Douglas Riblet, *Director*
Edward Scollins, *Director*
EMP: 55 **EST:** 1948
SALES: 10MM **Privately Held**
SIC: 3679 7389 Mfg Electronic Components Business Services

(G-13338)
MIDWAY UNITED LIMITED
21a Highland Cir (02494-3011)
PHONE..................................781 400-1742
▼ **EMP:** 500
SALES (est): 29.7MM **Privately Held**
SIC: 2491 Wood Preserving

(G-13339)
MIMOCO INC
475 Hillside Ave Ste 1 (02494-1200)
PHONE..................................617 783-1100
Evan Blaustein, *President*
Mimobot Izzy, *Manager*
Scott Seraydarian, *Director*
EMP: 15
SALES (est): 3.1MM **Privately Held**
SIC: 3577 5045 5734 Mfg Computer Peripheral Equipment Whol Computers/Peripherals Ret Computers/Software

(G-13340)
NEEDHAM CERTIFIED WELDING CORP
225 Highland Ave Rear (02494-3045)
P.O. Box 647 (02494-0012)
PHONE..................................781 444-7470
Flavia Ciriello, *President*
Carlo Ciriello, *Treasurer*
EMP: 4
SQ FT: 6,000
SALES (est): 685.9K **Privately Held**
WEB: www.needhambusiness.com
SIC: 3446 Mfg Architectural Metalwork

(G-13341)
ON SITE PRINTING & COPYING
679 Highland Ave (02494-2221)
PHONE..................................781 449-1871
Mekund Mehta, *President*
Dhira Mehta, *Manager*
EMP: 5
SALES (est): 545.9K **Privately Held**
WEB: www.on-siteprinting.com
SIC: 2759 2752 Commercial Printing Lithographic Commercial Printing

(G-13342)
PARAMETRIC HOLDINGS INC
140 Kendrick St (02494-2739)
PHONE..................................781 370-5000
James E Heppelmann, *President*
EMP: 3
SALES (est): 75.2K
SALES (corp-wide): 1.2B **Publicly Held**
SIC: 7372 Prepackaged Software Services
PA: Ptc Inc.
121 Seaport Blvd
Boston MA 02210
781 370-5000

(G-13343)
PATHFIRE INC
75 2nd Ave Ste 720 (02494-2826)
PHONE..................................972 581-2000
Scott Ginsburg, *Principal*
EMP: 5
SALES (est): 539.1K **Privately Held**
SIC: 2836 Mfg Biological Products

(G-13344)
SOLARONE SOLUTIONS INC (PA)
220 Reservoir St Ste 19 (02494-3133)
PHONE..................................339 225-4530
Moneer H Azzam, *President*
Nathanael Shepherd, *Treasurer*
David Gonzalez, *CTO*
◆ **EMP:** 11
SQ FT: 2,700
SALES (est): 1.6MM **Privately Held**
WEB: www.solarone.net
SIC: 3648 Mfg Lighting Equipment

(G-13345)
SUD-CHEMIE PROTECH INC
32 Fremont St Ste 1 (02494-2936)
PHONE..................................781 444-5188
Amiram Bar Ilan, *President*
Frank Wathan, *Treasurer*
▲ **EMP:** 30
SQ FT: 30,000
SALES (est): 8.9MM
SALES (corp-wide): 42.5MM **Privately Held**
SIC: 3822 2819 Mfg Environmental Controls Mfg Industrial Inorganic Chemicals
HQ: Sud-Chemie & Co. Limited Partnership
1600 W Hill St
Louisville KY 40210
502 634-7200

New Bedford
Bristol County

(G-13346)
A & R MACHINING TOOL & DIE
259 Samuel Barnet Blvd B (02745-1214)
PHONE..................................508 985-0916
Kevin Richard, *President*
EMP: 3
SQ FT: 2,100
SALES: 400K **Privately Held**
WEB: www.a-rsettingtools.com
SIC: 3312 Machine Shop/Tool & Die

(G-13347)
ABC DISPOSAL SERVICE INC
Also Called: ABC Disposal Welding Shop
994 Nash Rd (02746-1300)
P.O. Box 50540 (02745-0018)
PHONE..................................508 990-1911
Steve Camara, *Branch Mgr*
EMP: 26
SALES (corp-wide): 57.5MM **Privately Held**
SIC: 7692 Welding Repair
PA: Abc Disposal Service, Inc.
1245 Shawmut Ave
New Bedford MA 02746
508 995-0544

(G-13348)
ACCUSONIC TECHNOLOGIES (DH)
259 Samuel Barnet Blvd (02745-1214)
PHONE..................................508 495-6600
Guy Miller, *Engineer*
John Trofatter,
▲ **EMP:** 10 **EST:** 1961
SALES (est): 2.8MM
SALES (corp-wide): 2.4B **Publicly Held**
SIC: 3823 3829 3812 Mfg Process Control Instruments Mfg Measuring/Controlling Devices Mfg Search/Navigation Equipment
HQ: Ads Llc
340 The Bridge St Ste 204
Huntsville AL 35806
256 430-3366

(G-13349)
ACUSHNET COMPANY
Also Called: Titleist & Footjoy Worldwide
700 Belleville Ave (02745-6010)
P.O. Box 965, Fairhaven (02719-0965)
PHONE..................................508 979-2000
Dale Shenk, *Exec VP*
Cindy Jeffers, *Purchasing*
Kimberly Francis, *Marketing Mgr*
Jim Arruda, *Manager*
Ted Ratcliffe, *Network Mgr*
EMP: 2300 **Publicly Held**
WEB: www.titleist.com
SIC: 3949 Mfg Sporting/Athletic Goods
HQ: Acushnet Company
333 Bridge St
Fairhaven MA 02719
508 979-2000

(G-13350)
ACUSHNET COMPANY
215 Duchaine Blvd (02745-1209)
PHONE..................................508 979-2000
Daniel Lampinski, *Technical Mgr*
James Rotondo, *Engineer*
Walter Uihlein, *Branch Mgr*
Daniel Kirichok, *Technical Staff*
EMP: 40 **Publicly Held**
WEB: www.titleist.com
SIC: 3949 Mfg Sporting/Athletic Goods
HQ: Acushnet Company
333 Bridge St
Fairhaven MA 02719
508 979-2000

(G-13351)
ACUSHNET COMPANY
Also Called: Titleist
256 Samuel Barnet Blvd (02745-1215)
P.O. Box 965 (02741-0965)
PHONE..................................508 979-2156
Michael Kramer, *Manager*
Eric Lastowka, *Technical Staff*
EMP: 40 **Publicly Held**
WEB: www.titleist.com
SIC: 3949 Mfg Sporting/Athletic Goods
HQ: Acushnet Company
333 Bridge St
Fairhaven MA 02719
508 979-2000

(G-13352)
ACUSHNET RUBBER COMPANY INC
Also Called: Precix
744 Belleville Ave (02745-6010)
PHONE..................................508 998-4000
Marcio Lima, *CEO*
EMP: 400
SQ FT: 120,000
SALES (est): 124.8MM
SALES (corp-wide): 138.7MM **Privately Held**
WEB: www.precix.com
SIC: 3053 3061 2821 Mfg Gaskets/Packing/Sealing Devices Mfg Mechanical Rubber Goods Mfg Plastic Materials/Resins
PA: Zd Usa Holdings, Inc.
744 Belleville Ave
New Bedford MA 02745
508 998-4000

(G-13353)
AFC CABLE SYSTEMS INC
260 Duchaine Blvd (02745-1222)
PHONE..................................508 998-8277
Richard McGrail, *Branch Mgr*
EMP: 130 **Publicly Held**
WEB: www.afcweb.com
SIC: 3357 Nonferrous Wiredrawing/Insulating
HQ: Afc Cable Systems, Inc.
16100 Lathrop Ave
Harvey IL 60426
508 998-1131

(G-13354)
AHEAD LLC
270 Samuel Barnet Blvd (02745-1219)
PHONE..................................508 985-9898
Roy Jesus, *Opers Mgr*
Barbara Casagrande, *Opers Staff*
Bill Hermanson, *Sales Staff*
Anne Broholm,
Chantel Cardoso, *Administration*
◆ **EMP:** 303
SALES (est): 52MM
SALES (corp-wide): 662.3MM **Privately Held**
SIC: 2253 Knit Outerwear Mill
HQ: New Wave Group Ab
Kungsportsavenyen 10
Goteborg 411 3
317 128-900

(G-13355)
ALL PRO TINT
429 Allen St (02740-2112)
PHONE..................................508 992-8468
Donald Ouimette, *Principal*
EMP: 4
SALES (est): 322.2K **Privately Held**
SIC: 3211 Trade Contractor

(G-13356)
ALL SECURITY CO INC
771 Kempton St (02740-2544)
PHONE..................................508 993-4271
Paul Wesley, *President*
Christine Wesley, *Vice Pres*
EMP: 13
SQ FT: 2,652
SALES (est): 2.3MM **Privately Held**
SIC: 3699 7699 5731 Mfg Elec Mach/Equip/Supp Repair Services Ret Radio/Tv/Electronics

(G-13357)
ALLPAGE INC
54 Conduit St (02745-6016)
PHONE..................................508 995-6614
Paula Chainay, *President*
Kenneth Chainay, *Owner*
Brian Chainay, *Manager*
EMP: 3
SALES: 350K **Privately Held**
SIC: 3599 Mfg Industrial Machinery

(G-13358)
AMETEK INC
50 Welby Rd (02745-1100)
PHONE..................................508 998-4335
Michael Toro, *Vice Pres*
Paul Charpentier, *Design Engr*
Alvin Ng, *Sales Staff*
Susan Curado, *Branch Mgr*
EMP: 7
SALES (corp-wide): 4.8B **Publicly Held**
SIC: 3674 Mfg Process Control Instruments
PA: Ametek, Inc.
1100 Cassatt Rd
Berwyn PA 19312
610 647-2121

(G-13359)
ART SWISS CORPORATION
1357 E Rodney French Blvd (02744-2124)
PHONE..................................508 999-3281
Kenneth Joblon, *President*
EMP: 15
SQ FT: 10,000
SALES (est): 1MM **Privately Held**
WEB: www.brittanyusa.com
SIC: 2759 3555 Commercial Printing Mfg Printing Trades Machinery

(G-13360)
BAKER PARTS INC
Also Called: Bpi
135 Potter St (02740-4636)
P.O. Box 3942, Westport (02790-0299)
PHONE..................................508 636-3121
James C Watson, *President*
Todd Watson, *Vice Pres*
Rebecca W Fuentes, *Opers Dir*
Craig Fortini, *Purchasing*
Deborah J Watson, *Treasurer*
◆ **EMP:** 6
SQ FT: 10,000
SALES (est): 1.7MM **Privately Held**
WEB: www.bakerparts.com
SIC: 3556 5084 Mfg Food Products Machinery Whol Industrial Equipment

(G-13361)
BIG G SEAFOOD INC
48 Antonio Costa Ave (02740-7346)
PHONE..................................508 994-5113
Olivia Varao, *President*
George Smith, *Vice Pres*
EMP: 7
SQ FT: 1,200
SALES: 490K **Privately Held**
SIC: 2092 Cook And Process Conchs

(G-13362)
BIONETIKS CO
145 Union St Apt 8 (02740-6374)
PHONE..................................415 343-4990
Jorge Franco, *Principal*
EMP: 5
SALES (est): 137.3K **Privately Held**
SIC: 7372 Prepackaged Software Services

(G-13363)
BLUE FLEET WELDING SERVICE
Also Called: Sole Proprietorship
102 Wamsutta St (02740-6822)
PHONE..................................508 997-5513
Paul Lenieux, *Owner*
EMP: 11
SQ FT: 3,200
SALES: 100K **Privately Held**
SIC: 7692 Welding Repair

(G-13364)
BREWER BANNER DESIGNS
77 Forest St (02740-4850)
PHONE..................................508 996-6006
Alice P Brewer, *Owner*
EMP: 3
SALES: 200K **Privately Held**
WEB: www.brewerbanner.com
SIC: 2399 Ret Misc Merchandise

(G-13365)
BRITTANY GLOBAL TECH CORP
1357 E Rodney French Blvd (02744-2124)
PHONE..................................508 999-3281
Kenneth Joblon, *President*
◆ **EMP:** 89
SQ FT: 400,000
SALES (est): 33MM **Privately Held**
SIC: 2269 Finishing Plant

(G-13366)
BRODEUR MACHINE COMPANY INC
62 Wood St (02745-6248)
PHONE..................................508 995-2662
Mark A Brodeur, *Principal*
Lee Kissinger, *Vice Pres*
Tom Chartier, *Buyer*
Dennis Bravo, *Supervisor*
Markpaul Soares, *Info Tech Mgr*
EMP: 30
SALES (est): 6MM **Privately Held**
SIC: 3599 Mfg Metal Stampings

(G-13367)
BRODEUR MACHINE COMPANY BUS TR
Also Called: High Technology Coating Div
62 Wood St (02745-6248)
PHONE..................................508 995-2662
Mark Brodeur, *CEO*
Raymond Brodeur, *President*
Yvonne Sylvia, *Clerk*
EMP: 58 **EST:** 1922
SQ FT: 53,000

GEOGRAPHIC

SALES (est): 8.1MM **Privately Held**
WEB: www.brodeurmachine.com
SIC: 3469 7699 Mfg Metal Stampings Repair Services

(G-13368)
BUTLER ARCHITECTURAL WDWKG INC
200 Theodore Rice Blvd (02745-1212)
PHONE..................................508 985-9980
William D Butler, *President*
EMP: 13
SALES: 6MM **Privately Held**
SIC: 2499 Mfg Wood Products

(G-13369)
C P BOURG INC (PA)
Also Called: Bourg Collaters System
50 Samuel Barnet Blvd (02745-1285)
PHONE..................................508 998-2171
Christian P Bourg, *President*
James Tressler, *General Mgr*
Philippe Lambert Mr, *Vice Pres*
Donald J Schroeder, *Vice Pres*
Johanne Bourg Thibault, *Vice Pres*
◆ **EMP:** 54
SQ FT: 36,000
SALES (est): 12.4MM **Privately Held**
SIC: 3579 5044 Mfg Office Machines Whol Office Equipment

(G-13370)
CHAMBERLAIN MANUFACTURING CORP
New Bedford Div
117 King St (02745-5096)
PHONE..................................508 996-5621
James C Goncalo, *Branch Mgr*
EMP: 280
SALES (corp-wide): 1.4B **Privately Held**
WEB: www.chamberlin.com
SIC: 3483 Mfg Ammunition
HQ: Chamberlain Manufacturing Corporation
300 Windsor Dr
Oak Brook IL 60523
630 279-3600

(G-13371)
CMS ENTERPRISE INC
255 Popes Is (02740-7232)
PHONE..................................508 995-2372
Susan Ponte, *Principal*
EMP: 3
SALES (est): 211.2K **Privately Held**
SIC: 2048 Mfg Prepared Feeds

(G-13372)
COATERS INC
305 Nash Rd Unit 1 (02746-1800)
PHONE..................................508 996-5700
Paul Lubin, *President*
Philip Patrick, *Vice Pres*
Simon Lubin, *Treasurer*
EMP: 45 **EST:** 1934
SQ FT: 245,000
SALES (est): 5.1MM **Privately Held**
SIC: 2295 Mfg Coated Fabrics

(G-13373)
COLD ATLANTIC SEAFOOD INC
38 Bethel St (02740-6241)
PHONE..................................508 996-3352
Fax: 508 994-8308
EMP: 3
SALES (est): 210K **Privately Held**
SIC: 2092 Fresh & Frozen Seafood Processing

(G-13374)
CRAFT CORRUGATED BOX INC
4674 Acushnet Ave (02745-4736)
P.O. Box 50070 (02745-0003)
PHONE..................................508 998-2115
Ronald Mardula, *President*
EMP: 10 **EST:** 1964
SQ FT: 20,000
SALES (est): 1.8MM **Privately Held**
SIC: 2653 Mfg Corrugated/Solid Fiber Boxes

(G-13375)
CRYSTAL ICE CO INC
178 Front St (02740-7291)
PHONE..................................508 997-7522
Joseph E Swift, *President*
Robert F Swift, *Treasurer*
EMP: 18
SQ FT: 10,000
SALES: 2.5MM **Privately Held**
WEB: www.crystaliceco.com
SIC: 2097 Mfg Ice

(G-13376)
D J BASS INC
Also Called: Bass Ready Rooter
84 Bates St (02745-6008)
PHONE..................................508 678-4499
Dennis Bastarache, *President*
EMP: 7
SALES (est): 1.1MM **Privately Held**
WEB: www.bassreddy.com
SIC: 2842 Drain Cleaning Service

(G-13377)
DAVICO INC
Also Called: Davico Manufacturing
95 Brook St (02746-1782)
PHONE..................................508 998-1150
Raymond Surprenant, *President*
▲ **EMP:** 10
SQ FT: 5,000
SALES (est): 1.7MM **Privately Held**
WEB: www.davicomfg.com
SIC: 3714 Mfg Motor Vehicle Parts/Accessories

(G-13378)
DECO INTERIOR FINISHES INC
189 Popes Is (02740-7252)
P.O. Box 70099, North Dartmouth (02747-0099)
PHONE..................................508 994-9436
David Shea, *President*
EMP: 4
SQ FT: 1,200
SALES (est): 463K **Privately Held**
WEB: www.difinc.com
SIC: 2221 Installation Of Wall Fabric

(G-13379)
DION SIGNS AND SERVICE INC
125 Samuel Barnet Blvd (02745-1204)
PHONE..................................401 724-4459
Raymond P Dion, *President*
Rionald M Dion, *Vice Pres*
Richard S Dion, *Treasurer*
EMP: 10
SALES (est): 1.8MM
SALES (corp-wide): 6.4MM **Privately Held**
WEB: www.dionsigns.com
SIC: 3646 7389 Makes Electric Signs For Commercial Concerns
PA: Poyant Signs, Inc.
125 Samuel Barnet Blvd
New Bedford MA 02745
800 544-0961

(G-13380)
DOCKSIDE REPAIRS INC
14 Hervey Tichon Ave (02740-7348)
PHONE..................................508 993-6730
Roy Enoksen, *President*
EMP: 12
SQ FT: 1,000
SALES (est): 2MM **Privately Held**
SIC: 7692 Welding Shop

(G-13381)
EAST COAST FABRICATION INC
137 Popes Is (02740-7252)
PHONE..................................508 990-7918
Charles M Quinn Jr, *President*
▲ **EMP:** 5
SALES (est): 332.7K **Privately Held**
SIC: 3599 Mfg Industrial Machinery

(G-13382)
EASTER SEALS MASSACHUSETTS
256 Union St (02740-5948)
PHONE..................................508 992-3128
EMP: 16
SALES (corp-wide): 11.9MM **Privately Held**
SIC: 3842 Mfg Surgical Appliances/Supplies
PA: Easter Seals Massachusetts, Inc
484 Main St Ste 600
Worcester MA 01608
508 757-2756

(G-13383)
EDGEWATER MARINE INDS LLC
Also Called: Richardson's Maptech
90 Hatch St Unit 1 (02745-6000)
PHONE..................................508 992-6555
Lee Estes,
EMP: 25
SALES (est): 539K **Privately Held**
SIC: 2741 7389 Misc Publishing Business Services

(G-13384)
EPEC LLC (PA)
Also Called: Epec Engineered Technologies
176 Samuel Barnet Blvd (02745)
PHONE..................................508 995-5171
Rich Gregorski, *President*
Al Wright, *President*
Angie Brown, *General Mgr*
Sunny Wong, *Business Mgr*
Anton Beck, *Project Mgr*
▲ **EMP:** 90 **EST:** 1952
SQ FT: 60,000
SALES (est): 19.5MM **Privately Held**
SIC: 3672 Mfg Printed Circuit Boards

(G-13385)
FIBERSPAR LINEPIPE LLC
800 Purchase St Ste 502 (02740-6354)
PHONE..................................281 854-2636
Bonnie Moran, *Branch Mgr*
EMP: 4
SALES (corp-wide): 8.4B **Publicly Held**
SIC: 3498 Mfg Fabricated Pipe/Fittings
HQ: Fiberspar Linepipe Llc
12239 Fm 529 Rd
Houston TX 77041

(G-13386)
FINICKY PET FOOD INC
68 Blackmer St (02744-2614)
PHONE..................................508 991-8448
William F Schofield Sr, *CEO*
William F Schofield Jr, *President*
EMP: 25
SQ FT: 3,000
SALES (est): 4.4MM **Privately Held**
SIC: 2048 Mfg Prepared Feeds

(G-13387)
FIVE STAR MANUFACTURING INC
163 Samuel Barnet Blvd (02745-1220)
PHONE..................................508 998-1404
David A Cabral, *President*
Gualter A Massa, *Treasurer*
John Camara, *Technical Staff*
John P Camara, *Admin Sec*
EMP: 58
SALES (est): 4MM **Privately Held**
SIC: 3841 Mfg Surgical/Medical Instruments

(G-13388)
FIVE STAR SURGICAL INC
Also Called: Five Star Companies
163 Samuel Barnet Blvd (02745-1220)
PHONE..................................508 998-1404
John P Camara, *President*
Gualter A Massa, *Treasurer*
David A Cabral, *Admin Sec*
EMP: 94
SQ FT: 20,000
SALES (est): 15.8MM **Privately Held**
WEB: www.5starsurgical.com
SIC: 3841 Mfg Surgical/Medical Instruments

(G-13389)
FRINGE FACTORY
119 Coggeshall St (02746-2443)
PHONE..................................508 992-7563
Micheal Fournier, *Partner*
Michael Fournier, *Partner*
Paul Fournier, *Partner*
EMP: 6
SQ FT: 10,000
SALES (est): 430K **Privately Held**
WEB: www.thefringefactory.com
SIC: 2241 Narrow Fabric Mill

(G-13390)
GEC DURHAM INDUSTRIES INC (PA)
255 Samuel Barnet Blvd (02745-1220)
PHONE..................................508 995-2636
J Douglas Russel, *President*
EMP: 40
SALES (est): 38.4MM **Privately Held**
SIC: 3612 Mfg Transformers

(G-13391)
GOLD LINE CONNECTOR INC
Also Called: Gold Line Manufacturing
263 Brook St Unit 2 (02745-5275)
PHONE..................................508 999-5656
EMP: 19
SALES (corp-wide): 2.2MM **Privately Held**
WEB: www.gold-line.com
SIC: 3825 Mfg Audio Test Equipment Coaxial Connectors
PA: Gold Line Connector Inc
40 Great Pasture Rd
Redding CT 06896
203 938-2588

(G-13392)
H LOEB CORPORATION
419 Sawyer St Unit 2 (02746-5605)
PHONE..................................508 996-3745
Geoffrey Faucher, *President*
Julius Shaw, *Treasurer*
▲ **EMP:** 20 **EST:** 1948
SQ FT: 36,000
SALES (est): 4.8MM **Privately Held**
WEB: www.hloeb.com
SIC: 3644 3083 2675 Mfg Nonconductive Wiring Devices Mfg Laminated Plastic Plate/Sheet Mfg Die-Cut Paper/Paperboard

(G-13393)
HCC AEGIS INC (DH)
Also Called: Ametek Aegis
50 Welby Rd (02745-1100)
PHONE..................................508 998-3141
Timothy N Jones, *President*
Alan Ferreira, *General Mgr*
William J Burke, *Principal*
Gregory Myers, *Principal*
Kathryn E Sena, *Principal*
EMP: 28
SQ FT: 95,000
SALES (est): 35.1MM
SALES (corp-wide): 4.8B **Publicly Held**
WEB: www.hccaegis.com
SIC: 3674 Mfg Semiconductors/Related Devices
HQ: Hcc Industries Inc.
4232 Temple City Blvd
Rosemead CA 91770
626 443-8933

(G-13394)
HERCULES SLR (US) INC (PA)
44 South St (02740-7221)
PHONE..................................508 993-0010
Christos Giannou, *President*
▲ **EMP:** 19
SALES (est): 2.6MM **Privately Held**
SIC: 3531 5088 5551 Mfg Whol Ret Commercial Marine Products

(G-13395)
HORACIOS WELDING & SHTMTL INC
64 John Vertente Blvd (02745-1207)
PHONE..................................508 985-9940
Horacio B Tavares, *President*
EMP: 15
SQ FT: 45,000
SALES (est): 4MM **Privately Held**
SIC: 7692 Welding Repair

(G-13396)
I N I SCREEN PRINTING
2812 Acushnet Ave (02745-3411)
PHONE..................................774 206-1341
Edson Pereira, *Principal*
EMP: 4
SALES (est): 361.4K **Privately Held**
SIC: 2759 Commercial Printing

(G-13397)
INCIDENT CONTROL SYSTEMS LLC
Also Called: Revolution Armor
92 Gifford St 33 (02744-2611)
PHONE..................................508 984-8820
James Mitchell, *Mng Member*
EMP: 5
SALES: 1.5MM **Privately Held**
SIC: 3462 Mfg Iron/Steel Forgings

(G-13398)
J CARVALHO LLC
166 Essex St (02745-3501)
PHONE..................................774 206-1435
John Carvalho, *Principal*
EMP: 3
SALES (est): 297.5K **Privately Held**
SIC: 2499 Mfg Wood Products

(G-13399)
JA APPAREL CORP
689 Belleville Ave (02745-6011)
PHONE..................................580 990-4580
EMP: 8
SALES (corp-wide): 3.3B **Publicly Held**
SIC: 2311 Mfg Men's/Boy's Suits/Coats
HQ: Ja Apparel Corp.
6380 Rogerdale Rd
Houston TX 10019
877 986-9669

(G-13400)
JOHN E RUGGLES & CO
123 Sawyer St Unit 1 (02746-5403)
P.O. Box 8179 (02742-8179)
PHONE..................................508 992-9766
John E Ruggles, *Owner*
EMP: 4
SQ FT: 25,000
SALES: 330K **Privately Held**
SIC: 2298 Mfg Cordage/Twine

(G-13401)
JOSEPH ABBOUD MFG CORP (DH)
689 Belleville Ave (02745-6011)
PHONE..................................508 999-1301
Anthony Sapienza, *President*
Eric Spiel, *CFO*
Bill Nunes, *Manager*
▲ **EMP:** 500
SQ FT: 208,000
SALES (est): 73.2MM
SALES (corp-wide): 3.2B **Publicly Held**
SIC: 2311 Mfg Men's/Boy's Suits/Coats
HQ: The Men's Wearhouse Inc
6380 Rogerdale Rd
Houston TX 77072
281 776-7000

(G-13402)
JOSEPH ABBOUD MFG CORP
11 Belleville Rd (02745-5906)
PHONE..................................508 961-1726
Joseph Abboud, *Principal*
EMP: 5
SALES (corp-wide): 3.2B **Publicly Held**
SIC: 2311 Mfg Men's/Boy's Suits/Coats
HQ: Joseph Abboud Manufacturing Corp.
689 Belleville Ave
New Bedford MA 02745
508 999-1301

(G-13403)
KETCHAM SUPPLY CO INC
111 Myrtle St (02740-7029)
PHONE..................................508 997-4787
Heather Ketcham, *President*
EMP: 12
SQ FT: 25,000
SALES (est): 721.8K **Privately Held**
SIC: 3429 3496 Hardware, Nec

(G-13404)
KETCHAM TRAPS
111 Myrtle St (02740-7029)
PHONE..................................508 997-4787
Robert Ketcham, *Owner*
▲ **EMP:** 7
SQ FT: 11,000
SALES (est): 921.4K **Privately Held**
WEB: www.lobstering.com
SIC: 3429 5199 Mfg Hardware Whol Non-durable Goods

(G-13405)
KIRBY GEORGE JR PAINT CO INC
163 Mount Vernon St (02740-4610)
PHONE..................................508 997-9008
George Kirby III, *CEO*
George Kirby IV, *Vice Pres*
EMP: 3 **EST:** 1846
SQ FT: 2,500
SALES: 150K **Privately Held**
SIC: 2851 Mfg Paints/Allied Products

(G-13406)
KYLER SEAFOOD INC
Also Called: Kyler's
2 Washburn St (02740-7336)
PHONE..................................508 984-5150
Jeff Nanfelt, *President*
Billy Arruda, *Exec VP*
Steve Souza, *Controller*
Ruth Marshman, *Accountant*
Ted Depatie, *Sales Associate*
▼ **EMP:** 100
SQ FT: 35,000
SALES (est): 16.1MM **Privately Held**
WEB: www.kylerseafood.com
SIC: 2092 Mfg Fresh/Frozen Packaged Fish

(G-13407)
L & S INDUSTRIES INC (PA)
32 Lambeth St (02745-1003)
P.O. Box 50097 (02745-0004)
PHONE..................................508 995-4654
Jeanne-Marie Boylan, *President*
Dean Boylan, *Vice Pres*
EMP: 25
SQ FT: 8,400
SALES (est): 3.4MM **Privately Held**
SIC: 3273 Mfg Ready-Mixed Concrete

(G-13408)
LISBON SAUSAGE CO INC
Also Called: Amaral's Linguica
433 S 2nd St (02740-5764)
P.O. Box 2028 (02741-2028)
PHONE..................................508 993-7645
Antonio Rodrigues, *President*
EMP: 18
SQ FT: 1,800
SALES (est): 2MM **Privately Held**
SIC: 2013 5147 Mfg & Whol Sausage

(G-13409)
LOCAL MEDIA GROUP INC
Also Called: Standard Times
25 Elm St (02740-6228)
P.O. Box 5912 (02742-5912)
PHONE..................................508 997-7411
William T Kennedy, *Principal*
EMP: 260
SQ FT: 25,000
SALES (corp-wide): 1.5B **Publicly Held**
WEB: www.ottaway.com
SIC: 2711 7313 Newspapers-Publishing/Printing Advertising Representative
HQ: Local Media Group, Inc.
40 Mulberry St
Middletown NY 10940
845 341-1100

(G-13410)
LOCAL MEDIA GROUP INC
Also Called: Middleboro Gazette
25 Elm St (02740-6228)
PHONE..................................508 947-1760
Jon Høglof, *Editor*
Jane Lopes, *Manager*
EMP: 6
SQ FT: 1,716
SALES (corp-wide): 1.5B **Publicly Held**
WEB: www.ottaway.com
SIC: 2711 Newspapers-Publishing/Printing
HQ: Local Media Group, Inc.
40 Mulberry St
Middletown NY 10940
845 341-1100

(G-13411)
LORENZOS BAKERY LLC
1533 Acushnet Ave (02746-2223)
PHONE..................................508 287-9974
Lorenzo N Vazquez, *Principal*
Lorenzo Vazquez, *Principal*
EMP: 6
SALES (est): 219.6K **Privately Held**
SIC: 2051 Mfg Bread/Related Prdts

(G-13412)
M & R SCREEN PRINTING INC
95 Rodney French Blvd (02744-1603)
P.O. Box 160, East Freetown (02717-0160)
PHONE..................................508 996-0419
John B Macaroco, *President*
John Macaroco, *President*
Peter S Russell, *Treasurer*
EMP: 39
SQ FT: 4,000
SALES (est): 4.2MM **Privately Held**
WEB: www.mandrscreenprinting.com
SIC: 2759 Commercial Printing

(G-13413)
M F FLEY INCRPRTD-NEW BDFORD
Also Called: Foley Fish
77 Wright St (02740-7250)
P.O. Box 1806 (02741-1806)
PHONE..................................508 997-0773
Michael Foley, *President*
Laura Foley Ramsden, *Principal*
Linda Foley, *Vice Pres*
Peter Barnard Ramsden, *Admin Sec*
EMP: 40
SQ FT: 28,053
SALES (est): 6.2MM
SALES (corp-wide): 54.2MM **Privately Held**
WEB: www.foleyfish.com
SIC: 2092 Mfg Fresh/Frozen Packaged Fish
PA: M. F. Foley Company
24 W Howell St
Boston MA 02125
508 997-0773

(G-13414)
MADEWELL MANUFACTURING CO INC
651 Orchard St (02744-1008)
PHONE..................................508 997-0768
Jay Kivowitz, *President*
Haskell Kivowitz, *Chairman*
Thelma Kivowitz, *Treasurer*
EMP: 3
SQ FT: 5,000
SALES (est): 270K **Privately Held**
SIC: 2329 2339 2326 Mfg Men's/Boy's Clothing Mfg Women's/Misses' Outerwear Mfg Men's/Boy's Work Clothing

(G-13415)
MANOMET MANUFACTURING INC
194 Riverside Ave (02746-5428)
PHONE..................................508 997-1795
Edward Fitzsimmons, *President*
EMP: 3
SALES (est): 161.5K **Privately Held**
SIC: 3999 Mfg Misc Products

(G-13416)
MARTHAS SEASTREAK VINEYARD LLC
Also Called: New England Fast Ferry
49 State Pier (02740-7254)
PHONE..................................617 896-0293
EMP: 7
SALES (est): 729.1K **Privately Held**
SIC: 2084 Mfg Wines/Brandy/Spirits

(G-13417)
MAXIMUM INC
30 Samuel Barnet Blvd (02745-1205)
PHONE..................................508 995-2200
Peter Kilgore, *President*
Edward Rogerson, *Treasurer*
William Rogerson, *Admin Sec*
EMP: 11
SQ FT: 6,000
SALES (est): 1.9MM
SALES (corp-wide): 18MM **Privately Held**
WEB: www.maximum-inc.com
SIC: 3829 Mfg Measuring/Controlling Devices
PA: Imtra Corporation
30 Samuel Barnet Blvd
New Bedford MA 02745
508 995-7000

(G-13418)
MORGAN ADVANCED CERAMICS INC
225 Theodore Rice Blvd (02745-1213)
PHONE..................................508 995-1725
John Stang, *General Mgr*
Brian Rocnoy, *Plant Mgr*
EMP: 184
SALES (corp-wide): 1.3B **Privately Held**
WEB: www.morganelectroceramics.com
SIC: 2899 3251 Mfg Chemical Preparations Mfg Brick/Structural Tile
HQ: Morgan Advanced Materials Inc.
2425 Whipple Rd
Hayward CA 94544

(G-13419)
N B BAKING CO
98 County St (02744-1134)
PHONE..................................508 992-5413
EMP: 4
SALES (est): 154.2K **Privately Held**
SIC: 2051 Mfg Bread/Related Products

(G-13420)
NEW BEDFORD SALCHICHARIA INC (PA)
6 Rockdale Ave (02740-1071)
PHONE..................................508 992-6257
Antonio J Umbelina, *President*
Carlos A Brizida, *Treasurer*
EMP: 4
SQ FT: 3,200
SALES (est): 520.9K **Privately Held**
SIC: 2013 Mfg Prepared Meats

(G-13421)
NEW BEDFORD SCALE CO INC
144 Francis St (02740-2538)
PHONE..................................508 997-6730
Jim Stpierre, *President*
Gary Pelletier, *Treasurer*
EMP: 7
SQ FT: 2,200
SALES (est): 1.2MM **Privately Held**
WEB: www.nbscale.com
SIC: 3596 7699 Mfg Scales/Balances-Nonlaboratory Repair Services

(G-13422)
NEW ENGLAND CUSTOM WOOD WKG
Also Called: New England Custom Woodworking
350 North St (02740-4011)
PHONE..................................508 991-8038
Chris Ouellette, *President*
Melissa Oullette, *Vice Pres*
EMP: 4 **EST:** 1998
SALES: 71K **Privately Held**
SIC: 2431 Millwork

(G-13423)
NEW ENGLAND FENCEWRIGHTS INC
249 Brownell Ave (02740-1658)
PHONE..................................508 999-3337
EMP: 6
SALES (est): 370.3K **Privately Held**
SIC: 2499 Mfg Wood Products

(G-13424)
NEW ENGLAND PLASTICS CORP
126 Duchaine Blvd (02745-1201)
PHONE..................................508 995-7334
James B Osborne, *Opers-Prdtn-Mfg*
EMP: 45
SALES (corp-wide): 16.5MM **Privately Held**
SIC: 3089 3081 Mfg Plastic Products Mfg Unsupported Plastic Film/Sheet
PA: New England Plastics Corporation
310 Salem St Ste 2
Woburn MA 01801
781 933-6004

(G-13425)
NEW ENGLAND WATER JET CUTTING
84 Gifford St (02744-2615)
PHONE..................................508 993-9235
Peter Rodrick, *CEO*

GEOGRAPHIC

Roland Letendre, *Principal*
EMP: 3
SALES (est): 225.1K **Privately Held**
WEB: www.newaterjet.com
SIC: 3549 3599 2675 2282 Mfg Metal-working Mach Mfg Industrial Machinery Mfg Die-Cut Paper/Board Throwing/Winding Mill

(G-13426)
NFI LLC
Also Called: Nameplates For Industry
213 Theodore Rice Blvd (02745-1218)
PHONE..................................508 998-9021
Marcia La Belle, *Vice Pres*
Marcia Labelle, *Vice Pres*
Susan Rudnick, *CFO*
Maryanne Hodgkins, *Manager*
Renaud Megard,
EMP: 44
SQ FT: 14,000
SALES (est): 8MM **Privately Held**
WEB: www.nameplatesforindustry.com
SIC: 2759 Commercial Printing

(G-13427)
NICHE INC
Also Called: Barnstable Riding
57 Cove St (02744-2409)
PHONE..................................508 990-4202
Roland Letendre, *President*
Peter Roderick, *Treasurer*
▲ **EMP:** 50
SQ FT: 1,000,000
SALES (est): 8.6MM **Privately Held**
WEB: www.barnstableriding.com
SIC: 3172 3751 3199 2399 Mfg Personal Leather Gds Mfg Motorcycles/Bicycles Mfg Leather Goods Mfg Fabrctd Textile Pdts Mfg Mens/Boys Clothing

(G-13428)
NORTH COAST SEA-FOODS CORP
43 Blackmer St (02744-2613)
PHONE..................................508 997-0766
EMP: 50
SALES (corp-wide): 60.3MM **Privately Held**
SIC: 2092 Mfg Fresh/Frozen Packaged Fish
PA: North Coast Sea-Foods Corp.
5 Drydock Ave
Boston MA 02210
617 345-4400

(G-13429)
NORTH EAST SILICON TECH INC
11 David St (02744-2310)
PHONE..................................508 999-2001
Robert J Weeks, *President*
Chris Weeks, *Vice Pres*
Christopher L Weeks, *Vice Pres*
▲ **EMP:** 65
SQ FT: 30,000
SALES (est): 11.9MM **Privately Held**
WEB: www.nestecsilicon.com
SIC: 3674 Mfg Semiconductors/Related Devices

(G-13430)
NORTHERN PELAGIC GROUP LLC
4 Fish Is (02740-7226)
PHONE..................................508 979-1171
Brady Schofield, *Mng Member*
▼ **EMP:** 20
SQ FT: 25,000
SALES (est): 4.2MM **Privately Held**
WEB: www.norpel.com
SIC: 2092 Mfg Fresh/Frozen Packaged Fish

(G-13431)
NUTEX INDUSTRIES INC
127 Rodney French Blvd # 4 (02744-1623)
P.O. Box 40219 (02744-0016)
PHONE..................................508 993-2501
Andrei Klein, *President*
EMP: 29
SQ FT: 83,000
SALES: 2.5MM **Privately Held**
WEB: www.nutexindustries.com
SIC: 2241 Narrow Fabric Mill

(G-13432)
OCEAN CLIFF CORPORATION
362 S Front St (02740-5745)
PHONE..................................508 990-7900
J Gregory White, *President*
EMP: 6
SQ FT: 10,000
SALES: 1.5MM **Privately Held**
SIC: 2087 Mfg Flavor Extracts

(G-13433)
OCEAN MARINE FABRICATING
201 1/2 Popes Is (02740-7232)
PHONE..................................508 999-5554
Stephen Shurtleff, *Owner*
EMP: 4
SALES (est): 308.3K **Privately Held**
SIC: 3355 Mfg Aluminum Extruded Products

(G-13434)
PACKAGING PRODUCTS CORPORATION (PA)
Also Called: Arctic Pack
198 Herman Melville Blvd (02740-7344)
PHONE..................................508 997-5150
Theodore E Heidenreich Jr, *Ch of Bd*
Robert G Heidenreich, *President*
Theodore E Heidenreich III, *President*
Tony Cardoso, *Opers Staff*
Jonathan Mather, *Production*
▼ **EMP:** 19
SQ FT: 18,000
SALES (est): 4.3MM **Privately Held**
SIC: 3081 3086 5199 Mfg Unsupported Plastic Film/Sheet Mfg Plastic Foam Products Whol Nondurable Goods

(G-13435)
PARALLEL PRODUCTS OF NENG (DH)
969 Shawmut Ave (02746-1365)
PHONE..................................508 884-5100
Eugene W Kiesel, *President*
Timothy Cusson, *Vice Pres*
David Kenney, *Treasurer*
EMP: 5
SALES (est): 4.8MM
SALES (corp-wide): 49.8MM **Privately Held**
SIC: 2869 3089 Manufactures Industrial Organic Chemicals Specializing In Denatured Industrial Alcohols (Non-Beverage) (100)
HQ: Parallel Products Of Kentucky, Inc
401 Industry Rd Ste 100
Louisville KY 40208
502 471-2444

(G-13436)
PARAMOUNT CORP
Also Called: Oberon Company
22 Logan St (02740-7376)
P.O. Box 61008 (02746-0008)
PHONE..................................508 999-4442
Jack Hirschmann, *President*
Zac Twight, *VP Sales*
Coleen Gonsalves, *Sales Staff*
Jim Pollard, *Sales Staff*
Jack Evans, *Manager*
EMP: 50
SALES (est): 10.7MM **Privately Held**
SIC: 3851 Mfg Ophthalmic Goods

(G-13437)
PEQUOD INC
Also Called: Rose Alley Ale House
94 Front St (02740-7262)
PHONE..................................508 858-5123
Howard Mallowes IV, *Treasurer*
EMP: 5
SALES (est): 653.6K **Privately Held**
SIC: 3589 Mfg Service Industry Machinery

(G-13438)
PLACES TO GO LLC
1 Wamsutta St (02740-7369)
P.O. Box 87081, South Dartmouth (02748-0700)
PHONE..................................774 202-7756
Edward M Pacheco, *Principal*
EMP: 7 **EST:** 2011
SALES (est): 997.9K **Privately Held**
SIC: 3799 Mfg Transportation Equipment

(G-13439)
PLATING TECHNOLOGY INC
Also Called: Star Plating
41 Coffin Ave (02746-2407)
PHONE..................................508 996-4006
John S Thompson, *President*
William D Roeder, *Vice Pres*
EMP: 40 **EST:** 1955
SQ FT: 10,000
SALES (est): 5.7MM **Privately Held**
WEB: www.starplating.net
SIC: 3471 Plating/Polishing Service

(G-13440)
POLYNEER INC
259 Samuel Barnet Blvd D (02745-1214)
PHONE..................................508 998-5225
Paolo Belini, *President*
Nancy Mitchell, *Office Mgr*
▲ **EMP:** 40
SQ FT: 20,000
SALES (est): 5MM **Privately Held**
WEB: www.polyneer.com
SIC: 3069 8711 Mfg Fabricated Rubber Products Engineering Services

(G-13441)
POWDER PRO POWDER COATING INC
195 Riverside Ave (02746)
PHONE..................................508 991-5999
Antone Salgado, *Owner*
Michael Staab, *Manager*
EMP: 4
SALES (est): 320.7K **Privately Held**
WEB: www.powder-pro.net
SIC: 3479 Coating/Engraving Svcs

(G-13442)
POYANT SIGNS INC (PA)
125 Samuel Barnet Blvd (02745-1204)
PHONE..................................800 544-0961
Leonard M Poyant, *CEO*
Richard Poyant, *President*
Erik Tracey, *Chief*
Ruben Bernardo, *Opers Staff*
Victor Gonsalves, *CFO*
EMP: 48 **EST:** 1938
SQ FT: 50,000
SALES (est): 6.4MM **Privately Held**
WEB: www.poyantsigns.com
SIC: 3993 Mfg Signs/Advertising Specialties

(G-13443)
PRECISION ORTHOT & PROSTHETICS
203 Popes Is (02740-7232)
PHONE..................................508 991-5577
Mathew Hebert, *President*
Matthew E Hebert, *Officer*
EMP: 5
SALES (est): 663.6K **Privately Held**
SIC: 3842 Mfg Surgical Appliances/Supplies

(G-13444)
REAL GOODS SOLAR INC
50 Conduit St (02745-6016)
PHONE..................................508 992-1416
EMP: 125 **Publicly Held**
SIC: 3433 Plumbing/Heating/Air Cond Contractor
PA: Real Goods Solar, Inc.
110 16th St Ste 300
Denver CO 80202

(G-13445)
RICHARD CANTWELL WOODWORKING
611 Belleville Ave (02745-5982)
PHONE..................................508 984-7921
William Whitman, *President*
EMP: 3
SALES (est): 463.6K **Privately Held**
SIC: 2431 Mfg Millwork

(G-13446)
ROBERT EMMET COMPANY INC
51 Chancery St (02740-3503)
PHONE..................................508 997-2651
Thomas E Reilly, *President*
Mary E Reilly, *President*
Thomas Reilly, *Director*
▲ **EMP:** 6
SALES (est): 960.8K **Privately Held**
SIC: 3499 Mfg Pewter Glass Silver Gold Brass Ware Specializing In Irish Goods

(G-13447)
SCRIMSHAW SCREENPRINTING
1587 Purchase St (02740-6817)
PHONE..................................508 617-7498
Shane Mackie, *Owner*
EMP: 3 **EST:** 2015
SALES (est): 118K **Privately Held**
SIC: 2759 Commercial Printing

(G-13448)
SEA FUELS MARINE
465 N Front St (02746-2242)
PHONE..................................508 992-2323
EMP: 6
SALES (est): 748.9K **Privately Held**
SIC: 2869 Mfg Industrial Organic Chemicals

(G-13449)
SEA WATCH INTERNATIONAL LTD
15 Antonio Costa Ave (02740-7347)
PHONE..................................508 984-1406
John Miller, *General Mgr*
EMP: 70
SALES (corp-wide): 114.7MM **Privately Held**
WEB: www.seaclam.com
SIC: 2092 Mfg Fresh/Frozen Packaged Fish
PA: Sea Watch International, Ltd.
8978 Glebe Park Dr
Easton MD 21601
410 822-7501

(G-13450)
SHARROCKS ENGLISH BAKERY INC
135 Potter St (02740-4636)
P.O. Box 1135, Marion (02738-0021)
PHONE..................................508 997-5710
Henry Dejesus, *President*
Sarah Dejesus, *General Mgr*
Judy Dejesus, *Vice Pres*
EMP: 9
SALES (est): 1.2MM **Privately Held**
SIC: 2052 Retail Bakery

(G-13451)
SPINNER PUBLICATIONS INC
164 William St (02740-6022)
P.O. Box 1801 (02741-1801)
PHONE..................................508 994-4564
Tracy Furtata, *Principal*
Susan Grace, *Mktg Dir*
Joseph Thomas, *Exec Dir*
EMP: 6
SALES (est): 39.6K **Privately Held**
WEB: www.spinnerpub.com
SIC: 2731 Books-Publishing/Printing

(G-13452)
STANDARD MODERN COMPANY
186 Duchaine Blvd (02745-1201)
PHONE..................................774 425-3537
Ben Couto, *IT/INT Sup*
EMP: 6
SALES (est): 750.4K **Privately Held**
SIC: 2752 Lithographic Commercial Printing

(G-13453)
SYMMETRY MEDICAL INC
61 John Vertente Blvd (02745-1202)
PHONE..................................508 998-1104
Patrick Heffron, *VP Bus Dvlpt*
Jay Nunes, *Branch Mgr*
Cristina Jorge, *Administration*
EMP: 250
SQ FT: 14,000
SALES (corp-wide): 696.7MM **Privately Held**
WEB: www.symmetrymedical.com
SIC: 3841 Mfg Surgical/Medical Instruments
HQ: Symmetry Medical Inc.
3724 N State Road 15
Warsaw IN 46582

(G-13454)
TNCO INC
61 John Vertente Blvd (02745-1202)
PHONE.....................................781 447-6661
Karin Gilman, *President*
Roger M Burke, *Vice Pres*
Frank Difrancesco, *Vice Pres*
EMP: 60 **EST:** 1964
SQ FT: 25,000
SALES (est): 6MM **Privately Held**
SIC: 3841 3545 Mfg Surgical/Medical Instruments Mfg Machine Tool Accessories

(G-13455)
TOMRA MASS LLC
969 Shawmut Ave (02746-1365)
PHONE.....................................203 395-3484
Kenney Ciccketti,
EMP: 35
SALES (est): 4.2MM
SALES (corp-wide): 936.9MM **Privately Held**
SIC: 2611 4953 Pulp Mill Refuse Systems
HQ: Tomra Of North America (Inc)
1 Corporate Dr Ste 710
Shelton CT 06484

(G-13456)
UNDER COVER INC
138 Hatch St (02745-6025)
PHONE.....................................508 997-7600
Kelli W Arsenault, *President*
Peter C Arsenault, *Treasurer*
Kelli Arsenault, *Sales Staff*
EMP: 10
SQ FT: 200
SALES: 500K **Privately Held**
SIC: 2393 Mfg Textile Bags

(G-13457)
VICTORIA H BRADSHAW
Also Called: Hiller Printing
686 Belleville Ave (02745-6035)
PHONE.....................................508 992-1702
Victoria Bradshaw, *Owner*
EMP: 4
SQ FT: 3,500
SALES (est): 194.7K **Privately Held**
SIC: 2752 Lithographic Commercial Printing

(G-13458)
VULPLEX INCORPORATED
305 Nash Rd (02746-5868)
PHONE.....................................508 996-6787
Simon Lubin, *President*
Paul Lubin, *President*
EMP: 42
SQ FT: 50,000
SALES (est): 2.8MM **Privately Held**
SIC: 2295 2297 2241 Mfg Coated Fabrics Mfg Nonwoven Fabrics Narrow Fabric Mill

(G-13459)
WOOD GEEK INC
685 Orchard St (02744-1017)
PHONE.....................................508 858-5282
Frederick A Miller Jr, *President*
EMP: 9
SQ FT: 6,000
SALES: 750K **Privately Held**
SIC: 2511 Mfg Wood Household Furniture

(G-13460)
ZD USA HOLDINGS INC (PA)
744 Belleville Ave (02745-6010)
PHONE.....................................508 998 4000
David Slutz, *CEO*
EMP: 120
SALES (est): 138.7MM **Privately Held**
SIC: 3053 Mfg Gaskets/Packing/Sealing Devices

New Braintree
Worcester County

(G-13461)
WALKER MACHINE
1290 W Brookfield Rd (01531-1553)
PHONE.....................................508 867-8097
Randall Walker, *Owner*
Joan Walker, *Co-Owner*
EMP: 3
SALES (est): 271.3K **Privately Held**
SIC: 3599 Mfg Industrial Machinery

Newbury
Essex County

(G-13462)
AIRFLOW DIRECTION INC
2 Livingston Ln (01951-1136)
PHONE.....................................978 462-9995
Brian Wiseman, *President*
▲ **EMP:** 5
SALES: 300K **Privately Held**
WEB: www.airflowdirection.com
SIC: 3823 Mfg Process Control Instruments

(G-13463)
PJS TO YOUR DOOR LLC
71 Green St (01951-1707)
PHONE.....................................978 462-0699
EMP: 3
SALES (est): 135.4K **Privately Held**
SIC: 3442 Mfg Metal Doors/Sash/Trim

(G-13464)
POWERHOUSE BOTANIC DISTILLERY
184 High Rd (01951-2212)
PHONE.....................................978 930-8281
EMP: 3
SALES (est): 109.1K **Privately Held**
SIC: 2085 Mfg Distilled/Blended Liquor

(G-13465)
SALT MARSH CANVAS
Also Called: Marine Canvas Shop
10 Bittersweet Ln (01951-1101)
PHONE.....................................978 462-0070
Sarah Goddard Rinkaus, *President*
EMP: 4
SALES (est): 271.5K **Privately Held**
SIC: 2211 Cotton Broadwoven Fabric Mill

(G-13466)
SHUTTERS R US
22 S Pond St (01951-1220)
PHONE.....................................978 376-0201
Susan Becker, *Principal*
EMP: 3
SALES (est): 147.8K **Privately Held**
SIC: 3442 Mfg Metal Doors/Sash/Trim

Newburyport
Essex County

(G-13467)
ABARISCAN INC
78 Lime St (01950-2909)
PHONE.....................................978 462-0284
Steven W Krusemark, *President*
EMP: 5 **EST:** 2014
SALES: 100K **Privately Held**
SIC: 3577 5043 Mfg Computer Peripheral Equipment Whol Photo Equipment/Supplies

(G-13468)
ALFA LAVAL INC
Also Called: Alfa Laval Thermal-Food Ctr
111 Parker St (01950-4011)
PHONE.....................................978 465-5777
Craig Martin, *Manager*
EMP: 25
SQ FT: 15,200
SALES (corp-wide): 4.2B **Privately Held**
SIC: 3443 3556 Mfg Fabricated Plate Work Mfg Food Products Machinery
HQ: Alfa Laval Inc.
5400 Intl Trade Dr
Richmond VA 23231
866 253-2528

(G-13469)
ARWOOD MACHINE CORPORATION
Also Called: AMC
95 Parker St Ste 4 (01950-4034)
PHONE.....................................978 463-3777
Michael Munday, *President*
Daniel Sedler, *Vice Pres*
David Munday, *VP Opers*
Anthony Marino, *Mfg Mgr*
Ellen Dana, *Purch Agent*
EMP: 92 **EST:** 1966
SQ FT: 82,000
SALES: 13.3MM **Privately Held**
WEB: www.arwoodmachine.com
SIC: 3599 Mfg Industrial Machinery

(G-13470)
AW AIRFLO INDUSTRIES INC
Also Called: Precision Metal Fabrication
52 Parker St (01950-4056)
PHONE.....................................978 465-6260
Leo A Perreault, *President*
EMP: 20
SQ FT: 20,000
SALES (est): 4.2MM **Privately Held**
WEB: www.awairflo.com
SIC: 3444 Mfg Sheet Metalwork

(G-13471)
B & G CABINET
253 Low St Ste 8 (01950-3510)
PHONE.....................................978 465-6455
John Burtruccio, *Partner*
Jean Lanham, *Office Admin*
EMP: 13
SALES (est): 2.3MM **Privately Held**
WEB: www.bgcabinet.com
SIC: 2434 Mfg Wood Kitchen Cabinets

(G-13472)
BERKSHIRE MNUFACTURED PDTS INC
116 Parker St (01950-4008)
PHONE.....................................978 462-8161
George Psyhojos, *President*
Brian Kelly, *Vice Pres*
Jim Moroney, *Engineer*
Raymond Ngo, *Engineer*
Chris Corey, *Cust Mgr*
EMP: 150
SQ FT: 35,000
SALES (est): 42.4MM **Privately Held**
WEB: www.berkshiremfp.com
SIC: 3469 3599 3544 3471 Mfg Metal Stampings Mfg Industrial Machinery Mfg Dies/Tools/Jigs/Fixt Plating/Polishing Svcs

(G-13473)
BIXBY INTERNATIONAL CORP
1 Preble Rd (01950-4042)
PHONE.....................................978 462-4100
Daniel S Rocconi, *President*
Robert Mc Lellan, *President*
Christopher M Fraser, *Corp Secy*
Chris Vanremoortel, *Engineer*
Rob Law, *Senior Engr*
▲ **EMP:** 60 **EST:** 1940
SQ FT: 90,000
SALES (est): 19.7MM **Privately Held**
WEB: www.bixbyintl.com
SIC: 3083 3089 Mfg Laminated Plastic Plate/Sheet Mfg Plastic Products

(G-13474)
BRADFORD & BIGELOW INC
3 Perkins Way (01950-4007)
PHONE.....................................978 904-3112
John Galligan, *President*
Adam Gates, *Business Mgr*
Stephen Pompeo, *Business Mgr*
Richard Dunn, *Exec VP*
Rick Dunn, *Exec VP*
▲ **EMP:** 115 **EST:** 1947
SQ FT: 150,000
SALES (est): 44.5MM **Privately Held**
WEB: www.bradford-bigelow.com
SIC: 2752 Lithographic Commercial Printing

(G-13475)
BUCKLEGUYCOM LLC
15 Graf Rd (01950-4014)
PHONE.....................................978 213-9989
Peter W Harriss, *Mng Member*
EMP: 7
SALES: 1MM **Privately Held**
SIC: 3965 Mfg Fasteners/Buttons/Pins

(G-13476)
C F JAMESON & CO INC
69 Purchase St (01950-3109)
P.O. Box 5197, Haverhill (01835-0197)
PHONE.....................................978 462-4097
Benjamin J Jameson, *President*
Pravin Patel, *Vice Pres*
Arthur C Jameson, *Treasurer*
Jonny Jones, *Accountant*
EMP: 14 **EST:** 1925
SQ FT: 13,000
SALES (est): 1.8MM **Privately Held**
WEB: www.cfjameson.com
SIC: 2851 Mfg Paints/Allied Products

(G-13477)
CAREER PRESS INC (PA)
Also Called: New Page Books
65 Parker St Ste 7 (01950-4600)
PHONE.....................................201 848-0310
Ron Fry, *President*
Kirsten Dalley, *Editor*
Anne Brooks, *Vice Pres*
Deborah Donnell, *Marketing Staff*
◆ **EMP:** 23
SQ FT: 19,000
SALES (est): 2MM **Privately Held**
WEB: www.careerpress.com
SIC: 2731 Misc Publishing

(G-13478)
COMDEC INCORPORATED
25 Hale St (01950-3599)
PHONE.....................................978 462-3399
Steven A Meredith, *President*
▲ **EMP:** 31 **EST:** 1982
SQ FT: 48,000
SALES (est): 4MM **Privately Held**
WEB: www.comdecinc.com
SIC: 2759 Commercial Printing

(G-13479)
COMMONWEALTH BIOFUEL
77 Parker St (01950-4000)
PHONE.....................................978 881-0478
EMP: 3
SALES (est): 177.1K **Privately Held**
SIC: 2869 Mfg Industrial Organic Chemicals

(G-13480)
CRYSTAL ENGINEERING CO INC
2 Stanley Tucker Dr (01950-4039)
PHONE.....................................978 465-7007
Michael R Trotta, *President*
Peter Kershaw, *COO*
Timothy Barrett, *Engineer*
Robert Bouchard, *Engineer*
George Hunt, *Sales Staff*
EMP: 28 **EST:** 1956
SQ FT: 2,600
SALES (est): 6.5MM **Privately Held**
WEB: www.crystalengineering.com
SIC: 3469 3452 Mfg Metal Stampings Mfg Bolts/Screws/Rivets

(G-13481)
DEHAAS ADVERTISING & DESIGN
10 Dorothy E Lucey Dr (01950-1781)
PHONE.....................................978 462-1997
Debbie Dehaas, *President*
EMP: 3 **EST:** 1985
SALES (est): 259.1K **Privately Held**
WEB: www.dehaasdesign.com
SIC: 3993 Mfg Signs/Advertising Specialties

(G-13482)
DIANNES FINE DESSERTS INC (PA)
4 Graf Rd (01950-4015)
PHONE.....................................978 463-3832
Mike Knowles, *CEO*
Daniel Scales, *President*
Dixie Raxter, *Division Mgr*
Tom Lundquist, *CFO*
Peter Franggos, *Controller*
EMP: 190
SQ FT: 90,000
SALES (est): 139.9MM **Privately Held**
SIC: 2053 Mfg Frozen Bakery Products

GEOGRAPHIC

(G-13483)
DIANNES FINE DESSERTS INC
1 Perry Way (01950)
PHONE..................................978 463-3881
Thomas Lundquist, *CFO*
EMP: 200
SALES (corp-wide): 139.9MM **Privately Held**
SIC: 2053 Mfg Frozen Bakery Products
PA: Dianne's Fine Desserts, Inc.
4 Graf Rd
Newburyport MA 01950
978 463-3832

(G-13484)
EAST CAST WLDG FABRICATION LLC
104 Parker St (01950-4063)
PHONE..................................978 465-2338
Andrew Laurence, *Principal*
Ron April, *Principal*
Larry Scates, *Purchasing*
EMP: 30
SALES (est): 3.2MM **Privately Held**
SIC: 7692 Welding Repair

(G-13485)
EBARA TECHNOLOGIES INC
69 Parker St B (01950-4012)
PHONE..................................978 465-1983
Mark Perry, *Vice Pres*
EMP: 4 **Privately Held**
WEB: www.ebaratech.com
SIC: 3563 Mfg Vacuum Pumps
HQ: Ebara Technologies Incorporated
51 Main Ave
Sacramento CA 95838
916 920-5451

(G-13486)
ELECTRONIC PRODUCTS INDS INC
85 Parker St (01950-4095)
PHONE..................................978 462-8101
Christopher Mosher, *President*
EMP: 46 **EST:** 2017
SQ FT: 26,500
SALES (est): 4.7MM **Privately Held**
SIC: 3674 Manufactures Semiconductors/Related Devices

(G-13487)
EPI II INC
Also Called: Industrial Realty Trust
30 Green St (01950-2639)
PHONE..................................978 462-1514
Joseph J Urbanetti, *President*
Donald C Griffin, *Clerk*
EMP: 65
SQ FT: 8,000
SALES (est): 10.1MM **Privately Held**
SIC: 3674 Mfg Electronic Semiconductors & Accessories

(G-13488)
FINESSE SOLUTIONS INC
5 Perry Way (01950-4009)
PHONE..................................978 255-1296
EMP: 5
SALES (corp-wide): 24.3B **Publicly Held**
SIC: 3823 Mfg Process Control Instruments
HQ: Finesse Solutions, Inc.
3501 Leonard Ct
Santa Clara CA 95054
408 570-9000

(G-13489)
FLEXAUST COMPANY INC
40r Merrimac St Ste 401w (01950-2064)
PHONE..................................978 465-0445
Michael Obrien, *Vice Pres*
EMP: 5
SALES (corp-wide): 216.4MM **Privately Held**
SIC: 3052 Mfg Rubber/Plastic Hose/Belting
HQ: Flexaust Company Inc
1200 Prospect St Ste 325
La Jolla CA 92037
619 232-8429

(G-13490)
FOILMARK INC (HQ)
Also Called: I T W Foils
5 Malcolm Hoyt Dr (01950-4082)
PHONE..................................978 225-8200
Frank J Olsen Jr, *President*
Philip Leibel, *Treasurer*
▲ **EMP:** 91
SALES (est): 38.8MM
SALES (corp-wide): 14.7B **Publicly Held**
SIC: 3497 3549 3544 Mfg Metal Foil/Leaf Mfg Metalworking Machinery Mfg Dies/Tools/Jigs/Fixtures
PA: Illinois Tool Works Inc.
155 Harlem Ave
Glenview IL 60025
847 724-7500

(G-13491)
FOX BROTHERS FURNITURE STUDIO
39 Liberty St (01950-2830)
PHONE..................................978 462-7726
Henry Fox, *President*
EMP: 3
SQ FT: 4,000
SALES: 250K **Privately Held**
WEB: www.foxbros.com
SIC: 2511 2521 Mfg Wood Household And Some Office Furniture

(G-13492)
FUEL TRAINING STUDIO LLC
75 Merrimac St (01950-2540)
PHONE..................................617 694-5489
Jeanne Carter, *Co-Founder*
EMP: 5
SALES (est): 667.7K **Privately Held**
SIC: 2869 Mfg Industrial Organic Chemicals

(G-13493)
FUNCTIONAL COATINGS LLC
Also Called: Hero Coatings
13 Malcolm Hoyt Dr (01950-4017)
PHONE..................................978 462-0746
David P Lynch, *Vice Pres*
Stephen R Lynch,
David Lynch,
▲ **EMP:** 80
SQ FT: 20,000
SALES (est): 7MM **Privately Held**
WEB: www.functionalcoatings.com
SIC: 2891 3554 Mfg Adhesives/Sealants Mfg Paper Industrial Machinery

(G-13494)
GEONAUTICS MANUFACTURING INC
506 Merrimac St (01950-1700)
PHONE..................................978 462-7161
Tim Tracy, *President*
EMP: 25 **EST:** 1960
SQ FT: 25,000
SALES (est): 3.1MM **Privately Held**
WEB: www.geonauticsmfg.com
SIC: 3083 3544 3086 3451 Mfg Lamnatd Plstc Plates Mfg Dies/Tools/Jigs/Fixt Mfg Plastic Foam Prdts Mfg Screw Machine Prdts Mfg Carbon/Graphite Prdt

(G-13495)
HARBORSIDE PRINTING CO INC
Also Called: Coastal Printing
3 Graf Rd Ste 5 (01950-4601)
PHONE..................................978 462-2026
Micheal R Morin, *President*
Doreen Dern, *Admin Sec*
EMP: 11
SALES: 7.8MM **Privately Held**
WEB: www.harborprint.com
SIC: 2752 Offset Printing

(G-13496)
HAWTAN LEATHERS LLC
75 Parker St (01950-4000)
PHONE..................................978 465-3791
Daniel A Gallagher Jr,
Lisa C Gallagher,
◆ **EMP:** 105
SALES (est): 14.6MM **Privately Held**
SIC: 3111 5199 Leather Tanning/Finishing Whol Nondurable Goods

(G-13497)
HERO COATINGS INC
13 Malcolm Hoyt Dr (01950-4017)
PHONE..................................978 462-0746
Stephen Lynch, *President*
David P Lynch, *Corp Secy*
EMP: 9
SQ FT: 20,000
SALES (est): 2MM **Privately Held**
WEB: www.herocoatings.com
SIC: 2891 Mfg Adhesives/Sealants

(G-13498)
HONEYWELL ROBERT WARNER
14 Hawthorne Rd (01950-3338)
PHONE..................................978 358-8080
Robert Warner, *Owner*
EMP: 3
SALES (est): 145K **Privately Held**
SIC: 3724 Mfg Aircraft Engines/Parts

(G-13499)
IAN MARIE INC
Also Called: Journeyman Press, The
11 Malcolm Hoyt Dr (01950-4017)
PHONE..................................978 463-6742
Dana Thoms, *President*
Sheryl Richards, *Purch Mgr*
Scott Vaughan, *Director*
EMP: 34 **EST:** 2014
SALES (est): 4.6MM **Privately Held**
SIC: 2741 Misc Publishing

(G-13500)
INNOCOR FOAM TECHNICAL
122 Parker St (01950-4008)
PHONE..................................978 462-5400
Michael C Thompson, *CEO*
Chris Lacorata, *Principal*
EMP: 17
SALES (est): 1.5MM
SALES (corp-wide): 238.1MM **Privately Held**
SIC: 3086 Mfg Plastic Foam Products
HQ: Innocor Foam Technologies, Llc
200 Schulz Dr Ste 2
Red Bank NJ 07701

(G-13501)
INOVAR PACKAGING GROUP LLC
Also Called: Labelprint America
8 Opportunity Way (01950-4043)
PHONE..................................978 463-4004
Robin Hamilton, *General Mgr*
EMP: 24
SALES (corp-wide): 3B **Privately Held**
SIC: 2759 Commercial Printing
HQ: Inovar Packaging Group, Llc
10470 Miller Rd
Dallas TX 75238
817 277-6666

(G-13502)
IVES EEG SOLUTIONS LLC
25 Storey Ave (01950-1869)
PHONE..................................978 358-8006
Susan Phelan, *Principal*
Patrick Phelan, *Vice Pres*
EMP: 4 **EST:** 2010
SALES (est): 210K **Privately Held**
SIC: 3841 Mfg Surgical/Medical Instruments

(G-13503)
KEIVER WILLARD-LUMBER CORP
11 Graf Rd 13 (01950-4091)
PHONE..................................978 462-7193
Robert D Keiver, *President*
Patricia Heintzelman, *Corp Secy*
Kevin Barlow, *Vice Pres*
Karl Gray, *Vice Pres*
Bruce Arlington, *Sales Staff*
EMP: 71
SALES (est): 12.2MM **Privately Held**
WEB: www.keiver-willard.com
SIC: 2431 5031 Mfg Millwork Whol Lumber/Plywood/Millwork

(G-13504)
KLEENLINE LLC
6 Opportunity Way Rear (01950-4043)
PHONE..................................978 463-0827
Jim Laverdiere, *President*
Mark W Anderson, *Manager*
William M Shult, *Manager*
EMP: 55
SALES (est): 13.1MM
SALES (corp-wide): 587.9MM **Privately Held**
WEB: www.kleenline.com
SIC: 3535 Mfg Conveyors/Equipment
PA: Pro Mach, Inc.
50 E Rivercntr Blvd 180
Covington KY 41011
513 831-8778

(G-13505)
KLONE LAB LLC
115 Water St Ste A (01950-3081)
PHONE..................................978 378-3434
David Slauson, *Opers Staff*
Karen Parady, *Finance Mgr*
Marcy Maglio, *Sales Mgr*
Kelly Palma, *Sales Staff*
Erin Gerrity, *Director*
EMP: 7 **EST:** 2016
SALES (est): 705.3K **Privately Held**
SIC: 3021 Mfg Rubber/Plastic Footwear

(G-13506)
LABELPRINT AMERICA INC
8 Opportunity Way (01950-4043)
PHONE..................................978 463-4004
Antonio Yemma, *President*
EMP: 29
SQ FT: 21,000
SALES (est): 3.9MM **Privately Held**
SIC: 2759 Commercial Printing

(G-13507)
LAKE MANUFACTURING CO INC
6 Opportunity Way (01950-4043)
PHONE..................................978 465-1617
Robert Lake, *President*
EMP: 14
SQ FT: 10,000
SALES (est): 2.2MM **Privately Held**
WEB: www.lakemfg.com
SIC: 3599 Mfg Industrial Machinery

(G-13508)
LAVANT GARDE INC
Perkins Way Unit 1 (01950)
PHONE..................................805 522-0045
Hayel Said, *CEO*
EMP: 4
SALES (est): 344.8K **Privately Held**
WEB: www.lavantgarde.com
SIC: 2844 5122 Mfg Toilet Preparations Whol Drugs/Sundries

(G-13509)
MACDIARMID MACHINE CORP
7 Perry Way Ste 13 (01950-4002)
PHONE..................................978 465-3546
Scott Macdiarmid, *President*
EMP: 10
SQ FT: 6,000
SALES (est): 1.8MM **Privately Held**
SIC: 3599 Mfg Industrial Machinery

(G-13510)
MARK RICHEY WDWKG & DESIGN INC
40 Parker St (01950-4092)
PHONE..................................978 499-3800
Mark Richey, *President*
Greg Porfido, *COO*
Chris Plante, *Foreman/Supr*
Brian Hawkes, *Project Engr*
Grace A Parisi, *Controller*
▲ **EMP:** 79
SQ FT: 70,000
SALES: 7.7MM **Privately Held**
WEB: www.markrichey.com
SIC: 2431 Mfg Millwork

(G-13511)
MERSEN USA EP CORP (DH)
374 Merrimac St (01950-1930)
PHONE..................................805 351-8400
Gerhard Doerr, *President*
Tom Woodruff, *Treasurer*
◆ **EMP:** 80
SQ FT: 175,000

SALES (est): 28.7MM
SALES (corp-wide): 1.9MM Privately Held
WEB: www.astrocosmos.com
SIC: 3443 3315 5051 Mfg Fabricated Plate Wrk Mfg Steel Wire/Rltd Prdt Metals Service Center
HQ: Mersen Usa St. Marys-Pa Corp.
215 Stackpole St
Saint Marys PA 15857
814 781-1234

(G-13512)
METZYS TAQUERIA LLC
17 55th St (01950-4453)
PHONE..................................978 992-1451
Anthony Leone, *Opers Staff*
Erik Metzdorf,
EMP: 3
SALES (est): 538.5K Privately Held
SIC: 2599 5812 Eating Place Mfg Furniture/Fixtures

(G-13513)
MICROMETAL TECHNOLOGIES INC (PA)
5 New Pasture Rd (01950-4040)
PHONE..................................978 462-3600
Thomas F Burke, *President*
EMP: 10
SQ FT: 7,000
SALES (est): 1.3MM Privately Held
SIC: 3679 Mfr Electronic Materials

(G-13514)
MIDDLESEX GENERAL INDUSTRIES
2 New Pasture Rd Ste 7 (01950-4054)
PHONE..................................781 935-8870
Daniel Morin, *President*
George W Horn, *President*
Adrian L Pyke, *President*
Dan Morian, *Manager*
EMP: 35
SQ FT: 14,000
SALES (est): 6.9MM Privately Held
WEB: www.midsx.com
SIC: 3825 Mfg Electrical Measuring Instruments

(G-13515)
MINUTEMAN PRESS
188 Route 1 Unit E (01950-4086)
PHONE..................................978 465-2242
Sumner Misenheimer, *Owner*
EMP: 5
SQ FT: 2,000
SALES (est): 439K Privately Held
SIC: 2752 2791 2789 Lithographic Commercial Printing Typesetting Services Bookbinding/Related Work

(G-13516)
MTI-MILLIREN TECHNOLOGIES INC
2 New Pasture Rd Ste 10 (01950-4054)
PHONE..................................978 465-6064
Bryan T Milliren, *President*
Marcel Filimon, *Technology*
EMP: 42
SQ FT: 25,000
SALES (est): 7.3MM Privately Held
SIC: 3679 3825 Mfg Electronic Components Mfg Electrical Measuring Instruments

(G-13517)
NAUGLER CO INC
Also Called: Naugler Engineering
5 Perry Way Ste 1 (01950-4009)
PHONE..................................978 463-9199
Robert C Naugler, *President*
EMP: 5 EST: 1955
SQ FT: 3,200
SALES: 198.9K Privately Held
WEB: www.naugler.com
SIC: 3568 3714 Mfg Flexible Couplings & Universal Joints

(G-13518)
NORTHEAST E D M INC
4 Mulliken Way Ste 3 (01950-4145)
PHONE..................................978 462-4663
Jennifer Molin, *President*
EMP: 8
SQ FT: 2,000
SALES (est): 1.2MM Privately Held
WEB: www.northeastedm.com
SIC: 3599 Machine Shop Jobbing & Repair

(G-13519)
OLIVE NEWBURYPORT OIL
50 Water St Ste 403 (01950-2866)
PHONE..................................978 462-7700
Karen Shernan, *Owner*
Katie Shernan, *Co-Owner*
EMP: 5 EST: 2012
SALES (est): 198.3K Privately Held
SIC: 2079 Mfg Edible Fats/Oils

(G-13520)
PACKAGING SPECIALTIES INC
3 Opportunity Way (01950-4044)
PHONE..................................978 462-1300
Gary Swerling, *President*
Philip G Ives, *President*
Ray Faneuf, *Treasurer*
Adam Fischer, *Sales Staff*
Albert Wencl, *Admin Sec*
▲ EMP: 58
SQ FT: 38,000
SALES (est): 14.3MM Privately Held
WEB: www.pack-spec.com
SIC: 2621 5199 2657 2652 Paper Mill Whol Nondurable Goods Mfg Folding Paperbrd Box Mfg Setup Paperboard Box

(G-13521)
POLYCARBON INDUSTRIES INC (DH)
Also Called: PCI Synthesis
9 Opportunity Way (01950-4044)
PHONE..................................978 462-5555
Edward S Price, *President*
Paul Sulloway, *COO*
Rajesh Shukla, *Vice Pres*
Lynn Laroche, *QC Mgr*
Raj Shukla, *Research*
▲ EMP: 100
SQ FT: 60,000
SALES (est): 18.5MM
SALES (corp-wide): 7.5MM Privately Held
WEB: www.pcisynthesis.com
SIC: 2834 Mfg Pharmaceutical Preparations
HQ: Seqens
21 Ecully Parc
Ecully 69130
426 991-800

(G-13522)
POLYONICS CORPORATION
24 Graf Rd (01950-4015)
PHONE..................................978 462-3600
Thomas F Burke, *President*
▲ EMP: 10 EST: 1982
SQ FT: 8,000
SALES: 1MM Privately Held
SIC: 3679 Mfr Electronic Materials
PA: Micrometal Technologies Inc
5 New Pasture Rd
Newburyport MA 01950

(G-13523)
PRODUCT RESOURCES LLC
4 Mulliken Way (01950-4145)
PHONE..................................978 524-8500
Jerry Mace, *COO*
Jennifer Sacchetti, *Purch Mgr*
Jennifer Popp, *Purchasing*
Michael Dragonas, *Engineer*
Nick Loy, *Engineer*
▲ EMP: 30
SQ FT: 30,000
SALES: 6.5MM Privately Held
WEB: www.pridocs.com
SIC: 3625 3822 3699 8711 Mfg Relay/Indstl Control Mfg Environmntl Controls Mfg Elec Mach/Equip/Supp Engineering Services

(G-13524)
PROTECH ASSOCIATES INC
4 Court St (01950-2503)
P.O. Box 846, West Newbury (01985-0846)
PHONE..................................978 462-1241
Janice Walsh, *President*
Chris Jerace, *Vice Pres*
EMP: 3
SALES (est): 180K Privately Held
SIC: 2842 Mfg Polish/Sanitation Goods

(G-13525)
QUALITY SOLUTIONS INC (PA)
Also Called: Firebrand Technologies
44 Merrimac St Ste 22 (01950-2580)
PHONE..................................978 465-7755
Francis P Toolan Jr, *President*
Barbara Blanchette, *QC Mgr*
Linda Adler, *Sales Staff*
Steve Rutberg, *Sales Staff*
Lindsey L Rudnickas, *Marketing Staff*
EMP: 27
SALES (est): 5.8MM Privately Held
SIC: 2741 7372 Misc Publishing Prepackaged Software Services

(G-13526)
RADAR TECHNOLOGY INC
2 New Pasture Rd (01950-4054)
PHONE..................................978 463-6064
Bryan Milliren, *President*
EMP: 20
SQ FT: 15,000
SALES (est): 681.8K Privately Held
WEB: www.radartechinc.com
SIC: 3812 3625 Mfg Search/Navigation Equipment Mfg Relays/Industrial Controls

(G-13527)
REDWHEEL/WEISER LLC (PA)
65 Parker St Ste 7 (01950-4600)
PHONE..................................978 465-0504
Jan Johnson, *Publisher*
Pat Bryce, *Buyer*
Rosemary Herbert, *Manager*
Michael Kerber,
Janice Johnson,
▲ EMP: 7 EST: 1926
SQ FT: 2,600
SALES (est): 2.4MM Privately Held
WEB: www.redwheelweiser.com
SIC: 2731 5192 Books-Publishing/Printing Whol Books/Newspapers

(G-13528)
REEL EASY INC
68 Curzon Mill Rd (01950-6254)
PHONE..................................978 476-7187
Edward S Fontes, *President*
Jeffrey Fontes, *Admin Sec*
EMP: 4
SALES: 300K Privately Held
SIC: 3949 5091 5941 Mfg Sporting/Athletic Goods Whol Sporting/Recreational Goods Ret Sporting Goods/Bicycles

(G-13529)
RENAISSANCE INTERNATIONAL
Also Called: Attar Software USA
204 High St (01950-3824)
PHONE..................................978 465-5111
Robert Keller, *President*
Clare Keller, *Treasurer*
David Poutry, *Admin Sec*
EMP: 4
SALES (est): 387.7K Privately Held
WEB: www.intellicrafters.com
SIC: 7372 7379 7371 Prepackaged Software Services Computer Related Services Custom Computer Programing

(G-13530)
RIVERWALK BREWING
40 Parker St Ste 4 (01950-4093)
PHONE..................................978 499-2337
Elizabeth Sanderson, *Principal*
EMP: 12 EST: 2016
SALES (est): 1.8MM Privately Held
SIC: 2082 Drinking Place

(G-13531)
ROCHESTER ELECTRONICS LLC (PA)
16 Malcolm Hoyt Dr (01950-4018)
PHONE..................................978 462-9332
Al Frugaletti, *President*
Dennis Martin, *General Mgr*
Thomas Gerrish, *Vice Pres*
Donald Amundson, *Engineer*
William Brown, *Engineer*
◆ EMP: 175 EST: 2005
SQ FT: 265,000
SALES (est): 45.9MM Privately Held
WEB: www.rocelec.com
SIC: 3674 5065 Mfg Semiconductors/Related Devices Whol Electronic Parts/Equipment

(G-13532)
ROCHESTER ELECTRONICS LLC
Also Called: Warehouse
18 Malcolm Hoyt Dr (01950-4018)
PHONE..................................978 462-1248
EMP: 3
SALES (est): 200.1K
SALES (corp-wide): 45.9MM Privately Held
SIC: 3674 Mfg Semiconductors/Related Devices
PA: Rochester Electronics, Llc
16 Malcolm Hoyt Dr
Newburyport MA 01950
978 462-9332

(G-13533)
SCREENCO PRINTING INC
4 Malcolm Hoyt Dr (01950-4018)
PHONE..................................978 465-1211
Stephen Elworthy, *President*
Michelle Doyle, *Controller*
EMP: 6 EST: 1998
SQ FT: 3,500
SALES: 400K Privately Held
WEB: www.screenco.net
SIC: 2752 2269 Lithographic Commercial Printing Finishing Plant

(G-13534)
SPEEDBOARD USA INC
4 Malcolm Hoyt Dr (01950-4018)
PHONE..................................978 462-2700
Robert Blair, *President*
EMP: 7 EST: 2011
SALES: 100K Privately Held
SIC: 2493 3644 Mfg Reconstituted Wood Products Mfg Nonconductive Wiring Devices/ Design Speedboards

(G-13535)
SPRAY MAINE INC
104 Parker St (01950-4063)
PHONE..................................207 384-2273
Christopher Donahue, *President*
John Perrone, *Clerk*
EMP: 15
SALES (est): 1.5MM Privately Held
SIC: 3479 7336 Painting Of Metal Products & Silk Screen Printing

(G-13536)
STANDARD MACHINES INC
25 Hale St (01950-3599)
PHONE..................................978 462-4999
Steven A Meredith, *Principal*
EMP: 5
SALES (est): 466.9K Privately Held
SIC: 7372 Prepackaged Software Services

(G-13537)
STREM CHEMICALS INCORPORATED
7 Mulliken Way (01950-4019)
PHONE..................................978 499-1600
Michael E Strem, *President*
Ephraim Honig, *COO*
Catherine Casagrande, *Purchasing*
Adam B Paton, *Admin Sec*
▲ EMP: 60 EST: 1964
SQ FT: 29,000
SALES (est): 20.1MM Privately Held
SIC: 2819 2869 Mfg Industrial Inorganic Chemicals Mfg Industrial Organic Chemicals

(G-13538)
TALON ENGINEERING
65 Parker St Ste 9 (01950-4600)
PHONE..................................978 465-5571
Rick Wessant, *President*
Linda Wessant, *Vice Pres*
EMP: 5
SALES (est): 671.7K Privately Held
SIC: 3599 Machine Shop

GEOGRAPHIC

(G-13539)
THE CRICKET SYSTEM INC
Also Called: Visible Good
5 Perkins Way Ste 2 (01950-4504)
PHONE....617 905-1420
John Rossi, *CEO*
Michael Sabourin, *COO*
Tina Newman, *CFO*
EMP: 5
SALES: 995K **Privately Held**
SIC: 3448 Mfg Prefabricated Metal Buildings

(G-13540)
THERMAL TECHNIC INC
13a Tremont St (01950-2809)
P.O. Box 597, Tesuque NM (87574-0597)
PHONE....978 270-5674
Douglas M McTernan, *Principal*
Humberto Bastidas, *Sales Staff*
EMP: 5 **EST:** 2015
SALES (est): 493.9K **Privately Held**
SIC: 3398 Metal Heat Treating

(G-13541)
THOMAS MACHINE WORKS INC
9 New Pasture Rd (01950-4040)
PHONE....978 462-7182
Joseph Casey, *President*
EMP: 9 **EST:** 1973
SQ FT: 12,000
SALES: 1MM **Privately Held**
WEB: www.thomasmachine.com
SIC: 3545 Mfg Machine Tool Accessories

(G-13542)
TRAILJOURNALS LLC
64 Carter St Apt 2 (01950-2234)
PHONE....978 358-7536
Mathew Olsen, *Principal*
EMP: 3
SALES (est): 195.3K **Privately Held**
SIC: 2721 Periodicals-Publishing/Printing

(G-13543)
TSHB INC
11 Malcolm Hoyt Dr (01950-4017)
PHONE....978 465-8950
Dana Thoms, *President*
EMP: 45
SQ FT: 48,000
SALES (est): 7.6MM **Privately Held**
WEB: www.jpress.com
SIC: 2752 Lithographic Commercial Printing

(G-13544)
UFP TECHNOLOGIES INC (PA)
100 Hale St (01950-3504)
PHONE....978 352-2200
R Jeffrey Bailly, *Ch of Bd*
Mitchell C Rock, *Senior VP*
William David Smith, *Senior VP*
Daniel J Shaw Jr, *Vice Pres*
Tom Goodwin, *Prdtn Mgr*
EMP: 36 **EST:** 1963
SQ FT: 183,000
SALES: 190.4MM **Publicly Held**
WEB: www.ufpt.com
SIC: 3086 Mfg Packaging And Shipping Materials & Padding Foamed Plastics

(G-13545)
ULTRACLAD CORPORATION
10 Perry Way (01950-4001)
PHONE....978 358-7945
Joseph C Runkle, *President*
EMP: 7
SQ FT: 11,000
SALES: 3MM **Privately Held**
SIC: 3544 8731 Mfg Dies/Tools/Jigs/Fixtures Commercial Physical Research

(G-13546)
UNION SPECIALTIES INC
3 Malcolm Hoyt Dr (01950-4084)
PHONE....978 465-1717
William J Greene, *President*
Kevin Rodden, *Vice Pres*
Joe Marshall, *Purchasing*
Marshall Thomas, *Engineer*
John M Sullivan, *CFO*
◆ **EMP:** 33
SQ FT: 32,000
SALES (est): 10.8MM **Privately Held**
WEB: www.unionspecialties.com
SIC: 2843 2891 2851 2842 Mfg Surface Active Agent Mfg Adhesives/Sealants Mfg Paints/Allied Prdts Mfg Polish/Sanitation Gd

(G-13547)
UNTHA SHREDDING TECH AMER INC
Also Called: Untha Shredding Tech Amer
10 Perry Way (01950-4001)
PHONE....978 465-0083
EMP: 4
SALES (corp-wide): 355.8K **Privately Held**
SIC: 3589 Mfg Service Industry Machinery
HQ: Untha Shredding Technology America Inc.
1 Lafayette Rd Unit 4
Hampton NH 03842
603 601-2304

(G-13548)
VARIAN SEMICDTR EQP ASSOC INC
4 Stanley Tucker Dr (01950-4039)
PHONE....978 463-1500
Dave Holbrook, *Manager*
EMP: 110
SALES (corp-wide): 14.6B **Publicly Held**
SIC: 3559 8249 Mfg Misc Industry Machinery Vocational School
HQ: Varian Semiconductor Equipment Associates, Inc.
35 Dory Rd
Gloucester MA 01930
978 282-2000

(G-13549)
WILMINGTON RESEARCH & DEV CORP
Also Called: Wrd Innovative Controls
50 Parker St Ste 3 (01950-4068)
PHONE....978 499-0100
Stephen B Boyd, *President*
Bruce Vogel, *VP Sales*
EMP: 6
SQ FT: 5,000
SALES (est): 1.1MM **Privately Held**
WEB: www.wrdcorp.com
SIC: 3625 7389 3823 Mfg Relays/Industrial Controls Business Services Mfg Process Control Instruments

Newton
Middlesex County

(G-13550)
3WYC INC
117 Wallace St (02461-1924)
PHONE....617 584-7767
MEI Xue, *CEO*
EMP: 3 **EST:** 2014
SALES (est): 656.1K **Privately Held**
SIC: 7372 7389 Educational Consultant

(G-13551)
A S P ENTERPRISES INC
Also Called: Signs By Tomorrow
227 California St (02458-1063)
PHONE....617 244-2762
Nicholas Papakyrikos, *President*
EMP: 3
SQ FT: 3,000
SALES (est): 409.1K **Privately Held**
SIC: 3993 Signsadv Specs

(G-13552)
AA GLOBAL PRINTING INC
22 Parker Ave (02459-2662)
PHONE....617 527-7629
Aron Blume, *President*
Adam Gould, *Director*
EMP: 4
SALES (est): 101.5K **Privately Held**
SIC: 2752 Lithographic Commercial Printing

(G-13553)
ACER THERAPEUTICS INC (PA)
300 Washington St Ste 351 (02458-1655)
PHONE....844 902-6100
Stephen J Aselage, *Ch of Bd*
Chris Schelling, *President*
Harry S Palmin, *COO*
William Andrews, *Chief Mktg Ofcr*
Donald R Joseph,
EMP: 3
SQ FT: 2,760
SALES (est): 3.6MM **Publicly Held**
WEB: www.pharmafrontierscorp.com
SIC: 2834 8731 Pharmaceutical Preparations Biotechnical Research

(G-13554)
ACUITYBIO CORPORATION
200 Upland Rd (02460-2423)
PHONE....617 515-9671
Mark W Grinstaff, *Director*
Alain J Hanover, *Director*
EMP: 4
SALES (est): 381.6K **Privately Held**
SIC: 3841 Mfg Surgical/Medical Instruments

(G-13555)
ADOBE SYSTEMS INCORPORATED
275 Washington St Ste 300 (02458-1630)
PHONE....617 467-6760
EMP: 67
SALES (corp-wide): 9B **Publicly Held**
SIC: 7372 Prepackaged Software Services
PA: Adobe Inc.
345 Park Ave
San Jose CA 95110
408 536-6000

(G-13556)
ADVANCE SYSTEMS INC
79a Chapel St (02458-1010)
PHONE....888 238-8704
Gareth Corcoran, *CEO*
Robert Parks, *Sales Staff*
EMP: 10
SALES (est): 898.8K **Privately Held**
SIC: 7372 Prepackaged Software Services

(G-13557)
ALCRESTA THERAPEUTICS INC
1 Newton Executive Park # 100 (02462-1493)
PHONE....617 431-3600
Daniel Orlando, *CEO*
Alexey Margolin, *Ch of Bd*
Robert Gallotto, *President*
Steve Dubin, *Principal*
David Brown, *Vice Pres*
EMP: 28
SALES (est): 6.2MM **Privately Held**
SIC: 2869 Mfg Industrial Organic Chemicals

(G-13558)
ALLENA PHARMACEUTICALS INC (PA)
1 Newton Executive Park # 202 (02462-1493)
PHONE....617 467-4577
Alexey Margolin, *Ch of Bd*
Louis Brenner, *President*
Edward Wholihan, *CFO*
Axel Bolte, *Bd of Directors*
EMP: 32
SQ FT: 7,795
SALES (est): 3.4MM **Publicly Held**
SIC: 2834 2836 Pharmaceutical Preparations And Mfg Biological Products

(G-13559)
ALLY AUTOMOTIVE INC
16 Dalby St Ste 2 (02458-1031)
PHONE....734 604-2257
EMP: 5
SALES: 30K **Privately Held**
SIC: 3711 Mfg Motor Vehicle/Car Bodies

(G-13560)
ALM WORKS INC (PA)
181 Wells Ave Ste 204 (02459-3344)
PHONE....617 600-4369
Ekaterina Malykh, *Principal*
Mikhail Babushkin, *Principal*
Igor Sereda, *Principal*
EMP: 3
SQ FT: 3,094
SALES (est): 205.4K **Privately Held**
SIC: 7372 Prepackaged Software

(G-13561)
AMBROSE D CEDRONE LODGE 1069
196 Adams St (02458-1203)
PHONE....617 460-4664
Paul Camilli, *President*
EMP: 3 **EST:** 2017
SALES: 22.4K **Privately Held**
SIC: 3721 Mfg Aircraft

(G-13562)
ARGOSY PUBLISHING INC (PA)
109 Oak St Ste 102 (02464-1493)
PHONE....617 527-9999
Andrew Bowditch, *CEO*
Maite Suarez-Rivas, *Exec VP*
Kate O'Riordan, *Project Mgr*
Matthew Bowditch, *CFO*
Robb Kneebone, *Sales Mgr*
EMP: 20
SQ FT: 18,000
SALES (est): 6.3MM **Privately Held**
WEB: www.argosypublishing.com
SIC: 2791 7336 2731 2396 Typesetting Services Coml Art/Graphic Design Book-Publishing/Printing Mfg Auto/Apparel Trim

(G-13563)
ARTIGIANO STAINED GLASS
1238 Chestnut St (02464-1482)
PHONE....617 244-0141
Carmello Iriti, *Owner*
EMP: 4
SALES (est): 240.2K **Privately Held**
WEB: www.artigianostainedglass.com
SIC: 3231 Mfg Products-Purchased Glass

(G-13564)
ATHIGO
61 Chapel St (02458-1010)
PHONE....617 410-8834
EMP: 4
SALES: 100K **Privately Held**
SIC: 7372 Prepackaged Software Services

(G-13565)
BARCLAY WATER MANAGEMENT INC
55 Chapel St Ste 400 (02458-1075)
PHONE....617 926-3400
William J Brett, *President*
Joseph J Berns, *Vice Pres*
Donald Carney Jr, *Vice Pres*
Michael F Davidson, *Vice Pres*
Roland A Dion, *Vice Pres*
EMP: 80
SQ FT: 26,000
SALES (est): 10.1MM
SALES (corp-wide): 30.4MM **Privately Held**
WEB: www.barclaywm.com
SIC: 2899 Mfg Chemical Preparations
PA: Barclay Water Management, Inc.
55 Chapel St Ste 400
Newton MA
617 926-3400

(G-13566)
BARRETT TECHNOLOGY LLC
73 Chapel St Ste D (02458-1088)
PHONE....617 252-9000
William Townsend, *Mng Member*
EMP: 25 **EST:** 2015
SALES (est): 190.3K **Privately Held**
SIC: 3569 8731 3829 General Industrial Machinery, Nec, Nsk

(G-13567)
BETTER BOTTLING SOLUTIONS LLC
25 Harrington St (02460-1525)
PHONE....219 308-5616
EMP: 3
SALES (est): 167.8K **Privately Held**
SIC: 2086 Mfg Bottled/Canned Soft Drinks

(G-13568)
BIOMED SOFTWARE INC
72 Kensington St (02460-1312)
PHONE....617 513-1298
John McCall, *President*
EMP: 4 **EST:** 1998
SALES: 290K **Privately Held**
WEB: www.biomedsoftware.com
SIC: 7372 Prepackaged Software Services

▲ = Import ▼=Export
◆ =Import/Export

(G-13569)
BIOSENSICS LLC
57 Chapel St Ste 200 (02458-1080)
PHONE..................................888 589-6213
Joseph Gwin, *Vice Pres*
Nima Shokrollahi, *Sr Software Eng*
Neda Movaghar,
EMP: 5
SALES (est): 720.7K **Privately Held**
SIC: 3845 Research And Develops Wearable Sensors

(G-13570)
BIOTECH DIAGNOSTICS
109 Lovett Rd (02459-3107)
PHONE..................................617 332-8787
Vithal Jathar, *President*
EMP: 3
SALES (est): 189K **Privately Held**
SIC: 3829 Mfg Measuring/Controlling Devices

(G-13571)
BONAMAR CORP
1105 Washington St (02465-2119)
PHONE..................................617 965-3400
Marc Nussbaum, *Manager*
EMP: 15
SALES (corp-wide): 21.3MM **Privately Held**
SIC: 2092 Mfg Fresh/Frozen Packaged Fish
PA: Bonamar, Corp.
200 E Broward Blvd # 1010
Fort Lauderdale FL 33301
305 718-9850

(G-13572)
BOSTON TRANSTEC LLC
481 Dudley Rd (02459-2810)
PHONE..................................617 930-6088
Tengiz Tkebuchava, *Principal*
Robert Whiting, *Principal*
EMP: 4 **EST:** 2009
SALES (est): 334.3K **Privately Held**
SIC: 3841 Mfg Surgical/Medical Instruments

(G-13573)
BRIDGEME LLC
273 Otis St (02465-2531)
PHONE..................................617 310-4801
Benjamin Bloomstone, *Managing Prtnr*
EMP: 6
SQ FT: 100
SALES (est): 242K **Privately Held**
SIC: 7372 Prepackaged Software Services

(G-13574)
CASPI CARDS AND ART
137 Lowell Ave (02460-1521)
P.O. Box 600220 (02460-0002)
PHONE..................................617 964-8888
Mickie Caspi, *Owner*
Micha K Caspi, *Owner*
▲ **EMP:** 5
SALES (est): 500K **Privately Held**
WEB: www.caspi.com
SIC: 2771 Mfg Greeting Cards

(G-13575)
CEACO INC
Also Called: Gamewright
70 Bridge St Ste 200 (02458-1141)
PHONE..................................617 926-8080
Carol J Glazer, *President*
Trudi Lazarus, *Senior VP*
Allison Yada, *Vice Pres*
Cindy Basque, *CFO*
Julie Mandello, *Accounting Mgr*
▲ **EMP:** 8
SQ FT: 11,000
SALES (est): 1.8MM **Privately Held**
WEB: www.ceaco.com
SIC: 3944 Mfg Games/Toys

(G-13576)
CELEROS INC
Also Called: Celeros Separations
1188 Centre St Ste 1 (02459-1556)
PHONE..................................248 478-2800
Scott Coleridge, *CEO*
Mark Norige, *President*
Robert Cutler, *COO*
Kathleen Okolita, *Admin Sec*
EMP: 25
SQ FT: 17,000
SALES (est): 3.5MM **Privately Held**
SIC: 3559 Mfg Misc Industry Machinery

(G-13577)
CHEETAH MEDICAL INC (PA)
1320 Centre St Ste 400 (02459-2400)
PHONE..................................617 964-0613
Chris Hutchison, *President*
EMP: 29 **EST:** 2010
SALES (est): 9.2MM **Privately Held**
SIC: 3841 Mfg Surgical/Medical Instruments

(G-13578)
CHELSEA INDUSTRIES INC (HQ)
46a Glen Ave (02459-2066)
PHONE..................................617 232-6060
Ronald G Casty, *Ch of Bd*
Emil S Bernstein, *Treasurer*
▲ **EMP:** 6 **EST:** 1926
SQ FT: 185,000
SALES (est): 31.6MM
SALES (corp-wide): 49.8MM **Privately Held**
SIC: 3535 Mfg Conveyors/Equipment

(G-13579)
CHESHIRE SOFTWARE INC
1170 Walnut St (02461-1224)
P.O. Box 67487, Chestnut Hill (02467-0006)
PHONE..................................617 527-4000
Joshua Wright, *President*
Jim Farmelant, *Software Engr*
EMP: 10
SALES (est): 890K **Privately Held**
WEB: www.cheshire.com
SIC: 7372 Prepackaged And Customized Software Services

(G-13580)
CMIO MAGAZINE PUBLICATIONS
152 Washington St (02458-2250)
PHONE..................................617 851-6671
Alex Johnas, *Owner*
EMP: 5
SALES (est): 220K **Privately Held**
SIC: 2721 Periodicals-Publishing/Printing

(G-13581)
COLLABORATIVE MED CONCEPT LLC
Also Called: CMC
43 Ruane Rd (02465-2627)
PHONE..................................603 494-6056
Dennis Werger,
EMP: 3 **Privately Held**
SIC: 3841 Mfg Surgical/Medical Instruments

(G-13582)
COUNTRY STANDARD TIME
54 Ballard St (02459-1251)
PHONE..................................617 969-0331
Jeffrey Remz, *Owner*
EMP: 30
SALES (est): 1.1MM **Privately Held**
WEB: www.countrystandardtime.com
SIC: 2721 Periodicals-Publishing/Printing

(G-13583)
COURAGE THERAPEUTICS INC
64 Homer St (02459-1517)
PHONE..................................617 216-9921
Dan Housman, *CEO*
Fred Mermelstein, *Principal*
EMP: 8
SALES (est): 340K **Privately Held**
SIC: 2834 Mfg Pharmaceutical Preparations

(G-13584)
CRAZY FOAM INTERNATIONAL LLC
181 Wells Ave Ste 105 (02459-3344)
PHONE..................................781 985-5048
Joshua Fink, *CEO*
Atef Halaka, *COO*
Frank Klisanich, *Vice Pres*
EMP: 7
SQ FT: 3,500
SALES (est): 1.1MM **Privately Held**
SIC: 2841 Mfg Soap/Other Detergents

(G-13585)
CYBERARK SOFTWARE INC (HQ)
60 Wells Ave Ste 103 (02459-3257)
PHONE..................................617 965-1544
Udi Mokady, *Ch of Bd*
Ehud Mokady, *President*
Alon Cohen, *Chairman*
Chris Hughes, *COO*
Clarence Hinton, *Senior VP*
EMP: 21
SQ FT: 1,000
SALES (est): 36.5MM
SALES (corp-wide): 75.6MM **Privately Held**
WEB: www.cyber-ark.com
SIC: 7372 Prepackaged Software Services
PA: Cyberark Software Ltd.
9 Hapsagot
Petah Tikva
391 800-00

(G-13586)
DUKE RIVER ENGINEERING CO
30 Ossipee Rd (02464-1444)
PHONE..................................617 965-7255
Jeffrey Thumm, *President*
EMP: 7
SQ FT: 3,000
SALES (est): 562.8K **Privately Held**
SIC: 3826 Developer Of Medical Devises

(G-13587)
EMC CORPORATION
95 Wells Ave Ste 215 (02459-3241)
PHONE..................................617 618-3400
Marc Burckin, *President*
Kumar Thirumal, *Principal*
John Conway, *Vice Pres*
Sandra Morais, *Business Anlyst*
Janet Piazza, *Program Mgr*
EMP: 250
SALES (corp-wide): 90.6B **Publicly Held**
WEB: www.emc.com
SIC: 3572 7372 Mfg Computer Storage Devices Prepackaged Software Services
HQ: Emc Corporation
176 South St
Hopkinton MA 01748
508 435-1000

(G-13588)
EMC TEST DESIGN LLC
521 California St (02460-1210)
P.O. Box 600532 (02460-0005)
PHONE..................................508 292-1833
Roman Litovsky,
EMP: 11
SALES (est): 1MM **Privately Held**
WEB: www.emctd.com
SIC: 3825 Mfg Electrical Measuring Instruments

(G-13589)
ENLIVITY CORPORATION
345 Upland Ave (02461-2028)
PHONE..................................617 964-5237
Gillian Isabelle, *Principal*
EMP: 6
SALES (est): 542.8K **Privately Held**
SIC: 2834 Mfg Pharmaceutical Preparations

(G-13590)
ER ENTERPRISES LLC
51 Winchester St Ste 203 (02461-1704)
PHONE..................................617 296-9140
François Fermin,
EMP: 4
SALES (est): 470.8K **Privately Held**
SIC: 3695 Mfg Magnetic/Optical Recording Media

(G-13591)
EXTEND BIOSCIENCES INC
90 Bridge St Ste 100 (02458-1119)
P.O. Box 400927, Cambridge (02140-0010)
PHONE..................................732 599-8580
Tarik Soliman, *CEO*
Laura Hales, *COO*
EMP: 4
SALES (est): 396K **Privately Held**
SIC: 2836 Biological Products Except Diagnostic

(G-13592)
FAMILIES AND WEALTH LLC
1075 Washington St (02465-2185)
PHONE..................................617 558-5800
Thomas F Gorman, *Principal*
EMP: 3
SALES (est): 128.1K **Privately Held**
SIC: 2711 Newspapers-Publishing/Printing

(G-13593)
FOCAL POINT OPTICIANS INC (PA)
882 Walnut St (02459-1799)
PHONE..................................617 965-2770
Joanne Azzoto-Zafron, *President*
EMP: 5
SQ FT: 1,000
SALES (est): 517K **Privately Held**
SIC: 3851 5999 Mfg Ophthalmic Goods Ret Misc Merchandise

(G-13594)
GCKM MACHINES
14 Hawthorn St (02458-1215)
PHONE..................................617 584-6266
Michael Borghesani, *Vice Pres*
EMP: 4
SALES (est): 241.1K **Privately Held**
SIC: 3531 Mfg Construction Machinery

(G-13595)
GENERAL ELECTRIC COMPANY
1 Gateway Ctr Ste 251 (02458-2802)
PHONE..................................617 608-6008
Kuo Nah, *Branch Mgr*
EMP: 220
SALES (corp-wide): 121.6B **Publicly Held**
SIC: 3643 Mfg Conductive Wiring Devices
PA: General Electric Company
5 Necco St
Boston MA 02210
617 443-3000

(G-13596)
GINGER SOFTWARE INC
128 Chestnut St (02465-2539)
PHONE..................................617 755-0160
Yael K Zangvil, *President*
Ziv Isaiah, *Principal*
David Noy, *Principal*
Alex Ben-ARI, *Vice Pres*
Miki Feldman-Simon, *Vice Pres*
EMP: 20
SALES (est): 1.2MM **Privately Held**
SIC: 7372 Prepackaged Software Services

(G-13597)
GRAPHIC ARTS FINISHERS INC
185 Countryside Rd (02459-2918)
PHONE..................................617 241-9292
Morris Greenbaum, *CEO*
Alan Greenbaum, *President*
David Greenbaum, *Treasurer*
Mark Greenbaum, *Treasurer*
Michael Greenbaum, *Director*
▲ **EMP:** 30 **EST:** 1957
SQ FT: 60,000
SALES: 6MM **Privately Held**
SIC: 2631 Paperboard Mill

(G-13598)
H C STARCK INC (HQ)
45 Industrial Pl (02461-1951)
PHONE..................................617 630-5800
Andreas Mader, *CEO*
Jens Kn LL, *COO*
Richard E Howard, *Treasurer*
Paul A Leblanc, *Treasurer*
Michael Rei, *CTO*
◆ **EMP:** 150
SQ FT: 300,000
SALES (est): 120.6MM
SALES (corp-wide): 355.8K **Privately Held**
WEB: www.hcstarck.com
SIC: 3339 3356 3313 Primary Nonferrous Metal Producer Nonferrous Rolling/Drawing Mfg Electrometallurgical Prdts-Ex Steel

GEOGRAPHIC

(G-13599)
HEARTBREAK HILL RUNNING CO INC
638 Commonwealth Ave (02459-1644)
PHONE..................................617 467-4487
Dan Fitzgerald, *Branch Mgr*
EMP: 5
SALES (est): 336.5K
SALES (corp-wide): 614.6K **Privately Held**
SIC: 3949 Ret Sporting Goods/Bicycles
PA: Heartbreak Hill Running Company, Inc.
652 Tremont St
Boston MA 02118
617 391-0897

(G-13600)
HELMICK & SCHECHTER INC
447 Lowell Ave Apt 3 (02460-2116)
PHONE..................................617 332-2433
Ralph Helmick, *President*
Stuart Schechter, *Treasurer*
EMP: 5
SALES: 806.9K **Privately Held**
WEB: www.handsart.net
SIC: 3299 8412 Mfg Nonmetallic Mineral Products Museum/Art Gallery

(G-13601)
HID GLOBAL CORPORATION
1320 Centre St Ste 201a (02459-2456)
PHONE..................................617 581-6200
EMP: 108
SALES (corp-wide): 8.8B **Privately Held**
SIC: 3825 Mfg Electrical Measuring Instruments
HQ: Hid Global Corporation
611 Center Ridge Dr
Austin TX 78753
800 237-7769

(G-13602)
HOMEPORTFOLIO INC
Also Called: Building Blocks
288 Walnut St Ste 500 (02460-1994)
PHONE..................................617 559-1197
Dale Williams, *President*
Steven Schneider, *CFO*
EMP: 94
SQ FT: 20,000
SALES (est): 6.3MM **Privately Held**
WEB: www.homeportfolio.com
SIC: 7372 7374 7375 Prepackaged Software Services Data Processing/Preparation Information Retrieval Services

(G-13603)
I MAKE NEWS
1254 Chestnut St (02464-1451)
PHONE..................................617 864-4400
Kathleen Goodwin, *Principal*
EMP: 4
SALES (est): 195.5K **Privately Held**
SIC: 2711 Newspapers-Publishing/Printing

(G-13604)
INDUSTRIAL VIDEO & CTRL CO LLC
330 Nevada St (02460-1458)
PHONE..................................617 467-3059
Norman Fast, *President*
Sarah Nguyen, *Partner*
Gregory Santos, *Business Mgr*
Bill Richards, *Vice Pres*
Ric Bonnell, *Engineer*
◆ **EMP:** 21
SQ FT: 4,000
SALES: 6MM **Privately Held**
WEB: www.ivcco.com
SIC: 3651 Mfg Home Audio/Video Equipment

(G-13605)
INNOPAD INC
50 Winchester Rd (02458-1985)
PHONE..................................978 253-4204
John Aodeborgh, *President*
▲ **EMP:** 6
SALES (est): 878.1K **Privately Held**
SIC: 3559 Mfg Misc Industry Machinery

(G-13606)
KARYOPHARM THERAPEUTICS INC (PA)
85 Wells Ave Fl 2 (02459-3298)
PHONE..................................617 658-0600
Michael G Kauffman, *CEO*
Derek Magdziak, *Chairman*
Christopher B Primiano, *Exec VP*
Christopher Primiano, *Exec VP*
Anand Varadan, *Exec VP*
EMP: 154
SQ FT: 62,143
SALES: 30.3MM **Publicly Held**
SIC: 2834 Pharmaceutical Preparations

(G-13607)
KAYAKU ADVANCED MATERIALS INC
20 Ossipee Rd (02464-1444)
PHONE..................................617 965-5511
Paul Boisvert, *Opers Mgr*
Marcel McQuiggan, *Mfg Mgr*
Bridgid Wanjala, *Research*
EMP: 14 **Privately Held**
SIC: 2899 Mfg Chemical Preparations
PA: Kayaku Advanced Materials, Inc.
200 Flanders Rd
Westborough MA 01581

(G-13608)
KEENA CORPORATION
21 Barnstable Rd (02465-2925)
PHONE..................................617 928-3493
Harvey Epstein, *President*
EMP: 6
SALES (est): 555.3K
SALES (corp-wide): 957.8K **Privately Held**
SIC: 2672 Mfg Coated/Laminated Paper
PA: Keena Corporation
25 Lenglen Rd Ste 4
Newton MA
617 244-9800

(G-13609)
LIBERTY ENGINEERING INC
26 Farwell St (02460-1071)
PHONE..................................617 965-6644
Dennis Chevalier, *President*
Renee Percy, *Senior Buyer*
EMP: 30
SQ FT: 16,000
SALES (est): 5.8MM **Privately Held**
SIC: 3679 Mfg Electronic Components

(G-13610)
LIFE IMAGE INC
Also Called: Lifeimage
1 Gteway Ctr St Ste 200 (02458)
PHONE..................................617 244-8411
Matthew A Michela, *CEO*
Hamid Tabatabaie, *Exec VP*
Frank D Brilliant, *Senior VP*
Janak Joshi, *Senior VP*
Nate Bechtel, *Vice Pres*
EMP: 60
SALES (est): 12.8MM **Privately Held**
SIC: 7372 Prepackaged Software Services

(G-13611)
LUMICELL INC
275 Washington St Ste 200 (02458-1630)
PHONE..................................617 404-1001
Kelly Londy, *CEO*
Jorge Ferrer, *Vice Pres*
Kevin Hershberger, *CFO*
Bill Johnson, *CFO*
Felix Geissler, *Chief Mktg Ofcr*
EMP: 3
SALES (est): 487.7K **Privately Held**
SIC: 3845 Mfg Electromedical Equipment

(G-13612)
MANAGEMENT ROUNDTABLE INC
321 Walnut St Ste 222 (02460-1927)
PHONE..................................781 891-8080
Alex Cooper, *President*
Stewart Maws, *Chairman*
Jacqueline Cooper, *Exec VP*
EMP: 3 **EST:** 1980
SALES: 200K **Privately Held**
SIC: 2721 8249 Periodicals-Publishing/Printing Vocational School

(G-13613)
MEGA-POWER INC
Also Called: Associated Power Products
44 Oak St Ste 1 (02464-1462)
PHONE..................................800 982-4339
Steven Dworkin, *President*
EMP: 6
SQ FT: 6,000
SALES: 15.2MM **Privately Held**
SIC: 3691 Mfg Storage Batteries

(G-13614)
METTLER-TOLEDO INTL INC
150 Wells Ave (02459-3302)
PHONE..................................800 472-4646
EMP: 3
SALES (corp-wide): 2.9B **Publicly Held**
SIC: 3596 3821 3826 3823 Mfg Scale/Balance-Nonlab Mfg Lab Apparatus/Furn Mfg Analytical Instr Mfg Process Cntrl Instr
PA: Mettler-Toledo International Inc.
1900 Polaris Pkwy Fl 6
Columbus OH 43240
614 438-4511

(G-13615)
MINUTEMAN PRESS INTL INC
1383 Washington St (02465-2003)
PHONE..................................617 244-7001
Michael Hurley, *Owner*
EMP: 9
SALES (corp-wide): 23.4MM **Privately Held**
SIC: 2752 Comm Prtg Litho
PA: Minuteman Press International, Inc.
61 Executive Blvd
Farmingdale NY 11735
631 249-1370

(G-13616)
NAHAS SELIM
Also Called: SMIth&press
56 Ripley St (02459-2207)
PHONE..................................617 595-8808
Selim Nahas, *Owner*
Stacy Nahas, *Principal*
EMP: 3
SALES (est): 50.3K **Privately Held**
SIC: 2731 Books-Publishing/Printing

(G-13617)
NCR CORPORATION
180 Wells Ave (02459-3328)
PHONE..................................617 558-2000
Santu Rohhegi, *Branch Mgr*
Matthew Robinson, *Manager*
EMP: 150
SALES (corp-wide): 6.4B **Publicly Held**
WEB: www.ncr.com
SIC: 3578 7699 8741 Mfg Calculating Equipment Repair Services Management Services
PA: Ncr Corporation
864 Spring St Nw
Atlanta GA 30308
937 445-5000

(G-13618)
NEWTON-WELLESLEY HEALTH CARE
2014 Washington St (02462-1607)
P.O. Box 9127, Charlestown (02129-9127)
PHONE..................................617 726-2142
Fax: 617 244-9347
EMP: 13
SALES (corp-wide): 173.5MM **Privately Held**
SIC: 3829 Mfg Measuring/Controlling Devices
PA: Newton-Wellesley Health Care System, Inc.
2014 Washington St
Newton MA 02462
617 243-6000

(G-13619)
NONANTUM BOXING CLUB LLC
75 Adams St (02458-1126)
PHONE..................................617 340-3700
Nicole Starck, *Principal*
EMP: 4 **EST:** 2008
SALES (est): 324.5K **Privately Held**
SIC: 3949 Mfg Sporting/Athletic Goods

(G-13620)
NORCROSS CORPORATION
255 Newtonville Ave Ste 1 (02458-1898)
PHONE..................................617 969-7020
Robert Norcross Jr, *President*
EMP: 6
SQ FT: 12,000
SALES (est): 937.5K **Privately Held**
WEB: www.viscosity.com
SIC: 3823 Mfg Process Control Instruments

(G-13621)
NOVELSAT INC
25 Tanglewood Rd (02459-2849)
PHONE..................................617 658-1419
Tuvia Feldman, *Chairman*
Benny Glazer, *Vice Pres*
Kobi Shitrit, *Manager*
Josef Berger, *Director*
EMP: 14
SALES (est): 1.6MM **Privately Held**
SIC: 3663 Mfg Radio/Tv Communication Equipment

(G-13622)
ORAM CORPORATE ADVISORS
189 Wells Ave Ste 100 (02459-3355)
PHONE..................................617 701-7430
Ryan Barrett, *CEO*
EMP: 5
SALES (est): 494.1K **Privately Held**
SIC: 3571 Mfg Electronic Computers

(G-13623)
PAYTRONIX SYSTEMS INC (PA)
80 Bridge St Ste 400 (02458-1119)
PHONE..................................617 649-3300
Andrew Robbins, *President*
Eddie Ayala, *Sales Staff*
Terri Burton, *Sales Staff*
Kimberly Otocki, *Marketing Staff*
Ted Plaisted, *Manager*
EMP: 70
SALES (est): 11.7MM **Privately Held**
WEB: www.paytronix.com
SIC: 7372 Prepackaged Software Services

(G-13624)
PB & J DISCOVERIES LLC
113 Belmont St (02460)
PHONE..................................617 903-7253
Jeremi Rabson, *Partner*
EMP: 3 **EST:** 2010
SALES (est): 152.4K **Privately Held**
SIC: 2399 Mfg Fabricated Textile Products

(G-13625)
PHARMA MODELS LLC
700 Centre St (02458-2329)
PHONE..................................617 630-1729
Brynmor Watkins, *Principal*
EMP: 3
SALES (est): 264.6K **Privately Held**
SIC: 2834 Mfg Pharmaceutical Preparations

(G-13626)
PHOTONVIEW TECHNOLOGIES
500 Lowell Ave (02460-2353)
PHONE..................................781 366-4836
Mengxi Zhang, *President*
Thomas Wang, *Co-Owner*
EMP: 5
SALES (est): 198.4K **Privately Held**
SIC: 3845 Mfg Electromedical Equipment

(G-13627)
POWER OBJECT INC
123 Ridge Ave (02459-2506)
PHONE..................................617 630-5701
Martin Shiu, *President*
Martis Shiu, *President*
EMP: 27 **EST:** 1998
SALES (est): 2.4MM **Privately Held**
SIC: 7372 Prepackaged Software Services

(G-13628)
QUANTTUS INC
2 Newton Executive Park # 104 (02462-1434)
PHONE..................................617 401-2648
Shahid Azim, *CEO*
EMP: 9
SALES (est): 1.7MM **Privately Held**
SIC: 3845 Mfg Electromedical Equipment

(G-13629)
RELX INC
Also Called: Lexisnexis
313 Washington St Ste 401 (02458-1659)
PHONE....617 558-4925
Yvette Politis, *Counsel*
Michael F Walsh, *Vice Pres*
EMP: 53
SALES (corp-wide): 9.8B **Privately Held**
SIC: 2721 Periodicals
HQ: Relx Inc.
230 Park Ave Ste 700
New York NY 10169
212 309-8100

(G-13630)
RICHARDS ARKLAY S CO INC
72 Winchester St (02461-1720)
PHONE....617 527-4385
Lincoln K Richards, *President*
Gerhard Richards, *Exec VP*
▲ **EMP:** 20 **EST:** 1938
SQ FT: 7,000
SALES (est): 3.5MM **Privately Held**
WEB: www.asrichards.com
SIC: 3823 Mfg Process Control Instruments

(G-13631)
RIGHT SUBMISSION LLC
59 High St (02464-1238)
PHONE....617 407-9076
Marek Nowosielski-Slepowron, *CEO*
Juan Serna, *President*
Juan Carlos Serna, *President*
EMP: 4
SALES (est): 144K **Privately Held**
SIC: 7372 Prepackaged Software Services

(G-13632)
SAW MILL BROOK LLC
16 Sycamore Rd (02459-3102)
PHONE....617 332-5793
Fani Sotiriadis, *Principal*
EMP: 3
SALES (est): 215.6K **Privately Held**
SIC: 2421 Sawmill/Planing Mill

(G-13633)
SCOTT GRUSBY LLC
26 Jerome Ave (02465-1105)
PHONE....617 538-9112
Scott Grusby, *Principal*
EMP: 3 **EST:** 2009
SALES (est): 160K **Privately Held**
SIC: 2499 Mfg Wood Products

(G-13634)
SECOND WIND SYSTEMS INC
15 Riverdale Ave (02458-1057)
PHONE....617 581-6090
Enda Bloomer, *Principal*
Allison Scuderi, *Information Mgr*
EMP: 11
SALES (est): 1.4MM **Privately Held**
SIC: 3829 Mfg Measuring/Controlling Devices

(G-13635)
SECURELYTIX INC
2 Newton Executive Park # 104
(02462-1434)
PHONE....617 283-5227
Lou Madge, *CEO*
Carrie Gates, *Co-Owner*
EMP: 3
SQ FT: 800
SALES (est): 71.1K **Privately Held**
SIC: 7372 7373 Prepackaged Software Services Computer Systems Design

(G-13636)
SEMANTIC OBJECTS LLC
25 Cabot St (02458-2501)
PHONE....617 272-0955
Amit Phansalkar, *CEO*
Shashi Kant, *President*
EMP: 11
SALES (est): 408K **Privately Held**
SIC: 7372 7389 Prepackaged Software Services

(G-13637)
SHUFRO SECURITY COMPANY INC
Also Called: Shufro Engineering Labs
1231 Washington St (02460)
P.O. Box 600393 (02460-0004)
PHONE....617 244-3355
Richard Shufro, *President*
EMP: 8
SALES (est): 1.3MM **Privately Held**
WEB: www.shufro.com
SIC: 3669 1731 Mfg Communications Equipment Electrical Contractor

(G-13638)
SILICON MICRO DISPLAY INC
1126 Beacon St Ste 2 (02461-1151)
PHONE....617 433-7630
Paul Jin, *President*
EMP: 3 **EST:** 2012
SALES (est): 279.9K **Privately Held**
SIC: 3577 Mfg Computer Peripheral Equipment

(G-13639)
SPATTER INC
21 Randolph St (02461-1308)
PHONE....617 510-0498
Ori Spigelman, *CEO*
Suzy Peled-Spigelman, *Vice Pres*
Yehuda Orr, *Development*
EMP: 8 **EST:** 2013
SALES (est): 507K **Privately Held**
SIC: 7372 Prepackaged Software

(G-13640)
STAR VACCINE INC
45 Irving St (02459-1611)
PHONE....617 584-5483
Yi Le, *President*
EMP: 3
SALES: 200K **Privately Held**
SIC: 2836 Mfg Biological Products

(G-13641)
STUART KARON
Also Called: Spiral Software
248 Park St (02458-2313)
PHONE....802 649-1911
Stuart Karon, *Owner*
EMP: 4
SALES (est): 204.9K **Privately Held**
SIC: 7372 Prepackaged Software Services

(G-13642)
SYSAID TECHNOLOGIES INC
128 Chestnut St (02465-2539)
PHONE....800 686-7047
Sarah Lahav, *CEO*
Israel Lifshitz, *Chairman*
EMP: 15
SALES (est): 1.1MM **Privately Held**
SIC: 7372 Prepackaged Software Services

(G-13643)
TASK PRINTING INC
Also Called: Signal Graphics Printing
441 Centre St (02458-2063)
PHONE....617 332-4414
Teresa Greco, *President*
Anthony Greco, *Treasurer*
EMP: 6
SQ FT: 1,600
SALES (est): 898.8K **Privately Held**
SIC: 2752 7334 Lithographic Commercial Printing Photocopying Services

(G-13644)
TRADERN FINE WOODWORKING INC
175 California St (02458-1093)
PHONE....617 393-3733
David Bogue, *Principal*
EMP: 4
SALES (est): 512.8K **Privately Held**
SIC: 2431 Mfg Millwork

(G-13645)
USA RENEWABLE LLC
22 Considine Rd (02459-3604)
PHONE....617 319-7237
Yury Babchenko, *Co-Owner*
Lilya Ivanova, *Co-Owner*
Alex Sukharevsky,
EMP: 5
SALES (est): 330K **Privately Held**
SIC: 3841 2835 8731 Mfg Surgical/Med Instr Mfg Diagnostic Substance Coml Physical Research Plumbing/Heat/Ac Contr Bus Servs Non-Comcl Site

(G-13646)
VACCA SIGN SERVICE INC
Also Called: Vacca Sign & Awning Service
69 Adams St Rear (02458-1126)
PHONE....617 332-3111
EMP: 4
SALES (est): 227.3K **Privately Held**
SIC: 3993 Mfg Signs/Advertising Specialties

(G-13647)
VAISALA INC
15 Riverdale Ave (02458-1057)
PHONE....617 467-1500
Scott Sternberg, *CEO*
Richard Schoonenberg, *Project Mgr*
Jen Clay, *Manager*
EMP: 60
SALES (corp-wide): 276.9MM **Privately Held**
SIC: 3829 Mfg Measuring/Controlling Devices
HQ: Vaisala Inc.
194 S Taylor Ave
Louisville CO 80027
303 499-1701

(G-13648)
VBLEARNING LLC
109 Oak St Ste 203 (02464-1493)
PHONE....617 527-9999
EMP: 23 **EST:** 2015
SALES (est): 427.2K **Privately Held**
SIC: 7372 Prepackaged Software Services

(G-13649)
VINDOR MUSIC INC
12 Salisbury Rd (02458-1948)
PHONE....617 984-9831
Fernando Trias, *President*
EMP: 4
SALES: 25K **Privately Held**
SIC: 3931 7372 Mfg Musical Instruments Prepackaged Software Services

(G-13650)
VISITOR GUIDE PUBLISHING INC
19 Jacobs Ter (02459-2818)
PHONE....617 542-5283
Boris Charolle, *President*
Jay Sweet, *Vice Pres*
Simon Shendelman, *Art Dir*
Mike Alvich, *Surgery Dir*
EMP: 6
SQ FT: 1,300
SALES: 2MM **Privately Held**
SIC: 2741 Guide Publishing

(G-13651)
VITAL SIGNS
44 Joseph Rd (02460-1122)
PHONE....617 645-3946
Mike Viscomi, *Principal*
EMP: 3
SALES (est): 166.2K **Privately Held**
SIC: 3993 Mfg Signs/Advertising Specialties

(G-13652)
VITALSENSORS TECHNOLOGIES LLC
29 Glenwood Ave (02459-2533)
PHONE....978 635-0450
Robert K O'Leary,
Peter Kent,
Rene Martinez,
EMP: 15
SQ FT: 3,500
SALES (est): 2.1MM **Privately Held**
WEB: www.vitalsensorstech.com
SIC: 3674 Mfg Semiconductors/Related Devices

(G-13653)
VIVIDO NATURAL LLC
22 Keefe Ave Ste 1 (02464-1317)
PHONE....617 630-0131
Amine Sabbagh,
▲ **EMP:** 10
SQ FT: 1,500
SALES: 500K **Privately Held**
SIC: 2099 Mfg Food Preparations

(G-13654)
WELLCOIN INC
11 Drumlin Rd (02459-2806)
PHONE....617 512-8617
Glenn Laffel, *CEO*
JP Pollak, *Chief Engr*
Daniela Retelny, *Product Mgr*
EMP: 7
SALES (est): 445.4K **Privately Held**
SIC: 7372 Prepackaged Software Services

(G-13655)
YOUNG AUTHORS FOUNDATION INC
Also Called: TEEN INK
437 Newtonville Ave Ste 1 (02460-1934)
P.O. Box 610030 (02461-0030)
PHONE....617 964-6800
John Meyer, *President*
Emily Sperber, *Editor*
EMP: 6
SALES: 652.7K **Privately Held**
WEB: www.collegemadness.com
SIC: 2721 5942 Periodicals-Publishing/Printing Ret Books

Newton Centre
Middlesex County

(G-13656)
MOBILE MONITOR TECH LLC
831 Beacon St Ste 202 (02459-1822)
PHONE....617 965-5057
Frederic Macdonald, *CEO*
Lawrence M Pensack, *President*
Jeffrey Simmons, *Treasurer*
▲ **EMP:** 3
SALES (est): 286.4K **Privately Held**
WEB: www.mmt2.com
SIC: 3577 Mfg Computer Peripheral Equipment

Newton Upper Falls
Middlesex County

(G-13657)
CHANGE LOGIC
233 Needham St Ste 300 (02464-1502)
PHONE....617 274-8661
Andrew Binns, *Principal*
EMP: 10 **EST:** 2010
SALES (est): 1.1MM **Privately Held**
SIC: 2992 Mfg Lubricating Oils/Greases

(G-13658)
SCION MEDICAL TECHOLOGIES LLC
90 Oak St 1 (02464-1439)
PHONE....617 455-5186
Joseph Siletto,
EMP: 8 **EST:** 2012
SALES (est): 620K **Privately Held**
SIC: 3841 Mfg Surgical/Medical Instruments

Norfolk
Norfolk County

(G-13659)
CAMGER COATINGS SYSTEMS INC
364 Main St (02056-1249)
PHONE....508 528-5787
Daniel C Iannuzzi, *President*
Tim Sheridan, *Purch Mgr*
Thomas Meisner, *Treasurer*
Guido Beschi, *Accounting Mgr*
Tom Walker, *Sales Staff*
EMP: 35
SQ FT: 70,000
SALES (est): 10.1MM **Privately Held**
SIC: 2851 Mfg Paints/Allied Products

(G-13660)
GUARDIAN INDUS PDTS INC MASS
150 Dedham St (02056-1665)
PHONE..................................508 384-0060
Paul Shepard, *President*
Madeleine Hutnak, *Office Mgr*
EMP: 8
SALES (est): 1.3MM **Privately Held**
WEB: www.floorfixer.com
SIC: 3081 5169 Manufactures And Wholesales Industrial Protective Coatings Specializing In Wall And Floor Coverings

(G-13661)
H E MOORE CORP (PA)
45 Lakeshore Dr (02056-1262)
PHONE..................................617 268-1262
Douglas Moore, *President*
EMP: 3
SQ FT: 5,000
SALES (est): 370K **Privately Held**
SIC: 3599 Mfg Industrial Machinery

(G-13662)
HAMLIN CABINETS CORP
112 Pond St (02056-1610)
PHONE..................................508 384-8371
Brian Hamlin, *President*
Kevin Hamlin, *Vice Pres*
Roy Hamlin, *Treasurer*
EMP: 9
SQ FT: 7,000
SALES (est): 1.2MM **Privately Held**
WEB: www.hamlincabinet.com
SIC: 2434 Mfg Kitchen And Bathroom Cabinets Made Of Wood

(G-13663)
LONGWORTH VENTURE PARTNERS LP (PA)
17 Chickadee Dr (02056-1740)
PHONE..................................781 663-3600
Paul Margolis, *Senior Partner*
William Sheehan, *Principal*
EMP: 40
SALES (est): 2.4MM **Privately Held**
WEB: www.longworth.com
SIC: 7372 6726 Prepackaged Software Services Closed-End Investment Office

(G-13664)
STAFFORD MANUFACTURING CORP
91 Holbrook St (02056-1812)
PHONE..................................978 657-8000
EMP: 3 **EST:** 2018
SALES (est): 142.6K **Privately Held**
SIC: 3568 Mfg Power Transmission Equipment

(G-13665)
T I S SOFTWARE CORP
9 Noon Hill Ave (02056-1118)
PHONE..................................508 528-9027
Tariq Siddiqui, *President*
EMP: 3
SALES (est): 137.3K **Privately Held**
SIC: 7372 Prepackaged Software Services

(G-13666)
TAKLITE LLC
8 Shire Dr Ste 3 (02056-1583)
PHONE..................................508 298-8331
Miklos Sahin-Toth, *Principal*
EMP: 4 **EST:** 2015
SALES (est): 449.7K **Privately Held**
SIC: 3648 Mfg Lighting Equipment

North Adams
Berkshire County

(G-13667)
AIR-TITE HOLDERS INC
1560 Curran Hwy (01247-3900)
PHONE..................................413 664-2730
Glenn Therrien, *President*
Ann Therrien, *Treasurer*
▲ **EMP:** 16
SQ FT: 27,000
SALES (est): 2.5MM **Privately Held**
WEB: www.airtiteholders.com
SIC: 3089 Mfg Plastic Products

(G-13668)
BECKS PRINTING CO
16 Protection Ave (01247-2251)
PHONE..................................413 664-7411
John Haskins, *Owner*
EMP: 5
SQ FT: 1,200
SALES (est): 598.6K **Privately Held**
WEB: www.becksprinting.com
SIC: 2752 Lithographic Commercial Printing

(G-13669)
BERKMATICS INC
59 Demond Ave (01247-3240)
P.O. Box 1839 (01247-1839)
PHONE..................................413 664-6152
Arthur Wylde, *Ch of Bd*
Douglas Wylde, *President*
Audie Wylde, *Vice Pres*
Russell Wylde, *Vice Pres*
EMP: 10 **EST:** 1940
SQ FT: 15,000
SALES: 900K **Privately Held**
SIC: 3451 Mfg Automatic Screw Machine Products

(G-13670)
BOXCAR MEDIA LLC
102 Main St (01247-3402)
PHONE..................................413 663-3384
Jim Shaker, *CFO*
Osmin F Olivarez, *Mng Member*
Paul Renaud, *Director*
EMP: 40
SQ FT: 5,000
SALES (est): 2.8MM **Privately Held**
SIC: 2741 7372 Web Design Printing And Publishing

(G-13671)
CORDMASTER ENGINEERING CO INC
Also Called: Cme
1544 Curran Hwy (01247-3900)
PHONE..................................413 664-9371
Bernard J Laroche, *President*
Luis Teixeira, *President*
Hugh M Daley, *Exec VP*
Carl Van Krese, *Manager*
EMP: 20
SQ FT: 10,000
SALES (est): 4.4MM **Privately Held**
WEB: www.cordmaster.com
SIC: 3643 3613 3625 3699 Mfg Conductive Wire Dvcs Mfg Elec Mach/Equip/Supp Mfg Switchgear/Boards Mfg Relay/Indstl Control Injection Molding Of Plasti

(G-13672)
CRANE & CO INC
1466 Curran Hwy (01247-3964)
P.O. Box 897 (01247-0897)
PHONE..................................413 664-4321
Steve Nelson, *Branch Mgr*
EMP: 108
SALES (corp-wide): 3.3B **Publicly Held**
SIC: 2621 Paper Mill
HQ: Crane & Co., Inc.
1 Beacon St Ste 1702
Boston MA 02108
617 648-3799

(G-13673)
CRANE STATIONERY LLC
1466 Curran Hwy (01247-3964)
PHONE..................................413 664-2256
John P Macy, *Principal*
EMP: 700
SQ FT: 70,656
SALES (est): 120MM
SALES (corp-wide): 240.1MM **Privately Held**
SIC: 2621 Paper Mill
PA: Mohawk Fine Papers Inc.
465 Saratoga St
Cohoes NY 12047
518 237-1740

(G-13674)
DENAULT INC
Also Called: Deerfield Machine & Tool Co
79 Walden St (01247-3328)
P.O. Box 777 (01247-0777)
PHONE..................................413 664-6771
Alfred Denault, *President*
Teresa D Denault, *Vice Pres*
EMP: 7
SQ FT: 5,576
SALES (est): 1MM **Privately Held**
WEB: www.denault.com
SIC: 3599 Machine Shop

(G-13675)
GHP MEDIA INC
Also Called: Excelsior Printing
123 Mass Moca Way (01247-2411)
PHONE..................................413 663-3771
Steve Bortner, *Vice Pres*
Joseph Lavalla, *Vice Pres*
Marc Server, *Vice Pres*
John Vesia, *Vice Pres*
Cheryl Vincent, *Client Mgr*
EMP: 60 **Privately Held**
SIC: 2752 2796 2791 2789 Lithographic Coml Print Platemaking Services Typesetting Services Bookbinding/Related Work Commercial Printing
PA: Ghp Media Inc.
475 Heffernan Dr
West Haven CT 06516

(G-13676)
HOTROD HOTLINE
106 Main St (01247-3402)
PHONE..................................208 562-0470
Edward Lawford, *Owner*
EMP: 5
SALES (est): 270K **Privately Held**
WEB: www.hotrodhotline.com
SIC: 2721 Periodicals-Publishing/Printing

(G-13677)
L HEWITT RAND
55 Chenaille Ter (01247-3013)
PHONE..................................413 664-8171
Rand Hewitt, *Principal*
EMP: 3
SALES (est): 259.1K **Privately Held**
SIC: 3131 Mfg Footwear Cut Stock

(G-13678)
LAMB PRINTING COMPANY INC
48 Cherry St (01247-4202)
PHONE..................................413 662-2495
William Lamb, *Ch of Bd*
Kenneth Lamb, *President*
Roberta Lamb, *Treasurer*
EMP: 3
SQ FT: 5,500
SALES: 300K **Privately Held**
SIC: 2752 2759 Offset Printing

(G-13679)
MARY ANN CAPRONI
Also Called: Caproni Sugar Bush
452 Walker St (01247-2883)
PHONE..................................413 663-7330
Mary Ann Caproni, *Owner*
EMP: 3
SALES (est): 99.5K **Privately Held**
SIC: 2099 Mfg Food Preparations

(G-13680)
MCC MATERIALS INC
243 Union St (01247-3564)
PHONE..................................860 309-9491
Irving Slavid, *President*
EMP: 5
SALES (est): 340K **Privately Held**
SIC: 3281 Mfg Cut Stone/Products

(G-13681)
MEEHAN ELECTRONICS CORPORATION
Also Called: Mec
1544 Curran Hwy (01247-3900)
PHONE..................................413 664-9371
Bernard J Laroche, *President*
Hugh M Daley, *Corp Secy*
◆ **EMP:** 16
SQ FT: 10,000
SALES (est): 2.1MM **Privately Held**
WEB: www.meehanelectronics.com
SIC: 3679 Mfg Electronic Components

(G-13682)
MORRISON BERKSHIRE INC
865 Church St (01247-4126)
P.O. Box 958 (01247-0958)
PHONE..................................413 663-6501
Jim White, *President*
Richard Pellerin, *Vice Pres*
Dick Pelleran, *Plant Mgr*
Todd Stjacques, *Engineer*
Steve Doyle, *Controller*
◆ **EMP:** 50
SQ FT: 130,000
SALES (est): 11.7MM **Privately Held**
WEB: www.morrisonberkshire.com
SIC: 3599 Mfg Industrial Machinery

(G-13683)
NORTH POINT BRANDS LLC
Also Called: Cheeky Fishing
60 Roberts Dr E (01247-3254)
PHONE..................................339 707-3017
Ted Upton, *CEO*
Peter Crommett, *Principal*
EMP: 5
SALES (est): 404.9K **Privately Held**
SIC: 3949 Mfg Sporting/Athletic Goods

(G-13684)
NORTHERN BERKSHIRE PREGNANCY
98 Church St Ste 1 (01247-4364)
PHONE..................................413 346-4291
Paula W Labonte, *Principal*
EMP: 6 **EST:** 2012
SALES: 77K **Privately Held**
SIC: 2835 Mfg Diagnostic Substances

(G-13685)
STOREY PUBLISHING LLC (HQ)
210 Mass Moca Way (01247-2426)
PHONE..................................413 346-2100
Sarah Guare, *Editor*
Lisa Hiley, *Editor*
Carleen Madigan, *Editor*
Emily Spiegelman, *Editor*
Regina Velazquez, *Production*
▲ **EMP:** 40
SQ FT: 17,000
SALES (est): 10.2MM
SALES (corp-wide): 92.7MM **Privately Held**
WEB: www.storey.com
SIC: 2731 5192 5961 Book-Publishing/Printing Whol Books/Newspapers
PA: Workman Publishing Co. Inc.
225 Varick St Fl 9
New York NY 10014
212 254-5900

North Andover
Essex County

(G-13686)
ADVANCE REPRODUCTIONS CORP
100 Flagship Dr (01845-6193)
PHONE..................................978 685-2911
Thomas J Nigrelli, *President*
Paul Nigrelli, *Vice Pres*
Aaron Crear, *Regl Sales Mgr*
▼ **EMP:** 70
SQ FT: 37,000
SALES (est): 15.2MM **Privately Held**
WEB: www.advancerepro.com
SIC: 3861 Mfg Photographic Equipment/Supplies

(G-13687)
ADVANCED RESEARCH DEVELOPMENT
Also Called: Ard
805 Turnpike St Ste 1 (01845-6122)
PHONE..................................781 285-8721
Alvin Marks, *Principal*
EMP: 3
SALES (est): 376.7K **Privately Held**
SIC: 3842 Mfg Surgical Appliances/Supplies

▲ = Import ▼=Export
◆ =Import/Export

(G-13688)
AERO SURVEILLANCE INC
800 Turnpike St Ste 300 (01845-6156)
PHONE..................................978 691-5832
Philippe Roy, *President*
Olivier Bourgeois, *CFO*
EMP: 3 **EST:** 2011
SALES (est): 285.9K **Privately Held**
SIC: 3812 Mfg Search/Navigation Equipment

(G-13689)
AMASTAN TECHNOLOGIES INC
25 Commerce Way Ste 1 (01845-1002)
PHONE..................................978 258-1645
Aaron Bent, *CEO*
Frank Roberts, *President*
EMP: 11
SALES (est): 2.2MM **Privately Held**
SIC: 2899 Mfg Chemical Preparations

(G-13690)
ANDOVER PUBLISHING COMPANY
Also Called: Andover Townsmen
100 Turnpike St (01845-5033)
P.O. Box 1986, Andover (01810-0186)
PHONE..................................978 475-7000
Irving E Rogers III, *President*
Bill Burt, *Editor*
Rosemary Ford, *Assoc Editor*
EMP: 20
SQ FT: 5,000
SALES (est): 926.2K **Privately Held**
WEB: www.andovertownsman.com
SIC: 2711 Newspapers-Publishing/Printing

(G-13691)
ARIES SYSTEMS CORPORATION
50 High St Ste 21 (01845-2620)
PHONE..................................978 975-7570
Lyndon S Holmes, *President*
Richard Wynne, *Vice Pres*
Kenneth Fogarty, *Treasurer*
Michael Di Natale, *Business Anlyst*
Stacey Lavelle, *Business Anlyst*
EMP: 25
SALES (est): 4.7MM
SALES (corp-wide): 9.8B **Privately Held**
WEB: www.extralib.com
SIC: 7372 7371 Prepackaged Software Services Custom Computer Programming
HQ: Elsevier Inc.
230 Park Ave Fl 8
New York NY 10169
212 989-5800

(G-13692)
ATS FINISHING INC
2350 Turnpike St (01845-6347)
PHONE..................................978 975-0957
James Smetanka, *President*
Jim Ellis, *Director*
EMP: 3
SALES (est): 196.7K **Privately Held**
SIC: 3999 Industrial/Commercial/Finishing

(G-13693)
BROLECO INC (PA)
200 Sutton St Ste 226 (01845-1651)
PHONE..................................978 689-3200
Joel Brother, *President*
Mary Gandolfo, *Info Tech Mgr*
Theodore B Brother, *Director*
▲ **EMP:** 5 **EST:** 1974
SQ FT: 5,000
SALES (est): 916K **Privately Held**
SIC: 3111 Leather Tanning/Finishing

(G-13694)
CENTRAL METAL FINISHING INC
80 Flagship Dr (01845-6106)
PHONE..................................978 291-0500
Carol Shibles, *President*
Melissa Boule, *Engineer*
Ted Jabczanka, *Supervisor*
Matt Cox, *Director*
EMP: 120
SQ FT: 41,000
SALES (est): 17.3MM **Privately Held**
WEB: www.cenmet.com
SIC: 3471 Plating/Polishing Service

(G-13695)
COLOR CHANGE TECHNOLOGY INC
30 Massachusetts Ave (01845-3458)
PHONE..................................978 377-0050
Chris Wyres, *CEO*
Charles Pemble, *Treasurer*
EMP: 4
SALES (est): 253.1K **Privately Held**
SIC: 2816 Mfg Inorganic Pigments

(G-13696)
CRAIG AAR
800 Turnpike St Ste 300 (01845-6156)
PHONE..................................978 691-0024
Frank Marchesini, *General Mgr*
Kris Kimbrough, *Principal*
Tomasz Wilk, *Executive*
EMP: 5 **EST:** 2000
SALES (est): 442.6K **Privately Held**
SIC: 3812 Mfg Search/Navigation Equipment

(G-13697)
DAWNS SIGN TECH INCORPORATED
33 Flagship Dr (01845-6103)
PHONE..................................978 208-0012
David Arthur Pease, *Director*
EMP: 3
SALES (est): 295.8K **Privately Held**
SIC: 3993 Mfg Signs/Advertising Specialties

(G-13698)
EAGLE-TRIBUNE PUBLISHING CO (DH)
Also Called: Andover Townsman
100 Turnpike St (01845-5033)
PHONE..................................978 946-2000
Donna J Barrett, *President*
Al Gepler, *Publisher*
Thomas J Lindley III, *Admin Sec*
EMP: 200
SQ FT: 100,000
SALES (est): 127.5MM **Privately Held**
WEB: www.eagletribune.com
SIC: 2711 Newspapers-Publishing/Printing
HQ: Newspaper Holding, Inc.
425 Locust St
Johnstown PA 15901
814 532-5102

(G-13699)
EAGLE-TRIBUNE PUBLISHING CO
Also Called: Eagle Tribune, The
100 Turnpike St (01845-5033)
P.O. Box 1986, Andover (01810-0186)
PHONE..................................978 946-2000
Bill Cantwell, *Editor*
Ken Johnson, *Editor*
David N Olson, *Editor*
Ed Wholley, *Advt Staff*
Karen Andreas, *Branch Mgr*
EMP: 71 **Privately Held**
WEB: www.clintonnc.com
SIC: 2711 Newspapers-Publishing/Printing
HQ: Eagle-Tribune Publishing Company
100 Turnpike St
North Andover MA 01845
978 946-2000

(G-13700)
ECRM INCORPORATED (PA)
Also Called: Ecrm Imaging Systems
25 Commerce Way Ste 1 (01845-1002)
PHONE..................................800 537-3276
Richard Black, *CEO*
William R Givens, *Ch of Bd*
Joe Chevalier, *Vice Pres*
Dave Connor, *Vice Pres*
Tony Lang, *Mfg Staff*
▲ **EMP:** 100
SQ FT: 101,786
SALES (est): 25.8MM **Privately Held**
SIC: 3555 Mfg Printing Trades Machinery

(G-13701)
EKEYS4 CARS
8 Marblehead St (01845-2332)
PHONE..................................978 655-3135
Jim Broadhurst, *Owner*
EMP: 4
SALES (est): 280K **Privately Held**
SIC: 3699 7699 Mfg Electrical Equipment/Supplies Repair Services

(G-13702)
ENVIROCARE CORPORATION (PA)
167 Coventry Ln (01845-2131)
PHONE..................................978 658-0123
Robert Seidewand, *President*
Barbara Cloonan, *Manager*
EMP: 6
SQ FT: 6,000
SALES: 1.2MM **Privately Held**
WEB: www.envirocarecorp.com
SIC: 3999 Mfg Misc Products

(G-13703)
FIDELIS EMC
149 Lancaster Rd (01845-2148)
PHONE..................................978 655-3390
Steve Cheche, *Principal*
EMP: 3 **EST:** 2015
SALES (est): 99.1K **Privately Held**
SIC: 3572 Mfg Computer Storage Devices

(G-13704)
FLAGSHIP PRESS INC
150 Flagship Dr (01845-6117)
PHONE..................................978 975-3100
Jeffrey N Poor, *CEO*
Charles N Poor, *President*
Roy Workman, *President*
Carol A Poor, *Corp Secy*
Jeff Poor, *COO*
EMP: 129 **EST:** 1950
SQ FT: 63,000
SALES (est): 37.4MM **Privately Held**
WEB: www.flagshippress.com
SIC: 2752 2791 2789 Lithographic Commercial Printing Typesetting Services Bookbinding/Related Work

(G-13705)
FLAME LAMINATING CORPORATION (PA)
2350 Turnpike St Bldg B (01845-6347)
PHONE..................................978 725-9527
Joseph Di Grazia, *President*
Eric Digrazia, *President*
Joel Digrazia, *Admin Sec*
▲ **EMP:** 15
SQ FT: 40,000
SALES (est): 3.1MM **Privately Held**
WEB: www.flamelaminatingcorp.com
SIC: 2295 Mfg Coated Fabrics

(G-13706)
FROZEN BATTERS INC
Also Called: Bake-N-Joy Foods
351 Willow St (01845-5921)
PHONE..................................508 683-1414
Judith F Ogan, *Principal*
Gary M Ogan, *Vice Pres*
George Fregone, *Vice Pres*
Steven M Weinstein, *Vice Pres*
Robert M Ogan, *Treasurer*
EMP: 100 **EST:** 1982
SQ FT: 30,000
SALES (est): 14.7MM **Privately Held**
SIC: 2051 Mfg Bread/Related Products

(G-13707)
GEFRAN INC (DH)
400 Willow St (01845-5934)
PHONE..................................781 729-5249
Mark Caldwell, *CEO*
Christian Pampallona, *General Mgr*
Andrea Franceschetti, *Vice Chairman*
Dave Campbell, *Opers Mgr*
Kevin Sellers, *Mfg Mgr*
◆ **EMP:** 45 **EST:** 1982
SALES (est): 7.6MM **Privately Held**
WEB: www.sieiamerica.com
SIC: 3566 3625 Mfg Speed Changers/Drives Mfg Relays/Industrial Controls
HQ: Gefran Spa
Via Sebina 74
Provaglio D'iseo BS 25050
029 676-01

(G-13708)
GEFRAN ISI INC
400 Willow St (01845-5934)
PHONE..................................781 729-0842
Ennio Franceshetti, *President*
Mark Caldwell, *Treasurer*
Robert Vivier, *Controller*
EMP: 29
SALES (est): 4.4MM **Privately Held**
WEB: www.gefran.com
SIC: 3823 3829 Mfg Process Control Instruments Mfg Measuring/Controlling Devices
HQ: Gefran Spa
Via Sebina 74
Provaglio D'iseo BS 25050
029 676-01

(G-13709)
HOME GROWN LACROSSE LLC
400 Osgood St (01845-2905)
PHONE..................................978 208-2300
Bryan J Brazill, *Mng Member*
EMP: 4
SALES (est): 354K **Privately Held**
SIC: 3949 Mfg Sporting/Athletic Goods

(G-13710)
INTERNTONAL MICRO PHOTONIX INC
120 Willow St (01845-5918)
PHONE..................................978 685-3800
Francis S Maldari, *Principal*
EMP: 9 **EST:** 2011
SALES (est): 1.1MM **Privately Held**
SIC: 3661 Mfg Telephone/Telegraph Apparatus

(G-13711)
IVENIX INC
50 High St Ste 50 # 50 (01845-2620)
PHONE..................................978 775-8050
Jorgen B Hansen, *CEO*
Janice Clements-Skelto, *Vice Pres*
George Gray, *Vice Pres*
Steve Schiefen, *Project Dir*
Carolyn Malleck, *Treasurer*
EMP: 41
SQ FT: 2,500
SALES (est): 9.9MM **Privately Held**
WEB: www.fluidnet.net
SIC: 3841 Mfg Surgical/Medical Instruments

(G-13712)
JG MANUFACTURING CORP
1980 Turnpike St Ste 3 (01845-6396)
PHONE..................................978 681-8400
George Hallett, *President*
EMP: 4
SQ FT: 3,000
SALES (est): 500K **Privately Held**
SIC: 3599 Machine Shop

(G-13713)
JOHNSON MATTHEY PHRM MTLS INC
Also Called: Johnson Matthey Phrm Svcs
70 Flagship Dr (01845-6126)
PHONE..................................978 784-5000
Thomas Saulnier, *Manager*
EMP: 35
SALES (corp-wide): 13.8B **Privately Held**
WEB: www.jmpharmaservices.com
SIC: 2833 8731 2834 Mfg Medicinal/Botanical Products Commercial Physical Research Mfg Pharmaceutical Preparations
HQ: Johnson Matthey Pharmaceutical Materials Inc
25 Patton Rd
Devens MA 01434
978 784-5000

(G-13714)
KETTLEPIZZA LLC
1755 Osgood St (01845-1028)
PHONE..................................888 205-1931
Laurie Bradshaw, *General Mgr*
George Peters, *Vice Pres*
Alfred F Contarino Jr,
EMP: 5
SALES: 1.2MM **Privately Held**
SIC: 3631 Eating Place

(G-13715)
L-COM INC (DH)
Also Called: L-Com Global Connectivity
50 High St (01845-2620)
PHONE..................................978 682-6936
Terry Jarnigan, *President*

Nick Nash, *President*
Brian Macdonald, *Corp Secy*
Zig Woronko, *COO*
Chris Long, *Senior VP*
▲ **EMP:** 90 **EST:** 1983
SALES (est): 123.9MM **Privately Held**
WEB: www.l-com.com
SIC: 3678 3577 3357 Mfg Electronic Connectors Mfg Computer Peripheral Equipment Nonferrous Wiredrawing/Insulating
HQ: Infinite Electronics, Inc.
17792 Fitch
Irvine CA 92614
949 261-1920

(G-13716)
LASERCRAZE
1580 Osgood St Ste 2210 (01845-1038)
PHONE..................................978 689-7700
Curt Bellavance, *Exec Dir*
EMP: 40
SALES (est): 3.1MM **Privately Held**
SIC: 2759 Commercial Printing

(G-13717)
LEAP YEAR PUBLISHING LLC
16 High St Ste 300 (01845-2656)
PHONE..................................978 688-9900
Enno Tjalsma, *Mng Member*
▲ **EMP:** 13
SALES (est): 2.5MM **Privately Held**
WEB: www.leapyearpublishing.com
SIC: 2759 3944 2754 Commercial Printing Mfg Games/Toys Gravure Commercial Printing

(G-13718)
MICROWAVE ENGINEERING CORP
1551 Osgood St (01845-1041)
PHONE..................................978 685-2776
Suzanne Wright, *President*
Chris Holman, *Vice Pres*
Hong Chau, *VP Opers*
Linda Williams, *Production*
Maurice Aghion, *VP Engrg*
▲ **EMP:** 80
SQ FT: 60,000
SALES (est): 14.3MM **Privately Held**
SIC: 3679 3678 3677 3663 Mfg Elec Components Mfg Elec Connectors Mfg Elec Coil/Transfrmrs Mfg Radio/Tv Comm Equip

(G-13719)
NEWMIND ROBOTICS LLC
44 Royal Crest Dr Apt 6 (01845-6557)
PHONE..................................239 322-2997
Nathan George,
EMP: 5
SALES (est): 202.2K **Privately Held**
SIC: 3728 Mfg Aircraft Parts/Equipment

(G-13720)
NORTH ANDOVER FLIGHT ACADEMY
Also Called: Boston Helicopters
492 Sutton St (01845-1505)
P.O. Box 776 (01845-0776)
PHONE..................................978 689-7600
John McGroerty, *Owner*
EMP: 5 **EST:** 2008
SALES (est): 415.3K **Privately Held**
SIC: 3699 Mfg Electrical Equipment/Supplies

(G-13721)
OPTICAL METROLOGY INC
Also Called: Optimet
1600 Osgood St Ste 1-150 (01845-1048)
PHONE..................................978 657-6303
Carl Burns, *President*
EMP: 3
SALES (est): 190K **Privately Held**
WEB: www.optimet.com
SIC: 3827 Mfg Optical Instruments/Lenses

(G-13722)
ORION ENTERPRISES INC (HQ)
Also Called: Orion Fittings
1600 Osgood St Ste 2005 (01845-1059)
PHONE..................................913 342-1653
John Mc Coy, *President*
Bill Mc Coy, *Vice Pres*
James B Mc Coy, *Vice Pres*
Clay Reeder, *Treasurer*
Joseph Mc Coy, *Admin Sec*
◆ **EMP:** 110
SQ FT: 93,000
SALES (est): 29.5MM
SALES (corp-wide): 1.5B **Publicly Held**
SIC: 3084 5074 3432 3089 Mfg Plastic Pipe Whol Plumbing Equip/Supp Mfg Plumbing Fxtr Fittng Mfg Plastic Products
PA: Watts Water Technologies, Inc.
815 Chestnut St
North Andover MA 01845
978 688-1811

(G-13723)
ORION FITTINGS INC
815 Chestnut St (01845-6009)
PHONE..................................978 689-6150
Paula Adkins, *Controller*
Debbie Stotz, *Executive*
EMP: 4
SALES (est): 297K **Privately Held**
SIC: 3084 Mfg Plastic Pipe

(G-13724)
PIPE DREAM CUPCAKES LLC
195 Amberville Rd (01845-3378)
PHONE..................................978 397-6470
Nadine Lee Levin, *Principal*
EMP: 6 **EST:** 2011
SALES (est): 302.2K **Privately Held**
SIC: 2051 Mfg Bread/Related Products

(G-13725)
PRESSUE TECHNIQUES
39 Flagship Dr (01845-6103)
PHONE..................................978 686-2211
Peter P Rubenstein, *Principal*
EMP: 3 **EST:** 2012
SALES (est): 357.6K **Privately Held**
SIC: 3728 Mfg Aircraft Parts/Equipment

(G-13726)
PRIDECRAFT INC
109 Sutton St (01845-1610)
PHONE..................................978 685-2831
John Disalvo, *President*
Paul Disalvo, *Vice Pres*
EMP: 6
SQ FT: 15,000
SALES (est): 600K **Privately Held**
WEB: www.pridecraftinc.com
SIC: 2499 2511 8711 Mfg Wood Products & Household Furniture & Engineering Service

(G-13727)
PROTEIN PRODUCTS INC
76 Carlton Ln (01845-5603)
PHONE..................................508 954-6020
Peter Noble, *President*
Chris Gorski, *Corp Secy*
▲ **EMP:** 3
SALES (est): 302.3K **Privately Held**
WEB: www.proteinpro.com
SIC: 2075 Soybean Oil Mill

(G-13728)
SOLUSOFT INC
300 Willow St (01845-5910)
PHONE..................................978 375-6021
Kiran Thakrar, *President*
Jay Ruparelia, *Opers Mgr*
Chiman Patel, *Shareholder*
EMP: 25 **EST:** 1994
SQ FT: 20,000
SALES (est): 2MM **Privately Held**
SIC: 7372 7371 Prepackaged Software Services Custom Computer Programing

(G-13729)
ST REGIS SPORTSWEAR LTD
3 Ironwood Rd (01845-2126)
PHONE..................................518 725-6767
Martin Krieger, *President*
Priscilla Blood, *Admin Sec*
EMP: 9
SALES (est): 1.2MM **Privately Held**
SIC: 2281 Yarn Spinning Mill

(G-13730)
THOUGHT ONE LLC
194 Gray St (01845-6302)
P.O. Box 26946, Salt Lake City UT (84126-0946)
PHONE..................................408 623-3278
Andrey Mishin,
Kenneth Breur,
Galina Mishin,
EMP: 3
SALES: 2MM **Privately Held**
SIC: 3674 Mfg Semiconductors/Related Devices

(G-13731)
TIMELINX SOFTWARE LLC
800 Turnpike St Ste 300 (01845-6156)
PHONE..................................978 662-1171
Mark E Engelberg,
EMP: 5
SQ FT: 1,000
SALES (est): 900K **Privately Held**
SIC: 7372 Prepackaged Software Services

(G-13732)
TROEMNER
1600 Osgood St Ste E213 (01845-1060)
PHONE..................................978 655-3377
Steven Butler, *Principal*
EMP: 3
SALES (est): 184.7K **Privately Held**
SIC: 3821 Mfg Lab Apparatus/Furniture

(G-13733)
UNADILLA ANTENNAS MFGCO
8 Marblehead St Ste B (01845-2332)
P.O. Box 4215, Andover (01810-0814)
PHONE..................................978 975-2711
EMP: 6
SQ FT: 7,500
SALES (est): 835.8K **Privately Held**
SIC: 3663 Mfg Radio/Tv Communication Equipment

(G-13734)
UNITED PLASTIC FABRICATING INC (PA)
165 Flagship Dr (01845-6119)
PHONE..................................978 975-4520
F Joseph Lingel, *President*
Bryan Curley, *Vice Pres*
Alexander Callahan, *Marketing Staff*
Brian Huberdeau, *Manager*
Richard P McGonnell, *Director*
EMP: 100
SQ FT: 40,000
SALES (est): 24.4MM **Privately Held**
WEB: www.polytanker.com
SIC: 3089 3083 Mfg Plastic Products Mfg Laminated Plastic Plate/Sheet

(G-13735)
UNIVERSAL PHARMA TECH LLC
70 Flagship Dr Ste 3 (01845-6126)
PHONE..................................978 975-7216
Bob Byron, *General Mgr*
EMP: 13
SQ FT: 10,000
SALES (est): 1.3MM **Privately Held**
SIC: 3559 8731 Mfg Separation Equipment & Does Contract Research & Development

(G-13736)
VERIONIX INC
251 Granville Ln (01845-4905)
PHONE..................................978 682-5671
Chris Doughty, *President*
EMP: 3
SALES: 500K **Privately Held**
WEB: www.verionix.com
SIC: 3823 Mfg Pressure Measurement Industrial Instruments

(G-13737)
WATTS REGULATOR CO (HQ)
815 Chestnut St (01845-6098)
PHONE..................................978 689-6000
Munish Nanda, *President*
Marc Lieberman, *Principal*
Dwain Dehmlow, *Vice Pres*
William C McCartney, *CFO*
Timothy M Macphee, *Treasurer*
◆ **EMP:** 230
SQ FT: 35,000
SALES (est): 456.4MM
SALES (corp-wide): 1.5B **Publicly Held**
WEB: www.wattsreg.com
SIC: 3491 3494 Mfg Industrial Valves Mfg Valves/Pipe Fittings
PA: Watts Water Technologies, Inc.
815 Chestnut St
North Andover MA 01845
978 688-1811

(G-13738)
WATTS REGULATOR CO
1600 Osgood St (01845-1048)
PHONE..................................978 688-1811
John Colton, *Branch Mgr*
EMP: 650
SALES (corp-wide): 1.5B **Publicly Held**
SIC: 3491 Mfg Industrial Valves
HQ: Watts Regulator Co.
815 Chestnut St
North Andover MA 01845
978 689-6000

(G-13739)
WATTS WATER TECHNOLOGIES INC (PA)
815 Chestnut St (01845-6009)
PHONE..................................978 688-1811
W Craig Kissel, *Ch of Bd*
Robert J Pagano Jr, *President*
Elie A Melhem, *President*
Munish Nanda, *President*
Kenneth R Lepage, *Exec VP*
◆ **EMP:** 140
SALES: 1.5B **Publicly Held**
WEB: www.wattsind.com
SIC: 3494 3491 Mfg Valves/Pipe Fittings Mfg Industrial Valves

(G-13740)
WIN ENTERPRISES INC
300 Willow St Ste 2 (01845-5912)
PHONE..................................978 688-2000
Chiman L Patel, *President*
Dave Burke, *Vice Pres*
Mark Goulet, *Vice Pres*
Richard Lattime, *Safety Mgr*
Shawn Reynolds, *Engineer*
▲ **EMP:** 50
SQ FT: 21,000
SALES (est): 11.7MM **Privately Held**
WEB: www.win-ent.com
SIC: 3571 Whol Computers/Peripherals

North Attleboro
Bristol County

(G-13741)
A G INDUSTRIES INC
75 Chestnut St (02760-2301)
PHONE..................................508 695-4219
Alan Greenleaf, *President*
EMP: 4
SQ FT: 9,340
SALES (est): 680.3K **Privately Held**
SIC: 3441 Structural Metal Fabrication

(G-13742)
ACRYLINE INC
324 S Washington St (02760-2155)
PHONE..................................508 695-0060
Russell H Baker Jr, *President*
Anne Baker, *Clerk*
EMP: 30 **EST:** 1976
SQ FT: 33,000
SALES (est): 2.2MM **Privately Held**
WEB: www.acryline.com
SIC: 3993 Mfg Signs/Advertising Specialties

(G-13743)
AERC REMOVALS LLC
11 Robert Toner Blvd (02763-1174)
PHONE..................................774 218-4212
EMP: 4 **EST:** 2010
SALES (est): 336.8K **Privately Held**
SIC: 3442 Mfg Metal Doors/Sash/Trim

(G-13744)
ALUMA-CAST CORP
136 May St (02760-4324)
P.O. Box 3068 (02761-3068)
PHONE..................................508 399-6650
Eric Packer, *President*
Scott Welton, *Vice Pres*
EMP: 4
SALES (est): 275.5K **Privately Held**
SIC: 3949 Mfg Golf Clubs

(G-13745)
APOTHECARY PRODUCTS LLC
Also Called: Health Enterprises
90 George Leven Dr (02760-3580)
PHONE..................................508 695-0727
EMP: 20
SALES (corp-wide): 115.7MM **Privately Held**
SIC: 3999 3842 3069 3089 Mfg Misc Products Mfg Surgical Appliances Mfg Fabrcatd Rubber Prdt Mfg Plastic Products
PA: Apothecary Products, Llc
11750 12th Ave S
Burnsville MN 55337
800 328-2742

(G-13746)
ARTCRAFT CO INC
200 John L Dietsch Blvd (02763-1077)
P.O. Box E, Attleboro Falls (02763-0415)
PHONE..................................508 695-4042
John R Dumochel, *President*
Brian Rotchford, *Vice Pres*
Scott Shreve, *Vice Pres*
Bob Houle, *Prdtn Mgr*
Barbara Peloquin, *Controller*
▲ **EMP:** 69 **EST:** 1939
SQ FT: 45,000
SALES (est): 12.2MM **Privately Held**
WEB: www.artcraft.com
SIC: 2752 Lithographic Commercial Printing

(G-13747)
ASHWORTH ASSOC MFG WHL JWELERS
Also Called: Ashworth Awards
41 Richards Ave (02760-1609)
P.O. Box 831 (02761-0831)
PHONE..................................508 695-1900
Daniel Ashworth, *President*
Kim Ashworth, *Vice Pres*
Luke Baiungo, *Accounts Exec*
Sally Gregory, *Accounts Exec*
Gretchen Siano, *Accounts Exec*
▲ **EMP:** 11
SQ FT: 6,000
SALES (est): 1.1MM **Privately Held**
WEB: www.ashworthawards.com
SIC: 3961 3911 Mfg Costume Jewelry Mfg Precious Metal Jewelry

(G-13748)
ASPELL SAGGERS LLC
60 James St (02760-3109)
PHONE..................................508 216-3264
Graham Saggers, *Principal*
▲ **EMP:** 3
SALES (est): 64K **Privately Held**
SIC: 3255 Mfg Clay Refractories

(G-13749)
BARBER ELC ENCLOSURES MFG INC
30 Chestnut St (02760-2304)
PHONE..................................508 699-4872
Linda Thibault, *President*
Michael Yidiaris, *Opers Mgr*
Jim Chapman, *Sales Mgr*
EMP: 22
SALES (est): 2.6MM **Privately Held**
SIC: 3469 Mfg Metal Stampings

(G-13750)
BORO SAND & STONE CORP (PA)
192 Plain St (02760-4124)
PHONE..................................508 699-2911
Thomas P Walsh, *President*
EMP: 46
SQ FT: 3,000
SALES: 10MM **Privately Held**
SIC: 3273 5032 Mfg Ready-Mixed Concrete Whol Brick/Stone Matrls

(G-13751)
CAB SCREEN PRINTING
32 Reardons Field Ln (02763-1163)
PHONE..................................508 695-8421
Susan Harris, *Owner*
EMP: 3
SALES: 70K **Privately Held**
SIC: 2752 Lithographic Commercial Printing

(G-13752)
CHECON CORPORATION (PA)
30 Larsen Way (02763-1055)
PHONE..................................508 643-0940
Donald E Conaway, *Ch of Bd*
D Allen Conaway, *President*
Judith S Conaway, *President*
Patty Phillippino, *Prdtn Mgr*
Ted Therrian, *Prdtn Mgr*
EMP: 120 **EST:** 1960
SQ FT: 42,000
SALES (est): 29.5MM **Privately Held**
WEB: www.checon.com
SIC: 3643 Mfg Conductive Wiring Devices

(G-13753)
CLARKIE INDUSTRIES
182 Grant St (02760-2411)
PHONE..................................508 404-0202
David Clark, *Owner*
EMP: 10
SALES (est): 400K **Privately Held**
SIC: 2393 Mfg Textile Bags

(G-13754)
CUSTOM CRAFTED ENTERPRISES
123 John L Dietsch Sq (02763-1027)
PHONE..................................508 695-2878
Richard Cavallaro, *President*
Cheryl Cavallaro, *Treasurer*
EMP: 5
SQ FT: 6,000
SALES (est): 370K **Privately Held**
SIC: 2329 2339 Manufactures Men's And Women's Athletic Uniforms

(G-13755)
EPOXALOT JEWELRY
38 Peck St (02760-3140)
PHONE..................................508 699-0767
Charles Garnett, *Owner*
Joann Garnett, *Co-Owner*
EMP: 6
SQ FT: 6,000
SALES (est): 366.7K **Privately Held**
SIC: 3479 Coating/Engraving Service

(G-13756)
FULLER BOX CO INC (PA)
150 Chestnut St (02760-3205)
P.O. Box 9 (02761-0009)
PHONE..................................508 695-2525
Peter C Fuller, *President*
Thomas Mercer, *Vice Pres*
David Whitty, *Vice Pres*
Jonathan Backner, *CFO*
Alvin R Fuller, *Admin Sec*
▲ **EMP:** 100 **EST:** 1944
SQ FT: 52,000
SALES (est): 33.2MM **Privately Held**
WEB: www.fullerbox.com
SIC: 2675 3172 3086 2657 Mfg Die-Cut Paper/Board Mfg Personal Leather Gds Mfg Plastic Foam Prdts Mfg Folding Paperbrd Box

(G-13757)
GARNER LEACH INC
262 Broad St (02760-1154)
P.O. Box 3249 (02761-3249)
PHONE..................................508 695-9395
Armand Iskenderian, *President*
EMP: 80
SALES (corp-wide): 225.3B **Publicly Held**
SIC: 3356 Nonferrous Rolling/Drawing
HQ: Leachgarner, Inc.
49 Pearl St
Attleboro MA 02703
508 222-7400

(G-13758)
GREENWOOD EMRGNCY VEHICLES LLC (HQ)
530 John Dietsch Blvd (02763-1080)
PHONE..................................508 695-7138
Mark Macdonald, *President*
Barbara Horigan, *Purch Agent*
Jerry Kassner, *VP Finance*
EMP: 75
SALES: 43MM
SALES (corp-wide): 4.5MM **Privately Held**
SIC: 3537 5087 5012 3711 Wholesale Auto/Motor Vehicles/Firefighting Equipment Manufacture Indstl Truck/Tractor & Motor Vehicle Bodies
PA: Emergency Vehicles Holdings, Llc
30 Monument Sq Ste 302
Concord MA 01742
617 956-1336

(G-13759)
HYDROTECH SERVICES INC
38b George Leven Dr (02760-3580)
P.O. Box 2368, Plainville (02762-0299)
PHONE..................................508 699-5977
Jeffrey Woods, *President*
EMP: 12
SALES (est): 1.7MM **Privately Held**
WEB: www.hydrotechservices.com
SIC: 3589 Mfg Water Treatment Equipment

(G-13760)
K W BRISTOL CO INC
4 Bruce Ave (02760-2302)
P.O. Box 748 (02761-0748)
PHONE..................................508 699-4742
Ronald R Deauregard, *President*
EMP: 4
SQ FT: 12,000
SALES (est): 411.6K **Privately Held**
SIC: 3599 3961 Machine Shop & Manufactures Keychains

(G-13761)
KIDPUB PRESS LLC
433 Smith St (02760-2422)
PHONE..................................617 407-2337
Perry Donham, *Principal*
EMP: 4 **EST:** 2010
SALES (est): 269.3K **Privately Held**
SIC: 2741 Misc Publishing

(G-13762)
MEDIA SCOPE INTERNATIONAL INC
Also Called: Mediascope International
51 Stoddard Dr (02760-3408)
PHONE..................................508 643-2988
EMP: 4 **EST:** 1998
SALES (est): 320K **Privately Held**
WEB: www.media-scope.com
SIC: 3695 Mfg Magnetic/Optical Recording Media

(G-13763)
METALOR TECHNOLOGIES USA CORP (DH)
255 John L Dietsch Blvd (02763-1069)
PHONE..................................508 699-8800
Yuxing Shang, *President*
Michelle Wheeler, *Regional Mgr*
Robert Stiles, *Counsel*
Cheryl Mello, *Exec VP*
Stephen Chapman, *Vice Pres*
▲ **EMP:** 165
SQ FT: 35,000
SALES (est): 40.6MM **Privately Held**
SIC: 3339 3341 Primary Nonfrs Mtl Prdcr Secndry Nonfrs Mtl Prdcr
HQ: Metalor Technologies International Sa
Rue Des Perveuils 8
Marin-Epagnier NE 2074
327 206-111

(G-13764)
METALOR USA REFINING CORP (DH)
255 John L Dietsch Blvd (02763-1069)
P.O. Box 225 (02761-0225)
PHONE..................................508 699-8800
Laurence Drummond, *President*
Michael Mooiman, *General Mgr*
Antoine Demontmolline, *CFO*
Todd Kropp, *CFO*
Nicolas Carrera, *Treasurer*
▲ **EMP:** 130
SQ FT: 65,000
SALES (est): 20.2MM **Privately Held**
WEB: www.metalorjewelry.com
SIC: 3341 3339 2819 Secondary Nonferrous Metal Producer Primary Nonferrous Metal Producer Mfg Industrial Inorganic Chemicals
HQ: Metalor Technologies Usa Corp
255 John L Dietsch Blvd
North Attleboro MA 02763
508 699-8800

(G-13765)
MINI-SYSTEMS INC (PA)
Also Called: MINI-SYSTEMS THIN FILM DIV
20 David Rd (02760-2102)
P.O. Box 69 (02761-0069)
PHONE..................................508 695-1420
Glen E Robertson, *President*
Elaine Ryan, *Admin Sec*
EMP: 200
SQ FT: 17,000
SALES: 14MM **Privately Held**
WEB: www.mini-systemsinc.com
SIC: 3676 3674 3672 3651 Mfg Electronic Resistors Mfg Semiconductors/Dvcs Mfg Printed Circuit Brds Mfg Home Audio/Video Eqp

(G-13766)
MODULEASE CORPORATION
212 Mount Hope St (02760-3908)
P.O. Box 932 (02761-0932)
PHONE..................................508 695-4145
Linda Prewandowski, *President*
Mark Gaboury, *Director*
EMP: 5 **EST:** 2008
SALES (est): 805.5K **Privately Held**
SIC: 2452 Modular Building

(G-13767)
NEEDLETECH PRODUCTS INC
452 John L Dietsch Blvd (02763-1079)
PHONE..................................508 431-4000
Francis J Tarallo, *President*
EMP: 165
SALES (est): 1.8MM
SALES (corp-wide): 93.9MM **Privately Held**
WEB: www.needletech.com
SIC: 3841 Mfg Surgical/Medical Instruments
HQ: Theragenics Corporation
5203 Bristol Indus Way
Buford GA 30518
770 271-0233

(G-13768)
NELMED CORPORATION
1 Thyme Ln (02760-6415)
PHONE..................................508 695-8817
EMP: 3
SQ FT: 1,500
SALES (est): 260K **Privately Held**
WEB: www.nelmed.com
SIC: 3841 Mfg Medical Products

(G-13769)
NEW ENGLAND STAINED GLASS
478 Old Post Rd (02760-4233)
P.O. Box 1095 (02761-1095)
PHONE..................................508 699-6965
James Donahue, *Owner*
EMP: 3
SQ FT: 6,432
SALES (est): 229.1K **Privately Held**
WEB: www.newenglandstainedglass.com
SIC: 3231 1793 Mfg Products-Purchased Glass Glass/Glazing Contractor

(G-13770)
OPTAMARK LLC (PA)
Also Called: Optamark Prtg & Mktg Companies
865 E Washington St (02760-1873)
PHONE..................................508 643-1017
Krupal Puchhadiya, *CFO*
Tarang Gosalia, *Mng Member*
EMP: 4 **EST:** 2011
SALES (est): 320.5K **Privately Held**
SIC: 2759 2752 Commercial Printing Lithographic Commercial Printing

(G-13771)
PETER THRASHER
Also Called: Triboro Supply
93 S Washington St (02760-2273)
EMP: 3
SALES (est): 21K **Privately Held**
SIC: 3714 5531 Mfg And Ret Exhaust Parts

GEOGRAPHIC

(G-13772)
POLY-TECH DIAMOND CO INC
4 East St (02760-2307)
P.O. Box 6 (02761-0006)
PHONE..........508 695-3561
Timothy Phipps, *President*
Matt Ringuette, *Manager*
EMP: 11
SQ FT: 6,200
SALES (est): 1.8MM **Privately Held**
WEB: www.polytechdiamond.com
SIC: **3545** Mfg Diamond Cutting Tools

(G-13773)
POLYMETALLURGICAL LLC
262 Broad St (02760-1154)
PHONE..........508 695-9312
John A Manzi, *President*
Thomas Burray, *Treasurer*
Carl Pallister, *Sales Dir*
Mark A Dingley, *Admin Sec*
EMP: 36
SQ FT: 58,000
SALES (est): 4.8MM
SALES (corp-wide): 770.6MM **Publicly Held**
WEB: www.polymet.com
SIC: **3479** 3496 3341 Coating/Engraving Service Mfg Misc Fabricated Wire Products Secondary Nonferrous Metal Producer
HQ: Brainin-Advance Industries Llc
48 Frank Mossberg Dr
Attleboro MA 02703
508 226-1200

(G-13774)
PREMIER ROLL & TOOL INC
10 Alice Agnew Dr (02763-1099)
PHONE..........508 695-2551
Maurice Udelson, *President*
Keith Udelson, *Vice Pres*
Joyce Udelson, *Treasurer*
EMP: 7
SQ FT: 7,800
SALES (est): 1MM **Privately Held**
SIC: **3316** 3544 Mfg Steel Rolls Machine Tools & Dies

(G-13775)
REKLAW MACHINE INC
142 Old Post Rd (02760-4216)
PHONE..........508 699-9255
Samuel G Walker, *President*
Fran Walker, *Vice Pres*
EMP: 6 **EST:** 1971
SQ FT: 4,500
SALES: 310K **Privately Held**
SIC: **3599** Mfg Industrial Machinery

(G-13776)
ROGER JETTE SILVERSMITHS INC
52 Orne St (02760)
P.O. Box 613 (02761-0613)
PHONE..........508 695-5555
Roger Jette, *President*
EMP: 6
SQ FT: 5,000
SALES: 10MM **Privately Held**
SIC: **3914** Silversmith

(G-13777)
RSJ LLC
Also Called: Rogerjettesilversmiths
52 Orne St (02760-2445)
P.O. Box 613 (02761-0613)
PHONE..........508 695-5555
Roger O Jette, *Owner*
EMP: 3 **EST:** 2009
SALES (est): 102.5K **Privately Held**
SIC: **3471** 7699 Plating/Polishing Service Repair Services

(G-13778)
S M ENGINEERING CO INC
Also Called: SM Heat Treating
83 Chestnut St (02760-2301)
P.O. Box 948 (02761-0948)
PHONE..........508 699-4484
Barbara Morin, *Vice Pres*
EMP: 15 **EST:** 1954
SQ FT: 30,000
SALES (est): 3MM **Privately Held**
WEB: www.sm-furnaces.com
SIC: **3567** 3398 Mfg Industrial Furnaces/Ovens Metal Heat Treating

(G-13779)
SIGNET PRODUCTS CORPORATION
521 Mount Hope St (02760-2611)
PHONE..........650 592-3575
Ross A Davies, *President*
EMP: 4
SALES (est): 108.9K **Privately Held**
SIC: **3674** Mfg Semiconductors/Related Devices

(G-13780)
SIR SPEEDY INC
865 E Washington St (02760-1873)
PHONE..........508 643-1016
Nisha Gonseales, *Owner*
EMP: 3
SALES (corp-wide): 19.9MM **Privately Held**
SIC: **2752** Comm Prtg Litho
HQ: Sir Speedy, Inc.
26722 Plaza
Mission Viejo CA 92691
949 348-5000

(G-13781)
STAR ENGINEERING INC
1 Vaillancourt Dr (02763-1054)
PHONE..........508 316-1492
Victor Neagoe, *President*
Paul Gigliotti, *Purch Mgr*
Bill Sharp, *Project Engr*
Michael Coleman, *CFO*
Gerry Latremouille, *Program Mgr*
EMP: 30
SQ FT: 16,000
SALES: 5MM **Privately Held**
WEB: www.starengineeringinc.com
SIC: **3679** 8711 Mfg Electronic Components Engineering Services

(G-13782)
STAY SHARP TOOL COMPANY INC
229 West St (02760-1148)
P.O. Box 1069 (02761-1069)
PHONE..........508 699-6990
William White, *President*
Paula White, *Admin Sec*
EMP: 5
SQ FT: 8,000
SALES (est): 637.1K **Privately Held**
WEB: www.staysharp.com
SIC: **3469** Mfg Metal Stampings

(G-13783)
TANTAR CORP
Also Called: Optamark Printing & Marketing
865 E Washington St (02760-1873)
PHONE..........508 643-1017
Pranshu Jain, *CTO*
Nisha Gosalia, *Director*
EMP: 3
SALES (est): 350.5K **Privately Held**
SIC: **2752** Lithographic Commercial Printing

(G-13784)
THERAPEUTIC INNOVATIONS INC
13 Dexter St Unit 7 (02760-1730)
P.O. Box 464, Malden (02148-0009)
PHONE..........347 754-0252
Solomon Mensah, *CEO*
EMP: 6
SALES (est): 331.3K **Privately Held**
SIC: **3841** 7389 Mfg Surgical/Medical Instruments

(G-13785)
TUTTI FRUTTI
999 S Washington St (02760-3656)
PHONE..........508 695-7795
EMP: 3
SALES (est): 166.4K **Privately Held**
SIC: **2026** Mfg Fluid Milk

(G-13786)
WISE MOUTH INC
84 Bank St (02760-1621)
PHONE..........508 345-2559
Lei Nichols, *President*
EMP: 6 **EST:** 2017
SALES (est): 632K **Privately Held**
SIC: **2086** Mfg Bottled/Canned Soft Drinks

(G-13787)
WR SHARPLES CO INC
211 John L Dietsch Sq (02763-1027)
PHONE..........508 695-5656
Daniel R Sharples, *President*
Helen I Sharples, *Treasurer*
Bud Marcello, *Sales Staff*
EMP: 20
SQ FT: 15,000
SALES (est): 3.4MM **Privately Held**
WEB: www.sharplesdie.com
SIC: **3544** Mfg Dies/Tools/Jigs/Fixtures

North Billerica
Middlesex County

(G-13788)
ACCENT PRINTING INC
99 Chelmsford Rd Rear 13 (01862-1351)
PHONE..........781 487-9300
Dilip Mirchandani, *President*
Brian Fisher, *Prdtn Mgr*
EMP: 6
SALES (est): 1MM **Privately Held**
SIC: **2752** Lithographic Commercial Printing

(G-13789)
ACCUSEMBLE ELECTRONICS INC
5 Esquire Rd (01862-2522)
PHONE..........978 584-0072
Deborah Bayley, *President*
Clarke Bayley, *Vice Pres*
EMP: 12 **EST:** 1979
SQ FT: 12,000
SALES (est): 2.3MM **Privately Held**
WEB: www.accusemble.com
SIC: **3672** Engineering Services

(G-13790)
ADG PRINTING INCORPORATED
306 Boston Rd Ste 3 (01862-2600)
PHONE..........978 667-9285
Ralph Papa, *President*
Bob Papa, *CFO*
EMP: 3
SALES (est): 320K **Privately Held**
SIC: **2752** Lithographic Commercial Printing

(G-13791)
ALLIED FABRICATION INC
18 Republic Rd (01862-2504)
PHONE..........978 667-5901
Kenneth Gillis, *President*
EMP: 3
SALES: 320K **Privately Held**
SIC: **3441** 1799 Structural Metal Fabrication Trade Contractor

(G-13792)
ALPINE PRECISION LLC
23 Sullivan Rd (01862-2003)
PHONE..........978 667-6333
Marie Faranna, *Office Mgr*
Brian Fjeld,
EMP: 10
SQ FT: 6,000
SALES: 2.7MM **Privately Held**
WEB: www.alpineprecision.com
SIC: **3599** Mfg Industrial Machinery

(G-13793)
ANTHEM MUSIC GROUP INC
2 Sterling Rd Unit 2 # 2 (01862-2595)
PHONE..........978 667-3224
David Kilkenny, *President*
Jay Maschmeier, *Safety Dir*
Brent Beech, *Director*
▲ **EMP:** 4
SALES (est): 397.1K **Privately Held**
SIC: **3931** Mfg Musical Instruments

(G-13794)
AVED ELECTRONICS LLC
95 Billerica Ave (01862-1231)
PHONE..........978 453-6393
Ralph P Santosuosso, *President*
Pendleton Dottie, *Engineer*
Deryl Santosuosso, *Admin Sec*
▲ **EMP:** 90 **EST:** 1979
SQ FT: 15,000
SALES (est): 40MM
SALES (corp-wide): 48.2MM **Privately Held**
WEB: www.aved.com
SIC: **3679** Mfg Electronic Components
PA: Lithion Power Group Ltd
333 7 Ave Sw Unit 970
Calgary AB T2P 2
587 349-5468

(G-13795)
BAKER COMMODITIES INC
Also Called: Corenco Div
134 Billerica Ave (01862-1234)
P.O. Box 132 (01862-0132)
PHONE..........978 454-8811
Joe Huelsman, *Principal*
EMP: 100
SQ FT: 10,000
SALES (corp-wide): 153.6MM **Privately Held**
WEB: www.bakercommodities.com
SIC: **2077** 2076 2079 Mfg Animal/Marine Fat/Oil Vegetable Oil Mill Mfg Edible Fats/Oils
PA: Baker Commodities, Inc.
4020 Bandini Blvd
Vernon CA 90058
323 268-2801

(G-13796)
BNZ MATERIALS INC
400 Iron Horse Park (01862-1616)
PHONE..........978 663-3401
Norman Scheffer, *Research*
Norman S Scheffer, *Research*
Richard A Beyer, *Branch Mgr*
Gwen Whitbeck,
EMP: 40
SALES (corp-wide): 47MM **Privately Held**
WEB: www.bnzmaterials.com
SIC: **3255** 2493 3821 3469 Mfg Clay Refractories Mfg Reconstd Wood Prdts
PA: Bnz Materials, Inc.
6901 S Pierce St Ste 180
Littleton CO 80128
303 978-1199

(G-13797)
BOSTON AND MAINE CORPORATION (HQ)
Also Called: Panam Railways
1700 Iron Horse Park (01862-1641)
PHONE..........978 663-1130
David A Fink, *Ch of Bd*
David Armstrong, *President*
Eric Lawer, *CFO*
EMP: 200 **EST:** 1833
SQ FT: 60,000
SALES (est): 114MM
SALES (corp-wide): 202.3MM **Privately Held**
SIC: **3531** Mfg Construction Machinery
PA: Pan Am Railways, Inc.
1700 Iron Horse Park
North Billerica MA 01862
978 663-1129

(G-13798)
BRANSON ULTRASONICS CORP
267 Boston Rd Ste 4 (01862-2310)
PHONE..........978 262-9040
Steve Galligan, *Manager*
EMP: 41
SALES (corp-wide): 18.3B **Publicly Held**
SIC: **3699** Mfg Electrical Equipment/Supplies
HQ: Branson Ultrasonics Corporation
41 Eagle Rd Ste 1
Danbury CT 06810
203 796-0400

(G-13799)
BRUNSWICK ENCLOSURE COMPANY
25 Sullivan Rd Ste 6 (01862-2020)
PHONE..................................978 670-1124
Steven Jovellas, *President*
EMP: 8
SQ FT: 2,500
SALES (est): 1.2MM **Privately Held**
SIC: 3442 Mfg Commercial Aluminum Windows & Doors

(G-13800)
BTU INTERNATIONAL INC (HQ)
23 Esquire Rd (01862-2530)
PHONE..................................978 667-4111
Paul J Van Der Wansem, *Ch of Bd*
Peter J Tallian, *COO*
James M Griffin, *Vice Pres*
Hongliang LI, *Prdtn Mgr*
David Bloom, *Engineer*
◆ **EMP:** 132
SQ FT: 150,000
SALES: 47.7MM
SALES (corp-wide): 85MM **Publicly Held**
WEB: www.btu.com
SIC: 3559 Whol Industrial Equipment
PA: Amtech Systems, Inc.
131 S Clark Dr
Tempe AZ 85281
480 967-5146

(G-13801)
BTU OVERSEAS LTD (DH)
23 Esquire Rd (01862-2530)
PHONE..................................978 667-4111
EMP: 3
SALES (est): 654.5K
SALES (corp-wide): 85MM **Publicly Held**
SIC: 3823 Mfg Process Control Instruments
HQ: Btu International, Inc.
23 Esquire Rd
North Billerica MA 01862
978 667-4111

(G-13802)
CLEANBASINS INC
Also Called: Sewerman
272 Rangeway Rd (01862-2014)
P.O. Box 366, Billerica (01821-0366)
PHONE..................................978 670-5838
Brian Macdonald, *President*
EMP: 4
SALES: 600K **Privately Held**
WEB: www.cleanbasins.com
SIC: 1389 3589 Cleaning Services

(G-13803)
CONCEPT MACHINING INC
25 Sullivan Rd Ste 7 (01862-2020)
PHONE..................................978 663-4999
Bob Volpe, *President*
EMP: 5
SQ FT: 4,000
SALES: 1MM **Privately Held**
WEB: www.conceptmachininginc.com
SIC: 3599 Mfg Industrial Machinery

(G-13804)
CONTOUR SEMICONDUCTOR INC
85 Rangeway Rd Ste 1 (01862-2105)
P.O. Box 729, Bolton (01740-0729)
PHONE..................................978 670-4100
Saul Zales, *CEO*
Dan Shepard, *President*
Tom Trent, *Vice Pres*
Christopher Wentworth, *Vice Pres*
EMP: 10
SALES (est): 1.5MM **Privately Held**
WEB: www.contoursemi.com
SIC: 3674 Mfg Semiconductors/Related Devices

(G-13805)
CURRICULUM ASSOCIATES LLC (PA)
153 Rangeway Rd (01862-2013)
PHONE..................................978 667-8000
Andrew Smith, *President*
Woody Paik, *Senior VP*
Adam Chace, *Vice Pres*
Derek Dorzaio, *Vice Pres*
Fred Ferguson, *Vice Pres*
▲ **EMP:** 500
SQ FT: 78,000
SALES (est): 14MM **Privately Held**
SIC: 2731 2741 Books-Publishing/Printing Misc Publishing

(G-13806)
DANTE CONFECTION
19 Sterling Rd Ste 6 (01862-2524)
PHONE..................................978 262-2242
Santi Falcone, *Owner*
Marissa Falcone, *Co-Owner*
EMP: 3
SALES (est): 250.1K **Privately Held**
WEB: www.danteconfection.com
SIC: 2064 Ret Candy/Confectionery

(G-13807)
DIAMOND USA INC (HQ)
85 Rangeway Rd Ste 3 (01862-2105)
PHONE..................................978 256-6544
Erwin Kammerer, *CEO*
Lisa Valente, *Treasurer*
Hans Gerber, *Director*
EMP: 20
SQ FT: 10,000
SALES: 10MM
SALES (corp-wide): 88.2MM **Privately Held**
WEB: www.diamond-fo.com
SIC: 3229 Mfg Fiber Optic
PA: Diamond Sa
Via Dei Patrizi 5
Losone Tl 6616
583 074-545

(G-13808)
DIECAST MANUFACTURER (PA)
67 Faulkner St (01862-1501)
PHONE..................................978 667-6784
Dieter D Marlock, *Partner*
Rob S Martin, *Partner*
William Martin, *Vice Pres*
EMP: 3
SQ FT: 2,500
SALES (est): 12.8MM **Privately Held**
SIC: 3542 Mfg Machine Tools-Forming

(G-13809)
DIGITAL GRAPHICS INC
101 Billerica Ave Bldg 6n (01862-1271)
PHONE..................................781 270-3670
Jim Dadmun, *President*
Bob Novelli, *CFO*
EMP: 45
SQ FT: 15,000
SALES (est): 4.7MM **Privately Held**
SIC: 2752 7336 2759 Lithographic Commercial Printing Commercial Art/Graphic Design Commercial Printing

(G-13810)
E F JELD CO INC
152 Rangeway Rd (01862-2010)
PHONE..................................978 667-1416
Edward Fjeld, *CEO*
Mark B Reynolds, *President*
Donald Pascucci, *Vice Pres*
Thomas M Fjeld, *Treasurer*
Arthur Fraser, *Treasurer*
EMP: 8 **EST:** 1972
SQ FT: 7,000
SALES (est): 920K **Privately Held**
WEB: www.efjeld.com
SIC: 3826 Mfg Analytical Instruments

(G-13811)
E I DU PONT DE NEMOURS & CO
Also Called: Dupont
331 Treble Cove Rd (01862-2849)
PHONE..................................978 663-7113
Donald Kiepert, *Branch Mgr*
EMP: 31
SALES (corp-wide): 30.6B **Publicly Held**
WEB: www.dupont.com
SIC: 2819 Mfg Industrial Inorganic Chemicals
HQ: E. I. Du Pont De Nemours And Company
974 Centre Rd Bldg 735
Wilmington DE 19805
302 485-3000

(G-13812)
E&D MACHINING INC
19 Sterling Rd Ste 5a (01862-2524)
PHONE..................................978 667-4848
James Morin, *President*
EMP: 4 **EST:** 1997
SALES (est): 448.2K **Privately Held**
SIC: 3599 Mfg Industrial Machinery

(G-13813)
EXCELL SOLUTIONS INC
18 Esquire Rd (01862-2502)
PHONE..................................978 663-6100
Marie Lennartz, *President*
George Kendall, *General Mgr*
Aaron Blais, *Manager*
Christopher Dionne, *Manager*
Clayton Lennartz, *Info Tech Mgr*
EMP: 9
SQ FT: 6,000
SALES (est): 1.6MM **Privately Held**
SIC: 3444 Mfg Sheet Metalwork

(G-13814)
FLIR SYSTEMS INC
Also Called: Flir Surveillance, Inc.
25 Esquire Rd (01862-2501)
PHONE..................................978 901-8000
Jeff Glover, *Credit Mgr*
EMP: 250
SALES (corp-wide): 1.7B **Publicly Held**
SIC: 3861 Manufacturing Of Manufacturer Of Photo Equipment
PA: Flir Systems, Inc.
27700 Sw Parkway Ave
Wilsonville OR 97070
503 498-3547

(G-13815)
FLIR SYSTEMS-BOSTON INC (HQ)
Also Called: Inframetrics
25 Esquire Rd (01862-2501)
PHONE..................................978 901-8000
Andrew C Teich, *CEO*
Kevin Tucker, *General Mgr*
Pete Smart, *Regional Mgr*
Rudy Machuca, *Business Mgr*
Jon Allan, *Engineer*
EMP: 300
SQ FT: 70,000
SALES (est): 77.5MM
SALES (corp-wide): 1.7B **Publicly Held**
WEB: www.flirsystems.com
SIC: 3823 3674 3812 Mfg Process Control Instruments Mfg Semiconductors/Related Devices Mfg Search/Navigation Equipment
PA: Flir Systems, Inc.
27700 Sw Parkway Ave
Wilsonville OR 97070
503 498-3547

(G-13816)
FRANKLIN ROBOTICS INC
85 Rangeway Rd Ste 3 (01862-2105)
PHONE..................................617 513-7666
Rory Mackean, *CEO*
Joe Jones, *CTO*
EMP: 4
SQ FT: 1,200
SALES: 400K **Privately Held**
SIC: 3569 Mfg General Industrial Machinery

(G-13817)
FUNCTIONAL ASSESSMENT TECH INC
Also Called: Fasstech
76 Treble Cove Rd Ste 3 (01862-2232)
PHONE..................................978 663-2800
Lee Brody, *COO*
Stephen Andress, *Admin Sec*
EMP: 18
SQ FT: 12,000
SALES (est): 2MM **Privately Held**
WEB: www.fasstech.com
SIC: 3841 Mfg Surgical/Medical Instruments
PA: Srs Medical Systems, Inc.
76 Treble Cove Rd Ste 3
North Billerica MA 01862

(G-13818)
GALVANIC APPLIED SCIENCES
101 Billerica Ave 5-104 (01862-1256)
PHONE..................................978 848-2701
Helen Cornett, *CEO*
Jack Cotter, *General Mgr*
EMP: 13
SALES (est): 3.5MM
SALES (corp-wide): 15.9MM **Privately Held**
SIC: 3826 Mfg Analytical Instruments
PA: Galvanic Applied Sciences Inc
7000 Fisher Rd Se
Calgary AB T2H 0
403 252-8470

(G-13819)
GEAR/TRONICS INC
100 Chelmsford Rd (01862-1396)
PHONE..................................781 933-1400
Robert Doherty, *President*
EMP: 23
SQ FT: 25,000
SALES (est): 1.6MM **Privately Held**
SIC: 3334 Primary Aluminum Producer

(G-13820)
GEAR/TRONICS INDUSTRIES INC
Also Called: X-4 Tool Div
100 Chelmsford Rd (01862-1328)
P.O. Box 376 (01862-0376)
PHONE..................................781 933-1400
Richard L Duffy, *President*
Jane Ann Hughes, *Admin Sec*
EMP: 53 **EST:** 1923
SQ FT: 73,000
SALES (est): 13.1MM **Privately Held**
WEB: www.geartronics.com
SIC: 3566 3549 Mfg Speed Changers/Drives Mfg Metalworking Machinery

(G-13821)
GEM WELDING
12 Republic Rd (01862-2504)
PHONE..................................978 362-3873
George Macallister, *President*
EMP: 8 **EST:** 2015
SALES (est): 360K **Privately Held**
SIC: 7692 Welding Repair

(G-13822)
GENERAL MANUFACTURING CORP
154 Rangeway Rd (01862-2010)
PHONE..................................978 667-5514
Ted Barrett, *President*
Edward M Barrett, *President*
EMP: 30
SQ FT: 12,000
SALES (est): 6.2MM **Privately Held**
SIC: 3679 Mfg Electronic Components

(G-13823)
HARPER BROS PRINTING INC
25 Sullivan Rd Ste 3 (01862-2020)
PHONE..................................978 667-9459
Richard Harper, *President*
EMP: 5
SALES (est): 602.8K **Privately Held**
WEB: www.harperbrothers.com
SIC: 2752 Lithographic Commercial Printing

(G-13824)
HYDROCISION INC
267 Boston Rd Ste 28 (01862-2310)
PHONE..................................978 474-9300
Alain Tranchemontagne, *CEO*
Howard Donnelly, *President*
Paul Kowalski, *Vice Pres*
Patricia Vanblarcom, *CFO*
Francis M Galasso, *Treasurer*
EMP: 30
SQ FT: 7,500
SALES (est): 4.5MM **Privately Held**
SIC: 3841 Mfg Surgical/Medical Instruments

(G-13825)
HYDRONICS MANUFACTURING INC
150 Rangeway Rd (01862-2010)
PHONE..................................978 528-4335
Joachim Fiedrich, *President*

Marie Fiedrich, *Corp Secy*
Richard Brockman, *CFO*
EMP: 7 **EST:** 2008
SALES (est): 1.4MM **Privately Held**
SIC: 2426 Hardwood Dimension/Floor Mill

(G-13826)
INDUSTRIAL FLOOR COVERING INC
148 Rangeway Rd Unit Cd (01862-2010)
PHONE..................................978 362-8655
Jennifer Grech, *President*
Walter Dupont, *Treasurer*
EMP: 8
SALES (est): 1.6MM **Privately Held**
SIC: 3996 1752 Mfg Hard Floor Coverings Floor Laying Contractor

(G-13827)
INFINITE ELECTRONICS INTL INC
Also Called: Radio Waves
495r Billerica Ave (01862-1205)
PHONE..................................978 459-8800
Frank Hall, *Engineer*
EMP: 4 **Privately Held**
SIC: 3663 Whol Electronic Parts/Equipment
HQ: Infinite Electronics International, Inc.
17792 Fitch
Irvine CA 92614
949 261-1920

(G-13828)
INTEGRA LUXTEC INC
85 Rangeway Rd Ste 1 (01862-2105)
PHONE..................................508 835-9700
Stewart Essig, *CEO*
Joanne Dion, *Buyer*
EMP: 67
SQ FT: 25,000
SALES (est): 8.9MM **Publicly Held**
WEB: www.lxuhc.com
SIC: 3841 Mfg Surgical/Medical Instruments
PA: Integra Lifesciences Holdings Corporation
311 Enterprise Dr
Plainsboro NJ 08536

(G-13829)
JOHN A KACHAGIAN
Also Called: Aram Machine Co
34 Sullivan Rd Ste 15 (01862-2000)
PHONE..................................978 663-8511
John A Kachagian, *Owner*
EMP: 4
SQ FT: 4,500
SALES (est): 376.4K **Privately Held**
SIC: 3599 Mfg Industrial Machinery

(G-13830)
KILDER CORPORATION
Also Called: Lamintd Plas Dstrs Fbricators
7 Executive Park Dr (01862-1318)
PHONE..................................978 663-8800
John R Sabatino, *President*
John Sabatino, *CTO*
EMP: 30
SQ FT: 20,000
SALES (est): 6.6MM **Privately Held**
WEB: www.laminatedplastics.com
SIC: 3082 5162 Mfg Plastic Profile Shapes Whol Plastic Materials/Shapes

(G-13831)
LANTHEUS HOLDINGS INC (PA)
331 Treble Cove Rd (01862-2849)
PHONE..................................978 671-8001
Brian Markison, *Ch of Bd*
Mary Anne Heino, *President*
John Bolla, *COO*
Michael Duffy, *Senior VP*
Etienne Montagut, *Senior VP*
EMP: 41
SQ FT: 578,000
SALES: 343.3MM **Publicly Held**
SIC: 2835 2834 Mfg Diagnostic Substances Mfg Pharmaceutical Preparations

(G-13832)
LANTHEUS MEDICAL IMAGING INC (HQ)
331 Treble Cove Rd (01862-2849)
PHONE..................................800 362-2668
Mary A Heino, *President*
Peter Card, *President*
John Bolla, *Vice Pres*
Timothy G Healey, *Vice Pres*
Carol Walker, *Vice Pres*
▲ **EMP:** 277
SALES (est): 110.8MM
SALES (corp-wide): 343.3MM **Publicly Held**
SIC: 2834 3841 Mfg Pharmaceutical Preparations Mfg Surgical/Medical Instruments
PA: Lantheus Holdings, Inc.
331 Treble Cove Rd
North Billerica MA 01862
978 671-8001

(G-13833)
LANTHEUS MI INTERMEDIATE INC
331 Treble Cove Rd (01862-2849)
PHONE..................................978 671-8001
Jeffrey Bailey, *President*
John K Bakewell, *CFO*
EMP: 519
SALES: 301.6MM **Privately Held**
SIC: 3841 2834 Medical Apparatus Pharmaceutical Preparations

(G-13834)
LENNARTZ ENTERPRISES LLC
Also Called: Palace Manufacturing Co
18 Esquire Rd (01862-2502)
PHONE..................................978 663-6100
Clayton Lennartz, *Marketing Mgr*
Marie Lennartz, *Mng Member*
George Kendall, *Executive*
EMP: 14
SALES: 1.7MM **Privately Held**
SIC: 3599 Mfg Industrial Machinery

(G-13835)
LEX-AIRE PRODUCTS INC
34 Sullivan Rd Ste 2 (01862-2000)
PHONE..................................978 663-7202
William H Copp, *President*
Elizabeth Copp, *Treasurer*
EMP: 3
SQ FT: 3,900
SALES (est): 475.1K **Privately Held**
SIC: 3563 Mfg Spray Painting Equip

(G-13836)
LOUIS C MORIN COMPANY INC
19 Sterling Rd Ste 4 (01862-2524)
PHONE..................................978 670-1222
Louis Morin, *President*
EMP: 14 **EST:** 1964
SALES (est): 2MM **Privately Held**
SIC: 3451 Mfg Screw Machine Products

(G-13837)
M C TEST SERVICE INC
Also Called: Mc Assembly
101 Billerica Ave Bldg 7 (01862-1256)
PHONE..................................781 218-7550
George Moore, *Branch Mgr*
EMP: 12
SALES (corp-wide): 216.1MM **Privately Held**
SIC: 3672 Mfg Printed Circuit Boards
HQ: M C Test Service, Inc.
425 North Dr
Melbourne FL 32934
321 253-0541

(G-13838)
MAGELLAN DIAGNOSTICS INC
101 Billerica Ave Ste 4-2 (01862-1268)
PHONE..................................978 856-2345
Amy Winslow, *President*
Norman Sheppard, *Vice Pres*
Janine Leblanc, *Finance*
Jennifer Zonderman, *Sales Staff*
Catherine Lufkin, *Marketing Staff*
EMP: 50
SQ FT: 23,000
SALES (est): 10.9MM
SALES (corp-wide): 201MM **Publicly Held**
SIC: 3826 8071 Mfg Analytical Instruments Medical Laboratory
HQ: Magellan Biosciences, Inc.
101 Billerica Ave Ste 4-2
North Billerica MA 01862
978 856-2345

(G-13839)
MASS VAC INC
Also Called: Mv Products Division
247 Rangeway Rd (01862-2017)
P.O. Box 359 (01862-0359)
PHONE..................................978 667-2393
Herbert R Gatti, *President*
David Rolph, *General Mgr*
Curt Paden, *Sales Staff*
EMP: 30
SQ FT: 13,100
SALES (est): 5.4MM **Privately Held**
WEB: www.massvac.com
SIC: 3563 7699 5084 3561 Mfg Air/Gas Compressors Repair Services Whol Industrial Equip Mfg Pumps/Pumping Equip

(G-13840)
MC ASSEMBLY INTERNATIONAL LLC
101 Billerica Ave Bldg 7 (01862-1256)
PHONE..................................781 729-1073
Ron Barilone, *Division Mgr*
EMP: 300
SALES (corp-wide): 216.1MM **Privately Held**
SIC: 3672 Mfg Printed Circuit Boards
HQ: Mc Assembly International, Llc
425 North Dr
Melbourne FL 32934

(G-13841)
MEDICAL-TECHNICAL GASES INC
Also Called: Med-Tech
8 Executive Park Dr (01862-1319)
PHONE..................................781 395-1946
Ramesh Kapur, *President*
EMP: 20
SQ FT: 15,000
SALES (est): 3.3MM **Privately Held**
WEB: www.medtechgases.com
SIC: 3841 Mfg Surgical/Medical Instruments

(G-13842)
MENICON AMERICA INC
76 Treble Cove Rd Ste 3 (01862-2232)
PHONE..................................781 609-2042
Scott J Orphanos, *President*
▲ **EMP:** 6
SALES (est): 1.2MM **Privately Held**
SIC: 3851 Mfg Ophthalmic Goods
PA: Menicon Co., Ltd.
3-21-19, Aoi, Naka-Ku
Nagoya AIC 460-0

(G-13843)
METROBLITY OPTICAL SYSTEMS INC
101 Billerica Ave Bldg 7 (01862-1256)
PHONE..................................781 255-5300
Alexander Saunders, *President*
James Baldwin, *Principal*
Robert Degan, *Chairman*
Peter Bennett, *Admin Sec*
▲ **EMP:** 58
SQ FT: 40,895
SALES: 11.7MM **Privately Held**
WEB: www.metrobility.com
SIC: 3577 Mfg Data Communication Equipment Specifically Connectivity Products For Local Wide And Metropolitan Area Networking Systems

(G-13844)
MFG ELECTRONICS INC
70 Treble Cove Rd Ste 1 (01862-2228)
PHONE..................................978 671-5490
Dennis Buchenholz, *President*
Dennis Bubhenholz, *President*
Jessica Bubhenholz, *Shareholder*
Michael Bubhenholz, *Shareholder*
EMP: 8
SALES (est): 1.4MM **Privately Held**
WEB: www.mfge.com
SIC: 3672 Mfg Printed Circuit Boards

(G-13845)
MICROWAVE CMPNENTS SPECIALISTS
Also Called: MCS
34 Sullivan Rd Ste 10 (01862-2000)
P.O. Box 138, Nutting Lake (01865-0138)
PHONE..................................978 667-1215
Berardo A Parisse Jr, *President*
Paula Parisse, *Clerk*
EMP: 12
SQ FT: 5,400
SALES (est): 1.1MM **Privately Held**
SIC: 3599 Machine Shop

(G-13846)
MIKES PRECISION MACHINE INC
14 Hadley St (01862-2605)
PHONE..................................978 667-9793
Mike Rosa, *President*
EMP: 7
SQ FT: 1,788
SALES (est): 945.7K **Privately Held**
SIC: 3599 Machine Shop

(G-13847)
MRSI SYSTEMS LLC
101 Billerica Ave Bldg 3 (01862-1270)
PHONE..................................978 667-9449
Michael Chalsen, *President*
Daniel Crowley, *Vice Pres*
Yi Qian, *Vice Pres*
Larry Faranda, *Engineer*
Manoj Walvekar, *Engineer*
EMP: 44
SQ FT: 41,000
SALES (est): 13.2MM
SALES (corp-wide): 398MM **Privately Held**
SIC: 3565 Operates As A Manufacturer Of Packaging Machinery Specializing In Turnkey Die Bonding And Dispensing Systems
PA: Mycronic Ab (Publ)
Nytorpsvagen 9
Taby 183 7
863 852-00

(G-13848)
MUNSEY SCREW MACHINE PRODUCTS
3 Executive Park Dr Ste 3 # 3 (01862-1347)
PHONE..................................978 667-4053
Kenneth Munsey, *President*
EMP: 5
SQ FT: 10,000
SALES (est): 528.8K **Privately Held**
SIC: 3451 Mfg Screw Machine Products

(G-13849)
NISSIN ION EQUIPMENT USA INC
34 Sullivan Rd (01862-2000)
PHONE..................................978 362-2590
EMP: 11 **Privately Held**
SIC: 3674 Mfg Semiconductors/Related Devices
HQ: Nissin Ion Equipment Usa, Inc.
8701 N Mopac Expy
Austin TX 78759
512 340-1423

(G-13850)
OMNI GLASS INC
Also Called: Omniglass
55 High St Ste 4 (01862-1637)
PHONE..................................978 667-6664
Donald Wilson, *President*
Kevin Reynolds, *Vice Pres*
EMP: 4
SQ FT: 3,200
SALES (est): 462.6K **Privately Held**
WEB: www.omniglass.net
SIC: 3229 3231 Mfg Pressed/Blown Glass Mfg Products-Purchased Glass

(G-13851)
P T P MACHINING INC
25 Sullivan Rd Ste 7 (01862-2020)
PHONE..................................800 872-3400
Peter Norton, *President*
EMP: 5
SQ FT: 2,000
SALES: 600K **Privately Held**
SIC: 3599 Machine Shop

(G-13852)
PACE INDUSTRIES LLC
Cambridge Division
67 Faulkner St (01862-1501)
PHONE..................................978 667-8400
William T Donovan, *Branch Mgr*
EMP: 244
SALES (corp-wide): 101.3MM **Privately Held**
SIC: 3363 3364 3365 3369 Mfg Aluminum Die-Casting Mfg Nonfrs Die-Castings Aluminum Foundry Nonferrous Metal Foundry
HQ: Pace Industries, Llc
481 S Shiloh Dr
Fayetteville AR 72704
479 443-1455

(G-13853)
PEAK SCIENTIFIC INC (DH)
19 Sterling Rd Ste 1 (01862-2524)
PHONE..................................866 647-1649
Robin Macgeachy, *President*
June Macgeachy, *Admin Sec*
EMP: 26
SALES: 5MM
SALES (corp-wide): 81.3MM **Privately Held**
SIC: 3621 Mfg Motors/Generators
HQ: Peak Scientific Instruments Limited
Unit 11 Fountain Crescent Inchinnan
Business Park
Renfrew PA4 9
141 812-8100

(G-13854)
PEAK SCIENTIFIC INSTRUMENTS
19 Sterling Rd Ste 5 (01862-2524)
PHONE..................................978 262-1384
Steven Macgeachy, *Vice Pres*
EMP: 36
SALES (est): 3.2MM
SALES (corp-wide): 81.3MM **Privately Held**
SIC: 3569 Mfg General Industrial Machinery
HQ: Peak Scientific Instruments Limited
Unit 11 Fountain Crescent Inchinnan
Business Park
Renfrew PA4 9
141 812-8100

(G-13855)
PERKINELMER HLTH SCIENCES INC
331 Treble Cove Rd (01862-2849)
PHONE..................................617 350-9024
Steve Humphrey, *Manager*
James Deberadinis, *Manager*
EMP: 40
SALES (corp-wide): 2.7B **Publicly Held**
SIC: 3826 Mfg Analytical Instruments
HQ: Perkinelmer Health Sciences, Inc.
940 Winter St
Waltham MA 02451
781 663-6900

(G-13856)
PLASTIC CONCEPTS INC
2 Sterling Rd Unit 2 # 2 (01862-2595)
P.O. Box 355, Billerica (01821-0355)
PHONE..................................978 663-7996
Michael Thompson, *President*
EMP: 20
SQ FT: 15,000
SALES: 2MM **Privately Held**
WEB: www.plastic-concepts.com
SIC: 3089 5162 Mfg Plastic Products Whol Plastic Materials/Shapes

(G-13857)
R F INTEGRATION INC (PA)
85 Rangeway Rd Ste 1 (01862-2105)
PHONE..................................978 654-6770
Patrick O'Sullivan, *President*
Ray Maroney, *Director*
EMP: 12
SQ FT: 3,200
SALES (est): 2MM **Privately Held**
WEB: www.rfintegration.com
SIC: 3674 Integrated Circuit Design For Wireless Communications

(G-13858)
RAYTHEON COMPANY
90 Salem Rd (01862-2700)
PHONE..................................978 313-0201
EMP: 3
SALES (corp-wide): 27B **Publicly Held**
SIC: 3812 3663 3761 Mfg Aerospace/Defense Products & Services
PA: Raytheon Company
870 Winter St
Waltham MA 02451
781 522-3000

(G-13859)
RD CONTRACTORS INC
Also Called: R D Fence Co
220 Boston Rd (01862-2309)
PHONE..................................978 667-6545
Richard Snydeman, *President*
William J Snydeman, *Treasurer*
EMP: 14
SQ FT: 2,200
SALES: 1.5MM **Privately Held**
SIC: 2499 5211 Mfg & Ret Wood Fences

(G-13860)
REA ASSOCIATES INC
325 Boston Rd (01862-2622)
PHONE..................................209 521-2727
Michael REA, *CEO*
EMP: 8 **EST:** 1962
SQ FT: 8,000
SALES (est): 1.1MM **Privately Held**
WEB: www.reaassociates.com
SIC: 3679 Mfg Microwave Components

(G-13861)
REE MACHINE WORKS INC
34 Sullivan Rd Ste 7 (01862-2000)
PHONE..................................978 663-9105
Mark Gordon, *President*
EMP: 7
SALES: 790K **Privately Held**
SIC: 3599 Mfg Industrial Machinery

(G-13862)
ROBERTSON-CHASE FIBERS LLC
16 Esquire Rd Ste 2 (01862-2528)
PHONE..................................978 453-2837
Elizabeth Perry, *Mng Member*
▲ **EMP:** 15
SQ FT: 30,000
SALES (est): 1.6MM **Privately Held**
WEB: www.classiceliteyarns.com
SIC: 2281 Yarn Spinning Mill

(G-13863)
SEMILAB USA LLC
101 Billerica Ave Bldg 5 (01862-1271)
PHONE..................................508 647-8400
Chris Moore, *CEO*
Han Chang, *General Mgr*
Amy Mueller, *Controller*
EMP: 19
SALES (corp-wide): 10.8MM **Privately Held**
SIC: 3826 Mfg Capital Equipment/Semiconductor Industry
PA: Semilab Usa Llc
10770 N 46th St Ste E700
Tampa FL 33617
813 977-2244

(G-13864)
SIGN EFFECTS INC
Also Called: Signeffects
29 High St (01862-2414)
PHONE..................................978 663-0787
David Demeo, *Manager*
EMP: 4 **Privately Held**
WEB: www.sign-effects.com
SIC: 3993 Mfg Signs/Advertising Specialties
PA: Sign Effects Inc
29 High St
North Billerica MA 01862

(G-13865)
SOFTWARE CONCEPTS INC
3 Survey Cir Ste 2 (01862-2149)
PHONE..................................978 584-0400
Stephen L Cataldo, *President*
Robert M Dicicco, *Treasurer*
Mitzi Dicicco, *Mktg Coord*
Joe Aucone, *Prgrmr*
Joseph Aucone, *Shareholder*
EMP: 10
SQ FT: 4,600
SALES (est): 1MM **Privately Held**
WEB: www.sci400.com
SIC: 7372 Prepackaged Software Services

(G-13866)
SPECIALIZED COATING SERVICES
16 Esquire Rd Unit A (01862-2527)
PHONE..................................978 362-0346
Jim Carr, *General Mgr*
EMP: 3
SALES (est): 209.7K **Privately Held**
SIC: 3471 Plating/Polishing Service

(G-13867)
SRS MEDICAL CORP
76 Treble Cove Rd Ste 3 (01862-2232)
PHONE..................................978 663-2800
EMP: 8 **Privately Held**
SIC: 3841 Mfg Surgical/Medical Instruments
HQ: Srs Medical Corp.
8672p 154th Ave Ne
Redmond WA 98052
425 882-1101

(G-13868)
SRS MEDICAL SYSTEMS INC (PA)
76 Treble Cove Rd Ste 3 (01862-2232)
PHONE..................................978 663-2800
Lee Brody, *CEO*
Kevin M Connolly, *President*
David Mahoney, *Vice Pres*
Carolyn Evans, *Administration*
◆ **EMP:** 28
SQ FT: 12,500
SALES (est): 6.7MM **Privately Held**
SIC: 3841 Mfg Surgical/Medical Instruments

(G-13869)
STANDEX INTERNATIONAL CORP
Spincraft Division
500 Iron Horse Park (01862-1617)
PHONE..................................978 667-2771
Rick Paul, *President*
Len Paolillo, *Vice Pres*
Debra Chaplin, *Materials Mgr*
Jonathan Silva, *Engineer*
Joseph Juliano, *Controller*
EMP: 55
SALES (corp-wide): 791.5MM **Publicly Held**
SIC: 3599 7692 3469 3444 Mfg Industrial Machinery Welding Repair Mfg Metal Stampings Mfg Sheet Metalwork Structural Metal Fabrctn
PA: Standex International Corporation
11 Keewaydin Dr Ste 300
Salem NH 03079
603 893-9701

(G-13870)
STATIC CLEAN INTERNATIONAL
267 Boston Rd Ste 8 (01862-2310)
PHONE..................................781 229-7799
Jim Patterson, *President*
Chuck Dignan, *Opers Mgr*
Karen Patterson, *Treasurer*
Chuck Dufner, *Executive*
▲ **EMP:** 10
SQ FT: 3,000
SALES (est): 2.3MM **Privately Held**
WEB: www.staticclean.com
SIC: 3699 5065 Mfg Electrical Equipment/Supplies Whol Electronic Parts/Equipment

(G-13871)
TEVTECH LLC
100 Billerica Ave (01862-1234)
PHONE..................................978 667-4557
Alex Teverovsky, *Mng Member*
John Decosta,
Jim McDonald,
EMP: 13
SQ FT: 15,000
SALES (est): 3.4MM **Privately Held**
WEB: www.tevtechllc.com
SIC: 3567 Mfg Industrial Furnaces/Ovens

(G-13872)
THERAGENICS CORPORATION
19 Sterling Rd Ste 4 (01862-2524)
PHONE..................................978 528-4307
David Evans, *Controller*
EMP: 3
SALES (corp-wide): 93.9MM **Privately Held**
SIC: 2834 Pharmaceutical Preparations
HQ: Theragenics Corporation
5203 Bristol Indus Way
Buford GA 30518
770 271-0233

(G-13873)
TRANS-MATE LLC
13 Sterling Rd (01862-2518)
PHONE..................................800 867-9274
Steven Stockman, *President*
EMP: 20
SQ FT: 40,000
SALES (est): 6.9MM
SALES (corp-wide): 166MM **Privately Held**
WEB: www.trans-mate.com
SIC: 2999 2841 Manufactures Petroleum/Coal Products Soap/Other Detergents
HQ: Niteo Products, Llc
5949 Sherry Ln Ste 540
Dallas TX 75225
214 245-5000

(G-13874)
TRANSITION AUTOMATION INC
101 Billerica Ave Bldg 5 (01862-1271)
PHONE..................................978 670-5500
Mark Curtin, *President*
EMP: 12
SQ FT: 8,500
SALES: 2.8MM **Privately Held**
WEB: www.transitionautomation.com
SIC: 3555 Mfg Of Screen Printing Equipment

(G-13875)
URSA NAVIGATION SOLUTIONS INC
Also Called: Ursanav
85 Rangeway Rd Ste 110 (01862-2141)
PHONE..................................781 538-5299
Charles Schue, *CEO*
Stephen Bartlett, *Vice Pres*
EMP: 8
SQ FT: 9,300
SALES (est): 985.4K **Privately Held**
SIC: 3812 Mfg Search/Navigation Equipment

(G-13876)
WELFAB INC
100 Rangeway Rd (01862-2133)
PHONE..................................978 667-0180
Bruce Martin, *President*
Bonnie Martin, *Treasurer*
EMP: 35
SQ FT: 33,000
SALES (est): 8.7MM **Privately Held**
WEB: www.welfab.com
SIC: 3441 7692 3444 Structural Metal Fabrication Welding Repair Mfg Sheet Metalwork

(G-13877)
WILLIAM CLEMENTS
Also Called: William Clements Boatbuilder
18 Mount Pleasant St (01862-1212)
P.O. Box 87 (01862-0087)
PHONE..................................978 663-3103
William Clements, *Owner*
EMP: 6

GEOGRAPHIC

SALES (est): 387.6K **Privately Held**
WEB: www.boatbldr.com
SIC: 3732 Boatbuilding/Repairing

(G-13878)
WOODWORKING MACHINERY SERVICES
11 Esquire Rd Ste 2 (01862-2523)
P.O. Box 465, Wilmington (01887-0465)
PHONE..................................978 663-8488
Michael R Kane, *President*
Frank J Aiesi, *Vice Pres*
EMP: 3
SQ FT: 1,500
SALES (est): 457.9K **Privately Held**
SIC: 3553 7699 Mfg Woodworking Machinery Repair Services

(G-13879)
WORLD SLEEP PRODUCTS INC
Also Called: Englander
12 Esquire Rd (01862-2502)
P.O. Box 2126, Corsicana TX (75151-2126)
PHONE..................................978 667-6648
Charles Warshaver, *President*
Hugh Oxnard, *Vice Pres*
Mark Savel, *Vice Pres*
▼ **EMP:** 75
SQ FT: 1,000
SALES (est): 6.6MM **Privately Held**
WEB: www.worldsleepproducts.com
SIC: 2515 Mfg Mattresses/Bedsprings

North Brookfield
Worcester County

(G-13880)
FT SMITH TRCKG & EXCVTG INC
Also Called: F T Smith Sand & Gravel
53 Brooks Pond Rd (01535-2201)
P.O. Box 333 (01535-0333)
PHONE..................................508 867-0400
Frederick T Smith III, *President*
EMP: 3
SQ FT: 300
SALES (est): 485.8K **Privately Held**
SIC: 1442 Construction Sand/Gravel

(G-13881)
HD BENNETT MACHINE CO INC
3 Crooks Cross Rd (01535)
PHONE..................................508 867-0154
Hudson Bennett, *President*
Jessica Bennett, *Vice Pres*
EMP: 6
SALES: 450K **Privately Held**
SIC: 3469 Mfg Metal Stampings

(G-13882)
TECHNO BLOC
70 E Brookfield Rd (01535-1712)
PHONE..................................774 449-8400
EMP: 5 **EST:** 2011
SALES (est): 457.6K **Privately Held**
SIC: 3291 Mfg Abrasive Products

(G-13883)
VIBRAM CORPORATION (DH)
18 School St (01535-1937)
PHONE..................................508 867-6494
Kevin Donahue, *Ch of Bd*
Eric A Rosen, *President*
Dan Hibbard, *Engineer*
Craig Bibeau, *Manager*
James M Barkoskie, *Admin Sec*
▲ **EMP:** 238 **EST:** 1916
SQ FT: 33,000
SALES (est): 35MM
SALES (corp-wide): 160.3MM **Privately Held**
WEB: www.vibram.com
SIC: 3069 5087 Mfg Fabrcatd Rubber Prdt Whol Svc Estblshmt Equip
HQ: Vibram Corporation
9 Damonmill Sq Fl 2
Concord MA 01742
978 318-0000

North Chelmsford
Middlesex County

(G-13884)
AMICUS HLTHCARE LVING CTRS LLC
2 Technology Dr (01863-2400)
PHONE..................................978 934-0000
Jerimiah Terrant, *President*
EMP: 50
SALES (corp-wide): 15MM **Privately Held**
SIC: 3674 8051 8052 Mfg Semiconductors/Related Devices Skilled Nursing Care Facility Intermediate Care Facility
PA: Amicus Healthcare Living Centers Llc
133 Blakely Rd Ste 211
Colchester VT 05446
802 658-5250

(G-13885)
BARE BONES SOFTWARE INC
73 Princeton St Ste 206 (01863-1581)
PHONE..................................978 251-0500
Richard M Siegel, *President*
Patrick Woolsey, *COO*
Vicky Wong, *Sales Staff*
EMP: 10
SQ FT: 1,200
SALES (est): 969.5K **Privately Held**
WEB: www.barebones.com
SIC: 7372 Prepackaged Software Services

(G-13886)
BOOK-MART PRESS INC
15 Wellman Ave (01863-1334)
PHONE..................................978 251-6000
Gary S Gluckow, *President*
Michelle S Gluckow, *Vice Pres*
Harriette Gluckow, *Treasurer*
EMP: 95
SQ FT: 80,000
SALES (est): 7.3MM **Privately Held**
SIC: 2732 Book Printing

(G-13887)
COURIER COMMUNICATIONS LLC (HQ)
Also Called: Raven Ventures LLC
15 Wellman Ave (01863-1334)
PHONE..................................978 251-6000
Anthony F Caruso, *Vice Pres*
Peter Clifford, *Vice Pres*
Steve Franzino, *Vice Pres*
Yvonne Hurlbutt, *Vice Pres*
Shannon Ryson, *Vice Pres*
EMP: 13
SALES (est): 108.6MM
SALES (corp-wide): 3.8B **Publicly Held**
SIC: 2731 Book Manufacturer & Content Management
PA: Lsc Communications, Inc.
191 N Wacker Dr Ste 1400
Chicago IL 60606
773 272-9200

(G-13888)
COURIER COMPANIES INC (PA)
15 Wellman Ave (01863-1334)
PHONE..................................978 251-6000
James F Conway III, *Ch of Bd*
Joseph Brennan, *President*
Justin Shawn, *President*
Peter D Tobin, *Exec VP*
Clarence Strowbridge, *Vice Pres*
EMP: 20
SQ FT: 65,000
SALES (est): 2.5MM **Privately Held**
WEB: www.couriercompanies.com
SIC: 2732 5192 Book Printing Whol Books/Newspapers

(G-13889)
COURIER INTL HOLDINGS LLC
15 Wellman Ave (01863-1334)
PHONE..................................978 251-6000
EMP: 3
SALES (est): 67.9K
SALES (corp-wide): 6.8B **Publicly Held**
SIC: 2732 Book Printing
PA: R. R. Donnelley & Sons Company
35 W Wacker Dr
Chicago IL 60601
312 326-8000

(G-13890)
COURIER NEW MEDIA INC (DH)
Also Called: Courier Epic
15 Wellman Ave (01863-1334)
PHONE..................................978 251-3945
James F Conway III, *President*
William Topaz, *Vice Pres*
Robert P Story Jr, *Treasurer*
Lee Cochrane, *Asst Treas*
Mary Gail Mc Carthy, *Admin Sec*
EMP: 21
SALES (est): 6.7MM
SALES (corp-wide): 3.8B **Publicly Held**
SIC: 2731 2732 Books-Publishing/Printing Book Printing
HQ: Courier Communications Llc
15 Wellman Ave
North Chelmsford MA 01863
978 251-6000

(G-13891)
COURTSMART DIGITAL SYSTEMS INC
51 Middlesex St Unit 128 (01863-1566)
PHONE..................................978 251-3300
Andrew Treinis, *President*
Nelson Reis, *Technology*
EMP: 32
SALES (est): 9MM **Privately Held**
SIC: 3663 3651 3679 3669 Mfg Radio/Tv Comm Equip Mfg Home Audio/Video Eqp

(G-13892)
DATA PLUS INCORPORATED
55 Middlesex St Unit 219 (01863-1570)
PHONE..................................978 888-6300
Bruce Bensetler, *President*
EMP: 10
SQ FT: 3,282
SALES (est): 1.3MM **Privately Held**
WEB: www.dphs.com
SIC: 7372 Prepackaged Software Srvcs

(G-13893)
ESKILL CORPORATION
7 Technology Dr Ste 101 (01863-2441)
PHONE..................................978 649-8010
Eric Friedman, *CEO*
Rj Nichols, *Partner*
EMP: 15
SQ FT: 1,000
SALES (est): 1.5MM **Privately Held**
WEB: www.eskill.com
SIC: 7372 Prepackaged Software Services

(G-13894)
EXETER ANALYTICAL INC (PA)
7 Doris Dr Ste 6a (01863-1237)
PHONE..................................978 251-1411
Paul Brockman, *President*
Leslie Beauregard, *Office Mgr*
▲ **EMP:** 12
SQ FT: 2,500
SALES (est): 1.2MM **Privately Held**
WEB: www.eai1.com
SIC: 3821 Mfg Lab Apparatus/Furniture

(G-13895)
HARDRIC LABORATORIES INC
55 Middlesex St (01863-1569)
P.O. Box 129 (01863-0129)
PHONE..................................978 251-1702
Richard Charbonnier, *President*
Peter N Richard, *Admin Sec*
EMP: 38
SQ FT: 19,435
SALES (est): 8.3MM **Privately Held**
WEB: www.hardric.com
SIC: 3827 3728 3699 3231 Mfg Optical Instr/Lens Mfg Aircraft Parts/Equip Mfg Elec Mach/Equip/Supp Mfg Prdt-Purchased Glass

(G-13896)
IBC COMMUNICATIONS INC
6 Stonehill Rd (01863-1010)
PHONE..................................978 455-9692
EMP: 3
SALES (est): 163.3K **Privately Held**
WEB: www.choiceswireless.com
SIC: 3669 Mfg Communications Equipment

(G-13897)
IMPERIAL IMAGE INC
55 Middlesex St (01863-1569)
PHONE..................................978 251-0420
Deborah Boivin, *CEO*
Anthony Demarco, *President*
Cindi Page, *Executive*
EMP: 11
SQ FT: 10,000
SALES (est): 2.1MM **Privately Held**
WEB: www.imperial-image.com
SIC: 2752 2759 Lithographic Commercial Printing Commercial Printing

(G-13898)
JR GRADY COMPANY LLC
63 Middlesex St Ste 7 (01863-1584)
PHONE..................................978 458-3662
John Raymond, *Principal*
EMP: 5
SALES: 500K **Privately Held**
SIC: 3535 Mfg Conveyors/Equipment

(G-13899)
KELLER PRODUCTS INC
180 Middlesex St (01863-2060)
PHONE..................................978 264-1911
Richard Strauss, *President*
Jonathan Strauss, *Vice Pres*
EMP: 10
SQ FT: 3,500
SALES: 1.5MM **Privately Held**
WEB: www.kellerfilters.com
SIC: 3589 Mfr Water Filters & Oil/Water Separators

(G-13900)
LE MASURIER GRANITE QUARRY
Ledge Rd (01863)
P.O. Box 71 (01863-0071)
PHONE..................................978 251-3841
John L Le Masurier, *President*
EMP: 3 **EST:** 1944
SQ FT: 3,000
SALES (est): 349.1K **Privately Held**
SIC: 1411 Granite Quarry

(G-13901)
LINEAR TECHNOLOGY LLC
15 Research Pl (01863-2412)
PHONE..................................978 656-4750
Steven Martin, *Design Engr*
Joseph Silk, *Branch Mgr*
Brian Shaffer, *Technology*
EMP: 7
SQ FT: 29,856
SALES (corp-wide): 5.9B **Publicly Held**
SIC: 3674 Mfg Semiconductors/Related Devices
HQ: Linear Technology Llc
1630 Mccarthy Blvd
Milpitas CA 95035
408 432-1900

(G-13902)
LSC COMMUNICATIONS INC
Also Called: North Chelmsford Digital
15 Wellman Ave (01863-1334)
PHONE..................................978 251-6000
Kathy Baker, *Purch Mgr*
Faaez Khateeb, *Engineer*
Douglas Toler, *Supervisor*
EMP: 67
SALES (corp-wide): 3.8B **Publicly Held**
SIC: 2732 Print And Office Products
PA: Lsc Communications, Inc.
191 N Wacker Dr Ste 1400
Chicago IL 60606
773 272-9200

(G-13903)
MAXIM INTEGRATED PRODUCTS INC
8 Technology Dr (01863-2400)
PHONE..................................978 934-7600
Monica Gilbert, *Principal*
EMP: 528

SALES (corp-wide): 2.3B **Publicly Held**
WEB: www.maxim-ic.com
SIC: 3674 Mfg Semiconductors/Related Devices
PA: Maxim Integrated Products, Inc.
160 Rio Robles
San Jose CA 95134
408 601-1000

(G-13904)
METAL FISH LLC
100 Wotton St (01863-1336)
PHONE..................................978 930-0637
William Shambley, *President*
EMP: 3
SALES (est): 234.7K **Privately Held**
SIC: 3599 Mfg Industrial Machinery

(G-13905)
NONWOVENS INC
100 Wotton St (01863-1336)
P.O. Box 921 (01863-0921)
PHONE..................................978 251-8612
Clifford E Dallmeyer, *President*
Brian Dallmeyer, *Vice Pres*
Margo A Dallmeyer, *Vice Pres*
▲ **EMP:** 16
SQ FT: 160,000
SALES: 2MM **Privately Held**
WEB: www.nonwovens.com
SIC: 2297 Mfg Nonwoven Fabrics

(G-13906)
P A G INDUSTRIES INC
70 Princeton St Ste 2 (01863-1577)
PHONE..................................978 265-5610
Paul A Gurski, *President*
Mary Cathleen Pantanella, *Vice Pres*
EMP: 10
SALES (est): 1.5MM **Privately Held**
WEB: www.pagind.com
SIC: 3432 Mfg Plumbing Fixture Fittings

(G-13907)
PICKEN PRINTING INC
10 Middlesex St (01863-1783)
P.O. Box 909 (01863-0909)
PHONE..................................978 251-0730
Peter Picken, *President*
Lewel Picken, *Clerk*
EMP: 24 **EST:** 1918
SQ FT: 5,000
SALES (est): 2.8MM **Privately Held**
SIC: 2752 2791 2789 Lithographic Commercial Printing Typesetting Services Bookbinding/Related Work

(G-13908)
PLASTIC DESIGN INC
180 Middlesex St Ste 2 (01863-2060)
PHONE..................................978 251-4830
Errol Flynn, *President*
Daryl Flynn, *Co-President*
Kurt Flynn, *Co-President*
Bob Payne, *Plant Mgr*
Marilyn Flynn, *Treasurer*
EMP: 30 **EST:** 1977
SQ FT: 23,000
SALES: 6.1MM **Privately Held**
WEB: www.plasticdesigninc.com
SIC: 2821 5162 Mfg Plastic Materials/Resins Whol Plastic Materials/Shapes

(G-13909)
ROBERTS PROTOTYPE MACHINING
108 Middlesex St Ste 12 (01863-2047)
PHONE..................................978 251-4200
Raymond Roberts, *Owner*
EMP: 5
SALES (est): 313.1K **Privately Held**
SIC: 3599 Mfg Industrial Machinery

(G-13910)
SCIENTIFIC SOLUTIONS INC
55 Middlesex St Unit 210 (01863-1570)
PHONE..................................978 251-4554
John Noto, *President*
Steven Berg, *President*
EMP: 10
SALES (est): 1.6MM **Privately Held**
WEB: www.sci-sol.com
SIC: 3827 8731 Mfg Optical Instruments/Lenses Commercial Physical Research

(G-13911)
TECHLAW INC
7 Technology Dr Ste 202 (01863-2441)
PHONE..................................617 918-8612
EMP: 4
SALES (corp-wide): 36.2MM **Privately Held**
SIC: 3812 Search And Navigation Equipment, Nsk
HQ: Techlaw, Inc.
14500 Avion Pkwy Ste 300
Chantilly VA 20151
703 818-1000

(G-13912)
VELOXITY ONE LLC
51 Middlesex St Unit 110 (01863-1566)
PHONE..................................855 844-5060
Krassimir Popov, *CEO*
Latchezar Popov, *CFO*
EMP: 3 **EST:** 2014
SQ FT: 6,500
SALES (est): 374K **Privately Held**
SIC: 3571 Electronic Computers

(G-13913)
WELCH WELDING AND TRCK EQP INC
Also Called: Welch Welding and Truck Eqp
164 Middlesex St (01863-2028)
PHONE..................................978 251-8726
Bradford Welch, *President*
EMP: 20
SQ FT: 6,000
SALES (est): 2.3MM **Privately Held**
WEB: www.hitchconnection.com
SIC: 7692 3446 3444 Welding Repair Truck Accessories

(G-13914)
WELCH WELDING INC
162 Middlesex St (01863)
PHONE..................................978 251-8726
Richard Welch, *Principal*
EMP: 4
SALES (est): 187.7K **Privately Held**
SIC: 7692 Welding Repair

North Dartmouth
Bristol County

(G-13915)
A & A JEWELERS INC
279 State Rd (02747-4322)
PHONE..................................508 992-5320
Alexander Nasrawi, *President*
Mandy Burgo, *Office Mgr*
▲ **EMP:** 7
SALES (est): 397.2K **Privately Held**
SIC: 3911 7631 Mfg & Repairs Jewelry

(G-13916)
CAPE COD CUPOLA CO INC
78 State Rd (02747-2922)
PHONE..................................508 994-2119
John E Bernier Jr, *President*
EMP: 6 **EST:** 1939
SQ FT: 2,100
SALES (est): 935.3K **Privately Held**
WEB: www.capecodcupola.com
SIC: 2431 3443 3599 Mfg Millwork Mfg Fabricated Plate Wrk Mfg Industrial Machinery Whol Durable Goods

(G-13917)
CLARIS VISION LLC
51 State Rd (02747-3319)
PHONE..................................508 994-1400
Marcello Celentano, *CEO*
Beth Baker, *Ophthalmology*
Paul Jandron, *Software Engr*
EMP: 7 **EST:** 2015
SALES (est): 137.2K **Privately Held**
SIC: 3851 Mfg Ophthalmic Goods

(G-13918)
DEN MAR CORPORATION
1005 Reed Rd (02747-1567)
PHONE..................................508 999-3295
Henry Martin Jr, *President*
EMP: 17 **EST:** 1971
SQ FT: 56,000
SALES (est): 3.5MM **Privately Held**
SIC: 3589 Mfg Service Industry Machinery

(G-13919)
EAST COAST INTERIORS INC
4 Ledgewood Blvd (02747-1229)
PHONE..................................508 995-4200
David Boswell, *President*
Raymond Silva, *Opers Mgr*
Carol Silveira, *Office Admin*
EMP: 18
SQ FT: 15,000
SALES: 1.2MM **Privately Held**
SIC: 2431 Mfg Millwork

(G-13920)
GASPARS SAUSAGE CO INC
384 Faunce Corner Rd (02747-1257)
PHONE..................................508 998-2012
Charles R Gaspar, *President*
Robert A Gaspar, *Vice Pres*
Tobias A Gaspar, *Treasurer*
▲ **EMP:** 47
SQ FT: 34,000
SALES (est): 7.4MM **Privately Held**
WEB: www.gasparssausage.com
SIC: 2013 Mfg Prepared Meats

(G-13921)
GINSCO INC
Also Called: New York Bagel Co
272 State Rd (02747-4312)
PHONE..................................508 990-3350
Steve Ginsberg, *Owner*
EMP: 10
SALES (est): 728.5K
SALES (corp-wide): 3.6MM **Privately Held**
SIC: 2051 Mfg Bread/Related Products
PA: Ginsco Inc
1706 President Ave
Fall River MA 02720
508 677-4767

(G-13922)
JC CLOCKS COMPANY INC
9 Ventura Dr (02747-1244)
PHONE..................................508 998-8442
Emanuel Correia, *President*
EMP: 21
SQ FT: 9,000
SALES (est): 2.2MM **Privately Held**
SIC: 2434 2431 2521 Mfg Wood Kitchen Cabinet Mfg Millwork Mfg Wood Office Furn

(G-13923)
JOSEPH K DELANO SAWMILL INC
158 Cross Rd (02747-1902)
PHONE..................................508 994-8752
John Delano, *President*
EMP: 3
SALES: 200K **Privately Held**
SIC: 2421 Sawmill/Planing Mill

(G-13924)
MARBUO INC
Also Called: Minuteman Press
634 State Rd Unit E2 (02747-1818)
PHONE..................................508 994-7700
William P Martin, *President*
EMP: 6
SALES (est): 543.9K **Privately Held**
SIC: 2752 Comm Prtg Litho

(G-13925)
SIVS OIL INC
197 State Rd (02747-2649)
PHONE..................................508 951-0528
Paul S Dias, *President*
EMP: 3
SALES (est): 406.6K **Privately Held**
SIC: 1382 Oil/Gas Exploration Services

(G-13926)
STATE ROAD CEMENT BLOCK CO
656 State Rd (02747-1894)
PHONE..................................508 993-9473
Richard Bono, *President*
Paul Bono, *Vice Pres*
EMP: 8 **EST:** 1947
SQ FT: 3,500
SALES (est): 1.4MM **Privately Held**
WEB: www.stateroadcement.com
SIC: 3271 5032 Mfg Concrete Block/Brick Whol Brick/Stone Material

(G-13927)
STEELE & ROWE INC
190 Chase Rd (02747-1004)
PHONE..................................508 993-6413
Robery Steele, *President*
Emily Steele, *Vice Pres*
EMP: 3 **EST:** 1962
SQ FT: 1,500
SALES (est): 272.1K **Privately Held**
SIC: 2394 Mfg Canvas/Related Products

(G-13928)
TRINITY PRESS INC
199 Pine Island Rd (02747-1322)
PHONE..................................508 998-1072
George S Bailey, *President*
Michael Kehoe, *Corp Secy*
EMP: 5
SQ FT: 5,000
SALES: 645K **Privately Held**
WEB: www.trinitypressinc.com
SIC: 2752 Lithographic Commercial Printing

North Dighton
Bristol County

(G-13929)
AVILA TEXTILES INC
620 Spring St (02764-1363)
P.O. Box 897 (02764-0881)
PHONE..................................508 828-5882
Manuel Avila, *President*
◆ **EMP:** 7
SQ FT: 24,000
SALES (est): 900K **Privately Held**
SIC: 2241 Narrow Fabric Mill

(G-13930)
BOSTON SASH & MILLWORK INC
667 Spring St (02764-1359)
P.O. Box 345 (02764-0345)
PHONE..................................508 880-8808
Robert A Raimondi Jr, *President*
Liz Harrington, *CFO*
EMP: 17
SQ FT: 24,200
SALES (est): 2.2MM **Privately Held**
SIC: 2431 Whol Lumber/Plywood/Millwork

(G-13931)
GILTRON INC
620 Spring St 90-1 (02764-1363)
P.O. Box 914 (02764-0881)
PHONE..................................508 359-4310
A Stanley Pittman, *President*
Stanley Pittman, *President*
Alfred S Pittman Jr, *Vice Pres*
EMP: 6 **EST:** 1951
SQ FT: 9,500
SALES (est): 910.3K **Privately Held**
WEB: www.giltron.com
SIC: 3545 7699 5063 5084 Mfg Induction Heating Equipment & Designs & Make Tools & Accessories For Such Equipment

(G-13932)
INTEPLAST GROUP CORPORATION
Also Called: Ibs - Interplast Group
455 Somerset Ave (02764-1811)
P.O. Box 562, Swansea (02777-0562)
PHONE..................................508 880-7640
EMP: 17 **Privately Held**
SIC: 3081 Whol Nondurable Goods
PA: Inteplast Group Corporation
9 Peach Tree Hill Rd
Livingston NJ 07039

(G-13933)
PRECAST VAULT CO INC
Also Called: Lee Burial Vaults
131 Autumn St (02764-1379)
PHONE..................................508 252-4886
Mark Riccardi, *Branch Mgr*
EMP: 5

SALES (corp-wide): 700K **Privately Held**
SIC: 3272 Mfg Concrete Products
PA: Precast Vault Co Inc
131 Adams St
Braintree MA 02184
508 252-4886

(G-13934)
PRECISION IMAGES INC
620 Spring St (02764-1363)
PHONE..................................508 824-6200
Laureen A Therriault, *President*
EMP: 6
SALES (est): 542.8K **Privately Held**
SIC: 2759 Commercial Printing

(G-13935)
PRYSMIAN CBLES SYSTEMS USA LLC
Also Called: Draka Cableteq
22 Joseph Warner Blvd (02764)
PHONE..................................508 822-5444
EMP: 213 **Privately Held**
SIC: 3357 Nonferrous Wiredrawing/Insulating
HQ: Prysmian Cables And Systems Usa, Llc
4 Tesseneer Dr
Highland Heights KY 41076
859 572-8000

(G-13936)
PRYSMIAN CBLES SYSTEMS USA LLC
Also Called: Draka Cableteq USA
20 Joseph E Warner Blvd (02764-1300)
PHONE..................................508 822-5444
▲ **EMP:** 5 **Privately Held**
SIC: 3315 Mfg Steel Wire/Related Products
HQ: Prysmian Cables And Systems Usa, Llc
4 Tesseneer Dr
Highland Heights KY 41076
859 572-8000

(G-13937)
TAUNTON STOVE COMPANY INC
Also Called: Tasco Engineering
490 Somerset Ave Ste 490 # 490
(02764-1810)
P.O. Box 198 (02764-0198)
PHONE..................................508 823-0786
Clifford Bodge, *President*
Bruce Bodge, *Vice Pres*
Barbara Bodge, *Shareholder*
John F Brady, *Clerk*
▲ **EMP:** 34 **EST:** 1950
SQ FT: 27,000
SALES (est): 6.4MM **Privately Held**
WEB: www.tauntonstove.com
SIC: 3444 3599 3631 3429 Mfg Sheet Metalwork Mfg Industrial Machinery Mfg Household Cook Equip Mfg Hardware

(G-13938)
WORLD PUBLICATIONS INC
455 Somerset Ave (02764-1811)
PHONE..................................508 880-5555
Jeffrey M Press, *President*
Gail Press, *President*
EMP: 4
SALES (est): 359.8K **Privately Held**
SIC: 2741 Misc Publishing

(G-13939)
ZATEC LLC
620 Spring St (02764-1363)
P.O. Box 588 (02764-0588)
PHONE..................................508 880-3388
Michael Gobeille, *Technical Staff*
Charles Bruckman,
Jennifer Lyle, *Admin Asst*
▲ **EMP:** 50
SQ FT: 35,000
SALES (est): 7.9MM **Privately Held**
WEB: www.zatecinc.com
SIC: 3081 Mfg Unsupported Plastic Film/Sheet

North Easton
Bristol County

(G-13940)
AKA MCHLNGELO STRBUILDER LLC
31 Randall St (02356-2236)
PHONE..................................508 238-9054
Joshua P Jacobs, *Owner*
Jacobs Mary, *VP Sales*
EMP: 150
SALES (est): 7.6MM **Privately Held**
WEB: www.akastairs.com
SIC: 2431 Mfg Millwork

(G-13941)
AMERICAN HEALTH RESOURCES INC
28 Hillington Dr (02356-2652)
PHONE..................................508 588-7700
EMP: 4
SALES (est): 376.7K **Privately Held**
SIC: 2761 8099 Mfg Manifold Business Forms Health/Allied Services

(G-13942)
BALAJI INTERNATIONAL INC
2 Oak Leaf Ln (02356-3629)
PHONE..................................508 472-1953
Raj Gupta, *President*
EMP: 3
SALES (est): 467.7K **Privately Held**
SIC: 3826 Mfg Analytical Instruments

(G-13943)
BENSON ENTERPRISES INC
87 Union St (02356-1013)
PHONE..................................508 583-5401
Wayne E Benson, *President*
Wayne Benson, *President*
EMP: 11
SALES (est): 1.9MM **Privately Held**
WEB: www.bensonent.com
SIC: 3272 1711 1794 Mfg Septic Tanks & Pre Cast Manholes Installs Septic Tanks & Cesspools And Excavation Contractor

(G-13944)
BEON HOME INC
8 Barberry Ln (02356-3614)
PHONE..................................617 600-8329
Alexei Erchak, *CEO*
Arvind Baliga, *COO*
Martin Forest, *Research*
EMP: 6
SQ FT: 1,200
SALES: 200K **Privately Held**
SIC: 3699 3229 Mfg Electrical Equipment/Supplies Mfg Pressed/Blown Glass

(G-13945)
GERALD F DALTON & SONS INC
51 Rockland St (02356-2501)
PHONE..................................508 238-5374
Gerald F Dalton, *President*
EMP: 3 **EST:** 2001
SALES (est): 261.2K **Privately Held**
SIC: 3444 Mfg Sheet Metalwork

(G-13946)
GRAYSTONE LIMITED LLC (PA)
Also Called: Bluewater Farms
50 Oliver St Ste 102 (02356-1467)
P.O. Box 402 (02356-0402)
PHONE..................................855 356-1027
Scott Simmons, *VP Sales*
Michael Dubuc,
Craig Canning,
Brendan Moquin,
EMP: 4
SQ FT: 1,200
SALES: 8MM **Privately Held**
SIC: 2033 Mfg Canned Fruits/Vegetables

(G-13947)
HILLIARDS HOUSE CANDY INC (PA)
316 Main St (02356-1107)
PHONE..................................508 238-6231
Charles McCarthy, *President*
Judith McCarthy, *Treasurer*
EMP: 60
SQ FT: 8,500
SALES (est): 8.3MM **Privately Held**
WEB: www.hilliardscandy.com
SIC: 2064 5441 5451 2066 Mfg Candy/Confectionery Ret Candy/Confectionery Ret Dairy Products Mfg Chocolate/Cocoa Prdt

(G-13948)
J-A INDUSTRIES INCORPORATED
6 Eleanore Strasse (02356-2687)
PHONE..................................508 297-1648
Christine Vella, *President*
EMP: 3
SQ FT: 4,500
SALES (est): 348K **Privately Held**
SIC: 3339 5013 7533 Primary Nonferrous Metal Producer Whol Auto Parts/Supplies Auto Exhaust Repair

(G-13949)
NEWSTAMP LIGHTING CORP
Also Called: Newstamp Lighting Co
227 Bay Rd (02356-2673)
P.O. Box 189 (02356-0189)
PHONE..................................508 238-7073
Sandra Zeitsiff, *President*
EMP: 10
SQ FT: 17,000
SALES (est): 3.1MM **Privately Held**
WEB: www.newstamplighting.com
SIC: 3645 3646 3494 3444 Mfg Residentl Light Fixt Mfg Coml Light Fixtures Mfg Valves/Pipe Fittings Mfg Sheet Metalwork Mfg Hardware

(G-13950)
NORTH EASTON COMPANIES INC
23 Wedgewood Dr (02356-1356)
PHONE..................................774 259-0172
Alex Daigneault, *President*
EMP: 3
SALES: 950K **Privately Held**
SIC: 3451 Mfg Screw Machine Products

(G-13951)
NORTH EASTON MACHINE CO INC
218 Elm St (02356-1115)
P.O. Box 178 (02356-0178)
PHONE..................................508 238-6219
Jon Holbrook, *President*
Lillian Holbrook, *Treasurer*
EMP: 18
SQ FT: 15,000
SALES (est): 4MM **Privately Held**
WEB: www.northeastonmachine.com
SIC: 3451 Mfg Screw Machine Products

(G-13952)
SLUSH CONNECTION INC
Also Called: Ronnie's Olde Fashioned Slush
109 Chestnut St (02356-3612)
PHONE..................................508 230-3788
Ronald Imbornone, *President*
EMP: 5
SQ FT: 3,000
SALES: 2.3MM **Privately Held**
SIC: 2024 Mfg Ice Cream/Frozen Desert

North Falmouth
Barnstable County

(G-13953)
QUARTERLY UPDATE
32 Quail Hollow Rd (02556-3013)
PHONE..................................508 540-0848
Robert M Reece, *Principal*
EMP: 3 **EST:** 2011
SALES (est): 137K **Privately Held**
SIC: 2721 Periodicals-Publishing/Printing

(G-13954)
TELEDYNE BENTHOS INC (HQ)
49 Edgerton Dr (02556-2821)
PHONE..................................508 563-1000
Thomas W Altshuler PHD, *President*
James R Kearbey, *Vice Pres*
Francis E Dunne Jr, *CFO*
Pamela Falotico, *Human Res Dir*
Melissa Rossi, *Marketing Staff*
▲ **EMP:** 119 **EST:** 1962
SQ FT: 26,000
SALES (est): 18.9MM
SALES (corp-wide): 2.9B **Publicly Held**
WEB: www.benthos.com
SIC: 3812 Mfg Search/Navigation Equipment
PA: Teledyne Technologies Inc
1049 Camino Dos Rios
Thousand Oaks CA 91360
805 373-4545

(G-13955)
TELEDYNE INSTRUMENTS INC
Also Called: Teledyne Benthos
49 Edgerton Dr (02556-2821)
PHONE..................................508 563-1000
Bob Leclaire, *Sales Staff*
Thomas W Altshuler, *Branch Mgr*
Alan Sanborn, *Manager*
EMP: 15
SALES (corp-wide): 2.9B **Publicly Held**
SIC: 3812 Mfg Search/Navigation Equipment
HQ: Teledyne Instruments, Inc.
1049 Camino Dos Rios
Thousand Oaks CA 91360
805 373-4545

(G-13956)
TELEDYNE INSTRUMENTS INC
Teledyne Webb Research
49 Edgerton Dr (02556-2821)
PHONE..................................508 563-1000
Bob Melvin, *President*
Daniel H Webb, *General Mgr*
Marc Bamberger, *Engineer*
Robert Melvin, *Engineer*
Pamela Falotico, *Human Resources*
EMP: 35
SALES (corp-wide): 2.9B **Publicly Held**
WEB: www.teledyne.com
SIC: 3829 Mfg Measuring/Controlling Devices
HQ: Teledyne Instruments, Inc.
1049 Camino Dos Rios
Thousand Oaks CA 91360
805 373-4545

(G-13957)
TELEDYNE INSTRUMENTS INC
Also Called: Teledyne Webb Research
49 Edgerton Dr (02556-2821)
PHONE..................................508 548-2077
Louise Mitchell, *Vice Pres*
EMP: 50
SALES (corp-wide): 2.9B **Publicly Held**
SIC: 3699 Mfg Electrical Equipment/Supplies
HQ: Teledyne Instruments, Inc.
1049 Camino Dos Rios
Thousand Oaks CA 91360
805 373-4545

North Grafton
Worcester County

(G-13958)
ALL STEEL FABRICATING INC
84 Creeper Hill Rd (01536-1400)
P.O. Box 597 (01536-0597)
PHONE..................................508 839-4471
James Magill, *President*
James Magill Jr, *Vice Pres*
Kevin H Magill, *Vice Pres*
Angela Magill, *Treasurer*
EMP: 30
SQ FT: 30,000
SALES (est): 7.8MM **Privately Held**
WEB: www.allsteelfab.com
SIC: 3441 3443 Structural Metal Fabrication Mfg Fabricated Plate Work

(G-13959)
DAUPHINAIS & SON INC
8 Shrewsbury St (01536-1526)
PHONE..................................508 839-9258
Joanne Dauphinais, *President*
EMP: 3 **EST:** 2012
SALES (est): 194.6K **Privately Held**
SIC: 3273 Mfg Ready-Mixed Concrete

(G-13960)
FDA GROUP LLC
3 Bridle Ridge Dr (01536-2204)
PHONE..................................413 330-7476
Nicholas Capman, *Principal*
Timothy Lamm, *Vice Pres*
EMP: 11
SALES (est): 1.3MM **Privately Held**
SIC: 2834 5047 Mfg Pharmaceutical Preparations Whol Medical/Hospital Equipment

(G-13961)
JCB INC
Also Called: Bottle & Cork
197 Worcester St (01536-1528)
PHONE..................................508 839-5550
Biasini John, *President*
EMP: 5
SALES (est): 385.7K **Privately Held**
SIC: 3565 Manufactures Bottles

(G-13962)
LANGSTROM METALS INC
84 Creeper Hill Rd (01536-1433)
PHONE..................................508 839-5224
Jim Magill, *President*
EMP: 4
SALES (est): 233.1K **Privately Held**
SIC: 3369 Nonferrous Metal Foundry

(G-13963)
LINCOLN PRECISION MACHINING CO
Also Called: Lincoln Hoist
121 Creeper Hill Rd (01536-1437)
P.O. Box 458 (01536-0458)
PHONE..................................508 839-2175
David Hallen, *President*
Richard Hallen, *Treasurer*
Doris E Hallen, *Asst Treas*
▲ **EMP:** 25
SQ FT: 20,000
SALES (est): 5.4MM **Privately Held**
WEB: www.lincoln-precision.com
SIC: 3599 Mfg Industrial Machinery

(G-13964)
PRIMARY COLORS INC
9 Millennium Dr (01536-1862)
PHONE..................................508 839-3202
Judy Mickleson, *President*
Jim Brown, *Sales Dir*
EMP: 24
SQ FT: 40,000
SALES (est): 6.8MM **Privately Held**
WEB: www.primarycolorsinc.com
SIC: 2865 Mfg Cyclic Crudes/Intermediates/Dyes

(G-13965)
SUNSHINE SIGN COMPANY INC
121 Westboro Rd (01536-1809)
PHONE..................................508 839-5588
David R Glispin, *President*
Harry Novelle, *Project Mgr*
EMP: 130
SQ FT: 10,000
SALES: 3.8MM **Privately Held**
WEB: www.sunshinesign.com
SIC: 3993 Mfg Signs/Advertising Specialties

(G-13966)
VERRILLON INC
15 Centennial Dr (01536-1860)
PHONE..................................508 890-7100
Abdel Soufiane PHD, *President*
Gary Churchill, *Vice Pres*
▲ **EMP:** 30
SQ FT: 50,000
SALES (est): 5.8MM **Privately Held**
WEB: www.verrillon.com
SIC: 3674 Mfg Semiconductors/Related Devices
HQ: Afl Telecommunications Llc
170 Ridgeview Center Dr
Duncan SC 29334
864 433-0333

(G-13967)
WASHINGTON MILLS CERAMIC CORP (DH)
20 N Main St (01536-1522)
PHONE..................................508 839-6511
Jack Williams, *Vice Pres*
Jo Ann Wood, *Manager*
◆ **EMP:** 389
SQ FT: 57,000
SALES (est): 28MM
SALES (corp-wide): 175.7MM **Privately Held**
SIC: 3291 Mfg Abrasive Tumbling Stones
HQ: Washington Mills North Grafton, Inc.
20 N Main St
North Grafton MA 01536
508 839-6511

(G-13968)
WASHINGTON MILLS N GRAFTON INC (HQ)
20 N Main St (01536-1522)
P.O. Box 428 (01536-0428)
PHONE..................................508 839-6511
Peter H Williams, *President*
Bruce Vigneaux, *Mayor*
Alden F L Harris II, *Treasurer*
Nancy E Gates, *Admin Sec*
William Decelle, *Maintence Staff*
◆ **EMP:** 100
SQ FT: 126,000
SALES (est): 83.1MM
SALES (corp-wide): 175.7MM **Privately Held**
SIC: 3291 Mfg Abrasive Products
PA: Washington Mills Group, Inc.
20 N Main St
North Grafton MA 01536
508 839-6511

(G-13969)
WYMAN-GORDON COMPANY (DH)
244 Worcester St (01536-1200)
PHONE..................................508 839-8252
Kenneth D Buck, *President*
Roger P Becker, *Vice Pres*
Steven C Blackmore, *Treasurer*
Shawn R Hagel, *Director*
Roger A Cooke, *Admin Sec*
◆ **EMP:** 400 **EST:** 1883
SQ FT: 514,000
SALES (est): 1.2B
SALES (corp-wide): 225.3B **Publicly Held**
WEB: www.dropdies.com
SIC: 3462 3324 3728 3317 Mfg Iron/Steel Forgings Steel Investment Foundry
HQ: Precision Castparts Corp.
4650 Sw Mcdam Ave Ste 300
Portland OR 97239
503 946-4800

North Oxford
Worcester County

(G-13970)
CROCKER ARCHITECTURAL SHTMTL
129 Southbridge Rd (01537-1210)
PHONE..................................508 987-9900
Christine Crocker Lusignan, *President*
James Hubert Jr, *Project Mgr*
Madeline Crocker, *Treasurer*
EMP: 40
SQ FT: 12,000
SALES (est): 10.6MM **Privately Held**
WEB: www.crockerarchitectural.com
SIC: 3444 1761 Mfg Sheet Metalwork Roofing/Siding Contractor

(G-13971)
CUSTOM CONVYRS FABRICATION INC
140 Southbridge Rd (01537-1168)
P.O. Box 751 (01537-0751)
PHONE..................................508 922-0283
Wendell Barnes, *President*
EMP: 12
SALES (est): 1.5MM **Privately Held**
SIC: 3496 Mfg Misc Fabricated Wire Products

(G-13972)
MYRIAD ENGINEERING CO INC
96 Southbridge Rd (01537-1205)
PHONE..................................508 731-6416
Dennis Allard, *President*
Donna Allard, *Vice Pres*
Ashley Allard, *Director*
EMP: 11
SALES: 1.5MM **Privately Held**
SIC: 3599 Mfg Industrial Machinery

(G-13973)
PIONEER CONSOLIDATED CORP
Also Called: Pioneer Cover All
96 Southbridge Rd (01537-1205)
P.O. Box 186, Middlesboro KY (40965-0186)
PHONE..................................508 987-8438
Linny Braver, *President*
EMP: 30
SQ FT: 16,000
SALES (est): 3.3MM **Privately Held**
SIC: 2394 3564 Mfg Canvas/Related Products Mfg Blowers/Fans

(G-13974)
R P WOODWORKING INC
4 Pioneer Dr (01537-1219)
PHONE..................................508 987-3722
Richard Desplaines Jr, *Owner*
EMP: 4 **EST:** 2010
SALES (est): 561.6K **Privately Held**
SIC: 2431 Mfg Millwork

(G-13975)
SWISS PRECISION PRODUCTS INC (DH)
627 Main St (01537-1305)
PHONE..................................508 987-8003
Jay Athanes, *President*
EMP: 27
SQ FT: 15,000
SALES (est): 3.3MM
SALES (corp-wide): 548.1MM **Publicly Held**
SIC: 3599 3841 3494 Mfg Industrial Machinery Mfg Surgical/Med Instr Mfg Valves/Pipe Fittings
HQ: Stratos International, Inc.
299 Johnson Ave Sw
Waseca MN 56093
507 833-8822

(G-13976)
WEYMOUTH BRAIDED RUG CO INC
Also Called: North Oxford Mills
5 Clara Barton Rd (01537)
P.O. Box 576 (01537-0576)
PHONE..................................508 987-8525
Robert Mack, *President*
Lois Edinberg, *Clerk*
EMP: 4 **EST:** 1964
SQ FT: 5,000
SALES (est): 539.1K **Privately Held**
SIC: 2273 5713 5211 Mfg Carpets/Rugs Ret Floor Covering Ret Lumber/Building Materials

North Quincy
Norfolk County

(G-13977)
INDUSTRIAL HEAT TREATING INC
Also Called: I H T
22 Densmore St 26 (02171-1785)
P.O. Box 98 (02171-0002)
PHONE..................................617 328-1010
Lynne Davis, *President*
EMP: 24
SQ FT: 48,000
SALES (est): 8MM **Privately Held**
WEB: www.indht.com
SIC: 3398 Metal Heat Treating

North Reading
Middlesex County

(G-13978)
B F M MINI GOLF DRIVING RANGE
327 Main St (01864-1326)
PHONE..................................978 664-9276
Elizabeth Carvarlo, *Owner*
EMP: 10
SALES (est): 597.7K **Privately Held**
SIC: 3949 Mfg Sporting/Athletic Goods

(G-13979)
BIG POND WIRELESS LLC
Also Called: Radio Systems
1230 Furnace Brook Pkwy (01864)
PHONE..................................781 593-2321
David Pamp, *General Mgr*
Robert Leonard,
EMP: 7
SQ FT: 3,000
SALES (est): 741K **Privately Held**
WEB: www.colonialradio.com
SIC: 3663 5063 Mfg Radio/Tv Communication Equipment Whol Electrical Equipment

(G-13980)
CHOICE WOODWORKING INC
25 Nutter Rd (01864-2144)
PHONE..................................978 207-0289
Nicholas Biagiotti, *Principal*
EMP: 4
SALES (est): 579.5K **Privately Held**
SIC: 2431 Mfg Millwork

(G-13981)
CREATIVE MOTION TECHNOLOGY
Also Called: CM Technology
45 Main St (01864-2204)
PHONE..................................978 664-6218
James O'Rourke, *Principal*
Mary Emerson, *Sales Staff*
EMP: 6
SALES: 500K **Privately Held**
SIC: 3621 Mfg Motors/Generators

(G-13982)
G S DAVIDSON CO INC
55 Concord St (01864-2640)
PHONE..................................617 389-4000
Gerald S Davidson, *President*
EMP: 5 **EST:** 1978
SQ FT: 3,500
SALES (est): 664.5K **Privately Held**
WEB: www.gsdavidson.com
SIC: 3429 Mfg Hardware

(G-13983)
GREAT OAK PUBLICATIONS INC
Also Called: North Reading Transcript
7 Bow St Ste 2 (01864-2534)
P.O. Box 7 (01864-0007)
PHONE..................................978 664-4761
Albert E Silvia Sr, *President*
Frances Silvia, *Treasurer*
Albert Silvia Jr, *Manager*
EMP: 15
SQ FT: 1,600
SALES (est): 785.1K **Privately Held**
SIC: 2711 Newspapers-Publishing/Printing

(G-13984)
HEFFRON ASPHALT CORP (PA)
Also Called: Heffron Materials
68 Winter St (01864-2203)
P.O. Box 162, Wilmington (01887-0162)
PHONE..................................781 935-1455
Milton Heffron Sr, *Ch of Bd*
Kenneth Heffron, *Director*
Anna Heffron, *Clerk*
EMP: 7 **EST:** 1943
SQ FT: 375
SALES (est): 1.2MM **Privately Held**
SIC: 2951 1611 5032 Mfg Asphalt Paving Mix & Contractor & Whol Sand & Gravel

GEOGRAPHIC

(G-13985)
IMMEDIA SEMICONDUCTOR INC
Also Called: Blink
100 Riverpark Dr Fl 1 (01864-2649)
PHONE..................................978 296-4950
Peter Besen, *CEO*
Don Shulsinger, *Vice Pres*
EMP: 15
SALES (est): 526K **Publicly Held**
SIC: 3674 Mfg Semiconductors/Related Devices
PA: Amazon.Com, Inc.
410 Terry Ave N
Seattle WA 98109

(G-13986)
LOST SOCK CORPORATION
26 Hillview Rd (01864-1321)
PHONE..................................978 664-0730
John Dobbyn, *Principal*
EMP: 3
SALES (est): 198.9K **Privately Held**
SIC: 2252 Mfg Hosiery

(G-13987)
MASS PRINTING & FORMS INC
352 Park St Ste 202w (01864-2156)
PHONE..................................781 396-1970
Andrew Pallotta, *President*
Jason Coombs, *VP Opers*
Julie Webster, *Controller*
Bill Crowley, *VP Sales*
EMP: 7
SQ FT: 2,000
SALES (est): 1.2MM **Privately Held**
WEB: www.massprinting.com
SIC: 2752 Lithographic Commercial Printing

(G-13988)
NORTH SHORE PRINTING INC
281 Main St (01864-1301)
PHONE..................................978 664-2609
Robert Killian, *President*
Cynthia Killian, *Treasurer*
EMP: 5
SALES (est): 661.2K **Privately Held**
WEB: www.northshoreprint.com
SIC: 2752 7334 Lithographic Commercial Printing Photocopying Services

(G-13989)
SHIRE HUMN GNTIC THERAPIES INC
200 Riverpark Dr (01864-2621)
PHONE..................................781 482-0883
EMP: 10
SALES (corp-wide): 15.1B **Privately Held**
SIC: 2834 Mfg Pharmaceutical Preparations
HQ: Shire Human Genetic Therapies, Inc.
300 Shire Way
Lexington MA 02421
617 349-0200

(G-13990)
TERADYNE INC (PA)
600 Riverpark Dr (01864-2634)
PHONE..................................978 370-2700
Roy A Vallee, *Ch of Bd*
Mark E Jagiela, *President*
Bradford B Robbins, *President*
Gregory S Smith, *President*
Walter G Vahey, *President*
▲ **EMP:** 277 **EST:** 1960
SQ FT: 422,000
SALES: 2.1B **Publicly Held**
WEB: www.teradyne.com
SIC: 3825 3643 3674 Mfg Automatic Test Equipment

(G-13991)
TERADYNE INC
500 Riverpark Dr (01864-2615)
PHONE..................................978 370-2700
John Wood, *Vice Pres*
Rich Homestead, *Manager*
EMP: 260
SALES (corp-wide): 2.1B **Publicly Held**
WEB: www.teradyne.com
SIC: 3825 Mfg Automatic Test Equipment
PA: Teradyne, Inc.
600 Riverpark Dr
North Reading MA 01864
978 370-2700

(G-13992)
TOWN OF NORTH READING
235 North St (01864-1260)
PHONE..................................978 664-6027
Martin Tilton, *Branch Mgr*
EMP: 39 **Privately Held**
SIC: 2721 Periodicals-Publishing/Printing
PA: Town Of North Reading
235 North St Ofc
North Reading MA 01864
978 664-6010

(G-13993)
VEHO TECH INC
13 Greene St (01864-2011)
PHONE..................................617 909-6026
EMP: 3
SALES (est): 71.1K **Privately Held**
SIC: 7372 4789 Prepackaged Software

(G-13994)
WILSONART INTL HOLDINGS LLC
29 Concord St (01864-2601)
PHONE..................................978 664-5230
Harry Fedden, *Manager*
EMP: 30
SALES (corp-wide): 4.1B **Privately Held**
WEB: www.wilsonart.com
SIC: 2821 2541 Mfg Plastic Materials/Resins Mfg Wood Partitions/Fixtures
HQ: Wilsonart International Holdings Llc
2501 Wilsonart Dr
Temple TX 76504
254 207-7000

North Uxbridge
Worcester County

(G-13995)
L W TANK REPAIR INCORPORATED
410 N Main St (01538)
P.O. Box 308 (01538-0308)
PHONE..................................508 234-6000
Leonard J Wiersma, *President*
Brent Wiersma, *Treasurer*
EMP: 18 **EST:** 1969
SQ FT: 12,500
SALES (est): 3.2MM **Privately Held**
WEB: www.lwtank.com
SIC: 7692 Welding Repair

North Weymouth
Norfolk County

(G-13996)
BAYVIEW GRAPHICS
21 Bayview St (02191-1207)
PHONE..................................781 878-3340
Micheal Buccalla, *Owner*
EMP: 3
SALES: 140K **Privately Held**
SIC: 2759 Commercial Printing

Northampton
Hampshire County

(G-13997)
BEN & BLLS CHCLAT EMPORIUM INC (PA)
143 Main St (01060-3434)
PHONE..................................413 584-5695
Ben Coggins, *President*
Robert Koury, *Treasurer*
EMP: 10 **EST:** 1952
SQ FT: 1,200
SALES (est): 1.3MM **Privately Held**
SIC: 2064 5441 Mfg And Retails Candy

(G-13998)
CEDAR CHEST INC
150 Main St Ste 1 (01060-3461)
PHONE..................................413 584-3860
Philip Hueber, *Principal*
Donna Allen, *Finance Mgr*
EMP: 15
SALES (est): 2.1MM **Privately Held**
SIC: 2511 Mfg Wood Household Furniture

(G-13999)
COCA-COLA REFRESHMENTS USA INC
45 Industrial Dr (01060-2394)
PHONE..................................413 586-8450
Tabitha Hyytinen, *Purch Mgr*
EMP: 73
SALES (corp-wide): 31.8B **Publicly Held**
SIC: 2086 2087 Mfg Bottled/Canned Soft Drinks Mfg Flavor Extracts/Syrup
HQ: Coca-Cola Refreshments Usa, Inc.
2500 Windy Ridge Pkwy Se
Atlanta GA 30339
770 989-3000

(G-14000)
COMPANY OF COCA-COLA BOTTLING
45 Industrial Dr (01060-2326)
PHONE..................................413 586-8450
Dirk Lunsford, *Branch Mgr*
EMP: 92 **Privately Held**
WEB: www.coke.com
SIC: 2086 2033 Mfg Bottled/Canned Soft Drinks Mfg Canned Fruits/Vegetables
HQ: Coca-Cola Bottling Company Of Southeastern New England, Inc.
150 Waterford Parkway S
Waterford CT 06385
860 443-2816

(G-14001)
CONTACT QUARTERLY
Also Called: Contact Edition
221 Pine St Ste 112 (01062-1262)
P.O. Box 603 (01061-0603)
PHONE..................................413 586-1181
Nancy Stark Smith, *Director*
EMP: 4
SALES (est): 218.7K **Privately Held**
WEB: www.contactquarterly.com
SIC: 2721 Periodicals-Publishing/Printing

(G-14002)
COUNCIL ON INTL PUB AFFIRS INC (PA)
Also Called: Boot Strap Press
3 Mont View Ave (01060-3320)
PHONE..................................212 972-9878
Ward Morehouse, *President*
▲ **EMP:** 8
SALES: 93.9K **Privately Held**
SIC: 2731 Books Publisher

(G-14003)
CRAIG F BRADFORD
Also Called: Bradford Woodworking
190 Industrial Dr Ste 1 (01060-2068)
PHONE..................................413 586-4500
Craig Bradford, *Owner*
EMP: 3 **EST:** 1977
SALES: 200K **Privately Held**
SIC: 2511 2431 2434 Mfg Wood Household Furn Mfg Millwork

(G-14004)
DIPWELL COMPANY INC
82 Industrial Dr Unit 3 (01060-2389)
PHONE..................................413 587-4673
Lynn P Alstadt, *President*
Karen Lynn Alstadt, *Vice Pres*
Brian Baird, *Treasurer*
EMP: 8
SALES (est): 1.1MM **Privately Held**
SIC: 3914 Mfg Silverware/Plated Ware

(G-14005)
EDWARD ELGAR PUBLISHING INC
9 Dewey Ct (01060-3815)
PHONE..................................413 584-5551
Edward Elgar, *President*
Fiona Briden, *Publisher*
Cathleen Tenero, *Sales Staff*
Siobhan Tripp, *Marketing Staff*
Jean Bond, *Office Mgr*
▲ **EMP:** 7
SALES (est): 714.8K **Privately Held**
SIC: 2731 Books-Publishing/Printing

(G-14006)
ERIC CARLE LLC
Also Called: Eric Carle Studio
84 North St (01060-3214)
PHONE..................................413 586-2046
Eric Carle, *President*
EMP: 3
SQ FT: 1,700
SALES (est): 22.3K **Privately Held**
WEB: www.eric-carle.com
SIC: 2731 Books-Publishing/Printing

(G-14007)
HARDIGG INDUSTRIES INC
Also Called: Hardigg Case Center
99 Industrial Dr Ste 1 (01060-2375)
PHONE..................................413 665-2163
Ron Swerdorski, *Manager*
EMP: 9
SALES (corp-wide): 208.2MM **Privately Held**
WEB: www.hardigg.com
SIC: 2449 Mfg Wood Containers
HQ: Hardigg Industries, Inc.
147 N Main St
South Deerfield MA 01373
413 665-2163

(G-14008)
HEAVENLY CHOCOLATE
Also Called: Bryce
150 Main St (01060-3598)
PHONE..................................413 586-0038
Bud Stockwell, *Owner*
EMP: 20
SALES (est): 957K **Privately Held**
SIC: 2066 Ret Candy/Confectionery

(G-14009)
L3 TECHNOLOGIES INC
L3 Keo
50 Prince St (01060-3635)
PHONE..................................413 586-2330
Bill Taylor, *President*
Jim Tierney, *President*
Jim Geller, *Human Res Dir*
Doug Jones, *Mktg Dir*
Michael Wall, *Branch Mgr*
EMP: 600
SQ FT: 8,000
SALES (corp-wide): 6.8B **Publicly Held**
WEB: www.kollmorgen.com
SIC: 3621 3625 3827 3812 Mfg Motors/Generators Mfg Relay/Indstl Control Mfg Optical Instr/Lens Mfg Search/Navgatn Equip Mfg Electromedical Equip
HQ: L3 Technologies, Inc.
600 3rd Ave Fl 34
New York NY 10016
212 697-1111

(G-14010)
LINK ENTERPRISES CORP
Also Called: Rigstar Rigging
82 Industrial Dr (01060-2384)
PHONE..................................413 585-9869
Steven E Kendall, *President*
EMP: 4
SALES (est): 564K **Privately Held**
SIC: 2298 1799 Mfg Cordage/Twine Trade Contractor

(G-14011)
MACHINEMETRICS INC
47 Pleasant St (01060-3984)
PHONE..................................413 341-5747
Lauzier Jacob, *CFO*
Graham Immerman, *Mktg Dir*
Christina Gay, *Marketing Staff*
Jacob Lauzier, *CTO*
Justin Aquadro, *Sr Software Eng*
EMP: 8
SALES (est): 740.3K **Privately Held**
SIC: 7372 Prepackaged Software Services

(G-14012)
MICROCAL LLC
22 Industrial Dr E (01060-2395)
PHONE..................................413 586-7720
EMP: 3 **EST:** 2016
SALES (est): 114.7K **Privately Held**
SIC: 3821 Mfg Lab Apparatus/Furniture

(G-14013)
MIKE ORZEL LOGGING
150 Federal St (01062-2718)
PHONE.................................413 320-3367
EMP: 3
SALES (est): 191.6K **Privately Held**
SIC: 2411 Logging

(G-14014)
OLIVE NORTHAMPTON OIL CO
150 Main St Ste 14 (01060-3131)
PHONE.................................413 537-7357
Jason Martin, *President*
EMP: 3
SALES (est): 113.4K **Privately Held**
SIC: 2079 Ret Misc Foods

(G-14015)
ORTHOTICS PROSTHETICS LABS INC
241 King St Ste 123 (01060-2344)
PHONE.................................413 585-8622
James Hass, *Branch Mgr*
EMP: 5
SALES (est): 383K
SALES (corp-wide): 1.5MM **Privately Held**
SIC: 3842 5999 Mfg Surgical Appliances/Supplies Ret Misc Merchandise
PA: Orthotics & Prosthetics Laboratories, Inc.
300 Birnie Ave Ste 303
Springfield MA 01107
413 737-2404

(G-14016)
PACIFIC PRINTING INC
19 Damon Rd (01060-1899)
PHONE.................................413 585-5700
Timothy Banister, *President*
Tracy Banister, *Treasurer*
EMP: 7
SQ FT: 8,000
SALES (est): 1.1MM **Privately Held**
SIC: 2261 2262 2759 2284 Cotton Finishing Plant Manmade Fabric Fnshg Plt Commercial Printing Thread Mill

(G-14017)
PACKAGING CORPORATION AMERICA
Also Called: PCA
525 Mount Tom Rd (01060-4261)
PHONE.................................413 584-6132
Robert Park, *General Mgr*
EMP: 86
SALES (corp-wide): 7B **Publicly Held**
SIC: 2653 Mfg Corrugated/Solid Fiber Boxes
PA: Packaging Corporation Of America
1 N Field Ct
Lake Forest IL 60045
847 482-3000

(G-14018)
PHILLIPS ENTERPRISES INC
149 Easthampton Rd (01060-4103)
PHONE.................................413 586-5860
William Phillips, *President*
Jim Dean, *General Mgr*
Julee Clement, *Administration*
▲ **EMP**: 18
SQ FT: 65,000
SALES (est): 5.2MM **Privately Held**
WEB: www.phillipsenterprises.com
SIC: 2541 2542 Mfg Wood Partitions/Fixt Mfg Nonwd Partition/Fixt

(G-14019)
PIONEER VLY EDUCTL PRESS INC
Also Called: Pioneer Valley Books
155 Industrial Dr (01060-2326)
PHONE.................................413 727-3573
Michele Dufresne, *President*
Nick Dufresne, *Vice Pres*
Bob Dufresne, *Treasurer*
Lauri Yanis, *Sales Staff*
Matthew Dufresne, *Admin Sec*
▲ **EMP**: 17
SALES: 5MM **Privately Held**
WEB: www.pvep.com
SIC: 2731 Whol Books/Newspapers

(G-14020)
SAINT-GOBAIN CERAMICS PLAS INC
175 Industrial Dr (01060-2326)
PHONE.................................413 586-8167
Terry Thibault, *Opers Mgr*
Arun Kumar, *Marketing Mgr*
EMP: 15
SALES (corp-wide): 209.1MM **Privately Held**
WEB: www.sgceramics.com
SIC: 3297 Mfg Nonclay Refractories
HQ: Saint-Gobain Ceramics & Plastics, Inc.
750 E Swedesford Rd
Valley Forge PA 19482
-

(G-14021)
SMJ METAL CO INC
Also Called: Ralph's Blacksmith Shop
36 Smith St (01060-3823)
PHONE.................................413 586-3535
Arthur D Grodd, *President*
Jeffrey J Payne, *Purch Mgr*
EMP: 50
SQ FT: 5,400
SALES (est): 11MM **Privately Held**
SIC: 3441 Structural Metal Fabrication

(G-14022)
TEMP-PRO INCORPORATED
200 Industrial Dr (01060-2380)
P.O. Box 89 (01061-0089)
PHONE.................................413 584-3165
Rodolfo Jacobson, *President*
Nancy Hubbard, *Purch Mgr*
Dawn Dube, *Purchasing*
Nancy Harding, *Treasurer*
▲ **EMP**: 35
SQ FT: 60,000
SALES (est): 9.5MM **Privately Held**
WEB: www.temp-pro.com
SIC: 3823 Mfg Process Control Instruments

(G-14023)
TRAVEL MEDICINE INC
369 Pleasant St (01060-3914)
P.O. Box 359 (01061-0359)
PHONE.................................413 584-0381
Stuart R Rose MD, *CEO*
Waltraud P Rose, *Treasurer*
EMP: 4
SALES (est): 498.6K **Privately Held**
WEB: www.travmed.com
SIC: 2721 5961 Publisher In An International Travel Health Guide & Mail Order Of Travel Medical Equipment

(G-14024)
VALLEY ADVOCATE
115 Conz St Ste 2 (01060-4445)
PHONE.................................413 584-0003
Patty Desroche, *Principal*
EMP: 3
SALES (est): 30.2K **Privately Held**
SIC: 2711 Newspapers-Publishing/Printing

(G-14025)
VCA INC
209 Earle St (01060-3643)
PHONE.................................413 587-2750
Bruce Volz, *President*
Anthony Clarke, *Treasurer*
Catharine Nguyen, *Human Res Mgr*
Donald Brakey, *Manager*
EMP: 30
SQ FT: 10,000
SALES (est): 2MM **Privately Held**
WEB: www.vca-inc.com
SIC: 2531 2431 2517 2511 Mfg Public Building Furn Mfg Millwork Mfg Wd Tv/Radio Cabinets Mfg Wood Household Furn

(G-14026)
WALRUS ENTERPRISES LLC
30 Aldrich St (01060-2215)
P.O. Box 1502 (01061-1502)
PHONE.................................413 387-4387
Renato Bartoli, *Principal*
Anna VA Polesny,
▲ **EMP**: 9
SALES (est): 1.2MM **Privately Held**
WEB: www.coloredsmoke.com
SIC: 2865 Mfg Cyclic Crudes/Intermediates/Dyes

(G-14027)
WRIGHT ARCHITECTURAL MLLWK CORP
115 Industrial Dr (01060-2326)
PHONE.................................413 586-3528
Walter K Price, *President*
Michael D Buell, *Treasurer*
EMP: 30
SQ FT: 20,150
SALES (est): 5.9MM **Privately Held**
WEB: www.wrightmw.com
SIC: 2431 Mfg Millwork

Northborough
Worcester County

(G-14028)
A T S CASES INC
172 Otis St Ste 4 (01532-2415)
P.O. Box 723 (01532-0723)
PHONE.................................508 393-9110
Ronald Orlando, *President*
Michael H Orlando, *Principal*
EMP: 8
SQ FT: 26,000
SALES (est): 1.4MM **Privately Held**
WEB: www.atscases.com
SIC: 3161 Mfg Luggage - Carrying Cases

(G-14029)
ASPEN AEROGELS INC (PA)
30 Forbes Rd Bldg B (01532-2501)
PHONE.................................508 691-1111
Mark L Noetzel, *Ch of Bd*
Donald R Young, *President*
Gregg R Landes, *Senior VP*
Corby C Whitaker, *Senior VP*
Jeffrey A Ball, *Vice Pres*
EMP: 216
SQ FT: 51,650
SALES: 104.3MM **Publicly Held**
WEB: www.aerogel.com
SIC: 2899 Mfg Insulating Compounds

(G-14030)
CAMAR CORP
55 Church St (01532-1439)
PHONE.................................508 845-9263
James A Mercanti, *President*
Barbara Mercanti, *Clerk*
EMP: 10 **EST**: 1974
SQ FT: 20,000
SALES (est): 1.7MM **Privately Held**
WEB: www.camarcorp.com
SIC: 3511 Mfg Turbines/Generator Sets

(G-14031)
CRAMARO TARPAULIN SYSTEMS INC
51 Sw Cutoff (01532-2111)
PHONE.................................508 393-3062
David Feitler, *Admin Sec*
EMP: 9
SQ FT: 3,000
SALES (corp-wide): 28.4MM **Privately Held**
WEB: www.cramarotarps.com
SIC: 2394 Mfg Canvas Related Products
PA: Cramaro Tarpaulin Systems Inc
600 North Dr
Melbourne FL 32934
321 757-7611

(G-14032)
CUSTOM COMPUTER SYSTEMS INC
36 Woodland Rd (01532-1865)
PHONE.................................508 393-8899
Raul Garciarivera, *President*
EMP: 6
SALES (est): 858.4K **Privately Held**
WEB: www.ccsnet.com
SIC: 3672 7373 Mfg Printed Circuit Boards

(G-14033)
EXPANSION OPPORTUNITIES INC
Also Called: Viewpoint Sign & Awning
35 Lyman St Ste 1 (01532-2076)
PHONE.................................508 303-8200
Jeffrey A Kwass, *President*
Sean Donovan, *Project Mgr*
Jack Floyd, *Project Mgr*
Dave Randa, *Treasurer*
Lauren Keenan-Aradi, *Office Mgr*
EMP: 48
SQ FT: 18,000
SALES (est): 3.9MM **Privately Held**
WEB: www.vwpoint.com
SIC: 3993 2394 3444 Mfg Signs/Advertising Specialties Mfg Canvas/Related Products Mfg Sheet Metalwork

(G-14034)
GENZYME CORPORATION
11 Forbes Rd (01532-2501)
PHONE.................................508 351-2699
Robert C Chaves, *Principal*
EMP: 93 **Privately Held**
SIC: 2834 Mfg Pharmaceutical Preparations
HQ: Genzyme Corporation
50 Binney St
Cambridge MA 02142
617 252-7500

(G-14035)
HARRYS MACHINED PARTS
15 Belmont St (01532-2416)
P.O. Box 861 (01532-0861)
PHONE.................................508 366-1455
Rick Stetson, *Owner*
EMP: 3
SQ FT: 2,100
SALES (est): 214.8K **Privately Held**
SIC: 3599 Mfg Industrial Machinery

(G-14036)
HOSOKAWA ALPINE AMERICAN INC
455 Whitney St (01532-2503)
PHONE.................................508 655-1123
David Nunes, *President*
Robert Hitchins, *Vice Pres*
Donald Brophy, *Treasurer*
Ben McNally, *Controller*
Thomas Valorie, *Admin Sec*
▲ **EMP**: 19
SALES: 60MM **Privately Held**
SIC: 3229 Mfg Pressed/Blown Glass
PA: Hosokawa Micron Corporation
1-9, Tajika, Shodai
Hirakata OSK 573-1
-

(G-14037)
HOSOKAWA MICRON INTERNATIONAL
Also Called: Hosokawa Alpine American Div
455 Whitney St (01532-2503)
PHONE.................................508 655-1123
David Nunes, *President*
EMP: 16 **Privately Held**
WEB: www.hosokawa.com
SIC: 3559 2393 8711 5044 Mfg Misc Industry Mach Mfg Textile Bags Engineering Services Whol Office Equipment
HQ: Hosokawa Micron International Inc.
10 Chatham Rd
Summit NJ 07901
908 273-6360

(G-14038)
MATEC INSTRUMENT COMPANIES INC (PA)
56 Hudson St Ste 3 (01532-1968)
PHONE.................................508 393-0155
Kenneth Bishop, *President*
David Walling, *Treasurer*
Kim Goyette, *Asst Controller*
▲ **EMP**: 37 **EST**: 1964
SQ FT: 20,000
SALES (est): 6.5MM **Privately Held**
WEB: www.matec.com
SIC: 3829 3826 3825 3699 Mfg Measure/Control Dvcs Mfg Analytical Instr Mfg Elec Measuring Instr Mfg Elec Mach/Equip/Supp

GEOGRAPHIC

(G-14039)
MOTION TECHNOLOGY INC
10 Forbes Rd (01532-2501)
PHONE....................508 460-9800
Bill McMahon, *President*
William McMahon, *President*
Diane Darling, *Corp Secy*
Meagan Gregoire, *Marketing Mgr*
Bess Wightman, *Marketing Staff*
▲ **EMP:** 30
SQ FT: 22,000
SALES (est): 7MM **Privately Held**
WEB: mtiproducts.com/
SIC: 3589 Mfg Service Industry Machinery

(G-14040)
NEWCORR PACKAGING INC
66 Lyman St (01532-2062)
P.O. Box 29 (01532-0029)
PHONE....................508 393-9256
Hans Koch, *President*
Theodore Romanow, *Clerk*
▲ **EMP:** 60
SQ FT: 110,000
SALES (est): 20.5MM **Privately Held**
SIC: 2653 Mfg Corrugated/Solid Fiber Boxes

(G-14041)
NIROGYONE THERAPEUTICS LLC
10 Laurel Ave (01532-1670)
PHONE....................508 439-2197
Vincent Sandanayaka, *Principal*
EMP: 3 **EST:** 2013
SALES (est): 179.8K **Privately Held**
SIC: 2834 Mfg Pharmaceutical Preparations

(G-14042)
ON GRADE USA
276 W Main St Rear (01532-2165)
PHONE....................508 351-9480
James Flanders, *Partner*
Brian Brady, *Partner*
EMP: 4
SQ FT: 2,000
SALES (est): 280K **Privately Held**
SIC: 3829 Mfg Measuring/Controlling Devices

(G-14043)
PALL NORTHBOROUGH (DH)
50 Bearfoot Rd Ste 1 (01532-1551)
P.O. Box 5630, Cortland NY (13045-5630)
PHONE....................978 263-9888
Eric Krasnoff, *Ch of Bd*
John Rozembersky, *Vice Pres*
▲ **EMP:** 7
SQ FT: 30,000
SALES (est): 5.4MM
SALES (corp-wide): 19.8B **Publicly Held**
WEB: www.pall.com
SIC: 3821 3564 Mfg Lab Apparatus/Furniture Mfg Blowers/Fans
HQ: Pall Corporation
25 Harbor Park Dr
Port Washington NY 11050
516 484-5400

(G-14044)
PONGO SOFTWARE LLC
Also Called: Pongo Resume
168 E Main St (01532-1604)
PHONE....................508 393-4528
Rodney Capron Jr,
EMP: 5
SALES (est): 580K **Privately Held**
SIC: 7372 Prepackaged Software Services

(G-14045)
POWER SYSTEMS INTEGRITY INC
Also Called: PSI
100 Otis St Ste 6 (01532-2438)
PHONE....................508 393-1655
Harold Marsden, *President*
Aaron Cooledge, *CFO*
EMP: 7
SQ FT: 3,000
SALES (est): 1.1MM **Privately Held**
WEB: www.psinteg.com
SIC: 3571 3577 3825 3548 Mfg Electronic Computers Mfg Computer Peripherals Mfg Elec Measuring Instr Mfg Welding Apparatus Mfg Switchgear/Boards

(G-14046)
SAINT-GOBAIN CERAMICS PLAS INC
9 Goddard Rd (01532-1545)
PHONE....................508 351-7754
Rakesh Kapoor, *Manager*
EMP: 285
SALES (corp-wide): 209.1MM **Privately Held**
WEB: www.sgceramics.com
SIC: 2821 Mfg Industrial Inorganic Chemicals
HQ: Saint-Gobain Ceramics & Plastics, Inc.
750 E Swedesford Rd
Valley Forge PA 19482
-

(G-14047)
SAINT-GOBAIN CORPORATION
9 Goddard Rd (01532-1545)
PHONE....................508 351-7112
George M Brown, *Principal*
EMP: 47
SALES (corp-wide): 209.1MM **Privately Held**
SIC: 3269 2891 3221 Mfg Pottery Products
HQ: Saint-Gobain Corporation
20 Moores Rd
Malvern PA 19355
-

(G-14048)
STERIS CORPORATION
435 Whitney St (01532-1147)
PHONE....................508 393-9323
Ray Fife, *Production*
EMP: 5 **Privately Held**
SIC: 3841 Mfg Surgical Appliances/Supplies
HQ: Steris Corporation
5960 Heisley Rd
Mentor OH 44060
440 354-2600

(G-14049)
SUNDRUM SOLAR INC
Also Called: Mgi Energy
15 Hillside Rd (01532-2401)
PHONE....................508 740-6256
Michael Intrieri, *CEO*
EMP: 8
SALES (est): 269.1K **Privately Held**
SIC: 3433 Hybrid Solar Energy Gereration

(G-14050)
TELEFLUENT COMMUNICATIONS INC
104 Otis St Ste 22 (01532-2440)
PHONE....................508 393-0005
John K Esler, *President*
Eric H Karp, *Admin Sec*
EMP: 14
SALES (est): 2.2MM **Privately Held**
SIC: 3645 Mfg Residential Lighting Fixtures

(G-14051)
TOMANDTIM ENTERPRISES LLC
Also Called: HB Printing
75 W Main St (01532-1880)
P.O. Box 4787, Framingham (01704-4787)
PHONE....................508 380-5550
Timothy N Hostage,
Tom Hostage,
EMP: 7
SQ FT: 1,800
SALES: 850K **Privately Held**
SIC: 2759 Commercial Printing

(G-14052)
TOOLMEX INDUS SOLUTIONS INC (PA)
34 Talbot Rd (01532-2010)
PHONE....................508 653-5110
Arkadiusz Kielb, *CEO*
Michael L Clifford, *Corp Secy*
Lukas Kielb, *Vice Pres*
David McGuire, *Purchasing*
Carrie Richard, *Purchasing*
▲ **EMP:** 56
SQ FT: 37,000
SALES (est): 12.4MM **Privately Held**
WEB: www.toolmex.com
SIC: 3829 3541 5084 3545 Mfg Measure/Control Dvcs Mfg Machine Tool-Cutting Whol Industrial Equip Mfg Machine Tool Access Whol Electrical Equip

Northbridge
Worcester County

(G-14053)
AMBUR MACHINE CO INC
2376 Providence Rd (01534-1086)
P.O. Box 516 (01534-0516)
PHONE....................508 234-6341
Nancy Frieswick, *President*
EMP: 5 **EST:** 1971
SQ FT: 2,000
SALES (est): 701.6K **Privately Held**
SIC: 3599 Mfg Industrial Machinery

(G-14054)
CAYA CONSTRUCTION CO
76 Sutton St (01534)
PHONE....................508 234-5082
Gerard Caya, *Owner*
EMP: 6
SQ FT: 3,328
SALES (est): 573.1K **Privately Held**
SIC: 3531 1771 Mfg Construction Machinery Concrete Contractor

(G-14055)
EQUINATURE LLC
Also Called: Equinature Products
1961 Quaker St (01534-1209)
PHONE....................774 217-8057
Christine Taylor, *Mng Member*
EMP: 6
SALES (est): 404.1K **Privately Held**
SIC: 2399 Manufacture Horse Care Products

(G-14056)
FORTIS LLC
76 Sutton St Unit 151 (01534-4409)
PHONE....................617 600-4178
David Downey, *President*
EMP: 3
SALES (est): 314.8K **Privately Held**
SIC: 3561 Mfg Pumps/Pumping Equipment

(G-14057)
MAINLINE ENERGY SYSTEMS INC
Also Called: Mainline Heating & Supply
95 June St (01534-1184)
PHONE....................860 429-9663
Michael Wytenus, *President*
EMP: 5
SALES (est): 907.4K **Privately Held**
SIC: 3433 Alternative Heating Store Wood Stoves And Inserts Pellet Stoves And Inserts Coal Stoves Gas Stoves And Fireplaces

(G-14058)
POLYFOAM CORP
2355 Providence Rd (01534-1085)
P.O. Box 906 (01534-0906)
PHONE....................508 234-6323
Henry W Coz, *CEO*
Thomas L Coz, *President*
Donna Boissonneault, *COO*
Sandi Tetreau, *Purch Agent*
Mark Matthews, *Manager*
▲ **EMP:** 80 **EST:** 1974
SQ FT: 400,000
SALES (est): 17.9MM **Privately Held**
WEB: www.polyfoamcorp.com
SIC: 3086 Mfg Plastic Materials/Resins

(G-14059)
Q6 INTEGRATION INC
126 Clubhouse Ln (01534-1281)
PHONE....................508 266-0638
James Cusick, *President*
EMP: 3
SALES (est): 242.2K **Privately Held**
SIC: 3599 Mfg Industrial Machinery

(G-14060)
RIVERDALE MILLS CORPORATION
Also Called: Aquamesh
130 Riverdale St (01534-1381)
P.O. Box 920 (01534-0920)
PHONE....................508 234-8715
James Knott Sr, *Ch of Bd*
James Knott Jr, *President*
Larry Walsh, *Vice Pres*
Debra Krikorian, *CFO*
Angela Fredette, *Human Res Mgr*
◆ **EMP:** 150
SQ FT: 392,000
SALES (est): 55.9MM **Privately Held**
WEB: www.riverdale.com
SIC: 3496 3423 Mfg Misc Fabricated Wire Products Mfg Hand/Edge Tools

(G-14061)
SIMPLY DESIGNS & PRINTING
2236 Providence Rd (01534-1255)
P.O. Box 458 (01534-0458)
PHONE....................508 234-3424
Diane Rivard, *Owner*
EMP: 3
SALES (est): 195.3K **Privately Held**
SIC: 2759 Commercial Printing

(G-14062)
TENT CONNECTION INC
Also Called: American Folding Table Mfg
1682 Providence Rd (01534-2208)
PHONE....................508 234-8746
Paul E Tonry, *President*
Edmond Tonry, *Principal*
Marie Tonry, *Principal*
EMP: 9
SQ FT: 4,000
SALES (est): 873.5K **Privately Held**
WEB: www.tentconnection.com
SIC: 2394 7359 Mfg Canvas/Related Products Equipment Rental/Leasing

Northfield
Franklin County

(G-14063)
FISHER LOGGING
275 S Mountain Rd (01360-9682)
PHONE....................413 498-2615
Charles Fisher, *President*
EMP: 3
SALES (est): 136.7K **Privately Held**
SIC: 2411 Logging

(G-14064)
MICHAEL HUMPHRIES WDWKG INC
158 Birnam Rd (01360-9528)
P.O. Box 33 (01360-0033)
PHONE....................413 498-0018
Michael Humphries, *President*
EMP: 8
SALES (est): 1.4MM **Privately Held**
SIC: 2499 Mfg Wood Products

(G-14065)
MICHAEL HUMPHRIES WOODWORKING
105 Main St (01360-1064)
PHONE....................413 498-2187
David Koester, *Branch Mgr*
EMP: 3
SALES (est): 196.1K
SALES (corp-wide): 1.2MM **Privately Held**
WEB: www.michaelhumphries.com
SIC: 2431 Mfg Millwork
PA: Michael Humphries Woodworking Inc
77 White Rd
Warwick MA
978 544-2694

(G-14066)
SEVERANCES SUGARHOUSE
286 Capt Beers Plain Rd (01360-9529)
PHONE....................413 498-2032
Milton Severance, *Owner*
EMP: 12

▲ = Import ▼=Export
◆ =Import/Export

SALES (est): 430K Privately Held
SIC: 2099 Mfg Food Preparations

(G-14067)
SISSON ENGINEERING CORP
330 Old Wendell Rd (01360-9675)
PHONE....413 498-2840
Cody Sisson, *CEO*
Kathy Chilik, *Principal*
Jeanne Sisson, *Corp Secy*
Max Parohich, *Manager*
EMP: 23
SQ FT: 18,000
SALES (est): 3.1MM Privately Held
WEB: www.sissoncorp.com
SIC: 3599 Mfg Industrial Machinery

(G-14068)
TRI STATE PRECISION INC
1 Ashuelot Rd (01360-9665)
PHONE....413 498-2961
Brian D Bordner, *President*
Brenda L Bordner, *Treasurer*
EMP: 3
SQ FT: 7,000
SALES (est): 439.8K Privately Held
WEB: www.tri-state.com
SIC: 3545 Mfg Industrial Machinery

Norton
Bristol County

(G-14069)
138 BARROWS STREET REALTY INC
138 Barrows St (02766-3123)
PHONE....508 285-2904
EMP: 55 EST: 1951
SQ FT: 105,000
SALES (est): 5.8MM Privately Held
WEB: www.tweave.com
SIC: 2221 2231 2241 2211 Manmad Brdwv Fabric Mill Wool Brdwv Fabric Mill Narrow Fabric Mill Cotton Brdwv Fabric Mill

(G-14070)
AMAZING GLAZE
41 New Taunton Ave (02766-3206)
PHONE....508 285-7234
EMP: 3 EST: 2008
SALES (est): 165.6K Privately Held
SIC: 3272 Mfg Concrete Products

(G-14071)
AXIS-SHIELD POC AS
15 Commerce Way Ste E (02766-3330)
PHONE....508 285-4870
John Sperzel, *President*
Fabio Rota, *Research*
Steve Grossman, *Admin Sec*
EMP: 32
SALES (est): 6.1MM Privately Held
SIC: 2835 Mfg Diagnostic Substances

(G-14072)
BROTHERS MACHINING CORP
364 Reservoir St (02766-1507)
PHONE....508 286-9136
Christopher Neufell, *Principal*
EMP: 3 EST: 2008
SALES (est): 304.2K Privately Held
SIC: 3599 Mfg Industrial Machinery

(G-14073)
CPS TECHNOLOGIES CORP
111 S Worcester St (02766-2102)
PHONE....508 222-0614
Francis J Hughes Jr, *Ch of Bd*
Grant C Bennett, *President*
Thomas E Breen, *Senior VP*
Kipp Standley, *Engineer*
David Valle, *Design Engr*
EMP: 143
SQ FT: 38,000
SALES: 21.5MM Privately Held
WEB: www.alsic.com
SIC: 3674 Mfg Advanced Ceramic Components

(G-14074)
CREATIVE IMPRINTS INC
Also Called: C I Medical
15 Commerce Way Ste A (02766-3329)
PHONE....508 285-7650
Clifford A Garnett, *CEO*
Marc A Cohen, *President*
▼ EMP: 20
SQ FT: 20,000
SALES (est): 5.4MM Privately Held
WEB: www.cimedical.com
SIC: 2752 5085 Lithographic Commercial Printing Whol Industrial Supplies

(G-14075)
CROWN POLY INC
19 Country Club Way (02766-1155)
PHONE....781 883-4979
EMP: 3
SALES (est): 188.6K Privately Held
SIC: 2673 Mfg Bags-Plastic/Coated Paper

(G-14076)
DATA TRANSLATION INC (PA)
10 Commerce Way Ste E (02766-3321)
PHONE....508 481-3700
Alfred A Molinari, *President*
Ellen W Harpin, *Vice Pres*
Andreas C Randow, *Vice Pres*
Jeffrey M Cronin, *VP Opers*
Michael A Dipoto, *VP Finance*
EMP: 53
SQ FT: 100,000
SALES (est): 11.4MM Privately Held
WEB: www.datx.com
SIC: 7372 3577 Prepackaged Software Services Mfg Computer Peripheral Equipment

(G-14077)
FULL CIRCLE PADDING INC
253 Mansfield Ave Unit 5 (02766-1377)
P.O. Box 388 (02766-0388)
PHONE....508 285-2500
Charles Rogers III, *President*
Colin Rogers, *Vice Pres*
Kathy McHugh, *IT/INT Sup*
EMP: 18
SQ FT: 6,000
SALES: 1.4MM Privately Held
WEB: www.fullcirclepadding.com
SIC: 2299 5091 5941 Mfg Textile Goods Whol Sporting/Recreational Goods Ret Sporting Goods/Bicycles

(G-14078)
GREG ASSELIN STUDIOS LTD
Also Called: Graphic Awards & Trophy
27 Walker St (02766-1113)
PHONE....508 222-7361
Greg Asselin, *Owner*
EMP: 5
SQ FT: 10,000
SALES (est): 325.9K Privately Held
SIC: 3914 Mfg Silverware/Plated Ware

(G-14079)
JEWELRY CREATIONS
123 Reservoir St (02766-2201)
P.O. Box 177, Attleboro (02703-0003)
PHONE....508 285-4230
John Silva, *Owner*
EMP: 4
SQ FT: 6,000
SALES (est): 234.5K Privately Held
WEB: www.swcreations.net
SIC: 3911 3089 3914 Mfg Precious Metal Jewelry Mfg Plastic Products Mfg Silverware/Plated Ware

(G-14080)
JP SEALCOATING INC
6 Gentian Rd (02766-1624)
PHONE....508 954-3510
Rhonda Pietersen, *Principal*
EMP: 4
SALES (est): 300.3K Privately Held
SIC: 2891 Mfg Adhesives/Sealants

(G-14081)
MEASUREMENT COMPUTING CORP (HQ)
10 Commerce Way Ste C1 (02766-3321)
P.O. Box 842604, Boston (02284-2604)
PHONE....508 946-5100
Peter Anderson, *General Mgr*
Bill Kennedy, *Vice Pres*
William Kennedy, *Vice Pres*
Cliff Cox, *Buyer*
Susan Bickford, *Credit Staff*
▲ EMP: 55
SALES: 15MM
SALES (corp-wide): 1.3B Publicly Held
WEB: www.measurementcomputing.com
SIC: 3672 7372 Mfg Printed Circuit Boards Prepackaged Software Services
PA: National Instruments Corporation
11500 N Mopac Expy
Austin TX 78759
512 683-0100

(G-14082)
MEDICAL DEVICE BUS SVCS INC
15 Commerce Way (02766-3329)
PHONE....508 828-2726
Mary Ellen Fayad, *Human Resources*
Don Grilli, *Branch Mgr*
EMP: 100
SALES (corp-wide): 81.5B Publicly Held
SIC: 3842 Mfg Surgical Appliances/Supplies
HQ: Medical Device Business Services, Inc.
700 Orthopaedic Dr
Warsaw IN 46582

(G-14083)
MONTIONES BISCOTTI (PA)
253 Mansfield Ave (02766-1381)
PHONE....508 285-7004
Mary Montione, *Owner*
EMP: 15
SALES (est): 903K Privately Held
SIC: 2051 5947 Mfg Bread/Related Products Ret Gifts/Novelties

(G-14084)
NEW ENGLAND PHOTOCONDUCTOR
Also Called: N E P
253 Mansfield Ave (02766-1381)
P.O. Box M (02766-0927)
PHONE....508 285-5561
Paul M Brennan, *President*
Richard Brennan, *Opers Mgr*
EMP: 12
SQ FT: 4,500
SALES (est): 1.9MM Privately Held
WEB: www.nepcorp.com
SIC: 3826 Mfg Analytical Instruments

(G-14085)
OUTLAW AUDIO LLC
10b Commerce Way Ste B (02766-3313)
P.O. Box 975, Easton (02334-0975)
PHONE....508 286-4110
Peter Tribeman,
Diane Bielski,
Jonathan Lederman,
▲ EMP: 10
SALES (est): 1.8MM Privately Held
WEB: www.outlawaudio.com
SIC: 3651 Mfg Home Audio/Video Equipment

(G-14086)
RHEE GOLD COMPANY
155 Pine St (02766-3303)
P.O. Box 2150 (02766-0929)
PHONE....508 285-6650
Rhee Coldman, *President*
EMP: 12
SALES (est): 1.3MM Privately Held
WEB: www.rheegold.com
SIC: 2721 7941 Periodicals-Publishing/Printing Sports Club/Manager/Promoter

(G-14087)
SAFE PROCESS SYSTEMS INC
54 S Washington St (02766-2906)
PHONE....508 285-5109
Donald Cybulski, *Principal*
EMP: 3
SALES (est): 219.1K Privately Held
SIC: 3625 Mfg Relays/Industrial Controls

(G-14088)
SCIENCE SERUM LLC
194 John Scott Blvd (02766-2615)
PHONE....508 369-7733
Neil Goldman, *Principal*
EMP: 3 EST: 2016
SALES (est): 90K Privately Held
SIC: 2836 Mfg Biological Products

(G-14089)
SINCLAIR MANUFACTURING CO LLC
12 S Worcester St (02766-2012)
P.O. Box 398, Chartley (02712-0398)
PHONE....508 222-7440
William Hubbard, *President*
EMP: 63 EST: 1943
SQ FT: 50,000
SALES (est): 8MM
SALES (corp-wide): 67.1MM Privately Held
WEB: www.sinclairmfg.com
SIC: 3679 Mfg Electronic Components
PA: Hermetic Solutions Group Inc.
4000 State Route 66 # 310
Tinton Falls NJ 07753
732 722-8780

(G-14090)
SOUTH SHORE MILLWORK INC
7 Maple St (02766-2605)
PHONE....508 226-5500
Jeffrey P Burton, *President*
Joseph Roth, *COO*
Chris Ferland, *Project Mgr*
Gerald Whalen, *Project Mgr*
Shawn Cafferty, *Engineer*
▼ EMP: 70
SQ FT: 60,000
SALES (est): 12.8MM Privately Held
WEB: www.southshoremillwork.com
SIC: 2431 2499 Mfg Millwork Mfg Wood Products

(G-14091)
VALENTINE TOOL & STAMPING INC
171 W Main St (02766-1232)
P.O. Box 469 (02766-0469)
PHONE....508 285-6911
Charles Valentine Jr, *President*
Charles C Valentine Jr, *President*
Lawrence Valentine, *Vice Pres*
Phil Murphy, *Mfg Staff*
Virginia Welton, *Asst Treas*
EMP: 19 EST: 1954
SQ FT: 35,000
SALES (est): 4MM Privately Held
WEB: www.valentineflyreel.com
SIC: 3469 3861 3542 Mfg Metal Stampings Mfg Photographic Equipment/Supplies Mfg Machine Tools-Forming

(G-14092)
VW QUALITY COATING
62 Cross St (02766-2319)
PHONE....617 963-6503
Joseph Van Wart, *Principal*
EMP: 10
SALES (est): 1MM Privately Held
SIC: 3479 Coating/Engraving Service

(G-14093)
WB ENGINEERING INC
Also Called: Presto Lifts
50 Commerce Way (02766-3322)
PHONE....508 952-4000
Lisa Ramsey, *Manager*
EMP: 50
SALES (corp-wide): 81.4MM Privately Held
WEB: www.lifttable.com
SIC: 3537 Mfg Industrial Trucks
HQ: W.B. Engineering, Inc.
11 Gray Rd
Falmouth ME 04105
207 878-0700

GEOGRAPHIC

Norwell
Plymouth County

(G-14094)
ARBORTECH TOOLS USA CORP
45r Washington St (02061-1715)
PHONE..................................866 517-7869
Kevin Ross Inkster, *President*
David Kormanec, *Sales Staff*
Joe Tuohy, *Manager*
EMP: 3
SALES (est): 182.8K **Privately Held**
SIC: 3423 Mfg Hand/Edge Tools

(G-14095)
AT&T INC
10 Washington St (02061-1749)
PHONE..................................781 878-8169
EMP: 5
SALES (corp-wide): 170.7B **Publicly Held**
SIC: 3663 Mfg Radio/Tv Communication Equipment
PA: At&T Inc.
208 S Akard St
Dallas TX 75202
210 821-4105

(G-14096)
AVEDIS ZILDJIAN CO (PA)
22 Longwater Dr (02061-1612)
PHONE..................................781 871-2200
Craigie A Zildjian, *President*
Brad Baker, *Vice Pres*
Andy Schlosser, *Vice Pres*
Joe Testa, *Vice Pres*
Art Collins, *Plant Mgr*
◆ **EMP:** 130
SQ FT: 66,000
SALES (est): 22.4MM **Privately Held**
WEB: www.zildjian.com
SIC: 3931 Mfg Musical Instruments

(G-14097)
BLACKTRACE INC
156 Norwell Ave (02061-1212)
PHONE..................................617 848-1211
Richard Gray, *President*
Andrew Lovatt, *COO*
EMP: 8
SALES (est): 2MM
SALES (corp-wide): 15.5MM **Privately Held**
SIC: 3821 Mfg Lab Apparatus/Furniture
PA: Blacktrace Holdings Limited
Unit 3, Anglian Business Park
Royston HERTS SG8 5
176 325-2149

(G-14098)
BROOKS ASSOCIATES INC (PA)
300 Longwater Dr Unit 3 (02061-1662)
P.O. Box 85, Accord (02018-0085)
PHONE..................................781 871-3400
Joe Klier Jr, *President*
Peter Klier, *CFO*
Michael Klier, *Admin Sec*
Joe Sarli, *Technician*
EMP: 7 **EST:** 1985
SQ FT: 3,000
SALES (est): 1.5MM **Privately Held**
WEB: www.brooksmachinery.com
SIC: 3599 Mfg Industrial Machinery

(G-14099)
CABINET HOUSE LLC
33 Tara Dr (02061-2622)
PHONE..................................781 424-2259
Gregory A Hayes, *Principal*
EMP: 4
SALES (est): 204.7K **Privately Held**
SIC: 2434 Mfg Wood Kitchen Cabinets

(G-14100)
CONCERT MEDICAL LLC
77 Accord Park Dr Ste A3 (02061-1623)
PHONE..................................781 261-7400
Normand P Collard, *Principal*
Patrick J Kinney Jr, *Principal*
Howard W Donnelly, *Mng Member*
George A Adaniya,
Paul J Dobson,
▲ **EMP:** 23
SALES (est): 4.8MM **Privately Held**
SIC: 3841 Mfg Surgical/Medical Instruments

(G-14101)
COUNTRY LIFE LLC
335 Washington St Ste 3 (02061-1900)
PHONE..................................781 659-1321
Jill Carney, *Office Mgr*
EMP: 3 **Privately Held**
SIC: 2833 Mfg Medicinal/Botanical Products
HQ: Country Life, Llc
180 Vanderbilt Motor Pkwy
Hauppauge NY 11788
631 232-5400

(G-14102)
EAST COAST PUBLICATIONS INC (PA)
Also Called: New England Real Estate Jurnl
17 Accord Park Dr Ste 207 (02061-1629)
P.O. Box 55, Accord (02018-0055)
PHONE..................................781 878-4540
Thomas Murray, *CEO*
Tony McDonald, *Partner*
Shirley Crivelli, *Publisher*
Jeff Keller, *Publisher*
Patti Stone, *Publisher*
EMP: 26
SQ FT: 8,000
SALES (est): 1.8MM **Privately Held**
WEB: www.rejournal.com
SIC: 2711 6531 2721 Newspapers-Publishing/Printing Real Estate Agent/Manager Periodicals-Publishing/Printing

(G-14103)
GATEHOUSE MEDIA LLC
600 Cordwainer Dr (02061-1644)
PHONE..................................781 829-9305
Jim Piasecki, *CEO*
Mark Hathaway, *Engineer*
Rodgers Mnas, *Manager*
Sara Deuth, *Executive Asst*
Nicole Barnwell, *Technician*
EMP: 49
SALES (corp-wide): 1.5B **Publicly Held**
SIC: 2711 Newspapers-Publishing/Printing
HQ: Gatehouse Media, Llc
175 Sullys Trl Fl 3
Pittsford NY 14534
585 598-0030

(G-14104)
IMAGE RESOLUTIONS INC
382 Washington St Unit 2 (02061-2070)
PHONE..................................781 659-0900
Phyllis Wenzel, *President*
Bill Wenzel, *Vice Pres*
EMP: 6
SQ FT: 3,000
SALES: 900K **Privately Held**
WEB: www.imageresolutions.com
SIC: 2759 Commercial Printing

(G-14105)
LARSON WORLDWIDE INC
95 Mount Blue St (02061-1015)
PHONE..................................781 659-2115
Robert A Larson, *President*
Susan Corcoran, *Vice Pres*
EMP: 4
SALES: 400K **Privately Held**
WEB: www.larsonworldwide.com
SIC: 2741 8249 8748 7389 Publisher Of A Newsletter Conducts Symposioums & Industry Specialist Consultant & Promoters Of Trade Shows

(G-14106)
LIDDELL BROTHERS INC
61 Accord Park Dr (02061-1614)
PHONE..................................781 293-2100
Garrett Liddell, *President*
Jacob Liddell, *Vice Pres*
Michelle Hood, *Manager*
EMP: 25
SQ FT: 17,000
SALES (est): 2.5MM **Privately Held**
WEB: www.liddellbrothers.com
SIC: 3993 1611 Mfg Signs/Advertising Specialties Highway/Street Construction

(G-14107)
MARUHO HTSUJYO INNOVATIONS INC (PA)
55 Accord Park Dr (02061-1665)
PHONE..................................617 653-1617
John F Rousseau Jr, *President*
Thomas E Hancock, *Vice Pres*
Ryoai Imai, *Director*
Atsushi Sugita, *Director*
EMP: 15
SALES (est): 6.3MM **Privately Held**
SIC: 3565 3841 Mfg Packaging Machinery Mfg Surgical/Medical Instruments

(G-14108)
NEW ENGLAND RUNNER
320 Washington St (02061-1700)
PHONE..................................781 987-1730
EMP: 3
SALES (est): 116K **Privately Held**
SIC: 2711 Newspapers-Publishing/Printing

(G-14109)
NOW PUBLISHERS INC
167 Washington St Ste 20 (02061-1797)
P.O. Box 1024, Hanover (02339-1001)
PHONE..................................781 871-0245
Zachary Rolnik, *President*
Tanya Capawana, *Marketing Staff*
EMP: 4
SALES (est): 289.1K **Privately Held**
SIC: 2721 Periodicals-Publishing/Printing

(G-14110)
PARTYLITE WORLDWIDE LLC (DH)
600 Cordwainer Dr Ste 202 (02061-1644)
PHONE..................................888 999-5706
Harry Slatkin, *CEO*
Robert B Goergen Jr, *President*
Kathleen Luce, *President*
Lisa Parketny, *President*
Martin K Hler, *General Mgr*
◆ **EMP:** 250
SQ FT: 1,000
SALES (est): 340.5MM
SALES (corp-wide): 2.4B **Publicly Held**
SIC: 3999 5961 Mfg Misc Products Ret Mail-Order House
HQ: Partylite, Inc.
59 Armstrong Rd
Plymouth MA 02360
203 661-1926

(G-14111)
PETERSON AND NASH INC
846 Main St (02061-2320)
PHONE..................................781 826-9085
Wayne Peterson, *President*
Marie Peterson, *Co-Owner*
EMP: 39 **EST:** 1939
SQ FT: 11,000
SALES (est): 1.4MM **Privately Held**
SIC: 3423 3541 Mfg Hand/Edge Tools Mfg Machine Tools-Cutting

(G-14112)
SULLIVAN MANUFACTURING COMPANY
Also Called: Sullivan Tire
41 Accord Park Dr (02061-1614)
PHONE..................................781 982-1550
Robert D Sullivan, *President*
David M Sullivan, *Vice Pres*
Mehtab Kazmi, *Manager*
Lynn A Sawiski, *Admin Sec*
EMP: 20
SQ FT: 6,500
SALES: 5.2MM
SALES (corp-wide): 272.2MM **Privately Held**
SIC: 3011 Mfg Tires/Inner Tubes
PA: Sullivan Investment Co., Inc.
41 Accord Park Dr
Norwell MA 02061
781 982-1550

(G-14113)
W P MOORE CO INC
249 High St (02061-1833)
PHONE..................................781 878-9566
William Moore, *President*
EMP: 5
SQ FT: 4,000
SALES (est): 615.2K **Privately Held**
SIC: 3599 Mfg Industrial Machinery

(G-14114)
WALPOLE WOODWORKERS INC
183 Washington St (02061-1752)
PHONE..................................781 681-9099
Patricia Suarez, *Branch Mgr*
EMP: 4
SALES (corp-wide): 83.9MM **Privately Held**
WEB: www.walpolewoodworkers.com
SIC: 2499 5211 5712 2452 Mfg Wood Products Ret Lumber/Building Mtrl Ret Furniture Mfg Prefabrcatd Wd Bldgs Mfg Prefab Metal Bldgs
PA: Walpole Outdoors Llc
100 Rver Ridge Dr Ste 302
Norwood MA 02062
508 668-2800

Norwood
Norfolk County

(G-14115)
269 WALPOLE STREET LLC
269 Walpole St (02062-3251)
PHONE..................................781 762-1128
Donald L Simi, *Manager*
EMP: 5
SQ FT: 7,591
SALES (est): 405.4K **Privately Held**
SIC: 2911 Petroleum Refiner

(G-14116)
ABBAS SHAHRESTANAKI
61 Endicott St (02062-3046)
PHONE..................................617 548-0986
Abbas Shahrestanaki, *Principal*
EMP: 4
SALES (est): 292.6K **Privately Held**
SIC: 2431 Mfg Millwork

(G-14117)
ABSOLUTE METAL FINISHING INC
90 Morse St (02062-4326)
PHONE..................................781 551-8235
Michael Deneen Jr, *President*
Sandra Emery, *QC Mgr*
EMP: 27
SQ FT: 10,000
SALES (est): 3.2MM **Privately Held**
WEB: www.absolutemetal.com
SIC: 3471 Plating/Polishing Service

(G-14118)
ACE RESULT LLC
343 Vanderbilt Ave (02062-5007)
PHONE..................................612 559-3838
Boukay Sung,
EMP: 3
SALES (est): 99.4K **Privately Held**
SIC: 2519 Mfg Household Furniture

(G-14119)
ADINA INC (PA)
90 Kerry Pl Ste 5 (02062-4765)
PHONE..................................781 762-4477
V Zev Rejman, *President*
EMP: 20
SQ FT: 11,000
SALES (est): 3MM **Privately Held**
WEB: www.adinadesign.com
SIC: 3961 3911 Mfg Costume Jewelry Mfg Precious Metal Jewelry

(G-14120)
ADMET INC
51 Morgan Dr Ste 15 (02062-5091)
PHONE..................................781 769-0850
Richard Gedney, *President*
Gennadiy Komm, *Project Mgr*
Mark Sousa, *Purch Mgr*
Maria Conway, *Buyer*
Mark Kennedy, *Engineer*
▲ **EMP:** 7
SALES (est): 2.1MM **Privately Held**
WEB: www.admet.com
SIC: 3829 Mfg Measuring/Controlling Devices

(G-14121)
ADVANCED GRAPHICS INC
470 Washington St Ste 20 (02062-2349)
PHONE..........781 551-0550
Charles Spiegel, *President*
Jason Spiegel, *Exec VP*
EMP: 4
SQ FT: 1,200
SALES (est): 739.7K **Privately Held**
WEB: www.adv-graphics.com
SIC: 2759 Commercial Printing

(G-14122)
ADVANCED INSTRUMENTS LLC (PA)
2 Technology Way Ste 1 (02062-2630)
PHONE..........781 320-9000
John L Coughlin, *President*
Pete Emond, *President*
Dianne Walters, *General Mgr*
Robert Mello, *COO*
Peter Costas, *Vice Pres*
▲ **EMP:** 94
SQ FT: 55,000
SALES (est): 19.5MM **Privately Held**
WEB: www.aicompanies.com
SIC: 3826 Mfg Analytical Instruments

(G-14123)
ADVANCED THERMAL SOLUTIONS INC (PA)
89 Access Rd Ste 27 (02062-5234)
PHONE..........781 769-2800
Kaveh Aza, *President*
Kaveh Azar, *President*
Sharon Koss, *Vice Pres*
Rebecca O'Day, *Vice Pres*
Andrea Koss, *Marketing Staff*
▲ **EMP:** 40
SQ FT: 15,000
SALES (est): 8.5MM **Privately Held**
WEB: www.qats.com
SIC: 3823 3829 3826 Mfg Process Control Instruments Mfg Measuring/Controlling Devices Mfg Analytical Instruments

(G-14124)
ALDRICH MARBLE & GRANITE CO
Also Called: Aldrich Stone
83 Morse St Ste 3 (02062-4350)
PHONE..........781 762-6111
Thomas J Aldrich, *President*
Glen Murrey, *Vice Pres*
EMP: 23
SQ FT: 17,000
SALES (est): 2.2MM **Privately Held**
WEB: www.aldrichstone.com
SIC: 3281 5032 5713 Marble & Granite Fabrication

(G-14125)
ALTAIR AVIONICS CORPORATION
249 Vanderbilt Ave Ste 1 (02062-5033)
PHONE..........781 762-8600
Doug Thompson, *President*
David Keenan, *Vice Pres*
Donald Simoneau, *Finance*
Jeff Coleman, *Manager*
Donna Driscoll, *Manager*
EMP: 40
SQ FT: 13,000
SALES (est): 4MM
SALES (corp-wide): 66.5B **Publicly Held**
WEB: www.altairavionics.com
SIC: 3812 Mfg Search/Navigation Equipment
PA: United Technologies Corporation
10 Farm Springs Rd
Farmington CT 06032
860 728-7000

(G-14126)
AMERICAD TECHNOLOGY CORPORAT
700 Pleasant St (02062-4632)
P.O. Box 314 (02062-0314)
PHONE..........781 551-8220
Mark Haslett, *President*
EMP: 35
SQ FT: 19,000
SALES (est): 6.2MM **Privately Held**
WEB: www.americadtech.com
SIC: 3089 Mfg Plastic Products

(G-14127)
AMERICAN BATTERY COMPANY LLC
930 Washington St (02062-3412)
PHONE..........781 440-0325
Robert P Marotto,
▲ **EMP:** 7
SALES (est): 878.3K **Privately Held**
SIC: 3691 Mfg Storage Batteries

(G-14128)
AMERICAN COPY PRINT
Also Called: American Copyprint
1502 Boston Providence Tp (02062-4643)
PHONE..........781 769-9077
Sudhair Shah, *Owner*
EMP: 4
SQ FT: 2,500
SALES (est): 270K **Privately Held**
WEB: www.american-copyprint.com
SIC: 2752 Lithographic Commercial Printing

(G-14129)
AMERICAN INK & OIL CORPORATION
61 Endicott St Ste 33 (02062-3052)
PHONE..........781 762-0026
Henry G Levinson, *President*
EMP: 5 **EST:** 1931
SQ FT: 10,000
SALES: 1.6MM **Privately Held**
WEB: www.aminkoil.com
SIC: 2899 Mfg Chemical Preparations

(G-14130)
ANALOG DEVICES INC (PA)
1 Technology Way (02062-2666)
P.O. Box 9106 (02062-9106)
PHONE..........781 329-4700
Ray Stata, *Ch of Bd*
Vincent Roche, *President*
Martin Cotter, *Senior VP*
Joseph Hassett, *Senior VP*
Gregory Henderson, *Senior VP*
◆ **EMP:** 1000 **EST:** 1965
SQ FT: 130,000
SALES: 5.9B **Publicly Held**
WEB: www.analog.com
SIC: 3674 Mfg Integrated Circuits

(G-14131)
ANALOG DEVICES INTL INC (HQ)
1 Technology Way (02062-2666)
PHONE..........781 329-4700
Joseph E Mc Donough, *President*
EMP: 15
SQ FT: 74,300
SALES (est): 65.6MM
SALES (corp-wide): 5.9B **Publicly Held**
SIC: 3674 3825 Mfg Semiconductors/Related Devices Mfg Electrical Measuring Instruments
PA: Analog Devices, Inc.
1 Technology Way
Norwood MA 02062
781 329-4700

(G-14132)
APOGEE TECHNOLOGY INC (PA)
Also Called: (A DEVELOPMENT STAGE COMPANY)
129 Morgan Dr (02062-5014)
PHONE..........781 551-9450
Herbert M Stein, *Ch of Bd*
Craig A Dubitsky, *Principal*
Arthur S Reynolds, *Principal*
Sheryl B Stein, *Principal*
Alan W Tuck, *Principal*
EMP: 6
SQ FT: 5,000
SALES (est): 65K **Privately Held**
SIC: 3841 Mfg Surgical/Medical Instruments

(G-14133)
APPLIED PLASTICS CO INC
25 Endicott St (02062-3006)
P.O. Box 128 (02062-0128)
PHONE..........781 762-1881
Thomas Barrett, *CEO*
Dave B Ring, *Ch of Bd*
EMP: 30
SQ FT: 12,400
SALES: 12.9MM **Privately Held**
WEB: www.appliedplastics.com
SIC: 3479 Coating/Engraving Service

(G-14134)
ARTECH HOUSE INC (HQ)
685 Canton St (02062-2608)
PHONE..........781 769-9750
William M Bazzy, *President*
Christopher Ernst, *COO*
Kate Skypeck, *Sales Staff*
Gergana Spasova, *Business Anlyst*
EMP: 12
SQ FT: 8,000
SALES (est): 3.7MM
SALES (corp-wide): 12.2MM **Privately Held**
WEB: www.artechhouse.com
SIC: 2731 7372 7812 Book Publishers
PA: Horizon House Publications Inc.
685 Canton St
Norwood MA 02062
781 769-9750

(G-14135)
ASD-LIGHTING CORP
625 University Ave (02062-2642)
PHONE..........781 739-3977
EMP: 5
SALES (est): 667.4K **Privately Held**
SIC: 3646 Mfg Commercial Lighting Fixtures

(G-14136)
ATLANTIC POLY INC
86 Morse St (02062-4326)
PHONE..........781 769-4260
John B Maslowski, *President*
John Powers, *Sales Executive*
EMP: 18
SQ FT: 38,000
SALES (est): 2.9MM **Privately Held**
SIC: 3081 5162 Mfg Unsupported Plastic Film/Sheet Whol Plastic Materials/Shapes

(G-14137)
BBCG LLC
Also Called: Vantage Graphics
273 Lenox St Ste 8 (02062-3497)
PHONE..........617 796-8800
Bon Chan, *President*
Gary Chow, *Vice Chairman*
Benjamin Chow, *Treasurer*
EMP: 4
SQ FT: 5,000
SALES (est): 600K **Privately Held**
WEB: www.vangraph.com
SIC: 2752 7336 7334 Lithographic Commercial Printing Commercial Art/Graphic Design Photocopying Services

(G-14138)
BOSTON EXECUTIVE HELICOPTERS
209 Access Rd (02062-5247)
PHONE..........781 603-6186
Christopher Donovan, *Owner*
EMP: 3 **EST:** 2014
SALES (est): 255.6K **Privately Held**
SIC: 3721 Airport/Airport Services

(G-14139)
CARITAS PET IMAGING LLC
800 Washington St Ste 1 (02062-3487)
PHONE..........508 259-8919
Robert E Guyon, *Principal*
EMP: 5
SALES: 4.9MM **Privately Held**
SIC: 3845 Mfg Electromedical Equipment

(G-14140)
CASTLE ISLAND BREWING CO LLC
31 Astor Ave (02062-5016)
PHONE..........781 951-2029
Adam Romanow, *Mng Member*
EMP: 40
SALES (est): 3.2MM **Privately Held**
SIC: 2082 Mfg Malt Beverages

(G-14141)
CHACO INC
Also Called: Print Central
99 Central St (02062-3544)
P.O. Box 245 (02062-0245)
PHONE..........781 769-5557
Joseph Chafets, *President*
EMP: 5
SQ FT: 1,200
SALES (est): 429.6K **Privately Held**
SIC: 2752 2791 2789 Lithographic Commercial Printing Typesetting Services Bookbinding/Related Work

(G-14142)
CONSEAL INTERNATIONAL INC
90 Kerry Pl Ste 2 (02062-4765)
PHONE..........781 278-0010
Stephen C Perry, *President*
EMP: 4
SQ FT: 8,000
SALES (est): 957.9K **Privately Held**
WEB: www.servomexinc.com
SIC: 2899 2834 Mfg Chemical Preparations Mfg Pharmaceutical Preparations

(G-14143)
CONTEMPORARY CABINET DESIGNS
416 Lenox St Ste B (02062-3465)
PHONE..........781 769-7979
R Clark Kinton, *President*
Walter J White Jr, *Treasurer*
Debra Kinton, *Clerk*
Susan White, *Clerk*
EMP: 4
SQ FT: 4,200
SALES: 300K **Privately Held**
SIC: 2521 2431 Mfg Wood Office Furniture Mfg Millwork

(G-14144)
CORBUS PHARMACEUTICALS INC
500 River Ridge Dr # 200 (02062-5154)
PHONE..........617 963-1000
Mark A Tepper, *President*
Sumner Burstein, *Principal*
Robert Zurier, *Principal*
Greg Coulter, *Vice Pres*
Edward Monaghan, *Vice Pres*
EMP: 9
SALES (est): 1.6MM
SALES (corp-wide): 4.8MM **Publicly Held**
SIC: 2834 Mfg Pharmaceutical Preparations
PA: Corbus Pharmaceuticals Holdings, Inc.
500 River Ridge Dr
Norwood MA 02062
617 963-0100

(G-14145)
CORBUS PHRMCTCALS HOLDINGS INC (PA)
500 River Ridge Dr (02062-5045)
PHONE..........617 963-0100
Yuval Cohen, *CEO*
Alan Holmer, *Ch of Bd*
Mark Tepper, *President*
Robert Discordia, *Vice Pres*
Ross Lobell, *Vice Pres*
EMP: 21
SALES: 4.8MM **Publicly Held**
SIC: 2834 Pharmaceutical Preparations

(G-14146)
CORPORATE PRESS
89 Access Rd Ste 17 (02062-5234)
PHONE..........781 769-6656
Michael Kadetsky, *Partner*
Steven B Brown, *Partner*
EMP: 10
SQ FT: 4,500
SALES (est): 1.1MM **Privately Held**
SIC: 2752 2741 Lithographic Commercial Printing Misc Publishing

(G-14147)
ECOLAB INC
1 Edgewater Dr Ste 210 (02062-7607)
PHONE..........781 688-2100
Todd Goble, *General Mgr*
Paula Palmi, *Vice Pres*
EMP: 55

SALES (corp-wide): 14.6B **Publicly Held**
WEB: www.ecolab.com
SIC: 2841 Whol Chemicals/Products
PA: Ecolab Inc.
1 Ecolab Pl
Saint Paul MN 55102
800 232-6522

(G-14148)
ENGINRED PLAS SLTONS GROUP INC
Also Called: Epsg
76 Astor Ave Ste 101 (02062-5099)
PHONE....................................781 762-3913
Erik Larson, *President*
▲ **EMP:** 5
SQ FT: 6,000
SALES (est): 2.5MM
SALES (corp-wide): 31.3MM **Privately Held**
WEB: www.epsginc.com
SIC: 3089 8711 Mfg Plastic Products Engineering Services
PA: Polymer Technologies, Inc.
420 Corporate Blvd
Newark DE 19702
302 738-9001

(G-14149)
ENTERADE USA
100 Rver Ridge Dr Ste 112 (02062)
PHONE....................................781 352-5450
Sarah Bate, *Office Mgr*
Steve Gatto, *Mng Member*
EMP: 12
SALES (est): 808.5K **Privately Held**
SIC: 2086 Mfg Bottled/Canned Soft Drinks

(G-14150)
ENTERPRISE NEWSMEDIA LLC
Also Called: Norwood Bulletin
1091 Washington St (02062-4416)
PHONE....................................781 769-5535
Matt Cook, *Branch Mgr*
EMP: 10
SALES (corp-wide): 1.5B **Publicly Held**
WEB: www.enterprisenewsmedia.com
SIC: 2711 Newspapers-Publishing/Printing
HQ: Enterprise Newsmedia, Llc
400 Crown Colony Dr
Quincy MA 02169
585 598-0030

(G-14151)
EUROPEAN CABINET DESIGN INC
2 Sumner St (02062-4612)
PHONE....................................781 769-7100
Tony Colobraro, *President*
Luigi Sellito, *Vice Pres*
EMP: 4
SALES (est): 350K **Privately Held**
SIC: 2434 Mfg Wood Kitchen Cabinets

(G-14152)
EXCEL GRAPHIX
35 Arnold Rd (02062-4788)
PHONE....................................781 642-6736
Fax: 781 642-6737
EMP: 5
SALES (est): 489.1K **Privately Held**
WEB: www.excelgraphix.com
SIC: 2759 Commercial Printing

(G-14153)
FUEL SOURCE INC
960 Providence Hwy (02062)
PHONE....................................781 469-8449
Ziad Saba, *Principal*
EMP: 4
SALES (est): 365.1K **Privately Held**
SIC: 2869 Mfg Industrial Organic Chemicals

(G-14154)
FURLONGS COTTAGE CANDIES
1355 Bston Prvidence Tpke (02062-5055)
PHONE....................................781 762-4124
Gail Ghelfi, *President*
Albert Ghelfi, *Chairman*
Kenneth Thrasher, *Vice Pres*
Doris Thrasher, *Treasurer*
EMP: 11
SQ FT: 2,500
SALES (est): 530K **Privately Held**
SIC: 2064 5441 5812 Mfg & Ret Candies & Operates A Soda Fountain

(G-14155)
GEORGIA-PACIFIC LLC
315 Norwood Park S Ste 1 (02062-4681)
PHONE....................................781 440-3600
EMP: 3
SALES (corp-wide): 40.6B **Privately Held**
WEB: www.gp.com
SIC: 2631 2421 2611 2431 Paperboard Mill Sawmill/Planing Mill Pulp Mill Mfg Millwork
HQ: Georgia-Pacific Llc
133 Peachtree St Nw
Atlanta GA 30303
404 652-4000

(G-14156)
GOLDMAN-KOLBER INC
185 Dean St Ste 204 (02062-4552)
PHONE....................................781 769-6362
David Steinhauer, *President*
Susan L Steinhauer, *Vice Pres*
Lori Grady, *Mktg Dir*
EMP: 25 **EST:** 1919
SQ FT: 3,800
SALES (est): 2.9MM **Privately Held**
WEB: www.goldmankolber.com
SIC: 3911 Mfg Precious Metal Jewelry

(G-14157)
HOME MARKET FOODS INC (PA)
140 Morgan Dr Ste 100 (02062-5076)
PHONE....................................781 948-1500
Douglas K Atamian, *CEO*
Wesley L Atamian, *President*
Rocky Schroeder, *Vice Pres*
Mike Weiermiller, *Vice Pres*
Kartik Patel, *Prdtn Mgr*
EMP: 150
SQ FT: 85,000
SALES (est): 426.4MM **Privately Held**
WEB: www.homemarketfoods.com
SIC: 2013 Mfg Prepared Meats

(G-14158)
HORIZON HOUSE PUBLICATIONS INC (PA)
Also Called: Signal Integrity Journal
685 Canton St (02062-2608)
PHONE....................................781 769-9750
William Bazzy, *CEO*
Ivar Anderson Bazzy, *President*
Carl Sheffres, *Editor*
Barbara Walsh, *Editor*
Jared Bazzy, *Vice Pres*
EMP: 53
SQ FT: 26,061
SALES: 12.2MM **Privately Held**
WEB: www.telecoms-mag.com
SIC: 2721 2731 5192 8748 Periodical-Publish/Print Book-Publishing/Printing Whol Books/Newspapers Business Consulting Svcs

(G-14159)
I & I SLING INC
1400 Boston Providence Tp (02062-5044)
P.O. Box 101 (02062-0101)
PHONE....................................781 575-0600
Scott Woodward, *Manager*
EMP: 80
SALES (corp-wide): 16.8MM **Privately Held**
SIC: 2298 Mfg Cordage/Twine
PA: I & I Sling, Inc.
205 Bridgewater Rd
Aston PA 19014
800 874-3539

(G-14160)
ILLINOIS TOOL WORKS INC
Instron A Div Ill Tl Works
825 University Ave (02062-2643)
PHONE....................................781 828-2500
Bob Chartrand, *Vice Pres*
Jim Schepp, *Production*
Martin Blenkhorn, *Engineer*
Lorenzo Majno, *VP Mktg*
Steve Martindale, *Branch Mgr*
EMP: 300
SALES (corp-wide): 14.7B **Publicly Held**
SIC: 3829 3826 Mfg Measuring/Controlling Devices Mfg Analytical Instruments
PA: Illinois Tool Works Inc.
155 Harlem Ave
Glenview IL 60025
847 724-7500

(G-14161)
INGLESIDE CORPORATION
Also Called: Printmaster
89 Access Rd Ste 17 (02062-5234)
PHONE....................................781 769-6656
Tim Connors, *President*
EMP: 9
SQ FT: 1,000
SALES: 1,000K **Privately Held**
SIC: 2752 Lithographic Commercial Printing

(G-14162)
INPHOTONICS INC
111 Downey St (02062-2612)
PHONE....................................781 440-0202
A C Makrides, *President*
Anthony J Medaglia, *Admin Sec*
EMP: 10
SALES: 1,000K **Privately Held**
WEB: www.inphotonics.com
SIC: 3821 Mfg Lab Apparatus/Furniture

(G-14163)
INSTANT SIGN CENTER
1400 Boston Providence Tp (02062-5158)
PHONE....................................781 278-0150
Jay Con, *Owner*
John Geenan, *Principal*
Mike Collari, *Accounts Exec*
Jay Kahn, *Sales Staff*
EMP: 6
SALES (est): 600.5K **Privately Held**
SIC: 3993 Mfg Signs/Advertising Specialties

(G-14164)
INSTRON APPLICATIONS LAB
825 University Ave (02062-2643)
PHONE....................................800 564-8378
EMP: 3 **EST:** 2017
SALES (est): 114.7K **Privately Held**
SIC: 3821 Mfg Measuring/Controlling Devices

(G-14165)
INSTRON JAPAN COMPANY LTD
825 University Ave (02062-2643)
PHONE....................................781 828-2500
Steven Martindale, *President*
EMP: 450
SALES (est): 32.1MM
SALES (corp-wide): 14.7B **Publicly Held**
SIC: 3829 Mfg Measuring/Controlling Devices
PA: Illinois Tool Works Inc.
155 Harlem Ave
Glenview IL 60025
847 724-7500

(G-14166)
INTERNATIONAL FOOD PRODUCTS
Also Called: Sabra Foods
422 Walpole St Ste B (02062-3072)
PHONE....................................781 769-6666
Pierre Saroufim, *President*
Dorothy Saroufim, *Shareholder*
EMP: 7
SQ FT: 5,000
SALES (est): 892.8K **Privately Held**
SIC: 2099 Mfg Food Preparations

(G-14167)
ITW INSTRON
825 University Ave (02062-2643)
PHONE....................................781 762-3216
EMP: 5
SALES (est): 449.4K **Privately Held**
SIC: 3829 Mfg Measuring/Controlling Devices

(G-14168)
K INT L WOODWORKING
59 Earle St (02062-1504)
PHONE....................................781 440-0512
Franjo Katic, *Principal*
EMP: 4 **EST:** 2008
SALES (est): 424.3K **Privately Held**
SIC: 2431 Mfg Millwork

(G-14169)
KAMWELD TECHNOLOGIES INC
Also Called: Kam Weld Technologies
90 Access Rd (02062-5237)
PHONE....................................781 762-6922
Kaveh Azar, *President*
Sharon Koss, *Vice Pres*
EMP: 10
SALES (est): 1.3MM **Privately Held**
WEB: www.kamweld.com
SIC: 3548 Whol Industrial Equipment

(G-14170)
KEYSTONE PRINTING INK CO
180 Kerry Pl Ste C (02062-4735)
PHONE....................................781 762-6974
Jim Linskey, *Manager*
EMP: 8
SALES (corp-wide): 3.1MM **Privately Held**
WEB: www.keystoneink.com
SIC: 2893 Mfg Printing Ink
PA: Keystone Printing Ink Co.
2700 Roberts Ave
Philadelphia PA 19129
215 228-8100

(G-14171)
KITCHENS & BATH OF NORWOOD
520 Boston Providence (02062-4946)
PHONE....................................781 255-1448
Tom Dacosta, *Owner*
EMP: 3
SALES (est): 211.9K **Privately Held**
SIC: 2434 Mfg Wood Kitchen Cabinets

(G-14172)
KREATE & PRINT INC
14 Central St (02062-3504)
PHONE....................................781 255-0505
Kashmira Vora, *President*
Premal Vora, *Treasurer*
EMP: 3
SQ FT: 1,600
SALES (est): 412.5K **Privately Held**
SIC: 2759 7334 Commercial Printing

(G-14173)
L T X INTERNATIONAL INC
Also Called: LTX Credence
825 University Ave (02062-2643)
PHONE....................................781 461-1000
David Tacelli, *CEO*
Roger W Blethen, *Ch of Bd*
Mark Gallenberger, *COO*
Tam Pham, *Design Engr*
Mark J Gallenberger, *CFO*
EMP: 100
SALES (est): 14.9MM
SALES (corp-wide): 451.7MM **Publicly Held**
WEB: www.ltx.com
SIC: 3825 7629 7373 3674 Mfg Elec Measuring Instr Electrical Repair Computer Systems Design Mfg Semiconductors/Dvcs
HQ: Xcerra Corporation
825 University Ave
Norwood MA 02062
781 461-1000

(G-14174)
LAWRENCE INSTRON CORPORATION
825 University Ave (02062-2643)
PHONE....................................781 828-2500
Steven Martindale, *CEO*
John Reskusich, *General Mgr*
Michael Boyd, *Business Mgr*
Kerry Rosado, *Opers Dir*
Paul Ekholm, *Opers Mgr*
◆ **EMP:** 200
SALES (est): 70.3MM **Privately Held**
SIC: 3829 Mfg Measuring/Controlling Devices

(G-14175)
LIQUIDSKY TECHNOLOGIES INC (PA)
89 Access Rd (02062-5229)
PHONE....................................857 389-9893

EMP: 10
SALES (est): 1.1MM Privately Held
SIC: 3694 Mfg Engine Electrical Equipment

(G-14176)
MANUFCTRING RESOURCE GROUP INC
Also Called: Mrg
930 Washington St (02062-3412)
PHONE....781 440-9700
Robert Marotto, *President*
Joseph F Prior, *President*
Robin Gonzales, *Vice Pres*
James McKenna, *Vice Pres*
Debbie Cunniff, *Office Mgr*
EMP: 140
SQ FT: 45,000
SALES: 18MM Privately Held
WEB: www.mrg-inc.com
SIC: 3625 Mfg Relays/Industrial Controls

(G-14177)
MEGANUTRA INC (PA)
128 Carnegie Row Ste 107 (02062-5162)
PHONE....781 762-9600
Yao Lin, *President*
EMP: 7
SALES (est): 1.1MM Privately Held
SIC: 2023 Mfg Dry/Evaporated Dairy Products

(G-14178)
METROPOLITAN CAB DISTRS CORP (PA)
Also Called: Metropltan Cbinets Countertops
505 University Ave (02062-2636)
PHONE....781 949-8900
Stuart Elfland, *President*
Bryan Dempsey, *Project Mgr*
Elfland Samantha, *VP Sls/Mktg*
Sean Rodgers, *Human Res Dir*
Scott Donoghue, *Sales Staff*
▲ EMP: 5
SQ FT: 85,000
SALES (est): 30.4MM Privately Held
WEB: www.metcabinet.com
SIC: 2434 2541 Mfg Wood Kitchen Cabinets Mfg Wood Partitions/Fixtures

(G-14179)
MICRON CORPORATION
89 Access Rd Ste 5 (02062-5234)
PHONE....781 769-5771
William C Theos, *President*
James W Theos, *President*
Chuck Theos, *General Mgr*
Charles W Theos, *Vice Pres*
Eleftheria Theos, *Admin Sec*
EMP: 23
SQ FT: 5,000
SALES: 3.9MM Privately Held
WEB: www.microncorp.com
SIC: 3672 Mfg Printed Circuit Boards

(G-14180)
MYSTIC SCENIC STUDIOS INC
Also Called: Mystic Millwork
293 Lenox St (02062-3462)
PHONE....781 440-0914
Jim Ray, *President*
Dunacn Maio, *General Mgr*
James J Fitzgerald, *Vice Pres*
Michael McKenna, *Vice Pres*
Jonathan Hondorp, *CFO*
EMP: 100
SQ FT: 100,000
SALES (est): 16.1MM Privately Held
WEB: www.mysticmillwork.com
SIC: 3999 3993 7389 Mfg Misc Products Mfg Signs/Advertising Specialties Business Services

(G-14181)
NEOGENIX LLC (PA)
588 Pleasant St Ste 2 (02062-4553)
PHONE....781 702-6732
Lawrence Cali, *Vice Pres*
Srinivasan Sarangapan,
Srinivasan Sarangapani,
EMP: 3
SALES (est): 511.7K Privately Held
SIC: 3842 Mfg Surgical Appliances/Supplies

(G-14182)
NEW ENGLAND PARTNERSHIP INC
Also Called: New England Coffee Company
30 Walpole St (02062-3356)
PHONE....800 225-3537
James M Kaloyanides, *President*
Chuck Kozubal, *President*
James Kaloyanides Jr, *Vice Pres*
John C Kaloyanides, *Vice Pres*
Michael Poore Mr, *Vice Pres*
▼ EMP: 200 EST: 1916
SQ FT: 90,000
SALES (est): 1.4MM
SALES (corp-wide): 358.5MM Privately Held
WEB: www.necoffeeco.com
SIC: 2095 5149 Mfg Roasted Coffee Whol Groceries
HQ: Reily Foods Company
400 Poydras St Fl 10
New Orleans LA 70130
-

(G-14183)
NEWPRO DESIGNS INC (HQ)
90 Kerry Pl Ste 5 (02062-4765)
PHONE....781 762-4477
V Zev Rejman, *President*
EMP: 20
SQ FT: 11,000
SALES (est): 1.7MM
SALES (corp-wide): 3MM Privately Held
SIC: 3961 3911 Mfg Costume & Silver Jewelry
PA: Adina Inc.
90 Kerry Pl Ste 5
Norwood MA 02062
781 762-4477

(G-14184)
NORWOOD SHEET METAL CORP
744 Bston Prvdnce Tpke St (02062-5291)
P.O. Box 309 (02062-0309)
PHONE....781 762-0720
Orlando J Germano Jr, *President*
Mary A Frederick, *Corp Secy*
EMP: 10
SQ FT: 4,800
SALES: 660K Privately Held
SIC: 3444 Mfg Sheet Metalwork

(G-14185)
NORWOOD WOODWORKING INC
640 Pleasant St Ste 1 (02062-4573)
PHONE....781 762-8367
Henry J Cullen Jr, *President*
Andy Lemus, *Manager*
EMP: 3
SALES (est): 368.8K Privately Held
SIC: 2541 Mfg Wood Partitions/Fixtures

(G-14186)
OLYMPIC ADHESIVES INC (PA)
670 Canton St (02062-2671)
PHONE....800 829-1871
John E Murray, *CEO*
Mark E Corndell, *President*
Darryl Hanson, *Division Mgr*
Stephen P Hopkins, *Exec VP*
Stephen Hopkins, *Exec VP*
◆ EMP: 49
SQ FT: 60,000
SALES (est): 15.5MM Privately Held
SIC: 2891 Mfg Adhesives/Sealants

(G-14187)
OMARC LLC
588 Pleasant St Ste 2 (02062-4553)
PHONE....781 702-6732
Srinivasan Sarangapani,
EMP: 3
SQ FT: 1,500
SALES (est): 262.4K Privately Held
WEB: www.omarc.com
SIC: 3841 Whol Medical/Hospital Equipment
PA: Neogenix, Llc
588 Pleasant St Ste 2
Norwood MA 02062
-

(G-14188)
PPI/TIME ZERO INC
Also Called: New Age Ems
1400 Boston Providence Tp (02062-5015)
PHONE....508 226-6090
Dana Pittman, *President*
EMP: 30
SALES (corp-wide): 69.1MM Privately Held
SIC: 3672 Mfg Printed Circuit Boards
HQ: Ppi/Time Zero, Inc.
11 Madison Rd
Fairfield NJ 07004
973 278-6500

(G-14189)
PULSE NETWORK INC
Also Called: Tpni
10 Oceana Way (02062-2610)
PHONE....781 688-8000
Stephen Saber, *Ch of Bd*
Nicholas Saber, *President*
John Saber, *CIO*
Robin Phillips, *Director*
▲ EMP: 18
SQ FT: 10,000
SALES: 2.3MM Privately Held
SIC: 7372 Prepackaged Software Services

(G-14190)
PURATOS CORPORATION
83 Morse St (02062-4351)
PHONE....781 688-8560
EMP: 3
SALES (est): 188.6K Privately Held
SIC: 2099 Mfg Food Preparations

(G-14191)
RARE BEAUTY BRANDS INC
Also Called: Patchology
83 Morse St Ste 8a (02062-4351)
PHONE....888 243-0646
Chris Hobson, *President*
Marc Shores, *Vice Pres*
Kathy St Clair, *Vice Pres*
Michael Jordan, *VP Opers*
Michele Zyla, *Controller*
EMP: 51
SALES (est): 3.1MM Privately Held
SIC: 2844 5122 Mfg Toilet Preparations Whol Drugs/Sundries

(G-14192)
REGAL PRESS INCORPORATED (PA)
79 Astor Ave (02062-5016)
P.O. Box 126 (02062-0126)
PHONE....781 769-3900
William N Duffey Jr, *President*
▼ EMP: 120
SQ FT: 150,000
SALES (est): 19.3MM Privately Held
WEB: www.regalpress.com
SIC: 2752 2761 2672 2759 Lithographic Coml Print Mfg Manifold Bus Forms Mfg Coat/Laminated Paper

(G-14193)
REMTEC INCORPORATED
5 Endicott St (02062-3042)
PHONE....781 762-5732
Paul Kurth, *Branch Mgr*
EMP: 6
SALES (est): 465.4K Privately Held
WEB: www.remtecinc.com
SIC: 3672 Mfg Multi-Layer Plated Copper On Ceramic
PA: Remtec, Incorporated
100 Morse St Ste 7
Norwood MA 02062
-

(G-14194)
REMTEC INCORPORATED (PA)
Also Called: TEC Mark Plating
100 Morse St Ste 7 (02062-4679)
PHONE....781 762-9191
Nahum Rapoport, *President*
Mike Hipsman, *Vice Pres*
Charles Ahern, *CFO*
Chuck Ahern, *CFO*
Jayne Nistad, *Accounts Mgr*
EMP: 35
SQ FT: 15,000
SALES (est): 8MM Privately Held
WEB: www.remtecinc.com
SIC: 3671 Mfg Electron Tubes

(G-14195)
REST ENSURED MEDICAL INC
661 Pleasant St Ste 99 (02062-4682)
PHONE....603 225-2860
Andrew Cook, *President*
EMP: 8
SALES (est): 1.1MM Privately Held
SIC: 3841 Mfg Surgical/Medical Instruments

(G-14196)
REVOLUTION COMPOSITES LLC
340 Vanderbilt Ave (02062-5008)
PHONE....781 255-1111
David Dahlheimer, *Mfg Staff*
Timothy Reardon, *Director*
Jeremy Torman, *Director*
EMP: 6
SQ FT: 6,000
SALES: 500K Privately Held
SIC: 2241 Narrow Fabric Mill

(G-14197)
ROGERS CABINETS
604 Pleasant St (02062-4604)
PHONE....781 762-5700
EMP: 3
SQ FT: 4,900
SALES (est): 226.5K Privately Held
SIC: 2542 Partitions And Fixtures, Except Wood, Nsk

(G-14198)
SIEMENS HLTHCARE DGNOSTICS INC
115 Norwood Park S (02062-4633)
PHONE....781 551-7000
Tom Dimarzo, *Branch Mgr*
Jonathan Shipman, *Manager*
Richard Horrigan, *Director*
EMP: 200
SQ FT: 42,000
SALES (corp-wide): 96.9B Privately Held
WEB: www.dpcweb.com
SIC: 3841 Mfg Surgical/Medical Instruments
HQ: Siemens Healthcare Diagnostics Inc.
511 Benedict Ave
Tarrytown NY 10591
914 631-8000

(G-14199)
SIEMENS HLTHCARE DGNOSTICS INC
2 Edgewater Dr (02062-4637)
PHONE....781 269-3000
Svein Gjelsvik, *Engineer*
Sandra Capen, *Manager*
Robert Seiche, *Software Engr*
Bill Thorpe, *Software Engr*
Sandra C Capen, *Exec Dir*
EMP: 200
SALES (corp-wide): 96.9B Privately Held
WEB: www.dpcweb.com
SIC: 3826 Mfg Blood Gases Testing Machines
HQ: Siemens Healthcare Diagnostics Inc.
511 Benedict Ave
Tarrytown NY 10591
914 631-8000

(G-14200)
SKILLSOFT CORPORATION
100 River Ridge Dr # 104 (02062-5036)
PHONE....800 899-1038
EMP: 5
SALES (corp-wide): 352.2K Privately Held
SIC: 7372 Prepackaged Software Services
HQ: Skillsoft Corporation
300 Innovative Way # 201
Nashua NH 03062
603 324-3000

(G-14201)
SPX CORPORATION
595 Pleasant St (02062-4603)
PHONE....704 752-4400
EMP: 19

GEOGRAPHIC

SALES (corp-wide): 1.5B **Publicly Held**
WEB: www.spx.com
SIC: 3443 Mfg Fabricated Plate Work
PA: Spx Corporation
13320a Balntyn Corp Pl
Charlotte NC 28277
980 474-3700

(G-14202)
SUN COUNTRY FOODS INC (HQ)
1 Edgewater Dr Ste 200 (02062-4669)
P.O. Box 88176, Seattle WA (98138-2176)
PHONE..................................855 824-7645
John Heily, *President*
Michael Morin, *CFO*
Michael Castle, *Treasurer*
Andy Heily, *Director*
EMP: 21 **EST:** 2011
SQ FT: 80,000
SALES (est): 1.7MM
SALES (corp-wide): 222.4MM **Privately Held**
SIC: 2099 Mfg Food Preparations
PA: Continental Mills, Inc.
18100 Andover Park W
Tukwila WA 98188
206 816-7000

(G-14203)
TE CONNECTIVITY CORPORATION
62 Nahatan St (02062-5717)
PHONE..................................781 278-5273
Al Dadah, *Manager*
EMP: 281
SALES (corp-wide): 13.9B **Privately Held**
WEB: www.raychem.com
SIC: 3678 Mfg Electronic Connectors
HQ: Te Connectivity Corporation
1050 Westlakes Dr
Berwyn PA 19312
610 893-9800

(G-14204)
UNIVERSAL CARBURETOR INC
Also Called: Universal Auto Service
544 Pleasant St (02062-4504)
PHONE..................................781 762-3771
Joseph Kalalas, *President*
William Kalalas, *Shareholder*
EMP: 3
SQ FT: 7,000
SALES (est): 230K **Privately Held**
SIC: 3592 7538 7539 Rebuilds And Repairs Carburetors

(G-14205)
WILLIAMS MACHINE
20 Railroad Ave (02062-4238)
P.O. Box 537, Foxboro (02035-0537)
PHONE..................................781 762-1342
Scott Williams, *Owner*
EMP: 3
SALES (est): 273.5K **Privately Held**
SIC: 3599 Mfg Industrial Machinery

(G-14206)
XCERRA CORPORATION (HQ)
825 University Ave (02062-2643)
PHONE..................................781 461-1000
David G Tacelli, *President*
Mark J Gallenberger, *COO*
Neil Kelly, *Vice Pres*
Tim Alton, *Engineer*
Theresa Russell, *Engineer*
EMP: 213
SQ FT: 56,400
SALES: 390.7MM
SALES (corp-wide): 451.7MM **Publicly Held**
WEB: www.ltx.com
SIC: 3825 3429 Mfg Electrical Measuring Instruments Mfg Hardware
PA: Cohu, Inc.
12367 Crosthwaite Cir
Poway CA 92064
858 848-8100

(G-14207)
XCERRA CORPORATION
825 University Ave (02062-2643)
PHONE..................................781 461-1000
EMP: 141
SALES (corp-wide): 451.7MM **Publicly Held**
WEB: www.ltx.com
SIC: 3825 Mfg Semiconductor Test Equipment
HQ: Xcerra Corporation
825 University Ave
Norwood MA 02062
781 461-1000

(G-14208)
XCERRA CORPORATION
825 University Ave (02062-2643)
PHONE..................................781 461-1000
David Tacelli, *Manager*
EMP: 30
SALES (corp-wide): 451.7MM **Publicly Held**
WEB: www.ltx.com
SIC: 3825 3674 7629 7373 Mfg Elec Measuring Instr Mfg Semiconductors/Dvcs Electrical Repair Computer Systems Design
HQ: Xcerra Corporation
825 University Ave
Norwood MA 02062
781 461-1000

Oak Bluffs
Dukes County

(G-14209)
BASEMENT DESIGNS INC
Also Called: Broadway Station
110 California Ave (02557)
PHONE..................................508 693-4442
John Peter Hall, *President*
Helen Hall, *Treasurer*
EMP: 3
SALES (est): 230K **Privately Held**
SIC: 2759 Commercial Printing

(G-14210)
DA ROSAS
Also Called: Martha's Vineyard Printing Co
46 Circuit Ave (02557)
P.O. Box 1668 (02557-1668)
PHONE..................................508 693-0110
Antonio G Da Rosa III, *President*
Dennis P Da Rosa, *Vice Pres*
Lucinda A Da Rosa Barrett, *Treasurer*
EMP: 15
SQ FT: 13,000
SALES (est): 2.2MM **Privately Held**
SIC: 2752 5943 5112 Offset Printing & Ret Office Forms & Supplies

(G-14211)
ROUGELUXE APOTHECARY INC
21 Kennebec Ave (02557)
P.O. Box 1566 (02557-1566)
PHONE..................................508 696-0900
Kathryn H Magistrini, *President*
Louis E Magistrini, *Treasurer*
EMP: 3
SQ FT: 1,000
SALES (est): 140K **Privately Held**
SIC: 2844 Mfg Toilet Preparations

Oakham
Worcester County

(G-14212)
FORWARD ENTERPRISES INC
182 Crawford Rd (01068-9715)
PHONE..................................508 882-0265
Paul Davis, *President*
Victoria Davis, *Principal*
EMP: 3
SALES: 500K **Privately Held**
SIC: 2411 Logging

Orange
Franklin County

(G-14213)
ATHOL SCREW MACHINE PRODUCTS
123 New Athol Rd (01364-9619)
P.O. Box 182, Athol (01331-0182)
PHONE..................................978 249-8072
Skip Hayward, *Co-Owner*
Dan Hayward, *Co-Owner*
EMP: 5
SQ FT: 3,200
SALES (est): 231K **Privately Held**
SIC: 3451 Mfg Screw Machine Products

(G-14214)
DEXTER INNVATIVE SOLUTIONS LLC
61 E River St (01364-1801)
PHONE..................................978 544-2751
David Scarfe, *Manager*
Thomas Leboeuf,
EMP: 4
SQ FT: 27,000
SALES (est): 532.2K **Privately Held**
SIC: 3541 Mfg Machine Tools-Cutting

(G-14215)
ECHO INDUSTRIES INC
61 R W Moore Ave (01364-6415)
PHONE..................................978 544-7000
Maynard H Southard, *CEO*
Bret H Bero, *President*
Carolyn Fontaine, *Buyer*
EMP: 20
SQ FT: 25,000
SALES (est): 3.7MM **Privately Held**
WEB: www.echoindustries.com
SIC: 3469 3356 3355 3423 Mfg Metal Stampings Nonferrous Rollng/Drawng Aluminum Rolling/Drawing Mfg Hand/Edge Tools

(G-14216)
EROLLS INC
158 Gov Dukakis Dr (01364-2033)
PHONE..................................978 544-0100
Jim Spooner, *President*
Paul Stansel, *Vice Pres*
EMP: 11 **EST:** 2000
SALES (est): 1.8MM **Privately Held**
WEB: www.erolls.net
SIC: 2679 Mfg Converted Paper Products

(G-14217)
HEYES FOREST PRODUCTS INC
34 Daniel Shays Hwy (01364-2026)
PHONE..................................978 544-8801
Fred L Heyes, *President*
EMP: 8 **EST:** 1971
SQ FT: 46,000
SALES (est): 1.2MM **Privately Held**
WEB: www.heyesforest.com
SIC: 2421 1629 3553 Sawmill/Planing Mill Heavy Construction Mfg Woodworking Machinery

(G-14218)
HI-DE LINERS INC
131 W Main St (01364-1150)
P.O. Box 555 (01364-0555)
PHONE..................................978 544-7801
William Dillion, *President*
Kevin Cooke, *Prdtn Mgr*
Bill Thiem, *Maintence Staff*
EMP: 21
SQ FT: 17,000
SALES (est): 5.7MM **Privately Held**
SIC: 2673 Mfg Bags-Plastic/Coated Paper

(G-14219)
INTERFACE PRCSION BNCHWRKS INC
150 Quabbin Blvd (01364-6412)
P.O. Box 425 (01364-0425)
PHONE..................................978 544-8866
Carl Bittenbender, *President*
Donald Schlicke, *Exec Dir*
EMP: 5
SQ FT: 16,000
SALES: 175.6K **Privately Held**
SIC: 3679 Mfg Electronic Components

(G-14220)
LEAVITT MACHINE CO
Also Called: Dexter Precision Products
24 E River St (01364-2207)
PHONE..................................978 544-3872
David Coolidge, *President*
EMP: 3 **EST:** 1890
SQ FT: 35,000
SALES: 500K **Privately Held**
WEB: www.leavitt-dexter.com
SIC: 3541 3545 3569 Mfg Valve Reseating Machines Lathe Chucks Steam Trap & Automatic Air Separator Machines

(G-14221)
MBW INCORPORATED
184 Gov Dukakis Dr (01364-2033)
P.O. Box 423 (01364-0423)
PHONE..................................978 544-6462
James B Jones, *President*
Mary Elisabeth L Jones, *Vice Pres*
Wendy Jones, *Vice Pres*
George D Jones III, *Treasurer*
▲ **EMP:** 140
SQ FT: 30,000
SALES (est): 21.4MM **Privately Held**
SIC: 2679 Mfg Converted Paper Products

(G-14222)
PHA INDUSTRIES INC
153 Quabbin Blvd (01364-6413)
PHONE..................................978 544-8770
Joseph Carbone, *President*
Mike Carbone, *Vice Pres*
John Siegman, *Research*
EMP: 17
SALES (est): 1.7MM **Privately Held**
SIC: 3999 Mfg Misc Products

(G-14223)
QUABBIN INC
158 Gov Dukakis Dr (01364-2033)
PHONE..................................978 544-3872
Mark F Leboeuf, *President*
Thomas J Leboeuf, *Vice Pres*
EMP: 17
SQ FT: 33,000
SALES (est): 3MM **Privately Held**
SIC: 3545 3599 Mfg Machine Tool Accessories Mfg Industrial Machinery

(G-14224)
REGAL SPORTING TECHNOLOGIES
100 Prentiss St (01364-1823)
PHONE..................................978 544-6571
Donald Barnes, *President*
EMP: 4
SALES (est): 304.3K **Privately Held**
SIC: 3949 Mfg Fly Fishing Gear

(G-14225)
REGEN POWER SYSTEMS LLC
113 Michael Ln (01364-6400)
PHONE..................................203 328-3045
EMP: 3
SQ FT: 800
SALES: 1MM **Privately Held**
SIC: 3621 Mfg Motors/Generators

(G-14226)
RIVETO MANUFACTURING CO
36 S Main St (01364-1248)
P.O. Box 297 (01364-0297)
PHONE..................................978 544-2171
John B Stevenson, *President*
EMP: 40
SQ FT: 40,000
SALES (est): 4.8MM **Privately Held**
WEB: www.slencil.com
SIC: 3951 Mfg Ball Point Pens & Parts

(G-14227)
RODNEY HUNT-FONTAINE INC (DH)
46 Mill St (01364-1251)
PHONE..................................978 544-2511
Kerry Gahm, *President*
Howard Lederman, *Vice Pres*
Devon Lawrence, *Project Engr*
Robert Kennedy, *Treasurer*
John A Kemp, *Human Resources*

◆ **EMP:** 135 **EST:** 1840
SQ FT: 318,000
SALES (est): 37.1MM **Publicly Held**
WEB: www.rodneyhunt.com
SIC: **3491** 3322 3728 3494 Mfg Industrial Valves Malleable Iron Foundry Mfg Aircraft Parts/Equip Mfg Valves/Pipe Fittings Structural Metal Fabrctn
HQ: Rexnord Llc
3001 W Canal St
Milwaukee WI 53208
414 342-3131

(G-14228)
SEAMAN PAPER COMPANY MASS INC
184 Gov Dukakis Dr (01364-2033)
PHONE....................................978 544-2455
Frank Hogan, *Manager*
EMP: 7
SALES (corp-wide): 44.6MM **Privately Held**
WEB: www.satinwrap.com
SIC: **2621** Paper Mill
PA: Seaman Paper Company Of Massachusetts, Inc.
35 Wilkins Rd
Gardner MA 01440
978 632-1513

(G-14229)
THOMAS J DOANE
59 Ward Rd (01364-9750)
PHONE....................................978 821-2361
Thomas J Doane, *Principal*
EMP: 3 **EST:** 2009
SALES (est): 143K **Privately Held**
SIC: **2411** Logging

Orleans
Barnstable County

(G-14230)
BERGER CORPORATION
2 Lots Hollow Rd (02653)
PHONE....................................508 255-3267
Robert Berger, *President*
EMP: 3
SQ FT: 10,000
SALES: 700K **Privately Held**
SIC: **2431** 5712 Mfg Millwork Ret Furniture

(G-14231)
CAPE COD READY MIX INC
300 Rt 6a (02653-3114)
P.O. Box 399 (02653-0399)
PHONE....................................508 255-4600
Christopher W Our, *President*
Peter Joy, *General Mgr*
EMP: 24 **EST:** 1997
SALES (est): 5MM **Privately Held**
WEB: www.capecodreadymix.com
SIC: **3273** Mfg Ready-Mixed Concrete

(G-14232)
COMMUNITY OF JESUS INC (PA)
5 Bay View Dr (02653-2206)
P.O. Box 1094 (02653-1094)
PHONE....................................508 255-1094
Betty Pugsley, *President*
Hollis Shackelford, *Treasurer*
Lillian Miao, *Director*
▲ **EMP:** 72
SALES (est): 8.6MM **Privately Held**
SIC: **2731** 8661 2721 7819 Book-Publishing/Printing Religious Organization Periodical-Publish/Print Motion Picture Services

(G-14233)
FIBERGLAS FABRICATIONS
36 Giddiah Hill Rd (02653)
PHONE....................................508 255-9409
Robert H Reynolds, *President*
EMP: 3
SQ FT: 2,400
SALES: 134.5K **Privately Held**
SIC: **3732** Boatbuilding/Repairing

(G-14234)
HARWICH ORACLE
Also Called: Register, The
5 Namskaket Rd (02653-3202)
PHONE....................................508 247-3200
Mark Skayla, *Chief*
EMP: 35
SALES (est): 1MM **Privately Held**
SIC: **2711** Newspapers-Publishing/Printing

(G-14235)
HERSEY CLUTCH CO
Also Called: Protek-Sure
8 Commerce Dr (02653-4014)
P.O. Box 328 (02653-0328)
PHONE....................................508 255-2533
Richard Hersey, *Owner*
EMP: 10 **EST:** 1964
SQ FT: 7,200
SALES (est): 1MM **Privately Held**
WEB: www.herseyclutch.com
SIC: **3568** 3566 Mfg Power Transmission Equipment Mfg Speed Changers/Drives

(G-14236)
NAUSET LANTERN SHOP
52 Rt 6a (02653-2412)
P.O. Box 1198 (02653-1198)
PHONE....................................508 255-1009
Michael Joly, *Owner*
EMP: 5
SQ FT: 3,000
SALES: 125K **Privately Held**
WEB: www.nausetlanternshop.com
SIC: **3648** 5719 5961 Mfg Lighting Equipment Ret Misc Homefurnishings Ret Mail-Order House

(G-14237)
NAUSET OPTICAL
9 West Rd Ste 12 (02653-3200)
PHONE....................................508 255-6394
Paul Heard, *Owner*
EMP: 3
SALES (est): 190K **Privately Held**
SIC: **3851** 5995 Mfg Ophthalmic Goods Ret Optical Goods

(G-14238)
NICKERSON STONECRAFTERS OF CAO
300 Rt 6a (02653-3114)
P.O. Box 399 (02653-0399)
PHONE....................................508 255-8600
Walter Burnie, *President*
Bob Legge, *Principal*
Bruce Macgregor, *Vice Pres*
Sandy Allen, *Controller*
EMP: 7
SQ FT: 1,400
SALES (est): 707.7K **Privately Held**
SIC: **3281** Mfg Cut Stone/Products

(G-14239)
OUTDOOR OUTFITTERS INC
Also Called: Goose Hummock Shop
15 Rt 6a (02653-2437)
P.O. Box 57 (02653-0057)
PHONE....................................508 255-0455
Michael Macaskill, *President*
EMP: 20
SQ FT: 12,000
SALES (est): 2.7MM **Privately Held**
WEB: www.goose.com
SIC: **3949** 5091 Mfg Sporting/Athletic Goods Whol Sporting/Recreational Goods

(G-14240)
PLEASANT BAY BOAT SPAR CO LLC
80 Rayber Rd (02653-4015)
P.O. Box 1174 (02653-1174)
PHONE....................................508 240-0058
EMP: 5 **EST:** 1999
SQ FT: 4,800
SALES: 450K **Privately Held**
WEB: www.marinerestoration.com
SIC: **3732** Boatbuilding/Repairing

(G-14241)
SAVVY ON MAIN
50 Main St (02653-2441)
P.O. Box 2068 (02653-6068)
PHONE....................................508 255-5076
Gloria Peretz, *Principal*
Janis Higgins, *Principal*
Michael Peretz, *Principal*
EMP: 9
SALES (est): 1MM **Privately Held**
SIC: **2389** Mfg Apparel/Accessories

(G-14242)
THOMPSONS PRINTING INC
51 Finlay Rd (02653-3320)
PHONE....................................508 255-0099
Charles O Thompson, *President*
Susan Thompson, *Vice Pres*
EMP: 12
SQ FT: 8,000
SALES (est): 1.4MM **Privately Held**
WEB: www.thompsonsprinting.com
SIC: **2752** Commercial Offset Printer

(G-14243)
TRUE WORDS TORTILLAS INC
136 Rt 6a (02653-3264)
PHONE....................................508 255-3338
EMP: 6
SALES (est): 537.5K **Privately Held**
SIC: **2099** Mfg Food Preparations

(G-14244)
W S WALCOTT INC
Also Called: Sir Speedy
180 Hilltop Plz Rr 6 (02653)
PHONE....................................508 240-0882
Thomas Spollen, *President*
Linda Phillips, *Vice Pres*
EMP: 8
SQ FT: 1,600
SALES (est): 810K **Privately Held**
SIC: **2752** Comm Prtg Litho

(G-14245)
WAFER INSPECTION SERVICES INC
Woodland Dr (02653)
PHONE....................................508 944-2851
Albert Ng, *Branch Mgr*
EMP: 5
SALES (corp-wide): 850K **Privately Held**
WEB: www.waferinspectionservices.com
SIC: **3826** 5084 7359 7389 Semiconductor Sales And Service For Capital Equipment From Kla-Tencor Applied Materials Teradyne
PA: Wafer Inspection Services Inc
2 Firethorn Ln
Sandwich MA 02563
508 944-2851

Osterville
Barnstable County

(G-14246)
BRIDGE PUBLISHING LLC
155 Smoke Valley Rd (02655-1822)
PHONE....................................508 681-8914
Gardner Bridge, *Principal*
EMP: 3
SALES (est): 106.4K **Privately Held**
SIC: **2711** Newspapers-Publishing/Printing

(G-14247)
GENEISIS SPRINKLER SYSTEMS
21 Fir Ln (02655-1312)
PHONE....................................508 428-1842
Gregory Straticoglu, *Owner*
EMP: 5
SALES (est): 261.8K **Privately Held**
SIC: **3494** Mfg/Distribute Sprinklers Systems

(G-14248)
GLASS BY PETZE
130 Westwind Cir (02655-1376)
P.O. Box 406 (02655-0406)
PHONE....................................508 428-0971
EMP: 10
SALES (est): 409.7K **Privately Held**
SIC: **3221** 3231 Mfg Glass Containers Mfg Products-Purchased Glass

(G-14249)
NJF PACKAGING ENTERPRISE
245 Westwind Cir (02655-1367)
PHONE....................................508 428-1255
EMP: 4
SALES (est): 413.3K **Privately Held**
SIC: **2631** Paperboard Mill

Otis
Berkshire County

(G-14250)
TONLINO & SONS LLC
1678 Monterey Rd (01253-9691)
P.O. Box 190 (01253-0190)
PHONE....................................413 329-8083
Jake Tonlino,
John Tonlino,
Kimberly Tonlino,
EMP: 3
SALES: 200K **Privately Held**
SIC: **1429** Crushed/Broken Stone

Oxford
Worcester County

(G-14251)
A B ENGINEERING & CO
Also Called: AB Engineering & Company
3 Old Cudworth Rd (01540-2842)
P.O. Box 690 (01540-0690)
PHONE....................................508 987-0318
Alfred Beland, *President*
Alfred E Beland, *President*
EMP: 9
SQ FT: 55,000
SALES (est): 2.9MM **Privately Held**
WEB: www.ajeceng.com
SIC: **3559** Mfg Industrial Machinery

(G-14252)
ADVANCE PLASTICS INC
27 Industrial Park Rd E (01540-2858)
P.O. Box 94, Dudley (01571-0094)
PHONE....................................508 987-7235
Mark Hattabaugh, *President*
EMP: 7
SQ FT: 4,500
SALES (est): 773.1K **Privately Held**
SIC: **3089** Mfg Plastic Products

(G-14253)
BARTON RICE CORPORATION
12 Hawksley Rd (01540-2856)
PHONE....................................508 966-2194
Robert L Couture, *President*
EMP: 4
SQ FT: 25,000
SALES (est): 597K **Privately Held**
SIC: **3554** Mfg Paper Pulp Mill Machinery

(G-14254)
BONSAL AMERICAN INC
Old Webster Rd (01540)
PHONE....................................508 987-8188
Michael Carmevele, *Manager*
EMP: 35
SALES (corp-wide): 29.7B **Privately Held**
WEB: www.bonsalamerican.com
SIC: **3531** 3272 Mfg Construction Machinery Mfg Concrete Products
HQ: Bonsal American, Inc.
625 Griffith Rd Ste 100
Charlotte NC 28217
704 525-1621

(G-14255)
BUTLERS RV SERVICES CORP
Also Called: Kosco Oil
254 Sutton Ave (01540-1824)
PHONE....................................508 987-0234
James Butler Jr, *Vice Pres*
EMP: 4
SQ FT: 4,800
SALES: 2.7MM **Privately Held**
SIC: **3715** Mfg Truck Trailers

(G-14256)
CHASE CORPORATION
24 Dana Rd (01540-1704)
PHONE....................................508 731-2710
EMP: 11

GEOGRAPHIC

SALES (corp-wide): 281.3MM **Publicly Held**
SIC: 3644 3479 3672 Mfg Nonconductv Wire Dvc Coating/Engraving Svcs Mfg Printed Circuit Brds
PA: Chase Corporation
295 University Ave
Westwood MA 02090
781 332-0700

(G-14257)
CONVIBER INC
2 Hawksley Rd Unit F (01540-2863)
PHONE..................................724 274-6300
Frank Puchechelli, *Principal*
EMP: 4
SALES (corp-wide): 13.3MM **Privately Held**
WEB: www.conviber.com
SIC: 3535 Whol Industrial Supplies
PA: Conviber, Inc.
644 Garfield St
Springdale PA 15144
724 274-6300

(G-14258)
DAVID PACKARD COMPANY INC
15 Industrial Park Rd E (01540-2858)
P.O. Box 594 (01540-0594)
PHONE..................................508 987-2998
Kathleen Packard, *Principal*
Matt Dipietro, *Opers Mgr*
EMP: 8
SQ FT: 10,000
SALES (est): 1.4MM **Privately Held**
WEB: www.david-packard-company.com
SIC: 3599 Mfg Industrial Machinery

(G-14259)
EPV PLASTICS CORPORATION
2 Hawksley Rd Unit A (01540-2863)
P.O. Box 660 (01540-0660)
PHONE..................................508 987-2595
Leonard P Montione, *President*
▲ **EMP:** 6
SQ FT: 21,000
SALES (est): 1.1MM **Privately Held**
WEB: www.epvplastics.com
SIC: 3081 5162 Mfg Unsupported Plastic Film/Sheet Whol Plastic Materials/Shapes

(G-14260)
ETAWIZ LLC
1 Maid Marion St (01540-2434)
PHONE..................................774 823-5156
Kevin Anderson,
EMP: 4
SALES (est): 128.7K **Privately Held**
SIC: 7372 Prepackaged Software Services

(G-14261)
FLAGG PALMER PRECAST INC
1 Industrial Park Rd W (01540-2849)
P.O. Box 421, West Barnstable (02668-0421)
PHONE..................................508 987-3400
Frank Maki, *President*
Tam Toowl, *Admin Sec*
EMP: 9
SQ FT: 6,000
SALES (est): 1MM **Privately Held**
SIC: 3272 Mfg Concrete Products

(G-14262)
FX GROUP
2 Hawksley Rd Unit B (01540-2863)
PHONE..................................508 987-1366
Brian Anger, *Principal*
▲ **EMP:** 5
SALES (est): 710.3K **Privately Held**
SIC: 2542 Mfg Partitions/Fixtures-Non-wood

(G-14263)
IPG PHOTONICS CORPORATION (PA)
50 Old Webster Rd (01540-2706)
PHONE..................................508 373-1100
Valentin P Gapontsev, *Ch of Bd*
Trevor D Ness, *Senior VP*
Alexander Ovtchinnikov, *Senior VP*
Felix Stukalin, *Senior VP*
Igor Samartsev, *CTO*
▲ **EMP:** 277
SQ FT: 427,300
SALES: 1.4B **Publicly Held**
SIC: 3699 3229 3674 Mfg Fiber Lasers And Other Components

(G-14264)
L & L CONCRETE PRODUCTS INC
28 Linwood St (01540-2846)
P.O. Box 516, Webster (01570-0516)
PHONE..................................508 987-8175
Louis A Esposito Jr, *President*
Emilia Esposito, *Admin Sec*
EMP: 12 **EST:** 1940
SQ FT: 6,000
SALES (est): 1.6MM **Privately Held**
SIC: 3272 Mfg Concrete Products

(G-14265)
LEGGETT & PLATT INCORPORATED
Also Called: Oxford Spring 5301
23 Dana Rd (01540-1703)
P.O. Box 719 (01540-0719)
PHONE..................................508 987-8706
Maik Breckwoldt, *Vice Pres*
Paul Napieralski, *Branch Mgr*
Kevin Schofield, *Manager*
Bob Thompson, *Executive*
Belinda Clark, *Administration*
EMP: 30
SALES (corp-wide): 4.2B **Publicly Held**
WEB: www.leggett.com
SIC: 2515 2514 5085 3495 Mfg Mattress/Bedsprings
PA: Leggett & Platt, Incorporated
1 Leggett Rd
Carthage MO 64836
417 358-8131

(G-14266)
LELANITE CORPORATION
Also Called: De Ross Pallet Co
Town Forest Rd (01540)
P.O. Box 160, Webster (01570-0160)
PHONE..................................508 987-1771
Bernie Ray, *Manager*
EMP: 6
SALES (corp-wide): 6.8MM **Privately Held**
WEB: www.lelanite.com
SIC: 2448 Mfg Wood Pallets/Skids
PA: Lelanite Corporation
1 Cudworth Rd
Webster MA 01570
508 987-2637

(G-14267)
LINE BORE INDUSTRIES INC
3 Harlan Dr (01540-2840)
PHONE..................................508 987-6509
Charles Dickson Jr, *President*
Cheryl Dickson, *Vice Pres*
Betty Dickson, *Clerk*
EMP: 10
SQ FT: 8,500
SALES (est): 1.6MM **Privately Held**
WEB: www.linebore.com
SIC: 3599 Mfg Electric Housings

(G-14268)
MAGNETIC TECHNOLOGIES LTD
43 Town Forest Rd (01540-2845)
P.O. Box 257 (01540-0257)
PHONE..................................508 987-3303
John E Deluca, *President*
Greg Podstawka, *VP Engrg*
Karen J Deluca, *Admin Sec*
▲ **EMP:** 15
SQ FT: 13,000
SALES (est): 4.2MM **Privately Held**
WEB: www.magnetictech.com
SIC: 3568 3625 Mfg Power Transmission Equipment Mfg Relays/Industrial Controls

(G-14269)
MATKIM INDUSTRIES INC
2 Hawksley Rd Unit D (01540-2863)
P.O. Box 168 (01540-0168)
PHONE..................................508 987-3599
Matt Shenker, *President*
EMP: 40
SQ FT: 20,000
SALES (est): 8.3MM **Privately Held**
SIC: 3644 Mfg Nonconductive Wiring Devices

(G-14270)
NORDIC SHIELD PLASTIC CORP
Also Called: 2 Hawksley Drive
2 Hawksley Rd Unit E (01540-2863)
P.O. Box 561 (01540-0561)
PHONE..................................508 987-5361
Leonard P Montione, *Principal*
▲ **EMP:** 6
SALES (est): 2MM **Privately Held**
SIC: 3081 Mfg Plastic Products

(G-14271)
OXFORD ASPHALT INC
Also Called: Oxford Asphalt Mfg & Pav
190 Old Webster Rd (01540-2024)
PHONE..................................508 987-0321
Anthony Amorello, *President*
John Amorello, *Treasurer*
Joseph Amorello, *Treasurer*
EMP: 5
SQ FT: 2,000
SALES (est): 722.6K **Privately Held**
SIC: 2951 Mfg Asphalt

(G-14272)
RJ MARINE INDUSTRIES
Also Called: Shoreside Docks
1 Hawksley Rd (01540-2856)
P.O. Box 143, Charlton Depot (01509-0143)
PHONE..................................508 248-9933
Ray Johnson, *Owner*
EMP: 9
SQ FT: 7,000
SALES: 1.1MM **Privately Held**
WEB: www.shoresidedocks.com
SIC: 3429 Mfg Hardware

(G-14273)
S LANE JOHN & SON INCORPORATED
Off Clara Barton (01540)
P.O. Box 781, North Oxford (01537-0781)
PHONE..................................508 987-3959
Joseph Dirienzo, *Manager*
EMP: 10
SALES (corp-wide): 24.1MM **Privately Held**
SIC: 1422 5032 Crushed/Broken Limestone Whol Brick/Stone Material
PA: S Lane John & Son Incorporated
730 E Mountain Rd
Westfield MA 01085
413 568-8986

(G-14274)
SWISSTURN/USA INC
21 Dana Rd (01540-1709)
PHONE..................................508 987-6211
Kenneth J Mandile, *President*
Diane M Mandile, *Admin Sec*
EMP: 55
SQ FT: 25,000
SALES (est): 10MM **Privately Held**
WEB: www.swissturn.com
SIC: 3451 Mfg Screw Machine Products

(G-14275)
TEC ENGINEERING CORP
31 Town Forest Rd (01540-2868)
PHONE..................................508 987-0231
Maurice Minardi, *President*
Todd Stpierre, *Natl Sales Mgr*
EMP: 16
SQ FT: 31,000
SALES (est): 5.3MM **Privately Held**
WEB: www.teceng.net
SIC: 3535 3559 5084 Mfg Conveyors/Equipment Mfg Misc Industry Mach Whol Industrial Equip

(G-14276)
VENMILL INDUSTRIES INC
36 Town Forest Rd (01540-2839)
PHONE..................................508 363-0410
Michael U Schmidt, *President*
Karen Brady, *Accounting Mgr*
Pam Olson, *Bookkeeper*
Peter Tam, *Director*
Robert Treadwell, *Director*
▲ **EMP:** 20
SALES (est): 4.1MM **Privately Held**
WEB: www.venmill.com
SIC: 3651 Mfg Home Audio/Video Equipment

Palmer
Hampden County

(G-14277)
ADAPTAS SOLUTIONS (PA)
7 3rd St (01069-1542)
PHONE..................................413 284-9975
Jay Ray, *President*
Laura Jean Ray, *Vice Pres*
Patricia Roy, *Treasurer*
Kevin Topor, *Treasurer*
▲ **EMP:** 65
SQ FT: 3,000
SALES (est): 13.3MM **Privately Held**
WEB: www.detechinc.com
SIC: 3671 Mfg Electron Tubes

(G-14278)
AMERICA CABLE ASSEMBLIES INC (PA)
21 Wilbraham St Unit A12 (01069-9526)
PHONE..................................413 283-2515
Charles McCarthy, *President*
EMP: 3
SALES (est): 881.2K **Privately Held**
WEB: www.americancableassemblies.com
SIC: 3357 Nonferrous Wiredrawing/Insulating

(G-14279)
AMERICAN DRY ICE CORPORATION (PA)
Also Called: American Carbonation
19 2nd St (01069-1536)
P.O. Box 719 (01069-0719)
PHONE..................................413 283-9906
Robert Koerner, *President*
George Koerner, *Treasurer*
EMP: 13
SQ FT: 5,600
SALES (est): 4.4MM **Privately Held**
SIC: 2097 Mfg Ice

(G-14280)
BENOIT & COMPANY
1240 Park St (01069-1664)
P.O. Box 660 (01069-0660)
PHONE..................................413 283-8348
George Benoit, *Owner*
EMP: 6
SALES (est): 359.2K **Privately Held**
SIC: 3089 Plastics Products, Nec, Nsk

(G-14281)
BLTEES
21 Wilbraham St Unit A4 (01069-9659)
PHONE..................................413 289-0050
David Mahoney, *Principal*
EMP: 3
SALES (est): 227.7K **Privately Held**
SIC: 2759 Commercial Printing

(G-14282)
C & C THERMOFORMING INC
111 Breckenridge St Ste A (01069-1621)
PHONE..................................413 289-1900
Willard Cutler Jr, *President*
Kathleen Kelley, *Manager*
EMP: 5
SQ FT: 15,000
SALES (est): 773.8K **Privately Held**
WEB: www.candcthermoforming.com
SIC: 3089 Mfg Plastic Products

(G-14283)
CDILED LLC
21 Wilbraham St (01069-9605)
P.O. Box 932 (01069-0932)
PHONE..................................413 530-2921
Stanley Turek, *Principal*
Paul Caron, *Director*
EMP: 3 **EST:** 2017
SALES (est): 156.3K **Privately Held**
SIC: 3646 Mfg Commercial Lighting Fixtures

(G-14284)
CEMENT WELL CONCRETE PRODUCTS
104 Mason St (01069-2210)
PHONE..................................413 283-8450
Peter Wojtowicz, *President*

▲ = Import ▼=Export
◆ =Import/Export

Paulette Wojtowicz, *Vice Pres*
EMP: 4 **EST:** 1953
SQ FT: 2,160
SALES: 200K **Privately Held**
WEB:
www.cementwellconcreteproducts.com
SIC: 3272 Mfg Prefabricated Concrete Products

(G-14285)
CONTECH ENGNERED SOLUTIONS LLC
41 Fenton St (01069-1800)
PHONE..................................413 283-7611
Lamar Patterson, *Plant Mgr*
Dan Steffeck, *Branch Mgr*
EMP: 40
SQ FT: 25,000 **Privately Held**
SIC: 3443 Mfg Fabricated Plate Work
HQ: Contech Engineered Solutions Llc
9025 Centre Pointe Dr # 400
West Chester OH 45069
513 645-7000

(G-14286)
DUBLIN STEEL CORPORATION
95 2nd St (01069-1543)
PHONE..................................413 289-1218
Shannon Danylieko, *President*
Donald Duffy, *Treasurer*
EMP: 20
SQ FT: 8,400
SALES (est): 5.1MM **Privately Held**
WEB: www.dublinsteel.net
SIC: 3441 Structural Metal Fabrication

(G-14287)
ESSITY
Also Called: Molnycke
1st St (01069)
P.O. Box 720 (01069-0720)
PHONE..................................413 289-1221
Art Whitman, *Controller*
EMP: 75
SALES (corp-wide): 12.4B **Privately Held**
SIC: 2676 Mfg Disposable Briefs
HQ: Essity North America Inc.
2929 Arch St Ste 2600
Philadelphia PA 19104

(G-14288)
LIGNETICS NEW ENGLAND INC
21 Wilbraham St Unit B13 (01069-9685)
P.O. Box 532, Jaffrey NH (03452-0532)
PHONE..................................413 284-1050
Richard Walch, *Manager*
Steve Walker, *Exec Dir*
EMP: 8
SALES (corp-wide): 28MM **Privately Held**
WEB: www.pelletheat.com
SIC: 2448 Bag Wood Pellet
HQ: Lignetics Of New England, Inc.
1075 E S Boulder Rd
Louisville CO 80027
303 802-5400

(G-14289)
NOVACEL INC (DH)
21 3rd St (01069-1542)
PHONE..................................413 283-3468
Laurent Derolez, *CEO*
David Anderson, *President*
Richard Karane, *Principal*
Michael Story, *CFO*
William Dopp, *Treasurer*
▲ **EMP:** 50
SQ FT: 250,000
SALES (est): 58.7MM
SALES (corp-wide): 4MM **Privately Held**
WEB: www.novacelonline.com
SIC: 2671 Mfg Packaging Paper/Film
HQ: Novacel
27 Rue Du Docteur Emile Bataille
Deville-Les-Rouen 76250
232 827-222

(G-14290)
PAINT TOWN INC
21 Wilbraham St Unit A2 (01069-9659)
PHONE..................................413 283-2245
John W Bromage Jr, *President*
Josh Bromage, *Teacher*
EMP: 5
SALES (est): 556.4K **Privately Held**
SIC: 3993 Mfg Signs/Advertising Specialties

(G-14291)
PALMER FOUNDRY INC
22 Mount Dumplin Rd (01069-1128)
P.O. Box 955 (01069-0955)
PHONE..................................413 283-2976
David Logan, *CEO*
Jim Lagrant, *President*
Robert Logan, *President*
Dennis Hayden, *Vice Pres*
Robert Fontaine, *Opers Mgr*
EMP: 70 **EST:** 1951
SQ FT: 51,000
SALES (est): 16.5MM **Privately Held**
WEB: www.palmerfoundry.com
SIC: 3366 Copper Foundry

(G-14292)
PHILLIPS PACKAGING
1633 N Main St (01069-1041)
PHONE..................................413 289-1070
Scott Phillips, *Owner*
EMP: 4
SQ FT: 8,000
SALES (est): 543.1K **Privately Held**
SIC: 2653 Mfg Corrugated/Solid Fiber Boxes

(G-14293)
POLYMER CORPORATION
Also Called: Polymer Injection Molding
1 3rd St (01069-1542)
PHONE..................................413 267-5524
Pat Bowles, *Purch Agent*
James F Ryan, *Branch Mgr*
Paula Martin, *Technician*
EMP: 38
SALES (corp-wide): 73.3MM **Privately Held**
WEB: www.polymerdesign.com
SIC: 3089 Mfg Plastic Products
HQ: Polymer Corporation
180 Pleasant St
Rockland MA 02370
781 871-4606

(G-14294)
PROFILES INCORPORATED
7 First St (01069)
P.O. Box 850 (01069-0850)
PHONE..................................413 283-7790
Jeff Buck, *President*
Thomas Allard, *Vice Pres*
Dean Kiley, *CFO*
▲ **EMP:** 35 **EST:** 1962
SQ FT: 75,000
SALES (est): 10.6MM
SALES (corp-wide): 770.6MM **Publicly Held**
WEB: www.profiles-inc.com
SIC: 3315 3496 Mfg Steel Wire/Related Products Mfg Misc Fabricated Wire Products
PA: Nn, Inc.
6210 Ardrey Kell Rd
Charlotte NC 28277
980 264-4300

(G-14295)
SANDERSON-MACLEOD INCORPORATED
1199 S Main St (01069-1855)
P.O. Box 50 (01069-0050)
PHONE..................................413 283-3481
Eric Sanderson, *President*
Mark Borsari, *President*
Linda Mitchell, *Vice Pres*
James Pascale, *Vice Pres*
Chris Breyare, *Plant Mgr*
▲ **EMP:** 115 **EST:** 1961
SQ FT: 84,000
SALES (est): 18MM **Privately Held**
WEB: www.sandersonmacleod.com
SIC: 3991 3351 3315 2221 Mfg Brooms/Brushes Copper Rolling/Drawing Mfg Steel Wire/Rltd Prdt Manmad Brdwv Fabric Mill

(G-14296)
SHEDWORKS INC
Also Called: Quabbin Vly Frmng Cmpnents Div
8 3rd St (01069-1541)
PHONE..................................413 284-1600
Wayne L Buxton, *President*
Edward J Ryan Jr, *Admin Sec*
EMP: 5
SALES (est): 46.1K **Privately Held**
SIC: 2421 Sawmill/Planing Mill

(G-14297)
TMI INDUSTRIES INC
Also Called: Thorndike Mills
25 Ware St (01069-1514)
P.O. Box 968 (01069-0968)
PHONE..................................413 283-9021
Mitchell Garabedian, *President*
Edward Garabedian, *Treasurer*
Marilyn Madsen, *Bookkeeper*
Anna Garabedian, *Asst Treas*
Karen Garabedian, *Sales Staff*
▲ **EMP:** 44
SQ FT: 50,000
SALES (est): 5.8MM **Privately Held**
WEB: www.thorndikemills.com
SIC: 2273 7389 5713 Mfg Braided Rugs

(G-14298)
TURLEY PUBLICATIONS INC (PA)
24 Water St (01069-1862)
PHONE..................................800 824-6548
Keith P Turley, *Principal*
Lisa Connell, *Editor*
Dave Forbes, *Editor*
Kathy Mitchell, *Editor*
Corrina Warton, *Human Res Dir*
EMP: 150
SQ FT: 15,000
SALES (est): 54.3MM **Privately Held**
WEB: www.turley.com
SIC: 2711 2741 Newspapers-Publishing/Printing Misc Publishing

(G-14299)
UNICORE LLC
6 Chamber Rd (01069)
P.O. Box 324 (01069-0324)
PHONE..................................413 284-9995
Robert Yahn Jr, *Mng Member*
EMP: 20 **EST:** 1999
SQ FT: 20,000
SALES (est): 3.3MM **Privately Held**
SIC: 2821 Mfg Plastic Materials/Resins

(G-14300)
VARTANIAN CUSTOM CABINETS
10 2nd St (01069-1534)
PHONE..................................413 283-3438
John N Vartanian, *President*
Aram P Vartanian, *CFO*
Debra Vartanian, *Admin Sec*
EMP: 13
SQ FT: 15,000
SALES (est): 1.7MM **Privately Held**
WEB: www.vartaniancabinets.com
SIC: 2434 Mfg Wood Kitchen Cabinets

Paxton
Worcester County

(G-14301)
FARRAR PRESS INC
707 Pleasant St (01612-1026)
PHONE..................................508 799-9874
Scott Farrar, *President*
EMP: 4
SQ FT: 2,000
SALES: 125K **Privately Held**
SIC: 2752 Offset Printers

(G-14302)
NORTHEAST OUTDOORS INC
Also Called: NORTHEAST BIG BUCK CLUB
390 Marshall St (01612-1228)
PHONE..................................508 752-8762
Jeffrey E Brown, *President*
EMP: 12
SALES: 93.9K **Privately Held**
WEB: www.bigbuckclub.com
SIC: 2721 7997 Membership Hunting Club Periodicals-Publishing/Printing

(G-14303)
VINYL APPROACH
12 Walnut St (01612-1515)
PHONE..................................508 755-5279
Mark A Lewis, *Principal*
EMP: 3 **EST:** 2010
SALES (est): 210.3K **Privately Held**
SIC: 3993 Mfg Signs/Advertising Specialties

Peabody
Essex County

(G-14304)
A & A INDUSTRIES INC
320 Jubilee Dr (01960-4030)
PHONE..................................978 977-9660
Aurelian Mardiros, *President*
Anahid Mardiros, *Vice Pres*
Charles Toomajian, *Admin Sec*
▲ **EMP:** 32
SQ FT: 120,000
SALES: 8.7MM **Privately Held**
WEB: www.aandaindustries.com
SIC: 3599 Mfg Industrial Machinery

(G-14305)
ABOUT-FACE KITCHENS INC
27 Walnut St Ste 1h (01960-5679)
PHONE..................................978 532-0212
Ray Pasciuto, *President*
Raymond Pasciuto, *CFO*
EMP: 4
SALES (est): 399.3K **Privately Held**
WEB: www.aboutfacekitchens.com
SIC: 2434 1799 Mfg Wood Kitchen Cabinets Trade Contractor

(G-14306)
ACME SIGN CORPORATION
3 Lakeland Park Dr (01960-3835)
PHONE..................................978 535-6600
Brian Brinkers, *President*
EMP: 3
SQ FT: 10,000
SALES (est): 422.7K **Privately Held**
WEB: www.acmesigncorp.com
SIC: 3993 Mfg Signs/Advertising Specialties

(G-14307)
ADHESIVE PACKAGING SPC INC (DH)
Also Called: APS
103 Foster St (01960-5933)
P.O. Box 31 (01960-0831)
PHONE..................................800 222-1117
Stephen J Buchanan, *President*
Theodore Clark, *President*
Stephen Buchanan, *General Mgr*
Gary A Stenke, *Corp Secy*
Mike Redman, *Vice Pres*
EMP: 50
SQ FT: 35,000
SALES (est): 11.9MM
SALES (corp-wide): 3B **Publicly Held**
SIC: 2671 Mfg Packaging Paper/Film
HQ: Royal Adhesives And Sealants Llc
2001 W Washington St
South Bend IN 46628
574 246-5000

(G-14308)
AES CORPORATION
285 Newbury St Ste 1 (01960-7468)
P.O. Box 2093 (01960-7093)
PHONE..................................978 535-7310
Michael Sherman, *CEO*
Gary Shottes, *President*
Bill Goretkin, *General Mgr*
Owais Hassan, *Vice Pres*
Hacker Todd, *Vice Pres*
◆ **EMP:** 53 **EST:** 1974
SQ FT: 26,500
SALES (est): 16.2MM **Privately Held**
WEB: www.aes-intellinet.com
SIC: 3699 7382 Mfg Electrical Equipment/Supplies Security Systems Services

GEOGRAPHIC

(G-14309)
ALLIANCE LEATHER FINISHING
58 Pulaski St Ste 2 (01960-1829)
PHONE..................................978 531-6771
Michael Listro, *Vice Pres*
Manny Veiga, *Admin Sec*
▲ **EMP:** 17
SQ FT: 4,000
SALES: 2.3MM **Privately Held**
SIC: **3172** 3111 Mfg Personal Leather Goods Leather Tanning/Finishing

(G-14310)
AMPHENOL PCD INC
2 Technology Dr (01960-7907)
PHONE..................................978 921-1531
EMP: 4
SALES (corp-wide): 8.2B **Publicly Held**
SIC: **3625** Mfg Relays/Industrial Controls
HQ: Amphenol Pcd, Inc.
72 Cherry Hill Dr Ste 2
Beverly MA 01915

(G-14311)
ANALOGIC CORPORATION (HQ)
8 Centennial Dr (01960-7987)
PHONE..................................978 326-4000
Fred B Parks, *President*
Mervat Faltas, *Senior VP*
Brooks West, *Senior VP*
Jim Dacosta, *Vice Pres*
Yash Singh, *Vice Pres*
▲ **EMP:** 1000 **EST:** 1967
SQ FT: 514,000
SALES (est): 393.9MM
SALES (corp-wide): 396.1MM **Privately Held**
WEB: www.analogic.com
SIC: **3825** 3812 Manufacturing Electrical Measuring Instruments & Medical/Hospital Equipment
PA: Anlg Holding Company, Inc.
8 Centennial Dr
Peabody MA 01960
978 326-4000

(G-14312)
ANALOGIC CORPORATION
Analogic Measurement & Control
8 Centennial Dr (01960-7987)
PHONE..................................978 977-3000
Andrew Toth, *Manager*
EMP: 10
SALES (corp-wide): 396.1MM **Privately Held**
WEB: www.analogic.com
SIC: **3825** Mfg Electrical Measuring Instruments
HQ: Analogic Corporation
8 Centennial Dr
Peabody MA 01960
978 326-4000

(G-14313)
AP PLASTICS LLC
103 Foster St (01960-5933)
PHONE..................................800 222-1117
Stephen J Buchanan, *Manager*
EMP: 4
SALES (est): 297.9K
SALES (corp-wide): 3B **Publicly Held**
SIC: **2891** Mfg Adhesives/Sealants
PA: H.B. Fuller Company
1200 Willow Lake Blvd
Saint Paul MN 55110
651 236-5900

(G-14314)
ATLANTIC AUTO & TRCK PARTS LLC
245 Newbury St Rm 1 (01960-1315)
PHONE..................................978 535-6777
Dick Ziemlak, *President*
Jeff Clarke, *Vice Pres*
EMP: 8
SALES: 950K **Privately Held**
SIC: **3089** Mfg Plastic Products

(G-14315)
BELDEN INC
210 Andover St Unit 48 (01960-1647)
PHONE..................................978 573-0908
Mike Green, *Branch Mgr*
EMP: 239
SALES (corp-wide): 2.5B **Publicly Held**
SIC: **3357** Mfg High-Speed Electronic Cables
PA: Belden Inc.
1 N Brentwood Blvd Fl 15
Saint Louis MO 63105
314 854-8000

(G-14316)
BOSTON PROCESS TECH INC
10 Technology Dr Ste 1a (01960-7976)
PHONE..................................978 854-5579
Jian Zhang, *President*
EMP: 12
SQ FT: 5,700
SALES (est): 4MM **Privately Held**
SIC: **3559** 3674 Mfg Misc Industry Machinery Mfg Semiconductors/Related Devices

(G-14317)
BRANCH OLIVE OIL COMPANY LLC
210 Andover St (01960-1647)
PHONE..................................781 775-8788
Jerry Knox, *Principal*
EMP: 7 **EST:** 2016
SALES (est): 133.7K **Privately Held**
SIC: **2079** Mfg Edible Fats/Oils

(G-14318)
C S I KEYBOARDS INC
56 Pulaski St Unit 1 (01960-1830)
PHONE..................................978 532-8181
Peter J Castner, *President*
Gary Brown, *Vice Pres*
▲ **EMP:** 36
SQ FT: 20,000
SALES (est): 7.4MM **Privately Held**
WEB: www.csikeyboards.com
SIC: **3575** 3643 3577 Mfg Computer Terminals Mfg Conductive Wiring Devices Mfg Computer Peripheral Equipment

(G-14319)
CALENDAR PRESS INC
28 Winter St (01960-5942)
P.O. Box 191 (01960-0991)
PHONE..................................978 531-1860
Catherine Trainor, *President*
George Trainor, *Vice Pres*
John Trainor, *VP Human Res*
EMP: 30
SQ FT: 16,200
SALES (est): 4.8MM **Privately Held**
WEB: www.calendarpressinc.com
SIC: **2752** Lithographic Commercial Printing

(G-14320)
CAPE POND ICE COMPANY
26 Walnut St (01960-5673)
PHONE..................................978 531-4853
Scott Memhard, *Owner*
EMP: 4
SALES (corp-wide): 1.5MM **Privately Held**
SIC: **2097** Mfg Ice
PA: Cape Pond Ice Company
104 Commercial St
Gloucester MA 01930
978 283-0174

(G-14321)
COGENT ENGINEERING INC
119 Foster St Bldg 8 (01960-5933)
PHONE..................................978 977-3310
Joseph Kracunas, *President*
Deborah Kracunas, *Treasurer*
EMP: 9
SQ FT: 18,000
SALES (est): 957K **Privately Held**
SIC: **3599** Mfg Industrial Machinery

(G-14322)
COLONIAL MACHINE COMPANY
16 Albert Rd (01960-2515)
PHONE..................................781 233-0026
Charles H Kelley, *Owner*
EMP: 3
SQ FT: 2,000
SALES: 250K **Privately Held**
SIC: **3599** Mfg Industrial Machinery

(G-14323)
COLONIAL ORNAMENTAL IRON WORKS
77 Walnut St Ste 3 (01960-5691)
PHONE..................................978 531-1474
William Katsapetses, *Owner*
William Katsepetses, *Owner*
EMP: 4
SQ FT: 5,000
SALES (est): 400K **Privately Held**
SIC: **3446** Mfg Architectural & Ornamental Metalwork

(G-14324)
COMMUNICATION INK INC
140 Summit St (01960-5156)
P.O. Box 3373 (01961-3373)
PHONE..................................978 977-4595
Ray Hendrickson, *President*
Bridget Timmins, *President*
Liane Woods, *Supervisor*
Sandy Gallagher, *CTO*
EMP: 12
SALES (est): 880K **Privately Held**
WEB: www.chrbook.com
SIC: **2741** 7331 Misc Publishing Direct Mail Advertising Services

(G-14325)
COMPONENT HNDNG INSPCTN PCKN
Also Called: Chips
83 Pine St Ste 13 (01960-3635)
PHONE..................................978 535-3997
Paul Cunningham, *President*
EMP: 3
SQ FT: 8,000
SALES (est): 484.3K **Privately Held**
SIC: **3674** Mfg Semiconductors/Related Devices

(G-14326)
CREATIVE PUBLISHING CORP AMER (PA)
2 1st Ave Ste 103 (01960-4960)
PHONE..................................978 532-5880
Richard H Ayer, *President*
EMP: 39 **EST:** 1980
SQ FT: 9,000
SALES (est): 2.8MM **Privately Held**
WEB: www.cpcadvertising.com
SIC: **2711** 7336 2791 Newspapers-Publishing/Printing Commercial Art/Graphic Design Typesetting Services

(G-14327)
CYBTEK INC
147 Summit St Ste 3b3 (01960-5173)
PHONE..................................978 532-7110
Adam Williams, *CEO*
EMP: 5 **EST:** 2009
SQ FT: 2,000
SALES (est): 697.9K **Privately Held**
SIC: **7372** 7378 Prepackaged Software Services Computer Maintenance/Repair

(G-14328)
D F CARTER CO INC
147 Summit St Ste 7 (01960-5173)
PHONE..................................978 977-0444
Robert D Carter, *President*
Carl Caret, *Corp Secy*
Carol Carter, *Treasurer*
EMP: 11
SQ FT: 6,500
SALES (est): 1.2MM **Privately Held**
SIC: **3599** Machine Shop

(G-14329)
DESERT HARVEST SOLAR FARM LLC
2 Centennial Dr Ste 4f (01960-7919)
PHONE..................................978 531-2222
EMP: 3
SALES (est): 175.2K **Privately Held**
SIC: **3674** Semiconductors And Related Devices, Nsk

(G-14330)
DESK TOP GRAPHICS INC (HQ)
Also Called: Spire Express
1 1st Ave (01960-4963)
PHONE..................................617 832-1927
Eric Dyer, *President*
Isaac Dyer, *Exec VP*
Rick Theder, *Exec VP*
▲ **EMP:** 23
SQ FT: 80,000
SALES (est): 10.9MM
SALES (corp-wide): 72.7MM **Privately Held**
SIC: **2796** 2752 7336 7374 Platemaking Services Lithographic Coml Print Coml Art/Graphic Design Data Processing/Prep Typesetting Services
PA: Digipress, Inc.
1 1st Ave
Peabody MA 01960
617 832-1927

(G-14331)
DIGIPRESS INC (PA)
Also Called: Spire
1 1st Ave (01960-4963)
PHONE..................................617 832-1927
Eric W Dyer, *President*
Isaac C Dyer, *Corp Secy*
Rick Theder, *Director*
EMP: 150
SQ FT: 80,000
SALES (est): 72.7MM **Privately Held**
SIC: **2752** Lithographic Commercial Printing

(G-14332)
ECONOMY COUPON & PRINTING INC
Also Called: Economy Printing
11 Mason St (01960-5943)
PHONE..................................781 279-8555
Peter Anastasia, *President*
EMP: 4
SQ FT: 3,500
SALES (est): 580.2K **Privately Held**
WEB: www.ecprint.net
SIC: **2752** 7336 2759 Lithographic Commercial Printing Commercial Art/Graphic Design Commercial Printing

(G-14333)
EMGA FOODS LLC
Also Called: Mozzarella House
26 Walnut St (01960-5673)
PHONE..................................978 532-0000
Giuseppe Argentieri, *Mng Member*
EMP: 6
SQ FT: 5,000
SALES: 700K **Privately Held**
SIC: **2022** Ret Dairy Products

(G-14334)
ESSEX COUNTY BREWING CO LLC
58 Pulaski St Bldg A (01960-1800)
PHONE..................................978 587-2254
Paul E Donhauser, *CEO*
EMP: 8
SALES (est): 235.3K **Privately Held**
SIC: **2082** Mfg Malt Beverages

(G-14335)
FURNITURE DESIGN SERVICES INC
119 Foster St Bldg 13 (01960-5933)
PHONE..................................978 531-3250
Chris Rice, *President*
EMP: 11
SALES (est): 1.4MM **Privately Held**
SIC: **2434** Mfg Wood Kitchen Cabinets

(G-14336)
GOODRICH CORPORATION
Also Called: UTC Aerospace Systems
5th St (01960)
P.O. Box 3369 (01961-3369)
PHONE..................................978 532-2350
Alan Douglas, *Engineer*
David Turner, *Engineer*
Brian Naslund, *Design Engr*
Michael Stewart, *Branch Mgr*
EMP: 150
SALES (corp-wide): 66.5B **Publicly Held**
WEB: www.bfgoodrich.com
SIC: **3728** Mfg Aircraft Parts/Equipment
HQ: Goodrich Corporation
2730 W Tyvola Rd 4
Charlotte NC 28217
704 423-7000

▲ = Import ▼=Export
◆ =Import/Export

(G-14337)
GREYLOCK PRESS LLC
6 Granite Road Ext (01960-6521)
PHONE..................................978 530-1740
Beth Johnson, *Principal*
EMP: 3 **EST:** 2015
SALES (est): 76.2K **Privately Held**
SIC: 2711 Newspapers-Publishing/Printing

(G-14338)
HARMONIC DRIVE LLC (HQ)
247 Lynnfield St (01960-4904)
PHONE..................................978 532-1800
Steve Foley, *Facilities Mgr*
Henry Kim, *Engineer*
Mel Hallah, *Sales Staff*
Linda Votano, *Sales Staff*
Tetsuo Ikuta,
▲ **EMP:** 74
SQ FT: 34,300
SALES (est): 18.5MM **Privately Held**
WEB: www.harmonic-drive.com
SIC: 3566 Mfg Speed Changers/Drives

(G-14339)
HENDRICKSON PUBLISHERS LLC
140 Summit St (01960-5156)
P.O. Box 3473 (01961-3473)
PHONE..................................978 532-6546
Kris Orlando, *Sales Executive*
Stephen J Hendrickson,
Ray E Hendrickson,
David L Townsley,
▲ **EMP:** 13
SQ FT: 3,000
SALES (est): 2MM **Privately Held**
WEB: www.hendricksonpublishers.net
SIC: 2731 Books-Publishing/Printing

(G-14340)
HENDRICKSON PUBLISHERS INC
140 Summit St (01960-5156)
P.O. Box 3473 (01961-3473)
PHONE 800 358-3111
Bev Devoe, *Sales Staff*
Meg Lynch, *Marketing Staff*
EMP: 3
SALES (est): 44.3K **Privately Held**
SIC: 2731 Books-Publishing/Printing

(G-14341)
HIGH LINER FOODS USA INC
801 Jubilee Dr (01960-4061)
PHONE..................................978 977-5305
EMP: 133
SALES (corp-wide): 1B **Privately Held**
SIC: 2092 Mfg Fresh/Frozen Packaged Fish
HQ: High Liner Foods (Usa) Incorporated
1 Highliner Ave
Portsmouth NH 03801
603 431-6865

(G-14342)
HP HOOD LLC
18 Blackstone St (01960-1002)
PHONE..................................978 535-3385
Joseph Hood, *Principal*
Julie Biviano, *Business Mgr*
Keith Sturgis, *Opers Mgr*
Roger Cairns, *Warehouse Mgr*
Fred Baker, *Maint Spvr*
EMP: 14
SALES (est): 1.3MM **Privately Held**
SIC: 2026 Mfg Fluid Milk

(G-14343)
INTERNATIONAL LIGHT TECH INC
Also Called: Gilway Technical Lamp
10 Technology Dr Ste 2 (01960-7976)
PHONE..................................978 818-6180
Thomas Connolly, *CEO*
Holly Wallace, *Vice Pres*
Michelle M Collins, *Purchasing*
Michael T O Connor, *CFO*
Brehon S Griswold, *Treasurer*
▲ **EMP:** 21 **EST:** 1963
SQ FT: 17,000
SALES (est): 6.4MM **Privately Held**
WEB: www.intl-lighttech.com
SIC: 3641 3826 3999 3829 Mfg Electric Lamps Mfg Analytical Instr Mfg Misc Products Mfg Measure/Control Dvcs Mfg Coml Light Fixtures

(G-14344)
JAMES G HACHEY INC
Also Called: In Building Cellular
1r Newbury St Ste 309 (01960-3816)
PHONE..................................781 229-6400
James Hachey, *President*
Diane Hachey, *Finance Mgr*
EMP: 5
SALES (est): 1MM **Privately Held**
WEB: www.inbuildingcellular.com
SIC: 3825 4812 4813 Mfg Electrical Measuring Instruments Radiotelephone Communication Telephone Communications

(G-14345)
JEOL USA INC (HQ)
11 Dearborn Rd (01960-3862)
P.O. Box 6043 (01961-6043)
PHONE..................................978 535-5900
Peter Genovese, *President*
Hideaki Arima, *Vice Pres*
Masuru Iwatani, *Vice Pres*
Robert Pohorenec, *Vice Pres*
Barbara Lear, *Prdtn Mgr*
▲ **EMP:** 120
SQ FT: 30,000
SALES (est): 68.6MM **Privately Held**
WEB: www.jeolusa.com
SIC: 3826 Mfg Analytical Instruments

(G-14346)
JOHN COVEY
Also Called: Covey Engineering
6 Cobb Ave (01960-3610)
P.O. Box 2026 (01960-7026)
PHONE..................................978 535-4681
John Covey, *Owner*
EMP: 12
SQ FT: 3,000
SALES (est): 1.1MM **Privately Held**
SIC: 3599 Machine Shop

(G-14347)
KING KALIPERS INC
58 Pulaski St Ste 21 (01960-1893)
PHONE..................................978 977-4994
J D Lindsey, *President*
Dj Robert, *Vice Pres*
Lois Bergin, *Manager*
▲ **EMP:** 26
SQ FT: 27,000
SALES (est): 4.3MM **Privately Held**
WEB: www.kaliper.com
SIC: 3714 Rebuilds Motor Vehicle Disc Brakes

(G-14348)
KONDELIN ASSOCIATES INC (HQ)
Also Called: Oxford Graphics
10 Centennial Dr Ste 105 (01960-7900)
PHONE..................................978 281-3663
Robert Simko, *CEO*
EMP: 15
SQ FT: 10,000
SALES (est): 2.3MM
SALES (corp-wide): 238MM **Privately Held**
WEB: www.oxfordgraphicsinc.com
SIC: 2759 2752 Commercial Printing Lithographic Commercial Printing
PA: Resource Label Group, Llc
147 Seaboard Ln
Franklin TN 37067
615 661-5900

(G-14349)
KSG ENTERPRISES INC
Also Called: Finelines
77 Walnut St Ste 8 (01960-5691)
PHONE..................................978 977-7357
Karen S Gilman, *President*
EMP: 17
SQ FT: 4,000
SALES (est): 1.5MM **Privately Held**
SIC: 2392 2391 Mfg Household Furnishings Mfg Curtains/Draperies

(G-14350)
LASER PROCESS MFG INC
2 Centennial Dr Ste 6 (01960-7919)
PHONE..................................978 531-6003
Lynn O'Malley, *CEO*
J Charles Rivers, *President*
Jeff Gibson, *Vice Pres*
Matthew Henry, *Accounts Exec*
Ryan Cronin, *Art Dir*
EMP: 12
SQ FT: 7,000
SALES (est): 1.3MM **Privately Held**
WEB: www.laserprocessmfg.com
SIC: 3599 Mfg Industrial Machinery

(G-14351)
LAWRENCE METAL FORMING CORP
7 Lakeland Park Dr (01960-3835)
P.O. Box 2215 (01960-7215)
PHONE..................................978 535-1200
Stefan Costa, *President*
Paul Costa, *Treasurer*
EMP: 15
SALES (est): 2.2MM **Privately Held**
SIC: 3498 Fabricates Pipes & Tubes

(G-14352)
LIBERATED IMAGES INC
119 Foster St (01960-5933)
PHONE..................................978 532-1880
Chris Wren, *Principal*
EMP: 3 **EST:** 2008
SALES (est): 227.7K **Privately Held**
SIC: 2759 Commercial Printing

(G-14353)
LJL ENTERPRISES INC
20 Webster St Fl 4 (01960-4465)
P.O. Box 804, Marblehead (01945-0804)
PHONE..................................781 639-2714
Arthur Michaels, *President*
EMP: 5
SALES (est): 576.2K **Privately Held**
SIC: 2331 2335 2337 2339 Mfg Women/Misses Blouses Mfg Women/Misses Dresses Mfg Women/Miss Suit/Coat Mfg Women/Miss Outerwear Mfg Women/Miss Underwear

(G-14354)
M/K SYSTEMS INC
300 Andover St Unit 213 (01960-1526)
PHONE..................................978 857-9228
Andrew Taylor Kallmes, *President*
EMP: 7
SALES: 400K **Privately Held**
SIC: 3821 Mfg Lab Apparatus/Furniture

(G-14355)
MICROPLASMIC CORPORATION
17 Esquire Dr (01960-1704)
PHONE..................................978 548-9762
Fax: 978 531-3671
EMP: 4
SALES (est): 330K **Privately Held**
WEB: www.microplasmic.com
SIC: 2851 8734 Ceramic Coating Process For Titanium Aluminum And Metal Machinery/Parts Also Research And Development Of Coating Processes

(G-14356)
NEW ENGLAND LASER INC
1 Centennial Dr Ste 1 # 1 (01960-7920)
PHONE..................................978 587-3914
Michael McCullock, *President*
Gayle Vyn, *Treasurer*
Fredrick Vyn, *Admin Sec*
EMP: 3
SALES (est): 627.7K **Privately Held**
WEB: www.nelp.com
SIC: 3444 Mfg Sheet Metalwork

(G-14357)
NORTH AMERICAN STEEL CORP
1 Gwinnett Rd (01960-3512)
PHONE..................................978 535-7587
Steven Rayworth, *President*
EMP: 3
SALES (est): 394.9K **Privately Held**
SIC: 3441 Structural Metal Fabrication

(G-14358)
NORTH SHORE LABORATORIES CORP
Also Called: Safety Seals
44 Endicott St (01960-3122)
P.O. Box 568 (01960-7568)
PHONE..................................978 531-5954
Robert A Niconchuk, *President*
Susan Pelletier, *Admin Sec*
▲ **EMP:** 11 **EST:** 1964
SALES: 2.6MM **Privately Held**
SIC: 3714 7389 Mfg Motor Vehicle Parts/Accessories

(G-14359)
PALAKA CORP
Also Called: Supper Time USA
18 Northfield Rd (01960-1632)
PHONE..................................978 531-6252
Peggy Weiser, *President*
EMP: 6
SALES (est): 370K **Privately Held**
SIC: 2099 Mfg Food Preparations

(G-14360)
PALMER MANUFACTURING CO LLC
1 2nd St Ste 1 # 1 (01960-4958)
PHONE..................................781 321-0480
EMP: 3
SALES (corp-wide): 368.2MM **Privately Held**
SIC: 3724 Mfg Aircraft Engines/Parts
HQ: Palmer Manufacturing Co., Llc.
243 Medford St
Malden MA 02148
781 321-0480

(G-14361)
PARADIGM PRCISION HOLDINGS LLC
1 2nd St (01960-4957)
PHONE..................................978 278-7100
John Russell, *Branch Mgr*
EMP: 15
SALES (corp-wide): 368.2MM **Privately Held**
SIC: 3724 Manufactures Aircraft Engines Or Parts
HQ: Paradigm Precision Holdings, Llc
404 W Guadalupe Rd
Tempe AZ 85283

(G-14362)
PINPOINT LASER SYSTEMS INC
56 Pulaski St Unit 5 (01960-1830)
PHONE..................................978 532-8001
Albert M Creighton, *President*
Vin Barsalou, *Mfg Mgr*
Bryan Blair, *Engineer*
Rosemary Belt, *Marketing Mgr*
EMP: 20
SQ FT: 5,000
SALES (est): 3.9MM **Privately Held**
WEB: www.pinlaser.com
SIC: 3821 3829 Mfg Lab Apparatus/Furniture Mfg Measuring/Controlling Devices

(G-14363)
PRATTVILLE MACHINE & TL CO INC
240 Jubilee Dr Fl 2 (01960-4062)
PHONE..................................978 538-5229
John Russo, *President*
Vinny Spinali, *General Mgr*
Veronica Russo, *Purch Mgr*
Veronica Ruo, *Purchasing*
Steve Evans, *QC Mgr*
EMP: 80
SQ FT: 48,000
SALES (est): 16.2MM **Privately Held**
WEB: www.prattvillemachine.com
SIC: 3599 Mfg Industrial Machinery

(G-14364)
RELIABLE SCREW MCH PDTS INC
119r Foster St Bldg 6-2 (01960-5951)
PHONE..................................978 531-0520
Robert Scorzoni, *President*
Debra Scorzoni, *Senior VP*
▼ **EMP:** 6
SQ FT: 10,000

GEOGRAPHIC

SALES (est): 580K **Privately Held**
SIC: 3451 Mfg Screw Machine Products

(G-14365)
RIVERSIDE ENGINEERING CO INC
12 County St (01960-5208)
PHONE..................................978 531-1556
Bruce Madden, *President*
EMP: 7
SQ FT: 3,500
SALES (est): 745.8K **Privately Held**
SIC: 3599 Job Machine Shop

(G-14366)
ROUSSELOT PEABODY INC
227 Washington St (01960-5423)
PHONE..................................978 573-3700
Larry Jeske, *President*
Kathy Olbrich, *Principal*
Catherine Duffty, *Engineer*
Stephen Smith, *Treasurer*
Sean McHugh, *CIO*
◆ **EMP:** 18 **EST:** 1930
SQ FT: 480,000
SALES (est): 6MM **Privately Held**
SIC: 2899 Mfg Chemical Preparations
HQ: Rousselot Dubuque Inc
2350 Kerper Blvd
Dubuque IA 52001
888 455-3556

(G-14367)
ROYAL STAMP WORKS INC
19 Centennial Dr (01960-7901)
P.O. Box 3172 (01961-3172)
PHONE..................................978 531-5555
Anne Distefano, *President*
EMP: 5
SQ FT: 2,000
SALES (est): 380K **Privately Held**
SIC: 3953 Mfg Marking Devices

(G-14368)
S & S STATUARY
8 Patricia Rd (01960-3473)
PHONE..................................978 535-5837
Sharon Vitali, *Owner*
EMP: 3
SQ FT: 9,000
SALES (est): 170K **Privately Held**
SIC: 3299 Mfg Statues

(G-14369)
SEMINEX CORPORATION
100 Corporate Pl Ste 302 (01960-3809)
PHONE..................................978 326-7700
David Bean, *CEO*
Patricia Robinson, *Vice Pres*
Neal Stoker, *Vice Pres*
Matthew Hamersprom, *Design Engr*
EMP: 6
SQ FT: 2,000
SALES: 3MM **Privately Held**
WEB: www.seminex.com
SIC: 3674 Mfg Semiconductors/Related Devices

(G-14370)
SOLVENT KLEENE INC
119 Foster St Bldg 6 (01960-5933)
PHONE..................................978 531-2279
Itamar Kutai, *President*
Adams Don, *Purchasing*
Jeffrey J Krugman, *Treasurer*
EMP: 15
SQ FT: 22,000
SALES (est): 2.9MM **Privately Held**
WEB: www.solventkleene.com
SIC: 2911 2865 Petroleum Refiner Mfg Cyclic Crudes/Intermediates/Dyes

(G-14371)
SPECIALIZED TURNING INC
147 Summit St Ste 7 (01960-5173)
PHONE..................................978 977-0444
Harold E Holm Jr, *President*
EMP: 30
SALES (est): 6.7MM **Privately Held**
WEB: www.specializedturning.com
SIC: 3451 Mfg S Crew Machine Products

(G-14372)
STAHL (USA) INC (DH)
13 Corwin St (01960-5107)
PHONE..................................978 968-1382
Huub Van Beijeren, *CEO*
Ron Dawley, *Controller*
▲ **EMP:** 36
SQ FT: 6,223,120
SALES (est): 6.1MM
SALES (corp-wide): 971.4MM **Privately Held**
WEB: www.stahlusa.com
SIC: 2891 Mfg Adhesives/Sealants
HQ: Stahl Holdings B.V.
Sluisweg 10
Waalwijk 5145
416 689-111

(G-14373)
SUBURBAN PUBLISHING CORP
Also Called: Suburban Real Estate News
2 1st Ave Ste 103 (01960-4960)
PHONE..................................978 818-6300
Richard H Ayer, *President*
EMP: 15 **EST:** 1979
SQ FT: 9,000
SALES (est): 872.2K
SALES (corp-wide): 2.8MM **Privately Held**
WEB: www.suburbanpublishing.com
SIC: 2711 2721 Newspaper Publishing
PA: Creative Publishing Corporation Of America
2 1st Ave Ste 103
Peabody MA 01960
978 532-5880

(G-14374)
SWAROVSKI US HOLDING LIMITED
210 Andover St (01960-1647)
PHONE..................................978 531-4582
Jill Russell, *President*
EMP: 4
SALES (corp-wide): 4.7B **Privately Held**
SIC: 3961 Mfg Costume Jewelry
HQ: Swarovski U.S. Holding Limited
1 Kenney Dr
Cranston RI 02920
401 463-6400

(G-14375)
TECHFILM SERVICES INC
103 Foster St (01960-5933)
PHONE..................................978 531-3300
Stephen Buchanan, *President*
Barbara Nelson, *Treasurer*
EMP: 5
SQ FT: 12,000
SALES (est): 456.3K **Privately Held**
WEB: www.adhesivepackaging.com
SIC: 2891 Mfg Adhesives/Sealants

(G-14376)
TECHNICAL MANUFACTURING CORP (HQ)
Also Called: Tmcs
15 Centennial Dr (01960-7993)
PHONE..................................978 532-6330
Bruce P Wilson, *President*
Robert S Feit, *Vice Pres*
Keith J Kowalski, *Vice Pres*
Igor Kordunsky, *Research*
Justin Nealey, *Engineer*
▲ **EMP:** 80
SQ FT: 50,000
SALES (est): 24.2MM
SALES (corp-wide): 4.8B **Publicly Held**
SIC: 3829 Mfg Measuring/Controlling Devices
PA: Ametek, Inc.
1100 Cassatt Rd
Berwyn PA 19312
610 647-2121

(G-14377)
THRIFTCO SPEEDI-PRINT CENTER
Also Called: Thriftco Printing
56 Pulaski St Unit 7 (01960-1830)
PHONE..................................978 531-5546
Barry Sinewitz, *President*
Linda Gaeta, *Vice Pres*
EMP: 4
SALES (est): 440K **Privately Held**
SIC: 2752 Lithographic Commercial Printing

(G-14378)
TLC VISION (USA) CORPORATION
201 Andover St (01960-1603)
PHONE..................................978 531-4114
EMP: 23
SALES (corp-wide): 1.2B **Privately Held**
SIC: 2591 Mfg Drapery Hardware/Blinds
HQ: Tlc Vision (Usa) Corporation
16305 Swingley Ridge Rd # 300
Chesterfield MO 63017
636 534-2300

(G-14379)
TRU TECHNOLOGIES INC
245 Lynnfield St (01960-5049)
PHONE..................................978 532-0775
Linda Moulton, *CEO*
EMP: 146
SALES (est): 9.1MM **Privately Held**
SIC: 3679 3812 3643 3678 Mfg Electronic Components Search/Navigation Equip Conductive Wiring Devices & Electronic Connectors

(G-14380)
TUCKER ENGINEERING INC
4 5th St (01960-4916)
PHONE..................................978 532-5900
Donald A Tucker, *President*
Tina M Tucker, *Treasurer*
EMP: 38
SQ FT: 12,000
SALES (est): 6.6MM **Privately Held**
WEB: www.tuckereng.com
SIC: 3599 Mfg Industrial Machinery

(G-14381)
VORTEX INC
4 Dearborn Rd (01960-3804)
PHONE..................................978 535-8721
Vito P Martello, *President*
Jay McNulty, *General Mgr*
David Allen, *Vice Pres*
▲ **EMP:** 65
SQ FT: 25,000
SALES (est): 12.2MM **Privately Held**
WEB: www.vortexmetal.com
SIC: 3444 3312 Mfg Sheet Metalwork Blast Furnace-Steel Works

(G-14382)
WHITECAP COMPOSITES INC
147 Summit St (01960-5174)
PHONE..................................978 278-5718
Ben Parker, *President*
Paul Zimmerman, *Corp Secy*
▲ **EMP:** 6 **EST:** 2011
SQ FT: 10,000
SALES (est): 914.6K **Privately Held**
SIC: 2221 2295 3732 Manmad Brdwv Fabric Mill Mfg Coated Fabrics Boatbuilding/Repairing

(G-14383)
WINCHESTER INTERCONNECT CORP
245 Lynnfield St (01960-5049)
PHONE..................................978 532-0775
Stephen Eccles, *General Mgr*
Shannon Williams, *Accounting Mgr*
Ana Berrellez, *Manager*
Jacqui Benko, *Analyst*
EMP: 65
SALES (corp-wide): 16.6B **Privately Held**
SIC: 3678 Mfg Electronic Connectors
HQ: Winchester Interconnect Corporation
68 Water St
Norwalk CT 06854
-

(G-14384)
WINCHESTER INTERCONNECT CORP
245 Lynnfield St (01960-5049)
PHONE..................................978 532-0775
Stephen Eccles, *General Mgr*
EMP: 65
SALES (corp-wide): 16.6B **Privately Held**
WEB: www.micross.com
SIC: 3678 Mfg Electronic Connectors
HQ: Winchester Interconnect Corporation
68 Water St
Norwalk CT 06854
-

(G-14385)
WINCHSTER INTERCONNECT RF CORP (HQ)
245 Lynnfield St (01960-5049)
P.O. Box 842464, Boston (02284-2464)
PHONE..................................978 532-0775
Timothy S O'Neil, *President*
Anthony Martiniello, *Admin Sec*
▼ **EMP:** 65
SQ FT: 40,000
SALES: 20MM **Privately Held**
WEB: www.trucorporation.com
SIC: 3643 3678 Mfg Conductive Wiring Devices Mfg Electronic Connectors

(G-14386)
WIND TUNNEL HEATING & AC LLC
20 State St (01960-6141)
PHONE..................................978 977-7783
Stephen Defreitas, *Principal*
EMP: 4 **EST:** 2008
SALES (est): 501.4K **Privately Held**
SIC: 3443 Mfg Fabricated Plate Work

(G-14387)
WOODMAN PRECISION ENGINEERING
119 Foster St (01960-5933)
PHONE..................................978 538-9544
Chris Ahordini, *President*
EMP: 10
SALES: 1MM **Privately Held**
SIC: 3599 Machine Shop Jobbing & Repair

Pelham
Hampshire County

(G-14388)
HUMAN RESOURCE DEV PRESS (PA)
Also Called: Hrd Press
22 Amherst Rd (01002-9709)
PHONE..................................413 253-3488
Robert R Carkhuff, *President*
Robert W Carkhuff, *Publisher*
Richard Croteau, *CFO*
EMP: 21
SQ FT: 6,000
SALES (est): 2.4MM **Privately Held**
WEB: www.hrdpress.com
SIC: 2731 7812 7371 Publisher Of Training Materials In Books Video And Computer Software

Pembroke
Plymouth County

(G-14389)
AB-WEY MACHINE & DIE CO INC
51 School St (02359-3407)
P.O. Box 567, Hanson (02341-0567)
PHONE..................................781 294-8031
Anthony Delacono, *President*
Raymond J Sylvester, *Clerk*
EMP: 15 **EST:** 1967
SQ FT: 18,000
SALES (est): 2.5MM **Privately Held**
WEB: www.abweymachine.com
SIC: 3599 3542 Mfg Industrial Machinery Mfg Machine Tools-Forming

(G-14390)
ALLIANCE BOOK MFG CO INC
221 Mattakeesett St (02359)
PHONE..................................781 294-0802
EMP: 3
SQ FT: 5,000
SALES (est): 210K **Privately Held**
WEB: www.alliancebookmfg.com
SIC: 2789 Bookbinding Of Hard Covered Books

(G-14391)
ANTENNA RESEARCH ASSOC INC
Seavey Engineering
28 Riverside Dr Ste 2 (02359-4947)
PHONE.................................781 829-4740
Sean Walsh, *General Mgr*
EMP: 37
SQ FT: 39,850
SALES (corp-wide): 22MM **Privately Held**
SIC: 3663 Mfg Radio/Tv Communication Equipment
PA: Antenna Research Associates, Inc.
11850 Baltimore Ave Ste H
Beltsville MD 20705
301 937-8888

(G-14392)
APPLE MILL HOLDING COMPANY INC
Also Called: Sunrise
720 Washington St (02359-2324)
PHONE.................................781 826-9706
Henry C Appleton, *President*
Leah Donner, *Office Mgr*
Sherri Pond, *Executive*
EMP: 11
SQ FT: 20,000
SALES (est): 1.8MM **Privately Held**
WEB: www.sunrisesystems.com
SIC: 3993 3674 Mfg Signs/Advertising Specialties Mfg Semiconductors/Related Devices
PA: Sunrise Systems Electronics Co. Inc.
720 Washington St
Pembroke MA 02359
781 826-9706

(G-14393)
BELCO FUEL COMPANY INC
38 Mountain Ash Ln (02359-2006)
PHONE.................................781 331-6521
Tony Borrelli, *Principal*
EMP: 4
SALES (est): 355.4K **Privately Held**
SIC: 2869 Mfg Industrial Organic Chemicals

(G-14394)
CHERRY HILL CONSTRUCTION CORP
722 Washington St (02359-2324)
P.O. Box 6, North Pembroke (02358-0006)
PHONE.................................781 826-6886
Jim McGill, *President*
EMP: 7
SQ FT: 3,000
SALES (est): 402.6K **Privately Held**
WEB: www.cherryhillpool.com
SIC: 3949 Sales & Installation Of Swimming Pools

(G-14395)
CHIC LLC
Also Called: Leon Levin
2 Corporate Park Dr (02359)
PHONE.................................781 312-7800
Charles Godfrey,
▲ **EMP:** 3 **EST:** 1999
SALES (est): 335.5K **Privately Held**
SIC: 2335 Mfg Women's/Misses' Dresses

(G-14396)
D & H PRINT MANAGEMENT LTD
300 Oak St Ste 1925 (02359-1984)
PHONE.................................781 829-0209
Mark Hunt, *President*
EMP: 5
SALES (est): 570K **Privately Held**
WEB: www.dhprint.com
SIC: 2759 Commercial Printing

(G-14397)
DATANATIONAL CORPORATION
Also Called: Wti Systems
100 Schoosett St Ste 2a (02359-1875)
PHONE.................................781 826-3400
Robert M Raymond, *President*
Joseph E Kaminski III, *President*
EMP: 12
SQ FT: 2,000
SALES (est): 1MM **Privately Held**
WEB: www.datanationalcorp.com
SIC: 7372 Prepackaged Software Services

(G-14398)
DDS SERVICES LTD
30 Oak St (02359-1915)
P.O. Box 562, Green Harbor (02041-0562)
PHONE.................................781 837-3997
Deborah A Deady, *President*
EMP: 6
SALES (est): 452.5K **Privately Held**
SIC: 3471 Plating/Polishing Service

(G-14399)
DIMARK PRECISION MACHINING
745 Washington St (02359-2341)
P.O. Box 317, North Pembroke (02358-0317)
PHONE.................................781 447-7990
James Porter, *President*
John Porter, *Corp Secy*
Richard Lawrence, *Vice Pres*
EMP: 17
SQ FT: 8,500
SALES (est): 2.6MM **Privately Held**
SIC: 3599 Mfg Industrial Machinery

(G-14400)
DOLLY PLOW INC
Also Called: New England Installations
53 Mattakeesett St (02359-2512)
PHONE.................................781 293-9828
Albert Petrell Jr, *President*
EMP: 4
SALES (est): 350K **Privately Held**
SIC: 3799 Mfg Transportation Equipment

(G-14401)
DUROMAR INC
706 Washington St (02359-2324)
PHONE.................................781 826-2525
A Wesley Langeland, *President*
Jonathan Otto Proctor, *Vice Pres*
EMP: 6
SQ FT: 5,000
SALES (est): 1.3MM **Privately Held**
WEB: www.duromar.com
SIC: 2851 Coating/Engraving Service

(G-14402)
E S RITCHIE & SONS INC
Also Called: Richie Navigation
243 Oak St (02359-1980)
P.O. Box 548 (02359-0548)
PHONE.................................781 826-5131
Jonathan Sherman, *President*
Greg Urquhart, *Facilities Mgr*
Tom Reiber, *Purch Mgr*
Patrick Lonergan, *Technical Mgr*
EMP: 35 **EST:** 1850
SQ FT: 22,500
SALES (est): 12.3MM **Privately Held**
WEB: www.ritchienavigation.com
SIC: 3812 Mfg Search/Navigation Equipment

(G-14403)
EASTERN INDUSTRIAL PRODUCTS
737 Washington St (02359-2341)
P.O. Box 1150 (02359-1150)
PHONE.................................781 826-9511
Daniel P Spurling, *President*
Susan Spurling, *Clerk*
EMP: 18
SQ FT: 9,300
SALES (est): 3.3MM **Privately Held**
WEB: www.easternindustrialproducts.com
SIC: 3053 Mfg Gaskets/Packing/Sealing Devices

(G-14404)
FCI OPHTHALMICS INC
30 Corporate Park Dr # 310 (02359-2071)
PHONE.................................781 826-9060
Jean-Pierre Desseignes, *President*
Susan Gaines, *Accountant*
EMP: 7
SALES (est): 1.2MM
SALES (corp-wide): 449.3K **Privately Held**
WEB: www.meditec.zeiss.com
SIC: 3841 Mfg Surgical/Medical Instruments
HQ: Carl Zeiss Meditec Ag
Goschwitzer Str. 51-52
Jena 07745
364 122-00

(G-14405)
FLOC LLC
125 Church St Ste 90-136 (02359-1929)
PHONE.................................617 823-5798
Aaron Dasilva, *CEO*
EMP: 3
SALES: 25K **Privately Held**
SIC: 7372 7389 Prepackaged Software Services Business Serv Non-Commercial Site

(G-14406)
GEORGE PUBLISHING COMPANY
167 Elm St (02359-2015)
PHONE.................................781 826-4996
Fredrick George, *Owner*
EMP: 4 **EST:** 2013
SALES (est): 267.6K **Privately Held**
SIC: 2741 Misc Publishing

(G-14407)
GROUND SUPPORT PRODUCTS CORP
Also Called: Gsp Worldwide
42 Winter St Ste 5 (02359-4958)
PHONE.................................860 491-3348
Katherine Hunt, *President*
Christina Hunt, *Admin Sec*
▲ **EMP:** 4
SALES (est): 39.5K **Privately Held**
WEB: www.airportgse.com
SIC: 3728 Mfg Aircraft Parts/Equipment

(G-14408)
HORNER MILLWORK CORP
55 Corporate Park Dr # 1 (02359-1959)
PHONE.................................781 826-7770
Peter D Humphrey, *Branch Mgr*
EMP: 22
SALES (corp-wide): 48.2MM **Privately Held**
WEB: www.hornermillwork.com
SIC: 2431 Mfg Millwork
PA: Horner Millwork Corp.
1255 Grand Army Hwy
Somerset MA 02726
508 679-6479

(G-14409)
HOYLU INC
Also Called: Hoylu Boston
50 Corporate Park Dr # 270 (02359-1998)
PHONE.................................877 554-6958
Zach Hurvitz, *Sales Staff*
EMP: 5
SALES (corp-wide): 1.2MM **Privately Held**
SIC: 7372 Prepackaged Software Services
PA: Hoylu, Inc.
720 4th Ave Ste 220
Kirkland WA 98033
425 269-3299

(G-14410)
I V I CORP
265 Oak St (02359-1980)
PHONE.................................781 826-3195
George J Mackertich, *President*
George J Mac Kertich, *President*
▲ **EMP:** 10
SQ FT: 20,000
SALES (est): 1.5MM **Privately Held**
WEB: www.ivicorp.com
SIC: 3567 Mfg Industrial Furnaces/Ovens

(G-14411)
INTERCEPT BOAT CORP
171 Mattakeesett St Ste 9 (02359-2539)
PHONE.................................781 294-8100
Amy W Lincoln, *CEO*
Amy Lincoln -operations Manage, *Manager*
EMP: 3
SALES (est): 417.1K **Privately Held**
WEB: www.interceptboats.com
SIC: 3732 Boatbuilding/Repairing

(G-14412)
JLC TECH LLC
370 Corporate Park Dr (02359-4969)
PHONE.................................781 826-8162
Silvio Porciatti, *Principal*
Joanne Protasewich, *Opers Staff*
Nick Konarski, *Sales Staff*
Ted McDermott, *Sales Staff*
Chantel Betterton, *Marketing Staff*
▲ **EMP:** 20 **EST:** 2013
SALES (est): 2.6MM **Privately Held**
SIC: 3646 Mfg Commercial Lighting Fixtures

(G-14413)
KENT FABRICATIONS INC
171 Mattakeesett St (02359-2539)
PHONE.................................339 244-4533
Raymond A Miller, *President*
Mark Amorello, *Treasurer*
EMP: 8
SALES (est): 1.8MM **Privately Held**
SIC: 3441 Structural Metal Fabrication

(G-14414)
KEVIN BONNEY
Also Called: K B Welding
79 Water St (02359-1947)
PHONE.................................781 826-6439
Kevin Bonney, *Owner*
EMP: 3
SQ FT: 300
SALES (est): 394.9K **Privately Held**
SIC: 3444 Mfg Sheet Metalwork

(G-14415)
LASER LABS INC
70 Corporate Park Dr # 1245 (02359-4901)
PHONE.................................781 826-4138
EMP: 3
SALES (est): 103K **Privately Held**
SIC: 3812 3825 Mfg Search/Navigation Equipment Mfg Electrical Measuring Instruments

(G-14416)
MACKENZIE MACHINE & DESIGN INC
171 Mattakeesett St Ste 2 (02359-2539)
PHONE.................................339 933-8157
Neal Mackenzie, *President*
EMP: 17 **EST:** 1959
SQ FT: 5,000
SALES (est): 2.4MM **Privately Held**
SIC: 3599 Mfg Industrial Machinery

(G-14417)
MOBLE INTERNET ACCESS INC
300 Oak St Ste 1010 (02359-1984)
P.O. Box 47, Chatham (02633-0047)
PHONE.................................978 273-2390
Peter Gruol, *President*
EMP: 5
SALES (est): 328.2K **Privately Held**
SIC: 3663 Mfg Radio/Tv Communication Equipment

(G-14418)
NEW ENGLAND SHRLINES COMPANIES
704 Washington St (02359-2324)
PHONE.................................781 826-0140
Roger Morton, *President*
Monica Puentes, *Administration*
EMP: 10
SALES (est): 1.4MM **Privately Held**
SIC: 2431 5031 Mfg & Wholesales Millwork

(G-14419)
NEW ENGLAND SOLAR HOT WTR INC
54 Corporate Park Dr # 510 (02359-2051)
PHONE.................................781 536-8633
Bruce Dike, *President*
▲ **EMP:** 3
SALES (est): 316.1K **Privately Held**
SIC: 3433 Mfg Heating Equipment-Non-electric

(G-14420)
NORTH RIVER GRAPHICS INC
100 Corporate Park Dr # 1730 (02359-4964)
PHONE.................................781 826-6866
Mary Hill, *President*
Jeffrey Hill, *Treasurer*
EMP: 9
SALES (est): 1.6MM **Privately Held**
SIC: 2752 Lithographic Commercial Printing

GEOGRAPHIC

(G-14421)
NUVELUTION PHARMA INC
31 Schoosett St (02359-1877)
PHONE..................................781 924-1148
Ronald Martell, *President*
Milena Kanova-Petrova, *Senior VP*
EMP: 5
SALES (est): 272.5K **Privately Held**
SIC: 2834 Mfg Pharmaceutical Preparations

(G-14422)
PROSTRONG INC
300 Oak St Ste 1120 (02359)
PHONE..................................781 829-0000
Doris Crary, *President*
Frank Busch, *Vice Pres*
EMP: 5
SQ FT: 3,000
SALES (est): 1.6MM **Privately Held**
WEB: www.prostrong.com
SIC: 2844 7231 Mfg Toilet Preparations Beauty Shop

(G-14423)
PROTECTOWIRE CO INC
60 Washington St (02359-1833)
PHONE..................................781 826-3878
Carol M Sullivan, *Ch of Bd*
Andrew K Sullivan, *President*
Gary P Fields, *Exec VP*
Brian Harrington, *Prdtn Mgr*
Matt Eppich, *Purch Mgr*
EMP: 30 **EST:** 1936
SALES (est): 6.3MM **Privately Held**
WEB: www.protectowire.com
SIC: 3669 Mfg Communications Equipment

(G-14424)
RICHARD GILBERT
Also Called: Engineered Precision Products
52 Adams Ave (02359-2456)
PHONE..................................508 337-8774
EMP: 3 **EST:** 2003
SALES (est): 160K **Privately Held**
SIC: 3599 Machine Shop Jobbing And Repair

(G-14425)
SCIDYNE
649 School St (02359-3632)
PHONE..................................781 293-3059
Mark Durgin, *Owner*
EMP: 11
SALES (est): 1.6MM **Privately Held**
WEB: www.scidyne.com
SIC: 3571 Mfg Electronic Computers

(G-14426)
SFJ PHARMA
31 Schoosett St (02359-1877)
PHONE..................................781 924-1148
EMP: 3
SALES (est): 226.6K **Privately Held**
SIC: 2834 Mfg Pharmaceutical Preparations

(G-14427)
SOUTH SHORE CUSTOM PRINTS
85 Mattakeesett St (02359-2511)
PHONE..................................781 293-8300
Mark Stodart, *Owner*
EMP: 3 **EST:** 2012
SALES (est): 191.7K **Privately Held**
SIC: 2752 Lithographic Commercial Printing

(G-14428)
SUNRISE SYSTEMS ELEC CO INC (PA)
720 Washington St (02359-2324)
PHONE..................................781 826-9706
Eric Harrington, *President*
Zack Farahmand, *Admin Sec*
EMP: 8
SALES (est): 1.8MM **Privately Held**
SIC: 3993 3674 Mfg Signs/Advertising Specialties Mfg Semiconductors/Related Devices

(G-14429)
TRADEMARK PRINT INC
300 Oak St Ste 1925 (02359)
PHONE..................................781 829-0209
Stephen R Erickson, *President*
Shane M Davis, *Treasurer*
EMP: 4
SALES (est): 590.9K **Privately Held**
SIC: 2752 Lithographic Commercial Printing

(G-14430)
TURNING POINT INDUSTRY FL
160 Corporate Park Dr (02359-2086)
PHONE..................................239 340-1942
Thomas F Minisce, *Principal*
▲ **EMP:** 4
SALES (est): 404.5K **Privately Held**
SIC: 3429 3432 Mfg Hardware Mfg Plumbing Fixture Fittings

(G-14431)
UNIVERSAL TIPPING CO INC
11 Parker Rd (02359-3002)
PHONE..................................781 826-5135
Bill H Barr, *President*
Norma Barr, *Treasurer*
EMP: 4
SQ FT: 7,500
SALES: 350K **Privately Held**
SIC: 3089 Mfg Plastic Products

(G-14432)
VENLO COMPANY
125 Church St Unit 90-411 (02359-1929)
PHONE..................................781 826-0485
Thomas O'Brien, *Principal*
▲ **EMP:** 3 **EST:** 2009
SALES (est): 363.6K **Privately Held**
SIC: 3199 Mfg Leather Goods

(G-14433)
WOOD DECOR INC
300 Oak St (02359)
PHONE..................................781 826-4954
Joe Hicks, *Manager*
EMP: 7
SALES (est): 27.8K **Privately Held**
SIC: 2499 Mfg Wood Products

(G-14434)
YANKEE TRADER SEAFOOD LTD
1610 Corporate Park (02359)
PHONE..................................781 829-4350
Stephanie Hernan, *CEO*
Lisa Hellar, *President*
Alex Hernan, *Director*
EMP: 12
SQ FT: 8,800
SALES (est): 3.2MM **Privately Held**
WEB: www.yankeetraderseafood.com
SIC: 2099 Mfg Food Preparations

Pepperell
Middlesex County

(G-14435)
ABSOLUTE MANUFACTURING INC
24 Lomar Park Ste F (01463-1489)
PHONE..................................978 433-0760
Dave Gosselin, *President*
EMP: 8
SALES (est): 1.3MM **Privately Held**
SIC: 3599 Mfg Industrial Machinery

(G-14436)
ASTRON INC (PA)
Also Called: Circle Wire
21 Lomar Park (01463-1416)
PHONE..................................978 433-9500
David M Abbot, *Ch of Bd*
Mark Mathews, *President*
Albert A Polmonari, *President*
John H Kellogg, *Treasurer*
Miller Ruth, *Administration*
EMP: 26 **EST:** 1906
SQ FT: 28,000
SALES (est): 5.5MM **Privately Held**
WEB: www.astronstamping.com
SIC: 3469 3452 Mfg Metal Stampings Mfg Bolts/Screws/Rivets

(G-14437)
BURTON FRAME AND TRAILER INC
106 Brookline St (01463-1141)
P.O. Box 317 (01463-0317)
PHONE..................................978 433-2051
David Burton, *President*
EMP: 4
SQ FT: 7,500
SALES (est): 459.1K **Privately Held**
SIC: 7692 5521 Welding Repair Ret Used Automobiles

(G-14438)
HITEC PRODUCTS INC
4 Lomar Park (01463-1416)
PHONE..................................978 772-6963
Vincent P Wnuk, *President*
Stephen P Wnuk Jr, *Treasurer*
EMP: 14
SALES (est): 2.2MM **Privately Held**
WEB: www.hitecprod.com
SIC: 3829 Mfg Measuring/Controlling Devices

(G-14439)
J & J MUSIC BOXES INC
10 Lomar Park (01463-1486)
P.O. Box 1508, Jensen Beach FL (34958-1508)
PHONE..................................978 433-5686
EMP: 10
SALES (est): 710K **Privately Held**
SIC: 3999 Mfg Music Boxes

(G-14440)
KEYSTONE PRECISION & ENGRG
16 Lomar Park Ste 3 (01463-1449)
PHONE..................................978 433-8484
Anthony Serino, *President*
Robert E Stanieich, *Vice Pres*
EMP: 20
SQ FT: 6,300
SALES (est): 2.1MM **Privately Held**
SIC: 3599 Precision Machine Shop

(G-14441)
KEYSTONE PRECISION INC
16 Lomar Park Ste 3 (01463-1449)
PHONE..................................978 433-8484
Ronald V Long, *President*
Ethel Long, *Clerk*
EMP: 9
SQ FT: 4,300
SALES: 627.8K **Privately Held**
SIC: 3679 Mfg Industrial Machinery

(G-14442)
LUMACERA INNOVATIVE MTLS INC
83 East St (01463-1302)
PHONE..................................978 302-6475
Brian Lacourse, *President*
EMP: 3
SALES (est): 217.1K **Privately Held**
SIC: 1459 Clay/Related Mineral Mining

(G-14443)
NORTH BRIDGE WOODWORKING
Also Called: THOMAS CONWAY, DBA NORTH BRIDGE WOODWORKING
7 Lomar Park Unit 2 (01463-1473)
PHONE..................................978 433-0148
EMP: 3
SQ FT: 2,600
SALES (est): 225.7K **Privately Held**
WEB: www.northbridgewoodworking.com
SIC: 2499 Mfg Wood Products

(G-14444)
PEPPERELL BRAIDING COMPANY INC (PA)
22 Lowell St (01463-1703)
P.O. Box 1487 (01463-3487)
PHONE..................................978 433-2133
William P Slivinski, *President*
Thomas J Murray Jr, *Vice Pres*
Sandra J Lavalley, *Admin Sec*
▲ **EMP:** 30
SQ FT: 18,500
SALES (est): 13.5MM **Privately Held**
WEB: www.pepperell.com
SIC: 3089 2241 2298 Mfg Plastic Products Narrow Fabric Mill Mfg Cordage/Twine

(G-14445)
PEPPERELL INTERNATIONAL
34 Prospect St (01463-1540)
PHONE..................................508 878-7987
EMP: 7
SALES (est): 987.1K **Privately Held**
SIC: 2821 Mfg Plastic Materials/Resins

(G-14446)
THERMOCERMET
4 Lomar Park (01463-1416)
PHONE..................................978 425-0404
Vince Wnuk, *Owner*
EMP: 3
SALES (est): 170K **Privately Held**
SIC: 3542 Mfg Machine Tools-Forming

Pinehurst
Middlesex County

(G-14447)
BILLERICA BACKSTAGE REHEARSAL
749 Boston Rd (01866)
P.O. Box 158 (01866-0158)
PHONE..................................978 670-1133
Tory Turco, *Owner*
EMP: 3 **EST:** 1997
SALES (est): 96.3K **Privately Held**
SIC: 3949 Mfg Sporting/Athletic Goods

Pittsfield
Berkshire County

(G-14448)
ADVANCE MACHINE & TOOL INC
50 Greenway St (01201-6604)
PHONE..................................413 499-4900
Michael Wasuk, *President*
Dave McDermott, *Vice Pres*
Alan Pavoni, *Vice Pres*
EMP: 10
SQ FT: 6,000
SALES (est): 1.4MM **Privately Held**
WEB: www.advancemachinetool.com
SIC: 3599 Machining

(G-14449)
AGI POLYMATRIX LLC (HQ)
Also Called: Amaray
45 Downing Industrial Par (01201-3812)
PHONE..................................413 499-3550
Steve Ploof, *CFO*
◆ **EMP:** 80 **EST:** 2010
SQ FT: 83,000
SALES: 90MM
SALES (corp-wide): 2.9B **Privately Held**
WEB: www.polymatrix.com
SIC: 3089 Mfg Plastic Products
PA: Atlas Holdings, Llc
100 Northfield St
Greenwich CT 06830
203 622-9138

(G-14450)
ALDAM PRESS INC
163 South St Ste 4 (01201-6880)
PHONE..................................413 443-2800
Paul James Aldam, *President*
Alicia Marie Aldam, *Admin Sec*
EMP: 3
SALES (est): 276.8K **Privately Held**
SIC: 2752 Lithographic Commercial Printing

(G-14451)
AMARAY PLASTICS
45 Downing Industrial Par (01201-3812)
PHONE..................................413 499-3550
EMP: 13
SALES (est): 2.1MM **Privately Held**
SIC: 3089 Mfg Plastic Products

(G-14452)
APEX RESOURCE TECHNOLOGIES INC
Also Called: Inanycase.com
17 Downing Three Park 2b (01201-3966)
PHONE..................................413 442-1414
Donna L Rochel, *President*
Donna Rochelo, *Corp Secy*
Don Rochelo, *COO*
Peter Crowe, *Design Engr*
David Hall, *CFO*
▲ **EMP:** 60
SQ FT: 12,000
SALES (est): 12.5MM **Privately Held**
SIC: 3089 Mfg Plastic Products

(G-14453)
ARACES INCORPORATED
570 East St (01201-5309)
PHONE..................................413 499-9997
EMP: 4
SALES (est): 332K **Privately Held**
SIC: 3714 Mfg Motor Vehicle Parts/Accessories

(G-14454)
ARMOR HOLDINGS PROTECH DIV
1595 East St (01201-3807)
PHONE..................................413 445-4000
John Bird, *CEO*
EMP: 4
SALES (est): 290K **Privately Held**
SIC: 3312 Body Armor Mf

(G-14455)
BALDERDASH CELLARS
502 East St Ste B (01201-5370)
PHONE..................................413 464-4629
Christian Hanson, *Owner*
EMP: 3 **EST:** 2013
SALES (est): 173K **Privately Held**
SIC: 2084 Mfg Wines/Brandy/Spirits

(G-14456)
BERKSHIRE CONCRETE CORP (HQ)
550 Cheshire Rd (01201-1823)
P.O. Box 1145 (01202-1145)
PHONE..................................413 443-4734
Perri C Petricca, *President*
Robert Petricca, *Exec VP*
Basil A Petricca, *Treasurer*
EMP: 205
SQ FT: 2,000
SALES (est): 17.1MM
SALES (corp-wide): 126.9MM **Privately Held**
WEB: www.unistresscorp.com
SIC: 3273 5211 1442 Mfg Ready-Mixed Concrete Ret Lumber/Building Materials Construction Sand/Gravel
PA: Petricca Industries, Inc.
550 Cheshire Rd
Pittsfield MA 01201
413 499-1441

(G-14457)
BERKSHIRE CUSTOM COATING INC
50 Downing Industrial Par (01201-3836)
PHONE..................................413 442-3757
Kevin Ploss, *President*
Doug Smith, *Vice Pres*
Lorraine Ploss, *Treasurer*
EMP: 35
SQ FT: 15,000
SALES (est): 1.7MM **Privately Held**
WEB: www.berkshirecustomcoating.com
SIC: 3479 Coating/Engraving Service

(G-14458)
BERKSHIRE MTN BKY PIZZA CAFE
Also Called: Berkshire Mtn Bky Pizza Cafe
180 Elm St Ste A (01201-6500)
PHONE..................................413 464-9394
Richard Bourdon, *Principal*
EMP: 6
SALES (est): 450K **Privately Held**
SIC: 2051 5812 Mfg Bread/Related Products Eating Place

(G-14459)
BERKSHIRE PRECISION TOOL LLC
9 Betnr Industrial Dr (01201-7899)
PHONE..................................413 499-3875
William F Coyle Jr, *CEO*
Gabi Radu, *Research*
Ryan Davine, *Manager*
Dan Holmes, *Manager*
Gerhard Tschabitzer, *Manager*
EMP: 40
SALES (est): 6.8MM
SALES (corp-wide): 21.8MM **Privately Held**
SIC: 3545 Mfg Metal Cutting Tools
PA: Harpoint Holdings, Inc
200 Front St
Millersburg PA 17061
717 692-2113

(G-14460)
BERKSHIRE SCREEN
95 Davis St (01201-2544)
PHONE..................................413 212-8360
Harold Boland, *Owner*
EMP: 3 **EST:** 2010
SALES (est): 195.1K **Privately Held**
SIC: 3353 Mfg Aluminum Sheet/Foil

(G-14461)
BERKSHIRE TOTES FOR TOTS INC
89 Egremont Ave (01201-7207)
PHONE..................................413 442-7048
Amy Tanner, *Principal*
EMP: 3
SALES (est): 101.2K **Privately Held**
SIC: 2711 Newspapers-Publishing/Printing

(G-14462)
CALLAHAN SIGN LLC
Also Called: Callahan Sign Company
8 Federico Dr Unit B (01201-5518)
P.O. Box 744 (01202-0744)
PHONE..................................413 443-5931
James Callahan, *CEO*
Barry Callahan, *Business Mgr*
Grayson Callahan, *Manager*
EMP: 6
SQ FT: 2,500
SALES (est): 791.1K **Privately Held**
WEB: www.callahansign.com
SIC: 3993 Mfg Signs/Advertising Specialties

(G-14463)
CHARLES MCCANN
Also Called: Iron Man Machine
27 Hungerford St (01201-7717)
PHONE..................................413 442-3922
Charles McCann, *Owner*
EMP: 3
SQ FT: 3,000
SALES (est): 360.3K **Privately Held**
SIC: 3599 Mfg Industrial Machinery

(G-14464)
CHEYNE AWNING & SIGN CO
275 Hungerford St (01201-7812)
PHONE..................................413 442-4742
Toll Free:..................................877 -
Timothy Harrigan, *Owner*
EMP: 4
SALES (est): 337.4K **Privately Held**
SIC: 2394 3993 Mfg Canvas/Related Products Mfg Signs/Advertising Specialties

(G-14465)
COURIER PRINTING INC
26 1st St (01201-6212)
PHONE..................................413 442-3242
Terry C Lampiasi, *President*
Angel Lampiasi, *Treasurer*
EMP: 4 **EST:** 1930
SQ FT: 2,800
SALES: 375K **Privately Held**
SIC: 2759 2752 7334 4822 Letterpress Printing Thermography Offset Printing Photocopier & Fax Service

(G-14466)
CRANE & CO INC
Also Called: Purchasing Dept
66 Downing Industrial Par (01201)
PHONE..................................413 684-6856
Jerry Rudd, *Manager*
EMP: 15
SALES (corp-wide): 3.3B **Publicly Held**
WEB: www.crane.com
SIC: 2621 Paper Mill
HQ: Crane & Co., Inc.
1 Beacon St Ste 1702
Boston MA 02108
617 648-3799

(G-14467)
CRANE & CO INC
17 Downing Industrial Par (01201-3811)
PHONE..................................413 684-2600
Richard Kendall, *Branch Mgr*
EMP: 108
SALES (corp-wide): 3.3B **Publicly Held**
SIC: 2621 Paper Mill
HQ: Crane & Co., Inc.
1 Beacon St Ste 1702
Boston MA 02108
617 648-3799

(G-14468)
CURTIL NORTH AMERICA LLC
12 Betnr Industrial Dr (01201-7831)
PHONE..................................661 294-0030
Bertrand Curtil, *President*
EMP: 3 **EST:** 2010
SALES (est): 256.3K **Privately Held**
SIC: 3724 Mfg Aircraft Engines/Parts

(G-14469)
ELEGANT STITCHES INC
237 1st St (01201-4725)
PHONE..................................413 447-9452
Alfred Enchill, *President*
Sherwood Enchill, *Corp Secy*
Vivian Enchill, *Vice Pres*
EMP: 3
SALES: 350K **Privately Held**
WEB: www.elegantstitches.net
SIC: 2395 2759 Pleating/Stitching Services Commercial Printing

(G-14470)
GENERAL DYNAMICS CORPORATION
100 Plastics Ave (01201-3985)
PHONE..................................413 494-2313
Fred Ratzel, *Regional Mgr*
Michael Arace, *Engineer*
Casey Comisky, *Engineer*
Dean Creighton, *Engineer*
David Dickhaus, *Engineer*
EMP: 5
SALES (corp-wide): 36.1B **Publicly Held**
SIC: 3812 Mfg Search/Navigation Equipment
PA: General Dynamics Corporation
11011 Sunset Hills Rd
Reston VA 20190
703 876-3000

(G-14471)
GENERAL DYNAMICS DEF
100 Plastics Ave (01201-3985)
PHONE..................................413 494-1110
Nicholas D Chabraja, *President*
Luis Coelho, *Project Mgr*
Asquith Bailey, *Engineer*
Michael Johnson, *Engineer*
Rick Palma, *Engineer*
▲ **EMP:** 1900 **EST:** 1996
SALES (est): 172.5MM
SALES (corp-wide): 36.1B **Publicly Held**
SIC: 3812 3795 3625 Mfg Search/Navigation Equipment Mfg Tanks/Tank Components Mfg Relays/Industrial Controls
PA: General Dynamics Corporation
11011 Sunset Hills Rd
Reston VA 20190
703 876-3000

(G-14472)
GENERAL DYNMICS MSSION SYSTEMS
100 Plastics Ave (01201-3632)
PHONE..................................413 494-1110
Rick Lohr, *Engineer*
Steve Zdon, *Engineer*
George Ferry, *Program Mgr*
Gerald Wergland, *Manager*
Eric Cahoon, *IT/INT Sup*
EMP: 746
SALES (corp-wide): 36.1B **Publicly Held**
SIC: 3669 3812 Mfg Command & Control Intelligence Surveillance Reconnaissance & Information Equipment
HQ: General Dynamics Mission Systems, Inc.
12450 Fair Lakes Cir # 200
Fairfax VA 22033
703 263-2800

(G-14473)
GEORGE WESTON BAKERIES
703 W Housatonic St (01201-6678)
PHONE..................................413 443-6095
Jim Terry, *Principal*
EMP: 4
SALES (est): 176.6K **Privately Held**
SIC: 2051 Mfg Bread/Related Products

(G-14474)
GRAPHIC IMPACT SIGNS INC
575 Dalton Ave (01201-2908)
PHONE..................................413 499-0382
John Renzi, *President*
Nancy Renzi, *Vice Pres*
EMP: 30 **EST:** 1951
SQ FT: 17,600
SALES (est): 4.6MM **Privately Held**
WEB: www.gisigns.com
SIC: 3993 1799 Mfg Signs/Advertising Specialties Trade Contractor

(G-14475)
HALLOWELL ENGRG & MFG CORP
Also Called: Hallowell EMC
239 West St (01201-5847)
PHONE..................................413 445-4263
W Stetson Hallowell, *President*
Sam Zeygerman, *Technical Staff*
EMP: 9
SALES (est): 720K **Privately Held**
WEB: www.hallowell.com
SIC: 3841 Mfg Anesthesia Ventilators For Veterinarians

(G-14476)
HI-TECH MOLD & TOOL INC
1 Technology Dr W (01201-8222)
PHONE..................................413 443-9184
William Kristensen, *President*
▲ **EMP:** 120
SQ FT: 72,000
SALES: 18.4MM **Privately Held**
WEB: www.hitechmoldtool.com
SIC: 3544 Mfg Dies/Tools/Jigs/Fixtures

(G-14477)
INTEGRATED CLEAN TECH INC
25 Ontario St (01201-5678)
PHONE..................................413 281-2555
Myron Ritrosky, *President*
EMP: 3
SALES: 800K **Privately Held**
SIC: 3433 Mfg Heating Equipment-Non-electric

(G-14478)
JOHNS BUILDING SUPPLY CO INC
891 Crane Ave Ste 1 (01201-1764)
PHONE..................................413 442-7846
William Koziara, *President*
EMP: 10
SQ FT: 5,000
SALES (est): 2.2MM **Privately Held**
SIC: 3271 5211 Mfg Concrete Block/Brick Ret Lumber/Building Materials

(G-14479)
KWIK MART
Also Called: Chicos Wine and Spirits
1245 W Housatonic St (01201-7525)
PHONE..................................413 464-7902
EMP: 4
SALES (est): 255.8K **Privately Held**
SIC: 2084 Mfg Wines/Brandy/Spirits

(G-14480)
LAKEWOOD INDUSTRIES INC
Also Called: Lakewood Mold
40 Downing Industrial Par (01201-3806)
PHONE..................................413 499-3550
George F Rufo Jr, *President*
EMP: 100 **EST:** 1962
SQ FT: 25,000
SALES (est): 10MM **Privately Held**
SIC: **3089** 3544 Mfg Plastic Products Mfg Dies/Tools/Jigs/Fixtures

(G-14481)
LANDER INC
20 Keeler St Bldg D (01201-1597)
P.O. Box 679 (01202-0679)
PHONE..................................413 448-8734
William J Lander, *President*
EMP: 10 **EST:** 1981
SQ FT: 1,600
SALES: 340K **Privately Held**
WEB: www.landerinc.com
SIC: **3599** Mfg Industrial Machinery

(G-14482)
LAURIN PUBLISHING CO INC (PA)
Also Called: Photonics Media
100 West St (01201-5779)
P.O. Box 4949 (01202-4949)
PHONE..................................413 499-0514
Teddi C Laurin, *CEO*
Thomas F Laurin, *President*
Francis Laurin, *Principal*
Ralph Cianflone Jr, *Admin Sec*
EMP: 65
SQ FT: 20,000
SALES (est): 9.8MM **Privately Held**
WEB: www.photonics.com
SIC: **2721** 2741 Periodical-Publish/Print Misc Publishing

(G-14483)
LENCO INDUSTRIES INC
Also Called: Lenco Armored Vehicles
10 Betnr Industrial Dr (01201-7831)
PHONE..................................413 443-7359
Leonard W Light, *President*
Diane Light, *Vice Pres*
Tom Bailey, *Purch Agent*
Steve Mix, *Technical Mgr*
Marissa Light, *VP Finance*
◆ **EMP:** 60
SQ FT: 65,000
SALES (est): 19.5MM **Privately Held**
WEB: www.lencoarmor.com
SIC: **3711** Mfg Motor Vehicle/Car Bodies

(G-14484)
LENOX LUMBER CO
325 Partridge Rd (01201-1777)
PHONE..................................413 637-2744
Peter F Borgnis, *Owner*
EMP: 15 **EST:** 1981
SALES (est): 1.2MM **Privately Held**
SIC: **2421** 2411 2448 Sawmill/Planing Mill Logging Mfg Wood Pallets/Skids

(G-14485)
LOCKHEED MARTIN CORPORATION
75 S Church St Ste 401 (01201-6185)
PHONE..................................413 236-3400
Vance Coffman, *Branch Mgr*
EMP: 435 **Publicly Held**
WEB: www.lockheedmartin.com
SIC: **3812** Mfg Search/Navigation Equipment
PA: Lockheed Martin Corporation
6801 Rockledge Dr
Bethesda MD 20817

(G-14486)
LTI SMART GLASS INC
Also Called: LTI Group
14 Federico Dr (01201-5518)
PHONE..................................413 637-5001
Jeff Besse, *President*
Jeffrey E Besse, *President*
Alvin Beal, *Prdtn Dir*
Vicki Moulen, *Purchasing*
John H Martino, *Admin Sec*
▲ **EMP:** 100
SQ FT: 100,000
SALES (est): 22.9MM **Privately Held**
WEB: www.ltismartglass.com
SIC: **3211** 3231 Mfg Flat Glass Mfg Products-Purchased Glass

(G-14487)
M J GORDON COMPANY INC
141 North St 302 (01201-5156)
P.O. Box 4441 (01202-4441)
PHONE..................................413 448-6066
Allan B Gordon, *President*
Joann Gordon, *Corp Secy*
EMP: 3
SQ FT: 2,000
SALES (est): 377K **Privately Held**
WEB: www.mjgordonco.com
SIC: **2813** 2992 Mfg Aerosols & Carnauba Wax

(G-14488)
MAGNUS MOLDING INC
1995 East St (01201-3850)
PHONE..................................413 443-1192
David Pedrotti, *President*
EMP: 27
SQ FT: 20,000
SALES (est): 5MM
SALES (corp-wide): 13.5MM **Privately Held**
WEB: www.magnusmolding.com
SIC: **3089** 3544 Mfg Plastic Products Mfg Dies/Tools/Jigs/Fixtures
PA: Modern Mold & Tool, Inc.
1995 East St
Pittsfield MA 01201
413 443-1192

(G-14489)
MANUTECH INDUSTRIES
17 Taconic Park Dr (01201-2682)
PHONE..................................413 447-7794
Jeff Thompson, *Partner*
Graham Thompson, *Partner*
EMP: 3
SQ FT: 2,500
SALES: 400K **Privately Held**
WEB: www.manutechindustries.com
SIC: **3599** Machine Shop

(G-14490)
MILLERS PETROLEUM SYSTEMS INC
875 Crane Ave (01201-1709)
PHONE..................................413 499-2134
Dennis Miller, *President*
EMP: 8
SQ FT: 6,000
SALES: 1.2MM **Privately Held**
WEB: www.millerspetroleum.com
SIC: **3559** 1799 Mfg Misc Industry Machinery Trade Contractor

(G-14491)
MODERN MOLD & TOOL INC (PA)
Also Called: Magnus Molding
1995 East St (01201-3894)
PHONE..................................413 443-1192
David J Pedrotti, *President*
John Ciullu, *Vice Pres*
EMP: 25 **EST:** 1951
SQ FT: 15,000
SALES (est): 13.5MM **Privately Held**
SIC: **3089** 3544 Mfg Plastic Products Mfg Dies/Tools/Jigs/Fixtures

(G-14492)
MOLDMASTER ENGINEERING INC
187 Newell St (01201-5465)
P.O. Box 1161 (01202-1161)
PHONE..................................413 442-5793
Thomas F Kushi Jr, *President*
Timothy Kushi, *Vice Pres*
Paul Butler, *Engineer*
Kevin B Kushi, *Admin Sec*
EMP: 40 **EST:** 1945
SQ FT: 30,000
SALES (est): 6.9MM **Privately Held**
WEB: www.moldmaster.com
SIC: **3089** 3544 Mfg Plastic Products Mfg Dies/Tools/Jigs/Fixtures

(G-14493)
NANOMOLECULARDX
105 Elm St (01201-6554)
PHONE..................................518 588-7815
Patrick Muraca, *CEO*
Michael Dicesare, *COO*
EMP: 10
SALES (est): 873.9K **Privately Held**
SIC: **3825** Mfg Electrical Measuring Instruments

(G-14494)
NEENAH TECHNICAL MATERIALS
1080 Dalton Ave (01201-2902)
PHONE..................................413 684-7488
▲ **EMP:** 6
SALES (est): 493.8K **Privately Held**
SIC: **2297** Business Services

(G-14495)
NEENAH TECHNICAL MATERIALS INC
Technical Materials Division
448 Hubbard Ave (01201-3822)
PHONE..................................413 684-7874
Shawn Littrell, *Director*
EMP: 104
SALES (corp-wide): 1B **Publicly Held**
SIC: **2621** 5943 2752 Paper Mill Ret Stationery Lithographic Commercial Printing
HQ: Neenah Technical Materials, Inc.
Ashuelot Park Ii 448 Hbbr
Dalton MA 01226
678 518-3343

(G-14496)
NEW ENGLAND NEWSPAPERS INC (DH)
Also Called: Town Crier, The
75 S Church St Ste L1 (01201-6140)
PHONE..................................413 447-7311
W Dean Singleton, *CEO*
Kevin Corrado, *President*
Joseph James Lodovic IV, *Vice Pres*
James McDougald, *Treasurer*
Catheryn Wandrei, *Human Res Dir*
EMP: 200
SQ FT: 25,000
SALES (est): 58.1MM
SALES (corp-wide): 4.2B **Privately Held**
WEB: www.berkshireeagle.com
SIC: **2711** Newspapers-Publishing/Printing

(G-14497)
O W LANDERGREN INC
1500 W Housatonic St (01201-7500)
PHONE..................................413 442-5632
Arthur E Goodrich, *Director*
Paul W Polidoro, *Director*
Mark R Pratt, *Director*
George A Goodrich, *Admin Sec*
▲ **EMP:** 33 **EST:** 1956
SQ FT: 25,000
SALES (est): 5.9MM **Privately Held**
WEB: www.owlandergren.com
SIC: **3469** 7692 3599 3441 Mfg Metal Stampings Welding Repair Mfg Industrial Machinery Structural Metal Fabrctn

(G-14498)
PEN RO MOLD AND TOOL INC
Also Called: Pen Ro Group
343 Pecks Rd Ste 5 (01201-1352)
PHONE..................................413 499-0464
Rick Arena, *President*
▲ **EMP:** 28 **EST:** 1966
SQ FT: 40,000
SALES (est): 4.9MM **Privately Held**
WEB: www.pen-ro.com
SIC: **3544** 3089 Mfg Dies/Tools/Jigs/Fixtures Mfg Plastic Products

(G-14499)
PITTSFIELD GAZETTE INC
10 Wendell Avenue Ext # 101
(01201-6284)
P.O. Box 2236 (01202-2236)
PHONE..................................413 443-2010
Jonathan Levine, *President*
EMP: 4
SALES (est): 230K **Privately Held**
WEB: www.pittsfieldgazette.com
SIC: **2711** 8611 Newspapers-Publishing/Printing Business Association

(G-14500)
PITTSFIELD PLASTICS ENGRG INC
Also Called: Precision Spools
1510 W Housatonic St (01201-7508)
P.O. Box 1246 (01202-1246)
PHONE..................................413 442-0067
Thomas Walker, *CEO*
Duncan Cooper, *Vice Pres*
Brandin Quail, *Purch Agent*
Thomas Holmes, *Shareholder*
▲ **EMP:** 100
SQ FT: 36,000
SALES (est): 25.8MM **Privately Held**
WEB: www.pittsplas.com
SIC: **3089** 3544 Mfg Plastic Products Mfg Dies/Tools/Jigs/Fixtures

(G-14501)
PITTSFIELD RYE BAKERY INC
1010 South St (01201-8225)
P.O. Box 637 (01202-0637)
PHONE..................................413 443-9141
Arnold Robbins, *President*
Rick Robbins, *Treasurer*
Linda Robbins, *Admin Sec*
EMP: 28 **EST:** 1937
SQ FT: 3,000
SALES (est): 6.3MM **Privately Held**
SIC: **2051** Mfg Bread/Related Prdts

(G-14502)
PRAKTIKATALYST PHARMA LLC
25 Juliana Dr (01201-8439)
PHONE..................................413 442-1857
Kenneth S Wheelock Esq, *Principal*
EMP: 3
SALES (est): 157K **Privately Held**
SIC: **2834** Business Services At Non-Commercial Site

(G-14503)
PYRAMID MOLD INC
495 Churchill St (01201-1237)
PHONE..................................413 442-6198
Francis Curro, *President*
EMP: 6
SQ FT: 2,700
SALES: 719.8K **Privately Held**
WEB: www.pyramidmoldinc.com
SIC: **3544** Mfg Dies/Tools/Jigs/Fixtures

(G-14504)
QUALITY PRINTING COMPANY INC
3 Federico Dr (01201-5518)
P.O. Box 632 (01202-0632)
PHONE..................................413 442-4166
John Di Santis, *President*
Robert King, *General Mgr*
Nicholas E Disantis, *Vice Pres*
EMP: 51 **EST:** 1963
SQ FT: 20,000
SALES (est): 9.3MM **Privately Held**
WEB: www.qualprint.com
SIC: **2752** Lithographic Commercial Printing

(G-14505)
RAYTHEON COMPANY
540 Merrill Rd (01201-3714)
PHONE..................................413 494-8042
EMP: 5
SALES (corp-wide): 27B **Publicly Held**
SIC: **3812** Mfg Search/Navigation Equipment
PA: Raytheon Company
870 Winter St
Waltham MA 02451
781 522-3000

(G-14506)
SABIC US HOLDINGS LP
1 Plastics Ave (01201-3697)
PHONE..................................413 448-7110
Frank Bagala, *General Mgr*
Matthew Prater, *Counsel*
Ralph Chapman, *Project Mgr*
David Gulino, *Project Mgr*
Brian Whitman, *Project Mgr*
▼ **EMP:** 11000
SALES: 118.7K **Privately Held**
SIC: **2821** Mfg Plastic Materials/Resins

HQ: Saudi Basic Industries Corporation (Sabic)
Exit 8, North Ring Road, P. O. Box 5101
Riyadh 11422
112 258-000

(G-14507)
SAMPCO INC (PA)
56 Downing Pkwy (01201)
PHONE..................................413 442-4043
Michael O Ryan, *President*
Jeffrey Podell, *Vice Pres*
John Brown, *Production*
▲ **EMP:** 125
SQ FT: 40,000
SALES (est): 72.5MM **Privately Held**
SIC: 2599 7389 Mfg Furniture/Fixtures Business Services

(G-14508)
SHIRE CITY HERBALS INC
15 Commercial St (01201-5321)
PHONE..................................413 344-4740
Amy Huebner, *Principal*
EMP: 18 **EST:** 2011
SALES (est): 2.6MM **Privately Held**
SIC: 2099 Mfg Food Preparations

(G-14509)
STATIFLO INTERNATIONAL LTD
75 S Church St Ste 6f (01201-6135)
PHONE..................................413 684-9911
EMP: 5
SALES (est): 704.4K **Privately Held**
SIC: 3531 Mfg Construction Machinery

(G-14510)
STONE COMPANY
2 Westview Rd (01201-8021)
PHONE..................................413 442-1447
Pat Carhart, *Manager*
EMP: 6
SALES (est): 405.3K **Privately Held**
SIC: 1423 Crushed/Broken Granite

(G-14511)
STUART ALLYN CO INC
17 Taconic Park Dr Ste 2 (01201-2682)
P.O. Box 2342 (01202-2342)
PHONE..................................413 443-7306
Stuart A Scace, *President*
Allyn Scace, *Vice Pres*
Marcia Scace, *Treasurer*
Peter Gerard, *Admin Sec*
EMP: 7
SQ FT: 4,000
SALES: 650K **Privately Held**
WEB: www.stuartallyn.com
SIC: 3544 3089 Manufactures Industrial Molds And Dies And Provides Injection Molding Of Plastics

(G-14512)
UNISTRESS CORP
550 Cheshire Rd (01201-1823)
P.O. Box 1145 (01202-1145)
PHONE..................................413 499-1441
Perri C Petricca, *President*
Ronald Deangelis, *Vice Pres*
Beth Mitchell, *Vice Pres*
Saul Shenkman, *Vice Pres*
Chadwick Kasten, *Treasurer*
▲ **EMP:** 300
SQ FT: 90,000
SALES (est): 28MM
SALES (corp-wide): 126.9MM **Privately Held**
SIC: 3272 Mfg Concrete Products
PA: Petricca Industries, Inc.
550 Cheshire Rd
Pittsfield MA 01201
413 499-1441

(G-14513)
WOHRLES FOODS INC (PA)
1619 East St (01201-3857)
P.O. Box 224 (01202-0224)
PHONE..................................413 442-1518
Walter Pickwell, *President*
Jon Pickwell, *Vice Pres*
Barbara Pickwell, *Treasurer*
Lynn Kessler, *Admin Sec*
EMP: 35 **EST:** 1952
SQ FT: 25,000
SALES (est): 6.5MM **Privately Held**
SIC: 2013 5147 5142 5141 Mfg Prepared Meats Whol Meats/Products Whol Packaged Frzn Goods Whol General Groceries Whol Fish/Seafoods

Plainville
Norfolk County

(G-14514)
A & J TOOL FINDINGS CO INC
6 W Bacon St (02762)
P.O. Box 1655 (02762-0655)
PHONE..................................508 695-6631
Albert J Beyersdorfer, *President*
Hope Bryant, *Exec VP*
EMP: 16
SQ FT: 12,000
SALES (est): 1.8MM **Privately Held**
SIC: 3915 Mfg Precious Metal Jewelry

(G-14515)
ATCO PLASTICS INC
31 W Bacon St (02762-2418)
PHONE..................................508 695-3573
Ralph P Schlenker, *President*
William F Machen, *Clerk*
▲ **EMP:** 60 **EST:** 1955
SQ FT: 40,000
SALES (est): 7.5MM **Privately Held**
SIC: 3089 3544 Mfg Plastic Products Mfg Dies/Tools/Jigs/Fixtures

(G-14516)
BUILDING ENVELOPE SYSTEMS LLC
Also Called: Team Bes
20 High St (02762-1000)
PHONE..................................508 381-0429
Brett Miller, *CEO*
Sandy Sharp, *Admin Asst*
EMP: 60 **EST:** 2011
SALES (est): 697.5K **Privately Held**
SIC: 3449 Mfg Misc Structural Metalwork

(G-14517)
DESCO ELECTRONICS INC
36 Bacon Sq (02762-2067)
PHONE..................................508 643-1950
Angela Frankudakis, *President*
George Hrabushi, *VP Sales*
EMP: 12
SQ FT: 7,100
SALES: 800K **Privately Held**
SIC: 3679 Mfg Electronic Components

(G-14518)
ELECTRO-FIX INC
300 South St (02762-1529)
P.O. Box 1775 (02762-0775)
PHONE..................................508 695-0228
Thomas Kade, *President*
John Kade, *Treasurer*
Richard Andrew, *Regl Sales Mgr*
Carl Costa, *Director*
EMP: 22
SQ FT: 20,000
SALES (est): 4.7MM **Privately Held**
WEB: www.electro-fix.com
SIC: 3825 3829 Mfg Electrical Measuring Instruments Mfg Measuring/Controlling Devices

(G-14519)
GASKIN MANUFACTURING CORP
Also Called: Swiss Technology New England
17 Cross St Unit 8 (02762-1531)
PHONE..................................508 695-8949
Shawn Gaskin, *President*
EMP: 11
SALES (est): 916.9K **Privately Held**
SIC: 3599 Mfg Industrial Machinery

(G-14520)
HILSINGER COMPANY PARENT LLC (PA)
Also Called: Hilco Vision
33 W Bacon St (02762-2418)
P.O. Box 1538 (02762-0538)
PHONE..................................508 699-4406
Robert Nahmias, *President*
Bud Chatfield, *Business Mgr*
Norman Nelson, *Vice Pres*
Erick Boger, *Plant Mgr*
Frank Balou, *Safety Mgr*
▲ **EMP:** 236 **EST:** 2003
SQ FT: 70,000
SALES (est): 26.2MM **Privately Held**
WEB: www.hilco.com
SIC: 3827 3851 Mfg Optical Instruments/Lenses And Mfg Ophthalmic Goods

(G-14521)
HILSINGER HOLDINGS INC
33 W Bacon St (02762-2418)
PHONE..................................508 699-4406
Robert Nahmias, *President*
◆ **EMP:** 250
SALES: 10MM
SALES (corp-wide): 22.4MM **Privately Held**
WEB: www.hilco-usa.com
SIC: 3851 3827 Mfg Ophthalmic Goods Mfg Optical Instruments/Lenses
PA: Pnc Equity Partners Lp
620 Liberty Ave
Pittsburgh PA 15222
412 914-0175

(G-14522)
HMH RELIGIOUS MFG INC
11 Mirimichi St (02762-1710)
PHONE..................................508 699-9464
Alexis Dean, *President*
EMP: 10
SALES (est): 784.2K **Privately Held**
SIC: 3999 Mfg Misc Products

(G-14523)
J MASSE SIGN
5 Madison St Unit B (02762-1317)
PHONE..................................508 695-0534
Jason Masse, *Owner*
EMP: 3
SALES (est): 211.7K **Privately Held**
SIC: 3993 Mfg Signs/Advertising Specialties

(G-14524)
LAKESIDE MANAGEMENT CORP
3 Belcher St (02762-1303)
PHONE..................................508 695-3252
Gerard Lorusso, *President*
EMP: 20
SALES (est): 1.2MM **Privately Held**
SIC: 1442 Construction Sand/Gravel

(G-14525)
LANDFIL GAS PRODCRS OF PLNVLLE
3 Belcher St (02762-1303)
PHONE..................................508 695-3252
Henry G Grilli, *Principal*
EMP: 3
SALES (est): 199.2K **Privately Held**
SIC: 1311 Crude Petroleum/Natural Gas Production

(G-14526)
LEWICKI & SONS EXCAVATING INC
15 Wilmarth Ln (02762-1116)
PHONE..................................508 695-0122
Stan Lewicki, *President*
Carol Lewicki,
Fredrick Lewicki,
Joesph Lewicki,
Thomas Lewicki,
EMP: 8
SQ FT: 10,000
SALES (est): 1.1MM **Privately Held**
SIC: 3531 1542 Mfg Construction Machinery Nonresidential Construction

(G-14527)
LORUSSO CORP (PA)
3 Belcher St (02762-1303)
PHONE..................................508 668-6520
Gerard C Lorusso, *President*
Henry Grill, *CFO*
▲ **EMP:** 50
SQ FT: 5,000
SALES (est): 16.4MM **Privately Held**
WEB: www.lorussocorp.com
SIC: 2951 1442 3272 Mfg Asphalt Mixtr/Blocks Construction Sand/Gravel Mfg Concrete Products

(G-14528)
MINI-SYSTEMS INC
Electronic Package Division
168 E Bacon St (02762-2107)
P.O. Box 1597 (02762-0597)
PHONE..................................508 695-2000
Robert Lemar, *Opers-Prdtn-Mfg*
EMP: 30
SALES (est): 3MM
SALES (corp-wide): 14MM **Privately Held**
WEB: www.mini-systemsinc.com
SIC: 3231 3676 3825 3674 Mfg Prdt-Purchased Glass Mfg Electronic Resistors Mfg Elec Measuring Instr Mfg Semiconductors/Dvcs Mfg Conductive Wire Dvcs
PA: Mini-Systems, Inc.
20 David Rd
North Attleboro MA 02760
508 695-1420

(G-14529)
MORSE READY MIX LLC
24 Cross St (02762-1402)
P.O. Box 2189 (02762-0296)
PHONE..................................508 809-4644
EMP: 35
SALES (est): 7.2MM **Privately Held**
SIC: 3273 Mfg Ready-Mixed Concrete

(G-14530)
NEW ENGLAND METALFORM INC
380 South St (02762-1529)
PHONE..................................508 695-9340
Herman Krobath, *President*
Robert Gagliardo, *Vice Pres*
EMP: 36
SQ FT: 16,500
SALES (est): 7MM **Privately Held**
WEB: www.nemetalform.com
SIC: 3469 3444 Manufacture Metal Stampings Manufacture Sheet Metalwork

(G-14531)
NORFOLK ASPHALT COMPANY INC
3 Belcher St (02762-1303)
PHONE..................................508 668-3100
Gerard Lorusso, *President*
Dave Laflamme, *Vice Pres*
EMP: 20 **EST:** 1941
SQ FT: 5,000
SALES (est): 2MM
SALES (corp-wide): 16.4MM **Privately Held**
WEB: www.lorussocorp.com
SIC: 2951 Mfg Asphalt Mixtures/Blocks
PA: Lorusso Corp.
3 Belcher St
Plainville MA 02762
508 668-6520

(G-14532)
NORTH AMERICAN AUTO EQUIPMENT
86 Washington St Unit D2 (02762-2189)
PHONE..................................866 607-4022
Richard Nickerson, *President*
◆ **EMP:** 3
SALES (est): 508.6K **Privately Held**
SIC: 3559 Mfg Misc Industry Machinery

(G-14533)
PLAINVILLE STOCK COMPANY
104 South St (02762-2052)
P.O. Box 1628 (02762-0628)
PHONE..................................508 699-4434
William Weisman, *President*
Robert Weisman, *Treasurer*
EMP: 60
SQ FT: 23,000
SALES (est): 5.4MM **Privately Held**
WEB: www.plainvillestock.com
SIC: 3911 Mfg Precious Metal Jewelry

(G-14534)
SCG SIGNS
72 Taunton St Ste 202 (02762-2132)
PHONE..................................781 297-9400
Michael I Bass, *President*
Steve Bass, *VP Sales*
EMP: 3

GEOGRAPHIC

SALES (est): 269.5K **Privately Held**
SIC: 3993 Mfg Signs/Advertising Specialties

(G-14535)
SEMCO MACHINE CORP
14 High St (02762-1114)
PHONE....508 384-8303
Fred F Holmes, *President*
Miriam Holmes, *Treasurer*
EMP: 24
SALES (est): 4.1MM **Privately Held**
WEB: www.camtrac.com
SIC: 3599 Mfg Industrial Machinery

(G-14536)
TITUS ENGRAVING & STONESETTING
Also Called: Ledor Jewelry
44 Washington St Unit 1 (02762-5111)
P.O. Box 2369 (02762-0299)
PHONE....508 695-6842
Dana L Titus, *President*
Suzanne Titus, *Admin Sec*
EMP: 30
SALES (est): 2.7MM **Privately Held**
WEB: www.ledorjewelry.com
SIC: 3479 Coating/Engraving Service

(G-14537)
TRIAD INC
44 Washington St (02762-5111)
PHONE....508 695-2247
Andrew P Harney, *President*
Dana Titus, *Vice Pres*
Shirley H Harney, *Treasurer*
EMP: 7
SQ FT: 3,300
SALES (est): 299.6K **Privately Held**
SIC: 7692 3548 Welding Repair Mfg Welding Apparatus

(G-14538)
WINER WOODWORKING
54 Walnut St (02762-1421)
PHONE....508 695-5871
Peter Winer, *President*
EMP: 4
SALES (est): 239K **Privately Held**
SIC: 2431 Mfg Millwork

Plymouth
Plymouth County

(G-14539)
AERONAUTICA WINDPOWER LLC
11 Resnik Rd (02360-5469)
PHONE....508 732-8945
Walter Wunder, *President*
Mike Hunkins, *Director*
Jordan Debus, *Technician*
Stephen Hrkach, *Technician*
Matthew Glynn,
▲ **EMP:** 24
SALES (est): 5.9MM **Privately Held**
SIC: 3511 Mfg Turbines/Generator Sets

(G-14540)
AGIS INC
214 S Meadow Rd (02360-4740)
PHONE....508 591-8400
Peter Krukiel, *President*
Marlene Krukiel, *President*
EMP: 3
SALES (est): 561.3K **Privately Held**
SIC: 3599 Mfg Industrial Machinery

(G-14541)
AGWEY METAL DESIGNS INC
206 S Meadow Rd (02360-4740)
PHONE....508 747-1037
Bruce Morrison, *President*
Walter Morrison, *Vice Pres*
Cori Morrison, *Treasurer*
EMP: 8
SQ FT: 7,200
SALES (est): 1.1MM **Privately Held**
WEB: www.agweymetaldesigns.com
SIC: 3444 Metal Stamping

(G-14542)
AMERICAN JOURNAL TRNSP
116 Court St Ste 4 (02360-8710)
PHONE....508 927-4183
Bill Burban, *Principal*
Monica Grier, *Sales Staff*
Brendan Dugan, *Director*
EMP: 5
SALES (est): 337.6K **Privately Held**
SIC: 2741 Periodicals-Publishing/Printing

(G-14543)
AUTOCAM MEDICAL INC
24 Aldrin Rd (02360-4804)
PHONE....508 830-1442
John C Kennedy, *President*
EMP: 22
SQ FT: 13,323
SALES (est): 4.7MM **Privately Held**
SIC: 3841 Mfg Surgical/Medical Instruments

(G-14544)
AUTOMATECH INC (PA)
138 Industrial Park Rd (02360-7243)
PHONE....508 830-0088
Tom Schiller, *President*
Kirsten Currier, *Sales Staff*
Dave Osborn, *Software Dev*
Henry Bacher, *Shareholder*
Jack Nedleman, *Shareholder*
EMP: 8
SQ FT: 12,000
SALES (est): 4.9MM **Privately Held**
SIC: 7372 7379 Prepackaged Software Services Computer Related Services

(G-14545)
BLADE TECH SYSTEMS INC
Also Called: Flexo Concepts
100 Armstrong Rd Ste 103 (02360-7219)
PHONE....508 830-9506
Kevin McLaughlin, *President*
Maria McLaughlin, *Corp Secy*
▲ **EMP:** 7
SQ FT: 5,000
SALES (est): 1.6MM **Privately Held**
WEB: www.flexoconcepts.com
SIC: 3555 Mfg Printing Trades Machinery

(G-14546)
C & H AIR INC
246 S Meadow Rd Ste 29 (02360-4789)
PHONE....508 746-5511
Peter Conner, *President*
Gail Conner, *Vice Pres*
EMP: 6
SALES (est): 530K **Privately Held**
SIC: 3721 Aircraft Sales

(G-14547)
C S H INDUSTRIES INC
15 Appollo 11 Rd (02360-4877)
PHONE....508 747-1990
James A Hassan, *President*
Samuel Peter Hassan, *Sales Staff*
EMP: 25
SQ FT: 10,000
SALES (est): 4.8MM **Privately Held**
WEB: www.cshindustries.com
SIC: 3444 Mfg Sheet Metalwork

(G-14548)
CAPEWAY BEARING & MACHINE INC
100 Camelot Dr (02360-3016)
PHONE....508 747-2800
Kenneth Renaud, *CEO*
EMP: 3
SQ FT: 4,000
SALES (est): 485.5K **Privately Held**
SIC: 3714 5063 5085 Mfg Of Drive Shafts & A Whol Of Bearings & Transmission Supplies

(G-14549)
CAPEWAY WELDING INC
9 Appollo 11 Rd (02360-4866)
PHONE....508 747-6666
Ronald Peck, *President*
Douglas Peck, *Vice Pres*
Alice Peck, *Admin Sec*
EMP: 10
SQ FT: 16,000
SALES: 650K **Privately Held**
SIC: 7692 3599 Welding Repair Mfg Industrial Machinery

(G-14550)
CDF CORPORATION (PA)
77 Industrial Park Rd (02360-4868)
PHONE....508 747-5858
Joseph J Sullivan Jr, *President*
Tom McCarthy, *General Mgr*
Joseph J Sullivan Sr, *Principal*
Leigh Vaughn, *Regional Mgr*
Marcia I Sullivan, *Vice Pres*
◆ **EMP:** 98
SQ FT: 155,000
SALES (est): 24.7MM **Privately Held**
WEB: www.cdf-liners.com
SIC: 3089 3081 2821 Mfg Plastic Products Mfg Unsupported Plastic Film/Sheet Mfg Plastic Materials/Resins

(G-14551)
COOL GEAR INTERNATIONAL LLC
10 Cordage Park Cir # 212 (02360-7333)
PHONE....508 830-3440
Henry Roth, *Exec VP*
Chris Hoyt, *Controller*
▲ **EMP:** 60
SALES (est): 11.8MM **Privately Held**
SIC: 3089 Mfg Plastic Products
HQ: Igloo Products Corp.
777 Igloo Rd
Katy TX 77494
281 394-6800

(G-14552)
DIECAST CONNECTIONS CO INC
10 Cordage Park Cir # 222 (02360-7318)
PHONE....413 592-8444
Beth Zastawny, *President*
William Gillespie, *Vice Pres*
William Douglas Gillespie, *Director*
▲ **EMP:** 125
SQ FT: 15,000
SALES (est): 20.3MM **Privately Held**
SIC: 3363 Mfg Aluminum Die-Castings

(G-14553)
ELECTRA DYNE COMPANY INC
56 Jordan Rd (02360-3005)
P.O. Box 1344 (02362-1344)
PHONE....508 746-3270
Peter Mac Caferri, *President*
Judy Mac Caferri, *President*
Michael Maccaferri, *Software Dev*
Larry Mackenzie, *Technician*
EMP: 5
SALES: 350K **Privately Held**
WEB: www.electra-dyne.com
SIC: 3621 Mfg Of 12 Volt Motor Hauling System

(G-14554)
ELECTROPOLISHING SYSTEMS INC
24 Aldrin Rd (02360-4804)
PHONE....508 830-1717
Alan Ryalls, *President*
Chuck Snell, *Production*
Jim Dennehy, *Research*
Jennifer Ryalls, *Treasurer*
EMP: 50
SQ FT: 40,000
SALES: 8MM **Privately Held**
WEB: www.electropolishingsystems.com
SIC: 3471 Plating/Polishing Service

(G-14555)
ENCORE CROWN & BRIDGE INC
Also Called: Encore Dental Laboratory
37 Industrial Park Rd (02360-4868)
PHONE....508 746-6025
EMP: 27
SALES (est): 4.4MM **Privately Held**
SIC: 3843 8072 Dental Laboratory Mfg Dental Equipment/Supplies

(G-14556)
EURODUNA AMERICAS INC
81 Sanderson Dr (02360-1453)
PHONE....508 888-2710
Tony Shepherd, *President*
Karina Dubbeldam, *Principal*
Nils Dubbeldam, *Director*
▲ **EMP:** 4
SALES (est): 261.4K **Privately Held**
SIC: 2048 Mfg Prepared Feeds

(G-14557)
FINAL FORGE LLC
246 S Meadow Rd Ste 13 (02360-4775)
PHONE....857 244-0764
David Rogers,
EMP: 3
SALES (est): 104.1K **Privately Held**
SIC: 3089 3949 8711 Mfg Plastic Products Mfg Sporting/Athletic Goods Engineering Services

(G-14558)
FOCAL POINT TECHNOLOGIES
15 Richards Rd (02360-4871)
PHONE....508 830-9716
Jonathan C Metters, *President*
EMP: 4 **EST:** 1997
SALES: 400K **Privately Held**
WEB: www.fptlasers.com
SIC: 3479 Engraving Service

(G-14559)
G & G SILK SCREENING
187 Court St (02360-4004)
PHONE....508 830-1075
Joseph Gallant, *Owner*
EMP: 7
SQ FT: 2,800
SALES (est): 750K **Privately Held**
SIC: 2759 2395 Commercial Printing Pleating/Stitching Services

(G-14560)
G T C FALCON INC
130 Industrial Park Rd (02360-7243)
PHONE....508 746-0200
Gerald Leto, *President*
EMP: 10
SQ FT: 5,200
SALES: 1MM **Privately Held**
WEB: www.gtcfalcon.com
SIC: 3829 Mfg Measuring/Controlling Devices

(G-14561)
INDEPENDENT FERMENTATIONS
Also Called: Indieferm
127 Camelot Dr Ste 3 (02360-3039)
PHONE....508 789-9940
Paul Nixon, *Principal*
EMP: 7
SQ FT: 1,600
SALES (est): 496.5K **Privately Held**
SIC: 2082 Mfg Malt Beverages

(G-14562)
MAYFLOWER BREWING COMPANY LLC
12 Resnik Rd (02360-7245)
PHONE....508 746-2674
Derek Conway, *Manager*
Andrew Brosseau,
EMP: 20
SQ FT: 12,000
SALES (est): 3.2MM **Privately Held**
SIC: 2082 Drinking Place

(G-14563)
MCGIRR GRAPHICS INCORPORATED
19 Richards Rd (02360-4871)
PHONE....508 747-6400
EMP: 3 **EST:** 2012
SALES (est): 180.8K **Privately Held**
SIC: 2752 Lithographic Commercial Printing

(G-14564)
MCGIRR GRAPHICS INCORPORATED
19 Richards Rd (02360-4871)
PHONE....508 747-6400
James McGirr, *President*
Graham McGirr, *Vice Pres*
Al Havens, *Consultant*
EMP: 25
SQ FT: 6,000
SALES (est): 4.5MM **Privately Held**
WEB: www.cranberrygraphics.com
SIC: 2759 2752 Commercial Printing Lithographic Commercial Printing

▲ = Import ▼=Export
◆ =Import/Export

(G-14565)
MEDICAL MONOFILAMENT MFG LLC
121 Camelot Dr Ste 2 (02360-3037)
PHONE..........508 746-7877
Michelle Hardiman,
Alexa Fox,
EMP: 5
SALES (est): 859.3K **Privately Held**
WEB: www.medicalmonofilament.com
SIC: 3841 Mfg Of A Medical Diagnostic Tool

(G-14566)
MICROCUT INC
8 Aldrin Rd (02360-4804)
PHONE..........781 582-8090
Joseph G Dennehy, *President*
▼ **EMP:** 7
SQ FT: 7,500
SALES (est): 1MM **Privately Held**
WEB: www.microcutusa.com
SIC: 3545 Mfg Machine Tool Accessories

(G-14567)
N S R METAL WORKS
5 Raffaele Rd Ste 2 (02360-3017)
PHONE..........508 732-0190
Robert Burr, *Owner*
EMP: 3
SQ FT: 3,276
SALES (est): 600K **Privately Held**
SIC: 3446 Mfg Architectural Metalwork

(G-14568)
NORTHEAST PRINTING & GRAPHICS
179 Court St (02360-4053)
P.O. Box 6364 (02362-6364)
PHONE..........508 746-8689
Mark Stafford, *President*
EMP: 5
SQ FT: 3,300
SALES: 270K **Privately Held**
SIC: 2759 Commercial Printing

(G-14569)
NORTHICE
Also Called: North Taste
624 Long Pond Rd (02360-2612)
PHONE..........781 985-5225
Jerry Levine, *Vice Pres*
EMP: 10
SALES (est): 538.1K **Privately Held**
WEB: www.northice.com
SIC: 2087 Mfg Flavor Extracts/Syrup

(G-14570)
ORTHOTIC SOLUTIONS INC
2277 State Rd Ste 5 (02360-7111)
PHONE..........774 205-2278
Pamela A Hoaglund, *President*
EMP: 3
SALES (est): 257.9K **Privately Held**
WEB: www.orthoticsolutionsinc.com
SIC: 3842 Mfg Surgical Appliances/Supplies

(G-14571)
OUTRAGEOUS LURES LLC
118 Long Pond Rd Ste C (02360-2662)
PHONE..........347 509-8610
Owen Nannarone, *CEO*
EMP: 5
SALES (est): 145.4K **Privately Held**
SIC: 3949 Mfg Sporting/Athletic Goods

(G-14572)
PARTYLITE INC (HQ)
59 Armstrong Rd (02360-7206)
PHONE..........203 661-1926
Harry Slatkin, *CEO*
Dan Chad, *COO*
Mark Bono, *VP Finance*
Glenn Pike, *Corp Comm Staff*
Jose Ramos, *Technology*
◆ **EMP:** 95 **EST:** 1977
SALES (est): 2.3B
SALES (corp-wide): 2.4B **Publicly Held**
WEB: www.blythindustries.com
SIC: 2023 3999 3641 5199 Mfg Dry/Evap Dairy Prdts Mfg Misc Products Mfg Electric Lamps Whol Nondurable Goods
PA: The Carlyle Group L P
1001 Pennsylvania Ave Nw 220s
Washington DC 20004
202 729-5626

(G-14573)
PILGRIM INNOVATIVE PLAS LLC
127 Industrial Park Rd (02360-7242)
PHONE..........508 732-0297
Joseph Ostiguy, *Engineer*
Joel Nickerson, *Mng Member*
Jena Landry, *Admin Mgr*
EMP: 12
SQ FT: 16,400
SALES (est): 2.3MM **Privately Held**
WEB: www.pipllc.com
SIC: 3089 Mfg Plastic Products

(G-14574)
PLYMOUTH AWNING CO
4 Brookside Ave (02360-2925)
PHONE..........508 746-3740
Jane Ross-Anderson, *Owner*
EMP: 3
SQ FT: 3,000
SALES: 200K **Privately Held**
SIC: 3444 5999 Mfg Sheet Metalwork Ret Misc Merchandise

(G-14575)
PLYMOUTH BAY WINERY
114 Water St (02360-3864)
P.O. Box 1161 (02362-1161)
PHONE..........508 746-2100
Kathy Cherry, *Owner*
EMP: 5
SALES (est): 216.1K **Privately Held**
WEB: www.plymouthbaywinery.com
SIC: 2084 5812 Mfg Wines/Brandy/Spirits Eating Place

(G-14576)
POWDER HORN PRESS INC (PA)
301 Court St Apt 1 (02360-4324)
PHONE..........508 746-8777
Bridgette Anderson, *President*
Dawn Mackechnie, *Senior VP*
Richard Anderson Jr, *Treasurer*
EMP: 7
SQ FT: 1,000
SALES (est): 1MM **Privately Held**
WEB: www.powderhornpress.com
SIC: 2752 Lithographic Commercial Printing

(G-14577)
PRAZI USA INC
214 S Meadow Rd Rear S (02360-4740)
P.O. Box 1165 (02362-1165)
PHONE..........508 747-1490
Robert E Cumings Jr, *President*
▲ **EMP:** 5
SQ FT: 3,200
SALES (est): 838.9K **Privately Held**
WEB: www.praziusa.com
SIC: 3531 5084 Mfg Construction Machinery Whol Industrial Equipment

(G-14578)
R B MACHINE CO INC
Also Called: Standard Repair Co Division
5 Raffaele Rd (02360-3017)
PHONE..........508 830-0567
Robert Burr, *President*
Dorothy Burr, *Treasurer*
EMP: 7
SQ FT: 4,200
SALES (est): 973.3K **Privately Held**
SIC: 3599 Mfg Industrial Machinery

(G-14579)
REKLIST LLC
94 Carver Rd (02360-5281)
PHONE..........215 518-1637
Daniel Levy,
EMP: 3
SALES (est): 71.1K **Privately Held**
SIC: 7372 Prepackaged Software Services

(G-14580)
RICHARDS MICRO-TOOL LLC
Also Called: Cutting Edge Technologies
250 Cherry St (02360-4876)
PHONE..........508 746-6900
Eli Crotzer, *President*
EMP: 40
SQ FT: 25,000
SALES (est): 7.8MM
SALES (corp-wide): 724.3MM **Privately Held**
WEB: www.richardsmicrotool.com
SIC: 3545 Mfg Machine Tool Accessories
HQ: Arch Global Precision Llc
2600 S Telg Rd Ste 180
Bloomfield Hills MI 48302
734 266-6900

(G-14581)
S & M FUELS INC
86 Sandwich St (02360-3334)
PHONE..........508 746-1495
Sameh Kanan, *Principal*
EMP: 5
SALES (est): 312.3K **Privately Held**
SIC: 2869 Mfg Industrial Organic Chemicals

(G-14582)
SEABURY SPLASH INC
10 Cordage Park Cir # 212 (02360-7318)
PHONE..........508 830-3440
Donna J Roth, *President*
Henry M Roth, *Treasurer*
◆ **EMP:** 45
SALES (est): 5.1MM **Privately Held**
WEB: www.coolgearinc.com
SIC: 3089 Mfg Plastic Products

(G-14583)
SMARTPAK EQUINE LLC (DH)
40 Grissom Rd Ste 500 (02360-7251)
PHONE..........774 773-1100
Rebecca Goss, *Vice Pres*
David Mulvey, *Vice Pres*
Dodd Corby, *VP Opers*
Kevin Wilson, *Prdtn Mgr*
Carolyn Goudreau, *Senior Buyer*
▲ **EMP:** 100
SQ FT: 65,000
SALES (est): 43MM
SALES (corp-wide): 13.2B **Publicly Held**
WEB: www.smartpakequine.com
SIC: 2048 5199 5999 Mfg Prepared Feeds Whol Nondurable Goods Ret Misc Merchandise
HQ: Butler Animal Health Supply Llc
400 Metro Pl N Ste 100
Dublin OH 43017
614 761-9095

(G-14584)
SOUTH SHORE DSTLESS BLASTG LLC
12 Cedarhill Park Dr 1 (02360-2243)
PHONE..........508 789-4575
Bradford Simmons, *Mng Member*
EMP: 5
SQ FT: 1,250
SALES (est): 161.2K **Privately Held**
SIC: 3471 Plating/Polishing Service

(G-14585)
STELLAR MEDICAL PUBLICATIONS
20 North St Ste 1 (02360-3380)
PHONE..........508 732-6767
David Newcombe, *Principal*
Nancy Nicklas, *Assoc Editor*
EMP: 3
SALES (est): 269.9K **Privately Held**
SIC: 2721 Periodicals-Publishing/Printing

(G-14586)
SWIFT-CUT AUTOMATION USA INC
212 S Meadow Rd Ste 6 (02360-5450)
PHONE..........888 572-1160
Neil Smith, *President*
Scott Wirtanen, *Vice Pres*
Peter Macneill, *Treasurer*
EMP: 4
SQ FT: 5,000
SALES (est): 72K **Privately Held**
SIC: 3541 Mfg Machine Tools-Cutting
PA: Swift-Cut Automation Limited
1 Lancaster Park
Burton-On-Trent STAFFS
154 347-3300

(G-14587)
TECH-ETCH INC (PA)
45 Aldrin Rd (02360-4886)
PHONE..........508 747-0300
George E Keeler, *President*
Richard P Balonis, *Vice Pres*
Richard R Balonis, *Vice Pres*
Kiernan P Kearney, *Vice Pres*
Kiernan Kearney, *Vice Pres*
EMP: 450 **EST:** 1964
SQ FT: 120,000
SALES (est): 112.4MM **Privately Held**
WEB: www.techetch.com
SIC: 3469 3672 3479 Mfg Metal Stampings Mfg Printed Circuit Boards Coating/Engraving Service

(G-14588)
THREE JAKES
Also Called: Three Jakes Screenprinting
116 Long Pond Rd (02360-2663)
PHONE..........781 706-6886
Nathan Torrance, *Partner*
EMP: 3
SALES (est): 117.2K **Privately Held**
SIC: 2759 Commercial Printing

(G-14589)
VACUUM PROCESS TECHNOLOGY LLC
70 Industrial Park Rd (02360-4829)
PHONE..........508 732-7200
Ralf Faber, *President*
Carl Nielsen, *Vice Pres*
Joseph Patrinostro, *Engineer*
Matthew Makein, *Project Engr*
Katie Wilson, *Admin Asst*
EMP: 35
SQ FT: 36,000
SALES (est): 7.4MM **Privately Held**
WEB: www.vptec.com
SIC: 3826 8711 3827 Mfg Analytical Instruments Engineering Services Mfg Optical Instruments/Lenses

GEOGRAPHIC

Plympton
Plymouth County

(G-14590)
ARISE AIR INC
120 Palmer Rd (02367-1202)
PHONE..........888 359-2747
Bryan Ellis, *President*
EMP: 25
SALES (est): 2.1MM **Privately Held**
WEB: www.ariseair.com
SIC: 3721 Mfg Aircraft

(G-14591)
FIRST QUALITY METAL PRODUCTS
171 Palmer Rd Ste D (02367-1212)
PHONE..........781 585-5820
Paul Goyett, *President*
EMP: 9
SALES (est): 1.2MM **Privately Held**
SIC: 3444 Mfg Sheet Metalwork

(G-14592)
LITECONTROL CORPORATION
Also Called: Lite Control
65 Spring St (02367-1701)
PHONE..........781 294-0100
Adrian R Grundy, *COO*
Nicholas Sealey, *Facilities Mgr*
Colleen Scioscia, *Production*
Charles Moylan, *QC Mgr*
Tim Farrell, *Design Engr Mgr*
▲ **EMP:** 205 **EST:** 1936
SQ FT: 180,000
SALES (est): 46MM
SALES (corp-wide): 4.4B **Publicly Held**
WEB: www.litecontrol.com
SIC: 3646 Mfg Commercial Lighting Fixtures
HQ: Newco Lighting, Inc.
40 Waterview Dr
Shelton CT 06484
475 882-4000

(G-14593)
SPECIALTY PRTRS F BUSH SON CO
79 Upland Rd (02367-1602)
P.O. Box 95 (02367-0095)
PHONE....781 585-9444
Frank Bush, *President*
EMP: 4
SQ FT: 700
SALES (est): 230K **Privately Held**
SIC: 2759 Graphic Art Finishing

Pocasset
Barnstable County

(G-14594)
CAPE COD SWEETS LLC
Also Called: Cape Cod Provisions
31 Jonathan Bourne Dr # 1 (02559-4919)
P.O. Box 278, West Wareham (02576-0278)
PHONE....508 564-5840
Craig Canning, *President*
Kristine Esdale, *Marketing Staff*
EMP: 10 **EST:** 2016
SALES (est): 377.2K **Privately Held**
SIC: 2066 Mfg Chocolate/Cocoa Products

(G-14595)
GLOBAL INTERCONNECT INC
11 Jonathan Bourne Dr (02559-4917)
PHONE....508 563-6306
Stephen R Bates, *President*
Sarah Ciampa, *Vice Pres*
Robert Gray, *Vice Pres*
▲ **EMP:** 75
SQ FT: 20,000
SALES (est): 14.9MM **Privately Held**
WEB: www.globalinterconnect.com
SIC: 3678 3679 Mfg Electronic Connectors Mfg Electronic Components

(G-14596)
HYDROID INC (PA)
1 Henry Dr (02559-1415)
PHONE....508 563-6565
Duane Fotheringham, *President*
Graham Lester, *Senior VP*
Julie Ferland, *Vice Pres*
Tom Reynolds, *Vice Pres*
Luca Mastrangelo, *Project Mgr*
◆ **EMP:** 167
SALES (est): 32.2MM **Privately Held**
SIC: 3812 3625 3531 Mfg Search/Navigation Equipment Mfg Relays/Industrial Controls Mfg Construction Machinery

(G-14597)
HYDROID LLC
1 Henry Dr (02559-1415)
PHONE....508 563-6565
Lorna Bandstra, *General Mgr*
Jeff Payne, *General Mgr*
Bruno Umbro, *General Mgr*
Dennis Grace, *Vice Pres*
Paulo Cabral, *Software Engr*
EMP: 37
SQ FT: 2,070
SALES (est): 37MM
SALES (corp-wide): 1.5B **Privately Held**
WEB: www.hydroid.com
SIC: 3731 Shipbuilding/Repairing
HQ: Simrad North America Inc
19210 33rd Ave W Ste A
Lynnwood WA 98036

(G-14598)
IMAGE FACTORY
50 Portside Dr (02559-1928)
PHONE....508 295-3876
Nancy Sawyer, *Owner*
EMP: 9
SALES (est): 733.9K **Privately Held**
SIC: 2389 2759 5137 5651 Mfg Apparel/Accessories Commercial Printing Whol Women/Child Clothng Ret Family Clothing

(G-14599)
IMAGE SOURCE INTERNATIONAL INC
53a Portside Dr (02559-2147)
PHONE....508 801-9252
Patrick J Downes, *President*
A Michael Storlazzi, *Treasurer*
▲ **EMP:** 29
SQ FT: 5,000
SALES (est): 3.1MM **Privately Held**
SIC: 2741 Misc Publishing

(G-14600)
POCASSET MACHINE CORPORATION
7 Commerce Park Rd (02559-2298)
P.O. Box 3088 (02559-3088)
PHONE....508 563-5572
Barry M Kent, *President*
Christopher T Kent, *Vice Pres*
Mark Pierce, *Foreman/Supr*
Victoria J Kent, *Treasurer*
Donna Kent, *Director*
▲ **EMP:** 29
SALES (est): 5.1MM **Privately Held**
WEB: www.pocassetmachine.com
SIC: 3469 3599 3061 Mfg Metal Stampings Mfg Industrial Machinery Mfg Mechanical Rubber Goods

(G-14601)
SHAW WOODWORKING INC
150 Highland Ave (02559)
PHONE....508 563-1242
James R Shaw, *President*
Vicki Shaw, *Vice Pres*
EMP: 7
SQ FT: 3,500
SALES: 1MM **Privately Held**
SIC: 2431 Mfg Millwork

(G-14602)
WENAUMET BLUFFS BOAT WORKS INC
239 Barlows Landing Rd (02559)
P.O. Box 1270 (02559-1270)
PHONE....888 224-9942
David Arch, *President*
Allan Sherrard Arch, *Principal*
EMP: 3
SALES (est): 195K **Privately Held**
SIC: 3732 Boatbuilding/Repairing

(G-14603)
WIGGIN MEANS PRECAST CO INC
79 Barlows Landing Rd (02559-1914)
P.O. Box 1507 (02559-1507)
PHONE....508 564-6776
Mark Ricciardi, *President*
Brian Ricciardi, *Treasurer*
EMP: 8
SALES (est): 1.2MM **Privately Held**
SIC: 3272 Mfg Concrete Products

(G-14604)
WIGGIN PRECAST CORP
79 Barlows Landing Rd (02559)
P.O. Box 1138 (02559-1138)
PHONE....508 564-6776
Daniel Wiggin, *President*
EMP: 15
SALES (est): 1.7MM **Privately Held**
SIC: 3272 Mfg Concrete Products

Princeton
Worcester County

(G-14605)
INDUSTRIAL PALLET LLC
29 Gregory Rd (01541-1110)
PHONE....860 234-0962
Joseph Obrien, *Owner*
EMP: 4
SALES (est): 145K **Privately Held**
SIC: 2448 Mfg Wood Pallets/Skids

(G-14606)
LAWRENCE SIGLER
Also Called: Sigler Machine Co
314 Ball Hill Rd (01541-1706)
PHONE....978 464-2027
Lawrence J Sigler, *Owner*
EMP: 8
SQ FT: 7,500
SALES: 627.6K **Privately Held**
SIC: 3599 3553 3549 Mfg Industrial Machinery Mfg Woodworking Machinery Mfg Metalworking Machinery

Provincetown
Barnstable County

(G-14607)
B & B MFG CO
186 Bradford St (02657-2427)
PHONE....508 487-0858
Marcene Marcoux, *Principal*
EMP: 3
SALES (est): 200.6K **Privately Held**
SIC: 3999 Mfg Misc Products

(G-14608)
PROVINCETOWN ARTS PRESS INC (PA)
650 Commercial St (02657-1725)
PHONE....508 487-3167
Dean Pappas, *President*
Jason Shinder, *Vice Pres*
Paul Andich, *Treasurer*
◆ **EMP:** 5
SALES: 161K **Privately Held**
WEB: www.ellendudley.com
SIC: 2721 Periodicals-Publishing/Printing

(G-14609)
SHOP THERAPY IMPORTS
20 Province Rd (02657-1240)
PHONE....508 487-8970
Patti Tronolone, *Owner*
▲ **EMP:** 6
SALES (est): 685.2K **Privately Held**
SIC: 2321 2331 2369 5137 Mfg Men/Boys Furnishings Mfg Women/Misses Blouses Mfg Girl/Child Outerwear Whol Women/Child Clothng

(G-14610)
TIN CAN ALLEY
269 Commercial St (02657-2201)
PHONE....508 487-1648
Larry Hendershot, *Principal*
EMP: 4
SALES (est): 356.1K **Privately Held**
SIC: 3411 Mfg Metal Cans

(G-14611)
WOODARD & CURRAN INC
200 Route 6 (02657-1252)
PHONE....508 487-5474
EMP: 3
SALES (corp-wide): 147MM **Privately Held**
SIC: 3589 Mfg Service Industry Machinery
PA: Woodard & Curran, Inc.
41 Hutchins Dr
Portland ME 04102
800 426-4262

Quincy
Norfolk County

(G-14612)
A F MURPHY DIE & MCH CO INC
Also Called: Mdm
430 Hancock St (02171-2409)
P.O. Box 127, North Quincy (02171-0003)
PHONE....617 328-3820
John F Murphy III, *President*
EMP: 6 **EST:** 1907
SQ FT: 17,000
SALES (est): 952.9K **Privately Held**
SIC: 3469 Mfg Metal Stampings

(G-14613)
ACORN OVERHEAD DOOR
249 Governors Rd (02169-1111)
PHONE....508 378-0441
Bob Metzler, *Owner*
Tina Metzler, *Owner*
EMP: 4
SALES (est): 115.6K **Privately Held**
SIC: 3535 Mfg Conveyors/Equipment

(G-14614)
BAY STATE MILLING COMPANY (PA)
100 Congress St Ste 2 (02169-0906)
PHONE....617 328-4423
Brian G Rothwell, *CEO*
Bernard J Rothwell III, *Chairman*
Peter Levangie, *COO*
James D Wilmes, *Exec VP*
Doug Dewitt, *Vice Pres*
◆ **EMP:** 40
SQ FT: 35,000
SALES (est): 154.8MM **Privately Held**
WEB: www.bsm.com
SIC: 2041 Mfg Flour/Grain Mill Prooducts

(G-14615)
BETH VENETO
Also Called: Ginger Bettys
215 Samoset Ave Ste 15 (02169-2446)
PHONE....617 472-4729
Beth Veneto, *Owner*
EMP: 4
SALES (est): 298.4K **Privately Held**
WEB: www.gingerbettys.com
SIC: 2051 Mfg Bread/Related Products

(G-14616)
BIOENERGY INTERNATIONAL LLC
Also Called: Myri
3 Batterymarch Park # 301 (02169-7500)
PHONE....617 657-5200
Stephen J Gatto, *Mng Member*
EMP: 80
SALES (est): 11.3MM **Privately Held**
WEB: www.bioenergyinternational.com
SIC: 2865 Mfg Cyclic Crudes/Intermediates/Dyes

(G-14617)
BOSTON SCIENTIFIC CORPORATION
Also Called: Customer Fulfillment Center
500 Commander Shea Blvd (02171-1518)
PHONE....617 689-6000
Steve Theisen, *Prdtn Mgr*
Jackie Drinkwater, *Purchasing*
Rick Barlow, *Manager*
Daniel Cooke, *Manager*
Linda Downey, *Manager*
EMP: 285
SALES (corp-wide): 9.8B **Publicly Held**
WEB: www.bsci.com
SIC: 3841 Mfg Surgical/Medical Instruments
PA: Boston Scientific Corporation
300 Boston Scientific Way
Marlborough MA 01752
508 683-4000

(G-14618)
BRAVO MASLOW LLC
2 Cityview Ln Apt 605 (02169-4657)
PHONE....912 580-0044
Juan Bravo,
EMP: 6
SALES (est): 216.7K **Privately Held**
SIC: 2389 Mfg Apparel/Accessories

(G-14619)
CONSTELLATION BRANDS INC
1 Batterymarch Park (02169-7454)
PHONE....617 249-5082
EMP: 3
SALES (corp-wide): 8.1B **Publicly Held**
SIC: 2084 Mfg Wines/Brandy/Spirits
PA: Constellation Brands, Inc.
207 High Point Dr # 100
Victor NY 14564
585 678-7100

(G-14620)
DRIGGIN SANDRA DBA EXTRA EXTRA
Also Called: Extra Extra Daily
21 Mayor Thomas J Mcgrath (02169-5351)
PHONE....617 773-6996
Sandra Driggin, *Owner*
Debbie Previti, *Exec Dir*
EMP: 25

SALES (est): 724K Privately Held
WEB: www.extraextra.biz
SIC: 2711 2741 Newspapers-Publishing/Printing Misc Publishing

(G-14621)
EMD SERONO INC
4 Batterymarch Park # 200 (02169-7468)
PHONE....781 261-7500
Scott Smith, Manager
Shelly Frazier, Admin Asst
Barbara Miller, Admin Asst
EMP: 9
SALES (corp-wide): 16.4B Privately Held
SIC: 2834 Mfg Pharmaceutical Preparations
HQ: Emd Serono, Inc.
1 Technology Pl
Rockland MA 02370
781 982-9000

(G-14622)
EMD SERONO BIOTECH CENTER INC
4 Batterymarch Park Ste 2 (02169-7468)
PHONE....978 294-1100
Michael Leva, Vice Pres
EMP: 25
SALES (corp-wide): 16.4B Privately Held
SIC: 2834 Mfg Pharmaceutical Preparations
HQ: Emd Serono Biotech Center, Inc.
1 Technology Pl
Rockland MA 02370
800 283-8088

(G-14623)
ENTERPRISE NEWSMEDIA LLC (HQ)
400 Crown Colony Dr (02169-0930)
PHONE....585 598-0030
Kirk Davis, Mng Member
Garrett J Cummings,
EMP: 6
SALES (est): 59.3MM
SALES (corp-wide): 1.5B Publicly Held
WEB: www.enterprisenewsmedia.com
SIC: 2711 Newspapers-Publishing/Printing
PA: Gannett Co., Inc.
7950 Jones Branch Dr
Mc Lean VA 22102
703 854-6000

(G-14624)
EXCEL TOOL & DIE CO INC
69 Sumner St (02169-7036)
PHONE....617 472-0473
Richard Wicklund, President
Alan Wicklund, Vice Pres
EMP: 8 EST: 1952
SQ FT: 12,000
SALES: 1.2MM Privately Held
WEB: www.exceltool-die.com
SIC: 3469 Mfg Metal Stampings

(G-14625)
FEELEYS COMPANY INC
232 Water St 238 (02169-6539)
PHONE....617 773-1711
Stephen A Feeley, President
James J Feeley Jr, President
Stephen Feeley, Treasurer
Marcia Feeley Dyment, Clerk
EMP: 7 EST: 1954
SQ FT: 40,000
SALES: 1MM Privately Held
SIC: 3479 Coating/Engraving Service

(G-14626)
FOXROCK GRANITE LLC
100 Newport Ave (02171)
PHONE....617 249-8015
Jason T Ward, Principal
EMP: 6 EST: 2015
SALES (est): 122K Privately Held
SIC: 3281 Cut Stone And Stone Products

(G-14627)
GALAXY SOFTWARE INC
200 Falls Blvd Unit B301 (02169-8186)
PHONE....617 773-7790
Gary Dunne, Vice Pres
EMP: 7
SALES (est): 465K Privately Held
WEB: www.galaxysoftware.com
SIC: 7372 Prepackaged Software Services

(G-14628)
GENERAL DYNAMICS MISSION SYSTE
553 South St (02169-7318)
PHONE....617 715-7000
Chris Marzilli, President
Kevin Hopkins, Engineer
Mary Lepage, Engineer
Tim Mondeau, Engineer
Chris Murphy, Engineer
▲ EMP: 99
SQ FT: 9,600
SALES (est): 18MM
SALES (corp-wide): 36.1B Publicly Held
WEB: www.bluefinrobotics.com
SIC: 3812 Mfg Search/Navigation Equipment
HQ: General Dynamics Mission Systems, Inc.
12450 Fair Lakes Cir # 200
Fairfax VA 22033
703 263-2800

(G-14629)
GOLDEN MANET PRESS INC
86 Robertson St (02169-1217)
PHONE....617 773-2423
Lance Peterson, President
EMP: 5 EST: 1962
SQ FT: 2,500
SALES (est): 814K Privately Held
WEB: www.gmpress.net
SIC: 2752 2759 Offset Printing

(G-14630)
GRANITE PRINT LLC
90 Palmer St (02169-3308)
PHONE....617 479-5777
Paula Rowe,
EMP: 4
SALES: 600K Privately Held
SIC: 2752 Lithographic Commercial Printing

(G-14631)
HANCOCK ELECTRIC MTR SVCS INC
231 Willard St (02169-1513)
PHONE....617 472-5789
Ken Thompson, President
Carol Thompson, Treasurer
Scott Thompson, Administration
EMP: 6
SQ FT: 2,400
SALES: 1.5MM Privately Held
SIC: 7694 5063 Electric Motor Sales & Service

(G-14632)
HOPPS COMPANY
20 Braintree Ave (02169-3221)
PHONE....617 481-1379
Matthew D Hopps, Principal
EMP: 3 EST: 2010
SALES (est): 204.1K Privately Held
SIC: 2013 Mfg Prepared Meats

(G-14633)
IMPRESSIONS PLUS INC
89 Penn St (02169)
PHONE....617 479-5777
Paula M Rowe, President
Timothy Scott, CFO
EMP: 16
SQ FT: 7,000
SALES: 1.3MM Privately Held
SIC: 2752 7336 Commercial Offset Printing & Design Service

(G-14634)
INDIAN RIVER SAND LLC
200 Falls Blvd Unit E308 (02169-8192)
PHONE....413 977-0646
Derrick Hale,
Joseph Gogal,
EMP: 5
SALES (est): 130.6K Privately Held
SIC: 1442 Construction Sand/Gravel

(G-14635)
INTELLIGENT COMPRESSION TECH
1250 Hancock St Ste 701n (02169-4335)
PHONE....617 773-3369
Michael Slygh, President
Bob Eastwood, Vice Pres
Peter Lepeska, Vice Pres
George Wilson, CFO
William Sebastian, CTO
EMP: 20
SALES (est): 1.5MM
SALES (corp-wide): 2B Publicly Held
WEB: www.ictcompress.com
SIC: 7372 Prepackaged Software Services
PA: Viasat, Inc.
6155 El Camino Real
Carlsbad CA 92009
760 476-2200

(G-14636)
INTELYCARE INC
1515 Hancock St Ste 203 (02169-5230)
PHONE....617 971-8344
John Shagoury, President
Ike Nnah, Principal
EMP: 10
SALES (est): 116.4K Privately Held
SIC: 7372 Prepackaged Software Services

(G-14637)
MAKING YOUR MARK INC
121 Liberty St (02169-7639)
PHONE....617 479-0999
John Delano, President
Don Fraser, Vice Pres
EMP: 7
SQ FT: 4,000
SALES (est): 711.5K Privately Held
SIC: 3953 Mfg Marking Devices

(G-14638)
MARINE BIOPRODUCTS
39 Broad St (02169-4689)
PHONE....617 847-1426
E James Irio, Owner
EMP: 5
SALES (est): 254K Privately Held
SIC: 2077 Mfg Animal/Marine Fat/Oil

(G-14639)
MERLINONE INC (PA)
17 Whitney Rd (02169-4309)
PHONE....617 328-6645
David Tenenbaum, President
Jan Tenenbaum, Vice Pres
Brian Marotta, Opers Staff
Mindy Hreczuck, Engineer
Shevawn Hardesty, CFO
EMP: 20
SQ FT: 1,200
SALES (est): 3MM Privately Held
WEB: www.merlin-net.com
SIC: 7372 Prepackaged Software Services

(G-14640)
MODERN GRAPHICS INC
28 Glendale Rd (02169-1937)
PHONE....781 331-5000
Louis Akory, President
Akoury Louis, Info Tech Dir
EMP: 10 EST: 1972
SQ FT: 3,500
SALES: 2MM Privately Held
WEB: www.moderngraphicsinc.com
SIC: 2791 7336 Typesetting Services Commercial Art/Graphic Design

(G-14641)
MYRIANT LAKE PROVIDENCE INC
3 Batterymarch Park Fl 3 # 3 (02169-7500)
PHONE....617 657-5200
Ralph Tapia, Principal
Sam Chan, Manager
EMP: 40
SALES (est): 7.3MM Privately Held
SIC: 2869 Mfg Industrial Organic Chemicals

(G-14642)
NEW ENGLAND WORLDWIDE EXPORT
Also Called: Interior Design Center
247 Water St (02169-6533)
PHONE....617 472-0251
Khamis Sidahmed, Owner
EMP: 9
SQ FT: 2,200
SALES (est): 650K Privately Held
SIC: 2211 5714 Cotton Broadwoven Fabric Mill Ret Draperies/Upholstery

(G-14643)
OFFSET PREP INC
91 Newbury Ave (02171-1937)
PHONE....617 472-7887
Marianne Smith, President
EMP: 5
SQ FT: 4,000
SALES (est): 501K Privately Held
WEB: www.offsetprep.com
SIC: 2759 Lithographic Commercial Printing

(G-14644)
PATHEER INC (PA)
180 Old Colony Ave # 200 (02170-3875)
PHONE....888 968-5936
Akash Savdharia, Principal
EMP: 4
SALES (est): 452.1K Privately Held
SIC: 7372 Prepackaged Software Services

(G-14645)
PAUL H MURPHY & CO INC
634 Willard St (02169-7415)
PHONE....617 472-7707
Paul H Murphy Sr, President
Barry Wallenmaier, Accountant
Anna Murphy, Human Res Mgr
Angela Martin, Officer
EMP: 10
SQ FT: 8,000
SALES (est): 1.5MM Privately Held
WEB: www.phmurphyandcompany.com
SIC: 2759 Lithographic Commercial Printing

(G-14646)
POS CENTER INC
5 Beale St (02170-2702)
PHONE....617 797-5026
Jian Ji LI, Principal
EMP: 5
SALES (est): 435.8K Privately Held
SIC: 7372 Prepackaged Software Services

(G-14647)
PRECISION WOODWORKING
50 Samoset Ave (02169-2324)
PHONE....617 479-7604
John G O'Shea, Principal
EMP: 4
SALES (est): 366.3K Privately Held
SIC: 2431 Mfg Millwork

(G-14648)
PRESIDENT PRESS INC
100 Columbia St (02169-7552)
PHONE....617 773-1235
John Eckblom, President
Bert Eckblom, Admin Sec
EMP: 12 EST: 1934
SQ FT: 7,000
SALES: 1.5MM Privately Held
SIC: 2752 Offset Printing

(G-14649)
QUALITY METAL CRAFT INC
135 Old Colony Ave (02170-3896)
PHONE....617 479-7374
Mark Chagnon, President
Margaret Chagnon, Admin Sec
EMP: 5
SQ FT: 10,000
SALES (est): 1.1MM Privately Held
SIC: 3444 Mfg Sheet Metalwork

(G-14650)
QUARTERLY REVIEW OF WINES
Also Called: Quarterly Review Wines Mag
22 Safford St (02171-2602)
PHONE....781 721-0525
EMP: 25
SALES (est): 1.6MM Privately Held
WEB: www.qrw.com
SIC: 2721 5812 Periodicals-Publishing/Printing Eating Place

(G-14651)
QUINCY STEEL & WELDING CO INC
444 Sea St (02169-2705)
PHONE....617 472-1180
Ann M Sheptyck, President
Stephen J Sheptyck Jr, Treasurer
Brunt Richardson, Clerk

EMP: 5
SQ FT: 10,000
SALES (est): 679.6K **Privately Held**
SIC: 3444 7692 Sheet Metal Fabrication & Welding

(G-14652)
QUINCY SUN PUBLISHING CO INC
1372 Hancock St Ste 102 (02169-5190)
PHONE..................................617 471-3100
Henry W Bosworth Jr, *President*
Dorothy Bosworth, *Clerk*
EMP: 10
SQ FT: 3,000
SALES (est): 554.9K **Privately Held**
SIC: 2711 Newspapers-Publishing/Printing

(G-14653)
RAYTHEON COMPANY
465 Centre St (02169-7530)
PHONE..................................781 522-3000
Nicole Jordan, *Project Mgr*
Chris Maniates, *QC Mgr*
Arthur Webb, *Engineer*
Bruce Hunter, *Manager*
Carrie Brown, *Manager*
EMP: 500
SALES (corp-wide): 27B **Publicly Held**
SIC: 3674 Mfg Hybrid Integrated Circuits
PA: Raytheon Company
870 Winter St
Waltham MA 02451
781 522-3000

(G-14654)
RHEINWERK PUBLISHING INC
Also Called: Galileo Press, Inc.
2 Heritage Dr Ste 305 (02171-2165)
PHONE..................................781 228-5070
Rainer Kaltenecker, *President*
Aja Walkes, *Marketing Mgr*
Florian Vimniak, *Director*
EMP: 10
SALES (est): 1MM
SALES (corp-wide): 16.6MM **Privately Held**
SIC: 2741 Misc Publishing
PA: Rheinwerk Verlag Gmbh
Rheinwerkallee 4
Bonn 53227
228 421-500

(G-14655)
SIGNAL GRAPHICS 225
17 Foster St (02169-5307)
PHONE..................................617 472-1700
Rui Pontes, *Owner*
EMP: 6
SALES (est): 650.2K **Privately Held**
SIC: 2752 Lithographic Commercial Printing

(G-14656)
SIT INC
41 Franklin St (02169-4947)
PHONE..................................617 479-7796
Peter Aiello, *President*
◆ **EMP:** 4
SQ FT: 4,000
SALES (est): 461.8K **Privately Held**
WEB: www.sit.com
SIC: 2511 Mfg Wood Household Furniture

(G-14657)
SOUTH SHORE PLATING CO INC
28 Forest Ave (02169-1011)
PHONE..................................617 773-8064
Richard W Deady Jr, *President*
Anna Deady, *Treasurer*
Shannon Lipman, *Clerk*
EMP: 4 **EST:** 1945
SQ FT: 3,000
SALES (est): 452.1K **Privately Held**
WEB: www.southshoreplating.com
SIC: 3471 Electroplating Polishing & Finishing Metals & Formed Products

(G-14658)
SPRUCE MOUNTAIN WIND LLC
549 South St (02169-7318)
PHONE..................................617 890-0600
Jay M Cashman, *Principal*
EMP: 4 **EST:** 2009
SALES (est): 295.6K **Privately Held**
SIC: 3621 Mfg Motors/Generators

(G-14659)
STEARNS PERRY & SMITH CO INC
33 Fayette St Ste 1 (02171-2655)
PHONE..................................617 423-4775
Charles Smith, *President*
Barbara Smith, *Principal*
Paul Smith, *Principal*
Ralph Young, *Treasurer*
EMP: 9
SQ FT: 8,000
SALES (est): 1MM **Privately Held**
SIC: 7694 Electric Motor Repair

(G-14660)
STRAN & COMPANY INC (PA)
Also Called: Stran Promotional Solutions
2 Heritage Dr Ste 600 (02171-2168)
PHONE..................................617 822-6950
Andrew C Stranberg, *President*
Andy J Shape, *President*
Randolph Birney, *Vice Pres*
Rob Haughey, *Vice Pres*
Mike Friedman, *CFO*
◆ **EMP:** 30 **EST:** 1994
SQ FT: 20,000
SALES: 25MM **Privately Held**
WEB: www.stran.com
SIC: 3999 Mfg Misc Products

(G-14661)
THAI NOODLE BAR
501 Washington St (02169-5834)
PHONE..................................617 689-8847
Jittipong Rakritikul, *President*
EMP: 3
SALES (est): 97.9K **Privately Held**
SIC: 2098 Mfg Macaroni/Spaghetti

(G-14662)
TWIN RIVERS TECH HOLDINGS INC
Also Called: Twin Rivers Technologies U.S.
780 Washington St (02169-7356)
PHONE..................................617 472-9200
Scott Chatlin, *CEO*
John Ward, *Vice Pres*
EMP: 120
SALES (est): 10.3MM **Privately Held**
SIC: 2819 Mfg Industrial Inorganic Chemicals

(G-14663)
TWIN RIVERS TECH LTD PARTNR
780 Washington St (02169-7356)
PHONE..................................617 472-9200
Paul Angelico, *President*
John Gilbride, *Project Mgr*
Albert Sharlow, *Opers Mgr*
Trisha Prasinos, *Traffic Mgr*
Hasni Ahmad, *Opers Staff*
EMP: 98 **EST:** 2015
SALES (est): 32.6MM **Privately Held**
SIC: 2869 Mfg Industrial Organic Chemicals

(G-14664)
TWIN RIVERS TECH MFG CORP
780 Washington St (02169-7356)
PHONE..................................888 929-8780
Dato M E Mavani Abdullah, *Director*
EMP: 9
SALES (est): 248.6K **Privately Held**
SIC: 2819 Mfg Industrial Inorganic Chemicals
PA: Fgv Holdings Berhad
Level 42 Menara Felda
Kuala Lumpur KLP 50088
-

(G-14665)
UNITED PROSTHETICS INC
300 Congress St Ste 404a (02169-0907)
PHONE..................................617 773-7140
Brandon Green, *Director*
EMP: 3
SALES (est): 312.7K **Privately Held**
SIC: 3842 Ret Misc Merchandise

(G-14666)
VERDE LLC
95 Suomi Rd (02169-4810)
PHONE..................................617 955-2402
Nick Ni, *Mktg Dir*
Haiming Li, *Mng Member*
EMP: 7
SALES (est): 380.7K **Privately Held**
SIC: 2813 Mfg Industrial Gases

(G-14667)
VIVAGENE BIOTECH INC
2 Eustis St (02170-2303)
PHONE..................................617 302-4398
Xiaoqing Liu, *President*
EMP: 3
SALES (est): 170K **Privately Held**
SIC: 2836 Mfg Biological Products

Randolph
Norfolk County

(G-14668)
ACCURATE METAL FINISHING CORP
414 South St (02368-5338)
PHONE..................................781 963-7300
Allyn Ryalls III, *President*
Donna J Derringer, *Treasurer*
EMP: 30
SQ FT: 22,000
SALES (est): 3.9MM **Privately Held**
WEB: www.accuratemetalfinishing.com
SIC: 3471 Plating/Polishing Service

(G-14669)
ADONAI SPRING WATER INC
31 West St Unit 4 (02368-4036)
PHONE..................................844 273-7672
EMP: 5
SALES: 1MM **Privately Held**
SIC: 2086 Mfg Bottled/Canned Soft Drinks

(G-14670)
ALLOY FABRICATORS OF NENG
39 York Ave (02368-1891)
PHONE..................................781 986-6400
Christian G Dietz III, *President*
Royal Mulkern, *General Mgr*
Christian Dietz, *Vice Pres*
Royal C Mulkern, *Admin Sec*
▼ **EMP:** 14
SQ FT: 15,000
SALES (est): 3MM **Privately Held**
WEB: www.alloyfabne.com
SIC: 3443 3499 Mfg Fabricated Plate Work Mfg Misc Fabricated Metal Products

(G-14671)
BREWERS LEDGE INC
Also Called: Brewer Fitness
87 York Ave (02368-1827)
PHONE..................................781 961-5200
W Conant Brewer, *President*
George Brewer, *Vice Pres*
EMP: 6
SQ FT: 9,500
SALES: 910K **Privately Held**
WEB: www.brewersledge.net
SIC: 3949 Mfg Climbing Machines

(G-14672)
CAMBRIDGEPORT
21 Pacella Park Dr (02368-1755)
PHONE..................................781 302-3347
Filip Silipov, *Principal*
Jeffrey Levine, *Engineer*
EMP: 6
SALES (est): 1.2MM **Privately Held**
SIC: 3444 Mfg Sheet Metalwork

(G-14673)
CHASE CORPORATION
19 Highland Ave (02368-4540)
PHONE..................................781 963-2600
Mark Rovczar, *General Mgr*
EMP: 50
SALES (corp-wide): 281.3MM **Publicly Held**
WEB: www.chasecorp.com
SIC: 3069 3081 2899 3644 Mfg Fabrcatd Rubber Prdt Mfg Unsupport Plstc Film Mfg Chemical Preparation Mfg Noncondu ctv Wire Dvc Nonfrs Wiredrwng/Insltng
PA: Chase Corporation
295 University Ave
Westwood MA 02090
781 332-0700

(G-14674)
CHEN HSI PIN
25 Warren St (02368-4015)
PHONE..................................781 986-7900
Hsi-Pin Chen, *Principal*
EMP: 3
SALES (est): 144.6K **Privately Held**
SIC: 3452 Mfg Bolts/Screws/Rivets

(G-14675)
CURRYS LEATHER SHOP INC
Also Called: Curry's Leather Products
314 High St (02368-1634)
PHONE..................................781 963-0679
Robert Curry, *President*
Jennifer V Curry, *Office Mgr*
▲ **EMP:** 12 **EST:** 1946
SALES (est): 1.7MM **Privately Held**
WEB: www.curysleather.com
SIC: 3161 3999 3172 3199 Mfg Luggage Mfg Misc Products Mfg Personal Leather Gds

(G-14676)
DORMAKABA USA INC
480 S Main St (02368-5223)
PHONE..................................781 963-0182
John Mounelaphom, *Branch Mgr*
EMP: 35
SALES (corp-wide): 2.8B **Privately Held**
SIC: 3429 Mfg Hardware
HQ: Dormakaba Usa Inc.
100 Dorma Dr
Reamstown PA 17567
717 336-3881

(G-14677)
ECONOCORP INC
72 Pacella Park Dr (02368-1791)
PHONE..................................781 986-7500
Wayne Goldberg, *President*
Mark Jacobson, *Vice Pres*
Jack Bowers, *Mfg Mgr*
Justin Kirkpatrick, *Export Mgr*
Alfonso Posada, *Sales Mgr*
▲ **EMP:** 50 **EST:** 1955
SQ FT: 20,000
SALES (est): 19.3MM **Privately Held**
SIC: 3565 Mfg Packaging Machinery

(G-14678)
ELECTROSTAT
24 Petipas Ln (02368-4919)
PHONE..................................781 885-2135
Barbara Pulli, *Principal*
EMP: 3 **EST:** 2010
SALES (est): 148.8K **Privately Held**
SIC: 3471 Plating/Polishing Service

(G-14679)
EXXONMOBIL OIL CORPORATION
93 Mazzeo Dr (02368-3401)
PHONE..................................781 963-7252
Kelline Lopez, *Branch Mgr*
EMP: 4
SALES (corp-wide): 290.2B **Publicly Held**
SIC: 1311 2911 4613 5171 Petro/Natural Gas Prodn Petroleum Refining Refined Petrol Pipeline Petroleum Bulk Station
HQ: Exxonmobil Oil Corporation
2805 Sycamore St
Beaumont TX 77701
-

(G-14680)
FAST MAILING
55 Teed Dr (02368-4201)
P.O. Box 1298 (02368-1298)
PHONE..................................617 605-8693
Scott Trabucco, *Owner*
EMP: 9
SALES (est): 847.9K **Privately Held**
SIC: 2759 Direct Mail Advertising Services

(G-14681)
FLEXCON INDUSTRIES INC
300 Pond St Ste 1 (02368-2664)
P.O. Box 782 (02368-0782)
PHONE..................................781 986-2424
George L Simas Jr, *Principal*
George Simas, *Vice Pres*
Lisa Shola, *Traffic Mgr*
Matt Kearney, *Engineer*

▲ = Import ▼=Export
◆ =Import/Export

George L Simas, *Finance Other*
▲ **EMP:** 125
SQ FT: 150,000
SALES (est): 45.1MM **Privately Held**
WEB: www.flexconind.com
SIC: 3443 Mfg Fabricated Plate Work

(G-14682)
FOWLER PRINTING AND GRAPHICS
132 York Ave (02368-1845)
PHONE..................................781 986-8900
Joanne Brennan, *President*
EMP: 14
SQ FT: 16,000
SALES (est): 2.3MM **Privately Held**
WEB: www.fowlerprinting.com
SIC: 2752 Lithographic Commercial Printing

(G-14683)
GATEHOUSE MEDIA MASS I INC
Also Called: Wellesley Townsman
15 Pacella Park Dr (02368-1780)
PHONE..................................781 235-4000
Cathy Brauner, *Manager*
EMP: 125
SALES (corp-wide): 1.5B **Publicly Held**
SIC: 2711 Newspapers-Publishing/Printing
HQ: Gatehouse Media Massachusetts I, Inc.
48 Dunham Rd
Beverly MA 01915
585 598-0030

(G-14684)
HOLBROOK SUN INC
15 Pacella Park Dr # 200 (02368-1780)
PHONE..................................781 767-4000
Greg Rush, *CEO*
Cathy Conley, *Principal*
EMP: 11
SALES (est): 357.3K **Privately Held**
SIC: 2711 Newspapers

(G-14685)
HORLICK COMPANY INC
91 Pacella Park Dr (02368-1755)
PHONE..................................781 963-0090
William A Nesbitt, *President*
Shawn D Hennessey, *Vice Pres*
Shawn Hennessey, *Branch Mgr*
Cynthia Beach, *CTO*
Karen Stroup, *Maintence Staff*
▲ **EMP:** 8 **EST:** 1992
SQ FT: 23,500
SALES (est): 2.1MM **Privately Held**
WEB: www.horlick.com
SIC: 3621 3625 Mfg Motors/Generators Mfg Relays/Industrial Controls

(G-14686)
HYTEX INDUSTRIES INC
Also Called: Hytex Decorative Textiles
58 York Ave (02368-1898)
PHONE..................................781 963-4400
Jeremiah J McQuillen, *President*
Richard N Blosz, *President*
Paula L Lewis, *Vice Pres*
Rick Rigazio, *Vice Pres*
Alan N Horwitz, *Director*
▲ **EMP:** 21 **EST:** 1959
SQ FT: 30,000
SALES (est): 5.3MM **Privately Held**
WEB: www.hytex.com
SIC: 3081 3089 3069 Mfg Unsupport Plstc Film Mfg Plastic Products Mfg Fabrcatd Rubber Prdt

(G-14687)
INTEGRATED DYNAMICS ENGRG INC (HQ)
68 Mazzeo Dr (02368-3402)
PHONE..................................781 326-5700
Heidi S Shippell-Heiland, *President*
Jack Hughes, *General Mgr*
Erik Zantinge, *Vice Pres*
Steve Shedd, *Mfg Staff*
Sam Milgrom, *Buyer*
EMP: 34
SQ FT: 10,000
SALES (est): 3.9MM
SALES (corp-wide): 3B **Privately Held**
WEB: www.ideworld.com
SIC: 3829 Mfg Measuring/Controlling Devices
PA: Aalberts N.V.
Stadsplateau 18
Utrecht
303 079-300

(G-14688)
INTEGRITY GRAPHICS LLC
21 Mazzeo Dr Ste 101 (02368-3448)
PHONE..................................339 987-5533
Peter Stefans,
John Pastuszak,
EMP: 6
SALES (est): 630.7K **Privately Held**
SIC: 2759 Commercial Printing

(G-14689)
MD STETSON COMPANY INC
92 York Ave (02368-1828)
PHONE..................................781 986-6161
Michael J Glass, *President*
Andrea Glass, *Principal*
Arnie Chace, *Regional Mgr*
Andrew Glass, *Sales Staff*
Fran Lisbon, *Sales Staff*
EMP: 45
SQ FT: 60,000
SALES (est): 14.6MM **Privately Held**
WEB: www.mdstetson.com
SIC: 2842 5169 2899 2819 Mfg Polish/Sanitation Gd Whol Chemicals/Products Mfg Chemical Preparation Mfg Indstl Inorgan Chem

(G-14690)
MELVILLE CANDY CORPORATION
Also Called: Melville Old Time Candy & Pdts
28 York Ave (02368-1828)
PHONE..................................800 638-8063
Gary Newcomb Melville, *President*
Joseph Melville, *Corp Secy*
Scott Griffin, *QC Mgr*
Craig Warner, *Manager*
Hillary McLaughlin, *Creative Dir*
EMP: 22
SQ FT: 4,000
SALES (est): 4.8MM **Privately Held**
SIC: 2064 Mfg Candy/Confectionery

(G-14691)
NEW-COM METAL PRODUCTS CORP
29 Teed Dr (02368-4201)
PHONE..................................781 767-7520
William Puleo, *President*
Anthony Puleo, *Corp Secy*
Nathaniel Lee, *Engineer*
Jane Dulong, *Controller*
EMP: 22
SQ FT: 21,000
SALES (est): 5.5MM **Privately Held**
SIC: 3444 Mfg Sheet Metalwork

(G-14692)
PEPSI
Also Called: Pepsico
663 North St (02368-4317)
PHONE..................................781 986-5249
▼ **EMP:** 5
SALES (est): 305.7K **Privately Held**
SIC: 2086 Carb Sft Drnkbtlcn

(G-14693)
PEPSICO INC
663 North St (02368-4317)
PHONE..................................781 767-6622
Bill Rousseau, *Sales Staff*
EMP: 191
SALES (corp-wide): 64.6B **Publicly Held**
SIC: 2086 Carb Sft Drnkbtlcn
PA: Pepsico, Inc.
700 Anderson Hill Rd
Purchase NY 10577
914 253-2000

(G-14694)
PROGRESSIVE MARBLE FABRICATION
43 York Ave (02368-1827)
PHONE..................................781 963-6029
Carmelo Maisano, *President*
Mike Manzo, *Administration*
EMP: 5
SQ FT: 10,000
SALES: 500K **Privately Held**
WEB: www.progressivemarble.com
SIC: 3281 Mfg Cut Stone & Stone Products Marble & Granite

(G-14695)
RANDOLPH ENGINEERING INC
Also Called: Randolph Sunglasses
26 Thomas Patten Dr (02368-3902)
PHONE..................................781 961-6070
Peter M Waszkiewicz, *CEO*
Richard Waszkiewicz, *President*
Stanislaw J Zaleski, *Treasurer*
Richard Zaleski, *Admin Sec*
▲ **EMP:** 40
SQ FT: 22,000
SALES (est): 7.6MM **Privately Held**
WEB: www.randolphusa.com
SIC: 3851 Mfg Ophthalmic Goods

(G-14696)
RETAIL SALES INC
75 York Ave Ste A (02368-1841)
PHONE..................................781 963-8169
Fax: 781 963-8217
EMP: 5
SALES (corp-wide): 121.9MM **Privately Held**
SIC: 2711 Newspapers-Publishing/Printing
HQ: Retail Sales Inc
135 Morrissey Blvd
Boston MA 02125
617 929-2000

(G-14697)
SAVIN PRODUCTS COMPANY INC
214 High St (02368-1837)
P.O. Box 323 (02368-0323)
PHONE..................................781 961-2743
Margaret Ambrosia, *President*
EMP: 11
SQ FT: 10,000
SALES (est): 2.3MM **Privately Held**
WEB: www.savinproducts.com
SIC: 2842 5169 Mfg Polish/Sanitation Goods Whol Chemicals/Products

(G-14698)
STACYS PITA CHIP COMPANY INC
1 Posturepedic Dr (02368)
PHONE..................................781 961-2800
Stacy Madison, *President*
Thomas Salcito, *Treasurer*
Linda Wimberly, *Admin Sec*
▼ **EMP:** 100
SQ FT: 17,500
SALES (est): 18.2MM
SALES (corp-wide): 64.6B **Publicly Held**
WEB: www.pepsico.com
SIC: 2096 Mfg Potato Chips/Snacks
PA: Pepsico, Inc.
700 Anderson Hill Rd
Purchase NY 10577
914 253-2000

(G-14699)
TRELLEBORG OFFSHORE BOSTON INC
24 Teed Dr (02368-4202)
PHONE..................................774 719-1400
Robert Kelly, *President*
Raymond Hobem, *Vice Pres*
Victoria Samples, *Engineer*
Leo Quinlan, *Accounting Mgr*
Greg Atkinson, *Credit Staff*
▲ **EMP:** 54
SALES (est): 22.6MM
SALES (corp-wide): 3.5B **Privately Held**
SIC: 2819 3086 Mfg Industrial Inorganic Chemicals Mfg Plastic Foam Products
HQ: Trelleborg Offshore Uk Limited
Stanley Way
Skelmersdale LANCS WN8 8
169 571-2000

(G-14700)
ULTRA FILTRONICS LTD
91 York Ave (02368-1827)
PHONE..................................781 961-4775
Eugene Dennen Jr, *President*
Ronald Hostetter, *Treasurer*
Kathleen McCurdy Dennen, *Admin Sec*
EMP: 5
SALES (est): 999.3K **Privately Held**
SIC: 3569 Mfg General Industrial Machinery

(G-14701)
VENT-RITE VALVE CORP (PA)
Also Called: Skidmore Co
300 Pond St (02368-2664)
P.O. Box 783 (02368-0783)
PHONE..................................781 986-2000
Thomas J Swan Jr, *President*
Michael Kennedy, *CFO*
Joseph Swan, *Treasurer*
▲ **EMP:** 40
SQ FT: 200
SALES (est): 5.4MM **Privately Held**
WEB: www.skidmorepump.com
SIC: 3443 3491 Mfg Fabricated Plate Work Mfg Industrial Valves

(G-14702)
WEYMOUTH NEWS
15 Pacella Park Dr # 120 (02368-1700)
PHONE..................................781 337-1944
Brian Parrelli, *Owner*
EMP: 3
SALES (est): 161.7K **Privately Held**
WEB: www.weymouthnews.com
SIC: 2711 Newspapers-Publishing/Printing

(G-14703)
ZIPRINT CENTERS INC
217 N Main St (02368-4635)
PHONE..................................781 963-2250
Scott G Roberts, *President*
EMP: 7
SQ FT: 1,800
SALES (est): 750K **Privately Held**
WEB: www.ziprintcenters.com
SIC: 2752 Offset Printing

Raynham
Bristol County

(G-14704)
AGGREGATE INDS - NORTHEAST REG
1500 King Philip St (02767-1448)
PHONE..................................508 822-7120
Dominique Mantica, *Manager*
EMP: 4
SALES (corp-wide): 4.5B **Privately Held**
SIC: 2951 1611 Mfg Asphalt Mixtures/Blocks Highway/Street Construction
HQ: Aggregate Industries - Northeast Region, Inc
1715 Brdwy
Saugus MA 01906
781 941-7200

(G-14705)
ARTS INTERNATIONAL WHOLESALE
104 Forge River Pkwy (02767-1465)
PHONE..................................508 822-7181
Arthur Cabral, *Owner*
EMP: 8
SQ FT: 9,980
SALES (est): 516.3K **Privately Held**
SIC: 2051 Mfg Bread/Related Products

(G-14706)
C H BABB CO INC
Also Called: Babbco
445 Paramount Dr (02767-5178)
PHONE..................................508 977-0600
Foran William C, *President*
Ruy Ferreira, *Project Mgr*
Paul Novello, *Prdtn Mgr*
Frank Twiss, *Facilities Mgr*
Jared Leite, *Purch Mgr*
▲ **EMP:** 40
SQ FT: 75,000
SALES (est): 14.9MM **Privately Held**
WEB: www.chbabb.com
SIC: 3556 Mfg Food Products Machinery

(G-14707)
CONSTRUCTION SOURCE MGT LLC
33 Commercial St (02767-5361)
PHONE..................................508 484-5100

GEOGRAPHIC

John C Kelly, *Mng Member*
EMP: 8
SALES (est): 992.9K **Privately Held**
SIC: 1442 Construction Sand/Gravel

(G-14708)
CRUE BREW BREWERY LLC
293 Whippoorwill Dr (02767-1198)
PHONE..................................508 272-6090
Kevin Merritt, *Mng Member*
EMP: 3
SALES: 350K **Privately Held**
SIC: 2082 7389 Mfg Malt Beverages Business Serv Non-Commercial Site

(G-14709)
DEPUY MITEK LLC
325 Paramount Dr (02767-5199)
PHONE..................................508 880-8100
Ian Lawson, *President*
Kevin McKenney, *Manager*
Gregory Maloblocki, *Director*
James Paiva, *Director*
▲ **EMP:** 398
SALES (est): 598.3K
SALES (corp-wide): 81.5B **Publicly Held**
WEB: www.depuy.com
SIC: 3841 Mfg Surgical/Medical Instruments
PA: Johnson & Johnson
1 Johnson And Johnson Plz
New Brunswick NJ 08933
732 524-0400

(G-14710)
DEPUY SPINE LLC (HQ)
325 Paramount Dr (02767-5199)
PHONE..................................508 880-8100
Max M Reinhardt, *President*
Ruth Forstadt, *Project Mgr*
Tienli Lin, *Project Mgr*
Eileen Dunne, *Buyer*
Joseph Mooney, *Engineer*
▲ **EMP:** 350
SQ FT: 280,000
SALES (est): 79.8MM
SALES (corp-wide): 81.5B **Publicly Held**
WEB: www.depuyspine.com
SIC: 3842 Mfg Surgical Appliances/Supplies
PA: Johnson & Johnson
1 Johnson And Johnson Plz
New Brunswick NJ 08933
732 524-0400

(G-14711)
DEPUY SYNTHES PRODUCTS INC (DH)
325 Paramount Dr (02767-5199)
PHONE..................................508 880-8100
Martin Fitchett, *President*
Paul Randall, *Engineer*
EMP: 59
SALES (est): 19.1MM
SALES (corp-wide): 81.5B **Publicly Held**
SIC: 3841 Mfg Medical/Hospital Equipment Research & Development
HQ: Depuy Spine, Llc
325 Paramount Dr
Raynham MA 02767
508 880-8100

(G-14712)
DEPUY SYNTHES SALES INC
Codman Neuro
325 Paramount Dr (02767-5199)
PHONE..................................508 880-8100
Lacey Elberg, *Administration*
EMP: 5
SALES (corp-wide): 81.5B **Publicly Held**
SIC: 3841 Manufactures Surgical Or Medical Instruments
HQ: Depuy Synthes Sales Inc
325 Paramount Dr
Raynham MA 02767
508 880-8100

(G-14713)
DEPUY SYNTHES SALES INC
Depuy Synthes Spine
325 Paramount Dr (02767-5199)
PHONE..................................508 880-8100
EMP: 11
SALES (corp-wide): 81.5B **Publicly Held**
SIC: 3842 Manufactures Surgical Appliances Or Supplies
HQ: Depuy Synthes Sales Inc
325 Paramount Dr
Raynham MA 02767
508 880-8100

(G-14714)
ELECTROCHEM SOLUTIONS INC
670 Paramount Dr (02767-5411)
PHONE..................................781 575-0800
Paul Oliveira, *Production*
Gerard Lozzi, *QC Mgr*
Gregory Decker, *Engineer*
Dave Field, *Engineer*
Roman Kozlov, *Engineer*
EMP: 120
SALES (corp-wide): 1.2B **Publicly Held**
WEB: www.eacnet.com
SIC: 3692 5063 5065 Mfg Primary Batteries Whol Electrical Equipment Whol Electronic Parts/Equipment
HQ: Electrochem Solutions, Inc.
10000 Wehrle Dr
Clarence NY 14031
-

(G-14715)
GEORGE R KING
Also Called: Proforma Platinum Group
27 Gretchen Way (02767-5163)
PHONE..................................508 821-3826
George R King, *Owner*
EMP: 3
SALES (est): 150K **Privately Held**
SIC: 2759 Commercial Printing

(G-14716)
ILLINOIS TOOL WORKS INC
166 Stoneybrook Rd (02767-1792)
PHONE..................................508 821-9828
Scott Balutis, *Manager*
EMP: 94
SALES (corp-wide): 14.7B **Publicly Held**
SIC: 3089 Mfg Plastic & Metal Components & Fasteners
PA: Illinois Tool Works Inc.
155 Harlem Ave
Glenview IL 60025
847 724-7500

(G-14717)
MEDICAL DEVICE BUS SVCS INC
Also Called: Johnson & Johnson
325 Paramount Dr (02767-5199)
PHONE..................................508 880-8100
Max Reinhardt, *Vice Pres*
Kathy Burkard, *Project Mgr*
Vickie Cady, *Project Mgr*
Kathy Irvine, *Project Mgr*
William Roosa, *Opers Mgr*
EMP: 48
SALES (corp-wide): 81.5B **Publicly Held**
SIC: 3841 Mfg Surgical/Medical Instruments
HQ: Medical Device Business Services, Inc.
700 Orthopaedic Dr
Warsaw IN 46582
-

(G-14718)
MEGA NA INC
175 Paramount Dr Unit 302 (02767-1066)
PHONE..................................781 784-7684
Lucio De Risi, *CEO*
Daniel Hebda, *COO*
Luca De Risi, *Vice Pres*
Henri-Louis De Vilmorin, *Vice Pres*
Sebastien Rey, *Vice Pres*
EMP: 29
SQ FT: 3,422
SALES: 10.2MM
SALES (corp-wide): 884.7K **Privately Held**
WEB: www.mega.com
SIC: 7372 Prepackaged Software Services
PA: Mega International Srl
Via Della Spiga 36
Milano MI 20121
027 800-19

(G-14719)
METTLER PACKAGING LLC
90 New State Hwy Ste 1 (02767-5461)
PHONE..................................508 738-2201
Michael Mettler,
▲ **EMP:** 4
SQ FT: 1,000
SALES (est): 834.7K
SALES (corp-wide): 19.6MM **Privately Held**
WEB: www.papier-mettler.com
SIC: 2673 Mfg Bags-Plastic/Coated Paper
PA: Papier - Mettler Inhaber Michael Mettler
Hochwaldstr. 22
Morbach 54497
653 379-0

(G-14720)
MODULAR AIR FILTRATION SYSTEMS
450 Richmond St (02767-5301)
PHONE..................................508 823-4900
William Lovenbury, *President*
Robert Lovenbury, *Treasurer*
EMP: 20
SALES (est): 1.4MM **Privately Held**
SIC: 3677 Mfg Electronic Coils/Transformers

(G-14721)
NORTHERN AIR INC
450 Richmond St (02767-5301)
PHONE..................................508 823-4900
Bill Lovenbury, *President*
Sharon Whitfield, *Office Mgr*
EMP: 5
SALES (est): 951.8K **Privately Held**
SIC: 3564 Mfg Blowers/Fans

(G-14722)
NOUVEAU PACKAGING LLC
65 Ryan Dr Unit F1 (02767-1974)
PHONE..................................508 880-0300
Beverly King, *Mng Member*
Charles R King,
EMP: 3
SQ FT: 6,500
SALES: 2MM **Privately Held**
SIC: 2679 Whol Nondurable Goods

(G-14723)
OMNI LIFE SCIENCE INC (HQ)
480 Paramount Dr (02767-1085)
PHONE..................................508 824-2444
Rick Epstein, *CEO*
George B Cipollett, *CEO*
David Lorenzi, *President*
David L Lasalle, *COO*
Carl Knobloch, *Vice Pres*
▲ **EMP:** 35
SQ FT: 12,000
SALES (est): 5.3MM **Privately Held**
WEB: www.omnils.com
SIC: 3842 Mfg Surgical Appliances/Supplies

(G-14724)
OMNILIFE SCIENCE INC
175 Paramount Dr Unit 5 (02767-1065)
PHONE..................................508 824-2444
George Cipolletti, *President*
Richard D Nikolaev, *Branch Mgr*
EMP: 4 **Privately Held**
WEB: www.omnils.com
SIC: 3841 Mfg Surgical/Medical Instruments
HQ: Omni Life Science, Inc.
480 Paramount Dr
Raynham MA 02767
508 824-2444

(G-14725)
PIN STOP
87 Lakeview Dr (02767-1612)
PHONE..................................508 824-1886
Colleen Dwyer, *Principal*
EMP: 3
SALES (est): 224.4K **Privately Held**
SIC: 3452 Mfg Bolts/Screws/Rivets

(G-14726)
POWERWASH CO
40 Gatsby Dr (02767-8075)
P.O. Box 636, Raynham Center (02768-0636)
PHONE..................................508 823-9274
Derek McGovorn, *Owner*
EMP: 3
SALES: 100K **Privately Held**
SIC: 2842 Mfg Polish/Sanitation Goods

(G-14727)
PRO-TECH ORTHOPEDICS INC
95 Ryan Dr Ste 8 (02767-1992)
PHONE..................................508 821-9600
Thomas Kimball, *President*
Martin Andersson, *Vice Pres*
EMP: 10
SALES: 1.2MM **Privately Held**
SIC: 3842 Mfg Surgical Appliances/Supplies

(G-14728)
RAYNHAM TOOL & DIE INC
150 Broadway (02767-1414)
P.O. Box 307, Raynham Center (02768-0307)
PHONE..................................508 822-4489
Leo Champagne, *President*
EMP: 3
SQ FT: 1,800
SALES: 750K **Privately Held**
SIC: 3544 3599 Mfg Dies/Tools/Jigs/Fixtures Mfg Industrial Machinery

(G-14729)
RYAN IRON WORKS INC
1830 Broadway (02767-1967)
P.O. Box 159 (02767-0159)
PHONE..................................508 821-2058
Howard F Shea, *President*
John Shea, *President*
Lawrence W Kelley, *Exec VP*
Paul Berube, *Vice Pres*
Farid Rifai, *Engineer*
EMP: 50
SQ FT: 65,000
SALES (est): 12.2MM **Privately Held**
WEB: www.ryanornamental.com
SIC: 3446 Mfg Architectural Metalwork

(G-14730)
SIGN A RAMA
Also Called: Sign-A-Rama
1470 New State Hwy # 21 (02767-5420)
PHONE..................................508 822-7533
Mike Nelken, *Owner*
EMP: 3
SQ FT: 1,800
SALES (est): 270.4K **Privately Held**
WEB: www.signaramaraynham.com
SIC: 3993 Signsadv Specs

(G-14731)
SUNRISE TECHNOLOGIES LLC
54 Commercial St Ste 2 (02767-1300)
PHONE..................................508 884-9732
Vance Spillman,
▼ **EMP:** 15
SALES (est): 3.8MM **Privately Held**
SIC: 3648 Mfg Lighting Equipment

(G-14732)
TECHNICAL SERVICES INC
263 South St E (02767-5129)
PHONE..................................781 389-8342
Sean Riley, *Principal*
EMP: 4
SALES (est): 484.1K **Privately Held**
SIC: 3672 Mfg Printed Circuit Boards

Reading
Middlesex County

(G-14733)
DAILY WOBURN TIMES INC
Also Called: The Daily Times & Chronicle
531 Main St (01867-3134)
P.O. Box 240 (01867-0340)
PHONE..................................781 944-2200
EMP: 20
SQ FT: 4,600
SALES (corp-wide): 7MM **Privately Held**
SIC: 2711 Newspapers-Publishing/Printing
PA: Daily Woburn Times Inc
1 Arrow Dr
Woburn MA 01801
781 933-3700

(G-14734)
FRAEN CORPORATION (PA)
80 New Crossing Rd (01867-3291)
PHONE..................................781 205-5300
Nicholas Scarfo, *CEO*

Nicodemo Scarfo, *CEO*
Brenda Demarco, *Prdtn Mgr*
Laurena McDermott, *Prdtn Mgr*
Dave Perkins, *Purch Mgr*
▲ **EMP:** 120 **EST:** 1924
SQ FT: 65,000
SALES (est): 23.4MM **Privately Held**
WEB: www.fraen.com
SIC: 3469 3451 3089 3873 Mfg Metal Stampings Mfg Screw Machine Prdts Mfg Plastic Products Mfg Watches/Clocks/Parts Mfg Elec Components

(G-14735)
FRAEN MECHATRONICS LLC
80 New Crossing Rd (01867-3254)
PHONE....................................781 439-5934
John Lambert, *CEO*
EMP: 3
SALES (est): 121.3K **Privately Held**
SIC: 3621 Mfg Motors/Generators

(G-14736)
HEAD 2 TOE
167 Pleasant St (01867-2759)
P.O. Box 508 (01867-0708)
PHONE....................................781 944-0286
Patricia Griffin, *President*
EMP: 10
SALES (est): 626.9K **Privately Held**
SIC: 2842 Mfg Polish/Sanitation Goods

(G-14737)
HEATMAKER PARTS & SERVICE
95 Main St (01867-3972)
P.O. Box 310, Lynnfield (01940-0310)
PHONE....................................617 930-0036
Craig Rinaldi, *Owner*
EMP: 4
SALES (est): 166.8K **Privately Held**
SIC: 3433 Mfg Heating Equipment-Non-electric

(G-14738)
PGC ACQUISITION LLC
Also Called: Pairpoint Crystal
74 Pleasant St (01867-3018)
P.O. Box 515, Sagamore (02561-0515)
PHONE....................................508 888-2344
Tom Fiocco, *President*
Tomas J Fiocco, *Principal*
EMP: 13
SQ FT: 35,000
SALES (est): 1.9MM **Privately Held**
WEB: www.pairpoint.com
SIC: 3229 5719 5023 5199 Mfg Pressed/Blown Glass Ret Misc Homefurnishings Whol Homefurnishings Whol Nondurable Goods

(G-14739)
POSITION HEALTH INC
123 Haven St Ste 2689 (01867-2952)
PHONE....................................617 549-2403
EMP: 3
SQ FT: 1,000
SALES (est): 95K **Privately Held**
SIC: 7372 Prepackaged Software Services

(G-14740)
RICHARDSONS ICE CREAM
50 Walkers Brook Dr (01867-3224)
PHONE....................................781 944-9121
Chris Richardson, *Principal*
EMP: 3
SALES (est): 146.9K **Privately Held**
SIC: 2024 5812 Mfg Ice Cream/Frozen Desert Eating Place

(G-14741)
ROGER A REED INC
Also Called: Reed Wax
167 Pleasant St (01867-2759)
P.O. Box 508 (01867-0708)
PHONE....................................781 944-4640
Patricia Griffin, *President*
EMP: 24 **EST:** 1939
SALES (est): 4.3MM **Privately Held**
WEB: www.reedwax.com
SIC: 2842 Mfg Polish/Sanitation Goods

(G-14742)
S W KEATS COMPANY
85 Libby Ave (01867-1942)
PHONE....................................781 935-4282
Samuel Keats, *Owner*
EMP: 3
SQ FT: 1,750
SALES (est): 200.1K **Privately Held**
SIC: 3599 Mfg Industrial Machinery

(G-14743)
SIGNS SOLUTIONS UNLIMITED
53 Tamarack Rd (01867-1842)
PHONE....................................781 942-0111
Jill M Carrera, *Principal*
EMP: 5
SALES (est): 446.6K **Privately Held**
SIC: 3993 Mfg Signs/Advertising Specialties

(G-14744)
WILLETT INSTITUTE OF FINANCE
16 Red Gate Ln (01867-3856)
PHONE....................................617 247-3030
Edward R Willett, *CEO*
Paul Langone, *President*
EMP: 3
SALES (est): 206.7K **Privately Held**
SIC: 2731 8299 Publishes Training Books In Finance & Management & Offers Training Programs In Finance & Management

Rehoboth
Bristol County

(G-14745)
BIMBO BAKERIES USA INC
63 Fall River Ave (02769-1009)
PHONE....................................508 336-7735
Pat McGowan, *Manager*
EMP: 127 **Privately Held**
SIC: 2053 Mfg Frozen Bakery Products
HQ: Bimbo Bakeries Usa, Inc
255 Business Center Dr # 200
Horsham PA 19044
215 347-5500

(G-14746)
BRADLEY OIL COMPANY
513 Winthrop St (02769-1205)
PHONE....................................508 336-4400
David Bradley, *Principal*
EMP: 3 **EST:** 2010
SALES (est): 154.4K **Privately Held**
SIC: 1311 Crude Petroleum/Natural Gas Production

(G-14747)
BREED NUTRITION INC
5 Old Bliss St (02769-1929)
PHONE....................................508 840-3888
Carl Morris, *Co-Owner*
Paul Risotti, *Co-Owner*
Stewart Willits, *Co-Owner*
EMP: 3 **EST:** 2016
SALES (est): 91.3K **Privately Held**
SIC: 2023 7999 5499 Mfg Dry/Evaporated Dairy Products Amusement/Recreation Services Ret Misc Foods

(G-14748)
EXCALIBUR WELDING AND PIPING
45 Providence St (02769-1615)
PHONE....................................401 241-0548
EMP: 8
SALES (est): 88.7K **Privately Held**
SIC: 7692 Welding Repair

(G-14749)
FASTSIGNS OF ATTLEBORO
5 Greenwood Dr (02769-2243)
PHONE....................................508 699-6699
Joe Tavares, *Owner*
EMP: 3
SALES (est): 263.6K **Privately Held**
SIC: 3993 Signsadv Specs

(G-14750)
HASS BROS INC
Also Called: JPS and Sons
190 Providence St (02769-1023)
PHONE....................................508 336-9323
Joseph A Hass Jr, *President*
John R Hass, *Vice Pres*
EMP: 5 **EST:** 1905
SALES: 250K **Privately Held**
SIC: 2011 0212 Meat Packing Plant Beef Cattle-Except Feedlot

(G-14751)
J & K SALES COMPANY INC
Also Called: Komor Mfg Co
225 Pleasant St (02769-1617)
PHONE....................................508 252-6235
Henry Jablecki, *Ch of Bd*
Michael Jablecki, *President*
Stephen Jablecki, *Vice Pres*
Katherine Tardiff, *Treasurer*
Mary Maguire, *Admin Sec*
EMP: 40 **EST:** 1946
SQ FT: 110,000
SALES (est): 3.4MM **Privately Held**
WEB: www.jksalescompany.com
SIC: 3961 Mfg Non-Precious Metal Children's' Costume Jewelry

(G-14752)
KND MACHINE CO
61 Blanding Rd (02769-1115)
PHONE....................................508 336-5509
Nicholas Digiammo, *Owner*
EMP: 4
SALES: 750K **Privately Held**
SIC: 3732 Manufacturer /Cnc Machined Custom Parts

(G-14753)
NANTUCKET PAVERS INC
71 Fall River Ave (02769-1009)
PHONE....................................508 336-5800
John P Ferreira, *President*
▲ **EMP:** 11
SALES (est): 1.5MM **Privately Held**
WEB: www.nantucketpavers.com
SIC: 3272 Mfg Concrete Products

(G-14754)
NEW ENGLAND GRAVEL HAULERS
38 Winthrop St (02769-2653)
PHONE....................................508 922-4518
James Barishian, *Principal*
EMP: 5
SALES (est): 385.2K **Privately Held**
SIC: 1442 Construction Sand/Gravel

(G-14755)
NORTHEAST EMS ENTERPRISES
1 Apple Valley Dr (02769-1334)
PHONE....................................508 252-6584
Randy Silveira, *President*
EMP: 4
SALES (est): 501.1K **Privately Held**
SIC: 3841 Retails Medical Equipment

(G-14756)
OLDCASTLE INFRASTRUCTURE INC
Also Called: Rotondo Precast
41 Almeida Rd (02769-1007)
PHONE....................................508 336-7600
Chris Fowler, *Manager*
EMP: 60
SALES (corp-wide): 29.7B **Privately Held**
WEB: www.oldcastle-precast.com
SIC: 3272 1711 Mfg Concrete Products Plumbing/Heating/Air Cond Contractor
HQ: Oldcastle Infrastructure, Inc.
7000 Cntl Prkaway Ste 800
Atlanta GA 30328
470 602-2000

(G-14757)
OLDCASTLE PRECAST INC
41 Almeida Rd (02769-1007)
PHONE....................................508 867-8312
EMP: 50
SALES (corp-wide): 24.2B **Privately Held**
SIC: 3272 5211 Mfg Concrete Products Ret Lumber/Building Materials
HQ: Oldcastle Precast, Inc.
1002 15th St Sw Ste 110
Auburn WA 30328
253 833-2777

(G-14758)
QUARRY BROTHERS INCORPORATED
466 Winthrop St (02769-1301)
PHONE....................................508 252-9922
Adam C Stephens, *President*
EMP: 6
SALES (est): 685K **Privately Held**
SIC: 3281 Mfg Cut Stone/Products

(G-14759)
RHODE ISLAND SHEET METAL
30 Palmer Meadow Ln (02769-1138)
PHONE....................................508 557-1140
Thomas Gravel, *Principal*
EMP: 3
SALES (est): 394.9K **Privately Held**
SIC: 3444 Mfg Sheet Metalwork

(G-14760)
ROBERT RUSSELL CO INC
38 Park St (02769-2712)
PHONE....................................508 226-4140
Robert Russell Sr, *President*
Robert Russell Jr, *Treasurer*
Claire Russell, *Clerk*
▲ **EMP:** 4
SQ FT: 8,200
SALES (est): 587.6K **Privately Held**
SIC: 3441 1796 Rebuild Machines & Mfg Fabricated Steel

(G-14761)
TARGET MARKETING GROUP INC
Also Called: Rehoboth Reporter
72 Rocky Hill Rd (02769-1415)
P.O. Box 170 (02769-0170)
PHONE....................................508 252-6575
Richard R Georgia, *President*
Barbara Georgia, *Vice Pres*
EMP: 5
SALES (est): 344K **Privately Held**
WEB: www.rehobothreporter.com
SIC: 2711 Newspapers-Publishing/Printing

(G-14762)
WAYNES SHEET METAL INC
157 Tremont St (02769-2818)
PHONE....................................508 431-8057
Wayne Gaudreau, *President*
Margaret Gardrue, *Treasurer*
EMP: 7
SALES (est): 600K **Privately Held**
SIC: 3444 Fabrication & Install Mfg Sheet Metalwork

Revere
Suffolk County

(G-14763)
ATLANTIC ANIMAL HEALTH INC
Also Called: Squire Laboratories
100 Mill St (02151-5300)
PHONE....................................781 289-9600
Eugene Salerno, *President*
◆ **EMP:** 6 **EST:** 1967
SQ FT: 10,000
SALES: 1MM **Privately Held**
SIC: 2834 Mfg Veterinary Pharmaceuticals

(G-14764)
BELLOFATTO ELECTRICAL
Also Called: Signal Cnstr Insul Mintainence
26 Geneva St (02151-2124)
PHONE....................................781 284-4164
George T Bellofatto, *Owner*
Mr George Tbellofatto, *Owner*
EMP: 6
SQ FT: 15,000
SALES (est): 270K **Privately Held**
SIC: 3669 Install/Repair Traffic Signal And Sports Park Lighting Security Systems Cctv Camera Systems Intelligent Transportation Systems

(G-14765)
DURANT PRFMCE COATINGS INC
112 Railroad Ave (02151-4085)
PHONE....................................781 289-1400
Ronald A Yanetti, *President*

GEOGRAPHIC

Al Losanno, *Vice Pres*
Marilyn Yanetti, *Vice Pres*
EMP: 12 **EST:** 1950
SQ FT: 19,000
SALES (est): 5.5MM **Privately Held**
WEB: www.durantpaints.com
SIC: 2851 5231 Mfg Paints/Allied Prdts Ret Paint/Glass/Wallppr

(G-14766)
HERGON DESIGN INC
188 Lincoln St (02151-5706)
PHONE.................................781 286-0663
Klacson Santos, *President*
▲ **EMP:** 4
SALES (est): 429.3K **Privately Held**
WEB: www.hergon.com
SIC: 3299 7389 Mfg Nonmetallic Mineral Products Business Services At Non-Commercial Site

(G-14767)
INDEPENDANT NEWSPAPER GROUP
Also Called: Chelsea Record
385 Broadway Ste 105 (02151-3049)
PHONE.................................781 485-0588
Stephen Quigley, *President*
EMP: 40 **EST:** 2001
SALES (est): 4MM **Privately Held**
WEB: www.reverejournal.com
SIC: 2759 2711 Commercial Printing Newspapers-Publishing/Printing

(G-14768)
INDEPENDENT NEWSPAPER GROUP
Also Called: Beacon Hill Times, The
385 Broadway (02151-3033)
PHONE.................................781 485-0588
Karen Cord Taylor, *President*
Jacqueline Freeman, *Editor*
Susan McWhinney-Morse, *Vice Pres*
Stephen Quigley, *Manager*
EMP: 30
SALES (est): 1.3MM **Privately Held**
WEB: www.beaconhilltimes.com
SIC: 2711 Newspapers-Publishing/Printing

(G-14769)
JB SPORTS LLC
Also Called: Flexi Brace
121 Morris St (02151-1029)
PHONE.................................617 930-3044
Jalmar Araujo, *Owner*
▲ **EMP:** 4
SQ FT: 1,500
SALES: 1.5MM **Privately Held**
SIC: 3949 Mfg Sporting/Athletic Goods

(G-14770)
L & J LEATHERS MANUFACTURING
Also Called: Bikers Outfitters, The
1039 Broadway (02151-1308)
PHONE.................................781 289-6466
Lisa Darian, *Owner*
EMP: 3
SQ FT: 16,000
SALES (est): 341.1K **Privately Held**
WEB: www.bikersoutfitter.com
SIC: 3161 2386 5699 Mfg & Ret Leather Motorcycle Accessories

(G-14771)
MADISON GROUP INC
Also Called: Madison Nobile Media
1330 Broadway (02151-1363)
P.O. Box 251 (02151-0008)
PHONE.................................781 853-0029
Kevin Chiles, *President*
EMP: 5
SQ FT: 4,000
SALES: 1.2MM **Privately Held**
WEB: www.madisonprint.com
SIC: 2759 7311 Commercial Printing Advertising Agency

(G-14772)
MAGAZINE COLUMBIANO
545 Malden St (02151-1861)
PHONE.................................617 365-3182
Marino Velasquez, *Owner*
EMP: 3
SALES (est): 83.3K **Privately Held**
SIC: 2721 Periodicals-Publishing/Printing

(G-14773)
MC KINNON PRINTING CO INC
101 Naples Rd (02151-1301)
PHONE.................................781 592-3677
Carl R Rosa, *President*
Marie T Rosa, *Clerk*
EMP: 3
SALES (est): 317.6K **Privately Held**
SIC: 2759 2752 Commercial Printing Lithographic Commercial Printing

(G-14774)
OMNI-TROL INDUSTRIES INC
15 Whitmore Rd (02151-5916)
P.O. Box 249 (02151-0008)
PHONE.................................781 284-8000
Anthony Pesce, *President*
Stephen Stickney, *Treasurer*
Sidney I Kramer, *Clerk*
EMP: 13
SQ FT: 25,000
SALES (est): 1.6MM
SALES (corp-wide): 2.3MM **Privately Held**
WEB: www.whitmorcompany.com
SIC: 3589 Builds Water Purification Equipment
PA: The Whitmor Company Inc
15 Whitmore Rd
Revere MA 02151
781 284-8000

(G-14775)
REVERE INDEPENDENT
385 Broadway Ste 105 (02151-3049)
PHONE.................................781 485-0588
Steven Quigley, *Partner*
Josh Resnek, *Editor*
EMP: 20
SALES (est): 848.8K **Privately Held**
WEB: www.revereindependent.com
SIC: 2711 Newspapers-Publishing/Printing

(G-14776)
SWEETHEARTS CANDY CO LLC
135 American Legion Hwy (02151-2405)
P.O. Box 1390, Lynnfield (01940-5390)
PHONE.................................781 485-4500
C Dean Metropoulos,
EMP: 500
SALES (est): 10.8MM **Privately Held**
SIC: 2064 2066 Manufactures Candy/Confectionery And Chocolate/Cocoa Products

(G-14777)
VITO WHEEL MUSIC MORE
105 Thornton St (02151-5104)
PHONE.................................781 241-9476
Vito Colon, *Principal*
EMP: 3
SALES (est): 239.5K **Privately Held**
SIC: 3312 Blast Furnace-Steel Works

(G-14778)
WHITMOR COMPANY INC (PA)
15 Whitmore Rd (02151-5916)
P.O. Box 249 (02151-0008)
PHONE.................................781 284-8000
Anthony Pesce, *President*
Stephen Stickney, *Vice Pres*
Ettore De Francesto, *Human Resources*
EMP: 14 **EST:** 1942
SQ FT: 25,000
SALES (est): 2.3MM **Privately Held**
WEB: www.whitmorcompany.com
SIC: 3613 5084 Mfg Power Switchboards & Parts Whol Industrial Machinery & Equipment

Richmond
Berkshire County

(G-14779)
GRANT LARKIN
937 Summit Rd (01254)
P.O. Box 203 (01254-0203)
PHONE.................................413 698-2599
Matt Larkin, *Partner*
Elaine Grant, *Partner*
EMP: 3
SALES (est): 297.1K **Privately Held**
SIC: 3429 5932 7389 Interior Design & Antique Sales

(G-14780)
GROVE STREET ENTERPRISES INC
Also Called: Hilltop Orchard
508 Canaan Rd (01254-5116)
P.O. Box 189 (01254-0189)
PHONE.................................413 698-3301
Wendy Vittori, *Corp Secy*
John Vittori, *Vice Pres*
EMP: 15
SQ FT: 2,500
SALES (est): 2.2MM **Privately Held**
SIC: 2084 Mfg Wines/Brandy/Spirits

Rochdale
Worcester County

(G-14781)
KEMP TECHNOLOGIES INC
7 Virginia Dr (01542-1201)
PHONE.................................631 418-8407
Dolores Farrell, *Principal*
EMP: 5
SALES (est): 277.1K **Privately Held**
SIC: 3577 7371 Mfg Computer Peripheral Equipment Custom Computer Programing

(G-14782)
LAIRD WOODWORKING INC
863 Pleasant St (01542-1126)
PHONE.................................508 892-8877
James F Laird, *Principal*
EMP: 5
SALES (est): 435.4K **Privately Held**
SIC: 2431 Mfg Millwork

(G-14783)
STEEL PRODUCTS CORPORATION (PA)
105 Huntoon Memorial Hwy (01542-1305)
P.O. Box 51 (01542-0051)
PHONE.................................508 892-4770
Charles A Olson, *President*
Gary Donahue, *Treasurer*
Gary Donohue, *Sales Mgr*
EMP: 6 **EST:** 1953
SQ FT: 6,000
SALES (est): 1MM **Privately Held**
WEB: www.steelproducts.com
SIC: 2821 2851 Mfg Plastic Materials/Resins Mfg Paints/Allied Products

Rochester
Plymouth County

(G-14784)
CAPTAIN BONNEYS CREAMERY
267 New Bedford Rd (02770-1520)
PHONE.................................774 218-3586
EMP: 3 **EST:** 2012
SALES (est): 148.6K **Privately Held**
SIC: 2021 Mfg Creamery Butter

(G-14785)
DRS DEVELOPMENT LLC
10 Marion Rd (02770-4123)
PHONE.................................774 271-0533
George B Dornblaser Jr, *Principal*
EMP: 3
SALES (est): 190.5K **Privately Held**
SIC: 3674 Mfg Semiconductors/Related Devices

(G-14786)
FOAMACTION SPORTS LLC
298 Neck Rd (02770-1706)
PHONE.................................508 887-3721
Michael Andrew Gleick, *Principal*
EMP: 4
SALES (est): 266.7K **Privately Held**
SIC: 3949 Mfg Sporting/Athletic Goods

(G-14787)
GREY FORCE COOLING
214 Neck Rd (02770-1306)
PHONE.................................508 441-1753
Nathan Johnston, *Owner*
EMP: 5
SQ FT: 1,200
SALES (est): 324.1K **Privately Held**
SIC: 3577 Mfg Computer Cooling Systems

Rockland
Plymouth County

(G-14788)
3M COMPANY
30 Commerce Rd (02370-1053)
PHONE.................................781 871-1400
Glen Stanley, *Design Engr*
EMP: 14
SALES (corp-wide): 32.7B **Publicly Held**
SIC: 2891 Mfg Adhesives/Sealants
PA: 3m Company
3m Center
Saint Paul MN 55144
651 733-1110

(G-14789)
AIRXCHANGE INC
85 Longwater Dr (02370-1093)
PHONE.................................781 871-4816
Donald Steele, *President*
Richard Taft, *Senior VP*
James Connell, *Vice Pres*
Jim Connell, *Vice Pres*
Dr Lawrence Hoagland, *Vice Pres*
▲ **EMP:** 65
SQ FT: 35,000
SALES (est): 17.2MM **Privately Held**
WEB: www.airxchange.com
SIC: 3585 Mfg Refrigeration/Heating Equipment

(G-14790)
APPAREL 2000 LLC
40 Reservoir Park Dr D (02370-1099)
PHONE.................................781 740-6204
Robert Mazzola, *Principal*
Pat Mokman,
EMP: 5 **EST:** 1998
SALES: 500K **Privately Held**
WEB: www.apparel2000.net
SIC: 2395 Pleating/Stitching Services

(G-14791)
ARBO MACHINE CO INC
45 Union St (02370-1919)
PHONE.................................781 871-3449
Aram Onbashian Jr, *President*
EMP: 9 **EST:** 1963
SQ FT: 3,500
SALES (est): 1.1MM **Privately Held**
SIC: 3599 Machine Shop Jobbing

(G-14792)
ARBORWAY METAL FINISHING INC
Also Called: AMF Technologies
401 Vfw Dr (02370-1176)
P.O. Box 537, Accord (02018-0537)
PHONE.................................781 982-0137
Thomas J O'Mara, *President*
Susan M O'Mara, *Clerk*
EMP: 14
SQ FT: 12,000
SALES (est): 1.4MM **Privately Held**
WEB: www.amftechnologies.com
SIC: 3471 Plating/Polishing Service

(G-14793)
BENDON GEAR & MACHINE INC
100 Weymouth St Ste A1 (02370-1145)
PHONE.................................781 878-8100
S George Belezos, *President*
Douglas Truessel, *Vice Pres*
Russ Molly, *Production*
Christopher P Belezos, *Treasurer*
June Smey, *Manager*
EMP: 29 **EST:** 1951
SQ FT: 26,000
SALES (est): 5.6MM **Privately Held**
WEB: www.bendongear.com
SIC: 3599 3566 Machine Shop

(G-14794)
BOSTON ATMTC SPRNKLR FBRCATION
10 Commerce Rd 2 (02370-1053)
PHONE.....781 681-5122
John Cokinos, *President*
EMP: 3
SQ FT: 30,000
SALES (est): 314.5K **Privately Held**
SIC: 3432 Mfg Sprinkler Pipes

(G-14795)
CAPEWAY PRINTING & COPY CENTER
71 Reservoir Park Dr (02370-1060)
PHONE.....781 878-1600
Jim Grady, *President*
EMP: 7
SALES: 1MM **Privately Held**
SIC: 2752 Offset Printing

(G-14796)
CREATIVE SUCCESS ALLIANCE CORP
100 Weymouth St Ste D2 (02370-1145)
PHONE.....781 878-7114
David Lindahl, *CEO*
Tammy Beckwith, *CFO*
EMP: 33
SALES (est): 667.7K **Privately Held**
SIC: 2741 6099 Misc Publishing Depository Banking Services

(G-14797)
CUSTOM QUALITY SILK SCREEN
333 Weymouth St Ste 5 (02370-1144)
PHONE.....781 878-0760
Brian Sigal, *Owner*
EMP: 6
SALES (est): 495K **Privately Held**
SIC: 2759 Commercial Printing

(G-14798)
E J WHITE FUEL
89 Spring St (02370-2616)
PHONE.....781 878-0802
EMP: 3 **EST:** 2011
SALES (est): 165.1K **Privately Held**
SIC: 2869 Mfg Industrial Organic Chemicals

(G-14799)
EMD SERONO INC (DH)
Also Called: EMD Pharmaceuticals
1 Technology Pl (02370-1071)
PHONE.....781 982-9000
James Hoyes, *President*
Rehan Verjee, *President*
Bruce Gaumond, *Principal*
Meeta Gulyani, *Exec VP*
Allene Diaz, *Senior VP*
▲ **EMP:** 625
SQ FT: 60,000
SALES (est): 220.3MM
SALES (corp-wide): 16.4B **Privately Held**
WEB: www.serono.com
SIC: 2834 Mfg Pharmaceutical Preparations
HQ: Merck Serono Sa

Coinsins VD 1267
584 322-000

(G-14800)
EMD SERONO BIOTECH CENTER INC (HQ)
1 Technology Pl (02370-1071)
PHONE.....800 283-8088
James Hoyes, *President*
Dr Steve Arkinstall, *Senior VP*
Dr Thorsten Eickenhorst, *Senior VP*
Devin Smith, *Vice Pres*
Ying Zheng, *Associate Dir*
EMP: 82
SALES (est): 9MM
SALES (corp-wide): 16.4B **Privately Held**
WEB: www.merck.de
SIC: 2834 Mfg Pharmaceutical Preparations
PA: Merck Kg Auf Aktien
Frankfurter Str. 250
Darmstadt 64293
615 172-0

(G-14801)
EMD SERONO HOLDING INC
1 Technology Pl (02370-1071)
PHONE.....781 982-9000
Lisa Costantino, *Principal*
EMP: 31
SALES (est): 197.8K
SALES (corp-wide): 16.4B **Privately Held**
SIC: 2834 Pharmaceutical Preparations
HQ: Emd Serono, Inc.
1 Technology Pl
Rockland MA 02370
781 982-9000

(G-14802)
EMD SERONO RESEARCH INST INC (HQ)
1 Technology Pl (02370-1071)
PHONE.....781 982-9000
James Hoyes, *President*
Steve Arkinstall, *Senior VP*
Thorsten Eickenhorst, *Senior VP*
Devin Smith, *Vice Pres*
Lisa Costantino, *CFO*
EMP: 20
SALES (est): 7.4MM
SALES (corp-wide): 16.4B **Privately Held**
SIC: 2834 Mfg Pharmaceutical Preparations
PA: Merck Kg Auf Aktien
Frankfurter Str. 250
Darmstadt 64293
615 172-0

(G-14803)
FLINT GROUP US LLC
45 Reservoir Park Dr (02370-1056)
PHONE.....781 763-0600
Glenn Hicks, *Branch Mgr*
Steve Doherty, *Manager*
EMP: 19
SALES (corp-wide): 2.6MM **Privately Held**
SIC: 2893 Mfg Printing Ink
HQ: Flint Group Us Llc
17177 N Laurel Park Dr # 300
Livonia MI 48152
734 781-4600

(G-14804)
GTA-NHT INC (HQ)
Also Called. Venture Tape
30 Commerce Rd (02370-1053)
PHONE.....781 331-5900
Mark Hurowitz, *President*
Manuel Pardo, *Treasurer*
Gerry Mc Govern, *VP Finance*
M M Dai, *Admin Sec*
◆ **EMP:** 180
SQ FT: 134,000
SALES (est): 55.4MM
SALES (corp-wide): 32.7B **Publicly Held**
SIC: 2672 3842 2671 2295 Mfg Coat/Laminated Paper Mfg Surgical Appliances Mfg Packaging Paper/Film Mfg Coated Fabrics Narrow Fabric Mill
PA: 3m Company
3m Center
Saint Paul MN 55144
651 733-1110

(G-14805)
H H ARNOLD CO INC
529 Liberty St (02370-1239)
P.O. Box 526 (02370-0526)
PHONE.....781 878-0346
William Arnold, *President*
John B Arnold, *President*
William G Arnold, *President*
Richard Arnold, *Vice Pres*
EMP: 25 **EST:** 1902
SQ FT: 36,000
SALES: 2MM **Privately Held**
WEB: www.hharnold.com
SIC: 3599 Mfg Industrial Machinery

(G-14806)
HAULAWAY DUMPSTER DISPOSAL
800 Hingham St (02370-1074)
PHONE.....781 871-1234
EMP: 5
SALES (est): 425.8K **Privately Held**
SIC: 3443 Mfg Fabricated Plate Work

(G-14807)
ICE EFFECTS
83 E Water St Ste 15 (02370-1834)
PHONE.....781 871-7070
Steve Rose, *Owner*
EMP: 4
SALES (est): 258K **Privately Held**
SIC: 2024 Mfg Ice Cream/Frozen Desert

(G-14808)
ILLINOIS TOOL WORKS INC
ITW Tacc
56 Air Station Indus Park (02370-1138)
PHONE.....781 878-7015
Craig Waters, *Principal*
Jim Dube, *Prdtn Mgr*
Carlos Deandrade, *Manager*
EMP: 93
SALES (corp-wide): 14.7B **Publicly Held**
SIC: 2891 Mfg Adhesives/Sealants
PA: Illinois Tool Works Inc.
155 Harlem Ave
Glenview IL 60025
847 724-7500

(G-14809)
ITW PLYMERS SALANTS N AMER INC
56 Air Station Indus Park (02370-1138)
PHONE.....781 681-0418
Darla Martin, *Accountant*
EMP: 36
SALES (corp-wide): 1.5B **Publicly Held**
SIC: 2891 Mfg Adhesives/Sealants
HQ: Itw Polymers Sealants North America Inc.
111 S Nursery Rd
Irving TX 75060
972 438-9111

(G-14810)
J JOY ASSOCIATES INC
273 Weymouth St Ste 2 (02370-1143)
PHONE.....781 871-1569
David Joy, *President*
EMP: 5
SQ FT: 3,200
SALES (est): 606K **Privately Held**
SIC: 2752 Lithographic Commercial Printing

(G-14811)
LAMITECH
800 Hingham St Ste 200 (02370-1067)
PHONE.....781 878-7708
Andrew Londergran, *Manager*
EMP: 13
SALES (est): 1MM **Privately Held**
WEB: www.lamitech.com
SIC: 2631 Paperboard Mill

(G-14812)
MASS SIGN & DECAL INC
443 Webster St Ste 2 (02370-1294)
PHONE.....781 878-7446
Thomas P Healy Jr, *President*
EMP: 6
SQ FT: 6,000
SALES (est): 805.3K **Privately Held**
SIC: 3993 1799 5999 2399 Mfg Signs/Ad Specialties Special Trade Contractor

(G-14813)
MERIT MEDICAL SYSTEMS INC (HQ)
1050 Hingham St Fl 1 (02370-1076)
PHONE.....781 681-7900
Fred Lampropoulos, *President*
Arlin Nelson, *COO*
Willard W Hennemann, *Vice Pres*
Kent Stanger, *CFO*
Martin Stephens, *VP Sales*
EMP: 13
SQ FT: 13,000
SALES (est): 1.2MM
SALES (corp-wide): 882.7MM **Publicly Held**
WEB: www.biospheremed.com
SIC: 3841 Mfg Surgical/Medical Instruments
PA: Merit Medical Systems, Inc.
1600 W Merit Pkwy
South Jordan UT 84095
801 253-1600

(G-14814)
MIJA INDUSTRIES INC
11 Commerce Rd Ste C (02370-1080)
PHONE.....781 871-5629
John J Mc Sheffrey, *President*
Michaella Mc Sheffrey, *Vice Pres*
Penny Almeida, *Personnel*
▲ **EMP:** 40
SQ FT: 48,000
SALES (est): 10MM **Privately Held**
SIC: 3823 Mfg Process Control Instruments

(G-14815)
MORSE DIVING INC
199 Weymouth St Ste 4 (02370-1142)
PHONE.....781 733-1511
Kenneth Downey, *President*
Donna Downey, *Vice Pres*
EMP: 5
SALES: 300K **Privately Held**
SIC: 3949 Ret Sporting Goods/Bicycles

(G-14816)
MSC MANUFACTURING INC
12 Industrial Way (02370)
PHONE.....781 888-8587
Elizabeth Nasrey, *President*
Elizabeth Lopez, *President*
Roland Nasrey, *Vice Pres*
EMP: 5
SALES: 600K **Privately Held**
SIC: 3728 Mfg Aircraft Parts/Equipment

(G-14817)
MULTEC COMMUNICATIONS
319 Centre Ave Ste 166 (02370-2613)
PHONE.....781 294-4992
Brian M Stephens, *Owner*
Laura Goherty, *Manager*
EMP: 5
SQ FT: 1,500
SALES: 500K **Privately Held**
WEB: www.rfwiz.com
SIC: 3669 7622 Mfg Communications Equipment Radio/Television Repair

(G-14818)
PARADIGM BIODEVICES INC
800 Hingham St Ste 207s (02370-1079)
P.O. Box 518, Norwell (02061-0518)
PHONE.....781 982-9950
Michael O'Neill, *President*
Susan O'Neill, *Treasurer*
Bob Maloney, *Controller*
Garrett De Borst, *Sales Dir*
EMP: 7
SALES (est): 953.7K **Privately Held**
WEB: www.paradigmbiodevices.com
SIC: 3841 Mfg Surgical/Medical Instruments

(G-14819)
POLYMER CORPORATION (HQ)
Also Called: Polymer Liquid Resin Casting
180 Pleasant St (02370-1229)
PHONE.....781 871-4606
Robert Underwood, *President*
R David Bergonia, *Corp Secy*
Robert L Underwood, *Corp Secy*
James Ryan, *Senior VP*
Joseph S Higdon, *VP Mfg*
▲ **EMP:** 60
SQ FT: 25,000
SALES (est): 18.8MM
SALES (corp-wide): 73.3MM **Privately Held**
WEB: www.polymerdesign.com
SIC: 3089 5162 Mfg Plastic Products Whol Plastic Materials/Shapes
PA: North American Fund Iii, Lp
135 S La Salle St # 3225
Chicago IL 60603
312 332-4950

(G-14820)
PRIOR SCIENTIFIC INC (HQ)
80 Reservoir Park Dr (02370-1062)
PHONE.....781 878-8442
Thomas Freda, *Principal*
Mark Cherwek, *VP Admin*
Jeff Davis, *Engineer*
Suzanne Leary, *Asst Controller*
Dennis Doherty, *Natl Sales Mgr*
EMP: 16
SQ FT: 9,000

GEOGRAPHIC

SALES (est): 2.8MM
SALES (corp-wide): 21.5MM **Privately Held**
WEB: www.prior.com
SIC: 3827 3829 Mfg Optical Instruments/Lenses & Measuring/Controlling Devices
PA: Prior Scientific Instruments Limited
Unit 3-4 Fielding Industrial Estate,
Wilbraham Road
Cambridge CAMBS CB21
122 388-1711

(G-14821)
REGIONAL SPT MEDIA GROUP LLC
Also Called: Hockey Magazine, The
800 Hingham St (02370-1074)
PHONE..................................781 871-9271
EMP: 9
SALES: 600K **Privately Held**
SIC: 2721 Magazine Publishing

(G-14822)
ROCKLAND EQUIPMENT COMPANY LLC
171 Vfw Dr (02370-1129)
PHONE..................................781 871-4400
Robert Delmonico,
Derek Delmonico,
EMP: 10
SALES (est): 1.3MM **Privately Held**
SIC: 3531 Mfg Construction Machinery

(G-14823)
RUSSARD INC
160 Pleasant St (02370-1272)
PHONE..................................781 986-4545
Donna White, *President*
Steven White, *Principal*
EMP: 15
SQ FT: 10,000
SALES (est): 1.9MM **Privately Held**
WEB: www.russard.com
SIC: 3599 Mfg Industrial Machinery

(G-14824)
SERONO INC
1 Technology Pl (02370-1071)
PHONE..................................781 681-2137
Dawne Green, *Principal*
EMP: 10
SALES (est): 1.7MM **Privately Held**
SIC: 2834 Mfg Pharmaceutical Preparations

(G-14825)
SERONO LABORATORIES INC
1 Technology Pl (02370-1071)
PHONE..................................781 681-2288
EMP: 79
SALES (est): 501.5K
SALES (corp-wide): 18B **Privately Held**
SIC: 2834 Mfg Pharmaceutical Preparations
HQ: Emd Serono, Inc.
1 Technology Pl
Rockland MA 02370
781 982-9000

(G-14826)
SOUTHSTERN MTAL FBRICATORS INC
Air Station Industrial Pa (02370)
P.O. Box 362 (02370-0362)
PHONE..................................781 878-1505
Russell J Anderson III, *President*
Elio D Roffo, *Vice Pres*
Ronald Mavilia, *Treasurer*
EMP: 30
SQ FT: 80,000
SALES (est): 5.9MM **Privately Held**
WEB: www.southeasternmetal.com
SIC: 3446 3441 Mfg Architectural Metalwork Structural Metal Fabrication

(G-14827)
SSIDM INC
800 Hingham St Ste 200 (02370-1067)
P.O. Box 453, Marshfield Hills (02051-0453)
PHONE..................................781 871-7677
Leslie A Jones, *President*
EMP: 5
SQ FT: 700
SALES (est): 470K **Privately Held**
SIC: 3822 Mfg Environmental Controls

(G-14828)
STATIC TECHNOLOGIES CORP
Also Called: Static Control
138 Weymouth St (02370-1136)
PHONE..................................781 871-8962
EMP: 12
SQ FT: 14,000
SALES (est): 850K **Privately Held**
WEB: www.static-tech.com
SIC: 3822 Mfg Environmental Controls

(G-14829)
T & T MACHINE PRODUCTS INC
254 Beech St (02370-2749)
P.O. Box 430 (02370-0430)
PHONE..................................781 878-3861
Anthony F Muscillo, *President*
Thomas Brown, *Treasurer*
EMP: 10
SALES (est): 1.7MM **Privately Held**
WEB: www.ne.mediaone.net
SIC: 3643 3229 3841 Mfg Electronic Connectors Specializing In Cable Connectors And Fiber Optics Strands

(G-14830)
TIMOTHY SILLS
Also Called: Pallet Removal
64 Summer St (02370-2708)
PHONE..................................781 635-8193
Timothy Sills, *Principal*
EMP: 3
SALES (est): 212.5K **Privately Held**
SIC: 2448 Mfg Wood Pallets/Skids

(G-14831)
TUBULAR AUTOMOTIVE & ENGRG
248 Weymouth St (02370-1139)
P.O. Box 279 (02370-0279)
PHONE..................................781 878-9875
Daniel Walker, *President*
David Walker, *Vice Pres*
EMP: 4 **EST:** 1963
SQ FT: 3,000
SALES (est): 370K **Privately Held**
SIC: 3714 Manufactures Exhaust Systems

(G-14832)
UNIVERSAL WILDE INC
403 Vfw Dr (02370-1170)
PHONE..................................781 251-2700
Bob Canzano, *Sales Staff*
Shawn Gill, *Branch Mgr*
EMP: 146 **Privately Held**
WEB: www.mgraphics.net
SIC: 2752 Lithographic Commercial Printing
PA: Universal Wilde, Inc.
26 Dartmouth St Ste 1
Westwood MA 02090

(G-14833)
YOGAPIPE INC
800 Hingham St Ste 200n (02370-1079)
PHONE..................................844 964-2747
Andrew Gallagher, *CEO*
Greg Carr, *President*
EMP: 7 **EST:** 2016
SQ FT: 400
SALES: 3MM **Privately Held**
SIC: 3444 Mfg Sheet Metalwork

Rockport
Essex County

(G-14834)
B/E AEROSPACE INC
31 Pooles Ln (01966-1431)
PHONE..................................978 546-1331
Amin J Khoury, *Ch of Bd*
EMP: 3
SALES (corp-wide): 66.5B **Publicly Held**
SIC: 2531 3728 3647 Manufacturing Aircraft Interior Parts
HQ: B/E Aerospace, Inc.
1400 Corporate Center Way
Wellington FL 33414
561 791-5000

(G-14835)
GREEN HERON HLTH SOLUTIONS INC
47a High St (01966-2103)
PHONE..................................978 309-8118
EMP: 5
SALES: 200K **Privately Held**
SIC: 3841 Mfg Surgical/Medical Instruments

(G-14836)
IMPULSE PACKAGING INC
34 Eden Rd (01966-2335)
PHONE..................................401 434-5588
EMP: 20
SQ FT: 2,000
SALES (est): 3MM **Privately Held**
SIC: 3469 5944 Mfg Metal Stampings Ret Jewelry

Roslindale
Suffolk County

(G-14837)
ALEXS UGLY SAUCE LLC
57 Prospect Ave (02131-2625)
P.O. Box 302262, Jamaica Plain (02130-0048)
PHONE..................................617 300-0180
A M Bourgeois, *Mng Member*
Alexander M Bourgeois, *Mng Member*
EMP: 3
SALES (est): 210.5K **Privately Held**
SIC: 2035 Mfg Pickles/Sauces/Dressing

(G-14838)
HARVEY BRAVMAN
Also Called: Advanced Digital Replication
4394 Washington St (02131-3422)
PHONE..................................617 323-9969
Harvey Bravman, *Owner*
EMP: 3
SALES: 1.5MM **Privately Held**
WEB: www.mediareplication.com
SIC: 3652 Mfg Compact Discs

(G-14839)
MYSDISPENSERS INC
511 Beech St (02131-4904)
PHONE..................................617 327-1124
Yury Sherman, *Principal*
EMP: 7 **EST:** 2015
SALES (est): 420K **Privately Held**
SIC: 3089 Mfg Plastic Products

(G-14840)
NOLAS FRESH FOODS LLC
99 Walter St (02131-1504)
PHONE..................................617 283-2644
Sherie L Grillon, *Principal*
EMP: 3
SALES (est): 293.4K **Privately Held**
SIC: 2099 5812 Mfg Food Preparations Eating Place

(G-14841)
PETER GALBERT
7 Gardenside St (02131-3710)
PHONE..................................978 660-5580
Peter Galbert, *Chairman*
EMP: 3
SALES (est): 283K **Privately Held**
SIC: 2511 Mfg Wood Household Furniture

(G-14842)
PURITAN ICECREAM INC
3895 Washington St (02131-1221)
PHONE..................................617 524-7500
Steve Rando, *Manager*
EMP: 5
SALES (est): 494.3K **Privately Held**
SIC: 2024 Mfg Ice Cream/Frozen Desert

(G-14843)
SIGN POST LLC
4190 Washington St (02131-1731)
PHONE..................................617 469-4400
Richard S Caplan,
Barbara L Caplan,
EMP: 3
SALES: 196.2K **Privately Held**
SIC: 3993 5099 Mfg Signs/Advertising Specialties Whol Durable Goods

(G-14844)
W & G GAS SERVICES LLC
103 Mount Hope St (02131)
PHONE..................................617 327-2515
Jaquiline Darajani,
EMP: 5
SALES (est): 131.6K **Privately Held**
SIC: 1389 Oil/Gas Field Services

(G-14845)
W C CANNIFF & SONS INC
Also Called: Canniff Monument
531 Cummins Hwy (02131-3943)
P.O. Box 170065, Boston (02117-0074)
PHONE..................................617 323-3690
Edward C Canniff Jr, *President*
EMP: 15
SALES (corp-wide): 1.1MM **Privately Held**
WEB: www.canniffmonuments.com
SIC: 3281 Mfg Cut Stone/Products
PA: W C Canniff & Sons Inc
531 Cummins Hwy
Boston MA 02131
617 323-3690

Rowley
Essex County

(G-14846)
BETTER MAINTENANCE SHEET METAL
48 Railroad Ave (01969-1206)
P.O. Box 35 (01969-0035)
PHONE..................................978 948-7067
Gerard St Jacques, *Owner*
EMP: 5
SALES (est): 414.4K **Privately Held**
SIC: 3444 Mfg Sheet Metalwork

(G-14847)
CAPCO CRANE & HOIST INC
58 Forest Ridge Dr (01969-2143)
PHONE..................................978 948-2998
Anthony Caputo III, *President*
James G Couturier, *Treasurer*
David F Caputo, *Admin Sec*
▲ **EMP:** 24
SQ FT: 12,000
SALES (est): 10.6MM **Privately Held**
WEB: www.capcocrane.com
SIC: 3536 Mfg Hoists/Cranes/Monorails

(G-14848)
CAPONE IRON CORPORATION
20 Turcotte Memorial Dr (01969-1706)
P.O. Box 706 (01969-3706)
PHONE..................................978 948-8000
Stephen J Capone, *President*
Gary D Capone, *Vice Pres*
EMP: 35
SQ FT: 33,000
SALES (est): 10.1MM **Privately Held**
SIC: 3441 Structural Metal Fabrication

(G-14849)
CASSIDY BROS FORGE INC
282 Newburyport Tpke (01969-2009)
PHONE..................................978 948-7303
Maurice Cassidy, *President*
Peter Cassidy, *Vice Pres*
Vincent Paul Cassidy, *Vice Pres*
EMP: 20
SQ FT: 15,000
SALES (est): 3.5MM **Privately Held**
SIC: 3446 Mfg Architectural Metalwork

(G-14850)
CHASSIS ENGINEERING LLC
445 Newburyport Tpke (01969-1728)
PHONE..................................978 948-0826
Edmund Berk Jr,
Leanne Berk,
Richard Gilbert,
June Peterson,
EMP: 14
SQ FT: 12,800
SALES: 1MM **Privately Held**
WEB: www.chassis-engineering.com
SIC: 3679 Mfg Electronic Components

(G-14851)
CHOICE GRAPHICS INC
140 Central St Ste 4 (01969-1327)
PHONE..................................978 948-2789
Jon Keith Harris, *President*
Christina Harris, *Vice Pres*
Keith Harris, *Bd of Directors*
EMP: 7
SQ FT: 2,400
SALES (est): 1MM **Privately Held**
WEB: www.partnerwithchoice.com
SIC: 2752 Commercial Offset Printing

(G-14852)
DEFIANCE GRAPHICS CORP
140 Central St (01969-1301)
P.O. Box 313 (01969-0783)
PHONE..................................978 948-2789
Paul Tardiff, *President*
Beverly Tardiff, *Vice Pres*
EMP: 10
SQ FT: 6,000
SALES (est): 947.1K **Privately Held**
SIC: 2759 2752 Commercial Printing Lithographic Commercial Printing

(G-14853)
F L C MACHINED PRODUCTS CO
47 Main St (01969-1803)
PHONE..................................978 948-7525
Jeffrey Carnevale, *President*
Frederick L Carnevale, *Treasurer*
EMP: 5
SQ FT: 4,000
SALES (est): 450K **Privately Held**
SIC: 3599 Job Machine Shop

(G-14854)
GENERAL PRODUCTS & GEAR CORP
Also Called: GP&g
120 Haverhill St (01969-2112)
PHONE..................................978 948-8146
Quinton Schaffer, *President*
EMP: 8 **EST:** 1952
SQ FT: 15,000
SALES (est): 600K **Privately Held**
WEB: www.gpgc.com
SIC: 3599 Industrial Machinery

(G-14855)
KNEELAND BROS INC
51 Wethersfield St (01969-1715)
PHONE..................................978 948-3919
Roy D Kneeland, *President*
EMP: 15 **EST:** 1962
SQ FT: 1,000
SALES (est): 1.5MM **Privately Held**
SIC: 2091 Mfg Canned/Cured Fish/Seafood

(G-14856)
MARDON MANUFACTURING COMPANY
237r Main St (01969-1502)
PHONE..................................978 948-7040
Donald Thurston, *Owner*
EMP: 3
SALES (est): 50K **Privately Held**
WEB: www.mardonmfg.com
SIC: 3541 Mfg Machine Tools-Cutting

(G-14857)
MICHELL INSTRUMENTS INC
319 Newburyport Tpke # 207 (01969-1754)
P.O. Box 11241, Hauppauge NY (11788-0703)
PHONE..................................978 484-0005
Nigel Futter, *President*
Melissa Ambrose, *Corp Secy*
Daniel Kot, *Engineer*
EMP: 6
SALES (est): 1.6MM
SALES (corp-wide): 177.9K **Privately Held**
WEB: www.michell.com/us
SIC: 3823 Mfg Process Control Instruments
HQ: Michell Instruments Limited
Unit 48 Lancaster Way Business Park
Ely CAMBS CB6 3
135 365-8000

(G-14858)
MILACRON MARKETING COMPANY LLC
428 Newburyport Tpke (01969-1761)
PHONE..................................978 238-7100
Steven Morris, *General Mgr*
EMP: 30 **Publicly Held**
SIC: 3089 Mfg Plastic Products
HQ: Milacron Marketing Company Llc
4165 Half Acre Rd
Batavia OH 45103

(G-14859)
MODERN HERITAGE LLC
237 Wethersfield St (01969-1710)
PHONE..................................781 913-8261
Steve Slade, *Principal*
EMP: 4 **EST:** 2015
SALES (est): 421.8K **Privately Held**
SIC: 2431 Mfg Millwork

(G-14860)
MVK SILT SOCK
250 Main St (01969-1512)
PHONE..................................978 204-9483
Micheal Kovalchuk, *President*
EMP: 5 **EST:** 2013
SALES (est): 229.8K **Privately Held**
SIC: 2252 Mfg Hosiery

(G-14861)
NORTHEAST METALS TECH LLC
289 Newburyport Tpke (01969-2008)
PHONE..................................978 948-2633
Anthony J Bowes,
EMP: 8
SALES (est): 1MM **Privately Held**
SIC: 3398 Metal Heat Treating

(G-14862)
OCEAN LURES LLC
4 Ice Pond Dr (01969-2337)
PHONE..................................978 618-1982
Paul Rogato, *Principal*
EMP: 3
SALES (est): 168.9K **Privately Held**
SIC: 3949 Mfg Sporting/Athletic Goods

(G-14863)
RAMCO MACHINE LLC
27 Turcotte Memorial Dr (01969-1706)
PHONE..................................978 948-3778
Brian M Goodwin, *Office Mgr*
Randolph Jezowski,
Carolyn Jezowski,
Mike Jezowski,
EMP: 29
SQ FT: 24,000
SALES (est): 6MM **Privately Held**
SIC: 3541 Mfg Machine Tools-Cutting

(G-14864)
ROWLEY READY MIX INC
Also Called: Rowley Concrete
84 Central St (01969-1701)
P.O. Box 321 (01969-0771)
PHONE..................................978 948-2544
Downey H Shea Jr, *President*
EMP: 15 **EST:** 1948
SQ FT: 500
SALES (est): 2.8MM **Privately Held**
SIC: 3273 5211 Mfg Ready-Mixed Concrete Ret Lumber/Building Materials

(G-14865)
S M B MACHINE CO
79 Boxford Rd (01969-2419)
PHONE..................................978 948-7624
Stephen Blunda, *Owner*
EMP: 3
SALES (est): 319.9K **Privately Held**
SIC: 3599 Machine Shop

(G-14866)
SERIGRAPHICS UNLIMITED
108 Newburyport Tpke (01969-2135)
PHONE..................................978 356-4896
Richard Scott, *Owner*
EMP: 6
SQ FT: 3,600
SALES (est): 501.5K **Privately Held**
SIC: 2262 2791 2396 Manmade Fiber & Silk Finishing Plant Typesetting Services Mfg Auto/Apparel Trimming

(G-14867)
TOWN COMMON INC
77 Wethersfield St (01969-1713)
PHONE..................................978 948-8696
Marc Malazalli, *President*
EMP: 10
SQ FT: 2,287
SALES (est): 479.8K **Privately Held**
SIC: 2711 Newspapers-Publishing/Printing

(G-14868)
WINFREYS OLDE ENGLISH FDGE INC (PA)
Also Called: Winfrey's Fudge & Candy
40 Newburyport Tpke Ste 1 (01969-2106)
PHONE..................................978 948-7448
Christine Winfrey, *President*
Stuart Winfrey, *Treasurer*
EMP: 16
SQ FT: 10,000
SALES: 1.2MM **Privately Held**
WEB: www.winfreys.com
SIC: 2064 2066 Mfg Candy/Confectionery Mfg Chocolate/Cocoa Products

(G-14869)
WINNINGHOFF BOATS INC
55 Warehouse Ln (01969-1508)
PHONE..................................978 948-2314
Jack Winninghoff, *President*
Warren C Jepson, *Vice Pres*
EMP: 10 **EST:** 1976
SQ FT: 7,500
SALES: 1MM **Privately Held**
WEB: www.winninghoff.com
SIC: 3732 Boatbuilding & Repairing

Roxbury
Suffolk County

(G-14870)
BULLY BOY DISTILLERS
35 Cedric St (02119-3001)
PHONE..................................617 442-6000
David Saltonstall Willis, *Principal*
▲ **EMP:** 3
SALES (est): 331.8K **Privately Held**
SIC: 2085 Mfg Distilled/Blended Liquor

(G-14871)
CITY FRESH FOODS INC
69 Shirley St (02119-3066)
P.O. Box 255698, Uphams Corner (02125-5698)
PHONE..................................617 606-7123
Sheldon Lloyd, *CEO*
EMP: 80
SALES (est): 4.9MM **Privately Held**
SIC: 2099 Mfg Food Preparations

(G-14872)
CITY FRESH FOODS INC
77 Shirley St (02119-3035)
P.O. Box 255698, Uphams Corner (02125-5698)
PHONE..................................617 606-7123
Glynn Lloyd, *President*
Sheldon Lloyd, *Vice Pres*
EMP: 80
SQ FT: 150,000
SALES (est): 12.4MM **Privately Held**
WEB: www.cityfreshfoods.com
SIC: 2099 Mfg Food Preparations

(G-14873)
JEAN CHARLES BLONDINE
Also Called: Delice
28 Mount Pleasant Ave (02119-3348)
PHONE..................................857 247-9369
Blondine Jean Charles, *Owner*
EMP: 5
SALES (est): 159.1K **Privately Held**
SIC: 2051 Mfg Bread/Related Products

(G-14874)
LIBERTY CONSTRUCTION SVCS LLC
65 Allerton St (02119-2901)
PHONE..................................617 602-4001
Kevin Chin, *President*
Robert Arcari, *Superintendent*
Brett Szabo, *COO*
Marshall Felix, *Vice Pres*
He Jeanette, *Vice Pres*
EMP: 80
SALES (est): 33.4MM **Privately Held**
SIC: 1389 Oil/Gas Field Services

(G-14875)
PHOTON BOUNCE
19 Elmore St (02119-3625)
PHONE..................................617 708-1231
Gina Brooks, *Principal*
EMP: 3
SALES (est): 152.5K **Privately Held**
SIC: 3661 Mfg Telephone/Telegraph Apparatus

Royalston
Worcester County

(G-14876)
QUABBIN INC
11 Falls Rd (01368-8927)
PHONE..................................978 249-8891
Tom Leboeuf, *Owner*
EMP: 3
SALES (est): 167.7K **Privately Held**
SIC: 3599 Mfg Industrial Machinery

Russell
Hampden County

(G-14877)
COUNTRYSIDE WOODCRAFT
665 Huntington Rd (01071-9525)
P.O. Box 439 (01071-0439)
PHONE..................................413 862-3276
Jerald Reinford, *Partner*
Ronald Hess, *Partner*
EMP: 18
SQ FT: 13,580
SALES (est): 2.1MM **Privately Held**
SIC: 2511 Mfg Wood Household Furniture

(G-14878)
SCAPIN SAND & GRAVEL INC
260 Blandford Rd (01071-9777)
PHONE..................................413 568-0091
Anthony Scapin, *Principal*
EMP: 6 **EST:** 2008
SALES (est): 471.3K **Privately Held**
SIC: 1442 Construction Sand/Gravel

Rutland
Worcester County

(G-14879)
AL WOODWORKING
173 Pleasantdale Rd (01543-1231)
PHONE..................................508 886-2883
Andre Louis G Larose, *Principal*
EMP: 4
SALES (est): 357.9K **Privately Held**
SIC: 2431 Mfg Millwork

(G-14880)
BRIGGS LUMBER PRODUCTS
336 E County Rd (01543-2034)
P.O. Box 203 (01543-0203)
PHONE..................................508 886-2054
EMP: 11
SQ FT: 10,000
SALES (est): 1.1MM **Privately Held**
SIC: 2448 Mfg Wood Pallets/Skids

(G-14881)
FIRST PLACE WELDING INC
Also Called: Towbandit
183 E County Rd (01543-2061)
PHONE..................................508 886-4762
Christopher R Curtis, *President*
Chris Curtis, *Principal*
Jaime Tice, *Vice Pres*
EMP: 6
SALES (est): 1.1MM **Privately Held**
SIC: 7692 Welding Repair

(G-14882)
JLP SERVICES INC
6 Kenwood Dr (01543-1215)
PHONE..................................508 667-5498
Jennifer Petrila, *President*
◆ **EMP:** 3
SALES: 65K **Privately Held**
SIC: 3441 Structural Metal Fabrication

Sagamore
Barnstable County

(G-14883)
BAE SYSTEMS TECH SOL SRVC INC
1 Flat Rock Hill Rd (02561-5000)
P.O. Box 305 (02561-0305)
PHONE..................................508 833-9562
EMP: 5
SALES (corp-wide): 22.1B **Privately Held**
SIC: 3812 Mfg Search/Navigation Equipment
HQ: Bae Systems Technology Solutions & Services Inc.
520 Gaither Rd
Rockville MD 20850
703 847-5820

(G-14884)
NATUREX-DBS LLC
Also Called: Fruitaceuticals
39 Pleasant St (02561)
PHONE..................................774 247-0022
Douglas Klaiber,
EMP: 6
SALES (est): 893.1K **Privately Held**
SIC: 2833 Mfg Medicinal/Botanical Products
HQ: Naturex Inc.
375 Huyler St
South Hackensack NJ 07606
201 440-5000

Sagamore Beach
Barnstable County

(G-14885)
CREATIVE HYDRONICS INTL INC
Also Called: Neatheat
42 Diandy Rd (02562-2422)
PHONE..................................508 524-3535
Craig Coe, *President*
EMP: 3 **EST:** 2010
SALES (est): 449.7K **Privately Held**
SIC: 3433 5074 Mfg Heating Equipment-Nonelectric Whol Plumbing Equipment/Supplies

(G-14886)
PUBLISHERS DESIGN & PROD SVCS
349 Old Plymouth Rd (02562-2367)
P.O. Box 1480 (02562-1480)
PHONE..................................508 833-8300
Mark Bergeron, *President*
Peter Chamberlain, *Sales Staff*
EMP: 12 **EST:** 1988
SALES (est): 630K **Privately Held**
WEB: www.pdps.com
SIC: 2791 7338 7336 Typesetting Services Secretarial/Court Reporting Commercial Art/Graphic Design

(G-14887)
SOUTHEASTERN MILLWORK CO INC
150 State Rd (02562)
PHONE..................................508 888-6038
Charles S Cooper, *Principal*
Tom Duggan, *Treasurer*
EMP: 13
SALES (est): 1.6MM **Privately Held**
SIC: 2431 Mfg Millwork

Salem
Essex County

(G-14888)
3 POTATO 4 LLC
Also Called: 3p4
2 E India Square Mall (01970-3700)
PHONE..................................978 744-0948
EMP: 3
SALES (est): 230.6K **Privately Held**
SIC: 2096 Mfg Potato Chips/Snacks

(G-14889)
ACCUPROBE CORPORATION
35 Congress St Ste 201 (01970-7315)
PHONE..................................978 745-7878
Madhukar Reddy, *Branch Mgr*
EMP: 25
SQ FT: 7,000
SALES (corp-wide): 103.9K **Privately Held**
SIC: 3674 Mfg Semiconductors/Related Devices
PA: Accuprobe Corporation
5 Eliot Rd
Lexington MA
-

(G-14890)
AMERICAL SERGICAL COMPANY
45 Congress St (01970-5579)
PHONE..................................781 592-7200
Barbara Greenspan, *Treasurer*
EMP: 8
SALES (est): 623.5K **Privately Held**
SIC: 3842 Mfg Surgical Appliances/Supplies

(G-14891)
AMERICAN SURGICAL COMPANY LLC
45 Congress St Ste 153 (01970-5998)
PHONE..................................781 592-7200
Geoff Piasio, *Sales Staff*
Sasha Sylvia, *Office Mgr*
Roger Piasio, *Mng Member*
Erik Piasio,
EMP: 50
SQ FT: 11,000
SALES (est): 9.7MM **Privately Held**
SIC: 3842 Mfg Surgical/Medical Instruments

(G-14892)
ANTERION THERAPEUTICS INC
1 Loring Ave Ste B117 (01970-4533)
PHONE..................................617 240-0324
Robert Leonard, *CEO*
EMP: 3 **EST:** 2008
SALES (est): 240K **Privately Held**
SIC: 2834 Mfg Pharmaceutical Preparations/ Research

(G-14893)
APOGEE MACHINING SERVICES INC
97 Canal St (01970-4839)
PHONE..................................978 740-4689
James J Brown, *President*
▼ **EMP:** 5
SQ FT: 4,000
SALES (est): 613.9K **Privately Held**
SIC: 3599 Machine Shop

(G-14894)
ATLANTIS WOODWORKING INC
283 Derby St (01970-3600)
PHONE..................................978 745-5312
Michael Lowe, *President*
David Valcovic, *Clerk*
EMP: 3
SQ FT: 1,200
SALES (est): 323.5K **Privately Held**
SIC: 2431 Custom Woodworking

(G-14895)
ATOMIC CAFE (PA)
45 Mason St Ste 1 (01970-2266)
PHONE..................................978 910-0489
Andrew Mahoney, *Principal*
EMP: 15
SALES (est): 1.8MM **Privately Held**
SIC: 2095 Mfg Roasted Coffee

(G-14896)
AUTODESK INC
120 Washington St Ste 202 (01970-3545)
PHONE..................................855 646-4868
Don Henrich, *Branch Mgr*
EMP: 38
SALES (corp-wide): 2.5B **Publicly Held**
SIC: 7372 Prepackaged Software Services
PA: Autodesk, Inc.
111 Mcinnis Pkwy
San Rafael CA 94903
415 507-5000

(G-14897)
BEMATEK SYSTEMS INC
96 Swampscott Rd Ste 7 (01970-7004)
P.O. Box 264, Beverly (01915-0005)
PHONE..................................978 744-5816
David R Ekstrom, *President*
Elizabeth Ekstrom, *Vice Pres*
EMP: 5 **EST:** 1981
SQ FT: 11,000
SALES: 700K **Privately Held**
WEB: www.bematek.com
SIC: 3556 Mfg Food Products Machinery

(G-14898)
BRISTOL BAY LLC
70 Washington St Ste 310 (01970-3520)
PHONE..................................978 744-4272
George C Vernet, *Principal*
EMP: 8 **EST:** 2016
SALES (est): 865.1K **Privately Held**
SIC: 2621 Paper Mill

(G-14899)
BURNHAM ASSOCIATES INC
14 Franklin St (01970-2504)
PHONE..................................978 745-1788
Craig Burnham, *President*
Cindy Burnham, *Treasurer*
Cynthia Burnham, *Treasurer*
EMP: 15
SALES: 2MM **Privately Held**
WEB: www.burnhamassociates.com
SIC: 3944 1629 Mfg Games/Toys Heavy Construction

(G-14900)
CABOT HERITAGE CORP
Also Called: Cabot Market Letter
176 North St (01970-1648)
P.O. Box 2049 (01970-6249)
PHONE..................................978 745-5532
Timothy W Lutts, *President*
EMP: 20
SQ FT: 2,000
SALES (est): 1.7MM **Privately Held**
WEB: www.cabot.net
SIC: 2721 Newsletter Publishing

(G-14901)
CAPTAIN DUSTYS ICE CREAM
143 Derby St (01970-5639)
PHONE..................................978 744-0777
Lisa Barlett, *Owner*
EMP: 4 **EST:** 2010
SALES (est): 194.3K **Privately Held**
SIC: 2024 Mfg Ice Cream/Frozen Desert

(G-14902)
COLONIAL KEY & ENGRAVING
Also Called: Colonial Engravers
1 Florence St Ste 2 (01970-4977)
PHONE..................................978 745-8237
Paul Connely, *Partner*
EMP: 4
SALES (est): 418.2K **Privately Held**
WEB: www.colonialengravers.com
SIC: 2759 5947 Commercial Printing Ret Gifts/Novelties

(G-14903)
CREATIVE INK
Also Called: AlphaGraphics
167 Boston St (01970-1430)
PHONE..................................978 741-2244
Fax: 978 740-0501
EMP: 4
SALES (est): 178.6K **Privately Held**
SIC: 2752 Comm Prtg Litho

(G-14904)
CROW HAVEN CORNER INC
125 Essex St (01970-3706)
PHONE..................................978 745-8763
Laurie Stathopoulos, *Principal*
EMP: 4
SALES (est): 230.6K **Privately Held**
SIC: 3999 Mfg Misc Products

(G-14905)
DEACON GILES INC
75 Canal St (01970-4886)
PHONE..................................781 883-8256
Ian Hunter, *CEO*
Dawn McDonald, *Mng Member*
EMP: 7
SALES (est): 619K **Privately Held**
SIC: 2085 Mfg Distilled/Blended Liquor

(G-14906)
DESIGN COPY PRINTERS INC
Also Called: Creative Ink
167 Boston St (01970-1430)
PHONE..................................978 741-2244
David Zion, *President*
Beth A Zion, *President*
EMP: 4
SQ FT: 2,200
SALES (est): 42.5K **Privately Held**
SIC: 2752 Lithographic Commercial Printing

(G-14907)
DOYLE SAILMAKERS INC (PA)
96 Swampscott Rd Ste 8 (01970-7004)
PHONE..................................978 740-5950
Robert Doyle, *President*
John Curtis, *Opers Mgr*
Will Pingree, *Prdtn Mgr*
▲ **EMP:** 30 **EST:** 1982
SQ FT: 12,000
SALES (est): 6.2MM **Privately Held**
WEB: www.doylesails.com
SIC: 2394 Mfg Canvas/Related Products

(G-14908)
EAB TESTING INC
27 Congress St Ste 305-18 (01970-5510)
PHONE..................................978 548-7626
Andrew Barnes, *President*
EMP: 3
SALES: 40K **Privately Held**
SIC: 3534 Mfg Elevators/Escalators

(G-14909)
ENDODYNAMIX INC
121 Loring Ave Ste 910 (01970-4491)
PHONE..................................978 740-0400
Pavel Menn, *President*
EMP: 11
SALES (est): 1.1MM
SALES (corp-wide): 859.6MM **Publicly Held**
SIC: 3841 Mfg Surgical/Medical Instruments
PA: Conmed Corporation
525 French Rd
Utica NY 13502
315 797-8375

(G-14910)
EXCELITAS TECHNOLOGIES CORP
35 Congress St Ste 2021 (01970-7314)
PHONE..................................800 775-6786
Jim Roche, *Branch Mgr*
EMP: 150
SALES (corp-wide): 1.2B **Privately Held**
SIC: 3677 3679 Mfg Electronic Coils/Transformers Mfg Electronic Components
HQ: Excelitas Technologies Corp.
200 West St
Waltham MA 02451
-

(G-14911)
FALMER ASSOCIATES INC
Also Called: Falmer Thermal Spray
96 Swampscott Rd Ste 10 (01970-7004)
PHONE..................................978 745-4000
Stacy Ames, *President*
EMP: 5
SQ FT: 7,000

▲ = Import ▼=Export
◆ =Import/Export

SALES: 653K **Privately Held**
WEB: www.falmer.com
SIC: 3479 Metal Coating & Engraving

(G-14912)
FOOTPRINT PWR ACQUISITIONS LLC
24 Fort Ave (01970-5623)
PHONE..................................978 740-8411
Peter Furniss, *Principal*
EMP: 9
SALES (est): 1.1MM **Privately Held**
SIC: 2752 Lithographic Commercial Printing

(G-14913)
G&E STEEL FABRICATORS INC
4 Florence St Unit 5 (01970-4884)
PHONE..................................978 741-0391
Gino Ciasullo, *President*
Anthony Ciasullo, *Project Mgr*
▲ **EMP:** 11
SQ FT: 3,000
SALES (est): 500K **Privately Held**
WEB: www.gandesteel.com
SIC: 3446 Mfg Architectural Metalwork

(G-14914)
GARDNER MATTRESS CORPORATION (PA)
254 Canal St (01970-4596)
PHONE..................................978 744-1810
Gardner P Sisk, *President*
EMP: 16
SQ FT: 20,000
SALES (est): 2.2MM **Privately Held**
WEB: www.gardnermattress.com
SIC: 2515 Mfg Mattresses/Bedsprings

(G-14915)
GILLIANS FOODS INC
45 Congress St Ste 106 (01970-5598)
PHONE..................................781 586-0086
Robert W Otolo, *President*
Bob Otolo, *Principal*
▲ **EMP:** 30
SQ FT: 30,000
SALES: 3MM **Privately Held**
WEB: www.gilliansfoods.com
SIC: 2099 Mfg Food Preparations

(G-14916)
GT ADVANCED TECHNOLOGIES INC
35 Congress St Ste 251 (01970-5592)
PHONE..................................978 498-4294
Jim Roche, *Branch Mgr*
EMP: 4 **Privately Held**
SIC: 3674 Mfg Semiconductors/Related Devices
PA: Gt Advanced Technologies Inc.
5 Wentworth Dr Ste 1
Hudson NH 03051
-

(G-14917)
GTAT CORPORATION
27 Congress St (01970-7309)
PHONE..................................978 745-0088
Hoil Kim, *Vice Pres*
Raja Bal, *CFO*
Leila Penzner,
Tom Gutierrez,
EMP: 27 **EST:** 2010
SALES (est): 412.7K **Privately Held**
SIC: 3827 Mfg Semiconductors/Related Devices
PA: Gt Advanced Technologies Inc.
5 Wentworth Dr Ste 1
Hudson NH 03051
-

(G-14918)
H&H PROPELLER SHOP INC (PA)
0 Essex St (01970-5246)
PHONE..................................978 744-3806
John A Pelletier, *President*
Laurence Martin, *Vice Pres*
William Clemens, *Treasurer*
Robert L Telletier, *Admin Sec*
▲ **EMP:** 50 **EST:** 1951
SALES (est): 7.3MM **Privately Held**
WEB: www.proprecon.com
SIC: 3714 Mfg Motor Vehicle Parts/Accessories

(G-14919)
HENDRICK MANUFACTURING CORP (PA)
32 Commercial St (01970-3917)
PHONE..................................781 631-4400
Daniel P Wiggin, *President*
Jeffrey Grant, *Vice Pres*
Linda K Wiggin, *CFO*
Linda Wiggin, *Treasurer*
Whitney Wiggin, *Mktg Dir*
▲ **EMP:** 19 **EST:** 1952
SQ FT: 10,000
SALES (est): 3.3MM **Privately Held**
WEB: www.hendrickmfg.net
SIC: 3541 2599 3564 Mfg Machine Tools-Cutting Mfg Furniture/Fixtures Mfg Blowers/Fans

(G-14920)
HEX
246 Essex St Frnt (01970-3412)
PHONE..................................978 666-0765
Jay Hexner, *Principal*
EMP: 3
SALES (est): 120K **Privately Held**
SIC: 3999 Mfg Misc Products

(G-14921)
HIGGINSON BOOK COMPANY
10 Colonial Rd (01970-2943)
P.O. Box 778 (01970-0878)
PHONE..................................978 745-7170
Nicole Schulte, *Principal*
EMP: 6 **EST:** 2013
SALES (est): 172.9K **Privately Held**
SIC: 2731 Books-Publishing/Printing

(G-14922)
HOLMES STAMP COMPANY
Also Called: Corporate Connection
128 Margin St (01970-3312)
PHONE..................................978 744-1051
Aimee Noel, *Branch Mgr*
EMP: 6
SALES (corp-wide): 3.2MM **Privately Held**
SIC: 3953 Mfg & Ret Marking Products
PA: Holmes Stamp Company
2021 Saint Augustine Rd E
Jacksonville FL 32207
904 396-2291

(G-14923)
JACQUELINES WHOLESALE BKY INC
Also Called: Jacquelines Gourmet Cookies
96 Swampscott Rd Ste 1 (01970-7004)
PHONE..................................978 744-8600
Marc Hazel, *President*
Keith Knearem, *Plant Mgr*
Maria Bourguignon, *Purch Mgr*
Lucille Freddo, *QC Mgr*
Alexandra Libby, *Research*
EMP: 85 **EST:** 2000
SQ FT: 150,000
SALES (est): 35.8MM **Privately Held**
WEB: www.jacquelinesbakery.com
SIC: 2051 Mfg Bread/Related Products

(G-14924)
JD SOFTWARE INC
27 Congress St Ste 505 (01970-5523)
PHONE..................................888 419-9998
Lhassan Oubala, *President*
Matthew Poussard, *Software Engr*
EMP: 9
SQ FT: 3,000
SALES: 750K **Privately Held**
SIC: 7372 Prepackaged Software Services

(G-14925)
JEWISH JOURNAL
Also Called: Journal Jewish
27 Congress St Ste 501 (01970-5577)
PHONE..................................978 745-4111
Yulia Zhorov, *Editor*
Marcy Grand, *Accounts Exec*
Lois Kaplan, *Sales Staff*
Gerald Posner, *Supervisor*
EMP: 10
SALES: 612.7K **Privately Held**
WEB: www.jewishjournal.org
SIC: 2711 Newspapers-Publishing/Printing

(G-14926)
JPH GRAPHICS LLC
Also Called: Shirts Illustrated
87 Canal St (01970-4839)
PHONE..................................978 744-7873
Julie Lazzaro,
EMP: 6
SQ FT: 6,000
SALES: 500K **Privately Held**
SIC: 2396 2395 5699 Custom Screen Printing & Embroidering & Ret Sportswear

(G-14927)
KERR LEATHERS INC
63 Jefferson Ave (01970-2956)
PHONE..................................978 852-0660
Hugh Kerr, *Owner*
▲ **EMP:** 20
SALES (est): 2MM **Privately Held**
WEB: www.kerrleathers.com
SIC: 3199 5137 5139 Mfg Leather Goods Whol Women/Child Clothng

(G-14928)
MALIK EMBOSSING CORP
28 Varney St (01970-1932)
PHONE..................................978 745-6060
Frank Malik, *President*
▲ **EMP:** 5
SQ FT: 20,000
SALES (est): 420K **Privately Held**
SIC: 3111 6531 Leather Embosser

(G-14929)
MIXFIT INC
26 Aborn St (01970-1104)
PHONE..................................617 902-8082
Reza Zanjani, *President*
Ashfin Islam, *Vice Pres*
EMP: 7 **EST:** 2015
SALES (est): 172.6K **Privately Held**
SIC: 7372 Prepackaged Software Services

(G-14930)
MOST CARDIO INCORPORATED
121 Loring Ave Ste 600 (01970-4475)
PHONE..................................978 594-1614
Henri De Guillebon, *Principal*
EMP: 3 **EST:** 2012
SALES (est): 323.7K **Privately Held**
SIC: 3841 Mfg Surgical/Medical Instruments

(G-14931)
MOSTMED INC
Also Called: Interdynamics
121 Loring Ave Ste 920 (01970-4474)
PHONE..................................978 740-0400
Pavel Menn, *CEO*
Bill Bookwalltei, *Ch of Bd*
EMP: 5
SALES (est): 651.4K **Privately Held**
SIC: 3491 Mfg Industrial Valves

(G-14932)
NORTH SHORE JEWISH PRESS LTD
Also Called: Jewish Journal, The
27 Congress St Ste 501 (01970-5577)
PHONE..................................978 745-4111
Izzy Adams, *President*
EMP: 10
SALES: 603.6K **Privately Held**
SIC: 2711 Newspapers-Publishing/Printing

(G-14933)
OLSEN & SILK ABRASIVES
35 Congress St (01970-5529)
P.O. Box 8467 (01971-8467)
PHONE..................................978 744-4720
Peter Silk, *Partner*
EMP: 4
SQ FT: 3,000 **Privately Held**
SIC: 3291 Mfg Tungsten Carbide Abrasives

(G-14934)
PAGE STREET PUBLISHING COMPANY
27 Congress St Ste 105 (01970-5577)
PHONE..................................978 594-8758
William Kiester, *Principal*
Sarah Monroe, *Editor*
Elizabeth Seise, *Editor*
Thomas Frank, *Prdtn Dir*
Pattianne Folta, *CFO*
◆ **EMP:** 13
SALES: 2MM **Privately Held**
SIC: 2731 Books-Publishing/Printing

(G-14935)
PIRATE DOG BRAND LLC
4 Florence St Unit 3 (01970-4884)
PHONE..................................978 745-4786
Eric G Glass, *Principal*
EMP: 7
SALES (est): 481.8K **Privately Held**
SIC: 2085 Mfg Distilled/Blended Liquor

(G-14936)
POWELL AND MAHONEY LLC
39 Norman St (01970-3380)
PHONE..................................978 745-4332
Mark E Mahoney, *Principal*
EMP: 6 **EST:** 2012
SALES (est): 430.6K **Privately Held**
SIC: 2087 Mfg Flavor Extracts/Syrup

(G-14937)
PULEOS DAIRY
376 Highland Ave (01970-1744)
PHONE..................................978 590-7611
Charles Puleo Jr, *Owner*
EMP: 3
SQ FT: 2,400
SALES (est): 243.9K **Privately Held**
WEB: www.puleosdairy.com
SIC: 2026 2024 Mfg Fluid Milk Mfg Ice Cream/Frozen Desert

(G-14938)
ROBERT MURPHY
10 Colonial Rd Ste 5 (01970-2943)
PHONE..................................978 745-7170
Robert Murphy, *Owner*
▲ **EMP:** 35
SALES (est): 1.8MM **Privately Held**
WEB: www.higginsonbooks.com
SIC: 2731 2789 2752 Books-Publishing/Printing Bookbinding/Related Work Lithographic Commercial Printing

(G-14939)
ROLLS BATTERY OF NEW ENGLAND
7 Oak St (01970-2219)
PHONE..................................978 745-3333
Joseph McGinnis, *Partner*
Dana Shorey, *Partner*
EMP: 5
SQ FT: 5,000
SALES: 1MM **Privately Held**
WEB: www.rollsbatteryne.net
SIC: 3691 Mfg Batteries

(G-14940)
SALEM HOUSE PRESS
Also Called: Norge Forge Press
11 Beacon St (01970-4101)
P.O. Box 249 (01970-0249)
PHONE..................................978 578-9238
EMP: 25 **EST:** 2004
SALES (est): 627.2K **Privately Held**
SIC: 2731 Books-Publishing

(G-14941)
SALEMS OLD FSHONED CANDIES INC
93 Canal St (01970-4839)
P.O. Box 389 (01970-0489)
PHONE..................................978 744-3242
Freeman Corkum, *President*
EMP: 18
SQ FT: 13,000
SALES (est): 1.7MM **Privately Held**
SIC: 2064 Mfg Candy

(G-14942)
SCARLET LTR PRESS GALLERY LLC
Also Called: Scarlet Letter Press, The
10 Colonial Rd Ste 14 (01970-2947)
PHONE..................................978 741-1850
Joshua Devries,
EMP: 4
SALES (est): 187K **Privately Held**
SIC: 2741 Misc Publishing

(G-14943)
SLESAR BROS BREWING CO INC
Also Called: Salem Beer Works
278 Derby St (01970-3635)
PHONE..................................978 745-2337
Steve Slesar, *Vice Pres*
EMP: 40 **Privately Held**
SIC: 2082 5812 Mfg Malt Beverages Eating Place
PA: Slesar Bros. Brewing Company, Inc.
110 Canal St
Boston MA

(G-14944)
STAN RAY PRODUCTS CO
8 Roslyn St (01970-4621)
P.O. Box 1398, Marblehead (01945-5398)
PHONE..................................978 594-0667
William H Goodwin III, *President*
EMP: 3
SALES (est): 133.6K **Privately Held**
SIC: 3949 Mfg Sporting/Athletic Goods

(G-14945)
THERMAL CIRCUITS INC
1 Technology Way (01970-7000)
PHONE..................................978 745-1162
Anthony A Klein, *President*
David M Abbot, *COO*
John H Kellogg, *Treasurer*
▲ **EMP:** 150
SQ FT: 52,000
SALES (est): 36.7MM **Privately Held**
WEB: www.thermalcircuits.com
SIC: 3699 3433 3585 Mfg Electrical Equipment/Supplies Mfg Heating Equipment-Nonelectric Mfg Refrigeration/Heating Equipment

(G-14946)
TITAN ADVNCED ENRGY SLTONS INC
35 Congress St Ste 2251 (01970-5529)
PHONE..................................561 654-5558
Shawn Murphy, *CEO*
◆ **EMP:** 16
SALES (est): 559.8K **Privately Held**
SIC: 3691 Mfg Storage Batteries

(G-14947)
TROPICAL PRODUCTS INC
220 Highland Ave (01970-1842)
PHONE..................................978 740-5665
Edward Berman, *President*
▲ **EMP:** 45
SQ FT: 50,000
SALES (est): 10.7MM **Privately Held**
WEB: www.tropicalproducts.net
SIC: 2844 Mfg Toilet Preparations

Salisbury
Essex County

(G-14948)
AMERICAN SHEET METAL LLC
4 Fanaras Dr (01952-1443)
PHONE..................................978 578-8360
James Levasseur, *Principal*
EMP: 20
SALES (est): 5.5MM **Privately Held**
SIC: 3444 Mfg Sheet Metalwork

(G-14949)
CULVER COMPANY LLC
104 Bridge Rd (01952-2410)
PHONE..................................978 463-1700
Francis Culver Jr, *Mng Member*
Kristen Van Dine, *Director*
Brennan Culver,
EMP: 17
SALES (est): 1.8MM **Privately Held**
SIC: 2741 Misc Publishing

(G-14950)
EASTERN MASS MACHINED PRODUCTS
164 Elm St (01952-1805)
PHONE..................................978 462-9301
Jack E Hillman Sr, *President*
Alex Beijer, *General Mgr*
EMP: 14
SQ FT: 2,000
SALES (est): 2.3MM **Privately Held**
SIC: 3599 Mfg Industrial Machinery

(G-14951)
HUNTS SEAFOOD INC
17 North End Blvd Ste A (01952-2202)
PHONE..................................978 255-2636
Edwin Hunt Sr, *President*
EMP: 8
SQ FT: 2,400
SALES (est): 688.2K **Privately Held**
SIC: 2092 5146 Shucks & Whol Clams

(G-14952)
LC TECHNOLOGY SOLUTIONS INC
2c Fanaras Dr (01952-1443)
PHONE..................................978 255-1620
Peter M Calandra Jr, *President*
EMP: 7
SALES (est): 1.7MM **Privately Held**
SIC: 3821 Mfg Lab Apparatus/Furniture

(G-14953)
MOBILE MINI INC
77 Bridge Rd (01952-2409)
PHONE..................................866 344-4092
Carrie Bryson, *Manager*
EMP: 20
SALES (corp-wide): 593.2MM **Publicly Held**
SIC: 3448 Mfg And Leases Prefabricated Portable Buildings
PA: Mobile Mini, Inc.
4646 E Van Buren St # 400
Phoenix AZ 85008
480 894-6311

(G-14954)
N2BM NUTRITION INC
Also Called: Need To Build Muscle
10b Elm St (01952-1930)
PHONE..................................978 241-2851
Ricardo Vallejo, *President*
EMP: 5 **EST:** 2013
SALES (est): 286K **Privately Held**
SIC: 2048 Mfg Prepared Feeds

(G-14955)
PV ENGINEERING & MFG INC
88 Rabbit Rd (01952-1312)
PHONE..................................978 465-1221
Vicky Vlismas, *President*
Peter Vlismas, *Vice Pres*
Nicholas Vlismas, *Treasurer*
EMP: 22
SQ FT: 17,000
SALES (est): 4.2MM **Privately Held**
WEB: www.pvengineering.net
SIC: 3599 Mfg Industrial Machinery

(G-14956)
SIGNS BY DOUG
213 Lafayette Rd (01952-1545)
PHONE..................................978 463-2222
Doug Hanson, *Principal*
EMP: 3
SALES (est): 18.4K **Privately Held**
WEB: www.signsbydoug.com
SIC: 3993 Mfg Signs/Advertising Specialties

(G-14957)
TH GLENNON CO INC
25 Fanaras Dr (01952-1444)
PHONE..................................978 465-7222
Brian R Shea, *President*
Rocky Berry, *Vice Pres*
Peter Brady Jr, *Director*
Cathleen E Shea, *Director*
◆ **EMP:** 20
SQ FT: 15,000
SALES (est): 10.1MM **Privately Held**
WEB: www.mulchcolorjet.com
SIC: 2851 Mfg Paints/Allied Products

(G-14958)
VAUGHN THERMAL CORPORATION
26 Old Elm St (01952-1898)
P.O. Box 5431 (01952-0431)
PHONE..................................978 462-6683
Ian Bratt, *President*
Ken Ladd, *Vice Pres*
Joe Copeland, *Prdtn Mgr*
Jimmy Valliere, *Production*
Jim Leonard, *Engineer*
▲ **EMP:** 40 **EST:** 1988
SALES (est): 11.3MM
SALES (corp-wide): 9.1MM **Privately Held**
SIC: 3639 3634 Mfg Household Appliances Mfg Electric Housewares/Fans
PA: Heh Holdings Llc
45 Seymour St
Stratford CT

(G-14959)
VYNORIUS PRESTRESS INC
Also Called: Vynorius Companies, The
150 Elm St (01952-1805)
PHONE..................................978 462-7765
William Vynorius, *President*
Michael Barth, *Vice Pres*
Micheal Barth, *Vice Pres*
Mary Lou Vynorius, *Vice Pres*
Tracy Vynorius Harris, *Treasurer*
EMP: 10
SALES (est): 1.9MM **Privately Held**
SIC: 3271 Mfg Concrete Block/Brick

Sandisfield
Berkshire County

(G-14960)
EZEQUELLE LOGGING INC
165 Sandisfield Rd (01255-9619)
PHONE..................................413 258-0265
James A Ezequelle, *President*
EMP: 3
SALES (est): 195.9K **Privately Held**
SIC: 2411 Logging

Sandwich
Barnstable County

(G-14961)
BILLARD CORPORATION
Also Called: Express Company
290 Route 130 Unit 1 (02563-2366)
PHONE..................................508 888-4964
Charles Billard, *President*
EMP: 4
SQ FT: 4,000
SALES: 5MM **Privately Held**
SIC: 2759 7331 Commercial Printing Direct Mail Advertising Services

(G-14962)
BOSTON SAND & GRAVEL COMPANY
Also Called: Lawrence Ready-Mix
181 Kiahs Way (02563)
P.O. Box 2096 (02563-8096)
PHONE..................................508 888-8002
Jack Greeley, *Manager*
EMP: 10
SALES (corp-wide): 121MM **Privately Held**
WEB: www.bostonsand.com
SIC: 3273 Mfg Ready-Mixed Concrete
PA: Boston Sand & Gravel Company Inc
100 N Washington St Fl 2
Boston MA 02114
617 227-9000

(G-14963)
BUILDERS SUPPLY OF CAPE COD
18 Jan Sebastian Dr (02563-2380)
PHONE..................................508 888-0444
Nicholas Papadopoulo, *Owner*
Elaine Papadopoulos, *Owner*
Katina Papadopoulos, *Owner*
EMP: 3
SQ FT: 12,000
SALES (est): 369.1K **Privately Held**
SIC: 2431 5211 Mfg Millwork Ret Lumber/Building Materials

(G-14964)
COCA COLA BTLG CO OF CAPE COD
Also Called: Coca-Cola
370 Route 130 (02563-2302)
P.O. Box 779 (02563-0779)
PHONE..................................508 888-0001
John Kayajan, *President*
John La Flamme, *VP Sales*
Stephen Sinclair, *Clerk*
EMP: 75 **EST:** 1939
SQ FT: 75,000
SALES (est): 8.7MM **Privately Held**
SIC: 2086 Mfg Bottled/Canned Soft Drinks

(G-14965)
COCA-COLA BOTTLING COMPANY
370 Route 130 (02563-2302)
PHONE..................................508 888-0001
Gina Devlin, *Branch Mgr*
EMP: 75 **Privately Held**
SIC: 2086 5149 Mfg Bottled/Canned Soft Drinks Whol Groceries
HQ: Coca-Cola Beverages Northeast, Inc.
1 Executive Park Dr # 330
Bedford NH 03110
603 627-7871

(G-14966)
COLONIAL BLACKSMITH
5 Christina Ln (02563-2907)
PHONE..................................508 420-5326
Jim Ciborowski, *President*
EMP: 3
SALES (est): 190K **Privately Held**
SIC: 3446 Mfg Architectural Metalwork

(G-14967)
EASTERN WOODS MUSIC PUBLISHING
159 Cotuit Rd (02563-2655)
P.O. Box 648, Forestdale (02644-0701)
PHONE..................................508 238-3270
Peter Janson, *Owner*
EMP: 3
SALES (est): 31.2K **Privately Held**
WEB: www.easternwoodsmusic.com
SIC: 2741 Misc Publishing

(G-14968)
GONCO INC (PA)
Also Called: Cape Cod Textile
338 Route 130 (02563-2302)
PHONE..................................508 833-3900
Stephen D Gonneville, *President*
EMP: 9
SQ FT: 8,000
SALES (est): 1MM **Privately Held**
WEB: www.babybib.net
SIC: 2395 2261 2385 Pleating/Stitching Services Cotton Finishing Plant Mfg Waterproof Outerwear

(G-14969)
HERITAGE PRESS INC
Also Called: Heritage Print Solutions
335 Cotuit Rd Unit 3 (02563-5123)
P.O. Box 653 (02563-0653)
PHONE..................................508 888-2111
Dominic Macone Jr, *President*
▲ **EMP:** 3
SQ FT: 3,200
SALES: 783K **Privately Held**
WEB: www.heritagepresscapecod.com
SIC: 2752 5199 Lithographic Commercial Printing Whol Nondurable Goods

(G-14970)
JP LILLIS ENTERPRISES INC (PA)
Also Called: Polar Cap Ice Co
7 Jan Sebastian Dr (02563-2325)
PHONE..................................508 888-8394
Joseph P Lillis, *President*
Robert White, *Treasurer*

Philip Castleman, *Admin Sec*
EMP: 15
SQ FT: 12,000
SALES (est): 8.3MM **Privately Held**
WEB: www.capecodice.com
SIC: 2097 Mfg Ice

(G-14971)
OR-6 LLC
49 Boardley Rd (02563-2617)
PHONE.................................617 515-1909
Tracy Thorpe, *CEO*
Wade Goolishian, *COO*
EMP: 3
SALES (est): 263.9K **Privately Held**
SIC: 3842 Mfg Surgical Appliances/Supplies

(G-14972)
PID ANALYZERS LLC
Also Called: Hnu
2 Washington Cir Ste 4 (02563-2376)
PHONE.................................774 413-5281
Scott Pierce, *Sales Mgr*
Jennifer L Driscoll, *Mng Member*
Steven Brown, *Webmaster*
Jennifer L Maclachlan,
EMP: 10
SALES (est): 1.6MM **Privately Held**
SIC: 3823 Mfg Process Control Instruments

(G-14973)
SANDWICH LANTERN
17 Jan Sebastian Dr Ste 1 (02563-2362)
PHONE.................................508 833-0515
Steve Sherman, *Owner*
EMP: 5
SQ FT: 3,000
SALES: 550K **Privately Held**
WEB: www.sandwichlantern.com
SIC: 3645 Mfg Residential Lighting Fixtures

(G-14974)
TRIPLE CROWN CBNETS MLLWK CORP
12b Jan Sebastian Dr (02563-2324)
PHONE.................................508 833-6500
Kevin Fitzpatrick, *President*
Wayne Paciocco, *Vice Pres*
EMP: 7
SALES (est): 610K **Privately Held**
SIC: 2431 2434 Mfg Millwork Mfg Wood Kitchen Cabinets

Saugus
Essex County

(G-14975)
AGGREGATE INDS - NORTHEAST REG
1715 Broadway Ste 1 (01906-4704)
PHONE.................................781 941-7200
Bradley Smith, *Manager*
EMP: 5
SALES (corp-wide): 4.5B **Privately Held**
SIC: 2951 3273 1429 1611 Mfg Asphalt Mixtr/Blocks Mfg Ready-Mixed Concrete Crushed/Broken Stone Highway/Street Cnstn
HQ: Aggregate Industries - Northeast Region, Inc
1715 Brdwy
Saugus MA 01906
781 941-7200

(G-14976)
AGGREGATE INDUSTRIES - MWR INC
1715 Broadway Ste 1 (01906-4704)
PHONE.................................781 941-7200
EMP: 27
SALES (corp-wide): 4.5B **Privately Held**
SIC: 3273 Central-Mixed Concrete
HQ: Aggregate Industries - Mwr, Inc.
2815 Dodd Rd
Eagan MN 55121
651 683-0600

(G-14977)
AGGREGATE INDUSTRIES - MWR INC
1831 Broadway (01906-4155)
PHONE.................................781 231-3400
Robert Peckham, *President*
EMP: 60
SALES (corp-wide): 4.5B **Privately Held**
SIC: 3273 Mfg Ready-Mixed Concrete
HQ: Aggregate Industries - Mwr, Inc.
2815 Dodd Rd
Eagan MN 55121
651 683-0600

(G-14978)
AGGREGATE INDUSTRIES - MWR INC
1715 Broadway Ste 1 (01906-4704)
PHONE.................................781 941-3108
Marco Rodriquez, *Plant Mgr*
Brett Dahl, *Purchasing*
Robert Anderson, *Manager*
Warren Jarvis, *Technology*
Edmund Capodilupo, *Officer*
EMP: 35
SALES (corp-wide): 4.5B **Privately Held**
SIC: 3273 Mfg Ready-Mixed Concrete Asphalt Bituminous Concrete Sand Gravel & Crushed Stone & Bituminous Concrete Contractor
HQ: Aggregate Industries - Mwr, Inc.
2815 Dodd Rd
Eagan MN 55121
651 683-0600

(G-14979)
COUNTER CULTURE
60 Main St (01906-3353)
PHONE.................................781 439-9810
Chris Galvin, *Principal*
EMP: 3
SALES (est): 217.4K **Privately Held**
SIC: 3131 Mfg Footwear Cut Stock

(G-14980)
EASTERN METAL INDUSTRIES INC
910 Broadway Rear (01906-3236)
PHONE.................................781 231-5220
Gabriel Pasquale, *President*
EMP: 10
SQ FT: 14,000
SALES (est): 1.6MM **Privately Held**
SIC: 3441 Structural Metal Fabrication

(G-14981)
FOOT LOCKER RETAIL INC
1201 Broadway (01906-4274)
PHONE.................................781 231-0142
Anthony Squillante, *Manager*
EMP: 7
SALES (corp-wide): 7.9B **Publicly Held**
SIC: 3949 Mfg Sporting/Athletic Goods
HQ: Foot Locker Retail, Inc.
330 W 34th St
New York NY 10001
800 991-6815

(G-14982)
GARDEN WORLD INC
24r Bennett Hwy Ste 3 (01906-5500)
PHONE.................................781 233-9510
Joseph M Dinapoli, *President*
EMP: 3
SALES (est): 394.3K **Privately Held**
SIC: 2875 Mfg Fertilizers-Mix

(G-14983)
GMF ENGINEERING INC
Also Called: Park Press Printers
15 Main St (01906-2347)
PHONE.................................781 233-0315
Gebrael M Farhat, *President*
EMP: 8
SALES (est): 1.5MM **Privately Held**
SIC: 2752 Lithographic Commercial Printing

(G-14984)
HAMILTON ELEVATOR INTERIORS
6 Belair St (01906-3004)
PHONE.................................781 233-9540
Glenn Bowie, *President*
EMP: 12
SALES (est): 683.7K **Privately Held**
SIC: 3534 Mfg Elevators/Escalators

(G-14985)
HERB CON MACHINE COMPANY INC
6 Bow Street Ext (01906-1106)
PHONE.................................781 233-2755
Herbert J Comeau Jr, *President*
EMP: 4
SALES (est): 519K **Privately Held**
SIC: 3559 7692 Mfg Misc Industry Machinery Welding Repair

(G-14986)
HUNTER ASSOCIATES INC
Also Called: Auto Hunter Magazine
92 Walnut St Ste 3 (01906-1949)
P.O. Box 13, Lynnfield (01940-0013)
PHONE.................................781 233-9100
Thomas Lemberger, *President*
EMP: 40
SQ FT: 4,000
SALES (est): 3MM **Privately Held**
WEB: www.autohunteronline.com
SIC: 2721 Magazine Publisher

(G-14987)
IONSENSE INC
999 Broadway Ste 404 (01906-4510)
PHONE.................................781 231-1739
Brian Musselman, *President*
Curtis Lintvedt, *CFO*
EMP: 14
SQ FT: 6,000
SALES: 2.3MM **Privately Held**
SIC: 3826 Mfg Analytical Instruments

(G-14988)
J & B METAL PRODUCTS COMPANY
341 Central St (01906-2375)
P.O. Box 1318 (01906-0618)
PHONE.................................781 233-7506
Frederick Moore, *President*
EMP: 4
SQ FT: 10,000
SALES (est): 445.8K **Privately Held**
SIC: 3444 Sheet Metal Work

(G-14989)
JD DESIGN LLC
184 Broadway Ste 11 (01906-1099)
PHONE.................................781 941-2066
Joseph J Diruzzo,
EMP: 4
SQ FT: 1,600
SALES: 200K **Privately Held**
SIC: 3993 Mfg Signs/Advertising Specialties

(G-14990)
LAMB & RITCHIE COMPANY INC
90 Broadway (01906-1091)
PHONE.................................781 941-2700
David A Ritchie, *President*
▲ **EMP:** 40 **EST:** 1872
SQ FT: 86,000
SALES (est): 10.2MM **Privately Held**
WEB: www.lambritchie.com
SIC: 3444 Mfg Sheet Metalwork

(G-14991)
NEVRON PLASTICS INC
Also Called: Nevron Plastics and Metals
124 Ballard St (01906-1799)
PHONE.................................781 233-1310
Thomas Jarosz, *President*
EMP: 15 **EST:** 1965
SQ FT: 58,000
SALES (est): 4.1MM **Privately Held**
SIC: 3441 3089 Fabrication Of Plastics And Metal

(G-14992)
NEW ENGLAND BLAZERS
4 Hickory Ln (01906-3160)
PHONE.................................617 448-3709
Paul Cowan, *Principal*
EMP: 3 **EST:** 2016
SALES (est): 190.9K **Privately Held**
SIC: 3842 Mfg Surgical Appliances/Supplies

(G-14993)
OLD SCHOOL APPAREL
341 Central St Ste A (01906-2375)
PHONE.................................781 231-0753
Rebecca Allison, *Principal*
EMP: 3
SALES (est): 289.2K **Privately Held**
SIC: 2759 Commercial Printing

(G-14994)
RED OAK WINNERY LLC
6 Fox Hollow Dr (01906-3170)
PHONE.................................781 558-1702
Frank Spadafora, *President*
EMP: 4
SALES (est): 209.9K **Privately Held**
SIC: 2084 Mfg Wines/Brandy/Spirits

(G-14995)
RUSSOS INC
329 Main St (01906-3143)
PHONE.................................781 233-1737
Vincent J Vannah, *CEO*
Joanne Vannah, *President*
EMP: 19 **EST:** 1954
SQ FT: 1,200
SALES (est): 419.8K **Privately Held**
WEB: www.russoscandy.com
SIC: 2064 2024 5441 5451 Mfg Candy/Confectionery Mfg Ice Cream/Desserts Ret Candy/Confectionery Ret Dairy Products Mfg Chocolate/Cocoa Prdt

(G-14996)
SHARP SERVICES INC
222 Central St (01906-2107)
P.O. Box 1364 (01906-0664)
PHONE.................................781 854-3334
Paul Maganbini, *Owner*
EMP: 7
SALES (est): 959.5K **Privately Held**
SIC: 3556 Mfg Food Products Machinery

(G-14997)
SNYDER MACHINE CO INC
9 Thomas St Unit C9 (01906-3293)
PHONE.................................781 233-2080
Henry R Snyder, *President*
▼ **EMP:** 17 **EST:** 1962
SQ FT: 16,000
SALES: 2MM **Privately Held**
SIC: 3599 3554 Machine Shop Jobbing & Repair

(G-14998)
SONNYS PIZZA INC
Also Called: Delvec
3 Fox Hollow Dr (01906-3171)
PHONE.................................617 381-1900
Joseph B De Luca, *President*
Maria-Elena De Luca, *Treasurer*
EMP: 15
SQ FT: 12,000
SALES: 1.1MM **Privately Held**
SIC: 2099 Mfr Pizzas

(G-14999)
SPEEDWAY LLC
240 Broadway (01906-1264)
PHONE.................................781 233-5491
John Hess, *Owner*
EMP: 66 **Publicly Held**
SIC: 1311 Oil & Gas Refining
HQ: Speedway Llc
500 Speedway Dr
Enon OH 45323
937 864-3000

(G-15000)
SULLIVAN APPLE CIDER
34 Prospect St (01906-2155)
PHONE.................................781 233-7090
Paul F Sullivan, *Principal*
EMP: 3
SALES (est): 131.9K **Privately Held**
SIC: 2082 Mfg Malt Beverages

(G-15001)
VINEGAR HILL LLC
20 Main St (01906-2340)
PHONE.................................781 233-3190
Kevin F Procopio, *Manager*
EMP: 3
SALES (est): 142.6K **Privately Held**
SIC: 2099 Mfg Food Preparations

(G-15002)
W J ROBERTS CO INC
181 Central St (01906-2031)
P.O. Box 1146 (01906-0346)
PHONE..................................781 233-8176
William J Roberts, *President*
EMP: 25
SQ FT: 11,011
SALES (est): 4MM **Privately Held**
WEB: www.wjroberts.com
SIC: 3599 3699 3643 3429 Mfg Industrial Machinery Mfg Elec Mach/Equip/Supp Mfg Conductive Wire Dvcs Mfg Hardware

Savoy
Berkshire County

(G-15003)
S & S MACHINE AND WELDING INC
128 Windsor Rd (01256-9211)
PHONE..................................413 743-5714
Fred Sawyer, *President*
Allen Sawyer, *Principal*
Richard Sawyer, *Principal*
Gwen Deblois, *Admin Sec*
▼ **EMP:** 9
SQ FT: 2,800
SALES (est): 900K **Privately Held**
SIC: 3599 Mfg Industrial Machinery

Scituate
Plymouth County

(G-15004)
A TO Z BOATWORKS INC
12 Chief Jstce Cshng Hwy (02066-4408)
PHONE..................................781 545-6632
Charlie Allen, *Owner*
EMP: 6
SALES (est): 737.3K **Privately Held**
SIC: 3732 Boatbuilding/Repairing

(G-15005)
AJA INTERNATIONAL INC
809 Country Way (02066-1700)
P.O. Box 246 (02060-0246)
PHONE..................................781 545-7365
William Hale, *President*
Linda Tardie, *Vice Pres*
William M Provost, *Treasurer*
Michael R Hale, *Admin Sec*
James Hannon, *Asst Sec*
EMP: 47
SQ FT: 3,200
SALES (est): 10.1MM **Privately Held**
WEB: www.ajaint.com
SIC: 3829 3821 Mfg Measuring/Controlling Devices Mfg Lab Apparatus/Furniture

(G-15006)
BRADFORD DISTILLERY LLC (PA)
604 First Parish Rd (02066-3207)
PHONE..................................781 378-2491
Robert Bradford Rohla, *Principal*
EMP: 3
SALES (est): 699.3K **Privately Held**
SIC: 2085 Mfg Distilled/Blended Liquor

(G-15007)
BUCKLEY CO INC
31 Hollycrest Rd (02066-3016)
PHONE..................................781 545-7975
Stephen E Buckley, *President*
EMP: 3
SQ FT: 45,000
SALES (est): 452.5K **Privately Held**
WEB: www.buckleyrack.com
SIC: 2542 Mfg Partitions/Fixtures-Nonwood

(G-15008)
CISCO SYSTEMS INC
10 Fox Vine Ln (02066-2053)
PHONE..................................978 936-1246
EMP: 3
SALES (corp-wide): 51.9B **Publicly Held**
SIC: 3577 Mfg Computer Peripheral Equipment
PA: Cisco Systems, Inc.
170 W Tasman Dr
San Jose CA 95134
408 526-4000

(G-15009)
MARK KEUP
105 Front St (02066-1315)
PHONE..................................781 544-4610
EMP: 5
SALES (est): 261K
SALES (corp-wide): 252.9K **Privately Held**
SIC: 3949 Mfg Sporting/Athletic Goods
PA: Mark Keup
376 Gannett Rd
Scituate MA 02066
781 544-9283

(G-15010)
PICKWICK
59 Glades Rd (02066-1647)
PHONE..................................781 545-0884
EMP: 3
SALES (est): 163.5K **Privately Held**
SIC: 2321 Mfg Men's/Boy's Furnishings

(G-15011)
SAFVE INC
24 Ladds Way (02066-1921)
PHONE..................................781 545-3546
Shirley Young, *President*
EMP: 8
SALES: 95K **Privately Held**
SIC: 3589 7389 Mfg Service Industry Machinery Business Services

(G-15012)
SCITUATE CASEWORKS INC
7 Sangay Ln (02066-4727)
PHONE..................................781 534-4167
Erik Knapp, *President*
EMP: 3
SALES (est): 296.5K **Privately Held**
SIC: 3523 Mfg Farm Machinery/Equipment

(G-15013)
SCITUATE CONCRETE PIPE CORP
1 Buckeye Ln (02066-1924)
P.O. Box 870 (02066-0870)
PHONE..................................781 545-0564
William E Hoffman, *President*
Richard W Hoffman, *Treasurer*
EMP: 40 **EST:** 1959
SALES (est): 7.3MM **Privately Held**
WEB: www.scituatecompanies.com
SIC: 3272 Mfg Concrete Products

(G-15014)
SOUTH SHORE MANUFACTURING INC
Also Called: Jack's Machine Company
647 First Parish Rd (02066-3106)
PHONE..................................781 447-9264
Patrick Johnson, *President*
EMP: 10 **EST:** 2015
SQ FT: 10,000
SALES (est): 740.7K **Privately Held**
SIC: 3599 Mfg Industrial Machinery

(G-15015)
STACIS STITCHES LLC
761 Country Way (02066-1847)
PHONE..................................781 206-7478
William Joseph Carey III,
EMP: 3
SALES (est): 170.8K **Privately Held**
SIC: 2211 Cotton Broadwoven Fabric Mill

(G-15016)
THEN & NOW PUBLISHING
421 1st St Paris Rd (02066)
P.O. Box 5, Norwell (02061-0005)
PHONE..................................781 378-2013
Arthur J Roberts, *Owner*
EMP: 12
SALES (est): 578.8K **Privately Held**
SIC: 2741 Misc Publishing

Seekonk
Bristol County

(G-15017)
ADAPTIVE MOBILITY EQUIPMENT
Also Called: AME
1551 Fall River Ave (02771-3710)
PHONE..................................508 336-2556
Dennis Koshanek, *President*
Susan Koshanek, *Vice Pres*
EMP: 6
SALES (est): 1.7MM **Privately Held**
WEB: www.amemobility.com
SIC: 3842 5511 Conversion Vans Etc For Disabled People

(G-15018)
BACK STREET INC
Also Called: Fastsigns
128 Highland Ave (02771-5806)
PHONE..................................508 336-6333
Karen Martins, *President*
EMP: 6
SALES: 500K **Privately Held**
SIC: 3993 Signsadv Specs

(G-15019)
BIG DOG DISPOSAL INC
72 Pond St (02771-3915)
P.O. Box 886, North Attleboro (02761-0886)
PHONE..................................508 695-9539
Brian A Dasilva, *Principal*
EMP: 7
SALES (est): 667.6K **Privately Held**
SIC: 3089 3443 Mfg Plastic Products Mfg Fabricated Plate Work

(G-15020)
COUNTRYSIDE SIGNS
Also Called: Mmd Art Service
102 Pond St Unit F1 (02771-3941)
PHONE..................................508 761-9530
Michael Szczoczarz, *Owner*
EMP: 4
SALES: 250K **Privately Held**
SIC: 3993 Mfg Signs/Advertising Specialties

(G-15021)
DRIVEWAY MEDICS LLC
10 Vista Ct (02771-2319)
PHONE..................................508 761-6921
Jason Adamonis, *Vice Pres*
EMP: 5
SALES (est): 492.3K **Privately Held**
SIC: 2952 Mfg Asphalt Felts/Coatings

(G-15022)
FLAG & GIFT STORE LTD
79 Pheasant Ridge Rd (02771-2718)
PHONE..................................508 675-6400
Karen Azza, *President*
EMP: 5
SALES (est): 410K **Privately Held**
SIC: 2399 Mfg Fabricated Textile Products

(G-15023)
H & W TEST PRODUCTS INC
58 Industrial Ct (02771-2017)
PHONE..................................508 336-3200
Gordon R Hutton, *President*
Steven A Whitcomb, *President*
Warren Joubert, *Prdtn Mgr*
Julie Blaydes, *Office Mgr*
EMP: 12
SQ FT: 6,000
SALES (est): 2.1MM **Privately Held**
SIC: 3825 Mfg Electrical Measuring Instruments

(G-15024)
HYDRO QUIP INC (PA)
108 Pond St (02771-3915)
PHONE..................................508 399-5771
Louis Silvio, *President*
Tim Auclair, *Manager*
Gordon Clarke, *Technology*
EMP: 6
SALES (est): 1.6MM **Privately Held**
WEB: www.hydroquipinc.com
SIC: 3589 5084 Mfg Service Industry Machinery Whol Industrial Equipment

(G-15025)
KORNER BAGEL PARTNERSHIP
Also Called: Krazy Korner Bagel & Deli
23 Circle Dr (02771-3724)
PHONE..................................508 336-5204
Betty Delude, *Partner*
Richard Coty, *Partner*
EMP: 20
SALES (est): 1.4MM **Privately Held**
SIC: 2051 5461 5812 Mfg Bread/Related Products Retail Bakery Eating Place

(G-15026)
LITTLE KIDS INC
1015 Newman Ave (02771-4411)
PHONE..................................401 454-7600
James D Engle, *President*
Richard Engle, *Vice Pres*
Andrew March, *Project Mgr*
John Davies, *Research*
Mary Kue, *Business Anlyst*
▲ **EMP:** 39
SQ FT: 74,000
SALES (est): 10.2MM **Privately Held**
WEB: www.littlekidsinc.com
SIC: 3944 3089 Mfg Games/Toys Mfg Plastic Products

(G-15027)
MICRO ELECTRONICS INC
1005 Newman Ave (02771-4411)
PHONE..................................508 761-9161
Gary Perrino, *President*
EMP: 10
SQ FT: 2,700
SALES (est): 1MM **Privately Held**
WEB: www.microstrip.com
SIC: 3549 Mfg Fiber Optic Stripping Tools

(G-15028)
MINUTEMAN PRESS
294 Taunton Ave (02771-5231)
PHONE..................................508 336-3050
Bob Frechette, *Owner*
EMP: 5
SQ FT: 1,100
SALES (est): 430.7K **Privately Held**
SIC: 2752 Comm Prtg Litho

(G-15029)
MODERN TRACTOR & TRUCK SERVICE
400 Pine St (02771-2698)
PHONE..................................508 761-4425
Steven S Howitt, *President*
Shirley Howitt, *Clerk*
EMP: 5
SQ FT: 5,500
SALES: 333.2K **Privately Held**
SIC: 1389 7359 0711 Underground Storage Tank Removal

(G-15030)
MRF ENTERPRISES INC
Also Called: Minuteman Press
294 Taunton Ave (02771-5231)
PHONE..................................508 336-3050
Marc R Frechette, *President*
EMP: 5
SALES (est): 421.2K **Privately Held**
SIC: 2752 Comm Prtg Litho

(G-15031)
NC CONVERTING INC
32 Hollister Rd (02771-2002)
PHONE..................................508 336-6510
Natalino V Chiavettone, *President*
EMP: 7
SQ FT: 1,800
SALES (est): 1.1MM **Privately Held**
SIC: 3549 Mfg Metalworking Machinery

(G-15032)
NU CHROME CORP
32 Industrial Ct (02771-2017)
P.O. Box 362 (02771-0362)
PHONE..................................508 557-1418
Don Kemp, *President*
EMP: 15
SQ FT: 40,000

▲ = Import ▼=Export
◆ =Import/Export

SALES (est): 1.5MM Privately Held
SIC: 3471 Rechroming Of Automobile Trim

(G-15033)
PHILLIP IPPOLITO
Also Called: Ippolito Stonecraft
1970 Fall River Ave (02771-2037)
PHONE....................................508 336-9616
Phillip Ippolito, *Owner*
▲ EMP: 10
SQ FT: 6,000
SALES (est): 1.4MM Privately Held
SIC: 3281 5211 Mfg Cut Stone/Products Ret Lumber/Building Materials

(G-15034)
PHOENIX INC
257 Pine St (02771-2601)
PHONE....................................508 399-7100
Robert C Fuller, *President*
Steven Fuller, *Vice Pres*
▲ EMP: 38 EST: 1974
SQ FT: 65,000
SALES (est): 2.2MM Privately Held
WEB: www.phoenix-inc.com
SIC: 3541 Mfg Machine Tools-Cutting

(G-15035)
QCI INC
257 Pine St (02771-2601)
PHONE....................................508 399-8983
Nick Korentis, *President*
Teresa Korentis, *Treasurer*
EMP: 18
SALES (est): 3MM Privately Held
WEB: www.qcieng.com
SIC: 3634 Mfg Electric Housewares/Fans

(G-15036)
SEEKONK MANUFACTURING CO INC
Also Called: SEEKONK PRECISION TOOLS
87 Perrin Ave (02771-4195)
PHONE....................................508 761-8284
Frederick Dobras, *President*
Cindy Richard, *Vice Pres*
EMP: 21
SQ FT: 40,000
SALES: 4.2MM Privately Held
WEB: www.seekonk.com
SIC: 3423 Mfg Hand/Edge Tools

(G-15037)
SIGNS & SITES INC
20 Commerce Way Ste 10 (02771-5823)
PHONE....................................508 336-5858
David Mitchell, *President*
Jared Walker, *Graphic Designe*
EMP: 3
SALES (est): 306.2K Privately Held
SIC: 3993 Mfg Signs/Advertising Specialties

(G-15038)
STATELINE FUEL
1587 Fall River Ave (02771-3749)
PHONE....................................508 336-0665
Stephen J Ferreira M, *Principal*
EMP: 5
SALES (est): 679.2K Privately Held
SIC: 2869 Mfg Industrial Organic Chemicals

(G-15039)
TCI AMERICA INC
21 Industrial Ct (02771-2016)
PHONE....................................508 336-6633
Kathleen Hayes, *President*
Michael Young, *Vice Pres*
EMP: 22
SALES (est): 2MM Privately Held
SIC: 2741 7389 Internet Publishing And Broadcasting Misc Publishing Business Services

(G-15040)
TCI PRESS INC
21 Industrial Ct (02771-2016)
PHONE....................................508 336-6633
Mark D Hayes, *President*
Steve Dicaprio, *Vice Pres*
Annette Tessier, *Bookkeeper*
Annmarie Fillion, *Officer*
Kathleen M Hayes, *Admin Sec*
EMP: 50
SQ FT: 20,000
SALES (est): 7MM Privately Held
WEB: www.tcipress.com
SIC: 2752 Lithographic Commercial Printing

(G-15041)
TELCO COMMUNICATIONS INC
Also Called: TCI
21 Industrial Ct (02771-2026)
PHONE....................................508 336-6633
Mark Hayes, *President*
Kathleen Hayes, *Vice Pres*
EMP: 35
SQ FT: 14,000
SALES (est): 3.2MM Privately Held
SIC: 2721 7389 Publishers Of Periodicals

(G-15042)
TILLOTSON CORPORATION (PA)
Also Called: Best Manufacturing
1539 Fall River Ave Ste 1 (02771-3748)
PHONE....................................781 402-1731
Bill Alico, *President*
Thomas S Deans, *President*
Everett A Pearson, *Vice Pres*
Rick Tillotson, *Vice Pres*
Grafton Corbett III, *Treasurer*
◆ EMP: 10
SALES (est): 44.4MM Privately Held
WEB: www.bestglove.com
SIC: 3069 Mfg Fabricated Rubber Products

(G-15043)
TILLOTSON RUBBER CO INC
1539 Fall River Ave (02771-3748)
PHONE....................................781 402-1731
Grafton Corbett, *Asst Treas*
Frederick Tillotson, *Director*
EMP: 7
SQ FT: 50,000
SALES (est): 998.6K
SALES (corp-wide): 44.4MM Privately Held
SIC: 3842 Mfg Examiners & Surgical Gloves & Specialty Rubber Products
PA: Tillotson Corporation
1539 Fall River Ave Ste 1
Seekonk MA 02771
781 402-1731

(G-15044)
WRIGHT TRAILERS INC
1825 Fall River Ave (02771-2007)
PHONE....................................508 336-8530
Daniel D Wright, *President*
Susan M Wright, *Treasurer*
Steven T Wright, *Director*
Jenn C Caron, *Admin Sec*
EMP: 16
SQ FT: 22,000
SALES (est): 3.3MM Privately Held
WEB: www.wrightparts.com
SIC: 3799 7539 Mfg Transportation Equipment Automotive Repair

Sharon
Norfolk County

(G-15045)
ADVANCED PRINT SOLUTIONS INC (PA)
45 Bishop Rd (02067-2408)
PHONE....................................508 655-8434
Benjamin Zibrak, *President*
EMP: 6
SALES (est): 654K Privately Held
SIC: 2752 Lithographic Commercial Printing

(G-15046)
BANACEK INVSTGTONS SRCH RECOVE
1075 Providence Hwy (02067-1671)
P.O. Box 6054, Chandler AZ (85246-6054)
PHONE....................................781 784-1400
Gene Irwin, *Principal*
EMP: 3
SALES (est): 346.1K Privately Held
SIC: 3599 Mfg Industrial Machinery

(G-15047)
CHARLES RIVER APPAREL INC
1205 Providence Hwy (02067-1671)
PHONE....................................781 793-5300
Barry S Lipsett, *President*
Ross Dohrmann, *Regional Mgr*
Walter I Lipsett, *Exec VP*
Tracy Lehnen, *Vice Pres*
Jennifer Wilson, *Vice Pres*
◆ EMP: 70
SQ FT: 130,000
SALES (est): 11.3MM Privately Held
WEB: www.charlesriverapparel.com
SIC: 2311 2339 2369 Mfg Men's/Boy's Suits/Coats Mfg Women's/Misses' Outerwear Mfg Girl/Youth Outerwear

(G-15048)
CJ CORRADO & SONS INC
Also Called: Natick Center Graphics
45 Bishop Rd (02067-2408)
PHONE....................................508 655-8434
Clifford J Corrado, *President*
EMP: 4
SALES (est): 498.8K
SALES (corp-wide): 654K Privately Held
WEB: www.natickcentergraphics.com
SIC: 2752 7334 Offset Printing & Copying
PA: Advanced Print Solutions, Inc.
45 Bishop Rd
Sharon MA 02067
508 655-8434

(G-15049)
DH CUSTOM WOODWORKS
68 Ames St (02067-2107)
PHONE....................................781 784-5951
EMP: 4
SALES (est): 282.8K Privately Held
SIC: 2431 Mfg Millwork

(G-15050)
GATEHOUSE MEDIA MASS I INC
Also Called: Tanscript Newspapers
2 Commercial St (02067-1659)
PHONE....................................781 487-7200
Asa Cole, *Branch Mgr*
EMP: 111
SALES (corp-wide): 1.5B Publicly Held
SIC: 2759 Newspaper Publishing Company
HQ: Gatehouse Media Massachusetts I, Inc.
48 Dunham Rd
Beverly MA 01915
585 598-0030

(G-15051)
HIGHLAND INSTRUMENTS
2 Manns Hill Cres (02067-2267)
P.O. Box 381933, Cambridge (02238-1933)
PHONE....................................617 504-6031
Tim Wagner, *Principal*
EMP: 5
SALES (est): 309.5K Privately Held
WEB: www.highlandinstruments.com
SIC: 3845 Brain Stimulation R&D

(G-15052)
INDUSTRIAL METAL PDTS CO INC
Also Called: Inmetal
15 Merchant St (02067-1614)
PHONE....................................781 762-3330
Evelyn E Hurlbut, *President*
Criag Perry, *Finance*
Chris Robinson, *Technology*
Craig A Perry, *Admin Sec*
EMP: 84
SQ FT: 25,000
SALES (est): 18.9MM Privately Held
WEB: www.inmetal.com
SIC: 3444 3441 Mfg Sheet Metalwork Structural Metal Fabrication

(G-15053)
MINI POPS INC
19 Robin Rd (02067-2112)
PHONE....................................781 436-5864
Arieh L Taube, *President*
EMP: 7
SALES (est): 455.5K Privately Held
SIC: 2064 Mfg Candy/Confectionery

(G-15054)
NOVAGENESIS
77 Norwood St (02067-1262)
PHONE....................................781 784-1149
Marjorie Newman, *President*
Martin Newman, *Principal*
EMP: 25
SQ FT: 1,000
SALES (est): 4MM Privately Held
WEB: www.quessence.com
SIC: 2844 Mfg Toilet Preparations

(G-15055)
PCB CONNECT INC
1 Merchant St (02067-1662)
PHONE....................................781 806-5670
William M Hackett, *CEO*
Jonas Pettersson, *President*
EMP: 3
SALES (est): 156.2K Privately Held
SIC: 3672 Mfg Printed Circuit Boards

(G-15056)
SENIOR OPERATIONS LLC
Also Called: Metal Bellows
1075 Providence Hwy (02067-1671)
PHONE....................................781 784-1400
John Cory, *Chief Engr*
Dan Cordeiro, *Engineer*
Jason Bacchiocchi, *Project Engr*
Daniel Nyren, *Project Engr*
Joyce Wegrzyn, *Project Engr*
EMP: 200
SQ FT: 70,000
SALES (corp-wide): 1.4B Privately Held
SIC: 3599 Mfg Industrial Machinery
HQ: Senior Operations Llc
300 E Devon Ave
Bartlett IL 60103
630 372-3500

(G-15057)
SHARON ASSOCIATES
7 King Phillip Rd (02067-2976)
PHONE....................................781 784-2455
Mark Gelb, *Owner*
EMP: 4
SALES (est): 190K Privately Held
WEB: www.sharonassociates.com
SIC: 3634 Mfg Electric Housewares/Fans

(G-15058)
SWEETHEARTS THREE INC
24 Pond St (02067-2038)
PHONE....................................781 784-5193
Karen Schwab, *President*
EMP: 3
SQ FT: 1,000
SALES (est): 231.1K Privately Held
WEB: www.sweetheartsthree.com
SIC: 2066 5441 Mfg Chocolate/Cocoa Products Ret Candy/Confectionery

Sheffield
Berkshire County

(G-15059)
DEK TILLETT LTD
Also Called: Tillett's
1373 Boardman St (01257-9519)
PHONE....................................413 229-8764
Kathleen Tillett, *President*
Dek Tillet, *President*
EMP: 6 EST: 1970
SALES (est): 691.2K Privately Held
SIC: 2299 2339 Mfg Textile Goods Mfg Women's/Misses' Outerwear

(G-15060)
GRANEY JOHN F METAL DESIGN LLC
Also Called: Graney Metal Designs
1920 N Main St (01257-9562)
P.O. Box 994, Great Barrington (01230-0994)
PHONE....................................413 528-6744
John F Graney, *President*
Laurel Graney, *Vice Pres*
Ian Ramsey, *Manager*
EMP: 6
SQ FT: 2,000

SALES: 650K **Privately Held**
WEB: www.graneymetaldesign.com
SIC: 2514 3446 5712 5211 Mfg & Ret Forged & Fabricated Iron Copper & Brass Interior & Exterior Furniture Gates & Railings

(G-15061)
JIM LOVEJOY CABINETMAKER
75 Main St (01257-9555)
PHONE..................................413 229-9008
Jim Lovejoy, *Owner*
EMP: 3 **EST:** 2003
SALES: 300K **Privately Held**
WEB: www.jimlovejoycabinetmaker.com
SIC: 2434 Mfg Wood Kitchen Cabinets

(G-15062)
PLASKOLITE LLC
113 Silver St (01257)
PHONE..................................800 628-5084
Don Shultz, *Branch Mgr*
EMP: 159
SALES (corp-wide): 294.5MM **Privately Held**
SIC: 2821 Mfg Plastic Materials/Resins
PA: Plaskolite, Llc
400 W Nationwide Blvd # 400
Columbus OH 43215
614 294-3281

(G-15063)
PLASKOLITE LLC
Also Called: Sheffield Plastic Division
119 Salisbury Rd (01257-9706)
PHONE..................................800 628-5084
Don Shultz, *Branch Mgr*
EMP: 120
SALES (corp-wide): 294.5MM **Privately Held**
SIC: 2821 Mfg Plastic Materials/Resins
PA: Plaskolite, Llc
400 W Nationwide Blvd # 400
Columbus OH 43215
614 294-3281

(G-15064)
PLASKOLITE MASSACHUSETTS LLC
119 Salisbury Rd (01257-9706)
PHONE..................................413 229-8711
Mitchell P Grindley, *President*
Richard J Larkin, *CFO*
EMP: 140
SALES (est): 4.2MM
SALES (corp-wide): 294.5MM **Privately Held**
SIC: 2821 Mfg Plastic Materials/Resins
PA: Plaskolite, Llc
400 W Nationwide Blvd # 400
Columbus OH 43215
614 294-3281

(G-15065)
SHEFFIELD POTTERY INC
995 N Main St (01257-9579)
P.O. Box 399 (01257-0399)
PHONE..................................413 229-7700
John Cowen, *President*
Patricia Buteux, *Vice Pres*
Suzy Colpitts, *Sales Mgr*
Tim Heffernan, *Marketing Staff*
▼ **EMP:** 25 **EST:** 1946
SQ FT: 37,000
SALES (est): 4.3MM **Privately Held**
WEB: www.sheffield-pottery.com
SIC: 3269 5719 3999 1459 Mfg Pottery Products Ret Misc Homefurnishings Mfg Misc Products Clay/Related Mineral Mng

Shelburne Falls
Franklin County

(G-15066)
BRIAN SUMMER
Also Called: Sun & Moon Originals
46 Conway St Ste B (01370-1421)
PHONE..................................413 625-9990
Brian Summer, *Owner*
EMP: 6
SALES (est): 300K **Privately Held**
WEB: www.sunandmoonoriginals.com
SIC: 2392 Amusement/Recreation Services

(G-15067)
DAVID W WALLACE
Also Called: Bittersweet Herb Farm
635 Mohawk Trl (01370-9775)
PHONE..................................413 625-6523
David W Wallace, *Owner*
EMP: 8
SALES (est): 704.6K **Privately Held**
WEB: www.bittersweetherbfarm.com
SIC: 3999 5961 5947 5499 Mfg Mail Order Service & Ret Of Novelties Including Potpourri Herbal Dips & Blends Vinegar's & Gift Baskets

(G-15068)
DICK MULLER DESIGNER/CRAFTSMAN
21 High St (01370-1205)
PHONE..................................413 625-0016
Richard Muller, *Owner*
Dianne Muller, *Co-Owner*
EMP: 4
SALES (est): 239.7K **Privately Held**
SIC: 3171 2387 3172 5632 Mfg Women's Handbags/Purses Mfg Apparel Belts Mfg Personal Leather Goods Ret Women's Accessories Ret Luggage/Leather Good

(G-15069)
EDDIES WHEELS INC
140 State St (01370-1020)
PHONE..................................413 625-0033
Leslie Grinnell, *President*
▲ **EMP:** 14
SALES (est): 1.7MM **Privately Held**
WEB: www.eddieswheels.com
SIC: 3842 Mfg Surgical Appliances/Supplies

(G-15070)
EI-ENVRNMENTAL INTEGRATION LLC
278 Old Greenfield Rd (01370-9661)
PHONE..................................413 219-9547
Thor A Holbek, *Manager*
EMP: 3 **EST:** 2010
SALES (est): 368.3K **Privately Held**
SIC: 3663 Mfg Radio/Tv Communication Equipment

(G-15071)
INDEPENDENT NEWS
12 Main St Ste 1 (01370-1161)
PHONE..................................413 522-5046
EMP: 3 **EST:** 2015
SALES (est): 103.3K **Privately Held**
SIC: 2711 Newspapers-Publishing/Printing

(G-15072)
JOSH SMPSON CNTEMPORARY GL INC
30 Frank Williams Rd (01370-9724)
PHONE..................................413 625-6145
Josiah Simpson, *President*
Jacqui Proctor, *Marketing Staff*
EMP: 10
SQ FT: 6,000
SALES (est): 1.4MM **Privately Held**
WEB: www.joshsimpson.com
SIC: 3229 Mfg Blown Glass & Glassware

(G-15073)
LAMSON AND GOODNOW LLC
Also Called: Lamson and Goodnow Mfg
45 Conway St (01370-1420)
P.O. Box 846, Westfield (01086-0846)
PHONE..................................413 625-0201
Brian J Hayes, *Principal*
▲ **EMP:** 20
SQ FT: 26,000
SALES (est): 3.7MM **Privately Held**
WEB: www.lamsonsharp.com
SIC: 3421 3089 3423 Whol Homefurnishings Whol Professional Equipment

(G-15074)
LAMSON AND GOODNOW MFG CO
Also Called: Lamsonsharp
45 Conway St (01370-1420)
PHONE..................................413 625-6311
J Ross Anderson, *CEO*
▲ **EMP:** 20 **EST:** 1837
SQ FT: 30,000
SALES (est): 5.8MM **Privately Held**
SIC: 3421 3423 Mfg Cutlery Mfg Hand/Edge Tools Mfg Lab Apparatus/Furn

(G-15075)
RAE JS
2231 Mohawk Trl (01370)
PHONE..................................413 625-9228
EMP: 5
SALES (est): 577.9K **Privately Held**
SIC: 7692 Welding Repair

(G-15076)
YOUNG & CONSTANTIN N RIVER GL (PA)
Deerfield Ave (01370)
PHONE..................................413 625-6422
Toll Free:..866 -
Kathleen Young, *President*
EMP: 5
SALES (est): 986.7K **Privately Held**
SIC: 3229 Mfg Pressed/Blown Glass

Sherborn
Middlesex County

(G-15077)
ASIAN ART SOCIETY NEW ENGLAND
50 Old Orchard Rd (01770-1036)
PHONE..................................781 250-6311
Steve Daskin, *President*
EMP: 3
SALES: 4.3K **Privately Held**
SIC: 3999 Mfg Misc Products

(G-15078)
COMPOSITE COMPANY INC
19 Kendall Ave (01770-1321)
PHONE..................................508 651-1681
Gary L Hawkins, *President*
John Hawkins, *Treasurer*
EMP: 8
SQ FT: 2,000
SALES (est): 1.1MM **Privately Held**
SIC: 7692 Welding Repair

(G-15079)
SKYLIGHT NAVIGATION TECHNOLOGY
19 Peckham Hill Rd (01770-1605)
PHONE..................................508 655-7516
Michael Perlmutter, *Owner*
EMP: 3
SALES (est): 206.7K **Privately Held**
SIC: 3827 Optical Instruments

Shirley
Middlesex County

(G-15080)
AMPAC ENTERPRISES INC
Also Called: All Star Sporting Goods
1 Main St (01464-2838)
P.O. Box 1356 (01464-1356)
PHONE..................................978 425-6266
Stanley M Jurga, *President*
Wilson Herrera, *CFO*
◆ **EMP:** 65
SQ FT: 24,000
SALES (est): 4.5MM **Privately Held**
SIC: 3949 5091 Mfg Sporting/Athletic Goods Whol Sporting/Recreational Goods

(G-15081)
BEMIS ASSOCIATES INC (PA)
1 Bemis Way (01464-2527)
PHONE..................................978 425-6761
Stephen Howard, *CEO*
Michael Johansen, *President*
Dave Riggert, *Vice Pres*
Lori Nowakowski, *Purch Agent*
Jacqueline Creran, *Engineer*
◆ **EMP:** 170
SQ FT: 160,000
SALES (est): 92.2MM **Privately Held**
WEB: www.bemisheatseal.com
SIC: 2891 2851 3479 Mfg Adhesives/Sealants Mfg Paints/Allied Products Coating/Engraving Service

(G-15082)
BEMIS ASSOCIATES INC
100 Ayer Rd (01464-2518)
PHONE..................................978 425-6761
Stephen Howard, *Manager*
EMP: 120
SALES (corp-wide): 92.2MM **Privately Held**
WEB: www.bemisheatseal.com
SIC: 2891 2851 Mfg Adhesives/Sealants Mfg Paints/Allied Products
PA: Bemis Associates, Inc.
1 Bemis Way
Shirley MA 01464
978 425-6761

(G-15083)
EXALPHA BIOLOGICALS INC
2 Shaker Rd Ste B101 (01464-2535)
PHONE..................................978 425-1370
John Castracane, *President*
Earl Madorsky, *Vice Pres*
Fred Reynold PHD, *VP Bus Dvlpt*
EMP: 4
SALES (est): 420K **Privately Held**
WEB: www.exalpha.com
SIC: 3841 Mfg Surgical/Medical Instruments

(G-15084)
GYS TECH LLC
Also Called: Cardan Robotics
Phoenix Pk 2 Shker Rd Ste Phoenix Park (01464)
PHONE..................................530 613-9233
Adeline Harris, *CEO*
EMP: 13
SALES (est): 1.6MM
SALES (corp-wide): 13.6B **Publicly Held**
SIC: 3845 Mfg Electromedical Equipment
PA: Stryker Corporation
2825 Airview Blvd
Portage MI 49002
269 389-4934

(G-15085)
HARVARD MANUFACTURING INC
2 Shaker Rd Ste C104 (01464-2561)
PHONE..................................978 425-5375
Charles Delong, *President*
EMP: 4
SQ FT: 2,500
SALES (est): 363.4K **Privately Held**
SIC: 3545 Manufactures Machine Tools Attachments And Accessories Specializing In Precision Cnc Machining

(G-15086)
HERFCO INC
9 Great Rd (01464-2898)
PHONE..................................978 772-4758
James K Farnsworth, *President*
EMP: 22
SQ FT: 20,500
SALES (est): 4MM **Privately Held**
WEB: www.herfco.com
SIC: 3444 Mfg Sheet Metalwork

(G-15087)
IMAGE SOFTWARE SERVICES INC
Also Called: ISS
2 Shaker Rd Ste D103 (01464-2551)
PHONE..................................978 425-3600
Jeffrey W Schwarz, *President*
Andrea Willette, *Vice Pres*
EMP: 35
SQ FT: 2,000
SALES (est): 1.4MM **Privately Held**
WEB: www.imagesoftwareservices.net
SIC: 2759 2741 3652 Commercial Printing Misc Publishing Mfg Prerecorded Records/Tapes

▲ = Import ▼=Export
◆ =Import/Export

(G-15088)
KCB SOLUTIONS LLC
900 Mount Laurel Cir (01464-2422)
PHONE..................................978 425-0400
Ralph Nilsson, *President*
Eddie Wiencko, *Engineer*
EMP: 16
SALES (est): 3.6MM **Privately Held**
SIC: 3674 Mfg Semiconductors/Related Devices

(G-15089)
MCELROY ELECTRONICS CORP
27 Fredonian St 33 (01464-2836)
P.O. Box 488 (01464-0488)
PHONE..................................978 425-4055
John C Mc Elroy Jr, *President*
Daniel L Mc Elroy, *Vice Pres*
Mark Mc Elroy, *Vice Pres*
EMP: 12 **EST:** 1957
SQ FT: 7,500
SALES (est): 1.5MM **Privately Held**
WEB: www.mcelroyelectronics.com
SIC: 3612 Mfg Transformer Terminations

(G-15090)
MOBIUS IMAGING LLC
2 Shaker Rd Ste F100 (01464-2535)
PHONE..................................978 796-5068
Eugene A Gregerson, *President*
▲ **EMP:** 84
SQ FT: 30,000
SALES (est): 23MM
SALES (corp-wide): 13.6B **Publicly Held**
SIC: 3841 Mfg Surgical/Medical Instruments
PA: Stryker Corporation
2825 Airview Blvd
Portage MI 49002
269 389-4934

(G-15091)
NANOPTEK CORPORATION
2 Shaker Rd (01464-2525)
PHONE..................................978 460-7107
John M Guerra, *CEO*
EMP: 4
SALES (est): 350K **Privately Held**
SIC: 3827 8731 Mfg Optical Instruments/Lenses Commercial Physical Research

(G-15092)
POLAR CONTROLS INC
2 Shaker Rd Ste F220 (01464-2555)
PHONE..................................978 425-2233
Adam Cohen, *President*
Josh Tang, *Vice Pres*
Celeste Lawrence, *Engineer*
EMP: 8
SQ FT: 5,000
SALES (est): 1.4MM **Privately Held**
WEB: www.polarcontrols.com
SIC: 3699 Mfg Electronic Equipment

(G-15093)
SCINTITECH INC
1000 Mt Lurel Cir Shirley (01464)
PHONE..................................978 425-0800
Vadim Gayshan, *President*
◆ **EMP:** 4
SQ FT: 7,000
SALES: 1.8MM **Privately Held**
SIC: 3829 Mfg Measuring/Controlling Devices

(G-15094)
THERMO-FAB CORPORATION
76 Walker Rd (01464-2921)
PHONE..................................978 425-2311
Tom King, *President*
Heather Buyak, *Office Mgr*
Donna Lozeau, *Info Tech Mgr*
Yi Chong, *Technology*
Mike Vitols, *Athletic Dir*
▲ **EMP:** 35
SQ FT: 21,000
SALES (est): 7.3MM **Privately Held**
WEB: www.thermofab.com
SIC: 3089 3469 Mfg Plastic Products Mfg Metal Stampings

(G-15095)
TIER 7 COMMUNICATIONS
41 Holden Rd (01464-2114)
PHONE..................................978 425-9543
Thomas Oldfield, *President*
EMP: 7
SALES: 700K **Privately Held**
SIC: 3674 Mfg Semiconductors/Related Devices

(G-15096)
TPE SOLUTIONS INC (PA)
Also Called: Nexprene
3 Patterson Rd Ste 2 (01464-2907)
PHONE..................................978 425-3033
Jonas Angus, *President*
Mary Elaine Dunn-Angus, *Treasurer*
◆ **EMP:** 6
SQ FT: 60,000
SALES: 14MM **Privately Held**
WEB: www.tpesinc.com
SIC: 2821 Mfg Plastic Materials/Resins

Shrewsbury
Worcester County

(G-15097)
ACTEGA NORTH AMERICA INC
Also Called: Actega Wit
577 Hartford Tpke Ste C (01545-4387)
PHONE..................................508 845-6600
Joseph Rieck, *Manager*
EMP: 5
SALES (corp-wide): 385.1K **Privately Held**
WEB: www.waterinktech.com
SIC: 2893 Mfg Printing Ink
HQ: Actega North America, Inc.
950 S Chester Ave Ste B2
Delran NJ 08075
856 829-6300

(G-15098)
AGGREGATE INDUSTRIES - MWR INC
651 Lake St (01545-4662)
PHONE..................................508 754-4709
Richie Kilpoyne, *Manager*
EMP: 3
SALES (corp-wide): 4.5B **Privately Held**
SIC: 3273 Mfg Ready-Mixed Concrete
HQ: Aggregate Industries - Mwr, Inc.
2815 Dodd Rd
Eagan MN 55121
651 683-0600

(G-15099)
ALS OIL SERVICE
307 Hartford Tpke (01545-4024)
PHONE..................................508 853-2539
Edward A Flynn Jr, *Manager*
EMP: 5
SALES (est): 416.6K **Privately Held**
SIC: 1382 Oil/Gas Exploration Services

(G-15100)
AMERICAN METAL POLISHING
14 Commerce Rd (01545-4398)
PHONE..................................978 726-7752
George Beer, *Principal*
EMP: 3
SALES (est): 106.4K **Privately Held**
SIC: 3471 Plating/Polishing Service

(G-15101)
AMERICAS BEST DEFENSE
274 South St (01545-4397)
PHONE..................................774 745-5809
EMP: 3 **EST:** 2017
SALES (est): 174.4K **Privately Held**
SIC: 3812 Mfg Search/Navigation Equipment

(G-15102)
ANOMET PRODUCTS INC
830 Boston Tpke (01545-3386)
PHONE..................................508 842-0174
Terence Wong, *President*
Bob Gallant, *General Mgr*
David Kokidko, *General Mgr*
James Wong, *Corp Secy*
Dan Lambert, *Engineer*
EMP: 35 **EST:** 1976
SQ FT: 32,000
SALES (est): 5.9MM **Privately Held**
WEB: www.anometproducts.com
SIC: 3471 3643 3357 Plating/Polishing Service Mfg Conductive Wiring Devices Nonferrous Wiredrawing/Insulating

(G-15103)
ATLANTIC VISION INC
810 Boston Tpke Ste 2 (01545-3389)
PHONE..................................508 845-8401
Kathleen McDonough, *President*
▲ **EMP:** 8
SQ FT: 10,000
SALES (est): 1.6MM **Privately Held**
WEB: www.atlanticvision.com
SIC: 3827 5049 Mfg Optical Instruments/Lenses Whol Professional Equipment

(G-15104)
BLACK DIAMOND DRILL GRINDERS
17 Viking Ter (01545-4579)
PHONE..................................978 465-3799
Ha Phung, *President*
Frank Kiritsy, *Vice Pres*
▲ **EMP:** 10
SQ FT: 6,500
SALES (est): 750K **Privately Held**
WEB: www.blackdiamondgrinder.com
SIC: 3599 5084 Mfg Industrial Machinery Whol Industrial Equipment

(G-15105)
BOSTON MEDICAL PRODUCTS INC
70 Chestnut St (01545-4101)
PHONE..................................508 898-9300
Stuart K Montgomery, *President*
Michael Warren, *QC Mgr*
Marcus A Eisenhut, *Treasurer*
John Duquette, *Natl Sales Mgr*
Gabriele Meissner, *Admin Sec*
EMP: 25
SQ FT: 16,000
SALES (est): 5.1MM
SALES (corp-wide): 3.3MM **Privately Held**
WEB: www.bosmed.com
SIC: 3842 5047 Mfg Surgical Appliances/Supplies Whol Medical/Hospital Equipment
PA: Bess Ag
Gustav-Krone-Str. 7
Berlin 14167
308 169-0990

(G-15106)
CASSA FLOOR DESIGN INC
420 Boston Tpke (01545-3464)
PHONE..................................508 845-0600
Amarildo Soares, *President*
David Cassanelli, *Treasurer*
EMP: 17
SALES (est): 928K **Privately Held**
SIC: 3281 Mfg Cut Stone/Products

(G-15107)
DEJA BREW INC
510 Boston Tpke (01545-5973)
PHONE..................................508 842-8991
Ray Schavone, *President*
EMP: 7
SQ FT: 2,700
SALES (est): 910.2K **Privately Held**
WEB: www.deja-brew.com
SIC: 2082 Mfg Malt Beverages

(G-15108)
DONAHUE INDUSTRIES INC
5 Industrial Dr (01545-5835)
PHONE..................................508 845-6501
Judith L Donahue, *President*
Walter Laptewicz, *Vice Pres*
EMP: 25 **EST:** 1973
SQ FT: 23,000
SALES (est): 5.1MM **Privately Held**
WEB: www.donahueindustries.com
SIC: 3421 3452 3089 3541 Mfg Cutlery Mfg Bolts/Screws/Rivets Mfg Plastic Products Mfg Machine Tool-Cutting

(G-15109)
DUVA DISTRIBUTORS INC
479 Hartford Tpke (01545-4002)
P.O. Box 560 (01545-0560)
PHONE..................................508 841-8182
Christopher Duva, *President*
EMP: 30
SQ FT: 13,000
SALES (est): 2.9MM **Privately Held**
SIC: 2051 Mfg Bread/Related Products

(G-15110)
EMBROIDERY PLACE
10 Broushane Cir (01545-2050)
PHONE..................................508 842-5311
Colleen Gardner, *Owner*
EMP: 8
SALES: 150K **Privately Held**
SIC: 2395 Pleating/Stitching Services

(G-15111)
EPS POLYMER DISTRIBUTION INC
165 Memorial Dr Ste D (01545-6208)
PHONE..................................508 925-5932
Edward Smith, *President*
Joan Powers, *Vice Pres*
EMP: 3
SQ FT: 3,600
SALES (est): 648.4K **Privately Held**
WEB: www.epspolymer.com
SIC: 2821 Mfg Plastic Materials/Resins

(G-15112)
FITIVITY INC
15 Meadowsweet Rd (01545-6604)
PHONE..................................508 308-5822
Guy Pistone, *CEO*
EMP: 6
SALES: 127.7K **Privately Held**
SIC: 7372 Prepackaged Software Services

(G-15113)
FREESTYLE SYSTEMS LLC
238 Cherry St Ste 1 (01545-4085)
PHONE..................................508 845-4911
Michelle Tank,
Michael Hopper,
▲ **EMP:** 7
SALES (est): 1MM **Privately Held**
WEB: www.freestylesystems.com
SIC: 3999 Mfg Misc Products

(G-15114)
GALLANT MACHINE WORKS INC
6 Ek Ct (01545-4573)
PHONE..................................508 799-2919
Eric K Tessier, *President*
EMP: 10
SALES (est): 1.2MM **Privately Held**
SIC: 3599 Mfg Industrial Machinery

(G-15115)
GREEN DRAGON BINDERY INC
265 Boylston St (01545-1921)
PHONE..................................508 842-8250
Barbara Carpenter, *President*
EMP: 5 **EST:** 1963
SALES (est): 523K **Privately Held**
WEB: www.greendragonbindery.com
SIC: 2789 Bookbinding/Related Work

(G-15116)
HEBERT RETAIL LLC
Also Called: Hebert Candies
574 Hartford Tpke (01545-4048)
PHONE..................................508 845-8051
Sheila Shechtman, *CEO*
Richard Shechtman, *Exec VP*
Corey Mastrapasqua, *Graphic Designe*
EMP: 60
SQ FT: 65,000
SALES (est): 9MM
SALES (corp-wide): 33.6MM **Privately Held**
SIC: 2064 5441 Mfg Candy/Confectionery Ret Candy/Confectionery
PA: American Gourmet Group, Llc
574 Hartford Tpke
Shrewsbury MA 01545
860 761-6500

GEOGRAPHIC

(G-15117)
INDUSTRIAL POLYMERS & CHEM INC (PA)
508 Boston Tpke (01545-5997)
PHONE..................................508 845-6112
Susan M Dacey, *CEO*
Robert Desrosiers, *President*
Clarence Gary, *Production*
Lisa Joppas, *Administration*
▲ **EMP:** 30 **EST:** 1959
SQ FT: 35,000
SALES (est): 4.2MM **Privately Held**
SIC: 2295 Mfg Coated Fabrics

(G-15118)
INSTRUMENT & VALVE SERVICES CO
238 Cherry St Ste D (01545-4085)
PHONE..................................508 842-7000
Cris Carter, *Manager*
EMP: 8
SALES (corp-wide): 18.3B **Publicly Held**
WEB: www.instrum3nt.com
SIC: 3823 Mfg Process Control Instruments
HQ: Instrument & Valve Services Company
205 S Center St
Marshalltown IA 50158

(G-15119)
IPAC FABRICS INC
508 Boston Tpke (01545-5970)
PHONE..................................508 845-6112
Susan Dacey, *President*
Joan Dacey-Seib, *Treasurer*
EMP: 3
SQ FT: 35,000
SALES (est): 210K **Privately Held**
SIC: 2295 Mfg Resin Coated Fabrics

(G-15120)
JNP COFFEE LLC
8 Kalamat Farms Cir (01545-1656)
P.O. Box 576 (01545-0576)
PHONE..................................858 518-7437
EMP: 3
SALES (est): 258K **Privately Held**
SIC: 2095 Mfg Roasted Coffee

(G-15121)
LFR CHASSIS INC
20 Sewall St (01545-1329)
PHONE..................................508 425-3117
Rob Fuller, *Principal*
EMP: 4
SALES (est): 475.7K **Privately Held**
SIC: 3714 Mfg Motor Vehicle Parts/Accessories

(G-15122)
MARK D SKIEST
4 Parker Rd (01545-5126)
PHONE..................................508 754-0639
Mark D Skiest, *Principal*
EMP: 5
SALES (est): 497.2K **Privately Held**
SIC: 3713 Mfg Truck/Bus Bodies

(G-15123)
MINDFUL ELEMENTS LLC
112 South St (01545-3032)
PHONE..................................508 845-2833
EMP: 3 **EST:** 2008
SALES (est): 177.5K **Privately Held**
SIC: 2819 Mfg Industrial Inorganic Chemicals

(G-15124)
MITCHELL DIFFERENTIAL INC
384 Hartford Tpke (01545-4023)
PHONE..................................508 755-3790
Daniel J Mitchell, *President*
EMP: 3
SALES (est): 333.1K **Privately Held**
SIC: 3711 Mfg Motor Vehicle/Car Bodies

(G-15125)
NELES USA INC (DH)
Also Called: Field Sytems Division
44 Bowditch Dr (01545-1719)
PHONE..................................508 852-0200
John Quinlivan, *President*
Jerry Mitchell, *President*
Florentinina Dan, *Business Anlyst*
Kathy Martin, *Marketing Staff*
Keith Hill, *Manager*
▲ **EMP:** 239
SALES (est): 116.4MM
SALES (corp-wide): 3.5B **Privately Held**
SIC: 3592 Mfg Carburetors/Pistons/Rings

(G-15126)
NELES USA INC
Also Called: Metso Automation
44 Bowditch Dr (01545-1719)
PHONE..................................508 852-0200
Susan Prior, *Principal*
David Escobar, *Sales Mgr*
Mike Poff, *Manager*
Bob Vickowski, *Manager*
Steve Obermann, *Senior Mgr*
EMP: 4
SALES (corp-wide): 3.5B **Privately Held**
SIC: 3592 Mfg Carburetors/Pistons/Rings
HQ: Neles Usa Inc
44 Bowditch Dr
Shrewsbury MA 01545
508 852-0200

(G-15127)
NELES USA INC
42 Bowditch Dr (01545-1719)
PHONE..................................508 852-0200
Chris Van Laar, *Branch Mgr*
Marina Vahlberg, *Info Tech Mgr*
EMP: 14
SALES (corp-wide): 3.5B **Privately Held**
SIC: 3592 Mfg Carburetors/Pistons/Rings
HQ: Neles Usa Inc
44 Bowditch Dr
Shrewsbury MA 01545
508 852-0200

(G-15128)
PHADEAN ENGINEERING CO INC
44 Summer St (01545-5645)
P.O. Box 611 (01545-8611)
PHONE..................................888 204-0900
Donna Cina, *President*
EMP: 3 **EST:** 1946
SALES (est): 240K **Privately Held**
SIC: 3089 8711 Mfg Plastic Oilers

(G-15129)
PRECISION STONE WORKS INC
224 Cherry St Ste C (01545-4673)
PHONE..................................774 261-4420
Leonardo De Souza Carvalho, *Admin Sec*
EMP: 4
SALES (est): 210.1K **Privately Held**
SIC: 1411 Dimension Stone Quarry

(G-15130)
SEAGATE TECHNOLOGY LLC
333 South St (01545-7807)
PHONE..................................508 770-3111
John J Gannon, *Manager*
EMP: 240 **Privately Held**
SIC: 3572 Mfg Computer Storage Devices
HQ: Seagate Technology Llc
10200 S De Anza Blvd
Cupertino CA 95014
408 658-1000

(G-15131)
SERVICE ORIENTED SALES INC
Also Called: Sourcing Opportunities
775 Hartford Tpke Ste 2 (01545-4105)
PHONE..................................508 845-3330
Susan Ondovic, *President*
◆ **EMP:** 5
SALES (est): 515.2K **Privately Held**
WEB: www.sourcing-opps.com
SIC: 3441 Structural Metal Fabrication

(G-15132)
SHREWSBURY NATIONAL PRESS
298 Boston Tpke Ste 3 (01545-3871)
PHONE..................................508 756-7502
Martis Bania, *President*
EMP: 6
SQ FT: 30,000
SALES (est): 250K **Privately Held**
SIC: 2752 2759 Lithographic Commercial Printing Commercial Printing

(G-15133)
STONEY INDUSTRIES INC
89 School St (01545-5022)
PHONE..................................508 845-6731
Stan Stoney, *Principal*
EMP: 3
SALES (est): 248.7K **Privately Held**
SIC: 3999 Mfg Misc Products

(G-15134)
VALENTE BACKHOE SERVICE LLC
1 Temple Ct (01545-2171)
PHONE..................................508 754-7013
Paul Valente, *Principal*
EMP: 4
SALES (est): 481K **Privately Held**
SIC: 3531 Mfg Construction Machinery

(G-15135)
VASOTECH INC
55 Plainfield Ave (01545-5736)
PHONE..................................617 686-2770
Tim Wu, *President*
EMP: 3
SALES (est): 247.1K **Privately Held**
SIC: 3845 Mfg Electromedical Equipment

(G-15136)
VIVID ENGINEERING
415 Boston Tpke Ste 305 (01545-3415)
PHONE..................................508 842-0165
David Johnson, *Owner*
EMP: 5
SALES (est): 550K **Privately Held**
SIC: 3577 Mfg Computer Peripheral Equipment

(G-15137)
WELD ENGINEERING CO INC
34 Fruit St (01545-3200)
PHONE..................................508 842-2224
Thomas Less, *President*
◆ **EMP:** 25
SALES (est): 4.7MM **Privately Held**
WEB: www.weldengineering.com
SIC: 3548 5084 3564 Welding Apparatus, Nsk

(G-15138)
ZEXEN TECHNOLOGY LLC
238 Cherry St Ste C (01545-4085)
PHONE..................................508 786-9928
Bo Zhang, *President*
▲ **EMP:** 4
SQ FT: 3,000
SALES: 500K **Privately Held**
SIC: 3629 Distributes And Sales Electric Motors And Machine Parts

(G-15139)
ZYCAL BIOCEUTICALS MFG LLC
3 Turning Leaf Cir (01545-5484)
PHONE..................................888 779-9225
Elaine Ann Fankhauser, *Administration*
EMP: 39
SALES (corp-wide): 817K **Privately Held**
SIC: 3999 Mfg Misc Products
PA: Zycal Bioceuticals Manufacturing Llc
5a Executive Dr
Toms River NJ 08755
888 779-9225

Shutesbury
Franklin County

(G-15140)
N E M T R LLC
29 Highland Dr (01072-9736)
PHONE..................................413 259-1444
Peter Gees, *President*
EMP: 4
SQ FT: 4,000
SALES: 300K **Privately Held**
SIC: 3541 8734 Mfg Machine Tools-Cutting Testing Laboratory

Siasconset
Nantucket County

(G-15141)
NANTUCKET CHRONICLE LLC
39 Low Beach Rd (02564)
PHONE..................................508 257-6683
EMP: 3 **EST:** 2013
SALES (est): 145K **Privately Held**
SIC: 2711 Newspapers-Publishing/Printing

Somerset
Bristol County

(G-15142)
CONCENTRIC FABRICATION LLC
179 Riverside Ave (02725-2842)
PHONE..................................774 955-5692
Derek Riley, *Principal*
EMP: 3 **EST:** 2014
SALES (est): 432K **Privately Held**
SIC: 3446 Mfg Architectural Metalwork

(G-15143)
COUNTY STREET ICE CREAM CORP
2977 County St (02726-3904)
PHONE..................................508 674-3357
John J Hodnett, *Principal*
EMP: 5
SALES (est): 317.7K **Privately Held**
SIC: 2024 Mfg Ice Cream/Frozen Desert

(G-15144)
FORTIER BOATS INC
34 Riverside Ave (02725-2869)
PHONE..................................508 673-5253
EMP: 5
SQ FT: 12,000
SALES (est): 856.4K **Privately Held**
SIC: 3732 Boatbuilding/Repairing

(G-15145)
KICKEMUIT INDUSTRIES LLC
177 Riverside Ave (02725-2842)
PHONE..................................508 675-0594
Mark Pearson,
EMP: 4
SQ FT: 14,000
SALES (est): 600.8K **Privately Held**
SIC: 2821 Mfg Plastic Materials/Resins

(G-15146)
LENMARINE INC
1 Main St (02726-5631)
PHONE..................................508 678-1234
Steven Wanderson, *Opers Staff*
EMP: 15
SALES (corp-wide): 2.8MM **Privately Held**
SIC: 2621 Paper Mill
PA: Lenmarine, Inc.
99 Poppasquash Rd Unit 1
Bristol RI 02809
401 253-2200

(G-15147)
N FERRARA INC
10 Riverside Ave (02725-2869)
PHONE..................................508 679-2440
Nicola Ferrara, *President*
Liana Ferrara, *Clerk*
EMP: 10
SQ FT: 20,000
SALES: 1MM **Privately Held**
SIC: 3547 5084 Mfg Rolling Mill Machinery

(G-15148)
SPINDLE CITY PRECIOUS METALS
161 Wilbur Ave (02725-2058)
PHONE..................................508 567-1597
EMP: 8
SALES (est): 917.6K **Privately Held**
SIC: 3339 Primary Nonferrous Metal Producer

▲ = Import ▼=Export
◆ =Import/Export

(G-15149)
TAMER INDUSTRIES INC
185 Riverside Ave (02725-2842)
PHONE..................................508 677-0900
Atwell B Hedly, *President*
Jeffrey Hedly, *President*
Debbie Le Vesque, *Office Mgr*
EMP: 100
SALES (est): 19.8MM **Privately Held**
WEB: www.tamerind.com
SIC: 3444 Mfg Sheet Metalwork

Somerville
Middlesex County

(G-15150)
3 LITTLE FIGS LLC
278 Highland Ave B (02143-1338)
PHONE..................................617 623-3447
Katie E Rooney, *Principal*
EMP: 4
SALES (est): 263.6K **Privately Held**
SIC: 2051 Mfg Bread/Related Products

(G-15151)
ALBERT CAPONE (PA)
Also Called: Capone Foods
14 Bow St (02143-2915)
PHONE..................................617 629-2296
Albert Capone, *Owner*
Ashley Capone, *Sales Staff*
EMP: 7
SQ FT: 4,000
SALES (est): 857.5K **Privately Held**
WEB: www.caponefoods.com
SIC: 2099 5149 5143 2098 Mfg Food Preparations Whol Groceries Whol Dairy Products Mfg Macaroni/Spaghetti

(G-15152)
ALLSTON-BRIGHTON TAB
20 Holland St (02144-2700)
PHONE..................................617 629-3387
EMP: 3 **EST:** 2010
SALES (est): 150.5K **Privately Held**
SIC: 3661 Mfg Telephone/Telegraph Apparatus

(G-15153)
ALTAEROS ENERGIES INC
28 Dane St (02143-3237)
PHONE..................................617 908-8464
Ryan Holy, *Business Mgr*
Adam Rein, *Vice Pres*
EMP: 4
SALES (est): 59.2K **Privately Held**
SIC: 3511 Mfg Misc Products

(G-15154)
AMES SAFETY ENVELOPE COMPANY (DH)
Also Called: Ames Color File Div
12 Tyler St (02143-3241)
PHONE..................................617 684-1000
Kurt Ramsauer, *President*
Robert Ainold, *Vice Pres*
Steve Diforge, *Vice Pres*
Tim Donnhue, *Treasurer*
◆ **EMP:** 75 **EST:** 1919
SQ FT: 270,000
SALES (est): 20.9MM **Privately Held**
WEB: www.amespage.com
SIC: 2675 5112 Manufactures Die-Cut Paper And Paperboard Wholesale Stationery And Office Supplies
HQ: Tab Products Co. Llc
605 4th St
Mayville WI 53050
920 387-3131

(G-15155)
ARCHITECTURAL OPENINGS INC
16 Garfield Ave (02145-2105)
PHONE..................................617 776-9223
Stephen Kearns, *President*
▲ **EMP:** 17
SQ FT: 10,000
SALES: 838K **Privately Held**
WEB: www.archop.com
SIC: 2431 Mfg Millwork

(G-15156)
ARMADA LOGISTICS INC
Also Called: Odyn
48 Grove St Ste 201 (02144-2500)
PHONE..................................855 727-6232
Eric Gilmore, *CEO*
EMP: 4
SALES (est): 228.2K
SALES (corp-wide): 2.9MM **Privately Held**
SIC: 7372 4731 Prepackaged Software Services Freight Transportation Arrangement
PA: Turvo, Inc.
200 S Mathilda Ave
Sunnyvale CA 94086
650 830-3508

(G-15157)
ART SHIRT CO
228 Lowell St (02144-2638)
PHONE..................................617 625-2636
Gilbert Ricci, *Owner*
EMP: 3
SALES (est): 216.9K **Privately Held**
SIC: 2759 Commercial Printing

(G-15158)
BILL MARTEL
Also Called: Martel Binding
2 Bradley St Ste S8 (02145-2969)
PHONE..................................617 776-1040
EMP: 6
SQ FT: 4,000
SALES (est): 381.5K **Privately Held**
SIC: 2789 Bookbinding & Related Work

(G-15159)
BIOPHYSICAL DEVICES INC
27 Columbus Ave (02143-2018)
PHONE..................................617 629-0304
Peter Sisk, *CEO*
EMP: 3
SALES (est): 168.1K **Privately Held**
SIC: 3679 7389 Mfg Electronic Components

(G-15160)
BOMAS MACHINE SPECIALTIES INC
334 Washington St (02143-3812)
PHONE..................................617 628-3831
Joseph Annese, *President*
Mary Annese, *Treasurer*
Teresea Annese, *Treasurer*
EMP: 10
SQ FT: 7,000
SALES (est): 1.6MM **Privately Held**
WEB: www.bomas.com
SIC: 3851 Optical Grinding Service

(G-15161)
BRAZILIAN TIMES
311 Broadway (02145-1933)
P.O. Box 447 (02143-0006)
PHONE..................................617 625-5559
Edison Paiva, *Owner*
EMP: 6
SALES (est): 277.4K **Privately Held**
SIC: 2711 Newspapers-Publishing/Printing

(G-15162)
BRYAN ONCOR INC
141 Powder House Blvd (02144-1613)
PHONE..................................617 957-9858
Christopher Adams, *CEO*
EMP: 7
SQ FT: 1,000
SALES: 2.5MM **Privately Held**
SIC: 2834 Mfg Pharmaceutical Preparations

(G-15163)
CAMBRIDGE ELECTRONICS LABORATO
20 Chester St (02144-3005)
PHONE..................................617 629-2805
Jeffrey Race, *Principal*
EMP: 4
SALES (est): 401K **Privately Held**
SIC: 3661 Mfg Telephone/Telegraph Apparatus

(G-15164)
CANDLEWICK PRESS INC
99 Dover St Ste 3 (02144-2816)
PHONE..................................617 661-3330
Karen Lotz, *President*
Sarah Sherman, *Production*
Hilary Berkman, *Treasurer*
Emily M Marchand, *Admin Sec*
▲ **EMP:** 88
SQ FT: 28,000
SALES (est): 8.3MM
SALES (corp-wide): 99.9MM **Privately Held**
WEB: www.candlewick-press.com
SIC: 2731 Books-Publishing/Printing
PA: Walker Books Limited
87 Vauxhall Walk
London SE11
207 793-0909

(G-15165)
CARRICK PHARMACEUTICALS INC
16 Highland Rd (02144-2311)
PHONE..................................617 623-0525
Ted Miller, *CEO*
EMP: 3
SALES (est): 171.1K **Privately Held**
SIC: 2834 Mfg Pharmaceutical Preparations

(G-15166)
CLYPD INC
212 Elm St Ste 4 (02144-2959)
PHONE..................................617 800-9481
Joshua Summers, *CEO*
Doug Hurd, *Exec VP*
Jason Burke, *Vice Pres*
Rae Holly, *Vice Pres*
EMP: 28
SALES (est): 3.3MM **Privately Held**
SIC: 7372 Prepackaged Software

(G-15167)
COSTUME WORKS INC
36 Alston St (02143-2102)
PHONE..................................617 623-7510
Elizabeth Perlman, *President*
EMP: 11
SQ FT: 3,700
SALES: 600K **Privately Held**
WEB: www.costumeworksinc.com
SIC: 2389 Mfg Theatrical Costumes

(G-15168)
DEMOSTHENES GREEK-AM DEMO
218 Somerville Ave (02143-3416)
PHONE..................................617 628-7766
Chris Kakambouras, *Principal*
EMP: 4
SALES (est): 138.7K **Privately Held**
SIC: 2711 Newspapers-Publishing/Printing

(G-15169)
DIAKOSMISIS CORPORATION
561 Windsor St Ste B301 (02143-4158)
P.O. Box 356 (02143-0009)
PHONE..................................617 776-7714
Arthur Stamatopulos, *President*
George Montialagre, *Foreman/Supr*
EMP: 8
SQ FT: 6,000
SALES (est): 1.1MM **Privately Held**
WEB: www.diak.com
SIC: 2541 2434 Mfg Wood Partitions/Fixtures Mfg Wood Kitchen Cabinets

(G-15170)
EVERGAGE INC
212 Elm St Ste 4 (02144-2959)
PHONE..................................888 310-0589
Karl Wirth, *CEO*
Josh Baumrind, *Partner*
Laura Saati, *Vice Pres*
Oleg Rekutin, *Engineer*
Cait Gorges, *Sales Dir*
EMP: 70
SQ FT: 5,000
SALES (est): 3.2MM **Privately Held**
SIC: 7372 Prepackaged Software Services

(G-15171)
FINCH THERAPEUTICS INC
200 Innerbelt Rd Ste 400 (02143-4456)
PHONE..................................617 229-6499
Mark Smith, *President*
Andrew Noh, *Treasurer*
James Burgess, *Director*
EMP: 9
SALES (est): 168.9K **Privately Held**
SIC: 3844 Mfg X-Ray Apparatus/Tubes

(G-15172)
FLAGRAPHICS INC
30 Alston St (02143-2102)
P.O. Box 108 (02143-0002)
PHONE..................................617 776-7549
Antonio G Lafuente, *President*
Jen Travassos, *Office Mgr*
EMP: 20
SQ FT: 18,349
SALES: 1.1MM **Privately Held**
WEB: www.flagraphics.com
SIC: 2399 3446 2499 3089 Mfg Flags Banners & Metal Wooden And Fiberglass Flagpoles

(G-15173)
FLEMING & SON CORP
Also Called: Fleming Printing
40 White St (02144-3213)
PHONE..................................617 623-3047
Gary F Shea, *President*
Ed Ryan, *Vice Pres*
Stan Boliver, *Director*
EMP: 13 **EST:** 1938
SQ FT: 5,000
SALES (est): 1.9MM **Privately Held**
WEB: www.flemingprinting.com
SIC: 2752 Lithographic Commercial Printing

(G-15174)
FORMLABS INC (PA)
35 Medford St Ste 201 (02143-4237)
PHONE..................................617 932-5227
Maxim Lobovsky, *President*
Marlou De Jong, *Opers Mgr*
Luke Plummer, *Research*
Craig Broady, *Engineer*
Zach Brown, *Engineer*
◆ **EMP:** 400
SQ FT: 300
SALES (est): 7.6MM **Privately Held**
SIC: 2759 Commercial Printing

(G-15175)
GANGI PRINTING INC
17 Kensington Ave (02145-2106)
P.O. Box 632 (02143-0008)
PHONE..................................617 776-6071
Steven Gangi, *CEO*
Susan Gangi, *President*
Stephen L Gangi, *COO*
EMP: 11
SQ FT: 5,000
SALES (est): 668.5K **Privately Held**
WEB: www.gangiprinting.com
SIC: 2752 Lithographic Commercial Printing

(G-15176)
GATEHOUSE MEDIA MASS I INC
Also Called: Cambridge Chronicle
20 40 Holland St (02144)
PHONE..................................617 629-3381
Catherine Powers, *Director*
EMP: 8
SALES (corp-wide): 1.5B **Publicly Held**
SIC: 2711 Newspapers-Publishing/Printing
HQ: Gatehouse Media Massachusetts I, Inc.
48 Dunham Rd
Beverly MA 01915
585 598-0030

(G-15177)
GEOMETRIC INFORMATICS INC
387 Somerville Ave Apt 2 (02143-2951)
P.O. Box 325 (02143-0009)
PHONE..................................617 440-1078
Shing-Tunt Yau, *President*
Xian Feng, *Principal*
Yalin Wang, *Principal*
WEI Han, *Research*
Dale Royer, *Senior Engr*
EMP: 9

GEOGRAPHIC

SALES (est): 161K **Privately Held**
SIC: 7372 Prepackaged Software Services

(G-15178)
GEOORBITAL INC
17 Rev Nzreno Prperzi Way (02143-3228)
PHONE..................................617 651-1102
Michael Burtov, *CEO*
EMP: 15 **EST:** 2014
SQ FT: 2,000
SALES (est): 1.7MM **Privately Held**
SIC: 3714 Mfg Motor Vehicle Parts/Accessories

(G-15179)
GROVE LABS INC
28 Dane St (02143-3237)
PHONE..................................703 608-8178
Gabriel Blanchet, *CEO*
James Byron, *Chief Engr*
EMP: 13 **EST:** 2013
SALES (est): 1.6MM **Privately Held**
SIC: 3699 7371 Mfg Electrical Equipment/Supplies Custom Computer Programing

(G-15180)
GUY T PIRO & SONS
Also Called: Piro Printing
483 Medford St (02145-2699)
PHONE..................................617 776-2840
Marc Piro, *Owner*
EMP: 5
SQ FT: 1,500
SALES (est): 418.9K **Privately Held**
SIC: 2752 Lithographic Commercial Printing

(G-15181)
HEILA TECHNOLOGIES INC
444 Somerville Ave Ste 2 (02143-3270)
PHONE..................................954 829-4839
Francisco Morocz, *CEO*
EMP: 3 **EST:** 2015
SQ FT: 140
SALES: 370K **Privately Held**
SIC: 3674 Mfg Semiconductors/Related Devices

(G-15182)
HELIX POWER CORPORATION
28 Dane St (02143-3237)
PHONE..................................781 718-7282
Matthew Lazarewicz, *President*
Donald Bender, *Vice Pres*
EMP: 3
SALES (est): 191.7K **Privately Held**
SIC: 3629 Mfg Electrical Industrial Apparatus

(G-15183)
HOME HEATING SERVICES CORP
2 Alpine St (02144-2790)
P.O. Box 207 (02143-0902)
PHONE..................................617 625-8255
Peter Dupuis, *Owner*
EMP: 32
SALES (est): 1.2MM **Privately Held**
SIC: 1389 Oil/Gas Field Services

(G-15184)
INTERNATIONAL PRESS OF BOSTON
387 Somerville Ave Apt 3 (02143-2951)
PHONE..................................617 623-3016
Shing Tung Yao, *President*
Brian Bianchini, *General Mgr*
EMP: 5
SQ FT: 1,000
SALES (est): 519.6K **Privately Held**
SIC: 2731 Books-Publishing/Printing

(G-15185)
INTERNTONAL SCIENCE FOUNDATION
385 Somerville Ave (02143-2932)
PHONE..................................703 869-1853
Bong Lian, *Principal*
EMP: 5
SALES (est): 179.9K **Privately Held**
SIC: 2741 Misc Publishing

(G-15186)
ITEXT SOFTWARE CORP
265 Medford St Ste 500 (02143-1963)
PHONE..................................617 982-2646
Bruno Lowagie, *President*
Ingeborg Willaert, *CFO*
EMP: 8 **EST:** 2009
SALES (est): 1.2MM **Privately Held**
SIC: 7372 Prepackaged Software Services

(G-15187)
J P MORIARTY & CO INC
Also Called: JP Moriarty Millwork
22 Clifton St Ste 1 (02144-2577)
PHONE..................................617 628-3000
John P Moriarty, *President*
EMP: 6
SQ FT: 18,000
SALES (est): 825.5K **Privately Held**
WEB: www.jpmoriarty.com
SIC: 2431 Mfg Custom Wood Doors Wood Windows Wood Moldings & Millwork

(G-15188)
JAMES A KILEY COMPANY
15 Linwood St (02143-2112)
PHONE..................................617 776-0344
John C Kiley, *President*
James Kiley Jr, *Vice Pres*
Timothy Kiley, *Vice Pres*
John Colbert, *Purchasing*
EMP: 45 **EST:** 1890
SQ FT: 40,000
SALES (est): 9.3MM **Privately Held**
SIC: 3713 Mfg Truck/Bus Bodies

(G-15189)
LABMINDS INC
285 Washington St Ste 3 (02143-3339)
PHONE..................................844 956-8327
Ville Lehtonen, *CEO*
Jochen Klingelhoefer, *Vice Pres*
Ricklef Wohlers, *Vice Pres*
Michal Wozny, *Vice Pres*
EMP: 9 **EST:** 2013
SALES (est): 1.3MM **Privately Held**
SIC: 3821 Mfg Lab Apparatus/Furniture
PA: Labminds Ltd
Penrose House 67 Hightown Road
Banbury OXON
800 086-8771

(G-15190)
LEVELTRIGGER INC
212 Elm St (02144-2958)
PHONE..................................650 468-1098
Puneet Batra, *Principal*
Renee Bochman, *COO*
EMP: 3
SALES (est): 237K **Privately Held**
SIC: 7372 Prepackaged Software Services

(G-15191)
LOTO LIGHTING LLC
1 Fitchburg St Apt C305 (02143-2194)
PHONE..................................617 776-3115
Thomas Devlin, *Mng Member*
EMP: 5
SALES (est): 731.4K **Privately Held**
SIC: 3646 Mfg Commercial Lighting Fixtures

(G-15192)
MAGIQ TECHNOLOGIES INC (PA)
11 Ward St Ste 300 (02143-4214)
PHONE..................................617 661-8300
Bob Gelfond, *CEO*
Audrius Berzanskis, *COO*
Andrew Hammond, *Vice Pres*
Michael Lagasse, *Vice Pres*
Steven Bookman, *CFO*
▲ **EMP:** 12
SALES (est): 1.2MM **Privately Held**
WEB: www.magiqtech.com
SIC: 3699 Mfg Electrical Equipment & Supplies

(G-15193)
MAGPIE INDUSTRIES LLC
416 Highland Ave (02144-2511)
PHONE..................................617 623-3330
David Sakowski, *Mng Member*
EMP: 7
SALES (est): 392.5K **Privately Held**
SIC: 3999 Mfg Misc Products

(G-15194)
MANGE LLC
30 Summer St Apt 1 (02143-1986)
PHONE..................................917 880-2104
Christopher Spivak, *Mng Member*
▼ **EMP:** 8
SALES: 120K **Privately Held**
SIC: 2099 5149 Mfg Food Preparations Whol Groceries

(G-15195)
MASSACHUSETTS ENVELOPE CO INC (PA)
Also Called: Grossman Marketing Group
30 Cobble Hill Rd (02143-4412)
P.O. Box 100 (02143-0002)
PHONE..................................617 623-8000
David Grossman, *President*
Ben Grossman, *Principal*
Thomas Cummings, *Vice Pres*
Maureen McGoldrick, *Vice Pres*
Doug Smith, *CFO*
EMP: 40 **EST:** 1910
SALES (est): 12.1MM **Privately Held**
WEB: www.massenvplus.com
SIC: 2759 5112 8741 7331 Commercial Printing Whol Stationery/Offc Sup Management Services

(G-15196)
MASTER PRINTING & SIGNS
60 Union Sq (02143-3032)
PHONE..................................617 623-8270
Angelica Menatti, *Owner*
Nilson Rigonatti, *Co-Owner*
EMP: 3
SQ FT: 3,000
SALES (est): 224.2K **Privately Held**
SIC: 2752 7336 Lithographic Commercial Printing Commercial Art/Graphic Design

(G-15197)
MCINTIRE BRASS WORKS INC
14 Horace St (02143-4207)
PHONE..................................617 547-1819
Elaine Anthony, *President*
Arthur Anthony, *Vice Pres*
EMP: 7
SQ FT: 2,000
SALES (est): 1MM **Privately Held**
WEB: www.slidepole.com
SIC: 3351 3569 Mfg Bronze Pipes And Firefighting Or Related Equipment

(G-15198)
MENON LABORATORIES INC
28 Dane St (02143-3237)
PHONE..................................339 224-2787
Latika Menon, *Ch of Bd*
Eugen Panaitescu, *Info Tech Dir*
EMP: 3 **EST:** 2013
SALES (est): 210K **Privately Held**
SIC: 2819 Mfg Industrial Inorganic Chemicals

(G-15199)
MICRO-LEADS INC
255 Elm St Ste 300 (02144-2957)
PHONE..................................617 299-0295
Bryan McLaughlin, *President*
EMP: 6
SALES (est): 150.9K **Privately Held**
SIC: 3845 Mfg Electromedical Equipment

(G-15200)
MULTI TOUCH SURFACE INC
25 Lewis St Apt 3 (02143-3805)
PHONE..................................408 634-9224
EMP: 50 **EST:** 2012
SALES (est): 5.1MM **Privately Held**
SIC: 3577 Mfg Computer Peripheral Equipment

(G-15201)
MYSTIC VALLEY FOUNDRY INC
14 Horace St (02143-4298)
PHONE..................................617 547-1819
Arthur Anthony, *President*
Lara Anthony, *Treasurer*
EMP: 7
SQ FT: 10,000
SALES (est): 1.1MM **Privately Held**
SIC: 3366 3363 3365 Mfg Aluminum Die-Castings Copper Foundry Aluminum Foundry

(G-15202)
NORTHAST PRFORMER PUBLICATIONS
Also Called: Northeast Performer Magazine
24 Dane St (02143-3202)
P.O. Box 348 (02143-0009)
PHONE..................................617 627-9200
EMP: 3
SALES (est): 255K **Privately Held**
WEB: www.performermag.com
SIC: 2721 Periodicals-Publishing/Printing

(G-15203)
PERCEPTIVE AUTOMATA INC (PA)
230 Somerville Ave 2 (02143-3406)
PHONE..................................617 299-1296
Kshitij Misra, *CEO*
EMP: 13
SALES (est): 4.1MM **Privately Held**
SIC: 7372 Prepackaged Software Services

(G-15204)
PERFORMER PUBLICATIONS INC
24 Dane St (02143-3202)
P.O. Box 348 (02143-0009)
PHONE..................................617 627-9200
William House, *CEO*
EMP: 8
SALES (est): 586.9K **Privately Held**
SIC: 2741 Misc Publishing

(G-15205)
PETER FORG MANUFACTURING CO
50 Park St (02143-3614)
P.O. Box 433 (02143-0006)
PHONE..................................617 625-0337
Donald Forg, *President*
David Forg, *Vice Pres*
EMP: 18 **EST:** 1881
SQ FT: 30,000
SALES (est): 2.7MM **Privately Held**
WEB: www.peterforg.com
SIC: 3469 Mfg Metal Stampings

(G-15206)
PSG FRAMING INC
130 Broadway (02145-3201)
PHONE..................................617 261-1817
Bernard Pucker, *President*
Archie Agan, *Accounting Mgr*
Suzanne Pucker, *Admin Sec*
EMP: 19
SQ FT: 9,800
SALES: 2MM **Privately Held**
SIC: 2499 Mfg Wood Products

(G-15207)
PUCKER GALLERY INC
Also Called: Psg Framing
130 Broadway Rear (02145-3201)
PHONE..................................617 261-1817
J Watkins, *Manager*
EMP: 15
SALES (corp-wide): 1.6MM **Privately Held**
WEB: www.puckergallery.com
SIC: 3952 4225 Mfg Lead Pencils/Art Goods General Warehouse/Storage
PA: Pucker Gallery, Inc
240 Newbury St Ste 3
Boston MA 02116
617 267-9473

(G-15208)
QRSTS LLC
Also Called: R.A.w
561 Windsor St Ste B101 (02143-4144)
PHONE..................................617 625-3335
Peter Rinneg, *Mng Member*
EMP: 8
SALES (est): 719.2K **Privately Held**
WEB: www.qrsts.com
SIC: 2759 Commercial Printing

▲ = Import ▼=Export
◆ =Import/Export

(G-15209)
RELIABLE SHADE & SCREEN CO
14 Sterling St 2 (02144-1117)
PHONE.................................617 776-9538
Fax: 617 547-9222
EMP: 3
SQ FT: 3,000
SALES (est): 311.1K Privately Held
SIC: 3442 2591 Mfg Metal Doors/Sash/Trim Mfg Drapery Hardware/Blinds

(G-15210)
RIGHTHAND ROBOTICS INC
237 Washington St (02143-3019)
PHONE.................................617 501-0085
Leif Jentoft, President
Victoria Coleman, Engineer
Yuli Friedman, Engineer
Parker Heyl, Design Engr
John Sullivan, Electrical Engi
EMP: 3
SALES (est): 467.7K Privately Held
SIC: 3569 7389 Mfg General Industrial Machinery

(G-15211)
ROGERS FOAM AUTOMOTIVE CORP
20 Vernon St Ste 1 (02145-3699)
PHONE.................................617 623-3010
William Tee, Branch Mgr
EMP: 10
SALES (corp-wide): 194.7MM Privately Held
SIC: 3086 Mfg Plastic Foam Products
HQ: Rogers Foam Automotive Corporation
501 W Kearsley St
Flint MI 48503
810 820-6323

(G-15212)
ROGERS FOAM CORPORATION (PA)
20 Vernon St Ste 1 (02145-3699)
PHONE.................................617 623-3010
David P Marotta, President
Mathew Rogers, Chairman
Sharod Hulsoor, Traffic Mgr
Gerardo Arneros, Engineer
Joseph Marenghi, Info Tech Mgr
◆ EMP: 350 EST: 1947
SQ FT: 140,500
SALES (est): 194.7MM Privately Held
WEB: www.rogersfoam.com
SIC: 3086 Mfg Plastic Foam Products

(G-15213)
ROSENOFF REPORTS INC
Also Called: Realist, The
26a Aberdeen Rd (02144-3255)
PHONE.................................617 628-7783
Alan Rosenoff, President
EMP: 3
SALES (est): 205.5K Privately Held
SIC: 2721 Periodicals-Publishing/Printing

(G-15214)
SEFACOR INC
30 Murdock St Apt 1 (02145-3543)
PHONE.................................617 471-0176
Anupam Dopeniya, CEO
EMP: 5
SALES (est): 556.7K Privately Held
WEB: www.sefacor.com
SIC: 2834 Biotechnology

(G-15215)
SKELMIR LLC
55 Davis Sq 2 (02144-2908)
PHONE.................................617 625-1551
Graham Nice, VP Bus Dvlpt
Kristin O'Donnell, Office Mgr
David Burrage, Software Engr
Craig Gwydir, Software Engr
Art Mellor, Software Engr
EMP: 10
SQ FT: 1,200
SALES: 1.1MM Privately Held
WEB: www.skelmer.com
SIC: 7372 Prepackaged Software Services

(G-15216)
SOMERVILLE NEWS
699 Broadway (02144-2223)
PHONE.................................617 666-4010
Neil W McCabe, Principal
EMP: 3
SALES: 120K Privately Held
SIC: 2711 Newspapers-Publishing/Printing

(G-15217)
SOMERVILLE OFFICE
344 Somerville Ave (02143-2918)
PHONE.................................617 776-0738
Joseph A Curtatone, Mayor
EMP: 3
SALES (est): 131.9K Privately Held
SIC: 2053 Mfg Frozen Bakery Products

(G-15218)
SOMERVILLE ORNAMENTAL IR WORKS
7 George St (02145-3467)
PHONE.................................617 666-8872
Maria Lorusso, President
Elio A Lorusso, Treasurer
EMP: 9 EST: 1996
SALES: 200K Privately Held
SIC: 3446 Mfg Custom Iron Work

(G-15219)
SOMERVILLE SCIENCE AND TECH
15 Ward St (02143-4228)
PHONE.................................617 628-3150
Jonah Jacob, Principal
Pmp Valenti, Project Mgr
EMP: 4 EST: 2010
SALES (est): 232.8K Privately Held
SIC: 3674 Mfg Semiconductors/Related Devices

(G-15220)
SRP SIGNS
Also Called: SRP Sign & Awning
236 Pearl St (02145-3926)
PHONE.................................617 623-6222
Stuart Pitchel, Owner
Mary Finigan, Admin Sec
EMP: 5
SALES (est): 391.4K Privately Held
WEB: www.srpsigns.com
SIC: 3993 Mfg Signs/Advertising Specialties

(G-15221)
T O C FINISHING CORP
22 Clifton St (02144-2560)
PHONE.................................617 623-3310
Timothy J Harney, President
John McGrath, General Mgr
EMP: 14
SQ FT: 9,000
SALES: 1MM Privately Held
SIC: 3599 Metal Finishings

(G-15222)
TECHNOLOGY ORGANIZATION INC
76 Highland Ave (02143-1724)
PHONE.................................617 623-4488
Susan E Schur, President
EMP: 4
SALES (est): 187.9K Privately Held
SIC: 2711 8611 Newspapers-Publishing/Printing Business Association

(G-15223)
THREE RING BINDERS
11 Miller St Ste 205a (02143-3595)
PHONE.................................617 354-4084
Amy Lapidow, Owner
EMP: 3
SALES (est): 175.2K Privately Held
SIC: 2789 Bookbinding/Related Work

(G-15224)
TRACER TECHNOLOGIES INC
Also Called: Eco Division
20 Assembly Square Dr (02145-1307)
PHONE.................................617 776-6410
Fraser M Walsh, President
Peter Polsonetti, Senior Engr
Roisin Doyle, Executive
▲ EMP: 36
SQ FT: 10,000
SALES: 11MM Privately Held
WEB: www.tracer-eco.com
SIC: 3691 8731 Mfg Storage Batteries Commercial Physical Research

(G-15225)
TRI STAR PRINTING & GRAPHICS
33 Park St (02143-3254)
PHONE.................................617 666-4480
Ping Jiang, President
EMP: 8
SQ FT: 3,207
SALES (est): 983K Privately Held
SIC: 2752 7334 Lithographic Commercial Printing Photocopying Services

(G-15226)
TULIP INTERFACES INC (PA)
561 Windsor St B402 (02143-4131)
PHONE.................................833 468-8547
Natan Linder, President
Mason Glidden, Engineer
Rony Kubat, Admin Sec
EMP: 4
SALES (est): 1.2MM Privately Held
SIC: 7372 Prepackaged Software Services

(G-15227)
VIA SCIENCE INC (PA)
100 Dover St (02144-2811)
PHONE.................................857 600-2171
Colin Gounden, CEO
Katherine Ravanis, Senior VP
EMP: 7
SALES (est): 1.8MM Privately Held
SIC: 7372 Prepackaged Software Services

(G-15228)
VIDEOIQ INC
450 Artisan Way Ste 200 (02145-1262)
PHONE.................................781 222-3069
Alexander Fernandes, Ch of Bd
Annita Tanini, Corp Secy
Bryan Schmode, COO
Danny Kam, Exec VP
Pedro Simoes, Senior VP
▲ EMP: 32
SQ FT: 10,000
SALES (est): 6MM Privately Held
WEB: www.videoiq.net
SIC: 3699 8731 7382 Mfg Electrical Equipment/Supplies Commercial Physical Research Security Systems Services

(G-15229)
VOXEL8 INC
21 Rev Nazareno Properzi (02143-3222)
PHONE.................................916 396-3714
Jennifer Lewis, President
EMP: 16 EST: 2014
SALES (est): 2.8MM Privately Held
SIC: 3577 7371 Mfg Computer Peripheral Equipment Custom Computer Programing

(G-15230)
WATERTOWN PRINTERS INC
21 Mcgrath Hwy Ste 3 (02143-4219)
PHONE.................................781 893-9400
Bradley Geilfuss, President
John H Geilfuss, Treasurer
Son Hui Geilfuss, Director
EMP: 7
SQ FT: 6,000
SALES (est): 547.4K Privately Held
SIC: 2759 Commercial Printing

(G-15231)
WAVESENSE INC
444 Somerville Ave (02143-3260)
PHONE.................................917 488-9677
Tarik Bolat, CEO
EMP: 5
SALES (est): 203.2K Privately Held
SIC: 3812 Mfg Search/Navigation Equipment

(G-15232)
WHITMORE FAMILY ENTPS LLC
Also Called: Taza Chocolate
561 Windsor St Ste B206 (02143-4189)
PHONE.................................617 623-0804
Barbara Reilly, COO
Amanda Lydon, Human Res Mgr
Sarah K Mastrangelo, Human Res Mgr
Sarah Kirnie, Human Resources
Suhayl Ramirez, Marketing Staff
◆ EMP: 15
SQ FT: 1,200
SALES (est): 3.4MM Privately Held
SIC: 2066 Whol Groceries

(G-15233)
WISDOM PUBLICATIONS INC (PA)
199 Elm St (02144-3195)
PHONE.................................617 776-7416
Timothy Mc Neill, President
Laura Cunningham, Production
Lydia Anderson, Marketing Staff
Aitken Daniel, Commissioner
▲ EMP: 8
SQ FT: 1,491
SALES: 1.8MM Privately Held
WEB: www.wisdompubs.org
SIC: 2731 Books-Publishing/Printing

South Barre
Worcester County

(G-15234)
290 INDUSTRIAL STITCHING INC
49 Main St (01074-7728)
PHONE.................................978 355-0271
Shoua Her, Director
EMP: 4
SALES (est): 230.4K Privately Held
SIC: 2395 Pleating/Stitching Services

South Carver
Plymouth County

(G-15235)
OCEAN SPRAY CRANBERRIES INC
60 Federal Rd (02366)
P.O. Box 38 (02366-0038)
PHONE.................................508 866-5306
Norman Rose, Manager
EMP: 4
SALES (corp-wide): 1.6B Privately Held
WEB: www.oceanspraycrantastics.com
SIC: 2033 Mfg Canned Fruits/Vegetables
PA: Ocean Spray Cranberries, Inc.
1 Ocean Spray Dr
Middleboro MA 02349
508 946-1000

South Dartmouth
Bristol County

(G-15236)
BIRDS & BEANS LLC
27 Summer St (02748-3828)
PHONE.................................857 233-2722
William Wilson, Principal
EMP: 3
SALES (est): 211.4K Privately Held
SIC: 2095 Mfg Roasted Coffee

(G-15237)
DARTMOUTH FEEDERS & TRAPS INC
53 Russells Mills Rd (02748-1757)
PHONE.................................774 202-6594
John Sullivan, President
Geraldine Sullivan, Vice Pres
EMP: 3
SQ FT: 1,000
SALES: 200K Privately Held
WEB: www.dartmouthfeeders.com
SIC: 2449 5261 Mfg Wood Containers Ret Nursery/Garden Supplies

(G-15238)
DOYLE SAILMAKERS INC
Also Called: Doyle Manchester Sailmakers
278 Elm St (02748-3420)
PHONE.................................508 992-6322
Bill Ribar, Manager
EMP: 5

SALES (corp-wide): 6.2MM **Privately Held**
WEB: www.doylesails.com
SIC: 2394 7699 Mfg & Repair Sail For Sailboats
PA: Doyle Sailmakers, Inc
96 Swampscott Rd Ste 8
Salem MA 01970
978 740-5950

(G-15239)
EARLY AMERICAN INDUSTRIES ASSN
167 Bakerville Rd (02748-1174)
PHONE..................................508 439-2215
Elton Hall, *President*
John Watson, *Principal*
Elton W Hall, *Exec Dir*
EMP: 4
SALES: 180.7K **Privately Held**
WEB: www.eaiainfo.org
SIC: 2721 2741 Journal And Newsletter Publications

(G-15240)
MARSHALL MARINE CORP
55 Shipyard Ln (02748-2115)
PHONE..................................508 994-0414
Geoff Marshall, *President*
Jo-Ann Taylor, *Office Mgr*
▼ **EMP:** 11
SQ FT: 10,000
SALES (est): 1.4MM **Privately Held**
WEB: www.marshallcat.com
SIC: 3732 4493 Mfg Fiberglass Boats

(G-15241)
P STRAKER LTD
Also Called: Penny Straker Gardens
8 Middle St (02748-3428)
PHONE..................................508 996-4804
Penelope Straker, *President*
EMP: 7
SQ FT: 1,500
SALES (est): 500K **Privately Held**
SIC: 2741 5949 Publishes Patterns & Ret Yarns

(G-15242)
PHOENIX SHEET METAL
53 Cove Rd (02748-2736)
PHONE..................................508 994-4046
Stephen Contois, *Owner*
EMP: 8
SQ FT: 800
SALES: 640K **Privately Held**
SIC: 3444 1761 Mfg Sheet Metalwork Roofing/Siding Contractor

(G-15243)
SALGADO SAND & GRAVEL INC
779 Russells Mills Rd (02748-1172)
PHONE..................................774 202-2626
Jaime M Salgado, *Principal*
EMP: 6
SALES (est): 290K **Privately Held**
SIC: 1442 Construction Sand/Gravel

South Deerfield
Franklin County

(G-15244)
1 CALL DOES IT ALL AND THEN
Also Called: One Call Does It All
85 State Rd (01373-9653)
PHONE..................................413 584-5381
Mark Battey, *President*
Joy Battey, *Corp Secy*
EMP: 3
SALES (est): 320K **Privately Held**
SIC: 3443 7389 4953 Mfg Fabricated Plate Work Business Services Refuse System

(G-15245)
BARKER STEEL LLC
Also Called: Harris Steel
73 Old State Rd (01373-9758)
P.O. Box 221 (01373-0221)
PHONE..................................413 665-2381
Paul Benoit, *QC Mgr*
Brian Luippold, *Branch Mgr*
EMP: 27
SALES (corp-wide): 25B **Publicly Held**
WEB: www.barker.com
SIC: 3441 Structural Metal Fabrication
HQ: Barker Steel Llc
55 Sumner St Ste 1
Milford MA 01757
800 363-3953

(G-15246)
BERKSHIRE BREWING COMPANY INC (PA)
12 Railroad St (01373-1034)
P.O. Box 251 (01373-0251)
PHONE..................................413 665-6600
Christopher T Lalli, *President*
Gary Bogoff, *Treasurer*
Clay Cummings, *Technology*
▲ **EMP:** 14
SQ FT: 7,000
SALES (est): 3.6MM **Privately Held**
SIC: 2082 Mfg Malt Beverages

(G-15247)
CHANNING BETE COMPANY INC (PA)
Also Called: Channing-Bete
1 Community Pl (01373-7328)
P.O. Box 908, Greenfield (01302-0908)
PHONE..................................413 665-7611
Channing L Bete, *Ch of Bd*
Michael G Bete, *President*
Michael Wasilauski, *Editor*
J Michael Cahill, *Exec VP*
Kim M Canuel, *Vice Pres*
◆ **EMP:** 289
SALES (est): 47MM **Privately Held**
WEB: www.channing-bete.com
SIC: 2731 7812 2732 Book-Publishing/Printing Motion Pict/Video Prodtn Book Printing

(G-15248)
COVESTRO LLC
8 Fairview Way (01373-9674)
P.O. Box 186 (01373-0186)
PHONE..................................412 777-2000
Shaun Gaus, *General Mgr*
EMP: 68
SALES (corp-wide): 16.2B **Privately Held**
SIC: 2822 3081 Mfg Synthetic Rubber Mfg Unsupported Plastic Film/Sheet
HQ: Covestro Llc
1 Covestro Cir
Pittsburgh PA 15205
412 413-2000

(G-15249)
G AND W PRECISION
226 Greenfield Rd (01373)
PHONE..................................413 397-3361
Gary N Stone, *Principal*
EMP: 3
SALES (est): 228K **Privately Held**
SIC: 3089 Mfg Plastic Products

(G-15250)
HABITAT POST & BEAM INC
Also Called: Habitat Virtual Village
21 Elm St (01373)
PHONE..................................413 665-4006
Peter D May, *President*
Huckle May, *Vice Pres*
EMP: 20
SQ FT: 2,860
SALES (est): 2.9MM **Privately Held**
WEB: www.soulsport.com
SIC: 2452 Mfg Prefabricated Wood Buildings

(G-15251)
PELICAN PRODUCTS INC
147 N Main St (01373-1026)
PHONE..................................413 665-2163
Joe Eckerle, *President*
Mike Bousquet, *Controller*
Jim Rooney, *Sales Mgr*
Mark Case, *Branch Mgr*
EMP: 21
SALES (corp-wide): 208.2MM **Privately Held**
SIC: 3648 Mfg Lighting Equipment
PA: Pelican Products, Inc.
23215 Early Ave
Torrance CA 90505
310 326-4700

(G-15252)
PILOT PRECISION PROPERTIES LLC
15 Merrigan Way (01373-1106)
PHONE..................................413 350-5200
Eric Hagopian, *Mng Member*
EMP: 3
SALES (est): 182.2K **Privately Held**
SIC: 3545 Holding Company

(G-15253)
POLAR FOCUS INC
20 Industrial Dr E (01373-7301)
P.O. Box 3, Hadley (01035-0003)
PHONE..................................413 665-2044
Michael Akret, *CEO*
Kathy Patrician, *Treasurer*
Steve Schrems, *Assistant*
EMP: 5
SALES (est): 677.1K **Privately Held**
SIC: 2295 Mfg Coated Fabrics

(G-15254)
PRO PEL PLASTECH INC
4 Industrial Dr E (01373-7301)
PHONE..................................413 665-2282
Joseph H Nickerson IV, *President*
EMP: 6
SALES (corp-wide): 5MM **Privately Held**
SIC: 3089 Mfg Plastic Products
PA: Pro Pel Plastech, Inc.
378 Long Plain Rd
South Deerfield MA 01373
413 665-3379

(G-15255)
PRO PEL PLASTECH INC (PA)
378 Long Plain Rd (01373-9642)
P.O. Box 165 (01373-0165)
PHONE..................................413 665-3379
Joseph H Nickerson IV, *President*
Marcia L Nickerson, *Admin Sec*
Karl Mosher, *Maintence Staff*
EMP: 40
SQ FT: 32,500
SALES (est): 5MM **Privately Held**
WEB: www.pro-pel.com
SIC: 3089 Mfg Plastic Products

(G-15256)
SMITHS INTERCONNECT INC
Also Called: Satcom Division
5 6 North St (01373)
P.O. Box 109 (01373-0109)
PHONE..................................413 665-0965
Robert A White, *General Mgr*
Rob Sumner, *Info Tech Mgr*
Mark Duncan, *Technician*
EMP: 27
SALES (corp-wide): 3.1B **Privately Held**
SIC: 3663 Mfg Radio/Tv Communication Equipment
HQ: Smiths Interconnect, Inc.
4726 Eisenhower Blvd
Tampa FL 33634
813 901-7200

(G-15257)
TECHNOMAD ASSOCIATES LLC
37 Harvard St Ste 2 (01373)
PHONE..................................413 665-6704
Rodger Von Kries,
EMP: 7 **Privately Held**
WEB: www.technomad.com
SIC: 3651 Mfg Home Audio/Video Equipment
PA: Technomad Associates, Llc
5 Tina Dr
South Deerfield MA 01373

(G-15258)
TECHNOMAD ASSOCIATES LLC (PA)
5 Tina Dr (01373-1032)
P.O. Box 273 (01373-0273)
PHONE..................................413 665-6704
Karl Von Kries, *President*
Rodger Von Kries, *President*
Steve Schilling, *CFO*
Joe Morris, *CIO*
▲ **EMP:** 9
SQ FT: 1,000
SALES (est): 1.7MM **Privately Held**
WEB: www.technomad.com
SIC: 3651 Mfg Home Audio/Video Equipment

(G-15259)
WORTHINGTON ASSEMBLY INC
14 Industrial Dr E Unit 2 (01373-7338)
PHONE..................................413 397-8265
Neil C Scanlon, *President*
Barbara Quinn, *Partner*
Tom Quinn, *Partner*
Rafal Dybacki, *CFO*
Peter Connor, *Admin Sec*
EMP: 15
SQ FT: 2,000
SALES (est): 3.7MM **Privately Held**
SIC: 3672 Assembles Printed Circuit Boards

(G-15260)
YANKEE CANDLE COMPANY INC (DH)
16 Yankee Candle Way (01373-7325)
P.O. Box 110 (01373-0110)
PHONE..................................413 665-8306
Hope Margala, *CEO*
Dana Springfield, *General Mgr*
Amy Torres, *District Mgr*
James A Perley, *COO*
Richard R Ruffolo, *Senior VP*
◆ **EMP:** 200
SQ FT: 90,000
SALES (est): 1.4B
SALES (corp-wide): 8.6B **Publicly Held**
WEB: www.yankeecandle.com
SIC: 3999 2899 5999 Mfg Misc Products Mfg Chemical Preparations Ret Misc Merchandise

(G-15261)
YANKEE CANDLE INVESTMENTS LLC (DH)
16 Yankee Candle Way (01373-7325)
PHONE..................................413 665-8306
Harlan M Kent, *CEO*
Martha S Lacroix, *Exec VP*
James A Perley, *Exec VP*
Gregory W Hunt, *CFO*
EMP: 9
SALES (est): 844.1MM
SALES (corp-wide): 8.6B **Publicly Held**
SIC: 3999 5999 Manufactures And Retails Candles

(G-15262)
YANKEE HOLDING CORP (DH)
16 Yankee Candle Way (01373-7325)
PHONE..................................413 665-8306
Craig W Rydin, *Ch of Bd*
James A Perley, *Exec VP*
Lisa K McCarthy, *CFO*
Martha S Lacroix, *Officer*
EMP: 9
SQ FT: 75,000
SALES (est): 1.4B
SALES (corp-wide): 8.6B **Publicly Held**
SIC: 3999 2899 Mfg Misc Products Mfg Chemical Preparation

(G-15263)
YCC HOLDINGS LLC
16 Yankee Candle Way (01373-7325)
PHONE..................................413 665-8306
Lisa K McCarthy, *Treasurer*
EMP: 5185
SQ FT: 75,000
SALES: 844.1MM
SALES (corp-wide): 8.6B **Publicly Held**
SIC: 3999 2899 5999 Mfg Misc Products Mfg Chemical Preparations Ret Misc Merchandise
HQ: Yankee Candle Investments Llc
16 Yankee Candle Way
South Deerfield MA 01373

South Dennis
Barnstable County

(G-15264)
AGGREGATE INDS - NORTHEAST REG
230 Great Western Rd (02660-3715)
PHONE...508 398-8865
Robert Nardone, *Branch Mgr*
EMP: 6
SALES (corp-wide): 4.5B **Privately Held**
SIC: 3273 Mfg Ready-Mixed Concrete
HQ: Aggregate Industries - Northeast Region, Inc
1715 Brdwy
Saugus MA 01906
781 941-7200

(G-15265)
BASS RIVER MARINE CANVAS LLC
239 Great Western Rd (02660-3819)
PHONE...781 856-5145
Diane J Kelley Miss, *Principal*
EMP: 4
SALES (est): 176.5K **Privately Held**
SIC: 2211 Cotton Broadwoven Fabric Mill

(G-15266)
SANDCASTLE PUBLISHING LLC
434 Route 134 (02660-3433)
PHONE...508 398-3100
Jeffrey H Heth, *Principal*
EMP: 4
SALES (est): 278.7K **Privately Held**
SIC: 2741 Misc Publishing

(G-15267)
TREE CO INC
239 Great Western Rd (02660-3819)
PHONE...508 432-7529
Michael Mann, *Principal*
EMP: 3
SALES (est): 288.6K **Privately Held**
SIC: 2411 Logging

South Easton
Bristol County

(G-15268)
ACON INC
22 Bristol Dr (02375-1108)
PHONE...508 230-8022
C W Lin, *President*
Jean Lin, *Treasurer*
▲ **EMP:** 10
SQ FT: 17,000
SALES (est): 3.7MM **Privately Held**
WEB: www.aconinc.com
SIC: 3679 Mfg Electronic Components

(G-15269)
AIR ENERGY GROUP LLC
6 Norfolk Ave (02375-1156)
PHONE...508 230-9445
Fares Kabbani,
▲ **EMP:** 31
SQ FT: 20,000
SALES: 10MM **Privately Held**
WEB: www.airenergy.com
SIC: 3563 Whol Industrial Equipment

(G-15270)
BEE INTERNATIONAL INC
46 Eastman St Ste 5 (02375-1297)
PHONE...508 238-5558
Tal Shechter, *President*
Deborah Shechter, *Treasurer*
▲ **EMP:** 41
SQ FT: 3,000
SALES (est): 9.4MM
SALES (corp-wide): 5.1MM **Privately Held**
WEB: www.beei.com
SIC: 3561 5084 Mfg Pumps/Pumping Equipment Whol Industrial Equipment
PA: Bee (Best Emulsifying Equipment) International Ltd.
Migdal Haemek
Migdal Haemek

(G-15271)
BORO SAND & STONE CORP
87 Eastman St (02375-6200)
PHONE...508 238-7222
Thomas Walsh, *Corp Comm Staff*
Bruce Cusick, *Manager*
EMP: 4
SQ FT: 11,220
SALES (corp-wide): 10MM **Privately Held**
SIC: 3273 Mfg Ready-Mixed Concrete
PA: Boro Sand & Stone Corp.
192 Plain St
North Attleboro MA 02760
508 699-2911

(G-15272)
C AND M MICRO-TOOL INC
18 Plymouth Dr (02375-1163)
PHONE...508 230-3535
Carmen Tropeano, *President*
Ciro Tropeano, *Vice Pres*
EMP: 25
SQ FT: 16,000
SALES: 400K
SALES (corp-wide): 4.3MM **Privately Held**
WEB: www.ptgspecials.com
SIC: 3541 Mfg Machine Tools-Cutting
PA: Professional Tool Grinding Co., Inc.
18 Plymouth Dr
South Easton MA 02375
508 230-3535

(G-15273)
CASE ASSEMBLY SOLUTIONS INC
Also Called: Treetop
19 Norfolk Ave Ste B (02375-1911)
PHONE...508 238-5665
Gregory Cronin, *President*
Jay Sullivan, *Treasurer*
Jerome J Sullivan Jr, *Treasurer*
▲ **EMP:** 29
SQ FT: 18,000
SALES (est): 6.9MM **Privately Held**
WEB: www.case-assembly.com
SIC: 3672 3679 Mfg Printed Circuit Boards Mfg Electronic Components

(G-15274)
CONNECTED AUTOMOTIVE
Also Called: Cas of New England
87 Eastman St (02375-6200)
PHONE...508 238-5855
John P Jenkins, *President*
EMP: 25
SQ FT: 7,500
SALES (est): 4.9MM **Privately Held**
SIC: 3825 5013 7371 Mfg Elec Measuring Instr Whol Auto Parts/Supplies Computer Programming Svc

(G-15275)
CUE INC
19 Norfolk Ave Ste D (02375-1911)
PHONE...617 591-9500
Paul Zecchi, *Ch of Bd*
Sam Millen, *President*
▲ **EMP:** 10
SALES (est): 814.5K **Privately Held**
SIC: 3651 Mfg Home Audio/Video Equipment

(G-15276)
DEANGELIS IRON WORK INC
305 Depot St (02375-1535)
P.O. Box 350 (02375-0350)
PHONE...508 238-4310
Richard J Davis Jr, *President*
Harry M Dodakian, *Vice Pres*
Christopher S Conne, *Treasurer*
Donald R Jacobs, *Admin Sec*
EMP: 35 **EST:** 1978
SQ FT: 18,600
SALES (est): 8.8MM **Privately Held**
WEB: www.deangelisiron.com
SIC: 3446 Mfg Architectural Mtlwrk

(G-15277)
FORTE TECHNOLOGY INC
58 Norfolk Ave Ste 4 (02375-1940)
PHONE...508 297-2363
Patricia R White, *President*
Mark Dmohowski, *Engineer*
▼ **EMP:** 10 **EST:** 1956
SQ FT: 7,200
SALES (est): 2.3MM **Privately Held**
SIC: 3829 Mfg Measuring/Controlling Devices

(G-15278)
HANGER PROSTHETHICS & ORTHOTIC
67 Belmont St (02375-1103)
PHONE...508 238-6760
Shanie Scott, *President*
Vinit Asar, *President*
Sam Liang, *President*
EMP: 4
SALES (est): 216.6K **Privately Held**
SIC: 3842 Mfg Surgical Appliances/Supplies

(G-15279)
ID GRAPHICS GROUP INC
Also Called: ID Sign Group
9 Bristol Dr (02375-1109)
P.O. Box 506 (02375-0506)
PHONE...508 238-8500
Timothy Fisher, *President*
Jacquelyn Churchill, *Treasurer*
EMP: 20
SQ FT: 6,000
SALES (est): 3MM **Privately Held**
SIC: 3993 3089 2796 Mfg Signs/Advertising Specialties Mfg Plastic Products Platemaking Services

(G-15280)
INTERNATIONAL COIL INC
Also Called: I C I
8 Norfolk Ave Unit 2 (02375-1156)
P.O. Box 668 (02375-0668)
PHONE...508 580-8515
Jorge Machadinho, *President*
Johnny Teixeira, *Treasurer*
Jose Estrela, *Clerk*
▲ **EMP:** 20
SQ FT: 13,000
SALES: 2MM **Privately Held**
WEB: www.internationalcoil.com
SIC: 3612 Mfg Transformers

(G-15281)
INTERNATIONAL SOLE & LEA CORP
520 Depot St (02375-1545)
PHONE...508 588-0905
EMP: 10 **EST:** 1941
SQ FT: 12,000
SALES (est): 660K **Privately Held**
SIC: 3131 Mfg Shoe Soles Heels & Counters

(G-15282)
INTERSTATE MAT CORPORATION
32 Norfolk Ave Ste 4 (02375-1941)
P.O. Box 331 (02375-0331)
PHONE...508 238-0116
Victor M Cucinotta Jr, *President*
EMP: 6
SQ FT: 20,000
SALES (est): 986.6K **Privately Held**
SIC: 3069 Mfg Fabricated Rubber Products

(G-15283)
JIM HALUCK
Also Called: Signs By Tomorrow
65 Belmont St (02375-1103)
PHONE...508 230-8901
Jim Haluck, *Owner*
EMP: 5
SALES: 300K **Privately Held**
SIC: 3993 Signsadv Specs

(G-15284)
LION LABELS INC
15 Hampden Dr (02375-1159)
P.O. Box 820 (02375-0820)
PHONE...508 230-8211
Michael Berke, *President*
Jerome M Berke, *President*
Tami Decelles, *CFO*
Nina Berke, *Treasurer*
Edward Page, *Mktg Dir*
EMP: 24 **EST:** 1966
SQ FT: 29,000
SALES (est): 6.5MM **Privately Held**
WEB: www.lionlabels.com
SIC: 2672 2752 Mfg Coated/Laminated Paper Lithographic Commercial Printing

(G-15285)
MACDONALD CABINET &
580 Washington St (02375-1184)
PHONE...508 346-3221
Laurence W Macdonald, *President*
Susan G Macdonald, *Corp Secy*
Larry Macdonald, *Vice Pres*
Joan Mazzaferro, *Project Mgr*
EMP: 3
SQ FT: 1,200
SALES (est): 630.3K **Privately Held**
SIC: 2434 Mfg Wood Kitchen Cabinets

(G-15286)
POP TOPS COMPANY INC
Also Called: Pop Tops Sportswear
10 Plymouth Dr (02375-1192)
PHONE...508 580-2580
James Fine, *President*
Jonathan Fine, *Vice Pres*
EMP: 30
SQ FT: 10,000
SALES (est): 4.2MM **Privately Held**
WEB: www.poptopssportswear.com
SIC: 2395 2329 2339 Pleating/Stitching Services Mfg Men's/Boy's Clothing Mfg Women's/Misses' Outerwear

(G-15287)
POWER PROS CONSULTING GROUP
20 Hampden Dr Ste 4 (02375-1180)
PHONE...508 238-6629
Michael Schuster, *President*
EMP: 6
SQ FT: 1,400
SALES (est): 426.1K **Privately Held**
WEB: www.pwrpros.com
SIC: 7372 Prepackaged Software Services

(G-15288)
PRESSURE BIOSCIENCES INC
Also Called: PBI
14 Norfolk Ave (02375-1907)
PHONE...508 230-1828
Jeffrey N Peterson, *Ch of Bd*
Richard T Schumacher, *President*
Edmund Ting, *Senior VP*
Alexander Lazarev, *Vice Pres*
Joseph L Damasio Jr, *CFO*
EMP: 19
SALES: 2.4MM **Privately Held**
WEB: www.pressurebiosciences.com
SIC: 3841 Mfg Pressure Cycling Technology Equipment

(G-15289)
PROF TOOL GRIND INC
Also Called: Professional Tool Grinding
18 Plymouth Dr (02375-1163)
PHONE...508 230-3535
Carmen Tropeano, *President*
EMP: 25
SALES: 3.9MM
SALES (corp-wide): 4.3MM **Privately Held**
WEB: www.ptgspecials.com
SIC: 3541 Mfg Cutting Tools
PA: Professional Tool Grinding Co., Inc.
18 Plymouth Dr
South Easton MA 02375
508 230-3535

(G-15290)
PROFESSIONAL TL GRINDING INC (PA)
18 Plymouth Dr (02375-1163)
PHONE...508 230-3535
Carmen Tropeano, *President*
Ciro Tropeano, *Vice Pres*
David Tropeano, *Vice Pres*
Kevin Provencal, *Engineer*
EMP: 26
SQ FT: 16,000

GEOGRAPHIC

SALES (est): 4.3MM **Privately Held**
WEB: www.ptgspecials.com
SIC: 3541 Mfg Machine Tools-Cutting

(G-15291)
RIVKIND ASSOCIATES INC (PA)
30 Twin Brooks Dr (02375-6206)
PHONE.................................781 269-2415
Melvin Rivkind, *CEO*
Kenneth Rivkind, *President*
David Kovner, *Vice Pres*
EMP: 11
SQ FT: 15,000
SALES (est): 1.3MM **Privately Held**
WEB: www.rivkind.com
SIC: 2752 7331 Lithographic Commercial Printing Direct Mail Advertising Services

(G-15292)
SHAW GLASS HOLDINGS LLC
Also Called: Solar Seal
55 Bristol Dr Ste 1 (02375-1195)
PHONE.................................508 238-0112
Frederick P Shaw, *President*
▲ **EMP:** 110
SQ FT: 100,000
SALES (est): 32MM
SALES (corp-wide): 99.5MM **Privately Held**
SIC: 3211 Mfg Flat Glass
PA: Consolidated Glass Holdings, Inc.
500 Grant Ave Ste 201
East Butler PA 16029
866 412-6977

(G-15293)
THERMAL FLUIDS INC
93 Kevins Way (02375-1284)
P.O. Box 1071, Easton (02334-1071)
PHONE.................................508 238-9660
Scott Kudcey, *President*
Scot Kudcey, *President*
EMP: 5
SALES: 1.2MM **Privately Held**
SIC: 2819 Mfg Speciality Chemicals

(G-15294)
VIAMED CORP
15d Plymouth Dr D (02375-1164)
PHONE.................................508 238-0220
Gary Lewis, *President*
EMP: 13
SQ FT: 7,500
SALES (est): 1.8MM **Privately Held**
SIC: 3841 3496 Mfg Surgical/Medical Instruments Mfg Misc Fabricated Wire Products

(G-15295)
WELDING CRAFTSMEN CO INC
63 Norfolk Ave (02375-1190)
PHONE.................................508 230-7878
Paul Raynard, *President*
EMP: 15 **EST:** 1977
SQ FT: 16,000
SALES (est): 2.6MM **Privately Held**
WEB: www.weldingcraftsmen.com
SIC: 3444 7692 Mfg Sheet Metalwork Welding Repair

South Grafton
Worcester County

(G-15296)
ATLANTIC TURTLE TOP INC
127 Ferry St (01560-1344)
PHONE.................................508 839-1711
Robert G Flynn Sr, *President*
William Flynn, *Vice Pres*
Madeline D Flynn, *Treasurer*
EMP: 3
SALES (est): 477.9K **Privately Held**
WEB: www.atlanticturtletop.com
SIC: 3711 Mfg Motor Vehicle/Car Bodies

(G-15297)
HUESON CORP
134 Ferry St (01560-1390)
P.O. Box 231, Northbridge (01534-0231)
PHONE.................................508 234-6372
Daniel J Hughes, *President*
Walter Hagstrom, *Engineer*
Jack A Hughes, *Treasurer*
Patty Arsenault, *Office Mgr*
▲ **EMP:** 11
SQ FT: 24,000
SALES (est): 3.8MM **Privately Held**
WEB: www.huesonwire.com
SIC: 3357 Nonferrous Wiredrawing/Insulating

(G-15298)
RICHMAND TEXTILES INC
20 Milford Rd (01560-1208)
PHONE.................................508 839-6600
Armand Gariepy Jr, *President*
Richard Plasse, *Treasurer*
EMP: 14
SQ FT: 14,500
SALES (est): 798.6K **Privately Held**
SIC: 2231 Weavers Of Textile Fabrics

(G-15299)
TEMP-FLEX LLC
26 Milford Rd (01560-1208)
PHONE.................................508 839-3120
Raymond Baril, *President*
Rick Black, *Vice Pres*
Kris Lower, *Vice Pres*
Ann Marie Gonyea, *Bookkeeper*
Dan Laforest,
▲ **EMP:** 70
SALES (est): 15.1MM
SALES (corp-wide): 40.6B **Privately Held**
WEB: www.tempflex.com
SIC: 3315 3357 Mfg Steel Wire/Related Products Nonferrous Wiredrawing/Insulating
HQ: Molex, Llc
2222 Wellington Ct
Lisle IL 60532
630 969-4550

South Hadley
Hampshire County

(G-15300)
CANSON INC
21 Industrial Dr (01075-2621)
PHONE.................................413 538-9250
James J Allery, *President*
Sonja M Stewart, *Treasurer*
Robert Toth, *VP Mktg*
Kevin Beckerdite, *Manager*
Eric Joan, *Director*
◆ **EMP:** 100 **EST:** 1928
SQ FT: 110,000
SALES (est): 35.6MM **Privately Held**
WEB: www.canson-us.com
SIC: 2679 5199 Mfg Converted Paper Products Whol Nondurable Goods
HQ: Latame 2
Canson International
Herouville Saint Clair
-

(G-15301)
DENTAL STUDIOS OF WESTERN MASS
120 Lyman St (01075-1927)
PHONE.................................413 787-9920
Toll Free:.................................888 -
Dennis Croll, *President*
Louise M Croll, *Corp Secy*
EMP: 4
SALES (est): 357.7K **Privately Held**
WEB: www.dentalstudios.com
SIC: 3466 8021 Mfg Crowns/Closures Dentist's Office

(G-15302)
EIS WIRE & CABLE INC
775 New Ludlow Rd (01075-2625)
PHONE.................................413 536-0152
Nicholas J Moceri, *President*
Thomas L Depetrillo, *Chairman*
Roy St Andre, *Exec VP*
William Ten Kate, *Engineer*
Armand Mayotte, *CFO*
EMP: 55
SQ FT: 125,000
SALES (est): 23.3MM **Privately Held**
WEB: www.eiswire.com
SIC: 3357 Nonferrous Wiredrawing/Insulating

(G-15303)
GGS CUSTOM METALS INC
Also Called: Gg Inks
785 New Ludlow Rd (01075-2625)
PHONE.................................413 315-4344
Gerry-Paul Geoffrion, *Principal*
EMP: 19
SALES (est): 2.7MM **Privately Held**
SIC: 2752 Lithographic Commercial Printing

(G-15304)
GIANNETTI MFG SERVICES INC
28 Michael Dr (01075-3024)
PHONE.................................413 532-9736
Leonard J Giannetti, *President*
EMP: 3
SQ FT: 2,000
SALES (est): 50K **Privately Held**
SIC: 2754 Gravure Commercial Printing

(G-15305)
KNIGHT MACHINE & TOOL CO INC
11 Industrial Dr (01075-2621)
PHONE.................................413 532-2507
Gary T O'Brien, *President*
EMP: 10
SQ FT: 3,500
SALES (est): 1.6MM **Privately Held**
WEB: www.knightmachine.net
SIC: 3599 Machine Shop Jobbing And Repair

(G-15306)
LYMAN CONRAD (PA)
Also Called: American Canvas & Aluminum
228 Lathrop St (01075-3309)
P.O. Box 667, Westfield (01086-0667)
PHONE.................................413 538-8200
Lyman Conrad, *Owner*
EMP: 25
SQ FT: 4,000
SALES (est): 1.4MM **Privately Held**
SIC: 2394 3089 3444 7299 Mfg Canvas Vinyl And Metal Awnings And Does Contract Stitching

(G-15307)
MEDALCO METALS INC (PA)
23 College St Ste 3 (01075-1414)
PHONE.................................413 586-6010
Dwight Klepacki, *President*
Lawrence Dansky, *Vice Pres*
Michael W Hogan, *Director*
▲ **EMP:** 12
SQ FT: 46,000
SALES (est): 4.9MM **Privately Held**
SIC: 3364 Mfg Nonferrous Die-Castings

(G-15308)
PIONEER VALLEY PLATING CO
51 San Souci Dr (01075-1378)
PHONE.................................413 535-1424
David Hampson, *Owner*
EMP: 3
SQ FT: 4,000
SALES (est): 160K **Privately Held**
SIC: 3471 Plating/Polishing Service

(G-15309)
PROFESSIONAL LITHOGRAPHY INC
630 New Ludlow Rd (01075-2693)
PHONE.................................413 532-9473
Walter J Les, *President*
Paul Vinciguerra, *Vice Pres*
Shirley Les, *Clerk*
EMP: 29 **EST:** 1961
SQ FT: 25,000
SALES (est): 1.2MM **Privately Held**
SIC: 2759 2791 2789 Commercial Printing Typesetting Services

(G-15310)
QUALITY LOOSE LEAF CO
Also Called: Yvon, Russel
62 Lyman St (01075-2378)
PHONE.................................413 534-5891
Russell Yvon, *Owner*
EMP: 5
SALES (est): 389.6K **Privately Held**
SIC: 2782 Mfg Looseleaf Binders

(G-15311)
TECH FAB INC
1 W Main St Ste B (01075-2798)
PHONE.................................413 532-9022
W Ken Cordes, *President*
Laurie McKemmie, *Office Mgr*
EMP: 20 **EST:** 1945
SQ FT: 20,000
SALES (est): 2.4MM **Privately Held**
SIC: 3469 3444 Mfg Metal Stampings Mfg Sheet Metalwork

(G-15312)
VERICO TECHNOLOGY LLC
Also Called: Precision Litho
749 New Ludlow Rd (01075-2625)
PHONE.................................413 539-9111
EMP: 250
SALES (corp-wide): 132.7MM **Privately Held**
SIC: 3555 Mfg Printing Trades Machinery
HQ: Verico Technology Llc
230 Shaker Rd
Enfield CT 06082
800 492-7286

(G-15313)
YANKEE PRINTING GROUP INC
630 New Ludlow Rd (01075-2669)
PHONE.................................413 532-9513
Harold L Davis Jr, *President*
Richard R Davis, *Vice Pres*
Kathryn Trudeau, *Director*
Richard Davis, *Executive*
EMP: 25
SQ FT: 30,000
SALES (est): 3.5MM **Privately Held**
SIC: 2759 2752 2675 2791 Commercial Printing Lithographic Coml Print Mfg Die-Cut Paper/Board Typesetting Services

South Hamilton
Essex County

(G-15314)
DANVERSBANK
Also Called: Hamilton Branch
25 Railroad Ave (01982-2218)
PHONE.................................978 468-2243
Marcia Crateau, *Principal*
EMP: 7 **EST:** 2010
SALES (est): 187.5K **Privately Held**
SIC: 3578 Mfg Calculating Equipment

South Lancaster
Worcester County

(G-15315)
ATLANTIC BOOKBINDERS INC
87 Flagg St (01561)
PHONE.................................978 365-4524
David Bruso, *President*
Susan Bruso, *Corp Secy*
Timothy Paddock, *Treasurer*
EMP: 7
SQ FT: 10,000
SALES (est): 644.5K **Privately Held**
WEB: www.atlanticbookbinders.com
SIC: 2789 2782 Bookbinding/Related Work Mfg Blankbooks/Binders

(G-15316)
BESTWAY OF NEW ENGLAND INC
840 Sterling Rd (01561)
P.O. Box 1286 (01561-1286)
PHONE.................................978 368-7667
Karl D Ochs, *President*
EMP: 10
SQ FT: 33,000
SALES (est): 158.8K
SALES (corp-wide): 38.9MM **Privately Held**
WEB: www.bestwayone.com
SIC: 2491 Wood Preserving
PA: Bestway Enterprises Inc.
3877 Luker Rd
Cortland NY 13045
607 753-8261

(G-15317)
DAVINCI BIOMEDICAL RES PDTS
40 Maple Ave (01561)
P.O. Box 1125 (01561-1125)
PHONE..................................978 368-3477
Joseph Villani, *President*
EMP: 6
SALES (est): 1.3MM **Privately Held**
WEB: www.davincibiomed.com
SIC: 3821 Manufacture Research Devices

(G-15318)
JAMES MONROE WIRE & CABLE CORP (PA)
767 Sterling Rd (01561)
P.O. Box 1203 (01561-1203)
PHONE..................................978 368-0131
David Fisher, *President*
Terry McInnes, *Sales Staff*
Ted Munro, *Sales Staff*
Brendan Tally, *Sales Staff*
William Blair, *Director*
▲ **EMP:** 80
SQ FT: 185,000
SALES (est): 23.7MM **Privately Held**
WEB: www.jamesmonroewire.com
SIC: 3315 3357 5063 Mfg Steel Wire/Related Products Nonferrous Wiredrawing/Insulating Whol Electrical Equipment

South Lee
Berkshire County

(G-15319)
ONYX SPECIALTY PAPERS INC
40 Willow St (01260)
P.O. Box 188 (01260-0188)
PHONE..................................413 243-1231
Patricia C Begrowicz, *President*
Molly Hines, *Technical Staff*
Christopher R Mathews, *Admin Sec*
◆ **EMP:** 137
SALES (est): 49.4MM **Privately Held**
SIC: 2621 Paper Mill

South Walpole
Norfolk County

(G-15320)
RCO RENOVATIONS INC
2 Willow St (02071-1036)
P.O. Box 217 (02071-0217)
PHONE..................................508 668-5524
Richard Ollis, *President*
EMP: 3
SALES (est): 301.7K **Privately Held**
SIC: 1389 Oil/Gas Field Services

South Weymouth
Norfolk County

(G-15321)
LEVAGGIS CANDIES
1186 Main St (02190-1559)
PHONE..................................781 335-1231
James Puopolo, *Owner*
EMP: 6 **EST:** 1947
SALES (est): 303.5K **Privately Held**
SIC: 2066 5441 Mfg Chocolate/Cocoa Products Ret Candy/Confectionery

(G-15322)
STONE DESIGN MARBLE & GRAN CO
1235 Main St (02190-1515)
PHONE..................................781 331-3000
Hoa Thanh Vu, *President*
▲ **EMP:** 7
SQ FT: 3,080
SALES (est): 811.8K **Privately Held**
SIC: 3281 5032 Marble Manufacturer And Wholesaler

(G-15323)
W M GULLIKSEN MFG CO INC (PA)
30 Fairway Lndg (02190-4203)
PHONE..................................617 323-5750
Chester A Gillis, *President*
Kim Greenlaw, *Clerk*
EMP: 27 **EST:** 1927
SALES (est): 3.3MM **Privately Held**
WEB: www.gulliksen.com
SIC: 3089 3544 Mfg Plastic Products Mfg Dies/Tools/Jigs/Fixtures

South Yarmouth
Barnstable County

(G-15324)
ACME-SHOREY PRECAST CO INC
351 Whites Path (02664-1214)
P.O. Box 374, North Falmouth (02556-0374)
PHONE..................................508 430-0956
Dennis Lajoie, *General Mgr*
EMP: 20
SALES (corp-wide): 3.8MM **Privately Held**
SIC: 3272 Mfg Concrete Products
PA: Acme-Shorey Precast Co., Inc.
36 Great Western Rd
Harwich MA 02645
508 432-0530

(G-15325)
BREWER ELECTRIC & UTILITIES IN
110 Old Town House Rd (02664-1661)
PHONE..................................508 771-2040
James Riley, *President*
Scott Ventura, *Manager*
EMP: 25
SALES (est): 2.5MM **Privately Held**
SIC: 3825 1731 Mfg Electrical Measuring Instruments Electrical Contractor

(G-15326)
CAPE COD FENCE CO
20 N Main St (02664-3150)
PHONE..................................508 398-2293
Dewitt Davenport, *Branch Mgr*
EMP: 12
SALES (corp-wide): 2.3MM **Privately Held**
SIC: 2499 Mfg Wood Products
PA: Cape Cod Fence Co
1093 Route 28
South Yarmouth MA 02664
508 398-6041

(G-15327)
CHURCHILL COATINGS CORPORATION
243 Pleasant St (02664-4558)
PHONE..................................508 394-6573
Beth Howder, *Administration*
EMP: 4
SALES (est): 256K **Privately Held**
SIC: 3479 Coating/Engraving Service

(G-15328)
CLASSIC LETTER PRESS INC
77 Diane Ave (02664-1907)
PHONE..................................508 221-7496
Robert Manahl, *President*
Patricia Manahl, *Vice Pres*
EMP: 3
SQ FT: 1,800
SALES: 210K **Privately Held**
SIC: 2759 Letter Press Shop

(G-15329)
FOUR SEASONS TRATTORIA INC
1077 Route 28 (02664-4105)
PHONE..................................508 760-6600
Jose Fernandez, *Principal*
EMP: 3
SALES (est): 262.7K **Privately Held**
SIC: 2759 Commercial Printing

(G-15330)
MIKES MACHINE CO INC
24 Commonwealth Ave (02664-1248)
PHONE..................................508 619-3168
Michael Asci, *President*
Lisa Asci, *Treasurer*
EMP: 3
SALES (est): 310K **Privately Held**
SIC: 3599 Mfg Industrial Machinery

(G-15331)
MTI UNIFIED COMMUNICATIONS LLC
5 Dupont Ave Unit 5-5 (02664-1203)
P.O. Box 174 (02664-0174)
PHONE..................................774 352-1110
Lauren F Mahoney, *Mng Member*
EMP: 3
SQ FT: 2,500
SALES (est): 250K **Privately Held**
SIC: 3577 4813 4899 1731 Mfg Computer Peripherals Telephone Communications Communication Services Electrical Contractor

(G-15332)
OF CAPE COD INCORPORATED
Also Called: Sign-A-Rama
12 Whites Path Ste 6 (02664-1222)
PHONE..................................508 398-9100
James McDermott, *President*
Victoria McDermott, *Vice Pres*
EMP: 4
SQ FT: 1,200
SALES: 500K **Privately Held**
SIC: 3993 Signsadv Specs

(G-15333)
PLYMOUTH SIGN CO INC
63 Old Main St (02664-6007)
P.O. Box 134 (02664-0134)
PHONE..................................508 398-2721
George Caggiano, *President*
EMP: 5
SQ FT: 3,600
SALES: 1MM **Privately Held**
WEB: www.plymouthsign.com
SIC: 3993 Mfg Signs/Advertising Specialties

(G-15334)
SURTAN MANUFACTURING CO
Also Called: The Cape Cod Sandal
1198 Route 28 Unit E (02664-4488)
PHONE..................................508 394-4099
Richard Surabian, *Partner*
Stephen Surabian, *Partner*
EMP: 5 **EST:** 1968
SQ FT: 3,700
SALES: 250K **Privately Held**
SIC: 3171 3143 3144 2387 Mfg Womens Handbag/Purse Mfg Men's Footwear Mfg Women's Footwear Mfg Apparel Belts Ret Luggage/Leather Good

(G-15335)
WINKIR INSTANT PRINTING INC
23 Whites Path Ste R (02664-1236)
PHONE..................................508 398-9748
Ralph H Braman, *President*
Barbara A Braman, *Treasurer*
EMP: 5 **EST:** 1981
SALES (est): 696.5K **Privately Held**
WEB: www.winkirprinting.com
SIC: 2752 Lithographic Commercial Printing

(G-15336)
YANKEE CRAFTERS WAMPUM JEWELRY
48 N Main St (02664-3149)
P.O. Box 296 (02664-0296)
PHONE..................................508 394-0575
Janet Rounseville, *President*
EMP: 3
SQ FT: 2,000
SALES: 120K **Privately Held**
SIC: 3961 5944 Mfg & Retails Costume Jewelry

Southampton
Hampshire County

(G-15337)
CHAMPAGNE TABLES & PET PDTS
15 Old County Rd (01073-9604)
PHONE..................................413 527-4370
Phillip Champagne, *Owner*
EMP: 5
SQ FT: 3,500
SALES (est): 337K **Privately Held**
WEB: www.champagnetables.com
SIC: 3999 5999 Mfg Misc Products Ret Misc Merchandise

(G-15338)
GRAPHICS SOURCE CO
18 Pequot Rd (01073-9587)
P.O. Box 51885, Indian Orchard (01151-5885)
PHONE..................................413 543-0700
Lee Deshais, *Owner*
EMP: 13
SALES (est): 1.8MM **Privately Held**
SIC: 2679 Commercial Printing

(G-15339)
HOLLAND WOODWORKING
224 Pomeroy Meadow Rd (01073-9458)
PHONE..................................413 527-6588
Roger Bishop, *Owner*
Paula Kareda, *Manager*
EMP: 3
SALES (est): 241.4K **Privately Held**
SIC: 2499 Mfg Wood Products

(G-15340)
LYMAN SHEET METAL CO INC
281 College Hwy (01073-9625)
P.O. Box 215 (01073-0215)
PHONE..................................413 527-0848
Kevin West, *President*
Glenn West, *Vice Pres*
Keith West, *Vice Pres*
Myrna West, *Vice Pres*
EMP: 7 **EST:** 1894
SQ FT: 2,700
SALES (est): 1.1MM **Privately Held**
SIC: 3444 Mfg Sheet Metalwork

(G-15341)
MOUNTAIN VIEW MACHINE
26 Pleasant St (01073-9557)
PHONE..................................413 527-6837
Peter Girouard, *Owner*
EMP: 3 **EST:** 1996
SALES (est): 237.9K **Privately Held**
WEB: www.mountainviewmachine.com
SIC: 3599 Mfg Industrial Machinery

Southborough
Worcester County

(G-15342)
AMORSA THERAPEUTICS INC
7 Banfill Ln (01772-1719)
PHONE..................................508 571-8240
Joseph Blanchard, *CEO*
Anita Gupta, *Principal*
Alex Nivorozhkin, *COO*
Michael Palfreyman, *Officer*
EMP: 5 **EST:** 2013
SALES (est): 225.8K **Privately Held**
SIC: 2834 Mfg Pharmaceutical Preparations

(G-15343)
ASHLAND CABINET CORP
7 Turnpike Rd (01772-2107)
PHONE..................................508 303-8100
Matt Di Pilato, *President*
Brian Bush, *Treasurer*
EMP: 7
SALES (est): 906.9K **Privately Held**
WEB: www.ashlandcabinet.com
SIC: 2434 Mfg Wood Kitchen Cabinets

(G-15344)
BALLARD UNMANNED SYSTEMS INC
Also Called: Protonex Technology Corp
153 Northboro Rd Ste 1 (01772-1034)
PHONE....................................508 687-4970
Paul Osenar, *President*
David A Ierardi, *Vice Pres*
Phil Robinson, *Vice Pres*
Greg Sipriano, *Vice Pres*
Christopher Bonni, *Engineer*
EMP: 15
SQ FT: 12,000
SALES (est): 9MM
SALES (corp-wide): 96.5MM **Privately Held**
SIC: 3629 Mfg Electrical Industrial Apparatus
PA: Ballard Power Systems Inc
9000 Glenlyon Pky
Burnaby BC V5J 5
604 454-0900

(G-15345)
BIODIRECTION INC
144 Trnpike Rd Sthborough Southborough (01772)
PHONE....................................508 599-2400
Sharad Joshi, *President*
Brian McGlynn, *Exec VP*
David Bastable, *Director*
Stephen Brackett, *Director*
Robert Mercier, *Director*
EMP: 21 **EST:** 2010
SALES (est): 1.1MM **Privately Held**
SIC: 3841 Mfg Surgical/Medical Instruments

(G-15346)
BIQ LLC
37 Valley Rd (01772-1306)
P.O. Box 464 (01772-0464)
PHONE....................................508 485-9896
Matthew Paulson, *President*
Eric Strovink,
EMP: 3
SALES (est): 157.7K
SALES (corp-wide): 102MM **Privately Held**
SIC: 7372 Prepackaged Software Services
PA: Opera Solutions, Llc
10 Exchange Pl Fl 11
Jersey City NJ 07302
646 520-4320

(G-15347)
BLACK ICE PUBLISHERS
130 Main St (01772-1432)
P.O. Box 448 (01772-0448)
PHONE....................................508 481-0910
Bruce A King, *Owner*
EMP: 3 **EST:** 1972
SALES (est): 130K **Privately Held**
SIC: 2741 2731 Misc Publishing Books-Publishing/Printing

(G-15348)
BLOCK ENGINEERING LLC
132 Turnpike Rd Ste 110 (01772-2129)
PHONE....................................508 480-9643
Petros A Kotidis, *CEO*
Anish Goyal, *Vice Pres*
George Baker,
EMP: 20
SALES (est): 4.2MM **Privately Held**
WEB: www.blockeng.com
SIC: 3826 Mfg Analytical Instruments

(G-15349)
BLOCK MEMS LLC
132 Turnpike Rd Ste 110 (01772-2129)
PHONE....................................508 251-3100
Daniel J Cavicchio Jr, *Mng Member*
George M Baker,
EMP: 15
SALES (est): 2.4MM **Privately Held**
SIC: 3824 Mfg Fluid Meter/Counting Devices

(G-15350)
BOLLYWOOD DELIGHTS INC
6 Lynbrook Rd (01772-1428)
PHONE....................................508 740-1908
Manpreet Khurana, *Principal*
EMP: 8
SALES (est): 498.9K **Privately Held**
SIC: 2051 Mfg Bread/Related Products

(G-15351)
BRAINWAVE SCIENCE LLC
Also Called: Brain Fingerprinting Tech
257 Turnpike Rd Ste 220 (01772-1791)
PHONE....................................774 760-1678
Krishna Ika, *President*
Thierry Maison, *Principal*
Bijendra Malik, *Principal*
EMP: 6
SALES (est): 460K **Privately Held**
SIC: 3845 Mfg Electromedical Equipment

(G-15352)
CAMBEX CORPORATION
337 Turnpike Rd Ste 200 (01772-1760)
P.O. Box 79 (01772-0079)
PHONE....................................508 217-4508
Joseph Kruy, *Branch Mgr*
EMP: 5
SALES (corp-wide): 5.7MM **Publicly Held**
SIC: 3572 Mfg Computer Storage Devices
PA: Cambex Corporation
115 Flanders Rd
Westborough MA 01581
508 983-1200

(G-15353)
D-LEW INC
Also Called: Quikprint
216 Boston Rd (01772-1301)
PHONE....................................508 481-7709
Darryl Lewis, *President*
EMP: 3
SQ FT: 2,000
SALES: 500K **Privately Held**
SIC: 2752 Lithographic Commercial Printing

(G-15354)
DEVICE TECHNOLOGIES INC
Also Called: Dti
155 Northboro Rd Ste 8 (01772-1033)
PHONE....................................508 229-2000
Nicholas B Petri, *President*
Ogden Petri, *Vice Pres*
Gloria Amorelli, *Executive*
◆ **EMP:** 20
SQ FT: 23,000
SALES (est): 5MM **Privately Held**
WEB: www.devicetec.com
SIC: 3429 3451 3495 3061 Mfg Hardware Mfg Screw Machine Prdts Mfg Wire Springs Mfg Mechanical Rubber Gd

(G-15355)
DOUGHERTY TOOL COMPANY INC
148 Marlboro Rd (01772-1212)
PHONE....................................508 485-5566
William Dougherty, *President*
Carla Dougherty, *Clerk*
EMP: 8
SQ FT: 10,000
SALES (est): 1.1MM **Privately Held**
SIC: 3599 Machine Shop

(G-15356)
EMC CORPORATION
21 Coslin Dr Bldg 4 (01772-1771)
PHONE....................................508 382-7556
EMP: 9
SALES (corp-wide): 90.6B **Publicly Held**
SIC: 3572 7372 7371 3577 Mfg Computer Storage Dvc Prepackaged Software Svc Computer Programming Svc Mfg Computer Peripherals
HQ: Emc Corporation
176 South St
Hopkinton MA 01748
508 435-1000

(G-15357)
FIT AMERICA INC
150 Cordaville Rd Ste 100 (01772-1848)
P.O. Box 5387, Frisco CO (80443-5387)
PHONE....................................309 839-1695
Carl Fruth, *President*
Alexandra Auer, *Admin Sec*
EMP: 9
SQ FT: 1,000
SALES (est): 18.9MM
SALES (corp-wide): 25.4MM **Privately Held**
SIC: 3544 3313 3253 2759 Mfg Dies/Tools/Jigs/Fixt Mfg Elctrometlrgcl Prdts Mfg Ceramic Wall/Fl Tile Commercial Printing
PA: Fit Ag
Am Grohberg 1
Lupburg 92331
949 294-290

(G-15358)
GTXCEL INC
144 Turnpike Rd Ste 140 (01772-2121)
PHONE....................................508 804-3092
Peter E Stilson, *CEO*
EMP: 17 **EST:** 2014
SALES (est): 1.9MM **Privately Held**
SIC: 2741 Misc Publishing

(G-15359)
GYRUS ACMI LLC (DH)
Also Called: Olympus Surgical Tech Amer
136 Turnpike Rd Ste 300 (01772-2118)
PHONE....................................508 804-2600
Roy Davis, *CEO*
Phil Ryan, *Vice Pres*
David Hazerjian, *Purchasing*
Joe Green, *Engineer*
Simon Shaw, *CFO*
▲ **EMP:** 150 **EST:** 1987
SALES (est): 245.3MM **Privately Held**
SIC: 3841 5047 Mfg Surgical/Medical Instruments Whol Medical/Hospital Equipment
HQ: Olympus Corporation Of The Americas
3500 Corp Pkwy
Center Valley PA 18034
484 896-5000

(G-15360)
HEWLETT PACKARD HP AUTONOMY SO
120 Turnpike Rd (01772-2104)
PHONE....................................508 476-0000
EMP: 99 **EST:** 1871
SALES (est): 5.4MM **Privately Held**
SIC: 3714 Mfg Motor Vehicle Parts/Accessories

(G-15361)
HONEYWELL INTERNATIONAL INC
250 Turnpike Rd (01772-1742)
PHONE....................................508 490-7100
EMP: 114
SALES (corp-wide): 41.8B **Publicly Held**
WEB: www.honeywell.com
SIC: 3724 Mfg Aircraft Engines/Parts
PA: Honeywell International Inc.
300 S Tryon St
Charlotte NC 28202
973 455-2000

(G-15362)
JLG TECHNOLOGIES LLC
371 Turnpike Rd Ste 200 (01772-1747)
PHONE....................................508 424-2338
Jay L Gainsboro, *President*
EMP: 6
SALES (est): 869.5K
SALES (corp-wide): 330.7MM **Privately Held**
SIC: 3699 Security Control Equipment And Systems
PA: Securus Technologies, Inc.
4000 International Pkwy
Carrollton TX 75007
972 241-1535

(G-15363)
NOVOTECHNIK US INC
155 Northboro Rd Ste 31 (01772-1033)
PHONE....................................508 485-2244
Matt Pietro, *President*
EMP: 7
SQ FT: 7,000
SALES: 4.9MM
SALES (corp-wide): 30.9MM **Privately Held**
WEB: www.novotechnik.com
SIC: 3825 Mfg Electrical Measuring Instruments
PA: Novotechnik Messwertaufnehmer Ohg
Horbstr. 12
Ostfildern 73760
711 448-90

(G-15364)
SEMICONSOFT INC
83 Pine Hill Rd (01772-1313)
PHONE....................................617 388-6832
Leo Asinovski, *President*
EMP: 10
SQ FT: 2,000
SALES (est): 650K **Privately Held**
SIC: 3829 Mfg Measuring/Controlling Devices

(G-15365)
SEVCON INC (HQ)
155 Northboro Rd Ste 1 (01772-1033)
PHONE....................................508 281-5500
Matthew Boyle, *President*
Paul N Farquhar, *CFO*
▲ **EMP:** 37
SQ FT: 13,500
SALES: 49.8MM
SALES (corp-wide): 10.5B **Publicly Held**
WEB: www.sevcon.com
SIC: 3714 3674 Mfg Motor Vehicle Parts/Accessories Mfg Semiconductors/Related Devices
PA: Borgwarner Inc.
3850 Hamlin Rd
Auburn Hills MI 48326
248 754-9200

(G-15366)
SEVCON USA INC
155 Northboro Rd Ste 1 (01772-1033)
PHONE....................................508 281-5500
Matt Boyle, *President*
▲ **EMP:** 14
SQ FT: 12,000
SALES (est): 8MM
SALES (corp-wide): 10.5B **Publicly Held**
WEB: www.sevcon-us.com
SIC: 3621 Mfg Motors/Generators
HQ: Sevcon, Inc.
155 Northboro Rd Ste 1
Southborough MA 01772
508 281-5500

(G-15367)
SPIRENT COMMUNICATIONS INC
5 Crystal Pond Rd (01772-1758)
PHONE....................................774 463-0281
EMP: 6
SALES (corp-wide): 476.9MM **Privately Held**
SIC: 3825 Communication Services
HQ: Spirent Communications Inc.
27349 Agoura Rd
Calabasas CA 91301
818 676-2300

(G-15368)
SYNER-G PHARMA CONSULTING LLC
371 Trnpike Rd 2 Pk Cntl (01772)
PHONE....................................508 460-9700
Prabu Nambiar, *Mng Member*
EMP: 9 **EST:** 2007
SALES (est): 1.2MM **Privately Held**
SIC: 2834 Mfg Pharmaceutical Preparations

(G-15369)
TETHERX INC
41 Darlene Dr (01772-2058)
PHONE....................................508 308-7845
Chris Pierson, *Vice Pres*
EMP: 4
SALES (est): 424.5K **Privately Held**
SIC: 3841 Surgical And Medical Instruments

(G-15370)
VECTURA INCORPORATED
371 Turnpike Rd Ste 120 (01772-1747)
PHONE....................................508 573-5700
EMP: 4
SALES (est): 315.7K **Privately Held**
SIC: 2834 Mfg Pharmaceutical Preparations

(G-15371)
VHP FLIGHT SYSTEMS LLC
36 Clifford Rd (01772-1502)
PHONE..................................508 229-2615
James Prater,
EMP: 3 **EST:** 2005
SALES (est): 106.2K **Privately Held**
SIC: 3721 Mfg Aircraft

(G-15372)
WEBCO ENGINEERING INC
155 Northboro Rd Ste 20 (01772-1033)
PHONE..................................508 303-0500
Roger Mc Clelland, *President*
Roland Hill, *Vice Pres*
Robert Preddy, *Sales Dir*
EMP: 19
SQ FT: 15,622
SALES (est): 3.7MM **Privately Held**
WEB: www.webcoeng.com
SIC: 3554 7699 Mfg Paper Industrial Machinery Repair Services

Southbridge
Worcester County

(G-15373)
59 BEECHER STREET LLC
59 Beecher St (01550-2655)
PHONE..................................631 734-6200
Joseph P Marinelli Jr, *Principal*
EMP: 4
SALES (est): 227.3K **Privately Held**
SIC: 2084 Mfg Wines/Brandy/Spirits

(G-15374)
A & M TOOL & DIE COMPANY INC
Also Called: Saga Packaging Machinery Div
64 Mill St Ste 1 (01550-0017)
PHONE..................................508 764-3241
Alvino Aliberti, *President*
Guido Jacques, *Vice Pres*
Robert Jacques, *Treasurer*
Robert G Caprera, *Admin Sec*
EMP: 50 **EST:** 1948
SQ FT: 250,000
SALES (est): 10.6MM **Privately Held**
WEB: www.am-tool.com
SIC: 3544 3565 Mfg Dies/Tools/Jigs/Fixtures Mfg Packaging Machinery

(G-15375)
ALLTEC LASER TECHNOLOGY
50 Optical Dr (01550-2584)
PHONE..................................508 765-6666
Jeanine McElroy, *Principal*
EMP: 10
SALES (est): 1.1MM **Privately Held**
SIC: 2759 Commercial Printing

(G-15376)
BERMER PRECISION PRODUCTS LLC
94 Ashland Ave (01550-2804)
PHONE..................................508 764-2521
Jacob B Szugda,
EMP: 5
SALES (est): 488.4K **Privately Held**
SIC: 3544 Mfg Dies/Tools/Jigs/Fixtures

(G-15377)
BERMER TOOL & DIE INC
81 Ashland Ave (01550-2803)
P.O. Box 159 (01550 0159)
PHONE..................................508 764-2521
John Szugda, *President*
EMP: 28
SQ FT: 33,000
SALES (est): 4.5MM **Privately Held**
SIC: 3544 Mfg Dies/Tools/Jigs/Fixtures

(G-15378)
CREATEK-STONE INC
833 Main St Ste 2 (01550-1119)
PHONE..................................888 786-6389
Albert C West Jr, *President*
James W Schoepfer, *Vice Pres*
▼ **EMP:** 9
SQ FT: 6,700
SALES (est): 904.5K **Privately Held**
SIC: 3999 Mfg Misc Products

(G-15379)
DEGREASING DEVICES CO
105 Dresser St (01550-2436)
PHONE..................................508 765-0045
Roderick P Murphy, *President*
Jean Murphy, *Vice Pres*
▲ **EMP:** 9
SQ FT: 8,000
SALES: 1.5MM **Privately Held**
WEB: www.degreasingdevices.com
SIC: 3559 3677 3699 5084 Mfr & Whol Industrial Cleaning Equipment

(G-15380)
DEXTER-RUSSELL INC
44 River St (01550-1834)
P.O. Box 983122, Boston (02298-3122)
PHONE..................................800 343-6042
Richard B Hardy, *Ch.of Bd*
Kevin Clark, *Vice Pres*
Craig M Giguere, *Treasurer*
April Ullrich, *Human Res Mgr*
Stephen Clarke, *Sales Staff*
▲ **EMP:** 125
SQ FT: 160,000
SALES (est): 27.7MM
SALES (corp-wide): 106.8K **Privately Held**
WEB: www.dexter-russell.com
SIC: 3421 3423 Mfg Cutlery Mfg Hand/Edge Tools
PA: Hyde Group, Inc.
54 Eastford Rd
Southbridge MA 01550
800 872-4933

(G-15381)
ELEMENT PRECISION LLC
10 Cabot St (01550-2683)
PHONE..................................774 318-1777
EMP: 6 **EST:** 2016
SALES (est): 715.4K **Privately Held**
SIC: 2819 Industrial Inorganic Chemicals, Nec

(G-15382)
FALL PREVENTION ALARMS INC
186 Hamilton St (01550-1881)
PHONE..................................508 765-5050
Kevin R Keith, *President*
Beverly Bibbo, *Vice Pres*
EMP: 7
SALES: 500K **Privately Held**
SIC: 3669 Mfg Communications Equipment

(G-15383)
FUSED FIBEROPTICS LLC
79 Golf St (01550-2866)
PHONE..................................508 765-1652
Thomas A Dowling, *Managing Prtnr*
Robert F Dowling Jr, *Managing Prtnr*
EMP: 13
SQ FT: 14,000
SALES (est): 1.6MM **Privately Held**
WEB: www.fusedfiberoptics.com
SIC: 3229 Mfg Fiberoptic Components

(G-15384)
HARDLINE HEAT TREATING INC
134 Ashland Ave (01550-2804)
PHONE..................................508 764-6669
Robert Chalue, *President*
▲ **EMP:** 30
SALES: 4MM **Privately Held**
WEB: www.hardlineheattreating.com
SIC: 3398 Metal Heat Treating

(G-15385)
HYDE GROUP INC (PA)
Also Called: Hyde Tools
54 Eastford Rd (01550-3604)
P.O. Box 1875 (01550-1875)
PHONE..................................800 872-4933
Rob Scoble, *President*
Richard R Clemence, *Vice Pres*
Paul Yanka, *Prdtn Mgr*
Tim Oshea, *Engineer*
Eric Wilhelm, *Engineer*
◆ **EMP:** 130 **EST:** 1881
SQ FT: 200,000
SALES: 106.8K **Privately Held**
WEB: www.hydetools.com
SIC: 3421 5199 3423 Mfg Cutlery Whol Nondurable Goods Mfg Hand/Edge Tools

(G-15386)
HYDE TOOLS
54 Eastford Rd (01550-3604)
PHONE..................................508 764-4344
Robert Scoble, *President*
Joseph Anzalotti, *Vice Pres*
Corie Talbot, *Vice Pres*
EMP: 4
SALES (est): 369.4K **Privately Held**
SIC: 3423 Hand And Edge Tools, Nec

(G-15387)
ITALIAN CHOPPERS LLC
64 High St (01550-1706)
PHONE..................................508 648-6816
Mark Montani, *Manager*
EMP: 3
SALES (est): 311.3K **Privately Held**
SIC: 3751 Mfg Motorcycles/Bicycles

(G-15388)
J I MORRIS COMPANY
394 Elm St (01550-3067)
PHONE..................................508 764-4394
John B Dirlam, *President*
Paul A Mills, *Vice Pres*
Peter B Dirlam, *Treasurer*
EMP: 9 **EST:** 1920
SQ FT: 100,000
SALES (est): 1.4MM **Privately Held**
WEB: www.morris01550.com
SIC: 3545 3452 3544 Mfg Machine Tool Accessories Mfg Bolts/Screws/Rivets Mfg Dies/Tools/Jigs/Fixtures

(G-15389)
J P MFG INC
13 Lovely St (01550-1799)
PHONE..................................508 764-2538
Gloria Kania, *President*
Edmond Kuzdzal, *Vice Pres*
EMP: 22
SQ FT: 10,000
SALES (est): 4.1MM **Privately Held**
WEB: www.jpmfg.com
SIC: 3827 Mfg Optical Instruments/Lenses

(G-15390)
K & K THERMOFORMING INC
380 Elm St (01550-3028)
PHONE..................................508 764-7700
David A Keller, *President*
EMP: 21
SALES: 3.3MM **Privately Held**
WEB: www.kplastic.com
SIC: 2671 Mfg Packaging Paper/Film

(G-15391)
LAVALLEE MACHINERY INC
831 Main St (01550-1169)
PHONE..................................508 764-2896
David Lavallee, *President*
Beverly Lavallee, *Clerk*
EMP: 7
SQ FT: 10,000
SALES: 700K **Privately Held**
SIC: 3599 Machine Shop Jobbing & Repair

(G-15392)
LENSMASTER OPTICAL COMPANY
28 Sandersdale Rd Ste 1 (01550-2861)
PHONE..................................508 764-4958
David Hmielowski, *President*
EMP: 3
SQ FT: 7,600
SALES (est): 238.7K **Privately Held**
WEB: www.lensmastertooling.com
SIC: 3851 Ret Optical Goods

(G-15393)
LSA CLEANPART LLC
Also Called: Cleanpart-East
10 Cabot St Ste 100 (01550-2683)
PHONE..................................508 765-4848
EMP: 7
SALES (corp-wide): 14.1MM **Privately Held**
SIC: 3544 3471 Mfg Dies/Tools/Jigs/Fixtures Plating/Polishing Service
HQ: Lsa Cleanpart, Llc
1610 Berryessa Rd Ste B
Santa Clara CA 95054

(G-15394)
MBI GRAPHICS & PRINTING CORP
97 Worcester St (01550-3409)
P.O. Box 733, Fiskdale (01518-0733)
PHONE..................................508 765-0658
Martin Bania, *President*
Jane Bania, *Vice Pres*
EMP: 10
SQ FT: 3,200
SALES: 900K **Privately Held**
WEB: www.mbigraphics.com
SIC: 2752 5044 Lithographic Commercial Printing Whol Office Equipment

(G-15395)
MBS FABRICATION INC (PA)
270 Ashland Ave (01550-3103)
PHONE..................................508 765-0900
Carleton Macgillivray, *President*
David Macgillivray, *Vice Pres*
Brenda Macgillivray, *Treasurer*
Carol Macgillivray, *Admin Sec*
EMP: 15
SALES (est): 3.3MM **Privately Held**
SIC: 3441 Structural Metal Fabrication

(G-15396)
MERCHANTS FABRICATION INC (PA)
23 Golf St (01550-2809)
PHONE..................................508 784-6700
Mark Richard Fisher, *President*
Melissa Tremblay, *Office Mgr*
EMP: 7
SALES (est): 990.6K **Privately Held**
SIC: 3443 Mfg Fabricated Plate Wrk

(G-15397)
OPTIM INC
64 Mill St (01550-1175)
PHONE..................................508 765-5879
EMP: 5
SALES (est): 330K **Privately Held**
SIC: 3599 Mfg Industrial Machinery

(G-15398)
OPTIMUM TECHNOLOGIES INC
114 Pleasant St (01550-1236)
PHONE..................................508 765-8100
EMP: 10
SQ FT: 5,300
SALES (est): 2.7MM **Privately Held**
WEB: www.optech.org
SIC: 3827 8711 Mfg Optical Instruments/Lenses Engineering Services

(G-15399)
PATRIOT CUSTOMS INCORPORATED
134 Ashland Ave (01550-2804)
PHONE..................................508 764-7342
Christopher Twine, *Owner*
EMP: 3
SQ FT: 1,250
SALES (est): 354.2K **Privately Held**
WEB: www.patriotprinting.net
SIC: 2752 Lithographic Commercial Printing

(G-15400)
SCHOTT NORTH AMERICA INC
Also Called: Schott Lighting and Imaging
122 Charlton St (01550-1914)
PHONE..................................508 765-3300
Donald A Miller, *President*
Gerald J Fine, *President*
Ottmar Ernst, *Vice Pres*
Jim Triba, *QC Mgr*
Daniel Bedoya, *Engineer*
EMP: 220
SALES (est): 38.9MM
SALES (corp-wide): 449.3K **Privately Held**
SIC: 3229 Mfg Pressed/Blown Glass
HQ: Schott Corporation
555 Taxter Rd Ste 470
Elmsford NY 10523
914 831-2200

(G-15401)
SCHOTT NORTH AMERICA INC
Schott Fiber Optics
122 Charlton St (01550-1914)
PHONE..................................508 765-9744

GEOGRAPHIC

Donald Miller, *Manager*
EMP: 99
SALES (corp-wide): 449.3K **Privately Held**
WEB: www.us.schott.com
SIC: 3229 Mfg Fiber Optics
HQ: Schott North America, Inc.
555 Taxter Rd Ste 470
Elmsford NY 10523
914 831-2200

(G-15402)
SCHOTT NORTH AMERICA INC
Also Called: Schott Electronic Packaging
15 Wells St Ste 1 (01550-4503)
PHONE..................................508 765-7450
Andreas Becker, *Ch of Bd*
EMP: 65
SALES (est): 9.2MM
SALES (corp-wide): 449.3K **Privately Held**
WEB: www.us.schott.com
SIC: 3679 3643 3053 Mfg Electronic Components Mfg Conductive Wiring Devices Mfg Gaskets/Packing/Sealing Devices
HQ: Schott North America, Inc.
555 Taxter Rd Ste 470
Elmsford NY 10523
914 831-2200

(G-15403)
SIMONDS INCORPORATED
248 Elm St (01550-2616)
P.O. Box 100 (01550-0100)
PHONE..................................508 764-3235
Joan Logee, *President*
Jamie Muller, *Vice Pres*
Alisha Desrochers, *Prdtn Mgr*
▲ **EMP:** 17
SQ FT: 9,600
SALES: 3MM **Privately Held**
WEB: www.simonds-inc.com
SIC: 3546 Mfg Hand/Edge Tools

(G-15404)
SIMSAK MACHINE & TOOL CO INC
28 Sandersdale Rd Ste 1 (01550-2860)
PHONE..................................508 764-4958
David Hmielowski, *President*
Jan Hmielowski, *Treasurer*
EMP: 5 **EST:** 1970
SQ FT: 4,000
SALES (est): 420K **Privately Held**
SIC: 3542 3544 Manufactures Machine Tools Injection Molds Jigs And Gauges

(G-15405)
STONEBRIDGE PRESS INC (PA)
Also Called: Southbridge News
25 Elm St (01550-2647)
P.O. Box 90 (01550-0090)
PHONE..................................508 764-4325
Frank Chilinski, *President*
John Coots, *President*
David S Cutler, *Vice Pres*
Ron Tramblay, *CFO*
Sandy Lapensee, *Executive*
EMP: 50
SALES (est): 5.1MM **Privately Held**
WEB: www.townclassified.com
SIC: 2711 Newspapers-Publishing/Printing

(G-15406)
SUPERIOR CAKE PRODUCTS INC
94 Ashland Ave (01550-2804)
PHONE..................................508 764-3276
Kevin P McCafferty, *CEO*
Michael Faucher, *President*
Christopher T Smith, *President*
Vincent Martelli, *CFO*
Rick Buchanan, *Finance Dir*
EMP: 70
SQ FT: 80,000
SALES (est): 16.4MM
SALES (corp-wide): 850.3MM **Publicly Held**
SIC: 2051 Mfg Bread/Related Products
HQ: Hostess Brands, Llc
1 E Armour Blvd
Kansas City MO 64111
816 701-4600

(G-15407)
UNITED LENS COMPANY INC
259 Worcester St (01550-1376)
PHONE..................................508 765-5421
William R Lannon, *CEO*
Paul J Digregorio, *Vice Pres*
Justin Blouin, *Prdtn Mgr*
Hong Lee, *Prdtn Mgr*
Kevin Labarge, *Production*
▲ **EMP:** 150
SQ FT: 150,000
SALES (est): 22.2MM **Privately Held**
WEB: www.unitedlens.com
SIC: 3827 Mfg Optical Instruments/Lenses

(G-15408)
VOCERO HISPANO NEWSPAPER INC
44 Hamilton St (01550-3706)
PHONE..................................508 792-1942
Pablo Santiago, *President*
EMP: 7
SALES (est): 439.2K **Privately Held**
WEB: www.vocerohispano.com
SIC: 2711 7311 8742 7313 Newspapers-Publish/Print Advertising Agency Mgmt Consulting Svcs Advertising Rep

(G-15409)
WORCESTER TLEGRAM GAZETTE CORP
39 Elm St Ste 2 (01550-2644)
PHONE..................................508 764-2519
Fax: 508 764-2774
EMP: 10
SALES (corp-wide): 1.5B **Publicly Held**
SIC: 2711 Newspapers-Publishing/Printing
HQ: Worcester Telegram & Gazette Corporation
20 Franklin St
Worcester MA 01608
508 793-9100

Southfield
Berkshire County

(G-15410)
CUESPORT INC
1415 Canaan Southfield Rd (01259-9764)
PHONE..................................413 229-6626
Norman P Stalker, *President*
Donna M Stalker, *Treasurer*
Frederick J Mali, *Shareholder*
EMP: 9 **EST:** 1963
SALES: 250K **Privately Held**
SIC: 3949 Mfg Billiard Cues

Southwick
Hampden County

(G-15411)
B & E TOOL COMPANY INC
Also Called: B&E Precision Arcft Components
10 Hudson Dr (01077-9546)
P.O. Box 40 (01077-0040)
PHONE..................................413 569-5585
Robert Quaglia, *CEO*
▲ **EMP:** 78 **EST:** 1950
SQ FT: 35,000
SALES (est): 27.6MM
SALES (corp-wide): 220.2MM **Privately Held**
WEB: www.betool.com
SIC: 3728 Mfg Aircraft Parts/Equipment
PA: Cadence Aerospace, Llc
3150 E Miraloma Ave
Anaheim CA 92806
949 877-3630

(G-15412)
BUILDERS CHOICE KITCHEN & BATH
796 College Hwy (01077-9690)
PHONE..................................413 569-9802
Gerald Pohner, *President*
EMP: 3
SQ FT: 2,500
SALES (est): 432.6K **Privately Held**
SIC: 2434 Mfg Wood Kitchen Cabinets

(G-15413)
FERRARI CLASSICS CORPORATION
Also Called: Screamin Stevens
120 Berkshire Ave (01077-9651)
PHONE..................................413 569-6179
Steven Ferrari, *President*
Virginia Ferrari, *Vice Pres*
EMP: 4
SQ FT: 5,000
SALES: 200K **Privately Held**
SIC: 3944 Mfg Games/Toys

(G-15414)
JULIE CECCHINI
Also Called: Terra Americana
74 Tannery Rd (01077-9770)
PHONE..................................413 562-2042
Julie Cecchini, *Owner*
EMP: 10
SALES (est): 690.9K **Privately Held**
SIC: 2052 Food Mfg

(G-15415)
KELLOGG BROS INC
377 N Loomis St (01077-9692)
P.O. Box 1162 (01077-1162)
PHONE..................................413 569-6029
Seth Kellogg, *President*
Constance Kellogg, *Treasurer*
Tanya C Kellogg, *Clerk*
EMP: 8
SQ FT: 5,000
SALES: 944K **Privately Held**
SIC: 3272 5211 Mfg Concrete Septic Tanks & Ret Concrete

(G-15416)
NITOR CORP
5 Whalley Way (01077-9222)
PHONE..................................413 998-0510
Stephen K Phillips, *Principal*
EMP: 3 **EST:** 2010
SALES (est): 415.9K **Privately Held**
SIC: 2759 Commercial Printing

(G-15417)
SAWMILL PARK
1 Saw Mill Park (01077-9212)
PHONE..................................413 569-3393
Deb Mc Cann, *Principal*
EMP: 3
SALES (est): 257K **Privately Held**
SIC: 2421 6513 Sawmill/Planing Mill Apartment Building Operator

(G-15418)
T J BARK MULCH INC
25 Sam West Rd (01077-9734)
P.O. Box 1168 (01077-1168)
PHONE..................................413 569-2400
James Oleksak, *President*
EMP: 11
SALES (est): 1.4MM **Privately Held**
SIC: 2499 Mfg Wood Products

(G-15419)
TOVA INDUSTRIES INC
Also Called: D & S Manufacturing
10 Hudson Dr (01077-9546)
P.O. Box 1133 (01077-1133)
PHONE..................................413 569-5688
John Wilander, *President*
Paul Tobias, *COO*
Jack Tarnauskas, *QC Mgr*
Eva Fuller, *Engineer*
Craig Lebeau, *Engineer*
EMP: 15 **EST:** 1976
SQ FT: 8,000
SALES (est): 2.8MM **Privately Held**
WEB: www.dsmfgtova.com
SIC: 3599 Machine Shop

(G-15420)
WESTERN MASS RENDERING CO INC
94 Foster Rd (01077-9522)
PHONE..................................413 569-6265
David Plakias, *President*
EMP: 30
SQ FT: 23,000
SALES (est): 4.6MM **Privately Held**
WEB: www.wmrco.com
SIC: 2077 Recycling Waste

(G-15421)
WGI INC
34 Hudson Dr (01077-9546)
P.O. Box 1130 (01077-1130)
PHONE..................................413 569-9444
Frederick Filios, *President*
Larry Sears, *COO*
Rebecca Totti, *Vice Pres*
David Norton, *CFO*
Theresa Thomas, *CFO*
EMP: 135
SQ FT: 73,000
SALES (est): 37.4MM **Privately Held**
SIC: 3492 3724 3568 3769 Mfg Fluid Power Valves Mfg Aircraft Engine/Part Mfg Power Transmsn Equip Mfg Space Vehicle Equip Mfg Motor Vehicle Bodies

(G-15422)
WHALLEY PRECISION INC
28 Hudson Dr (01077-9546)
PHONE..................................413 569-1400
John Whalley, *President*
David Whalley, *Vice Pres*
▲ **EMP:** 17
SQ FT: 17,000
SALES (est): 3.3MM **Privately Held**
WEB: www.whalleyprecision.com
SIC: 3599 Mfg Industrial Machinery

(G-15423)
WHIP CITY TOOL & DIE CORP
813 College Hwy (01077-9690)
P.O. Box 99 (01077-0099)
PHONE..................................413 569-5528
Brian M Iserman, *President*
Nathan A Kane, *Vice Pres*
Bonnie White, *Manager*
▼ **EMP:** 24
SQ FT: 17,500
SALES (est): 5.4MM **Privately Held**
WEB: www.whipcitytool.com
SIC: 3544 Mfg Dies/Tools/Jigs/Fixtures

Spencer
Worcester County

(G-15424)
ADVANCED MFG TECH INC
Also Called: Amt
2 Bixby Rd (01562-2402)
PHONE..................................508 885-0249
Doug Roesch, *President*
EMP: 5
SQ FT: 10,000
SALES: 1.1MM **Privately Held**
SIC: 3544 Mfg Dies/Tools/Jigs/Fixtures

(G-15425)
AUCOINS PRESS INC
104 Main St (01562-2140)
P.O. Box 643 (01562-0643)
PHONE..................................508 885-0800
Donna M Aucoin, *President*
EMP: 4
SALES (est): 426.7K **Privately Held**
SIC: 2752 2759 Lithographic Commercial Printing Commercial Printing

(G-15426)
AUCOINS PRINTING
37 Mcdonald St (01562-2545)
PHONE..................................508 885-3595
Ronald Aucoin, *Owner*
EMP: 3
SALES (est): 153.2K **Privately Held**
SIC: 2759 Lithographic Commercial Printing

(G-15427)
CONSTANT VELOCITY MFG LLC
221 N Spencer Rd (01562-1234)
PHONE..................................508 735-3399
Charles McGrath, *Principal*
EMP: 3
SALES (est): 129.2K **Privately Held**
SIC: 3999 Mfg Misc Products

(G-15428)
DIENES CORPORATION
27 W Main St (01562-2498)
PHONE..................................508 885-6301
William Shea, *President*

▲ = Import ▼=Export
◆ =Import/Export

Kenneth Jaillet, *Vice Pres*
▲ **EMP:** 40
SQ FT: 34,000
SALES (est): 9.6MM
SALES (corp-wide): 605.7K **Privately Held**
WEB: www.dienesusa.com
SIC: 3545 Mfg Machine Tool Accessories
HQ: Supe-Dienes Gmbh
Kolner Str. 7
Overath 51491
220 660-50

(G-15429)
FLEXCON COMPANY INC (PA)
1 Flexcon Industrial Park (01562-2643)
PHONE....................................508 885-8200
Neil McDonough, *CEO*
Linda Rieo, *President*
Lavon Winkler, *President*
Aziz Gdihi, *Vice Pres*
Dan Twining, *Vice Pres*
◆ **EMP:** 700
SQ FT: 30,000
SALES (est): 333.1MM **Privately Held**
WEB: www.flexcon.com
SIC: 3081 2891 Mfg Unsupported Plastic Film/Sheet Mfg Adhesives/Sealants

(G-15430)
FLEXCON INDUSTRIAL LLC (HQ)
1 S Spencer Rd (01562-2643)
PHONE....................................210 798-1900
Neil McDonoughm, *President*
Morgan Ebin, *Vice Pres*
▲ **EMP:** 37
SALES (est): 20.2MM
SALES (corp-wide): 333.1MM **Privately Held**
SIC: 3086 Mfg Plastic Foam Products
PA: Flexcon Company, Inc.
1 Flexcon Industrial Park
Spencer MA 01562
508 885-8200

(G-15431)
GODIN LAND CLEARING
Also Called: Timber Leasing
28 Marble Rd (01562-2830)
PHONE....................................508 885-9666
Toll Free:....................................888 -
Roger Godin, *Owner*
EMP: 4
SALES (est): 320.7K **Privately Held**
SIC: 2411 Logging

(G-15432)
LEVEILLEE ARCHTCTRAL MLLWK INC
23 S Spencer Rd (01562-2629)
PHONE....................................508 885-9731
Richard J Leveillee, *President*
EMP: 10
SALES: 950K **Privately Held**
SIC: 2431 Mfg Millwork

(G-15433)
MERCURY WIRE PRODUCTS INC
1 Mercury Dr (01562-1999)
PHONE....................................508 885-6363
Robert K Yard, *President*
Christopher Yard, *Vice Pres*
Raymond Ainsworth, *Engineer*
Jesus Mendoza, *Engineer*
Perry Harrison, *CFO*
▼ **EMP:** 135
SQ FT: 65,000
SALES (est): 56.1MM **Privately Held**
WEB: www.mercurywire.com
SIC: 3357 Nonferrous Wiredrawing/Insulating

(G-15434)
REVO BIOLOGICS INC
300 Charlton Rd (01562-3138)
PHONE....................................508 370-5451
EMP: 50
SALES (corp-wide): 4.2MM **Privately Held**
SIC: 2836 6794 Mfg Biological Products Patent Owner/Lessor
HQ: Revo Biologics, Inc.
175 Crossing Blvd
Framingham MA 01702

(G-15435)
ROBERT KOWALSKI
Also Called: Kowalski Furinture Design
22 Cherry St (01562-2111)
PHONE....................................508 885-5392
EMP: 4
SQ FT: 1,500
SALES (est): 161.7K **Privately Held**
SIC: 2511 Wood Household Furniture, Nsk

(G-15436)
SPENCER INDUSTRIAL PAINTING
60 Wire Village Rd (01562-1439)
PHONE....................................508 885-5406
Arnold W Beer, *President*
EMP: 8
SQ FT: 2,000
SALES (est): 540K **Privately Held**
SIC: 3479 Painting Of Metal Products

(G-15437)
SUNFIELD SOLAR
22 Treadwell Dr (01562-1321)
PHONE....................................508 885-3300
EMP: 3
SALES (est): 150K **Privately Held**
SIC: 3433 Mfg Heating Equipment-Nonelectric

Springfield
Hampden County

(G-15438)
A G MILLER COMPANY INC
53 Batavia St (01109-3893)
PHONE....................................413 732-9297
Rick Miller, *President*
Ernestine Amiller, *Admin Sec*
▲ **EMP:** 43
SQ FT: 40,000
SALES (est): 9.1MM **Privately Held**
WEB: www.agmiller.com
SIC: 3444 Mfg Sheet Metalwork

(G-15439)
ACCENT ON INDUSTRIAL METAL INC
179 Page Blvd (01104-3035)
PHONE....................................413 785-1654
David M Tassinari, *President*
David T Tassinari, *Manager*
EMP: 10 **EST:** 1980
SQ FT: 25,000
SALES (est): 1.9MM **Privately Held**
WEB: www.accentindustrial.com
SIC: 3369 Nonferrous Metal Foundry

(G-15440)
ACE SIGNS INC
477 Cottage St (01104-3290)
P.O. Box 3374 (01101-3374)
PHONE....................................413 739-3814
James Carlin Sr, *President*
James Carlin Jr, *Vice Pres*
Cathy Smith, *Treasurer*
Jim Manzi, *Graphic Designe*
EMP: 10
SQ FT: 11,000
SALES: 1.3MM **Privately Held**
WEB: www.acesigns.com
SIC: 3993 Mfg Signs/Advertising Specialties

(G-15441)
AERO - BOND CORP
1 Allen St Ste 212 (01108-1953)
P.O. Box 80269 (01138-0269)
PHONE....................................413 734-2224
Surya Kodali, *President*
Anuraag K Kodali, *President*
Kirti R Kodali, *Director*
EMP: 10
SQ FT: 4,800
SALES (est): 1.7MM **Privately Held**
WEB: www.aerobondcorp.com
SIC: 3724 Mfg Aircraft Engines/Parts

(G-15442)
AEROBOND COMPOSITES LLC
1 Allen St Ste 201 (01108-1953)
PHONE....................................413 734-2224
EMP: 20
SALES (est): 746.7K **Privately Held**
SIC: 3728 Aircraft Parts And Equipment, Nec, Nsk

(G-15443)
AGNOLI SIGN COMPANY INC
722 Worthington St (01105-1115)
P.O. Box 1055 (01101-1055)
PHONE....................................413 732-5111
Donald G Agnoli, *President*
EMP: 20 **EST:** 1930
SQ FT: 20,000
SALES: 2MM **Privately Held**
WEB: www.agnolisign.com
SIC: 3993 Mfg Signs/Advertising Specialties

(G-15444)
ALLIANCE UPHOLSTERY INC
143 Main St (01105-2405)
PHONE....................................413 731-7857
Evan Cohen, *President*
Simon Skolnick, *Treasurer*
EMP: 4
SQ FT: 3,000
SALES (est): 332.7K **Privately Held**
SIC: 2512 7641 Mfg Upholstered Household Furniture Reupholstery/Furniture Repair

(G-15445)
AMERICAN OUTDOOR BRANDS CORP (PA)
2100 Roosevelt Ave (01104-1606)
PHONE....................................800 331-0852
Robert L Scott, *Vice Ch Bd*
P James Debney, *President*
Brian D Murphy, *President*
Mark P Smith, *President*
Lane Tobiassen, *President*
EMP: 724
SALES: 638.2MM **Publicly Held**
SIC: 3482 Mfg Small Arms Ammunition

(G-15446)
APMAR USA INC
175 Progress Ave (01104-3230)
PHONE....................................413 781-5261
Gary Aprahamian, *President*
Judith Mary Marciano, *Principal*
Emmanuel Tsitsirides, *Prdtn Mgr*
Marc Boudreau, *Sales Mgr*
EMP: 5
SALES (est): 813.7K **Privately Held**
SIC: 3471 Plating/Polishing Service

(G-15447)
APPLE STEEL RULE DIE CO INC
88 Industry Ave Ste C (01104-3367)
PHONE....................................414 353-2444
Barbara Wanbold, *Branch Mgr*
Bill Lesperance, *Technical Staff*
EMP: 20
SALES (corp-wide): 9.3MM **Privately Held**
WEB: www.appledie.com
SIC: 3544 Mfg Dies/Tools/Jigs/Fixtures
PA: Apple Steel Rule Die Co., Inc.
7817 W Clinton Ave
Milwaukee WI 53223
414 353-2444

(G-15448)
ASTENJOHNSON INC
40 Progress Ave (01104-3231)
PHONE....................................413 733-6603
Don Cappell, *Branch Mgr*
EMP: 146
SALES (corp-wide): 542.1MM **Privately Held**
SIC: 2221 Manmade Broadwoven Fabric Mill
PA: Astenjohnson, Inc.
4399 Corporate Rd
North Charleston SC 29405
843 747-7800

(G-15449)
ATHLETIC EMBLEM & LETTERING CO
Also Called: Hampden Hat & Cap Co Division
189 Taylor St (01105-1747)
PHONE....................................413 734-0415
Michael Godek, *President*
EMP: 15
SQ FT: 20,000
SALES (est): 1.7MM **Privately Held**
WEB: www.athleticemblem.com
SIC: 2399 2353 2395 Mfg Emblems Badges Banners & Baseball Caps

(G-15450)
BAY STATE CAST PRODUCTS INC
41 Brookdale Dr (01104-3269)
PHONE....................................413 736-1028
Peter Maziarz, *President*
Thomas Maziarz, *Vice Pres*
EMP: 8
SQ FT: 14,500
SALES: 1.4MM **Privately Held**
SIC: 3544 Mfg Dies/Tools/Jigs/Fixtures

(G-15451)
BENCHMARK CARBIDE
616 Dwight St (01104-3409)
PHONE....................................800 523-8570
Steve Layher, *Principal*
EMP: 6 **EST:** 2012
SALES (est): 92.7K **Privately Held**
SIC: 2819 Mfg Industrial Inorganic Chemicals

(G-15452)
BIG DADDY BOOMERANGS LLC
88 Coral Rd (01118-2402)
PHONE....................................413 297-7079
Jeffrey N Lebeau, *Principal*
EMP: 4
SALES (est): 173.1K **Privately Held**
SIC: 3949 Mfg Sporting/Athletic Goods

(G-15453)
BILL WILLARD INC
Also Called: Willard's Concrete
1350 Main St Ste 1505 (01103-1664)
PHONE....................................413 584-1054
Fax: 413 584-1754
EMP: 8
SALES (est): 950.9K
SALES (corp-wide): 1.9MM **Privately Held**
SIC: 3273 Mfg Ready-Mixed Concrete
PA: Bill Willard Inc
1350 Main St Ste 1505
Springfield MA
413 584-1802

(G-15454)
BIO-CATALYTIC ENTERPRISES INC
1 Allen St Ste 201 (01108-1953)
PHONE....................................413 739-9148
Donald Watson, *President*
Tracy Carman, *Vice Pres*
EMP: 20
SALES (est): 12.2K **Privately Held**
SIC: 2869 Mfg Industrial Organic Chemicals

(G-15455)
BLUE RHINO OF NE
1709 Page Blvd (01104-1753)
PHONE....................................413 781-3694
Drabik John, *Principal*
EMP: 8
SALES (est): 850.7K **Privately Held**
SIC: 2911 Petroleum Refiner

(G-15456)
BOULEVARD MACHINE & GEAR INC
785 Page Blvd (01104-3036)
PHONE....................................413 788-6466
Susan Kasa, *President*
Kazimierz Kasa, *Vice Pres*
EMP: 23
SQ FT: 10,000
SALES (est): 5.4MM **Privately Held**
WEB: www.boulevardmachine.com
SIC: 3599 3462 Mfg Industrial Machinery Mfg Iron/Steel Forgings

(G-15457)
BUSINESS WEST
Also Called: Business West On Line
1441 Main St Ste 604 (01103-1449)
PHONE....................................413 781-8600
John Gormally, *Owner*
Stephen Krevalin, *Managing Prtnr*

George O'Brien, *Editor*
Melissa Hallock, *Sales Staff*
Shannon Bliven, *Mktg Coord*
EMP: 9
SALES (est): 588.2K **Privately Held**
WEB: www.businesswest.com
SIC: 2711 Newspapers-Publishing/Printing

(G-15458)
CARL FISHER CO INC
42 Wilcox St (01105-2399)
P.O. Box 2209 (01101-2209)
PHONE..................................413 736-3661
Ronald Fisher, *President*
Douglas Fisher, *Treasurer*
EMP: 40
SQ FT: 20,000
SALES (est): 6.8MM **Privately Held**
SIC: 3441 3444 Mfg Sheet Metalwork Structural Metal Fabrication

(G-15459)
CELLASSIST LLC (PA)
54 Hobson St (01109-1112)
PHONE..................................413 559-1256
Seth Berggren, *Electrical Engi*
Hendalee Wilson,
Michael Deschamps,
EMP: 5
SALES (est): 511.7K **Privately Held**
SIC: 3663 Mfg Radio/Tv Communication Equipment

(G-15460)
CHICOPEE VISION CENTER INC
Also Called: 16 Acres Optical
1907 Wilbraham Rd (01129-1822)
PHONE..................................413 796-7570
William E Dyke Jr, *President*
EMP: 18
SALES (est): 1.5MM **Privately Held**
SIC: 3851 Mfg Eyeglasses & Contact Lenses

(G-15461)
CONDON MFG CO INC
310 Verge St (01129-1197)
PHONE..................................413 543-1250
Kenneth Condon, *President*
Gregg Condon, *Treasurer*
Joanne Evans, *Admin Sec*
EMP: 17 **EST:** 1946
SQ FT: 8,100
SALES (est): 2.5MM **Privately Held**
WEB: www.condonmfg.com
SIC: 3491 3451 Mfg Industrial Valves Mfg Screw Machine Products

(G-15462)
CRAFTMENS CORNER
940 Boston Rd (01119-1316)
PHONE..................................413 782-3783
Gary Bellucci, *Owner*
EMP: 5
SALES (est): 420.3K **Privately Held**
SIC: 3199 Mfg Leather Goods

(G-15463)
CRRC MA CORPORATION
655 Page Blvd (01104-3013)
PHONE..................................617 415-7190
Mark Smith, *General Mgr*
EMP: 7
SALES (corp-wide): 31.1B **Privately Held**
SIC: 3743 Mfg Railroad Equipment
HQ: Crrc Ma Corporation
108 Myrtle St Ste 3
Quincy MA 02171
617 415-7180

(G-15464)
CUMMINS INC
177 Rocus St Ste 1 (01104-3479)
PHONE..................................413 737-2659
Dan Leigh, *General Mgr*
Danny Leigh, *Branch Mgr*
EMP: 9
SALES (corp-wide): 23.7B **Publicly Held**
WEB: www.cummins.com
SIC: 3519 Mfg Motor Vehicle Parts/Accessories
PA: Cummins Inc.
500 Jackson St
Columbus IN 47201
812 377-5000

(G-15465)
CURTIS UNIVERSAL JOINT CO INC
4 Birnie Ave (01107-1191)
PHONE..................................413 737-0281
Glenn Beauregard, *General Mgr*
▲ **EMP:** 35 **EST:** 1935
SQ FT: 30,000
SALES (est): 8MM **Privately Held**
WEB: www.curtisuniversal.com
SIC: 3568 Mfg Power Transmission Equipment

(G-15466)
CUSTOM CARBIDE CORP
616 Dwight St (01104-3462)
PHONE..................................413 732-7470
Paul Y St Louis, *President*
EMP: 12
SQ FT: 6,500
SALES (est): 2MM **Privately Held**
WEB: www.ridgecarbidetool.com
SIC: 3545 Mfg Machine Tools-Cutting

(G-15467)
DONCASTERS INC
Storms Forge Division
160 Cottage St (01104-3250)
PHONE..................................413 785-1801
Paul Hopkins, *Opers Mgr*
David Simm, *Branch Mgr*
Dave Smith, *Info Tech Mgr*
EMP: 90
SALES (corp-wide): 604.8MM **Privately Held**
SIC: 3325 3462 Steel Foundry Mfg Iron/Steel Forgings
HQ: Doncasters Inc.
835 Poquonnock Rd
Groton CT 06340

(G-15468)
ELECTRO-TERM INC
Also Called: Electro-Term/Hollingsworth
50 Warehouse St (01118-1058)
PHONE..................................413 734-6469
Walt Rustic, *CEO*
Thomas Dancy, *President*
Andrea Gagne, *Treasurer*
Robert Block, *Sales Mgr*
Craig Allen, *Manager*
EMP: 74
SQ FT: 48,000
SALES (est): 7.4MM **Privately Held**
SIC: 3643 3678 Mfg Conductive Wiring Devices Mfg Electronic Connectors

(G-15469)
ELY TOOL INC
455 Cottage St (01104-4005)
PHONE..................................413 732-2347
Edward L Young, *President*
Halina ME, *Finance*
EMP: 34
SQ FT: 10,000
SALES (est): 5.9MM **Privately Held**
WEB: www.young-ely.com
SIC: 3545 Mfg Machine Tool Accessories

(G-15470)
EXXONMOBIL PIPELINE COMPANY
145 Albany St (01105-1001)
PHONE..................................413 736-1881
Mike D Censo, *Manager*
EMP: 3
SALES (est): 176.8K **Privately Held**
SIC: 2911 Petroleum Refiner

(G-15471)
GRAPHIC EXCELLENCE LLC
Also Called: Sir Speedy
1441 Main St (01103-1406)
PHONE..................................413 733-6691
Traci Conners, *Mng Member*
Michael Conners,
EMP: 7 **EST:** 1973
SQ FT: 3,200
SALES: 850K **Privately Held**
SIC: 2752 Comm Prtg Litho

(G-15472)
GRASSETTI SALES ASSOCIATES
Also Called: Roberts Manufacturing Company
160 Progress Ave (01104-3232)
PHONE..................................413 737-2283
Robert A Grassetti, *President*
EMP: 9 **EST:** 1975
SALES (est): 1.3MM **Privately Held**
SIC: 3599 Machine Shop

(G-15473)
GREEN SOLAR LLC
933 E Columbus Ave (01105-2509)
PHONE..................................413 552-4114
EMP: 3
SALES (est): 116.1K **Privately Held**
SIC: 2211 Broadwoven Fabric Mills, Cotton

(G-15474)
HANGER PRSTHETCS & ORTHO INC
1985 Main St (01103-1095)
PHONE..................................413 734-0002
Thomas Kirk, *CEO*
Tom Mesick, *Director*
EMP: 4
SALES (corp-wide): 1B **Publicly Held**
SIC: 3842 Mfg Surgical Appliances/Supplies
HQ: Hanger Prosthetics & Orthotics, Inc.
10910 Domain Dr Ste 300
Austin TX 78758
512 777-3800

(G-15475)
HEDGE HOG INDUSTRIES
86 Princeton St (01109-3427)
PHONE..................................413 363-2528
Mike Serricchio, *Principal*
EMP: 3
SALES (est): 154K **Privately Held**
SIC: 3999 Mfg Misc Products

(G-15476)
HITPOINT INC (PA)
1350 Main St Ste 1300 (01103-6107)
P.O. Box 476, Greenfield (01302-0476)
PHONE..................................508 314-6070
Aaron St John, *CEO*
Paul Hake, *President*
Steve Victorino, *CFO*
EMP: 18
SQ FT: 2,400
SALES (est): 5.6MM **Privately Held**
SIC: 3944 Mfg Games/Toys

(G-15477)
HORIZON SHEET METAL INC
109 Cadwell Dr (01104-1705)
PHONE..................................413 734-6966
Peggy Grodd, *President*
Gerald A Desjardins, *President*
Craig Gallagher, *Materials Mgr*
Gary Fortier, *Engineer*
Philip C Schultz, *CFO*
EMP: 55
SQ FT: 45,000
SALES: 6MM **Privately Held**
WEB: www.horizonsmi.com
SIC: 3444 Mfg Sheet Metalwork

(G-15478)
INEOS MELAMINES LLC
730b Worcester St (01151-1022)
PHONE..................................413 730-3811
Scott Hansen, *Opers Staff*
Jeanne Visser, *Engineer*
Denise Martinez, *Accountant*
Charles Lyon,
◆ **EMP:** 42
SALES (est): 12.1MM
SALES (corp-wide): 352.2K **Privately Held**
SIC: 2821 Mfg Plastic Materials/Resins
HQ: Ineos Group Ag
Avenue Des Uttins 3
Rolle VD
216 277-040

(G-15479)
INTEMPO SOFTWARE INC (PA)
191 Chestnut St Fl 5 (01103-1571)
PHONE..................................800 950-2221
Matt Hopp, *General Mgr*
Deanna Freeman, *Manager*
Jeff Loomis, *Director*
EMP: 15
SQ FT: 5,000
SALES (est): 3MM **Privately Held**
SIC: 7372 Prepackaged Software Services

(G-15480)
INTERNTNAL BR-TECH SLTIONS INC (PA)
225 Armory St (01104-2425)
PHONE..................................413 739-2271
Jonathan Waitt, *President*
EMP: 14
SQ FT: 5,500
SALES (est): 1.9MM **Privately Held**
SIC: 3699 Mfg Electrical Equipment/Supplies

(G-15481)
JOSEPH FREEDMAN CO INC (PA)
115 Stevens St (01104-3120)
PHONE..................................888 677-7818
John Freedman, *President*
Ernest Gagnon Jr, *Vice Pres*
Kirk Stillman, *Opers Mgr*
Don George, *CFO*
Donald George, *CFO*
EMP: 55 **EST:** 1891
SQ FT: 120,000
SALES (est): 24.5MM **Privately Held**
SIC: 3355 Aluminum Rolling/Drawing

(G-15482)
JOSEPH FREEDMAN CO INC
40 Albany St (01105-1002)
PHONE..................................413 781-4444
John Freedman, *Branch Mgr*
EMP: 31
SALES (corp-wide): 24.5MM **Privately Held**
SIC: 3355 Mfg Aluminum Wire & Cable
PA: Joseph Freedman Co., Inc.
115 Stevens St
Springfield MA 01104
888 677-7818

(G-15483)
K & W MACHINE WORKS
146 Verge St (01129-1124)
PHONE..................................413 543-3329
Fax: 413 543-3329
EMP: 5
SQ FT: 2,028
SALES: 500K **Privately Held**
SIC: 3599 7692 Mfg Industrial Machinery Welding Repair

(G-15484)
KIELB WELDING ENTERPRISES
Also Called: Advance Welding
150 Brookdale Dr (01104-3208)
PHONE..................................413 734-4544
Kaz Kielb, *President*
Christopher Kielb, *Vice Pres*
EMP: 10 **EST:** 1978
SQ FT: 10,000
SALES (est): 860K **Privately Held**
WEB: www.theperfectweld.com
SIC: 7692 Welding & Fabricating Service

(G-15485)
LOVEJOY CURTIS LLC
4 Birnie Ave (01107-1129)
PHONE..................................413 737-0281
EMP: 25
SALES (corp-wide): 3.5B **Publicly Held**
SIC: 3568 Mfg Power Transmission Equipment
HQ: Lovejoy Curtis Llc
200 Lovejoy Ave
South Haven MI 49090
269 637-5132

(G-15486)
LUSTER-ON PRODUCTS INC
54 Waltham Ave (01109-3398)
P.O. Box 90247 (01139-0247)
PHONE..................................413 739-2541
Paul R Lane, *President*
Alexander J Price, *Treasurer*
Jaime Camacho, *Technical Staff*
Catherine P Rogers, *Admin Sec*
▲ **EMP:** 18 **EST:** 1968
SQ FT: 75,000

SALES (est): 4.5MM **Privately Held**
WEB: www.luster-on.com
SIC: 2899 5084 8711 Mfg Chemical Preparations Whol Industrial Equipment Engineering Services

(G-15487)
MANUFCTRERS PATTERN FNDRY CORP
25 Mill River Ln (01105-2415)
P.O. Box 468, East Longmeadow (01028-0468)
PHONE..................................413 732-8117
Fax: 413 739-1326
EMP: 6 **EST:** 1938
SQ FT: 17,000
SALES: 800K **Privately Held**
SIC: 3469 3543 Mfg Metal And Wood Industrial Patterns And Aluminum And Bronze Industrial Castings

(G-15488)
MEREDITH CORPORATION
Also Called: Four M Studios
1300 Liberty St (01104-1153)
PHONE..................................413 733-4040
EMP: 3
SALES (corp-wide): 3.1B **Publicly Held**
SIC: 2721 Periodicals-Publishing/Printing
PA: Meredith Corporation
1716 Locust St
Des Moines IA 50309
515 284-3000

(G-15489)
MERRIAM-WEBSTER INCORPORATED (DH)
47 Federal St (01105-1230)
P.O. Box 281 (01102-0281)
PHONE..................................413 734-3134
John M Morse, *President*
Peter Sokolowski, *Editor*
Matt Dube, *Vice Pres*
Judith G Recke, *Vice Pres*
Jed Santoro, *Vice Pres*
▲ **EMP:** 186
SQ FT: 35,000
SALES (est): 18.3MM
SALES (corp-wide): 2.6MM **Privately Held**
WEB: www.merriam-webster.com
SIC: 2731 2741 Books-Publishing/Printing Misc Publishing
HQ: Encyclopaedia Britannica, Inc.
325 N Lasalle St Ste 200
Chicago IL 60654
312 347-7000

(G-15490)
MITCHELL MACHINE INCORPORATED (PA)
224 Hancock St (01109-4399)
P.O. Box 90128 (01139-0128)
PHONE..................................413 739-9693
John Mitchell, *President*
Francis Mitchell, *Vice Pres*
Steve Delong, *Engineer*
Jeff Kiratsoulis, *Engineer*
Frank Mitchell, *CFO*
EMP: 25
SQ FT: 30,000
SALES (est): 4.9MM **Privately Held**
WEB: www.mitchellmachine.com
SIC: 3554 3559 3548 Mfg Paper Industrial Machinery Mfg Misc Industry Machinery Mfg Welding Apparatus

(G-15491)
MPINGO MULTI CASTING
146 Chestnut St (01103-1576)
PHONE..................................413 241-2500
EMP: 4
SALES (est): 258.1K **Privately Held**
SIC: 3369 Nonferrous Metal Foundry

(G-15492)
NASH MFG & GRINDING SVCS
572 Saint James Ave (01109-3832)
P.O. Box 1266, Holyoke (01041-1266)
PHONE..................................413 301-5416
Matthew Nash, *President*
Jan Lee Nash, *Vice Pres*
EMP: 11
SQ FT: 2,100
SALES: 300K **Privately Held**
WEB: www.nashmanufacturing.com
SIC: 3599 Machine Shop

(G-15493)
NORTH END OIL SERVICE CO INC
1003 Saint James Ave (01104-2148)
PHONE..................................413 734-7057
Julio C Feliciano, *Principal*
EMP: 4
SALES (est): 313.5K **Privately Held**
SIC: 1389 Oil/Gas Field Services

(G-15494)
NORTHERN TOOL MFG CO INC
170 Progress Ave (01104-3232)
PHONE..................................413 732-5549
George Frigo, *President*
Mary Breglio, *Treasurer*
EMP: 18 **EST:** 1952
SQ FT: 15,000
SALES: 1.5MM **Privately Held**
WEB: www.northerntoolmfg.com
SIC: 3089 Mfg Plastic Products

(G-15495)
NUFORJ LLC
1350 Main St (01103-1628)
PHONE..................................413 530-0349
Rudy Vogel, *Partner*
Donald Deptowicz, *Principal*
EMP: 14
SALES (est): 571.5K **Privately Held**
SIC: 3599 Mfg Industrial Machinery

(G-15496)
OUT & ABOUT MAGAZINE
21 Kay St (01109-1310)
PHONE..................................413 783-6704
Gerald Anchors Jr, *Principal*
John Finco, *Marketing Staff*
EMP: 3
SALES (est): 104.4K **Privately Held**
SIC: 2721 Periodicals-Publishing/Printing

(G-15497)
P&G GRAPHIC SOLUTIONS INC
Also Called: Sign-A-Rama
784 Page Blvd (01104-3025)
PHONE..................................413 731-9213
Gene Niksa, *President*
EMP: 4 **EST:** 2008
SALES: 500K **Privately Held**
SIC: 3993 Signsadv Specs

(G-15498)
POLY-METAL FINISHING INC
1 Allen St Ste 218 (01108-1953)
P.O. Box 80049 (01138-0049)
PHONE..................................413 781-4535
Jason Kudelka, *President*
Tim Kellogg, *Prdtn Mgr*
Paul Laquerre, *Prdtn Mgr*
EMP: 70 **EST:** 1971
SQ FT: 40,000
SALES (est): 9.8MM **Privately Held**
WEB: www.poly-metal.com
SIC: 3471 3479 Plating/Polishing Service Coating/Engraving Service

(G-15499)
PPI/TIME ZERO INC
140 Carando Dr (01104-3296)
PHONE..................................781 881-2400
Frank Roda, *Branch Mgr*
EMP: 6
SALES (corp-wide): 69.1MM **Privately Held**
SIC: 3672 Printed Circuit Boards
HQ: Ppi/Time Zero, Inc.
11 Madison Rd
Fairfield NJ 07004
973 278-6500

(G-15500)
REFCO MANUFACTURING US INC
66 Industry Ave Ste 8 (01104-3285)
PHONE..................................413 746-3094
Manfred Ulrich, *President*
Steve Seacord, *Vice Pres*
▲ **EMP:** 6
SALES (est): 1.2MM
SALES (corp-wide): 543.8MM **Privately Held**
SIC: 3585 Mfg Refrigeration/Heating Equipment
HQ: Refco Manufacturing Ltd.
Industriestrasse 11
Hitzkirch LU 6285
419 197-282

(G-15501)
RELEVANT ENERGY CONCEPTS INC
1833 Roosevelt Ave (01109-2439)
PHONE..................................413 733-7692
Debra Tolliver, *Principal*
EMP: 4
SALES (est): 306.1K **Privately Held**
SIC: 3825 1771 Mfg Electrical Measuring Instruments Concrete Contractor

(G-15502)
REPUBLICAN COMPANY (HQ)
Also Called: Springfield Newspaper
1860 Main St (01103-1073)
PHONE..................................413 788-1000
David B Evans, *President*
Robyn Newhouse, *Publisher*
Joe Deburro, *Editor*
Robbin Jones, *Counsel*
Michael Newhouse, *Vice Pres*
EMP: 623 **EST:** 1878
SQ FT: 200,000
SALES (est): 132.5MM
SALES (corp-wide): 5.4B **Privately Held**
WEB: www.union-news.com
SIC: 2711 Newspapers-Publishing/Printing
PA: Advance Publications, Inc.
1 World Trade Ctr Fl 43
New York NY 10007
718 981-1234

(G-15503)
ROBERTS & SONS PRINTING INC
1791 Boston Rd (01129-1129)
PHONE..................................413 283-9356
George Roberts, *President*
Jeffrey Roberts, *Vice Pres*
Diana Roberts, *Treasurer*
Stephen Manning, *Clerk*
EMP: 7 **EST:** 1980
SALES: 392K **Privately Held**
SIC: 2759 2752 Commercial Printing Lithographic Commercial Printing

(G-15504)
SEND PYMETS TO WASHER WIZZARDS
34 Cambridge St (01109-3004)
PHONE..................................413 733-2739
James Lafleur, *Principal*
EMP: 3
SALES (est): 201.9K **Privately Held**
SIC: 3452 Mfg Bolts/Screws/Rivets

(G-15505)
SMITHFIELD DIRECT LLC
Carando
20 Carando Dr (01104-3212)
P.O. Box 491 (01102-0491)
PHONE..................................413 781-5620
Donald Kimdle, *Manager*
EMP: 300
SQ FT: 160,000 **Privately Held**
WEB: www.farmlandfoods.com
SIC: 2013 2011 Mfg Prepared Meats Meat Packing Plant
HQ: Smithfield Direct, Llc
4225 Naperville Rd # 600
Lisle IL 60532

(G-15506)
SMITHFIELD FOODS INC
Also Called: Carando Foods
20 Carando Dr (01104-3212)
P.O. Box 491 (01102-0491)
PHONE..................................413 781-5620
Al Ferentino, *Marketing Staff*
EMP: 721 **Privately Held**
SIC: 2011 Meat Packing Plant
HQ: Smithfield Foods, Inc.
200 Commerce St
Smithfield VA 23430
757 365-3000

(G-15507)
SOLUTIA INC
730 Worcester St (01151-1022)
P.O. Box 51975, Indian Orchard (01151-5975)
PHONE..................................413 788-6911
Jack Mayusky, *Branch Mgr*
EMP: 750 **Publicly Held**
SIC: 2821 Mfg Plastic Materials/Resins
HQ: Solutia Inc.
575 Maryville Centre Dr
Saint Louis MO 63141
423 229-2000

(G-15508)
SPIRIG ADVANCED TECH INCIES
Also Called: Sat
144 Oakland St (01108-1738)
PHONE..................................413 788-6191
Ernest Spirig, *President*
Laurie Topjian, *General Mgr*
▲ **EMP:** 3
SQ FT: 1,500
SALES: 350K **Privately Held**
WEB: www.spirig.com
SIC: 3699 3822 Mfg Electronic Devices & Temperature Control Devices

(G-15509)
SPRINGFIELD LABEL TAPE CO INC
430 Saint James Ave (01109-3830)
PHONE..................................413 733-6634
Howard Libowitz, *President*
Charles Libowitz, *Treasurer*
EMP: 34 **EST:** 1963
SQ FT: 20,000
SALES (est): 7.5MM **Privately Held**
WEB: www.springfieldlabel.com
SIC: 2672 Lithographic Commercial Printing

(G-15510)
SUFFIELD POULTRY INC
Also Called: Royal Harvest Foods
90 Avocado St (01104-3304)
PHONE..................................413 737-8392
James Vallides, *President*
Lynne Vallides, *Admin Sec*
EMP: 3
SQ FT: 40,000
SALES (est): 401K **Privately Held**
WEB: www.royalharv.com
SIC: 2015 5144 5142 Poultry Processing Whol Poultry/Products Whol Packaged Frozen Goods

(G-15511)
SUPER BRUSH LLC
800 Worcester St (01151-1042)
PHONE..................................413 543-1442
Roger Allen Sheeks, *Mng Member*
Cathy Desorcy, *Manager*
EMP: 95 **EST:** 1964
SQ FT: 40,000
SALES (est): 17.5MM **Privately Held**
WEB: www.superbrush.com
SIC: 3089 Mfg Foam Applicators And Swabs

(G-15512)
THIBAULT FUEL OIL
215 Albany St (01105-1019)
P.O. Box 319, West Springfield (01090-0319)
PHONE..................................413 782-9577
Butch Thibault, *President*
EMP: 7
SALES (est): 942.3K **Privately Held**
SIC: 2911 Petroleum Refiner

(G-15513)
THOMPSON/CENTER ARMS CO INC (HQ)
2100 Roosevelt Ave (01104-1606)
PHONE..................................800 331-0852
Peter James Debney, *President*
William F Spengler, *Treasurer*
◆ **EMP:** 32

GEOGRAPHIC

SALES (est): 17.3MM
SALES (corp-wide): 638.2MM Publicly Held
WEB: www.thompsoninvestmentcasting.com
SIC: 3484 Mfg Small Arms
PA: American Outdoor Brands Corporation
2100 Roosevelt Ave
Springfield MA 01104
800 331-0852

(G-15514)
THORN INDUSTRIES INC
732 Cottage St (01104-4207)
PHONE..................................413 737-2464
John Hicks, *President*
Steven J Hicks, *General Mgr*
EMP: 12
SQ FT: 2,100
SALES (est): 1.8MM Privately Held
WEB: www.thornind.com
SIC: 3599 Mfg Industrial Machinery

(G-15515)
TITEFLEX COMMERCIAL INC
603 Hendee St (01104-3003)
PHONE..................................413 739-5631
William T Smith, *President*
Robert M Speer, *Corp Secy*
◆ EMP: 14
SQ FT: 110,000
SALES (est): 1.9MM
SALES (corp-wide): 3.1B Privately Held
SIC: 3599 3052 Manufacturing Industrial Machinery And Rubber/Plastic Hose/Belting
PA: Smiths Group Plc
4th Floor
London SW1Y
207 004-1600

(G-15516)
TITEFLEX CORPORATION (HQ)
603 Hendee St (01104-3034)
PHONE..................................413 739-5631
Pat McCaffrey, *President*
Patrick Henry, *Vice Pres*
Jeff McDonald, *Opers Mgr*
Justina Sawyer, *Purchasing*
Christopher Bruce, *Engineer*
▲ EMP: 345
SQ FT: 280,000
SALES (est): 141.8MM
SALES (corp-wide): 3.1B Privately Held
WEB: www.titeflex.com
SIC: 3052 3599 Mfg Rubber/Plastic Hose/Belting Mfg Industrial Machinery
PA: Smiths Group Plc
4th Floor
London SW1Y
207 004-1600

(G-15517)
TITEFLEX CORPORATION
Also Called: Titeflex Teflon & Metal Hose
603 Hendee St (01104-3034)
PHONE..................................413 781-0008
Tom Bassett, *Branch Mgr*
EMP: 25
SALES (corp-wide): 3.1B Privately Held
WEB: www.titeflex.com
SIC: 2821 Mfg Plastic Materials/Resins
HQ: Titeflex Corporation
603 Hendee St
Springfield MA 01104
413 739-5631

(G-15518)
TRIDENT ALLOYS INC
181 Abbe Ave (01107-1073)
PHONE..................................413 737-1477
James H Galaska, *President*
EMP: 26 EST: 1979
SQ FT: 27,500
SALES (est): 4.2MM Privately Held
WEB: www.tridentalloysinc.com
SIC: 3325 3369 Steel Foundry Nonferrous Metal Foundry

(G-15519)
TRUCK BUYER INC
33 Oakdale St (01104-1733)
PHONE..................................413 273-9993
Alan J Salem, *President*
Joan Salem, *Treasurer*
▼ EMP: 4 EST: 1999
SALES: 300K Privately Held
SIC: 3537 Mfg Industrial Trucks/Tractors

(G-15520)
UNIVERSAL TOOL CO INC
33 Rose Pl (01104-3198)
PHONE..................................413 732-4807
John M Piane Jr, *President*
▲ EMP: 41 EST: 1928
SQ FT: 12,000
SALES (est): 5.7MM Privately Held
SIC: 3469 Mfg Metal Stampings

(G-15521)
VALLEY PLATING INC 8-1-80
412 Albany St (01105-1049)
PHONE..................................413 788-7375
John Wietecha, *President*
Dennis Chaffee, *Treasurer*
Nicole Krstyen, *Human Res Mgr*
Jessica Gambino, *Admin Asst*
Christopher Belinda, *Maintence Staff*
EMP: 75
SQ FT: 39,000
SALES (est): 10.6MM Privately Held
WEB: www.valleyplatinginc.com
SIC: 3471 Plating/Polishing Service

(G-15522)
W S SIGN DESIGN CORP
884 Alden St (01109-2647)
PHONE..................................413 241-6916
Ronald E Whitaker, *President*
EMP: 4
SQ FT: 6,000
SALES: 1MM Privately Held
WEB: www.wssign-design.com
SIC: 3993 7389 Mfg Signs/Advertising Specialties Business Services

(G-15523)
WASTE MGMT INC
Also Called: Rrt of Springfield Mass Inc
84 Birnie Ave (01107-1129)
PHONE..................................413 747-9294
Jimmy Rodriguez, *Manager*
Mike Moores, *Manager*
EMP: 30
SALES (est): 4.3MM
SALES (corp-wide): 14.9B Publicly Held
WEB: www.wastemanagement.com
SIC: 3559 Mfg Misc Industry Machinery
HQ: Waste Management Holdings Inc
1001 Fannin St Ste 4000
Houston TX 77002
713 512-6200

(G-15524)
WEB CLOSEOUT
360 El Paso St (01104-2955)
PHONE..................................413 222-8302
Mike Sarrage, *President*
EMP: 20
SALES (est): 1MM Privately Held
WEB: www.webcloseout.com
SIC: 2741 Misc Publishing

(G-15525)
WESTROCK CONTAINER LLC
320 Parker St (01129-1026)
P.O. Box 842159, Boston (02284-2159)
PHONE..................................413 733-2211
Dan Kazes, *Branch Mgr*
EMP: 76
SALES (corp-wide): 18.2B Publicly Held
SIC: 2653 Mfg Corrugated/Solid Fiber Boxes
HQ: Westrock Container, Llc
1601 Blairs Ferry Rd Ne
Cedar Rapids IA 52402
319 393-3610

(G-15526)
WESTROCK CP LLC
320 Parker St (01129-1026)
PHONE..................................413 543-2311
Barry Roberts, *Manager*
EMP: 101
SALES (corp-wide): 18.2B Publicly Held
SIC: 2653 Mfg Corrugated/Solid Fiber Boxes
HQ: Westrock Cp, Llc
1000 Abernathy Rd
Atlanta GA 30328

(G-15527)
WESTROCK MWV LLC
Envelope Division
2001 Roosevelt Ave (01104-1657)
P.O. Box 3300 (01102-3300)
PHONE..................................413 736-7211
Barry Levenson, *Branch Mgr*
EMP: 600
SALES (corp-wide): 18.2B Publicly Held
WEB: www.meadwestvaco.com
SIC: 2631 2677 2671 Paperboard Mill Mfg Envelopes Mfg Packaging Paper/Film
HQ: Westrock Mwv, Llc
501 S 5th St
Richmond VA 23219
804 444-1000

(G-15528)
WESTROCK RKT COMPANY
320 Parker St (01129-1026)
PHONE..................................413 543-7300
EMP: 3
SALES (corp-wide): 18.2B Publicly Held
SIC: 2653 2652 2631 Mfg Corrugated/Fiber Box Mfg Setup Paperboard Box Paperboard Mill
HQ: Westrock Rkt, Llc
1000 Abernathy Rd Ste 125
Atlanta GA 30328
770 448-2193

(G-15529)
ZATO INC
Also Called: Zato Health
1350 Main St Ste 502 (01103-1676)
PHONE..................................617 834-8105
John Holbrook, *CEO*
EMP: 3
SALES (est): 202.8K Privately Held
SIC: 7372 7389 Prepackaged Software Services

(G-15530)
ZEPKAS ANTIGUES
121 Wildwood Ave (01118-1955)
PHONE..................................413 782-2964
Joseph Zepka, *Owner*
EMP: 3
SALES: 89K Privately Held
SIC: 3944 Mfg Games/Toys

Sterling
Worcester County

(G-15531)
AGENCY SYSTEMS GROUP
20 Kilburn Rd (01564-2116)
PHONE..................................978 422-8479
Mario Balducci, *Owner*
EMP: 5
SALES: 550K Privately Held
SIC: 3823 Mfg Computer Interface Equipment For Industrial Process Control

(G-15532)
AGRIUM ADVANCED TECH US INC
18 Legate Hill Rd (01564-2312)
P.O. Box 607 (01564-0607)
PHONE..................................978 422-3331
John Allen, *Branch Mgr*
EMP: 3 Privately Held
SIC: 2873 Mfg Nitrogenous Fertilizers
HQ: Agrium Advanced Technologies (U.S.) Inc.
2915 Rocky Mountain Ave # 400
Loveland CO 80538

(G-15533)
ALTEC NORTHEAST LLC
44 Chocksett Rd (01564-2355)
PHONE..................................508 320-9041
Lee Styslinger III,
▲ EMP: 13
SALES (est): 2.7MM
SALES (corp-wide): 764.3MM Privately Held
SIC: 3531 3536 3713 Mfg Construction Mach Mfg Hoist/Crane/Monorail Mfg Truck/Bus Bodies
HQ: Altec Industries, Inc.
210 Inverness Center Dr
Birmingham AL 35242
205 991-7733

(G-15534)
ALTO TECHNOLOGIES CORPORATION (PA)
Also Called: Alto Aviation
86 Leominster Rd (01564-2114)
P.O. Box 399 (01564-0399)
PHONE..................................978 422-9071
Donald Hamilton, *President*
Kevin Hayes, *Vice Pres*
Steve Scarlata, *Vice Pres*
Eugenio Penate, *Electrical Engi*
Janess Don, *Technical Staff*
▲ EMP: 15
SQ FT: 38,000
SALES (est): 4.6MM Privately Held
WEB: www.altoaviation.com
SIC: 3651 Mfg Home Audio/Video Equipment

(G-15535)
ANDERSON POWER PRODUCTS INC (HQ)
13 Pratts Junction Rd (01564-2305)
PHONE..................................978 422-3600
Nick Shkordoff, *President*
Jeffrey S Burkhardt, *Vice Pres*
John Mc Carthy, *Plant Mgr*
Michael Hole, *Regl Sales Mgr*
▲ EMP: 74
SALES (est): 20MM
SALES (corp-wide): 342.5MM Privately Held
SIC: 3829 5065 3678 3643 Mfg Measure/Control Dvcs Whol Electronic Parts Mfg Elec Connectors Mfg Conductive Wire Dvcs Mfg Dies/Tools/Jigs/Fixt
PA: Ideal Industries, Inc.
1375 Park Ave
Sycamore IL 60178
815 895-5181

(G-15536)
BILLY HILL TUBS LLC
47 Chocksett Rd (01564-2353)
PHONE..................................978 422-8800
Russell H Mason, *Principal*
EMP: 5 EST: 2011
SALES (est): 278.1K Privately Held
SIC: 3089 Mfg Plastic Products

(G-15537)
BIOMEDICAL POLYMERS INC
16 Chocksett Rd (01564-2336)
PHONE..................................978 632-2555
Michael T Faulkner, *President*
Steve Duval, *General Mgr*
John Bellorado, *VP Mfg*
James Lucier, *Inv Control Mgr*
Pamela Rogers, *Buyer*
▲ EMP: 60
SALES (est): 16.2MM Privately Held
WEB: www.biomedicalpolymers.com
SIC: 3089 Mfg Plastic Products

(G-15538)
CONTINENTAL STONE MBL GRAN INC
Also Called: Continental Stone, Inc.
287 Leominster Rd (01564-2151)
Rural Route 12, Leominster (01453)
PHONE..................................978 422-8700
Manoel Leite, *President*
▲ EMP: 22
SQ FT: 10,000
SALES: 2MM Privately Held
SIC: 3281 Mfg Cut Stone/Products

(G-15539)
HENDRICKSON ADVERTISING INC
118 Leominster Rd (01564-2113)
P.O. Box 471 (01564-0471)
PHONE..................................978 422-8087
Glenn Hendrickson, *President*
Elizabeth Hendrickson, *Clerk*
EMP: 5 EST: 1954
SQ FT: 5,400

SALES (est): 564.2K Privately Held
SIC: 2261 2759 5961 Screen Printing Of Cotton Broadwoven Fabrics And Other Screen Printing Services Also Mail Orders Screen Printed Novelties

(G-15540)
IDEAL INDUSTRIES INC
Anderson Power Products
13 Pratts Junction Rd (01564-2305)
PHONE..................................978 422-3600
James A Colony, *President*
EMP: 138
SALES (corp-wide): 342.5MM Privately Held
WEB: www.idealindustries.com
SIC: 3829 5065 3678 3643 Mfg Measure/Control Dvcs Whol Electronic Parts Mfg Elec Connectors Mfg Conductive Wire Dvcs Mfg Dies/Tools/Jigs/Fixt
PA: Ideal Industries, Inc.
1375 Park Ave
Sycamore IL 60178
815 895-5181

(G-15541)
KYLE EQUIPMENT CO INC
14 Legate Hill Rd (01564-2312)
P.O. Box 658 (01564-0658)
PHONE..................................978 422-8448
Charles F Kyle, *President*
Sean Kyle, *Vice Pres*
EMP: 7
SQ FT: 8,500
SALES (est): 1.3MM Privately Held
SIC: 3533 Mfg Oil/Gas Field Machinery

(G-15542)
NEW ENGLAND BLINDS
7 Honeycrisp Way (01564-1559)
PHONE..................................508 868-5399
Susan Pikor, *Owner*
EMP: 3
SALES: 500K Privately Held
SIC: 2591 Ret Misc Homefurnishings

(G-15543)
S KYLE EQUIPMENT LLC
Also Called: Skyquip
7 Crowley Rd (01564-2413)
P.O. Box 658 (01564-0658)
PHONE..................................978 422-8448
Sean Kyle, *President*
EMP: 4 EST: 2014
SQ FT: 3,600
SALES (est): 465.5K Privately Held
SIC: 3533 Mfg Oil/Gas Field Machinery

(G-15544)
SIGLER MACHINE CO
3 Northeast Blvd (01564-2339)
PHONE..................................978 422-7868
Lawrence Sigler, *Owner*
EMP: 10
SALES (est): 1MM Privately Held
WEB: www.siglermachine.com
SIC: 3599 Mfg Industrial Machinery

(G-15545)
SPACE AGE ELECTRONICS INC (PA)
58 Chocksett Rd (01564-2354)
PHONE..................................800 486-1723
Eugene H Mongeau, *Chairman*
Mike Madden, *Business Mgr*
Steve Busa, *Materials Mgr*
Mike Lynch, *Mfg Staff*
Deb Beauregard, *Purchasing*
EMP: 25
SQ FT: 75,000
SALES (est): 9.1MM Privately Held
WEB: www.1sae.com
SIC: 3669 Mfg Communications Equipment

(G-15546)
STERLING CONCRETE CORP
194 Worcester Rd (01564)
PHONE..................................978 422-8282
George Defalco, *President*
EMP: 10
SALES (est): 2.5MM Privately Held
SIC: 3273 Mfg Ready-Mixed Concrete

(G-15547)
STERLING PEAT INC
Also Called: Sterling Peat & Loam
64 Greenland Rd (01564-2606)
PHONE..................................978 422-8294
John C Kristoff, *President*
EMP: 3 EST: 1934
SALES: 125K Privately Held
SIC: 1499 0213 0212 Nonmetallic Mineral Mining Hog Farm Or Feedlot Beef Cattle-Except Feedlot

(G-15548)
WACHUSETT PRECAST INC
74 Pratts Junction Rd (01564-2304)
P.O. Box 901 (01564-0901)
PHONE..................................978 422-3311
David J Dugan, *President*
EMP: 4
SQ FT: 8,000
SALES (est): 680.8K Privately Held
SIC: 3272 5032 5999 Mfg Concrete Products Whol Brick/Stone Material Ret Misc Merchandise

(G-15549)
WEETABIX COMPANY INC
12 Industrial Dr (01564)
PHONE..................................978 422-2905
EMP: 6
SALES (corp-wide): 401.7MM Privately Held
WEB: www.weetabixusa.com
SIC: 2043 Mfg Cereal
HQ: The Weetabix Company Inc
20802 Kensington Blvd
Lakeville MN 55044
978 365-1000

(G-15550)
WIREWAY/HUSKY CORP
Pratts Junction Rd (01564)
P.O. Box 645, Denver NC (28037-0645)
PHONE..................................978 422-6716
Mark Stuart, *Manager*
EMP: 32
SALES (corp-wide): 27.1MM Privately Held
WEB: www.wirewayhusky.com
SIC: 3496 3444 Mfg Misc Fabricated Wire Products Mfg Sheet Metalwork
PA: Wireway/Husky Corp.
6146 Denver Indus Pk Rd
Denver NC 28037
704 483-1135

Stockbridge
Berkshire County

(G-15551)
RTR TECHNOLOGIES INC (PA)
Also Called: R T R
48 Main St (01262-9701)
P.O. Box 67 (01262-0067)
PHONE..................................413 298-0025
Rosalie Berger, *CEO*
Rosalie B Berger, *President*
Ted Howley, *Purch Mgr*
Jack Straub, *Sales Staff*
Craig Berger, *Director*
▲ EMP: 15
SQ FT: 2,800
SALES (est): 10.2MM Privately Held
WEB: www.rtrtechnologies.com
SIC: 3743 Mfg Railroad Equipment

Stoneham
Middlesex County

(G-15552)
ACTION APPAREL INC (PA)
100a Maple St (02180-3143)
PHONE..................................781 224-0777
John Losco Jr, *President*
Ginny Desimone, *Office Mgr*
EMP: 14
SQ FT: 6,500
SALES: 3.1MM Privately Held
SIC: 2261 5137 Cotton Finishing Plant Whol Women's/Child's Clothing

(G-15553)
ALLAN PONN
Also Called: Ponn Rubber Co
38 Montvale Ave (02180-2446)
P.O. Box 817, Georgetown (01833-0817)
PHONE..................................781 438-4338
Allan Ponn, *Owner*
EMP: 5
SQ FT: 1,800
SALES: 400K Privately Held
SIC: 3069 Mfg Rubberized Products

(G-15554)
AMKOR TECHNOLOGY INC
105 Central St Ste 2300 (02180-1206)
PHONE..................................781 438-7800
Ron Simon, *CEO*
Nicole Hablutzel, *Technical Staff*
Craig Landry, *Technical Staff*
EMP: 9
SALES (corp-wide): 4.3B Publicly Held
WEB: www.amkor.com
SIC: 3674 Mfg Semiconductors/Related Devices
PA: Amkor Technology, Inc.
2045 E Innovation Cir
Tempe AZ 85284
480 821-5000

(G-15555)
B & D PRECISION INC
41 Elm St Ste 7 (02180-1660)
PHONE..................................781 438-8644
Dennis Dillon, *President*
Bruce A Bower, *Clerk*
EMP: 3
SQ FT: 2,000
SALES (est): 331.2K Privately Held
SIC: 3541 3544 Mfg Machine Tools & Dies

(G-15556)
BATEMAN & SLADE INC
263 Main St Ste 3 (02180-3565)
PHONE..................................617 423-5556
George David Bateman, *President*
EMP: 5
SALES (est): 618.1K Privately Held
WEB: www.batemanslade.com
SIC: 2752 Lithographic Commercial Printing

(G-15557)
CIRCADIAN INFORMATION
2 Main St Ste 310 (02180-3336)
PHONE..................................781 439-6326
Martin Moore-Ede, *General Ptnr*
EMP: 10
SALES (est): 397.4K Privately Held
SIC: 2741 Miscellaneous Publishing, Nsk

(G-15558)
CRIMSON PRESS
16 Spencer St (02180-2616)
PHONE..................................781 914-3111
Richard Flewelling, *President*
EMP: 4
SALES (est): 254.8K Privately Held
SIC: 2741 Misc Publishing

(G-15559)
CUSTOM ATMATED PROSTHETICS LLC (DH)
Also Called: Cap
85 Maple St Ste 1 (02180-3197)
PHONE..................................781 279-2771
Robert Nazzal, *CEO*
Robert Cohen, *President*
EMP: 9
SALES (est): 2.7MM
SALES (corp-wide): 13.2B Publicly Held
SIC: 3843 Manufactures Dental Equipment/Supplies
HQ: Zahn Dental Co Inc
135 Duryea Rd
Melville NY 11747
631 843-5500

(G-15560)
DRC PRECISION MACHINING CO
74 Maple St Ste B (02180-3130)
PHONE..................................781 438-4500
John Darcy, *President*
EMP: 3
SALES: 220.3K Privately Held
SIC: 3545 Mfg Precision Equipment Machine Shop

(G-15561)
EAST COAST SIGN COMPANY
125 North St (02180-2151)
PHONE..................................781 858-9382
Andrew Puopolo, *Principal*
EMP: 5
SALES (est): 398.5K Privately Held
SIC: 3993 Mfg Signs/Advertising Specialties

(G-15562)
ESCALON DIGITAL SOLUTIONS INC
Also Called: Sonomedescalon
91 Montvale Ave Ste 320 (02180-3623)
PHONE..................................610 688-6830
Richard J Depiano Jr, *CEO*
Mark Wallace, *COO*
Matt Carnevale, *Exec VP*
Robert O'Connor, *CFO*
EMP: 13
SALES (est): 1.1MM Privately Held
SIC: 3841 Mfg Surgical/Medical Instruments

(G-15563)
EXSTAR
4 Manison St Ste A (02180-3126)
PHONE..................................339 293-9334
Charles Discioscio, *Principal*
EMP: 14
SALES (est): 2.9MM Privately Held
SIC: 3643 Mfg Conductive Wiring Devices

(G-15564)
FREEDA S FOODS LLC
3 Citation Ave (02180-1905)
PHONE..................................781 662-6474
Alfina Guevara, *Principal*
EMP: 3 EST: 2012
SALES (est): 165.7K Privately Held
SIC: 2099 Mfg Food Preparations

(G-15565)
IDS IMAGING DEV SYSTEMS INC
92 Montvale Ave Ste 2950 (02180-3651)
PHONE..................................781 787-0048
Daniel Seiler, *COO*
Robin Deturck, *Sales Staff*
EMP: 11
SQ FT: 2,500
SALES (est): 1.7MM
SALES (corp-wide): 66.7MM Privately Held
SIC: 3829 5043 Mfg Measuring/Controlling Devices Whol Photo Equipment/Supplies
HQ: Ids Imaging Development Systems Gmbh
Dimbacher Str. 6-8
Obersulm 74182
713 496-1960

(G-15566)
LPI PRINTING AND GRAPHIC INC
Also Called: Ontraget Promotional
18 Spencer St (02180-2616)
PHONE..................................781 438-5400
William D Joseph, *President*
EMP: 25
SQ FT: 16,000
SALES (est): 2.9MM Privately Held
WEB: www.lpiprinting.com
SIC: 2741 2752 2791 2789 Misc Publishing Lithographic Coml Print Typesetting Services Bookbinding/Related Work

(G-15567)
MARK TODISCO
Also Called: Gamit Signs
24 Spencer St (02180-2616)
PHONE..................................781 438-5280
Mark Todisco, *Owner*
EMP: 5 EST: 1974
SQ FT: 4,000
SALES (est): 492.6K Privately Held
WEB: www.gamitsigns.com
SIC: 3993 Mfg Signs/Advertising Specialties

(G-15568)
MUNDOS CRAZY MUSIC PUBG CORP
21 Whipple Ave (02180-1358)
PHONE..................................781 438-1704
Keith Doyle, *Principal*
EMP: 4 **EST:** 2010
SALES (est): 180.9K **Privately Held**
SIC: 2741 Misc Publishing

(G-15569)
NORTHEAST MANUFACTURING CO INC
35 Spencer St (02180-2615)
PHONE..................................781 438-3022
Chris Lobdell, *President*
Patricia Richards, *Shareholder*
EMP: 31
SQ FT: 12,000
SALES (est): 5.6MM **Privately Held**
WEB: www.northeastmfg.com
SIC: 3599 Mfg Industrial Machinery

(G-15570)
PHARMACEUTICAL STRTGS STFNG LL
477 Main St (02180-2602)
PHONE..................................781 835-2300
Nicholas J Lento,
EMP: 99
SQ FT: 1,700
SALES (est): 9.8MM **Privately Held**
SIC: 2834 Mfg Pharmaceutical Preparations

(G-15571)
QUEUES ENFORTH DEVELOPMENT INC
Also Called: QED
92 Montvale Ave Ste 4300 (02180-3625)
PHONE..................................781 870-1100
David D Varney, *President*
John Olson, *Vice Pres*
Kevin Hanron, *Manager*
Martin Graney, *Network Mgr*
EMP: 13
SQ FT: 2,600
SALES (est): 2.4MM **Privately Held**
WEB: www.qed.com
SIC: 3695 Mfg Magnetic/Optical Recording Media

(G-15572)
WESCO BUILDING & DESIGN INC
271 Main St Ste G01 (02180-3591)
PHONE..................................781 279-0490
Benjamin J Caggiano Jr, *Vice Pres*
EMP: 25
SQ FT: 2,000
SALES (est): 2.3MM **Privately Held**
SIC: 2431 6552 1542 Mfg Millwork Subdivider/Developer Nonresidential Construction

(G-15573)
WESCOR LTD (PA)
271 Main St Ste G01 (02180-3591)
PHONE..................................781 279-0490
Benjamin J Caggiano Jr, *President*
EMP: 19
SQ FT: 2,000
SALES (est): 3.1MM **Privately Held**
SIC: 2431 6552 1542 Mfg Millwork Subdivider/Developer Nonresidential Construction

Stoughton
Norfolk County

(G-15574)
AGGREGATE INDS - NORTHEAST REG
1101 Turnpike St (02072-1160)
PHONE..................................781 344-1100
Bill Donovan, *President*
EMP: 3
SALES (corp-wide): 4.5B **Privately Held**
SIC: 3273 Mfg Ready-Mixed Concrete
HQ: Aggregate Industries - Northeast Region, Inc
1715 Brdwy
Saugus MA 01906
781 941-7200

(G-15575)
AGGREGATE INDUSTRIES - MWR INC
1101 Turnpike St (02072-1160)
PHONE..................................781 344-1100
Bill Donovan, *Manager*
EMP: 25
SALES (corp-wide): 4.5B **Privately Held**
SIC: 3273 Mfg Ready-Mixed Concrete
HQ: Aggregate Industries - Mwr, Inc.
2815 Dodd Rd
Eagan MN 55121
651 683-0600

(G-15576)
AIRY TECHNOLOGY INC
31 Tosca Dr Ste 8 (02072-1500)
PHONE..................................781 341-1850
Adam Giandomenico, *President*
EMP: 5
SALES (est): 590.9K
SALES (corp-wide): 2.9MM **Privately Held**
SIC: 2899 Operates As A Manufacturer Of Chemical Preparations Specializing In Food Contamination Testing Or Screening Kits
PA: Particles Plus, Inc.
31 Tosca Dr Ste 8
Stoughton MA 02072
781 341-6898

(G-15577)
ALBERT BASSE ASSOCIATES INC
175 Campanelli Pkwy (02072-3743)
PHONE..................................781 344-3555
Ellen B Dietz, *CEO*
Albert Chip Basse, *President*
Albert Basse, *President*
Ronald J Frisch, *Principal*
Edwin E Basse, *Vice Pres*
EMP: 45 **EST:** 1928
SQ FT: 30,000
SALES (est): 8.4MM **Privately Held**
WEB: www.albertbasse.com
SIC: 2759 Commercial Printing

(G-15578)
ALCOA GLOBAL FASTENERS INC
44 Campanelli Pkwy (02072-3704)
PHONE..................................412 553-4545
Carl A Annese Jr, *Vice Pres*
Mike Shaw, *Maintence Staff*
▲ **EMP:** 27 **EST:** 1949
SQ FT: 110,000
SALES (est): 6.5MM
SALES (corp-wide): 14B **Publicly Held**
WEB: alcoafasteningsystems.com
SIC: 3542 3452 Mfg Machine Tools-Forming Mfg Bolts/Screws/Rivets
HQ: Arconic Global Fasteners & Rings, Inc.
3990a Heritage Oak Ct
Simi Valley CA 93063
805 527-3600

(G-15579)
ALPHA CHEMICAL SERVICES INC
Also Called: A C S
46 Morton St (02072-2829)
P.O. Box 431 (02072-0431)
PHONE..................................781 344-8688
Mark Juckett, *CEO*
Elise Dauksevicz, *President*
Brian Jacobson, *Treasurer*
Tony Mancari, *Sales Staff*
Nicole Dauksevicz, *Technical Staff*
EMP: 35
SQ FT: 34,000
SALES (est): 10.6MM **Privately Held**
SIC: 2842 2841 Mfg Polish/Sanitation Goods Mfg Soap/Other Detergents

(G-15580)
ANGSTROM ADVANCED INC
95 Mill St (02072-1422)
PHONE..................................781 519-4765
Haiming LI, *President*
Nick Ni, *General Mgr*
Haining Ni, *Marketing Staff*
Christina Wang, *Assistant*
▲ **EMP:** 100
SQ FT: 20,000
SALES (est): 20.8MM **Privately Held**
WEB: www.angstromadvanced.com
SIC: 3569 3827 Mfg General Industrial Machinery Mfg Optical Instruments/Lenses

(G-15581)
ARTISAN INDUSTRIES INC
44 Campanelli Pkwy (02072-3704)
PHONE..................................781 893-6800
Timothy L Davis, *President*
Anthony J Agostino, *Treasurer*
James M Donovan, *Admin Sec*
◆ **EMP:** 100 **EST:** 1934
SQ FT: 114,000
SALES (est): 35MM **Privately Held**
WEB: www.artisanind.com
SIC: 3559 3449 3563 3643 Mfg Misc Industry Mach Mfg Misc Structural Mtl Mfg Air/Gas Compressors Mfg Conductive Wire Dvcs

(G-15582)
AVON FOOD COMPANY LLC
30 James Massey Ln (02072-5015)
PHONE..................................781 341-4981
Stephen G Anastos,
Heidi Anastos,
EMP: 12
SALES: 0 **Privately Held**
SIC: 2099 Mfg Food Preparations

(G-15583)
CAMELOT ENTERPRISES INC (PA)
213 Turnpike St Ste 1 (02072-3769)
PHONE..................................781 341-9100
Elliot Kaplan, *President*
Neil Kaplan, *Opers Staff*
EMP: 12
SQ FT: 15,000
SALES (est): 1.1MM **Privately Held**
WEB: www.camelotemb.com
SIC: 2395 Pleating/Stitching Services

(G-15584)
COLLEGIUM PHARMACEUTICAL INC
100 Technology Center Dr # 300 (02072-4747)
PHONE..................................781 713-3699
Michael T Heffernan, *Ch of Bd*
Joseph Ciaffoni, *President*
Alison B Fleming, *Exec VP*
Shirley R Kuhlmann, *Exec VP*
John Weet, *Vice Pres*
EMP: 250
SQ FT: 19,335
SALES: 280.4MM **Privately Held**
WEB: www.collegiumpharma.com
SIC: 2834 Pharmaceutical Preparations

(G-15585)
CYN OIL CORPORATION
Also Called: Cyn Environmental Services
1771 Washington St (02072-3397)
P.O. Box 119 (02072-0119)
PHONE..................................781 341-8074
Laurie Lapworth, *Manager*
EMP: 90
SALES (corp-wide): 70.4MM **Privately Held**
WEB: www.cynenv.com
SIC: 1389 Oil/Gas Field Services
PA: Cyn Oil Corporation
100 Tosca Dr
Stoughton MA 02072
800 622-6365

(G-15586)
ELECTRNIC SHTMTAL CRFTSMEN INC
120 Central St (02072-1148)
PHONE..................................781 341-3260
Marc Levine, *President*
Richard Levine, *Vice Pres*
Mark Todaro, *Engineer*
Linda Kearney, *Office Mgr*
▼ **EMP:** 25
SQ FT: 20,000
SALES (est): 4.5MM **Privately Held**
WEB: www.escinc.biz
SIC: 3444 Mfg Sheet Metal Work

(G-15587)
ENO MASSACHUSETTS
200 Tosca Dr (02072-1506)
PHONE..................................781 297-7331
Lisa Lawhon, *President*
EMP: 5 **EST:** 1997
SALES (est): 382.3K **Privately Held**
SIC: 2084 Mfg Wines/Brandy/Spirits

(G-15588)
ENVIE COMPANY INC
5 Cabot Pl (02072-4624)
PHONE..................................866 700-6410
EMP: 5
SALES: 1.4MM **Privately Held**
SIC: 2741 Internet Publishing And Broadcasting

(G-15589)
ESSENTIAL LIFE SOLUTIONS LTD
308 Tosca Dr (02072-1516)
PHONE..................................781 341-7240
E Daniel Yukon, *President*
EMP: 6
SALES (est): 610K **Privately Held**
SIC: 3561 Mfg Pumps/Pumping Equipment

(G-15590)
F H PETERSON MACHINE CORP
143 South St (02072-3715)
P.O. Box 617 (02072-0617)
PHONE..................................781 341-4930
Stanley B Urban, *President*
Jonathan A Berard, *Vice Pres*
Wilbur Boss, *Vice Pres*
Jill Kaminsky, *Admin Sec*
Venus Waterhouse, *Admin Sec*
EMP: 60 **EST:** 1957
SQ FT: 28,000
SALES (est): 12.2MM **Privately Held**
WEB: www.fhpetersonmachine.com
SIC: 3599 Mfg Industrial Machinery

(G-15591)
FC PHILLIPS INC
471 Washington St (02072-4203)
P.O. Box 780 (02072-0780)
PHONE..................................781 344-9400
Craig R Snow, *President*
Steve N Ramondi, *QC Mgr*
Brian R Snow, *Treasurer*
Walter Bobkaitis, *Traffic Dir*
Marjorie P Snow, *Admin Sec*
EMP: 50 **EST:** 1911
SQ FT: 35,000
SALES (est): 8MM **Privately Held**
WEB: www.fcphillips.com
SIC: 3451 Mfg Precision Machined Products & Detachable Spikes

(G-15592)
FIRST IMPRESSION PRINTING INC
178 Tosca Dr (02072-1511)
PHONE..................................781 344-8855
Mark Reed, *President*
EMP: 7 **EST:** 1998
SQ FT: 5,400
SALES: 748.1K **Privately Held**
WEB: www.myprinter.us
SIC: 2759 Commercial Printing

(G-15593)
GLOBE COMPOSITE SOLUTIONS LLC
200 Shuman Ave Ste 100 (02072-3766)
P.O. Box 393 (02072-0393)
PHONE..................................781 871-3700
Carl Forsythe, *CEO*
Michael Dyson, *President*
William Clement, *CFO*
EMP: 50 **EST:** 2002
SQ FT: 72,000
SALES (est): 14.6MM
SALES (corp-wide): 812.9MM **Publicly Held**
SIC: 2655 Mfg Fiber Cans/Drums

PA: Esco Technologies Inc.
9900 Clayton Rd Ste A
Saint Louis MO 63124
314 213-7200

(G-15594)
GLOBE COMPOSITE SOLUTIONS LTD
200 Shuman Ave (02072-3766)
PHONE..................................781 871-3700
Carl Forsythe, *Principal*
Scott Hruzd, *VP Opers*
Jim Texiera, *QC Mgr*
Matthew Samperi, *Design Engr*
Miriam Kiesel, *Manager*
EMP: 59
SALES (corp-wide): 13MM **Privately Held**
SIC: 3089 Mfg Plastic Products
PA: Globe Composite Solutions, Ltd.
4925 Grnvlle Ave Ste 1400
Dallas TX 75206
781 681-6838

(G-15595)
H & C SALES INC
107 Tosca Dr (02072-1505)
P.O. Box 113, Sharon (02067-0113)
PHONE..................................781 344-6445
Howard Robinson, *President*
EMP: 5
SQ FT: 4,000
SALES (est): 705.6K **Privately Held**
SIC: 2621 Whol Packaging For The Confectionery Trade

(G-15596)
HO TOY NOODLES INC (PA)
1490 Central St (02072-4414)
PHONE..................................617 426-0247
Jeffrey Wong, *President*
Gordon Wong, *Vice Pres*
Barry Wong, *Treasurer*
▲ **EMP:** 17
SQ FT: 1,000
SALES (est): 2.6MM **Privately Held**
SIC: 2098 2052 Mfg Macaroni/Spaghetti Mfg Cookies/Crackers

(G-15597)
HONORCRAFT LLC
292 Page St Ste A (02072-1136)
P.O. Box 385 (02072-0385)
PHONE..................................781 341-0410
Andrew Hopkin, *President*
Irene Clenott, *Office Mgr*
EMP: 24 **EST:** 2015
SQ FT: 18,752
SALES (est): 1.5MM **Privately Held**
SIC: 3555 3993 Mfg Printing Trades Machinery Mfg Signs/Advertising Specialties

(G-15598)
INTERNATIONAL EVENT PRODUCTS
Also Called: Iep
1490 Central St Ste D (02072-4414)
P.O. Box 521 (02072-0521)
PHONE..................................781 341-0929
Lawrence A Green, *President*
Filomena Felix, *President*
Jenna Cefary, *Vice Pres*
▲ **EMP:** 4
SALES (est): 810K **Privately Held**
SIC: 3262 Mfg Vitreous China Tableware

(G-15599)
JAMES E COFRAN
Also Called: C & P Precision Machine Co
106 Cabral Cir (02072-3553)
PHONE..................................781 341-0897
James E Cofran, *Owner*
EMP: 5
SQ FT: 1,250
SALES (est): 326.5K **Privately Held**
SIC: 3599 Machine Shop

(G-15600)
KALMAN ELECTRIC MOTORS INC
471 Page St (02072-1141)
PHONE..................................781 341-4900
Howard Kalman, *President*
EMP: 6
SQ FT: 6,000
SALES: 1MM **Privately Held**
SIC: 7694 7629 5063 5085 Repairs Electric Motors & Power Tools & Wholesales Electric Motors & Power Tools

(G-15601)
KOCHMAN REIDT & HAIGH INC
471 Page St Ste 8 (02072-1141)
PHONE..................................781 573-1500
Paul Reidt, *President*
William Kochman, *Vice Pres*
James Kochman, *Treasurer*
Alan Haigh, *Asst Treas*
EMP: 42 **EST:** 1991
SQ FT: 20,000
SALES (est): 6.1MM **Privately Held**
WEB: www.cabinetmakers.com
SIC: 2541 2434 Mfg Wood Partitions/Fixtures Mfg Wood Kitchen Cabinets

(G-15602)
LALLY COLUMN CORP
138 Plain Dr (02072-3994)
PHONE..................................508 828-5997
Barry Paul Gill, *President*
EMP: 3 **EST:** 1994
SALES (est): 441K **Privately Held**
SIC: 3441 Structural Metal Fabrication

(G-15603)
MACHINE INCORPORATED
879 Turnpike St (02072-1114)
PHONE..................................781 297-3700
Richard Mileika, *President*
Hans Pohlmann, *Engineer*
EMP: 20
SQ FT: 15,000
SALES (est): 1.1MM **Privately Held**
WEB: www.machineinc.com
SIC: 3599 Mfg Industrial Machinery

(G-15604)
MANDES INC
593 Washington St (02072-4207)
PHONE..................................781 344-6915
George Michaelidis, *President*
EMP: 4
SALES (est): 401.3K **Privately Held**
SIC: 3421 Mfg Cutlery

(G-15605)
MARVER MED INC
1063 Turnpike St (02072-1160)
P.O. Box 258 (02072-0258)
PHONE..................................781 341-9372
Steven J Tallarida, *President*
Jon T Tallarida, *Corp Secy*
Scott Spillane, *Opers Staff*
Christopher Laplante, *CFO*
Stan Korona, *Manager*
EMP: 10
SQ FT: 5,000
SALES (est): 1.2MM **Privately Held**
SIC: 3451 3599 Mfg Screw Machine Products Mfg Industrial Machinery

(G-15606)
MASSACHUSETTS BAY TECH INC
Also Called: Mbt
378 Page St Ste 7 (02072-1124)
PHONE..................................781 344-8809
Brian Fallon, *President*
Charles Fallon, *Vice Pres*
▼ **EMP:** 19
SQ FT: 12,000
SALES (est): 3.2MM **Privately Held**
SIC: 3674 Mfg Semiconductors & Related Devices

(G-15607)
MESSER LLC
Also Called: Boc Gases
97 Maple St (02072-1105)
PHONE..................................781 341-4575
Frank Mulrooney, *Branch Mgr*
Tom Brady, *Manager*
Thomas Dumican, *Manager*
Thomas Hunt, *Manager*
Dan Poirier, *Manager*
EMP: 10
SALES (corp-wide): 1.4B **Privately Held**
SIC: 2813 Natural Gas Distribution
HQ: Messer Llc
200 Somerset Corp Blvd # 7000
Bridgewater NJ 08807
908 464-8100

(G-15608)
MILANI INDUSTRIES INC
61 Marys Way (02072-2227)
PHONE..................................781 344-3377
Patricia Milani, *Principal*
EMP: 3
SALES (est): 164.6K **Privately Held**
SIC: 3999 Mfg Misc Products

(G-15609)
NATIONAL SERVICE SYSTEMS INC
Also Called: National System
1600 Washington St (02072-3347)
P.O. Box 113 (02072-0113)
PHONE..................................781 344-6504
Patricia Fossella, *President*
Robert Fossella, *President*
EMP: 6 **EST:** 1978
SQ FT: 8,000
SALES (est): 964.2K **Privately Held**
SIC: 3442 1751 Mfg Metal Doors/Sash/Trim Carpentry Contractor

(G-15610)
NEENAH FOUNDRY COMPANY
1595 Central St (02072-1694)
PHONE..................................781 344-1711
Rick Friel, *Branch Mgr*
EMP: 3
SALES (corp-wide): 420.7MM **Privately Held**
SIC: 3321 Gray/Ductile Iron Foundry
HQ: Neenah Foundry Company
2121 Brooks Ave
Neenah WI 54956
920 725-7000

(G-15611)
NEUTRASAFE CORPORATION
421 Page St Ste 1 (02072-1107)
PHONE..................................781 616-3951
Dorothy Bernasconi, *President*
Michael Bernasconi, *Vice Pres*
EMP: 5
SALES (est): 514.7K **Privately Held**
SIC: 3433 Mfg Heating Equipment-Nonelectric

(G-15612)
OFFICE MANAGEMENT SYSTEMS
84 Central Dr (02072-1805)
P.O. Box 704 (02072-0704)
PHONE..................................617 921-2966
Caroline Gagan, *Principal*
EMP: 3
SALES (est): 321.5K **Privately Held**
SIC: 2752 Lithographic Commercial Printing

(G-15613)
PARTICLES PLUS INC (PA)
31 Tosca Dr Ste 8 (02072-1500)
PHONE..................................781 341-6898
Adam Giandomenico, *President*
Jim Akey, *Sales Mgr*
David Pariseau, *CTO*
EMP: 17
SALES (est): 2.9MM **Privately Held**
SIC: 3826 Mfg Analytical Instruments

(G-15614)
PEARSON MACHINE COMPANY LLC
81 Tosca Dr (02072-1501)
PHONE..................................781 341-9416
John V Pell,
Irene Pearson Pell,
John P Pell,
EMP: 5
SQ FT: 3,000
SALES (est): 571.5K **Privately Held**
SIC: 3599 Mfg Industrial Machinery

(G-15615)
PERKINS BROTHERS CORP
Also Called: Perkins Pre-Coat
92 Evans Dr (02072-4421)
PHONE..................................781 858-3031
John E S Perkins, *President*
William S C Perkins, *Admin Sec*
EMP: 20
SQ FT: 25,000
SALES (est): 2.4MM
SALES (corp-wide): 222.7MM **Privately Held**
SIC: 2439 Mfg Structural Wood Members
PA: Maibec Inc
1984 5e Rue Bureau 202
Levis QC G6W 5
418 830-8855

(G-15616)
PRECIOUS ALLOY REFINING LLC
1595 Central St (02072-1694)
PHONE..................................774 296-5000
Sean Patrick Coyne, *Principal*
EMP: 4 **EST:** 2014
SALES (est): 359.7K **Privately Held**
SIC: 3341 Secondary Nonferrous Metal Producer

(G-15617)
PRIMO MEDICAL GROUP INC (PA)
75 Mill St (02072-1422)
PHONE..................................781 297-5700
Steven Tallarida, *Ch of Bd*
Frank Fedorowicz, *COO*
Jon Tallarida, *Senior VP*
Laurie Bourgeois, *Vice Pres*
Kenneth Eliasen, *Vice Pres*
EMP: 150 **EST:** 1953
SQ FT: 70,000
SALES (est): 47.3MM **Privately Held**
WEB: www.stdmed.com
SIC: 3841 Mfg Surgical/Medical Instruments

(G-15618)
RO 59 INC
1 Cabot Pl Ste 3 (02072-4606)
PHONE..................................781 341-1222
Ronald Bender, *President*
Oscar Levine PHD, *Treasurer*
EMP: 9
SQ FT: 3,000
SALES: 3MM **Privately Held**
SIC: 2899 2992 Mfg Lubricating Surface Coatings

(G-15619)
S&S INDUSTRIES INC (PA)
1551 Central St (02072-1686)
PHONE..................................914 885-1500
Joseph Horta, *President*
Hugo Duarte, *Vice Pres*
◆ **EMP:** 15 **EST:** 1946
SQ FT: 10,000
SALES (est): 13.9MM **Privately Held**
SIC: 3315 3496 Mfg Steel Wire/Related Products Mfg Misc Fabricated Wire Products

(G-15620)
SAMAR CO INC
220 Cushing St (02072-2341)
PHONE..................................781 297-7264
William J Selby, *President*
William Selby, *President*
Ronald Selby, *Treasurer*
▲ **EMP:** 85
SQ FT: 50,000
SALES (est): 14.5MM **Privately Held**
SIC: 3052 3083 3082 Mfg Rubber/Plastic Hose/Belting Mfg Laminated Plastic Plate/Sheet Mfg Plastic Profile Shapes

(G-15621)
SICK INC (DH)
800 Technology Center Dr # 5
(02072-4721)
PHONE..................................781 302-2500
Alberto Bertomeu, *President*
Hermann Miedel, *General Mgr*
Robert Bauer, *Chairman*
Matthew Cody, *Engineer*
Anna Grimley, *Engineer*
EMP: 11
SQ FT: 46,000
SALES (est): 8MM
SALES (corp-wide): 1B **Privately Held**
SIC: 3625 Mfg Relays/Industrial Controls

GEOGRAPHIC

HQ: Sick, Inc
6900 W 110th St
Minneapolis MN 55438
952 941-6780

(G-15622)
SPOONTIQUES INC
111 Island St (02072-1401)
PHONE...781 344-9530
Ken Sawyer, *President*
Nancy Snapper, *Info Tech Mgr*
Erin Bruno, *Graphic Designe*
◆ **EMP:** 60
SQ FT: 65,000
SALES (est): 10.2MM **Privately Held**
WEB: www.spoontiques.com
SIC: 3499 Mfg Misc Fabricated Metal Products

(G-15623)
STD MANUFACTURING INC
1063 Turnpike St (02072-1160)
P.O. Box 420 (02072-0420)
PHONE...781 828-4400
Dave Elich, *General Mgr*
Steve Tallarida, *Principal*
Francis Federowicz, *COO*
Stephen Deane, *Vice Pres*
Doug Darcy, *Mfg Staff*
EMP: 9
SALES (est): 637.2K **Privately Held**
SIC: 3999 Mfg Misc Products

(G-15624)
SUPERLATIVE PRINTING INC
4 Cabot Pl Ste 3 (02072-4613)
PHONE...781 341-9000
Frank Frazier, *Sales Staff*
Sally Mong, *Officer*
EMP: 15
SQ FT: 988
SALES (est): 1.6MM **Privately Held**
SIC: 2752 Lithographic Commercial Printing

(G-15625)
SX INDUSTRIES INC (PA)
1551 Central St (02072-1686)
PHONE...781 828-7111
Michael Fink, *Ch of Bd*
Stephen Fink, *President*
▲ **EMP:** 30 **EST:** 1944
SQ FT: 38,000
SALES (est): 6.9MM **Privately Held**
WEB: www.sxindustries.com
SIC: 3131 6512 3444 3356 Mfg Footwear Cut Stock Nonresdentl Bldg Operatr Mfg Sheet Metalwork Nonferrous Rollng/Drawng

(G-15626)
TIMCO CORPORATION
Also Called: Sx Industries
1551 Central St (02072-1686)
P.O. Box 332, Weymouth (02188-0002)
PHONE...781 821-1041
Tim O'Hara, *President*
▲ **EMP:** 40
SALES (est): 236.8K **Privately Held**
SIC: 3469 Mfg Metal Stampings

(G-15627)
USER-FRIENDLY RECYCLING LLC
186 Tosca Dr (02072-1511)
P.O. Box 631 (02072-0631)
PHONE...781 269-5021
David Spiegelman,
EMP: 6
SALES: 800K **Privately Held**
SIC: 3559 Mfg Misc Industry Machinery

(G-15628)
WEBTEAMWORK
25 Pondview Ln (02072-1077)
PHONE...781 344-8373
EMP: 6
SALES: 500K **Privately Held**
SIC: 7372 Prepackaged Software Services

Stow
Middlesex County

(G-15629)
ADANAC SOFTWARE INC
174 Barton Rd (01775-1527)
PHONE...978 562-3466
Dirk Hart, *President*
EMP: 3
SALES (est): 169.3K **Privately Held**
SIC: 7372 Prepackaged Software Services

(G-15630)
ADVANCE MACHINE CO INC
49 White Pond Rd (01775-1323)
PHONE...978 897-5808
Ronald W Jagiello, *President*
EMP: 4
SQ FT: 7,000
SALES: 300K **Privately Held**
SIC: 3599 Machine Shop

(G-15631)
BLACK AND WHITE PRINTING
501 Gleasondale Rd Ste 9 (01775-1495)
PHONE...401 265-7811
Dan Ramos, *Principal*
EMP: 3
SALES (est): 158.6K **Privately Held**
SIC: 2759 Commercial Printing

(G-15632)
HYDRO-TEST PRODUCTS INC
85 Hudson Rd (01775-1254)
PHONE...978 897-4647
Douglas B Sagar, *President*
▼ **EMP:** 14
SQ FT: 10,000
SALES: 4MM **Privately Held**
WEB: www.hydro-test.com
SIC: 3548 3949 3999 3569 Mfg Welding Apparatus Mfg Sport/Athletic Goods Mfg Misc Products Mfg General Indstl Mach Mfg Industrial Gases

(G-15633)
MINUTE MAN AIRFIELD
302 Boxboro Rd (01775-2101)
PHONE...978 897-3933
Donald McPherson, *Owner*
EMP: 11
SALES: 100K **Privately Held**
SIC: 2752 Lithographic Commercial Printing

(G-15634)
NASHOBA VALLEY EXTRACT LLC
15 Sudbury Rd (01775-1511)
PHONE...978 201-5245
Timothy A Gagnon, *Principal*
EMP: 3
SALES (est): 233.8K **Privately Held**
SIC: 2836 Mfg Biological Products

(G-15635)
RADIUS MEDICAL TECH INC
46 Edson St (01775-1236)
PHONE...978 263-4466
Maureen Finlayson, *President*
EMP: 11
SALES (est): 1.3MM **Privately Held**
WEB: www.radiusmed.com
SIC: 3841 Mfg Surgical/Medical Instruments

Sturbridge
Worcester County

(G-15636)
1817 SHOPPE INC (PA)
Also Called: Seraph, The
420 Main St Ste 1 (01566-1359)
P.O. Box 500 (01566-0500)
PHONE...508 347-2241
Alexandra Pifer, *President*
Michael Pifer, *Treasurer*
▲ **EMP:** 5
SQ FT: 6,000
SALES (est): 1MM **Privately Held**
WEB: www.theseraph.com
SIC: 2512 5712 Mfg Upholstered Household Furniture Ret Furniture

(G-15637)
ALSCO INDUSTRIES INC
174 Charlton Rd (01566-1505)
P.O. Box 1168 (01566-3168)
PHONE...508 347-1199
Allan J Rieser, *CEO*
Stephen M Rieser, *President*
Lisa Berthiaume, *Executive*
▲ **EMP:** 70
SQ FT: 65,000
SALES (est): 20MM **Privately Held**
SIC: 3089 3544 Mfg Plastic Products Mfg Dies/Tools/Jigs/Fixtures

(G-15638)
ARLAND TOOL & MFG INC (PA)
421 Main St (01566-1055)
P.O. Box 207 (01566-0207)
PHONE...508 347-3368
William Gagnon, *President*
Gerald Gagnon, *Facilities Mgr*
Mike Golinski, *Purch Agent*
Justin Mahaney, *Engineer*
Melissa Baker, *CFO*
◆ **EMP:** 100 **EST:** 1950
SQ FT: 80,000
SALES (est): 22.7MM **Privately Held**
WEB: www.arland.com
SIC: 3599 Mfg Industrial Machinery

(G-15639)
JOURNAL OF ANTQ & COLLECTIBLES
Also Called: Brimfield Flemarket.com
46 Hall Rd (01566-1279)
P.O. Box 950 (01566-2950)
PHONE...508 347-1960
Jody Young, *President*
Maxine Lome, *Publisher*
Joe Michaelik, *CFO*
Pat Rainka, *Sales Staff*
EMP: 12
SALES (est): 540K **Privately Held**
SIC: 2759 Commercial Printing

(G-15640)
LIGHT ENGINES LLC
29 Library Ln S (01566-1093)
PHONE...508 347-3647
Patrick McGarrah,
Alexander Shishov,
EMP: 4
SQ FT: 4,000
SALES (est): 366.3K **Privately Held**
SIC: 3646 Mfg Commercial Lighting Fixtures

(G-15641)
OFS BRIGHTWAVE LLC
50 Hall Rd (01566-1279)
PHONE...508 347-2261
Patrice Dubois, *Principal*
EMP: 9
SALES (est): 1.2MM **Privately Held**
SIC: 3357 Nonferrous Wiredrawing/Insulating

(G-15642)
OFS FITEL LLC
50 Hall Rd (01566-1299)
PHONE...508 347-2261
Debbie Bleanger, *Branch Mgr*
EMP: 49 **Privately Held**
WEB: www.ofsoptics.com
SIC: 3357 Nonferrous Wiredrawing/Insulating
HQ: Ofs Fitel Llc
2000 Northeast Expy
Norcross GA 30071
888 342-3743

(G-15643)
OPTIM LLC
64 Technology Park Rd (01566-1253)
PHONE...508 347-5100
Jeff Barrett, *CEO*
Robert V Griffin, *Treasurer*
Jo Ann Sleeper, *Controller*
Mike Day, *Executive*
EMP: 50 **EST:** 1979
SQ FT: 11,000
SALES (est): 10.6MM **Privately Held**
WEB: www.optimnet.com
SIC: 3841 Mfg Surgical/Medical Instruments

(G-15644)
PEGASUS GLASSWORKS INC
66 Technology Park Rd (01566-1253)
P.O. Box 255 (01566-0255)
PHONE...508 347-5656
Peter Graves, *President*
▲ **EMP:** 10
SQ FT: 15,000
SALES (est): 1.1MM **Privately Held**
WEB: www.pegasusglassworks.com
SIC: 3229 Mfg Products-Purchased Glass

(G-15645)
PENWELL
Also Called: Editorial Ofc Indtrl Lser Solt
15 Country Hill Rd (01566-1061)
P.O. Box 245 (01566-0245)
PHONE...508 347-8245
David Belforte, *Principal*
EMP: 8 **EST:** 1986
SALES (est): 419.9K **Privately Held**
SIC: 2721 Periodicals-Publishing/Printing

(G-15646)
PHOTONIS SCIENTIFIC INC (DH)
Also Called: Photonis Usa, Inc.
660 Main St (01518-1259)
P.O. Box 1159 (01566-3159)
PHONE...508 347-4000
Roland Minnier, *President*
Bruce Laprade, *Vice Pres*
Steve Ritzau, *Research*
Butch Langevin, *Engineer*
Margaret M Cooley, *Marketing Staff*
EMP: 51
SALES (est): 8.2MM
SALES (corp-wide): 177.9K **Privately Held**
SIC: 3679 3829 3826 3812 Mfg Elec Components Mfg Measure/Control Dvcs Mfg Analytical Instr Mfg Search/Navgatn Equip Mfg Electron Tubes
HQ: Photonis Defense, Inc.
1000 New Holland Ave
Lancaster PA 17601
717 295-6000

(G-15647)
SOUTHBRIDGE SHTMTL WORKS INC
441 Main St (01566-1055)
P.O. Box 517 (01566-0517)
PHONE...508 347-7800
John Q Colognesi, *President*
Louis E Colognesi Jr, *President*
Joanne Baldridge, *Enginr/R&D Asst*
Edward L Colognesi, *Treasurer*
Ernest Colognesi, *Treasurer*
▲ **EMP:** 50 **EST:** 1959
SQ FT: 60,000
SALES (est): 11.4MM **Privately Held**
WEB: www.ssmwusa.com
SIC: 3444 Mfg Sheet Metalwork

(G-15648)
SPEC-ELEC PLATING CORP
Also Called: Special Electronics Plating
101 Colonial Dr (01566-2302)
PHONE...508 347-7255
Mike Cournoyer, *President*
EMP: 4
SALES (est): 304.7K **Privately Held**
SIC: 3471 Plating/Polishing Service

(G-15649)
SPOTLITEUSA LLC
31 Audubon Way (01566-2323)
PHONE...508 347-2627
Steven Chojnicki, *General Mgr*
Anne Chojnicki, *Mng Member*
EMP: 3
SALES: 500K **Privately Held**
SIC: 1311 Crude Petroleum/Natural Gas Production

Sudbury
Middlesex County

(G-15650)
ABBEY WATER TREATMENT INC
419 Concord Rd (01776-1822)
PHONE..........978 443-5001
William Cossar, *President*
Maureen Cloonan, *Clerk*
EMP: 6
SALES (est): 680.4K **Privately Held**
SIC: 3589 Business Services

(G-15651)
ACOUSTIC MAGIC INC
35 Peakham Rd (01776-2942)
PHONE..........978 440-9384
Bernard R Feingold, *CEO*
EMP: 6
SALES (est): 911.7K **Privately Held**
WEB: www.acousticmagic.com
SIC: 3651 Mfg Microphones

(G-15652)
ALLENA LABS
142 North Rd Ste B (01776-1142)
PHONE..........617 467-4577
EMP: 3 **EST:** 2016
SALES (est): 261.7K **Privately Held**
SIC: 2834 Mfg Pharmaceutical Preparations

(G-15653)
BENU BIOPHARMA INC
50 Lands End Ln (01776-3436)
PHONE..........508 208-5634
Dennis I Goldberg, *Principal*
Eric M Morrel, *Vice Pres*
EMP: 6
SALES (est): 497.7K **Privately Held**
SIC: 2834 Mfg Pharmaceutical Preparations

(G-15654)
BOSTON DESIGN GUIDE INC
277 Concord Rd (01776-2342)
PHONE..........978 443-9886
Melanie Kaplan, *President*
Carly Stewart, *Editor*
EMP: 15
SALES (est): 1.5MM **Privately Held**
WEB: www.bostondesignguide.com
SIC: 2721 Periodicals-Publishing/Printing

(G-15655)
DJ MICROLAMINATES INC
490 Boston Post Rd (01776-3367)
PHONE..........978 261-3188
Donald W Johnson, *President*
EMP: 5
SALES (est): 816.7K **Privately Held**
SIC: 2821 Mfg Plastic Materials/Resins

(G-15656)
DRINK MAPLE INC
144 North Rd Ste 1050 (01776-1179)
PHONE..........978 610-6408
Rose Jeff, *Principal*
EMP: 7 **EST:** 2015
SALES (est): 333.8K **Privately Held**
SIC: 2087 Mfg Flavor Extracts/Syrup

(G-15657)
FOOTSIZER LLC
365 Boston Post Rd # 300 (01776-3023)
PHONE..........617 337-3537
Scott Bradley,
EMP: 4 **EST:** 2014
SQ FT: 1,200
SALES: 50K **Privately Held**
SIC: 7372 Prepackaged Software Services

(G-15658)
INFORMATION SERVER CO
Also Called: Tisco
3 Camperdown Ln (01776-1687)
PHONE..........978 443-1871
Pascal Cleve, *Ch of Bd*
EMP: 3 **EST:** 1993
SALES (est): 176.6K **Privately Held**
WEB: www.tisco.com
SIC: 3695 Software / Semi Conductor Ip

(G-15659)
INSPECTROLOGY LLC
142 North Rd Ste N (01776-1149)
PHONE..........978 212-3100
Marty Mastovich, *Marketing Mgr*
Neil Casa, *Mng Member*
Michael J Kessler,
Paul C Knutrud,
▲ **EMP:** 24
SALES (est): 1.8MM **Privately Held**
SIC: 3825 Mfg Electrical Measuring Instruments

(G-15660)
INSPEEDCOM LLC
10 Hudson Rd (01776-1737)
PHONE..........978 397-6813
Albert E Barrett Jr,
Lorenzo Majno,
EMP: 3
SALES: 140K **Privately Held**
SIC: 3999 Mfg Weather Products

(G-15661)
IVA CORPORATION
142 North Rd Ste R (01776-1142)
PHONE..........978 443-5800
Paul Birkner, *Engineer*
David A Birkner, *Treasurer*
EMP: 5
SQ FT: 2,500
SALES: 1.5MM **Privately Held**
WEB: www.ivacorp.com
SIC: 3577 5045 7389 Mfg Computer Peripheral Equipment Whol Computers/Peripherals Business Services

(G-15662)
LEGENDS & HEROES
Also Called: Skineez Skin Care Wear
365 Astin Post Rd Ste 210 (01776)
PHONE..........617 571-6990
Michelle Moran, *Owner*
EMP: 30 **EST:** 2010
SALES (est): 10MM **Privately Held**
SIC: 2253 Knit Outerwear Mill

(G-15663)
METHODS 3D INC
65 Union Ave (01776-2277)
PHONE..........978 443-5388
Don Miller, *General Mgr*
Paul Johnston, *Principal*
Carol Colaianni, *CFO*
EMP: 14
SALES (est): 986.3K **Privately Held**
SIC: 3569 Mfg General Industrial Machinery

(G-15664)
NS CONVERTERS LLC
400 Boston Post Rd 2d (01776-3009)
PHONE..........508 628-1501
▲ **EMP:** 4
SALES (est): 627.4K **Privately Held**
WEB: www.nsconverters.com
SIC: 2521 Mfg Wood Office Furniture

(G-15665)
OPED INC
383 Boston Post Rd Ste 2 (01776-3050)
PHONE..........781 891-6733
Stephan Habermeyer, *CEO*
Elaine Marten, *Principal*
▲ **EMP:** 8
SALES (est): 590K **Privately Held**
SIC: 3842 Mfg Surgical Appliances/Supplies

(G-15666)
QUALTRE INC (HQ)
Also Called: Panasnic DVC Slutions Lab Mass
144 North Rd Ste 2250 (01776-1162)
PHONE..........508 658-8360
Edgar Masri, *President*
Farrokh Ayazi, *CTO*
EMP: 24
SQ FT: 5,500
SALES (est): 2.3MM **Privately Held**
WEB: www.qualtre.com
SIC: 3812 Manufactures Search/Navigation Equipment

(G-15667)
R G J ASSOCIATES INC
Also Called: Williamsville Products
11 Hop Brook Ln (01776-2010)
PHONE..........978 443-7642
EMP: 7
SALES (est): 550K **Privately Held**
SIC: 2842 Mfg Furniture & Wood Care Products

(G-15668)
SOLX INC
98 Ruddock Rd (01776-1318)
PHONE..........978 808-6926
Doug P Adams, *President*
EMP: 5
SQ FT: 4,000
SALES: 360K **Privately Held**
SIC: 3845 Mfg Electromedical Equipment

(G-15669)
TOUCHPOINT SOFTWARE CORP
490 Boston Post Rd Ste 5 (01776-3367)
PHONE..........978 443-0094
Ed Marney, *President*
Myles McDonough, *Vice Pres*
EMP: 18
SQ FT: 3,500
SALES (est): 778.5K **Privately Held**
WEB: www.touchpointcorp.com
SIC: 7372 Prepackaged Software Services

(G-15670)
UVTECH SYSTEMS INC
490 Boston Post Rd (01776-3367)
PHONE..........978 440-7282
David Elliott, *President*
Jill Elmstrom Mann, *Admin Sec*
EMP: 8
SQ FT: 2,000
SALES (est): 1.4MM **Privately Held**
WEB: www.uvtechsystems.com
SIC: 3589 Mfg Service Industry Machinery

(G-15671)
VANGUARD SOLAR INC
365 Boston Post Rd # 303 (01776-3023)
PHONE..........508 361-1463
John W Palmer, *President*
George J Pilla, *CFO*
Dennis J Flood, *CTO*
EMP: 3 **EST:** 2007
SALES (est): 262.4K **Privately Held**
SIC: 3674 Mfg Semiconductors/Related Devices
PA: Natcore Technology, Inc.
189 N Water St Ste 700
Rochester NY 14604

(G-15672)
VEROSOUND INC
128 Powder Mill Rd (01776-1055)
PHONE..........978 440-7898
Jing Jiang Wen, *President*
EMP: 3
SALES: 0 **Privately Held**
SIC: 3826 Mfg Analytical Instruments

(G-15673)
VIRICOR INC
98 Ruddock Rd (01776-1318)
PHONE..........508 733-5537
Doug Adams, *CEO*
EMP: 3
SALES (est): 230K **Privately Held**
SIC: 3829 Mfg Measuring/Controlling Devices

(G-15674)
YAMAHA UNFIED CMMNICATIONS INC (HQ)
144 North Rd Ste 3250 (01776-1169)
PHONE..........978 610-4040
Jean Pierre Carney, *President*
Nick Emoto, *President*
Mark Reid, *President*
Martin Bodley, *Corp Secy*
Peter Hemme, *CFO*
▲ **EMP:** 69
SQ FT: 15,000
SALES (est): 15.6MM **Privately Held**
WEB: www.revolabs.com
SIC: 3651 Mfg Home Audio/Video Equipment

Sunderland
Franklin County

(G-15675)
K S E INC
665 Amherst Rd Ste 1 (01375-5911)
P.O. Box 368, Amherst (01004-0368)
PHONE..........413 549-5506
James R Kittrell, *President*
G R Kittrell, *Vice Pres*
Carl Dupre, *Engineer*
Timothy Moriarty, *Engineer*
David Gerrish, *Manager*
EMP: 12
SQ FT: 11,000
SALES (est): 950K **Privately Held**
WEB: www.kse.net
SIC: 3564 8734 5049 Mfr Air Pollution Control Equipment Does Product Development & Testing And Whol Radon Test Kits

(G-15676)
SINAUER ASSOCIATES INC
23 Plumtree Rd (01375-9468)
P.O. Box 407 (01375-0407)
PHONE..........413 549-4300
Andrew Sinauer, *President*
Dean Scudder, *Vice Pres*
▲ **EMP:** 26
SQ FT: 6,000
SALES: 4.3MM **Privately Held**
WEB: www.sinauer.com
SIC: 2731 7812 7372 Textbook Publisher Video And Cd Rom Production

(G-15677)
TREW CORP (PA)
Amherst Rd (01375)
P.O. Box 395 (01375-0395)
PHONE..........413 665-4051
Paul H Warner Jr, *President*
Robert H Warner Jr, *Treasurer*
EMP: 3 **EST:** 1965
SQ FT: 1,800
SALES (est): 1.2MM **Privately Held**
SIC: 2951 Mfg Bituminous Concrete & Traprock

Sutton
Worcester County

(G-15678)
900 INDUSTRIES INC
16 Deborah Dr (01590-2510)
PHONE..........508 865-9600
Mary McNamara, *President*
Mary Mc Namara, *President*
Greta Heath, *Opers Mgr*
Paul F Mc Namara, *Treasurer*
Paul McNamara, *Treasurer*
▲ **EMP:** 5 **EST:** 1984
SQ FT: 10,000
SALES (est): 1.2MM **Privately Held**
WEB: www.900industries.com
SIC: 3569 Mfg General Industrial Machinery

(G-15679)
ATLAS BOX AND CRATING CO INC (PA)
Also Called: Atlas Global Solutions
223 Wrcster Prvdence Tpke (01590-2905)
PHONE..........508 865-1155
Arthur Mahassel, *President*
Lori Mahassel, *Admin Sec*
◆ **EMP:** 250
SALES (est): 99MM **Privately Held**
WEB: www.atlasbox.net
SIC: 2441 2448 2653 Mfg Wood Boxes/Shook Mfg Wood Pallets/Skids Mfg Corrugated/Solid Fiber Boxes

(G-15680)
CHEVALIER ASSOCIATES INC
Also Called: Bride & Groom
176 Worcester Prov Tpke 101a (01590-1901)
PHONE..........508 770-0092
Richard E Chevalier, *President*

GEOGRAPHIC

Lisa Dayne, *Editor*
Lyndsay Saulnier, *Marketing Staff*
EMP: 4
SALES (est): 28.9K **Privately Held**
WEB: www.originalweddingexpo.com
SIC: 2721 Periodicals-Publishing/Printing

(G-15681)
CREATIVE STRANDS
3 Boston Rd Ste 7 (01590-3800)
PHONE..................................508 865-1141
Linda M Little, *Principal*
EMP: 3
SALES (est): 162.7K **Privately Held**
SIC: 3999 Mfg Misc Products

(G-15682)
ENTEC POLYMERS
166 Stone School Rd (01590-3725)
PHONE..................................508 865-2001
Ken Pen, *Manager*
EMP: 5 **EST:** 2007
SALES (est): 457.5K **Privately Held**
SIC: 2821 Mfg Plastic Materials/Resins

(G-15683)
INDUSOL INC
11 Depot St (01590-3825)
P.O. Box 723 (01590-0723)
PHONE..................................508 865-9516
John J Connor II, *President*
John W Baldwin, *Treasurer*
EMP: 25 **EST:** 1950
SQ FT: 120,000
SALES (est): 5.7MM **Privately Held**
WEB: www.indusolinc.com
SIC: 2821 2891 Mfg Plastic Materials/Resins Mfg Adhesives/Sealants

(G-15684)
INTERSTATE GASKET COMPANY INC
55 Gilmore Dr (01590-2745)
PHONE..................................508 234-5500
Edward Z Savickas, *Ch of Bd*
John Savickas, *President*
Richard Dearborn, *Clerk*
EMP: 13
SQ FT: 12,000
SALES (est): 1.7MM **Privately Held**
WEB: www.interstate-gasket.com
SIC: 3053 Mfg Gaskets/Packing/Sealing Devices

(G-15685)
INTERSTATE SPECIALTY PDTS INC
Also Called: Isp
55 Gilmore Dr (01590-2745)
PHONE..................................800 984-1811
John Savickas, *President*
▲ **EMP:** 20
SQ FT: 6,000
SALES (est): 5MM **Privately Held**
WEB: www.interstatesp.com
SIC: 3423 Mfg Gaskets/Packing/Sealing Devices

(G-15686)
LANOCO SPECIALTY WIRE PDTS INC
7 John Rd (01590-2509)
PHONE..................................508 865-1500
Thomas O'Connor, *President*
John Lannon, *Treasurer*
▲ **EMP:** 12
SQ FT: 13,000
SALES (est): 1.7MM **Privately Held**
WEB: www.lanoco.com
SIC: 3315 3496 Mfg Steel Wire/Related Products Mfg Misc Fabricated Wire Products

(G-15687)
MAYFIELD PLASTICS INC
68 Providence Rd (01590-3813)
PHONE..................................508 865-8150
Ronald G Cross, *President*
A Gordon Cross, *Vice Pres*
Alexander W Samoiloff, *Vice Pres*
Lee Baker, *Foreman/Supr*
Matthew Paquette, *Engineer*
EMP: 43 **EST:** 1972
SQ FT: 60,000
SALES (est): 8.9MM
SALES (corp-wide): 21.3MM **Privately Held**
WEB: www.mayfieldplastics.com
SIC: 3089 Mfg Plastic Products
PA: Universal Plastics Corporation
75 Whiting Farms Rd
Holyoke MA 01040
413 592-4791

(G-15688)
PACKAGE INDUSTRIES INC
Also Called: Package Steel Buildings
15 Harback Rd (01590-2521)
PHONE..................................508 865-5871
Daniel E Moroney, *President*
Howard Hatch, *Opers Mgr*
Todd Zastawny, *Engineer*
Miriam Sanderson, *Treasurer*
Becky Seguin, *Manager*
EMP: 45
SQ FT: 100,000
SALES (est): 14.5MM **Privately Held**
WEB: www.packagesteel.com
SIC: 3448 Mfg Prefabricated Metal Buildings

(G-15689)
PACKAGE STEEL SYSTEMS INC
15 Harback Rd (01590-2521)
PHONE..................................508 865-5871
Robert Fisette, *President*
Zach McAyn III, *Treasurer*
EMP: 40
SQ FT: 80,000
SALES: 10MM **Privately Held**
SIC: 3441 Structural Metal Fabrication

(G-15690)
POLYVINYL FILMS INC
19 Depot St (01590-3825)
P.O. Box 753 (01590-0753)
PHONE..................................508 865-3558
John W Baldwin, *President*
Maria H Connor, *Treasurer*
John Baldwin, *Executive*
Robert N Baldwin, *Admin Sec*
◆ **EMP:** 95 **EST:** 1954
SQ FT: 120,000
SALES (est): 31.5MM **Privately Held**
WEB: www.stretchtite.com
SIC: 3081 Mfg Unsupported Plastic Film/Sheet

(G-15691)
S RALPH CROSS AND SONS INC
68 Providence Rd (01590-3813)
PHONE..................................508 865-8112
Ronald G Cross, *President*
A Gordon Cross, *Vice Pres*
Stanley R Cross Jr, *Vice Pres*
Sandra E Wondolowski, *Treasurer*
EMP: 43 **EST:** 1946
SQ FT: 60,000
SALES (est): 564.8K **Privately Held**
SIC: 3544 3543 Mfg Dies/Tools/Jigs/Fixtures Mfg Industrial Patterns

(G-15692)
SOURCE INTERNATIONAL CORP
17 Gilmore Dr (01590-2745)
PHONE..................................508 842-5555
U Karl Mueller, *President*
David L McGlynn, *Director*
▲ **EMP:** 29
SQ FT: 100,000
SALES (est): 8.9MM **Privately Held**
WEB: www.sourceseating.com
SIC: 2521 2522 Mfg Wood Office Furniture Mfg Office Furniture-Nonwood

(G-15693)
TAFT SOUND
3 Carrier Ln (01590-1620)
PHONE..................................508 476-2662
Phillip Davidson, *Owner*
EMP: 4
SALES (est): 238.2K **Privately Held**
WEB: www.taftsound.com
SIC: 3651 Mfg Home Audio/Video Equipment

(G-15694)
UNIFIED2 GLOBL PACKG GROUP LLC
223 Wrcster Prvdence Tpke (01590-2905)
PHONE..................................508 865-1155
Arthur Mahassel, *President*
EMP: 650
SALES (est): 111.6MM **Privately Held**
SIC: 2441 2448 2653 Mfg Wood Boxes/Shook Mfg Wood Pallets/Skids Mfg Corrugated/Solid Fiber Boxes

(G-15695)
VAILLANCOURT FOLK ART INC
9 Main St Ste 1h (01590-1660)
PHONE..................................508 476-3601
Gary Vaillancourt, *President*
Judi Vaillancourt, *Vice Pres*
▲ **EMP:** 30
SQ FT: 7,000
SALES (est): 3.3MM **Privately Held**
SIC: 3269 3229 5947 Mfg Chalk Ware Figurine Collectibles Glass Ornaments & Christmas Dinnerware

(G-15696)
WINDLE INDUSTRIES INC
94 Singletary Ave (01590-1839)
PHONE..................................508 865-5773
Terrence B Windle, *President*
EMP: 15
SQ FT: 150,000
SALES (est): 896.3K **Privately Held**
SIC: 2299 2282 Mfg Textile Goods Throwing/Winding Mill

Swampscott
Essex County

(G-15697)
FEIN ACADEMY LLC
21 Bay View Dr (01907-2626)
PHONE..................................978 495-0777
Reuven Fein,
Yulia Fein,
EMP: 5
SALES (est): 361.2K **Privately Held**
SIC: 7372 Educational Software

(G-15698)
LAB PUBLICATIONS LLC
47 Paradise Rd (01907-1958)
PHONE..................................781 598-9779
Leslie Breen, *Principal*
EMP: 4
SALES (est): 264.5K **Privately Held**
SIC: 2741 Misc Publishing

(G-15699)
QUEST SOFTWARE INC
45 New Ocean St (01907-1840)
PHONE..................................781 592-0752
Andrew Tripodi, *Branch Mgr*
David Swanson, *Manager*
EMP: 30
SALES (corp-wide): 1.3B **Privately Held**
SIC: 7372 Prepackaged Software Services
HQ: Quest Software, Inc.
4 Polaris Way
Aliso Viejo CA 92656
949 754-8000

(G-15700)
SWAMPSCOTT FUEL INC
197 Essex St (01907-1150)
PHONE..................................781 592-1065
Richard Elkhoury, *Principal*
EMP: 3
SALES (est): 198.9K **Privately Held**
SIC: 2869 Mfg Industrial Organic Chemicals

(G-15701)
VEEAM SOFTWARE CORPORATION
45 New Ocean St (01907-1840)
PHONE..................................781 592-0752
EMP: 3
SALES (corp-wide): 21MM **Privately Held**
SIC: 7372 Prepackaged Software Services
HQ: Veeam Software Corporation
8800 Lyra Dr Ste 350
Columbus OH 43240

Swansea
Bristol County

(G-15702)
A & S TACKLE CORP
724 Locust St (02777-3525)
PHONE..................................508 679-8122
Steven D Abdow, *President*
Steven Abdow, *President*
▲ **EMP:** 6
SALES (est): 474.5K **Privately Held**
SIC: 3949 Mfg Sporting/Athletic Goods

(G-15703)
COMPU-GARD INC
1432 Gar Hwy (02777-4291)
P.O. Box 469 (02777-0469)
PHONE..................................508 679-8845
Peter Leite, *President*
EMP: 21
SQ FT: 30,000
SALES (est): 4MM **Privately Held**
WEB: www.compu-gard.com
SIC: 3699 Mfg Electrical Equipment/Supplies

(G-15704)
CONVEYTREX LLC
1658 Gar Hwy (02777-3934)
PHONE..................................508 812-4333
Matthew K Westfield, *Principal*
EMP: 4 **EST:** 2009
SALES (est): 398.7K **Privately Held**
SIC: 3535 Mfg Conveyors/Equipment

(G-15705)
ISOTEK CORPORATION
Also Called: Isabellenhuette USA
1199 Gar Hwy (02777-4262)
PHONE..................................508 673-2900
Felix Heusler, *Ch of Bd*
Thomas Sojda, *President*
▲ **EMP:** 7
SQ FT: 1,100
SALES (est): 1.5MM
SALES (corp-wide): 188.7MM **Privately Held**
WEB: www.isotekcorp.com
SIC: 3676 Mfg Electronic Resistors
PA: Isabellenhutte Heusler Gmbh & Co. Kg
Eibacher Weg 3-5
Dillenburg 35683
277 193-40

(G-15706)
LAWSON HEMPHILL INC
1658 Grnd Army Rpblc Hwy (02777)
PHONE..................................508 679-5364
John Sullivan, *President*
Phillip Walmsley, *Engineer*
Patrick Sullivan, *Treasurer*
EMP: 9
SALES (est): 622.8K **Privately Held**
SIC: 2426 Hardwood Dimension/Floor Mill

(G-15707)
LOUIE AND TEDS BLACKTOP INC
105 Buffington St (02777-4822)
PHONE..................................508 678-4948
Louie Rebello, *President*
Deodato F Rebello, *Treasurer*
EMP: 10
SALES (est): 847.5K **Privately Held**
SIC: 3531 1629 8711 1622 Concrete Contractor

(G-15708)
MALONE BROTHERS INC
1699 Gar Hwy (02777-3901)
P.O. Box 358 (02777-0358)
PHONE..................................508 379-3662
Russell Malone, *President*
Thomas Malone, *Vice Pres*
EMP: 5
SALES (est): 777K **Privately Held**
SIC: 3444 Mfg Sheet Metalwork

(G-15709)
NAT CHIAVETTIONE INC
Also Called: Nat's Garage
702 Warren Ave (02777-3343)
PHONE.................................508 336-4142
Nat Chiavettione, *President*
EMP: 3
SALES: 500K **Privately Held**
SIC: 3599 Mfr Race Engines

(G-15710)
NEW ENGLAND RE BULLTIN
Also Called: New England Publishing Group
1610 Gar Hwy (02777-3947)
P.O. Box 357 (02777-0357)
PHONE.................................508 675-8884
Tr Brankco, *President*
EMP: 10
SALES (est): 920K **Privately Held**
WEB: www.nehomefinder.com
SIC: 2721 Periodicals-Publishing/Printing

(G-15711)
OBS WOODCRAFTS INC
314 Swansom Rd (02777-4945)
PHONE.................................508 679-0480
Michael O'Brien, *President*
Muriel O'Brien, *Treasurer*
EMP: 10 **EST:** 1977
SQ FT: 7,300
SALES (est): 1.2MM **Privately Held**
SIC: 2499 Mfg Wood Products

(G-15712)
P G L INDUSTRIES INC
1432 Gar Hwy (02777-4291)
P.O. Box 469 (02777-0469)
PHONE.................................508 679-8845
Peter G Leite, *President*
EMP: 22
SQ FT: 20,000
SALES (est): 4.2MM **Privately Held**
WEB: www.pglindustries.com
SIC: 3444 Mfg Sheet Metalwork

(G-15713)
POWER SOLUTIONS LLC (PA)
8 Filko Ave Unit 5 (02777-3445)
P.O. Box 100, Barrington RI (02806-0100)
PHONE.................................800 876-9373
Guy Lacerte, *President*
EMP: 10
SQ FT: 6,000
SALES (est): 1.9MM **Privately Held**
WEB: www.power-solutions.com
SIC: 3691 5065 Mfg Storage Batteries Whol Electronic Parts/Equipment

(G-15714)
SAFE CONVEYOR INCORPORATED
1658 Gar Hwy Ste 2 (02777-3934)
PHONE.................................774 688-9109
Gregory A Ferguson, *President*
EMP: 3
SALES (est): 303.9K **Privately Held**
SIC: 3535 Mfg Conveyors/Equipment

(G-15715)
SHAWMUT METAL PRODUCTS INC
1914 Gar Hwy (02777-3930)
P.O. Box 543 (02777-0543)
PHONE.................................508 379-0803
Kevin Kelly, *President*
Francis Kelly Jr, *Treasurer*
EMP: 38
SQ FT: 20,000
SALES (est): 9.3MM **Privately Held**
WEB: www.shawmutmetal.com
SIC: 3441 Structural Metal Fabrication

(G-15716)
STAR PICKLING CORP
941 Wood St (02777-3550)
PHONE.................................508 672-8535
Joseph C Castro, *President*
Vivian Castro, *Treasurer*
EMP: 14 **EST:** 1956
SQ FT: 34,000
SALES: 1.2MM **Privately Held**
SIC: 2035 Mfg Pickled Foodstuffs

(G-15717)
TESTING MACHINES INC
1658 Gar Hwy Ste 6 (02777-3934)
PHONE.................................302 613-5600
Dean Ross, *Manager*
EMP: 5
SALES (corp-wide): 13.4MM **Privately Held**
WEB: www.testingmachines.com
SIC: 3829 5084 Mfg Measuring/Controlling Devices Whol Industrial Equipment
PA: Testing Machines, Inc.
40 Mccullough Dr Unit A
New Castle DE 19720
302 613-5600

(G-15718)
TRUE MACHINE CO INC
2222 Gar Hwy (02777-3907)
PHONE.................................508 379-0329
Louis Pestana, *President*
Paul C Croteau, *Manager*
EMP: 7
SALES: 2MM **Privately Held**
WEB: www.truemachine.com
SIC: 3469 3541 7389 Mfg Metal Stampings Mfg Machine Tool-Cutting Business Services Bus Servs Non-Comcl Site

Taunton
Bristol County

(G-15719)
AD-A-DAY COMPANY INC
245 W Water St (02780-4844)
P.O. Box 950 (02780-0950)
PHONE.................................508 824-8676
Merrill N Cross, *President*
Ben Deptula, *Facilities Mgr*
EMP: 41 **EST:** 1944
SQ FT: 75,000
SALES (est): 5.7MM **Privately Held**
WEB: www.ad-a-day.com
SIC: 2759 3993 2741 5199 Commercial Printing Mfg Signs/Ad Specialties Misc Publishing Whol Nondurable Goods

(G-15720)
AGGREGATE INDS - NORTHEAST REG
203 Fremont St (02780-1214)
PHONE.................................508 821-9508
Joe Kenn, *Branch Mgr*
EMP: 15
SALES (corp-wide): 4.5B **Privately Held**
SIC: 1429 5032 Crushed/Broken Stone Whol Brick/Stone Material
HQ: Aggregate Industries - Northeast Region, Inc
1715 Brdwy
Saugus MA 01906
781 941-7200

(G-15721)
AIPCO INC
Also Called: American Insulated Panel Co
75 John Hancock Rd (02780-1096)
PHONE.................................508 823-7003
John J Lynch, *President*
Judith Lynch, *Treasurer*
EMP: 35
SQ FT: 35,000
SALES (est): 6.6MM **Privately Held**
SIC: 3585 Mfg Refrigeration/Heating Equipment

(G-15722)
ALEKSANDR S YASKOVICH
Also Called: Budget Printing Center
40 Weir St (02780-3916)
PHONE.................................508 822-7267
Aleksandr S Yaskovich, *Owner*
EMP: 4
SQ FT: 1,200
SALES (est): 363.4K **Privately Held**
SIC: 2752 7334 Lithographic Commercial Printing Photocopying Services

(G-15723)
ALEXANDER MOLES
306 Winthrop St (02780-4355)
PHONE.................................508 823-8864
Alexander Moles, *Owner*
Linda Moles, *Co-Owner*
EMP: 5
SALES (est): 203.2K **Privately Held**
SIC: 3589 1629 Mfg Service Industry Machinery Heavy Construction

(G-15724)
ALLIANCE CABLE CORP
201 Alfred Lord Blvd (02780-7617)
P.O. Box 1199 (02780-0972)
PHONE.................................508 824-5896
John Duryea, *President*
George Hudson, *Treasurer*
EMP: 50
SQ FT: 14,000
SALES (est): 4.4MM **Privately Held**
SIC: 3315 3357 Mfg Steel Wire/Related Products Nonferrous Wiredrawing/Insulating

(G-15725)
APPLIED COMPUTER ENGINEERING (PA)
500 Myles Standish Blvd # 1 (02780-1079)
PHONE.................................508 824-4630
Chao P Yang, *President*
Anting Yang, *Vice Pres*
EMP: 6
SQ FT: 1,000
SALES: 238.7K **Privately Held**
WEB: www.gridstat.com
SIC: 7372 Prepackaged Software Services

(G-15726)
ARGOS CORPORATION
84 Independence Dr (02780-7363)
PHONE.................................508 828-5900
John Cicalis, *President*
Perry Cicalis, *Treasurer*
EMP: 10
SQ FT: 13,000
SALES (est): 1.7MM **Privately Held**
WEB: www.argosco.com
SIC: 3082 Mfg Plastic Profile Shapes

(G-15727)
ASURE SOFTWARE INC
30 Robert W Boyden Rd 500b (02780-7838)
PHONE.................................512 437-2700
Todd Luttinger, *Vice Pres*
EMP: 5
SALES (corp-wide): 88.9MM **Publicly Held**
WEB: www.forgent.com
SIC: 7372 Prepackaged Software Services
PA: Asure Software, Inc.
3700 N Capital Of Texas H
Austin TX 78746
512 437-2700

(G-15728)
AUTOMATIC MACHINE PDTS SLS CO
400 Constitution Dr (02780-7360)
PHONE.................................508 822-4226
John S Holden Jr, *Ch of Bd*
John S Holden III, *President*
▲ **EMP:** 63
SALES (est): 13.9MM **Privately Held**
WEB: www.ampcomp.com
SIC: 3494 3451 Mfg Valves/Pipe Fittings Mfg Screw Machine Products

(G-15729)
AUTOMATIC MACHINE PRODUCTS CO
400 Constitution Dr (02780-7360)
PHONE.................................508 822-4226
John Holden III, *President*
Larry Drake, *QC Mgr*
Cheryl L Holden, *Admin Sec*
Cheryl Holden, *Admin Sec*
▲ **EMP:** 23
SALES (est): 5MM **Privately Held**
SIC: 3451 Mfg Screw Machine Products

(G-15730)
B & J MANUFACTURING CORP
Also Called: Bates & Klinke
55 Constitution Dr (02780-1071)
PHONE.................................508 822-1990
Stephen Benson, *President*
Gregory Benson, *Vice Pres*
Peter Benson, *Vice Pres*
EMP: 60
SQ FT: 36,000
SALES (est): 12.8MM **Privately Held**
WEB: www.bjmfg.com
SIC: 3499 3471 Mfg Misc Fabricated Metal Products Plating/Polishing Service

(G-15731)
B LUKA SIGNS INC
39 Tremont St (02780-3015)
PHONE.................................508 822-9022
Sergio Bento, *Principal*
EMP: 5
SALES (est): 517.9K **Privately Held**
SIC: 3993 Mfg Signs/Advertising Specialties

(G-15732)
BAY STATE CRUCIBLE CO
740 W Water St (02780-5003)
P.O. Box 407 (02780-0407)
PHONE.................................508 824-5121
Bradford Tripp, *President*
Nancy Tripp, *Admin Sec*
EMP: 21
SQ FT: 55,000
SALES (est): 3.1MM **Privately Held**
WEB: www.baystatecrucible.com
SIC: 3297 Mfg Nonclay Refractories

(G-15733)
BOSTON ORTHOTICS INC
30 Rob W Boyden Rd 1100 (02780)
PHONE.................................508 821-7655
David Macelhiney, *President*
EMP: 22 **EST:** 1997
SQ FT: 6,000
SALES (est): 3.5MM **Privately Held**
SIC: 3842 Ret Misc Merchandise

(G-15734)
BRAND DIELECTRICS INC
30 Robert W Boyden Rd 900a (02780-7833)
PHONE.................................508 828-1200
Charles Bostiwick, *Vice Pres*
Richard Lotz, *Treasurer*
EMP: 4
SQ FT: 8,000
SALES (est): 573.5K **Privately Held**
WEB: www.branddielectrics.com
SIC: 3084 Mfg Plastic Pipe

(G-15735)
CENTRAL GARDEN & PET COMPANY
Also Called: New England Pottery
125 John Hancock Rd Ste 5 (02780-1055)
PHONE.................................508 884-5426
Mike Jones, *Branch Mgr*
EMP: 40
SALES (corp-wide): 2.3B **Publicly Held**
SIC: 3269 5199 Whol Nondurable Goods
PA: Central Garden & Pet Company
1340 Treat Blvd Ste 600
Walnut Creek CA 94597
925 948-4000

(G-15736)
CERAMIC PROCESS SYSTEMS
111 Worcester St (02780-2088)
PHONE.................................508 222-0614
Grant Bennett, *Principal*
Mark Occhionero, *Vice Pres*
Michael Staab, *Manager*
Kathleen Flanagan, *Data Admn*
EMP: 9 **EST:** 2007
SALES (est): 1.1MM **Privately Held**
SIC: 3674 Mfg Semiconductors/Related Devices

(G-15737)
COLONIAL BRASS COMPANY
42 Connie St (02780-5128)
PHONE.................................508 947-1098
Daniel Moriarty, *President*
Christopher McVay, *Bd of Directors*
EMP: 5 **EST:** 1913
SQ FT: 7,500
SALES (est): 402.2K **Privately Held**
SIC: 3993 Ret Misc Merchandise

(G-15738)
CONTROLS FOR AUTOMATION INC
25 Constitution Dr (02780-1071)
PHONE..................................508 802-6005
David S Mochi, *President*
Charlotte Russell, *Purch Mgr*
Dennis Salisbury, *CFO*
Glen Gardner, *Marketing Staff*
Rob Russell, *Manager*
▲ **EMP:** 25
SQ FT: 25,000
SALES (est): 17MM **Privately Held**
WEB: www.gocfa.com
SIC: 3492 Mfg Fluid Power Valves/Fittings

(G-15739)
DA COSTA AWNINGS & CANVAS SPC
Also Called: Da Costa Awning Co
16 Winter St (02780-1975)
PHONE..................................508 822-4944
Antone Da Costa, *Owner*
EMP: 4 **EST:** 1960
SQ FT: 1,500
SALES (est): 210K **Privately Held**
SIC: 2394 5211 Mfg Awnings & Ret Aluminum Doors & Windows

(G-15740)
DARRELL WHEATON
Also Called: Circuit Design
200 Myles Standish Blvd # 3 (02780-7371)
PHONE..................................508 824-1669
Darrell Wheaton, *Owner*
EMP: 3
SQ FT: 600
SALES (est): 220K **Privately Held**
WEB: www.circuit-design-us.com
SIC: 3672 Mfg Printed Circuit Boards

(G-15741)
DAVOL/TAUNTON PRINTING INC
330 Winthrop St Ste 3 (02780-7103)
PHONE..................................508 824-4305
John W Leddy, *President*
Catherine J Leddy, *Shareholder*
EMP: 11 **EST:** 1858
SQ FT: 14,000
SALES (est): 1.2MM **Privately Held**
SIC: 2752 2759 Offset Printing

(G-15742)
DIAL FABRICS CO INC
20 Cushman St (02780-4204)
P.O. Box 590 (02780-0590)
PHONE..................................508 822-5333
Sergio Cardoza, *President*
Delfina Cardoza, *Principal*
EMP: 26 **EST:** 1979
SQ FT: 55,000
SALES (est): 2MM **Privately Held**
SIC: 2241 5949 Narrow Fabric Mill Ret Sewing Supplies/Fabrics

(G-15743)
DIAMOND PLATED TECHNOLOGY INC
Also Called: Cut Rite Instruments
28 Godfrey St (02780-4815)
PHONE..................................508 823-2711
Matthew B Hooper, *President*
Nicole Michael, *Admin Sec*
EMP: 4
SALES (est): 211.9K **Privately Held**
SIC: 3291 Mfg Abrasive Products

(G-15744)
DIVERSITECH CORPORATION
Also Called: Quick-Sling
391 W Water St (02780-4899)
PHONE..................................800 699-0453
Kelli Johnson, *Branch Mgr*
EMP: 9
SALES (corp-wide): 35.5MM **Privately Held**
SIC: 3272 Mfg Concrete Products
HQ: Diversitech Corporation
6650 Sugarloaf Pkwy # 100
Duluth GA 30097
678 542-3600

(G-15745)
DRAKA FIBRE TECHNOLOGY
761 Warner Blvd (02780-4343)
PHONE..................................508 822-0246
Dan Costa, *Principal*
EMP: 4
SALES (est): 266.6K **Privately Held**
SIC: 3357 Nonferrous Wiredrawing/Insulating

(G-15746)
EASTERN DIAGNOSTIC IMAGING
Also Called: E D I
597 Winthrop St (02780-2166)
PHONE..................................508 828-2970
Stephen Walsh, *President*
Paul Gonyea, *Vice Pres*
Gary Shaw, *Vice Pres*
Jim Perdikis, *Accounting Mgr*
Daniel Bond, *Sales Mgr*
◆ **EMP:** 12
SQ FT: 12,000
SALES (est): 1.4MM **Privately Held**
WEB: www.easterndiagnostic.com
SIC: 3844 Whol Medical/Hospital Equipment

(G-15747)
EDSON CORPORATION
Also Called: Foundry Div of Edson
9 2nd St (02780-4820)
PHONE..................................508 822-0100
Bruce Perry, *Manager*
EMP: 5
SQ FT: 6,000
SALES (corp-wide): 4.1MM **Privately Held**
WEB: www.edsonpumps.com
SIC: 3369 Nonferrous Metal Foundry
PA: The Edson Corporation
146 Duchaine Blvd
New Bedford MA 02745
508 995-9711

(G-15748)
EMD MILLIPORE CORPORATION
530 John Hancock Rd (02780-7379)
PHONE..................................781 533-5754
Joshua Batcoiffe, *Branch Mgr*
EMP: 317
SALES (corp-wide): 16.4B **Privately Held**
SIC: 3826 Mfg Analytical Instr Mfg Biological Products Mfg Diagnostic Substance
HQ: Emd Millipore Corporation
400 Summit Dr
Burlington MA 01803
781 533-6000

(G-15749)
ESP SOLUTIONS SERVICES LLC
580 Myles Standish Blvd # 2 (02780-1081)
PHONE..................................508 285-0017
Christine Noonan, *CEO*
Matthew Noonan, *Mng Member*
EMP: 38
SQ FT: 22,000
SALES: 2.5MM **Privately Held**
SIC: 2395 2396 Pleating/Stitching Services Mfg Auto/Apparel Trimming

(G-15750)
FULL LINE GRAPHICS INC
68 Cheryl Cir (02780-4385)
PHONE..................................508 238-1914
Aaron Leppo, *President*
EMP: 4
SALES (est): 492.6K **Privately Held**
WEB: www.flg.net
SIC: 2752 Lithographic Commercial Printing

(G-15751)
GABCON WELDING & CNSTR CO
Also Called: All American Septic & Sewer
15 Hamilton St (02780-2455)
PHONE..................................508 822-2220
George Bumila Jr, *Owner*
EMP: 75
SALES (est): 963.4K **Privately Held**
WEB: www.gabcons.com
SIC: 7692 Welding Repair Trade Contractor

(G-15752)
GATEHOUSE MEDIA LLC
Also Called: Taughton Daily Gazette
5 Cohannet St (02780-3903)
PHONE..................................508 880-9000
Sean Burke, *Principal*
Rebecca Hyman, *Editor*
EMP: 50
SALES (corp-wide): 1.5B **Publicly Held**
WEB: www.gatehousemedia.com
SIC: 2711 Newspapers-Publishing/Printing
HQ: Gatehouse Media, Llc
175 Sullys Trl Fl 3
Pittsford NY 14534
585 598-0030

(G-15753)
GENERAL DYNAMICS
425 John Quincy Adams Rd (02780-7397)
PHONE..................................508 880-4521
Gerald J Demuro, *President*
Myron Wagner, *Vice Pres*
Roberta Macdonald, *Senior Buyer*
Joseph Frias, *Purchasing*
John Medas, *Purchasing*
EMP: 58 **EST:** 2011
SALES (est): 12.4MM **Privately Held**
SIC: 3663 Radio And Tv Communications Equipment,Nsk

(G-15754)
GENERAL DYNAMICS MISSION
400 John Quincy Adams Rd (02780-1083)
PHONE..................................508 880-4000
Gregg Klawson, *General Mgr*
Jeff Rand, *Project Mgr*
Brendan Almeida, *Engineer*
Dave Berry, *Engineer*
Harry Dunham, *Engineer*
EMP: 1000
SALES (corp-wide): 36.1B **Publicly Held**
SIC: 3571 Mfg Electronic Computers
HQ: General Dynamics Mission Systems, Inc.
12450 Fair Lakes Cir # 200
Fairfax VA 22033
703 263-2800

(G-15755)
GENERAL DYNMICS MSSION SYSTEMS
20 Constitution Dr (02780-1070)
PHONE..................................508 880-4000
Walter Benson, *Branch Mgr*
Donna Truman, *Software Engr*
EMP: 5
SALES (corp-wide): 36.1B **Publicly Held**
SIC: 3661 Mfg Telecommunication & Information Technology
HQ: General Dynamics Mission Systems, Inc.
12450 Fair Lakes Cir # 200
Fairfax VA 22033
703 263-2800

(G-15756)
GREEN BROTHERS FABRICATING
15 4th St (02780-4812)
PHONE..................................508 880-3608
Joshua Green, *President*
Brett Green, *Treasurer*
EMP: 25
SALES: 220K **Privately Held**
WEB: www.greenbrothersfabrication.com
SIC: 3444 3699 3443 3469 Mfg Sheet Metalwork Mfg Elec Mach/Equip/Supp Mfg Fabricated Plate Wrk Mfg Metal Stampings Mfg Prefab Metal Bldgs

(G-15757)
HARODITE INDUSTRIES INC (PA)
66 South St (02780-4357)
PHONE..................................508 824-6961
Michael P Albert, *Ch of Bd*
Aaron M Albert, *President*
Gabriel Alves, *Prdtn Mgr*
John Rodrigues, *Controller*
Tommy Bridges, *Chief Mktg Ofcr*
◆ **EMP:** 70 **EST:** 1930
SQ FT: 200,000
SALES (est): 19.5MM **Privately Held**
WEB: www.harotex.com
SIC: 2221 Manmade Broadwoven Fabric Mill

(G-15758)
IMPERIAL POOLS INC
90 John Hancock Rd (02780-1047)
PHONE..................................508 339-3830
Tamayo Ray, *Branch Mgr*
Rafael Tamayo, *Branch Mgr*
EMP: 12
SALES (corp-wide): 70.3MM **Privately Held**
SIC: 3949 Mfg Sporting/Athletic Goods
PA: Imperial Pools, Inc.
33 Wade Rd
Latham NY 12110
518 786-1200

(G-15759)
IQE KC LLC
200 John Hancock Rd (02780-7320)
PHONE..................................508 824-6696
Angela Foley, *Purchasing*
William M Kurtz,
Andrew W Nelson,
Brian Schoonover,
EMP: 82
SALES (est): 20.9MM **Privately Held**
SIC: 3674 Mfg Semiconductors/Related Devices

(G-15760)
JMS MANUFACTURING INC
Also Called: Bee Fiberglass
22 5th St Unit 8 (02780-7038)
PHONE..................................508 675-1141
Jose Sousa, *President*
EMP: 15 **EST:** 1950
SQ FT: 30,000
SALES (est): 1.4MM **Privately Held**
WEB: www.beefiberglass.com
SIC: 3089 Manufactures Plastics Products

(G-15761)
KDO LLC
8 Broadway Ave (02780-1845)
PHONE..................................508 802-1347
Kevin D Oliveira, *Principal*
EMP: 5
SALES (est): 360.7K **Privately Held**
SIC: 2951 Asphalt Paving Mixtures And Blocks, Nsk

(G-15762)
KMS MACHINE WORKS INC
447 Winthrop St (02780-2154)
PHONE..................................508 822-3151
Charles Cronan, *President*
Michael Cronan, *Vice Pres*
Frances Cronan, *Admin Sec*
Fred Drake, *Maintence Staff*
Frances Cronin, *Clerk*
EMP: 19
SQ FT: 7,500
SALES (est): 3.8MM **Privately Held**
WEB: www.kmsmachine.com
SIC: 3599 Mfg Industrial Machinery

(G-15763)
MAXON PRECISION MOTORS INC (HQ)
125 Dever Rd (02780-7910)
PHONE..................................508 677-0520
Chris Blake, *President*
Greg Hayman, *CFO*
Roger Hess, *Sales Engr*
Paul McGrath, *Sales Engr*
Biren Patel, *Sales Engr*
◆ **EMP:** 42
SALES (est): 10.2MM
SALES (corp-wide): 533.9MM **Privately Held**
WEB: www.maxonmotor.com
SIC: 3625 3566 3621 7694 Mfg Relay/Indstl Control Mfg Speed Changer/Drives Mfg Motors/Generators Armature Rewinding
PA: Interelectric Ag
Brunigstrasse 220
Sachseln OW
416 661-500

(G-15764)
MCCABE SAND & GRAVEL CO INC
120 Berkley St (02780-4900)
PHONE..................................508 823-0771
Gregory R Keelan, *President*
Kayla Lopes, *Treasurer*
Kelly A Keelan, *Director*
Jill A Zajac, *Admin Sec*
EMP: 25
SQ FT: 18,000
SALES (est): 3.5MM **Privately Held**
SIC: 3273 5032 Mfg Ready-Mixed Concrete Whol Brick/Stone Material

(G-15765)
MICHAEL M ALMEIDA
Also Called: Future Graphics
330 Winthrop St Unit 1 (02780-7103)
PHONE..................................508 823-4957
Michael M Almeida, *Owner*
EMP: 3
SQ FT: 3,000
SALES (est): 262.4K **Privately Held**
WEB: www.futuregraphicsco.com
SIC: 2752 2791 Lithographic Commercial Printing Typesetting Services

(G-15766)
MS WHEELCHAIR MASS FOUNDATION
19 Scadding St (02780-6874)
PHONE..................................774 501-1185
Autumn Grant, *Principal*
EMP: 3
SALES (est): 220K **Privately Held**
SIC: 3842 Mfg Surgical Appliances/Supplies

(G-15767)
NABSON INC
45 Independence Dr (02780-1090)
PHONE..................................617 323-1101
James Calabrese, *President*
EMP: 7
SALES (est): 2.8MM **Privately Held**
WEB: www.nabson.net
SIC: 3678 5065 Mfg Electronic Connectors Whol Electronic Parts/Equipment

(G-15768)
NESTLE
455 John Hancock Rd (02780-7372)
PHONE..................................508 828-3954
EMP: 8
SALES (est): 501.9K **Privately Held**
SIC: 2038 Mfg Frozen Specialties

(G-15769)
NUMOTION
300 Myles Standish Blvd (02780-7364)
PHONE..................................401 681-2153
EMP: 3
SALES (est): 234.2K **Privately Held**
SIC: 3842 Mfg Surgical Appliances/Supplies

(G-15770)
OHLSON PACKAGING LLC (DH)
490 Constitution Dr (02780-7389)
PHONE..................................508 977-0004
John Ohlson Jr, *President*
Kevi Ohlson, *CFO*
Mike Marchand, *Finance Mgr*
James Mackenzie, *Manager*
Karl Chambers, *Director*
▲ **EMP:** 12
SQ FT: 14,000
SALES (est): 8.1MM
SALES (corp-wide): 855.2MM **Privately Held**
WEB: www.ohlsonpack.com
SIC: 3565 4783 Mfg Packaging Machinery Packing/Crating Service

(G-15771)
PARICON TECHNOLOGIES CORP
500 Myles Standish Blvd (02780-1079)
PHONE..................................508 823-0876
Toll Free:..................................877 -
Roger Weiss, *President*
Julie Fontaine, *Office Mgr*
Everett Simons, *Officer*
EMP: 14
SALES (est): 2.2MM **Privately Held**
WEB: www.paricon-tech.com
SIC: 3678 3679 Mfg Electronic Connectors Mfg Electronic Components

(G-15772)
PRECISION CIRCUIT CORPORATION
580 Myles Standish Blvd # 2 (02780-1081)
PHONE..................................508 479-8843
EMP: 3
SALES (est): 175.7K **Privately Held**
SIC: 3672 Mfg Printed Circuit Boards

(G-15773)
PRIMARY GRAPHICS CORPORATION
175 W Water St (02780-4844)
PHONE..................................781 575-0411
Anthony F Goodwin, *President*
Michael Goodwin, *Treasurer*
James Goodwin, *Admin Sec*
EMP: 17
SQ FT: 10,000
SALES (est): 2.5MM **Privately Held**
WEB: www.primary-graphics.com
SIC: 2759 Lithographic Commercial Printing

(G-15774)
PROFESSNAL CNTRACT STRLIZATION
Also Called: P C S
40 Myles Standish Blvd (02780-1026)
PHONE..................................508 822-5524
Gary Cranston, *President*
Marie Cranston, *Clerk*
▲ **EMP:** 10
SQ FT: 33,000
SALES (est): 1MM **Privately Held**
WEB: www.pcsinc.org
SIC: 3841 Mfg Surgical/Medical Instruments

(G-15775)
PRYSMIAN CBLES SYSTEMS USA LLC
761 Joseph Warner Blvd (02780-4343)
PHONE..................................508 822-0246
Kevin Sullivan, *Branch Mgr*
EMP: 7 **Privately Held**
SIC: 3357 Nonferrous Wiredrawing/Insulating
HQ: Prysmian Cables And Systems Usa, Llc
4 Tesseneer Dr
Highland Heights KY 41076
859 572-8000

(G-15776)
QG LLC
Worldcolor Taunton Retail
1133 County St (02780-3712)
PHONE..................................508 828-4400
Ted Gilly, *Branch Mgr*
EMP: 473
SALES (corp-wide): 4.1B **Publicly Held**
WEB: www.qwdys.com
SIC: 2752 Lithographic Commercial Printing
HQ: Qg, Llc
N61w23044 Harrys Way
Sussex WI 53089

(G-15777)
QUAD/GRAPHICS INC
50 John Hancock Rd (02780-1045)
PHONE..................................508 692-3100
John Gregg, *Project Mgr*
Dave Baptista, *Production*
Grant Lees, *Software Engr*
Ryan Reed, *Software Engr*
Erik Walke, *Technician*
EMP: 463
SALES (corp-wide): 4.1B **Publicly Held**
SIC: 2752 Lithographic Commercial Printing
PA: Quad/Graphics Inc.
N61w23044 Harrys Way
Sussex WI 53089
414 566-6000

(G-15778)
REDI-MIX SERVICES INCORPORATED
120 Berkley St (02780-4984)
PHONE..................................508 823-0771
Joseph Tutsch Jr, *Principal*
EMP: 4
SALES (est): 298.2K **Privately Held**
SIC: 3251 3273 5169 Mfg Brick/Structural Tile Mfg Ready-Mixed Concrete Whol Chemicals/Products

(G-15779)
RENS WELDING & FABRICATING
988 Crane Ave S Ste 1 (02780-7811)
PHONE..................................508 828-1702
Rens Hayes III, *President*
Joan Hayes, *Office Mgr*
F H Rens III, *Admin Sec*
EMP: 12
SQ FT: 50,000
SALES (est): 2.1MM **Privately Held**
SIC: 7692 3446 3441 Welding Repair Mfg Architectural Metalwork Structural Metal Fabrication

(G-15780)
RI KNITTING CO INC
20 Cushman St (02780-4204)
PHONE..................................508 822-5333
Ronald Fish, *President*
Scott Gauvin, *President*
Bryan Gardner, *Treasurer*
Chuck Gauvin, *Credit Mgr*
Alicia Lopez, *Admin Sec*
EMP: 38
SQ FT: 48,000
SALES (est): 4.5MM **Privately Held**
WEB: www.riknitting.com
SIC: 2241 Narrow Fabric Mill

(G-15781)
RYAN TOOL CO INC
336 Weir St 2 (02780-4234)
PHONE..................................508 822-6576
Robert Ryan, *President*
Doris Ryan, *Treasurer*
EMP: 3
SQ FT: 10,000
SALES (est): 308.5K **Privately Held**
WEB: www.ryantoolcompany.com
SIC: 3599 3569 Mfg Industrial Machinery Mfg General Industrial Machinery

(G-15782)
S & E FUELS INC
113 Dean St (02780-2717)
PHONE..................................617 407-9977
Sameh Kanan, *Principal*
EMP: 4
SALES (est): 322.7K **Privately Held**
SIC: 2869 Mfg Industrial Organic Chemicals

(G-15783)
SAINT-GOBAIN PRFMCE PLAS CORP
700 Joseph E Warner Blvd (02780)
PHONE..................................508 823-7701
Jim Fricks, *Branch Mgr*
EMP: 118
SALES (corp-wide): 209.1MM **Privately Held**
SIC: 2821 Mfg Plastic Materials/Resins
HQ: Saint-Gobain Performance Plastics Corporation
31500 Solon Rd
Solon OH 44139
440 836-6900

(G-15784)
SIL-MED CORPORATION
700 Warner Blvd (02780-4345)
PHONE..................................508 823-7701
Patrick Culley, *Principal*
EMP: 71
SQ FT: 22,000
SALES (est): 6.1MM
SALES (corp-wide): 209.1MM **Privately Held**
WEB: www.sil-med.com
SIC: 3841 Mfg Surgical/Medical Instruments
HQ: Saint-Gobain Performance Plastics Corporation
31500 Solon Rd
Solon OH 44139
440 836-6900

(G-15785)
SILVER CITY ALUMINUM CORP
704 W Water St (02780-5078)
PHONE..................................508 824-8631
Ronald Xavier, *President*
Jean Kingsley Souza, *Manager*
EMP: 60
SQ FT: 45,000
SALES (est): 16.2MM **Privately Held**
WEB: www.scaluminum.com
SIC: 3354 Mfg Aluminum Extruded Products

(G-15786)
SMARTCO SERVICES LLC
200 Myles Standish Blvd A (02780-7371)
PHONE..................................508 880-0816
Susan Gallant, *Vice Pres*
Bill Buker, *Technology*
Kyle Davies, *Technology*
Bryan Klugh,
EMP: 30
SQ FT: 250
SALES (est): 2.5MM **Privately Held**
SIC: 7372 Prepackaged Software Services

(G-15787)
STAR PRINTING CORP
Also Called: Pilgrim Plastics
10 Mozzone Blvd (02780-3751)
PHONE..................................508 583-9046
Mark Abrams, *President*
Neal Abrams, *Vice Pres*
Patty Chase, *Cust Mgr*
◆ **EMP:** 40 **EST:** 1946
SALES (est): 6.6MM **Privately Held**
WEB: www.starprintingcorp.com
SIC: 2752 Lithographic Commercial Printing

(G-15788)
TAUNTON MA
155 Myles Standish Blvd (02780-7325)
PHONE..................................774 226-0681
EMP: 3
SALES (est): 128.9K **Privately Held**
SIC: 2711 Newspapers-Publishing/Printing

(G-15789)
TAUNTON VENETIAN BLIND INC
Also Called: Coronet Awning Company
27 Main St (02780-2732)
P.O. Box 347 (02780-0347)
PHONE..................................508 822-7548
Donald Hotte, *President*
EMP: 3 **EST:** 1950
SQ FT: 2,400
SALES (est): 280K **Privately Held**
SIC: 2591 3444 Mfg Window Coverings & Venetian Blinds & Metal Awnings

(G-15790)
THEODORES
4 County St (02780-3502)
PHONE..................................508 409-1421
EMP: 5 **EST:** 2009
SALES (est): 452.8K **Privately Held**
SIC: 3679 Electronic Components, Nec, Nsk

(G-15791)
TRIBE MEDITERRANEAN FOODS INC
110 Prince Henry Dr (02780-7385)
P.O. Box 2178, Wilkes Barre PA (18703-2178)
PHONE..................................774 961-0000
John McGuckin, *CEO*
▲ **EMP:** 70
SQ FT: 70,000
SALES (est): 15.8MM
SALES (corp-wide): 113.5MM **Privately Held**
SIC: 2026 2022 2099 Manufactures Fluid Milk Manufactures Cheese Manufactures Food Preparations
PA: Lakeview Farms, Llc
1600 Gressel Dr
Delphos OH 45833
419 695-9925

GEOGRAPHIC

(G-15792)
TROPICANA PRODUCTS INC
305 Constitution Dr Ste 2 (02780-7391)
PHONE..................................508 821-2056
Robert Florio, *Manager*
EMP: 25
SALES (corp-wide): 64.6B **Publicly Held**
WEB: www.tropicana.com/biz
SIC: 2033 2086 2037 2048 Mfg Fresh & Packaged Citrus Fruit Juices Soft Drinks & Frozen Citrus Concentrate
HQ: Tropicana Products, Inc.
1001 13th Ave E
Bradenton FL 34208
941 747-4461

(G-15793)
UNICUS PHARMACEUTICALS LLC
30 Robert W Boyden Rd (02780-7833)
PHONE..................................508 659-7002
Pinaki Majhi, *CEO*
EMP: 20
SALES (est): 150.3K **Privately Held**
SIC: 2834 Mfg Pharmaceutical Preparations

(G-15794)
UNITED CITRUS PRODUCTS CO
195 Constitution Dr (02780-7388)
PHONE..................................800 229-7300
EMP: 7
SALES (est): 680K **Privately Held**
SIC: 2099 Mfg Food Preparations

(G-15795)
UNITED TECHNOLOGIES CORP
30 Robert W Boyden Rd 1200a (02780-7833)
PHONE..................................508 942-8883
EMP: 255
SALES (corp-wide): 66.5B **Publicly Held**
SIC: 3724 Mfg Aircraft Engines/Parts
PA: United Technologies Corporation
10 Farm Springs Rd
Farmington CT 06032
860 728-7000

(G-15796)
V&S TAUNTON GALVANIZING LLC
585 John Hancock Rd (02780-7336)
PHONE..................................508 828-9499
Werner Niehaus,
Brian Miller,
EMP: 35
SALES (est): 6MM **Privately Held**
SIC: 3479 Coating/Engraving Service

(G-15797)
VIRGINIA STAINLESS
700 W Water St (02780-5003)
PHONE..................................508 880-5498
EMP: 4
SALES (est): 276K **Privately Held**
SIC: 3498 Mfg Fabricated Pipe/Fittings

(G-15798)
WATERS TECHNOLOGIES CORP
177 Robert Treat Paine Dr (02780-7266)
PHONE..................................508 482-5223
Derrick St Laurent, *Safety Mgr*
Clay Lucas, *Purch Mgr*
Mike Glynn, *Branch Mgr*
Jim Lachapelle, *Admin Asst*
EMP: 10
SQ FT: 5,000 **Publicly Held**
SIC: 3826 Mfg Analytical Instruments
HQ: Waters Technologies Corporation,
34 Maple St
Milford MA 01757
508 478-2000

(G-15799)
WESTERBEKE CORPORATION (PA)
150 John Hancock Rd (02780-7319)
PHONE..................................508 977-4273
John H Westerbeke Jr, *President*
John Westerbeke, *COO*
Paul Ayers, *Purch Mgr*
Dennis Durkee, *Purch Mgr*
Greg Haidemenos, *CFO*
◆ **EMP:** 45 **EST:** 1934
SQ FT: 110,000
SALES (est): 11.4MM **Privately Held**
WEB: www.westerbeke.com
SIC: 3519 Mfg Internal Combustion Engines

(G-15800)
WOLLASTON FOUNDRY
Also Called: Wallaston Foundry and Machine
36 Allison Ave (02780-6958)
PHONE..................................508 884-3400
Mark Cafarella, *President*
EMP: 6
SALES (est): 1.2MM **Privately Held**
SIC: 3569 Mfg General Industrial Machinery

(G-15801)
WYRMWOOD INC
144 W Britannia St (02780-1634)
PHONE..................................508 837-0057
Douglas Costello, *President*
EMP: 8
SALES (est): 1.4MM **Privately Held**
SIC: 3944 Mfg Games/Toys

Teaticket
Barnstable County

(G-15802)
PACKAGING DEVICES INC (PA)
61 Homestead Ln (02536-5715)
P.O. Box 443, Falmouth (02541-0443)
PHONE..................................508 548-0224
Paul Ronsetti, *President*
Charles Alexander, *Vice Pres*
Carol Ronsetti, *Admin Sec*
EMP: 19
SALES (est): 990K **Privately Held**
WEB: www.packagingdevices.com
SIC: 2671 3565 3544 Mfg Packaging Paper/Film Mfg Packaging Machinery Mfg Dies/Tools/Jigs/Fixtures

Templeton
Worcester County

(G-15803)
JBM SERVICE INC
686 Patriots Rd (01468-1243)
P.O. Box 295 (01468-0295)
PHONE..................................978 939-8004
Teresa Gagne, *President*
EMP: 70
SALES (est): 9.7MM **Privately Held**
SIC: 2448 Mfg Wood Pallets/Skids

(G-15804)
R H LE MIEUR CORP
638 Patriots Rd (01468-1301)
PHONE..................................978 939-8741
Robert Le Mieur, *President*
Edith Lemieur, *Treasurer*
EMP: 16
SQ FT: 6,000
SALES (est): 1.6MM **Privately Held**
SIC: 2511 Mfg Furniture Reproductions Specializing In Wooden Chairs & Tables

(G-15805)
SPACE AGE ELECTRONICS INC
283 Baldwinville Rd (01468-1443)
PHONE..................................978 652-5421
Eugene H Mongeau, *Branch Mgr*
EMP: 25
SALES (corp-wide): 9.1MM **Privately Held**
WEB: www.1sae.com
SIC: 3669 Mfg Of Communication Equipment
PA: Space Age Electronics, Inc.
58 Chocksett Rd
Sterling MA 01564
800 486-1723

Tewksbury
Middlesex County

(G-15806)
ASCENT AEROSYSTEMS LLC
1061 East St (01876-1464)
PHONE..................................330 554-6334
Jan Peter Fuchs,
EMP: 3
SALES (est): 262.5K **Privately Held**
SIC: 3721 Mfg Drones

(G-15807)
ATLEE CORP
30 Commerce Way Ste 2 (01876-1776)
PHONE..................................978 681-1003
David J Healy, *President*
David Healy, *President*
EMP: 3
SALES (est): 167.4K **Privately Held**
SIC: 3469 Mfg Metal Stampings

(G-15808)
AXYGEN BIOSCIENCE INC
836 North St (01876-1256)
PHONE..................................978 442-2200
EMP: 1200
SALES (est): 39MM
SALES (corp-wide): 11.2B **Publicly Held**
SIC: 3089 Mfg Plastic Products
PA: Corning Incorporated
1 Riverfront Plz
Corning NY 14831
607 974-9000

(G-15809)
C & D SIGNS INC
Also Called: Metro Sign & Awning
170 Lorum St (01876-1700)
PHONE..................................978 851-2424
Brian A Chipman, *President*
Tom Dunn, *Vice Pres*
Corey Fischer, *Vice Pres*
Rebecca Hubbard, *Sales Staff*
Elena Berry, *Sales Executive*
EMP: 35
SQ FT: 3,000
SALES: 4.5MM **Privately Held**
WEB: www.metrosignandawning.com
SIC: 3993 Mfg Signs/Advertising Specialties

(G-15810)
CAMBRIDGE ISOTOPE LABS INC (DH)
Also Called: Cambridge Isotope Labs
3 Highwood Dr (01876-1147)
PHONE..................................978 749-8000
Cliff Caldwell, *CEO*
Joel C Bradley, *Ch of Bd*
Peter E Dodwell, *President*
Steven Igo, *Vice Pres*
Mike Steiger, *Plant Mgr*
▲ **EMP:** 85
SQ FT: 45,000
SALES (est): 19.2MM **Privately Held**
WEB: www.isotope.com
SIC: 2869 Mfg Industrial Organic Chemicals

(G-15811)
COLE SIGN CO
1615 Shawsheen St Ste 5 (01876-1551)
PHONE..................................978 851-5502
Gary Cole, *Owner*
EMP: 3
SALES (est): 206.8K **Privately Held**
SIC: 3993 Mfg Signs/Advertising Specialties

(G-15812)
COMPUTER MANAGEMENT CONS
500 Clark Rd Ste 3a (01876-1639)
PHONE..................................603 595-0850
EMP: 5
SALES (est): 380K **Privately Held**
SIC: 7372 Prepackaged Software Services

(G-15813)
CUSTOM GLASS AND ALUM CO INC
120 Lumber Ln Unit 4 (01876-1489)
PHONE..................................978 640-5800
Rita Curtis, *President*
EMP: 8
SALES (est): 657.5K **Privately Held**
SIC: 3211 Mfg Glass

(G-15814)
DELAWARE VALLEY CORP
600 Woburn St (01876-3441)
PHONE..................................978 459-6932
Tim Curtis, *Branch Mgr*
EMP: 34
SALES (corp-wide): 10.9MM **Privately Held**
WEB: www.delawarevalleycorp.com
SIC: 2297 3429 2273 Mfg Nonwoven Fabrics Mfg Hardware Mfg Carpets/Rugs
PA: Delaware Valley Corp.
500 Broadway
Lawrence MA 01841
978 688-6995

(G-15815)
DURAFLOW LLC
120 Lumber Ln Unit 15 (01876-1489)
PHONE..................................978 851-7439
Bill Matheson, *General Mgr*
David Spann, *Sales Engr*
Joseph Lander, *Mng Member*
Kathy Cioffi, *Director*
William F Matheson,
EMP: 15
SQ FT: 8,000
SALES (est): 3.6MM **Privately Held**
SIC: 2899 3589 Wastewater Discharge Compliance Process Materials Recovery And Water Recycle

(G-15816)
EDWARDS VACUUMS INC
1 Highwood Dr Ste 101 (01876-1156)
PHONE..................................978 753-3647
Chris Hill, *Principal*
EMP: 3
SALES (est): 241.3K **Privately Held**
SIC: 3589 Mfg Service Industry Machinery

(G-15817)
EVOQUA WATER TECHNOLOGIES LLC
558 Clark Rd (01876-1631)
PHONE..................................978 863-4600
Malcolm Kinnaird, *Division Pres*
EMP: 50
SALES (corp-wide): 1.4B **Publicly Held**
SIC: 3589 3569 3823 3826 Mfg Svc Industry Mach Mfg General Indstl Mach
HQ: Evoqua Water Technologies Llc
210 6th Ave Ste 3300
Pittsburgh PA 15222
724 772-0044

(G-15818)
HOODCO SYSTEMS INC
30 Barry Dr (01876-2252)
PHONE..................................978 851-7473
Michael Ovalle, *President*
EMP: 13
SALES: 1.2MM **Privately Held**
SIC: 3444 Mfg Sheet Metalwork

(G-15819)
INFINEON TECH AMERICAS CORP
1 Highwood Dr Ste 302 (01876-1156)
PHONE..................................978 640-3893
EMP: 6
SALES (corp-wide): 8.3B **Privately Held**
SIC: 3674 Mfg Semiconductors/Related Devices
HQ: Infineon Technologies Americas Corp.
101 N Pacific Coast Hwy
El Segundo CA 90245
310 726-8000

(G-15820)
MARINE POLYMER TECH INC (PA)
159 Lorum St (01876-1716)
PHONE..................................781 270-3200
Sergio Finkielsztein, *President*

▲ = Import ▼=Export
◆ =Import/Export

John Vournakis, *Vice Pres*
Eduardo Finkielszteon, *CFO*
Marco Finkielsztein, *Treasurer*
EMP: 35
SQ FT: 40,000
SALES: 10.1MM **Privately Held**
WEB: www.webmpt.com
SIC: 3842 Mfg Surgical Appliances/Supplies

(G-15821)
MARK DYKEMAN
Also Called: Dykeman Welding & Fabrication
805 Chandler St (01876-3709)
PHONE..................................978 691-1100
Mark Dykeman, *Owner*
EMP: 4
SALES (est): 410K **Privately Held**
SIC: 3312 Blast Furnace-Steel Works

(G-15822)
MEGATECH CORPORATION
525 Woburn St Ste 3 (01876-3432)
PHONE..................................978 937-9600
Vahan V Basmajian, *President*
Varant Z Basmajian, *Vice Pres*
Dan Hettler, *Mkta Coord*
Varant Basmajian, *Technology*
▲ **EMP:** 16
SQ FT: 20,000
SALES (est): 2MM **Privately Held**
WEB: www.megatechcorp.com
SIC: 3999 2741 Mfg Misc Products Misc Publishing

(G-15823)
MICROSEMI CORPORATION
890 East St Ste 3 (01876-1476)
PHONE..................................978 232-3793
EMP: 3
SALES (corp-wide): 5.3B **Publicly Held**
SIC: 3674 Mfg Semiconductors & Devices
HQ: Microsemi Corporation
1 Enterprise
Aliso Viejo CA 92656
949 380-6100

(G-15824)
MIKE GATH
Also Called: Gath Signs
509 Main St (01876-1818)
PHONE..................................978 851-4373
Mike Gath, *Owner*
EMP: 3
SALES (est): 290.8K **Privately Held**
SIC: 3993 Mfg Signs/Advertising Specialties

(G-15825)
PINE AND BAKER MFG INC
Also Called: Pine and Baker, Inc.
166 Lorum St (01876-1700)
PHONE..................................978 851-1215
Philip S Baker, *President*
EMP: 14 **EST:** 1939
SQ FT: 22,000
SALES (est): 132.8K **Privately Held**
SIC: 3651 2426 2499 Mfg Hi-Fidelity Speaker Systems Furniture Cabinets & Wooden Garden Fences

(G-15826)
PINE BAKER INC
166 Lorum St (01876-1700)
PHONE..................................978 851-1215
EMP: 8
SALES (est): 1MM **Privately Held**
SIC: 2499 1751 Mfg Wood Products Carpentry Contractor

(G-15827)
POWER GRAPHICS PRINTING
Also Called: Powergraphics Printing
1921 Main St Ste 4 (01876-2189)
PHONE..................................978 851-8988
Patrick Powers, *Owner*
EMP: 4
SQ FT: 1,500
SALES: 300K **Privately Held**
SIC: 2759 2789 2752 Commercial Printing Bookbinding/Related Work Lithographic Commercial Printing

(G-15828)
RAYTHEON COMPANY
50 Apple Hill Dr (01876-1198)
PHONE..................................978 858-5000
Richard Beltson, *President*
Emmanuel Perrotti, *Principal*
John Evicci, *Engineer*
Bruce Hatton, *Engineer*
Howard Kornstein, *Engineer*
EMP: 10
SALES (corp-wide): 27B **Publicly Held**
SIC: 3812 Mfg Search/Navigation Equipment
PA: Raytheon Company
870 Winter St
Waltham MA 02451
781 522-3000

(G-15829)
RAYTHEON COMPANY
50 Apple Hill Dr (01876-1198)
PHONE..................................978 858-5000
Dan Smith, *President*
EMP: 135
SALES (corp-wide): 27B **Publicly Held**
SIC: 3812 3761 3769 Mfg Search/Navgatn Equip Mfg Missiles/Space Vehcl Mfg Space Vehicle Equip
PA: Raytheon Company
870 Winter St
Waltham MA 02451
781 522-3000

(G-15830)
RAYTHEON COMPANY
50 Apple Hill Dr (01876-1198)
P.O. Box 1201 (01876-0901)
PHONE..................................978 858-4700
Christine Connors, *Manager*
EMP: 132
SALES (corp-wide): 27B **Publicly Held**
SIC: 3812 Mfg Search/Navigation Equipment
PA: Raytheon Company
870 Winter St
Waltham MA 02451
781 522-3000

(G-15831)
RAYTHEON SYSTEMS SUPPORT CO (HQ)
50 Apple Hill Dr (01876-1198)
PHONE..................................978 851-2134
Daniel J Crowley, *President*
EMP: 8
SALES (est): 5.3MM
SALES (corp-wide): 27B **Publicly Held**
SIC: 3812 Mfg Defense Systems
PA: Raytheon Company
870 Winter St
Waltham MA 02451
781 522-3000

(G-15832)
READYS WINDOW PRODUCTS INC
98 N Billerica Rd (01876-3510)
PHONE..................................978 851-3963
Linda M Ready, *President*
Frederick J Ready, *Treasurer*
EMP: 4
SQ FT: 3,500
SALES: 160K **Privately Held**
SIC: 2394 5999 5039 Mfg Canvas/Related Products Ret Misc Merchandise Whol Construction Materials

(G-15833)
RYCA INC
1768 Main St Ste 2 (01876-4752)
PHONE..................................978 851-3265
Candida M Connors, *Principal*
EMP: 4
SALES (est): 484.8K **Privately Held**
SIC: 3714 Mfg Motor Vehicle Parts/Accessories

(G-15834)
SANDYS MACHINE
24 Towanda Rd (01876-2356)
PHONE..................................978 970-1800
Steve Agnatovech, *Owner*
EMP: 3
SALES (est): 298.6K **Privately Held**
SIC: 3549 Mfg Metalworking Machinery

(G-15835)
SMART MODULAR TECHNOLOGIES INC
2 Highwood Dr Ste 101 (01876-1100)
PHONE..................................978 221-3513
EMP: 8
SALES (corp-wide): 1.2B **Publicly Held**
SIC: 3577 Mfg Computer Peripheral Equipment
HQ: Smart Modular Technologies Inc.
39870 Eureka Dr
Newark CA 94560

(G-15836)
SPRING MANUFACTURING CORP
2235 Main St (01876-3029)
P.O. Box 300 (01876-0300)
PHONE..................................978 658-7396
Roger A Desmarais, *President*
Rose Gilfeather, *Office Mgr*
EMP: 11
SQ FT: 11,000
SALES (est): 1.8MM **Privately Held**
WEB: www.springmancorp.com
SIC: 3495 Mfg Precision Springs

(G-15837)
STARKWEATHER ENGINEERING INC
1615 Shawsheen St Ste 14 (01876-1551)
PHONE..................................978 858-3700
Douglas A Starkweather, *President*
Sarah A Starkweather, *Vice Pres*
EMP: 10
SQ FT: 4,000
SALES (est): 1.3MM **Privately Held**
SIC: 3441 1799 Structural Metal Fabrication Trade Contractor

(G-15838)
STEPHEN GOULD CORPORATION
30 Commerce Way Ste 1 (01876-1776)
PHONE..................................978 851-2500
Luke Vitas, *Sales Mgr*
Zack Vitas, *Sales Mgr*
Denise Donahue, *Accounts Mgr*
Matt Lopiano, *Sales Staff*
Steve Potoff, *Sales Staff*
EMP: 25
SALES (corp-wide): 678.7MM **Privately Held**
WEB: www.stephengould.com
SIC: 2657 7336 Mfg Folding Paperboard Boxes Commercial Art/Graphic Design
PA: Stephen Gould Corporation
35 S Jefferson Rd
Whippany NJ 07981
877 557-5337

(G-15839)
STRAIGHTLINE EXCAVATION CORP
86 Lee St (01876-2032)
PHONE..................................978 858-0800
Dominic J Pellegrino, *President*
EMP: 3
SALES (est): 1.2MM **Privately Held**
SIC: 3531 Plows Construction Excavating And Grading

(G-15840)
STRONG ELECTRIC
100 Country Club Dr (01876-1635)
PHONE..................................855 709-0701
EMP: 3 **EST:** 2015
SALES (est): 223.4K **Privately Held**
SIC: 3089 Mfg Plastic Products

(G-15841)
TEWKSBURY WELDING INC
Also Called: Tewksbury Welding Service
285 Beech St (01876-4031)
P.O. Box 360 (01876-0360)
PHONE..................................978 851-7401
Donald McLaren, *President*
EMP: 5
SALES (est): 1.1MM **Privately Held**
SIC: 7692 Welding Repair

(G-15842)
THERMO ELECTRON KARLSRUHE GMBH
2 Radcliff Rd (01876-1182)
PHONE..................................978 513-3724
John Quigley, *Branch Mgr*
EMP: 4
SALES (corp-wide): 177.9K **Privately Held**
SIC: 3829 Mfg Measuring/Controlling Devices
HQ: Thermo Electron (Karlsruhe) Gmbh
Dieselstr. 4
Karlsruhe 76227
721 409-40

(G-15843)
THERMO FISHER SCIENTIFIC INC
2 Radcliff Rd (01876-1182)
PHONE..................................781 622-1000
EMP: 5
SALES (corp-wide): 24.3B **Publicly Held**
SIC: 3826 Mfg Analytical Instruments
PA: Thermo Fisher Scientific Inc.
168 3rd Ave
Waltham MA 02451
781 622-1000

(G-15844)
THERMO KEYTEK LLC
2 Radcliff Rd (01876-1182)
P.O. Box 712117, Cincinnati OH (45271-2117)
PHONE..................................978 275-0800
Gordon Woodfall,
Steve Ha,
▼ **EMP:** 100 **EST:** 2005
SALES (est): 15.7MM
SALES (corp-wide): 24.3B **Publicly Held**
WEB: www.thermo.com
SIC: 3826 Mfg Analytical Instruments
PA: Thermo Fisher Scientific Inc.
168 3rd Ave
Waltham MA 02451
781 622-1000

(G-15845)
THERMO SCNTFIC PRTBLE ANLYTCAL (HQ)
2 Radcliff Rd (01876-1182)
PHONE..................................978 657-5555
Daryoosh Vakhshoori, *CEO*
Lisa Witte, *President*
Doug Kahn, *Principal*
Kevin O'Brien, *Vice Pres*
Maura Fitzpatrick, *Admin Sec*
▲ **EMP:** 190
SQ FT: 45,000
SALES (est): 45MM
SALES (corp-wide): 24.3B **Publicly Held**
WEB: www.ahuracorp.com
SIC: 3826 Mfg Analytical Instruments
PA: Thermo Fisher Scientific Inc.
168 3rd Ave
Waltham MA 02451
781 622-1000

(G-15846)
V & G IRON WORKS INC
1500 Shawsheen St (01876-1562)
PHONE..................................978 851-9191
Virgilio Bancarotta, *President*
Rosaria Bancarotta, *Treasurer*
EMP: 15
SQ FT: 12,000
SALES (est): 3.8MM **Privately Held**
SIC: 3499 Mfg Misc Fabricated Metal Products

(G-15847)
VASCA INC
3 Highwood Dr (01876-1147)
PHONE..................................978 640-0431
Bernard E Lyons, *President*
▲ **EMP:** 43
SALES (est): 4.1MM **Privately Held**
SIC: 3845 3841 Mfg Electromedical Equipment Mfg Surgical/Medical Instruments

GEOGRAPHIC

(G-15848)
WELLPET LLC (PA)
200 Ames Pond Dr Ste 200 # 200 (01876-1291)
PHONE..................................877 869-2971
Ernie Huber, *Vice Pres*
Nick Deldon, *CFO*
Bill McDonald, *CFO*
John Iaquinta, *Accountant*
Mike Desautels, *Sales Staff*
▲ **EMP:** 90
SQ FT: 60,000
SALES (est): 85.6MM **Privately Held**
WEB: www.omhpet.com
SIC: 2047 Mfg Dog/Cat Food

(G-15849)
WICKED CORNHOLE
1875 Main St Ste 5 (01876-4720)
PHONE..................................978 851-7600
Bruce Taylor, *Principal*
EMP: 3
SALES (est): 271.5K **Privately Held**
SIC: 3944 Mfg Games/Toys

Thorndike
Hampden County

(G-15850)
O C WHITE COMPANY
4226 Church St (01079-7728)
PHONE..................................413 289-1751
Richard May Sr, *President*
▲ **EMP:** 21 **EST:** 1893
SQ FT: 13,500
SALES (est): 4.8MM **Privately Held**
WEB: www.ocwhite.com
SIC: 3646 Mfg Commercial Lighting Fixtures

Three Rivers
Hampden County

(G-15851)
MILLENNIUM DIE GROUP INC
Also Called: Stan-Allen Co.
2022 Bridge St (01080-1055)
P.O. Box 128 (01080-0128)
PHONE..................................413 283-3500
Richard Sweeting, *President*
John Pangetti, *Vice Pres*
Earl Quinn, *Vice Pres*
Larry Humiston, *Cust Mgr*
EMP: 20
SALES (est): 3.4MM **Privately Held**
WEB: www.millenniumdie.com
SIC: 3544 Mfg Dies/Tools/Jigs/Fixtures

Topsfield
Essex County

(G-15852)
ADVANCE DATA TECHNOLOGY INC
132 Washington St (01983-1625)
P.O. Box 1207, Gloucester (01931-1207)
PHONE..................................978 801-4376
Scott Gaskell, *President*
John Gaskell, *Treasurer*
Raymond D Tarr, *Admin Sec*
EMP: 18
SQ FT: 3,000
SALES (est): 1.9MM **Privately Held**
WEB: www.adtmemory.com
SIC: 3674 5065 Mfg Semiconductors/Related Devices Whol Electronic Parts/Equipment

(G-15853)
ALTERNATIVE SCREEN PRINTING
426 Boston St Ste 150 (01983-1216)
PHONE..................................978 887-9927
Fax: 978 887-8799
▲ **EMP:** 10
SQ FT: 10,000
SALES (est): 650K **Privately Held**
SIC: 2759 Screen Printing

(G-15854)
COMTECH PST CORP
Hill Engineering
417 Boston St (01983-1218)
PHONE..................................978 887-5754
Scott Schneider, *Manager*
EMP: 12
SALES (corp-wide): 671.8MM **Publicly Held**
WEB: www.comtechpst.com
SIC: 3663 3613 Mfg Radio/Tv Communication Equipment Mfg Switchgear/Switchboards
HQ: Comtech Pst Corp.
105 Baylis Rd
Melville NY 11747
631 777-8900

(G-15855)
CULLINAN MANUFACTURING INC
Also Called: N&N Manufacturing Co
25 Howlett St (01983-1409)
PHONE..................................978 465-1110
Richard Cullinan, *President*
EMP: 25
SQ FT: 5,600
SALES (est): 3MM **Privately Held**
SIC: 3679 Mfg Electronic Components

(G-15856)
DIAMOND SOLAR GROUP LLC
460 Boston St Ste 1 (01983-1223)
PHONE..................................978 808-9288
Manny Sieradzki,
EMP: 20
SALES (est): 1.5MM **Privately Held**
SIC: 3699 Mfg Electrical Equipment/Supplies

(G-15857)
ENGEMENT COMPANY INC
58 Main St Ste 2 (01983-1840)
PHONE..................................978 561-3008
Kennth P Dzierzek, *President*
EMP: 5
SALES (est): 616.3K **Privately Held**
SIC: 3825 Mfg Electrical Measuring Instruments

(G-15858)
EVANS INDUSTRIES INC
249 Boston St (01983-2295)
P.O. Box 169 (01983-0269)
PHONE..................................978 887-8561
Kendall Evans, *President*
▲ **EMP:** 30 **EST:** 1965
SQ FT: 12,000
SALES (est): 6.2MM **Privately Held**
WEB: www.evansindustries.com
SIC: 3599 Mfg Industrial Machinery

(G-15859)
FAIRVIEW MACHINE COMPANY INC
Also Called: FMC
427 Boston St (01983-1238)
PHONE..................................978 887-2141
Armand F Lauzon Jr, *CEO*
Michael C Moulton, *Ch of Bd*
Donna Costello, *CFO*
EMP: 50 **EST:** 1962
SQ FT: 25,000
SALES (est): 10.1MM **Privately Held**
SIC: 3599 Mfg Industrial Machinery

(G-15860)
GLAXOSMITHKLINE LLC
37 Grove St (01983-1709)
PHONE..................................978 853-6490
EMP: 27
SALES (corp-wide): 40.6B **Privately Held**
SIC: 2834 Mfg Pharmaceutical Preparations
HQ: Glaxosmithkline Llc
5 Crescent Dr
Philadelphia PA 19112
215 751-4000

(G-15861)
GRAHAM WHITEHEAD & MANGER CO (PA)
Also Called: Exact Components
462 Boston St Ste 2-1 (01983-1242)
PHONE..................................203 922-9225
Lyle Graham, *President*
Robert Manger Jr, *Treasurer*
EMP: 5
SALES (est): 450.1K **Privately Held**
SIC: 3315 Mfg Steel Wire/Related Products

(G-15862)
N&N MANUFACTURING INC (PA)
25 Howlett St (01983-1409)
PHONE..................................978 465-1110
John E Nault, *President*
▲ **EMP:** 18
SQ FT: 20,000
SALES (est): 3.6MM **Privately Held**
SIC: 3679 Mfg Electronic Components

(G-15863)
NEW ENGLAND CARBIDE INC
Also Called: Newcarb
428 Boston St Ste A (01983-1216)
PHONE..................................978 887-0313
Eamonn McDonnell, *President*
Andrew De Bernardo, *Treasurer*
Noeleen McDonnell, *Director*
EMP: 10
SQ FT: 10,000
SALES (est): 1.3MM **Privately Held**
WEB: www.newenglandcarbide.com
SIC: 3545 Mfg Machine Tool Accessories

(G-15864)
ORBITAL BIOSCIENCES LLC (PA)
4 Winsor Ln (01983-1511)
PHONE..................................978 887-5077
William F Bowers,
Linda Bowers,
EMP: 5
SALES (est): 250K **Privately Held**
WEB: www.orbio.com
SIC: 3677 Develops & Mfr Laboratory Separation Products Specializing In Filtration

(G-15865)
SI TECH INC
218 Boston St Ste 105 (01983-2210)
PHONE..................................978 887-3550
Norman Noriega, *President*
Ingrid Desilvestre, *Principal*
Nelson Desilvestre, *Vice Pres*
EMP: 5
SALES: 1.3MM **Privately Held**
SIC: 3674 Mfg Semiconductors/Related Devices

(G-15866)
TEKTRON INC
424 Boston St Ste B (01983-1216)
PHONE..................................978 887-0091
Philip Tanzella, *President*
Frank V Tanzella, *Vice Pres*
Karen Tanzella, *Clerk*
EMP: 10
SQ FT: 6,000
SALES: 1MM **Privately Held**
SIC: 3613 3545 3625 3599 Mfg Switchgear/Boards Mfg Machine Tool Access Mfg Relay/Indstl Control Mfg Industrial Machinery

(G-15867)
TRIREME MANUFACTURING CO INC
245 Boston St (01983-2215)
PHONE..................................978 887-2132
John Tsiplakis, *President*
EMP: 21
SQ FT: 13,000
SALES (est): 5.6MM **Privately Held**
SIC: 3511 Mfg Turbines/Generator Sets

Townsend
Middlesex County

(G-15868)
ASYMMETRICAL DEFENSE LLC
155 N End Rd (01469-1122)
PHONE..................................978 597-6078
Bret Lentine, *Principal*
EMP: 3 **EST:** 2016
SALES (est): 161.9K **Privately Held**
SIC: 3812 Mfg Search/Navigation Equipment

(G-15869)
CAM ENGINEERING INC
8 Jefts St (01469-1275)
PHONE..................................978 300-5073
Binh Pham, *President*
EMP: 4
SQ FT: 3,500
SALES (est): 360K **Privately Held**
SIC: 3599 Precision Machinery & Mfg

(G-15870)
CN CUSTOM CABINETS INC
365 Main St (01469-1029)
PHONE..................................978 300-5531
Marvin G Calderon, *President*
Eliud O Calderon, *Admin Sec*
EMP: 5
SQ FT: 52,000
SALES (est): 761.8K **Privately Held**
SIC: 2541 Mfg Wood Partitions/Fixtures

(G-15871)
DELUXE CORPORATION
12 South St (01469-1302)
P.O. Box 643 (01469-0643)
PHONE..................................978 597-8715
Sharon Quinn, *Branch Mgr*
EMP: 248
SALES (corp-wide): 2B **Publicly Held**
WEB: www.dlx.com
SIC: 2782 Mfg Blankbooks/Binders
PA: Deluxe Corporation
3680 Victoria St N
Shoreview MN 55126
651 483-7111

(G-15872)
F R MAHONY ASSOCIATES
41 Bayberry Hill Rd (01474-1120)
PHONE..................................978 597-0703
Keith Dobie, *President*
EMP: 22 **EST:** 2001
SALES (est): 1MM **Privately Held**
SIC: 3589 Mfg Service Industry Machinery

(G-15873)
RADIO ENGINEERING ASSOC INC
79 Tyler Rd (01469-1204)
PHONE..................................978 597-0010
Stephen Cloutier, *President*
EMP: 3
SQ FT: 1,400
SALES: 40K **Privately Held**
WEB: www.radioengineeringassociates.com
SIC: 3663 8711 Engineering Services

(G-15874)
TLS PRINTING LLC
84 Tyler Rd (01469-1203)
PHONE..................................508 234-2344
David G Foster,
Richard L Bloniasz Jr,
James R Russell,
EMP: 13
SQ FT: 38,000
SALES (est): 2.4MM **Privately Held**
WEB: www.tlsprinting.com
SIC: 2679 Lithographic Commercial Printing

▲ = Import ▼=Export
◆ =Import/Export

Turners Falls
Franklin County

(G-15875)
CHARTER NEX FILMS INC
18 Industrial Blvd (01376-1608)
PHONE..................................413 863-3171
Kathy Bolhous, *Branch Mgr*
EMP: 6 **Privately Held**
SIC: 3081 Mfg Unsupported Plastic Film/Sheet
HQ: Charter Nex Films, Inc.
1264 E High St
Milton WI 53563

(G-15876)
COLD RIVER MINING INC
17 Masonic Ave (01376-2515)
P.O. Box 501 (01376-0501)
PHONE..................................413 863-5445
Rob Houchens, *President*
▲ **EMP:** 9 **EST:** 2008
SALES (est): 1.4MM **Privately Held**
SIC: 3915 Mfg Jewelers' Materials

(G-15877)
FRANKLIN AREA SURVIVAL CENTER
96 4th St (01376-1307)
PHONE..................................413 863-9549
Faigh Rockwood, *President*
Ed Peramba, *Principal*
EMP: 16
SALES: 185.6K **Privately Held**
SIC: 2099 Mfg Food Preparations

(G-15878)
HEAT FAB INC
130 Industrial Blvd (01376-1607)
PHONE..................................413 863-2242
Jerry Nolan, *CFO*
Marcus McCrary,
EMP: 100
SALES (est): 18.1MM **Privately Held**
WEB: www.heatfab.com
SIC: 3444 3443 3564 Mfg Sheet Metal-work Mfg Fabricated Plate Wrk Mfg Blowers/Fans

(G-15879)
HILLSIDE PLASTICS INC
Also Called: Sugarhill Containers
262 Millers Falls Rd (01376-1613)
PHONE..................................413 863-2222
Peter M Haas, *President*
Peter Haas, *General Mgr*
Brian Kucenski, *Engineer*
Kathryn L Colby, *Treasurer*
Alan H Blanker, *Admin Sec*
EMP: 211
SQ FT: 47,000
SALES (est): 43.3MM **Privately Held**
WEB: www.hillsideplastics.com
SIC: 3089 Mfg Plastic Products
PA: Carr Management, Inc.
1 Tara Blvd Ste 303
Nashua NH 03062

(G-15880)
JUDD WIRE INC (DH)
124 Turnpike Rd (01376-2699)
PHONE..................................413 863-9402
James Koulgeorge, *President*
Denise Mankowsky, *Purchasing*
Judd Wire, *Research*
▲ **EMP:** 258
SQ FT: 472,000
SALES (est): 50.6MM **Privately Held**
WEB: www.juddwire.com
SIC: 3357 Nonferrous Wiredrawing/Insulating
HQ: Sumitomo Electric U.S.A., Inc.
21241 S Wstn Ave Ste 120
Torrance CA 90501
310 782-0227

(G-15881)
MAYHEW STEEL PRODUCTS INC (PA)
Also Called: Mayhew Tools
199 Industrial Blvd (01376-1611)
PHONE..................................413 625-6351
John C Lawless, *President*
William S Lawless, *Vice Pres*
Doug Pratt, *Maint Spvr*
Debbie Powell, *Production*
Eric Mills, *VP Sales*
▲ **EMP:** 31 **EST:** 1856
SQ FT: 28,565
SALES (est): 4.8MM **Privately Held**
WEB: www.mayhew.com
SIC: 3423 Mfg Hand/Edge Tools

(G-15882)
MONTAGUE INDUSTRIES INC
Also Called: Montague Machine Company
15 Rastallis St (01376-8901)
P.O. Box 777 (01376-0777)
PHONE..................................413 863-4301
S Jay Pierce, *CEO*
Judith A Pierce, *President*
Les Johnston, *Admin Sec*
EMP: 26
SQ FT: 52,000
SALES: 3.1MM **Privately Held**
SIC: 3599 3554 Mfg Industrial Machinery Mfg Paper Industrial Machinery

(G-15883)
MONTAGUE REPORTER INCORPORATED
177 Avenue A (01376-1210)
PHONE..................................413 863-8666
Wesley Blixt, *Owner*
EMP: 3
SALES: 97.7K **Privately Held**
SIC: 2711 Newspapers-Publishing/Printing

(G-15884)
NEW ENGLAND EXTRUSION INC
18 Industrial Blvd (01376-1608)
PHONE..................................413 863-3171
Cathy Bolhous, *President*
▼ **EMP:** 180
SQ FT: 105,000
SALES (est): 21.9MM **Privately Held**
WEB: www.nex-films.com
SIC: 3081 Mfg Unsupported Plastic Film/Sheet
HQ: Charter Nex Holding Company
1264 E High St
Milton WI 53563

(G-15885)
SIMONS STAMPS INC
320 Avenue A (01376-1826)
PHONE..................................413 863-6800
Simon Alciere, *President*
EMP: 14
SALES: 850K **Privately Held**
WEB: www.simonstamp.com
SIC: 3069 5099 5999 Mfg Fabricated Rubber Products Whol Durable Goods Ret Misc Merchandise

Tyngsboro
Middlesex County

(G-15886)
BP FLY CORPORATION (PA)
Also Called: Beacon Power
65 Middlesex Rd (01879-2041)
PHONE..................................978 649-9114
Barry R Brits, *President*
James M Spiezio, *Corp Secy*
Judith F Judson, *Vice Pres*
Matthew L Lazarewicz, *Vice Pres*
EMP: 46
SQ FT: 103,000
SALES (est): 7.8MM **Privately Held**
WEB: www.beaconpower.com
SIC: 3612 Mfg Transformers

(G-15887)
C & C MACHINE INC
78 Progress Ave (01879-1436)
P.O. Box 490 (01879-0490)
PHONE..................................978 649-0285
Ernie Cote, *President*
Paul Hearu, *General Mgr*
Ernest D Cote Jr, *Co-President*
James Cote, *Vice Pres*
EMP: 37
SQ FT: 15,000
SALES: 3.5MM **Privately Held**
WEB: www.ccmachineusa.com
SIC: 3599 Mfg Industrial Machinery

(G-15888)
DJ WHOLESALE CLUB INC
Also Called: Xmix
3 Westech Dr (01879-2720)
PHONE..................................978 649-2525
Larry Clawson, *President*
Theresa Clawson, *Founder*
Neil Petricone, *Marketing Mgr*
EMP: 9
SQ FT: 3,000
SALES (est): 991.5K **Privately Held**
WEB: www.djwholesaleclub.com
SIC: 3652 Direct Marketing Company

(G-15889)
ICS CORP
100 Business Park Dr # 13 (01879-1071)
PHONE..................................978 362-0057
Roger Fritz, *CEO*
Landon Fritz, *Vice Pres*
EMP: 4
SALES (est): 780.6K **Privately Held**
SIC: 3625 Mfg Relays/Industrial Controls

(G-15890)
INDUSTRIAL LBLING SYSTEMS CORP
100 Business Park Dr (01879-1071)
PHONE..................................978 649-7004
James J Blouin, *President*
Serhat Kotak, *Vice Pres*
Gregory Frederick, *Technical Mgr*
▼ **EMP:** 20
SQ FT: 10,000
SALES (est): 1.9MM **Privately Held**
WEB: www.ils-barcode.com
SIC: 2396 2672 2671 Mfg Auto/Apparel Trimming Mfg Coated/Laminated Paper Mfg Packaging Paper/Film

(G-15891)
INVENTRONICS INC
130 Middlesex Rd Ste 14 (01879-2725)
PHONE..................................978 649-9040
Paul Sanderson, *President*
Albert Sanderson, *President*
EMP: 5
SQ FT: 1,200
SALES (est): 793.5K **Privately Held**
WEB: www.accu-tuner.com
SIC: 3825 8742 Mfg Microprocessor Controlled Pitch Measuring Equipment

(G-15892)
L & L RACE CARS
47 Frost Rd (01879-1128)
PHONE..................................978 420-7852
Steven Landry, *Owner*
EMP: 4
SALES: 275K **Privately Held**
SIC: 3444 Metal Fabrication

(G-15893)
LEGACY MEDICAL SOLUTIONS LLC
90 Progress Ave 3 (01879-1436)
PHONE..................................978 655-6007
Joel Hughes,
EMP: 3
SALES (est): 713.1K **Privately Held**
SIC: 3841 Mfg Surgical/Medical Instruments

(G-15894)
M-TECH
67 Westech Dr (01879-2720)
PHONE..................................978 649-4563
Mark Bernett, *Owner*
EMP: 5 **EST:** 1984
SQ FT: 1,800
SALES: 300K **Privately Held**
WEB: www.m-tech.com
SIC: 3599 Mfg Industrial Machinery

(G-15895)
MASSACHUSETTS CONTROL CTR INC
40 Westech Dr (01879-2720)
PHONE..................................978 649-1128
Anthony J Deehan, *Branch Mgr*
EMP: 3
SALES (corp-wide): 12.9MM **Privately Held**
SIC: 3585 5075 5722 Mfg Refrigeration/Heating Equipment Whol Heat/Air Cond Equipment/Supplies Ret Household Appliances
PA: Massachusetts Control Center, Inc.
77 Dudley St
Arlington MA 02476
781 646-1128

(G-15896)
METAL PROCESSING CO INC
75 Westech Dr (01879-2720)
PHONE..................................978 649-1289
Robin Perry, *President*
Michael J Perry, *Treasurer*
◆ **EMP:** 8
SQ FT: 4,000
SALES: 1.6MM **Privately Held**
WEB: www.metproco.com
SIC: 3679 3398 Mfg Hermetic Seals & Heat Treating

(G-15897)
NEW ENGLAND CRANE INC
500 Potash Hill Rd Unit 1 (01879-2797)
PHONE..................................207 782-7353
George Frost, *Branch Mgr*
EMP: 4
SALES (est): 442.7K
SALES (corp-wide): 1.2MM **Privately Held**
SIC: 3536 Mfg Hoists/Cranes/Monorails
PA: New England Crane, Inc
70 Commercial St Ste 1
Lewiston ME 04240
207 782-7353

(G-15898)
PAWSITIVELY YUMMY
440 Middlesex Rd (01879-1070)
PHONE..................................603 889-3181
Lisa A Shapiro, *Principal*
EMP: 3
SALES (est): 185.7K **Privately Held**
SIC: 3999 Mfg Misc Products

(G-15899)
PICONICS INC
26 Cummings Rd (01879-1498)
PHONE..................................978 649-7501
Stephen A Slenker, *Ch of Bd*
Stephen A Slenkerr, *Ch of Bd*
Brian Goodhue, *Engineer*
Marie A Slenker, *Treasurer*
▲ **EMP:** 45 **EST:** 1964
SQ FT: 28,000
SALES (est): 8.2MM **Privately Held**
WEB: www.piconics.com
SIC: 3674 Mfg Semiconductors/Related Devices

(G-15900)
PRECISION TECHNOLOGIES INC
42 Westech Dr (01879-2720)
P.O. Box 610 (01879-0610)
PHONE..................................978 649-8715
Bryan Subsick, *CEO*
Walter Subsick, *Corp Secy*
Susan Galligan, *Purch Agent*
▲ **EMP:** 32
SQ FT: 11,000
SALES (est): 5.6MM **Privately Held**
WEB: www.precision-techno.com
SIC: 3599 Mfg Industrial Machinery

(G-15901)
SZR FUEL LLC
46 Anderson Dr (01879-2453)
PHONE..................................978 649-2409
Simon Raad, *Principal*
EMP: 3 **EST:** 2010
SALES (est): 259.9K **Privately Held**
SIC: 2869 Mfg Industrial Organic Chemicals

(G-15902)
TESCO ASSOCIATES INC
500 Businema Pk Dr Unit 1 (01879)
PHONE....................................978 649-5527
G Lawrence Thatcher, *President*
EMP: 15
SQ FT: 4,800
SALES (est): 5MM **Privately Held**
WEB: www.tescoassociates.com
SIC: 3842 Mfg Surgical Appliances/Supplies

Upton
Worcester County

(G-15903)
ADVANTCRAFT INC
11 Juniper Rd (01568-1479)
P.O. Box 465 (01568-0465)
PHONE....................................508 498-4644
John J Kokoszka, *President*
EMP: 4
SQ FT: 600
SALES: 200K **Privately Held**
SIC: 3446 7359 Mfg Architectural Metalwork Equipment Rental/Leasing

(G-15904)
ARISTOCRAT PRODUCTS INC
17 Taft St Ste 1 (01568-1136)
PHONE....................................508 529-3471
Paul Flaherty, *President*
EMP: 8
SQ FT: 4,000
SALES (est): 819.2K **Privately Held**
WEB: www.aristocratproducts.com
SIC: 2053 Mfg Frozen Pies

(G-15905)
BRC DEVELOPMENT LLC
Also Called: Everyday Speech
28 Rockwood Ln (01568-1692)
PHONE....................................774 245-7750
Caleb Brunell, *CEO*
EMP: 3
SALES (est): 172.9K **Privately Held**
SIC: 7372 Prepackaged Software Services

(G-15906)
COOK FOREST PRODUCTS INC
Also Called: Cook Company
252 Milford St (01568-1325)
PHONE....................................508 634-3300
Douglas Cook, *President*
EMP: 22
SQ FT: 4,000
SALES (est): 3.2MM **Privately Held**
SIC: 2499 1629 2421 Mfg Wood Products Heavy Construction Sawmill/Planing Mill

(G-15907)
K M T MACHINING
41 Grove St (01568-1337)
P.O. Box 99 (01568-0099)
PHONE....................................508 529-6953
Mike Tetreault, *Owner*
EMP: 3 **EST:** 1996
SALES (est): 239.4K **Privately Held**
SIC: 3599 Mfg Industrial Machinery

(G-15908)
KIRSTEIN PER
Also Called: Nanotech Consulting
158 East St (01568-1212)
PHONE....................................508 473-9673
Per Kirstein, *Owner*
EMP: 3
SALES (est): 300K **Privately Held**
SIC: 3826 Mfg Analytical Instruments

(G-15909)
MODELTRONIX
13 Grove St (01568-1359)
PHONE....................................508 529-3567
Walter Ramsey, *Owner*
EMP: 3
SALES: 450K **Privately Held**
SIC: 3812 Mfg Search/Navigation Equipment

(G-15910)
TATTERSALL MACHINING INC
190 Milford St (01568-1313)
P.O. Box 1019 (01568-6019)
PHONE....................................508 529-2300
Bruce Tattersall, *President*
EMP: 13
SQ FT: 6,000
SALES (est): 1.8MM **Privately Held**
WEB: www.tattersallmachining.com
SIC: 3599 Mfg Industrial Machinery

(G-15911)
TOWN CRIER PUBLICATIONS INC
Also Called: Upton & Mendon Town Crier
48 Mechanic St (01568-1578)
PHONE....................................508 529-7791
Alfred Holman, *President*
Marilyn Holman, *Owner*
EMP: 18
SALES: 500K **Privately Held**
WEB: www.utcnews.com
SIC: 2711 Newspapers-Publishing/Printing

Uxbridge
Worcester County

(G-15912)
A & J INDUSTRIES LLC
56 Industrial Dr (01569-2279)
PHONE....................................508 278-4531
Al Prindle,
John Gaudett,
▲ **EMP:** 12
SALES (est): 2.9MM **Privately Held**
SIC: 3089 Mfg Plastic Products

(G-15913)
AA WHITE COMPANY
867 Quaker Hwy Unit A (01569-2252)
PHONE....................................508 779-0821
Anna Picard, *CEO*
EMP: 12 **EST:** 1865
SQ FT: 8,000
SALES (est): 1.2MM **Privately Held**
WEB: www.aawhite.com
SIC: 3953 Mfg Marking Devices

(G-15914)
AVIATION WELDING
73 Commerce Dr (01569-2280)
PHONE....................................508 278-3041
Robert N Allen, *Principal*
EMP: 5
SALES (est): 667K **Privately Held**
SIC: 7692 Welding Repair

(G-15915)
EXTREME PROTOCOL SOLUTIONS INC
10 River Rd Ste 102e (01569-2259)
PHONE....................................508 278-3600
Roger Gagnon, *President*
Colin Carufel, *Vice Pres*
David Deming, *Shareholder*
Brent Burkholder, *Admin Sec*
EMP: 5
SQ FT: 4,000
SALES: 720K **Privately Held**
WEB: www.extremeprotocol.com
SIC: 7372 Prepackaged Software Services

(G-15916)
FITNESS EM LLC
660 Douglas St (01569-2171)
P.O. Box 422, Manchaug (01526-0422)
PHONE....................................508 278-3209
Michael Savage, *CEO*
Donna Savage, *President*
Jack Lasey, *COO*
Robert Bostwick, *Exec VP*
Eric McGourty, *CFO*
▲ **EMP:** 34
SQ FT: 5,000
SALES (est): 5.3MM **Privately Held**
WEB: www.fitnessem.com
SIC: 3949 5091 5046 Mfg Sporting/Athletic Goods Whol Sporting/Recreational Goods Whol Commercial Equipment

(G-15917)
FOAM CONCEPTS INC
44 Rivulet St (01569-3134)
P.O. Box 410 (01569-0410)
PHONE....................................508 278-7255
Mark Villamaino, *President*
Philip Michaelson, *Vice Pres*
◆ **EMP:** 30
SQ FT: 80,000
SALES (est): 4.4MM **Privately Held**
WEB: www.foamconcepts.com
SIC: 3086 Mfg Plastic Foam Products

(G-15918)
HEARTWOOD CABINETMAKERS LLC
51 N Main St (01569-1719)
PHONE....................................508 634-2004
Christopher J Goddard, *Principal*
EMP: 4
SALES (est): 372.5K **Privately Held**
SIC: 2434 Mfg Wood Kitchen Cabinets

(G-15919)
HEAT-FLO INC
15 Megan Ct (01569-2272)
P.O. Box 612 (01569-0612)
PHONE....................................508 278-2400
George Celorier, *President*
▲ **EMP:** 8
SALES (est): 1.9MM **Privately Held**
WEB: www.heat-flo.com
SIC: 3585 7389 Mfg Refrigeration/Heating Equipment Business Services At Non-Commercial Site

(G-15920)
INDUSTRIAL FOUNDRY CORPORATION
Elmdale Rd (01569)
PHONE....................................508 278-5523
Russell McLean, *President*
Craig Mc Lean, *Shareholder*
Keith Mc Lean, *Clerk*
EMP: 9 **EST:** 1961
SQ FT: 12,000
SALES (est): 1.6MM **Privately Held**
SIC: 3365 3364 Aluminum Foundry Mfg Nonferrous Die-Castings

(G-15921)
IRADION LASER INC
1 Technology Dr (01569-2282)
PHONE....................................401 762-5100
Claudia Reygadas, *Purchasing*
Clifford E Morrow, *Director*
▼ **EMP:** 6
SQ FT: 9,000
SALES (est): 1.6MM **Privately Held**
SIC: 3699 Mfg Electrical Equipment/Supplies

(G-15922)
JUMBO DONUTS
5 Douglas St (01569-1814)
PHONE....................................508 278-9977
Roda Macomus, *Manager*
EMP: 15 **EST:** 1998
SALES (est): 1.3MM **Privately Held**
SIC: 2051 Mfg Bread/Related Products

(G-15923)
LAMPIN CORPORATION (PA)
38 River Rd (01569-2245)
P.O. Box 327 (01569-0327)
PHONE....................................508 278-2422
William Dibenedetto, *CEO*
Robin Leclaire, *President*
EMP: 27 **EST:** 1982
SQ FT: 22,000
SALES (est): 3.8MM **Privately Held**
WEB: www.lampin.com
SIC: 3462 3873 3568 3566 Mfg Iron/Steel Forgings Mfg Watches/Clocks/Parts Mfg Power Transmsn Equip Mfg Speed Changer/Drives

(G-15924)
LENZE AMERICAS CORPORATION (DH)
630 Douglas St (01569-2001)
PHONE....................................508 278-9100
Ralph Rosas III, *President*
Ines Oppermann, *President*
Jane Watson, *Regional Mgr*
Daniel Repp, *Business Mgr*
John Uzzolino, *Business Mgr*
▲ **EMP:** 59
SALES: 95.9MM
SALES (corp-wide): 26.5MM **Privately Held**
SIC: 3566 Mfg Speed Changers/Drives
HQ: Lenze Se (Societas Europaea)
Hans-Lenze-Str. 1
Aerzen 31855
515 482-0

(G-15925)
LINCOLN ELECTRIC HOLDINGS INC
6 N Main St Ste 205 (01569-1871)
PHONE....................................508 366-7070
John Stropki, *President*
EMP: 275
SALES (corp-wide): 3B **Publicly Held**
SIC: 3548 Whol Industrial Supplies
PA: Lincoln Electric Holdings, Inc.
22801 Saint Clair Ave
Cleveland OH 44117
216 481-8100

(G-15926)
NORFOLK IRON WORKS INC
227 River Rd (01569-2246)
PHONE....................................508 482-9162
EMP: 3
SQ FT: 5,200
SALES (est): 543.9K **Privately Held**
SIC: 3446 Mfg Metal Stairs And Railings

(G-15927)
NORTHEAST TWR SVC
64 Acorn Dr (01569-2161)
PHONE....................................508 533-1620
Robert Hadden, *President*
EMP: 4
SALES (est): 270.5K **Privately Held**
SIC: 3585 Mfg Refrigeration/Heating Equipment

(G-15928)
PRECISION ENGINEERING INC
29 Industrial Dr (01569-2273)
P.O. Box 546 (01569-0546)
PHONE....................................508 278-5700
Liora K Stone, *President*
Peter F Stone, *Admin Sec*
EMP: 50
SQ FT: 40,000
SALES (est): 13.6MM **Privately Held**
WEB: www.precisionengineering.com
SIC: 3444 Mfg Sheet Metalwork

(G-15929)
PRECISION TAPE & LABEL CO INC
322 West St (01569-2007)
P.O. Box 566 (01569-0566)
PHONE....................................508 278-7700
N Secord-Voellings, *President*
Nicolle Secord-Voellings, *President*
Deborah Secord, *Vice Pres*
Voellings Nicolle, *VP Prdtn*
EMP: 10
SQ FT: 10,000
SALES (est): 1.8MM **Privately Held**
WEB: www.precisiontapeandlabel.com
SIC: 2672 Mfg Coated/Laminated Paper

(G-15930)
STRICKLAND K WHEELOCK
Also Called: Wheelock Textile
46 Pleasant St (01569-1854)
PHONE....................................508 265-2896
Strickland K Wheelock, *Owner*
EMP: 5 **EST:** 2010
SALES: 1.5MM **Privately Held**
SIC: 2299 Mfg Textile Goods

(G-15931)
THERMAL SEAL INSULATING GL INC
47 Industrial Dr (01569-2273)
PHONE....................................508 278-4243
Ann M Oliveira, *President*
EMP: 10
SQ FT: 4,000
SALES (est): 1.5MM **Privately Held**
SIC: 3211 Mfg Flat Glass

(G-15932)
TOWN OF UXBRIDGE
Also Called: Uxbridge Dpw Dept
80 River Rd (01569-2271)
PHONE..................................508 278-2887
William Buma, *Manager*
EMP: 4 **Privately Held**
WEB: www.uxbridgepolice.com
SIC: 3589 Mfg Service Industry Machinery
PA: Town Of Uxbridge
21 S Main St
Uxbridge MA 01569
508 278-8600

Vineyard Haven
Dukes County

(G-15933)
MARTHAS VINEYARD TIMES
30 Beach Rd (02568-5582)
P.O. Box 518 (02568-0518)
PHONE..................................508 693-6100
Doug Cabral, *President*
Chris Roberts, *Sales Staff*
Jim Osborn, *Manager*
EMP: 18
SALES (est): 990.2K **Privately Held**
WEB: www.mvtimes.com
SIC: 2711 Newspaper

(G-15934)
MIX
Also Called: Hometown Design Mix
4 Union St (02568)
PHONE..................................508 693-8240
EMP: 3
SALES: 75K **Privately Held**
SIC: 3273 Mfg Ready-Mixed Concrete

(G-15935)
TISBURY PRINTER INC
39 Lagoon Pond Rd (02568)
P.O. Box 1674 (02568-0909)
PHONE..................................508 693-4222
T Christopher Decker, *President*
Cornelia Hubbard Decker, *Treasurer*
Janet Holladay, *Officer*
EMP: 10
SQ FT: 2,000
SALES (est): 1.1MM **Privately Held**
WEB: www.tisburyprinter.com
SIC: 2752 Lithographic Commercial Printing

Waban
Middlesex County

(G-15936)
FIRST MAGAZINE LLC
49 Helene Rd (02468-1024)
PHONE..................................617 965-0504
Rudolph Peselman, *Principal*
EMP: 3
SALES (est): 133.3K **Privately Held**
SIC: 2721 Periodicals-Publishing/Printing

(G-15937)
KOAN BIOTHERAPEUTICS INC
15 Laura Rd (02468-2163)
PHONE..................................617 968-7882
Shadi Aryanpour, *President*
Mikyung Yu, *Principal*
EMP: 4
SALES (est): 172.3K **Privately Held**
SIC: 2836 Mfg Biological Products

(G-15938)
MATTHEW ASSOCIATES INC
92 Crofton Rd (02468-2115)
PHONE..................................617 965-6126
Howard Budovsky, *President*
Jaynee Budovshey, *Treasurer*
EMP: 3
SALES (est): 299.7K **Privately Held**
SIC: 3679 Mfg Electronic Components

(G-15939)
STATE HOUSE NEWS
37 Holly Rd (02468-1411)
PHONE..................................617 969-9175
EMP: 3
SALES (est): 125.2K **Privately Held**
SIC: 2711 Newspapers-Publishing/Printing

Wakefield
Middlesex County

(G-15940)
ALL CITY SCREEN PRINTING INC
Also Called: T Stop
983 Main St (01880-3927)
PHONE..................................781 665-0000
Rod Faulkner, *President*
Nancy Faulkner, *Treasurer*
EMP: 9
SQ FT: 4,500
SALES (est): 1.1MM **Privately Held**
SIC: 2759 2395 Commercial Printing Pleating/Stitching Services

(G-15941)
ANALYSIS TECH INC
Also Called: Anatech
6 Whittemore Ter (01880-2252)
P.O. Box 326 (01880-0726)
PHONE..................................781 224-1223
John W Sofia, *President*
EMP: 4
SQ FT: 3,000
SALES (est): 739.4K **Privately Held**
SIC: 3825 Mfg Electrical Measuring Instruments

(G-15942)
BARNARD DIE INC
Also Called: Barnard Water Jet Cutting
431 Water St Frnt (01880-3516)
PHONE..................................781 246-3117
Douglas Barnard, *President*
Gary Barnard, *Treasurer*
EMP: 10 **EST:** 1976
SQ FT: 4,200
SALES: 650K **Privately Held**
WEB: www.barnarddie.com
SIC: 3544 Mfg Steel Rule Cutting Dies

(G-15943)
BATTEN BROS INC
Also Called: Batten Sign
893 Main St (01880-3999)
PHONE..................................781 245-4800
Richard E Batten, *President*
Edward Batten, *Manager*
John Connors, *Manager*
EMP: 14
SQ FT: 8,000
SALES (est): 1.6MM **Privately Held**
WEB: www.battensign.com
SIC: 3993 Mfg Electric Signs

(G-15944)
BERTOLDO INC
Also Called: Bertoldo Engraving
43 Wiley St (01880-3518)
PHONE..................................781 324-9145
Nicolas Martone, *President*
Patricia T Martone, *Director*
EMP: 5
SALES: 320K **Privately Held**
SIC: 3479 3089 Engraving Of Metal & Plastic

(G-15945)
CARDIOVASCULAR INSTRUMENT
Also Called: Cinco Medical
102 Foundry St (01880-3204)
P.O. Box 188 (01880-0288)
PHONE..................................781 245-7799
A Edward Urkiewicz, *President*
Ann Urkiewicz, *Vice Pres*
EMP: 12
SQ FT: 20,000
SALES (est): 1.6MM **Privately Held**
WEB: www.cinco7799.com
SIC: 3845 Mfg Electromedical Apparatus

(G-15946)
COMMTANK CARES INC
84 New Salem St (01880-1906)
PHONE..................................781 224-1021
Kevin Hoag, *Principal*
EMP: 5 **EST:** 2013
SALES (est): 294.8K **Privately Held**
SIC: 1389 Oil/Gas Field Services

(G-15947)
D S GREENE CO INC
431 Water St (01880-3516)
P.O. Box 239 (01880-0339)
PHONE..................................781 245-2644
Donald S Greene Jr, *President*
Helen M Greene, *Clerk*
EMP: 8 **EST:** 1952
SQ FT: 15,000
SALES (est): 1MM **Privately Held**
SIC: 3599 Machine Shop

(G-15948)
DAVID CORPORATION (PA)
301 Edgewater Pl Ste 116 (01880-1249)
PHONE..................................781 587-3008
Mark Dorn, *President*
Kyle G Caswell, *Senior VP*
EMP: 50
SALES (est): 7MM **Privately Held**
SIC: 7372 5734 7373 Prepackaged Software Services Retails Computers And Software Computer Systems Design

(G-15949)
DAVINCI GROUP
6 Cowdry Ln (01880-1577)
PHONE..................................781 391-6009
Mark Birchem, *President*
Qinglin Zeng, *Software Dev*
EMP: 5 **EST:** 1995
SALES (est): 486K **Privately Held**
WEB: www.davincigroupinc.com
SIC: 7372 Prepackaged Software Services

(G-15950)
DIAMOND STL & FABRICATION LLC
80 New Salem St Ste 9 (01880-1900)
PHONE..................................781 245-3255
Jeffrey A Cook,
Jeffrey M Cook,
EMP: 3
SALES: 250K **Privately Held**
SIC: 3441 Structural Metal Fabrication

(G-15951)
E & J GALLO WINERY
401 Edgewater Pl Ste 195 (01880-6200)
PHONE..................................781 213-5050
Lisa Martel, *Manager*
EMP: 38
SALES (corp-wide): 2.4B **Privately Held**
SIC: 2084 Mfg Wines/Brandy/Spirits
PA: E. & J. Gallo Winery
600 Yosemite Blvd
Modesto CA 95354
209 341-3111

(G-15952)
FITZ MACHINE INC
4 Railroad Ave Ste 5 (01880-3225)
PHONE..................................781 245-5966
Kathleen Fitzgerald, *CEO*
Edward Fitzgerald, *Vice Pres*
EMP: 14 **EST:** 1994
SQ FT: 5,000
SALES: 1.4MM **Privately Held**
WEB: www.fitzmachine.com
SIC: 3599 Mfg Industrial Machinery

(G-15953)
FUEL GYM LLC
385 Main St (01880-3060)
P.O. Box 277 (01880-0577)
PHONE..................................781 315-8001
EMP: 3 **EST:** 2010
SALES (est): 213.1K **Privately Held**
SIC: 2869 Mfg Industrial Organic Chemicals

(G-15954)
HIGH VOLTAGE ENGINEERING CORP
401 Edgewater Pl Ste 680 (01880-6228)
PHONE..................................781 224-1001
Philip M Martineau, *CEO*
Clifford Press, *Ch of Bd*
Laurence S Levy, *Vice Pres*
Joseph McHugh, *CFO*
Charles A Schultz Jr, *CFO*
EMP: 18 **EST:** 1946
SQ FT: 5,350
SALES (est): 3.5MM **Privately Held**
SIC: 3825 3625 3826 3824 Mfg Industrial Instruments

(G-15955)
IMAGE POLYMERS COMPANY (DH)
384 Lowell St Ste 207 (01880-1986)
PHONE..................................978 296-0194
Akira Misawa, *President*
▲ **EMP:** 8
SALES (est): 3.8MM **Privately Held**
SIC: 2821 Mfg Plastic Materials/Resins
HQ: Mitsui Chemicals America, Inc.
800 Westchester Ave N607
Rye Brook NY 10573
914 253-0777

(G-15956)
INFORMATION BUILDERS INC
500 Edgewater Dr Ste 568 (01880-6222)
PHONE..................................781 224-7660
Bill Holland, *Sales Staff*
Scott Sutherland, *Branch Mgr*
Joe Walsh, *Manager*
EMP: 50
SALES (corp-wide): 232.8MM **Privately Held**
WEB: www.informationbuilders.com
SIC: 7372 Prepackaged Software Services
PA: Information Builders, Inc.
2 Penn Plz Fl 28
New York NY 10121
212 736-4433

(G-15957)
LLOYD LABS
24 Fitch Ct (01880-1932)
P.O. Box 256 (01880-0556)
PHONE..................................781 224-0083
Richard Funchion, *Principal*
EMP: 3
SALES (est): 187.2K **Privately Held**
SIC: 2834 Mfg Pharmaceutical Preparations

(G-15958)
MAIN INDUSTRIAL TIRES LTD (PA)
107 Audubon Rd Ste 2 (01880-1245)
PHONE..................................713 676-0251
Terry Lindbergh, *President*
Rachel Revilla, *Director*
▲ **EMP:** 17
SQ FT: 45,000
SALES (est): 27.9MM **Privately Held**
SIC: 3011 Mfg Tires/Inner Tubes

(G-15959)
MAINE RUBBER INTERNATIONAL
Also Called: Maine Tire
107 Audubon Rd Ste 2 (01880-1245)
PHONE..................................877 648-1949
Terry Lindbergh, *CEO*
Ken Hebert, *CFO*
EMP: 125 **EST:** 1951
SQ FT: 8,500
SALES (est): 12.1MM **Privately Held**
SIC: 3011 Mfg Tires/Inner Tubes
PA: Main Industrial Tires Ltd
107 Audubon Rd Ste 2
Wakefield MA 01880

(G-15960)
MARANATHA INDUSTRIES INC (PA)
Also Called: Industrial Chemical
24 Fitch Ct (01880-1932)
P.O. Box 256 (01880-0556)
PHONE..................................781 245-0038
Richard Funchion, *President*
▲ **EMP:** 10
SQ FT: 9,500
SALES (est): 2.5MM **Privately Held**
SIC: 2842 2899 Mfg Polish/Sanitation Goods Mfg Chemical Preparations

(G-15961)
METAL IMPROVEMENT COMPANY LLC
Also Called: Curtiss Wright Surface Tech
1 Nablus Rd (01880-1991)
PHONE..................................781 246-3848
Kelly Hoffman, *Branch Mgr*
EMP: 15
SALES (corp-wide): 2.4B **Publicly Held**
WEB: www.mic-houston.com
SIC: 3398 Metal Heat Treating
HQ: Metal Improvement Company, Llc
80 E Rte 4 Ste 310
Paramus NJ 07652
201 843-7800

(G-15962)
MYSTIC INDUSTRIES CORP
474 Main St (01880-3320)
P.O. Box 296 (01880-0696)
PHONE..................................781 245-1950
Joel K Marcus, *President*
Andrew Marcus, *Vice Pres*
Peter D Marcus, *Treasurer*
Peter Marcus, *Treasurer*
◆ **EMP:** 15
SQ FT: 31,000
SALES (est): 1.9MM **Privately Held**
WEB: www.mysticindustries.com
SIC: 3999 5199 Mfg Misc Products Whol Nondurable Goods

(G-15963)
NATGUN CORPORATION (HQ)
11 Teal Rd (01880-1223)
PHONE..................................781 224-5180
Charles E Crowley, *CEO*
Christine Delaney, *Senior Buyer*
Matt Nedella, *Project Engr*
Donald Paula, *CFO*
Joe Pappo, *Manager*
EMP: 190 **EST:** 1929
SQ FT: 13,800
SALES (est): 48MM **Privately Held**
WEB: www.natgun.com
SIC: 3795 Mfg Tanks/Tank Components

(G-15964)
NE CHOICE CABINET
85 Farm St (01880-3549)
PHONE..................................781 245-3800
Edward M Greeley, *CEO*
EMP: 4
SALES (est): 303.1K **Privately Held**
SIC: 2434 Mfg Wood Kitchen Cabinets

(G-15965)
NORTHEAST PLASTICS INC
5 Del Carmine St (01880-3402)
PHONE..................................781 245-5512
Jean Leach, *President*
Robert Shiebler, *Vice Pres*
EMP: 19
SQ FT: 9,000
SALES (est): 3.8MM **Privately Held**
WEB: www.northeastplastics.com
SIC: 3089 3544 Mfg Plastic Products Mfg Dies/Tools/Jigs/Fixtures

(G-15966)
NOVA INSTRUMENTS LLC (PA)
500 Edgewater Dr (01880-6229)
PHONE..................................781 897-1200
Jim Barbookles, *CEO*
Jean-Marc Muller, *President*
EMP: 7
SALES (est): 3.1MM **Privately Held**
SIC: 3826 Mfg Analytical Instruments

(G-15967)
PAUL K GUILLOW INC
40 New Salem St (01880-1979)
P.O. Box 229 (01880-0329)
PHONE..................................781 245-5255
Thomas G Barker, *President*
Thomas Barker, *Vice Pres*
Tom Maguire, *Plant Mgr*
James D Conniff, *Treasurer*
Alson G Smith, *Director*
▲ **EMP:** 50 **EST:** 1926
SQ FT: 65,475
SALES (est): 7.7MM **Privately Held**
WEB: www.guillow.com
SIC: 3944 Mfg Games/Toys

(G-15968)
PERSIMMON TECHNOLOGIES CORP
200 Harvard Mill Sq (01880-3238)
PHONE..................................781 587-0677
Michael W Pippins, *President*
Mark Hanna, *Vice Pres*
Martin Hosek, *Vice Pres*
Al Chin, *Senior Buyer*
Scott Wilkas, *Manager*
EMP: 11
SQ FT: 12,000
SALES (est): 4MM **Privately Held**
SIC: 3569 Mfg General Industrial Machinery
PA: Sumitomo Heavy Industries, Ltd.
2-1-1, Osaki
Shinagawa-Ku TKY 141-0
-

(G-15969)
PICIS CLINICAL SOLUTIONS INC (DH)
100 Quannapowitt Pkwy # 405
(01880-1319)
PHONE..................................336 397-5336
Jeff Bender, *CEO*
Mark D Crockett MD, *President*
Dan McCarthy, *President*
Steve Hammond, *Exec VP*
Marcus Perez, *Exec VP*
EMP: 180
SQ FT: 50,000
SALES (est): 63.6MM
SALES (corp-wide): 3B **Privately Held**
WEB: www.picis.com
SIC: 7372 7371 Prepackaged Software Services Custom Computer Programing
HQ: N. Harris Computer Corporation
1 Antares Dr Suite 400
Nepean ON K2E 8
613 226-5511

(G-15970)
PMWEB INC
1 Pope St (01880-2179)
PHONE..................................617 207-7080
Marc Jaude, *President*
Chris Wagner, *Vice Pres*
Michael Vernon, *Admin Sec*
EMP: 100 **EST:** 2006
SQ FT: 15,000
SALES: 10MM **Privately Held**
WEB: www.pmweb.com
SIC: 7372 7371 Prepackaged Software Services Custom Computer Programing

(G-15971)
PRECISE TIME AND FREQUENCY LLC
50l Audubon Rd (01880-1203)
PHONE..................................781 245-9090
Michael J Ferrantino Sr, *Mng Member*
EMP: 5
SQ FT: 4,000
SALES (est): 303.2K
SALES (corp-wide): 24.8MM **Publicly Held**
SIC: 3825 Manufactures Electrical Measuring Instruments
PA: Lgl Group, Inc.
2525 Shader Rd
Orlando FL 32804
407 298-2000

(G-15972)
PREMIUM SUND SLUTIONS AMER LLC (PA)
Also Called: Pss
301 Edgewater Pl Ste 100 (01880-1281)
PHONE..................................781 968-5511
Debra Ricker,
EMP: 13 **EST:** 2013
SALES (est): 22.5MM **Privately Held**
SIC: 3651 Mfg Home Audio/Video Equipment

(G-15973)
PROTOM INTERNATIONAL INC
500 Edgewater Dr Ste 522 (01880-6254)
PHONE..................................781 245-3964
Dan Raymond, *Vice Pres*
Emad Lababidi, *Branch Mgr*
EMP: 35 **Privately Held**
SIC: 3844 Mfg X-Ray Apparatus/Tubes
PA: Protom International, Inc.
610 Parker Sq
Flower Mound TX 75028
-

(G-15974)
SDL XYENTERPRISE LLC (PA)
201 Edgewater Dr Ste 225 (01880-6216)
PHONE..................................781 756-4400
Dominic Lavelle, *CEO*
Lori Brittain, *Director*
Kevin Keating, *Director*
EMP: 145
SQ FT: 20,000
SALES (est): 12.5MM **Privately Held**
WEB: www.xyenterprise.com
SIC: 7372 7378 7371 Computer Maintenance/Repair Custom Computer Programing Prepackaged Software Services

(G-15975)
SECURITY DEVICES INTL INC
107 Audubon Rd Ste 201 (01880-1245)
PHONE..................................905 582-6402
Bryan Ganz, *Ch of Bd*
Rakesh Malhotra, *Treasurer*
Jim Dunfey, *Controller*
Lisa Klein,
EMP: 4
SALES: 250.2K **Privately Held**
SIC: 3699 Mfg Electrical Equipment/Supplies

(G-15976)
SPEC LINES
4 Railroad Ave Ste 2 (01880-3225)
PHONE..................................781 245-0044
Frank Forrant, *President*
Mark Forrant, *President*
Paul Mellor, *Treasurer*
EMP: 5
SALES (est): 510K **Privately Held**
WEB: www.speclines.net
SIC: 3646 Mfg Industrial & Institutional Electrical Lighting Equipment

(G-15977)
STANDEX INTERNATIONAL CORP
Innovent Standex Engrv Group
107 Audubon Rd (01880-1266)
PHONE..................................978 538-0808
Casper Prong, *Branch Mgr*
EMP: 5
SALES (corp-wide): 791.5MM **Publicly Held**
SIC: 3545 Mfg Machine Tool Accessories
PA: Standex International Corporation
11 Keewaydin Dr Ste 300
Salem NH 03079
603 893-9701

(G-15978)
STEM SOLUTIONS LLC
Also Called: Labfitout
301 Edgewater Pl Ste 100 (01880-1281)
P.O. Box 259 (01880-0459)
PHONE..................................617 826-6111
Lisa Stpeter, *President*
Kathleen Broderick, *President*
James Broderick, *Vice Pres*
EMP: 9
SALES (est): 9MM **Privately Held**
SIC: 3821 Mfg Lab Apparatus/Furniture

(G-15979)
SWEET CREATIONS
23 Water St Ste R (01880-3043)
PHONE..................................781 246-0836
Donald Tyler, *Owner*
EMP: 20
SQ FT: 2,800
SALES: 590K **Privately Held**
SIC: 2051 2052 Whol And Ret Bakery

(G-15980)
TA INSTRUMENTS-WATERS LLC (PA)
Also Called: Lasercomp Ta
107 Audubon Rd Ste 140 (01880-1245)
PHONE..................................781 233-1717
Andrzej Brzezinski, *President*
Eva Rudowska, *Clerk*
EMP: 10
SALES (est): 1.5MM **Privately Held**
WEB: www.lasercomp.com
SIC: 3826 Mfg Analytical Instruments

(G-15981)
THRIVE BIOSCIENCE INC
11 Audubon Rd (01880-1256)
PHONE..................................978 720-8048
Gary Magnant, *CEO*
Brian Foley, *Vice Pres*
Tom Farb, *CFO*
Alan Blanchard, *Officer*
EMP: 8
SQ FT: 7,252
SALES (est): 1.3MM **Privately Held**
SIC: 3826 Mfg Analytical Instruments

(G-15982)
VICTOR MICROWAVE INC
38 W Water St (01880-2999)
PHONE..................................781 245-4472
Robert Parks, *President*
EMP: 12
SQ FT: 16,000
SALES (est): 2MM **Privately Held**
SIC: 3679 3825 3663 Mfg Microwave Components

(G-15983)
WAKEFIELD ITEM CO
Also Called: Wakefield Daily Item
26 Albion St (01880-2803)
PHONE..................................781 245-0080
Robert P Dolbeare, *President*
◆ **EMP:** 35 **EST:** 1922
SQ FT: 4,000
SALES (est): 2MM **Privately Held**
WEB: www.wakefielditem.com
SIC: 2711 2752 Newspapers-Publishing/Printing Lithographic Commercial Printing

(G-15984)
WESTROCK CP LLC
Also Called: Smurfit Stone
365 Audubon Rd (01880-1204)
PHONE..................................781 245-8600
Donald Roy, *Branch Mgr*
EMP: 100
SQ FT: 144,000
SALES (corp-wide): 18.2B **Publicly Held**
WEB: www.jefferson-smurfit.com
SIC: 2653 Mfg Corrugated/Solid Fiber Boxes
HQ: Westrock Cp, Llc
1000 Abernathy Rd
Atlanta GA 30328
-

(G-15985)
WILLIAM BLANCHARD CO INC
Also Called: Blanchard Awnings
486 Main St (01880-3320)
PHONE..................................781 245-8050
Allen Young, *President*
Colin Young, *Treasurer*
Thomas Young, *Clerk*
EMP: 10 **EST:** 1915
SQ FT: 6,000
SALES (est): 1MM **Privately Held**
SIC: 2394 Mfg Canvas/Related Products

Walpole
Norfolk County

(G-15986)
3 PLAY INC (PA)
Also Called: Eurosled
1600 Providence Hwy Ste 1 (02081-2551)
PHONE..................................781 205-4820
Marc P Hauser, *President*
◆ **EMP:** 9
SALES (est): 1.1MM **Privately Held**
SIC: 3949 5941 Mfg Sporting/Athletic Goods Ret Sporting Goods/Bicycles

(G-15987)
ACUMENTRICS RUPS LLC
10 Walpole Park S (02081-2523)
PHONE..................................617 932-7877
John Cerulli, *CEO*
Bill Owens, *VP Engrg*
Tyler Dawbin, *Technical Staff*

▲ = Import ▼=Export
◆ =Import/Export

EMP: 30
SALES (est): 5MM Privately Held
SIC: 3629 3679 Mfg Elec Indstl Equip Mfg Elec Components

(G-15988)
ATREX ENERGY INC (PA)
19 Walpole Park S (02081-2570)
PHONE....781 461-8251
Gary Simon, *CEO*
Michael J Gagnon, *Vice Pres*
Duoc Nguyen, *Mfg Spvr*
Andy Barnett, *Engineer*
Ed Portmann, *Engineer*
▲ EMP: 45
SQ FT: 40,000
SALES (est): 13MM Privately Held
WEB: www.acumentrics.com
SIC: 3629 3612 7372 3677 Mfg Elec Indstl Equip Mfg Transformers Prepackaged Software Svc Mfg Elec Coil/Transfrmrs

(G-15989)
BAKER HGHES OLFLD OPRTIONS LLC
1600 Providence Hwy Ste 4 (02081-2551)
PHONE....508 668-0400
Tim Davis, *President*
EMP: 200
SALES (corp-wide): 22.8B Publicly Held
WEB: www.bot.bhi-net.com
SIC: 1389 Oil/Gas Field Services
HQ: Baker Hughes Oilfield Operations Llc
17021 Aldine Westfield Rd
Houston TX 77073
713 879-1000

(G-15990)
BOSTON TRAILER MANUFACTURING
1 Production Rd (02081-1310)
PHONE....508 668-2242
Roland A Garrant, *President*
Rocco Taddeo, *Treasurer*
EMP: 42
SQ FT: 16,000
SALES (est): 2MM Privately Held
SIC: 3715 7539 7538 3792 Mfg Truck Trailers Automotive Repair General Auto Repair Mfg Trailers/Campers Mfg Truck/Bus Bodies

(G-15991)
CNE MACHINE COMPANY
2000 Main St Ste 7 (02081-1426)
PHONE....508 668-4110
Desmond Quinn, *Owner*
EMP: 3
SALES (est): 247.2K Privately Held
SIC: 3599 Mfg Industrial Machinery

(G-15992)
GOLD WATER TECHNOLOGY INC
25 Walpole Park S (02081-2522)
P.O. Box 827, Westwood (02090-0827)
PHONE....781 551-3590
Judy Lo, *President*
Frank Lo, *Prdtn Mgr*
EMP: 9
SALES (est): 737.3K Privately Held
WEB: www.goldwater.com
SIC: 3944 Mfg Games/Toys

(G-15993)
HIGH VOLTAGE MAINTENANCE CORP
Also Called: Vertiv
24 Walpole Park S Ste 3 (02081-2541)
PHONE....508 668-9205
Jeffrey Freelove, *Manager*
EMP: 12
SALES (corp-wide): 2.9B Privately Held
WEB: www.hvmcorp.com
SIC: 3823 Mfg Process Control Instruments
HQ: High Voltage Maintenance Corporation
5100 Energy Dr
Dayton OH 45414
937 278-0811

(G-15994)
INKIFY LLC
25 Walpole Park S Ste 8 (02081-2522)
PHONE....617 304-6642
Carlos A Lobato, *Principal*
EMP: 3 EST: 2016
SALES (est): 301.6K Privately Held
SIC: 2759 Commercial Printing

(G-15995)
ISLAND DESSERTS LLC
24 Walpole Park S Ste 1 (02081-2541)
PHONE....508 660-2200
Robert F Leavitt,
EMP: 65
SALES (est): 7.7MM Privately Held
SIC: 2099 Mfg Food Preparations

(G-15996)
J & M CABINET SHOP INC
2050 Main St (02081-1413)
PHONE....508 660-6660
Morton Balduf, *President*
Paul G Patterson, *Vice Pres*
EMP: 16 EST: 1974
SQ FT: 8,000
SALES (est): 1.6MM Privately Held
SIC: 2434 Mfg Wooden & Formica Kitchen Cabinets & Countertops

(G-15997)
KINETIC FUEL LLC
31 Lavender Ln (02081-3763)
PHONE....508 668-8278
Julie Nicoletti, *Principal*
EMP: 4
SALES (est): 394.5K Privately Held
SIC: 2869 Mfg Industrial Organic Chemicals

(G-15998)
KW STEEL STRUCTURES LLC
50 School St (02081-3532)
P.O. Box 253, Canton (02021-0253)
PHONE....857 342-7838
Nancy Webster, *Mng Member*
EMP: 6 EST: 2013
SALES (est): 958.5K Privately Held
SIC: 3441 Structural Metal Fabrication

(G-15999)
M V MASON ELEC INC
442 High Plain St (02081-4250)
PHONE....508 668-6200
Matthew V Dimarco, *Principal*
EMP: 3
SALES (est): 207.3K Privately Held
SIC: 3677 Mfg Electronic Coils/Transformers

(G-16000)
MASS MACHINE INC
24 Walpole Park S Ste 14 (02081-2541)
PHONE....781 467-3550
Peter Watson, *President*
EMP: 14
SQ FT: 8,000
SALES (est): 1.8MM Privately Held
SIC: 3599 Mfg Industrial Machinery

(G-16001)
MASSACHUSETTS MACHINE WORKS
24 Walpole Park S Ste 14 (02081-2541)
PHONE....781 467-3550
Leroy Seamore, *President*
Peter Watson, *Human Res Mgr*
EMP: 17
SALES: 1MM Privately Held
WEB: www.massmachine.com
SIC: 3599 Mfg Industrial Machinery

(G-16002)
MICREX CORPORATION
17 Industrial Rd (02081-1304)
PHONE....508 660-1900
Richard C Walton, *Ch of Bd*
Peter Smith, *Vice Pres*
Susan Olsen Ms, *Admin Sec*
▲ EMP: 16
SQ FT: 20,000
SALES (est): 2.8MM Privately Held
WEB: www.micrex.com
SIC: 3554 3552 Mfg Paper Industrial Machinery Mfg Textile Machinery

(G-16003)
MOHAWK INDUSTRIES INC
15 Walpole Park S Ste 8 (02081-2561)
PHONE....508 660-8935
Marty Smith, *Branch Mgr*
EMP: 156
SALES (corp-wide): 9.9B Publicly Held
WEB: www.mohawkind.com
SIC: 2273 Mfg Carpets/Rugs
PA: Mohawk Industries, Inc.
160 S Industrial Blvd
Calhoun GA 30701
706 629-7721

(G-16004)
MV MASON ELECTRONICS INC
Also Called: A F I Med Electronic Eqp Repai
486 High Plain St (02081-4250)
PHONE....508 668-6200
Matthew De Marco, *President*
Millicent Di Marco, *Clerk*
EMP: 3 EST: 1979
SQ FT: 1,700
SALES (est): 390.4K Privately Held
WEB: www.mvmason.com
SIC: 3677 Mfg Electronic Coils/Transformers

(G-16005)
NORTH AMRCN FLTRATION MASS INC
Also Called: Mass Transfer Systems
23 Walpole Park S Ste 12 (02081-2559)
PHONE....508 660-9016
Dave Painter, *President*
Steven Friedman, *Vice Pres*
◆ EMP: 16 EST: 1997
SQ FT: 20,000
SALES (est): 3.4MM Privately Held
WEB: www.sanborntechnologies.com
SIC: 3589 Mfg Service Industry Machinery
PA: North American Filtration Inc
Old Augusta Rd Hwy 70
Denmark SC 29042

(G-16006)
PEC DETAILING CO INC
33 Delcor Dr (02081-3343)
PHONE....508 660-8954
Paul E Crockett, *President*
Mary Jean Crockett, *Corp Secy*
EMP: 4
SQ FT: 900
SALES (est): 460.6K Privately Held
SIC: 3441 8711 Structural Metal Fabrication Engineering Services

(G-16007)
PRIDEMAXX FINE WOOD CABINETRY
1034 East St (02081-2984)
PHONE....508 527-8700
EMP: 4 EST: 2012
SALES (est): 318.9K Privately Held
SIC: 2434 Mfg Wood Kitchen Cabinets

(G-16008)
RAYMOND THIBAULT
155 N Pough Rd (02081)
PHONE....508 281-5500
Raymond Thibault, *Owner*
EMP: 3
SALES (est): 156.3K Privately Held
SIC: 3621 Mfg Motors/Generators

(G-16009)
ROLLS-ROYCE MARINE NORTH AMER (DH)
110 Norfolk St (02081-1704)
PHONE....508 668-9610
Don Roussinos, *President*
Walter Roy, *Purchasing*
Steven Lacey, *Engineer*
Nate Mills, *Engineer*
Brian Dore, *Human Resources*
◆ EMP: 150
SQ FT: 18,000
SALES (est): 73.2MM
SALES (corp-wide): 20.7B Privately Held
SIC: 3599 3446 3429 Mfg Industrial Machinery Mfg Architectural Metalwork Mfg Hardware
HQ: Rolls-Royce North America Holdings Inc.
1875 Explorer St Ste 200
Reston VA 20190
703 834-1700

(G-16010)
S M LORUSSO & SONS INC (PA)
Also Called: Wrentham Quarry Div
331 West St (02081-1608)
P.O. Box 230 (02081-0230)
PHONE....508 668-2600
Antonio J Lorusso Jr, *President*
James Lorusso, *Vice Pres*
Samuel Lorusso, *Vice Pres*
Joseph Stafford, *Vice Pres*
Steve Stafford, *Vice Pres*
EMP: 30 EST: 1938
SQ FT: 4,400
SALES (est): 29.4MM Privately Held
SIC: 1442 Construction Sand/Gravel

(G-16011)
SHAWMUT ENGINEERING CO
87 West St (02081-1819)
PHONE....508 850-9500
Kendall Nygren, *President*
Lindsey Nygren, *Co-Owner*
EMP: 10 EST: 1920
SQ FT: 23,000
SALES: 620K Privately Held
SIC: 3469 Mfg Metal Stampings

(G-16012)
SOFTMEDIA INC
27 Crane Rd (02081-4353)
PHONE....978 528-3266
Dennis M Riley, *President*
EMP: 4
SALES: 400K Privately Held
WEB: www.softmediainc.com
SIC: 7372 Software Programming Services

(G-16013)
TAC LIFE SYSTEMS LLC
44 Heritage Dr (02081-2240)
PHONE....617 719-8797
Peter Giannopoulos, *Principal*
Jash Delisle, *Principal*
Leo Manning, *Principal*
Frank Noguiera, *Principal*
EMP: 4
SALES (est): 208.5K Privately Held
SIC: 2821 Mfg Plastic Materials/Resins

(G-16014)
TOOLING RESEARCH INC (PA)
Also Called: Valcom Division
81 Diamond St (02081-3495)
P.O. Box 306 (02081-0306)
PHONE....508 668-1950
Milton F Florest Jr, *President*
Ann E Florest, *Vice Pres*
Ann Florest, *Vice Pres*
EMP: 12
SQ FT: 15,000
SALES (est): 1.7MM Privately Held
WEB: www.tooling-research.com
SIC: 3555 3565 Contract Mfg & Special Machine Designs

(G-16015)
U-HAUL CO OF MASSACHUSETTS
1 Production Rd (02081-1310)
PHONE....508 668-2242
Rocco Taddeo, *Treasurer*
Don Miller, *Manager*
EMP: 12
SALES (corp-wide): 3.7B Publicly Held
SIC: 3715 7539 7538 7513 Mfg Truck Trailers Automotive Repair General Auto Repair Truck Rental/Leasing
HQ: U-Haul Co Of Massachusetts Inc
151 Linwood St
Somerville MA

(G-16016)
US STANDARD BRANDS INC
44 Heritage Dr (02081-2240)
PHONE....617 719-8796
Georgia Giannopoulos, *President*
EMP: 4

SALES: 50K **Privately Held**
SIC: 3999 5999 Mfg Misc Products Ret Misc Merchandise

(G-16017)
WALPOLE PRINT WORKS INC
430 High Plain St (02081-4263)
PHONE..................................508 668-0247
Thomas Scotti, *President*
EMP: 5
SQ FT: 1,400
SALES (est): 430K **Privately Held**
SIC: 2752 Lithographic Commercial Printing

(G-16018)
WONDER TABLITZ CORPORATION
4 Walpole Park S Ste 3 (02081-2562)
PHONE..................................508 660-0011
Andrew Schultz, *President*
William Schultz, *Treasurer*
EMP: 5
SQ FT: 4,000
SALES (est): 490.1K **Privately Held**
WEB: www.wondertablitz.com
SIC: 2842 Mfg Polish/Sanitation Goods

Waltham
Middlesex County

(G-16019)
A B & D MACHINING INC
Also Called: Comptronics
56 Clematis Ave (02453-7013)
PHONE..................................781 891-4120
Ralph Moccia, *President*
Diane Moccia, *Vice Pres*
Bethany Moccia, *Treasurer*
EMP: 6 **EST:** 1982
SQ FT: 3,800
SALES (est): 549.9K **Privately Held**
SIC: 3599 Mfg Industrial Machinery

(G-16020)
A123 SYSTEMS LLC
200 West St (02451-1121)
PHONE..................................617 778-5700
Sam Trinch, *Exec VP*
Todd McAllister, *Opers Staff*
Jaime Acevedo, *Engineer*
Jerry Amey, *Engineer*
Rod Bustamante, *Engineer*
EMP: 108
SALES (corp-wide): 10.8MM **Privately Held**
SIC: 3691 5063 Mfg Storage Batteries Whol Electrical Equipment
HQ: A123 Systems Llc
27101 Cabaret Dr
Novi MI 48377
248 412-9249

(G-16021)
ACCUFAB INC
81 Rumford Ave (02453-3846)
PHONE..................................781 894-5737
James Hagberg, *President*
George Hagberg, *CFO*
EMP: 3
SQ FT: 8,000
SALES: 500K **Privately Held**
SIC: 3444 Mfg Sheet Metalwork

(G-16022)
ACKLES STEEL & IRON COMPANY
12 Sun St (02453-4102)
P.O. Box 540363 (02454-0363)
PHONE..................................781 893-6818
William Ackles, *President*
Richard Ackles, *President*
Andrew Ackles, *Vice Pres*
William P Ackles, *Vice Pres*
EMP: 16
SQ FT: 5,500
SALES: 5.5MM **Privately Held**
WEB: www.acklessteel.com
SIC: 3312 2431 Blast Furnace-Steel Works Mfg Millwork

(G-16023)
ACTON METAL PROCESSING CORP
41 Athletic Field Rd (02451-4617)
P.O. Box 540671 (02454-0671)
PHONE..................................781 893-5890
Ruppert Flagg, *President*
Todd Walsh, *Vice Pres*
EMP: 28
SQ FT: 15,400
SALES (est): 2.9MM **Privately Held**
SIC: 3471 Plating/Polishing Service

(G-16024)
ACTRONICS INCORPORATED
166 Bear Hill Rd (02451-1073)
PHONE..................................781 890-7030
Paul Boudreau, *Vice Pres*
EMP: 13
SQ FT: 10,000
SALES: 2MM **Privately Held**
WEB: www.actronics.com
SIC: 3724 3728 Aircraft Parts Manufacturing

(G-16025)
AEROSPACE FABRICATORS INC
116 Harvard St (02453-4112)
P.O. Box 540574 (02454-0574)
PHONE..................................781 899-4535
Raymond T Richard, *President*
Mark Richard, *Vice Pres*
Concetta Richard, *Clerk*
EMP: 8
SQ FT: 6,500
SALES (est): 1.3MM **Privately Held**
SIC: 3444 Mfg Sheet Metalwork

(G-16026)
AGGREGATE INDS - NORTHEAST REG
537 South St Rear (02453-2720)
P.O. Box 39, Burlington (01803-0062)
PHONE..................................781 893-7562
EMP: 15
SALES (corp-wide): 26.4B **Privately Held**
SIC: 3273 5032 Mfg Ready-Mixed Concrete Whol Brick/Stone Material
HQ: Aggregate Industries - Northeast Region, Inc
1715 Brdwy
Saugus MA 01906
781 941-7200

(G-16027)
ALBANY MOLECULAR RESEARCH INC
201 Jones Rd Ste 300 (02451-1618)
PHONE..................................781 672-4530
Elizabeth Jean Sanders, *President*
EMP: 10
SALES (corp-wide): 137.4MM **Privately Held**
SIC: 2833 Mfg Medicinal/Botanical Products
HQ: Albany Molecular Research, Inc.
26 Corporate Cir
Albany NY 12203

(G-16028)
ALERE US HOLDINGS LLC
51 Sawyer Rd (02453-3448)
PHONE..................................781 647-3900
David A Teitel, *President*
EMP: 4
SALES (est): 286K
SALES (corp-wide): 30.5B **Publicly Held**
SIC: 2835 Mfg Diagnostic Substances
HQ: Alere Inc.
51 Sawyer Rd Ste 200
Waltham MA 02453
781 647-3900

(G-16029)
ALKERMES INC (HQ)
852 Winter St (02451-1420)
PHONE..................................781 609-6000
Richard Pops, *CEO*
Glen Wheeler, *Principal*
Dennis Bucceri, *Vice Pres*
Rebecca Peterson, *Vice Pres*
Sal Pignio, *Vice Pres*
▲ **EMP:** 277
SALES (est): 177.7MM **Privately Held**
WEB: www.alkermes.com
SIC: 2834 8731 Pharmaceutical Preparations Biotechnical Commercial Research Services

(G-16030)
ALKERMES CNTRLLED THERAPEUTICS
Also Called: Acti
852 Winter St (02451-1420)
PHONE..................................877 706-0510
Richard F Pops, *CEO*
Michael A Wall, *Ch of Bd*
David Broecker, *President*
James Andolsek, *Business Mgr*
Dennis Britt, *Business Mgr*
EMP: 66
SQ FT: 90,000
SALES (est): 11.1MM **Privately Held**
WEB: www.alkermes.com
SIC: 2834 Mfg Pharmaceutical Preparations
HQ: Alkermes, Inc.
852 Winter St
Waltham MA 02451
781 609-6000

(G-16031)
ALLURE SECURITY TECHNOLOGY INC
200 5th Ave Ste 4010 (02451-8758)
P.O. Box 470, New York NY (10024-0470)
PHONE..................................877 669-8883
Salvatore Stolfo, *Ch of Bd*
Salvatore J Stolfo, *President*
EMP: 4
SALES (est): 265.7K **Privately Held**
SIC: 7372 Prepackaged Software Services

(G-16032)
AMAG PHARMACEUTICALS INC (PA)
1100 Winter St (02451-1427)
PHONE..................................617 498-3300
Gino Santini, *Ch of Bd*
Ted Myles, *COO*
Elizabeth Bolgiano, *Exec VP*
J Alan Butcher, *Exec VP*
Joseph D Vittiglio, *Exec VP*
EMP: 257
SALES: 474MM **Publicly Held**
WEB: www.advancedmagnetics.com
SIC: 2834 2835 Pharmaceutical Preparations

(G-16033)
ANDREW ALLIANCE USA INC
135 Beaver St Ste 402 (02452-8463)
PHONE..................................617 797-9071
Piero Zucchelli, *CEO*
EMP: 3
SALES (est): 328.1K **Privately Held**
SIC: 3821 Mfg Lab Apparatus/Furniture

(G-16034)
APELLIS PHARMACEUTICALS INC (PA)
100 5th Ave (02451-8703)
PHONE..................................617 977-5700
Gerald Chan, *Ch of Bd*
Cedric Francois, *President*
Pascal Deschatelets, *COO*
Thomas Lackner, *Senior VP*
Ahmad Sadr, *Senior VP*
EMP: 38
SQ FT: 7,125
SALES (est): 18.5MM **Publicly Held**
SIC: 2834 Pharmaceutical Preparation

(G-16035)
APOGENT TECHNOLOGIES INC
81 Wyman St (02451-1223)
PHONE..................................781 622-1300
Seth H Hoogasian, *President*
Anthony Smith, *Treasurer*
EMP: 7200
SALES (est): 196MM
SALES (corp-wide): 24.3B **Publicly Held**
SIC: 3229 3843 3821 Mfg Pressed/Blown Glass Mfg Dental Equip/Supply
HQ: Fisher Scientific International Llc
81 Wyman St
Waltham MA 02451
781 622-1000

(G-16036)
ARM INC
100 5th Ave Fl 5 (02451-8727)
PHONE..................................978 264-7300
EMP: 4 **Privately Held**
SIC: 3674 Mfg Semiconductors/Related Devices
HQ: Arm, Inc.
150 Rose Orchard Way
San Jose CA 95134

(G-16037)
ARRAKIS THERAPEUTICS INC
830 Winter St Ste 1 (02451-1477)
PHONE..................................617 913-0348
Michael Gilman, *CEO*
Katrine Bosley, *Ch of Bd*
James Barsoum, *Senior VP*
Gnanasambandam Kumaravel, *Vice Pres*
Heather Lounsbury, *Vice Pres*
EMP: 6
SALES (est): 276.1K **Privately Held**
SIC: 2899 Mfg Chemical Preparations

(G-16038)
ARVEST PRESS INC
252r Calvary St (02453-8366)
PHONE..................................781 894-4844
Mayda Chaprazian, *President*
Alex Kouchakdjian, *President*
Harout Chaprazian, *Treasurer*
EMP: 6 **EST:** 1983
SQ FT: 8,000
SALES: 1.4MM **Privately Held**
WEB: www.arvestpress.com
SIC: 2752 Lithographic Commercial Printing

(G-16039)
AUTOMEC INC
82 Calvary St (02453-5918)
PHONE..................................781 893-3403
James Ofria, *President*
Rick Hersey, *Prdtn Mgr*
Linda Jones, *Treasurer*
Doug Flynn, *Cust Mgr*
Betty Panaggio, *Office Mgr*
◆ **EMP:** 24
SALES (est): 4MM **Privately Held**
WEB: www.automec.com
SIC: 3549 3545 Mfg Metalworking Machinery & Machine Tool Accessories

(G-16040)
AVEDRO INC (HQ)
201 Jones Rd (02451-1600)
PHONE..................................781 768-3400
Reza Zadno, *President*
Desmond Adler, *Vice Pres*
John Frantzis, *Vice Pres*
Chris Cocomazzi, *Engineer*
Thomas E Griffin, *CFO*
▼ **EMP:** 93
SQ FT: 27,000
SALES: 27.6MM
SALES (corp-wide): 181.2MM **Publicly Held**
SIC: 2834 5048 3841 Mfg Pharmaceutical Preparations Whol Ophthalmic Goods Mfg Surgical/Medical Instruments
PA: Glaukos Corporation
229 Avenida Fabricante
San Clemente CA 92672
949 367-9600

(G-16041)
BATTERY VENTURES VI LP
930 Winter St Ste 2500 (02451-1516)
PHONE..................................781 577-1000
Cornel Faucher, *Partner*
Matt Niehaus, *Partner*
Neeraj Agrawal, *General Ptnr*
Michael Brown, *General Ptnr*
Tom Crotty, *General Ptnr*
EMP: 750
SALES (est): 28.5MM **Privately Held**
SIC: 7372 Prepackaged Software Services

(G-16042)
BBC PRINTING AND PRODUCTS INC
21 Hill Rd (02451-1715)
PHONE..................................781 647-4646
Vasken Basmajian, *President*
Sheila Basmajian, *Clerk*

▲ = Import ▼=Export
◆ =Import/Export

EMP: 8
SQ FT: 22,000
SALES: 1MM **Privately Held**
WEB: www.bbcprintingproducts.com
SIC: 2679 2759 2752 Mfg Paperboard Menu Covers & Prints Menus & Full Service Printer

(G-16043)
BEAVER-VISITEC INTL HOLDINGS (PA)
411 Waverley Oaks Rd # 229 (02452-8422)
PHONE....................................847 739-3219
Tom Kapfer, *President*
Meghan Lutz, *Sales Staff*
EMP: 12
SALES (est): 28.4MM **Privately Held**
SIC: 3841 Ophthalmic Instrument And Apparatus Manufacture

(G-16044)
BEAVER-VISITEC INTL INC (HQ)
500 Totten Pond Rd # 500 (02451-1924)
PHONE....................................781 906-8080
Dana G Mead Jr, *President*
Ray Cusano, *Engineer*
Shervin Korangy, *CFO*
Raymond Dohr, *Sales Staff*
Meghan Lutz, *Sales Staff*
▲ EMP: 200 EST: 1932
SQ FT: 63,000
SALES (est): 43.7MM
SALES (corp-wide): 243.1MM **Privately Held**
SIC: 3841 3851 Mfg Surgical/Medical Instruments Mfg Ophthalmic Goods
PA: Roundtable Healthcare Partners, Lp
272 E Deerpath Ste 350
Lake Forest IL 60045
847 739-3200

(G-16045)
BEAVER-VISITEC INTL INC
411 Waverley Oaks Rd # 229 (02452-8422)
PHONE....................................847 739-3219
Tom Kapfer, *President*
EMP: 8
SALES (corp-wide): 243.1MM **Privately Held**
SIC: 3841 Mfg Surgical/Medical Instruments
HQ: Beaver-Visitec International, Inc.
500 Totten Pond Rd # 500
Waltham MA 02451
781 906-8080

(G-16046)
BENNETT GODING & COOPER INC
738 Main St (02451-0616)
PHONE....................................978 682-8868
Michael A Cooper, *Principal*
EMP: 3
SALES (est): 280.6K **Privately Held**
SIC: 2295 Mfg Coated Fabrics

(G-16047)
BIGTINCAN MOBILE PTY LTD
260 Charles St Ste 101 (02453-3529)
PHONE....................................617 981-7557
Patrick Welch, *Chief Mktg Ofcr*
Geoff Cohen, *Exec Dir*
EMP: 4 **Privately Held**
SIC: 7372 Prepackaged Software Services
HQ: Bigtincan Mobile Pty Ltd
L 20 320 Pitt St
Sydney NSW 2000

(G-16048)
BIOVERATIV INC (DH)
225 2nd Ave (02451-1122)
PHONE....................................781 663-4400
John G Cox, *CEO*
Theron Harpole, *Facilities Mgr*
Sarah Sturtevant, *Research*
Benjamin Vieira, *Research*
Rick Bodmer, *Engineer*
EMP: 56 EST: 2016
SQ FT: 125,000
SALES: 1.1B **Privately Held**
SIC: 2834 Manufactures Pharmaceutical Preparations
HQ: Blink Acquisition Corp.
225 2nd Ave
Waltham MA 02451
781 663-4400

(G-16049)
BLUESNAP INC (PA)
800 South St Ste 640 (02453-1492)
PHONE....................................781 790-5013
Ralph Dangelmaier, *President*
Jeff Coppolo, *Vice Pres*
Kimberly Rowell, *Marketing Staff*
EMP: 25
SQ FT: 7,000
SALES: 19.6MM **Privately Held**
SIC: 7372 Prepackaged Software Services

(G-16050)
BOSTON TAG AND LABEL INC
296 Newton St Ste 4 (02453-0458)
PHONE....................................781 893-9080
Peter Kates, *President*
EMP: 3
SQ FT: 700
SALES: 750K **Privately Held**
WEB: www.bostontag.com
SIC: 2759 Commercial Printing

(G-16051)
BOYNTON MACHINE COMPANY INC
101 Clematis Ave Ste 6 (02453-7035)
PHONE....................................781 899-9900
Mark Boynton, *President*
EMP: 50
SQ FT: 3,000
SALES (est): 7.5MM **Privately Held**
WEB: www.houmachamber.com
SIC: 3599 Machine Shop Jobbing & Repair

(G-16052)
BROOKLINE PRINT CENTER
85 River St Ste 7 (02453-8352)
PHONE....................................617 926-0300
Daniel Winter, *Owner*
EMP: 5
SALES (est): 369.6K **Privately Held**
WEB: www.brooklineprintcenter.com
SIC: 2752 Lithographic Commercial Printing

(G-16053)
BRUNO DIDUCA
Also Called: Alpha Press
57 Harvard St (02453-4280)
PHONE....................................781 894-5300
Bruno Diduca, *Owner*
Bruno Di Duca, *Manager*
EMP: 9
SQ FT: 7,000
SALES (est): 690.6K **Privately Held**
WEB: www.alphapress.com
SIC: 2752 6531 Commercial Printing, Lithographic

(G-16054)
C & J CLARK AMERICA INC (DH)
Also Called: Bostonian Shoe Co
60 Tower Rd (02451-1022)
PHONE....................................617 964-1222
Gary Champion, *President*
Chris Caswell, *Vice Pres*
Sharon Schuler, *Vice Pres*
Isaac Otero, *Store Mgr*
Maureen Grady, *Treasurer*
◆ EMP: 330 EST: 1977
SQ FT: 30,000
SALES (est): 685.1MM **Privately Held**
WEB: www.clarks.com
SIC: 3143 5139 5661 Mfg Men's Footwear Whol Footwear Ret Shoes
HQ: Clarks Americas Inc.
60 Tower Rd
Waltham MA 02451
617 796-5000

(G-16055)
C & J CLARK LATIN AMERICA
60 Tower Rd (02451-1022)
PHONE....................................617 243-4100
Maureen Grady, *President*
Rick Almeida, *Vice Pres*
Scott Bracci, *Vice Pres*
Don Brady, *Vice Pres*
Sharon Schuler, *Vice Pres*
EMP: 19
SQ FT: 30,000
SALES (est): 2.9MM **Privately Held**
SIC: 3143 5661 5139 Mfg Men's Footwear Ret Shoes Whol Footwear

(G-16056)
C & K COMPONENTS LLC (PA)
1601 Trapelo Rd Ste 178 (02451-7356)
PHONE....................................617 969-3700
Tom Schultz, *CEO*
Ted Arnstein, *Senior VP*
Phillip Gregory, *Engineer*
Kathy Lino, *Controller*
Patrick Egan, *Regl Sales Mgr*
▲ EMP: 67 EST: 1957
SALES (est): 15.3MM **Privately Held**
WEB: www.ittcannon.com
SIC: 3679 3678 3643 3613 Mfg Elec Components Mfg Elec Connectors Mfg Conductive Wire Dvcs Mfg Switchgear/Boards

(G-16057)
C & M TOOL AND DIE LLC
36 Rumford Ave (02453-3845)
PHONE....................................781 893-1880
Carlo Libertini,
Mark Libertini,
EMP: 4
SQ FT: 4,500
SALES (est): 467.2K **Privately Held**
SIC: 3544 Mfg Dies/Tools/Jigs/Fixtures

(G-16058)
C & M TOOL AND MFG INC
39 Emerson Rd (02451-4613)
PHONE....................................781 899-1709
Angelo Libertini, *President*
Paul Donnelly, *CFO*
EMP: 5
SALES: 950K **Privately Held**
SIC: 3469 Mfg Metal Stampings

(G-16059)
CAMBRDGE SUND MGT HOLDINGS LLC (DH)
404 Wyman St Ste 200 (02451-1242)
PHONE....................................781 547-7100
Christopher Calisi, *CEO*
Rob Claus, *Vice Pres*
Faruk Bursal, *Engineer*
Meir Mechtinger, *Engineer*
EMP: 4
SQ FT: 11,500
SALES (est): 14.9MM
SALES (corp-wide): 11.4MM **Privately Held**
SIC: 3669 Mfg Communications Equipment
HQ: Biamp Systems, Llc
9300 Sw Gemini Dr
Beaverton OR 97008
503 641-7287

(G-16060)
CARA ARMOUR
80 Trapelo Rd (02452-6327)
PHONE....................................781 899-7297
Cara Armour, *Principal*
EMP: 3
SALES (est): 155.6K **Privately Held**
SIC: 3999 Mfg Misc Products

(G-16061)
CARBIDE SPECIALITIES
38 Guinan St (02451-4367)
P.O. Box 541389 (02454-1389)
PHONE....................................781 899-1300
John Reynolds, *Owner*
EMP: 4
SALES: 200K **Privately Held**
WEB: www.ccatools.com
SIC: 3599 Mfg Industrial Machinery

(G-16062)
CARBON BLACK INC (DH)
1100 Winter St Ste 4900 (02451-1461)
PHONE....................................617 393-7400
Patrick Morley, *President*
EMP: 350
SQ FT: 81,991
SALES: 209.7MM
SALES (corp-wide): 90.6B **Publicly Held**
WEB: www.bit9.com
SIC: 7372 Prepackaged Software Services
HQ: Vmware, Inc.
3401 Hillview Ave
Palo Alto CA 94304
650 427-5000

(G-16063)
CARBON BLACK FEDERAL INC
1100 Winter St Ste 4900 (02451-1461)
PHONE....................................617 393-7400
Mark Sullivan, *Principal*
Roman Brozyna, *Principal*
EMP: 4
SALES (est): 223.5K
SALES (corp-wide): 90.6B **Publicly Held**
SIC: 7372 Prepackaged Software Services
HQ: Carbon Black, Inc.
1100 Winter St Ste 4900
Waltham MA 02451
617 393-7400

(G-16064)
CAZENA INC
1601 Trapelo Rd Ste 205 (02451-7340)
PHONE....................................781 897-6380
Prat Moghe, *CEO*
Daniel Hayes, *CFO*
EMP: 30
SQ FT: 7,300
SALES (est): 3MM **Privately Held**
SIC: 7372 Prepackaged Software Services

(G-16065)
CERNER CORPORATION
Also Called: Cerner DHT
51 Sawyer Rd Ste 600 (02453-3493)
PHONE....................................781 434-2200
Mary Pappas, *Research*
Neal Thurman, *Program Mgr*
EMP: 53
SALES (corp-wide): 5.3B **Publicly Held**
WEB: www.cerner.com
SIC: 7372 Prepackaged Software Services
PA: Cerner Corporation
2800 Rock Creek Pkwy
Kansas City MO 64117
816 201-1024

(G-16066)
CHEBLI ARCHITECTURAL WOODWORK
50 Sun St (02453-4154)
PHONE....................................781 642-0733
Abdo Chebli, *President*
EMP: 5
SQ FT: 8,000
SALES: 700K **Privately Held**
SIC: 2431 Mfg Millwork

(G-16067)
CIMPRESS USA INCORPORATED (DH)
275 Wyman St Ste 100 (02451-1218)
PHONE....................................866 614-8002
Robert Keane, *President*
Trynka Shineman, *Principal*
Michelle Kang, *Project Mgr*
Akshay Kusumgar, *Project Mgr*
Patrick McLean, *Project Mgr*
▼ EMP: 277
SALES (est): 712.4MM
SALES (corp-wide): 2.7B **Privately Held**
SIC: 2752 Lithographic Commercial Printing
HQ: Vistaprint B.V.
Hudsonweg 8
Venlo 5928
778 507-700

(G-16068)
CITIUS PRINTING & GRAPHICS LLC
20 Clematis Ave (02453-7011)
PHONE....................................781 547-5550
George Perry,
Robert Kashian,
EMP: 9
SQ FT: 6,000
SALES (est): 1.7MM **Privately Held**
WEB: www.citiusprint.com
SIC: 2752 Lithographic Commercial Printing

GEOGRAPHIC

(G-16069)
CLEMATIS MACHINE & FIXTURE CO
42 Clematis Ave (02453-7013)
P.O. Box 540421 (02454-0421)
PHONE.................................781 894-0777
William Thompson, *President*
William Thompson Jr, *Vice Pres*
EMP: 15 **EST:** 1945
SQ FT: 5,500
SALES: 1.6MM **Privately Held**
SIC: 3599 Machine Shop

(G-16070)
CLEVER GREEN CABINETS LLC
738 Main St (02451-0616)
PHONE.................................508 963-6776
Jonathan Taylor, *Principal*
EMP: 4
SALES (est): 344.2K **Privately Held**
SIC: 2434 Mfg Wood Kitchen Cabinets

(G-16071)
COMMONWEALTH FUEL CORP
281 Eastern Ave (02451)
P.O. Box 246, Allston (02134-0003)
PHONE.................................617 884-5444
Bob Mac William, *Principal*
EMP: 6
SALES (est): 646K **Privately Held**
SIC: 2869 Mfg Industrial Organic Chemicals

(G-16072)
COMMONWLTH VENTR FUNDING GROUP (PA)
391 Totten Pond Rd # 402 (02451-2006)
P.O. Box 3009, Wakefield (01880-0771)
PHONE.................................781 684-0095
Thomas Conway, *President*
William Booth, *Vice Pres*
EMP: 11
SQ FT: 2,000
SALES (est): 36.6MM **Privately Held**
WEB: www.cvfg.com
SIC: 3713 Mfg Truck/Bus Bodies

(G-16073)
COMPANY OF COCA-COLA BOTTLING
80 2nd Ave (02451-1108)
PHONE.................................781 672-8624
Jim Heruny, *Sales/Mktg Mgr*
EMP: 45 **Privately Held**
WEB: www.coke.com
SIC: 2086 5149 Mfg Bottled/Canned Soft Drinks Whol Groceries
HQ: Coca-Cola Bottling Company Of Southeastern New England, Inc.
150 Waterford Parkway S
Waterford CT 06385
860 443-2816

(G-16074)
COMPANY OF COCA-COLA BOTTLING
275 Wyman St (02451-1200)
PHONE.................................617 622-5400
EMP: 4
SALES (corp-wide): 16.6B **Privately Held**
SIC: 2086 Carb Sft Drnkbtlcn
HQ: Coca-Cola Bottling Company Of Southeastern New England, Inc.
150 Waterford Parkway S
Waterford CT 06385
860 443-2816

(G-16075)
CONNECTRN INC
203 Crescent St Ste 403 (02453-3420)
PHONE.................................781 223-2852
Idriz Limaj, *CEO*
Michael Wood, *President*
Agron Ademi, *Architect*
EMP: 3
SALES (est): 155.1K **Privately Held**
SIC: 7372 Prepackaged Software Services

(G-16076)
CORINDUS INC
309 Waverley Oaks Rd # 105 (02452-8443)
PHONE.................................508 653-3335
Mark Toland, *CEO*
Tal Wenderoe, *Exec VP*
Jim Desisto, *Vice Pres*
Robert Elden, *Engineer*
Eric Klem, *Engineer*
▲ **EMP:** 50
SQ FT: 9,000
SALES (est): 5MM
SALES (corp-wide): 10.7MM **Privately Held**
WEB: www.corindus.com
SIC: 3826 Mfg Analytical Instruments
PA: Corindus Vascular Robotics, Inc.
309 Waverly Oaks Rd # 10
Waltham MA 02452
508 653-3335

(G-16077)
CORINDUS VASCULAR ROBOTICS INC (PA)
309 Waverly Oaks Rd # 10 (02452-8443)
PHONE.................................508 653-3335
Jeffrey C Lightcap, *Ch of Bd*
Mark J Toland, *President*
Douglas Teany, *COO*
Chris Cain, *Vice Pres*
Matt Lemay, *Vice Pres*
EMP: 34 **EST:** 2011
SQ FT: 26,402
SALES: 10.7MM **Privately Held**
SIC: 3841 Surgical & Medical Instruments & Apparatus

(G-16078)
COUNTEREDGE LLC
108 Clematis Ave Unit 2 (02453-7064)
PHONE.................................781 891-0050
Vincent Pizzi, *Mng Member*
▲ **EMP:** 14
SALES (est): 2.3MM **Privately Held**
SIC: 3131 Mfg Footwear Cut Stock

(G-16079)
DATA ASSOCIATES BUSINESS TRUST
280 Bear Hill Rd (02451-1098)
P.O. Box 267, Weston (02493-0006)
PHONE.................................781 890-0110
Mark Deangelis, *President*
Joanne Deangelis, *Principal*
Joseph St Martin, *CFO*
▼ **EMP:** 30
SQ FT: 16,000
SALES (est): 4.8MM **Privately Held**
WEB: www.dataassociates.com
SIC: 2759 Commercial Printing

(G-16080)
DATANYZE INC (DH)
170 Data Dr (02451-2222)
PHONE.................................415 237-3434
Ilya Semin, *CEO*
Jason Vargas, *Managing Dir*
Dara Warner, *Opers Staff*
Stephen Frost, *Accounts Exec*
Kevin Toth, *Manager*
EMP: 25 **EST:** 2014
SALES (est): 183.5K **Privately Held**
SIC: 2741 7379 Internet Publishing And Broadcasting Computer Related Svc
HQ: Zoom Information, Llc
170 Data Dr
Waltham MA 02451
781 693-7500

(G-16081)
DECIPHERA PHARMACEUTICALS LLC
200 Smith St (02451-0099)
PHONE.................................781 209-6400
Michael D Taylor, *President*
Daniel L Flynn, *Founder*
Thomas P Kelly, *CFO*
Oliver Rosen, *Chief Mktg Ofcr*
EMP: 5
SALES (est): 876.3K
SALES (corp-wide): 18.7MM **Publicly Held**
SIC: 2834 Pharmaceutical Preparations
PA: Deciphera Pharmaceuticals, Inc.
200 Smith St Rm 1
Waltham MA 02451
781 209-6400

(G-16082)
DECIPHERA PHARMACEUTICALS INC (PA)
200 Smith St Rm 1 (02451-0006)
PHONE.................................781 209-6400
Steven Hoerter, *CEO*
James A Bristol, *Ch of Bd*
Daniel L Flynn, *Exec VP*
Thomas P Kelly, *CFO*
Daniel C Martin, *Ch Credit Ofcr*
EMP: 26
SQ FT: 45,000
SALES (est): 18.7MM **Publicly Held**
SIC: 2834 Pharmaceutical Preparations

(G-16083)
DEFENSE LOGICS LLC
66 Stow St (02453-1637)
PHONE.................................781 330-9195
A P Mathew, *CEO*
EMP: 5
SALES (est): 165.6K **Privately Held**
SIC: 7372 Prepackaged Software Services

(G-16084)
DENTSPLY IH INC (HQ)
Also Called: Dentsply Implants
590 Lincoln St (02451-2173)
PHONE.................................781 890-6800
Scott A Root, *President*
Valerie Curry, *District Mgr*
Tracy Henderson, *District Mgr*
Jim Bailey, *CFO*
Manish Sachdeva, *Administration*
▲ **EMP:** 200
SQ FT: 16,000
SALES (est): 44.7MM
SALES (corp-wide): 3.9B **Publicly Held**
WEB: www.astratechusa.com
SIC: 3841 Mfg Surgical/Medical Instruments
PA: Dentsply Sirona Inc.
13320 Bllntyne Crprtate P
Charlotte NC 28277
844 848-0137

(G-16085)
DESCAL INC
Also Called: Sir Speedy
1275 Main St Ste 1 (02451-1762)
PHONE.................................781 736-9400
Patricia Sands, *President*
EMP: 8
SQ FT: 8,000
SALES: 1MM **Privately Held**
WEB: www.descal.com
SIC: 2752 Comm Prtg Litho

(G-16086)
DESK TOP SOLUTIONS INC
Also Called: Microprint
335 Bear Hill Rd (02451-1006)
PHONE.................................781 890-7500
Brian Solov, *President*
EMP: 15
SALES (est): 2.5MM **Privately Held**
WEB: www.mprint.com
SIC: 2759 Commercial Printing

(G-16087)
DIGITAL COGNITION TECH INC
210 Bear Hill Rd Ste 301 (02451-1025)
PHONE.................................617 433-1777
Nancy Briefs, *CEO*
Antonia Holway, *Senior VP*
Allison Byers, *Vice Pres*
Irma Dishnica, *Controller*
EMP: 22
SALES: 94.4K **Privately Held**
SIC: 3841 Mfg Surgical/Medical Instruments

(G-16088)
DIGITAL GUARDIAN INC (PA)
275 Wyman St Ste 250 (02451-1265)
PHONE.................................781 788-8180
MO Rosen, *President*
Ben Cody, *Senior VP*
Debra Danielson, *Senior VP*
Mark Stevens, *Senior VP*
Frank Aneiros, *Vice Pres*
▼ **EMP:** 21
SQ FT: 32,000
SALES (est): 81.2MM **Privately Held**
WEB: www.verdasys.com
SIC: 7372 Prepackaged Software Services

(G-16089)
DOCBOX INC
760 Main St 2-4 (02451-0625)
PHONE.................................978 987-2569
Tracy Rausch, *President*
John Howse, *General Mgr*
Jere McLucas, *Engineer*
Bobby Shah, *CFO*
Michael Szwaja, *Software Engr*
EMP: 12
SALES (est): 1.4MM **Privately Held**
SIC: 3845 Mfg Electromedical Equipment

(G-16090)
DOVER MICROSYSTEMS INC
203 Crescent St Ste 108 (02453-3420)
PHONE.................................781 577-0300
Jothy Rosenberg, *CEO*
EMP: 9
SQ FT: 2,000
SALES (est): 485.4K **Privately Held**
SIC: 3674 Mfg Semiconductors/Related Devices

(G-16091)
DRAPE IT INC
131 Lexington St (02452-4636)
P.O. Box 541597 (02454-1597)
PHONE.................................781 209-1912
Joseph Marucci II, *President*
Sally Marucci, *Treasurer*
Joe Marucci, *Executive*
EMP: 10
SQ FT: 7,000
SALES (est): 1.1MM **Privately Held**
SIC: 2391 Mfg Curtains/Draperies

(G-16092)
DSK ENGINEERING AND TECHNOLOGY
180 Elm St Ste 201 (02453-5368)
P.O. Box 924, Palmer (01069-0924)
PHONE.................................413 289-6485
Rita Pensyl, *President*
Karen Cutone, *Vice Pres*
Denis Pensyl, *Vice Pres*
EMP: 6
SQ FT: 2,200
SALES (est): 735.1K **Privately Held**
WEB: www.dskengineering.com
SIC: 3679 3612 8711 Design Power Supplies And Power Transformers & Electrical Engineering

(G-16093)
DYNATRACE INC (PA)
1601 Trapelo Rd Ste 116 (02451-7351)
PHONE.................................781 530-1000
John Van Siclen, *CEO*
Bernd Greifeneder, *Senior VP*
Stephen J Pace, *Senior VP*
EMP: 4
SQ FT: 40,000
SALES: 430.9MM **Publicly Held**
SIC: 7372 Prepackaged Software Services

(G-16094)
DYNATRACE HOLDINGS LLC (HQ)
1601 Trapelo Rd Ste 116 (02451-7351)
PHONE.................................781 530-1000
John Van Siclen, *CEO*
EMP: 200
SALES (est): 53.3MM
SALES (corp-wide): 430.9MM **Publicly Held**
SIC: 7372 5045 Prepackaged Software Services Whol Computers/Peripherals
PA: Dynatrace, Inc.
1601 Trapelo Rd Ste 116
Waltham MA 02451
781 530-1000

(G-16095)
DYNATRACE INTERNATIONAL LLC (DH)
1601 Trapelo Rd Ste 116 (02451-7351)
PHONE.................................781 530-1000
H A Jllos, *Senior VP*
Rich Royer, *Accounts Mgr*
Joseph A Nathan, *Mng Member*
Paul A Czarnik, *CTO*
John Bellow, *MIS Dir*
EMP: 3

SALES (est): 1.1MM
SALES (corp-wide): 430.9MM **Publicly Held**
SIC: 7372 Prepackaged Software Srvcs
HQ: Dynatrace Holdings Llc
1601 Trapelo Rd Ste 116
Waltham MA 02451
781 530-1000

(G-16096)
ELLUCIAN
230 3rd Ave (02451-7528)
PHONE..................................781 672-1800
Erica Schuppert, *Consultant*
Matt Dobosh, *Director*
EMP: 3
SALES (est): 175.7K **Privately Held**
SIC: 7372 Prepackaged Software Services

(G-16097)
EMD MILLIPORE CORPORATION
300 2nd Ave (02451-1102)
PHONE..................................781 533-5858
EMP: 317
SALES (corp-wide): 16.4B **Privately Held**
SIC: 3826 Mfg Analytical Instruments
HQ: Emd Millipore Corporation
400 Summit Dr
Burlington MA 01803
781 533-6000

(G-16098)
ENSIGN-BICKFORD INDUSTRIES INC
1601 Trapelo Rd Ste 284 (02451-7357)
PHONE..................................781 693-1870
EMP: 5
SALES (corp-wide): 185.7MM **Privately Held**
SIC: 2892 Mfg Explosives
PA: Ensign-Bickford Industries, Inc.
125 Powder Forest Drive 3 Flr 3
Simsbury CT 80202
860 843-2000

(G-16099)
ENTASIS THRPUTICS HOLDINGS INC (PA)
35 Gatehouse Dr (02451-1215)
PHONE..................................781 810-0120
Nicholas Galakatos, *Ch of Bd*
Manoussos Perros, *President*
Michael Gutch, *CFO*
David Altarac, *Chief Mktg Ofcr*
Elizabeth Keiley, *General Counsel*
EMP: 5
SQ FT: 20,062
SALES: 5MM **Publicly Held**
SIC: 2834 Pharmaceutical Preparations

(G-16100)
EVEREST HALTHCARE HOLDINGS INC (DH)
920 Winter St (02451-1521)
PHONE..................................781 699-9000
Ronald J Kuerbitz, *President*
EMP: 3
SALES (est): 5.5MM
SALES (corp-wide): 18.3B **Privately Held**
SIC: 3841 Mfg Surgical/Medical Instruments

(G-16101)
EVEREST HEALTHCARE TEXAS HOLDG
920 Winter St (02451-1521)
PHONE..................................781 699-9000
EMP: 4
SALES (est): 204.4K
SALES (corp-wide): 16.6B **Privately Held**
SIC: 3841 Mfg Surgical/Medical Instruments
HQ: Fresenius Medical Care Holdings, Inc.
920 Winter St
Waltham MA 02451

(G-16102)
EXCELITAS TECH HOLDG CORP
200 West St Ste E403 (02451-1121)
PHONE..................................781 522-5914
David Nislick, *CEO*
Joel Falcone, *Exec VP*
Michael Messier, *Exec VP*
James RAO, *Exec VP*
Jim RAO, *Exec VP*
EMP: 10
SALES (est): 1.2B **Privately Held**
SIC: 3648 3845 Mfg Lighting Equipment Mfg Electromedical Equipment
PA: Excelitas Technologies Holdings Llc
200 West St Ste E403
Waltham MA 02451

(G-16103)
EXCELITAS TECH HOLDINGS LLC (PA)
200 West St Ste E403 (02451-1121)
PHONE..................................781 522-5900
Marc Reuss, *Exec VP*
Guy Antley, *Sales Staff*
David Nislick,
EMP: 10
SALES (est): 600.6MM **Privately Held**
SIC: 3648 Mfg Lighting Equipment

(G-16104)
EXCELITAS TECHNOLOGIES CORP (DH)
200 West St (02451-1121)
PHONE..................................781 522-5910
David Nislick, *CEO*
EMP: 30
SALES (est): 1.2B
SALES (corp-wide): 1.2B **Privately Held**
SIC: 3674 3827 3648 3679 Mfg Semiconductors/Dvcs Mfg Optical Instr/Lens Mfg Lighting Equipment Mfg Elec Components
HQ: Exc Holdings Ii Corp.
666 5th Ave Fl 36
New York NY 10103
212 644-5900

(G-16105)
EYEGATE PHARMACEUTICALS INC (PA)
271 Waverly Oaks Rd # 10 (02452-8469)
PHONE..................................781 788-9043
Paul Chaney, *Ch of Bd*
Stephen From, *President*
Brenda Mann, *Vice Pres*
Lisa Brandano, *Opers Staff*
Michael Manzo, *VP Engrg*
EMP: 11
SQ FT: 4,516
SALES: 1.6MM **Publicly Held**
SIC: 2834 Pharmaceutical Preparations

(G-16106)
FABTRON CORPORATION
80 Calvary St (02453-5952)
PHONE..................................781 891-4430
Clifford L Derick Jr, *President*
Brian Derick, *Opers Mgr*
EMP: 35
SQ FT: 33,000
SALES (est): 5.9MM **Privately Held**
WEB: www.fabtron.net
SIC: 3444 Mfg Sheet Metalwork

(G-16107)
FISHER SCIENTIFIC INTL LLC (HQ)
81 Wyman St (02451-1223)
PHONE..................................781 622-1000
Seth H Hoogasian, *President*
Dan Lovaas, *Regional Mgr*
Jeffrey Jochims, *Vice Pres*
Alan Malus, *Vice Pres*
Anthony H Smith, *Vice Pres*
◆ **EMP:** 125
SQ FT: 25,000
SALES (est): 3.3B
SALES (corp-wide): 24.3B **Publicly Held**
WEB: www.fisher1.com
SIC: 2869 3821 5169 5049 Mfg Industl Organic Chem Mfg Lab Apparatus/Furn Whol Chemicals/Products
PA: Thermo Fisher Scientific Inc.
168 3rd Ave
Waltham MA 02451
781 622-1000

(G-16108)
FMS NEW YORK SERVICES LLC (DH)
920 Winter St (02451-1521)
PHONE..................................781 699-9000
William J Valle, *President*
EMP: 6
SALES (est): 3.4MM
SALES (corp-wide): 18.3B **Privately Held**
SIC: 3841 Mfg Surgical/Medical Instruments

(G-16109)
FORTRESS BIOTECH INC
95 Sawyer Rd Ste 110 (02453-3471)
PHONE..................................781 652-4500
EMP: 10 **Publicly Held**
SIC: 2834 Mfg Pharmaceutical Preparations
PA: Fortress Biotech, Inc.
2 Gansevoort St Fl 9
New York NY 10014

(G-16110)
FRESENIUS MED CARE HLDINGS INC (DH)
Also Called: Fresenius Medical Care N Amer
920 Winter St (02451-1521)
PHONE..................................781 699-9000
Ronald Kuerbitz, *CEO*
William Valle, *President*
Ron Castle, *Senior VP*
Douglas Kott, *Senior VP*
ARI Chompre, *Vice Pres*
◆ **EMP:** 600
SQ FT: 200,000
SALES (est): 10.3B
SALES (corp-wide): 18.3B **Privately Held**
WEB: www.fmcna.com
SIC: 3841 8092 Mfg Surgical/Medical Instruments Kidney Dialysis Centers

(G-16111)
FRESENIUS MED CARE RNAL THRPIE
920 Winter St (02451-1521)
PHONE..................................781 699-9000
Ronald J Kuerbitz,
EMP: 4
SALES (est): 184.4K
SALES (corp-wide): 18.3B **Privately Held**
SIC: 3841 Mfg Surgical/Medical Instruments
HQ: Fresenius Medical Care Holdings, Inc.
920 Winter St
Waltham MA 02451

(G-16112)
FRESENIUS MED CARE VNTURES LLC (DH)
920 Winter St (02451-1521)
PHONE..................................781 699-9000
Jim Barsanti, *Manager*
EMP: 8
SALES (est): 101.8MM
SALES (corp-wide): 18.3B **Privately Held**
SIC: 3841 Mfg Surgical/Medical Instruments

(G-16113)
FRESENIUS MED CARE W WLLOW LLC
920 Winter St (02451-1521)
PHONE..................................781 699-9000
EMP: 11
SALES (corp-wide): 16.6B **Privately Held**
SIC: 3841 Mfg Surgical/Medical Instruments
HQ: Fresenius Medical Care West Willow, Llc
1485 Richardson Dr # 100
Richardson TX 75075

(G-16114)
FRESENIUS MED SVCS GROUP LLC
920 Winter St Ste 3142 (02451-1521)
PHONE..................................781 699-9000
Ronald Kuerbitz, *CEO*
William Valle, *President*
Douglas Kott, *Senior VP*
Angelo Moesslang, *CFO*
Mark Fawcett, *Treasurer*
EMP: 7
SALES (est): 224.8K
SALES (corp-wide): 18.3B **Privately Held**
SIC: 3841 8092 Mfg Surgical/Medical Instruments Kidney Dialysis Centers
HQ: Fresenius Medical Care Holdings, Inc.
920 Winter St
Waltham MA 02451

(G-16115)
FRESENIUS MEDICAL CARE NORTH (DH)
920 Winter St Ste A (02451-1519)
PHONE..................................781 699-9000
Ronald J Kuerbtiz, *President*
William Fink, *Vice Pres*
Peter E Gladitsch, *CFO*
Maxine Rotigliano, *Director*
EMP: 57
SALES (est): 10.3B
SALES (corp-wide): 18.3B **Privately Held**
SIC: 3841 Mfg Surgical/Medical Instruments
HQ: Fresenius Medical Care Beteiligungsges. Mbh
Else-Kroner-Str. 1
Bad Homburg 61352
617 260-90

(G-16116)
FRESENIUS USA MARKETING INC (DH)
920 Winter St (02451-1521)
PHONE..................................781 699-9000
Mark Costanzo, *President*
EMP: 19
SALES (est): 4.2MM
SALES (corp-wide): 18.3B **Privately Held**
SIC: 3841 Mfg Surgical/Medical Instruments

(G-16117)
G FINKENBEINER INC
33 Rumford Ave (02453-3894)
PHONE..................................781 899-3138
Thomas Hession, *President*
Diane Hession, *Vice Pres*
EMP: 4
SQ FT: 4,500
SALES: 700K **Privately Held**
WEB: www.finkenbeiner.com
SIC: 3229 3931 Mfg Pressed/Blown Glass Mfg Musical Instruments

(G-16118)
GENERAL FLUIDICS CORPORATION
1601 Trapelo Rd (02451-7333)
PHONE..................................617 543-3114
Robert Granier, *President*
EMP: 6
SALES (est): 540.3K **Privately Held**
SIC: 3826 Mfg Analytical Instruments

(G-16119)
GENERATION FOUR INC
Also Called: Minuteman Press
713 Main St (02451-0609)
PHONE..................................781 899-3180
John Fantasia, *President*
Julie Fantasia, *Principal*
EMP: 8
SQ FT: 3,000
SALES (est): 1MM **Privately Held**
WEB: www.generationfour.com
SIC: 2752 2791 2789 Lithographic Commercial Printing Typesetting Services Bookbinding/Related Work

(G-16120)
GENZYME CORPORATION
153 2nd Ave (02451-1122)
PHONE..................................781 487-5728
Edmund Sybertz, *CEO*
Scott Clark, *Project Mgr*
Yang Wang, *Research*
Jin Zhao, *Research*
EMP: 93 **Privately Held**
SIC: 2835 Mfg Diagnostic Substance
HQ: Genzyme Corporation
50 Binney St
Cambridge MA 02142
617 252-7500

GEOGRAPHIC

(G-16121)
GOT INTERFACE
135 Beaver St Ste 206 (02452-8463)
PHONE....781 547-5700
Daniel Skiba, *President*
EMP: 11
SALES (est): 1.8MM **Privately Held**
SIC: 3823 Nonclassified Establishment

(G-16122)
GRAPHISOFT NORTH AMERICA INC
60 Hickory Dr Ste 101 (02451-1013)
PHONE....617 485-4219
Steve Benford, *Managing Dir*
Tibor SA Rdy, *Info Tech Dir*
Tibor SA - Rdy, *Info Tech Dir*
Eric Stromberg, *Administration*
EMP: 35
SQ FT: 2,662
SALES (est): 5.1MM **Privately Held**
SIC: 7372 Prepackaged Software Services

(G-16123)
H & T SPECIALTY CO INC
56 Clematis Ave (02453-7013)
P.O. Box 540185 (02454-0185)
PHONE....781 893-3866
Gary Jenks, *President*
EMP: 11 **EST:** 1951
SQ FT: 6,400
SALES: 1.3MM **Privately Held**
SIC: 3679 3599 Machine Shop

(G-16124)
HARVARD INSTANT PRINTING
36 Elm St (02453-5360)
P.O. Box 2431, Framingham (01703-2431)
PHONE....781 893-2622
Steve Privitera, *Owner*
Paula Privitera, *Treasurer*
EMP: 5 **EST:** 1978
SQ FT: 3,000
SALES (est): 441K **Privately Held**
SIC: 2752 2791 Offset Printing & Typesetting

(G-16125)
HEINRICH LLC
156 Bishops Forest Dr (02452-8807)
PHONE....781 891-9591
Patricia Heinrich, *Principal*
EMP: 3
SALES (est): 185.4K **Privately Held**
SIC: 2298 Mfg Cordage/Twine

(G-16126)
HEMEDEX INC
564 Main St Ste 300 (02452-5568)
PHONE....617 577-1759
Fredrick H Bowman, *CEO*
Stefanie Blair, *Opers Staff*
Stefanie Cantin, *Business Dir*
EMP: 14
SQ FT: 6,500
SALES (est): 2.2MM **Privately Held**
WEB: www.hemedex.com
SIC: 3841 Mfg Surgical/Medical Instruments

(G-16127)
HOME INTENSIVE CARE INC
920 Winter St (02451-1521)
PHONE....781 699-9000
Rice Powell, *Director*
EMP: 4
SALES (est): 240.5K
SALES (corp-wide): 18.3B **Privately Held**
SIC: 3841 Mfg Surgical/Medical Instruments
HQ: Fresenius Medical Care Holdings, Inc.
920 Winter St
Waltham MA 02451

(G-16128)
ILIOS INC
Also Called: Ilios Dynamics
45 1st Ave (02451-1105)
PHONE....781 466-6481
John N Hatsopoulos, *CEO*
David A Garrison, *CFO*
Joseph Gehret, *CTO*
EMP: 3
SALES (est): 286.8K
SALES (corp-wide): 35.8MM **Publicly Held**
SIC: 3585 Manufacturing Refrigeration/Heating Equipment
PA: Tecogen Inc.
45 1st Ave
Waltham MA 02451
781 622-1120

(G-16129)
IMAGING W VAREX HOLDINGS INC
940 Winter St (02451-1457)
PHONE....781 663-6900
Sunny Sanyal, *CEO*
Kim Honeysett, *Senior VP*
Clarence Verhoef, *CFO*
EMP: 3
SALES (est): 7.2MM
SALES (corp-wide): 780.6MM **Publicly Held**
SIC: 3826 Mfg Analytical Instruments
PA: Varex Imaging Corporation
1678 S Pioneer Rd
Salt Lake City UT 84104
801 972-5000

(G-16130)
IMMUNOGEN INC (PA)
830 Winter St (02451-1477)
PHONE....781 895-0600
Stephen C McCluski, *Ch of Bd*
Mark J Enyedy, *President*
Craig Barrows, *Exec VP*
Richard J Gregory, *Exec VP*
Blaine H McKee, *Exec VP*
EMP: 189
SQ FT: 110,000
SALES: 53.4MM **Publicly Held**
WEB: www.immunogen.com
SIC: 2834 Pharmaceutical Preparations

(G-16131)
IMMUNOGEN SECURITIES CORP
830 Winter St Ste 6 (02451-1477)
PHONE....617 995-2500
Gregory D Perry, *Principal*
Paul Sorgi, *Plant Mgr*
Jennifer Coccia, *Research*
Barbara Leece, *Research*
Carol Hausner, *Finance Mgr*
EMP: 29
SALES (est): 3.1MM
SALES (corp-wide): 53.4MM **Publicly Held**
SIC: 2834 Management Investment
PA: Immunogen, Inc.
830 Winter St
Waltham MA 02451
781 895-0600

(G-16132)
INDUSTRIAL BIOMEDICAL SENSORS
Also Called: I B S
1377 Main St (02451-1644)
PHONE....781 891-4201
Sanlu Y Chang, *President*
Kuo Chang PHD, *Treasurer*
EMP: 10
SQ FT: 5,000
SALES (est): 950K **Privately Held**
WEB: www.ibs-corp.com
SIC: 3823 3571 3365 Mfg Industrial/Medical Instruments Electronic Biosensors And Aerospace Products

(G-16133)
INFOBIONIC INC
200 5th Ave Ste 4030 (02451-8758)
PHONE....978 674-8304
Stuart Long, *CEO*
Dave Maccutcheon, *COO*
Paul McEwan, *CFO*
Jennifer Kennedy, *Accounting Mgr*
EMP: 26 **EST:** 2011
SQ FT: 9,000
SALES (est): 1.6MM **Privately Held**
SIC: 3845 Mfg Electromedical Equipment

(G-16134)
INFOLIBRIA INC
271 Waverley Oaks Rd (02452-8469)
PHONE....781 392-2200
Ian C Yates PHD, *President*
David L Hoey, *Vice Pres*
Kevin Lewis, *Vice Pres*
Joseph Otto, *Vice Pres*
Peter S Rood, *Vice Pres*
EMP: 85
SALES (est): 6.6MM **Privately Held**
WEB: www.infolibria.com
SIC: 3823 Mfg Process Control Instruments

(G-16135)
INSTRUMENTATION & CONTROL TECH
Also Called: I C T
738 Main St Ste 219 (02451-0616)
PHONE....781 273-5052
EMP: 17
SQ FT: 1,000
SALES: 750K **Privately Held**
SIC: 3823 Mfg Process Control Instruments

(G-16136)
K2W LLC
Also Called: Onguard
30 Grant St (02453-4202)
PHONE....617 818-2613
Kerry Wu,
EMP: 4
SALES (est): 273K **Privately Held**
SIC: 3081 Mfg Unsupported Plastic Film/Sheet

(G-16137)
KELTRON CORPORATION (HQ)
101 1st Ave Ste 4a (02451-1160)
PHONE....781 894-8710
David S Wilbourn, *President*
Dave Blanken, *President*
Lisa Korklan, *Vice Pres*
Patti Caira, *Mfg Mgr*
David Ritter, *Sales Mgr*
EMP: 21
SQ FT: 18,000
SALES: 3.5MM
SALES (corp-wide): 33.3MM **Privately Held**
WEB: www.keltroncorp.com
SIC: 3669 Mfg Communications Equipment
PA: Valcom, Inc.
5614 Hollins Rd
Roanoke VA 24019
540 427-3900

(G-16138)
KM FOODS INC
47 Graymore Rd (02451-2201)
PHONE....781 894-7616
Joseph T Maguire, *Principal*
EMP: 6
SALES (est): 301K **Privately Held**
SIC: 2099 Mfg Food Preparations

(G-16139)
KNOWLEDGE MANAGEMENT ASSOC LLC
Also Called: Metal Graphic
77 Rumford Ave Ste 2 (02453-3872)
PHONE....781 250-2001
David Goldstein, *Mng Member*
▼ **EMP:** 9
SALES (est): 1.2MM **Privately Held**
WEB: www.kmainc.com
SIC: 7372 Prepackaged Software Services

(G-16140)
KODA INDUSTRIES INDIANA LLC
51 Sawyer Rd Ste 420 (02453-3488)
PHONE....781 891-3066
Bill Leaver, *CFO*
EMP: 97
SALES (est): 9.9MM
SALES (corp-wide): 52.4MM **Privately Held**
SIC: 3585 5075 Mfg Refrigeration/Heating Equipment Whol Heat/Air Cond Equipment/Supplies
PA: Koda Enterprises Group, Llc
51 Sawyer Rd Ste 420
Waltham MA 02453
781 891-0467

(G-16141)
KRONOS INCORPORATED
200 West St Ste 4a (02451-1154)
PHONE....978 947-2990
EMP: 60
SALES (corp-wide): 1B **Privately Held**
SIC: 7372 Prepackaged Software Services
HQ: Kronos Incorporated
900 Chelmsford St # 312
Lowell MA 01851
978 250-9800

(G-16142)
L-TRONICS INC
195 Fox Rd Unit 111 (02451-0213)
PHONE....781 893-6672
Daniel Leone, *President*
EMP: 5 **EST:** 2010
SALES (est): 413.9K **Privately Held**
SIC: 3672 Mfg Printed Circuit Boards

(G-16143)
L-TRONICS INC
30 Clematis Ave Ste 2 (02453-7069)
PHONE....781 893-6672
Daniel Leone, *President*
Milagro Leone, *Treasurer*
Peter Brown, *Admin Sec*
▲ **EMP:** 25
SQ FT: 5,000
SALES (est): 6.5MM **Privately Held**
WEB: www.l-tronics.com
SIC: 3672 Mfg Printed Circuit Boards

(G-16144)
LECTRO ENGINEERING INC
39 Calvary St Fl 2 (02453-5974)
PHONE....781 891-9640
Joseph D Georgianna, *President*
EMP: 10
SALES (est): 1.5MM **Privately Held**
SIC: 3444 Mfg Sheet Metalwork

(G-16145)
LIGHT METAL PLATERS LLC
70 Clematis Ave (02453-7013)
P.O. Box 540150 (02454-0150)
PHONE....781 899-8855
Steven Delorey, *President*
Phyllis Gauthier, *Treasurer*
▲ **EMP:** 20 **EST:** 1960
SQ FT: 7,600
SALES (est): 2.4MM **Privately Held**
WEB: www.lightmetalplaters.com
SIC: 3471 3479 7336 2396 Plating/Polishing Svcs Coating/Engraving Svcs Coml Art/Graphic Design Mfg Auto/Apparel Trim

(G-16146)
MACLELLAN CO
121 Felton St (02453-4139)
PHONE....781 891-5462
Peter Maclellan Sr, *Owner*
EMP: 6
SQ FT: 2,000
SALES (est): 292.8K **Privately Held**
SIC: 3471 Plating/Polishing Service

(G-16147)
MARIE DEPROFIO
Also Called: Unlimited Plant Care Service
11 Harrington Rd (02452-4720)
PHONE....781 894-9793
Marie Deprofio, *Owner*
Steven Deprofio, *Co-Owner*
EMP: 7
SALES: 350K **Privately Held**
SIC: 2431 Interior Landscaping

(G-16148)
MASSACHUSETTS MEDICAL SOCIETY (PA)
Also Called: New England Journal Medicine
860 Winter St (02451-1411)
PHONE....781 893-4610
Dale Magee, *President*
Emily Dulude, *General Mgr*
Matthew O'Rourke, *General Mgr*
Julie Ingelfinger, *Editor*
Pam Miller, *Editor*
EMP: 450 **EST:** 1781
SQ FT: 202,000

SALES (est): 135.2MM Privately Held
SIC: 2721 8621 Periodicals-Publishing/Printing Professional Organization

(G-16149)
MATERIALISE DENTAL INC
590 Lincoln St (02451-2173)
PHONE....................443 557-0121
Barbara Sterner, *Principal*
EMP: 28
SALES (est): 2.7MM Privately Held
SIC: 7372 Prepackaged Software Services

(G-16150)
MINDEDGE INC
271 Waverley Oaks Rd (02452-8469)
PHONE....................781 250-1805
Jefferson Flanders, *CEO*
Rachel Cerbone, *Editor*
Amanda Malgeri, *Editor*
Eric Weil, *Editor*
Jack Birolini, *Manager*
EMP: 11
SQ FT: 4,000
SALES (est): 931.7K Privately Held
WEB: www.mindedge.com
SIC: 7372 Prepackaged Software Services

(G-16151)
MINERVA NEUROSCIENCES INC (PA)
1601 Trapelo Rd Ste 284 (02451-7357)
PHONE....................617 600-7373
Remy Luthringer, *CEO*
Marc D Beer, *Ch of Bd*
Rick Russell, *President*
Joseph Reilly, *COO*
Frederick Ahlholm, *Senior VP*
EMP: 11
SQ FT: 4,043
SALES (est): 2.1MM Publicly Held
SIC: 2834 Pharmaceutical Preparations

(G-16152)
MJ RESEARCH INC (HQ)
245 Winter St Ste 100 (02451-8709)
PHONE....................510 724-7000
John D Finney, *President*
Michael J Finney, *Treasurer*
EMP: 150
SQ FT: 84,000
SALES (est): 24.6MM
SALES (corp-wide): 2.2B Publicly Held
SIC: 3823 Mfg Process Control Instruments
PA: Bio-Rad Laboratories, Inc.
1000 Alfred Nobel Dr
Hercules CA 94547
510 724-7000

(G-16153)
MODUS MEDIA INC
1601 Trapelo Rd Ste 170 (02451-7353)
PHONE....................781 663-5000
Terence M Leahy, *Ch of Bd*
Daniel Beck, *President*
W Kendal Southerland, *President*
David Tanner, *President*
Leo S Vannoni, *Treasurer*
EMP: 26
SALES (est): 5.3MM
SALES (corp-wide): 819.8MM Publicly Held
WEB: www.modusmedia.com
SIC: 2752 2789 5045 7371 Lithographic Coml Print Bookbinding/Related Work Whol Computer/Peripheral Computer Programming Svc Computer Related Svcs
PA: Steel Connect, Inc.
1601 Trapelo Rd Ste 170
Waltham MA 02451
781 663-5001

(G-16154)
NABS INC
Also Called: Nabs Bindery
180 Elm St Ste 5 (02453-5334)
PHONE....................781 899-7719
Nuccia Arsenault, *President*
Paul Arsenault, *Clerk*
EMP: 11
SQ FT: 5,500
SALES (est): 1.3MM Privately Held
WEB: www.nabsbindery.com
SIC: 2789 Bookbinding/Related Work

(G-16155)
NANOENTEK INC
240 Bear Hill Rd Ste 101 (02451-1026)
PHONE....................781 472-2558
Woo Chul Jung, *President*
EMP: 3 Privately Held
SIC: 3841 Mfg Surgical/Medical Instruments
PA: Nanoentek Inc.
5 Digital-Ro 26-Gil, Guro-Gu
Seoul 08389

(G-16156)
NANOLAB INC
22 Bedford St (02453)
PHONE....................781 609-2722
David Carnahan, *President*
Krzysztof Kempa, *Vice Pres*
EMP: 5
SQ FT: 3,770
SALES (est): 869.8K Privately Held
WEB: www.nano-lab.com
SIC: 3624 Mfg Carbon/Graphite Products

(G-16157)
NANOSEMI INC
200 5th Ave Ste 2020 (02451-8733)
PHONE....................781 472-2832
Helen Kim, *President*
Zohaib Mahmood, *Technical Staff*
EMP: 26
SALES (est): 2.8MM Privately Held
SIC: 3679 Mfg Electronic Components

(G-16158)
NETCRACKER TECHNOLOGY CORP (HQ)
95 Sawyer Rd (02453-3464)
PHONE....................781 419-3300
Andrew Feinberg, *President*
Alena Astafyeva, *Partner*
Pamela Benson, *Partner*
Vaidhianathan Bharadwaj, *Partner*
Dowlath Bibi, *Partner*
EMP: 134
SQ FT: 45,000
SALES (est): 287.4MM Privately Held
WEB: www.netcracker.com
SIC: 7372 Prepackaged Software Services

(G-16159)
NEUROMETRIX INC (PA)
1000 Winter St (02451-1436)
PHONE....................781 890-9989
Shai N Gozani, *Ch of Bd*
Marc Cryan, *Engineer*
Francis X McGillin, *Ch Credit Ofcr*
Alison Bogusz, *Sales Staff*
Emily Adekore, *Marketing Mgr*
EMP: 42
SQ FT: 12,000
SALES: 16MM Publicly Held
WEB: www.neurometrix.com
SIC: 3841 Mfg Medical & Surgical Devices

(G-16160)
NOCION THERAPEUTICS INC
100 Beaver St Ste 301 (02453-8400)
PHONE....................781 812-6176
Stephanie Gillis, *Administration*
EMP: 7
SALES (est): 304.1K Privately Held
SIC: 2834 Mfg Pharmaceutical Preparations

(G-16161)
NORTHPOINT PRINTING SVCS INC
230 2nd Ave Ste 3 (02451-1140)
PHONE....................781 895-1900
John Allekian, *President*
EMP: 12
SQ FT: 1,300
SALES (est): 1.1MM Privately Held
SIC: 2759 Lithographic Commercial Printing

(G-16162)
NOVA BIOMEDICAL CORPORATION (PA)
200 Prospect St (02453-3465)
PHONE....................781 894-0800
Francis Manganaro, *President*
Jeff Dubois, *Vice Pres*
Mark Hobbs, *Accounts Mgr*
Amy Ryan, *Accounts Exec*
Mike Ford, *Sales Staff*
▲ EMP: 621 EST: 1976
SQ FT: 220,000
SALES (est): 309.9MM Privately Held
WEB: www.novabiomedical.com
SIC: 2833 3826 Mfg Medicinal/Botanical Products Mfg Analytical Instruments

(G-16163)
NUTRASWEET COMPANY
500 Totten Pond Rd 6 (02451-1916)
PHONE....................706 303-5600
◆ EMP: 27
SALES (est): 7.7MM Privately Held
SIC: 2869 Mfg Industrial Organic Chemicals

(G-16164)
NUTRASWEET COMPANY
500 Totten Pond Rd Ste 61 (02451-1924)
PHONE....................706 303-5600
William Defer, *Exec VP*
Marsha Ludlow, *Purchasing*
EMP: 50 Privately Held
SIC: 2869 Mfg Industrial Organic Chemicals
HQ: The Nutrasweet Company
222 Merchandise Mart Plz # 936
Chicago IL 60654
312 873-5000

(G-16165)
OATSYSTEMS INC
309 Waverley Oaks Rd # 306
(02452-8451)
PHONE....................781 907-6100
Michael George, *CEO*
Bob Lentz, *Senior VP*
Eric Fischer, *Vice Pres*
Sanjay Sarma, *Vice Pres*
Karl Waldman, *Vice Pres*
EMP: 65
SQ FT: 7,500
SALES (est): 4.9MM Privately Held
WEB: www.oatsystems.com
SIC: 7372 Prepackaged Software Services

(G-16166)
ONCOMED PHRM SVCS MA INC
150 Bear Hill Rd (02451-1028)
PHONE....................781 209-5470
Burt Zweigenhaft, *Principal*
Bill Foxx, *Director*
EMP: 9
SALES (est): 1.1MM Privately Held
SIC: 2834 Mfg Pharmaceutical Preparations

(G-16167)
OPENCLINICA LLC
460 Totten Pond Rd (02451-1991)
PHONE....................617 621-8585
Michael Collins, *CEO*
Brittany Stark, *Project Mgr*
Denise Drinkwater, *Finance*
Tia Tep, *Human Resources*
Krikor Krumlian, *CTO*
EMP: 25
SALES (est): 3.9MM Privately Held
SIC: 3821 Mfg Lab Apparatus/Furniture

(G-16168)
ORACLE AMERICA INC
580 Winter St (02451)
PHONE....................781 672-4280
Michael Donley, *Branch Mgr*
EMP: 187
SALES (corp-wide): 39.5B Publicly Held
SIC: 7372 Prepackaged Software Services
HQ: Oracle America, Inc.
500 Oracle Pkwy
Redwood City CA 94065
650 506-7000

(G-16169)
OSPREY COMPLIANCE SOFTWARE LLC
275 2nd Ave Ste 2 (02451-1159)
PHONE....................888 677-7394
EMP: 4
SALES (est): 44.8K
SALES (corp-wide): 1.1MM Privately Held
SIC: 7372 Prepackaged Software Services
PA: Steele Compliance Solutions, Inc.
1350 Treat Blvd Ste 230
Walnut Creek CA 94597
415 692-5000

(G-16170)
PALLEON PHARMA INC
266 2nd Ave Ste 202 (02451-1168)
PHONE....................857 285-5904
Ll Peng, *Principal*
EMP: 9
SALES (est): 1.2MM Privately Held
SIC: 2834 Mfg Pharmaceutical Preparations

(G-16171)
PERKINELMER INC (PA)
940 Winter St (02451-1457)
PHONE....................781 663-6900
Robert F Friel, *Ch of Bd*
Joel S Goldberg, *Senior VP*
Daniel R Tereau, *Senior VP*
Tajinder Vohra, *Senior VP*
David Blackett, *Vice Pres*
▲ EMP: 120 EST: 1947
SQ FT: 54,667
SALES: 2.7B Publicly Held
WEB: www.perkinelmer.com
SIC: 3845 3826 Mfg Electromedical Equipment Mfg Analytical Instruments

(G-16172)
PERKINELMER HLTH SCIENCES INC (DH)
940 Winter St (02451-1457)
PHONE....................781 663-6900
Robert F Friel, *President*
Scott P Kennedy, *Treasurer*
▲ EMP: 200
SQ FT: 25,000
SALES (est): 197.1MM
SALES (corp-wide): 2.7B Publicly Held
SIC: 3821 Mfg Lab Apparatus/Furniture

(G-16173)
PERSPECTA SVCS & SOLUTIONS INC (DH)
Also Called: Qinetiq North America, Inc.
350 2nd Ave Bldg 1 (02451-1104)
PHONE....................781 684-4000
Dr Andrew Rogers, *President*
Jeff Yorsz, *President*
Dr Richard Wiesman, *Exec VP*
Doug Ounanian, *Vice Pres*
Robert Polutchko, *Vice Pres*
EMP: 50
SALES (est): 12.6MM Privately Held
SIC: 3812 8731 Mfg Search/Navigation Equipment Commercial Physical Research
HQ: Qinetiq Us Holdings, Inc.
5885 Trinity Pkwy Ste 130
Centreville VA 20120
202 429-6630

(G-16174)
PLATAINE INC
465 Waverley Oaks Rd # 420
(02452-8496)
PHONE....................336 905-0900
Clay Bolick, *Vice Pres*
Harry Druck, *Vice Pres*
EMP: 9
SALES (est): 196.1K Privately Held
SIC: 7372 Prepackaged Software Services

(G-16175)
PLATING FOR ELECTRONICS INC
94 Calvary St (02453-5920)
P.O. Box 540536 (02454-0536)
PHONE....................781 893-2368
Stephen J Davino, *President*
Phillip J Davino, *Vice Pres*
Michael A Davino, *Treasurer*
EMP: 44
SQ FT: 19,000
SALES (est): 5.2MM Privately Held
WEB: www.p4e.com
SIC: 3471 Plating/Polishing Service

GEOGRAPHIC

(G-16176)
PRAECIS PHARMACEUTICALS INC
830 Winter St Ste 1 (02451-1477)
PHONE....................781 795-4100
Malcolm L Gefter, *Ch of Bd*
Kevin F McLaughlin, *President*
Richard W Wagner, *Exec VP*
O Prem Das, *Senior VP*
Edward C English, *CFO*
EMP: 78
SQ FT: 65,000
SALES (est): 9.7MM
SALES (corp-wide): 40.6B **Privately Held**
WEB: www.praecis.com
SIC: 2834 Bio Technological Research & Development And Mfg Pharmaceutical Preparations
HQ: Glaxosmithkline Holdings (Americas) Inc.
1105 N Market St
Wilmington DE 19801
302 984-6932

(G-16177)
PRESTIGE CUSTOM MIRROR & GLASS
182 High St (02453-5914)
PHONE....................781 647-0878
Phillip Wallace, *President*
EMP: 12
SALES (est): 790K **Privately Held**
WEB: www.prestigecustommirrorandglass.com
SIC: 3231 1793 Mfg & Installs Custom Shower Doors & Mirrors

(G-16178)
PRIMEVIGILANCE INC
1601 Trapelo Rd (02451-7333)
PHONE....................781 703-5540
Aleksandra Seisert, *Office Mgr*
EMP: 6
SALES: 0 **Privately Held**
SIC: 3821 Mfg Lab Apparatus/Furniture

(G-16179)
PTC INC
230 3rd Ave (02451-7528)
PHONE....................617 792-7622
C R Harrison, *President*
EMP: 150
SALES (corp-wide): 1.2B **Publicly Held**
WEB: www.ptc.com
SIC: 7372 Prepackaged Software Services
PA: Ptc Inc.
121 Seaport Blvd
Boston MA 02210
781 370-5000

(G-16180)
QUEEN SCREW & MFG INC
60 Farwell St (02453-8378)
PHONE....................781 894-8110
Domenic De Julio, *President*
Peter Babigian, *Vice Pres*
Michael De Julio, *Treasurer*
Peter Babieian, *Human Res Mgr*
Gloria Babigian, *Shareholder*
EMP: 55 **EST:** 1966
SQ FT: 13,500
SALES (est): 9.4MM **Privately Held**
WEB: www.queenscrew.com
SIC: 3599 Mfg Industrial Machinery

(G-16181)
R & H COMMUNICATIONS INC (PA)
Also Called: Allegra Print and Imaging
187 Lexington St Ste 4 (02452-4601)
PHONE....................781 893-6221
Ruth Cretella, *President*
Henry A Cretella, *Treasurer*
EMP: 12
SQ FT: 2,100
SALES (est): 1.7MM **Privately Held**
WEB: www.rhcommunications.com
SIC: 2752 7334 2791 2789 Lithographic Coml Print Photocopying Service Typesetting Services Bookbinding/Related Work

(G-16182)
R L HACHEY COMPANY
16 Pine Hill Cir (02451-2128)
PHONE....................781 891-4237
Russell Hachey, *Owner*
EMP: 4
SQ FT: 2,888
SALES: 94K **Privately Held**
SIC: 3599 Mfg Industrial Machinery

(G-16183)
RADIUS HEALTH INC (PA)
950 Winter St (02451-1424)
PHONE....................617 551-4000
Jesper Hoiland, *President*
Tina Wallace, *Regional Mgr*
Joseph Kelly, *Senior VP*
Kate Hermans, *Vice Pres*
Jamal Saeh, *Vice Pres*
EMP: 91
SQ FT: 26,553
SALES: 99.2MM **Publicly Held**
SIC: 2834 8731 Pharmaceutical Preparations

(G-16184)
RAYTHEON COMPANY (PA)
870 Winter St (02451-1449)
P.O. Box 660425, Dallas TX (75266-0425)
PHONE....................781 522-3000
Thomas A Kennedy, *Ch of Bd*
Rebecca R Rhoads, *President*
David C Wajsgras, *President*
Martin Fette, *Principal*
Michael Blumberg, *Chairman*
EMP: 450 **EST:** 1922
SQ FT: 955,967
SALES: 27B **Publicly Held**
SIC: 3812 3663 3761 Mfg Aerospace/Defense Products & Services

(G-16185)
RAYTHEON INTERNATIONAL INC (PA)
870 Winter St (02451-1449)
PHONE....................781 522-3000
John D Harris II, *CEO*
Thomas A Vecchiolla, *President*
Richard A Goglia, *Treasurer*
Robert B Shanks, *Admin Sec*
EMP: 8
SALES (est): 5.1MM **Privately Held**
SIC: 3812 3769 Mfg Search/Navigation Equipment Mfg Space Vehicle Equipment

(G-16186)
RED SPOT PRINTING
182 Newton St (02453-8653)
PHONE....................781 894-2211
Philip Di Duca, *Owner*
EMP: 3
SQ FT: 2,800
SALES (est): 400K **Privately Held**
SIC: 2752 Lithographic Commercial Printing

(G-16187)
REPLIGEN CORPORATION (PA)
41 Seyon St Ste 100 (02453-8358)
PHONE....................781 250-0111
Karen A Dawes, *Ch of Bd*
Tony J Hunt, *President*
Ralf Kuriyel, *Senior VP*
John Bonham-Carter, *Vice Pres*
Marc Centrella, *Vice Pres*
EMP: 275
SQ FT: 76,000
SALES: 194MM **Publicly Held**
WEB: www.repligen.com
SIC: 2836 Mfg Biological Products

(G-16188)
REVULYTICS INC (PA)
130 Turner St (02453-8901)
PHONE....................781 398-3400
Joseph Noonan, *CEO*
Martha Stuart, *Vice Pres*
Kevin Ball, *VP Finance*
Kathleen Fleming, *Asst Controller*
Kathy Simpson, *Asst Controller*
EMP: 50
SALES (est): 7.1MM **Privately Held**
SIC: 7372 Prepackaged Software Services

(G-16189)
RICHARD H BIRD & CO INC
Also Called: Bird Precision
1 Spruce St (02453-4316)
P.O. Box 540569 (02454-0569)
PHONE....................781 894-0160
Carl J Cunningham, *President*
EMP: 39 **EST:** 1913
SQ FT: 12,400
SALES: 8.6MM **Privately Held**
WEB: www.birdprecision.com
SIC: 3915 Mfg Jewelers' Materials

(G-16190)
ROTEK INSTRUMENT CORP
390 Main St (02452-6640)
P.O. Box 540504 (02454-0504)
PHONE....................781 899-4611
Paul Lualdi, *President*
Rose-Ann West, *Corp Secy*
Paul Abercrombie, *Mfg Mgr*
Lawrence Weissbach, *QC Dir*
Paul C Lualdi, *MIS Staff*
EMP: 20
SQ FT: 6,150
SALES (est): 3.1MM **Privately Held**
WEB: www.rotek.com
SIC: 3825 3829 Mfg Electrical Measuring Instruments Mfg Measuring/Controlling Devices

(G-16191)
SAUCONY INC (DH)
Also Called: Hyde Athletic Industries
500 Totten Pond Rd Ste 1 (02451-1927)
PHONE....................617 824-6000
John H Fisher, *Ch of Bd*
Charles A Gottesman, *Vice Ch Bd*
Michael Umana, *COO*
Michael Jeppesen, *Senior VP*
Samuel S Ward, *Senior VP*
▲ **EMP:** 125 **EST:** 1912
SQ FT: 141,000
SALES (est): 49.2MM
SALES (corp-wide): 2.2B **Publicly Held**
WEB: www.sauconyinc.com
SIC: 3149 3143 3144 2329 Mfg Footwear-Ex Rubber Mfg Men's Footwear
HQ: The Stride Rite Corporation
500 Totten Pond Rd Ste 1
Waltham MA 02451
617 824-6000

(G-16192)
SHIRE HUMN GNTIC THERAPIES INC
Also Called: Shire Pharmaceuticals
1100 Winter St Fl 3 (02451-1473)
PHONE....................781 862-1561
EMP: 7
SALES (corp-wide): 15.1B **Privately Held**
SIC: 2834 Mfg Pharmaceutical Preparations
HQ: Shire Human Genetic Therapies, Inc.
300 Shire Way
Lexington MA 02421
617 349-0200

(G-16193)
SIEMENS INDUSTRY SOFTWARE INC
200 5th Ave Fl 5 (02451-8704)
PHONE....................781 250-6800
EMP: 8
SALES (corp-wide): 96.9B **Privately Held**
SIC: 7372 Prepackaged Software Services
HQ: Siemens Industry Software Inc.
5800 Granite Pkwy Ste 600
Plano TX 75024
972 987-3000

(G-16194)
SIERRA PRESS INC
713 Main St (02451-0609)
PHONE....................617 923-4150
Garo Masrof, *President*
Greg Masrof, *Clerk*
EMP: 3
SQ FT: 800
SALES (est): 330K **Privately Held**
WEB: www.sierrapress.com
SIC: 2752 Offset Printing

(G-16195)
SNOWBOUND SOFTWARE CORPORATION
309 Waverly Oaks Rd # 401 (02452-8460)
PHONE....................617 607-2000
Simon Wieczner, *CEO*
James Palo, *President*
Dan Magnarelli, *Regional Mgr*
Robert Amidon, *Engineer*
Susan Parent, *Finance*
EMP: 100
SQ FT: 15,000
SALES: 18MM **Privately Held**
WEB: www.snowbound.com
SIC: 7372 Prepackaged Software Services

(G-16196)
SOBI INC
890 Winter St Ste 200 (02451-1493)
PHONE....................610 228-2040
Lyn Wiesinger, *CEO*
Jeff Henderson, *Vice Pres*
Michael Keavany, *Vice Pres*
Kevin Springman, *Vice Pres*
Dean Pioch, *Sales Staff*
EMP: 20
SALES (est): 4.8MM
SALES (corp-wide): 962.1MM **Privately Held**
SIC: 2834 5122 Mfg Pharmaceutical Preparations Mfg Pharmaceutical Preparations Whol Drugs/Sundries
PA: Swedish Orphan Biovitrum Ab (Publ)
Tomtebodavagen 23a
Solna 171 6
869 720-00

(G-16197)
SOFTWARE LEVERAGE INC
465 Waverley Oaks Rd # 103 (02452-8465)
PHONE....................781 894-3399
John M Gilbert, *President*
EMP: 4
SQ FT: 1,500
SALES (est): 373.5K **Privately Held**
WEB: www.sli.com
SIC: 7372 Prepackaged Software Services

(G-16198)
SOJOURNIX INC
400 Totten Pond Rd # 115 (02451-2040)
PHONE....................781 864-1111
Daniel S Grau, *CEO*
EMP: 4
SALES (est): 346.7K **Privately Held**
SIC: 2834 Mfg Pharmaceutical Preparations

(G-16199)
SPIDLE CORP
Also Called: Super Faraday Labs
519 Main St (02452-5524)
PHONE....................617 448-7386
Adrian Pearce Spidle Jr, *CEO*
EMP: 3
SALES (est): 86.5K **Privately Held**
SIC: 2741 Internet Publishing And Broadcasting

(G-16200)
SSH GOVERNMENT SOLUTIONS INC
460 Totten Pond Rd # 460 (02451-1991)
PHONE....................781 247-2124
Matt McKenna, *President*
Matthew McKenna, *President*
Jyrki Lalla, *Treasurer*
Warren Browne, *Finance*
Markku Karppi, *Admin Sec*
EMP: 4
SQ FT: 5,000
SALES (est): 212.1K **Privately Held**
SIC: 7372 Prepackaged Software Services

(G-16201)
STARFISH STORAGE CORPORATION
271 Waverley Oaks Rd # 301 (02452-8469)
PHONE....................781 250-3000
Deena Berton, *President*
Deena A Berton, *Principal*
Joseph Hickson,
EMP: 9

▲ = Import ▼=Export
◆ =Import/Export

SALES (est): 439.4K Privately Held
SIC: 7372 Prepackaged Software

(G-16202)
STRAWBRRY HL GRND DELIGHTS LLC
39 Emerson Rd Ste 104 (02451-4614)
PHONE....617 319-3557
Henry M Zunino, *Principal*
EMP: 3
SALES (est): 276.5K Privately Held
SIC: 2064 Mfg Candy/Confectionery

(G-16203)
SWISS CONCEPT INC
Also Called: Concept Manufacturing Company
77 Felton St (02453-4120)
P.O. Box 6109, Holliston (01746-6109)
PHONE....781 894-1281
Chu Moy, *President*
EMP: 8
SQ FT: 3,000
SALES: 950K Privately Held
SIC: 3599 Mfg Industrial Machinery

(G-16204)
SYNDAX PHARMACEUTICALS INC (PA)
35 Gatehouse Dr Fl 3 (02451-1215)
PHONE....781 419-1400
Briggs W Morrison, *CEO*
Dennis G Podlesak, *Ch of Bd*
Michael A Metzger, *President*
Michael L Meyers, *Senior VP*
Miranda Mc Rees, *Vice Pres*
EMP: 18
SQ FT: 4,712
SALES: 1.5MM Publicly Held
SIC: 2834 Pharmaceutical Preparations

(G-16205)
SYNDAX SECURITIES CORPORATION
35 Gatehouse Dr (02451-1215)
PHONE....781 472-2985
Richard P Shea, *Principal*
EMP: 3
SALES (est): 171.4K Privately Held
SIC: 2834 Mfg Pharmaceutical Preparations

(G-16206)
TECHNICAL PUBLICATIONS INC
Also Called: Tpi Solutions Ink
45 Calvary St (02453-5974)
PHONE....781 899-0263
James W Spurrell, *President*
Diana Spurrell, *Clerk*
EMP: 10 EST: 1962
SQ FT: 8,000
SALES (est): 1.5MM Privately Held
SIC: 2752 Offset Printing

(G-16207)
TECOGEN INC (PA)
45 1st Ave (02451-1105)
PHONE....781 622-1120
Benjamin M Locke, *CEO*
Angelina M Galiteva, *Ch of Bd*
Robert A Panora, *President*
Jeffrey Glick, *Vice Pres*
Mary Mariano, *Purch Mgr*
▲ EMP: 27
SQ FT: 43,000
SALES: 35.8MM Publicly Held
WEB: www.tecogen.com
SIC: 3585 7623 Refrigeration Service/Repair Mfg Refrigeration/Heating Equipment

(G-16208)
TEGO INC
460 Totten Pond Rd # 720 (02451-1850)
PHONE....781 547-5680
Timothy Butler, *CEO*
Laverne Cerfolio, *Vice Pres*
Jessica Solimini, *Administration*
▼ EMP: 9
SQ FT: 9,000
SALES (est): 1.8MM Privately Held
SIC: 3674 Mfg Semiconductors/Related Devices

(G-16209)
TELOME INC
1393 Main St (02451-1632)
PHONE....617 383-7565
Preston Estep, *CEO*
EMP: 9
SQ FT: 3,800
SALES (est): 638.6K Privately Held
SIC: 2835 Mfg Diagnostic Substances

(G-16210)
TESARO INC (HQ)
1000 Winter St Ste 3300 (02451-1230)
PHONE....339 970-0900
Leon O Moulder Jr, *CEO*
Mary Lynne Hedley, *President*
Heidi Booth, *Area Mgr*
Todd Boudreau, *Area Mgr*
Colleen Chapman, *Area Mgr*
EMP: 117
SQ FT: 260,000
SALES: 223.3MM
SALES (corp-wide): 40.6B Privately Held
SIC: 2834 Mfg Pharmaceutical Preparations
PA: Glaxosmithkline Plc
G S K House
Brentford MIDDX TW8 9
208 047-5000

(G-16211)
TESARO SECURITIES CORPORATION
1000 Winter St (02451-1436)
PHONE....339 970-0900
Gregory Covino, *Director*
Mary Lynne Hedley, *Director*
Jerald Korn, *Director*
EMP: 598
SALES (est): 20.4MM
SALES (corp-wide): 40.6B Privately Held
SIC: 2834 Mfg Pharmaceutical Preparations
HQ: Tesaro, Inc.
1000 Winter St Ste 3300
Waltham MA 02451

(G-16212)
THERMEDETEC INC
Also Called: Thermo Detection
21 Hickory Dr 4 (02451-1034)
PHONE....508 520-0430
Anne Pol, *Senior VP*
Kenneth Apicerno, *Treasurer*
EMP: 800
SQ FT: 34,250
SALES (est): 72MM
SALES (corp-wide): 24.3B Publicly Held
SIC: 3823 Mfg Industrial Instruments
PA: Thermo Fisher Scientific Inc.
168 3rd Ave
Waltham MA 02451
781 622-1000

(G-16213)
THERMO FISHER SCIENTIFIC INC (PA)
168 3rd Ave (02451-7551)
PHONE....781 622-1000
Marc N Casper, *President*
Michael A Boxer, *Senior VP*
Peter E Hornstra, *Vice Pres*
EMP: 210
SQ FT: 127,000
SALES: 24.3B Publicly Held
WEB: www.thermo.com
SIC: 3826 3845 3823 3629 Mfg Analytical Instruments

(G-16214)
THERMO INSTRUMENT SYSTEMS INC
81 Wyman St (02451-1223)
PHONE....781 622-1000
Marizn E Dekkers, *President*
Dave Brinkley, *Sales Staff*
EMP: 4
SALES (est): 490K Privately Held
SIC: 3829 Mfg Measuring/Controlling Devices

(G-16215)
THRYV INC
201 Jones Rd Ste 1 (02451-1613)
PHONE....972 453-7000
EMP: 27
SALES (corp-wide): 1.6B Privately Held
SIC: 2741 Misc Publishing
PA: Thryv, Inc.
2200 W Airfield Dr
Dfw Airport TX 75261
972 453-7000

(G-16216)
TOUCH INC
27 Spring St (02451-4431)
PHONE....781 894-8133
George Simpson, *President*
Ira S Bernstein, *Vice Pres*
EMP: 15
SQ FT: 4,000
SALES (est): 1.9MM Privately Held
WEB: www.the-touch.com
SIC: 3911 Mfg Precious Metal Jewelry

(G-16217)
TRIKINETICS INC
56 Emerson Rd (02451-4608)
PHONE....781 891-6110
Mark Spencer, *President*
Sergio Simunovic, *Vice Pres*
EMP: 6
SALES (est): 1MM Privately Held
WEB: www.trikinetics.com
SIC: 3599 Mfg Industrial Machinery

(G-16218)
UPTODATE INC (DH)
230 3rd Ave Ste 1000 (02451-7560)
PHONE....781 392-2000
Arvind Subramanian, *President*
Ted Post, *Chief*
Denise Basow, *Vice Pres*
David A Del Toro, *Vice Pres*
Steve M Kerscher, *Vice Pres*
EMP: 60
SALES (est): 22.5MM
SALES (corp-wide): 4.7B Privately Held
WEB: www.uptodate.com
SIC: 7372 8011 Prepackaged Software Services Medical Doctor's Office
HQ: Wolters Kluwer Health, Inc.
2001 Market St Ste 5
Philadelphia PA 19103
215 521-8300

(G-16219)
VIACELL INC (DH)
Also Called: Viacord
940 Winter St (02451-1457)
PHONE....617 914-3400
Vaughn M Kailian, *Ch of Bd*
Marc D Beer, *President*
James Corbett, *President*
Mary T Thistle, *Senior VP*
Morey Kraus, *Vice Pres*
EMP: 42
SALES (est): 11.5MM
SALES (corp-wide): 2.7B Publicly Held
WEB: www.viacord.com
SIC: 2834 Mfg Pharmaceutical Preparations

(G-16220)
VISITREND LLC
80 Hope Ave Apt 402 (02453-2746)
PHONE....857 919-2372
John T Langton PHD, *Mng Member*
EMP: 10
SALES (est): 560.3K Privately Held
SIC: 7372 Prepackaged Software Services

(G-16221)
VISTERRA INC
275 2nd Ave (02451-1159)
PHONE....617 498-1070
Brian Pereira, *President*
Greg Babcock, *Vice Pres*
Jean Bender, *Vice Pres*
Jennifer Dupee, *Opers Staff*
Emily Helger, *Research*
EMP: 42
SQ FT: 14,500
SALES (est): 2.7MM Privately Held
SIC: 2834 Mfg Pharmaceutical Preparations
HQ: Otsuka America, Inc.
1 Embarcadero Ctr # 2020
San Francisco CA 94111
415 986-5300

(G-16222)
WALDEN SERVICES INC
3 Roseanna Park Dr (02452-0311)
PHONE....781 642-7653
Nina Schultz, *President*
Louis Vitiello, *Treasurer*
EMP: 4
SALES (est): 316.6K Privately Held
WEB: www.waldenservices.com
SIC: 7372 Business Services

(G-16223)
WEST ST INTRMDATE HLDINGS CORP (PA)
195 West St (02451-1111)
PHONE....781 434-5051
Michelle Graham, *Vice Pres*
Brian Wueste, *Director*
EMP: 15
SALES (est): 2.4B Privately Held
SIC: 2834 Mfg Pharmaceutical Preparations

(G-16224)
WOLTERS KLUWER FINCL SVCS INC
130 Turner St Bldg 34 (02453-8901)
PHONE....978 263-1212
Steve Tsang, *Branch Mgr*
EMP: 300
SALES (corp-wide): 4.7B Privately Held
SIC: 2761 8111 Mfg Manifold Bus Forms Legal Services Office
HQ: Wolters Kluwer Financial Services, Inc.
100 S 5th St Ste 700
Minneapolis MN 55402

(G-16225)
WORMTOWN ATOMIC PROPULSION
303 Bear Hill Rd (02451-1016)
PHONE....781 487-7777
Richard B Livingston, *President*
Ellen Livingston, *Treasurer*
EMP: 5
SQ FT: 15,000
SALES (est): 439.4K Privately Held
SIC: 3764 Atomic Propulsion Systems

(G-16226)
ZERO POROSITY CASTING INC
411 Waverley Oaks Rd (02452-8448)
PHONE....781 373-1951
Arpine Azizian, *Principal*
EMP: 12
SALES (est): 1.5MM Privately Held
SIC: 3911 Mfg Precious Metal Jewelry

(G-16227)
ZOOM INFORMATION LLC (HQ)
170 Data Dr (02451-2222)
PHONE....781 693-7500
Derek Schoettle, *CEO*
Aileen McHugh, *Engineer*
Donna Angelucci, *Accountant*
Abby Bilbo, *Finance*
Alex Harrah, *Sales Mgr*
EMP: 85
SALES (est): 19.7MM Privately Held
WEB: www.eliyon.com
SIC: 2741 Internet Publishing And Broadcasting

Ware
Hampshire County

(G-16228)
AXIS CNC INCORPORATED
39 Gould Rd (01082-9809)
PHONE....413 967-6803
Daniel G Larzazs, *Principal*
Colin Chrabaszcz, *Opers Mgr*
EMP: 14
SALES (est): 1.9MM Privately Held
SIC: 3599 Mfg Industrial Machinery

GEOGRAPHIC

(G-16229)
BAGROUT INC
44 Monroe St (01082-1608)
PHONE..................................413 949-0743
Betty Grout, *President*
EMP: 3
SALES (est): 293.5K **Privately Held**
SIC: 3171 Mfg Women's Handbags/Purses

(G-16230)
BIZ TEK PRINTING AND MKTG LLC
Also Called: BT Copy & Printing Center
5 North St Ste 7 (01082-1003)
P.O. Box 50, Sturbridge (01566-0050)
PHONE..................................508 248-3377
Dennis Craig,
EMP: 5
SQ FT: 2,500
SALES: 700K **Privately Held**
SIC: 2752 Lithographic Commercial Printing

(G-16231)
CYCLE ENGINEERING INC
132 Gilbertville Rd (01082-9201)
PHONE..................................413 967-3818
Rodney Polak, *President*
EMP: 5
SQ FT: 1,100
SALES (est): 125K **Privately Held**
SIC: 3544 Mfg Tools Dies And Automated Equipment

(G-16232)
DR BESSETTE NATURALS
71 Greenwich Rd (01082-9331)
PHONE..................................413 277-6188
EMP: 3
SALES (est): 300.4K **Privately Held**
SIC: 2841 Mfg Soap/Other Detergents

(G-16233)
ECLIPSE MFG INC
44 Pleasant St (01082-1220)
PHONE..................................920 457-2311
EMP: 25
SQ FT: 12,200
SALES: 750K **Privately Held**
SIC: 3648 Mfg Lighting Equipment

(G-16234)
JOSEPH LOTUFF SR
Also Called: Ware Sportswear
44 E Main St (01082-1385)
P.O. Box 420 (01082-0420)
PHONE..................................413 967-5964
Ric Lotuff, *Owner*
Joseph Lotuff Sr, *Owner*
EMP: 40
SALES (est): 2.7MM **Privately Held**
WEB: www.berkshireblanket.com
SIC: 2231 5621 Wool Broadwoven Fabric Mill Ret Women's Clothing

(G-16235)
KANZAKI SPECIALTY PAPERS INC (DH)
20 Cummings St (01082-1716)
PHONE..................................413 967-6204
Stephen P Hefner, *President*
Stephen Hefner, *Vice Pres*
Joshua Polak, *Vice Pres*
Peter Sawosi, *Vice Pres*
Erik Wattu, *Administration*
◆ **EMP:** 205
SQ FT: 300,000
SALES (est): 105.2MM **Privately Held**
WEB: www.kanzakiusa.com
SIC: 2621 Paper Mill

(G-16236)
QUABBIN WIRE & CABLE CO INC (PA)
10 Maple St (01082-1597)
PHONE..................................413 967-6281
Paul Engel, *President*
Debi Engel, *Exec VP*
Stacy Gilmour, *Vice Pres*
Daniel G Griswold, *Vice Pres*
George Melnik, *Vice Pres*
EMP: 75
SQ FT: 140,000
SALES (est): 17MM **Privately Held**
WEB: www.quabbin.com
SIC: 3643 3357 Nonferrous Wiredrawing/Insulating Mfg Conductive Wiring Devices

(G-16237)
STARCHEM INC (PA)
85 Beaver Rd (01082-9496)
PHONE..................................413 967-8700
Stanley Jurkowski, *President*
EMP: 8
SALES (est): 1.3MM **Privately Held**
SIC: 2841 5169 Mfg Soap/Other Detergents Whol Chemicals/Products

(G-16238)
THREE FAYS POWER LLC
189 River Rd (01082-9409)
PHONE..................................413 427-2665
Karen Fay, *Principal*
William Db Fay, *Mng Member*
Celeste Fay,
William Fay,
EMP: 3 **EST:** 2012
SALES: 125K **Privately Held**
SIC: 3999 Mfg Misc Products

(G-16239)
TURLEY PUBLICATIONS INC
Also Called: New England Antiques Journal
80 Main St (01082-1318)
PHONE..................................413 967-3505
Doug Turley, *Vice Pres*
Pamela Moen, *Branch Mgr*
EMP: 4
SALES (corp-wide): 54.3MM **Privately Held**
WEB: www.turley.com
SIC: 2711 2721 Newspapers-Publishing/Printing Periodicals-Publishing/Printing
PA: Turley Publications, Inc.
24 Water St
Palmer MA 01069
800 824-6548

Wareham
Plymouth County

(G-16240)
BBB & MACHINE INC
1 Thatcher Ln (02571-1076)
PHONE..................................508 273-0050
Kevin Allaire, *CEO*
EMP: 3
SALES (est): 367.8K **Privately Held**
SIC: 3599 Mfg Industrial Machinery

(G-16241)
BEETLE INC
3 Thatcher Ln (02571-1076)
PHONE..................................508 295-8585
William Womack, *President*
Michelle Buonitonto, *Corp Secy*
EMP: 7
SALES: 300K **Privately Held**
WEB: www.beetlecat.com
SIC: 3732 Boatbuilding/Repairing

(G-16242)
CAPE COD SHIPBUILDING CO
7 Narrows Rd (02571-1630)
P.O. Box 152 (02571-0152)
PHONE..................................508 295-3550
Gordon L Goodwin, *President*
Wendy Goodwin, *Vice Pres*
▼ **EMP:** 18 **EST:** 1899
SQ FT: 20,000
SALES (est): 3.2MM **Privately Held**
WEB: www.capecodshipbuilding.com
SIC: 3732 4492 4493 Mfg Repair Towing & Storage Of Sailboats

(G-16243)
CATAKI INTERNATIONAL INC
Also Called: Tak Systems
14 Kendrick Rd Ste 5 (02571-5020)
P.O. Box 939, East Wareham (02538-0939)
PHONE..................................508 295-9630
Michael Diesso, *President*
Cheryl Cavacas, *Vice Pres*
EMP: 21
SQ FT: 10,000
SALES (est): 2.1MM **Privately Held**
SIC: 3843 3069 7841 Manufactures Dental Medical And Veterinary Supplies

(G-16244)
DESIGN MARK INDUSTRIES INC
3 Kendrick Rd (02571-1077)
PHONE..................................800 451-3275
John Winzeler Jr, *President*
Mike Seidman, *Vice Pres*
Paul Pearson, *VP Engrg*
Steve Normandin, *Treasurer*
Spencer L Purinton, *Admin Sec*
EMP: 74
SQ FT: 19,000
SALES (est): 14.8MM **Privately Held**
WEB: www.design-mark.com
SIC: 2759 3089 3679 Commercial Printing Mfg Plastic Products Mfg Electronic Components
PA: Nfi Corp.
213 Theodore Rice Blvd
New Bedford MA 02745
508 998-9021

(G-16245)
DOROTHY COXS CANDIES INC
Also Called: Dorothy Cox Chocolates
8 Kendrick Rd Unit 4-5 (02571-1079)
PHONE..................................774 678-0654
Francis J Cox Jr, *President*
Francis J Cox Sr, *Vice Pres*
Geraldine Cox, *Treasurer*
EMP: 20
SQ FT: 8,200
SALES (est): 3.5MM **Privately Held**
WEB: www.dorothycox.com
SIC: 2064 5441 2066 Mfg Candy/Confectionery Ret Candy/Confectionery Mfg Chocolate/Cocoa Products

(G-16246)
ELECTRO-PREP INC
Also Called: Greenwood Associates
14 Kendrick Rd Ste 3 (02571-5020)
PHONE..................................508 291-2880
Skip Sullivan, *President*
Edward S Sullivan, *Treasurer*
Richard Sullivan, *Treasurer*
Casey A Sullivan, *Admin Sec*
EMP: 19
SQ FT: 6,000
SALES (est): 5.3MM **Privately Held**
WEB: www.electroprep.com
SIC: 3496 5045 Mfg Misc Fabricated Wire Products Whol Computers/Peripherals

(G-16247)
GATEHOUSE MEDIA MASS I INC
Also Called: Wareham Courier
24 Sandwich Rd (02571-1668)
PHONE..................................508 295-1190
Al Becker, *Branch Mgr*
EMP: 35
SALES (corp-wide): 1.5B **Publicly Held**
SIC: 2711 Newspapers-Publishing/Printing
HQ: Gatehouse Media Massachusetts I, Inc.
48 Dunham Rd
Beverly MA 01915
585 598-0030

(G-16248)
GATEWAY PRINTING
174 Main St (02571-2112)
PHONE..................................508 295-0505
Robert C Forrest, *Partner*
Deborah A Forrest, *Partner*
EMP: 4
SQ FT: 1,600
SALES (est): 389K **Privately Held**
SIC: 2752 Lithographic Commercial Printing

(G-16249)
HI-WAY CONCRETE PDTS CO INC
2746 Cranberry Hwy (02571-1042)
PHONE..................................508 295-0834
Richard J Vicino, *CEO*
Michael J Vicino, *COO*
Fran Vicino, *Vice Pres*
Francis C Vicino Jr, *Vice Pres*
Kristine R Monast, *CFO*
EMP: 25 **EST:** 1954
SQ FT: 9,600
SALES (est): 4.5MM **Privately Held**
SIC: 3271 3281 3251 Mfg Concrete Block/Brick Mfg Cut Stone/Products Mfg Brick/Structural Tile

(G-16250)
HOSTAR MAR TRNSPT SYSTEMS INC
1 Kendrick Rd (02571-1077)
PHONE..................................508 295-2900
Patricia B Stimson, *President*
Dwight S Stimson III, *COO*
Dwight Stimson, *COO*
▼ **EMP:** 27
SQ FT: 28,000
SALES: 5MM **Privately Held**
WEB: www.hostarmarine.com
SIC: 3799 3537 2599 3569 Mfg Transportation Equip Mfg Indstl Truck/Tractor Mfg Furniture/Fixtures Mfg General Indstl Mach Mfg Fluid Power Pump/Mtr

(G-16251)
J & J TECHNOLOGIES INC
18 Kendrick Rd (02571-1079)
PHONE..................................508 291-3803
James Ayars, *President*
Jim Ayars, *President*
Dave Goble, *Engineer*
Jack McNally, *Treasurer*
Colin Reddy, *Sales Staff*
EMP: 70
SQ FT: 30,000
SALES (est): 18.6MM **Privately Held**
WEB: www.jjtech.tv
SIC: 3672 Mfg Printed Circuit Boards

(G-16252)
M A D SIGNS
2510 Cranberry Hwy Ste 6 (02571-1019)
PHONE..................................508 273-7887
EMP: 3 **EST:** 2012
SALES (est): 144K **Privately Held**
SIC: 2711 Newspapers-Publishing/Printing

(G-16253)
NAVIONICS INC
6 Thatcher Ln (02571-1076)
PHONE..................................508 291-6000
Giuseppe Carnevali, *Ch of Bd*
Bob Moshiri, *Vice Pres*
Daniele Palma, *Treasurer*
Ilaria Gonnella, *Controller*
Rochelle Correiro, *Sales Staff*
▲ **EMP:** 27
SALES (est): 5.4MM
SALES (corp-wide): 261.7K **Privately Held**
WEB: www.navionics.com
SIC: 3812 Mfg Search/Navigation Equipment
HQ: Navionics Srl
Via Fondacci 269
Massarosa LU 55054
058 432-9114

(G-16254)
PROJECT RESOURCES INC
16 Kendrick Rd Ste 6 (02571-1067)
PHONE..................................508 295-7444
Carlo Dipersio, *President*
Joan Dipersio, *Clerk*
EMP: 15
SQ FT: 7,500
SALES (est): 2.4MM **Privately Held**
WEB: www.pri-projectresources.com
SIC: 3577 3613 Mfg Computer Peripheral Equipment Mfg Switchgear/Switchboards

(G-16255)
TREGO INC
5 Little Brook Rd (02571)
P.O. Box 579, West Wareham (02576-0579)
PHONE..................................508 291-3816
Michael Smead, *President*
EMP: 7 **EST:** 1951
SQ FT: 15,500
SALES (est): 1MM **Privately Held**
SIC: 3678 Mfg Electronic Connectors

(G-16256)
V POWER EQUIPMENT LLC
297 Charge Pond Rd (02571-1108)
PHONE....................................508 273-7596
Glen Viera,
EMP: 10
SALES (est): 222K **Privately Held**
SIC: 3714 3563 Mfg Motor Vehicle Parts/Accessories Mfg Air/Gas Compressors

(G-16257)
VIABELLA HOLDINGS LLC
Also Called: Mhgc
9 Kendrick Rd (02571-1077)
PHONE....................................800 688-9998
Mark Salkovitz, *President*
◆ **EMP:** 10
SALES (est): 175.3K **Privately Held**
SIC: 2771 2678 Mfg Greeting Cards Mfg Stationery Products

(G-16258)
VISIONAID INC
11 Kendrick Rd (02571-1077)
P.O. Box 752310, Memphis TN (38175-2310)
PHONE....................................508 295-3300
Daniel McCarthy, *President*
Ken Duffie, *Vice Pres*
Timothy Flaherty, *Vice Pres*
Calum Maclachlan, *Treasurer*
◆ **EMP:** 48 **EST:** 1943
SQ FT: 34,000
SALES (est): 7.7MM
SALES (corp-wide): 79.6MM **Privately Held**
WEB: www.visionaidinc.com
SIC: 3851 3842 2834 Manufacturing Ophthalmic Goods Surgical Appliances And Pharmaceutical Preps
HQ: Radians, Inc.
5305 Distriplex Farms Dr
Memphis TN 38141
901 388-7776

Warren
Worcester County

(G-16259)
AWL ASSOC
2345b Main St (01083-7932)
P.O. Box 4 (01083-0004)
PHONE....................................413 436-9600
Albert Lalashius, *Owner*
EMP: 3 **EST:** 1990
SALES (est): 220K **Privately Held**
SIC: 3599 Mfg Industrial Machinery

(G-16260)
CIRCOR NAVAL SOLUTIONS LLC (HQ)
82 Bridge St (01083-2144)
P.O. Box 5020, Monroe NC (28111-5020)
PHONE....................................413 436-7711
Darryl Mayhorn, *CEO*
◆ **EMP:** 57
SQ FT: 200,000
SALES (est): 17.2MM
SALES (corp-wide): 1.1B **Publicly Held**
SIC: 3561 5084 Mfg Pumps/Pumping Equipment Whol Industrial Equipment
PA: Circor International, Inc.
30 Corporate Dr Ste 200
Burlington MA 01803
781 270-1200

(G-16261)
PORTLAND VALVE LLC (HQ)
82 Bridge St (01083-2144)
P.O. Box 5020, Monroe NC (28111-5020)
PHONE....................................704 289-6511
Darryl Mayhorn, *CEO*
▲ **EMP:** 21
SQ FT: 36,000
SALES (est): 5.7MM
SALES (corp-wide): 1.1B **Publicly Held**
SIC: 3492 3599 3494 Manufactrues Fluid Power Valves/Fittings Industrial Machinery And Valves/Pipe Fittings
PA: Circor International, Inc.
30 Corporate Dr Ste 200
Burlington MA 01803
781 270-1200

(G-16262)
PORTLAND VALVE LLC
90 Industrial Way (01083)
PHONE....................................978 284-4000
EMP: 4
SALES (corp-wide): 3.6B **Publicly Held**
SIC: 3492 Mfg Fluid Power Valves/Fittings
HQ: Portland Valve Llc
82 Bridges Ave
Warren MA 01083
413 436-7711

Watertown
Middlesex County

(G-16263)
ADVANCED MECHANICAL TECH INC (PA)
Also Called: Amti
176 Waltham St (02472-4800)
PHONE....................................617 923-4174
Bruce F White, *President*
Gary M Blanchard, *Vice Pres*
Albert Drueding, *Director*
Fred W Ruland, *Admin Sec*
EMP: 33 **EST:** 1976
SQ FT: 23,000
SALES (est): 7.7MM **Privately Held**
SIC: 3829 3825 8733 Mfg Measuring/Controlling Devices Mfg Electrical Measuring Instruments Noncommercial Research Organization

(G-16264)
AGGREGATE INDS - NORTHEAST REG
48 Coolidge Ave (02472-2815)
PHONE....................................617 924-8550
Robert Peckham, *Principal*
EMP: 5
SQ FT: 1,200
SALES (corp-wide): 4.5B **Privately Held**
SIC: 3273 Mfg Ready-Mixed Concrete
HQ: Aggregate Industries - Northeast Region, Inc
1715 Brdwy
Saugus MA 01906
781 941-7200

(G-16265)
AILERON THERAPEUTICS INC
490 Arsenal Way Ste 210 (02472-2988)
PHONE....................................774 444-0704
Jeffrey A Bailey, *Ch of Bd*
Manuel C Alves Aivado, *President*
Richard J Wanstall, *CFO*
Kira A Nelson, *VP Finance*
Vojislav Vukovic, *Chief Mktg Ofcr*
EMP: 23
SALES (est): 1.8MM **Privately Held**
SIC: 2834 8731 Pharmaceutical Preparations Biotechnical Research

(G-16266)
ALDATU BIOSCIENCES INC
201 Dexter Ave (02472-4228)
PHONE....................................978 705-1036
David Raiser, *CEO*
Iain Macleod, *Treasurer*
EMP: 5
SALES (est): 225.8K **Privately Held**
SIC: 2835 Mfg Diagnostic Substances

(G-16267)
AM TECHNOLOGIES INC
108 Water St (02472-4696)
PHONE....................................617 926-7920
Andrew Mashulam, *Principal*
EMP: 3
SALES (est): 210K **Privately Held**
SIC: 3579 Mfg Office Machines

(G-16268)
AMBERGEN INC (PA)
313 Pleasant St Ste 4 (02472-2491)
PHONE....................................617 923-9990
Kenneth Rothschild, *President*
Rashel Batelman, *Admin Sec*
EMP: 15
SQ FT: 5,000
SALES: 1.9MM **Privately Held**
WEB: www.ambergen.com
SIC: 2836 Mfg Biological Products

(G-16269)
ARCHITCTRAL GRAPHICS SIGNS INC
73 Oakland St (02472-2251)
PHONE....................................617 924-0070
Susan Tanner, *President*
E Stephen Tanner, *Treasurer*
EMP: 6
SALES: 450K **Privately Held**
SIC: 3993 Mfg Signs/Advertising Specialties

(G-16270)
ATHENAHEALTH INC (HQ)
311 Arsenal St Ste 14 (02472-2785)
PHONE....................................617 402-1000
Robert E Segert, *CEO*
Diane Bartoli, *General Mgr*
Victoria Bartolome, *Business Mgr*
Ashley Ward, *Business Mgr*
Josh Gray, *Vice Pres*
EMP: 148
SQ FT: 551,984
SALES: 1.2B **Privately Held**
WEB: www.athenahealth.com
SIC: 7372 Prepackaged Software Svc
PA: Athenahealth Holding Corp.
311 Arsenal St Ste 14
Watertown MA 02472
617 402-1000

(G-16271)
BAIKAR ASSOCIATION INC (PA)
Also Called: Armenian Mirror-Spectator
755 Mount Auburn St (02472-1509)
PHONE....................................617 924-4420
Dr Artin Arzoumanian, *President*
Dr Armen Demerjian, *Treasurer*
EMP: 12
SALES: 219.3K **Privately Held**
SIC: 2731 2732 2711 Publishers & Newspaper Periodicals

(G-16272)
BALANCETEK CORPORATION
18 Winsor Ave (02472-1460)
PHONE....................................781 910-9706
John Vittal, *Vice Pres*
Lewis M Nashner, *Director*
David R Pierson, *Director*
Conrad Wall III, *Director*
Susan Dorn, *Shareholder*
EMP: 6
SALES (est): 365.2K **Privately Held**
SIC: 3841 Mfg Surgical/Medical Instruments

(G-16273)
BLOOM & COMPANY INC
694 Mount Auburn St (02472-3572)
PHONE....................................617 923-1526
Richard Bloom, *President*
George Bloom, *Vice Pres*
EMP: 18 **EST:** 1955
SQ FT: 5,000
SALES (est): 1.4MM **Privately Held**
WEB: www.bloomandcompany.com
SIC: 2391 7389 Contract Interior Design Installation And Manufacture Of Window Treatments For The Commercial And Healthcare Industries

(G-16274)
BOSTON SCIENTIFIC CORPORATION
Medi-Tech
480 Pleasant St (02472-2463)
PHONE....................................617 972-4000
Peter Nicholas, *Manager*
Bob Lane, *Master*
EMP: 285
SALES (corp-wide): 9.8B **Publicly Held**
WEB: www.bsci.com
SIC: 3841 Mfg/Distribution Of Medical Devices
PA: Boston Scientific Corporation
300 Boston Scientific Way
Marlborough MA 01752
508 683-4000

(G-16275)
BOSTON TURNING WORKS
120 Elm St (02472-2966)
PHONE....................................617 924-4747
Peter Maguire, *Owner*
EMP: 4
SQ FT: 6,000
SALES (est): 450K **Privately Held**
WEB: www.bostonturningworks.com
SIC: 2499 2431 Mfg Wood Products Mfg Millwork

(G-16276)
CHARLESBRIDGE PUBLISHING INC (PA)
Also Called: Imagine Publishing
85 Main St Ste 5 (02472-4411)
PHONE....................................617 926-0329
Brent H Farmer, *President*
Donald Robb, *Vice Pres*
Mary Sabia, *Vice Pres*
Brian Walker, *Vice Pres*
Rachel Doody, *Sales Staff*
▲ **EMP:** 32 **EST:** 1980
SQ FT: 6,000
SALES (est): 3.3MM **Privately Held**
WEB: www.charlesbridge.com
SIC: 2741 2731 Misc Publishing Books-Publishing/Printing

(G-16277)
DEMANDQ INC
480 Pleasant St Ste B110 (02472-2462)
PHONE....................................617 401-2165
Edison Almeida, *CEO*
Jon Stahl, *COO*
Jerry Ventura, *Vice Pres*
Leo Su, *Engineer*
Jim Godwin, *Executive*
EMP: 4
SALES: 200K **Privately Held**
SIC: 3822 Mfg Environmental Controls

(G-16278)
DIELECTRIC PRODUCTS
178 Orchard St (02472-1817)
PHONE....................................617 924-5688
Gerard Gilkie, *Owner*
EMP: 6
SQ FT: 4,000
SALES: 250K **Privately Held**
SIC: 3567 Mfg Dielectric Heating Equipment

(G-16279)
DOBLE ENGINEERING COMPANY (HQ)
85 Walnut St (02472-4037)
PHONE....................................617 926-4900
David B Zabetakis, *President*
Richard Heywood, *Managing Dir*
Don Angell, *Vice Pres*
Julie Brown, *Vice Pres*
Jay Cunningham, *Vice Pres*
▲ **EMP:** 13
SQ FT: 85,000
SALES (est): 165.7MM
SALES (corp-wide): 812.9MM **Publicly Held**
WEB: www.doble.com
SIC: 3825 7359 3829 3826 Mfg Elec Measuring Instr Equipment Rental/Leasing Mfg Measure/Control Dvcs Mfg Analytical Instr
PA: Esco Technologies Inc.
9900 Clayton Rd Ste A
Saint Louis MO 63124
314 213-7200

(G-16280)
EASTGATE SYSTEMS INC
134 Main St Ste 2a (02472-4416)
PHONE....................................617 924-9044
Mark Bernstein, *President*
Linda J Thorsen, *Principal*
Meryl R Cohen, *Treasurer*
EMP: 4
SQ FT: 1,500
SALES (est): 421.5K **Privately Held**
SIC: 7372 2731 Prepackaged Software Services Books-Publishing/Printing

GEOGRAPHIC

(G-16281)
ELITE
129a Galen St (02472-4507)
PHONE..................................617 407-9300
Anna Kupelian, *Owner*
EMP: 3
SQ FT: 600
SALES (est): 103K **Privately Held**
SIC: 2759 Engraving Service

(G-16282)
ENANTA PHARMACEUTICALS INC
500 Arsenal St (02472-2806)
PHONE..................................617 607-0800
Bruce L A Carter, *Ch of Bd*
Jay R Luly, *President*
Yat Sun or, *Senior VP*
Jeffrey Higgins, *Opers Mgr*
Jiang Long, *Research*
EMP: 89
SQ FT: 49,000
SALES: 205.2MM **Privately Held**
WEB: www.enanta.com
SIC: 2834 8731 Pharmaceutical Preparations Biotechnical Research

(G-16283)
EVEREST HERALD LTD PARTNERSHIP
25 Norseman Ave (02472-1527)
PHONE..................................617 744-0620
Khatiwada Shesh, *Principal*
EMP: 3
SALES (est): 112.9K **Privately Held**
SIC: 2711 Newspapers-Publishing/Printing

(G-16284)
EXERGEN CORPORATION
400 Pleasant St (02472-2691)
PHONE..................................617 923-9900
Francesco Pompei, *President*
Bart Van Liempd, *General Mgr*
Henry L Anthony, *Vice Pres*
Roger Nelson, *Senior Engr*
Janette Lee, *Design Engr*
◆ **EMP:** 100
SQ FT: 37,000
SALES (est): 29.1MM **Privately Held**
WEB: www.exergen.com
SIC: 3826 8711 Mfg Analytical Instruments Engineering Services

(G-16285)
EXTRA VIRGIN FOODS INC
Also Called: Extra Virgin Foods Company
71 Arlington St (02472-4274)
PHONE..................................617 407-9161
Paul Hatziiliades, *President*
EMP: 9
SALES (est): 3.2MM **Privately Held**
SIC: 2079 2022 Mfg Edible Fats/Oils Mfg Cheese

(G-16286)
EYE POINT PHARMAC
400 Pleasant St (02472-2691)
PHONE..................................617 926-5000
EMP: 3
SALES (est): 157.7K
SALES (corp-wide): 2.9MM **Publicly Held**
SIC: 3826 Analytical Instruments
PA: Eyepoint Pharmaceuticals, Inc.
480 Pleasant St Ste B300
Watertown MA 02472
617 926-5000

(G-16287)
EYEPOINT PHARMACEUTICALS INC (PA)
480 Pleasant St Ste B300 (02472-2468)
PHONE..................................617 926-5000
Goran Ando, *Ch of Bd*
Nancy Lurker, *President*
Ron Honig, *Senior VP*
Hong Guo, *Vice Pres*
George O Elston, *CFO*
EMP: 44
SQ FT: 20,240
SALES: 2.9MM **Publicly Held**
WEB: www.psivida.com
SIC: 3841 3826 Mfg Surgical And Medical Instruments Laboratory Analytical Instruments

(G-16288)
FLUID MANAGEMENT SYSTEMS INC
Also Called: F M S
580 Pleasant St (02472-2408)
PHONE..................................617 393-2396
Hamid Shirkhan, *President*
Jim Ceven, *Engineer*
Amanda Garcia, *Accountant*
Matthew Falkenstein, *Technical Staff*
EMP: 25
SQ FT: 25,000
SALES: 2.5MM **Privately Held**
WEB: www.forspace.com
SIC: 3826 Mfg Analytical Instruments

(G-16289)
HAIRENIK ASSOCIATION INC
80 Bigelow Ave (02472-2012)
PHONE..................................617 926-3974
Pearl Teague, *President*
Asted Kotchikian, *President*
Khatchig Mouradian, *Editor*
Vicken Aprahamian, *Div Sub Head*
Khajak Megerdichian, *Clerk*
EMP: 10
SQ FT: 2,028
SALES (est): 510K **Privately Held**
SIC: 2711 Newspapers-Publishing/Printing

(G-16290)
HARRINGTON AIR SYSTEMS LLC
80 Rosedale Rd (02472-2234)
PHONE..................................781 341-1999
Rick Donohue, *Vice Pres*
Joseph Cannistraro,
David Cannistraro,
EMP: 21
SALES (est): 2.6MM **Privately Held**
SIC: 3444 1711 Manufacturing Sheet Metalwork Plumbing/Heating/Air Cond Contractor

(G-16291)
IGGYS BREAD LTD
Also Called: Iggys Bread of The World
205 Arlington St Ste 4 (02472-2046)
PHONE..................................617 491-7600
Mark Menezes, *Manager*
EMP: 20 **Privately Held**
WEB: www.iggysbread.com
SIC: 2051 Mfg Bread/Related Products
PA: Iggy's Bread Ltd.
130 Fawcett St
Cambridge MA 02138

(G-16292)
INTELLIGENT BUS ENTRMT INC
480 Pleasant St Ste C210 (02472-2596)
PHONE..................................617 519-4172
Adam Sodowick, *CEO*
EMP: 19
SALES (est): 1.7MM **Privately Held**
WEB: www.trueoffice.com
SIC: 7372 7379 Prepackaged Software Services Computer Related Services

(G-16293)
KALA PHARMACEUTICALS INC
490 Arsenal Way Ste 120 (02472-2988)
PHONE..................................781 996-5252
Mark Iwicki, *Ch of Bd*
Susan Coultas, *Vice Pres*
Mary Reumuth, *CFO*
Kim Brazzell, *Chief Mktg Ofcr*
Patrick Bedell, *Exec Dir*
EMP: 37
SQ FT: 66,052
SALES (est): 4.4MM **Privately Held**
SIC: 2834 Mfg Pharmaceutical Preparations

(G-16294)
LEXITEK INC
50 Hunt St Ste 120 (02472-4625)
PHONE..................................781 431-9604
Steven Ebstein, *President*
Chwenyuan Ku, *Principal*
EMP: 3
SQ FT: 3,000
SALES (est): 415.7K **Privately Held**
WEB: www.lexitek.com
SIC: 3827 Mfg Optical Instruments/Lenses

(G-16295)
LIFEADY INC
72 Winsor Ave (02472-1460)
PHONE..................................781 632-1296
Mark Steinwinter, *President*
Eamon Kearns, *COO*
Olu Brown, *Chief Engr*
EMP: 3
SALES (est): 71.1K **Privately Held**
SIC: 7372 7389 Prepackaged Software Services

(G-16296)
LUCK INDUSTRIAL SALES INC
46 Quincy St (02472-1802)
PHONE..................................617 924-0728
Randy Luck, *President*
EMP: 3
SALES: 490K **Privately Held**
WEB: www.luckindustrialsales.com
SIC: 3535 Mfg Conveyors/Equipment

(G-16297)
MARKARIAN ELECTRIC LLC
586 Pleasant St Ste 5 (02472-2678)
PHONE..................................617 393-9700
Eric A Markarian, *Principal*
EMP: 7
SALES (est): 1.3MM **Privately Held**
SIC: 3699 1731 Mfg Electrical Equipment/Supplies Electrical Contractor

(G-16298)
MARKFORGED INC (PA)
480 Pleasant St (02472-2463)
PHONE..................................866 496-1805
Greg Mark, *CEO*
Darcey Harrison, *Vice Pres*
Assaf Zipori, *Vice Pres*
Brian Nadeau, *VP Engrg*
Alexander Crease, *Engineer*
EMP: 150
SALES (est): 3.6MM **Privately Held**
SIC: 3599 Mfg Industrial Machinery

(G-16299)
MARKFORGED INC
85 School St (02472-4251)
PHONE..................................617 666-1935
EMP: 60
SALES (corp-wide): 3.6MM **Privately Held**
SIC: 3599 Mfg Industrial Machinery
PA: Markforged, Inc.
480 Pleasant St
Watertown MA 02472
866 496-1805

(G-16300)
MCDERMOTT PALLOTTA INC
Also Called: Evans & Faulkner
376 Arsenal St (02472-2892)
PHONE..................................617 924-2318
Thomas J McDermott, *President*
Marylouise Pallotta-Mcdermott, *Treasurer*
EMP: 5
SQ FT: 6,500
SALES (est): 616.9K **Privately Held**
SIC: 2791 2789 2752 Typesetting Services Bookbinding/Related Work Lithographic Commercial Printing

(G-16301)
METALLIUM INC
11 Duff St (02472-3001)
PHONE..................................508 728-9074
David W Hamric, *Principal*
EMP: 3
SALES (est): 202.7K **Privately Held**
SIC: 2819 Mfg Industrial Inorganic Chemicals

(G-16302)
MONADNOCK ASSOCIATES INC (PA)
3 Brook St (02472-2314)
PHONE..................................617 924-7032
Stephen Burakoff, *President*
Mark Perreault, *CFO*
Carl Bindman, *Treasurer*
EMP: 10
SALES (est): 957.2K **Privately Held**
SIC: 7372 6211 Prepackaged Software Investment Banking

(G-16303)
NEWLY WEDS FOODS INC
70 Grove St 80 (02472-2829)
PHONE..................................617 926-7600
John Lincoln, *Plant Mgr*
Dave Curran, *Purch Mgr*
Craig Logan, *Maintence Staff*
EMP: 80
SQ FT: 180,000
SALES (corp-wide): 128.2MM **Privately Held**
WEB: www.newlywedsfoods.com
SIC: 2051 2099 Mfg Bread/Related Products Mfg Food Preparations
PA: Newly Weds Foods, Inc.
4140 W Fullerton Ave
Chicago IL 60639
773 489-7000

(G-16304)
P & M BRICK & BLOCK INC
213 Arlington St (02472-2004)
PHONE..................................617 924-6020
Michael P Pirolli Jr, *President*
John Pirolli, *Vice Pres*
Robert A Pirolli, *Treasurer*
Frank K Sheehan, *Clerk*
▲ **EMP:** 8
SQ FT: 16,000
SALES: 1MM **Privately Held**
SIC: 3271 5211 Mfg Concrete Block/Brick Ret Lumber/Building Materials

(G-16305)
PAULSON ELECTRIC
75 Partridge St (02472-1628)
PHONE..................................617 926-5661
Carl Paulson, *Principal*
EMP: 5
SALES (est): 378.2K **Privately Held**
SIC: 3993 Mfg Signs/Advertising Specialties

(G-16306)
PETER YOUNG COMPANY
Also Called: A A Mono Rite Acct Brd Sys
11 Boyd St (02472-2534)
P.O. Box 66, Brookline (02446-0001)
PHONE..................................617 923-1101
Peter Young, *President*
EMP: 6
SQ FT: 9,104
SALES (est): 452.4K **Privately Held**
SIC: 2759 Business Forms Printing

(G-16307)
PHARMA LAUNCHER LLC
290 Pleasant St Apt 219 (02472-2430)
PHONE..................................508 812-0850
Katherine Tsaioun, *President*
EMP: 3
SALES (est): 157K **Privately Held**
SIC: 2834 Business Services, Nec, Nsk

(G-16308)
PULPDENT CORPORATION
80 Oakland St (02472-2202)
P.O. Box 780 (02471-0780)
PHONE..................................617 926-6666
Harold Berk, *President*
Kenneth J Berk, *Corp Secy*
Frederick Berk, *Vice Pres*
▲ **EMP:** 80
SQ FT: 60,000
SALES (est): 15.3MM **Privately Held**
WEB: www.pulpdent.com
SIC: 3843 Mfg Dental Equipment/Supplies

(G-16309)
Q-BIZ SOLUTIONS LLC
480 Pleasant St Ste B200 (02472-2518)
PHONE..................................617 212-7684
Jayne Thompson,
Nield Montgomery,
EMP: 3
SALES (est): 55.8K **Privately Held**
SIC: 7372 Prepackaged Software Services
PA: Dynamo Software, Inc.
480 Pleasant St Ste B200
Watertown MA 02472

(G-16310)
RADIATION MONITORING DVCS INC (HQ)
44 Hunt St Ste 2 (02472-4699)
PHONE..................................617 668-6800
Kanai Shah, *President*
Kent Riley, *Principal*
Michael Squillante, *Vice Pres*
EMP: 29
SQ FT: 10,000
SALES (est): 13.4MM
SALES (corp-wide): 43.7MM **Privately Held**
WEB: www.rmdinc.com
SIC: 3829 3845 Manufactures Measuring/Controlling Devices And Electromedical Equipment
PA: Dynasil Corporation Of America
313 Washington St Ste 403
Newton MA 02458
617 668-6855

(G-16311)
RESPIRATORY MOTION INC
80 Coolidge Hill Rd (02472-5003)
PHONE..................................508 954-2706
Jenny E Freeman, *President*
Kevin Hughes, *Vice Pres*
Malcolm Bock, *VP Engrg*
Shelby Morss, *QC Mgr*
Matthew McGuire, *Research*
EMP: 20
SALES: 700K **Privately Held**
SIC: 3845 Mfg Electromedical Equipment

(G-16312)
RMD INSTRUMENTS CORP
44 Hunt St Ste 2 (02472-4624)
PHONE..................................617 668-6900
Gerald Entine, *President*
▲ **EMP:** 35
SALES (est): 5.6MM **Privately Held**
SIC: 3829 Mfg Measuring/Controlling Devices

(G-16313)
SALT WOODS LLC
19 Calvin Rd (02472-2001)
PHONE..................................617 744-9401
Daniel Crossman, *Principal*
EMP: 3 **EST:** 2014
SALES (est): 124.6K **Privately Held**
SIC: 2899 Mfg Chemical Preparations

(G-16314)
SELECTA BIOSCIENCES INC (PA)
480 Arsenal Way Ste 1 (02472-2896)
PHONE..................................617 923-1400
Carsten Brunn, *CEO*
Omid Farokhzad, *Ch of Bd*
Werner Cautreels, *President*
Carrie S Cox, *Chairman*
Lloyd Johnston, *COO*
EMP: 45
SQ FT: 27,833
SALES: 903K **Publicly Held**
SIC: 2834 Mfg Pharmaceutical Preparations

(G-16315)
SEVEN CYCLES INC
125 Walnut St Ste 206 (02472-4050)
PHONE..................................617 923-7774
Robert Vandermark, *President*
EMP: 25
SQ FT: 7,000
SALES (est): 4.1MM **Privately Held**
WEB: www.sevencycles.com
SIC: 3751 Ret Sporting Goods/Bicycles

(G-16316)
SIGNWORKS GROUP INC
60 Arsenal St Ste 2 (02472-2659)
PHONE..................................617 924-0292
Bernard Lebow, *President*
Yvonne McAdow, *Project Mgr*
Jim Treacy, *Sales Staff*
EMP: 12
SQ FT: 3,000
SALES (est): 1.5MM **Privately Held**
WEB: www.signworksgroup.com
SIC: 3993 Mfg Sales And Service Intand Ext Signage

(G-16317)
SOCOMEC INC (DH)
9 Galen St Ste 120 (02472-4521)
PHONE..................................617 245-0447
Michael Krumenacker, *CEO*
John Cascio, *Treasurer*
Paul Smith, *Sales Staff*
Linn Steve, *Manager*
Thomas H Thorelli, *Admin Sec*
▲ **EMP:** 11
SQ FT: 15,000
SALES (est): 4MM
SALES (corp-wide): 3.1MM **Privately Held**
SIC: 3679 5065 3699 Mfg Electronic Components Whol Electronic Parts/Equipment Mfg Electrical Equipment/Supplies
HQ: Socomec
1 A 4
Benfeld 67230
388 574-141

(G-16318)
SPRING WATER ASSOCIATES USA
Also Called: Summit Springs
31 Oakley Rd (02472-1305)
P.O. Box 1446, Concord (01742-1446)
PHONE..................................978 371-0138
Sahag Bukruian, *President*
Christine Bukruian, *Vice Pres*
Tanya Bukruian, *Admin Sec*
EMP: 6
SQ FT: 1,000
SALES: 1.3MM **Privately Held**
SIC: 2086 Mfg Bottled/Canned Soft Drinks

(G-16319)
SQZ BIOTECHNOLOGIES COMPANY
134 Coolidge Ave (02472-2971)
PHONE..................................617 758-8672
Agustin Lopez Marquez, *CEO*
Volker Herrmann, *President*
Armon Sharei, *Chairman*
Amy Merino, *Research*
Teri Loxam, *CFO*
EMP: 5
SALES: 430K **Privately Held**
SIC: 3841 7389 Mfg Surgical/Medical Instruments Business Services At Non-Commercial Site

(G-16320)
TARVEDA THERAPEUTICS INC
134 Coolidge Ave (02472-2971)
PHONE..................................617 923-4100
Drew Fromkin, *President*
Steven A Hamburger, *Vice Pres*
Sudha Kadiyala, *Vice Pres*
Laura MEI, *Vice Pres*
Brian Roberts, *CFO*
EMP: 30
SALES (est): 6.6MM **Privately Held**
SIC: 2834 Mfg Pharmaceutical Preparations

(G-16321)
TETRAPHASE PHARMACEUTICALS INC (PA)
480 Arsenal Way Ste 2 (02472-2895)
PHONE..................................617 715-3600
Leonard Patrick Gage, *Ch of Bd*
Larry Edwards, *President*
Maria Stahl, *Senior VP*
Christopher Watt, *Senior VP*
Larry Tsai, *Chief Mktg Ofcr*
EMP: 65
SQ FT: 37,438
SALES: 18.9MM **Publicly Held**
WEB: www.tetraphasepharma.com
SIC: 2834 2833 Pharmaceutical Preparations Antibiotics

(G-16322)
THERMA-FLOW INC
Also Called: Everhot
191 Arlington St (02472-2003)
P.O. Box 416 (02471-0416)
PHONE..................................617 924-3877
Edwin Hill, *President*
Robert Suffredini, *CFO*
Bob Suffredini, *Treasurer*
▲ **EMP:** 25
SQ FT: 33,000
SALES (est): 5.9MM **Privately Held**
WEB: www.tfi-everhot.com
SIC: 3443 3639 Mfg Fabricated Plate Work Mfg Household Appliances

(G-16323)
THREE TWINS PRODUCTIONS INC
18 Bridge St (02472-4811)
PHONE..................................617 926-0377
Michael Gilarde, *President*
Thomas Gilarde, *Vice Pres*
Vincent Gilarde, *Treasurer*
EMP: 12
SQ FT: 3,200
SALES (est): 1.3MM **Privately Held**
SIC: 2759 7389 Screen Printers & Embroidering

(G-16324)
TOM SNYDER PRODUCTIONS INC (HQ)
100 Talcott Ave Ste 6 (02472-5715)
PHONE..................................617 600-2145
Rick Abrams, *President*
Stacey Pusey, *Director*
EMP: 100
SQ FT: 14,500
SALES (est): 21.1MM
SALES (corp-wide): 1.6B **Publicly Held**
WEB: www.classroomdiscussions.com
SIC: 7372 7371 7331 Prepackaged Software Services Custom Computer Programing Direct Mail Advertising Services
PA: Scholastic Corporation
557 Broadway Lbby 1
New York NY 10012
212 343-6100

(G-16325)
TRANS METRICS INC (HQ)
180 Dexter Ave (02472-4202)
P.O. Box 9143 (02471-9143)
PHONE..................................617 926-1000
David Reis, *President*
Peter Godfrey, *Vice Pres*
Brian Hallihan, *VP Finance*
EMP: 15
SQ FT: 100,000
SALES (est): 1.5MM
SALES (corp-wide): 39.4MM **Privately Held**
WEB: www.trans-metrics.com
SIC: 3829 5084 Mfg Measuring/Controlling Devices Whol Industrial Equipment
PA: United Electric Controls Company
180 Dexter Ave
Watertown MA 02472
617 923-6900

(G-16326)
UMECH TECHNOLOGIES LLC
25 Clarendon St (02472-2813)
PHONE..................................617 923-2942
Abraham McCallister, *Principal*
Cameron Abnet, *Vice Pres*
EMP: 4 **EST:** 2000
SALES (est): 408.8K **Privately Held**
SIC: 3643 Mfg Micro-Electrical Mechanical Systems Testers

(G-16327)
UNITED ELECTRIC CONTROLS CO
Also Called: Trans Metrics Division
180 Dexter Ave (02472-4200)
P.O. Box B (02472)
PHONE..................................617 926-1000
David Reis, *CEO*
Levon Khatchadourian, *Technical Staff*
EMP: 99
SALES (corp-wide): 39.4MM **Privately Held**
WEB: www.ueonline.com
SIC: 3823 Mfg Process Control Instruments
PA: United Electric Controls Company
180 Dexter Ave
Watertown MA 02472
617 923-6900

(G-16328)
UNITED MARBLE FABRICATORS INC
10 Munroe Ave (02472-2834)
PHONE..................................617 926-6226
Thomas Kilfoyle, *President*
▲ **EMP:** 6
SQ FT: 4,000
SALES (est): 2MM **Privately Held**
SIC: 3281 Mfg Granite And Marble Products

(G-16329)
VIROGEN CORP
200 Dexter Ave (02472-4238)
PHONE..................................617 926-9167
EMP: 4
SQ FT: 1,500
SALES (est): 360K **Privately Held**
WEB: www.virogen.com
SIC: 3826 Analytical Instruments, Nsk

(G-16330)
WINDGAP MEDICAL INC
200 Dexter Ave Ste 2 (02472-4244)
PHONE..................................617 440-3311
Chris Stepanian, *President*
Brent Buchine, *Chairman*
Julia Bradsher, *Adv Board Mem*
EMP: 5 **EST:** 2012
SQ FT: 500
SALES: 400K **Privately Held**
SIC: 3841 5122 Mfg Surgical/Medical Instruments Whol Drugs/Sundries

(G-16331)
WITRICITY CORPORATION (PA)
57 Water St (02472-4603)
PHONE..................................617 926-2700
Alex Gruzen, *CEO*
Steve Chen, *Vice Pres*
David Schatz, *Vice Pres*
Donald R Peck, *CFO*
Morris Kesler, *CTO*
EMP: 15
SALES (est): 3.2MM **Privately Held**
SIC: 3559 7389 Mfg Misc Industry Machinery Business Services

Wayland
Middlesex County

(G-16332)
ANNOVATION BIOPHARMA INC
2 Dairy Farm Ln (01778-2817)
PHONE..................................617 724-0343
David Grayzel MD, *CEO*
EMP: 5
SALES (est): 180.5K
SALES (corp-wide): 6.1MM **Privately Held**
SIC: 3841 2834 Develops Pharmaceutical Products In The Field Of Anesthesia Sedation And Sleep
PA: The Medicines Company
8 Sylvan Way
Parsippany NJ 07054
973 290-6000

(G-16333)
ARTQUICK CORP
72 Oxbow Rd (01778-1009)
PHONE..................................508 358-4864
George Dergalis, *President*
EMP: 3
SALES (est): 18.3K **Privately Held**
SIC: 2741 Misc Publishing

(G-16334)
AURIGA MEASUREMENT SYSTEMS (PA)
Also Called: Auriga Microwave
302 Willow Brook Dr (01778-5123)
PHONE..................................978 452-7700
Ted Lewis, *Vice Pres*
Yusuke Tajima, *Chief Engr*
Bruce L Cohen,
Michael Menzer,
EMP: 5
SQ FT: 14,000

GEOGRAPHIC

SALES (est): 3.2MM Privately Held
WEB: www.aurigamicrowave.com
SIC: 3663 3825 3812 Mfg Radio/Tv Communication Equipment Mfg Electrical Measuring Instruments Mfg Search/Navigation Equipment

(G-16335)
CITY PBLCATIONS GREATER BOSTON
18 Lake Shore Dr (01778-4104)
PHONE..................................617 549-7622
Christopher Howard, *Owner*
EMP: 7
SALES (est): 400K Privately Held
SIC: 7372 8742 Prepackaged Software Services Management Consulting Services

(G-16336)
SMPRETTY INC
Also Called: Style ME Pretty
97 Lincoln Rd (01778-1303)
PHONE..................................508 358-1639
Tait Larson, *President*
EMP: 7
SALES: 1MM Privately Held
SIC: 2741 7389 Internet Publishing And Broadcasting

(G-16337)
WAYLAND SUDBURY SEPTAGE
490 Boston Post Rd (01778-1831)
P.O. Box 71 (01778-0071)
PHONE..................................508 358-7328
EMP: 3
SALES (est): 278.9K Privately Held
SIC: 3589 Mfg Service Industry Machinery

Webster
Worcester County

(G-16338)
ALUMI-NEX MOLD INC
155 Chase Ave (01570-4325)
PHONE..................................508 949-2200
John Walker Jr, *President*
EMP: 14
SQ FT: 6,000
SALES (est): 1.9MM Privately Held
SIC: 3544 3089 Mfg Dies/Tools/Jigs/Fixtures Mfg Plastic Products

(G-16339)
ANGLO SILVER LINER CO
21 Pearl St (01570-2223)
P.O. Box 899 (01570-0899)
PHONE..................................508 943-1440
Dilip Mehta, *President*
Joe Tone, *President*
EMP: 18
SQ FT: 60,000
SALES (est): 1.1MM Privately Held
SIC: 2221 Mfg Textile Fabrics

(G-16340)
CM MURPHY WELDING INC ✪
75 Lakeside Ave (01570-3591)
PHONE..................................508 868-8511
EMP: 8 EST: 2019
SALES (est): 88.7K Privately Held
SIC: 7692 Welding Repair

(G-16341)
DG MARSHALL ASSOCIATES INC
11 Old Worcester Rd (01570-2112)
PHONE..................................508 943-2394
John Murphy, *Engineer*
Bob Lapan, *Design Engr*
Brett Napierata, *Sales Mgr*
Jim Marshall, *Manager*
EMP: 24
SALES (est): 6.4MM Privately Held
SIC: 3535 Mfg Conveyors/Equipment

(G-16342)
HAZARD MARINE A DIV LTD INDS
4 Town Forest Rd (01570-3165)
PHONE..................................508 943-7531
Dean R Hazard, *President*
EMP: 6
SALES (est): 953.3K Privately Held
SIC: 3732 7699 Boatbuilding/Repairing Repair Services

(G-16343)
HT MACHINE CO INC
15 Town Forest Rd (01570-3112)
PHONE..................................508 949-1105
Steven Leighton, *President*
Thomas L Holden, *Treasurer*
Kathryn J Holden, *Admin Sec*
EMP: 17 EST: 1969
SQ FT: 10,000
SALES (est): 3.3MM Privately Held
WEB: www.htmachine.com
SIC: 3599 Mfg Industrial Machinery

(G-16344)
JAF CORPORATION
Also Called: Atlas Screen Process
37 Market St (01570-2246)
PHONE..................................508 943-8519
Gregory Furey, *President*
EMP: 3 EST: 1961
SQ FT: 5,000
SALES: 300K Privately Held
SIC: 3552 3555 Mfg Textile Machinery Mfg Printing Trades Machinery

(G-16345)
JEFFCO FIBRES INC (PA)
12 Park St (01570-2888)
P.O. Box 816 (01570-0816)
PHONE..................................508 943-0440
Jeffrey H Lonstein, *President*
Blanche Lonstein, *Corp Secy*
Wayne Ushman, *Director*
◆ EMP: 140 EST: 1971
SQ FT: 200,000
SALES: 75MM Privately Held
SIC: 3086 5199 Mfg Fibre Foam Products Whol Nondurable Goods

(G-16346)
LELANITE CORPORATION (PA)
1 Cudworth Rd (01570-3102)
P.O. Box 160 (01570-0160)
PHONE..................................508 987-2637
Richard G Perry, *President*
Marc Frieden, *Engineer*
Karen Perry, *Admin Sec*
EMP: 42 EST: 1956
SQ FT: 106,000
SALES (est): 6.8MM Privately Held
WEB: www.lelanite.com
SIC: 3086 2448 Mfg Plastic Foam Products Mfg Wood Pallets/Skids

(G-16347)
LINX CONSULTING LLC
Also Called: Raymond L Martin
661 S Main St Ste 7 (01570-2280)
PHONE..................................508 461-6333
Raymond Martin, *Mng Member*
EMP: 10
SQ FT: 6,000
SALES (est): 1.4MM Privately Held
SIC: 3663 8741 Wireless Antenna Assembly Project Management

(G-16348)
LOUIS RICHARDS
Also Called: Classic Millwork Design Co
661 S Main St Ste 1 (01570-2280)
PHONE..................................508 671-9017
Louis Richards, *Owner*
EMP: 5
SQ FT: 7,000
SALES (est): 764.2K Privately Held
SIC: 2431 Mfg Millwork

(G-16349)
PLASMA GIKEN LIMITED COMPANY
6 Viking Rd (01570-3156)
PHONE..................................508 640-7708
EMP: 5 EST: 2012
SALES (est): 340K Privately Held
SIC: 2836 Mfg Biological Products

(G-16350)
SB MARKETERS INC
14 Mark Ave (01570-3569)
PHONE..................................508 943-7162
EMP: 3
SALES (est): 156.7K Privately Held
SIC: 3845 Mfg Electromedical Equipment

(G-16351)
STEVES PUBLICATION SVC
80 Thompson Rd (01570-1400)
P.O. Box 30247, Worcester (01603-0247)
PHONE..................................508 671-9192
Steve Place, *Principal*
EMP: 4 EST: 2008
SALES (est): 230.8K Privately Held
SIC: 2741 Misc Publishing

(G-16352)
TELETRAK ENVMTL SYSTEMS INC (PA)
2 Sutton Rd (01570)
PHONE..................................508 949-2430
Gerd Reinig, *Ch of Bd*
EMP: 5
SQ FT: 1,300
SALES (est): 492.2K Privately Held
SIC: 3599 3563 Mfg Industrial Machinery Mfg Air/Gas Compressors

(G-16353)
THIN LINE DEFENSE LLC
28 Town Forest Rd (01570-3162)
PHONE..................................774 696-5285
Joshua Collins, *Principal*
EMP: 3
SALES (est): 172K Privately Held
SIC: 3812 Mfg Search/Navigation Equipment

(G-16354)
YANKEE SHOPPER
Also Called: Patriot Newspaper
168 Gore Rd (01570-6814)
PHONE..................................508 943-8784
Paul Odonnell, *Owner*
EMP: 10
SALES (est): 340K Privately Held
SIC: 2711 Newspapers-Publishing/Printing

(G-16355)
ZMETRA CLARSPAN STRUCTURES LLC
2 Old Worcester Rd (01570-2109)
P.O. Box 218 (01570-0218)
PHONE..................................508 943-0940
Joseph Zmetra, *Principal*
Ronald Zmetra,
EMP: 7 EST: 2014
SQ FT: 45,000
SALES: 1MM Privately Held
SIC: 2394 Mfg Canvas/Related Products

Wellesley
Norfolk County

(G-16356)
ACLARA SOFTWARE INC
Also Called: Nexus Energyguide
16 Laurel Ave Ste 100 (02481-7531)
PHONE..................................781 283-9160
Harvey Michaels, *CEO*
Martin Flusberg, *President*
▲ EMP: 92
SQ FT: 15,000
SALES (est): 6.5MM
SALES (corp-wide): 812.9MM Publicly Held
WEB: www.nexusenergy.com
SIC: 7372 Prepackaged Software Services
PA: Esco Technologies Inc.
9900 Clayton Rd Ste A
Saint Louis MO 63124
314 213-7200

(G-16357)
ACLARA TECHNOLOGIES LLC
16 Laurel Ave Ste 100 (02481-7531)
PHONE..................................781 694-3300
Harvey Michaels, *CEO*
Randy Bell, *VP Opers*
Lyn Salvo, *Human Res Dir*
Mike Frankland, *Manager*
Jason Khourie, *Software Engr*
EMP: 40
SALES (corp-wide): 4.4B Publicly Held
SIC: 3824 3825 3829 7371 Mfg Fluid Meters/Devices Mfg Elec Measuring Instr Mfg Measure/Control Dvcs Computer Programming Svc Computer Systems Design
HQ: Aclara Technologies Llc
77 West Port Plz Ste 500
Saint Louis MO 63146
314 895-6400

(G-16358)
ALFRESCO SOFTWARE INC (PA)
100 Worcester St Ste 203 (02481-3628)
PHONE..................................888 317-3395
Bernadette Nixon, *CEO*
Doug Dennerline, *CEO*
Paul Holmes-Higgin, *President*
Bob Pritchard, *Senior VP*
Kamil Chaudhary, *Vice Pres*
EMP: 80
SALES (est): 29.1MM Privately Held
SIC: 7372 Prepackaged Software Services

(G-16359)
AMERICAN BILTRITE INC (PA)
57 River St Ste 302 (02481-2097)
PHONE..................................781 237-6655
Roger S Marcus, *Ch of Bd*
Richard G Marcus, *President*
William Marcus, *Exec VP*
Posnak Bonnie, *Vice Pres*
Bob Gentilucci, *Vice Pres*
◆ EMP: 7 EST: 1908
SQ FT: 10,000
SALES (est): 63.6MM Publicly Held
WEB: www.ambilt.com
SIC: 3069 2672 2241 3961 Mfg Fabrcatd Rubber Prdt

(G-16360)
ARCHITECTURAL KITCHENS INC
310b Washington St (02481-4929)
P.O. Box 189, Berlin (01503-0189)
PHONE..................................781 239-9750
William J Prachnick, *President*
EMP: 8
SQ FT: 1,400
SALES (est): 1.1MM Privately Held
SIC: 2434 Mfg Wood Kitchen Cabinets

(G-16361)
AURORA IMAGING TECHNOLOGY INC
165 Worcester St (02481-3615)
PHONE..................................617 522-6900
Elaine McCarthy, *Manager*
EMP: 3
SALES (corp-wide): 13.1MM Privately Held
WEB: www.auroramri.com
SIC: 3555 Mfg Printing Trades Machinery
PA: Aurora Imaging Technology Inc
8 Electronics Ave Ste 1
Danvers MA 01923
877 975-7530

(G-16362)
AVTEC INDUSTRIES INC
5 Bacon St (02482-5701)
PHONE..................................978 562-2300
Allen Herring, *Vice Pres*
John Rowen, *Vice Pres*
EMP: 3
SQ FT: 5,000
SALES (est): 466.9K Privately Held
WEB: www.avtecindustries.com
SIC: 2899 Mfg Flame Retardant Chemicals

(G-16363)
BARBER WALTERS INDUSTRIES LLC
142 Oakland St (02481-5323)
PHONE..................................781 241-5433
Walter Jones,
EMP: 5
SALES (est): 150.7K Privately Held
SIC: 3999 Mfg Misc Products

(G-16364)
BONESUPPORT INC
60 William St Ste 330 (02481-3824)
PHONE..................................781 772-1756

Fredrik Lindberg, *CEO*
Offer Nonhoff, *CFO*
Zeljko Radovancevic, *Director*
EMP: 9
SALES (est): 956.1K **Privately Held**
SIC: 3842 Mfg Surgical Appliances/Supplies

(G-16365)
CLOZEX MEDICAL INC
36 Washington St Ste 220 (02481-1933)
PHONE..................................781 237-1673
Michael Lebner, *President*
EMP: 9
SALES (est): 1MM **Privately Held**
WEB: www.clozex.com
SIC: 3845 Mfg Electromedical Equipment

(G-16366)
COLEY PHARMACEUTICAL GROUP INC
93 Worcester St Ste 101 (02481-3609)
PHONE..................................781 431-9000
Robert L Bratzler PHD, *President*
Arthur M Krieg MD, *Exec VP*
Ferdinand E Massari MD, *Senior VP*
Charles H Abdalian Jr, *CFO*
EMP: 130
SQ FT: 18,500
SALES (est): 8.6MM
SALES (corp-wide): 53.6B **Publicly Held**
WEB: www.coleypharma.com
SIC: 2834 Pharmaceutical Preparations
PA: Pfizer Inc.
235 E 42nd St Rm 107
New York NY 10017
212 733-2323

(G-16367)
INANOVATE INC
56 Beechwood Rd (02482-2333)
PHONE..................................617 610-1712
Robert Nelson, *Administration*
EMP: 4
SALES (est): 453.8K **Privately Held**
SIC: 3845 Mfg Electromedical Equipment

(G-16368)
JOEL GOLDSMITH BAGNAL INC
101 Central St (02482-5729)
PHONE..................................781 235-8266
Paul Sudman, *President*
EMP: 3
SQ FT: 1,200
SALES (est): 170K **Privately Held**
WEB: www.joelbagnal.com
SIC: 3961 5944 Mfg Custom Made Jewelry & Ret Fine Jewelry

(G-16369)
KEYNECTUP INC
30 Grove St (02482-7707)
P.O. Box 812838 (02482-0025)
PHONE..................................781 325-3414
Douglas Chrystall, *CEO*
EMP: 7
SQ FT: 800
SALES (est): 200K **Privately Held**
SIC: 7372 Prepackaged Software Services

(G-16370)
LEADERCLIPS INC
17 Pembroke Rd (02482-7441)
PHONE..................................248 808-1093
EMP: 5
SALES (est): 345.8K **Privately Held**
SIC: 7372 7389 Prepackaged Software Services

(G-16371)
M B S SERVICES INC
37 Bay State Rd (02481-3244)
PHONE..................................781 431-0945
Mark Dente, *Owner*
EMP: 3
SALES (est): 197.7K **Privately Held**
WEB: www.mbss-inc.com
SIC: 7372 Prepackaged Software Services

(G-16372)
MEDCOOL INC
30 Washington St (02481-1929)
PHONE..................................617 512-4530
Helen Maslocka, *CEO*
EMP: 3
SALES (est): 191.6K **Privately Held**
SIC: 3845 Medical Devices

(G-16373)
MIX AND COMPANY LTD
Also Called: Mix & Company
68 Central St (02482-5806)
PHONE..................................781 235-0028
EMP: 15
SALES (corp-wide): 7.8MM **Privately Held**
SIC: 3273 Mfg Ready-Mixed Concrete
PA: Mix And Company, Ltd.
21 Drydock Ave
Boston MA 02210
617 443-4001

(G-16374)
NANO-AUDIO
21 Pine Plain Rd (02481-1143)
PHONE..................................781 416-5096
Steve Derezinski, *Principal*
EMP: 3
SALES (est): 175.2K **Privately Held**
WEB: www.nano-audio.com
SIC: 3674 Manufacturer

(G-16375)
NEMUCORE MED INNOVATIONS INC
Also Called: Nmi
33 Kirkland Cir (02481-4812)
PHONE..................................617 943-9983
Timothy P Coleman, *CEO*
Susan Keyes, *Vice Pres*
Nicole Stephenson, *Opers Staff*
EMP: 9
SALES (est): 1.3MM **Privately Held**
SIC: 2834 Mfg Pharmaceutical Preparations / Nano-Medicine Development

(G-16376)
NEOTRON INC
5 Hayden Pl (02481-5517)
PHONE..................................781 239-3461
Steven Paul Ahlen, *CEO*
EMP: 5
SALES (est): 388.5K **Privately Held**
SIC: 3829 Mfg Measuring/Controlling Devices

(G-16377)
OAK GROUP INC
892 Worcester St Ste 250 (02482-3794)
P.O. Box 812863 (02482-0026)
PHONE..................................781 943-2200
David Maltz, *President*
EMP: 20
SQ FT: 2,500
SALES (est): 1.5MM **Privately Held**
WEB: www.oakgroup.com
SIC: 7372 Prepackaged Software Services

(G-16378)
OASISWORKS INC
14 Mica Ln Ste 204 (02481-1708)
PHONE..................................617 329-5588
EMP: 5
SALES: 6MM **Privately Held**
SIC: 7372 Prepackaged Software Services

(G-16379)
PACE ASSOCIATES INC
Also Called: Printsmith Needham
370 Weston Rd (02482-2339)
PHONE..................................781 433-0639
Peter A Ciesluk, *President*
EMP: 5
SALES: 450K **Privately Held**
SIC: 2752 Lithographic Commercial Printing

(G-16380)
PERKINELMER HOLDINGS INC (HQ)
940 Winter St (02481)
PHONE..................................781 663-6900
Gregory Summe, *CEO*
Gail Fons, *Program Mgr*
EMP: 3
SQ FT: 53,400
SALES (est): 346.7MM
SALES (corp-wide): 2.7B **Publicly Held**
SIC: 3826 Mfg Analytical Instruments
PA: Perkinelmer, Inc.
940 Winter St
Waltham MA 02451
781 663-6900

(G-16381)
PLUMRIVER LLC
94 Edmunds Rd (02481-2940)
PHONE..................................781 431-7477
Henry White, *Branch Mgr*
EMP: 30
SALES (corp-wide): 5.7MM **Privately Held**
SIC: 7372 Prepackaged Software Services
PA: Plumriver Llc
1257 E College Ave
State College PA 16801
781 577-9575

(G-16382)
R R VENTURE
25 Paine St (02481-6003)
PHONE..................................781 431-6170
Richard Siber, *Principal*
EMP: 4
SALES (est): 320.8K **Privately Held**
SIC: 3949 Mfg Sporting/Athletic Goods

(G-16383)
RACHIOTEK LLC
70 Walnut St (02481-2135)
PHONE..................................407 923-0721
Craig Corrance, *CEO*
Michele Lucey, *Vice Pres*
EMP: 5
SQ FT: 2,000
SALES (est): 300.4K **Privately Held**
SIC: 3841 5047 Mfg Surgical/Medical Instruments Whol Medical/Hospital Equipment

(G-16384)
RWWI HOLDINGS LLC
55 William St Ste 240 (02481-4003)
PHONE..................................781 239-0700
EMP: 360
SALES (est): 9.6MM **Privately Held**
SIC: 7372 Prepackaged Software

(G-16385)
RY KY INC
21 Cunningham Rd (02481-7620)
PHONE..................................781 235-4581
Jacqueline Anne Sullivan, *Principal*
EMP: 3
SALES (est): 309.4K **Privately Held**
SIC: 2531 Mfg Public Building Furniture

(G-16386)
SANO LLC
14 Thackeray Rd 1c (02481-3409)
PHONE..................................617 290-3348
Paul Hayre,
EMP: 3
SALES (est): 247.7K **Privately Held**
SIC: 2835 Mfg Diagnostic Substances

(G-16387)
SHERBORN MARKET INC
29 Grantland Rd (02481-7607)
P.O. Box 81237 (02481-0002)
PHONE..................................781 489-5006
Alexander Weatherall, *Principal*
EMP: 3 **EST:** 2010
SALES (est): 314.5K **Privately Held**
SIC: 2869 Mfg Industrial Organic Chemicals

(G-16388)
SUZHOU-CHEM INC
396 Washington St Ste 318 (02481-6209)
PHONE..................................781 433-8618
Joan Ni, *President*
EMP: 6
SALES: 10MM **Privately Held**
SIC: 2834 Mfg Pharmaceutical Preparations

(G-16389)
SYNERTIDE PHARMACEUTICALS INC
88 Kingsbury St (02481-4847)
PHONE..................................801 671-1329
Zhaolin Wang, *Principal*
EMP: 3
SALES (est): 155.5K **Privately Held**
SIC: 2834 Mfg Pharmaceutical Preparations

(G-16390)
TW LIGHTING INCORPORATED (PA)
396 Washington St 277 (02481-6209)
P.O. Box 250, Newton Upper Falls (02464-0002)
PHONE..................................617 830-6755
Tony Chen, *President*
Scott Nassa, *Vice Pres*
WEI Ye, *Treasurer*
Tori Flagg-Durkin, *Administration*
▲ **EMP:** 9 **EST:** 2011
SALES (est): 1.3MM **Privately Held**
SIC: 3648 Mfg Lighting Equipment

(G-16391)
VACCINE TECHNOLOGIES INC (PA)
15 S Woodside Ave (02482-2300)
PHONE..................................781 489-3388
Yichen Lu, *President*
Huyen Cao, *Vice Pres*
EMP: 4
SALES (est): 540K **Privately Held**
SIC: 2836 Mfg Biological Products

(G-16392)
VOX COMMUNICATIONS GROUP LLC
70 Walnut St (02481-2135)
PHONE..................................781 239-8018
Bruce Danziger,
EMP: 75
SALES: 950K **Privately Held**
SIC: 3663 Radio Broadcasting

(G-16393)
WATSON PRINTING CO INC
Also Called: David Rich Co
118 Cedar St Ste 2 (02481-3596)
PHONE..................................781 237-1336
Andrew T Watson, *President*
Tara Kelley, *Manager*
EMP: 7
SQ FT: 2,000
SALES (est): 1MM **Privately Held**
WEB: www.watsonprinting.com
SIC: 2752 Lithographic Commercial Printing

(G-16394)
WINDSOR PRESS INC
356 Washington St (02481-6206)
P.O. Box 81245, Wellesley Hills (02481-0401)
PHONE..................................781 235-0265
Salvatore De Fazio III, *President*
James Fullerton, *Clerk*
EMP: 3 **EST:** 1929
SALES (est): 350.3K **Privately Held**
SIC: 2752 Offset Printing

Wellesley Hills
Norfolk County

(G-16395)
AMERICAN OPTICS LIMITED
34 Washington St Ste 200 (02481-1903)
PHONE..................................905 631-5377
Larry Hicks, *President*
David Pierce, *CFO*
EMP: 10
SALES (est): 414.8K **Privately Held**
SIC: 3845 3841 5047 Mfg Electromedical Equip Mfg Surgical/Med Instr Whol Med/Hospital Equip

(G-16396)
CENSA PHARMACEUTICALS INC (PA)
65 William St Ste 200 (02481-3808)
PHONE..................................617 225-7700
Jonathan Reis, *CEO*
Jennifer Becker, *Office Admin*
Chris Schelling, *Director*
EMP: 13

SALES (est): 4MM **Privately Held**
SIC: 2834 Mfg Pharmaceutical Preparations

(G-16397)
GLOBAL ADVANCED METALS USA INC (PA)
100 Worcester St Ste 200 (02481-3628)
PHONE..................................781 996-7300
Andrew O'Donovan, *CEO*
Steve Krause, *President*
EMP: 53
SALES (est): 23.3MM **Privately Held**
SIC: 3339 Primary Nonferrous Metal Producer

(G-16398)
LIFE+GEAR INC
Also Called: Pacific Pathway
21 Cushing Rd (02481-2903)
PHONE..................................858 755-2099
Nicholas Connor, *CEO*
Dennis Bertken, *President*
Greg Simko, *Principal*
Joyce Ip, *Purch Mgr*
▲ **EMP:** 33
SQ FT: 6,800
SALES (est): 6.1MM **Privately Held**
WEB: www.lifegear.com
SIC: 3949 5099 Mfg Lighting Equipment Whol Durable Goods Mfg Sport/Athletic Goods

(G-16399)
PAPERS & PRESENTS
10 Lanark Rd (02481-3029)
PHONE..................................781 235-1079
Caroline McCoy, *Owner*
Ilana Reis, *Program Dir*
EMP: 5
SALES (est): 415.7K **Privately Held**
SIC: 2759 Retails Stationery

(G-16400)
UROLAZE INC
192 Worcester St (02481-5507)
PHONE..................................413 374-5006
Thomas W McMahon, *President*
Tim Driscoll, *Vice Pres*
Timothy Driscoll, *Treasurer*
Roger S Wyner, *Director*
EMP: 3 **EST:** 2013
SALES (est): 321.8K **Privately Held**
SIC: 3699 Mfg Electrical Equipment/Supplies

Wellfleet
Barnstable County

(G-16401)
COPY CAPS
50 Somerset Ave (02667-8036)
PHONE..................................508 349-1300
Bruce Einhorn, *Owner*
EMP: 3
SQ FT: 1,000
SALES (est): 96K **Privately Held**
SIC: 2395 Pleating/Stitching Services

(G-16402)
SALT WELLFLEET
55 Commercial St (02667)
P.O. Box 106, South Wellfleet (02663-0106)
PHONE..................................508 237-4415
EMP: 3 **EST:** 2014
SALES (est): 121.5K **Privately Held**
SIC: 2339 Mfg Women's/Misses' Outerwear

Wenham
Essex County

(G-16403)
MOCKTAIL BEVERAGES INC
88 Walnut Rd (01984-1611)
PHONE..................................855 662-5824
William D Gamelli, *President*
Henry W Newman, *Treasurer*
James B Dowla, *Director*
Mark Guthrie, *Bd of Directors*
EMP: 4
SALES: 140K **Privately Held**
SIC: 2086 7389 Mfg Bottled/Canned Soft Drinks Business Serv Non-Commercial Site

West Barnstable
Barnstable County

(G-16404)
BARNSTABLE BRACELET
160 Percival Dr (02668-1233)
PHONE..................................508 362-1630
Karen Francis, *Principal*
EMP: 3
SALES (est): 202.3K **Privately Held**
SIC: 3961 Mfg Costume Jewelry

(G-16405)
CAPE SETUPS LLC
1611 Main St (02668-1122)
PHONE..................................508 375-6444
Diane Mailloux, *Partner*
Jeremy Mailloux, *Partner*
EMP: 6
SQ FT: 2,000
SALES (est): 790K **Privately Held**
WEB: www.capesetups.com
SIC: 3571 7373 Mfg Computers & Integrates Computer Systems

(G-16406)
E M CROSBY BOAT WORKS
48 Lombard Ave (02668-1333)
P.O. Box 551 (02668-0551)
PHONE..................................508 362-7100
Edward Crosby, *Owner*
EMP: 5
SALES (est): 683.9K **Privately Held**
SIC: 3732 Boatbuilding/Repairing

(G-16407)
EXIT FIVE GALLERY
Also Called: Exit 5 Gallery
1085 Main St (02668-1152)
PHONE..................................508 375-1011
Junichi Sawayanagi, *President*
Linda King, *Principal*
Sandra Sawayanagi, *Treasurer*
EMP: 3
SALES (est): 160K **Privately Held**
SIC: 3952 8412 7699 Mfg Lead Pencils/Art Goods Museum/Art Gallery Repair Services

West Boxford
Essex County

(G-16408)
STONE HOUSE FARM INC
Also Called: Nason's Stone House Farm
276 Washington St (01885)
P.O. Box 44 (01885-0044)
PHONE..................................978 352-2323
James H Nason, *President*
EMP: 8
SQ FT: 1,200
SALES: 400K **Privately Held**
SIC: 2053 5461 Mfg Frozen Bakery Products Retail Bakery

West Boylston
Worcester County

(G-16409)
ATLAS PRESS WORCESTER INC
211 Shrewsbury St Ste 1 (01583-2127)
PHONE..................................508 835-9440
Alan R Cooper, *President*
EMP: 6 **EST:** 1932
SQ FT: 8,000
SALES: 703.2K **Privately Held**
WEB: www.atlaspress.com
SIC: 2752 Lithographic Commercial Printing

(G-16410)
C & C METALS ENGINEERING INC
104 Hartwell St (01583-2410)
PHONE..................................508 835-9011
Anthony Conklin, *President*
Rick Cobiski Jr, *Vice Pres*
Richard J Cobiski Jr, *Admin Sec*
EMP: 34
SQ FT: 14,000
SALES (est): 7.3MM **Privately Held**
WEB: www.ccmetalsinc.com
SIC: 3599 Mfg Industrial Machinery

(G-16411)
CENTRAL COATING TECH INC
165 Shrewsbury St (01583-2198)
PHONE..................................508 835-6225
Robert Killion, *CEO*
James Ambrose, *President*
Allen Favreau, *Facilities Mgr*
Daniel Licht, *Engineer*
Kathleen Garland, *Accounting Mgr*
EMP: 80
SQ FT: 35,000
SALES (est): 10.5MM **Privately Held**
WEB: www.centralcoating.com
SIC: 3479 Coating/Engraving Service

(G-16412)
CENTRAL MASS INSTALLATIONS
250 Worcester St Unit 6 (01583-1758)
PHONE..................................508 612-3092
Jose Vargas, *Owner*
EMP: 4
SALES: 650K **Privately Held**
SIC: 2542 Mfg Partitions/Fixtures-Nonwood

(G-16413)
CURTIS INDUSTRIES LLC (PA)
Also Called: Curtis Tractor Cab
70 Hartwell St (01583-2408)
PHONE..................................508 853-2200
Randy Ploof, *Business Mgr*
Marty Robinson, *Engineer*
Todd Brown, *Design Engr*
Michael Orrell, *Design Engr*
John Davis, *Sales Staff*
▲ **EMP:** 10 **EST:** 1968
SQ FT: 168,000
SALES (est): 32.6MM **Privately Held**
WEB: www.curtiscab.com
SIC: 3713 3714 Mfg Truck/Bus Bodies Mfg Motor Vehicle Parts/Accessories

(G-16414)
DIAS INFRARED CORP
75 Sterling St (01583-1218)
PHONE..................................845 987-8152
Philip Gregor, *CEO*
EMP: 6
SALES (est): 396.2K **Privately Held**
SIC: 3823 Mfg Process Control Instruments

(G-16415)
DUNCAN M GILLIES CO INC
66 Central St (01583-1653)
P.O. Box 355 (01583-0355)
PHONE..................................508 835-4445
Duncan H Gillies, *President*
Mark Spencer, *Vice Pres*
Marjorie P Gillies, *Treasurer*
Rita L Spencer, *Shareholder*
Edward C Maher, *Clerk*
EMP: 5
SQ FT: 7,000
SALES (est): 600.7K **Privately Held**
SIC: 3953 Mfg Marking Devices

(G-16416)
H O WIRE CO INC
215 Shrewsbury St (01583-2107)
PHONE..................................508 243-7177
Rand Daniels III, *President*
EMP: 11
SALES: 3MM **Privately Held**
SIC: 3471 Plating Of Metals And Formed Products

(G-16417)
HEMENWAY & ASSOCIATES
127 Worcester St (01583-1715)
PHONE..................................508 835-2859
Lance Hemenway, *Owner*
EMP: 6
SQ FT: 2,500
SALES: 680K **Privately Held**
SIC: 3999 Mfg Misc Products

(G-16418)
ISUN INTERNATIONAL GROUP LLC
235 W Boylston St Ste A (01583-1754)
PHONE..................................508 835-9000
John McDaniel,
Brian Johnson,
Ben Paharik,
▲ **EMP:** 5
SALES (est): 1.4MM **Privately Held**
WEB: www.isungroup.com
SIC: 3448 Mfg Prefabricated Metal Buildings

(G-16419)
JEN REN CORPORATION
Also Called: Action Press
45 Sterling St Ste 11 (01583-1201)
PHONE..................................508 835-3331
Peter Iannacchino, *President*
EMP: 3
SALES: 375K **Privately Held**
SIC: 2752 Lithographic Commercial Printing

(G-16420)
JOHNS MANVILLE CORPORATION
Also Called: Johns Manville
10 Bunkerhill Pkwy (01583-2004)
PHONE..................................774 261-8500
EMP: 126
SALES (corp-wide): 225.3B **Publicly Held**
SIC: 2952 Mfg Asphalt Felts/Coatings
HQ: Johns Manville Corporation
717 17th St Ste 800
Denver CO 80202
303 978-2000

(G-16421)
LOWELL CORPORATION
Also Called: Porter-Ferguson
65 Hartwell St (01583-2407)
PHONE..................................508 835-2900
David S Cummings, *President*
Paul Di Pierro, *Sls & Mktg Exec*
▲ **EMP:** 32
SQ FT: 34,000
SALES (est): 6.8MM **Privately Held**
WEB: www.lowellcorp.com
SIC: 3423 Mfg Hand/Edge Tools

(G-16422)
MCNAMARA FABRICATING CO INC
215 Shrewsbury St (01583-2107)
PHONE..................................774 243-7425
Timothy Walsh, *President*
EMP: 11
SALES (est): 2.2MM **Privately Held**
WEB: www.mac-fab.com
SIC: 3443 7692 Mfg Fabricated Plate Work Welding Repair

(G-16423)
NEW TEK DESIGN GROUP INC
18 Worcester St (01583-1413)
PHONE..................................508 835-4544
David Amato, *Vice Pres*
Mark Euler, *Vice Pres*
EMP: 14
SALES: 1.3MM **Privately Held**
WEB: www.newtekdesigngroup.com
SIC: 2759 Commercial Printing

(G-16424)
ONE OFF APPAREL INC
18 Worcester St (01583-1413)
PHONE..................................508 835-8883
Jeffrey Lavin, *President*
EMP: 3
SALES (est): 300.3K **Privately Held**
SIC: 2759 Commercial Printing

(G-16425)
PALOMAR PRINTING
232 W Boylston St (01583-1729)
PHONE..................................508 856-7237
Jill Murray-Wildt, *Owner*
EMP: 3
SALES (est): 376.5K **Privately Held**
WEB: www.palomarprinting.com
SIC: 2752 Commercial Printing

(G-16426)
PARDI MFG INC
185 Shrewsbury St (01583-2105)
P.O. Box 60356, Worcester (01606-0356)
PHONE..................................508 835-7887
Steve Pelleran, *President*
EMP: 5
SQ FT: 4,500
SALES (est): 820.1K **Privately Held**
SIC: 3822 Mfg Temperature Controls Devices Specializing In Aquastat Immersion Wells

(G-16427)
PRECISION MACHINE & GEAR INC
Also Called: PMG
104 Hartwell St (01583-2410)
PHONE..................................508 835-7888
Jaimal Tuteja, *President*
EMP: 5
SQ FT: 400
SALES (est): 758.6K **Privately Held**
SIC: 3599 Mfg Industrial Machinery

West Bridgewater
Plymouth County

(G-16428)
AMERICAN DRONE SOLUTIONS LLC
50 Brooks Pl (02379-1145)
PHONE..................................413 306-9427
Douglas Campbell,
EMP: 20 **EST:** 2017
SALES (est): 821.4K **Privately Held**
SIC: 3721 Mfg Aircraft

(G-16429)
ATLANTIC RES MKTG SYSTEMS INC
Also Called: Arms
230 W Center St (02379-1620)
PHONE..................................508 584-7816
Richard E Swan, *President*
Sharon Swan, *Vice Pres*
EMP: 12
SQ FT: 26,000
SALES (est): 1.4MM **Privately Held**
WEB: www.armsmounts.com
SIC: 3827 5961 3429 Mfg Optical Instruments/Lenses Ret Mail-Order House Mfg Hardware

(G-16430)
AUTOMOTIVE MACH SHOP SUP
630 N Main St (02379-1233)
PHONE..................................508 586-6706
Ed Shenan, *Principal*
EMP: 3 **EST:** 1999
SALES (est): 220K **Privately Held**
SIC: 3559 Mfg Misc Industry Machinery

(G-16431)
BAIRD & BARTLETT COI NC
319 Manley St (02379-1034)
PHONE..................................508 588-9400
Fax: 508 586-3028
EMP: 3
SALES (est): 202.5K **Privately Held**
SIC: 2631 Paperboard Mill

(G-16432)
BATH SYSTEMS MASSACHUSETTS INC
25 Turnpike St (02379-1004)
PHONE..................................508 521-2700
Glenn Cotton, *President*
Brian Cotton, *Principal*
EMP: 10
SALES (est): 925.7K **Privately Held**
SIC: 3443 Mfg Fabricated Plate Work

(G-16433)
CAST COAT INC
354 West St Ste 1 (02379-1498)
PHONE..................................508 587-4502
Robert Lothrop, *President*
Jeffrey S Lothrop, *Vice Pres*
Clydette Lothrop, *Clerk*
EMP: 5
SQ FT: 4,000
SALES (est): 785.2K **Privately Held**
WEB: www.cast-coat.com
SIC: 2851 3479 Mfg Paints/Allied Products Coating/Engraving Service

(G-16434)
CCS MARINE INC
Also Called: Surfaceworx
124 Turnpike St Ste 12 (02379-1046)
PHONE..................................508 587-8877
Mark Ellis, *President*
Sam Devito, *Opers Mgr*
EMP: 6
SQ FT: 5,000
SALES (est): 1.3MM **Privately Held**
WEB: www.surfaceworx.com
SIC: 2851 Mfg Paints/Allied Products

(G-16435)
CORY MANUFACTURING INC
343 Manley St (02379-1094)
PHONE..................................508 680-2111
Matthew Berk, *President*
EMP: 8
SALES (est): 661.5K **Privately Held**
SIC: 3999 Mfg Misc Products

(G-16436)
DC SCAFFOLD INC
400 West St Ste 2 (02379-1095)
PHONE..................................508 580-5100
John Degrenier, *President*
EMP: 12
SALES (est): 1.9MM **Privately Held**
SIC: 3446 Mfg Architectural Metalwork

(G-16437)
DOCUPRINT EXPRESS LTD
1 Bert Dr Ste 14 (02379-1060)
PHONE..................................508 895-9090
David Parness, *Owner*
EMP: 5 **EST:** 1992
SALES (est): 470.7K **Privately Held**
SIC: 2759 Commercial Printing

(G-16438)
DOUBLE E COMPANY LLC (PA)
Also Called: Web Handling Equipment
319 Manley St Ste 301 (02379-1034)
PHONE..................................508 588-8099
Bryan Gregory, *President*
Mark Peretti, *Vice Pres*
Trina Campbell, *Purch Agent*
Michael V Deurse, *Engineer*
Jeffrey V Cura, *CFO*
◆ **EMP:** 150
SQ FT: 65,000
SALES (est): 38.6MM **Privately Held**
WEB: www.doubleeusa.com
SIC: 3545 3568 Mfg Machine Tool Accessories Mfg Power Transmission Equipment

(G-16439)
DRAPER METALS
652 W Rear Center St (02379)
P.O. Box 365 (02379-0365)
PHONE..................................508 584-4617
Joseph Draheim, *Owner*
Joseph Drahein, *Owner*
EMP: 4
SQ FT: 5,000
SALES (est): 1MM **Privately Held**
SIC: 3312 Blast Furnace-Steel Works

(G-16440)
E H METALCRAFT COMPANY INC
396 West St (02379-1015)
PHONE..................................508 580-0870
Ralph Hansen, *President*
EMP: 5
SQ FT: 5,000
SALES (est): 631.1K **Privately Held**
SIC: 3541 Mfg Machine Tools-Cutting

(G-16441)
HESS CORPORATION
244 W Center St (02379-1627)
PHONE..................................508 580-6530
EMP: 15
SALES (corp-wide): 11.4B **Publicly Held**
SIC: 1311 Exploration & Production Of Crude Oil & Natural Gas
PA: Hess Corporation
1185 Ave Of The Americas
New York NY 10036
212 997-8500

(G-16442)
JIMSAN ENTERPRISES INC
Also Called: Hilliard's Chocolate System
275 E Center St (02379-1813)
PHONE..................................508 587-3666
James Bourne, *President*
Sandra Bourne, *Clerk*
EMP: 9
SQ FT: 6,000
SALES (est): 1.6MM **Privately Held**
WEB: www.hilliardschocolate.com
SIC: 3556 Mfg Machines For Coating Candies

(G-16443)
LOPESDZINE
1 Bert Dr Ste 3 (02379-1025)
PHONE..................................508 857-0121
Joseph Lopes, *Owner*
EMP: 3
SALES (est): 226.3K **Privately Held**
SIC: 2759 Commercial Printing

(G-16444)
MASTER-HALCO INC
63 Manley St (02379-1016)
PHONE..................................508 583-7474
Joe Meade, *Manager*
EMP: 25 **Privately Held**
WEB: www.fenceonline.com
SIC: 3315 Trade Contractor
HQ: Master-Halco, Inc.
3010 Lbj Fwy Ste 800
Dallas TX 75234
972 714-7300

(G-16445)
MEDITERRANEAN CUSTOM CABINETS
318 Manley St Ste 1 (02379-1087)
PHONE..................................508 588-5498
Harry Mitoulis, *President*
EMP: 4
SQ FT: 7,000
SALES: 600K **Privately Held**
SIC: 2434 Mfg Wood Kitchen Cabinets

(G-16446)
MOBILE MINI INC
125 Manley St (02379-1001)
PHONE..................................508 427-5395
Jared Chernick, *Branch Mgr*
EMP: 10
SALES (corp-wide): 593.2MM **Publicly Held**
WEB: www.mobilemini.com
SIC: 3448 Mfg Prefabricated Metal Buildings
PA: Mobile Mini, Inc.
4646 E Van Buren St # 400
Phoenix AZ 85008
480 894-6311

(G-16447)
MOLD MAKERS INC
Also Called: Moldmakers
1 Old West St (02379-1453)
PHONE..................................508 588-4212
Raymond Bissonnette, *President*
Tracy Mead, *Finance Mgr*
Jody Mead, *Manager*
EMP: 5
SQ FT: 2,800
SALES (est): 500K **Privately Held**
WEB: www.moldmakers-inc.com
SIC: 3544 Mfg Industrial Molds

(G-16448)
ON THE SPOT
120 S Main St (02379-1739)
PHONE..................................508 583-6070
Thomas A McGuane, *Owner*
EMP: 3
SALES (est): 329.5K **Privately Held**
SIC: 3444 Mfg Aluminum Gutters

(G-16449)
PARKWAY MANUFACTURING CO INC
1 Bert Dr Ste 11 (02379-1059)
PHONE..................................508 559-6686
Thomas Accuavatti, *President*
Valerie Acciavatti, *Treasurer*
James E Bailey, *Clerk*
EMP: 7
SQ FT: 1,500
SALES (est): 684.2K **Privately Held**
SIC: 3599 Mfg Industrial Machinery

(G-16450)
PRETORIUS ELECTRIC
Also Called: Pretorius Electric and Sign
267a S Main St (02379-1777)
P.O. Box 654, Brockton (02303-0654)
PHONE..................................508 326-9492
Rich Pretorius, *Mng Member*
EMP: 5
SALES (est): 374.2K **Privately Held**
SIC: 3993 1731 Mfg Signs/Advertising Specialties Electrical Contractor

(G-16451)
REXA INC
Also Called: Rexa Electraulic Actuation
4 Manley St (02379-1017)
PHONE..................................508 584-1199
Takashi Ikegaya, *President*
Etsuko Ikegaya, *Corp Secy*
Kristen Smith, *Buyer*
Chad Ballard, *Engineer*
Kenneth Garron, *Finance Mgr*
◆ **EMP:** 99
SQ FT: 48,358
SALES (est): 32.3MM **Privately Held**
SIC: 3625 Mfg Relays/Industrial Controls
HQ: Nihon Koso Co., Ltd.
1-16-7, Nihombashi
Chuo-Ku TKY 103-0

(G-16452)
SHARP MANUFACTURING INC
415 N Elm St (02379-1119)
PHONE..................................508 583-4080
Steven Madonna, *President*
Susan Madonna, *Corp Secy*
EMP: 8
SQ FT: 7,500
SALES (est): 980K **Privately Held**
SIC: 3599 Machine Shop

(G-16453)
SHAWMUT LLC (PA)
208 Manley St (02379-1044)
PHONE..................................508 588-3300
James H Wyner, *CEO*
Anna Burke, *COO*
Sherri Harrington, *Vice Pres*
Louis Desousa, *Purch Mgr*
Greg Carey, *Engineer*
▲ **EMP:** 130
SQ FT: 140,000
SALES (est): 185.1MM **Privately Held**
WEB: www.darlexx.com
SIC: 2295 Mfg Coated Fabrics

(G-16454)
SKEW PRODUCTS INCORPORATED
Also Called: Spec Tools
4 Bert Dr Ste 6 (02379-1038)
PHONE..................................508 580-5800
John A Badiali, *President*
Cheryl A Badiali, *Corp Secy*
Bud Badiali, *Engineer*
▲ **EMP:** 22
SQ FT: 5,000
SALES (est): 3.1MM **Privately Held**
SIC: 3423 Mfg Hand/Edge Tools

(G-16455)
SMART MANUFACTURING
55 Turnpike St Ste 7 (02379-1090)
PHONE..................................508 219-0327
EMP: 3
SALES (est): 285.1K **Privately Held**
SIC: 3599 Mfg Industrial Machinery

GEOGRAPHIC

(G-16456)
SPIRUS MEDICAL LLC
375 West St (02379-1014)
PHONE..................................781 297-7220
Ross Garofalo, *Principal*
EMP: 3
SALES (est): 368.8K **Privately Held**
SIC: 3841 Mfg Surgical/Medical Instruments

(G-16457)
STD PRECISION GEAR & INSTR INC
318 Manley St Ste 5 (02379-1087)
PHONE..................................508 580-0035
James Manning, *President*
David Weekley, *Engineer*
Steven Tallarida, *Treasurer*
Jon T Tallarida, *Admin Sec*
EMP: 35
SQ FT: 8,000
SALES: 1.2MM **Privately Held**
WEB: www.stdgear.com
SIC: 3566 Mfg Speed Changers/Drives

(G-16458)
SUNBURST ELECTRONIC MANUFACTUR (PA)
Also Called: Sunburst Ems
70 Pleasant St (02379-1506)
PHONE..................................508 580-1881
Andrew Chase, *President*
David Sarcione, *Business Mgr*
Tara Sullivan, *Buyer*
Ken Chasse, *QC Mgr*
Toan Nguyen, *Engineer*
▲ **EMP:** 74
SQ FT: 36,000
SALES (est): 16.9MM **Privately Held**
WEB: www.sunburstems.com
SIC: 3672 3679 Mfg Printed Circuit Boards Mfg Electronic Components

(G-16459)
TMH MACHINING & WELDING CORP
124 Turnpike St Ste 15 (02379-1071)
PHONE..................................508 580-6899
Antonio Hruzd, *President*
EMP: 14
SALES: 1.8MM **Privately Held**
SIC: 3599 Mfg Industrial Machinery

(G-16460)
TPI INDUSTRIES LLC
208 Manley St (02379-1044)
PHONE..................................508 588-3300
James Wyner, *Branch Mgr*
EMP: 4
SALES (corp-wide): 185.1MM **Privately Held**
SIC: 2295 Mfg Coated Fabrics
HQ: Tpi Industries, Llc
265 Ballard Rd
Middletown NY 10941
845 692-2820

(G-16461)
TWIN LEATHER CO INC
24 Jason Way (02379-1292)
PHONE..................................508 583-3485
Richmond Castano, *President*
EMP: 5 **EST:** 1949
SALES: 150K **Privately Held**
WEB: www.twinleather.com
SIC: 3053 3131 3021 3111 Mfg Gasket/Packing/Seals Mfg Footwear Cut Stock Mfg Rubber/Plstc Ftwear Leather Tanning/Finshng

(G-16462)
US DISCOUNT PRODUCTS LLC
354 West St Ste 4 (02379-1475)
PHONE..................................877 841-5782
Nick Mirrione, *Manager*
Charles Mirrione, *Manager*
▲ **EMP:** 4 **EST:** 2011
SALES (est): 400.1K **Privately Held**
SIC: 3423 3523 3531 Mfg Hand/Edge Tools Mfg Farm Machinery/Equipment Mfg Construction Machinery

(G-16463)
US SHEETMETAL INC
420 West St (02379-1072)
PHONE..................................508 427-0500
John Martin Neilan, *President*
Christina Neilan, *Treasurer*
EMP: 7 **EST:** 2001
SALES (est): 1.2MM **Privately Held**
SIC: 3444 Mfg Sheet Metalwork

West Brookfield
Worcester County

(G-16464)
ARLAND TOOL & MFG INC
45 Freight House Rd (01585)
PHONE..................................508 867-3085
Meliisa Baker, *Branch Mgr*
EMP: 15
SALES (corp-wide): 22.7MM **Privately Held**
WEB: www.arland.com
SIC: 3599 Mfg Industrial Machinery
PA: Arland Tool & Mfg, Inc.
421 Main St
Sturbridge MA 01566
508 347-3368

(G-16465)
BROOKFIELD WIRE COMPANY INC (HQ)
231 E Main St (01585)
PHONE..................................508 867-6474
Anthony J Defino, *President*
Leonard M Defino, *President*
Francis P Defino, *Vice Pres*
▲ **EMP:** 30
SQ FT: 48,000
SALES (est): 9.9MM **Privately Held**
WEB: www.brookfieldwire.com
SIC: 3315 3357 Mfg Steel Wire/Related Products Nonferrous Wiredrawing/Insulating

(G-16466)
CONCRETE BLOCK INSULATING SYST
Also Called: Cbis
25 Freight House Rd (01585-3132)
P.O. Box 1000 (01585-1000)
PHONE..................................508 867-4241
Dave Nickerson, *CEO*
Daniel Prouty, *Treasurer*
H James Law, *Director*
Joanne N Middleton, *Director*
EMP: 20
SQ FT: 60,000
SALES (est): 4.1MM **Privately Held**
WEB: www.cbisinc.com
SIC: 3086 Mfg Plastic Foam Products

(G-16467)
COPE & SCRIBE INCORPORATED
29 Rodman St (01585-2810)
PHONE..................................508 410-7100
George Stephens Garwood, *President*
EMP: 5
SQ FT: 2,500
SALES: 760K **Privately Held**
SIC: 2434 Mfg Wood Kitchen Cabinets

(G-16468)
CROSBY MACHINE COMPANY INC
17 Freight House Rd (01585-3132)
P.O. Box 682 (01585-0682)
PHONE..................................508 867-3121
Russell Crosby, *President*
Russell C Crosby, *Manager*
EMP: 4
SQ FT: 22,000
SALES: 500K **Privately Held**
WEB: www.rcrosby.com
SIC: 3559 3444 Mfg Misc Industry Machinery Mfg Sheet Metalwork

(G-16469)
GAVITT WIRE AND CABLE CO INC
62 Central St (01585-3140)
PHONE..................................508 867-6476
Harold R Chesson III, *President*
Bruce Gaudreau, *Safety Mgr*
Dave Dunican, *Maint Spvr*
Lisa A Baker, *Treasurer*
Cindy Baxter, *Manager*
EMP: 55 **EST:** 1923
SQ FT: 60,000
SALES (est): 15.6MM **Privately Held**
WEB: www.gavitt.com
SIC: 3357 Nonferrous Wiredrawing/Insulating

(G-16470)
GREMARCO INDUSTRIES INC
131 E Main St (01585-2909)
P.O. Box 1041 (01585-1041)
PHONE..................................508 867-5244
Gregory L Deotte, *President*
Mary J Deotte, *Vice Pres*
▲ **EMP:** 17
SALES (est): 4.1MM **Privately Held**
WEB: www.gremarco.com
SIC: 3564 Mfg Industrial/Commercial Filters

(G-16471)
MCCARTHY BROS FUEL CO INC
33 Lakeshore Dr (01585-2764)
PHONE..................................508 867-5515
Joseph Bonvie, *Principal*
EMP: 4
SALES (est): 297.4K **Privately Held**
SIC: 2869 Mfg Industrial Organic Chemicals

(G-16472)
MRSE
Also Called: Massachstts Rebuild Svc Export
192 W Main St (01585-2728)
P.O. Box 827 (01585-0827)
PHONE..................................508 867-5083
Frank Gaumond, *Vice Pres*
Steve Mansur, *Vice Pres*
William Holmes, *Engineer*
EMP: 11
SQ FT: 14,000
SALES (est): 2.4MM **Privately Held**
WEB: www.mrse.com
SIC: 3541 5085 Mfg Machine Tools-Cutting Whol Industrial Supplies

(G-16473)
QUIRK WIRE CO INC
Also Called: Wirecraft Products
146 E Main St (01585-2901)
PHONE..................................508 867-3155
Peter Schlichting, *President*
Mary A Falardeau, *CFO*
Mary Falardeau, *CFO*
Diana Gould, *Manager*
Karen Shepard, *Admin Asst*
▲ **EMP:** 39 **EST:** 1978
SQ FT: 20,000
SALES (est): 12.1MM **Privately Held**
WEB: www.quirkwire.com
SIC: 3357 3496 3315 Nonferrous Wiredrawing/Insulating Mfg Misc Fabricated Wire Products Mfg Steel Wire/Related Products

West Chatham
Barnstable County

(G-16474)
JAM & JELLY CHATHAM
Also Called: Chatham Jam & Jelly Shop
10 Vineyard Ave (02669)
P.O. Box 214 (02669-0214)
PHONE..................................508 945-3052
Carol Cummings, *Owner*
Carole Cummings, *Owner*
Robin Cummings, *Owner*
EMP: 5
SALES (est): 130K **Privately Held**
SIC: 2033 5499 Mfg Canned Fruits/Vegetables Ret Misc Foods

West Dennis
Barnstable County

(G-16475)
ELEMENT LLC
Also Called: Fresh Interiors
581 Main St (02670-2264)
PHONE..................................508 394-3032
Richard McLaughoin,
EMP: 3 **EST:** 2009
SALES (est): 482.5K **Privately Held**
SIC: 2819 Mfg Industrial Inorganic Chemicals

(G-16476)
TURN WRIGHT MACHINE WORK
791 Main St (02670-2709)
P.O. Box 1477 (02670-1477)
PHONE..................................508 394-0724
Keith Fenner, *Partner*
Vanessa Fenner, *Partner*
EMP: 4
SALES (est): 426.3K **Privately Held**
SIC: 3599 Mfg Industrial Machinery

West Falmouth
Barnstable County

(G-16477)
ACME PRECAST CO INC
509 Thomas B Landers Rd (02574)
P.O. Box 374, North Falmouth (02556-0374)
PHONE..................................508 548-9607
Walter E Stone, *President*
EMP: 30
SQ FT: 1,500
SALES (est): 4.3MM **Privately Held**
SIC: 3272 1711 7699 Mfg Installs And Cleans Cesspools & Septic Tanks

(G-16478)
ENTERPRISE PUBLICATIONS
Also Called: Press Room, The
35 Technology Park Dr (02574)
PHONE..................................508 457-9180
EMP: 7
SALES (corp-wide): 6MM **Privately Held**
SIC: 2711 Newspapers-Publishing/Printing
PA: Enterprise Publications
50 Depot Ave
Falmouth MA 02540
508 548-4700

West Groton
Middlesex County

(G-16479)
CANNER INCORPORATED
Also Called: Carvers' Guild
1 Cannery Row (01472)
P.O. Box 198 (01472-0198)
PHONE..................................978 448-3063
Carl Canner, *President*
Carol Canner, *Clerk*
EMP: 19
SQ FT: 25,000
SALES (est): 2.5MM **Privately Held**
WEB: www.carversguild.com
SIC: 3231 7641 2426 Mfg Of Decorative Glass Reupholstery/Furniture Repair Hardwood Dimension/Floor Mill

West Harwich
Barnstable County

(G-16480)
ARCTIC HOLDINGS LLC
Also Called: Coldtub
198 Route 28 (02671-1220)
PHONE..................................978 535-5351
Scott Burt, *Info Tech Mgr*
Dawn Burt,
EMP: 6
SQ FT: 15,000

SALES: 1.4MM Privately Held
WEB: www.arcticspasdepot.com
SIC: 3841 Mfg Surgical/Medical Instruments

(G-16481)
R E K MANAGEMENT INC
Also Called: A Printery
33 Route 28 (02671-1042)
PHONE 508 775-3005
EMP: 5
SQ FT: 3,200
SALES: 500K Privately Held
WEB: www.aprintery.com
SIC: 2752 7334 Lithographic Commercial Printing Photocopying Services

West Hatfield
Hampshire County

(G-16482)
BROCKWAY-SMITH COMPANY
125 Chestnut St (01088-9501)
P.O. Box 159, Hatfield (01038-0159)
PHONE 413 247-9674
Lou Guillette, *Branch Mgr*
EMP: 75
SALES (corp-wide): 160.3MM Privately Held
WEB: www.brosco.com
SIC: 2431 5031 Whol Lumber/Plywd/Millwk Mfg Millwork
PA: Brockway-Smith Company
35 Upton Dr Ste 100
Wilmington MA 01887
978 475-7100

(G-16483)
MILL VALLEY MOLDING INC
15 West St (01088-9516)
PHONE 413 247-9313
Ralph Healy, *President*
James K Patenaude, *Treasurer*
EMP: 75
SQ FT: 11,000
SALES (est): 7MM Privately Held
WEB: www.millvalleymolding.com
SIC: 3089 Mfg Plastic Products

(G-16484)
MILL VALLEY MOLDING LLC
Also Called: SCI Tech New England Molding
15 West St (01088-9516)
PHONE 413 247-9313
Leda Mahmoodi, *Principal*
EMP: 4
SALES (est): 362K Privately Held
SIC: 3089 Injection Molding

(G-16485)
RUDISON ROUTHIER ENGRG CO
32 West St (01088-9517)
PHONE 413 247-9341
Edward Routhier, *President*
Dennis Routhier, *Shareholder*
Louis Routhier Jr, *Shareholder*
EMP: 4 EST: 1962
SQ FT: 8,000
SALES (est): 516.4K Privately Held
SIC: 3555 3554 3312 Mfg Printing Trades Machinery Mfg Paper Industrial Machinery Blast Furnace-Steel Works

(G-16486)
VISION MACHINING INC
9 West St (01088 9516)
P.O. Box 709, North Hatfield (01066-0709)
PHONE 413 247-5678
Ross Poudrier, *President*
Gary V Galvagni, *Vice Pres*
Diane A Galvagni, *CFO*
EMP: 3
SQ FT: 1,200
SALES (est): 386.8K Privately Held
SIC: 3599 Mfg Industrial Machinery

(G-16487)
WHITEWATER LLC
15 West St (01088-9516)
PHONE 413 237-5032
Michael Damon, *Principal*
EMP: 5 EST: 2008
SALES (est): 679.3K Privately Held
SIC: 3544 Mfg Dies/Tools/Jigs/Fixtures

(G-16488)
WHITEWATER PLASTICS INC
15 West St (01088-9516)
P.O. Box 1524, Northampton (01061-1524)
PHONE 413 237-5032
Michael Damon, *President*
Diana Damon, *Corp Secy*
Bruce G Rosewarne, *Director*
EMP: 3 EST: 2016
SALES (est): 339.7K Privately Held
SIC: 3089 Mfg Plastic Products

West Newbury
Essex County

(G-16489)
ANDALUNA ENTERPRISES INC
Also Called: Newbury Port Olive Oil
159 Indian Hill St (01985-2228)
PHONE 617 335-3204
Karen Nelson Shernan, *CEO*
EMP: 8
SALES: 650K Privately Held
SIC: 2079 Mfg Edible Fats/Oils

(G-16490)
ELECTROLYZER CORP
22 Bachelor St (01985-1522)
PHONE 978 363-5349
Samuel B Coco, *Ch of Bd*
Duane Mayo, *President*
Donald Harper, *Vice Pres*
Patrick Lucci, *Vice Pres*
Barry Galler, *Opers Staff*
EMP: 7
SQ FT: 1,000
SALES (est): 870K Privately Held
WEB: www.electrolyzercorp.com
SIC: 3556 Mfg Food Products Machinery

(G-16491)
FOGG FLAVOR LABS LLC
59 Prospect St (01985-1008)
PHONE 978 808-1732
Gerald Azenaro, *Principal*
EMP: 6 EST: 2016
SALES (est): 627.8K Privately Held
SIC: 2099 Mfg Food Preparations

(G-16492)
OVERSEAS PROJECT ADVANCEMENT
61 Turkey Hill Rd (01985-2008)
PHONE 978 255-1816
Samson Shafir, *President*
EMP: 10 EST: 1992
SALES: 1.1MM Privately Held
SIC: 3674 Manufacturer

West Roxbury
Suffolk County

(G-16493)
ARMSTRONG PHARMACEUTICALS INC (HQ)
423 Lagrange St (02132-3314)
PHONE 617 323-7404
Jack Zhang, *CEO*
Mary Luo, *COO*
James Luo, *Vice Pres*
▲ EMP: 70 EST: 2001
SALES (est): 11.3MM
SALES (corp-wide): 294.6MM Publicly Held
WEB: www.armstrong-pharma.com
SIC: 2834 Mfg Pharmaceutical Preparations
PA: Amphastar Pharmaceuticals Inc
11570 6th St
Rancho Cucamonga CA 91730
909 980-9484

(G-16494)
EREVNOS CORPORATION
142 Keystone St (02132-5137)
PHONE 619 675-9536
Dennis Pantazatos, *CEO*
Maria Marmarinos, *President*
EMP: 5
SALES: 3K Privately Held
SIC: 7372 Prepackaged Software Services

(G-16495)
ETEC INC
Also Called: Electronic Test Energy Co
25 Worley St (02132-1713)
PHONE 617 477-4308
Mark R Ford Jr, *President*
Brian Clozzi, *Treasurer*
EMP: 20
SQ FT: 10,000
SALES: 5MM Privately Held
WEB: www.etec-inc.com
SIC: 3825 7389 Mfr Test Equipment & Service Semi Conductor Devices

(G-16496)
GRANDE BROTHERS INC
72 Martin St (02132-6433)
PHONE 617 323-6169
EMP: 6
SALES (est): 287.6K Privately Held
SIC: 2323 Mfg Men's/Boy's Neckwear

(G-16497)
IMPERIAL MONOGRAM COMPANY INC
Also Called: Imperial Embroidery
1733 Centre St (02132-1550)
PHONE 617 323-0100
Erik Grande, *President*
Nicholas Grande, *Vice Pres*
EMP: 6 EST: 1958
SQ FT: 2,400
SALES (est): 634.8K Privately Held
WEB: www.imperialusa.biz
SIC: 2395 Pleating/Stitching Services

(G-16498)
LASER LASER INC
1895 Centre St Ste 205 (02132-1933)
PHONE 617 615-2292
EMP: 4 EST: 2014
SALES (est): 163.3K Privately Held
SIC: 2782 Blankbooks And Looseleaf Binders, Nsk

(G-16499)
MODEM SRISMITHA
1811 Centre St (02132-1945)
PHONE 617 323-0080
Modem Srismitha, *President*
EMP: 3 EST: 2016
SALES (est): 123.8K Privately Held
SIC: 3661 Mfg Telephone/Telegraph Apparatus

(G-16500)
PRIMMBIOTECH INC
8 Rutledge St (02132-2624)
P.O. Box 425695, Cambridge (02142-0013)
PHONE 617 308-8135
Richard Stelluto, *President*
EMP: 3
SALES (est): 235.9K Privately Held
WEB: www.primmbiotech.com
SIC: 2836 Custom Research Services

(G-16501)
PROFILE NEWS
1895 Centre St Ste 10 (02132-1933)
PHONE 617 325-1515
Abe Tannous, *Owner*
EMP: 5
SALES (est): 377.8K Privately Held
SIC: 2711 Newspapers-Publishing/Printing

(G-16502)
RAYWATCH INC
107 Montclair Ave 2 (02132-7803)
PHONE 401 338-2211
Matthew Gagne, *CEO*
Erno Sajo, *Development*
Piotr Zygmanski, *Development*
EMP: 3
SALES (est): 181.3K Privately Held
SIC: 3829 Mfg Measuring/Controlling Devices

(G-16503)
SPLICE THERAPEUTICS INC
14 Curlew St (02132-4102)
PHONE 914 804-4136
Fabio Petrocca, *CEO*
Hagop Youssoufian, *Director*
David Martin, *Admin Sec*
EMP: 3
SALES (est): 193.2K Privately Held
SIC: 2834 Mfg Pharmaceutical Preparations

West Springfield
Hampden County

(G-16504)
ACUMEN DATA SYSTEMS INC
2223 Westfield St (01089-2000)
PHONE 413 737-4800
Ed Squires, *President*
Dan Coffey, *Vice Pres*
Paul Panosky, *Project Mgr*
EMP: 15
SQ FT: 5,500
SALES (est): 2MM Privately Held
WEB: www.acumendatasystems.com
SIC: 7372 Custom Computer Programing

(G-16505)
ADVANCED ELECTRONIC CONTROLS
94 Doty Cir (01089-1308)
PHONE 413 736-3625
Paul Denoncourt, *Owner*
EMP: 4
SALES (est): 461.2K Privately Held
SIC: 3679 Electrical Control Panels And Products

(G-16506)
AGRI-MARK INC
958 Riverdale St (01089-4621)
PHONE 413 732-4168
David King, *Prdtn Mgr*
Scott Werme, *Opers-Prdtn-Mfg*
Anthony Lucia, *Maintence Staff*
EMP: 100
SALES (corp-wide): 382MM Privately Held
WEB: www.agrimark.net
SIC: 2026 2021 Mfg Fluid Milk Mfg Creamery Butter
PA: Agri-Mark, Inc.
40 Shattuck Rd Ste 301
Andover MA 01810
978 552-5500

(G-16507)
ALDEN MEDICAL LLC (PA)
Also Called: Ciden Technologies
360 Cold Spring Ave Ste 1 (01089-3700)
PHONE 413 747-9717
Jessica Markel, *QA Dir*
Damon D'Amico, *Mng Member*
▲ EMP: 4
SQ FT: 3,000
SALES (est): 9.3MM Privately Held
WEB: www.aldenmedical.com
SIC: 2899 Mfg Chemical Preparations

(G-16508)
ARCH PARENT INC
1129 Riverdale St (01089-4615)
PHONE 413 504-1433
EMP: 3 Privately Held
SIC: 2752 Lithographic Commercial Printing
HQ: Arch Parent Inc.
9 W 57th St Fl 31
New York NY 10019
212 796-8500

(G-16509)
ATC GROUP SERVICES LLC
73 William Frank Dr (01089-3261)
PHONE 337 234-8777
Kelly Young, *Branch Mgr*
EMP: 30 Privately Held
SIC: 3826 Mfg Analytical Instruments
HQ: Atc Group Services Llc
5750 Johnston St Ste 400
Lafayette LA 70503
337 234-8777

GEOGRAPHIC

(G-16510)
ATLAS COPCO COMPRESSORS LLC
92 Interstate Dr (01089-4532)
PHONE..................................413 493-7290
Uew Fefraber, *Manager*
EMP: 19
SALES (corp-wide): 10B **Privately Held**
WEB: www.atlascopco.com
SIC: 3563 Mfg Air/Gas Compressors Mfg Motors/Generators
HQ: Atlas Copco Compressors Llc
300 Technology Center Way # 5
Rock Hill SC 29730
866 472-1015

(G-16511)
BART TRUCK EQUIPMENT LLC
358 River St (01089-3632)
PHONE..................................413 737-2766
James Diclementi, *President*
Christopher Diclementi, *Sales Mgr*
Therese Diclementi,
Timothy Diclementi,
EMP: 9
SALES (est): 950K **Privately Held**
SIC: 3713 Mfg Truck/Bus Bodies

(G-16512)
CLARK PAINT & VARNISH COMPANY
Also Called: Clark Paint Factory
966 Union St (01089-4234)
PHONE..................................413 733-3554
Andrew Raker, *President*
Marcia Raker, *Treasurer*
EMP: 6 **EST:** 1944
SQ FT: 10,000
SALES (est): 1.2MM **Privately Held**
WEB: www.clarkpaint.com
SIC: 2851 5231 Mfg Paints/Allied Products Ret Paint/Glass/Wallpaper

(G-16513)
COVERIS ADVANCED COATINGS
69 William Frank Dr (01089-3261)
PHONE..................................413 539-5547
Ed McCarron, *Vice Pres*
Kristina Tassistro Devine, *Production*
▲ **EMP:** 20
SQ FT: 3,000
SALES (est): 3.8MM
SALES (corp-wide): 2.2B **Privately Held**
WEB: www.intelicoat.com
SIC: 2671 2851 Mfg Packaging Paper/Film Mfg Paints/Allied Products
HQ: Transcontinental Ac Uk Ltd.
Ash Road North
Wrexham LL13
197 866-0241

(G-16514)
CYALUME TECHNOLOGIES INC (DH)
96 Windsor St (01089-3528)
PHONE..................................888 451-4885
Zivi Nedivi, *President*
Dale Baker, *COO*
Michael Bielonko, *CFO*
◆ **EMP:** 140
SALES: 33MM
SALES (corp-wide): 41.2MM **Publicly Held**
WEB: www.cyalume.com
SIC: 3648 Manufacturer Lighting Equipment

(G-16515)
DDFHKLT INC
Also Called: Graphic Printing Co
233 Western Ave (01089-3455)
P.O. Box 1164 (01090-1164)
PHONE..................................413 733-7441
EMP: 11
SQ FT: 10,000
SALES (est): 114.3K **Privately Held**
SIC: 2752 2789 Lithographic Commercial Printing Bookbinding/Related Work

(G-16516)
DIAMONDHEAD USA INC
622 Union St (01089-4111)
PHONE..................................413 537-4806
John Deluca, *Principal*
Deluca Dave, *Program Mgr*
Danine Ritucci, *Executive Asst*
EMP: 3 **EST:** 2013
SALES (est): 269.7K **Privately Held**
SIC: 3999 Mfg Misc Products

(G-16517)
EASTERN CAST HARDWARE CO INC
77 Heywood Ave (01089-3715)
PHONE..................................413 733-7690
John Depalma, *President*
Anne Depalma, *Clerk*
EMP: 6 **EST:** 1940
SQ FT: 12,000
SALES (est): 550K **Privately Held**
SIC: 3429 Mfg Metal Casket Hardware

(G-16518)
ELM INDUSTRIES INC
380 Union St Ste 67 (01089-4123)
P.O. Box 717 (01090-0717)
PHONE..................................413 734-7762
George W Martin, *President*
John F Martin, *Vice Pres*
Kenneth C Martin, *Vice Pres*
EMP: 20
SQ FT: 11,000
SALES (est): 2.6MM **Privately Held**
SIC: 3089 Mfg Plastic Products

(G-16519)
ESCOUNTERTOPS LLC
3 Century Way (01089-4235)
PHONE..................................413 732-8128
Benjamin Abel, *CEO*
EMP: 8
SALES (est): 239.8K **Privately Held**
SIC: 3281 Mfg Cut Stone/Products

(G-16520)
FEDERAL SPECIALTIES INC
140 Norman St (01089-5004)
PHONE..................................413 782-6900
Gordon Phelps, *President*
Peggy Phelps, *Treasurer*
EMP: 3 **EST:** 1967
SQ FT: 5,000
SALES: 389K **Privately Held**
SIC: 2394 5039 5211 Mfr & Whol Aluminum Canopies & Awnings And Whol & Ret Exterior Bldg Pdts

(G-16521)
FOUNTAIN PLATING COMPANY INC
492 Prospect Ave (01089-4596)
PHONE..................................413 781-4651
Nina Fountain, *President*
Laurence R Fountain, *Chairman*
Dexter Fountain, *Vice Pres*
Edgar Judd, *Plant Mgr*
Jeff Hotham, *Prdtn Mgr*
EMP: 95 **EST:** 1963
SQ FT: 70,000
SALES (est): 21.7MM **Privately Held**
WEB: www.fountain-plating.com
SIC: 3724 3471 Mfg Aircraft Engines/Parts Plating/Polishing Service

(G-16522)
FRG PUBLICATIONS
Also Called: Green Publishing
380 Union St Ste 100 (01089-4104)
PHONE..................................413 734-3411
Thomas Green, *President*
EMP: 14
SALES (est): 1MM **Privately Held**
SIC: 2741 Misc Publishing

(G-16523)
FUEL FIRST ELM INC
173 Elm St (01089-2726)
PHONE..................................413 732-5732
Sanjay Patel, *President*
EMP: 3
SALES (est): 182K **Privately Held**
SIC: 2869 Mfg Industrial Organic Chemicals

(G-16524)
HAYES PROSTHETIC INC
1309 Riverdale St (01089-4693)
PHONE..................................413 733-2287
Robert F Hayes, *President*
Brian Hayes, *Corp Secy*
EMP: 5
SQ FT: 3,000
SALES (est): 787.7K **Privately Held**
SIC: 3842 5999 Mfg Surgical Appliances/Supplies Ret Misc Merchandise

(G-16525)
IMPRINTED SPORTSWEAR INC
Also Called: T-Shirt Station
1458 Riverdale St Ste B (01089-4673)
PHONE..................................413 732-5271
Fred Aaron, *President*
EMP: 4
SALES (est): 442.9K **Privately Held**
WEB: www.t-shirtstation.com
SIC: 2396 7389 Screen Printing & Embroidery On Activewear

(G-16526)
INTELICOAT TECHNOLOGIES
69 William Frank Dr (01089-3261)
PHONE..................................413 536-7800
Bob Champigny, *President*
EMP: 4
SALES (est): 380K **Privately Held**
SIC: 3826 Mfg Analytical Instruments

(G-16527)
INTERNATIONAL BEAM WLDG CORP
63 Doty Cir (01089-1395)
PHONE..................................413 781-4368
William B Howe, *President*
Robin Colburs, *Manager*
Carol A Howe, *Clerk*
EMP: 10
SQ FT: 7,000
SALES (est): 954.1K **Privately Held**
SIC: 7692 Welding Repair

(G-16528)
LEISURE TIME CANVAS
140 Norman St (01089-5004)
PHONE..................................413 785-5500
John Vogel, *President*
Phyllis Hard, *Vice Pres*
EMP: 7
SQ FT: 70,000
SALES (est): 530K **Privately Held**
SIC: 2394 Mfg Canvas Products

(G-16529)
LETTERPRESS SERVICES INC
85 Phelon Ave (01089-3459)
PHONE..................................413 732-0399
John Spencer Barrett, *President*
Joseph C Barrett, *Officer*
EMP: 5
SQ FT: 3,700
SALES (est): 478.2K **Privately Held**
SIC: 2759 Commercial Printing

(G-16530)
MICON DIE CORPORATION
Also Called: Micon Steel Rule Die
85 Phelon Ave (01089-3459)
P.O. Box 11 (01090-0011)
PHONE..................................413 478-5029
Michael Condon, *President*
EMP: 3
SQ FT: 5,500
SALES: 250K **Privately Held**
SIC: 3544 Mfg Dies/Tools/Jigs/Fixtures

(G-16531)
MOUNT TOM BOX COMPANY INC
190 Interstate Dr (01089-4582)
PHONE..................................413 781-5300
David Strauss, *President*
EMP: 44
SQ FT: 65,000
SALES (est): 7.4MM **Privately Held**
WEB: www.mounttombox.com
SIC: 2653 Mfg Corrugated/Solid Fiber Boxes

(G-16532)
MTI SYSTEMS INC
Also Called: Manufactures Technologies
1111 Elm St Ste 6 (01089-1540)
PHONE..................................413 733-1972
Thomas Charkiewicz, *President*
Rene M Laviolette, *CFO*
Nancy Olechna, *Treasurer*
EMP: 28
SALES (est): 3.6MM **Privately Held**
WEB: www.mtisystems.com
SIC: 7372 7371 Prepackaged Software Services Custom Computer Programing

(G-16533)
MULTI SIGN INC
Also Called: Fastsigns
777 Riverdale St (01089-4611)
PHONE..................................413 732-9900
George Smarz, *President*
Melinda Martin, *Graphic Designe*
EMP: 4 **EST:** 1996
SALES (est): 372.5K **Privately Held**
SIC: 3993 Signsadv Specs

(G-16534)
NEENAH NORTHEAST LLC (HQ)
70 Front St (01089-3113)
PHONE..................................413 533-0699
Anthony Pd Maclaurin, *CEO*
Eric Schondorf, *Vice Pres*
Craig Thiel, *Vice Pres*
Matthew Levine, *Treasurer*
◆ **EMP:** 110
SALES (est): 141.1MM
SALES (corp-wide): 1B **Publicly Held**
SIC: 2631 Paperboard Mill
PA: Neenah, Inc.
3460 Preston Ridge Rd # 150
Alpharetta GA 30005
678 566-6500

(G-16535)
NORTEK INC
70 Doty Cir (01089-1394)
PHONE..................................413 781-4777
Bianca P Magnani, *President*
Raymond Santinello, *Vice Pres*
EMP: 20
SQ FT: 8,000
SALES: 2.2MM **Privately Held**
SIC: 3545 Mfg Machine Tool Accessories

(G-16536)
NUMERIC INC
Also Called: Numeric Machining Company
195 Wayside Ave (01089-1319)
PHONE..................................413 732-6544
Joseph McGovern, *President*
EMP: 10
SQ FT: 4,050
SALES (est): 1.3MM **Privately Held**
WEB: www.numeric.com
SIC: 3599 8721 Machine Shop & Billing Service

(G-16537)
ORANGE SHUTTER STUDIOS
85 Poplar Ave (01089-2926)
PHONE..................................413 544-8403
EMP: 3 **EST:** 2017
SALES (est): 143.2K **Privately Held**
SIC: 3442 Mfg Metal Doors/Sash/Trim

(G-16538)
OUIMETTE PRINTING INC
40 Kelso Ave (01089-3440)
PHONE..................................413 736-5926
David Ouimette, *President*
EMP: 4
SQ FT: 1,600
SALES (est): 450K **Privately Held**
WEB: www.ouimetteprinting.com
SIC: 2752 Offset Print Shop

(G-16539)
PACKAGE PRINTING COMPANY INC
33 Myron St (01089-1486)
P.O. Box 378 (01090-0378)
PHONE..................................413 736-2748
James G Barnhart, *President*
Robert Barnhart, *Admin Sec*
▲ **EMP:** 30
SQ FT: 30,000
SALES (est): 8MM **Privately Held**
SIC: 2671 2759 Mfg Packaging Paper/Film Commercial Printing

(G-16540)
PAPER PLUS INC
Also Called: Curry Copy Ctr W Springfield
91 Union St 1 (01089-3316)
PHONE.................................413 785-1363
Stephen C Lang, *President*
Beth Lang, *Clerk*
EMP: 6
SQ FT: 2,500
SALES (est): 630K **Privately Held**
SIC: 2752 7334 Printer & Photocopying Service

(G-16541)
PEERLESS HANDCUFF CO INC
181 Doty Cir (01089-1309)
PHONE.................................413 732-2156
Peter Gill, *President*
Bradford Gill, *Treasurer*
▲ **EMP:** 5
SQ FT: 3,000
SALES (est): 510K **Privately Held**
WEB: www.peerless.net
SIC: 3429 Mfg Handcuffs

(G-16542)
PHOTONICS N PICOQUANT AMER INC
9 Trinity Dr (01089-1825)
PHONE.................................413 562-6161
Rainer Erdmann, *President*
Alain Bourdon, *Vice Pres*
Danielle McCauley, *Info Tech Mgr*
EMP: 5 **EST:** 2008
SALES (est): 619.8K **Privately Held**
SIC: 3826 Mfg Analytical Instruments

(G-16543)
PIONEER PRECISION GRINDING
175 New Bridge St (01089)
P.O. Box 960 (01090-0960)
PHONE.................................413 739-3371
James M Upson, *President*
Gilbert M Upson, *Treasurer*
EMP: 15 **EST:** 1965
SQ FT: 3,000
SALES (est): 1.3MM **Privately Held**
SIC: 3599 Mfg Industrial Machinery

(G-16544)
PIONEER VALLEY PRINTING CO
62 Ely Ave (01089-2214)
PHONE.................................413 739-2855
Fax: 413 527-7266
EMP: 3
SQ FT: 3,000
SALES: 350K **Privately Held**
SIC: 2752 Offset Printing

(G-16545)
PIONEER VLY ORTHTICS PRSTHTICS
138 Doty Cir (01089-1310)
PHONE.................................413 788-9655
Frank H Twyeffort, *President*
EMP: 8 **EST:** 1978
SQ FT: 3,000
SALES (est): 992.4K **Privately Held**
SIC: 3842 7699 Mfg Surgical Appliances/Supplies Repair Services

(G-16546)
PLACON CORPORATION
1227 Union Street Ext (01089-4022)
PHONE.................................413 785-1553
Ed Kadlam, *General Mgr*
EMP: 120
SALES (corp-wide): 34.3MM **Privately Held**
SIC: 3089 Mfg Plastic Products
PA: Placon Corporation
6096 Mckee Rd
Fitchburg WI 53719
608 271-5634

(G-16547)
PRECISION COMPONENTS GROUP
190 Doty Cir (01089-1310)
PHONE.................................413 333-4184
Peter A Elias, *CEO*
Mark A Zadie, *Treasurer*
EMP: 3 **EST:** 2016
SALES (est): 173.8K **Privately Held**
SIC: 3728 3724 Mfg Aircraft Parts/Equip Mfg Aircraft Engine/Part

(G-16548)
PRO TOOL & MACHINE
349 Cold Spring Ave (01089-3757)
PHONE.................................413 732-8940
Mirek Guzek, *Owner*
EMP: 3
SALES (est): 200.1K **Privately Held**
SIC: 3599 Mfg Industrial Machinery

(G-16549)
PROSTHTIC ORTHTIC SLUTIONS LLC
66 Myron St (01089-1416)
PHONE.................................413 785-4047
Christian M Rogers,
EMP: 8
SALES (est): 1.1MM **Privately Held**
SIC: 3842 Mfg Surgical Appliances/Supplies

(G-16550)
Q PIN2S BILLIARDS
885 Riverdale St (01089-4612)
PHONE.................................413 285-7971
Dixie Willison, *Principal*
EMP: 5 **EST:** 2011
SALES (est): 365K **Privately Held**
SIC: 3452 Mfg Bolts/Screws/Rivets

(G-16551)
SHARP GRINDING CO INC
Also Called: Sharp Precision Grinding
168 Windsor St (01089-3530)
PHONE.................................413 737-8808
Gary R Pettazoni, *President*
EMP: 4
SQ FT: 4,000
SALES (est): 290K **Privately Held**
SIC: 3541 Mfg Machine Tools

(G-16552)
STEEL PANEL FOUNDATIONS LLC
Also Called: Spf
1111 Elm St Ste 33 (01089-1540)
PHONE.................................413 439-0218
Salvator Scuderi,
Deborah A Scuderi,
▲ **EMP:** 7
SALES (est): 487.9K **Privately Held**
SIC: 2515 Mfg Mattresses/Bedsprings

(G-16553)
STEVES SPORTS
94 Front St (01089-3113)
PHONE.................................413 746-1696
Steve Bordeaux, *Owner*
EMP: 4
SALES (est): 200K **Privately Held**
WEB: www.stevessports.com
SIC: 2759 Commercial Printing

(G-16554)
SULLIVAN PAPER COMPANY INC (PA)
42 Progress Ave (01089-3313)
P.O. Box 88 (01090-0088)
PHONE.................................413 827-7030
George R Sullivan, *CEO*
Joe Sullivan, *President*
Mike Sullivan, *President*
Richard Sullivan, *Chairman*
Roy Britten, *Vice Pres*
◆ **EMP:** 165 **EST:** 1939
SQ FT: 30,000
SALES (est): 56MM **Privately Held**
WEB: www.sullivanpaper.com
SIC: 2679 Mfg Converted Paper Products

(G-16555)
SUPREME BRASS & ALUM CASTINGS
210 Windsor St (01089-3532)
PHONE.................................413 737-4433
Dominique Rettura, *President*
EMP: 3
SQ FT: 5,000
SALES: 500K **Privately Held**
SIC: 3365 3366 Manufactures Aluminum Brass And Bronze Castings

(G-16556)
TROY INDUSTRIES INC
151 Capital Dr (01089-1354)
PHONE.................................413 788-4288
Steve P Troy, *CEO*
Andrew Finn, *President*
Eric Babski, *Design Engr*
Erhan Erden, *Technology*
Stephen Bartlett, *Technician*
EMP: 95
SQ FT: 3,000
SALES (est): 2.6MM **Privately Held**
WEB: www.troyind.com
SIC: 3489 Mfg Ordnance/Accessories

(G-16557)
TRUE PRECISION INC
17 Allston Ave (01089-3799)
PHONE.................................413 788-4226
Leo R La Flamme, *President*
Robert Serre, *Vice Pres*
EMP: 12
SQ FT: 2,200
SALES: 900K **Privately Held**
WEB: www.trueprecision.com
SIC: 3599 Mfg Industrial Machinery

(G-16558)
TRUE PRECISION INDUSTRIES INC
17 Allston Ave (01089-3799)
PHONE.................................413 788-4226
Richard Champigny, *President*
Michael Belisle, *Treasurer*
EMP: 15
SALES (est): 1.9MM **Privately Held**
SIC: 3599 Mfg Industrial Machinery

(G-16559)
UNITED INDUSTRIAL TEX PDTS INC (PA)
321 Main St (01089-3908)
PHONE.................................413 737-0095
Wayne Perry, *President*
Joanne Perry, *CFO*
Keith Perry, *Treasurer*
EMP: 34
SQ FT: 10,000
SALES: 3.9MM **Privately Held**
WEB: www.uitprod.com
SIC: 2394 2299 2393 Mfg Canvas/Related Products Mfg Textile Goods Mfg Textile Bags

(G-16560)
UNITED INDUSTRIAL TEX PDTS INC
136 Bliss St (01089-3435)
PHONE.................................413 737-0095
Wayne Perry, *President*
EMP: 4
SQ FT: 7,800
SALES (corp-wide): 3.9MM **Privately Held**
SIC: 2394 2299 2393 Mfg Canvas/Related Products Mfg Textile Goods Mfg Textile Bags
PA: United Industrial Textile Products, Inc.
321 Main St
West Springfield MA 01089
413 737-0095

(G-16561)
VALENTINE PLATING COMPANY INC
155 Allston Ave (01089-3796)
PHONE.................................413 732-0009
Steve Valentino Jr, *President*
Anthony Valentino, *Vice Pres*
EMP: 34 **EST:** 1965
SALES: 1.6MM **Privately Held**
SIC: 3471 Plating/Polishing Service

(G-16562)
VOGFORM TOOL & DIE CO INC
56 Doty Cir (01089-1308)
PHONE.................................413 737-6947
John Vogel, *President*
Elizabeth Vogel, *Treasurer*
EMP: 14
SQ FT: 9,000
SALES (est): 2.1MM **Privately Held**
WEB: www.vogform.com
SIC: 3545 Mfg Dies/Tools/Jigs/Fixtures

(G-16563)
WEST SPRINGFIELD RECORD INC
516 Main St (01089-3983)
P.O. Box 357 (01090-0357)
PHONE.................................413 736-1587
Marie Coburn, *President*
Thomas Coburn, *Editor*
EMP: 7 **EST:** 1951
SQ FT: 1,500
SALES (est): 443.4K **Privately Held**
SIC: 2711 Newspapers-Publishing/Printing

(G-16564)
WESTERN BRONZE INC
54 Western Ave (01089-3491)
PHONE.................................413 737-1319
Daniel Kotowitz, *President*
Nancy Kotowitz, *Manager*
EMP: 10
SQ FT: 12,000
SALES (est): 1.1MM **Privately Held**
WEB: www.westernbronze.com
SIC: 3366 Copper Foundry

(G-16565)
WESTERN MASS COPYING PRTG INC
Also Called: Copycat Print Shop
138 Memorial Ave Ste 1 (01089-4046)
PHONE.................................413 734-2679
Robert R Perrier, *President*
Steven J Beshara, *Admin Sec*
EMP: 5
SALES: 350K **Privately Held**
SIC: 2752 7334 Lithographic Commercial Printing Photocopying Services

West Townsend
Middlesex County

(G-16566)
CORONA FILMS INC
241 Dudley Rd (01474-1038)
P.O. Box 181 (01474-0181)
PHONE.................................978 597-6444
Brett Purvis, *President*
Gary Lahti, *Treasurer*
▲ **EMP:** 3
SQ FT: 6,400
SALES (est): 411.4K **Privately Held**
SIC: 2621 Paper Mill

West Wareham
Plymouth County

(G-16567)
CALORIQUE LLC
2380 Cranberry Hwy Unit 6 (02576-1229)
PHONE.................................508 291-2000
William D McCarthy, *Mng Member*
EMP: 14
SQ FT: 20,000
SALES (est): 815.1K **Privately Held**
SIC: 3567 Mfg Industrial Furnaces/Ovens

(G-16568)
COTTER MACHINE CO INC (PA)
7 Little Brook Rd (02576-1221)
P.O. Box 249 (02576-0249)
PHONE.................................508 291-7400
Gregory Cotter, *President*
EMP: 15
SQ FT: 10,000
SALES (est): 3.2MM **Privately Held**
SIC: 3599 Mfg Industrial Machinery

(G-16569)
EAST COAST FABRICATIONS
9 Acoaxet Ln (02576-1123)
P.O. Box 638 (02576-0638)
PHONE.................................508 295-1982
Gerald Johnson, *Owner*
EMP: 3
SALES (est): 225K **Privately Held**
SIC: 3441 Structural Metal Fabrication

(G-16570)
EDGEONE LLC
Also Called: Ore Offshore
4 Little Brook Rd (02576-1222)
P.O. Box 848 (02576-0848)
PHONE..................................508 291-0960
Steven Withrow, *Branch Mgr*
EMP: 9
SALES (corp-wide): 22.5MM **Privately Held**
WEB: www.edgeone.com
SIC: 3812 5049 Mfg Search/Navigation Equipment Whol Professional Equipment
PA: Edgeone Llc
4 Little Brook Rd
West Wareham MA 02576
508 291-0057

(G-16571)
EDGEONE LLC
Edgetech
4 Little Brook Rd (02576-1222)
PHONE..................................508 291-0057
Greg Macearhern, *Branch Mgr*
EMP: 65
SALES (corp-wide): 22.5MM **Privately Held**
WEB: www.edgeone.com
SIC: 3812 Mfg Analytical Instrument Mfg Search/Navigation Equipment
PA: Edgeone Llc
4 Little Brook Rd
West Wareham MA 02576
508 291-0057

(G-16572)
FIBERSPAR SPOOLABLE PRODUCTS (PA)
28 Pattersons Brook Rd (02576-1216)
PHONE..................................508 291-9000
Peter Quigley, *President*
▲ **EMP:** 25
SQ FT: 5,000
SALES (est): 2.2MM **Privately Held**
SIC: 3084 Mfg Plastic Pipe

(G-16573)
FRANKLIN FIXTURES INC (PA)
20 Pattersons Brook Rd # 1 (02576-1265)
PHONE..................................508 291-1475
James E Baylis, *President*
David Uhrik, *General Mgr*
David N Troe, *Vice Pres*
EMP: 29 **EST:** 1975
SQ FT: 45,000
SALES (est): 3.7MM **Privately Held**
WEB: www.franklinfixtures.com
SIC: 2541 Mfg Wood Partitions/Fixtures

(G-16574)
HAYDEN MANUFACTURING CO INC
50 Carver Rd (02576-1226)
PHONE..................................508 295-0497
Beverly St Jacques, *President*
Raymond St Jacques, *Treasurer*
David St Jacques, *Manager*
EMP: 7
SQ FT: 40,000
SALES (est): 887.9K **Privately Held**
WEB: www.haydenmfg.com
SIC: 3523 Mfg Farm Machinery/Equipment

(G-16575)
MAKE ARCHITECTURAL METALWORKING
2358 Cranberry Hwy (02576-1208)
PHONE..................................508 273-7603
Paul A Meneses, *Principal*
EMP: 14
SALES (est): 2.5MM **Privately Held**
SIC: 3446 Mfg Architectural Metalwork

(G-16576)
ROCHESTER BITUMINOUS PRODUCTS
83 Kings Hwy (02576-1501)
PHONE..................................508 295-8001
Ideal Batista, *President*
EMP: 6
SALES (est): 1.2MM **Privately Held**
WEB: www.rochesterbituminous.com
SIC: 2951 1611 Mfg Asphalt Mixtures/Blocks Highway/Street Construction

(G-16577)
TRINITY HEATING & AIR INC
Also Called: Trinity Solar Systems
20 Pattersons Brook Rd (02576-1265)
PHONE..................................508 291-0007
Jane McArdle, *Branch Mgr*
EMP: 80 **Privately Held**
SIC: 3433 Mfg Heating Equipment-Non-electric
PA: Trinity Heating & Air, Inc.
2211 Allenwood Rd
Wall Township NJ 07719
-

West Yarmouth
Barnstable County

(G-16578)
BAXTER INC
Also Called: Baxter Crane & Rigging
10 Bayview St (02673-8203)
PHONE..................................508 228-8136
Jonathan Baxter, *President*
▲ **EMP:** 8
SQ FT: 450
SALES (est): 760K **Privately Held**
WEB: www.baxtercrane.com
SIC: 7692 7353 5051 Welding Repair Heavy Construction Equipment Rental Metals Service Center

(G-16579)
LOCATION LUBE INC
164 Mid Tech Dr Unit H (02673-2527)
PHONE..................................508 888-5000
Rich Halverson, *President*
EMP: 3
SALES (est): 263.2K **Privately Held**
WEB: www.locationlube.com
SIC: 3569 Mfg Lubricating Equipment

(G-16580)
LOWER LIMB TECHNOLOGY LLC
191 Mid Tech Dr (02673-2581)
PHONE..................................508 775-0990
James F Tierney,
EMP: 10
SALES (est): 444.2K **Privately Held**
SIC: 3842 Mfg Surgical Appliances/Supplies

(G-16581)
ORTHOTIC & PROSTHETIC CTRS LLC
126b Mid Tech Dr (02673-2560)
PHONE..................................508 775-7151
James Tierney, *Mng Member*
EMP: 5
SALES (est): 536.9K **Privately Held**
WEB: www.oandpcenters.com
SIC: 3842 Mfg Surgical Appliances/Supplies

(G-16582)
SPINAL TECHNOLOGY INC (PA)
191 Mid Tech Dr (02673-2581)
PHONE..................................508 775-0990
James Tierney, *President*
James Benelli, *Vice Pres*
John Stacy, *Purch Agent*
Ariane St Claire, *CFO*
Michael Roy, *Cust Svc Mgr*
EMP: 70
SQ FT: 18,000
SALES (est): 13.1MM **Privately Held**
WEB: www.spinaltech.com
SIC: 3842 Mfg Surgical Appliances/Supplies

Westborough
Worcester County

(G-16583)
2 COOL PROMOS
1900 W Park Dr Ste 280 (01581-3919)
PHONE..................................508 351-9700
Jeff Michaelson, *Owner*
EMP: 3
SALES (est): 192.6K **Privately Held**
WEB: www.2coolpromos.com
SIC: 2711 5199 7311 Newspapers-Publishing/Printing Whol Nondurable Goods Advertising Agency

(G-16584)
3M TOUCH SYSTEMS INC
115 Flanders Rd (01581-1033)
PHONE..................................508 871-1840
Samuel Thomas, *Branch Mgr*
EMP: 158
SALES (corp-wide): 32.7B **Publicly Held**
WEB: www.dynapro.com
SIC: 3577 Mfg Computer Peripheral Equipment
HQ: 3m Touch Systems, Inc.
501 Griffin Brook Dr
Methuen MA 01844
978 659-9000

(G-16585)
AAF MICROSYSTEMS LTD
21 E Main St Ste 3 (01581-1467)
PHONE..................................508 366-9100
Jeffrey Pelland, *CEO*
Grace Carter, *Accountant*
EMP: 6
SALES (est): 552.5K **Privately Held**
SIC: 7372 Prepackaged Software Services

(G-16586)
ACCELA GRAPHICS NENG INC
74 Otis St (01581-3323)
P.O. Box 408 (01581-0408)
PHONE..................................508 366-5999
EMP: 8
SALES: 1.2MM **Privately Held**
SIC: 2759 7336 Commercial Printing Commercial Art/Graphic Design

(G-16587)
ACTUATE CORPORATION
25 Smith St (01581-1723)
PHONE..................................508 870-9822
Matt F Highsmith, *Branch Mgr*
EMP: 3
SALES (corp-wide): 2.8B **Privately Held**
SIC: 7372 Prepackaged Software Services
HQ: Actuate Corporation
951 Mariners Island Blvd # 7
San Mateo CA 94404
-

(G-16588)
AMERICAN MACHINE CO
58 Hopkinton Rd (01581-2126)
P.O. Box 253 (01581-0253)
PHONE..................................508 366-9634
Matthew D Manella, *President*
Bruce R Rososky Jr, *Vice Pres*
Bruce Rososky, *Human Res Mgr*
Darlene Manella, *Admin Sec*
EMP: 6
SQ FT: 1,200
SALES (est): 899.8K **Privately Held**
WEB: www.americanmachinecompany.com
SIC: 3599 Mfg Industrial Machinery

(G-16589)
APEX PRESS INC
122 Turnpike Rd (01581-2854)
PHONE..................................508 366-1110
Sheila A Gendreau, *President*
Raymond Gendreau J, *IT/INT Sup*
EMP: 18
SQ FT: 15,600
SALES: 1.2MM **Privately Held**
SIC: 2759 7334 2752 Commercial Printing Photocopying Services Lithographic Commercial Printing

(G-16590)
ATERNITY INC
200 Friberg Pkwy Ste 1004 (01581-3933)
PHONE..................................508 475-0414
EMP: 140
SQ FT: 9,800
SALES (est): 16.8MM **Privately Held**
SIC: 7372 Prepackaged Software Services

(G-16591)
AVERY DENNISON CORPORATION
1700 W Park Dr Ste 400 (01581-3915)
PHONE..................................508 948-3500
Whitten Ashlie, *Sales Staff*
Pat Harnois, *Manager*
Raymond Millette, *Technology*
EMP: 117
SALES (corp-wide): 7.1B **Publicly Held**
SIC: 2672 3081 3497 2678 Mfg Coat/Laminated Paper Mfg Unsupport Plstc Film Mfg Metal Foil/Leaf
PA: Avery Dennison Corporation
207 N Goode Ave
Glendale CA 91203
626 304-2000

(G-16592)
BAGDON ADVERTISING INC
Also Called: Community Advocate
32 South St (01581-1619)
P.O. Box 1574 (01581-6574)
PHONE..................................508 366-5500
David D Bagdon, *President*
Barbara Clifford, *Sales Staff*
EMP: 15
SQ FT: 3,600
SALES (est): 1MM **Privately Held**
WEB: www.communityadvocate.com
SIC: 2711 Newspapers-Publishing/Printing

(G-16593)
BEL POWER INC
2400 Computer Dr (01581-1887)
PHONE..................................508 870-9775
Howard Kaepplein, *President*
William Ng, *Vice Pres*
Bernie Schroter, *Vice Pres*
Andrew Demarco, *Engineer*
▲ **EMP:** 55
SQ FT: 22,000
SALES (est): 7.2MM
SALES (corp-wide): 548.1MM **Publicly Held**
SIC: 3629 Mfg Electrical Industrial Apparatus
PA: Bel Fuse Inc.
206 Van Vorst St
Jersey City NJ 07302
201 432-0463

(G-16594)
BOSSONNET INC
121 Flanders Rd (01581-1030)
PHONE..................................508 986-2308
Gilles Bossonnet, *CEO*
EMP: 3
SQ FT: 1,000
SALES (est): 138.2K **Privately Held**
SIC: 3599 Mfg Industrial Machinery

(G-16595)
BOSTON-POWER INC (PA)
2200 W Park Dr Ste 320 (01581-3961)
P.O. Box 798, Northborough (01532-0798)
PHONE..................................508 366-0885
Sonny Wu, *Ch of Bd*
Alex Pan, *President*
Eric Tu, *COO*
Jackie He, *Senior VP*
Simon Vieira-Ribeiro, *CFO*
▲ **EMP:** 54
SALES (est): 16.2MM **Privately Held**
WEB: www.boston-power.com
SIC: 3691 Mfg Storage Batteries

(G-16596)
BUSINESS RESOURCES INC
Also Called: Development Resources
1500 W Park Dr (01581-3936)
PHONE..................................508 433-4600
David Sears, *CEO*
EMP: 10
SQ FT: 3,500
SALES (est): 1.6MM **Privately Held**
SIC: 2759 Commercial Printing

(G-16597)
C2C SYSTEMS INC
112 Turnpike Rd Ste 111 (01581-2860)
PHONE..................................508 870-2205
David Hunt, *President*
EMP: 16
SQ FT: 2,500
SALES (est): 2MM **Privately Held**
SIC: 3695 7371 Mfg Magnetic & Optical Recording Media Custom Computer Programing

(G-16598)
CAMBEX CORPORATION (PA)
115 Flanders Rd (01581-1033)
PHONE..................................508 983-1200
Joseph F Kruy, *President*
Les Koch, *Vice Pres*
Lois P Lehberger, *Vice Pres*
EMP: 10
SQ FT: 15,000
SALES (est): 5.7MM **Publicly Held**
SIC: 3572 Mfg Computer Storage Devices

(G-16599)
CANAL TOYS USA LTD
1700 W Park Dr Ste 120 (01581-3941)
PHONE..................................508 366-9060
Bill Uzell, *CEO*
Patrick Krief, *CEO*
▲ **EMP:** 4
SALES (est): 646.3K **Privately Held**
SIC: 3944 Mfg Games/Toys

(G-16600)
CANVAS LINK INC
10 Old Flanders Rd (01581-1010)
PHONE..................................508 366-3323
EMP: 8
SQ FT: 1,500
SALES: 500K **Privately Held**
SIC: 2394 7371 Mfg Canvas/Related Products Custom Computer Programing

(G-16601)
CARLSTROM PRESSED METAL CO INC
65 Fisher St (01581-1898)
PHONE..................................508 366-4472
David M Carlstrom, *President*
EMP: 25 **EST:** 1950
SQ FT: 45,000
SALES (est): 4.8MM **Privately Held**
WEB: www.carlstrompm.com
SIC: 3469 Mfg Metal Stampings

(G-16602)
CGIT WESTBORO INC
30 Oak St (01581-3319)
PHONE..................................508 836-4000
Dana Perry, *CFO*
▲ **EMP:** 105
SQ FT: 36,578
SALES (est): 11.8MM
SALES (corp-wide): 927MM **Publicly Held**
WEB: www.cgit-westboro.com
SIC: 3613 3612 Mfg Switchgear/Switchboards Mfg Transformers
PA: Azz Inc.
3100 W 7th St Ste 500
Fort Worth TX 76107
817 810-0095

(G-16603)
CLEARESULT CONSULTING INC
50 Washington St Ste 3000 (01581-1169)
PHONE..................................508 836-9500
Aziz Virani, *Branch Mgr*
EMP: 6
SALES (corp-wide): 657MM **Privately Held**
SIC: 2741 Misc Publishing
PA: Clearesult Consulting Inc.
4301 Westbank Dr Ste A250
Austin TX 78746
512 327-9200

(G-16604)
COGHLIN COMPANIES INC (PA)
Also Called: Columbia Tech
27 Otis St (01581-3349)
PHONE..................................508 753-2354
James W Coghlin Sr, *CEO*
Christopher J Coghlin, *President*
Randy Ziffer, *President*
Madison Finlay, *COO*
Myron Waite, *Exec VP*
EMP: 150
SQ FT: 61,000
SALES (est): 144MM **Privately Held**
SIC: 3613 Mfg Switchgear/Switchboards

(G-16605)
COLUMBIA ELECTRICAL CONTRS INC
Also Called: Columbia Tech
27 Otis St Ste 300 (01581-3373)
PHONE..................................508 366-8297
Christopher J Coghlin, *President*
Christopher J Palermo, *CFO*
James W Coghlin Sr, *Treasurer*
▲ **EMP:** 240
SQ FT: 55,000
SALES: 138MM
SALES (corp-wide): 144MM **Privately Held**
WEB: www.columbiatech.com
SIC: 3613 Mfg Switchgear/Switchboards
PA: Coghlin Companies, Inc.
27 Otis St
Westborough MA 01581
508 753-2354

(G-16606)
COMPANY OF COCA-COLA BOTTLING
2 Sassacus Dr (01581-3348)
PHONE..................................508 836-5200
Mike Gillan, *Manager*
EMP: 20 **Privately Held**
WEB: www.coke.com
SIC: 2086 Carb Sft Drnkbtlcn
HQ: Coca-Cola Bottling Company Of Southeastern New England, Inc.
150 Waterford Parkway S
Waterford CT 06385
860 443-2816

(G-16607)
COMPONENT SOURCES INTL
121 Flanders Rd (01581-1030)
PHONE..................................508 986-2300
Stephen Doody, *President*
Chris Oneill, *CFO*
Arthur Cormier, *Sales Staff*
Brendan Obrien, *Sales Associate*
Ed D'Entremont, *VP Mktg*
EMP: 15
SQ FT: 3,000
SALES: 20MM **Privately Held**
WEB: www.compsources.com
SIC: 3541 3678 3643 Mfg Machine Tools-Cutting Mfg Electronic Connectors Mfg Conductive Wiring Devices

(G-16608)
CONMED CORPORATION
134 Flanders Rd (01581-1023)
PHONE..................................508 366-3668
Eugene R Corasanti, *CEO*
Ed McLean, *Engineer*
EMP: 142
SALES (corp-wide): 859.6MM **Publicly Held**
SIC: 3845 Mfg Surgical/Medical Instruments
PA: Conmed Corporation
525 French Rd
Utica NY 13502
315 797-8375

(G-16609)
CONNECTEDVIEW LLC
1 Research Dr Ste 310b (01581-3962)
PHONE..................................508 205-0243
Heather Litwin, *CFO*
Vipul Minocha,
Daniel Stouffer, *Graphic Designe*
EMP: 6
SALES (est): 346K **Privately Held**
SIC: 7372 Business Oriented Software

(G-16610)
CRANE DATA LLC
110 Turnpike Rd Ste 213 (01581-2863)
PHONE..................................508 439-4419
Peter G Crane,
EMP: 12 **EST:** 2006
SQ FT: 3,000
SALES: 897.6K **Privately Held**
SIC: 2721 8211 Periodicals-Publishing/Printing Elementary/Secondary School

(G-16611)
CSI MFG INC
121 Flanders Rd (01581-1030)
PHONE..................................508 986-2300
Stephen Doody, *President*
Michael Vinci, *Treasurer*
EMP: 20
SQ FT: 15,000
SALES: 3.2MM **Privately Held**
WEB: www.csimfg.com
SIC: 3559 Mfg Misc Industry Machinery

(G-16612)
DANAFILMS CORP
5 Otis St (01581-3311)
P.O. Box 624 (01581-0624)
PHONE..................................508 366-8884
Dale Brockman, *President*
David Young, *Vice Pres*
▲ **EMP:** 8
SALES (est): 250.3K **Privately Held**
SIC: 3081 Mfg Unsupported Plastic Film/Sheet
PA: Inteplast Group Corporation
9 Peach Tree Hill Rd
Livingston NJ 07039

(G-16613)
DECCO
108 Milk St (01581-1228)
PHONE..................................508 329-1391
Loroy Greenwalls, *President*
EMP: 4
SALES (est): 273.5K **Privately Held**
SIC: 2834 Mfg Pharmaceutical Preparations

(G-16614)
DECITEK CORP
145 Flanders Rd (01581-1031)
P.O. Box 930 (01581-5930)
PHONE..................................508 366-1011
Heng Seng, *President*
Seng Heng, *COO*
Cindy Richards, *Purchasing*
Betty Lacroix, *Finance Mgr*
EMP: 7
SQ FT: 5,000
SALES (est): 756.8K **Privately Held**
WEB: www.decitek.com
SIC: 3577 Mfg Computer Peripherals For Numerical Control Machines

(G-16615)
DETECTOGEN INC
5 Jacob Amsden Rd (01581-1766)
PHONE..................................508 330-1709
Maryellen Feeney, *CEO*
Antonio Campos-Neto, *Exec VP*
EMP: 4
SALES (est): 290K **Privately Held**
SIC: 2835 Mfg Diagnostic Substances

(G-16616)
ECLINICALWORKS LLC
114 Turnpike Rd (01581-2861)
PHONE..................................508 836-2700
Ryan Sullivan, *Vice Pres*
Heidi Cesarano, *Branch Mgr*
EMP: 46
SALES (corp-wide): 282.2MM **Privately Held**
SIC: 7372 Prepackaged Software Services
PA: Eclinicalworks, Llc
2 Technology Dr
Westborough MA 01581
508 475-0450

(G-16617)
EMSEAL JOINT SYSTEMS LTD
25 Bridle Ln (01581-2603)
PHONE..................................508 836-0280
Lester Hensley, *President*
Bashar Moussallieh, *Project Mgr*
Mike Lavallee, *Safety Mgr*
Walter Jones, *Engrg Mgr*
Timothy Fulham, *Treasurer*
◆ **EMP:** 50
SQ FT: 30,000
SALES (est): 13.8MM
SALES (corp-wide): 427.8MM **Privately Held**
WEB: www.emseal.com
SIC: 3568 2891 3441 3053 Manufactures Power Transmsn Equip Adhesives/Sealants Structural Metal Fabrctn Gasket/Packing/Seals
HQ: Sika Corporation
201 Polito Ave
Lyndhurst NJ 07071
201 933-8800

(G-16618)
FIBERON TECHNOLOGIES INC (PA)
287 Turnpike Rd (01581-2856)
PHONE..................................508 616-9500
Mark Johnson, *President*
Richard Dodakian, *Director*
Hsin Lee, *Director*
▲ **EMP:** 10
SALES (est): 1.6MM **Privately Held**
WEB: www.fiberon.com
SIC: 3661 Mfg Telephone/Telegraph Apparatus

(G-16619)
GENERAL ELECTRIC COMPANY
1400 Computer Dr Ste 3 (01581-1760)
PHONE..................................508 870-5200
EMP: 15
SALES (corp-wide): 121.6B **Publicly Held**
SIC: 3511 3612 3641 3632 Mfg Turbine/Genratr Sets Mfg Transformers
PA: General Electric Company
5 Necco St
Boston MA 02210
617 443-3000

(G-16620)
GENZYME CORPORATION
1 Research Dr Ste 200 (01581-3917)
P.O. Box 9322, Framingham (01701-9322)
PHONE..................................508 351-2600
Elizabeth Ruff, *Business Anlyst*
Ravi Balaji, *Technology*
David Caruso, *Analyst*
EMP: 216 **Privately Held**
SIC: 2834 Mfg Pharmaceutical Preparations
HQ: Genzyme Corporation
50 Binney St
Cambridge MA 02142
617 252-7500

(G-16621)
GENZYME CORPORATION
Also Called: Genzyme Genetics
3400 Computer Dr (01581-1771)
PHONE..................................508 898-9001
Leann Segler, *General Mgr*
Michael Minahan, *Senior VP*
David Fiandaca, *Manager*
Igor Levin, *Technology*
Narasimhan Nagan, *Director*
EMP: 26 **Privately Held**
WEB: www.genzyme.com
SIC: 2834 Mfg Pharmaceutical Preparations
HQ: Genzyme Corporation
50 Binney St
Cambridge MA 02142
617 252-7500

(G-16622)
GLOBAL LF SCNCES SLTONS USA LL
14 Walkup Dr (01581-1019)
PHONE..................................508 475-2000
Warren C Pniches, *Branch Mgr*
EMP: 4
SALES (corp-wide): 121.6B **Publicly Held**
SIC: 2834 Mfg Pharmaceutical Preparations
HQ: Global Life Sciences Solutions Usa Llc
100 Results Way
Marlborough MA 01752
800 526-3593

(G-16623)
H LAROSEE AND SONS INC
140 E Main St (01581-1769)
PHONE..................................978 562-9417

GEOGRAPHIC

Stephen G Larosee, *President*
Jr S Larosee, *Executive*
EMP: 22 **EST:** 1903
SQ FT: 4,000
SALES (est): 2.5MM **Privately Held**
SIC: 3471 Plating/Polishing Service

(G-16624)
HOPKINGTON INDEPENDENT
32 South St (01581-1619)
PHONE..................................508 435-5188
Sarah Duckett, *President*
EMP: 8
SALES (est): 530.1K **Privately Held**
WEB: www.hopkintonindependent.com
SIC: 2711 Newspapers-Publishing/Printing

(G-16625)
HUGARD INC
121 Flanders Rd (01581-1030)
PHONE..................................508 986-2300
Robert Hugard, *President*
Maurice Hugard, *Vice Pres*
Stephen Doody, *Shareholder*
▲ **EMP:** 4
SALES (est): 574.5K
SALES (corp-wide): 818K **Privately Held**
WEB: www.hugard.com
SIC: 3545 Precision Maching
PA: Hmr Finance
1380 Route De Montferrond
Magland 74300
-

(G-16626)
INTEPLAST ENGINEERED FILMS INC
5 Otis St (01581-3311)
PHONE..................................508 366-8884
Lee Seidel, *Branch Mgr*
EMP: 70
SALES (est): 2.5MM **Privately Held**
SIC: 2673 Bags: Plastic, Laminated, And Coated, Nsk
HQ: Inteplast Engineered Films Inc.
2875 Market St Ste 100
Garland TX 75041
800 373-9410

(G-16627)
J T GARDNER INC (PA)
Also Called: Curry Printing
190 Turnpike Rd (01581-2806)
PHONE..................................800 540-4993
Peter Gardner, *President*
Joseph Gardner, *Treasurer*
EMP: 23
SQ FT: 17,000
SALES: 4.5MM **Privately Held**
WEB: www.curryprinting.com
SIC: 2796 2752 2791 2789 Platemaking Services Lithographic Coml Print Typesetting Services Bookbinding/Related Work

(G-16628)
J T GARDNER INC
Also Called: Curry Printing & Copy Center
144 E Main St (01581-1769)
P.O. Box 603 (01581-0603)
PHONE..................................508 366-2679
Bob Gardner, *Manager*
EMP: 5
SALES (corp-wide): 4.5MM **Privately Held**
WEB: www.curryprinting.com
SIC: 2752 Lithographic Commercial Printing
PA: J. T. Gardner, Inc.
190 Turnpike Rd
Westborough MA 01581
800 540-4993

(G-16629)
KAYAKU ADVANCED MATERIALS INC (PA)
Also Called: Microchem
200 Flanders Rd (01581-1040)
PHONE..................................617 965-5511
Jeremiah J Cole Jr, *President*
John Ross, *Vice Pres*
Daniel Crosby, *Production*
Alisha Begin, *Engineer*
Milton Bernal, *Engineer*
EMP: 30
SALES (est): 17.1MM **Privately Held**
WEB: www.microchem.com
SIC: 2899 5049 Mfg Chemical Preparations Whol Professional Equipment

(G-16630)
KOPIN CORPORATION (PA)
125 North Dr (01581-3341)
PHONE..................................508 870-5959
John C C Fan, *Ch of Bd*
Sam Zeng, *General Mgr*
Bor-Yeu Tsaur, *Exec VP*
Hong Choi, *Vice Pres*
Bill Maffucci, *Vice Pres*
EMP: 175
SQ FT: 74,000
SALES: 24.4MM **Publicly Held**
WEB: www.kopin.com
SIC: 3674 Mfg Semiconductors/Related Devices

(G-16631)
KOPIN DISPLAY CORPORATION (PA)
125 North Dr (01581-3335)
PHONE..................................508 870-5959
John C Fan, *President*
Richard Sneider, *Admin Sec*
EMP: 7
SALES (est): 2.2MM **Privately Held**
SIC: 3674 Mfg Semiconductors/Related Devices

(G-16632)
LEHI SHEET METAL CORPORATION
245 Flanders Rd (01581-1034)
PHONE..................................508 366-8550
Gale J Bullen, *Corp Secy*
David J Bullen, *Treasurer*
EMP: 29 **EST:** 1978
SQ FT: 50,000
SALES (est): 5.9MM **Privately Held**
WEB: www.lehisheetmetal.com
SIC: 3444 Mfg Sheet Metalwork

(G-16633)
MACNEILL ENGINEERING CO INC
1700 W Park Dr Ste 310 (01581-3976)
PHONE..................................508 481-8830
Harris L Macneill, *President*
Nancy L Macneill, *Corp Secy*
▲ **EMP:** 50
SQ FT: 67,000
SALES (est): 7.5MM **Privately Held**
WEB: www.macneill.com
SIC: 3089 3949 3131 3021 Mfg Plastic Products Mfg Sport/Athletic Goods Mfg Footwear Cut Stock Mfg Rubber/Plstc Ftwear

(G-16634)
MICROCHIP TECHNOLOGY INC
Also Called: Microchip Technologies
112 Turnpike Rd Ste 100 (01581-2860)
PHONE..................................774 760-0087
Mike Fogerty, *Manager*
EMP: 166
SALES (corp-wide): 5.3B **Publicly Held**
SIC: 3674 Mfg Semiconductors/Related Devices
PA: Microchip Technology Inc
2355 W Chandler Blvd
Chandler AZ 85224
480 792-7200

(G-16635)
MICROS SYSTEMS INC
1800 W Park Dr Ste 250 (01581-3927)
PHONE..................................508 655-7500
Lyndon Daniels, *Branch Mgr*
EMP: 19
SALES (corp-wide): 39.5B **Publicly Held**
WEB: www.micros.com
SIC: 7372 Prepackaged Software Services
HQ: Micros Systems, Inc.
7031 Columbia Gateway Dr # 1
Columbia MD 21046
443 285-6000

(G-16636)
MICROWAVE CMPNENTS SYSTEMS INC
Also Called: MCS
131 Flanders Rd (01581-1031)
PHONE..................................508 466-8400
Vern Babigian, *President*
Peter Nacu, *Buyer*
Liz McKenna, *Finance Mgr*
Paul J Dube, *Admin Sec*
Jim Kittredge, *Admin Sec*
EMP: 11
SQ FT: 6,700
SALES (est): 1.8MM **Privately Held**
SIC: 3679 Mfg Electronic Components

(G-16637)
MURATA POWER SOLUTIONS INC (DH)
129 Flanders Rd (01581-1030)
PHONE..................................508 339-3000
Tatsuo Bizen, *President*
Walter Wong, *General Mgr*
Yoshitaka Kotera, *Vice Pres*
Steve Pimpis, *Vice Pres*
Janet Nye, *Senior Buyer*
▲ **EMP:** 135
SALES (est): 60.2MM **Privately Held**
WEB: www.datel.com
SIC: 3679 3672 3629 3825 Mfg Elec Components Mfg Printed Circuit Brds Mfg Elec Indstl Equip Mfg Elec Measuring Instr Mfg Semiconductors/Dvcs
HQ: Murata Electronics North America, Inc.
2200 Lake Park Dr Se
Smyrna GA 30080
770 436-1300

(G-16638)
MURATA PWR SLTONS PORTLAND LLC
129 Flanders Rd (01581-1030)
PHONE..................................508 339-3000
EMP: 3
SALES (est): 418K **Privately Held**
WEB: www.murata-ps.com
SIC: 3612 Mfg Transformers
PA: Murata Manufacturing Co.,Ltd.
1-10-1, Higashikotari
Nagaokakyo KYO 617-0
-

(G-16639)
NOREMAC MANUFACTURING CORP
62 Hopkinton Rd (01581-2126)
P.O. Box 867 (01581-0867)
PHONE..................................508 879-7514
Janice Connelly, *CEO*
Joseph Connelly, *President*
Reg Carruthers, *Controller*
Paul Senecal, *Financial Exec*
Janus M Connelly, *Admin Sec*
EMP: 30 **EST:** 1961
SQ FT: 6,400
SALES (est): 5.3MM **Privately Held**
WEB: www.noremacmach.com
SIC: 3599 7692 Mfg Industrial Machinery Welding Repair

(G-16640)
ONEPIN INC
2200 W Park Dr Ste 440 (01581-3961)
PHONE..................................508 475-1000
Feyzi Celik, *CEO*
Feyzi Elik, *President*
Christopher De Grace, *Vice Pres*
David Baum, *Director*
Kenneth Mabbs, *Director*
EMP: 23
SQ FT: 3,200
SALES (est): 2.7MM **Privately Held**
WEB: www.onepin.com
SIC: 7372 Prepackaged Software Services

(G-16641)
PALL CORPORATION
20 Walkup Dr (01581-1019)
PHONE..................................508 871-5394
Anne Jones, *Vice Pres*
Collins Michael, *Technical Mgr*
Scott Gordon, *Research*
Allen Steve, *Software Engr*
Tamas Bodogh, *IT/INT Sup*
EMP: 364
SALES (corp-wide): 19.8B **Publicly Held**
SIC: 3569 Mfg General Industrial Machinery
HQ: Pall Corporation
25 Harbor Park Dr
Port Washington NY 11050
516 484-5400

(G-16642)
PARATRONIX INC
200 Flanders Rd (01581-1040)
PHONE..................................508 222-8979
Lawrence Habershaw, *President*
Eleanor Habershaw, *Treasurer*
EMP: 18
SQ FT: 9,500
SALES (est): 2.2MM **Privately Held**
WEB: www.paratronix.com
SIC: 3479 Coating/Engraving Service
PA: Kayaku Advanced Materials, Inc.
200 Flanders Rd
Westborough MA 01581
-

(G-16643)
PHARMATRON INC
2400 Computer Dr (01581-1887)
PHONE..................................603 645-6766
Marc Amiet, *CEO*
EMP: 10
SQ FT: 4,000
SALES: 2MM **Privately Held**
WEB: www.pharmatron.com
SIC: 3825 Mfg Electrical Measuring Instruments

(G-16644)
PRINT RESOURCE
1500 W Park Dr Ste 215 (01581-3966)
PHONE..................................508 433-4660
David Sears, *Principal*
Lasantha Jayasinghe, *Vice Pres*
Anthony Lange, *Vice Pres*
Ben Przekop, *Business Dir*
EMP: 6
SALES (est): 101.6K **Privately Held**
SIC: 2752 Lithographic Commercial Printing

(G-16645)
RUCKUS WIRELESS INC
Also Called: Arris International
8 Technology Dr Ste 200 (01581-1756)
PHONE..................................508 870-1184
Steven S Birer, *Branch Mgr*
David Franklin, *Manager*
David Bowler, *Director*
EMP: 40 **Privately Held**
SIC: 3661 Mfg Telephone/Telegraph Apparatus
HQ: Ruckus Wireless, Inc.
350 W Java Dr
Sunnyvale CA 94089
650 265-4200

(G-16646)
SAVAGE COMPANIES
19 Walkup Dr (01581-1018)
PHONE..................................508 616-8772
John Agoritsas, *Director*
EMP: 5
SALES (corp-wide): 1B **Privately Held**
WEB: www.savageind.com
SIC: 3568 4213 Mfg Power Transmission Equipment Trucking Operator-Nonlocal
HQ: Savage Companies
901 W Legacy Center Way
Midvale UT 84047
801 944-6600

(G-16647)
SAVE ENERGY SYSTEMS INC
39 Blossom Ct (01581-3679)
PHONE..................................617 564-4442
Paul Laskow, *President*
Craig Yancich, *Sales Staff*
EMP: 5
SALES (est): 684.5K **Privately Held**
SIC: 3822 Mfg Environmental Controls

(G-16648)
SERVOMOTIVE CORPORATION
10 Mohawk Dr (01581-1821)
PHONE..................................508 726-9222
Anthony Linn, *President*
EMP: 3

▲ = Import ▼=Export
◆ =Import/Export

SALES: 30K Privately Held
SIC: 3577 Manufacture Motion Control Circuit Board

(G-16649)
SIMSOFT CORP
1 Butterfield Dr (01581-3947)
PHONE....508 366-5451
Devinder Rekhi, *President*
Barney Hart, *Manager*
EMP: 8
SALES: 3.5MM Privately Held
SIC: 7372 Prepackaged Software Services

(G-16650)
SPECTRIS INC (HQ)
117 Flanders Rd (01581-1042)
PHONE....508 768-6400
Clive Graeme Watson, *President*
Andrew Brock, *Engineer*
Raymond Donaldson, *Engineer*
Ben Pattison, *Engineer*
David Goldstein, *Asst Treas*
EMP: 19
SQ FT: 15,000
SALES (est): 338.5MM
SALES (corp-wide): 2.1B Privately Held
WEB: www.spectris.com
SIC: 3674 3829 3826 3821 Mfg Semiconductors/Dvcs Mfg Measure/Control Dvcs Mfg Analytical Instr Mfg Lab Apparatus/Furn
PA: Spectris Plc
Heritage House
Egham TW20
178 447-0470

(G-16651)
STEDT HYDRAULIC CRANE CORP
Also Called: Stetco
27 Washington St (01581-1052)
PHONE....508 366-9151
Fax: 508 870-1731
▲ EMP: 15
SQ FT: 22,000
SALES (est): 4.2MM
SALES (corp-wide): 6.8B Publicly Held
WEB: www.stetcoproducts.com
SIC: 3537 5084 1799 3594 Mfg Indstl Truck/Tractor Whol Industrial Equip Special Trade Contractor Mfg Fluid Power Pump/Mtr
HQ: Iowa Mold Tooling Co., Inc.
500 W Us Highway 18
Garner IA 50438
641 923-3711

(G-16652)
SYNOPSYS INC
1800 W Park Dr Ste 410 (01581-3926)
PHONE....508 870-6500
Mark Kahan, *Manager*
EMP: 8
SALES (corp-wide): 3.3B Publicly Held
WEB: www.opticalres.com
SIC: 7372 Optical & Illumination Product Design
PA: Synopsys, Inc.
690 E Middlefield Rd
Mountain View CA 94043
650 584-5000

(G-16653)
TAKASAGO ELECTRIC INC
Also Called: Takasago Fluidic Systems
1900 W Park Dr Ste 280 (01581-3919)
PHONE....508 983-1434
EMP: 4
SALES (est): 309.9K Privately Held
SIC: 3494 Mfg Valves/Pipe Fittings

(G-16654)
TATE LYLE INGRDNTS AMRICAS LLC
30 Walkup Dr (01581-1019)
P.O. Box 725 (01581-0725)
PHONE....508 366-8322
Wes McGill, *Manager*
EMP: 5
SALES (corp-wide): 3.5B Privately Held
WEB: www.aestaley.com
SIC: 2046 Corn Milling Products
HQ: Tate & Lyle Ingredients Americas Llc
2200 E Eldorado St
Decatur IL 62521
217 423-4411

(G-16655)
TERROIR WINES LLC
134 Flanders Rd (01581-1023)
PHONE....508 329-1626
Sheri Carl,
Gordon Alexander,
EMP: 3
SQ FT: 1,500
SALES (est): 500K Privately Held
SIC: 2084 Mfg Wines/Brandy/Spirits

(G-16656)
TFC ENTERPRISES LLC
Also Called: Beautyflame
4 Beeton Path (01581-3370)
PHONE....866 996-2701
Joseph I Minevich,
Igal Seagal,
EMP: 5
SALES (est): 418.4K Privately Held
WEB: www.BeautyFlame.com
SIC: 3272 Mfg Concrete Products

(G-16657)
WADSWORTH MEDICAL TECH INC
5 Harvest Way (01581-3647)
PHONE....508 789-6531
Andrew D Fox, *President*
EMP: 4
SALES (est): 327.4K Privately Held
SIC: 3842 Mfg Surgical Appliances/Supplies

(G-16658)
WELDSHIP INDUSTRIES INC
75 E Main St Fl 2 (01581-1420)
PHONE....508 898-0100
Robert Arcieri, *Principal*
EMP: 4
SALES (corp-wide): 3MM Privately Held
SIC: 2813 Mfg Industrial Gases
PA: Weldship Industries, Inc.
225 W 2nd St Unit 2
Bethlehem PA 18015
610 861-7330

Westfield
Hampden County

(G-16659)
360 RECYCLING LLC
100 Sgt Tm Dion Way (01085-1462)
PHONE....413 562-0193
Nathan Michalewicz, *Mng Member*
EMP: 10
SQ FT: 600
SALES (est): 441.7K Privately Held
SIC: 2875 Mfg Fertilizers-Mix Only

(G-16660)
40 UP TACKLE COMPANY INC
16 Union Ave Ste 5 (01085-2678)
P.O. Box 442 (01086-0442)
PHONE....413 562-0385
Bradlee Gage, *President*
Chester A Cook, *Treasurer*
Bradlee E Gage Jr, *Treasurer*
Alan D Cook, *Admin Sec*
▲ EMP: 5
SQ FT: 4,000
SALES: 180K Privately Held
SIC: 3949 Mfg Sporting/Athletic Goods

(G-16661)
A & A ARCHITECTURAL WDWKG INC
104 Mainline Dr Ste C (01085-3308)
PHONE....413 568-9914
David Armitage, *President*
EMP: 3
SQ FT: 2,700
SALES: 250K Privately Held
SIC: 3553 Mfg Woodworking Machinery

(G-16662)
A & D METAL INC
555 Southampton Rd (01085-1329)
PHONE....413 485-7505
Alexander Lewinski, *President*
EMP: 13
SQ FT: 24,000
SALES (est): 2.8MM Privately Held
WEB: www.admetal.com
SIC: 3444 Mfg Sheet Metalwork

(G-16663)
ACRALUBE INC
54b Mainline Dr (01085-3314)
PHONE....413 562-5019
Katherine Henderson, *Director*
EMP: 6
SALES (est): 413.2K Privately Held
SIC: 3479 Coating/Engraving Service

(G-16664)
ALLSTATE HOOD & DUCT INC
88 Notre Dame St (01085-1924)
PHONE....413 568-4663
Todd Duval, *President*
Kimberly Saletnik, *Treasurer*
EMP: 10
SALES (est): 1.2MM Privately Held
SIC: 3444 Mfg Sheet Metalwork

(G-16665)
AMPAC PACKAGING LLC
175 Ampad Rd (01085-5604)
PHONE....413 572-2658
Daniel Clauson, *Manager*
EMP: 4
SALES (corp-wide): 1.1B Privately Held
WEB: www.jencoat.com
SIC: 2671 Mfg Packaging Paper/Film
HQ: Ampac Packaging, Llc
12025 Tricon Rd
Cincinnati OH 45246
513 671-1777

(G-16666)
APPALACHIAN PRESS
11 Railroad Ave (01085-2403)
PHONE....413 568-2621
Michael Dion, *Principal*
EMP: 4
SALES (est): 241.6K Privately Held
SIC: 2759 Commercial Printing

(G-16667)
ARCHITECTS OF PACKAGING INC
11 Mainline Dr (01085-3313)
PHONE....413 568-3187
David H Small, *President*
Donald I Small, *Chairman*
Cheryl Dowd, *Accounts Exec*
Matt Bryant, *Webmaster*
EMP: 8
SQ FT: 22,000
SALES (est): 1.3MM Privately Held
WEB: www.architectsofpackaging.com
SIC: 3086 7389 Mfg Plastic Foam Products Business Services

(G-16668)
ATLAS BRASS & ALUMINUM CO
139 Meadow St (01085-3228)
PHONE....413 732-4604
Robert S Clark, *President*
EMP: 3 EST: 1935
SQ FT: 2,750
SALES: 1MM Privately Held
SIC: 3366 3363 Mfg Bronze & Aluminum Sand Castings

(G-16669)
ATLAS COPCO COMPRESSORS LLC
94 N Elm St Fl 4 (01085-1641)
P.O. Box 431 (01086-0431)
PHONE....518 765-3344
Christine Goodreau, *Branch Mgr*
EMP: 24
SALES (corp-wide): 10B Privately Held
SIC: 3563 Mfg Air/Gas Compressors
HQ: Atlas Copco Compressors Llc
300 Technology Center Way # 5
Rock Hill SC 29730
866 472-1015

(G-16670)
B&D PALLET BLDG & INDUS SUP
Also Called: B & D Pallet Co
997 Western Ave (01085-2527)
P.O. Box 1567 (01086-1567)
PHONE....413 568-9624
Richard Oleksak, *President*
Elizabeth Oleksak, *Vice Pres*
EMP: 18
SQ FT: 18,000
SALES (est): 2.8MM Privately Held
SIC: 2448 Mfg Wood Pallets/Skids

(G-16671)
BARKER STEEL LLC
287 Lockhouse Rd (01085-1235)
PHONE....413 568-7803
Tom Dechristopher, *Manager*
Ed Galenski, *Manager*
EMP: 35
SALES (corp-wide): 25B Publicly Held
WEB: www.barker.com
SIC: 3312 3449 3441 Blast Furnace-Steel Works Mfg Misc Structural Metalwork Structural Metal Fabrication
HQ: Barker Steel Llc
55 Sumner St Ste 1
Milford MA 01757
800 363-3953

(G-16672)
BEDARD SHEET METAL COMPANY
123 Summit Lock Rd Ste 2 (01085-1666)
PHONE....413 572-3774
Barbara Bedard, *President*
EMP: 7
SQ FT: 5,000
SALES (est): 930.1K Privately Held
SIC: 3444 Sheet Metal Fabricating And Customizing

(G-16673)
BERKSHIRE GROUP LTD
184 Falcon Dr (01085-1470)
P.O. Box 490 (01086-0490)
PHONE....413 562-7200
Gary Webster, *President*
Danine Ritucci, *Vice Pres*
Travis Wilson, *Design Engr*
EMP: 7 EST: 1997
SALES (est): 605K Privately Held
WEB: www.berkshiregroup.com
SIC: 3599 Mfg Custom Machinery

(G-16674)
BERN OPTICS INC
579 Southampton Rd Ste 1 (01085-1659)
PHONE....413 568-6800
Bernd Ho Gottschalk, *President*
Michael Vineyard, *Opers Mgr*
Erik Roberts, *Engineer*
EMP: 23
SQ FT: 7,500
SALES (est): 5.7MM Privately Held
WEB: www.bernoptics.com
SIC: 3827 Mfg Optical Instruments/Lenses

(G-16675)
BROOK POND MACHINING INC
170b Lockhouse Rd (01085-1236)
PHONE....413 562-7411
James L Edinger, *President*
Lisa J Edinger, *CFO*
EMP: 9
SQ FT: 6,000
SALES: 600K Privately Held
SIC: 3599 Mfg Industrial Machinery

(G-16676)
CALIBER COMPANY (PA)
Also Called: Savage Arms
100 Springdale Rd (01085-1987)
PHONE....413 642-4260
Miguel Lopez, *CFO*
Stephen M Nolan, *Director*
Scott D Chaplin, *Director*
Albert Kasper, *Director*
Robert Keller, *Director*
EMP: 18
SALES (est): 106.4MM Privately Held
SIC: 3484 Mfg Small Arms

(G-16677)
CEMEX MATERIALS LLC
Also Called: Westfield - Pipe
69 Neck Rd (01085-2419)
PHONE..................................413 562-3647
Greg Yazhbin, *Branch Mgr*
EMP: 37 **Privately Held**
SIC: 3273 Mfg Ready-Mixed Concrete
HQ: Cemex Materials Llc
1501 Belvedere Rd
West Palm Beach FL 33406
561 833-5555

(G-16678)
CIRCUIT SYSTEMS INC (PA)
Also Called: Dicronite Dry Lube
54 Mainline Dr Ste B (01085-3314)
PHONE..................................413 562-5019
Al Rhynard, *President*
Alyvin Rhynard, *Corp Secy*
William R Henderson, *Vice Pres*
▲ **EMP:** 15
SQ FT: 9,500
SALES (est): 2.1MM **Privately Held**
WEB: www.dicronite.com
SIC: 2992 Mfg Lubricating Oils/Greases

(G-16679)
COLUMBIA MANUFACTURING INC
1 Cycle St (01085-4400)
P.O. Box 1230 (01086-1230)
PHONE..................................413 562-3664
Kenneth W Howard, *President*
Donald A Bieker, *President*
Brian W Chiba, *Corp Secy*
Ali Salehi, *Vice Pres*
Bruce R Turcotte, *CFO*
◆ **EMP:** 65
SQ FT: 300,000
SALES (est): 13.3MM **Privately Held**
WEB: www.columbiamfginc.com
SIC: 2531 5091 Mfg Public Building Furniture Whol Sporting/Recreational Goods

(G-16680)
DION LABEL PRINTING INC
539 North Rd (01085-9774)
P.O. Box 1507 (01086-1507)
PHONE..................................413 568-3713
John J Dion Jr, *President*
Jane Dion, *Corp Secy*
Dave Dion, *Vice Pres*
◆ **EMP:** 82
SQ FT: 35,000
SALES: 14.6MM **Privately Held**
WEB: www.dionlabel.com
SIC: 2679 2752 Mfg Converted Paper Products Lithographic Commercial Printing

(G-16681)
ECHELON INDUSTRIES CORPORATION
53 Airport Rd (01085-1357)
PHONE..................................413 562-6659
Clayton Jarvis, *President*
EMP: 28
SALES (est): 1MM **Privately Held**
SIC: 3721 Mfg Aircraft

(G-16682)
EPICENTER
1 Arch Rd (01085-1795)
PHONE..................................413 568-1360
EMP: 11
SALES (est): 1MM **Privately Held**
SIC: 7372 Prepackaged Software Services

(G-16683)
EV RITE TOOL INC
132 Elm St (01085-2918)
P.O. Box 251 (01086-0251)
PHONE..................................413 568-1433
Everett Bacon, *President*
Eugene Bacon, *Vice Pres*
EMP: 6
SQ FT: 7,000
SALES (est): 610K **Privately Held**
SIC: 3599 Machine Shop

(G-16684)
G & H MANUFACTURING INC
455 North Rd (01085-9624)
PHONE..................................413 562-2035
William L Guertin Jr, *President*
Mark Gould, *Vice Pres*
Ed Brown, *Purch Mgr*
Susan J Molitoris, *Treasurer*
EMP: 4
SQ FT: 3,000
SALES: 500K **Privately Held**
WEB: www.ghmanufacturing.com
SIC: 3599 Job Machine Shop

(G-16685)
GTB INNOVATIVE SOLUTIONS INC
507 Southampton Rd Ste 1 (01085-1381)
PHONE..................................413 733-0146
Geraldine Cross, *President*
EMP: 10
SALES (est): 689K **Privately Held**
SIC: 3714 Mfg Motor Vehicle Parts/Accessories

(G-16686)
GULFSTREAM AEROSPACE CORP
33 Elise St (01085-1493)
PHONE..................................413 562-5866
David Ebel, *Branch Mgr*
EMP: 21
SALES (corp-wide): 36.1B **Publicly Held**
WEB: www.gulfstream.com
SIC: 3721 Mfg Aircraft
HQ: Gulfstream Aerospace Corporation
500 Gulfstream Rd
Savannah GA 31408
912 965-3000

(G-16687)
H B SMITH COMPANY INC
61 Union St Ste 7 (01085-2476)
PHONE..................................413 568-3148
Walter Pawlowski, *Treasurer*
Peter J Stasz, *Clerk*
EMP: 50 **EST:** 1853
SQ FT: 120,000
SALES (est): 6.4MM **Privately Held**
SIC: 3433 3567 Mfg Heating Equipment-Nonelectric Mfg Industrial Furnaces/Ovens

(G-16688)
HAMPTON DOOR COMPANY INC
14 Coleman Ave (01085-4460)
P.O. Box 1114 (01086-1114)
PHONE..................................413 568-5730
Donald Groleau, *President*
EMP: 5
SQ FT: 10,000
SALES (est): 751K **Privately Held**
WEB: www.hamptondoor.com
SIC: 3442 5211 Mfg Metal Doors/Sash/Trim Ret Lumber/Building Materials

(G-16689)
INDUSTRIAL CUTTING TOOLS INC
351 N Elm St (01085-1622)
P.O. Box 548 (01086-0548)
PHONE..................................413 562-2996
Felix McGrath, *President*
Jeanne Mc Grath, *Treasurer*
Robert Crowley, *Clerk*
EMP: 8 **EST:** 1981
SQ FT: 3,000
SALES (est): 570K **Privately Held**
SIC: 3545 Mfg Standard & Specialty Cutting Tools

(G-16690)
INSTRUMENT TECHNOLOGY INC
Also Called: ITI
33 Airport Rd (01085-1357)
P.O. Box 381 (01086-0381)
PHONE..................................413 562-3512
Gregory Carignan, *President*
Jeffrey Carignan, *Vice Pres*
Dawn A Thomas, *Vice Pres*
Michelle Clark, *Purchasing*
Nicoleta Negrut, *Design Engr*
EMP: 50
SQ FT: 25,000
SALES (est): 10.3MM **Privately Held**
WEB: www.scopes.com
SIC: 3827 Mfg Optical Instr/Lens
PA: Transom Shields Group, Llc

Wilmington DE
-

(G-16691)
JAN WOODWORKS RENOVATION
61 Bowdoin St (01085-4269)
PHONE..................................413 563-2534
Joseph Muto, *Owner*
EMP: 3
SALES: 270K **Privately Held**
SIC: 2431 1521 Mfg Millwork Single-Family House Construction

(G-16692)
JARVIS SURGICAL INC
53 Airport Rd (01085-1357)
PHONE..................................413 562-6659
Clayton Jarvis, *President*
James Goulet, *Engineer*
Robert C Danaher, *Admin Sec*
EMP: 20
SQ FT: 12,000
SALES (est): 4MM
SALES (corp-wide): 20.4MM **Privately Held**
WEB: www.jarvissurgical.com
SIC: 3841 Mfg Surgical/Medical Instruments
PA: Jarvis Group, Inc.
229 Buckingham St
Hartford CT
860 278-2353

(G-16693)
JEN-COAT INC (DH)
Also Called: Prolamina
132 N Elm St (01085-1644)
P.O. Box 274 (01086-0274)
PHONE..................................413 875-9855
Greg Tucker, *CEO*
Eric Bradford, *CFO*
Tony Marmo, *Manager*
◆ **EMP:** 230
SQ FT: 375,000
SALES (est): 110.6MM
SALES (corp-wide): 1.1B **Privately Held**
WEB: www.jencoat.com
SIC: 3554 Mfg Paper Industrial Machinery

(G-16694)
JOHN LATKA & CO INC
204 Southampton Rd (01085-1792)
PHONE..................................413 562-4374
Patricia Banas, *President*
EMP: 5
SQ FT: 6,700
SALES: 690K **Privately Held**
WEB: www.latkaprint.com
SIC: 2752 8742 Lithographic Coml Print Mgmt Consulting Svcs

(G-16695)
JOHNCARLO WOODWORKING INC
30 Clifton St (01085-3304)
P.O. Box 1385 (01086-1385)
PHONE..................................413 562-4002
Giancarlo Fiordalice, *President*
Peter Fiordalice, *Treasurer*
EMP: 12
SQ FT: 6,000
SALES (est): 1.9MM **Privately Held**
WEB: www.johncarlowoodworking.com
SIC: 2431 Mfg Millwork

(G-16696)
K & R MACHINE CO CORP
99 Springdale Rd (01085-1625)
PHONE..................................413 568-9335
EMP: 6
SALES (est): 410K **Privately Held**
SIC: 3599 Machine Shop

(G-16697)
LONGCAP LAMSON PRODUCTS LLC
79 Mainline Dr (01085-3313)
P.O. Box 846 (01086-0846)
PHONE..................................413 642-8135
David Sepavich, *Vice Pres*
EMP: 10
SALES (est): 1.4MM **Privately Held**
SIC: 3421 Mfg Cutlery

(G-16698)
MANUFACTURING TECH GROUP INC
Also Called: M T G
85 Servistar Indus Way (01085-5601)
PHONE..................................413 562-4337
Richard Carver, *President*
John Adam, *Vice Pres*
Daniel Rowe, *Engineer*
EMP: 53
SQ FT: 67,000
SALES (est): 9.5MM **Privately Held**
SIC: 3444 Mfg Sheet Metalwork

(G-16699)
MCNAIRN PACKAGING INC (PA)
6 Elise St (01085-1414)
PHONE..................................413 568-1989
Ken W A Miller, *President*
Judy Lightle, *Regional Mgr*
Bart Gogarty, *COO*
Terry Smith, *Exec VP*
Leonard Harris, *Production*
◆ **EMP:** 66
SQ FT: 103,000
SALES (est): 21.3MM **Privately Held**
WEB: www.mcnairnpackaging.com
SIC: 2621 Paper Mill

(G-16700)
MESTEK INC (PA)
Also Called: Dadanco - Mestek
260 N Elm St (01085-1614)
PHONE..................................470 898-4533
Stuart B Reed, *CEO*
Bill Rafferty, *Principal*
Jim David, *Vice Pres*
Richard Kessler, *Vice Pres*
Kurt Shea, *Vice Pres*
◆ **EMP:** 20
SQ FT: 200,000
SALES (est): 629.1MM **Privately Held**
SIC: 3585 3634 3549 3542 Mfg Refrig/Heat Equip Mfg Elec Housewares/Fans

(G-16701)
MESTEK INC
Wrens Division
260 N Elm St (01085-1614)
PHONE..................................413 564-5530
Bruce Dewey, *President*
EMP: 100
SALES (corp-wide): 629.1MM **Privately Held**
SIC: 3569 3585 Mfg General Industrial Machinery Mfg Refrigeration/Heating Equipment
PA: Mestek, Inc.
260 N Elm St
Westfield MA 01085
470 898-4533

(G-16702)
MESTEK INC
Sterling Radiator/Reed Nat Div
260 N Elm St (01085-1614)
P.O. Box 519 (01086-0519)
PHONE..................................413 568-9571
Amy Babikyan, *Natl Sales Mgr*
John E Reed, *Branch Mgr*
EMP: 400
SQ FT: 10,000
SALES (corp-wide): 629.1MM **Privately Held**
SIC: 3433 3444 3822 3549 Mfg Finned Tube Radiators
PA: Mestek, Inc.
260 N Elm St
Westfield MA 01085
470 898-4533

(G-16703)
MESTEK INC
260 N Elm St (01085-1614)
PHONE..................................413 568-9571
R Bruce Dewey, *President*
EMP: 3
SALES (corp-wide): 629.1MM **Privately Held**
SIC: 3446 Mfg Architectural Metalwork

PA: Mestek, Inc.
260 N Elm St
Westfield MA 01085
470 898-4533

(G-16704)
MICRO ABRASIVES CORPORATION
720 Southampton Rd (01085-1387)
P.O. Box 669 (01086-0669)
PHONE..................................413 562-3641
Robert E Nesin, *President*
Michael Keenan, *Vice Pres*
Douglas Stutz, *Vice Pres*
Debbie Ouellette, *Research*
◆ **EMP:** 36 **EST:** 1957
SQ FT: 125,000
SALES: 14MM **Privately Held**
WEB: www.microgrit.com
SIC: 3291 Mfg Abrasive Products

(G-16705)
MILLRITE MACHINE INC
587 Southampton Rd (01085-1329)
PHONE..................................413 562-9212
Robert Valcourt, *President*
Susan Valcourt, *Admin Sec*
Kerry Wyckoff,
EMP: 30
SQ FT: 10,000
SALES: 3.6MM **Privately Held**
SIC: 3599 Mfg Industrial Machinery

(G-16706)
MORTON BUILDINGS INC
563 Southampton Rd (01085-1329)
PHONE..................................413 562-7028
Carl Franz, *Branch Mgr*
EMP: 12
SQ FT: 5,932
SALES (corp-wide): 463.7MM **Privately Held**
WEB: www.mortonbuildings.com
SIC: 3448 Mfg Prefabricated Metal Buildings
PA: Morton Buildings, Inc.
252 W Adams St
Morton IL 61550
800 447-7436

(G-16707)
NES WORLDWIDE INC
3 Progress Ave (01085-1687)
PHONE..................................413 485-5038
John Balicki, *President*
Derek Case, *Partner*
Steve Martin, *Partner*
Ronald P Moussette, *Partner*
James Sleboda, *Treasurer*
▲ **EMP:** 24
SQ FT: 38,000
SALES (est): 5.2MM **Privately Held**
WEB: www.nesworldwide.com
SIC: 3555 Mfg Printing Trades Machinery

(G-16708)
NU-TRUSS INC
Also Called: Western Mass Truss
52 Steiger Dr (01085-4945)
P.O. Box 2197 (01086-2197)
PHONE..................................413 562-3861
Keith Cressotti, *President*
Robert Bigelow, *Treasurer*
Peter Howe, *Shareholder*
EMP: 14 **EST:** 1997
SALES: 900K **Privately Held**
SIC: 2439 Mfg Structural Wood Members

(G-16709)
OMNI MANUFACTURING CO INC
51 Church St (01085-2805)
P.O. Box 753 (01086-0753)
PHONE..................................413 568-6175
Walter C Daubitz, *President*
Susan M Daubitz, *Corp Secy*
EMP: 5
SQ FT: 2,000
SALES (est): 446.3K **Privately Held**
SIC: 3599 Mfg Industrial Machinery

(G-16710)
PACKAGING CORPORATION AMERICA
Also Called: PCA/Supply Services 302b
61 Turnpike Industrial Rd (01085-1646)
PHONE..................................413 562-0610
Ray Stowell, *Branch Mgr*
EMP: 4
SALES (corp-wide): 7B **Publicly Held**
WEB: www.packagingcorp.com
SIC: 2653 Mfg Corrugated/Solid Fiber Boxes
PA: Packaging Corporation Of America
1 N Field Ct
Lake Forest IL 60045
847 482-3000

(G-16711)
PARAGON MFG INC
61 Union St Ste 108 (01085-2490)
PHONE..................................413 562-7202
Steven P Beals, *President*
Karen L Beals, *President*
EMP: 15
SQ FT: 8,000
SALES (est): 2.9MM **Privately Held**
WEB: www.paragonmfg.com
SIC: 3599 Mfg Industrial Machinery

(G-16712)
PEERLESS PRECISION INC
22 Mainline Dr (01085-3314)
PHONE..................................413 562-2359
Larry A Maier, *President*
Joe Beavis, *Engineer*
Deborah Maier, *CFO*
Crystal Reyes, *Admin Asst*
EMP: 20
SQ FT: 6,600
SALES (est): 4MM **Privately Held**
WEB: www.peerlessprecision.com
SIC: 3599 Mfg Industrial Machinery

(G-16713)
PERFORMANCE TOOL INC
41 Jefferson St Ste 2 (01085-3086)
PHONE..................................413 568-6643
Fax: 413 562-5376
EMP: 4 **EST:** 1997
SALES (est): 270K **Privately Held**
SIC: 3599 Mfg Industrial Machinery

(G-16714)
PFR MACHINE CO
15 Ponders Hollow Rd (01085-4457)
PHONE..................................413 568-7603
Paul Ruszala, *Owner*
EMP: 5
SQ FT: 1,600
SALES (est): 350K **Privately Held**
SIC: 3599 Machine Shop

(G-16715)
PILGRIM CANDLE COMPANY INC (PA)
36 Union Ave (01085-2444)
PHONE..................................413 562-2635
Joseph Shibley, *President*
Rosemary Pagios, *Treasurer*
Donna Shibley, *Clerk*
▲ **EMP:** 20
SQ FT: 20,000 **Privately Held**
SIC: 3999 5999 5947 Mfg Misc Products Ret Misc Merchandise Ret Gifts/Novelties

(G-16716)
PRODUCTION HONING INC
327 N Elm St (01085-1622)
PHONE..................................413 568-9238
Albert Cassanelli, *Ch of Bd*
Daniel M Cassanelli, *President*
EMP: 3 **EST:** 1969
SQ FT: 6,400
SALES: 250K **Privately Held**
SIC: 3599 Machine Shop

(G-16717)
PROGRESS ENTERPRISES LLC
3 Progress Ave (01085-1687)
PHONE..................................413 562-2736
Steven Martin, *General Mgr*
John Balicki,
Ronald Moussette,
James Sleboda,
▲ **EMP:** 14
SALES (est): 2.5MM **Privately Held**
SIC: 3861 Mfg Photographic Equipment/Supplies

(G-16718)
PROLAMINA CORPORATION
Also Called: Prolamina Westfield Plant 2
175 Ampad Rd (01085-5604)
PHONE..................................413 562-2315
EMP: 8
SALES (corp-wide): 1.1B **Privately Held**
SIC: 2671 5199 Mfg Packaging Paper/Film Whol Nondurable Goods
HQ: Prolamina Corporation
132 N Elm St
Westfield MA 01085

(G-16719)
PUFFER INTERNATIONAL INC
24 Elm St Ste 2 (01085-2965)
PHONE..................................413 562-9100
EMP: 7
SALES (est): 678.2K
SALES (corp-wide): 350K **Privately Held**
SIC: 2752 Lithographic Commercial Printing
PA: Puffer International, Inc.
45 1/2 Union St
Easthampton MA 01027
413 527-1069

(G-16720)
PUFFER INTERNATIONAL INC
139 Meadow St (01085-3228)
PHONE..................................413 527-1069
Don Puffer, *Branch Mgr*
EMP: 4
SALES (est): 257.2K
SALES (corp-wide): 350K **Privately Held**
SIC: 2759 7334 Commercial Printing Photocopying Services
PA: Puffer International, Inc.
45 1/2 Union St
Easthampton MA 01027
413 527-1069

(G-16721)
QUALITY MACHINING CO INC
96b1 Mainline Dr (01085-3306)
P.O. Box 164 (01086-0164)
PHONE..................................413 562-0389
Henry Pluciennik, *President*
Olga Pluciennik, *Vice Pres*
EMP: 5 **EST:** 1976
SQ FT: 2,000
SALES: 150K **Privately Held**
SIC: 3599 Mfg Industrial Machinery

(G-16722)
QUALITY PACKAGING & GRAPHICS
280 Lockhouse Rd (01085-1236)
P.O. Box 1338 (01086-1338)
PHONE..................................413 568-1923
Robert Baker, *President*
EMP: 4
SQ FT: 13,000
SALES (est): 481.4K **Privately Held**
SIC: 2652 Mfg Setup Paperboard Boxes

(G-16723)
ROSELLIS MACHINE & MFG CO
248 Root Rd (01085-9828)
PHONE..................................413 562-4317
Nicholas A Roselli, *President*
Vincent Roselli, *Vice Pres*
EMP: 10
SQ FT: 3,000
SALES (est): 935K **Privately Held**
SIC: 3451 5941 Mfr Screw Machine Products

(G-16724)
RPM WOOD FINISHES GROUP INC
C C I Division
221 Union St (01085-2423)
PHONE..................................413 562-9655
Gina Auclair, *Manager*
Deb Lanier, *Manager*
EMP: 12
SALES (corp-wide): 5.5B **Publicly Held**
SIC: 2851 2893 3479 Mfg Paints/Allied Prdts/Printing Inks
HQ: Rpm Wood Finishes Group, Inc.
2220 Us Highway 70 Se # 100
Hickory NC 28602
828 261-0325

(G-16725)
S LANE JOHN & SON INCORPORATED (PA)
730 E Mountain Rd (01085-1805)
P.O. Box 125 (01086-0125)
PHONE..................................413 568-8986
Harry C Lane, *President*
Arthur F Turton, *Director*
Jonathan Lane, *Admin Sec*
EMP: 10 **EST:** 1890
SQ FT: 5,000
SALES (est): 24.1MM **Privately Held**
SIC: 1429 1442 Crushed/Broken Stone Construction Sand/Gravel

(G-16726)
SAVAGE ARMS INC (DH)
100 Springdale Rd Ste 1 (01085-1673)
PHONE..................................413 642-4135
Ronald Coburn, *Ch of Bd*
◆ **EMP:** 200
SQ FT: 336,000
SALES (est): 104.2MM
SALES (corp-wide): 106.4MM **Privately Held**
WEB: www.savagearms.com
SIC: 3484 Mfg Small Arms
HQ: Savage Sports Corporation
100 Springdale Rd
Westfield MA 01085
413 568-7001

(G-16727)
SAVAGE RANGE SYSTEMS INC
100 Springdale Rd (01085-1987)
PHONE..................................413 568-7001
Stephen M Nolan, *Director*
Scott D Chaplin, *Director*
Albert Kasper, *Director*
Robert Keller, *Director*
▼ **EMP:** 8
SQ FT: 336,000
SALES (est): 2.1MM
SALES (corp-wide): 106.4MM **Privately Held**
WEB: www.savagerangesystems.com
SIC: 3949 Mfg Sporting/Athletic Goods
HQ: Savage Sports Corporation
100 Springdale Rd
Westfield MA 01085
413 568-7001

(G-16728)
SAVAGE SPORTS CORPORATION (HQ)
100 Springdale Rd (01085-1987)
PHONE..................................413 568-7001
Ronald Coburn, *Ch of Bd*
Albert F Kasper, *President*
David Pacentini, *CFO*
EMP: 13
SQ FT: 336,000
SALES (est): 106.4MM **Privately Held**
SIC: 3484 Mfg Small Arms
PA: Caliber Company
100 Springdale Rd
Westfield MA 01085
413 642-4260

(G-16729)
SCHULTZ CO INC
Also Called: Wesco Manufacturing
18 Coleman Ave (01085-4404)
PHONE..................................413 568-1592
Richard Schultz, *President*
EMP: 3 **EST:** 1967
SQ FT: 6,600
SALES (est): 250K **Privately Held**
SIC: 3469 Mfg Metal Stampings

(G-16730)
SIGN SHOP INC
215 E Main St Ste 2 (01085-3326)
PHONE..................................413 562-1876
Monica Luberda, *President*
Michael Sobczyk, *Vice Pres*
EMP: 3
SQ FT: 2,500
SALES: 60K **Privately Held**
SIC: 3993 Mfg Signs/Advertising Specialties

GEOGRAPHIC

(G-16731)
SONICRON SYSTEMS CORPORATION
Also Called: Plastron Company
382 Suthampton Rd Ste 102 (01085)
P.O. Box 38 (01086-0038)
PHONE..................................413 562-5218
Ronald V Cecchini, *President*
Marcia Cecchini, *Treasurer*
EMP: 20
SQ FT: 16,000
SALES (est): 3.9MM **Privately Held**
WEB: www.sonicron.com
SIC: 3559 3089 3544 Mfg Misc Industry Machinery Mfg Plastic Products Mfg Dies/Tools/Jigs/Fixtures

(G-16732)
TELL TOOL INC
Also Called: Cadence Aerospace
35 Turnpike Industrial Rd (01085-1646)
PHONE..................................413 568-1671
David Smith, *President*
Robert Morin, *Vice Pres*
John O'Donnell, *Vice Pres*
Charles Fuller, *CFO*
Deborah Van Wright, *Info Tech Mgr*
EMP: 100
SQ FT: 60,000
SALES (est): 29.7MM
SALES (corp-wide): 220.2MM **Privately Held**
WEB: www.telltool.com
SIC: 3724 3769 Mfg Aircraft Engines/Parts Mfg Space Vehicle Equipment
HQ: Tell Tool Acquisition Inc.
35 Turnpike Industrial Rd
Westfield MA 01085
413 568-1671

(G-16733)
TELL TOOL ACQUISITION INC (HQ)
35 Turnpike Industrial Rd (01085-1646)
PHONE..................................413 568-1671
Edward Torres, *Vice Pres*
EMP: 4
SALES (est): 29.7MM
SALES (corp-wide): 220.2MM **Privately Held**
SIC: 3724 3769 Mfg Aircraft Engines/Parts Mfg Space Vehicle Equipment
PA: Cadence Aerospace, Llc
3150 E Miraloma Ave
Anaheim CA 92806
949 877-3630

(G-16734)
THERMAL DYNAMIX INC
15 E Silver St (01085-4420)
PHONE..................................413 562-1266
Peter Howe, *President*
John Horoschak, *Vice Pres*
James Lobik, *Clerk*
EMP: 4
SQ FT: 1,500
SALES: 1MM **Privately Held**
WEB: www.thermaldynamix.com
SIC: 3569 Mfg General Industrial Machinery

(G-16735)
TNT MANUFACTURING LLC
988 Southampton Rd Ste B (01085-2020)
PHONE..................................413 562-0690
Bernie Tetreault,
Laurie Tetreault,
EMP: 3
SQ FT: 1,200
SALES: 450K **Privately Held**
WEB: www.tntmanufacturing.net
SIC: 3561 Mfg Industrial Parts

(G-16736)
TRANSCON TECHNOLOGIES INC
Also Called: E C I
53 Mainline Dr (01085-3313)
P.O. Box 1536 (01086-1536)
PHONE..................................413 562-7684
Pablo A Nyarady, *President*
Bob Carrier, *Vice Pres*
Doug Crowe, *Technician*
EMP: 45
SQ FT: 35,000
SALES (est): 8.2MM **Privately Held**
WEB: www.eciworld.com
SIC: 3677 Mfg Electronic Coils/Transformers

(G-16737)
TRANSOM SCOPES INC
Also Called: Instrument Technology
33 Airport Rd (01085-1357)
P.O. Box 381 (01086-0381)
PHONE..................................413 562-3606
Hugh Dorrian, *CEO*
Jonathan Shields, *CFO*
EMP: 37
SALES (est): 1.4MM **Privately Held**
SIC: 3827 Mfg Optical Instruments/Lenses

(G-16738)
US TSUBAKI AUTOMOTIVE LLC
152 Apremont Way (01085-5301)
PHONE..................................413 593-1100
Tim Goble, *Branch Mgr*
EMP: 16 **Privately Held**
SIC: 3462 3568 3496 Mfg Iron/Steel Forgings Mfg Power Transmission Equipment Mfg Misc Fabricated Wire Products
HQ: U.S. Tsubaki Automotive, Llc
106 Lonczak St
Chicopee MA 01022

(G-16739)
VECTOR TOOL & DIE CORPORATION
317 Northwest Rd (01085-3931)
P.O. Box 1135 (01086-1135)
PHONE..................................413 562-1616
Michael Bernardara, *President*
Frank Bernardara, *President*
Carol Bernardara, *Treasurer*
EMP: 6
SALES: 500K **Privately Held**
SIC: 3544 Mfg Special Tools Dies Die Sets Jigs & Fixtures Jig Grinding & Wire Edm

(G-16740)
WATERWOOD CORPORATION
77 Servistar Indus Way (01085-5601)
PHONE..................................413 572-1010
Jack Chak Ki Fu, *Principal*
EMP: 23
SALES (est): 2.2MM **Privately Held**
SIC: 2038 Mfg Frozen Specialties

(G-16741)
WESTEK ARCHITECTURAL WDWKG INC
97 Servistar Indus Way (01085-5601)
PHONE..................................413 562-6363
Bruce Scheible, *President*
James Kotowicz, *Treasurer*
EMP: 16
SQ FT: 15,000
SALES (est): 2.9MM **Privately Held**
SIC: 2431 Mfg Millwork

(G-16742)
WESTFIELD CONCRETE INC
403 Paper Mill Rd (01085-1735)
PHONE..................................413 562-4814
Ron Dahle, *President*
EMP: 20
SALES (est): 1MM **Privately Held**
SIC: 3273 Mfg Ready-Mixed Concrete

(G-16743)
WESTFIELD ELECTROPLATING CO (PA)
Also Called: Wepco
68 N Elm St (01085-1690)
P.O. Box 298 (01086-0298)
PHONE..................................413 568-3716
Michael P Stolpinski, *President*
Jonathan M Stolpinski, *Vice Pres*
Lynn Poulin, *Controller*
Kenneth M Curran, *Director*
Lynn M Poulin, *Director*
EMP: 120 **EST:** 1946
SQ FT: 52,000
SALES (est): 18.1MM **Privately Held**
WEB: www.westfieldplating.com
SIC: 3471 3479 Plating/Polishing Service Coating/Engraving Service

(G-16744)
WESTFIELD GRINDING WHEEL CO
Also Called: Gaylord, Richard N
135 Apremont Way (01085-1303)
P.O. Box 798 (01086-0798)
PHONE..................................413 568-8634
Edward S Sauers, *President*
Gina Pellegrini, *Admin Asst*
▲ **EMP:** 30 **EST:** 1923
SQ FT: 29,500
SALES (est): 3.9MM **Privately Held**
WEB: www.westfieldgrinding.com
SIC: 3291 Mfg Grinding Wheels

(G-16745)
WESTFIELD NEWS GROUP LLC
62 School St (01085-2835)
PHONE..................................413 562-4181
Patrick Berry,
EMP: 42
SQ FT: 8,000
SALES (est): 2.1MM **Privately Held**
SIC: 2711 Newspapers-Publishing/Printing

(G-16746)
WESTFIELD NEWS PUBLISHING INC (DH)
Also Called: Westfield Evening News
64 School St (01085-2835)
PHONE..................................413 562-4181
Lawrence I Hebert, *President*
Lawrence Hebert, *Principal*
Navza Carols, *Principal*
Virginia L White, *Corp Secy*
E Carol Mazza, *Vice Pres*
EMP: 47
SQ FT: 14,000
SALES (est): 19.3MM
SALES (corp-wide): 3B **Publicly Held**
WEB: www.wenpub.com
SIC: 2711 2752 Newspapers-Publishing/Printing Lithographic Commercial Printing
HQ: Sinclair Television Of Capital District, Inc.
1000 Wilson Blvd Ste 2700
Arlington VA 22209
703 647-8700

(G-16747)
WESTFIELD TOOL & DIE INC
55 Arnold St Ste 101 (01085-2888)
P.O. Box 608 (01086-0608)
PHONE..................................413 562-2393
James Janisieski, *President*
John Simmitt, *Vice Pres*
EMP: 13 **EST:** 1961
SQ FT: 10,000
SALES (est): 1.7MM **Privately Held**
SIC: 3544 3542 Mfg Progressive Punch Press Dies & Four Slide Machine Tools

(G-16748)
WESTFIELD WHIP MFG CO
360 Elm St (01085-2922)
P.O. Box 425 (01086-0425)
PHONE..................................413 568-8244
Carol Ann Martin, *President*
Daniel R Seals, *Treasurer*
EMP: 14
SQ FT: 15,000
SALES (est): 1.8MM **Privately Held**
SIC: 3199 Mfg Whips

(G-16749)
WHIP CITY JERKY LLC
271 Elm St (01085-3360)
PHONE..................................413 568-2050
Anthony J Neuser, *Principal*
Tony Neuser, *Officer*
EMP: 4
SALES (est): 309.7K **Privately Held**
SIC: 2013 5421 Mfg Prepared Meats Ret Meat/Fish

Westford
Middlesex County

(G-16750)
ABBOTT
4 Robbins Rd (01886-4113)
PHONE..................................978 577-3467
EMP: 11
SALES (est): 1.6MM **Privately Held**
SIC: 2834 Mfg Pharmaceutical Preparations

(G-16751)
ACCUMET ENGINEERING INC
123 Oak Hill Rd (01886-1145)
PHONE..................................978 692-6180
Marie C Sexton, *Ch of Bd*
Gregory J Sexton, *President*
Susan Sullivan, *Principal*
June P Beauchesne, *Treasurer*
Bruce N Beauchesne, *Admin Sec*
EMP: 34 **EST:** 1979
SQ FT: 16,000
SALES (est): 7.9MM **Privately Held**
WEB: www.lsi-ma.com
SIC: 3599 Mfg Industrial Machinery

(G-16752)
ALDEN AND BRODEN CORPORATION
13 Blue Ridge Rd (01886-1910)
PHONE..................................603 882-0330
John Alden, *President*
Bob Alden, *Vice Pres*
EMP: 8 **EST:** 1978
SQ FT: 9,000
SALES: 850K **Privately Held**
WEB: www.alden-broden.com
SIC: 3555 2821 Mfg Printing Trades Machinery Mfg Plastic Materials/Resins

(G-16753)
ANOVA DATA INC
4 Technology Park Dr (01886-3140)
P.O. Box 729, Bolton (01740-0729)
PHONE..................................978 577-6600
John St Amand, *CEO*
Chip Boyle, *Vice Pres*
Kumar Kovvali, *Vice Pres*
Nerissa Robert, *Vice Pres*
Todd Warble, *Vice Pres*
EMP: 6
SALES (est): 152.6K **Privately Held**
SIC: 3825 3829 3826 Mfg Electrical Measuring Instruments Mfg Measuring/Controlling Devices Mfg Analytical Instruments

(G-16754)
AROMA SPA & LASER CENTER INC
225 Essex St (01886)
PHONE..................................978 685-8883
Edivaneia C Kwon, *President*
EMP: 3
SALES (est): 171.6K **Privately Held**
SIC: 3841 Mfg Surgical/Medical Instruments

(G-16755)
ARTEL VIDEO SYSTEMS CORP
5b Lyberty Way (01886-3617)
PHONE..................................978 263-5775
Mike Rizzo, *President*
Jeff Masucci, *CTO*
▼ **EMP:** 35
SQ FT: 17,000
SALES (est): 8.4MM **Privately Held**
WEB: www.newfoundtech.com
SIC: 3663 3651 3661 Mfg Radio/Tv Communication Equipment Mfg Home Audio/Video Equipment Mfg Telephone/Telegraph Apparatus

(G-16756)
BERGERON MACHINE INC
65 Powers Rd (01886-4110)
PHONE..................................978 577-6235
EMP: 15
SALES (est): 1MM **Privately Held**
SIC: 3315 Mfg Industrial Machinery

(G-16757)
BISCOM INC
10 Technology Park Dr # 102 (01886-3175)
PHONE..................................978 250-1800
Bill Ho, *CEO*
S K Ho, *Chairman*
Don Dunning, *COO*
Tom Bishop, *Exec VP*
Michael Gayowski, *Senior VP*
EMP: 67

SALES (est): 13.6MM Privately Held
WEB: www.biscom.com
SIC: 7372 3661 3571 Prepackaged Software Services Mfg Telephone/Telegraph Apparatus Mfg Electronic Computers

(G-16758)
BRITISH BEER COMPANY INC
149 Littleton Rd (01886-3121)
PHONE 978 577-6034
Gary Simon, *Branch Mgr*
EMP: 25
SALES (corp-wide): 4.1MM Privately Held
SIC: 2082 Mfg Malt Beverages
PA: British Beer Company, Inc.
15 Richards Rd A
Plymouth MA 02360
508 747-1776

(G-16759)
CAD TECH MACHINE INCORPORATED
7 Littleton Rd Ste D1 (01886-3131)
PHONE 978 692-0677
David Willoughby, *Owner*
EMP: 3
SALES (est): 273.6K Privately Held
SIC: 3599 Mfg Industrial Machinery

(G-16760)
CARNEGIE COMMUNICATIONS LLC
210 Littleton Rd Ste 100 (01886-3513)
PHONE 978 692-5092
Joe Moore, *CEO*
Meghan Dalesandro, *Exec VP*
Ilya Liberman, *Exec VP*
Deborah Millin, *Exec VP*
Alexa Poulin, *Exec VP*
EMP: 33
SALES (est): 5.4MM Privately Held
WEB: www.carnegiecomm.com
SIC: 2721 7319 7331 7311 Periodical-Publish/Print Advertising Services Direct Mail Ad Svcs Advertising Agency
PA: Carnegie Dartlet Llc
210 Littleton Rd Ste 100
Westford MA 01886
978 692-5092

(G-16761)
CARNEGIE DARTLET LLC (PA)
210 Littleton Rd Ste 100 (01886-3580)
PHONE 978 692-5092
Joseph Moore, *CEO*
Meghan Dalesandro, *COO*
Allison Brake, *Vice Pres*
Scott Ochander, *Chief Mktg Ofcr*
Tyler Borders, *CIO*
EMP: 3
SALES (est): 5.4MM Privately Held
SIC: 2721 7319 7331 7311 Periodical-Publish/Print Advertising Services Direct Mail Ad Svcs Advertising Agency

(G-16762)
CLARKWORKS MACHINE
496 Groton Rd Ste 5 (01886-1100)
PHONE 978 692-2556
Brad Clarke, *Owner*
EMP: 6
SALES (est): 665.5K Privately Held
SIC: 3599 Mfg Industrial Machinery

(G-16763)
CYNOSURE INC (HQ)
Also Called: Smartlipo
5 Carlisle Rd (01886-3601)
PHONE 978 256-4200
Michael R Davin, *President*
Timothy W Baker, *COO*
Douglas J Delaney, *Exec VP*
Douglas Delaney, *Exec VP*
Jorge Pinedo, *Exec VP*
▲ EMP: 277
SQ FT: 150,000
SALES (est): 351.1MM
SALES (corp-wide): 3.3B Publicly Held
WEB: www.cynosurelaser.com
SIC: 3845 Mfg Electromedical Equipment
PA: Hologic, Inc.
250 Campus Dr
Marlborough MA 01752
508 263-2900

(G-16764)
DINNER DAILY LLC
26 Colonial Dr (01886-4503)
P.O. Box 678 (01886-0020)
PHONE 978 392-5887
Laurin Mills, *Founder*
EMP: 5
SALES (est): 201.6K Privately Held
SIC: 2711 Newspapers-Publishing/Printing

(G-16765)
ELPAKCO INC (PA)
2 Carl Thompson Rd (01886-1561)
P.O. Box 72 (01886-0003)
PHONE 978 392-0400
John S Grant, *President*
Ryan Grant, *Sales Mgr*
▲ EMP: 21
SQ FT: 10,000
SALES (est): 2.5MM Privately Held
WEB: www.elpakco.com
SIC: 3678 5065 3674 Mfg Electronic Connectors Whol Electronic Parts/Equipment Mfg Semiconductors/Related Devices

(G-16766)
FILTER-KLEEN MANUFACTURING CO
3 Broadway St (01886)
P.O. Box 1319 (01886-4719)
PHONE 978 692-5137
Chris Franklyn, *President*
Troy Guilmette, *Opers Staff*
Joanne Guilmett, *Treasurer*
Janice D Kelley, *Clerk*
EMP: 18
SALES (est): 3.4MM Privately Held
SIC: 3569 Mfg General Industrial Machinery

(G-16767)
FLETCHER GRANITE LLC (DH)
535 Groton Rd (01886-1146)
PHONE 978 692-1312
Antonio C Ramos, *Mng Member*
EMP: 5
SALES (est): 2MM
SALES (corp-wide): 17.3MM Privately Held
WEB: www.fletchergranite.com
SIC: 1411 3281 3272 2951 Dimension Stone Quarry Mfg Cut Stone/Products Mfg Concrete Products Mfg Asphalt Mixtr/Blocks
HQ: Georgia Stone Industries Inc.
15 Branch Pike
Smithfield RI 02917
401 232-2040

(G-16768)
GENRAD INC
Also Called: Environmedics Div
7 Technology Park Dr (01886-3141)
PHONE 978 589-7000
Robert Dutkowsky, *Ch of Bd*
Paul Geere, *President*
Stephen Holford, *President*
Michael W Schraeder, *President*
Lori B Hannay, *Vice Pres*
EMP: 600
SQ FT: 230,000
SALES: 341.6MM
SALES (corp-wide): 2.1B Publicly Held
SIC: 3825 7629 Mfg & Services Electronic Test Equipment
PA: Teradyne, Inc.
600 Riverpark Dr
North Reading MA 01864
978 370-2700

(G-16769)
GO GREEN INDUSTRIES INC
2 Doris Rd (01886-1518)
PHONE 978 496-1881
Stephen Cuzziere, *Principal*
EMP: 3 EST: 2008
SALES (est): 197.4K Privately Held
SIC: 3999 Mfg Misc Products

(G-16770)
GOODRICH CORPORATION
9 Technology Park Dr (01886-3141)
PHONE 978 303-6700
Marcelo Macri, *Branch Mgr*
EMP: 13
SALES (corp-wide): 66.5B Publicly Held
SIC: 3721 Mfg Aircraft
HQ: Goodrich Corporation
2730 W Tyvola Rd 4
Charlotte NC 28217
704 423-7000

(G-16771)
GOODRICH CORPORATION
7 Technology Park Dr (01886-3141)
PHONE 978 303-6700
Kevin Raftery, *General Mgr*
Willliam Beiter, *General Mgr*
Virginia Berthel, *Principal*
Vinod Parameswara, *Engineer*
Charles Patras, *Engineer*
EMP: 700
SALES (corp-wide): 66.5B Publicly Held
WEB: www.bfgoodrich.com
SIC: 3724 3728 7372 Mfg Aircraft Engine/Part Mfg Aircraft Parts/Equip
HQ: Goodrich Corporation
2730 W Tyvola Rd 4
Charlotte NC 28217
704 423-7000

(G-16772)
HEURISTIC LABS INC
16 Byrne Ave (01886-1514)
PHONE 347 994-0299
Christofer Garner, *Principal*
Nicholas Armstrong-Crews, *Principal*
EMP: 5
SALES (est): 283.9K Privately Held
SIC: 7372 Prepackaged Software Services

(G-16773)
IDEAL CONCRETE BLOCK CO (PA)
Also Called: Pavers By Ideal
45 Powers Rd (01886-4111)
P.O. Box 747 (01886-0023)
PHONE 978 692-3076
John V Burgoyne Sr, *President*
James M Burgoyne, *Vice Pres*
Joseph Burgoyne III, *Vice Pres*
Lawrence Nicolai Sr, *Vice Pres*
Dennis Maney, *Purch Agent*
▲ EMP: 45 EST: 1923
SALES (est): 9.5MM Privately Held
WEB: www.idealconcreteblock.com
SIC: 3271 5032 Mfg Concrete Block/Brick Whol Brick/Stone Material

(G-16774)
KADANT INC (PA)
1 Technology Park Dr # 210 (01886-3139)
PHONE 978 776-2000
Jonathan W Painter, *President*
Stan Malton, *Managing Dir*
Mike Gerdin, *District Mgr*
Mike Six, *District Mgr*
Eric T Langevin, *Exec VP*
▲ EMP: 277
SQ FT: 15,000
SALES: 633.7MM Publicly Held
WEB: www.kadantaes.com
SIC: 3554 3321 2621 Paper Industries Machinery Pulp Fiber Granules And Iron Castings

(G-16775)
LAVELLE MACHINE & TOOL CO INC
485 Groton Rd (01886-1149)
P.O. Box 1558 (01886-4996)
PHONE 978 692-8825
Edwin Lavelle Jr, *President*
EMP: 35
SQ FT: 25,000
SALES (est): 6MM Privately Held
WEB: www.lavellemachine.com
SIC: 3599 Mfg Industrial Machinery

(G-16776)
LINDEN PHOTONICS INC
1 Park Dr Ste 10 (01886-3535)
PHONE 978 392-7985
Amaresh Mahapatra, *President*
EMP: 5
SQ FT: 3,600
SALES (est): 899.2K Privately Held
WEB: www.lindenphotonics.com
SIC: 3357 Nonferrous Wiredrawing/Insulating

(G-16777)
MACK TECHNOLOGIES INC (HQ)
27 Carlisle Rd (01886-3644)
PHONE 978 392-5500
John Kovach, *President*
Florence M Belnap, *Corp Secy*
Debbie Dalkas, *Human Res Mgr*
Donald S Kendall III, *Director*
▲ EMP: 200
SQ FT: 108,000
SALES (est): 165.4MM
SALES (corp-wide): 432.8MM Privately Held
WEB: www.macktech.com
SIC: 3577 3571 Mfg Computer Peripheral Equipment Mfg Electronic Computers
PA: Mack Group, Inc.
608 Warm Brook Rd
Arlington VT 05250
802 375-2511

(G-16778)
MATERION PRCSION OPTICS THIN F (DH)
2 Lyberty Way (01886-3616)
PHONE 978 692-7513
Thomas F Mauser, *Corp Secy*
Robert Naranjo, *Vice Pres*
Darren Brown, *Engineer*
▼ EMP: 10 EST: 1971
SQ FT: 125,000
SALES (est): 34.5MM
SALES (corp-wide): 1.2B Publicly Held
WEB: www.Materion.com
SIC: 3827 Mfg Optical Instruments/Lenses
HQ: Materion Advanced Materials Technologies And Services Inc.
2978 Main St
Buffalo NY 14214
800 327-1355

(G-16779)
MAY GRAPHICS & PRINTING INC
Also Called: Ledgeview Printing
359 Littleton Rd (01886-4065)
P.O. Box 724 (01886-0022)
PHONE 978 392-1302
Richard Maggio, *President*
EMP: 8
SQ FT: 3,000
SALES (est): 1.4MM Privately Held
WEB: www.ledgeviewprinting.com
SIC: 2752 Lithographic Commercial Printing

(G-16780)
NETWORK EQUIPMENT TECH INC (DH)
Also Called: Net.com
4 Technology Park Dr (01886-3140)
PHONE 510 713-7300
David Wagenseller, *President*
Frederick D Dalessio, *Principal*
C Nicholas Keating Jr, *Principal*
David R Laube, *Principal*
Francois P Le, *Vice Pres*
◆ EMP: 36
SQ FT: 97,747
SALES (est): 19.4MM
SALES (corp-wide): 618.5MM Publicly Held
WEB: www.net.com
SIC: 3577 Mfg Communication Equipments & Global Provider Networking Technology
HQ: Sonus Networks, Inc.
4 Technology Park Dr
Westford MA 01886
978 614-8100

(G-16781)
NEXTEK INC
2 Park Dr Ste 1 (01886-3525)
P.O. Box 385 (01886-0385)
PHONE 978 577-6214
Steve Russo, *President*
George Kauffman, *Admin Sec*
▲ EMP: 20
SQ FT: 3,500
SALES (est): 3.8MM Privately Held
WEB: www.nexteklightning.com
SIC: 3699 Mfg Electrical Equipment/Supplies

GEOGRAPHIC

(G-16782)
NORTHERN OUTDOOR LIGHTING
14 Bixby Ln (01886-2525)
PHONE..................................978 987-9845
William H Knowles, *Principal*
EMP: 5 **EST:** 2013
SALES (est): 411.2K **Privately Held**
SIC: 3648 Mfg Lighting Equipment

(G-16783)
PERFORMANCE MOTION DEVICES INC
1 Technology Park Dr # 5 (01886-3139)
PHONE..................................978 266-1210
Chuck Lewin, *President*
EMP: 20
SQ FT: 10,000
SALES (est): 5.9MM **Privately Held**
WEB: www.pmdcorp.com
SIC: 3625 3823 3674 Mfg Relays/Industrial Controls Mfg Process Control Instruments Mfg Semiconductors/Related Devices

(G-16784)
PFIZER INC
3 Starr Cir (01886-2934)
PHONE..................................978 799-8657
Eric Kibblehouse, *Director*
EMP: 3
SALES (corp-wide): 53.6B **Publicly Held**
SIC: 2834 Mfg Pharmaceutical Preparations
PA: Pfizer Inc.
235 E 42nd St Rm 107
New York NY 10017
212 733-2323

(G-16785)
PORTER SARGENT PUBLISHERS INC
2 Lan Dr Ste 100 (01886-3532)
PHONE..................................617 922-0076
J Katherine Sargent, *President*
John Yonce, *General Mgr*
John Buckley, *Assoc VP*
EMP: 7 **EST:** 1914
SALES (est): 623.2K **Privately Held**
WEB: www.portersargent.com
SIC: 2731 2741 Books-Publishing/Printing Misc Publishing

(G-16786)
PRINTING SOLUTIONS INC
6 Carlisle Rd Ste 6 # 6 (01886-3619)
PHONE..................................978 392-9903
Andre Lagasse, *President*
Don Lagasse, *Clerk*
EMP: 10
SQ FT: 15,000
SALES (est): 1.5MM **Privately Held**
WEB: www.printingsolutionsinc.com
SIC: 2752 Lithographic Commercial Printing

(G-16787)
RADENNA LLC
60 1/2 Cold Spring Rd (01886-2211)
PHONE..................................781 248-8826
Michael Filippov,
Alexey Zaparovanny,
EMP: 5
SALES (est): 419.2K **Privately Held**
SIC: 3812 Mfg Search/Navigation Equipment

(G-16788)
RED HAT INC
314 Little 10 Rd 10th (01886)
PHONE..................................978 392-1000
EMP: 15
SALES (corp-wide): 79.5B **Publicly Held**
SIC: 7372 Prepackaged Software Services
HQ: Red Hat, Inc.
100 E Davie St
Raleigh NC 27601
-

(G-16789)
RED HAT INC
3 Lan Dr Ste 100 (01886-3568)
PHONE..................................978 692-3113
Brian Stevens, *Manager*
EMP: 15
SALES (corp-wide): 79.5B **Publicly Held**
WEB: www.apacheweek.com
SIC: 7372 Operating Systems Software Development
HQ: Red Hat, Inc.
100 E Davie St
Raleigh NC 27601
-

(G-16790)
RIVERMEADOW SOFTWARE INC
319 Littleton Rd Ste 305 (01886-4100)
PHONE..................................617 448-4990
Partha Ghosh, *Principal*
Norem Soriano, *Manager*
EMP: 9
SALES (est): 1.1MM **Privately Held**
SIC: 7372 Prepackaged Software Services

(G-16791)
SECEON INC
238 Littleton Rd Ste 206 (01886-3531)
PHONE..................................978 923-0040
Ashish Tiwarn, *Engineer*
Gary Scott, *Treasurer*
Arun Gandhi, *Director*
EMP: 20
SALES: 2MM **Privately Held**
SIC: 7372 Prepackaged Software Services

(G-16792)
SHATTUCK PRCSION MACHINING INC
2 Park Dr Ste 7 (01886-3525)
PHONE..................................978 392-0848
Dale Shattuck, *President*
EMP: 4
SQ FT: 3,462
SALES (est): 212.7K **Privately Held**
SIC: 3599 Mfg Industrial Machinery

(G-16793)
SOFTWARE EXPERTS INC
4 Grey Fox Ln (01886-1913)
PHONE..................................978 692-5343
RAO Mallik, *President*
Malliareddy Karra, *Principal*
EMP: 14
SQ FT: 700
SALES (est): 806.3K **Privately Held**
WEB: www.softwareexperts.com
SIC: 7372 Prepackaged Software Services

(G-16794)
SUBURBAN MACHINE
Also Called: N/A
69 Broadway St (01886-2106)
PHONE..................................978 392-9100
Bruce Sthilaire, *President*
Bruce St Hilaire, *President*
EMP: 6
SALES: 1.1MM **Privately Held**
SIC: 3599 Mfg Industrial Machinery

(G-16795)
SYMETRICA INC
4 Lyberty Way A (01886-3616)
PHONE..................................508 718-5610
Heddwyn Lewis Davies, *President*
EMP: 10
SALES (est): 1.5MM **Privately Held**
WEB: www.symetrica.com
SIC: 3812 Mfg Search/Navigation Equipment

(G-16796)
TERRASONICS LLC
91 Depot St (01886-1314)
PHONE..................................978 692-3274
Susan Poniatowski,
EMP: 3
SALES (est): 266K **Privately Held**
WEB: www.terrasonics.com
SIC: 3699 Ultrasonic Process Equipment

(G-16797)
TEST REP ASSOCIATES INC
319 Littleton Rd Ste 104 (01886-4133)
PHONE..................................978 692-8000
Martin Heffler, *President*
Richard Saccetti, *Vice Pres*
Ron Fiume, *Admin Sec*
Connie O'Shea, *Administration*
EMP: 6
SALES (est): 508K **Privately Held**
WEB: www.testrep.com
SIC: 1389 Oil/Gas Field Services

(G-16798)
TRIJAY INC
149 Groton Rd (01886-1337)
PHONE..................................978 692-6104
David H Jewett, *President*
Dennis Jewett, *Treasurer*
EMP: 8
SQ FT: 15,000
SALES (est): 800K **Privately Held**
SIC: 3444 Sheet Metal Fabrication

(G-16799)
VITTAMED CORPORATION (PA)
25 Kirsi Cir (01886-2013)
PHONE..................................617 977-4536
Murph McKeon, *Finance Dir*
Theodoro Dagi, *Chief Mktg Ofcr*
EMP: 3
SALES (est): 307K **Privately Held**
SIC: 3845 Mfg Electromedical Equipment

(G-16800)
WESTFORD CHEMICAL CORPORATION
98 Concord Rd (01886-4025)
P.O. Box 798 (01886-0024)
PHONE..................................978 392-0689
Ronald Laroche, *President*
Steven Laroche, *Vice Pres*
EMP: 3
SQ FT: 2,800
SALES: 1.3MM **Privately Held**
WEB: www.biosolve.com
SIC: 2899 Mfg Chemical Preparations

Westhampton
Hampshire County

(G-16801)
MAITRI LEARNING LLC
131 Tob Hill Rd (01027-9615)
PHONE..................................413 529-2868
Julia Volkman,
EMP: 4
SALES (est): 299.8K **Privately Held**
SIC: 2731 Publishing

Westminster
Worcester County

(G-16802)
ANDERSON LOGGING AND LUMBER
36 Nichols St (01473-1441)
PHONE..................................978 874-2751
Scott Anderson, *Owner*
EMP: 4
SALES (est): 386.5K **Privately Held**
SIC: 2411 5211 Lumber Company

(G-16803)
BROGANS CUSTOM WOODWORKING
30 Main St (01473-1448)
PHONE..................................978 502-8013
Shane Brogan, *Principal*
EMP: 4 **EST:** 2010
SALES (est): 278.9K **Privately Held**
SIC: 2431 Mfg Millwork

(G-16804)
FITCHBURG WELDING CO INC
4 Depot Rd (01473-1220)
P.O. Box 467 (01473-0467)
PHONE..................................978 874-2911
Paul H Morin, *President*
Paul H Morin Jr, *Vice Pres*
Debbie Pelkey, *Human Res Mgr*
Jay Robbins, *Sales Mgr*
Norman J Courtemanche, *Admin Sec*
▼ **EMP:** 35 **EST:** 1935
SQ FT: 48,000
SALES (est): 9.6MM **Privately Held**
SIC: 3441 7692 Structural Metal Fabrication Welding Repair

(G-16805)
ILLINOIS TOOL WORKS INC
Also Called: ITW EF&c US
180 State Rd E (01473-1208)
PHONE..................................978 874-0151
Marcey Miller, *Branch Mgr*
EMP: 230
SALES (corp-wide): 14.7B **Publicly Held**
SIC: 3465 3089 Mfg Automotive Stampings Mfg Plastic Products
PA: Illinois Tool Works Inc.
155 Harlem Ave
Glenview IL 60025
847 724-7500

(G-16806)
J & B METAL FINISHING
1 Leominster St (01473)
P.O. Box 754 (01473-0754)
PHONE..................................978 874-5944
Bob Hilton, *Partner*
Joseph Macneil, *Partner*
EMP: 5
SQ FT: 5,000
SALES (est): 478.7K **Privately Held**
SIC: 3471 Plating/Polishing Service

(G-16807)
JARVENPAA & SONS
233 S Ashburnham Rd (01473-1106)
PHONE..................................978 874-2231
Eino W Jarvenpaa Jr, *Owner*
EMP: 5
SALES (est): 260K **Privately Held**
SIC: 2421 4151 Sawmill & School Bus Transportation

(G-16808)
MASSACHUSETTS NATURAL FERT INC
65 Bean Porridge Hill Rd (01473-1121)
P.O. Box 363 (01473-0363)
PHONE..................................978 874-0744
William Page, *President*
EMP: 7
SALES (est): 910K **Privately Held**
SIC: 2875 Mfg Fertilizers-Mix Only

(G-16809)
MAYHEW BASQUE PLASTICS LLC
100 Simplex Dr Ste 3 (01473-1482)
PHONE..................................978 537-5219
John C Lawless, *Mng Member*
Clifford Basque,
Gregory Basque,
William S Lawless,
▲ **EMP:** 16
SQ FT: 30,000
SALES: 1MM
SALES (corp-wide): 4.8MM **Privately Held**
WEB: www.basqueplastics.com
SIC: 3089 3544 Mfg Plastic Products Mfg Dies/Tools/Jigs/Fixtures
PA: Mayhew Steel Products, Inc.
199 Industrial Blvd
Turners Falls MA 01376
413 625-6351

(G-16810)
MILES KEDEX CO INC
1 Rowtier Rd (01473-1675)
PHONE..................................978 874-1403
Stephen A Muller, *President*
Charles A Gelinas Sr, *Admin Sec*
▲ **EMP:** 35
SQ FT: 35,000
SALES (est): 4.7MM **Privately Held**
WEB: www.mileskedex.com
SIC: 2295 2631 3172 Mfg Coated Fabrics Paperboard Mill Mfg Personal Leather Goods

(G-16811)
NEW ENGLAND EAGLE MACHINE INC
25 Theodore Dr Ste 3 (01473-1248)
P.O. Box 597, North Grafton (01536-0597)
PHONE..................................978 874-0017
Kevin Magill, *President*
James Magill Jr, *Vice Pres*
EMP: 5
SQ FT: 10,000

SALES (est): 525.2K Privately Held
SIC: 3599 Manufactures And Repair Industrial Machinery

(G-16812)
RANOR INC
1 Bella Dr (01473-1058)
PHONE..............978 874-0591
Alexander Shen, *CEO*
Joe Ciras, *Safety Mgr*
Karen Stone, *Production*
Tom Jankauskas, *QC Dir*
Dave Babeau, *Engineer*
▲ EMP: 98
SQ FT: 120,000
SALES (est): 16.7MM Publicly Held
SIC: 3441 3599 Structural Metal Fabrication Mfg Industrial Machinery
PA: Techprecision Corporation
1 Bella Dr
Westminster MA 01473

(G-16813)
SIMPLEX TIME RECORDER CO (DH)
Also Called: Tyco Acquisition Corp. Xxv NV
50 Technology Drive (01441-0001)
PHONE..............978 731-2500
Robert F Chauvin, *President*
Mark Altsman, *Business Mgr*
Michael Jenkins, *Business Mgr*
Anthony Morizio, *Business Mgr*
John Vozzy, *Business Mgr*
EMP: 211
SALES (est): 38.7MM Privately Held
SIC: 3669 Mfg Communications Equipment
HQ: Johnson Controls Fire Protection Lp
6600 Congress Ave
Boca Raton FL 33487
561 988-7200

(G-16814)
STR GRINNELL GP HOLDING LLC
50 Technology Dr (01441-0001)
PHONE..............978 731-2500
Jerry R Boggess, *President*
EMP: 25
SALES (est): 2.1MM Privately Held
WEB: www.comtec-alaska.com
SIC: 3579 Mfg Office Machines
HQ: Simplex Time Recorder Llc
50 Technology Dr
Westminster MA 01441

(G-16815)
TECHPRECISION CORPORATION (PA)
1 Bella Dr (01473-1058)
PHONE..............978 874-0591
Alexander Shen, *CEO*
Richard S McGowan, *Ch of Bd*
Thomas Sammons, *CFO*
Joseph Ciras, *Technical Staff*
▲ EMP: 3
SQ FT: 145,000
SALES: 16.7MM Publicly Held
SIC: 3599 3441 Mfg Industrial Machinery Structural Metal Fabrication

(G-16816)
TOWN OF WESTMINSTER
Also Called: Westminster Fire Department
7 South St (01473-1534)
PHONE..............978 874-2313
Brenton Macaloney, *Chief*
Ralph Leblanc, *Train & Dev Mgr*
EMP: 30 Privately Held
WEB: www.westminster-ma.org
SIC: 3569 Mfg General Industrial Machinery
PA: Town Of Westminster
11 South St
Westminster MA 01473
978 874-7400

(G-16817)
TWIN CITY MACHINING INC
4 Curtis Rd (01473-1221)
P.O. Box 467 (01473-0467)
PHONE..............978 874-1940
Mark Morin, *President*
Brian Morin, *Vice Pres*
Paul Morin, *Vice Pres*
▲ EMP: 9
SALES (est): 1.2MM Privately Held
SIC: 3599 Mfg Industrial Machinery

(G-16818)
TYCO SAFETY PRODUCTS US INC
91 Technology Dr (01441-0001)
PHONE..............800 435-3192
Mike Fieramosca, *Branch Mgr*
Cheryl Newton, *Technician*
EMP: 50 Privately Held
SIC: 3699 Mfg Electrical Equipment/Supplies
HQ: Tyco Safety Products Us, Inc.
6600 Congress Ave
Boca Raton FL 33487
561 912-6000

(G-16819)
UNIVERSAL HINGE CORP (PA)
18 Newton Rd (01473-1302)
PHONE..............603 935-9848
Edward Depietro, *CEO*
Roger Carr, *Manager*
EMP: 10
SALES (est): 1.1MM Privately Held
SIC: 3429 Mfg Hardware

(G-16820)
WACHUSETT BREWING COMPANY INC
175 State Rd E (01473-1681)
PHONE..............978 874-9965
Ned Lafortune, *President*
Christian McMahan, *President*
▲ EMP: 70
SQ FT: 10,000
SALES (est): 6.8MM Privately Held
WEB: www.wachusettbrew.com
SIC: 2082 Mfg Malt Beverages

(G-16821)
ZF ACTIVE SAFETY & ELEC US LLC
Also Called: TRW Fastening Systems
180 State Rd E (01473-1208)
PHONE..............978 874-0151
Melven Derek, *Branch Mgr*
Gary Skalaban, *Manager*
Carol Rakowski, *Director*
Dave Derby, *Clerk*
EMP: 21
SALES (corp-wide): 216.2K Privately Held
SIC: 3469 Mfg Motor Vehicle Parts/Accessories
HQ: Zf Active Safety & Electronics Us Llc
12001 Tech Center Dr
Livonia MI 48150
734 855-2600

Weston
Middlesex County

(G-16822)
BANNERAMA INSTANT SIGNS INC
10 Sibley Rd (02493-2550)
P.O. Box 3056, Framingham (01705-3056)
PHONE..............781 899-4744
David Curran, *President*
EMP: 4
SALES (est): 230K Privately Held
WEB: www.bannneramasigns.com
SIC: 2399 Mfg Fabricated Textile Products

(G-16823)
BOSTON BIOPHARMA LLC
30 Page Rd (02493-2127)
PHONE..............617 780-9300
Sonny Abraham, *Mng Member*
EMP: 4
SALES: 1MM Privately Held
SIC: 2834 Mfg Pharmaceutical Preparations

(G-16824)
COGNISCENT INC
410 Concord Rd (02493-1313)
PHONE..............508 863-0069
John S Kauer, *Chairman*
Joel White, *Exec VP*
EMP: 12
SALES: 1MM Privately Held
WEB: www.cogniscentinc.com
SIC: 3699 Mfg Electrical Equipment/Supplies

(G-16825)
EYEMAX LLC
74 Chestnut St (02493-1533)
PHONE..............781 424-9281
Elias Reichel, *President*
EMP: 3 EST: 2013
SALES (est): 189.2K Privately Held
SIC: 2834 Mfg Pharmaceutical Preparations

(G-16826)
GRANITE BROOK LLC
199 Church St (02493-2007)
P.O. Box 417 (02493-0906)
PHONE..............781 788-9700
Nicole Leone, *Manager*
Mike Leone,
Frank Leone,
EMP: 4
SALES (est): 472.9K Privately Held
SIC: 2499 Mfg Wood Products

(G-16827)
MASSACHUSETTS MTLS TECH LLC (PA)
12 Gowell Ln (02493-1648)
PHONE..............617 500-8325
Simon Bellemare, *President*
Steven Palkovic, *Vice Pres*
EMP: 4
SALES (est): 594.2K Privately Held
SIC: 3829 7389 Mfg Measuring/Controlling Devices Business Services

(G-16828)
NOXXON PHARMA INC
51 Fairview Rd (02493-2023)
PHONE..............617 232-0638
Don Munoz, *CFO*
EMP: 3
SALES (est): 166.4K Privately Held
SIC: 2834 Mfg Pharmaceutical Preparations

(G-16829)
PINESTREAM COMMUNICATIONS INC
52 Pine St (02493-1116)
PHONE..............781 893-6836
Cliff Hirsch, *President*
Marilyn Hirsch, *Administration*
EMP: 3 EST: 1997
SALES (est): 161.8K Privately Held
WEB: www.pinestream.com
SIC: 2711 Newspapers-Publishing/Printing

(G-16830)
PRIME NATIONAL PUBLISHING CORP
Also Called: Journal Emergency Management
470 Boston Post Rd Ste 1 (02493-1576)
PHONE..............781 899-2702
Eileen F Devito, *President*
Richard Devito, *Shareholder*
EMP: 15
SALES (est): 1.5MM Privately Held
WEB: www.pnpco.com
SIC: 2721 Periodicals-Publishing/Printing

(G-16831)
RHINE INC
51 Church St (02493-2003)
PHONE..............781 710-7121
Patricia Bee O'Neill, *Principal*
EMP: 3
SALES (est): 182.2K Privately Held
SIC: 3131 5139 5661 7389 Mfg Footwear Cut Stock Whol Footwear Ret Shoes Bus Servs Non-Comcl Site

(G-16832)
SYNOSTICS INC
3 Old Coach Rd (02493-2001)
PHONE..............781 248-5699
O Prem Das, *CEO*
E Fayelle Whelihan, *Principal*
EMP: 7
SALES (est): 459.4K Privately Held
SIC: 2834 Mfg Pharmaceutical Preparations

(G-16833)
THERASTAT LLC
44 Kings Grant Rd (02493-2158)
PHONE..............781 373-1865
Charles Keough, *President*
Nancy Hsiung,
EMP: 4
SALES (est): 189.6K Privately Held
SIC: 2835 Mfg Diagnostic Substances

(G-16834)
WESTON MEDICAL PUBLISHING LLC
470 Boston Post Rd (02493-1567)
PHONE..............781 899-2702
Richard A Devito Jr,
EMP: 3
SALES: 750K Privately Held
SIC: 2721 Periodicals-Publishing/Printing

Westport
Bristol County

(G-16835)
AMA ENGINEERING SMARTMOVE
683 American Legion Hwy (02790-4103)
PHONE..............508 636-7740
Paula Wright, *Sales Staff*
William A Wright,
EMP: 12
SALES: 3MM Privately Held
SIC: 3535 Mfg Conveyors

(G-16836)
BUZZARDS BAY BREWING INC
98 Horseneck Rd (02790-1399)
PHONE..............508 636-2288
Robert Russel, *President*
Carol Russel, *Treasurer*
Chris Atkinson, *Director*
Tim Coleman, *Director*
EMP: 9 EST: 1997
SQ FT: 13,251
SALES (est): 979.5K Privately Held
WEB: www.buzzardsbrew.com
SIC: 2082 5149 Mfg Malt Beverages Whol Groceries

(G-16837)
CAMARA METALWORKS
1126 American Legion Hwy (02790-1193)
PHONE..............508 636-7822
P Camara, *Owner*
EMP: 3 EST: 2001
SALES (est): 357.3K Privately Held
SIC: 3599 Mfg Industrial Machinery

(G-16838)
DARTMOUTH AWNING CO INC
Also Called: Bji Enterprises
45 Beeden Rd (02790-1162)
PHONE..............508 636-6838
Brad Gifford, *President*
EMP: 7
SALES: 325K Privately Held
WEB: www.buildtoday.com
SIC: 2394 5999 Mfg Canvas/Related Products Ret Misc Merchandise

(G-16839)
FOUR ELEMENTS SALON & SPA
875 State Rd Unit 2 (02790-2853)
PHONE..............508 672-3111
EMP: 3
SALES (est): 225.7K Privately Held
SIC: 2819 Mfg Industrial Inorganic Chemicals

GEOGRAPHIC

(G-16840)
GRATE PRODUCTS LLC
Also Called: Pioneer Basements
31 Sanford Rd (02790-3502)
PHONE..................................800 649-6140
Stephen F Andras, *Mng Member*
Deice Andras,
EMP: 6
SALES (est): 1MM **Privately Held**
SIC: 2899 Mfg Chemical Preparations

(G-16841)
HOWARTH SPECIALTY COMPANY
Also Called: Howarth Bkkping Income Tax Svc
37 E Briggs Rd (02790-2901)
PHONE..................................508 674-8950
Fax: 508 675-0020
EMP: 3
SALES (est): 140K **Privately Held**
SIC: 2759 7291 Commercial Printing Tax Return Preparation Services

(G-16842)
JR & SONS CONSTRUCTION
17 Sodom Rd (02790-4944)
PHONE..................................508 326-7884
Giovencio Reposo, *Owner*
EMP: 5
SALES (est): 350K **Privately Held**
SIC: 2951 Mfg Asphalt Mixtures/Blocks

(G-16843)
MARTINS CHEESE CO INC
221 Sodom Rd (02790-4926)
PHONE..................................508 636-2357
David Martin, *Owner*
EMP: 6
SQ FT: 1,500
SALES (est): 366.2K **Privately Held**
SIC: 2022 Mfg Cheese

(G-16844)
NEW ENGLAND ALPACA FIBER POOL
645 Sanford Rd (02790-4019)
P.O. Box 1398 (02790-0605)
PHONE..................................508 672-6032
Christopher Riley, *President*
EMP: 3
SALES (est): 388.3K **Privately Held**
SIC: 3559 Mfg Misc Industry Machinery

(G-16845)
PRECISION HANDLING DEVICES (PA)
Also Called: Silver Eagle
758b State Rd (02790-2838)
PHONE..................................508 679-5282
John D Hubbard II, *President*
Edward Viner, *Principal*
Gerald Hubbard, *Vice Pres*
Debbie Mickle, *Purch Mgr*
EMP: 10
SQ FT: 12,000
SALES (est): 721.1K **Privately Held**
WEB: www.precision-handling.com
SIC: 3577 8711 3951 3535 Mfg Computer Peripherals Engineering Services Mfg Pens/Mechncl Pencils Mfg Conveyors/Equipment

(G-16846)
SILVA WOODWORKING
337 American Legion Hwy (02790-4127)
PHONE..................................508 636-0059
Joe Silva, *Owner*
EMP: 4
SALES (est): 484.4K **Privately Held**
SIC: 2431 Mfg Millwork

(G-16847)
SMITHS MEDICAL ASD INC
47 Fallon Dr (02790-1208)
PHONE..................................508 636-6909
Luke Almeida, *Branch Mgr*
EMP: 3
SALES (corp-wide): 3.1B **Privately Held**
SIC: 3841 Mfg Surgical/Medical Instruments
HQ: Smiths Medical Asd, Inc.
6000 Nathan Ln N Ste 100
Plymouth MN 55442
763 383-3000

(G-16848)
SOUTHCOAST STONEWORKS INC
875 State Rd Unit 9 (02790-2853)
PHONE..................................774 319-5200
EMP: 15
SALES (est): 1MM **Privately Held**
SIC: 1411 Dimension Stone Quarry

(G-16849)
TRUE GRIT ABRASIVE INC
46 Westlook Ln (02790-1400)
PHONE..................................508 636-2008
Barbara Lizotte, *President*
Thomas Lizotte, *Vice Pres*
EMP: 10
SQ FT: 14,000
SALES (est): 1.3MM **Privately Held**
SIC: 3291 Mfg Abrasive Products

(G-16850)
VILLAGE SPORTS
737 State Rd (02790-2829)
PHONE..................................508 672-4284
Carol Oliver, *Principal*
EMP: 6
SALES (est): 476.3K **Privately Held**
SIC: 3949 Mfg Sporting/Athletic Goods

(G-16851)
WESTPORT ENVMTL SYSTEMS LP
251 Forge Rd (02790-5216)
PHONE..................................508 636-8811
Jean Hoyt Olinger, *Ch of Bd*
John Olinger, *President*
EMP: 65
SQ FT: 87,500
SALES (est): 6.7MM **Privately Held**
SIC: 3564 3556 Mfg Blowers/Fans Mfg Food Products Machinery

(G-16852)
WILLIAM MCCASKIE INC
197 Forge Rd (02790-1141)
PHONE..................................508 636-8845
Andrew J Bolton, *President*
David Bolton, *Treasurer*
▲ **EMP:** 8
SQ FT: 28,000
SALES (est): 1.7MM **Privately Held**
WEB: www.mccaskiereels.com
SIC: 3499 Mfg Metal Reels & Cable

(G-16853)
ZIBRA CORPORATION
640 American Legion Hwy (02790-4107)
PHONE..................................508 636-6606
Art Mc Kinley, *President*
EMP: 10
SQ FT: 4,200
SALES (est): 2MM **Privately Held**
WEB: www.zibracorp.com
SIC: 3827 Mfg Borescopes For Medical Applications

Westport Point
Bristol County

(G-16854)
F L TRIPP & SONS INC
Cherry & Webb Ln (02791)
P.O. Box 23 (02791-0023)
PHONE..................................508 636-4058
Richard Gemma, *President*
Carl Tripp, *President*
Harold F Tripp, *Vice Pres*
Rick Gemma, *Controller*
Russell M Tripp, *Clerk*
EMP: 20 **EST:** 1922
SQ FT: 3,150
SALES: 2.2MM **Privately Held**
WEB: www.fltripp.com
SIC: 3731 5551 4493 Shipbuilding/Repairing Ret Boats Marina Operation

Westwood
Norfolk County

(G-16855)
270 UNIVERSITY AVE LLC
270 University Ave (02090-2309)
PHONE..................................781 407-0836
Angela Pacini Fiori, *Principal*
EMP: 3
SALES (est): 138.9K **Privately Held**
SIC: 3281 Mfg Cut Stone/Products

(G-16856)
ABTELUM BIOMEDICAL INC
175 Briar Ln (02090-3410)
PHONE..................................781 367-1696
Nelson Ruiz-Opazo, *President*
Victoria Herrera, *COO*
Francis Carr, *Admin Sec*
EMP: 4
SALES (est): 171.3K **Privately Held**
SIC: 2834 Mfg Pharmaceutical Preparations

(G-16857)
ADE TECHNOLOGIES INC (HQ)
80 Wilson Way (02090-1806)
PHONE..................................781 467-3500
Robert C Abbe, *President*
Stephen Mac Leod, *Electrical Engi*
▲ **EMP:** 70
SALES (est): 5.9MM
SALES (corp-wide): 4.5B **Publicly Held**
SIC: 3829 3545 Mfg Measuring/Controlling Devices Mfg Machine Tool Accessories
PA: Kla Corporation
1 Technology Dr
Milpitas CA 95035
408 875-3000

(G-16858)
BLACK & DECKER (US) INC
377 University Ave (02090-2300)
PHONE..................................781 329-3407
Heidi Heiland, *VP Human Res*
Tom Celluci, *Manager*
EMP: 7
SALES (corp-wide): 13.9B **Publicly Held**
WEB: www.dewalt.com
SIC: 3546 Mfg Power-Driven Handtools
HQ: Black & Decker (U.S.) Inc.
1000 Stanley Dr
New Britain CT 06053
860 225-5111

(G-16859)
CAMBRIDGE SOUNDWORKS INC
Also Called: Warehouse
26 Dartmouth St (02090-2301)
PHONE..................................781 329-2777
Mike Mahoney, *Manager*
EMP: 4
SALES (corp-wide): 54.9MM **Privately Held**
WEB: www.clubhifi.com
SIC: 3651 Mfg Home Audio/Video Equipment
HQ: Cambridge Soundworks, Inc.
1630 Cimarron Plz
Stillwater OK 74075
405 742-6704

(G-16860)
CHASE CORP INC
295 University Ave (02090-2315)
PHONE..................................781 332-0700
Terry Jones, *Principal*
Jim Grady, *Production*
Lauren Fisher, *Buyer*
Luzmabel Ramirez, *Buyer*
Jeffrey Sargeant, *Research*
EMP: 6
SALES (est): 1.1MM **Privately Held**
SIC: 3644 3479 Mfg Nonconductive Wiring Devices Coating/Engraving Service

(G-16861)
CHASE CORPORATION (PA)
295 University Ave (02090-2315)
PHONE..................................781 332-0700
Peter R Chase, *Ch of Bd*
Adam P Chase, *President*
Jim Grady, *Production*
Luzmabel Ramirez, *Buyer*
Ken Dalton, *Purchasing*
EMP: 8 **EST:** 1946
SQ FT: 20,200
SALES: 281.3MM **Publicly Held**
WEB: www.chasecorp.com
SIC: 3644 3479 3672 Mfg Insulating Materials

(G-16862)
CHASE CORPORATION
Also Called: Chase Construction
295 University Ave (02090-2315)
PHONE..................................781 329-3259
Joel Dzekciorius, *Branch Mgr*
Steven Quinn, *Manager*
EMP: 12
SALES (corp-wide): 281.3MM **Publicly Held**
WEB: www.chasecorp.com
SIC: 3644 3479 3672 Mfg Nonconductive Wiring Devices Coating/Engraving Service Mfg Printed Circuit Boards
PA: Chase Corporation
295 University Ave
Westwood MA 02090
781 332-0700

(G-16863)
CHASE SPECIALITY COATING
295 University Ave (02090-2315)
PHONE..................................781 332-0700
Adam P Chase, *CEO*
EMP: 15 **EST:** 2016
SALES (est): 57.1K **Privately Held**
SIC: 2851 Mfg Paints/Allied Products

(G-16864)
DAWSON FORTE LLP
Also Called: Kinross Cashmere
47 Harvard St (02090)
PHONE..................................781 467-0170
Forte Dawson, *Branch Mgr*
EMP: 3
SALES (corp-wide): 7.5MM **Privately Held**
SIC: 2221 Manmade Broadwoven Fabric Mill
HQ: Dawson Forte, Llp
40 Shawmut Rd
Canton MA 02021
508 651-7910

(G-16865)
EPIDEMIC SOLUTIONS INC
7 Youngs Rd (02090-3024)
PHONE..................................504 722-3818
Joseph Insler, *President*
Ajoy Basu, *Vice Pres*
John Moustoukas, *Treasurer*
Michael Gilbert, *Director*
Scott Weiner, *Admin Sec*
EMP: 5
SQ FT: 1,500
SALES (est): 198.4K **Privately Held**
SIC: 3845 Electromedical Equipment

(G-16866)
GARY KELLNER
Also Called: Harvard Environmental Services
524 High St (02090-1606)
P.O. Box 2547 (02090-7547)
PHONE..................................781 329-0404
Gary Kellner, *Owner*
EMP: 3
SALES (est): 241.5K **Privately Held**
SIC: 3369 1799 Nonferrous Metal Foundry Trade Contractor

(G-16867)
GROZIER TECHNICAL SYSTEMS INC
11 Stanford Dr (02090-3317)
PHONE..................................781 762-4446
Richard Cann, *President*
EMP: 3
SALES (est): 259.6K **Privately Held**
WEB: www.grozier.com
SIC: 3829 Mfg Measuring/Controlling Devices

(G-16868)
HEARTLANDER SURGICAL INC
90 Wildwood Dr (02090-2735)
PHONE..................................781 320-9601
Paul Cashman, *Vice Pres*
EMP: 3
SALES (est): 185.5K **Privately Held**
SIC: 3845 Mfg Electromedical Equipment

(G-16869)
IDEX MPT INC (HQ)
Also Called: Fitzpatrick Company, The
90 Glacier Dr Ste 1000 (02090-1818)
PHONE..................................630 530-3333
Andrew Milner, *President*
Jerry Cain, *Engineer*
◆ **EMP:** 100 **EST:** 1912
SALES (est): 22.4MM
SALES (corp-wide): 2.4B **Publicly Held**
WEB: www.fitzmill.com
SIC: 3547 Mfg Rolling Mill Machinery
PA: Idex Corporation
1925 W Field Ct Ste 200
Lake Forest IL 60045
847 498-7070

(G-16870)
INEOQUEST TECHNOLOGIES INC (PA)
247 Station Dr Ste Ne2 (02090-2397)
PHONE..................................508 339-2497
Peter Dawson, *Ch of Bd*
Calvin Harrison, *President*
Ken Badeau, *Mfg Mgr*
Michelle Dickinson, *Opers Staff*
JD Doyle, *VP Engrg*
EMP: 109 **EST:** 2001
SALES (est): 25.5MM **Privately Held**
WEB: www.ineoquest.com
SIC: 3825 Mfg Electrical Measuring Instruments

(G-16871)
KLA CORPORATION
60 Glacier Dr Ste 4000 (02090-1800)
PHONE..................................978 843-7670
David Barnett, *Production*
Paul Sliney, *Branch Mgr*
EMP: 65
SALES (corp-wide): 4.5B **Publicly Held**
SIC: 3827 Mfg Optical Instruments/Lenses
PA: Kla Corporation
1 Technology Dr
Milpitas CA 95035
408 875-3000

(G-16872)
MEDICAL INFORMATION TECH INC (PA)
Meditech Cir (02090)
PHONE..................................781 821-3000
Lawrence A Polimeno, *Vice Ch Bd*
Howard Messing, *President*
Rich Caporale, *Regional Mgr*
Steve Devine, *Regional Mgr*
Robert Duquette, *Regional Mgr*
EMP: 148
SALES: 488.1MM **Privately Held**
WEB: www.meditech.com
SIC: 7372 Prepackaged Software Services

(G-16873)
MICROFLUIDICS INTL CORP
90 Glacier Dr Ste 1000 (02090-1818)
PHONE..................................617 969-5452
James N Little, *President*
EMP: 28
SALES (est): 9.1MM
SALES (corp-wide): 2.4B **Publicly Held**
WEB: www.mficcorp.com
SIC: 3559 3821 Mfg Misc Industry Machinery Mfg Lab Apparatus/Furniture
PA: Idex Corporation
1925 W Field Ct Ste 200
Lake Forest IL 60045
847 498-7070

(G-16874)
ROMANOW INC (PA)
Also Called: Romanow Container
346 University Ave (02090-2309)
PHONE..................................781 320-9200
Theodore Romanow, *President*
Kenneth Lozano, *President*
Dick Romanow, *Exec VP*
Randal S Noller, *Opers Staff*
Richard C Romanow, *Treasurer*
EMP: 120
SQ FT: 145,000
SALES (est): 22MM **Privately Held**
SIC: 2653 Mfg Corrugated/Solid Fiber Boxes

(G-16875)
ROMANOW PACKAGING LLC
Also Called: Perry Packaging
346 University Ave (02090-2309)
PHONE..................................781 320-8309
Ted Romanow, *President*
EMP: 126
SALES (est): 19.1MM
SALES (corp-wide): 22MM **Privately Held**
SIC: 2653 Mfg Corrugated Boxes
PA: Romanow, Inc.
346 University Ave
Westwood MA 02090
781 320-9200

(G-16876)
SURGICAL SPECIALTIES CORP (HQ)
Also Called: Angiotech
247 Station Dr Ste Ne1 (02090-2397)
PHONE..................................781 751-1000
Dan Croteau, *CEO*
Victor Diaz, *President*
Daniel J Sutherby, *CFO*
Mark Wagner, *Marketing Staff*
Day Dent, *Admin Sec*
EMP: 200 **EST:** 1996
SQ FT: 22,000
SALES (est): 67.3MM
SALES (corp-wide): 278.3MM **Privately Held**
WEB: www.sharpoint.com
SIC: 3842 3841 Mfg Surgical Appliances/Supplies Mfg Surgical/Medical Instruments
PA: Angiotech Pharmaceuticals, Inc
355 Burrard St Suite 1100
Vancouver BC V6C 2
604 221-7676

(G-16877)
SWAMPSCOTT FUEL INC
69 Peartree Dr (02090-2122)
PHONE..................................781 251-0993
Richard Elkhoury, *Principal*
EMP: 3
SALES (est): 130.4K **Privately Held**
SIC: 2869 Mfg Industrial Organic Chemicals

(G-16878)
T S X PRODUCTS CORPORATION
100 Lowder Brook Dr # 2500 (02090-1185)
PHONE..................................781 769-1800
David Vogel, *President*
EMP: 3
SALES (est): 249.8K **Privately Held**
SIC: 3661 Mfg Telecommunication Equipment

(G-16879)
TAPECOAT COMPANY
295 University Ave (02090-2315)
PHONE..................................781 332-0700
Peter R Chase, *Principal*
EMP: 3 **EST:** 2013
SALES (est): 329.9K **Privately Held**
SIC: 2821 Mfg Plastic Materials/Resins

(G-16880)
UNIVERSAL WILDE INC (PA)
26 Dartmouth St Ste 1 (02090-2332)
PHONE..................................781 251-2700
William Fitzgerald, *CEO*
Matt Holden, *President*
John Sisson, *President*
Tome Andrade, *Partner*
Bill Fitzgerald, *Principal*
▲ **EMP:** 150
SQ FT: 190,000
SALES (est): 243.4MM **Privately Held**
WEB: www.mgraphics.net
SIC: 2752 Lithographic Commercial Printing

(G-16881)
UNIVERSAL WILDE INC
Also Called: Acme Printing
26 Dartmouth St Ste 1 (02090-2332)
PHONE..................................978 658-0800
Patrick Romich, *CEO*
Kevin Buckley, *Sales Staff*
EMP: 146 **Privately Held**
SIC: 2752 2791 2789 Lithographic Commercial Printing Typesetting Services Bookbinding/Related Work
PA: Universal Wilde, Inc.
26 Dartmouth St Ste 1
Westwood MA 02090

(G-16882)
WESTWOOD YOUTH SOFTBALL INC
6 Winter Ter (02090-2927)
P.O. Box 202 (02090-0202)
PHONE..................................781 762-5185
Steve Goodrich, *Principal*
EMP: 4 **EST:** 2012
SALES (est): 254.4K **Privately Held**
SIC: 2869 Mfg Industrial Organic Chemicals

Weymouth
Norfolk County

(G-16883)
ADVANCED FRP SYSTEMS INC
106 Finnell Dr Ste 13 (02188-1114)
P.O. Box 1259, Plymouth (02362-1259)
PHONE..................................508 927-6915
Russell Esker Giudici, *President*
Peter Krukiel, *Treasurer*
EMP: 7
SQ FT: 5,000
SALES: 900K **Privately Held**
SIC: 2822 5198 Mfg Synthetic Rubber Whol Paints/Varnishes

(G-16884)
ATLANTIC TOOL COMPANY
18 Station St (02189-2208)
P.O. Box 890129 (02189-0003)
PHONE..................................781 331-5550
Joseph Wilson, *Owner*
EMP: 4
SALES (est): 290.3K **Privately Held**
SIC: 3599 Mfg Industrial Machinery

(G-16885)
BARREL HOUSE Z LLC
95 Woodrock Rd (02189-2335)
PHONE..................................339 207-7888
Russ Heissner, *Principal*
Mary Heissner, *Marketing Staff*
EMP: 3 **EST:** 2015
SALES (est): 135K **Privately Held**
SIC: 2082 Mfg Malt Beverages

(G-16886)
BRADY ENTERPRISES INC
45 Finnell Dr (02188-1110)
PHONE..................................781 337-7057
Marcio Bradley, *Branch Mgr*
EMP: 13
SALES (corp-wide): 21.1MM **Privately Held**
SIC: 2099 Mfg Food Preparations
PA: Brady Enterprises, Inc.
167 Moore Rd
East Weymouth MA 02189
781 682-6280

(G-16887)
ELECTRO SWITCH CORP
180 King Ave (02188-2927)
PHONE..................................781 607-3306
Sean Bell, *Engineer*
Anh Le, *Engineer*
Daniel Menard, *Engineer*
Erik Merck, *Engineer*
Paco Mowrey, *Engineer*
EMP: 175
SALES (corp-wide): 88.3MM **Privately Held**
WEB: www.electroswitch.com
SIC: 3613 3643 3625 3621 Mfg Switchgear/Boards Mfg Conductive Wire Dvcs Mfg Relay/Indstl Control Mfg Motors/Generators
HQ: Electro Switch Corp.
775 Pleasant St Ste 1
Weymouth MA 02189
781 335-1195

(G-16888)
ELERTS CORPORATION
1132 Main St Ste 300 (02190-1511)
PHONE..................................781 803-6362
Edward English, *CEO*
Delores Byrne, *Business Mgr*
Brad Anderson, *Vice Pres*
Christopher Russo, *Vice Pres*
Jeannie Andrews, *Sales Associate*
EMP: 15 **EST:** 2010
SALES (est): 1.3MM **Privately Held**
SIC: 7372 Prepackaged Software

(G-16889)
GATEHOUSE MEDIA MASS I INC
91 Washington St (02188-1702)
PHONE..................................781 682-4850
Cathy Conley, *Manager*
EMP: 4
SALES (corp-wide): 1.5B **Publicly Held**
SIC: 2711 Newspapers-Publishing/Printing
HQ: Gatehouse Media Massachusetts I, Inc.
48 Dunham Rd
Beverly MA 01915
585 598-0030

(G-16890)
INFORS USA INC
25 Mathewson Dr (02189-2345)
PHONE..................................781 335-3108
EMP: 3
SALES (est): 187K
SALES (corp-wide): 15.2MM **Privately Held**
SIC: 3821 Mfg Lab Apparatus/Furniture
HQ: Infors Usa Inc.
9070 Junction Dr Ste D
Annapolis Junction MD 20701
410 792-8007

(G-16891)
INFOTRENDS RESEARCH GROUP
Also Called: Infotrends Cap Ventures
97 Libbey Industrial Pkwy # 300 (02189-3110)
PHONE..................................781 616-2100
EMP: 25
SALES (est): 2.1MM
SALES (corp-wide): 57.3MM **Privately Held**
SIC: 3721 Mfg Aircraft
HQ: Infotrends, Inc.
97 Libbey Industrial Pkwy # 300
Weymouth MA 02189
781 616-2100

(G-16892)
INNOVATIVE MEDIA GROUP INC
Also Called: Signature Graphics & Signs
36 Finnell Dr Ste 3 (02188-1106)
PHONE..................................781 335-8773
Kathleen E Ready, *President*
Kathleen Ready, *Owner*
Richard Ready, *Treasurer*
EMP: 13
SQ FT: 1,800
SALES (est): 1.5MM **Privately Held**
SIC: 3993 Mfg Signs/Advertising Specialties

(G-16893)
MILLENNIUM PRINTING CORP
317 Libbey Pkwy (02189-3113)
PHONE..................................781 337-0002
Denise S Connors, *President*
Bill Crabtree, *Accounts Exec*
EMP: 6
SQ FT: 2,400
SALES (est): 1.8MM **Privately Held**
WEB: www.mpc02188.com
SIC: 2752 Lithographic Commercial Printing

(G-16894)
MOONEYTUNCO INC
Also Called: Merry Christmas From Heaven
65 Mathewson Dr Ste C (02189-2347)
PHONE....................................781 331-4445
John Mooney, *President*
EMP: 7
SALES (corp-wide): 1.9MM **Privately Held**
SIC: 3999 5199 Mfg Misc Products Whol Nondurable Goods
PA: Mooneytunco, Inc.
1023 Washington St
Weymouth MA 02189
781 331-5308

(G-16895)
NE STAINLESS STEEL FAB
86 Finnell Dr Ste 23 (02188-1100)
PHONE....................................781 335-0121
Jean Barry, *General Mgr*
Ed Travis, *Engineer*
EMP: 8 **EST:** 2010
SALES (est): 730K **Privately Held**
SIC: 3312 Blast Furnace-Steel Works

(G-16896)
PAUL M DEPALMA FUEL LLC
41 Cranberry Rd (02188-2710)
PHONE....................................781 812-0156
Paul M Depalma, *Principal*
EMP: 4 **EST:** 2012
SALES (est): 203.3K **Privately Held**
SIC: 2869 Mfg Industrial Organic Chemicals

(G-16897)
PIVOTAL AERO WIND TURBINES INC
555 Bridge St (02191-1825)
PHONE....................................781 803-2982
Johann Q Sammy, *President*
EMP: 4
SALES (est): 258.5K **Privately Held**
SIC: 3511 Mfg Turbines/Generator Sets

(G-16898)
PREMIER SERVICES INC
Also Called: Keezer Sportswear
106 Finnell Dr Ste 5 (02188-1114)
PHONE....................................781 335-9305
Robert Keezer, *President*
EMP: 4
SQ FT: 3,000
SALES (est): 502.8K **Privately Held**
WEB: www.keezersportswear.com
SIC: 2395 Imprint And Embroidery Apparel

(G-16899)
PYRAMID PRINTING AND ADVG INC
Also Called: Pyramid Printing and Digital
54 Mathewson Dr 60 (02189-2346)
PHONE....................................781 337-7609
Ronald Ciccolo, *President*
EMP: 22 **EST:** 1976
SQ FT: 15,000
SALES (est): 3.5MM **Privately Held**
WEB: www.pyramidprinting.net
SIC: 2752 2791 2789 Lithographic Commercial Printing Typesetting Services Bookbinding/Related Work

(G-16900)
QUAD/GRAPHICS INC
370 Libbey Industri (02189-3119)
PHONE....................................781 917-1601
Cameron Paul, *Manager*
EMP: 509
SALES (corp-wide): 4.1B **Publicly Held**
SIC: 2752 Lithographic Commercial Printing
PA: Quad/Graphics Inc.
N61w23044 Harrys Way
Sussex WI 53089
414 566-6000

(G-16901)
STAR LITHO INC
360 Libbey Indus Pkwy (02189-3133)
PHONE....................................781 340-9401
Ernest Chekoulias, *President*
Scott Chekoulias, *Treasurer*
Dorothy Chekoulias, *Clerk*
EMP: 25
SALES (est): 4.5MM **Privately Held**
SIC: 2752 Lithographic Commercial Printing

(G-16902)
TIEN VO CORP
311 North St (02191-1335)
PHONE....................................781 340-7245
EMP: 3
SALES (est): 174.5K **Privately Held**
SIC: 3356 Nonferrous Rolling/Drawing

(G-16903)
VERIFACTS
1285 Washington St Ste 1 (02189-2397)
PHONE....................................781 337-1717
EMP: 3
SALES (est): 175.3K **Privately Held**
SIC: 2721 Periodicals-Publishing/Printing

(G-16904)
WORLD NEWS FIRM INC
87 Knollwood Cir (02188-2210)
PHONE....................................781 335-0113
Patrick M O'Connor, *President*
EMP: 3
SALES (est): 167.9K **Privately Held**
SIC: 2711 Newspapers-Publishing/Printing

Whately
Franklin County

(G-16905)
G AND W PRECISION INC
199 Long Plain Rd C (01093-9703)
P.O. Box 203 (01093-0203)
PHONE....................................413 665-0983
Gary Stone, *President*
Walter Kellogg, *Treasurer*
EMP: 6
SQ FT: 4,500
SALES (est): 770.9K **Privately Held**
WEB: www.gwprecision.com
SIC: 3089 Mfg Plastic Products

(G-16906)
HI TUNES
Also Called: HI Tune Wax
207 River Rd (01093)
P.O. Box 8, South Deerfield (01373-0008)
PHONE....................................435 962-0405
Gregory Carlson, *Owner*
EMP: 10
SQ FT: 1,000
SALES (est): 250K **Privately Held**
SIC: 2842 Mfg Polish/Sanitation Goods

(G-16907)
NEW ENGLAND BROACH CO INC
199-A Long Plain Rd (01093)
P.O. Box 45 (01093-0045)
PHONE....................................413 665-7064
John Hassay, *President*
Peter McDonough, *Vice Pres*
Michael F Hassay Jr, *Treasurer*
EMP: 10
SQ FT: 9,300
SALES: 830K **Privately Held**
SIC: 3545 Mfg Machine Tool Accessories

Wheelwright
Worcester County

(G-16908)
RAITTO ENGINEERING & MFG INC
36 Mill St (01094-5001)
P.O. Box 125 (01094-0125)
PHONE....................................413 477-6637
Richard H Raitto, *President*
EMP: 5
SQ FT: 30,000
SALES (est): 766.8K **Privately Held**
WEB: www.raitto.com
SIC: 3089 3544 Custom Injection Molding Of Plastics & Mfg Molds

Whitinsville
Worcester County

(G-16909)
A S A P ENGRAVERS
211 Mason Rd (01588-1326)
PHONE....................................508 234-6974
Ray Jolie, *Owner*
EMP: 3 **EST:** 1985
SALES (est): 208.8K **Privately Held**
SIC: 3479 Coating/Engraving Service

(G-16910)
ALLEN-BAILEY TAG & LABEL INC
100 Main St Ste 103 (01588-2246)
PHONE....................................585 538-2324
Dick Manderville, *Manager*
EMP: 28
SALES (corp-wide): 16MM **Privately Held**
WEB: www.abtl.com
SIC: 2679 2672 2671 Mfg Converted Paper Prdt Mfg Coat/Laminated Paper Mfg Packaging Paper/Film
PA: Tag Allen-Bailey & Label Inc
716 Match Point Dr # 101
Virginia Beach VA 23462
585 538-2324

(G-16911)
BROZZIAN LLC
5 Sunset Dr (01588-1042)
PHONE....................................774 280-9338
Richard P Bedrosian, *Principal*
EMP: 3
SALES (est): 149.7K **Privately Held**
SIC: 2099 Mfg Food Preparations

(G-16912)
CREIGHTON KAYLA
315 Linwood Ave (01588-2313)
PHONE....................................508 612-0685
Kayla Creighton, *Principal*
EMP: 3 **EST:** 2011
SALES (est): 170.8K **Privately Held**
SIC: 3812 Mfg Search/Navigation Equipment

(G-16913)
HUTCHISON CO ADVG DISPLAY
369 Douglas Rd (01588-2022)
P.O. Box 486 (01588-0486)
PHONE....................................508 234-4681
Euan Hutchison, *Principal*
EMP: 4
SALES (est): 118.4K **Privately Held**
SIC: 3089 Mfg Plastic Products

(G-16914)
INFINITE KNOT LLC
Also Called: Contacts411
466 Carpenter Rd (01588-1346)
P.O. Box 390, Greens Farms CT (06838-0390)
PHONE....................................617 372-0707
Barry Gold, *Principal*
David Spier, *Exec VP*
Karen Sallick,
EMP: 4 **EST:** 2010
SALES (est): 247.1K **Privately Held**
SIC: 7372 7389 Prepackaged Software Services

(G-16915)
IRRIGATION AUTOMTN SYSTMS INC
1 Main St Ste 10 (01588-2201)
P.O. Box 552, Grafton (01519-0552)
PHONE....................................800 549-4551
Brett Niver, *President*
EMP: 3
SALES (est): 640K **Privately Held**
SIC: 3669 3822 Mfg Communications Equipment Mfg Environmental Controls

(G-16916)
LOUD TECHNOLOGIES INC
Eastern Acoustic Works
1 Main St Ste 1 # 1 (01588-2201)
PHONE....................................508 234-6158
Steven Desrosiers, *Engineer*
Frank Loyko, *Branch Mgr*
EMP: 212
SALES (corp-wide): 64.9MM **Privately Held**
SIC: 3651 3663 Mfg Home Audio/Video Eqp
PA: Loud Audio, Llc
16220 Wood Red Rd Ne
Woodinville WA 98072
425 892-6500

(G-16917)
OMNI CONTROL TECHNOLOGY INC
Also Called: Oct
1 Main St Ste 4 (01588-2201)
P.O. Box 444 (01588-0444)
PHONE....................................508 234-9121
Peter J Bedigian, *Principal*
Carol Jessing, *Production*
Daniel Whynot, *Purch Mgr*
Robert Legg, *Engineer*
Gerald Gowdy, *Electrical Engi*
EMP: 40
SQ FT: 7,500
SALES (est): 11MM
SALES (corp-wide): 2.3B **Privately Held**
WEB: www.omnicontroltech.com
SIC: 3625 Mfg Electrical & Electronic Control Equipment Systems
PA: Nibe Industrier Ab
Jarnvagsgatan 40
Markaryd 285 3
433 730-00

(G-16918)
STEVEN SPROTT
121 Cottage St 1 (01588-1460)
PHONE....................................774 276-6534
Steven Sprott, *Principal*
EMP: 3 **EST:** 2018
SALES (est): 106.3K **Privately Held**
SIC: 3621 Mfg Motors/Generators

(G-16919)
TOM BERKOWITZ TRUCKING INC (PA)
279 Douglas Rd (01588-2021)
P.O. Box 90 (01588-0090)
PHONE....................................508 234-2920
Tom Berkowitz, *President*
EMP: 22
SALES (est): 2.5MM **Privately Held**
SIC: 3713 5064 Mfg Truck/Bus Bodies Whol Appliances/Tv/Radio

Whitman
Plymouth County

(G-16920)
B & C TOOLING COMPANY INC
844 Bedford St (02382-1104)
PHONE....................................781 447-5292
John R Barr III, *President*
EMP: 5
SALES: 200K **Privately Held**
SIC: 3599 Mfg Industrial Machinery

(G-16921)
COMPUTRON METAL PRODUCTS INC
66 Pond St (02382-2163)
P.O. Box 167 (02382-0167)
PHONE....................................781 447-2265
Russell J Leone, *President*
Joseph Gillis, *Vice Pres*
EMP: 17
SQ FT: 10,000
SALES (est): 2.5MM **Privately Held**
WEB: www.computronmetal.com
SIC: 3444 Mfg Sheet Metalwork

(G-16922)
DIGITAL IMAGE FIDELITY LLC
25 South Ave (02382-2049)
P.O. Box 473 (02382-0473)
PHONE....................................508 577-8496
Ann M Sabin, *Sales Staff*
John Galvin,
Susan Galvin,
EMP: 3 **EST:** 1997
SALES: 600K **Privately Held**
SIC: 3663 Printing Press Presetting

▲ = Import ▼=Export
◆ =Import/Export

(G-16923)
DIMARK INCORPORATED
Also Called: Precision Machining
205 Commercial St (02382-2401)
P.O. Box 271 (02382-0271)
PHONE..................................781 447-7990
John W Brown, *President*
EMP: 20 **EST:** 1979
SALES (est): 2.9MM **Privately Held**
WEB: www.dimarkprecision.com
SIC: 3444 Sheet Metal Shop

(G-16924)
HARRY B HARDING & SON INC
Also Called: Harding Print
15 Colebrook Blvd (02382-2057)
P.O. Box 293 (02382-0293)
PHONE..................................781 447-3941
John D Campbell, *President*
John Walkey, *Treasurer*
EMP: 4 **EST:** 1891
SQ FT: 10,000
SALES (est): 1MM **Privately Held**
SIC: 2752 Lithographic Commercial Printing

(G-16925)
PRECISION PCB INC (PA)
7 Oakdale Farm Rd (02382-1657)
PHONE..................................781 447-6285
Joseph Drier III, *President*
EMP: 8
SQ FT: 3,400
SALES (est): 780.1K **Privately Held**
SIC: 3674 Mfg Semiconductors/Related Devices

(G-16926)
PRECISION PCB PRODUCTS INC
7 Oakdale Farm Rd (02382-1657)
PHONE..................................508 966-9484
Joseph Drier, *Shareholder*
Joseph Drier III, *Shareholder*
EMP: 8
SALES: 1.8MM **Privately Held**
WEB: www.precisionpcb.com
SIC: 3541 Mfg Machine Tools-Cutting

(G-16927)
R J SHEPHERD CO INC
7 Marble St (02382-2458)
P.O. Box 169 (02382-0169)
PHONE..................................781 447-5768
Terry Frechette, *President*
Paul Luippold, *Manager*
EMP: 3
SQ FT: 4,000
SALES (est): 613.9K **Privately Held**
SIC: 3949 Mfg Sporting/Athletic Goods

(G-16928)
S & T PRECISION PLATE CUTTING
205 Commercial St Rear (02382-2401)
PHONE..................................781 447-1084
Scott Augustson, *President*
EMP: 3 **EST:** 1984
SALES: 675K **Privately Held**
SIC: 3599 Mfg Industrial Machinery

(G-16929)
WATERTOWN ENGINEERING CORP
Also Called: Watertown Cremation Products
1200 Auburn St (02382-1728)
P.O. Box 308 (02382-0308)
PHONE..................................781 857-2555
Domenic Taverna, *President*
Mark Donovan, *President*
▲ **EMP:** 30
SQ FT: 12,000
SALES (est): 5.8MM **Privately Held**
WEB: www.watertownengineering.com
SIC: 3442 3272 Mfg Metal Doors/Sash/Trim Mfg Concrete Products

(G-16930)
WHITMAN CASTINGS INC (PA)
40 Raynor Ave (02382-2123)
P.O. Box 456 (02382-0456)
PHONE..................................781 447-4417
R Brian Ladner, *President*
James T Bruso, *Treasurer*
Francis Ladner, *Admin Sec*
Ronald Ladner, *Admin Sec*
EMP: 26
SQ FT: 40,000
SALES (est): 5.4MM **Privately Held**
WEB: www.whitmancastings.com
SIC: 3321 3542 3369 Gray/Ductile Iron Foundry Mfg Machine Tools-Forming Nonferrous Metal Foundry

(G-16931)
WHITMAN COMPANY INC
356 South Ave Ste 1 (02382-2062)
PHONE..................................781 447-2422
James P Lemonias, *Ch of Bd*
Peter J Lemonias, *President*
EMP: 30 **EST:** 1947
SQ FT: 45,000
SALES (est): 3.8MM **Privately Held**
WEB: www.metalfinishers.com
SIC: 3471 Plating/Polishing Service Plating/Polishing Service

(G-16932)
WHITMAN TOOL AND DIE CO INC
72 Raynor Ave (02382-2123)
P.O. Box 248 (02382-0248)
PHONE..................................781 447-0421
Paul Werthen, *Vice Pres*
Aly Werthen, *Vice Pres*
Steve Semas, *Purch Mgr*
Peter Werthen, *Purchasing*
Thomas Werthen, *Treasurer*
EMP: 33 **EST:** 1949
SQ FT: 31,000
SALES (est): 6.4MM **Privately Held**
WEB: www.whitmantool.com
SIC: 3469 3544 Mfg Metal Stampings Mfg Dies/Tools/Jigs/Fixtures

Wilbraham
Hampden County

(G-16933)
BIMBO BAKERIES USA INC
Also Called: Freihofer's Bakery Outlet
1964 Boston Rd Ste 3 (01095-1055)
PHONE..................................413 543-5328
Lynn Kandrotas, *Manager*
EMP: 5 **Privately Held**
SIC: 2051 Mfg Bread/Related Products
HQ: Bimbo Bakeries Usa, Inc
255 Business Center Dr # 200
Horsham PA 19044
215 347-5500

(G-16934)
CS-MA LLC
Also Called: Construction Service
2420 Boston Rd (01095-1106)
P.O. Box 966 (01095-0966)
PHONE..................................413 733-6631
Shaun P Carroll Jr,
Robert M Carroll,
Deb Spear,
EMP: 49
SQ FT: 800
SALES (est): 10.5MM **Privately Held**
SIC: 3273 Mfg Ready-Mixed Concrete

(G-16935)
DAUPHINAIS & SON INC
Also Called: Construction Service Division
2420 Boston Rd (01095-1106)
P.O. Box 966 (01095-0966)
PHONE..................................413 596-3964
Vincent Dauphinais, *Ch of Bd*
EMP: 10
SQ FT: 2,000
SALES (est): 1.7MM **Privately Held**
SIC: 3273 5211 5032 1741 Mfg Ready-Mixed Concrete Ret Lumber/Building Mtrl Whol Brick/Stone Matrls Masonry/Stone Contractor

(G-16936)
FLODESIGN SONICS INC
380 Main St (01095-1639)
PHONE..................................413 596-5900
Louis Masi, *CEO*
Stanley Kowalski III, *President*
Jeffery King, *Vice Pres*
Chris Leidel, *VP Opers*
Kathleen Mincieli, *VP Human Res*
EMP: 23
SALES (est): 5.5MM **Privately Held**
SIC: 3589 Mfg Service Industry Machinery

(G-16937)
FRANK L REED INC
Also Called: Utility Mfg Co
2443 Boston Rd (01095-1105)
P.O. Box 758 (01095-0758)
PHONE..................................413 596-3861
Loring Reed, *President*
Jay T Reed, *Vice Pres*
Jeffrey Reed, *Vice Pres*
▲ **EMP:** 20
SQ FT: 40,000
SALES (est): 4.2MM **Privately Held**
WEB: www.utilitymfg.com
SIC: 3315 3351 3496 3316 Mfg Steel Wire/Rltd Prdt Copper Rolling/Drawing Mfg Misc Fab Wire Prdts Mfg Cold-Rolled Steel

(G-16938)
GOOD CAUSE GREETINGS INC
30 W Colonial Rd (01095-2116)
PHONE..................................413 543-1515
Catherine Robbins, *CEO*
Ted Robbins, *Marketing Staff*
EMP: 6
SALES (est): 700K **Privately Held**
WEB: www.goodcausegreetings.com
SIC: 2771 Mfg Greeting Cards

(G-16939)
KEATING WILBERT VAULT COMPANY
1840 Boston Rd (01095-1001)
PHONE..................................413 543-1226
David A Dumala, *President*
EMP: 17 **EST:** 1976
SQ FT: 2,500
SALES (est): 3.2MM **Privately Held**
SIC: 3272 5087 Mfg Concrete Burial Vaults

(G-16940)
MATALLURGICAL PERSPECTIVES
4 Meeting House Ln (01095-1758)
PHONE..................................413 596-4283
James F R Grochmal, *Principal*
EMP: 3
SALES (est): 173K **Privately Held**
SIC: 3089 Mfg Plastic Products

(G-16941)
NORPIN MFG CO INC
2342 Boston Rd (01095-1104)
P.O. Box 1031 (01095-7031)
PHONE..................................413 599-1628
Norman T Pincince, *President*
Kenneth Pincince, *Vice Pres*
Mark Pincince, *Plant Mgr*
EMP: 14
SQ FT: 33,000
SALES (est): 3MM **Privately Held**
WEB: www.norpin.com
SIC: 3469 Mfg Metal Stampings

(G-16942)
OLIVE MANNYS OIL INC
1872 Boston Rd (01095-1003)
PHONE..................................413 233-2532
Barbara J Rovithis, *President*
EMP: 3
SALES (est): 91.3K **Privately Held**
SIC: 2079 Mfg Edible Fats/Oils

(G-16943)
THERMO PRODUCTS
2341 Boston Rd Ste A120b (01095-1367)
PHONE..................................413 279-1980
Robert Paquette, *President*
EMP: 4
SALES (est): 293.7K **Privately Held**
SIC: 3433 Mfg Heating Equipment-Non-electric

(G-16944)
WURSZT INC
2460 Boston Rd (01095-1249)
PHONE..................................413 599-4900
Greg S Wurszt, *Principal*
EMP: 5
SALES (est): 585.7K **Privately Held**
SIC: 3679 Mfg Electronic Components

(G-16945)
YANKEE ELECTRICAL MFG CO
600 Main St (01095-1611)
PHONE..................................413 596-8256
Alfred E Carpluk, *President*
Stephen Carpluk, *Vice Pres*
Stuart Carpluk, *Vice Pres*
Dolores Carpluk, *Treasurer*
EMP: 9
SQ FT: 30,000
SALES (est): 1MM **Privately Held**
SIC: 3674 Mfg Of Solid State Electronic Devices

Williamsburg
Hampshire County

(G-16946)
ACHESON COMPANY LLC
Also Called: Acheson Properties
6 Main St (01096)
PHONE..................................413 268-0246
EMP: 6 **EST:** 2007
SALES: 150K **Privately Held**
SIC: 1389 Oil/Gas Field Services

(G-16947)
BREWMASTERS BREWING SVCS LLC
4 Main St (01096-9428)
PHONE..................................413 268-2199
Dennis Michael Bates Jr,
Michael Gifford Charpentier,
EMP: 6
SALES (est): 185.1K **Privately Held**
SIC: 2082 Mfg Malt Beverages

(G-16948)
CJ SPRONG & CO INC
Also Called: C S Sprong & Co
1679 West Rd (01096-9745)
PHONE..................................413 628-4410
Constance Sprong, *President*
EMP: 5
SQ FT: 3,596
SALES (est): 540K **Privately Held**
WEB: www.cjsprong.com
SIC: 2519 5712 Mfg Household Furniture Ret Furniture

(G-16949)
CONWAY PALLET INC
270 Williamsburg Rd (01096-9740)
PHONE..................................413 268-3343
Harry A Culver, *President*
Bruce Culver, *Vice Pres*
Dana Culver, *Vice Pres*
EMP: 10
SALES (est): 690K **Privately Held**
SIC: 2448 Mfg Pallets & Skids

(G-16950)
DUFRESNES SUGAR HOUSE
113 Goshen Rd (01096-9733)
PHONE..................................413 268-7509
Keith Dufresne, *Principal*
EMP: 5
SALES (est): 422.6K **Privately Held**
SIC: 2099 Mfg Food Preparations

(G-16951)
JON GOODMAN
Also Called: Jon Goodman Photogravure
102 Petticoat Hill Rd (01096-9433)
PHONE..................................413 586-9650
Jon Goodman, *Owner*
EMP: 3
SALES: 180K **Privately Held**
SIC: 2754 Gravure Commercial Printing

(G-16952)
LASHWAY LOGGING INC
Also Called: Lashway Firewood Co
67 Main St (01096-9404)
P.O. Box 231 (01096-0231)
PHONE..................................413 268-3600
William J Lashway Jr, *President*
Bryan Lashway, *Vice Pres*
Lance Lashway, *Vice Pres*
Lee H Lashway, *Treasurer*

GEOGRAPHIC

EMP: 19 **EST:** 1965
SQ FT: 15,000
SALES: 20MM **Privately Held**
SIC: 2421 2499 2411 Sawmill/Planing Mill Mfg Wood Products Logging

(G-16953)
WILLIAMSBURG BLACKSMITHS INC
26 Williams St (01096-9427)
PHONE..................................413 268-7341
Elizabeth Tiley, *President*
EMP: 5
SQ FT: 8,000
SALES (est): 450K **Privately Held**
WEB: www.williamsburgblacksmiths.com
SIC: 3429 Mfg Household Hardware

Williamstown
Berkshire County

(G-16954)
BANCROFT CUSTOM WOODWORKS
3223 Hancock Rd (01267-9710)
PHONE..................................413 738-7001
Peter Gagliardi, *Principal*
EMP: 5
SALES (est): 558.3K **Privately Held**
SIC: 2431 Mfg Millwork

(G-16955)
BIOMASS COMMODITIES CORP
227 Adams Rd (01267-3233)
PHONE..................................413 458-5326
Averill Cook, *President*
Melisa Selgwerth, *Treasurer*
Carol Corrigan, *Admin Sec*
EMP: 5
SQ FT: 5,000
SALES: 800K **Privately Held**
SIC: 3826 Mfg Analytical Instruments

(G-16956)
BROUDE INTERNATIONAL EDITIONS
141 White Oaks Rd (01267-2291)
P.O. Box 547 (01267-0547)
PHONE..................................413 458-8131
Gwen Broude, *President*
Paul Opel, *Principal*
Ronald Broude, *Vice Pres*
▲ **EMP:** 3
SALES (est): 113.6K **Privately Held**
SIC: 2741 Publisher Of Music Books On Music & Other Publications

(G-16957)
JF GRIFFIN PUBLISHING LLC
148 Main St (01267-2604)
PHONE..................................413 458-4800
Stephen Statham, *Publisher*
Eli Garnish, *Editor*
Jeremy Garnish, *Prdtn Mgr*
Chris Sobolowski, *Art Dir*
Andrew T Kelly,
EMP: 6
SALES (est): 869.9K **Privately Held**
SIC: 2741 Misc Publishing

(G-16958)
MCCLELLAND PRESS INC (PA)
Also Called: Elder Printing & Supply Co Div
103 North St (01267-2042)
P.O. Box 485 (01267-0485)
PHONE..................................413 663-5750
John Elder, *President*
William Elder, *Treasurer*
William E Elder, *Treasurer*
EMP: 18
SQ FT: 10,000
SALES (est): 2.1MM **Privately Held**
SIC: 2752 5943 5947 5999 Offset Printing As Well As Retails Office Forms Office Supplies Greeting Cards Gifts Stationery And Business Machines

(G-16959)
PRINT SHOP
30 Spring St (01267-2853)
PHONE..................................413 458-6039
Elinor Goodwin, *Principal*
EMP: 3
SALES (est): 180K **Privately Held**
SIC: 2759 Lithographic Commercial Printing

(G-16960)
SHADOWBROOK CUSTOM CABINETRY
62 Stratton Rd (01267-2943)
PHONE..................................413 664-9590
Jeremy Broadwell, *Owner*
EMP: 4
SALES (est): 200.7K **Privately Held**
SIC: 2434 Mfg Wood Kitchen Cabinets

(G-16961)
STEINERFILM INC
Also Called: Steinerfilm USA
987 Simonds Rd (01267-2197)
PHONE..................................413 458-9525
Else Steiner, *Principal*
Robert C Rives, *Admin Sec*
▲ **EMP:** 160
SQ FT: 198,900
SALES (est): 26MM **Privately Held**
WEB: www.steinerfilm.com
SIC: 3675 Mfg Electronic Capacitors

Wilmington
Middlesex County

(G-16962)
ACCELLENT HOLDINGS CORP
100 Fordham Rd (01887-2168)
PHONE..................................978 570-6900
Ron Sparks, *President*
Stewart Fisher, *CFO*
EMP: 3667
SQ FT: 3,000
SALES (est): 182.1MM **Privately Held**
SIC: 3841 3679 3315 3552 Mfg Surgical/Med Instr Mfg Elec Components Mfg Steel Wire/Rltd Prdt Mfg Textile Machinery Mfg Steel Pipe/Tubes

(G-16963)
ACCELLENT LLC (DH)
Also Called: Lake Region Medical
100 Fordham Rd Bldg C (01887-2168)
PHONE..................................978 570-6900
Robert E Kirby, *President*
Franco Torres, *Engineer*
Jeremy A Friedman, *CFO*
Moises Hernandez, *Technology*
▲ **EMP:** 200
SALES (est): 343.4MM
SALES (corp-wide): 1.2B **Publicly Held**
SIC: 3841 8711 Mfg Surgical/Medical Instruments Engineering Services

(G-16964)
ACCU PACKAGING INC
210 Andover St Ste 3 (01887-1229)
PHONE..................................978 447-5590
Richard Harris, *President*
Kerry Bolis, *Finance Mgr*
EMP: 6
SALES (est): 874.9K **Privately Held**
WEB: www.accu-packaging.com
SIC: 2671 Custom Packaging Of Resin Systems

(G-16965)
ADA FABRICATORS INC
323 Andover St Ste 3 (01887-1035)
P.O. Box 179, North Billerica (01862-0179)
PHONE..................................978 262-9900
John P Flaherty, *President*
William Scott Ober, *Vice Pres*
EMP: 20
SQ FT: 25,000
SALES (est): 3.6MM **Privately Held**
SIC: 3537 1542 Mfg Industrial Trucks/Tractors Nonresidential Construction

(G-16966)
ADVANCED IMAGING INC
234 Ballardvale St (01887-1054)
PHONE..................................978 658-7776
John Macnamara, *President*
Patricia Phipps, *Info Tech Mgr*
EMP: 28
SQ FT: 20,000
SALES: 4.5MM **Privately Held**
WEB: www.advdigital.com
SIC: 2759 Commercial Printing

(G-16967)
ADVANSOURCE BIOMATERIALS CORP
Also Called: Chronoflex
229 Andover St (01887-1088)
PHONE..................................978 657-0075
▲ **EMP:** 11
SQ FT: 26,000
SALES: 3.3MM **Privately Held**
WEB: www.cardiotech-inc.com
SIC: 3841 Mfg Surgical & Medical Instruments

(G-16968)
AERIAL ACOUSTICS CORPORATION
100 Research Dr Ste 4 (01887-4406)
PHONE..................................978 988-1600
Michael Kelly, *President*
David Marshall, *Vice Pres*
▲ **EMP:** 10
SQ FT: 10,000
SALES (est): 1.7MM **Privately Held**
WEB: www.aerialacoustics.com
SIC: 3651 5064 Mfg Home Audio/Video Equipment Whol Appliances/Tv/Radio

(G-16969)
AGFA CORPORATION
Also Called: AGFA Finance Group
200 Ballardvale St (01887-1074)
PHONE..................................978 658-5600
Raymond A Melillo, *General Mgr*
Jonathan Ashton, *VP Opers*
Jef Gerardts, *Project Mgr*
Matt Ketko, *Project Mgr*
Cathy Wall, *Opers Mgr*
EMP: 300
SQ FT: 7,500
SALES (corp-wide): 479.1MM **Privately Held**
SIC: 3861 Mfg Photographic Equipment/Supplies
HQ: Agfa Corporation
611 River Dr Ste 305
Elmwood Park NJ 07407
800 540-2432

(G-16970)
ALL AMERICAN EMBROIDERY INC
Also Called: A A E,
789 Woburn St Ste 2 (01887-4619)
PHONE..................................978 657-0414
Toll Free:..888 -
Eric Knowlton, *President*
EMP: 4
SALES (est): 256.2K **Privately Held**
WEB: www.aaeapparel.com
SIC: 2395 3993 2211 2759 Pleating/Stitching Svcs Mfg Signs/Ad Specialties Cotton Brdwv Fabric Mill Commercial Printing

(G-16971)
ALLCOAT TECHNOLOGY INC
100 Eames St (01887-3371)
PHONE..................................978 988-0880
Michael Lombard, *President*
Corine Parigian, *Vice Pres*
Tyrone Tufts, *Research*
Kurt Bimmler, *Technical Staff*
EMP: 40
SQ FT: 90,000
SALES (est): 11.6MM **Privately Held**
SIC: 2822 2891 Mfg Synthetic Rubber Mfg Adhesives/Sealants

(G-16972)
ALLSTAR FOUNDATION FOR UREA CY
125 Federal St (01887-2568)
PHONE..................................978 658-5319
Michael Vestal, *President*
EMP: 3
SALES (est): 241K **Privately Held**
SIC: 2873 Mfg Nitrogenous Fertilizers

(G-16973)
AMETEK INC
Ametek Aerospace & Defense
50 Fordham Rd (01887-2190)
PHONE..................................978 988-4101
David Zappico, *President*
EMP: 68
SALES (corp-wide): 4.8B **Publicly Held**
SIC: 3621 3829 3825 3812 Mfg Motors/Generators Mfg Measure/Control Dvcs Mfg Elec Measuring Instr Mfg Search/Navgatn Equip
PA: Ametek, Inc.
1100 Cassatt Rd
Berwyn PA 19312
610 647-2121

(G-16974)
AMETEK AROSPC PWR HOLDINGS INC (HQ)
50 Fordham Rd (01887-2190)
PHONE..................................978 988-4771
Robert S Feit, *Senior VP*
Robert R Mandos, *Senior VP*
Richard Sherlock, *Opers Mgr*
Maximillian Morse, *Engineer*
Chris Prouty, *Engineer*
EMP: 105
SALES (est): 78.2MM
SALES (corp-wide): 4.8B **Publicly Held**
SIC: 3812 3724 Mfg Search/Navigation Equipment Mfg Aircraft Engines/Parts
PA: Ametek, Inc.
1100 Cassatt Rd
Berwyn PA 19312
610 647-2121

(G-16975)
ATC TECHNOLOGIES INC (PA)
30b Upton Dr (01887-4455)
PHONE..................................781 939-0725
Paul Kierce, *President*
Paul C Kierce, *President*
John T Kierce, *Admin Sec*
EMP: 11
SQ FT: 10,000
SALES (est): 3.9MM **Privately Held**
WEB: www.atctechnologiesinc.com
SIC: 3841 Mfg Surgical/Medical Instruments

(G-16976)
ATLANTIC STEEL FABRICATORS INC
238 Andover St (01887-1022)
PHONE..................................978 657-8292
Joe Ciccariello, *President*
▲ **EMP:** 6
SQ FT: 5,200
SALES (est): 1MM **Privately Held**
SIC: 3441 Structural Metal Fabrication

(G-16977)
AZORES CORP (DH)
16 Jonspin Rd (01887-1093)
PHONE..................................978 253-6200
Elvino M Da Silveira, *President*
Steve Gardner, *Vice Pres*
Dave Bushong, *Admin Sec*
▲ **EMP:** 14
SQ FT: 10,000
SALES (est): 4.2MM
SALES (corp-wide): 324.5MM **Publicly Held**
WEB: www.azorescorp.com
SIC: 3672 Mfg Printed Circuit Boards
HQ: Rudolph Technologies, Inc.
16 Jonspin Rd
Wilmington MA 01887
978 253-6200

(G-16978)
BACK BAY SIGN
65 Industrial Way (01887-3499)
PHONE..................................978 203-0570
Martin Aronovitz, *Owner*
EMP: 5
SALES (est): 286.7K **Privately Held**
SIC: 3993 Mfg Signs/Advertising Specialties

(G-16979)
BACK BAY SIGN LLC
65i Industrial Way (01887-3499)
PHONE..................................781 475-1001

John Garrant, *Opers Mgr*
Paul Desantis, *VP Sales*
Martin G Aronovitz,
EMP: 20
SQ FT: 18,000
SALES (est): 3.3MM **Privately Held**
WEB: www.backbaysign.com
SIC: 3993 Mfg Signs/Advertising Specialties

(G-16980)
BACKSEAT GORILLA APPLICATIONS
41 Garden Ave (01887-1846)
PHONE....................978 658-6161
Jonathan R Eaton, *Principal*
EMP: 3
SALES (est): 199.5K **Privately Held**
SIC: 3625 Mfg Relays/Industrial Controls

(G-16981)
BAUSCH & LOMB INCORPORATED
100 Research Dr Ste 2 (01887-4406)
PHONE....................978 658-6111
Ruta Subatis, *Manager*
EMP: 13
SALES (corp-wide): 8.3B **Privately Held**
WEB: www.bausch.com
SIC: 3851 Mfg Ophthalmic Goods
HQ: Bausch & Lomb Incorporated
400 Somerset Corp Blvd
Bridgewater NJ 08807
585 338-6000

(G-16982)
BENEVENTO ASPHALT CORP
900 Salem St (01887-1236)
P.O. Box 454 (01887-0454)
PHONE....................978 658-5300
Charles J Benevento, *President*
Mark Hemenway, *Opers Mgr*
William Schneider, *Opers Mgr*
EMP: 10
SALES (est): 3.5MM **Privately Held**
WEB: www.benevento.com
SIC: 1442 Construction Sand/Gravel

(G-16983)
BENEVENTO SAND & STONE CORP
Also Called: Benevento Asphalt
200 Salem St (01887)
P.O. Box 454 (01887-0454)
PHONE....................978 658-4762
Charlie Benevento, *President*
Tim Allard, *Manager*
EMP: 13 **EST:** 1954
SQ FT: 2,000
SALES (est): 4MM **Privately Held**
SIC: 1442 Construction Sand/Gravel

(G-16984)
BOC GROUP INC
301 Ballardvale St (01887-4440)
PHONE....................978 658-5410
Jim Gentilcore, *CEO*
EMP: 3 **EST:** 2008
SALES (est): 476K **Privately Held**
SIC: 3561 Mfg Pumps/Pumping Equipment

(G-16985)
BURLINGTON MACHINE INC
340b Fordham Rd (01887-2169)
PHONE....................978 284-6525
John P Haroutunian, *President*
EMP: 18
SQ FT: 5,000
SALES (est): 3.3MM **Privately Held**
WEB: www.burlingtonmachine.com
SIC: 3451 Mfg Screw Machine Products

(G-16986)
CADILLAC GAGE TEXTRON INC (HQ)
201 Lowell St (01887-4113)
PHONE....................978 657-5111
▲ **EMP:** 5 **EST:** 1986
SQ FT: 101,000
SALES (est): 4.6MM
SALES (corp-wide): 13.9B **Publicly Held**
SIC: 3711 3714 3483 Motor Vehicles And Car Bodies
PA: Textron Inc.
40 Westminster St
Providence RI 02903
401 421-2800

(G-16987)
CLEARMOTION INC
400 Research Dr (01887-4407)
PHONE....................617 313-0822
EMP: 4 **Privately Held**
SIC: 3714 Mfg Motor Vehicle Parts/Accessories
PA: Clearmotion, Inc.
805 Middlesex Tpke
Billerica MA 01821

(G-16988)
CONCRETE PDTS OF LONDONDERRY
773 Salem St (01887-1222)
PHONE....................978 658-2645
Brenda Shea Stratis, *President*
Ed Shea, *Vice Pres*
Edward F Shea, *Vice Pres*
EMP: 3 **EST:** 1962
SALES: 637.6K **Privately Held**
SIC: 3272 Mfg Prefabricated Concrete Housing Components Septic Tanks & Prefabricated Steps

(G-16989)
COOKES SKATE SUPPLIES INC
446 Main St (01887-3209)
PHONE....................978 657-7586
Scott Cooke, *President*
Michael Bedell, *Vice Pres*
EMP: 8
SQ FT: 10,000
SALES (est): 1.2MM **Privately Held**
WEB: www.cookesskatesupply.com
SIC: 3949 5941 Mfg Ice Skates & Ret Sports Equipment

(G-16990)
CURIRX INC
205 Lowell St 1c (01887-2972)
PHONE....................978 658-2962
Indu Javeri, *President*
Katherine Nguyen, *Research*
EMP: 3
SALES (est): 743.2K **Privately Held**
SIC: 2834 Mfg Pharmaceutical Preparations

(G-16991)
CUSTOM STITCH
379 Middlesex Ave (01887-2133)
PHONE....................978 988-1344
Susan Binkoski, *Owner*
EMP: 4
SALES (est): 236.2K **Privately Held**
WEB: www.customstitchonline.com
SIC: 2395 Embroidery Work

(G-16992)
CUTISPHARMA INC
841 Woburn St (01887-3414)
PHONE....................800 461-7449
Neal I Muni, *President*
Ronald L Scarboro, *COO*
EMP: 17
SALES (est): 3.7MM
SALES (corp-wide): 10.3MM **Privately Held**
WEB: www.cutispharma.com
SIC: 2834 Mfg Pharmaceutical Preparations
PA: Novaquest Capital Management Llc
4208 Six Forks Rd Ste 920
Raleigh NC 27609
919 459-8620

(G-16993)
DAILY WOBURN TIMES INC
Also Called: Town Crier
1 Arrow Dr (01887)
PHONE....................978 658-2346
Stu Neilson, *General Mgr*
EMP: 8
SALES (corp-wide): 7MM **Privately Held**
WEB: www.woburnonline.com
SIC: 2711 Newspapers-Publishing/Printing
PA: Daily Woburn Times Inc
1 Arrow Dr Ste 1 # 1
Woburn MA 01801
781 933-3700

(G-16994)
DIAMOND EXPRESS INC
155 West St Ste 3 (01887-3064)
PHONE....................781 284-9402
Vincent A Gemma, *President*
Binny Jemma, *President*
EMP: 22
SALES (est): 3.2MM **Privately Held**
SIC: 3915 Mfg Jewelers' Materials

(G-16995)
DONNELLEY FINANCIAL LLC
5 Cornell Pl (01887-2129)
PHONE....................978 251-4000
Jay Adams, *CFO*
EMP: 13
SALES (corp-wide): 963MM **Publicly Held**
WEB: www.bowne.com
SIC: 2752 Lithographic Commercial Printing
HQ: Donnelley Financial, Llc
35 W Wacker Dr
Chicago IL 60601
844 866-4337

(G-16996)
DSM COATING RESINS INC
730 Main St (01887-3366)
PHONE....................800 458-0014
Jeffrey Brule, *President*
EMP: 140
SALES (corp-wide): 10.2B **Privately Held**
SIC: 3479 2851 2821 5162 Coating/Engraving Svcs Mfg Paints/Allied Prdts Mfg Plstc Material/Resin Whol Plastic Mtrl/Shapes
HQ: Dsm Coating Resins, Inc
1472 Columbia Nitrogen Dr
Augusta GA

(G-16997)
DUCKHILL RIVER CORP
Also Called: Rapid Reproduction
520 Main St (01887-3244)
PHONE....................978 657-6186
Douglas Cioffi, *President*
EMP: 5
SQ FT: 4,000
SALES (est): 561.2K **Privately Held**
SIC: 2759 Lithographic Commercial Printing

(G-16998)
DUSA PHARMACEUTICALS INC (DH)
25 Upton Dr (01887-4409)
PHONE....................978 657-7500
Robert F Doman, *President*
William F O'Dell, *Exec VP*
David Fadness, *Vice Pres*
Michael J Todisco, *Vice Pres*
Richard Marcotte, *Buyer*
EMP: 91
SALES (est): 14.7MM
SALES (corp-wide): 1.3B **Privately Held**
WEB: www.dusapharma.com
SIC: 2834 Mfg Pharmaceutical Preparations
HQ: Sun Pharmaceutical Industries, Inc.
2 Independence Way
Princeton NJ 08540
609 495-2800

(G-16999)
E GS GAUGING INCORPORATED
200 Research Dr (01887-4442)
PHONE....................978 663-2300
Carter Watson, *Principal*
EMP: 4
SALES (est): 498.9K **Privately Held**
SIC: 3823 Mfg Process Control Instruments

(G-17000)
ECOLAB INC
240 Ballardvale St Ste D (01887-1060)
PHONE....................978 658-2423
Jim Martel, *Manager*
EMP: 11
SALES (corp-wide): 14.6B **Publicly Held**
WEB: www.ecolab.com
SIC: 2841 Whol Chemicals/Products
PA: Ecolab Inc.
1 Ecolab Pl
Saint Paul MN 55102
800 232-6522

(G-17001)
ENERGY SCIENCES INC
Also Called: Esi
42 Industrial Way Ste 1 (01887-3471)
PHONE....................978 694-9000
Tatsuyuki Kawajiri, *CEO*
Scott Desrosiers, *Project Mgr*
Joseph Cierniewski, *Engineer*
Richard Danton, *CFO*
Mike Swain, *Supervisor*
▲ **EMP:** 50 **EST:** 1971
SQ FT: 52,000
SALES (est): 16.1MM **Privately Held**
WEB: www.ebeam.com
SIC: 3565 Mfg Drying Equipment And Curing
PA: Iwasaki Electric Co.,Ltd.
1-1-7, Higashinihombashi
Chuo-Ku TKY 103-0

(G-17002)
FRITO-LAY NORTH AMERICA INC
337 Ballardvale St (01887-1042)
PHONE....................978 657-8344
EMP: 200
SALES (corp-wide): 64.6B **Publicly Held**
WEB: www.fritolay.com
SIC: 2096 5145 Mfg Potato Chips/Snacks Whol Confectionery
HQ: Frito-Lay North America, Inc.
7701 Legacy Dr
Plano TX 75024

(G-17003)
GAYNOR INDUSTRIES CORPORATION
98 Eames St (01887-3370)
PHONE....................978 658-5500
Scott Fallavollita, *President*
EMP: 4
SALES (est): 279.5K **Privately Held**
SIC: 3452 Mfg Bolts/Screws/Rivets

(G-17004)
IBC ADVANCED ALLOYS INC-BELAC
55 Jonspin Rd (01887-1020)
PHONE....................978 284-8900
Raymond L White III, *President*
EMP: 7
SALES (corp-wide): 15.7MM **Privately Held**
SIC: 3599 Mfg Industrial Machinery
PA: Ibc Advanced Alloys Corp
570 Granville St Unit 1200
Vancouver BC V6C 3
604 685-6263

(G-17005)
INNOVION CORPORATION
265 Ballardvale St (01887-1036)
PHONE....................978 267-4064
EMP: 3
SALES (corp-wide): 8MM **Privately Held**
SIC: 3674 Mfg Semiconductors/Related Devices
PA: Innovion Corporation
2121 Zanker Rd
San Jose CA 95131
408 763-7000

(G-17006)
INTELLGENT OFFICE INTRIORS LLC
5 Waltham St (01887-2347)
PHONE....................978 808-7884
Robert Azevedo, *Principal*
Rob Azevedo, *Sales Mgr*
EMP: 4
SALES (est): 497.9K **Privately Held**
SIC: 3469 Mfg Metal Stampings

GEOGRAPHIC

(G-17007)
ION TRACK INSTRUMENTS LLC
205 Lowell St (01887-2972)
PHONE....................978 658-3767
Anthony Jenkins,
Paul Eisenbraun,
Andrew Hawes,
Walter Kopek,
William McGann,
▲ **EMP:** 100
SQ FT: 20,000
SALES (est): 9.1MM **Privately Held**
SIC: 3699 3829 3825 Mfg Electrical Equipment/Supplies Mfg Measuring/Controlling Devices Mfg Electrical Measuring Instruments

(G-17008)
J G MACHINE CO INC
21 Concord St (01887-2131)
PHONE....................978 447-5279
John M Graney, *President*
EMP: 6 **EST:** 1964
SQ FT: 2,500
SALES (est): 484K **Privately Held**
WEB: www.jgmachineco.com
SIC: 3599 Mfg Industrial Machinery

(G-17009)
J K L CORP
Also Called: Sign Station
12 Bay St Ste 105 (01887-2945)
PHONE....................978 657-5575
Paul Hudson, *President*
EMP: 3
SQ FT: 1,500
SALES: 200K **Privately Held**
SIC: 3993 Mfg Signs/Advertising Specialties

(G-17010)
JJT ENGINEERING INC
Also Called: Rodco Engineering
3b Lopez Rd (01887-2563)
P.O. Box 51 (01887-0051)
PHONE....................978 657-4137
Frank J Mc Nally, *President*
Todd McNally, *Principal*
Judith A Mc Nally, *Treasurer*
EMP: 8
SQ FT: 10,000
SALES: 2MM **Privately Held**
WEB: www.jjtengineering.com
SIC: 3599 Mfg Industrial Machinery

(G-17011)
KENTRON TECHNOLOGIES INC
155 West St Ste 10 (01887-6010)
PHONE....................978 988-9100
Robert Goodman, *CEO*
Chris Karabatsos, *President*
Matthew Murphy, *COO*
Tom Mullen, *Vice Pres*
Michael Murphy, *Director*
EMP: 25
SALES (est): 2.2MM **Privately Held**
WEB: www.kentrontech.com
SIC: 3577 Mfg Computer Peripheral Equipment

(G-17012)
KIRKWOOD HOLDINGS INC (PA)
Also Called: Kirkwood Direct
904 Main St (01887-3319)
PHONE....................978 658-4200
Robert Coppinger, *President*
Artie Stanton, *President*
Edward Kelley, *Vice Pres*
Mike Radochia, *Vice Pres*
Eric Twark, *Vice Pres*
▲ **EMP:** 200
SQ FT: 48,000
SALES (est): 80.9MM **Privately Held**
WEB: www.kirkwoodprinting.com
SIC: 2752 2791 2789 2759 Lithographic Coml Print Typesetting Services Bookbinding/Related Work Commercial Printing

(G-17013)
KOCH SEPARATION SOLUTIONS INC (DH)
Also Called: Koch Membrane Systems, Inc.
850 Main St (01887-3367)
P.O. Box 9133, Chelsea (02150-9133)
PHONE....................978 694-7000
David H Koch, *Ch of Bd*
Manny Singh, *President*
Jack Cangiano, *Regional Mgr*
Mark Farrell, *COO*
David Ringland, *Senior Buyer*
◆ **EMP:** 200 **EST:** 1966
SQ FT: 122,000
SALES (est): 103.1MM
SALES (corp-wide): 40.6B **Privately Held**
WEB: www.kochmembrane.com
SIC: 3569 3564 Mfg General Industrial Machinery Mfg Blowers/Fans
HQ: Koch-Glitsch, Lp
4111 E 37th St N
Wichita KS 67220
316 828-5000

(G-17014)
L3 TECHNOLOGIES INC
L3 Ssg
65 Jonspin Rd (01887-1020)
PHONE....................978 694-9991
Daniel F Desmond, *President*
EMP: 150
SALES (corp-wide): 6.8B **Publicly Held**
SIC: 3827 Mfg Optical Instruments/Lenses
HQ: L3 Technologies, Inc.
600 3rd Ave Fl 34
New York NY 10016
212 697-1111

(G-17015)
LAKE REGION MANUFACTURING INC (HQ)
Also Called: Lake Region Medical
100 Fordham Rd Ste 3 (01887-2154)
PHONE....................952 361-2515
Joe Fleischhacker, *CEO*
Donald J Spence, *Ch of Bd*
Matthew Manley, *Technical Mgr*
Todd Beaupre, *Engineer*
Ben Kegley, *Engineer*
EMP: 890
SQ FT: 159,000
SALES (est): 240MM
SALES (corp-wide): 1.2B **Publicly Held**
WEB: www.lakergn.com
SIC: 3841 3845 Mfg Surgical/Medical Instruments Mfg Electromedical Equipment
PA: Integer Holdings Corporation
5830 Gran Pkwy Ste 1150
Plano TX 75024
214 618-5243

(G-17016)
LAKE REGION MEDICAL INC (HQ)
100 Fordham Rd Ste 3 (01887-2154)
PHONE....................978 570-6900
Donald J Spence, *President*
Ron Honig, *Vice Pres*
Richard E Johnson, *CFO*
▲ **EMP:** 45
SQ FT: 55,000
SALES (est): 469.8MM
SALES (corp-wide): 1.2B **Publicly Held**
WEB: www.deepdraw.com
SIC: 3841 Mfg Surgical/Medical Instruments
PA: Integer Holdings Corporation
5830 Gran Pkwy Ste 1150
Plano TX 75024
214 618-5243

(G-17017)
LANTOS TECHNOLOGIES INC
50 Concord St Ste E-300 (01887-2196)
PHONE....................781 443-7633
John Bojanowski, *CEO*
David Mackie, *President*
Xiaowei Chen, *Manager*
Rosemary Ocallaghan, *Administration*
Schmul Gniwisch,
EMP: 9
SALES (est): 1.6MM **Privately Held**
SIC: 3845 Mfg Electromedical Equipment

(G-17018)
LOADSPRING SOLUTIONS INC (PA)
187 Ballardvale St B210 (01887-1053)
PHONE....................978 685-9715
Eric Leighton, *President*
Al Marshall, *Exec VP*
Cameron Vixie, *Exec VP*
Rebecca Humphries, *Accountant*
Christopher Granzella, *Software Engr*
EMP: 17
SQ FT: 7,219
SALES (est): 18.3MM **Privately Held**
WEB: www.loadspring.com
SIC: 7372 Prepackaged Software Services

(G-17019)
LUBRIZOL GLOBAL MANAGEMENT
207 Lowell St (01887-2941)
PHONE....................978 642-5051
Kevin Macmaster, *Controller*
Ronald Conti, *Corp Comm Staff*
Michael Voltero, *Branch Mgr*
Craig Schuster, *Manager*
EMP: 53
SALES (corp-wide): 225.3B **Publicly Held**
WEB: www.pharma.noveoninc.com
SIC: 2899 5169 Mfg Process Control Instruments & Whol Chemicals
HQ: Lubrizol Global Management, Inc
9911 Brecksville Rd
Brecksville OH 44141
216 447-5000

(G-17020)
MARLOW WATSON INC (HQ)
Also Called: Watson-Marlow/Bredel Pumps
37 Upton Technology Park (01887)
P.O. Box 536285, Pittsburgh PA (15253-5904)
PHONE....................800 282-8823
James Whalen, *CEO*
Steven Lavargna, *President*
Rick Balek, *General Mgr*
Jo Weekes, *General Mgr*
William Mandel, *Vice Pres*
▲ **EMP:** 45
SQ FT: 25,000
SALES: 81MM
SALES (corp-wide): 1.5B **Privately Held**
WEB: www.watson-marlow.com
SIC: 3561 Whol Industrial Equipment
PA: Spirax-Sarco Engineering Plc
Charlton House
Cheltenham GLOS GL53
124 252-1361

(G-17021)
MEDSOURCE TECH HOLDINGS LLC (DH)
100 Fordham Rd Bldg C (01887-2168)
PHONE....................978 570-6900
Richard Effress, *Ch of Bd*
Daniel Croteau, *Vice Pres*
Jim Drill, *Vice Pres*
Joseph Caffarelli, *CFO*
William J Kullback, *CFO*
EMP: 17
SQ FT: 7,000
SALES (est): 56.2MM
SALES (corp-wide): 1.2B **Publicly Held**
WEB: www.medsourcetech.com
SIC: 3841 8711 Mfg Surgical/Medical Instruments Engineering Services
HQ: Accellent Llc
100 Fordham Rd Bldg C
Wilmington MA 01887
978 570-6900

(G-17022)
MEDSOURCE TECHNOLOGIES LLC (DH)
100 Fordham Rd Ste 1 (01887-2154)
PHONE....................978 570-6900
Diane Loudon,
EMP: 10 **EST:** 1970
SQ FT: 41,000
SALES (est): 28MM
SALES (corp-wide): 1.2B **Publicly Held**
WEB: www.medsourcetech.com
SIC: 3841 3842 Mfg Surgical/Medical Instruments Mfg Surgical Appliances/Supplies
HQ: Medsource Technologies Holdings, Llc
100 Fordham Rd Bldg C
Wilmington MA 01887
978 570-6900

(G-17023)
METAL IMPROVEMENT COMPANY LLC
Also Called: Curtiss-Wright Surface Tech
201 Ballardvale St (01887-1013)
PHONE....................978 658-0032
Tom Bacon, *Branch Mgr*
Patrick Addonizio, *Manager*
EMP: 40
SALES (corp-wide): 2.4B **Publicly Held**
SIC: 3398 Metal Heat Treating
HQ: Metal Improvement Company, Llc
80 E Rte 4 Ste 310
Paramus NJ 07652
201 843-7800

(G-17024)
MKS INSTRUMENTS INC
Also Called: M K S Astex Products
90 Industrial Way (01887-4610)
PHONE....................978 284-4000
Paul Loomis, *General Mgr*
Eric Snyder, *Vice Pres*
David Silva, *Buyer*
Arthur Derstepanian, *Engineer*
David Elms, *Engineer*
EMP: 150
SALES (corp-wide): 2B **Publicly Held**
WEB: www.mksinst.com
SIC: 3823 Mfg Vacuum Pressure & Flow Measuring Instruments
PA: Mks Instruments, Inc.
2 Tech Dr Ste 201
Andover MA 01810
978 645-5500

(G-17025)
MKS MSC INC
90 Industrial Way (01887-4610)
PHONE....................978 284-4000
John R Bertucci, *President*
Ann Von Sneidern, *Accounts Mgr*
EMP: 700
SALES (est): 53.4MM
SALES (corp-wide): 2B **Publicly Held**
WEB: www.mksinst.com
SIC: 3823 3491 3494 Mfg Process Cntrl Instr Mfg Industrial Valves Mfg Valves/Pipe Fittings
PA: Mks Instruments, Inc.
2 Tech Dr Ste 201
Andover MA 01810
978 645-5500

(G-17026)
MONKS MANUFACTURING CO INC
1 Upton Dr (01887-1018)
PHONE....................978 657-8282
Ian L Monks, *President*
Terry Monks, *Director*
Marie Smith, *Executive*
Lee Monks, *Clerk*
EMP: 21 **EST:** 1973
SQ FT: 12,000
SALES (est): 3MM **Privately Held**
WEB: www.monksmfg.com
SIC: 3599 Mfg Industrial Machinery

(G-17027)
MORTON & COMPANY INC
11 Eames St (01887-3391)
PHONE....................978 657-7726
David M Morton, *President*
Janice C Morton, *Shareholder*
John H Kimball Jr, *Clerk*
EMP: 35
SQ FT: 12,000
SALES (est): 4.9MM **Privately Held**
WEB: www.mortco.com
SIC: 3599 Mfg Industrial Machinery

(G-17028)
NESTLE USA INC
240 Ballardvale St (01887-1055)
PHONE....................978 988-2030
Gail Riesz, *Branch Mgr*
EMP: 139
SALES (corp-wide): 92.8B **Privately Held**
WEB: www.nestleusa.com
SIC: 2023 Mfg Dry/Evaporated Dairy Products

HQ: Nestle Usa, Inc.
1812 N Moore St Ste 118
Rosslyn VA 22209
818 549-6000

(G-17029)
NEU-TOOL DESIGN INC
Also Called: Bio-Mold Division
220 Ballardvale St Ste A (01887-1050)
PHONE..................................978 658-5881
John Neuman, *President*
Ed Lombardi, *Director*
Andy Kennedy, *Executive*
EMP: 20
SQ FT: 12,000
SALES (est): 3.4MM **Privately Held**
WEB: www.neu-tool.com
SIC: 3089 3544 Mfg Plastic Products Mfg Dies/Tools/Jigs/Fixtures

(G-17030)
NEWPORT CORPORATION
Also Called: Ophir Optics
90 Industrial Way (01887-4610)
PHONE..................................978 296-1306
Madeleine Arsaga, *Asst Sec*
Jeffrey Coyne, *Admin Sec*
EMP: 99
SALES (est): 9.1MM **Privately Held**
SIC: 3827 Mfg Optical Instruments/Lenses

(G-17031)
NOEVEON INC
207 Lowell St (01887-2941)
PHONE..................................978 642-5004
Michael Voltero, *Principal*
▲ **EMP:** 3
SALES (est): 270.5K **Privately Held**
SIC: 3679 Mfg Electronic Components

(G-17032)
ONTO INNOVATION INC (PA)
16 Jonspin Rd (01887-1093)
PHONE..................................978 253-6200
Michael P Plisinski, *CEO*
Christopher A Seams, *Ch of Bd*
Rodney Smedt, *Vice Pres*
Elizabeth Lawrence, *Engineer*
Summer Liu, *Engineer*
EMP: 277
SALES: 324.5MM **Publicly Held**
WEB: www.nanometrics.com
SIC: 3829 Mfg Measuring/Controlling Devices

(G-17033)
OPHIR OPTICS LLC
90 Industrial Way (01887-4610)
PHONE..................................978 657-6410
Lynne Fontaine, *General Mgr*
Ofer Ben-David, *Regl Sales Mgr*
Dennis Cope, *Mng Member*
◆ **EMP:** 110
SQ FT: 38,000
SALES (est): 16.1MM
SALES (corp-wide): 2B **Publicly Held**
WEB: www.ophiropt.com
SIC: 3827 Mfg Optical Instruments/Lenses
HQ: Newport Corporation
1791 Deere Ave
Irvine CA 92606
949 863-3144

(G-17034)
OPPORTUNITY/DISCOVERY LLC
220 Ballardvale St Ste C (01887-1050)
PHONE..................................781 301-1596
Al Magro, *President*
EMP: 6 **EST:** 2017
SALES (est): 359K **Privately Held**
SIC: 3841 Mfg Surgical/Medical Instruments

(G-17035)
OPTO-LINE INTERNATIONAL INC
265 Ballardvale St Ste 3 (01887-1036)
PHONE..................................978 658-7255
John Arnault, *President*
Paul Sumner, *COO*
John Sumner, *Treasurer*
EMP: 10
SQ FT: 10,000
SALES: 1.7MM **Privately Held**
WEB: www.opto-line.com
SIC: 3827 Mfg Optical Instruments/Lenses

(G-17036)
OSRAM SYLVANIA INC (HQ)
200 Ballardvale St # 305 (01887-1074)
PHONE..................................978 570-3000
Richard Leaman, *President*
Frank St Onge, *General Mgr*
Joerg Ayrle, *Senior VP*
Jeff Hunt, *Vice Pres*
Jane Running, *Vice Pres*
◆ **EMP:** 950 **EST:** 1993
SALES (est): 2.2B
SALES (corp-wide): 3.8B **Privately Held**
WEB: www.silvania.com
SIC: 3646 3641 3647 3643 Mfg Coml Light Fixtures Mfg Electric Lamps Mfg Vehicle Light Equip Mfg Conductive Wire Dvcs Mfg Nonclay Refractories
PA: Osram Licht Ag
Marcel-Breuer-Str. 6
Munchen 80807
896 213-0

(G-17037)
OSRAM SYLVANIA INC
200 Ballardvale St # 305 (01887-1074)
PHONE..................................978 750-3900
Jes Munk Hansen, *President*
EMP: 310
SALES (corp-wide): 3.8B **Privately Held**
WEB: www.sylvania.com
SIC: 3641 Mfg Electric Lamps
HQ: Osram Sylvania Inc
200 Ballardvale St # 305
Wilmington MA 01887
978 570-3000

(G-17038)
PRECISION PLASTICS INC
18 Dadant Dr (01887-2149)
PHONE..................................978 658-5345
Paul Logan, *Manager*
EMP: 5
SALES (est): 525.4K **Privately Held**
SIC: 3089 Mfg Plastic Products

(G-17039)
PREFERRED PUBLICATIONS INC
10 Fiorenza Dr (01887-4427)
PHONE..................................978 697-4180
Kenneth Dorothy, *President*
Nancy Dorothy, *Vice Pres*
EMP: 6 **EST:** 1981
SALES (est): 420.6K **Privately Held**
SIC: 2741 Misc Publishing

(G-17040)
PVD PRODUCTS INC
Also Called: P V D
35 Upton Dr Ste 200 (01887-1018)
PHONE..................................978 694-9455
James A Greer, *President*
EMP: 18
SQ FT: 7,500
SALES (est): 5.9MM **Privately Held**
WEB: www.pvdproducts.com
SIC: 3826 Mfg Analytical Instruments

(G-17041)
RIGAKU ANALYTICAL DEVICES INC
30 Upton Dr Ste 2 (01887-1017)
PHONE..................................781 328-1024
Melanie Fuller, *General Mgr*
Yoichi Yokomizo, *COO*
Alicia Kimsey, *Administration*
▲ **EMP:** 30
SQ FT: 6,000
SALES (est): 4.5MM **Privately Held**
SIC: 3812 3826 3823 Mfg Search/Navigation Equipment Mfg Analytical Instruments Mfg Process Control Instruments
HQ: Rigaku Corporation Of America
9009 New Trails Dr
The Woodlands TX 77381
281 362-2300

(G-17042)
RUDOLPH TECHNOLOGIES INC (HQ)
16 Jonspin Rd (01887-1093)
P.O. Box 860, Budd Lake NJ (07828-0860)
PHONE..................................978 253-6200
Michael P Plisinski, *CEO*
Elvino Da Silveira, *Vice Pres*
Robert A Koch, *Vice Pres*
Steven R Roth, *CFO*
EMP: 277 **EST:** 1940
SQ FT: 50,000
SALES: 273.7MM
SALES (corp-wide): 324.5MM **Publicly Held**
WEB: www.rudolphtech.com
SIC: 3829 Mfg Process Control Instruments Mfg Optical Instruments/Lenses Mfg Measuring/Controlling Devices
PA: Onto Innovation Inc.
16 Jonspin Rd
Wilmington MA 01887
978 253-6200

(G-17043)
SCREENPRINT/DOW INC
200 Research Dr Ste 6 (01887-4432)
PHONE..................................978 657-7290
Walter T Dowgiallo, *President*
Bill Donovan, *Senior VP*
Robert Boileau, *Vice Pres*
Dave Kern, *Opers Mgr*
Laura Bento, *Prdtn Mgr*
EMP: 74
SQ FT: 30,000
SALES (est): 28.2MM **Privately Held**
WEB: www.screenprintdow.com
SIC: 2679 Mfg Converted Paper Products

(G-17044)
SCULLY SIGNAL COMPANY (PA)
Also Called: Scully Data Systems
70 Industrial Way (01887-3479)
PHONE..................................617 692-8600
Katrina Scully Ohl, *President*
Robert G Scully, *Chairman*
Othniel Vizcaino, *Production*
James P Maselan, *Admin Sec*
Colleen McCune, *Assistant*
▲ **EMP:** 109
SQ FT: 70,000
SALES (est): 39.4MM **Privately Held**
WEB: www.scully.com
SIC: 3823 3494 7374 3825 Mfg Process Cntrl Instr Mfg Valves/Pipe Fittings Data Processing/Prep Mfg Elec Measuring Instr Mfg Relay/Indstl Control

(G-17045)
SMYTH COMPANIES LLC
271 Ballardvale St (01887-1081)
PHONE..................................800 776-1201
Domenic Mancini, *Manager*
EMP: 6 **Privately Held**
SIC: 2679 Mfg Converted Paper Products
HQ: Smyth Companies, Llc
1085 Snelling Ave N
Saint Paul MN 55108
651 646-4544

(G-17046)
SONOSYSTEMS N SCHUNK AMER CORP (DH)
250 Andover St (01887-1048)
PHONE..................................978 658-9400
David Norquist, *President*
William Harden, *Controller*
Gordon Kevin, *Sr Software Eng*
Stefan Trube, *Director*
David Da Rin, *Admin Sec*
▲ **EMP:** 31
SQ FT: 15,000
SALES (est): 3.8MM
SALES (corp-wide): 1.2B **Privately Held**
WEB: www.staplaultrasonics.com
SIC: 3699 Mfg Electrical Equipment/Supplies
HQ: Schunk Sonosystems Gmbh
Hauptstr. 95
Wettenberg 35435
641 803-0

(G-17047)
ST JUDE MEDICAL LLC
600 Research Dr Ste 1 (01887-4438)
PHONE..................................978 657-6519
Daniel Jstarks, *President*
Ana Vitorino, *Senior Buyer*
Arkady Pievsky, *Engineer*
EMP: 47
SALES (corp-wide): 30.5B **Publicly Held**
SIC: 2834 Mfg Pharmaceutical Preparations
HQ: St. Jude Medical, Llc
1 Saint Jude Medical Dr
Saint Paul MN 55117
651 756-2000

(G-17048)
STAFFORD MANUFACTURING CORP
256 Andover St (01887-1003)
P.O. Box 277, North Reading (01864-0277)
PHONE..................................978 657-8000
Arthur Stafford, *President*
Bill Fiegener, *Controller*
Jim Swiezynski, *Chief Mktg Ofcr*
Jarred Ayan, *Software Engr*
Wray G Falwell, *Technical Staff*
▲ **EMP:** 40 **EST:** 1975
SQ FT: 30,000
SALES (est): 10.2MM **Privately Held**
WEB: www.staffordmfg.com
SIC: 3568 Mfg Power Transmission Equipment

(G-17049)
STUFFED FOODS LLC
14 Jewel Dr Ste 3 (01887-3361)
PHONE..................................978 203-0370
David Robinson, *President*
David Gillen, *Vice Pres*
▲ **EMP:** 47
SALES (est): 5MM **Privately Held**
SIC: 2038 Mfg Frozen Specialties

(G-17050)
SYMBOTIC LLC
Also Called: Casepick Systems, LLC
200 Research Dr (01887-4442)
PHONE..................................978 284-2800
Richard Cohen, *Mng Member*
Rebecca Beck,
William M Boyd III,
Corey C Dufresne,
Foster D Hinshaw,
EMP: 8 **EST:** 2007
SALES (est): 2.1B
SALES (corp-wide): 3.9B **Privately Held**
SIC: 3549 Mfg Metalworking Machinery
PA: C&S Wholesale Grocers, Inc.
7 Corporate Dr
Keene NH 03431
603 354-7000

(G-17051)
TECOMET INC
301 Ballardvale St Ste 3 (01887-4405)
PHONE..................................978 642-2400
EMP: 85
SALES (corp-wide): 696.7MM **Privately Held**
SIC: 3841 3324 3365 3369 Mfg Surgical/Med Instr Steel Investment Foundry Aluminum Foundry Nonferrous Metal Foundry
PA: Tecomet Inc.
115 Eames St
Wilmington MA 01887
978 642-2400

(G-17052)
TECOMET INC (PA)
115 Eames St (01887-3380)
PHONE..................................978 642-2400
Victor Swint, *CEO*
Art Burghouwt, *President*
Dan Howell, *President*
Vlad Miskovic, *President*
Rick Roscizewski, *General Mgr*
EMP: 180
SALES (est): 696.7MM **Privately Held**
WEB: www.tecomet.com
SIC: 3841 3444 Manufacturer Of Surgical/Med Instr Manufacturer Of Sheet Metalwork

(G-17053)
TERADIODE INC
30 Upton Dr (01887-1017)
PHONE..................................978 988-1040
Parviz Tayebati, *President*
Bien Chann, *Vice Pres*
Robin Huang, *Vice Pres*
Damon Pender, *CFO*
Fred Leonberger, *Director*
▲ **EMP:** 75
SQ FT: 35,000

GEOGRAPHIC

SALES (est): 5.1MM **Privately Held**
SIC: 3699 Mfg Electrical Equipment/Supplies
PA: Panasonic Corporation
1006, Kadoma
Kadoma OSK 571-0

(G-17054)
TEXTRON SYSTEMS CORPORATION (DH)
Also Called: Textron Defense Systems
201 Lowell St (01887-4113)
PHONE....................................978 657-5111
▲ **EMP:** 45
SALES (est): 154.5MM
SALES (corp-wide): 13.9B **Publicly Held**
WEB: www.textronsystems.com
SIC: 3483 5088 Ammunition, Except For Small Arms, Nec
HQ: Textron Lycoming Corp
40 Westminster St
Providence RI 02903
401 421-2800

(G-17055)
THERMO FISHER SCIENTIFIC INC
Also Called: Thermo Keytek
200 Research Dr Ste 3 (01887-4432)
PHONE....................................978 275-0800
Howard Kopech, *Manager*
Flavio Chocala, *Officer*
Denise Modoono, *Executive Asst*
EMP: 75
SALES (corp-wide): 24.3B **Publicly Held**
WEB: www.thermo.com
SIC: 3845 3629 3823 3826 Mfg Electromedical Equip Mfg Elec Indstl Equip
PA: Thermo Fisher Scientific Inc.
168 3rd Ave
Waltham MA 02451
781 622-1000

(G-17056)
TNEMEC EAST INC
11 Upton Dr (01887-1018)
PHONE....................................978 988-9500
Harold Righter, *President*
Martin E Greenblat, *Clerk*
EMP: 21 **EST:** 1958
SQ FT: 6,000
SALES (est): 1.3MM **Privately Held**
SIC: 2851 Mfg Paints/Allied Products

(G-17057)
TRANE INC
181 Ballardvale St # 201 (01887-1191)
PHONE....................................978 737-3900
Colin Boosey, *Engineer*
Jack Borgschulte, *Branch Mgr*
Pat Butler, *Executive*
EMP: 100 **Privately Held**
SIC: 3585 Mfg Refrigeration/Heating Equipment
HQ: Trane Inc.
1 Centennial Ave Ste 101
Piscataway NJ 08854
732 652-7100

(G-17058)
TRAXON TECHNOLOGIES
200 Ballardvale St # 300 (01887-1075)
PHONE....................................201 508-1570
Terry H Oneal, *President*
EMP: 11
SALES (est): 1.8MM **Privately Held**
SIC: 3641 Mfg Electric Lamps

(G-17059)
TREXEL INC
Also Called: Axiomatics
100 Research Dr Ste 1 (01887-4406)
PHONE....................................781 932-0202
Stephen G Braig, *President*
Steve G Braig, *President*
Levi Kishbaugh, *President*
Petr Janik, *Vice Pres*
Brent Strawbridge, *Vice Pres*
EMP: 35 **EST:** 1982
SQ FT: 15,000
SALES (est): 7.1MM **Privately Held**
WEB: www.trexel.com
SIC: 3089 3086 Mfg Plastic Products Mfg Plastic Foam Products

(G-17060)
UNITED TOOL & MACHINE CORP
98 Eames St (01887-3392)
PHONE....................................978 658-5500
Scott Fallo, *President*
EMP: 24 **EST:** 1963
SQ FT: 15,000
SALES (est): 5.1MM **Privately Held**
SIC: 3469 3599 3544 Mfg Metal Stampings Mfg Industrial Machinery Mfg Dies/Tools/Jigs/Fixtures

(G-17061)
UNIVERSAL COLOR CORP INC
377 Ballardvale St Unit 1 (01887-1042)
PHONE....................................978 658-2300
Kevin T Coneeny, *President*
EMP: 14
SALES (est): 2.5MM **Privately Held**
SIC: 2893 5999 Mfg Printing Ink Ret Misc Merchandise

(G-17062)
UTI HOLDING COMPANY
100 Fordham Rd Bldg C (01887-2168)
PHONE....................................978 570-6900
EMP: 3
SALES (est): 322.4K
SALES (corp-wide): 1.4B **Publicly Held**
SIC: 3841 Mfg Surgical/Medical Instruments
HQ: Accellent Llc
100 Fordham Rd Bldg C
Wilmington MA 01887
978 570-6900

(G-17063)
VIANT AS&O HOLDINGS LLC
100 Fordham Rd (01887-2168)
PHONE....................................866 899-1392
Andrew Fritz, *President*
EMP: 3
SALES (est): 279.6K
SALES (corp-wide): 368.7MM **Privately Held**
SIC: 3841 Mfg Surgical/Medical Instruments
PA: Viant Medical Holdings, Inc.
2 Hampshire St
Foxborough MA 02035
480 553-6400

(G-17064)
WALPOLE WOODWORKERS INC
168 Lowell St (01887-2942)
PHONE....................................978 658-3373
Steven Schultz, *Branch Mgr*
EMP: 15
SALES (corp-wide): 83.9MM **Privately Held**
WEB: www.walpolewoodworkers.com
SIC: 2499 5712 2452 3448 Mfg Wood Products Ret Furniture Mfg Prefabrcatd Wd Bldgs Mfg Prefab Metal Bldgs Mfg Wood Household Furn
PA: Walpole Outdoors Llc
100 Rver Ridge Dr Ste 302
Norwood MA 02062
508 668-2800

(G-17065)
WASTE WATER EVAPORATORS INC
6 Marion St (01887-3132)
PHONE....................................978 256-3259
Sid Kerr, *Principal*
EMP: 6
SALES (est): 577.7K **Privately Held**
WEB: www.wastewaterevaporators.com
SIC: 3443 Mfg Waste Water Evaporators

(G-17066)
WILLIAMS SIGN ERECTION INC
20 Lowell St (01887-3203)
PHONE....................................978 658-3787
Janet Williams, *President*
EMP: 4
SQ FT: 2,500
SALES (est): 624.6K **Privately Held**
SIC: 3531 Mfg Signs/Advertising Specialties

(G-17067)
WILMINGTON PARTNERS LP
Also Called: Polymer Technology
100 Research Dr Ste 2 (01887-4406)
PHONE....................................978 658-6111
Charles River Laboratories, *Partner*
Ruta Suvatis, *Principal*
Robert F Thompson, *Principal*
▼ **EMP:** 250
SALES (est): 28.1MM
SALES (corp-wide): 8.3B **Privately Held**
WEB: www.ciudadoptica.com
SIC: 3851 2834 Mfg Ophthalmic Goods Mfg Pharmaceutical Preparations
HQ: Bausch & Lomb Incorporated
400 Somerset Corp Blvd
Bridgewater NJ 08807
585 338-6000

(G-17068)
WTD INC (PA)
Also Called: Screenprint
271 Ballardvale St (01887-1081)
PHONE....................................978 658-8200
Walter T Dowgiallo, *President*
Andrew Farquharson, *President*
Scott Boucher, *QC Mgr*
John Morrison, *CFO*
Mike Doherty, *Manager*
EMP: 65
SQ FT: 56,000
SALES (est): 8.2MM **Privately Held**
WEB: www.dowindustries.com
SIC: 2759 Commercial Printing

(G-17069)
XENON CORPORATION (PA)
37 Upton Dr Ste 2 (01887-4453)
PHONE....................................978 661-9033
Louis R Panico, *CEO*
Michael Gnaegy, *Vice Pres*
Neil Cameron, *Mfg Mgr*
Joseph Pinto, *Mfg Staff*
Ryan Hathaway, *Engineer*
▲ **EMP:** 28 **EST:** 1964
SQ FT: 7,608
SALES (est): 8.6MM **Privately Held**
WEB: www.xenoncorp.com
SIC: 3648 Mfg Lighting Equipment

(G-17070)
XOS TECHNOLOGIES INC (HQ)
Also Called: Xos Digital
181 Ballardvale St Ste 2 (01887-1189)
PHONE....................................978 447-5220
Matthew Bairos, *CEO*
Jack Lengyel, *President*
Dotty Keane, *Opers Mgr*
Steve Quinn, *CTO*
Steve Bayne,
EMP: 33
SQ FT: 10,000
SALES (est): 18.6MM **Privately Held**
WEB: www.xostech.com
SIC: 2741 7371 Internet Publishing And Broadcasting Custom Computer Programing

Winchendon
Worcester County

(G-17071)
BELLECRAFT WOODWORKING INC
540 River St (01475-1054)
PHONE....................................978 297-2672
Andre P Belletete, *President*
Thomas Belletete, *Vice Pres*
EMP: 27 **EST:** 1960
SQ FT: 37,500
SALES: 1.5MM **Privately Held**
SIC: 2511 Mfg Finished Pine Oak And Cherry Case Goods

(G-17072)
D A MFG CO LLC
261 Lincoln Ave (01475-1172)
P.O. Box 4 (01475-0004)
PHONE....................................978 297-1059
Curtis Burnham, *Mng Member*
Elaine Burnham,
EMP: 5
SQ FT: 3,000
SALES: 240K **Privately Held**
SIC: 2431 2441 Mfg Millwork Mfg Wood Boxes/Shook

(G-17073)
DAVID SEVIGNY INC
Also Called: Sevigny, David L Supplies
62 Hale St (01475-1009)
P.O. Box 418 (01475-0418)
PHONE....................................978 297-2775
Richard Sevigny, *Principal*
Patrick Allire, *Treasurer*
Cathline Sevigny, *Admin Sec*
EMP: 5
SQ FT: 6,000
SALES (est): 639.7K **Privately Held**
SIC: 3272 5993 Mfg Concrete Products Ret Tobacco Products

(G-17074)
DIEHL GRAPHICS CO
128 Maple St (01475-1347)
PHONE....................................978 297-1598
Ralph Diehl III, *Owner*
EMP: 3
SALES: 85K **Privately Held**
SIC: 2759 Commercial Printing

(G-17075)
F W LOMBARD COMPANY (PA)
246 Lakeview Dr (01475-2319)
PHONE....................................978 827-5333
Carl F Mellin Jr, *President*
Robert Joyal, *Vice Pres*
EMP: 30 **EST:** 1911
SQ FT: 30,000
SALES (est): 2.3MM **Privately Held**
WEB: www.fwlombard.com
SIC: 2521 Mfg Wooden Seating & Tables

(G-17076)
GOODSPEED MACHINE COMPANY
15 Summer Dr (01475-1645)
P.O. Box 129 (01475-0129)
PHONE....................................978 297-0296
John S Witt, *President*
Susan M Witt, *Principal*
▲ **EMP:** 3
SQ FT: 45,000
SALES (est): 504.7K **Privately Held**
SIC: 3553 5084 Mfg Woodworking Machinery Whol Industrial Equipment

(G-17077)
INEOS NOVA LCC
26 Belmont Ave (01475-1233)
PHONE....................................978 297-2265
Mark Price, *Principal*
EMP: 3
SALES (est): 244.1K **Privately Held**
SIC: 2821 Mfg Plastic Materials/Resins

(G-17078)
MYLEC INC (PA)
37 Commercial Dr (01475-3006)
P.O. Box 500, Winchendon Springs (01477)
PHONE....................................978 297-0089
Ricky Laperriere, *President*
Ricky P Laperriere, *President*
Tina Laperriere, *Vice Pres*
Becky Paul, *Credit Mgr*
Patrick Ruble, *Natl Sales Mgr*
▲ **EMP:** 60 **EST:** 1970
SQ FT: 140,000
SALES (est): 6.5MM **Privately Held**
WEB: www.mylec.com
SIC: 3949 Mfg Sporting/Athletic Goods Management Consulting Services

(G-17079)
R & P PLASTICS LLC
202 Spruce St (01475-1159)
PHONE....................................978 297-1115
John J Lavallee,
▲ **EMP:** 6
SQ FT: 50,000
SALES: 1.2MM **Privately Held**
SIC: 2673 Mfg Bags-Plastic/Coated Paper

(G-17080)
RAU BROTHERS INC
480 Central St (01475-1207)
PHONE....................................978 297-1381
Ottmar Rau, *President*

EMP: 6
SQ FT: 20,000
SALES (est): 460K Privately Held
SIC: 2541 Mfg Wood Partitions/Fixtures

(G-17081)
RELIABLE
77 Mill St (01475-1120)
PHONE....978 230-2689
Shane Walker, *Principal*
EMP: 3
SALES (est): 228.5K Privately Held
SIC: 3559 Mfg Misc Industry Machinery

(G-17082)
SALOOM FURNITURE CO INC
256 Murdock Ave (01475-1127)
PHONE....978 297-1901
Peter Saloom, *President*
Davide Berthiaume, *COO*
Roy Kvingedale, *Purch Mgr*
Roy Kvingedal, *Purch Agent*
Gloria J Heughins, *Engineer*
▲ EMP: 88
SQ FT: 80,000
SALES (est): 11.1MM Privately Held
WEB: www.saloom.com
SIC: 2511 Mfg Wood Household Furniture

Winchester
Middlesex County

(G-17083)
BITTID LLC
81 Walnut St (01890-2822)
PHONE....781 570-2077
Russell Lamontagne, *President*
EMP: 4 EST: 2016
SALES (est): 189.6K Privately Held
SIC: 2836 Mfg Biological Products

(G-17084)
BLANCHARD PRESS INC
249 Mystic Valley Pkwy (01890-3130)
PHONE....617 426-6690
John A Sutherland Jr, *CEO*
Robert Sutherland, *President*
Andrew Paraskos, *Vice Pres*
Ann Sutherland, *Clerk*
EMP: 10
SQ FT: 9,000
SALES (est): 1.3MM Privately Held
WEB: www.blanchardpress.com
SIC: 2752 7336 8742 Lithographic Commercial Printing Commercial Art/Graphic Design Management Consulting Services

(G-17085)
CARRIAGE HSE DEVELOPMENTS LLC
253 Swanton St (01890-1938)
PHONE....339 221-4253
Mario C Covino, *Mng Member*
EMP: 3
SALES (est): 283.3K Privately Held
SIC: 2541 7389 Mfg Wood Partitions/Fixtures Business Services

(G-17086)
DASEIN INC
109 Cambridge St (01890-3740)
PHONE....781 756-0380
Thomas Accardo, *President*
EMP: 3
SALES (est): 358.5K Privately Held
SIC: 2261 Cotton Finishing Plant

(G-17087)
FIRST PRINT INC
109 Cambridge St (01890-3740)
PHONE....781 729-7714
Thomas Accardo, *President*
Edna Accardo, *Treasurer*
EMP: 10
SALES (est): 644K Privately Held
WEB: www.firstprint.net
SIC: 2396 Silk Screen Printing On Fabrics

(G-17088)
INFORMATION GATEKEEPERS INC
72 Thornberry Rd (01890-3243)
P.O. Box 606 (01890-0806)
PHONE....617 782-5033
Paul Polishuk, *President*
Brian Mark, *Marketing Mgr*
Will Ashley, *Info Tech Dir*
EMP: 6
SQ FT: 7,000
SALES (est): 608.8K Privately Held
WEB: www.telecomcalendar.com
SIC: 2721 7389 2741 2731 Periodical-Publish/Print Business Services Misc Publishing Book-Publishing/Printing

(G-17089)
ITS A CORKER
29 Arthur St (01890-1604)
PHONE....781 729-9630
D Taylor-Smith, *Owner*
EMP: 3
SALES (est): 197.5K Privately Held
SIC: 2298 Mfg Cordage/Twine

(G-17090)
KEEFE PICCOLO COMPANY INC
54 Church St (01890-2501)
PHONE....781 369-1626
Jim Keefe, *President*
EMP: 3
SALES (est): 331.8K Privately Held
WEB: www.keefepiccolo.com
SIC: 3931 Mfg Musical Instruments

(G-17091)
LITHO-CRAFT INC
1 Lowell Ave (01890-1129)
P.O. Box 728 (01890-4128)
PHONE....781 729-1789
Andrew W Bosworth, *President*
Marie A Bosworth, *Treasurer*
Marie Bosworth, *Treasurer*
Karen Bosworth, *Clerk*
EMP: 15 EST: 1976
SQ FT: 5,200
SALES (est): 2MM Privately Held
WEB: www.litho-craft.com
SIC: 2752 Lithographic Commercial Printing

(G-17092)
MJW MASS INC
Also Called: M P I
37 East St (01890-1155)
P.O. Box 845563, Boston (02284-5563)
PHONE....781 721-0332
Edward J Alois, *President*
James R Hart, *Corp Secy*
Gerald Kerber, *Plant Mgr*
Terri West, *Traffic Mgr*
Michelle Sullivan, *Purch Mgr*
◆ EMP: 70
SQ FT: 37,500
SALES (est): 20.4MM Privately Held
WEB: www.webmpi.com
SIC: 3089 Mfg Plastic Products

(G-17093)
OLYMPIC SYSTEMS CORPORATION
15 Lowell Ave (01890-1194)
PHONE....781 721-2740
James Putney, *President*
Simon Bedigian, *President*
Peter G Johannsen, *Clerk*
EMP: 50
SQ FT: 20,000
SALES (est): 6.1MM Privately Held
WEB: www.olympicsystemscorp.com
SIC: 3599 Mfg Industrial Machinery

(G-17094)
PACOTHANE TECHNOLOGIES (PA)
37 East St (01890-1155)
PHONE....781 729-0927
Martin Wilheim, *Principal*
James Hart, *CFO*
◆ EMP: 25
SALES (est): 3.7MM Privately Held
SIC: 2621 Paper Mill

(G-17095)
PHILIP RS SORBETS
Also Called: Frozen Desserts
750 Main St (01890-4310)
PHONE....781 721-6330
Phili Rotondo, *President*
▲ EMP: 10
SQ FT: 3,500
SALES (est): 1.1MM Privately Held
SIC: 2024 Mfg Ice Cream/Frozen Desert

(G-17096)
SPARROWS LITTLE TECH LLC
176 Mystic Valley Pkwy (01890-2847)
PHONE....781 799-6442
Donna J Brezinski,
EMP: 4
SALES (est): 228.1K Privately Held
SIC: 3845 Mfg Electromedical Equipment

(G-17097)
STATE FUEL
74 Swanton St (01890-2041)
PHONE....781 438-5557
John Zero, *Principal*
EMP: 3 EST: 1996
SALES (est): 154.3K Privately Held
SIC: 2869 Mfg Industrial Organic Chemicals

(G-17098)
TECA-PRINT USA CORP
2a Lowell Ave (01890-1130)
PHONE....781 369-1084
Jean-Louis Dubuit, *President*
Aimee Dean, *Controller*
Liam Clancy, *Director*
EMP: 15
SQ FT: 13,000
SALES (est): 3.4MM Privately Held
WEB: www.teca-print.com
SIC: 3555 Mfg Printing Trades Machinery

(G-17099)
TRUMPIT INC (PA)
13 Briarwood Ln (01890-3869)
PHONE....617 650-9292
Vasileios Gianoukos, *CEO*
EMP: 4 EST: 2015
SALES (est): 673.7K Privately Held
SIC: 7372 Prepackaged Software Services

Winthrop
Suffolk County

(G-17100)
ONLINE PRINT RESOURCES
19 Moore St (02152-1320)
PHONE....617 539-3961
Robert Swanson, *Principal*
EMP: 3
SALES (est): 214.3K Privately Held
WEB: www.vestcom.com
SIC: 2752 Lithographic Commercial Printing

(G-17101)
VILLAGE NETMEDIA INC
Also Called: Journal Transcript Newspapers
39 Putnam St (02152-2903)
PHONE....617 846-3700
Christal Keefe, *Branch Mgr*
EMP: 3
SALES (corp-wide): 9.6MM Privately Held
WEB: www.jobsformaine.com
SIC: 2711 2721 Newspapers-Publishing/Printing Periodicals-Publishing/Printing
PA: Village Netmedia, Inc.
91 Camden St Ste 403
Rockland ME 04841
207 594-4401

Woburn
Middlesex County

(G-17102)
A & G CENTERLESS GRINDING INC
15 Linscott Rd (01801-2001)
PHONE....781 281-0007
Guy Agri, *President*
EMP: 18
SQ FT: 20,000
SALES: 4.7MM Privately Held
WEB: www.agcenterless.com
SIC: 3599 Mfg Industrial Machinery

(G-17103)
AA PHARMACEUTICALS INC
470 Wildwood Ave Ste 3 (01801-2082)
PHONE....617 935-1241
Dongli Chen, *President*
EMP: 5
SALES (est): 513.6K Privately Held
SIC: 2834 Mfg Pharmaceutical Preparations

(G-17104)
ABCLONAL-NEO INC
Also Called: Cambridge Proteome
395 W Cummings Park (01801-6335)
PHONE....617 412-1176
Pengcheng Zhu, *Chairman*
EMP: 10
SALES (est): 676.6K Privately Held
SIC: 2835 Diagnostic Substances, Nsk

(G-17105)
ABPRO CORPORATION
68 Cummings Park (01801-2124)
PHONE....617 225-0808
Ian Chan, *Ch of Bd*
Eugene Y Chan, *Vice Ch Bd*
Benjamin Ha, *Vice Ch Bd*
Adam S Mostafa, *CFO*
Shaun Murphy, *Systems Dir*
EMP: 42
SQ FT: 15,000
SALES: 2.2MM Privately Held
WEB: www.abpro-labs.com
SIC: 2834 2835 Pharmaceutical Preparations & Mfg Diagnostic Substances

(G-17106)
ACCOUNTING WEB
400 Tradecenter G755 (01801-7452)
PHONE....978 331-1243
Andrew North, *Publisher*
EMP: 80 EST: 1999
SALES (est): 1.4MM Privately Held
SIC: 2741 Misc Publishing

(G-17107)
ACI TECHNOLOGY INC
Also Called: Arise Computer
215 Salem St Ste J (01801-2061)
PHONE....781 937-9888
Allen Hsu, *President*
Andy Hsu, *Vice Pres*
Cindy Hsu, *Shareholder*
▲ EMP: 14
SQ FT: 10,000
SALES (est): 2MM Privately Held
SIC: 3823 Mfg Industrial Computer

(G-17108)
ACP WATERJET INC
325a New Boston St (01801-6231)
PHONE....800 951-5127
Carlos Eduardo T Fernandes, *President*
EMP: 25
SQ FT: 6,000
SALES: 750K Privately Held
SIC: 3541 Mfg Machine Tools-Cutting

(G-17109)
ADDILAT INC (PA)
70 Conn St (01801-5662)
PHONE....781 258-9963
Michael McGonigle, *CEO*
Michael Callahan, *CFO*
EMP: 3
SQ FT: 900

GEOGRAPHIC

SALES: 400K **Privately Held**
SIC: 3674 Mfg Semiconductors/Related Devices

(G-17110)
ADEPTIS INC
400 Tradecenter Ste 5900 (01801-7471)
PHONE..................................781 569-5996
Steve Nevins, *President*
EMP: 5
SALES (est): 319.3K **Privately Held**
WEB: www.adeptis.com
SIC: 7372 Prepackaged Software Services

(G-17111)
ADVANCED MEASUREMENT TECH INC
10e Commerce Way (01801-1044)
PHONE..................................781 938-7800
Ken Penaskovic, *Branch Mgr*
EMP: 95
SALES (corp-wide): 4.8B **Publicly Held**
WEB: www.buy-instruments.com
SIC: 3829 Mfg Measuring/Controlling Devices
HQ: Advanced Measurement Technology, Inc.
801 S Illinois Ave
Oak Ridge TN 37830
865 482-4411

(G-17112)
ADVANCED WELDING & DESIGN INC
6 Draper St (01801-4522)
PHONE..................................781 938-7644
John Canney, *President*
EMP: 16
SQ FT: 10,000
SALES (est): 1.9MM **Privately Held**
SIC: 7692 Welding Repair

(G-17113)
ADVISOR PERSPECTIVES INC
10 State St Fl 2nd (01801-6804)
P.O. Box 380, Lexington (02420-0004)
PHONE..................................781 376-0050
Robert Keith Huebscher, *President*
EMP: 99
SALES (est): 5.3MM **Privately Held**
SIC: 2741 Electronic Financial Newsletter

(G-17114)
AERO BRAZING CORP
223 New Boston St (01801-6214)
PHONE..................................781 933-7511
Richard G Mizzoni, *President*
Richard Mizzoni, *Vice Pres*
Nicholas Zajka, *Treasurer*
Metrophane Zajka, *Admin Sec*
EMP: 14 **EST:** 1974
SQ FT: 7,000
SALES (est): 1.7MM **Privately Held**
WEB: www.aerobrazing.com
SIC: 7692 Metal Brazing

(G-17115)
ALDEN HAUK INC
215 Salem St Ste 10 (01801-2070)
PHONE..................................781 281-0154
Geno A Impemba Jr, *President*
EMP: 12
SQ FT: 5,500
SALES: 750K **Privately Held**
WEB: www.aldenhauk.com
SIC: 2752 Lithographic Commercial Printing

(G-17116)
ALIVIA CAPITAL LLC (PA)
Also Called: Alivia Technology
400 Tradecenter Ste 5900 (01801-7471)
PHONE..................................781 569-5212
Kleber Gallardo, *Mng Member*
EMP: 8
SALES: 2MM **Privately Held**
SIC: 7372 Prepackaged Software Services

(G-17117)
ALMUSNET INC
400 Tradecenter Ste 4900 (01801-7468)
PHONE..................................781 933-1846
Kewan Khawaja, *President*
EMP: 40
SALES: 500K **Privately Held**
SIC: 7372 Prepackaged Software Services

(G-17118)
AMF OPTICAL SOLUTIONS LLC
30 Nashua St Ste 3 (01801-4566)
PHONE..................................781 933-6125
Robert Lafieniere, *President*
Jeff Kenton, *Mng Member*
EMP: 8
SQ FT: 10,000
SALES: 5MM **Privately Held**
SIC: 3827 5049 Mfg Optical Instruments/Lenses Whol Professional Equipment

(G-17119)
ANTHONY INDUSTRIES INC
5r Green St (01801-4392)
PHONE..................................781 305-3750
Marc Antetomaso, *Principal*
EMP: 8
SALES (est): 646.7K **Privately Held**
SIC: 3999 Mfg Misc Products

(G-17120)
ARBORJET INC
99 Blueberry Hill Rd (01801-5266)
PHONE..................................781 935-9070
Peter Wild, *President*
Kevin Brewer, *Vice Pres*
Bill Keogh, *Production*
John Manganiello, *Controller*
Joe Aiken, *Sales Staff*
EMP: 27
SQ FT: 6,000
SALES (est): 3.3MM **Privately Held**
WEB: www.arborjet.com
SIC: 3545 Mfg Machine Tool Accessories

(G-17121)
ARCAM CAD TO METAL INC
6 Gill St (01801-1721)
PHONE..................................781 281-1718
Eric Bert, *Principal*
EMP: 12
SALES (est): 2.1MM
SALES (corp-wide): 121.6B **Publicly Held**
SIC: 3365 3842 3444 3699 Aluminum Foundries
HQ: Arcam Ab
Krokslatts Fabriker 27a
Molndal 431 3
317 183-379

(G-17122)
ARISTON ENGRAVING & MACHINE CO
56 Dragon Ct (01801-1014)
PHONE..................................781 935-2328
Nicholas Pappas, *President*
George Geranis, *General Mgr*
EMP: 8
SQ FT: 6,500
SALES (est): 1MM **Privately Held**
WEB: www.aristonengraving.com
SIC: 3479 Mechanical Engraving

(G-17123)
ASE (US) INC
18 Commerce Way Ste 2900 (01801-1090)
PHONE..................................781 305-5900
Eric Leonard, *Sales Staff*
Chris Langhammer, *Branch Mgr*
EMP: 5 **Privately Held**
SIC: 3674 Mfg Semiconductors/Related Devices
HQ: Ase (U.S) Inc.
1255 E Arques Ave
Sunnyvale CA 94085
408 636-9500

(G-17124)
AXIOM MICRODEVICES INC
20 Sylvan Rd (01801-1845)
PHONE..................................781 376-3000
Brett Butler, *CEO*
David Kang, *President*
Donald McClymont, *President*
Bruce Warren, *CFO*
EMP: 4
SALES (est): 405.8K
SALES (corp-wide): 3.3B **Publicly Held**
WEB: www.axiom-micro.com
SIC: 3663 Mfg Radio/Tv Communication Equipment
PA: Skyworks Solutions, Inc.
20 Sylvan Rd
Woburn MA 01801
781 376-3000

(G-17125)
AZURITY PHARMACEUTICALS (PA)
8 Cabot Rd (01801-1190)
PHONE..................................855 379-0382
Neal I Muni, *President*
Ronald L Scarboro, *COO*
Se-SE Yennes, *Vice Pres*
Jean Kadera, *Executive*
EMP: 11
SALES (est): 1.8MM **Privately Held**
SIC: 2834 Mfg Pharmaceutical Preparations

(G-17126)
BALYO INC
78b Olympia Ave (01801-2057)
PHONE..................................781 281-7957
Denis Lussault, *President*
Robin Depesa, *Project Mgr*
EMP: 21
SQ FT: 14,000
SALES: 3MM
SALES (corp-wide): 5.6MM **Privately Held**
SIC: 3569 Mfg General Industrial Machinery
PA: Balyo
3 Rue Paul Mazy
Ivry-Sur-Seine 94200
155 264-310

(G-17127)
BARBOUR STOCKWELL INC
45 6th Rd (01801-1757)
PHONE..................................781 933-5200
Kenneth Maillar, *President*
Anthony Enos, *Vice Pres*
Robert Gautlier, *Vice Pres*
Joshua Prudden, *Engineer*
Tony Enos, *Info Tech Dir*
▲ **EMP:** 20 **EST:** 1858
SQ FT: 20,000
SALES (est): 3.6MM **Privately Held**
WEB: www.barbourstockwell.com
SIC: 3825 8734 Mfg Measuring Instruments Testing Laboratory

(G-17128)
BECTON DICKINSON AND COMPANY
Also Called: Bd Bioscience
6 Henshaw St (01801-4624)
PHONE..................................781 935-5115
Charles Crespi, *Branch Mgr*
EMP: 429
SALES (corp-wide): 15.9B **Publicly Held**
SIC: 3841 Mfg Surgical/Medical Instruments
PA: Becton, Dickinson And Company
1 Becton Dr
Franklin Lakes NJ 07417
201 847-6800

(G-17129)
BELMAR COMPANY
10 Draper St Ste 30 (01801-4559)
PHONE..................................781 935-2233
Joseph Bellitti, *Owner*
EMP: 5
SQ FT: 500
SALES (est): 474.1K **Privately Held**
SIC: 3599 Mfg Industrial Machinery

(G-17130)
BERGEN PIPE SUPPORTS INC (HQ)
Also Called: Pipe Supports Group
225 Merrimac St (01801-1756)
PHONE..................................781 935-9550
Danny Burns, *CEO*
James Bonetti, *President*
Mike Spellman, *President*
David Lynch, *Exec VP*
Donald Colkin, *Vice Pres*
EMP: 30 **EST:** 1964
SQ FT: 5,000
SALES (est): 12.6MM
SALES (corp-wide): 840.5MM **Privately Held**
WEB: www.bergenpower.com
SIC: 3498 Mfg Valves/Pipe Fittings
PA: Hill & Smith Holdings Plc
Westhaven House
Solihull W MIDLANDS B90 4
121 704-7430

(G-17131)
BEYOND SHAKER LLC
124a Cummings Park (01801)
PHONE..................................617 461-6608
Scott Rousseau,
EMP: 6
SALES (est): 387.3K **Privately Held**
SIC: 2099 Mfg Food Preparations

(G-17132)
BITFLOW INC
400 W Cummings Park # 5050 (01801-6524)
PHONE..................................781 932-2900
Avner A Butnaru, *CEO*
Reynold J Dodson, *President*
Brittany Calnen, *Sales Staff*
James W Moore, *Legal Staff*
EMP: 11
SQ FT: 5,163
SALES (est): 2.7MM **Privately Held**
WEB: www.bitflow.com
SIC: 3672 7371 Mfg Printed Circuit Boards Custom Computer Programing

(G-17133)
BLACK DIAMOND GROUP INC
Also Called: Work and Tactical Gear
300 Tradecenter Ste 5550 (01801-7434)
PHONE..................................781 932-4173
Alan Lunder, *CEO*
Robert Mills, *President*
Michael Teixeira, *Exec VP*
▲ **EMP:** 12
SALES (est): 2.2MM **Privately Held**
SIC: 3021 5139 Mfg Rubber/Plastic Footwear Whol Footwear

(G-17134)
BLUEZONE PRODUCTS INC
225 Wildwood Ave (01801-3140)
PHONE..................................781 937-0202
Karen Benedek, *CEO*
Phil Carbone, *President*
Raymond Chang, *Director*
Guichao Hua, *Director*
◆ **EMP:** 5
SALES: 1.2MM **Privately Held**
SIC: 3585 3822 Mfg Refrigeration/Heating Equipment Mfg Environmental Controls

(G-17135)
BOSTON AMERICA CORP
55 6th Rd Ste 8 (01801-1746)
PHONE..................................781 933-3535
Matthew Kavet, *President*
Susan Mewhiney, *Cust Mgr*
Rebecca Devries, *Creative Dir*
Michelle Mohnkern, *Graphic Designe*
◆ **EMP:** 15
SALES (est): 3.6MM **Privately Held**
SIC: 3499 Mfg Misc Fabricated Metal Products

(G-17136)
BOSTON M4 TECH LLC
500 W Cummings Park # 1500 (01801-6534)
PHONE..................................617 279-3172
Ali S ABO Laban, *Mng Member*
▲ **EMP:** 5 **EST:** 2012
SALES: 250K **Privately Held**
SIC: 3843 Mfg Dental Equipment/Supplies

(G-17137)
BOSTON WELDING & DESIGN INC
7 Micro Dr (01801-5701)
PHONE..................................781 932-0035
Robert Diorio, *President*
Evelyn Diorio, *Office Mgr*
EMP: 15
SQ FT: 20,000

SALES: 3MM Privately Held
SIC: 7692 Welding Repair

(G-17138)
BOSTONCOUNTERS LLC
78h Olympia Ave (01801-2057)
PHONE..................................781 281-1622
Jon Mancini, *Mng Member*
Todd Mancini, *Mng Member*
Cleider Marques, *Mng Member*
Scott McCollem, *Mng Member*
EMP: 4
SALES (est): 412.4K Privately Held
SIC: 2511 2514 Mfg Wood Household Furniture Mfg Metal Household Furniture

(G-17139)
BRANNEN BROTHERS-FLUTEMAKERS
Also Called: Brannen Flutes
58 Dragon Ct (01801-1014)
PHONE..................................781 935-9522
Bickford W Brannen, *President*
Birgitte M Flanders, *Admin Sec*
EMP: 28
SQ FT: 111,000
SALES (est): 4.6MM Privately Held
WEB: www.brannenflutes.com
SIC: 3931 Mfg Musical Instruments

(G-17140)
CADNEXUS INC
100 Tower Office Park K (01801-2127)
PHONE..................................781 281-2672
Ali Merchant, *President*
Kent Summers, *Director*
EMP: 5
SALES: 500K Privately Held
SIC: 7372 Prepackaged Software Services

(G-17141)
CDI METERS INC
3r Green St Ste 2 (01801-4366)
PHONE..................................508 867-3178
Roger Dennison, *President*
EMP: 3
SALES (est): 541.1K Privately Held
WEB: www.cdimeters.com
SIC: 3823 Mfg Process Control Instruments

(G-17142)
CENTRAL ADMXTURE PHRM SVCS INC
55 6th Rd (01801-1767)
PHONE..................................781 376-0032
Arthur Dahl, *Principal*
EMP: 30
SALES (corp-wide): 2.6MM Privately Held
WEB: www.capspharmacy.com
SIC: 2834 5122 Manufacture Pharmaceutical Preparations Wholesales Drugs/Sundries
HQ: Central Admixture Pharmacy Services, Inc.
2525 Mcgaw Ave
Irvine CA 92614

(G-17143)
CHARLES WEBB INC (PA)
Also Called: Charles Webb Desgr Woodworker
470 Wildwood Ave Ste 7 (01801-2082)
PHONE..................................781 569-0444
John Gross, *President*
Charles Webb, *Treasurer*
EMP: 25 EST: 1966
SQ FT: 30,000
SALES (est): 2.3MM Privately Held
SIC: 2511 5712 2521 2512 Mfg Wood Household Furn Ret Furniture Mfg Wood Office Furn Mfg Uphls Household Furn

(G-17144)
CLAYTON LLC
Also Called: Bluebird Graphic Sols
17 Everberg Rd Ste E (01801-1019)
PHONE..................................617 250-8500
Anthony Clayton,
Cynthia Clayton,
Kyle Wolfe, *Sr Associate*
EMP: 20
SQ FT: 8,500
SALES (est): 1.2MM Privately Held
SIC: 3993 3446 7336 Mfg Signs/Advertising Specialties Mfg Architectural Metalwork Commercial Art/Graphic Design

(G-17145)
CNH TECHNOLOGIES INC
10a Henshaw St (01801-4666)
PHONE..................................781 933-0362
Yi-Fong Wang, *President*
◆ EMP: 5
SALES (est): 792.6K Privately Held
WEB: www.cnhtechnologies.com
SIC: 2834 Mfg Pharmaceutical Preparations

(G-17146)
COATING APPLICATION TECH
219 New Boston St (01801-6214)
PHONE..................................781 491-0699
Robert R Withee, *CEO*
Joseph W Selbeck, *President*
EMP: 13 EST: 2010
SALES: 2.2MM Privately Held
SIC: 3479 Coating/Engraving Service

(G-17147)
CONANT CONTROLS INC
215 Salem St Ste K (01801-2061)
P.O. Box 310, Medford (02155-0004)
PHONE..................................781 395-2240
Stanley M Lewis, *President*
EMP: 14 EST: 1946
SQ FT: 15,000
SALES (est): 3MM Privately Held
WEB: www.conantcontrols.com
SIC: 3592 3494 3492 3491 Mfg Carburetors/Pistons Mfg Valves/Pipe Fittings Mfg Fluid Power Valves Mfg Industrial Valves

(G-17148)
CONNOISSEURS PRODUCTS CORP (PA)
17 Presidential Way (01801-1040)
PHONE..................................800 851-5333
Douglas Dorfman, *CEO*
Jonathan Dorfman, *Vice Pres*
◆ EMP: 100
SQ FT: 70,000
SALES (est): 19.7MM Privately Held
WEB: www.connoisseurs.com
SIC: 2842 Mfg Polish/Sanitation Goods

(G-17149)
CONNOLLY PRINTING LLC
17b Gill St (01801-1768)
PHONE..................................781 932-8885
Laura Connolly, *Cust Mgr*
Kevin Connolly, *Mng Member*
EMP: 6
SALES (est): 1MM Privately Held
SIC: 2752 Lithographic Commercial Printing

(G-17150)
CONTECH ENGNERED SOLUTIONS LLC
10 Tower Office Park (01801-2182)
PHONE..................................781 932-4201
Joe Williams, *Branch Mgr*
EMP: 10 Privately Held
SIC: 3443 Mfg Fabricated Plate Work
HQ: Contech Engineered Solutions Llc
9025 Centre Pointe Dr # 400
West Chester OH 45069
513 645-7000

(G-17151)
CONTINENTAL METAL PDTS CO INC
Also Called: Cmp
35 Olympia Ave (01801-2045)
P.O. Box 2295 (01888-0495)
PHONE..................................781 935-4400
Paul Siegal, *President*
Stephen Siegal, *Vice Pres*
EMP: 45 EST: 1948
SQ FT: 60,000
SALES (est): 8.1MM Privately Held
WEB: www.continentalmetal.com
SIC: 3842 3589 Mfg Surgical Appliances/Supplies Mfg Service Industry Machinery

(G-17152)
CONTINUUS PHARMACEUTICAL
25 Olympia Ave (01801-6307)
PHONE..................................781 281-0099
EMP: 5 EST: 2015
SALES (est): 539.6K Privately Held
SIC: 2834 Pharmaceutical Preparations

(G-17153)
CONTINUUS PHARMACEUTICALS INC
25r Olympia Ave (01801-6307)
PHONE..................................781 281-0226
Salvatore Mascia, *President*
Ridade Sayin, *Research*
Chuntian Hu, *Engineer*
Born Stephen, *Finance*
EMP: 14
SQ FT: 4,000
SALES (est): 3.4MM Privately Held
SIC: 2869 8732 Mfg Industrial Organic Chemicals Commercial Nonphysical Research

(G-17154)
COVARIS INC (PA)
14 Gill St Unit H (01801-1721)
PHONE..................................781 932-3959
James A Laugharn, *President*
Carl Beckett, *General Mgr*
Chris Devlin, *Vice Pres*
Maria Nassar, *Materials Mgr*
Argenis Gonzalez, *QC Mgr*
EMP: 40
SQ FT: 90,000
SALES (est): 7.8MM Privately Held
WEB: www.covarisinc.com
SIC: 3826 Mfg Analytical Instruments

(G-17155)
CROWN EQUIPMENT CORPORATION
Also Called: Crown Lift Trucks
2 Presidential Way (01801-1041)
PHONE..................................781 933-3366
Andy Crampton, *Branch Mgr*
EMP: 78
SALES (corp-wide): 4.2B Privately Held
SIC: 3537 Mfg Industrial Trucks/Tractors Whol Industrial Equipment
PA: Crown Equipment Corporation
44 S Washington St
New Bremen OH 45869
419 629-2311

(G-17156)
CUSTOM AROSPC COMPONENTS LLC
30 Nashua St Ste 3 (01801-4566)
PHONE..................................781 935-4940
Cosmo Pascuito, *CEO*
Carl Pasciuto, *President*
Michael Pascuito, *Vice Pres*
Joanna Dowling, *Mng Member*
Anna Pasciuto,
▼ EMP: 65
SQ FT: 42,000
SALES (est): 7.3MM
SALES (corp-wide): 12.6MM Privately Held
SIC: 3599 Mfg Industrial Machinery
PA: The Custom Group Inc
30 Nashua St Ste 3
Woburn MA 01801
781 935-4940

(G-17157)
CUSTOM MACHINE LLC
30 Nashua St Ste 2 (01801-4566)
PHONE..................................781 935-4940
Cosmo Pascuito, *CEO*
Carl Pasciuto, *President*
Joanna Dowling, *Vice Pres*
Michael Pascuito, *Vice Pres*
EMP: 15
SALES (est): 1.4MM
SALES (corp-wide): 12.6MM Privately Held
SIC: 3448 Mfg Prefabricated Metal Buildings
PA: The Custom Group Inc
30 Nashua St Ste 3
Woburn MA 01801
781 935-4940

(G-17158)
CUSTOM OFFICE FURN BOSTON INC
10 Atlantic Ave Ste 3 (01801-5188)
PHONE..................................781 933-9970
Timothy Mahoney, *President*
EMP: 15
SQ FT: 15,000
SALES (est): 1.9MM Privately Held
SIC: 2521 2522 Mfg Wood Office Furn

(G-17159)
CUSTOM PLASTICS MACHINING INC
9 Presidential Way Ste D (01801-1092)
PHONE..................................781 937-9700
Dan Smith, *President*
EMP: 4
SALES (est): 478.1K Privately Held
SIC: 3599 Mfg Industrial Machinery

(G-17160)
CUTANEA LIFE SCIENCES INC
120 Presidential Way # 330 (01801-1182)
PHONE..................................484 568-0100
Robert J Bitterman, *President*
Robert Ferrara, *CFO*
Carmine Augello, *Sales Staff*
Stacey Ewing, *Manager*
Jessica Pung, *Senior Mgr*
EMP: 30
SALES: 5MM Privately Held
SIC: 2834 Mfg Pharmaceutical Preparations Specializing In Skin Diseases
PA: Maruho Co., Ltd.
1-5-22, Nakatsu, Kita-Ku
Osaka OSK 531-0

(G-17161)
CYTA THERAPEUTICS INC
165 New Boston St (01801-6201)
PHONE..................................617 947-1416
Bernadette Fendrock, *CEO*
Steve Faraci, *Vice Pres*
EMP: 5
SALES (est): 340.2K Privately Held
SIC: 2834 Pharmaceutical Preparations

(G-17162)
DAILY WOBURN TIMES INC (PA)
Also Called: Daily Times Chronicle
1 Arrow Dr Ste 1 # 1 (01801-2252)
PHONE..................................781 933-3700
Peter Haggerty, *President*
Richard P Haggerty, *President*
James D Haggerty III, *Vice Pres*
EMP: 60 EST: 1901
SQ FT: 27,500
SALES (est): 7MM Privately Held
WEB: www.woburnonline.com
SIC: 2711 Newspapers-Publishing/Printing

(G-17163)
DAN-KAR PLASTICS PRODUCTS
192 New Boston St C (01801-6207)
P.O. Box 279, Reading (01867-0479)
PHONE..................................781 935-9221
Terrance Hahn, *President*
Katherine Hahn, *Vice Pres*
Kathryn Hahn, *Human Res Dir*
EMP: 6
SQ FT: 10,000
SALES (est): 984.5K Privately Held
WEB: www.dan-kar.com
SIC: 3821 3089 3356 Mfg Lab Apparatus/Furniture Mfg Plastic Products Nonferrous Rolling/Drawing

(G-17164)
DATA PRINT INC
18 Cranes Ct (01801-5604)
PHONE..................................781 935-3350
Ralph Wooldridge, *President*
Catherine Wooldridge, *Clerk*
EMP: 10
SQ FT: 10,000
SALES (est): 1.5MM Privately Held
WEB: www.dataprint.net
SIC: 2752 Offset Printing & Lithography

(G-17165)
DAVOL INC
160 New Boston St (01801-6204)
PHONE..................................781 932-5900

GEOGRAPHIC

Son Pho, *Engineer*
Kelly Behrentt, *Manager*
EMP: 22
SALES (corp-wide): 15.9B **Publicly Held**
WEB: www.perfixplug.com
SIC: 3841 Mfg Surgical/Medical Instruments
HQ: Davol Inc.
100 Crossings Blvd
Warwick RI 02886
401 825-8300

(G-17166)
DEARBORN CRANE AND ENGRG CO
110 Winn St Ste 205 (01801-2800)
PHONE..................................781 897-4100
Bernadette Grov-Wright, *Branch Mgr*
EMP: 4
SALES (corp-wide): 14MM **Privately Held**
SIC: 3536 Mfg Hoists/Cranes/Monorails
PA: Dearborn Crane And Engineering Company
1133 E 5th St
Mishawaka IN 46544
574 259-2444

(G-17167)
DG3 GROUP AMERICA INC
Also Called: Dg3 Digital Pubg Solutions
500 W Cummings Park # 4500
(01801-6503)
PHONE..................................617 241-5600
EMP: 8
SALES (corp-wide): 321.1MM **Privately Held**
SIC: 7372 Prepackaged Software Services
HQ: Dg3 Group America, Inc.
100 Burma Rd
Jersey City NJ 07305
201 793-5000

(G-17168)
DIGITAL VDEO CMMUNICATIONS INC
Also Called: D V C
500 W Cummings Park # 2000
(01801-6503)
PHONE..................................781 932-6882
Scott Adams, *President*
Chris Dixon, *President*
EMP: 4
SQ FT: 2,300
SALES (est): 490K **Privately Held**
WEB: www.digitalvideocommunications.com
SIC: 3699 Mfg Electrical Equipment/Supplies

(G-17169)
DOUGH CONNECTION CORPORATION
32a Holton St (01801-5205)
PHONE..................................877 693-6844
Mark Pesaturo, *President*
EMP: 7
SALES (est): 893K **Privately Held**
SIC: 2045 2099 Mfg Prepared Flour Mixes/Doughs Mfg Food Preparations

(G-17170)
DREWS LLC
10 Kennedy Rd (01801-3407)
PHONE..................................781 935-6045
Drew Starkweather, *President*
Jim Byrne, *Vice Pres*
EMP: 3
SALES (est): 123.5K **Privately Held**
SIC: 2032 5499 Mfg Canned Specialties Ret Misc Foods

(G-17171)
E V YEUELL INC
Also Called: Yeuell Name Plate & Label
17 Gill St (01801-1768)
PHONE..................................781 933-2984
Thomas W Barry, *President*
Judith A Hall, *Vice Pres*
Andrew F Hall III, *Treasurer*
EMP: 26 **EST:** 1963
SALES (est): 4.2MM **Privately Held**
WEB: www.yeuell.com
SIC: 2752 3479 3993 2671 Lithographic Coml Print Coating/Engraving Svcs Mfg Signs/Ad Specialties Mfg Packaging Paper/Film Mfg Auto/Apparel Trim

(G-17172)
EARLYSENSE INC
800 W Cummings Park # 6400
(01801-6358)
PHONE..................................781 373-3228
Avner Halperin, *President*
Tim O'Malley, *President*
Karissa Price-Rico, *COO*
Hadar Ritte, *Vice Pres*
Eric Puffer, *Senior Engr*
EMP: 13
SALES (est): 2.6MM
SALES (corp-wide): 5.2MM **Privately Held**
SIC: 3841 Mfg Surgical/Medical Instruments
PA: Earlysense Ltd
7 Jabotinsky
Ramat Gan 52520
375 223-30

(G-17173)
EASY WAY DRY CLEANERS INC
Also Called: Easy Way Cleaners
227 Main St (01801-5003)
PHONE..................................781 933-1473
Peter Kim, *President*
EMP: 5
SQ FT: 2,000
SALES (est): 399.1K **Privately Held**
SIC: 3633 7216 Mfg Home Laundry Equipment Drycleaning Plant

(G-17174)
ELECTRICAL SAFETY PRODUCTS LLC
375 Main St Bldg 100 (01801-5030)
PHONE..................................781 249-5007
EMP: 4
SQ FT: 2,500
SALES: 40.5K **Privately Held**
SIC: 3699 Electrical Contractor

(G-17175)
ELECTROCHEM INC
400 W Cummings Park # 5600
(01801-6510)
PHONE..................................781 938-5300
Radha Jalan, *President*
▼ **EMP:** 10
SQ FT: 5,000
SALES: 1.5MM **Privately Held**
WEB: www.fuelcell.com
SIC: 2813 R&D/Mfg Hydrogen Equipment

(G-17176)
ELKAY PLASTICS
101 Commerce Way (01801-1007)
PHONE..................................781 932-9800
Fax: 781 932-1796
EMP: 3 **EST:** 2000
SALES (est): 210.4K **Privately Held**
SIC: 3089 Mfg Plastic Products

(G-17177)
ENDOGEN INC
30 Commerce Way (01801-8503)
PHONE..................................617 225-0055
EMP: 72
SQ FT: 12,144
SALES (est): 4.1MM **Privately Held**
SIC: 2835 2836 8731 3841 Mfg Diagnostic Substance Mfg Biological Products Coml Physical Research Mfg Surgical/Med Instr
HQ: Perbio Science Ab
Arendalsvagen 30
Goteborg
422 690-90

(G-17178)
EPIC TECHNOLOGIES INC
500 W Cummings Park # 6950
(01801-6540)
PHONE..................................781 932-7870
James E Kohl, *President*
EMP: 16
SQ FT: 12,700
SALES (est): 3.4MM **Privately Held**
WEB: www.epic-tech.com
SIC: 3565 8742 Mfg Packaging Machinery Management Consulting Services

(G-17179)
FILTERED AIR SYSTEMS INC
100 Ashburton Ave Ste 3 (01801-1333)
PHONE..................................781 491-0508
Ryan Greene, *President*
Bryan Murphy, *Shareholder*
▲ **EMP:** 8
SQ FT: 7,400
SALES: 1.2MM **Privately Held**
WEB: www.filteredairsystems.com
SIC: 3589 Mfg Industrial Electrical Vacuum Cleaners & Sweepers

(G-17180)
FINE MAGAZINE
9 Fowle St (01801-5101)
PHONE..................................617 721-7372
John Smiroldo, *President*
EMP: 21
SALES (est): 1.4MM **Privately Held**
SIC: 2721 Periodicals-Publishing/Printing

(G-17181)
FIRST ELECTRIC MOTOR SVC INC
73 Olympia Ave (01801-2022)
PHONE..................................781 491-1100
James F Steenbruggen, *President*
EMP: 40
SQ FT: 17,000
SALES (est): 9.4MM **Privately Held**
SIC: 7694 5999 Armature Rewinding Ret Misc Merchandise

(G-17182)
FLOW GRINDING CORP (PA)
70 Conn St (01801-5662)
PHONE..................................781 933-5300
Winfield B Perry, *President*
Hubert A Perry Jr, *Exec VP*
Luke Perry, *Vice Pres*
▲ **EMP:** 5
SQ FT: 30,000
SALES (est): 2.5MM **Privately Held**
WEB: www.winbrogroup.com
SIC: 3541 Mfg Machine Tools-Cutting

(G-17183)
FLUENT TECHNOLOGIES INC
331 Montvale Ave Ste 300 (01801-4670)
PHONE..................................781 939-0900
Michael Zimmer, *President*
Jay Axson, *Principal*
Leslie Miller, *Accounts Mgr*
EMP: 16
SQ FT: 3,000
SALES (est): 1.2MM **Privately Held**
SIC: 2741 Misc Publishing

(G-17184)
FORWARD PHOTONICS LLC
500 W Cummings Park # 1900
(01801-6536)
PHONE..................................617 767-3519
Robin Huang, *CEO*
EMP: 10 **EST:** 2016
SALES (est): 530K **Privately Held**
SIC: 3674 Mfg Semiconductors/Related Devices

(G-17185)
FRAEN CORPORATION
324 New Boston St (01801-6211)
PHONE..................................781 937-8825
Charles R Fuller, *President*
Kenneth Donahue, *Vice Pres*
Scott McKenzie, *Manager*
EMP: 30
SALES (corp-wide): 23.4MM **Privately Held**
WEB: www.fraen.com
SIC: 3469 Mfg Metal Stampings
PA: Fraen Corporation
80 New Crossing Rd
Reading MA 01867
781 205-5300

(G-17186)
FRAEN MACHINING CORPORATION (PA)
Also Called: Swisstronics
324 New Boston St (01801-6211)
PHONE..................................781 205-5400
Peter W Fuller, *President*
Nicodemo Scarfo, *Treasurer*
Manuela Veiga, *Executive*
Charles R Fuller, *Clerk*
▲ **EMP:** 56
SQ FT: 36,000
SALES (est): 10.1MM **Privately Held**
WEB: www.swisstronics.com
SIC: 3451 Mfg Screw Machine Products

(G-17187)
FREQUENCY THERAPEUTICS INC (PA)
19 Presidential Way Fl 2 (01801-1184)
PHONE..................................866 389-1970
Marc A Cohen, *Ch of Bd*
David L Lucchino, *President*
Richard Mitrano, *VP Finance*
Dana Hilt, *Chief Mktg Ofcr*
Christopher R Loose, *Security Dir*
EMP: 13
SQ FT: 9,500
SALES (est): 471.6K **Publicly Held**
SIC: 2834 Pharmaceutical Preparations

(G-17188)
FRIDAY ENGINEERING INC
17 Everberg Rd (01801-1019)
PHONE..................................781 932-8686
Charles Shea, *President*
EMP: 7
SQ FT: 5,000
SALES: 370K **Privately Held**
SIC: 3599 Injection Molding And Machining

(G-17189)
FUSION OPTIX INC
17 Wheeling Ave (01801-2008)
PHONE..................................781 995-0805
Terence E Yeo, *CEO*
James Riley, *Admin Sec*
▲ **EMP:** 25
SQ FT: 14,000
SALES (est): 8.6MM **Privately Held**
WEB: www.fusionoptix.com
SIC: 3089 Mfg Plastic Products

(G-17190)
GENOA SAUSAGE CO INC
14 Industrial Pkwy (01801-1970)
PHONE..................................781 933-3115
Romuald Monkiewicz, *President*
EMP: 80
SALES (est): 6.3MM
SALES (corp-wide): 117.2MM **Privately Held**
WEB: www.kayem.com
SIC: 2013 Mfg Prepared Meats
PA: Kayem Foods, Inc.
75 Arlington St
Chelsea MA 02150
781 933-3115

(G-17191)
GENTEST CORPORATION
6 Henshaw St (01801-4624)
PHONE..................................781 935-5115
Charles Crespi, *President*
George Wayne, *Director*
EMP: 42
SQ FT: 12,000
SALES (est): 4.4MM **Privately Held**
SIC: 2834 8734 Mfg Research Reagents And Commercial Testing/Research Laboratory

(G-17192)
GERARD F SCALLEY
18 Dartmouth St (01801-1602)
PHONE..................................781 933-3009
Gerald Scalley, *Owner*
EMP: 4
SALES (est): 121.4K **Privately Held**
SIC: 2759 Commercial Printing

(G-17193)
GOTUIT MEDIA CORP
Also Called: Gotuit Video
400 Tradecenter Ste 3890 (01801-7462)
PHONE..................................801 592-5575
Mark Pascarella, *CEO*
EMP: 25
SALES (est): 2.7MM **Privately Held**
WEB: www.gotuit.com
SIC: **7372** Prepackaged Software Services

(G-17194)
GREGSTROM CORPORATION
64 Holton St (01801-5288)
P.O. Box 609 (01801-0709)
PHONE..................................781 935-6600
Paul J Didonato, *Ch of Bd*
Jeffrey Didonato, *President*
Judy Didonato, *Corp Secy*
Clark Boyce, *VP Sales*
▲ **EMP**: 75 **EST**: 1946
SALES (est): 16.1MM **Privately Held**
WEB: www.gregstrom.com
SIC: **3089** Mfg Plastic Products

(G-17195)
HANNAFORD & DUMAS CORPORATION
26 Conn St (01801-5662)
PHONE..................................781 503-0100
Steve Bryer, *President*
Michelle A Hannaford, *Corp Secy*
Tracy Gallagher, *Accounts Mgr*
Dick Ronan, *Accounts Mgr*
Keith Hagman, *Accounts Exec*
EMP: 35
SQ FT: 15,000
SALES (est): 7.7MM **Privately Held**
SIC: **2759** Commercial Printing

(G-17196)
HARTNETT CO INC
946 Main St (01801-1221)
PHONE..................................781 935-2600
Mary Hartnett, *President*
Christopher Hartnett, *Vice Pres*
EMP: 10
SQ FT: 5,000
SALES: 2.5MM **Privately Held**
SIC: **3999** Mfg Plaques Picture Laminated

(G-17197)
HARVEY INDUSTRIES INC
33 Commonwealth Ave (01801-1009)
PHONE..................................781 935-7990
Dave Deveuev, *Branch Mgr*
EMP: 50
SALES (corp-wide): 1.2B **Privately Held**
SIC: **3442** 5033 Mfg Metal Storm Doors And Windows And Whol Building Materials
PA: Harvey Industries, Inc.
1400 Main St Fl 3
Waltham MA 02451
800 598-5400

(G-17198)
HD LIFESCIENCES LLC
12 Gill St Ste 4500 (01801-1778)
PHONE..................................866 949-5433
Lucas Webb Diehl,
Ian Helmar,
Christopher Jones,
EMP: 6
SQ FT: 2,200
SALES: 3MM **Privately Held**
SIC: **3842** Mfg Surgical Appliances/Supplies

(G-17199)
HERLEY INDUSTRIES INC
Also Called: Herley New England
10 Sonar Dr (01801-5704)
PHONE..................................781 729-9450
Mark Tucci, *Vice Pres*
William R Wilson, *Vice Pres*
John Lagasse, *Plant Mgr*
Roy Dias, *Engineer*
Jim Sadin, *Engineer*
EMP: 125
SALES (corp-wide): 1B **Privately Held**
WEB: www.herley.com
SIC: **3679** Mfg Electronic Components
HQ: Herley Industries, Inc.
3061 Industry Dr
Lancaster PA 17603
717 397-2777

(G-17200)
II-VI PHOTONICS (US) INC (HQ)
Also Called: Aegis Semiconductor Security
78a Olympia Ave (01801-2057)
PHONE..................................781 938-1222
Fran Kramer, *President*
Jeffrey D Farmer, *General Mgr*
Craig Creaturo, *Treasurer*
Glenn D Bartolini, *Exec Dir*
David J Parent, *Exec Dir*
EMP: 45
SQ FT: 20,000
SALES (est): 6.1MM
SALES (corp-wide): 1.3B **Publicly Held**
WEB: www.aegis-semi.com
SIC: **3674** Mfg Semiconductors/Related Devices
PA: Ii-Vi Incorporated
375 Saxonburg Blvd
Saxonburg PA 16056
724 352-4455

(G-17201)
INFINITE GRAPHIC SOLUTIONS
15 Cranes Ct (01801-5603)
PHONE..................................781 938-6333
Frank Murphy, *President*
EMP: 6
SALES (est): 633.2K **Privately Held**
WEB: www.infinitegs.net
SIC: **2752** Lithographic Commercial Printing

(G-17202)
INNOVATIONS IN OPTICS INC
82 Cummings Park (01801-2125)
PHONE..................................781 933-4477
Thomas Brukilacchio, *President*
Kevin Carr, *Vice Pres*
Sarah H Brukilacchio, *CFO*
EMP: 4
SALES (est): 866.4K **Privately Held**
WEB: www.innovationsinoptics.com
SIC: **3827** Mfg Optical Instruments/Lenses

(G-17203)
INSULTAB INC
45 Industrial Pkwy Ste 1 (01801-1996)
PHONE..................................781 935-0800
Philip Cowen, *CEO*
Rose Saporito, *Sales Staff*
David Mariotti, *Info Tech Mgr*
▲ **EMP**: 80 **EST**: 1964
SQ FT: 90,000
SALES (est): 17.3MM
SALES (corp-wide): 7.9B **Privately Held**
WEB: www.insultab.com
SIC: **3082** 3083 Manufacturer Of Plastic Profile Shapes Mfg Laminated Plastic Plate/Sheet
HQ: Pexco Llc
6470 E Johns Rssng 430
Johns Creek GA 30097
770 777-8540

(G-17204)
INTAC INTERNATIONAL INC
15 Commonwealth Ave # 202
(01801-5193)
PHONE..................................781 272-4494
Daniel Restivo, *President*
Seth Hauben, *Marketing Mgr*
EMP: 26
SQ FT: 15,000
SALES (est): 2.3MM **Publicly Held**
WEB: www.intacinternational.com
SIC: **7372** 7371 Prepackaged Software Services Custom Computer Programing
PA: Remark Holdings, Inc.
3960 Howard Hughes Pkwy # 900
Las Vegas NV 89169

(G-17205)
INTEGRATED OPHTHALMIC SYS
596 Main St (01801-2924)
PHONE..................................617 571-8238
Matthew Carnevale, *President*
EMP: 5
SALES: 1MM **Privately Held**
SIC: **3841** Mfg Surgical/Medical Instruments

(G-17206)
INTERNATIONAL STONE INC
10 Ryan Rd (01801-2444)
PHONE..................................781 937-3300
Joanne Gemelarro, *President*
◆ **EMP**: 80
SQ FT: 30,000
SALES (est): 19.3MM **Privately Held**
SIC: **3441** 5032 3281 Structural Metal Fabrication Whol Brick/Stone Material Mfg Cut Stone/Products

(G-17207)
ITT CORPORATION
10 Mill St (01801-3310)
PHONE..................................781 932-5665
Tom Stagliano, *Branch Mgr*
EMP: 12
SALES (corp-wide): 2.7B **Publicly Held**
WEB: www.ittind.com
SIC: **3625** Mfg Relays/Industrial Controls
HQ: Itt Llc
1133 Westchester Ave N-100
White Plains NY 10604
914 641-2000

(G-17208)
JANIS RESEARCH COMPANY INC (PA)
225 Wildwood Ave (01801-3140)
PHONE..................................781 491-0888
Thomas G Pasakarnis, *President*
Susan Celikmen, *Vice Pres*
Dana Doo, *Opers Staff*
Dan Lugan, *Engineer*
Kerry Faulkner, *Design Engr*
▲ **EMP**: 67 **EST**: 1960
SQ FT: 17,500
SALES (est): 15.2MM **Privately Held**
SIC: **3826** Mfg Analytical Instruments

(G-17209)
JANIS RESEARCH COMPANY LLC
225 Wildwood Ave (01801-3140)
PHONE..................................781 491-0888
Thomas Pasakarnis, *Principal*
Michael Shanley, *Controller*
EMP: 60
SALES (est): 8.6MM
SALES (corp-wide): 15.2MM **Privately Held**
WEB: www.janis.com
SIC: **3826** Mfg Analytical Instruments
PA: Janis Research Company, Inc.
225 Wildwood Ave
Woburn MA 01801
781 491-0888

(G-17210)
JARICA INC
Also Called: Jack's Custom Woodworking
3 Aberjona Dr (01801-2043)
PHONE..................................781 935-1907
John A Hussey, *President*
EMP: 18
SQ FT: 3,000
SALES (est): 3.1MM **Privately Held**
WEB: www.jcwcountertops.com
SIC: **2452** 1799 2541 2821 Mfg Prefabrcatd Wd Bldgs Special Trade Contractor Mfg Wood Partitions/Fixt Mfg Plstc Material/Resin

(G-17211)
KOROLATH OF NEW ENGLAND INC (HQ)
310 Salem St (01801-2065)
PHONE..................................781 933-6004
Robert D Kearin, *President*
Michael P Famiglietti, *Treasurer*
EMP: 3 **EST**: 1962
SQ FT: 56,000
SALES (est): 1.9MM
SALES (corp-wide): 16.5MM **Privately Held**
WEB: www.korolath.com
SIC: **3089** Mfg Plastic Products
PA: New England Plastics Corporation
310 Salem St Ste 2
Woburn MA 01801
781 933-6004

(G-17212)
KRAFT HEINZ FOODS COMPANY
Also Called: Kraft Foods
1 Hill St (01801-4625)
PHONE..................................781 933-2800
Kathleen Pigott, *Opers-Prdtn-Mfg*
EMP: 250
SALES (corp-wide): 26.2B **Publicly Held**
WEB: www.kraftfoods.com
SIC: **2022** 2013 2095 Mfg Cheese Mfg Prepared Meats Mfg Roasted Coffee
HQ: Kraft Heinz Foods Company
1 Ppg Pl Fl 34
Pittsburgh PA 15222
412 456-5700

(G-17213)
LEGGETT & PLATT INCORPORATED
Also Called: Leggett & Platt 1010
3040 Junior Home Rd (01801)
PHONE..................................336 956-5000
Dean McGuire, *General Mgr*
EMP: 300
SQ FT: 6,000
SALES (corp-wide): 4.2B **Publicly Held**
WEB: www.leggett.com
SIC: **2515** Mfg Mattresses/Bedsprings
PA: Leggett & Platt, Incorporated
1 Leggett Rd
Carthage MO 64836
417 358-8131

(G-17214)
LIONANO INC
19 Presidential Way # 103 (01801-1184)
PHONE..................................607 216-8156
Yingchao Yu, *CEO*
EMP: 4
SQ FT: 500
SALES (est): 364.5K **Privately Held**
SIC: **3691** 8731 Mfg Batteries Commercial Physical Research

(G-17215)
LISA SIGNS INC
Also Called: Simply Sisters Silk Screening
2 Norwood Cir (01801-1272)
P.O. Box 130 (01801-0130)
PHONE..................................781 935-1821
Lisa Hurley, *President*
EMP: 3
SQ FT: 3,000
SALES (est): 287.3K **Privately Held**
SIC: **2759** 2395 Commercial Printing Pleating/Stitching Services

(G-17216)
LKM INDUSTRIES INC
44 6th Rd Ste 2 (01801-1784)
PHONE..................................781 935-9210
Salvi Colucciello, *President*
Ralph Colucciello, *Vice Pres*
John Colucciello, *Engineer*
William E Nunnelley, *Treasurer*
Maria Colucciello-Ros, *Info Tech Mgr*
EMP: 60 **EST**: 1978
SQ FT: 101,000
SALES (est): 18.4MM **Privately Held**
SIC: **3511** 3724 Mfg Turbines/Generator Sets Mfg Aircraft Engines/Parts

(G-17217)
LOGIN VSI INC
300 Tradecenter Ste 3460 (01801-1883)
PHONE..................................844 828-3693
Eric-Jan Van Leeuwen, *CEO*
EMP: 6
SALES (est): 772.2K **Privately Held**
SIC: **7372** Prepackaged Software Services

(G-17218)
LORD HOBO BREWING COMPANY LLC
5 Draper St (01801-4521)
PHONE..................................781 281-0809
Daniel Lanigan, *CEO*
EMP: 10
SALES (est): 1.1MM **Privately Held**
SIC: **2082** Mfg Malt Beverages

(G-17219)
LYMOL MEDICAL CORP (PA)
Also Called: Bryan
4 Plympton St (01801-2917)
PHONE.................................781 935-0004
Kim Abrano, *CEO*
EMP: 10
SQ FT: 4,000
SALES (est): 1.9MM **Privately Held**
WEB: www.bryancorp.com
SIC: 3841 Mfg Surgical/Medical Instruments

(G-17220)
LYTRON INCORPORATED
9 Forbes Rd (01801-2103)
PHONE.................................781 933-7300
EMP: 3
SALES (corp-wide): 642MM **Privately Held**
SIC: 3443 Mfg Fabricated Plate Work
HQ: Lytron Incorporated
55 Dragon Ct
Woburn MA 01801
781 933-7300

(G-17221)
M & K ENGINEERING INC
166 New Boston St (01801-6204)
PHONE.................................781 933-1760
Henry Bernardo, *President*
Keith Bernardo, *President*
Bibiana Bernardo, *CFO*
EMP: 45
SQ FT: 20,000
SALES (est): 9.1MM **Privately Held**
WEB: www.mkeng.com
SIC: 3599 Mfg Industrial Machinery

(G-17222)
MAGNOLIA OPTICAL TECH INC
52b Cummings Park Ste 314 (01801)
PHONE.................................781 376-1505
Ashok Sood, *CEO*
Yash R Puri, *Vice Pres*
EMP: 5 **EST:** 2000
SALES (est): 691K **Privately Held**
SIC: 3827 Mfg Optical Instruments/Lenses

(G-17223)
MASCON INC
5 Commonwealth Ave Unit 3 (01801-1032)
PHONE.................................781 938-5800
James Chen, *President*
Jeannie Chen, *Treasurer*
Susan Lee, *Accountant*
Michael Campbell, *Finance*
Bob Marino, *Technology*
◆ **EMP:** 25
SQ FT: 18,000
SALES (est): 3.8MM **Privately Held**
SIC: 3089 3363 Mfg Plastic Products Mfg Aluminum Die-Castings

(G-17224)
MASTERWORK
10 Draper St Ste 35 (01801-4560)
PHONE.................................781 995-3354
EMP: 5
SALES (est): 320K **Privately Held**
SIC: 2679 Mfg Converted Paper Products

(G-17225)
MBL INTERNATIONAL CORPORATION (DH)
15a Constitution Way (01801-1024)
PHONE.................................781 939-6964
Tim Lowery, *CEO*
Mike Carroll, *Vice Pres*
Sue Malas, *Opers Staff*
Marc Delcommenne, *Research*
Shinobu Kitamura, *Treasurer*
EMP: 12
SALES (est): 5.7MM **Privately Held**
SIC: 2834 5122 Mfg Pharmaceutical Preparations Whol Drugs/Sundries

(G-17226)
MCMANUS E VQ GP LLC
14 Winter Rd (01801-1226)
PHONE.................................781 935-2483
EMP: 3
SALES (est): 138.8K **Privately Held**
SIC: 3131 Footwear Cut Stock

(G-17227)
MEDIATEK USA INC
Also Called: Mediatek Woburn
120 Presidential Way (01801-1181)
PHONE.................................781 503-8000
Koh Hung Loh, *Principal*
EMP: 100
SALES (corp-wide): 75.8MM **Privately Held**
SIC: 3559 3674 Semiconductor Company-Systems On Chip For Wireless Communications And Connectivity
PA: Mediatek Usa Inc.
2840 Junction Ave
San Jose CA 95134
408 526-1899

(G-17228)
METRICK MANUFACTURING CO INC
Also Called: Metric Mfg
142 Bedford Rd Ste 3 (01801-3999)
PHONE.................................781 935-1331
Michael Metrick Jr, *President*
Anne Metrick, *Treasurer*
EMP: 3 **EST:** 1981
SQ FT: 3,000
SALES: 418K **Privately Held**
WEB: www.metrickmfg.com
SIC: 7692 3441 Welding & Steel Fabrication

(G-17229)
METRO GROUP INC
64 Cummings Park (01801-2124)
PHONE.................................781 932-9911
Michael Flayhive, *Branch Mgr*
EMP: 15
SALES (corp-wide): 21.4MM **Privately Held**
SIC: 3589 Mfg Service Industry Machinery
PA: Metro Group, Inc.
5023 23rd St
Long Island City NY 11101
718 729-7200

(G-17230)
MICROSCALE INC
800 W Cummings Park # 3350
(01801-6372)
PHONE.................................781 995-2245
Xingtao Wu, *President*
EMP: 5
SALES (est): 576.7K **Privately Held**
WEB: www.microscaleinc.com
SIC: 3674 Mfg Semiconductors/Related Devices

(G-17231)
MICROSS EXPRESS
400 W Cummings Park # 6900
(01801-6519)
PHONE.................................781 938-0866
Robert Sarkisian, *President*
EMP: 7
SALES (est): 286.4K **Privately Held**
SIC: 3674 Mfg Semiconductors/Related Devices

(G-17232)
MIDAS TECHNOLOGY INC
400 W Cummings Park # 6400
(01801-6533)
PHONE.................................781 938-0069
Kenneth D Towl, *President*
David F Barnes, *Director*
George Bloom, *Director*
▼ **EMP:** 50
SQ FT: 1,725
SALES (est): 5.8MM **Privately Held**
WEB: www.midastechnology.com
SIC: 3679 3599 Mfg Electronic Components Mfg Industrial Machinery

(G-17233)
MILLENNIUM RESEARCH LABS INC
Also Called: Mrl
160 New Boston St (01801-6204)
PHONE.................................781 935-0790
Nayantara Bhat, *President*
EMP: 5
SALES (est): 1.1MM **Privately Held**
WEB: www.mrl-online.com
SIC: 3826 Chemical Analysis Research & Development Methods Development And Validation

(G-17234)
MONOTYPE IMAGING INC (DH)
600 Unicorn Park Dr (01801-3376)
PHONE.................................781 970-6000
Douglas Shaw, *President*
▲ **EMP:** 90
SQ FT: 25,000
SALES (est): 52.9MM
SALES (corp-wide): 303.5MM **Privately Held**
WEB: www.monotypeimaging.com
SIC: 7372 7371 Prepackaged Software Services Custom Computer Programing

(G-17235)
NANOSURF INC
300 Tradecenter Ste 5450 (01801-7405)
PHONE.................................781 549-7361
URS Matter, *CEO*
Saju Nettikadan, *General Mgr*
EMP: 3
SQ FT: 1,600
SALES (est): 358.3K
SALES (corp-wide): 5.8MM **Privately Held**
SIC: 3826 Mfg Analytical Instruments
PA: Nanosurf Ag
Graubernstrasse 12
Liestal BL 4410
619 274-747

(G-17236)
NANTERO INC
25b Olympia Ave (01801-6307)
PHONE.................................781 932-5338
Greg Schmergel, *CEO*
Lee Cleveland, *Vice Pres*
Sohrab Kianian, *Vice Pres*
Thomas Bengtson, *Engineer*
Rinn Cleavelin, *Engineer*
EMP: 50
SALES (est): 10.7MM **Privately Held**
WEB: www.nram.com
SIC: 3674 Mfg Semiconductors/Related Devices

(G-17237)
NATALE CO SAFETYCARE LL
5 W Dexter Ave (01801-1617)
PHONE.................................781 933-7205
John Natale, *Owner*
EMP: 3
SALES (est): 240.5K **Privately Held**
SIC: 3312 Blast Furnace-Steel Works

(G-17238)
NELSON & POWER INC
5 Washington Ter (01801-3315)
PHONE.................................781 933-0679
EMP: 4 **EST:** 1938
SQ FT: 15,500
SALES: 387.1K **Privately Held**
SIC: 2431 Mfg Millwork

(G-17239)
NEO GREEN TECHNOLOGY CORP
Also Called: Neo Scientific
395 W Cummings Park (01801-6335)
PHONE.................................617 500-7103
▲ **EMP:** 5
SALES (est): 270.3K **Privately Held**
SIC: 3999 Mfg Misc Products

(G-17240)
NEUROGASTRX INCORPORATED
600 Unicorn Park Dr (01801-3376)
PHONE.................................781 730-4006
Jim O'Mara, *CEO*
EMP: 3 **EST:** 2016
SALES (est): 241.8K **Privately Held**
SIC: 2834 Mfg Pharmaceutical Preparations

(G-17241)
NEW ENGLAND DRAPERY ASSOC INC
Also Called: New England Drapery & Blind
5 Conn St Ste 2 (01801-5698)
PHONE.................................781 944-7536
Joseph Interrante, *President*
EMP: 5 **EST:** 1981
SQ FT: 4,000
SALES: 1MM **Privately Held**
SIC: 2591 5023 Mfg Drapery Hardware/Blinds Whol Homefurnishings

(G-17242)
NEW ENGLAND PET DISTR CTR LLC
268 W Cummings Park (01801-6346)
PHONE.................................781 937-3600
David Krydka,
EMP: 5
SALES: 3MM **Privately Held**
SIC: 2834 Mfg Pharmaceutical Preparations

(G-17243)
NEW ENGLAND PLASTICS CORP (PA)
310 Salem St Ste 2 (01801-2098)
PHONE.................................781 933-6004
Robert Kearin, *President*
Michael P Famiglietti, *Treasurer*
John Stewart, *Director*
EMP: 30
SQ FT: 60,000
SALES (est): 16.5MM **Privately Held**
SIC: 3081 3089 Mfg Unsupported Plastic Film/Sheet Mfg Plastic Products

(G-17244)
NEW OBJECTIVE INC
2 Constitution Way (01801-1293)
PHONE.................................781 933-9560
Gary Valaskovic, *President*
Emily Ehrenfeld, *Vice Pres*
Emily Ehrenfele, *Vice Pres*
Stanley Durand, *Prdtn Mgr*
EMP: 15
SQ FT: 9,000
SALES (est): 3.8MM **Privately Held**
WEB: www.newobjective.com
SIC: 3826 Mfg Analytical Instruments

(G-17245)
NEXTCEA INC
600 W Cummings Park # 6375
(01801-7241)
PHONE.................................800 225-1645
Frank Y Hsieh, *President*
Kelly Dunn, *Associate*
EMP: 3
SALES (est): 452.1K **Privately Held**
SIC: 2834 Mfg Pharmaceutical Preparations

(G-17246)
NOVA IDEA INC
124 Cummings Park (01801-2128)
PHONE.................................781 281-2183
Eduardo Dasilveira, *Principal*
EMP: 5
SALES (est): 395.5K **Privately Held**
SIC: 2269 2759 Finishing Plant Commercial Printing

(G-17247)
NOVA INSTRUMENTS CORPORATION (PA)
600 Unicorn Park Dr Ste 4 (01801-3343)
PHONE.................................781 897-1200
Jim Barbookles, *CEO*
EMP: 7
SALES (est): 2.7MM **Privately Held**
SIC: 3823 Mfg Process Control Instruments

(G-17248)
O & P IAM INC
400 W Cummings Park # 4950
(01801-6519)
PHONE.................................781 239-3331
Robert C Drillio, *Principal*
Sharon Drillio, *Vice Pres*
EMP: 6

SALES (est): 881.8K **Privately Held**
SIC: 3842 Mfg Surgical Appliances/Supplies

(G-17249)
OPKO DIAGNOSTICS LLC
Also Called: Fluidx
4 Constitution Way Ste E (01801-1042)
PHONE..................................781 933-8012
Phillip Frost, *CEO*
Michael Magliochetti, *President*
David Steinmiller, *COO*
Sophie Chheou, *QC Mgr*
Jason Taylor, *Senior Engr*
EMP: 6
SQ FT: 3,000
SALES (est): 850K **Publicly Held**
WEB: www.clarosdx.com
SIC: 3845 Mfg Electromedical Equipment
PA: Opko Health, Inc.
4400 Biscayne Blvd
Miami FL 33137

(G-17250)
OPTICRAFT INC
17d Everberg Rd (01801-1019)
PHONE..................................781 938-0456
Dennis McAllister, *President*
EMP: 20 **EST**: 1978
SQ FT: 6,700
SALES: 3MM **Privately Held**
WEB: www.opticraft.com
SIC: 3827 Mfg Optical Instruments/Lenses

(G-17251)
OPTOWARES INCORPORATED
15 Presidential Way (01801-1040)
PHONE..................................781 427-7106
Wayne Weimer, *President*
Jeanne Hladky, *Manager*
EMP: 11
SQ FT: 2,000
SALES (est): 1.9MM
SALES (corp-wide): 3.3MM **Privately Held**
SIC: 3699 Mfg Electrical Equipment/Supplies
PA: Photonwares Corporation
15 Presidential Way
Woburn MA 01801
781 935-1200

(G-17252)
OZZIE PRINTING INC
24b Conn St (01801-5662)
PHONE..................................978 657-9400
Steve A Aimbraino, *President*
EMP: 4
SALES (est): 230K **Privately Held**
WEB: www.ozzieprinting.com
SIC: 2752 Lithographic Commercial Printing

(G-17253)
PACOTHANE TECHNOLOGIES
76 Holton St (01801-5205)
PHONE..................................781 756-3163
Carl Papalano, *Manager*
EMP: 25
SALES (corp-wide): 3.7MM **Privately Held**
SIC: 2621 Paper Mill
PA: Pacothane Technologies
37 East St
Winchester MA 01890
781 729-0927

(G-17254)
PARAGRAPH 11 LLC
5 Draper St (01801-4521)
PHONE..................................781 281-1143
EMP: 3
SALES (est): 190K **Privately Held**
SIC: 2082 Mfg Malt Beverages

(G-17255)
PARKER-HANNIFIN CORPORATION
Also Called: Parker Hannifin Chomerics
70 Dragon Ct (01801-1014)
PHONE..................................781 939-4278
David Hill, *Branch Mgr*
EMP: 400
SALES (corp-wide): 14.3B **Publicly Held**
SIC: 3053 8734 Mfg Gaskets/Packing/Sealing Devices Testing Laboratory
PA: Parker-Hannifin Corporation
6035 Parkland Blvd
Cleveland OH 44124
216 896-3000

(G-17256)
PARKER-HANNIFIN CORPORATION
8 Commonwealth Ave (01801-1010)
PHONE..................................781 935-4850
EMP: 6
SALES (est): 447.5K **Privately Held**
SIC: 3053 Mfg Gaskets/Packing/Sealing Devices

(G-17257)
PARKER-HANNIFIN CORPORATION
Parker Chomerics Division
77 Dragon Ct (01801-1039)
PHONE..................................781 935-4850
Timothy Harned, *Principal*
Austin Sonny Carter, *Engineer*
Gavin Hawkes, *Design Engr*
CHI Wu, *Design Engr*
Carla Lynch, *Sales Staff*
EMP: 400
SALES (corp-wide): 14.3B **Publicly Held**
WEB: www.parker.com
SIC: 2891 3053 3444 Mfg Adhesives/Sealants Mfg Gaskets/Packing/Sealing Devices Mfg Sheet Metalwork
PA: Parker-Hannifin Corporation
6035 Parkland Blvd
Cleveland OH 44124
216 896-3000

(G-17258)
PATERSON GROUP INC
225 Merrimac St (01801-1756)
PHONE..................................781 935-7036
David P Lynch, *President*
Robert B Paterson, *Principal*
EMP: 250
SQ FT: 5,000
SALES (est): 18.7MM **Privately Held**
SIC: 3498 Mfg Fabricated Pipe/Fittings

(G-17259)
PEARL DIE CUTTING & FINISHING
110 Commerce Way Ste E (01801-1098)
PHONE..................................781 721-6900
Steven Rich, *Principal*
EMP: 14
SALES (est): 1.9MM **Privately Held**
SIC: 3544 Mfg Dies/Tools/Jigs/Fixtures

(G-17260)
PERCUSSION SOFTWARE INC
600 Unicorn Park Dr Ste 2 (01801-3343)
P.O. Box 767, Burlington (01803-5767)
PHONE..................................781 438-9900
Deidre Diamond, *CEO*
Barry Reynolds, *Ch of Bd*
Mark Somol, *President*
Dan Flanigan, *Vice Pres*
EMP: 150
SALES (est): 17MM **Privately Held**
WEB: www.percussionsoftware.com
SIC: 7372 Prepackaged Software Services

(G-17261)
PETNET SOLUTIONS INC
350 Wshington St Unit 268 (01801)
PHONE..................................865 218-2000
Doug Husa, *Branch Mgr*
EMP: 4
SALES (corp-wide): 96.9B **Privately Held**
SIC: 2835 Mfg Diagnostic Substances
HQ: Petnet Solutions, Inc.
810 Innovation Dr
Knoxville TN 37932
865 218-2000

(G-17262)
PHARYX INC
325 New Boston St Unit 6 (01801-6200)
PHONE..................................617 792-0524
Harry Lee, *President*
EMP: 3
SALES: 200K **Privately Held**
WEB: www.pharyx.com
SIC: 3821 Commercial Physical And Biological Research

(G-17263)
PHOTONWARES CORPORATION (PA)
15 Presidential Way (01801-1040)
PHONE..................................781 935-1200
Jing Zhao, *CEO*
Jeanne Hladky, *Manager*
EMP: 5
SQ FT: 80,000
SALES (est): 3.3MM **Privately Held**
SIC: 3699 Mfg Electrical Equipment/Supplies

(G-17264)
PIERCE BIOTECHNOLOGY INC
30 Commerce Way Ste 2 (01801-1059)
PHONE..................................781 622-1000
Karen Oppenheimer, *Sales Staff*
Perry Rieck, *Sales Staff*
Megann Tate, *Sales Staff*
Nicholas Oldford, *Business Anlyst*
Owen A Dempsey, *Manager*
EMP: 21
SALES (corp-wide): 24.3B **Publicly Held**
WEB: www.piercenet.com
SIC: 2835 2836 Mfg Diagnostic Substances
HQ: Pierce Biotechnology, Inc.
3747 N Meridian Rd
Rockford IL 61101
815 968-0747

(G-17265)
PIEZO SYSTEMS INC
65 Tower Office Park (01801-2113)
PHONE..................................781 933-4850
Robert E Carter, *President*
Richard S Kensley, *Treasurer*
Donald Murphy, *Manager*
EMP: 6
SQ FT: 8,000
SALES (est): 1MM **Privately Held**
WEB: www.piezo.com
SIC: 3679 Mfg Electronic Components

(G-17266)
PLASTIC FABRICATORS CORP
310 Salem St (01801-2065)
PHONE..................................781 933-6007
Robert Kearin, *President*
EMP: 3
SALES (est): 186.7K **Privately Held**
SIC: 3089 Mfg Plastic Products

(G-17267)
PONN MACHINE CUTTING CO
20 Cross St (01801-5606)
PHONE..................................781 937-3373
Abraham Ponn, *President*
John Connors, *Shareholder*
Richard Ponn, *Shareholder*
EMP: 12
SQ FT: 15,000
SALES (est): 1.7MM **Privately Held**
WEB: www.ponnmachine.com
SIC: 3069 Mfg Fabricated Rubber Products

(G-17268)
POROGEN CORPORATION (DH)
35a Cabot Rd (01801-1003)
PHONE..................................781 491-0807
Benjamin Bikson, *President*
Yong Ding, *Corp Secy*
EMP: 22
SQ FT: 30,000
SALES (est): 3MM
SALES (corp-wide): 121.9MM **Privately Held**
SIC: 3599 Manufacturer Industrial Machinery

(G-17269)
PRESS-IT LLC
84 Washington St (01801-4658)
PHONE..................................781 935-0035
Alan Kushinsky, *Principal*
EMP: 4
SALES (est): 352K **Privately Held**
SIC: 2741 Misc Publishing

(G-17270)
PRINT MANAGEMENT SYSTEMS INC
26 Conn St (01801-5662)
PHONE..................................781 944-1041
James G Lenox, *President*
EMP: 10
SALES (est): 1.2MM **Privately Held**
WEB: www.gopmsi.com
SIC: 2752 2759 Lithographic Commercial Printing Commercial Printing

(G-17271)
PTTGC INNOVATION AMERICA CORP (HQ)
45 Cummings Park (01801-2123)
PHONE..................................617 657-5234
Dennis McCullough, *President*
Adam Lerner, *Counsel*
Arne Philipp Duss, *Senior VP*
Regina Detore Paglia, *Senior VP*
Mark Shmorhun, *Vice Pres*
▲ **EMP**: 25
SALES (est): 13.1MM **Privately Held**
SIC: 2869 Mfg Industrial Organic Chemicals

(G-17272)
PUBLISHING SOLUTIONS GROUP INC
400 W Cummings Park # 2600
(01801-6596)
PHONE..................................617 274-9001
Lori Becker, *President*
Barbara T Flockhart, *CFO*
EMP: 14
SQ FT: 4,000
SALES: 1.3MM **Privately Held**
WEB: www.publishingsolutionsgroup.com
SIC: 2731 Books-Publishing/Printing

(G-17273)
PURE IMAGING
9 Fowle St (01801-5101)
PHONE..................................781 537-6992
Kenneth G Fettig, *Principal*
EMP: 5
SALES (est): 511.7K **Privately Held**
SIC: 2796 Platemaking Services

(G-17274)
PURPOSEENERGY INC (PA)
800 W Cummings Park # 3400
(01801-6551)
PHONE..................................617 202-9156
Eric Fitch, *President*
Todd Hasselbeck, *Vice Pres*
Jeffrey Garner, *Opers Staff*
John Keane, *Director*
Thomas Klein, *Director*
EMP: 3
SALES (est): 689.6K **Privately Held**
WEB: www.purposeenergy.com
SIC: 2869 Mfg Industrial Organic Chemicals

(G-17275)
QUAD/GRAPHICS INC
110 Commerce Way Ste F (01801-1098)
PHONE..................................781 231-7200
Maciej Romaniszyn, *Vice Pres*
Sara Paulsen, *Opers Staff*
Collin Tinsley, *Production*
Chris Vanek, *Production*
Pete Holler, *Technical Mgr*
EMP: 151
SALES (corp-wide): 4.1B **Publicly Held**
SIC: 2752 Lithographic Commercial Printing
PA: Quad/Graphics Inc.
N61w23044 Harrys Way
Sussex WI 53089
414 566-6000

(G-17276)
QUALITY LASER INC
36 6th Rd (01801-1758)
PHONE..................................617 479-7374
Brent Marks, *President*
EMP: 4
SALES (est): 161.3K **Privately Held**
SIC: 3441 Structural Metal Fabrication

GEOGRAPHIC

(G-17277)
QUANTANCE INC (PA)
20 Sylvan Rd (01801-1845)
PHONE..................................650 293-3300
Vikas Vinayak, *President*
Michael Girvan Lampe, *VP Sales*
Serge Drogi, *CTO*
EMP: 31
SALES (est): 12MM **Privately Held**
SIC: 3674 Mfg Semiconductors/Related Devices

(G-17278)
QUEST DRAPE
46 Cummings Park (01801-2123)
PHONE..................................781 859-0300
Lee Dunalp, *CEO*
James Dawson, *Opers Mgr*
EMP: 3 **EST:** 2015
SALES (est): 54.5K **Privately Held**
SIC: 2391 Curtains And Draperies, Nsk

(G-17279)
RAYTHEON COMPANY
235 Presidential Way (01801-1060)
PHONE..................................781 933-1863
Matthew Pollard, *Engineer*
Joan Trovato, *Manager*
Dana Cocozziello, *Manager*
Debi Horvath, *Consultant*
Terry Parker, *Technology*
EMP: 132
SALES (corp-wide): 27B **Publicly Held**
SIC: 3812 Nonclassified Establishment
PA: Raytheon Company
870 Winter St
Waltham MA 02451
781 522-3000

(G-17280)
RAYTHEON COMPANY
225 Presidential Way (01801-5143)
PHONE..................................339 645-6000
Cheryl Labreck, *Engineer*
Rob Weihmayer, *Branch Mgr*
Stacy J Speer, *Department Mgr*
Mark Gordon, *Technology*
EMP: 132
SALES (corp-wide): 27B **Publicly Held**
SIC: 3812 Mfg Search/Navigation Equipment
PA: Raytheon Company
870 Winter St
Waltham MA 02451
781 522-3000

(G-17281)
RAZOR TOOL INC
6 Adele Rd (01801-1911)
PHONE..................................781 654-1582
Antranig Mardiros, *President*
EMP: 3
SQ FT: 11,280
SALES: 300K **Privately Held**
SIC: 3545 Mfg Machine Tool Accessories

(G-17282)
REFORM BIOLOGICS LLC
12 Gill St Ste 4650 (01801-1743)
PHONE..................................617 871-2101
John Sorvillo, *CEO*
EMP: 11
SALES (est): 2.1MM **Privately Held**
SIC: 2834 Mfg Pharmaceutical Preparations

(G-17283)
REPLIMUNE GROUP INC
18 Commerce Way (01801-1051)
PHONE..................................781 995-2443
Philip Astley-Sparke, *Ch of Bd*
Robert Coffin, *President*
Colin Love, *COO*
Howard Kaufman, *Chief Mktg Ofcr*
EMP: 67
SQ FT: 4,000
SALES (est): 2.8MM **Privately Held**
SIC: 2836 Biological Products

(G-17284)
RESIN DESIGNS LLC (HQ)
11 State St (01801-2172)
PHONE..................................781 935-3133
Adam P Chase, *CEO*
Amy McCormick, *Project Mgr*
Donald Ames, *Finance Mgr*
Kris Hanson, *Technical Staff*
EMP: 50
SQ FT: 20,000
SALES (est): 9MM
SALES (corp-wide): 281.3MM **Publicly Held**
WEB: www.resindesigns.com
SIC: 2891 Mfg Adhesives/Sealants
PA: Chase Corporation
295 University Ave
Westwood MA 02090
781 332-0700

(G-17285)
RIVINIUS & SONS INC
225 Salem St (01801-2002)
PHONE..................................781 933-5620
Alan Crosbie, *President*
Forrest C Rivinius, *Treasurer*
EMP: 14 **EST:** 1953
SQ FT: 5,000
SALES (est): 2.9MM **Privately Held**
WEB: www.riviniusandsons.com
SIC: 3312 Blast Furnace-Steel Works

(G-17286)
RL CONTROLS LLC
2 Gill St (01801-1721)
PHONE..................................781 932-3349
Lena Walsh,
EMP: 20
SQ FT: 2,800
SALES (est): 7.7MM **Privately Held**
WEB: www.rlcontrols.com
SIC: 3743 7629 Mfg Railroad Equipment Electrical Repair

(G-17287)
S & T GLOBAL INC
470 Wildwood Ave Ste 3 (01801-2082)
PHONE..................................781 376-1774
Zhuang Su, *President*
EMP: 11
SALES (est): 1.8MM **Privately Held**
SIC: 2819 Mfg Industrial Inorganic Chemicals

(G-17288)
SAFECOR HEALTH LLC
317 New Boston St Ste 100 (01801-6231)
PHONE..................................781 933-8780
Stephen Fischbach, *CEO*
Mark Leney, *Vice Pres*
Laurel Lombardi, *Vice Pres*
Randy Young, *Opers Dir*
Paul Steadman, *Opers Staff*
EMP: 99 **EST:** 2008
SALES (est): 13.6MM **Privately Held**
SIC: 2834 Mfg Pharmaceutical Preparations

(G-17289)
SCHARN INDUSTRIES
9 Presidential Way (01801-8509)
PHONE..................................781 376-9777
Deborah Scharn, *Principal*
EMP: 15 **EST:** 2009
SALES (est): 1.2MM **Privately Held**
SIC: 3999 Mfg Misc Products

(G-17290)
SCHNEEBERGER INC (DH)
44 Sixth Rd (01801-1784)
PHONE..................................781 271-0140
Hans M Schneeberger, *CEO*
Adrian Fuchser, *Exec VP*
Donna Croak, *Admin Asst*
▲ **EMP:** 9
SQ FT: 8,000
SALES (est): 3.8MM
SALES (corp-wide): 392.5K **Privately Held**
WEB: www.schneeberger.com
SIC: 3829 Mfg Measuring/Controlling Devices
HQ: Schneeberger Ag Lineartechnik
St. Urbanstrasse 12
Roggwil BE 4914
629 184-111

(G-17291)
SCIAPS INC (PA)
7 Constitution Way (01801-1194)
PHONE..................................339 222-2585
Don Sackett, *President*
Gary Lortie, *CFO*
Dave Day, *CTO*
EMP: 25 **EST:** 2012
SALES (est): 6.6MM **Privately Held**
SIC: 3826 Mfg Analytical Instruments

(G-17292)
SENOPSYS LLC
800 W Cummings Park # 1500
(01801-6353)
PHONE..................................781 935-7450
Jeffrey Worthington,
EMP: 6
SALES (est): 757.3K **Privately Held**
SIC: 2834 Mfg Pharmaceutical Preparations

(G-17293)
SHEAR COLOR PRINTING INC
30d 6th Rd (01801-1758)
PHONE..................................781 376-9607
Joel Weitzman, *President*
Mark Sierra, *Accounts Exec*
Stewart Weitzman, *Admin Sec*
EMP: 23
SQ FT: 5,500
SALES (est): 4MM **Privately Held**
WEB: www.shearcolor.com
SIC: 2752 2754 Lithographic Commercial Printing Gravure Commercial Printing

(G-17294)
SHRUT & ASCH LEATHER CO INC
5 Cranes Ct (01801-5603)
PHONE..................................781 460-2288
Howard Shrut, *President*
▲ **EMP:** 4 **EST:** 1941
SQ FT: 13,500
SALES (est): 657K **Privately Held**
SIC: 3111 Leather Tanning/Finishing

(G-17295)
SIGNAL COMMUNICATIONS CORP
4 Wheeling Ave (01801-2009)
P.O. Box 2588 (01888-1188)
PHONE..................................781 933-0998
Robert Lapham, *President*
Nadim Farhat, *President*
John Reali, *Opers Staff*
EMP: 30
SQ FT: 17,000
SALES (est): 6.1MM
SALES (corp-wide): 48.7MM **Privately Held**
WEB: www.sigcom.com
SIC: 3669 3661 3644 Mfg Communications Equipment Mfg Telephone/Telegraph Apparatus Mfg Nonconductive Wiring Devices
PA: Gulf Industries, Inc.
70393 Bravo St
Covington LA 70433
985 892-6500

(G-17296)
SIGNS TO GO INC
Also Called: Fastsigns
400 W Cummings Park # 1975
(01801-6519)
PHONE..................................781 938-7700
Pankaj R Shah, *President*
Sunita P Shah, *Treasurer*
EMP: 5
SQ FT: 1,500
SALES (est): 590.8K **Privately Held**
SIC: 3993 Signsadv Specs

(G-17297)
SKYWORKS SOLUTIONS INC (PA)
20 Sylvan Rd (01801-1885)
PHONE..................................781 376-3000
Liam K Griffin, *President*
▲ **EMP:** 750 **EST:** 1962
SQ FT: 158,000
SALES: 3.3B **Publicly Held**
WEB: www.alphaind.com
SIC: 3674 Mfg Semiconductors/Related Devices

(G-17298)
SKYWORKS SOLUTIONS INC
Also Called: Skyworks Luxembourg S.A.R.L.
20 Sylvan Rd (01801-1885)
PHONE..................................781 935-5150
Ken Bushmich, *Manager*
EMP: 275
SALES (corp-wide): 3.3B **Publicly Held**
WEB: www.alphaind.com
SIC: 3679 3674 Mfg Electronic Components Mfg Semiconductors/Related Devices
PA: Skyworks Solutions, Inc.
20 Sylvan Rd
Woburn MA 01801
781 376-3000

(G-17299)
SOLIDENERGY SYSTEMS LLC
35 Cabot Rd (01801-1003)
PHONE..................................617 972-3412
Aseem Juneja, *Human Res Dir*
Qichao Hu, *Mng Member*
Singh Rajendra, *Associate*
EMP: 43
SALES (est): 3MM **Privately Held**
SIC: 3691 Mfg Storage Batteries

(G-17300)
SPLASH SHIELD INC
8 Cedar St Ste 61 (01801-6362)
P.O. Box 398, Danvers (01923-0698)
PHONE..................................781 935-8844
EMP: 3
SQ FT: 3,000
SALES (est): 356.2K **Privately Held**
SIC: 3086 Mfg Plastic Foam Products

(G-17301)
SQDM
100 Tower Office Park M (01801-2187)
PHONE..................................888 993-9674
Eric Borthwick, *Principal*
EMP: 3
SALES (est): 146K **Privately Held**
SIC: 7372 Prepackaged Software Services

(G-17302)
STONE DECOR GALLERIA INC
15 Normac Rd (01801-2012)
PHONE..................................781 937-9377
Santino Gamellaro, *President*
▲ **EMP:** 5
SALES (est): 376.8K **Privately Held**
SIC: 3281 5032 Mfg Cut Stone/Products Whol Brick/Stone Material

(G-17303)
STONE SURFACES INC
275 Salem St Ste 2 (01801-2168)
PHONE..................................781 270-4600
Pierre Rancourt, *President*
Dimitris Kampouris, *Vice Pres*
Nino Decarolis, *Opers Staff*
▲ **EMP:** 12
SQ FT: 7,000
SALES (est): 1.5MM **Privately Held**
SIC: 3281 Mfg Cut Stone/Products

(G-17304)
TECHNLOGY DEV CLLABORATIVE LLC
3r Green St Ste B (01801-4366)
PHONE..................................781 933-6116
Hubert Wright,
EMP: 6
SALES (est): 1MM **Privately Held**
SIC: 3823 Mfg Process Control Instruments

(G-17305)
TECOMET INC
170 New Boston St (01801-6204)
PHONE..................................781 782-6400
Robert Lynch, *Vice Pres*
Jesse Gordon, *Engineer*
Bob Lynch, *Manager*
EMP: 60
SALES (corp-wide): 696.7MM **Privately Held**
WEB: www.tecomet.com
SIC: 3599 3823 1629 4911 Mfg Industrial Machinery Mfg Process Cntrl Instr

▲ = Import ▼=Export
◆ =Import/Export

PA: Tecomet Inc.
115 Eames St
Wilmington MA 01887
978 642-2400

(G-17306)
TERADYNE INC
36 Cabot Rd (01801-1004)
PHONE..................................978 370-2700
Edward Hogan, *Branch Mgr*
EMP: 140
SALES (corp-wide): 2.1B **Publicly Held**
WEB: www.teradyne.com
SIC: 3825 3643 Mfg Automatic Test Equipment & Connecting Devices
PA: Teradyne, Inc.
600 Riverpark Dr
North Reading MA 01864
978 370-2700

(G-17307)
TERRAFUGIA INC
23 Rainin Rd Ste 2 (01801-4689)
PHONE..................................781 491-0812
Chao Jing, *CEO*
Kevin Colburn, *COO*
Dagny Dukach, *Opers Staff*
Rich Paolino, *Senior Buyer*
Andrew Sand, *Engineer*
EMP: 19 **EST:** 2017
SALES (est): 787K
SALES (corp-wide): 46.7B **Privately Held**
SIC: 3721 Manufactures Aircraft
PA: Zhejiang Geely Holding (Group) Co., Ltd.
No. 1760, Jiangling Road, Binjiang District
Hangzhou 31005

(G-17308)
TESSOLAR INC
10 State St Ste 1b (01801-6820)
PHONE..................................508 479-9818
Leslie Fritzemeier, *President*
EMP: 3
SALES (est): 382.3K **Privately Held**
SIC: 3674 Mfg Semiconductors/Related Devices

(G-17309)
TEXTHELP INC
600 Unicorn Park Dr Ste 2 (01801-3343)
PHONE..................................781 503-0421
Jack Dolan, *President*
Victoria Baird, *Business Mgr*
David Herr, *Vice Pres*
Erin Macdonald, *Opers Staff*
Andrew Sharp, *Engineer*
EMP: 6
SALES: 8.7MM **Privately Held**
WEB: www.texthelp.com
SIC: 7372 Prepackaged Software Services

(G-17310)
VACUUM BARRIER CORPORATION
4 Barten Ln (01801-5601)
P.O. Box 529 (01801-0529)
PHONE..................................781 933-3570
Russell W Blanton, *President*
Greg Rosinski, *COO*
David W Tucker, *Exec VP*
David Tucker, *Exec VP*
Eric Oconnell, *Engineer*
EMP: 40 **EST:** 1958
SQ FT: 32,000
SALES (est): 11.3MM **Privately Held**
WEB: www.vacuumbarrier.com
SIC: 3559 3812 Mfg Misc Industry Machinery Mfg Search/Navigation Equipment

(G-17311)
VAISALA INC
Also Called: Sigmet, Westford Operations
10d Gill St (01801-1721)
PHONE..................................508 574-1163
Richard E Passarelli Jr, *President*
Gary Frey, *Business Mgr*
Patty Federico, *Purch Agent*
Mikko Laakso, *Engrg Mgr*
Heikki Turtiainen, *Research*
EMP: 9
SALES (est): 1.5MM **Privately Held**
WEB: www.sigmet.com
SIC: 3812 Mfg Measuring/Controlling Devices

(G-17312)
VAISALA INC
10d Gill St (01801-1721)
PHONE..................................781 933-4500
Scott Sternberg, *President*
Heikki Turtiainen, *Research*
Robert Ireland, *Sales Mgr*
Sean Murphy, *Marketing Staff*
Gerald Ducharme, *Branch Mgr*
EMP: 50
SALES (corp-wide): 276.9MM **Privately Held**
WEB: www.vaisala.com
SIC: 3829 Mfg Measuring/Controlling Devices
HQ: Vaisala Inc.
194 S Taylor Ave
Louisville CO 80027
303 499-1701

(G-17313)
VIRIDIS3D LLC
10 Roessler Rd (01801-6208)
PHONE..................................781 305-4961
James F Bredt,
EMP: 6 **EST:** 2009
SALES (est): 364.6K **Privately Held**
SIC: 2759 Commercial Printing

(G-17314)
VIVID TECHNOLOGIES INC
10 Commerce Way (01801-1028)
PHONE..................................781 939-3986
Kristoph Krug, *Principal*
EMP: 3
SALES (est): 256.5K **Privately Held**
SIC: 3844 Mfg X-Ray Apparatus/Tubes

(G-17315)
WATERTECH INTERNATIONAL
12 Alfred St Ste 300 (01801-1915)
PHONE..................................781 592-8224
EMP: 5
SALES (est): 522.4K **Privately Held**
SIC: 3823 Mfg Process Control Instruments

(G-17316)
WATERTOWN IRONWORKS INC
47 Henshaw St (01801-4668)
PHONE..................................781 491-0229
Anthony Damico, *President*
Luigi D'Amico, *Treasurer*
Vera D'Amico, *Clerk*
EMP: 15
SQ FT: 6,000
SALES (est): 3.2MM **Privately Held**
SIC: 3446 Mfg Architectural Metalwork

(G-17317)
WAYNE KERR ELECTRONICS INC
165l New Boston St (01801-6201)
PHONE..................................781 938-8390
Luke Lien, *President*
EMP: 4 **EST:** 1982
SALES (est): 541.1K **Privately Held**
SIC: 3825 5065 Mfg Electrical Measuring Instruments Whol Electronic Parts/Equipment

(G-17318)
WESCOR LTD
5 Conn St (01801-5668)
PHONE..................................781 938-8686
Ben Caggiano, *Manager*
EMP: 6
SALES (corp-wide): 3.1MM **Privately Held**
SIC: 2499 Mfg Wood Products
PA: Wescor, Ltd.
271 Main St Ste G01
Stoneham MA 02180
781 279-0490

(G-17319)
WHOLESALE PRINTING INC
2 Cedar St Ste 2 # 2 (01801-6352)
PHONE..................................781 937-3357
John Struthers, *President*
Dan Ornae, *CFO*
EMP: 12
SQ FT: 1,600
SALES (est): 1.5MM **Privately Held**
WEB: www.wholesaleprintinginc.com
SIC: 2759 Lithographic Commercial Printing

(G-17320)
WIDHAM WOOD CORPORATION
13 Cranes Ct Rear (01801-5603)
PHONE..................................781 932-8572
James Kusch, *President*
Ann Kusch,
EMP: 4
SALES (est): 304K **Privately Held**
SIC: 2431 Mfg Millwork

(G-17321)
WINDHAM WOOD INTERIORS INC
13 Cranes Ct (01801-5603)
PHONE..................................781 932-8572
James Kusch, *President*
EMP: 7
SQ FT: 7,700
SALES (est): 785.2K **Privately Held**
SIC: 2431 Mfg Custom Millwork

(G-17322)
WINDSTREAM ENRGY SOLUTIONS LLC
10g Roessler Rd Ste 524 (01801-6272)
PHONE..................................781 333-5450
Vineet Malik,
▲ **EMP:** 6
SALES: 950K **Privately Held**
SIC: 3511 Mfg Turbines/Generator Sets

(G-17323)
WINFIELD BROOKS COMPANY INC
70 Conn St (01801-5693)
PHONE..................................781 933-5300
Winnfield Perry, *President*
Keith Perry, *Exec VP*
Dana Perry, *Director*
▲ **EMP:** 10 **EST:** 1951
SQ FT: 30,000
SALES (est): 1.9MM **Privately Held**
WEB: www.winbro.com
SIC: 2842 2992 2891 2851 Mfg Polish/Sanitation Gd Mfg Lubrictng Oil/Grease Mfg Adhesives/Sealants Mfg Paints/Allied Prdts
PA: Flow Grinding Corp.
70 Conn St
Woburn MA 01801

(G-17324)
WOTECH ASSOCIATES
26 Mayflower Rd (01801-5445)
PHONE..................................781 935-3787
Stanley Pomeranz, *Owner*
EMP: 4
SQ FT: 400
SALES: 100K **Privately Held**
SIC: 3678 5065 Designs & Man Electronic Systems & Imports And Exports Electronic Parts

(G-17325)
XYLEM WATER SOLUTIONS USA INC
78 Olympia Ave (01801-2057)
PHONE..................................781 935-6515
Brian McCarthy, *Branch Mgr*
Steve McCaughey, *Associate*
EMP: 8 **Publicly Held**
SIC: 3561 Mfg Pumps/Pumping Equipment
HQ: Xylem Water Solutions U.S.A., Inc.
4828 Prkwy Plz Blvd 200
Charlotte NC 28217

(G-17326)
YIELD10 BIOSCIENCE INC (PA)
Also Called: Metabolix
19 Presidential Way # 201 (01801-1184)
PHONE..................................617 583-1700
Robert L Van Nostrand, *Ch of Bd*
Joseph Shaulson, *President*
Lynne H Brum, *Vice Pres*
Johan Van, *Vice Pres*
Dawit Abreham, *Research*
◆ **EMP:** 68
SALES: 556K **Publicly Held**
WEB: www.metabolix.com
SIC: 2869 Industrial Organic Chemicals

Woods Hole
Barnstable County

(G-17327)
LUSCOMBE AVE WAITING ROOM
21 Luscombe Ave (02543-1013)
PHONE..................................508 299-8051
EMP: 14
SALES (est): 1MM **Privately Held**
SIC: 3731 Shipbuilding/Repairing

Worcester
Worcester County

(G-17328)
3CROSS BREWING COMPANY
26 Cambridge St (01603)
PHONE..................................508 615-8195
David Howland, *President*
EMP: 17
SALES (est): 2MM **Privately Held**
SIC: 2082 Mfg Malt Beverages

(G-17329)
A N C TOOL AND MANUFACTURING
49 Gardner St (01610-2507)
PHONE..................................508 757-0224
Fax: 508 757-9668
EMP: 7 **EST:** 1979
SQ FT: 15,000
SALES (est): 770K **Privately Held**
WEB: www.anctool.com
SIC: 3541 3429 Mfg Machine Parts And Tools And Mfg Locks And Related Hardware

(G-17330)
A SCHULMAN CUSTOM COMPOUNDING
53 Millbrook St Ste 2 (01606-2817)
PHONE..................................508 756-0002
Frank Hampton, *President*
Bernard Rzepka, *Principal*
Randall Youngsma, *Vice Pres*
Bill Mahoney, *Controller*
◆ **EMP:** 140
SQ FT: 116,000
SALES (est): 39.1MM
SALES (corp-wide): 39.1B **Privately Held**
WEB: www.ecmplastics.com
SIC: 3089 Mfg Plastic Products
HQ: A. Schulman, Inc.
3637 Ridgewood Rd
Fairlawn OH 44333
330 666-3751

(G-17331)
ABBOTT LABORATORIES
Also Called: Sodexo Abbott Bioresearch
100 Research Dr (01605-4314)
PHONE..................................508 849-2500
Catherine Tripp, *Branch Mgr*
EMP: 617
SALES (corp-wide): 30.5B **Publicly Held**
SIC: 2834 Mfg Pharmaceutical Preparations
PA: Abbott Laboratories
100 Abbott Park Rd
Abbott Park IL 60064
224 667-6100

(G-17332)
ABBVIE INC
Also Called: Abbvie Bioresearch Center
100 Research Dr (01605-4312)
PHONE..................................508 849-2500
Miles D White, *Ch of Bd*
Jochen Salfeld, *Vice Pres*
Shawn Cruz, *Project Mgr*
Eric Dominguez, *Project Mgr*
Paul Duggan, *Project Mgr*
EMP: 33

SALES (corp-wide): 32.7B **Publicly Held**
SIC: 2834 Mfg Pharmaceutical Preparations
PA: Abbvie Inc.
1 N Waukegan Rd
North Chicago IL 60064
847 932-7900

(G-17333)
ABSOLUTE HAITIAN CORPORATION (PA)
33 Southgate St (01610-1720)
PHONE..................................508 459-5372
Glenn Williams Frohring, *President*
Nathan K F Smith, *Treasurer*
Michael C Ortolano, *Admin Sec*
▲ **EMP:** 10
SALES (est): 3.2MM **Privately Held**
SIC: 3089 Mfg Plastic Products

(G-17334)
ACCUDIE INC
532 Franklin St (01604-2977)
PHONE..................................508 756-8482
Richard Duval, *President*
EMP: 5
SQ FT: 5,000
SALES: 350K **Privately Held**
SIC: 3544 Mfg Dies & Tools

(G-17335)
AERO TURBINE COMPONENTS INC
993 Millbury St (01607-2106)
PHONE..................................508 755-2121
Jon Adams, *President*
Steve Averka, *Treasurer*
EMP: 5
SQ FT: 4,841
SALES: 700K **Privately Held**
SIC: 3724 Airplane Turbine Compnents

(G-17336)
AMKOR INDUSTRIAL PRODUCTS INC
42 Lagrange St (01610-1536)
P.O. Box 167 (01614-0167)
PHONE..................................508 799-4970
EMP: 22
SALES (corp-wide): 2.4MM **Privately Held**
SIC: 3469 3592 3451 Mfg Metal Stampings Mfg Carburetors/Pistons/Rings Mfg Screw Machine Products
PA: Amkor Industrial Products Inc
90 Madison St Ste 407
Worcester MA
508 799-4970

(G-17337)
AMPLICEA THERAPEUTICS INC
53 Hancock Hill Dr (01609-1543)
PHONE..................................617 515-6755
Leslie J Williams, *CEO*
EMP: 3
SALES (est): 181.1K **Privately Held**
SIC: 2834 Pharmaceutical Preparations

(G-17338)
ANCHOR LABS GROUP INC
95 Prescott St (01605-1717)
PHONE..................................508 500-9157
Samuel Baumgarten, *President*
EMP: 4
SALES (est): 98.3K **Privately Held**
SIC: 7372 Prepackaged Software Services

(G-17339)
ANGEL GUARD PRODUCTS INC
120 Goddard Memorial Dr (01603-1260)
PHONE..................................508 791-1073
James Badgio, *President*
Fred Cormier, *President*
Scot Peterson, *Vice Pres*
▲ **EMP:** 9
SQ FT: 7,000
SALES (est): 1.2MM **Privately Held**
WEB: www.angelguardproducts.com
SIC: 3991 3842 8732 Mfg Brushes A Snow Removal Device For Cars & Personal Safety Equipment An Ice Rescue Device & Commercial Research

(G-17340)
APPLIED PLASTIC TECHNOLOGY INC
169 Fremont St (01603-2352)
PHONE..................................508 752-5924
Frank Beckerer, *CEO*
Jim Morin, *President*
Kathy Brady, *Vice Pres*
Randy Guertin, *Vice Pres*
◆ **EMP:** 32 **EST:** 1978
SQ FT: 55,000
SALES (est): 6MM **Privately Held**
WEB: www.aplastic.com
SIC: 3089 Mfg Plastic Products

(G-17341)
AQUA BIO COMPLIANCE CORP
44 Richmond Ave (01602-1533)
PHONE..................................508 798-2966
EMP: 4
SALES (est): 296.8K **Privately Held**
SIC: 2836 Mfg Biological Products

(G-17342)
ARMCO WOODWORKING & DISPLAY
115 Sw Cutoff (01604-2729)
PHONE..................................508 831-0990
Anthony Macaruso Jr, *President*
EMP: 6
SQ FT: 4,000
SALES (est): 520K **Privately Held**
SIC: 2541 Mfg Wood Partitions/Fixtures

(G-17343)
AUTO BODY SUPPLIES AND PAINT
90 Washington St (01610-2720)
PHONE..................................508 791-4111
EMP: 8
SALES (corp-wide): 13MM **Privately Held**
SIC: 3465 Automotive Stampings, Nsk
PA: Auto Body Supplies And Paint Inc
1205 Main St Ste 4
East Hartford CT 06108
860 528-9283

(G-17344)
BABCOCK POWER INC RESEARCH CTR
45 Mckeon Rd (01610-2325)
PHONE..................................508 792-4800
EMP: 5
SALES (est): 427.9K **Privately Held**
SIC: 3443 Mfg Fabricated Plate Work

(G-17345)
BASEMENT LLC
316 Main St Unit 1 (01608-1553)
PHONE..................................508 762-9080
Roger Bachour, *President*
EMP: 5
SALES (est): 119.8K **Privately Held**
SIC: 2082 Mfg Malt Beverages

(G-17346)
BATTERY RESOURCERS LLC
54 Rockdale St (01606-1928)
PHONE..................................206 948-6325
Diran Apelian, *Co-Owner*
Yan Wang, *Co-Owner*
Eric Gratz, *Chief Engr*
EMP: 4 **EST:** 2015
SALES (est): 147.9K **Privately Held**
SIC: 3691 Mfg Storage Batteries

(G-17347)
BELDEN INC
Also Called: Telecast Fiber Systems
324 Clark St (01606-1214)
PHONE..................................508 754-4858
Charles Raines, *Accountant*
Ernst Balzora-Rivert, *Finance*
Chris D Minico, *Director*
Matthew Miles, *Technician*
EMP: 239
SALES (corp-wide): 2.5B **Publicly Held**
SIC: 3357 Nonferrous Wiredrawing/Insulating
PA: Belden Inc.
1 N Brentwood Blvd Fl 15
Saint Louis MO 63105
314 854-8000

(G-17348)
BLACK OXIDE CO INC
100 Grand St Ste 3 (01610-1647)
P.O. Box 304, Spencer (01562-0304)
PHONE..................................508 757-0340
David Brooks, *President*
EMP: 3 **EST:** 1959
SQ FT: 1,600
SALES (est): 332.7K **Privately Held**
SIC: 3559 3471 Mfg Misc Industry Machinery Plating/Polishing Service

(G-17349)
BODYCOTE THERMAL PROC INC
284 Grove St (01605-3908)
PHONE..................................508 754-1724
Mike Sakelakos, *General Mgr*
Michael Harrison, *General Mgr*
Ankit Patel, *General Mgr*
Donald Richardson, *General Mgr*
George Landa, *Opers Mgr*
EMP: 30
SQ FT: 5,000
SALES (corp-wide): 960MM **Privately Held**
SIC: 3398 Metal Heat Treating
HQ: Bodycote Thermal Processing, Inc.
12700 Park Central Dr # 700
Dallas TX 75251
214 904-2420

(G-17350)
BOSTON ATLANTIC CORP
Also Called: Boston Atlantic Gasket and Rbr
7 Harris Ct (01610)
PHONE..................................508 754-4076
Carl Benander, *President*
EMP: 12
SQ FT: 16,000
SALES (est): 2MM **Privately Held**
SIC: 3053 5085 Mfg Gaskets/Packing/Sealing Devices Whol Industrial Supplies

(G-17351)
BP LUBRICANTS USA INC
692 Millbury St 94 (01607)
PHONE..................................508 791-3201
Jay Camball, *Manager*
EMP: 5
SALES (corp-wide): 298.7B **Privately Held**
SIC: 2992 Manufacturer Of Lubricants
HQ: Bp Lubricants Usa Inc.
1500 Valley Rd
Wayne NJ 07470
973 633-2200

(G-17352)
CADRUS THERAPEUTICS INC
67 Millbrook St Ste 422 (01606-2845)
PHONE..................................508 344-9719
David Easson, *President*
EMP: 4
SALES (est): 235.8K **Privately Held**
SIC: 2834 Mfg Pharmaceutical Preparations

(G-17353)
CAMPAIGNSTHATWINCOM LLC
210 Park Ave 210 # 210 (01609-2246)
PHONE..................................508 667-6365
Don Shortman, *Partner*
Mark Carron,
EMP: 4
SALES (est): 800K **Privately Held**
SIC: 2759 7389 Commercial Printing Business Services

(G-17354)
CENTRAL STEEL RULE DIE INC
46 W Mountain St (01606-1397)
PHONE..................................508 853-2663
George Harris, *President*
Chris Harris, *Vice Pres*
Kim Harkins, *Admin Sec*
EMP: 4
SQ FT: 1,200
SALES (est): 471.4K **Privately Held**
SIC: 3312 Blast Furnace-Steel Works

(G-17355)
CHILMARK ARCHTCTURAL WDWKG LLC
705 Plantation St (01605-2061)
PHONE..................................508 856-9200
Nicki Goodnow, *Owner*
Adria Polleta, *Co-Owner*
EMP: 10 **EST:** 1992
SALES (est): 1.5MM **Privately Held**
WEB: www.chilmarkwoodworking.com
SIC: 2431 Mfg Millwork

(G-17356)
CITY WELDING & FABRICATION INC
10 Ararat St Ste 1 (01606-3315)
PHONE..................................508 853-6000
Paul Curci, *President*
EMP: 20
SQ FT: 1,500
SALES (est): 2.7MM **Privately Held**
SIC: 7692 Welding Repair

(G-17357)
COHENS UNITED BAKING INC
26 Washburn St (01610-2638)
PHONE..................................508 754-0232
James H Lloyd, *President*
EMP: 5 **EST:** 1957
SQ FT: 1,500
SALES (est): 401.2K **Privately Held**
SIC: 2051 Mfg Bread/Related Products

(G-17358)
CONCEPT TOOLING INC
242 Stafford St (01603-1142)
PHONE..................................508 754-6466
Scott Roberge, *President*
Steven Hebert, *Vice Pres*
EMP: 5
SQ FT: 3,500
SALES (est): 505.1K **Privately Held**
SIC: 3599 Precision Job Shop

(G-17359)
CONTINENTAL WOODCRAFT INC (PA)
Also Called: Continental Consolidated Inds
7 Coppage Dr (01603-1252)
PHONE..................................508 581-9560
Paul Hamlon, *President*
EMP: 26
SALES (est): 5.8MM **Privately Held**
WEB: www.continentalconsolidated.com
SIC: 2541 2542 2431 Mfg Wood Parti-tions/Fixt

(G-17360)
COORSTEK INC
Also Called: Coorstek Worcester
5 Norton Dr (01606-2679)
PHONE..................................774 317-2600
Matthew Simpson, *Engineer*
Andy Duncan, *Branch Mgr*
Richard Hengst, *Manager*
EMP: 310
SALES (corp-wide): 407.6MM **Privately Held**
SIC: 3264 3053 3081 3082 Mfg Porcelain Elc Supply Mfg Gasket/Packing/Seals Mfg Unsupport Plstc Film Mfg Plstc Profile Shapes Mfg Machine Tool Access
HQ: Coorstek, Inc.
14143 Denver West Pkwy # 400
Lakewood CO 80401
303 271-7000

(G-17361)
CROMPTON PARK ORAL SURGERY & I
59 Quinsigamond Ave (01610-1867)
PHONE..................................508 799-2550
W David Kelly,
EMP: 6
SALES (est): 660K **Privately Held**
SIC: 3842 Dental Implants

(G-17362)
DAVID CLARK COMPANY INC (PA)
360 Franklin St (01604-4900)
P.O. Box 15054 (01615-0054)
PHONE..................................508 756-6216
Darald R Libby, *Ch of Bd*

Robert A Vincent, *President*
John W Bassick, *Exec VP*
John Bassick, *Exec VP*
James T Bergin, *Vice Pres*
▲ **EMP:** 240 **EST:** 2006
SQ FT: 277,000
SALES (est): 68.7MM **Privately Held**
WEB: www.davidclark.com
SIC: 3663 3842 3841 Mfg Radio/Tv Communication Equipment Mfg Surgical Appliances/Supplies Mfg Surgical/Medical Instruments

(G-17363)
DAVIS CORP OF WORCESTER INC (PA)
Also Called: Davis Publications
50 Portland St (01608-2013)
PHONE..................................508 754-7201
Wyatt R Wade, *President*
Missy Nicholson, *Editor*
Mark W Davis, *Chairman*
Julian Wade, *Vice Pres*
Thomas Lucci, *CFO*
◆ **EMP:** 24 **EST:** 1856
SQ FT: 85,000
SALES: 6.8K **Privately Held**
WEB: www.davis-art.com
SIC: 2731 2721 Books-Publishing/Printing Periodicals-Publishing/Printing

(G-17364)
DAVIS PUBLICATIONS INC
Also Called: Davis Art Images
50 Portland St Fl 3 (01608-2013)
PHONE..................................508 754-7201
Mark Davis, *Ch of Bd*
Julian Wade, *President*
Julian D Wade, *President*
Mary Smith, *Accounts Mgr*
Laura Flavin, *Director*
EMP: 33 **EST:** 1958
SQ FT: 50,000
SALES (est): 5.8MM
SALES (corp-wide): 6.8K **Privately Held**
WEB: www.davispublications.com
SIC: 2721 Periodicals-Publishing/Printing
PA: Davis Corp Of Worcester, Inc.
50 Portland St
Worcester MA 01608
508 754-7201

(G-17365)
DKD SOLUTIONS INC
Also Called: Ruby Electric
77 E Worcester St (01604-3648)
PHONE..................................508 762-9114
Donald R Juozaitis, *President*
EMP: 9
SALES (est): 1.5MM **Privately Held**
SIC: 3621 Mfg Motors/Generators

(G-17366)
DOCUMENTS ON DEMAND INC
Also Called: AlphaGraphics
184 Main St (01608-1146)
PHONE..................................508 793-0956
Raymond H Mantyla Jr, *President*
EMP: 11
SALES (est): 1.8MM **Privately Held**
SIC: 2752 Comm Prtg Litho

(G-17367)
DSS CIRCUITS INC
29 Oriental St (01605-4008)
PHONE..................................508 852-8061
Wayne Truchsess, *President*
EMP: 4
SALES (est): 455.4K **Privately Held**
SIC: 3679 Mfg Electronic Components

(G-17368)
E R S RESOURCES
95 Prescott Pl (01605)
PHONE..................................508 421-3434
Fax: 508 421-5209
EMP: 3
SALES (est): 193K **Privately Held**
SIC: 3999 Mfg Misc Products

(G-17369)
EATON FARM CONFECTIONERS INC
370 Main St Ste 1200 (01608-1724)
PHONE..................................508 865-5235
Lynwood H Eaton, *President*
Nicholas C Marro, *Vice Pres*
Bertha A Eaton, *Treasurer*
EMP: 8
SQ FT: 8,000
SALES: 800K **Privately Held**
WEB: www.eatonfarmcandies.com
SIC: 2064 Mfg Candy/Confectionery

(G-17370)
ELECTRODES INCORPORATED
218 Franklin St (01604-5019)
PHONE..................................508 757-2295
Ronald Giloespie, *Manager*
EMP: 3
SALES (corp-wide): 23.3MM **Privately Held**
WEB: www.electrodes-inc.com
SIC: 3624 Manufacturers Representative Of Graphite Electrodes
PA: Electrodes, Incorporated
260a Quarry Rd
Milford CT 06460
954 803-4736

(G-17371)
ELECTROWEAVE INC
425 Shrewsbury St (01604-1638)
PHONE..................................508 752-8932
Beatrice Andrews, *President*
Thomas P Andrews, *Vice Pres*
Paul Mc Allister, *Clerk*
EMP: 4
SQ FT: 20,000
SALES (est): 290K **Privately Held**
WEB: www.electroweave.com
SIC: 3315 3643 3357 Mfg Steel Wire/Related Products Mfg Conductive Wiring Devices Nonferrous Wiredrawing/Insulating

(G-17372)
ETC COMPONENTS USA INC
346 Franklin St (01604-5503)
P.O. Box 3522 (01613-3522)
PHONE..................................508 353-7075
John Bremner Sharp, *President*
▲ **EMP:** 3
SALES (est): 371.2K **Privately Held**
SIC: 3679 Mfg Electronic Components

(G-17373)
FASTCAST CONSORTIUM INC
Also Called: Kervick Entreprises
40 Rockdale St (01606-1908)
PHONE..................................508 853-4500
Paul Kervick, *CEO*
Robert Kervick, *President*
EMP: 150
SALES (est): 6.6MM **Privately Held**
SIC: 3069 Business Consortium

(G-17374)
FEDHAL FOODS INC
560 Lincoln St (01605-1927)
PHONE..................................508 595-9178
EMP: 3
SALES (est): 198.3K **Privately Held**
SIC: 2099 Mfg Food Preparations

(G-17375)
FLEX-O-GRAPHIC PRTG PLATE INC
33 Arctic St Ste 4 (01604-4931)
PHONE..................................508 752-8100
John Carlson, *President*
EMP: 25 **EST:** 1956
SQ FT: 20,000
SALES (est): 3MM **Privately Held**
SIC: 2796 Platemaking Services

(G-17376)
FLEX-REST INC
7 Brookfield St (01605-3901)
PHONE..................................508 797-4046
Frederic Ambrose, *President*
David Hawley, *Vice Pres*
EMP: 3
SQ FT: 700
SALES (est): 260K **Privately Held**
WEB: www.flexdesks.com
SIC: 2522 Mfg Keyboard Holders

(G-17377)
FORM ROLL DIE CORP (PA)
217 Stafford St (01603-1198)
PHONE..................................508 755-2010
Mildred Mason, *President*
Jon Maki, *Engineer*
Diane Generelli, *Treasurer*
Marie Mason, *Shareholder*
Richard Mason, *Shareholder*
▼ **EMP:** 31
SQ FT: 14,000
SALES: 4.4MM **Privately Held**
WEB: www.formrolldie.com
SIC: 3545 3542 Mfg Machine Tools & Accessories

(G-17378)
FORM ROLL DIE CORP
Also Called: Stafford Special Tool
88 Webster Pl (01603-1920)
PHONE..................................508 755-5302
Richard Mason, *Branch Mgr*
EMP: 12
SALES (corp-wide): 4.4MM **Privately Held**
WEB: www.formrolldie.com
SIC: 3542 3599 Mfg Machine Tools-Forming Mfg Industrial Machinery
PA: Form Roll Die Corp
217 Stafford St
Worcester MA 01603
508 755-2010

(G-17379)
FRANK E LASHUA INC (PA)
Also Called: Fel Tech Hammer Division
1 Pullman St (01606-3310)
PHONE..................................508 552-0023
Frank Lashua, *President*
▲ **EMP:** 5
SQ FT: 6,000
SALES: 1.5MM **Privately Held**
SIC: 3541 Mfg Machine Tools-Cutting

(G-17380)
GEISEL SOFTWARE INC
67 Millbrook St Ste 520 (01606-2846)
PHONE..................................508 853-5310
Brian J Geisel, *President*
EMP: 12
SALES (est): 541.7K **Privately Held**
SIC: 7372 Prepackaged Software Services

(G-17381)
GENERAL WIRE PRODUCTS INC
425 Shrewsbury St (01604-1638)
PHONE..................................508 752-8260
Thomas P Andrews, *President*
Beatrice Andrews, *Vice Pres*
Thomas P Andrews Jr, *Vice Pres*
EMP: 24
SQ FT: 30,000
SALES (est): 7.2MM **Privately Held**
WEB: www.generalwireproducts.com
SIC: 3357 3643 3496 3315 Nonfrs Wire-drwng/Insltng Mfg Conductive Wire Dvcs Mfg Misc Fab Wire Prdts Mfg Steel Wire/Rltd Prdt
PA: United Wire & Cable Corporation
425 Shrewsbury St
Worcester MA 01604
508 757-3872

(G-17382)
GILLIES W TECHNOLOGIES LLC
250 Barber Ave (01606-2495)
P.O. Box 60329 (01606-0329)
PHONE..................................508 852-2502
Mark Spencer, *Exec VP*
Martin Rosenberger, *Officer*
▲ **EMP:** 8 **EST:** 1997
SALES: 1.3MM **Privately Held**
WEB: www.wgillies.com
SIC: 2796 3555 Platemaking Services Mfg Printing Trades Machinery

(G-17383)
GINSENG UP CORPORATION (PA)
16 Plum St (01604-3600)
PHONE..................................508 799-6178
Sang Kil Han, *President*
◆ **EMP:** 8 **EST:** 1981
SQ FT: 1,000
SALES (est): 4.5MM **Privately Held**
WEB: www.ginsengup.com
SIC: 2086 Mfg Bottled/Canned Soft Drinks

(G-17384)
GLSYNTHESIS INC
298 Highland St (01602-2130)
PHONE..................................508 754-6700
Jan Chen, *CEO*
George Wright, *President*
▲ **EMP:** 23 **EST:** 1996
SQ FT: 10,000
SALES (est): 3.3MM **Privately Held**
WEB: www.glsynthesis.com
SIC: 2834 Mfg Pharmaceutical Preparations

(G-17385)
GRAFTON NEWS HOLDINGS LLC
Also Called: Grafton News, The
100 Front St Ste 500 (01608-1440)
P.O. Box 457, North Grafton (01536-0457)
PHONE..................................508 839-2259
Charles Bolack, *Owner*
Don Clark,
EMP: 3
SALES (est): 164.6K **Privately Held**
SIC: 2711 Newspapers-Publishing/Printing

(G-17386)
GUERTIN GRAPHICS & AWARDS INC
136 Southbridge St (01608-2010)
PHONE..................................508 754-0200
John Guertin, *President*
EMP: 12
SALES (est): 389.8K **Privately Held**
SIC: 2759 5999 Commercial Printing Ret Misc Merchandise

(G-17387)
GUIDING CHANNELS CO
93 Longmeadow Ave (01606-2148)
PHONE..................................508 853-0781
Ken Daigle, *Owner*
EMP: 3
SALES: 150K **Privately Held**
SIC: 2741 Misc Publishing

(G-17388)
HAMILTON SIGN & DESIGN INC
545 Sw Cutoff (01607-1766)
PHONE..................................508 459-9731
Ronald S Hamilton, *Principal*
EMP: 3
SALES (est): 253.5K **Privately Held**
SIC: 3993 Mfg Signs/Advertising Specialties

(G-17389)
HEARST COMMUNICATIONS INC
Also Called: Telegram & Gazette
100 Front St Ste 500 (01608-1440)
PHONE..................................508 793-9100
Christopher Stevens, *President*
Christine Ortoleva, *Finance Dir*
Bruce Bennet, *Manager*
EMP: 200
SALES (corp-wide): 8.3B **Privately Held**
WEB: www.telegram.com
SIC: 2711 7313 Newspapers-Publishing/Printing Advertising Representative
HQ: Hearst Communications, Inc.
300 W 57th St
New York NY 10019
212 649-2000

(G-17390)
HOWARD PRODUCTS INCORPORATED
7 Brookfield St (01605-3988)
PHONE..................................508 757-2440
David Hawley, *President*
Bradford F Hawley, *Shareholder*
EMP: 16
SQ FT: 11,000
SALES (est): 3MM **Privately Held**
WEB: www.howardproducts.com
SIC: 3444 Mfg Sheet Metalwork

(G-17391)
INDEPENENT PLATING CO
35 New St (01605-3324)
PHONE..................................508 756-0301
Charles D Flanagan, *President*
EMP: 25

SALES (est): 1.5MM **Privately Held**
SIC: 3471 3479 Plating/Polishing Service Coating/Engraving Service

(G-17392)
INFINITY
346 Franklin St Ste 2 (01604-5503)
PHONE..................................508 753-1981
Melissa Evans, *Principal*
EMP: 3
SALES (est): 254.4K **Privately Held**
SIC: 3567 Mfg Industrial Furnaces/Ovens

(G-17393)
INSIGNIA ATHLETICS LLC
60 Fremont St (01603-2355)
PHONE..................................508 756-3633
Robert J Devaney, *Principal*
David Cartagena, *Warehouse Mgr*
EMP: 3
SALES (est): 289.4K **Privately Held**
SIC: 3949 Mfg Sporting/Athletic Goods

(G-17394)
INTERNATIONAL CRMIC ENGRG CORP (PA)
235 Brooks St (01606-3307)
PHONE..................................508 853-4700
Merrill W Higgins, *CEO*
Jonathan Higgins, *President*
Blair Sharleville, *Buyer*
Meaghan Merrill, *Engineer*
Andrew Higgins, *VP Sales*
EMP: 49
SQ FT: 10,000
SALES (est): 5.7MM **Privately Held**
WEB: www.intlceramics.com
SIC: 3299 Mfg Nonmetallic Mineral Products

(G-17395)
J F OMALLEY WELDING CO
Also Called: O'Malley J F Welding
1177 Millbury St (01607-1414)
PHONE..................................508 791-8671
EMP: 5
SALES (est): 326.3K **Privately Held**
SIC: 7692 7629 Welding Repair Electrical Repair

(G-17396)
J T GARDNER INC
Also Called: Curry Printing
165 Southbridge St (01608-2045)
PHONE..................................508 751-6600
EMP: 5
SALES (corp-wide): 4.5MM **Privately Held**
SIC: 2752 2791 2796 2789 Commercial Printing, Lithographic
PA: J. T. Gardner, Inc.
190 Turnpike Rd
Westborough MA 01581
800 540-4993

(G-17397)
JEFFERSON RUBBER WORKS INC
Also Called: Jefferson Rubber Products
17 Coppage Dr (01603-1252)
PHONE..................................508 791-3600
David F Pentland, *Ch of Bd*
David Donovan, *Info Tech Mgr*
▲ **EMP:** 100
SQ FT: 30,000
SALES (est): 17.8MM **Privately Held**
WEB: www.jeffersonrubber.com
SIC: 3069 3061 Mfg Fabricated Rubber Products Mfg Mechanical Rubber Goods

(G-17398)
KAHR ARMS INC
130 Goddard Memorial Dr (01603-1260)
PHONE..................................508 635-1414
Justine Moon, *President*
Manfred Moik, *Purchasing*
Keith Tomizawa, *Engineer*
Don Kuwahara, *Sales Staff*
Leo Mattern, *Administration*
EMP: 23
SALES (est): 4.3MM **Privately Held**
SIC: 3484 Mfg Small Arms

(G-17399)
KERVICK FAMILY FOUNDATION INC
40 Rockdale St (01606-1908)
PHONE..................................508 853-4500
Paul J Kervick, *Ch of Bd*
Robert B Kervick, *President*
Kevin M Kervick, *Exec VP*
Joseph Dynof, *Treasurer*
Deborah Emmons, *Asst Treas*
EMP: 3 **EST:** 1905
SQ FT: 160,000
SALES: 20MM **Privately Held**
SIC: 3462 3463 2752 3324 Mfg Iron/Steel Forgings Mfg Nonferrous Forgings Lithographic Coml Print Steel Investment Foundry Nonferrous Metal Foundry

(G-17400)
KILLEEN MACHINE AND TL CO INC
33 Hermon St (01610-1592)
PHONE..................................508 754-1714
Gene A Degre, *Principal*
Karen Zawalich, *Sales Staff*
Aline Doucet, *Director*
EMP: 59 **EST:** 1924
SQ FT: 74,000
SALES (est): 14.6MM **Privately Held**
SIC: 3469 Mfg Metal Stampings

(G-17401)
KINEFAC CORPORATION
Also Called: Kinepower Company Division
156 Goddard Memorial Dr (01603-1262)
PHONE..................................508 754-6901
Noel P Greis, *President*
Richard J Koral, *Vice Pres*
Richard Koral, *Vice Pres*
Ronaold Gagnon, *Project Mgr*
Ronald Zacek, *Prdtn Mgr*
▲ **EMP:** 55
SQ FT: 57,500
SALES (est): 13.7MM **Privately Held**
WEB: www.kinefac.com
SIC: 3541 3542 5085 3547 Mfg Machine Tool-Cutting Mfg Machine Tool-Forming Whol Industrial Supplies Mfg Rolling Mill Mach

(G-17402)
KT ACQUISITION LLC
Also Called: Komtek Technologies
40 Rockdale St (01606-1908)
PHONE..................................508 853-4500
Robert Kervick, *CEO*
EMP: 70
SALES: 12MM **Privately Held**
SIC: 3366 3542 Copper Foundry Mfg Machine Tools-Forming

(G-17403)
L & J OF NEW ENGLAND INC
15 Sagamore Rd Ste 2 (01605-3991)
PHONE..................................508 756-8080
Duncan Leith, *President*
EMP: 38
SQ FT: 30,000
SALES (est): 5MM **Privately Held**
WEB: www.ljne.com
SIC: 3471 3479 2759 Plating/Polishing Service Coating/Engraving Service Commercial Printing

(G-17404)
L & J SCREEN PRINTERS INC
15 Sagamore Rd (01605-3914)
PHONE..................................508 791-7320
Gretchen Prunier, *President*
Duncan Leith, *Vice Pres*
Don Leith, *Treasurer*
EMP: 8
SQ FT: 3,000
SALES (est): 600K **Privately Held**
SIC: 2759 Screen Printing On Metal

(G-17405)
L & R MANUFACTURING CO INC
340 Tacoma St (01605-3538)
PHONE..................................508 853-0562
Robert M Ritter, *President*
John A Erickson Jr, *Clerk*
EMP: 18
SQ FT: 15,000
SALES (est): 3.3MM **Privately Held**
SIC: 3498 Manufacturer Of Tubular Metal Products

(G-17406)
L HARDY COMPANY INC (PA)
17 Mill St (01603-2075)
P.O. Box 30277 (01603-0277)
PHONE..................................508 757-3480
Norman Monks, *President*
◆ **EMP:** 10
SQ FT: 30,000
SALES (est): 3.5MM **Privately Held**
WEB: www.leatherknives.com
SIC: 3545 Mfg Machine Tool Accessories

(G-17407)
LETS GO TECHNOLOGY INC (PA)
Also Called: New England Low Vision
799 W Boylston St (01606-3071)
PHONE..................................508 853-8200
Scott V Krug, *President*
Michelle Perkins, *Technology*
Erin Davis, *Administration*
EMP: 11
SALES: 99K **Privately Held**
SIC: 3851 8042 Manufactures Ophthalmic Goods Optometrist's Office

(G-17408)
LUTCO BEARINGS INC
677 Cambridge St Ste 1 (01610-2664)
PHONE..................................508 756-6296
John C Stowe, *President*
Steven Noone, *CFO*
Daniel A Ferry, *Marketing Staff*
EMP: 100 **EST:** 1945
SQ FT: 80,000
SALES (est): 13.9MM **Privately Held**
WEB: www.lutco.com
SIC: 3451 Mfg Screw Machine Products

(G-17409)
LYONS SIGNS INC
1454 Grafton St (01604-2720)
PHONE..................................508 754-2501
John Lyons, *President*
Patrice Lyons, *Vice Pres*
EMP: 3
SQ FT: 7,000
SALES (est): 361.3K **Privately Held**
SIC: 3993 Mfg Signs/Advertising Specialties

(G-17410)
MADISON CABLE CORPORATION
125 Goddard Memorial Dr (01603-1233)
PHONE..................................508 752-2884
Nicolas Marinelarena, *CFO*
▲ **EMP:** 213 **EST:** 1970
SQ FT: 180,000
SALES (est): 33.3MM
SALES (corp-wide): 13.9B **Privately Held**
WEB: www.madisoncable.com
SIC: 3357 3643 3577 Nonferrous Wiredrawing/Insulating Mfg Conductive Wiring Devices Mfg Computer Peripheral Equipment
HQ: Te Connectivity Corporation
1050 Westlakes Dr
Berwyn PA 19312
610 893-9800

(G-17411)
MAGMOTOR TECHNOLOGIES INC
10 Coppage Dr (01603-1252)
PHONE..................................508 835-4305
Aryan Papoli, *CEO*
Willigar Jamie, *Sales Mgr*
▲ **EMP:** 11 **EST:** 1979
SQ FT: 44,000
SALES (est): 3.2MM **Privately Held**
WEB: www.inverpower.com
SIC: 3714 3823 Mfg Motor Vehicle Parts/Accessories Mfg Process Control Instruments

(G-17412)
MEGAWAVE CORPORATION
234 Brooks St 3 (01606-3300)
PHONE..................................978 615-7200
Steven Best, *Principal*
John Benham, *Principal*
Allison Parent, *Engineer*
Marshall W Cross, *Treasurer*
EMP: 5
SALES (est): 626.8K **Privately Held**
WEB: www.megawave.com
SIC: 3812 Mfg Search/Navigation Equipment

(G-17413)
METACOG INC
55 Linden St (01609-4612)
PHONE..................................508 798-6100
Victoria Porras, *CEO*
Doug Stein, *CTO*
EMP: 9 **EST:** 2014
SQ FT: 250
SALES (est): 362.8K
SALES (corp-wide): 68.4MM **Privately Held**
SIC: 7372 8732 Prepackaged Software Services Commercial Nonphysical Research
PA: The Computing Technology Industry Association Inc
3500 Lacey Rd Ste 100
Downers Grove IL 60515
630 678-8300

(G-17414)
MICRO ARC WELDING SERVICE
33 Pullman St (01606-3310)
PHONE..................................508 852-6125
Scott Malkasian, *Owner*
EMP: 6
SQ FT: 200
SALES (est): 477.4K **Privately Held**
WEB: www.microarcwelding.com
SIC: 7692 Micro Welding Service

(G-17415)
MICRO TECH MFG INC
100 Grand St Ste 1 (01610-1677)
PHONE..................................508 752-5212
Theodore M Jasiewicz, *President*
T J Jasiewicz, *Vice Pres*
Marie Jasiewicz, *Treasurer*
EMP: 15 **EST:** 1965
SQ FT: 12,000
SALES (est): 1.9MM **Privately Held**
SIC: 3599 Mfg Industrial Machinery

(G-17416)
MICROBIOTIX INC
1 Innovation Dr Ste 14 (01605-4332)
PHONE..................................508 757-2800
Terry Bowlin, *President*
Shire Biochem, *Shareholder*
EMP: 25
SQ FT: 10,739
SALES (est): 5.2MM **Privately Held**
WEB: www.microbiotix.com
SIC: 2833 Pharmaceutical Research & Development

(G-17417)
MICROMETALS TECH CORP
12 Jacques St (01603-1926)
PHONE..................................508 792-1615
Bogdan Mlynarski, *President*
Wanda Mlynarski, *Admin Sec*
EMP: 10
SQ FT: 10,000
SALES (est): 1.5MM **Privately Held**
SIC: 3469 Mfg Machine Parts

(G-17418)
MINDSCIENCES INC
45 Hickory Dr (01609-1016)
PHONE..................................516 658-2985
Judson Brewer,
EMP: 3
SALES (est): 176.9K **Privately Held**
SIC: 3845 Mfg Electromedical Equipment

(G-17419)
MINIKE CARD CARE
532 W Boylston St (01606-2027)
PHONE..................................508 853-4490
James McCullough, *Owner*
Bryan McCullough, *Co-Owner*
EMP: 6
SALES (est): 357.1K **Privately Held**
SIC: 2754 Gravure Commercial Printing

(G-17420)
MINUTEMAN PRESS WORCESTER INC
122 Green St Ste 1 (01604-4143)
PHONE..................................508 757-5450
Bill Feinberg, *President*
EMP: 5
SQ FT: 2,200
SALES: 1.6MM **Privately Held**
SIC: 2752 Comm Prtg Litho

(G-17421)
MODERN MFG INC WORCESTER
Also Called: Modern Architechtural Glazing
12 Brussels St (01610-2940)
PHONE..................................508 791-7151
Richard F Uras, *President*
Donna Bolte, *Treasurer*
EMP: 20 **EST:** 1952
SQ FT: 40,000
SALES (est): 3.9MM **Privately Held**
WEB: www.modernglazing.com
SIC: 3442 3231 Mfg Frames Glass Products

(G-17422)
MODERN SHEETMETAL INC
243 Stafford St Ste 2 (01603-1168)
PHONE..................................508 798-6665
Ped Mrugala, *President*
EMP: 6
SQ FT: 2,000
SALES (est): 800.1K **Privately Held**
SIC: 3444 1761 Mfg Sheet Metalwork & Sheetmetal Contractor

(G-17423)
MOLE HOLLOW CANDLES LIMITED
5 Wheeler Ave (01609-1707)
PHONE..................................508 756-7415
David Ja Dunn, *President*
Beth W Dunn, *Corp Secy*
EMP: 30
SQ FT: 5,000
SALES (est): 2.4MM **Privately Held**
WEB: www.molehollowcandle.com
SIC: 3999 5999 5199 Mfg Retails & Whol Candles

(G-17424)
MORGAN ENTERPRISES INC
110 Blackstone River Rd (01607-1489)
P.O. Box 70316 (01607-0316)
PHONE..................................985 377-3216
Dustin Morgan, *Principal*
EMP: 3
SALES (est): 360K **Privately Held**
SIC: 2759 Commercial Printing

(G-17425)
MR SANDLESS CENTRAL MASS
191 Fairhaven Rd (01606-3134)
PHONE..................................508 864-6517
Frank Pupillo, *Owner*
EMP: 3 **EST:** 2014
SALES: 200K **Privately Held**
SIC: 2426 1771 1751 Hardwood Dimension/Floor Mill Concrete Contractor Carpentry Contractor

(G-17426)
MRS MACKS BAKERY INC
1393 Grafton St Ste 5 (01604-2733)
PHONE..................................508 753-0610
Shawn McAvey, *President*
Grainne McAvey, *President*
EMP: 7
SQ FT: 3,000
SALES (est): 828.3K **Privately Held**
SIC: 2051 5812 Mfg Bread/Related Products Eating Place

(G-17427)
NED ACQUISITION CORP
18 Grafton St (01604-4934)
PHONE..................................508 798-8546
Brad Wyatt, *President*
Rene Blais, *Manager*
EMP: 50
SALES (est): 4.4MM **Privately Held**
SIC: 3545 Mfg Machine Tool Accessories

(G-17428)
NELES USA INC
28 Bowditch Dr (01605-2005)
PHONE..................................508 852-0200
EMP: 7
SALES (corp-wide): 3.5B **Privately Held**
SIC: 3592 Whol Industrial Equipment
HQ: Neles Usa Inc
44 Bowditch Dr
Shrewsbury MA 01545
508 852-0200

(G-17429)
NEW ENGLAND BUSINESS MEDIA LLC (PA)
Also Called: Worcester Business Journal
172 Shrewsbury St Ste 1 (01604-4636)
PHONE..................................508 755-8004
Mary Rogers, *Controller*
Kim Vautour, *Human Res Mgr*
Peter R Stanton, *Mng Member*
Peter Stanton, *Mng Member*
Joseph R Zwiebel, *Mng Member*
EMP: 22
SQ FT: 12,000
SALES (est): 2.4MM **Privately Held**
WEB: www.mainebiz.biz
SIC: 2711 2721 Newspapers-Publishing/Printing Periodicals-Publishing/Printing

(G-17430)
NEW ENGLAND INDUS COATINGS
Also Called: N E Industrial Coatings
50 Lagrange St (01610-1536)
PHONE..................................508 754-1066
Scott Crandell, *President*
Robert Joly, *Treasurer*
EMP: 5
SQ FT: 12,000
SALES: 575K **Privately Held**
SIC: 3479 Applies Coatings To Metal & Formed Industrial Products

(G-17431)
NEW ENGLAND ORTHOTIC & PROST
Also Called: Neops
405 Grove St Ste 2 (01605-1270)
PHONE..................................508 890-8808
Art Shea, *Director*
EMP: 3
SALES (corp-wide): 25.6MM **Privately Held**
WEB: www.neops.com
SIC: 3842 Mfg Surgical Appliances/Supplies
PA: New England Orthotic And Prosthetic Systems, Llc
33 Business Park Dr Ste 3
Branford CT 06405
203 483-8488

(G-17432)
NEW ENGLAND SIGN GROUP INC
Also Called: Kay Gee Sign and Graphics Co
33 Arctic St (01604-4932)
PHONE..................................508 832-3471
Kari Lunden, *President*
Michael Hannigan, *Vice Pres*
Norm Picard, *Vice Pres*
Chris Podles, *Shareholder*
EMP: 25 **EST:** 2015
SALES: 3MM **Privately Held**
SIC: 3993 Mfg Signs/Advertising Specialties

(G-17433)
NEW ENGLAND SUGARS LLC
1120 Millbury St (01607-1415)
PHONE..................................508 792-3801
John Yonover,
EMP: 3
SALES (est): 232.5K **Privately Held**
SIC: 2061 Mfg Raw Cane Sugar

(G-17434)
NEW METHOD PLATING CO INC
43 Hammond St (01610-1523)
PHONE..................................508 754-2671
Ralph J Capalbo Jr, *President*
Capalbo Christopher, *Director*
EMP: 26
SQ FT: 25,000
SALES (est): 2.9MM **Privately Held**
WEB: www.newmethodplating.com
SIC: 3471 Plating/Polishing Service

(G-17435)
NRZ COMPANIES INC
774 W Boylston St (01606-3041)
PHONE..................................508 856-7237
Samuel Wildt, *President*
EMP: 4 **EST:** 2016
SALES (est): 115.8K **Privately Held**
SIC: 2396 Mfg Auto/Apparel Trimming

(G-17436)
OLAF PHARMACEUTICAL INC
1 Innovation Dr (01605-4307)
PHONE..................................508 755-3570
Fax: 508 755-5792
EMP: 5 **EST:** 2011
SALES (est): 500K **Privately Held**
SIC: 2834 Mfg Pharmaceutical Preparations

(G-17437)
OROURKE WELDING INC
Also Called: A-1 Auto Frame
851 Millbury St (01607)
PHONE..................................508 755-6360
John O'Rourke, *President*
EMP: 5
SALES (est): 346.8K **Privately Held**
SIC: 7692 Welding Repair

(G-17438)
PADCO INC
19 Wells St (01604-1727)
PHONE..................................508 753-8486
Joseph A Padavano, *President*
Carolyn Padavano, *Treasurer*
EMP: 15
SALES (est): 2MM **Privately Held**
WEB: www.padcomusa.com
SIC: 2541 Mfg Cabinets

(G-17439)
PAGIO INC
84 Winter St (01604-5036)
PHONE..................................508 756-5006
Paul Giorgio, *Owner*
Donna Roberson, *Editor*
EMP: 3 **EST:** 2004
SALES (est): 304.6K **Privately Held**
SIC: 2721 Periodicals-Publishing/Printing

(G-17440)
PHIO PHARMACEUTICALS CORP
60 Prescott St Ste 8 (01605-2661)
PHONE..................................508 767-3861
Geert Cauwenbergh, *Branch Mgr*
EMP: 4
SALES (corp-wide): 138K **Publicly Held**
SIC: 2834 Mfg Pharmaceutical Preparations
PA: Phio Pharmaceuticals Corp.
257 Simarano Dr Ste 101
Marlborough MA 01752
508 767-3681

(G-17441)
PILGRIM TOOL & DIE INC
565 Southbridge St (01610-1727)
PHONE..................................508 753-0190
Robert J Graham Jr, *President*
Micheal Graham, *Vice Pres*
Jean Graham, *Clerk*
EMP: 7 **EST:** 1989
SQ FT: 5,000
SALES (est): 822.4K **Privately Held**
WEB: www.pilgrimhearth.com
SIC: 3544 Mfg Molds & Dies

(G-17442)
POBCO INC
99 Hope Ave (01603-2298)
PHONE..................................508 791-6376
Stephen P Johnson, *President*
David W Johnson, *Vice Pres*
Thomas G Johnson, *Vice Pres*
Lisa K Khoury, *Treasurer*
▼ **EMP:** 20 **EST:** 1929
SQ FT: 20,000
SALES (est): 4MM **Privately Held**
WEB: www.pobcoplastics.com
SIC: 3089 2499 Mfg Plastic Products Mfg Wood Products

(G-17443)
POLAR CORP (PA)
Also Called: Polar Beverages
1001 Southbridge St (01610-2218)
P.O. Box 15011 (01615-0011)
PHONE..................................508 753-6383
Ralph D Crowley Jr, *President*
Stephen Carey, *Vice Pres*
James Doyle, *Vice Pres*
Daniel Oconnor, *Vice Pres*
Jim Robert, *Opers Mgr*
▼ **EMP:** 700
SQ FT: 350,000
SALES (est): 404.9MM **Privately Held**
WEB: www.polarbev.com
SIC: 2086 5149 Mfg Soft Drinks Whol Groceries

(G-17444)
POWER GUIDE MARKETING INC (PA)
540 W Boylston St Rear (01606-2074)
P.O. Box 13, Fitzwilliam NH (03447-0013)
PHONE..................................508 853-7357
Ronald Josephson, *President*
Richard Lupoin, *Senior VP*
Lind Josephson, *Admin Sec*
EMP: 5 **EST:** 1997
SQ FT: 750
SALES (est): 961.4K **Privately Held**
WEB: www.power-guide.com
SIC: 3679 Mfg Electronic Components

(G-17445)
PREMATECH LLC
Also Called: Prematech Advanced Ceramics
160 Goddard Memorial Dr (01603-1260)
PHONE..................................508 791-9549
Mona Lynn Pappafava, *President*
James Vazvo, *CFO*
Jennifer Prematech, *Sales Staff*
Marcy Pappafava,
EMP: 35 **EST:** 2004
SQ FT: 26,000
SALES (est): 5.8MM **Privately Held**
WEB: www.prematechac.com
SIC: 3291 Mfg Abrasive Products

(G-17446)
PREMATECHNOLIGIES LLC
Prematech Advanced Ceramics
160 Goddard Memorial Dr (01603-1260)
PHONE..................................508 791-9549
John Killem, *Mng Member*
EMP: 40
SALES (est): 3.8MM
SALES (corp-wide): 3MM **Privately Held**
SIC: 3599 Mfg Industrial Machinery
PA: Prematechnoligies Llc
Garden St
Greensburg PA

(G-17447)
PRIMETALS TECHNOLOGIES USA LLC
40 Crescent St (01605-2404)
PHONE..................................508 755-6111
EMP: 17 **Privately Held**
SIC: 3312 Blast Furnace-Steel Works
HQ: Primetals Technologies Usa Llc
5895 Windward Pkwy Fl 2
Alpharetta GA 30005
770 740-3800

(G-17448)
QUICK STOP PRINTING
340 Shrewsbury St (01604-4615)
PHONE..................................508 797-4788
Edward Massei Jr, *Owner*
EMP: 5
SQ FT: 3,648
SALES (est): 593.8K **Privately Held**
WEB: www.quickstopprinting.com
SIC: 2759 Commercial Printing

(G-17449)
RAND-WHITNEY CONTAINER BOARD L
1 Rand Whitney Way (01607-1890)
P.O. Box 336, Montville CT (06353-0336)
PHONE..................................860 848-1900
Robert Kraft, *Partner*
Jim Wood, *General Mgr*
Rory Herlihy, *Opers Mgr*
Madeline Smith, *Production*
Guy Joseph, *Engineer*
EMP: 100
SQ FT: 120,000
SALES (est): 35.9MM **Privately Held**
WEB: www.rwcb.com
SIC: 2631 Paperboard Mill
PA: Kraft Group Llc
1 Patriot Pl
Foxboro MA 02035

(G-17450)
RAND-WHITNEY CONTAINER LLC (DH)
1 Rand Whitney Way (01607-1890)
PHONE..................................508 890-7000
Robert K Kraft, *President*
Rick Dumais, *General Mgr*
Aaron Manderbach, *District Mgr*
Andrew Veroneau, *Business Mgr*
Rob Desantis, *Project Mgr*
EMP: 175
SQ FT: 300,000
SALES (est): 90MM **Privately Held**
SIC: 2653 2631 Mfg Corrugated/Solid Fiber Boxes Paperboard Mill
HQ: Rand-Whitney Group Llc
1 Rand Whitney Way
Worcester MA 01607
508 791-2301

(G-17451)
RAND-WHITNEY CONTAINER LLC
Also Called: Rand Whitney-Greenwood St
2 Rand Whitney Way (01607-1890)
PHONE..................................774 420-2425
EMP: 4 **Privately Held**
SIC: 2653 Mfg Corrugated/Solid Fiber Boxes
HQ: Rand-Whitney Container Llc
1 Rand Whitney Way
Worcester MA 01607
508 890-7000

(G-17452)
RAND-WHITNEY GROUP LLC (HQ)
1 Rand Whitney Way (01607-1890)
PHONE..................................508 791-2301
Drew Nason, *Prdtn Mgr*
Robert K Kraft,
John McNabb Jr, *Administration*
EMP: 145
SQ FT: 200,000
SALES (est): 218.7MM **Privately Held**
SIC: 2653 2657 2631 Mfg Corrugated/Solid Fiber Boxes Mfg Folding Paperboard Boxes Paperboard Mill

(G-17453)
READY 2 RUN GRAPHICS SIGNS INC
240 Barber Ave Ste R (01606-2479)
PHONE..................................508 459-9977
David Winchester, *President*
EMP: 4
SALES: 200K **Privately Held**
SIC: 3993 Mfg Signs/Advertising Specialties

(G-17454)
REDEMPTION ROCK BREWERY CO
Also Called: Redemption Rock Brewing Co
333 Shrewsbury St (01604-4081)
PHONE..................................978 660-5526
Danielle Babineau, *CEO*
Kevin Kirkness, *General Mgr*
Gregory Carlson, *Prdtn Mgr*
Daniel Carlson, *Marketing Staff*
EMP: 4
SALES (est): 169.6K **Privately Held**
SIC: 2082 Mfg Malt Beverages

(G-17455)
REDI-LETTERS EXPRESS LLC
1051 Millbury St Ste B (01607-1479)
PHONE..................................508 340-3284
Ralph A St Germain Jr, *President*
EMP: 3
SALES (est): 197K **Privately Held**
SIC: 3993 5046 Manufactures Signs And Advertising Specialties Wholesales Commercial Equipment Specializing In Electrical Signs

(G-17456)
REED MACHINERY INC (PA)
10a New Bond St (01606-2615)
PHONE..................................508 595-9090
James D Flanagan, *President*
Steven Copeland, *Vice Pres*
Brian Faucher, *Vice Pres*
Adam Kettles, *VP Bus Dvlpt*
Jeffrey T Hoffman, *Treasurer*
▲ **EMP:** 18
SQ FT: 25,000
SALES (est): 3.5MM **Privately Held**
SIC: 3545 Mfg Machine Tool Accessories

(G-17457)
REINFORCED STRUCTURES FOR ELEC
50 Suffolk St (01604-4091)
PHONE..................................508 754-5316
James Romeo, *President*
Edward Romeo, *President*
Wendy Romeo, *Principal*
Robert Romeo, *Chairman*
Blunk Terry, *Engineer*
EMP: 27 **EST:** 1970
SQ FT: 10,000
SALES (est): 3.5MM **Privately Held**
SIC: 2821 3678 3674 3644 Mfg Plstc Material/Resin Mfg Elec Connectors Mfg Semiconductors/Dvcs Mfg Nonconductv Wire Dvc

(G-17458)
RELIABLE PLATING CO INC
Also Called: Electroplating Co
523 Southbridge St (01610-1715)
PHONE..................................508 755-9434
George H Sogigian, *President*
Harry G Sogigian, *Vice Pres*
Ann Avakian, *Admin Sec*
EMP: 5
SQ FT: 3,000
SALES (est): 320K **Privately Held**
SIC: 3471 Electroplating & Anodizing Service

(G-17459)
RILEY POWER INC
Also Called: Reiley Power
5 Neponset St (01606-2714)
PHONE..................................508 852-7100
EMP: 166
SQ FT: 10,000
SALES (corp-wide): 627.7MM **Privately Held**
SIC: 3433 3443 Mfg Heating Equipment-Nonelectric Mfg Fabricated Plate Work
HQ: Riley Power Inc.
5 Neponset St
Worcester MA 01752
508 852-7100

(G-17460)
ROGER TOOL AND DIE COMPANY INC
33 Pullman St (01606-3310)
PHONE..................................508 853-3757
Steven Malkasian, *President*
Alicia Merritt, *Business Mgr*
Mark Malkasian, *Vice Pres*
Trudy Bratkon, *Office Mgr*
EMP: 8
SQ FT: 6,000
SALES (est): 1.4MM **Privately Held**
WEB: www.rogertool.com
SIC: 3559 Mfg Misc Industry Machinery

(G-17461)
S I HOWARD GLASS COMPANY INC
Also Called: Howard S I Glass Co
379 Sw Cutoff (01604-2713)
PHONE..................................508 753-8146
Earl R Farmer Jr, *President*
Jason Perch, *Vice Pres*
▲ **EMP:** 25
SQ FT: 24,000
SALES (est): 5.4MM **Privately Held**
WEB: www.howardglass.com
SIC: 3827 Mfg Optical Instruments/Lenses

(G-17462)
SAEILO INC
130 Goddard Memorial Dr (01603-1260)
PHONE..................................508 799-9809
Sam Wada, *Manager*
EMP: 20
SALES (corp-wide): 30MM **Privately Held**
WEB: www.kahrshop.com
SIC: 3599 Contract Machine Shop
HQ: Saeilo, Inc.
105 Kahr Ave
Greeley PA 18425

(G-17463)
SAEILO USA INC
Kahr Arms
130 Goddard Memorial Dr (01603-1260)
PHONE..................................508 795-3919
Soji Wada, *Division Mgr*
EMP: 20 **Privately Held**
WEB: www.kahr.com
SIC: 3484 Mfg Fire Arms
HQ: Saeilo Usa Inc
105 Kahr Ave
Greeley PA 18425
845 735-6500

(G-17464)
SAINT-GOBAIN ABRASIVES INC (DH)
Also Called: Bonded Abrasives
1 New Bond St (01606-2614)
P.O. Box 15008 (01615-0008)
PHONE..................................508 795-5000
Patrick Millot, *CEO*
John Crowe, *President*
John R Mesher, *Vice Pres*
Steven F Messmer, *Vice Pres*
M Shawn Puccio, *Vice Pres*
◆ **EMP:** 2500
SALES (est): 2.4B
SALES (corp-wide): 209.1MM **Privately Held**
WEB: www.sgabrasives.com
SIC: 3291 3559 3545 3297 Mfg Abrasive Products Mfg Misc Industry Mach

(G-17465)
SAINT-GOBAIN CERAMICS PLAS INC
Also Called: Saint-Gobain Ceramic Materials
1 New Bond St (01606-2614)
PHONE..................................508 795-5000
Howard Wallar, *Manager*
EMP: 85
SALES (corp-wide): 209.1MM **Privately Held**
WEB: www.sgceramics.com
SIC: 3291 Mfg Industrial Inorganic Chemicals
HQ: Saint-Gobain Ceramics & Plastics, Inc.
750 E Swedesford Rd
Valley Forge PA 19482

(G-17466)
SAINT-GOBAIN CERAMICS PLAS INC
351 Stores St (01606)
PHONE..................................508 795-5000
EMP: 4
SALES (corp-wide): 209.1MM **Privately Held**
SIC: 2819 Mfg Industrial Inorganic Chemicals
HQ: Saint-Gobain Ceramics & Plastics, Inc.
750 E Swedesford Rd
Valley Forge PA 19482

(G-17467)
SAINT-GOBAIN PRFMCE PLAS CORP
717 Plantation St (01605-2039)
PHONE..................................508 852-3072
Bob Caleski, *Principal*
Timmithy Mayfield, *Principal*
Rob Watterman, *Principal*
John Nolan, *Manager*
EMP: 50
SALES (corp-wide): 209.1MM **Privately Held**
SIC: 3089 3053 3357 3496 Mfg Plastic Products Mfg Gasket/Packing/Seals Nonfrs Wiredrwng/Insltng Mfg Misc Fab Wire Prdts Mfg Fabrcatd Rubber Prdt
HQ: Saint-Gobain Performance Plastics Corporation
31500 Solon Rd
Solon OH 44139
440 836-6900

(G-17468)
SANCHEZ OCTAVIO STORAGE
Also Called: Printing Depot
9 Short St (01604-3320)
PHONE..................................508 853-3309
Octavio Sanchez, *Owner*
EMP: 5 **EST:** 2007
SALES: 300K **Privately Held**
SIC: 2759 Commercial Printing

(G-17469)
SANCLIFF INC
Also Called: Dykrex Wire Die Machinery Div
97 Temple St (01604-5029)
P.O. Box 2444 (01613-2444)
PHONE..................................508 795-0747
William G Drumm, *President*
EMP: 13
SQ FT: 23,000
SALES: 1.3MM **Privately Held**
WEB: www.sancliff.com
SIC: 3544 3699 3559 Mfg Dies/Tools/Jigs/Fixtures Mfg Electrical Equipment/Supplies Mfg Misc Industry Machinery

(G-17470)
SEALCOATING
110 Blackstone River Rd (01607-1489)
PHONE..................................508 926-8080
EMP: 3
SALES (est): 134.6K **Privately Held**
SIC: 2951 Highway/Street Construction

(G-17471)
SEM-TEC INC
47 Lagrange St (01610-1595)
PHONE..................................508 798-8551
Joseph M Krosoczka, *President*
Steven Krosoczka, *Treasurer*
▲ **EMP:** 50
SQ FT: 100,000
SALES (est): 8.7MM **Privately Held**
SIC: 3399 3494 Mfg Primary Metal Products Mfg Valves/Pipe Fittings

(G-17472)
SERRATO SIGN CO
Also Called: Serrato Signs
15 Dewey St (01609-2909)
PHONE..................................508 756-7004
Andrew Serrato, *Owner*
EMP: 8 **EST:** 1946
SQ FT: 6,000
SALES (est): 905.3K **Privately Held**
WEB: www.serratosigns.com
SIC: 3993 7389 Mfg Signs/Advertising Specialties Business Services

(G-17473)
SIEMENS INDUSTRY INC
40 Crescent St (01605-2404)
PHONE..................................508 849-6519
Eric Main, *Purchasing*
EMP: 87
SALES (corp-wide): 96.9B **Privately Held**
SIC: 3822 Mfg Environmental Controls
HQ: Siemens Industry, Inc.
1000 Deerfield Pkwy
Buffalo Grove IL 60089
847 215-1000

(G-17474)
SJOGREN INDUSTRIES INC
982 Southbridge St (01610-2219)
PHONE..................................508 987-3206
Carl Sjogren, *Principal*
EMP: 18

SALES (est): 132.4K Privately Held
SIC: 3999 Mfg Misc Products

(G-17475)
SLIDEWAYS INC
705 Plantation St Ste 1 (01605-2062)
PHONE.................................508 854-0799
Thomas Sioui, *CEO*
Glenn T Priest, *Vice Pres*
Paul Lamalva,
▲ EMP: 21
SQ FT: 9,000
SALES (est): 2MM Privately Held
WEB: www.slideways.com
SIC: 3089 Mfg Nonmetallic Bearings & Wear Components

(G-17476)
SMI MA INC
Also Called: Saeilo Manufacturing Inds
130 Goddard Memorial Dr (01603-1260)
PHONE.................................508 799-9809
Sam Wada, *President*
Kuniko Gomi, *Treasurer*
Keith Tomizawa, *Admin Sec*
EMP: 50
SQ FT: 20,000
SALES (est): 6.1MM
SALES (corp-wide): 30MM Privately Held
SIC: 3599 Mfg Industrial Machinery
PA: Saeilo Enterprises Inc
105 Kahr Ave
Greeley PA 18425
845 735-6500

(G-17477)
SOUTHWEST ASIAN INCORPORATED
55 Millbrook St Ste 4 (01606-2804)
PHONE.................................508 753-7126
Tha Lam, *Owner*
EMP: 8
SALES (est): 988.3K Privately Held
SIC: 3663 3629 Mfg Radio/Tv Communication Equipment Mfg Electrical Industrial Apparatus

(G-17478)
ST CYR INC
Also Called: St Cyr Salon Spa
235 Park Ave (01609-1965)
PHONE.................................508 752-2222
Robert C Cyr, *President*
EMP: 27
SQ FT: 5,000
SALES (est): 4.4MM Privately Held
WEB: www.stcyrsalon.com
SIC: 2844 7231 Mfg Toilet Preparations Beauty Shop

(G-17479)
ST PIERRE MANUFACTURING CORP
Also Called: St Pierre Chain & Wire Rope
317 E Mountain St (01606-1298)
PHONE.................................508 853-8010
Henry G St Pierre, *President*
Edward J St Pierre, *Treasurer*
Matthew Finizio, *Sales Staff*
Nanette St Pierre, *Marketing Staff*
Sue Chambers, *Technology*
▲ EMP: 30 EST: 1966
SQ FT: 45,000
SALES (est): 8.7MM Privately Held
WEB: www.stpierreusa.com
SIC: 3462 3536 3499 5084 Mfg Iron/Steel Forgings Mfg Hoist/Crane/Monorail Mfg Misc Fab Metal Prdts Whol Industrial Equip Mfg Misc Fab Wire Prdts

(G-17480)
STAFFORD WIRE SPECIALTY INC
243 Stafford St Ste 1 (01603-1168)
PHONE.................................508 799-6124
Ted Lundberg, *CEO*
EMP: 4
SQ FT: 15,000
SALES (est): 839.9K Privately Held
SIC: 3315 Mfg Misc Fabricated Wire Products

(G-17481)
STANDARD LOCK WASHER & MFG CO
Also Called: Valve Components Division
1451 Grafton St (01604-2718)
P.O. Box 397 (01613-0397)
PHONE.................................508 757-4508
Alfred E Barry Sr, *President*
EMP: 30 EST: 1938
SQ FT: 28,000
SALES (est): 4.6MM Privately Held
WEB: www.stanlok.com
SIC: 3452 5085 Mfg Industrial Fasteners

(G-17482)
STANLOK CORPORATION
1451 Grafton St (01604-2718)
P.O. Box 2735 (01613-2735)
PHONE.................................508 757-4508
Al Barry, *President*
▲ EMP: 25 EST: 1968
SALES (est): 2MM Privately Held
WEB: www.nutsinc.com
SIC: 3452 Mfg Bolts/Screws/Rivets

(G-17483)
SUMMIT FORMS
456 W Boylston St (01606-3225)
P.O. Box 60300 (01606-0300)
PHONE.................................508 853-6838
Paul Conner, *Principal*
EMP: 5 EST: 1986
SALES (est): 695.3K Privately Held
SIC: 2752 Lithographic Commercial Printing

(G-17484)
SUNRISE PROSTHETICS ORTHOTICS (PA)
10 Harvard St (01609-2831)
PHONE.................................508 753-4738
Karen Lynch, *CEO*
John Gannon, *Info Tech Dir*
Linette Martinez, *Info Tech Dir*
EMP: 7
SALES (est): 940.3K Privately Held
SIC: 3842 Mfg Surgical Appliances/Supplies

(G-17485)
TABLE TALK PIES INC (PA)
Also Called: Pieco Holdings
120 Washington St Ste 1 (01610-2751)
PHONE.................................508 438-1556
Christos Cocaine, *President*
Harry Kokkinis, *Vice Pres*
James Cumming, *Plant Mgr*
Greg Diezel, *Plant Mgr*
Dino Suffoletto, *Production*
▼ EMP: 60
SQ FT: 164,000
SALES (est): 19.9MM Privately Held
WEB: www.tabletalkpie.com
SIC: 2051 Mfg Bread/Related Products

(G-17486)
TE CONNECTIVITY CORPORATION
Madison Cable
125 Goddard Memorial Dr (01603-1233)
PHONE.................................717 592-4299
Chuck Grant, *Branch Mgr*
EMP: 281
SALES (corp-wide): 13.9B Privately Held
WEB: www.raychem.com
SIC: 3678 3643 Manufactures Electronic And Electrical Connection Devices And Current Carrying Devices
HQ: Te Connectivity Corporation
1050 Westlakes Dr
Berwyn PA 19312
610 893-9800

(G-17487)
TERECON CORP (PA)
55 Carter Rd (01609-1037)
P.O. Box 528, Saunderstown RI (02874-0528)
PHONE.................................508 791-1875
Joseph Concordia, *President*
EMP: 4
SALES (est): 343.2K Privately Held
SIC: 2899 Mfg Chemical Preparations

(G-17488)
THERMOPLASTICS CO INC
24 Woodward St (01610-2942)
PHONE.................................508 754-4668
G Peter Murphy, *President*
EMP: 20 EST: 1973
SQ FT: 33,000
SALES (est): 4.2MM Privately Held
WEB: www.thermoplasticsco.com
SIC: 3559 7699 5084 Mfg Parts For Plastic Working Machinery & Repairs Machinery

(G-17489)
TOPSALL MACHINE TOOL CO INC
33 Bullard Ave (01605-1643)
PHONE.................................508 755-0332
Paul Huikku, *President*
Robert Huikku, *Treasurer*
Richard Toppin, *Clerk*
EMP: 4 EST: 1981
SALES (est): 483.8K Privately Held
WEB: www.topsallmachine.com
SIC: 3621 3559 Mfrs Pelletizing Rotors For Plastics Industry

(G-17490)
TRI-STAR SPORTSWEAR INC
1051 Millbury St Ste A (01607-1479)
PHONE.................................508 799-4117
Paul Mahassel, *President*
EMP: 5
SQ FT: 4,000
SALES (est): 398.1K Privately Held
SIC: 2395 Embroidered Sportswear

(G-17491)
TRICAB (USA) INC
15 Coppage Dr (01603-1252)
PHONE.................................508 421-4680
Allan Greenfield, *President*
Michael Armstrong, *Admin Sec*
▲ EMP: 50
SALES (est): 15.7MM Privately Held
SIC: 3357 Nonferrous Wiredrawing/Insulating
HQ: Tricab (Australia) Pty Ltd
33 Prohasky St
Port Melbourne VIC 3207

(G-17492)
UMASS MEM MRI IMAGING CTR LLC
Also Called: Shields Mri At Umass Memorial
214 Shrewsbury St (01604-4629)
PHONE.................................508 756-7300
Jeffrey Ronner,
EMP: 20
SALES (est): 1MM Privately Held
SIC: 3826 8011 Mfg Analytical Instruments Medical Doctor's Office

(G-17493)
UNITED METAL FABRICATORS INC
1021 Southbridge St (01610-2218)
PHONE.................................508 754-1800
Theodore Polenski Jr, *President*
Bob Maska, *Principal*
Pat Cirillo, *Treasurer*
EMP: 10
SQ FT: 14,000
SALES (est): 1.3MM Privately Held
SIC: 3443 3599 3444 Mfg Sheet Metalwork Enclosures And Weldments And Does Machining

(G-17494)
UNITED WIRE & CABLE CORP (PA)
425 Shrewsbury St (01604-1690)
PHONE.................................508 757-3872
Thomas P Andrews, *President*
Beatrice Andrews, *Vice Pres*
EMP: 3
SQ FT: 23,000
SALES (est): 7.2MM Privately Held
SIC: 3357 5051 Mfr & Whol Wire

(G-17495)
UNIVERSAL BUSINESS FORMS INC
759 Salisbury St (01609-1124)
PHONE.................................508 852-5520
Keith D Mooradian, *President*
EMP: 3
SQ FT: 1,800
SALES (est): 349.2K Privately Held
SIC: 2752 Lithographic Commercial Printing

(G-17496)
VALKYRIE COMPANY INC (PA)
Also Called: Abas Accessories
60 Fremont St (01603-2396)
PHONE.................................508 756-3633
James J Devaney, *President*
Marty Nathan, *CFO*
Bill Devaney, *Med Doctor*
▲ EMP: 100
SQ FT: 118,000
SALES (est): 13.2MM Privately Held
WEB: www.valkyriemfg.com
SIC: 3172 Mfg Personal Leather Goods

(G-17497)
VALKYRIE COMPANY INC
Also Called: Basco Leather Goods
60 Fremont St (01603-2396)
PHONE.................................508 756-3633
James J Devaney, *President*
EMP: 60
SALES (corp-wide): 13.2MM Privately Held
WEB: www.valkyriemfg.com
SIC: 3172 Manufactures Leather Goods
PA: The Valkyrie Company Inc
60 Fremont St
Worcester MA 01603
508 756-3633

(G-17498)
VANGY TOOL COMPANY INC
621 Millbury St (01607-1019)
PHONE.................................508 754-2669
Michael A Ottaviano, *President*
Paul T Ottaviano, *Vice Pres*
Paul Ottaviano, *Vice Pres*
Sandra Mitchell, *Clerk*
EMP: 9 EST: 1956
SQ FT: 9,000
SALES (est): 1.1MM Privately Held
WEB: www.vangytool.com
SIC: 3599 2671 Mfg Industrial Machinery Mfg Packaging Paper/Film

(G-17499)
VELLUMOID INC
54 Rockdale St (01606-1993)
PHONE.................................508 853-2500
Peter A Parseghian, *President*
Stephen C Parseghian, *Vice Pres*
James A Dupre, *Treasurer*
Robert S Hight, *Admin Sec*
▲ EMP: 40
SQ FT: 100,000
SALES (est): 5.9MM Privately Held
WEB: www.vellumoid.com
SIC: 3053 Mfg Gaskets/Packing/Sealing Devices

(G-17500)
VICTORY PRODUCTIONS INC
55 Linden St Ste 2 (01609-4612)
PHONE.................................508 755-0051
Victoria Porras, *President*
Michael Avidon, *Editor*
Brendan Irsfeld, *Editor*
Richard Pickering, *COO*
Robert Oliva, *Vice Pres*
EMP: 50
SQ FT: 9,560
SALES (est): 5.5MM Privately Held
SIC: 2731 Books-Publishing/Printing

(G-17501)
VISIMARK INC (PA)
Also Called: Durable Technologies
33 Arctic St Ste 2 (01604-4989)
P.O. Box 2570 (01613-2570)
PHONE.................................866 344-7721
Kari Lunden, *President*
Chris Podles, *Vice Pres*
Christopher Podles, *Vice Pres*
◆ EMP: 34

GEOGRAPHIC

SQ FT: 8,000
SALES: 3.4MM **Privately Held**
WEB: www.visimarkinc.com
SIC: 3953 Mfg Marking Devices

(G-17502)
VISION DYNAMICS LLC
799 W Boylston St Ste 1 (01606-3071)
PHONE..................................203 271-1944
Charlie Collins, *CEO*
Scott V Krug, *President*
EMP: 7
SQ FT: 2,000
SALES (est): 882K
SALES (corp-wide): 99K **Privately Held**
WEB: www.visiondynamics.com
SIC: 3851 8042 Manufactures Ophthalmic Goods Optometrist's Office
PA: Let's Go Technology, Inc.
799 W Boylston St
Worcester MA 01606
508 853-8200

(G-17503)
WALKER MAGNETICS GROUP INC
60 Solferino St Ste A (01604-1784)
PHONE..................................774 670-1423
Mark Calderan, *Vice Pres*
Bob Arruda, *Engineer*
Ken Jankowski, *Engineer*
Brad Perch, *Engineer*
John Kuhnash, *CFO*
EMP: 16
SALES (corp-wide): 116.9MM **Privately Held**
SIC: 3823 Mfg Process Control Instruments
HQ: Walker Magnetics Group, Inc.
600 Day Hill Rd
Windsor CT 06095
508 853-3232

(G-17504)
WILLIAM SEVER INC
61 Sever St (01609-2165)
PHONE..................................617 651-2483
Brien Walton, *Principal*
Timothy Loew, *Exec Dir*
EMP: 10 **EST:** 2016
SALES (est): 268.4K **Privately Held**
SIC: 7372 Prepackaged Software Services

(G-17505)
WORCESTER MANUFACTURING INC
Also Called: Worcester Chrome Furniture
35 New St (01605-3324)
PHONE..................................508 756-0301
Michael Nahorniak, *President*
John Nahorniak, *Vice Pres*
Pamela Nahorniak, *Vice Pres*
EMP: 45
SQ FT: 140,000
SALES (est): 10.8MM **Privately Held**
WEB: www.cdfschoolfurn.com
SIC: 3498 3496 3479 3471 Mfg Fabrctd Pipe/Fitting Mfg Misc Fab Wire Prdts Coating/Engraving Svcs Plating/Polishing Svcs Mfg Metal Stampings

(G-17506)
WORCESTER PUBLISHING
101 Water St (01604-5033)
PHONE..................................508 749-3166
Craig I Thornton, *Principal*
EMP: 4
SALES (est): 188.8K **Privately Held**
SIC: 2711 Newspapers-Publishing/Printing

(G-17507)
WORCESTER TLEGRAM GAZETTE CORP (HQ)
Also Called: Community Shopper
100 Front St Fl 20 (01608-1402)
PHONE..................................508 793-9100
Paul Provost, *Publisher*
Victor Infante, *Editor*
Jody Ryan, *Sales Staff*
Brittany Prendiville, *Mktg Coord*
Bruce Gaultney, *Administration*
EMP: 400
SQ FT: 150,000
SALES (est): 43.5MM
SALES (corp-wide): 1.7B **Publicly Held**
SIC: 2711 Newspapers-Publishing/Printing
PA: The New York Times Company
620 8th Ave Bsmt 1
New York NY 10018
212 556-1234

(G-17508)
WORCESTER TLEGRAM GAZETTE CORP
Also Called: Coulter Press
100 Front St Fl 20 (01608-1425)
PHONE..................................978 368-0176
Gary Hutner, *Manager*
EMP: 20
SALES (corp-wide): 1.7B **Publicly Held**
SIC: 2711 Newspapers-Publishing/Printing
HQ: Worcester Telegram & Gazette Corporation
100 Front St Fl 20
Worcester MA 01608
508 793-9100

(G-17509)
WRIGHT G F STEEL & WIRE CO
Also Called: Wright Wire
243 Stafford St (01603-1168)
PHONE..................................508 363-2718
EMP: 30 **EST:** 1921
SQ FT: 292,000
SALES (est): 2.8MM **Privately Held**
SIC: 3496 Mfg Wire Fencing

(G-17510)
WRIGHT LINE LLC (HQ)
Also Called: Eaton Wright Line
160 Gold Star Blvd (01606-2791)
PHONE..................................508 852-4300
Edward D Bednarcik, *CEO*
Pete Rumsey, *Senior VP*
Steve Bloch, *Vice Pres*
Joseph White Sr, *CFO*
Carl Cottuli, *VP Mktg*
◆ **EMP:** 122 **EST:** 1934
SQ FT: 241,000
SALES (est): 71.5MM **Privately Held**
WEB: www.wrightline.com
SIC: 3821 3577 2521 2522 Mfg Lab Apparatus/Furn Mfg Computer Peripherals Mfg Wood Office Furn Mfg Nonwood Office Furn

(G-17511)
WYMAN-GORDON COMPANY
80 Hermon St (01610-4010)
PHONE..................................508 839-8253
Paul Rossi, *Manager*
EMP: 100
SALES (corp-wide): 225.3B **Publicly Held**
WEB: www.dropdies.com
SIC: 3462 3463 Mfg Iron/Steel Forgings Mfg Nonferrous Forgings
HQ: Wyman-Gordon Company
244 Worcester St
North Grafton MA 01536
508 839-8252

(G-17512)
YOWAY LLC (PA)
395 Park Ave Ste 2 (01610-1057)
PHONE..................................508 459-0611
Long Dang, *Principal*
EMP: 4
SALES (est): 699.3K **Privately Held**
SIC: 2026 Mfg Fluid Milk

Wrentham
Norfolk County

(G-17513)
AGGREGATE INDS - NORTHEAST REG
400 Green St (02093-1736)
PHONE..................................508 384-3161
Alan Chabot, *Plant Mgr*
Bob Ferris, *Manager*
EMP: 30
SALES (corp-wide): 4.5B **Privately Held**
SIC: 1429 2951 Crushed/Broken Stone Mfg Asphalt Mixtures/Blocks
HQ: Aggregate Industries - Northeast Region, Inc
1715 Brdwy
Saugus MA 01906
781 941-7200

(G-17514)
ALPHAMED INCORPORATED
150 Ellery St (02093-2513)
PHONE..................................774 571-9415
Robert C Ferris, *CEO*
Judith Lidsky, *Vice Pres*
Herbert A Moore, *Admin Sec*
Carl F Barnes, *Asst Sec*
EMP: 3
SALES: 1MM **Privately Held**
WEB: www.alphamed.biz
SIC: 2819 7389 Mfg Industrial Inorganic Chemicals

(G-17515)
BACON INDUSTRIES INC
65 Warren Dr (02093-1003)
PHONE..................................508 384-0780
Wayne Coburn, *Controller*
EMP: 15
SQ FT: 10,000
SALES (est): 2.6MM **Privately Held**
SIC: 2891 3089 Mfg Adhesives/Sealants Mfg Plastic Products

(G-17516)
BARDON TRIMOUNT INC
400 Green St (02093-1736)
PHONE..................................508 384-3161
Robert Ferris, *Principal*
EMP: 3
SALES (est): 145.5K **Privately Held**
SIC: 1429 Crushed/Broken Stone

(G-17517)
CAPSTAN ATLANTIC
10 Cushing Dr (02093-1153)
PHONE..................................508 384-3100
Mark Paullin, *President*
EMP: 250
SQ FT: 22,000
SALES (est): 10.3MM **Privately Held**
SIC: 3499 Mfg Misc Fabricated Metal Products

(G-17518)
EAST COAST FILTER INC
560 Washington St Ste 3 (02093-1697)
PHONE..................................716 649-2326
Kevin Zagrodny, *Principal*
▲ **EMP:** 9
SALES (est): 796K **Privately Held**
SIC: 3569 Mfg General Industrial Machinery

(G-17519)
ELIZABETH ARDEN INC
1 Premium Outlet Blvd (02093-1570)
PHONE..................................508 384-9018
EMP: 3 **Publicly Held**
SIC: 2844 Mfg Toilet Preparations
HQ: Elizabeth Arden, Inc.
880 Sw 145th Ave Ste 200
Pembroke Pines FL 33027

(G-17520)
ER LEWIN INC
25 Cushing Dr (02093-1154)
PHONE..................................508 384-0363
Fax: 508 384-0373
▼ **EMP:** 25
SQ FT: 30,000
SALES: 4MM **Privately Held**
WEB: www.erlewin.com
SIC: 3442 Metal Doors, Sash, And Trim, Nsk

(G-17521)
GOREMOTE
1 Premium Outlet Blvd (02093-1570)
PHONE..................................508 384-0139
EMP: 3
SALES (est): 177.1K **Privately Held**
SIC: 3643 Mfg Conductive Wiring Devices

(G-17522)
GRAVEL PUBLIC HOUSE
36 South St (02093-1527)
P.O. Box 762 (02093-0762)
PHONE..................................508 384-0888
EMP: 3
SALES (est): 79.9K **Privately Held**
SIC: 1442 Construction Sand/Gravel

(G-17523)
INGLESIDE CORPORATION
38 South St (02093-1527)
PHONE..................................774 847-9386
Tim Connors, *Owner*
EMP: 5
SALES (est): 308.2K **Privately Held**
SIC: 2752 Lithographic Commercial Printing

(G-17524)
JOHNSON CONTROLS INC
78 South St (02093-2119)
PHONE..................................508 384-0018
EMP: 40 **Privately Held**
SIC: 3822 3829 Mfg Environmental Controls Mfg Measuring/Controlling Devices
HQ: Johnson Controls Inc
5757 N Green Bay Ave
Milwaukee WI 53209
414 524-1200

(G-17525)
LESTAGE
360 Spring St (02093-1833)
PHONE..................................508 695-7038
Richard Lestage, *Partner*
Garner Lestage, *Partner*
EMP: 3
SALES (est): 186.5K **Privately Held**
SIC: 3911 Mfg Precious Metal Jewelry

(G-17526)
MUNICIPAL GRAPHICS INC
30 Commercial Dr (02093-1941)
PHONE..................................508 384-0925
Jill Arnold, *President*
Christopher Arnold, *Admin Sec*
EMP: 4
SQ FT: 3,000
SALES: 450K **Privately Held**
WEB: www.advertee.net
SIC: 3993 Mfg Signs/Advertising Specialties

(G-17527)
PVH CORP
475 Washington St Ste 6 (02093-1100)
PHONE..................................508 384-0070
EMP: 12
SALES (corp-wide): 9.6B **Publicly Held**
SIC: 2321 2331 2253 3143 Mfg Whol & Ret Branded/Licensed Apparel
PA: Pvh Corp.
200 Madison Ave Bsmt 1
New York NY 10016
212 381-3500

(G-17528)
S M LORUSSO & SONS INC
Also Called: Lorusso, SM & Son
128 East St (02093-1315)
PHONE..................................508 384-3587
Billy Higgins, *Manager*
EMP: 5
SALES (corp-wide): 29.4MM **Privately Held**
SIC: 1442 Construction Sand/Gravel
PA: S. M. Lorusso & Sons, Inc.
331 West St
Walpole MA 02081
508 668-2600

Yarmouth Port
Barnstable County

(G-17529)
CHARR CUSTOM BOAT COMPANY
20 Corporation Rd (02675-1701)
PHONE..................................508 375-0028
Robert Bodurtha, *Manager*
EMP: 3

SALES (est): 446.4K Privately Held
SIC: 3732 Boatbuilding/Repairing

(G-17530)
MAGWEN DIAMOND PDTS INC
10 Knollwood Dr (02675-2064)
PHONE....................508 375-9152
George Wennerberg, *Owner*
EMP: 6 EST: 1970
SALES (est): 290K Privately Held
SIC: 3545 Mfg Machine Tool Accessories

(G-17531)
SOCIETY FOR MARINE MAMMALOGY
290 Summer St (02675-1734)
PHONE....................508 744-2276
Ann Pabst, *President*
Kathleen Moore, *Treasurer*
Tara Cox, *Admin Sec*
EMP: 4
SALES: 199.3K Privately Held
SIC: 2721 2731 Periodicals-Publishing/Printing Books-Publishing/Printing

(G-17532)
TALIN BOOKBINDERY
947 Route 6a (02675-2171)
PHONE....................508 362-8144
Pamela Talin, *Partner*
James Talin, *Partner*
EMP: 3
SALES (est): 218.4K Privately Held
SIC: 2789 Bookbinding/Related Work

(G-17533)
WENDI C SMITH
Also Called: Harvest of Barnstable
89 Willow St (02675-1753)
PHONE....................508 362-4595
Wendi C Smith, *Owner*
EMP: 12
SQ FT: 1,200
SALES (est): 536.4K Privately Held
WEB: www.wendismithequineservices.com
SIC: 3999 5992 Mfg Misc Products Ret Florist

NEW HAMPSHIRE

Albany
Carroll County

(G-17534)
ALVIN J COLEMAN & SON INC
Also Called: Coleman Concrete Division
9 Nh Route 113 (03818-7443)
PHONE....................603 447-3056
Curtis Coleman, *Branch Mgr*
EMP: 50
SALES (corp-wide): 36.8MM Privately Held
WEB: www.colemanconcrete.com
SIC: 3273 Ready Mix Concrete
PA: J Coleman Alvin & Son Inc
9 Nh Route 113
Albany NH 03818
603 447-5936

(G-17535)
AMBIX MANUFACTURING INC
1369 Nh Route 16 (03818-7328)
P.O. Box 55, Freedom (03836-0055)
PHONE....................603 452-5247
Melissa Florio, *Vice Pres*
▲ EMP: 10
SALES: 1MM Privately Held
SIC: 3089 Mfg Plastic Products

(G-17536)
COLEMAN CONCRETE INC
9 Nh Route 113 (03818-7320)
PHONE....................603 447-5936
Curtis D Coleman, *President*
Mary Ellen Wesley, *Controller*
EMP: 38
SALES: 950K Privately Held
SIC: 3273 Mfg Ready-Mixed Concrete

Alexandria
Grafton County

(G-17537)
LAURENCE SHARPE
208 Plumer Hill Rd (03222-6702)
PHONE....................603 744-8175
Laurence Sharpe, *Owner*
EMP: 3
SALES (est): 150K Privately Held
SIC: 2411 1794 Logging Excavation Contractor

Allenstown
Merrimack County

(G-17538)
COMPLETE CVRAGE WODPRIMING LLC
288 Pinewood Rd (03275-2343)
PHONE....................603 485-1122
Kenneth Roy,
EMP: 3
SALES (est): 405.9K Privately Held
SIC: 2431 Mfg Millwork

(G-17539)
MATERIALS RESEARCH FRNCS INC
Also Called: M R F
65 Pinewood Rd Unit 2 (03275-2346)
PHONE....................603 485-2394
▼ EMP: 19
SQ FT: 17,304
SALES: 4.6MM Privately Held
WEB: www.mrf-furnaces.com
SIC: 3821 3567 Laboratory Apparatus And Furniture

(G-17540)
PERFECT FIT INDUSTRIES LLC
Hodgson Thomas & Sons Division
25 Canal St (03275-1601)
PHONE....................603 485-7161
Jeff Scott, *Manager*
EMP: 9 Privately Held
WEB: www.perfectfitindustries.com
SIC: 2392 2391 Mfg Bedroom Furnishings
HQ: Perfect Fit Industries, Llc
8501 Tower Point Dr Ste C
Charlotte NC 28227

(G-17541)
RECYCLING MECHANICAL NENG LLC
44 Ferry St (03275-1622)
PHONE....................603 268-8028
Jason White, *Sales Staff*
Russ Bennett, *Sales Staff*
EMP: 10
SQ FT: 9,600
SALES (est): 1.5MM Privately Held
WEB: www.recmech.com
SIC: 3443 7692 Mfg Fabricated Plate Work Welding Repair

Alstead
Cheshire County

(G-17542)
FULLER MACHINE CO INC
5 Gilsum Mine Rd (03602-3909)
PHONE....................603 835-6559
Larry Wilson, *President*
EMP: 14
SQ FT: 2,500
SALES (est): 2.3MM Privately Held
SIC: 3599 Machine Shop Jobbing & Repair

(G-17543)
UNITED TOOL & STAMPING CO INC
6 Ben Molesky Dr (03602)
PHONE....................603 352-2585
Dennis Molesky, *President*
EMP: 5 EST: 1957
SQ FT: 5,000
SALES (est): 388.7K Privately Held
SIC: 3469 Mfg Metal Stampings

Alton
Belknap County

(G-17544)
ALCOR-USA LLC
220 Stockbridge Corner Rd (03809-5238)
PHONE....................603 398-1564
Gary Dudman, *President*
Cory Dudman, *Exec VP*
EMP: 3
SALES (est): 181.7K Privately Held
SIC: 2329 Mfg Men's/Boy's Clothing

(G-17545)
BAY STATE SWISS CAM DESIGN
286 Henry Wilson Hwy (03809-4908)
P.O. Box 1259 (03809-1259)
PHONE....................603 859-7552
Tom Chagnon, *Owner*
EMP: 3
SALES (est): 277.1K Privately Held
SIC: 3451 Mfg Screw Machine Products

(G-17546)
HILLSGROVE MACHINE INC
45 Dudley Rd (03809-5215)
P.O. Box 249 (03809-0249)
PHONE....................603 776-5090
Daniel Hillsgrove, *President*
Dan Hillsgrove, *Vice Pres*
EMP: 10
SQ FT: 7,000
SALES (est): 1.8MM Privately Held
WEB: www.hillsgrove-machine.com
SIC: 3599 Machine Shop

(G-17547)
SKMR CONSTRUCTION LLC
Also Called: Shipping Containers Neng
42 Stage Coach Rd (03809-4857)
PHONE....................603 520-0117
Thomas Fry, *Mng Member*
EMP: 6
SQ FT: 144
SALES: 600K Privately Held
SIC: 3443 Industrial Building Construction

Amherst
Hills County

(G-17548)
SCARZELLO & ASSOCS INC
3 Carol Ann Ln (03031-3335)
PHONE....................603 673-7746
Steven Scarzello, *President*
Peter Scarzello, *Treasurer*
EMP: 3
SALES (est): 290K Privately Held
SIC: 3089 Mfg Plastic Products

Amherst
Hillsborough County

(G-17549)
AEROSAT AVIONICS LLC
60 State Route 101a (03031-2213)
PHONE....................603 943-8680
Dennis Ferguson, *CEO*
David Kopf, *President*
Skip Feher, *Vice Pres*
William McNary, *Vice Pres*
D Grayson Allen, *Mng Member*
EMP: 75
SQ FT: 2,000
SALES (est): 17.3MM Privately Held
WEB: www.aerosat.com
SIC: 3663 Mfg Radio/Tv Communication Equipment
PA: As Liquidation I Company Inc.
62 State Route 101a 2b
Amherst NH 03031

(G-17550)
AMERICAN PRINTING INC
6 Columbia Dr Unit B (03031-2354)
PHONE....................603 880-0277
Roger Martineau, *President*
Beverly Martineau, *VP Mktg*
EMP: 14
SALES (est): 1.4MM Privately Held
WEB: www.amerprinting.com
SIC: 2752 Lithographic Commercial Printing

(G-17551)
ARMSTRONG INDUSTRIES INC
27 Old Milford Rd (03031-3072)
PHONE....................715 629-1632
Jeffrey Armstrong, *Principal*
EMP: 3 EST: 2016
SALES (est): 144.3K Privately Held
SIC: 3999 Mfg Misc Products

(G-17552)
AS LIQUIDATION I COMPANY INC (PA)
62 State Route 101a 2b (03031-2278)
PHONE....................603 879-0205
Dennis Ferguson, *CEO*
David H Rowe, *Ch of Bd*
Mike Barrett, *President*
Richard Anderson, *Vice Pres*
Skip Feher, *Vice Pres*
EMP: 76
SALES (est): 5.7MM Privately Held
SIC: 3669 8711 Aviation Engineering

(G-17553)
CABLE ASSEMBLIES INC
13 Columbia Dr Unit 17 (03031-2358)
PHONE....................603 889-4090
Mark Britton, *President*
Karen Britton, *Vice Pres*
EMP: 10
SQ FT: 3,600
SALES: 1.9MM Privately Held
WEB: www.kilroys.net
SIC: 3357 Nonferrous Wiredrawing/Insulating

(G-17554)
CITADEL COMPUTER CORPORATION
16 Columbia Dr (03031-2304)
P.O. Box 965, Milford (03055-0965)
PHONE....................603 672-5500
Gregory Walker, *President*
Kevin Berube, *Engineer*
EMP: 5
SALES (est): 1MM Privately Held
WEB: www.citadelcomputer.com
SIC: 3571 Whol Computers/Peripherals

(G-17555)
CLASSIC SIGNS INC
13 Columbia Dr Unit 16 (03031-2331)
PHONE....................603 883-0384
Paul Tripp, *President*
George Gagnon, *Vice Pres*
William Mc Namara, *Vice Pres*
EMP: 17
SQ FT: 5,000
SALES (est): 2.1MM Privately Held
SIC: 3993 Mfg Signs/Advertising Specialties

(G-17556)
DEVTECH PET INC (PA)
12 Howe Dr (03031-2314)
PHONE....................603 889-8311
Martin H Beck, *President*
▲ EMP: 35 EST: 1999
SALES (est): 6.8MM Privately Held
WEB: www.devtechlabs.com
SIC: 3085 Mfg Plastic Bottles

(G-17557)
DIACOM CORPORATION
5 Howe Dr (03031-2315)
PHONE....................603 880-1900
Scott Rafferty, *President*
Bob Doyle, *Vice Pres*
Mike Grywalski, *Engineer*
Todd Holbrook, *Engineer*
Bob Fortin, *Project Engr*
▲ EMP: 90
SQ FT: 30,000

GEOGRAPHIC

SALES (est): 18MM **Privately Held**
WEB: www.diacom.com
SIC: 3069 Mfg Fabricated Rubber Products

(G-17558)
EAST COAST CONCRETE PDTS LLC
5 Northern Blvd Ste 15 (03031-2325)
PHONE..................................603 883-3042
Dave Schwanke,
EMP: 3
SALES (est): 215.4K **Privately Held**
SIC: 3272 Mfg Concrete Products

(G-17559)
EMA SERVICES INC
105 State Route 101a # 6 (03031-2245)
PHONE..................................978 251-4044
EMP: 20
SQ FT: 5,000
SALES (est): 4.3MM **Privately Held**
SIC: 3672 Mfg Printed Circuit Boards

(G-17560)
EXOTHERMICS INC
14 Columbia Dr (03031-2304)
PHONE..................................603 821-5660
Stephen G Dipietro, *President*
Sharon Krawiecki, *Director*
EMP: 15
SQ FT: 25,400
SALES: 6.1MM **Privately Held**
WEB: www.exothermicsinc.com
SIC: 3728 3764 8731 Mfg Aircraft Parts/Equipment Mfg Space Propulsion Units/Parts Commercial Physical Research

(G-17561)
EXPRESS ASSEMBLYPRODUCTS LLC
10 Northern Blvd Ste 14b (03031-2336)
PHONE..................................603 424-5590
Michael Dechambeau, *Mng Member*
EMP: 10
SQ FT: 2,400
SALES: 10MM **Privately Held**
WEB: www.expressassembly.com
SIC: 3541 5072 Mfg & Whol Assembly Tools

(G-17562)
FINETECH
60 State Route 101a (03031-2213)
PHONE..................................603 627-8989
Neil O'Brien, *Branch Mgr*
EMP: 3
SALES (corp-wide): 826.1K **Privately Held**
SIC: 3674 Mfg Semiconductors & Related Devices
HQ: Finetech
560 E Germann Rd Ste 103
Gilbert AZ 85297
480 893-1630

(G-17563)
FREDERICKS PASTRIES (PA)
109 State Route 101a # 4 (03031-2291)
PHONE..................................603 882-7725
Toll Free:..877 -
Sue Roberts, *Owner*
EMP: 4
SQ FT: 5,670
SALES (est): 782.3K **Privately Held**
WEB: www.pastry.net
SIC: 2051 5149 5461 2064 Mfg Whol & Ret Bakery Of Pastries & Candy

(G-17564)
GLACIER COMPUTER LLC
10 Northern Blvd Ste 2 (03031-2328)
PHONE..................................603 882-1560
Dan Poisson, *Engineer*
Rodney Mitchell, *Branch Mgr*
EMP: 15
SALES (est): 1.8MM
SALES (corp-wide): 2.9MM **Privately Held**
WEB: www.glaciercomputer.com
SIC: 3571 5734 Mfg Electronic Computers Ret Computers/Software
PA: Glacier Computer, L.L.C.
46 Bridge St Ste 1
New Milford CT 06776
860 355-7552

(G-17565)
GREENFIELD INDUSTRIES INC
Also Called: Fabricated Metals
5 Manhattan Dr (03031-2303)
PHONE..................................603 883-6423
Linda Greenfield, *President*
Richard Greenfield, *Vice Pres*
Shirley Greenfield Keating, *Vice Pres*
James Greenfield, *Treasurer*
EMP: 5
SALES (est): 665.5K **Privately Held**
SIC: 3441 3446 3444 3443 Structural Metal Fabrctn Mfg Architectural Mtlwrk Mfg Sheet Metalwork Mfg Fabricated Plate Wrk

(G-17566)
GTIMD LLC
Also Called: Gtimd Catheter Solutions
6 Columbia Dr (03031-2343)
PHONE..................................603 880-0277
Eran Levit, *Administration*
EMP: 11 **EST:** 2016
SALES (est): 1.3MM **Privately Held**
SIC: 3841 Mfg Surgical/Medical Instruments

(G-17567)
GUILD OPTICAL ASSOCIATES INC
11 Columbia Dr Unit 13 (03031-2317)
PHONE..................................603 889-6247
Mark Breda, *President*
EMP: 18
SQ FT: 20,000
SALES (est): 2.9MM **Privately Held**
WEB: www.guildoptics.com
SIC: 3211 3827 Mfg Optical Instruments/Lenses Mfg Flat Glass

(G-17568)
H&M METALS LLC
9a Columbia Dr (03031-2364)
PHONE..................................603 889-8320
Janice Zeimetz, *Buyer*
Robert Hendrickson, *Sales Executive*
David Medina,
Lori Pelletier,
◆ **EMP:** 80 **EST:** 1972
SQ FT: 98,000
SALES (est): 17.6MM **Privately Held**
WEB: www.hmmetals.net
SIC: 3444 Mfg Sheet Metalwork

(G-17569)
JMK INC
15 Caldwell Dr (03031-2345)
PHONE..................................603 886-4100
James W Kennedy, *President*
Mary Kennedy, *Treasurer*
EMP: 25
SQ FT: 12,000
SALES (est): 4.5MM **Privately Held**
WEB: www.jmkfilters.com
SIC: 3677 Mfg Electronic Coils/Transformers

(G-17570)
JR POIRIER TOOL & MACHINE CO
4 Manhattan Dr (03031-2303)
PHONE..................................603 882-9279
Jim Poirier, *Owner*
Jim Poirer, *Owner*
EMP: 13
SQ FT: 10,000
SALES (est): 1.5MM **Privately Held**
WEB: www.poiriertool.com
SIC: 3599 Machine Shop Jobbing And Repair

(G-17571)
KINEX CAPPERS LLC (PA)
13 Columbia Dr Unit 4 (03031-2319)
PHONE..................................603 883-2400
Lawrence Joseph Quinlan,
▼ **EMP:** 10
SALES (est): 989.9K **Privately Held**
WEB: www.kinexcappers.com
SIC: 3466 Mfg Crowns/Closures

(G-17572)
MANUFACTURING SERVICES GROUP
Also Called: M S G
105 State Route 101a # 6 (03031-2244)
PHONE..................................603 883-1022
Raymond Rose, *President*
EMP: 12
SQ FT: 3,000
SALES: 5MM **Privately Held**
SIC: 3672 Mfg Printed Circuit Boards

(G-17573)
MARK ALLEN CABINETRY LLC
13 Columbia Dr Unit 3 (03031-2319)
PHONE..................................603 491-7570
EMP: 8
SALES (corp-wide): 915.3K **Privately Held**
SIC: 2434 Mfg Wood Kitchen Cabinets
PA: Mark Allen Cabinetry Llc
232 Route 13
Brookline NH 03033
603 321-3163

(G-17574)
MARMON UTILITY LLC
116 State Route 101a (03031-2265)
PHONE..................................603 673-2040
EMP: 7
SALES (corp-wide): 225.3B **Publicly Held**
SIC: 3357 Nonferrous Wiredrawing/Insulating
HQ: Marmon Utility Llc
53 Old Wilton Rd
Milford NH 03055
603 673-2040

(G-17575)
MAXILON LABORATORIES INC
105 State Route 101a # 8 (03031-2244)
P.O. Box 850, Hollis (03049-0850)
PHONE..................................603 594-9300
Peter R Ebner, *President*
EMP: 7
SALES (est): 900.9K **Privately Held**
WEB: www.maxilon.com
SIC: 3841 Mfg Surgical/Medical Instruments

(G-17576)
MOBILEROBOTS INC
Also Called: Adept Mobilerobots
10 Columbia Dr (03031-2341)
PHONE..................................603 881-7960
Jeanne Dietsch, *President*
Brian Ewing, *General Mgr*
▲ **EMP:** 26
SQ FT: 12,700
SALES (est): 6.6MM **Privately Held**
WEB: www.mobilerobots.com
SIC: 3569 3999 Mfg General Industrial Machinery Mfg Misc Products

(G-17577)
MONARCH INTERNATIONAL INC
Also Called: Monarch Monitoring
15 Columbia Dr (03031-2305)
PHONE..................................603 883-3390
Kenneth Grabeau, *President*
Alan Wolfson, *Vice Pres*
Alan Woolfson, *Vice Pres*
Dennis Sanville, *Purch Mgr*
Brianna Niquette, *Buyer*
▲ **EMP:** 40
SQ FT: 33,000
SALES (est): 9.6MM **Privately Held**
WEB: www.monarchinstrument.com
SIC: 3824 3825 3845 3823 Mfg Fluid Meters/Devices Mfg Elec Measuring Instr Mfg Electromedical Equip Mfg Process Cntrl Instr Mfg Electronic Computers

(G-17578)
NET RESULTS IN CAD INC
1 Overlook Dr Ste 1 # 1 (03031-2800)
P.O. Box 22, West Chesterfield (03466-0022)
PHONE..................................603 249-9995
Edmund Gosciminski, *President*
EMP: 3
SALES (est): 366.7K **Privately Held**
WEB: www.netresultsincad.com
SIC: 3672 8711 Mfg Printed Circuit Boards Engineering Services

(G-17579)
NORTHEAST SAND & GRAVEL
17 Old Nashua Rd Ste 14 (03031-2839)
PHONE..................................603 213-6133
EMP: 3
SALES (est): 137.2K **Privately Held**
SIC: 1442 Construction Sand/Gravel

(G-17580)
ODHNER HOLOGRAPHICS
5 Lake Front St (03031-1831)
PHONE..................................603 673-8651
Jeff Odhner, *Owner*
EMP: 4
SALES (est): 270K **Privately Held**
WEB: www.stabilock.com
SIC: 3679 Mfg Electronic Components

(G-17581)
POLY-JECT INC
8 Manhattan Dr (03031-2342)
PHONE..................................603 882-6570
Steven Thibeault, *President*
David Chouinard, *Prdtn Mgr*
▲ **EMP:** 20
SQ FT: 26,000
SALES (est): 5.4MM **Privately Held**
WEB: www.polyject.com
SIC: 3089 Mfg Plastic Products

(G-17582)
PROFESSNAL SFTWR FOR NRSES INC
4 Limbo Ln (03031-1869)
PHONE..................................800 889-7627
Sharon C Redes, *President*
Peter Redes, *Vice Pres*
Wanda Roscoe, *Technical Staff*
Tami Lynn Redes, *Director*
Paula Jean Sidore, *Director*
EMP: 14
SALES (est): 1.6MM **Privately Held**
SIC: 7372 Prepackaged Software Services

(G-17583)
R H MURPHY CO INC
3 Howe Dr Ste 3 # 3 (03031-2362)
PHONE..................................603 889-2255
Robert H Murphy, *President*
Carol Murphy, *Corp Secy*
Roland Gosselin, *Vice Pres*
Tom Solon, *Sales Staff*
Roy Maston, *Info Tech Dir*
EMP: 5
SQ FT: 9,000
SALES (est): 490K **Privately Held**
WEB: www.rhmurphy.com
SIC: 3089 Mfg & Designs Packaging Plastic Trays For Shipping Of Semiconductors

(G-17584)
RESIN SYSTEMS CORPORATION
62 State Route 101a Ste 1 (03031-2295)
PHONE..................................603 673-1234
Daniel B Prawdzik Sr, *President*
EMP: 53
SQ FT: 15,000
SALES (est): 11.6MM **Privately Held**
WEB: www.resinsystems.com
SIC: 3089 Mfg Plastic Products

(G-17585)
RME FILTERS INC
98 State Route 101a (03031-2273)
P.O. Box 838 (03031-0838)
PHONE..................................603 595-4573
Roger Martin, *President*
Richard A Secor, *Treasurer*
EMP: 10
SQ FT: 1,500
SALES: 550K **Privately Held**
WEB: www.rmefilters.com
SIC: 3677 5065 Mfg Electronic Coils/Transformers Whol Electronic Parts/Equipment

(G-17586)
RONTEX AMERICA INC
1 Caldwell Dr (03031-2310)
PHONE..................................603 883-5076
Craig Haley, *President*
◆ **EMP:** 29
SQ FT: 30,000
SALES (est): 5.3MM **Privately Held**
SIC: 2297 Mfg Nonwoven Fabrics

(G-17587)
S & S MACHINE LLC
11 Caldwell Dr Ste 4 (03031-2321)
PHONE....................................603 204-5542
Robin Samuelson,
EMP: 17 **EST:** 2011
SALES (est): 3.3MM **Privately Held**
SIC: 3599 Mfg Industrial Machinery

(G-17588)
SOLID EARTH TECHNOLOGIES INC
3 Howe Dr Ste 3 # 3 (03031-2348)
PHONE....................................603 882-5319
Matt Stacy, *President*
EMP: 7
SALES (est): 1.6MM **Privately Held**
WEB: www.solidearthtech.com
SIC: 3493 Mfg Steel Springs-Nonwire

(G-17589)
SUMAKE NORTH AMERICA LLC
10 Northern Blvd Ste 13 (03031-2328)
PHONE....................................603 402-2924
Brant Mullens, *Sales Staff*
Michael Dechambeau,
EMP: 4 **EST:** 2014
SALES (est): 106.9K **Privately Held**
SIC: 3621 Mfg Motors/Generators

(G-17590)
UNITED SENSOR CORP
3 Northern Blvd Ste B2 (03031-2326)
PHONE....................................603 672-0909
Adam Rakiey, *President*
Andrew Rakiey, *Mng Member*
Christopher Rakiey, *Mng Member*
Nancy Rakiey, *Admin Sec*
EMP: 10
SQ FT: 5,000
SALES (est): 1.9MM **Privately Held**
WEB: www.unitedsensorcorp.com
SIC: 3829 Mfg Pitot Probes And Various Pressure Sensing Probes

(G-17591)
WILLIAMS & HUSSEY MCH CO INC
105 State Route 101a # 4 (03031-2245)
P.O. Box 1308 (03031-1308)
PHONE....................................603 732-0219
Stephen Carter, *President*
Sheila Nourse, *General Mgr*
EMP: 14
SQ FT: 10,000
SALES (est): 2.9MM **Privately Held**
WEB: www.williamsnhussey.com
SIC: 3553 3541 Mfg Woodworking Machinery Mfg Machine Tools-Cutting

Antrim
Hillsborough County

(G-17592)
BAKER SALMON CHRISTOPHER
Also Called: Old Hancock Glassworks
375 Keene Rd (03440-3105)
PHONE....................................603 588-4000
C Bakersalmon, *Owner*
EMP: 3
SQ FT: 3,200
SALES (est): 161.3K **Privately Held**
SIC: 3231 Mfg Products-Purchased Glass

(G-17593)
BRAILSFORD & COMPANY INC
15 Elm Ave (03440-3707)
P.O. Box 459 (03440-0459)
PHONE....................................603 588-2880
Robert Drummond, *President*
Betsy Drummond, *Owner*
Kr Smith, *Shareholder*
EMP: 25 **EST:** 1944
SQ FT: 7,600
SALES (est): 4.1MM **Privately Held**
WEB: www.brailsfordco.com
SIC: 3699 3561 3826 3564 Mfg Elec Mach/Equip/Supp Mfg Pumps/Pumping Equip Mfg Analytical Instr Mfg Blowers/Fans

(G-17594)
COGWORKS LTD
10 Water St (03440-3923)
PHONE....................................603 588-3333
Ian Johnson, *President*
Rob Howard, *Admin Sec*
EMP: 5
SQ FT: 6,000
SALES (est): 550K **Privately Held**
SIC: 2431 Mfg Wooden Products

(G-17595)
LEMIRE R & SONS LLC
Also Called: Lemire R & Sons Logging
237 Elm Ave (03440-3709)
PHONE....................................603 588-3718
Roland Lemire Jr, *Partner*
EMP: 6
SALES (est): 792.9K **Privately Held**
SIC: 2411 Logging Contractor

(G-17596)
MAINELINE GRAPHICS LLC
1 High St (03440)
P.O. Box 301 (03440-0301)
PHONE....................................603 588-3177
Laura Maine,
David Maine,
EMP: 7
SALES: 300K **Privately Held**
WEB: www.maineline.us
SIC: 3993 7336 Mfg Signs/Advertising Specialties Commercial Art/Graphic Design

(G-17597)
RILEY MOUNTAIN PRODUCTS INC
Also Called: Artek
10 Water St (03440-3923)
P.O. Box 550 (03440-0550)
PHONE....................................603 588-7234
William A Prokop, *President*
EMP: 12
SQ FT: 6,000
SALES (est): 1.1MM **Privately Held**
SIC: 3083 2499 Mfg Laminated Plastic Plate/Sheet Mfg Wood Products

Ashland
Grafton County

(G-17598)
ELPAKCO INC
Main St (03217)
PHONE....................................603 968-9950
Scott Golden, *Branch Mgr*
EMP: 9
SALES (corp-wide): 2.5MM **Privately Held**
WEB: www.elpakco.com
SIC: 3599 Mfg Industrial Machinery
PA: Elpakco, Inc.
2 Carl Thompson Rd
Westford MA 01886
978 392-0400

(G-17599)
FREUDENBERG-NOK GENERAL PARTNR
Also Called: Fredenberg-Nok Seals Division
125 Main St (03217)
PHONE....................................603 968-7187
Carsten Mueller, *Manager*
EMP: 120
SALES (corp-wide): 10.5B **Privately Held**
WEB: www.freudenberg-nok.com
SIC: 3544 3053 Mfg Dies/Tools/Jigs/Fixtures Mfg Gaskets/Packing/Sealing Devices
HQ: Freudenberg-Nok General Partnership
47774 W Anchor Ct
Plymouth MI 48170
734 451-0020

(G-17600)
MONEYSWORTH & BEST USA INC
1 Cedar Ln (03217)
PHONE....................................603 968-3301
Deborah French, *President*
Nora Gulesserian, *Treasurer*
EMP: 35
SALES (est): 1MM **Privately Held**
SIC: 2499 Mfg Wood Products

(G-17601)
ROCHESTER SHOE TREE CO INC (PA)
1 Cedar Ln (03217)
PHONE....................................603 968-3301
Debra French, *President*
▲ **EMP:** 70 **EST:** 1922
SQ FT: 3,000
SALES (est): 12.1MM **Privately Held**
WEB: www.rstco.com
SIC: 2842 2499 Mfg Polish/Sanitation Goods Mfg Wood Products

Atkinson
Rockingham County

(G-17602)
ACCELERATOR SYSTEMS INC
Also Called: D Moore Associates
3 Commerce Dr Ste 303 (03811-2175)
PHONE....................................603 898-6010
Douglas M Moore, *President*
Mary Howie, *Admin Sec*
EMP: 3
SQ FT: 3,600
SALES (est): 491.7K **Privately Held**
WEB: www.acceleratorsystems.com
SIC: 3679 Mfg Electronic Components

(G-17603)
COGENT MFG SOLUTIONS LLC
Also Called: Atlantic Microtool
115 Fieldstone Ln (03811-2371)
P.O. Box 95 (03811-0095)
PHONE....................................603 898-3212
Bruce A Siemering, *President*
Bruce Siemering, *President*
Neil Robinson, *Vice Pres*
EMP: 4
SALES: 2MM **Privately Held**
SIC: 3672 7389 Cutting Tool Mfg

(G-17604)
HUTCHINSON MACHINE
Also Called: Precision Machine Shop
12 Industrial Way Unit 7 (03811-2384)
PHONE....................................603 329-9545
John D Hutchinson, *Owner*
EMP: 3 **EST:** 1998
SQ FT: 2,100
SALES (est): 304.6K **Privately Held**
SIC: 3599 3523 Mfg Industrial Machinery Mfg Farm Machinery/Equipment

(G-17605)
LORAL PRESS INC
7 Main St (03811-2516)
P.O. Box 327 (03811-0327)
PHONE....................................603 362-5549
Alan D La Branche, *President*
Dianne Camara, *Controller*
EMP: 6 **EST:** 1979
SQ FT: 4,500
SALES (est): 863.5K **Privately Held**
SIC: 2752 Lithographic Commercial Printing

(G-17606)
NORTHEAST METAL SPINNING INC
13 Industrial Way (03011-2194)
PHONE....................................603 898-2232
Brian Castle, *President*
Cheryll Castle, *Corp Secy*
EMP: 6
SQ FT: 7,200
SALES: 1MM **Privately Held**
WEB: www.nemetalspinning.com
SIC: 3469 Spins Metal For The Trade

(G-17607)
SEMICONDUCTOR CIRCUITS INC (PA)
14c Industrial Way (03811-2194)
PHONE....................................603 893-2330
Teddi Ritchie, *President*
Nancy Pond, *Accountant*
▲ **EMP:** 14
SQ FT: 24,000
SALES (est): 3.2MM **Privately Held**
WEB: www.dcdc.com
SIC: 3679 Mfg Electronic Components

Auburn
Rockingham County

(G-17608)
BRI-WELD INDUSTRIES LLC
55 Gold Ledge Ave (03032-3602)
PHONE....................................603 622-9480
Brian D Potter,
EMP: 10
SQ FT: 8,200
SALES (est): 1.6MM **Privately Held**
SIC: 7692 1799 7532 Welding Repair Trade Contractor Auto Body Repair/Painting

(G-17609)
FOREST MANUFACTURING CORP
Also Called: Trickett Woodworks Company
8 Grey Point Ave (03032-3630)
PHONE....................................603 647-6991
Paul Trickett, *President*
Chris Trickett, *Vice Pres*
EMP: 10
SQ FT: 10,000
SALES (est): 1.9MM **Privately Held**
WEB: www.trickettwoodworks.com
SIC: 2431 Mfg Millwork

(G-17610)
GARVIN INDUSTRIES INC
81 Priscilla Ln (03032-3724)
PHONE....................................603 647-5410
Forrest Garvin, *President*
Bertha Garvin, *Vice Pres*
EMP: 7
SQ FT: 10,000
SALES (est): 1MM **Privately Held**
WEB: www.garvinind.com
SIC: 3444 Mfg Sheet Metalwork

(G-17611)
INDABA HOLDINGS CORP
Also Called: NH Signs
66 Gold Ledge Ave (03032-3602)
PHONE....................................603 437-1200
Peter March, *President*
Noeleen March, *Vice Pres*
EMP: 10
SQ FT: 4,000
SALES (est): 1.3MM **Privately Held**
WEB: www.nhsigns.com
SIC: 3993 7389 Mfg Design Service & Install Signs

(G-17612)
K & B ROCK CRUSHING LLC
20 Commercial Ct (03032-3725)
PHONE....................................603 622-1188
Keith A Babb,
Keith Babb,
EMP: 9 **EST:** 2001
SQ FT: 45,000
SALES: 2.7MM **Privately Held**
SIC: 1429 Crushed/Broken Stone

(G-17613)
SIMPLIPROTECTED LLC
50 Westminster Ln (03032-3840)
PHONE....................................603 669-7465
Jeffrey Pratt, *Principal*
EMP: 3
SALES (est): 143.6K **Privately Held**
SIC: 3577 7372 7389 Mfg Computer Peripheral Equipment Prepackaged Software Services

(G-17614)
YANKEE CRAFTSMAN INC
Also Called: The Sonus Company
261 Old Candia Rd (03032-3902)
P.O. Box 55, Candia (03034-0055)
PHONE....................................603 483-5900
Peter Bowman, *President*
EMP: 3
SQ FT: 5,400

GEOGRAPHIC

SALES (est): 378.9K **Privately Held**
WEB: www.precisionhills.com
SIC: 2431 2541 Mfg Millwork Mfg Wood Partitions/Fixtures

Barnstead
Belknap County

(G-17615)
BREEZY HILL LUMBER CO
78 Province Rd (03218-4061)
PHONE..................................603 496-8870
Eddie Watson, *President*
EMP: 14
SALES (est): 1.2MM **Privately Held**
SIC: 2421 Sawmill/Planing Mill

(G-17616)
LIBERTY MACHINE LLC
409 Parade Rd (03218-3676)
PHONE..................................603 435-6613
James Russell,
EMP: 3
SALES (est): 377K **Privately Held**
SIC: 3599 Mfg Industrial Machinery

(G-17617)
STEVE LEIGHTON
Also Called: Leighton Logging
801 Province Rd (03218)
PHONE..................................603 664-2378
Steve Leighton, *Owner*
EMP: 3
SALES (est): 258K **Privately Held**
WEB: www.stevenleighton.com
SIC: 2411 Logging

Barrington
Strafford County

(G-17618)
GOSOLAR NH LLC
232 Cales Hwy (03825)
PHONE..................................603 948-1189
Dakota Viel, *Warehouse Mgr*
Jake Ottolini, *Mng Member*
EMP: 25 **EST:** 2015
SALES (est): 1.5MM **Privately Held**
SIC: 3674 Mfg Semiconductors/Related Devices

(G-17619)
J W PRECISION COMPANY INC
373 Route 4 (03825)
P.O. Box 668 (03825-0668)
PHONE..................................603 868-6574
Wendy Mousette, *President*
EMP: 4
SQ FT: 1,080
SALES: 300K **Privately Held**
SIC: 3599 Mfg Industrial Machinery

(G-17620)
PBS PLASTICS INC
219 Old Concord Tpke (03825-5155)
PHONE..................................603 868-1717
Andrew Salach, *President*
Kurt Bertram, *Vice Pres*
Craig Croteau, *Opers Mgr*
EMP: 10
SQ FT: 10,000
SALES (est): 2.1MM **Privately Held**
WEB: www.pbsplastics.com
SIC: 3089 Mfg Plastic Products

(G-17621)
QUALITY FABRICATORS LLC
246 Calef Hwy (03825-7233)
P.O. Box 332 (03825-0332)
PHONE..................................603 905-9012
Richard Clare,
EMP: 8
SALES (est): 1.1MM **Privately Held**
SIC: 3441 Structural Metal Fabrication

(G-17622)
RICHARD TOWNSEND
Also Called: Townsend Systems
43 Hall Rd (03825-3209)
PHONE..................................603 664-5987
Richard Townsend, *Owner*
EMP: 3
SALES: 1.2MM **Privately Held**
SIC: 3663 Mfg Satellite Control Systems

(G-17623)
SEPARETT-USA
50 Commerce Way (03825-3544)
P.O. Box 226 (03825-0226)
PHONE..................................603 682-0963
EMP: 3
SALES (est): 182K **Privately Held**
SIC: 3089 Mfg Plastic Products

(G-17624)
TURBOCAM INC
38 Redemption Rd (03825-7486)
PHONE..................................603 905-0200
Marian Noronha, *Branch Mgr*
EMP: 3
SALES (corp-wide): 92MM **Privately Held**
SIC: 3599 Mfg Industrial Machinery
PA: Turbocam, Inc.
607 Calef Hwy Ste 200
Barrington NH 03825
603 905-0200

(G-17625)
TURBOCAM INC (PA)
Also Called: Turbocam International
607 Calef Hwy Ste 200 (03825-5539)
PHONE..................................603 905-0200
Marian Noronha, *President*
Tim Noronha, *General Mgr*
John Bressoud, *Vice Pres*
Robert Bujeaud, *Vice Pres*
Rene Allen, *Buyer*
▲ **EMP:** 233
SQ FT: 32,000
SALES (est): 92MM **Privately Held**
WEB: www.turbocam.com
SIC: 3599 Mfg Industrial Machinery

(G-17626)
TURBOCAM ATMTED PROD SYSTEMS I (HQ)
Also Called: Taps
607 Calef Hwy Ste 100 (03825-5539)
PHONE..................................603 905-0220
Marian Noronha, *President*
John Bressoud, *General Mgr*
Rob Bujeaud, *Vice Pres*
Ollie Sexton, *Vice Pres*
Doug Patteson, *CFO*
◆ **EMP:** 46
SALES (est): 22.8MM
SALES (corp-wide): 92MM **Privately Held**
SIC: 3462 Mfg Iron/Steel Forgings
PA: Turbocam, Inc.
607 Calef Hwy Ste 200
Barrington NH 03825
603 905-0200

Bartlett
Carroll County

(G-17627)
PEG KEARSARGE CO INC
Also Called: Pegco Process Labs
14 Mill St (03812)
PHONE..................................603 374-2341
Paul W Soares, *President*
EMP: 7 **EST:** 1878
SQ FT: 20,000
SALES (est): 544.5K **Privately Held**
SIC: 2843 2499 2842 3471 Mfg Surface Active Agent Mfg Wood Products

Bedford
Hills County

(G-17628)
NEAT AS A PIN
40 Palomino Ln (03110-6445)
PHONE..................................603 627-3504
EMP: 3
SALES (est): 171.5K **Privately Held**
SIC: 3452 Mfg Bolts/Screws/Rivets

Bedford
Hillsborough County

(G-17629)
ALIGNREVENUE INC
Also Called: Alignmeeting
3 Old Mill Rd (03110-4519)
PHONE..................................603 566-4117
Richard Pratte, *CEO*
EMP: 3 **Privately Held**
SIC: 7372 Prepackaged Software Services

(G-17630)
ALLEGRA PRINT & IMAGING
128 S River Rd Ste 2 (03110-6720)
PHONE..................................603 622-3821
Steve Chaisson, *Co-Owner*
EMP: 4 **EST:** 2006
SALES (est): 349.9K **Privately Held**
SIC: 2752 Lithographic Commercial Printing

(G-17631)
ASSURED COMPUTING TECHNOLOGIES
19 Harvey Rd Unit 13-15 (03110-6810)
PHONE..................................603 627-8728
EMP: 9
SQ FT: 1,000
SALES: 500K **Privately Held**
WEB: www.assuredcomptech.com
SIC: 3575 5932 3993 8713 Mfg Computer Terminals Ret Used Merchandise Mfg Signs/Ad Specialties Security System Svcs

(G-17632)
BESHEER STUDIOS
Also Called: Besheer Artile Studios
27 Mcintosh Ln (03110-4417)
P.O. Box 10456 (03110-0456)
PHONE..................................603 472-5288
Kenneth Besheer, *Owner*
EMP: 3
SALES: 500K **Privately Held**
SIC: 3253 Mfg Ceramic Wall/Floor Tile

(G-17633)
BROEN-LAB INC
15 Constitution Dr # 122 (03110-6042)
PHONE..................................205 956-9444
Tommy Peddycord, *President*
Mogens Laursen, *Vice Pres*
James M Murray, *CPA*
▲ **EMP:** 11
SQ FT: 7,500
SALES (est): 1.9MM
SALES (corp-wide): 3B **Privately Held**
WEB: www.broeninc.com
SIC: 3491 Mfg Industrial Valves
HQ: Broen A/S
Skovvej 30
Assens 5610
647 120-95

(G-17634)
BROOK HOLLOW SAND & GRAVEL
317 S River Rd (03110-6829)
PHONE..................................603 231-0238
Robert S Lamontagne, *President*
EMP: 3
SALES (est): 220K **Privately Held**
SIC: 1442 Construction Sand/Gravel

(G-17635)
CENTURY ROBOTICS LLC
548 Donald St Ste 12 (03110-5953)
PHONE..................................603 540-2576
EMP: 3 **EST:** 2017
SALES (est): 155.7K **Privately Held**
SIC: 3089 Mfg Plastic Products

(G-17636)
COMPRESSOR ENERGY SERVICES LLC
49 Church Rd (03110-5425)
PHONE..................................603 491-2200
Jeffrey K Wright, *Mng Member*
EMP: 6
SQ FT: 2,000
SALES: 1MM **Privately Held**
SIC: 3563 Mfg Air/Gas Compressors

(G-17637)
CRANE PAYMENT SOLUTIONS INC (HQ)
1 Executive Park Dr # 202 (03110-6913)
PHONE..................................603 685-6999
Bradley L Ellis, *President*
◆ **EMP:** 27
SQ FT: 18,000
SALES (est): 5.4MM
SALES (corp-wide): 3.3B **Publicly Held**
WEB: www.telequipcorp.com
SIC: 3578 Mfg Calculating Equipment
PA: Crane Co.
100 1st Stamford Pl # 300
Stamford CT 06902
203 363-7300

(G-17638)
DEBORAH FROST
Also Called: ACS
20 Commerce Park North # 106
(03110-6911)
PHONE..................................603 882-3100
Deborah Frost, *President*
▲ **EMP:** 10
SALES (est): 652.5K **Privately Held**
SIC: 3661 Mfg Telephone/Telegraph Apparatus

(G-17639)
EAGLE TEST SYSTEMS INC
2 Commerce Dr Ste 102 (03110-6803)
PHONE..................................603 624-5757
Edward Aten, *Branch Mgr*
EMP: 13
SALES (corp-wide): 2.1B **Publicly Held**
WEB: www.eagletest.com
SIC: 3825 Mfg Electrical Measuring Instruments
HQ: Eagle Test Systems, Inc.
2200 Millbrook Dr
Buffalo Grove IL 60089
847 367-8282

(G-17640)
FERROTEC (USA) CORPORATION (HQ)
33 Constitution Dr (03110-6000)
PHONE..................................603 472-6800
Eiji Miyamaga, *CEO*
Nigel Hunton, *President*
Robert Otey, *President*
Akira Yamamura, *Chairman*
Barry Moskoitz, *Vice Pres*
◆ **EMP:** 90
SQ FT: 55,000
SALES (est): 51.5MM **Privately Held**
WEB: www.ferrotec.com
SIC: 3568 3053 Mfg Power Transmission Equipment Mfg Gaskets/Packing/Sealing Devices

(G-17641)
FLEXOGRPHIC PRINT SLUTIONS LLC
1 Hardy Rd 306 (03110-4915)
PHONE..................................603 570-6339
Mark Lalonde, *President*
EMP: 4 **EST:** 2014
SQ FT: 1,000
SALES (est): 227.6K **Privately Held**
SIC: 2679 Mfg Converted Paper Products

(G-17642)
GENERAL KINETICS LLC
10 Commerce Park North # 6 (03110-6905)
PHONE..................................603 627-8547
Scott Martimeau, *President*
William T Larkins, *President*
John Laplante, *CTO*
EMP: 4
SQ FT: 10,980
SALES (est): 682.9K
SALES (corp-wide): 15.6MM **Privately Held**
WEB: www.activeshock.com
SIC: 3714 Mfg Motor Vehicle Parts/Accessories

PA: General Kinetics Engineering Corporation
110 East Dr
Brampton ON L6T 1
905 458-0888

(G-17643)
GONE BAKING LLC
64 Settlers Ct (03110-4546)
PHONE..................................603 305-6026
Steven Cohen Esq, *Administration*
EMP: 3 **EST:** 2012
SALES (est): 163.4K **Privately Held**
SIC: 2051 Mfg Bread/Related Products

(G-17644)
HAIGH-FARR INC
43 Harvey Rd (03110-6805)
PHONE..................................603 644-6170
David P Farr, *CEO*
George I Farr, *President*
Cindy Gruca, *President*
Don Dutremble, *VP Mfg*
Terry Cole, *QC Mgr*
EMP: 14
SQ FT: 30,000
SALES (est): 3.8MM **Privately Held**
WEB: www.haigh-farr.com
SIC: 3663 8711 8733 Mfg Radio/Tv Communication Equipment Engineering Services Noncommercial Research Organization

(G-17645)
IBIS LLC
Also Called: Miedge
10 Corporate Dr Ste 100 (03110-5956)
PHONE..................................603 471-0951
Richard Lowner, *Managing Prtnr*
Mark J Smith, *Mng Member*
Darin Vick, *Officer*
EMP: 20 **EST:** 2010
SALES (est): 1.6MM
SALES (corp-wide): 47.7MM **Privately Held**
SIC: 7372 Prepackaged Software Services
PA: Zywave, Inc.
10100 W Innovation Dr # 300
Milwaukee WI 53226
414 454-6100

(G-17646)
INSTY-PRINTS OF BEDFORD INC
25 S River Rd (03110-6708)
PHONE..................................603 622-3821
Lawrence Goldberg, *President*
Lynn Goldberg, *Treasurer*
EMP: 7
SQ FT: 1,354
SALES: 600K **Privately Held**
SIC: 2752 7336 Lithographic Commercial Printing Commercial Art/Graphic Design

(G-17647)
JUST NATURALS & COMPANY LLC
5 Cotton Cir (03110-4658)
PHONE..................................603 471-0944
Karen Girardo, *Principal*
EMP: 4 **EST:** 2008
SALES (est): 419.3K **Privately Held**
SIC: 2844 Mfg Toilet Preparations

(G-17648)
JUTRAS SIGNS INC
Also Called: Jutras Signs & Flags
30 Harvey Rd Unit 8 (03110-6818)
PHONE..................................603 622-2344
Cathy Champagne, *President*
EMP: 25
SQ FT: 18,000
SALES (est): 3.3MM **Privately Held**
WEB: www.jutrassigns.com
SIC: 3993 1611 Mfg Signs/Advertising Specialties Highway/Street Construction

(G-17649)
KANA SOFTWARE INC
10 Corporate Dr Ste 2206 (03110-5956)
PHONE..................................650 614-8300
EMP: 4 **Publicly Held**
SIC: 7372 Prepackaged Software Services
HQ: Kana Software, Inc.
2550 Walsh Ave Ste 120
Santa Clara CA 95051
650 614-8300

(G-17650)
KENTICO SOFTWARE LLC
15 Constitution Dr Ste 2g (03110-6075)
PHONE..................................866 328-8998
Eric C Webb, *Mng Member*
Eric Webb, *Director*
EMP: 31 **EST:** 2008
SALES (est): 799K **Privately Held**
SIC: 7372 Custom Computer Programing
PA: Kentico Software S.R.O.
Nove Sady 996/25
Brno - Stare Brno 60200

(G-17651)
LYOPHILIZATION SVCS NENG INC
Also Called: Lsne
25 Commerce Dr (03110-6835)
PHONE..................................603 668-5763
Myron Dittmer, *Branch Mgr*
EMP: 20
SALES (corp-wide): 6.5MM **Privately Held**
SIC: 2836 Mfg Biological Products
PA: Lyophilization Services Of New England, Inc.
1 Sundial Ave Ste 112
Manchester NH 03103
603 626-5763

(G-17652)
LYOPHILIZATION SVCS NENG INC
19 Harvey Rd Ste 5&7 (03110-6810)
PHONE..................................603 626-9559
Myron Dittmer, *Branch Mgr*
EMP: 19
SALES (corp-wide): 6.5MM **Privately Held**
SIC: 2836 Mfg Biological Products
PA: Lyophilization Services Of New England, Inc.
1 Sundial Ave Ste 112
Manchester NH 03103
603 626-5763

(G-17653)
MAX PHARMACEUTICAL LLC
238 Joppa Hill Rd (03110-4207)
PHONE..................................603 472-2813
Frederick J Foley, *Manager*
EMP: 3
SALES (est): 240.2K **Privately Held**
SIC: 2834 Mfg Pharmaceutical Preparations

(G-17654)
MICROELECTRODES INC
40 Harvey Rd (03110-6805)
PHONE..................................603 668-0692
Normand C Hebert, *President*
Marc Hebert, *Admin Sec*
EMP: 8
SQ FT: 5,200
SALES: 750K **Privately Held**
WEB: www.microelectrodes.com
SIC: 3826 Mfg Analytical Instruments

(G-17655)
MONOPLEX EYE PROSTHETICS LLC
169 S River Rd Unit 14a (03110-6972)
PHONE..................................603 622-5200
Peter Kazanovicz, *Manager*
EMP: 3
SALES (est): 191.9K **Privately Held**
SIC: 3842 Mfg Surgical Appliances/Supplies

(G-17656)
NATIONAL METER INDUSTRIES INC
10 Commerce Park North 11a (03110-6920)
PHONE..................................603 669-5790
Louis A Deberadinis, *President*
Stephen Deberadinis, *Vice Pres*
Donald Deberadinis, *Treasurer*
EMP: 8
SQ FT: 4,120
SALES (est): 1.1MM **Privately Held**
WEB: www.national-meter.com
SIC: 3612 Mfg Killowatt Electronic Meters

(G-17657)
OPTICS 1 INC
2 Cooper Ln (03110-5966)
PHONE..................................603 296-0469
Julien Apollon,
EMP: 7
SALES (corp-wide): 807.3MM **Privately Held**
WEB: www.optics1.com
SIC: 3827 Optical Instruments And Lenses
HQ: Optics 1, Inc.
2 Cooper Ln
Bedford NH 03110
603 296-0469

(G-17658)
OPTICS 1 INC (DH)
2 Cooper Ln (03110-5966)
PHONE..................................603 296-0469
Arturo Andrade, *Business Mgr*
Jose Andrade, *Business Mgr*
Mark Belanger, *Exec VP*
Jon Aldrich, *Opers Staff*
Seth Chapman, *Engineer*
EMP: 16
SQ FT: 15,000
SALES (est): 10.1MM
SALES (corp-wide): 807.3MM **Privately Held**
WEB: www.optics1.com
SIC: 3827 Mfg Optical Instruments/Lenses
HQ: Safran Vectronix Ag
Max Schmidheiny-Strasse 202
Heerbrugg SG 9435
717 267-200

(G-17659)
PARAMOUNT PUBLISHING INC/
24 S Hills Dr (03110-4920)
PHONE..................................603 472-3528
Frank Zito, *President*
EMP: 3
SALES (est): 199.7K **Privately Held**
SIC: 2741 Misc Publishing

(G-17660)
POWERBOX (USA) INC
15 Constitution Dr Ste 1a (03110-6002)
PHONE..................................303 439-7211
Troy Talbert, *CEO*
T O Mannerford, *Ch of Bd*
Mark Motsinger, *President*
Rich Trompeter, *President*
Jim Rosica, *COO*
▲ **EMP:** 6
SQ FT: 5,100
SALES (est): 914.1K
SALES (corp-wide): 3.3MM **Privately Held**
WEB: www.powerboxusa.com
SIC: 3469 Mfg Metal Stampings
PA: Powerbox International Ab
Industrigatan 8
Gnesta 646 3
158 703-10

(G-17661)
SDC SOLUTIONS INC
35 Constitution Dr Ste 99 (03110-6025)
PHONE..................................603 629-4242
Joseph Jarnutowsky, *President*
EMP: 40
SALES (est): 4.1MM **Privately Held**
WEB: www.sdcsolutions.com
SIC: 7372 Mfg Mission Critical Communications Solutions Software

(G-17662)
SEGWAY INC (DH)
14 Technology Dr (03110-6908)
PHONE..................................603 222-6000
Rodney C Keller Jr, *President*
Mary P Savage, *COO*
Jason Barton, *Vice Pres*
Francis Bridges, *Vice Pres*
Gene Northam, *Vice Pres*
◆ **EMP:** 103
SQ FT: 200,000
SALES (est): 22.4MM
SALES (corp-wide): 5MM **Privately Held**
WEB: www.segway.com
SIC: 3751 Mfg Motorcycles/Bicycles
HQ: Nunn Bo (Tianjin) Technology Co., Ltd.
No.3, Tianrui Road, Qiche Industries Park, Wu Qing District
Tianjin 30170
225 968-6633

(G-17663)
SIERRA NEVADA CORPORATION
43 Constitution Dr # 202 (03110-6083)
PHONE..................................775 331-0222
Fatih Ozmen, *CEO*
EMP: 257
SALES (corp-wide): 1.9B **Privately Held**
SIC: 3812 3728 Mfg Search/Navigation Equipment Mfg Aircraft Parts/Equipment
PA: Sierra Nevada Corporation
444 Salomon Cir
Sparks NV 89434
775 331-0222

(G-17664)
SPRAYING SYSTEMS CO
174 Route 101 (03110-5417)
P.O. Box 5046, Manchester (03108-5046)
PHONE..................................603 471-0505
John Sowden, *Sales Staff*
John Sowdenm, *Manager*
EMP: 10
SALES (corp-wide): 264.7MM **Privately Held**
WEB: www.spray.com
SIC: 3499 Mfg Misc Fabricated Metal Products
PA: Spraying Systems Co.
200 W North Ave
Glendale Heights IL 60139
630 665-5000

(G-17665)
TRAVELBRAINS INC
14 Tether Rd (03110-5660)
PHONE..................................603 471-0127
Paul C Davis, *President*
Catherin Davis, *Vice Pres*
Victor J Davis, *CTO*
▲ **EMP:** 3
SALES (est): 198.2K **Privately Held**
WEB: www.travelbrains.com
SIC: 2731 Books-Publishing/Printing

(G-17666)
VISUAL POLYMER TECH LLC
91 Brick Mill Rd (03110-5145)
PHONE..................................603 488-5064
Gregory Caldwell, *Mng Member*
▲ **EMP:** 12
SALES (est): 1.4MM **Privately Held**
WEB: www.visualpolymer.com
SIC: 3087 Custom Compounding-Purchased Resins

(G-17667)
WHOLISTIC PET ORGANICS LLC
341 Route 101 (03110-5104)
PHONE..................................603 472-8300
Ryan Phillips, *General Mgr*
John Phillips, *Mng Member*
Sarah Phillips, *Manager*
EMP: 7
SALES: 650K **Privately Held**
SIC: 2047 2048 Mfg Animal Food Mfg Prepared Feeds

(G-17668)
Z-FLEX (US) INC
20 Commerce Park North # 107 (03110-6900)
PHONE..................................603 669-5136
Ian Donnelly, *President*
▲ **EMP:** 25
SQ FT: 40,000
SALES (est): 4.6MM
SALES (corp-wide): 49.3MM **Privately Held**
WEB: www.z-flex.com
SIC: 3259 Mfg Structural Clay Products
HQ: Z-Flex Realty, Inc.
20 Commerce Park North # 107
Bedford NH 03110

GEOGRAPHIC

Belmont
Belknap County

(G-17669)
AFL TELECOMMUNICATIONS LLC
16 Eastgate Park Dr (03220-3604)
PHONE..................................603 528-7780
Sean Adam, *Branch Mgr*
Kim Huckaby, *Data Proc Staff*
EMP: 50 **Privately Held**
SIC: 3357 Nonferrous Wiredrawing/Insulating
HQ: Afl Telecommunications Llc
170 Ridgeview Center Dr
Duncan SC 29334
864 433-0333

(G-17670)
AVERY DENNISON CORPORATION
Also Called: Avery Dnnson Dgtal Ink Sltions
7 Fruite St Unit 7 # 7 (03220-3544)
PHONE..................................603 217-4144
Adam Tourville, *Manager*
EMP: 32
SALES (corp-wide): 7.1B **Publicly Held**
SIC: 2672 Mfg Coated/Laminated Paper
PA: Avery Dennison Corporation
207 N Goode Ave
Glendale CA 91203
626 304-2000

(G-17671)
BOSTON FOG LLC
18 Walnut St (03220-3838)
PHONE..................................888 846-4145
John Vallerand,
Barry Franks,
Paul Quaranto,
EMP: 3
SALES (est): 225.3K **Privately Held**
SIC: 2879 Mfg Agricultural Chemicals

(G-17672)
COCA-COLA BOTTLING COMPANY
495 Depot St (03220)
P.O. Box 809 (03220-0809)
PHONE..................................603 267-8834
Donna Merrill, *Branch Mgr*
EMP: 100 **Privately Held**
SIC: 2086 8741 Mfg Bottled/Canned Soft Drinks Management Services
HQ: Coca-Cola Beverages Northeast, Inc.
1 Executive Park Dr # 330
Bedford NH 03110
603 627-7871

(G-17673)
HAMILTON PRECISION LLC
274 Jamestown Rd (03220-4321)
PHONE..................................603 524-7622
Mark Hamilton, *Mng Member*
EMP: 4
SQ FT: 2,100
SALES: 500K **Privately Held**
SIC: 3544 Manufacturers Precision Tools And Dies

(G-17674)
INK MILL CORP
7 Fruite St G (03220-3544)
PHONE..................................603 217-4144
Kevin Dyer, *CEO*
◆ **EMP:** 13
SALES (est): 3.2MM
SALES (corp-wide): 7.1B **Publicly Held**
WEB: www.inkmillcorp.com
SIC: 2893 Mfg Printing Ink
PA: Avery Dennison Corporation
207 N Goode Ave
Glendale CA 91203
626 304-2000

(G-17675)
INOFAB-NNOVATION INFABRICATION
46 Aiden Cir (03220-4054)
PHONE..................................603 491-2946
Nicholas Kaminski, *Principal*
EMP: 3
SALES (est): 244.1K **Privately Held**
SIC: 3089 Mfg Plastic Products

(G-17676)
JORGENSEN TOOL & STAMPING INC
23 Fruite St (03220-3501)
PHONE..................................603 524-5813
Richard Jorgensen, *President*
Peter Hudson, *QC Mgr*
Sandra Jorgensen, *Asst Treas*
EMP: 35
SQ FT: 8,000
SALES (est): 6.3MM **Privately Held**
SIC: 3599 3469 Mfg Industrial Machinery Mfg Metal Stampings

(G-17677)
LEPAGE BAKERIES PARK ST LLC
Also Called: Country Kitchen
438 Union Rd (03220-3833)
PHONE..................................603 524-9104
Kenneth Ouellette, *Manager*
EMP: 11
SALES (corp-wide): 3.9B **Publicly Held**
WEB: www.lbck.com
SIC: 2051 Mfg Bread/Related Products
HQ: Lepage Bakeries Park Street Llc
11 Adamian Dr
Auburn ME 04210
207 783-9161

(G-17678)
MILPOWER SOURCE INC
7 Field Ln (03220-4621)
P.O. Box 810 (03220-0810)
PHONE..................................603 267-8865
Tomer Eshed, *General Mgr*
EMP: 65
SALES (corp-wide): 10.2MM **Privately Held**
SIC: 3629 Mfg Electrical Industrial Apparatus
PA: Milpower Source Inc.
7 Field Ln
Belmont NH 03220
603 267-8865

(G-17679)
PETER PIERCE
Also Called: Peter Pierce Logging
390 Durrell Mountain Rd (03220-3314)
PHONE..................................603 524-8312
Peter Pierce, *Owner*
EMP: 3
SALES (est): 185.9K **Privately Held**
SIC: 2411 1794 Logging Excavation Contractor

(G-17680)
PICHES SKI SHOP INC
Also Called: Piches Screen Printing & EMB
282 Daniel Webster Hwy (03220-3038)
PHONE..................................603 524-4413
Rob Bolduc Jr, *President*
EMP: 12
SALES (corp-wide): 5.1MM **Privately Held**
SIC: 2759 Commercial Printing
PA: Piche's Ski Shop, Inc.
318 Gilford Ave
Gilford NH 03249
603 524-2068

(G-17681)
PROVINCE KILN DRIED FIREWOOD
428 South Rd (03220-4420)
PHONE..................................603 524-4447
Brian R Hutchins, *Administration*
EMP: 4
SALES (est): 432.1K **Privately Held**
SIC: 3559 Mfg Misc Industry Machinery

(G-17682)
REDIMIX COMPANIES INC (DH)
3 Eastgate Park Dr (03220-3603)
PHONE..................................603 524-4434
Dave Bissonette, *President*
EMP: 50
SQ FT: 30,000
SALES (est): 7.5MM
SALES (corp-wide): 29.7B **Privately Held**
SIC: 3273 Mfg Ready-Mixed Concrete

(G-17683)
SILVER LAKE FABRICATION
28 Gardners Grove Rd (03220-4308)
PHONE..................................603 630-5658
Aaron Leclerc, *Executive*
EMP: 3 **EST:** 2010
SALES (est): 203.8K **Privately Held**
SIC: 3842 Mfg Surgical Appliances/Supplies

(G-17684)
SWISSET TOOL COMPANY INC
32 Eastgate Park Dr (03220-3604)
PHONE..................................603 524-0082
Dave Sanborn, *President*
Douglas Sanborn, *Vice Pres*
Kristina Sanborn, *Executive Asst*
EMP: 6
SQ FT: 3,500
SALES: 1MM **Privately Held**
WEB: www.swissettool.com
SIC: 3545 Mfg Machine Tool Accessories

(G-17685)
TEL -TUK ENTERPRISES LLC
Also Called: Tel-Tuk Construction
4 Dearborn St (03220-4156)
PHONE..................................603 267-1966
Richard Tucker,
Francis A Tellier,
EMP: 3
SALES (est): 360K **Privately Held**
SIC: 3531 3545 Mfg Construction Machinery Mfg Machine Tool Accessories

(G-17686)
WILCOM INC
73 Daniel Webster Hwy (03220-3028)
P.O. Box 508, Laconia (03247-0508)
PHONE..................................603 524-2622
Dennis McCarthy, *President*
John Helenek, *CFO*
Sandy Jordan, *Sales Dir*
▲ **EMP:** 26
SQ FT: 47,000
SALES (est): 6.3MM **Privately Held**
WEB: www.wilcominc.com
SIC: 3823 3825 Manufacturing Process Control Instruments Manufacturing Electrical Measuring Instruments

Bennington
Hillsborough County

(G-17687)
ANTRIM CONTROLS & SYSTEMS
76 N Bennington Rd (03442-4500)
PHONE..................................603 588-6297
Jim Bronson, *Principal*
EMP: 4
SALES (est): 434.4K **Privately Held**
SIC: 3625 Mfg Relays/Industrial Controls

(G-17688)
DH HARDWICK & SONS INC
301 Francestown Rd (03442)
P.O. Box 430, Antrim (03440-0430)
PHONE..................................603 588-6618
Teresa Hardwick, *President*
EMP: 30
SALES: 5MM **Privately Held**
SIC: 2411 1629 5211 Logging Heavy Construction Ret Lumber/Building Materials

(G-17689)
MONADNOCK PAPER MILLS INC (PA)
117 Antrim Rd (03442-4205)
PHONE..................................603 588-3311
Richard G Verney, *President*
Chris Benincasa, *Vice Pres*
Joe Fletcher, *Vice Pres*
Robert McDonald, *VP Mfg*
Keith Blanc, *Maint Spvr*
▼ **EMP:** 140 **EST:** 1819
SQ FT: 300,000
SALES: 78.1MM **Privately Held**
WEB: www.mpm.com
SIC: 2621 5085 Paper Mill Whol Industrial Supplies

Berlin
Coos County

(G-17690)
3D LOGGING CO INC
302 Howard St (03570-3746)
PHONE..................................603 915-3020
Richard Eastman, *President*
EMP: 19
SALES (est): 1.6MM **Privately Held**
SIC: 2411 Logging Services

(G-17691)
ALPINE MACHINE CO INC
355 Goebel St (03570-2318)
PHONE..................................603 752-1441
Raymond Labrecque, *President*
Scott Legendre, *Corp Secy*
Dana Legendre, *Vice Pres*
EMP: 19
SQ FT: 9,000
SALES (est): 3.6MM **Privately Held**
SIC: 3599 3441 Mfg Industrial Machinery Structural Metal Fabrication

(G-17692)
BERLIN DAILY SUN
Also Called: Conway Daily Sun
164 Main St Ste 1 (03570-2477)
PHONE..................................603 752-5858
Mark Garang, *Partner*
EMP: 5
SALES (est): 211.1K **Privately Held**
SIC: 2711 Newspapers-Publishing/Printing

(G-17693)
BFMC LLC
Also Called: Berlin Foundary & Achine Co
489 Goebel St (03570-2338)
P.O. Box 127 (03570-0127)
PHONE..................................603 752-4550
Gary A Hamel,
▼ **EMP:** 20 **EST:** 1904
SQ FT: 60,000
SALES: 2.1MM **Privately Held**
WEB: www.berlinfoundry.com
SIC: 3554 3599 Mfg Paper Industries Machinery Mfg Industrial Machinery

(G-17694)
CROSS MACHINE INC
167 Glen Ave (03570-1905)
P.O. Box 529 (03570-0529)
PHONE..................................603 752-6111
Richard Fournier, *President*
EMP: 19
SQ FT: 11,200
SALES (est): 5.7MM **Privately Held**
WEB: www.crossmachine.com
SIC: 3441 Structural Metal Fabrication

(G-17695)
DEFLEX INNOVATIONS INC
22 Jericho Rd (03570-1314)
PHONE..................................603 215-6738
Karyne Jacques, *Director*
EMP: 3 **EST:** 2017
SALES (est): 174.5K **Privately Held**
SIC: 3089 Mfg Plastic Products

(G-17696)
GORHAM BRICK & BLOCK INC
331 Western Ave (03570-1016)
PHONE..................................603 752-3631
Steve Buckovitch, *President*
Frank Di Neen, *CPA*
Patty Buckovitch, *Admin Sec*
EMP: 4
SQ FT: 450
SALES (est): 331.2K **Privately Held**
SIC: 3271 Mfg Concrete Block/Brick

(G-17697)
GUITABEC USA INC
42 Industrial Park Dr (03570-3555)
PHONE..................................603 752-1432
Robert Godin, *President*
▲ **EMP:** 32
SALES (est): 3.5MM **Privately Held**
SIC: 3931 Mfg Guitars

(G-17698)
JIMTOWN SAND AND GRAVEL INC
1803 Riverside Dr (03570-3143)
PHONE..................603 752-4622
Arthur R Couture, *President*
EMP: 3
SALES (est): 358.1K **Privately Held**
SIC: 1442 Construction Sand/Gravel

(G-17699)
LESSARD & SONS LOGGING INC
Also Called: Lessard & Sons Trucking
1775 Hutchins St (03570-3509)
PHONE..................603 752-5767
Lessard Clement, *President*
Allen Lessard, *Vice Pres*
EMP: 3
SALES (est): 250K **Privately Held**
SIC: 2411 Logging Contractor

(G-17700)
SMITH & TOWN PRINTERS LLC
42 Main St (03570-2459)
PHONE..................603 752-2150
Rachel Godbout, *Mng Member*
Matthew Godbout,
Michael Godbout,
EMP: 9
SQ FT: 3,500
SALES (est): 1.2MM **Privately Held**
WEB: www.smithandtownprinters.com
SIC: 2752 2791 2759 Lithographic Commercial Printing Typesetting Services Commercial Printing

(G-17701)
STORAGE CONCEPTS
1 Francis St (03570-1542)
PHONE..................603 752-1111
Norman R Richards, *Owner*
EMP: 5
SALES (est): 312.5K **Privately Held**
SIC: 2599 Mfg Furniture/Fixtures

Boscawen
Merrimack County

(G-17702)
CHARLES SMITH STEEL LLC
115 N Main St (03303-1106)
PHONE..................603 753-9844
Charles Smith Jr, *President*
EMP: 9
SALES (est): 1.9MM **Privately Held**
SIC: 3441 Structural Metal Fabrication

(G-17703)
ELEKTRISOLA INCORPORATED (PA)
126 High St (03303-2809)
PHONE..................603 796-2114
Oliver Schildbach, *CEO*
Detlef Schildbach, *President*
David Dimartino, *Vice Pres*
George P Downing, *Vice Pres*
Terry Smith, *Vice Pres*
▲ **EMP:** 175 **EST:** 1975
SALES (est): 30MM **Privately Held**
WEB: www.elektrisola.com
SIC: 3496 3357 Mfg Misc Fabricated Wire Products Nonferrous Wiredrawing/Insulating

(G-17704)
KSD CUSTOM WOOD PRODUCTS INC
102 High St (03303-2602)
PHONE..................603 796-2951
Kim Doubleday, *President*
EMP: 21
SQ FT: 35,000
SALES (est): 3.6MM **Privately Held**
WEB: www.ksdcwp.com
SIC: 2431 Mfg Millwork

(G-17705)
PAGE BELTING COMPANY INC
104 High St (03303-2602)
PHONE..................603 796-2463
Mark Coen, *President*
EMP: 46 **EST:** 1868
SQ FT: 40,000
SALES (est): 6.8MM **Privately Held**
WEB: www.pagebelting.com
SIC: 3199 Mfg Leather Goods

Bow
Merrimack County

(G-17706)
ABSOLUTE RSTRTION SLANT SLTONS
3 Tallwood Dr Ste 3 # 3 (03304-3301)
PHONE..................603 518-5864
Eric Boelzner, *Principal*
EMP: 4
SALES (est): 404.4K **Privately Held**
SIC: 2891 Mfg Adhesives/Sealants

(G-17707)
ATLANTIC AIR PRODUCTS MFG LLC
814 Route 3a (03304-4018)
PHONE..................603 410-3900
Sara Jordan, *Human Resources*
Skip Creamer, *Mng Member*
EMP: 10
SALES (est): 1.1MM **Privately Held**
WEB: www.atlanticairproducts.com
SIC: 3444 Mfg Sheet Metalwork

(G-17708)
BOVIE SCREEN PROCESS PRTG INC
4 Northeast Ave (03304-3407)
P.O. Box 720, Concord (03302-0720)
PHONE..................603 224-0651
David Lee Gintzler, *President*
Jean Drew, *Cust Mgr*
EMP: 50 **EST:** 2015
SQ FT: 31,000
SALES (est): 4MM **Privately Held**
WEB: www.bovie.com
SIC: 2759 Commercial Printing

(G-17709)
CENTROID WIRE AND CABLE LLC
155 River Rd Unit 28 (03304-3361)
PHONE..................603 227-0900
Rod Davidson,
Bob Phelan,
Mike Phelan,
EMP: 3
SQ FT: 3,500
SALES (est): 357.9K **Privately Held**
SIC: 3496 Mfg Misc Fabricated Wire Products

(G-17710)
CONPROCO CORP
655 River Rd (03304-3367)
PHONE..................603 743-5800
Christopher D Brown, *Branch Mgr*
EMP: 4
SALES (corp-wide): 47.7MM **Privately Held**
WEB: www.conproco.com
SIC: 3272 1799 1741 3281 Mfg Concrete Products Special Trade Contractor & Mfg Cut Stone Products And Hydraulic Cement
PA: Conproco Corp.
388 High St
Somersworth NH 03878
603 743-5800

(G-17711)
ENE SYSTEMS OF NH INC
155 River Rd Unit 10 (03304-3362)
PHONE..................603 856-0330
Paul O'Brien, *President*
Richard Olson, *Vice Pres*
EMP: 8
SQ FT: 2,600
SALES (est): 1.5MM
SALES (corp-wide): 46.2MM **Privately Held**
WEB: www.procontrolsinc.com
SIC: 3822 Manufacturing Environmental Controls
PA: Ene Systems, Inc.
480 Neponset St Ste 11d
Canton MA 02021
781 828-6770

(G-17712)
ENSIO RESOURCES INC
Also Called: Patriot Glass
431 River Rd (03304-3351)
P.O. Box 279, Bellevue WA (98009-0279)
PHONE..................603 224-0221
Mark Ensio, *President*
EMP: 5
SALES (est): 576.8K **Privately Held**
SIC: 1481 Nonmetallic Mineral Services

(G-17713)
EVANS PRINTING CO
155 River Rd Unit 15 (03304-3362)
PHONE..................603 856-8238
John Holman, *CEO*
Robert Holman, *President*
EMP: 8 **EST:** 1930
SQ FT: 12,000
SALES (est): 1.1MM **Privately Held**
WEB: www.evansprinting.com
SIC: 2752 2759 Commercial Offset Printing

(G-17714)
G P 2 TECHNOLOGIES INC
Also Called: Gp2 Technologies
157 River Rd Unit 18 (03304-3362)
PHONE..................603 226-0336
Thomas Porat, *President*
Thurlow Greene, *Vice Pres*
Jerry Peterson, *Vice Pres*
Gerald Peterson, *VP Opers*
EMP: 8
SQ FT: 9,600
SALES (est): 1.4MM **Privately Held**
WEB: www.gp2tech.com
SIC: 3555 Mfg Machinery

(G-17715)
GS BLODGETT CORPORATION
509 Route 3a (03304-3102)
P.O. Box 501, Concord (03302-0501)
PHONE..................603 225-5688
Joe McAuley, *Sales Staff*
Bob Granger, *Branch Mgr*
EMP: 259
SALES (corp-wide): 2.7B **Publicly Held**
SIC: 3589 Mfg Commercial Cooking Equipment
HQ: G.S. Blodgett Corporation
42 Allen Martin Dr
Essex Junction VT 05452
802 860-3700

(G-17716)
HIGH SPEED TECHNOLOGIES INC
1357 Route 3a 9 (03304-4029)
PHONE..................603 483-0333
Ralph Frisella, *President*
EMP: 25
SALES (est): 3.7MM **Privately Held**
WEB: www.highspeedtechnologies.com
SIC: 3549 Mfg Metalworking Machinery

(G-17717)
JEMBOW INC
92 Woodhill Rd (03304-5310)
PHONE..................603 774-6055
EMP: 3
SALES (est): 200K **Privately Held**
SIC: 2262 2759 Manmade Fiber & Silk Finishing Plant Commercial Printing

(G-17718)
KALWALL CORPORATION
Also Called: Kal-Lite Division
40 River Rd (03304)
PHONE..................603 224-6881
William Dannhauer, *Principal*
Nancy Garneau, *Project Dir*
Jeff Hicks, *Opers Mgr*
John Graham, *Research*
EMP: 80
SALES (corp-wide): 147.8MM **Privately Held**
WEB: www.kalwall.com
SIC: 3089 Mfg Plastic Products
PA: Kalwall Corporation
1111 Candia Rd
Manchester NH 03109
603 627-3861

(G-17719)
KELLER PRODUCTS INCORPORATED
164 River Rd (03304-3353)
PHONE..................603 224-5502
Duston Shost, *Marketing Staff*
Dustin Shost, *Branch Mgr*
EMP: 30
SALES (corp-wide): 9.1MM **Privately Held**
WEB: www.kellerzone.com
SIC: 2821 2431 Mfg Plastic Materials/Resins Mfg Millwork
PA: Keller Products, Incorporated
41 Union St
Manchester NH 03103

(G-17720)
KOFFEE KUP BAKERY INC
28 Dunklee Rd Ste 3 (03304-3319)
PHONE..................603 225-6149
Birt Blais, *Branch Mgr*
EMP: 4
SALES (corp-wide): 30.8MM **Privately Held**
WEB: www.koffeekupbakery.biz
SIC: 2051 Mfg Bread/Related Products
PA: Koffee Kup Bakery, Inc.
59 Rathe Rd Ste A
Colchester VT 05446
802 863-2696

(G-17721)
LINE-X MERRIMACK VALLEY LLC
617 Route 3a (03304-3320)
PHONE..................603 224-7792
Steven A Owen,
EMP: 3
SALES: 800K **Privately Held**
WEB: www.linexofmv.com
SIC: 3792 5013 Mfg Travel Trailers/Campers Whol Auto Parts/Supplies

(G-17722)
METZGER/MCGUIRE INC
807 Route 3a (03304-4019)
P.O. Box 2217, Concord (03302-2217)
PHONE..................603 224-6122
Scott C Metzger, *President*
Michelle R McKinnon, *Vice Pres*
Craig N Metzger, *Vice Pres*
Ray Lawler, *Manager*
Jim Marchillo, *Technical Staff*
EMP: 20
SQ FT: 6,000
SALES (est): 4.5MM **Privately Held**
WEB: www.metzgermcguire.com
SIC: 2821 Mfg Plastic Materials/Resins

(G-17723)
NEW HAMPSHIRE BINDERY INC
81 Dow Rd (03304-3607)
PHONE..................603 224-0441
Thomas Ives, *President*
Suzanne Ives, *Vice Pres*
EMP: 13 **EST:** 1934
SQ FT: 13,333
SALES (est): 1.7MM **Privately Held**
WEB: www.nhbindery.com
SIC: 2789 Bookbinding/Related Work

(G-17724)
NORTH EAST CERAMIC STUDIO INC
2 Noyes Ln (03304-3338)
PHONE..................603 225-9310
Richard A Goduti, *President*
Donald Goduti, *Clerk*
▲ **EMP:** 7 **EST:** 1972
SALES (est): 450K **Privately Held**
SIC: 3843 Dental Laboratory

(G-17725)
PAVELOK
10 Dunklee Rd Ste 35 (03304-3305)
PHONE..................603 225-7283
Delavan Cate, *Principal*

GEOGRAPHIC

EMP: 4 **EST:** 2010
SALES (est): 231.8K **Privately Held**
SIC: 3423 Mfg Hand/Edge Tools

(G-17726)
PEN & INC
Also Called: Copper Maid
155 River Rd Unit 8 (03304-3362)
P.O. Box 2646, Concord (03302-2646)
PHONE..................................603 225-7522
Mason Newick, *President*
EMP: 5
SALES: 250K **Privately Held**
SIC: 2771 Mfg Greeting Cards

(G-17727)
PITCO FRIALATOR INC (HQ)
Also Called: Magic Kitch'n
553 Route 3a (03304-3215)
P.O. Box 501, Concord (03302-0501)
PHONE..................................603 225-6684
Tim Fitzgerald, *CEO*
Mark Lang, *President*
Roger McGhee, *President*
Karl Searl, *President*
Cheryl Gagnon, *Senior Buyer*
▲ **EMP:** 310 **EST:** 1918
SQ FT: 100,000
SALES: 155MM
SALES (corp-wide): 2.7B **Publicly Held**
WEB: www.blodgett.com
SIC: 3589 Mfg Service Industry Machinery
PA: The Middleby Corporation
1400 Toastmaster Dr
Elgin IL 60120
847 741-3300

(G-17728)
PLASTECH MACHINING FABRICATION
25 Dunklee Rd (03304-3308)
PHONE..................................603 228-7601
Louis Ferriero, *President*
EMP: 10 **EST:** 1997
SQ FT: 7,000
SALES: 1.2MM **Privately Held**
WEB: www.plastechfab.com
SIC: 3599 Machine Shop

(G-17729)
RIVERVIEW LABS INC
Also Called: Beverly Hills Hlth & Buty Pdts
24 Dunklee Rd Ste 14 (03304-3332)
PHONE..................................603 715-2759
David Mobed, *President*
EMP: 4
SALES: 450K **Privately Held**
SIC: 2844 Mfg Toilet Preparations

(G-17730)
S CAMEROTA & SONS INC
Also Called: Camerota Truck Parts
865 Route 3a (03304-4019)
P.O. Box 1134, Enfield CT (06083-1134)
PHONE..................................603 228-9343
John Pilvelis, *Branch Mgr*
Joe Audet, *Manager*
EMP: 6
SALES (corp-wide): 111MM **Privately Held**
WEB: www.camerota.com
SIC: 3714 5531 Mfg Motor Vehicle Parts/Accessories Ret Auto/Home Supplies
PA: S. Camerota & Sons, Inc.
245 Shaker Rd
Enfield CT 06082
860 763-0896

(G-17731)
SAWTECH SCIENTIFIC INC
14 Dow Rd Unit A (03304-3600)
PHONE..................................603 228-1811
Thomas Bennett, *President*
EMP: 6
SQ FT: 7,500
SALES (est): 1.1MM **Privately Held**
WEB: www.sawtechscientific.com
SIC: 3549 3553 3599 Mfg Metalworking Machinery Mfg Woodworking Machinery Mfg Industrial Machinery

(G-17732)
SUPERIOR ICE CREAM EQP LLC
155 River Rd Unit 9 (03304-3362)
PHONE..................................603 225-4207
Kevin McCan, *Mng Member*
EMP: 15 **EST:** 2017
SQ FT: 4,000
SALES: 4MM **Privately Held**
SIC: 3556 Mfg Food Products Machinery

(G-17733)
SUPERIOR NOVELTY EQUIPMENT
155 River Rd Unit 12 (03304-3362)
PHONE..................................603 225-4207
Kevin McCann, *President*
▲ **EMP:** 3
SQ FT: 1,800
SALES: 700K **Privately Held**
SIC: 3556 Mfg Food Products Machinery

(G-17734)
SYNTEGRATECH INCORPORATED
33 Tonga Dr (03304-4819)
PHONE..................................603 225-4008
D Mark Read, *President*
Patricia Tanner, *Treasurer*
Thomas Platt, *Admin Sec*
EMP: 6
SQ FT: 2,600
SALES (est): 610K **Privately Held**
WEB: www.syntegratech.com
SIC: 3577 Mfg Computer Peripheral Equipment

(G-17735)
UNIQUE MECHANICAL SERVICES INC
Also Called: U M S
162 W Main St (03304)
PHONE..................................603 856-0057
Beverly Skillings, *Vice Pres*
EMP: 9
SQ FT: 5,000
SALES (est): 1.5MM **Privately Held**
SIC: 3317 Mfg Steel Pipe/Tubes

(G-17736)
YARRA DESIGN & FABRICATION LLC
Also Called: Concord Awning & Canvas
1 Tallwood Dr (03304-3302)
PHONE..................................603 224-6880
Denise Sandberg, *President*
EMP: 13
SQ FT: 6,000
SALES: 933.8K **Privately Held**
WEB: www.concordawning.com
SIC: 2394 1799 Mfg Canvas/Related Products Trade Contractor

(G-17737)
YOUNG FURNITURE MFG INC
161 River Rd (03304-3343)
PHONE..................................603 224-8830
Andrew N Young, *President*
Thomas A Young, *Vice Pres*
Kenneth E Young, *Treasurer*
Jason Young, *Office Mgr*
Betty Young, *Admin Sec*
EMP: 28
SQ FT: 20,000
SALES (est): 3.5MM **Privately Held**
SIC: 2434 Mfg Wood Kitchen Cabinets

(G-17738)
Z-TECH LLC
56 Dow Rd (03304-3608)
PHONE..................................603 228-1305
Paul Russo, *CFO*
◆ **EMP:** 30
SQ FT: 33,000
SALES (est): 7.5MM **Privately Held**
WEB: www.z-techzirconia.com
SIC: 2819 2869 Mfg Industrial Inorganic Chemicals Mfg Industrial Organic Chemicals

Bradford
Merrimack County

(G-17739)
BRADFORD MACHINE INC
8 Bacon Rd (03221-3500)
P.O. Box 109 (03221-0109)
PHONE..................................603 938-2355
David Long, *President*
EMP: 3
SALES (est): 210K **Privately Held**
SIC: 3599 Machine Shop

(G-17740)
C W MOCK LOGGING
142 Fairgrounds Rd (03221-3125)
PHONE..................................603 938-6096
Christopher Wmock, *Principal*
EMP: 3
SALES (est): 202.9K **Privately Held**
SIC: 2411 Logging

(G-17741)
COLONIAL WOODWORKING INC
65 Main St (03221)
P.O. Box 342 (03221-0342)
PHONE..................................603 938-5131
Paul Saxby, *President*
EMP: 18 **EST:** 1975
SQ FT: 12,000
SALES (est): 2.5MM **Privately Held**
SIC: 2431 Mfg Millwork

(G-17742)
TENSOR COMMUNICATIONS SYSTEMS
159 Day Pond Rd (03221-3400)
PHONE..................................603 938-5206
John Gadoury, *Owner*
EMP: 6
SALES (est): 500K **Privately Held**
WEB: www.tensor-cs.com
SIC: 3663 8748 Communication Consultant & Manufactures Microwave Communication Equipment

Brentwood
Rockingham County

(G-17743)
ADVANCED CUSTOM CABINETS INC
13 Prescott Rd (03833-6502)
PHONE..................................603 772-6211
Joseph Ready, *President*
EMP: 21
SQ FT: 8,600
SALES (est): 2.6MM **Privately Held**
SIC: 2541 2434 1751 Mfg Wood Partitions/Fixtures Mfg Wood Kitchen Cabinets Carpentry Contractor

(G-17744)
ASPHALT RECOVERY TECH LLC
Also Called: Art
50 Pine Rd (03833-6509)
PHONE..................................603 778-1449
Robert Zickell,
EMP: 4
SALES (est): 306.3K **Privately Held**
WEB: www.asphalttechgroup.com
SIC: 2951 Mfg Asphalt Mixtures/Blocks

(G-17745)
ASSOCIATED TRAINING SVCS LLC
Also Called: Associated Training Svcs of NW
5 Industrial Dr (03833-6543)
PHONE..................................603 772-9002
Ralph Delvecchio, *Manager*
EMP: 5
SALES (est): 520.8K **Privately Held**
SIC: 3699 Heavy Equipment Training Services

(G-17746)
AUTO ELECTRIC SERVICE LLC
191 Crawley Falls Rd A8 (03833-6034)
PHONE..................................603 642-5990
Kurt Colligan, *Owner*
EMP: 4
SALES (est): 464.1K **Privately Held**
SIC: 3699 7539 Mfg Electrical Equipment/Supplies Automotive Repair

(G-17747)
CKM COATINGS
191 Crawley Falls Rd # 12 (03833-6035)
PHONE..................................603 642-5728
Chris Merrill, *Principal*
EMP: 4
SALES (est): 356.2K **Privately Held**
SIC: 3479 Coating/Engraving Service

(G-17748)
DHF LLC
424 Route 125 Unit 6 (03833-6641)
PHONE..................................603 778-2440
Christopher Phillips, *Vice Pres*
EMP: 4
SALES (est): 315.1K **Privately Held**
SIC: 3069 Mfg Fabricated Rubber Products

(G-17749)
FASTRAX SIGNS INC
67 Route 27 (03833-6647)
PHONE..................................603 775-7500
Shawn Nordin, *President*
EMP: 7
SALES: 200K **Privately Held**
SIC: 3993 Mfg Signs/Advertising Specialties

(G-17750)
GLASS PRO INC
364 Middle Rd (03833-6017)
PHONE..................................603 436-2882
Daniel Pearson, *Principal*
EMP: 3
SALES (est): 292.5K **Privately Held**
SIC: 3231 Mfg Products-Purchased Glass

(G-17751)
HARD CORE SPRAL TUBE WNDERS IN
50 Pine Rd (03833-6509)
PHONE..................................603 775-0230
Carter Soper, *President*
Mathew Soper, *Vice Pres*
Taylor Soper, *Shareholder*
EMP: 9
SQ FT: 7,500
SALES (est): 2.1MM **Privately Held**
SIC: 2655 Mfg Fiber Cans/Drums

(G-17752)
MTI POLYEXE CORPORATION
50 Pine Rd (03833-6509)
PHONE..................................603 778-1449
Michael Sullivan, *Vice Pres*
Ed Dalrymple, *Manager*
EMP: 16 **EST:** 2015
SALES (est): 3.8MM **Privately Held**
SIC: 2821 Mfg Plastic Materials/Resins

(G-17753)
OMNI TECHNOLOGIES CORP
195 Route 125 (03833-6026)
PHONE..................................603 679-2211
David Faxon, *CFO*
EMP: 3
SALES (est): 127.2K **Privately Held**
SIC: 3399 Mfg Primary Metal Products

(G-17754)
POLYEXE CORPORATION
50 Pine Rd (03833-6509)
PHONE..................................603 778-1143
Thomas J Zickell, *President*
William Thalheimer, *Treasurer*
Ed McCusker, *Supervisor*
Nat Bockh, *Director*
Edmund Nangini, *Admin Sec*
EMP: 20
SQ FT: 3,500
SALES: 3.2MM **Privately Held**
SIC: 2821 Mfg Plastic Materials/Resins

(G-17755)
POOLE SHEET METAL & WLDG INC
35 Commercial Dr 1 (03833-6630)
PHONE..................................603 679-3860
Ken Poole, *President*
EMP: 4
SQ FT: 6,000
SALES: 800K **Privately Held**
WEB: www.poolesheetmetal.com
SIC: 3444 Mfg Sheet Metalwork

(G-17756)
QUIKRETE COMPANIES LLC
44 Jubal Martin Rd (03833-6549)
PHONE..................................603 778-2123
Lynn Allen, *Manager*
EMP: 40 **Privately Held**
WEB: www.quikrete.com
SIC: 3272 Mfg Concrete Products
HQ: The Quikrete Companies Llc
5 Concourse Pkwy Ste 1900
Atlanta GA 30328
404 634-9100

(G-17757)
RECYCLED ASP SHINGLE TECH LLC
Also Called: Ras-Tech
50 Pine Rd (03833-6509)
PHONE..................................603 778-1449
Thomas Zickell, *Mng Member*
Robert Zickell,
EMP: 6
SQ FT: 1,000
SALES (est): 1MM **Privately Held**
SIC: 2951 Mfg Asphalt Mixtures/Blocks

(G-17758)
STARKEY WELDING CRANE SERVICE
444 Route 125 (03833-6610)
PHONE..................................603 679-2553
Charles A Starkey, *Owner*
EMP: 7
SALES: 950K **Privately Held**
SIC: 7692 7389 Welding Repair Business Services

(G-17759)
STINGRAY MANUFACTURING LLC
187c Route 125 Unit C5 (03833)
P.O. Box 1581, Raymond (03077-3581)
PHONE..................................603 642-8987
Jonathan Davies, *Mng Member*
EMP: 3
SQ FT: 2,800
SALES: 250K **Privately Held**
SIC: 3599 Mfg Industrial Machinery

(G-17760)
SUNRISE FOODS INCORPORATED
25 Pine St (03833-2720)
P.O. Box 601 (03833-0601)
PHONE..................................603 772-4420
Kevin Johnston, *President*
EMP: 10
SQ FT: 12,000
SALES (est): 691.4K **Privately Held**
SIC: 2087 5143 Mfg Of Flavoring Extracts And Flavoring Syrups & Whol Of Specialty Cheeses

(G-17761)
WAYNE MANUFACTURING INDS LLC
13 Prescott Rd (03833-6502)
PHONE..................................978 416-0899
Wayne Donohue,
EMP: 22
SALES (est): 2MM **Privately Held**
SIC: 3086 Mfg Plastic Foam Products

Bristol
Grafton County

(G-17762)
CORBEIL ENTERPRISES INC
Also Called: Machine Shop, The
12 Bristol Rd (03222)
P.O. Box 633 (03222-0633)
PHONE..................................603 744-2867
Ruth Corbeil, *President*
Walter Corbeil, *Vice Pres*
Diane Williams, *Director*
Pat Keniston, *Admin Sec*
EMP: 13
SQ FT: 6,600
SALES: 900K **Privately Held**
SIC: 3599 7999 7622 Machine Shop Jobbing & Repair

(G-17763)
FREUDENBERG-NOK GENERAL PARTNR
Also Called: Bps Division
450 Pleasant St (03222-3012)
PHONE..................................603 934-7800
Glenn Anderson, *Manager*
Dave Szacik, *Manager*
EMP: 145
SALES (corp-wide): 10.5B **Privately Held**
WEB: www.freudenberg-nok.com
SIC: 3053 Mfg Gaskets/Packing/Sealing Devices
HQ: Freudenberg-Nok General Partnership
47774 W Anchor Ct
Plymouth MI 48170
734 451-0020

(G-17764)
FREUDENBERG-NOK GENERAL PARTNR
Also Called: Components Division
450 Pleasant St (03222-3012)
P.O. Box 2001 (03222-2001)
PHONE..................................603 744-0371
Gregory Keenan, *Manager*
EMP: 300
SALES (corp-wide): 10.5B **Privately Held**
WEB: www.freudenberg-nok.com
SIC: 3053 Mfg Gaskets/Packing/Sealing Devices
HQ: Freudenberg-Nok General Partnership
47774 W Anchor Ct
Plymouth MI 48170
734 451-0020

(G-17765)
GARRETT G GILPATRIC
231 Peaked Hill Rd (03222-3333)
PHONE..................................603 744-3286
Garrett G Gilpatric, *Principal*
EMP: 3
SALES (est): 251.9K **Privately Held**
SIC: 2411 Logging

(G-17766)
GREEN MOUNTAIN MARINADES
191 Dick Brown Rd (03222-5307)
PHONE..................................802 434-3731
Dave Lasch, *Principal*
EMP: 3
SALES (est): 158.4K **Privately Held**
SIC: 2013 Mfg Prepared Meats

(G-17767)
GRIST FOR MILL LLC
Also Called: Mill Fudge Factory, The
2 Central St (03222-3134)
PHONE..................................603 744-0405
Noah Munro, *Owner*
Kristen Vaccaro, *General Mgr*
Linda Carmichael,
David Munro,
EMP: 16 **EST:** 2006
SALES: 250K **Privately Held**
SIC: 2064 7929 5812 Mfg Candy/Confectionery Entertainer/Entertainment Group Eating Place

(G-17768)
NEWFOUND WOOD WORKS INC (PA)
67 Danforth Brook Rd (03222-3414)
PHONE..................................603 744-6872
Rose Woodyard, *President*
Michael Vermouth, *President*
Alan Mann, *Vice Pres*
EMP: 5
SQ FT: 4,320
SALES (est): 401.6K **Privately Held**
WEB: www.newfound.com
SIC: 2431 Mfg Canoe & Kayak Kits

Brookline
Hills County

(G-17769)
A F FUELS
102 Route 13 (03033-2527)
PHONE..................................603 672-7010
EMP: 3 **EST:** 2011
SALES (est): 245K **Privately Held**
SIC: 2869 Mfg Industrial Organic Chemicals

Brookline
Hillsborough County

(G-17770)
ERMEL PRECISION MACHINING INC
24 Route 13 (03033-2002)
PHONE..................................603 673-7336
Marcus Ermel, *President*
EMP: 3
SQ FT: 3,500
SALES (est): 416.4K **Privately Held**
SIC: 3599 Mfg Industrial Machinery

(G-17771)
I R SOURCES INC
28 Old Milford Rd (03033-2417)
PHONE..................................603 672-0582
Mark Knights, *President*
EMP: 3
SALES (est): 396.6K **Privately Held**
SIC: 3699 Mfg Electrical Equipment/Supplies

(G-17772)
MARK ALLEN CABINETRY LLC (PA)
Also Called: Cabinet Maker
232 Route 13 (03033-2404)
PHONE..................................603 321-3163
Mark Allen Guay, *Administration*
EMP: 7
SALES (est): 915.3K **Privately Held**
SIC: 2434 Mfg Wood Kitchen Cabinets

(G-17773)
SUPERIOR STEEL FABRICATORS INC
46 Route 13 (03033-2002)
P.O. Box 116 (03033-0116)
PHONE..................................603 673-7509
P Donald Hoard, *President*
Jeffrey Crocker, *Admin Sec*
EMP: 15
SQ FT: 10,000
SALES (est): 2.6MM **Privately Held**
SIC: 3446 3441 Mfg Architectural Metalwork Structural Metal Fabrication

(G-17774)
VALDE SYSTEMS INC
4 Hobart Hill Rd (03033-2531)
PHONE..................................603 577-1728
Matthew Linder, *President*
▼ **EMP:** 8
SALES (est): 690K **Privately Held**
WEB: www.valdesystems.com
SIC: 3823 Mfg Process Control Instrument

Campton
Grafton County

(G-17775)
BRN CORPORATION
Also Called: Transfer Technologies
3279 Us Route 3 (03223)
PHONE..................................603 726-3800
Langdon Brauns, *President*
Robert L Brauns, *Systems Analyst*
EMP: 4
SALES (est): 32.2K **Privately Held**
WEB: www.brncorp.com
SIC: 2752 3061 Lithographic Commercial Printing Mfg Mechanical Rubber Goods

(G-17776)
EVERGREEN EMBROIDERY
239 Riverside Dr (03223-4651)
P.O. Box 1536 (03223-1536)
PHONE..................................603 726-4271
Donna F Minickiello, *Partner*
Faust Minickiello, *Partner*
EMP: 12
SALES (est): 970.1K **Privately Held**
SIC: 2395 Pleating/Stitching Services

(G-17777)
GRANITE STATE LOG HOMES INC (PA)
Also Called: Lumber Outlet
17 King Rd (03223-4229)
PHONE..................................603 536-4949
Debbie Macdonald, *President*
EMP: 12
SQ FT: 3,000 **Privately Held**
WEB: www.logkitsnow.com
SIC: 2452 5211 Mfg Prefabricated Wood Buildings Ret Lumber/Building Materials

Canaan
Grafton County

(G-17778)
F C HAMMOND & SON LBR CO INC
Also Called: Hammond Lumber
11 Hammonds Way (03741)
P.O. Box 17 (03741-0017)
PHONE..................................603 523-4353
Fred Hammond, *President*
Tamra Hammond, *Vice Pres*
EMP: 10 **EST:** 1945
SQ FT: 2,000
SALES: 890K **Privately Held**
WEB: www.hammondgrinding.com
SIC: 2421 5031 Sawmill & Whol Lumber Materials

(G-17779)
INOV8V ENERGY LLC
738 Goose Pond Rd (03741-7539)
PHONE..................................603 632-7333
Kevin McCullough, *Mng Member*
EMP: 3
SALES: 1.2MM **Privately Held**
SIC: 1321 Natural Gas Liquids Production

Candia
Rockingham County

(G-17780)
CARRINGTON INTERNATIONAL LLC
293 High St (03034-2717)
PHONE..................................603 867-8957
Stephen Frost,
EMP: 5
SALES: 500K **Privately Held**
SIC: 2731 Books-Publishing/Printing

(G-17781)
EASTERN TIME DESIGN INC
Also Called: Powertronics
143 Raymond Rd (03034-2133)
PHONE..................................603 483-5876
Lawrence P Stacy, *President*

Steven Liggett, *Shareholder*
Michael St Laurent, *Shareholder*
EMP: 11
SQ FT: 2,200
SALES (est): 2MM **Privately Held**
SIC: 3825 Mfg Electrical Measuring Instruments

(G-17782)
ERIMAR SYSTEM INTEGRATION
39 Hemlock Dr (03034-2211)
PHONE..................................603 483-4000
Gary York, *President*
EMP: 3
SALES (est): 394.8K **Privately Held**
SIC: 3599 Mfg Industrial Machinery

(G-17783)
EWE KIDS INC
1 Tower Hill Rd (03034-2219)
PHONE..................................603 483-0984
Russell J Dann, *President*
EMP: 3
SALES (est): 189.3K **Privately Held**
WEB: www.ewekids.com
SIC: 3999 Mfg Misc Products

(G-17784)
GKS SERVICE COMPANY INC
196 Brown Rd (03034-2601)
P.O. Box 413 (03034-0413)
PHONE..................................603 483-2122
Gregory K Saunders,
EMP: 4
SQ FT: 1,800
SALES (est): 638.6K **Privately Held**
SIC: 2514 Mfg Metal Household Furniture

(G-17785)
GRAPHIC CONSUMER SERVICES INC
208 Brown Rd (03034-2623)
P.O. Box 368 (03034-0368)
PHONE..................................603 483-5355
Rene Bouthiette, *President*
Richard Bouthiette, *Vice Pres*
Norma Bouthiette, *Treasurer*
EMP: 3
SALES (est): 412.4K **Privately Held**
WEB: www.graphicsnh.com
SIC: 2752 2791 7336 Offset Printing

Canterbury
Merrimack County

(G-17786)
SUNNYSIDE MAPLES
130 Asby Rd (03224-2704)
PHONE..................................603 848-7091
EMP: 3 **EST:** 2015
SALES (est): 147.9K **Privately Held**
SIC: 2099 Mfg Food Preparations

Center Barnstead
Belknap County

(G-17787)
ADAM BURTT TREE AND LOG LLC
39 Chapelle Rd (03225-3409)
PHONE..................................603 269-2019
Adam W Burtt, *Administration*
EMP: 3
SALES (est): 33.8K **Privately Held**
SIC: 2411 Logging

(G-17788)
CMD LOGGING
520 N Barnstead Rd (03225-3947)
PHONE..................................603 986-5055
EMP: 6 **EST:** 2014
SALES (est): 282.7K **Privately Held**
SIC: 2411 Logging

(G-17789)
GOURMET OILS AND VINEGARS NENG
21 Maple St (03225-3601)
PHONE..................................603 269-2271
Mark Sargent, *Principal*
EMP: 3
SALES (est): 136.4K **Privately Held**
SIC: 2099 Mfg Food Preparations

(G-17790)
OUR TOWN PUBLISHING INC
Also Called: Apraxis Software
1080 N Barnstead Rd (03225-3962)
P.O. Box 220 (03225-0220)
PHONE..................................603 776-2500
Daniel Barraford, *President*
EMP: 6
SALES (est): 380K **Privately Held**
WEB: www.otchoice.com
SIC: 2741 8611 Misc Publishing Business Association

Center Conway
Carroll County

(G-17791)
ARTHURS MEMORIALS INC
875 Eastman Rd (03813)
PHONE..................................603 356-5398
Jeffrey Lang, *President*
EMP: 3
SALES (est): 424.6K **Privately Held**
SIC: 3272 Mfg Concrete Products

(G-17792)
AUSTIN MEDICAL PRODUCTS INC
66 Eastern Ave (03813-4422)
PHONE..................................603 356-7004
William Brown III, *President*
Crystal Brown, *Admin Sec*
▼ **EMP:** 5
SQ FT: 3,000
SALES (est): 887.4K **Privately Held**
WEB: www.ampatch.com
SIC: 3842 5047 Mfg Surgical Appliances/Supplies Whol Medical/Hospital Equipment

(G-17793)
CERAMCO INC
1467 E Main St (03813-4169)
P.O. Box 300 (03813-0300)
PHONE..................................603 447-2090
Thomas Henriksen, *President*
Jim McMahon, *General Mgr*
▲ **EMP:** 20
SQ FT: 10,350
SALES: 2MM **Privately Held**
WEB: www.ceramcoceramics.com
SIC: 3264 3299 Mfg Porcelain Electrical Suppplies Mfg Nonmetallic Mineral Products

(G-17794)
DISCOUNT BEVERAGES PLUS CIG
1130 Eastman Rd (03813-4221)
P.O. Box 3273, North Conway (03860-3273)
PHONE..................................603 356-8844
Mark Keenan, *Owner*
EMP: 3
SALES (est): 272.2K **Privately Held**
SIC: 2086 5921 Mfg Bottled/Canned Soft Drinks Ret Alcoholic Beverages

(G-17795)
EMERLYN SOFTWARE LLC
1620 E Main St 209 (03813-4117)
P.O. Box 2358, North Conway (03860-2358)
PHONE..................................603 447-6130
Calvin Hunsicker,
EMP: 5
SALES (est): 408.6K **Privately Held**
WEB: www.emerlyn.com
SIC: 7372 Prepackaged Software Services

(G-17796)
EMM PRECISION INC
619 E Conway Rd (03813-4057)
P.O. Box 2410, Conway (03818-2410)
PHONE..................................603 356-8892
Charles Gagnon, *President*
Judith Gagnon, *Vice Pres*
Jeanne Graves, *Executive*
EMP: 10
SQ FT: 8,000
SALES: 1.4MM **Privately Held**
WEB: www.emmprecision.com
SIC: 3599 Machine Shop

(G-17797)
FADDEN CHIPPING & LOGGING INC
Also Called: Fadden Trucking
1708 E Conway Rd (03813-4007)
P.O. Box 243, Conway (03818-0243)
PHONE..................................603 939-2462
Thomas A Fadden, *President*
Vicki Graves, *Vice Pres*
EMP: 10
SALES: 1.5MM **Privately Held**
SIC: 2411 Logging Camp Mfg Wood Chips

(G-17798)
GARLAND LUMBER COMPANY INC
636 E Conway Rd (03813-4004)
P.O. Box 3184, North Conway (03860-3184)
PHONE..................................603 356-5636
Roger L Garland Sr, *President*
Roger Garland Jr, *Vice Pres*
Jacqueline M Garland, *Admin Sec*
EMP: 30
SQ FT: 2,500
SALES (est): 4.1MM **Privately Held**
SIC: 2411 1794 4959 Logging Excavation Contractor Sanitary Services

(G-17799)
GARLAND TRANSPORTATION CORP
636 E Conway Rd (03813-4004)
PHONE..................................603 356-5636
Roger L Garland Jr, *Administration*
EMP: 3
SALES (est): 272.6K **Privately Held**
SIC: 2411 Logging

(G-17800)
HOMEGROWN LUMBER
230 Heath Rd (03813-4101)
PHONE..................................603 447-3800
Steven Morrill, *Owner*
EMP: 6
SALES (est): 525.2K **Privately Held**
WEB: www.homegrownlumber.com
SIC: 2421 Sawmill/Planing Mill

(G-17801)
LUPINE INC
16 Lupine Ln (03813-4431)
P.O. Box 1600, Conway (03818-1600)
PHONE..................................603 356-7371
David Jensen, *President*
Scott Badger, *Vice Pres*
Valerie Jensen, *Treasurer*
Tracy McCarthy, *Marketing Staff*
Michael Mulvey, *Technician*
▲ **EMP:** 76
SQ FT: 25,000
SALES (est): 7.4MM **Privately Held**
WEB: www.lupinepet.com
SIC: 3999 2399 Mfg Misc Products Mfg Fabrctd Textile Pdts

Center Ossipee
Carroll County

(G-17802)
BEECH RIVER MILL
30 Route 16b (03814-6824)
PHONE..................................603 539-2636
Donald Ouellette, *Owner*
Beverly Ouellette, *Treasurer*
▼ **EMP:** 5
SALES (est): 690.7K **Privately Held**
WEB: www.beechrivermill.com
SIC: 2431 5211 Mfg Millwork Custom Shutters & Shutter Products

(G-17803)
EFFICIENCY PLUS
49 Leavitt Rd (03814-6326)
PHONE..................................603 539-8125
Arthur Butland, *Principal*
EMP: 3
SALES (est): 229.9K **Privately Held**
SIC: 3433 Mfg Heating Equipment-Non-electric

(G-17804)
MITEE-BITE PRODUCTS LLC
340 Route 16b (03814-6841)
P.O. Box 430 (03814-0430)
PHONE..................................603 539-4538
Richard Porter, *President*
EMP: 16
SQ FT: 10,000
SALES (est): 3.3MM **Privately Held**
SIC: 3429 Mfg Hardware

(G-17805)
OSSIPEE CHIPPING INC
400 Route 25 E (03814-6404)
PHONE..................................603 539-5097
Marco Carrier, *President*
EMP: 3
SALES (est): 5MM **Privately Held**
SIC: 2421 Sawmill/Planing Mill

(G-17806)
TOP KAYAKER GEO ODYSSEY LLC
1805 Route 16 (03814-6119)
PHONE..................................603 651-1036
Tom Holtey, *Managing Prtnr*
EMP: 5
SALES (est): 233.8K **Privately Held**
SIC: 2741 5961 Misc Publishing Ret Mail-Order House

Center Sandwich
Carroll County

(G-17807)
NORTHWIND TIMBER
Also Called: Northwind Wood
379 N Sandwich Rd (03227)
P.O. Box 423 (03227-0423)
PHONE..................................603 284-6123
Thomas Thiel, *Owner*
EMP: 4
SALES: 110K **Privately Held**
SIC: 3931 Mfg Musical Instruments

Center Tuftonboro
Carroll County

(G-17808)
LANCE WILLIAMS & SON LOGGING &
157 Ledge Hill Rd (03816-5353)
PHONE..................................603 569-3349
Lance Williams, *Principal*
EMP: 6
SALES (est): 549.4K **Privately Held**
SIC: 2411 Logging

Charlestown
Sullivan County

(G-17809)
AGCO CORPORATION
72 Hammond Acres (03603-4713)
PHONE..................................603 826-4664
Lisa Chamberlain, *Manager*
EMP: 3
SALES (corp-wide): 9.3B **Publicly Held**
WEB: www.agcocorp.com
SIC: 3523 Mfg Farm Machinery/Equipment
PA: Agco Corporation
4205 River Green Pkwy
Duluth GA 30096
770 813-9200

(G-17810)
AMERICAN MARINE PRODUCTS INC
73 Southwest St (03603-4499)
P.O. Box 1200 (03603-1200)
PHONE..................................954 782-1400
Richard Prull, *President*
EMP: 25

SQ FT: 30,000
SALES (est): 4.1MM **Privately Held**
WEB: www.americanmarine.com
SIC: 3231 3083 3732 Mfg Products-Purchased Glass Mfg Laminated Plastic Plate/Sheet Boatbuilding/Repairing

(G-17811)
BOMAR INC
Also Called: Pompanette
73 Southwest St (03603-4499)
P.O. Box 1200 (03603-1200)
PHONE..................................603 826-5781
Richard Truell, *President*
James Bailey, *CFO*
Paul Hazen, *Finance Mgr*
Ric Stpierre, *Director*
◆ **EMP:** 100
SALES (est): 7.9MM **Privately Held**
SIC: 3543 3471 3429 3369 Mfg Industrial Patterns Plating/Polishing Svcs Mfg Hardware Nonferrous Metal Foundry

(G-17812)
CORCORAN MACHINE CO
76 Weeks Rd (03603-5315)
PHONE..................................603 445-5258
Ken Corcoran, *Owner*
EMP: 3 **EST:** 1997
SALES: 100K **Privately Held**
SIC: 3599 Mfg Industrial Machinery

(G-17813)
DESIGN STANDARDS CORP
957 Claremont Rd (03603-4666)
P.O. Box 1620 (03603-1620)
PHONE..................................603 826-7744
Laurence Crainich, *President*
Bob Allman, *General Mgr*
Frank Lopez, *General Mgr*
Tom Carignan, *Engineer*
Brian Larose, *Engineer*
▲ **EMP:** 72
SALES (est): 17.8MM **Privately Held**
WEB: www.designstandards.com
SIC: 3469 3841 Mfg Metal Stampings Mfg Surgical/Medical Instruments

(G-17814)
GKN AEROSPACE NEW ENGLAND INC
1105 River Rd (03603-4176)
PHONE..................................603 542-5135
Daniel Meredith, *General Mgr*
Steve Neuser, *Branch Mgr*
EMP: 70
SALES (corp-wide): 11.3B **Privately Held**
SIC: 3724 3999 3599 Mfg Aircraft Engines/Parts Mfg Misc Products Mfg Industrial Machinery
HQ: Gkn Aerospace New England, Inc.
273 Adams St
Manchester CT 06042

(G-17815)
GREEN MOUNTAIN GLASS LLC
3 Depot St (03603)
P.O. Box 916 (03603-0916)
PHONE..................................603 826-4660
Mark Ledvina,
Kathryn King,
EMP: 8
SQ FT: 3,000
SALES (est): 763.8K **Privately Held**
WEB: www.greenmountainglass.com
SIC: 3211 Glass/Glazing Contractor

(G-17816)
JSP FABRICATION INC
49 Hammond Rd (03603-4763)
P.O. Box 382 (03603-0382)
PHONE..................................603 826-3868
Joseph Pickul, *President*
Robert J Pickul, *Vice Pres*
Patricia Pickul, *Treasurer*
EMP: 3
SALES: 220K **Privately Held**
SIC: 3444 Mfg Sheet Metalwork

(G-17817)
NEWPORT SAND & GRAVEL CO INC
Also Called: Carroll Concrete Co
368 Springfield Rd (03603-4742)
PHONE..................................603 826-4444
Colin Nelson, *Manager*
EMP: 8
SALES (corp-wide): 44MM **Privately Held**
SIC: 3273 Mfg Ready-Mixed Concrete
PA: Newport Sand & Gravel Co., Inc.
8 Reeds Mill Rd
Newport NH 03773
603 298-0199

(G-17818)
OPTICAL SOLUTIONS INC
Also Called: OSI
26 Bull Run (03603-4346)
PHONE..................................603 826-4411
Bradley J Piccirillo, *President*
Holly Piccirillo, *Treasurer*
EMP: 9
SQ FT: 8,960
SALES (est): 1.6MM **Privately Held**
WEB: www.opticalsolutionsinc.com
SIC: 3827 5049 Mfg Optical Instruments/Lenses Whol Professional Equipment

(G-17819)
POMPANETTE LLC (PA)
Also Called: Gray Enterprises
73 Southwest St (03603-4499)
P.O. Box 1200 (03603-1200)
PHONE..................................717 569-2300
Nicole Leonard, *Purch Agent*
Scott Gilbert, *Engineer*
Bob Touton, *Sales Mgr*
Devon Burbank, *Sales Staff*
Richard Truell, *Mng Member*
◆ **EMP:** 70
SQ FT: 100,000
SALES (est): 24.8MM **Privately Held**
WEB: www.pompanette.com
SIC: 3429 Mfg Hardware

(G-17820)
W H M INDUSTRIES INC
Hemlock Rd (03603)
P.O. Box 1468 (03603-1468)
PHONE..................................603 835-6015
Wilhelm H Meyerose, *President*
Betty Meyerose, *Vice Pres*
EMP: 6
SQ FT: 16,000
SALES (est): 784.5K **Privately Held**
SIC: 3544 Mfg Dies/Tools/Jigs/Fixtures

(G-17821)
WHELEN ENGINEERING CO
Also Called: Plastics Group of Whelen, The
99 Ceda Rd (03603-4597)
PHONE..................................860 526-9504
John Olson, *President*
George Whelen IV, *Exec VP*
Brian Boardman, *Plant Mgr*
Jim Blundon, *Engineer*
Jacob Chamberlain, *Engineer*
▲ **EMP:** 38
SQ FT: 32,000
SALES (est): 9MM
SALES (corp-wide): 175MM **Privately Held**
SIC: 3544 Mfg Dies/Tools/Jigs/Fixtures
PA: Whelen Engineering Company, Inc.
51 Winthrop Rd
Chester CT 06412
860 526-9504

Chatham
Carroll County

(G-17822)
LOG HOUSE DESIGNS INC (PA)
184 Butter Hill Rd (03813-5302)
PHONE..................................603 694-3373
D Kenyon King, *President*
Janice Purslow, *Vice Pres*
EMP: 32
SQ FT: 6,000
SALES (est): 2.5MM **Privately Held**
SIC: 2385 Mfg Waterproof Outerwear

Chester
Rockingham County

(G-17823)
CHESTER FOREST PRODUCTS INC
143 Halls Village Rd (03036-4214)
PHONE..................................603 887-4123
Richard D Lewis, *President*
Sue Lewis, *Treasurer*
EMP: 5
SALES (est): 410K **Privately Held**
SIC: 2421 Sawmill

(G-17824)
CUSTOM WOODWORKING BRENTWOOD
10 Edwards Mill Rd (03036-4154)
PHONE..................................603 887-6766
Paul Faxon, *President*
EMP: 6
SQ FT: 4,500
SALES: 530K **Privately Held**
SIC: 2434 Mfg Wood Kitchen Cabinets

(G-17825)
SALTWHISTLE TECHNOLOGY LLC
96 Lane Rd (03036-4048)
PHONE..................................603 887-3161
Dennis Glynn,
EMP: 3
SALES: 1,000K **Privately Held**
WEB: www.saltwhistletechnology.com
SIC: 3669 Mfg Communications Equipment

(G-17826)
STONE MACHINE CO INC
45 E Derry Rd (03036-4318)
P.O. Box 368 (03036-0368)
PHONE..................................603 887-4287
Frank Camillieri, *President*
Chris Stone, *Vice Pres*
Malcolm R Stone, *Treasurer*
EMP: 18
SQ FT: 8,400
SALES (est): 3.3MM **Privately Held**
WEB: www.stonemachine.com
SIC: 3599 7692 Mfg Industrial Machinery Welding Repair

(G-17827)
WATER WORKS SUPPLY CORP
220 Old Sandown Rd (03036-4122)
PHONE..................................781 322-1238
Jim Johnston, *Manager*
EMP: 5
SALES (corp-wide): 5.3MM **Privately Held**
WEB: www.wwscorp.com
SIC: 3599 5051 5074 Whol Gate Valves Tube & Iron Fittings Hydrants & Pipes & Machine Shop
PA: Water Works Supply Corp.
869 Eastern Ave
Malden MA
781 322-1238

Chesterfield
Cheshire County

(G-17828)
DUNN WOODWORKS
168 Friedsam Dr (03443-3807)
P.O. Box 182 (03443-0182)
PHONE..................................603 363-4180
Ray Dunn, *Owner*
EMP: 4
SALES: 200K **Privately Held**
SIC: 2431 Mfg Millwork

Chichester
Merrimack County

(G-17829)
INSPECTCHECK LLC
160 Dover Rd Unit 6 (03258-6537)
PHONE..................................603 223-0003
Mike Desmond, *Manager*
Stephen Exner,
Scott Precourt,
Scott A Precourt,
EMP: 3 **EST:** 2012
SALES (est): 167.4K **Privately Held**
SIC: 7372 Prepackaged Software Services

(G-17830)
SPEEDWAY LLC
135 Dover Rd (03258-6518)
PHONE..................................603 798-3154
EMP: 74 **Publicly Held**
SIC: 1311 Oil & Gas Refining
HQ: Speedway Llc
500 Speedway Dr
Enon OH 45323
937 864-3000

Chocorua
Carroll County

(G-17831)
HYDROCAD SFTWR SOLUTIONS LLC
216 Chocorua Mountain Hwy (03817-4402)
P.O. Box 477 (03817-0477)
PHONE..................................603 323-8666
Peter Smart, *CEO*
EMP: 4
SALES (est): 171.6K **Privately Held**
SIC: 7372 Prepackaged Software

(G-17832)
SWIFT RIVER WOOD PRODUCTS
358 White Mountain Hwy (03817-4600)
P.O. Box 500 (03817-0500)
PHONE..................................603 323-3317
Tim Brown, *Owner*
EMP: 4
SQ FT: 3,400
SALES: 190K **Privately Held**
SIC: 2511 2426 Mfg Wood Household Furniture Hardwood Dimension/Floor Mill

Claremont
Sullivan County

(G-17833)
3 D WELDING
18 Old Newport Rd (03743-4353)
P.O. Box 942 (03743-0942)
PHONE..................................603 543-0866
Richard Barrette, *Partner*
Steve Ward, *Partner*
EMP: 3
SALES (est): 150K **Privately Held**
SIC: 7692 Welding Repair

(G-17834)
AMERICAN BRUSH COMPANY INC
112 Industrial Blvd (03743-5123)
P.O. Box 1490 (03743-1490)
PHONE..................................603 542-9951
Allen Benson, *CEO*
Brent Swenson, *President*
Mark Saji, *CFO*
EMP: 14 **EST:** 1913
SQ FT: 116,000
SALES (est): 2.3MM **Privately Held**
SIC: 3991 Mfg Brooms/Brushes
HQ: Linzer Products Corp.
248 Wyandanch Ave
West Babylon NY 11704
631 253-3333

(G-17835)
APC PAPER COMPANY INC (PA)
Also Called: APC Paper Group
130 Sullivan St (03743-5210)
PHONE..................................603 542-0411
Francis M Tarantino, *President*
Paul F Mallet, *Vice Pres*
Dave Harris, *Opers Staff*
Brian Mallet, *Purchasing*
Tracy Spaulding, *Executive*
▲ **EMP:** 64
SQ FT: 83,000
SALES (est): 12.5MM **Privately Held**
WEB: www.apcpaper.com
SIC: 2621 Paper Mill

(G-17836)
BOURDONS INSTITUTIONAL SLS INC
85 Plains Rd (03743-4527)
PHONE..................................603 542-8709
Daniel Desmarais, *President*
Charles Aiken, *Treasurer*
▲ **EMP:** 23
SQ FT: 45,000
SALES: 3.8MM **Privately Held**
WEB: www.bourdons.com
SIC: 2515 Mfg Mattresses/Bedsprings

(G-17837)
BUTCHER BLOCK INC
Also Called: North Country Smokehouse
19 Syd Clarke Dr (03743-5608)
PHONE..................................800 258-4304
Aaron Corbett, *CEO*
Michael Satzow, *President*
Janean Butterfield, *Sales Staff*
Bonnie Johnson, *Office Mgr*
EMP: 20
SQ FT: 15,000
SALES (est): 4.7MM **Privately Held**
WEB: www.ncsmokehouse.com
SIC: 2013 5961 Mfg Prepared Meats Ret Mail-Order House

(G-17838)
CAFE REFUGEE INC
2 Stewart Ave (03743-5924)
PHONE..................................603 499-7415
EMP: 3 **EST:** 2012
SALES (est): 120K **Privately Held**
SIC: 2731 8249 8742 8748 Book-Publishing/Printing Vocational School Mgmt Consulting Svcs Business Consulting Svcs Computer Systems Design

(G-17839)
CANAM BRIDGES US INC
386 River Rd (03743-5671)
PHONE..................................603 542-5202
EMP: 20
SALES (est): 4.3MM
SALES (corp-wide): 177.9K **Privately Held**
SIC: 3441 5051 Structural Metal Fabrication Metals Service Center
HQ: Groupe Canam Inc
11505 1re Av Bureau 500
Saint-Georges QC G5Y 7
418 228-8031

(G-17840)
CARBON FELT INC
98 Plains Rd (03743-4525)
PHONE..................................603 542-0202
Zhonglei Jin, *President*
Brad Reagan, *Opers Mgr*
John Anders, *Office Mgr*
EMP: 10
SQ FT: 165,000
SALES: 40MM **Privately Held**
SIC: 2299 Mfg Textile Goods

(G-17841)
CASCADED PURCHASE HOLDINGS INC (PA)
Also Called: New Hampshire Industries
35 Connctcut Rver Bend Rd (03743)
PHONE..................................603 448-1090
John Batten, *President*
Timothy Fulham, *Director*
James Liberty, *Director*
▲ **EMP:** 115
SQ FT: 42,000
SALES (est): 33.7MM **Privately Held**
WEB: www.nhipulleys.com
SIC: 3429 Mfg Hardware

(G-17842)
CNC NORTH INC
16 Industrial Blvd (03743-5122)
P.O. Box 1395 (03743-1395)
PHONE..................................603 542-3361
Patrick Joseph Harrington, *President*
Gary Caravella, *Vice Pres*
Robert Hawkins, *Admin Sec*
▲ **EMP:** 9
SALES (est): 1.8MM **Privately Held**
SIC: 3541 Mfg Machine Tools-Cutting

(G-17843)
CONNECTCUT PRCSION CSTINGS INC
20 Wentworth Pl (03743-4403)
PHONE..................................603 542-3373
Ronald Morello Jr, *President*
Annette Morello, *Vice Pres*
EMP: 7
SQ FT: 8,500
SALES: 2.4MM **Privately Held**
WEB: www.ctprecisioncastings.com
SIC: 3363 Mfg Aluminum Die-Castings

(G-17844)
COSTA PRECISION MFG CORP (PA)
59 Plains Rd (03743-4526)
P.O. Box 990 (03743-0990)
PHONE..................................603 542-5229
Richard Zielinski, *President*
Richard M Zielinski, *Vice Pres*
Martin A Zielinski, *Treasurer*
EMP: 40
SQ FT: 32,000
SALES (est): 7.6MM **Privately Held**
WEB: www.costaprecision.com
SIC: 3599 3544 Mfg Industrial Machinery Mfg Dies/Tools/Jigs/Fixtures

(G-17845)
CROWN POINT CABINETRY CORP
462 River Rd (03743-5653)
P.O. Box 1560 (03743-1560)
PHONE..................................603 542-1273
Brian D Stowell, *President*
Rebecca C Stowell, *Vice Pres*
Rebecca Stowell, *Treasurer*
▼ **EMP:** 97
SQ FT: 100,000
SALES (est): 10.7MM **Privately Held**
SIC: 2434 Mfg Wood Kitchen Cabinets

(G-17846)
CROWN POINT REALTY CORP INC
153 Charlestown Rd (03743-5616)
P.O. Box 1560 (03743-1560)
PHONE..................................603 543-1208
Brian Stowell, *Principal*
Rebecca Stowell, *Treasurer*
Richard Dechaine, *Shareholder*
Patricia Paquette, *Shareholder*
Jeff Stowell, *Shareholder*
EMP: 96
SQ FT: 18,200
SALES (est): 8.2MM **Privately Held**
WEB: www.crownpointcabinetry.com
SIC: 2517 2434 Mfg Wood Tv/Radio Cabinets Mfg Wood Kitchen Cabinets

(G-17847)
DIVERSIFIED ENTERPRISES-ADT
101 Mulberry St Ste 2n (03743-2612)
PHONE..................................603 543-0038
Russell E Smith, *Owner*
EMP: 7
SQ FT: 3,500
SALES (est): 903.1K **Privately Held**
WEB: www.polysurfacesbookstore.com
SIC: 3826 2899 Mfg Analytical Instruments Mfg Chemical Preparations

(G-17848)
DOOLITTLES PRINT SERVE INC
84 Elm St (03743-4915)
PHONE..................................603 543-0700
Michael Stankevich, *President*
Debra Bond, *Vice Pres*
EMP: 3
SALES (est): 259.5K **Privately Held**
SIC: 2741 2759 7334 Misc Publishing Commercial Printing Photocopying Services

(G-17849)
EAGLE PUBLICATIONS INC
Also Called: Eagle Times
45 Crescent St (03743-2220)
PHONE..................................603 543-3100
Harry Hartman, *President*
Amanda Quimby, *Sales Staff*
EMP: 21
SQ FT: 22,500
SALES (est): 1.6MM **Privately Held**
SIC: 2711 2752 Newspapers-Publishing/Printing Lithographic Commercial Printing

(G-17850)
FLAT ROCK TILE AND STONE
181 Washington St (03743-5509)
PHONE..................................603 542-0678
Rick Michlaenoic, *Owner*
EMP: 3
SALES (est): 308.5K **Privately Held**
SIC: 1411 Dimension Stone Quarry

(G-17851)
FULLING MILL FLY FISHING LLC
329 River Rd (03743-5650)
PHONE..................................603 542-5480
Valerie Dodge, *Office Mgr*
EMP: 5
SALES (est): 532K **Privately Held**
WEB: www.fullingmill.com
SIC: 3949 Whol Sporting/Recreational Goods
HQ: Fulling Mill Limited
Unit 8 Fairlawn Enterprise Park Bonehurst Road
Redhill
129 377-8600

(G-17852)
GREEN MOUNTAIN METALS OF VT
2 Wentworth Pl (03743-4403)
PHONE..................................603 542-0005
Robert P Morin, *President*
Deborah C Morin, *Vice Pres*
EMP: 18
SQ FT: 12,000
SALES (est): 3MM **Privately Held**
SIC: 3451 Mfg Screw Machine Products

(G-17853)
LAKE MACHINE CO INC
12 Balcom Pl (03743-4400)
P.O. Box 1088 (03743-1088)
PHONE..................................603 542-8884
Edgar Grallert, *President*
▲ **EMP:** 10
SQ FT: 5,000
SALES (est): 1.7MM **Privately Held**
SIC: 3599 Mfg Industrial Machinery

(G-17854)
MATRIX AEROSPACE CORP
421 River Rd (03743-5652)
PHONE..................................603 542-0191
Ed Farris, *President*
Thomas A Hillebrand, *Vice Pres*
EMP: 65
SQ FT: 7,500
SALES (est): 20MM **Privately Held**
SIC: 3728 Mfg Aircraft Parts/Equipment

(G-17855)
MIKROS MANUFACTURING INC
24 Colonel Ashley Ln (03743-4424)
PHONE..................................603 690-2020
Javier A Valenzuela, *President*
▲ **EMP:** 42
SQ FT: 15,000
SALES (est): 6MM **Privately Held**
WEB: www.mikros.net
SIC: 3599 8731 Mfg Industrial Machinery Commercial Physical Research

(G-17856)
OLDENBURG GROUP INC
169 Pleasant St Ste 3 (03743-3190)
PHONE..................................603 542-9548
Ward Morrison, *Branch Mgr*
EMP: 143 **Privately Held**
SIC: 3532 Mfg Mining Machinery
PA: Oldenburg Group Inc
1648 Mcgrathiana Pkwy # 100
Lexington KY 40511

(G-17857)
OLDENBURG GROUP INCORPORATED
423 River Rd (03743-5652)
PHONE..................................603 542-9548
Paul Donovan, *Business Mgr*
Tom Dellosatto, *Branch Mgr*
EMP: 40
SALES (corp-wide): 112.1MM **Privately Held**
WEB: www.oldenburggroup.com
SIC: 3532 Mfg Drill & Blast Mining Equipment
PA: Oldenburg Group Incorporated
1717 W Civic Dr
Milwaukee WI 53209
414 354-6600

(G-17858)
PACLANTIC INC
Also Called: Paclantic Boot Company
91 Main St Ste C (03743-4841)
PHONE..................................603 542-8600
Stephen F Bonner, *President*
Stephen Moss, *Director*
▲ **EMP:** 6
SALES: 2MM **Privately Held**
SIC: 3089 3442 3021 Mfg Plastic Products Mfg Metal Doors/Sash/Trim Mfg Rubber/Plastic Footwear

(G-17859)
RALPH L OSGOOD INC
Also Called: Osgood Welding
144 Grissom Ln (03743-5635)
P.O. Box 63, Ascutney VT (05030-0063)
PHONE..................................603 543-1703
Kevin Osgood, *President*
Ralph Osgood, *President*
Debbie Osgood, *Corp Secy*
Janice Osgood, *Treasurer*
EMP: 18
SALES: 320K **Privately Held**
SIC: 7692 7538 Welding Repair Truck Engine Repair

(G-17860)
SCOTT G REED TRUCK SVCS INC
287 Washington St (03743-5516)
P.O. Box 989 (03743-0989)
PHONE..................................603 542-5032
Scott G Reed, *President*
EMP: 15
SQ FT: 4,800
SALES (est): 3.5MM **Privately Held**
WEB: www.sgreed.com
SIC: 3715 7538 5531 Mfg Truck Trailers Truck Engine Repair Services Ret Automotive Parts

(G-17861)
THERMACUT INC
153 Charlestown Rd (03743-5616)
PHONE..................................603 543-0585
Richard Mann, *President*
Kevin Bonneau, *President*
Jean Wilson, *Purchasing*
Keith Grenier, *Sales Mgr*
Jesse Minckler, *Regl Sales Mgr*
▲ **EMP:** 30
SQ FT: 50,000
SALES (est): 5.6MM
SALES (corp-wide): 322.5MM **Privately Held**
WEB: www.tatras.com
SIC: 3541 Mfg Machine Tools-Cutting
HQ: Thermacut Gmbh
Essener Str. 1
Wilnsdorf 57234
273 940-330

(G-17862)
TIMBERPEG EAST INC (PA)
61 Plains Rd (03743-4526)
PHONE..................................603 542-7762
Robert Britton, *President*
Jordan Silverstein, *Exec VP*

EMP: 25
SQ FT: 40,000
SALES (est): 4MM Privately Held
SIC: 2452 1521 Mfg Prefabricated Wood Buildings Single-Family House Construction

(G-17863)
VAN DORN AND CURTISS
178 Broad St (03743-2626)
P.O. Box 829 (03743-0829)
PHONE....603 542-3081
Thomas P Connair, *Principal*
EMP: 3
SALES (est): 193.8K Privately Held
SIC: 3411 Mfg Metal Cans

(G-17864)
WH SILVERSTEIN INC
Also Called: Timberpeg
61 Plains Rd (03743-4526)
PHONE....603 542-5418
William Silverstein, *President*
Teressa Prucha, *CFO*
John Harper, *Sales Mgr*
Jim Driesch, *Manager*
EMP: 40
SALES (est): 7.7MM Privately Held
SIC: 2452 Mfg Prefabricated Wood Buildings

(G-17865)
YANKEE BARN HOMES INC
61 Plains Rd (03743-4526)
PHONE....603 863-4545
Tony Hanslin, *President*
Sean Marsh, *Engineer*
Holly Ostrander, *Manager*
Kerri Terwilliger, *Business Dir*
Samantha Hosking, *Administration*
EMP: 60
SQ FT: 10,000
SALES (est): 9.3MM Privately Held
WEB: www.yankeebarnhomes.com
SIC: 2452 Mfg Prefabricated Wood Buildings

Colebrook
Coos County

(G-17866)
D & E SCREW MACHINE PDTS INC
34 Bill Bromage Dr (03576-2016)
P.O. Box 38 (03576-0038)
PHONE....508 658-7344
Leslie Ann Eldridge, *President*
EMP: 14
SALES: 950K Privately Held
SIC: 3451 Screw Machine Products

(G-17867)
DANS LOGGING & CONSTRUCTION
219 Reed Rd (03576-3815)
PHONE....603 237-4040
Daniel Outmette, *Owner*
EMP: 5
SALES (est): 383.9K Privately Held
SIC: 2411 Logging

(G-17868)
G M L OF NH INC
104 Titus Hill Rd (03576-3614)
P.O. Box 37 (03576-0037)
PHONE....603 237-5231
Michael Grandmaison, *President*
Christa Howe, *Admin Sec*
EMP: 6
SALES (est): 452.7K Privately Held
SIC: 2411 Logging

(G-17869)
G&S LOGGING
12 Lombard St (03576-3244)
PHONE....603 237-4929
Clyde Gray, *Principal*
EMP: 3
SALES (est): 215K Privately Held
SIC: 2411 Logging

(G-17870)
GILLES CHAMPAGNE
Edwards St (03576)
P.O. Box 10 (03576-0010)
PHONE....603 237-5272
Gilles Champagne, *Owner*
EMP: 7
SALES (est): 424K Privately Held
WEB: www.gilleschampagnephotography.com
SIC: 2411 Logging

(G-17871)
HEALTHCO INTERNATIONAL LLC
1 Wilderness Rd (03576-3331)
PHONE....603 255-3771
Thomas N Tillotson, *Manager*
▲ EMP: 15
SQ FT: 80,000
SALES (est): 1.8MM Privately Held
SIC: 3842 Glove Manufacturer

(G-17872)
J R LOGGING INC
41 Spring St (03576-2701)
PHONE....603 237-8010
Jack Riendeau, *President*
Gaston J Riendeau,
EMP: 5
SALES (est): 370K Privately Held
SIC: 2411 Logging

(G-17873)
LIEBL PRINTING CO
15 Forbes Hill Rd (03576-3801)
PHONE....603 237-8650
David West, *Owner*
Wendy Haywood-West, *Co-Owner*
EMP: 6
SQ FT: 5,000
SALES: 490K Privately Held
SIC: 2759 Lithographic Commercial Printing

(G-17874)
NEWS & SENTINEL INC
6 Bridge St (03576-3033)
P.O. Box 39 (03576-0039)
PHONE....603 237-5501
Karen Ladd, *President*
Melissa Shaw, *Director*
Butch Ladd, *Admin Sec*
EMP: 12 EST: 1957
SQ FT: 6,000
SALES (est): 890.3K Privately Held
WEB: www.colbsent.com
SIC: 2711 Newspapers-Publishing/Printing

(G-17875)
PREPCO INC
6 Sanel Dr (03576-3635)
P.O. Box 380 (03576-0380)
PHONE....603 237-4080
Peter Weiner, *President*
Peter J Weiner, *President*
Gary Bergeron, *QC Mgr*
Hilda Weiner, *Treasurer*
EMP: 9
SQ FT: 3,500
SALES: 2MM Privately Held
WEB: www.prepco.com
SIC: 3841 Mfg Surgical/Medical Instruments

(G-17876)
THE GREAT N WOODS ASSOC/ BLIND
23 Gould St (03576-3056)
PHONE....603 490-9877
Louis Leon-Guerrero, *President*
Rick Tillotson, *Admin Sec*
EMP: 9
SALES (est): 539K Privately Held
SIC: 3842 Mfg Surgical Appliances/Supplies

(G-17877)
W CRAIG WASHBURN
Also Called: C W Timber
45 Diamond Pond Rd (03576-3500)
PHONE....603 237-8403
W Craig Washburn, *Owner*
Lisa Washburn, *Bookkeeper*
EMP: 7 EST: 1988
SALES: 853K Privately Held
SIC: 2411 Logging

(G-17878)
WELOG INC
11 Skyline Dr (03576-3649)
PHONE....603 237-8277
Malcolm Washburn, *President*
Donna Washburn, *Admin Sec*
EMP: 12
SALES (est): 1.8MM Privately Held
WEB: www.hyha.com
SIC: 2411 1794 Logging & Excavating Contractor

Concord
Merrimack County

(G-17879)
ACARA HOLDINGS LLC
Also Called: Business Card Express
162 Pembroke Rd (03301-5767)
P.O. Box 287, Derry (03038-0287)
PHONE....603 434-3175
Ronald Hauff, *Owner*
Carl Lehmann, *Credit Staff*
EMP: 17
SQ FT: 11,000
SALES (est): 4.2MM Privately Held
WEB: www.bcecards.com
SIC: 2759 Commercial Printing

(G-17880)
ADVANTAGE PLASTIC PRODUCTS INC
38 Henniker St (03301-8528)
PHONE....603 227-9540
Joel Beaudette, *Principal*
▲ EMP: 28 EST: 2008
SALES (est): 5.5MM Privately Held
SIC: 3089 Mfg Plastic Products

(G-17881)
ADVANTAGE SIGNS INC
128 Hall St Ste C (03301-3451)
PHONE....603 224-7446
Russell Aubertin, *President*
Cheryl Dolin, *Vice Pres*
EMP: 5
SQ FT: 3,000
SALES (est): 668.1K Privately Held
WEB: www.advantagesigns.net
SIC: 3993 7532 Mfg Signs/Advertising Specialties Auto Body Repair/Painting

(G-17882)
ALL AMERICAN WALLS AND PAVERS
1 N Curtisville Rd (03301-5907)
PHONE....603 219-0822
Debbie A Kobzik, *Principal*
EMP: 4
SALES (est): 527.8K Privately Held
SIC: 3531 Mfg Construction Machinery

(G-17883)
ARGYLE ASSOCIATES INC
Also Called: New Hampshire Print Mail Svcs
30 Terrill Park Dr (03301-5257)
PHONE....603 226-4300
Kevin Boyarsky, *President*
EMP: 23
SALES (est): 2.4MM Privately Held
SIC: 2759 Commercial Printing

(G-17884)
BITTWARE INC (DH)
Also Called: Bittware Fpga Cmpt Systems
45 S Main St Ste L100 (03301-4800)
PHONE....603 226-0404
Jeffry Milrod, *President*
Craig Lund, *General Mgr*
Jeff Avitabile, *Mfg Staff*
Darren Taylor, *VP Sls/Mktg*
Chad Hamilton, *Development*
EMP: 31
SQ FT: 15,000
SALES (est): 9.9MM
SALES (corp-wide): 40.6B Privately Held
WEB: www.bittware.com
SIC: 3613 Manuafctures Switchgear/Switchboards
HQ: Molex, Llc
2222 Wellington Ct
Lisle IL 60532
630 969-4550

(G-17885)
BOYCE HIGHLANDS FURN CO INC
14 Whitney Rd (03301-1831)
PHONE....603 753-1042
John Lentine, *President*
Robert Lowe, *Vice Pres*
Brien Murphy, *Vice Pres*
EMP: 34 EST: 1977
SALES (est): 6.8MM Privately Held
WEB: www.boycehighlands.com
SIC: 2431 Mfg Millwork

(G-17886)
BRIANS MACHINE SHOP LLC
27 Industrial Park Dr # 1 (03301-8523)
PHONE....603 224-4333
Glenda Lemoine,
Brian Lemoine,
EMP: 7
SALES (est): 887.3K Privately Held
SIC: 3599 Mfg Industrial Machinery

(G-17887)
BRIDGE & BYRON INC
Also Called: Bridge Byron Printers
45 S State St (03301-3729)
PHONE....603 225-5221
Robert Rainbill, *President*
EMP: 8 EST: 1926
SQ FT: 5,000
SALES (est): 690K Privately Held
WEB: www.bridgeandbyron.com
SIC: 2752 Offset Printing

(G-17888)
CAPITAL ORTHTICS PRSTHTICS LLC (PA)
246 Pleasant St Ste 200 (03301-2548)
PHONE....603 226-0106
George Rogers, *Mng Member*
EMP: 9
SALES (est): 1.2MM Privately Held
SIC: 3842 Ret Misc Merchandise

(G-17889)
CAPITOL COPY INC
1 Eagle Sq Ste 15 (03301-4903)
PHONE....603 226-2679
Kenneth Kreis Sr, *President*
Jennifer Kreis, *Treasurer*
EMP: 6
SQ FT: 4,000
SALES (est): 855.2K Privately Held
WEB: www.capitolcopy.com
SIC: 2789 2759 2752 7334 Photocopying Service Bookbinding/Related Work Commercial Printing Lithographic Coml Print

(G-17890)
CAPITOL DISTRIBUTORS INC
114 Hall St (03301-3425)
P.O. Box 1148 (03302-1148)
PHONE....603 224-3348
John Shea, *CEO*
EMP: 4
SALES (est): 200.1K Privately Held
SIC: 2082 Mfg Malt Beverages

(G-17891)
CB VENTURES LLC
162 Pembroke Rd (03301-5767)
PHONE....603 434-3175
David K Fries Esq, *Administration*
Carl Lehmann,
EMP: 17
SALES (est): 1.3MM Privately Held
SIC: 2759 Commercial Printing

(G-17892)
CHANNELBIND INTERNATIONAL CORP (PA)
45 Centre St (03301-4205)
PHONE....864 579-7072
Thomas Hoffmeister, *President*
EMP: 23 EST: 1999
SALES (est): 945.8K Privately Held
SIC: 2789 Bookbinding/Related Work

GEOGRAPHIC

(G-17893)
CHARLES LEONARD STEEL SVCS LLC
Also Called: Clss
183 Pembroke Rd (03301-5768)
PHONE..................................603 225-0211
Charles B Fenderson, *Principal*
Leonard J Severini, *Principal*
Wendy Crowley, *Controller*
EMP: 13
SALES (est): 1.5MM **Privately Held**
SIC: 3441 Structural Metal Fabrication

(G-17894)
COMPUTYPE INC
Also Called: Identification Concepts
38 Locke Rd Ste 4 (03301-5422)
PHONE..................................603 225-5500
Don Gilbert, *Manager*
EMP: 15
SALES (corp-wide): 89MM **Privately Held**
WEB: www.computype.com
SIC: 2759 3565 2679 Commercial Printing Mfg Packaging Machinery Mfg Converted Paper Products
PA: Computype, Inc.
2285 County Road C W
Saint Paul MN 55113
651 633-0633

(G-17895)
CONCORD LITHO GROUP INC (PA)
92 Old Turnpike Rd (03301-7305)
PHONE..................................603 224-1202
Peter Cook, *CEO*
James D Cook, *Ch of Bd*
Walter Herrick, *Vice Pres*
Marlin Kaufman, *CFO*
Kristy Erickson, *Credit Mgr*
EMP: 110 **EST:** 1958
SQ FT: 210,000
SALES (est): 46.8MM **Privately Held**
WEB: www.concordlitho.com
SIC: 2752 Lithographic Commercial Printing

(G-17896)
CONCORD PHOTO ENGRAVING CO
12 Commercial St (03301-5031)
P.O. Box 1355 (03302-1355)
PHONE..................................603 225-3681
Peter Otto, *President*
Max Otto, *Vice Pres*
Shelley Otto, *VP Sales*
Tina Simpson, *Graphic Designe*
▲ **EMP:** 15 **EST:** 1932
SQ FT: 3,600
SALES (est): 1.9MM **Privately Held**
WEB: www.concordengraving.com
SIC: 2796 Mfg Photo Engraving Plates Flexographic Art & Printing Plates

(G-17897)
CRUCIAL CMPONENT MACHINING LLC
27 Industrial Park Dr # 5 (03301-8523)
PHONE..................................603 223-0012
Dan Labonville,
EMP: 3
SALES (est): 354.7K **Privately Held**
SIC: 3599 Mfg Industrial Machinery

(G-17898)
E CRANE COMPUTING INC
16 Centre St Ste 3 (03301-6321)
PHONE..................................603 226-4041
Phillip Wallingford, *President*
EMP: 3
SALES: 500K **Privately Held**
WEB: www.ecrane.com
SIC: 3695 Mfg Magnetic/Optical Recording Media

(G-17899)
ELECTROPAC CO INC
70 Pembroke Rd Ste 1 (03301-5753)
PHONE..................................603 622-3711
Raymond R Boissoneau, *President*
EMP: 42
SQ FT: 75,000
SALES (est): 7.4MM **Privately Held**
WEB: www.electropac.com
SIC: 3672 Mfg Printed Circuit Boards

(G-17900)
EXACOM INC
99 Airport Rd Ste 3 (03301-7301)
PHONE..................................603 228-0706
Helmut Koch, *President*
William Haskett, *Vice Pres*
Edward Huggins, *Vice Pres*
Jim Kirkland, *Sales Mgr*
Mark Woody, *Manager*
EMP: 20
SQ FT: 26,400
SALES (est): 5.5MM **Privately Held**
WEB: www.exacom.com
SIC: 3661 1731 Mfg Telephone/Telegraph Apparatus Electrical Contractor

(G-17901)
FABWORX SOLUTIONS INC
10 Ferry St Ste 136 (03301-5084)
PHONE..................................603 224-9679
Thomas Mulcahy, *Principal*
EMP: 4
SALES (est): 318K **Privately Held**
SIC: 3535 Mfg Conveyors/Equipment

(G-17902)
FLAG-WORKS OVER AMERICA LLC
6 N Main St (03301-4910)
PHONE..................................603 225-2530
Patrick Page,
EMP: 4
SQ FT: 4,000
SALES (est): 250K **Privately Held**
WEB: www.flag-works.com
SIC: 2399 5999 3446 Mfg & Ret Flagpoles

(G-17903)
GRANITE STATE CANDY SHOPPE LLC (PA)
13 Warren St (03301-4045)
PHONE..................................603 225-2591
Constantine Bart,
June Bart,
Michael Bart,
EMP: 15
SQ FT: 13,000
SALES (est): 2.4MM **Privately Held**
WEB: www.granitestatecandyshoppe.com
SIC: 2064 5145 5149 5441 Mfg Whol Ret And Mail Order Of Confectionery Specializing In Chocolate

(G-17904)
GRAPHIC PACKAGING INTL LLC
Also Called: Smurfit-Stone
80 Commercial St (03301-5031)
PHONE..................................603 230-5100
Jim Stanley, *Branch Mgr*
Dan Schoenenberger, *Manager*
EMP: 188 **Publicly Held**
SIC: 2631 2657 2652 Paperboard Mill Mfg Folding Paperboard Boxes Mfg Setup Paperboard Boxes
HQ: Graphic Packaging International, Llc
1500 Riveredge Pkwy # 100
Atlanta GA 30328

(G-17905)
GRAPHIC PACKAGING INTL LLC
80 Commercial St (03301-5031)
PHONE..................................603 230-5486
Jane Lucas, *Branch Mgr*
EMP: 21 **Publicly Held**
SIC: 2631 Whol Nondurable Goods
HQ: Graphic Packaging International, Llc
1500 Riveredge Pkwy # 100
Atlanta GA 30328

(G-17906)
GRAPHIC PACKAGING INTL LLC
Also Called: Laporte Division
80 Commercial St (03301-5031)
PHONE..................................603 230-5100
Mike Haney, *Branch Mgr*
EMP: 84 **Publicly Held**
SIC: 2631 2652 Paperboard Mill Mfg Setup Paperboard Boxes
HQ: Graphic Packaging International, Llc
1500 Riveredge Pkwy # 100
Atlanta GA 30328

(G-17907)
GRAPHIC PACKAGING INTL LLC
Also Called: Southfield Carton
80 Commercial St (03301-5031)
PHONE..................................603 224-2333
Rodney Alexander, *President*
EMP: 80
SQ FT: 6,000 **Publicly Held**
SIC: 2657 2631 Mfg Folding Paperboard Boxes Paperboard Mill
HQ: Graphic Packaging International, Llc
1500 Riveredge Pkwy # 100
Atlanta GA 30328

(G-17908)
HOPTO INC (PA)
6 Loudon Rd Ste 200 (03301-5321)
PHONE..................................800 472-7466
Jonathon Richard Skeels, *President*
EMP: 14
SQ FT: 2,527
SALES: 3.1MM **Publicly Held**
WEB: www.graphon.com
SIC: 7372 Prepackaged Software Services

(G-17909)
HOYT ELEC INSTR WORKS INC
23 Meter St (03303-1894)
PHONE..................................603 753-6321
Donald E Hall, *President*
Andrew Hoyt, *Vice Pres*
S Michael Trela, *Treasurer*
▲ **EMP:** 54 **EST:** 1904
SQ FT: 30,000
SALES (est): 11.4MM **Privately Held**
WEB: www.hoytmeter.com
SIC: 3825 3613 Mfg Electrical Measuring Instruments Mfg Switchgear/Switchboards

(G-17910)
IF I ONLY HAD A NICKEL
7 Jordan Ave (03301-2716)
PHONE..................................603 225-3972
Elizabeth A Pearson, *Owner*
EMP: 3
SALES (est): 172.4K **Privately Held**
SIC: 3356 Nonferrous Rolling/Drawing

(G-17911)
LAD WELDING & FABRICATION
33 Fisherville Rd (03303-4134)
PHONE..................................603 228-6617
William Bodah, *President*
EMP: 12
SQ FT: 11,000
SALES (est): 1.7MM **Privately Held**
WEB: www.ladwelding.com
SIC: 3444 1799 Mfg Sheet Metalwork Trade Contractor

(G-17912)
LAND AND SEA INC
25 Henniker St (03301-8528)
PHONE..................................603 226-3966
Robert M Bergeron, *President*
Virginia V Bergeron, *Admin Sec*
◆ **EMP:** 55 **EST:** 1981
SQ FT: 48,560
SALES (est): 12.1MM **Privately Held**
WEB: www.land-and-sea.com
SIC: 3559 Mfg Misc Industry Machinery

(G-17913)
MACHINE CRAFT COMPANY INC
114 Hall St (03301-3425)
P.O. Box 3665 (03302-3665)
PHONE..................................603 225-0958
Kim Jennison, *President*
Janette Jennison, *Treasurer*
▲ **EMP:** 15 **EST:** 1980
SQ FT: 10,000
SALES (est): 3.1MM **Privately Held**
SIC: 3599 Mfg Industrial Machinery

(G-17914)
MELLEN COMPANY INC (PA)
40 Chenell Dr (03301-8544)
PHONE..................................603 228-2929
Jonathan Y Mellen, *President*
Lisa Walter, *COO*
Lisa Yacopucci Walters, *Controller*
Larry Desorbo, *Sales Mgr*
Jonathan Mellen, *Branch Mgr*
EMP: 25
SQ FT: 20,000
SALES (est): 3.4MM **Privately Held**
WEB: www.mellencompany.com
SIC: 3567 Mfg Industrial Furnaces/Ovens

(G-17915)
NELSON ROBOTICS CORP
26 Monroe St (03301-3619)
PHONE..................................603 856-7421
Isaiah Nelson, *President*
EMP: 4
SALES (est): 271.6K **Privately Held**
SIC: 3823 Mfg Process Control Instruments

(G-17916)
NEW ENGLAND BRACE CO INC (PA)
2 Greenwood Ave (03301-3927)
PHONE..................................508 588-6060
Paul W Guimond, *President*
Karen M Acton, *Vice Pres*
EMP: 14 **EST:** 1945
SQ FT: 8,000
SALES (est): 5MM **Privately Held**
WEB: www.nebrace.com
SIC: 3842 Mfg Surgical Appliances/Supplies

(G-17917)
NEWSPAPERS NEW ENGLAND INC (PA)
Also Called: Valley News
1 Monitor Dr (03301-1834)
P.O. Box 1177 (03302-1177)
PHONE..................................603 224-5301
George W Wilson, *President*
Aaron Julien, *President*
Harry Green, *Prdtn Dir*
Amy Fifield, *Project Engr*
Scott Graff, *CFO*
▲ **EMP:** 5 **EST:** 1923
SQ FT: 75,000
SALES (est): 80.7MM **Privately Held**
WEB: www.cmonitor.com
SIC: 2711 Newspapers-Publishing/Printing

(G-17918)
NEWSPAPERS OF NEW HAMPSHIRE (HQ)
Also Called: Monadnock Ledger
1 Monitor Dr (03301-1834)
P.O. Box 1177 (03302-1177)
PHONE..................................603 224-5301
George W Wilson, *President*
Geoidi Wilson, *President*
EMP: 171
SQ FT: 75,000
SALES (est): 26.7MM
SALES (corp-wide): 80.7MM **Privately Held**
WEB: www.concordmonitor.com
SIC: 2711 Newspapers-Publishing/Printing
PA: Newspapers Of New England, Inc.
1 Monitor Dr
Concord NH 03301
603 224-5301

(G-17919)
NHRPA
172 Pembroke Rd (03301-5791)
PHONE..................................603 340-5583
Keith Hickey, *Principal*
EMP: 5
SALES (est): 120.3K **Privately Held**
SIC: 2531 Mfg Public Building Furniture

(G-17920)
OAKWOOD CABINETRY
26 Thayer Pond Rd (03301-7516)
PHONE..................................603 927-4713
Holly Edgecomb-Lamb, *Manager*
Donald Edgecomb, *Administration*
EMP: 4
SALES (est): 416.7K **Privately Held**
SIC: 2434 Mfg Wood Kitchen Cabinets

▲ = Import ▼=Export
◆ =Import/Export

(G-17921)
ONSITE DRUG TESTING NENG
2 Industrial Park Dr # 2 (03301-8520)
PHONE....603 226-3858
Kimberly Reid, *Owner*
EMP: 7
SALES: 700K **Privately Held**
SIC: 2899 Mfg Chemical Preparations

(G-17922)
PATSYS BUS SALES AND SERVICE
31 Hall St (03301-3415)
PHONE....603 226-2222
Joseph R Alosa, *President*
EMP: 10
SALES (est): 821.3K **Privately Held**
WEB: www.alosa.com
SIC: 3711 Mfg Motor Vehicle/Car Bodies

(G-17923)
PITCO FRIALATOR INC
10 Ferry St (03301-5022)
PHONE....603 225-6684
▲ **EMP:** 4 **EST:** 1981
SALES (est): 430K **Privately Held**
SIC: 3589 Mfg Service Industry Machinery

(G-17924)
PRAXAIR SURFACE TECH INC
146 Pembroke Rd Ste 1 (03301-5706)
PHONE....603 224-9585
Greg Tucker, *General Mgr*
Bernie St Onge, *Engineer*
Scott Fogg, *Corp Comm Staff*
EMP: 70 **Privately Held**
SIC: 3563 3542 Mfg Air/Gas Compressors Mfg Machine Tools-Forming
HQ: Praxair Surface Technologies, Inc.
1500 Polco St
Indianapolis IN 46222
317 240-2500

(G-17925)
QUALITY PRESS INC
126 Hall St Ste I (03301-3447)
PHONE....603 889-7211
Drake Daniels, *President*
EMP: 5
SALES (est): 410K **Privately Held**
WEB: www.qualitypressincnh.com
SIC: 2752 Lithographic Commercial Printing

(G-17926)
REGIONAL MFG SPECIALISTS INC
Also Called: Agile Magnetics
24 Chenell Dr (03301-8529)
PHONE....800 805-8991
James Atwood, *CEO*
Peter Hayden, *Opers Mgr*
Sharon Rock, *Cust Mgr*
▲ **EMP:** 80
SALES (est): 8.8MM
SALES (corp-wide): 791.5MM **Publicly Held**
WEB: www.regionalmfg.com
SIC: 3612 Mfg Transformers
PA: Standex International Corporation
11 Keewaydin Dr Ste 300
Salem NH 03079
603 893-9701

(G-17927)
SAY IT IN STITCHES INC
128 Hall St Ste B (03301-3440)
PHONE....603 224-6470
Ruth Coneys, *President*
Steve Coneys, *Vice Pres*
EMP: 9
SQ FT: 6,000
SALES (est): 776.6K **Privately Held**
WEB: www.stitchesnh.com
SIC: 2395 2396 5949 2759 Pleating/Stitching Svcs Mfg Auto/Apparel Trim Ret Sewing Supplies/Fbrc Commercial Printing

(G-17928)
SCRAPPIN SOUL SISTERS
3 Lawrence Street Ext (03301-5320)
PHONE....603 717-7136
Jackie Young, *Mng Member*
Michael Bourbeau,
EMP: 4
SALES (est): 363.3K **Privately Held**
SIC: 2782 Mfg Blankbooks/Binders

(G-17929)
SIGNS HAPPEN INC
Also Called: Sign-A-Rama
190 Manchester St Frnt (03301-5180)
PHONE....603 225-4081
Dave Hazen, *President*
Linda Stevens, *Treasurer*
EMP: 3
SQ FT: 1,500
SALES (est): 200K **Privately Held**
WEB: www.signshappen.com
SIC: 3993 Signsadv Specs

(G-17930)
SIMPLY FOOTWEAR UTAH LLC
Also Called: Simply Birkenstock
8 S Main St (03301-4809)
P.O. Box 130, New Hampton (03256-0130)
PHONE....603 715-2259
Charles Moulton,
Frank Clay,
EMP: 3 **EST:** 2011
SALES (est): 355.1K **Privately Held**
SIC: 3021 Mfg Rubber/Plastic Footwear

(G-17931)
STATE MILITARY RESERVATION
1 Minuteman Way (03301-5607)
PHONE....603 225-1230
William Dearborn, *Principal*
EMP: 3
SALES (est): 223.5K **Privately Held**
SIC: 2711 Newspapers-Publishing/Printing

(G-17932)
STOWE WOODWARD LLC
Also Called: Stowe Woodward Co-Div SW Ind
60 Old Turnpike Rd (03301-5242)
PHONE....603 224-6300
Brian Ridge, *Manager*
EMP: 25
SALES (corp-wide): 6.6B **Privately Held**
SIC: 3069 Mfg Rubber Roll Covering
HQ: Stowe Woodward Llc
8537 Six Forks Rd Ste 300
Raleigh NC 27615

(G-17933)
SWENSON GRANITE COMPANY LLC (DH)
369 N State St (03301-3233)
PHONE....603 225-4322
Robert Pope, *President*
Dennis Ames, *Store Mgr*
Bill Bonneau, *Store Mgr*
John Doherty, *Store Mgr*
Paul Dyer, *Store Mgr*
▲ **EMP:** 50 **EST:** 1883
SQ FT: 10,000
SALES (est): 54.6MM
SALES (corp-wide): 2.1MM **Privately Held**
WEB: www.swensongranite.com
SIC: 3281 1411 Manufactures Cut Stone/Products Dimension Stone Quarry
HQ: Polycor Inc
76 Rue Saint-Paul Bureau 100
Quebec QC G1K 3
418 692-4695

(G-17934)
TAFA INCORPORATED (DH)
Also Called: Praxair Surface
146 Pembroke Rd Ste 1 (03301-5735)
PHONE....603 224-9585
Tim Moser, *President*
▲ **EMP:** 49 **EST:** 1976
SQ FT: 35,625
SALES (est): 11.3MM **Privately Held**
SIC: 3563 3542 Mfg Air/Gas Compressors Mfg Machine Tools-Forming
HQ: Praxair, Inc.
10 Riverview Dr
Danbury CT 06810
203 837-2000

(G-17935)
TEDDYS TEES INC
9 Perley St (03301-3674)
PHONE....603 226-2762
Steven Story, *President*
Charlene Story, *Admin Sec*
EMP: 8
SQ FT: 17,000
SALES (est): 1.2MM **Privately Held**
SIC: 2752 Commercial Printing

(G-17936)
TOWN & COUNTRY REPROGRAPHICS
230 N Main St (03301-5051)
PHONE....603 225-9521
Dan Byron, *Owner*
EMP: 10
SALES (est): 1.1MM **Privately Held**
SIC: 2752 Lithographic Commercial Printing

(G-17937)
TRI-STATE IRON WORKS INC
24 Industrial Park Dr (03301-8512)
PHONE....603 228-0020
Kenneth McLaren, *President*
EMP: 30
SQ FT: 4,000
SALES (est): 6.7MM **Privately Held**
WEB: www.tristateiron.com
SIC: 3441 Structural Metal Fabrication

(G-17938)
VENTRICOM WIRELESS TECH
58 Mandevilla Ln (03301-2414)
PHONE....603 226-0025
Bob Hildreth, *Owner*
EMP: 5 **EST:** 1994
SALES (est): 519.2K **Privately Held**
SIC: 2752 Lithographic Commercial Printing

(G-17939)
WALNUT BOTTOM INC
Also Called: Concord Print Sltions Copy Svc
30 Terrill Park Dr (03301-5257)
PHONE....603 224-6606
Linda Jaggard, *President*
EMP: 3
SALES (est): 240K **Privately Held**
WEB: www.printingnh.com
SIC: 2752 2789 Lithographic Commercial Printing Bookbinding/Related Work

(G-17940)
WHITE MOUNTAIN IMAGING
46 Chenell Dr (03301-8538)
PHONE....603 228-2630
Rick Mc Donald, *Manager*
EMP: 12
SALES (corp-wide): 28MM **Privately Held**
WEB: www.wmi-t2.com
SIC: 3559 5047 Mfg Misc Industry Machinery Whol Medical/Hospital Equipment
PA: White Mountain Imaging
1617 Battle St
Webster NH 03303
603 648-2124

Contoocook
Merrimack County

(G-17941)
BRYANT GROUP INC
Also Called: Military Art China
28 Riverside Dr (03229-3147)
P.O. Box 808 (03229-0808)
PHONE....603 746-1166
Matthew Bryant, *President*
▲ **EMP:** 12
SQ FT: 8,000
SALES (est): 890K **Privately Held**
WEB: www.milart.com
SIC: 3999 Mfg Misc Products

(G-17942)
CHUCK ROSE INC
100 Chase Farm Rd (03229-2900)
PHONE....603 746-2311
Charles Rose, *Principal*
EMP: 14
SALES (est): 1.7MM **Privately Held**
SIC: 2411 Logging

(G-17943)
CONCORD MONITOR
44 S Shore Dr (03229-3214)
PHONE....603 224-5301
Elaine P Loft, *Principal*
EMP: 3
SALES (est): 99.2K **Privately Held**
SIC: 2711 Newspapers-Publishing/Printing

(G-17944)
EXCALIBUR SHELVING SYSTEMS INC
292 Burnham Intervale Rd (03229-3300)
P.O. Box 498 (03229-0498)
PHONE....603 746-6200
John Herrick, *President*
Theresa Werring, *Manager*
Philip Taub, *Admin Sec*
▼ **EMP:** 43 **EST:** 1982
SQ FT: 50,000
SALES (est): 8.7MM **Privately Held**
SIC: 2541 Mfg Wood Partitions/Fixtures

(G-17945)
HERRICK MILL WORK INC
290 Burnham Intervale Rd (03229-3300)
P.O. Box 495 (03229-0495)
PHONE....603 746-5092
John L Herrick, *President*
Joanne Herrick, *Treasurer*
Don Gartrell, *Admin Sec*
EMP: 39
SQ FT: 25,000
SALES (est): 3.1MM **Privately Held**
SIC: 2441 2541 2499 2435 Mfg Wood Boxes/Shooks Mfg Wood Partitions/Fixt Mfg Wood Products Mfg Hrdwd Veneer/Plywood Mfg Millwork

(G-17946)
MARKLIN CANDLE DESIGN LLC
28 Riverside Dr (03229-3147)
P.O. Box 182 (03229-0182)
PHONE....603 746-2211
Christine Marklin, *Vice Pres*
Martin G Marklin, *Mng Member*
EMP: 15
SALES (est): 2.1MM **Privately Held**
WEB: www.marklincandle.com
SIC: 3999 Manufactures Candles

(G-17947)
PROTOTEK SHTMTAL FBRCATION LLC (PA)
Also Called: Prototek Manufacturing
244 Burnham Intervale Rd (03229-3300)
PHONE....603 746-2001
William Gress, *CEO*
Brian Francoeur, *President*
Bob Carberry, *Purch Mgr*
Pj Swett, *Engineer*
Chad Magoon, *Sales Mgr*
◆ **EMP:** 61 **EST:** 1987
SQ FT: 40,000
SALES (est): 13.3MM **Privately Held**
WEB: www.prototek.com
SIC: 3444 Mfg Sheet Metalwork

(G-17948)
SKYTRANS MFG LLC
106 Burnham Intervale Rd (03229)
P.O. Box 216 (03229-0216)
PHONE....802 230-7783
Jeremy L Pendleton, *Mng Member*
Daniel E Pendleton, *Mng Member*
EMP: 17
SALES (est): 2.7MM **Privately Held**
SIC: 3599 4119 Mfg Industrial Machinery Local Passenger Transportation

(G-17949)
STANDARD MACHINE & ARMS
35 Tyler Rd (03229-3093)
PHONE....603 746-3562
Steven T Micucci, *Owner*
EMP: 3 **EST:** 1986
SALES (est): 170K **Privately Held**
WEB: www.archery1.com
SIC: 3599 3444 Mfg Industrial Machinery Mfg Sheet Metalwork

GEOGRAPHIC

Conway
Carroll County

(G-17950)
BARN DOOR SCREEN PRINTERS
56 Pleasant St (03818-6151)
PHONE..................................603 447-5369
David C Peterson, *Administration*
EMP: 7
SALES (est): 660.9K **Privately Held**
SIC: 2752 Lithographic Commercial Printing

(G-17951)
CHUCK ROAST EQUIPMENT INC (PA)
90 Odell Hill Rd (03818-4401)
P.O. Box 1450 (03818-1450)
PHONE..................................603 447-5492
Charles Henderson, *President*
Lloyd Henderson, *Admin Sec*
EMP: 25
SQ FT: 16,000
SALES (est): 3.2MM **Privately Held**
WEB: www.chuckroast.com
SIC: 2329 2339 5621 5611 Mfg Mens/Boys Clothing Mfg Women/Miss Outerwear Ret Women's Clothing Ret Men's/Boy's Clothing Ret Childs/Infants Wear

(G-17952)
GEMINI SIGNS & DESIGN LTD
226 W Main St (03818-6141)
P.O. Box 1451 (03818-1451)
PHONE..................................603 447-3336
Jonathan Goodwin, *President*
Kathy Baker, *Bookkeeper*
EMP: 4
SQ FT: 4,200
SALES: 300K **Privately Held**
WEB: www.geminisigns.net
SIC: 2499 3993 Mfg Wood Products Mfg Signs/Advertising Specialties

(G-17953)
GREEN MTN RIFLE BARREL CO INC
Also Called: Green Mountain Custom Barrels
153 W Main St (03818-6143)
P.O. Box 2670 (03818-2670)
PHONE..................................603 447-1095
Holly Nordholm Meanley, *President*
Jeffrey Whiting, *Engineer*
▼ **EMP:** 10
SALES (est): 2.4MM
SALES (corp-wide): 94.2MM **Privately Held**
WEB: www.gmriflebarrel.com
SIC: 3484 3482 Mfg Small Arms Mfg Small Arms Ammunition
HQ: Modern Muzzleloading, Inc.
213 Dennis St
Athens TN 37303
866 518-4181

(G-17954)
JOHN J MARR
Also Called: Town & Country
Main St Rr 113 (03818)
P.O. Box 400, Center Conway (03813-0400)
PHONE..................................603 939-2698
John J Marr, *Owner*
EMP: 18
SQ FT: 22,000
SALES (est): 2MM **Privately Held**
SIC: 3443 2431 3648 5719 Mfg Fabricated Plate Work Mfg Millwork Mfg Lighting Equipment Ret Misc Homefurnishings

(G-17955)
MARGARET QUINT LOGGING
161 Jack Frost Ln (03818-6217)
PHONE..................................603 447-3957
P Quint, *Principal*
EMP: 3
SALES (est): 198.5K **Privately Held**
SIC: 2411 Logging

(G-17956)
NEW ENGLAND EMBROIDERY COMPANY
Rr 16 (03818)
P.O. Box 332 (03818-0332)
PHONE..................................603 447-3878
Robert E Dunham, *President*
Ann Larson, *Principal*
EMP: 5
SQ FT: 4,000
SALES (est): 431K **Privately Held**
SIC: 2395 Pleating/Stitching Services

(G-17957)
PETER MARQUES
Also Called: Tentsmith
87 Main St (03818-6166)
P.O. Box 1748 (03818-1748)
PHONE..................................603 447-2344
Peter Marques, *Owner*
EMP: 7
SQ FT: 3,000
SALES (est): 633.3K **Privately Held**
WEB: www.tentsmiths.com
SIC: 2394 Mfg Canvas/Related Products

(G-17958)
TEE ENTERPRISES
Rr 16 (03818)
P.O. Box 1700 (03818-1700)
PHONE..................................603 447-5662
Carl Thibodeau, *Owner*
EMP: 19
SQ FT: 10,000
SALES (est): 2.3MM **Privately Held**
WEB: www.teeenterprises.com
SIC: 3599 Machine Shop

(G-17959)
TMC BOOKS LLC
731 Tasker Hill Rd (03818-5220)
PHONE..................................603 447-5589
Peter Lewis, *Partner*
Frank Hubbell, *Partner*
Tbr Walsh, *Partner*
EMP: 3
SALES (est): 149.5K **Privately Held**
SIC: 2731 Books-Publishing/Printing

Cornish
Sullivan County

(G-17960)
FRED C WELD INC
Also Called: Fred C Weld Logging
102 Root Hill Rd (03745-4711)
PHONE..................................603 675-6147
Fred C Weld, *President*
Susan Weld, *Vice Pres*
EMP: 3
SALES: 500K **Privately Held**
SIC: 2411 Logging Contractor

(G-17961)
J R LIGGETT LTD INC
973 Nh Route 12a (03745-4115)
PHONE..................................603 675-2055
James R Liggett, *President*
Diane E Miller, *Treasurer*
▲ **EMP:** 7
SQ FT: 2,500
SALES (est): 570.7K **Privately Held**
WEB: www.jrliggett.com
SIC: 2841 2844 Mfg Soap/Other Detergents Mfg Toilet Preparations

(G-17962)
LARRY DINGEE
Also Called: Dingee Machine Co
195 Nh Route 120 (03745-4316)
P.O. Box 162, Cornish Flat (03746-0162)
PHONE..................................603 542-9682
Larry Dingee, *Owner*
EMP: 7
SQ FT: 7,000
SALES: 1MM **Privately Held**
SIC: 3711 7532 3714 3713 Mfg Motor Vehicle Bodies Auto Body Repair/Paint Mfg Motor Vehicle Parts Mfg Truck/Bus Bodies

Danbury
Merrimack County

(G-17963)
DAVCO
1397 Us Route 4 (03230-4529)
PHONE..................................603 768-3517
Richard Davis, *Principal*
EMP: 4 **EST:** 2010
SALES (est): 362.3K **Privately Held**
SIC: 3699 Mfg Electrical Equipment/Supplies

(G-17964)
HANNAN TECHNOLOGIES LLC
208 Dean Rd (03230)
P.O. Box 69 (03230-0069)
PHONE..................................603 768-5656
Wayne A Cote,
EMP: 5
SALES (est): 161K **Privately Held**
SIC: 3999 Mfg Misc Products

(G-17965)
SMITH RIVER SAND & GRAVEL LLC
289 Ragged Mountain Rd (03230-4324)
PHONE..................................603 768-3330
James D Phelps, *Principal*
EMP: 3
SALES (est): 136.5K **Privately Held**
SIC: 1442 Construction Sand/Gravel

(G-17966)
WALLACE BUILDING PRODUCTS CORP
40 Wallace Ln (03230-4437)
P.O. Box 194 (03230-0194)
PHONE..................................603 768-5402
John D Tauriello, *President*
James Doiron, *Manager*
EMP: 25
SQ FT: 20,000
SALES (est): 8.3MM **Privately Held**
WEB: www.williamcwallaceprefab.com
SIC: 2452 Mfg Prefabricated Wood Buildings

Danville
Rockingham County

(G-17967)
BROWN DOG SOFTWARE INC
24 Colby Rd (03819-5103)
P.O. Box 147, Hampton (03843-0147)
PHONE..................................603 382-2713
Robert Chase II, *Principal*
EMP: 5
SALES (est): 395.9K **Privately Held**
SIC: 7372 Prepackaged Software Services

(G-17968)
EYEPVIDEO SYSTEMS LLC
25 Olde Rd (03819-3225)
PHONE..................................603 382-2547
Brendan Daly,
EMP: 4
SALES (est): 761.4K **Privately Held**
WEB: www.eyepvideo.com
SIC: 3674 Integrator Dealer And Manufacturer Network Video Systems

(G-17969)
POST WOODWORKING INC
Also Called: Storage With Style
163 Kingston Rd (03819-3230)
PHONE..................................603 382-4951
Mark Post, *President*
Paul D P Riley Jr, *Vice Pres*
Phil Curtin, *Admin Sec*
EMP: 25
SQ FT: 4,500
SALES (est): 6.3MM **Privately Held**
WEB: www.postwoodworking.com
SIC: 2452 Mfg Prefabricated Wood Buildings

Deerfield
Rockingham County

(G-17970)
MICRO METAL COMPONENTS INC
19 Brown Rd (03037-1524)
PHONE..................................603 463-5986
Cindy Webb, *President*
Forrest Webb, *Chairman*
Janet R Webb, *Treasurer*
EMP: 6
SQ FT: 2,000
SALES (est): 720.6K **Privately Held**
SIC: 3679 Mfg Receiving Antennas

Derry
Rockingham County

(G-17971)
APRIOMED INC
45 S Main St Unit 2 (03038-2144)
PHONE..................................603 421-0875
Joseph F Cerami III, *President*
Renee Collier, *Sales Staff*
EMP: 3
SALES (est): 390.6K **Privately Held**
SIC: 3841 Mfg Surgical/Medical Instruments

(G-17972)
BIOSAN LABORATORIES INC
Also Called: Megafood
8 Bowers Rd (03038-4279)
P.O. Box 5244, Manchester (03108-5244)
PHONE..................................603 437-0861
Carl Jackson, *President*
Richard Lafond, *Vice Pres*
Kaitlin Sullivan, *Purch Agent*
Elsa Pombeiro, *CFO*
Laura Goldberg, *VP Sales*
EMP: 42
SALES (est): 8.6MM **Privately Held**
WEB: www.biosan.net
SIC: 2834 Mfg Pharmaceutical Preparations

(G-17973)
BOXFORD DESIGNS LLC
55 Walnut Hill Rd (03038-5021)
PHONE..................................603 216-2399
Harry Zoglio,
EMP: 4
SALES (est): 282.9K **Privately Held**
SIC: 3674 Mfg Semiconductors/Related Devices

(G-17974)
C SOMMER SOFTWARE LLC
11 Symphony Ln (03038-5307)
PHONE..................................603 432-6225
Charles Sommer, *Principal*
EMP: 3
SALES (est): 123.4K **Privately Held**
SIC: 7372 Prepackaged Software Services

(G-17975)
CABINET MASTERS INC
4 Beaver Lake Rd (03038-5116)
PHONE..................................603 425-6428
Donald Jorgensen, *President*
Rod Daily, *Vice Pres*
EMP: 3
SALES (est): 329.6K **Privately Held**
SIC: 2434 1521 Mfg Wood Kitchen Cabinets Single-Family House Construction

(G-17976)
CIRCUIT EXPRESS INC
16 Westgate Rd (03038-3736)
PHONE..................................603 537-9392
Antonio Silva, *President*
EMP: 3
SALES (est): 174.9K **Privately Held**
SIC: 3672 Mfg Printed Circuit Boards

(G-17977)
DATAPAQ INC
3 Corporate Park Dr # 1 (03038-2281)
PHONE..................................603 537-2680

Michael E White, *President*
Susan Walsh, *Admin Sec*
EMP: 25
SQ FT: 8,000
SALES (est): 2.9MM
SALES (corp-wide): 6.4B **Publicly Held**
WEB: www.datapaq.com
SIC: 3823 5049 Mfg Process Control Instruments Whol Professional Equipment
HQ: Fluke Electronics Corporation
6920 Seaway Blvd
Everett WA 98203
425 347-6100

(G-17978)
EAGLE-TRIBUNE PUBLISHING CO
Also Called: Derry News
46 W Broadway (03038-2329)
PHONE..................................603 437-7000
Cathy Dicampo, *Branch Mgr*
EMP: 71 **Privately Held**
SIC: 2711 Newspapers-Publishing/Printing
HQ: Eagle-Tribune Publishing Company
100 Turnpike St
North Andover MA 01845
978 946-2000

(G-17979)
FIREYE INC (DH)
3 Manchester Rd (03038-3008)
PHONE..................................603 432-4100
Gerald Slocum, *President*
John Devine, *Vice Pres*
Sarah B Fjelstul, *Treasurer*
Laura L Martinage, *Treasurer*
Diane Andrews, *Admin Sec*
▲ **EMP:** 190
SQ FT: 80,000
SALES (est): 44.8MM
SALES (corp-wide): 66.5B **Publicly Held**
WEB: www.fireye.com
SIC: 3669 3842 3812 Mfg Communications Equipment Mfg Surgical Appliances/Supplies Mfg Search/Navigation Equipment
HQ: Kidde Fire Protection Inc.
350 E Union St
West Chester PA 19382
610 363-1400

(G-17980)
GOOD HUES CUSTOM POWDR COATING
227 Rockingham Rd (03038-4519)
PHONE..................................603 434-8034
Thomas Vallante, *Owner*
EMP: 4
SALES (est): 271.4K **Privately Held**
SIC: 3479 Coating/Engraving Service

(G-17981)
HAWK QUALITY PRODUCTS INC
125 Rockingham Rd (03038-4153)
P.O. Box 885 (03038-0885)
PHONE..................................603 432-3319
Jeff Hawkes, *President*
Randy Hawkes, *Vice Pres*
Betty Hawkes, *Treasurer*
EMP: 15
SQ FT: 10,000
SALES: 1.5MM **Privately Held**
WEB: www.hawkquality.com
SIC: 3599 Machine Shop Jobbing & Repair

(G-17982)
HEIDI JOS LLC
55 Crystal Ave (03038-1702)
PHONE..................................603 774-5375
Michael Tanner, *Principal*
EMP: 3
SALES (est): 124.5K **Privately Held**
SIC: 2013 Mfg Prepared Meats

(G-17983)
INTELITEK INC
18 Tsienneto Rd (03038-1505)
PHONE..................................800 221-2763
Brenda Quinn, *President*
Yael Amitay, *Vice Pres*
Ronen Kalif, *VP Opers*
Ziv Shpringer, *CFO*
Deborah Connors, *Office Mgr*
▲ **EMP:** 40
SQ FT: 30,000
SALES (est): 8.3MM
SALES (corp-wide): 4.3MM **Privately Held**
WEB: www.intelitek.com
SIC: 3451 Mfg Screw Machine Products
PA: Robogroup T.E.K. Ltd
13 Hamelacha
Rosh Haayin 48091
390 041-11

(G-17984)
KARL GSCHWIND MACHINEWORKS LLC
6 Tinkham Ave (03038-1408)
PHONE..................................603 434-4211
Karl Gschwind, *President*
Robert Allen, *Mng Member*
EMP: 12 **EST:** 1964
SQ FT: 5,000
SALES (est): 1.9MM **Privately Held**
SIC: 3599 Mfg Industrial Machinery

(G-17985)
KINDELAN WOODWORKING
179 Rockingham Rd (03038-4518)
PHONE..................................603 434-3253
Robert Kersey, *Owner*
EMP: 3
SQ FT: 5,000
SALES (est): 256.2K **Privately Held**
WEB: www.kindelanwoodworking.com
SIC: 2431 Mfg Millwork

(G-17986)
LEFT-TEES DESIGNS BAYOU LLC
15 W Broadway Ste 2 (03038-2368)
P.O. Box 1055, Merrimack (03054-1055)
PHONE..................................603 437-6630
William J Pomer,
William Pomer,
EMP: 13
SQ FT: 4,500
SALES: 450K **Privately Held**
WEB: www.left-tees.com
SIC: 2759 Commercial Printing

(G-17987)
LIQUID BLUE INC
6 Linlew Dr (03038-3002)
PHONE..................................401 333-6200
Paul Roidoulis, *President*
▲ **EMP:** 100
SALES: 13.4MM **Privately Held**
WEB: www.liquidblue.com
SIC: 2261 2396 Cotton Finishing Plant Mfg Auto/Apparel Trimming

(G-17988)
MARTEL ELECTRONICS CORP
3 Corporate Park Dr # 1 (03038-2281)
PHONE..................................603 434-6033
David Devries, *CEO*
Thomas C Fatur, *President*
David M Devries, *Treasurer*
William Modlin, *VP Sales*
James F McFaden, *Admin Sec*
▲ **EMP:** 29
SQ FT: 10,000
SALES (est): 6.2MM
SALES (corp-wide): 6.4B **Publicly Held**
WEB: www.martelcorp.com
SIC: 3825 5084 Mfg Electrical Measuring Instruments Whol Industrial Equipment
HQ: Fluke Corporation
6920 Seaway Blvd
Everett WA 98203
425 347 6100

(G-17989)
NAKED NUTRIENT BY DESEO LLC
55 Crystal Ave Unit 7 (03038-1702)
PHONE..................................646 809-4943
Amanda Sweetman,
EMP: 3
SALES (est): 91.3K **Privately Held**
SIC: 2023 Mfg Dry/Evaporated Dairy Products

(G-17990)
NEL-TECH LABS INCORPORATED
Also Called: N T L
4 Ash Street Ext (03038-2274)
P.O. Box 1631 (03038-6631)
PHONE..................................603 425-1096
Scott Stapleford, *President*
Virginia Stapleford, *Corp Secy*
Gary Stapleford, *Director*
Linda Lukens, *Admin Sec*
EMP: 18
SQ FT: 12,000
SALES (est): 3.6MM **Privately Held**
WEB: www.nel-techlabs.com
SIC: 3669 3661 3651 3577 Mfg Communications Equip Mfg Telephone/Graph Eqip Mfg Home Audio/Video Eqp Mfg Computer Peripherals

(G-17991)
NEURAXIS LLC
Also Called: Thompson SCI
16 Route 111 Ste 2 (03038-4142)
PHONE..................................603 912-5306
John Sullivan,
Michael Drnek,
EMP: 4 **EST:** 2012
SALES (est): 322.6K **Privately Held**
SIC: 3841 Mfg Surgical/Medical Instruments

(G-17992)
NUTFIELD CABINETRY LLC
8 Shelly Dr (03038-5736)
PHONE..................................603 498-6252
EMP: 3 **EST:** 2016
SALES (est): 133.3K **Privately Held**
SIC: 2434 Mfg Wood Kitchen Cabinets

(G-17993)
PICA MFG SOLUTIONS INC
4 Ash Street Ext Unit 3 (03038-2274)
PHONE..................................603 845-3258
Rich Shevelow, *President*
Mark Pare, *COO*
Steven Goldberg, *CFO*
▲ **EMP:** 35
SQ FT: 7,000
SALES (est): 36.4MM **Privately Held**
WEB: www.picasales.com
SIC: 3672 3559 Mfg Printed Circuit Boards Mfg Misc Industry Machinery

(G-17994)
PRECISION TOOL & MOLDING LLC
Also Called: Precision Tool and Die
22 Manchester Rd Unit 10 (03038-3032)
PHONE..................................603 437-6685
Michael Driscoll, *Owner*
▼ **EMP:** 51
SALES: 10MM
SALES (corp-wide): 186.3MM **Privately Held**
WEB: www.precisiontoolanddie.net
SIC: 3089 Mfg Plastic Products
HQ: Ctp Carrera, Inc.
600 Depot St
Latrobe PA 15650
724 539-6995

(G-17995)
PURE ELEMENT
8 Birch St (03038-2171)
PHONE..................................603 235-4373
Cindy Osborn, *Principal*
EMP: 4 **EST:** 2007
SALES (est): 272.9K **Privately Held**
SIC: 2819 Mfg Industrial Inorganic Chemicals

(G-17996)
SPEEDWAY LLC
50 Birch St (03038-2715)
PHONE..................................603 434-9702
David A Hatch, *Branch Mgr*
EMP: 15 **Publicly Held**
WEB: www.hess.com
SIC: 1311 Exploration & Production Of Crude Oil & Natural Gas
HQ: Speedway Llc
500 Speedway Dr
Enon OH 45323
937 864-3000

(G-17997)
SPIRAL AIR MANUFACTURING INC
1 B St (03038-1723)
P.O. Box 395, Hudson (03051-0395)
PHONE..................................603 624-6647
David Quintiliani, *President*
EMP: 9
SQ FT: 17,000
SALES (est): 1.3MM **Privately Held**
WEB: www.spiral-air.com
SIC: 3444 Mfg Sheet Metalwork

(G-17998)
STENTECH INC (HQ)
22 Manchester Rd Unit 8b (03038-3066)
PHONE..................................603 505-4470
Sibthain Mirza Akbar, *President*
▲ **EMP:** 13
SALES (est): 3.8MM
SALES (corp-wide): 11.2MM **Privately Held**
SIC: 2675 Mfg Solder Paste Tencils
PA: 1359470 Ontario Inc.
138 Anderson Ave Unit 6
Markham ON L6E 1
905 472-7773

(G-17999)
STENTECH PHOTO STENCIL LLC
22 Manchester Rd Unit 8b (03038-3066)
PHONE..................................719 287-7934
Sip Akbar, *President*
Kim Nanney, *CFO*
EMP: 15
SALES: 4MM **Privately Held**
SIC: 2675 Mfg Die-Cut Paper/Paperboard

(G-18000)
TOTAL PACKAGING CONCEPTS INC
115 Franklin Street Ext (03038-1455)
P.O. Box 368, Atkinson (03811-0368)
PHONE..................................603 432-4651
Milton C Dadoly, *President*
Joyce E Dadoly, *Admin Sec*
EMP: 15
SQ FT: 32,000
SALES (est): 3.8MM **Privately Held**
SIC: 2653 Mfg Corrugated/Solid Fiber Boxes

(G-18001)
US GOLD AND DIAMOND EXCH LLC (PA)
64 Crystal Ave (03038-1710)
PHONE..................................603 300-8888
James J Halpin,
EMP: 9
SALES (est): 3.3MM **Privately Held**
SIC: 1041 6799 Gold Ore Mining Investor

Dover
Strafford County

(G-18002)
7TH SETTLEMENT BREWERY LLC
47 Washington St (03820-3877)
PHONE..................................603 534-5292
Joshua Henry,
David Boynton,
EMP: 20
SALES (est): 3.7MM **Privately Held**
SIC: 2082 5812 Mfg Malt Beverages Eating Place

(G-18003)
ADHESIVE INNOVATIONS LLC
Washington Ctr Ste 204 (03820)
PHONE..................................877 589-0544
John K Burnham, *Principal*
▲ **EMP:** 4
SALES (est): 267.3K **Privately Held**
SIC: 2891 Mfg Adhesives/Sealants

(G-18004)
AFFINITY LED LIGHT LLC
Also Called: Affinity Led Lighting
1 Washington St Ste 5121 (03820-3977)
PHONE..................................978 378-5338

Steven R Lieber, *Mng Member*
▲ **EMP:** 4 **EST:** 2013
SALES (est): 297.6K **Privately Held**
SIC: 3646 Mfg Commercial Lighting Fixtures

(G-18005)
ANDERSON WELDING LLC
3 Dean Dr (03820-5613)
PHONE..................................603 996-6225
Jesse Anderson, *Principal*
EMP: 8
SALES (est): 88.7K **Privately Held**
SIC: 7692 Welding Repair

(G-18006)
ATECH DESIGNS INC
77 Spur Rd (03820-9110)
PHONE..................................603 926-8216
Karl Leinsing, *President*
EMP: 4
SQ FT: 3,000
SALES: 2MM **Privately Held**
WEB: www.atechdesigns.com
SIC: 3841 Mfg Surgical/Medical Instruments

(G-18007)
BAVEC LLC
6 Jefferson Dr (03820-2824)
PHONE..................................603 290-5285
Glenn Bacon,
EMP: 3
SALES (est): 318.7K **Privately Held**
SIC: 3842 7389 Mfg Surgical Appliances/Supplies

(G-18008)
BAYHEAD PRODUCTS CORPORATION
173 Crosby Rd (03820-4356)
PHONE..................................603 742-3000
Elissa Moore, *President*
Gregory Moore, *Vice Pres*
Cory Ash, *Safety Mgr*
Marcia Thomas, *Sales Staff*
EMP: 25
SALES (est): 6.1MM **Privately Held**
WEB: www.bayheadproducts.com
SIC: 3089 Mfg Plastic Products

(G-18009)
BOOTH FELT CO INC
Also Called: JB Dawn Products
1 Progress Dr Ste 1 # 1 (03820-5537)
PHONE..................................603 330-3334
John Poster, *President*
M L Landegger, *Admin Sec*
EMP: 8 **EST:** 1904
SALES (est): 607K **Privately Held**
WEB: www.boothfelt.com
SIC: 2299 3296 3053 2842 Mfg Textile Goods Mfg Mineral Wool Mfg Gasket/Packing/Seals Mfg Polish/Sanitation Gd Mfg Nonwoven Fabrics

(G-18010)
BOULDER TECHNOLOGIES LLC
6 Faraday Dr (03820-5033)
PHONE..................................603 740-8402
Derrick Levine,
Joe Chalafour,
Holly Labreck,
▲ **EMP:** 6
SALES (est): 957.3K **Privately Held**
WEB: www.boulderic.com
SIC: 3572 Mfg Computer Storage Devices

(G-18011)
CALLING ALL CARGO LLC
69 Venture Dr Unit 4 (03820-5930)
P.O. Box 2034 (03821-2034)
PHONE..................................603 740-1900
Michael Carlton, *Mng Member*
Jessica Smith, *Administration*
EMP: 10
SQ FT: 2,500
SALES: 125K **Privately Held**
WEB: www.callingallcargo.com
SIC: 2298 Mfg Cordage/Twine

(G-18012)
CHAUVIN ARNOUX INC (PA)
Also Called: Aemc Instruments
15 Faraday Dr (03820-4383)
PHONE..................................603 749-6434
Winthrop D Smith, *President*
▲ **EMP:** 50
SALES (est): 11.5MM **Privately Held**
WEB: www.chauvinarnoux.com
SIC: 3829 Mfg Measuring/Controlling Devices

(G-18013)
CHISLETTS BOATING & DESIGN LLC
35 Industrial Park (03820-4332)
PHONE..................................603 755-6815
Cameron Chislett,
EMP: 12
SALES: 1MM **Privately Held**
SIC: 3732 Boatbuilding/Repairing

(G-18014)
CONTRACT MFG TECH LLC
2 Crescent Ave (03820-2715)
PHONE..................................603 692-4488
Brian Kelley, *Mng Member*
EMP: 6
SQ FT: 1,500
SALES (est): 1.1MM **Privately Held**
WEB: www.contract-mfg-tech.com
SIC: 2672 Mfg Paper Feeding Devices

(G-18015)
COSTELLO/APRIL DESIGN INC
Also Called: C/A Design
180 Crosby Rd (03820-4334)
PHONE..................................603 749-6755
Michael M Costello, *President*
John Catizone, *Vice Pres*
Robert April, *Treasurer*
Daniel C Hoefle, *Admin Sec*
EMP: 47
SALES: 6.4MM **Privately Held**
WEB: www.c-a-design.com
SIC: 3711 3469 Mfg Motor Vehicle/Car Bodies Mfg Metal Stampings
PA: The Heico Companies L L C
70 W Madison St Ste 5600
Chicago IL 60602

(G-18016)
CRAMER FABRICS INC
20 Venture Dr (03820-5912)
PHONE..................................603 742-3838
Hans Cramer, *President*
Tara Frank, *Treasurer*
Mark Ragust, *Manager*
Joanne Studebaker, *IT/INT Sup*
Johannes Cramer, *Director*
◆ **EMP:** 45
SQ FT: 60,000
SALES (est): 11.1MM
SALES (corp-wide): 177.9K **Privately Held**
WEB: www.cramerfabrics.com
SIC: 2221 2297 Manmade Broadwoven Fabric Mill Mfg Nonwoven Fabrics
PA: C. Cramer Beteiligungs-Gmbh
Domring 4-10
Warstein
290 288-0

(G-18017)
D F RICHARD INC
Also Called: D. F. Richard Energy
124 Broadway (03820-3238)
P.O. Box 669 (03821-0669)
PHONE..................................603 742-2020
Richard Card, *CEO*
Robert A Richard, *President*
Raymond J Richard, *Vice Pres*
Daniel Richard, *Business Anlyst*
Anita S Corain, *Admin Sec*
EMP: 60
SQ FT: 15,000
SALES: 30MM **Privately Held**
SIC: 1382 Oil/Gas Exploration Services

(G-18018)
DAILY FANTASY SPT RANKINGS LLC
175 Mount Vernon St (03820-2716)
PHONE..................................609 273-8408
Douglas Norrie, *Administration*
EMP: 3
SALES (est): 106.6K **Privately Held**
SIC: 2711 Newspapers-Publishing/Printing

(G-18019)
DMI TECHNOLOGY CORP (PA)
1 Progress Dr (03820-5450)
PHONE..................................603 742-3330
James Elsner, *President*
Logan D Delany Jr, *Chairman*
John Arico, *Administration*
EMP: 14
SALES (est): 126.2MM **Privately Held**
WEB: www.dmitechnology.com
SIC: 3625 3621 Mfg Relays/Industrial Controls Mfg Motors/Generators

(G-18020)
EDDEFY INC
7 Riverside Dr (03820-4654)
PHONE..................................802 989-1934
Joyce Bettencourt, *Principal*
Jennifer Heyning, *Principal*
Shabnam Ozlati, *Principal*
Teal Furnholm,
EMP: 4 **EST:** 2013
SALES (est): 182.8K **Privately Held**
SIC: 7372 Prepackaged Software Services

(G-18021)
ELECTROCRAFT NEW HAMPSHIRE INC (DH)
1 Progress Dr (03820-5537)
PHONE..................................603 742-3330
James Elsner, *President*
John Arico, *Administration*
▲ **EMP:** 28
SQ FT: 120,000
SALES (est): 8.1MM
SALES (corp-wide): 126.2MM **Privately Held**
WEB: www.easternairdevices.com
SIC: 3621 3825 3694 3625 Mfg Motors/Generators Mfg Elec Measuring Instr Mfg Engine Elec Equip Mfg Relay/Indstl Control Mfg Speed Changer/Drives
HQ: Electrocraft, Inc.
2 Marin Way Ste 3
Stratham NH 03885
855 697-7966

(G-18022)
FORWARD MERCH LLC
Also Called: Jsr Merchandising
111 Venture Dr (03820-5915)
PHONE..................................603 742-4377
Masessa Tiffini,
EMP: 3
SALES (est): 457.5K **Privately Held**
SIC: 2759 5961 Commercial Printing Ret Mail-Order House

(G-18023)
GES CONTROL SYSTEMS INC
Also Called: Graphis Electrical Controls
22 Grandview Dr (03820-8300)
PHONE..................................905 336-5517
Dave Sodel, *Manager*
EMP: 6
SALES (corp-wide): 5.3MM **Privately Held**
WEB: www.gescontrols.com
SIC: 2621 Press Controls
PA: Ges Control Systems Inc
3375 North Service Rd Unit C7
Burlington ON L7N 3
905 336-5517

(G-18024)
GREEN MOUNTAIN RISK MGT LLC
660 Central Ave Ste 201 (03820-3435)
PHONE..................................802 683-8586
Frank Santin, *CEO*
Randal Schaetzke, *Administration*
EMP: 10
SALES (est): 623.7K **Privately Held**
SIC: 3482 Mfg Small Arms Ammunition

(G-18025)
GRIP POD SYSTEMS INTL LLC
77 Childs Dr (03820-5121)
PHONE..................................239 233-3694
Joseph Gaddini, *Mng Member*
EMP: 5
SALES: 2MM **Privately Held**
SIC: 3484 Mfg Small Arms

(G-18026)
HAMPSHIRE CONTROLS CORPORATION
1 Grove St (03820-3314)
P.O. Box 516 (03821-0516)
PHONE..................................603 749-9424
Dianne Rush, *President*
David Laub, *General Mgr*
Linda Stewart, *Programmer Anys*
EMP: 12 **EST:** 1976
SQ FT: 7,225
SALES: 830K **Privately Held**
WEB: www.hampshirecontrols.com
SIC: 3625 3829 3822 Mfg Relays/Industrial Controls Mfg Measuring/Controlling Devices Mfg Environmental Controls

(G-18027)
HARVEYS BAKERIES
6 Progress Dr (03820-5450)
PHONE..................................603 749-5149
Brad Guillemette, *Owner*
EMP: 4
SALES (est): 243.6K **Privately Held**
SIC: 2051 Mfg Bread/Related Products

(G-18028)
HM MACHINE LLC
44 Venture Dr (03820-5912)
PHONE..................................603 948-1178
Andrew John Hussey, *Owner*
EMP: 5
SALES (est): 916.6K **Privately Held**
SIC: 3599 Mfg Industrial Machinery

(G-18029)
HM MACHINE LLC
5 Faraday Dr (03820-5024)
PHONE..................................603 617-3450
Sarah Hussey, *Principal*
EMP: 7
SALES (est): 772.3K **Privately Held**
SIC: 3599 Mfg Industrial Machinery

(G-18030)
IWORX SYSTEMS INC
62 Littleworth Rd (03820-4330)
PHONE..................................603 742-2492
Ashish More, *President*
Karen Mitchell, *Dir Ops-Prd-Mfg*
Shelly Thompson, *Engineer*
Christine Weston, *Technical Staff*
Sarah More, *Admin Sec*
EMP: 17
SQ FT: 8,000
SALES (est): 3MM **Privately Held**
SIC: 3825 Mfg Electrical Measuring Instruments

(G-18031)
J & E SPECIALTY INC
519 Central Ave (03820-3420)
PHONE..................................603 742-6357
John Cabral, *President*
Elaine Cabral, *Treasurer*
Stephen Roberts, *Admin Sec*
EMP: 6
SQ FT: 5,000
SALES: 380K **Privately Held**
SIC: 3471 Plating/Polishing Service

(G-18032)
JACKSON BOND ENTERPRISES LLC
39 Industrial Park (03820-4332)
PHONE..................................603 742-2350
Bruce A Bond,
EMP: 6
SALES (est): 1MM **Privately Held**
WEB: www.jacksonbondllc.com
SIC: 2299 Mfg Textile Goods

(G-18033)
JUST RIGHT AWNINGS & SIGNS
7 Industrial Park (03820-4332)
PHONE..................................603 740-8416
Rick Spurlin, *President*
EMP: 6
SQ FT: 8,000
SALES (est): 674.9K **Privately Held**
SIC: 2394 1799 Mfg Canvas/Related Products Trade Contractor

(G-18034)
LEOPARD SNOW PUBLISHING LLC
171 Durham Rd (03820-4396)
PHONE....603 742-7714
Marc Estes, *Principal*
EMP: 4 **EST:** 2015
SALES (est): 73.2K **Privately Held**
SIC: 2741 Misc Publishing

(G-18035)
LITTLE ACRE GOURMET FOODS
7 W Knox Marsh Rd (03820-4346)
PHONE....603 749-7227
William Ahrens, *Owner*
EMP: 3
SALES (est): 202.7K **Privately Held**
SIC: 2099 Mfg Food Preparations

(G-18036)
MFB HOLDINGS LLC
Also Called: Blouin Display
27 Production Dr (03820-5917)
P.O. Box 10, Rollinsford (03869-0010)
PHONE....603 742-0104
David Zoia, *Mng Member*
Adam Zoia, *Mng Member*
Katie St Pierre, *Manager*
▲ **EMP:** 40 **EST:** 1948
SQ FT: 42,000
SALES (est): 8.8MM **Privately Held**
WEB: www.mfblouin.com
SIC: 3446 Mfg Architectural Metalwork

(G-18037)
MG PRINT AND PROMOTIONS
1 Washington St Ste 501 (03820-3848)
P.O. Box 1161 (03821-1161)
PHONE....603 343-2534
James Munro, *Owner*
EMP: 4 **EST:** 2015
SALES (est): 171.1K **Privately Held**
SIC: 2752 2759 Lithographic Commercial Printing Commercial Printing

(G-18038)
NEW ENGLAND HOMES INC
277 Locust St (03820-4009)
PHONE....603 436-8830
Daniel J Donahue, *President*
Kathi Mann, *Treasurer*
Stephen Pica, *Regl Sales Mgr*
EMP: 85 **EST:** 1961
SQ FT: 9,000
SALES (est): 10.8MM **Privately Held**
WEB: www.newenglandhomes.net
SIC: 2452 Mfg Prefabricated Wood Buildings

(G-18039)
NEW ENGLAND INNOVATIONS CORP
Also Called: North East Products
4 Progress Dr (03820-5450)
PHONE....603 742-6247
Philip Sidmore, *President*
Evelyn Sidmore, *Vice Pres*
EMP: 12
SQ FT: 13,000
SALES (est): 2.3MM **Privately Held**
SIC: 3599 Machine Shop

(G-18040)
NISHI ENTERPRISES INC
442 Central Ave (03820-3425)
PHONE....603 749-0113
Jonathan West, *President*
EMP: 4
SQ FT: 2,000
SALES (est): 534.8K **Privately Held**
WEB: www.cochecoprintworks.com
SIC: 2759 Commercial Printing

(G-18041)
NORTH COUNTRY TRACTOR INC
Also Called: John Deere Authorized Dealer
10 Littleworth Rd (03820-4329)
PHONE....603 742-5488
Robert Gonyou, *Owner*
EMP: 15
SALES (est): 1.9MM **Privately Held**
SIC: 3524 5082 Mfg Lawn/Garden Equipment Whol Construction/Mining Equipment
PA: North Country Tractor, Inc.
149 Sheep Davis Rd
Pembroke NH 03275

(G-18042)
NORTH EAST CUTTING DIE CORP
29 Industrial Park (03820-4332)
P.O. Box 2238, Hampton (03843-2238)
PHONE....603 436-8952
Mark Geller, *President*
EMP: 20
SQ FT: 10,000
SALES (est): 3.3MM **Privately Held**
WEB: www.necuttingdie.com
SIC: 3599 3544 Mfg Industrial Machinery Mfg Dies/Tools/Jigs/Fixtures

(G-18043)
NWARE TECHNOLOGIES INC
6 Old Rochester Rd # 202 (03820-2028)
PHONE....603 617-3760
Dany Parent, *President*
EMP: 6
SALES (est): 560K **Privately Held**
WEB: www.nwaretech.com
SIC: 7372 Prepackaged Software Services

(G-18044)
PAGEPRO WIRELESS
332 Central Ave (03820-4133)
P.O. Box 262 (03821-0262)
PHONE....603 749-5600
Toll Free:....888 -
Kenneth S Chu, *Owner*
EMP: 4
SALES (est): 421.1K **Privately Held**
WEB: www.pageprowireless.com
SIC: 3661 Mfg Telephone/Telegraph Apparatus

(G-18045)
PENTAIR RSDNTIAL FLTRATION LLC
Also Called: Fibredyne
47 Crosby Rd (03820-4340)
PHONE....603 749-1610
James Donnelly, *President*
▲ **EMP:** 15
SALES (est): 3.6MM
SALES (corp-wide): 18.3B **Publicly Held**
WEB: www.fibredyne.com
SIC: 3589 Mfg Service Industry Machinery
HQ: Sta-Rite Industries, Llc
293 S Wright St
Delavan WI 53115
888 782-7483

(G-18046)
POPZUP LLC
1 Washington St Ste 5110 (03820-3977)
PHONE....978 502-1737
Marty Lapham, *Principal*
EMP: 3
SALES (est): 191.4K **Privately Held**
SIC: 2099 Mfg Food Preparations

(G-18047)
PROMETHEUS GROUP OF NH LTD
1 Washington St Ste 3171 (03820-2234)
PHONE....800 442-2325
Richard Poore, *President*
Patricia Quintana, *COO*
Michael Ives, *CFO*
▲ **EMP:** 10
SQ FT: 3,700
SALES (est): 2MM **Privately Held**
WEB: www.theprogrp.com
SIC: 3841 Mfg Surgical/Medical Instruments

(G-18048)
R F HUNTER CO INC
113 Crosby Rd Ste 9 (03820-4389)
PHONE....603 742-9565
Paul Santoro, *President*
Martha Santoro, *Vice Pres*
▲ **EMP:** 8
SQ FT: 5,000
SALES (est): 930K **Privately Held**
WEB: www.rfhunter.com
SIC: 3569 Mfg General Industrial Machinery

(G-18049)
RAND-WHITNEY CONTAINER LLC
15 Stonewall Dr (03820-5531)
PHONE....603 822-7300
EMP: 150 **Privately Held**
SIC: 2653 Mfg Corrugated/Solid Fiber Boxes
HQ: Rand-Whitney Container Llc
1 Rand Whitney Way
Worcester MA 01607
508 890-7000

(G-18050)
RELYCO SALES INC
121 Broadway (03820-3250)
P.O. Box 1229 (03821-1229)
PHONE....603 742-0999
Michael R Steinberg, *CEO*
Bruce Steinberg, *President*
Susan Sayers, *Partner*
Emily Harris, *Vice Pres*
Laurie Steinberg, *Vice Pres*
EMP: 40
SQ FT: 13,500
SALES (est): 9.1MM **Privately Held**
WEB: www.relyco.com
SIC: 2759 5112 5044 Commercial Printing Whol Stationery/Office Supplies Whol Office Equipment

(G-18051)
SALMON FALLS WOODWORKS LLC
38 Littleworth Rd (03820-4329)
PHONE....603 740-6060
Fred Loucks, *Mng Member*
EMP: 14
SALES (est): 2.3MM **Privately Held**
SIC: 2431 Mfg Millwork

(G-18052)
SEACOAST REDIMIX CONCRETE LLC (PA)
349 Mast Rd (03820-5518)
PHONE....603 742-4441
D Bissonnette,
Dave Bissonnette,
Mark Bissonnette,
EMP: 18
SQ FT: 1,500
SALES (est): 1.9MM **Privately Held**
SIC: 3273 5211 Mfg/Ret Ready- Mixed Concrete

(G-18053)
SPECIALTY TEXTILE PRODUCTS LLC
Also Called: Spectex
1 Progress Dr (03820-5537)
PHONE....603 330-3334
Victor Pisinski,
▲ **EMP:** 18
SALES (est): 3MM **Privately Held**
WEB: www.spectex.net
SIC: 2299 Mfg Textile Goods

(G-18054)
SPECTEX LLC
1 Progress Dr Ste 1 # 1 (03820-5537)
PHONE....603 330-3334
Victor Pisinski,
Steve Rossi,
EMP: 19
SALES (est): 6.5MM **Privately Held**
SIC: 3554 Mfg Paper Industrial Machinery

(G-18055)
SUNDANCE SIGN & DESIGN
89 Oak St (03820-3582)
PHONE....603 742-1517
Michael Leary, *Partner*
EMP: 3
SQ FT: 1,400
SALES (est): 375.1K **Privately Held**
WEB: www.autumnsun.com
SIC: 3993 Mfg Signs/Advertising Specialties

(G-18056)
SYNAP INC
77 Fourth St (03820-2900)
PHONE....888 572-1150
Shelby Brewer, *President*
EMP: 7 **EST:** 2014
SALES (est): 256.4K **Privately Held**
SIC: 7372 7389 Prepackaged Software Services Business Services At Non-Commercial Site

(G-18057)
TALL SHIP DISTILLERY LLC
32 Crosby Rd Ste 5 (03820-8313)
PHONE....603 842-0098
EMP: 6
SALES (est): 434.3K **Privately Held**
SIC: 2085 Mfg Distilled/Blended Liquor

(G-18058)
TANORAMA SUNTANNING CENTER
827 Central Ave (03820-2577)
PHONE....603 742-1600
Robert Ashe, *Owner*
EMP: 3
SALES (est): 180K **Privately Held**
SIC: 3648 Mfg Lighting Equipment

(G-18059)
TERRACOTTA PASTA CO (PA)
1 Washington St Ste 206 (03820-3848)
PHONE....603 749-2288
Kevin Cambridge, *Owner*
EMP: 3 **EST:** 1999
SALES (est): 493.4K **Privately Held**
SIC: 2099 Mfr Pasta

(G-18060)
THUNDERBOLT INNOVATION LLC
53 Washington St Ste 300 (03820-4081)
PHONE....888 335-6234
Sean Hussey, *CEO*
EMP: 4
SALES: 150K **Privately Held**
SIC: 7372 Prepackaged Software Services

(G-18061)
TICKED OFF INC
97 Spruce Ln (03820-4542)
PHONE....603 742-0925
Richard Hebbard, *President*
Mary Hebbard, *Vice Pres*
EMP: 8
SALES (est): 1.3MM **Privately Held**
WEB: www.tickedoff.com
SIC: 2833 3841 Mfg Medicinal/Botanical Products Mfg Surgical/Medical Instruments

(G-18062)
TURBOCAM AUTOMATED PRODUCTION
5 Faraday Dr (03820-5024)
PHONE....603 905-0240
EMP: 3
SALES (corp-wide): 92MM **Privately Held**
SIC: 3462 Mfg Iron/Steel Forgings
HQ: Turbocam Automated Production Systems, Inc.
607 Calef Hwy Ste 100
Barrington NH 03825
603 905-0220

(G-18063)
TURBOCAM ENERGY SOLUTIONS LLC
5 Faraday Dr (03820-5024)
PHONE....603 905-0200
James Noronha, *President*
D Douglas Patteson, *CFO*
▲ **EMP:** 45
SALES (est): 8.9MM **Privately Held**
SIC: 3398 Metal Heat Treating

(G-18064)
URASEAL INC
Also Called: Accenus
1 Washington St Ste 5126 (03820-3977)
PHONE....603 749-1004
John Burnham, *President*
Mike Devaney, *Chairman*
EMP: 18
SQ FT: 42,000
SALES (est): 4.1MM **Privately Held**
WEB: www.uraseal.com
SIC: 3661 Mfg Telephone/Telegraph Apparatus

GEOGRAPHIC

(G-18065)
VIGILANT INCOPORATED
85 Industrial Park (03820-4332)
PHONE..................................603 285-0400
Charles T Griffiths, *President*
James A Brown, *Vice Pres*
Andrea Donahue, *Sales Staff*
Natasha Morin, *Sales Staff*
Lisa Pinault, *Sales Staff*
◆ **EMP:** 45
SQ FT: 46,000
SALES (est): 7.2MM **Privately Held**
WEB: www.vigilantinc.com
SIC: 2499 Mfg Wood Products

(G-18066)
VISHAY HIREL SYSTEMS LLC
140 Crosby Rd (03820-4334)
PHONE..................................603 742-4375
Gary Bates, *Manager*
EMP: 95
SALES (corp-wide): 3B **Publicly Held**
SIC: 3677 3612 Mfg Electronic Coils/Transformers Mfg Transformers
HQ: Vishay Hirel Systems Llc
7767 Elm Creek Blvd N # 305
Maple Grove MN 55369
952 544-1344

(G-18067)
WELCH FLUOROCARBON INC
113 Crosby Rd Ste 10 (03820-4370)
PHONE..................................603 742-0164
Evan Welch, *President*
Tim Towle, *Vice Pres*
Tiffany Hall, *Mfg Staff*
Sondra Boyd, *Buyer*
Seth Welch, *Sales Executive*
EMP: 30
SQ FT: 7,800
SALES (est): 7.7MM **Privately Held**
WEB: www.welchfluorocarbon.com
SIC: 3089 Mfg Plastic Products

Dublin
Cheshire County

(G-18068)
HELMERS PUBLISHING INC
Also Called: Desktop Engineering Magazine
1283 Main St (03444-8242)
PHONE..................................603 563-1631
Stephen Robbins, *President*
David L Andrews, *Publisher*
Donna McLain, *COO*
Tom Conlon, *Vice Pres*
Darlene Sweeney, *Prdtn Dir*
EMP: 25 **EST:** 1979
SALES (est): 2.5MM **Privately Held**
WEB: www.deskeng.com
SIC: 2721 2741 2731 7389 Periodical-Publish/Print Misc Publishing Book-Publishing/Printing Business Services

(G-18069)
YANKEE PUBLISHING INCORPORATED (PA)
Also Called: Yankee Magazine
1121 Main St (03444-8246)
P.O. Box 520 (03444-0520)
PHONE..................................603 563-8111
James Trowbridge, *President*
Judson D Hale Sr, *Chairman*
Paul Belliveau, *Vice Pres*
Jody Bugbee, *Vice Pres*
Judson D Hale Jr, *Vice Pres*
EMP: 50 **EST:** 1935
SQ FT: 15,200
SALES (est): 16.6MM **Privately Held**
WEB: www.almanac.com
SIC: 2721 Misc Publishing

Dummer
Coos County

(G-18070)
GAGNE & SONS LOGGING CO LLC
146 Ferry Rd (03588-5338)
PHONE..................................603 449-2255
Frederick Gagne,
Lorraine Gagne,
EMP: 4
SALES (est): 1MM **Privately Held**
SIC: 2411 Logging Contractor

(G-18071)
PAT GAGNE LOGGING
236 Ferry Rd (03588-5340)
PHONE..................................603 449-2479
Patrick Gagne, *Principal*
EMP: 3
SALES (est): 122.5K **Privately Held**
SIC: 2411 Logging

Dunbarton
Merrimack County

(G-18072)
ALTERNATIVE FUEL SYSTEMS E LLC
19 Twist Hill Rd (03046-4323)
PHONE..................................603 231-1942
Scott H Zepp, *Principal*
EMP: 3
SALES (est): 225K **Privately Held**
SIC: 2869 Mfg Industrial Organic Chemicals

(G-18073)
MARCOU CONSTRUCTION COMPANY
250 Mansion Rd (03046-4608)
PHONE..................................603 774-6511
Beverly Marcou, *Owner*
James Marcou, *Vice Pres*
Louis F Marcou Jr, *Vice Pres*
Joanne Magoon, *Treasurer*
EMP: 5
SALES (est): 1.3MM **Privately Held**
SIC: 1429 Crushed Stone

(G-18074)
STITCH THIS
11 White Tail Ln (03046-4108)
PHONE..................................603 774-0736
Wanda Dutton, *Principal*
EMP: 3
SALES (est): 107K **Privately Held**
SIC: 2395 Pleating/Stitching Services

Durham
Strafford County

(G-18075)
BMED HOLDING LLC
Also Called: Dpal Technologies
16 Strafford Ave (03824-1908)
PHONE..................................603 868-1888
F William Hersman,
EMP: 3
SALES: 100K **Privately Held**
SIC: 3845 Mfg Electromedical Equipment

(G-18076)
ECO SERVICES LLC
Also Called: Separett USA
23 Durham Point Rd (03824-3100)
P.O. Box 226, Barrington (03825-0226)
PHONE..................................603 682-0963
James Siedenburg, *Mng Member*
EMP: 5
SALES: 2.2MM **Privately Held**
SIC: 3088 5999 5099 8742 Mfg Plstc Plumbing Fixtr Ret Misc Merchandise Whol Durable Goods Mgmt Consulting Svcs

(G-18077)
MAC OBSERVER INC
18 Denbow Rd Ste 101 (03824-3105)
P.O. Box 859 (03824-0859)
PHONE..................................603 868-2030
Dave Hamilton, *President*
Lisa Hamilton, *Editor*
EMP: 4
SALES (est): 400K **Privately Held**
SIC: 2741 Newsletter Publishing

(G-18078)
MANROLAND GOSS WEB SYSTEMS AMR (DH)
121 Technology Dr Ste 1 (03824-4725)
PHONE..................................603 750-6600
Alexander Wassermann, *CEO*
Greg Blue, *Vice Pres*
Dave Soden, *Vice Pres*
Dirk Rauh, *CFO*
Nicole Vinet, *VP Finance*
◆ **EMP:** 500
SQ FT: 500,000
SALES (est): 200.3MM
SALES (corp-wide): 360.4K **Privately Held**
WEB: www.gossinternational.com
SIC: 3555 7699 Mfg Printing Trades Machinery Repair Services
HQ: Manroland Goss Web Systems Gmbh
Alois-Senefelder-Allee 1
Augsburg 86153
821 424-0

(G-18079)
PAINE PUBLISHING LLC
51 Durham Point Rd (03824-3100)
PHONE..................................603 682-0735
Katie Delahaye Paine, *Principal*
EMP: 5
SALES (est): 390K **Privately Held**
SIC: 2721 Periodicals-Publishing/Printing

East Hampstead
Rockingham County

(G-18080)
ACE MACHINE INC
563 Rte 111 (03826)
P.O. Box 869 (03826-0869)
PHONE..................................603 329-6716
Bruce De Boyes, *President*
EMP: 14
SQ FT: 3,800
SALES (est): 1.2MM **Privately Held**
WEB: www.ace-machine.com
SIC: 3599 Machine Shop Jobbing & Repair

(G-18081)
CZ MACHINE INC
Also Called: C Z Machine Shop
110 Hunt Rd (03826)
PHONE..................................603 382-4259
Mike Czeremin, *President*
Rudi Czeremin, *Vice Pres*
Doris Kendal, *Admin Sec*
EMP: 7
SQ FT: 6,000
SALES (est): 783.4K **Privately Held**
SIC: 3599 Machine Shop

(G-18082)
RAM PRINTING INCORPORATED (PA)
Also Called: Hampstead Copy Center
Rr 111 (03826)
P.O. Box 900 (03826-0900)
PHONE..................................603 382-7045
Walter Zaremba, *President*
Buddy Zaremba, *Treasurer*
EMP: 46
SQ FT: 7,000
SALES (est): 10.2MM **Privately Held**
WEB: www.ramprinting.com
SIC: 2752 7334 2791 Lithographic Commercial Printing Photocopying Services Typesetting Services

(G-18083)
RAM PRINTING INCORPORATED
Also Called: Hampstead Copy Center
3 Commerce Park Dr (03826-2459)
P.O. Box 10 (03826-0010)
PHONE..................................603 382-3400
Jeff Grover, *Manager*
EMP: 4
SALES (est): 343.7K
SALES (corp-wide): 10.2MM **Privately Held**
WEB: www.ramprinting.com
SIC: 2752 Lithographic Commercial Printing
PA: Ram Printing Incorporated
Rr 111
East Hampstead NH 03826
603 382-7045

East Kingston
Rockingham County

(G-18084)
BIG DADDY BREWS LLC
1 Bioteau Dr (03827-2040)
PHONE..................................603 569-5647
Robert Levine, *Principal*
EMP: 3 **EST:** 2016
SALES (est): 88.3K **Privately Held**
SIC: 2082 Mfg Malt Beverages

(G-18085)
CHEMCAGE US LLC
97 Giles Rd (03827-2009)
PHONE..................................617 504-9548
Charles Farmer, *Principal*
EMP: 3
SALES (est): 88K **Privately Held**
SIC: 2834 7389 Mfg Pharmaceutical Preparations Business Services At Non-Commercial Site

(G-18086)
DODGE WOODWORKING LLC
7 Cove Rd (03827-2120)
PHONE..................................603 642-6188
Lewis Dodge, *Principal*
EMP: 4
SALES (est): 268K **Privately Held**
SIC: 2431 Mfg Millwork

(G-18087)
KAV MACHINE COMPANY INC
7 Orchard Ln (03827-2072)
P.O. Box 85, Plaistow (03865-0085)
PHONE..................................603 642-5251
Raymond Viglione, *President*
Beverley Viglione, *Treasurer*
EMP: 6
SQ FT: 3,200
SALES (est): 728.8K **Privately Held**
SIC: 3599 Mfg Industrial Machinery

(G-18088)
MSM PROTEIN TECHNOLOGIES INC
97 Giles Rd (03827-2009)
PHONE..................................617 504-9548
Tajib A Mirzabekov, *President*
C Davis Farmer Jr, *Treasurer*
David I Kreimer, *Admin Sec*
EMP: 11
SALES (est): 902.1K **Privately Held**
SIC: 2834 Mfg Pharmaceutical Preparations

(G-18089)
NEWBAMA STEEL INC
213 Haverhill Rd (03827-2136)
P.O. Box 1108, Plaistow (03865-1108)
PHONE..................................603 382-2261
Angeline L Kinnon, *President*
Peter Kinnon, *Vice Pres*
EMP: 6
SQ FT: 7,500
SALES (est): 544.5K **Privately Held**
WEB: www.newbamasteel.com
SIC: 3449 Mfg Misc Structural Metalwork

(G-18090)
QUALITY BABBITTING SERVICES
25 Pheasant Run (03827-2051)
PHONE..................................603 642-7147
Robert Staves, *President*
EMP: 3
SALES: 375K **Privately Held**
WEB: www.babbitting.net
SIC: 3366 Repair Babbit Bearings

(G-18091)
RSI METAL FABRICATION LLC
213 Haverhill Rd Bldg 9 (03827-2136)
P.O. Box 479 (03827-0479)
PHONE..................................603 382-8367
Joshua Winter, *Manager*
EMP: 4 **EST:** 2013

SALES (est): 233K Privately Held
SIC: 3312 Blast Furnace-Steel Works

(G-18092)
TRI C MANUFACTURING INC
33 Haverhill Rd (03827-2110)
PHONE..............603 642-8448
George Chauncey, *President*
Michael Carey, *Treasurer*
EMP: 8
SQ FT: 2,500
SALES (est): 1.1MM Privately Held
SIC: 3444 Manufacturing Of Industrial Sheet Metalwork And The Installation Of Duct Work

East Swanzey
Cheshire County

(G-18093)
LANE CONSTRUCTION CORPORATION
Also Called: Cold River Materials
Oliver Hl Rd Off Rte 32 S (03446)
P.O. Box 908, Walpole (03608-0908)
PHONE..............603 352-2006
Rick Raynor, *Manager*
EMP: 4
SALES (corp-wide): 3.2B Privately Held
WEB: www.laneconstruct.com
SIC: 1442 Construction Sand/Gravel
HQ: The Lane Construction Corporation
90 Fieldstone Ct
Cheshire CT 06410
203 235-3351

East Wakefield
Carroll County

(G-18094)
BUTCH EATON LOGGING & TRUCKI
1496 Province Lake Rd (03830-3965)
PHONE..............603 522-3894
Ronald W Eaton III, *Principal*
EMP: 3 EST: 2010
SALES (est): 241.4K Privately Held
SIC: 2411 Logging

Effingham
Carroll County

(G-18095)
J B A PRODUCTS
234 Granite Rd (03882-8655)
PHONE..............603 539-5034
Brenda Augenti, *Owner*
EMP: 3
SALES (est): 157.3K Privately Held
SIC: 2393 Mfg Textile Bags

(G-18096)
PINE RIVER LOGGING
314 Hutchens Pond Rd (03882-8220)
PHONE..............603 833-1340
Ross Wright, *Principal*
EMP: 3
SALES (est): 244K Privately Held
SIC: 2411 Logging

Enfield
Grafton County

(G-18097)
ENERTGETIC BALTIC MI
80 Baltic St (03748-3162)
P.O. Box 10 (03748-0010)
PHONE..............603 252-0804
Timothy Taylor, *President*
EMP: 4
SALES: 85K Privately Held
SIC: 3699 Mfg Electrical Equipment/Supplies

(G-18098)
ENFIELD PUBLISHING & DIST CO
234 May St (03748)
P.O. Box 699 (03748-0699)
PHONE..............603 632-7377
Linda Jones, *Owner*
▲ EMP: 5
SALES (est): 338.8K Privately Held
WEB: www.editionstechnip.com
SIC: 2731 Books-Publishing/Printing

Epping
Rockingham County

(G-18099)
FLEXI-DOOR CORPORATION
Also Called: Door Craft
277 Pleasant St (03042-2112)
PHONE..............603 679-2286
Joseph Piotrowski, *President*
Gary Piotrowski, *Vice Pres*
EMP: 5
SQ FT: 4,000
SALES (est): 542.3K Privately Held
SIC: 3089 Mfg Awnings & Vinyl Strip Doors

(G-18100)
L & M SHEDS LLC
66 N River Rd (03042-3408)
PHONE..............603 679-5243
Mercell Bernier, *Mng Member*
Linda Bernier,
Mark Bernier,
EMP: 5
SALES (est): 496.7K Privately Held
SIC: 2511 0782 2452 Mfg Wood Household Furniture Lawn/Garden Services Mfg Prefabricated Wood Buildings

(G-18101)
MALCOLM BRADSHER CO INC
181 Exeter Rd (03042-2216)
PHONE..............603 679-3888
Malcolm Bradsher, *President*
EMP: 6
SALES (est): 802.5K Privately Held
SIC: 1442 Construction Sand/Gravel

(G-18102)
SEYMOUR WOODWORKING
479 Calef Hwy (03042)
PHONE..............603 679-2055
James Seymour, *President*
EMP: 3 EST: 1988
SALES (est): 600K Privately Held
SIC: 2499 Mfg Wood Products

(G-18103)
STARCRAFTS PUBLISHING LLC
68a Fogg Rd (03042-3405)
PHONE..............603 734-5303
Maria Simms,
EMP: 3
SALES (est): 271.7K Privately Held
SIC: 2741 Misc Publishing

Epsom
Merrimack County

(G-18104)
BEAUMAC COMPANY INC
382 Suncook Valley Hwy (03234-4243)
PHONE..............603 736-9321
David W Beaucher, *President*
EMP: 12
SQ FT: 23,000
SALES (est): 3.1MM Privately Held
WEB: www.beaumac.com
SIC: 3599 Mfg Industrial Machinery

(G-18105)
CHESTER BRALEY
25 Howards Ln (03234-4500)
PHONE..............239 841-0019
Chester Braley, *Principal*
EMP: 4 EST: 2009
SALES (est): 186.8K Privately Held
SIC: 2431 Mfg Millwork

(G-18106)
LOUDON SCREEN PRINTING INC
1929 Dover Rd (03234-4128)
PHONE..............603 736-9420
EMP: 4
SALES (est): 600K Privately Held
SIC: 3993 2759 Mfg Signs/Advertising Specialties Commercial Printing

(G-18107)
NEWSTRESS INC
1640 Dover Rd (03234)
P.O. Box 330 (03234-0330)
PHONE..............603 736-9000
Nishan Nahikian, *President*
EMP: 25 EST: 1972
SQ FT: 22,000
SALES (est): 3.7MM Privately Held
SIC: 3272 Mfg Concrete Products

Errol
Coos County

(G-18108)
B HALL & SONS LOGGING INC
63 Hall Rd (03579-6655)
P.O. Box 299 (03579-0299)
PHONE..............603 482-7741
Richard Hall, *President*
Neil Hall, *Vice Pres*
Sandra Hall, *Treasurer*
EMP: 3
SALES (est): 410.1K Privately Held
SIC: 2411 Logging

(G-18109)
BEAR COUNTRY POWERSPORTS LLC
54 Main St (03579)
P.O. Box 332 (03579-0332)
PHONE..............603 482-3370
Kathleen Gingras,
EMP: 8
SALES (est): 872.1K Privately Held
SIC: 3792 Mfg Travel Trailers/Campers

Exeter
Rockingham County

(G-18110)
ANVIL INTERNATIONAL LLC (HQ)
2 Holland Way (03833-2937)
PHONE..............603 418-2800
Jason Hild, *CEO*
Dean Taylor, *Vice Pres*
▲ EMP: 27
SALES (est): 648.3MM Privately Held
WEB: www.anvilint.com
SIC: 3498 3321 3317 3494 Mfg Fabrctd Pipe/Fitting Gray/Ductile Iron Fndry Mfg Steel Pipe/Tubes Mfg Valves/Pipe Fittings Mfg Hardware

(G-18111)
BAUER HOCKEY LLC
100 Domain Dr Ste 1 (03833-2996)
PHONE..............603 430-2111
Paul Dachsteiner, *President*
Julie Zaleski, *Treasurer*
Michelle Hanson, *Admin Sec*
EMP: 152
SQ FT: 67,000
SALES (est): 3.4MM
SALES (corp-wide): 2.6MM Privately Held
SIC: 3949 Mfg Sporting/Athletic Goods
HQ: Bce Acquisition Us, Inc.
100 Domain Dr
Exeter NH 03833
603 430-2111

(G-18112)
BCE ACQUISITION US INC (HQ)
100 Domain Dr (03833-4801)
PHONE..............603 430-2111
Paul Dachsteiner, *President*
Julie Zaleski, *Treasurer*
Michelle Hanson, *Admin Sec*
EMP: 3
SQ FT: 67,000
SALES (est): 18MM
SALES (corp-wide): 2.6MM Privately Held
SIC: 3949 6719 Mfg Sporting/Athletic Goods Holding Company

(G-18113)
BENTLEY PHARMACEUTICALS INC (HQ)
2 Holland Way (03833-2937)
PHONE..............603 658-6100
James R Murphy, *Ch of Bd*
John A Sedor, *President*
David C Brush, *Vice Pres*
Fred Feldman, *Research*
Richard P Lindsay, *CFO*
EMP: 13
SQ FT: 15,700
SALES (est): 26.9MM
SALES (corp-wide): 5.4B Privately Held
WEB: www.bentleypharm.com
SIC: 2834 Mfg Pharmaceutical Preparations
PA: Teva Pharmaceutical Industries Limited
5 Bazel
Petah Tikva 49510
392 672-67

(G-18114)
BPS DIAMOND SPORTS INC
100 Domain Dr (03833-4801)
PHONE..............253 891-8377
Don Cooper, *Director*
Brian J Fox, *Risk Mgmt Dir*
▲ EMP: 9 EST: 2013
SALES (est): 979.7K
SALES (corp-wide): 149.6MM Privately Held
SIC: 3949 Mfg Sporting/Athletic Goods
PA: Old Bh Inc.
100 Domain Dr
Exeter NH 03833
603 430-2111

(G-18115)
C3I INC
8 Commerce Way (03833-4588)
PHONE..............603 929-9989
Charles J Wagner, *President*
Michael Curry, *Principal*
James Cook, *Director*
Dillon Lucier, *Officer*
EMP: 20
SQ FT: 10,000
SALES (est): 3.4MM Privately Held
SIC: 3812 5065 Mfg Search/Navigation Equipment Whol Electronic Parts/Equipment

(G-18116)
COBHAM
Also Called: Cobham Antenna Systems
32 Industrial Dr (03833-4557)
PHONE..............603 418-9786
EMP: 5
SALES (est): 515.5K Privately Held
SIC: 3812 Mfg Search/Navigation Equipment

(G-18117)
COBHAM EXETER INC
11 Continental Dr (03833-4564)
PHONE..............603 775-5200
John McNulla, *CEO*
Rick Pierson, *President*
Brian McLaughlin, *Engineer*
Richard Gregorio, *CFO*
Thomas Smith, *Program Mgr*
EMP: 454
SQ FT: 165,000
SALES (est): 122.4MM
SALES (corp-wide): 2.4B Privately Held
WEB: www.contmicro.com
SIC: 3679 Mfg Electronic Components
HQ: Cobham Aes Holdings Inc.
2121 Crystal Dr Ste 625
Arlington VA 22202

(G-18118)
CONTINTENTIAL MICROWAVE
32 Industrial Dr (03833-4557)
PHONE..............603 775-5200
Marc Lapasset, *General Mgr*
Richard Gregorio, *CFO*

GEOGRAPHIC

EMP: 8
SALES (est): 1MM **Privately Held**
SIC: 3812 Mfg Search/Navigation Equipment

(G-18119)
DUTCH OPHTHALMIC USA INC
10 Continental Dr Bldg 1 (03833-7507)
PHONE..................................603 778-6929
Gr Vijfvinkel, *President*
Susan Pizon, *General Mgr*
Jessica Hardy, *Info Tech Mgr*
EMP: 10
SQ FT: 4,500
SALES (est): 2.3MM **Privately Held**
SIC: 3841 Mfg Surgical/Medical Instruments

(G-18120)
EXETER CABINET COMPANY INC
16 Kingston Rd Unit 5 (03833-4300)
P.O. Box 457 (03833-0457)
PHONE..................................603 778-8113
Patrick E Castonguay, *President*
Faye Castonguay, *Admin Sec*
EMP: 6
SQ FT: 11,000
SALES (est): 679.8K **Privately Held**
SIC: 2434 Mfg Wooden Cabinets

(G-18121)
FLUID EQP SOLUTIONS NENG LLC
7 Walters Way (03833-4592)
P.O. Box 87, Amesbury MA (01913-0002)
PHONE..................................855 337-6633
Ben McLaughlin, *Sales Engr*
Benjamin McLaughlin, *Mng Member*
EMP: 5 **EST:** 2012
SALES (est): 334.6K **Privately Held**
SIC: 3443 Mfg Fabricated Plate Work

(G-18122)
GARY BLAKE CAR BUFFS
58 Portsmouth Ave (03833-2109)
PHONE..................................603 778-0563
Peter Obuchon, *Manager*
EMP: 6 **EST:** 2001
SALES (est): 460K **Privately Held**
WEB: www.garyblakemotorcars.com
SIC: 3541 Mfg Machine Tools-Cutting

(G-18123)
GREAT BAY GAZETTE
6 2nd St (03833-4719)
PHONE..................................603 793-2620
Natalie Healy, *Principal*
EMP: 3
SALES (est): 126.7K **Privately Held**
SIC: 2711 Newspapers-Publishing/Printing

(G-18124)
IPOTEC LLC
41 Industrial Park Dr (03833)
PHONE..................................603 778-2882
Alan P Randle, *President*
Ken Eudenbach, *Opers Staff*
▲ **EMP:** 6
SQ FT: 5,000
SALES (est): 1MM **Privately Held**
WEB: www.ipotec.com
SIC: 2822 Mfg Elastomer Components

(G-18125)
NEW HAMPSHIRE MACHINE PRODUCTS
10 Kingston Rd (03833-4320)
P.O. Box 975 (03833-0975)
PHONE..................................603 772-4404
Barbara Michaud, *President*
Owen Baril, *Chairman*
EMP: 8 **EST:** 1975
SQ FT: 5,000
SALES (est): 600K **Privately Held**
WEB: www.newhampshiremachineproducts.com
SIC: 3451 Mfg Precision Screw Machine Products

(G-18126)
OLD BH INC (PA)
100 Domain Dr (03833-4801)
PHONE..................................603 430-2111
Kevin Davis, *President*
Julie Zaleski, *Controller*
Jennifer Hutchinson, *Asst Treas*
Matt Hayes, *Sales Staff*
Darryl Hughes, *Mktg Dir*
◆ **EMP:** 195
SQ FT: 350,000
SALES (est): 149.6MM **Privately Held**
SIC: 3949 Mfg Sporting/Athletic Goods

(G-18127)
OSRAM SYLVANIA INC
Also Called: Chemical & Metallurgical Div
131 Portsmouth Ave (03833-2105)
PHONE..................................603 772-4331
David Lamprey, *Opers-Prdtn-Mfg*
Frank St Ong, *Marketing Staff*
EMP: 100
SALES (corp-wide): 3.8B **Privately Held**
WEB: www.sylvania.com
SIC: 3641 3671 3643 3433 Mfg Nonclay Refractories Mfg Electron Tubes Mfg Conductive Wire Dvcs Mfg Heat Equip-Nonelec
HQ: Osram Sylvania Inc
200 Ballardvale St # 305
Wilmington MA 01887
978 570-3000

(G-18128)
OSRAM SYLVANIA INC
Also Called: General Lighting Division
131 Portsmouth Ave (03833-2140)
PHONE..................................603 669-5350
EMP: 200
SALES (corp-wide): 4.8B **Privately Held**
SIC: 3641 Mfg Electric Lamps
HQ: Osram Sylvania Inc
200 Ballardvale St # 305
Wilmington MA 01887
978 570-3000

(G-18129)
PSJL CORPORATION
41 Industrial Dr (03833-4597)
PHONE..................................978 313-2550
Darion Upton, *Principal*
EMP: 52
SALES (corp-wide): 67.5MM **Privately Held**
SIC: 3577 Mfg Computer Peripheral Equipment
PA: Psjl Corporation
780 Boston Rd Ste 4
Billerica MA 01821
978 313-2500

(G-18130)
RIVER CITY SOFTWARE LLC
108 Kingston Rd (03833-4328)
P.O. Box 128 (03833-0128)
PHONE..................................603 686-5525
Michelle Berk, *Office Mgr*
Anthony Berke,
EMP: 6
SQ FT: 2,000
SALES: 200K **Privately Held**
WEB: www.rivercitysoftware.com
SIC: 7372 8748 Prepackaged Software Services Business Consulting Services

(G-18131)
SEAPOINT SENSORS INC
45 Water St Frnt (03833-2465)
P.O. Box 368 (03833-0368)
PHONE..................................603 642-4921
Jeffrey Mather, *President*
EMP: 3
SALES: 200K **Privately Held**
WEB: www.seapoint.com
SIC: 3812 Mfg Search/Navigation Equipment

(G-18132)
SIG SAUER INC
12 Industrial Dr (03833-4557)
PHONE..................................603 610-3000
Ron Cohen, *CEO*
EMP: 99
SALES (corp-wide): 583.5K **Privately Held**
SIC: 3484 Mfg Small Arms
HQ: Sig Sauer Inc.
72 Pease Blvd
Newington NH 03801
603 610-3000

(G-18133)
TBD BRANDS LLC
Also Called: Yoghund
7 Beech Hill Rd (03833-4502)
PHONE..................................603 775-7772
Jody T Rodgers, *Mng Member*
EMP: 5
SALES (est): 1.6MM **Privately Held**
SIC: 2047 5149 Mfg Dog/Cat Food Whol Groceries

(G-18134)
UNARCO MATERIAL HANDLING INC
1 Hampton Rd Unit 106 (03833-4891)
PHONE..................................603 772-2070
Bill Morisson, *Manager*
EMP: 25
SALES (corp-wide): 4.1B **Privately Held**
WEB: www.unarcorack.com
SIC: 3823 3824 3577 Mfg Process Control Instruments Mfg Fluid Meter/Counting Devices Mfg Computer Peripheral Equipment
HQ: Unarco Material Handling, Inc.
701 16th Ave E
Springfield TN 37172

(G-18135)
VAPOTHERM INC (PA)
100 Domain Dr Ste 102 (03833-4904)
PHONE..................................603 658-0011
James Liken, *Ch of Bd*
Joseph Army, *President*
David Blouin, *Vice Pres*
John Coolidge, *Vice Pres*
Marc Davidson, *Vice Pres*
▲ **EMP:** 298 **EST:** 1993
SALES: 42.3MM **Publicly Held**
SIC: 3841 Mfg Surgical/Medical Instruments

(G-18136)
VELOCITY MANUFACTURING INC
41 Industrial Dr Ste 1 (03833-4570)
PHONE..................................603 773-2386
Jim Laird, *Vice Pres*
Kristi Smith, *Controller*
Mehdi Ali, *Manager*
EMP: 50
SQ FT: 20,000
SALES (est): 8.2MM
SALES (corp-wide): 128.7MM **Privately Held**
WEB: www.velocitymfginc.com
SIC: 3679 Manufactures Wire Harnesses
PA: Integrated Cable Assembly Holdings, Inc.
6401 S Country Club Rd # 101
Tucson AZ 85706
520 290-9987

(G-18137)
WALL INDUSTRIES INC
37 Industrial Dr Ste 3 (03833-7519)
PHONE..................................603 778-2300
James F McCann Jr, *President*
James M Bunt, *Treasurer*
Kevin E McCann, *Admin Sec*
▲ **EMP:** 45 **EST:** 1960
SQ FT: 70,000
SALES: 11MM
SALES (corp-wide): 4.7B **Publicly Held**
WEB: www.wallindustries.com
SIC: 3621 3612 Mfg Motors/Generators Mfg Transformers
PA: Continental Resources, Inc.
20 N Broadway
Oklahoma City OK 73102
405 234-9000

(G-18138)
WE CORK ENTERPRISES INC
16 Kingston Rd Unit 6 (03833-4300)
PHONE..................................603 778-8558
Ann Wicander, *President*
Elizabeth Wicander, *Vice Pres*
Hjalmar Wicander, *Shareholder*
▲ **EMP:** 5
SALES (est): 751.7K **Privately Held**
WEB: www.wecork.com
SIC: 2499 Mfg Wood Products

Farmington
Strafford County

(G-18139)
ANDREW J FOSS COMPANY INC
100 Cocheco Rd (03835-3804)
PHONE..................................603 755-2515
John Cardinal, *President*
Emmanuel Krasner, *Admin Sec*
EMP: 11 **EST:** 1963
SQ FT: 20,000
SALES (est): 2.1MM **Privately Held**
WEB: www.ajfoss.com
SIC: 3272 Mfg Concrete Products

(G-18140)
ARTEMAS INDUSTRIES INC
20 Sarah Greenfield Way (03835-3709)
PHONE..................................603 755-9777
Donald W Cammet, *President*
Donald W Cammett, *President*
Michelle S Cammett, *Corp Secy*
David Dugal, *Vice Pres*
EMP: 7
SQ FT: 5,000
SALES: 300K **Privately Held**
SIC: 3599 Mfg Industrial Machinery

(G-18141)
ENERGY RESOURCES GROUP INC (PA)
23 Commerce Pkwy (03835-4101)
PHONE..................................603 335-2535
Carrie Hurn, *President*
Joe Ferris, *Project Mgr*
Scott Gagne, *Manager*
Keith B Frisbee, *Director*
Holly A Baron, *Admin Sec*
▲ **EMP:** 24
SQ FT: 1,600,000
SALES (est): 6.2MM **Privately Held**
WEB: www.ergincorp.com
SIC: 3511 Mfg Turbines/Generator Sets

(G-18142)
H R P PRODUCTS INC
101 Nh Route 11 (03835-3838)
P.O. Box 190, Somersworth (03878-0190)
PHONE..................................603 330-3757
Luke Janetos, *President*
Louise M Janetos, *Treasurer*
EMP: 11
SQ FT: 5,000
SALES (est): 1.1MM **Privately Held**
WEB: www.hrpsports.com
SIC: 3949 2329 Mfg Protective Jackets Used For Motorcycle Racing & Contract Stitching Of Athletic Protective Gear

(G-18143)
J J PLANK CORPORATION
Also Called: Spencer-Johnston Co
16 Plank Industrial Dr (03835-3811)
P.O. Box 1955, Appleton WI (54912-1955)
PHONE..................................920 733-4479
Chuck Chase, *Branch Mgr*
EMP: 6
SQ FT: 17,600
SALES (corp-wide): 6.6B **Privately Held**
WEB: www.jjplank.com
SIC: 3554 7699 3531 Mfg Paper Industrial Machinery Repair Services Mfg Construction Machinery
HQ: J. J. Plank Corporation
728 Watermark Ct
Neenah WI 54956
920 733-4479

(G-18144)
SCHAEFERROLLS INC
Also Called: Paper Mill and Indus Rbr Pdts
23 Plank Industrial Dr (03835-3811)
P.O. Box 697 (03835-0697)
PHONE..................................603 335-1786
John Fisher, *CEO*
Jeanine Lewis, *Treasurer*
Russell Shillaber, *Admin Sec*
▲ **EMP:** 22
SQ FT: 38,000

SALES (est): 5.4MM Privately Held
WEB: www.samcorolls.com
SIC: 3069 Mfg Fabricated Rubber Products

(G-18145)
SENECA MACHINE
317 Main St (03835-3772)
PHONE....603 755-8900
Gary Feroz, *Owner*
EMP: 3
SQ FT: 14,500
SALES (est): 377.4K Privately Held
SIC: 3599 Mfg Jobbing Or Repair Machine

(G-18146)
WHITE MOUNTAIN PLOWING
67 Glen St (03835-3334)
PHONE....603 817-0913
Chris Pycko, *Principal*
EMP: 3
SALES (est): 305.3K Privately Held
SIC: 2851 Mfg Paints/Allied Products

Fitzwilliam
Cheshire County

(G-18147)
ABTECH INC
126 Rte 12 N (03447)
P.O. Box 509 (03447-0509)
PHONE....603 585-7106
Kenneth Abbott, *President*
William Abbott, *Vice Pres*
EMP: 24
SALES (est): 1.2MM Privately Held
WEB: www.abtechmfg.com
SIC: 3599 Mfg Industrial Machinery

(G-18148)
DAVES SITEWORK AND SAWMILL
850 Templeton Tpke (03447-3387)
PHONE....603 313-0787
David S Loock, *Owner*
EMP: 4
SALES (est): 161.5K Privately Held
SIC: 2421 Sawmill/Planing Mill

(G-18149)
DUXBURY COMPOSITE PRODUCTS
57 Creamery Rd (03447)
P.O. Box 429 (03447-0429)
PHONE....603 585-9100
Daniel Scheerer, *President*
EMP: 21
SALES (est): 600.4K Privately Held
SIC: 3296 Mfg Mineral Wool

(G-18150)
LORETO PUBLICATIONS INC
139a Tully Brook Rd (03447)
P.O. Box 603 (03447-0603)
PHONE....603 239-6671
Doug Bershaw, *President*
▲ EMP: 6
SALES: 170.7K Privately Held
SIC: 2731 Books-Publishing/Printing

(G-18151)
MONADNOCK GRINDING LLC
98 Royalston Rd (03447-3440)
P.O. Box 152 (03447-0152)
PHONE....603 585-7275
Darnell Favreau, *Principal*
EMP: 7 EST: 2007
SALES (est): 708.8K Privately Held
SIC: 3599 Mfg Industrial Machinery

(G-18152)
PLP COMPOSITE TECHNOLOGIES
57 Creamery Rd (03447-3528)
P.O. Box 429 (03447-0429)
PHONE....603 585-9100
William Bazley, *President*
▲ EMP: 34
SALES (est): 5.5MM Privately Held
WEB: www.plpcomp.com
SIC: 3089 3446 Mfg Plastic Products Mfg Architectural Metalwork

(G-18153)
TOMMILA BROTHERS INC
487 Nh (03447)
P.O. Box 12 (03447-0012)
PHONE....603 242-7774
John W Tommila, *CEO*
Chuck Nolan, *Vice Pres*
EMP: 10 EST: 1936
SQ FT: 800
SALES (est): 1.7MM Privately Held
SIC: 2421 5211 5031 2431 Sawmill/Planing Mill Ret Lumber/Building Mtrl Whol Lumber/Plywd/Millwk Mfg Millwork

Franconia
Grafton County

(G-18154)
SECRET SOCK SOCIETY
170 Beechwood Ln (03580-5109)
PHONE....603 443-3208
Nancy Annunziato, *President*
EMP: 3 EST: 2014
SALES: 8K Privately Held
SIC: 2252 Mfg Hosiery

Franklin
Merrimack County

(G-18155)
ACME STAPLE COMPANY INC
87 Hill Rd (03235-1108)
PHONE....603 934-2320
Richard L Gold, *President*
Dawn Landry, *COO*
Onno Boswinkel, *Vice Pres*
Thomas R Gold, *Vice Pres*
Mark Billeci, *Sales Mgr*
▲ EMP: 15 EST: 1982
SQ FT: 44,000
SALES (est): 3.3MM Privately Held
WEB: www.acmestaple.com
SIC: 3315 3579 Mfg Steel Wire/Related Products Mfg Office Machines

(G-18156)
CENTURY MAGNETICS INTL
20 Canal St Ste 401 (03235-1602)
PHONE....603 934-4931
Jim Klingensmith, *President*
James Klingensmith, *President*
Richard Osgood, *CFO*
EMP: 16
SQ FT: 10,000
SALES (est): 1MM Privately Held
SIC: 3612 Mfg Of Magnetic Components Transformers

(G-18157)
ENTECH MANUFACTURING LLC
234 Hill Rd (03235-1120)
PHONE....603 934-1288
Vito Tropiano, *Mng Member*
Jutta Tropiano,
EMP: 6
SQ FT: 4,600
SALES (est): 723.4K Privately Held
SIC: 3599 Machine Shop

(G-18158)
INSULFAB PLASTICS INC
155 N Main St (03235-1026)
PHONE....603 934-2770
Charles A Pauwels, *Branch Mgr*
EMP: 10
SALES (est): 1.9MM
SALES (corp-wide): 26.5MM Privately Held
WEB: www.insulfab.com
SIC: 3089 Mfg Plastic Products
PA: Insulfab Plastics, Inc.
834 Hayne St
Spartanburg SC 29301
864 582-7506

(G-18159)
LONG RANGE LLC
26 Cannery St (03235)
PHONE....603 934-3009
Neil Chadwick, *Mng Member*
Neal Chatwick,
EMP: 5
SQ FT: 5,500
SALES (est): 803.5K Privately Held
SIC: 3679 Mfg Electronic Components

(G-18160)
MCBEY JOHN
Also Called: McBey Machines
55 Industrial Park Dr (03235-2507)
P.O. Box 128 (03235-0128)
PHONE....603 934-2858
John McBey, *Owner*
EMP: 5
SQ FT: 4,000
SALES (est): 266.2K Privately Held
SIC: 3599 Machine Shop

(G-18161)
PATRIOT FOUNDRY & CASTINGS LLC
324 Hill Rd (03235-1141)
P.O. Box 298 (03235-0298)
PHONE....603 934-3919
Gregory Davall, *Mng Member*
Chris Leuteritz,
Debra Leuteritz,
EMP: 15
SALES: 950K Privately Held
SIC: 3365 Aluminum Foundry

(G-18162)
PCC STRUCTURALS GROTON
PCC Strcturals Alum Operations
35 Industrial Park Dr (03235-2507)
PHONE....603 286-4301
EMP: 6
SALES (corp-wide): 225.3B Publicly Held
SIC: 3324 Steel Investment Foundry
HQ: Pcc Structurals Groton
839 Poquonnock Rd
Groton CT 06340
860 405-3700

(G-18163)
PERFORMANCE CHEMICALS LLC
40 Industrial Park Dr (03235-2507)
P.O. Box 9 (03235-0009)
PHONE....603 228-1200
Michael R Currier,
Joe Goguen, *Maintence Staff*
EMP: 10
SALES (est): 1.9MM Privately Held
WEB: www.performancechemicals.com
SIC: 2899 Whol Chemicals/Products

(G-18164)
SODA SHOPPE OF FRANKLIN
901 Central St (03235-2049)
PHONE....603 934-0100
Cory Keith, *Principal*
EMP: 10
SALES (est): 1.3MM Privately Held
SIC: 2024 5812 Mfg Ice Cream/Frozen Desert Eating Place

(G-18165)
STENCILS ONLINE LLC
70 Industrial Park Dr # 7 (03235-2520)
PHONE....603 934-5034
Bridgett Gauthier, *Sales Mgr*
Fred McAllister, *Mng Member*
▲ EMP: 6
SALES (est): 881.3K Privately Held
WEB: www.stencilsonline.com
SIC: 2675 7389 5961 Mfg Die-Cut Paper/Paperboard Business Services At Non-Commercial Site Electronic Shopping

(G-18166)
WATTS REGULATOR CO
Webster Valve Company
583 S Main St (03235-1559)
PHONE....603 934-5110
Kent Sargent, *General Mgr*
Bertagna Peter, *Senior Engr*
EMP: 600
SALES (corp-wide): 1.5B Publicly Held
WEB: www.wattsreg.com
SIC: 3491 3364 3593 Mfg Industrial Valves Mfg Nonferrous Die-Castings Mfg Fluid Power Cylinders
HQ: Watts Regulator Co.
815 Chestnut St
North Andover MA 01845
978 689-6000

(G-18167)
WATTS WATER TECHNOLOGIES INC
583 S Main St (03235-1559)
PHONE....603 934-1369
Roy Meier, *General Mgr*
Bryan Anderson, *Principal*
Rene Danjou, *Prgrmr*
EMP: 55
SALES (corp-wide): 1.5B Publicly Held
SIC: 3491 Mfg Industrial Valves
PA: Watts Water Technologies, Inc.
815 Chestnut St
North Andover MA 01845
978 688-1811

(G-18168)
WATTS WATER TECHNOLOGIES INC
Watts Regulator
20 Industrial Park Dr (03235)
PHONE....603 934-1367
Bryan Anderson, *Principal*
EMP: 38
SALES (corp-wide): 1.5B Publicly Held
SIC: 3491 Mfg Industrial Valves
PA: Watts Water Technologies, Inc.
815 Chestnut St
North Andover MA 01845
978 688-1811

(G-18169)
WYMAN-GORDON COMPANY
35 Industrial Park Dr (03235-2507)
PHONE....603 934-6630
Mike Fillion, *Branch Mgr*
EMP: 50
SALES (corp-wide): 225.3B Publicly Held
WEB: www.dropdies.com
SIC: 3363 Aluminum Casting
HQ: Wyman-Gordon Company
244 Worcester St
North Grafton MA 01536
508 839-8252

(G-18170)
YDC PRECISION MACHINE INC
518 North Rd (03235-5434)
PHONE....603 934-6200
Yvan D Cote, *President*
Rose Cote, *Vice Pres*
EMP: 3
SALES: 200K Privately Held
WEB: www.ydcmachining.com
SIC: 3599 Mfg Industrial Machinery

Freedom
Carroll County

(G-18171)
UNDERGROUND PRESS
516 Huckins Rd (03836-4421)
P.O. Box 601, West Ossipee (03890-0601)
PHONE....603 323-2022
Mike Lavoie, *Owner*
EMP: 4
SALES (est): 387.4K Privately Held
SIC: 2752 Lithographic Commercial Printing

(G-18172)
VIER ECK MACHINE AND TOOL INC
277 W Bay Rd (03836-4512)
PHONE....603 860-1616
Robert Barber, *President*
Robert Barker, *President*
EMP: 3
SALES: 100K Privately Held
SIC: 3599 Machine Shop

GEOGRAPHIC

Fremont
Rockingham County

(G-18173)
ALL NATURES ELEMENTS
190 Scribner Rd (03044-3405)
PHONE..................................603 427-3535
EMP: 3 **EST:** 2013
SALES (est): 154.1K **Privately Held**
SIC: 2819 Industrial Inorganic Chemicals, Nec

(G-18174)
BEST MACHINE INC
79 Beede Hill Rd (03044-3247)
PHONE..................................603 895-4018
Mark Woodman, *President*
Cheryl Woodman, *Director*
EMP: 7
SQ FT: 2,500
SALES (est): 1.2MM **Privately Held**
WEB: www.bestmachineinc.com
SIC: 3291 3599 Mfg Of Metal Products For Industrial Machinery Repair Of Industrial Equipment

(G-18175)
COPP LOGGING LLC
27 Danville Rd (03044-3518)
PHONE..................................603 479-4828
Allen E Copp, *Administration*
EMP: 3 **EST:** 2010
SALES (est): 246.5K **Privately Held**
SIC: 2411 Logging

(G-18176)
FREMONT MACHINE & TOOL CO INC
Also Called: FREMONT ENGINEERING
810 Main St (03044-3585)
PHONE..................................603 895-9445
David Lambert, *President*
Roland Lambert Jr, *Vice Pres*
EMP: 9
SQ FT: 1,400
SALES: 534.9K **Privately Held**
SIC: 3541 Mfg Machine Tools-Cutting

(G-18177)
ION PHYSICS CORP
373 Main St (03044)
P.O. Box 165 (03044-0165)
PHONE..................................603 895-5100
Helmuti Milde, *President*
Charles Salisbury, *Vice Pres*
Leslie F Milde, *Treasurer*
Helmut Milde, *Info Tech Mgr*
EMP: 8
SQ FT: 3,000
SALES (est): 87.3K **Privately Held**
WEB: www.ionphysics.com
SIC: 3825 8731 3621 Mfg Electrical Measuring Instruments Commercial Physical Research Mfg Motors/Generators

(G-18178)
PRECISION DEPANELING MCHS LLC
326 Main St Unit 11 (03044-3440)
PHONE..................................540 248-1381
Thomas Nisbet,
EMP: 10
SQ FT: 7,000
SALES (est): 1.8MM
SALES (corp-wide): 3.5MM **Privately Held**
SIC: 3544 3549 Mfg Dies/Tools/Jigs/Fixtures Mfg Metalworking Machinery
PA: Precision Placement Machines, Inc.
326 Main St Unit 11
Fremont NH 03044
603 895-5112

(G-18179)
PRECISION PLACEMENT MCHS INC (PA)
326 Main St Unit 11 (03044-3440)
PHONE..................................603 895-5112
Thomas Nisbet, *President*
▲ **EMP:** 17
SQ FT: 15,000
SALES (est): 3.5MM **Privately Held**
SIC: 3672 Mfg Printed Circuit Boards

(G-18180)
ROBERT A COLLINS
Also Called: Collins Pattern & Mold
130 Scribner Rd (03044-3405)
PHONE..................................603 895-2345
Robert A Collins, *Owner*
EMP: 3 **EST:** 1963
SQ FT: 9,000
SALES: 350K **Privately Held**
SIC: 3086 3469 Mfg Plastic Foam Products Mfg Metal Stampings

(G-18181)
UNITED MCH & TL DESIGN CO INC
18 River Rd (03044-3577)
P.O. Box 168 (03044-0168)
PHONE..................................603 642-3601
George Lufkin Jr, *President*
Barbara Lufkin, *Treasurer*
EMP: 35
SQ FT: 28,000
SALES (est): 8MM **Privately Held**
SIC: 3429 Mfg Industrial Machinery

Gilford
Belknap County

(G-18182)
AMG-AWETIS MFG GROUP CORP
18 Colonial Dr (03249-6401)
PHONE..................................603 286-1645
Jeans Frank, *CEO*
Arthur Rabert, *Opers Staff*
EMP: 10
SALES: 5MM
SALES (corp-wide): 933.7K **Privately Held**
SIC: 3599 Industrial Machinery And Automation Manufacturing
HQ: Awetis Gmbh
Dr.-Werner-Freyberg-Str. 7
Laudenbach 69514
620 180-6390

(G-18183)
CORE ASSEMBLIES INC
21 Meadowbrook Ln Unit 4 (03249-6305)
PHONE..................................603 293-0270
Cory Navoy, *President*
EMP: 15
SQ FT: 4,800
SALES: 1.7MM **Privately Held**
WEB: www.coreassemblies.com
SIC: 3599 3443 3672 Mfg Industrial Machinery Mfg Fabricated Plate Wrk Mfg Printed Circuit Brds

(G-18184)
DANIEL WHEELER
Also Called: Native Sun Studio
180 Stark St (03249-6435)
PHONE..................................603 528-6363
EMP: 3
SQ FT: 1,500
SALES: 375K **Privately Held**
SIC: 3231 Mfg Products-Purchased Glass

(G-18185)
DGF INDSTRIAL INNVATIONS GROUP
25 Waterford Pl (03249-6661)
P.O. Box 7532, Laconia (03247-7532)
PHONE..................................603 528-6591
Gisele Lambert, *President*
Douglas L Lambert, *General Mgr*
EMP: 15
SALES (est): 1.1MM **Privately Held**
WEB: www.dgfindustrial.com
SIC: 3599 7699 3444 3356 Mfg Industrial Machinery Repair Services Mfg Sheet Metalwork Nonferrous Rollng/Drawng

(G-18186)
DIGITAL PRINTER SERVICE
159 Mountain Dr (03249-6796)
PHONE..................................860 395-7942
Steven Verrilli, *President*
EMP: 3
SALES (est): 343.5K **Privately Held**
SIC: 2752 Lithographic Commercial Printing

(G-18187)
EAST COAST WELDING
1979 Lake Shore Rd (03249-7657)
PHONE..................................603 293-8384
Allan Fasshauer, *Owner*
EMP: 4
SALES (est): 404.1K **Privately Held**
SIC: 7692 Welding Repair

(G-18188)
HERRMANN PEPI CRYSTAL INC
3 Waterford Pl (03249-6322)
PHONE..................................603 528-1020
Pepi Herrmann, *President*
Katharina Herrmann, *Vice Pres*
EMP: 4
SALES (est): 260K **Privately Held**
WEB: www.handcut.com
SIC: 3229 5999 Art Studio Creating Crystal Art Pieces And Retailing The Same

(G-18189)
HOWARD PRECISION INC
Also Called: Hpi
359 Hounsell Ave (03249-6922)
PHONE..................................603 293-8012
Joseph D Howard, *President*
Carole Howard, *Vice Pres*
EMP: 18
SQ FT: 9,000
SALES: 600K **Privately Held**
SIC: 3599 Mfg Industrial Machinery

(G-18190)
LEVASSEUR PRECISION INC
13 Artisan Ct Unit A (03249-6320)
P.O. Box 7361, Laconia (03247-7361)
PHONE..................................603 524-6766
Richard Levasseur, *President*
Sara J Levasseur, *Vice Pres*
Scott Levasseur, *Opers Mgr*
EMP: 4
SQ FT: 5,000
SALES: 165K **Privately Held**
WEB: www.levasseurprecision.com
SIC: 3599 Mfg Industrial Machinery

(G-18191)
METZ ELECTRONICS CORP
Also Called: M E C
7 Countryside Dr (03249-6405)
PHONE..................................603 524-8806
EMP: 30
SQ FT: 15,000
SALES (est): 4.8MM **Privately Held**
WEB: www.metzelectronics.com
SIC: 3672 3679 Mfg Printed Circuit Boards Mfg Electronic Components

(G-18192)
SPECIAL PROJECTS GROUP LLC
221 Intervale Rd B2 (03249-7435)
P.O. Box 7283, Laconia (03247-7283)
PHONE..................................603 391-9700
Mark Richardson,
EMP: 7
SALES (est): 310K **Privately Held**
SIC: 3732 7532 Boatbuilding/Repairing Auto Body Repair/Painting

Gilmanton
Belknap County

(G-18193)
L R FUEL SYSTEMS
151 South Rd (03237-4945)
PHONE..................................603 848-3835
EMP: 3
SALES (est): 184.1K **Privately Held**
SIC: 2869 Mfg Industrial Organic Chemicals

(G-18194)
SUNNYSIDE MAPLES INC
554 Meadow Pond Rd (03237-5138)
PHONE..................................603 783-9961
Elaine Moore, *President*
EMP: 3
SALES (est): 236.5K **Privately Held**
SIC: 2099 Wholesale Maple Syrup & Products

Gilsum
Cheshire County

(G-18195)
AVOCUS PUBLISHING INC
4 White Brook Rd (03448)
P.O. Box 89 (03448-0089)
PHONE..................................603 357-0236
Ernest Peter, *President*
EMP: 9
SALES (est): 534K **Privately Held**
WEB: www.avocus.com
SIC: 2731 Books-Publishing/Printing

(G-18196)
WS BADGER COMPANY INC
768 Route 10 (03448-7503)
P.O. Box 58 (03448-0058)
PHONE..................................603 357-2958
William Whyte, *President*
Kathleen Schwerin, *Vice Pres*
Emily Schwerin-Whyte, *Treasurer*
Rebecca Hamilton, *Admin Sec*
▲ **EMP:** 31
SALES (est): 9MM **Privately Held**
WEB: www.badgerbalm.com
SIC: 2844 Mfg Toilet Preparations

Goffstown
Hillsborough County

(G-18197)
ACCURATE BRAZING CORPORATION (HQ)
36 Cote Ave Ste 5 (03045-5261)
PHONE..................................603 945-3750
Steven Francis, *President*
Rebecca Vernier, *Enginr/R&D Asst*
Leo Francis, *Treasurer*
Frank Little, *Finance Mgr*
Hazen Earle, *Manager*
EMP: 47
SQ FT: 10,000
SALES: 20MM
SALES (corp-wide): 3B **Privately Held**
WEB: www.accuratebrazing.com
SIC: 3398 Metal Heat Treating
PA: Aalberts N.V.
Stadsplateau 18
Utrecht
303 079-300

(G-18198)
CONCEPT TOOL AND DESIGN INC
28 Daniel Plummer Rd # 9 (03045-2552)
PHONE..................................603 622-0216
Dale Caron, *President*
EMP: 6
SQ FT: 3,200
SALES (est): 1MM **Privately Held**
WEB: www.concepttoolandesign.com
SIC: 3089 Mfg Plastic Products

(G-18199)
DAVID R BURL
56 N Mast St (03045-1712)
PHONE..................................603 235-2661
David R Burl, *Principal*
EMP: 6
SALES (est): 501.9K **Privately Held**
SIC: 2411 Logging

(G-18200)
FEATURE PRODUCTS LTD
18 Cote Ave Ste 13 (03045-5241)
PHONE..................................603 669-0800
David Still, *President*
Lee Still, *Senior VP*
Hank Lippisch, *Engineer*
Ronald Stewart, *Sales Staff*
▲ **EMP:** 8
SQ FT: 10,000
SALES (est): 925.6K **Privately Held**
SIC: 3469 Mfg Metal Stampings-Offshore Manufacturing Representative Firm

(G-18201)
G & G TOOL & DIE CORP
36 Cote Ave Ste 3 (03045-5261)
PHONE..................................603 625-9744
Leo Gosselin, *President*
Joseph Gaffney, *Vice Pres*
Joseph Gaffney Jr, *Treasurer*
EMP: 3 **EST:** 1978
SQ FT: 1,200
SALES: 200K **Privately Held**
SIC: 3089 Mfg Plastic Injection Molds

(G-18202)
G&R INDUSTRIES INC
4 Cote Ave Ste 9 (03045-5293)
PHONE..................................603 626-3071
Bob Gonsilves, *President*
EMP: 4
SALES (est): 346.7K **Privately Held**
SIC: 3999 Mfg Misc Products

(G-18203)
HAPPY HOUSE AMUSEMENT INC
70 Depot St (03045-1755)
P.O. Box 120 (03045-0120)
PHONE..................................603 497-4151
Raymond Blondeau Sr, *President*
▲ **EMP:** 50
SQ FT: 36,000
SALES (est): 4.3MM **Privately Held**
SIC: 3999 7993 5091 Manufactures And Rents Coin-Operated Amusement Machines And Wholesales Billiard Equipment Dartboards And Supplies

(G-18204)
HAWKES MOTORSPORTS LLC
129a S Mast St (03045-6101)
PHONE..................................603 660-9864
Austin Hawkes,
EMP: 4
SALES: 200K **Privately Held**
SIC: 3537 Mfg Industrial Trucks/Tractors

(G-18205)
JUST COUNTERS
28 Daniel Plummer Rd # 3 (03045-2570)
PHONE..................................603 627-2027
John Laughlin, *Owner*
EMP: 5
SALES (est): 522.1K **Privately Held**
SIC: 2541 Mfg Wood Partitions/Fixtures

(G-18206)
NEW HAMPSHIRE STAMPING CO INC
9 Lance Ln Ste 2 (03045-5263)
PHONE..................................603 641-1234
Robert La Rochelle, *President*
Andrew Hill, *Treasurer*
Bruce Marrisson, *Controller*
EMP: 25
SQ FT: 15,000
SALES (est): 4.6MM **Privately Held**
WEB: www.nhstamp.com
SIC: 3469 3087 3312 Mfg Metal Stampings Custom Compounding-Purchased Resins Blast Furnace-Steel Works

(G-18207)
NEW HAMPSHIRE STL ERECTORS INC
17 Lamy Dr (03045-5219)
P.O. Box 4226, Manchester (03108-4226)
PHONE..................................603 668-3464
Mark A Ginnard, *President*
EMP: 50
SQ FT: 20,200
SALES (est): 8.7MM **Privately Held**
SIC: 3446 1791 3441 Mfg Architectural Mtlwrk Structural Steel Erectn Structural Metal Fabrctn

(G-18208)
NEW HMPSHIRE STL FBRCATORS INC
17 Lamy Dr (03045-5219)
P.O. Box 4226, Manchester (03108-4226)
PHONE..................................603 668-3464
Mark A Ginnard, *President*
Russell Hilliard, *VP Sales*
Daniel Dineen, *Sr Project Mgr*
EMP: 40
SALES (est): 9.4MM **Privately Held**
SIC: 3441 Structural Metal Fabrication

(G-18209)
PLASTIC TECHNIQUES INC
27 Springfield Rd (03045-5232)
P.O. Box 250 (03045-0250)
PHONE..................................603 622-5570
Gossett Mc Rae, *CEO*
Marcel Pelletier, *Engrg Dir*
Chris McRae, *Manager*
EMP: 27
SQ FT: 50,000
SALES (est): 5.2MM **Privately Held**
SIC: 3089 3646 3535 Mfg Plastic Products Mfg Commercial Lighting Fixtures Mfg Conveyors/Equipment

Gorham
Coos County

(G-18210)
ALBRITE SIGNS LLC
20 Libby St (03581-1300)
P.O. Box 68 (03581-0068)
PHONE..................................603 466-5192
Ryan Christopher,
Valerie Christopher,
EMP: 3 **EST:** 1999
SALES (est): 251.4K **Privately Held**
SIC: 3993 Mfg Signs/Advertising Specialties

(G-18211)
CREATIVE THREADS LLC
43a Dublin St (03581-1517)
P.O. Box 150 (03581-0150)
PHONE..................................603 466-2752
Tracey Drouin,
EMP: 3
SQ FT: 960
SALES: 150K **Privately Held**
SIC: 2395 Pleating/Stitching Services

(G-18212)
GORHAM SAND & GRAVEL
42 Lancaster Rd (03581-1411)
PHONE..................................603 466-2291
Roger Martin, *Manager*
EMP: 20
SALES (est): 677.2K **Privately Held**
SIC: 1442 Construction Sand/Gravel

(G-18213)
KEL LOG INC
Also Called: Kelly Trucking
580 Main St (03581-4908)
PHONE..................................603 752-2000
Michael Kelley, *President*
EMP: 25
SALES (corp-wide): 3.2MM **Privately Held**
SIC: 2411 Logging
PA: Kel Log Inc
743 E Side River Rd
Milan NH 03588
603 752-2000

(G-18214)
LABONVILLE INC
Also Called: Labonville Safety
500 Main St Trlr 21 (03581-4905)
PHONE..................................603 752-3221
Ronald Dannault, *Manager*
EMP: 20
SALES (corp-wide): 10.5MM **Privately Held**
WEB: www.labonville.com
SIC: 3842 2326 Mfg Surgical Appliances/Supplies Mfg Men's/Boy's Work Clothing
PA: Labonville, Inc.
504 Main St
Gorham NH 03581
603 752-4030

Goshen
Sullivan County

(G-18215)
PHOENIX RESOURCES
193 Lempster Coach Rd (03752-3508)
PHONE..................................603 863-9096
Richard Costello, *President*
EMP: 3
SALES: 3MM **Privately Held**
WEB: www.phoenixpwb.com
SIC: 3679 8711 8748 7373 Mfg Elec Components Engineering Services Business Consulting Svcs Computer Systems Design

Grafton
Grafton County

(G-18216)
J & D WELDING
377 Kinsman Rd (03240-3614)
PHONE..................................603 523-7695
Jeff Johnston, *President*
EMP: 3
SALES (est): 77.1K **Privately Held**
SIC: 7692 Welding Repair

Grantham
Sullivan County

(G-18217)
TOPEK LLC
Also Called: Yankee Barn Home
131 Yankee Barn Rd (03753-3243)
PHONE..................................603 863-2400
Grace Kemp, *Controller*
Jeffrey Rosen, *Creative Dir*
Paul Marinelli,
EMP: 15 **EST:** 2011
SALES: 3MM **Privately Held**
SIC: 2451 Mfg Mobile Homes

Greenfield
Hillsborough County

(G-18218)
AMERICAN STEEL FABRICATORS INC
328 Sawmill Rd (03047-4130)
P.O. Box 185 (03047-0185)
PHONE..................................603 547-6311
Mark S Carter, *President*
EMP: 37
SQ FT: 28,000
SALES (est): 8.5MM **Privately Held**
SIC: 3441 Structural Metal Fabrication

Greenland
Rockingham County

(G-18219)
ADVANCED CONCRETE TECH INC-NH
Also Called: A C T
300 Portsmouth Ave (03840-2220)
PHONE..................................603 431-5661
Max Hoene, *President*
▲ **EMP:** 7
SQ FT: 4,000
SALES (est): 1.2MM
SALES (corp-wide): 43MM **Privately Held**
WEB: www.concretebiz.com
SIC: 3531 Mfg Construction Machinery
PA: Wiggert & Co. Gmbh
Wachhausstr. 3b
Karlsruhe 76227
721 943-460

(G-18220)
ANSON SAILMAKERS INC
Also Called: Sailmaking Support Systems
588 Portsmouth Ave (03840-2225)
P.O. Box 606 (03840-0606)
PHONE..................................603 431-6676
Jeff Andersen, *President*
Pamela Andersen, *Vice Pres*
EMP: 4
SALES (est): 36.9K **Privately Held**
WEB: www.hfflag.com
SIC: 2394 Mfg Canvas/Related Products

(G-18221)
ARENS STONEWORKS INC
434 Portsmouth Ave (03840-2222)
P.O. Box 550 (03840-0550)
PHONE..................................603 436-8000
Robert Arens, *CEO*
Amy Ryan, *Vice Pres*
EMP: 12
SALES (est): 1.3MM **Privately Held**
SIC: 3281 Mfg Cut Stone/Products

(G-18222)
COAST TO COAST FF & E INSTALLA
2 Spring Hill Rd (03840-2600)
PHONE..................................603 433-0164
Mark St Pierre, *President*
Sherry St Pierre, *Vice Pres*
▲ **EMP:** 12
SALES (est): 1.7MM **Privately Held**
SIC: 2599 1796 Mfg Furniture/Fixtures Building Equipment Installation

(G-18223)
DEBORAH LUDINGTON
Also Called: Sweet Grass Farm
16 Autumn Pond Park (03840-2426)
PHONE..................................603 766-1651
Deborah Ludington, *Owner*
Debbie Ludington, *Principal*
▲ **EMP:** 3
SQ FT: 2,400
SALES (est): 414.2K **Privately Held**
SIC: 2841 Manufacture Soap And Body-care Products

(G-18224)
NOVEL IRON WORKS INC
250 Ocean Rd (03840-2431)
PHONE..................................603 436-7950
Hollie Noveletsky, *CEO*
Josh Rosenthal, *President*
Thomas Heaney, *Exec VP*
Keith Moreau, *Vice Pres*
EMP: 110
SQ FT: 120,000
SALES (est): 35.7MM **Privately Held**
WEB: www.noveliron.com
SIC: 3441 Structural Metal Fabrication

(G-18225)
ZAX SIGNAGE CORP
6 Autumn Pond Park (03840-2425)
PHONE..................................603 319-6178
EMP: 3
SALES (est): 233.7K **Privately Held**
SIC: 3993 Mfg Signs/Advertising Specialties

Greenville
Hills County

(G-18226)
PITCHERVILLE SAND & GRAV CORP
36 Brown Dr (03048-3343)
PHONE..................................603 878-0035
EMP: 5
SALES (est): 450.5K **Privately Held**
SIC: 1442 Construction Sand/Gravel

Greenville
Hillsborough County

(G-18227)
MONADNOCK LAND CLEARING
Also Called: Monadnock Land Clearing & Chip
932 Fitchburg Rd (03048-3340)
P.O. Box 547 (03048-0547)
PHONE..................................603 878-2803
Hermel Pelletier, *President*
Joseph Lyle Brundige, *Vice Pres*
EMP: 7
SQ FT: 800
SALES (est): 862.5K **Privately Held**
WEB: www.monadnocklandclearing.com
SIC: 2411 1629 Logging Land Clearing

(G-18228)
NORTHEAST DRILL SUPPLY
36a Brown Dr (03048-3343)
PHONE..................................603 878-0998
Gerald E Parker, *Principal*
EMP: 3
SALES: 1.5MM **Privately Held**
SIC: 3533 Mfg Oil/Gas Field Machinery

(G-18229)
OLD DUTCH MUSTARD CO INC
Also Called: Pilgrim Foods Co
68 Old Wilton Rd (03048-3100)
P.O. Box 547 (03048-0547)
PHONE..................................516 466-0522
Denice Blanchard, *Safety Dir*
Charles Santich, *Manager*
EMP: 55
SALES (corp-wide): 15.2MM **Privately Held**
SIC: 2099 2033 2035 Mfg Food Preparations Mfg Canned Fruits/Vegtbl Mfg Pickles/Sauces
PA: Old Dutch Mustard Co. Inc.
98 Cuttermill Rd Ste 260s
Great Neck NY 11021
516 466-0522

(G-18230)
WILLIAM N LAMARRE CON PDTS INC
87 Adams Hill Rd (03048-3000)
P.O. Box 333 (03048-0333)
PHONE..................................603 878-1340
Jean L Lamarre, *President*
William N Lamarre, *Vice Pres*
William La Marre, *VP Sales*
Marie J Joerger, *Admin Sec*
EMP: 19
SQ FT: 18,500
SALES (est): 3.2MM **Privately Held**
SIC: 3272 Mfg Concrete Products

Groveton
Coos County

(G-18231)
CARON FABRICATION LLC
Also Called: Auto/Truck Repair
115 Lancaster Rd (03582-4018)
PHONE..................................603 631-0025
Christopher Caron, *Mng Member*
EMP: 4
SALES: 600K **Privately Held**
SIC: 7692 Structural Metal Fabrication

(G-18232)
PERRAS LUMBER CO INC
45 Perras Rd (03582)
P.O. Box 129 (03582-0129)
PHONE..................................603 636-1830
Robert Perras, *President*
EMP: 37
SQ FT: 125,000
SALES: 5.1MM **Privately Held**
SIC: 2421 Sawmill/Planing Mill Ret Lumber/Building Materials Ret Hardware

(G-18233)
PRIMA AMERICA CORPORATION
248 State St (03582-4036)
P.O. Box 274 (03582-0274)
PHONE..................................603 631-5407
David Auger, *Manager*
▲ **EMP:** 20
SALES (est): 950K **Privately Held**
SIC: 2911 Petroleum Refiner

(G-18234)
RICHARD DUPUIS LOGGING INC
107 Thompson Rd (03582-4315)
PHONE..................................603 636-2986
Richard Dupuis, *President*
Richrd Dupuis, *President*
Joel Dupuis, *Vice Pres*
Tracy Dupuis, *Vice Pres*
EMP: 3
SALES (est): 361.2K **Privately Held**
SIC: 2411 Logging

Guild
Sullivan County

(G-18235)
FRANK WIGGINS (PA)
Also Called: Z & W Machine Tool Company
501 Sunapee St (03754)
P.O. Box 140 (03754-0140)
PHONE..................................603 863-3151
Frank Wiggins, *Owner*
Paul Spanos, *Supervisor*
EMP: 4
SQ FT: 2,000
SALES: 400K **Privately Held**
SIC: 3599 Machine Shop

Hampstead
Rockingham County

(G-18236)
ATKINSON THIN FILM SYSTEMS
Also Called: Atfsi
25 Garland Dr (03841-2337)
PHONE..................................603 329-7322
John H Bradshaw III, *President*
EMP: 4
SQ FT: 15,000
SALES (est): 502.7K **Privately Held**
WEB: www.sputtercoat.com
SIC: 3479 Coating/Engraving Service

(G-18237)
BARLOW ARCHITECTURAL MLLWK LLC
30 Gigante Dr (03841-2310)
PHONE..................................603 329-6026
Wayne Barlow, *Manager*
▲ **EMP:** 25
SALES (est): 4.6MM **Privately Held**
SIC: 2499 Mfg Wood Products

(G-18238)
BLUE DAWG PWR WASH SOUTHERN NH
567 Main St (03841-2000)
PHONE..................................603 498-9473
EMP: 3
SALES (est): 167.5K **Privately Held**
SIC: 3572 Mfg Computer Storage Devices

(G-18239)
DESIGN CONSULTANTS ASSOCIATES
1 Owens Ct (03841-2400)
PHONE..................................603 329-4541
Martha Richardson, *President*
Norman Guevin, *President*
Gene Tenney, *Opers Staff*
EMP: 11
SQ FT: 7,600
SALES: 300K **Privately Held**
SIC: 3677 8711 Mfg Electronic Power Supply Transformers & Electrical Or Electronic Engineering Service

(G-18240)
IMED MFG
9 Gigante Dr (03841-2405)
PHONE..................................603 489-5184
EMP: 3 **EST:** 2015
SALES (est): 250.3K **Privately Held**
SIC: 3999 Mfg Misc Products

(G-18241)
LEUSIN MICROWAVE LLC
6 Gigante Dr (03841-2310)
P.O. Box 894 (03841-0894)
PHONE..................................603 329-7270
Antoine Assaf, *Manager*
EMP: 10
SALES (est): 1.5MM **Privately Held**
SIC: 3825 Mfg Electrical Measuring Instruments

(G-18242)
M & A ADVNCED DESIGN CNSTR INC (PA)
1 Gigante Dr (03841-2310)
PHONE..................................603 329-9515
Theresa Allen, *President*
Bob Allen, *Vice Pres*
Robert Allen, *Vice Pres*
EMP: 7
SQ FT: 6,000
SALES (est): 4.6MM **Privately Held**
SIC: 3569 7699 Mfg General Industrial Machinery Repair Services

(G-18243)
MEM-CO FITTINGS INC
45 Gigante Dr (03841-2310)
PHONE..................................603 329-9633
Ray Joseph, *President*
EMP: 6
SALES (est): 720.6K **Privately Held**
SIC: 3494 Mfg Valves/Pipe Fittings

(G-18244)
METAL SUPPLIERS ONLINE LLC
35 Gigante Dr (03841-2310)
P.O. Box 711 (03841-0711)
PHONE..................................603 329-0101
Alan Gamble, *CEO*
Barbara Edington,
EMP: 5
SQ FT: 3,000
SALES (est): 2.2MM **Privately Held**
WEB: www.suppliersonline.com
SIC: 1081 Metal Mining Services

(G-18245)
NCAB GROUP USA INC (PA)
10 Starwood Dr (03841-2339)
PHONE..................................603 329-4551
Steve Strevens, *General Mgr*
Martin Magnusson, *Managing Dir*
Slobodan Shokoski, *Managing Dir*
Rikard Wallin, *Managing Dir*
David M Wolff, *Managing Dir*
▲ **EMP:** 30
SALES (est): 5.9MM **Privately Held**
SIC: 3672 Mfg Printed Circuit Boards

(G-18246)
NORTHEAST CABINET DESIGNS LLC
2 Mary E Clark Dr Ste 2 # 2 (03841-5206)
PHONE..................................603 329-3465
Gary Batryn, *Principal*
EMP: 3 **EST:** 2010
SALES (est): 418.8K **Privately Held**
SIC: 2434 Mfg Wood Kitchen Cabinets

(G-18247)
OMEGA LABORATORIES INC
8 Gigante Dr (03841-2310)
PHONE..................................978 768-7771
Jack Moon, *President*
EMP: 11
SQ FT: 12,000
SALES (est): 1.2MM **Privately Held**
WEB: www.omegalaboratories.com
SIC: 3825 Mfg Microwave Test Equipment

(G-18248)
PF PRO FNSHG SILKSCREENING INC
13 Gigante Dr (03841-2310)
PHONE..................................603 329-8344
Frances M Beaudry, *President*
Richard D Beaudry, *Vice Pres*
EMP: 7
SQ FT: 6,000
SALES (est): 600K **Privately Held**
WEB: www.profinishinginc.com
SIC: 3479 7336 Powder And Liquid Coating And Silk Screening

(G-18249)
RICKSS MOTORSPORT ELECTRICS
48 Gigante Dr (03841-2310)
PHONE..................................603 329-9901
Rick Shaw, *President*
Donna Shaw, *Vice Pres*
Amanda Basnett, *Marketing Mgr*
▲ **EMP:** 8
SALES (est): 1.2MM **Privately Held**
WEB: www.ricksmotorsportelectrics.com
SIC: 3694 Mfg Engine Electrical Equipment

(G-18250)
TEAM SOLUTIONS MACHINING INC
17 Gigante Dr (03841-2403)
PHONE..................................978 420-2389
EMP: 3
SQ FT: 5,000
SALES: 500K **Privately Held**
SIC: 3545 Machine Tool Accessories

(G-18251)
WDW MACHINE INC
17 Gigante Dr Ste 1 (03841-2403)
PHONE..................................603 329-9604
Wilbur Webster Jr, *President*
EMP: 7
SQ FT: 4,000
SALES (est): 1.1MM **Privately Held**
WEB: www.wdwmachine.com
SIC: 3599 Mfg Industrial Machinery

Hampton
Rockingham County

(G-18252)
ADHESIVE TECHNOLOGIES INC (PA)
Also Called: Ad-Tech
3 Merrill Industrial Dr (03842-1995)
PHONE..................................603 926-1616
Peter S Melendy, *President*
Pete Baussmann, *Vice Pres*
Joe Sordillo, *Research*
Gerardus Briels, *Director*
Daniel G Smith, *Admin Sec*
◆ **EMP:** 25
SQ FT: 26,000
SALES (est): 11.9MM **Privately Held**
WEB: www.adhesivetech.com
SIC: 2891 3546 Mfg Adhesives/Sealants Mfg Power-Driven Handtools

(G-18253)
ALLIED WHEELCHAIR
725 Lafayette Rd Ste 3 (03842-1295)
PHONE..................................603 601-8174
Richard A Dearborn, *Owner*
EMP: 3
SALES (est): 318.9K **Privately Held**
SIC: 3842 Mfg Surgical Appliances/Supplies

(G-18254)
AQUA TITE INNOVATIVE SOLUTIONS
1 Liberty Ln E Ste 117 (03842-1840)
PHONE..................................603 431-5555
Brian Rix, *Owner*
Fred Sullivan, *Vice Pres*
EMP: 5
SALES (est): 673.3K **Privately Held**
SIC: 2842 2891 Mfg Polish/Sanitation Gd Mfg Adhesives/Sealants

(G-18255)
ARDENT CONCEPTS INC
4 Merrill Industrial Dr # 8 (03842-1943)
P.O. Box 1822 (03843-1822)
PHONE..................................603 474-1760
Gordon Vinther, *President*

▲ = Import ▼=Export
◆ =Import/Export

David Emma, *President*
Steve Cleveland, *Vice Pres*
EMP: 6
SQ FT: 2,500
SALES (est): 1.4MM
SALES (corp-wide): 8.2B **Publicly Held**
WEB: www.ardentconcepts.com
SIC: 3674 Manufacturer & Wholesaler Of Semiconduction Test Equipment
PA: Amphenol Corporation
358 Hall Ave
Wallingford CT 06492
203 265-8900

(G-18256)
B/E AEROSPACE INC
94 Tide Mill Rd (03842-2705)
PHONE..................................603 926-5700
Amin J Khoury, *Ch of Bd*
Edward Gager, *President*
Kevin Kadamus, *Sr Project Mgr*
EMP: 5
SALES (corp-wide): 66.5B **Publicly Held**
SIC: 2531 3728 3647 Manufacturing Aircraft Interior Parts
HQ: B/E Aerospace, Inc.
1400 Corporate Center Way
Wellington FL 33414
561 791-5000

(G-18257)
BARBARA BROWNIE LLC
22 Watsons Ln (03842-1212)
PHONE..................................603 601-2886
Barbara Freedman, *Principal*
EMP: 4
SALES (est): 202.2K **Privately Held**
SIC: 2051 Mfg Bread/Related Products

(G-18258)
BC NICHOLS MACHINE LLC
7 Kershaw Ave Ste 2 (03842-3323)
P.O. Box 248 (03843-0248)
PHONE..................................603 926-2333
Randy Currier, *Mng Member*
EMP: 6
SALES (est): 974K **Privately Held**
SIC: 3559 Mfg Misc Industry Machinery

(G-18259)
BRAZONICS INC (DH)
94 Tide Mill Rd (03842-2705)
PHONE..................................603 758-6237
Mike Mastergeorge, *President*
Kenn Bevins, *General Mgr*
EMP: 100
SQ FT: 36,000
SALES (est): 24.6MM
SALES (corp-wide): 66.5B **Publicly Held**
WEB: www.brazonics.com
SIC: 3728 Mfg Aircraft Parts/Equipment
HQ: B/E Aerospace, Inc.
1400 Corporate Center Way
Wellington FL 33414
561 791-5000

(G-18260)
CHEM QUEST INC
1 Liberty Ln E Ste 212 (03842-1840)
PHONE..................................207 856-2993
Fax: 207 854-3842
EMP: 4
SQ FT: 1,500
SALES (est): 560.3K **Privately Held**
WEB: www.chem-quest.com
SIC: 2841 2842 Mfg Soap/Other Detergents Mfg Polish/Sanitation Goods

(G-18261)
CHEMTRADE CHEMICALS US LLC
239 Drakeside Rd (03842-1804)
PHONE..................................603 926-0191
Gia Oei, *Branch Mgr*
EMP: 11
SALES (corp-wide): 1.2B **Privately Held**
SIC: 2819 Mfg Industrial Inorganic Chemicals
HQ: Chemtrade Chemicals Us Llc
90 E Halsey Rd
Parsippany NJ 07054

(G-18262)
ENDUR ID INC
8 Merrill Industrial Dr # 4 (03842-4901)
PHONE..................................603 758-1488
Robert Chadwick, *President*
Sharon Chadwick, *Vice Pres*
EMP: 4
SALES: 500K **Privately Held**
WEB: www.endurid.com
SIC: 3999 Mfg Misc Products

(G-18263)
FLEX-PRINT-LABELS
10 Merrill Industrial Dr (03842-1979)
PHONE..................................603 929-3088
Robert J Zakian, *Vice Pres*
John Cardellicchio, *Vice Pres*
Mike Labrecque, *Opers Mgr*
Edward Paquette, *CFO*
Kim McClain, *Accounting Mgr*
▲ **EMP:** 47
SQ FT: 40,000
SALES (est): 8.1MM **Privately Held**
WEB: www.labelsinc.com
SIC: 2759 3565 Commercial Printing Mfg Packaging Machinery

(G-18264)
HAMPTON SAND AND GRAVEL
564 Lafayette Rd (03842-3347)
PHONE..................................603 601-2275
Thomas Fortin, *Principal*
EMP: 3
SALES (est): 130K **Privately Held**
SIC: 1442 Construction Sand/Gravel

(G-18265)
INGENVEN FLRPLYMER SLUTIONS LL
70 High St (03842-2207)
PHONE..................................603 601-0877
David P Midgley, *Principal*
EMP: 3
SALES (est): 261.1K **Privately Held**
SIC: 3449 Mfg Misc Structural Metalwork

(G-18266)
LAFAYETTE DISTRIBUTORS CPL INC
369 Lafayette Rd (03842-2223)
PHONE..................................603 430-9405
Joe Salema, *President*
Tony Salema, *COO*
EMP: 38
SALES (est): 4.4MM **Privately Held**
SIC: 2051 Ret And Whol Of Donuts

(G-18267)
MIKROLAR INC
7 Scott Rd Ste 5 (03842-1173)
PHONE..................................603 617-2508
Michael Fortier, *President*
EMP: 8
SALES (est): 990K **Privately Held**
SIC: 3569 Mfg General Industrial Machinery

(G-18268)
PROTRACKER SOFTWARE INC
6 Merrill Industrial Dr # 7 (03842-1970)
P.O. Box 514 (03843-0514)
PHONE..................................603 926-8085
Warren J Mackensen, *President*
EMP: 7
SALES (est): 532.9K **Privately Held**
WEB: www.protracker.com
SIC: 7372 Prepackaged Software Services

(G-18269)
Q A TECHNOLOGY COMPANY INC
110 Towle Farm Rd (03842-1805)
PHONE..................................603 926-1193
Dave Coe, *President*
John Sproul, *Prdtn Mgr*
Jill Pelletier, *Buyer*
Steve Ergmann, *Engineer*
Matt Parker, *Design Engr*
EMP: 75
SQ FT: 83,000
SALES (est): 24.1MM **Privately Held**
WEB: www.qatech.com
SIC: 3825 3678 3643 Mfg Electrical Measuring Instruments Mfg Electronic Connectors Mfg Conductive Wiring Devices

(G-18270)
ROWE MACHINE CO
143 N Shore Rd (03842-1463)
PHONE..................................603 926-0029
Marc Rowe, *Owner*
Nancy Rowe, *Co-Owner*
EMP: 10
SQ FT: 6,000
SALES (est): 1MM **Privately Held**
WEB: www.rowemachine.com
SIC: 3599 5571 Mfg Industrial Machinery Ret Motorcycles

(G-18271)
SEA HAGG DISTILLERY
12 Willow Ln (03842-1481)
PHONE..................................603 380-4022
Heather Hughes, *Principal*
EMP: 8
SALES (est): 694.6K **Privately Held**
SIC: 2085 Mfg Distilled/Blended Liquor

(G-18272)
SLEEPNET CORP
5 Merrill Industrial Dr (03842-1980)
PHONE..................................603 758-6600
Thomas Moulton, *CEO*
Ann Melvin, *Purchasing*
June Brewster, *Finance*
▲ **EMP:** 24
SQ FT: 15,000
SALES (est): 3.6MM **Privately Held**
WEB: www.sleep-net.com
SIC: 3845 Mfg Electromedical Equipment

(G-18273)
TELEDYNE INSTRUMENTS INC
Also Called: Teledyne D.G. O Brien
1 Lafayette Rd Unit 1 # 1 (03842-2627)
PHONE..................................603 474-5571
EMP: 75
SALES (corp-wide): 2.9B **Publicly Held**
SIC: 3823 Mfg Process Control Instruments
HQ: Teledyne Instruments, Inc.
1049 Camino Dos Rios
Thousand Oaks CA 91360
805 373-4545

(G-18274)
TOM JAMES COMPANY
4 Merrill Industrial Dr (03842-1943)
PHONE..................................603 601-6944
EMP: 11
SALES (corp-wide): 492.1MM **Privately Held**
SIC: 2311 Mfg Mens/Boys Suit/Coats
PA: Tom James Company
263 Seaboard Ln
Franklin TN 37067
615 771-1122

(G-18275)
TSI GROUP INC (DH)
Also Called: Thermal Solutions
94 Tide Mill Rd (03842-2705)
PHONE..................................603 964-0296
Gregory R Tucker, *CEO*
E J Mondor, *President*
Kevin Rowan, *President*
Dale Jessick, *Exec VP*
David K Helms, *CFO*
EMP: 20
SQ FT: 3,000
SALES (est): 101.1MM
SALES (corp-wide): 66.5B **Publicly Held**
SIC: 3599 3398 3443 3444 Mfg Industrial Machinery Metal Heat Treating
HQ: B/E Aerospace, Inc.
1400 Corporate Center Way
Wellington FL 33414
561 791-5000

(G-18276)
U S ARTISTIC EMBROIDERY INC
416 High St (03842-2311)
PHONE..................................603 929-0505
EMP: 3
SALES: 250K **Privately Held**
SIC: 2395 Custom Embroidery

(G-18277)
VISIBLE LIGHT INC
24 Stickney Ter Ste 6 (03842-4902)
PHONE..................................603 926-6049
Philip J Infurna, *Owner*
Annette Russo, *Project Mgr*
Louie Robinson, *Opers Mgr*
Rich Hayes, *Sales Staff*
Steve Schmitt, *Sales Staff*
EMP: 3
SALES (est): 387K **Privately Held**
SIC: 3645 Mfg Residential Lighting Fixtures

(G-18278)
VISIBLE LIGHT INC
6 Merrill Industrial Dr # 11 (03842-1970)
PHONE..................................603 926-6049
Phil Infurna, *President*
Stacy Melanson, *Sales Staff*
EMP: 9
SALES (est): 1MM **Privately Held**
SIC: 3648 Mfg Lighting Equipment

(G-18279)
VISUAL INSPECTION PRODUCTS
7 Kershaw Ave Ste 3 (03842-3323)
P.O. Box 328 (03843-0328)
PHONE..................................603 929-4414
Ron Arriel, *Owner*
EMP: 3
SQ FT: 7,000
SALES: 300K **Privately Held**
WEB: www.vipcharts.com
SIC: 2789 Mfg Optical Charts

(G-18280)
WHITES WELDING CO INC
6 Kershaw Ave (03842-3352)
PHONE..................................603 926-2261
Mark George, *President*
EMP: 5
SQ FT: 2,000
SALES (est): 363.5K **Privately Held**
SIC: 7692 Welding Repair

Hampton Falls
Rockingham County

(G-18281)
AQUA SYSTEMS INC (PA)
289 Exeter Rd (03844-2011)
P.O. Box 181 (03844-0181)
PHONE..................................603 778-8796
Ernest M Cherry Jr, *President*
▲ **EMP:** 8
SALES: 2MM **Privately Held**
WEB: www.aquasystemsinc.com
SIC: 3443 7389 Mfg Fabricated Plate Work Business Serv Non-Commercial Site

(G-18282)
FAVORITE FUELS LLC
1 Crank Rd (03844-2102)
P.O. Box 395 (03844-0395)
PHONE..................................603 967-4889
John Alkire, *Principal*
EMP: 5 **EST:** 2010
SALES (est): 660.6K **Privately Held**
SIC: 2869 Mfg Industrial Organic Chemicals

(G-18283)
KENSINGTON GROUP INCORPORATED
Also Called: Imagewise
113 Lafayette Rd (03844-2305)
P.O. Box 1080, Hampton (03843-1080)
PHONE..................................603 926-6742
Lawrence Crampsey Jr, *President*
Eric Lindsay, *Vice Pres*
▲ **EMP:** 17
SQ FT: 9,000

SALES (est): 1.9MM **Privately Held**
WEB: www.medicaldocservices.com
SIC: 2741 2752 2791 2731 Misc Publishing Lithographic Coml Print Typesetting Services Book-Publishing/Printing Book Printing

Hancock
Hillsborough County

(G-18284)
DANIEL JOHNSTON & CO INC
19 Boutwell Rd (03449-4400)
PHONE..................................603 525-9330
Daniel Johnston, *President*
David Johnston, *Partner*
EMP: 3
SALES: 2MM **Privately Held**
WEB: www.danieljohnston.com
SIC: 1389 Oil/Gas Field Services

(G-18285)
MAIN STREET CHEESE LLC
37 Main St (03449-5321)
P.O. Box 185 (03449-0185)
PHONE..................................603 525-3300
Sarah Laeng-Gilliatt, *President*
EMP: 3
SALES (est): 159.8K **Privately Held**
SIC: 2026 Mfg Fluid Milk

Hanover
Grafton County

(G-18286)
DARTMOUTH INC
Also Called: DARTMOUTH, THE
6175 Robinson Hall (03755-3507)
PHONE..................................603 646-2600
Rdex Tejera, *CEO*
EMP: 25
SALES: 143.6K **Privately Held**
WEB: www.thedartmouth.com
SIC: 2711 Newspapers-Publishing/Printing

(G-18287)
DARTMOUTH UNDYING INC
14 Dunster Dr (03755-2704)
PHONE..................................603 643-2143
EMP: 4
SALES: 10.1K **Privately Held**
SIC: 2329 Mfg Men's/Boy's Clothing

(G-18288)
GRAVEL HILL PARTNERS LLC
34 Macdonald Dr (03755-1627)
PHONE..................................603 277-9074
Ryan Johnson, *Bd of Directors*
EMP: 3 **EST:** 2013
SALES (est): 123.7K **Privately Held**
SIC: 1442 Construction Sand/Gravel

(G-18289)
HONES LLC
12 South St Ste 3 (03755-2163)
PHONE..................................603 643-4223
W Joseph Maloney, *Principal*
EMP: 3
SALES (est): 166.7K **Privately Held**
SIC: 3291 Mfg Abrasive Products

(G-18290)
HYPERTHERM INC (PA)
21 Great Hollow Rd (03755-3124)
P.O. Box 5010 (03755-5010)
PHONE..................................603 643-3441
Richard W Couch Jr, *Ch of Bd*
Evan Smith, *President*
Aaron Brandt, *General Mgr*
Tommy Hanchette, *District Mgr*
Barbara Couch, *Vice Pres*
◆ **EMP:** 1100
SQ FT: 155,000
SALES (est): 458.8MM **Privately Held**
WEB: www.hypertherm.com
SIC: 3541 Mfg Machine Tools-Cutting

(G-18291)
HYPERTHERM INC
1 Etna Rd (03755-3121)
PHONE..................................603 643-3441
Evan Smith, *Branch Mgr*
EMP: 14
SALES (corp-wide): 458.8MM **Privately Held**
SIC: 3541 Mfg Machine Tools-Cutting
PA: Hypertherm, Inc.
21 Great Hollow Rd
Hanover NH 03755
603 643-3441

(G-18292)
HYPERTHERM INC
9 Great Hollow Rd (03755-3122)
PHONE..................................603 643-3441
EMP: 5
SALES (corp-wide): 458.8MM **Privately Held**
SIC: 3541 Mfg Machine Tools- Cutting
PA: Hypertherm, Inc.
21 Great Hollow Rd
Hanover NH 03755
603 643-3441

(G-18293)
INDEPENDENT ROWING NEWS INC
53 S Main St Ste 201 (03755-2022)
PHONE..................................603 448-5090
Charles Davis, *Publisher*
Chip Davis, *Publisher*
EMP: 6
SALES (est): 381.8K **Privately Held**
SIC: 2711 Newspapers-Publishing/Printing

(G-18294)
IOMETRY INC
9 Morrison Rd (03755-1629)
PHONE..................................603 643-5670
Steven Reinitz, *Principal*
Alexander Slocum, *Principal*
EMP: 3
SALES (est): 145.2K **Privately Held**
SIC: 3841 Mfg Surgical/Medical Instruments

(G-18295)
MORANO GELATO INC
55 S Main St (03755-2047)
PHONE..................................603 643-4233
Morgan Morano, *President*
EMP: 7
SALES (est): 618.4K **Privately Held**
SIC: 2024 Eating Place

(G-18296)
ROBES DANA WOOD CRAFTSMEN (PA)
3 Great Hollow Rd (03755-3122)
PHONE..................................603 643-9355
Caroline Cannon, *President*
Martha S Robes, *Vice Pres*
Gregory R Russell, *Vice Pres*
Caleb J Wood, *Vice Pres*
EMP: 5
SQ FT: 6,000
SALES (est): 1.1MM **Privately Held**
WEB: www.danarobes.com
SIC: 2426 Hardwood Dimension/Floor Mill

(G-18297)
SHERIDAN NH
69 Lyme Rd (03755-1293)
PHONE..................................603 643-2220
EMP: 3 **EST:** 2016
SALES (est): 131.2K **Privately Held**
SIC: 2752 Lithographic Commercial Printing

(G-18298)
STEERFORTH PRESS LLC
25 Lebanon St Frnt (03755-2182)
PHONE..................................603 643-4787
▲ **EMP:** 5
SQ FT: 1,000
SALES (est): 553K **Privately Held**
WEB: www.steerforth.com
SIC: 2741 Miscellaneous Publishing, Nsk

(G-18299)
THAYER MACHINE SHOP
8000 Cummings Hall (03755-8001)
PHONE..................................603 646-3261
Edmond Cooley, *Principal*
EMP: 3 **EST:** 2008
SALES (est): 228.1K **Privately Held**
SIC: 3599 Mfg Industrial Machinery

(G-18300)
VAN LEER JODI
38 Goodfellow Rd (03755-4800)
PHONE..................................603 643-3034
Jodi Vanleer, *Principal*
EMP: 3
SALES (est): 215.9K **Privately Held**
SIC: 3412 Mfg Metal Barrels/Pails

Harrisville
Cheshire County

(G-18301)
E-Z CRETE LLC
250 Hancock Rd (03450-5204)
PHONE..................................603 313-6462
Brice Raynor, *Principal*
EMP: 5
SALES (est): 544.9K **Privately Held**
SIC: 3272 Mfg Concrete Products

(G-18302)
HARRISVILLE DESIGNS INC (PA)
69 Main St Fl 2 (03450)
PHONE..................................603 827-3333
John Colony III, *President*
Patricia Colony, *Vice Pres*
Sharon Wilder, *Prdtn Mgr*
Erin Hammerstedt, *Exec Dir*
▲ **EMP:** 7
SQ FT: 6,000
SALES (est): 3.9MM **Privately Held**
WEB: www.harrisville.com
SIC: 3552 2281 5199 5949 Mfg Textile Machinery Yarn Spinning Mill Whol Nondurable Goods Ret Sewing Supplies/Fbrc

Henniker
Merrimack County

(G-18303)
CONTOOCOOK RIVER LUMBER INC
54 Main St (03242)
P.O. Box 2089 (03242-2089)
PHONE..................................603 428-3636
David Herrick, *President*
Marlo Herrick, *Vice Pres*
EMP: 20
SALES (est): 1.6MM **Privately Held**
SIC: 2421 Sawmill/Planing Mill

(G-18304)
COUSINEAU LUMBER INC
Also Called: Cousineau Forest Products
1310 Old Concord Rd (03242-3546)
PHONE..................................603 428-7155
Curtis Richmond, *Manager*
EMP: 5
SALES (corp-wide): 11MM **Privately Held**
SIC: 2421 Sawmill/Planing Mill
PA: Cousineau Lumber, Inc.
845 Us Route 2 E Ste 2e
Wilton ME 04294
207 645-4448

(G-18305)
GOSS LUMBER CO INC
841 Flanders Rd (03242-6395)
PHONE..................................603 428-3363
Donald Goss Jr, *President*
Lyne Mors, *Office Mgr*
Robert Howard III, *Admin Sec*
EMP: 9
SQ FT: 3,360
SALES: 1MM **Privately Held**
SIC: 2421 5211 Sawmill/Planing Mill Ret Lumber/Building Materials

(G-18306)
GRANITE STATE FOREST PRODUCTS
1104 Old Concord Rd (03242-3542)
PHONE..................................603 428-7890
Richard A French Jr, *President*
Deb Tickle, *Manager*
EMP: 6
SQ FT: 10,000
SALES (est): 92.4K **Privately Held**
WEB: www.gsfp.com
SIC: 2421 2441 Sawmill/Planing Mill Mfg Wood Boxes/Shook

(G-18307)
MICHIE CORPORATION
Also Called: Henniker Redi-Mix
173 Buxton Industrial Dr (03242-3559)
P.O. Box 870 (03242-0870)
PHONE..................................603 428-7426
Alan Michie, *President*
Pamela Michie, *Vice Pres*
Stuart Michie, *Vice Pres*
Pam Michie, *Treasurer*
Jessica Michie, *Office Mgr*
EMP: 75
SQ FT: 7,000
SALES (est): 13.7MM **Privately Held**
WEB: www.michiecorp.com
SIC: 3272 3273 1794 1442 Mfg Concrete Products Mfg Ready-Mixed Concrete Excavation Contractor Construction Sand/Gravel

(G-18308)
N H CENTRAL CONCRETE CORP
4 Bradford Rd (03242)
P.O. Box 840 (03242-0840)
PHONE..................................603 428-7900
Ronald D Goss, *President*
Wayne Patenaude, *Corp Secy*
Rodney Patenaude, *Vice Pres*
Doug Parker, *Manager*
EMP: 15
SALES (est): 1.9MM **Privately Held**
SIC: 3272 Mfg Ready-Mixed Concrete

(G-18309)
PAT TRAP INC
632 Western Ave (03242-3491)
PHONE..................................603 428-3396
Stuart Patenaude, *President*
Amy Patenaude, *Vice Pres*
Katherine Patenaude, *Treasurer*
EMP: 9 **EST:** 1983
SALES (est): 1.2MM **Privately Held**
WEB: www.pattrap.com
SIC: 3949 Mfg Sporting/Athletic Goods

(G-18310)
PATENAUDE LUMBER COMPANY INC
628 Rush Rd (03242-3187)
P.O. Box 627 (03242-0627)
PHONE..................................603 428-3224
Rodney Patenaude, *President*
Ronald Goss, *Vice Pres*
Kathleen Goss, *Treasurer*
Tracy Goss, *Office Mgr*
Caroline Patenaude, *Admin Sec*
◆ **EMP:** 25
SALES (est): 3.8MM **Privately Held**
SIC: 2421 Sawmill/Planing Mill

(G-18311)
QUILTED THREADS LLC
116 Main St (03242-3275)
P.O. Box 778 (03242-0778)
PHONE..................................603 428-6622
Rebecca S Weber, *Mng Member*
EMP: 9
SALES (est): 714K **Privately Held**
WEB: www.quiltedthreads.com
SIC: 2395 Ret Sewing Supplies/Fabrics

Hillsboro
Hillsborough County

(G-18312)
ALL SIGNS STEVE MAIN
17 Holman St (03244-5418)
PHONE..................................603 464-5455
Stephen Main, *Owner*
EMP: 4
SALES: 98K **Privately Held**
SIC: 3993 Mfg Signs/Advertising Specialties

▲ = Import ▼=Export
◆ =Import/Export

(G-18313)
HAFFORDLOGGING
553 W Main St (03244-5210)
PHONE..................................603 478-0142
EMP: 6 **EST:** 2008
SALES (est): 330K **Privately Held**
SIC: 2411 Logging

Hillsborough
Hillsborough County

(G-18314)
BARETT AND GOULD INC
31 Norton Dr (03244)
PHONE..................................603 464-6400
Toll Free:..................................888 -
Robert A Gould, *President*
EMP: 17 **EST:** 1952
SALES (est): 2.9MM **Privately Held**
WEB: www.barettandgould.com
SIC: 3444 3469 Mfg Sheet Metalwork Mfg Metal Stampings

(G-18315)
GATES MOORE LIGHTING
224 Bible Hill Rd (03244-4809)
PHONE..................................203 847-3231
Patricia Moore, *Owner*
EMP: 3
SALES: 85K **Privately Held**
WEB: www.gatesmoorelighting.com
SIC: 3645 3648 Mfg Residential Lighting Fixtures Lighting Equipment

(G-18316)
GRANITE QUILL PUBLISHERS
246 W Main St (03244-5251)
P.O. Box 1190 (03244-1190)
PHONE..................................603 464-3388
Joyce Bosse, *Partner*
Leigh Bosse, *Partner*
EMP: 6
SALES (est): 30.7K **Privately Held**
SIC: 2711 Newspapers-Publishing/Printing

(G-18317)
OSRAM SYLVANIA INC
Also Called: Automotive & Miniature Ltg
275 W Main St (03244-5233)
PHONE..................................603 464-7235
Ben Sucy, *Branch Mgr*
EMP: 300
SQ FT: 135,000
SALES (corp-wide): 3.8B **Privately Held**
WEB: www.sylvania.com
SIC: 3641 3714 Mfg Electric Lamps Mfg Motor Vehicle Parts/Accessories
HQ: Osram Sylvania Inc
200 Ballardvale St # 305
Wilmington MA 01887
978 570-3000

(G-18318)
RICKS TRUCK & TRAILER REPAIR
39 Merrill Rd (03244-4922)
P.O. Box 515 (03244-0515)
PHONE..................................603 464-3636
Gordon Mellen, *Owner*
EMP: 3
SQ FT: 3,000
SALES (est): 361.8K **Privately Held**
SIC: 3715 7539 7699 Mfg Truck Trailers Automotive Repair Repair Services

Hinsdale
Cheshire County

(G-18319)
CONTINENTAL CABLE LLC
Also Called: Gbg Industries
253 Monument Rd (03451-2033)
PHONE..................................800 229-5131
Gary Preston, *COO*
Brian Nadeau, *Vice Pres*
Tom McKenney, *Engineer*
Alaine Williams, *Controller*
Alissa Hunt, *Human Res Dir*
▲ **EMP:** 56
SQ FT: 51,000
SALES (est): 11.4MM
SALES (corp-wide): 44.7MM **Privately Held**
WEB: www.gbgindustries.com
SIC: 3496 3644 3728 Mfg Misc Fabricated Wire Products Mfg Nonconductive Wiring Devices Mfg Aircraft Parts/Equipment
PA: Cables Ben-Mor Inc, Les
1105 Rue Lemire
Saint-Hyacinthe QC J2T 1
450 778-0022

(G-18320)
HCP PACKAGING USA INC
370 Monument Rd (03451-2040)
PHONE..................................603 256-3141
Andrew Drummond, *Prdtn Mgr*
George Benegger, *Branch Mgr*
EMP: 150
SALES (corp-wide): 19.7MM **Privately Held**
WEB: www.hcp-usa.com
SIC: 3089 Mfg Plastic Products
PA: Hcp Packaging Usa, Inc.
1 Waterview Dr Ste 102
Shelton CT 06484
203 924-2408

(G-18321)
SONG EVEN
15 Old Brattleboro Rd (03451-2045)
PHONE..................................603 256-6018
Cynthia Marble, *Partner*
EMP: 4
SALES (est): 400K **Privately Held**
SIC: 3911 5094 Mfg Precious Metal Jewelry Whol Jewelry/Precious Stones

Holderness
Grafton County

(G-18322)
ACTON CUSTOM ENTERPRISES
33 Wildwood Dr (03245-5754)
PHONE..................................603 279-0241
Nicholas Acton, *Owner*
EMP: 6
SALES (est): 446.7K **Privately Held**
SIC: 3465 Mfg Automotive Stampings

(G-18323)
MEGAPRINT INC
1177 Nh Route 175 (03245-5031)
P.O. Box 87, Plymouth (03264-0087)
PHONE..................................603 536-2900
Jay Buckley, *President*
Cindy Reed, *Purchasing*
Connie Steiner, *Controller*
Carolyn Soucy, *Sales Mgr*
Dave Cote, *Graphic Designe*
EMP: 16
SQ FT: 4,800
SALES: 2MM **Privately Held**
SIC: 2759 Printing Service

Hollis
Hillsborough County

(G-18324)
AEROPLAS CORP INTERNATIONAL
265b Proctor Hill Rd (03049 6427)
PHONE..................................603 465-7300
Thomas C Walton, *President*
EMP: 3
SQ FT: 7,500
SALES (est): 225.4K **Privately Held**
SIC: 2821 Manufactures Polymer Resins

(G-18325)
ALEXANDER LAN INC
175 Broad St (03049-6028)
PHONE..................................603 880-8800
Dirk A D Smith, *President*
EMP: 10
SQ FT: 1,600
SALES (est): 822.8K **Privately Held**
WEB: www.alexander.com
SIC: 7372 Prepackaged Software Services

(G-18326)
BASIS AUDIO INC
26 Clinton Dr Ste 116 (03049-6578)
PHONE..................................603 889-4776
Jolanta Conti, *President*
EMP: 4
SQ FT: 4,000
SALES (est): 662.9K **Privately Held**
WEB: www.basisaudio.com
SIC: 3651 Mfg Home Audio/Video Equipment

(G-18327)
BURNS INDUSTRIES INCORPORATED
34 Pepperell Rd (03049-6411)
PHONE..................................603 881-8336
Rhonda Burns, *President*
Stephen J Burns, *Director*
▲ **EMP:** 3
SQ FT: 5,000
SALES (est): 946.8K **Privately Held**
SIC: 3699 7629 4841 Mfg Electrical Equipment/Supplies Electrical Repair Cable/Pay Television Service

(G-18328)
DALE VISHAY ELECTRONICS LLC
Also Called: Vishay Ultrasource
22 Clinton Dr (03049-6595)
PHONE..................................603 881-7799
EMP: 100
SALES (corp-wide): 3B **Publicly Held**
SIC: 3674 Mfg Semiconductors/Related Devices
HQ: Dale Vishay Electronics Llc
1122 23rd St
Columbus NE 68601
605 665-9301

(G-18329)
DEVPROTEK INC
4 Clinton Dr (03049-6595)
PHONE..................................603 577-5557
Les Scenna, *President*
EMP: 8 **EST:** 2000
SQ FT: 3,000
SALES (est): 1.4MM **Privately Held**
WEB: www.devprotek.com
SIC: 3569 Mfg General Industrial Machinery

(G-18330)
DIAMOND CASTING AND MCH CO INC
95 Proctor Hill Rd (03049)
PHONE..................................603 465-2263
Gerald Letendre, *President*
Greg Rockwell, *Project Mgr*
EMP: 45
SQ FT: 80,000
SALES (est): 9.4MM **Privately Held**
WEB: www.diamondcasting.com
SIC: 3363 3365 3599 3369 Mfg Aluminum Die-Casting Aluminum Foundry Mfg Industrial Machinery Nonferrous Metal Foundry Mfg Nonfrs Die-Castings

(G-18331)
ENVIRONMENTAL TEST PDTS LLC (PA)
29 Shipley Dr (03049-6029)
PHONE..................................603 924-5010
Rob Gual, *President*
Chris Peahl, *COO*
Eric Peahl, *Vice Pres*
EMP: 7
SQ FT: 2,000
SALES (est): 254.1K **Privately Held**
WEB: www.etpproducts.com
SIC: 3826 Mfg & Assemble Environmental Testing Equipment

(G-18332)
HOLLIS LINE MACHINE CO INC (PA)
295 S Merrimack Rd (03049-6242)
PHONE..................................603 465-2251
John Siergiewicz Jr, *President*
Jamie Gauthier, *Foreman/Supr*
Ken Cogswell, *Engineer*
▲ **EMP:** 50
SQ FT: 18,000
SALES (est): 7.8MM **Privately Held**
WEB: www.hollisline.com
SIC: 7692 3599 3567 Welding Repair Mfg Industrial Machinery Mfg Industrial Furnaces/Ovens

(G-18333)
INFINIZONE CORP
99 Pine Hill Rd (03049-5941)
P.O. Box 131, Nashua (03061-0131)
PHONE..................................603 465-2917
Jonathan Orr, *President*
EMP: 10
SALES: 500K **Privately Held**
WEB: www.infinizone.com
SIC: 7372 7371 Prepackaged Software Services Custom Computer Programing

(G-18334)
MICROMATICS MACHINE CO INC
9 Clinton Dr (03049-6595)
PHONE..................................603 889-2115
Anita Brown, *President*
EMP: 14
SQ FT: 20,000
SALES: 3.8MM **Privately Held**
SIC: 3599 Mfg Industrial Machinery

(G-18335)
NEXTMOVE TECHNOLOGIES LLC
1 Kerk St (03049-6442)
PHONE..................................603 654-1280
Scott Cheyne,
Charles B Brown,
EMP: 7
SALES (est): 1.2MM **Privately Held**
SIC: 3669 Mfg Communications Equipment

(G-18336)
PARKER-HANNIFIN CORPORATION
Parker Precision Fluidics
26 Clinton Dr Ste 103 (03049-6579)
PHONE..................................603 595-1500
Jonathan Desousa, *Business Mgr*
Glenn Taylor, *Engineer*
Joel Verrecchia, *Engineer*
Jim Heselton, *Branch Mgr*
Hank Fitzsimmons, *Manager*
EMP: 150
SALES (corp-wide): 14.3B **Publicly Held**
WEB: www.parker.com
SIC: 3823 3492 Mfg Process Control Instruments Mfg Fluid Power Valves/Fittings
PA: Parker-Hannifin Corporation
6035 Parkland Blvd
Cleveland OH 44124
216 896-3000

(G-18337)
PARKER-HANNIFIN CORPORATION
Also Called: Pneutronics Division
26 Clinton Dr Ste 103 (03049-6579)
PHONE..................................973 575-4844
Donald Washkewicz, *President*
Harry Wang, *Engineer*
EMP: 50
SALES (corp-wide): 14.3B **Publicly Held**
WEB: www.parker.com
SIC: 3491 3492 Mfg Industrial Valves Mfg Fluid Power Valves/Fittings
PA: Parker-Hannifin Corporation
6035 Parkland Blvd
Cleveland OH 44124
216 896-3000

(G-18338)
PNEUCLEUS TECHNOLOGIES LLC
19a Clinton Dr (03049-6595)
PHONE..................................603 921-5300
EMP: 5 **EST:** 2017
SALES (est): 583.4K **Privately Held**
SIC: 3823 Mfg Process Control Instruments

(G-18339)
PURITAN PRESS INC (PA)
Also Called: Puritan Capital
95 Runnells Bridge Rd (03049-6535)
PHONE..................................603 889-4500
Kurt Peterson, *President*

GEOGRAPHIC

Michael Ames, *Vice Pres*
Jay Stewart, *Vice Pres*
Rene Valiquet, *CFO*
EMP: 50
SQ FT: 30,600
SALES (est): 15.9MM **Privately Held**
WEB: www.puritanpress.com
SIC: 2752 2759 2791 7331 Lithographic Coml Print Commercial Printing Typesetting Services Direct Mail Ad Svcs

(G-18340)
VALLEY WELDING & FABG INC
261 Proctor Hill Rd (03049-6427)
P.O. Box 894 (03049-0894)
PHONE..................................603 465-3266
Carolyn A Valley, *President*
Loren J Valley, *President*
Larry Valley, *Vice Pres*
EMP: 20
SQ FT: 15,000
SALES (est): 4.2MM **Privately Held**
WEB: www.valleyweld.com
SIC: 3444 7692 3443 3441 Mfg Sheet Metalwork Welding Repair Mfg Fabricated Plate Wrk Structural Metal Fabrctn

Hooksett
Merrimack County

(G-18341)
ADVANCED RADON MITIGATION INC
180 Londonderry Tpke # 1 (03106-1969)
PHONE..................................603 644-1207
Robin D Gelinas, *President*
EMP: 4
SQ FT: 4,000
SALES (est): 803K **Privately Held**
WEB: www.advancedradonmitigation.com
SIC: 3589 Mfg Service Industry Machinery

(G-18342)
ALS PRECISION MACHINING LLC
1356 Hooksett Rd (03106-1816)
PHONE..................................603 647-1075
Alain Demers,
EMP: 5
SQ FT: 140
SALES (est): 453.7K **Privately Held**
SIC: 3599 Mfg Industrial Machinery

(G-18343)
BIMBO BAKERIES USA INC
Also Called: Freihofer's Bakery Outlet
3 E Point Dr (03106-2019)
PHONE..................................603 626-7405
Shawn McKenna, *Branch Mgr*
EMP: 20 **Privately Held**
SIC: 2051 Mfg Bread/Related Products
HQ: Bimbo Bakeries Usa, Inc
255 Business Center Dr # 200
Horsham PA 19044
215 347-5500

(G-18344)
BURTON WIRE & CABLE INC
4 Brookside West (03106-2518)
PHONE..................................603 624-2427
Burton A Hyman, *President*
◆ **EMP:** 12
SQ FT: 10,000
SALES (est): 4.4MM **Privately Held**
SIC: 3357 Nonferrous Wiredrawing/Insulating

(G-18345)
C & O BOX & PRINTING COMPANY
Also Called: C & O Box Co
84 Pheasant Hill Rd (03106-1720)
PHONE..................................508 881-1760
Thomas O Cleveland, *President*
Brenda Cleveland, *Corp Secy*
EMP: 3 **EST:** 1952
SQ FT: 4,500
SALES: 300K **Privately Held**
SIC: 2652 2759 2752 Mfg Setup Paperboard Boxes Commercial Printing Lithographic Commercial Printing

(G-18346)
CHASE ELECTRIC MOTORS LLC
Also Called: Wright Electric Motors
78 Londonderry Tpke G1 (03106-2000)
PHONE..................................603 669-2565
Mark R Chase,
EMP: 8
SQ FT: 3,600
SALES (est): 750K **Privately Held**
SIC: 7694 7629 5063 5999 Armature Rewinding Electrical Repair Whol Electrical Equip

(G-18347)
COBRA PRECISION MACHINING CORP
3 Craneway (03106-2194)
PHONE..................................603 434-8424
David Granquist, *President*
EMP: 7 **EST:** 2013
SALES: 1.3MM **Privately Held**
SIC: 3491 3545 3469 Mfg Industrial Valves Mfg Machine Tool Accessories Mfg Metal Stampings

(G-18348)
DUTILE GLINES & HIGGINS INC
146 Londonderry Tpke # 12 (03106-1966)
P.O. Box 5638, Manchester (03108-5638)
PHONE..................................603 622-0452
David Dutile, *President*
Robert Glines, *Treasurer*
EMP: 10
SQ FT: 6,000
SALES (est): 1.9MM **Privately Held**
SIC: 3823 3674 3577 3571 Mfg Process Cntrl Instr Mfg Semiconductors/Dvcs Mfg Computer Peripherals Mfg Electronic Computers

(G-18349)
FIRE PROTECTION TEAM LLC
78 Londonderry Tpke 10 (03106-2000)
PHONE..................................603 641-2550
Kacey Prishwalko,
Jodie Arnold, *Assistant*
EMP: 4
SALES (est): 544.3K **Privately Held**
SIC: 3569 General Industrial Machinery, Nec, Nsk

(G-18350)
FIRST IMPRESSIONS EMBROIDERY
1261 Hooksett Rd Ste 1 (03106-1094)
PHONE..................................603 606-1400
Scott Lavigne, *Owner*
EMP: 3
SALES (est): 147.1K **Privately Held**
SIC: 2395 2262 Pleating/Stitching Services Manmade Fiber & Silk Finishing Plant

(G-18351)
GENERAL ELECTRIC COMPANY
31 Industrial Park Dr (03106-1851)
PHONE..................................603 666-8300
Jing Huang, *Plant Mgr*
Stephen Carter, *Engineer*
Zachary Gamache, *Engineer*
Don Lowe, *Engineer*
Christian Garvin, *Human Res Mgr*
EMP: 695
SALES (corp-wide): 121.6B **Publicly Held**
SIC: 3724 3728 3714 Mfg Aircraft Engines/Parts Mfg Aircraft Parts/Equipment Mfg Motor Vehicle Parts/Accessories
PA: General Electric Company
5 Necco St
Boston MA 02210
617 443-3000

(G-18352)
LEW A CUMMINGS CO INC
Also Called: Cummings Printing Company
4 Peters Brook Dr (03106-1822)
P.O. Box 16495 (03106-6490)
PHONE..................................603 625-6901
John L Cummings, *President*
Norma J Shea, *Treasurer*
Andrea Hecker, *Representative*
EMP: 106
SQ FT: 84,000
SALES: 20.7MM **Privately Held**
WEB: www.cummingsprinting.com
SIC: 2752 Lithographic Commercial Printing

(G-18353)
MACY INDUSTRIES INC
5 Lehoux Dr (03106-1836)
PHONE..................................603 623-5568
Nicholas Mercier, *CEO*
Melissa Glennon, *Administration*
EMP: 40
SQ FT: 13,875
SALES: 4.8MM **Privately Held**
WEB: www.macyindustries.com
SIC: 3444 7699 Mfg Sheet Metalwork Repair Services

(G-18354)
PREMIER PACKAGING LLC
47 Post Rd (03106-1725)
PHONE..................................603 485-7465
EMP: 4
SALES (est): 68.4K **Privately Held**
SIC: 7372 Prepackaged Software Services

(G-18355)
PRO-CUT CNC MACHINE INC
7 Lehoux Dr (03106-1836)
PHONE..................................603 623-5533
Marcel Labonville, *President*
Dan Labonville, *Vice Pres*
EMP: 3
SQ FT: 2,400
SALES: 500K **Privately Held**
SIC: 3599 Mfg Industrial Machinery

(G-18356)
PSI WATER SYSTEMS INC (PA)
Also Called: Encon Evaporators
1368 Hooksett Rd (03106-1823)
PHONE..................................603 624-5110
Mark J Fregeau, *President*
EMP: 20
SALES (est): 4.7MM **Privately Held**
WEB: www.evaporator.com
SIC: 3569 Mfg General Industrial Machinery

(G-18357)
RAN/ALL METAL TECHNOLOGY INC
7a E Point Dr (03106-2019)
P.O. Box 16419 (03106-6419)
PHONE..................................603 668-1907
James Oriani, *President*
Kevin Mullen, *Vice Pres*
▼ **EMP:** 9
SQ FT: 12,000
SALES: 2.8MM **Privately Held**
SIC: 3444 Mfg Sheet Metalwork

(G-18358)
RB GRAPHICS INC
Also Called: Signature Press & Blue Prtg
45 Londonderry Tpke (03106-2046)
P.O. Box 16328 (03106-6328)
PHONE..................................603 624-4025
R William Baker, *President*
Dan Bouchard, *General Mgr*
EMP: 9
SALES (est): 1.3MM **Privately Held**
SIC: 2752 2759 7334 2789 Lithographic Coml Print Commercial Printing Photocopying Service Bookbinding/Related Work

(G-18359)
RIMOL GREENHOUSE SYSTEMS INC
40 Londonderry Tpke 2d (03106-1914)
PHONE..................................603 629-9004
Robert Rimol, *President*
Bob Rimol, *Owner*
Karen Rimol, *Vice Pres*
Matt Connell, *Sales Mgr*
John Wells, *Sales Staff*
EMP: 10
SQ FT: 6,000
SALES: 7MM **Privately Held**
WEB: www.rimol.com
SIC: 3448 5191 Mfg Prefabricated Metal Buildings Whol Farm Supplies

(G-18360)
SIGN GALLERY
101 West River Rd (03106-2626)
PHONE..................................603 622-7212
Janet Tuttle, *Owner*
EMP: 4
SQ FT: 4,000
SALES (est): 220K **Privately Held**
SIC: 3993 5999 Mfg Signs/Advertising Specialties Ret Misc Merchandise

(G-18361)
YOUR OIL TOOLS LLC
78 Londonderry Tpke D5 (03106-2027)
PHONE..................................701 645-8665
M Steven Kesserling, *Administration*
EMP: 4
SALES (est): 213.2K **Privately Held**
SIC: 1311 Crude Petroleum/Natural Gas Production

Hopkinton
Merrimack County

(G-18362)
HMC CORPORATION (PA)
284 Maple St (03229-3339)
PHONE..................................603 746-3399
Peter R Taylor, *President*
▲ **EMP:** 35 **EST:** 1952
SQ FT: 30,000
SALES (est): 5.4MM **Privately Held**
WEB: www.hmccorp.com
SIC: 3553 5084 Mfg Woodworking Machinery Whol Industrial Equipment

(G-18363)
HOUSE OF LAURILA
1138 Hopkinton Rd (03229-2636)
P.O. Box 162, Contoocook (03229-0162)
PHONE..................................603 224-8123
Annette Frye, *Owner*
EMP: 3
SQ FT: 250
SALES: 15K **Privately Held**
SIC: 2842 Mfg Leather Dressings

(G-18364)
PETROFIBER CORPORATION (PA)
1994 Maple St (03229-3330)
PHONE..................................603 627-0416
Bill Delafonto, *President*
Anthony Dinapoli, *Treasurer*
EMP: 4
SALES (est): 471.5K **Privately Held**
SIC: 2611 Pulp Mill

Hudson
Hills County

(G-18365)
LOCKED IN STEEL
Also Called: Perfections Group
16 Abbott St (03051-4004)
PHONE..................................603 233-8299
▼ **EMP:** 5
SQ FT: 2,500
SALES (est): 240K **Privately Held**
SIC: 3499 Mfg Misc Fabricated Metal Products

(G-18366)
MERCURY SYSTEMS INC
Also Called: McE - Monroe
267 Lowell Rd Ste A (03051-4937)
PHONE..................................203 792-7474
EMP: 8
SALES (corp-wide): 234.8MM **Publicly Held**
SIC: 3721 3625 Mfg Aircraft Mfg Relays/Industrial Controls
PA: Mercury Systems, Inc.
201 Riverneck Rd
Chelmsford MA 01810
978 256-1300

(G-18367)
SCHUL INTERNATIONAL CO INC
34 Executive Dr (03051-4919)
PHONE..................................603 889-6872
EMP: 3
SALES (est): 123.2K **Privately Held**
SIC: 2891 Adhesives And Sealants, Nsk

Hudson
Hillsborough County

(G-18368)
603 MANUFACTURING LLC
21 Park Ave (03051-3985)
PHONE..................................603 578-9876
Phil Lausier, *President*
Cynthia Coneeny, *Controller*
EMP: 9
SALES (est): 266.1K
SALES (corp-wide): 7.1MM **Privately Held**
SIC: 3679 Mfg Electronic Components
PA: Rf Logic, Llc
21 Park Ave
Hudson NH 03051
603 578-9876

(G-18369)
ADAX MACHINE CO INC
5 Flagstone Dr (03051-4905)
PHONE..................................603 598-6777
Joseph R Williams, *President*
EMP: 20
SQ FT: 20,000
SALES (est): 3.5MM **Privately Held**
WEB: www.adaxmachine.com
SIC: 3599 Mfg Industrial Machinery

(G-18370)
ADVANCED FITNES COMPONENTS LLC
17 Hampshire Dr Ste 18 (03051-4940)
PHONE..................................603 595-1967
Bala Vatti,
Kevin Groder,
Deepak Vatti,
EMP: 14
SALES (est): 1.1MM **Privately Held**
WEB: www.afc-llc.com
SIC: 3949 Mfg And Market Fitness Equipment

(G-18371)
AIREX CORPORATION
17 Executive Dr (03051-4914)
PHONE..................................603 821-3065
William R Carroll, *President*
Greg Wearly, *General Mgr*
Amie Marion, *Admin Asst*
Robert Young, *Technician*
EMP: 40
SQ FT: 53,000
SALES (est): 7.6MM **Privately Held**
WEB: www.airexco.com
SIC: 3564 Mfg Blowers/Fans

(G-18372)
ALCO CONSTRUCTION INC
5 Christine Dr Unit 5-G (03051-3026)
PHONE..................................603 305-8493
Helene Grondin, *President*
Alex Pare, *Vice Pres*
EMP: 6 **EST:** 2006
SQ FT: 400
SALES: 1MM **Privately Held**
SIC: 2542 1751 5032 1742 Mfg Nonwd Partition/Fixt Carpentry Contractor Whol Brick/Stone Matrls Drywall/Insulation Contr

(G-18373)
AMERICAN IR SOLUTIONS LLC
Also Called: Airs
1 Wall St (03051-3983)
P.O. Box 1509, Nashua (03061-1509)
PHONE..................................662 626-2477
Daniel Manitakos, *President*
Leo Monea, *IT/INT Sup*
EMP: 7
SQ FT: 3,000
SALES (est): 918K **Privately Held**
SIC: 3812 Mfg Search/Navigation Equipment

(G-18374)
APRIL METALWORKS
31 Sagamore Park Rd (03051-4915)
PHONE..................................603 883-1510
John Glanton, *President*
EMP: 4
SALES (est): 615.4K **Privately Held**
SIC: 3444 Mfg Sheet Metalwork

(G-18375)
ATRIUM MEDICAL CORPORATION
29 Flagstone Dr (03051-4920)
PHONE..................................603 880-1433
EMP: 6
SALES (corp-wide): 58.7MM **Privately Held**
SIC: 3842 Mfg Surgical Appliances/Supplies
HQ: Atrium Medical Corporation
40 Continental Blvd
Merrimack NH 03054
603 880-1433

(G-18376)
BAE SYSTEMS INFO & ELEC SYS
65 River Rd (03051-5244)
P.O. Box 868, Nashua (03061-0868)
PHONE..................................603 885-4321
David Logan, *Vice Pres*
David Cates, *Engineer*
Dharmarajan Viswanathan, *Cust Mgr*
EMP: 753
SALES (corp-wide): 22.1B **Privately Held**
WEB: www.iesi.na.baesystems.com
SIC: 3679 3812 8731 Mfg Electronic Components Mfg Search/Navigation Equipment Commercial Physical Research
HQ: Bae Systems Information And Electronic Systems Integration Inc.
65 Spit Brook Rd
Nashua NH 03060
603 885-4321

(G-18377)
BARLO SIGNS INTERNATIONAL INC
158 Greeley St (03051-3422)
PHONE..................................603 880-8949
Arthur Bartlett, *President*
Pamela Bartlett, *Corp Secy*
Annie St Peters, *Director*
▲ **EMP:** 70
SQ FT: 15,000
SALES (est): 11.8MM **Privately Held**
WEB: www.barlosigns.com
SIC: 3993 7699 Mfg Signs/Advertising Specialties Repair Services

(G-18378)
C & M MACHINE PRODUCTS INC
25 Flagstone Dr (03051-4920)
PHONE..................................603 594-8100
Paul Villemaire, *CEO*
Daniel Villemaire, *President*
Gene F Gfantozzi, *Vice Pres*
Robert Rzasa, *CFO*
Lori Lanzillo, *Human Res Mgr*
▲ **EMP:** 90
SQ FT: 100,000
SALES (est): 31.3MM **Privately Held**
WEB: www.cm-machineproducts.com
SIC: 3599 Mfg Industrial Machinery

(G-18379)
CEI FLOWMASTER PRODUCTS LLC
18 Park Ave (03051-3934)
PHONE..................................603 880-0094
John S Gilchrist Jr,
EMP: 4 **EST:** 2008
SALES (est): 375.7K **Privately Held**
SIC: 3824 Mfg Fluid Meter/Counting Devices

(G-18380)
CONCRETE SYSTEMS INC
Also Called: Cleco Manufacturing
14 Park Ave (03051-3934)
PHONE..................................603 886-5472
Donna Cassidy, *Principal*
Antoni Thel, *Chief Engr*
Steven Clark, *Design Engr*
EMP: 60
SALES (corp-wide): 55.3MM **Privately Held**
SIC: 3448 3272 Mfg Prefabricated Metal Buildings Mfg Concrete Products
PA: Concrete Systems, Inc.
9 Commercial St
Hudson NH 03051
603 889-4163

(G-18381)
CYCLONES ARENA
20 Constitution Dr (03051-3986)
PHONE..................................603 880-4424
Wes Dolloff, *Owner*
Bill Flanagan, *Director*
EMP: 10
SALES (est): 1.1MM **Privately Held**
SIC: 3674 Mfg Semiconductors/Related Devices

(G-18382)
D M PRINTING SERVICE INC
3 Central St (03051-4204)
P.O. Box 216 (03051-0216)
PHONE..................................603 883-1897
Dennis Mc Guire, *President*
EMP: 3
SQ FT: 1,500
SALES (est): 366.8K **Privately Held**
SIC: 2752 2759 Lithographic Commercial Printing Commercial Printing

(G-18383)
DANIEL PRESTON
Also Called: New England Solid Surfaces
7 Industrial Dr (03051-3914)
P.O. Box 727 (03051-0727)
PHONE..................................603 579-0525
Daniel C Preston, *Owner*
EMP: 5
SQ FT: 5,000
SALES (est): 430.2K **Privately Held**
SIC: 2541 Mfg Wood Partitions/Fixtures

(G-18384)
DENNIS THOMPSON
Also Called: T N T Precision
315 Derry Rd Ste 14 (03051-3051)
PHONE..................................603 595-6813
Dennis Thompson, *Owner*
EMP: 8
SALES (est): 1.1MM **Privately Held**
SIC: 3599 Mfg Industrial Machinery

(G-18385)
DETROIT FORMING INC
Also Called: D F I
15 Sagamore Park Rd (03051-4901)
PHONE..................................603 598-2767
Donna Nagle, *Manager*
EMP: 3
SALES (corp-wide): 78.4MM **Privately Held**
WEB: www.detroitforming.net
SIC: 3089 Mfg Plastic Products
PA: Detroit Forming, Inc.
19100 W 8 Mile Rd
Southfield MI 48075
248 352-8108

(G-18386)
DR GUILBEAULT AIR COMPRSR LLC
17 Park Ave (03051-3985)
PHONE..................................603 598 0891
Raeann Pacheco, *Office Mgr*
Don Guilbeault, *Mng Member*
EMP: 25
SALES (est): 3MM **Privately Held**
SIC: 3563 Mfg Air/Gas Compressors

(G-18387)
DURO-FIBER CO INC
11 Park Ave (03051-3985)
PHONE..................................603 881-4200
John A Hatfield, *President*
Bob Folk, *General Mgr*
Rob Johnson, *Plant Mgr*
EMP: 12
SQ FT: 18,000
SALES (est): 1.9MM **Privately Held**
SIC: 2221 Manmade Broadwoven Fabric Mill

(G-18388)
E PRINT INC
10 Rebel Rd (03051-3025)
PHONE..................................603 594-0009
Ben Maurias, *President*
Hiltrud Bennett, *President*
Debra Maurias, *Admin Sec*
EMP: 8
SQ FT: 3,000
SALES (est): 907.5K **Privately Held**
WEB: www.eprintinc.com
SIC: 2752 7336 5199 Lithographic Commercial Printing Commercial Art/Graphic Design Whol Nondurable Goods

(G-18389)
EVERETT CHARLES TECH LLC
Also Called: Circuitest Services
7 Park Ave (03051-3985)
PHONE..................................603 882-2621
EMP: 6
SALES (corp-wide): 451.7MM **Publicly Held**
WEB: www.ectinfo.com
SIC: 3825 8734 Mfg Electrical Measuring Instruments Testing Laboratory
HQ: Everett Charles Technologies, Llc
14570 Meyer Canyon Dr # 100
Fontana CA 92336
909 625-5551

(G-18390)
FARO TECHNOLOGIES INC
1 Wall St Ste 105 (03051-3983)
PHONE..................................603 893-6200
Simon Raab, *Principal*
EMP: 5
SALES (corp-wide): 403.6MM **Publicly Held**
SIC: 3699 Mfg Electrical Equipment/Supplies
PA: Faro Technologies, Inc.
250 Technology Park
Lake Mary FL 32746
407 333-9911

(G-18391)
FWM INC
11 Friars Dr (03051-4900)
PHONE..................................603 578-3366
Michael J Barry, *President*
Don Barry, *General Mgr*
EMP: 37
SQ FT: 50,000
SALES (est): 8.4MM **Privately Held**
SIC: 3441 3599 Structural Metal Fabrication Mfg Industrial Machinery

(G-18392)
GILCHRIST METAL FABG CO INC (PA)
18 Park Ave (03051-3934)
PHONE..................................603 889-2600
John S Gilchrist Jr, *President*
Stuart Gilchrist, *General Mgr*
Jack Gilchrist, *Principal*
Paul Shapiro, *Vice Pres*
Don Johnson, *Project Mgr*
EMP: 36
SQ FT: 70,000
SALES: 6.6MM **Privately Held**
WEB: www.gmfco.com
SIC: 3443 3444 3441 Mfg Fabricated Plate Work Mfg Sheet Metalwork Structural Metal Fabrication

(G-18393)
GRANITE STATE PLASTICS INC
37 Executive Dr (03051-4903)
PHONE..................................603 669-6715
Steven W Lunder, *President*
Jenn Hayden, *Office Mgr*
John B Emory, *Admin Sec*
▲ **EMP:** 35
SQ FT: 25,000
SALES (est): 8.9MM **Privately Held**
WEB: www.granitestateplastics.com
SIC: 3089 Mfg Plastic Products

(G-18394)
GT ADVANCED TECHNOLOGIES INC (PA)
Also Called: Gtat
5 Wentworth Dr Ste 1 (03051-4929)
PHONE..................................603 883-5200

GEOGRAPHIC

Greg Knight, *CEO*
Matthew E Massengill, *Ch of Bd*
Daniel W Squiller, *Exec VP*
Mark Bentham, *Vice Pres*
Joe Loiselle, *Vice Pres*
▲ **EMP:** 114
SQ FT: 106,000
SALES (est): 167.5MM **Privately Held**
SIC: 3674 Mfg Semiconductors/Related Devices

(G-18395)
GT ADVANCED TECHNOLOGIES LTD
5 Wentworth Dr (03051-4929)
PHONE..................................603 883-5200
EMP: 3
SALES (est): 171.4K **Privately Held**
SIC: 3674 Mfg Semiconductors/Related Devices

(G-18396)
GTAT CORPORATION (HQ)
5 Wentworth Dr 1 (03051-4929)
PHONE..................................603 883-5200
Greg Knight, *President*
Kurt Schmid, *President*
Dan Squiller, *COO*
Jeffrey J Ford, *Vice Pres*
Joe Loiselle, *Vice Pres*
▲ **EMP:** 217
SQ FT: 100,000
SALES (est): 89.3MM **Privately Held**
WEB: www.gtsolar.com
SIC: 3674 3567 Mfg Semiconductors/Related Devices Mfg Industrial Furnaces/Ovens

(G-18397)
HAMMAMATSU CORPORATION
20 Sunland Dr (03051-3209)
PHONE..................................603 883-3888
EMP: 3 **EST:** 2002
SALES (est): 200K **Privately Held**
SIC: 3679 Mfg Electronic Components

(G-18398)
INCON INC
21 Flagstone Dr (03051-4920)
PHONE..................................603 595-0550
Robert J Butler, *CEO*
Ted Schultz, *President*
Steven Camerino, *Admin Sec*
EMP: 49
SQ FT: 32,000
SALES (est): 8.6MM **Privately Held**
WEB: www.inconconnector.com
SIC: 3678 Mfg Electronic Connectors

(G-18399)
INNOVATIVE PRODUCTS & EQP INC
20 Executive Dr (03051-4902)
PHONE..................................603 246-5858
Dale R Beaver, *President*
Richard Brownstein, *Vice Pres*
Eric Peterson, *Vice Pres*
Kevin G Prince, *Treasurer*
Christina Mechalides, *Admin Sec*
▲ **EMP:** 39
SQ FT: 30,000
SALES: 6MM **Privately Held**
SIC: 3569 Mfg General Industrial Machinery

(G-18400)
INSIDE TRACK CABLING INC
18 West Rd (03051-3019)
PHONE..................................603 886-8013
Aaron Ives, *President*
Tammy Bieren, *Vice Pres*
Tammy Gagnon, *Vice Pres*
EMP: 30
SQ FT: 88,000
SALES (est): 6MM **Privately Held**
WEB: www.insidetrackcabling.com
SIC: 3643 Mfg Conductive Wiring Devices

(G-18401)
INTEGRA BIOSCIENCES CORP
2 Wentworth Dr (03051-4918)
PHONE..................................603 578-5800
Gary Nelson, *President*
Alexander Studer, *Business Mgr*
Chris Lacroix, *Engineer*
David Laroche, *Engineer*
Nick Pyzocha, *Engineer*
▲ **EMP:** 15
SQ FT: 5,000
SALES (est): 5.1MM
SALES (corp-wide): 2MM **Privately Held**
WEB: www.viaflo.com
SIC: 3826 Mfg Analytical Instruments
HQ: Integra Biosciences Holding Ag
Tardisstrasse 201
Zizers GR 7205
812 869-530

(G-18402)
INTERCONNECT TECHNOLOGY INC
Also Called: ITI
3 Christine Dr (03051-3026)
PHONE..................................603 883-3116
EMP: 11
SQ FT: 6,400
SALES (est): 2.2MM **Privately Held**
SIC: 3613 3569 Mfg Switchgear/Switchboards Mfg General Industrial Machinery

(G-18403)
JET-CO PRECISION MACHINING
Also Called: Jetco
286 Lowell Rd (03051-5299)
PHONE..................................603 882-7958
Gerard E Jette, *President*
Diane Petrain, *Treasurer*
EMP: 4
SALES (est): 300K **Privately Held**
SIC: 3599 Machine Shop

(G-18404)
JMD INDUSTRIES INC
1 Park Ave (03051-3928)
PHONE..................................603 882-3198
James M Dedeus, *President*
Janet Dedeus, *Treasurer*
Mike Seidl, *Manager*
Alicia Mecca, *Admin Asst*
EMP: 40 **EST:** 1978
SQ FT: 20,000
SALES (est): 5.9MM **Privately Held**
WEB: www.twirlytowels.com
SIC: 3471 Plating/Polishing Service

(G-18405)
KASE PRINTING INC
13 Hampshire Dr Ste 12 (03051-4948)
PHONE..................................603 883-9223
John Koumantzelis, *President*
John Bishop, *President*
Jean Koumantzelis, *VP Admin*
Paula Dupuis, *Cust Mgr*
Mike Ribaudo, *Marketing Staff*
EMP: 46
SQ FT: 9,000
SALES (est): 9.5MM **Privately Held**
WEB: www.kaseprinting.com
SIC: 2752 Lithographic Commercial Printing

(G-18406)
KELLEY BROS NEW ENGLAND LLC (HQ)
17 Hampshire Dr Ste 20 (03051-4940)
PHONE..................................603 881-5559
Scott D Kelley, *Mng Member*
EMP: 13
SQ FT: 6,000
SALES (est): 2.9MM
SALES (corp-wide): 43.1MM **Privately Held**
SIC: 2431 Mfg Millwork
PA: Kelley Brothers, Llc
317 E Brighton Ave
Syracuse NY 13210
800 856-2550

(G-18407)
KM HOLDING INC
120 Derry St (03051-3712)
P.O. Box 240 (03051-0240)
PHONE..................................603 566-2704
Jonathan Kane, *President*
EMP: 15
SALES (est): 2.7MM **Privately Held**
WEB: www.computeroptics.com
SIC: 3827 Mfg Optical Instruments/Lenses

(G-18408)
KRETETEK INDUSTRIES LLC
66 River Rd (03051-5225)
PHONE..................................603 402-3073
Jessica Moore, *Mng Member*
EMP: 10
SALES (est): 66.7K **Privately Held**
SIC: 2851 Mfg Paints/Allied Products

(G-18409)
LANMARK CONTROLS INC
1 Wall St Ste C-103 (03051-3983)
PHONE..................................978 264-0200
EMP: 5
SALES (est): 1.8MM
SALES (corp-wide): 403.6MM **Publicly Held**
SIC: 7372 Prepackaged Software Services
PA: Faro Technologies, Inc.
250 Technology Park
Lake Mary FL 32746
407 333-9911

(G-18410)
LEPAGE BAKERIES PARK ST LLC
Also Called: Country Kitchen
2 Security Dr (03051-5246)
PHONE..................................603 880-4446
Tim Jackson, *Manager*
EMP: 30
SALES (corp-wide): 3.9B **Publicly Held**
SIC: 2051 Mfg Bread/Related Products
HQ: Lepage Bakeries Park Street Llc
11 Adamian Dr
Auburn ME 04210
207 783-9161

(G-18411)
LIFE IS GOOD (PA)
15 Hudson Park Dr (03051-3989)
PHONE..................................603 594-6100
Albert Jacobs, *CEO*
Tom Hassell, *Vice Pres*
Erica Figueiras, *Marketing Staff*
Ryan Keleher, *Department Mgr*
Michelle Deane, *Manager*
▲ **EMP:** 61 **EST:** 1994
SALES (est): 25.9MM **Privately Held**
SIC: 2759 Commercial Printing

(G-18412)
LIFE IS GOOD WHOLESALE INC
Also Called: Life Is Good Design Center
15 Hudson Park Dr (03051-3989)
PHONE..................................603 594-6100
Albert Jacobs, *President*
Roy Hefferman, *COO*
Robert Romano, *Vice Pres*
Shaun White, *Vice Pres*
John Jacobs, *Ch Credit Ofcr*
◆ **EMP:** 100
SQ FT: 150,000
SALES (est): 19.4MM
SALES (corp-wide): 25.9MM **Privately Held**
SIC: 2261 Cotton Finishing Plant
PA: The Life Is Good Company
51 Melcher St Ste 901
Boston MA 02210
617 867-8900

(G-18413)
MASIMO SEMICONDUCTOR INC
25 Sagamore Park Rd (03051-4901)
PHONE..................................603 595-8900
Mark P De Raad, *President*
Daryl Pulver, *Engineer*
Xuebing Zhang, *Engineer*
EMP: 30
SALES (est): 6.3MM **Privately Held**
SIC: 3674 Mfg Semiconductors/Related Devices

(G-18414)
MERCURY SYSTEMS INC
267 Lowell Rd Ste 101 (03051-4937)
PHONE..................................603 883-2900
Kevin Beals, *CEO*
Mike Caffelle, *Controller*
EMP: 120
SALES (corp-wide): 654.7MM **Publicly Held**
SIC: 3672 Mfg Printed Circuit Boards
PA: Mercury Systems, Inc.
50 Minuteman Rd
Andover MA 01810
978 256-1300

(G-18415)
MODERN METAL SOLUTIONS LLC
12 Park Ave (03051-3927)
PHONE..................................603 402-3022
Eleanor Dahar,
EMP: 6
SALES (est): 449.9K **Privately Held**
SIC: 3412 Mfg Metal Barrels/Pails

(G-18416)
MORGAN ADVANCED CERAMICS INC
4 Park Ave (03051-3927)
PHONE..................................603 598-9122
Jon Stang, *Branch Mgr*
EMP: 40
SALES (corp-wide): 1.3B **Privately Held**
WEB: www.morganelectroceramics.com
SIC: 3251 Mfg Abrasive Products
HQ: Morgan Advanced Materials Inc.
2425 Whipple Rd
Hayward CA 94544

(G-18417)
MRPC NORTHEAST LLC
Also Called: Johnson Precision
12 Executive Dr (03051-4939)
PHONE..................................603 880-3616
Greg Riemer, *Mng Member*
▲ **EMP:** 33
SALES (est): 8MM
SALES (corp-wide): 28MM **Privately Held**
SIC: 3089 3544 Mfg Plastic Products Mfg Dies/Tools/Jigs/Fixtures
PA: Molded Rubber & Plastic Corporation
13161 W Glendale Ave
Butler WI 53007
262 781-7122

(G-18418)
NASHUA FABRICATION CO INC
7 Security Dr (03051-5246)
PHONE..................................603 889-2181
Micheal Bernazani, *President*
Henry Bernazani, *Vice Pres*
Jane Noyes, *Treasurer*
Jeffrey H Mazerolle, *Admin Sec*
EMP: 18
SQ FT: 20,000
SALES (est): 3.6MM **Privately Held**
WEB: www.nashuafab.com
SIC: 3444 3713 Mfg Sheet Metalwork Mfg Truck/Bus Bodies

(G-18419)
NASHUA SAND & GRAVEL LLC
22 West Rd (03051-3019)
PHONE..................................603 459-8662
EMP: 3
SQ FT: 218
SALES (est): 219.6K **Privately Held**
SIC: 1442 Construction Sand/Gravel

(G-18420)
NEW ENGLAND SIGNS & AWNGS LLC
315 Derry Rd Ste 3 (03051-3050)
PHONE..................................603 235-7205
Robert McIntyre,
EMP: 4
SQ FT: 3,000
SALES: 600K **Privately Held**
SIC: 3089 3993 Mfg Plastic Products Mfg Signs/Advertising Specialties

(G-18421)
OCEAN INDUSTRIES LLC
Also Called: Acu Gage Systems
12 Park Ave (03051-3927)
PHONE..................................603 622-2481
John A Kane,
Lisa Caron,
▲ **EMP:** 5
SQ FT: 10,300

SALES (est): 1MM **Privately Held**
WEB: www.acu-gage.com
SIC: 3825 Mfg Electrical Measuring Instruments

(G-18422)
OMNI COMPONENTS CORP (PA)
46 River Rd Ste 1 (03051-5239)
PHONE..................................603 882-4467
William Holka, *President*
Frank Stone, *Exec VP*
Larry Cuneo, *Vice Pres*
Adam Baney, *Engineer*
Mike Norton, *Engineer*
EMP: 52
SQ FT: 37,000
SALES (est): 11.3MM **Privately Held**
SIC: 3999 3451 Mfg Misc Products Mfg Screw Machine Products

(G-18423)
ONLINE DEFENSE PRODUCTS LLC
142 Lowell Rd Unit 17385 (03051-4938)
PHONE..................................603 845-3211
Nathan C Sprague, *Administration*
EMP: 3
SALES (est): 251.4K **Privately Held**
SIC: 3812 Mfg Search/Navigation Equipment

(G-18424)
OPTI-SCIENCES INC
8 Winn Ave (03051-4547)
PHONE..................................603 883-4400
William Berzins, *President*
Raymond Russotti, *Vice Pres*
Jeff Kay, *Marketing Staff*
EMP: 5
SALES (est): 1MM **Privately Held**
WEB: www.optisci.com
SIC: 3826 5049 5999 Mfg Analytical Instruments Whol Professional Equipment Ret Misc Merchandise

(G-18425)
PARKER-HANNIFIN CORPORATION
Also Called: Chomerics Division
16 Flagstone Dr (03051-4904)
PHONE..................................603 880-4807
Shawne Deary, *Corp Comm Staff*
David Hill, *Branch Mgr*
EMP: 105
SQ FT: 25,000
SALES (corp-wide): 14.3B **Publicly Held**
WEB: www.parker.com
SIC: 3479 Coats & Laminates Plastic Film To Metals
PA: Parker-Hannifin Corporation
6035 Parkland Blvd
Cleveland OH 44124
216 896-3000

(G-18426)
PGC WIRE & CABLE LLC
17 Hampshire Dr Ste 1 (03051-4940)
PHONE..................................603 821-7300
Michael Moore, *Manager*
Thomas A Pursch,
EMP: 14 **EST:** 2012
SALES (est): 729.1K **Privately Held**
SIC: 3679 Mfg Electronic Components

(G-18427)
PNEUTEK INC
17 Friars Dr Ste D (03051-4926)
PHONE..................................603 595-0302
Harry M Haytayan, *President*
Karen Puthill, *Vice Pres*
Dave Persad, *CTO*
▲ **EMP:** 10
SQ FT: 45,000
SALES (est): 1.5MM **Privately Held**
WEB: www.pneutek.com
SIC: 3546 Mfg Power-Driven Handtools

(G-18428)
PRINCETON TECHNOLOGY CORP
33 Constitution Dr (03051-3986)
PHONE..................................603 595-1987
Craig E Norton, *CEO*
Wayne C Norton, *President*
John Dawson, *Project Mgr*
Maureen Abbott, *Buyer*
Brasil Amy, *Buyer*
EMP: 88
SQ FT: 20,000
SALES (est): 25.9MM **Privately Held**
WEB: www.princetontech.com
SIC: 3672 3679 Mfg Printed Circuit Boards Mfg Electronic Components

(G-18429)
PROTO PART INC
71 Pine Rd Unit F (03051-5322)
PHONE..................................603 883-6531
Kendall Roche, *President*
EMP: 13
SQ FT: 12,000
SALES (est): 2.2MM **Privately Held**
WEB: www.protopart.com
SIC: 3089 Mfg Plastic Products

(G-18430)
PTP MACHINING
21 West Rd (03051-3019)
PHONE..................................603 204-5446
Peter Norton, *Owner*
EMP: 5
SALES (est): 501.8K **Privately Held**
SIC: 3599 Mfg Industrial Machinery

(G-18431)
QESIDYNE INC
4 Candy Ln Unit 1 (03051-3062)
PHONE..................................603 883-3116
Kevin Susi, *President*
Jonathan Susi, *Treasurer*
EMP: 6
SQ FT: 6,000
SALES (est): 111.3K **Privately Held**
SIC: 3672 3845 3812 3823 Mfg Printed Circuit Brds Mfg Electromedical Equip Mfg Search/Navgatn Equip Mfg Process Cntrl Instr Mfg Surgical/Med Instr

(G-18432)
RDF CORPORATION
23 Elm Ave (03051-3224)
PHONE..................................603 882-5195
Naresh Puri, *President*
Tiger Wang, *Mfg Mgr*
Laura McCormack, *Senior Buyer*
Anthony Amato, *Engineer*
Ryan Matocha, *Engineer*
EMP: 69
SQ FT: 16,000
SALES (est): 16.3MM **Privately Held**
WEB: www.rdfcorp.com
SIC: 3829 Mfg Measuring/Controlling Devices

(G-18433)
RED BRICK CLOTHING CO
17 Dracut Rd Unit A (03051-5079)
PHONE..................................603 882-4100
Marie Mayotte, *Owner*
Richard Mayotte, *Controller*
Keith Mayotte, *Admin Sec*
EMP: 4
SALES (est): 614.1K **Privately Held**
WEB: www.redbrickclothingco.com
SIC: 2759 Commercial Printing

(G-18434)
REEDS FERRY SMALL BUILDINGS
3 Tracy Ln (03051-3031)
PHONE..................................603 883-1362
Timothy G Carleton, *President*
Steven Carleton, *Vice Pres*
EMP: 62
SALES (est): 3.1MM **Privately Held**
WEB: www.reedsferry.com
SIC: 2452 Mfg Prefabricated Wood Buildings

(G-18435)
RF LOGIC LLC (PA)
21 Park Ave (03051-3985)
PHONE..................................603 578-9876
Cindy Coneeny, *Human Resources*
Phil Lausier, *Mng Member*
Tarnya Baillio, *Technology*
EMP: 43
SQ FT: 20,000
SALES (est): 7.1MM **Privately Held**
WEB: www.rflogic.net
SIC: 3679 Mfg Electronic Components

(G-18436)
ROBINSON PRECISION TOOLS CORP
315 Derry Rd Ste 15 (03051-3051)
PHONE..................................603 889-1625
Dana Robinson, *President*
EMP: 10
SQ FT: 3,000
SALES (est): 671.1K **Privately Held**
SIC: 3599 Mfg Industrial Machinery

(G-18437)
SEMIKRON INC (HQ)
11 Executive Dr (03051-4914)
P.O. Box 66 (03051-0066)
PHONE..................................603 883-8102
Thomas O'Reilley, *President*
Andy Camardo, *Area Mgr*
Tom Rantala, *Area Mgr*
Sung-Sik Moon, *Business Mgr*
Lisa Danzinger, *Purch Mgr*
▲ **EMP:** 38
SQ FT: 54,000
SALES (est): 5.7MM
SALES (corp-wide): 546.2MM **Privately Held**
WEB: www.semikron.com
SIC: 3674 Mfg Semiconductors/Related Devices
PA: Semikron International Dr. Fritz Martin Gmbh & Co. Kg
Sigmundstr. 200
Nurnberg 90431
911 655-90

(G-18438)
SONIC MANUFACTURING CO INC
35 Sagamore Park Rd (03051-4915)
PHONE..................................603 882-1020
Thomas Glasheen, *Principal*
EMP: 34
SALES (est): 8.2MM **Privately Held**
SIC: 3672 Mfg Printed Circuit Boards

(G-18439)
SPARTON TECHNOLOGY CORP
8 Hampshire Dr (03051-4921)
PHONE..................................603 880-3692
Victor Breton, *President*
Michael S Breton, *Treasurer*
▲ **EMP:** 75
SQ FT: 80,000
SALES (est): 15MM **Privately Held**
WEB: www.spartontechnology.com
SIC: 3599 3444 Mfg Industrial Machinery Mfg Sheet Metalwork

(G-18440)
STATE PATTERN WORKS
3 Winn Ave (03051-4548)
PHONE..................................603 882-0701
Phillip Durand, *Partner*
Raymond Durand, *Partner*
EMP: 3
SQ FT: 2,700
SALES: 150K **Privately Held**
SIC: 3469 Mfg Metal Stampings

(G-18441)
STEAM TURBINE 4 U
5 Demery Rd (03051-5105)
PHONE..................................603 465-8881
EMP: 3 **EST:** 2015
SALES (est): 133.9K **Privately Held**
SIC: 3511 Mfg Turbines/Generator Sets

(G-18442)
STEEL ELEMENTS INTL LLC
3 Security Dr (03051-5246)
PHONE..................................603 466-2500
Scott Coulombe,
Kevin Cormier,
▼ **EMP:** 4
SALES (est): 440K **Privately Held**
SIC: 3441 Structural Metal Fabrication

(G-18443)
SUPERIOR SHEET METAL LLC
14 Flagstone Dr (03051-4904)
PHONE..................................603 577-8620
W Douglas Fox,
EMP: 16
SALES: 3.9MM **Privately Held**
WEB: www.superiorsm.com
SIC: 3444 Mfg Sheet Metalwork

(G-18444)
SYNTECH MICROWAVE INC
8 Rebel Rd (03051-3041)
PHONE..................................603 880-9767
Matthew Mason, *President*
EMP: 6
SALES (est): 945.9K **Privately Held**
WEB: www.syntechmicrowave.com
SIC: 3663 Mfg Rf Micro Wave Radio Components

(G-18445)
TECHNICAL MACHINE COMPONENTS
4 Security Dr (03051-5246)
PHONE..................................603 880-0444
Kevin Gervais, *President*
Gary McNiff, *Corp Secy*
EMP: 14
SQ FT: 10,000
SALES (est): 1.2MM **Privately Held**
WEB: www.technicalmachine.com
SIC: 3599 3444 Machining Precision Machine Shop

(G-18446)
TELEDYNE INSTRS LEEMAN LABS
110 Lowell Rd (03051-4806)
PHONE..................................603 521-3299
Peter G Brown, *General Mgr*
EMP: 70
SALES (est): 6.9MM
SALES (corp-wide): 2.9B **Publicly Held**
WEB: www.teledyne.com
SIC: 3826 Mfg Analytical Instruments
PA: Teledyne Technologies Inc
1049 Camino Dos Rios
Thousand Oaks CA 91360
805 373-4545

(G-18447)
TELEDYNE INSTRUMENTS INC
Teledyne Tekmar
110 Lowell Rd (03051-4806)
PHONE..................................603 886-8400
Peter Brown, *General Mgr*
EMP: 65
SALES (corp-wide): 2.9B **Publicly Held**
SIC: 3826 Mfg Analytical Instruments
HQ: Teledyne Instruments, Inc.
1049 Camino Dos Rios
Thousand Oaks CA 91360
805 373-4545

(G-18448)
THERMO FISHER SCIENTIFIC INC
22 Friars Dr (03051-4900)
PHONE..................................603 595-0505
Julie Procaccini, *Branch Mgr*
EMP: 4
SALES (corp-wide): 24.3B **Publicly Held**
SIC: 3826 Mfg Analytical Instruments
PA: Thermo Fisher Scientific Inc.
168 3rd Ave
Waltham MA 02451
781 622-1000

(G-18449)
VALID MFG INC
13 Hampshire Dr Ste 3 (03051-4948)
PHONE..................................603 880-0948
Sol Huot, *Materials Mgr*
Chet Khiev, *Director*
EMP: 10
SALES (est): 661.4K **Privately Held**
SIC: 3999 Mfg Misc Products

(G-18450)
VARITRON TECHNOLOGIES USA INC
Also Called: Varitron Hudson
12 Executive Dr Ste 2 (03051-4939)
PHONE..................................603 577-8855
Michel Farley, *President*
Jonathan Saunders, *Vice Pres*
EMP: 40
SQ FT: 15,000

SALES: 10MM
SALES (corp-wide): 87MM **Privately Held**
WEB: www.altronicsmfg.com
SIC: 3672 Mfg Printed Circuit Boards
PA: Groupe Varitron Inc
4811 Ch De La Savane
Saint-Hubert QC J3Y 9
450 926-1778

(G-18451)
W K HILLQUIST INC
37 Executive Dr (03051-4903)
PHONE..................................603 595-7790
Warren K Hillquist, *President*
Michael Torpey, *Vice Pres*
▲ **EMP:** 50
SQ FT: 36,000
SALES (est): 13.4MM **Privately Held**
WEB: www.wkhillquist.com
SIC: 3089 Mfg Plastic Products

(G-18452)
WIKOFF COLOR CORPORATION
4 Hampshire Dr (03051-4921)
PHONE..................................603 864-6456
Al Provost, *Prdtn Mgr*
Ryan Lomme, *Branch Mgr*
Bruce Stapleton, *Admin Sec*
EMP: 10
SALES (corp-wide): 145.1MM **Privately Held**
WEB: www.wikoff.com
SIC: 2893 Mfg Printing Ink
PA: Wikoff Color Corporation
1886 Merritt Rd
Fort Mill SC 29715
803 548-2210

(G-18453)
WOOD VISIONS INC
66b Old Derry Rd (03051-3016)
P.O. Box 815, Derry (03038-0815)
PHONE..................................603 595-9663
Patrick Patterson, *President*
David Rugh, *Vice Pres*
EMP: 4
SQ FT: 4,500
SALES (est): 447.6K **Privately Held**
WEB: www.woodvisions1.com
SIC: 2499 Mfg Outdoor Wooden Products

Intervale
Carroll County

(G-18454)
DONALD A JHNSON FINE WDWKG LLC
199 Dundee Rd (03845-6145)
PHONE..................................603 356-9080
Donald A Johnson,
EMP: 3
SALES (est): 325K **Privately Held**
SIC: 2431 1751 Mfg Millwork Carpentry Contractor

(G-18455)
PETER LIMMER & SONS INC
Rr 16 Box A (03845)
P.O. Box 88 (03845-0088)
PHONE..................................603 356-5378
Peter S Limmer, *President*
Karl Limmer, *Vice Pres*
▲ **EMP:** 3
SQ FT: 2,400
SALES (est): 378.9K **Privately Held**
WEB: www.limmerboot.com
SIC: 3143 3144 Mfg Men's Footwear Mfg Women's Footwear

Jaffrey
Cheshire County

(G-18456)
APOLLO STEEL LLC
52 Fitzgerald Dr (03452-6616)
P.O. Box 329 (03452-0329)
PHONE..................................603 532-1156
Clifton Gerard Pelissier,
John Demartin,
EMP: 5
SALES (est): 1.6MM **Privately Held**
SIC: 3441 Structural Metal Fabrication

(G-18457)
ATLAS PYROVISION ENTERTAINMENT (PA)
136 Old Sharon Rd (03452-5854)
P.O. Box 498 (03452-0498)
PHONE..................................603 532-8324
Stephen Pelkey, *President*
EMP: 26 **EST:** 2014
SALES (est): 15.4MM **Privately Held**
SIC: 2899 Mfg Chemical Preparations

(G-18458)
D C SPEENEY SONS PYROTECHNICS
531 North St (03452-5518)
P.O. Box 478 (03452-0478)
PHONE..................................603 532-9323
Eugene Speeney, *President*
Shelia Bergerom, *Vice Pres*
Lionel Bergerom, *Treasurer*
Nancy Speeney, *Admin Sec*
Francis Quinlan, *Clerk*
EMP: 6
SALES: 250K **Privately Held**
SIC: 2899 Mfg Fireworks

(G-18459)
D D BEAN & SONS CO (PA)
207 Peterborough St (03452-5868)
P.O. Box 348 (03452-0348)
PHONE..................................603 532-8311
Delcie David Bean, *President*
Christopher Vernon Bean, *Corp Secy*
Mark Crane Bean, *Vice Pres*
◆ **EMP:** 68 **EST:** 1938
SQ FT: 70,000
SALES (est): 16.1MM **Privately Held**
WEB: www.ddbean.com
SIC: 3999 Mfg Misc Products

(G-18460)
DAVID R GODINE PUBLISHER INC
426 Nutting Rd (03452-5745)
P.O. Box 450 (03452-0450)
PHONE..................................603 532-4100
David R Godine, *President*
EMP: 8
SALES (corp-wide): 939.9K **Privately Held**
WEB: www.blacksparrowpress.com
SIC: 2731 Books-Publishing/Printing
PA: David R. Godine, Publisher, Inc.
15 Court Sq Ste 320
Boston MA 02108
617 451-9600

(G-18461)
DIVERSIFIED DECORATING SALES
32 Fitzgerald Dr (03452-6616)
P.O. Box 386, Peterborough (03458-0386)
PHONE..................................603 532-4557
Richard S Shell, *President*
Murray R Wigsten, *Treasurer*
Jeffrey Crocker, *Clerk*
EMP: 6
SQ FT: 3,200
SALES (est): 1.1MM **Privately Held**
WEB: www.diversifieddecorating.com
SIC: 2822 Manufactures Stamp Rubber For Printers

(G-18462)
EMD MILLIPORE CORPORATION
11 Prescott Rd (03452-6636)
PHONE..................................603 532-8711
Marco Berardi, *QA Dir*
David Corliss, *Design Engr*
Grace McGlynn, *Manager*
Jill Fopiano, *Manager*
Steve Ringer, *Supervisor*
EMP: 400
SALES (corp-wide): 16.4B **Privately Held**
WEB: www.millipore.com
SIC: 3826 Mfg Analytical Instruments
HQ: Emd Millipore Corporation
400 Summit Dr
Burlington MA 01803
781 533-6000

(G-18463)
ENVIRONMENTAL TEST PDTS LLC
45 Knight St 1 (03452-5835)
PHONE..................................603 593-5268
Eric Peahl, *Branch Mgr*
EMP: 3
SALES (est): 379.4K
SALES (corp-wide): 254.1K **Privately Held**
WEB: www.etpproducts.com
SIC: 3826 Mfg & Assemble Environmental Testing Equipment
PA: Environmental Test Products Llc
29 Shipley Dr
Hollis NH 03049
603 924-5010

(G-18464)
GENTLE MACHINE CO LLC
39 Hadley Rd (03452-5817)
P.O. Box 425 (03452-0425)
PHONE..................................603 532-9363
Daniel Gentle,
Bev Gentle,
EMP: 3
SALES: 160K **Privately Held**
SIC: 3599 Mfg Industrial Machinery

(G-18465)
GRAPHICAST INC
36 Knight St (03452-5833)
P.O. Box 430 (03452-0430)
PHONE..................................603 532-4481
Walter A Zanchuk, *President*
David Gregory, *QC Mgr*
▼ **EMP:** 30 **EST:** 1978
SQ FT: 13,200
SALES: 2.7MM **Privately Held**
WEB: www.graphicast.com
SIC: 3369 Nonferrous Metal Foundry

(G-18466)
HIGH STANDARD INC
81 Turnpike Rd (03452-6669)
PHONE..................................603 532-8000
Mitchell Bargeron, *Manager*
EMP: 4 **Privately Held**
WEB: www.hsipanels.com
SIC: 3281 Mfg Cut Stone/Products
HQ: High Standard, Inc.
81 Fitzgerald Dr
Jaffrey NH 03452
603 532-8000

(G-18467)
HMD INC
Also Called: Medical Device Fabrication
81 Turnpike Rd (03452-6669)
PHONE..................................603 532-5757
Thomas Coneys, *President*
EMP: 35
SALES (est): 6.6MM **Privately Held**
WEB: www.medefab.com
SIC: 3841 Mfg Surgical/Medical Instruments

(G-18468)
JEBA GRAPHICS LLC
Also Called: Savron Graphics
32 Fitzgerald Dr (03452-6616)
P.O. Box 250 (03452-0250)
PHONE..................................603 532-7726
Robert Crowley, *Principal*
EMP: 3
SALES (est): 378.6K **Privately Held**
SIC: 2752 Lithographic Commercial Printing

(G-18469)
JOHNSON ABRASIVES CO INC
49 Fitzgerald Dr (03452-6615)
PHONE..................................603 532-4434
Elizabeth Johnson, *Ch of Bd*
Courtland Johnson, *President*
Charles Johnson, *Vice Pres*
▲ **EMP:** 40 **EST:** 1971
SQ FT: 4,000
SALES (est): 5.2MM **Privately Held**
WEB: www.johnsonabrasives.com
SIC: 3291 Mfg Abrasive Products

(G-18470)
KING MANUFACTURING CO INC
295 Squantum Rd (03452-6654)
PHONE..................................603 532-6455
William Stewart, *President*
Donald Stewart, *Vice Pres*
Joseph Hoppock, *Admin Sec*
EMP: 11
SQ FT: 25,000
SALES (est): 890K **Privately Held**
SIC: 3315 Mfg Staples Steel

(G-18471)
LIGNETICS NEW ENGLAND INC
141 Old Sharon Rd (03452-5850)
PHONE..................................603 532-4666
Joe Powers, *Plant Mgr*
Tony Woods, *Director*
EMP: 15
SALES (corp-wide): 28MM **Privately Held**
SIC: 2448 Mfg Wood Pallets/Skids
HQ: Lignetics Of New England, Inc.
1075 E S Boulder Rd
Louisville CO 80027
303 802-5400

(G-18472)
LIGNETICS NEW ENGLAND INC
415 Squantum Rd (03452-6655)
PHONE..................................603 532-4666
EMP: 30
SALES (corp-wide): 28MM **Privately Held**
SIC: 2448 Mfg Wood Pallets/Skids
HQ: Lignetics Of New England, Inc.
1075 E S Boulder Rd
Louisville CO 80027
303 802-5400

(G-18473)
MICROCATHETER COMPONENTS LLC
82 Fitzgerald Dr Unit 1a (03452-6706)
P.O. Box 456 (03452-0456)
PHONE..................................603 532-0345
Mary Karen Wirein, *Mng Member*
Diane Sukuda, *Mng Member*
EMP: 5 **EST:** 2015
SQ FT: 3,000
SALES: 500K **Privately Held**
SIC: 3841 Mfg Surgical/Medical Instruments

(G-18474)
MONADNOCK LOG HOME SVCS LLC
24 Red Gate Rd (03452-6202)
PHONE..................................603 876-4800
John Finnell, *Sales Staff*
Bradly Hamilton, *Manager*
Robert H Colgate,
Bob McKelvey,
EMP: 12
SALES (est): 1.9MM **Privately Held**
WEB: www.monadnockloghomes.com
SIC: 2452 Mfg Prefabricated Wood Buildings

(G-18475)
PUZZLE HOUSE
426 Nutting Rd (03452-5745)
PHONE..................................603 532-4442
Sarah Kurzon, *Owner*
▲ **EMP:** 10
SALES (est): 654.6K **Privately Held**
WEB: www.puzzlehouse.com
SIC: 3944 Mfg Games/Toys

(G-18476)
SAVRON GRAPHICS INC (PA)
4 Stratton Rd (03452-6663)
P.O. Box 250 (03452-0250)
PHONE..................................603 532-7726
Gregory R Lawn, *President*
Selma Lawn, *Treasurer*
Jeffrey Crocker, *Admin Sec*
EMP: 7
SQ FT: 3,000
SALES (est): 2MM **Privately Held**
WEB: www.savrongraphics.com
SIC: 2752 5112 Lithographic Commercial Printing

(G-18477)
SORBY & SON HEATING
21 Erin Ln (03452-5716)
PHONE..................................603 532-7214
Timothy Sorby, *Owner*
EMP: 5
SALES (est): 303.7K **Privately Held**
SIC: 1389 Oil/Gas Field Services

(G-18478)
SWING LABELS INC
81 Fitzgerald Dr (03452-6615)
PHONE..................................978 425-0855
Matt Cannon, *President*
EMP: 3
SALES (est): 614.5K **Privately Held**
WEB: www.swinglabels.com
SIC: 2679 Mfg Converted Paper Products

(G-18479)
TELEFLEX INCORPORATED
50 Plantation Dr (03452-6631)
PHONE..................................603 532-7706
Fred Preiss, *Vice Pres*
Kenneth Belluch, *Engineer*
Stephen Gildea, *Engineer*
Robert Jackson, *Engineer*
Laurie Jones, *Engineer*
EMP: 23
SALES (corp-wide): 2.4B **Publicly Held**
SIC: 3599 3841 3083 3082 Mfg Industrial Machinery Mfg Surgical/Med Instr Mfg Lamnatd Plstc Plates Mfg Plstc Profile Shapes
PA: Teleflex Incorporated
550 E Swedesford Rd # 400
Wayne PA 19087
610 225-6800

(G-18480)
TFX MEDICAL INCORPORATED
50 Plantation Dr (03452-6631)
PHONE..................................603 532-7706
R Ernest Waaser, *President*
C Jeffrey Jacobs, *Treasurer*
Kevin K Gordon, *Director*
Cynthia Sharo, *Admin Sec*
EMP: 325
SQ FT: 60,000
SALES (est): 44MM
SALES (corp-wide): 2.4B **Publicly Held**
WEB: www.tfx.com
SIC: 3599 3841 3083 3082 Mfg Industrial Machinery Mfg Surgical/Med Instr Mfg Lamnatd Plstc Plates Mfg Plstc Profile Shapes
PA: Teleflex Incorporated
550 E Swedesford Rd # 400
Wayne PA 19087
610 225-6800

(G-18481)
WEIDNER SERVICES LLC
5 Saw Mill Dr (03452-5946)
P.O. Box 752, Rindge (03461-0752)
PHONE..................................603 532-4833
Maureen Reider, *Principal*
James Weidner, *Mng Member*
EMP: 13
SALES (est): 967K **Privately Held**
SIC: 7692 Welding Repair

Jefferson
Coos County

(G-18482)
CHERRY POND DESIGNS INC
Also Called: Cherry Pond Furniture
716 Meadows Rd (03583-6847)
PHONE..................................603 586-7795
Peter Guest Jr, *President*
Peter Guest Sr, *Chairman*
EMP: 10
SQ FT: 10,000
SALES (est): 1.3MM **Privately Held**
WEB: www.cherryponddesigns.com
SIC: 2511 5961 Mfg Wood Household Furniture Ret Mail-Order House

(G-18483)
FORREST P HICKS II
Also Called: Hicks Loggings
28 Meadows Rd (03583-6838)
P.O. Box 125 (03583-0125)
PHONE..................................603 586-9819
Forrest P Hicks II, *Owner*
EMP: 5
SALES (est): 607.5K **Privately Held**
SIC: 2411 Logging

(G-18484)
INGERSON TRANSPORTATION
36 Alderbrook Dr (03583-6533)
PHONE..................................603 586-4335
Douglas Ingerson, *Partner*
Mitchell Ingerson, *Partner*
EMP: 9
SALES: 500K **Privately Held**
SIC: 2499 Mfg Mulch

(G-18485)
JOSSELYNS SAWMILL INC
243 Bailey Rd (03583-6506)
PHONE..................................603 586-4507
Keith Josselyn, *President*
EMP: 4
SALES (est): 581.6K **Privately Held**
WEB: www.josselyns.com
SIC: 2421 Sawmill/Planing Mill

(G-18486)
SDS LOGGING INC
180 Presidential Hwy (03583-6730)
PHONE..................................603 586-7098
EMP: 5
SALES (corp-wide): 1.1MM **Privately Held**
SIC: 2411 Logging
PA: Sds Logging Inc

Whitefield NH 03598
603 481-0208

(G-18487)
TREELINE TIMBER
11 Nevers Ln (03583-6800)
PHONE..................................603 586-7725
Craig Crukay, *Owner*
EMP: 8
SALES (est): 490K **Privately Held**
SIC: 2411 Logging

Keene
Cheshire County

(G-18488)
1911 OFFICE LLC
20 Central Sq (03431-3795)
P.O. Box 323 (03431-0323)
PHONE..................................603 352-2448
Rosamond P Delori, *Administration*
EMP: 4
SALES (est): 319.7K **Privately Held**
SIC: 3634 Mfg Electric Housewares/Fans

(G-18489)
603 OPTX INC
80 Krif Rd Unit 14 (03431-4737)
PHONE..................................603 357-4900
Shawn Voisine, *President*
EMP: 4
SALES (est): 509.2K **Privately Held**
SIC: 3827 Mfg Optical Instruments/Lenses

(G-18490)
ALERT PRODUCTS
95 Krif Rd (03431-4718)
PHONE..................................603 357-3331
Stephen Neary, *Vice Pres*
EMP: 4 **EST:** 2000
SALES (est): 236.2K **Privately Held**
WEB: www.alertproducts.com
SIC: 3699 Mfg Electrical Equipment/Supplies

(G-18491)
AMETEK PRECITECH INC (HQ)
44 Black Brook Rd (03431-5044)
PHONE..................................603 357-2510
Bruce P Wilson, *President*
Dan Johnson, *Vice Pres*
Daniel W Lawrence, *Vice Pres*
William J Burke, *Treasurer*
Kathryn E Sena, *Admin Sec*
▲ **EMP:** 100
SQ FT: 63,000
SALES (est): 20.5MM
SALES (corp-wide): 4.8B **Publicly Held**
WEB: www.precitech.com
SIC: 3552 3545 3827 3568 Mfg Textile Machinery Mfg Machine Tool Access Mfg Optical Instr/Lens Mfg Power Transmsn Equip Mfg Machine Tool-Cutting
PA: Ametek, Inc.
1100 Cassatt Rd
Berwyn PA 19312
610 647-2121

(G-18492)
ARIEL INSTANT PRINTING
26 Roxbury St (03431-3265)
PHONE..................................603 352-3663
Stephen Bunn, *Owner*
EMP: 3
SQ FT: 1,600
SALES (est): 261.9K **Privately Held**
SIC: 2752 Lithographic Commercial Printing

(G-18493)
ARZOL CORP
Also Called: Arzol Chemical Company
12 Norway Ave Ste 2 (03431-3740)
PHONE..................................603 352-5242
William H Hollister, *President*
Martha Hollister, *Vice Pres*
Heather M Hollister, *Director*
EMP: 4
SALES (est): 330K **Privately Held**
SIC: 2819 3842 Mfg Industrial Inorganic Chemicals Mfg Surgical Appliances/Supplies

(G-18494)
BACKPORCH PUBLISHING
16 Russell St (03431-2341)
PHONE..................................603 357-8761
Marcia Duffy, *Principal*
EMP: 4
SALES (est): 232.4K **Privately Held**
SIC: 2741 Misc Publishing

(G-18495)
BANK & BUSINESS FORMS INC
6 Kingsbury St (03431-3825)
P.O. Box 422 (03431-0422)
PHONE..................................603 357-0567
Lawrence Besserer, *President*
EMP: 5
SALES (est): 330K **Privately Held**
SIC: 2759 2782 2761 2752 Commercial Printing Mfg Blankbooks/Binders Mfg Manifold Bus Forms Lithographic Coml Print

(G-18496)
CONNELL COMMUNICATIONS INC
149 Emerald St Unit O (03431-3684)
PHONE..................................603 924-7271
T James Connell, *President*
EMP: 50
SQ FT: 24,000
SALES (est): 6.3MM
SALES (corp-wide): 1.7B **Privately Held**
WEB: www.tasteforlife.com
SIC: 2721 2741 Periodicals-Publishing/Printing Misc Publishing
HQ: Idg Communications, Inc.
5 Speen St
Framingham MA 01701
508 872-8200

(G-18497)
CORNING INCORPORATED
69 Island St Ste T (03431-3507)
PHONE..................................603 357-7662
Kevan Taylor, *Branch Mgr*
EMP: 120
SALES (corp-wide): 11.2B **Publicly Held**
SIC: 3229 Mfg Pressed/Blown Glass
PA: Corning Incorporated
1 Riverfront Plz
Corning NY 14831
607 974-9000

(G-18498)
COUNTER TECH INC
180 Emerald St Ste 50 (03431-3616)
PHONE..................................603 352-1882
Alan Whetmore, *President*
Charles Tifford, *Vice Pres*
EMP: 3
SQ FT: 5,000
SALES: 500K **Privately Held**
SIC: 2541 Mfg Custom Counter Tops

(G-18499)
CURRY COPY CENTER OF KEENE
Also Called: Curry Printing & Office Sups
7 Emerald St Apt 204 (03431-3661)
PHONE..................................603 352-9542
Arlene Fitz Simon, *President*
Steve Bragdon, *Admin Sec*
EMP: 5
SQ FT: 5,000
SALES (est): 686.6K **Privately Held**
SIC: 2752 5943 Offset Printing & Ret Office Supplies

(G-18500)
E-Z CRETE LLC
502 Winchester St (03431-3918)
PHONE..................................603 313-6462
Brice Raynor, *Principal*
EMP: 3
SALES (est): 167K **Privately Held**
SIC: 3272 Mfg Concrete Products

(G-18501)
ELECTRONIC IMAGING MTLS INC
20 Forge St (03431-5038)
PHONE..................................603 357-1459
Alex Henkel, *President*
Heather Bell, *Vice Pres*
Larry Ames, *Production*
Jillian Bishop, *Marketing Staff*
Cheryl Carignan, *Supervisor*
EMP: 40
SQ FT: 20,000
SALES (est): 4.8MM **Privately Held**
WEB: www.eiminc.com
SIC: 2759 2672 Commercial Printing Mfg Coated/Laminated Paper

(G-18502)
EVS NEW HAMPSHIRE INC
Also Called: Holden
50 Optical Ave (03431-4319)
PHONE..................................603 352-3000
Scott Berkowitz, *President*
EMP: 75
SQ FT: 30,000
SALES (est): 12.3MM
SALES (corp-wide): 26.2MM **Privately Held**
SIC: 3444 Mfg Sheet Metalwork
PA: Electronic Visions Systems Inc
1 Kenner Ct
Riverdale NJ 07457
973 839-4432

(G-18503)
FILTRINE MANUFACTURING CO INC (PA)
15 Kit St (03431-5911)
PHONE..................................603 352-5500
Peter Hansel, *President*
John Hansel, *Chairman*
Charles Hansel, *Vice Pres*
Turner Hansel, *Vice Pres*
▼ **EMP:** 80 **EST:** 1901
SALES (est): 8.6MM **Privately Held**
WEB: www.filtrine.com
SIC: 3585 3589 Mfg Refrigeration/Heating Equipment Mfg Service Industry Machinery

(G-18504)
GEMGRAPHICS INC
415 Marlboro St (03431-4310)
PHONE..................................603 352-7112
Steve Myre, *President*
EMP: 3
SALES (est): 393.7K **Privately Held**
SIC: 2752 Lithographic Commercial Printing

GEOGRAPHIC

(G-18505)
GEMINI FIRFIELD SCREENPRINTING
149 Emerald St Unit N (03431-3662)
PHONE.................................603 357-3847
Steve Myre, *President*
Ronald Rzasa, *Vice Pres*
EMP: 7
SQ FT: 4,000
SALES (est): 500K **Privately Held**
WEB: www.geminiscreenprint.com
SIC: 2261 Textile & Industrial Screenprinting

(G-18506)
GS PRECISION INC-KEENE DIV
18 Bradco St (03431-3996)
PHONE.................................603 355-1166
Ray Anderson, *President*
Claus Knappe, *Chairman*
Edward Hewey, *Vice Pres*
Tyler Goodnow, *Sales Staff*
EMP: 90
SQ FT: 65,000
SALES (est): 19.5MM
SALES (corp-wide): 121.9MM **Privately Held**
WEB: www.knappe-koester.com
SIC: 3599 Mfg Industrial Machinery
PA: G. S. Precision, Inc.
101 John Seitz Dr
Brattleboro VT 05301
802 257-5200

(G-18507)
JANOS TECHNOLOGY INC
55 Black Brook Rd (03431-5044)
PHONE.................................603 757-0070
Jonathan Hildrey, *CFO*
Karen Bays, *Administration*
EMP: 8
SALES (est): 219.3K **Privately Held**
SIC: 3827 Optical Instruments And Lenses

(G-18508)
JANOS TECHNOLOGY LLC
55 Black Brook Rd (03431-5044)
PHONE.................................603 757-0070
Jonathan Hildrey, *Finance*
◆ **EMP:** 175
SQ FT: 35,000
SALES (est): 18.7MM
SALES (corp-wide): 6.4B **Publicly Held**
WEB: www.janostech.com
SIC: 3827 Mfg Optical Instruments/Lenses
HQ: Fluke Electronics Corporation
6920 Seaway Blvd
Everett WA 98203
425 347-6100

(G-18509)
KEEBOWIL INC (PA)
Also Called: Solar Source
353 West St (03431-2442)
P.O. Box 523 (03431-0523)
PHONE.................................603 352-4232
Robert W Therrien, *President*
Gordon Ayotte, *Division Mgr*
Alex Kossakoski, *Exec VP*
Bob Hardy, *Vice Pres*
Robert Lefebvre, *Vice Pres*
EMP: 100 **EST:** 1932
SQ FT: 35,000
SALES (est): 39.7MM **Privately Held**
WEB: www.melanson.com
SIC: 3444 1761 Mfg Sheet Metalwork Roofing/Siding Contractor

(G-18510)
KEENE GAS CORPORATION
Also Called: Cornerstone Propane
64 Main St Ste A (03431-3701)
PHONE.................................603 352-4134
Bobbi Duval, *Principal*
Tim Ball, *Manager*
EMP: 18
SALES (est): 1.4MM **Privately Held**
SIC: 1321 Natural Gas Liquids Production

(G-18511)
KEENE PUBLISHING CORPORATION
Also Called: Keene Sentinel
60 West St (03431-3373)
P.O. Box 546 (03431-0546)
PHONE.................................603 352-1234
Terrence L Williams, *President*
Kevin Pearson, *Editor*
Cecily Weisburgh, *Editor*
Kelvin Parker, *Opers Staff*
Michael Breshears, *Sales Mgr*
EMP: 100 **EST:** 1992
SQ FT: 22,800
SALES (est): 8.8MM **Privately Held**
WEB: www.keenenh.com
SIC: 2711 Newspapers-Publishing/Printing

(G-18512)
KENNEDY INFORMATION LLC
24 Railroad St (03431-3744)
P.O. Box 190, Sullivan (03445-0190)
PHONE.................................603 357-8100
Daniel Houder, *President*
John Yoder, *Consultant*
Chad Robinson, *Research Analys*
EMP: 33 **EST:** 1970
SALES (est): 3.9MM
SALES (corp-wide): 1.8B **Privately Held**
SIC: 2741 Misc Publishing
HQ: The Bureau Of National Affairs Inc
1801 S Bell St Ste Cn110
Arlington VA 22202
703 341-3000

(G-18513)
KISERS ORTHO PROSTHETIC SERV (PA)
25 Avon St (03431-3510)
PHONE.................................603 357-7666
Michael Kiser, *President*
Frances Kiser, *Vice Pres*
EMP: 5
SALES (est): 583.8K **Privately Held**
SIC: 3842 5999 Mfg Surgical Appliances/Supplies Ret Misc Merchandise

(G-18514)
MAPLE NUT KITCHEN LLC
43 Darling Rd (03431-4939)
PHONE.................................603 354-3219
Leanna Houle, *Sales Staff*
Vivian Cubilla-Lindblom, *Mng Member*
EMP: 3 **EST:** 2014
SALES (est): 83K **Privately Held**
SIC: 2064 Mfg Candy/Confectionery

(G-18515)
MILLWORK MASTERS LTD (PA)
69 Island St Ste B (03431-3507)
PHONE.................................603 358-3038
Peter Bringer, *President*
EMP: 12
SQ FT: 4,980
SALES (est): 1.1MM **Privately Held**
SIC: 2431 5031 5211 Mfg Millwork Whol Lumber/Plywd/Millwk

(G-18516)
MILTRONICS MFG SVCS INC
95 Krif Rd (03431-4718)
PHONE.................................603 352-3333
Anton M Neary, *President*
Jim Fischer, *Vice Pres*
Matthew W Neary, *Deputy Dir*
Elisabeth G R Neary, *Admin Sec*
EMP: 15
SQ FT: 10,000
SALES: 1.5MM **Privately Held**
WEB: www.miltronics.com
SIC: 3679 Mfg Electronic Components

(G-18517)
MOUNTAIN CORPORATION (PA)
59 Optical Ave (03431-4320)
P.O. Box 686 (03431-0686)
PHONE.................................603 355-2272
Kenny Ballard, *CEO*
Michael Krinsky, *President*
Sherri Hudson, *Sales Staff*
Randy Patrick, *Director*
▼ **EMP:** 180
SQ FT: 100,000
SALES (est): 50.1MM **Privately Held**
SIC: 2253 5961 Knit Outerwear Mill Electronic Shopping

(G-18518)
MPB CORPORATION (HQ)
Also Called: Timken Super Precision
7 Optical Ave (03431-4348)
P.O. Box 607 (03431-0607)
PHONE.................................603 352-0310
Erik Paulhardt, *President*
Phillip Fracassa, *Vice Pres*
Ronald N Cushing, *Engineer*
Ronald Cushing, *Engineer*
Paul Hartwell, *Engineer*
▲ **EMP:** 675 **EST:** 1941
SQ FT: 178,800
SALES (est): 260.1MM
SALES (corp-wide): 3.5B **Publicly Held**
SIC: 3562 6061 Mfg Ball/Roller Bearings Federal Credit Union
PA: The Timken Company
4500 Mount Pleasant St Nw
North Canton OH 44720
234 262-3000

(G-18519)
MULTI-MED INC
26 Victoria Ct (03431-4218)
PHONE.................................603 357-8733
Alan Reid, *President*
L Ernest Reid, *Treasurer*
EMP: 50
SALES (est): 6MM **Privately Held**
WEB: www.multimedinc.com
SIC: 3841 Mfg Surgical/Medical Instruments

(G-18520)
NEW HAMPSHIRE FORGE INC
15 Forge St (03431-5037)
P.O. Box 423 (03431-0423)
PHONE.................................603 357-5692
J Robert Hof, *President*
Phillip Hof, *Vice Pres*
Pamela Hof, *Treasurer*
Stephen Bragdon, *Admin Sec*
▲ **EMP:** 25 **EST:** 1980
SQ FT: 5,000
SALES (est): 3.3MM **Privately Held**
SIC: 3462 Mfg Steel Forgings

(G-18521)
PHILS TREE SERVICE AND LOG
34 Dale Dr (03431-5005)
PHONE.................................603 352-0202
Philip Davis, *Principal*
EMP: 4
SALES (est): 272.3K **Privately Held**
SIC: 2411 Logging

(G-18522)
PITNEY BOWES INC
640 Marlboro St Ste 5 (03431-4049)
PHONE.................................603 352-7766
Rich Lawrey, *Manager*
EMP: 20
SALES (corp-wide): 3.5B **Publicly Held**
SIC: 3579 7359 Mfg Office Machines Equipment Rental/Leasing
PA: Pitney Bowes Inc.
3001 Summer St Ste 3
Stamford CT 06905
203 356-5000

(G-18523)
SAMSON MANUFACTURING CORP
32 Optical Ave (03431-4319)
PHONE.................................603 355-3903
Scott W Samson, *President*
Susan O'Brien, *Comptroller*
EMP: 24
SQ FT: 10,000
SALES (est): 4.3MM **Privately Held**
SIC: 3469 Mfg Metal Stampings

(G-18524)
SHAKOUR PUBLISHERS INC
Also Called: Monadnock Shopper News
445 West St (03431-2448)
P.O. Box 487 (03431-0487)
PHONE.................................603 352-5250
Mitchell G Shakour, *President*
Jack Cami, *Accounts Exec*
Marilyn Weir, *Accounts Exec*
EMP: 20
SQ FT: 2,000
SALES (est): 1.5MM **Privately Held**
WEB: www.shoppernews.com
SIC: 2711 Newspapers-Publishing/Printing

(G-18525)
SIMS PORTEX INC
10 Bowman Dr (03431-5043)
PHONE.................................603 352-3812
John Beauregard, *Principal*
Tanya Fratto, *Bd of Directors*
EMP: 11
SALES (est): 1.2MM **Privately Held**
SIC: 3841 Mfg Surgical/Medical Instruments

(G-18526)
SMITHS MEDICAL ASD INC
Production Ave (03431)
PHONE.................................603 352-3812
Thomas Westra, *VP Finance*
EMP: 20
SALES (corp-wide): 3.1B **Privately Held**
WEB: www.smith-medical.com
SIC: 3841 Mfg Surgical/Medical Instruments
HQ: Smiths Medical Asd, Inc.
6000 Nathan Ln N Ste 100
Plymouth MN 55442
763 383-3000

(G-18527)
SMITHS MEDICAL ASD INC
10 Bowman Dr (03431-5036)
PHONE.................................603 352-3812
Lynn Ziman, *Principal*
Lisa Huckins, *Engineer*
EMP: 43
SALES (corp-wide): 3.1B **Privately Held**
WEB: www.smith-medical.com
SIC: 3841 Mfg Surgical/Medical Instruments
HQ: Smiths Medical Asd, Inc.
6000 Nathan Ln N Ste 100
Plymouth MN 55442
763 383-3000

(G-18528)
STA FIT FOR WOMEN LLC
815 Court St (03431-1712)
PHONE.................................603 357-8880
EMP: 3
SALES (est): 170K **Privately Held**
SIC: 3841 Mfg Surgical/Medical Instruments

(G-18529)
STINGRAY OPTICS LLC
17a Bradco St (03431-3900)
PHONE.................................603 358-5577
Matt Snow, *President*
Troy Palmer, *Engineer*
Loren Blaisdell, *Manager*
Christopher Alexay,
EMP: 16
SQ FT: 12,800
SALES: 16MM
SALES (corp-wide): 163.5MM **Privately Held**
WEB: www.stingrayoptics.com
SIC: 3827 Manufacturer Of Optical Instruments Or Lenses
HQ: Em4 Inc
7 Oak Park Dr
Bedford MA 01730
781 275-7501

(G-18530)
STONEMAN CUSTOM JEWELERS
82 Washington St Ste 2 (03431-3194)
PHONE.................................603 352-0811
John Oconnor, *Owner*
EMP: 3
SQ FT: 500
SALES: 235K **Privately Held**
SIC: 3911 5944 7631 Mfg Precious Metal Jewelry Ret Jewelry Watch/Clock/Jewelry Repair

(G-18531)
SUNSET TOOL INC
58 Optical Ave (03431-4319)
PHONE.................................603 355-2246
Richard E Hall, *President*

Jane Hall, *CFO*
EMP: 20
SQ FT: 11,000
SALES (est): 2.8MM **Privately Held**
WEB: www.sunsettoolinc.com
SIC: 3544 3469 3599 Mfg Dies/Tools/Jigs/Fixtures Mfg Metal Stampings Mfg Industrial Machinery

(G-18532)
SURRY LICENSING LLC
7 Corporate Dr (03431-5042)
PHONE.................................603 354-7000
Richard B Cohen,
Timothy D Ludlow,
Michael F Newbold,
EMP: 4
SALES (est): 217.7K **Privately Held**
SIC: 2086 Mfg Bottled/Canned Soft Drinks

(G-18533)
TIDLAND CORPORATION
11 Bradco St (03431-3900)
PHONE.................................603 352-1696
Victor Kissell, *Manager*
EMP: 60
SALES (corp-wide): 2.9B **Privately Held**
WEB: www.tidland.com
SIC: 3554 3324 3568 Mfg Paper Indstl Mach Steel Investment Foundry Mfg Power Transmsn Equip
HQ: Tidland Corporation
2305 Se 8th Ave
Camas WA 98607
360 834-2345

(G-18534)
WHITNEY BROS CO
Also Called: Whitney Learning Materials
93 Railroad St (03431-3742)
P.O. Box 644 (03431-0644)
PHONE.................................603 352-2610
David Stabler, *President*
Mike Jablonski, *Vice Pres*
Lee Gray, *Receiver*
Brian Vaillancourt, *Sales Dir*
▲ **EMP:** 40 **EST:** 1904
SQ FT: 83,000
SALES: 4MM **Privately Held**
WEB: www.whitneybros.com
SIC: 2531 2511 Mfg Public Building Furn Mfg Wood Household Furn

Kensington
Rockingham County

(G-18535)
COUNTY COMMUNICATIONS
207 Amesbury Rd (03833-5723)
PHONE.................................603 394-7070
EMP: 3
SALES (est): 168.9K **Privately Held**
SIC: 3663 Mfg Radio/Tv Communication Equipment

(G-18536)
DAN DAILEY INC
Also Called: Dailey-Mc Neil
2 North Rd (03833-5605)
PHONE.................................603 778-2303
Daniel Dailey, *President*
Linda Mc Neil, *Treasurer*
EMP: 10
SALES (est): 982.4K **Privately Held**
SIC: 3231 Mfg Products-Purchased Glass

(G-18537)
VIKING WLDG & FABRICATION LLC
243 Amesbury Rd Ste 1 (03833-5703)
PHONE.................................603 394-7887
Donald Johnson, *General Mgr*
Robin Johnson, *Office Mgr*
Donald Johnson,
EMP: 8
SALES: 750K **Privately Held**
WEB: www.vikingwelding.com
SIC: 3441 3732 Structural Metal Fabrication Boatbuilding/Repairing

Kingston
Rockingham County

(G-18538)
AH NELSEN ASSOCIATES LLC
23 Sunshine Dr Ste 23 # 23 (03848-3544)
PHONE.................................603 716-6687
Albert H Nelsen IV, *Administration*
EMP: 3 **EST:** 2012
SALES: 250K **Privately Held**
SIC: 3269 Mfg Pottery Products

(G-18539)
AMERICAN CANVAS COMPANY LLC
63 Route 125 Ste 1 (03848-3589)
PHONE.................................603 642-6665
Travis McConnell, *Mng Member*
EMP: 4
SALES: 1MM **Privately Held**
WEB: www.americancanvasproducts.com
SIC: 2394 5199 5999 Mfg Canvas/Related Products Whol Nondurable Goods Ret Misc Merchandise

(G-18540)
APONOS MEDICAL CORPORATION
17 Route 125 Bldg A7 (03848-3583)
PHONE.................................603 347-8229
Ken Spector, *President*
EMP: 5
SALES (est): 346.4K **Privately Held**
SIC: 3841 Mfg Surgical/Medical Instruments

(G-18541)
CARRIAGE TOWNE NEWS
14 Church St (03848-3068)
P.O. Box 100 (03848-0100)
PHONE.................................603 642-4499
Al Getler, *President*
EMP: 7
SQ FT: 900
SALES (est): 214K **Privately Held**
WEB: www.carriagetownenews.com
SIC: 2711 Newspapers-Publishing/Printing

(G-18542)
CNC DESIGN & COUNSULTING LLC
63 Route 125 Ste 4 (03848-3589)
P.O. Box 222, Newmarket (03857-0222)
PHONE.................................603 686-5437
Laurence Morgano, *Mng Member*
EMP: 5
SQ FT: 2,000
SALES: 165K **Privately Held**
SIC: 3312 3599 General Machining

(G-18543)
EAST COAST METAL WORKS CO INC
21 Route 125 Unit 2 (03848-3593)
PHONE.................................603 642-9600
Tom Diorio, *President*
EMP: 7
SALES (est): 800K **Privately Held**
SIC: 3441 1799 7692 3444 Structural Metal Fabrctn Special Trade Contractor Welding Repair Mfg Sheet Metalwork

(G-18544)
HOMESTEAD KITCHEN CENTRE LLC
53 Church St Unit 18 (03848-3077)
PHONE.................................603 642-8022
Michele Lorraine Lovering, *Principal*
EMP: 4 **EST:** 2007
SALES (est): 548.8K **Privately Held**
SIC: 3553 Mfg Woodworking Machinery

(G-18545)
MASS CHASSIS
68 Route 125 (03848-3562)
PHONE.................................603 642-8967
Pat Murphy, *Owner*
EMP: 17
SALES (est): 443.8K **Privately Held**
SIC: 7692 Welding Repair

(G-18546)
TORROMEO INDUSTRIES INC
Also Called: Kingston Materials
18 Dorre Rd (03848-3412)
PHONE.................................603 642-5564
Paula Torromeo, *Manager*
EMP: 30
SALES (corp-wide): 10MM **Privately Held**
SIC: 3273 5032 Mfg Ready-Mixed Concrete Whol Brick/Stone Material
PA: Torromeo Industries, Inc.
33 Old Ferry Rd
Methuen MA 01844
978 686-5634

(G-18547)
ULTIMATE GLASS SERVICES LLC
17 Route 125 Unit 12 (03848-3586)
PHONE.................................603 642-3375
Joe Cutrona,
Kara Cutrona,
EMP: 3
SALES (est): 251.5K **Privately Held**
WEB: www.ultimateglassservices.com
SIC: 3231 Mfg Products-Purchased Glass

(G-18548)
WARDS WOODWORKING INC
16 Route 125 (03848-3529)
PHONE.................................603 642-7300
David J Damphousse, *Principal*
EMP: 4
SALES (est): 428.2K **Privately Held**
WEB: www.wardssheds.com
SIC: 2431 Mfg Millwork

Laconia
Belknap County

(G-18549)
AAVID CORPORATION
1 Aavid Cir (03246)
PHONE.................................603 528-3400
Alan W Wong, *President*
Christopher G Boehm, *President*
EMP: 3000
SALES (est): 228.8MM **Privately Held**
SIC: 3679 Mfg Electronic Components

(G-18550)
ACCELLENT ENDOSCOPY INC
45 Lexington Dr (03246-2935)
PHONE.................................603 528-1211
Don Spence, *President*
EMP: 110
SQ FT: 40,000
SALES (est): 12.3MM
SALES (corp-wide): 1.2B **Publicly Held**
SIC: 3841 Mfg Surgical/Medical Instruments
HQ: Accellent Llc
100 Fordham Rd Bldg C
Wilmington MA 01887
978 570-6900

(G-18551)
ACI - PCB INC
254 Court St Ste A (03246-5600)
PHONE.................................603 528-7711
Jeffrey A Holt, *Principal*
EMP: 5 **EST:** 2012
SALES (est): 520.8K **Privately Held**
SIC: 3672 Mfg Printed Circuit Boards

(G-18552)
ADDITIVE CIRCUITS INC
254 Court St Ste A (03246-5600)
PHONE.................................603 366-1578
Arthur Desmarais, *President*
EMP: 3
SALES (est): 220K **Privately Held**
SIC: 3679 Mfg Electronic Components

(G-18553)
AEROWELD INC
49 Blaisdell Ave (03246-4405)
PHONE.................................603 524-8121
Allen Richardson, *President*
Janette Richardson, *Vice Pres*
EMP: 10
SQ FT: 14,000
SALES (est): 1.3MM **Privately Held**
WEB: www.aeroweld-nh.com
SIC: 3724 3599 Mfg Aircraft Engines/Parts Mfg Industrial Machinery

(G-18554)
AKA TOOL INC
477 Province Rd Ste 1 (03246-1383)
PHONE.................................603 524-1868
Steven Jorgensen, *President*
EMP: 7 **EST:** 2006
SALES (est): 1.2MM **Privately Held**
SIC: 3599 Mfg Industrial Machinery

(G-18555)
ALGERS LEO NH ELC MTRS
459 Province Rd (03246-1331)
PHONE.................................603 524-3729
Thomas Bates, *President*
Karen Bates, *Treasurer*
EMP: 9
SALES (est): 1.8MM **Privately Held**
SIC: 7694 5063 Armature Rewinding Whol Electrical Equipment

(G-18556)
AMATEX CORPORATION
45 Primrose Dr S (03246-2901)
PHONE.................................603 524-2552
Michael De Angelo, *Safety Dir*
Peter Croceau, *Manager*
EMP: 27
SALES (corp-wide): 14.2MM **Privately Held**
WEB: www.amatex.com
SIC: 2221 3053 Manmade Broadwoven Fabric Mill Mfg Gaskets/Packing/Sealing Devices
PA: Amatex Corporation
1032 Stanbridge St
Norristown PA 19401
610 277-6100

(G-18557)
BARON MACHINE COMPANY INC
40 Primrose Dr S (03246-3927)
PHONE.................................603 524-6800
Kim E Baron, *President*
Jeremy Baron, *Vice Pres*
Michael Sanborn, *Purchasing*
Sue Gavarny, *Controller*
Lee Mattson, *Admin Sec*
EMP: 70 **EST:** 1956
SQ FT: 45,000
SALES (est): 11.8MM **Privately Held**
WEB: www.baronmachine.com
SIC: 7692 3599 Welding Repair Mfg Industrial Machinery

(G-18558)
BIG DADDYS SIGNS FLORIDA INC
24 Lexington Dr (03246-3945)
PHONE.................................800 535-2139
Steven Zwicker, *Principal*
EMP: 3
SALES (est): 135.2K **Privately Held**
SIC: 3993 Mfg Signs/Advertising Specialties

(G-18559)
BODYCOTE THERMAL PROC INC
187 Water St (03246-3351)
PHONE.................................603 524-7886
Dean Huffman, *General Mgr*
EMP: 21
SALES (corp-wide): 960MM **Privately Held**
SIC: 3398 Heat Treating & Grazing Of Metal Parts
HQ: Bodycote Thermal Processing, Inc.
12700 Park Central Dr # 700
Dallas TX 75251
214 904-2420

(G-18560)
BOULIA-GORRELL LUMBER CO INC
176 Fair St (03246-3322)
PHONE.................................603 524-1300
John A Veazey, *President*
Charles Veazey, *Vice Pres*
Sally McGarry, *Treasurer*

GEOGRAPHIC

Linda Laurent, *Manager*
EMP: 18 **EST:** 1866
SQ FT: 10,000
SALES (est): 2.6MM **Privately Held**
WEB: www.bogolumber.com
SIC: 2431 5211 Mfg Millwork Ret Lumber/Building Materials

(G-18561)
BURNS MACHINE LLC
516 Province Rd (03246-1329)
PHONE..................................603 524-4080
Michele A Welch, *Treasurer*
Glenn S Welch,
EMP: 23
SALES (est): 4.5MM **Privately Held**
SIC: 3599 Mfg Industrial Machinery

(G-18562)
CHESHIRE OPTICAL INC
53c Davis Pl (03246-2761)
PHONE..................................603 352-0602
Diane Castonguay, *Director*
EMP: 3
SALES (est): 224.6K **Privately Held**
SIC: 3827 Mfg Optical Instruments/Lenses

(G-18563)
COOPER PRODUCTS INC
210 Fair St (03246-3366)
PHONE..................................603 524-3367
Marcio Lima, *CEO*
Grant Massey, *General Mgr*
Don Avery, *Purch Mgr*
Andrew Nichols, *QC Mgr*
Kathleen Flon Grenier, *Treasurer*
▲ **EMP:** 44
SQ FT: 33,000
SALES: 5.5MM
SALES (corp-wide): 1.7B **Privately Held**
WEB: www.cooperproducts.com
SIC: 3061 3053 Mfg Mechanical Rubber Gd Mfg Gasket/Packing/Seals
HQ: Zhongding Sealing Parts (Usa), Inc.
400 Detroit Ave
Monroe MI 48162
734 241-8870

(G-18564)
FRONEK ANCHOR DARLING ENTP
86 Doris Ray Ct (03246-5509)
PHONE..................................603 528-1931
Durga Agrawal, *President*
EMP: 10
SALES: 1MM
SALES (corp-wide): 163.2MM **Privately Held**
WEB: www.pepindia.com
SIC: 3494 8711 3441 Manufacure Valves/Pipes Fittings Engineering Services
PA: Piping Technology & Products, Inc.
3701 Holmes Rd
Houston TX 77051
800 787-5914

(G-18565)
HAMPSHIRE HARDWOODS LLC
53 Captains Walk (03246-4083)
PHONE..................................603 434-1144
Charles R Boelig, *Mng Member*
EMP: 4
SALES: 1.2MM **Privately Held**
SIC: 3996 2431 Mfg Hard Floor Coverings Mfg Millwork

(G-18566)
HEBERT FOUNDRY & MACHINE INC
Also Called: Hebert Foundry & Machine Co
113 Fair St (03246-3321)
PHONE..................................603 524-2065
Richard Hebert, *President*
Dave Plummer, *Partner*
Donald Hebert, *Vice Pres*
Jennifer Hebert, *Vice Pres*
EMP: 35 **EST:** 1950
SQ FT: 60,000
SALES (est): 5.8MM
SALES (corp-wide): 4.2MM **Privately Held**
SIC: 3366 Copper Foundry
PA: The Hebert Manufacturing Company
113 Fair St
Laconia NH 03246
603 524-2065

(G-18567)
HEBERT MANUFACTURING COMPANY (PA)
113 Fair St (03246-3321)
PHONE..................................603 524-2065
Richard Hebert, *President*
Donald Hebert, *Vice Pres*
John Lull, *Admin Sec*
EMP: 55 **EST:** 1912
SQ FT: 52,000
SALES: 4.2MM **Privately Held**
SIC: 3364 3363 Mfg Nonferrous Die-Castings Mfg Aluminum Die-Castings

(G-18568)
INFRA RED TECHNOLOGY INC
Also Called: I R T
60 Bay St Ste 7 (03246-3309)
PHONE..................................603 524-1177
Edward Fortuna, *President*
Nancy Fortuna, *Treasurer*
EMP: 3
SQ FT: 5,248
SALES: 180K **Privately Held**
SIC: 3567 Designs Builds & Refurbishes Infrared And Wave Soddering Machines

(G-18569)
KELLERHAUS INC
259 Endicott St N (03246-1736)
P.O. Box 5337 (03247-5337)
PHONE..................................603 366-4466
Bettina Potter, *CEO*
Dave Allen, *President*
Kathleen Donohoe, *Admin Sec*
EMP: 30
SQ FT: 1,800
SALES (est): 1.9MM **Privately Held**
WEB: www.kellerhaus.com
SIC: 2024 2064 5947 Mfg Ice Cream Frozen Dessert & Candy & Ret Gifts

(G-18570)
LACONIA MAGNETICS INC
Prescott Hill Rd (03246)
P.O. Box 1457 (03247-1457)
PHONE..................................603 528-2766
Michael Southworth, *President*
Debbie Southworth, *Vice Pres*
EMP: 35
SQ FT: 10,000
SALES (est): 7.9MM **Privately Held**
SIC: 3677 3612 Mfg Electronic Coils/Transformers Mfg Transformers

(G-18571)
LAKE REGION MEDICAL INC
Also Called: Accellent Laconia
45 Lexington Dr (03246-2935)
PHONE..................................603 528-1211
Dawn Jones, *Branch Mgr*
EMP: 90
SALES (corp-wide): 1.2B **Publicly Held**
SIC: 3841 Mfg Surgical/Medical Instruments
HQ: Lake Region Medical, Inc.
100 Fordham Rd Ste 3
Wilmington MA 01887

(G-18572)
LAKES REGION NEWS CLUB INC
Also Called: Laconia Daily Sun
1127 Union Ave (03246-2126)
PHONE..................................603 527-9299
Edward J Engler, *President*
Edward Engler, *President*
Crystal Furnee, *Sales Staff*
Ginger Kozlowski, *Manager*
EMP: 6
SALES (est): 295.1K **Privately Held**
WEB: www.laconiadailysun.com
SIC: 2711 Newspapers-Publishing/Printing

(G-18573)
LAKES REGION TUBULAR PDTS INC
Also Called: Scotia Technology
51 Growth Rd (03246-1318)
P.O. Box 1190 (03247-1190)
PHONE..................................603 528-2838
David F Bonisteel, *President*
EMP: 47
SQ FT: 48,000
SALES (est): 16.7MM
SALES (corp-wide): 40.2MM **Privately Held**
WEB: www.scotia-tech.com
SIC: 3728 Mfg Aircraft Parts/Equipment
PA: United Flexible, Inc.
815 Forestwood Dr
Romeoville IL 60446
815 886-1140

(G-18574)
LEWIS AND SAUNDERS
144 Lexington Dr (03246-3077)
PHONE..................................603 528-1871
Graham Thomas, *Principal*
EMP: 3 **EST:** 2010
SALES (est): 370.9K **Privately Held**
SIC: 3812 Mfg Search/Navigation Equipment

(G-18575)
METZ COMMUNICATION CORPORATION
151c Elm St (03246-2367)
PHONE..................................603 528-2590
▲ **EMP:** 3
SQ FT: 10,000
SALES (est): 343.2K **Privately Held**
WEB: www.metzcommunication.com
SIC: 3663 Antennas For Marine Ham Commercial Use

(G-18576)
MILLS INDUSTRIES INC
167 Water St (03246-3351)
P.O. Box 1459 (03247-1459)
PHONE..................................603 528-4217
Michael Mills, *President*
EMP: 12 **EST:** 1972
SQ FT: 30,000
SALES: 2MM **Privately Held**
WEB: www.millsind.com
SIC: 3089 2653 Mfg Plastic & Corrugated Boxes

(G-18577)
NEW HMPSHIRE BALL BEARINGS INC
Astro Division
155 Lexington Dr (03246-2937)
PHONE..................................603 524-0004
Tracy Cathcart, *General Mgr*
Chris Rawnsley, *Vice Pres*
Susan Cote, *Buyer*
Jon Osier, *Engineer*
Kevin Quinn, *Engineer*
EMP: 500 **Privately Held**
WEB: www.nhbb.com
SIC: 3562 3366 3312 Mfg Ball/Roller Bearings Copper Foundry Blast Furnace-Steel Works
HQ: New Hampshire Ball Bearings, Inc.
175 Jaffrey Rd
Peterborough NH 03458
603 924-3311

(G-18578)
ON THE BALL CUTNHAUL
N Main St (03246)
PHONE..................................603 851-3283
Michael Vertone,
EMP: 3
SALES (est): 115.3K **Privately Held**
SIC: 2411 Logging

(G-18579)
ORION ENTRANCE CONTROL INC
76a Lexington Dr (03246-2934)
PHONE..................................603 527-4187
Steven Caroselli, *President*
Jerry Waldron, *Opers Mgr*
Chuck Waldron, *Purchasing*
Nancy Chase, *Marketing Mgr*
EMP: 43
SALES (est): 1.3MM **Privately Held**
SIC: 3699 Security Systems Services

(G-18580)
OUTDOOR ENHANCEMENTS LLC
Also Called: Eased Edges
343 Court St (03246-3651)
PHONE..................................603 524-8090
Brian Flanders, *Mng Member*
EMP: 3
SQ FT: 400
SALES (est): 54K **Privately Held**
WEB: www.outdoorenhancements.com
SIC: 2421 Sawmill/Planing Mill

(G-18581)
R & J TOOL INC (PA)
945 Scenic Rd (03246-1807)
P.O. Box 712 (03247-0712)
PHONE..................................603 366-4925
Robert Laflamme, *President*
EMP: 9
SALES (est): 1.3MM **Privately Held**
SIC: 3545 8742 Mfg Machine Tool Accessories Management Consulting Services

(G-18582)
R & K MACHINE
53 Blaisdell Ave (03246-4405)
PHONE..................................603 528-0221
Melissa A Hil, *Owner*
EMP: 6
SALES (est): 756.1K **Privately Held**
SIC: 3599 Mfg Industrial Machinery

(G-18583)
RIPLEY ODM LLC
143 Lake St Ste 1e (03246-2129)
PHONE..................................603 524-8350
Michael Schneider, *Principal*
Walter Shepherd, *Finance Dir*
EMP: 5
SQ FT: 3,000
SALES (est): 971.6K
SALES (corp-wide): 4.9MM **Privately Held**
WEB: www.odm-inc.com
SIC: 3661 Mfg Telephone/Telegraph Apparatus
PA: Ripley Tools, Llc
46 Nooks Hill Rd
Cromwell CT 06416
860 635-2200

(G-18584)
RUSSELL PRECISION
252 Hillcrest Dr (03246-1929)
PHONE..................................603 524-3772
EMP: 5
SALES (est): 360K **Privately Held**
SIC: 3545 Mfg Machine Tool Accessories

(G-18585)
SCREW-MATIC CORPORATION
10 Primrose Dr S (03246-2940)
PHONE..................................603 293-8850
Mark J Mc Carthy, *Branch Mgr*
EMP: 10
SALES (corp-wide): 8.8MM **Privately Held**
SIC: 3728 Mfg Aircraft Parts/Equipment
PA: Screw-Matic Corporation
1 Chase Park Rd
Seabrook NH 03874
978 356-6200

(G-18586)
SMALL BITES CUPCAKES
135 Franklin St (03246-2325)
PHONE..................................603 387-6333
EMP: 4
SALES (est): 180.8K **Privately Held**
SIC: 2051 Bread, Cake, And Related Products

(G-18587)
SMITHS TBLAR SYSTMS-LCONIA INC
Also Called: Titeflex Aerospace
93 Lexington Dr (03246-2935)
PHONE..................................603 524-2064
William T Smith, *President*
Randall Ferland, *Vice Pres*
Patrick D McCaffrey, *Vice Pres*

Robert M Speer, *Vice Pres*
Roxanne Laughy, *Mfg Spvr*
▲ **EMP:** 300 **EST:** 1913
SQ FT: 84,000
SALES (est): 109.1MM
SALES (corp-wide): 3.1B **Privately Held**
WEB: www.lewisandsaunders.com
SIC: 3463 3498 8734 7692 Mfg Nonferrous Forgings Mfg Fabrctd Pipe/Fitting Testing Laboratory Welding Repair Structural Metal Fabrctn
PA: Smiths Group Plc
4th Floor
London SW1Y
207 004-1600

(G-18588)
STAMPING TECHNOLOGIES INC
20 Growth Rd (03246-1318)
PHONE..................................603 524-5958
Mark St Gelais, *President*
Johanna St Gelais, *Vice Pres*
EMP: 16
SQ FT: 8,000
SALES (est): 1.6MM **Privately Held**
WEB: www.stampingtec.com
SIC: 3469 3312 3544 Mfg Metal Stampings Blast Furnace-Steel Work Mfg Dies/Tools/Jigs/Fixt

(G-18589)
TITEFLEX CORPORATION
93 Lexington Dr (03246-2935)
PHONE..................................603 524-2064
William Schaffer, *Purchasing*
Mark Rennie, *Research*
Tyler McGrath, *Engineer*
Carlene Marcotte, *Sales Mgr*
Bob Burns, *Branch Mgr*
EMP: 14
SALES (corp-wide): 3.1B **Privately Held**
SIC: 3724 Mfg Aircraft Engines/Parts
HQ: Titeflex Corporation
603 Hendee St
Springfield MA 01104
413 739-5631

(G-18590)
TYLERGRAPHICS INC
14 Lexington Dr Ste 2 (03246-3946)
PHONE..................................603 524-6625
Wade Heberling, *President*
EMP: 8
SALES (est): 1MM **Privately Held**
WEB: www.tylergraphics.com
SIC: 2759 Lithographic Commercial Printing

(G-18591)
VANTASTIC INC
Also Called: Body Covers
94 Primrose Dr N (03246-3074)
PHONE..................................603 524-1419
Sarah Gray, *President*
Aaron Gray, *Vice Pres*
EMP: 5
SALES (est): 680.4K **Privately Held**
WEB: www.body-covers.com
SIC: 2396 2759 Screen Printers

(G-18592)
VILLAGE WEST PUBLISHING INC
Also Called: Hearth Warming
Village W Cntry Clb 403 (03246)
P.O. Box 1288 (03247-1288)
PHONE..................................603 528-4285
Richard Wright, *President*
Susan Salls, *Treasurer*
EMP: 13
SQ FT: 3,900
SALES: 2.2MM **Privately Held**
WEB: www.hearthandhome.com
SIC: 2721 Magazine Publishers

(G-18593)
WEIRS PUBLISHING COMPANY INC
Also Called: Weirs Times
515 Endicott St N (03246-1725)
P.O. Box 5458 (03247-5458)
PHONE..................................888 308-8463
David Lawton, *President*
Sandra Lawton, *Treasurer*
Donna Lawton, *Accounts Exec*
Debra Bennett, *Sales Staff*
EMP: 10
SALES (est): 998.1K **Privately Held**
WEB: www.weirs.com
SIC: 2711 Newspapers-Publishing/Printing

(G-18594)
WERNER PRECISION MACHINE CORP
60 Bay St Ste 1 (03246-3309)
PHONE..................................603 524-0570
Dianne Knauss, *President*
Werner Knauss, *Vice Pres*
EMP: 6
SQ FT: 5,000
SALES (est): 480K **Privately Held**
SIC: 3599 Machine Shop Jobbing & Repair

(G-18595)
WINNISQUAM PRINTING INC
Also Called: Winnisquam Printing & Copying
71 Beacon St W A (03246-3460)
PHONE..................................603 524-2803
Rich Higginbotham, *President*
EMP: 5
SALES (est): 666.9K **Privately Held**
SIC: 2752 Lithographic Commercial Printing

Lancaster
Coos County

(G-18596)
A B EXCAVATING INC
653 Main St (03584-3612)
PHONE..................................603 788-5110
Allen Bouthillier, *President*
Kyle Bouthillier, *Admin Sec*
EMP: 20
SALES: 7MM **Privately Held**
SIC: 2411 1611 1623 1629 Logging Highway/Street Cnstn Water/Sewer/Utility Cnst Heavy Construction

(G-18597)
BURT GENERAL REPAIR & WELDING
Also Called: Burt's Repair
330 Portland St (03584-3318)
PHONE..................................603 788-4821
Burt Gilbert, *Owner*
EMP: 3
SALES (est): 209.4K **Privately Held**
SIC: 7692 Welding Repair

(G-18598)
CABOT HILL NATURALS INC
Also Called: Dent Herb Company
62 Bridge St (03584-3102)
PHONE..................................800 747-4372
David C Hill, *President*
Tyler Rancourt, *Vice Pres*
Gregg Karlins, *Sales Staff*
EMP: 11
SALES (est): 1.6MM **Privately Held**
SIC: 2844 Mfg Toilet Preparations

(G-18599)
COHOS COUNTERS LLC
272 Main St (03584-3039)
PHONE..................................603 788-4928
Donald L Crane, *Mng Member*
Donald Crane, *Mng Member*
Kendra Bell,
EMP: 3
SALES (est): 189.8K **Privately Held**
SIC: 3131 Mfg Footwear Cut Stock

(G-18600)
ED SANDERS
Also Called: Edsanders.com
36 Bunker Hill St (03584-3009)
PHONE..................................603 788-3626
Ed Sanders, *Owner*
EMP: 3
SALES: 160K **Privately Held**
WEB: www.edsanders.com
SIC: 2992 Mfg Lubricating Oils/Greases

(G-18601)
LOG CABIN BLDG CO & SAWMILL
3 Walker Dr (03584-3270)
P.O. Box 72 (03584-0072)
PHONE..................................603 788-3036
EMP: 3
SALES (est): 310K **Privately Held**
SIC: 2452 Mfg Prefabricated Wood Buildings

(G-18602)
MOUNT WASHINGTON VLY MTN EAR
79 Main St (03584-3027)
PHONE..................................603 447-6336
Ryan Corneau, *General Mgr*
EMP: 9
SQ FT: 2,000
SALES (est): 470K **Privately Held**
WEB: www.salmonpress.com
SIC: 2711 Newspapers Publishing Only Not Printed On Site

(G-18603)
PAK 2000 INC
16 Page Hill Rd (03584-3618)
PHONE..................................603 569-3700
Bob Coggelshall, *Manager*
Laura Morse, *Supervisor*
EMP: 55
SALES (corp-wide): 42.8MM **Privately Held**
WEB: www.pak2000.com
SIC: 2674 2673 2671 Mfg Bags-Uncoated Paper Mfg Bags-Plastic/Coated Paper Mfg Packaging Paper/Film
PA: Pak 2000, Inc.
189 Govenor Wentworth Hwy
Mirror Lake NH 03853
603 569-3700

(G-18604)
PERRAS PALLET LLC
44 Perras Rd (03584-4218)
PHONE..................................603 631-1169
Robert Perras,
EMP: 4
SALES (est): 210K **Privately Held**
SIC: 2448 Mfg Wood Pallets/Skids

(G-18605)
SOUTHWORTH TIMBER FRAMES INC
273 Garland Rd (03584-3409)
PHONE..................................603 788-2619
Benjamin Southworth, *President*
Dana Southworth, *Treasurer*
EMP: 6
SALES: 1MM **Privately Held**
SIC: 2439 2452 Mfg Structural Wood Members Mfg Prefabricated Wood Buildings

(G-18606)
TRIVIDIA MFG SOLUTIONS (DH)
Also Called: P.J. Noyes
89 Bridge St (03584-3103)
PHONE..................................603 788-2848
Scott Verner, *President*
Chrystal Chase, *Principal*
Tracey Morrill, *Principal*
Steve Skinner, *Principal*
Dennis Wogaman, *COO*
▲ **EMP:** 103 **EST:** 1868
SQ FT: 35,000
SALES (est): 18.5MM
SALES (corp-wide): 223.3MM **Privately Held**
WEB: www.pjnoyes.com
SIC: 2834 2844 2048 Mfg Pharmaceutical Preparations Mfg Toilet Preparations Mfg Prepared Feeds
HQ: Trividia Health, Inc.
2400 Nw 55th Ct
Fort Lauderdale FL 33309
954 677-8201

(G-18607)
TRIVIDIA MFG SOLUTIONS
248 Main St (03584-3038)
PHONE..................................603 788-4952
Dennis Wogaman, *COO*
EMP: 6
SALES (corp-wide): 223.3MM **Privately Held**
SIC: 2834 2844 2048 Mfg Pharmaceutical Preparations Mfg Toilet Preparations Mfg Prepared Feeds
HQ: Trividia Manufacturing Solutions, Inc
89 Bridge St
Lancaster NH 03584
603 788-2848

(G-18608)
ULTRAMAR INC
Also Called: Johnson Ultramar Fuel Service
440 Glen Ave (03584)
P.O. Box 447, Berlin (03570-0447)
PHONE..................................603 788-2771
Larry Tatlin, *Manager*
EMP: 12
SALES (corp-wide): 117B **Publicly Held**
WEB: www.divi.com
SIC: 2911 Petroleum Refiner
HQ: Ultramar Inc.
1 Valero Way
San Antonio TX 78249
210 345-2000

Landaff
Grafton County

(G-18609)
STOCKLEY TRUCKING INC
Also Called: Stockley Storage
405 S Main St (03585-5221)
PHONE..................................603 838-2860
Clayton Stockley, *President*
Michael Stockley, *Vice Pres*
Linda Stockley, *Admin Sec*
EMP: 9
SALES (est): 1MM **Privately Held**
SIC: 2411 Logging

Langdon
Cheshire County

(G-18610)
ATLANTIC SPORTS INTERNATIONAL
157 Village Rd (03602-8240)
P.O. Box 490, Alstead (03602-0490)
PHONE..................................603 835-6948
Kurt Meyerrose, *President*
Laurie K Meyerrose, *Vice Pres*
EMP: 4
SALES: 230K **Privately Held**
WEB: www.atlanticsportsintl.com
SIC: 3544 3949 Manufacture Custom Molding & Dies & Snow Skiing & Scuba Diving Equipment

(G-18611)
NOISE REDUCTION PRODUCTS INC
97 Lower Cemetery Rd (03602-8702)
P.O. Box 58, Alstead (03602-0058)
PHONE..................................603 835-6400
Thomas Esslinger, *President*
Jane Esslinger, *Treasurer*
EMP: 6
SALES: 750K **Privately Held**
WEB: www.noisereductionproducts.com
SIC: 3444 Mfg Sheet Metal Machine Guards

Lebanon
Grafton County

(G-18612)
ANSYS INC
10 Cavendish Ct (03766-1441)
PHONE..................................603 653-8005
John Widmann, *Research*
Brian Bell, *Engineer*
Erik Ferguson, *Engineer*
Erling Eklund, *Sls & Mktg Exec*
Kristen Secaur, *Controller*
EMP: 6

GEOGRAPHIC

SALES (corp-wide): 1.2B **Publicly Held**
WEB: www.ansys.com
SIC: 7372 Prepackaged Software Services
PA: Ansys, Inc.
2600 Ansys Dr
Canonsburg PA 15317
884 462-6797

(G-18613)
AVITIDE INC
16 Cavendish Ct Ste 151 (03766-1441)
PHONE..................................603 965-2100
Kevin Isett, *CEO*
Sarah McDonald, *Opers Mgr*
Grant Espie, *Mfg Staff*
Scott Kennedy, *CFO*
Warren Kett, *Security Dir*
EMP: 34
SALES: 1.5MM **Privately Held**
SIC: 2836 Mfg Biological Products

(G-18614)
BARRE TILE INC
187 Mechanic St (03766-1509)
PHONE..................................802 476-0912
Bill Clark, *Manager*
EMP: 10
SALES (corp-wide): 3.2MM **Privately Held**
WEB: www.barretile.com
SIC: 3281 5084 5211 Mfg Cut Stone/Products Whol Industrial Equip Ret Lumber/Building Mtrl
PA: Barre Tile, Inc.
889 S Barre Rd
South Barre VT 05670
802 476-0912

(G-18615)
BIMBO BAKERIES USA INC
Freihofer's Bakery Outlet
91 Mechanic St (03766-1519)
PHONE..................................603 448-4227
Heidi Gray, *Branch Mgr*
EMP: 18 **Privately Held**
SIC: 2051 Mfg Bread/Related Products
HQ: Bimbo Bakeries Usa, Inc
255 Business Center Dr # 200
Horsham PA 19044
215 347-5500

(G-18616)
BOND OPTICS LLC
76 Etna Rd (03766-1403)
P.O. Box 422 (03766-0422)
PHONE..................................603 448-2300
Jen Churchill, *Human Resources*
Arn Warren, *CTO*
Leonard A Guaraldi Jr,
EMP: 50
SQ FT: 50,000
SALES (est): 11.5MM **Privately Held**
WEB: www.bondoptics.com
SIC: 3827 Mfg Optical Instruments/Lenses

(G-18617)
C-R CONTROL SYSTEMS INC
85 Mechanic St Unit B2 (03766-1533)
PHONE..................................603 727-9149
Robert Seidler Jr, *President*
◆ **EMP:** 5 **EST:** 1962
SQ FT: 2,600
SALES (est): 590K **Privately Held**
WEB: www.crconsys.com
SIC: 3812 3625 Mfg Navigational Systems & Instruments

(G-18618)
CENTRIC SOFTWARE INC
115 Etna Rd Fl 2 (03766-1429)
PHONE..................................603 448-3009
Paul Landry, *Branch Mgr*
EMP: 6
SALES (corp-wide): 20.7MM **Privately Held**
WEB: www.centricsoftware.com
SIC: 7372 8742 Prepackaged Software Services Management Consulting Services
PA: Centric Software, Inc.
655 Campbell Technology P
Campbell CA 95008
408 574-7802

(G-18619)
CONNECTCUT RVER VLY YLLOW PGES
103 Hanover St Ste 9 (03766-1098)
PHONE..................................603 727-4700
Shawn Mason, *Owner*
EMP: 7
SALES (est): 501.2K **Privately Held**
SIC: 2741 Misc Publishing

(G-18620)
CREATIVE LTG DESIGNS DECOR LLC
227 Mechanic St Ste 2 (03766-1518)
PHONE..................................603 448-2066
Brian Horan, *Mng Member*
Lois Horan,
EMP: 3 **EST:** 2008
SQ FT: 4,000
SALES (est): 460.1K **Privately Held**
SIC: 3645 Mfg Residential Lighting Fixtures

(G-18621)
ELEMENT HANOVER - LEBANON
25 Foothill St (03766-1416)
PHONE..................................603 646-8108
EMP: 8
SALES (est): 1MM **Privately Held**
SIC: 2819 Industrial Inorganic Chemicals, Nec

(G-18622)
FRONTIER DESIGN GROUP LLC
31 Old Etna Rd Ste N5 (03766-1933)
PHONE..................................603 448-6283
Lauren Breindel, *Director*
Noah Sheinbaum, *Director*
Charles Hitchcock, *Executive*
Barry Braksick,
EMP: 8
SQ FT: 1,500
SALES (est): 650K **Privately Held**
SIC: 3679 Mfg Electronic Components

(G-18623)
FUJIFILM DIMATIX INC
109 Etna Rd (03766-1467)
PHONE..................................603 443-5300
John Batterton, *President*
Richard Leggett, *Senior Buyer*
Pete Clark, *Buyer*
Jeffery Hines, *Purchasing*
Fred Amidon, *Engineer*
EMP: 186 **Privately Held**
SIC: 3577 Mfg Computer Peripheral Equipment
HQ: Fujifilm Dimatix, Inc.
2250 Martin Ave
Santa Clara CA 95050
408 565-9150

(G-18624)
GEOKON LLC
48 Spencer St (03766-1363)
PHONE..................................603 448-1562
Ed Rice, *Purch Agent*
Colin Judd, *Engineer*
Jessica Dworak, *Credit Staff*
John Flynn, *Sales Engr*
Matt Sullivan, *Sales Engr*
◆ **EMP:** 100
SQ FT: 25,000
SALES: 30.8MM **Privately Held**
WEB: www.geokon.com
SIC: 3829 Mfg Measuring/Controlling Devices

(G-18625)
IMAGENE TECHNOLOGY INC
85 Mechanic St (03766-1537)
P.O. Box 667, Hanover (03755-0667)
PHONE..................................603 448-9940
Timothy Chow, *Exec Dir*
EMP: 18
SQ FT: 2,000
SALES: 2MM **Privately Held**
WEB: www.imagenetechnology.com
SIC: 3841 Mfg Surgical/Medical Instruments

(G-18626)
JUST REWARDS INC
Also Called: American Speedy Printing
443 Miracle Mile Ste 3 (03766-2672)
PHONE..................................603 448-6800
Glenn E Fuller, *President*
Beverly Fuller, *Vice Pres*
EMP: 4
SQ FT: 2,500
SALES (est): 387.5K **Privately Held**
SIC: 2752 Offset Printing

(G-18627)
LIFELINE SYSTEMS COMPANY
1 Medical Center Dr (03756-1000)
PHONE..................................603 653-1610
Karen Coffey, *Principal*
EMP: 3
SALES (corp-wide): 20.1B **Privately Held**
SIC: 3669 Services-Misc
HQ: Lifeline Systems Company
111 Lawrence St
Framingham MA 01702
508 988-1000

(G-18628)
LODESTONE BIOMEDICAL LLC
16 Cavendish Ct (03766-1441)
PHONE..................................617 686-5517
Solomon Diamond,
Bradley Ficko,
Lidia Valdes,
EMP: 3 **EST:** 2015
SALES (est): 245K **Privately Held**
SIC: 3841 Mfg Surgical/Medical Instruments

(G-18629)
LUMINESCENT SYSTEMS INC
4 Lucent Dr (03766-1439)
PHONE..................................603 643-7766
Peter J Gundermann, *President*
Edward Wozniak, *President*
Ron Girouard, *Director*
EMP: 125
SALES (corp-wide): 803.2MM **Publicly Held**
SIC: 3648 3641 Mfg Lighting Equipment Mfg Electric Lamps
HQ: Luminescent Systems, Inc.
130 Commerce Way
East Aurora NY 14052
716 655-0800

(G-18630)
MPB CORPORATION
336 Mechanic St (03766-2614)
PHONE..................................603 448-3000
Rober Baulman, *General Mgr*
EMP: 400
SALES (corp-wide): 3.5B **Publicly Held**
SIC: 3562 3568 Mfg Ball/Roller Bearings Mfg Power Transmission Equipment
HQ: Mpb Corporation
7 Optical Ave
Keene NH 03431
603 352-0310

(G-18631)
MPB CORPORATION
334 Mechanic St (03766)
PHONE..................................603 448-3000
EMP: 4
SALES (corp-wide): 3.5B **Publicly Held**
SIC: 3562 Mfg Ball/Roller Bearings
HQ: Mpb Corporation
7 Optical Ave
Keene NH 03431
603 352-0310

(G-18632)
MYTURNCOM PBC
Also Called: 2111 Hearst Ave
16 Cavendish Ct (03766-1441)
PHONE..................................206 552-8488
Gene Homicki, *CEO*
J Patrick Dunn, *Treasurer*
Nancy Deschenes, *Admin Sec*
EMP: 5 **EST:** 2013
SALES (est): 294.8K **Privately Held**
SIC: 7372 7371 Prepackaged Software

(G-18633)
NEW ENGLAND INDUSTRIES INC
Also Called: Nei Stamping
85 Etna Rd (03766-1466)
PHONE..................................603 448-5330
Michael B Landgraf, *Principal*
EMP: 42 **EST:** 1952
SQ FT: 51,000
SALES (est): 13.7MM **Privately Held**
WEB: www.neistamping.com
SIC: 3469 3544 Mfg Metal Stampings Mfg Dies/Tools/Jigs/Fixtures

(G-18634)
NJM PACKAGING LLC (HQ)
77 Bank St (03766-1771)
PHONE..................................603 448-0300
Michael Lapierre, *President*
James Moretti, *CFO*
Claude Desforges, *Sales Mgr*
Marla Labreche-Stallm, *Marketing Mgr*
Charles Lapierre, *Director*
EMP: 10
SQ FT: 170,000
SALES (est): 2.4MM
SALES (corp-wide): 587.9MM **Privately Held**
WEB: www.njmcli.com
SIC: 3565 Mfg Packaging Machinery
PA: Pro Mach, Inc.
50 E Rivercntr Blvd 180
Covington KY 41011
513 831-8778

(G-18635)
SIGNALQUEST LLC
10 Water St Ste 425 (03766-4200)
PHONE..................................603 448-6266
Whitmore B Kelley Jr, *CEO*
David Capotosto, *Opers Mgr*
John Miramonti, *Engineer*
Elizabeth Ewaschuk, *Finance*
Jason Topolewski, *Technician*
EMP: 20
SALES (est): 4.5MM **Privately Held**
WEB: www.signalquest.com
SIC: 3674 Mfg Semiconductors/Related Devices

(G-18636)
SIMBEX LLC
10 Water St Ste 410 (03766-1604)
PHONE..................................603 448-2367
Richard Bolander, *Engineer*
David Johnson, *Engineer*
Kathy Karr, *Human Res Mgr*
Spencer Brugger, *Technical Staff*
Aaron Jordan, *IT/INT Sup*
EMP: 26
SQ FT: 60,000
SALES (est): 3.9MM **Privately Held**
WEB: www.simbex.com
SIC: 3949 8711 8731 Mfg Sporting/Athletic Goods Engineering Services Commercial Physical Research

(G-18637)
STEALTH BIOLOGICS LLC
16 Cavendish Ct Rm 229 (03766-1441)
PHONE..................................603 643-5134
Karl E Griswold,
EMP: 3
SALES (est): 200.4K
SALES (corp-wide): 119.6K **Privately Held**
SIC: 2834 Mfg Pharmaceutical Preparations
PA: Occulo Holdings Llc
16 Cavendish Ct Rm 229
Lebanon NH 03766
802 359-7597

(G-18638)
TIMKEN COMPANY
Also Called: Lebanon Prcision Bearing Plant
336 Mechanic St (03766-2614)
P.O. Box 306, Alstead (03602-0306)
PHONE..................................603 443-5281
Tony King, *Buyer*
Jennifer Gross, *Controller*
Mark Stangl, *Sales Mgr*
John Carr, *Manager*
David Cadwell, *Manager*
EMP: 650

SALES (corp-wide): 3.5B Publicly Held
WEB: www.timken.com
SIC: 3562 Mfg Ball/Roller Bearings
PA: The Timken Company
4500 Mount Pleasant St Nw
North Canton OH 44720
234 262-3000

(G-18639)
TOP STITCH EMBROIDERY INC
233 Mascoma St (03766-2656)
PHONE 603 448-2931
Tracy Pelletier, *President*
EMP: 3
SALES (est): 276K Privately Held
SIC: 2395 Pleating/Stitching Services

(G-18640)
VALLEY SIGNS
Also Called: Compu Signs
22 Fairview Ave (03766-1265)
PHONE 603 252-1977
David Cook, *President*
Patricia J Cook, *Treasurer*
EMP: 6
SQ FT: 5,000
SALES: 400K Privately Held
SIC: 3993 1799 7374 Mfg Installs & Services Signs & Computer Graphic

(G-18641)
WHITMAN COMMUNICATIONS INC
10 Water St (03766-1630)
P.O. Box 1156 (03766-4156)
PHONE 603 448-2600
Stephen Whitman, *Chairman*
Carolyn Whitman, *Shareholder*
EMP: 24
SQ FT: 15,000
SALES: 2.5MM Privately Held
SIC: 2752 2791 Photo-Offset Printing Srvcs Typesetting Srvcs

Lee
Strafford County

(G-18642)
AMERICAN BUSINESS SERVICE
45 Harvey Mill Rd (03861-6302)
P.O. Box 732, Epping (03042-0732)
PHONE 603 659-2912
Anita Lowther, *President*
EMP: 5
SALES: 300K Privately Held
SIC: 3575 Manfactures Computers

(G-18643)
FLAG HILL DISTILLERY LLC
297 N River Rd (03861-6213)
PHONE 603 659-2949
Frank Walter Reinhold Jr, *Principal*
EMP: 4 EST: 2012
SALES (est): 344.8K Privately Held
SIC: 2084 Mfg Wines/Brandy/Spirits

(G-18644)
FLAG HILL WINERY & VINYRD LLC
297 N River Rd (03861-6213)
PHONE 603 659-2949
Frank Reinhold Jr, *President*
Linda Reinhold, *Vice Pres*
Christa C Phaneuf, *Manager*
EMP: 9
SALES (est): 560.6K Privately Held
SIC: 2084 Mfg Wines/Brandy/Spirits

Lincoln
Grafton County

(G-18645)
BURNDY LLC
Connector Road Route 3 (03251)
PHONE 603 745-8114
Dan Owens, *Production*
Jerry Heckman, *Director*
EMP: 180
SALES (corp-wide): 4.4B Publicly Held
WEB: www.fciconnect.com
SIC: 3643 Mfg Conductive Wiring Devices
HQ: Burndy Llc
47 E Industrial Park Dr
Manchester NH 03109

(G-18646)
BURNDY LLC
34 Bern Dibner Dr (03251-4202)
PHONE 603 745-8114
EMP: 7
SALES (corp-wide): 4.4B Publicly Held
SIC: 3643 Mfg Conductive Wiring Devices
HQ: Burndy Llc
47 E Industrial Park Dr
Manchester NH 03109

(G-18647)
QUIK LOC INC
Also Called: Quick-Loc
21 Arthur Salem Way (03251)
P.O. Box 665 (03251-0665)
PHONE 603 745-7008
Kevin Sullivan, *President*
Louise Sullivan, *Clerk*
EMP: 4
SALES (est): 759.7K Privately Held
WEB: www.quikloc.com
SIC: 3568 Mfg Power Transmission Equipment

Lisbon
Grafton County

(G-18648)
DCI INC (PA)
265 S Main St (03585-6217)
PHONE 603 838-6544
Henry A Kober, *President*
C Amos Kober, *Vice Pres*
Elizabeth Kober, *Vice Pres*
Jacob David Kober, *Vice Pres*
Jeff Mc Kelvey, *Plant Mgr*
◆ EMP: 100 EST: 1975
SQ FT: 50,000
SALES (est): 76.6MM Privately Held
SIC: 2531 5023 Mfg Public Building Furn Whol Homefurnishings

(G-18649)
MJM HOLDINGS INC (PA)
130 N Main St (03585-6603)
P.O. Box 264 (03585-0264)
PHONE 603 838-6624
Wendell W Jesseman, *President*
Richard C Johns, *Vice Pres*
Robert F Meserve, *Vice Pres*
Bette Liveston, *Human Res Dir*
Jim Trudell, *Manager*
EMP: 5 EST: 1871
SQ FT: 335,000
SALES: 75MM Privately Held
SIC: 3357 Nonferrous Wiredrawing & Insulating Work

(G-18650)
NEW ENGLAND WIRE TECH CORP (HQ)
130 N Main St (03585-6603)
P.O. Box 264 (03585-0264)
PHONE 603 838-6624
Richard Johns, *President*
Wendell W Jesseman, *Chairman*
Bob Meserve, *Vice Pres*
Robert Meserve, *Vice Pres*
Sean Bliss, *Production*
▲ EMP: 348 EST: 1898
SQ FT: 335,000
SALES: 63MM
SALES (corp-wide): 75MM Privately Held
WEB: www.newenglandwire.com
SIC: 3357 Nonferrous Wiredrawing/Insulating
PA: Mjm Holdings, Inc.
130 N Main St
Lisbon NH 03585
603 838-6624

Litchfield
Hillsborough County

(G-18651)
BURLODGE USA INC
24 Pearson St (03052-1094)
PHONE 336 776-1010
Neil Kirven, *President*
▲ EMP: 13
SQ FT: 15,000
SALES (est): 2.7MM
SALES (corp-wide): 2.6MM Privately Held
WEB: www.burlodgeusa.com
SIC: 3556 Mfg Food Products Machinery
HQ: Ali Group North America Corporation
101 Corporate Woods Pkwy
Vernon Hills IL 60061
847 215-6565

(G-18652)
NEW ENGLAND SMALL TUBE CORP
Also Called: Nest
480 Charles Bancroft Hwy # 3 (03052-1090)
PHONE 603 429-1600
Patrick M Algeo, *President*
Jack Algeo, *President*
Alan Law, *Opers Staff*
Lori Nelson, *Design Engr*
Colleen Ellif, *CFO*
EMP: 70
SQ FT: 20,000
SALES (est): 15.7MM Privately Held
WEB: www.nesmalltube.com
SIC: 3498 5051 3841 Mfg Fabricated Pipe/Fittings Metals Service Center Mfg Surgical/Medical Instruments

Littleton
Grafton County

(G-18653)
27TH EXPOSURE LLC
Also Called: Foto Factory
53 Main St (03561-4017)
P.O. Box 519 (03561-0519)
PHONE 603 444-5800
Art Tighe, *Opers Staff*
EMP: 5
SALES (est): 717.4K Privately Held
SIC: 3861 5946 7384 Mfg Photographic Equipment/Supplies Ret Cameras/Photography Supplies Photofinishing Laboratory

(G-18654)
APPALACHIAN STITCHING CO LLC (PA)
90 Badger St (03561-4111)
PHONE 603 444-4422
Scott Manning,
Douglas Elkins,
Pamela Manning,
▲ EMP: 35 EST: 2002
SQ FT: 20,000
SALES (est): 6.5MM Privately Held
WEB: www.appalachianstitching.com
SIC: 3172 Mfg Personal Leather Goods

(G-18655)
BURNDY LLC
150 Burndy Rd (03561-3957)
PHONE 603 444-6781
Larry Blaisdell, *Maint Spvr*
Parker Martel, *Engineer*
Robert Thibolt, *Branch Mgr*
Fred Chisolm, *Executive*
EMP: 200
SALES (corp-wide): 4.4B Publicly Held
WEB: www.fciconnect.com
SIC: 3678 3643 3546 Mfg Electronic Connectors Mfg Conductive Wiring Devices Mfg Power-Driven Handtools
HQ: Burndy Llc
47 E Industrial Park Dr
Manchester NH 03109

(G-18656)
CALEDONIAN RECORD PUBG CO INC
263 Main St (03561-4021)
PHONE 603 444-7141
Todd Smith, *Manager*
EMP: 8
SALES (corp-wide): 8.7MM Privately Held
WEB: www.caledonian-record.com
SIC: 2711 Newspapers-Publishing/Printing
PA: Caledonian Record Publishing Company, Inc.
190 Federal St
Saint Johnsbury VT 05819
802 748-8121

(G-18657)
DEPOT MILLWORKS
54 Cottage St (03561-5716)
PHONE 603 444-1656
Stephen Maciver, *Owner*
EMP: 3
SALES: 100K Privately Held
SIC: 2431 Mfg Millwork

(G-18658)
EMBRODERY BY EVRYTHING PER LLC
42 Cottage St (03561-5731)
PHONE 603 444-0130
Pat Beck,
Andrew Beck,
EMP: 5
SALES (est): 200K Privately Held
SIC: 2395 2759 Pleating/Stitching Services Commercial Printing

(G-18659)
FCI ELECTRICAL-BRUNDY PRODUCTS
150 Burndy Rd (03561-3957)
PHONE 603 444-6781
Betsy Babcock, *Principal*
EMP: 3 EST: 2010
SALES (est): 193K Privately Held
SIC: 3643 Mfg Conductive Wiring Devices

(G-18660)
GENFOOT AMERICA INC
673 Industrial Park Rd (03561-3953)
PHONE 603 575-5114
Frank Disensi, *Branch Mgr*
EMP: 100
SALES (corp-wide): 1.3MM Privately Held
SIC: 3089 3021 Mfg Plastic Products Mfg Rubber/Plstc Ftwear
HQ: Genfoot America, Inc
1940 55e Av
Lachine QC
514 341-3950

(G-18661)
HARRISON PUBLISHING HOUSE INC
Also Called: Bradford Price Book
995 Industrial Park Rd (03561-3956)
P.O. Box 320 (03561-0320)
PHONE 603 444-0820
David F McPhaul, *President*
Willard Martin, *Admin Sec*
EMP: 25 EST: 1912
SQ FT: 14,000
SALES (est): 3.2MM Privately Held
WEB: www.hphguide.com
SIC: 2721 2752 Periodicals-Publishing/Printing Lithographic Commercial Printing

(G-18662)
LITTLETON MILLWORK INC
44 Lafayette Ave (03561-5707)
PHONE 603 444-2677
Mitchell Greaves, *President*
EMP: 20 EST: 1967
SQ FT: 14,000
SALES (est): 2.9MM Privately Held
SIC: 2431 Mfg Millwork

(G-18663)
MOUNTAIN FIREWOOD KILN
1536 Broomstick Hill Rd (03561-5231)
PHONE 603 444-6954
Bill Latulip, *Owner*

GEOGRAPHIC

EMP: 3
SALES (est): 274.6K **Privately Held**
SIC: 3559 Mfg Misc Industry Machinery

(G-18664)
RONNIE MARVIN ENTERPRISES
33 Hillview Ter (03561-4807)
PHONE..................................603 444-5017
Rodney Marvin, *Partner*
Judith Marvin, *Partner*
EMP: 3
SALES (est): 328.8K **Privately Held**
SIC: 2542 4225 Mfg Partitions/Fixtures-Nonwood General Warehouse/Storage

(G-18665)
SABBOW AND CO INC
Wtc Granite Industries
390 Highland Ave (03561-4232)
PHONE..................................603 444-6724
Rick Hinck, *Branch Mgr*
EMP: 14
SALES (corp-wide): 25.6MM **Privately Held**
SIC: 3272 Mfg Concrete Products
PA: Sabbow And Co., Inc.
77 Regional Dr
Concord NH 03301
603 225-5169

(G-18666)
SHERWIN DODGE PRINTERS INC
365 Union St (03561-5619)
P.O. Box 481 (03561-0481)
PHONE..................................603 444-6552
Douglas Garfield, *President*
Kevin Emerson, *Graphic Designe*
EMP: 10
SQ FT: 15,000
SALES (est): 1.4MM **Privately Held**
WEB: www.sherwindodgeprinters.com
SIC: 2759 Lithographic Commercial Printing

(G-18667)
TENDER CORPORATION (PA)
944 Industrial Park Rd (03561-3956)
PHONE..................................603 444-5464
Christopher Heye, *CEO*
Gary Kiedaisch, *Ch of Bd*
Richard Tuttle, *President*
Sharon Bush, *Vice Pres*
John Gaulin, *Vice Pres*
◆ **EMP:** 100
SALES (est): 24.4MM **Privately Held**
WEB: www.tendercorp.com
SIC: 2879 2834 Mfg Agricultural Chemicals Mfg Pharmaceutical Preparations

(G-18668)
WHITE MOUNTAIN BIODIESEL LLC
83 Elm St (03561-4706)
PHONE..................................603 444-0335
Wayne W Presby, *Branch Mgr*
EMP: 8
SALES (corp-wide): 4.2MM **Privately Held**
SIC: 2911 Petroleum Refiner
PA: White Mountain Biodiesel Llc
35 Business Park Rd
North Haverhill NH 03774
603 728-7351

Londonderry
Rockingham County

(G-18669)
A SWEET AS SUGAR LIFE-CUPCAKES
173 Pillsbury Rd (03053-3223)
PHONE..................................603 591-8957
Victoria Johnson, *Administration*
EMP: 3
SALES (est): 124.3K **Privately Held**
SIC: 2051 Mfg Bread/Related Products

(G-18670)
ACME SALES
4 King George Dr (03053-2816)
PHONE..................................603 434-8826
Oz Peters, *President*
Clark Peters, *Vice Pres*
EMP: 5
SQ FT: 1,100
SALES: 700K **Privately Held**
SIC: 3494 Represent Mfg In Plumbing And Heating Industry

(G-18671)
ADMIX INC
Also Called: Advanced Mixing Technologies
144 Harvey Rd (03053-7449)
PHONE..................................603 627-2340
Mike Rizzo, *CEO*
Bob Hines, *COO*
Eric Therriault, *Vice Pres*
Bob Trottier, *Vice Pres*
Rob Lemon, *Project Mgr*
EMP: 30
SQ FT: 15,000
SALES (est): 10.8MM **Privately Held**
WEB: www.admix.com
SIC: 3556 3559 3531 Mfg Food Prdts Mach Mfg Misc Industry Mach Mfg Construction Mach

(G-18672)
ADVANTAGE MOLD INC
576 Mammoth Rd Ste 23 (03053-2151)
PHONE..................................603 647-6678
Peter J Matarozzo, *President*
Edward Hall, *Vice Pres*
Daniel Matarozzo, *Vice Pres*
EMP: 8 **EST:** 1997
SQ FT: 6,600
SALES (est): 1.2MM **Privately Held**
WEB: www.advantagemoldinc.com
SIC: 3089 Mfg Plastic Products

(G-18673)
AERATION TECHNOLOGIES INC
3 Commercial Ln Ste F (03053-2200)
PHONE..................................603 434-3539
Russell Sullivan, *Manager*
EMP: 3
SALES (corp-wide): 432.9K **Privately Held**
SIC: 3599 8711 Mfg Industrial Machinery Engineering Services
PA: Aeration Technologies Inc
11 Bartlet St
Andover MA
978 475-6385

(G-18674)
AL CU MET INC
3 Planeview Dr (03053-2307)
PHONE..................................603 432-6220
Russell Wilmarth, *CEO*
Mark Richardson, *President*
EMP: 45
SQ FT: 35,000
SALES (est): 13.4MM **Privately Held**
WEB: www.alcumet.com
SIC: 3369 Nonferrous Metal Foundry

(G-18675)
ALLIED ORTHOTIC INC
3 Commercial Ln Ste E (03053-2200)
PHONE..................................603 434-7722
Michael Michaud, *President*
Theresa Young, *Office Mgr*
EMP: 7
SQ FT: 4,800
SALES: 650K **Privately Held**
SIC: 3842 Mfg Surgical Appliances/Supplies

(G-18676)
ANTHONY GALLUZZO CORP
Also Called: Benjamin Chase Co
14 Liberty Dr (03053-2251)
PHONE..................................603 432-2681
Joseph Galluzzo, *President*
David Galluzzo, *Vice Pres*
Anthony Galluzzo Jr, *CFO*
EMP: 30
SQ FT: 34,000
SALES (est): 5MM **Privately Held**
WEB: www.anthonygalluzzocorp.com
SIC: 2499 2511 2431 Mfg Wood Products Mfg Wood Household Furniture Mfg Millwork

(G-18677)
ARC MAINTENANCE MACHINING
14 Tinker Ave Unit 2 (03053-2030)
PHONE..................................603 626-8046
David Webber, *President*
EMP: 8
SQ FT: 11,000
SALES (est): 275.2K **Privately Held**
WEB: www.aerorepaircorp.com
SIC: 7692 Welding Repair

(G-18678)
BAE SYSTEMS INFO & ELEC SYS
2 Industrial Dr (03053-2010)
PHONE..................................603 647-5367
Mark Patton, *Branch Mgr*
EMP: 4
SALES (corp-wide): 22.1B **Privately Held**
SIC: 3812 Mfg Search/Navigation Equipment
HQ: Bae Systems Information And Electronic Systems Integration Inc.
65 Spit Brook Rd
Nashua NH 03060
603 885-4321

(G-18679)
BBT NORTH AMERICA CORPORATION
50 Wentworth Ave (03053-7475)
PHONE..................................603 552-1100
Mike Tarmy, *Supervisor*
Angel Miller,
EMP: 3
SALES (est): 97.2K **Privately Held**
SIC: 3433 Mfg Heating Equipment-Nonelectric

(G-18680)
BOB BEAN COMPANY INC
Also Called: Minuteman Press
44 Nashua Rd Unit 2 (03053-3450)
PHONE..................................603 818-4390
Bob Bean, *President*
EMP: 4
SALES (est): 421K **Privately Held**
SIC: 2752 Comm Prtg Litho

(G-18681)
BURNDY LLC
47 Industrial Dr (03053)
PHONE..................................603 647-5000
Michele Foster, *Editor*
Lang James, *Sales Staff*
Kevin Ryan, *Branch Mgr*
EMP: 150
SALES (corp-wide): 4.4B **Publicly Held**
WEB: www.fciconnect.com
SIC: 3643 Mfg Electrical Connectors
HQ: Burndy Llc
47 E Industrial Park Dr
Manchester NH 03109

(G-18682)
BURNDY LLC
7 Aviation Park Dr (03053-2380)
PHONE..................................603 647-5119
Rod Ruland, *President*
EMP: 160
SALES (corp-wide): 4.4B **Publicly Held**
SIC: 3643 Mfg Conductive Wiring Devices
HQ: Burndy Llc
47 E Industrial Park Dr
Manchester NH 03109

(G-18683)
CAMERA WORKS INC
Also Called: Yourplayingcards.com
34 Londonderry Rd Unit A2 (03053-3351)
P.O. Box 882, Salem (03079-0882)
PHONE..................................603 898-7175
John Rowland, *President*
David Beaulieu, *Vice Pres*
▲ **EMP:** 6
SALES (est): 780.2K **Privately Held**
WEB: www.cameraworksnh.com
SIC: 2759 Commercial Printing

(G-18684)
CARR TOOL CO INC
19 Tinker Ave Unit 2 (03053-2031)
PHONE..................................603 669-0177
Donald Carr Jr, *President*
Irene Carr, *Treasurer*
EMP: 10
SALES: 1.5MM **Privately Held**
WEB: www.carrtoolcoinc.com
SIC: 3599 Mfg Industrial Machinery

(G-18685)
COCA-COLA BOTTLING COMPANY
7 Symmes Dr (03053-2102)
PHONE..................................603 437-3530
Richard Neal, *Branch Mgr*
EMP: 75 **Privately Held**
SIC: 2086 5149 Mfg Bottled/Canned Soft Drinks Whol Groceries
HQ: Coca-Cola Beverages Northeast, Inc.
1 Executive Park Dr # 330
Bedford NH 03110
603 627-7871

(G-18686)
CONCRETE SYSTEMS INC
15 Independence Dr (03053-2248)
PHONE..................................603 432-1840
Walter Siryk, *President*
EMP: 10
SALES (corp-wide): 55.3MM **Privately Held**
WEB: www.csigroup.com
SIC: 3272 3448 Mfg Concrete Products Mfg Prefabricated Metal Buildings
PA: Concrete Systems, Inc.
9 Commercial St
Hudson NH 03051
603 889-4163

(G-18687)
CONSOLIDATED CONTAINER CO LLC
27 Industrial Dr (03053-2009)
PHONE..................................603 329-6747
Tom Brewer, *Manager*
EMP: 38
SALES (corp-wide): 14B **Publicly Held**
SIC: 3089 Mfg Plastic Products
HQ: Consolidated Container Company, Llc
2500 Windy Ridge Pkwy Se # 1400
Atlanta GA 30339
678 742-4600

(G-18688)
CONSOLIDATED CONTAINER CO LLC
Also Called: Shelburne Plastics
27 Industrial Dr (03053-2009)
PHONE..................................603 624-6055
Lou Lacourse, *Manager*
EMP: 20
SALES (corp-wide): 14B **Publicly Held**
WEB: www.shelburneplastics.com
SIC: 3089 Mfg Plastic Products
HQ: Consolidated Container Company, Llc
2500 Windy Ridge Pkwy Se # 1400
Atlanta GA 30339
678 742-4600

(G-18689)
CRAWFORD SFTWR CONSULTING INC
1e Commons Dr Unit 26 (03053-3478)
PHONE..................................603 537-9630
Steven Carr, *President*
EMP: 7 **EST:** 2001
SQ FT: 1,000
SALES: 10MM **Privately Held**
WEB: www.crawford-software.com
SIC: 7372 Prepackaged Software Services

(G-18690)
CYTYC CORPORATION
2 E Perimeter Rd (03053-2020)
PHONE..................................603 668-7688
David Batt, *Manager*
EMP: 35
SALES (corp-wide): 3.3B **Publicly Held**
WEB: www.cytyc.com
SIC: 3841 Surgical And Medical Instruments

▲ = Import ▼=Export
◆ =Import/Export

HQ: Cytyc Corporation
250 Campus Dr
Marlborough MA 01752
508 263-2900

(G-18691)
D M F MACHINE CO INC
Also Called: Dmf Engineering
48 Harvey Rd (03053-7413)
PHONE..................................603 434-4945
Carl Bryson, *President*
Robert Bryson, *Vice Pres*
EMP: 5 **EST:** 1966
SQ FT: 3,000
SALES: 400K **Privately Held**
SIC: 3599 7692 Mfg Industrial Machinery Welding Repair

(G-18692)
DUAL CONTROL INC
8 Delta Dr Unit D (03053-2349)
PHONE..................................603 627-4114
EMP: 5
SALES (est): 318.3K **Privately Held**
SIC: 3699 Mfg Electrical Equipment/Supplies

(G-18693)
EASTERN METALS INC
4 Old Nashua Rd (03053-3616)
P.O. Box 772 (03053-0772)
PHONE..................................603 818-8639
EMP: 7
SALES (est): 25.5K **Privately Held**
SIC: 3399 1761 Mfg Primary Metal Products Roofing/Siding Contractor

(G-18694)
EBNER FURNACES
51 Harvey Rd Unit C (03053-7414)
PHONE..................................603 552-3806
David Dow, *President*
▲ **EMP:** 3 **EST:** 2012
SALES (est): 403.4K **Privately Held**
SIC: 3567 Mfg Industrial Furnaces/Ovens

(G-18695)
ELECTRONICS FOR IMAGING INC
12 Innovatiion Way (03053-2052)
PHONE..................................603 279-4635
EMP: 10
SALES (est): 1.2MM
SALES (corp-wide): 1B **Privately Held**
SIC: 2759 3955 Commercial Printing Mfg Carbon Paper/Ink Ribbons
HQ: Electronics For Imaging, Inc.
6750 Dumbarton Cir
Fremont CA 94555
650 357-3500

(G-18696)
ENVIRO-TOTE INC
15 Industrial Dr (03053-2009)
PHONE..................................603 647-7171
Nancy Sampo, *President*
Marilyn J Lee, *Treasurer*
▲ **EMP:** 38
SQ FT: 10,500
SALES (est): 4.4MM **Privately Held**
WEB: www.enviro-tote.com
SIC: 2393 2394 Mfg Textile Bags Mfg Canvas/Related Products

(G-18697)
FELTON INC
7 Burton Dr (03053-7435)
PHONE..................................603 425-0200
Ben Boehm, *CEO*
Daniel Boehm, *President*
Mark Godfrey, *Treasurer*
Travis McGrath, *Accountant*
▲ **EMP:** 75 **EST:** 1842
SQ FT: 75,000
SALES: 12.6MM **Privately Held**
WEB: www.feltonbrush.com
SIC: 3991 3496 3053 Mfg Brooms/Brushes Mfg Misc Fabricated Wire Products Mfg Gaskets/Packing/Sealing Devices

(G-18698)
FELTON BRUSH
7 Burton Dr (03053-7435)
PHONE..................................603 425-0200
EMP: 13
SALES (est): 1.7MM **Privately Held**
SIC: 3991 Mfg Brooms/Brushes

(G-18699)
FINISHIELD CORP
5 George Ave (03053-2017)
PHONE..................................603 641-2164
Roger Jubinville, *President*
Peter Vetri, *Treasurer*
EMP: 30
SALES (est): 3MM **Privately Held**
SIC: 3471 Plating/Polishing Service

(G-18700)
FLEX TECHNOLOGY INCORPORATED
6 George Ave (03053-2016)
PHONE..................................603 883-1500
James J Gale Jr, *President*
Collen Gale, *Treasurer*
EMP: 38
SQ FT: 280,000
SALES (est): 3.3MM **Privately Held**
SIC: 3672 Manufactures Flexible Circuit Boards

(G-18701)
HAROLD ESTEY LUMBER INC
9 Old Nashua Rd (03053-3617)
PHONE..................................603 432-5184
Harold Estey, *President*
Arlene Estey, *Vice Pres*
Thomas Estey, *Admin Sec*
EMP: 4
SALES: 300K **Privately Held**
SIC: 2421 5211 Sawmill

(G-18702)
HOLOGIC INC
2 E Perimeter Rd (03053-2020)
PHONE..................................603 668-7688
Suzanne Werneke, *Branch Mgr*
EMP: 195
SALES (corp-wide): 3.3B **Publicly Held**
SIC: 3844 Mfg Medical Diagnostic And Medical Imaging Equipment
PA: Hologic, Inc.
250 Campus Dr
Marlborough MA 01752
508 263-2900

(G-18703)
HUBBELL INCORPORATED
7 Aviation Park Dr (03053-2380)
P.O. Box 9507, Manchester (03108-9507)
PHONE..................................800 346-4175
Mary Shand, *Branch Mgr*
EMP: 75
SALES (corp-wide): 4.4B **Publicly Held**
WEB: www.fciconnect.com
SIC: 3643 5063 Mfg Conductive Wiring Devices Whol Electrical Equipment
PA: Hubbell Incorporated
40 Waterview Dr
Shelton CT 06484
475 882-4000

(G-18704)
INSULECTRO
8 Akira Way (03053-2037)
PHONE..................................603 629-4403
Kevin Miller, *Manager*
EMP: 40
SALES (corp-wide): 128.6MM **Privately Held**
SIC: 3672 5065 Mfg Printed Circuit Boards Whol Electronic Parts/Equipment
PA: Insulectro
20362 Windrow Dr Ste 100
Lake Forest CA 92630
949 587-3200

(G-18705)
IPN INDUSTRIES INC
8 Ricker Ave (03053-2001)
PHONE..................................603 623-8626
Arnaud Moor, *President*
EMP: 6
SQ FT: 8,000
SALES (est): 550K **Privately Held**
SIC: 2891 Mfg Adhesives/Sealants

(G-18706)
KANU INC
33 Londonderry Rd Unit 12 (03053-6601)
PHONE..................................603 437-6311
Kanu Patel, *President*
Robert Schafer, *Exec VP*
Mary Pinale,
EMP: 4
SALES (est): 606K **Privately Held**
SIC: 2844 Mfg Hair Care Products

(G-18707)
KAYCEE GROUP
21 Bear Meadow Rd (03053-2672)
PHONE..................................603 505-5754
Manu Kaycee, *Principal*
EMP: 3
SALES (est): 178.4K **Privately Held**
SIC: 3577 Mfg Computer Peripheral Equipment

(G-18708)
KENT NUTRITION GROUP INC
Blue Seal Feeds
15 Buttrick Rd (03053-3305)
PHONE..................................603 437-3400
EMP: 19
SALES (corp-wide): 332MM **Privately Held**
SIC: 2048 2047 Mfg Prepared Feeds Mfg Dog/Cat Food
HQ: Kent Nutrition Group, Inc.
1600 Oregon St
Muscatine IA 52761
563 264-4211

(G-18709)
KLUBER LUBRIC NORTH AMERCIA LP
32 Industrial Dr (03053-2008)
PHONE..................................603 647-4104
Dieter Becker, *President*
Hugh Benson, *Manager*
Toby Porter, *Manager*
EMP: 7
SALES (est): 1.2MM **Privately Held**
SIC: 2992 Mfg Lubricating Oils/Greases

(G-18710)
KLUBER LUBRICATION N AMER LP
32 Industrial Dr (03053-2008)
PHONE..................................800 447-2238
Edward Janes, *Plant Mgr*
Richard Miezkowski, *Plant Mgr*
Georg Sixt, *Plant Mgr*
Jolene Stevens, *Plant Mgr*
Steven Brochu, *Engineer*
EMP: 6
SALES (corp-wide): 10.5B **Privately Held**
WEB: www.kluberna.com
SIC: 2992 Mfg Lubricating Oils/Greases
HQ: Kluber Lubrication Na Lp
32 Industrial Dr
Londonderry NH 03053
603 647-4104

(G-18711)
KLUBER LUBRICATION NA LP (DH)
32 Industrial Dr (03053-2008)
PHONE..................................603 647-4104
Ralf Kraeme, *CEO*
Adrian Markusic, *VP Mfg*
David Dostal, *Sales Engr*
◆ **EMP:** 70
SQ FT: 55,000
SALES (est): 38.7MM
SALES (corp-wide): 10.5B **Privately Held**
WEB: www.kluberna.com
SIC: 2992 Mfg Lubricating Oils/Greases
HQ: Kluber Lubrication Munchen Se & Co. Kg
Geisenhausenerstr. 7
Munchen 81379
897 876-0

(G-18712)
LASER PROJECTION TECHNOLOGIES
8 Delta Dr Unit 9 (03053-2349)
PHONE..................................603 421-0209
Steven P Kaufman, *CEO*
EMP: 20
SALES (est): 3.1MM **Privately Held**
SIC: 3699 Mfg Electrical Equipment/Supplies

(G-18713)
LIBERTY ENRGY UTLITIES NH CORP (DH)
Also Called: Liberty Utilities
15 Buttrick Rd (03053-3305)
PHONE..................................905 287-2061
Victor Del Vecchio, *President*
Mark Smith, *Vice Pres*
Mary Young, *Vice Pres*
Jeffrey McChristian, *Opers Mgr*
Carol Carbonneau, *Opers Staff*
EMP: 69 **EST:** 2011
SALES: 194.3K
SALES (corp-wide): 1.6B **Privately Held**
SIC: 1311 Crude Petroleum/Natural Gas Production
HQ: Liberty Utilities Co.
12725 W Indian School Rd
Avondale AZ 85392
905 465-4500

(G-18714)
LINEAR & METRIC CO
37 Harvey Rd (03053-7412)
P.O. Box 233 (03053-0233)
PHONE..................................603 432-1700
Leonard Galvin Jr, *Owner*
EMP: 20
SQ FT: 10,000
SALES (est): 3.4MM **Privately Held**
SIC: 3599 Mfg Industrial Machinery

(G-18715)
LITCHFIELD SAND & GRAVEL
1 Continental Dr (03053-3199)
PHONE..................................603 424-6515
Jason Mattress, *Manager*
EMP: 3
SALES (est): 278.6K **Privately Held**
SIC: 1442 Construction Sand/Gravel

(G-18716)
MACOM TECH SLTONS HOLDINGS INC
Also Called: Cobham Metelics
54 Grenier Field Rd (03053-2046)
PHONE..................................603 641-3800
Francis Kwan, *General Mgr*
Brian Sailor, *CFO*
EMP: 78 **Publicly Held**
SIC: 3674 Mfg Semiconductors/Related Devices
PA: Macom Technology Solutions Holdings, Inc.
100 Chelmsford St
Lowell MA 01851

(G-18717)
MAPLELEAF SOFTWARE INC
254 Nashua Rd (03053-3652)
PHONE..................................603 413-0419
Dan Jozwick, *Principal*
EMP: 5
SALES (est): 411.1K **Privately Held**
SIC: 7372 Prepackaged Software Services

(G-18718)
MARTIN D MARGUERITE
Also Called: Embroidery Creat Londonderry
80 Nashua Rd Ste 15 (03053-3419)
PHONE..................................603 421-9654
Marguerite D Martin, *Owner*
EMP: 3 **EST:** 1996
SALES (est): 222.8K **Privately Held**
WEB: www.margueritemartinnyc.com
SIC: 2395 Pleating/Stitching Services

(G-18719)
MEDINA PLATING CORP
17 Kestree Dr (03053-4009)
PHONE..................................330 725-4155
Shawn Ritchie, *President*
Susan Kohanski, *Corp Secy*
Stephanie Miller, *Controller*
EMP: 28
SALES: 7MM **Privately Held**
WEB: www.medinaplating.com
SIC: 3471 Plating/Polishing Service

(G-18720)
MERECO TECHNOLOGIES GROUP INC (HQ)
8 Ricker Ave (03053-2001)
PHONE..................................401 822-9300

GEOGRAPHIC

Philip M Papoojian, *COO*
Richard J Land, *Admin Sec*
EMP: 28
SQ FT: 37,000
SALES (est): 4.6MM
SALES (corp-wide): 5.2MM **Privately Held**
SIC: 2891 Operates As A Manufacturer Of Adhesives And Sealants Specializing In Epoxy Adhesives
PA: Protex International
6 Rue Barbes
Levallois Perret 92300
181 930-072

(G-18721)
METAL WORKS INC
24 Industrial Dr (03053-2008)
PHONE.................................603 332-9323
Fred Pierce, *President*
Thomas Masiero, *COO*
David Staffiere, *Vice Pres*
EMP: 80
SQ FT: 60,000
SALES (est): 17.7MM **Privately Held**
WEB: www.metalworks-inc.com
SIC: 3444 Mfg Sheet Metalwork

(G-18722)
MICHELES SWEET SHOPPE LLC
Also Called: Michele's Totally Awesome Gour
123 Nashua Rd Unit 14 (03053-3454)
P.O. Box 4251, Concord (03302-4251)
PHONE.................................603 425-2946
Michele Holbrook,
EMP: 4
SALES (est): 297.2K **Privately Held**
SIC: 2096 5441 Mfg Potato Chips/Snacks Ret Candy/Confectionery

(G-18723)
MICRO TECH PRODUCTION MCH CO
1 Commercial Ln (03053-2242)
P.O. Box 870, Derry (03038-0870)
PHONE.................................603 434-1743
Robert Tufts, *President*
Thomas Tufts, *Treasurer*
EMP: 10 **EST:** 1968
SQ FT: 3,000
SALES: 1MM **Privately Held**
SIC: 3599 Machine Shop Jobbing & Repair

(G-18724)
MOONLIGHT MEADERY LLC
Also Called: Hidden Moon Brewing
23 Londonderry Rd Unit 17 (03053-3314)
PHONE.................................603 216-2162
Michael Fairbrother, *General Mgr*
Ben Fairbrother, *Sales Staff*
M Frbrother, *Manager*
EMP: 10
SALES: 1.1MM **Privately Held**
SIC: 2084 Mfg Wines/Brandy/Spirits

(G-18725)
MTS ASSOCIATES LONDONDERRY LLC
Also Called: Murray's Auto Recycling Center
55 Hall Rd (03053-2306)
PHONE.................................603 425-2562
Dave McCurdy, *President*
Edward Dudek, *General Mgr*
EMP: 8
SALES (corp-wide): 6MM **Privately Held**
WEB: www.mtsassociates.com
SIC: 3559 Mfg Misc Industry Machinery
PA: Mts Associates Of Londonderry, L.L.C.
15 Cross Rd
Hooksett NH 03106
603 623-7470

(G-18726)
MUSHIELD COMPANY INC
9 Ricker Ave (03053-2027)
P.O. Box 5045, Manchester (03108-5045)
PHONE.................................603 666-4433
David Grilli, *President*
Robert Joy, *Vice Pres*
Lara Blanchette, *Engineer*
Ron Shepherd, *Engineer*
Brett Joy, *Design Engr*
EMP: 20
SQ FT: 20,000
SALES (est): 5.5MM **Privately Held**
WEB: www.mushield.com
SIC: 3559 3398 3469 Mfg Misc Industry Machinery Metal Heat Treating Mfg Metal Stampings

(G-18727)
NEW HAMPSHIRE PRECISION MET (PA)
15 Industrial Dr (03053-2009)
PHONE.................................603 668-6777
J Emile Poirier, *President*
Joanna Poirier, *Treasurer*
Mark E Poirier, *Director*
John F Griffin Jr, *Admin Sec*
EMP: 45
SQ FT: 31,000
SALES (est): 6.8MM **Privately Held**
WEB: www.nhprecision.com
SIC: 3444 Mfg Sheet Metalwork

(G-18728)
NHP STRATHAM INC
Also Called: New Hampshire Prcsn Metal
15 Industrial Dr (03053-2009)
PHONE.................................603 668-6777
Emile Poirier, *Owner*
EMP: 50
SALES (est): 5.5MM **Privately Held**
SIC: 3444 Mfg Sheet Metalwork

(G-18729)
NU-CAST INC
29 Grenier Field Rd (03053-2015)
PHONE.................................603 432-1600
D Donald Mc Kitterick, *President*
John Bowkett, *Senior VP*
EMP: 130
SQ FT: 40,000
SALES (est): 24.5MM **Privately Held**
WEB: www.nucast.net
SIC: 3365 Aluminum Foundry

(G-18730)
NUTFIELD PUBLISHING LLC
2 Litchfield Rd (03053-2625)
PHONE.................................603 537-2760
Deb Paul,
EMP: 9
SALES (est): 716.6K **Privately Held**
SIC: 2741 Misc Publishing

(G-18731)
PRATT & WHITNEY
Also Called: Pratt & Whitney Aircraft Nelc
52 Pettengill Rd (03053-2050)
PHONE.................................800 742-5877
EMP: 3
SALES (est): 359.7K **Privately Held**
SIC: 3724 Mfg Aircraft Engines/Parts

(G-18732)
PRO STAR PRCSION MACHINING LLC
438 Kelly Ave (03053-2023)
PHONE.................................603 518-8570
Kevin Harriman,
Brian Cote,
Joanne O'Brien,
EMP: 3
SQ FT: 14,400
SALES (est): 120.4K **Privately Held**
SIC: 3599 Mfg Industrial Machinery

(G-18733)
PROTAVIC AMERICA INC
8 Ricker Ave (03053-2001)
PHONE.................................603 623-8624
Arnaud Moor, *President*
Benedicte Moor, *Treasurer*
EMP: 9
SALES (est): 2.4MM
SALES (corp-wide): 5.2MM **Privately Held**
SIC: 2891 Mfg Adhesives/Sealants
PA: Protex International
6 Rue Barbes
Levallois-Perret 92300
181 930-072

(G-18734)
ROB GEOFFROY
Also Called: Geoffroy Labs
176 Litchfield Rd (03053-7423)
PHONE.................................603 425-2517
EMP: 6
SALES (est): 280K **Privately Held**
WEB: www.geoffroylabs.com
SIC: 3679 3569 3674 Mfg Elec Components Mfg General Indstl Mach Mfg Semiconductors/Dvcs

(G-18735)
SEMIGEN INC
54 Grenier Field Rd (03053-2046)
PHONE.................................603 624-8311
James Morgan, *President*
Larry Chudd, *Corp Secy*
Paul Richard, *Engineer*
EMP: 25
SALES (est): 5.5MM **Privately Held**
SIC: 3827 3559 Mfg Optical Instruments/Lenses Mfg Misc Industry Machinery

(G-18736)
SIS-USA INC
Also Called: SIS Ergo
55 Wentworth Ave (03053-7476)
PHONE.................................603 432-4495
Scott McPartlin, *President*
Nick Tetreault, *Engineer*
◆ **EMP:** 15
SQ FT: 36,000
SALES: 13.2MM
SALES (corp-wide): 63.5K **Privately Held**
WEB: www.sis-usa-inc.com
SIC: 2522 Mfg Office Furniture-Nonwood
HQ: Midform Holding Aps
Fjordvej 116
Kolding
644 104-07

(G-18737)
SITEONE LANDSCAPE SUPPLY LLC
Also Called: John Deere Authorized Dealer
3 Aviation Park Dr (03053-2387)
PHONE.................................603 425-2572
EMP: 3
SALES (corp-wide): 2.1B **Publicly Held**
SIC: 3523 5082 Mfg Farm Machinery/Equipment Whol Construction/Mining Equipment
HQ: Siteone Landscape Supply, Llc
300 Colonial Center Pkwy # 600
Roswell GA 30076
770 255-2100

(G-18738)
SJM ETRONICS LLC
5 Clark Rd (03053-2124)
PHONE.................................603 512-3821
Stephen J Martel, *Owner*
EMP: 4
SALES (est): 448.8K **Privately Held**
SIC: 3621 Mfg Motors/Generators

(G-18739)
STITCHES BY KAYO INC
Also Called: Embroidme of Londonderry NH
44 Nashua Rd Unit 11 (03053-3473)
PHONE.................................603 965-0158
EMP: 3 **EST:** 2012
SALES: 250K **Privately Held**
SIC: 2395 Pleating/Stitching Services

(G-18740)
SYAM SOFTWARE INC
12 Lantern Ln (03053-3905)
PHONE.................................603 598-9575
Nick Thickins, *CEO*
James Parker, *Vice Pres*
Robert Wiener, *Accounts Exec*
Michael Daniele, *CTO*
Cory Nickerson, *Technology*
EMP: 12
SALES: 1MM **Privately Held**
WEB: www.syamsoftware.com
SIC: 7372 Prepackaged Software Services

(G-18741)
TEXTILES COATED INCORPORATED (PA)
Also Called: Textiles Coated International
6 George Ave (03053-2016)
PHONE.................................603 296-2221
John W Tippett, *CEO*
Bobbi Malloy, *Buyer*
Alina Bobar, *IT/INT Sup*
▲ **EMP:** 90
SQ FT: 85,000
SALES (est): 19.6MM **Privately Held**
WEB: www.textilescoated.com
SIC: 2821 2295 3081 2299 Mfg Plstc Material/Resin Mfg Coated Fabrics Mfg Unsupport Plstc Film Mfg Textile Goods Mfg Plastic Products

(G-18742)
UNI-CAST LLC
11 Industrial Dr (03053-2011)
PHONE.................................603 625-5761
Henri Fine, *President*
Jon Coleman, *QC Mgr*
Brandon Rouleau, *Sales Engr*
▲ **EMP:** 150
SQ FT: 44,000
SALES (est): 30.9MM **Privately Held**
WEB: www.uni-cast.com
SIC: 3365 Aluminum Foundry

(G-18743)
UPCYCLE SOLUTIONS INC
Also Called: North American Metals
7 Delta Dr (03053-2348)
PHONE.................................603 809-6843
William Dorazio, *President*
EMP: 3
SALES: 4.4MM **Privately Held**
SIC: 3444 4953 Mfg Sheet Metalwork Refuse System

(G-18744)
UPS SCS PRATT & WHITNEY
52 Pettengill Rd (03053-2050)
PHONE.................................860 565-0353
EMP: 5
SALES (est): 163.4K **Privately Held**
SIC: 3365 Aluminum Foundries

(G-18745)
WIRE BELT COMPANY OF AMERICA (PA)
154 Harvey Rd (03053-7473)
PHONE.................................603 644-2500
David Greer, *President*
F Wade Greer Jr, *Chairman*
Keith Martin, *Business Mgr*
Robert Greer, *Corp Secy*
David Maestri, *Vice Pres*
▲ **EMP:** 88 **EST:** 1947
SQ FT: 35,500
SALES (est): 17.3MM **Privately Held**
WEB: www.wirebelt.com
SIC: 3496 Mfg Misc Fabricated Wire Products

(G-18746)
WOODWORKS ARCHITECTURAL MLLWK
16 N Wentworth Ave (03053-7438)
PHONE.................................603 432-4050
Gary Bergeron, *President*
Michele Bergeron, *Vice Pres*
Ken St Jean, *Plant Mgr*
Mark Lickteig, *Project Mgr*
Ward Blodgett, *CFO*
EMP: 44
SQ FT: 75,000
SALES (est): 8.1MM **Privately Held**
WEB: www.woodworkslondonderry.com
SIC: 2431 Mfg Millwork

Loudon
Merrimack County

(G-18747)
CONCORD SAND AND GRAVEL INC
14 Presby Ln (03307-1628)
P.O. Box 1133, Concord (03302-1133)
PHONE.................................603 435-6787
Robert Cole, *President*
Levi Ladd, *Vice Pres*
EMP: 4
SQ FT: 900
SALES (est): 411.3K **Privately Held**
SIC: 1442 1429 Construction Sand/Gravel Crushed/Broken Stone

▲ = Import ▼=Export
◆ =Import/Export

(G-18748)
HIGH TECH HARVESTING LLC
7333 Oak Hill Rd (03307-0811)
PHONE..........603 229-0750
Todd Carmichael, *Mng Member*
Michael Barrett,
EMP: 3
SALES (est): 373.6K **Privately Held**
SIC: 2411 Logging

(G-18749)
JASON S LANDRY
263 Route 129 (03307-1337)
PHONE..........603 783-1154
Jason S Landry, *Principal*
EMP: 3
SALES (est): 247.5K **Privately Held**
SIC: 2411 Logging

(G-18750)
MAGOON LOGGING LLC
863 Route 129 (03307-1406)
PHONE..........603 435-9918
Matthew Magoon,
Jamie Magoon,
EMP: 4
SALES (est): 260K **Privately Held**
SIC: 2411 Logging

(G-18751)
NORTHERN DESIGN PRECAST INC
51 International Dr (03307-1210)
P.O. Box 7305, Laconia (03247-7305)
PHONE..........603 783-8989
Bradley J Thompson, *President*
Lee W Mattson, *Admin Sec*
EMP: 28
SQ FT: 2,500
SALES (est): 5MM **Privately Held**
WEB: www.ndprecast.com
SIC: 3272 8712 5211 Mfg Concrete Products Architectural Services Ret Lumber/Building Materials

(G-18752)
PLAN TECH INC
7031 Shaker Rd Unit J (03307-1111)
PHONE..........603 783-4767
David Stewart, *President*
Alan Cushing, *Vice Pres*
Norman Theriault, *Vice Pres*
Melanie Patten, *Production*
Linda Theriault, *Admin Sec*
EMP: 23
SQ FT: 28,000
SALES (est): 3.4MM **Privately Held**
WEB: www.plantech.com
SIC: 3089 2821 Mfg Plastic Products Mfg Plastic Materials/Resins

Lyme
Grafton County

(G-18753)
CENTER FOR NORTHERN WOODLANDS
16 On The Cmn (03768)
P.O. Box 270 (03768-0270)
PHONE..........802 439-6292
Elise Tillinghast, *Exec Dir*
EMP: 6
SQ FT: 3,700
SALES: 787.2K **Privately Held**
WEB: www.northernwoodlands.com
SIC: 2721 8299 Periodicals-Publishing/Printing School/Educational Services

(G-18754)
LYME GREEN HEAT
135 Mud Turtle Pond Rd (03768)
P.O. Box 152 (03768-0152)
PHONE..........603 359-8837
Morton Bailey, *Principal*
Sarah Pushee, *Sales Staff*
EMP: 3
SALES (est): 227.9K **Privately Held**
SIC: 3585 Mfg Refrigeration/Heating Equipment

(G-18755)
MAT GAME SET
51 Pinnacle Rd (03768-3317)
PHONE..........603 277-9763
Susan Valence, *Owner*
EMP: 6
SALES (est): 729.7K **Privately Held**
SIC: 2339 Mfg Women's/Misses' Outerwear

(G-18756)
SNOMATIC CONTROLS & ENGRG INC
4 Britton Ln (03768-3113)
PHONE..........603 795-2900
Scott Barthold, *President*
EMP: 5
SQ FT: 1,200
SALES (est): 622K **Privately Held**
SIC: 3585 Mfg Refrigeration/Heating Equipment

Lyndeborough
Hillsborough County

(G-18757)
BALLISTIC FLUID TECHNOLOGIES (PA)
352 Center Rd Unit 3 (03082-6526)
PHONE..........603 654-3065
Kempton F Philbrook, *Principal*
EMP: 3
SALES (est): 314.2K **Privately Held**
WEB: www.ballisticfluid.com
SIC: 3492 Mfg Fluid Power Valves/Fittings

(G-18758)
FOUR SAPS SUGAR SHACK CORP
10 Fredette Dr (03082-5812)
PHONE..........603 858-5159
Ken Begley, *President*
Derik Comtois, *Vice Pres*
Winfred Van Mourik, *Marketing Staff*
EMP: 3
SQ FT: 600
SALES (est): 120K **Privately Held**
SIC: 2099 Mfg Food Preparations

(G-18759)
NADEAU LOGGING
Also Called: Morning Star Farm
649 Forest Rd (03082-6007)
PHONE..........603 654-2594
EMP: 3
SALES (est): 210.8K **Privately Held**
SIC: 2411 Logging

Madbury
Strafford County

(G-18760)
APPLIED TOOL & DESIGN LLC
1 Mill Hill Rd (03823-7555)
PHONE..........603 740-2954
Joseph Stewart, *Mng Member*
Linda Stewart,
EMP: 3
SALES (est): 198K **Privately Held**
SIC: 3599 Machine Shop

(G-18761)
TAYLOR EGG PRODUCTS INC
242 Littleworth Rd (03823-7547)
PHONE..........603 742-1050
William Taylor, *President*
EMP: 20 **EST:** 1970
SQ FT: 23,000
SALES (est): 3.3MM
SALES (corp-wide): 29.4MM **Privately Held**
SIC: 2015 Mfg Of Canned Eggs
PA: Siegel Egg Co, Inc.
90 Salem Rd Ste 3
North Billerica MA 01862
978 528-2000

(G-18762)
VERTAL US INC
18a French Cross Rd (03823-7707)
PHONE..........603 490-1711
Julie Deslauriers, *CEO*
John Clifford, *COO*
Claude Beaule, *Chief Engr*
EMP: 3
SQ FT: 1,500
SALES (est): 174.6K **Privately Held**
SIC: 3599 Mfg Industrial Machinery

Madison
Carroll County

(G-18763)
MACLEAN PRECISION MCH CO INC
1928 Village Rd (03849)
P.O. Box 70 (03849-0070)
PHONE..........603 367-9011
Douglas Folsom, *President*
Deb Folsom, *General Mgr*
Pauline Maclean, *Treasurer*
EMP: 42
SQ FT: 12,000
SALES (est): 7.1MM **Privately Held**
WEB: www.macleanprecision.com
SIC: 3599 Mfg Industrial Machinery

(G-18764)
MADISON LUMBER MILL INC
71 Marcella Dr Rr 41 (03849)
P.O. Box 224, West Ossipee (03890-0224)
PHONE..........603 539-4145
Kim R Moore, *President*
James Smith, *Mfg Staff*
James T Smith, *Admin Sec*
EMP: 55
SALES (est): 10.2MM **Privately Held**
WEB: www.madisonlm.com
SIC: 2421 Sawmill/Planing Mill

(G-18765)
WILLOWTOYS
196 E Madison Rd (03849-5831)
PHONE..........603 367-4657
Joseph Martin, *Owner*
EMP: 3 **EST:** 2010
SALES (est): 218.3K **Privately Held**
SIC: 3944 Mfg Games/Toys

Manchester
Hills County

(G-18766)
DISTILLATION TECH PDTS LLC
285 Lindstrom Ln (03104-4793)
PHONE..........603 935-7070
EMP: 3 **EST:** 2012
SALES (est): 231.4K **Privately Held**
SIC: 3674 Mfg Semiconductors/Related Devices

(G-18767)
JCPTRADING INC
35 Elm St (03101-2719)
PHONE..........603 880-7042
EMP: 6
SALES (est): 1MM **Privately Held**
WEB: www.jcptrading.com
SIC: 3851 Mfg Ophthalmic Goods

(G-18768)
KEYSTONE PRESS LLC
9 Old Falls Rd (03103-3622)
PHONE..........603 622-5222
EMP: 15
SQ FT: 7,700
SALES (est): 1.4MM **Privately Held**
SIC: 2752 Commercial Offset Printing

(G-18769)
PUTNAM RF MACHINING LLC
720 Union St (03104-3676)
PHONE..........603 623-0700
EMP: 5
SALES: 950K **Privately Held**
SIC: 3334 Primary Aluminum Producer

(G-18770)
SUNSHINE SCOOPS LLC
210 Lowell St (03104-4979)
PHONE..........603 668-0992
EMP: 3 **EST:** 2010
SALES (est): 170.4K **Privately Held**
SIC: 2024 Mfg Ice Cream/Frozen Desert

Manchester
Hillsborough County

(G-18771)
ADVANCE CONCRETE FORM INC
Also Called: Advance Form & Supply
241 Pepsi Rd (03109-5320)
PHONE..........603 669-4496
Bernard Cancel, *Manager*
EMP: 7
SALES (corp-wide): 6.9MM **Privately Held**
WEB: www.advanceconcreteform.com
SIC: 3444 Mfg Concrete Forms
PA: Advance Concrete Form, Inc.
5102 Pflaum Rd
Madison WI 53718
608 222-8684

(G-18772)
ADVANCED CNC MACHINE INC
722 E Indus Pk Dr Unit 15 (03109-5628)
PHONE..........603 625-6631
Lane A Fraser, *President*
EMP: 16
SQ FT: 1,200
SALES (est): 1.2MM **Privately Held**
SIC: 3599 Machine Shop Jobbing And Repair

(G-18773)
AERO DEFENSE INTERNATIONAL LLC
400 Bedford St Ste 136 (03101-1195)
PHONE..........603 644-0305
Stephen Adler, *Principal*
EMP: 8 **EST:** 2007
SALES (est): 1.2MM **Privately Held**
SIC: 3812 Mfg Search/Navigation Equipment

(G-18774)
ALLARD NAZARIAN GROUP INC (PA)
Also Called: Granite State Manufacturing
124 Joliette St (03102-3017)
PHONE..........603 668-1900
John R Allard, *CEO*
Michael Allard, *Vice Pres*
Douglas Thomson, *Vice Pres*
Joel Miley, *Project Engr*
Younes Nazarian, *Treasurer*
EMP: 145
SQ FT: 73,484
SALES (est): 38.2MM **Privately Held**
WEB: www.gogsmgo.com
SIC: 3812 3829 3599 3566 Mfg Search/Navgatn Equip Mfg Measure/Control Dvcs Mfg Industrial Machinery Mfg Speed Changer/Drives

(G-18775)
ALLARD NAZARIAN GROUP INC
Also Called: Snow-Nbstedt Pwr Transmissions
111 Joliette St Ste 9 (03102-3018)
PHONE..........603 314-0017
Lee Tack, *Branch Mgr*
EMP: 11
SALES (corp-wide): 38.2MM **Privately Held**
SIC: 3812 3714 Mfg Search/Navigation Equipment Mfg Motor Vehicle Parts/Accessories
PA: Allard Nazarian Group, Inc.
124 Joliette St
Manchester NH 03102
603 668-1900

(G-18776)
ALLEGRO MICROSYSTEMS INC
Also Called: Sanken North America Inc.
955 Perimeter Rd (03103-3353)
PHONE..................................508 853-5000
Dennis H Fitzgerald, *President*
Bassem Nahas, *Design Engr Mgr*
Marvin Ng, *Engineer*
Roland Radius, *Engineer*
Michael Saltmarsh, *Engineer*
EMP: 5
SALES (est): 189K **Privately Held**
SIC: 3674 Mfg Semiconductors/Related Devices
PA: Sanken Electric Co., Ltd.
3-6-3, Kitano
Niiza STM 352-0

(G-18777)
ALLEGRO MICROSYSTEMS LLC (HQ)
955 Perimeter Rd (03103-3353)
P.O. Box 11155, Boston MA (02211-1155)
PHONE..................................603 626-2300
Ravi Vig, *CEO*
Judi Harrington, *Business Mgr*
Yoshihiro Suzuki, *Exec VP*
Vimal Gupta, *Vice Pres*
Andre G Labrecque, *Vice Pres*
◆ **EMP:** 500
SQ FT: 250,000
SALES: 652.7MM **Privately Held**
SIC: 3674 Mfg Semiconductors/Related Devices

(G-18778)
ALPHAGRAPHICS PNTSHP OF FUTURE
88 Harvey Rd (03103-3307)
PHONE..................................603 645-0002
Timothy J Hurley, *Owner*
Fred Holdsworth, *Owner*
EMP: 6
SALES (est): 800K **Privately Held**
SIC: 2752 Comm Prtg Litho

(G-18779)
ANCO SIGNS & STAMPS INC
749 E Industrial Park Dr (03109-5618)
P.O. Box 4576 (03108-4576)
PHONE..................................603 669-3779
Linda Tyrrell, *President*
Kevin Lyons, *Treasurer*
Steven Tyrrell Sr, *Director*
Linda Lyons, *Admin Sec*
EMP: 6
SQ FT: 3,000
SALES (est): 652.5K **Privately Held**
WEB: www.anco-nh.com
SIC: 3953 3993 5999 Mfg Marking Devices Mfg Signs Banners Flags

(G-18780)
ASSEMBLY SPECIALISTS INC
Also Called: A S I
8030 S Willow St Unit 3-4 (03103-2388)
PHONE..................................603 624-9563
EMP: 15
SQ FT: 5,000
SALES (est): 2.8MM **Privately Held**
WEB: www.asi-cables.com
SIC: 3549 Mfg Metalworking Machinery

(G-18781)
ASSURETEC HOLDINGS INC (PA)
62 Lowell St Ste 4 (03101-1607)
PHONE..................................603 641-8443
R Bruce Reeves, *Ch of Bd*
Gary Olin, *Vice Pres*
Kenneth Gorton, *Admin Sec*
EMP: 3
SQ FT: 5,600
SALES (est): 1.8MM **Privately Held**
SIC: 7372 Prepackaged Software Services

(G-18782)
ASTRONICS AEROSAT CORPORATION
220 Hackett Hill Rd (03102-8994)
PHONE..................................603 879-0205
Dennis Ferguson, *CEO*
Matthew Harrah, *Exec VP*
EMP: 100
SQ FT: 28,500
SALES (est): 23.2MM
SALES (corp-wide): 803.2MM **Publicly Held**
SIC: 3669 8711 Mfg Communications Equipment Engineering Services
PA: Astronics Corporation
130 Commerce Way
East Aurora NY 14052
716 805-1599

(G-18783)
AT COMM CORP
150 Dow St Ste 404 (03101-1254)
PHONE..................................603 624-4424
Bob Boyd, *Principal*
EMP: 12
SALES (corp-wide): 1.8MM **Privately Held**
WEB: www.atcomm.com
SIC: 3661 8731 Mfg & Develops Telephone Mgmt Devices
PA: At Comm Corporation
907 Burkhart Ave
San Leandro CA 94579
650 375-8188

(G-18784)
BAKER GRAPHICS INC
Also Called: Curry Copy and Printing Center
143 Middle St Ste 1 (03101-1978)
PHONE..................................603 625-5427
Sandy Baker, *President*
EMP: 7
SQ FT: 3,500
SALES (est): 510K **Privately Held**
SIC: 2752 7334 Offset Printing

(G-18785)
BANTRY COMPONENTS INC
Also Called: Krl Electronics
160 Bouchard St (03103-3315)
PHONE..................................603 668-3210
Verna Perry, *CEO*
Teresa Churillo, *CFO*
Terry Pihl, *Systems Staff*
EMP: 50 **EST:** 1969
SQ FT: 17,000
SALES (est): 9.8MM **Privately Held**
WEB: www.krlbantry.com
SIC: 3825 3823 3674 3577 Mfg Elec Measuring Instr Mfg Process Cntrl Instr Mfg Semiconductors/Dvcs Mfg Computer Peripherals Mfg Electronic Resistors

(G-18786)
BELISLE MACHINE WORKS INC
180 Revere Ave (03109-4442)
PHONE..................................603 669-8902
Richard Belisle, *President*
EMP: 3
SQ FT: 3,800
SALES (est): 325K **Privately Held**
SIC: 3599 Machine Shop

(G-18787)
BETTER LIFE LLC
8030 S Willow St Unit 1-4 (03103-2327)
PHONE..................................603 647-0077
Dennis Pidek,
EMP: 4
SALES (est): 320.5K **Privately Held**
SIC: 2395 2262 Embroidery & Silk Screening Svcs

(G-18788)
BLANCHARD CONTACT LENS INC
8025 S Willow St Ste 211 (03103-2311)
PHONE..................................800 367-4009
John Blanchard, *President*
Pierre Blanchard, *Vice Pres*
Gilles Castonguay, *Treasurer*
EMP: 10
SALES (est): 1.4MM **Privately Held**
WEB: www.blanchardlab.com
SIC: 3851 Ret Optical Goods

(G-18789)
BOLES ENTERPRISES INC
Also Called: Coloniel Printing
143 Middle St Ste 1 (03101-1978)
PHONE..................................603 622-4282
Curtis M Boles, *President*
Luke O'Neill, *Principal*
EMP: 9 **EST:** 1973
SQ FT: 4,000
SALES (est): 900K **Privately Held**
SIC: 2752 7334 Commercial Offset Printing Including Continuous Business Forms

(G-18790)
BRIGADE TACTICAL CORP
400 Bedford St Ste Sw05 (03101-1195)
PHONE..................................603 682-7063
Brian Bowersox, *President*
EMP: 3
SQ FT: 900
SALES (est): 114.3K **Privately Held**
SIC: 3484 Mfg Small Arms

(G-18791)
BURNDY AMERICAS INC (HQ)
47 E Industrial Pk Dr (03109-5311)
PHONE..................................603 647-5000
Rodd Ruland, *President*
Ray Lavoie, *Engineer*
EMP: 9
SALES (est): 252.7MM
SALES (corp-wide): 4.4B **Publicly Held**
SIC: 3643 5063 Mfg Conductive Wiring Devices Whol Electrical Equipment
PA: Hubbell Incorporated
40 Waterview Dr
Shelton CT 06484
475 882-4000

(G-18792)
BURNDY AMERICAS INTL HOLDG LLC
47 E Industrial Pk Dr (03109-5311)
PHONE..................................603 647-5000
Rodd Ruland, *President*
EMP: 642
SALES (est): 20.7MM
SALES (corp-wide): 4.4B **Publicly Held**
SIC: 3643 5063 Mfg Conductive Wiring Devices Whol Electrical Equip
HQ: Burndy Americas Inc
47 E Industrial Pk Dr
Manchester NH 03109

(G-18793)
BURNDY LLC (DH)
47 E Industrial Park Dr (03109-5311)
PHONE..................................603 647-5000
Lorraine Paquette, *General Mgr*
Jackie Sylvia, *General Mgr*
Lee Herron, *Vice Pres*
Kevin Ryan, *Vice Pres*
Alan Beck, *Plant Mgr*
◆ **EMP:** 277
SALES (est): 231.9MM
SALES (corp-wide): 4.4B **Publicly Held**
SIC: 3643 5063 Mfg Conductive Wiring Devices Whol Electrical Equipment

(G-18794)
CABINETS FOR LESS LLC
679 Mast Rd (03102-1417)
PHONE..................................603 935-7551
Zumra Gutierrez, *Principal*
EMP: 5
SALES (est): 598.1K **Privately Held**
SIC: 2434 5211 3253 5023 Mfg Wood Kitchen Cabinet Ret Lumber/Building Mtrl Mfg Ceramic Wall/Fl Tile Whol Homefurnishings

(G-18795)
CAPITAL ORTHTICS PRSTHTICS LLC
15 Nelson St (03103-2706)
PHONE..................................603 425-0106
George Rogers, *Branch Mgr*
EMP: 9
SALES (est): 1MM
SALES (corp-wide): 1.2MM **Privately Held**
SIC: 3842 Mfg Surgical Appliances/Supplies
PA: Capital Orthotics Prosthetics Llc
246 Pleasant St Ste 200
Concord NH 03301
603 226-0106

(G-18796)
CARLISLE PUBLICATIONS
40 Cascade Cir (03103-6905)
PHONE..................................603 622-4056
Gary Carkin, *Owner*
EMP: 3
SALES (est): 144K **Privately Held**
WEB: www.carlislepublications.com
SIC: 2741 Misc Publishing

(G-18797)
CCA GLOBAL PARTNERS INC
Also Called: Bizunite
670 North Commercial St # 300 (03101-1138)
PHONE..................................603 626-0333
Jason Larson, *Vice Pres*
Dan Pramis, *Consultant*
EMP: 11
SALES (corp-wide): 66.6MM **Privately Held**
SIC: 7372 Prepackaged Software Services
PA: Cca Global Partners, Inc.
4301 Earth City Expy
Earth City MO 63045
800 466-6984

(G-18798)
CHUCKLES INC
Also Called: Sukesha
11925 S Willow St (03103-2329)
P.O. Box 5126 (03108-5126)
PHONE..................................603 669-4228
Charles P Frank, *President*
◆ **EMP:** 25
SALES (est): 5.4MM **Privately Held**
WEB: www.allnutrient.com
SIC: 2844 Mfg Toilet Preparations

(G-18799)
CLARIOS
Also Called: Johnson Controls
915 Holt Ave Unit 7 (03109-5606)
PHONE..................................603 222-2400
EMP: 3 **Privately Held**
SIC: 2531 Mfg Public Building Furniture
HQ: Johnson Controls Inc
5757 N Green Bay Ave
Milwaukee WI 53209
414 524-1200

(G-18800)
COCA-COLA BOTTLING COMPANY
99 Eddy Rd (03102-3226)
PHONE..................................603 623-6033
Mark Francoeur, *Manager*
EMP: 52 **Privately Held**
SIC: 2086 Carb Sft Drnkbtlcn
HQ: Coca-Cola Beverages Northeast, Inc.
1 Executive Park Dr # 330
Bedford NH 03110
603 627-7871

(G-18801)
COMBAT WEAPONS DEVELOPMENT LLC
322 Circle Rd (03103-3124)
PHONE..................................603 978-0244
Joe Follansbee, *President*
EMP: 4
SALES (est): 172.4K **Privately Held**
SIC: 3489 Mfg Ordnance/Accessories

(G-18802)
CONEST SOFTWARE SYSTEMS INC
592 Harvey Rd (03103-3320)
P.O. Box 947, Londonderry (03053-0947)
PHONE..................................603 437-9353
Jim Beaumont, *President*
EMP: 30
SALES (est): 129.1K **Privately Held**
SIC: 7372 Prepackaged Software Services

(G-18803)
CONNEXIENT LLC
33 S Coml St Ste 302 (03101)
P.O. Box 10782, Bedford (03110-0782)
PHONE..................................603 669-1300
Mark Green, *CEO*
EMP: 12 **EST:** 2012
SALES (est): 695.9K **Privately Held**
SIC: 7372 Prepackaged Software Services

(G-18804)
CONSTRCTION SUMMARY OF NH MAIN
734 Chestnut St (03104-3001)
PHONE..................................603 627-8856

▲ = Import ▼=Export
◆ =Import/Export

Robert Morin, *President*
EMP: 9
SQ FT: 600
SALES (est): 875.3K **Privately Held**
WEB: www.constructionsummary.com
SIC: 2741 2711 Misc Publishing Newspapers-Publishing/Printing

(G-18805)
CORFIN INDUSTRIES LLC
1050 Perimeter Rd (03103-3303)
PHONE..................................603 893-9900
Donald Tyler, *President*
EMP: 80
SQ FT: 25,000
SALES (est): 18.8MM **Privately Held**
WEB: www.corfin.com
SIC: 3674 Mfg Semiconductors/Related Devices
PA: Corfin Industries Inc.
7b Raymond Ave Ste 7
Salem NH 03079
603 893-9900

(G-18806)
CORFLEX INC (PA)
669 E Industrial Pk Dr (03109-5625)
PHONE..................................603 623-3344
Theodore Lorenzetti Jr, *President*
Paul Lorenzetti, *Treasurer*
Scott Foley, *Executive*
▲ **EMP:** 40
SALES (est): 6MM **Privately Held**
WEB: www.corflex.com
SIC: 3842 8011 Mfg Surgical Appliances/Supplies Medical Doctor's Office

(G-18807)
COUNTER PRO INC
210 Lincoln St (03103-5030)
PHONE..................................603 647-2444
Leigh Paulsen, *President*
EMP: 15
SQ FT: 40,000
SALES: 2.5MM **Privately Held**
WEB: www.counterproinc.com
SIC: 2434 Mfg Wood Kitchen Cabinets

(G-18808)
COURRIER GRAPHICS INC
Also Called: Fastsigns
1875 S Willow St Ste B2 (03103-2382)
PHONE..................................603 626-7012
Richard Stgeorge, *President*
EMP: 3 **EST:** 1996
SALES (est): 416.5K **Privately Held**
SIC: 3993 Signsadv Specs

(G-18809)
DICHTOMATIK AMERICAS LP
100 Commercial St (03101-1126)
PHONE..................................603 628-7030
EMP: 4
SALES (est): 257.8K **Privately Held**
SIC: 2891 3053 5085 Mfg Adhesives/Sealants Mfg Gaskets/Packing/Sealing Devices Whol Industrial Supplies

(G-18810)
DISTILLERY NETWORK INC
21 W Auburn St Ste 30 (03101-2386)
PHONE..................................603 997-6786
Jonathan Zajac, *President*
Phillip Le Clerc, *Manager*
EMP: 5
SQ FT: 3,500
SALES (est): 187.8K **Privately Held**
SIC: 3556 Mfg Food Products Machinery

(G-18811)
DOCUMENT ARCHIVES IMAGING LLC
451 Pepsi Rd Ste C (03109-5317)
PHONE..................................603 656-5209
Jeff Stone, *Mng Member*
EMP: 5
SALES (est): 638.1K **Privately Held**
WEB: www.dai-nh.com
SIC: 3577 Mfg Computer Peripheral Equipment

(G-18812)
DOGGIE PASSPORT
214 Heathrow Ave (03104-6477)
PHONE..................................603 315-8243
Catherine Miller, *Owner*
▼ **EMP:** 4
SALES (est): 177.7K **Privately Held**
SIC: 1389 Construction Repair & Dismantling Srvcs

(G-18813)
DR BIRON INCORPORATED (PA)
Also Called: Keystone Press
9 Old Falls Rd (03103-3622)
PHONE..................................603 622-5222
Daniel Biron, *President*
EMP: 12 **EST:** 1915
SQ FT: 11,000
SALES (est): 2.2MM **Privately Held**
WEB: www.keystonepress.com
SIC: 2752 Lithographic Commercial Printing

(G-18814)
DUNN INDUSTRIES INC
123 Abby Rd (03103-3306)
PHONE..................................603 666-4800
Duane Dunn, *President*
EMP: 24
SQ FT: 16,000
SALES (est): 5.2MM
SALES (corp-wide): 1.1B **Privately Held**
WEB: www.dunnindustries.com
SIC: 3089 Mfg Plastic Products
PA: Tekni-Plex, Inc.
460 E Swedesford Rd # 3000
Wayne PA 19087
484 690-1520

(G-18815)
ELTEK USA INC
250 Commercial St # 2022 (03101-1142)
PHONE..................................603 421-0020
James Barry, *President*
EMP: 4
SQ FT: 3,000
SALES (est): 503.1K
SALES (corp-wide): 231.1K **Privately Held**
SIC: 3672 Mfg Printed Circuit Boards
HQ: Eltek Ltd
20 Gellis
Petah Tikva 49279
393 950-50

(G-18816)
ENERGY TODAY INC
373 S Willow St 254 (03103-5751)
PHONE..................................603 425-8933
Thomas Makmann, *President*
EMP: 4
SALES (est): 326.3K **Privately Held**
SIC: 1382 Oil And Gas Services
PA: Qed Connect, Inc.
373 S Willow St
Manchester NH 03103

(G-18817)
EOUTREACH SOLUTIONS LLC
Also Called: Customscoop
835 Hanover St Ste 204 (03104-5401)
PHONE..................................603 410-5000
Steven Bracy, *Exec Dir*
EMP: 14
SALES (est): 940.2K **Privately Held**
WEB: www.customscoop.com
SIC: 2711 Online New Outlet Company

(G-18818)
EQUIPOIS LLC
124 Joliette St (03102-3017)
PHONE..................................603 668-1900
Glenn Lawton, *President*
EMP: 5
SQ FT: 3,000
SALES (est): 500K **Privately Held**
SIC: 3569 Mfg General Industrial Machinery

(G-18819)
ERWIN PRECISION INC
Also Called: Epi
150 Dow St Ste 7 (03101-1270)
PHONE..................................603 623-2333
David Erwin, *President*
EMP: 5
SALES (est): 633.1K **Privately Held**
SIC: 3599 7692 Mfg Industrial Machinery Welding Repair

(G-18820)
EXECUTIVE WINE & SPIRITS INC
34 1st Ave (03104-1534)
PHONE..................................603 647-8048
EMP: 35
SALES (est): 1.8MM **Privately Held**
SIC: 2084 Mfg Wines/Brandy/Spirits

(G-18821)
EXPEDIENCE SOFTWARE LLC
1087 Elm St Ste 249 (03101-1819)
PHONE..................................978 378-5330
Melissa Mabon, *President*
Diane Loudenback, *Vice Pres*
Sharon Coddington, *Manager*
Brooke Savage, *Shareholder*
EMP: 25
SALES (est): 297.3K **Privately Held**
SIC: 7372 Prepackaged Software Services

(G-18822)
FIRST SIGN & CORPORATE IMAGE
107 Hollis St (03101-1235)
PHONE..................................603 627-0003
Scott Aubertin, *President*
EMP: 6
SALES (est): 429K **Privately Held**
SIC: 3993 Mfg Signs/Advertising Specialties

(G-18823)
FLASH CARD INC
44 Huse Rd (03103-3086)
PHONE..................................603 625-0803
Thomas Sansoucie, *President*
Sylvia Sansoucie, *Vice Pres*
Roger Sansoucie, *Treasurer*
EMP: 3
SALES: 100K **Privately Held**
WEB: www.showboards.com
SIC: 2791 Typesetting Services

(G-18824)
GARAVENTA U S A INC
999 Candia Rd Bldg 2 (03109-5210)
PHONE..................................603 669-6553
James Hunt, *Manager*
EMP: 4
SALES (corp-wide): 5.9MM **Privately Held**
WEB: www.garaventa-florida.com
SIC: 3999 Mfg Misc Products
HQ: Garaventa U S A, Inc.
225 W Depot St
Antioch IL 60002
847 395-9988

(G-18825)
GENERAL CABLE INDUSTRIES INC
Also Called: Manchester, NH Plant
345 Mcgregor St (03102-3222)
PHONE..................................603 668-1620
Tim Grass, *Manager*
Kurt Dion, *Info Tech Mgr*
EMP: 250 **Privately Held**
WEB: www.generalcable.com
SIC: 3496 3357 Mfg Misc Fabricated Wire Products Nonferrous Wiredrawing/Insulating
HQ: General Cable Industries, Inc.
4 Tesseneer Dr
Highland Heights KY 41076

(G-18826)
GENTEX CORPORATION
645 Harvey Rd Ste 1 (03103-3342)
PHONE..................................603 657-1200
Sherry Correia, *Human Res Mgr*
Mark Smith, *Branch Mgr*
Andy Veneri, *Program Mgr*
EMP: 180
SQ FT: 10,000
SALES (corp-wide): 143.3MM **Privately Held**
WEB: www.gentex.net
SIC: 3651 Mfg Home Audio/Video Equipment
PA: Gentex Corporation
324 Main St
Simpson PA 18407
570 282-3550

(G-18827)
GERLACH SHEET METAL
303 W Haven Rd (03104-2831)
PHONE..................................603 782-6136
EMP: 4
SALES (est): 591.2K **Privately Held**
SIC: 3444 Mfg Sheet Metalwork

(G-18828)
GLOBAL PLASTICS LLC (HQ)
99 Middle St Ste 1 (03101-1955)
PHONE..................................603 782-2835
Christopher Guimond,
◆ **EMP:** 10
SQ FT: 20,000
SALES (est): 106.2MM
SALES (corp-wide): 106.5MM **Privately Held**
SIC: 2821 Mfg Plastic Materials/Resins

(G-18829)
GRANITE STATE STAMPS INC
8025 S Willow St Ste 102 (03103-2311)
P.O. Box 5252 (03108-5252)
PHONE..................................603 669-9322
R Bruce Hale, *President*
Lynn Hale, *Vice Pres*
Kelly Hale, *Treasurer*
EMP: 11
SQ FT: 5,000
SALES (est): 1.4MM **Privately Held**
WEB: www.granitestatestamps.com
SIC: 3953 3993 Mfg Hand Stamps And Engraved Signs

(G-18830)
GREATER MANCHESTER SPORTS
35 Benjamin St (03109-4319)
PHONE..................................603 627-3892
Charlie Newton, *Owner*
EMP: 3
SALES (est): 126.8K **Privately Held**
SIC: 2711 Newspapers-Publishing/Printing

(G-18831)
GROLEN COMMUNICATIONS INC
814 Elm St Ste 101 (03101-2130)
PHONE..................................603 645-0101
Jon M Gross, *President*
John Gross, *Vice Pres*
Dave Stringer, *Opers Staff*
Edward J Lennon, *Treasurer*
EMP: 6
SQ FT: 9,500
SALES (est): 560K **Privately Held**
SIC: 3571 7375 8243 4813 Mfg Electronic Computers Information Retrieval Services

(G-18832)
HARVEY INDUSTRIES INC
725 Huse Rd (03103-2302)
PHONE..................................603 622-4232
Peter Gent, *Opers-Prdtn-Mfg*
EMP: 300
SALES (corp-wide): 1.2B **Privately Held**
SIC: 3442 Mfg Metal Doors/Sash/Trim
PA: Harvey Industries, Inc.
1400 Main St Fl 3
Waltham MA 02451
800 598-5400

(G-18833)
HINDSIGHT IMAGING INC
3 Waterford Way Unit 112 (03102-8113)
PHONE..................................607 793-3762
Arsen Hajian, *CEO*
EMP: 4 **EST:** 2015
SALES (est): 240K **Privately Held**
SIC: 3826 Mfg Analytical Instruments

(G-18834)
HIPPOPRESS LLC (PA)
Also Called: Qol Publications
49 Hollis St (03101-1239)
PHONE..................................603 625-1855
Jody Reese,
EMP: 35 **EST:** 2000

SALES (est): 2.2MM **Privately Held**
WEB: www.hippopress.com
SIC: 2711 Newspapers-Publishing/Printing

(G-18835)
HITACHI CABLE AMERICA INC
Performance Cable Systems
900 Holt Ave (03109-5604)
PHONE....................................603 669-4347
Mike Pruzin, *General Mgr*
Phil Facendola, *Design Engr*
Edward Austin, *Human Res Mgr*
Lucille Marston, *Info Tech Dir*
John Saggio, *Technician*
EMP: 175 **Privately Held**
SIC: 3357 Nonferrous Wiredrawing/Insulating
HQ: Hitachi Cable America Inc.
2 Manhattanville Rd # 301
Purchase NY 10577
914 694-9200

(G-18836)
HOLMRIS US INC
250 Commercial St # 2008 (03101-1142)
PHONE....................................603 232-3490
Michael Brandt, *President*
EMP: 4
SALES (est): 188.1K **Privately Held**
SIC: 2599 5712 Mfg Furniture/Fixtures Ret Furniture

(G-18837)
HOWARDS FUEL CO INC
24 Jane St (03104-5056)
P.O. Box 547, Pelham (03076-0547)
PHONE....................................603 635-9955
Howard Augenstein, *Owner*
EMP: 3 **EST:** 2008
SALES (est): 150K **Privately Held**
SIC: 2869 Mfg Industrial Organic Chemicals

(G-18838)
HUBBELL INCORPORATED
47 E Industrial Park Dr (03109-5311)
PHONE....................................603 647-5000
Lisa Robinson, *Opers Mgr*
Charles Ackerman, *Branch Mgr*
EMP: 147
SALES (corp-wide): 4.4B **Publicly Held**
SIC: 3643 3678 3694 Mfg Conductive Wiring Devices Mfg Electronic Connectors Mfg Engine Electrical Equipment
PA: Hubbell Incorporated
40 Waterview Dr
Shelton CT 06484
475 882-4000

(G-18839)
HUBSCRUB CO INC
1015 Candia Rd Unit 1 (03109-5253)
PHONE....................................603 624-4243
Karl Soderquist, *President*
EMP: 3
SQ FT: 7,200
SALES (est): 290K **Privately Held**
WEB: www.hubscrub.com
SIC: 3589 Mfg Automated Cleaning Systems

(G-18840)
HURLEY INK LLC
Also Called: AlphaGraphics
8 Perimeter Rd (03103-3307)
PHONE....................................603 645-0002
Paula Hurley, *Technology*
Timothy J Hurley,
EMP: 4
SQ FT: 2,500
SALES: 800K **Privately Held**
SIC: 2752 7334 Lithographic Commercial Printing Photocopying Services

(G-18841)
HYCON INC
349 E Industrial Park Dr (03109-5313)
PHONE....................................603 644-1414
Eero Hyvonen, *President*
Mika Hyvonen, *Treasurer*
Gregory Michaels, *Admin Sec*
EMP: 4
SQ FT: 24,500
SALES: 500K **Privately Held**
WEB: www.naplasticsltd.com
SIC: 3559 3613 8711 Mfg Misc Industry Machinery Mfg Switchgear/Switchboards Engineering Services

(G-18842)
INDUSTRIAL MARINE ELEC INC
Also Called: Production Process
8025 S Willow St Ste 207 (03103-2311)
PHONE....................................603 434-2309
Karl Ritzinger, *President*
Carolyn Ritzinger, *Treasurer*
EMP: 10
SALES (est): 1.8MM **Privately Held**
SIC: 3823 Mfg Process Control Instruments

(G-18843)
INTEGRATED DEICING SVCS LLC (DH)
Also Called: IDS
175 Ammon Dr (03103-3311)
PHONE....................................603 647-1717
Roger Langille, *President*
Scott Cummings, *General Mgr*
Bill Downing, *General Mgr*
Kevin Gill, *General Mgr*
Russell Herrington, *General Mgr*
EMP: 338
SQ FT: 1,800
SALES (est): 197.4MM
SALES (corp-wide): 95.2MM **Privately Held**
WEB: www.deicingsolutions.com
SIC: 3728 4581 Mfg Aircraft Parts/Equipment Airport/Airport Services
HQ: Inland Technologies Canada Incorporated
14 Queen St
Truro NS B2N 2
902 895-6346

(G-18844)
INTEGRATED DEICING SVCS LLC
175 Ammon Dr Unit 106 (03103-3311)
PHONE....................................603 647-1717
EMP: 219
SALES (corp-wide): 95.2MM **Privately Held**
SIC: 3728 Mfg Aircraft Parts/Equipment
HQ: Integrated Deicing Services, Llc
175 Ammon Dr
Manchester NH 03103
603 647-1717

(G-18845)
ITNH INC
150 Dow St (03101-1227)
PHONE....................................603 669-6900
Sasson Shemesh, *President*
Micheal Terlizzi, *Vice Pres*
Jacob Gilon, *CFO*
▲ **EMP:** 14
SQ FT: 10,000
SALES (est): 3.7MM **Privately Held**
WEB: www.itnh.com
SIC: 2752 Lithographic Commercial Printing

(G-18846)
J & D MACHINE
728 E Indus Pk Dr Unit 5 (03109-5631)
PHONE....................................603 624-9717
John Ambrose, *Owner*
EMP: 6
SQ FT: 4,000
SALES (est): 850K **Privately Held**
SIC: 3599 Mfg Industrial Machinery

(G-18847)
J & R LANGLEY CO INC
169 S Main St (03102-4498)
PHONE....................................603 622-9653
Robert R Schmidt, *President*
Kate Roop, *Principal*
Jennifer Jachowicz, *Sales Staff*
EMP: 15 **EST:** 1949
SQ FT: 10,000
SALES (est): 1.7MM **Privately Held**
WEB: www.jrlangley.com
SIC: 2391 5719 5023 Mfg Curtains/Drapery Ret Misc Homefurnishings Whol Homefurnishings

(G-18848)
JANICE MILLER
Also Called: Jaymill
150 Dow St Ste 4 (03101-1258)
PHONE....................................603 629-9995
Janice Miller, *President*
EMP: 7
SALES (est): 533.7K **Privately Held**
WEB: www.jaymil.com
SIC: 2511 Furniture

(G-18849)
JCP TRADING INC
Also Called: Venom Imaging
35 Elm St (03101-2719)
PHONE....................................603 232-0967
Jeff Polleck, *President*
EMP: 5
SQ FT: 8,800
SALES: 2.4MM **Privately Held**
SIC: 3751 Mfg Motorcycles/Bicycles

(G-18850)
JEWELL INSTRUMENTS LLC (PA)
Also Called: Modutec
850 Perimeter Rd (03103-3324)
PHONE....................................603 669-5121
Meyrick Mancebo, *General Mgr*
Mindy Forest, *Purch Mgr*
Neal Duffield, *Engineer*
Kyle Gagnon, *Engineer*
David Ramsey, *Engineer*
▲ **EMP:** 220
SQ FT: 60,000
SALES (est): 56.6MM **Privately Held**
WEB: www.jewellinstruments.com
SIC: 3823 Mfg Process Control Instruments

(G-18851)
JON SHAFTS & STUFF
347 Massabesic St (03103-3634)
PHONE....................................603 518-5033
Jon Larochelle, *Owner*
EMP: 4
SQ FT: 5,000
SALES (est): 356.9K **Privately Held**
SIC: 3714 7538 Mfg Motor Vehicle Parts General Auto Repair

(G-18852)
JP SERCEL ASSOCIATES INC
Also Called: Jpsa
220 Hackett Hill Rd (03102-8994)
PHONE....................................603 595-7048
Jeff Sercel, *President*
Kathy J Sercel, *Treasurer*
EMP: 90
SQ FT: 35,000
SALES (est): 13.1MM
SALES (corp-wide): 1.4B **Publicly Held**
WEB: www.jpsalaser.com
SIC: 3569 3699 Mfg General Industrial Machinery Mfg Electrical Equipment/Supplies
PA: Ipg Photonics Corporation
50 Old Webster Rd
Oxford MA 01540
508 373-1100

(G-18853)
JTC PRECISION SWISS INC
850 E Indus Pk Dr Ste 1 (03109-5635)
PHONE....................................603 935-9830
John Cieslik, *Principal*
EMP: 3
SALES (est): 443.5K **Privately Held**
SIC: 3451 Mfg Screw Machine Products

(G-18854)
KALWALL CORPORATION (PA)
1111 Candia Rd (03109-5211)
P.O. Box 237 (03105-0237)
PHONE....................................603 627-3861
Richard Keller, *President*
Katherine Garfield, *Corp Secy*
Amelia S Keller, *Vice Pres*
Sean Sullivan, *Materials Mgr*
Robert Busby, *Senior Engr*
◆ **EMP:** 450 **EST:** 1955
SQ FT: 100,000
SALES (est): 147.8MM **Privately Held**
WEB: www.kalwall.com
SIC: 3089 3083 Mfg Fiberglass Translucent Building Panels & Sheets

(G-18855)
KIMARK SPECIALTY BOX COMPANY
34 Beech St (03103-5612)
PHONE....................................603 668-1336
EMP: 26 **EST:** 1966
SQ FT: 25,000
SALES (est): 3.4MM **Privately Held**
WEB: www.kimarkbox.com
SIC: 3544 2657 Special Dies,Tools,Jigs,And Fixtures, Nsk

(G-18856)
KINNE ELECTRIC SERVICE COMPANY
155 Webster St (03104-2604)
PHONE....................................603 622-0441
Robert Morin, *President*
Debra Morin, *Corp Secy*
EMP: 5
SQ FT: 2,500
SALES (est): 785.1K **Privately Held**
SIC: 3694 Mfg Engine Electrical Equipment

(G-18857)
LADESCO INC
150 Dow St Ste 401 (03101-1241)
PHONE....................................603 623-3772
Wayne Trombly, *President*
Stephen Darling, *Prdtn Mgr*
Bernie Lavoie, *Engineer*
EMP: 150
SQ FT: 65,000
SALES (est): 15.7MM **Privately Held**
WEB: www.ladescoinc.com
SIC: 3677 Mfg Electronic Coils/Transformers

(G-18858)
LAIRD TECHNOLOGIES INC
1 Perimeter Rd Ste 1 # 1 (03103-3340)
PHONE....................................603 627-7877
Adam Alevy, *Vice Pres*
EMP: 10
SALES (corp-wide): 177.9K **Privately Held**
SIC: 3469 3663 Mfg Metal Stampings Mfg Radio/Tv Communication Equipment
HQ: Laird Technologies, Inc.
16401 Swingley Ridge Rd # 700
Chesterfield MO 63017
636 898-6000

(G-18859)
LANGER ASSOCIATES INC
55 South Commercial St B2 (03101-2606)
P.O. Box 1390, Merrimack (03054-1390)
PHONE....................................603 626-4388
Herbert Langer, *President*
EMP: 25
SQ FT: 1,500
SALES (est): 3.9MM **Privately Held**
WEB: www.langerplace.com
SIC: 3086 6531 Mfg Plastic Foam Products Real Estate Agent/Manager

(G-18860)
LARCHMONT ENGINEERING INC
180 Zachary Rd Ste 3 (03109-5623)
P.O. Box 6095 (03108-6095)
PHONE....................................603 622-8825
EMP: 3
SALES (corp-wide): 1.8MM **Privately Held**
WEB: www.larchmontengineering.com
SIC: 3523 3585 3561 Mfg Farm Machinery/Equipment Mfg Refrigeration/Heating Equipment Mfg Pumps/Pumping Equipment
PA: Larchmont Engineering, Inc.
12 Revere St
Lexington MA 02420
978 250-1260

(G-18861)
LASER GROUP PUBLISHING INC
177 E Industrial Park Dr (03109-5321)
P.O. Box 276, Nashua (03061-0276)
PHONE....................................603 880-8909
Jodi Valcourt, *President*
EMP: 10

SALES (est): 574.3K Privately Held
WEB: www.apartmentguide.com
SIC: 2721 Periodicals-Publishing/Printing
HQ: Consumer Source Inc.
3585 Engrg Dr Ste 100
Norcross GA 30092
678 421-3000

(G-18862)
LAWRENCE FAY
Also Called: Fay Electric Motors
93 Depot Rd (03103-6803)
PHONE....................603 668-3811
Wayne Fay, *Owner*
EMP: 5
SQ FT: 2,300
SALES (est): 448.1K Privately Held
WEB: www.fayelectricmotors.com
SIC: 7694 5063 Electric Motor Repair And Whol The Same

(G-18863)
LBRY INC
521 Pine St (03104-6058)
PHONE....................267 210-4292
Joshua Finer, *COO*
EMP: 5
SALES (est): 157.9K Privately Held
SIC: 2741 7389 Internet Publishing And Broadcasting

(G-18864)
LIBERTY PRESS INC
660 Mast Rd (03102-1218)
PHONE....................603 641-1991
J Claude Laroche, *President*
Randy Dufford, *Vice Pres*
EMP: 3
SALES (est): 382.1K Privately Held
SIC: 2752 Lithographic Commercial Printing

(G-18865)
LIVE WIRE MARKETING CORP
Also Called: Push603radio.com
26 Massabesic St (03103-4214)
PHONE....................603 969-8771
Marie Bertrand, *President*
Robesteur St Felix, *Vice Pres*
EMP: 3
SALES (est): 129.6K Privately Held
SIC: 2741 Internet Publishing And Broadcasting

(G-18866)
LYOPHILIZATION SVCS NENG INC (PA)
Also Called: L S N E
1 Sundial Ave Ste 112 (03103-7209)
PHONE....................603 626-5763
Matthew J Halvorsen, *President*
Shawn Cain, *COO*
Bob Haggerty, *Senior VP*
John Halvorsen, *Vice Pres*
Joe Hechavarria, *Vice Pres*
EMP: 17 EST: 1996
SQ FT: 10,000
SALES (est): 6.5MM Privately Held
WEB: www.lyophilization.com
SIC: 2836 2834 Mfg Biological Products Mfg Pharmaceutical Preparations

(G-18867)
MARMON AEROSPACE & DEFENSE LLC
Also Called: Rscc Aerospace & Defense
680 Hayward St (03103-4420)
PHONE....................603 622 3500
Tim Grass, *President*
Mike Dube, *Vice Pres*
▲ EMP: 75
SQ FT: 100,000
SALES (est): 19.7MM
SALES (corp-wide): 225.3B Publicly Held
SIC: 3357 Nonferrous Wiredrawing/Insulating
HQ: Marmon Energy Services Company
181 W Madison St Ste 2600
Chicago IL 60602
312 372-9500

(G-18868)
MAVERICK PHOTONICS LLC
2107 Elm St (03104-2316)
PHONE....................603 540-4434
Dane Hileman,
EMP: 4
SALES (est): 212.3K Privately Held
SIC: 3661 Mfg Telephone/Telegraph Apparatus

(G-18869)
MCLEAN COMMUNICATIONS LLC
50 Dow St (03101-1211)
PHONE....................603 624-1442
Sharron McCarthy, *President*
Ernesto Burden, *Vice Pres*
Angela Lebrun, *Sales Staff*
EMP: 82
SALES (est): 4.4MM
SALES (corp-wide): 16.6MM Privately Held
SIC: 2711 Newspapers-Publishing/Printing
PA: Yankee Publishing Incorporated
1121 Main St
Dublin NH 03444
603 563-8111

(G-18870)
MEASURED AIR PERFORMANCE LLC
250 Commercial St # 2015 (03101-1118)
PHONE....................603 606-8350
Steven Graves, *President*
EMP: 4
SQ FT: 2,400
SALES (est): 455.5K Privately Held
SIC: 3564 Mfg Blowers/Fans

(G-18871)
MICHAEL PERRA INC
640 Harvard St Ste 2 (03103-4481)
PHONE....................603 644-2110
Michael Perra, *President*
Randall Mikami, *Vice Pres*
EMP: 15
SQ FT: 21,000
SALES (est): 1.6MM Privately Held
SIC: 2511 Mfg Custom Wood Furniture

(G-18872)
MICROFAB INC
180 Zachary Rd Ste 1 (03109-5623)
PHONE....................603 621-9522
Wayne M Stauss, *President*
John Kelley, *Vice Pres*
EMP: 6 EST: 1999
SQ FT: 5,000
SALES: 1.4MM Privately Held
WEB: www.microfabinc.net
SIC: 3679 Mfg Electronic Components

(G-18873)
MICROSEMI CORPORATION
48 Abby Rd (03103-3314)
PHONE....................978 232-3793
EMP: 121
SALES (corp-wide): 5.3B Publicly Held
SIC: 3674 Mfg Semiconductors/Related Devices
HQ: Microsemi Corporation
1 Enterprise
Aliso Viejo CA 92656
949 380-6100

(G-18874)
MILL CITY LEATHER WORKS
31 Lavista St (03103-3935)
PHONE....................603 935-9974
EMP: 3
SALES (est): 223.2K Privately Held
SIC: 2431 Mfg Millwork

(G-18875)
MILLENNIUM PRECISION LLC
234 Abby Rd (03103-3332)
PHONE....................603 644-1555
Sean C Duclos, *President*
Eric K Filiatrault, *General Mgr*
Al Murelli, *Sales Mgr*
EMP: 5 EST: 2005
SALES (est): 1.1MM Privately Held
WEB: www.millenniumprecision.com
SIC: 3599 Mfg Industrial Machinery

(G-18876)
MITCH ROSEN EXTRAORDINARY GUNL
540 North Commercial St (03101-1122)
PHONE....................603 647-2971
Mitch Rosen, *Partner*
Nancy Rosen,
EMP: 10
SALES (est): 1.4MM Privately Held
SIC: 3199 Mfg Leather Goods

(G-18877)
MKIND INC
Also Called: Right Height Manufacturing
150 Dow St Ste 4 (03101-1258)
PHONE....................603 493-6882
Diane Kind, *President*
Michael Kind, *Vice Pres*
EMP: 8
SALES: 3.3MM Privately Held
SIC: 2522 5021 Mfg Office Furniture-Nonwood Whol Furniture

(G-18878)
MOTORWAY ENGINEERING INC
85 Hancock St (03101-2820)
PHONE....................603 668-6315
Joseph Johns, *President*
EMP: 10
SQ FT: 12,000
SALES: 2MM Privately Held
SIC: 3829 3751 Mfg Measuring/Controlling Devices Mfg Motorcycles/Bicycles

(G-18879)
MSN CORPORATION
Also Called: Budd Foods
431 Somerville St (03103-5129)
PHONE....................603 623-3528
Leo T Sprecher, *President*
Curtis J Marcott, *Corp Secy*
Fred Hayes, *VP Opers*
Richard Poole, *Purchasing*
EMP: 100
SQ FT: 30,000
SALES (est): 17.5MM Privately Held
WEB: www.chickenpies.com
SIC: 2013 2099 Mfg Prepared Meats Mfg Food Preparations

(G-18880)
MURRONEYS PRINTING INC
Also Called: McKeena Printing
2626 Brown Ave Ste 4 (03103-6835)
PHONE....................603 623-4677
Fred McKenna, *President*
EMP: 4
SQ FT: 3,800
SALES: 250K Privately Held
SIC: 2752 Lithographic Commercial Printing

(G-18881)
MY-T-MAN SCREEN PRINTING INC
540 North Commercial St (03101-1122)
PHONE....................603 622-7740
EMP: 12
SQ FT: 6,000
SALES: 750K Privately Held
WEB: www.mytman.com
SIC: 2262 7336 Screen Printing

(G-18882)
NEIGHBORHOOD NEWS
Also Called: Goffstown News
100 William Loeb Dr (03109-5309)
PHONE....................603 206-7800
Nackey Loeb, *President*
Terry Clark, *Accountant*
Lynn Kempf, *Accountant*
EMP: 30
SQ FT: 4,000
SALES (est): 1.9MM Privately Held
WEB: www.bowtimes.com
SIC: 2711 Newspapers-Publishing/Printing

(G-18883)
NEW ENGLAND BRAIDING CO INC
610 Gold St (03103-4005)
P.O. Box 4917 (03108-4917)
PHONE....................603 669-1987
Sally L Champlin, *President*
Jeff Zellers, *Admin Sec*
▲ EMP: 12
SQ FT: 17,000
SALES (est): 1.9MM Privately Held
SIC: 3053 Mfg Gaskets/Packing/Sealing Devices

(G-18884)
NEW HAMPSHIRE PLASTICS LLC
1 Bouchard St (03103-3313)
PHONE....................603 669-8523
Michael Desmarais, *President*
Gertrude Desmarais, *Vice Pres*
Mark Pimentel, *VP Opers*
Richard Desmarais, *CFO*
John Rioux, *Controller*
EMP: 75
SQ FT: 155,000
SALES (est): 33MM Privately Held
WEB: www.nhplastics.com
SIC: 2821 Mfg Plastic Materials/Resins

(G-18885)
NEW HAMPSHIRECOM
1662 Elm St Ste 100 (03101-1243)
PHONE....................603 314-0447
Dan O'Brien, *Principal*
EMP: 5 EST: 2011
SALES (est): 166.3K Privately Held
SIC: 2711 Newspapers-Publishing/Printing

(G-18886)
NEXT STEP BNICS PRSTHETICS INC (PA)
155 Dow St Ste 200 (03101-1299)
PHONE....................603 668-3831
Matthew J Albuquerque, *President*
Andrea Couture, *Manager*
EMP: 18
SQ FT: 7,500
SALES (est): 3.1MM Privately Held
WEB: www.nextstepoandp.com
SIC: 3842 Mfg Surgical Appliances/Supplies

(G-18887)
NORTH AMERICAN PLASTICS LTD
349 E Industrial Prk Dr (03109-5313)
PHONE....................603 644-1660
Eero J Hyvonen, *President*
Mika E Hyvonen, *Treasurer*
EMP: 20
SQ FT: 24,500
SALES (est): 3.9MM Privately Held
SIC: 3089 Mfg Plastic Products

(G-18888)
NORTHSTAR DIRECT LLC
249 Gay St (03103-6819)
P.O. Box 4352 (03108-4352)
PHONE....................603 627-3334
Tom Crowley, *COO*
Steve Arpaia, *Vice Pres*
Rich Morelli, *Vice Pres*
Cathy Klose, *Mng Member*
EMP: 10
SQ FT: 24,000
SALES (est): 2MM Privately Held
SIC: 2759 Commercial Printing

(G-18889)
NOUVEAU INTERIORS LLC
Also Called: Newbo Interiors
60 Rogers St (03103-5070)
PHONE....................603 398-1732
John Reuter,
EMP: 5
SQ FT: 7,000
SALES (est): 450K Privately Held
SIC: 2522 1799 7389 Mfg Office Furniture-Nonwood Trade Contractor Business Services

(G-18890)
NYLON CORPORATION AMERICA INC
Also Called: N Y C O A
333 Sundial Ave (03103-7216)
PHONE....................603 627-5150
Gregory Biederman, *Principal*
Paul Kennedy, *Business Mgr*
Pratik Shah, *Vice Pres*
Rita Markos, *Human Res Mgr*
◆ EMP: 60

GEOGRAPHIC

SQ FT: 150,000
SALES (est): 16.9MM
SALES (corp-wide): 30.1MM **Privately Held**
WEB: www.nycoa.net
SIC: 2821 Mfg Plastic Materials/Resins
PA: Metapoint Partners, A Limited Partnership
108 Beach St
Manchester MA 01944
978 531-1398

(G-18891)
NYLTECH NORTH AMERICA
333 Sundial Ave (03103-7216)
PHONE..................................603 627-5150
Anita Gladysz, *Cust Mgr*
EMP: 3 **EST:** 2013
SALES (est): 248.2K **Privately Held**
SIC: 2821 Mfg Plastic Materials/Resins

(G-18892)
OCEAN PREMIER SEAFOOD INC
174 Calef Rd Ste 1 (03103-6409)
PHONE..................................603 206-4787
EMP: 3 **EST:** 2013
SALES (est): 68.6K **Privately Held**
SIC: 2092 Mfg Fresh/Frozen Packaged Fish

(G-18893)
OLDCASTLE MATERIALS INC
1 Sundial Ave Ste 310 (03103-7299)
PHONE..................................603 669-2373
David Bissonnette, *Branch Mgr*
EMP: 9
SALES (corp-wide): 29.7B **Privately Held**
SIC: 3273 Mfg Ready-Mixed Concrete
HQ: Oldcastle Materials, Inc.
900 Ashwood Pkwy Ste 700
Atlanta GA 30338
-

(G-18894)
OLIVE LAKONIAN OIL LLC
561 Spruce St (03103-3527)
PHONE..................................603 264-5025
Panagiota Papastathis, *Principal*
EMP: 3 **EST:** 2015
SALES (est): 110.5K **Privately Held**
SIC: 2079 Mfg Edible Fats/Oils

(G-18895)
ON PINS & NEEDLES
20 Allen St (03102-5111)
PHONE..................................603 625-6573
EMP: 3
SALES (est): 158.4K **Privately Held**
SIC: 3452 Mfg Bolts/Screws/Rivets

(G-18896)
ORACLE CORPORATION
150 Dow St Ste 301 (03101-1254)
PHONE..................................603 668-4998
Victor Kuarsingh, *Engineer*
Dan Walulik, *Finance*
Brian Drouin, *Administration*
EMP: 44
SALES (corp-wide): 39.5B **Publicly Held**
SIC: 7372 Prepackaged Software Services
PA: Oracle Corporation
500 Oracle Pkwy
Redwood City CA 94065
650 506-7000

(G-18897)
PAPER THERMOMETER CO INC
62 Colin Dr (03103-3328)
P.O. Box 129, Greenfield (03047-0129)
PHONE..................................603 547-2034
Joseph D Loconti, *President*
Cathleen Duerig, *Principal*
Jo Anne Garvey, *Treasurer*
EMP: 6 **EST:** 1951
SALES (est): 665.5K **Privately Held**
SIC: 3823 Mfg Industrial Temperature Measurement Instruments Industrial Process Type

(G-18898)
PARAGON ELECTRONIC SYSTEMS
255 Coolidge Ave (03102-3206)
PHONE..................................603 645-7630
Chris Pearson, *President*
Jeff Ruthier, *President*
Bill McLaughlin, *Sales Engr*
EMP: 14
SQ FT: 3,000
SALES (est): 1.8MM **Privately Held**
WEB: www.paragonelect.com
SIC: 3674 Mfg Semiconductors/Related Devices

(G-18899)
PEPSI-COLA METRO BTLG CO INC
127 Pepsi Rd (03109-5305)
PHONE..................................603 625-5764
Dan Loura, *Branch Mgr*
EMP: 100
SALES (corp-wide): 64.6B **Publicly Held**
WEB: www.joy-of-cola.com
SIC: 2086 Mfg Bottled/Canned Soft Drinks
HQ: Pepsi-Cola Metropolitan Bottling Company, Inc.
1111 Westchester Ave
White Plains NY 10604
914 767-6000

(G-18900)
PERIMETER ACQUISITION CORP (HQ)
Also Called: Perimeter Technology
540 North Commercial St (03101-1122)
P.O. Box 16576, Hooksett (03106-6576)
PHONE..................................603 645-1616
Michael Dobbins, *President*
Kevin Rook, *Treasurer*
Gerome Artigliere, *Asst Treas*
EMP: 14
SQ FT: 20,000
SALES (est): 2.3MM
SALES (corp-wide): 151K **Privately Held**
WEB: www.perimetertechnology.com
SIC: 7372 Prepackaged Software Services

(G-18901)
PLAY TO WIN INC
183 Hayward St (03103-5504)
PHONE..................................603 669-6770
Evangelos Dusaitis, *President*
Gregory T Uliasz, *Admin Sec*
EMP: 4
SQ FT: 38,000
SALES (est): 499K **Privately Held**
SIC: 3599 Mfg Industrial Machinery

(G-18902)
PNE ENERGY SUPPLY LLC
1087 Elm St Ste 414 (03101-1853)
PHONE..................................603 413-6602
Megan McLaughlin, *Opers Staff*
Howard Plant, *Mng Member*
EMP: 3
SALES (est): 242.6K **Privately Held**
SIC: 3612 Mfg Transformers

(G-18903)
POLY-VAC INC
Also Called: Symmetry Medical Manufacturing
253 Abby Rd (03103-3333)
PHONE..................................603 647-7822
Barry Parker, *General Mgr*
Steve Geiger, *Opers Mgr*
Ryan Haas, *Safety Mgr*
Kevin Soper, *Production*
Shirley Goodwin, *Buyer*
EMP: 170
SALES (est): 30.2MM
SALES (corp-wide): 696.7MM **Privately Held**
WEB: www.symmetrymedical.com
SIC: 3842 3826 Mfg Surgical Appliances/Supplies Mfg Analytical Instruments
HQ: Symmetry Medical Inc.
3724 N State Road 15
Warsaw IN 46582
-

(G-18904)
PRECISION LETTER CORPORATION
396 Pepsi Rd (03109-5303)
PHONE..................................603 625-9625
Robert Elrick, *President*
▲ **EMP:** 18
SQ FT: 10,000
SALES (est): 1.8MM **Privately Held**
WEB: www.precisionletter.com
SIC: 3089 3993 Mfg Acrylic & Metal Letters & Panels

(G-18905)
PRINTERS SQUARE INC
Also Called: Talient Action Group
105 Faltin Dr (03103-5755)
PHONE..................................603 623-0802
Sean Owen, *President*
EMP: 16
SQ FT: 2,600
SALES (est): 2.6MM **Privately Held**
SIC: 2752 7311 Lithographic Commercial Printing Advertising Agency

(G-18906)
PRO DOUGH INC
8030 S Willow St Unit 2-7 (03103-2321)
PHONE..................................603 623-6844
Tim Gyorda, *CEO*
EMP: 11
SALES (est): 1.1MM **Privately Held**
SIC: 2041 5812 Mfg Flour/Grain Mill Prooducts Eating Place

(G-18907)
QUEEN CITY EXAMINER
112 Auburn St (03103-6239)
PHONE..................................603 289-6835
Glenn Rj Ouellette, *Principal*
EMP: 3
SALES (est): 136.5K **Privately Held**
SIC: 2711 Newspapers-Publishing/Printing

(G-18908)
QUEEN CITY SOUNDS INC
Also Called: Macdonald Associates
419 Somerville St (03103-5135)
PHONE..................................603 668-4306
Robert Bullard, *President*
Pauline Bullard, *Vice Pres*
EMP: 4
SALES (est): 427.7K **Privately Held**
WEB: www.queencitysound.com
SIC: 3498 Mfg Fabricated Pipe/Fittings

(G-18909)
RCD COMPONENTS LLC (HQ)
520 E Industrial Park (03109-5316)
PHONE..................................603 666-4627
Louis M Arcidy, *President*
Alfred C Arcidy, *Vice Pres*
Mark A Arcidy, *Vice Pres*
Maria L Grisanzio, *Vice Pres*
Michael J Arcidy, *CFO*
◆ **EMP:** 100
SQ FT: 48,000
SALES (est): 17.1MM
SALES (corp-wide): 18.7MM **Privately Held**
WEB: www.rcd-comp.com
SIC: 3676 3677 3829 Mfg Electronic Resistors Mfg Electronic Coils/Transformers Mfg Measuring/Controlling Devices
PA: Gowanda Holdings, Llc
1 Magnetic Pkwy
Gowanda NY 14070
716 532-2234

(G-18910)
RETRIEVE LLC
Also Called: Retrieve Technologies
50 Commercial St Ste 35s (03101)
PHONE..................................603 413-0022
Dave Arnold, *CEO*
John Rogers, *CFO*
Robert Curtis, *Sales Dir*
Francis Kelleher, *Marketing Staff*
John Bennett, *Manager*
EMP: 45
SALES (est): 4.2MM **Privately Held**
SIC: 7372 Prepackaged Software Services

(G-18911)
RGM ENTERPRISES INC
Also Called: Spillers Repro Graphics
880 2nd St (03102-5214)
PHONE..................................603 644-3336
Josh Szasranski, *Manager*
Chris Martel, *Manager*
EMP: 4
SALES (corp-wide): 5.6MM **Privately Held**
WEB: www.spillersusa.com
SIC: 2759 Commercial Printing
PA: Rgm Enterprises, Inc.
34 Lexington St
Lewiston ME 04240
207 784-1571

(G-18912)
RSCC WIRE & CABLE LLC
680 Hayward St (03103-4420)
PHONE..................................603 622-3500
Demitri Maistrellis, *President*
EMP: 80
SALES (corp-wide): 225.3B **Publicly Held**
SIC: 3357 Insulating Of Non Ferrous Wire And Cable
HQ: Rscc Wire & Cable Llc
20 Bradley Park Rd
East Granby CT 06026
-

(G-18913)
RX GREEN SOLUTIONS LLC
873 Page St Fl 2 (03109-4637)
P.O. Box 3213 (03105-3213)
PHONE..................................603 769-3450
Wes Matelich, *COO*
Chip Provost, *Sales Staff*
Todd Brady, *Mng Member*
EMP: 18 **EST:** 2011
SALES (est): 2.1MM **Privately Held**
SIC: 2875 Mfg Fertilizers-Mix Only

(G-18914)
SANMINA CORPORATION
140 Abby Rd (03103-3319)
PHONE..................................603 621-1800
Rob Walker, *Vice Pres*
Jose Carraskuillo, *Plant Mgr*
Nancy Flynn, *Senior Buyer*
Craig Giroux, *Engineer*
Doug Schancer, *Design Engr*
EMP: 124 **Publicly Held**
WEB: www.sanmina.com
SIC: 3672 Mfg Printed Circuit Boards
PA: Sanmina Corporation
2700 N 1st St
San Jose CA 95134
-

(G-18915)
SANT BANI PRESS INC
60 Buckley Cir Ste 3 (03109-5236)
PHONE..................................603 286-3114
Joseph Gelbard, *President*
Richard Shannon, *Vice Pres*
EMP: 12
SQ FT: 8,000
SALES (est): 747.6K
SALES (corp-wide): 3.2MM **Privately Held**
WEB: www.santbanipress.com
SIC: 2752 Offset Commercial Printing
PA: Morgan Press, Inc.
60 Buckley Cir Ste 3
Manchester NH
603 624-8660

(G-18916)
SAVVY WORKSHOP
55 South Commercial St (03101-2606)
PHONE..................................603 792-0080
Lisa Landry, *President*
Joseph Landry, *Vice Pres*
EMP: 7 **EST:** 1998
SQ FT: 2,000
SALES (est): 1MM **Privately Held**
WEB: www.printsavvy.com
SIC: 2759 7336 Commercial Printing Commercial Art/Graphic Design

(G-18917)
SCANSMART LLC
66 Valentine Dr (03103-2362)
PHONE..................................603 664-7773
Celest Dakoulas,
EMP: 3
SALES (est): 160K **Privately Held**
WEB: www.scansmart-usa.com
SIC: 2791 Typesetting Services

▲ = Import ▼=Export
◆ =Import/Export

(G-18918)
SCHLEUNIGER INC (DH)
87 Colin Dr (03103-3330)
PHONE..................................603 627-4860
Christoph Schupbach, *CEO*
Darren Teasck, *President*
Stefan Breu, *COO*
Jorg Gutowski, *CFO*
▲ **EMP:** 40
SQ FT: 42,000
SALES (est): 15.1MM
SALES (corp-wide): 1.2B **Privately Held**
WEB: www.schleuniger.com
SIC: 3569 Mfg General Industrial Machinery
HQ: Schleuniger Holding Ag
Bierigutstrasse 9
Thun BE 3608
333 340-333

(G-18919)
SCREEN PRINTED SPECIAL TS
18 Lake Ave (03101-2406)
PHONE..................................603 622-2901
Donald York, *Owner*
EMP: 3
SQ FT: 1,500
SALES (est): 272.4K **Privately Held**
SIC: 2261 7389 Screen Printing & Embroidery Of Garments Specializing In Athletic Wear And All Textiles

(G-18920)
SECRET GUIDE TO COMPUTERS
Also Called: Russ Walter Publishing
196 Tiffany Ln (03104-4782)
PHONE..................................603 666-6644
Russell Walter, *Owner*
▼ **EMP:** 3
SALES: 14.8K **Privately Held**
WEB: www.secretguide.net
SIC: 2731 7389 Books-Publishing/Printing Business Serv Non-Commercial Site

(G-18921)
SEMPER FI POWER SUPPLY INC
21 W Auburn St Ste 29 (03101-2386)
PHONE..................................603 656-9729
David Pitts, *President*
▲ **EMP:** 12
SQ FT: 15,000
SALES (est): 1.6MM **Privately Held**
WEB: www.semperfipowersupply.com
SIC: 3612 Mfg Power Transformers

(G-18922)
SIGN EXPRESS LLC
120 Edmond St (03102-1438)
PHONE..................................603 606-1279
Roland Paradis, *Owner*
EMP: 4
SALES (est): 202.8K **Privately Held**
SIC: 2741 Misc Publishing

(G-18923)
SIGNIFY NORTH AMERICA CORP
386 Commercial St (03101)
PHONE..................................603 645-6061
Leverda Wallace, *Surgery Dir*
EMP: 190
SALES (corp-wide): 7B **Privately Held**
SIC: 3646 Mfg Commercial Lighting Fixtures
HQ: Signify North America Corporation
200 Franklin Square Dr
Somerset NJ 08873
732 563-3000

(G-18924)
SILVER GRAPHICS
200 Gay St Ste 1 (03103-7098)
PHONE..................................603 669-6955
Bertram Silver, *Owner*
EMP: 3
SALES: 150K **Privately Held**
WEB: www.silvergraphicsllc.com
SIC: 2395 Pleating/Stitching Services

(G-18925)
SIR SPEEDY
41 Elm St (03101-2719)
PHONE..................................603 625-6868
Richard Stonner, *Partner*
Doreen Stonner, *Partner*
Jason Stonner, *Finance*
Rick Stonner, *Sales Staff*
EMP: 5
SQ FT: 1,800
SALES (est): 762.3K **Privately Held**
SIC: 2752 Comm Prtg Litho

(G-18926)
SOPHIA INSTITUTE
525 Greeley St (03102-2340)
P.O. Box 5284 (03108-5284)
PHONE..................................603 641-9344
EMP: 8
SALES: 2.1MM **Privately Held**
SIC: 2741 Misc Publishing

(G-18927)
SOUHEGAN MANAGEMENT CORP
Also Called: Pie Guy, The
99 Faltin Dr (03103-5755)
PHONE..................................603 898-8868
Christopher Burnley, *President*
EMP: 40
SALES (est): 10MM **Privately Held**
SIC: 2051 Mfg Bread/Related Products

(G-18928)
SPECTRUM MARKETING DBALOGO LOC
95 Eddy Rd Ste 101 (03102-3258)
PHONE..................................603 644-4800
Matt Provost, *Owner*
▲ **EMP:** 7
SALES (est): 942.2K **Privately Held**
SIC: 2241 2759 Narrow Fabric Mills, Nsk

(G-18929)
SQUARE SPOT PUBLISHING LLC
79 Pleasant St Ste 2 (03101-2319)
P.O. Box 999, Middlebury VT (05753-0999)
PHONE..................................603 625-6003
Kara N Sweeney Esq, *Administration*
EMP: 4
SALES (est): 265K **Privately Held**
SIC: 2741 Misc Publishing

(G-18930)
STERALON INC
7 Perimeter Rd Ste 10 (03103-3343)
PHONE..................................603 296-0490
Carol Jones, *President*
EMP: 3
SALES (est): 349.2K **Privately Held**
WEB: www.steralon.com
SIC: 3841 Mfg Surgical/Medical Instruments

(G-18931)
SULEYS SOCCER CENTER
1525 S Willow St Unit 3 (03103-3209)
PHONE..................................603 668-7227
Suley Doemmez, *Owner*
EMP: 4
SALES (est): 370.6K **Privately Held**
SIC: 2759 5941 Commercial Printing Ret Sporting Goods/Bicycles

(G-18932)
SUMMIT PACKAGING SYSTEMS INC (PA)
Also Called: SPS
400 Gay St (03103-6817)
P.O. Box 5304 (03108-5304)
PHONE..................................603 669-5410
Gordon C Gilroy, *President*
Kyle Kienia, *Safety Mgr*
Michael Conway, *CFO*
Scott N Gilroy, *Treasurer*
Scott Gilroy, *Treasurer*
◆ **EMP:** 400 **EST:** 1975
SQ FT: 200,000
SALES (est): 149.7MM **Privately Held**
WEB: www.summitpkg.com
SIC: 3499 3089 Mfg Misc Fabricated Metal Products Mfg Plastic Products

(G-18933)
SUNGARD INSURANCE SYSTEMS INC
250 Commercial St # 4004 (03101-1142)
PHONE..................................603 641-3636
William Gray, *Manager*
EMP: 3
SALES (corp-wide): 8.4B **Publicly Held**
WEB: www.sungardinsurance.com
SIC: 7372 7371 Prepackaged Software Services Custom Computer Programing
HQ: Sungard Insurance Systems Inc.
3150 Holcomb Bridge Rd
Norcross GA 30071
678 942-2500

(G-18934)
SWANSONS DIE CO INC
141 Queen City Ave (03101-7121)
PHONE..................................603 623-3832
William Swanson, *President*
Janice Swanson, *Corp Secy*
Judith Cassidy, *Treasurer*
Stephen Cohen, *Admin Sec*
EMP: 35
SQ FT: 4,000
SALES (est): 4MM **Privately Held**
WEB: www.swansondie.com
SIC: 3544 3423 Mfg Dies/Tools/Jigs/Fixtures Mfg Hand/Edge Tools

(G-18935)
TALIENT ACTION GROUP
105 Faltin Dr (03103-5755)
PHONE..................................603 703-0795
Sean Owen, *Owner*
EMP: 20
SALES (est): 297.4K **Privately Held**
SIC: 2759 Commercial Printing

(G-18936)
TEAMEDA INC
1001 Elm St 305 (03101-1828)
PHONE..................................603 656-5200
Guy D Haas, *President*
EMP: 7
SALES: 850K **Privately Held**
WEB: www.teameda.com
SIC: 7372 Prepackaged Software Services

(G-18937)
TECHLOK INC
125 Ray St (03104-2538)
PHONE..................................617 902-0322
EMP: 6
SALES (est): 310K **Privately Held**
SIC: 7372 Prepackaged Software

(G-18938)
TEMCO TOOL COMPANY INC
800 Holt Ave (03109-5601)
P.O. Box 5031 (03108-5031)
PHONE..................................603 622-6989
Norman Paul Gagne, *President*
Colleen Ann Gagne, *Treasurer*
EMP: 36 **EST:** 1963
SQ FT: 28,000
SALES (est): 11.8MM **Privately Held**
WEB: www.temcotool.com
SIC: 3544 Mfg Dies/Tools/Jigs/Fixtures

(G-18939)
TEXAS INSTRUMENTS INCORPORATED
50 Phillippe Cote St # 100 (03101-3105)
PHONE..................................603 222-8500
Martin Cardella, *Engineer*
Paul Casparro, *Engineer*
Alberto Jimeno, *Engineer*
Illya Kovarik, *Engineer*
Sean Meehan, *Engineer*
EMP: 10
SALES (corp-wide): 15.7B **Publicly Held**
SIC: 3674 Mfg Semiconductors & Related Devices
PA: Texas Instruments Incorporated
12500 Ti Blvd
Dallas TX 75243
214 479-3773

(G-18940)
TEXTILES COATED INCORPORATED
200 Bouchard St (03103-3309)
P.O. Box 5768 (03108-5768)
PHONE..................................603 296-2221
John W Tippett, *CEO*
EMP: 175
SALES (corp-wide): 19.6MM **Privately Held**
SIC: 2821 2295 Mfg Plastic Materials/Resins Mfg Coated Fabrics
PA: Textiles Coated, Incorporated
6 George Ave
Londonderry NH 03053
603 296-2221

(G-18941)
THIBCO INC
41 Alpheus St (03103-5706)
PHONE..................................603 623-3011
Gerard L Thibodeau, *President*
Richard E Bellerose, *Vice Pres*
EMP: 40
SALES (est): 4.2MM **Privately Held**
WEB: www.thibco.com
SIC: 2431 1751 Carpentry Contractor Mfg Millwork

(G-18942)
TOLLES COMMUNICATIONS CORP
103 Bay St (03104-3007)
PHONE..................................603 627-9500
Irvin Tolles, *President*
EMP: 7
SQ FT: 1,600
SALES (est): 316.3K **Privately Held**
SIC: 2711 7389 Newspapers-Publishing/Printing Business Services

(G-18943)
TYLER TECHNOLOGIES INC
Advanced Data Systems
307 Highlander Way (03103-7405)
PHONE..................................800 288-8167
Gene Richardson, *Branch Mgr*
EMP: 4
SALES (corp-wide): 935.2MM **Publicly Held**
WEB: www.tylertechnologies.com
SIC: 7372 Prepackaged Software Services
PA: Tyler Technologies, Inc.
5101 Tennyson Pkwy
Plano TX 75024
972 713-3700

(G-18944)
UNION LEADER CORPORATION (PA)
Also Called: New Hampshire Union Leader
100 William Loeb Dr (03109-5309)
P.O. Box 9555 (03108-9555)
PHONE..................................603 668-4321
Joseph W McQuaid, *President*
Susan Clark, *Editor*
Jennifer Lord, *Editor*
Tom Lynch, *Editor*
Matt Sartwell, *Editor*
EMP: 324 **EST:** 1946
SQ FT: 167,000
SALES (est): 40.9MM **Privately Held**
WEB: www.unionleader.com
SIC: 2711 Newspapers-Publishing/Printing

(G-18945)
UNITRODE CORPORATION (HQ)
50 Phillippe Cote St # 100 (03101-3105)
PHONE..................................603 222-8500
Edward H Browder, *President*
James Noon, *Principal*
Allan R Campbell, *Senior VP*
EMP: 500 **EST:** 1960
SQ FT: 174,400
SALES (est): 51.1MM
SALES (corp-wide): 15.7B **Publicly Held**
WEB: www.uicc.com
SIC: 3674 Mfg Integrated Circuits
PA: Texas Instruments Incorporated
12500 Ti Blvd
Dallas TX 75243
214 479-3773

(G-18946)
UNIVERSAL HINGE CORP
114 Bay St Ste 100 (03104-3000)
PHONE..................................603 935-9848
E Depietro, *Branch Mgr*
EMP: 6
SALES (est): 539.4K
SALES (corp-wide): 1.1MM **Privately Held**
SIC: 3429 Mfg Hardware
PA: Universal Hinge Corp.
18 Newton Rd
Westminster MA 01473
603 935-9848

GEOGRAPHIC

(G-18947)
UNIVERSAL SYSTEMS USA INC
21 W Auburn St Ste 22 (03101-2386)
PHONE..................................603 222-9070
James Haythornthwait, *CEO*
EMP: 12
SALES (est): 2MM **Privately Held**
SIC: 2821 Mfg Plastic Materials/Resins

(G-18948)
VELCRO INC (HQ)
95 Sundial Ave (03103-7230)
P.O. Box 4806 (03108-4806)
PHONE..................................603 669-4880
Alain Zijlstra, *President*
A John Holton, *President*
Michael Cina, *Engineer*
Evan Leonard, *Engineer*
Fraser Cameron, *Treasurer*
◆ **EMP:** 650
SQ FT: 300,000
SALES (est): 290MM **Privately Held**
SIC: 2241 Narrow Fabric Mill

(G-18949)
VELCRO USA INC (DH)
95 Sundial Ave (03103-7230)
PHONE..................................603 669-4880
Scott M Filion, *President*
Thomas Potterfield, *Principal*
Boris P Hadshi, *Vice Pres*
Samantha O'Neil, *Vice Pres*
Mike Morrison, *Plant Mgr*
◆ **EMP:** 800
SQ FT: 400,000
SALES (est): 290MM **Privately Held**
WEB: www.velcro.com
SIC: 2241 3965 Narrow Fabric Mill Mfg Fasteners/Buttons/Pins
HQ: Velcro, Inc.
95 Sundial Ave
Manchester NH 03103
603 669-4880

(G-18950)
VIBRAC LLC (PA)
1050 Perimeter Rd Ste 600 (03103-3355)
P.O. Box 840, Amherst (03031-0840)
PHONE..................................603 882-6777
Thomas Rogers, *President*
Robert Searle, *Vice Pres*
◆ **EMP:** 13
SQ FT: 10,000
SALES (est): 1.4MM **Privately Held**
WEB: www.vibrac.com
SIC: 3829 Mfg Measuring/Controlling Devices

(G-18951)
VICOR CORPORATION
Also Called: Granite Power Technologies
540 N Coml St Ste 210 (03101)
PHONE..................................603 623-3222
Tom Duff, *Manager*
EMP: 16
SALES (corp-wide): 291.2MM **Publicly Held**
WEB: www.vicoreurope.com
SIC: 3629 Mfg Power Conversion Devices
PA: Vicor Corporation
25 Frontage Rd
Andover MA 01810
978 470-2900

(G-18952)
VIRTUAL PUBLISHING LLC
103 Bay St (03104-3007)
PHONE..................................603 627-9500
Irv Tolles, *Owner*
EMP: 12
SALES (est): 550.6K **Privately Held**
SIC: 2741 Misc Publishing

(G-18953)
VISION WINE & SPIRITS LLC
540 N Coml St Ste 311 (03101)
PHONE..................................781 278-2000
Dean Williams, *General Mgr*
Dan Lasner, *Mng Member*
▲ **EMP:** 15
SALES: 15MM
SALES (corp-wide): 25.5MM **Privately Held**
SIC: 2084 Mfg Wines/Brandy/Spirits
PA: Martignetti Companies, Inc.
500 John Hancock Rd
Taunton MA 02780
800 862-4585

(G-18954)
WAVELINK LLC
800 Holt Ave (03109-5601)
P.O. Box 4358 (03108-4358)
PHONE..................................603 606-7489
Norman Gagne, *Mng Member*
Colleen Gagne,
▲ **EMP:** 10
SALES (est): 1.5MM **Privately Held**
SIC: 3678 Mfg Industrial Machinery

(G-18955)
WHITE MOUNTAIN DISTILLERY LLC
2072 Elm St (03104-2315)
PHONE..................................603 391-1306
Stefan Windler, *Principal*
EMP: 6
SALES (est): 513.2K **Privately Held**
SIC: 2085 Mfg Distilled/Blended Liquor

(G-18956)
XAVIER CORPORATION
124 Plymouth St (03102-4100)
PHONE..................................603 668-8892
Daniel Morin, *President*
EMP: 3
SQ FT: 1,500
SALES: 90K **Privately Held**
SIC: 3822 Mfg Thermostats

(G-18957)
XCALIBUR COMMUNICATIONS
95 Charlotte St (03103-7032)
PHONE..................................603 625-9555
EMP: 4 **EST:** 2005
SALES: 250K **Privately Held**
WEB: www.xcaliburcommunications.com
SIC: 3825 Mfg Electrical Measuring Instruments

(G-18958)
XMA CORPORATION
Also Called: Omni Spectra
7 Perimeter Rd Ste 2 (03103-3343)
PHONE..................................603 222-2256
Marc Smith, *President*
Debbi Leuteritz, *Purchasing*
Peter F Richard, *Finance*
Kelley Carr, *Director*
Bruce W Cooper, *Admin Sec*
▲ **EMP:** 30
SQ FT: 10,000
SALES (est): 6.6MM **Privately Held**
WEB: www.xmacorp.com
SIC: 3678 Mfg Electronic Connectors

Marlborough
Cheshire County

(G-18959)
ELECTRONICS AID INC
32 Roxbury Rd (03455-2215)
P.O. Box 325 (03455-0325)
PHONE..................................603 876-4161
Joel Seavey, *General Mgr*
Carroll Willson, *Vice Pres*
EMP: 9
SQ FT: 5,500
SALES (est): 143.6K **Privately Held**
WEB: www.electronicsaidinc.com
SIC: 3672 3679 3678 3699 Mfg Printed Circuit Boards Mfg Electronic Components Mfg Electronic Connectors Mfg Elec Mach/Equip/Supp

(G-18960)
INKBERRY
107 Main St (03455-2132)
PHONE..................................603 876-4880
Ronald Yantiss, *Owner*
EMP: 6
SALES (est): 250K **Privately Held**
WEB: www.inkberry.com
SIC: 2499 Mfg Wood Products

(G-18961)
KING & CO ARCHITECTURAL WDWKG
Also Called: King & Co Architectural Wdwkg
8 Roxbury Rd (03455-2215)
PHONE..................................603 876-4900
Robert C King, *Owner*
Nate Clay, *Opers Staff*
EMP: 4
SQ FT: 1,400
SALES (est): 503.4K **Privately Held**
WEB: www.kingstair.com
SIC: 2434 2431 Mfg Wood Kitchen Cabinets Mfg Millwork

(G-18962)
MIKE SEQUORE
Also Called: M H S Architectural Millwork
7 Roxbury Rd (03455-2217)
PHONE..................................603 876-4634
Mike Sequore, *Owner*
EMP: 3
SQ FT: 3,500
SALES (est): 251.1K **Privately Held**
SIC: 2499 5211 Mfg Custom Millwork

(G-18963)
MOUNTAIN CORPORATION
10 Wilcox Ct (03455)
PHONE..................................603 876-3630
Michael Krinsky, *Manager*
EMP: 65
SALES (corp-wide): 50.1MM **Privately Held**
SIC: 2253 2396 Knit Outerwear Mill/ Tee Shirts
PA: The Mountain Corporation
59 Optical Ave
Keene NH 03431
603 355-2272

(G-18964)
PHYSICAL MEASUREMENT TECH
4 Ling St (03455-2427)
P.O. Box 400 (03455-0400)
PHONE..................................603 876-9990
Gregory Lorsbach, *President*
Heidi Bushway, *Vice Pres*
EMP: 7
SALES (est): 700K **Privately Held**
WEB: www.pmtvib.com
SIC: 3825 Mfg Electrical Measuring Instruments

Marlow
Cheshire County

(G-18965)
AUDIO ACCESSORIES INC
Also Called: Audio Line
25 Mill St (03456-6340)
P.O. Box 360 (03456-0360)
PHONE..................................603 446-3335
MB Hall, *President*
Timothy Symonds, *Vice Pres*
David Hall, *Treasurer*
Homer S Bradley Jr, *Admin Sec*
▲ **EMP:** 40 **EST:** 1946
SQ FT: 12,000
SALES (est): 6.6MM **Privately Held**
WEB: www.patchbays.com
SIC: 3663 Mfg Radio/Tv Communication Equipment

(G-18966)
BRAZEN INNOVATIONS INC
40 Davis Dr (03456-6412)
P.O. Box 30 (03456-0030)
PHONE..................................603 446-7919
Edith Stearns, *President*
Dan Stearns, *Vice Pres*
▲ **EMP:** 5
SALES (est): 690.2K **Privately Held**
WEB: www.brazeninnovations.com
SIC: 7692 3398 Welding Repair Metal Heat Treating

Mason
Hillsborough County

(G-18967)
GRANITE STATE CASTING
127 Fitchburg Rd (03048-4717)
P.O. Box 33, Greenville (03048-0033)
PHONE..................................603 878-2759
James Roddy, *Partner*
Thomas Dalton, *Partner*
John Roddy Jr, *Partner*
EMP: 8
SQ FT: 8,000
SALES (est): 900K **Privately Held**
SIC: 3365 3366 Aluminum Foundry Copper Foundry

(G-18968)
HAMCO TANK SYSTEMS LLC
815 Hurricane Hill Rd (03048-3904)
PHONE..................................603 878-0585
Jeff Hamel,
EMP: 6
SALES (est): 381K **Privately Held**
WEB: www.hamcotanksystems.com
SIC: 1389 5112 Oil/Gas Field Services And Sales

(G-18969)
MAILLET CONSTRUCTION
129 Campbell Mill Rd (03048-4902)
P.O. Box 492, New Ipswich (03071-0492)
PHONE..................................603 582-2810
Eric Maillet, *President*
EMP: 5
SALES (est): 510K **Privately Held**
SIC: 1389 1711 1794 1761 Oil/Gas Field Services Plumbing/Heat/Ac Contr Excavation Contractor Roofing/Siding Contr

(G-18970)
MASON GRAPEVINE LLC
Also Called: Mason Grapevine, The
780 Starch Mill Rd (03048-4003)
PHONE..................................603 878-4272
Pamela Lassen,
EMP: 3
SALES (est): 137.1K **Privately Held**
SIC: 2711 Newspapers-Publishing/Printing

Meredith
Belknap County

(G-18971)
BLISS LOGGING
47 Old Center Harbor Rd (03253-6405)
PHONE..................................603 279-5674
P Bliss, *Principal*
EMP: 3
SALES (est): 257.7K **Privately Held**
SIC: 2411 Logging

(G-18972)
COMSTOCK INDUSTRIES INC
Foundry Ave (03253)
PHONE..................................603 279-7045
Richard Dwight Comstock Jr, *President*
Kathleen Mae Comstock, *Vice Pres*
EMP: 35
SQ FT: 17,400
SALES (est): 7.3MM **Privately Held**
WEB: www.comstockindustries.com
SIC: 3599 3089 3544 Mfg Industrial Machinery Mfg Plastic Products Mfg Dies/Tools/Jigs/Fixtures

(G-18973)
DISCERNING PALATE LLC (PA)
Also Called: Genuine Local
21 Corliss Hill Rd (03253-5203)
PHONE..................................603 279-8600
Mary Macdonald, *CEO*
Gavin Macdonald, *Principal*
EMP: 3 **EST:** 2016
SALES (est): 363.6K **Privately Held**
SIC: 2099 Mfg Food Preparations

(G-18974)
HERMIT WOODS INC
72 Main St (03253-5841)
PHONE..................................603 253-7968
Kenneth Hardcastle, *Treasurer*
EMP: 4
SALES (est): 217.5K **Privately Held**
SIC: 2084 Mfg Wines/Brandy/Spirits

(G-18975)
MISS PRINT
1 Meredith Center Rd (03253-7605)
PHONE..................................603 279-5939
Paul Bradley, *Owner*
EMP: 3
SALES (est): 238.9K **Privately Held**
SIC: 2752 Lithographic Commercial Printing

(G-18976)
OMNI SIGNS LLC
6 Wall St (03253-6006)
PHONE..................................603 279-1492
Paul Euiler, *Principal*
Beth Euiler,
EMP: 4
SQ FT: 3,000
SALES: 220K **Privately Held**
SIC: 3993 Mfg Signs

(G-18977)
REMCON-NORTH CORPORATION
7-9 Enterprise Ct (03253)
P.O. Box 957 (03253-0957)
PHONE..................................603 279-7091
Marie P Remson, *President*
EMP: 57 **EST:** 1966
SQ FT: 31,000
SALES (est): 9.2MM **Privately Held**
WEB: www.remcon-north.com
SIC: 3679 Mfg Electronic Components

(G-18978)
SALMON PRESS LLC (PA)
Also Called: Berlyn Reporter
5 Water St (03253-6233)
P.O. Box 729 (03253-0729)
PHONE..................................603 279-4516
John Coots, *Mng Member*
David Cutler,
EMP: 15
SALES (est): 5.3MM **Privately Held**
WEB: www.courier-littletonnh.com
SIC: 2711 Newspapers-Publishing/Printing

(G-18979)
SIBS LLC
Also Called: Kohv Eyewear
114 Upper Mile Point Dr (03253-5740)
PHONE..................................781 864-7498
Bryan S Biederman,
Nathaniel Dutile,
EMP: 3 **EST:** 2015
SALES (est): 133.6K **Privately Held**
SIC: 3851 5099 Mfg Ophthalmic Goods Whol Durable Goods

(G-18980)
TRIANGLE SHEET METAL INC
170 Waukewan St (03253-6023)
P.O. Box 955 (03253-0955)
PHONE..................................603 393-6770
Steven Brady, *President*
EMP: 3
SALES: 200K **Privately Held**
SIC: 3444 Mfg Sheet Metalwork

(G-18981)
TUCKER MOUNTAIN HOMES INC
Also Called: Rustic Renditions
26 Tucker Mountain Rd (03253-4825)
P.O. Box 1754 (03253-1754)
PHONE..................................603 279-4320
Lionel Moureir, *President*
EMP: 3
SALES (est): 299K **Privately Held**
SIC: 3423 2452 1799 Mfg Hand/Edge Tools Mfg Prefabricated Wood Buildings Trade Contractor

(G-18982)
WINNEPESAUKEE FORGE INC
5 Winona Rd (03253-6010)
P.O. Box 928 (03253-0928)
PHONE..................................603 279-5492
David Little, *President*
Heidi Little, *Vice Pres*
EMP: 3
SQ FT: 4,000
SALES: 250K **Privately Held**
WEB: www.irontable.com
SIC: 2514 2591 Mfg Metal Household Furniture Mfg Drapery Hardware/Blinds

Meriden
Sullivan County

(G-18983)
GARFIELDS SMOKEHOUSE INC
163 Main St (03770-5307)
P.O. Box 236 (03770-0236)
PHONE..................................603 469-3225
Elizabeth Taylor, *President*
Bill Taylor, *Vice Pres*
EMP: 3
SALES (est): 323K **Privately Held**
WEB: www.garfieldsmokehouse.com
SIC: 2022 2013 Mfg Cheese Mfg Prepared Meats

Merrimack
Hillsborough County

(G-18984)
ACE WELDING CO INC
715a Daniel Webster Hwy (03054-2713)
P.O. Box 695 (03054-0695)
PHONE..................................603 424-9936
Brian Robinson, *President*
Mary Robinson, *Corp Secy*
EMP: 28
SQ FT: 4,000
SALES (est): 6.2MM **Privately Held**
WEB: www.aceweldingnh.com
SIC: 3441 7692 Structural Metal Fabrication Welding Repair

(G-18985)
ATC POWER SYSTEMS INC
45 Depot St (03054-3427)
PHONE..................................603 429-0391
Joel Bedell, *President*
Rhonda Rafferty, *Purch Agent*
John Leonard, *Treasurer*
Glen Bouchard, *Controller*
Beau Valentin, *Executive*
EMP: 28
SQ FT: 15,000
SALES (est): 5.7MM **Privately Held**
WEB: www.atcpower.com
SIC: 3679 Mfg Electronic Components

(G-18986)
ATRIUM MEDICAL CORPORATION (HQ)
40 Continental Blvd (03054-4332)
PHONE..................................603 880-1433
Steve Herweck, *CEO*
Trevor Carlton, *President*
Ted Karwoski, *Vice Pres*
Bruce Aldrich, *Engineer*
Brian Burgess, *Engineer*
◆ **EMP:** 275 **EST:** 1981
SQ FT: 135,000
SALES (est): 101.9MM
SALES (corp-wide): 58.7MM **Privately Held**
WEB: www.atriummed.com
SIC: 3842 3841 Mfg Surgical Appliances/Supplies Mfg Surgical/Medical Instruments
PA: Getinge Holding B.V. & Co. Kg
Kehler Str. 31
Rastatt 76437
722 293-20

(G-18987)
AURIGA PIV TECH INC
30 Daniel Webster Hwy (03054-4822)
PHONE..................................603 402-2955
Christos Tsironis, *President*
EMP: 7 **EST:** 2016
SALES (est): 935K **Privately Held**
SIC: 3825 5084 Mfg Electrical Measuring Instruments Whol Industrial Equipment

(G-18988)
AVILITE CORP
59 Daniel Webster Hwy # 100
(03054-4877)
PHONE..................................603 626-4388
Robert Gamache, *President*
Herbert Langer, *Vice Pres*
Jan Langer, *Treasurer*
John Monson, *Admin Sec*
▲ **EMP:** 9
SQ FT: 50,000
SALES (est): 1.5MM **Privately Held**
SIC: 2821 3312 Mfg Plastic Materials/Resins Blast Furnace-Steel Works

(G-18989)
BAE SYSTEMS INFO & ELEC SYS
130 Daniel Webster Hwy (03054)
P.O. Box 868, Nashua (03061-0868)
PHONE..................................603 885-4321
Dr Jerry Wohletz, *Vice Pres*
William Watson, *Chief Engr*
Edward Brabant, *Engineer*
Macy Chu, *Engineer*
Takuya Otani, *Engineer*
EMP: 495
SALES (corp-wide): 22.1B **Privately Held**
WEB: www.iesi.na.baesystems.com
SIC: 3812 Mfg Aircraft Self-Protection Systems
HQ: Bae Systems Information And Electronic Systems Integration Inc.
65 Spit Brook Rd
Nashua NH 03060
603 885-4321

(G-18990)
BAE SYSTEMS INFO & ELEC SYS
144 Daniel Webster Hwy # 24
(03054-4898)
P.O. Box 868, Nashua (03061-0868)
PHONE..................................603 885-4321
Paul Markwardt, *Vice Pres*
William Breen, *Engineer*
Sean Morrell, *Engineer*
Joanne Routhier, *Sales Mgr*
Donna Phelps, *Contract Mgr*
EMP: 295
SALES (corp-wide): 22.1B **Privately Held**
WEB: www.iesi.na.baesystems.com
SIC: 3728 3679 Mfg Of Radio And Tv Antennas
HQ: Bae Systems Information And Electronic Systems Integration Inc.
65 Spit Brook Rd
Nashua NH 03060
603 885-4321

(G-18991)
CELESTICA LLC
Also Called: Celestica Arden Hills
11 Continental Blvd # 103 (03054-4341)
PHONE..................................603 657-3000
Steve Delaney, *Branch Mgr*
EMP: 600
SALES (corp-wide): 23.7B **Privately Held**
SIC: 3672 Assembles Printed Circuit Boards & Other Electronic Product Assembly
HQ: Celestica Llc
11 Continental Blvd # 103
Merrimack NH 03054

(G-18992)
CIRCUIT TECHNOLOGY INC
Also Called: Cirtech
6a Continental Blvd (03054-4302)
PHONE..................................603 424-2200
Beverly Parker, *CEO*
Clare O Parker, *President*
Bradley Parker, *COO*
Ronald Parker, *Vice Pres*
Mark Curran, *Purch Agent*
EMP: 65
SQ FT: 15,000
SALES (est): 19.2MM **Privately Held**
WEB: www.circuittec.com
SIC: 3672 Mfg Printed Circuit Boards

(G-18993)
COLT REFINING INC (PA)
12a Star Dr (03054-4470)
PHONE..................................603 429-9966
Harvey J Gottlieb, *President*
Mitch Coughlin, *Principal*
Rob Layman, *Business Mgr*
Jim Maher, *Vice Pres*
Michael Amoroso, *Prdtn Mgr*
◆ **EMP:** 49
SQ FT: 24,000
SALES (est): 5.9MM **Privately Held**
WEB: www.coltrefining.com
SIC: 3339 5093 3341 Primary Nonferrous Metal Producer Whol Scrap/Waste Material Secondary Nonferrous Metal Producer

(G-18994)
CPM ACQUISITION CORP
18 Continental Blvd (03054-4302)
PHONE..................................319 232-8444
Doug Ostrich, *CFO*
Phil Bergeron, *Branch Mgr*
EMP: 36 **Privately Held**
WEB: www.betaraven.com
SIC: 3523 3547 Mfg Farm Machinery/Equipment Mfg Rolling Mill Machinery
HQ: Cpm Acquisition Corp.
2975 Airline Cir
Waterloo IA 50703
319 232-8444

(G-18995)
CPM ACQUISITION CORP
Also Called: CPM U.S.A. Merr
18 Continental Blvd (03054-4302)
PHONE..................................603 423-6300
Ted Waitman, *Branch Mgr*
EMP: 36 **Privately Held**
WEB: www.betaraven.com
SIC: 3523 3547 Mfg Farm Machinery/Equipment Mfg Rolling Mill Machinery
HQ: Cpm Acquisition Corp.
2975 Airline Cir
Waterloo IA 50703
319 232-8444

(G-18996)
CUBIC WAFER INC
10 Al Paul Ln Ste 204 (03054-5801)
PHONE..................................603 546-0600
Clarence Yu, *Principal*
EMP: 4
SALES (est): 322.8K **Privately Held**
SIC: 3674 Mfg Semiconductors/Related Devices

(G-18997)
DALAU INCORPORATED
19 Star Dr Unit 6 (03054-4439)
PHONE..................................603 670-1031
David J Sage, *President*
Mark L Sage, *General Mgr*
Graham S Jaggs, *Treasurer*
▲ **EMP:** 6
SQ FT: 5,000
SALES (est): 1.1MM **Privately Held**
WEB: www.dalau.com
SIC: 2821 Mfg Plastic Materials/Resins
PA: Dalau Limited
Ford Road
Clacton-On-Sea
125 522-0220

(G-18998)
EL-OP US INC
220 Daniel Webster Hwy (03054-4898)
PHONE..................................603 889-2500
Michael Rukin, *Ch of Bd*
Roger J Sutherland, *President*
EMP: 400
SQ FT: 351,458
SALES (est): 47.7MM
SALES (corp-wide): 1B **Privately Held**
WEB: www.kollsman.com
SIC: 3812 3629 Mfg Search/Navigation Equipment Mfg Electrical Industrial Apparatus

GEOGRAPHIC

HQ: Efw Inc.
4700 Marine Creek Pkwy
Fort Worth TX 76179
-

(G-18999)
ELBIT SYSTEMS OF AMERICA LLC
220 Daniel Webster Hwy (03054-4898)
PHONE..................................603 889-2500
Jamie Knight, *Engineer*
Lam T Tran, *Sales Associate*
Robert Bragdon, *Branch Mgr*
Diane Giroux, *Manager*
EMP: 15
SALES (corp-wide): 1B **Privately Held**
SIC: 3827 Mfg Optical Instruments/Lenses
HQ: Elbit Systems Of America, Llc
4700 Marine Creek Pkwy
Fort Worth TX 76179
-

(G-19000)
FINITE SURFACE MOUNT TECH LLC
Also Called: Finite Smt
33 Elm St Ste B (03054-6400)
PHONE..................................603 423-0300
EMP: 3
SALES: 500K **Privately Held**
SIC: 3672 3679 Mfg Printed Circuit Boards Mfg Electronic Components

(G-19001)
GALLERIA STONE
714 Daniel Webster Hwy (03054-7205)
PHONE..................................603 424-2884
EMP: 3
SALES (est): 155K **Privately Held**
SIC: 3281 Mfg Cut Stone/Products

(G-19002)
GEORGE GORDON ASSOCIATES INC
12 Continental Blvd (03054-4302)
PHONE..................................603 424-5204
Donald R Belanger, *President*
Robert Bisbee, *Vice Pres*
Ron Downing, *Vice Pres*
Kimberly Butler, *Office Mgr*
EMP: 15
SQ FT: 25,000
SALES (est): 3.7MM **Privately Held**
WEB: www.ggapack.com
SIC: 3565 Mfg Packaging Machinery

(G-19003)
GETINGE GROUP LOGIS AMERI LLC
Also Called: Getinge AB
40 Continental Blvd (03054-4332)
PHONE..................................603 880-1433
Mattias Perjos, *CEO*
Steve Emery, *Finance*
Scott Dabbene, *Manager*
Wade Fox, *Director*
EMP: 700
SALES (est): 95.3K **Privately Held**
SIC: 3841 Mfg Surgical/Medical Instruments

(G-19004)
GT ADVANCED CZ LLC
243 Daniel Webster Hwy (03054-4807)
PHONE..................................603 883-5200
EMP: 3
SALES (est): 235K **Privately Held**
SIC: 3674 Mfg Semiconductors/Related Devices

(G-19005)
H F STAPLES & CO INC
Also Called: Miricle Wood
9 Webb Dr Ste 5 (03054-4876)
P.O. Box 956 (03054-0956)
PHONE..................................603 889-8600
James Stratton, *President*
Thomas Stratton, *Vice Pres*
EMP: 6 **EST:** 1897
SALES (est): 780K **Privately Held**
WEB: www.hfstaples.com
SIC: 2851 Mfg Paints/Allied Products

(G-19006)
HANESBRANDS INC
80 Premium Outlets Blvd # 365 (03054-4780)
PHONE..................................603 424-6737
EMP: 10
SALES (corp-wide): 6.8B **Publicly Held**
SIC: 2253 Ret Family Clothing
PA: Hanesbrands Inc.
1000 E Hanes Mill Rd
Winston Salem NC 27105
336 519-8080

(G-19007)
INSOURCE DESIGN & MFG TECH LLC
39 Depot St (03054-3427)
PHONE..................................603 718-8228
Mario Bartoli, *Mng Member*
EMP: 4
SALES (est): 647.4K **Privately Held**
SIC: 3663 8711 7389 3728 Mfg Radio/Tv Comm Equip Engineering Services Business Services Mfg Aircraft Parts/Equip Machine & Other Job Shop Work

(G-19008)
ITAG LLC
11 Marty Dr (03054-2964)
PHONE..................................603 429-8436
Daniel Baloche, *CEO*
EMP: 12
SALES (est): 850K **Privately Held**
WEB: www.itag.com
SIC: 7372 Prepackaged Software Services

(G-19009)
KEYSPIN MANUFACTURING
21 Continental Blvd (03054-4303)
PHONE..................................603 420-8508
Elizabeth Cacciola, *Administration*
EMP: 3
SALES (est): 233.6K **Privately Held**
SIC: 3999 Mfg Misc Products

(G-19010)
KMC SYSTEMS INC
220 Daniel Webster Hwy (03054-4898)
PHONE..................................866 742-0442
Ron Jellison, *Vice Pres*
Real Madore, *Mfg Dir*
▲ **EMP:** 100
SQ FT: 160,000
SALES (est): 21.6MM
SALES (corp-wide): 1B **Privately Held**
WEB: www.kmcsystems.com
SIC: 3812 3841 3629 Mfg Search/Navigation Equipment Mfg Surgical/Medical Instruments Mfg Electrical Industrial Apparatus
HQ: Kollsman, Inc.
220 Daniel Webster Hwy
Merrimack NH 03054
-

(G-19011)
KOLLSMAN INC (DH)
220 Daniel Webster Hwy (03054-4837)
P.O. Box 490 (03054-0490)
PHONE..................................603 889-2500
Ranaan Horowitz, *President*
Yuval Ramon, *COO*
Cheryl Colby, *Administration*
EMP: 520
SQ FT: 348,500
SALES (est): 123.5MM
SALES (corp-wide): 1B **Privately Held**
SIC: 3812 3629 Mfg Search/Navigation Equipment Mfg Electrical Industrial Apparatus

(G-19012)
LOCKHEED MARTIN CORPORATION
Also Called: Sanders- A Lockheed Martin Co
144 Daniel Webster Hwy (03054-4898)
PHONE..................................603 885-5295
Doug Cummings, *General Mgr*
EMP: 10 **Publicly Held**
WEB: www.lockheedmartin.com
SIC: 3812 Mfg Search/Navigation Equipment
PA: Lockheed Martin Corporation
6801 Rockledge Dr
Bethesda MD 20817
-

(G-19013)
MACHINED INTEGRATIONS LLC
1507 Columbia Cir (03054-4164)
P.O. Box 396 (03054-0396)
PHONE..................................603 420-8871
Dennis Tetip, *Mng Member*
EMP: 3 **EST:** 2013
SALES (est): 364K **Privately Held**
SIC: 3599 Mfg Industrial Machinery

(G-19014)
MERRIMACK MICRO LLC
76 Jessica Dr (03054-3570)
PHONE..................................603 809-4183
Lillian Carol Merriman, *President*
EMP: 5
SALES (est): 523.2K **Privately Held**
SIC: 3672 Mfg Printed Circuit Boards

(G-19015)
NASHUA CORPORATION
Also Called: Specialty Coated Products
59 Daniel Webster Hwy A (03054-4858)
PHONE..................................603 880-1110
Fax: 603 880-1281
EMP: 276 **Publicly Held**
SIC: 2679 2672 Mfg Converted Paper Products Mfg Coated/Laminated Paper
HQ: Nashua Corporation
59 Daniel Webster Hwy A
Merrimack NH 03054
603 880-1100

(G-19016)
NAVICO INC
10 Al Paul Ln Ste 101 (03054-5801)
PHONE..................................603 324-2042
Louis Chemi, *Branch Mgr*
Stephen Furr, *Manager*
EMP: 30
SALES (corp-wide): 343.8MM **Privately Held**
SIC: 3669 Mfg Communications Equipment
HQ: Navico Holding As
Nyaskaiveien 2
Egersund 4374
477 039-06

(G-19017)
NORTHEAST FUEL SYSTEMS LLC
53 Turbine Way Ste 47 (03054-4129)
PHONE..................................603 365-4103
Kenneth Foote, *President*
William Foote,
EMP: 4 **EST:** 2015
SALES (est): 219.4K **Privately Held**
SIC: 3724 Aircraft Engines And Engine Parts

(G-19018)
OZTEK CORP
11 Continental Blvd # 104 (03054-4341)
PHONE..................................603 546-0090
John O'Connor, *President*
David Zendzian, *Vice Pres*
Jay Goodell, *Design Engr*
Dave Zendzian, *CTO*
Thomas O'Reilly, *Director*
EMP: 11
SQ FT: 11,800
SALES (est): 3.5MM **Privately Held**
WEB: www.oztekcorp.com
SIC: 3829 Mfg Measuring/Controlling Devices

(G-19019)
PAPERGRAPHICS PRINT & COPY
4 John Tyler St Ste A (03054-4800)
PHONE..................................603 880-1835
Frank Lagana, *President*
Beatrice B Figler, *Vice Pres*
Linda Lagana, *Vice Pres*
John Borlaug, *Prdtn Mgr*
Harry Stamas, *Executive*
EMP: 15 **EST:** 1982
SQ FT: 7,000
SALES (est): 2.7MM **Privately Held**
WEB: www.papergraphicsonline.com
SIC: 2752 7334 5112 Lithographic Commercial Printing Photocopying Services Whol Stationery/Office Supplies

(G-19020)
PATON DATA COMPANY
19 Peaslee Rd (03054-4516)
PHONE..................................603 598-8070
Irving Paton, *Owner*
EMP: 3
SALES (est): 199K **Privately Held**
WEB: www.patondata.com
SIC: 7372 Prepackaged Software Services

(G-19021)
PIGEON HOLD TARGETS
75 Baboosic Lake Rd (03054-3509)
PHONE..................................603 420-8839
EMP: 3
SALES (est): 157.8K **Privately Held**
SIC: 3949 Mfg Sporting/Athletic Goods

(G-19022)
PJ DIVERSIFIED MACHINING INC
12b Star Dr Ste 3 (03054-4415)
PHONE..................................603 459-8655
Paula Demers, *Principal*
Joanne M Demers, *Principal*
Paul Demers, *Vice Pres*
George Demers, *Manager*
EMP: 8
SQ FT: 2,500
SALES: 897.1K **Privately Held**
SIC: 3599 Mfg Industrial Machinery

(G-19023)
POWERFAB INC
715a Daniel Webster Hwy (03054-2713)
P.O. Box 130 (03054-0130)
PHONE..................................603 424-3900
Mary Robinson, *President*
Warren Manning, *Sales Staff*
EMP: 4
SQ FT: 1,000
SALES (est): 701.3K **Privately Held**
SIC: 3441 Structural Metal Fabrication

(G-19024)
PRODWAYS
316 Daniel Webster Hwy (03054-4115)
PHONE..................................763 568-7966
Alban D'Hallium, *CEO*
Yves-Marie Hillion, *Treasurer*
Elizabeth Smith, *Office Mgr*
EMP: 8
SALES (est): 465.8K **Privately Held**
SIC: 3555 Mfg Printing Trades Machinery

(G-19025)
ROBERT VEINOT
Also Called: PC Whizdom
11 Plasic Rd (03054-7006)
PHONE..................................603 424-1799
EMP: 3
SQ FT: 1,800
SALES: 350K **Privately Held**
SIC: 3571 5734 5045 7378 Custom Building Sales Service And Networking Of Ibm Compatible Computers

(G-19026)
RYMSA MICRO COMMUNICATIONS (PA)
Also Called: Verizon Business
15 Caron St (03054-4428)
P.O. Box 1206, Windham ME (04062-1206)
PHONE..................................603 429-0800
Ramon Guira Arderiu, *President*
Dennis Lampman, *Manager*
Paul D Smith, *Director*
Donald R Stacy, *Admin Sec*
▲ **EMP:** 26 **EST:** 1966
SQ FT: 2,400
SALES (est): 2.8MM **Privately Held**
WEB: www.mcibroadcast.com
SIC: 3663 Mfg Radio/Tv Communication Equipment

(G-19027)
SAINT-GOBAIN PRFMCE PLAS CORP
701 Daniel Webster Hwy (03054-2713)
PHONE..................................603 424-9000

Robert C Ayotte, *CEO*
EMP: 250
SALES (corp-wide): 209.1MM **Privately Held**
SIC: 2821 Mfg Plastic Materials/Resins
HQ: Saint-Gobain Performance Plastics Corporation
31500 Solon Rd
Solon OH 44139
440 836-6900

(G-19028)
SEACHANGE THERAPEUTICS INC
66 Jessica Dr (03054-3570)
P.O. Box 1387 (03054-1387)
PHONE..................................603 424-6009
Jeannine Richardson, *Principal*
EMP: 3
SALES (est): 196.8K **Privately Held**
SIC: 2834 Mfg Pharmaceutical Preparations

(G-19029)
SEQUA CORPORATION
Kollsman Manufacturing
220 Daniel Webster Hwy (03054-4898)
PHONE..................................603 889-2500
Randy Moore, *President*
EMP: 6
SALES (corp-wide): 2.4B **Publicly Held**
WEB: www.sequa.com
SIC: 3812 Mfg Avionics & Electro-Optics
HQ: Sequa Corporation
3999 Rca Blvd
Palm Beach Gardens FL 33410
561 935-3571

(G-19030)
SOLIDSCAPE INC
316 Daniel Webster Hwy (03054-4115)
PHONE..................................603 424-0590
Michael Varanka, *President*
Fabio Esposito, *President*
William Dahl, *Vice Pres*
Zeke Harkleroad, *Vice Pres*
Paul Maloney, *Vice Pres*
▲ **EMP:** 49
SQ FT: 38,678
SALES (est): 11.5MM
SALES (corp-wide): 190.7MM **Privately Held**
WEB: www.solid-scape.com
SIC: 3542 Mfg Machine Tools-Forming
HQ: Stratasys, Inc.
7665 Commerce Way
Eden Prairie MN 55344
952 937-3000

(G-19031)
SONESYS LLC
21 Continental Blvd (03054-4303)
PHONE..................................603 423-9000
Louis Gargasz,
Joerg Laves,
EMP: 10
SQ FT: 3,000
SALES (est): 610K **Privately Held**
SIC: 3679 Mfg Electronic Components

(G-19032)
SPACE OPTICS RESEARCH LABS LLC
15 Caron St (03054-4428)
PHONE..................................978 250-8640
Sandra Scannell, *Business Mgr*
Robert Scannell,
EMP: 14
SQ FT: 16,000
SALES: 2.5MM **Privately Held**
WEB: www.sorl.com
SIC: 3827 Mfg Optical Instruments/Lenses

(G-19033)
SPRAYING SYSTEMS CO
243 Daniel Webster Hwy (03054-4807)
PHONE..................................603 517-1854
Michel Thenin, *General Mgr*
Robert Brooks, *Manager*
EMP: 35
SALES (corp-wide): 264.7MM **Privately Held**
WEB: www.spray.com
SIC: 3499 Mfg Misc Fabricated Metal Products
PA: Spraying Systems Co.
200 W North Ave
Glendale Heights IL 60139
630 665-5000

(G-19034)
STAMP NEWS PUBLISHING INC
42 Sentry Way (03054-4407)
PHONE..................................603 424-7556
John Dunn, *Principal*
Elaine Dunn, *Marketing Mgr*
EMP: 3
SALES (est): 227.3K **Privately Held**
SIC: 2741 Misc Publishing

(G-19035)
TABLES OF STONE (PA)
759 Daniel Webster Hwy (03054-2741)
PHONE..................................603 424-7577
Timothy Simkin, *Owner*
Sonya Simkin, *Co-Owner*
EMP: 3
SALES (est): 275.9K **Privately Held**
WEB: www.tablesofstone.net
SIC: 1423 5032 Fabrication Import & Installation Of Natural Stone

(G-19036)
TECH NH INC (PA)
8 Continental Blvd (03054-4302)
P.O. Box 476 (03054-0476)
PHONE..................................603 424-4404
Richard C Grosky, *President*
Roger Somers, *COO*
Greg Gardner, *Plant Mgr*
Greg Gradner, *Plant Mgr*
Anna Exner, *Purch Mgr*
▲ **EMP:** 67
SQ FT: 25,400
SALES (est): 11.3MM **Privately Held**
WEB: www.technh.com
SIC: 3089 8711 Mfg Plastic Products Engineering Services

(G-19037)
TEXAS INSTRUMENTS INCORPORATED
7 Continental Blvd (03054-4339)
PHONE..................................603 429-6079
EMP: 170
SALES (corp-wide): 12.2B **Publicly Held**
SIC: 3674 8711 Mfg Semiconductors/Related Devices Engineering Services
PA: Texas Instruments Incorporated
12500 Ti Blvd
Dallas TX 75243
214 479-3773

(G-19038)
TYLER TECHNOLOGIES INC
10 Al Paul Ln Ste 202 (03054-5801)
PHONE..................................603 578-6745
EMP: 22
SALES (corp-wide): 935.2MM **Publicly Held**
SIC: 7372 Prepackaged Software Services
PA: Tyler Technologies, Inc.
5101 Tennyson Pkwy
Plano TX 75024
972 713-3700

Middleton
Carroll County

(G-19039)
DIJITIZED COMMUNICATIONS INC
58 Route 153 (03887-6106)
PHONE..................................603 473-2144
Dan Trautman, *President*
Nancy Trautman, *Vice Pres*
Nancy M Trautman, *Vice Pres*
Christian Trautman, *Admin Sec*
EMP: 5
SQ FT: 500
SALES: 125K **Privately Held**
WEB: www.dijitized.com
SIC: 3822 7379 Mfg Environmental Controls Computer Related Services

Milan
Coos County

(G-19040)
KEL LOG INC (PA)
743 E Side River Rd (03588-3517)
PHONE..................................603 752-2000
Michael P Kelley, *President*
Susan S Kelley, *Vice Pres*
Margaret Vien, *Asst Treas*
Peter Bornstein, *Admin Sec*
EMP: 30
SALES (est): 3.2MM **Privately Held**
SIC: 2411 Logging Contractor

(G-19041)
NEW ENGLAND VLTS MONUMENTS LLC
8 Laurel Ln (03588-3534)
PHONE..................................603 449-2165
Dana Brouillece, *Mng Member*
EMP: 8
SALES (est): 860.7K **Privately Held**
SIC: 3272 Mfg Concrete Products

Milford
Hillsborough County

(G-19042)
AEGIS HOLDINGS LLC
Also Called: Aegis Container
Riverway W (03055)
P.O. Box 257 (03055-0257)
PHONE..................................603 673-8900
Craig A Meader, *Mng Member*
EMP: 25
SALES (est): 5.2MM **Privately Held**
SIC: 2653 Mfg Corrugated/Solid Fiber Boxes

(G-19043)
AETNA INSULATED WIRE LLC
53 Old Wilton Rd (03055-3119)
PHONE..................................757 460-3381
Gregory J Smith, *President*
Gregory Smith, *President*
Jeff Lovett, *General Mgr*
Walt Smith, *General Mgr*
Vincent Victa, *Controller*
▼ **EMP:** 116
SQ FT: 320,000
SALES (est): 32.6MM
SALES (corp-wide): 225.3B **Publicly Held**
WEB: www.aetnawire.com/
SIC: 3357 3351 Nonferrous Wiredrawing/Insulating Copper Rolling/Drawing
HQ: Marmon Holdings, Inc.
181 W Madison St Ste 2600
Chicago IL 60602
312 372-9500

(G-19044)
AIRMAR TECHNOLOGY CORP (PA)
35 Meadowbrook Dr (03055-4617)
PHONE..................................603 673-9570
Stephen Boucher, *CEO*
Karl T Krantz, *President*
Ted Krantz, *President*
Matt Boucher, *Vice Pres*
Jennifer Matsis, *Vice Pres*
◆ **EMP:** 260
SQ FT: 75,000
SALES (est): 47.8MM **Privately Held**
SIC: 3825 3829 3541 Mfg Electrical Measuring Instruments Mfg Measuring/Controlling Devices Mfg Machine Tools-Cutting

(G-19045)
AIRMAR TECHNOLOGY CORP
40 Meadowbrook Dr (03055)
PHONE..................................603 673-9570
Dee Dee Tower, *Principal*
EMP: 15
SALES (corp-wide): 47.8MM **Privately Held**
SIC: 3825 1541 Instruments To Measure Electricity
PA: Airmar Technology Corp.
35 Meadowbrook Dr
Milford NH 03055
603 673-9570

(G-19046)
ALENE CANDLES LLC (PA)
51 Scarborough Ln (03055-3117)
PHONE..................................603 673-5050
Shyam Gunasekaran, *Engineer*
Ted Goldberg, *VP Bus Dvlpt*
Andy James, *CFO*
Sarah Ozana, *Accounting Mgr*
Marty Remle, *Technology*
◆ **EMP:** 140
SQ FT: 75,000
SALES (est): 59.8MM **Privately Held**
WEB: www.alene.com
SIC: 3999 Mfg Misc Products

(G-19047)
AMHERST LABEL INC
15 Westchester Dr (03055-3056)
P.O. Box 596 (03055-0596)
PHONE..................................603 673-7849
Nick Calvetti, *President*
Nye Hornor, *Vice Pres*
Peter Lippitt, *Accountant*
Ruth Sterling, *Marketing Mgr*
David Sturm, *Admin Sec*
EMP: 43
SQ FT: 35,000
SALES (est): 7.9MM **Privately Held**
WEB: www.amherstlabel.com
SIC: 2759 Commercial Printing

(G-19048)
BARLOW WOOD PRODUCTS
119 Melendy Rd (03055-3417)
PHONE..................................603 673-2642
Paul Barlow, *Owner*
EMP: 5
SQ FT: 5,000
SALES (est): 320K **Privately Held**
SIC: 2448 Mfg Wood Pallets & Skids

(G-19049)
CIRTRONICS CORPORATION
528 Route 13 S Ste 130 (03055-3480)
P.O. Box 130 (03055-0130)
PHONE..................................603 249-9190
Dave Patterson, *President*
Robert C McCray, *Chairman*
Skip Tately, *Business Mgr*
Nancy Lynch, *COO*
George Mandragouras, *COO*
▲ **EMP:** 135
SQ FT: 170,000
SALES (est): 41.6MM **Privately Held**
WEB: www.cirtronics.com
SIC: 3672 Mfg Printed Circuit Boards

(G-19050)
CNI CORP
Also Called: Computer Network Integrators
468 Route 13 S Ste A (03055-3488)
PHONE..................................603 249-5075
Jon Dickinson, *President*
Scott Snow, *President*
Robert Howard, *Admin Sec*
EMP: 9
SQ FT: 4,800
SALES: 3MM **Privately Held**
WEB: www.cnicorp.com
SIC: 7372 7371 Prepackaged Software Services Custom Computer Programing

(G-19051)
CONTROLLED FLUIDICS LLC
18 Hollow Oak Ln (03055-4270)
PHONE..................................603 673-4323
Thomas Rolff, *Principal*
Laura Murphy, *Executive Asst*
EMP: 18 **EST:** 2011
SALES: 3.3MM **Privately Held**
SIC: 3599 Mfg Industrial Machinery

(G-19052)
COORSTEK INC
Also Called: Coorstek Milford
47 Powers St (03055-4928)
PHONE..................................603 673-7560

John Henrion, *Controller*
Dean Croucher, *Branch Mgr*
EMP: 100
SALES (corp-wide): 407.6MM **Privately Held**
SIC: 3264 Mfg Porcelain Electrical Supplies
HQ: Coorstek, Inc.
14143 Denver West Pkwy # 400
Lakewood CO 80401
303 271-7000

(G-19053)
COTE MACHINE
281 Mason Rd (03055-4611)
PHONE..................................603 673-0211
Maurice Cote, *Owner*
EMP: 4
SALES (est): 370.5K **Privately Held**
SIC: 3544 Mfg Dies/Tools/Jigs/Fixtures

(G-19054)
CUPCAKE ROWE LLC
25 Wyman Ln (03055-3577)
PHONE..................................603 673-0489
EMP: 4
SALES (est): 188.6K **Privately Held**
SIC: 2051 Mfg Bread/Related Products

(G-19055)
DEGREE CONTROLS INC (PA)
18 Meadowbrook Dr (03055-4612)
PHONE..................................603 672-8900
Jagat Sisodia, *President*
Rajesh Nair, *Chairman*
Eric N Birch, *Vice Pres*
Phillip Daniels, *Vice Pres*
William Langille, *Vice Pres*
▲ **EMP:** 50
SQ FT: 25,000
SALES (est): 9.8MM **Privately Held**
WEB: www.degreec.com
SIC: 3822 Mfg Environmental Controls

(G-19056)
GARDOC INC (DH)
Also Called: Spear Systems
86 Powers St (03055-4927)
PHONE..................................603 673-6400
Randall Spear, *President*
EMP: 12
SQ FT: 35,000
SALES (est): 911.4K
SALES (corp-wide): 1.7B **Privately Held**
WEB: www.spearlabel.com
SIC: 2672 Mfg Coated/Laminated Paper
HQ: Spear Usa Inc.
5510 Courseview Dr
Mason OH 45040
513 459-1100

(G-19057)
GRANITE STATE CONCRETE CO INC
408 Elm St (03055-4305)
P.O. Box 185 (03055-0185)
PHONE..................................603 673-3327
John Mac Lellan III, *President*
EMP: 25
SQ FT: 2,000
SALES (est): 2.1MM
SALES (corp-wide): 20.9MM **Privately Held**
SIC: 3273 1442 Mfg Ready-Mixed Concrete Construction Sand/Gravel
PA: J. G. Maclellan Concrete Co., Inc.
180 Phoenix Ave
Lowell MA 01852
978 458-1223

(G-19058)
HAYDON KERK MTION SLUTIONS INC
Also Called: Kerk Motion Products
56 Meadowbrook Dr (03055)
PHONE..................................603 465-7227
John Norris, *CEO*
EMP: 80
SQ FT: 29,000
SALES (est): 20.8MM **Privately Held**
WEB: www.kerkmotion.com
SIC: 3452 Mfg Bolts/Screws/Rivets Mfg Bolts/Screws/Rivets

(G-19059)
HI-TECH FABRICATORS INC
10 Scarborough Ln (03055-3117)
PHONE..................................603 672-3766
Paul Bailey, *President*
Ann Bailey, *Vice Pres*
EMP: 15
SQ FT: 12,000
SALES (est): 2MM **Privately Held**
WEB: www.hitechfabricators.com
SIC: 3444 Precision Sheet Metal Work

(G-19060)
HITCHINER MANUFACTURING CO INC (PA)
594 Elm St (03055-4306)
PHONE..................................603 673-1100
Mark Damien, *President*
John H Morison III, *Chairman*
Adrian Arce, *Vice Pres*
Scott Biederman, *Vice Pres*
Bruce Ebright, *Vice Pres*
◆ **EMP:** 1843
SQ FT: 220,000
SALES: 253.1MM **Privately Held**
WEB: www.hitchiner.com
SIC: 3324 Steel Investment Foundry

(G-19061)
HITCHINER MANUFACTURING CO INC
Also Called: Hitchiner Ferrous USA Division
1 Scarborough Ln (03055-3117)
PHONE..................................603 673-1100
Jason Mays, *Manager*
EMP: 96
SALES (corp-wide): 253.1MM **Privately Held**
WEB: www.hitchiner.com
SIC: 3324 3363 Mfg Precision Investment Steel Ferrous Castings
PA: Hitchiner Manufacturing Co., Inc.
594 Elm St
Milford NH 03055
603 673-1100

(G-19062)
HITCHINER MANUFACTURING CO INC
117 Old Wilton Rd (03055-3134)
PHONE..................................603 732-1935
Sandra Buckler, *Engineer*
Angela Delorfano, *Administration*
EMP: 209
SALES (corp-wide): 253.1MM **Privately Held**
SIC: 3324 Steel Investment Foundry
PA: Hitchiner Manufacturing Co., Inc.
594 Elm St
Milford NH 03055
603 673-1100

(G-19063)
HITCHINER MANUFACTURING CO INC
Also Called: Hitchiner Plant 1
Hitchiner Way (03055)
PHONE..................................603 673-1100
Jason Mays, *Manager*
EMP: 317
SALES (corp-wide): 253.1MM **Privately Held**
WEB: www.hitchiner.com
SIC: 3324 3363 Mfg Precision Investment Steel Ferrous Castings
PA: Hitchiner Manufacturing Co., Inc.
594 Elm St
Milford NH 03055
603 673-1100

(G-19064)
HOLLIS LINE MACHINE CO INC
128 Old Wilton Rd (03055-3118)
PHONE..................................603 465-2251
Tim Gregory, *Manager*
EMP: 30
SALES (corp-wide): 7.8MM **Privately Held**
WEB: www.hollisline.com
SIC: 3599 Mfg Industrial Machinery
PA: Hollis Line Machine Co., Inc.
295 S Merrimack Rd
Hollis NH 03049
603 465-2251

(G-19065)
HY-TEN DIE & DEVELOPMENT CORP
Also Called: Hy-Ten Plastics
38 Powers St (03055-4982)
PHONE..................................603 673-1611
Udo Fritsch, *Ch of Bd*
Franz Fritsch, *President*
Joseph Stone, *QC Mgr*
Trisha Maclaren, *Cust Mgr*
Fred Rice, *Manager*
EMP: 50
SQ FT: 35,000
SALES (est): 11MM **Privately Held**
WEB: www.hy-ten.com
SIC: 3089 3544 Mfg Plastic Products Mfg Dies/Tools/Jigs/Fixtures

(G-19066)
JENEX INC
172b South St (03055-3785)
P.O. Box 1219, Amherst (03031-1219)
PHONE..................................603 672-2600
Lennert Johnson, *President*
▲ **EMP:** 5
SQ FT: 3,000
SALES (est): 535.6K **Privately Held**
WEB: www.jenex.com
SIC: 3949 Mfg Sporting/Athletic Goods

(G-19067)
JENSEN CABINET CO
27 Dearborn St (03055-4021)
P.O. Box 69, Brookline (03033-0069)
PHONE..................................603 554-8363
Kent Jensen, *Owner*
EMP: 3
SALES: 200K **Privately Held**
SIC: 2499 2434 Mfg Wood Products Mfg Wood Kitchen Cabinets

(G-19068)
MARMON UTILITY
53 Old Wilton Rd (03055-3119)
PHONE..................................603 249-1302
Tony S Lopez, *President*
EMP: 5 **EST:** 2010
SALES (est): 748.8K **Privately Held**
SIC: 2298 Mfg Cordage/Twine

(G-19069)
MARMON UTILITY LLC (DH)
53 Old Wilton Rd (03055-3119)
PHONE..................................603 673-2040
Edward Ferry,
◆ **EMP:** 200
SQ FT: 175,000
SALES (est): 112.1MM
SALES (corp-wide): 225.3B **Publicly Held**
WEB: www.hendrix-wc.com
SIC: 3357 Nonferrous Wiredrawing/Insulating
HQ: Marmon Holdings, Inc.
181 W Madison St Ste 2600
Chicago IL 60602
312 372-9500

(G-19070)
NELSON AIR CORPORATION
559 Route 13 S (03055-3425)
P.O. Box 2 (03055-0002)
PHONE..................................603 673-3908
Bradley Engel, *President*
EMP: 5
SQ FT: 5,000
SALES: 500K **Privately Held**
SIC: 3568 Mfg Air Bearings

(G-19071)
NH WOODWORKS LLC
70 Powers St (03055-4927)
PHONE..................................603 361-4727
Andrew W Sutherland,
EMP: 5 **EST:** 2011
SALES: 300K **Privately Held**
SIC: 2431 Mfg Millwork

(G-19072)
PLASTI-CLIP CORPORATION
Also Called: Precision Design
38 Perry Rd (03055-4308)
PHONE..................................603 672-1166
Daniel Faneuf, *President*
EMP: 10 **EST:** 1978
SQ FT: 6,800
SALES (est): 1.2MM **Privately Held**
SIC: 3083 3496 Mfg Laminated Plastic Plate/Sheet Mfg Misc Fabricated Wire Products

(G-19073)
RAPID MOLD EVOLUTION
27 Ox Brook Woods Rd (03055-3444)
PHONE..................................603 673-1027
Bob Edmonds, *President*
EMP: 3 **EST:** 2017
SALES (est): 184K **Privately Held**
SIC: 3089 Mfg Plastic Products

(G-19074)
SAINT-GOBAIN ABRASIVES INC
47 Powers St (03055-4928)
PHONE..................................603 673-7560
Guy Morin, *Manager*
EMP: 300
SALES (corp-wide): 209.1MM **Privately Held**
WEB: www.sgabrasives.com
SIC: 2221 Fiberglass Fabrics
HQ: Saint-Gobain Abrasives, Inc.
1 New Bond St
Worcester MA 01606
508 795-5000

(G-19075)
SAINT-GOBAIN CERAMICS PLAS INC
Also Called: Saint-Gobain Crystals
33 Powers St (03055-4928)
PHONE..................................603 673-5831
Jeff Rioux, *Manager*
EMP: 100
SALES (corp-wide): 209.1MM **Privately Held**
WEB: www.sgceramics.com
SIC: 2819 Mfg Industrial Inorganic Chemicals
HQ: Saint-Gobain Ceramics & Plastics, Inc.
750 E Swedesford Rd
Valley Forge PA 19482

(G-19076)
SAINT-GOBAIN GLASS CORPORATION
Also Called: Saint-Gobain Igniter Products
47 Powers St (03055-4928)
PHONE..................................603 673-7560
Dean Croucher, *Branch Mgr*
EMP: 10
SALES (corp-wide): 209.1MM **Privately Held**
SIC: 3674 Mfg Semiconductors/Related Devices
HQ: Saint-Gobain Glass Corporation
20 Moores Rd
Malvern PA 19355
484 595-9430

(G-19077)
SAPHIKON INC
33 Powers St (03055-8901)
PHONE..................................603 672-7221
Jacques Nadra, *Ch of Bd*
George B Amoss, *Vice Pres*
F Lee Faust, *Vice Pres*
David L Mascarin, *Vice Pres*
John R Mesher, *Vice Pres*
EMP: 99
SQ FT: 31,000
SALES (est): 5MM
SALES (corp-wide): 209.1MM **Privately Held**
WEB: www.sgceramics.com
SIC: 3299 Mfg Synthetic Stones Including Industrial Sapphires And Other Single Crystal Material
HQ: Saint-Gobain Ceramics & Plastics, Inc.
750 E Swedesford Rd
Valley Forge PA 19482

(G-19078)
SPEAR GROUP HOLDINGS
Also Called: Spear New Hampshire
48 Powers St (03055-4927)
PHONE..................................603 673-6400
Nick Noyes, *Branch Mgr*
EMP: 50 **Privately Held**
WEB: www.spearsystems.com

▲ = Import ▼=Export
◆ =Import/Export

SIC: 2672 2759 Mfg Coated/Laminated Paper Commercial Printing
HQ: Spear Group Holdings Limited
Christopher Grey Court
Cwmbran NP44
163 362-7600

(G-19079)
SPEAR USA INC
86 Powers St (03055-4927)
PHONE..................................513 459-1100
EMP: 5
SALES (corp-wide): 1.7B Privately Held
SIC: 2759 Commercial Printing
HQ: Spear Usa Inc.
5510 Courseview Dr
Mason OH 45040
513 459-1100

(G-19080)
TRELLBORG PIPE SALS MLFORD INC (DH)
250 Elm St (03055-4758)
P.O. Box 301 (03055-0301)
PHONE..................................800 626-2180
Randy L Snyder, *President*
Robert Peacock, *CFO*
◆ EMP: 120
SQ FT: 66,000
SALES (est): 13.5MM
SALES (corp-wide): 3.5B Privately Held
SIC: 3053 3531 3541 3498 Mfg Gasket/Packing/Seals Mfg Construction Mach Mfg Machine Tool-Cutting Mfg Fabrctd Pipe/Fitting Mfg Hand/Edge Tools
HQ: Trelleborg Pipe Seals Lelystad B.V.
Pascallaan 80
Lelystad 8218
320 267-979

(G-19081)
TRELLBORG PIPE SALS MLFORD INC
279 Riverway W (03055)
PHONE..................................603 673-8680
EMP: 3
SALES (corp-wide): 3.5B Privately Held
SIC: 3053 Mfg Gaskets/Packing/Sealing Devices
HQ: Trelleborg Pipe Seals Milford, Inc.
250 Elm St
Milford NH 03055
800 626-2180

(G-19082)
WILKINS LUMBER CO INC
495 Mont Vernon Rd (03055)
P.O. Box 393, Amherst (03031-0393)
PHONE..................................603 673-2545
Tom Wilkins, *President*
Sally Wilkins, *Vice Pres*
EMP: 9
SQ FT: 5,000
SALES (est): 1.5MM Privately Held
WEB: www.wilkinsfamily.org
SIC: 2421 5211 Sawmill/Planing Mill Ret Lumber/Building Materials

(G-19083)
WIREWINDERS INC
Also Called: Wire Winders
151 Mont Vernon Rd (03055-4125)
P.O. Box 187 (03055-0187)
PHONE..................................603 673-1763
Michael Gaudette, *President*
EMP: 7
SQ FT: 6,000
SALES: 1.1MM Privately Held
WEB: www.wirewinders.com
SIC: 7694 Coil Winding Service

Milton
Strafford County

(G-19084)
EASTERN BOATS INC
11 Industrial Way (03851-4335)
P.O. Box 1040 (03851-1040)
PHONE..................................603 652-9213
Robert Bourdeau, *President*
Cheryl Randall, *Admin Sec*
EMP: 37
SQ FT: 1,200
SALES (est): 9MM Privately Held
WEB: www.easternboats.com
SIC: 3732 5551 Boatbuilding/Repairing Ret Boats

(G-19085)
EVERGREEN CABINETRY LLC
44 Evergreen Valley Rd (03851-4509)
PHONE..................................603 833-6881
Kathy Russ, *Administration*
EMP: 3
SALES (est): 179.7K
SALES (corp-wide): 224.6K Privately Held
SIC: 2434 Mfg Wood Kitchen Cabinets
PA: Evergreen Cabinetry Llc
16 Commerce Way
Milton NH
603 833-6881

(G-19086)
INDEX PACKAGING INC
Also Called: Index Millwork
1055 White Mountain Hwy (03851-4443)
PHONE..................................603 350-0018
Bruce Lander, *President*
William M Lander, *Exec VP*
Todd Miller, *Opers Mgr*
Craig Abbott, *Buyer*
Kristin Masta, *Purchasing*
▼ EMP: 160
SQ FT: 120,000
SALES (est): 29.7MM Privately Held
WEB: www.indexpackaging.com
SIC: 2449 3086 3412 2441 Mfg Wood Containers Mfg Plastic Foam Prdts Mfg Metal Barrels/Pails Mfg Wood Boxes/Shooks Mfg Millwork

(G-19087)
PROLINE PRODUCTS LLC
34 Industrial Way (03851-4336)
PHONE..................................603 652-7337
Thomas Murtagh,
EMP: 5
SQ FT: 14,000
SALES (est): 560K Privately Held
WEB: www.prolineproducts.com
SIC: 3799 3715 Mfg Transportation Equipment Mfg Truck Trailers

(G-19088)
TOOL SPECIALTIES MFG CO LLC
343 Farmington Rd (03851-4826)
PHONE..................................603 652-9346
Phillip L Boucher,
Barbara Boucher,
EMP: 5
SQ FT: 2,900
SALES: 780K Privately Held
SIC: 3599 Mfg Industrial Machinery

Monroe
Grafton County

(G-19089)
BUNNELL ROCKY LOG & FOREST MGT
523 Littleton Rd (03771-3214)
PHONE..................................603 638-4983
Rocky Bunnell, *Owner*
EMP: 3
SALES (est): 307.7K Privately Held
SIC: 2411 4213 Logging Trucking Operator-Nonlocal

(G-19090)
HB LOGGING LLC
523 Littleton Rd (03771-3214)
PHONE..................................603 638-4983
Heath Bunnell, *Principal*
EMP: 6
SALES (est): 809.6K Privately Held
SIC: 2411 Logging

(G-19091)
PETE AND GERRYS ORGANICS LLC
140 Buffum Rd (03771-3114)
PHONE..................................603 638-2827
Randy McBey, *Purch Agent*
Jesse Laflamme, *Mng Member*
▲ EMP: 30
SALES (est): 12.1MM Privately Held
WEB: www.peteandgerrys.com
SIC: 2015 Poultry Processing

Mont Vernon
Hillsborough County

(G-19092)
CELLAR CRAFTS
73 Old Milford Rd (03057-1812)
PHONE..................................603 673-3615
Rosalie Philbrick, *Owner*
EMP: 3
SALES (est): 241.7K Privately Held
WEB: www.cellarcraft.com
SIC: 2421 Sawmill/Planing Mill

(G-19093)
PICKUP PATROL LLC
2 Wallace Ln (03057-1117)
PHONE..................................603 310-9120
Maria Edvalson, *CEO*
Daniel Brackett, *Chief Engr*
Eric Edvalson, *Chief Engr*
Catherine Edvalson, *Mktg Dir*
Candee Noorda, *Marketing Staff*
EMP: 8 EST: 2014
SALES (est): 247.7K Privately Held
SIC: 7372 Prepackaged Software Services

(G-19094)
WILBUR TECHNICAL SERVICES LLC
97 S Main St (03057-1621)
P.O. Box 397 (03057-0397)
PHONE..................................603 880-7100
Nancy Wilbur, *CEO*
EMP: 8
SALES (est): 1.2MM Privately Held
SIC: 3826 Service Scientific Instrumentation

Moultonborough
Carroll County

(G-19095)
CG ROXANE LLC
455 Ossipee Rd (03254)
P.O. Box 657 (03254-0657)
PHONE..................................603 476-8844
Jim Sullivan, *Engineer*
Mark Wiggins, *Manager*
EMP: 35
SALES (corp-wide): 168.7MM Privately Held
WEB: www.cgroxane.com
SIC: 2086 7999 Mfg Bottled/Canned Soft Drinks Amusement/Recreation Services
PA: Cg Roxane Llc
1210 State Hwy 395
Olancha CA 93549
760 764-2885

(G-19096)
ELAN PUBLISHING COMPANY INC
72 Whittier Hwy Unit 3 (03254-3686)
P.O. Box 683, Meredith (03253-0683)
PHONE..................................603 253-6002
Thomas A Power, *CEO*
Sylvia Detscher, *President*
Robin West, *Finance Mgr*
EMP: 44
SQ FT: 20,000
SALES (est): 4MM Privately Held
WEB: www.elanpublish.com
SIC: 2731 Books-Publishing/Printing

(G-19097)
ELECTRCAL INSTLLATIONS INC EII
397 Whittier Hwy (03254-3629)
PHONE..................................603 253-4525
Darlene Fritz, *President*
Charles Fritz, *Vice Pres*
Charles L Fritz Jr, *Vice Pres*
James P Fritz, *Vice Pres*
Jim Fritz, *Vice Pres*
EMP: 35
SQ FT: 2,500
SALES: 9.3MM Privately Held
WEB: www.electricalinstallations.com
SIC: 3613 1731 Mfg Switchgear/Switchboards Electrical Contractor

(G-19098)
STATIM PHARMACEUTICALS INC
58 Bean Rd (03254-3101)
PHONE..................................650 305-0657
Bruce Cohen, *CEO*
Edward Schnipper, *Chief Mktg Ofcr*
EMP: 3
SALES (est): 123.2K Privately Held
SIC: 2834 Mfg Pharmaceutical Preparations

Nashua
Hills County

(G-19099)
ADVANCED CONSULTING
8 Corona Ave (03063-3107)
PHONE..................................603 882-5529
Benjamin M Mikulis, *Principal*
EMP: 3
SALES (est): 122.3K Privately Held
SIC: 3674 Consulting

(G-19100)
CVI GROUP INC (PA)
Also Called: Centorr Vaccum Industries
55 Northstern Blvd Unit 2 (03062)
PHONE..................................603 595-7233
EMP: 4
SQ FT: 40,000
SALES: 22.5MM Privately Held
WEB: www.cvigroup.com
SIC: 3567 Mfg Industrial Furnaces/Ovens

(G-19101)
PREFORMS PLUS
3 Capitol St (03063-1003)
PHONE..................................603 889-8311
EMP: 4 EST: 2014
SALES (est): 247.6K Privately Held
SIC: 3085 Plastics Bottles

Nashua
Hillsborough County

(G-19102)
494 AMHERST ST LLC
494 Amherst St (03063-1224)
PHONE..................................470 430-4608
Juan Antonio Solis, *Mng Member*
Luis Angel, *Mng Member*
EMP: 5
SALES (est): 139.9K Privately Held
SIC: 2032 Mfg Canned Specialties

(G-19103)
ABBOTT LABORATORIES
20 Trafalgar Sq Ste 459 (03063-4907)
PHONE..................................603 891-3380
Philip Posa Jr, *Manager*
EMP: 617
SALES (corp-wide): 30.5B Publicly Held
WEB: www.abbott.com
SIC: 2834 Pharmaceutical Preparation
PA: Abbott Laboratories
100 Abbott Park Rd
Abbott Park IL 60064
224 667-6100

(G-19104)
ADVANCED CIRCUIT TECHNOLO
91 Northeastern Blvd (03062-3141)
PHONE..................................603 880-6000
Linda Weston, *Principal*
EMP: 13
SALES (est): 1.6MM Privately Held
SIC: 3672 Mfg Printed Circuit Boards

(G-19105)
AKKEN INC
98 Spit Brook Rd Ste 402 (03062-5737)
PHONE..................................866 590-6695
Giridhar Akkineni, *CEO*

Satish Arukala, *Director*
EMP: 51
SQ FT: 6,000
SALES (est): 5.7MM **Privately Held**
SIC: 7372 Prepackaged Software Services

(G-19106)
AKUMINA INC
Also Called: Inc, Akumina
30 Temple St Ste 301 (03060-2414)
PHONE..................................603 318-8269
Ed Rogers, *CEO*
Ali Riaz, *Ch of Bd*
David Maffei, *President*
Tahlor Dicicco, *Vice Pres*
John Dibartolomeo, *CFO*
EMP: 23
SALES (est): 419.7K **Privately Held**
SIC: 7372 Prepackaged Software Services

(G-19107)
ALACRON INC
71 Spit Brook Rd Ste 200 (03060-5636)
PHONE..................................603 891-2750
Joseph A Sgro, *CEO*
Paul Stanton, *President*
Gabor Szakacs, *Engineer*
EMP: 10
SQ FT: 10,000
SALES: 3.6MM **Privately Held**
WEB: www.alacron.com
SIC: 3571 Mfg Electronic Computers

(G-19108)
ALBERT LANDRY
Also Called: L & L Fabricators
100 Factory St Ste E1 (03060-9305)
PHONE..................................603 883-1919
Albert Landry, *Owner*
EMP: 5
SQ FT: 6,800
SALES (est): 509.7K **Privately Held**
SIC: 3444 Mfg Sheet Metalwork

(G-19109)
ALL SEASONS
165 Ledge St (03060-3061)
PHONE..................................603 560-7777
EMP: 3 **EST:** 2012
SALES (est): 160K **Privately Held**
SIC: 3552 Mfg Textile Machinery

(G-19110)
ALLEN SYSTEMS GROUP INC
30 Temple St Fl 6 (03060-3483)
PHONE..................................239 435-2200
Jeremy Davis, *Branch Mgr*
EMP: 55
SALES (corp-wide): 245.5MM **Privately Held**
WEB: www.asg.com
SIC: 7372 Systems And Applications Management Software
PA: Asg Technologies Group, Inc.
708 Goodlette Rd N
Naples FL 34102
239 435-2200

(G-19111)
ALPHA GRAPH PRINTSHOP
Also Called: AlphaGraphics
97 Main St Ste 1 (03060-2751)
PHONE..................................603 595-1444
Mary Sue Orpin, *Partner*
David Orpin, *Partner*
EMP: 13
SQ FT: 5,500
SALES: 1.4MM **Privately Held**
SIC: 2752 7334 Lithographic Commercial Printing Photocopying Services

(G-19112)
AMBER HOLDING INC (DH)
107 Northeastern Blvd (03062-1916)
PHONE..................................603 324-3000
Charles E Moran, *President*
John Ambrose, *General Mgr*
Heide Abelli, *Vice Pres*
Reegan Fitzpatrick, *Vice Pres*
Jodi Gorodesky, *Vice Pres*
EMP: 23
SALES (est): 4.8MM
SALES (corp-wide): 352.2K **Privately Held**
SIC: 7372 Prepackaged Software Services
HQ: Skillsoft Corporation
300 Innovative Way # 201
Nashua NH 03062
603 324-3000

(G-19113)
AMPHENOL CORPORATION
Also Called: Amphenol Printed Circuits
91 Northeastern Blvd (03062-3141)
PHONE..................................603 879-3000
Tom Pursch, *Manager*
Bob McGrath, *Senior Mgr*
EMP: 400
SALES (corp-wide): 8.2B **Publicly Held**
SIC: 3672 Mfg Printed Circuit Boards
PA: Amphenol Corporation
358 Hall Ave
Wallingford CT 06492
203 265-8900

(G-19114)
AMPHENOL CORPORATION
Amphenol TCS
200 Innovative Way # 201 (03062-5740)
PHONE..................................603 879-3000
Patricia Burns, *Vice Pres*
John Treanor, *Vice Pres*
Albert Chen, *Engineer*
John Dunham, *Engineer*
Gerry Grassett, *Engineer*
EMP: 345
SALES (corp-wide): 8.2B **Publicly Held**
SIC: 3678 3643 3661 3496 Mfg Elec Connectors Mfg Conductive Wire Dvcs Mfg Telephone/Graph Eqip Mfg Misc Fab Wire Prdts Nonfrs Wiredrwng/Insltng
PA: Amphenol Corporation
358 Hall Ave
Wallingford CT 06492
203 265-8900

(G-19115)
AMPHENOL PRINTED CIRCUITS INC
Also Called: APC Phno
91 Northeastern Blvd (03062-3141)
PHONE..................................603 324-4500
R Adam Norwitt, *President*
Wendy Moody, *Program Mgr*
Edward C Wetmore, *Admin Sec*
Sovanna Hin, *Technician*
▲ **EMP:** 2200
SQ FT: 50,000
SALES (est): 228.8MM
SALES (corp-wide): 8.2B **Publicly Held**
WEB: www.act-flexcircuit.com
SIC: 3679 3678 3672 3357 Mfg Elec Components Mfg Elec Connectors Mfg Printed Circuit Brds Nonfrs Wiredrwng/Insltng
PA: Amphenol Corporation
358 Hall Ave
Wallingford CT 06492
203 265-8900

(G-19116)
AQYR TECHNOLOGIES INC
12 Murphy Dr Ste 200 (03062-1949)
PHONE..................................603 402-6099
Carl D'Alessandro, *President*
Donald Nadreau, *Vice Pres*
Shawn Augustine, *Engineer*
Scott Weber, *Engineer*
Kimberly Dickey, *Treasurer*
EMP: 25
SALES (est): 6MM
SALES (corp-wide): 18.2MM **Privately Held**
SIC: 3663 Mfg Radio/Tv Communication Equipment
PA: Windmill International, Inc.
12 Murphy Dr Ste 200
Nashua NH 03062
603 888-5502

(G-19117)
ARC TECHNOLOGY SOLUTIONS LLC
165 Ledge St Ste 4 (03060-3061)
PHONE..................................603 883-3027
Kenneth Collins, *President*
Allan Baldvins, *Vice Pres*
Richard Martin, *Vice Pres*
Kevin Hughes, *Engineer*
W Robert Nichols II, *CFO*
EMP: 33
SQ FT: 15,000
SALES (est): 11.8MM **Privately Held**
WEB: www.arcserv.com
SIC: 3825 3812 3829 8711 Mfg Elec Measuring Instr Mfg Search/Navgatn Equip Mfg Measure/Control Dvcs Engineering Services

(G-19118)
AUTAJON PACKG - BOSTON CORP
Also Called: Two C Pack
100 Northwest Blvd (03063-4006)
PHONE..................................603 595-0700
Patrick Pagani, *COO*
▲ **EMP:** 100
SQ FT: 350,000
SALES (est): 26.7MM
SALES (corp-wide): 6.9MM **Privately Held**
SIC: 2657 Whol Nondurable Goods
HQ: Autajon Cs
Petit Pelican Petit Pelican
Montelimar 26200
475 002-000

(G-19119)
AUTOVIRT INC
12 Murphy Dr (03062-1903)
PHONE..................................603 546-2900
Josh Klein, *CEO*
Klavs Landberg, *CTO*
EMP: 9 **EST:** 2007
SALES (est): 815.6K **Privately Held**
SIC: 7372 Prepackaged Software Services

(G-19120)
BAE SYSTEMS ELCTRONIC SOLUTION
65 Spit Brook Rd (03060-6909)
PHONE..................................603 885-3653
Thomas Arseneault, *President*
Donna Ryan, *Engineer*
David Cadorette, *Director*
EMP: 12
SALES (est): 1.3MM **Privately Held**
SIC: 3812 Mfg Search/Navigation Equipment

(G-19121)
BAE SYSTEMS INFO & ELEC SYS (DH)
65 Spit Brook Rd (03060-6909)
P.O. Box 868 (03061-0868)
PHONE..................................603 885-4321
Terry Crimmins, *CEO*
Martin Bennett, *General Mgr*
Maria Bustamante, *Vice Pres*
Kenneth Chu, *Vice Pres*
Clive Marchant, *Vice Pres*
EMP: 277 **EST:** 1951
SQ FT: 622,000
SALES (est): 2.4B
SALES (corp-wide): 22.1B **Privately Held**
WEB: www.iesi.na.baesystems.com
SIC: 3812 Mfg Search/Navigation Equipment

(G-19122)
BAE SYSTEMS INFO & ELEC SYS
95 Canal St (03064-2813)
P.O. Box 868 (03061-0868)
PHONE..................................603 885-4321
Brian Walters, *Vice Pres*
EMP: 336
SALES (corp-wide): 22.1B **Privately Held**
WEB: www.iesi.na.baesystems.com
SIC: 3812 Mfg Search/Navigation Equipment
HQ: Bae Systems Information And Electronic Systems Integration Inc.
65 Spit Brook Rd
Nashua NH 03060
603 885-4321

(G-19123)
BAE SYSTEMS INFO & ELEC SYS
65 Spit Brook Rd (03060-6909)
PHONE..................................603 885-3653
Zev Fixler, *Engineer*
EMP: 133
SALES (corp-wide): 22.1B **Privately Held**
WEB: www.iesi.na.baesystems.com
SIC: 3812 Navigational Systems & Equipment
HQ: Bae Systems Information And Electronic Systems Integration Inc.
65 Spit Brook Rd
Nashua NH 03060
603 885-4321

(G-19124)
BAE SYSTEMS INFO & ELEC SYS
9 Canal St (03064-2804)
PHONE..................................603 885-3770
Robert Brown, *Engineer*
Keith Kuczkowski, *Engineer*
Todd Marshall, *Engineer*
Kam Mun, *Engineer*
Larry Glennon, *Program Mgr*
EMP: 8
SALES (corp-wide): 22.1B **Privately Held**
SIC: 3728 3812 Mfg Search/Navgatn Equip
HQ: Bae Systems Information And Electronic Systems Integration Inc.
65 Spit Brook Rd
Nashua NH 03060
603 885-4321

(G-19125)
BAUSCH ARTICULATING PAPERS INC
12 Murphy Dr Unit 4 (03062-1930)
PHONE..................................603 883-2155
Ronald Joseph Kraus, *President*
Donna Kraus, *Vice Pres*
Karen Baker, *Office Mgr*
EMP: 4
SALES (est): 320K **Privately Held**
SIC: 3843 Whol Medical/Hospital Equipment

(G-19126)
BENCHMARK ELECTRONICS INC
100 Innovative Way # 100 (03062-5748)
PHONE..................................603 879-7000
Arthur Ryan, *Safety Mgr*
Cathy Schuyler, *Buyer*
Roy Lewis, *Engineer*
Elaine Ouellette, *Train & Dev Mgr*
Gerry Leo, *Branch Mgr*
EMP: 350
SALES (corp-wide): 2.5B **Publicly Held**
WEB: www.bench.com
SIC: 3672 Mfg Printed Circuit Boards
PA: Benchmark Electronics, Inc.
56 S Rockford Dr
Tempe AZ 85281
623 300-7000

(G-19127)
BLANCHARD PRINTING
16 Pinebrook Rd (03062-2240)
PHONE..................................603 891-1505
J Barrile, *Principal*
EMP: 4
SALES (est): 343.5K **Privately Held**
SIC: 2752 Lithographic Commercial Printing

(G-19128)
BOBOS INDOOR PLAYGROUND
522 Amherst St (03063-1019)
PHONE..................................603 718-8721
Adam Razzaboni, *Principal*
EMP: 4 **EST:** 2010
SALES (est): 250.5K **Privately Held**
SIC: 3949 Mfg Sporting/Athletic Goods

(G-19129)
BOSTON BILLOWS INC
55 Lake St Ste 7 (03060-4516)
PHONE..................................603 598-1200
Eric Skoug, *President*
Kim Igoe, *Vice Pres*
EMP: 8
SALES (est): 480K **Privately Held**
WEB: www.bostonbillows.com
SIC: 2392 Mfg Household Furnishings

(G-19130)
BRONZE CRAFT CORPORATION
37 Will St (03060-6002)
P.O. Box 788 (03061-0788)
PHONE..................................603 883-7747
Jack Atkinson, *Ch of Bd*
James J Bernard, *President*
James R Lajeunesse, *Vice Pres*
Gerald Bell, *Treasurer*
Beverly J Coelho, *Admin Sec*
▲ **EMP:** 60 **EST:** 1944
SQ FT: 55,000
SALES (est): 8.8MM **Privately Held**
WEB: www.bronzecraft.com
SIC: 3365 3366 3429 Aluminum Foundrycopper Foundry Mfg Hardware

(G-19131)
CARR MANAGEMENT INC (PA)
Also Called: Plastic Industries
1 Tara Blvd Ste 303 (03062-2809)
PHONE..................................603 888-1315
Beth Muscato, *CEO*
Andrew Carr, *Ch of Bd*
Gary Perry, *Vice Pres*
Robert Pearson, *CFO*
EMP: 12
SALES (est): 66.4MM **Privately Held**
SIC: 3085 Mfg Plastic Bottles

(G-19132)
CENTORR/VACUUM INDUSTRIES LLC (PA)
55 Northstern Blvd Unit 2 (03062)
PHONE..................................603 595-7233
William Nareski, *President*
Stephen Hewitt, *Vice Pres*
Kyle Melendy, *Engineer*
Ernest Morin, *Engineer*
Matthew Paul, *Engineer*
EMP: 44 **EST:** 1962
SQ FT: 40,000
SALES (est): 13.1MM **Privately Held**
WEB: www.centorr.com
SIC: 3567 Mfg Industrial Furnaces/Ovens

(G-19133)
CIRCUIT CONNECT INC
4 State St (03063-1012)
PHONE..................................603 880-7447
Richard Clutz, *President*
Mark Sites, *President*
Tim Kansler, *VP Engrg*
Marsha Matzkin, *VP Finance*
Charlene Carignan, *Accountant*
▲ **EMP:** 40
SQ FT: 28,000
SALES (est): 6.9MM **Privately Held**
WEB: www.circuit-connect.com
SIC: 3672 Mfg Printed Circuit Boards

(G-19134)
CLEAR ALIGN LLC
Clear Align North
24 Simon St (03060-3025)
PHONE..................................603 889-2116
Jonathan Kane, *CTO*
EMP: 15
SALES (corp-wide): 14.4MM **Privately Held**
SIC: 3827 Mfg Optical Instruments/Lenses
PA: Clear Align Llc
2550 Boulevard Of The Gen
Eagleville PA 19403
484 956-0510

(G-19135)
COLLINS PRECISION MACHINING
55 Lake St Ste 7 (03060-4516)
P.O. Box 1205 (03061-1205)
PHONE..................................603 882-2474
Michael Collins, *President*
EMP: 3
SQ FT: 2,030
SALES: 100K **Privately Held**
SIC: 3599 Mfg Industrial Machinery

(G-19136)
COLONIAL ELECTRONIC MFRS INC
1 Chestnut St Ste 203 (03060-9307)
PHONE..................................603 881-8244
Steven Holzman, *President*
Janet Holzman, *Vice Pres*
Martika Tetreault, *Buyer*
Mary R Berger, *Office Mgr*
Donna Demanche, *Planning*
▲ **EMP:** 45
SQ FT: 15,000
SALES (est): 11MM **Privately Held**
WEB: www.ceminc.net
SIC: 3672 Mfg Printed Circuit Boards

(G-19137)
COLORMARK INC
25 Progress Ave Ste A (03062-1942)
PHONE..................................603 595-2244
Robert J Marsh Jr, *President*
Jack Marsh, *COO*
EMP: 13
SQ FT: 6,250
SALES (est): 2.2MM **Privately Held**
SIC: 2672 Mfg Tapes & Labels

(G-19138)
CPH PROGRAM & MACHINE TOOL DES
134 Haines St 17 (03060-4093)
PHONE..................................603 716-3849
Christopher Hudon, *Administration*
EMP: 11
SALES (est): 1.5MM **Privately Held**
SIC: 3599 Mfg Industrial Machinery

(G-19139)
CRANE SECURITY TECH INC
Also Called: Crane Currency
1 Cellu Dr (03063-1008)
PHONE..................................603 881-1860
Stephen P Defalco, *President*
Gerald J Gartner, *President*
Stephen Curdo, *Vice Pres*
Melissa Kollman, *Purchasing*
Tom Bruneau, *Project Engr*
▲ **EMP:** 35
SQ FT: 12,700
SALES (est): 12MM
SALES (corp-wide): 3.3B **Publicly Held**
WEB: www.crane.com
SIC: 2621 Paper Mill
HQ: Crane & Co., Inc.
1 Beacon St Ste 1702
Boston MA 02108
617 648-3799

(G-19140)
CRITICAL PRCESS FILTRATION INC (PA)
1 Chestnut St Ste 221 (03060-9306)
PHONE..................................603 595-0140
Fred Arbogast, *CEO*
Kristen Ramalho, *President*
▲ **EMP:** 33 **EST:** 1998
SQ FT: 50,000
SALES (est): 4.4MM **Privately Held**
SIC: 2834 Mfg Pharmaceutical Preparations

(G-19141)
CUSTOM MANUFACTURING SVCS INC
Also Called: CMS
235 Main Dunstable Rd (03062-1904)
PHONE..................................603 883-1355
Susan A Beem, *President*
Raymond Durand, *Vice Pres*
David Persall, *Vice Pres*
Jean Karen, *Prdtn Mgr*
Derek Long, *Purch Dir*
▲ **EMP:** 40 **EST:** 1976
SQ FT: 13,500
SALES (est): 9.5MM **Privately Held**
WEB: www.cms-inc.org
SIC: 3672 3663 3679 3812 Mfg Printed Circuit Brds Mfg Radio/Tv Comm Equip Mfg Elec Components Mfg Search/Navgatn Equip Mfg Communications Equip

(G-19142)
D D G FABRICATION
29 Crown St (03060-6486)
PHONE..................................603 883-9292
Robert Moncada, *Principal*
EMP: 8
SALES (est): 971.1K **Privately Held**
SIC: 3444 Mfg Sheet Metalwork

(G-19143)
DELL INC
300 Innovative Way # 301 (03062-5746)
PHONE..................................603 579-9630
EMP: 150
SALES (corp-wide): 90.6B **Publicly Held**
SIC: 3571 Mfg Electronic Computers
HQ: Dell Inc.
1 Dell Way
Round Rock TX 78682
800 289-3355

(G-19144)
DELTA EDUCATION LLC
Also Called: Cpo Science
80 Northwest Blvd (03063-4067)
P.O. Box 3000 (03061-3000)
PHONE..................................800 258-1302
Steven Korte, *President*
Karen Moore, *Sales Staff*
Eileen Patrick, *Manager*
Ken Wesson, *Consultant*
▲ **EMP:** 300
SQ FT: 350,000
SALES (est): 41.2MM
SALES (corp-wide): 673.4MM **Publicly Held**
WEB: www.delta-edu.com
SIC: 3944 Mfg Games/Toys
PA: School Specialty, Inc.
W6316 Design Dr
Greenville WI 54942
920 734-5712

(G-19145)
DENALI SOFTWARE INC
154 Broad St Ste 1535 (03063-3205)
PHONE..................................603 566-0991
EMP: 3
SALES (corp-wide): 2.1B **Publicly Held**
SIC: 7372 Prepackaged Software Services
HQ: Denali Software, Inc.
2655 Seely Ave
San Jose CA 95134

(G-19146)
DISPERSION SERVICES LLC
25 Front St Ste 201 (03064-2696)
PHONE..................................603 577-9520
Rick Keirstead, *Purchasing*
William Lynch, *Mng Member*
Cheryl Lynch, *Admin Sec*
EMP: 6
SQ FT: 10,000
SALES (est): 710K **Privately Held**
WEB: www.dispersionservices.com
SIC: 2899 Mfg Chemical Preparations

(G-19147)
DREAMTECH WATER SOLUTIONS LLC
159 Main St Ste 100 (03060-2725)
PHONE..................................603 513-7829
William Taveras, *Manager*
EMP: 3
SALES (est): 122K **Privately Held**
SIC: 3589 Mfg Service Industry Machinery

(G-19148)
ELLAB INC
74 Northeastern Blvd (03062-3192)
PHONE..................................603 417-3363
EMP: 4
SALES (corp-wide): 449K **Privately Held**
SIC: 3823 Mfg Process Control Instruments
HQ: Ellab Inc
303 E 17th Ave Ste 10
Denver CO 80203
303 425-3370

(G-19149)
ELMO MOTION CONTROL INC
42 Technology Way (03060-3245)
PHONE..................................603 821-9979
John McLaughlin, *CEO*
James Anderson, *Engineer*
Kris Libby, *Engineer*
Lester Shaw, *Engineer*
EMP: 15
SALES (est): 3.6MM
SALES (corp-wide): 33.1MM **Privately Held**
WEB: www.elmomc.com
SIC: 3541 Mfg Machine Tools-Cutting
PA: Elmo Motion Control Limited
60 Amal
Petah Tikva 49513
392 923-00

(G-19150)
EPISERVER INC (DH)
542 Amherst St (03063-1016)
PHONE..................................603 594-0249
Bill Rogers, *CEO*
June Morris, *Senior VP*
Ben Schilens, *Senior VP*
David Ryan, *Vice Pres*
Shelley Svien, *Opers Staff*
EMP: 109 **EST:** 1998
SQ FT: 27,000
SALES (est): 57.5MM **Privately Held**
WEB: www.ektron.com
SIC: 7372 Prepackaged Software Services
HQ: Episerver Ab
Regeringsgatan 67
Stockholm 111 5
855 582-700

(G-19151)
EVERETT CHARLES TECH LLC
Also Called: APJ Test Consulting
41 Simon St Ste 1b (03060-3091)
PHONE..................................603 882-2621
EMP: 30
SALES (corp-wide): 451.7MM **Publicly Held**
SIC: 3825 Mfg Electrical Measuring Instruments
HQ: Everett Charles Technologies, Llc
14570 Meyer Canyon Dr # 100
Fontana CA 92336
909 625-5551

(G-19152)
EXTECH INSTRUMENTS CORPORATION
9 Townsend W (03063-1233)
PHONE..................................887 439-8324
Gerald W Blakeley III, *President*
Scott Pantalone Sr, *President*
Lucy M Blakeley, *Treasurer*
Elise Pantalone, *Treasurer*
▲ **EMP:** 79
SQ FT: 30,000
SALES (est): 13.6MM
SALES (corp-wide): 1.7B **Publicly Held**
SIC: 3825 3823 3577 Mfg Elec Measuring Instr Mfg Process Cntrl Instr Mfg Computer Peripherals
PA: Flir Systems, Inc.
27700 Sw Parkway Ave
Wilsonville OR 97070
503 498-3547

(G-19153)
FAB BRAZE CORP (PA)
5 Progress Ave (03062-1908)
PHONE..................................781 893-6777
Gordon Riblet, *President*
Stanley Berensen, *Clerk*
EMP: 3 **EST:** 1944
SQ FT: 6,000
SALES (est): 2.8MM **Privately Held**
SIC: 3559 3599 Machine Shop & Foundry

(G-19154)
FASTVISION LLC
71 Spit Brook Rd Ste 201 (03060-5636)
PHONE..................................603 891-4317
Joseph Sgro,
Paul Stanton,
EMP: 12
SQ FT: 10,000
SALES (est): 1.5MM **Privately Held**
WEB: www.fast-vision.com
SIC: 3861 Wholesale Imaging Cameras

(G-19155)
FDR CENTER FOR PROST
39 Simon St Ste 7 (03060-3046)
PHONE..................................603 595-9255
Paul Harney, *President*
EMP: 4
SALES (est): 622.7K **Privately Held**
SIC: 3842 Mfg Surgical Appliances/Supplies

GEOGRAPHIC

(G-19156)
FERRITE MICROWAVE TECH LLC
165 Ledge St Ste 2 (03060-3061)
PHONE....................................603 881-5234
Peter Tibbetts, *CEO*
Jim Welch, *Mfg Staff*
Marianne Lemieux, *Buyer*
Ken Mathis, *Engineer*
Mike Zeadow, *Engineer*
◆ **EMP:** 45
SQ FT: 43,700
SALES (est): 10.1MM **Privately Held**
WEB: www.ferriteinc.com
SIC: 3679 Mfg Electronic Components

(G-19157)
FIBEROPTIC RESALE CORP
21 Technology Way Ste 4e5 (03060-3245)
PHONE....................................603 496-1258
George Kyrias, *President*
EMP: 4
SALES (est): 525K **Privately Held**
SIC: 3357 Nonferrous Wiredrawing/Insulating

(G-19158)
FISHING HOT SPOTS INC
9 Townsend W (03063-1233)
P.O. Box 1167, Rhinelander WI (54501-1167)
PHONE....................................715 365-5555
George Swierczyski, *President*
Cooke Bausmann, *Vice Pres*
Brandt Brown, *Research*
Dawn Richter, *Director*
EMP: 8
SQ FT: 9,000
SALES (est): 1MM **Privately Held**
WEB: www.fishingmaps.net
SIC: 2741 2731 Misc Publishing Books-Publishing/Printing

(G-19159)
FLIR COMMERCIAL SYSTEMS INC
9 Townsend W Ste 1 (03063-1233)
PHONE....................................603 324-7824
Tom Scanllan, *Manager*
EMP: 200
SALES (corp-wide): 1.7B **Publicly Held**
SIC: 3861 Mfg Analytical Instruments
HQ: Flir Commercial Systems, Inc.
6769 Hollister Ave # 100
Goleta CA 93117

(G-19160)
FLIR MARITIME US INC
9 Townsend W (03063-1233)
PHONE....................................603 324-7900
Trudy Nault, *Opers Staff*
Kevin Murphy, *Controller*
Kim Johnson, *Credit Staff*
Tony Tiscio, *Sales Staff*
◆ **EMP:** 45 **EST:** 2001
SQ FT: 18,000
SALES (est): 8.9MM
SALES (corp-wide): 1.7B **Publicly Held**
WEB: www.raymarine.com
SIC: 3812 Mfg Search/Navigation Equipment
HQ: Raymarine Holdings Limited
Marine House
Fareham HANTS
239 269-3611

(G-19161)
FLIR SYSTEMS INC
9 Townsend W Ste 1 (03063-1233)
PHONE....................................603 324-7783
Lisa West Kerblom, *Branch Mgr*
EMP: 150
SALES (corp-wide): 1.7B **Publicly Held**
SIC: 3861 Mfg Analytical Instruments
PA: Flir Systems, Inc.
27700 Sw Parkway Ave
Wilsonville OR 97070
503 498-3547

(G-19162)
FLIR SYSTEMS INC
Also Called: Concrete Sol. Prod. Contact or
9 Townsend W Ste 1 (03063-1233)
PHONE....................................866 636-4487
Andrew C Teich, *CEO*
Earl Lewis, *Ch of Bd*
Todd M Duchene, *Senior VP*
Thomas A Surran, *Senior VP*
William W Davis, *Admin Sec*
EMP: 7
SALES (est): 651.8K **Privately Held**
SIC: 3812 3826 Mfg Search/Navigation Equipment Mfg Analytical Instruments

(G-19163)
FOUNDATION ARMOR LLC
472 Amherst St Unit 14 (03063-1204)
PHONE....................................866 306-0246
Tanya Willette,
Eric Schifone,
EMP: 15 **EST:** 2012
SQ FT: 10,000
SALES (est): 2.8MM **Privately Held**
SIC: 2851 Mfg Paints/Allied Products

(G-19164)
FUSER TECHNOLOGIES CORP
472 Amherst St Unit 22 (03063-1204)
PHONE....................................603 886-5186
Robert P Broden Jr, *President*
EMP: 3
SALES (est): 391K **Privately Held**
SIC: 3861 Mfg Photocopier Parts

(G-19165)
GENERAL DYNAMICS MISSION
24 Simon St (03060-3025)
PHONE....................................603 864-6300
Arcelia Garcia, *Administration*
EMP: 218
SALES (corp-wide): 36.1B **Publicly Held**
SIC: 3827 3851 Mfg Optical Instruments/Lenses Mfg Ophthalmic Goods
HQ: General Dynamics Mission Systems, Inc.
12450 Fair Lakes Cir # 200
Fairfax VA 22033
703 263-2800

(G-19166)
GENERATOR POWER SOLUTIONS NENG
29 Dickerman St (03060-5054)
PHONE....................................603 577-1766
Donna Sanders, *Owner*
Patrick Sanders, *Co-Owner*
EMP: 3
SALES: 170K **Privately Held**
SIC: 3621 Mfg Motors/Generators

(G-19167)
GEOPHYSICAL SURVEY SYSTEMS INC (DH)
Also Called: Gssi
40 Simon St Ste 1 (03060-3075)
PHONE....................................603 893-1109
Christopher C Hawekotte, *President*
Lorayne Pincence, *Prdtn Mgr*
Peter Masters, *Engineer*
Chris Plumlee, *Engineer*
Donald K Walczyk, *Treasurer*
EMP: 80
SQ FT: 30,000
SALES: 22.9MM **Privately Held**
WEB: www.geophysical.com
SIC: 3829 Mfg Measuring/Controlling Devices

(G-19168)
GL&V USA INC (HQ)
1 Cellu Dr Ste 200 (03063-1008)
PHONE....................................603 882-2711
Richard Verreault, *President*
David Dube, *Business Mgr*
Jose Santiago, *Business Mgr*
Glen Hicks, *Purch Mgr*
Nicole Guidoboni, *Buyer*
◆ **EMP:** 277 **EST:** 2000
SALES: 110MM **Privately Held**
WEB: www.glv.com
SIC: 3554 Mfg Paper Industrial Machinery
PA: Gl&V Us Corporation
175 Crystal St
Lenox MA 01240
413 637-2424

(G-19169)
GL&V USA INC
1 Cellu Dr Ste 200 (03063-1008)
PHONE....................................603 882-2711
Steven Shartrand, *Branch Mgr*
EMP: 75
SALES (corp-wide): 110MM **Privately Held**
WEB: www.glv.com
SIC: 3554 3826 Mfg Paper Industrial Machinery Mfg Analytical Instruments
HQ: Gl&V Usa Inc.
1 Cellu Dr Ste 200
Nashua NH 03063
603 882-2711

(G-19170)
GORILLA CIRCUITS
207 Main St (03060-2963)
PHONE....................................603 864-0283
EMP: 16
SALES (corp-wide): 36.2MM **Privately Held**
SIC: 3672 Mfg Printed Circuit Boards
PA: Gorilla Circuits
1445 Oakland Rd
San Jose CA 95112
408 294-9897

(G-19171)
GRANITE STATE FINISHING INC
141 Canal St Unit 2 (03064-2879)
PHONE....................................603 880-4130
Gary Gostanian, *President*
Joann Gostanian, *Vice Pres*
EMP: 5
SQ FT: 20,000
SALES (est): 585.3K **Privately Held**
SIC: 3479 7336 Coating/Engraving Service Commercial Art/Graphic Design

(G-19172)
GREENERD PRESS & MCH CO LLC (PA)
41 Crown St (03060-6349)
P.O. Box 886 (03061-0886)
PHONE....................................603 889-4101
Jerry Letendre,
Dafney Phua,
▲ **EMP:** 20 **EST:** 1962
SQ FT: 27,000
SALES (est): 6.1MM **Privately Held**
WEB: www.greenerd.com
SIC: 3542 Mfg Machine Tools-Forming

(G-19173)
GTAT CORPORATION
20 Trafalgar Sq (03063-1985)
PHONE....................................603 883-5200
EMP: 5 **Privately Held**
SIC: 3674 3567 Mfg Semiconductors/Related Devices Mfg Industrial Furnaces/Ovens
HQ: Gtat Corporation
5 Wentworth Dr 1
Hudson NH 03051

(G-19174)
GUARDIAN TECHNOLOGIES INC
4 Townsend W (03063-4220)
PHONE....................................603 594-0430
Mark Monreou, *Manager*
EMP: 3
SALES (est): 178K **Privately Held**
SIC: 3672 Mfg Printed Circuit Boards

(G-19175)
H6 SYSTEMS INCORPORATED
Also Called: H 6
55 Lake St Ste 11 (03060-4516)
PHONE....................................603 880-4190
Michael W Hunter, *President*
EMP: 4
SQ FT: 2,000
SALES: 2MM **Privately Held**
WEB: www.h6systems.com
SIC: 3825 Mfg Instruments For Measuring & Testing Of Electricity & Electrical Signals

(G-19176)
HAMPSHIRE CHEMICAL CORP (DH)
2 E Spit Brook Rd (03060)
PHONE....................................603 888-2320
James Mc Ilvenny, *President*
Roger R Gaudette, *Engrg Dir*
Patrick J Mc Mahon, *Business Dir*
Cheryl Corbett, *Admin Sec*
▼ **EMP:** 20
SQ FT: 50,000
SALES (est): 23.1MM
SALES (corp-wide): 61B **Publicly Held**
SIC: 2869 2899 2891 2851 Mfg Industl Organic Chem Mfg Chemical Preparation Mfg Adhesives/Sealants Mfg Paints/Allied Prdts Mfg Indstl Inorgan Chem
HQ: The Dow Chemical Company
2211 H H Dow Way
Midland MI 48642
989 636-1000

(G-19177)
HERBERT MOSHER
Also Called: Framery, The
60 Main St Ste 2 (03060-2720)
PHONE....................................603 882-4357
Herbert Mosher, *Owner*
EMP: 3 **EST:** 1976
SQ FT: 2,000
SALES (est): 250.1K **Privately Held**
SIC: 2499 7999 7699 Mfg Wood Products Amusement/Recreation Services Repair Services

(G-19178)
HIGHLAND TOOL CO INC
20 Simon St (03060-3096)
PHONE....................................603 882-6907
Donald Boulia, *President*
William Boula, *Vice Pres*
EMP: 15 **EST:** 1952
SQ FT: 10,000
SALES (est): 2.5MM **Privately Held**
SIC: 3599 Mfg Industrial Machinery

(G-19179)
HOLLIS CONTROLS INC (PA)
131 Daniel Webster Hwy (03060-5224)
PHONE....................................603 595-2482
Thomas Duff, *President*
Linda Duff, *Treasurer*
EMP: 6
SALES: 491.8K **Privately Held**
SIC: 3625 3629 Mfg Relays/Industrial Controls Mfg Electrical Industrial Apparatus

(G-19180)
HUNTLEY BENARD INDUSTRIES INC
5 Pine Street Ext (03060-3248)
PHONE....................................603 943-7813
EMP: 3
SALES (est): 106.6K **Privately Held**
SIC: 3999 Mfg Misc Products

(G-19181)
ICAD INC (PA)
98 Spit Brook Rd Ste 100 (03062-5734)
PHONE....................................603 882-5200
Michael Klein, *Ch of Bd*
Stacey Stevens, *Exec VP*
Kamal Gogineni, *Vice Pres*
Sergei Fotin, *Research*
Hrishikesh Haldankar, *Research*
EMP: 119
SQ FT: 11,000
SALES: 25.6MM **Publicly Held**
WEB: www.icadmed.com
SIC: 3841 2834 Mfg Surgical/Medical Instruments Pharmaceutical Preparations

(G-19182)
ID TECHNOLOGY LLC
Winco ID
237 Main Dunstable Rd (03062-1904)
PHONE....................................603 598-1553
Stan Kosidlo, *Branch Mgr*
EMP: 3
SALES (corp-wide): 587.9MM **Privately Held**
SIC: 3565 Mfg Packaging Machinery

HQ: Id Technology Llc
5051 N Sylvania Ave # 405
Fort Worth TX 76137
817 626-7779

(G-19183)
IE CHEMICAL SYSTEMS INC
402 S Main St (03060-5043)
PHONE..................................603 888-4777
Gary Bergeron, *President*
EMP: 10
SQ FT: 1,000
SALES (est): 1.2MM **Privately Held**
SIC: 3625 Chemical Automated Systems

(G-19184)
IMCOR INC
74 Northeastrn Blvd 19a (03062)
PHONE..................................603 886-4300
Robert S Ura, *President*
Kenneth H Ura, *Vice Pres*
Stephen Ura, *Vice Pres*
EMP: 5
SQ FT: 2,400
SALES (est): 282.6K **Privately Held**
SIC: 3842 Dental Implant Manufacturer

(G-19185)
IMPELLIMAX INC
165 Ledge St Ste 3 (03060-3061)
PHONE..................................603 886-9569
David Robbins, *CEO*
Carl Lueders, *CFO*
Beth Robbins, *Office Mgr*
▲ **EMP:** 13
SQ FT: 8,592
SALES (est): 808K
SALES (corp-wide): 5.3MM **Privately Held**
WEB: www.impellimax.com
SIC: 3674 Mfg Semiconductors/Related Devices
HQ: Monzite Corporation
165 Ledge St
Nashua NH 03060
617 429-7050

(G-19186)
IN THE MIX
2 Vernon St (03064-2672)
PHONE..................................603 557-2078
Michael L Laws Esq, *Principal*
EMP: 3 **EST:** 2015
SALES (est): 228.2K **Privately Held**
SIC: 3273 Mfg Ready-Mixed Concrete

(G-19187)
INCREDIBREW INC
112 Daniel Webster Hwy # 1 (03060-5243)
PHONE..................................603 891-2477
David Williams, *President*
Tim Sadler, *CTO*
EMP: 4
SALES (est): 360K **Privately Held**
WEB: www.incredibrew.com
SIC: 2082 5149 Mfg Malt Beverages Whol Groceries

(G-19188)
INNOVATIVE TEST SOLUTIONS LLC
41 Simon St Ste 2f (03060-3091)
PHONE..................................603 288-0280
Donald Chin, *Mng Member*
EMP: 8
SALES (est): 500K **Privately Held**
SIC: 3825 Mfg Electrical Measuring Instruments

(G-19189)
INTEGRITY LASER INC
6 Spruce St Unit 2 (03060-3518)
PHONE..................................603 930-1413
Jeff Muster, *President*
EMP: 3
SALES: 750K **Privately Held**
SIC: 3999 Mfg Misc Products

(G-19190)
INTERACTIVE SYSTEMS INC
Also Called: ISI-Exeter
61 Spit Brook Rd Ste 406 (03060-5614)
PHONE..................................603 318-7700
C Brown Lingamfelter, *President*
Dennis Charles, *Vice Pres*
EMP: 14
SQ FT: 3,000
SALES (est): 3MM **Privately Held**
WEB: www.isilink.com
SIC: 7372 Prepackaged Software Services

(G-19191)
IPG PHOTONICS CORPORATION
200 Innovative Way # 1390 (03062-5741)
PHONE..................................603 518-3200
Jeffrey Sercel,
EMP: 23
SALES (corp-wide): 1.4B **Publicly Held**
SIC: 3699 Mfg Electrical Equipment/Supplies
PA: Ipg Photonics Corporation
50 Old Webster Rd
Oxford MA 01540
508 373-1100

(G-19192)
K6 MANUFACTURING INC
15 Macdonald Dr (03062-1855)
PHONE..................................603 888-4669
Bob Krikwood, *President*
Mary Kirkwood, *Treasurer*
EMP: 6
SALES: 260K **Privately Held**
WEB: www.k6mfg.com
SIC: 3599 Mfg Industrial Machinery

(G-19193)
KELLEY BROS NEW ENGLAND LLC
16 Celina Ave (03063-1024)
PHONE..................................603 748-0274
Ken McNamara, *Manager*
EMP: 3
SALES (corp-wide): 43.1MM **Privately Held**
SIC: 2431 Mfg Millwork
HQ: Kelley Bros. Of New England, Llc
17 Hampshire Dr Ste 20
Hudson NH 03051
603 881-5559

(G-19194)
KEVIN S BOGHIGIAN
Also Called: Mountain Ridge Pet Supply
141 Canal St Unit 4 (03064-2879)
P.O. Box 3073 (03061-3073)
PHONE..................................603 883-0236
Kevin S Boghigian, *Owner*
EMP: 8
SALES (est): 505K **Privately Held**
SIC: 3999 Manufacturer Of Pet Supplies

(G-19195)
L3HARRIS TECHNOLOGIES INC
85 Northwest Blvd (03063-4013)
PHONE..................................603 689-1450
Marilyn Meddles, *Branch Mgr*
EMP: 25
SALES (corp-wide): 6.8B **Publicly Held**
SIC: 3823 3812 Engineering Services
PA: L3harris Technologies, Inc.
1025 W Nasa Blvd
Melbourne FL 32919
321 727-9100

(G-19196)
L3HARRIS TECHNOLOGIES INC
Exelis
85 Northwest Blvd Ste B (03063-4013)
PHONE..................................603 689-1450
Steve Partello, *Branch Mgr*
EMP: 30
SALES (corp-wide): 6.8B **Publicly Held**
WEB: www.ittind.com
SIC: 3625 Mfg Relays/Industrial Controls
PA: L3harris Technologies, Inc.
1025 W Nasa Blvd
Melbourne FL 32919
321 727-9100

(G-19197)
LASER ADVANTAGE LLC
4 Townsend W Ste 2 (03063-4220)
PHONE..................................603 886-9464
Michael R Lynch,
Gary Adams,
EMP: 13
SALES (est): 2MM **Privately Held**
WEB: www.laseradvantage.com
SIC: 3699 Mfg Laser Systems & Equipment

(G-19198)
LCM GROUP INC
3 Taggart Dr Ste C (03060-5592)
PHONE..................................603 888-1248
Lena MEI, *President*
EMP: 3
SQ FT: 700
SALES: 250K **Privately Held**
SIC: 7372 7379 Prepackaged Software Services Computer Related Services

(G-19199)
LOCKHEED MARTIN CORPORATION
410 Amherst St Ste 200 (03063-1238)
P.O. Box 868 (03061-0868)
PHONE..................................603 885-4321
Douglas Coleman, *Vice Pres*
EMP: 435 **Publicly Held**
WEB: www.lockheedmartin.com
SIC: 3812 Mfg Search/Navigation Equipment
PA: Lockheed Martin Corporation
6801 Rockledge Dr
Bethesda MD 20817

(G-19200)
LOCKHEED MARTIN CORPORATION
95 Canal St (03064-2813)
P.O. Box 868 (03061-0868)
PHONE..................................603 885-4321
Galen Ho, *President*
Robert Schaefer, *Principal*
Jacquot Huynh, *Electrical Engi*
EMP: 1261 **Publicly Held**
WEB: www.lockheedmartin.com
SIC: 3812 Mfg Search/Navigation Equipment
PA: Lockheed Martin Corporation
6801 Rockledge Dr
Bethesda MD 20817

(G-19201)
LYCO ENTERPRISES INC
171 Taylor St (03060-5156)
PHONE..................................603 888-2640
Peter Lyons, *President*
EMP: 3
SALES: 550K **Privately Held**
SIC: 3822 Mfg Environmental Controls

(G-19202)
M & M GLASS BLOWING CO INC
Also Called: M & M Glassblowing
2 Townsend W Ste 11a (03063-1277)
PHONE..................................603 598-8195
Wayne Martin, *President*
Susan Martin, *Treasurer*
EMP: 7
SQ FT: 2,400
SALES: 800K **Privately Held**
WEB: www.mmglassblowing.com
SIC: 3229 Manufactures Blown Glass For The Scientific Field

(G-19203)
M J C MACHINE INC
2 W Otterson St (03060-4508)
P.O. Box 1036 (03061-1036)
PHONE..................................603 889-0300
Fax: 603 889-7144
EMP: 11
SQ FT: 8,000
SALES: 2.5MM **Privately Held**
WEB: www.mjcmachine.com
SIC: 3599 Custom Machine Shop

(G-19204)
MASS DESIGN INC (PA)
41 Simon St Ste 2c (03060-3091)
PHONE..................................603 886-6460
Anthony Bourassa, *President*
Paul Boduch, *Vice Pres*
Neil Chulada, *Opers Mgr*
Steve St Pierre, *QC Mgr*
Kanaan Yaseen, *Info Tech Mgr*
EMP: 55
SQ FT: 45,000
SALES (est): 9.2MM **Privately Held**
WEB: www.massdesign.com
SIC: 3672 Mfg Printed Circuit Boards

(G-19205)
MASSAGE CHAIRS FOR LESS
3 Cardinal Cir (03063-3301)
PHONE..................................603 882-7580
Scott Philo, *Owner*
▲ **EMP:** 6
SALES (est): 518.5K **Privately Held**
SIC: 2515 Mfg Mattresses/Bedsprings

(G-19206)
MELEXIS INC
15 Trafalgar Sq Ste 100 (03063-1968)
PHONE..................................603 223-2362
Rudi Dewinter, *President*
Terry Campaniello, *Sales Executive*
EMP: 20
SQ FT: 8,000
SALES (est): 4.4MM
SALES (corp-wide): 183.7K **Privately Held**
WEB: www.melexis.com
SIC: 3674 Mfg Semiconductors/Related Devices
HQ: Melexis
Rozendaalstraat 12
Ieper 8900
572 261-31

(G-19207)
MEVATEC CORP
65 Spit Brook Rd (03060-6909)
PHONE..................................603 885-4321
David Harrold, *Vice Pres*
Leslie Jelalian, *Vice Pres*
Clive Marchant, *Vice Pres*
David Darden, *Project Mgr*
John Labrosse, *Project Mgr*
EMP: 14
SALES (est): 813.9K **Privately Held**
SIC: 3812 Mfg Search/Navigation Equipment

(G-19208)
MINUTEMAN PRESS INTL INC
217 W Hollis St (03060-3094)
PHONE..................................603 718-1439
Charles King, *Branch Mgr*
EMP: 4
SALES (corp-wide): 23.4MM **Privately Held**
SIC: 2752 Comm Prtg Litho
PA: Minuteman Press International, Inc.
61 Executive Blvd
Farmingdale NY 11735
631 249-1370

(G-19209)
MONZITE CORPORATION (HQ)
165 Ledge St (03060-3061)
PHONE..................................617 429-7050
David Robbins, *CEO*
Carl Lueders, *CFO*
▲ **EMP:** 12
SQ FT: 7,800
SALES (est): 1.4MM
SALES (corp-wide): 5.3MM **Privately Held**
SIC: 3679 Manufacturer Of Electronic Components
PA: Omni-Lite Industries Canada Inc
205 5 Ave Sw Suite 1600
Calgary AB
403 298-0331

(G-19210)
MORIN ENGINE SERVICES LLC
151 W Hollis St (03060-3147)
PHONE..................................603 880-3009
John J Morin,
EMP: 6 **EST:** 2008
SALES (est): 785.7K **Privately Held**
SIC: 3714 Mfg Motor Vehicle Parts/Accessories

(G-19211)
N KAMENSKE & CO INC
19 Fairhaven Rd (03060-5305)
PHONE..................................603 888-1007
Allan B Silber, *President*
Kenneth Silber, *Vice Pres*
EMP: 9
SQ FT: 5,000
SALES (est): 650K **Privately Held**
SIC: 3341 Secondary Brass & Bronze Smelting & Refining

GEOGRAPHIC

(G-19212)
NASHUA CIRCUITS INC
29 Crown St (03060-6486)
PHONE..................................603 882-1773
Robert Moncada, *President*
Paul Linehan, *Vice Pres*
Doreen Ouellette, *Engineer*
Roberta Moncada, *Controller*
EMP: 47
SQ FT: 75,000
SALES (est): 6.2MM **Privately Held**
WEB: www.ncipcb.com
SIC: 3672 Mfg Printed Circuit Boards

(G-19213)
NASHUA FOUNDRIES INC
5 Foundry St (03060-3412)
P.O. Box 552 (03061-0552)
PHONE..................................603 882-4811
Peter J Lyons, *President*
Deborah Gourdeau, *Bookkeeper*
Colleen Dupre, *Admin Sec*
EMP: 35 **EST:** 1863
SQ FT: 40,000
SALES (est): 6.3MM **Privately Held**
WEB: www.nashuafoundries.com
SIC: 3321 Gray/Ductile Iron Foundry

(G-19214)
NE DUMPSTER
20 C St (03060-3532)
PHONE..................................603 438-6402
EMP: 3
SALES (est): 195.1K **Privately Held**
SIC: 3443 Mfg Fabricated Plate Work

(G-19215)
NEW HAMPSHIRE OPTICAL SYS INC
10 N Southwood Dr (03063-1819)
PHONE..................................603 391-2909
James Carmichael, *Mng Member*
EMP: 3
SALES: 750K **Privately Held**
SIC: 3229 Clec And Dark Fiber Provider

(G-19216)
NEXUS TECHNOLOGY INC
78 Northastern Blvd Ste 2 (03062)
PHONE..................................877 595-8116
Rob Shelsky, *President*
EMP: 15
SALES (est): 2.9MM **Privately Held**
SIC: 3829 Mfg Measuring/Controlling Devices

(G-19217)
NH RAPID MACHINING LLC
22 Charron Ave (03063-1733)
PHONE..................................603 821-5200
Tom Pursch, *COO*
James Hall, *Production*
Bill Trussell, *Engineer*
Dave Willette, *Engineer*
Scott Trecartin, *Project Engr*
EMP: 8
SQ FT: 300
SALES (est): 2.6MM **Privately Held**
SIC: 3599 Mfg Industrial Machinery

(G-19218)
NORTHEAST CUSTOM CHROME NASHUA
123 Tolles St (03064-2447)
P.O. Box 481 (03061-0481)
PHONE..................................603 566-6165
EMP: 5 **EST:** 2008
SALES (est): 403.4K **Privately Held**
SIC: 3471 Plating/Polishing Service

(G-19219)
NORTHEAST NDT INC
379 Amherst St Ste 208 (03063-1226)
PHONE..................................603 595-4227
Richard Jandrew, *President*
EMP: 3
SALES: 150K **Privately Held**
SIC: 3829 Mfg Measuring/Controlling Devices

(G-19220)
NORTHEAST SILK SCREEN INC
78 Northastern Blvd Ste 1 (03062)
PHONE..................................603 883-6933
Edward Davis, *President*
Ed Davis, *Research*
Veronica A Lawrence, *Treasurer*
EMP: 5
SQ FT: 2,400
SALES (est): 620K **Privately Held**
WEB: www.northeastsilkscreen.com
SIC: 2759 Commercial Printing

(G-19221)
NTP SOFTWARE OF CA INC (PA)
427 Amherst St Ut381 (03063-1258)
PHONE..................................603 641-6937
Dave Crocker, *President*
Bruce Schwartz, *Treasurer*
EMP: 8 **EST:** 1996
SALES (est): 1.8MM **Privately Held**
SIC: 7372 Prepackaged Software Services

(G-19222)
OGDEN NEWSPAPERS NH LLC
Also Called: Telegraph, The
110 Main St Ste 1 (03060-2723)
PHONE..................................603 882-2741
Robert M Nutting,
EMP: 6 **EST:** 2013
SALES (est): 21.3K **Privately Held**
SIC: 2711 Newspapers-Publishing/Printing

(G-19223)
OMRON MICROSCAN SYSTEMS INC
486 Amherst St (03063-1282)
PHONE..................................603 598-8400
F H Van Alstyne, *Branch Mgr*
EMP: 9
SALES (corp-wide): 2.1B **Privately Held**
SIC: 3577 Mfg Computer Peripheral Equipment
HQ: Omron Microscan Systems, Inc.
700 Sw 39th St Ste 100
Renton WA 98057
425 226-5700

(G-19224)
OPTIMUM BINDERY SVCS OF NENG
Also Called: Optimum Bindery Services Neng
120 Nrthstern Blvd Unit 1 (03062)
PHONE..................................603 886-3889
Frank Frisoni, *President*
Joseph Frisoni, *Vice Pres*
EMP: 20
SQ FT: 21,000
SALES (est): 2.6MM **Privately Held**
WEB: www.optimumbindery.com
SIC: 2789 Manufactures Bindings Only

(G-19225)
ORACLE SYSTEMS CORPORATION
1 Oracle Dr Ste 1 # 1 (03062-2833)
PHONE..................................603 897-3000
Jeff Denham, *General Mgr*
Michael Fleck, *Principal*
Andre Basque, *Engineer*
Brett Fishberg, *Technology*
Fengting Chen, *Technical Staff*
EMP: 373
SALES (corp-wide): 39.5B **Publicly Held**
WEB: www.forcecapital.com
SIC: 7372 8731 7374 Prepackaged Software Services Commercial Physical Research Data Processing/Preparation
HQ: Oracle Systems Corporation
500 Oracle Pkwy
Redwood City CA 94065
650 506-7000

(G-19226)
P & D MACHINE INC
29 Mason St (03060-3457)
PHONE..................................603 883-1814
Phillup Lachaince, *President*
EMP: 5
SALES: 250K **Privately Held**
SIC: 3599 Mfg Industrial Machinery

(G-19227)
PASSIFORA PERSONAL PRODUCTS
5 Booth St (03060-4204)
PHONE..................................603 809-6762
Michael Parsons, *CEO*
EMP: 5
SALES: 500K **Privately Held**
SIC: 2676 Mfg Sanitary Paper Products

(G-19228)
PENNWELL CORPORATION
Computer Graphics World
98 Spit Brook Rd (03062-5737)
PHONE..................................603 891-9425
Mark Sinklestcin, *CEO*
EMP: 230 **Privately Held**
SIC: 2721 Periodicals-Publishing/Printing
HQ: Pennwell Corporation
110 S Hartford Ave # 200
Tulsa OK 74120
918 835-3161

(G-19229)
PENNWELL CORPORATION
Also Called: Laser Focus World
98 Spit Brook Rd (03062-5737)
P.O. Box 3004, Tulsa OK (74101-3004)
PHONE..................................603 891-0123
Adam Japko, *President*
EMP: 150 **Privately Held**
SIC: 2721 Periodicals-Publishing/Printing
HQ: Pennwell Corporation
110 S Hartford Ave # 200
Tulsa OK 74120
918 835-3161

(G-19230)
PERUSE SOFTWARE INC
436 Amherst St Ste 222 (03063-1276)
PHONE..................................603 626-0061
Michael Hogan, *CEO*
EMP: 7
SALES: 1MM **Privately Held**
SIC: 7372 Prepackaged Software Services

(G-19231)
PFEIFFER VACUUM INC (DH)
24 Trafalgar Sq (03063-1988)
PHONE..................................603 578-6500
Guillaume Kreziak, *President*
Michael Monroe, *Exec VP*
Howard Anderson, *Vice Pres*
Jim Schlesinger, *Safety Mgr*
Mindy Kosiavelon, *Purch Mgr*
▲ **EMP:** 35
SQ FT: 24,000
SALES (est): 226.6MM
SALES (corp-wide): 603.5MM **Privately Held**
SIC: 3561 Mfg Pumps/Pumping Equipment
HQ: Pfeiffer Vacuum Technology Ag
Berliner Str. 43
ABlar 35614
644 180-20

(G-19232)
PHARIO SOLUTION
11 Northeastern Blvd # 340 (03062-3139)
PHONE..................................603 821-3804
David Soucy, *Manager*
EMP: 4
SALES (est): 198.6K **Privately Held**
SIC: 7372 Prepackaged Software Services

(G-19233)
PHOENIX SCREEN PRINTING
61 Bridge St (03060-3533)
PHONE..................................603 578-9599
Scott Macconnell, *Partner*
Caryn Case, *Manager*
EMP: 12
SALES: 950K **Privately Held**
WEB: www.phoenixscreenprinting.com
SIC: 2759 Commercial Printing

(G-19234)
PLASTIC INDUSTRIES INC (HQ)
1 Tara Blvd (03062-2809)
PHONE..................................603 888-1315
Beth Muscato, *President*
▲ **EMP:** 85
SQ FT: 80,000
SALES (est): 11.1MM **Privately Held**
SIC: 3085 Mfg Plastic Bottles

(G-19235)
POLYMER TECHNOLOGIES LLC
4 Bud Way Ste 14 (03063-1740)
PHONE..................................603 883-4002
Ronald F Bogardus, *Owner*
Michael Bogardus, *Mng Member*
EMP: 5
SQ FT: 3,000
SALES: 1MM **Privately Held**
SIC: 2821 2891 8732 Mfg Polymerization Plastics & Adhesives & Is A Research & Development Company

(G-19236)
POWDERED METAL TECHNOLOGY CORP
Also Called: Advanced Specialty Metals
76 Northwest Blvd 29-A (03063)
PHONE..................................617 642-4135
Gerald Hoolahan, *CEO*
EMP: 12
SQ FT: 2,000
SALES (est): 1.2MM **Privately Held**
SIC: 3399 Mfg Powder Metals & Steel Additives

(G-19237)
PRECISION MODEL-FAB INC
134 Haines St Unit A (03060-4094)
PHONE..................................603 883-6680
Darnell Favreau, *President*
EMP: 4
SALES: 600K **Privately Held**
SIC: 3599 Jobbing & Repair Machine Shop

(G-19238)
PRESSTEK OVERSEAS CORP (DH)
200 Innovative Way (03062-5740)
PHONE..................................603 595-7000
Jeffrey A Beck, *Principal*
EMP: 4
SALES (est): 833.4K
SALES (corp-wide): 112.4MM **Privately Held**
WEB: www.presstek.com
SIC: 3555 Whol Industrial Equipment
HQ: Verico Technology Llc
230 Shaker Rd
Enfield CT 06082
800 492-7286

(G-19239)
PRINT FACTORY INC
15 Factory St (03060-3310)
PHONE..................................603 880-4519
John Chasse, *President*
Gloria Chasse, *Vice Pres*
EMP: 6 **EST:** 1980
SQ FT: 1,000
SALES (est): 650K **Privately Held**
WEB: www.printfactory.com
SIC: 2752 2791 7334 Offset Printing & Typesetting

(G-19240)
PRO AXIS MACHINING
25 Front St Ste 101c (03064-2696)
PHONE..................................603 595-1616
Robert Dufour, *President*
EMP: 3
SALES (est): 305.4K **Privately Held**
SIC: 3599 Mfg Industrial Machinery

(G-19241)
PROTEQ SOLUTIONS LLC
76 Northeastern Blvd 38a (03062-3185)
PHONE..................................603 888-6630
Charles Freihofer, *Mng Member*
EMP: 11
SALES: 840K **Privately Held**
SIC: 3829 Mfg Measuring/Controlling Devices

(G-19242)
QMAGIQ LLC
22 Cotton Rd Ste 180 (03063-4219)
PHONE..................................603 821-3092
Kim Beech, *Engineer*
Ross Faska, *Engineer*
Mani Sundaram,
Axel Reisenger,
EMP: 7
SQ FT: 2,534
SALES: 1.2MM **Privately Held**
WEB: www.qmagiq.com
SIC: 3674 Sensor Chip Manufacturer

(G-19243)
RACING MART FUELS LLC
27 Canal St (03064-2802)
PHONE..................................508 878-7664

EMP: 5
SALES (est): 380.8K **Privately Held**
SIC: 2869 Mfg Industrial Organic Chemicals

(G-19244)
RAPID FINISHING CORP
43 Simon St (03060-3029)
PHONE..................................603 889-4234
Barbara A O'Halloran, *President*
EMP: 40
SQ FT: 21,000
SALES (est): 3.7MM **Privately Held**
WEB: www.rapidfinishing.com
SIC: 3479 7336 2396 Coating/Engraving Service Commercial Art/Graphic Design Mfg Auto/Apparel Trimming

(G-19245)
RAPID GROUP
15 Charron Ave (03063-1734)
PHONE..................................603 821-7300
Jay Jacobs, *Principal*
Joelle Stone, *Human Res Mgr*
Charlie Dillow, *Regl Sales Mgr*
Doug Girard, *Regl Sales Mgr*
Joe Largy, *Regl Sales Mgr*
EMP: 14
SALES (est): 1.9MM **Privately Held**
SIC: 3444 Mfg Sheet Metalwork

(G-19246)
RAPID MANUFACTURING GROUP LLC
15 Charron Ave (03063-1734)
PHONE..................................603 402-4020
James Jacobs, *President*
Leonard Morrissey, *President*
Thomas Pursch, *COO*
EMP: 300
SALES (est): 7.2MM
SALES (corp-wide): 445.6MM **Publicly Held**
SIC: 3444 Mfg Sheet Metalwork
PA: Proto Labs, Inc.
5540 Pioneer Creek Dr
Maple Plain MN 55359
763 479-3680

(G-19247)
RAPID SHEET METAL LLC
15 Charron Ave (03063-1734)
PHONE..................................603 821-5300
James L Jacobs II, *President*
Tom Pursch, *COO*
EMP: 72
SQ FT: 25,000
SALES (est): 18.2MM **Privately Held**
WEB: www.rapidsheetmetal.com
SIC: 3444 Mfg Sheet Metalwork

(G-19248)
REGDOX SOLUTIONS INC
1 Tara Blvd Ste 300 (03062-2809)
PHONE..................................978 264-4460
William L Obrien, *President*
William Obrien, *COO*
EMP: 100
SALES (est): 5.8MM
SALES (corp-wide): 100.9MM **Privately Held**
SIC: 7372 Prepackaged Software Services
HQ: Brainloop Ag
Franziskanerstr. 14
Munchen 81669
894 446-990

(G-19249)
RENAISSANCE GLASSWORKS INC
3 Pine St Ste 1 (03060-3278)
PHONE..................................603 882-1779
Mark Frank, *President*
Kathleen Frank, *Vice Pres*
EMP: 3
SQ FT: 2,000
SALES (est): 151.7K **Privately Held**
SIC: 3231 5999 3211 Mfr Stain Glass Products & Retails Art Supplies

(G-19250)
RESEARCH IN MOTION RF INC (HQ)
22 Technology Way Fl 5 (03060-3245)
PHONE..................................603 598-8880
Ralph Pini, *President*
Paul Pelski, *General Mgr*
Tom Lambalot, *COO*
Greg Mendiola, *Senior VP*
David Laks, *VP Opers*
▲ **EMP:** 24
SQ FT: 12,000
SALES (est): 5MM
SALES (corp-wide): 904MM **Privately Held**
WEB: www.phasedarray.com
SIC: 3812 3663 Mfg Search/Navigation Equipment Mfg Radio/Tv Communication Equipment
PA: Blackberry Limited
2200 University Ave E
Waterloo ON N2K 0
519 888-7465

(G-19251)
RESONETICS LLC (PA)
26 Whipple St (03060-3044)
PHONE..................................603 886-6772
Tom Burns, *CEO*
Diwakar Ramanathan, *Business Mgr*
David Fogaren, *Senior VP*
Glenn Ogura, *Senior VP*
Demian Backs, *Vice Pres*
EMP: 172
SALES (est): 41.3MM **Privately Held**
SIC: 3845 Mfg Electromedical Equipment

(G-19252)
RH LABORATORIES INC
1 Tanguay Ave (03063-1711)
PHONE..................................603 459-5900
Benjamin Robinson, *CEO*
Stephen M Robinson, *President*
Frank Holt, *Vice Pres*
Bob Savinelli, *Purch Agent*
EMP: 40
SQ FT: 18,000
SALES (est): 7.4MM **Privately Held**
WEB: www.rh-labs.com
SIC: 3679 Mfg Electronic Components

(G-19253)
RICHARD ARIKIAN
Also Called: New England Water Systems
339 Broad St (03063-3035)
P.O. Box 3303 (03061-3303)
PHONE..................................603 881-5427
Richard Arikian, *Owner*
EMP: 3
SQ FT: 900
SALES: 297K **Privately Held**
SIC: 3589 Water Purification Equipment Household Type

(G-19254)
RIPANO STONEWORKS LTD
90 E Hollis St (03060-6370)
PHONE..................................603 886-6655
Richard Laliberte, *President*
Richard Lucien Laliberte, *President*
George Larocque, *Finance Other*
Patty Wieczerzak, *Office Mgr*
EMP: 27
SQ FT: 32,000
SALES (est): 3.2MM **Privately Held**
WEB: www.ripano.com
SIC: 3281 5999 1799 Mfg Cut Stone & Stone Products Ret Monuments & Tombstones Counter Top Installation

(G-19255)
ROLL TIDE OF NH LLC
Also Called: Crdn of Greater New Hampshire
4 Townsend W Ste 13 (03063-4220)
PHONE..................................603 417-2498
Leah Roxanne Lampognana, *Mng Member*
Thomas Lampognana,
EMP: 3
SQ FT: 3,000
SALES (est): 123.2K **Privately Held**
SIC: 2842 Mfg Polish/Sanitation Goods

(G-19256)
S M SERVICES INC
14 Progress Ave (03062-1924)
PHONE..................................603 883-3381
Tim Powell, *Principal*
EMP: 4
SALES (est): 299.8K **Privately Held**
SIC: 2299 Mfg Textile Goods

(G-19257)
SAHARA HEATERS MFG CO
Also Called: Sahara Heating Systems
22 Pinehurst Ave (03062-3238)
PHONE..................................603 888-7351
Ileene Adams, *President*
Rodney Adams, *Vice Pres*
Raeleen Adams, *Treasurer*
▲ **EMP:** 4
SALES: 1MM **Privately Held**
WEB: www.saharaindustries.com
SIC: 3634 3567 Mfg Electric Housewares/Fans Mfg Industrial Furnaces/Ovens

(G-19258)
SEAMARK INTERNATIONAL LLC
16 Celina Ave Unit 5 (03063-1037)
PHONE..................................603 546-0100
John Lobsitz,
▲ **EMP:** 18
SQ FT: 6,000
SALES (est): 5.6MM **Privately Held**
WEB: www.seamarkonline.com
SIC: 3577 Mfg Computer Peripheral Equipment

(G-19259)
SEMPCO INC
Also Called: Educational Instrument
51 Lake St Ste 7 (03060-4513)
P.O. Box 3262 (03061-3262)
PHONE..................................603 889-1830
Dongsup Ro, *President*
▲ **EMP:** 30
SQ FT: 18,000
SALES: 1.6MM **Privately Held**
WEB: www.sempcoinc.com
SIC: 3944 Mfg Games/Toys

(G-19260)
SENSEAR INC
20 Trafalgar Sq Ste 472 (03063-4907)
PHONE..................................603 589-4072
Justin Miller, *President*
Sarah Kramer, *Principal*
Shannon Kruckow, *Office Mgr*
EMP: 8
SALES (est): 1.1MM
SALES (corp-wide): 220.8K **Privately Held**
SIC: 3661 5065 Mfg & Whol Communication Headsets
HQ: Sensear Pty Ltd
199 Great Eastern Hwy
Belmont WA 6104

(G-19261)
SILICON SENSE INC
110 Daniel Webster Hwy # 217 (03060-5252)
PHONE..................................603 891-4248
Dawn Jennings, *President*
James Meriano, *Vice Pres*
EMP: 3
SQ FT: 750
SALES (est): 555.1K **Privately Held**
WEB: www.siliconsense.com
SIC: 3674 8742 3827 Mfg Semiconductors/Related Devices Management Consulting Services Mfg Optical Instruments/Lenses

(G-19262)
SKILLSOFT CORPORATION (DH)
300 Innovative Way # 201 (03062-5746)
PHONE..................................603 324-3000
Bill Donoghue, *CEO*
Chad Gaydos, *COO*
Anthony Barbone, *Senior VP*
Joe Dawe, *Senior VP*
Murali Sastry, *Senior VP*
EMP: 130
SQ FT: 68,755
SALES (est): 600.2MM
SALES (corp-wide): 352.2K **Privately Held**
WEB: www.skillsoft.com
SIC: 7372 Prepackaged Software Services

(G-19263)
SPECIALTY TRUSS INC
12 Mercier Ln (03062-1606)
PHONE..................................603 886-5523
Marco Labonte, *President*
Clermont Labonte, *Vice Pres*
EMP: 6
SALES (est): 341.2K **Privately Held**
SIC: 2439 Mfg Structural Wood Members

(G-19264)
SPIRE TECHNOLOGY SOLUTIONS LLC
Also Called: Apex Plastics
3 Capitol St (03063-1003)
PHONE..................................603 594-0005
David Fanning, *President*
EMP: 10 **EST:** 2016
SALES (est): 557.8K **Privately Held**
SIC: 3643 Mfg Conductive Wiring Devices

(G-19265)
SSI INVESTMENTS I LIMITED (DH)
107 Northeastern Blvd (03062-1916)
PHONE..................................603 324-3000
Charles E Moran, *President*
EMP: 3
SALES (est): 413.5MM
SALES (corp-wide): 352.2K **Privately Held**
SIC: 7372 Prepackaged Software
HQ: Skillsoft Corporation
300 Innovative Way # 201
Nashua NH 03062
603 324-3000

(G-19266)
SSI INVESTMENTS II LIMITED
107 Northeastern Blvd (03062-1916)
PHONE..................................603 324-3000
Charles E Moran, *President*
Jerald A Nine Jr, *COO*
Colm M Darcy, *Exec VP*
Mark A Townsend, *Exec VP*
Thomas J McDonald, *CFO*
EMP: 1103
SALES: 413.5MM
SALES (corp-wide): 352.2K **Privately Held**
SIC: 7372 Prepackaged Software
HQ: Ssi Investments I Limited
107 Northeastern Blvd
Nashua NH 03062

(G-19267)
STAR MACHINE INC
17 Airport Rd Ste 4 (03063-1707)
PHONE..................................603 882-1423
Richard Hickey, *President*
Kirk Boudreau, *Vice Pres*
EMP: 6
SQ FT: 1,800
SALES (est): 866.8K **Privately Held**
SIC: 3599 Machine Shop

(G-19268)
SWEENEY METAL FABRICATORS INC
15 Progress Ave (03062-1923)
PHONE..................................603 881-8720
John Sweeney, *President*
Cheri Sweeney, *Office Mgr*
EMP: 15
SALES (est): 2.2MM **Privately Held**
WEB: www.sweeneymetal.com
SIC: 3444 Mfg Sheet Metalwork

(G-19269)
SYNCHRO STARS SST
17 Mahogany Dr (03062-1228)
PHONE..................................603 493-4762
EMP: 4 **EST:** 2013
SALES (est): 295.3K **Privately Held**
SIC: 3621 Mfg Motors/Generators

(G-19270)
TAGGART ICE INC
8 Taggart Dr (03060-5506)
PHONE..................................603 888-4630
Jodie Ruonala, *President*
Ronald Ruonala, *Vice Pres*
Chris Beagle, *Treasurer*
EMP: 18 **EST:** 1945
SQ FT: 12,800
SALES (est): 2.9MM **Privately Held**
SIC: 2097 5199 Mfg Ice Whol Nondurable Goods

GEOGRAPHIC

(G-19271)
TELEGRAPH PUBLISHING COMPANY (HQ)
Also Called: Telegraph, The
110 Main St 1 (03060-2723)
PHONE..................................603 594-6472
William Mc Lean III, *Ch of Bd*
Andrew T Bickford, *President*
Matthew Burdette, *Chief*
Joe Biden, *Vice Pres*
Charles Catherwood, *Treasurer*
EMP: 200 **EST:** 1832
SQ FT: 76,000
SALES (est): 25MM
SALES (corp-wide): 25.6MM **Privately Held**
SIC: 2711 2759 Newspapers-Publishing/Printing Commercial Printing
PA: Independent Publications, Inc.
945 E Haverford Rd Ste A
Bryn Mawr PA
610 527-6330

(G-19272)
TEST MSRMENT INSTRMNTATION INC
Also Called: TMI
1 Chestnut St Ste 40 (03060-9311)
PHONE..................................603 882-8610
Michael Colavitos, *President*
EMP: 3
SALES (est): 503.9K **Privately Held**
WEB: www.tmiio.com
SIC: 3672 Mfg Printed Circuit Boards Mfg Process Control Instruments

(G-19273)
TEXTNOLOGY CORP
15 Trafalgar Sq Ste 203 (03063-1968)
PHONE..................................603 465-8398
Elizabeth Kosis, *President*
Ronald Nadeau, *VP Mktg*
EMP: 15
SALES (est): 1MM **Privately Held**
WEB: www.textcorp.com
SIC: 2741 7336 7374 7389 Publishing Foreign Language Translation Graphic Design And Web Site Design

(G-19274)
TOTAL AIR SUPPLY INC
171 E Hollis St (03060-6319)
PHONE..................................603 889-0100
Ben Quintiliani, *President*
Sue Quintiliani, *Vice Pres*
Holly Smith, *Sales Staff*
EMP: 42
SQ FT: 30,000
SALES (est): 14MM **Privately Held**
SIC: 3444 5075 Whol Heat/A C Equip/Supp Mfg Sheet Metalwork

(G-19275)
TRIMARAN PHARMA INC
115 Hawthorne Village Rd (03062-2278)
PHONE..................................508 577-7110
Walter Piskorski, *CEO*
Frank Bymaster, *Vice Pres*
Timothy Hsu, *Vice Pres*
EMP: 3
SALES (est): 146.2K **Privately Held**
SIC: 2834 Mfg Pharmaceutical Preparations

(G-19276)
TWO IN ONE MANUFACTURING INC
51 Lake St Ste 4 (03060-4513)
PHONE..................................603 595-8212
Mui Nguyen, *President*
Lee Nguyen, *Vice Pres*
EMP: 50
SQ FT: 13,000
SALES (est): 3.5MM **Privately Held**
WEB: www.twoinonemanufacturing.com
SIC: 3674 3672 3676 3944 Assembly Of Electronic Components & Educational Toys & Engineering Services

(G-19277)
VALLUM CORPORATION
61 Spit Brook Rd Ste 200 (03060-5614)
PHONE..................................603 577-1989
EMP: 3
SALES (est): 330.7K **Privately Held**
SIC: 3841 Mfg Surgical/Medical Instruments

(G-19278)
VALMET INC (HQ)
Also Called: Glv US Holding Inc
1 Cellu Dr (03063-1008)
PHONE..................................603 882-2711
Laurent Verreault, *President*
Frank Merchel, *Business Mgr*
Richard Verreauot, *Vice Pres*
Dennis Gagne, *Buyer*
Claude Legere, *Engineer*
EMP: 4
SALES (est): 53.1MM
SALES (corp-wide): 1.5MM **Privately Held**
SIC: 3554 Mfg Paper Industrial Machinery
PA: Investissements 5c Inc
3100 Rue Westinghouse
Trois-Rivieres QC
819 371-8282

(G-19279)
VASCULAR TECHNOLOGY INC
12 Murphy Dr Unit C (03062-1930)
PHONE..................................603 594-9700
Nilendu Srivastava, *President*
Gary Douglas, *Vice Pres*
David Regan, *Vice Pres*
Rachana Suchdev, *Director*
Megan Thayer, *Admin Sec*
EMP: 30
SQ FT: 9,700
SALES: 3.3MM **Privately Held**
WEB: www.vti-online.com
SIC: 3841 Mfg Surgical & Medical Instruments

(G-19280)
VCK BEST MACHINING LLC
4 Townsend W Ste 8 (03063-4220)
PHONE..................................603 880-8858
Kenneth Dow, *Mng Member*
EMP: 14
SQ FT: 6,000
SALES: 1.8MM **Privately Held**
SIC: 3599 Mfg Industrial Machinery

(G-19281)
VERICO TECHNOLOGY LLC
200 Innovative Way (03062-5740)
PHONE..................................603 402-7573
Sean Downey, *Branch Mgr*
EMP: 250
SALES (corp-wide): 112.4MM **Privately Held**
WEB: www.presstek.com
SIC: 3861 3555 Mfg Printing Trades Machinery Mfg Photographic Equipment/Supplies
HQ: Verico Technology Llc
230 Shaker Rd
Enfield CT 06082
800 492-7286

(G-19282)
VERTICAL DREAMS
25 E Otterson St (03060-3941)
PHONE..................................603 943-7571
Corey Heibert, *Owner*
EMP: 5
SALES (est): 361.6K
SALES (corp-wide): 178.8K **Privately Held**
SIC: 2591 Mfg Drapery Hardware/Blinds
PA: Vertical Dreams
250 Commercial St # 5001
Manchester NH 03101
603 625-6919

(G-19283)
W H BAGSHAW CO INC
1 Pine Street Ext Ste 135 (03060-3214)
PHONE..................................603 883-7758
Arron Bagshaw, *President*
Peter Brennan, *General Mgr*
Adria Bagshaw, *Vice Pres*
Jason Lafrance, *Mfg Staff*
Fred Osterholtz, *Sales Engr*
EMP: 28 **EST:** 1870
SQ FT: 100,000
SALES (est): 5.7MM **Privately Held**
WEB: www.whbagshaw.com
SIC: 3965 Mfg Fasteners/Buttons/Pins

(G-19284)
WATER STREET PRINTING LLC
97 Main St (03060-2751)
PHONE..................................603 595-1444
David Colin Orpin, *Principal*
EMP: 13
SALES (est): 512.3K **Privately Held**
SIC: 2752 Lithographic Commercial Printing

(G-19285)
WF HOLDINGS INC (PA)
3 E Spit Brook Rd (03060-5710)
PHONE..................................603 888-5443
Robert F Worthen, *President*
Jim Dodos, *Plant Engr*
Eileen Morin, *Treasurer*
David S Worthen, *Treasurer*
Brenna Gase, *Marketing Staff*
◆ **EMP:** 4
SQ FT: 73,000
SALES: 66.2MM **Privately Held**
SIC: 2891 2295 Mfg Adhesives & Sealants Coated Fabrics

(G-19286)
WHITE BIRCH BREWING LLC
460 Amherst St Ste 2 (03063-1220)
PHONE..................................603 402-4444
William Herlicka,
EMP: 19 **EST:** 2009
SALES (est): 2.2MM **Privately Held**
SIC: 2082 Drinking Place

(G-19287)
WIND RIVER SYSTEMS INC
10 Tara Blvd Ste 130 (03062-2800)
PHONE..................................603 897-2000
Ed Marks, *Manager*
EMP: 25 **Privately Held**
WEB: www.windriver.com
SIC: 7372 Prepackaged Software Services
HQ: Wind River Systems, Inc.
500 Wind River Way
Alameda CA 94501
510 748-4100

(G-19288)
WORTHEN INDUSTRIES INC (HQ)
Also Called: UPACO ADHESIVES
3 E Spit Brook Rd (03060-5783)
PHONE..................................603 888-5443
David S Worthen, *President*
Eric Boyce, *Plant Mgr*
Danny Carlson, *Plant Mgr*
Steve Gilcreast, *Plant Mgr*
Robert Rouleau, *Materials Mgr*
◆ **EMP:** 75 **EST:** 1957
SQ FT: 69,000
SALES: 112.6MM
SALES (corp-wide): 66.2MM **Privately Held**
SIC: 2891 Mfg Adhesives/Sealants
PA: Wf Holdings, Inc.
3 E Spit Brook Rd
Nashua NH 03060
603 888-5443

(G-19289)
WORTHEN INDUSTRIES INC
Also Called: Nylco Division
34 Cellu Dr (03063-1009)
PHONE..................................603 886-0973
Liwen Xu, *Opers Staff*
Jeff Tamplin, *Mfg Staff*
Mike Montplaisir, *Technician*
EMP: 16
SALES (corp-wide): 66.2MM **Privately Held**
SIC: 2891 2295 Mfg Adhesives & Coated Fabrics
HQ: Worthen Industries, Inc.
3 E Spit Brook Rd
Nashua NH 03060
603 888-5443

(G-19290)
XILINX INC
10 Tara Blvd Ste 410 (03062-2800)
PHONE..................................603 891-1096
Jim Ball, *Branch Mgr*
EMP: 14
SALES (corp-wide): 3B **Publicly Held**
WEB: www.xilinx.com
SIC: 3674 Mfg Semiconductors/Related Devices
PA: Xilinx, Inc.
2100 All Programable
San Jose CA 95124
408 559-7778

(G-19291)
YOGIBO LLC (PA)
16 Celina Ave Unit 13 (03063-1023)
PHONE..................................603 595-0207
Brock Wilson, *District Mgr*
Mike Lawrence, *Controller*
Giora Liran, *Marketing Staff*
Alexandra Marques, *Manager*
Mary Pat Joseph, *Director*
▲ **EMP:** 25
SQ FT: 10,000
SALES (est): 49.9MM **Privately Held**
SIC: 2519 Ret Furniture

New Boston
Hillsborough County

(G-19292)
CODE BRIEFCASE
77 Beard Rd (03070-3726)
PHONE..................................603 487-2381
Daniel Chamberlain, *Owner*
EMP: 3
SALES (est): 245.2K **Privately Held**
SIC: 3161 Mfg Luggage

(G-19293)
JON STRONG LOW IMPACT LOG LLC
141 Riverdale Rd (03070-4204)
PHONE..................................603 487-5298
Biron L Bedard Esq, *Administration*
EMP: 3
SALES (est): 221.7K **Privately Held**
SIC: 2411 Logging

(G-19294)
NEW BOSTON BULLETIN
74 Thornton Rd (03070-4706)
PHONE..................................603 487-5200
Brandy Mitroff, *Owner*
EMP: 5
SALES (est): 241.2K **Privately Held**
SIC: 2711 Newspapers-Publishing/Printing

(G-19295)
NORTHEAST WLDG BRIDGE REPR LLC
58 Riverdale Rd (03070-4201)
PHONE..................................603 396-8549
EMP: 8
SALES (est): 88.7K **Privately Held**
SIC: 7692 Welding Repair

(G-19296)
PROCRAFT CORPORATION
416 River Rd (03070)
P.O. Box 298 (03070-0298)
PHONE..................................603 487-2080
Jim Wilcoxen, *President*
Laurie Wilcoxen, *Treasurer*
EMP: 14
SQ FT: 10,000
SALES (est): 1.7MM **Privately Held**
WEB: www.procraftcorp.com
SIC: 2431 1751 Mfg Millwork Carpentry Contractor

(G-19297)
RETCOMP INC
2nd New Hampshire Tpke S (03070)
PHONE..................................603 487-5010
Loretta Caterino, *President*
Diane Drew, *Vice Pres*
EMP: 25
SQ FT: 2,750
SALES (est): 800K **Privately Held**
WEB: www.retcomp.com
SIC: 3672 3357 Mfg Printed Circuit Boards Nonferrous Wiredrawing/Insulating

(G-19298)
STRONG H J G BROS GRAV CORP
143 Riverdale Rd (03070-4204)
PHONE..................................603 487-5551
Bo Strong, *Principal*
EMP: 3
SALES (est): 163K **Privately Held**
SIC: 1442 Construction Sand/Gravel

(G-19299)
YANKEE SHUTTER CO
Also Called: Yankee Insulation
480 Bedford Rd (03070-5015)
PHONE..................................603 487-2400
Mark Richmond, *Owner*
EMP: 4
SALES (est): 336.8K **Privately Held**
WEB: www.yankeeshutter.com
SIC: 2431 Mfg Millwork

New Durham
Strafford County

(G-19300)
BOLSTRIDGE LOGGING LLC
159 Brackett Rd (03855-2329)
PHONE..................................603 859-8241
Larry Bolstridge, *Mng Member*
EMP: 5
SALES (est): 526.8K **Privately Held**
SIC: 2411 3531 5099 Logging Mfg Construction Machinery Whol Durable Goods

New Hampton
Belknap County

(G-19301)
ALAN T SEELER INC
Also Called: Ats Precision
87 Nh Route 132 N (03256-4103)
P.O. Box 778 (03256-0778)
PHONE..................................603 744-3736
John Seeler, *President*
Elizabeth Putnam, *Corp Secy*
Arthur Paradis, *Mktg Dir*
EMP: 12
SQ FT: 5,550
SALES (est): 1.8MM **Privately Held**
WEB: www.atsprecision.com
SIC: 3469 3494 Mfg Metal Stampings Mfg Valves/Pipe Fittings

New Ipswich
Hillsborough County

(G-19302)
AIRLINX COMMUNICATIONS INC
111 Old Country Rd (03071)
P.O. Box 253, Greenville (03048-0253)
PHONE..................................603 878-1926
Tjalling Hoiska, *President*
Elaine Hoiska, *CFO*
EMP: 15
SQ FT: 10,000
SALES (est): 2MM **Privately Held**
WEB: www.airlinx.com
SIC: 3663 Mfg Radio/Tv Communication Equipment

(G-19303)
D L S DETAILING
755 Turnpike Rd (03071-3840)
PHONE..................................603 878-2554
David Somero, *Owner*
EMP: 3
SALES: 130K **Privately Held**
SIC: 3315 Mfg Steel Wire/Related Products

(G-19304)
DAVIS VILLAGE SOLUTIONS LLC
167 Davis Village Rd (03071-3805)
P.O. Box 379 (03071-0379)
PHONE..................................603 878-3662
David Somero,
EMP: 3
SALES (est): 237.3K **Privately Held**
SIC: 3519 3537 3799 3599 Mfg Intrnl Cmbstn Engine Mfg Indstl Truck/Tractor Mfg Transportation Equip Mfg Industrial Machinery Mfg Construction Mach

(G-19305)
HIBERNIAN MACHINE TOOL SERVICE
948 Turnpike Rd (03071-3121)
PHONE..................................603 878-1917
Clemence Martin, *Owner*
EMP: 3
SALES (est): 273.9K **Privately Held**
SIC: 3599 Mfg Industrial Machinery

(G-19306)
KEY INDUSTRIES
65 Turnpike Rd Unit B (03071-3524)
P.O. Box 403 (03071-0403)
PHONE..................................603 369-9634
Matthew Salmonson, *Principal*
EMP: 3
SALES (est): 173.4K **Privately Held**
SIC: 3999 Mfg Misc Products

(G-19307)
NORTHEAST SAND AND GRAVEL LLC
214 Appleton Rd (03071-3206)
P.O. Box 497 (03071-0497)
PHONE..................................603 305-9429
EMP: 3
SALES (est): 182.3K **Privately Held**
SIC: 1442 Construction Sand/Gravel

(G-19308)
OAKRIDGE SIGN AND GRAPHICS LLC
42 Poor Farm Rd (03071-3830)
P.O. Box 252 (03071-0252)
PHONE..................................603 878-1183
Robert Cooke, *Mng Member*
EMP: 4
SALES (est): 499.1K **Privately Held**
WEB: www.oakridgesign.com
SIC: 3993 Mfg Signs/Advertising Specialties

(G-19309)
OPTICAL FIBER SYSTEMS INC
829b Turnpike Rd (03071)
P.O. Box 186 (03071-0186)
PHONE..................................603 291-0345
Frederic Durville, *President*
EMP: 4
SQ FT: 1,200
SALES: 147.9K **Privately Held**
WEB: www.opticalfibersystems.com
SIC: 3357 3825 Nonferrous Wiredrawing/Insulating Mfg Electrical Measuring Instruments

(G-19310)
PORTER MANUFACTURING
371 Turnpike Rd (03071-3640)
PHONE..................................603 303-6846
Melvin Porter, *Principal*
EMP: 3
SALES (est): 135K **Privately Held**
SIC: 3999 Mfg Misc Products

(G-19311)
WARWICK MILLS INC (PA)
Also Called: Turtle Skin
301 Turnpike Rd (03071-3639)
P.O. Box 409 (03071-0409)
PHONE..................................603 291-1000
Charles A Howland, *President*
Virginia Houston Howland, *Vice Pres*
Eric Sadowski, *Purch Mgr*
Charles Howland, *Chief Engr*
Timothy Smith, *Engineer*
▲ **EMP:** 120 **EST:** 1989
SQ FT: 1,000
SALES (est): 19.7MM **Privately Held**
WEB: www.warwickmills.com
SIC: 2221 Manmade Broadwoven Fabric Mill

New London
Merrimack County

(G-19312)
2D MATERIAL TECHNOLOGIES LLC
84 Todd Farm Ln (03257)
P.O. Box 2232 (03257-2232)
PHONE..................................603 763-4791
David Steinmiller, *CEO*
Michael Reeve, *COO*
Douglas Adamson, *CTO*
EMP: 3
SALES (est): 121.3K **Privately Held**
SIC: 3624 7389 Mfg Carbon/Graphite Products

(G-19313)
AVIAN TECHNOLOGIES LLC
116 Newport Rd Ste 4-6b (03257-5416)
P.O. Box 716, Sunapee (03782-0716)
PHONE..................................603 526-2420
Kathryn Springesteen, *CFO*
Kathy Springsteen, *CFO*
Art Springstein, *Mng Member*
EMP: 5
SQ FT: 1,200
SALES: 1.6MM **Privately Held**
WEB: www.aviantechnologies.com
SIC: 3229 Mfg Pressed/Blown Glass

(G-19314)
CCM LOGGING LAND CLEARING LLC
369 Burnt Hill Rd (03257-5306)
P.O. Box 160 (03257-0160)
PHONE..................................603 387-1853
Matt Michie, *Principal*
EMP: 3 **EST:** 2017
SALES (est): 199.1K **Privately Held**
SIC: 2411 Logging

(G-19315)
DURGIN AND CROWELL LBR CO INC
231 Fisher Corner Rd (03257-6550)
P.O. Box 160 (03257-0160)
PHONE..................................603 763-2860
Peter Crowell, *President*
BJ Manning, *Sales Executive*
B Manning, *Admin Sec*
EMP: 120
SQ FT: 10,000
SALES (est): 22.5MM **Privately Held**
SIC: 2421 Sawmill/Planing Mill

(G-19316)
ECHO COMMUNICATIONS INC
Also Called: Country Press
59 Pleasant St (03257-5564)
P.O. Box 2300 (03257-2300)
PHONE..................................603 526-6006
Katharyn Hoke, *President*
Howard Hoke, *Vice Pres*
EMP: 20
SQ FT: 8,000
SALES (est): 3.8MM **Privately Held**
WEB: www.echocominc.com
SIC: 2752 7331 2791 2721 Lithographic Coml Print Direct Mail Ad Svcs Typesetting Services Periodical-Publish/Print

Newfields
Rockingham County

(G-19317)
HUTCHINSON SEALING SYSTEMS INC
171 Exeter Rd 169 (03856-8225)
P.O. Box 169 (03856-0169)
PHONE..................................603 772-3771
Robert Nadeau, *Branch Mgr*
Shelley Lake, *Executive*
EMP: 150
SALES (corp-wide): 8.1B **Publicly Held**
SIC: 3069 Mfg Automotive Rubber Products
HQ: Hutchinson Sealing Systems, Inc.
3201 Cross Creek Pkwy
Auburn Hills MI 48326
248 375-3720

(G-19318)
PRINTED MATTER INC
27 Pleasant St (03856-8320)
P.O. Box 970 (03856-0970)
PHONE..................................603 778-2990
EMP: 26
SQ FT: 15,000
SALES: 3MM **Privately Held**
SIC: 2396 2759 Commercial Printing Mfg Auto/Apparel Trimming

(G-19319)
PROVENCAL MANUFACTURING INC (PA)
12 New Rd (03856-8405)
PHONE..................................603 772-6716
Scott Provencal, *President*
James Daughty, *Vice Pres*
EMP: 3
SQ FT: 5,000
SALES (est): 443.4K **Privately Held**
SIC: 3679 3613 Mfg Electrical Equip

(G-19320)
THOMAS H CONNER
Also Called: Conner Bottling Works
120 Exeter Rd (03856-8222)
P.O. Box 171 (03856-0171)
PHONE..................................603 778-0322
Thomas H Conner, *Owner*
EMP: 9
SALES (est): 1MM **Privately Held**
SIC: 2086 Mfg Carbonated Beverages

Newington
Rockingham County

(G-19321)
ATCO-AIRCRAFT TECHNICAL CO
521 Shattuck Way Ste 1 (03801-7872)
PHONE..................................603 433-0081
David Lancaster, *President*
Mary Elizabeth Lancaster, *Vice Pres*
Richard Longley, *Manager*
EMP: 5
SQ FT: 1,600
SALES (est): 1MM **Privately Held**
WEB: www.atco.net
SIC: 3728 Mfg Aircraft Parts/Equipment

(G-19322)
GEORGIA-PACIFIC LLC
170 Shattuck Way (03801-7868)
PHONE..................................603 433-8000
James Jenkins, *Branch Mgr*
Mary Holton, *Property Mgr*
EMP: 150
SALES (corp-wide): 40.6B **Privately Held**
WEB: www.gp.com
SIC: 3275 Mfg Gypsum Products
HQ: Georgia-Pacific Llc
133 Peachtree St Nw
Atlanta GA 30303
404 652-4000

(G-19323)
OWL SEPARATION SYSTEMS LLC
Also Called: Thermo Fisher Scientific
25 Nimble Hill Rd (03801-2760)
PHONE..................................603 559-9297
Stephen Norton, *President*
Bill Pelchat, *Engineer*
William Pelchat, *Engineer*
Joe Stocker, *Engineer*
John Borsella, *Sales Staff*
▲ **EMP:** 50 **EST:** 1995
SQ FT: 30,000
SALES (est): 8.7MM
SALES (corp-wide): 24.3B **Publicly Held**
WEB: www.owlsci.com
SIC: 3821 Mfg Lab Apparatus/Furniture
HQ: Fisher Scientific International Llc
81 Wyman St
Waltham MA 02451
781 622-1000

(G-19324)
PORTSMOUTH SIGN COMPANY
19 Nimble Hill Rd (03801-2727)
PHONE....................................603 436-0047
Dianna Getman, *Owner*
EMP: 5
SALES (est): 387.3K **Privately Held**
SIC: 3993 Mfg Signs/Advertising Specialties

(G-19325)
SIG SAUER INC (DH)
72 Pease Blvd (03801-6801)
PHONE....................................603 610-3000
Ron Cohen, *President*
David Oconnor, *Regional Mgr*
Tom Jankiewicz, *Exec VP*
Jeff Powers, *Vice Pres*
Steven Shawver, *Vice Pres*
◆ **EMP:** 245
SQ FT: 400,000
SALES (est): 306.4MM
SALES (corp-wide): 583.5K **Privately Held**
WEB: www.sigarms.com
SIC: 3484 7999 Mfg Small Arms Amusement/Recreation Services
HQ: Sig Sauer Beteiligungs Gmbh
Hollefeldstr. 46
Emsdetten
435 147-10

(G-19326)
SUBCOM LLC
100 Piscataqua Dr (03801-8002)
PHONE....................................603 436-6100
Michael Dumont, *Branch Mgr*
EMP: 72
SALES (corp-wide): 41MM **Privately Held**
SIC: 3661 Mfg Telephone/Telegraph Apparatus
HQ: Subcom, Llc
250 Industrial Way W
Eatontown NJ 07724
732 578-7000

(G-19327)
SUBCOM CABLE SYSTEMS LLC
100 Piscataqua Dr (03801-8002)
PHONE....................................603 436-6100
Jonathan J Dufour, *General Mgr*
Thomas Aaron,
▲ **EMP:** 275 **EST:** 1840
SQ FT: 693,000
SALES (est): 164.9MM
SALES (corp-wide): 41MM **Privately Held**
WEB: www.tycotelecom.com
SIC: 3357 Nonferrous Wiredrawing/Insulating
HQ: Subcom, Llc
250 Industrial Way W
Eatontown NJ 07724
732 578-7000

(G-19328)
THERMO NESLAB LLC
25 Nimble Hill Rd (03801-2794)
PHONE....................................603 436-9444
Seth H Hoogasian, *President*
Mike Aronson, *Vice Pres*
Mark Sinclair, *Mng Member*
Dennis O'Brien,
▲ **EMP:** 225
SQ FT: 120,000
SALES (est): 29.7MM
SALES (corp-wide): 24.3B **Publicly Held**
SIC: 3821 Mfg Lab Apparatus/Furniture
PA: Thermo Fisher Scientific Inc.
168 3rd Ave
Waltham MA 02451
781 622-1000

(G-19329)
WILCOX INDUSTRIES CORP (PA)
25 Piscataqua Dr (03801-7816)
PHONE....................................603 431-1331
James Teetzel, *CEO*
Laurie Teetzel, *COO*
Kim Brennan, *Vice Pres*
Scott Payette, *Vice Pres*
Brian Fritz, *Plant Mgr*
EMP: 130 **EST:** 1995
SQ FT: 33,000
SALES (est): 23.8MM **Privately Held**
SIC: 3699 3827 Mfg Electrical Equipment/Supplies Mfg Optical Instruments/Lenses

Newmarket
Rockingham County

(G-19330)
BAILEYWORKS INC
Also Called: Bailey Works
55 Main St 213 (03857-1666)
PHONE....................................603 292-6485
Toni Smith, *Owner*
EMP: 3
SALES: 250K **Privately Held**
WEB: www.baileyworks.com
SIC: 3161 5611 2393 Mfg Luggage Ret Men's/Boy's Clothing Mfg Textile Bags

(G-19331)
CHICK TRUCKING INC
Also Called: Newmarket Sand & Gravel
Rr 152 (03857)
PHONE....................................603 659-3566
William Chick, *President*
Dwight Chick, *Superintendent*
Doug Chick, *Plant Supt*
Barbara Chick, *Treasurer*
EMP: 7
SQ FT: 480
SALES (est): 595K **Privately Held**
WEB: www.chickchat.ivillage.com
SIC: 1442 Sand & Gravel Processing Plant

(G-19332)
COASTAL INFLATABLES LLC
16 Swampscott St (03857)
P.O. Box 222, Newfields (03856-0222)
PHONE....................................603 490-7606
James Woodsun,
▲ **EMP:** 3 **EST:** 2010
SALES: 200K **Privately Held**
SIC: 3089 Mfg Plastic Products

(G-19333)
EIGENLIGHT CORPORATION
13 Water St Apt B (03857-2091)
PHONE....................................603 692-9200
Craig Poole, *President*
Janice Poole, *President*
EMP: 30
SQ FT: 15,000
SALES (est): 5.6MM **Privately Held**
WEB: www.eigenlight.com
SIC: 3674 Mfg Semiconductors/Related Devices

(G-19334)
GUTERMANN INC
55 Main St Apt 409 (03857-1676)
PHONE....................................603 200-0340
Steven E Gilham, *President*
Cameron Keyes, *Director*
EMP: 4
SALES (est): 245.9K
SALES (corp-wide): 807.5K **Privately Held**
SIC: 3599 Mfg Industrial Machinery
PA: Gutermann Ag
Sihlbruggstrasse 140
Baar ZG 6340
417 606-033

(G-19335)
HAGAN DESIGN AND MACHINE INC
8 Forbes Rd (03857-2059)
PHONE....................................603 292-1101
Jonathan Hagan, *President*
Paul Hagan, *Vice Pres*
EMP: 4
SQ FT: 8,000
SALES (est): 619.4K **Privately Held**
WEB: www.hagandesign.com
SIC: 3599 7539 Mfg Industrial Machinery Automotive Repair

(G-19336)
LAMPREY RIVER SCREEN PRINT
25 N Main St (03857-1217)
PHONE....................................603 659-9959
Daniel Baffett, *President*
Daniel Baffestt, *President*
EMP: 3
SQ FT: 1,800
SALES (est): 261.9K **Privately Held**
SIC: 2759 Commercial Printing

(G-19337)
PROFILE METAL FORMING INC (HQ)
10 Forbes Rd (03857-2059)
PHONE....................................603 659-8323
George Donovan Jr, *CEO*
Bill Donovan, *General Mgr*
EMP: 31
SALES (est): 4.4MM
SALES (corp-wide): 17.1MM **Privately Held**
WEB: www.profilemetal-ray.com
SIC: 3444 Mfg Sheet Metalwork
PA: Profile Holdings, Inc.
370 Republic Dr
Mc Kenzie TN 38201
731 352-5341

(G-19338)
RUSSOUND/FMP INC
1 Forbes Rd Ste 1 # 1 (03857-2074)
PHONE....................................603 659-5170
Joe Brouillet, *CEO*
Maureen Baldwin, *President*
Charlie Porritt, *Vice Pres*
William Ramsdell, *Engineer*
Michelle Gorneau, *Controller*
◆ **EMP:** 150 **EST:** 1971
SQ FT: 36,000
SALES (est): 27.2MM **Privately Held**
SIC: 3651 5731 3612 Mfg Home Audio/Video Equipment Ret Radio/Tv/Electronics Mfg Transformers

(G-19339)
S & H PRECISION MFG CO INC (PA)
10 Forbes Rd (03857-2059)
PHONE....................................603 659-8323
George Donovan, *President*
Norman French, *Corp Secy*
EMP: 34
SALES (est): 1.8MM **Privately Held**
SIC: 3444 Mfg Sheet Metalwork

(G-19340)
SEACOAST MACHINE COMPANY LLC
80a Exeter Rd (03857-2031)
PHONE....................................603 659-3404
Richard Bajger, *Owner*
Jan Bajger,
EMP: 8
SQ FT: 5,700
SALES: 200K **Privately Held**
SIC: 3599 Mfg Industrial Machinery

(G-19341)
SEACOAST SCREEN PRINTING
5 Forbes Rd (03857-2060)
PHONE....................................603 758-6398
Brian Toohey, *Executive*
EMP: 3
SALES (est): 313.8K **Privately Held**
SIC: 2759 Commercial Printing

Newport
Sullivan County

(G-19342)
AMERIFORGE GROUP INC
AF Gloenco
452 Sunapee St (03773-1488)
PHONE....................................603 863-1270
Tom Hahnal, *Systems Mgr*
EMP: 50
SALES (corp-wide): 278.3MM **Privately Held**
WEB: www.ameri-forgegroup.com
SIC: 3469 3599 Mfg Metal Stampings Mfg Industrial Machinery
PA: Ameriforge Group Inc.
945 Bunker Hill Rd # 500
Houston TX 77024
713 393-4200

(G-19343)
CARROLL CONCRETE CO INC
Also Called: Newport Sand and Gravel
8 Reeds Mill Rd (03773-1249)
PHONE....................................603 863-1765
Shaun P Carroll, *President*
Michael Feeney, *Vice Pres*
EMP: 10
SALES (est): 1.4MM **Privately Held**
SIC: 3273 Mfg Ready-Mixed Concrete

(G-19344)
DALES PAINT N PLACE INC
449 Sunapee St Ste 6 (03773-5410)
PHONE....................................603 863-5050
Chad Hemingway, *President*
Dale Flewelling, *Vice Pres*
EMP: 3
SALES (est): 291.5K **Privately Held**
SIC: 3993 7312 Mfg Signs/Advertising Specialties Outdoor Advertising Services

(G-19345)
EICHENAUER INC
Also Called: Hartford
292 Sunapee St (03773-1232)
PHONE....................................603 863-1454
Donald Campbell, *President*
◆ **EMP:** 50 **EST:** 1951
SQ FT: 25,000
SALES (est): 9MM
SALES (corp-wide): 64.9MM **Privately Held**
WEB: www.advancedheaters.com
SIC: 3634 Mfg Electric Housewares/Fans
PA: Eichenauer Heizelemente Gmbh & Co. Kg
Industriestr. 1
Hatzenbuhl 76770
727 570-20

(G-19346)
ENDICOTT CUSTOM MACHINE LLC
462 Sunapee St (03773-1488)
PHONE....................................603 865-1323
Tad W Charles,
EMP: 5
SQ FT: 3,300
SALES (est): 334.6K **Privately Held**
SIC: 3599 Mfg Industrial Machinery

(G-19347)
FRANK WIGGINS
79 Bascom Rd (03773)
P.O. Box 157 (03773-0157)
PHONE....................................603 863-1537
Frank Wiggins, *Branch Mgr*
EMP: 3
SALES (corp-wide): 400K **Privately Held**
SIC: 3599 Mfg Industrial Machinery
PA: Frank Wiggins
501 Sunapee St
Guild NH 03754
603 863-3151

(G-19348)
LATVA MACHINE INC
Also Called: Lm
744 John Stark Hwy (03773-2607)
PHONE....................................603 863-5155
Mitchell William Latva, *President*
Tammy Craig, *Administration*
Larry Lussier, *Maintence Staff*
EMP: 50
SQ FT: 28,000
SALES (est): 11.6MM **Privately Held**
WEB: www.latva.com
SIC: 3599 Mfg Industrial Machinery

(G-19349)
LE WEED & SON LLC (PA)
187 S Main St (03773-1817)
P.O. Box 509 (03773-0509)
PHONE....................................603 863-1540
Wayne M Weed,
Dianne Boucher,
EMP: 10 **EST:** 1946
SQ FT: 15,000
SALES (est): 1.9MM **Privately Held**
SIC: 3273 Mfg Ready-Mixed Concrete

(G-19350)
MANNA MIX
5 Schoolhouse Rd (03773-1971)
PHONE.................................213 519-0719
EMP: 3
SALES (est): 157.3K **Privately Held**
SIC: 2099 Mfg Food Preparations

(G-19351)
NEWPORT CONCRETE BLOCK CO
Also Called: L E Weed and Son
187 S Main St (03773-1817)
P.O. Box 509 (03773-0509)
PHONE.................................603 863-1540
Wayne Weed, *Partner*
Diane Bouche, *Partner*
EMP: 10
SALES (est): 941.3K **Privately Held**
SIC: 3273 Mfg Ready-Mixed Concrete

(G-19352)
NEWPORT SAND & GRAVEL CO INC (PA)
Also Called: Carroll Concrete
8 Reeds Mill Rd (03773-1249)
P.O. Box 1000 (03773-1000)
PHONE.................................603 298-0199
Shaun P Carroll Sr, *President*
Bob Carroll, *General Mgr*
Michael Feeney, *Admin Sec*
Deborah Spear, *Admin Sec*
EMP: 15
SQ FT: 1,620
SALES (est): 44MM **Privately Held**
SIC: 3273 3297 Mfg Ready-Mixed Concrete Mfg Nonclay Refractories

(G-19353)
POLLUTION RESEARCH & DEV CORP (PA)
Also Called: Matrix Air
475 Sunapee St Ste 4 (03773-1490)
PHONE.................................603 863-7553
Tracy Nangeroni, *President*
Michael Nangeroni, *Vice Pres*
EMP: 13
SQ FT: 20,000
SALES (est): 1.3MM **Privately Held**
WEB: www.pollutionresearch.com
SIC: 3564 1711 Mfg Industrial Air Purification & Dust / Fume Collecting Equipment Plumbing Heating Air-Conditioning Contractor

(G-19354)
R D S MACHINE INC (PA)
3 Putnam Rd (03773-3019)
PHONE.................................603 863-4131
Richard Sullivan, *President*
Dina Cody, *Admin Sec*
EMP: 26
SQ FT: 4,500
SALES (est): 9.4MM **Privately Held**
WEB: www.rdsmachine.com
SIC: 3599 Mfg Industrial Machinery

(G-19355)
R FILION MANUFACTURING INC
Also Called: Kasi Infrared
931 John Stark Hwy (03773-2614)
P.O. Box 895, Claremont (03743-0895)
PHONE.................................603 865-1893
Roger G Filion Jr, *President*
Susan M Filion, *Vice Pres*
Susan Filion, *Vice Pres*
EMP: 16
SQ FT: 12,000
SALES (est): 3.1MM **Privately Held**
SIC: 3433 5999 Mfg Heating Equipment-Nonelectric Ret Misc Merchandise

(G-19356)
RDS MACHINE LLC
248 N Main St (03773-3029)
PHONE.................................603 863-4131
Michael Monroe, *Principal*
EMP: 5
SALES (est): 280K **Privately Held**
SIC: 3599 Mfg Industrial Machinery

(G-19357)
ROYMAL INC
475 Sunapee St (03773-1490)
P.O. Box 658 (03773-0658)
PHONE.................................603 863-2410
Roy M Malool, *Ch of Bd*
Laura Stocker, *President*
Robert Brown, *Research*
Lorissa Nugisa, *CFO*
Larisa Nugisa, *Human Res Mgr*
▲ **EMP:** 25
SQ FT: 20,000
SALES (est): 5.7MM **Privately Held**
WEB: www.roymalinc.com
SIC: 2671 2851 Mfg Packaging Paper/Film Mfg Paints/Allied Products

(G-19358)
SHRINKFAST MARKETING
Also Called: Div of Bttnfeld Glcester Engrg
460 Sunapee St (03773-1488)
PHONE.................................603 863-7719
Chuck Milliken, *Manager*
Richard Thomas, *Manager*
▲ **EMP:** 60
SALES (est): 5.7MM **Privately Held**
WEB: www.ameriforge.com
SIC: 3081 Mfg Unsupported Plastic Film/Sheet

(G-19359)
STONE VAULT CO
57 Main St Apt 1 (03773-1572)
PHONE.................................603 863-2720
Sidney C Laquire Jr, *Owner*
EMP: 3
SQ FT: 4,500
SALES: 400K **Privately Held**
SIC: 3281 5999 Manufactures Cut Stone & Products & Retails Misc Merchandise

(G-19360)
STURM RUGER & COMPANY INC
Ruger Firearms
411 Sunapee St (03773-1542)
PHONE.................................603 863-2000
Thomas P Sullivan, *Branch Mgr*
EMP: 750
SALES (corp-wide): 495.6MM **Publicly Held**
WEB: www.ruger-firearms.com
SIC: 3484 Mfg Pistols And Firearms
PA: Sturm, Ruger & Company, Inc.
1 Lacey Pl
Southport CT 06890
203 259-7843

(G-19361)
STURM RUGER & COMPANY INC
Also Called: Ruger Records Dept
529 Sunapee St (03773-1491)
PHONE.................................603 865-2424
Mike Butler, *Branch Mgr*
Bob Hoefer, *Director*
Carter Chamberlin, *Administration*
EMP: 375
SALES (corp-wide): 495.6MM **Publicly Held**
SIC: 3484 3324 Mfg Small Arms Steel Investment Foundry
PA: Sturm, Ruger & Company, Inc.
1 Lacey Pl
Southport CT 06890
203 259-7843

(G-19362)
STURM RUGER & COMPANY INC
Pine Tree Castings
411 Sunapee St (03773-1542)
PHONE.................................603 863-3300
Thomas P Sullivan, *Vice Pres*
Ricky Shepard, *Engineer*
Adam Taylor, *Engineer*
Adam Kuper, *Branch Mgr*
David Carton, *Branch Mgr*
EMP: 200
SQ FT: 100,000
SALES (corp-wide): 495.6MM **Publicly Held**
WEB: www.ruger-firearms.com
SIC: 3484 3341 3324 Mfg Small Arms Secndry Nonfrs Mtl Prdcr Steel Investment Foundry
PA: Sturm, Ruger & Company, Inc.
1 Lacey Pl
Southport CT 06890
203 259-7843

(G-19363)
THOMAS JEWELRY DESIGN INC
11 Cross St (03773-1705)
PHONE.................................603 372-6102
Jean Thomas, *Vice Pres*
Scott Thomas, *Vice Pres*
EMP: 87
SQ FT: 14,000
SALES (est): 3.2MM **Privately Held**
SIC: 3911 5944 Mfg Precious Metal Jewelry Ret Jewelry

(G-19364)
WILTON PRESSED METALS
488 Oak St (03773-3013)
P.O. Box 909 (03773-0909)
PHONE.................................603 863-1488
T A Parssinen III, *Partner*
Corina Ouellette, *Manager*
EMP: 8
SQ FT: 5,000
SALES (est): 580K **Privately Held**
SIC: 3469 Mfg Metal Stampings

Newton
Rockingham County

(G-19365)
ELEMENTAL INNOVATION INC
Also Called: Halo Maritime Defense Systems
5 Puzzle Ln (03858-3717)
PHONE.................................603 259-4400
Eric Johnson, *CEO*
Justin Bishop, *President*
Daniel Ross, *COO*
Donald Breslauer, *Vice Pres*
Glenn Breslauer, *Vice Pres*
EMP: 12
SQ FT: 1,500
SALES (est): 997.6K **Privately Held**
WEB: www.elementalinnovation.com
SIC: 3429 Mfg Hardware

(G-19366)
PAUL REVERE PRESS INC
5 Birch Rd (03858-3620)
PHONE.................................781 289-4031
Joseph Dilena, *President*
Joseph D Lena, *President*
EMP: 3
SALES (est): 310.3K **Privately Held**
WEB: www.revere.org
SIC: 2752 2759 Lithographic Commercial Printing Commercial Printing

(G-19367)
PRO DESIGN & MANUFACTURING
13 Elm St (03858-4414)
P.O. Box 415, Newton Junction (03859-0415)
PHONE.................................603 819-4131
Albert Johnson, *President*
John Johnson, *President*
EMP: 8
SALES (est): 710K **Privately Held**
SIC: 2221 Mfg Fiberglass

(G-19368)
PUREWOOD CABINETRY
6 W Main St (03858-3612)
PHONE.................................603 378-2001
Charlotte Scott, *Principal*
EMP: 3
SALES (est): 186.2K **Privately Held**
SIC: 2434 Mfg Wood Kitchen Cabinets

(G-19369)
SARRO MANUFACTURING INC
6 Puzzle Ln (03858-3722)
P.O. Box 104 (03858-0104)
PHONE.................................603 378-9161
Bruce A Sarro, *President*
EMP: 6
SQ FT: 5,600
SALES (est): 640K **Privately Held**
SIC: 3599 Mfg Industrial Machinery

(G-19370)
TEREX USA LLC
Also Called: Terex Environmental Equipment
22 Whittier St (03858-3524)
PHONE.................................603 382-0556
Heath Searles, *Sales Staff*
Neal Nowick, *Branch Mgr*
EMP: 90
SALES (corp-wide): 5.1B **Publicly Held**
SIC: 3541 Mfg Machine Tools-Cutting
HQ: Terex Usa, Llc
200 Nyala Farms Rd
Westport CT 06880
203 222-7170

North Conway
Carroll County

(G-19371)
AMERICAN CRYSTAL WORKS
27 Seavey St (03860-5357)
P.O. Box 102 (03860-0102)
PHONE.................................603 356-7879
Roger Cummings, *Owner*
EMP: 4
SALES (est): 311.9K **Privately Held**
SIC: 3231 Mfg Products-Purchased Glass

(G-19372)
BAVARIAN CHOCOLATE HAUS INC
2483 White Mountain Hwy (03860)
PHONE.................................603 356-2663
Lewis G Johnson, *Principal*
EMP: 4
SALES (est): 200K **Privately Held**
SIC: 2064 5441 Mfg Candy/Confectionery Ret Candy/Confectionery

(G-19373)
BLACK & DECKER CORPORATION
41 Settelers Grn (03860)
P.O. Box 41 (03860-0041)
PHONE.................................603 356-7595
EMP: 5
SALES (corp-wide): 11B **Publicly Held**
SIC: 3546 Mfg Power-Driven Handtools
HQ: The Black & Decker Corporation
701 E Joppa Rd
Towson MD 21286
410 716-3900

(G-19374)
BOUCHER COMPANY INC
19 Upper W Side Rd (03860)
PHONE.................................603 356-6455
Joseph Boucher, *President*
Laurie C Sawyer, *Vice Pres*
EMP: 4
SQ FT: 2,800
SALES: 340K **Privately Held**
WEB: www.boucherrealestate.com
SIC: 3599 Mfg Industrial Machinery

(G-19375)
C-V MACHINE COMPANY LLC
Also Called: Cv Machine Co & Hobby Shop
236 Kearsarge Rd (03860-5331)
P.O. Box 1132 (03860-1132)
PHONE.................................603 356-5189
Maureen C Seavey,
EMP: 3
SALES: 130K **Privately Held**
SIC: 3599 Mfg Industrial Machinery

(G-19376)
COUNTRY NEWS CLUB INC
Also Called: Conway Daily Sun
64 Seavey St (03860-5355)
P.O. Box 1940 (03860-1940)
PHONE.................................603 356-2999
Mark Guerringue, *President*
Jamie Gemmiti, *Editor*
Lloyd Jones, *Editor*
Adam Hirshan, *Vice Pres*
EMP: 40
SQ FT: 100,000
SALES (est): 2.5MM **Privately Held**
WEB: www.conwaydailysun.com
SIC: 2711 Newspapers-Publishing/Printing

GEOGRAPHIC

(G-19377)
NORTH CONWAY OLIVE OIL COMPANY
2730 White Mountain Hwy (03860)
PHONE..................................603 307-1066
William Kittredge, *President*
EMP: 3 **EST:** 2017
SALES (est): 91.3K **Privately Held**
SIC: 2079 Mfg Edible Fats/Oils

(G-19378)
P2K PRINTING LLC
Also Called: Minuteman Press
1305 White Mountain Hwy (03860-5155)
P.O. Box 1830 (03860-1830)
PHONE..................................603 356-2010
Patrick Kittle,
EMP: 7 **EST:** 1982
SQ FT: 3,500
SALES: 800K **Privately Held**
WEB: www.ncmmp.com
SIC: 2752 7334 7336 4783 Lithographic Coml Print Photocopying Service Coml Art/Graphic Design Packing/Crating Service

(G-19379)
STONEWALL KITCHEN LLC
Settlers Grn Green (03860)
PHONE..................................603 356-3342
EMP: 61 **Privately Held**
SIC: 2033 Ret Misc Foods
PA: Stonewall Kitchen, Llc
2 Stonewall Ln
York ME 03909

(G-19380)
VINTNERS CELLAR WINERY
1857 White Mountain Hwy (03860-5158)
P.O. Box 5002 (03860-5002)
PHONE..................................603 356-9463
Yvonne Staples, *Owner*
EMP: 3
SALES (est): 152.8K **Privately Held**
SIC: 2084 Mfg Wines/Brandy/Spirits

(G-19381)
WHITE MOUNTAIN CUPCAKERY LLC
2 Common Ct Unit D52 (03860-5439)
P.O. Box 523 (03860-0523)
PHONE..................................603 730-5140
Katherine Iannuzzi, *Manager*
EMP: 4
SALES (est): 238K **Privately Held**
SIC: 2051 Mfg Bread/Related Products

North Hampton
Rockingham County

(G-19382)
CROWN PROPERTIES & HM SLS LLC
203 Lafayette Rd (03862-2413)
P.O. Box 1627 (03862-1627)
PHONE..................................603 964-2005
Joe Roy, *Owner*
EMP: 4
SALES (est): 491.5K **Privately Held**
SIC: 2451 1531 Mfg Mobile Homes Operative Builders

(G-19383)
H&L INSTRUMENTS LLC
34 Post Rd (03862-2021)
P.O. Box 580 (03862-0580)
PHONE..................................603 964-1818
Bob Landman, *President*
Jeniffer Landman, *Owner*
Erwin Deal, *Principal*
Robert J Landman,
EMP: 10
SQ FT: 4,000
SALES (est): 970K **Privately Held**
WEB: www.hlinstruments.com
SIC: 3661 Mfr Fiberoptic Comm Equip Optical Comparators For Aircraft Engines & Semiconductor Wafers

(G-19384)
MARSPEC-ABERNAQUI-AMERICA
103 Exeter Rd (03862-2043)
P.O. Box 631 (03862-0631)
PHONE..................................603 964-4063
George Denoncourt, *President*
Gloria Denoncourt, *Treasurer*
EMP: 5
SQ FT: 5,000
SALES (est): 380K **Privately Held**
SIC: 3571 Light Manufacturer Of Fixed And Mobile Computer Network Operations Centers Emergency/Disaster Recovery Mobile Sh

(G-19385)
MORRIS AND BUTLER
3 Grandview Ter (03862-2116)
PHONE..................................603 918-0355
Edward Butler, *Owner*
Roz Fardi, *Co-Owner*
Susan Morris, *Co-Owner*
EMP: 60 **EST:** 2011
SALES (est): 2.4MM **Privately Held**
SIC: 3446 Mfg Architectural Metalwork

(G-19386)
PD & E ELECTRONICS LLC
180 Lafayette Rd Unit 13 (03862-2448)
PHONE..................................603 964-3165
Michael Nault,
EMP: 6
SALES (est): 1.4MM **Privately Held**
WEB: www.pdeelectronics.com
SIC: 3679 3672 3674 3677 Mfg Elec Components Mfg Printed Circuit Brds Mfg Semiconductors/Dvcs Mfg Elec Coil/Transfrmrs

(G-19387)
PROTECTIVE TECHNOLOGIES SVCS
216 Lafayette Rd Unit 201 (03862-2445)
PHONE..................................603 964-9421
Leo Crotty Jr, *President*
Robert Brown, *CFO*
EMP: 4
SQ FT: 4,000
SALES (est): 419.3K **Privately Held**
SIC: 3441 Manufactures Weather Shelter And Containment Products And Systems

(G-19388)
W5 CIRCUITS LLC
27 Hobbs Rd (03862-2121)
PHONE..................................603 964-6780
EMP: 3 **EST:** 2008
SALES (est): 180K **Privately Held**
SIC: 3679 Mfg Electronic Components

North Haverhill
Grafton County

(G-19389)
L E JACKSON COROPRATION
Also Called: Ice Cream Equipment Supply
2858 Drtmouth College Hwy (03774)
P.O. Box 398 (03774-0398)
PHONE..................................603 787-6036
Leigh Jackson, *President*
EMP: 3
SQ FT: 1,000
SALES (est): 390.5K **Privately Held**
SIC: 3556 Mfg Food Products Machinery

(G-19390)
TH LOGGING
2000 Briar Hill Rd (03774-4634)
PHONE..................................603 787-6235
Thomas Harris, *Principal*
EMP: 3
SALES (est): 219.2K **Privately Held**
SIC: 2411 Logging

(G-19391)
UPPER VALLEY PRESS INC
446 Benton Rd (03774-4611)
P.O. Box 459 (03774-0459)
PHONE..................................603 787-7000
Philip Hayward, *President*
Dennis Devaux, *Vice Pres*
Kevin Shelton, *Vice Pres*
Connie Smith, *Vice Pres*
Joe Lacasse, *Accounts Exec*
EMP: 80
SQ FT: 65,000
SALES (est): 14.1MM **Privately Held**
WEB: www.uvpress.com
SIC: 2752 7311 Lithographic Commercial Printing Advertising Agency

North Sutton
Merrimack County

(G-19392)
LABSPHERE INC
231 Shaker St (03260-5535)
P.O. Box 70 (03260-0070)
PHONE..................................603 927-4266
Scott Gish, *President*
Stephen Brooks, *Vice Pres*
John Johansen, *Vice Pres*
James Longacre, *Vice Pres*
Ray Ritter, *Vice Pres*
▲ **EMP:** 105
SQ FT: 33,000
SALES (est): 26.9MM
SALES (corp-wide): 1.5B **Privately Held**
WEB: www.labsphere.com
SIC: 3826 Mfg Analytical Instruments
PA: Halma Public Limited Company
Misbourne Court
Amersham BUCKS HP7 0
149 472-1111

North Swanzey
Cheshire County

(G-19393)
TILCON ARTHUR WHITCOMB INC (HQ)
28 Old Homestead Hwy (03431-4546)
P.O. Box 747, Keene (03431-0747)
PHONE..................................603 352-0101
Edward Silks, *Vice Pres*
EMP: 10 **EST:** 1933
SQ FT: 20,000
SALES (est): 3.3MM
SALES (corp-wide): 2.3MM **Privately Held**
WEB: www.arthurwhitcomb.com
SIC: 3273 1442 3271 5032 Mfg Ready-Mixed Concrete Construction Sand/Gravel Mfg Concrete Block/Brick Whol Brick/Stone Matrls
PA: Allan Block Corporation
7424 W 78th St
Minneapolis MN 55439
952 835-5309

North Walpole
Cheshire County

(G-19394)
J H DUNNING CORPORATION
Also Called: Vermont Custom Cabinetry
1 Dunning Dr (03609-1112)
PHONE..................................603 445-5591
Todd M Walker, *President*
EMP: 27 **EST:** 1906
SQ FT: 3,000
SALES (est): 5MM **Privately Held**
WEB: www.jhdunning.com
SIC: 2441 3993 2541 Mfg Wood Boxes/Shooks Mfg Signs/Ad Specialties

(G-19395)
LEN-TEX CORP
Also Called: Len-Tex Wallcoverings
18 Len Tex Ln (03609-1140)
PHONE..................................603 445-2342
Don Lennon, *President*
Charles Lennon, *Treasurer*
Richard Lennon, *Controller*
◆ **EMP:** 108
SQ FT: 59,000
SALES (est): 40.2MM **Privately Held**
WEB: www.lentexcorp.com
SIC: 2679 Mfg Converted Paper Products

(G-19396)
VERMONT CUSTOM WOOD PRODUCTS
Also Called: Vermont Custom Cabinetry
5 Dunning Dr (03609-1151)
PHONE..................................802 463-9930
Tom Westra, *President*
EMP: 13 **EST:** 1982
SALES: 1MM **Privately Held**
WEB: www.vermontcabinetry.com
SIC: 2511 2434 Mfg Wood Household Furniture Mfg Wood Kitchen Cabinets

(G-19397)
WOODSTONE COMPANY INC
Also Called: Vermont Glass
1164 Main St (03609-1153)
PHONE..................................603 445-2449
Robert Boylan, *Manager*
Tom Smidutz, *Manager*
EMP: 36
SALES (corp-wide): 5.3MM **Privately Held**
WEB: www.woodstone.com
SIC: 2431 Mfg Millwork
PA: The Woodstone Company Inc
17 Morse Brook Rd
Westminster VT 05158
802 722-9217

North Woodstock
Grafton County

(G-19398)
J H FADDENS & SONS
Also Called: Fadden Construction
99 Main St (03262)
PHONE..................................603 745-2406
Jim Fadden, *Owner*
EMP: 3
SALES: 30K **Privately Held**
WEB: www.nhmaplesyrup.com
SIC: 2099 1522 Mfg Food Preparations Residential Construction

(G-19399)
THH ASSOCIATES LLC
Also Called: True Colors Print & Design
800 Eastside Rd (03262-2762)
PHONE..................................603 536-3600
Terri Haas, *Mng Member*
Robin Sleeper, *Manager*
Tom Haas,
EMP: 11
SALES (est): 1.6MM **Privately Held**
WEB: www.truecolorsprint.com
SIC: 2752 Lithographic Commercial Printing

Northfield
Belknap County

(G-19400)
EPTAM PLASTICS LTD (PA)
Also Called: E. P. Tool & Machine
2 Riverside Business Park (03276)
PHONE..................................603 286-8009
Dana Waterman, *President*
Michelle Eggleston, *Production*
Charlie Pauwels, *Purchasing*
Matthew McKenna, *QC Mgr*
Gary Dane, *Engineer*
EMP: 100
SQ FT: 62,500
SALES (est): 18.7MM **Privately Held**
WEB: www.eptam.com
SIC: 3599 Mfg Industrial Machinery

(G-19401)
FREUDENBERG-NOK GENERAL PARTNR
Also Called: Tooling Tech Center
19 Axle Dr (03276-4001)
PHONE..................................603 286-1600
Bill Kobin, *Manager*
EMP: 100

▲ = Import ▼=Export ◆ =Import/Export

SALES (corp-wide): 10.5B **Privately Held**
WEB: www.freudenberg-nok.com
SIC: 3053 3714 5013 2821 Mfg Gasket/Packing/Seals Mfg Motor Vehicle Parts Whol Auto Parts/Supplies Mfg Plstc Material/Resin
HQ: Freudenberg-Nok General Partnership
47774 W Anchor Ct
Plymouth MI 48170
734 451-0020

(G-19402)
FREUDENBERG-NOK GENERAL PARTNR
6 Axle Dr (03276-4002)
PHONE..................................603 286-1600
EMP: 34
SALES (corp-wide): 10.5B **Privately Held**
SIC: 2821 3714 3053 3061 Mfg Plstc Material/Resin Mfg Motor Vehicle Parts Mfg Gasket/Packing/Seals Mfg Mechanical Rubber Gd
HQ: Freudenberg-Nok General Partnership
47774 W Anchor Ct
Plymouth MI 48170
734 451-0020

(G-19403)
JAMESTOWN INDUSTRIES INC
270 Tilton Rd Ste 4 (03276-4413)
PHONE..................................603 286-3301
Raymond Berthiaume, *President*
EMP: 5
SQ FT: 4,000
SALES (est): 482.5K **Privately Held**
SIC: 3544 Mfg Industrial Molds

(G-19404)
MAHERS WELDING SERVICE INC
103 Park St (03276-1548)
PHONE..................................603 286-4851
Richard Maher, *President*
Edgar McKean, *Admin Sec*
EMP: 3
SQ FT: 3,200
SALES: 250K **Privately Held**
SIC: 7692 Welding Repair

(G-19405)
MANNING BROTHERS WOOD PRODUCTS
27 Sargent St (03276-4017)
PHONE..................................603 286-4896
Dennis Manning, *President*
EMP: 4
SQ FT: 10,000
SALES: 500K **Privately Held**
SIC: 2441 Mfg Wooden Shipping Boxes

(G-19406)
MAPLE HEIGHTS FARM
133 Reservoir Rd (03276-4507)
PHONE..................................603 286-7942
EMP: 4 **EST:** 2000
SALES (est): 91K **Privately Held**
SIC: 2099 5191 5193 Mfg Food Preparations Whol Farm Supplies Whol Flowers/Florist Supplies

(G-19407)
PCC STRUCTURALS GROTON
Also Called: PCC Strcturals Alum Operations
24 Granite St (03276-1632)
P.O. Box 188, Tilton (03276-0188)
PHONE..................................603 286-4301
James Jordan,
EMP: 190
SQ FT: 110,000
SALES (corp-wide): 225.3B **Publicly Held**
SIC: 3369 Nonferrous Metal Foundry
HQ: Pcc Structurals Groton
839 Poquonnock Rd
Groton CT 06340
860 405-3700

(G-19408)
QUALITY CONTROLS INC
200 Tilton Rd (03276-4415)
PHONE..................................603 286-3321
Edmond C Young, *President*
Denise Armstrong, *CFO*
EMP: 45
SQ FT: 26,000
SALES (est): 8.9MM **Privately Held**
WEB: www.qcivalves.com
SIC: 3491 3593 3494 3492 Mfg Industrial Valves Mfg Fluid Power Cylinder Mfg Valves/Pipe Fittings Mfg Fluid Power Valves

(G-19409)
VERSATILE SUBCONTRACTING LLC
200 Tilton Rd Unit A (03276-4415)
PHONE..................................603 286-8081
James R Bickford, *Mng Member*
EMP: 8
SALES: 1MM **Privately Held**
SIC: 3679 Mfg Electronic Components

Northwood
Rockingham County

(G-19410)
AMERICAN CALAN INC
454 Jenness Pond Rd (03261-3110)
P.O. Box 307 (03261-0307)
PHONE..................................603 942-7711
Douglas V Briggs, *President*
Janet C Briggs, *Vice Pres*
George Stevens, *Vice Pres*
EMP: 4
SQ FT: 3,500
SALES: 554.4K **Privately Held**
WEB: www.americancalan.com
SIC: 3523 Mfg Poultry & Livestock Machinery

(G-19411)
AQUA SPECIALTIES
561 1st Nh Tpke (03261-3301)
PHONE..................................603 942-5671
Christian Kofer, *Owner*
EMP: 4
SALES (est): 454K **Privately Held**
SIC: 3823 Mfg Process Control Instruments

(G-19412)
HARDING METALS INC
42 Harding Dr (03261)
P.O. Box 418 (03261-0418)
PHONE..................................603 942-5573
Edwin Harding III, *President*
Joseph Harding, *Treasurer*
Anne Follett-Hogshea, *Controller*
Kevin Campbell, *Manager*
Rheal St Germain, *Manager*
▼ **EMP:** 35
SQ FT: 30,000
SALES: 11MM **Privately Held**
WEB: www.hardingmetals.com
SIC: 3339 5093 4953 3341 Primary Nonfrs Mtl Prdcr Whol Scrap/Waste Mat Refuse Systems Secndry Nonfrs Mtl Prdcr Blast Furnace-Steel Work

(G-19413)
P & M TOOL & DIE INC
Also Called: P&M Cnc Machining
372 1st Nh Tpke (03261-3408)
P.O. Box 649 (03261-0649)
PHONE..................................603 942-5636
Phillip W Mills, *President*
EMP: 4
SQ FT: 2,821
SALES (est): 650.9K **Privately Held**
SIC: 3599 Mfg Industrial Machinery

Nottingham
Rockingham County

(G-19414)
HAMPTON NORTH FISHERIES INC
163 Stevens Hill Rd (03290-4804)
PHONE..................................603 463-5874
Carol Stoddard, *Owner*
EMP: 4
SALES (est): 296.7K **Privately Held**
SIC: 3732 Boatbuilding/Repairing

(G-19415)
HUMAN BODY RECON COMPANY
11 Meindl Way (03290-4939)
P.O. Box 322, Raymond (03077-0322)
PHONE..................................603 895-2920
Janice Lyle, *Owner*
EMP: 5
SALES (est): 348.2K **Privately Held**
SIC: 2023 Mfg Dry/Evaporated Dairy Products

(G-19416)
JEWELL WOODWORKS LLC
79 Stage Rd (03290-5211)
PHONE..................................603 679-8025
Glenn A Jewell, *Principal*
EMP: 4
SALES (est): 362.2K **Privately Held**
SIC: 2431 Mfg Millwork

(G-19417)
TRI-STATE MFG SOLUTIONS LLC
124 Kennard Rd (03290-5803)
PHONE..................................508 769-2891
Scott Cafasso, *Mng Member*
EMP: 3
SALES (est): 120.4K **Privately Held**
SIC: 3531 Mfg Construction Machinery

(G-19418)
UAV - AMERICA INC
240 Stage Rd (03290)
P.O. Box 60 (03290-0060)
PHONE..................................603 389-6364
Jim Cooper, *Principal*
EMP: 8
SQ FT: 1,800
SALES (est): 606.1K **Privately Held**
SIC: 3721 Mfg Aircraft

Orange
Grafton County

(G-19419)
WALTER BUCKWOLD LOGGING
34 Cross Rd (03741-5101)
PHONE..................................603 523-9626
Walter R Buckwold, *Principal*
EMP: 6
SALES (est): 412.2K **Privately Held**
SIC: 2411 Logging

Orford
Grafton County

(G-19420)
EUPHONON CO
69 Archertown Rd (03777-4202)
P.O. Box 100 (03777-0100)
PHONE..................................603 353-4882
Judith Parker, *Owner*
EMP: 3
SALES (est): 130K **Privately Held**
SIC: 3931 5211 Mfg Musical Instruments Ret Lumber/Building Materials

(G-19421)
STACEY THOMSON
Also Called: Thomson Timber Harvstg & Trckg
53 Nh Route 10 (03777-4101)
P.O. Box 92 (03777-0092)
PHONE..................................603 353-9700
Stacey Thomson, *Owner*
Katherine Wright, *Administration*
EMP: 5
SALES (est): 595.5K **Privately Held**
SIC: 2411 1794 1795 5032 Logging Excavation Contractor Wrecking/Demolition Work Whol Brick/Stone Matrls Highway/Street Cnstn

Ossipee
Carroll County

(G-19422)
TECHNICOIL LLC
775 Route 16 (03864-7167)
PHONE..................................603 569-3100
Timothy Caravella, *CEO*
Dale Shields, *Opers Mgr*
Gregg Brown,
Pierre Villeneuve,
EMP: 18
SALES (est): 3.7MM **Privately Held**
SIC: 3677 Mfg Electronic Coils/Transformers

(G-19423)
TRACS CHILLERS LLC
790 Route 16 (03864-7166)
P.O. Box 21 (03864-0021)
PHONE..................................603 707-2241
Randy Willette,
EMP: 6
SALES (est): 245.2K **Privately Held**
SIC: 3443 Mfg Fabricated Plate Work

(G-19424)
TUFPAK INC
698 Browns Ridge Rd (03864-7354)
PHONE..................................603 539-4126
Joseph J Wadlinger, *President*
Michael Wadlinger, *Vice Pres*
Stephen Wadlinger, *Vice Pres*
Annette Fox, *Executive*
▲ **EMP:** 25 **EST:** 1976
SQ FT: 3,000
SALES (est): 9.8MM **Privately Held**
WEB: www.tufpak.com
SIC: 2673 2677 Mfg Bags-Plastic/Coated Paper Mfg Envelopes

Pelham
Hills County

(G-19425)
ANVIL MACHINE CO
Also Called: Anvil Precision Machine
72 Russell Dr (03076-5313)
PHONE..................................603 635-9009
EMP: 10
SALES: 400K **Privately Held**
SIC: 3599 Mfg Industrial Machinery

Pelham
Hillsborough County

(G-19426)
ALBERT LANGIN
Also Called: Mack Associates
19 Hayden Rd (03076-2204)
P.O. Box 723 (03076-0723)
PHONE..................................603 635-3560
Albert Langin, *Owner*
EMP: 6
SALES (est): 389.2K **Privately Held**
SIC: 3699 Mfg Electronic Equipment

(G-19427)
ALL SEASONS PRINTING & AWARDS
1 Industrial Park Dr # 20 (03076-2158)
PHONE..................................603 881-7106
Roger W Boisvert, *President*
Mark Boisvert, *Vice Pres*
David Boisvert, *Admin Sec*
EMP: 5
SQ FT: 3,500
SALES: 400K **Privately Held**
SIC: 2759 3914 7389 Screen Printing Mfg Trophies And Engraving Service

(G-19428)
ALPHA TECHNOLOGIES GROUP INC
33 Bridge St (03076-3475)
PHONE..................................603 635-2800
Johnny Blauchard, *Branch Mgr*

GEOGRAPHIC

EMP: 323
SALES (corp-wide): 21.8MM **Publicly Held**
WEB: www.nationalne.com
SIC: 3678 Manufactures Thermal Connectors
PA: Alpha Technologies Group, Inc.
11990 San Vicente Blvd # 350
Los Angeles CA 90049
310 566-4005

(G-19429)
C K PRODUCTIONS INC
Also Called: Body Rags
60a Pulpit Rock Rd (03076-3339)
PHONE..................................603 893-5069
Kenneth B Snow, *CEO*
▲ **EMP:** 41
SQ FT: 50,000
SALES (est): 5.9MM **Privately Held**
WEB: www.ckproductions.com
SIC: 2759 Commercial Printing

(G-19430)
DENNIS TRUDEL
Also Called: Dlt
72 Russell Dr Unit 3 (03076-5313)
PHONE..................................603 635-7208
Dennis Trudel, *Owner*
EMP: 3 **EST:** 2002
SQ FT: 1,200
SALES: 300K **Privately Held**
SIC: 3599 Mfg Industrial Machinery

(G-19431)
DIAMOND MUSIC CO
Also Called: Diamond Systems
5 Leonard Dr (03076-3320)
PHONE..................................603 635-2083
EMP: 3
SALES (corp-wide): 500K **Privately Held**
SIC: 3581 Mfg Vending Machines
PA: Diamond Music Co
125 Essex St
Lawrence MA 01840
978 686-6353

(G-19432)
ELECTRI-TEMP CORPORATION
10 Bridge St Unit 7 (03076-3424)
PHONE..................................603 422-2509
Brian Berger, *President*
EMP: 4
SQ FT: 1,450
SALES (est): 320K **Privately Held**
SIC: 3825 5049 Mfg Electrical Measuring Instruments Whol Professional Equipment

(G-19433)
FOLDER-GLR TECHL SVS GRP LLC
Also Called: Gluer-TEC
30 Pulpit Rock Rd (03076-3340)
P.O. Box 984 (03076-0984)
PHONE..................................603 635-7400
Michael Sutcliffe,
Brian Gamache,
Terence Shartles,
EMP: 7
SQ FT: 2,000
SALES: 1.3MM **Privately Held**
SIC: 3565 Mfg Packaging Machinery

(G-19434)
HAMMAR & SONS INC
71 Bridge St (03076-3479)
P.O. Box 184 (03076-0184)
PHONE..................................603 635-2292
Alrick Hammar Jr, *President*
Mary Hammar, *Treasurer*
Michael Hammer, *Admin Sec*
EMP: 21
SQ FT: 20,000
SALES (est): 2MM **Privately Held**
WEB: www.hammarandsons.com
SIC: 2262 7389 Silk Screen Printing & Sign Painting

(G-19435)
INK OUTSIDE BOX INCORPORATED
Also Called: Signs Now New Hampshire
71 Bridge St (03076-3479)
P.O. Box 184 (03076-0184)
PHONE..................................603 635-2292
Charles Raz, *President*
Rosemary Raz, *Treasurer*
EMP: 7
SQ FT: 4,480
SALES: 750K **Privately Held**
SIC: 3993 Mfg Signs/Advertising Specialties

(G-19436)
J T MANUFACTURING CORPORATION
60b Pulpit Rock Rd (03076-3339)
PHONE..................................603 821-5720
Frank Anastasi, *President*
Steve Anastasi, *Treasurer*
EMP: 40
SQ FT: 30,000
SALES (est): 6.7MM **Privately Held**
SIC: 3451 Mfg Screw Machine Products

(G-19437)
JIM CARR INC
100 Bridge St (03076-3422)
P.O. Box 385 (03076-0385)
PHONE..................................603 635-2821
Jim Carr, *President*
EMP: 5
SQ FT: 2,500
SALES (est): 387.2K **Privately Held**
SIC: 3999 5947 5094 5092 Mfg Misc Products Ret Gifts/Novelties Whol Jewelry/Precs Stone Whol Toys/Hobby Goods

(G-19438)
LEONARD PHILBRICK INC
Also Called: Pelham Machine & Tool Co
18 Atwood Rd (03076-3715)
PHONE..................................603 635-3500
Leonard Philbrick, *President*
EMP: 6 **EST:** 1979
SALES (est): 340K **Privately Held**
SIC: 3599 6512 Machine Shop & Commerical Real Estate Operator

(G-19439)
MEDICAL ISOTOPES INC
100 Bridge St (03076-3422)
PHONE..................................603 635-2255
Eric Stohler, *President*
EMP: 5
SALES (est): 1.1MM **Privately Held**
WEB: www.medicalisotopes.com
SIC: 2819 2833 2869 5169 Mfg Indstl Inorgan Chem Mfg Medicinal/Botanicals Mfg Industl Organic Chem Whol Chemicals/Products

(G-19440)
PELHAM PLASTICS INC
42 Dick Tracy Dr (03076-2154)
P.O. Box 997 (03076-0997)
PHONE..................................603 886-7226
John J Mackey, *President*
Steve Lee, *Business Mgr*
Randy Prior, *Engineer*
Pat Marino, *Financial Exec*
Hazel Laguna, *Technician*
EMP: 60
SQ FT: 31,000
SALES (est): 10.2MM **Privately Held**
WEB: www.pelhamplastics.com
SIC: 3089 Mfg Plastic Products

(G-19441)
PELL ENGINEERING AND MFG
29 Industrial Park Dr (03076-2136)
PHONE..................................603 598-6855
Armand Lagasse, *President*
Sylvia Lagasse, *Vice Pres*
Bill Mills, *Opers Mgr*
EMP: 13
SQ FT: 10,000
SALES (est): 1.8MM **Privately Held**
SIC: 3599 Machine Shop

(G-19442)
PHOTOMACHINING INC
4 Industrial Park Dr # 40 (03076-2163)
PHONE..................................603 882-9944
Ronald Schaeffer, *CEO*
John O'Connell, *President*
Ian Bergeson, *Engineer*
EMP: 15
SALES (est): 2.3MM **Privately Held**
WEB: www.photomachining.com
SIC: 3599 Mfg Industrial Machinery

(G-19443)
QUALITY COMPONENTS RP
5 Orchard Ln (03076-2503)
PHONE..................................603 864-8196
Arthur Lacroix, *Principal*
EMP: 4
SALES (est): 387.3K **Privately Held**
SIC: 3441 Structural Metal Fabrication

(G-19444)
RAYTHEON COMPANY
50 Bush Hill Rd (03076-3000)
PHONE..................................603 635-6800
Richard Desmarais, *Branch Mgr*
EMP: 25
SALES (corp-wide): 27B **Publicly Held**
SIC: 3812 Mfg Search/Navigation Equipment
PA: Raytheon Company
870 Winter St
Waltham MA 02451
781 522-3000

(G-19445)
ROLAND J SOUCY COMPANY LLC
52 Marsh Rd (03076-3135)
PHONE..................................603 635-3265
Roland Soucy, *President*
Theresa Soucy, *Treasurer*
EMP: 4
SQ FT: 4,000
SALES (est): 504.3K **Privately Held**
WEB: www.rjsoucy.com
SIC: 2431 3442 Mfg Millwork Mfg Metal Doors/Sash/Trim

(G-19446)
SCHUL INTERNATIONAL CO LLC
1 Industrial Park Dr # 14 (03076-2170)
PHONE..................................603 889-6872
Steve Robinson, *President*
▲ **EMP:** 15
SQ FT: 17,500
SALES (est): 3.2MM
SALES (corp-wide): 5.5B **Publicly Held**
WEB: www.schul.com
SIC: 2891 Mfg Adhesives/Sealants
HQ: Tremco Incorporated
3735 Green Rd
Beachwood OH 44122
216 292-5000

(G-19447)
SPECTRUM SERVICES
164 Jeremy Hill Rd (03076-2111)
PHONE..................................603 635-2439
Robert J Francis, *Owner*
EMP: 4
SALES: 500K **Privately Held**
SIC: 3825 Mfg Electrical Measuring Instruments

(G-19448)
SS & G LLC
Also Called: Gluertec
30 Pulpit Rock Rd (03076-3340)
P.O. Box 984 (03076-0984)
PHONE..................................603 635-7400
Brian Gamache, *Mng Member*
Micheal Sutcliffe,
EMP: 6
SQ FT: 1,500
SALES: 500K **Privately Held**
WEB: www.gluertec.com
SIC: 3565 Mfg Packaging Machinery

(G-19449)
TAYLOR & STEVENS CABINETRY
1 Industrial Park Dr # 24 (03076-2158)
PHONE..................................603 880-2022
Steve Jackson, *Owner*
EMP: 5
SALES (est): 320K **Privately Held**
SIC: 2434 Mfg Wood Kitchen Cabinets

(G-19450)
THREE NIGHT DELIVERY INC
4 Industrial Park Dr # 30 (03076-2163)
PHONE..................................603 595-6230
Robert L Wright, *President*
EMP: 4
SALES (est): 432.4K **Privately Held**
SIC: 3499 Mfg Misc Fabricated Metal Products

(G-19451)
TND INC
4 Industrial Park Dr # 30 (03076-2163)
PHONE..................................603 595-4795
Duane Masson, *Owner*
EMP: 4
SALES (est): 447.3K **Privately Held**
SIC: 3444 Mfg Sheet Metalwork

(G-19452)
UPNOVR INC
31 Pulpit Rock Rd Unit A (03076-3371)
P.O. Box 199 (03076-0199)
PHONE..................................603 625-8639
Alan Cady, *President*
▼ **EMP:** 20
SALES (est): 1.4MM **Privately Held**
SIC: 3446 Mfg Architectural Metalwork

(G-19453)
VETTE THERMAL SOLUTIONS LLC
Also Called: Vette North American Power Div
33 Bridge St (03076-3475)
PHONE..................................603 635-2800
Christopher Cutaia, *Manager*
EMP: 100 **Privately Held**
WEB: www.vettecorp.com
SIC: 3443 Mfg Fabricated Plate Work
HQ: Vette Thermal Solutions, Llc
14 Manchester Sq
Portsmouth NH 03801
603 635-2800

(G-19454)
WAKEFELD THERMAL SOLUTIONS INC (HQ)
Also Called: Wakefield-Vette
33 Bridge St (03076-3475)
PHONE..................................603 635-2800
Kevin Kreger, *President*
David Stone, *General Mgr*
Dan Bellerose, *Vice Pres*
Priscilla Gately, *Vice Pres*
Steve Lawson, *Vice Pres*
▲ **EMP:** 243 **EST:** 1993
SQ FT: 185,000
SALES (est): 90.7MM **Privately Held**
SIC: 3354 Mfg Aluminum Extruded Products

Pembroke
Merrimack County

(G-19455)
ACANA NORTHEAST INC
360 Commerce Way Unit 3 (03275)
PHONE..................................800 922-2629
Hugh Thomas Kane, *CEO*
EMP: 12 **EST:** 2012
SALES (est): 1.4MM **Privately Held**
SIC: 3556 Mfg Food Products Machinery

(G-19456)
C&S CHMCAL SPRTONS SENSORS LLC
338 N Pembroke Rd (03275-3604)
PHONE..................................603 491-9511
Casey Grenier,
EMP: 5
SALES (est): 305.8K **Privately Held**
SIC: 2835 Mfg Diagnostic Substances

(G-19457)
GLORIA JEAN PHOTOGRAPHY
347 Pembroke St (03275-3235)
PHONE..................................603 485-7176
Gloria Hillsgrove, *Owner*
EMP: 3
SALES (est): 145.4K **Privately Held**
SIC: 2771 Mfg Greeting Cards

(G-19458)
IZZY INDUSTRIES INC
701 Riverwood Dr (03275-3701)
PHONE..................................603 219-0596
Zach Morley, *Vice Pres*
▲ **EMP:** 10

SALES (est): 1MM Privately Held
SIC: 2326 Mfg Men's/Boy's Work Clothing

(G-19459)
NHRC LLC
415 4th Range Rd (03275-3311)
PHONE....603 485-2248
Peter Gialunis, *Principal*
Rich Cox, *Principal*
Jeff Gialunis, *Principal*
Jeff Ottrson, *Principal*
EMP: 10
SALES (est): 1MM Privately Held
WEB: www.nhrc.net
SIC: 3663 Mfg Radio/Tv Communication Equipment

(G-19460)
NORTHEAST INNOVATIONS INC
145 Sheep Davis Rd (03275-3710)
P.O. Box 120, Concord (03302-0120)
PHONE....603 226-4000
John Harrison, *President*
EMP: 10
SALES (est): 1.3MM Privately Held
WEB: www.neinnovations.com
SIC: 3661 Mfg Telephone Test Equipment

(G-19461)
ODDBALL BREWING CO
6 Glass St (03275-1512)
PHONE....603 210-5654
Mark Ferguson, *Principal*
EMP: 7 EST: 2014
SALES (est): 449.2K Privately Held
SIC: 2082 Mfg Malt Beverages

(G-19462)
PITCO FRIALATOR INC
39 Sheep Davis Rd (03275-3705)
PHONE....603 225-6684
EMP: 50
SALES (corp-wide): 2.7B Publicly Held
SIC: 3589 Mfg Service Industry Machinery
HQ: Pitco Frialator, Inc.
553 Route 3a
Bow NH 03304
603 225-6684

(G-19463)
RAINVILLE PRINTING ENTPS INC
272 Cross Rd (03275-2906)
PHONE....603 485-3422
Robert Rainville, *President*
EMP: 6
SALES (est): 278.4K Privately Held
SIC: 2752 Lithographic Commercial Printing

(G-19464)
WS DENNISON CABINETS INC
779 Silver Hills Dr (03275-4402)
PHONE....603 224-8434
Wayne George, *Principal*
EMP: 5
SALES (est): 20.6K Privately Held
SIC: 2434 Mfg Wood Kitchen Cabinets

Penacook
Merrimack County

(G-19465)
FIFE PACKAGING LLC
77 Merrimack St (03303-1710)
PHONE....603 753-2669
John D Pfeifle,
EMP: 30
SALES (est): 5.3MM Privately Held
SIC: 2675 Mfg Die-Cut Paper/Paperboard

Peterborough
Hills County

(G-19466)
CARUS PUBLISHING
20 Depot St Unit 310 (03458-1453)
PHONE....603 924-7209
▲ EMP: 9
SALES (est): 899.3K Privately Held
SIC: 2741 Misc Publishing

Peterborough
Hillsborough County

(G-19467)
BATTLE ROAD PRESS
216a Old Jaffrey Rd (03458-1825)
P.O. Box 454 (03458-0454)
PHONE....603 924-7600
Sarah Kurzon, *Owner*
▲ EMP: 5
SALES (est): 375.8K Privately Held
SIC: 2741 Misc Publishing

(G-19468)
BAUHAN PUBLISHING
44 Main St (03458-2445)
PHONE....603 567-4430
Sarah Bauhan, *Owner*
EMP: 4
SALES (est): 328K Privately Held
SIC: 2741 Misc Publishing

(G-19469)
CIM INDUSTRIES INC
23 Elm St Ste 2 (03458-1011)
PHONE....603 924-9481
Adam Chase, *President*
Richard Stephens, *Vice Pres*
EMP: 17
SQ FT: 25,000
SALES (est): 3.5MM
SALES (corp-wide): 281.3MM Publicly Held
WEB: www.cimind.com
SIC: 2899 Mfg Chemical Preparations
PA: Chase Corporation
295 University Ave
Westwood MA 02090
781 332-0700

(G-19470)
COLONIC CONNECTION
77 Hancock Rd Ste C (03458-1100)
PHONE....603 924-4449
Deborah Clark, *Principal*
EMP: 5
SALES (est): 248.8K Privately Held
SIC: 3845 Mfg Electromedical Equipment

(G-19471)
HAPPY BIRD BAKING COMPANY LLC
24 Long Hill Rd (03458-1811)
PHONE....603 759-0714
EMP: 4 EST: 2011
SALES (est): 175K Privately Held
SIC: 2051 Mfg Bread/Related Products

(G-19472)
HIDEN ANALYTICAL INC (DH)
75 Hancock Rd Ste H (03458-1118)
PHONE....603 924-5008
Ian Neale, *President*
Robert Blacas, *Treasurer*
Peter Hatton, *Director*
Fred Anderson, *Admin Sec*
EMP: 7 EST: 1995
SQ FT: 2,000
SALES: 4MM
SALES (corp-wide): 20.8MM Privately Held
WEB: www.hideninc.com
SIC: 3826 Mfg Analytical Instruments
HQ: Hiden Analytical Limited
420 Europa Boulevard
Warrington WA5 7
192 544-5225

(G-19473)
HYNDSIGHT VISION SYSTEMS INC
49 Vose Farm Rd Ste 120 (03458-2151)
P.O. Box 698 (03458-0698)
PHONE....603 924-1334
Melissa Thompson, *CEO*
▲ EMP: 6
SALES (est): 880.9K Privately Held
SIC: 3575 3861 Mfg Computer Terminals Mfg Photographic Equipment/Supplies

(G-19474)
IDEAL COMPOST COMPANY
439 Old Greenfield Rd (03458-1243)
PHONE....603 924-5050
Marshal Lombard, *President*
EMP: 3 EST: 1989
SALES (est): 406.4K Privately Held
WEB: www.idealcompost.com
SIC: 2875 Mfg Fertilizers-Mix Only

(G-19475)
LUCCI CORP
Also Called: Northeast Products
375 Jaffrey Rd Ste 7 (03458-1792)
PHONE....603 567-4301
Peter Luccisano, *President*
Joseph Luccisano, *Vice Pres*
▲ EMP: 15
SQ FT: 55,000
SALES (est): 2.3MM Privately Held
WEB: www.thermaseat.com
SIC: 2392 2531 Mfg Household Furnishings Mfg Public Building Furniture

(G-19476)
MICRO BENDS CORP
365 Jaffrey Rd (03458-1729)
PHONE....603 924-0022
Craig Rogozinski, *President*
Lisa Rogozinski, *Admin Sec*
EMP: 7
SQ FT: 8,400
SALES (est): 1.2MM Privately Held
SIC: 3498 5051 Mfg Fabricated Pipe/Fittings Metals Service Center

(G-19477)
MICROSPEC CORPORATION
327 Jaffrey Rd (03458-1729)
PHONE....603 924-4300
Timothy W Steele, *CEO*
Diane P Fukuda, *President*
Elizabeth Steele, *Vice Pres*
David Pugh, *Prdtn Mgr*
Christopher Stewart, *Prdtn Mgr*
▲ EMP: 20
SQ FT: 24,000
SALES (est): 6MM Privately Held
SIC: 3356 3357 Nonferrous Rolling/Drawing Nonferrous Wiredrawing/Insulating

(G-19478)
NEW HMPSHIRE BALL BEARINGS INC (DH)
Also Called: Nhbb
175 Jaffrey Rd (03458-1767)
PHONE....603 924-3311
Dan Lemieux, *President*
Sue Broderick, *General Mgr*
Richard Bardellini, *Exec VP*
Rich Bargellini, *Vice Pres*
Jim Geary, *Vice Pres*
▲ EMP: 335 EST: 1946
SALES: 264MM Privately Held
WEB: www.nhbb.com
SIC: 3562 Whol Industrial Supplies
HQ: Nmb (Usa) Inc.
9730 Independence Ave
Chatsworth CA 91311
818 709-1770

(G-19479)
NEW HMPSHIRE BALL BEARINGS INC
Also Called: Hitech Div
175 Jaffrey Rd (03458-1767)
PHONE....603 924-3311
Steven Morel, *Engineer*
Richard Reynells, *Branch Mgr*
EMP: 50 Privately Held
WEB: www.nhbb.com
SIC: 3562 5085 Mfg Ball/Roller Bearings Whol Industrial Supplies
HQ: New Hampshire Ball Bearings, Inc.
175 Jaffrey Rd
Peterborough NH 03458
603 924-3311

(G-19480)
NEWPORT SAND & GRAVEL CO INC
Also Called: Carroll Concrete Co
399 Jaffrey Rd (03458-1729)
PHONE....603 924-1999
Mark Luopa, *Manager*
EMP: 6
SALES (corp-wide): 44MM Privately Held
SIC: 3273 Mfg Ready-Mixed Concrete
PA: Newport Sand & Gravel Co., Inc.
8 Reeds Mill Rd
Newport NH 03773
603 298-0199

(G-19481)
NEWSPAPERS OF NEW HAMPSHIRE
Also Called: Monadnock Ledger
20 Grove St (03458-1470)
P.O. Box 36 (03458-0036)
PHONE....603 924-7172
Judy Tomlinson, *Sales Staff*
Geordie Wilson, *Manager*
EMP: 18
SALES (corp-wide): 80.7MM Privately Held
WEB: www.concordmonitor.com
SIC: 2711 Newspapers-Publishing/Printing
HQ: Newspapers Of New Hampshire Inc
1 Monitor Dr
Concord NH 03301
603 224-5301

(G-19482)
OLD DUBLIN ROAD INC
Also Called: Peterborough Basket Company
130 Grove St (03458-1756)
P.O. Box 120 (03458-0120)
PHONE....603 924-3861
Russell Dodds, *President*
Joan Dodds, *Vice Pres*
Wayne Dodds, *Vice Pres*
EMP: 60 EST: 1854
SQ FT: 36,000
SALES (est): 7.9MM Privately Held
WEB: www.peterborobasket.com
SIC: 2449 Mfg Wood Containers

(G-19483)
PETERBORO TOOL COMPANY INC
Upper Union St (03458)
P.O. Box 96, West Peterborough (03468-0096)
PHONE....603 924-3034
Kenneth Stockwell, *President*
James Poodiack, *Vice Pres*
EMP: 12
SQ FT: 8,000
SALES (est): 1.6MM Privately Held
WEB: www.ptool.com
SIC: 3599 Mfg Industrial Machinery

(G-19484)
PRECISION COMPONENTS INC
77 Hancock Rd Ste 1 (03458-1100)
PHONE....603 924-3597
Lucien Theriault, *President*
Barbara Theriault, *Corp Secy*
William Theriault, *Vice Pres*
EMP: 3
SQ FT: 3,600
SALES: 400K Privately Held
SIC: 3451 Mfg Screw Machine Products

(G-19485)
PYROMATE INC
270 Old Dublin Rd (03458-1337)
PHONE....603 924-4251
David M Lavoie, *President*
Jeffrey R Crocker, *Treasurer*
Karen E Lavoie, *Admin Sec*
EMP: 6
SALES (est): 680K Privately Held
WEB: www.pyromate.com
SIC: 3629 7389 Mfg Electrical Industrial Apparatus

(G-19486)
ROBERT TYSZKO OD PLLC
129 Wilton Rd (03458-1749)
PHONE....603 924-9591
Robert Tyszko, *Owner*
EMP: 3
SALES (est): 133K Privately Held
SIC: 3841 Optometrist's Office

GEOGRAPHIC

(G-19487)
SAVRON GRAPHICS INC
Also Called: Copies and More
19 Wilton Rd Ste 5 (03458-1799)
PHONE..................................603 924-7088
Dee McGrath, *Branch Mgr*
EMP: 3
SALES (corp-wide): 2MM **Privately Held**
WEB: www.savrongraphics.com
SIC: 2752 Commercial Printing
PA: Savron Graphics Inc
4 Stratton Rd
Jaffrey NH 03452
603 532-7726

(G-19488)
SIMON & SCHUSTER INC
Cobblestone Publishing
20 Depot St Unit 30 (03458-1453)
PHONE..................................603 924-7209
Lou Waryncia, *Manager*
EMP: 30
SALES (corp-wide): 25.9B **Publicly Held**
WEB: www.digonsite.com
SIC: 2721 2731 Publishes Educational Magazines And Teacher Resource Materials
HQ: Simon & Schuster, Inc.
1230 Ave Of The Americas
New York NY 10020
212 698-7000

(G-19489)
STERLING BUSINESS CORP
Also Called: Sterling Business Print & Mail
206 Concord St (03458-1209)
PHONE..................................603 924-9401
George Sterling, *President*
Loretta Sterling, *Treasurer*
EMP: 6
SQ FT: 7,500
SALES (est): 360K **Privately Held**
WEB: www.sbc.mv.com
SIC: 2752 7331 7338 7389 Mailing Service Secretarial Service & Answering Service

(G-19490)
STILLPOINT INTERNATIONAL INC
Also Called: STILLPOINT PUBLISHING
17 Eastridge Dr (03458-2147)
P.O. Box 477, Walpole (03608-0477)
PHONE..................................603 756-9281
EMP: 5
SQ FT: 3,000
SALES: 77.1K **Privately Held**
WEB: www.stillpoint.org
SIC: 2731 8661 Books-Publishing/Printing Religious Organization

(G-19491)
TRI-MED INC
Also Called: Tri Med Group
305 Union St (03458)
P.O. Box 432 (03458-0432)
PHONE..................................603 924-7211
Gregory Spitzfaden, *President*
Peter Jodoin, *Treasurer*
Andrew Lewis,
EMP: 5
SQ FT: 350
SALES (est): 852.3K **Privately Held**
WEB: www.tri-med.com
SIC: 3842 5047 Mfg Surgical Appliances/Supplies Whol Medical/Hospital Equipment

Piermont
Grafton County

(G-19492)
HUNTINGTON LOGGING
28 Arron Rd (03779-3102)
PHONE..................................603 272-9322
Jeffrey Huntington, *Principal*
EMP: 3
SALES (est): 235.7K **Privately Held**
SIC: 2411 Logging

(G-19493)
TRADITIONAL WOODWORKING LLC
164 River Rd (03779-3013)
PHONE..................................603 272-9324
Brian Henderson,
Brian F Henderson,
EMP: 3
SQ FT: 2,000
SALES (est): 390.3K **Privately Held**
SIC: 2431 Mfg Architectural Woodwork

Pittsburg
Coos County

(G-19494)
JORDAN ASSOCIATES
Also Called: Lancaster Herrald
Rr 145 (03592)
P.O. Box 263, Colebrook (03576-0263)
PHONE..................................603 246-8998
Charles Jordan, *Owner*
Donna Jordan, *Co-Owner*
EMP: 10
SALES (est): 292.2K **Privately Held**
SIC: 2711 7011 Newspapers-Publishing/Printing Hotel/Motel Operation

(G-19495)
ROY E AMEY
Also Called: R and L Amey
191 Tabor Rd (03592-5117)
PHONE..................................603 538-6913
Roy E Amey, *Owner*
EMP: 7
SALES (est): 508.4K **Privately Held**
SIC: 2411 Logging

(G-19496)
WARICK MANAGEMENT COMPANY INC
10 Farr Rd (03592-5169)
P.O. Box 339 (03592-0339)
PHONE..................................603 538-7112
Warren Chase, *President*
Richard Judd, *Admin Sec*
EMP: 7 **EST:** 1991
SALES (est): 872.5K **Privately Held**
SIC: 2411 Logging

Pittsfield
Merrimack County

(G-19497)
ALPHA DESIGN & COMPOSITION
47 Manchester St (03263-3401)
PHONE..................................603 435-8592
Norman Tuttle, *Owner*
EMP: 4
SALES (est): 190K **Privately Held**
SIC: 2791 Typesetting Services

(G-19498)
AMERICAN ENRGY INDPENDENCE LLC
Also Called: Americo
5 Main St (03263-3708)
PHONE..................................603 228-3611
Jack Shey,
Anthony P Giunta,
EMP: 5
SALES (est): 579.5K **Privately Held**
SIC: 2079 Mfg Edible Fats/Oils

(G-19499)
EVER BETTER EATING INC
Also Called: Rustic Crust
5 Main St (03263-3708)
P.O. Box 56 (03263-0056)
PHONE..................................603 435-5119
Bradford S Sterl, *President*
Bob Cheney, *Director*
▲ **EMP:** 100 **EST:** 1996
SQ FT: 12,000
SALES (est): 22.9MM **Privately Held**
WEB: www.rusticcrust.com
SIC: 2045 Mfg Prepared Flour Mixes/Doughs

(G-19500)
GLOBE MANUFACTURING CO LLC (DH)
37 Loudon Rd (03263-3604)
PHONE..................................603 435-8323
Donald D Welch II, *President*
John Cushman, *Regional Mgr*
Kurt Dittman, *Regional Mgr*
George E Freese III, *Senior VP*
Robert A Freese, *Senior VP*
EMP: 330 **EST:** 1887
SQ FT: 73,409
SALES (est): 60.1MM
SALES (corp-wide): 1.3B **Publicly Held**
WEB: www.globefiresuits.com
SIC: 3842 Mfg Surgical Appliances/Supplies

(G-19501)
INOFAB LLC
26 Broadway St (03263-3800)
PHONE..................................603 435-5082
Ted Nemetz, *Sales Staff*
Nicholas Kaminski,
EMP: 8
SALES (est): 732.1K **Privately Held**
SIC: 3448 3444 Mfg Prefabricated Metal Buildings Mfg Sheet Metalwork

(G-19502)
KENTEK CORPORATION
32 Broadway St (03263-3800)
PHONE..................................603 223-4900
Thomas Macmullin, *President*
EMP: 27
SQ FT: 15,000
SALES (est): 7MM **Privately Held**
WEB: www.kenteklaserstore.com
SIC: 3826 Mfg Analytical Instruments Mfg Electrical Equipment/Supplies

(G-19503)
MRP MANUFACTURING LLC
23 Catamount Rd (03263-3801)
P.O. Box 5 (03263-0005)
PHONE..................................603 435-5337
Mark Paulin,
EMP: 5
SQ FT: 1,000
SALES: 600K **Privately Held**
SIC: 3089 2396 3429 Mfg Plastic Products Mfg Auto/Apparel Trimming Mfg Hardware

(G-19504)
NOBLESPIRIT ENTP SFTWR LLC
51 Dowboro Rd (03263-3901)
PHONE..................................603 435-8218
Pauline Cortese, *Principal*
EMP: 3
SALES (est): 204.7K **Privately Held**
SIC: 7372 Prepackaged Software Services

(G-19505)
SUNCOOK VALLEY SUN INC
21 Broadway St (03263-3831)
P.O. Box 156 (03263-0156)
PHONE..................................603 435-6291
Arthur Morse, *President*
Elsie Morse, *Vice Pres*
EMP: 4
SALES (est): 337.6K **Privately Held**
SIC: 2711 Newspapers-Publishing/Printing

Plaistow
Rockingham County

(G-19506)
AAK POWER SUPPLY CORPORATION
73 Newton Rd Pmb 2 # 103 (03865-2424)
PHONE..................................603 382-2222
Patrice McColley, *President*
EMP: 10
SQ FT: 2,000
SALES: 100K **Privately Held**
SIC: 3629 Mfg Electrical Industrial Apparatus

(G-19507)
ASIA DIRECT LLC
91 Main St Ste 14 (03865-3012)
PHONE..................................603 382-9485
Paul Marcotte, *Mng Member*
Marion Marcotte,
Paul A Marcotte III,
Jennifer Rydeen,
▼ **EMP:** 500
SALES (est): 20.5MM **Privately Held**
WEB: www.asia-direct-us.com
SIC: 3679 Mfg Electronic Components

(G-19508)
BECKWOOD SERVICES INC
Also Called: Sparton Beckwood
27 Hale Spring Rd (03865-2314)
P.O. Box 985 (03865-0985)
PHONE..................................603 382-3840
Michael Woodbury, *COO*
Mike Woodbury, *COO*
James Adams, *CFO*
EMP: 75
SALES (est): 17.1MM
SALES (corp-wide): 374.9MM **Privately Held**
WEB: www.beckwood.com
SIC: 3625 3699 Mfg Relays/Industrial Controls Mfg Electrical Equipment/Supplies
HQ: Sparton Corporation
425 N Martingale Rd
Schaumburg IL 60173
847 762-5800

(G-19509)
BERUBE TOOL & DIE INC
34 Main St (03865-3050)
P.O. Box 1100 (03865-1100)
PHONE..................................603 382-2224
Roland Berube, *President*
Normand Berube, *Officer*
EMP: 7
SQ FT: 7,000
SALES (est): 1MM **Privately Held**
SIC: 3544 Mfg Tool & Die

(G-19510)
CARDINAL COMMUNICATIONS INC
23 Atkinson Depot Rd (03865-3138)
PHONE..................................603 382-4800
Joyce Driscoll, *Principal*
EMP: 3
SALES (est): 135.6K **Privately Held**
SIC: 2711 Newspapers-Publishing/Printing

(G-19511)
ENCO CONTAINER SERVICES INC
4 Wilder Dr Ste 7 (03865-4810)
P.O. Box 1770 (03865-1770)
PHONE..................................603 382-8481
EMP: 7
SQ FT: 16,000
SALES (est): 1.4MM **Privately Held**
WEB: www.encocontainer.com
SIC: 2621 Paper Mill

(G-19512)
ENCO INDUSTRIES INC
4 Wilder Dr Ste 7 (03865-4810)
P.O. Box 1770 (03865-1770)
PHONE..................................603 382-8481
Mike Rosa, *President*
▲ **EMP:** 18
SQ FT: 25,000
SALES (est): 4.4MM **Privately Held**
WEB: www.encoind.com
SIC: 2655 Mfg Fiber Cans/Drums

(G-19513)
ENVIROMART INDUSTRIES INC
4 Wilder Dr (03865-2856)
PHONE..................................603 378-0154
Brian Hughes, *General Mgr*
Richard Patterson, *Vice Pres*
Kaye Harper, *Admin Asst*
EMP: 7
SALES (est): 163.7K **Privately Held**
SIC: 3999 Mfg Misc Products

(G-19514)
ENVIRONMENTAL CONTAINER SVCS
Also Called: Enco
4 Wilder Dr Ste 7 (03865-4810)
P.O. Box 1770 (03865-1770)
PHONE..................................603 382-8481
Michael Rosa, *President*
Richard Patterson, *Vice Pres*
EMP: 7
SQ FT: 7,500
SALES: 2.4MM **Privately Held**
WEB: www.encogroup.com
SIC: 2655 Distribute Containers For Hazardous Waste
PA: General Environmental Corporation
33 Pine St
Exeter NH 03833

(G-19515)
ENVIRONMENTAL PACKG TECH INC
4 Wilder Dr Ste 7 (03865-4810)
P.O. Box 1770 (03865-1770)
PHONE..................................603 378-0340
Micheal Rosa, *President*
◆ **EMP:** 4
SALES (est): 32.5K **Privately Held**
WEB: www.enviropacktech.com
SIC: 2631 Paperboard Mill

(G-19516)
ENVIRONMENTAL SCIENCE TECH INC
Also Called: Est, Inc Government Services
4 Wilder Dr Ste 7 (03865-4810)
P.O. Box 1769 (03865-1769)
PHONE..................................603 378-0809
Michael Rosa, *CEO*
EMP: 10
SQ FT: 10,000
SALES (est): 960.1K **Privately Held**
SIC: 2653 Mfg Corrugated/Solid Fiber Boxes

(G-19517)
GRANITE STATE COVER AND CANVAS
144 Main St (03865-3014)
P.O. Box 1217 (03865-1217)
PHONE..................................603 382-5462
David Callahan, *CEO*
Robert Jubinville, *Admin Sec*
EMP: 14
SQ FT: 10,000
SALES: 3MM **Privately Held**
WEB: www.granitestatecover.com
SIC: 3715 Mfg Truck Trailers

(G-19518)
H&H CUSTOM METAL FABG INC
6 Duston Ave (03865-2203)
P.O. Box 457 (03865-0457)
PHONE..................................603 382-2818
Gary Lesiczka, *President*
Laurie Lesiczka, *Vice Pres*
EMP: 8
SALES (est): 1.3MM **Privately Held**
SIC: 3444 Mfg Sheet Metalwork

(G-19519)
LAGASSE & LEWIS LLC
38 Main St (03865-3066)
PHONE..................................603 382-5898
Harold Lewis,
Mark Lagasse,
EMP: 3
SALES (est): 238K **Privately Held**
SIC: 3721 Mfg Aircraft

(G-19520)
PLAISTOW CABINET CO INC
Also Called: Nmg
56 Newton Rd (03865-2408)
PHONE..................................603 382-1098
Norman Gallant, *President*
Michael Gallant, *Vice Pres*
Monique St Laurent, *Sales Staff*
EMP: 10
SALES (est): 1.2MM **Privately Held**
SIC: 2434 Mfg Wood Kitchen Cabinets

(G-19521)
QUALITY MACHINE INC
31 Kingston Rd (03865-2215)
PHONE..................................603 382-2334
Gary Cicale, *President*
Terri Cicale, *Accounting Dir*
EMP: 15
SALES (est): 2.4MM **Privately Held**
WEB: www.qualitymachine1.com
SIC: 3599 Mfg Industrial Machinery

(G-19522)
ROBERT CAIRNS COMPANY LLC
Also Called: Cairns Robert Company
2 Red Oak Dr Unit H (03865-2433)
PHONE..................................603 382-0044
Robert Cairns, *Owner*
EMP: 4
SALES (est): 459.8K **Privately Held**
SIC: 3827 3229 3211 Mfg Optical Instr/Lens Mfg Pressed/Blown Glass Mfg Flat Glass

(G-19523)
SCANDIA PLASTICS INC
55 Westville Rd (03865-2946)
P.O. Box 179 (03865-0179)
PHONE..................................603 382-6533
David R Hallett, *President*
Leon Boucher, *Vice Pres*
▲ **EMP:** 45
SQ FT: 62,000
SALES (est): 10.5MM
SALES (corp-wide): 7.9B **Privately Held**
WEB: www.scandia-nh.com
SIC: 2821 3083 Mfg Plastic Materials/Resins Mfg Laminated Plastic Plate/Sheet
HQ: Pexco Llc
6470 E Johns Rssng 430
Johns Creek GA 30097
770 777-8540

(G-19524)
SPARTON BECKWOOD LLC
27 Hale Spring Rd (03865-2314)
P.O. Box 985 (03865-0985)
PHONE..................................603 382-3840
EMP: 75 **EST:** 2013
SALES (est): 17.1MM
SALES (corp-wide): 374.9MM **Privately Held**
SIC: 3674 3672 Mfg Semiconductors/Related Devices Mfg Printed Circuit Boards
HQ: Sparton Corporation
425 N Martingale Rd
Schaumburg IL 60173
847 762-5800

(G-19525)
SUMMIT METAL FABRICATORS INC
144a Main St (03865-3014)
P.O. Box 1280 (03865-1280)
PHONE..................................603 328-2211
Joseph A Barbone, *President*
EMP: 68
SQ FT: 175,000
SALES (est): 6MM
SALES (corp-wide): 55.8MM **Privately Held**
SIC: 3441 Structural Metal Fabrication
PA: Methuen Construction Co., Inc.
144 Main St
Plaistow NH 03865
603 328-2222

(G-19526)
TACK-TILES BRAILLE SYSTEMS LLC
97 Forrest St (03865-2610)
P.O. Box 475 (03865-0475)
PHONE..................................603 382-1904
Kevin Murphy PHD,
Janice Murphy,
EMP: 3
SALES (est): 219.5K **Privately Held**
WEB: www.tack-tiles.com
SIC: 3999 Mfg Educational Aids For Visually Impaired

(G-19527)
WESSMARK NH LLC
2 Red Oak Dr (03865-2433)
PHONE..................................603 974-2932
Kenneth J Emonds,
EMP: 3
SALES (est): 228.8K **Privately Held**
SIC: 3672 Mfg Printed Circuit Boards

Plymouth
Grafton County

(G-19528)
COMPLEX MOLD & MACHINE
1137 Route 175 (03264)
PHONE..................................603 536-1221
George E Losefsky, *Partner*
Steven Curley, *Partner*
George Losefsky, *Partner*
Jonathan P Siek, *Partner*
EMP: 3
SQ FT: 2,400
SALES: 240K **Privately Held**
SIC: 3544 Manufacturer Of Special Dies And Tools Die Sets Jigs Fixtures And Primarily Industrial Molds

(G-19529)
NARRATIVE 1 SOFTWARE LLC
1 Bridge St Ste 301 (03264-1632)
PHONE..................................603 968-2233
EMP: 6
SALES (est): 296.3K **Privately Held**
SIC: 7372 Prepackaged Software Services

(G-19530)
PENNYSAVER
Also Called: Pennysaver The
607 Tenney Mountain Hwy # 137 (03264-3156)
PHONE..................................603 536-3160
Thomas Walrath, *President*
John H Sobetzer, *Co-President*
EMP: 9
SALES (est): 608.2K **Privately Held**
WEB: www.pennysavernh.com
SIC: 2711 Newspapers-Publishing/Printing

(G-19531)
VENTURE PRINT UNLIMITED INC
44 Main St (03264-1441)
PHONE..................................603 536-2410
Dawn Lemieux, *President*
EMP: 13
SQ FT: 500
SALES (est): 1.6MM **Privately Held**
SIC: 2759 7311 Commercial Printing

Portsmouth
Rockingham County

(G-19532)
ADVANCED DESIGN & MFG INC
Also Called: A D M
350 Heritage Ave Unit 3 (03801-8641)
PHONE..................................603 430-7573
Ron Raby, *President*
Caren Raby, *Vice Pres*
Deb Simon, *Purch Mgr*
Jeff Clark, *Clerk*
EMP: 50
SQ FT: 15,000
SALES (est): 9.4MM **Privately Held**
WEB: www.advanceddesign.com
SIC: 3679 Mfg Electronic Components

(G-19533)
AGGREGATE INDUSTRIES - MWR INC
650 Peverly Hill Rd (03801-5356)
PHONE..................................603 427-1137
Jonathan Oakes, *Branch Mgr*
EMP: 20
SALES (corp-wide): 4.5B **Privately Held**
SIC: 3273 Mfg Ready-Mixed Concrete
HQ: Aggregate Industries - Mwr, Inc.
2815 Dodd Rd
Eagan MN 55121
651 683-0600

(G-19534)
ALLIED TELESIS INC
15 Rye St (03801-6829)
PHONE..................................603 334-6058
EMP: 5 **Privately Held**
SIC: 3577 Mfg Computer Peripheral Equipment
HQ: Allied Telesis, Inc.
19800 North Creek Pkwy # 100
Bothell WA 98011
408 519-8700

(G-19535)
ALLTRAXX LLC
1950 Lafayette Rd Ste 202 (03801-8864)
PHONE..................................603 610-7179
Louis Altman,
Gina Aspinwall,
Jason Chute,
Len Corasaniti,
EMP: 5
SALES (est): 385.1K **Privately Held**
SIC: 3663 3669 Mfg Radio/Tv Comm Equip Mfg Communications Equip

(G-19536)
ANDY CROTEAU
285 Banfield Rd (03801-5601)
PHONE..................................603 436-8919
Andy Croteau, *Owner*
EMP: 3
SALES (est): 73.8K **Privately Held**
SIC: 7692 Welding Repair

(G-19537)
ANTRIM WIND ENERGY LLC
155 Fleet St (03801-4050)
PHONE..................................603 570-4842
John Kenworthy, *Exec Officer*
EMP: 3
SALES (est): 126K
SALES (corp-wide): 323.7K **Privately Held**
SIC: 3621 Mfg Motors/Generators
PA: Walden Green Energy Northeast Wind Llc
40 Worth St Fl 10
New York NY
646 527-7288

(G-19538)
AQUAWAVE OF NEW ENGLAND LLC
195 Nh Ave (03801-2816)
PHONE..................................603 431-8975
Jon P McMillan,
E Ingraham,
EMP: 12
SALES (est): 1.7MM **Privately Held**
SIC: 3589 Mfg Service Industry Machinery

(G-19539)
ASCA INC (PA)
112 Corporate Dr Ste 1 (03801-6890)
P.O. Box 1140 (03802-1140)
PHONE..................................603 433-6700
James Phelps, *President*
EMP: 34
SQ FT: 4,200
SALES (est): 4.2MM **Privately Held**
WEB: www.asca-design.com
SIC: 3446 Mfg Architectural Metalwork

(G-19540)
AURORA BIOSYSTEMS LLC
1 New Hampshire Ave (03801-2904)
PHONE..................................603 766-1947
Soenke Brunswieck, *CEO*
Scott Broughton, *Principal*
EMP: 3
SALES (est): 134.2K **Privately Held**
SIC: 2836 Mfg Biological Products

(G-19541)
AVID CORP
222 International Dr # 195 (03801-6818)
PHONE..................................603 559-9700
Mary Sheffer, *Principal*
EMP: 11
SALES (est): 2MM **Privately Held**
SIC: 3829 Mfg Measuring/Controlling Devices

(G-19542)
BAYCORP HOLDINGS LTD (PA)
953 Islington St Ste 22 (03801-4299)
PHONE..................................603 294-4850
Frank W Getman Jr, *President*
Raymond Faust, *COO*
Patrycia T Mitchell, *Treasurer*

GEOGRAPHIC

EMP: 13
SQ FT: 3,000
SALES (est): 3.7MM **Privately Held**
WEB: www.baycorpholdings.com
SIC: 2911 Petroleum Refiner

(G-19543)
BID2WIN SOFTWARE INC
Also Called: B2w
99 Bow St Ste 500 (03801-3846)
PHONE..................................800 336-3808
Paul J McKeon Jr, *CEO*
Lisa Clark, *Vice Pres*
Jeff Russell, *Vice Pres*
Bihari Srinivasan, *Vice Pres*
Tina Cochran, *Engineer*
EMP: 89
SQ FT: 22,160
SALES (est): 14.7MM **Privately Held**
WEB: www.bid2win.com
SIC: 7372 Prepackaged Software Services

(G-19544)
BIO GREEN
124 Heritage Ave Unit 15 (03801-5645)
PHONE..................................603 570-6159
Paul Grillo, *Regional Mgr*
EMP: 6
SALES (est): 591.8K **Privately Held**
SIC: 3443 Mfg Fabricated Plate Work

(G-19545)
BLUE TREE LLC
9 Sheafe St (03801-3817)
P.O. Box 148 (03802-0148)
PHONE..................................603 436-0831
Brian Smestad, *Administration*
▲ **EMP:** 3
SALES (est): 172.8K **Privately Held**
SIC: 2731 Books-Publishing/Printing

(G-19546)
BOSTON ENVIRONMENTAL LLC
600 State St Ste 7 (03801-4370)
PHONE..................................603 334-1000
Mike Hatch,
EMP: 14
SQ FT: 6,500
SALES (est): 2.6MM **Privately Held**
WEB: www.bostonenvironmental.com
SIC: 3443 Mfg Fabricated Plate Work

(G-19547)
BOTTOMLINE TECHNOLOGIES DE INC (PA)
325 Corporate Dr Ste 300 (03801-6847)
PHONE..................................603 436-0700
Robert A Eberle, *President*
John F Kelly, *General Mgr*
John Kelly, *General Mgr*
Jessica Pincomb Moran, *General Mgr*
Jessica Moran, *General Mgr*
EMP: 133
SQ FT: 85,000
SALES: 421.9MM **Publicly Held**
WEB: www.bottomline.com
SIC: 7372 Prepackaged Software Services

(G-19548)
CC1 INC
170 West Rd Ste 7 (03801-5663)
PHONE..................................603 319-2000
Richard D Lewis, *President*
James Lewis, *Vice Pres*
Robin Mills, *Vice Pres*
James E Lewis, *Admin Sec*
EMP: 25
SQ FT: 11,000
SALES (est): 5.3MM **Privately Held**
WEB: www.cc1inc.com
SIC: 3555 3829 3651 Mfg Printing Trades Machinery Mfg Measuring/Controlling Devices Mfg Home Audio/Video Equipment

(G-19549)
CELIOS CORPORATION
39 Sagamore Ave (03801-5526)
PHONE..................................978 877-2044
Brian Packard, *CEO*
Rob Stone, *CFO*
EMP: 6
SALES (est): 251.5K **Privately Held**
SIC: 3634 Mfg Electric Housewares/Fans

(G-19550)
CELLGENIX USA
1 Nh Ave (03801-2904)
PHONE..................................603 373-0408
Scott Broughton, *Director*
EMP: 4
SALES (est): 318.6K **Privately Held**
SIC: 2834 Mfg Pharmaceutical Preparations

(G-19551)
CHADWICK & TREFETHEN INC
50 Borthwick Ave (03801-4186)
PHONE..................................603 436-2568
David A Richards, *Ch of Bd*
David Bovee, *Vice Pres*
Janice Bakula, *Sales Mgr*
Jane Richards, *Clerk*
EMP: 10
SQ FT: 8,000
SALES: 700K **Privately Held**
WEB: www.chadwickreamers.com
SIC: 3423 Mfg Hand/Edge Tools

(G-19552)
CHASCO INC
Also Called: Four Seasons Fence
15 Banfield Rd Unit 6 (03801-5607)
PHONE..................................603 436-2141
Charles Kuehl, *President*
EMP: 15
SQ FT: 17,000
SALES (est): 1.5MM **Privately Held**
WEB: www.fourseasons1979.com
SIC: 2499 5211 Mfg Installs And Ret Cedar Fences & Other Cedar Outdoor Products

(G-19553)
CLARK PUBLISHING
44 Pearson St (03801-4834)
PHONE..................................603 431-1238
Theresa Wiseman, *Principal*
EMP: 3
SALES (est): 76.2K **Privately Held**
SIC: 2741 Misc Publishing

(G-19554)
CORE ELASTOMERS
170 West Rd Ste 2 (03801-5663)
PHONE..................................603 319-6912
Stephen H Roberts Esq, *Administration*
▲ **EMP:** 8
SALES (est): 1.2MM **Privately Held**
SIC: 2821 Mfg Plastic Materials/Resins

(G-19555)
CRAFT BREW ALLIANCE INC
35 Corporate Dr (03801-2847)
PHONE..................................603 430-8600
Jerry Prial, *President*
EMP: 52
SALES (corp-wide): 206.1MM **Publicly Held**
WEB: www.redhook.com
SIC: 2082 Ale Brewery
PA: Craft Brew Alliance, Inc.
929 N Russell St
Portland OR 97227
503 331-7270

(G-19556)
DAILY PORTSMOUTH
114 Crescent Way (03801-3480)
PHONE..................................603 767-1395
Philip Case Cohen, *Principal*
EMP: 5 **EST:** 2011
SALES (est): 197.7K **Privately Held**
SIC: 2711 Newspapers-Publishing/Printing

(G-19557)
DASAN ZHONE SOLUTIONS INC
112 Corporate Dr Ste 1 (03801-6890)
PHONE..................................510 777-7000
Sean Belanger, *Branch Mgr*
EMP: 50 **Publicly Held**
WEB: www.paradyne.com
SIC: 3577 Design & Manufacture Internet & Wide Area Connection Products
HQ: Dasan Zhone Solutions, Inc.
7195 Oakport St
Oakland CA 94621
510 777-7000

(G-19558)
ELECYR CORPORATION
871 Islington St Ste A100 (03801-4261)
PHONE..................................617 905-6800
EMP: 4
SALES (est): 320K **Privately Held**
SIC: 3629 Mfg Elec Indstl Equip

(G-19559)
ENERTRAC INC
100 Market St Unit 302 (03801-3760)
PHONE..................................603 821-0003
Steve Owens, *CEO*
Cham Morgan, *CFO*
EMP: 10
SALES (est): 1.5MM **Privately Held**
SIC: 3829 Mfg Measuring/Controlling Devices

(G-19560)
ERIE SCIENTIFIC LLC (DH)
Also Called: Erie Scientific Company
20 Post Rd (03801-5622)
PHONE..................................603 430-6859
Stephen K Wiatt, *Exec VP*
▲ **EMP:** 302
SQ FT: 120,000
SALES (est): 160.6MM
SALES (corp-wide): 24.3B **Publicly Held**
SIC: 3231 3821 3229 3221 Mfg Prdt-Purchased Glass Mfg Lab Apparatus/Furn Mfg Pressed/Blown Glass Mfg Glass Containers Mfg Flat Glass
HQ: Fisher Scientific International Llc
81 Wyman St
Waltham MA 02451
781 622-1000

(G-19561)
EV LAUNCHPAD LLC
1465 Woodbury Ave 384 (03801-3210)
PHONE..................................603 828-2919
James Penfold,
EMP: 10
SALES (est): 599.1K **Privately Held**
SIC: 3694 Mfg Engine Electrical Equipment

(G-19562)
EXTRUSION ALTERNATIVES INC
19 Post Rd (03801-5622)
PHONE..................................603 430-9600
Robert Pickett, *President*
Pete Panagakos, *Sales Staff*
Melissa Pickett, *Manager*
Tom Buswell, *Director*
EMP: 15
SALES (est): 2.3MM **Privately Held**
WEB: www.exaltcustomtubing.com
SIC: 3061 Mfg Surgical/Medical Instruments

(G-19563)
FLEXENERGY INC
Also Called: Flexenergy.com
30 Nh Ave (03801-2866)
PHONE..................................603 430-7000
Mark Schnepel, *President*
Robert Campbell, *Exec VP*
John Alday, *Vice Pres*
Mohammed Ebrahim, *Engineer*
Bob Livingston, *Engineer*
EMP: 90
SQ FT: 89,800
SALES (est): 15.1MM **Privately Held**
SIC: 3511 Mfg Turbines/Generator Sets
PA: Flexenergy Holdings, Llc
30 Nh Ave
Portsmouth NH 03801
603 430-7000

(G-19564)
FLEXENERGY HOLDINGS LLC (PA)
30 Nh Ave (03801-2866)
PHONE..................................603 430-7000
Mark Schnepel, *President*
EMP: 73 **EST:** 2013
SALES: 15.1MM **Privately Held**
SIC: 3511 Mfg Turbines/Generator Sets

(G-19565)
FOSTERS DAILY DMCRAT FSTRS SUN
111 Nh Ave (03801-2864)
PHONE..................................603 431-4888
Elaine Leduc, *Principal*
EMP: 4
SALES (est): 257.8K **Privately Held**
SIC: 2711 Newspapers-Publishing/Printing

(G-19566)
GALVION LTD (HQ)
200 International Dr # 250 (03801-6833)
PHONE..................................514 739-4444
Jonathan Blanshay, *President*
Craig Baden, *Principal*
EMP: 3
SALES (est): 2.6MM
SALES (corp-wide): 17.2MM **Privately Held**
SIC: 3851 Mfg Ophthalmic Goods
PA: Galvion Inc
3800 Rue Saint-Patrick Bureau 200
Montreal QC H4E 1
514 739-4444

(G-19567)
GLOBAL LAMINATES
300 Constitution Ave (03801-8609)
PHONE..................................603 373-8081
Bruce E Hurley, *Administration*
▲ **EMP:** 6
SALES (est): 722.6K **Privately Held**
SIC: 3089 Mfg Plastic Products

(G-19568)
GRANITE STATE PLASMA CUTTING
10 Pleasant St Ste 400 (03801-4551)
PHONE..................................603 536-4415
Raymond F Harmony, *President*
Marsha E Harmony, *President*
Raymond Harmony, *Vice Pres*
EMP: 35
SQ FT: 60,000
SALES (est): 8MM **Privately Held**
SIC: 3441 Structural Metal Fabrication

(G-19569)
GREAT RHYTHM BREWING CO LLC
229 Miller Ave (03801-5158)
P.O. Box 1624 (03802-1624)
PHONE..................................603 300-8588
Thomas Keane, *Principal*
EMP: 3
SALES (est): 346.9K **Privately Held**
SIC: 2082 Mfg Malt Beverages

(G-19570)
GREENWOOD PUBLISHING GROUP LLC
Heinemann Publishing
361 Hanover St (03801-3959)
P.O. Box 528 (03802-0097)
PHONE..................................603 431-7894
Bob Gokey, *Vice Pres*
Deanna Richardson, *Project Mgr*
Elizabeth Valway, *Production*
Pallavi Rayan, *Finance*
Terry Thomas, *Sales Dir*
EMP: 37
SALES (corp-wide): 1.3B **Publicly Held**
SIC: 2731 Books-Publishing/Printing
HQ: Greenwood Publishing Group, Llc
125 High St
Boston MA 02110
617 351-5000

(G-19571)
GUS & RUBY LETTERPRESS LLC
29 Congress St (03801-4004)
P.O. Box 344 (03802-0344)
PHONE..................................603 319-1717
Samantha Finigan, *Mng Member*
Riley Conaway, *Graphic Designe*
EMP: 3
SQ FT: 1,400
SALES (est): 309.3K **Privately Held**
SIC: 2759 Commercial Printing

(G-19572)
HANSA CONSULT NORTH AMER LLC
200 International Dr (03801-6833)
PHONE..................................603 422-8833
Karl M Overman, *Mng Member*
Joerg Hoehner,
Walter Phelps,
EMP: 12
SQ FT: 5,000
SALES (est): 2.7MM **Privately Held**
WEB: www.hcna-llc.com
SIC: 3822 Environment &Automation Services

(G-19573)
HARMONY METAL PRODUCTS NORTH
10 Pleasant St Ste 400 (03801-4551)
PHONE..................................603 536-6012
Raymond F Harmony, *President*
Marsha Harmony, *President*
Todd C Fahey, *Admin Sec*
EMP: 42 **EST:** 1964
SQ FT: 60,000
SALES (est): 9.5MM **Privately Held**
WEB: www.harmonymetal.com
SIC: 3499 Mfg Misc Fabricated Metal Products

(G-19574)
HAWTHORN CREATIVE GROUP LLC
33 Jewell Ct (03801-4990)
PHONE..................................603 610-0533
Dan Seitz, *Business Mgr*
Ben Morse, *Vice Pres*
Molly Patrick, *Vice Pres*
Jennifer Legacy, *Prdtn Mgr*
Jennifer Munro, *Prdtn Mgr*
EMP: 45
SQ FT: 6,000
SALES (est): 6.2MM **Privately Held**
SIC: 2741 Misc Publishing

(G-19575)
HOLASE INCORPORATED
75 Rochester Ave (03801-2852)
PHONE..................................603 397-0038
EMP: 4
SALES (est): 230K **Privately Held**
SIC: 3499 3842 3661 4899 Mfg Misc Fab Metal Products Mfg Surgical Appliances Mfg Telephone/Graphic Equip Communication Services

(G-19576)
HOUGHTON MIFFLIN HARCOURT CO
Also Called: Hmh
361 Hanover St (03801-3959)
PHONE..................................630 467-7000
EMP: 4
SALES (corp-wide): 1.3B **Publicly Held**
SIC: 3999 2731 Mfg Misc Products Books-Publishing/Printing
PA: Houghton Mifflin Harcourt Company
125 High St Ste 900
Boston MA 02110
617 351-5000

(G-19577)
IHEARTCOMMUNICATIONS INC
Also Called: Wheg.fm
815 Lafayette Rd (03801-5406)
PHONE..................................603 436-7300
Bob Greer, *Manager*
Kelly Brown, *Director*
Laura Boyce, *Social Dir*
EMP: 60 **Publicly Held**
SIC: 3663 Mfg Radio/Tv Communication Equipment
HQ: Iheartcommunications, Inc.
20880 Stone Oak Pkwy
San Antonio TX 78258
210 822-2828

(G-19578)
INFINITE IMAGING INC (PA)
933 Islington St (03801-4229)
PHONE..................................603 436-3030
William J Hurley, *Principal*
EMP: 26
SALES (est): 4.2MM **Privately Held**
SIC: 2752 Lithographic Commercial Printing

(G-19579)
INGU LLC
210 West Rd (03801-5639)
PHONE..................................603 770-5969
Jim Kane,
EMP: 10
SALES (est): 283.1K **Privately Held**
SIC: 3999 Mfg Misc Products

(G-19580)
IONBOND LLC
195 Nh Ave (03801-2816)
PHONE..................................603 610-4460
Corey Marcotte, *Branch Mgr*
EMP: 38 **Privately Held**
SIC: 3398 Coating/Engraving Service
HQ: Ionbond Llc
1823 E Whitcomb Ave
Madison Heights MI 48071

(G-19581)
ISHIGAKI USA LTD
280 Heritage Ave Unit J (03801-8619)
PHONE..................................603 433-3334
▲ **EMP:** 13
SALES (est): 1.9MM **Privately Held**
SIC: 3559 Mfg Misc Industry Machinery
PA: Ishigaki Co., Ltd.
1-6-5, Marunouchi
Chiyoda-Ku TKY 100-0

(G-19582)
JULIET MARINE SYSTEMS INC
101 Shattuck Way Ste 2 (03801-7876)
P.O. Box 21974 (03802-1974)
PHONE..................................603 319-8412
Gregory Sancoff, *President*
Curtis Lintvedt, *CFO*
EMP: 9
SALES (est): 1MM **Privately Held**
SIC: 3732 Boatbuilding/Repairing

(G-19583)
KELLEY SOLUTIONS INC
Also Called: Kelley Direct Solutions
210 West Rd Unit 7 (03801-5639)
PHONE..................................603 431-3881
Lisa Finneral, *President*
Shaun Kelly, *Principal*
EMP: 7
SQ FT: 2,210
SALES: 2.5MM **Privately Held**
WEB: www.kelleysolutions.com
SIC: 2752 5112 Lithographic Commercial Printing Whol Stationery/Office Supplies

(G-19584)
LANAIR RESEARCH & DEVELOPMENT
Also Called: Atco Lanair
521 Shattuck Way (03801-7872)
PHONE..................................603 433-6134
David Lancaster, *President*
Mary Liz Lancaster, *Vice Pres*
Richard Sorrentino, *Vice Pres*
EMP: 9 **EST:** 1996
SQ FT: 5,600
SALES (est): 873.6K **Privately Held**
WEB: www.lanairinc.com
SIC: 3728 Mfg Aircraft Parts/Equipment

(G-19585)
LEGACY GLOBAL SPORTS LP
290 Heritage Ave Unit 2 (03801-6874)
PHONE..................................603 373-7262
John St Pierre, *President*
Travis G Bezio, *Vice Pres*
Travis Bezio, *Vice Pres*
Mike Coleman, *Portfolio Mgr*
Phillip Passarelli, *Portfolio Mgr*
EMP: 3
SALES (est): 233K **Privately Held**
SIC: 2329 2339 Mfg Men's/Boy's Clothing Mfg Women's/Misses' Outerwear

(G-19586)
LIGHTHOUSE MANUFACTURING LLC
35 Mirona Road Ext (03801-5343)
PHONE..................................978 532-5999
Michael E Bean, *President*
J Charles Rivers, *Vice Pres*
EMP: 46 **EST:** 1974
SQ FT: 21,000
SALES (est): 8.2MM **Privately Held**
WEB: www.lighthousemfg.com
SIC: 3599 Mfg Industrial Machinery

(G-19587)
LOCAL MEDIA GROUP INC
Also Called: Seacoast Newspapers
111 New Hampshire Ave (03801-2864)
P.O. Box 119 (03802-0119)
PHONE..................................603 436-1800
John Tabor, *Manager*
EMP: 150
SALES (corp-wide): 1.5B **Publicly Held**
WEB: www.ottaway.com
SIC: 2711 Newspapers-Publishing/Printing
HQ: Local Media Group, Inc.
40 Mulberry St
Middletown NY 10940
845 341-1100

(G-19588)
LONZA BIOLOGICS INC
40 Goosebay Dr (03801)
PHONE..................................603 610-4696
EMP: 10
SALES (corp-wide): 5.6B **Privately Held**
SIC: 2834 Mfg Pharmaceutical Preparations
HQ: Lonza Biologics Inc.
101 International Dr
Portsmouth NH 03801
603 610-4500

(G-19589)
LONZA BIOLOGICS INC (DH)
101 International Dr (03801-2815)
PHONE..................................603 610-4500
Stephan Kutzer, *President*
Lindsey Kelley, *Project Mgr*
Katherine Leathers, *Mfg Mgr*
Rand Bussey, *Facilities Mgr*
William Deprofio, *Facilities Mgr*
▼ **EMP:** 277
SALES (est): 197.3MM
SALES (corp-wide): 5.6B **Privately Held**
WEB: www.lonza.com
SIC: 2834 Mfg Pharmaceutical Preparations
HQ: Lonza America Inc.
412 Mount Kemble Ave 200s
Morristown NJ 07960
201 316-9200

(G-19590)
LOYALTY BUILDERS INC (PA)
210 Commerce Way Ste 250 (03801-8203)
PHONE..................................603 610-8800
Peter Moloney, *CEO*
Leslie Parker, *CFO*
Mark Klein, *CTO*
EMP: 11 **EST:** 2011
SALES (est): 1.4MM **Privately Held**
SIC: 7372 Prepackaged Software Services

(G-19591)
LULULEMON USA INC
60 State St (03801-3824)
PHONE..................................603 431-0871
EMP: 6
SALES (corp-wide): 2.3B **Privately Held**
SIC: 2339 Mfg Women's/Misses' Outerwear
HQ: Lululemon Usa Inc.
2201 140th Ave E
Sumner WA 98390
604 732-6124

(G-19592)
ME AND OLLIES
2454 Lafayette Rd Ste 21 (03801-5619)
PHONE..................................603 319-1561
Roger Elkus, *Owner*
Aaron Veno, *Store Mgr*
EMP: 8
SALES (est): 642.6K **Privately Held**
SIC: 2051 Mfg Bread/Related Products

(G-19593)
MEETINGMATRIX INTL INC
195 Nh Ave (03801-2816)
PHONE..................................603 610-1600
EMP: 44
SQ FT: 6,600
SALES (est): 3.1MM
SALES (corp-wide): 5B **Privately Held**
WEB: www.meetingmatrix.com
SIC: 7372 Prepackaged Software
HQ: Amadeus Hospitality Americas, Inc.
75 Nh Ave Ste 300
Portsmouth NH 03801
603 436-7500

(G-19594)
MELVIN REISZ
Also Called: Summerwind Jewelers Goldsmiths
49 Market St (03801-2029)
PHONE..................................603 436-9188
Melvin Reisz, *Owner*
EMP: 6 **EST:** 1972
SALES: 1MM **Privately Held**
SIC: 3911 5944 Mfg & Ret Jewelry Precious Stones & Metal

(G-19595)
METAVAC LLC
20 Post Rd (03801-5622)
PHONE..................................631 207-2344
Michael J Kessler,
Robert Longo,
EMP: 46
SQ FT: 33,000
SALES (est): 6.6MM
SALES (corp-wide): 24.3B **Publicly Held**
WEB: www.medavac.com
SIC: 3826 Mfg Analytical Instruments
HQ: Fisher Scientific International Llc
81 Wyman St
Waltham MA 02451
781 622-1000

(G-19596)
MICRONICS FILTRATION LLC (HQ)
Also Called: Micronics Engineered Filtration
300 Constitution Ave # 201 (03801-8657)
PHONE..................................603 433-1299
Barry Hibble, *CEO*
Richard E Weiler, *President*
Julie A Pugh, *CFO*
◆ **EMP:** 119
SQ FT: 35,000
SALES (est): 19.3MM **Privately Held**
WEB: www.micronicsinc.com
SIC: 3569 5085 Mfg General Industrial Machinery Whol Industrial Supplies

(G-19597)
NEO MARKETS INC
953 Islington St Ste 22 (03801-4299)
PHONE..................................603 766-8716
EMP: 15
SQ FT: 3,000
SALES: 1MM **Privately Held**
SIC: 3823 Mfg Process Control Instruments

(G-19598)
NEW ENGLAND NAUTICAL LLC
1950 Lafayette Rd Ste 200 (03801-8864)
PHONE..................................603 601-3166
Glenn Callahan, *Mng Member*
EMP: 4
SQ FT: 1,000
SALES (est): 149.8K **Privately Held**
SIC: 3732 Boatbuilding/Repairing

(G-19599)
NEW ENGLAND PRINTING CORP
Also Called: PIP Printing
599 Lafayette Rd Ste 4 (03801-5409)
PHONE..................................603 431-0142
Alan Higginbotham, *President*
Steven Feld, *Admin Sec*
EMP: 10
SQ FT: 3,500
SALES (est): 1.3MM **Privately Held**
WEB: www.newenglandprinting.com
SIC: 2752 2796 2791 2789 Lithographic Coml Print Platemaking Services Typesetting Services Bookbinding/Related Work

(G-19600)
NEW HAMPSHIRE PROSTHETICS LLC
30 International Dr # 201 (03801-6812)
PHONE....................603 294-0010
Christopher Phillips, *Principal*
Christopher Croasdale,
EMP: 3 **EST:** 2013
SALES (est): 272.7K **Privately Held**
SIC: 3842 Mfg Surgical Appliances/Supplies

(G-19601)
NEWMARKET SOFTWARE SYSTEMS
75 Nh Ave Ste 300 (03801-2096)
PHONE....................603 436-7500
Sean Oneill, *Chairman*
EMP: 3
SALES (est): 326.8K **Privately Held**
SIC: 7372 Prepackaged Software Services

(G-19602)
OMADA TECHNOLOGIES LLC
36 Maplewood Ave (03801-3712)
PHONE....................603 944-7124
Richard Stover,
Matthew Keane,
EMP: 4
SALES: 2MM **Privately Held**
SIC: 7372 Prepackaged Software Services

(G-19603)
ON BOARD SOLUTIONS LLC
200 International Dr # 195 (03801-6835)
PHONE....................603 373-6500
Michael Chames,
EMP: 18
SALES (est): 1.5MM **Privately Held**
SIC: 3699 Mfg Electrical Equipment/Supplies

(G-19604)
OPTRIS IR SENSING LLC
200 International Dr # 170 (03801-6833)
PHONE....................603 766-6060
Tom Scanlon,
EMP: 5
SALES (est): 685.4K **Privately Held**
SIC: 3823 Mfg Process Control Instruments

(G-19605)
PARKER-HANNIFIN CORPORATION
Also Called: Parker Motor Design
15 Rye St Ste 307 (03801-6846)
PHONE....................603 433-6400
Timothy Harned, *Manager*
EMP: 3
SALES (corp-wide): 14.3B **Publicly Held**
WEB: www.parker.com
SIC: 3594 Mfg Fluid Power Pumps/Motors
PA: Parker-Hannifin Corporation
6035 Parkland Blvd
Cleveland OH 44124
216 896-3000

(G-19606)
PEAKED WIND POWER LLC
155 Fleet St (03801-4050)
PHONE....................603 570-4842
EMP: 3
SALES (est): 179.3K **Privately Held**
SIC: 3621 Mfg Motors/Generators

(G-19607)
PETER E RANDALL PUBLISHER LLC
5 Greenleaf Woods Dr (03801-5442)
P.O. Box 4542 (03802-4542)
PHONE....................603 431-5667
Deidre Randall, *Mng Member*
▲ **EMP:** 3
SQ FT: 450
SALES: 400K **Privately Held**
WEB: www.perpublisher.com
SIC: 2731 Books-Publishing/Printing

(G-19608)
PORTSMOUTH NAVAL SHIPYARD
Code 612 5 Bldg 153 6th (03804)
PHONE....................207 438-1000
EMP: 9
SALES (est): 363.7K **Privately Held**
SIC: 3731 Shipbuilding/Repairing

(G-19609)
POWERPLAY MANAGEMENT LLC
Also Called: Infinite Imaging
933 Islington St (03801-4229)
PHONE....................603 436-3030
Christopher Carrier, *Mng Member*
Christopher Oberg, *Mng Member*
EMP: 23
SQ FT: 4,000
SALES (est): 670.6K **Privately Held**
SIC: 2759 8742 3993 5199 Commercial Printing Mgmt Consulting Svcs Mfg Signs/Ad Specialties Whol Nondurable Goods

(G-19610)
PURELY ORGANIC PRODUCTS LLC
1 New Hampshire Ave # 125 (03801-2904)
PHONE....................212 826-9150
Robert Simmons, *Mng Member*
James Reinertson,
EMP: 3
SQ FT: 1,200
SALES: 1.4MM **Privately Held**
SIC: 2873 Mfg Nitrogenous Fertilizers

(G-19611)
Q LLC
4 Cutts St Unit 3 (03801-3784)
P.O. Box 6860 (03802-6860)
PHONE....................603 294-0047
Jessica Gauvin, *VP Bus Dvlpt*
Kevin Brittingham,
EMP: 9 **EST:** 2016
SQ FT: 12,000
SALES (est): 799.2K **Privately Held**
SIC: 3484 Mfg Small Arms

(G-19612)
RAMBLERS WAY FARM INC
100 Market St Unit 100 # 100
(03801-3797)
PHONE....................603 319-5141
EMP: 8 **Privately Held**
SIC: 2231 Wool Broadwoven Fabric Mill
PA: Rambler's Way Farm, Inc.
2 Storer St Ste 207
Kennebunk ME

(G-19613)
RED 23 HOLDINGS INC
Also Called: Port City Coffee Roasters
801 Islington St Ste 24 (03801-4254)
PHONE....................603 433-3011
Derek Laborie, *President*
EMP: 12
SQ FT: 1,500
SALES (est): 2MM
SALES (corp-wide): 2.1MM **Privately Held**
WEB: www.portcitycoffee.com
SIC: 2095 Coffee Roasting Service
PA: Carefree Group, Inc.
1029 5th St
Miami Beach FL 33139
866 800-1007

(G-19614)
REID PUBLICATION INC
Also Called: Homes and Land Magazine
2456 Lafayette Rd Ste 6 (03801-5624)
P.O. Box 1567 (03802-1567)
PHONE....................603 433-2200
Jim Reid, *President*
EMP: 5
SALES (est): 604.4K **Privately Held**
WEB: www.reidpublications.com
SIC: 2721 7319 Periodicals-Publishing/Printing Advertising Services

(G-19615)
RELX INC
361 Hanover St (03801-3959)
PHONE....................603 431-7894
John C Watson, *Principal*
EMP: 100
SALES (corp-wide): 9.8B **Privately Held**
WEB: www.lexis-nexis.com
SIC: 2721 Periodicals-Publishing/Printing
HQ: Relx Inc.
230 Park Ave Ste 700
New York NY 10169
212 309-8100

(G-19616)
ROLAND H RIPLEY & SON INC
59 Cass St (03801-4940)
PHONE....................603 436-1926
Roland Ripley, *President*
Marjorie Ripley, *Treasurer*
EMP: 4 **EST:** 1923
SQ FT: 10,000
SALES (est): 217.8K **Privately Held**
SIC: 3599 Machine Shop

(G-19617)
SCALLOPS MINERAL & SHELL EMPOR
65 Daniel St (03801-3810)
PHONE....................603 431-7658
Susan Hickey, *Owner*
EMP: 3
SALES (est): 234.6K **Privately Held**
SIC: 1429 Crushed/Broken Stone

(G-19618)
SEACOAST SHEARWATER DEV LLC
144 Washington St (03801-4670)
PHONE....................603 427-0000
Colby T Gamester Esq, *Principal*
EMP: 3
SALES (est): 103.8K **Privately Held**
SIC: 2711 Newspapers-Publishing/Printing

(G-19619)
SEACOAST TECHNOLOGIES INC
222 International Dr # 145 (03801-6817)
PHONE....................603 766-9800
EMP: 7 **EST:** 2000
SALES (est): 545.7K **Privately Held**
SIC: 3841 Surgical And Medical Instruments

(G-19620)
SHAUGHNESSY SEAGULL INC
195 Nh Ave (03801-2816)
PHONE....................603 433-4680
Cary Chaisson, *Co-Owner*
Stephen H Chaisson, *COO*
EMP: 5
SQ FT: 3,356
SALES: 1MM **Privately Held**
WEB: www.allegraportsmouth.com
SIC: 2752 Lithographic Commercial Printing

(G-19621)
SOUTHPORT MANAGEMENT GROUP LLC
Also Called: Sir Speedy
738 Islington St (03801-7217)
PHONE....................603 433-4664
Caytlinn Strickland, *Project Mgr*
Paul Lucy,
EMP: 8
SQ FT: 2,600
SALES (est): 1.6MM **Privately Held**
SIC: 2752 7334 2791 Lithographic Commercial Printing Photocopying Services Typesetting Services

(G-19622)
SPIRIT ADVISORY LLC
Also Called: Southport Printing Company
738 Islington St Ste C (03801-7217)
PHONE....................603 433-4664
Joshua Parison, *Owner*
EMP: 7
SQ FT: 3,092
SALES (est): 405.5K **Privately Held**
SIC: 2752 Lithographic Commercial Printing

(G-19623)
STENHOUSE PUBLISHERS
Also Called: Teachers Publishing Group
282 Corporate Dr Ste 1 (03801-8008)
PHONE....................207 253-1600
Dan Tobin, *President*
EMP: 15
SALES (est): 2.3MM
SALES (corp-wide): 157.3MM **Privately Held**
WEB: www.stenhouse.com
SIC: 2731 Books-Publishing/Printing
PA: Highlights For Children, Inc.
1800 Watermark Dr
Columbus OH 43215
614 486-0631

(G-19624)
TELEDYNE INSTRUMENTS INC
Also Called: Teledyne D.G. O'Brien
162 Corporate Dr Ste 100 (03801-6815)
PHONE....................603 474-5571
John Vanreenen, *Vice Pres*
Jane Smart, *VP Opers*
Patrick Barry, *Branch Mgr*
Daniel Thomas, *Technology*
Suzanne Blake, *Technician*
EMP: 228
SALES (corp-wide): 2.9B **Publicly Held**
WEB: www.teledynesolutions.com
SIC: 3643 3357 3621 3699 Mfg Conductive Wire Dvcs Nonfrs Wiredrwng/Insltng Mfg Motors/Generators Mfg Elec Mach/Equip/Supp Mfg Elec Connectors
HQ: Teledyne Instruments, Inc.
1049 Camino Dos Rios
Thousand Oaks CA 91360
805 373-4545

(G-19625)
THERMO FISHER SCIENTIFIC INC
23 Hampton St (03801-2874)
PHONE....................603 433-7676
Dan Fitzpatrick, *Manager*
EMP: 307
SALES (corp-wide): 24.3B **Publicly Held**
SIC: 3826 Mfg Analytical Instruments And Laboratory Products And Services
PA: Thermo Fisher Scientific Inc.
168 3rd Ave
Waltham MA 02451
781 622-1000

(G-19626)
THERMO FISHER SCIENTIFIC INC
6 Post Rd (03801-5622)
PHONE....................603 431-8410
EMP: 3
SALES (est): 196.2K **Privately Held**
SIC: 3826 Mfg Analytical Instruments

(G-19627)
UNITED STATES DEPT OF NAVY
Also Called: Portsmouth Naval Shipyard
Portsmouth Naval Shr (03804)
PHONE....................207 438-2714
Kevin McCoy, *Branch Mgr*
David R McCarthy, *Analyst*
EMP: 712 **Publicly Held**
SIC: 3731 9711 Shipbuilding/Repairing
HQ: United States Department Of The Navy
1200 Navy Pentagon
Washington DC 20350

(G-19628)
VERA ROASTING COMPANY
99 Bow St Ste 100e (03801-3995)
PHONE....................603 969-7970
Mark Galvin, *CEO*
Glen Miller, *Ch of Bd*
Evan Young, *Finance*
Chris Matrumalo, *Marketing Staff*
EMP: 7
SQ FT: 1,100
SALES (est): 280.1K **Privately Held**
SIC: 2095 5499 Roasted Coffee, Nsk

(G-19629)
VETTE THERMAL SOLUTIONS LLC (HQ)
Also Called: Wakefield-Vette
14 Manchester Sq (03801-8001)
PHONE....................603 635-2800
George P Dannecker, *President*
Jack Hillson, *COO*
Matthew Towse, *Admin Sec*
▲ **EMP:** 10

SALES (est): 11.5MM Privately Held
WEB: www.vettecorp.com
SIC: 3679 Mfg Electronic Components

(G-19630)
WAGZ INC (PA)
230 Commerce Way Ste 325 (03801-8201)
PHONE....603 570-6015
Terry Anderton, *CEO*
Joshua Jasper, *Vice Pres*
Michael Moreau, *VP Sales*
Colleen Baigle, *VP Mktg*
Samuel Stoddard, *CTO*
EMP: 14
SALES: 1.5MM Privately Held
SIC: 3571 7389 Mfg Electronic Computers

(G-19631)
WILLIAM J DEVANEY
230 Lafayette Rd Ste 2 (03801-5453)
PHONE....603 436-7603
William J Devaney, *Principal*
William Devaney, *Fmly & Gen Dent*
EMP: 4
SALES (est): 300.9K Privately Held
SIC: 3843 Mfg Dental Equipment/Supplies

(G-19632)
WOOD WORKS
855 Islington St Ste 123 (03801-4270)
PHONE....603 436-3805
William Clerk, *Partner*
EMP: 7
SALES (est): 770K Privately Held
WEB: www.thewoodworks.net
SIC: 2431 Mfg Millwork

Raymond
Rockingham County

(G-19633)
AGGREGATE INDUSTRIES - MWR INC
91 Chester Rd (03077-2019)
PHONE....603 243-3554
EMP: 18
SALES (corp-wide): 4.5B Privately Held
SIC: 3273 Mfg Ready-Mixed Concrete
HQ: Aggregate Industries - Mwr, Inc.
2815 Dodd Rd
Eagan MN 55121
651 683-0600

(G-19634)
AUTO-LOCK BROADHEAD CO LLC
59 Batchelder Rd (03077-2310)
PHONE....603 895-0502
Roger Franco,
EMP: 4
SALES (est): 125.1K Privately Held
SIC: 3999 Mfg Misc Products

(G-19635)
BE YOUNEEQ LLC
62 Langford Rd (03077-1704)
PHONE....603 244-3933
Raimundas Nutautas, *Mng Member*
EMP: 7
SALES (est): 382.8K Privately Held
SIC: 2771 Mfg Greeting Cards

(G-19636)
BORROUGHS CORPORATION
Also Called: Borroughs Manufacturing
22 Jennifer Ln (03077-2037)
PHONE....603 895-3991
Mark Debruyckere, *Manager*
EMP: 5
SALES (corp-wide): 51.5MM Privately Held
SIC: 2542 5712 Mfg Partitions/Fixtures-Nonwood Ret Furniture
PA: Borroughs Corporation
3002 N Burdick St
Kalamazoo MI 49004
800 748-0227

(G-19637)
BRENTWOOD BOX COMPANY INC
33 Lane Rd (03077-1800)
PHONE....603 895-0829
EMP: 3
SQ FT: 4,500
SALES: 250K Privately Held
SIC: 2449 Mfg Wood Containers

(G-19638)
HILLTOP COOPERATIVE
2 Parker Ave (03077-1347)
P.O. Box 371 (03077-0371)
PHONE....603 895-6476
Sandra Pike, *President*
Kathleen Dang, *Treasurer*
EMP: 5
SALES: 1,000K Privately Held
SIC: 2451 Mobile Homes, Nsk

(G-19639)
IMAGE FACTORY LLC
20 Chester Rd (03077-2015)
PHONE....603 895-3024
Gary Brown, *Owner*
EMP: 3 EST: 2001
SALES (est): 275K Privately Held
SIC: 3999 Mfg Misc Products

(G-19640)
MAX ROADS LLC
10 Twins Rd (03077-2665)
PHONE....603 895-5200
Bernadette Patterson,
EMP: 3 EST: 2002
SALES: 100K Privately Held
SIC: 3531 1794 Mfg Construction Machinery Excavation Contractor

(G-19641)
NORTEAST WOODWORKING INC
24 Old Manchester Rd (03077-2314)
P.O. Box 123 (03077-0123)
PHONE....603 895-4271
Richard Dubois, *President*
Warren Bain, *Vice Pres*
EMP: 3
SQ FT: 9,000
SALES: 250K Privately Held
SIC: 2431 Mfg Millwork

(G-19642)
NORTHEAST WOODWORKING PRODUCTS
24 Old Manchester Rd (03077-2314)
P.O. Box 123 (03077-0123)
PHONE....603 895-4271
Richard Dubois, *President*
EMP: 4 EST: 2001
SALES (est): 537.1K Privately Held
SIC: 2434 Mfg Wood Kitchen Cabinets

(G-19643)
PARKER & HARPER COMPANIES INC (PA)
Also Called: Gemini Valve
2 Otter Ct (03077-2506)
PHONE....603 895-4761
Daniel Packard, *President*
Ken Madden, *Vice Pres*
Harry Millette, *Vice Pres*
Daniel M Packard, *Treasurer*
Dennis F Gorman, *Admin Sec*
▲ EMP: 70
SQ FT: 70,000
SALES (est): 14MM Privately Held
WEB: www.geminivalve.com
SIC: 3494 3451 3643 3593 Mfg Valves/Pipe Fittings Mfg Screw Machine Prdts Mfg Conductive Wire Dvcs Mfg Fluid Power Cylinder

(G-19644)
ROYAL ADHESIVES & SEALANTS LLC
63 Epping St (03077-2621)
PHONE....860 788-3380
Ann Pecola, *Office Mgr*
EMP: 3
SALES (est): 123.2K Privately Held
SIC: 2891 Mfg Adhesives/Sealants

(G-19645)
SHOOKUS SPECIAL TOOLS INC
11 Center St (03077-2509)
P.O. Box 1027 (03077-1027)
PHONE....603 895-1200
Peter John Shookus, *President*
Lori C Shookus, *CFO*
EMP: 14
SQ FT: 16,000
SALES (est): 2.3MM Privately Held
WEB: www.shookustools.com
SIC: 3312 Contract Mfg Of Tool And Die Machine Parts

Rindge
Cheshire County

(G-19646)
AMERICAN KEDER INC (PA)
22 Perkins Rd (03461-5494)
P.O. Box 170107, Milwaukee WI (53217-8011)
PHONE....603 899-3233
Thomas Shields, *President*
J David Pozerycki, *Treasurer*
Gerhard Meisterjahn, *Shareholder*
Walter Mueller, *Shareholder*
▲ EMP: 8 EST: 2000
SQ FT: 8,000
SALES: 1.2MM Privately Held
WEB: www.keder.com
SIC: 3792 5199 Mfg Travel Trailers/Campers Whol Nondurable Goods

(G-19647)
BOUDRIEAU TOOL & DIE INC
1032 Nh Route 119 Unit 9 (03461-6008)
PHONE....603 899-5795
Dennis Boudrieau, *President*
Anne Boudrieau, *Corp Secy*
Scott Boudrieau, *Vice Pres*
EMP: 5
SQ FT: 3,200
SALES: 300K Privately Held
SIC: 3545 5999 Manufactures Tooling

(G-19648)
COLONIAL GREEN PRODUCTS LLC (PA)
1032 Nh Route 119 Unit 6 (03461-6008)
PHONE....603 532-7005
Chris Stewart,
EMP: 10
SQ FT: 4,000
SALES: 1.4MM Privately Held
SIC: 3296 Mfg Mineral Wool

(G-19649)
GRASON & ASSOCIATES LLC
1134 Nh Route 119 (03461)
P.O. Box 289 (03461-0289)
PHONE....603 899-3089
Rufus Grason, *Mng Member*
EMP: 3
SALES (est): 294.2K Privately Held
SIC: 3841 Mfg Surgical/Medical Instruments

(G-19650)
LEXINGTON DATA INCORPORATED
316 Main St (03461)
PHONE....603 899-5673
James Critser, *President*
EMP: 8
SALES (est): 605.4K Privately Held
SIC: 3571 Mfg Electronic Computers

Rochester
Strafford County

(G-19651)
ALBANY ENGNERED COMPOSITES INC
216 Airport Dr (03867-1718)
PHONE....603 330-5851
Brian Coffenberry, *President*
EMP: 55
SALES (corp-wide): 982.4MM Publicly Held
SIC: 2269 Finishing Plant
HQ: Albany Engineered Composites, Inc.
216 Airport Dr
Rochester NH 03867
603 330-5800

(G-19652)
ALBANY ENGNERED COMPOSITES INC
216 Airport Dr (03867-1718)
PHONE....603 330-5993
Steve Page, *Manager*
EMP: 15
SALES (corp-wide): 982.4MM Publicly Held
SIC: 2269 Finishing Plant
HQ: Albany Engineered Composites, Inc.
216 Airport Dr
Rochester NH 03867
603 330-5800

(G-19653)
ALBANY ENGNERED COMPOSITES INC
216 Airport Dr (03867-1718)
PHONE....603 330-5800
Joseph G Morone, *Branch Mgr*
EMP: 30
SALES (corp-wide): 982.4MM Publicly Held
SIC: 2269 Finishing Plant
HQ: Albany Engineered Composites, Inc.
216 Airport Dr
Rochester NH 03867
603 330-5800

(G-19654)
ALBANY ENGNERED COMPOSITES INC (HQ)
216 Airport Dr (03867-1718)
P.O. Box 1907, Albany NY (12201-1907)
PHONE....603 330-5800
Joseph G Morone, *CEO*
Greg Harwell, *President*
Rick Sharpe, *Senior VP*
Charles J Silva Jr, *Vice Pres*
Alex Roberts, *Opers Spvr*
◆ EMP: 120
SALES (est): 46.4MM
SALES (corp-wide): 982.4MM Publicly Held
SIC: 2269 Finishing Plant
PA: Albany International Corp.
216 Airport Dr
Rochester NH 03867
603 330-5850

(G-19655)
ALBANY INTERNATIONAL CORP (PA)
216 Airport Dr (03867-1718)
PHONE....603 330-5850
John C Standish, *Vice Ch Bd*
A William Higgins, *President*
Robert A Hansen, *Senior VP*
Bernd Nordhus-Westarp, *Vice Pres*
Dave Pawlick, *Vice Pres*
EMP: 100 EST: 1895
SALES: 982.4MM Publicly Held
WEB: www.albint.com
SIC: 2221 3496 2399 2899 Mfg Paper Broadwoven Fabrics Synthetic Materials Specialty Doors

(G-19656)
ALBANY INTERNATIONAL CORP
85 Innovation Dr (03867-1723)
PHONE....603 330-5993
EMP: 3
SALES (corp-wide): 982.4MM Publicly Held
SIC: 2221 Mfg Paper Broadwoven Fabrics
PA: Albany International Corp.
216 Airport Dr
Rochester NH 03867
603 330-5850

(G-19657)
ALBANY SAFRAN COMPOSITES LLC (HQ)
85 Innovation Dr (03867-1723)
P.O. Box 1907, Albany NY (12201-1907)
PHONE....603 330-5800

Joseph G Morone, *President*
Robert A Hansen, *Senior VP*
John B Cozzolino, *CFO*
▲ **EMP:** 32
SQ FT: 343,712
SALES (est): 16.2MM
SALES (corp-wide): 982.4MM **Publicly Held**
SIC: 3429 3728 Advanced 3d-Woven Composite Parts For Use In Aircraft And Rocket Engines
PA: Albany International Corp.
216 Airport Dr
Rochester NH 03867
603 330-5850

(G-19658)
AMERICAN BACON BOSTON FELT INC

31 Front St (03868-5823)
PHONE..................................603 332-7000
Wilson Pryne, *President*
◆ **EMP:** 50
SQ FT: 55,000
SALES (est): 8.6MM **Privately Held**
WEB: www.baconfelt.com
SIC: 2299 Mfg Textile Goods

(G-19659)
ASHLAND ELECTRIC PRODUCTS INC

10 Indl Way (03867)
PHONE..................................603 335-1100
Christophe Y Cloitre, *President*
Heather Ann Cloitre, *Treasurer*
EMP: 20
SQ FT: 20,000
SALES: 3.4MM **Privately Held**
WEB: www.ashlandelectric.com
SIC: 3621 Mfg Electric Motors

(G-19660)
ATHLETIC INNOVATION INC

54 Allen St Ste 2 (03867-1448)
PHONE..................................603 332-1212
Larry Sanders, *President*
Christopher Oby, *Vice Pres*
EMP: 4
SQ FT: 6,000
SALES: 300K **Privately Held**
SIC: 3949 Mfg Athletic Equipment

(G-19661)
AUGER ELECTRIC LLC

25 Hampshire Ave (03867-2012)
PHONE..................................603 335-5633
EMP: 4
SALES (est): 370K **Privately Held**
SIC: 3699 Mfg Electrical Equipment/Supplies

(G-19662)
BOSTON SAND & GRAVEL COMPANY

69 N Coast Rd (03868-8628)
PHONE..................................603 330-3999
Don Hayward, *Administration*
EMP: 102
SALES (corp-wide): 121MM **Privately Held**
SIC: 3273 Mfg Ready-Mixed Concrete
PA: Boston Sand & Gravel Company Inc
100 N Washington St Fl 2
Boston MA 02114
617 227-9000

(G-19663)
BRADFORD WHITE CORP

20 Industrial Way (03867-4296)
PHONE..................................603 332-0116
Jason Fifer, *Marketing Mgr*
EMP: 3 **EST:** 2016
SALES (est): 128K **Privately Held**
SIC: 3433 Mfg Heating Equipment-Non-electric

(G-19664)
CONTINENTAL BRAZE SUPPLY LLC

5 Sampson Rd (03867-4207)
P.O. Box 1836 (03866-1836)
PHONE..................................603 948-1016
George N Martin, *President*
Frank John Lickteig,
EMP: 3
SALES: 300K **Privately Held**
SIC: 2899 Mfg Chemical Preparations

(G-19665)
CONTITECH THERMOPOL LLC

35 Industrial Way Ste 204 (03867-6202)
PHONE..................................603 692-6300
Greg Mc Cloud, *Chairman*
EMP: 100
SALES (corp-wide): 49.2B **Privately Held**
SIC: 3052 2822 Mfg Rubber/Plastic Hose/Belting Mfg Synthetic Rubber
HQ: Contitech Thermopol Llc
9 Interstate Dr
Somersworth NH 03878

(G-19666)
CUSTOM BANNER & GRAPHICS LLC

184 Milton Rd (03868-8712)
PHONE..................................603 332-2067
R Clay Prewitt, *Mng Member*
EMP: 7
SQ FT: 8,000
SALES (est): 750K **Privately Held**
SIC: 2399 2269 2231 5131 Mfg Fabrctd Textile Pdts Finishing Plant Wool Brdwv Fabric Mill Whol Piece Goods/Notions

(G-19667)
DESCO INDUSTRIES INC

73 Allen St (03867-1403)
PHONE..................................603 332-0717
Chris Haas, *Manager*
EMP: 7
SALES (corp-wide): 66.3MM **Privately Held**
WEB: www.desco.com
SIC: 3629 Mfg Static Electricity Elimination Equipment
PA: Desco Industries, Inc.
3651 Walnut Ave
Chino CA 91710
909 627-8178

(G-19668)
DMR INDUSTRIES INC

181 Milton Rd (03868-8714)
PHONE..................................603 335-0325
Darrel Robinson, *President*
Marie Robinson, *Vice Pres*
EMP: 9
SQ FT: 7,000
SALES: 885K **Privately Held**
WEB: www.dmrindustries.com
SIC: 3599 Mfg Industrial Machinery

(G-19669)
ELDORADO STONE

36 Walnut St (03867-1017)
PHONE..................................617 947-6722
Carlton Cooper, *Principal*
EMP: 3
SALES (est): 180.5K **Privately Held**
SIC: 3272 Mfg Concrete Products

(G-19670)
GEORGE J FOSTER CO INC

90 N Main St (03867-1925)
PHONE..................................603 332-2200
Peter Scott, *Manager*
EMP: 3
SALES (est): 112.6K **Privately Held**
SIC: 2711 Newspapers-Publishing/Printing

(G-19671)
HUMPHREYS INDUSTRIAL PDTS INC

Also Called: Rubber Group, The
22 Nadeau Dr (03867-4637)
PHONE..................................603 692-5005
Robert Pruyn, *President*
Nadine Hayes, *Treasurer*
Peter F Burger, *Admin Sec*
▲ **EMP:** 54
SQ FT: 26,500
SALES (est): 9.3MM **Privately Held**
WEB: www.rubber-group.com
SIC: 3069 Mfg Fabricated Rubber Products

(G-19672)
INDEPENDENT COLOR PRESS LLC

189 Wakefield St (03867-1303)
P.O. Box 24 (03866-0024)
PHONE..................................603 539-5959
Ernest Carter,
EMP: 4 **EST:** 1970
SALES (est): 280K **Privately Held**
SIC: 2752 Lithographic Commercial Printing

(G-19673)
INTEC AUTOMATION INC

5 Sampson Rd (03867-4207)
P.O. Box 1653 (03866-1653)
PHONE..................................603 332-7733
Brian Keith Crossan, *President*
Corey Marcotte, *General Mgr*
Corey Margott, *Vice Pres*
Kate Crossan, *Purchasing*
EMP: 12
SALES (est): 2.5MM **Privately Held**
WEB: www.intecautomation.com
SIC: 3599 Mfg Industrial Machinery

(G-19674)
JAEGER USA INC

104 Pickering Rd (03867-4604)
PHONE..................................603 332-5816
John Simmers, *President*
Peter Burger, *Admin Sec*
▲ **EMP:** 18
SQ FT: 20,291
SALES (est): 3.5MM
SALES (corp-wide): 4.2MM **Privately Held**
WEB: www.ttweavers.com
SIC: 3199 1799 2295 Mfg Leather Goods Trade Contractor Mfg Coated Fabrics
HQ: Gebruder Jaeger Gmbh
Otto-Hahn-Str. 7
Wuppertal 42369
202 246-560

(G-19675)
JARVIS COMPANY INC (PA)

100 Jarvis Ave (03868-8811)
PHONE..................................603 332-9000
Marshall N Jarvis II, *President*
Robert Jarvis, *Sales Mgr*
Janice Brown, *Technology*
Kellie Loporcaro, *Assistant*
EMP: 100
SQ FT: 35,000
SALES (est): 26.9MM **Privately Held**
SIC: 3541 5084 Holding Company That Through Subsidiaries Mfg & Whol Machine Tools Metal Cutting Types

(G-19676)
JARVIS CUTTING TOOLS INC

100 Jarvis Ave (03868-8801)
PHONE..................................603 332-9000
Marshall Jarvis II, *President*
Tara Salonen, *Materials Mgr*
Bill Wortley, *Engineer*
Scott Graff, *CFO*
Debb Dube, *Human Res Mgr*
EMP: 75 **EST:** 1901
SQ FT: 30,000
SALES (est): 17.1MM
SALES (corp-wide): 26.9MM **Privately Held**
WEB: www.jarviscuttingtools.com
SIC: 3545 Mfg Machine Tool Accessories
PA: The Jarvis Company Inc
100 Jarvis Ave
Rochester NH 03868
603 332-9000

(G-19677)
LAARS HEATING SYSTEMS COMPANY

20 Industrial Way (03867-4296)
PHONE..................................603 335-6300
Bob Carnevale, *CEO*
Steven Bailey, *Principal*
William R Root, *Vice Pres*
Angelo Sinisi, *Vice Pres*
Cynthia Cindiphillips, *Director*
▲ **EMP:** 165
SQ FT: 100,000
SALES (est): 53MM
SALES (corp-wide): 222.6MM **Privately Held**
WEB: www.laarsheatingsystemscompany.com
SIC: 3443 Mfg Fabricated Plate Work
PA: Bradford White Corporation
725 Talamore Dr
Ambler PA 19002
215 641-9400

(G-19678)
LIBERTY RESEARCH CO INC (PA)

7 Nadeau Dr (03867-4637)
P.O. Box 160, Milan MI (48160-0160)
PHONE..................................603 332-2730
Derrick Perkins Jr, *President*
EMP: 16 **EST:** 1957
SQ FT: 40,000
SALES (est): 2.2MM **Privately Held**
WEB: www.libertyresearchco.com
SIC: 3451 Mfg Screw Machine Products

(G-19679)
NANTUCKET BEADBOARD CO INC

109 Chestnut Hill Rd (03867-5122)
P.O. Box 1676 (03866-1676)
PHONE..................................603 330-3338
Thomas Miller, *President*
Joanne Miller Macleod, *Vice Pres*
Carol A Galvin, *Admin Sec*
▼ **EMP:** 17 **EST:** 1998
SQ FT: 28,000
SALES (est): 4.4MM **Privately Held**
WEB: www.beadboard.com
SIC: 3429 Mfg Hardware

(G-19680)
NORTHEASTERN NONWOVENS INC

7 Amarosa Dr Unit 3 (03868-8638)
PHONE..................................603 332-5900
Michael Roche, *President*
Quentin Kampf, *Technical Mgr*
Jason Dill, *Engineer*
◆ **EMP:** 25
SQ FT: 50,000
SALES: 8MM **Privately Held**
SIC: 2297 Mfg Nonwoven Fabrics

(G-19681)
PASTURE HILL MILLWORK LLC

84 Estes Rd (03867-4232)
PHONE..................................603 335-4175
Doug Ham,
EMP: 3
SALES: 130K **Privately Held**
SIC: 2431 Mfg Millwork

(G-19682)
PATRIOT CYBER DEFENSE LLC

35 Walnut St (03867-1018)
PHONE..................................603 231-7000
Jennifer Caron, *Mng Member*
EMP: 4
SALES (est): 262.8K **Privately Held**
SIC: 3812 Mfg Search/Navigation Equipment

(G-19683)
ROCHESTER USA

73 Allen St (03867-1403)
PHONE..................................603 332-0717
Chris Haas, *Manager*
EMP: 4
SALES (est): 248.3K **Privately Held**
SIC: 3821 Mfg Lab Apparatus/Furniture

(G-19684)
ROKON INTERNATIONAL INC

50 Railroad Ave (03839-5229)
PHONE..................................603 335-3200
Thomas Blais, *President*
Bruce Osborne, *Admin Sec*
▲ **EMP:** 10
SQ FT: 15,800
SALES (est): 1.8MM **Privately Held**
WEB: www.rokon.com
SIC: 3799 Mfg Transportation Equipment

▲ = Import ▼=Export
◆ =Import/Export

(G-19685)
RP ABRASIVES & MACHINE INC
20 Spaulding Ave Unit 2 (03868-8730)
PHONE..................................603 335-2132
Joe Shean, *President*
Gerri Widener, *Bookkeeper*
EMP: 12
SALES (est): 1.6MM **Privately Held**
SIC: 3291 Mfg Abrasive Products

(G-19686)
SALMON PRESS LLC
Also Called: Rochester Times Newspaper
4 Union St (03867-1911)
PHONE..................................603 332-2300
Rich Piatt, *Branch Mgr*
EMP: 21
SALES (corp-wide): 5.3MM **Privately Held**
WEB: www.courier-littletonnh.com
SIC: 2711 Newspapers-Publishing/Printing
PA: Salmon Press Llc
5 Water St
Meredith NH 03253
603 279-4516

(G-19687)
SPAULDING COMPOSITES INC (PA)
55 Nadeau Dr (03867-4637)
PHONE..................................603 332-0555
Donnita Rockwell, *CEO*
Adam Stymiest, *QC Mgr*
Douglas R Keslin, *CFO*
Michael C Becker, *Controller*
Tammy Thibault, *Human Res Mgr*
◆ **EMP:** 70
SQ FT: 100,000
SALES: 12MM **Privately Held**
SIC: 3083 Mfg Laminated Plastic Plate/Sheet

(G-19688)
STUMP CITY CIDER
52 Bernard Rd (03868-5800)
PHONE..................................603 234-6288
EMP: 3 **EST:** 2013
SALES (est): 182.3K **Privately Held**
SIC: 2099 Mfg Food Preparations

(G-19689)
T K O PRINTING INC
189 Wakefield St (03867-1303)
PHONE..................................603 332-0511
Jim Graves, *President*
Stephanie Chick, *President*
Donna Potter, *Principal*
EMP: 4
SALES (est): 335.9K **Privately Held**
SIC: 2759 Print Shop

(G-19690)
THOMPSON/CENTER ARMS CO INC
400 N Main St (03867-4308)
PHONE..................................603 332-2394
EMP: 15
SALES (corp-wide): 638.2MM **Publicly Held**
SIC: 3484 Mfg Small Arms
HQ: Thompson/Center Arms Company, Inc.
2100 Roosevelt Ave
Springfield MA 01104
800 331-0852

Rollinsford
Strafford County

(G-19691)
JANCO INC (PA)
50 Goodwin Rd (03869-5002)
P.O. Box 857, Dover (03821-0857)
PHONE..................................603 742-0043
Mark P Janetos, *President*
Paul Janetos Jr, *Principal*
Louise Janetos, *Vice Pres*
Hitchcock Michael, *Engineer*
Kenneth H Swanson, *CFO*
EMP: 80 **EST:** 1959
SQ FT: 50,000
SALES (est): 16MM **Privately Held**
WEB: www.janco.com
SIC: 3089 Mfg Plastic Products

(G-19692)
JANCO ELECTRONICS INC
50 Goodwin Rd (03869-5002)
P.O. Box 1309, Dover (03821-1309)
PHONE..................................603 742-1581
Lewis E Janetos, *Ch of Bd*
Rusty Bruesch, *President*
Rollins L Janetos, *President*
John Bickford, *Corp Secy*
William Janetos, *Vice Pres*
EMP: 70
SQ FT: 40,000
SALES (est): 16.7MM **Privately Held**
WEB: www.janco-electronics.com
SIC: 3679 Mfg Electronic Components

(G-19693)
MANN PUBLISHING INCORPORATED
Also Called: Mann Publishing Group
710 Main St Fl 6 (03869)
P.O. Box 519, Greenland (03840-0519)
PHONE..................................603 601-0325
EMP: 16
SALES (est): 1MM **Privately Held**
WEB: www.mannpublishing.com
SIC: 2731 Book Publishing, Nsk

(G-19694)
NORTH COUNTRY HARD CIDER LLC
3 Front St Lowr Mill (03869-7001)
PHONE..................................603 834-9915
Silas Gordon, *Mng Member*
Ron Dixon, *Mng Member*
EMP: 6
SALES (est): 383.3K **Privately Held**
SIC: 2086 Mfg Bottled/Canned Soft Drinks

Rumney
Grafton County

(G-19695)
CERSOSIMO LUMBER COMPANY INC
3997 Rumney Route 25 (03266-3335)
PHONE..................................603 786-9482
Jim Brown, *Manager*
EMP: 22
SALES (corp-wide): 46.8MM **Privately Held**
WEB: www.cersosimolumber.com
SIC: 2421 Sawmill/Planing Mill
PA: Cersosimo Lumber Company, Inc.
1103 Vernon St
Brattleboro VT 05301
802 254-4508

(G-19696)
GROTON WIND LLC
590 Groton Hollow Rd (03266-3411)
PHONE..................................603 786-2862
Ryan Haley, *Plant Mgr*
EMP: 4
SALES (est): 208.5K **Privately Held**
SIC: 3621 Mfg Motors/Generators

(G-19697)
KELLY MANUFACTURING COMPANY
106 Water St (03266-3003)
P.O. Box 100 (03266-0100)
PHONE..................................603 786-9933
Edward Openshaw, *Owner*
EMP: 4
SQ FT: 4,500
SALES (est): 190K **Privately Held**
SIC: 3842 Mfg Crutches

(G-19698)
STONEWALL CABLE INC
126 Hawkensen Dr (03266-3548)
PHONE..................................603 536-1601
Jeffrey Paul Emery, *President*
Deborah J Emery, *Vice Pres*
Anthony Lamonica, *Marketing Staff*
Kim Sargent, *Manager*
Kim Leroux, *Executive Asst*
EMP: 65
SQ FT: 15,000
SALES (est): 15.8MM **Privately Held**
WEB: www.stonewallcable.com
SIC: 3357 Nonferrous Wiredrawing/Insulating

Rye
Rockingham County

(G-19699)
NAS FUELS LLC
Also Called: Atlantic Fuels
296 Lafayette Rd (03870)
P.O. Box 792 (03870-0792)
PHONE..................................603 964-6967
Rob Wilich,
EMP: 8
SALES (est): 374K **Privately Held**
SIC: 2869 Mfg Industrial Organic Chemicals

(G-19700)
OCEAN PUBLISHING
911 Ocean Blvd Apt 7 (03870-2800)
PHONE..................................603 812-5557
Tara Chase, *Owner*
EMP: 3
SQ FT: 700
SALES (est): 107K **Privately Held**
SIC: 2741 Misc Publishing

Salem
Rockingham County

(G-19701)
4POWER LLC
56 Stiles Rd Ste 101 (03079-4807)
P.O. Box 416, Windham (03087-0416)
PHONE..................................617 299-0068
Dr Arthur Pitara, *Director*
Dr Eugene Fitzgerald Jr,
E Arthur Fitzgerald,
Dr Steve Ringel,
EMP: 7
SQ FT: 1,400
SALES: 1MM **Privately Held**
SIC: 3674 8711 Research Development And Manufacturing Of Solar Cells

(G-19702)
603 SCREENPRINTING LLC
85 Lowell Rd (03079-4017)
PHONE..................................603 505-7693
Jeff Gartside,
EMP: 3
SALES (est): 170K **Privately Held**
SIC: 2759 Commercial Printing

(G-19703)
ADVANCED ENTP SYSTEMS CORP
Also Called: Utility Cloud
1 Stiles Rd Ste 302 (03079-4804)
PHONE..................................508 431-7607
Mark Moreau, *CEO*
EMP: 20
SALES (est): 208.1K **Privately Held**
WEB: myaesc.com
SIC: 7372 Prepackaged Software Services

(G-19704)
ADVANCED POLYMERICS INC
32 Hampshire Rd (03079-4204)
PHONE..................................603 328-8177
Stephen Jewitt, *President*
Kim Powers, *Vice Pres*
EMP: 9
SQ FT: 3,000
SALES: 500K **Privately Held**
SIC: 3479 Coating/Engraving Service

(G-19705)
ALLEN DATAGRAPH SYSTEMS INC
45a Northwestern Dr (03079-4809)
PHONE..................................603 216-6344
James Michael Elliott, *President*
Michael Elliott, *Principal*
Debby Elliott, *Exec VP*
▼ **EMP:** 31
SQ FT: 28,000
SALES: 5.3MM **Privately Held**
WEB: www.allendatagraph.com
SIC: 3577 3826 Mfg Computer Peripheral Equipment Mfg Analytical Instruments

(G-19706)
ANAREN CERAMICS INC
27 Northwestern Dr (03079-4844)
PHONE..................................603 898-2883
Raymond C Simione, *President*
Michael Skrzypek, *Engineer*
EMP: 75
SQ FT: 20,000
SALES (est): 12.9MM
SALES (corp-wide): 2.8B **Publicly Held**
WEB: www.anaren.com
SIC: 3672 3625 3679 Mfg Printed Circuit Boards Mfg Relays/Industrial Controls Mfg Electronic Components
HQ: Anaren, Inc.
6635 Kirkville Rd
East Syracuse NY 13057
315 432-8909

(G-19707)
ANDOVER CORPORATION
4 Commercial Dr (03079-2800)
PHONE..................................603 893-6888
John Cotton, *President*
Joshua Jones, *Engineer*
David Litwinovich, *Engineer*
Heidi Waring, *Executive*
▲ **EMP:** 49
SQ FT: 44,000
SALES (est): 11.2MM **Privately Held**
WEB: www.andcorp.com
SIC: 3827 Mfg Optical Instruments/Lenses

(G-19708)
AP EXTRUSION INC
10 Manor Pkwy Ste E (03079-4864)
PHONE..................................603 890-1086
John Brusseau, *President*
Mark Brusseau, *Vice Pres*
EMP: 14
SQ FT: 11,000
SALES (est): 2.5MM **Privately Held**
WEB: www.apextrusion.com
SIC: 2821 Mfg Plastic Materials/Resins

(G-19709)
AQUABACK TECHNOLOGIES INC
4 Raymond Ave Ste 8 (03079-2944)
PHONE..................................978 863-1000
William H Zebuhr, *CEO*
Scott Newquist, *CEO*
David Dussault, *COO*
EMP: 10
SALES (est): 2MM **Privately Held**
SIC: 3556 Mfg Food Products Machinery

(G-19710)
ATLANTIC MICROTOOL
91 Stiles Rd Ste 207 (03079-5804)
PHONE..................................603 898-3212
Neil Robinson, *Principal*
EMP: 4
SALES (est): 265.4K **Privately Held**
SIC: 3544 Mfg Dies/Tools/Jigs/Fixtures

(G-19711)
BE SEMICONDUCTOR INDS USA INC (HQ)
Also Called: Besi USA
14 Keewaydin Dr (03079-2839)
PHONE..................................603 626-4700
Richard Blickman, *CEO*
David Peacock, *President*
Stephen Shepard, *General Mgr*
▲ **EMP:** 33
SALES (est): 2.7MM
SALES (corp-wide): 582.5MM **Privately Held**
SIC: 3674 Mfg Semiconductors/Related Devices
PA: Be Semiconductor Industries N.V.
Ratio 6
Duiven 6921
263 194-500

(G-19712)
BEACON SALES ACQUISITION INC
Also Called: Applicator Sales & Service
15 Keewaydin Dr (03079-2840)
P.O. Box 10109, Portland ME (04104-0109)
PHONE.................................207 797-7950
Kevin Cini, *Branch Mgr*
EMP: 9
SALES (corp-wide): 7.1B **Publicly Held**
SIC: 3442 5031 5211 Mfg Metal Door/Sash/Trim Whol Lumber/Plywd/Millwk Ret Lumber/Building Mtrl
HQ: Beacon Sales Acquisition, Inc.
50 Webster Ave
Somerville MA 02143
877 645-7663

(G-19713)
BIO-CONCEPT LABORATORIES INC
13 Industrial Way (03079-2838)
PHONE.................................603 437-4990
Francis Smith, *President*
EMP: 20
SQ FT: 30,000
SALES (est): 6.1MM **Privately Held**
WEB: www.bioconcept.com
SIC: 2879 8731 Mfg Agricultural Chemicals Commercial Physical Research

(G-19714)
BOBBY OS FOODS LLC
21 Connell Dr (03079-2586)
PHONE.................................603 458-2502
Robert E Owaida, *Mng Member*
Robert Owaida, *Manager*
EMP: 5 **EST:** 2006
SQ FT: 2,400
SALES (est): 310K **Privately Held**
SIC: 2038 Mfg Frozen Specialties

(G-19715)
BOSTON BRACE INTERNATIONAL
Also Called: Boston Orthotics & Prosthetics
23 Stiles Rd Ste 218 (03079-2854)
PHONE.................................603 772-2388
Derek Ghostlaw, *District Mgr*
EMP: 6 **Privately Held**
SIC: 3842 Mfg Surgical Appliances/Supplies
PA: Boston Brace International, Inc.
20 Ledin Dr Ste 1
Avon MA 02322
-

(G-19716)
COHERENT INC
Also Called: Coherent Salem
32 Hampshire Rd (03079-4204)
PHONE.................................603 685-0900
Garry Rogerson, *Chairman*
Nancy Bedrosian, *Manager*
Zhan Kaijun, *Director*
EMP: 10
SALES (corp-wide): 1.4B **Publicly Held**
SIC: 3826 Mfg Analytical Instruments
PA: Coherent, Inc.
5100 Patrick Henry Dr
Santa Clara CA 95054
408 764-4000

(G-19717)
COLLINS LIGHTING & ASSOC LLC
17 Dawn St (03079-3231)
PHONE.................................603 893-1106
Gary F Collins, *Principal*
EMP: 3 **EST:** 2008
SALES (est): 316.7K **Privately Held**
SIC: 3645 Mfg Residential Lighting Fixtures

(G-19718)
CONNECTLEADER LLC
7 Stiles Rd Ste 102 (03079-4820)
PHONE.................................800 955-5040
Senraj Soundar, *President*
Sarah Hudson, *QC Mgr*
Latha Soundar, *Manager*
Anu Soundar, *Technology*
Chris Haigh, *Executive*
EMP: 140
SQ FT: 5,000
SALES (est): 9.9MM **Privately Held**
SIC: 7372 Prepackaged Software Services

(G-19719)
COOKING SOLUTIONS GROUP INC (HQ)
Also Called: Bki Worldwide
11 Keewaydin Dr Ste 300 (03079-2999)
PHONE.................................603 893-9701
David A Dunbar, *President*
EMP: 3
SALES (est): 116.6K
SALES (corp-wide): 2.7B **Publicly Held**
SIC: 3556 3631 Manufactures Food Products Machinery Manufactures Household Cooking Equipment
PA: The Middleby Corporation
1400 Toastmaster Dr
Elgin IL 60120
847 741-3300

(G-19720)
DATA ELECTRONIC DEVICES INC
Also Called: D S C
32 Northwestern Dr (03079-4810)
PHONE.................................603 893-2047
Udo H Fritsch, *CEO*
Victor R Giglio, *President*
Margaret Hannemann, *Exec VP*
Yvette Varney, *Controller*
Robert Leslie, *Admin Sec*
▲ **EMP:** 125 **EST:** 1966
SQ FT: 33,000
SALES (est): 49.7MM **Privately Held**
WEB: www.dataed.com
SIC: 3621 3679 3672 Mfg Motors/Generators Mfg Electronic Components Mfg Printed Circuit Boards

(G-19721)
DENNCO INC
21 Northwestern Dr (03079-4809)
PHONE.................................603 898-0004
James J Dennesen, *President*
Bob Leavitt, *CFO*
▲ **EMP:** 50
SALES (est): 4.6MM **Privately Held**
WEB: www.dencoinc.com
SIC: 3949 Mfg Sporting/Athletic Goods

(G-19722)
DM SEMICONDUCTOR COMPANY INC
24 Keewaydin Dr Ste 5 (03079-2860)
PHONE.................................603 898-7750
Norman R Macinnis Jr, *President*
EMP: 3
SALES (est): 344K **Privately Held**
WEB: www.dmsemi.com
SIC: 3444 Mfg Sheet Metalwork

(G-19723)
EDGE VELOCITY CORPORATION
68 Stiles Rd Ste G (03079-2818)
PHONE.................................603 912-5618
Paula Beauregard, *CEO*
Frank Knox, *CTO*
Gerald D'Avolico Jr, *Admin Sec*
EMP: 8
SQ FT: 1,700
SALES (est): 1.3MM **Privately Held**
WEB: www.edgevelocity.com
SIC: 3663 Mfg Radio/Tv Communication Equipment

(G-19724)
ELITE MANUFACTURING SVCS CORP
8 Industrial Way Ste B3 (03079-4857)
PHONE.................................978 688-6150
Richard Flynn, *President*
Liam Christopher Holt, *CTO*
EMP: 15 **EST:** 2015
SQ FT: 31,111
SALES: 1.4MM **Privately Held**
SIC: 3571 Mfg Electronic Computers

(G-19725)
ENTERASYS NETWORKS INC (HQ)
Also Called: Cabletron
9 Northstern Blvd Ste 300 (03079)
PHONE.................................603 952-5000
Ed Meyercord, *CEO*
Michael Fabiaschi, *President*
Chris Crowell, *Exec VP*
Ken Arola, *Vice Pres*
Frank Blohm, *Vice Pres*
▲ **EMP:** 60
SQ FT: 150,000
SALES (est): 120.3MM **Publicly Held**
WEB: www.enterasys.com
SIC: 3577 7373 3357 5045 Mfg Computer Peripherals Computer Systems Design Nonfrs Wiredrwng/Insltng

(G-19726)
EXTREME NETWORKS INC
9 Northeastern Blvd (03079-1996)
PHONE.................................603 952-5000
Scott Walker, *Project Mgr*
EMP: 15 **Publicly Held**
SIC: 3661 Mfg Telephone/Telegraph Apparatus
PA: Extreme Networks, Inc.
6480 Via Del Oro
San Jose CA 95119
-

(G-19727)
EZENIA INC (PA)
401 Main St Ste 205 (03079-2463)
PHONE.................................603 589-7600
Michael Fitzell, *President*
Dane A Donaldson, *Vice Pres*
Rene A Rodriguez, *Vice Pres*
Cecelia Moreno, *CFO*
EMP: 10
SALES: 1MM **Publicly Held**
WEB: www.ezenia.com
SIC: 3571 3661 7373 Mfg Electronic Computers Mfg Telephone/Telegraph Apparatus Computer Systems Design

(G-19728)
FABER FAMILY ASSOCIATES LPA (PA)
6 Northwestern Dr (03079-4810)
PHONE.................................603 681-0484
David Workman, *CEO*
EMP: 3
SALES (est): 136.4K **Privately Held**
SIC: 2821 Mfg Plastic Materials/Resins

(G-19729)
FABER INDUSTRIES LLC (HQ)
6 Northwestern Dr (03079-4810)
PHONE.................................603 681-0484
David Workman, *CEO*
Klaus Faber, *Ch of Bd*
Brenda Hood, *Controller*
▲ **EMP:** 12
SALES (est): 3.3MM
SALES (corp-wide): 136.4K **Privately Held**
SIC: 2821 Mfg Plastic Materials/Resins
PA: Faber Family Associates Lpa
6 Northwestern Dr
Salem NH 03079
603 681-0484

(G-19730)
FABER POLIVOL LLC (DH)
6 Northwestern Dr (03079-4810)
PHONE.................................603 681-0484
David Workman, *CEO*
Klaus Faber, *President*
EMP: 4
SALES (est): 597.4K
SALES (corp-wide): 136.4K **Privately Held**
SIC: 3089 Mfg Plastic Products

(G-19731)
FAST SIGNS
Also Called: Fastsigns
345 S Broadway (03079-4522)
PHONE.................................603 894-7446
Casey Condell, *Branch Mgr*
EMP: 4 **Privately Held**
SIC: 3993 Signsadv Specs
PA: Fast Signs
8373 Southwest Fwy
Houston TX 77074
-

(G-19732)
FBN PLASTICS INC
338 N Main St (03079-1286)
PHONE.................................603 894-4326
Richard Bell, *Principal*
EMP: 10
SALES (est): 1.3MM **Privately Held**
SIC: 3089 Mfg Plastic Products

(G-19733)
FIS SYSTEMS INTERNATIONAL LLC
Sungard
9 Northstern Blvd Ste 400 (03079)
PHONE.................................603 898-6185
EMP: 175
SALES (corp-wide): 8.4B **Publicly Held**
SIC: 7372 Prepackaged Software Services
HQ: Fis Systems International Llc
200 Campus Dr
Collegeville PA 19426
484 582-2000

(G-19734)
FIZZ TIME
Also Called: Bomb Cosmetics
11 Industrial Way Bldg C (03079-4840)
P.O. Box 442, Windham (03087-0442)
PHONE.................................603 870-0000
Toll Free:...877 -
Mark Stevens,
EMP: 10
SQ FT: 10,000
SALES (est): 671.8K **Privately Held**
WEB: www.fizztime.com
SIC: 2844 Man Cosmetics

(G-19735)
FLUKE ELECTRONICS CORPORATION
Also Called: Fluke Networks
87 Stiles Rd Ste 206 (03079-2899)
PHONE.................................603 537-2680
EMP: 8
SALES (corp-wide): 6.4B **Publicly Held**
SIC: 3825 3823 Mfg Elec Measuring Instr
HQ: Fluke Electronics Corporation
6920 Seaway Blvd
Everett WA 98203
425 347-6100

(G-19736)
FOXX LIFE SCIENCES LLC
6 Delaware Dr (03079-4033)
PHONE.................................603 890-3699
Imam Nethrapalli, *Vice Pres*
Brian Abbott, *Engineer*
Chhaya Lim, *Engineer*
Noella Rourke, *Finance*
Tara Lynch, *Human Res Mgr*
EMP: 18
SALES (est): 4.5MM **Privately Held**
SIC: 3085 Mfg Plastic Bottles

(G-19737)
FRUGAL PRINTER INC
Also Called: Proofing House Press
47a Northwestern Dr (03079-4809)
PHONE.................................603 894-6333
Matthew Hanna, *President*
Charles Miller, *Vice Pres*
John Borlaug, *Treasurer*
Jeff Hanson, *Admin Sec*
EMP: 12
SQ FT: 5,000
SALES: 1.5MM **Privately Held**
WEB: www.proofinghouse.com
SIC: 2752 Lithographic Commercial Printing

(G-19738)
G & A MACHINE INC
168 Lawrence Rd (03079-3910)
PHONE.................................603 894-6965
Michelle Alsup, *President*
Lyn Alsup, *Clerk*
EMP: 16
SALES (est): 1.9MM **Privately Held**
SIC: 3599 Mfg Industrial Machinery

(G-19739)
GPD OPTOELECTRONICS CORP
7 Manor Pkwy (03079-2842)
PHONE..................................603 894-6865
Oliver O Ward, *President*
William Dawson, *Vice Pres*
Rufus R Ward, *Vice Pres*
Rufus Ward, *Vice Pres*
Donald Voight, *Prdtn Mgr*
EMP: 30
SQ FT: 28,000
SALES (est): 5.7MM **Privately Held**
WEB: www.gpd-ir.com
SIC: 3674 Mfg Semiconductors/Related Devices

(G-19740)
GUIDEWIRE TECHNOLOGIES INC
26 Keewaydin Dr Ste A (03079-5803)
PHONE..................................603 894-4399
Douglas Curtis, *President*
Beth Newell, *Director*
EMP: 24
SQ FT: 13,000
SALES (est): 4MM **Privately Held**
WEB: www.guidewiretech.com
SIC: 3829 3827 3496 Medical Device Mfg

(G-19741)
HADCO CORPORATION (HQ)
12a Manor Pkwy (03079-2841)
PHONE..................................603 421-3400
Horace H Irvine II, *Ch of Bd*
Andrew E Lietz, *President*
Timothy P Losik, *CFO*
◆ **EMP:** 282
SQ FT: 122,750
SALES (est): 512.1MM **Publicly Held**
WEB: www.hadco.com
SIC: 3672 Mfg Printed Circuit Boards

(G-19742)
IFG INDUSTRIES LLC (DH)
6 Northwestern Dr (03079-4810)
PHONE..................................603 681-0484
David Workman, *CEO*
EMP: 4
SALES (est): 232.8K
SALES (corp-wide): 136.4K **Privately Held**
SIC: 3089 Mfg Plastic Products

(G-19743)
JAB MANUFACTURING LLC
51 Northwestern Dr Ste E (03079-4885)
P.O. Box 524 (03079-0524)
PHONE..................................603 328-8113
Faith Renee Brusseau, *Administration*
EMP: 7
SALES (est): 147.5K **Privately Held**
SIC: 3999 Mfg Misc Products

(G-19744)
KLEIN MARINE SYSTEMS INC
11 Klein Dr (03079-1249)
PHONE..................................603 893-6131
Guy M Malden, *CEO*
Robert P Capps, *Principal*
Frank Cobis, *Vice Pres*
▲ **EMP:** 76
SQ FT: 55,000
SALES (est): 14MM
SALES (corp-wide): 42.9MM **Publicly Held**
SIC: 3812 5065 Mfg Search/Navigation Equipment Whol Electronic Parts/Equipment
PA: Mitcham Industries, Inc.
2002 Timberloch Pl # 400
The Woodlands TX 77380
936 291-2277

(G-19745)
KUSA LLC
8 Industrial Way Ste D1 (03079-4873)
PHONE..................................603 912-5325
Dan Smith, *Sales Staff*
Giovanni Colasante, *Mng Member*
Raffaello Colasante,
▲ **EMP:** 6
SALES (est): 782.4K **Privately Held**
SIC: 3625 Mfg Relays/Industrial Controls

(G-19746)
LASER LIGHT ENGINES INC
8 Industrial Way Ste C6 (03079-4834)
PHONE..................................603 952-4550
Doug Darrow, *CEO*
David J Parent, *CFO*
EMP: 19
SALES (est): 3MM **Privately Held**
SIC: 3699 Mfg Electrical Equipment/Supplies

(G-19747)
LIGHTBLOCKS INC
32 Hampshire Rd (03079-4204)
PHONE..................................603 889-1115
Mary Wellington, *Ch of Bd*
Don Quinn, *Opers Staff*
Jennifer Simons, *Sales Dir*
EMP: 25
SQ FT: 31,118
SALES (est): 3.8MM **Privately Held**
WEB: www.lightblocks.com
SIC: 3299 Mfg Nonmetallic Mineral Products

(G-19748)
LONG ISLAND PIPE SUPPLY NH INC
Also Called: Long Island Pipe New Hampshire
50 Northwestern Dr Ste 6b (03079-5811)
PHONE..................................603 685-3200
Robert Moss, *President*
EMP: 10
SALES (est): 1.3MM **Privately Held**
SIC: 3498 Mfg Fabricated Pipe/Fittings

(G-19749)
MASQUERADE
4 Joanna Rd (03079-2018)
PHONE..................................603 275-0717
Donna Viau, *Owner*
EMP: 12 **EST:** 2011
SALES (est): 437.3K **Privately Held**
SIC: 2389 2392 Mfg Apparel/Accessories Mfg Household Furnishings

(G-19750)
MAYBROOK INC
8 Willow St Ste 2 (03079-2185)
PHONE..................................603 898-0811
Donald Francis, *Ch of Bd*
Alexander P Felson, *Vice Pres*
Katharine Felson, *Vice Pres*
Mike Lachance, *Manager*
▲ **EMP:** 11
SQ FT: 4,000
SALES (est): 1.2MM **Privately Held**
WEB: www.maybrook.com
SIC: 2844 Mfg Toilet Preparations

(G-19751)
MEMTEC CORPORATION
68 Stiles Rd Ste D (03079-2818)
PHONE..................................603 893-8080
Dennis P Garboski, *CEO*
Allen David,
EMP: 36 **EST:** 1962
SQ FT: 8,450
SALES (est): 7.2MM **Privately Held**
WEB: www.memteccorp.com
SIC: 3572 3845 3823 3812 Mfg Computer Storage Dvc Mfg Electromedical Equip Mfg Process Cntrl Instr Mfg Search/Navgatn Equip Mfg Computer Peripherals

(G-19752)
MICRO-PRECISION TECH INC
Also Called: M P
10 Manor Pkwy Ste C (03079-4864)
PHONE..................................603 893-7600
Etang Chen, *President*
Chris Chen, *Treasurer*
▲ **EMP:** 20
SQ FT: 8,545
SALES: 1.6MM **Privately Held**
WEB: www.micropt.com
SIC: 3674 Mfg Semiconductors/Related Devices

(G-19753)
MOVERAS LLC
22 Northwestern Dr (03079-4810)
PHONE..................................603 685-0404
Anthony Messina, *Controller*
Bret P Morrison, *Mng Member*
Mark Blanchard, *Technical Staff*
Aaron Golas, *Technical Staff*
EMP: 25
SALES (est): 7MM **Privately Held**
SIC: 3612 Mfg Transformers

(G-19754)
NATIONAL APERTURE INC
5 Northwestern Dr (03079-4809)
PHONE..................................603 893-7393
George Mauro, *CEO*
William Grenier, *President*
Charles Hawkins, *Vice Pres*
Donna Mauro, *Treasurer*
Joseph Tirella, *Technician*
EMP: 18
SQ FT: 5,600
SALES (est): 3.8MM **Privately Held**
WEB: www.nationalaperture.com
SIC: 3827 3829 Mfg Optical Instruments/Lenses Mfg Measuring/Controlling Devices

(G-19755)
NORA SYSTEMS INC (DH)
9 Northeastern Blvd (03079-1996)
PHONE..................................603 894-1021
Andreas Mueller, *President*
Tim Cole, *Vice Pres*
Heri Sontgerath, *Vice Pres*
Roy Kenny, *Warehouse Mgr*
Miriam Butscher, *Controller*
◆ **EMP:** 60
SQ FT: 100,000
SALES (est): 27.6MM
SALES (corp-wide): 2.6MM **Privately Held**
WEB: www.nora.com/us
SIC: 3069 Mfg Fabricated Rubber Products
HQ: Nora Systems Gmbh
Hohnerweg 2-4
Weinheim 69469
620 180-5666

(G-19756)
NORDSON MEDICAL (NH) INC (HQ)
Also Called: Vention Medical
29 Northwestern Dr (03079-4809)
PHONE..................................603 327-0600
Dan Croteau, *President*
Cheryl Morrissey, *Purch Agent*
Scott McCain, *Project Engr*
Elisia M Saab, *Financial Exec*
Robert Cook, *Manager*
▲ **EMP:** 115
SALES (est): 50.8MM
SALES (corp-wide): 2.2B **Publicly Held**
WEB: www.advpoly.com
SIC: 3082 3069 3083 Manufactures Plastic Profile Shapes Fabricated Rubber Products And Laminated Plastic Plate/Sheet
PA: Nordson Corporation
28601 Clemens Rd
Westlake OH 44145
440 892-1580

(G-19757)
ONVIO LLC
20 Northwestern Dr (03079-4810)
PHONE..................................603 685-0404
Bret P Morrison, *Mng Member*
EMP: 3
SALES (est): 93.7K **Privately Held**
SIC: 3545 Mfg Machine Tool Accessories

(G-19758)
ONVIO SERVO LLC
20 Northwestern Dr (03079-4810)
PHONE..................................603 685-0404
John D Amico, *President*
Bret P Morrison, *Mng Member*
David Workman,
▲ **EMP:** 28
SQ FT: 20,000
SALES (est): 7.5MM **Privately Held**
WEB: www.onviollc.com
SIC: 3566 Mfg Speed Changers/Drives

(G-19759)
ORIGINAL GOURMET FOOD CO LLC
52 Stiles Rd Ste 201 (03079-4807)
PHONE..................................603 894-1200
Richard A Alimenti, *President*
◆ **EMP:** 6
SQ FT: 1,200
SALES (est): 1.7MM **Privately Held**
WEB: www.ogfc.net
SIC: 2064 Mfg Candy/Confectionery

(G-19760)
PROFITKEY INTERNATIONAL INC
50 Stiles Rd (03079-2845)
PHONE..................................603 898-9800
Randy Keith, *President*
EMP: 25
SALES (est): 3.1MM **Privately Held**
WEB: www.profitkey.com
SIC: 7372 7379 7373 7371 Prepackaged Software Svc Computer Related Svcs Computer Systems Design Computer Programming Svc

(G-19761)
PROPHOTONIX LIMITED (PA)
13 Red Roof Ln Ste 200 (03079-2983)
PHONE..................................603 893-8778
Mark W Blodgett, *Ch of Bd*
Zita Jeske, *Engineer*
Karol Murphy, *Design Engr*
Edward Dolan, *CFO*
Timothy P Losik, *CFO*
EMP: 45 **EST:** 1951
SQ FT: 45,000
SALES (est): 20.4MM **Publicly Held**
WEB: www.stockeryale.com
SIC: 3827 3699 Mfg Optical Instruments/Lenses Mfg Electrical Equipment/Supplies

(G-19762)
RELX INC
8 Industrial Way Bldg C (03079-4873)
PHONE..................................603 898-9664
Margaret O'Neill, *Branch Mgr*
EMP: 35
SALES (corp-wide): 9.8B **Privately Held**
WEB: www.lexis-nexis.com
SIC: 2721 Periodicals-Publishing/Printing
HQ: Relx Inc.
230 Park Ave Ste 700
New York NY 10169
212 309-8100

(G-19763)
RICOR USA INC
200 Main St Ste 1 (03079-3149)
PHONE..................................603 718-8903
Bob Macleod, *President*
Nancy Ramos, *Manager*
EMP: 7
SALES: 950K **Privately Held**
SIC: 3999 Mfg Misc Products

(G-19764)
SABER MACHINE DESIGN CORP
50 Northwestern Dr Ste 9b (03079-5811)
PHONE..................................603 870-8190
Jeffrey Kling, *President*
EMP: 4
SALES (est): 550.2K **Privately Held**
WEB: www.sabermd.com
SIC: 3599 Mfg Industrial Machinery

(G-19765)
SAXON MANUFACTURING INC
50 Northwestern Dr Ste 9b (03079-5811)
PHONE..................................603 898-2499
Normand Beausoleil, *President*
EMP: 12 **EST:** 1954
SQ FT: 25,000
SALES: 1.1MM
SALES (corp-wide): 11.5MM **Privately Held**
SIC: 2439 Mfg Post Formed Counter Tops
PA: Prestolam Inc
2766 Rte Du President-Kennedy
Saint-Henri-De-Levis QC G0R 3
418 882-2242

GEOGRAPHIC

(G-19766)
SCOTT ELECTRONICS INC (PA)
5 Industrial Way Ste 2d (03079-4886)
PHONE..................................603 893-2845
John Metzemaekers, *President*
Cindy Goguen, *General Mgr*
Ken Morris, *General Mgr*
Jacqueline Metzemaekers, *Corp Secy*
Louise Elliott, *Exec VP*
EMP: 70
SALES (est): 24.1MM **Privately Held**
WEB: www.scottelec.com
SIC: 3679 Mfg Electronic Components

(G-19767)
SHIRT OUT OF LUCK LLC
45 Northwestern Dr (03079-4809)
PHONE..................................603 898-9002
Marc Brown, *Principal*
EMP: 6
SALES (est): 649.6K **Privately Held**
SIC: 2253 Knit Outerwear Mill

(G-19768)
SKEYETRAC LLC
70 N Broadway (03079-2102)
PHONE..................................603 898-8000
Michael Giuliano,
EMP: 10
SALES (est): 398.3K **Privately Held**
SIC: 3812 Mfg Search/Navigation Equipment

(G-19769)
STANDEX INTERNATIONAL CORP (PA)
11 Keewaydin Dr Ste 300 (03079-2999)
PHONE..................................603 893-9701
David Dunbar, *Ch of Bd*
Annemarie Bell, *Vice Pres*
Barbara Belongia, *Vice Pres*
Paul Burns, *Vice Pres*
Alan Glass, *Vice Pres*
EMP: 40
SALES: 791.5MM **Publicly Held**
WEB: www.standex.com
SIC: 3549 3675 3585 Mfg Metalworking Machinery Mfg Electronic Capacitors Mfg Refrigeration/Heating Equipment

(G-19770)
STATELINE REVIEW
236 N Broadway (03079-2195)
P.O. Box 2496 (03079-1150)
PHONE..................................603 898-2554
Leo Monfet, *Principal*
EMP: 5
SALES (est): 156.5K **Privately Held**
SIC: 2711 Newspapers-Publishing/Printing

(G-19771)
STELLAR MANUFACTURING INC
Also Called: Magnetometric Devices
10 Manor Pkwy Ste A (03079-4864)
PHONE..................................978 241-9537
David Gecks, *President*
Carole Burns, *Treasurer*
EMP: 27
SALES (est): 6.7MM **Privately Held**
WEB: www.stellarmanufacturing.com
SIC: 3679 3672 Mfg Electronic Components Mfg Printed Circuit Boards

(G-19772)
TMAX PUBLISHING LLC
85 Lowell Rd (03079-4017)
P.O. Box 2333 (03079-1148)
PHONE..................................603 505-7693
EMP: 4 **EST:** 2012
SALES (est): 303.4K **Privately Held**
SIC: 2741 Miscellaneous Publishing, Nsk

(G-19773)
TXC INC
8 Industrial Way Ste C7 (03079-4834)
PHONE..................................603 893-4999
Andrew Invirne, *President*
EMP: 10
SQ FT: 5,000
SALES (est): 1.2MM **Privately Held**
WEB: www.txcinc.com
SIC: 2752 Lithographic Commercial Printing

(G-19774)
U S PRODUCT LABELS INC
8c Industrial Way (03079)
PHONE..................................603 894-6020
Barbara Guzman, *President*
Bruce Menzies, *Vice Pres*
EMP: 4
SQ FT: 2,200
SALES (est): 400K **Privately Held**
SIC: 2759 Mfg Labels

(G-19775)
UNIVEX CORPORATION
3 Old Rockingham Rd (03079-2140)
PHONE..................................603 893-6191
John Tsiakos, *President*
Glen Orso, *Opers Staff*
Jim Trout, *Sales Staff*
Evan Priesel, *Marketing Mgr*
Shaun Giarrusso, *Manager*
▲ **EMP:** 60 **EST:** 1948
SQ FT: 42,000
SALES (est): 19.9MM **Privately Held**
WEB: www.univexcorp.com
SIC: 3556 Mfg Food Products Machinery

(G-19776)
UPTITE CO INC
1 Timothy Ln (03079-1882)
P.O. Box 769 (03079-0769)
PHONE..................................603 401-3856
Joseph Beshara, *Principal*
EMP: 3 **EST:** 2015
SALES (est): 90K **Privately Held**
SIC: 2834 Mfg Pharmaceutical Preparations

(G-19777)
VISIT WEI
43 Northwestern Dr (03079-4809)
PHONE..................................603 893-0900
Kelly Smith, *Opers Staff*
Martin Peralta, *Technology*
Matt Crevier, *Network Enginr*
Rachael Lee, *Administration*
EMP: 4
SALES (est): 114.4K **Privately Held**
SIC: 3572 Mfg Computer Storage Devices

(G-19778)
WILLIS & PHAM LLC
3 Scotts Ter (03079-2471)
PHONE..................................603 893-6029
John Pham, *President*
Ben Willis, *Vice Pres*
EMP: 3
SALES (est): 238.3K **Privately Held**
SIC: 3672 Mfg Printed Circuit Boards

(G-19779)
WITHROW INC
Also Called: Pie Guy The
9 Hemlock Ln (03079-4252)
PHONE..................................603 898-8868
Michael Withrow, *President*
Lisa Withrow, *Vice Pres*
EMP: 21
SQ FT: 8,000
SALES (est): 3.1MM **Privately Held**
SIC: 2051 Mfg Bread/Related Products

Salisbury
Merrimack County

(G-19780)
AG STRUCTURES LLC
96 Old Turnpike Rd (03268-5508)
PHONE..................................603 648-2987
James Mason, *Mng Member*
Lisa Mason, *Mng Member*
EMP: 9
SALES (est): 1.3MM **Privately Held**
SIC: 2452 Farm Building Agricultural Building

(G-19781)
JOHN C WHYTE
43 Mutton Rd (03268-5313)
P.O. Box 1284, Concord (03302-1284)
PHONE..................................603 530-1168
John Whyte, *Principal*
EMP: 6
SALES (est): 361K **Privately Held**
SIC: 2411 Logging

Sanbornville
Carroll County

(G-19782)
DALE E CRAWFORD
2453 Lovell Lake Rd (03872-4120)
PHONE..................................603 473-2738
Dale Crawford, *Principal*
EMP: 3
SALES (est): 315.3K **Privately Held**
SIC: 2411 Logging

(G-19783)
KINGSWOOD SALES INC
Also Called: Precision Roll
2499 White Mountain Hwy (03872-4426)
P.O. Box 255 (03872-0255)
PHONE..................................603 522-6636
Andrew Jacobson, *President*
EMP: 5
SQ FT: 3,000
SALES: 350K **Privately Held**
WEB: www.precisionroll.com
SIC: 3069 Mfg Fabricated Rubber Products

Sandown
Rockingham County

(G-19784)
HAIR DESIGNS BY DEBBIE TIN
144 North Rd (03873-2059)
PHONE..................................603 887-0643
EMP: 3
SALES (est): 216.1K **Privately Held**
SIC: 3356 Nonferrous Rolling/Drawing

(G-19785)
HLF INDUSTRIES
210 Fremont Rd (03873-2206)
PHONE..................................603 303-2425
Jeffrey Farrell, *Principal*
EMP: 3 **EST:** 2014
SALES (est): 141.6K **Privately Held**
SIC: 3999 Mfg Misc Products

(G-19786)
NEXVAC INC (PA)
56 Giordani Ln (03873-2639)
PHONE..................................603 887-0015
Gary J Bouchard, *President*
Frank Dibenedetto, *Vice Pres*
Peter Diforte, *CFO*
EMP: 15
SQ FT: 1,000
SALES (est): 1.4MM **Privately Held**
WEB: www.nexvac.com
SIC: 3563 7699 Manufactures Vaccum Pumps/Components And Hi-Tech Vaccum And Semiconductor Machinery Repair Services

(G-19787)
PIONEER METAL PRODUCTS INC
19 Pillsbury Rd (03873-2702)
PHONE..................................978 372-2100
EMP: 5
SQ FT: 4,250
SALES: 900K **Privately Held**
SIC: 3469 Metal Stampings

(G-19788)
WARD FABRICATION INC
7 Beechwood Rd (03873-2423)
PHONE..................................603 382-9700
Kelly Ward, *Owner*
EMP: 4
SALES: 380K **Privately Held**
SIC: 3449 3444 Mfg Misc Structural Metalwork Mfg Sheet Metalwork

(G-19789)
WHITE OAK FARMS
Also Called: Home of St Julien Macaroons
343 Main St (03873-2101)
PHONE..................................603 887-2233
James Price, *Owner*
EMP: 5
SALES (est): 475.3K **Privately Held**
WEB: www.macaroons.com
SIC: 2099 Mfg Food Preparations

Seabrook
Rockingham County

(G-19790)
ADHESIVE ENGINEERING & SUPPLY
15 Batchelder Rd (03874-4402)
P.O. Box 1445, Raymond (03077-3445)
PHONE..................................603 895-4028
James Yeames, *Owner*
EMP: 4
SALES (est): 373.3K **Privately Held**
SIC: 2891 Mfg Adhesives/Sealants

(G-19791)
AERO-DYNAMICS INC
Also Called: Aerodynamics Metal Finishing
142 Batchelder Rd (03874-4403)
PHONE..................................603 474-2547
Gregory Burizynski, *President*
John McDermott, *Treasurer*
Chris Basti, *Manager*
EMP: 25
SQ FT: 30,000
SALES (est): 3.4MM **Privately Held**
WEB:
www.aerodynamicsmetalfinishing.com
SIC: 3471 Plating/Polishing Service

(G-19792)
AMERIC AN NOVELTY INC
Also Called: Three Finger Seabrook Firewrks
692 Lafayette Rd (03874-4213)
P.O. Box 8607, Warwick RI (02888-0599)
PHONE..................................401 785-9850
Edward Dwyer, *President*
EMP: 3
SALES (est): 285.8K **Privately Held**
SIC: 2869 5999 2899 Mfg Industrial Organic Chemicals Ret Misc Merchandise Mfg Chemical Preparations

(G-19793)
BARTON CORPORATION SALISBURY
34 Folly Mill Rd Ste 4 (03874-4053)
P.O. Box 5787, Salisbury MA (01952-0787)
PHONE..................................603 760-2669
Kenneth Brown, *President*
EMP: 7
SALES (est): 1.4MM **Privately Held**
SIC: 2441 Mfg Wood Boxes/Shook

(G-19794)
BOCRA INDUSTRIES INC
140 Batchelder Rd (03874-4403)
PHONE..................................603 474-3598
Kirk Boswell, *President*
Richard Boswell, *President*
John Goodwin, *Foreman/Supr*
EMP: 22
SQ FT: 20,000
SALES (est): 3.3MM **Privately Held**
WEB: www.bocraindustries.com
SIC: 3545 3544 7692 Mfg Machine Tool Accessories Mfg Dies/Tools/Jigs/Fixtures Welding Repair

(G-19795)
BOND ADHESIVES & COATINGS CORP
Also Called: Bond Polymers International
896 Lafayette Rd (03874-4216)
P.O. Box 2458 (03874-2458)
PHONE..................................603 474-3811
John Nelson, *President*
Jay Osler, *Plant Mgr*
EMP: 5
SQ FT: 8,000
SALES (est): 1MM **Privately Held**
SIC: 2891 Mfg Adhesives/Sealants

(G-19796)
COCA-COLA BOTTLING COMPANY
118 Stard Rd (03874-4199)
PHONE....603 926-0404
Don Girard, *General Mgr*
EMP: 47 **Privately Held**
SIC: 2086 Carb Sft Drnkbtlcn
HQ: Coca-Cola Beverages Northeast, Inc.
1 Executive Park Dr # 330
Bedford NH 03110
603 627-7871

(G-19797)
COMMUNCTION CMPNENT FLTERS INC (PA)
Also Called: C C F
145 Batchelder Rd (03874-4402)
PHONE....603 294-4685
Dennis Nathan, *President*
Allen Cohen, *Vice Pres*
Jerry Towne, *Engineer*
▲ **EMP:** 4
SALES (est): 753.7K **Privately Held**
SIC: 3663 Mfg Radio/Tv Communication Equipment

(G-19798)
CXE EQUIPMENT SERVICES LLC
33 Beckman Lndg (03874-4289)
PHONE....603 437-2477
Norman E DOE,
Steven Barnes,
Frank Dunn,
EMP: 8 **EST:** 1997
SQ FT: 10,000
SALES (est): 1MM **Privately Held**
WEB: www.cxe-equip.com
SIC: 3674 Mfg Semi Conductors & Related Devices

(G-19799)
DYNA ROLL INC
146 Batchelder Rd (03874-4403)
PHONE....603 474-2547
Cara Burzynski, *President*
EMP: 3
SALES (est): 203.4K **Privately Held**
SIC: 3471 Plating/Polishing Service

(G-19800)
FAIRVIEW MILLWORK INC
344 State Route 107 (03874-4145)
PHONE....603 929-4449
Mark Guilmette, *Branch Mgr*
EMP: 6
SALES (corp-wide): 12.3MM **Privately Held**
SIC: 2431 Mfg Millwork
PA: Fairview Millwork, Inc.
100 Pearl St
Bridgewater MA 02324
508 697-6128

(G-19801)
GLOBAL PALLET & PACKAGING LLC
148 Batchelder Rd (03874-4403)
PHONE....603 969-6660
James W Geekie,
EMP: 8
SALES (est): 1.4MM **Privately Held**
SIC: 2448 Mfg Wood Pallets/Skids

(G-19802)
HALE BROTHERS INC
16 Stard Rd (03874-4125)
P.O. Box 368 (03874-0368)
PHONE....603 474-2511
Garrett Dolan, *President*
EMP: 3 **EST:** 1893
SQ FT: 6,400
SALES: 550K **Privately Held**
SIC: 3496 Mfg Misc Fabricated Wire Products

(G-19803)
HANNAH INTERNATIONAL FOODS INC
1 Depot Ln (03874-4492)
P.O. Box 458 (03874-0458)
PHONE....603 474-5805
George Hannah, *President*
Bill Louis, *General Mgr*
Bill St Louis, *Controller*
▲ **EMP:** 60
SALES (est): 13.8MM **Privately Held**
WEB: www.hannahfoods.net
SIC: 2099 Mfg Food Preparations

(G-19804)
HENKEL CORPORATION
167 Batchelder Rd (03874-4402)
PHONE....508 230-1100
Timothy Walsh, *Branch Mgr*
EMP: 202
SALES (corp-wide): 22B **Privately Held**
SIC: 2843 Whol Chemicals/Products
HQ: Henkel Us Operations Corporation
1 Henkel Way
Rocky Hill CT 06067
860 571-5100

(G-19805)
HENKEL LOCKTITE
1 Deer Xing (03874-4404)
PHONE....603 474-5541
Ken Gately, *Executive*
EMP: 3
SALES (est): 123.2K **Privately Held**
SIC: 2891 Mfg Adhesives/Sealants

(G-19806)
HURLEY PRECISION MACHINING LLC
19 Batchelder Rd (03874-4402)
PHONE....603 474-1879
Norman Hurley, *Mng Member*
EMP: 16
SQ FT: 5,200
SALES (est): 1MM **Privately Held**
WEB: www.hurley-eng.com
SIC: 3599 Mfg Industrial Machinery

(G-19807)
INFINITE CREATIVE ENTPS INC
Infinite Therapeutics
72 Stard Rd Unit 4 (03874-4598)
PHONE....603 910-5000
EMP: 5 **Privately Held**
SIC: 3634 Mfg Electric Housewares/Fans
PA: Infinite Creative Enterprises Inc.
72 Stard Rd Unit 4
Seabrook NH 03874

(G-19808)
JMSC ENTERPRISES INC
Also Called: Sprinker Innovations
95 Ledge Rd Unit 4 (03874-4333)
P.O. Box 365 (03874-0365)
PHONE....603 468-1010
Jim Beers, *President*
EMP: 4
SALES (est): 508.6K **Privately Held**
SIC: 3494 Mfg Valves/Pipe Fittings

(G-19809)
MARTIN INTL ENCLOSURES LLC
14 Woodworkers Way (03874-4327)
PHONE....603 474-2626
Mike Martin, *President*
Maura Dunigan, *Controller*
EMP: 40
SQ FT: 60,000
SALES (est): 8MM **Privately Held**
WEB: www.martinenclosures.com
SIC: 3444 Mfg Sheet Metalwork

(G-19810)
MICROVISION INC
20 London Ln (03874-4328)
P.O. Box 1651 (03874-1651)
PHONE....603 474-5566
Leonard M Kastrilevich, *President*
▼ **EMP:** 30
SQ FT: 15,000
SALES (est): 6.4MM **Privately Held**
WEB: www.micro-vision.net
SIC: 3829 Mfg Measuring/Controlling Devices

(G-19811)
NORTH EAST PRINTING MCHY INC
146 Batchelder Rd (03874-4403)
PHONE....603 474-7455
Joseph L Koravos II, *President*
Rosemary Koravos, *Business Mgr*
▼ **EMP:** 8
SQ FT: 8,000
SALES (est): 1.4MM **Privately Held**
WEB: www.nepminc.com
SIC: 2752 Lithographic Commercial Printing

(G-19812)
O BRIEN D G INC
1 Chase Park Rd (03874-4191)
PHONE....603 474-5571
Dan Beck, *Principal*
EMP: 10
SALES (est): 1.5MM **Privately Held**
SIC: 3643 Mfg Conductive Wiring Devices

(G-19813)
RIVERSIDE SPECIALTY FOODS INC
1 Depot Ln (03874-4492)
PHONE....603 474-5805
George Hannah, *President*
EMP: 3
SALES (est): 150K **Privately Held**
SIC: 2099 Mfg Food Preparations

(G-19814)
RUGGLES-KLINGEMANN MFG CO
34 Folly Mill Rd Ste 400 (03874-4053)
P.O. Box 1435 (03874-1435)
PHONE....603 474-8500
Robert Lord, *Principal*
EMP: 7
SALES (corp-wide): 2.5MM **Privately Held**
WEB: www.r-kmfg.com
SIC: 3491 Mfg Industrial Valves
PA: Ruggles-Klingemann Mfg Co
78 Water St
Beverly MA 01915
978 232-8300

(G-19815)
SCREEN GEMS INC
34 Folly Mill Rd Ste 2 (03874-4053)
P.O. Box 2275 (03874-2275)
PHONE....603 474-5353
Andrew P Skaff, *President*
William Skaff, *Corp Secy*
EMP: 12
SQ FT: 6,000
SALES: 2.1MM **Privately Held**
SIC: 2759 Commercial Printing

(G-19816)
SCREW-MATIC CORPORATION (PA)
1 Chase Park Rd (03874-4191)
PHONE....978 356-6200
Mark J McCarthy, *President*
John Andrews, *Vice Pres*
EMP: 35 **EST:** 1960
SQ FT: 14,000
SALES (est): 8.8MM **Privately Held**
WEB: www.screwmatic.com
SIC: 3728 Mfg Aircraft Parts/Equipment

(G-19817)
SEABROOK MEDICAL LLC
Also Called: Seabrook International, LLC
15 Woodworkers Way (03874-4327)
PHONE....603 474-1919
Paul Barck, *President*
Paul A Barck, *President*
George Denault, *Mfg Staff*
Nicholas Martin, *Engineer*
Elaine Healy, *Accountant*
EMP: 145
SQ FT: 55,000
SALES (est): 32.4MM
SALES (corp-wide): 724.3MM **Privately Held**
WEB: www.seabrookinternational.com
SIC: 3842 Manufacturer Of Surgical Appliances/Supplies
HQ: Arch Global Precision Llc
2600 S Telg Rd Ste 180
Bloomfield Hills MI 48302
734 266-6900

(G-19818)
SMARTFUEL AMERICA LLC
15 Batchelder Rd (03874-4402)
PHONE....603 474-5005
EMP: 8 **EST:** 2008
SALES (est): 1.3MM **Privately Held**
SIC: 2911 Petroleum Refiner

(G-19819)
SMOKY QUARTZ DISTILLERY LLC
14 Kimberly Dr (03874-4272)
P.O. Box 2758 (03874-2758)
PHONE....603 601-0342
Kevin Kurland, *Manager*
EMP: 7
SALES (est): 513.2K **Privately Held**
SIC: 2085 Mfg Distilled/Blended Liquor

(G-19820)
SWEENEY MANUFACTURING
103 Ledge Rd Unit 11 (03874-4347)
PHONE....603 814-4127
Colleen Sweeney, *Principal*
EMP: 3
SALES (est): 240.6K **Privately Held**
SIC: 3999 Mfg Misc Products

(G-19821)
SYPHERS MONUMENT DBA AFFORDABL
255 Lafayette Rd (03874-4512)
PHONE....603 468-3033
EMP: 3
SALES (est): 176.5K **Privately Held**
SIC: 3272 Ret Misc Merchandise

(G-19822)
WATER STRUCTURES LLC
60 Stard Rd (03874-4125)
P.O. Box 2938 (03874-2938)
PHONE....603 474-0615
Kim Noble, *Mng Member*
EMP: 5 **EST:** 1989
SQ FT: 7,000
SALES (est): 900K **Privately Held**
WEB: www.waterstructuresco.com
SIC: 3088 Mfg Plastic Plumbing Fixtures

(G-19823)
WILL-MOR MANUFACTURING INC
153 Batchelder Rd (03874-4402)
PHONE....603 474-8971
Fran Roman, *President*
Joe McLaughlin, *Purchasing*
Robert Rouillard, *Research*
Mike Kelly, *CFO*
Bryan Drew, *Manager*
EMP: 65 **EST:** 2009
SQ FT: 42,000
SALES (est): 16.6MM **Privately Held**
WEB: www.will-mor.com
SIC: 3545 7692 3444 Mfg Machine Tool Accessories Welding Repair Mfg Sheet Metalwork

Silver Lake
Carroll County

(G-19824)
NITEFIGHTER INTERNATIONAL
Also Called: Jogalite-Bikealite
114 High St (03875-5911)
P.O. Box 149 (03875-0149)
PHONE....603 367-4741
Huntington Barclay, *CEO*
Wendy Damon, *President*
Polly Hurteau, *CFO*
▲ **EMP:** 7
SQ FT: 14,000
SALES (est): 1MM **Privately Held**
SIC: 2329 2326 2339 2337 Mfg Mens/Boys Clothing Mfg Men/Boy Work Clothng Mfg Women/Miss Outerwear Mfg Women/Miss Suit/Coat

(G-19825)
RICHARDSON MFG CO INC
4 High St (03875)
P.O. Box 178 (03875-0178)
PHONE....603 367-9018
David Richardson, *President*
EMP: 8
SQ FT: 5,000

GEOGRAPHIC

SALES (est): 866.7K Privately Held
SIC: 3949 2339 2369 2329 Mfg Sporting And Athletic Goods Womens And Childrens Clothing And Outdoorswear

Somersworth
Strafford County

(G-19826)
ACLARA TECHNOLOGIES LLC
130 Main St (03878-3108)
PHONE..................................603 749-8376
Jason Subirana, *Vice Pres*
Daniel Sousa, *Mfg Staff*
Curt Crittenden, *Research*
Scott Brown, *Engineer*
John Roy, *Engineer*
EMP: 15
SALES (corp-wide): 4.4B **Publicly Held**
SIC: 3825 Mfg Electrical Measuring Instruments
HQ: Aclara Technologies Llc
77 West Port Plz Ste 500
Saint Louis MO 63146
314 895-6400

(G-19827)
AIREX LLC
15 Lilac Ln (03878-1432)
PHONE..................................603 841-2040
James C Sedgewick, *President*
Sarah Fagan, *Business Mgr*
Lindsay Badger, *Opers Staff*
Brian Cossette, *Engineer*
Brian Libby, *Engineer*
▲ **EMP:** 35 **EST:** 1950
SQ FT: 15,000
SALES (est): 4.8MM **Privately Held**
WEB: www.airex.com
SIC: 3612 Mfg Transformers

(G-19828)
BAM LAB LLC
186 Blackwater Rd (03878-1208)
PHONE..................................603 973-9388
Benjamin Baumann, *Principal*
EMP: 4 **EST:** 2012
SALES (est): 360.5K **Privately Held**
SIC: 2752 Lithographic Commercial Printing

(G-19829)
BIG DIPPER
Also Called: Roberge Sharon
222 Route 108 (03878-6518)
P.O. Box 247 (03878-0247)
PHONE..................................603 742-7075
EMP: 20
SALES (est): 1.2MM **Privately Held**
SIC: 2024 5451 Mfg Ice Cream/Frozen Desert Ret Dairy Products

(G-19830)
COLBY FOOTWEAR INC
364 Route 108 (03878-1589)
PHONE..................................603 332-2283
Matthew H Krassner, *President*
Burton S Silberstein, *Treasurer*
EMP: 250
SQ FT: 50,000
SALES (est): 23.9MM **Privately Held**
SIC: 3144 Mfg Women's Footwear Except Athletic

(G-19831)
CONPROCO CORP (PA)
388 High St (03878-1411)
PHONE..................................603 743-5800
Christopher D Brown, *President*
Christopher Brown, *President*
Paul Kfoury, *Admin Sec*
EMP: 18
SALES (est): 47.7MM **Privately Held**
WEB: www.conproco.com
SIC: 3255 3272 Mfg Clay Refractories Mfg Concrete Products

(G-19832)
CONTITECH THERMOPOL LLC
10 Interstate Dr (03878-1209)
PHONE..................................603 692-6300
EMP: 6
SALES (corp-wide): 49.2B **Privately Held**
SIC: 3052 2822 Mfg Rubber/Plastic Hose/Belting Mfg Synthetic Rubber
HQ: Contitech Thermopol Llc
9 Interstate Dr
Somersworth NH 03878

(G-19833)
CONTITECH THERMOPOL LLC (HQ)
9 Interstate Dr (03878-1210)
PHONE..................................603 692-6300
Greg Mc Cloud, *Chairman*
Edward Cotter,
▲ **EMP:** 7
SQ FT: 50,000
SALES (est): 50.7MM
SALES (corp-wide): 49.2B **Privately Held**
WEB: www.thermopolinternational.com
SIC: 3052 2822 Mfg Rubber/Plastic Hose/Belting Mfg Synthetic Rubber
PA: Continental Ag
Vahrenwalder Str. 9
Hannover 30165
511 938-01

(G-19834)
DEFENSE MANUFACTURERS INC
26 Willand Dr (03878-1400)
P.O. Box 757, Dover (03821-0757)
PHONE..................................603 332-4186
Dennis Ciotti, *President*
Melissa M Ciotti, *Treasurer*
Samuel R Reid, *Agent*
EMP: 3
SQ FT: 5,760
SALES: 1MM **Privately Held**
SIC: 3479 Mfg Stave Damping Modules For Submarines

(G-19835)
DIGITAL INK PRINTING LLC
72 High St (03878-2610)
PHONE..................................603 692-6002
Donna Barton,
EMP: 4
SALES: 300K **Privately Held**
SIC: 2759 Lithographic Commercial Printing

(G-19836)
ECO TOUCH INC
22 Canal St Unit 125 (03878-3264)
PHONE..................................603 319-1762
Anne Ruozzi, *CEO*
James Dudra, *Chief Mktg Ofcr*
EMP: 7
SALES (est): 660K **Privately Held**
WEB: www.ecotouch.net
SIC: 3714 Mfg Motor Vehicle Parts/Accessories

(G-19837)
FALL MACHINE COMPANY LLC
Also Called: F M C
10 Willand Dr (03878-1400)
PHONE..................................603 750-7100
Scott Dover,
Eli Azar,
Richard Fall,
Don Ronchi,
EMP: 81
SQ FT: 25,000
SALES (est): 19MM **Privately Held**
WEB: www.fallmachine.com
SIC: 3599 Mfg Industrial Machinery
PA: Aero Precision, Llc
2320 Commerce St
Tacoma WA 98402

(G-19838)
GE ENERGY MANAGEMENT SVCS INC
130 Main St (03878-3108)
PHONE..................................603 692-2100
Bill Rector, *Branch Mgr*
EMP: 200
SALES (corp-wide): 121.6B **Publicly Held**
SIC: 3677 Mfg Electronic Coils/Transformers
HQ: Ge Energy Management Services, Llc
4200 Wildwood Pkwy
Atlanta GA 30339
678 844-6000

(G-19839)
HANGER PRSTHETCS & ORTHO INC
7 Marsh Brook Dr Ste 201 (03878-6529)
PHONE..................................603 742-0334
Paul Jenkins, *Manager*
EMP: 5
SALES (corp-wide): 1B **Publicly Held**
SIC: 3842 Ret Misc Merchandise
HQ: Hanger Prosthetics & Orthotics, Inc.
10910 Domain Dr Ste 300
Austin TX 78758
512 777-3800

(G-19840)
HILLS PALLET COMPANY
362 Route 108 (03878-1646)
PHONE..................................603 988-8624
EMP: 4 **EST:** 2014
SALES (est): 237.9K **Privately Held**
SIC: 2448 Mfg Wood Pallets/Skids

(G-19841)
INTEGRATED DESIGN & MFG LLC
15 Interstate Dr (03878-1210)
PHONE..................................603 692-5563
Kathleen King, *Manager*
Jason Kyrousis,
Charles King,
EMP: 6
SQ FT: 5,100
SALES (est): 1MM **Privately Held**
WEB: www.idmnh.com
SIC: 3599 Mfg Industrial Machinery

(G-19842)
J-PAC LLC (HQ)
Also Called: J-Pac Medical
25 Centre Rd (03878-2927)
PHONE..................................603 692-9955
Mark Florence, *President*
Rick Crane, *Vice Pres*
Scott Benoit, *Transptn Dir*
William Morrison, *Mfg Staff*
Drew Garvey, *Project Engr*
EMP: 90
SQ FT: 60,000
SALES (est): 16.3MM **Privately Held**
WEB: www.j-pac.com
SIC: 2671 7389 Manufactures Packaging Paper/Film Business Services
PA: Torque Medical Holdings, Llc
437 Madison Ave
New York NY 10022
212 705-0143

(G-19843)
LABEL TECH INC
16 Interstate Dr (03878-1236)
PHONE..................................603 692-2005
Patrick Brady, *President*
EMP: 110
SQ FT: 38,000
SALES (est): 17.8MM **Privately Held**
WEB: www.labeltechinc.com
SIC: 2754 2672 2671 Gravure Commercial Printing Mfg Coated/Laminated Paper Mfg Packaging Paper/Film

(G-19844)
NEGM ELECTRIC LLC
302 Main St (03878-3003)
PHONE..................................603 692-4806
Michael A Negm, *Principal*
EMP: 6
SALES: 950K **Privately Held**
SIC: 3795 Electrical Contractor

(G-19845)
OMNI METALS COMPANY INC
14 Interstate Dr (03878-1238)
PHONE..................................603 692-6664
Gregory Merkley, *President*
Daniel Merkley, *Vice Pres*
EMP: 24
SQ FT: 20,000
SALES (est): 4.7MM **Privately Held**
WEB: www.omnimetalsco.com
SIC: 3444 2821 3479 Mfg Sheet Metalwork Mfg Plastic Materials/Resins Coating/Engraving Service

(G-19846)
RED FISH-BLUE FISH DYE WORKS
Also Called: Rfbf Dye Works
145 Green St (03878-2213)
PHONE..................................603 692-3900
Jeff Basseches, *President*
EMP: 15
SQ FT: 10,000
SALES (est): 1.8MM **Privately Held**
WEB: www.rfbfdyeworks.com
SIC: 2253 2759 Knit Outerwear Mill Commercial Printing

(G-19847)
REGAL SLEEVING & TUBING LLC
Also Called: Suflex
89 Crest Dr (03878-4405)
PHONE..................................603 659-5555
EMP: 41 **EST:** 2001
SQ FT: 100,000
SALES (est): 3.6MM **Privately Held**
WEB: www.suflex.com
SIC: 2295 Mfg Coated Fabrics

(G-19848)
RTD TECHNOLOGIES INC
360 Route 108 (03878-1589)
PHONE..................................603 692-5978
Marc Therrien, *President*
Raymond A Therrien, *President*
EMP: 8
SQ FT: 2,400
SALES (est): 1.2MM **Privately Held**
WEB: www.rtd-tech.com
SIC: 3544 Mfg Specialized Dies & Tools

(G-19849)
SUMNER PRINTING INC
433 Route 108 (03878-2043)
PHONE..................................603 692-7424
Michael Sumner Davis, *President*
Robert Parsons, *Exec VP*
Michael May, *Vice Pres*
▲ **EMP:** 40
SQ FT: 24,000
SALES (est): 8.8MM **Privately Held**
WEB: www.sumnerprinting.com
SIC: 2752 2759 2676 Lithographic Commercial Printing Commercial Printing Sanitary Paper Products And A Manufacturer Of Sanitary Paper Products
HQ: Hoffmaster Group, Inc.
2920 N Main St
Oshkosh WI 54901
920 235-9330

(G-19850)
THERMOPOL INC
13 Interstate Dr (03878-1210)
PHONE..................................603 692-6300
Shlomo Beitner, *President*
▲ **EMP:** 18 **EST:** 1992
SALES (est): 3.3MM **Privately Held**
SIC: 3536 Mfg Hoists/Cranes/Monorails

(G-19851)
TRI CAST INC (PA)
23 Interstate Dr (03878-1210)
PHONE..................................603 692-2480
Norman Briere, *President*
EMP: 10
SALES (est): 950.8K **Privately Held**
WEB: www.tricast.com
SIC: 3316 Mfg Cold-Rolled Steel Products

South Acworth
Sullivan County

(G-19852)
GAIL WILSON DESIGNS
420 Grout Hill Rd (03607-4203)
P.O. Box 611 (03607-0611)
PHONE..................................603 835-6551
Gail Wilson, *Owner*
EMP: 4

SALES (est): 75K Privately Held
WEB: www.gailwilsondesigns.com
SIC: 3944 Mfg Games/Toys

(G-19853)
MAYNARD & MAYNARD FURN MAKERS
Also Called: Cold River Furniture
21 Beryl Rd (03607)
PHONE..................603 835-2969
Peter Maynard, *Owner*
Marcie Maynard, *Co-Owner*
EMP: 3 EST: 1976
SALES (est): 160K Privately Held
WEB: www.coldriverfurniture.com
SIC: 2511 Mfg Wood Household Furniture

(G-19854)
R L BALLA INC
338 Beryl Mountain Rd (03607-4615)
P.O. Box 6 (03607-0006)
PHONE..................603 835-6529
Robert Balla, *President*
Lyle Balla, *Vice Pres*
John Balla, *Treasurer*
EMP: 15 EST: 1949
SALES: 2MM Privately Held
SIC: 2421 1794 Lumbermill & Excavation

South Hampton
Rockingham County

(G-19855)
CHATHAM FURN REPRODUCTIONS
39 Highland Rd (03827-3608)
PHONE..................603 394-0089
EMP: 38
SQ FT: 45,000
SALES (est): 2.3MM Privately Held
SIC: 2511 Mfg Wood Household Furniture

(G-19856)
NBR DIAMOND TOOL CORP
22 Exeter Rd Unit 2 (03827-3617)
PHONE..................603 394-2113
Nazareno B Renzi, *President*
EMP: 7
SQ FT: 2,000
SALES (est): 610K Privately Held
SIC: 3542 Diamond Precision Tooling

(G-19857)
TUFF CRETE CORPORATION
84 Exeter Rd (03827-3612)
PHONE..................603 485-1969
Elizabeth Watkins, *Principal*
EMP: 4
SALES: 750K Privately Held
SIC: 3272 Mfg Concrete Products

Spofford
Cheshire County

(G-19858)
THOMAS INSTRUMENTS INC
1453 Route 9 (03462-4256)
P.O. Box 50 (03462-0050)
PHONE..................603 363-4500
Lynn Thomas, *President*
Linda Thomas, *Vice Pres*
▲ EMP: 7
SQ FT: 20,000
SALES (est): 1MM
SALES (corp-wide): 6.5MM Privately Held
WEB: www.driller.com
SIC: 3629 3829 Mfg Blasting Machines & Seismographs & Lightning Detectors
PA: D & L Thomas Equipment Corporation
Of Spofford
1453 Route 9
Spofford NH 03462
603 363-4706

Stark
Coos County

(G-19859)
CLOUTIER SAND & GRAVEL
890 Northside Rd (03582)
PHONE..................603 636-1100
Albert Cloutier, *Principal*
EMP: 3
SALES (est): 217.3K Privately Held
SIC: 1442 Construction Sand/Gravel

Stewartstown
Coos County

(G-19860)
B P LOGGING
158 Creampoke Rd (03576-5412)
PHONE..................603 237-4131
EMP: 3 EST: 2010
SALES (est): 192.3K Privately Held
SIC: 2411 Burls, Wood

(G-19861)
CROSSKNOTS WOODWORKING
545 Hollow Rd (03576-5320)
PHONE..................603 237-8392
Cammy Cross, *Owner*
EMP: 4
SALES (est): 172.3K Privately Held
SIC: 2431 Mfg Millwork

(G-19862)
KHEOPS INTERNATIONAL INC (PA)
Also Called: Copper Lease
232 Us Route 3 (03576-5104)
P.O. Box 177, Colebrook (03576-0177)
PHONE..................603 237-8188
Mary Josee Viallant, *President*
Mary Gueymard, *Corp Secy*
Melanie Viallant, *Vice Pres*
▲ EMP: 24
SQ FT: 15,000
SALES (est): 2.6MM Privately Held
WEB: www.kheopsinternational.com
SIC: 3231 Mfg Products-Purchased Glass

(G-19863)
RANCLOES LOGGING LLC
822 Hollow Rd (03576-5331)
PHONE..................603 237-4474
David Rancloes, *Principal*
EMP: 6
SALES (est): 364.5K Privately Held
SIC: 2411 Logging

(G-19864)
SWR & SON LOGGING
597 Noyes Rd (03576-5556)
PHONE..................603 237-4158
Wendy Riendeau, *Owner*
EMP: 3
SALES (est): 244.1K Privately Held
SIC: 2411 Logging

Strafford
Strafford County

(G-19865)
AMI GRAPHICS INC (PA)
223 Drake Hill Rd (03884)
P.O. Box 157, Center Strafford (03815-0157)
PHONE..................603 664-7174
Peter Wensberg, *President*
Erik Wensberg, *Vice Pres*
Alexa Szilagyi, *Production*
Beth Kubiczki, *Info Tech Mgr*
Bryan Delaney, *Director*
EMP: 52
SQ FT: 37,000
SALES (est): 15.7MM Privately Held
WEB: www.amusementmedia.com
SIC: 2759 Commercial Printing

(G-19866)
STRAFFORD MACHINE INC
385 Province Rd (03884-6645)
P.O. Box 256 (03884-0256)
PHONE..................603 664-9758
Richard Oman, *President*
Richard Omand, *Owner*
EMP: 4
SQ FT: 7,200
SALES: 500K Privately Held
SIC: 3599 7692 Mfg Industrial Machinery Welding Repair

Stratham
Rockingham County

(G-19867)
ELECTROCRAFT INC (HQ)
2 Marin Way Ste 3 (03885-2613)
PHONE..................855 697-7966
James Elsner, *President*
Logan D Delany Jr, *Principal*
Jeff Porter, *Buyer*
Don Bolden, *Engineer*
Shannon Polcyn, *Engineer*
▲ EMP: 24
SALES (est): 122.2MM
SALES (corp-wide): 126.2MM Privately Held
SIC: 3625 3621 Mfg Relays/Industrial Controls Mfg Motors/Generators
PA: Dmi Technology Corp.
1 Progress Dr
Dover NH 03820
603 742-3330

(G-19868)
FASTRAX SIGNS
68 Portsmouth Ave (03885-2523)
P.O. Box 151 (03885-0151)
PHONE..................603 778-4799
Sean Nordin, *Owner*
EMP: 5 EST: 1995
SALES (est): 213.5K Privately Held
SIC: 3993 Mfg Signs/Advertising Specialties

(G-19869)
ITACONIX CORPORATION
2 Marin Way Ste 1 (03885-2613)
PHONE..................603 775-4400
Kevin Matthews, *CEO*
John Shaw, *President*
Robin Cridland, *CFO*
Laura Denner, *Director*
EMP: 10
SQ FT: 27,000
SALES (est): 1.8MM
SALES (corp-wide): 869.6K Privately Held
SIC: 2821 Mfg Plastic Materials/Resins
HQ: Itaconix (U.K.) Limited
1-2 Newtech Square
Deeside
-

(G-19870)
ITACONIX LLC
2 Marin Way (03885-2578)
PHONE..................603 775-4400
▲ EMP: 6
SALES (est): 600K Privately Held
SIC: 3589 Mfg Service Industry Machinery

(G-19871)
LINDT & SPRUNGLI (USA) INC (HQ)
1 Fine Chocolate Pl (03885-2592)
P.O. Box 276 (03885-0276)
PHONE..................603 778-8100
Daniel Studer, *CEO*
Jonathan Moenne, *General Mgr*
Roxanne Olsen, *General Mgr*
Priyam Thakur, *General Mgr*
Roberta Powell, *Vice Pres*
◆ EMP: 240
SQ FT: 122,000
SALES (est): 378.5MM
SALES (corp-wide): 4.4B Privately Held
WEB: www.lindtusa.com
SIC: 2066 5149 5441 Mfg Chocolate/Cocoa Products Whol Groceries Ret Candy/Confectionery
PA: Chocoladefabriken Lindt & Sprungli Ag
Seestrasse 204
Kilchberg ZH 8802
447 162-233

(G-19872)
M BRAUN INC
14 Marin Way (03885-2578)
PHONE..................603 773-9333
Christopher Chausse, *President*
Chris Chausse, *President*
Crae Hoffmaster, *Project Mgr*
Craig Picard, *Project Mgr*
Tom Battles, *Info Tech Dir*
▲ EMP: 57
SALES (est): 11.1MM
SALES (corp-wide): 1.9B Privately Held
WEB: www.mbraun.com
SIC: 3826 Mfg Analytical Instruments
HQ: M. Braun Inertgas-Systeme Gmbh
Dieselstr. 31
Garching B. Munchen 85748
893 266-90

(G-19873)
MALAGAR GROUP LLC
Also Called: Philbrick's Mobile Services
188 Bunker Hill Ave (03885-2435)
PHONE..................603 778-1372
Rick Philbrick,
EMP: 3
SALES (est): 289.5K Privately Held
SIC: 3511 Mfg Turbines/Generator Sets

(G-19874)
MBRAUN
14 Marin Way (03885-2578)
PHONE..................603 773-9333
Chris Chausse, *President*
Christopher Bartlett, *Mktg Dir*
▲ EMP: 64
SALES (est): 10.1MM Privately Held
SIC: 3845 Mfg Electromedical Equipment

(G-19875)
NEIGHBORHOOD BEER COMPANY INC
27 Chisholm Farm Dr (03885-2164)
PHONE..................603 418-7124
Joe Berwander, *President*
M O'Donnell, *Vice Pres*
Michael O'Donnell, *Vice Pres*
EMP: 5
SALES (est): 345.7K Privately Held
SIC: 2082 Mfg Malt Beverages

(G-19876)
TIMBERLAND LLC (HQ)
Also Called: Timberland Company, The
200 Domain Dr (03885-2575)
PHONE..................603 772-9500
Jim Pisani, *President*
Shawn Alderton, *District Mgr*
Theresa Walsh, *District Mgr*
Cindy Fotheringham, *Business Mgr*
Amy Hopkins, *Business Mgr*
◆ EMP: 500
SQ FT: 246,000
SALES (est): 1.5MM
SALES (corp-wide): 13.8B Publicly Held
WEB: www.timberland.com
SIC: 3144 2386 2329 2321 Mfg Women's Footwear Mfg Leather Clothing
PA: V.F. Corporation
105 Corporate Center Blvd
Greensboro NC 27408
336 424-6000

(G-19877)
WINGATE SALES ASSOCIATES LLC
2 College Rd Unit 1142 (03885-7633)
PHONE..................603 303-7189
Karen Lazerowich, *Principal*
EMP: 3
SALES (est): 475K Privately Held
SIC: 2599 5032 Mfg Furniture/Fixtures Whol Brick/Stone Material

GEOGRAPHIC

Sugar Hill
Grafton County

(G-19878)
POLLYS PANCAKE PARLOR
Also Called: Hildex Farm
672 Route 117 (03586-4222)
PHONE..................................603 823-5575
Roger H Aldrich, *President*
Dennis Cote, *Vice Pres*
Nancy D Aldrich, *Treasurer*
Katherine Cote, *Admin Sec*
EMP: 3 **EST:** 1900
SALES (est): 365.4K **Privately Held**
WEB: www.pollyspancakeparlor.com
SIC: 2099 5812 2064 2045 Mfg Food Preparations Eating Place Mfg Candy/Confectionery Mfg Prepared Flour Mixes

Sunapee
Sullivan County

(G-19879)
ARLINGTON SAMPLE BOOK CO INC (PA)
100 Fernwood Point Rd (03782-3100)
PHONE..................................603 763-9082
James S Nichol, *President*
▲ **EMP:** 6
SQ FT: 56,000
SALES (est): 1.1MM **Privately Held**
SIC: 2399 2621 Mfg Fabricated Textile Products Paper Mill

(G-19880)
COMMON SENSE MARKETING
Also Called: Common Sense Real Estate Guide
9 Central St (03782-2709)
P.O. Box 18 (03782-0018)
PHONE..................................603 763-2441
Ronald Garceau, *Owner*
EMP: 3
SQ FT: 1,800
SALES: 300K **Privately Held**
WEB: www.commonsensemarketing.com
SIC: 2721 Periodicals-Publishing/Printing

(G-19881)
INTERSTATE MANUFACTURING ASSOC
45 Lower Main St (03782-2912)
PHONE..................................603 863-4855
Fax: 603 863-3811
EMP: 6
SQ FT: 7,000
SALES: 600K **Privately Held**
SIC: 3599 Mfg Industrial Machinery

(G-19882)
MICRO-PRECISION INC (PA)
6 Main St (03782)
P.O. Box 714 (03782-0714)
PHONE..................................603 763-2394
John Wiggins, *President*
Norbert Beauchaine, *Vice Pres*
Charles Taylor, *Treasurer*
Robert Rossiter, *Shareholder*
EMP: 40 **EST:** 1961
SQ FT: 16,000
SALES (est): 6MM **Privately Held**
SIC: 3559 3812 Mfg Automotive Related Machinery

Surry
Cheshire County

(G-19883)
WOODARDS SUGAR HOUSE LLC
1200 Route 12a (03431-8212)
PHONE..................................603 358-3321
Katherine Woodard, *President*
EMP: 3
SALES (est): 108.1K **Privately Held**
SIC: 2099 Mfg Food Preparations

Swanzey
Cheshire County

(G-19884)
M & L ASPHALT SERVICES LLC
19 West St (03446-3318)
P.O. Box 297, West Swanzey (03469-0297)
PHONE..................................603 355-1230
Lawrence H Alley, *Mng Member*
EMP: 5 **EST:** 2010
SALES (est): 745.4K **Privately Held**
SIC: 2951 1611 Mfg Asphalt Mixtures/Blocks Highway/Street Construction

(G-19885)
MOLDPRO INC
36 Denman Thompson Hwy (03446-3003)
PHONE..................................603 357-2523
Gary Barnard, *President*
EMP: 30
SQ FT: 26,000
SALES (est): 356.2K **Privately Held**
WEB: www.moldproinc.com
SIC: 3544 3089 Mfg Dies/Tools/Jigs/Fixtures Mfg Plastic Products

(G-19886)
MOORE NNTECHNOLOGY SYSTEMS LLC (DH)
Also Called: Nanotechsys
230 Old Homestead Hwy (03446-2120)
PHONE..................................603 352-3030
Len Chaloux, *President*
Mark Boomgarden, *President*
Tom Dupell, *COO*
Bob Cassin, *Vice Pres*
Mitch Schadler, *Mng Member*
EMP: 63
SQ FT: 36,000
SALES: 23.8MM
SALES (corp-wide): 65.8MM **Privately Held**
WEB: www.nanotechsys.com
SIC: 3827 5084 Mfg Optical Instruments/Lenses Whol Industrial Equipment
HQ: Moore Tool Company, Inc.
800 Union Ave
Bridgeport CT 06607
203 366-3224

(G-19887)
NEOPA SIGNS
114 S Winchester St (03446-3212)
PHONE..................................603 352-3305
Ralph Randall, *Owner*
EMP: 3
SALES: 390K **Privately Held**
SIC: 3993 5999 Mfg Signs/Advertising Specialties Ret Misc Merchandise

(G-19888)
PRINTFUSION LLC
331 Flat Roof Mill Rd (03446-2707)
PHONE..................................603 283-0007
EMP: 3
SALES (est): 417.1K **Privately Held**
SIC: 2752 Commercial Printing, Lithographic

(G-19889)
SILVER DIRECT INC
351 Monadnock Hwy (03446-2135)
PHONE..................................603 355-8855
Pamela Wilder, *President*
EMP: 5
SQ FT: 3,000
SALES (est): 543.9K **Privately Held**
WEB: www.silverdirectinc.com
SIC: 2759 Commercial Printing

(G-19890)
TRUE NORTH NETWORKS LLC
15 Business Center Dr (03446-4400)
P.O. Box 10067 (03446-0067)
PHONE..................................603 624-6777
Denise C Thomas, *Mng Member*
Kris Glimenakis, *IT/INT Sup*
Steven James Ryder,
Suzanne Ruse, *Assistant*
EMP: 30
SALES (est): 1.1MM **Privately Held**
SIC: 3674 Mfg Semiconductors/Related Devices

Tamworth
Carroll County

(G-19891)
CREATIVE FILTRATION SYSTEMS
Also Called: Baker Bags
Rr 25 (03886)
P.O. Box 480 (03886-0480)
PHONE..................................603 323-2000
Mark Temkin, *President*
Gail Garland, *Manager*
EMP: 12 **EST:** 1972
SQ FT: 5,000
SALES: 1MM **Privately Held**
WEB: www.bakerbags.com
SIC: 3564 Mfg Blowers/Fans

(G-19892)
MONKEY-TRUNKS
1853 White Mountain Hwy (03886)
PHONE..................................603 367-4427
EMP: 3
SALES (est): 120K **Privately Held**
SIC: 3161 Mfg Luggage

(G-19893)
MOOSE MOUNTAIN LOGGING INC
55 Brewster Hill Rd (03886-5016)
P.O. Box 1125, Sanbornville (03872-1125)
PHONE..................................603 491-3667
Lance Maclean, *Principal*
EMP: 3
SALES (est): 209.8K **Privately Held**
SIC: 2411 Logging

(G-19894)
OSSIPEE MOUNTAIN LAND CO LLC
844 Whittier Rd (03886)
P.O. Box 599, West Ossipee (03890-0599)
PHONE..................................603 323-7677
Jeffery Coombs,
EMP: 30
SQ FT: 20,000
SALES (est): 1.4MM **Privately Held**
SIC: 2411 5099 Logging Whol Durable Goods

(G-19895)
UNISTAR CORPORATION
Junction Of Rtes 25 113 E (03886)
P.O. Box 463 (03886-0463)
PHONE..................................603 323-9327
Michael Dionne, *President*
EMP: 8
SQ FT: 4,000
SALES (est): 1.2MM **Privately Held**
SIC: 3599 Mfg Industrial Machinery

Temple
Hillsborough County

(G-19896)
BENS SUGAR SHACK
83 Webster Hwy (03084-4124)
PHONE..................................603 924-3177
Wendell Fisk, *Principal*
EMP: 7
SALES (est): 477.9K **Privately Held**
SIC: 2064 Mfg Candy/Confectionery

(G-19897)
GRANITE 3 LLC
24 Twillingate Rd (03084-4624)
PHONE..................................603 566-0339
Michael Barrett,
EMP: 6
SALES (est): 414.1K **Privately Held**
SIC: 3433 3822 7389 Mfg Heating Equipment-Nonelectric Mfg Environmental Controls

(G-19898)
NORTHROAD WOOD SIGNS
203 Old Revolutionary Rd (03084-4910)
PHONE..................................603 924-9330
Thomas B Hawkins, *Owner*
EMP: 5
SALES (est): 358.9K **Privately Held**
WEB: www.northroad.com
SIC: 3993 Mfg Signs/Advertising Specialties

(G-19899)
SOLAR-STREAM LLC
Also Called: Solar Stream
184 Hill Rd (03084-4710)
P.O. Box 48 (03084-0048)
PHONE..................................603 878-0066
Robert Wills,
Vivian Nicholl,
EMP: 3
SALES: 80K **Privately Held**
WEB: www.liujia.com
SIC: 3561 5084 Mfg Pumps/Pumping Equipment Whol Industrial Equipment

Thornton
Grafton County

(G-19900)
BETA ACQUISITION INC
Also Called: Comptus
202 Tamarack Rd (03285-6867)
PHONE..................................603 726-7500
Andrew White, *President*
EMP: 4
SALES (est): 515.3K **Privately Held**
SIC: 3829 7389 Mfg Measuring/Controlling Devices Business Services At Non-Commercial Site

(G-19901)
MARVEL SIGNS & DESIGNS LLC
2524 Nh Route 175 (03285-6252)
PHONE..................................603 726-4111
Rikki Ramsden, *Mng Member*
Jan Marvel,
Michelle Vaughn,
EMP: 4
SALES: 100K **Privately Held**
WEB: www.marvelsigns.com
SIC: 3993 Mfg Signs/Advertising Specialties

(G-19902)
SEAN BYRNES WELDING LLC
532 Upper Mad River Rd (03285-6447)
PHONE..................................603 726-4315
Sean Byrnes,
EMP: 3 **EST:** 2005
SALES (est): 532.3K **Privately Held**
SIC: 7692 Welding Repair

Tilton
Belknap County

(G-19903)
AMERICAN CUSTOM DESIGN WDWKG
168 Sanborn Rd (03276-5726)
P.O. Box 181 (03276-0181)
PHONE..................................603 286-3239
Bruce L Howard, *President*
EMP: 4
SALES (est): 412.1K **Privately Held**
SIC: 2431 Mfg Millwork

(G-19904)
BARCO MANUFACTURING INC
Also Called: Barco Engineering Co
505 W Main St (03276-5014)
PHONE..................................603 286-3324
David Barbuto, *President*
EMP: 30
SQ FT: 10,000
SALES (est): 2.5MM **Privately Held**
SIC: 3599 3451 Mfg Industrial Machinery Mfg Screw Machine Products

(G-19905)
FORGOTTEN TRADITIONS LLC
49 Silver Lake Rd (03276-5246)
PHONE..................................603 344-2231
Nathan J Searles,
EMP: 3
SALES (est): 160.8K **Privately Held**
SIC: 2099 Mfg Food Preparations

(G-19906)
INNOVATIVE PAPER TECH LLC
Also Called: 3M
1 Paper Trail (03276-5250)
P.O. Box 739 (03276-0739)
PHONE..................................603 286-4891
John Dicarlo, *President*
▼ **EMP:** 62
SALES (est): 11.8MM
SALES (corp-wide): 32.7B **Publicly Held**
WEB: www.mmm.com
SIC: 2621 Paper Mill
PA: 3m Company
3m Center
Saint Paul MN 55144
651 733-1110

(G-19907)
JR HINDS CONST SERV
60 Ridge Rd (03276-5810)
PHONE..................................603 496-2344
Jeffrey Rhinds, *Principal*
EMP: 5
SALES (est): 435.4K **Privately Held**
SIC: 3643 Mfg Conductive Wiring Devices

(G-19908)
NES EMBROIDERY INC
Also Called: Callahan, Robert
100 Autumn Dr Unit 2 (03276-5937)
PHONE..................................603 293-4664
Robert Callahan, *President*
▲ **EMP:** 12
SQ FT: 5,000
SALES (est): 710K **Privately Held**
WEB: www.nes-embroidery.com
SIC: 2395 2353 Embroidery Service

(G-19909)
PROFORMA PIPER PRINTING
600 Laconia Rd (03276-5322)
PHONE..................................603 934-5055
Craig Shufelt, *Owner*
EMP: 6 **EST:** 2013
SALES (est): 587.9K **Privately Held**
SIC: 2752 Lithographic Commercial Printing

(G-19910)
PROGEO GROUP INC
10 Timberline Dr (03276-5641)
PHONE..................................603 286-1942
Clark Gunness, *President*
EMP: 4
SALES (est): 300K **Privately Held**
SIC: 3599 Mfg Industrial Machinery

(G-19911)
SEALITE USA LLC
Also Called: Avlite Systems
61 Business Park Dr (03276-5821)
PHONE..................................603 737-1310
Pj Dillon, *Business Mgr*
Putaansuu Josh, *Engineer*
Deb Mercer, *Accountant*
Michael Walker, *Sales Staff*
Timothy Dining,
◆ **EMP:** 17
SALES (est): 1.3MM **Privately Held**
SIC: 3812 Mfg Search/Navigation Equipment

(G-19912)
SPINNAKER CONTRACT MFG INC
95 Business Park Dr (03276-5821)
PHONE..................................603 286-4366
Guy Nickerson, *President*
Pat Brough, *Vice Pres*
Clarke C Nickerson, *Vice Pres*
Jilian White, *Info Tech Mgr*
Gail Folden, *Technology*
▲ **EMP:** 65
SQ FT: 38,000
SALES: 20MM **Privately Held**
WEB: www.spinnakercontract.com
SIC: 3699 Mfg Electrical Equipment/Supplies

(G-19913)
YESCO SIGN AND LTG CONCORD
Also Called: Cmn Enterprises
322 W Main St Ste 127 (03276-5037)
PHONE..................................603 238-6988
Rick Nichols, *Mng Member*
EMP: 5
SALES (est): 320.1K **Privately Held**
SIC: 3993 Mfg Signs/Advertising Specialties

Troy
Cheshire County

(G-19914)
SURELL ACCESSORIES INC
198 N Main St (03465-2659)
P.O. Box 599 (03465-0599)
PHONE..................................603 242-7784
Darryl Meattey, *President*
Dan Meattey, *Sales Staff*
▲ **EMP:** 13 **EST:** 1979
SQ FT: 4,000
SALES: 1.7MM **Privately Held**
WEB: www.surellaccessories.com
SIC: 2371 2386 Mfg Fur Goods Mfg Leather Clothing

Walpole
Cheshire County

(G-19915)
BB WALPOLE LIQUIDATION NH INC
35 Main St (03608)
PHONE..................................603 756-2882
Yoon Chang, *Branch Mgr*
EMP: 3
SALES (est): 162.3K **Privately Held**
SIC: 2064 Mfg Candy/Confectionery
PA: Bb Walpole Liquidation Nh, Inc.
47 Main St Unit 1
Walpole NH 03608

(G-19916)
BB WALPOLE LIQUIDATION NH INC (PA)
Also Called: Burdick Chocolates
47 Main St Unit 1 (03608-9990)
P.O. Box 593 (03608-0593)
PHONE..................................603 756-3701
Paula Burdick, *President*
Bill Heleen, *Info Tech Mgr*
Shawn Doyle, *Technology*
◆ **EMP:** 85
SQ FT: 12,000
SALES (est): 13.2MM **Privately Held**
SIC: 2064 Mfg Candy/Confectionery

(G-19917)
BENSON WOODWORKING COMPANY INC
Also Called: Benson Woodhomes
6 Blackjack Xing (03608-4801)
PHONE..................................603 756-3600
Tedd Benson, *President*
Christine Benson, *Vice Pres*
Jeff Coleman, *Project Mgr*
Brad Moore, *Project Mgr*
Marilyn Taggart, *Sales Staff*
EMP: 80 **EST:** 1974
SQ FT: 12,500
SALES (est): 8.3MM **Privately Held**
SIC: 2452 2439 Mfg Prefabricated Wood Buildings Mfg Structural Wood Members

(G-19918)
CHAMBERLAIN MACHINE LLC
17 Huntington Ln (03608)
PHONE..................................603 756-2560
Robert E Boynton, *President*
Judith O Boynton, *Corp Secy*
Scott W Boynton, *Vice Pres*
◆ **EMP:** 47 **EST:** 1943
SQ FT: 50,000
SALES (est): 12.2MM **Privately Held**
WEB: www.chamberlainmachine.com
SIC: 3599 Mfg Industrial Machinery

(G-19919)
CURATOR
108 Wentworth Rd (03608-4818)
P.O. Box 985 (03608-0985)
PHONE..................................603 756-3888
Bronia Jenson, *President*
EMP: 3
SALES (est): 238.3K **Privately Held**
WEB: www.curatoronline.com
SIC: 2393 Mfgs Bags

(G-19920)
DIAMONDSHARP CORPORATION
20 Blanchard Brook Cir (03608-4406)
PHONE..................................603 445-2224
William Cadmus, *President*
Whitney Cadmus, *Director*
EMP: 4
SQ FT: 6,500
SALES (est): 376.1K **Privately Held**
WEB: www.diasharp.com
SIC: 3545 5085 Mfg Diamond Cutting Tools & Whls Industrial Diamonds Specializing In Diamond Powder

(G-19921)
HICKS MACHINE INC
65 Maplewood Cir (03608-4412)
P.O. Box 445 (03608-0445)
PHONE..................................603 756-3671
Randall Hicks, *President*
George M Kendall Jr, *Supervisor*
EMP: 22
SQ FT: 12,000
SALES: 3MM **Privately Held**
WEB: www.hicksmachine.com
SIC: 3599 Machine Shop Jobbing & Repair

(G-19922)
JONATHAN CLOWES SCULPTURE
98 March Hill Rd (03608-4616)
P.O. Box 365, Thomaston ME (04861-0365)
PHONE..................................603 835-6441
Jonathan Clowes, *Owner*
Evelyn Clowes, *Co-Owner*
EMP: 5
SQ FT: 4,000
SALES (est): 289.7K **Privately Held**
WEB: www.clowessculpture.com
SIC: 3299 Mfg Nonmetallic Mineral Products

(G-19923)
MARK WELCH
Also Called: Mark Welch Logging
713 River Rd (03608-4233)
PHONE..................................603 835-6347
Mark Welch, *Principal*
EMP: 3
SALES (est): 163.3K **Privately Held**
SIC: 2411 Logging

(G-19924)
SCOTT L NORTHCOTT
103 Cheney Hill Rd (03608-4302)
PHONE..................................603 756-4204
Scott L Northcott, *Owner*
Gail Golec, *Associate*
EMP: 5
SALES: 250K **Privately Held**
SIC: 2426 Hardwood Dimension/Floor Mill

(G-19925)
WALPOLE CABINETRY
5 Lambro Ln (03608-4856)
P.O. Box 364, Charlestown (03603-0364)
PHONE..................................603 826-4100
Thomas Perkins, *Owner*
EMP: 10
SQ FT: 2,000
SALES: 250K **Privately Held**
SIC: 2434 Mfg Wood Kitchen Cabinets

(G-19926)
WALPOLE CREAMERY LTD
532 Main St (03608-4470)
PHONE..................................603 445-5700
Robert Kasper Jr, *President*
EMP: 4
SALES (est): 219.7K **Privately Held**
SIC: 2024 5451 5963 Mfg Ice Cream/Frozen Desert Ret Dairy Products Direct Retail Sales

Warner
Merrimack County

(G-19927)
JEFF CUMMINGS SERVICES LLC
268 Bean Rd (03278-4202)
PHONE..................................603 456-3706
Jeffrey Cummings,
Suzanne Cummings,
EMP: 6
SALES (est): 644.5K **Privately Held**
SIC: 1381 5084 Oil/Gas Well Drilling Whol Industrial Equipment

(G-19928)
MADGETECH INC (PA)
6 Warner Rd (03278-4435)
PHONE..................................603 456-2011
Norman E Carlson, *President*
Jon Moriarty, *Mfg Dir*
Karl Hauck, *Senior Engr*
Suzan M Lehmann, *Admin Sec*
▼ **EMP:** 30
SQ FT: 6,400
SALES (est): 6.1MM **Privately Held**
WEB: www.madgetech.com
SIC: 3823 Mfg Process Control Instruments

(G-19929)
R C BRAYSHAW & CO INC (PA)
45 Waterloo St (03278-4221)
P.O. Box 91 (03278-0091)
PHONE..................................603 456-3101
Thomas C Brayshaw, *President*
Joshua Pincoske, *General Mgr*
Jim Newcomb, *Vice Pres*
Karen Wiggins, *Finance*
EMP: 28
SQ FT: 5,000
SALES (est): 6.6MM **Privately Held**
SIC: 2752 Lithographic Commercial Printing

(G-19930)
WARNER POWER ACQUISITION LLC (HQ)
40 Depot St (03278-4226)
PHONE..................................603 456-3111
Russ Ricker, *General Mgr*
Nick Hoiles, *Principal*
Souheil Benzerrouk, *Vice Pres*
Maryann Burout, *Vice Pres*
Kevin Shannon, *Vice Pres*
◆ **EMP:** 135 **EST:** 1999
SQ FT: 80,000
SALES (est): 39.7MM **Privately Held**
WEB: www.warnerpower.com
SIC: 3699 5063 Mfg Electrical Equipment/Supplies Whol Electrical Equipment
PA: Gti Power Acquisition, Llc
1500 Marion Ave
Grand Haven MI 49417
616 842-5430

(G-19931)
WARNER POWER CONVERSION LLC
40 Depot St (03278-4226)
PHONE..................................603 456-3111
Nick Hoiles, *CEO*
EMP: 150
SALES (est): 23.5MM
SALES (corp-wide): 39.7MM **Privately Held**
WEB: www.warnerpower.com
SIC: 3629 Mfg Electrical Industrial Apparatus

HQ: Warner Power Acquisition, Llc
40 Depot St
Warner NH 03278
603 456-3111

Weare
Hillsborough County

(G-19932)
BIG FOOTE CRUSHING LLC
1225 River Rd (03281-4719)
P.O. Box 4 (03281-0004)
PHONE..................................603 345-0695
EMP: 3
SALES (est): 369.9K **Privately Held**
SIC: 1442 Construction Sand/Gravel

(G-19933)
BRAZECOM INDUSTRIES LLC
45 B And B Ln (03281-5903)
PHONE..................................603 529-2080
Brandon Merron, *President*
Kim Merron, *Purchasing*
EMP: 9
SQ FT: 9,600
SALES (est): 1.1MM **Privately Held**
SIC: 3398 Metal Heat Treating

(G-19934)
J C B LEASING INC
14 B And B Ln (03281-5902)
PHONE..................................603 529-7974
Michael Brown, *President*
Scott Harrington, *Manager*
EMP: 60
SQ FT: 50,000
SALES: 1.5MM **Privately Held**
WEB: www.jcbcorporate.com
SIC: 3462 3531 1794 Mfg Iron/Steel Forgings Mfg Construction Machinery Excavation Contractor

(G-19935)
JMD DUCT FABRICATION LLC
25 Brown Ridge Rd (03281-5003)
PHONE..................................603 235-9314
Dan Cerullo, *Principal*
EMP: 6
SALES (est): 946.1K **Privately Held**
SIC: 3585 Mfg Refrigeration/Heating Equipment

(G-19936)
JR FRANK BOLTON
Also Called: Centre Machine
58 Carding Mill Rd (03281)
P.O. Box 76 (03281-0076)
PHONE..................................603 529-3633
Frank Bolton Jr, *Owner*
EMP: 3
SQ FT: 3,200
SALES (est): 326.4K **Privately Held**
SIC: 3544 Mfg Dies/Tools/Jigs/Fixtures

(G-19937)
KINGS CORNR WOODTURNING WDWKG
502 Barnard Hill Rd (03281-5102)
PHONE..................................603 529-0063
Michael Fonner, *Owner*
EMP: 3
SALES (est): 450K **Privately Held**
SIC: 2499 Mfg Wood Products

(G-19938)
MDS WELDING & FABRICATION
30 B And B Ln (03281-5965)
PHONE..................................603 660-0772
Matt Shapiro, *Executive*
EMP: 5
SALES (est): 644.7K **Privately Held**
SIC: 7692 Welding Repair

(G-19939)
RADIUS MFG & FABRICATION INC
164 Concord Stage Rd (03281-4611)
PHONE..................................603 529-0801
Daniel Demers, *President*
EMP: 5
SALES (est): 370.8K **Privately Held**
SIC: 3441 Structural Metal Fabrication

(G-19940)
SUSIE BZ NATURAL LIP BALM
17 Fieldstone Cir (03281-5610)
PHONE..................................603 529-7083
Suzanne E Leblanc, *Owner*
EMP: 3
SALES (est): 163.1K **Privately Held**
SIC: 2834 Mfg Pharmaceutical Preparations

(G-19941)
TANDEM KROSS LLC
Also Called: Tandemkross
490 S Stark Hwy (03281-5527)
PHONE..................................603 369-7060
Jen Ramsey, *General Mgr*
Danielle Gagnon, *Marketing Staff*
Jake Wyman,
Bryan Haaker,
EMP: 9
SALES (est): 611.7K **Privately Held**
SIC: 3484 5961 Mfg Small Arms Ret Mail-Order House

(G-19942)
VALHALLA CIRCUITS CORP
77 Gould Rd (03281-5916)
PHONE..................................603 854-3300
Paul Laliberte, *President*
EMP: 5
SALES (est): 346K **Privately Held**
SIC: 3672 Printed Circuit Boards

Webster
Merrimack County

(G-19943)
ADAM E MOCK AND SON LOGGING AN
1354 Pleasant St (03303-7611)
PHONE..................................603 648-2444
Adam E Mock, *Owner*
EMP: 5
SALES (est): 524.8K **Privately Held**
SIC: 2411 0212 Logging Beef Cattle-Except Feedlot

(G-19944)
MELLEN COMPANY INC
1260 Battle St (03303-7311)
PHONE..................................603 648-2121
Jonathan Mellen, *Branch Mgr*
EMP: 6
SALES (corp-wide): 3.4MM **Privately Held**
WEB: www.mellencompany.com
SIC: 3821 Mfg Lab Apparatus/Furniture
PA: The Mellen Company Inc
40 Chenell Dr
Concord NH 03301
603 228-2929

(G-19945)
SANTA CRUZ GUNLOCKS LLC
Also Called: STA Cruz Gun Locks
450 Tyler Rd (03303-7738)
PHONE..................................603 746-7740
Zsuzsa Tanos, *President*
David Tanos, *Managing Dir*
▲ **EMP:** 7
SALES: 4MM **Privately Held**
SIC: 3949 Mfg Gun Racks

Wentworth
Grafton County

(G-19946)
KING FOREST INDUSTRIES INC (PA)
53 E Side Rd (03282-3323)
P.O. Box 230 (03282-0230)
PHONE..................................603 764-5711
John King Jr, *President*
EMP: 65
SQ FT: 35,000
SALES (est): 12.5MM **Privately Held**
WEB: www.kingforest.com
SIC: 2421 Sawmill/Planing Mill

(G-19947)
PRECISION LUMBER INC
576 Buffalo Rd (03282-3417)
P.O. Box 158 (03282-0158)
PHONE..................................603 764-9450
Joe Robertie, *President*
Larry King, *Vice Pres*
EMP: 57
SQ FT: 1,800
SALES (est): 7.9MM **Privately Held**
SIC: 2426 2421 Sawmill/Planing Mill

West Lebanon
Grafton County

(G-19948)
CENTRICUT MANUFACTURING LLC
16 Airpark Rd (03784-1674)
PHONE..................................603 298-6191
Patrick Byrne, *Partner*
EMP: 45 **EST:** 1987
SALES (est): 3MM **Privately Held**
SIC: 3541 3548 Mfg Machine Tools-Cutting Mfg Welding Apparatus

(G-19949)
ELECTRONICS FOR IMAGING INC
Vutek
79 E Wilder Rd Ste 1 (03784-3101)
PHONE..................................603 279-6800
Scott Shinlever, *Manager*
EMP: 325
SALES (corp-wide): 1B **Privately Held**
WEB: www.vutek.com
SIC: 3555 5734 Mfg Printing Trades Machinery Ret Computers/Software
HQ: Electronics For Imaging, Inc.
6750 Dumbarton Cir
Fremont CA 94555
650 357-3500

(G-19950)
ENERGEX PELLET FUEL INC
20 Airpark Rd (03784-1740)
PHONE..................................603 298-7007
Bruce Lisle, *Principal*
EMP: 4
SALES (est): 389.3K **Privately Held**
SIC: 2869 Mfg Industrial Organic Chemicals

(G-19951)
FEDEX OFFICE & PRINT SVCS INC
267 Plainfield Rd (03784-2017)
PHONE..................................603 298-5891
Fax: 603 298-5923
EMP: 4
SALES (corp-wide): 47.4B **Publicly Held**
SIC: 2759 5099 7334 Commercial Printing Whol Durable Goods Photocopying Services
HQ: Fedex Office And Print Services, Inc.
7900 Legacy Dr
Dallas TX 75024
214 550-7000

(G-19952)
HD SUPPLY CONSTRUCTION SUPPLY
Also Called: A.H. Harris West Lebanon
17 Plaza Heights Rd # 3 (03784)
PHONE..................................603 298-6072
Jason Hill, *Branch Mgr*
EMP: 5 **Publicly Held**
SIC: 3444 7699 0782 Mfg Sheet Metalwork Repair Services Lawn/Garden Services
HQ: Hd Supply Construction Supply, Ltd (Lp)
3400 Cumberland Blvd Se
Atlanta GA 30339
770 852-9000

(G-19953)
HYERTHERM INC
20 Airpark Rd (03784-1740)
PHONE..................................603 643-3441
Bob Gendron, *Engineer*
EMP: 11
SALES (est): 1.3MM **Privately Held**
SIC: 3541 Mfg Machine Tools-Cutting

(G-19954)
INTOUCH SOFTWARE
37 Wildwood Dr (03784-3118)
PHONE..................................603 643-1952
EMP: 3 **EST:** 2014
SALES (est): 102.5K **Privately Held**
SIC: 7372 Prepackaged Software Services

(G-19955)
L L BEAN INC
8 Glen Rd Ste 29 (03784-1646)
PHONE..................................603 298-6975
Michael Stone, *Branch Mgr*
EMP: 6
SALES (corp-wide): 893MM **Privately Held**
SIC: 3949 Mfg Sporting/Athletic Goods
PA: L. L. Bean, Inc.
15 Casco St
Freeport ME 04033
207 552-2000

(G-19956)
LETTERMAN PRESS LLC
Also Called: Letter Man Press
1 Glen Rd Ste 222 (03784-1652)
PHONE..................................603 543-0500
Steve Nix, *Mng Member*
Janet Clayton,
Lee J Clayton,
EMP: 3 **EST:** 1959
SQ FT: 5,700
SALES: 250K **Privately Held**
SIC: 2752 2759 2791 2789 Lithographic Coml Print Commercial Printing Typesetting Services Bookbinding/Related Work

(G-19957)
MOTO TASSINARI INC
2 Technology Dr (03784-1671)
PHONE..................................603 298-6646
Steven Tassinari, *President*
Nick Turunen, *Engineer*
Scott Tassinari, *Treasurer*
Crystal Pringle, *Admin Sec*
▲ **EMP:** 10
SALES (est): 1.4MM **Privately Held**
WEB: www.vforce3.com
SIC: 3751 5571 Mfg Motorcycles/Bicycles Ret Motorcycles

(G-19958)
NOVO NORDISK US BIO PROD INC
9 Technology Dr (03784-1673)
PHONE..................................603 298-3169
Peter Gariepy, *Vice Pres*
EMP: 175 **EST:** 2014
SALES (est): 690.1K
SALES (corp-wide): 19.5B **Privately Held**
SIC: 2834 Mfg Pharmaceutical Preparations
HQ: Novo Nordisk Inc.
800 Scudders Mill Rd
Plainsboro NJ 08536
609 987-5800

(G-19959)
PRAECIS INC
6 Chambers Cir (03784-3103)
P.O. Box 5403, Hanover (03755-5403)
PHONE..................................603 277-9288
Nathaniel C Thompson, *Director*
EMP: 4
SALES (est): 566K **Privately Held**
SIC: 3823 Mfg Process Control Instruments

(G-19960)
PROGRESSIVE MANUFACTURING INC
20 Airpark Rd (03784-1674)
PHONE..................................603 298-5778
Patrick E Moynihan, *President*
EMP: 11
SALES (est): 2.4MM **Privately Held**
SIC: 3444 Mfg Sheet Metalwork

(G-19961)
ROCES NORTH AMERICA
10 Technology Dr Ste 1b (03784-1693)
PHONE..................................603 298-2137

▲ = Import ▼=Export
◆ =Import/Export

John Alarie, *Owner*
▲ **EMP:** 6
SALES (est): 576.5K **Privately Held**
SIC: 3949 Mfg Sporting/Athletic Goods

(G-19962)
THERMAL ARC INC
82 Benning St (03784-3405)
PHONE..................................800 462-2782
Paul D Melnuk, *Ch of Bd*
Patricia S Williams, *Vice Pres*
David L Dyckman, *CFO*
Steven W Fray, *VP Finance*
EMP: 100
SQ FT: 215,000
SALES (est): 880.1K
SALES (corp-wide): 3.6B **Publicly Held**
WEB: www.thermadyne.com
SIC: 3699 Mfg Electrical Equipment/Supplies
HQ: Thermal Dynamics Corporation
82 Benning St
West Lebanon NH 03784
603 298-5711

(G-19963)
THERMAL DYNAMICS CORPORATION (DH)
Also Called: Thermadyne
82 Benning St (03784-3403)
PHONE..................................603 298-5711
Paul D Melnuk, *Ch of Bd*
David L Dyckman, *Exec VP*
Patricia Williams, *Vice Pres*
Andrew Yamada, *Opers Mgr*
Steven W Fray, *VP Finance*
▲ **EMP:** 266 **EST:** 1917
SQ FT: 156,200
SALES (est): 37.9MM
SALES (corp-wide): 3.6B **Publicly Held**
WEB: www.thermadyne.com
SIC: 3541 5084 Mfg Machine Tools-Cutting Whol Industrial Equipment
HQ: Victor Equipment Company
2800 Airport Rd
Denton TX 76207
940 566-2000

West Nottingham
Rockingham County

(G-19964)
CUSTOM WELDING & FABRICATIONS
127 Old Turnpike Rd (03291)
P.O. Box 105, Nottingham (03290-0105)
PHONE..................................603 942-5170
Patrick Parenteau, *President*
EMP: 15
SQ FT: 5,000
SALES (est): 2.7MM **Privately Held**
WEB: www.customweldinginc.com
SIC: 3441 7692 3446 3444 Structural Metal Fabrctn Welding Repair Mfg Architectural Mtlwrk Mfg Sheet Metalwork Mfg Fabricated Plate Wrk

(G-19965)
DYER S DOCKING SYSTEMS CORP
404 Stage Rd (03291-6110)
PHONE..................................603 942-5122
John Dyer, *President*
Suzanne Dyer, *Shareholder*
Roland Morneau, *Admin Sec*
EMP: 12
SQ FT: 9,500
SALES (est): 1.3MM **Privately Held**
WEB: www.docksystem.com
SIC: 3448 Manufactures Aluminum Boat Docks

West Ossipee
Carroll County

(G-19966)
HOBBS TAVERN & BREWING CO LLC
2415 Route 16 (03890-6000)
P.O. Box 539 (03890-0539)
PHONE..................................603 539-2000
Nathan Deyesso, *Managing Prtnr*
Robert Finneron,
Charles Fisphbein,
EMP: 30
SQ FT: 12,500
SALES: 3.2MM **Privately Held**
SIC: 2082 5813 Mfg Malt Beverages Drinking Place

West Swanzey
Cheshire County

(G-19967)
PORT-O-LITE COMPANY INC
1 Railroad St (03469)
P.O. Box 630 (03469-0630)
PHONE..................................603 352-3205
Peter C Delaney, *President*
Marilyn Woods, *Vice Pres*
EMP: 10 **EST:** 1952
SQ FT: 80,000
SALES (est): 2.7MM **Privately Held**
SIC: 2431 Mfg Millwork

(G-19968)
RMA MANUFACTURING LLC
Also Called: Turmoil Manufacturing
735 W Swanzey Rd (03469)
P.O. Box 583 (03469-0583)
PHONE..................................603 352-0053
Ray Anderson, *Mng Member*
EMP: 20
SQ FT: 11,000
SALES (est): 2MM **Privately Held**
SIC: 3822 Mfg Environmental Controls

(G-19969)
TURMOIL INC
735 W Swanzey Rd (03469)
P.O. Box 583 (03469-0583)
PHONE..................................603 352-0053
John Parker-Hansel Jr, *President*
EMP: 20
SQ FT: 11,000
SALES (est): 4.7MM **Privately Held**
WEB: www.turmoilcoolers.com
SIC: 3822 Mfg Environmental Controls

Westmoreland
Cheshire County

(G-19970)
COX WOODWORKING INC
5 Route 63 (03467-4420)
PHONE..................................603 399-7704
Terry M Cox, *President*
Craig Stavseth, *Vice Pres*
EMP: 5
SALES: 385K **Privately Held**
SIC: 2431 Architectural Millwork

(G-19971)
EQUINOX SOFTWARE SYSTEMS INC
90 Overman Rd (03467-4101)
PHONE..................................603 399-9970
Thomas B Mc Connon, *President*
Rita-Marie Mc Connon, *Clerk*
EMP: 3
SALES (est): 228.7K **Privately Held**
WEB: www.equinoxsoftware.com
SIC: 7372 Prepackaged Software Services

Whitefield
Coos County

(G-19972)
PRESBY PLASTICS INC
143 Airport Rd (03598-3427)
PHONE..................................603 837-3826
David Presby, *President*
EMP: 25
SALES (est): 4MM **Privately Held**
WEB: www.presbyeco.com
SIC: 3089 Mfg Plastic Products

Wilmot
Merrimack County

(G-19973)
LEARNING STATION LLC
88 Stone Bridge Rd (03287-4625)
PHONE..................................603 496-7896
Andrew Friday,
EMP: 5
SALES (est): 219.7K **Privately Held**
SIC: 7372 Prepackaged Software

Wilton
Hillsborough County

(G-19974)
ALUMINUM CASTINGS INC
Also Called: General Machine & Foundry
4 Hampshire Hills Ln (03086)
P.O. Box 420, Hollis (03049-0420)
PHONE..................................603 654-9695
Robert Paro, *President*
Mark Paro, *Vice Pres*
EMP: 7
SQ FT: 43,000
SALES: 630.1K **Privately Held**
SIC: 3599 3544 Mfg Industrial Machinery Mfg Dies/Tools/Jigs/Fixtures

(G-19975)
ATLANTIC PREFAB INC (PA)
19 Stoney Brook Dr (03086-5025)
PHONE..................................603 668-2648
Michael Dion, *President*
Matthew Pudsey, *Prdtn Mgr*
EMP: 5
SALES (est): 1.8MM **Privately Held**
SIC: 2439 Mfg Structural Wood Members

(G-19976)
BURBAK COMPANIES
Also Called: Burbak Plastic
361 Forest Rd (03086-5136)
P.O. Box 669 (03086-0669)
PHONE..................................603 654-2291
Jerry Greene, *President*
Judy Collins, *Administration*
Becky Pellerin, *Administration*
EMP: 100
SQ FT: 30,000
SALES (est): 18.8MM **Privately Held**
WEB: www.burbak.com
SIC: 3089 3599 Mfg Plastic Products Mfg Industrial Machinery

(G-19977)
CUTTING TOOL TECHNOLOGIES INC
327 Forest Rd (03086-5135)
P.O. Box 720 (03086-0720)
PHONE..................................603 654-2550
Harold F Armstrong, *President*
Bruce K Bakaian, *Vice Pres*
Linda Bakaian, *Treasurer*
EMP: 7
SQ FT: 16,000
SALES (est): 1.1MM **Privately Held**
SIC: 3545 Mfg Industrial Machinery

(G-19978)
DIGITAL DEVICES INC
28 Howard St (03086-5424)
P.O. Box 718 (03086-0718)
PHONE..................................603 654-6240
Mary Jane Lamountain, *President*
Richard Koster, *Vice Pres*
Brian Koster, *Admin Sec*
EMP: 5
SQ FT: 12,000
SALES (est): 775.5K **Privately Held**
SIC: 3825 3824 Mfg Electrical Measuring Instruments Mfg Fluid Meter/Counting Devices

(G-19979)
E B FRYE & SON INC
Also Called: Frye's Measure Mill
12 Frye Mill Rd (03086-5010)
PHONE..................................603 654-6581
Harland H Savage Jr, *President*
EMP: 4 **EST:** 1858
SQ FT: 20,000
SALES (est): 1MM **Privately Held**
SIC: 2441 5947 5961 Mfg Wood Items Specializing In Reproduction Of Colonial & Shaker Gift Boxes & Ret Gift Shop & Mail Order House

GEOGRAPHIC

(G-19980)
EARTH SKY + WATER LLC
28 Howard St (03086-5424)
P.O. Box 60 (03086-0060)
PHONE..................................603 654-7649
EMP: 8 **EST:** 2008
SALES (est): 470.1K **Privately Held**
SIC: 2731 Books-Publishing/Printing

(G-19981)
KIMBALL PHYSICS INC
Also Called: K P I
311 Kimball Hill Rd (03086-5715)
PHONE..................................603 878-1616
Charles K Crawford, *President*
EMP: 40
SQ FT: 30,000
SALES (est): 10.1MM **Privately Held**
WEB: www.kimphys.com
SIC: 3821 3829 Mfg Lab Apparatus/Furniture Mfg Measuring/Controlling Devices

(G-19982)
MAPLE GUYS LLC
327 Forest Rd (03086)
P.O. Box 628 (03086-0628)
PHONE..................................603 654-2415
Christopher J Pheil,
Christopher Pfeil,
EMP: 3
SALES (est): 304.7K **Privately Held**
SIC: 2099 Mfg Food Preparations

(G-19983)
MCNALLY INDUSTRIES INC
Also Called: Merrill's Metal Shop
Tremont St (03086)
PHONE..................................603 654-5361
Steve McNally, *President*
Ronald R Smith, *Principal*
Susan McNally, *Admin Sec*
EMP: 6 **EST:** 1959
SQ FT: 3,000
SALES (est): 300K **Privately Held**
SIC: 3444 Sheet Metal Shop

(G-19984)
PROFFE PUBLISHING
6 Mountain Meadow Trl (03086-5340)
PHONE..................................603 654-1070
Jos Pluijmakers, *Administration*
EMP: 3
SALES (est): 50K **Privately Held**
SIC: 2741 Misc Publishing

(G-19985)
ROBERT NIXON
Also Called: Nixon Machine
328 Abbott Hill Rd (03086-8007)
PHONE..................................603 654-2285
Robert Nixon, *Owner*
EMP: 3
SALES: 125K **Privately Held**
SIC: 3544 Mfg Dies/Tools/Jigs/Fixtures

(G-19986)
ROSENCRNTZ GLDNSTERN BANKNOTES
6 Burns Hill Rd (03086)
P.O. Box 150, Milford (03055-0150)
PHONE..................................603 654-6160
Michael Zielie, *President*
Sandra Zielie, *Vice Pres*

▲ **EMP:** 12
SQ FT: 12,000
SALES (est): 1MM **Privately Held**
WEB: www.coolchecks.com
SIC: 2782 Mfg Blankbooks/Binders

(G-19987)
S & Q PRINTERS INC
Howard St (03086)
P.O. Box 1031 (03086-1031)
PHONE..................................603 654-2888
Linda Lombardo, *President*
▼ **EMP:** 7
SQ FT: 9,000
SALES (est): 885.4K **Privately Held**
WEB: www.sqprinters.com
SIC: 2752 Lithographic Commercial Printing

(G-19988)
SOUHEGAN WOOD PRODUCTS INC
10 Souhegan St (03086-8700)
P.O. Box 120 (03086-0120)
PHONE..................................603 654-2311
Randolph A Dunn, *President*
Elizabeth M Dunn, *Vice Pres*
Rhonda Stricklen, *Executive Asst*
▼ **EMP:** 18
SQ FT: 30,000
SALES (est): 3.2MM **Privately Held**
WEB: www.souheganwood.com
SIC: 2499 2493 Mfg Wood Products Mfg Reconstituted Wood Products

(G-19989)
SPECIAL HERMETIC PRODUCTS
Also Called: S H P
Riverview Mill 39 Souhgn (03086)
P.O. Box 269 (03086-0269)
PHONE..................................603 654-2002
Anthony Desantis, *President*
Lori Jensen, *Treasurer*
William C Sullivan, *Admin Sec*
EMP: 30
SQ FT: 15,000
SALES (est): 4.7MM **Privately Held**
WEB: www.shp-seals.com
SIC: 3679 3678 Mfg Electronic Components Mfg Electronic Connectors

(G-19990)
W S PACKAGING
Also Called: Label Art
1 Riverside Way (03086)
PHONE..................................603 654-6131
Thomas J Cobery, *President*
Terence Flaherty, *Senior VP*
Marie Anderson, *Vice Pres*
James Barry, *Vice Pres*
David M Lajoie, *Treasurer*
EMP: 205
SQ FT: 85,000
SALES (est): 28.7MM **Privately Held**
SIC: 2672 Mfg Coated/Laminated Paper

(G-19991)
WATERWEAR INC
Also Called: H2o Wear
24 Howard St (03086-5424)
P.O. Box 687 (03086-0687)
PHONE..................................603 654-5344
Richard P Lovett, *President*
▲ **EMP:** 25
SQ FT: 12,000
SALES (est): 2.7MM **Privately Held**
WEB: www.h2owear.com
SIC: 2339 2329 Mfg Women's/Misses' Outerwear Mfg Men's/Boy's Clothing

Winchester
Cheshire County

(G-19992)
INNOVATIVE MACHINE & SUP INC
40 Snow Rd (03470-2806)
PHONE..................................603 239-8082
Terry Haskins, *President*
Sandra Lapoint, *Treasurer*
Sandy Lapointe, *Treasurer*
EMP: 14
SQ FT: 12,000
SALES: 2MM **Privately Held**
SIC: 3599 Mfg Industrial Machinery

(G-19993)
MITCHELL SAND & GRAVEL LLC
20 Payne Rd (03470-2324)
PHONE..................................603 357-0881
EMP: 3
SALES (est): 405.4K **Privately Held**
SIC: 1442 Construction Sand/Gravel

(G-19994)
R L COOK TIMBER HARVESTING
811 Manning Hill Rd (03470-2720)
PHONE..................................603 239-6424
Douglas Cook, *President*
Douglas L Cook, *President*
Michael R Cook, *Vice Pres*
Sandra Cook, *Treasurer*
EMP: 4
SALES: 500K **Privately Held**
SIC: 2411 1794 Timber Harvesting And Gravel Excavation

(G-19995)
RESURRECTION DEFENSE LLC
71 Richmond Rd (03470-2428)
PHONE..................................603 313-1040
Zachary Nutting, *Principal*
EMP: 3 **EST:** 2016
SALES (est): 229.2K **Privately Held**
SIC: 3812 Mfg Search/Navigation Equipment

(G-19996)
THE KEENEY MANUFACTURING CO
Also Called: Plumb Pak
75 Plumb Pak Dr (03470-2928)
PHONE..................................603 239-6371
Gary Hill, *Manager*
EMP: 183
SALES (corp-wide): 132MM **Privately Held**
WEB: www.keeneymfg.com
SIC: 3432 Mfg Plumbing Fixture Fittings
PA: The Keeney Manufacturing Company
1170 Main St
Newington CT 06111
603 239-6371

(G-19997)
WINCHESTER PRECISION TECH LTD
41 Hildreth St (03470-3121)
PHONE..................................603 239-6326
Barry A Bordner, *President*
Jason Perron, *Vice Pres*
▲ **EMP:** 19
SQ FT: 33,000
SALES: 5MM **Privately Held**
WEB: www.winchesterroll.com
SIC: 3547 3599 3441 Mfg Rolling Mill Machinery Mfg Industrial Machinery Structural Metal Fabrication

Windham
Rockingham County

(G-19998)
AMERICAN POWER DESIGN INC
3 Industrial Dr Unit 6 (03087-2014)
PHONE..................................603 894-4446
Randy Normandin, *President*
Mark Ryan, *Chairman*
David Lutz, *Treasurer*
▲ **EMP:** 12
SQ FT: 4,500
SALES: 1.5MM **Privately Held**
WEB: www.apowerdesign.com
SIC: 3679 Mfg Electronic Components

(G-19999)
AMERICAN TINTER
5 Dublin Rd (03087-1531)
PHONE..................................603 458-6379
Corey Moore, *Principal*
EMP: 3
SALES (est): 269.1K **Privately Held**
SIC: 3211 Mfg Flat Glass

(G-20000)
AP DLEY CSTM LAMINATING CORP
6 Ledge Rd (03087-1509)
PHONE..................................603 437-6666
Arthur P Dailey, *President*
Sarah Costa, *Manager*
EMP: 20
SQ FT: 30,000
SALES (est): 4.4MM **Privately Held**
WEB: www.apdailey.com
SIC: 2431 7389 Mfg Millwork Business Services

(G-20001)
CET TECHNOLOGY LLC
27a Roulston Rd (03087-1210)
PHONE..................................603 894-6100
Jane Gilman, *Accountant*
Robert Mirabella,
Stephanie Plumlee, *Admin Sec*
▲ **EMP:** 11
SQ FT: 12,000
SALES: 1MM **Privately Held**
WEB: www.cettechnology.com
SIC: 3559 Mfg Electronic Component

(G-20002)
COLONIAL MEDICAL SUPPLY CO INC
31 Lowell Rd Unit 6 (03087-1858)
P.O. Box 554 (03087-0554)
PHONE..................................603 328-5130
Susan Fleming, *President*
EMP: 4
SALES (est): 644.8K **Privately Held**
WEB: www.colmedsupply.com
SIC: 3821 Mfg Lab Apparatus/Furniture

(G-20003)
CUSTOM DIE CUT INC
3 Lexington Rd Unit 1a (03087-5500)
PHONE..................................603 437-3090
Sal Yebba, *President*
Brian Reese, *Vice Pres*
Robin Yebba, *Vice Pres*
EMP: 7
SQ FT: 16,000
SALES: 1.5MM **Privately Held**
SIC: 2759 2675 2789 7389 Commercial Printing Mfg Die-Cut Paper/Board Bookbinding/Related Work Business Services

(G-20004)
EAGLE COPY CENTER
29 Beacon Hill Rd (03087-1102)
PHONE..................................603 225-3713
Effie Raft, *Owner*
Jason Raft, *Manager*
EMP: 3
SALES: 170K **Privately Held**
SIC: 2752 2759 2621 Lithographic Commercial Printing Commercial Printing Paper Mill

(G-20005)
EVERSOLVE LLC
8 Woodvue Rd (03087-2113)
PHONE..................................603 870-9739
Ioana Singureanu,
Keith Bagley,
EMP: 7
SALES (est): 316.9K **Privately Held**
SIC: 7372 Application Integration Software And Consulting

(G-20006)
GILL DESIGN INC
3 Industrial Dr Unit 5 (03087-2014)
PHONE..................................603 890-1237
Joanne Gill, *President*
Michael Gill, *Treasurer*
Milton Stewart, *Admin Sec*
EMP: 8
SALES (est): 1.3MM **Privately Held**
WEB: www.gilldsgn.com
SIC: 3679 8711 Mfg Electronic Components Engineering Services

(G-20007)
GRABBER CONSTRUCTION PDTS INC
Grabber Performance Group
10 Industrial Dr Unit 12 (03087-2018)
PHONE..................................603 890-0455
Ronald F Caterino, *Manager*
EMP: 15
SALES (corp-wide): 1.1B **Privately Held**
WEB: www.jwaorders.com
SIC: 3842 3648 Mfg Surgical Appliances/Supplies Mfg Lighting Equipment
HQ: Grabber Construction Products, Inc.
5255 W 11000 N Ste 100
Highland UT 84003
801 492-3880

(G-20008)
HOMEFREE LLC
10 Industrial Dr Unit 11 (03087-2018)
P.O. Box 491 (03087-0491)
PHONE..................................603 898-0172
Jill G Robbins,
EMP: 20
SQ FT: 9,000
SALES: 750K **Privately Held**
WEB: www.homefreetreats.com
SIC: 2052 Mfg Cookies/Crackers

(G-20009)
MICRO WELD FABTEC CORP
19 Spring St (03087-2382)
P.O. Box 344 (03087-0344)
PHONE..................................603 234-6531
John Lynch, *President*
Soraya Lynch, *Exec Dir*
EMP: 3
SALES (est): 350.5K **Privately Held**
SIC: 3498 7389 Mfg Fabricated Pipe/Fittings Business Services At Non-Commercial Site

(G-20010)
STROLID INC
8 Fletcher Rd (03087-2390)
PHONE..................................978 655-8550
Vinnie Micciche, *CEO*
Anthony Adamo, *Director*
Shawna Behen, *Director*
Josh Sack, *Director*
EMP: 12
SALES (est): 1MM **Privately Held**
SIC: 7372 Prepackaged Software Services

(G-20011)
SUMNER FANCY
Also Called: Salem Press
12 Telo Rd (03087-1151)
PHONE..................................603 893-3081
Sumner Fancy, *Owner*
Kevin Fancy, *Principal*
EMP: 5
SQ FT: 2,400
SALES (est): 306.5K **Privately Held**
WEB: www.auction-tix.com
SIC: 2759 2752 Commercial Printing Lithographic Commercial Printing

(G-20012)
TL SPORTS SALES INC
20 Clarke Farm Rd (03087-1851)
PHONE..................................603 577-1931
Thomas A Labonville, *Principal*
EMP: 3
SALES (est): 333.5K **Privately Held**
SIC: 2759 Commercial Printing

(G-20013)
UNITEC ENGINEERING INC
10 Collins Brook Rd (03087-1840)
PHONE..................................978 764-0553
John P Vincent, *President*
EMP: 17
SQ FT: 25,000
SALES (est): 1.9MM **Privately Held**
SIC: 3542 Mfg Machine Tools-Forming

(G-20014)
WHARF INDUSTRIES PRINTING INC
3 Lexington Rd Unit 2 (03087-5500)
P.O. Box 367 (03087-0367)
PHONE..................................603 421-2566
Michael Comeau, *President*
Jim Conway, *Sales Staff*
Linda Constantin, *Office Mgr*
Jill Mahan, *Graphic Designe*
EMP: 15
SALES (est): 3MM **Privately Held**
WEB: www.wharfindustries.com
SIC: 2752 Offset Printing

▲ = Import ▼=Export
◆ =Import/Export

Wolfeboro
Carroll County

(G-20015)
BLACKSMITH PRTG & COPY CTR LLC
90a Center St (03894)
P.O. Box 1754 (03894-1754)
PHONE..................................603 569-6300
Mark L Jacobs, *Partner*
Carol L Cloutier, *Partner*
J Victor Cloutier, *Partner*
Juliann C Jacobs, *Partner*
EMP: 4
SQ FT: 3,000
SALES: 204.3K **Privately Held**
WEB: www.blacksmithprinting.com
SIC: 2752 7334 Lithographic Commercial Printing Photocopying Services

(G-20016)
BUTTERNUTS GOOD DISHES INC
12 Railroad Ave (03894-4349)
P.O. Box 1041 (03894-1041)
PHONE..................................603 569-6869
Sally J Hunter, *President*
Suzanne Simmon, *Vice Pres*
EMP: 3
SQ FT: 1,200
SALES (est): 328.1K **Privately Held**
SIC: 3262 Mfg Vitreous China Tableware

(G-20017)
GI PLASTEK LLC
5 Wickers Dr (03894-4323)
PHONE..................................603 569-5100
Steve Ettore,
Perry Ashley,
Joel R Carpenter,
Lee Falgous,
Randy G Herman,
▲ **EMP:** 435
SALES (est): 57MM **Privately Held**
SIC: 3089 Mfg Plastic Products

(G-20018)
GI PLASTEK LTD PARTNERSHIP
5 Wickers Dr (03894-4323)
PHONE..................................603 569-5100
James Lyman, *Partner*
Perry Ashley, *Principal*
Walter Beinecke Jr, *Principal*
Wayne Donohue, *Principal*
Graham Gund, *Principal*
EMP: 435
SQ FT: 3,000
SALES (est): 47.8MM **Privately Held**
WEB: www.giplastek.com
SIC: 3089 Mfg Plastic Products

(G-20019)
GLOBAL FILTRATION SYSTEMS
615 Center St (03894-4815)
P.O. Box 2166 (03894-2166)
PHONE..................................603 651-8777
EMP: 6
SALES (est): 850.4K **Privately Held**
SIC: 3589 Mfg Service Industry Machinery

(G-20020)
IMAGE AWNINGS INC
509 S Main St (03894-4458)
PHONE..................................603 569-0680
Eric T Piper, *President*
Jim Kott, *Sales Mgr*
Amy O Piper, *Admin Sec*
EMP: 9
SQ FT: 5,000
SALES: 625K **Privately Held**
WEB: www.imageawnings.com
SIC: 2394 5999 Mfg Canvas/Related Products Ret Misc Merchandise

(G-20021)
KIMBALLS LUMBER CENTER LLC (PA)
Also Called: Kimball Wood Products
25 Varney Rd (03894-4351)
P.O. Box 725 (03894-0725)
PHONE..................................603 569-2477
Paul A Kimball,
EMP: 3
SQ FT: 1,800
SALES (est): 654K **Privately Held**
SIC: 2434 5031 5211 2511 Mfg Wood Kitchen Cabinet Whol Lumber/Plywd/Millwk Ret Lumber/Building Mtrl Mfg Wood Household Furn

(G-20022)
LINK METAL CORPORATION
45 Bay St (03894-4320)
P.O. Box 1512 (03894-1512)
PHONE..................................603 569-5085
Dianne Smallidge, *President*
Nancy Hersey, *Corp Secy*
D Scott Smallidge, *Vice Pres*
EMP: 6
SQ FT: 2,500
SALES: 370K **Privately Held**
SIC: 3451 Manufacture Manufacturing Industries Other

(G-20023)
NEEDHAM ELECTRIC SUPPLY LLC
26 Bay St (03894-4320)
PHONE..................................603 569-0643
Kevin Young, *Principal*
EMP: 6 **Publicly Held**
SIC: 3711 Mfg Motor Vehicle/Car Bodies
HQ: Needham Electric Supply, Llc
5 Shawmut Rd
Canton MA 02021
781 828-9494

(G-20024)
PSI MOLDED PLASTICS NH INC
Also Called: GI Plastek Wolfeboro
5 Wickers Dr (03894-4323)
PHONE..................................603 569-5100
Daniel H Mills, *President*
Rick Collopy, *Vice Pres*
Gerry Gajewski, *Vice Pres*
Steve So, *Vice Pres*
Tad Vaughn, *Vice Pres*
◆ **EMP:** 95
SALES: 25.9MM **Privately Held**
SIC: 3089 Mfg Plastic Products

(G-20025)
SWAFFIELD ENTERPRISES INC
Also Called: Kingswood Press, The
26 Mill St (03894-4353)
P.O. Box 506 (03894-0506)
PHONE..................................603 569-3017
William Swaffield, *President*
Becky Swaffield, *Treasurer*
EMP: 3 **EST:** 1950
SALES (est): 383.5K **Privately Held**
SIC: 2759 3861 Commercial Printing Mfg Photographic Equipment/Supplies

(G-20026)
THIBODEAU LOGGING & EXCAV LLC
6 Partridge Dr (03894-4025)
PHONE..................................603 953-5983
Raymond Thibodeau, *Principal*
EMP: 3
SALES (est): 322K **Privately Held**
SIC: 2411 Logging

(G-20027)
YMAA PUBLICATION CENTER INC
51 Mill St Unit 4 (03894-4361)
P.O. Box 480 (03894-0480)
PHONE..................................603 569-7988
Langley Barbara, *Ch of Bd*
David Ripianzi, *President*
EMP: 7
SALES: 1.2MM **Privately Held**
SIC: 2741 Misc Publishing

Wolfeboro Falls
Carroll County

(G-20028)
PANORAMIC PUBLISHING GROUP LLC
Also Called: Dinning Out -Main Coast
83 Center St (03896)
P.O. Box 119 (03896-0119)
PHONE..................................603 569-5257
Brad Lipe,
EMP: 10
SALES (est): 538.4K **Privately Held**
WEB: www.thelaker.com
SIC: 2711 Newspaper Publisher And Printer

Woodstock
Grafton County

(G-20029)
SPRAY FOAM DISTRS NENG INC
1366 Daniel Wecster Hwy (03293)
PHONE..................................603 745-3911
George Spanos, *President*
Jeff Bailey, *Technical Staff*
EMP: 20
SALES (est): 4.5MM **Privately Held**
SIC: 3612 3523 Mfg Transformers Mfg Farm Machinery/Equipment

Woodsville
Grafton County

(G-20030)
COVENTRY LOG HOMES
108 S Court St (03785-1022)
PHONE..................................603 747-8177
Jeff Elliott, *Principal*
Mark Elliott, *Vice Pres*
Brian Simano, *Prdtn Mgr*
Juanita Belyea, *Sales Staff*
Sean Franson, *Software Dev*
EMP: 30
SQ FT: 4,500
SALES: 3.7MM **Privately Held**
WEB: www.coventryloghomes.com
SIC: 2452 Mfg Prefabricated Wood Buildings

RHODE ISLAND

Ashaway
Washington County

(G-20031)
ASHAWAY LINE & TWINE MFG CO
24 Laurel St (02804-1515)
PHONE..................................401 377-2221
Pamela A Crandall, *President*
Kathryn Crandall, *Vice Pres*
Steven Crandall, *Vice Pres*
Mike McLaughlin, *Facilities Mgr*
Julian Crandall, *Supervisor*
▲ **EMP:** 80 **EST:** 1824
SQ FT: 10,000
SALES (est): 13.3MM **Privately Held**
WEB: www.ashawayusa.com
SIC: 2298 3949 3842 Mfg Cordage/Twine Mfg Sporting/Athletic Goods Mfg Surgical Appliances/Supplies

(G-20032)
BRANTNER AND ASSOCIATES INC
15 Gray Ln Ste 109 (02804-1210)
PHONE..................................401 326-9368
Brian Ravenelle, *Branch Mgr*
EMP: 4
SALES (corp-wide): 13.9B **Privately Held**
SIC: 3229 Mfg Pressed/Blown Glass
HQ: Brantner And Associates, Inc.
1700 Gillespie Way
El Cajon CA 92020
619 562-7070

(G-20033)
EAGLE INDUSTRIES INC
15 Gray Ln Ste 403 (02804-1210)
PHONE..................................401 596-8111
Daniel M Holdridge, *President*
James Holdridge Jr, *Vice Pres*
EMP: 20
SQ FT: 13,100
SALES (est): 4.6MM **Privately Held**
WEB: www.eagleelectric.com
SIC: 3555 8711 Mfg Printing Trades Machinery Engineering Services

(G-20034)
FINISH LINE SIGNS
28 Main St (02804-2228)
PHONE..................................401 377-8454
Brenda Ahern, *Principal*
EMP: 3
SALES (est): 202.4K **Privately Held**
SIC: 3993 Mfg Signs/Advertising Specialties

(G-20035)
GREENVILLE READY MIX INC
Skunk Hill Rd (02804)
PHONE..................................401 539-2333
Ron Gendron, *Principal*
EMP: 4
SALES (est): 318.6K **Privately Held**
SIC: 3273 Mfg Ready-Mixed Concrete

(G-20036)
HI TECH MCH & FABRICATION LLC
15 Gray Ln (02804-1209)
PHONE..................................866 972-2077
EMP: 20
SQ FT: 41,000
SALES (est): 4.3MM
SALES (corp-wide): 87.9B **Privately Held**
SIC: 3443 3469 Manufactures Fabricated Plate Work Metal Stampings
HQ: Hitachi Metals America, Ltd.
2 Manhattanville Rd # 301
Purchase NY 10577
914 694-9200

(G-20037)
HI TECH PROFILES INC
401 Main St (02804-1814)
PHONE..................................401 377-2040
Raymond Quinlan, *President*
Lydia Teixera, *Admin Sec*
▲ **EMP:** 24
SQ FT: 50,000
SALES: 4MM **Privately Held**
WEB: www.hitechprofiles.com
SIC: 3069 Mfg Fabricated Rubber Products

(G-20038)
HITACHI CABLE AMERICA INC
Also Called: High Performance Med Solutions
15 Gray Ln Ste 201 (02804-1210)
PHONE..................................401 315-5100
EMP: 150 **Privately Held**
SIC: 3082 3599 Mfg Unsupported Plastics Profile Shapes/Machine Shop
HQ: Hitachi Cable America Inc.
2 Manhattanville Rd # 301
Purchase NY 10577
914 694-9200

(G-20039)
PRESS TECH COMPANY INC
125 Main St (02804-2239)
P.O. Box 1059 (02804-0010)
PHONE..................................401 377-4800
David McCooey, *President*
William McCooey, *Vice Pres*
Steven McCooey, *Admin Sec*
▲ **EMP:** 4
SQ FT: 4,000
SALES: 1MM **Privately Held**
SIC: 3554 3555 Mfg Paper Industrial Machinery Mfg Printing Trades Machinery

(G-20040)
RICHARD D JOHNSON & SON INC
440 Main St (02804-1817)
PHONE..................................401 377-4312
Charles Johnson, *President*
Robert Johnson, *Vice Pres*
Karen Johnson, *Treasurer*
Richard Johnson, *Treasurer*
EMP: 5
SALES: 500K **Privately Held**
WEB: www.rdjinc.necoxmail.com
SIC: 3544 Mfg Extrusion Dies

(G-20041)
TE CONNCTVITY PHENIX OPTIX INC
15 Gray Ln Ste 301 (02804-1210)
PHONE..................................401 637-4600
Kevin Rock, *President*
EMP: 35
SQ FT: 15,000
SALES: 5.1MM
SALES (corp-wide): 13.9B **Privately Held**
SIC: 3229 Mfg Pressed/Blown Glass
HQ: Te Connectivity Mog Inc.
501 Oakside Ave
Redwood City CA 94063
650 361-5292

Barrington
Bristol County

(G-20042)
A BAILEYS LLC
Also Called: Medici Gelalto
57 Water Way (02806-4760)
PHONE..................................401 252-6002
Jean B Robertson, *President*
Jean Robertson,
Robert Robertson,
EMP: 3
SALES (est): 133.7K **Privately Held**
SIC: 2024 Mfg Ice Cream/Frozen Desert

(G-20043)
BROUILLETTE REALTY LLC
48 Barrington Ave (02806-2317)
PHONE..................................401 499-4867
Donald Brouillette, *Principal*
EMP: 4
SALES (est): 407.5K **Privately Held**
SIC: 2431 Mfg Millwork

(G-20044)
COMPONENT TECHNOLOGIES CORPORA
14 Grizwald Ave (02806)
P.O. Box 22 (02806-0022)
PHONE..................................401 965-2699
Leeds Mitchell, *Owner*
EMP: 4 **EST:** 2010
SALES (est): 263.8K **Privately Held**
SIC: 3369 Nonferrous Metal Foundry

(G-20045)
CORVUS PUBLISHING LLC
221 Washington Rd (02806-1840)
PHONE..................................401 595-8937
Geoffrey Licciardello, *Principal*
EMP: 3
SALES (est): 63.1K **Privately Held**
SIC: 2711 Newspapers-Publishing/Printing

(G-20046)
IMPERIA CORPORATION
306 Rumstick Rd (02806-4935)
PHONE..................................508 894-3000
Edwin S Barton III, *President*
EMP: 50
SQ FT: 48,000
SALES (est): 4.4MM **Privately Held**
WEB: www.imperiacabinet.com
SIC: 2434 2521 2431 Mfg Wood Kitchen Cabinets Mfg Wood Office Furniture Mfg Millwork

(G-20047)
JET ELECTRO-FINISHING CO INC
Also Called: Jet Electro Finishing
408 Middle Hwy (02806-2351)
P.O. Box 139 (02806-0139)
PHONE..................................401 728-5809
Derek Lightbrown, *President*
EMP: 4
SQ FT: 1,100
SALES (est): 451.4K **Privately Held**
WEB: www.jetelectrofinishing.com
SIC: 3471 Plating/Polishing Service

(G-20048)
N-M LETTERS INC
389 Nayatt Rd (02806-4309)
PHONE..................................401 245-5565
Judy Nelsonmintzer, *President*
Michael Mintzer, *Vice Pres*
EMP: 4
SQ FT: 1,800
SALES (est): 331K **Privately Held**
WEB: www.lettersmagazine.com
SIC: 2759 Commercial Printing

(G-20049)
NATIONAL CTHLIC BTHICS CTR INC
119 Bay Spring Ave (02806-1300)
PHONE..................................401 289-0680
EMP: 5
SALES (corp-wide): 1.6MM **Privately Held**
SIC: 2759 Commercial Printing
PA: National Catholic Bioethics Center, Inc.
6399 Drexel Rd
Philadelphia PA 19151
215 877-2660

(G-20050)
ORACLE CORPORATION
3 Veritas Way (02806-2751)
PHONE..................................401 245-1110
Dale Ritter, *Branch Mgr*
EMP: 302
SALES (corp-wide): 39.5B **Publicly Held**
SIC: 7372 Prepackaged Software Services
PA: Oracle Corporation
500 Oracle Pkwy
Redwood City CA 94065
650 506-7000

(G-20051)
PELLA CORPORATION
Also Called: Pella Window Door
39 Baron Rd (02806-4229)
PHONE..................................401 247-0309
EMP: 316
SALES (corp-wide): 1.7B **Privately Held**
SIC: 2431 Mfg Millwork
PA: Pella Corporation
102 Main St
Pella IA 50219
641 621-1000

(G-20052)
PRECISION ELECTROLYSIS NEEDLES
166 Bay Spring Ave (02806-1393)
PHONE..................................401 246-1155
Harry W Cary III, *President*
Joel Cary, *Personnel*
EMP: 10
SQ FT: 7,000
SALES (est): 1.1MM **Privately Held**
WEB: www.uniprobe.com
SIC: 3841 Mfg Surgical Needles Used For Electrolysis

(G-20053)
RHODE ISLAND FAMILY GUIDE
29 Chapin Rd (02806-4406)
P.O. Box 613, Wyoming (02898-0613)
PHONE..................................401 247-0850
Sheryl Rachmil-Etter, *Owner*
EMP: 5 **EST:** 1992
SALES (est): 356.4K **Privately Held**
SIC: 2731 7389 Books-Publishing/Printing

(G-20054)
RLCP INC
Also Called: Des Printing
262 New Meadow Rd (02806-3703)
PHONE..................................401 461-6560
Richard Holiday, *President*
EMP: 20
SQ FT: 15,000
SALES (est): 2.7MM **Privately Held**
SIC: 2759 Commercial Printing

(G-20055)
SIMPATICO SOFTWARE SYSTEMS
15 Blanding Ave (02806-1310)
PHONE..................................401 246-1358
EMP: 10
SALES (corp-wide): 1.5MM **Privately Held**
SIC: 7372 Prepackaged Software Services
PA: Simpatico Software Systems, Inc
20 Altieri Way Unit 3
Warwick RI 02886
401 558-0001

(G-20056)
SONG WIND INDUSTRIES INC
Also Called: Red Lessons Restaurant
6 Stratford Rd (02806-3618)
PHONE..................................401 245-7582
Walter Guertler, *Owner*
EMP: 22
SALES (est): 1.1MM **Privately Held**
SIC: 3999 5812 Mfg Misc Products Eating Place

(G-20057)
WHITESTONE PROVISION SUP CORP (PA)
Also Called: Three Sons Provision
4 Woodmont Ct (02806-4729)
PHONE..................................401 245-1346
John Dire, *President*
EMP: 4
SALES (est): 518.4K **Privately Held**
SIC: 2013 Mfg Prepared Meats

Block Island
Washington County

(G-20058)
MANISSES INC
Also Called: Block Island Times, The
1 Ocean Ave (02807)
P.O. Box 278 (02807-0278)
PHONE..................................401 466-2222
Fraser Lang, *President*
Betty Lang, *Principal*
Lars Trodson, *Editor*
EMP: 7
SQ FT: 400
SALES: 100K **Privately Held**
WEB: www.blockislandguide.com
SIC: 2711 Newspapers-Publishing/Printing

Bristol
Bristol County

(G-20059)
136 EXPRESS PRINTING INC
Also Called: 136 Express Prtg & Copy Ctr
380 Metacom Ave (02809-5152)
PHONE..................................401 253-0136
Richard Luiz, *President*
Lynn Luiz, *Treasurer*
EMP: 8
SALES (est): 580K **Privately Held**
SIC: 2752 Lithographic Commercial Printing

(G-20060)
ALDEN YACHTS CORPORATION
Also Called: Alden Yachts Brokerage
99 Poppasquash Rd Unit I (02809-1033)
PHONE..................................401 683-4200
David A Mac Farlane, *President*
EMP: 60
SALES (est): 7MM **Privately Held**
WEB: www.aldenyachts.com
SIC: 3732 4499 7389 4493 Boatbuilding/Repairing Water Transport Service Business Services Marina Operation

(G-20061)
ALTENLOH BRINCK & CO US INC
Also Called: Es Products
280 Franklin St (02809-3801)
PHONE..................................401 253-8600
Michael Murphy, *Branch Mgr*
EMP: 6
SALES (corp-wide): 370.6MM **Privately Held**
SIC: 3315 Mfg Steel Wire/Related Products
HQ: Altenloh, Brinck & Co. Us, Inc.
2105 Williams Co Rd 12 C
Bryan OH 43506

(G-20062)
APPLIED PLASTICS TECH INC
45 Broadcommon Rd (02809-2721)
P.O. Box 45 (02809-0045)
PHONE..................................401 253-0200
Jane Mac Intyre, *President*
Andrew K Mac Intyre, *Vice Pres*
Lionel Robitaille, *Engineer*
John Mac Intyre, *Treasurer*
Christie Keys, *Controller*
EMP: 35
SQ FT: 20,000
SALES (est): 6.9MM **Privately Held**
WEB: www.ptfeparts.com
SIC: 2821 Mfg Plastic Products

(G-20063)
AQUIDNECK CSTM COMPOSITES INC
69 Ballou Blvd (02809-2729)
PHONE..................................401 254-6911
William Koffler, *CEO*
Kyle A Borsare, *Vice Pres*
EMP: 5
SALES (est): 882.3K **Privately Held**
SIC: 3732 Boatbuilding/Repairing

(G-20064)
BERRY GLOBAL INC
51 Ballou Blvd (02809-2729)
PHONE..................................401 254-0600
Duarte Pimentel, *Principal*
Gina Catalano, *Manager*
EMP: 127 **Publicly Held**
SIC: 3089 Mfg Plastic Products
HQ: Berry Global, Inc.
101 Oakley St
Evansville IN 47710
812 424-2904

(G-20065)
BRISTOL CUSHIONS INC
31 Birchwood Dr (02809-4502)
PHONE..................................401 247-4499
Steve Starrett, *President*
EMP: 14
SQ FT: 7,200
SALES (est): 952.3K **Privately Held**
WEB: www.bristolcushions.com
SIC: 2392 3732 2591 Mfg Household Furnishings Boatbuilding/Repairing Mfg Drapery Hardware/Blinds

(G-20066)
BRISTOL PHOENIX
1 Bradford St (02809-1906)
PHONE..................................401 253-6000
Matt Hayes, *Owner*
EMP: 70
SALES (est): 1.7MM **Privately Held**
SIC: 2711 Newspapers-Publishing/Printing

(G-20067)
C & C FIBERGLASS COMPONENTS
75 Ballou Blvd (02809-2729)
PHONE..................................401 254-4342
Joseph Da Ponte, *President*
Cesar Daponte, *Prgrmr*
EMP: 14
SQ FT: 23,000
SALES (est): 2.4MM **Privately Held**
WEB: www.lemaboats.com
SIC: 3732 Repair Services

(G-20068)
CLEAR CARBON & COMPONENTS INC
108 Tupelo St (02809-2810)
PHONE....................................401 254-5085
Matthew Dunham, *President*
EMP: 12
SQ FT: 13,879
SALES (est): 2.1MM **Privately Held**
SIC: 3931 3543 3544 3624 Mfg Plastic Products Mfg Musical Instruments Mfg Industrial Patterns Mfg Dies/Tools/Jigs/Fixt Mfg Carbon/Graphite Prdt

(G-20069)
COMPOSITE ENERGY TECH INC
Also Called: Goetz Composites
52 Ballou Blvd (02809-2728)
PHONE....................................401 253-2670
Chase Hogoboom, *President*
EMP: 35
SQ FT: 38,000
SALES: 3MM **Privately Held**
SIC: 3624 Mfg Carbon/Graphite Products

(G-20070)
CORRADOS CANVAS & CUSHIONS INC
47 Gooding Ave (02809-2632)
PHONE....................................401 253-5511
Kevin Corrados, *President*
EMP: 3
SALES (est): 289.8K **Privately Held**
SIC: 2394 Mfg Canvas/Related Products

(G-20071)
COVALNCE SPCALTY ADHESIVES LLC
51 Ballou Blvd (02809-2729)
PHONE....................................401 253-2595
Andrew Gibson, *President*
Michele Forsell, *Exec VP*
Scott Lochotzki, *Technician*
EMP: 110 **Publicly Held**
WEB: www.6sens.com
SIC: 3089 Mfg Plastic Products
HQ: Covalence Specialty Adhesives Llc
101 Oakley St
Evansville IN 47710

(G-20072)
DAVIS PRESS
Also Called: Ideal Press
79 Sherry Ave (02809-2522)
PHONE....................................401 624-9331
Edward Davis, *Owner*
EMP: 5
SALES (est): 362.2K **Privately Held**
SIC: 2759 Commercial Printing

(G-20073)
EAST BAY MANUFACTURERS INC
400 Franklin St (02809-3827)
P.O. Box 436 (02809-0436)
PHONE....................................401 254-2960
Lou Victorino, *President*
▲ **EMP:** 14
SQ FT: 10,000
SALES: 1.7MM **Privately Held**
SIC: 3599 Mfg Industrial Machinery

(G-20074)
EAST PASSAGE BOATWRIGHTS INC
257 Franklin St Unit 8 (02809-3830)
PHONE....................................401 253-5535
C Richardson, *Vice Pres*
EMP: 4
SALES (est): 460.3K **Privately Held**
SIC: 3732 Boatbuilding/Repairing

(G-20075)
ELEMENT INDUSTRIES INC
Also Called: Gmt Composites
48 Ballou Blvd (02809-2728)
PHONE....................................401 253-8802
Jonathan Craig, *President*
Cathy Antone, *Human Res Mgr*
EMP: 10
SQ FT: 12,000
SALES: 1.5MM **Privately Held**
WEB: www.gmtcomposites.com
SIC: 3732 Boatbuilding/Repairing

(G-20076)
ELMCO/MPC TOOL COMPANY LLC (PA)
3 Peter Rd (02809-2621)
PHONE....................................401 253-3611
Steven Elmslie, *President*
Michael Reed, *Opers Mgr*
EMP: 4
SALES: 1.5MM **Privately Held**
SIC: 2653 Mfg Corrugated/Solid Fiber Boxes

(G-20077)
ERIC GOETZ CUSTOM SAILBOATS
15 Broadcommon Rd (02809-2721)
PHONE....................................401 253-2670
Eric Goetz, *President*
Peggy Clay, *Hum Res Coord*
◆ **EMP:** 35
SQ FT: 18,000
SALES (est): 5.7MM **Privately Held**
SIC: 3732 Boatbuilding/Repairing

(G-20078)
FISHERMENS DAILY CATCH LLC
70 Sherman Ave (02809-4543)
PHONE....................................401 252-1190
Vasco Rebelo,
EMP: 4
SALES (est): 112K **Privately Held**
SIC: 2711 Newspapers-Publishing/Printing

(G-20079)
FRIENDS HISTORIC BRISTOL INC
495 Hope St Unit 8 (02809-1849)
PHONE....................................401 451-2735
E Keith Maloney, *Ch of Bd*
Alex Papo, *Ch of Bd*
Robert Jacobus, *Director*
Susan Maloney, *Director*
Caroline Jacobus, *Administration*
EMP: 5
SALES (est): 261.9K **Privately Held**
SIC: 2621 Paper Mill

(G-20080)
FV MISTY BLUE LLC
16 Broadcommon Rd (02809-2722)
PHONE....................................609 884-3000
Daniel Cohen,
EMP: 4
SALES (est): 149.8K **Privately Held**
SIC: 3731 Shipbuilding/Repairing

(G-20081)
GALILEAN SEAFOOD INC
16 Broadcommon Rd (02809-2722)
PHONE....................................401 253-3030
Jerry Montopoli, *Ch of Bd*
Mark Montopoli, *President*
EMP: 95
SQ FT: 12,000
SALES (est): 10.6MM **Privately Held**
WEB: www.galileanseafoods.com
SIC: 2092 Mfg Fresh/Frozen Packaged Fish

(G-20082)
GREAT SOUPS INC
Also Called: Cooks Butlr Great Soups Sauces
67 Gooding Ave (02809-2603)
PHONE....................................401 253-3200
EMP: 10
SALES (est): 427.8K **Privately Held**
SIC: 2032 2035 Mfg Fresh Soups & Sauces

(G-20083)
GURIT (USA) INC
Also Called: Gurit Uk
115 Broadcommon Rd (02809-2714)
PHONE....................................401 396-5008
Damian Bannister, *President*
Lance Hill, *Sales Staff*
Sara Watson, *Marketing Staff*
▲ **EMP:** 30
SALES (est): 7.3MM
SALES (corp-wide): 431.7MM **Privately Held**
SIC: 2891 Mfg Adhesives/Sealants
PA: Gurit Holding Ag
Ebnaterstrasse 79
Wattwil SG
719 871-010

(G-20084)
HMC HOLDING CORPORATION (PA)
Also Called: Autospool
68 Buttonwood St (02809-3626)
PHONE....................................401 253-5501
J Michael Doherty, *Ch of Bd*
Peter Martin, *President*
Taras Chwalk, *Exec VP*
▲ **EMP:** 3
SQ FT: 22,000
SALES (est): 3.8MM **Privately Held**
SIC: 3599 Mfg Custom Machinery

(G-20085)
JADE ENGINEERED PLASTICS INC
121 Broadcommon Rd (02809-2714)
PHONE....................................401 253-4440
Steven M Holland, *President*
Lee Holland, *Vice Pres*
Mark Holland, *Vice Pres*
Matt Holland, *Sales Staff*
Lee G Holland, *Sales Executive*
▲ **EMP:** 78 **EST:** 1976
SQ FT: 21,200
SALES (est): 27MM **Privately Held**
WEB: www.jadeplastics.com
SIC: 3053 3089 Mfg Gaskets/Packing/Sealing Devices Mfg Plastic Products

(G-20086)
JOSEPH A THOMAS LTD
24 Broadcommon Rd (02809-2722)
P.O. Box 851 (02809-0998)
PHONE....................................401 253-1330
Joseph Strong, *President*
Ann Strong, *Vice Pres*
▲ **EMP:** 15
SQ FT: 4,800
SALES (est): 1.7MM **Privately Held**
SIC: 3291 3532 3423 Mfg Abrasive Wheels Drill Bits & Hand Tools

(G-20087)
KINDER INDUSTRIES INC
75 Tupelo St (02809-2842)
PHONE....................................401 253-7076
Phillip Kinder, *President*
William Kain, *Vice Pres*
Bill Teixeira, *Sales Mgr*
Jeff Popham, *Executive*
EMP: 12
SALES: 400K **Privately Held**
WEB: www.kinder-industries.com
SIC: 2211 2394 Cotton Broadwoven Fabric Mill Mfg Canvas/Related Products

(G-20088)
KMB INTERNATIONAL
8 Robin Dr (02809-4218)
P.O. Box 6823, Providence (02940-6823)
PHONE....................................401 253-6798
Manuel Furtado, *Owner*
EMP: 12
SALES: 350K **Privately Held**
SIC: 3961 Manufacture Jewelry

(G-20089)
LENMARINE INC (PA)
Also Called: Bristol Marine
99 Poppasquash Rd Unit 1 (02809-1018)
PHONE....................................401 253-2200
Andy Tyska, *President*
Nick King, *Vice Pres*
Chuck Kelley, *Manager*
Brendan Prior, *Manager*
▼ **EMP:** 25
SALES (est): 2.8MM **Privately Held**
WEB: www.bristolmarine.com
SIC: 3732 4493 Boatbuilding/Repairing Marina Operation

(G-20090)
LIGHTHOUSE PUBLICATIONS
30 Bradford St (02809-1907)
P.O. Box 568, Portsmouth (02871-0568)
PHONE....................................401 396-9888
Russell Piersons, *Branch Mgr*
EMP: 3
SALES (corp-wide): 380.1K **Privately Held**
SIC: 2759 Commercial Printing
PA: Lighthouse Publications
350 Kidds Hill Rd
Hyannis MA 02601
508 534-9291

(G-20091)
LUTHERS REPAIR SHOP INC
Also Called: Luther's Welding
500 Wood St (02809-2342)
PHONE....................................401 253-5550
Francis Luther Jr, *President*
Debra Luther, *Treasurer*
Ronald Gamon, *Admin Sec*
EMP: 10
SALES (est): 1.4MM **Privately Held**
WEB: www.lutherswelding.com
SIC: 3441 7692 Structural Metal Fabrication Welding Repair

(G-20092)
M F ENGINEERING COMPANY INC
7 Peter Rd (02809-2621)
P.O. Box 4 (02809-0004)
PHONE....................................401 253-6163
Paul Ferreira, *President*
EMP: 16
SQ FT: 8,750
SALES: 2MM **Privately Held**
WEB: www.mfeng.com
SIC: 3451 Mfg Screw Machine Parts

(G-20093)
MGB MACHINE INC
60 Magnolia St (02809-3333)
P.O. Box 114 (02809-0114)
PHONE....................................401 253-0055
Manuel G Botelho, *President*
EMP: 4
SQ FT: 3,000
SALES (est): 320K **Privately Held**
SIC: 3599 Machine Job Shop

(G-20094)
MOULDCAM INC
115 Broadcommon Rd (02809-2714)
PHONE....................................401 396-5522
John Barnitt, *President*
Jamie Mirima, *Shareholder*
▲ **EMP:** 8
SQ FT: 11,000
SALES (est): 1.3MM **Privately Held**
SIC: 3545 Mfg Machine Tool Accessories

(G-20095)
NEW YORK ACCESSORY GROUP INC
Also Called: I Shalom
500 Wood St Unit 21 (02809-2349)
PHONE....................................401 245-6096
Agnes Mc Laughlin, *Persnl Mgr*
Allen Ferreira, *Manager*
EMP: 65
SALES (corp-wide): 10.7MM **Privately Held**
SIC: 2389 5137 5136 2353 Mfg Apparel/Accessories Whol Women/Child Clothng Whol Mens/Boys Clothing Mfg Hats/Caps/Millinery Mfg Mens/Boys Neckwear
PA: New York Accessory Group, Inc.
411 5th Ave Fl 4
New York NY 10016
212 532-7911

(G-20096)
OUTERLMITS OFFSHORE POWERBOATS
3 Minturn Farm Rd (02809-4072)
PHONE....................................401 253-7300
Michael Fiore, *President*
Jason Cilio, *Opers Mgr*
Kathy Mazzarella, *Purch Mgr*
Donna Fiore, *Supervisor*
▲ **EMP:** 15

GEOGRAPHIC

SALES (est): 2.9MM **Privately Held**
WEB: www.outerlimitspowerboats.com
SIC: 3732 Boatbuilding/Repairing

(G-20097)
PAPER PACKAGING AND PANACHE
418 Hope St (02809-1806)
PHONE..................................401 253-2273
Linda Arruda, *President*
Robert Arruda, *Vice Pres*
EMP: 5
SQ FT: 1,000
SALES: 250K **Privately Held**
SIC: 2678 5947 Mfg Stationery Products Ret Gifts/Novelties

(G-20098)
PHOENIX-TIMES PUBLISHING CO
Also Called: East Bay Newspapers
1 Bradford St (02809-1906)
P.O. Box 90 (02809-0090)
PHONE..................................401 253-6000
Matthew D Hayes, *President*
EMP: 70
SQ FT: 16,000
SALES (est): 4.3MM **Privately Held**
SIC: 2711 Newspapers-Publishing/Printing

(G-20099)
POWERDOCKS LLC
1090 Hope St (02809-1133)
PHONE..................................401 253-3103
Anthony Baro, *Principal*
EMP: 3
SALES (est): 178.8K **Privately Held**
SIC: 3674 Mfg Semiconductors/Related Devices

(G-20100)
RILEY KITCHEN & BATH CO INC
369 Metacom Ave (02809-8523)
PHONE..................................401 253-2205
Michael D Riley, *President*
EMP: 3
SQ FT: 3,000
SALES (est): 330K **Privately Held**
SIC: 2434 Mfg Wood Kitchen Cabinets

(G-20101)
ROBIN INDUSTRIES INC
Also Called: Robin Rug
125 Thames St (02809-1815)
P.O. Box 656 (02809-0656)
PHONE..................................401 253-8350
Russell Karian, *President*
Gordon Karian, *Vice Pres*
EMP: 100 **EST:** 1962
SQ FT: 100,000
SALES (est): 8.8MM **Privately Held**
SIC: 2273 5713 Mfg Carpets/Rugs Ret Floor Covering

(G-20102)
SAINT-GOBAIN PRFMCE PLAS CORP
386 Metacom Ave (02809-5152)
PHONE..................................401 253-2000
J Michael Heller, *Finance*
David Hoague, *Manager*
EMP: 200
SALES (corp-wide): 209.1MM **Privately Held**
SIC: 3089 3229 Mfg Plastic Products Mfg Pressed/Blown Glass
HQ: Saint-Gobain Performance Plastics Corporation
31500 Solon Rd
Solon OH 44139
440 836-6900

(G-20103)
SHANNON BOAT COMPANY INC
Also Called: Shannon Yachts
19 Broadcommon Rd (02809-2768)
PHONE..................................401 253-2441
Walter Schulz, *President*
Morris Kellogg, *Vice Pres*
William Ramos, *Vice Pres*
EMP: 35
SQ FT: 23,000
SALES (est): 4.6MM **Privately Held**
WEB: www.shannonyachts.com
SIC: 3732 Boatbuilding/Repairing

(G-20104)
SYSTEMATICS INC
26 Burnside St (02809-2087)
PHONE..................................401 253-0050
David A Stewart, *President*
Flora C Stewart, *Vice Pres*
EMP: 3
SQ FT: 1,500
SALES: 180.3K **Privately Held**
WEB: www.systinc.com
SIC: 3823 Mfg Process Control Instruments

(G-20105)
THURSTON SAILS INC
112 Tupelo St (02809-2810)
PHONE..................................401 254-0970
Steven K Thurston, *President*
Edward M Thurston, *Vice Pres*
Phyllis Thurston, *Treasurer*
Neil Thurston, *Admin Sec*
▼ **EMP:** 11 **EST:** 1935
SQ FT: 15,000
SALES (est): 1.1MM **Privately Held**
WEB: www.marinemart.com
SIC: 2394 Mfg Custom Made Sails

(G-20106)
TRAFFIC SIGNS & SAFETY INC
70 Ballou Blvd (02809-2728)
PHONE..................................401 396-9840
Thomas F Coyne, *President*
Jay Coyne, *Vice Pres*
EMP: 5
SALES (est): 734K **Privately Held**
SIC: 3993 Mfg Signs/Advertising Specialties

(G-20107)
TRI-MACK PLASTICS MFG CORP
55 Broadcommon Rd 1 (02809-2730)
PHONE..................................401 253-2140
Edward Mack Jr, *President*
Nick Demello, *Project Engr*
Ilya Freydin, *Design Engr*
Mary Popham, *Treasurer*
Roy Teodoro, *Prgrmr*
EMP: 83
SALES (est): 27.5MM **Privately Held**
WEB: www.trimack.com
SIC: 3089 Mfg Plastic Products

(G-20108)
TXV AEROSPACE COMPOSITES LLC
55 Broadcommon Rd Unit 2 (02809-2730)
PHONE..................................425 785-0883
Timothy Herr, *Mng Member*
EMP: 20
SALES (est): 109.8K **Privately Held**
SIC: 2655 Mfg Fiber Cans/Drums

(G-20109)
WARWICK GROUP INC
Also Called: Printsource
8 Burke Rd (02809-3507)
PHONE..................................401 438-9451
EMP: 18 **EST:** 1969
SQ FT: 35,000
SALES (est): 2.4MM **Privately Held**
WEB: www.printsource.com
SIC: 2759 2752 2791 2789 Commercial Printing Lithographic Coml Print Typesetting Services Bookbinding/Related Work

(G-20110)
WESTFALL MANUFACTURING CO
15 Broadcommon Rd (02809-2721)
P.O. Box 7 (02809-0007)
PHONE..................................401 253-3799
Robert W Glanville, *President*
EMP: 10
SQ FT: 10,000
SALES (est): 2.2MM **Privately Held**
WEB: www.westfallmfg.com
SIC: 3589 Mfg Service Industry Machinery

(G-20111)
WOOD ST WOODWORKERS
274 Wood St (02809-3232)
PHONE..................................401 253-8257
EMP: 4
SALES (est): 255.4K **Privately Held**
SIC: 2431 Mfg Millwork

Central Falls
Providence County

(G-20112)
CENTRAL FALLS PROVISION CO
847 High St (02863-2347)
PHONE..................................401 725-7020
Paul Skoczylas, *President*
Mitchell Skoczylas, *Vice Pres*
EMP: 4 **EST:** 1928
SQ FT: 1,400
SALES (est): 380K **Privately Held**
SIC: 2013 Mfg Prepared Meats

(G-20113)
FULLER BOX CO INC
Also Called: Fuller Packaging
1152 High St (02863-1506)
P.O. Box 198 (02863-0198)
PHONE..................................401 725-4300
Peter Fuller, *President*
EMP: 75
SALES (corp-wide): 33.2MM **Privately Held**
WEB: www.fullerbox.com
SIC: 3069 2396 2653 2652 Mfg Fabrcatd Rubber Prdt Mfg Auto/Apparel Trim Mfg Corrugated/Fiber Box Mfg Setup Paperboard Box
PA: Fuller Box Co., Inc.
150 Chestnut St
North Attleboro MA 02760
508 695-2525

(G-20114)
GENERAL POLYMER INC
59 Foundry St (02863-2317)
PHONE..................................401 723-6660
Mark Lord, *President*
EMP: 8 **EST:** 1967
SQ FT: 70,000
SALES (est): 1.8MM **Privately Held**
SIC: 2851 Mfg Paints/Allied Products

(G-20115)
HOPE BUFFINTON PACKAGING INC
575 Lonsdale Ave (02863-2414)
P.O. Box 6250 (02863-0624)
PHONE..................................401 725-3646
Thomas Cavanagh, *CEO*
Gegory Yates, *President*
Douglas Yates, *Vice Pres*
EMP: 50
SALES (est): 7.2MM **Privately Held**
WEB: www.h-bpackaging.com
SIC: 2652 Mfg Setup Paperboard Boxes

(G-20116)
HOPE-BFFNTON PCKGING GROUP LLC
575 Lonsdale Ave (02863-2414)
P.O. Box 6250 (02863-0624)
PHONE..................................401 725-3646
Thomas Cavanagh,
Douglas Yates,
Gregory Yates,
▲ **EMP:** 15
SQ FT: 50,000
SALES (est): 2.9MM **Privately Held**
SIC: 2653 Mfg Corrugated/Solid Fiber Boxes

(G-20117)
K & W WEBBING COMPANY INC
403 Roosevelt Ave (02863-3129)
PHONE..................................401 725-4441
Jerzy Wec, *President*
Stanley Wec, *Treasurer*
Felicia Brasileiro, *VP Sales*
EMP: 18
SQ FT: 20,000
SALES (est): 2.1MM **Privately Held**
SIC: 2241 Narrow Fabric Mill

(G-20118)
LA CASONA RESTAURANT INC
Also Called: La Casona Bakery
768 Broad St (02863-2331)
PHONE..................................401 727-0002
Cristian Tabares, *President*
EMP: 4
SALES (est): 387.2K **Privately Held**
SIC: 2051 5812 Mfg Bread/Related Products Eating Place

(G-20119)
LEEDON WEBBING CO INC
86 Tremont St (02863-1439)
PHONE..................................401 722-1043
Robert Mackenzie, *President*
▲ **EMP:** 50 **EST:** 1941
SQ FT: 50,000
SALES (est): 7.7MM **Privately Held**
WEB: www.leedonwebbing.com
SIC: 2241 Narrow Fabric Mill

(G-20120)
METAL SPRAYING CO INC
900 Lonsdale Ave (02863-1617)
PHONE..................................401 725-2722
Fax: 401 727-0810
EMP: 3 **EST:** 1947
SQ FT: 2,300
SALES (est): 220K **Privately Held**
SIC: 3479 Coating/Engraving Service

(G-20121)
MURDOCK WEBBING COMPANY INC (PA)
27 Foundry St (02863-2348)
PHONE..................................401 724-3000
Craig Pilgrim, *CEO*
Don A De Angelis, *President*
Ed Brodeur, *CFO*
Vann Cummings, *Office Mgr*
▲ **EMP:** 133 **EST:** 1936
SQ FT: 280,000
SALES (est): 31.6MM **Privately Held**
WEB: www.mrdkweb.com
SIC: 2241 Narrow Fabric Mill

(G-20122)
OSRAM SYLVANIA INC
Also Called: Glass Technologies Division
1193 Broad St (02863-1514)
PHONE..................................401 723-1378
Steve Sander, *Manager*
EMP: 300
SQ FT: 50,000
SALES (corp-wide): 3.8B **Privately Held**
WEB: www.sylvania.com
SIC: 3641 3498 3369 Mfg Pressed/Blown Glass Mfg Electric Lamps Mfg Fabrctd Pipe/Fitting Nonferrous Metal Foundry
HQ: Osram Sylvania Inc
200 Ballardvale St # 305
Wilmington MA 01887
978 570-3000

(G-20123)
REED GOWDEY COMPANY
Also Called: Gowdey Reed
325 Illinois St (02863-1935)
PHONE..................................401 723-6114
James H Wilson, *Principal*
▲ **EMP:** 7 **EST:** 1834
SQ FT: 6,000
SALES (est): 439.2K **Privately Held**
WEB: www.gowdeyreed.com
SIC: 3552 Mfg Textile Machinery

(G-20124)
ROSCO LABORATORIES INC
Also Called: Rosco Glame
31 Walnut St (02863-2310)
PHONE..................................401 725-6765
Ray Peltier, *Opers-Prdtn-Mfg*
EMP: 6
SQ FT: 3,500 **Privately Held**
WEB: www.rosco.com
SIC: 2221 Manmade Broadwoven Fabric Mill
HQ: Rosco Laboratories, Inc.
52 Harbor View Ave
Stamford CT 06902
203 708-8900

(G-20125)
ROSCO MANUFACTURING LLC
500 High St (02863-3131)
PHONE..................................401 228-0120
Christopher D'Angelo, *Partner*
EMP: 30 **EST:** 2009
SALES (est): 6.2MM **Privately Held**
SIC: 3599 Mfg Industrial Machinery

(G-20126)
STOLBERGER INCORPORATED
1211 High St (02863-1505)
PHONE....401 724-8800
John Tomaz, *Vice Pres*
▲ **EMP:** 29
SALES (est): 5.7MM **Privately Held**
SIC: 3552 Mfg Textile Machinery

(G-20127)
TOP SHELL LLC
55 Conduit St Unit 1 (02863-1228)
PHONE....401 726-7890
Jack Parente, *Mng Member*
EMP: 11
SALES (est): 1MM **Privately Held**
SIC: 2099 Mfg Food Preparations

(G-20128)
VOGUE INDUSTRIES LTD PARTNR
Also Called: Safety Flag Company
82 Hadwin St (02863-1413)
P.O. Box 200 (02863-0200)
PHONE....401 722-0900
Norman E Bernson, *Managing Prtnr*
James Bernason, *Partner*
Jon Bernson, *General Mgr*
▲ **EMP:** 27
SQ FT: 6,000
SALES: 4MM **Privately Held**
WEB: www.safetyflag.com
SIC: 2399 5084 Mfg Fabricated Textile Products Whol Industrial Equipment

(G-20129)
WHITTET-HIGGINS COMPANY
33 Higginson Ave (02863-2412)
P.O. Box 8 (02863-0008)
PHONE....401 728-0700
Andrew A O Brown, *President*
David A Brown, *Corp Secy*
Susan O Brown, *Vice Pres*
Claire Mongeon, *Financial Exec*
EMP: 50
SQ FT: 38,000
SALES (est): 11.2MM **Privately Held**
WEB: www.whittet-higgins.com
SIC: 3568 Mfg Power Transmission Equipment

Charlestown
Washington County

(G-20130)
BEASLEY WOODWORKS LLC
22 Laurel Rd (02813-2713)
PHONE....401 529-5099
Cyrus Beasley, *Administration*
EMP: 4
SALES (est): 334.7K **Privately Held**
SIC: 2431 Mfg Millwork

(G-20131)
CASTER CRATIVE PHOTOGRAPHY LLC
280 Old Mill Rd (02813-3609)
PHONE....401 364-3545
Donna Caster, *Manager*
EMP: 5
SALES (est): 359.9K **Privately Held**
SIC: 3562 Mfg Ball/Roller Bearings

Chepachet
Providence County

(G-20132)
ADVANCED SELF DEFENSE
1020 Putnam Pike (02814-1465)
P.O. Box 246, Slatersville (02876-0246)
PHONE....401 486-8135
EMP: 3
SALES (est): 150K **Privately Held**
SIC: 3812 Mfg Search/Navigation Equipment

(G-20133)
C&M MFG CO INC
1879 Snake Hill Rd (02814-2514)
PHONE....401 232-9633
Christine L Deluca, *Principal*
EMP: 3
SALES (est): 199.9K **Privately Held**
SIC: 3999 Mfg Misc Products

(G-20134)
FROSTBITE CUPCAKES
230 Chestnut Oak Rd (02814-2145)
PHONE....508 801-6706
Leonard Mello, *Principal*
EMP: 8
SALES (est): 480.1K **Privately Held**
SIC: 2051 Mfg Bread/Related Products

(G-20135)
JOSEF CREATIONS INC (PA)
Also Called: Fairdeal Mfg Co
141 Jackson School Hse Rd (02814-1206)
P.O. Box 72796, Providence (02907-0796)
PHONE....401 421-4198
Michael R Impagliazzo, *President*
Deborah Impagliazzo, *Vice Pres*
Joseph Impagliazzo, *Admin Sec*
◆ **EMP:** 50 **EST:** 1952
SQ FT: 48,000
SALES (est): 4.7MM **Privately Held**
SIC: 3961 2399 3499 3993 Mfg Costume Jewelry Mfg Fabrctd Textile Pdts Mfg Misc Fab Metal Prdts Mfg Signs/Ad Specialties

Coventry
Kent County

(G-20136)
AQUA PHOENIX LIMITED
72 Wood Cove Dr (02816-6615)
PHONE....401 821-2732
EMP: 4
SALES (est): 280K **Privately Held**
SIC: 3592 Mfg Carburetors/Pistons/Rings

(G-20137)
ATLANTIC WATER MANAGEMENT
51 Fieldstone Dr (02816-8722)
P.O. Box 1511 (02816-0030)
PHONE....401 397-8200
Kevin Rabbitt, *General Mgr*
Lee Rabbitt, *Exec VP*
EMP: 3
SQ FT: 500
SALES: 1MM **Privately Held**
WEB: www.atlantic-water.com
SIC: 2899 Water Treatment Products Services And Eqiupment

(G-20138)
BENSON NEPTUNE INC (HQ)
Also Called: Neptune-Benson, LLC
6 Jefferson Dr (02816-6219)
PHONE....401 821-7140
Kenneth Rodi, *CEO*
◆ **EMP:** 40
SALES (est): 16.6MM
SALES (corp-wide): 1.4B **Publicly Held**
SIC: 3589 Mfg Service Industry Machinery
PA: Evoqua Water Technologies Corp.
210 6th Ave Ste 3300
Pittsburgh PA 15222
724 772-0044

(G-20139)
BI MEDICAL LLC
1372 Main St (02816-8436)
PHONE....866 246-3301
John Jarrell, *President*
Elizabeth Stone, *COO*
EMP: 7
SQ FT: 141,000
SALES (est): 422.9K **Privately Held**
SIC: 3841 2869 Mfg Surgical/Medical Instruments Mfg Industrial Organic Chemicals

(G-20140)
CAL CHEMICAL CORPORATION
592 Arnold Rd (02816-4108)
P.O. Box 1452 (02816-0027)
PHONE....401 821-0320
Charles Lamendola, *President*
Chris Lamendola, *CTO*
Joan Lamendola, *Admin Sec*
▲ **EMP:** 20 **EST:** 1961
SQ FT: 40,000
SALES (est): 3.8MM **Privately Held**
SIC: 2869 2819 Mfg Industrial Organic Chemicals Mfg Industrial Inorganic Chemicals

(G-20141)
CEDAR CRAFT FENCE CO
8 Doe Run (02816-4719)
PHONE....401 397-7765
EMP: 6 **EST:** 1957
SALES (est): 450K **Privately Held**
SIC: 2511 2499 5712 5211 Mfg & Ret Cedar Lawn Furniture & Cedar Fences

(G-20142)
COLONIAL MACHINE & TOOL CO INC
5 Salvas Ave (02816-4128)
PHONE....401 826-1883
Harry Masiello, *Owner*
Linda Masiello, *Vice Pres*
EMP: 40 **EST:** 1962
SQ FT: 31,500
SALES: 6MM **Privately Held**
SIC: 3599 Mfg Industrial Machinery

(G-20143)
CONSOLIDATED CONCRETE CORP
10 Reservoir Rd (02816-6400)
PHONE....401 828-4700
George Pesce, *Branch Mgr*
EMP: 5
SALES (corp-wide): 2.7MM **Privately Held**
SIC: 3273 Mfg Ready-Mixed Concrete
PA: Consolidated Concrete Corp.
835 Taunton Ave Unit 1
East Providence RI 02914
401 438-4700

(G-20144)
CUSTOM IRON WORKS INC
1600 Flat River Rd (02816-8904)
PHONE....401 826-3310
Jackie Grace, *President*
Brian Grace, *Vice Pres*
EMP: 10
SQ FT: 2,300
SALES: 1MM **Privately Held**
SIC: 3441 1796 3446 1799 Mfg Architectural Metalwork Trade Contractor

(G-20145)
DIONNE & SONS PIPING DYNAMICS
Also Called: Dionne & Sons Fuel Oil
599 Arnold Rd (02816-4134)
P.O. Box 369 (02816-0007)
PHONE....401 821-9266
Kathy Dionne, *President*
EMP: 5
SALES (est): 653K **Privately Held**
SIC: 1382 Oil/Gas Exploration Services

(G-20146)
ELI ENGINEERING CO INC
354 Hopkins Hill Rd (02816-6332)
PHONE....401 822-1494
Eric Eliason, *President*
Carl E Eliason, *Vice Pres*
Alyce Eliason, *Admin Sec*
EMP: 5
SQ FT: 2,400
SALES (est): 525.4K **Privately Held**
SIC: 3089 Mfg Plastic Products

(G-20147)
GARLAND INDUSTRIES INC
Also Called: Garland Writing Instruments
1 S Main St (02816-5719)
PHONE....401 821-1450
Fax: 401 823-7460
EMP: 30
SQ FT: 65,000
SALES (est): 3.4MM **Privately Held**
WEB: www.garlandpen.com
SIC: 3951 3952 Mfg Pens/Mechanical Pencils Mfg Lead Pencils/Art Goods

(G-20148)
HAWKINS MACHINE COMPANY INC
374 Hopkins Hill Rd (02816-6332)
P.O. Box 315 (02816-0006)
PHONE....401 828-1424
Charles Hawkins, *President*
EMP: 12
SQ FT: 7,500
SALES (est): 1.8MM **Privately Held**
SIC: 3599 Mfg Industrial Machinery

(G-20149)
J & J MACHINING
2059 Victory Hwy (02816-4523)
PHONE....401 397-2782
EMP: 3 **EST:** 2006
SALES (est): 130K **Privately Held**
SIC: 3541 Machining Services

(G-20150)
JIM CLIFT DESIGN INC
Also Called: Www.lapelpinplanet.com
5 Grandview St (02816-4117)
PHONE....401 823-9680
James Clift, *President*
Lynn F Clift, *Vice Pres*
EMP: 5
SQ FT: 4,200
SALES: 900K **Privately Held**
WEB: www.jimclift.com
SIC: 3961 Mfg Costume Jewelry

(G-20151)
JOJOSCUPCAKES LLC
77 Isle Of Capri Rd (02816-6924)
PHONE....401 297-4900
Joann Miller, *Principal*
EMP: 4
SALES (est): 226.1K **Privately Held**
SIC: 2051 Mfg Bread/Related Products

(G-20152)
LA BELLA BRIDE MAGAZINE
13 Northup Plat Rd (02816-6930)
PHONE....401 397-5795
EMP: 3
SALES (est): 174.2K **Privately Held**
SIC: 2721 Periodicals-Publishing/Printing

(G-20153)
LITTLE RHODY MACHINE REPAIR
7 Alice St (02816-7302)
PHONE....401 828-1919
Anita Weikman, *President*
EMP: 13
SQ FT: 6,000
SALES (est): 2.3MM **Privately Held**
WEB: www.lrmr.com
SIC: 3599 Machine Shop Jobbing & Repair Service

(G-20154)
MAGUIRE LACE & WARPING INC
Also Called: Maguire Lace Works
65 Stone St (02816-6153)
PHONE....401 821-1290
Joseph Maguire, *President*
Claire Maguire, *Vice Pres*
EMP: 4
SQ FT: 2,250
SALES (est): 330.4K **Privately Held**
SIC: 3552 2258 Mfg Textile Machinery Lace/Warp Knit Fabric Mill

(G-20155)
MASIELLO ENTERPRISES INC
Also Called: Durfee Enterprises
5 Salvas Ave (02816-4128)
PHONE....401 826-1883
Harry Masiello, *President*
Linda Masiello, *Vice Pres*
EMP: 45
SQ FT: 12,500
SALES (est): 4.2MM **Privately Held**
WEB: www.mercuryserver.com
SIC: 3469 3769 Mfg Metal Stampings Mfg Space Vehicle Equipment

(G-20156)
MIDLAND CO INC
91 Maple Valley Rd (02816-5076)
PHONE....401 397-4425
Louis E Guillemette, *President*

GEOGRAPHIC

Catherine Guillemette, *Vice Pres*
EMP: 3
SQ FT: 5,500
SALES (est): 250K **Privately Held**
SIC: 2258 3732 Mfr Lace & Builds Boats

(G-20157)
MILLER ELECTRIC MFG LLC
11 Grandview St (02816-4121)
PHONE..................................401 828-0087
EMP: 8
SALES (corp-wide): 14.7B **Publicly Held**
SIC: 3548 Mfg Welding Apparatus
HQ: Miller Electric Mfg. Llc
1635 W Spencer St
Appleton WI 54914
920 734-9821

(G-20158)
MTD INC
2471 Flat River Rd (02816-5101)
PHONE..................................401 397-5460
William Mossman, *President*
EMP: 3
SQ FT: 10,000
SALES (est): 200K **Privately Held**
SIC: 3544 Mfg Dies/Tools/Jigs/Fixtures

(G-20159)
MUNROE TOOL CO INC
134 Howard Ave (02816-7768)
PHONE..................................401 826-1040
John H Munroe, *President*
David J Munroe, *Vice Pres*
Mark W Satchell, *Vice Pres*
Gail B Munroe, *Admin Sec*
EMP: 4
SQ FT: 7,200
SALES: 264K **Privately Held**
SIC: 3599 Machine Shop Jobbing And Repair

(G-20160)
NORTHERN INDUSTRIES INC (PA)
429 Tiogue Ave (02816-5579)
PHONE..................................401 769-4305
Richard Bernard, *President*
Normand Champeau, *Admin Sec*
EMP: 8
SQ FT: 4,000
SALES (est): 1.3MM **Privately Held**
WEB: www.northerncoatings.com
SIC: 2851 2899 Mfg Paints/Allied Products Mfg Chemical Preparations

(G-20161)
NOVEMBER DEFENSE LLC
71 Teakwood Dr W (02816-8551)
PHONE..................................401 662-7902
Costantino Natale, *Principal*
EMP: 3
SALES (est): 139K **Privately Held**
SIC: 3812 Mfg Search/Navigation Equipment

(G-20162)
OCEAN STATE SCALE BALANCE LLC
31b Reservoir Rd (02816-6402)
P.O. Box 287, West Warwick (02893-0287)
PHONE..................................401 340-6622
Michael Pariseau,
EMP: 6
SALES (est): 966.8K **Privately Held**
SIC: 3596 Mfg Scales/Balances-Nonlaboratory

(G-20163)
R B L HOLDINGS INC
Also Called: Grate Technologies
6 Jefferson Dr (02816-6219)
PHONE..................................401 821-2200
Robert Lawson,
◆ **EMP:** 12
SQ FT: 10,000
SALES (est): 2.2MM **Privately Held**
SIC: 3089 2541 3272 Mfg Plastic Products Mfg Wood Partitions/Fixtures Mfg Concrete Products

(G-20164)
RHODES PHARMACEUTICALS LP
498 Washington St (02816-5467)
PHONE..................................401 262-9200
Vincent P Mancinelli, *President*
Robert Thebeau, *Vice Pres*
EMP: 13
SALES (est): 117.4MM **Privately Held**
WEB: www.rhodespharma.com
SIC: 2834 Mfg Pharmaceutical Preparations
HQ: Rhodes Associates L.P.
498 Washington St
Coventry RI

(G-20165)
STEVENS PUBLISHING INC
Also Called: Reminder, The
1049 Main St (02816-5706)
P.O. Box 33 (02816-0001)
PHONE..................................401 821-2216
Peter Stevens, *President*
EMP: 10 **EST:** 1954
SQ FT: 2,000
SALES (est): 1MM **Privately Held**
WEB: www.rireminder.com
SIC: 2741 2711 Misc Publishing Newspapers-Publishing/Printing

(G-20166)
TECHTRAK LLC
2435 Nsneck Hl Rd Ste A1b (02816)
PHONE..................................401 397-3983
Thomas Mulligan, *General Mgr*
Jean Ellen, *Technical Staff*
EMP: 7
SQ FT: 1,100
SALES: 2MM **Privately Held**
SIC: 2834 Mfg Pharmaceutical Preparations

(G-20167)
THOMAS ENGINEERING
9 Morin Ave (02816-7421)
PHONE..................................401 822-1235
Thomas Laboissonniere, *President*
Violette Laboissonniere, *Vice Pres*
Kevin V Vandewoestyne, *Plant Supt*
Gregory Vanasse, *Shareholder*
EMP: 7
SQ FT: 2,400
SALES (est): 884.2K **Privately Held**
SIC: 3599 Machine Shop

(G-20168)
TIFFANY PRINTING COMPANY
952 Tiogue Ave (02816-6304)
PHONE..................................401 828-5514
Linda Messina, *President*
Christopher Couture, *Vice Pres*
EMP: 4
SQ FT: 1,500
SALES (est): 419.1K **Privately Held**
WEB: www.tiffanyprinting.com
SIC: 2752 Offset Printing

(G-20169)
TIN MAN FABRICATION INC
161 Pilgrim Ave (02816-4217)
PHONE..................................401 822-4509
Steven Paige, *Principal*
EMP: 4
SALES (est): 372.8K **Privately Held**
SIC: 3356 Nonferrous Rolling/Drawing

(G-20170)
WUERSCH TIME INC
10 Monroe Dr (02816-6202)
PHONE..................................401 828-2525
Joseph Cairns, *President*
EMP: 5
SALES (est): 520.3K **Privately Held**
SIC: 3873 3829 Mfg Watches/Clocks/Parts Mfg Measuring/Controlling Devices

Cranston
Providence County

(G-20171)
ACCENT DISPLAY CORP
1655 Elmwood Ave Ste 9 (02910-4933)
PHONE..................................401 461-8787
Joseph Coury, *President*
Diane Coury, *Corp Secy*
▲ **EMP:** 47
SQ FT: 80,000
SALES (est): 7.4MM **Privately Held**
WEB: www.accentdisplay.com
SIC: 3993 Mfg Signs/Advertising Specialties

(G-20172)
ADI POLISHING INC
81 Calder St (02920-6501)
PHONE..................................401 942-3955
Angelo D Izzo, *President*
EMP: 5
SALES (est): 475.9K **Privately Held**
SIC: 3471 Plating/Polishing Service

(G-20173)
ALERT FIRE PROTECTION INC
40 Starline Way Unit 1 (02921-3446)
PHONE..................................401 261-8836
Alex Lermontov, *President*
EMP: 4
SALES (est): 300K **Privately Held**
SIC: 3569 Mfg General Industrial Machinery

(G-20174)
ALERT SOLUTIONS INC
201 Hillside Rd Ste 2 (02920-5667)
P.O. Box 20160 (02920-0942)
PHONE..................................401 427-2100
David Baeder, *President*
Paul Harrington, *Controller*
Nick Tavaglione, *Sales Mgr*
Crystal Kidd, *Accounts Mgr*
Matthew Puglise, *Accounts Exec*
EMP: 10
SQ FT: 3,000
SALES (est): 1.6MM
SALES (corp-wide): 2.9MM **Privately Held**
WEB: www.blimessaging.com
SIC: 2741 Internet Publishing And Broadcasting
PA: Catalyst Investors, L.P.
711 5th Ave Fl 6
New York NY 10022
212 863-4848

(G-20175)
ALEX AND ANI LLC (PA)
2000 Chapel View Blvd # 360
(02920-3040)
PHONE..................................401 633-1486
Harlan M Kent, *President*
Carolyn Rafaelian, *Principal*
Lisa Cosenza, *Regl Sales Mgr*
▼ **EMP:** 277
SQ FT: 20,000
SALES (est): 299.9MM **Privately Held**
SIC: 3915 5944 Mfg Jewelers' Materials Ret Jewelry

(G-20176)
ALLESCO INDUSTRIES INC (PA)
15 Amflex Dr (02921-2028)
PHONE..................................401 943-0680
Robert A Rotondo Sr, *President*
▲ **EMP:** 125 **EST:** 1999
SALES (est): 17.6MM **Privately Held**
WEB: www.allesco.net
SIC: 3452 5072 Holding Company

(G-20177)
ALLIED GROUP INC (PA)
25 Amflex Dr (02921-2073)
PHONE..................................401 461-1700
Raymond Amore, *CEO*
Robert C Clement, *President*
Barbara Camin, *Vice Pres*
Gene Gagne, *Purchasing*
Richard S Riley, *Treasurer*
EMP: 149 **EST:** 1946
SQ FT: 45,000
SALES (est): 24.8MM **Privately Held**
WEB: www.thealliedgrp.com
SIC: 2782 2761 2759 2671 Mfg Blankbooks/Binders Mfg Manifold Bus Forms Commercial Printing Mfg Packaging Paper/Film

(G-20178)
AMERICAN IRON & METAL USA INC (HQ)
25 Kenney Dr (02920-4443)
PHONE..................................401 463-5605
Herbert Black, *CEO*
Richard Black, *President*
Ronald Black, *Corp Secy*
◆ **EMP:** 41
SQ FT: 2,500
SALES (est): 250.2MM
SALES (corp-wide): 814.3MM **Privately Held**
SIC: 3356 8734 Nonferrous Rolling/Drawing Testing Laboratory
PA: Compagnie Americaine De Fer & Metaux Inc, La
9100 Boul Henri-Bourassa E
Montreal-Est QC H1E 2
514 494-2000

(G-20179)
AMERICAN RING CO INC
Also Called: American Plating
41 Wheatland Ave (02910-4004)
PHONE..................................401 467-4480
Joseph Calandrelli, *Manager*
EMP: 25
SQ FT: 10,000
SALES (corp-wide): 9.5MM **Privately Held**
WEB: www.firstcardco.com
SIC: 3471 Electroplating Of Metals
PA: American Ring Co., Inc.
19 Grosvenor Ave
East Providence RI 02914
401 438-9060

(G-20180)
AMERICAN-INTERNATIONAL TL INDS
99 Calder St (02920-6501)
PHONE..................................401 942-7855
Charles Zayat, *President*
Charles D Zayat Jr, *President*
Elaine Zayat, *Vice Pres*
Victoria Zayat, *Vice Pres*
▲ **EMP:** 4
SQ FT: 3,200
SALES (est): 326.5K **Privately Held**
WEB: www.aittool.com
SIC: 2851 5198 Mfg Paints/Allied Products Whol Paints/Varnishes

(G-20181)
AMSCO LTD INC
35 5th Ave (02910-4903)
PHONE..................................401 785-2860
EMP: 9
SQ FT: 5,500
SALES (est): 1.2MM **Privately Held**
WEB: www.amscoltd.com
SIC: 3961 Mfg Non-Precious Metal Jewelry

(G-20182)
ANCHOR CONCRETE
30 Budlong Rd (02920-6428)
PHONE..................................401 942-4800
Antonio Pezza, *Corp Secy*
EMP: 24 **EST:** 1923
SQ FT: 15,000
SALES (est): 3.3MM **Privately Held**
WEB: www.parkavecementblockco.com
SIC: 3271 3272 Mfg Concrete Block/Brick Mfg Concrete Products

(G-20183)
ANTON ENTERPRISES INC
430 Wellington Ave (02910-2935)
PHONE..................................401 781-3120
Donald Antonelli, *President*
Michael Antonelli, *Vice Pres*
EMP: 12
SQ FT: 1,800
SALES (est): 1.7MM **Privately Held**
WEB: www.antonent-inc.com
SIC: 3471 Plating/Polishing Service

(G-20184)
AUSTRIAN MACHINE CORP
Also Called: A M C Design and Manufacturing
25 Stamp Farm Rd (02921-3401)
PHONE....................................401 946-4090
Marjorie Kern, *President*
Kurt Kern, *Vice Pres*
Tom Costa, *IT/INT Sup*
David Machado, *Admin Sec*
EMP: 10
SQ FT: 15,000
SALES (est): 1.8MM **Privately Held**
WEB: www.austrianmachinecorp.com
SIC: 3555 Mfg Printing Trades Machinery

(G-20185)
AUTOMATIC FINDINGS
19 5th Ave (02910-4903)
PHONE....................................401 781-4810
Patrick Doran, *Partner*
EMP: 3
SQ FT: 4,000
SALES (est): 240K **Privately Held**
WEB: www.automaticfindings.com
SIC: 3915 Manufactures Jewelry Findings

(G-20186)
AVANTI JEWELRY INC
140 Comstock Pkwy Unit 5 (02921-2006)
PHONE....................................401 944-9430
Charles Albanese, *President*
Linda Albanese, *Vice Pres*
EMP: 15
SQ FT: 2,500
SALES (est): 1.8MM **Privately Held**
SIC: 3911 Mfg Precious Metal Jewelry

(G-20187)
B SIGN GRAPHICS INC
141 Rome Dr (02921-2123)
PHONE....................................401 943-6941
Peter Carpentier, *President*
Brenda Carpentier, *Vice Pres*
EMP: 3
SQ FT: 3,000
SALES (est): 311.1K **Privately Held**
WEB: www.bsg.necoxmail.com
SIC: 3993 Mfg Signs/Advertising Specialties

(G-20188)
BATES PLASTICS INC
60 Glen Rd (02920-7995)
PHONE....................................401 781-7711
EMP: 30 **EST:** 1969
SQ FT: 15,000
SALES (est): 282.6K **Privately Held**
SIC: 3089 Injection Molding Of Plastics

(G-20189)
BENNETTS SPORTS INC
900 Phenix Ave (02921-1133)
PHONE....................................401 943-7600
William Bennet, *CEO*
Jennifer Bennett, *Treasurer*
EMP: 5
SQ FT: 1,000
SALES: 800K **Privately Held**
WEB: www.bennettsports.com
SIC: 3949 Mfg Sporting/Athletic Goods

(G-20190)
BNR SUPPLIES
18 Gallup Ave (02910-3929)
PHONE....................................401 461-9132
Morris Rush, *Owner*
Silomena Rush, *Co-Owner*
EMP: 8
SALES: 500K **Privately Held**
SIC: 3841 Mfg Surgical/Medical Instruments

(G-20191)
BOBBY PINS
2208 Broad St (02905-3349)
PHONE....................................401 461-3400
Bobby Pins, *Principal*
EMP: 5 **EST:** 2011
SALES (est): 379.6K **Privately Held**
SIC: 3452 Mfg Bolts/Screws/Rivets

(G-20192)
C SJOBERG & SON INC
415 Station St (02910-2996)
P.O. Box 3583 (02910-0583)
PHONE....................................401 461-8220
Clifford W Sjoberg Jr, *President*
Timothy Sjoberg, *Vice Pres*
Joan Sjoberg, *Admin Sec*
EMP: 11 **EST:** 1946
SQ FT: 7,000
SALES (est): 1.1MM **Privately Held**
WEB: www.sjoberginc.com
SIC: 3469 Mfg Metal Stampings

(G-20193)
CADENCE SCIENCE INC
2080 Plainfield Pike (02921-2012)
PHONE....................................401 942-1031
Peter Harris, *Ch of Bd*
Alan Connor, *President*
Brian Plummer, *Vice Pres*
EMP: 200
SQ FT: 18,500
SALES: 32MM
SALES (corp-wide): 55MM **Privately Held**
WEB: www.olfablades.com
SIC: 3841 Mfg Surgical/Medical Instruments
PA: Cadence, Inc.
9 Technology Dr
Staunton VA 24401
540 248-2200

(G-20194)
CAPITOL STATIONERY COMPANY
1286 Cranston St (02920-6722)
PHONE....................................401 943-5333
Alexander P Agronick, *President*
EMP: 5
SQ FT: 7,000
SALES (est): 900K **Privately Held**
WEB: www.rioffice.com
SIC: 2754 5943 Gravure Commercial Printing Ret Stationery

(G-20195)
CARLOW ORTHPD & PROSTHETIC INC (PA)
1580 Pontiac Ave Ste 2 (02920-4487)
PHONE....................................203 483-8488
David Mahler, *President*
Warren Carlow, *President*
Linda Carlow, *Corp Secy*
EMP: 4 **EST:** 1972
SQ FT: 800
SALES (est): 499K **Privately Held**
SIC: 3842 Mfg Orthopedic Braces & Artificial Limbs

(G-20196)
CHEM-TAINER INDUSTRIES INC
Also Called: Todd Enterprises
530 Wellington Ave Ste 5 (02910-2950)
PHONE....................................401 467-2750
John Duffy, *CEO*
EMP: 70
SALES (corp-wide): 44.3MM **Privately Held**
WEB: www.chemtainer.com
SIC: 3089 3732 Mfg Plastic Products Boatbuilding/Repairing
PA: Chem-Tainer Industries Inc.
361 Neptune Ave
West Babylon NY 11704
631 422-8300

(G-20197)
COASTAL AQUACULTURAL SUPPLY
100 Glen Rd (02920-7947)
P.O. Box 8066 (02920-0066)
PHONE....................................401 467-9370
Brian Bowes, *President*
EMP: 5 **EST:** 1995
SALES (est): 307.7K **Privately Held**
WEB: www.coastalaquacultural.com
SIC: 3523 Mfg Farm Machinery/Equipment

(G-20198)
COCOFUEL
39 Ashburton Dr (02921-3410)
PHONE....................................401 209-8099
EMP: 6
SALES (est): 354.3K **Privately Held**
SIC: 2099 Mfg Food Preparations

(G-20199)
COLE CABINET CO INC
530 Wellington Ave (02910-2950)
PHONE....................................401 467-4343
Gene Orsi, *President*
EMP: 10
SQ FT: 5,000
SALES (est): 1.7MM **Privately Held**
WEB: www.colecabinets.com
SIC: 2541 5712 Mfg Wood Partitions/Fixtures Ret Furniture

(G-20200)
COOLEY INCORPORATED
5 Slater Rd (02920-4458)
PHONE....................................401 721-6374
Naresh Mehta, *Manager*
EMP: 20
SALES (corp-wide): 105.7MM **Privately Held**
WEB: www.cooleygroup.com
SIC: 2295 Mfg Coated Fabrics
HQ: Cooley, Incorporated
50 Esten Ave
Pawtucket RI 02860
401 724-9000

(G-20201)
COPY PRINT COMPANY
Also Called: Copy Print/Etc
176 N View Ave (02920-4809)
PHONE....................................401 228-3900
Lisa Nofi, *President*
EMP: 6
SQ FT: 13,000
SALES (est): 520K **Privately Held**
WEB: www.copyprint.net
SIC: 2752 7334 2791 2741 Commercial Printing Photocopying Typesetting And Desktop Publishing

(G-20202)
CRANSTON PRINT WORKS COMPANY (PA)
Also Called: C P W
1381 Cranston St (02920-6789)
PHONE....................................401 943-4800
Frederic Rockefeller Jr, *CEO*
James Thorpe, *Principal*
Fred Rockefeller, *Treasurer*
Mark Jones, *VP Finance*
Mary Shalkowski, *Asst Controller*
▲ **EMP:** 32
SQ FT: 400,000
SALES (est): 147.3MM **Privately Held**
WEB: www.cpw.com
SIC: 2261 2262 2899 Cotton Finishing Plant Manmade Fabric Fnshg Plt Mfg Chemical Preparation

(G-20203)
CRANSTON PRINT WORKS COMPANY
Also Called: Bercen Division
1381 Cranston St (02920-6789)
PHONE....................................800 525-0595
Jim Thorpe, *Branch Mgr*
EMP: 30
SALES (corp-wide): 147.3MM **Privately Held**
WEB: www.cpw.com
SIC: 2261 2262 Printer And Finisher Of Craft And Fashion Fabrics
PA: Cranston Print Works Company Inc
1381 Cranston St
Cranston RI 02920
401 943-4800

(G-20204)
CREATIVE DIGITAL INC
85 Wildflower Dr (02921-2327)
PHONE....................................401 942-0771
Joan Newell, *President*
Craig Newell, *Vice Pres*
EMP: 5
SQ FT: 1,400
SALES: 220K **Privately Held**
SIC: 2791 7384 8748 Typesetting Service Bureau & Film Processing

(G-20205)
CROSSTOWN PRESS INC
Also Called: Confidential Copy
829 Park Ave (02910-2037)
PHONE....................................401 941-4061
Steven H Levy, *President*
Bernard Levy, *Corp Secy*
EMP: 17
SQ FT: 8,000
SALES (est): 2.3MM **Privately Held**
WEB: www.crosstownpress.com
SIC: 2752 Lithographic Commercial Printing

(G-20206)
CUSTOM COMPOSITE MFG INC
21 Palmer Ave (02920-6533)
PHONE....................................401 275-2230
Barry McCoy, *President*
EMP: 3
SALES: 150K **Privately Held**
WEB: www.cc-mfg.com
SIC: 3842 Mfg Surgical Appliances/Supplies

(G-20207)
CX THIN FILMS LLC
1515 Elmwood Ave (02910-3800)
PHONE....................................401 461-5500
David Diraffaele,
EMP: 10
SALES (est): 398.2K **Privately Held**
SIC: 3676 Mfg Electronic Resistors

(G-20208)
DEAN MACHINE INCORPORATED
25 Sharpe Dr (02920-4402)
PHONE....................................401 919-5100
David Maynard, *President*
Paul Caito, *Vice Pres*
EMP: 25
SQ FT: 25,000
SALES (est): 4.4MM **Privately Held**
WEB: www.deanmachine.net
SIC: 3599 Mfg Industrial Machinery

(G-20209)
DESIGN FABRICATORS INC
72 Stamp Farm Rd (02921-3400)
PHONE....................................401 944-5294
Robin Degraide, *President*
EMP: 35
SQ FT: 37,500
SALES (est): 6.4MM **Privately Held**
SIC: 2431 Mfg Millwork

(G-20210)
DIFRUSCIA INDUSTRIES INC
1425 Cranston St (02920-6739)
PHONE....................................401 943-9900
Frank A Defruscio, *President*
EMP: 27
SQ FT: 29,000
SALES (est): 5.5MM **Privately Held**
WEB: www.difruscia.com
SIC: 3479 Coating/Engraving Service

(G-20211)
DIG RITE COMPANY INC
311 Pippin Orchard Rd (02921-3608)
PHONE....................................401 862-5895
Morris Maglioli, *President*
Tracy Pine, *Principal*
EMP: 3 **EST:** 2010
SALES (est): 141.7K **Privately Held**
SIC: 3531 1389 5082 Mfg Construction Machinery Oil/Gas Field Services Whol Construction/Mining Equipment

(G-20212)
DINA INC
357 Dyer Ave (02920-7008)
PHONE....................................401 942-9633
Lois Bordieri, *President*
John Bordieri, *Vice Pres*
EMP: 8 **EST:** 1972
SQ FT: 1,500
SALES (est): 650K **Privately Held**
WEB: www.dina-inc.com
SIC: 3961 5944 Mfg Costume Jewelry Ret Jewelry

(G-20213)
EAGLE PATTERN & CASTING CO
14 Oneida St (02920-7311)
PHONE....................................401 943-7154
Harry Constantino, *President*
EMP: 4
SQ FT: 10,000

GEOGRAPHIC

SALES: 300K **Privately Held**
SIC: 3543 Mfg Industrial Wood & Metal Patterns

(G-20214)
EASTERN SCREW COMPANY
15 Amflex Dr (02921-2028)
PHONE..................................401 943-0680
Robert Rotondo, *President*
▲ **EMP**: 125 **EST**: 1963
SQ FT: 42,000
SALES (est): 14MM
SALES (corp-wide): 17.6MM **Privately Held**
WEB: www.easternscrew.com
SIC: 3452 5072 Mfg Bolts/Screws/Rivets Whol Hardware
PA: Allesco Industries, Inc.
15 Amflex Dr
Cranston RI 02921
401 943-0680

(G-20215)
ELECTRO STANDARDS LAB INC
Also Called: Electro Standards Laboratories
36 Western Industrial Dr (02921-3403)
PHONE..................................401 946-1390
Raymond B Sepe, *President*
Kenneth Sepe, *Vice Pres*
Raymond B Sepe Jr, *Vice Pres*
Michael Sepe, *Treasurer*
Brenda Bucci, *CIO*
EMP: 63 **EST**: 1976
SQ FT: 25,000
SALES (est): 15.7MM **Privately Held**
WEB: www.electrostandards.com
SIC: 3577 8731 7373 3661 Mfg Computer Peripherals Coml Physical Research Computer Systems Design Mfg Telephone/Graph Eqip Mfg Misc Fab Wire Prdts

(G-20216)
ELMWOOD COUNTERTOP INC
50 Webb St (02920-7923)
PHONE..................................401 785-1677
Thomas Roselli, *President*
Thomas G Roselli, *President*
EMP: 9 **EST**: 1980
SQ FT: 6,000
SALES (est): 1.1MM **Privately Held**
WEB: www.elmwoodcountertop.com
SIC: 2541 Mfg Wood Partitions/Fixtures

(G-20217)
ENERGY MGT & CTRL SVCS INC
Also Called: EMC SERVICES
116 Budlong Rd (02920-6428)
PHONE..................................401 946-1440
James Jones, *President*
Wendy Roskowski, *Vice Pres*
EMP: 17
SQ FT: 3,200
SALES: 10.1MM **Privately Held**
WEB: www.emccontrols.net
SIC: 3822 5075 1731 Mfg Environmental Controls Whol Heat/Air Cond Equipment/Supplies Electrical Contractor

(G-20218)
ENPURE PROCESS SYSTEMS INC
54 Ingleside Ave (02905-2611)
PHONE..................................401 447-3976
Steven Bloom, *President*
Frederick Clark, *Vice Pres*
EMP: 4 **EST**: 2008
SQ FT: 3,000
SALES (est): 549.8K **Privately Held**
SIC: 3589 Mfg Service Industry Machinery

(G-20219)
EPOXIES INC
Also Called: Epoxies, Etc
21 Starline Way (02921-3407)
PHONE..................................401 946-5564
Michael Harrington, *President*
Paul Harrington, *Vice Pres*
EMP: 15
SQ FT: 15,000
SALES (est): 1.4MM **Privately Held**
SIC: 2891 2869 Mfg Adhesives/Sealants Mfg Industrial Organic Chemicals

(G-20220)
ESMOND MANUFACTURING COMPANY
169 N View Ave (02920-4832)
PHONE..................................401 942-9103
Jerry Dionne, *President*
EMP: 8
SQ FT: 6,000
SALES (est): 830K **Privately Held**
SIC: 3451 Mfg Automatic Screw Machine Products

(G-20221)
ESTATE AGENCY INC (PA)
Also Called: Bak Precision Industries
1001 Reservoir Ave (02910-5134)
PHONE..................................401 942-0700
Ralph Sacco III, *President*
Brad Sacco, *Treasurer*
EMP: 4 **EST**: 1956
SQ FT: 2,600
SALES (est): 375.7K **Privately Held**
WEB: www.theestateagency.com
SIC: 3599 Machine Shop

(G-20222)
ESTATE AGENCY INC
Also Called: Bak Precision Industries
25 Western Industrial Dr (02921-3406)
PHONE..................................401 946-5380
John Wetmore, *Foreman/Supr*
Ralph Sacco, *Systems Mgr*
EMP: 7
SALES (est): 736.6K
SALES (corp-wide): 375.7K **Privately Held**
WEB: www.theestateagency.com
SIC: 3545 Mfg Machine Tool Accessories
PA: The Estate Agency Inc
1001 Reservoir Ave
Cranston RI 02910
401 942-0700

(G-20223)
FACO METAL PRODUCTS INC
22 Thunder Trl (02921-2564)
PHONE..................................401 943-7127
William A Rose, *President*
Craig A Rose, *Vice Pres*
Kyle A Rose, *Treasurer*
EMP: 14
SQ FT: 20,000
SALES (est): 750K **Privately Held**
SIC: 3873 3469 Mfg Clock Hands & Metal Stampings

(G-20224)
FASANO CORP
333 Wellington Ave (02910-1338)
PHONE..................................401 785-9646
Albert Fasano, *President*
Ronald Fasano, *Vice Pres*
EMP: 5 **EST**: 1973
SQ FT: 4,400
SALES (est): 300K **Privately Held**
WEB: www.fasanocorp.com
SIC: 3451 Mfg Screw Machine Products

(G-20225)
FEDERAL ELECTRONICS INC
75 Stamp Farm Rd (02921-3401)
PHONE..................................401 944-6200
Romolo Evangelista, *President*
Richard Evangelista, *President*
Edward Evangelista, *Vice Pres*
EMP: 100
SQ FT: 42,000
SALES (est): 44MM **Privately Held**
WEB: www.federalelec.com
SIC: 3679 Mfg Electronic Components

(G-20226)
FIELDING MANUFACTURING INC
780 Wellington Ave (02910-2941)
PHONE..................................401 461-0400
Steven P Fielding, *President*
EMP: 45
SQ FT: 250,000
SALES (est): 9.8MM **Privately Held**
WEB: www.fieldingmfg.com
SIC: 3089 3544 3369 3364 Mfg Plastic Products Mfg Dies/Tools/Jigs/Fixt Nonferrous Metal Foundry Mfg Nonfrs Die-Castings

(G-20227)
FIELDING MFG ZINC DIECASTING
Also Called: Fielding Manufacturing
780 Wellington Ave (02910-2941)
PHONE..................................401 461-0400
Steven P Fielding, *President*
EMP: 55
SQ FT: 26,000
SALES (est): 7.5MM **Privately Held**
SIC: 3545 3364 Mfg Die-Casting Tools & Zinc Die-Castings

(G-20228)
FRI RESINS HOLDING COMPANY
Also Called: Epoxies, Etc
21 Starline Way (02921-3407)
PHONE..................................401 946-5564
Michael Harrington, *President*
Paul Harrington, *Vice Pres*
▲ **EMP**: 15
SQ FT: 20,000
SALES (est): 3.4MM
SALES (corp-wide): 45.6MM **Privately Held**
WEB: www.epoxies.com
SIC: 2891 2851 2869 Mfg Adhesives/Sealants Mfg Paints/Allied Products Mfg Industrial Organic Chemicals
PA: Meridian Adhesives Group Llc
100 Park Ave Fl 31
New York NY 10017
212 771-1717

(G-20229)
GANNON & SCOTT INC
33 Kenney Dr (02920-4480)
PHONE..................................401 463-5550
Ken Dionne, *CEO*
John Gannon, *President*
Gary Leonhardt, *Regional Mgr*
Lisa Spicuzza, *Purchasing*
David G Deuel, *CFO*
▲ **EMP**: 60
SQ FT: 40,000
SALES (est): 13.8MM **Privately Held**
WEB: www.gannon-scott.com
SIC: 3341 Secondary Nonferrous Metal Producer

(G-20230)
GASBARRE PRODUCTS INC
C I Hayes
81 Western Industrial Dr A (02921-3444)
PHONE..................................401 467-5200
Alex Gasbarre, *CEO*
Thomas Gasbarre, *President*
Mark Saline, *President*
Bob Brodeur, *Engineer*
Paul Chamberlain, *Sales Engr*
EMP: 10
SALES (corp-wide): 40MM **Privately Held**
WEB: www.gasbarre.com
SIC: 3567 3549 3542 Mfg Industrial Furnaces/Ovens Mfg Metalworking Machinery Mfg Machine Tools-Forming
PA: Gasbarre Products, Inc.
590 Division St
Du Bois PA 15801
814 371-3015

(G-20231)
GEM-CRAFT INC
1420 Elmwood Ave (02910-3847)
PHONE..................................401 854-1200
Ronald Verri, *President*
EMP: 20
SQ FT: 20,000
SALES (est): 2.6MM **Privately Held**
SIC: 3911 Mfg Precious Metal Jewelry

(G-20232)
GENNARO INC
1725 Pontiac Ave (02920-4477)
PHONE..................................401 632-4100
Steve Casinelli, *President*
John Wakim, *President*
Beverly Casinelli, *Corp Secy*
Sharon Rapoza, *Vice Pres*
▲ **EMP**: 15
SQ FT: 12,000
SALES (est): 2.8MM **Privately Held**
SIC: 3961 Mfg Costume Jewelry

(G-20233)
GREAT AMERICAN RECRTL EQP
24 Stafford Ct (02920-4464)
PHONE..................................401 463-5587
David Celani, *President*
▲ **EMP**: 32
SALES (est): 3.1MM **Privately Held**
WEB: www.greatamericanrec.com
SIC: 3949 Mfg Sporting/Athletic Goods

(G-20234)
GRENADE (USA) LLC
815 Reservoir Ave Ste 1a (02910-4442)
PHONE..................................401 944-3960
Gregg Madsen,
EMP: 5
SALES (est): 322.6K **Privately Held**
SIC: 3949 Mfg Sporting/Athletic Goods

(G-20235)
GRIND
1401 Park Ave Unit 1 (02920-6669)
PHONE..................................401 223-1212
Lori Vota, *Principal*
EMP: 3
SALES (est): 272.3K **Privately Held**
SIC: 3599 Mfg Industrial Machinery

(G-20236)
GRINNELL CABINET MAKERS INC
169 Mill St (02905-1017)
PHONE..................................401 781-1080
Scott Grinnell, *President*
EMP: 35
SQ FT: 80,000
SALES (est): 4.6MM **Privately Held**
WEB: www.grinnellcabinet.com
SIC: 2431 Mfg Millwork

(G-20237)
HOUSE OF STAINLESS INC
Also Called: Scott Brass
1637 Elmwood Ave (02910-4937)
PHONE..................................800 556-3470
Curt Burhoe, *President*
Jay Champi, *Accounts Mgr*
Richard Burkhart, *Admin Sec*
Richard Berg, *Representative*
▲ **EMP**: 35
SALES (est): 11.3MM **Privately Held**
SIC: 3351 Copper Rolling/Drawing

(G-20238)
HUDSON LIQUID ASPHALTS INC (PA)
2000 Chapel View Blvd # 380 (02920-3040)
PHONE..................................401 274-2200
Matthew J Gill, *President*
Francis J O'Brien, *President*
Tom Hudson, *Owner*
Edward R Lodge Jr, *Senior VP*
John J Hudson, *Vice Pres*
▲ **EMP**: 70
SALES (est): 28.6MM **Privately Held**
SIC: 2951 Mfg Asphalt Mixtures/Blocks

(G-20239)
HUDSON TERMINAL CORP
Also Called: Hudson Company
2000 Chapel View Blvd # 380 (02920-3040)
PHONE..................................401 941-0500
Denis Leamy, *Manager*
EMP: 8
SALES (corp-wide): 2.5MM **Privately Held**
SIC: 3531 Mfg Construction Machinery
PA: Hudson Terminal Corp.
29 Terminal Rd
Providence RI 02905
401 274-2200

(G-20240)
INTERIOR WDWKG SOLUTIONS INC
47 Pettaconsett Ave (02920-7914)
PHONE..................................401 261-6329
Brian Franco, *Principal*
▲ **EMP**: 4 **EST**: 2009
SALES (est): 456.3K **Privately Held**
SIC: 2431 Mfg Millwork

(G-20241)
IRA HOLTZ & ASSOCIATES
2220 Plainfield Pike 4w (02921-2031)
PHONE..................................401 521-8960
Ira Holtz, *President*
EMP: 3
SQ FT: 2,200
SALES (est): 393.2K **Privately Held**
SIC: 3961 Mfg Costume Jewelry

(G-20242)
ISELANN MOSS INDUSTRIES INC
41 Slater Rd (02920-4466)
PHONE..................................401 463-5950
Mark Wolstenholme, *President*
Gary Mason, *Treasurer*
EMP: 19 **EST:** 1969
SQ FT: 12,000
SALES (est): 3.5MM **Privately Held**
WEB: www.iselann-moss.com
SIC: 3069 Mfg Fabricated Rubber Products

(G-20243)
JAHRLING OCULAR PROSTHETICS
120 Dudley St Ste 202 (02905-2429)
PHONE..................................401 454-4168
Raymond Jahrling, *Branch Mgr*
EMP: 3
SQ FT: 720
SALES (est): 252.7K
SALES (corp-wide): 855.2K **Privately Held**
SIC: 3842 8011 Mfg Surgical Appliances/Supplies Medical Doctor's Office
PA: Jahrling Ocular Prosthetics Inc
50 Staniford St Fl 8
Boston MA 02114
617 523-2280

(G-20244)
JJI INTERNATIONAL INC
Also Called: Jolie Jewels
1 Weingeroff Blvd (02910-4009)
P.O. Box 603334, Providence (02906-0734)
PHONE..................................401 780-8668
Lisa Weingeroff, *President*
▲ **EMP:** 25
SALES (est): 4MM **Privately Held**
WEB: www.jjiinternational.com
SIC: 3961 Mfg Precious Metal Jewelry

(G-20245)
JMT EPOXY
25 Western Industrial Dr # 3 (02921-3406)
PHONE..................................401 331-9730
Joanne Gadwah, *Owner*
EMP: 4
SALES (est): 350.1K **Privately Held**
SIC: 2891 Mfg Adhesives/Sealants

(G-20246)
JOMAY INC
66 Libera St (02920-2525)
PHONE..................................401 944-5240
Joseph Lavallee, *President*
Marion Lavallee, *Vice Pres*
EMP: 12
SALES (est): 1.1MM **Privately Held**
SIC: 3911 5094 Mfg Precious Metal Jewelry Whol Jewelry/Precious Stones

(G-20247)
JRB ASSOCIATES INC
Also Called: G & A Plating & Polishing Co
2 2nd Ave (02910-4923)
PHONE..................................401 351-8693
Jim Brown, *President*
Doug James, *General Mgr*
Douglas James, *General Mgr*
EMP: 24
SALES (est): 2.3MM **Privately Held**
SIC: 3471 Plating/Polishing Service

(G-20248)
KINGSTON KRAFTS
15 Industrial Rd Unit 2 (02920-6771)
PHONE..................................401 272-0292
EMP: 3
SALES (est): 109.4K **Privately Held**
SIC: 2599 Mfg Furniture/Fixtures

(G-20249)
KIRK ELECTRONICS & PLASTIC
85 Glen Rd (02920-7913)
PHONE..................................401 467-8585
John Kirk, *President*
EMP: 3
SQ FT: 6,072
SALES (est): 265.5K **Privately Held**
SIC: 3643 Mfg Conductive Wiring Devices

(G-20250)
LANDA PRESSURE WASHERS OF RI
11 Comstock Pkwy (02921-2003)
PHONE..................................401 463-8303
David Mignacca, *President*
EMP: 6
SALES (est): 553.8K **Privately Held**
SIC: 3589 Mfg Service Industry Machinery

(G-20251)
LAVIGNE MANUFACTURING INC
15 Western Industrial Dr (02921-3402)
PHONE..................................401 490-4627
David T Lavigne, *President*
Daniel W Lavigne, *Vice Pres*
Daniel Lavigne, *Vice Pres*
Stuart Shechtman, *CFO*
Gerard E Lavigne, *Treasurer*
EMP: 110
SQ FT: 35,000
SALES (est): 20.5MM **Privately Held**
WEB: www.lavignemfg.com
SIC: 3599 Mfg Industrial Machinery

(G-20252)
LDB TOOL AND FINDINGS INC
Also Called: LDB Manufacturing
2380 Plainfield Pike (02921-2037)
PHONE..................................401 944-6000
Lorenzo Di Biasio Jr, *President*
Lawrence Kent, *Manager*
EMP: 5
SQ FT: 7,000
SALES (est): 480K **Privately Held**
SIC: 3496 3541 3569 Mfg Misc Fabricated Wire Products Mfg Machine Tools-Cutting Mfg General Industrial Machinery

(G-20253)
LEWIS GRAPHICS INC
269 Macklin St (02920-6521)
PHONE..................................401 943-8300
Fax: 401 943-8301
EMP: 9
SQ FT: 10,000
SALES: 1MM **Privately Held**
WEB: www.lewisgraphics.com
SIC: 2752 Commercial Printing Lithographic

(G-20254)
LIM JEWELRY
90 Libera St Ste 12 (02920-2500)
PHONE..................................401 946-9656
Rock Lim, *Owner*
EMP: 3
SALES: 250K **Privately Held**
SIC: 3911 Mfg Precious Metal Jewelry

(G-20255)
LINCOLN PACKING CO
7 Industrial Rd (02920-6796)
PHONE..................................401 943-0878
Giovanni A Colagiovanni, *CEO*
Vincent Colagiovanni, *Vice Pres*
EMP: 29 **EST:** 1957
SQ FT: 7,000
SALES (est): 6MM **Privately Held**
SIC: 2013 5147 2011 Mfg Prepared Meats Whol Meats/Products Meat Packing Plant

(G-20256)
LUV2BU INC
17 Yard St (02920-2332)
PHONE..................................401 612-9585
Sheryl Perretta, *President*
EMP: 9
SALES (est): 391.8K **Privately Held**
SIC: 3841 Mfg Surgical/Medical Instruments

(G-20257)
MAG JEWELRY CO INC
838 Dyer Ave (02920-6714)
PHONE..................................401 942-1840
Daniel J Magnanimi, *President*
EMP: 40 **EST:** 1951
SQ FT: 14,000
SALES (est): 7.5MM **Privately Held**
SIC: 3911 3961 Mfg Precious Metal Jewelry Mfg Costume Jewelry

(G-20258)
MALCO SAW CO INC
22 Field St (02920-7395)
PHONE..................................401 942-7380
Austin Livesey, *CEO*
Gregory Livesey, *President*
EMP: 7 **EST:** 1939
SALES (est): 780K **Privately Held**
WEB: www.malcosaw.com
SIC: 3425 3546 3541 Mfg Saw Blades/Handsaws Mfg Powerdriven Handtool Mfg Machine Tool-Cutting

(G-20259)
MARCELLO SAUSAGE CO
7 Industrial Rd (02920-6715)
PHONE..................................401 275-1952
EMP: 16
SQ FT: 3,000
SALES (est): 2MM **Privately Held**
SIC: 2013 Mfg Prepared Meats

(G-20260)
MEARTHANE PRODUCTS CORPORATION (PA)
16 Western Industrial Dr (02921-3405)
PHONE..................................401 946-4400
Kevin C Redmond, *CEO*
◆ **EMP:** 110 **EST:** 1965
SQ FT: 38,000
SALES (est): 22.2MM **Privately Held**
WEB: www.mearthane.com
SIC: 3089 3949 Mfg Plastic Products Mfg Sporting/Athletic Goods

(G-20261)
METHODS & MACHINING SVCS INC
140 Uxbridge St (02920-4811)
PHONE..................................401 942-5700
Leonard A Nulman, *President*
EMP: 3 **EST:** 1982
SQ FT: 3,000
SALES: 600K **Privately Held**
SIC: 3599 Machine Shop

(G-20262)
METRO INC (PA)
Also Called: Metro Home Video
1 Metro Park Dr (02910-4955)
PHONE..................................401 461-2200
Dennis Nichols, *President*
EMP: 50
SQ FT: 52,000
SALES (est): 8.7MM **Privately Held**
SIC: 2721 2731 5099 Periodicals-Publishing/Printing Books-Publishing/Printing Whol Durable Goods

(G-20263)
MILLWORK ONE INC
60 Kenney Dr (02920-4404)
PHONE..................................401 738-6990
John M Adams, *CEO*
John D Fish, *President*
Michael R McNulty Sr, *Vice Pres*
Scott Dematteo, *VP Mfg*
▲ **EMP:** 65
SQ FT: 45,000
SALES (est): 11.1MM
SALES (corp-wide): 12.2MM **Privately Held**
WEB: www.millworkone.com
SIC: 2431 Mfg Millwork
PA: Wood Bay Products Business Trust Inc
72 Taunton St
Plainville MA 02762
508 695-8033

(G-20264)
MINIATURE CASTING CORPORATION
21 Slater Rd (02920-4467)
PHONE..................................401 463-5090
Robert Piacitelli, *President*
Bill Tallman, *General Mgr*
EMP: 15 **EST:** 1962
SALES (est): 2.7MM **Privately Held**
WEB: www.minicast.com
SIC: 3364 Mfg Aluminum Die-Castings

(G-20265)
MORRIS & BROMS LLC
900 Wellington Ave (02910-3720)
P.O. Box 3727 (02910-0727)
PHONE..................................401 781-3134
Michael Archambault,
James Hines,
EMP: 16
SQ FT: 19,000
SALES: 1.3MM **Privately Held**
WEB: www.morrisandbroms.com
SIC: 3469 3444 Mfg Metal Stampings Mfg Sheet Metalwork

(G-20266)
NATALE & SONS CASTINGS
441 Niantic Ave (02910-1019)
PHONE..................................401 467-4744
Caroline Natale, *Owner*
John Natale, *Co-Owner*
EMP: 3
SQ FT: 1,350
SALES: 190K **Privately Held**
SIC: 3915 Mfg Jewelers' Materials

(G-20267)
NELIPAK CORPORATION (PA)
Also Called: Nelipak Healthcare Packaging
21 Amflex Dr (02921-2028)
PHONE..................................401 946-2699
Gregory Myers, *Ch of Bd*
Michael Kelly, *President*
Paul Treible, *VP Opers*
David McAndrew, *Opers Staff*
Jose Villafane, *Opers Staff*
▲ **EMP:** 80 **EST:** 1965
SQ FT: 60,000
SALES (est): 29.8MM **Privately Held**
WEB: www.alga.com
SIC: 3081 3083 2671 Mfg Unsupported Plastic Film/Sheet Mfg Laminated Plastic Plate/Sheet Mfg Packaging Paper/Film

(G-20268)
NEWPORT CREAMERY LLC
35 Sockanosset Cross Rd (02920-5535)
P.O. Box 8819 (02920-0819)
PHONE..................................401 946-4000
Nicholas Janikies, *President*
Leslie Rich, *Admin Sec*
EMP: 350
SALES (est): 29.8MM **Privately Held**
SIC: 2024 2013 5451 Mfg Ice Cream/Frozen Desert Mfg Prepared Meats Ret Dairy Products

(G-20269)
PACOS TACOS MOBILE MEX LLC
262 S Clarendon St (02910-3620)
PHONE..................................401 793-0515
Frank Mapes, *Principal*
EMP: 4
SALES (est): 283.2K **Privately Held**
SIC: 3421 Mfg Cutlery

(G-20270)
PEPSI-COLA METRO BTLG CO INC
24 Kenney Dr (02920-4404)
PHONE..................................401 468-3221
EMP: 81
SALES (corp-wide): 64.6B **Publicly Held**
SIC: 2086 Mfg Bottled/Canned Soft Drinks
HQ: Pepsi-Cola Metropolitan Bottling Company, Inc.
1111 Westchester Ave
White Plains NY 10604
914 767-6000

(G-20271)
PEPSI-COLA METRO BTLG CO INC
1400 Pontiac Ave (02920-4499)
PHONE..................................401 468-3300
Trevor Toolson, *Sales/Mktg Mgr*
EMP: 215
SQ FT: 15,000

GEOGRAPHIC

SALES (corp-wide): 64.6B **Publicly Held**
WEB: www.joy-of-cola.com
SIC: 2086 Mfg Bottled/Canned Soft Drinks
HQ: Pepsi-Cola Metropolitan Bottling Company, Inc.
1111 Westchester Ave
White Plains NY 10604
914 767-6000

(G-20272)
POLYFOAM CORPORATION
60 Glen Rd (02920-7947)
PHONE..................................401 781-3220
Thomas L Coz, *Principal*
EMP: 4
SALES (est): 321.8K **Privately Held**
SIC: 2821 Mfg Plastic Materials/Resins

(G-20273)
POWERDYNE INTERNATIONAL INC
145 Phenix Aveste 1 (02920)
PHONE..................................401 739-3300
James F O'Rourke, *CEO*
John M Faulhaber, *Ch of Bd*
Robert C Hemsen, *Vice Ch Bd*
Linda H Madison, *Corp Secy*
John Canham, *Officer*
EMP: 3
SQ FT: 1,000
SALES: 0 **Privately Held**
SIC: 3621 Mfg Electrical Generator

(G-20274)
PRODUCTION MACHINE SALES & SVC
74 Alton St (02910-3802)
P.O. Box 10240 (02910-0096)
PHONE..................................401 461-6830
Fax: 401 467-2659
EMP: 10
SALES: 500K **Privately Held**
SIC: 3469 Mfg Metal Stampings

(G-20275)
PROSYS FINISHING TECH INC
1420 Elmwood Ave (02910-3847)
PHONE..................................401 781-1011
▲ **EMP:** 5 **EST:** 1999
SALES (est): 995.8K **Privately Held**
SIC: 2819 Mfg Industrial Inorganic Chemicals

(G-20276)
R & D TL ENGRG FOUR-SLIDE PROD
Also Called: R & D Tl Engrg Four-Slide Prod
101 Libera St (02920-2525)
PHONE..................................401 942-9710
Richard Campopiano, *President*
Joseph A Agresti, *General Mgr*
EMP: 6
SQ FT: 3,600
SALES (est): 707.2K **Privately Held**
WEB: www.rdtoolengineering.com
SIC: 3469 3545 Mfg Metal Stampings Mfg Machine Tool Accessories

(G-20277)
R & R POLISHING CO INC
37 Fletcher Ave (02920-2522)
PHONE..................................401 831-6335
Anthony Riccio Jr, *President*
Peter Riccio, *Admin Sec*
EMP: 6
SQ FT: 1,400
SALES (est): 606.8K **Privately Held**
SIC: 3471 Plating/Polishing Service

(G-20278)
RESOURCES UNLIMITED INC
140 Comstock Pkwy (02921-2006)
PHONE..................................401 369-7329
Richard Butmarc, *President*
EMP: 15
SALES (est): 1.4MM **Privately Held**
SIC: 3993 Mfg Displays

(G-20279)
RHODE ISLAND LIMB CO (PA)
Also Called: Artificial Limb Co
1559 Elmwood Ave (02910-3853)
PHONE..................................401 941-6230
William Teoli, *President*
Elaine Teoli, *Vice Pres*
Jonathan Teoli, *Treasurer*
EMP: 7 **EST:** 1953
SQ FT: 2,000
SALES: 900K **Privately Held**
WEB: www.rilimb.com
SIC: 3842 5999 Mfg Surgical Appliances/Supplies Ret Misc Merchandise

(G-20280)
RIHANI PLASTICS INC
14 Suez St (02920-6517)
P.O. Box 8945 (02920-0988)
PHONE..................................401 942-7393
Ghaleb Rihani, *President*
EMP: 19
SQ FT: 30,000
SALES (est): 2.5MM **Privately Held**
SIC: 3069 Injection Molding Of Plastics

(G-20281)
ROLYN INC (PA)
Also Called: Chante
189 Macklin St (02920-6510)
PHONE..................................401 944-0844
Douglas Ricci, *President*
Anthony Rendine, *Vice Pres*
▲ **EMP:** 30 **EST:** 1963
SQ FT: 15,500
SALES (est): 1.8MM **Privately Held**
WEB: www.advancedcomfortsystems.com
SIC: 3911 3961 3915 Mfg Precious Metal Jewelry Mfg Costume Jewelry Mfg Jewelers' Materials

(G-20282)
SA FEOLE MASONRY SVCS INC
80 Angell Ave (02920-1610)
P.O. Box 20366 (02920-0944)
PHONE..................................401 273-2766
Karina Rossi, *President*
EMP: 5
SALES (est): 194.1K **Privately Held**
SIC: 2024 Mfg Ice Cream/Frozen Desert

(G-20283)
SAUGY INC
43 Ralls Dr (02920-3943)
PHONE..................................401 640-1879
Mary O'Brien, *President*
EMP: 3
SALES: 175K **Privately Held**
WEB: www.saugy.net
SIC: 2015 Poultry Frankfurters

(G-20284)
SCOPE DISPLAY & BOX CO INC (PA)
1840 Cranston St (02920-4139)
PHONE..................................401 942-7150
Victor Wilbert Jr, *President*
Stephen Wilbert, *Vice Pres*
EMP: 75
SQ FT: 35,000
SALES (est): 8.8MM **Privately Held**
WEB: www.scopedisplay.com
SIC: 3993 3999 2542 2541 Mfg Signs/Ad Specialties Mfg Misc Products Mfg Nonwd Partition/Fixt Mfg Wood Partitions/Fixt

(G-20285)
SIEMENS INDUSTRY INC
140 Pettaconsett Ave (02920-7918)
PHONE..................................401 942-2121
William Wilber, *Manager*
EMP: 40
SALES (corp-wide): 96.9B **Privately Held**
SIC: 3589 Mfg Sewage & Water Treatment Equipment
HQ: Siemens Industry, Inc.
1000 Deerfield Pkwy
Buffalo Grove IL 60089
847 215-1000

(G-20286)
SIR SPEEDY PRINTING INC
969 Park Ave (02910-3202)
PHONE..................................401 781-5650
Pat Welch, *President*
Fredrick Caffrey, *General Mgr*
EMP: 12
SQ FT: 3,000
SALES (est): 2.2MM **Privately Held**
WEB: www.sirspeedycranston.com
SIC: 2752 Comm Prtg Litho

(G-20287)
SPECTRUM THERMAL PROC LLC
818 Wellington Ave (02910)
PHONE..................................401 808-6249
Steve Egan, *General Mgr*
Richard Houghton Jr, *General Mgr*
Paul Squizzero, *CFO*
EMP: 18
SQ FT: 12,000
SALES (est): 3MM **Privately Held**
SIC: 3398 Metal Heat Treating

(G-20288)
SPEEDWAY LLC
473-479 Reservoir Ave (02910)
PHONE..................................401 941-4740
Joseph Rodrigues, *Manager*
EMP: 5
SQ FT: 646 **Publicly Held**
WEB: www.hess.com
SIC: 1311 Crude Petroleum/Natural Gas Production
HQ: Speedway Llc
500 Speedway Dr
Enon OH 45323
937 864-3000

(G-20289)
SPEEDY PETROLEUM INC
95 Warwick Ave (02905-3539)
PHONE..................................401 781-3350
Dikran Tashian, *President*
Maral Tashian, *Admin Sec*
EMP: 4
SALES (est): 726.8K **Privately Held**
SIC: 2999 Mfg Petroleum/Coal Products

(G-20290)
ST JOHN
727 Atwood Ave (02920-2523)
PHONE..................................401 944-0159
Wagih Ghobrial, *Principal*
EMP: 3
SALES (est): 225.1K **Privately Held**
SIC: 2339 Mfg Women's/Misses' Outerwear

(G-20291)
STAFFALL INC
1468 Elmwood Ave (02910-3847)
PHONE..................................401 461-5554
Ernest Crivellone, *President*
Diane Yingling, *Vice Pres*
Clementina Crivellone, *Admin Sec*
EMP: 22 **EST:** 1967
SQ FT: 22,000
SALES: 5MM **Privately Held**
WEB: www.staffall.com
SIC: 3679 Mfg Electronic Components

(G-20292)
STEVELLS JEWELRY INC
181 Macklin St (02920-6508)
PHONE..................................401 521-1930
Steven Antonelli, *President*
EMP: 4
SQ FT: 3,500
SALES: 500K **Privately Held**
SIC: 3369 Mfg White Metal Castings For The Jewelry Trade

(G-20293)
STYLECRAFT INC
1510 Pontiac Ave (02920-4488)
PHONE..................................401 463-9944
Neil Berman, *President*
▲ **EMP:** 58 **EST:** 1967
SQ FT: 18,000
SALES (est): 6.5MM **Privately Held**
WEB: www.corporatejewelry.com
SIC: 3911 3961 Mfg Precious Metal Jewelry Mfg Costume Jewelry

(G-20294)
SWAROVSKI DIGITAL BUSINESS USA
1 Kenney Dr (02920-4403)
PHONE..................................888 207-9873
Edward Capobianco, *CEO*
EMP: 3
SALES (est): 339.8K **Privately Held**
SIC: 3961 Mfg Costume Jewelry

(G-20295)
SWAROVSKI NORTH AMERICA LTD (DH)
Also Called: Signity Americas
1 Kenney Dr (02920-4403)
PHONE..................................401 463-6400
Daniel Cohen, *President*
Stephen Kahler, *Vice Pres*
John Simms, *Vice Pres*
Stephan Toljan, *Vice Pres*
Stacy Marks, *Opers Staff*
▲ **EMP:** 650
SQ FT: 179,000
SALES (est): 274.6MM
SALES (corp-wide): 4.7B **Privately Held**
SIC: 3961 5023 3231 Mfg Costume Jewelry Whol Homefurnishings Mfg Products-Purchased Glass
HQ: Swarovski U.S. Holding Limited
1 Kenney Dr
Cranston RI 02920
401 463-6400

(G-20296)
SWAROVSKI US HOLDING LIMITED (HQ)
1 Kenney Dr (02920-4403)
PHONE..................................401 463-6400
Daniel Cohen, *President*
Douglas Brown, *CFO*
Andrea Scicchitano, *Sales Staff*
Robert Mahan, *Manager*
Norman Orodenker, *Admin Sec*
EMP: 4
SQ FT: 40,000
SALES (est): 306.1MM
SALES (corp-wide): 4.7B **Privately Held**
SIC: 3961 3231 5048 5099 Mfg Costume Jewelry Mfg Prdt-Purchased Glass Whol Ophthalmic Goods Whol Durable Goods
PA: D. Swarovski Kg
SwarovskistraBe 30
Wattens 6112
522 450-00

(G-20297)
SYQWEST INC
30 Kenney Dr Ste 1 (02920-7962)
PHONE..................................401 432-7129
Robert Tarini, *CEO*
Micheal Curran, *President*
EMP: 30
SQ FT: 53,600
SALES: 10MM **Privately Held**
WEB: www.syqwestinc.com
SIC: 3812 Mfg Search/Navigation Equipment

(G-20298)
T O NAM SAUSAGE
444 Wellington Ave (02910-2935)
PHONE..................................401 941-9620
Pinhkeo Douangsanah, *Owner*
EMP: 3
SQ FT: 900
SALES: 150K **Privately Held**
SIC: 2013 Mfg Prepared Meats

(G-20299)
TACO INC (PA)
Also Called: Taco Comfort Solutions
1160 Cranston St (02920-7300)
PHONE..................................401 942-8000
John H White Jr, *President*
Wil Vandewiel, *President*
Bob Kleinschmidt, *Regional Mgr*
William Leuschen, *Regional Mgr*
Jeff North, *Regional Mgr*
◆ **EMP:** 375 **EST:** 1920
SQ FT: 120,000
SALES (est): 162.6MM **Privately Held**
WEB: www.taco-hvac.com
SIC: 3433 3561 3443 3822 Mfg Heat Equip-Nonelec Mfg Pumps/Pumping Equip Mfg Fabricated Plate Wrk Mfg Environmntl Controls

(G-20300)
TACO ELECTRONIC SOLUTIONS INC
1160 Cranston St (02920-7300)
PHONE..................................401 942-8000
Wil Vandewiel, *President*
Glenn Graham, *Treasurer*
John White, *Director*

Michael Martell, *Admin Sec*
EMP: 4
SALES (est): 150.8K **Privately Held**
SIC: 3571 Mfg Electronic Computers

(G-20301)
TECHNIC INC (PA)
47 Molter St (02910-1011)
P.O. Box 9650, Providence (02940-9650)
PHONE..................................401 781-6100
Hrant Shoushanian, *President*
Peter Sexton, *Business Mgr*
Alfred M Weisberg, *Exec VP*
Steve Schaefer, *Vice Pres*
Rob Schetty, *Vice Pres*
◆ **EMP:** 150 **EST:** 1944
SQ FT: 90,000
SALES (est): 125.5MM **Privately Held**
WEB: www.technic.com
SIC: 2899 3559 Mfg Chemical Preparations Mfg Misc Industry Machinery

(G-20302)
TIME PLATING INCORPORATED
30 Libera St (02920-2598)
PHONE..................................401 943-3020
Robert Di Meo, *President*
EMP: 5 **EST:** 1975
SQ FT: 4,500
SALES (est): 707.5K **Privately Held**
WEB: www.timeplating.com
SIC: 3471 Metal Plating

(G-20303)
TOTAL PLASTICS RESOURCES LLC
1518 Pontiac Ave (02920-4406)
PHONE..................................401 463-3090
John Quinn, *Branch Mgr*
EMP: 37
SALES (corp-wide): 863.9MM **Privately Held**
SIC: 3089 Mfg Plastic Products
HQ: Total Plastics Resources Llc
2810 N Burdick St Ste A
Kalamazoo MI 49004
269 344-0009

(G-20304)
TRANS-TEX LLC
117 Pettaconsett Ave (02920-7916)
PHONE..................................401 331-8483
Adrien Hebert, *Co-Owner*
Phillip Barr, *Co-Owner*
▲ **EMP:** 45
SQ FT: 19,000
SALES (est): 15.3MM **Privately Held**
WEB: www.trans-tex.com
SIC: 2672 Mfg Coated/Laminated Paper

(G-20305)
TRI-BRO TOOL COMPANY
1370 Elmwood Ave (02910-3889)
PHONE..................................401 781-6323
Thomas Walsh, *President*
Maggie Mullen, *Principal*
Edward Walsh, *Principal*
Robert Walsh, *Principal*
Christine McDermott, *Sales Staff*
EMP: 15 **EST:** 1946
SQ FT: 24,000
SALES (est): 1.6MM **Privately Held**
WEB: www.tri-bro.com
SIC: 3915 3544 Mfg Jewelers' Findings & Materials & Metal Forming & Metal Stamping Dies

(G-20306)
TWO SAINTS INC
81 Western Industrial Dr B (02921-3444)
PHONE..................................401 490-5500
Richard St Angelo, *CEO*
Richard Stangelo, *CEO*
▲ **EMP:** 10
SQ FT: 15,000
SALES (est): 530K **Privately Held**
SIC: 2511 Home Gift & Jewelry Accessories

(G-20307)
UNITED PLATING INC
2 2nd Ave (02910-4923)
PHONE..................................401 461-5857
Fax: 401 461-5370
EMP: 78 **EST:** 1965
SQ FT: 570
SALES (est): 8MM **Privately Held**
SIC: 3471 Electroplating

(G-20308)
URSCHEL TOOL CO
43 Navaho St (02907-3185)
PHONE..................................401 944-0600
Robert Ursillo, *President*
James R Ursillo, *President*
EMP: 15
SQ FT: 3,000
SALES: 2MM **Privately Held**
SIC: 3999 Mfg Misc Products

(G-20309)
WEI INC (PA)
33 Webb St (02920-7922)
PHONE..................................401 781-3904
Donald Waddington, *CEO*
John E Waddington, *President*
June Rocchio, *General Mgr*
EMP: 50
SALES (est): 8.1MM **Privately Held**
WEB: www.waddingtonelectronics.com
SIC: 3625 3613 3812 3674 Mfg Relay/Indstl Control Mfg Switchgear/Boards Mfg Search/Navgatn Equip Mfg Semiconductors/Dvcs

(G-20310)
WEI INC
25 Webb St (02920-7922)
PHONE..................................401 781-3904
Donald Waddington, *President*
John Waddington, *Vice Pres*
John Watington, *Vice Pres*
Jacquiline Alger, *Controller*
EMP: 10
SQ FT: 5,000
SALES (est): 534.9K
SALES (corp-wide): 8.1MM **Privately Held**
WEB: www.waddingtonelectronics.com
SIC: 3625 3613 Mfg Electronics
PA: Wei, Inc.
33 Webb St
Cranston RI 02920
401 781-3904

(G-20311)
WHEELER AVENUE LLC
Also Called: Ocean Laminating Films
999 Pontiac Ave Unit A (02920-7934)
PHONE..................................401 714-0996
Michael O'Connor, *Mng Member*
John McCormack,
▲ **EMP:** 5 **EST:** 2009
SQ FT: 8,000
SALES: 5MM **Privately Held**
SIC: 2671 Mfg Packaging Paper/Film

Cumberland
Providence County

(G-20312)
ABSORBENT SPECIALTY PDTS LLC
1 John C Dean Mem Blvd (02864-4801)
PHONE..................................401 722-1177
Erica Vincent, *Executive*
Carol Dancer,
◆ **EMP:** 14
SQ FT: 18,400
SALES (est): 1.1MM **Privately Held**
WEB: www.absorbsp.com
SIC: 2393 1629 2842 2679 Mfg Textile Bags Heavy Construction Mfg Polish/Sanitation Gd Mfg Converted Paper Prdt

(G-20313)
ALESIS LP
Also Called: Wavefront Semiconductor
200 Scenic View Dr (02864-1847)
PHONE..................................401 658-4032
Jan Wissmuller, *President*
John E O Donnell,
Gabrielle Koufman,
▲ **EMP:** 8
SALES (est): 740K
SALES (corp-wide): 1.4MM **Privately Held**
WEB: www.wavefrontsemi.com
SIC: 3931 Manufacturer Of Musical Instruments
PA: Inmusic, Llc
200 Scenic View Dr
Cumberland RI 02864
888 800-0681

(G-20314)
B & M PRINTING INC
1300 Mendon Rd (02864-4813)
PHONE..................................401 334-3190
Marguerite Y Girard, *President*
Bertrand C Girard, *Vice Pres*
EMP: 4
SQ FT: 1,500
SALES (est): 465.5K **Privately Held**
WEB: www.bmprintingweb.com
SIC: 2752 Lithographic Commercial Printing

(G-20315)
CALIBRATORS INC
38 Morning Glory Rd (02864-2391)
PHONE..................................401 769-0333
Michael Bruneault, *President*
EMP: 8
SQ FT: 20,000
SALES: 500K **Privately Held**
WEB: www.calibratorsinc.com
SIC: 3825 5084 3829 Mfg Electrical Measuring Instruments Whol Industrial Equipment Mfg Measuring/Controlling Devices

(G-20316)
CRUZ CONSTRUCTION COMPANY INC
23 Maple St Ste 6 (02864-8122)
PHONE..................................401 727-3770
Joseph Cruz, *President*
Dawn Cruz, *Vice Pres*
EMP: 10
SQ FT: 1,000
SALES (est): 2.1MM **Privately Held**
WEB: www.cruzconstruction.net
SIC: 2951 Mfg Asphalt Mixtures/Blocks

(G-20317)
CUMBERLAND FOUNDRY CO INC
310 W Wrentham Rd (02864-1005)
PHONE..................................401 658-3300
Albert Lucchetti, *President*
Thomas Lucchetti, *Vice Pres*
EMP: 38
SQ FT: 70,000
SALES (est): 8.8MM **Privately Held**
WEB: www.cumberlandfoundry.com
SIC: 3321 Gray/Ductile Iron Foundry

(G-20318)
D & B MACHINING INC
53 John St (02864-7713)
PHONE..................................401 726-2347
Rui Duarte, *President*
Tony Duarte, *Vice Pres*
Alice Duarte, *Treasurer*
Rui Duart, *Manager*
Aldora Duarte, *Exec Sec*
EMP: 40
SQ FT: 36,000
SALES (est): 6.2MM **Privately Held**
WEB: www.dbmachining.com
SIC: 3599 Mfg Industrial Machinery

(G-20319)
EAST COAST LAMINIATING COMPANY
362 Abbott Run Valley Rd (02864-3258)
PHONE..................................401 729-0097
Kenneth B White II, *President*
Lavonne White, *Vice Pres*
EMP: 4
SALES (est): 522.4K **Privately Held**
SIC: 3089 2431 Mfg Plastic Products Mfg Millwork

(G-20320)
ENVIRNMNTAL COMPLIANCE SYSTEMS
Also Called: E C S
3294 Mendon Rd (02864-2130)
PHONE..................................401 334-0306
Conrad Hamel, *President*
Steven Hamel, *Director*
EMP: 3
SQ FT: 2,000
SALES (est): 409.6K **Privately Held**
WEB: www.hamels.com
SIC: 3826 Mfg Analytical Instruments

(G-20321)
GIBBS LURES INC
1 Hatch St (02864-8203)
PHONE..................................401 726-2277
James P Griecci, *President*
Debra R Griecci, *Treasurer*
EMP: 4
SQ FT: 2,000
SALES (est): 240K **Privately Held**
WEB: www.gibbslures.com
SIC: 3949 Manufactures Artificial Salt Water Fishing Lures

(G-20322)
GOLDENROD WELDING INC
37 Elizabeth St (02864-7726)
P.O. Box 725, Chepachet (02814-0901)
PHONE..................................401 725-9248
Jack Hinkle, *Owner*
EMP: 5
SQ FT: 5,000
SALES (est): 210K **Privately Held**
SIC: 7692 Welding Repair

(G-20323)
GRASSROOTS OF NEW ENGLAND
202 Nate Whipple Hwy (02864-2221)
PHONE..................................401 333-1963
Joshua Imswiler, *President*
EMP: 5
SALES (est): 519.6K **Privately Held**
SIC: 3523 Mfg Farm Machinery/Equipment

(G-20324)
HERRICK & WHITE LTD
3 Flat St (02864-2335)
PHONE..................................401 658-0440
Kenneth E Bertram, *President*
Steven Brannigan, *Treasurer*
EMP: 100 **EST:** 1977
SQ FT: 50,000
SALES (est): 16.3MM **Privately Held**
WEB: www.herrick-white.com
SIC: 2542 2541 8712 Mfg Partitions/Fixtures-Nonwood Mfg Wood Partitions/Fixtures Architectural Services

(G-20325)
HINDLEY MANUFACTURING CO INC
9 Havens St (02864-8200)
P.O. Box 38 (02864-0038)
PHONE..................................401 722-2550
Charles J Hindley, *President*
Scott A Hindley, *Vice Pres*
Jack Silva, *Safety Dir*
Mike Ricciardi, *Site Mgr*
George Cloutier, *Purch Mgr*
◆ **EMP:** 80 **EST:** 1897
SQ FT: 110,000
SALES (est): 18.5MM **Privately Held**
WEB: www.hindley.com
SIC: 3496 3429 3452 Mfg Misc Fabricated Wire Products Mfg Hardware Mfg Bolts/Screws/Rivets

(G-20326)
HYSEN TECHNOLOGIES INC (PA)
1725 Mendon Rd Unit 205 (02864-4340)
PHONE..................................401 312-6500
Jay Chelo, *Owner*
EMP: 11
SALES (est): 936.2K **Privately Held**
SIC: 3663 Mfg Electronic Pagers

(G-20327)
ICE CREAM MACHINE CO
4288 Diamond Hill Rd (02864-1508)
PHONE..................................401 333-5053

GEOGRAPHIC

Kim Caron, *Owner*
EMP: 10 **EST:** 1977
SALES (est): 692.8K **Privately Held**
WEB: www.icecreampie.com
SIC: 2024 5421 Mfr & Ret Ice Cream

(G-20328)
IDS HIGHWAY SAFETY INC
136 Scott Rd (02864-2812)
P.O. Box 7604 (02864-0897)
PHONE..................................401 333-0740
Irene Ray, *President*
EMP: 5
SALES (est): 757.5K **Privately Held**
WEB: www.idsenterprises.net
SIC: 3679 7389 Mfg Electronic Components Business Services

(G-20329)
INTERNATIONAL JOURNAL OF ARTS
55 Farm Dr (02864-3565)
PHONE..................................401 333-1804
Joseph Bonnici, *Manager*
EMP: 5
SALES (est): 267.2K **Privately Held**
SIC: 2711 Newspapers-Publishing/Printing

(G-20330)
JOHNSON & JOHNSON
1300 Highland Corporate D (02864-8714)
PHONE..................................401 762-6751
EMP: 147
SALES (corp-wide): 81.5B **Publicly Held**
WEB: www.jnj.com
SIC: 3842 Mfg Surgical Appliances/Supplies
PA: Johnson & Johnson
1 Johnson And Johnson Plz
New Brunswick NJ 08933
732 524-0400

(G-20331)
NFA CORP
Hope Global Divison of Nfa
50 Martin St (02864-5335)
PHONE..................................401 333-8947
David Casty, *President*
EMP: 500
SQ FT: 125,000
SALES (corp-wide): 15.3MM **Privately Held**
WEB: www.hopeglobal.com
SIC: 2241 Narrow Fabric Mill
PA: Nfa Corp.
50 Martin St
Cumberland RI 02864
401 333-8990

(G-20332)
NFA CORP
Also Called: Novelty Plastics
50 Martin St (02864-5335)
P.O. Box 505807, Chelsea MA (02150-5807)
PHONE..................................401 333-8990
Norton Proman, *Branch Mgr*
EMP: 30
SQ FT: 61,000
SALES (corp-wide): 15.3MM **Privately Held**
WEB: www.hopeglobal.com
SIC: 2241 2631 Narrow Fabric Mill Paperboard Mill
PA: Nfa Corp.
50 Martin St
Cumberland RI 02864
401 333-8990

(G-20333)
NFA CORP
Hope Global Headquarters
50 Martin St (02864-5335)
PHONE..................................401 333-8990
Lisie Teoto, *CEO*
EMP: 500
SALES (corp-wide): 15.3MM **Privately Held**
WEB: www.hopeglobal.com
SIC: 2221 Mfg Of Textiles
PA: Nfa Corp.
50 Martin St
Cumberland RI 02864
401 333-8990

(G-20334)
NFA CORP
Also Called: Hope Global
50 Martin St (02864-5335)
PHONE..................................401 333-8990
Santiago Marcelino, *Vice Pres*
Karalee Tabron, *Vice Pres*
Joe Silva, *Plant Mgr*
Allan Gardner, *Engineer*
Connie Vitorino, *Human Res Mgr*
EMP: 400
SALES (corp-wide): 15.3MM **Privately Held**
WEB: www.hopeglobal.com
SIC: 2241 2257 Narrow Fabric Mill Weft Knit Fabric Mill
PA: Nfa Corp.
50 Martin St
Cumberland RI 02864
401 333-8990

(G-20335)
NUMARK INTERNATIONAL INC
200 Scenic View Dr (02864-1847)
PHONE..................................954 761-7550
John E O'Donnell, *President*
EMP: 10
SALES (est): 1MM **Privately Held**
SIC: 3674 Mfg Semiconductors/Related Devices

(G-20336)
OKONITE COMPANY
5 Industrial Rd (02864-4714)
PHONE..................................401 333-3500
Brad Detamore, *General Mgr*
John Elmini, *General Mgr*
Kate Guptill, *Human Res Mgr*
EMP: 80
SALES (corp-wide): 407MM **Privately Held**
WEB: www.okonite.com
SIC: 3357 3743 3661 Nonferrous Wiredrawing/Insulating Mfg Railroad Equipment Mfg Telephone/Telegraph Apparatus
PA: The Okonite Company Inc
102 Hilltop Rd
Ramsey NJ 07446
201 825-0300

(G-20337)
ORBETRON LLC
45 Industrial Rd Ste 208 (02864-4742)
P.O. Box 462, Lincoln (02865-0462)
PHONE..................................651 983-2872
Hank Gray, *Mng Member*
Roger Hultquist,
EMP: 4
SQ FT: 2,000
SALES: 219.4K **Privately Held**
SIC: 3824 3535 3596 3823 Mfg Fluid Meters/Devices Mfg Conveyors/Equipment Mfg Scale/Balance-Nonlab Mfg Process Cntrl Instr

(G-20338)
PEELED INC
Also Called: Peeled Snacks
30 Martin St Ste 3b1 (02864-5367)
PHONE..................................212 706-2001
Noha Waibsnaider, *President*
Cassie Abrams, *Principal*
Jessica Aquila, *Principal*
Ian Kelleher, *Principal*
Dawn Techow, *COO*
▲ **EMP:** 12
SALES (est): 6.7MM **Privately Held**
SIC: 2068 2034 Mfg Salted/Roasted Nuts/Seeds Mfg Dehydrated Fruits/Vegetables

(G-20339)
PLASTICS PLUS INC
Also Called: Envision
51 Abbott St Ste 1 (02864-8713)
P.O. Box 7129 (02864-0893)
PHONE..................................401 727-1447
Daniel J Smalley, *President*
▲ **EMP:** 45
SALES (est): 12.3MM **Privately Held**
WEB: www.plasticsplusinc.com
SIC: 3578 2541 Mfg Calculating Equipment Mfg Wood Partitions/Fixtures Mfg Wood Partitions/Fixtures

(G-20340)
POLYRACK NORTH AMERICA CORP
1600 Highland Corp Dr (02864)
PHONE..................................401 770-1500
Andreas C Rapp, *Principal*
▲ **EMP:** 5
SALES (est): 908.2K **Privately Held**
SIC: 3675 Manufacture Electronic Component

(G-20341)
RHODE ISLAND VENTILATING CO
29 Aurora Dr (02864-4607)
P.O. Box T, Lincoln (02865-0297)
PHONE..................................401 723-8920
Richard Saglio, *President*
EMP: 11 **EST:** 1960
SQ FT: 6,500
SALES (est): 1.2MM **Privately Held**
SIC: 3444 Fabricates & Installs Sheet Metal Specialties Not Stamped

(G-20342)
SEWRITE MFG INC
30 Martin St Ste 2a1 (02864-5350)
PHONE..................................401 334-3868
Ralph Sullivan, *President*
Joann Sullivan, *Vice Pres*
EMP: 6
SQ FT: 10,000
SALES (est): 554.9K **Privately Held**
SIC: 2395 Pleating/Stitching Services

(G-20343)
SWISSLINE PRECISION LLC
23 Ashton Pkwy Unit A (02864-4841)
PHONE..................................401 333-8888
Michael Chenevert, *President*
Gerard Hester, *Vice Pres*
Mike Chenevert, *Opers Staff*
Donna Ross, *Treasurer*
Paul Mellin, *Sales Mgr*
EMP: 65 **EST:** 2015
SQ FT: 30,000
SALES (est): 2.9MM **Privately Held**
SIC: 3451 Mfg Screw Machine Products

(G-20344)
SWISSLINE PRECISION MFG INC
23 Ashton Park Way Unit A (02864-4841)
PHONE..................................401 333-8888
David Chenevert, *President*
EMP: 59
SALES (est): 10.5MM **Privately Held**
SIC: 3541 Mfg Machine Tools-Cutting

(G-20345)
SWISSLINE PRODUCTS INC
23 Ashton Park Way Unit A (02864-4841)
PHONE..................................401 333-8888
David Chenevert, *President*
Raymond Barsalou, *Vice Pres*
EMP: 73
SQ FT: 30,000
SALES (est): 9.5MM **Privately Held**
WEB: www.swisslineprecision.com
SIC: 3599 3769 Mfg Industrial Machinery Mfg Space Vehicle Equipment

(G-20346)
TEDOR PHARMA INC
400 Highland Corporate Dr (02864-1788)
PHONE..................................401 658-5219
Theodore L Iorio, *President*
Matthew Iorio, *President*
Terry Novak, *COO*
Steven Tannenbaum, *Exec VP*
Laura Iorio, *Vice Pres*
▲ **EMP:** 41
SQ FT: 40,000
SALES (est): 11MM **Privately Held**
WEB: www.tedor.com
SIC: 2834 Mfg Pharmaceutical Preparations

(G-20347)
TEXCEL INC
18 Meeting St (02864-8323)
P.O. Box 6187, Providence (02940-6187)
PHONE..................................401 727-2113
John Pinkos, *President*
EMP: 15
SQ FT: 40,000
SALES (est): 2.5MM **Privately Held**
SIC: 3552 Mfg Textile Machinery

(G-20348)
TEXCEL INDUSTRIES INC
18 Meeting St (02864-8323)
P.O. Box 6187, Providence (02940-6187)
PHONE..................................401 727-2113
Joshua Teverow, *President*
Ricahrd Wasserman, *COO*
Jessica Wasserman, *Vice Pres*
EMP: 25
SALES (est): 2.7MM **Privately Held**
SIC: 2241 Narrow Fabric Mill

(G-20349)
TOSCANA EUROPEAN DAY SPA
3460 Mendon Rd Unit 4 (02864-2139)
PHONE..................................401 658-5277
Doina Mandrilla, *Owner*
EMP: 4
SALES (est): 441.1K **Privately Held**
WEB: www.toscanadayspa.com
SIC: 2844 Mfg Toilet Preparations

(G-20350)
WRIGHT INDUSTRIAL PRODUCTS CO
45 Industrial Rd (02864-4741)
PHONE..................................508 695-3924
James P Keegan, *President*
Betsy L Keegan, *Admin Sec*
EMP: 4
SQ FT: 6,000
SALES: 900K **Privately Held**
SIC: 3069 Mfg Rubber Rolls And Roll Coverings

East Greenwich
Kent County

(G-20351)
AIRGAS USA LLC
120 Telmore Rd (02818-1650)
PHONE..................................401 884-0201
Dennis Aubin, *Manager*
EMP: 4
SQ FT: 10,000
SALES (corp-wide): 121.9MM **Privately Held**
SIC: 2813 3569 3561 3511 Mfg Gases & Related Products
HQ: Airgas Usa, Llc
259 N Radnor Chester Rd
Radnor PA 19087
610 687-5253

(G-20352)
ALLEGRA PRINT & IMAGING
41 Rocky Hollow Rd (02818-3513)
PHONE..................................401 884-9280
Joan Reuter, *President*
Stanley R Reuter, *Treasurer*
EMP: 5
SQ FT: 2,200
SALES (est): 730.5K **Privately Held**
SIC: 2752 7334 4822 2791 Offset Print Shop & Copying Duplicating Facsimile And Typesetting Services

(G-20353)
BARDON INDUSTRIES INC
Also Called: Bardons Technology
3377 S County Trl (02818-1434)
P.O. Box 1657 (02818-0698)
PHONE..................................401 884-1814
Thomas Lydon, *President*
Thomas J Lydon Jr, *President*
Eileen A Barry, *Vice Pres*
EMP: 13
SQ FT: 4,000
SALES: 1.5MM **Privately Held**
WEB: www.bardonwaterservices.com
SIC: 2899 Mfg Chemical Preparations

(G-20354)
BMCO INDUSTRIES INC
4646 Post Rd Apt 1 (02818-4157)
PHONE..................................401 781-6884
Fax: 401 781-3840
EMP: 6 **EST:** 1973
SQ FT: 40,000

SALES: 1MM **Privately Held**
WEB: www.bmcoindustries.com
SIC: 3535 1796 Mfg Conveyors/Equipment Building Equipment Installation

(G-20355)
CABINET ASSEMBLY SYSTEMS CORP
Also Called: Cas America
1485 S County Trl Unit 4 (02818-1685)
PHONE..................................401 884-8556
Fax: 401 884-8557
EMP: 18
SQ FT: 12,000
SALES (est): 3.1MM **Privately Held**
WEB: www.casamerica.com
SIC: 2434 2521 Mfg Wood Kitchen Cabinets Mfg Wood Office Furniture

(G-20356)
CHERRY SEMICONDUCTOR CORP
2000 S County Trl (02818-1530)
PHONE..................................401 885-3600
Andrew F Durette, *Principal*
EMP: 6
SALES (est): 608.1K **Privately Held**
SIC: 3674 Mfg Semiconductors/Related Devices

(G-20357)
CHRONOMATIC INC
1503 S County Trl (02818-1695)
P.O. Box 610 (02818-0610)
PHONE..................................401 884-6361
Ann Marie Dasilva, *CEO*
EMP: 25 **EST:** 1963
SQ FT: 13,000
SALES: 4.5MM **Privately Held**
WEB: www.chronomaticinc.com
SIC: 3911 3961 Mfg Precious Metal Jewelry Mfg Costume Jewelry

(G-20358)
CLAYGROUND
5600 Post Rd Unit 109 (02818-3442)
PHONE..................................401 884-4888
Marie Carnevele, *Owner*
EMP: 6
SALES (est): 364.5K **Privately Held**
SIC: 3269 Mfg Pottery Products

(G-20359)
CUIVRE & CO LLC
Also Called: Duparquet Copper Cookware
5 Division St Bldg G (02818-3800)
PHONE..................................401 965-4569
James B Hamann,
EMP: 5
SALES (est): 183.6K **Privately Held**
SIC: 3449 Mfg Misc Structural Metalwork

(G-20360)
DEWETRON INC
2850 S County Trl Unit 1 (02818-1731)
PHONE..................................401 284-3750
Grant M Smith, *President*
Steve Dipalma, *Prdtn Mgr*
Susan M Smith, *CFO*
Jennifer Vazquez, *Marketing Mgr*
Elinor Donohoe, *Administration*
◆ **EMP:** 15 **EST:** 1997
SQ FT: 5,000
SALES (est): 4.5MM
SALES (corp-wide): 1.8B **Privately Held**
WEB: www.dewamerica.com
SIC: 3826 Mfg Analytical Instruments
HQ: Dewetron Deutschland Gmbh
Rudolf-Diesel-Str. 32
Ostfildern 73760
711 673-1006

(G-20361)
DOYLE SAILMAKERS INC
1 Division St Ste 1 # 1 (02818-3879)
PHONE..................................401 884-4227
Todd Johnston, *CEO*
EMP: 18
SALES (corp-wide): 6.2MM **Privately Held**
SIC: 2394 Mfg Canvas/Related Products
PA: Doyle Sailmakers, Inc
96 Swampscott Rd Ste 8
Salem MA 01970
978 740-5950

(G-20362)
DOYLE SAILS
Also Called: Doyle Sail Makers
1 Division St Ste 1 # 1 (02818-3879)
PHONE..................................401 884-4227
Todd Johnston, *CEO*
Ruth Johnston, *Vice Pres*
EMP: 6
SALES: 600K **Privately Held**
SIC: 2394 Mfg Canvas/Related Products

(G-20363)
EAGLEPICHER TECHNOLOGIES LLC
Also Called: Eaglepicher Yardney Division
2000 S County Trl (02818-1530)
PHONE..................................401 471-6580
Stuart Santee, *Senior Engr*
EMP: 15 **Privately Held**
SIC: 3691 Mfg Storage Batteries
PA: Eaglepicher Technologies, Llc
C & Porter St
Joplin MO 64801
-

(G-20364)
EAST GREENWICH SPINE AND SPORT
1351 S County Trl Ste 100 (02818-5079)
PHONE..................................401 886-5907
Matthew Joseph Smith, *President*
EMP: 15
SALES (est): 1.2MM **Privately Held**
SIC: 3949 Mfg Sporting/Athletic Goods

(G-20365)
EDWARD F BRIGGS DISPOSAL INC
Carrs Pond Rd (02818)
PHONE..................................401 294-6391
Edward Briggs, *Principal*
EMP: 4
SALES (est): 401.6K **Privately Held**
SIC: 3089 Mfg Plastic Products

(G-20366)
ENER-TEK INTERNATIONAL INC
2000 S County Trl (02818-1530)
PHONE..................................401 471-6580
Richard M Scibelli, *CEO*
Vincent A Yevoli, *President*
Janice T Donovan, *Corp Secy*
Jan Donovan, *Vice Pres*
EMP: 155
SALES (est): 9.3MM **Privately Held**
WEB: www.yardney.com
SIC: 3691 3692 8741 Mfg Storage Batteries Mfg Primary Batteries Management Services
PA: Eaglepicher Technologies, Llc
C & Porter St
Joplin MO 64801
-

(G-20367)
FORENSICSOFT INC
5700 Post Rd Unit 10 (02818-3455)
P.O. Box 727, North Kingstown (02852-0605)
PHONE..................................401 489-7559
John Dipippo, *President*
EMP: 6
SALES: 100K **Privately Held**
SIC: 7372 Software

(G-20368)
FORMEX INC
3305 S County Trl (02818-1477)
PHONE..................................401 885-9800
Edward Shea, *President*
EMP: 30
SALES (est): 4.4MM **Privately Held**
SIC: 3612 7692 3544 Mfg Transformers Welding Repair Mfg Dies/Tools/Jigs/Fixtures

(G-20369)
GREENE INDUSTRIES INC
65 Rocky Hollow Rd (02818-3513)
P.O. Box 66 (02818-0066)
PHONE..................................401 884-7530
Robert A Greene II, *President*
Allison Greene, *Vice Pres*
Robert Allen Greene, *Treasurer*
EMP: 5 **EST:** 1956
SQ FT: 5,000
SALES (est): 611.9K **Privately Held**
SIC: 2441 2448 5085 Mfr Wooden Boxes Pallets & Skids & Distributes Packaging Materials

(G-20370)
HOMELAND COMPANY
69 Highpoint Dr (02818-4209)
PHONE..................................401 884-2427
Robert L Jacob, *Owner*
EMP: 3
SALES (est): 160K **Privately Held**
WEB: www.homelandcompany.com
SIC: 2721 6531 Periodicals-Publishing/Printing Real Estate Agent/Manager

(G-20371)
LINESIDER BREWING COMPANY LLC
1485 S County Trl Ste 201 (02818-1747)
PHONE..................................401 398-7700
Jeremy Ruff, *Mng Member*
Daniel R Koppen,
EMP: 10
SQ FT: 4,200
SALES: 80K **Privately Held**
SIC: 2082 Mfg Malt Beverages

(G-20372)
MARKETPLACE INC CORPORATE
816 Middle Rd (02818-1807)
PHONE..................................401 336-3000
Neil Stamps, *President*
Chris Crawford, *Vice Pres*
EMP: 18
SQ FT: 6,800
SALES (est): 6.3MM **Privately Held**
WEB: www.tcmpi.com
SIC: 3911 Mfg Precious Metal Jewelry

(G-20373)
MERIDIAN PRINTING INC
1538 S County Trl (02818-1627)
PHONE..................................401 885-4882
Robert Nangle, *President*
Steven Lee, *Vice Pres*
▲ **EMP:** 59 **EST:** 1975
SQ FT: 30,000
SALES (est): 14.5MM **Privately Held**
SIC: 2752 Lithographic Commercial Printing

(G-20374)
NIPPON AMERICAN LIMITED
Also Called: Design Research Optics
3 Cedar Rock Mdws (02818-2443)
PHONE..................................401 885-7353
Mikiko Morimura, *President*
Bruce Sunderland, *Vice Pres*
EMP: 12
SALES: 5MM **Privately Held**
SIC: 3827 8299 Mfg Optical Instruments/Lenses School/Educational Services

(G-20375)
OCEAN STATE SOFTWARE LLC
151 Tanglewood Dr (02818-2228)
PHONE..................................202 695-8049
Ken Smith, *President*
EMP: 8
SALES (est): 484.5K **Privately Held**
SIC: 7372 7389 Prepackaged Software Services Business Services At Non-Commercial Site

(G-20376)
PASTA PATCH INC
183 Old Forge Rd (02818-4606)
PHONE..................................401 884-1234
Ferna Roarke, *President*
EMP: 11
SQ FT: 1,000
SALES: 350K **Privately Held**
SIC: 2098 Mfg Macaroni/Spaghetti

(G-20377)
PRINT SHOPS INC
70 Cliff St (02818-3228)
P.O. Box 1133 (02818-0965)
PHONE..................................401 885-1226
Kenneth Mills, *President*
Bernice Mills, *Vice Pres*
EMP: 10
SQ FT: 3,400
SALES (est): 1.7MM **Privately Held**
WEB: www.printshopsinc.com
SIC: 2752 Lithographic Commercial Printing

(G-20378)
S2S SURGICAL LLC
1503 S County Trl (02818-1695)
P.O. Box 722 (02818-0722)
PHONE..................................401 398-1933
Ann Marie Dasilva, *Mng Member*
Manuel Dasilva,
EMP: 6
SQ FT: 7,000
SALES: 1MM **Privately Held**
SIC: 3841 Mfg Surgical/Medical Instruments

(G-20379)
SEMICNDCTOR CMPNNTS INDS OF RI (DH)
Also Called: On Semiconductor
1900 S County Trl (02818-1631)
PHONE..................................401 885-3600
Keith Jackson, *CEO*
Marc St Jean, *Site Mgr*
Mary Macpersons, *Purch Agent*
Andy Laidler, *Engineer*
Jeremy Steele, *Engineer*
EMP: 968
SQ FT: 145,000
SALES (est): 34.7MM
SALES (corp-wide): 5.8B **Publicly Held**
SIC: 3674 Mfg Semiconductors/Related Devices
HQ: Semiconductor Components Industries, Llc
5005 E Mcdowell Rd
Phoenix AZ 85008
800 282-9855

(G-20380)
STANLEY BLACK & DECKER INC
Also Called: Stanley Tool
1 Briggs Dr (02818-1555)
PHONE..................................401 471-4280
Thomas J Mardo, *Branch Mgr*
EMP: 220
SALES (corp-wide): 13.9B **Publicly Held**
SIC: 3699 Mfg Electrical Equipment/Supplies
PA: Stanley Black & Decker, Inc.
1000 Stanley Dr
New Britain CT 06053
860 225-5111

(G-20381)
STANLEY FASTENING SYSTEMS LP (HQ)
2 Briggs Dr (02818-1555)
PHONE..................................401 884-2500
Stanley Works, *Managing Prtnr*
◆ **EMP:** 65
SALES (est): 198.5MM
SALES (corp-wide): 13.9B **Publicly Held**
SIC: 3399 3579 Mfg Primary Metal Products Mfg Office Machines
PA: Stanley Black & Decker, Inc.
1000 Stanley Dr
New Britain CT 06053
860 225-5111

(G-20382)
VACUUM PROCESSING SYSTEMS LLC
9 Mcgraw Ct (02818-2706)
PHONE..................................401 397-8578
Donald Gray, *President*
Joseph Schuttert, *Sales Mgr*
EMP: 3
SALES (est): 306.2K **Privately Held**
SIC: 3589 7389 Mfg Service Industry Machinery

GEOGRAPHIC

East Providence
Providence County

(G-20383)
A & H COMPOSITION AND PRTG INC
Also Called: Copy World
5 Almeida Ave (02914-1001)
PHONE....................401 438-1200
Anthony Andrade, *President*
EMP: 9 **EST:** 1971
SQ FT: 6,000
SALES (est): 868.9K **Privately Held**
SIC: 2752 2791 2789 Lithographic Commercial Printing Typesetting Services Bookbinding/Related Work

(G-20384)
A B MUNROE DAIRY INC
151 N Brow St (02914-4415)
PHONE....................401 438-4450
Robert C Armstrong Jr, *President*
Rick Gregoire, *Purch Mgr*
Elizabeth Armstrong, *Treasurer*
Bob Munro, *Sales Staff*
Joanne Pacheco, *Director*
EMP: 55 **EST:** 1881
SQ FT: 120,000
SALES (est): 9.5MM **Privately Held**
WEB: www.cowtruck.com
SIC: 2026 2038 Mfg Fluid Milk Mfg Frozen Specialties

(G-20385)
AMERICAN RING CO INC (PA)
19 Grosvenor Ave (02914-4569)
PHONE....................401 438-9060
Anthony Calandrelli, *President*
▲ **EMP:** 40
SQ FT: 56,000
SALES (est): 9.5MM **Privately Held**
WEB: www.firstcardco.com
SIC: 3961 3471 2675 Mfg Costume Jewelry Plating/Polishing Service Mfg Die-Cut Paper/Paperboard

(G-20386)
AMERICAN TROPHY & SUPPLY CO
110 Russell Ave (02914-3551)
PHONE....................401 438-3060
Kristen Gossler, *President*
EMP: 9 **EST:** 1951
SQ FT: 9,000
SALES (est): 1.2MM **Privately Held**
SIC: 3499 2759 3479 Mfg Metal Trophies Silk Screen Printing & Etching

(G-20387)
ANCO TOOL & DIE CO INC
30 Almeida Ave (02914-1097)
PHONE....................401 438-5860
John J Anterni Jr, *President*
Mary L Medeiros, *Corp Secy*
Milton Kaiser, *Prdtn Mgr*
EMP: 15 **EST:** 1959
SALES (est): 1.3MM **Privately Held**
SIC: 3089 Injection Molds

(G-20388)
ASPEN AEROGELS INC
3 Dexter Rd (02914-2045)
PHONE....................401 432-2612
Donald R Young, *Branch Mgr*
EMP: 14
SALES (corp-wide): 104.3MM **Publicly Held**
WEB: www.aerogel.com
SIC: 2899 8711 Mfg Chemical Preparations Engineering Services
PA: Aspen Aerogels, Inc.
30 Forbes Rd Bldg B
Northborough MA 01532
508 691-1111

(G-20389)
ASPEN AEROGELS RI LLC
3 Dexter Rd (02914-2045)
PHONE....................401 432-2612
Donald Young, *Principal*
EMP: 15
SALES (est): 1.8MM
SALES (corp-wide): 104.3MM **Publicly Held**
SIC: 2899 Mfg Chemical Preparations
PA: Aspen Aerogels, Inc.
30 Forbes Rd Bldg B
Northborough MA 01532
508 691-1111

(G-20390)
BARLOW DESIGNS INC
20 Commercial Way (02914-1000)
PHONE....................401 438-7925
Stephen B Barlow, *President*
Sally Barlow, *Vice Pres*
▲ **EMP:** 4 **EST:** 1978
SQ FT: 13,000
SALES (est): 868.6K **Privately Held**
WEB: www.barlowdesigns.com
SIC: 3961 3499 Mfg Costume Jewelry & Giftware Except Precious Metal

(G-20391)
BAZAR GROUP INC (PA)
Also Called: Imperial Pearl
795 Waterman Ave (02914-1713)
PHONE....................401 434-2595
Banice C Bazar, *President*
Nathan Magiera, *Inv Control Mgr*
Marc Alves, *Purchasing*
Josh Bazar, *Chief Mktg Ofcr*
Val Dasilva, *Manager*
▲ **EMP:** 25 **EST:** 1953
SQ FT: 30,000
SALES (est): 23.2MM **Privately Held**
WEB: www.imperial-deltah.com
SIC: 3961 3911 5094 Whol Jewelry/Precious Stones Mfg Costume Jewelry Mfg Precious Metal Jewelry

(G-20392)
BOSWORTH COMPANY
Also Called: Sea-Lect
930 Waterman Ave (02914-1337)
PHONE....................401 438-1110
Kenneth Bosworth, *President*
Nancy Bosworth, *Vice Pres*
Vincenza Wilson, *Marketing Staff*
EMP: 10 **EST:** 1982
SQ FT: 6,000
SALES (est): 2.2MM **Privately Held**
SIC: 3561 Manufactures Pumps And Valves

(G-20393)
BOYDCO INC (PA)
101 Commercial Way (02914-1024)
PHONE....................401 438-6900
David Speed, *President*
Eric Dewhirst, *Vice Pres*
Lee Sprague, *Vice Pres*
Rosemary Rapoza, *Accountant*
EMP: 18
SQ FT: 16,000
SALES (est): 2.1MM **Privately Held**
WEB: www.boydcoinc.com
SIC: 3561 Mfg Pumps/Pumping Equipment

(G-20394)
CAMIROB CORP
Also Called: B C T
30 Risho Ave (02914-1215)
PHONE....................401 435-4477
Carol Clarey, *President*
Michael Clarey, *Vice Pres*
Robert Clarey, *Admin Sec*
EMP: 20
SQ FT: 6,000
SALES (est): 3.4MM **Privately Held**
SIC: 2752 Comm Prtg Litho

(G-20395)
CARLA CORP
33 Sutton Ave (02914-3413)
P.O. Box 14192 (02914-0192)
PHONE....................401 438-7070
Ralph Fleming Jr, *Ch of Bd*
Ralph Fleming III, *President*
Brian Fleming, *Treasurer*
Peter Linardo, *MIS Dir*
EMP: 150 **EST:** 1965
SQ FT: 35,000
SALES (est): 20.4MM **Privately Held**
WEB: www.carlacorp.com
SIC: 3911 Mfg Precious Metal Jewelry

(G-20396)
CLAIRE STEWART LLC
800 Waterman Ave (02914-1728)
PHONE....................401 467-7400
Roderick Lichtenfels,
EMP: 150
SALES (est): 7.2MM
SALES (corp-wide): 27.2MM **Privately Held**
SIC: 3915 Mfg Jewelers' Materials
PA: W. R. Cobb Company
800 Waterman Ave
East Providence RI 02914
401 438-7000

(G-20397)
CLASSIC EMBROIDERY CO
855 Waterman Ave (02914-1700)
PHONE....................401 434-9632
Nancy Fontaine, *President*
Nancy J Fontaine, *Admin Sec*
EMP: 20
SQ FT: 10,000
SALES (est): 1.6MM **Privately Held**
SIC: 2395 2759 Pleating/Stitching Services Commercial Printing

(G-20398)
CLEMENT MACHINE TOOL CO INC
30 Central Ave (02914-4406)
PHONE....................401 438-7248
Thomas Clement, *President*
Larry Clement, *Vice Pres*
Albert Saunders,
EMP: 6 **EST:** 1976
SQ FT: 6,000
SALES: 350K **Privately Held**
SIC: 3599 Mfg Industrial Machinery

(G-20399)
CONSOLIDATED CONCRETE CORP (PA)
835 Taunton Ave Unit 1 (02914-1600)
PHONE....................401 438-4700
John R Pesce Jr, *President*
George Pesce, *Vice Pres*
EMP: 9 **EST:** 1957
SQ FT: 6,000
SALES (est): 2.7MM **Privately Held**
SIC: 3273 Mfg Ready-Mixed Concrete

(G-20400)
CONTRACT FUSION INC
99 Massasoit Ave (02914-2008)
PHONE....................401 438-1298
John Carter III, *President*
Letitia Carter, *Admin Sec*
EMP: 26
SQ FT: 14,000
SALES: 2.6MM **Privately Held**
WEB: www.contractfusion.com
SIC: 3599 5084 3915 3548 Mfg Industrial Machinery Whol Industrial Equip Mfg Jewelers' Materials Mfg Welding Apparatus

(G-20401)
CUSTOM & MILLER BOX COMPANY
25 Almeida Ave (02914-1001)
P.O. Box 2410, Pawtucket (02861-0410)
PHONE....................401 431-9007
David Strauss, *President*
EMP: 20
SQ FT: 40,000
SALES (est): 4.3MM
SALES (corp-wide): 59.1MM **Privately Held**
WEB: www.keycontainercorp.com
SIC: 2653 Mfg Corrugated/Solid Fiber Boxes
PA: Key Container Corporation
21 Campbell St
Pawtucket RI 02861
401 723-2000

(G-20402)
DAMA JEWELRY TECHNOLOGY INC
800 Waterman Ave (02914-1728)
PHONE....................401 272-6513
Marcos Fountoulakis, *President*
John Caito, *Exec VP*
▲ **EMP:** 30
SALES (est): 4.6MM **Privately Held**
SIC: 3915 3961 Mfg Jewelers' Materials Mfg Costume Jewelry

(G-20403)
DASKO IDENTIFICATION PRODUCTS
Also Called: Dasko Label
66 Commercial Way Unit 1 (02914-1003)
P.O. Box 546, Seekonk MA (02771-0546)
PHONE....................401 435-6500
Paul Movsesian, *Owner*
Bobby Brasil,
EMP: 12
SQ FT: 10,000
SALES (est): 3.9MM **Privately Held**
SIC: 3555 3993 2679 Mfg Printing Trades Machinery Mfg Signs/Advertising Specialties Mfg Converted Paper Products

(G-20404)
DEXTER ENTERPRISES CORP
Also Called: Dexter Co The
70 Waterman Ave (02914-4410)
PHONE....................401 434-2300
R S Dexter, *President*
EMP: 8
SALES (est): 636.3K **Privately Held**
SIC: 3993 7389 Mfg Signs/Advertising Specialties Business Services

(G-20405)
DEXTER SERVICE CENTER
80 Waterman Ave (02914-4410)
PHONE....................401 438-3900
Roy S Dexter, *President*
Kirk Dexter, *Corp Secy*
Brent Dexter, *Vice Pres*
EMP: 3
SQ FT: 25,000
SALES: 231.3K **Privately Held**
SIC: 7692 4959 7538 General Automotive & Truck Repair Welding Repair & Snow Removal

(G-20406)
DEXTER SIGN CO
Also Called: Dexter Crane Service
70 Waterman Ave (02914-4410)
PHONE....................401 434-1100
Roy S Dexter, *President*
Brent Dexter, *Vice Pres*
Kirk Dexter, *Treasurer*
EMP: 20 **EST:** 1945
SQ FT: 25,000
SALES (est): 2.1MM **Privately Held**
SIC: 3993 1542 7389 1731 Mfg Signs/Ad Specialties Nonresidential Cnstn Business Services Electrical Contractor

(G-20407)
DIGITAL PRINTING CONCEPTS INC
985 Waterman Ave (02914-1342)
PHONE....................401 431-2110
John Cummings, *President*
EMP: 3
SALES (est): 341.8K **Privately Held**
SIC: 2759 Commercial Printing

(G-20408)
EAST BAY ICE CO INC
1109 S Broadway (02914-4930)
PHONE....................401 434-7485
Robert Swift, *President*
EMP: 6
SQ FT: 18,000
SALES (est): 500K **Privately Held**
SIC: 2097 Mfg Ice

(G-20409)
EAST PROVIDENCE MOHAWKS
78 Vine St (02914-4317)
PHONE....................401 829-1411
Damian Ramos, *President*
EMP: 3
SALES (est): 62K **Privately Held**
SIC: 2273 Mfg Carpets/Rugs

(G-20410)
ENVIRONMENTAL CTRL SYSTEMS INC
Also Called: Aquas Group
830 Waterman Ave (02914-1728)
PHONE....................401 437-8612

▲ = Import ▼=Export
◆ =Import/Export

Nicholas Paolo Jr, *President*
Josh Berndt, *Project Engr*
EMP: 13
SQ FT: 2,234
SALES (est): 1.2MM **Privately Held**
SIC: 3559 Mfg Misc Industry Machinery

(G-20411)
EVANS CAPACITOR COMPANY
72 Boyd Ave (02914-1202)
PHONE..................................401 435-3555
Charles Dewey, *CEO*
David Evans, *President*
Mike Richard, *Opers Mgr*
Dave Zawacki, *Purch Mgr*
Tom Murphy, *QA Dir*
▼ **EMP:** 46
SQ FT: 5,000
SALES: 14.2MM **Privately Held**
WEB: www.evanscap.com
SIC: 3469 Mfg Metal Stampings

(G-20412)
EVANS FINDINGS COMPANY INC
Also Called: Evans Company
33 Eastern Ave (02914-2107)
PHONE..................................401 434-5600
Peter T Evans, *President*
Missy Golomb, *Purch Agent*
Tom Ramlow, *Sls & Mktg Exec*
Peter Evans, *CFO*
Missy Galob, *Accountant*
◆ **EMP:** 46 **EST:** 1945
SQ FT: 30,000
SALES: 11MM **Privately Held**
WEB: www.evanstechnology.com
SIC: 3469 3915 Mfg Metal Stampings Mfg Jewelers' Materials

(G-20413)
FERREIRA CONCRETE FORMS INC
7 Tallman Ave (02914-2022)
PHONE..................................401 639-0931
Mariano Ferreira, *President*
Sergio Ferreira, *Corp Secy*
EMP: 17
SQ FT: 17,000
SALES (est): 2.1MM **Privately Held**
SIC: 3271 Concrete Form Work

(G-20414)
FIRST CARD CO INC
79 Commercial Way (02914-1019)
PHONE..................................401 434-6140
Anthony Calandrelli, *President*
Ronald Marks,
Ronald J Marks,
▲ **EMP:** 28
SALES: 3MM **Privately Held**
SIC: 3911 Mfg Precious Metal Jewelry

(G-20415)
GRAPHIC INK INCORPORATED
629 Warren Ave (02914-2914)
PHONE..................................401 431-5081
Nelson Silva, *President*
Nelson Silvia, *President*
Hilda Allienello, *Vice Pres*
EMP: 16
SALES (est): 1.6MM **Privately Held**
WEB: www.graphicinkonline.com
SIC: 2759 Screen Printing

(G-20416)
GRIPNAIL CORPORATION
Also Called: Amtak Fasteners
97 Dexter Rd (02914-2045)
PHONE..................................401 431-1791
David Ashton, *President*
Christopher Ryding, *CFO*
▲ **EMP:** 35
SQ FT: 30,000
SALES (est): 7.8MM **Privately Held**
WEB: www.gripnail.com
SIC: 3429 3452 Mfg Hardware Mfg Bolts/Screws/Rivets

(G-20417)
GUIA COMMERCIAL PORTUGUES INC
100 Warren Ave (02914-5137)
P.O. Box 14331 (02914-0331)
PHONE..................................401 438-1740
David Dasilva, *President*
EMP: 7
SQ FT: 3,394
SALES (est): 295.7K **Privately Held**
SIC: 2741 Misc Publishing

(G-20418)
HALBRO AMERICA INC
885 Warren Ave (02914-1423)
PHONE..................................401 438-2727
Robert J Hoder, *President*
▲ **EMP:** 6
SQ FT: 2,000
SALES (est): 430K **Privately Held**
WEB: www.cleaningpro.com
SIC: 2321 Manufactures Rugby Shirts

(G-20419)
ILLUMINOSS MEDICAL INC
993 Waterman Ave (02914-1314)
PHONE..................................401 714-0008
Manny Avila, *CEO*
Dirk M Kuyper, *President*
Amy Orlick Berman, *Vice Pres*
Sara Money, *Production*
Lucy Doherty, *Office Mgr*
EMP: 13
SQ FT: 8,400
SALES (est): 2.4MM **Privately Held**
SIC: 3841 Mfg Surgical/Medical Instruments

(G-20420)
IMPERIAL-DELTAH INC
Also Called: Imperial Pearl Syndicate
795 Waterman Ave (02914-1713)
PHONE..................................401 434-2597
Banice Bazar, *President*
Jonathan Louttit, *Exec VP*
Todd Bazar, *Vice Pres*
Marsha Matteson, *Controller*
Alan Bergel, *Sales Staff*
▲ **EMP:** 100 **EST:** 1958
SALES (est): 12.1MM
SALES (corp-wide): 23.2MM **Privately Held**
WEB: www.pearls.com
SIC: 3911 5094 Mfg Precious Metal Jewelry Whol Jewelry/Precious Stones
PA: The Bazar Group Inc
795 Waterman Ave
East Providence RI 02914
401 434-2595

(G-20421)
ISM CAPITAL CORPORATION LTD
940 Waterman Ave (02914-1337)
PHONE..................................401 454-8519
Gregory Lucini, *President*
EMP: 3
SALES (est): 12.5K **Privately Held**
SIC: 3672 Mfg Printed Circuit Boards

(G-20422)
JH LYNCH & SONS INC
835 Taunton Ave (02914-1614)
PHONE..................................401 434-7100
Peter Lynch, *Manager*
EMP: 159
SALES (corp-wide): 95.6MM **Privately Held**
SIC: 2951 Mfg Asphalt Mixtures/Blocks
PA: J.H. Lynch & Sons, Inc.
50 Lynch Pl
Cumberland RI 02864
401 333-4300

(G-20423)
JMH INDUSTRIES INC
Also Called: Superior Glass
889 Waterman Ave (02914-1313)
PHONE..................................401 438-2500
Joe Horvath, *President*
EMP: 4 **EST:** 1992
SALES (est): 437.1K **Privately Held**
SIC: 3231 3211 Mfg Products-Purchased Glass Mfg Flat Glass

(G-20424)
JONES SAFETY EQUIPMENT COMPANY
Also Called: Jones & Company
325 Massasoit Ave (02914-2011)
PHONE..................................401 434-4010
Lawrence K Hey, *President*
Don Wylie, *Managing Prtnr*
Gail Griffin, *General Mgr*
Peter Skinner, *Exec VP*
Steve Bolan, *Vice Pres*
EMP: 7 **EST:** 1940
SQ FT: 5,000
SALES (est): 1.1MM **Privately Held**
SIC: 3851 Mfg Safety Goggles

(G-20425)
JONETTE JEWELRY COMPANY
Also Called: Satisfashion
373 Taunton Ave (02914-2610)
PHONE..................................401 438-1941
Gordon Lisker, *President*
EMP: 78
SQ FT: 18,000
SALES (est): 7.1MM **Privately Held**
SIC: 3961 Mfg Costume Jewelry

(G-20426)
KELLEY METAL CORP
115 Valley St (02914-4492)
PHONE..................................401 434-8795
John Kelly Jr, *President*
John Kelley III, *Vice Pres*
EMP: 10
SQ FT: 12,000
SALES (est): 1.2MM **Privately Held**
WEB: www.kellymetal.com
SIC: 3341 Secondary Smelting & Refining Of Nonferrous Metals

(G-20427)
L & B BEVERAGE INC
227 N Brow St Ste A (02914-4417)
PHONE..................................401 434-9991
Luis F Oliveria, *President*
▲ **EMP:** 4
SALES (est): 224.4K **Privately Held**
SIC: 2086 Manufacture Bottled/Canned Soft Drinks

(G-20428)
L F PEASE CO
Also Called: Pease Awning & Sunroom Co
21 Massasoit Ave (02914-4439)
P.O. Box 14205 (02914-0205)
PHONE..................................401 438-2850
Toll Free:..877 -
EMP: 12 **EST:** 1866
SQ FT: 25,000
SALES (est): 2MM **Privately Held**
SIC: 2431 2394 2591 3444 Millwork, Nsk

(G-20429)
LDC INC
22 First St (02914-5007)
PHONE..................................401 861-4667
Edward N Decristofaro, *President*
Jennifer Brousseau, *Exec VP*
▲ **EMP:** 10
SALES (est): 1.8MM **Privately Held**
WEB: www.ldcincorporated.com
SIC: 3544 3312 5944 5094 Mfg Dies/Tools/Jigs/Fixt Blast Furnace-Steel Work Ret Jewelry Whol Jewelry/Precs Stone

(G-20430)
LINDON GROUP INC
28 Sutton Ave (02914-3414)
PHONE..................................401 272-2081
Melinda F Penney, *President*
Dalita Tomellini, *Vice Pres*
Lindsay Pettinelli, *Sales Mgr*
▲ **EMP:** 4
SQ FT: 5,000
SALES (est): 1MM **Privately Held**
SIC: 3829 5039 Mfg Measuring/Controlling Devices Whol Construction Materials

(G-20431)
MATRIX I LLC
Also Called: Pep Micropep
1 Catamore Blvd Ste 3 (02914-1233)
PHONE..................................401 434-3040
Alan M Huffenus, *CEO*
John S Harker, *President*
EMP: 74
SQ FT: 65,000
SALES (est): 22.4MM
SALES (corp-wide): 770.6MM **Publicly Held**
SIC: 3089 3544 Mfg Plastic Products Mfg Dies/Tools/Jigs/Fixtures
HQ: Precision Engineered Products Llc
110 Frank Mossberg Dr
Attleboro MA 02703
508 226-5600

(G-20432)
MLS SCREW MACHINE CORP
10 Dexter Rd (02914-2004)
PHONE..................................401 435-3850
Maria Soares, *President*
Manuel Soares, *Vice Pres*
EMP: 5
SQ FT: 1,700
SALES: 75K **Privately Held**
SIC: 3452 Mfg Screws Bolts Fasteners And Other Machine Parts

(G-20433)
MORRIS TRANSPARENT BOX CO
945 Warren Ave (02914-1423)
PHONE..................................401 438-6116
Alfred T Morris Jr, *President*
Joan Morris, *Vice Pres*
Ann Morris, *Admin Sec*
EMP: 25
SQ FT: 20,000
SALES (est): 3.4MM **Privately Held**
SIC: 3089 5162 2671 Mfg Plastic Products Whol Plastic Materials/Shapes Mfg Packaging Paper/Film

(G-20434)
NARRAGANSETT BUS FORMS INC
21 Massasoit Ave (02914-4439)
P.O. Box 9448, Providence (02940-9448)
PHONE..................................401 331-2000
David Almeida, *CEO*
EMP: 20
SALES (est): 2.8MM **Privately Held**
SIC: 2752 Lithographic Commercial Printing

(G-20435)
NORDSON EFD LLC (HQ)
Also Called: E F D
40 Catamore Blvd (02914-1206)
PHONE..................................401 431-7000
Michael F Hilton, *President*
Joe Butz, *Area Mgr*
Gregory A Thaxton, *Senior VP*
Jeff Pembroke, *Vice Pres*
David Guiot, *Vice Pres*
▲ **EMP:** 212 **EST:** 1963
SQ FT: 115,000
SALES (est): 97.5MM
SALES (corp-wide): 2.2B **Publicly Held**
WEB: www.efd-inc.com
SIC: 3548 3586 3699 Mfg Welding Apparatus Mfg Measuring/Dispensing Pumps Mfg Electrical Equipment/Supplies
PA: Nordson Corporation
28601 Clemens Rd
Westlake OH 44145
440 892-1580

(G-20436)
NUMACO PACKAGING LLC
82 Boyd Ave (02914-1202)
PHONE..................................401 438-4952
Nicholas Titone, *President*
Jeff Brown, *COO*
Jason Titone, *Vice Pres*
▲ **EMP:** 10
SQ FT: 40,000
SALES (est): 2MM **Privately Held**
WEB: www.numaco.com
SIC: 3172 2652 3999 3545 Mfg Personal Leather Gds Mfg Setup Paperboard Box Mfg Misc Products Mfg Machine Tool Access

(G-20437)
OCEAN SIDE PUBLICATIONS
95 Putnam St (02914)
PHONE..................................401 331-8426
Guy Settipane, *President*
EMP: 4
SQ FT: 2,500
SALES (est): 307K **Privately Held**
SIC: 2731 2721 Books-Publishing/Printing Periodicals-Publishing/Printing

(G-20438)
OCEAN STATE CPL INC
40 Jordan St (02914-1214)
PHONE..................................401 431-0153
Robert Mongeon, *President*
Guido Petrosinelli, *Vice Pres*
Charles Coelho, *Admin Sec*
EMP: 110
SQ FT: 30,356
SALES (est): 16.3MM **Privately Held**
WEB: www.oceanstatecpl.com
SIC: 2053 Manufactures Bakery Products

(G-20439)
PARSONSKELLOGG LLC
Also Called: Driving Impressions
2290 Pawtucket Ave (02914-1710)
PHONE..................................401 438-0650
Tom Kellogg, *President*
Cameron Socha, *Opers Staff*
Pete McCormick, *CFO*
Joy Gothberg, *Finance*
Kristen Cambio, *Accounts Mgr*
EMP: 26
SQ FT: 21,000
SALES: 17.1MM **Privately Held**
WEB: www.parsonskellogg.com
SIC: 3949 7389 7319 Mfg Sporting/Athletic Goods Business Services Advertising Services

(G-20440)
PCS METRO
328 Warren Ave (02914-3841)
PHONE..................................401 574-6105
EMP: 4
SALES (est): 393.1K **Privately Held**
SIC: 3663 Mfg Radio/Tv Communication Equipment

(G-20441)
PG IMTECH OF CALIFORN
27 Dexter Rd (02914-2045)
PHONE..................................401 521-2490
Kenneth Shonk, *Administration*
EMP: 4
SALES (est): 299.3K **Privately Held**
SIC: 2851 Mfg Paints/Allied Products

(G-20442)
PITNEY BOWES INC
70 Catamore Blvd Ste 1 (02914-1218)
PHONE..................................401 435-8500
Nicolas Hage, *Manager*
EMP: 25
SALES (corp-wide): 3.5B **Publicly Held**
SIC: 3579 7359 Mfg Office Machines Equipment Rental/Leasing
PA: Pitney Bowes Inc.
3001 Summer St Ste 3
Stamford CT 06905
203 356-5000

(G-20443)
SE MASS DEVLOPMENT LLC
930 Waterman Ave (02914-1337)
PHONE..................................401 434-3329
EMP: 3 **EST:** 2009
SALES (est): 195.4K **Privately Held**
SIC: 3613 Mfg Switchgear/Switchboards

(G-20444)
SIGNATURE PRINTING INC
5 Almeida Ave (02914-1001)
PHONE..................................401 438-1200
Anthony Andrade, *President*
Daniel Paquette, *VP Bus Dvlpt*
EMP: 60
SQ FT: 1,500
SALES: 12.4MM **Privately Held**
SIC: 2752 Lithographic Commercial Printing

(G-20445)
TAHOE JEWELRY INC
20 J Medeiros Way (02914-1022)
PHONE..................................401 435-4114
John Medeiros, *President*
EMP: 30
SQ FT: 10,000
SALES (est): 4.2MM **Privately Held**
WEB: www.tahoejewelry.com
SIC: 3911 Mfg Precious Metal Jewelry

(G-20446)
TE CONNECTIVITY CORPORATION
Also Called: Tyco Elec Identification
76 Commercial Way (02914-1026)
P.O. Box 3608, Harrisburg PA (17105-3608)
PHONE..................................401 432-8200
Dennis Montefusco, *Manager*
EMP: 40
SALES (corp-wide): 13.9B **Privately Held**
WEB: www.raychem.com
SIC: 2672 3565 Mfg Labels & Labeling Equipment
HQ: Te Connectivity Corporation
1050 Westlakes Dr
Berwyn PA 19312
610 893-9800

(G-20447)
UP COUNTRY INC
76 Boyd Ave (02914-1202)
PHONE..................................401 431-2940
Alice M Nichols, *President*
▲ **EMP:** 22
SQ FT: 3,000
SALES (est): 2.6MM **Privately Held**
SIC: 3999 0752 Mfg Misc Products Animal Services

(G-20448)
W R COBB COMPANY (PA)
Also Called: Cobb/Ballou Findings
800 Waterman Ave (02914-1728)
PHONE..................................401 438-7000
Roderick Lichtenfels, *President*
Ralph Quackenbush, *Managing Dir*
Dror Galili, *Vice Pres*
Jay Gerber, *Vice Pres*
Karen Robinson, *Sales Staff*
▲ **EMP:** 150 **EST:** 1877
SQ FT: 30,000
SALES (est): 27.2MM **Privately Held**
WEB: www.wrcobb.com
SIC: 3915 Mfg Jewelers' Materials

(G-20449)
WHETSTONE WORKSHOP LLC
41 Dexter Rd (02914-2045)
PHONE..................................401 368-7410
Isaac Juodvalkis,
Maria Martinez,
EMP: 7
SQ FT: 7,500
SALES: 250K **Privately Held**
SIC: 3499 Mfg Misc Fabricated Metal Products

Exeter
Washington County

(G-20450)
HARDWOOD DESIGN INC
24 Dorset Mill Rd (02822-5026)
PHONE..................................401 294-2235
William Bivona, *President*
Robinson Berry, *Vice Pres*
Jake Olsted, *Manager*
EMP: 21
SQ FT: 12,000
SALES (est): 2.9MM **Privately Held**
WEB: www.hardwoodesign.com
SIC: 2431 2434 Mfg Millwork Mfg Wood Kitchen Cabinet

(G-20451)
HERITAGE CONCRETE CORP
535 South County Trl (02822-3405)
P.O. Box 553 (02822-0505)
PHONE..................................401 294-1524
Sharon Courtois, *President*
John Courtois, *Treasurer*
EMP: 10
SQ FT: 2,500
SALES (est): 1.1MM **Privately Held**
WEB: www.heritageconcrete.com
SIC: 3273 Mfg Ready Mixed Concrete

(G-20452)
MILLER FIREWOOD & LOGGING INC
1741 Ten Rod Rd (02822-1912)
PHONE..................................401 539-7707
Keil C Miller, *Principal*
EMP: 3
SALES (est): 233.8K **Privately Held**
SIC: 2411 Logging

(G-20453)
MOODY INVESTMENTS LLC
Also Called: Rovers Speacial Vehicles
716 South County Trl (02822-3404)
PHONE..................................401 423-0121
Richard Moody, *CEO*
EMP: 4
SALES: 1.2MM **Privately Held**
SIC: 3799 Vehicle Sales

Fiskeville
Providence County

(G-20454)
ARKWRIGHT ADVANCED COATING INC
Also Called: Sihl
538 Main St (02823)
P.O. Box 139 (02823-0139)
PHONE..................................401 821-1000
Diego Mosna, *CEO*
Chris McInerney, *Managing Dir*
Stephanie Provos, *Treasurer*
David Pachon, *Sales Staff*
◆ **EMP:** 110
SALES (est): 36.9MM
SALES (corp-wide): 950.8K **Privately Held**
WEB: www.arkwright.com
SIC: 2679 Mfg Converted Paper Products
PA: Diatec Holding Spa
Via Giosue' Carducci 11
Milano MI 20123
-

Forestdale
Providence County

(G-20455)
BELLOWS INC
194 School St (02824-1216)
P.O. Box 716 (02824-0716)
PHONE..................................401 766-5331
Mayana Bellows, *President*
Fredrick Bellows, *President*
EMP: 3
SALES (est): 240K **Privately Held**
SIC: 3199 Mfg Leather Goods

Foster
Providence County

(G-20456)
JOHNSON & JOHNSON
78 E Killingly Rd (02825-1432)
PHONE..................................401 647-1493
Tom Chrostek, *Manager*
EMP: 80
SALES (corp-wide): 81.5B **Publicly Held**
SIC: 2676 Mfg Consumer Products & Surgical Appliances
PA: Johnson & Johnson
1 Johnson And Johnson Plz
New Brunswick NJ 08933
732 524-0400

(G-20457)
MARK GOODWIN WOODEN BOWLS
63 Balcom Rd (02825-1324)
PHONE..................................866 478-4065
EMP: 3
SALES (est): 214.7K **Privately Held**
SIC: 2411 Logging

(G-20458)
NICKLE CREEK VINEYARD LLC
12 King Rd (02825-1339)
PHONE..................................401 369-3694
Sheri O'Connor, *Principal*
EMP: 5
SALES (est): 413.8K **Privately Held**
SIC: 2084 Mfg Wines/Brandy/Spirits

Glendale
Providence County

(G-20459)
BRUIN PLASTICS CO INC
61 Joslin Rd (02826-1633)
P.O. Box 700 (02826-0700)
PHONE..................................401 568-3081
Dennis E Angelone, *President*
Stephen M Angelone, *Vice Pres*
Brian Cardon, *Plant Supt*
Kevin Pettit, *Controller*
Tina Poxon, *Cust Mgr*
◆ **EMP:** 43 **EST:** 1964
SQ FT: 75,000
SALES: 7.4MM **Privately Held**
WEB: www.bruinplastics.com
SIC: 2295 Mfg Unsupported Plastic Film/Sheet

Greenville
Providence County

(G-20460)
A F F INC (PA)
Also Called: Fashion Accessories First
26 Lark Industrial Pkwy (02828-3009)
PHONE..................................401 949-3000
Arthur Fiorenzano, *President*
Nancy Landi, *Principal*
Joellen Quaglietta, *Principal*
Noel Bentley, *Vice Pres*
Frank Fiorenzano, *Vice Pres*
▲ **EMP:** 74
SQ FT: 22,000
SALES (est): 13.7MM **Privately Held**
WEB: www.faf.com
SIC: 3911 Mfg Precious Metal Jewelry

(G-20461)
ARTIC TOOL & ENGRG CO LLC
29 Lark Industrial Pkwy (02828-3024)
PHONE..................................401 785-2210
Michael Gamache, *CEO*
John Sousa, *General Mgr*
Bart Bauers, *CFO*
EMP: 13
SQ FT: 10,000
SALES (est): 2.2MM **Privately Held**
WEB: www.artictool.com
SIC: 3599 3469 7692 Mfg Industrial Machinery Mfg Metal Stampings Welding Repair
PA: The Carlyle Johnson Machine Company Llc
291 Boston Tpke
Bolton CT 06043
-

(G-20462)
ATOMIC LED INC
81 W Greenville Rd (02828-1507)
PHONE..................................401 265-0222
EMP: 4
SALES (est): 397.6K **Privately Held**
SIC: 3648 Mfg Lighting Equipment

(G-20463)
B FRESH
37 Lark Industrial Pkwy A (02828-3001)
PHONE..................................401 349-0001
Robert Thistle, *Principal*
EMP: 3
SALES (est): 144K **Privately Held**
SIC: 2064 Mfg Candy/Confectionery

(G-20464)
CAVANAGH COMPANY
610 Putnam Pike (02828-1438)
P.O. Box 953 (02828-0953)
PHONE..................................401 949-4000
Brian Cavanagh, *President*
Peter Cavanagh, *President*
Helene Cavanagh, *Corp Secy*
▲ **EMP:** 50 **EST:** 1941
SQ FT: 25,000
SALES (est): 8.6MM **Privately Held**
WEB: www.cavanaghco.com
SIC: 2051 Mfg Bread/Related Products

▲ = Import ▼=Export
◆ =Import/Export

(G-20465)
CREATIVE PINS BY LYNNE
6 Country Dr (02828-1902)
PHONE..................................401 949-3665
Lynne Gaudett, *Owner*
EMP: 3
SALES (est): 139.9K **Privately Held**
WEB: www.creativepins.net
SIC: 3911 Mfg Precious Metal Jewelry

(G-20466)
DAMICO MFG CO
22 Lark Industrial Pkwy C (02828-3042)
PHONE..................................401 949-0023
John Damico, *Principal*
EMP: 3
SQ FT: 2,000
SALES (est): 234.8K **Privately Held**
SIC: 3911 Mfg Precious Metal Jewelry

(G-20467)
HB PRECISION PRODUCTS
21 Lark Industrial Pkwy A (02828-3026)
P.O. Box 207, Slatersville (02876-0207)
PHONE..................................401 767-4340
Ronald Houle, *CEO*
Raymond Houle, *Vice Pres*
EMP: 10
SALES (est): 114.5K **Privately Held**
SIC: 3599 Mfg Industrial Machinery

(G-20468)
IMPRINT INC
Also Called: Imprint Industrial Service Co
22 Lark Industrial Pkwy E (02828-3042)
PHONE..................................401 949-1177
Margaret Chiovitti, *President*
Leslie Valiant, *Project Mgr*
EMP: 5 **EST:** 1996
SQ FT: 3,000
SALES (est): 658.3K **Privately Held**
WEB: www.imprint.com
SIC: 3555 5084 7699 Mfg Printing Equipment Whol Printing Equip & Supplies & Repairs Printing Equipment

(G-20469)
JACKSON BOOKBINDING CO INC
21 Lark Industrial Pkwy B (02828-3026)
PHONE..................................401 231-0800
Robert Jackson, *President*
William E Jackson Jr, *President*
Robert E Jackson, *Treasurer*
Ronald Jackson, *Asst Treas*
EMP: 15
SQ FT: 4,000
SALES (est): 1.4MM **Privately Held**
WEB: www.wejco.com
SIC: 2782 3469 3544 2789 Mfg Of Bookbinding Embossing Trade Binding Loose-Leaf Binders Foil Stamping & Die Cutting

(G-20470)
KERISSA CREATIONS INC
15 Lark Industrial Pkwy E (02828-3029)
P.O. Box 913 (02828-0913)
PHONE..................................401 949-3700
Marcus A Senerchia Jr, *President*
Sal Scetta, *Treasurer*
▲ **EMP:** 40 **EST:** 1982
SQ FT: 12,000
SALES (est): 6.1MM **Privately Held**
SIC: 3961 Mfg Precious Metal Jewelry

(G-20471)
PAVEMENT WAREHOUSE
11 Calista St (02828-2805)
P.O. Box 910 (02828-0910)
PHONE..................................401 233-3200
Charles Stanley, *Owner*
EMP: 3
SALES (est): 309K **Privately Held**
SIC: 2951 Mfg Asphalt Mixtures/Blocks

(G-20472)
RACHELS TABLE LLC
37 Lark Industrial Pkwy H (02828-3049)
PHONE..................................401 949-5333
Allyson Farrar, *President*
EMP: 3
SQ FT: 4,000
SALES (est): 293.6K **Privately Held**
SIC: 2032 Canned Specialties, Nsk

(G-20473)
REGENT CONTROLS INC
29 Lark Industrial Pkwy (02828-3024)
PHONE..................................203 732-6200
Lora C Murphy, *President*
H Clay Minor, *Vice Pres*
EMP: 11
SQ FT: 9,000
SALES (est): 1.9MM **Privately Held**
WEB: www.regentcontrols.com
SIC: 3625 Mfg Relays/Industrial Controls

(G-20474)
RICHARD CHIOVITTI
Also Called: Industrial Service Company
22 Lark Industrial Pkwy (02828-3053)
PHONE..................................401 949-1177
Richard Chiovitti Sr, *Owner*
EMP: 5
SQ FT: 3,000
SALES (est): 363.1K **Privately Held**
SIC: 3555 5084 7699 Mfg Printing Equipment Whol Printing Equip & Supplies & Repairs Printing Equipment

(G-20475)
SMITHFIED TIMES
543 Putnam Pike (02828-3017)
PHONE..................................401 232-9600
John J Tassoni Jr, *President*
EMP: 3 **EST:** 2016
SALES (est): 103.7K **Privately Held**
SIC: 2711 Newspapers-Publishing/Printing

(G-20476)
VIDEOLOGY IMGING SOLUTIONS INC (PA)
37 Lark Industrial Pkwy M (02828-3049)
PHONE..................................401 949-5332
Carol Ethier, *CEO*
Rick Nadeau, *Vice Pres*
Tim Wolfe, *Opers Mgr*
Paul Watkins, *Sales Staff*
Richard Haynes, *Manager*
▲ **EMP:** 36
SQ FT: 15,000
SALES (est): 4.4MM **Privately Held**
WEB: www.videologyinc.com
SIC: 3651 Mfg Home Audio/Video Equipment

Harrisville
Providence County

(G-20477)
ATLAS BARRELL & PALLET INC
50 Old Mill St (02830-1617)
PHONE..................................401 568-2900
Earl Handrigan, *President*
EMP: 55
SQ FT: 60,000
SALES (est): 7.2MM **Privately Held**
SIC: 2448 Mfg Wood Pallets/Skids

(G-20478)
DESNOYERS ENTERPRISES INC
Also Called: Compton Paper & Novelty
1160 Mount Pleasant Rd (02830-1736)
PHONE..................................800 922-4445
Armand Desnoyers, *President*
EMP: 6
SQ FT: 10,000
SALES (corp-wide): 2.8MM **Privately Held**
SIC: 3441 5113 Mfg Structural Steel & Whol Paper Products
PA: Desnoyers Enterprises Inc
1346 Newport Ave Unit 82
Attleboro MA 02703
508 639-5186

(G-20479)
GRAVEL ELECTRIC INC
27 Indigo Farm Rd (02830-1858)
PHONE..................................401 265-6041
Donald D Gravel, *President*
EMP: 3
SALES (est): 186.6K **Privately Held**
SIC: 1442 Construction Sand/Gravel

(G-20480)
HOMESPUN SAMPLAR
1716 Round Top Rd (02830-1013)
PHONE..................................401 732-3181
Linda McNalley, *Owner*
EMP: 3
SALES: 250K **Privately Held**
WEB: www.homespunsamplar.com
SIC: 3944 5949 Mfg Games/Toys Ret Sewing Supplies/Fabrics

Hope Valley
Washington County

(G-20481)
BUICK LLC
Also Called: Beadery Craft Products, The
106 Canonchet Rd (02832-1109)
P.O. Box 178 (02832-0178)
PHONE..................................401 539-2432
Joseph Ritacco, *Controller*
Steven Grahm, *Mng Member*
▲ **EMP:** 35
SQ FT: 28,000
SALES (est): 8MM **Privately Held**
WEB: www.thebeadery.com
SIC: 3999 Mfg Misc Products

(G-20482)
COASTAL PLASTICS INC
35 Mechanic St (02832-2017)
P.O. Box 477 (02832-0477)
PHONE..................................401 539-2446
Robert E Johnson, *President*
David Johnson, *Vice Pres*
Jane A Johnson, *Admin Sec*
EMP: 30
SQ FT: 28,000
SALES (est): 4.9MM **Privately Held**
SIC: 2821 Mfg Plastic Materials/Resins

(G-20483)
CRWW SPECIALTY COMPOSITES INC
49 Mechanic St (02832-2017)
P.O. Box 479 (02832-0479)
PHONE..................................401 539-8555
Craig Girdwood, *President*
EMP: 15
SQ FT: 20,000
SALES (est): 644.4K **Privately Held**
SIC: 2221 Manmade Broadwoven Fabric Mill

(G-20484)
DEE KAY DESIGNS INC (PA)
177 Skunk Hill Rd (02832-1211)
P.O. Box 448 (02832-0448)
PHONE..................................401 539-2400
Richard S Rakauskas, *President*
Charles Donnell, *Exec VP*
◆ **EMP:** 52
SQ FT: 50,000
SALES (est): 6.4MM **Privately Held**
WEB: www.kaydeedesigns.com
SIC: 2269 2261 5023 Finishing Plant Cotton Finishing Plant Whol Homefurnishings

(G-20485)
J TEFFT LOGGING & FIREWOO
33 Fenner Hill Rd (02832-1905)
PHONE..................................401 539-9838
Jason Tefft, *Principal*
EMP: 6
SALES (est): 585.4K **Privately Held**
SIC: 2411 Logging

(G-20486)
RAILING PRO INC
5 Summit Rd (02832-3217)
PHONE..................................401 539-7998
Steven McCaggart, *President*
EMP: 3
SALES: 700K **Privately Held**
WEB: www.railingpro.com
SIC: 3446 Mfg Architectural Metalwork

Hopkinton
Washington County

(G-20487)
JAMES THOMPSON NATIVE LUMBER
Also Called: Thompson Lumber
385 Woodville Rd (02833-1145)
P.O. Box 85 (02833-0085)
PHONE..................................401 377-2837
James Walter Thompson, *President*
EMP: 15 **EST:** 1958
SALES (est): 2.3MM **Privately Held**
SIC: 2421 2411 Sawmill/Planing Mill Logging

Jamestown
Newport County

(G-20488)
CLARK BOAT-YARD
110 Racquet Rd (02835-2929)
PHONE..................................401 423-3625
Sarah E Clark, *Owner*
Michael Clark, *Owner*
Rolf Gronneberg, *Principal*
EMP: 5
SQ FT: 2,000
SALES (est): 470.3K **Privately Held**
SIC: 3732 Marina Operation

(G-20489)
ENDLESS WAVE INC
11 Howland Ave (02835-1212)
PHONE..................................401 423-3400
Ronald F Dimauro, *Principal*
EMP: 4 **EST:** 2010
SALES (est): 305.8K **Privately Held**
SIC: 3949 Mfg Sporting/Athletic Goods

(G-20490)
F & S WOOD PRODUCTS
39 Frigate St (02835-1725)
PHONE..................................401 423-1048
EMP: 3
SALES (est): 210K **Privately Held**
SIC: 2426 Hardwood Dimension/Floor Mill

(G-20491)
ISLAND NEWS ENTERPRISE
Also Called: Jamestown Press
45 Narragansett Ave (02835-1150)
PHONE..................................401 423-3200
Jeff Mc Donough, *President*
Robert Berczuk, *Publisher*
Pat Holtzman, *Adv Mgr*
Jeffrey McDonough, *Manager*
EMP: 8
SALES: 600K **Privately Held**
WEB: www.jamestownpress.com
SIC: 2711 Newspapers-Publishing/Printing

(G-20492)
JAMESTOWN BOAT YARD INC
60 Racquet Rd (02835-2928)
P.O. Box 347 (02835-0347)
PHONE..................................401 423-0600
Clement Napolitano, *President*
Chris Ototowski, *Vice Pres*
Steve Devoe, *Treasurer*
Steve McInnis, *Admin Sec*
▲ **EMP:** 30
SQ FT: 132,000
SALES: 3MM **Privately Held**
WEB: www.jby.com
SIC: 3732 Marina Operation

(G-20493)
NORTHRUP & GIBSON ENTPS LLC
386 Beacon Ave (02835-2315)
PHONE..................................401 423-2152
Stephen Northrup, *Principal*
Shaun Gibson,
EMP: 4
SALES: 275K **Privately Held**
SIC: 3731 1542 Ship Repair & Commercial Construction

GEOGRAPHIC

(G-20494)
RICHARDSON LANDSCAPING CORP
25 Clarke St (02835-1303)
P.O. Box 354 (02835-0354)
PHONE....................401 423-1505
Dorothy Richardson, *President*
EMP: 5
SALES (est): 530K **Privately Held**
SIC: 2721 Periodicals-Publishing/Printing

Johnston
Providence County

(G-20495)
1ST CASTING COMPANY
64 Dyerville Ave (02919-4411)
PHONE....................401 272-0750
Jerry Traficante, *President*
EMP: 10
SQ FT: 4,400
SALES: 800K **Privately Held**
SIC: 3356 Drawing Of Precious & Non-Precious Metals

(G-20496)
A-1 POLISHING CO
8 Alcazar Ave (02919-4070)
PHONE....................401 751-8944
Allan Minande, *Principal*
EMP: 3
SALES (est): 108.8K **Privately Held**
SIC: 3471 Plating/Polishing Service

(G-20497)
ACCU RX INC
100 Federal Way (02919-4637)
P.O. Box 19223 (02919-0223)
PHONE....................401 454-2920
Nicholas Masi, *President*
Elaine Masi, *Vice Pres*
EMP: 50
SQ FT: 5,000
SALES (est): 3.2MM
SALES (corp-wide): 1.4MM **Privately Held**
WEB: www.crizal.com
SIC: 3851 Mfg Prescription Lenses
HQ: Essilor Laboratories Of America, Inc.
13515 N Stemmons Fwy
Dallas TX 75234
972 241-4141

(G-20498)
AG & G INC (PA)
Also Called: VIESTE ROSA
21 Mill St (02919-6817)
PHONE....................401 946-4330
Anthony Giarrusso, *President*
Angelo Giarrusso, *Vice Pres*
Frank Giarrusso, *Vice Pres*
Matthew Giarrusso, *Treasurer*
John Giarrusso, *Admin Sec*
▲ **EMP:** 33
SQ FT: 25,000
SALES: 11.9MM **Privately Held**
WEB: www.viesterosa.com
SIC: 3961 Mfg Costume Jewelry

(G-20499)
ALVITI LINK ALL INC
165 Dyerville Ave Unit 1 (02919-4400)
PHONE....................401 861-6656
Lucille Knight, *President*
Thomas C Plunkett, *Principal*
EMP: 7
SALES (est): 567.5K **Privately Held**
WEB: www.alvitilinkall.com
SIC: 3911 Mfg Precious Metal Jewelry

(G-20500)
ARDEN JEWELRY MFG CO
Also Called: Joan Imports
10 Industrial Ln (02919-3126)
PHONE....................401 274-9800
Steven Abrams, *President*
▲ **EMP:** 26 **EST:** 1940
SQ FT: 28,000
SALES (est): 3.2MM **Privately Held**
WEB: www.ardenjewelry.com
SIC: 3911 Mfg Precious Metal Jewelry

(G-20501)
BREN CORPORATION
1763 Plainfield Pike (02919-5940)
PHONE....................401 943-8200
Edmund D Cianciarulo, *President*
Natalie Cianciarulo, *Corp Secy*
EMP: 30 **EST:** 1973
SALES (est): 2.5MM **Privately Held**
SIC: 2386 3172 3171 Mfg Leather Clothing Mfg Personal Leather Goods Mfg Women's Handbags/Purses

(G-20502)
CARS REALTY LLC
17 Ferncrest Dr (02919-3503)
PHONE....................401 231-1389
Rosetta Bucci, *Mng Member*
Carmello Scuncio,
Susan Scuncio,
EMP: 4
SALES (est): 220K **Privately Held**
SIC: 2741 Misc Publishing

(G-20503)
CASE FUTURE CORPORATION INC
27 Mill St (02919-6800)
PHONE....................401 944-0402
Mario Cimarelli, *President*
▲ **EMP:** 23
SQ FT: 25,000
SALES (est): 3.6MM **Privately Held**
SIC: 3499 Mfg Hinged Metal Boxes/Packaging

(G-20504)
CLOOS WOODWORKING INC
8 Alcazar Ave (02919-4070)
PHONE....................401 528-8629
Francis A Cloos, *President*
EMP: 5
SALES (est): 478.8K **Privately Held**
SIC: 2431 Mfg Millwork

(G-20505)
D & D MODEL CLEANING & CASTING
2 Leah St (02919-5321)
PHONE....................401 274-4011
Domingos Dias, *President*
EMP: 6
SALES (est): 534.8K **Privately Held**
SIC: 3911 Whol Jewelry/Precious Stones

(G-20506)
DANGLERS INC
35 Oakdale Ave (02919-5320)
PHONE....................401 274-7742
Smith Noel, *President*
Christopher J Smith, *Treasurer*
EMP: 5
SQ FT: 2,000
SALES (est): 745.7K **Privately Held**
SIC: 3559 Mfg Electroplating Equipment

(G-20507)
DECORATORS SEWING SHOPPE INC
1 Salzillo St (02919-5234)
PHONE....................401 453-3500
Frank J Boffi, *President*
EMP: 4 **EST:** 1956
SQ FT: 10,000
SALES (est): 310K **Privately Held**
SIC: 2591 Mfg Window Treatments

(G-20508)
DEMAICH INDUSTRIES INC
70 Mill St (02919-6251)
PHONE....................401 944-3576
Douglas Hood, *President*
Claire Hood, *Vice Pres*
Paul Baffoni, *Sales Staff*
Mary A Arruda, *Manager*
EMP: 15
SQ FT: 10,000
SALES (est): 2.6MM **Privately Held**
WEB: www.demaich.com
SIC: 3469 3599 Mfg Metal Stampings Mfg Industrial Machinery

(G-20509)
DURA KOTE TECHNOLOGY LTD
2 Industrial Ln (02919-3126)
PHONE....................401 331-6460
Louis Francazio, *President*
Bob Ricci, *Vice Pres*
EMP: 10
SQ FT: 15,000
SALES (est): 800K **Privately Held**
WEB: www.durakotetech.com
SIC: 3471 E Coat Specialist/Plating/Polishing /Bead Blastingservice

(G-20510)
E & M ENTERPRISES INC
16 Sunnyside Ave (02919-5318)
PHONE....................401 274-7405
Ernest Motta, *President*
Robbin Motta, *Manager*
EMP: 10 **EST:** 2000
SQ FT: 9,000
SALES (est): 1.6MM **Privately Held**
SIC: 3599 Industrial Machinery, Nec, Nsk

(G-20511)
FRANK J NEWMAN & SON INC
44 Newman Ave (02919-4149)
PHONE....................401 231-0550
William J Newman, *President*
Annette L Amato, *Corp Secy*
EMP: 9
SQ FT: 8,000
SALES: 967K **Privately Held**
SIC: 3444 Mfg Sheet Metalwork

(G-20512)
FRED RICCI TOOL CO INC
Also Called: Chewbarka's Tags
165 Dyerville Ave Unit 2 (02919-4400)
PHONE....................401 464-9911
Frank Ricci, *President*
EMP: 10
SQ FT: 15,000
SALES: 1.2MM **Privately Held**
SIC: 3599 Manufacturer Identification Tags Toolmaker

(G-20513)
FUELING SERVICES LLC
Also Called: Whitco Ameritest
141 Shun Pike (02919-4514)
P.O. Box 41628, Providence (02940-1628)
PHONE....................401 764-0711
Mike Horkins, *CEO*
EMP: 16
SQ FT: 6,000
SALES (est): 895.4K **Privately Held**
SIC: 3559 Mfg Misc Industry Machinery

(G-20514)
G TANURY PLATING CO INC
100 Railroad Ave (02919-2407)
PHONE....................401 232-2330
George Tanury, *CEO*
Joseph L Traficante, *Vice Pres*
EMP: 65
SQ FT: 43,000
SALES (est): 7.1MM **Privately Held**
WEB: www.gtanury.com
SIC: 3471 Plating/Polishing Service

(G-20515)
GENERAL PLATING INC
16 Sunnyside Ave (02919-5318)
PHONE....................401 421-0219
Peter Dietrich, *President*
EMP: 5 **EST:** 1930
SQ FT: 5,500
SALES (est): 442.5K **Privately Held**
SIC: 3471 Mfg Electroplating Of Metals Formed Products

(G-20516)
INDUSTRIAL & COMMERCIAL FINSHG
Also Called: Icf
1339 Plainfield St (02919-6813)
PHONE....................401 942-4680
Ronald Patrick, *President*
EMP: 8
SQ FT: 5,000
SALES: 400K **Privately Held**
SIC: 3479 Coating/Engraving Service

(G-20517)
LEEMAR CASTING COMPANY INC
27 Mill St Unit 2 (02919-6800)
PHONE....................401 276-2844
EMP: 4
SALES: 350K **Privately Held**
SIC: 3324 Steel Investment Foundry

(G-20518)
LIMAGE INC
4 Industrial Ln (02919-3126)
PHONE....................401 369-7141
Thomas V Fiore, *President*
Patricia A Fiore, *Vice Pres*
▲ **EMP:** 50
SQ FT: 8,000
SALES (est): 6MM **Privately Held**
SIC: 3961 Mfg Costume Jewelry

(G-20519)
LOUIS PRESS INC
39 Greenville Ave Apt 1 (02919-4223)
PHONE....................401 351-9229
Louis Perrotta, *President*
Thomas Perrotta, *President*
EMP: 7
SQ FT: 1,800
SALES (est): 903.6K **Privately Held**
WEB: www.louispress.net
SIC: 2752 Lithographic Commercial Printing

(G-20520)
MARTINS SOLDERING
10 Alcazar Ave (02919-4069)
PHONE....................401 521-2280
John Martin, *Owner*
EMP: 7
SALES: 670K **Privately Held**
SIC: 3911 Mfg Precious Metal Jewelry

(G-20521)
MELONI TOOL CO INC
Also Called: Dama
25 Oakdale Ave (02919-5317)
PHONE....................401 272-6513
Dominic Meloni, *President*
▲ **EMP:** 8
SALES (est): 670K **Privately Held**
WEB: www.dama.net
SIC: 3542 3915 Mfg Machine Tools-Forming Mfg Jewelers' Materials

(G-20522)
MINUTEMAN PRESS OF JOHNSTON
1999 Plainfield Pike # 3 (02919-5725)
PHONE....................401 944-0667
David Buttery, *Partner*
Linda Buttery, *Partner*
EMP: 4
SALES (est): 381.4K **Privately Held**
WEB: www.minmanri.com
SIC: 2752 Comm Prtg Litho

(G-20523)
MODERN MANUFACTURING INC
Also Called: Modern Jewelry
47 Homeland St (02919-5170)
PHONE....................401 944-9230
▲ **EMP:** 10
SQ FT: 27,000
SALES (est): 1.2MM **Privately Held**
SIC: 3961 Mfg Of Costume Jewelry & Costume Novelties Except Precious Metal

(G-20524)
MORGAN MILL METALS LLC
25 Morgan Mill Rd (02919-6320)
PHONE....................401 270-9944
Brian Kroll, *Plant Supt*
Cheryl S McElroy, *CFO*
Cameron McElroy, *Mng Member*
EMP: 15
SQ FT: 5,000
SALES: 10MM **Privately Held**
SIC: 3341 Secondary Nonferrous Metal Producer

(G-20525)
NEW CANAAN STONE SERVICE LLC
2 Deer Run Trl (02919-1008)
PHONE....................401 829-8293
Angelo J Iafrate, *Principal*
EMP: 5
SALES (est): 348.2K **Privately Held**
SIC: 3272 Mfg Concrete Products

(G-20526)
NORTHERN RI CONSERVATION DST
2283 Hartford Ave (02919-1713)
PHONE..................................401 934-0840
Paul Dolan, *Principal*
Jean Lynch, *Chairman*
Norman Hammond, *Treasurer*
William Colburn, *Admin Sec*
EMP: 6
SALES (est): 125K **Privately Held**
SIC: 3823 Water Quality

(G-20527)
PACKAGING COMPANY LLC (PA)
Also Called: A H Mfg. Co.
1 Carding Ln (02919-4621)
P.O. Box 19720 (02919-0720)
PHONE..................................401 943-5040
Jeffrey A Feibelman, *CEO*
Diane Middlemiss, *Vice Pres*
Andy Feldman, *VP Sales*
Cathy Ward, *Cust Mgr*
Filomena Carlone, *Sales Staff*
▲ **EMP:** 86
SQ FT: 150,000
SALES (est): 64.8MM **Privately Held**
WEB: www.aandhusa.com
SIC: 2653 2671 Mfg Corrugated/Solid Fiber Boxes Mfg Packaging Paper/Film

(G-20528)
PAUL KING FOUNDRY INC
92 Allendale Ave (02919-2351)
PHONE..................................401 231-3120
Paul Cabanagh, *President*
Michelle Cavanagh, *Business Mgr*
▲ **EMP:** 9
SALES (est): 660K **Privately Held**
WEB: www.fineartcasting.com
SIC: 3366 Copper Foundry

(G-20529)
PHE INVESTMENTS LLC
Also Called: Ava Anderson
1 Carding Ln (02919-4621)
PHONE..................................401 289-2900
Ava Sprague Anderson, *CEO*
Kimberly Anderson, *President*
Frohman Anderson III, *Founder*
Robert Anderson, *COO*
Bob Manny, *COO*
EMP: 55
SQ FT: 120,000
SALES (est): 13.8MM **Privately Held**
SIC: 2834 Mfg Pharmaceutical Preparations

(G-20530)
PM COLORS INC
10 Industrial Ln (02919-3126)
PHONE..................................401 521-7280
Paul Mercier, *President*
Steven Abrams, *Vice Pres*
EMP: 5
SALES: 250K **Privately Held**
SIC: 3479 Coating/Engraving Service

(G-20531)
PROPRINT INC
1145 Atwood Ave (02919-4924)
PHONE..................................401 944-3855
Ronald De Stefano, *President*
David De Stefano, *Vice Pres*
Nancy De Stefano, *Admin Sec*
EMP: 15
SQ FT: 3,000
SALES (est): 1.8MM **Privately Held**
SIC: 2759 Commercial Printing

(G-20532)
PROVIDENCE CABLE CORPORATION
12 Peppermint Ln (02919-3056)
PHONE..................................401 632-7650
Laura A Weedon, *President*
EMP: 14
SALES (est): 1.3MM **Privately Held**
WEB: www.providencecable.com
SIC: 3357 Distributor Of Data Network Cables

(G-20533)
RAMTEL CORPORATION
115 Railroad Ave (02919-2441)
PHONE..................................401 231-3340
Robert Moio Jr, *President*
Eleanor A Kelly, *Treasurer*
EMP: 18
SALES (est): 3MM **Privately Held**
WEB: www.ramtel.com
SIC: 3661 Mfg Telephones

(G-20534)
REAL ESTATE JOURNAL OF RI INC
1343 Hartford Ave Ste 2 (02919-7145)
P.O. Box 8392, Cranston (02920-0392)
PHONE..................................401 831-7778
Ralph A Coppolino, *President*
Ralph Coppolino, *Owner*
EMP: 5
SQ FT: 1,500
SALES (est): 340.5K **Privately Held**
WEB: www.rejri.com
SIC: 2711 Publisher Of A Real Estate Newspaper Not Printed On Site

(G-20535)
RECOGNITION AWARDS
Also Called: EMBlem&badge
16 Sunnyside Ave (02919-5318)
PHONE..................................401 365-1265
Robbin Motta, *Owner*
EMP: 4
SALES: 200K **Privately Held**
SIC: 3999 Mfg Misc Products

(G-20536)
RHODE ISLAND CENTERLESS INC
24 Morgan Mill Rd (02919-6321)
PHONE..................................401 942-0403
David Bryan, *President*
Joyce Bryan, *Treasurer*
Debra Bryan, *Office Mgr*
Martin Bryan, *Shareholder*
EMP: 10
SQ FT: 7,500
SALES (est): 1MM **Privately Held**
SIC: 3291 Mfg Abrasive Products

(G-20537)
RHODE ISLAND PROVISION CO INC
Also Called: Little Rhody Brand
5 Day St (02919-4301)
PHONE..................................401 831-0815
Edward R Robalisky, *President*
David Rickett, *Vice Pres*
D Robalisky, *Treasurer*
EMP: 17
SQ FT: 10,000
SALES (est): 1.9MM **Privately Held**
SIC: 2013 Mfg Sausages & Frankfurters

(G-20538)
ROBERTS POLISHING CO
928 Plainfield St (02919-6728)
PHONE..................................401 946-8922
Robert Mallo, *Principal*
EMP: 3
SALES (est): 121K **Privately Held**
SIC: 3471 Plating/Polishing Service

(G-20539)
RVS & CO
387 George Waterman Rd (02919-2332)
PHONE..................................401 231-8200
Roger V Scungio, *President*
Melodie Betters, *General Mgr*
Jean Scungio, *Vice Pres*
EMP: 12 **EST:** 1980
SQ FT: 5,000
SALES (est): 1.8MM **Privately Held**
WEB: www.rvsandco.com
SIC: 3364 Mfg Nonferrous Die-Castings

(G-20540)
SAMIC MFG COMPANY
807 Hartford Ave (02919-5424)
PHONE..................................401 421-2400
Salvatore Piscione, *President*
Michael Tomeo, *Vice Pres*
Kevin Piscione, *Treasurer*
EMP: 7
SQ FT: 7,200
SALES (est): 500K **Privately Held**
SIC: 3469 3542 Manufactures Metal Stamping & Metal Forming Machine Tools

(G-20541)
SBWINSOR CREAMERY LLC
58 Pine Hill Ave (02919-1451)
PHONE..................................401 231-5113
Alan K Winsor, *Owner*
EMP: 3
SALES (est): 164.3K **Privately Held**
SIC: 2021 Mfg Creamery Butter

(G-20542)
STITCHS CUSTOM EMBROIDERY LLC
554 Killingly St (02919-5227)
PHONE..................................401 943-5900
Michelle Andrews, *President*
Leonard J Andrews, *Manager*
EMP: 5
SALES: 450K **Privately Held**
WEB: www.stitchsonline.com
SIC: 2395 Pleating/Stitching Services

(G-20543)
STUPELL INDUSTRIES LTD INC
14 Industrial Ln (02919-3126)
PHONE..................................401 831-5640
Robert Stupell, *President*
Todd Stupell, *Vice Pres*
Patricia Tobin, *Bookkeeper*
Mario Ajca, *Manager*
▲ **EMP:** 14
SQ FT: 12,000
SALES: 2MM **Privately Held**
WEB: www.stupellind.com
SIC: 2499 5023 2394 Mfg Wood Products Whol Homefurnishings Mfg Canvas/Related Products

(G-20544)
UBIO INC
1603 Plainfield Pike B5 (02919-6274)
PHONE..................................401 541-9172
John De Clemente, *CEO*
Lucille De Clemente, *President*
EMP: 40
SALES (est): 2.6MM **Privately Held**
WEB: www.ubio.com
SIC: 3961 Mfg Of Costume Jewelry

(G-20545)
UNIQUE PLATING CO
66 Mill St (02919-6251)
PHONE..................................401 943-7366
John Arakelian Jr, *President*
EMP: 8
SQ FT: 13,200
SALES (est): 909.7K **Privately Held**
SIC: 3471 Plating/Polishing Service

(G-20546)
UTILITY SYSTEMS INC
123 King Philip St (02919-4330)
P.O. Box 19120 (02919-0120)
PHONE..................................401 351-6681
Henry V Rosciti, *President*
EMP: 11 **EST:** 1995
SALES (est): 2MM **Privately Held**
SIC: 3713 Utlity

(G-20547)
VISCO PRODUCTS INC
7 Victory Ave (02919-5312)
PHONE..................................401 831-1665
Lawrence Viscolosi Jr, *President*
EMP: 5
SQ FT: 8,000
SALES (est): 560K **Privately Held**
SIC: 3442 Mfg Aluminum Weather Stripping Including Door Thresholds

Kenyon
Washington County

(G-20548)
KENYON INDUSTRIES INC
36 Sherman Ave (02836-1012)
P.O. Box 115, Shannock (02875-0115)
PHONE..................................401 364-7761
Joanne Bagley, *President*
Peggy Brunetti, *Purchasing*
Joseph Trumpetto, *Treasurer*
Brad Boss, *Sales Mgr*
Bernie Gilbert, *Sales Staff*
◆ **EMP:** 300
SQ FT: 330,000
SALES (est): 52.9MM **Privately Held**
WEB: www.brookwoodcos.com
SIC: 2262 2269 2295 Manmade Fiber & Silk Finishing Plant Finishing Plant Mfg Coated Fabrics
HQ: Brookwood Companies Incorporated
485 Madison Ave Ste 500
New York NY 10022
212 551-0100

Kingston
Washington County

(G-20549)
CELLINI INC (PA)
35 Roxanna Ln (02881-1227)
PHONE..................................212 594-3812
David Rooney, *President*
Paul Sellon, *Vice Pres*
Bradford Sellon Jr, *Treasurer*
EMP: 59
SQ FT: 21,000
SALES (est): 3.4MM **Privately Held**
WEB: www.celliniinc.com
SIC: 3911 Mfg Precious Metal Jewelry

(G-20550)
I COPY
99 Fortin Rd Ste 115 (02881-1427)
PHONE..................................401 788-8277
Larry Morse, *CEO*
EMP: 5
SALES (est): 711.3K **Privately Held**
WEB: www.icopy.com
SIC: 2752 Digital Printing & Photo Copying

(G-20551)
KEY GRAPHICS INC
Also Called: Allegra Print & Imaging No 196
7 Caitlin Ct (02881-1841)
PHONE..................................401 826-2425
Robert E Sweeney Jr, *President*
Samantha A Sweeney, *Vice Pres*
EMP: 8
SALES (est): 1MM **Privately Held**
SIC: 2752 Lithographic Commercial Printing

Lincoln
Providence County

(G-20552)
ACS INDUSTRIES INC (PA)
1 New England Way Unit 1 # 1 (02865-4285)
PHONE..................................401 769-4700
Steven Buckler, *President*
Peter Botvin, *Vice Pres*
Jeff Buckler, *Vice Pres*
Paul Pimentel, *CFO*
Wendy Sferrazza, *Admin Asst*
▲ **EMP:** 50
SQ FT: 20,000
SALES (est): 987.1MM **Privately Held**
WEB: www.acsindustries.com
SIC: 3291 3496 3312 3315 Mfg Abrasive Products Mfg Misc Fab Wire Prdts Blast Furnace-Steel Work Mfg Steel Wire/Rltd Prdt Mfg General Indstl Mach

(G-20553)
AF GROUP INC
24 Albion Rd Ste 210 (02865-3747)
PHONE..................................401 757-3910
Keith Lonergan, *President*
John Carroll, *Chairman*
▼ **EMP:** 150
SALES (est): 4.4MM **Privately Held**
SIC: 3842 Mfg Surgical Appliances/Supplies

(G-20554)
AMERICAN TOOL COMPANY
623 George Washington Hwy (02865-4245)
PHONE..................................401 333-0111

GEOGRAPHIC

Richard P Mc Cally, *President*
Diane U Mc Cally, *Vice Pres*
Paula Greene, *Bookkeeper*
EMP: 20 **EST:** 1917
SQ FT: 13,000
SALES (est): 3.8MM **Privately Held**
WEB: www.americantoolcompany.com
SIC: 3599 Mfg Industrial Machinery

(G-20555)
ANDON ELECTRONICS CORPORATION
4 Court Dr (02865-4203)
PHONE..................................401 333-0388
John Tate, *President*
Irene Small, *Vice Pres*
Scott Tate, *Vice Pres*
Fidel Estrada, *Engineer*
Floyd Stokes, *Engineer*
EMP: 35
SQ FT: 55,000
SALES (est): 7MM **Privately Held**
WEB: www.andonelect.com
SIC: 3679 5065 Mfg Electronic Components Whol Electronic Parts/Equipment

(G-20556)
ANTHONY CORRADO INC
Also Called: Corrado Block
125 Higginson Ave (02865-2700)
PHONE..................................401 723-7600
Alexander Saharian, *President*
EMP: 5
SQ FT: 40,000
SALES: 1.8MM **Privately Held**
SIC: 3271 Mfg Concrete Building Blocks & Bricks

(G-20557)
ARTVAC CORPORATION
17 New England Way (02865-4290)
PHONE..................................401 333-6120
Herbert Mershon, *President*
Richard Mayhew, *Treasurer*
Ray Hodges, *Executive*
Sol Mershon, *Shareholder*
▲ **EMP:** 35
SQ FT: 15,000
SALES (est): 2.9MM **Privately Held**
WEB: www.artvac.com
SIC: 3499 Mfg Misc Fabricated Metal Products

(G-20558)
BATES ABRASIVE PRODUCTS INC
Also Called: Marvel Abrasive Products
6 Carol Dr (02865-4402)
PHONE..................................773 586-8700
Leslie Branch, *President*
Barbara Branch, *Vice Pres*
▲ **EMP:** 35
SQ FT: 35,000
SALES (est): 3.1MM **Privately Held**
WEB: www.marvelabrasives.com
SIC: 3291 Mfg Abrasive Products

(G-20559)
BREEZE PUBLICATIONS INC
Also Called: Valley Breeze
6 Blckstone Vly Pl Ste 20 (02865-1179)
PHONE..................................401 334-9555
Tom Ward, *President*
Melanie Thibeault, *Editor*
Bruce McCabe, *Technology*
Bradford Poirier, *Exec Dir*
Donna Meehan, *Art Dir*
EMP: 50
SQ FT: 8,000
SALES (est): 3.1MM **Privately Held**
WEB: www.valleybreeze.com
SIC: 2711 Newspapers-Publishing/Printing

(G-20560)
CALISE & SONS BAKERY INC (PA)
2 Quality Dr (02865-4266)
PHONE..................................401 334-3444
Michael Calise, *President*
Robert L Calise, *Vice Pres*
Scott Cran, *Vice Pres*
Kimberlynn Swafford, *Engineer*
Peter Petrocelli, *Treasurer*
▲ **EMP:** 150
SQ FT: 67,000
SALES (est): 43.2MM **Privately Held**
WEB: www.calisebakery.com
SIC: 2051 Mfg Bread/Related Products

(G-20561)
CALISTA THERAPEUTICS INC
32 Riverside Dr (02865-1511)
PHONE..................................401 345-5979
Andrew Mallon, *President*
EMP: 5 **EST:** 2012
SALES (est): 441.1K **Privately Held**
SIC: 2834 Mfg Pharmaceutical Preparations

(G-20562)
CHEMART COMPANY
11 New England Way (02865-4289)
PHONE..................................401 333-9200
Richard Beaupre, *CEO*
Jeanette Berger, *Accounts Exec*
Carmen Lopera, *Technology*
EMP: 30
SALES (corp-wide): 13.6MM **Privately Held**
WEB: www.chemart.com
SIC: 3479 Photochemical Etching
PA: Chemart Company
15 New England Way
Lincoln RI 02865
401 333-9200

(G-20563)
CHEMART COMPANY (PA)
15 New England Way (02865-4252)
PHONE..................................401 333-9200
Richard E Beaupre, *President*
Nicholas Jones, *General Mgr*
Larry Lefebvre, *Vice Pres*
Ana Lopes, *Sales Mgr*
Aimee Degregory, *Accounts Mgr*
▲ **EMP:** 60
SQ FT: 55,000
SALES (est): 13.6MM **Privately Held**
WEB: www.chemart.com
SIC: 3479 3471 Coating/Engraving Service Plating/Polishing Service

(G-20564)
CHOKLIT MOLD LTD
23 Carrington St (02865-1702)
PHONE..................................401 725-7377
Richard Goyette, *President*
Lea Goyette, *Vice Pres*
EMP: 4
SALES (est): 558.6K **Privately Held**
WEB: www.choklitmolds.com
SIC: 3544 Mfg Dies/Tools/Jigs/Fixtures

(G-20565)
CONKLIN LIMESTONE COMPANY
25 Wilbur Rd (02865-5199)
PHONE..................................401 334-2330
Frederick Conklin, *President*
Fred E Conklin, *Vice Pres*
EMP: 5 **EST:** 1930
SQ FT: 1,200
SALES (est): 815.3K **Privately Held**
SIC: 1422 Quarrying Of Crushed & Broken Limestone

(G-20566)
CREST MANUFACTURING COMPANY
5 Hood Dr (02865-1103)
P.O. Box 368 (02865-0368)
PHONE..................................401 333-1350
Gary S Hood, *President*
Laura Hood, *Admin Sec*
EMP: 38 **EST:** 1953
SQ FT: 18,000
SALES: 1.9MM **Privately Held**
WEB: www.crestmfg.com
SIC: 3677 3469 3829 3823 Mfg Elec Coil/Transfrmrs Mfg Metal Stampings Mfg Measure/Control Dvcs Mfg Process Cntrl Instr

(G-20567)
DENISON PHARMACEUTICALS LLC
1 Powder Hill Rd (02865-4407)
PHONE..................................401 723-5500
C D Hill, *President*
Bradley Stone, *President*
Thomas Stone, *Vice Pres*
John Taggart, *Warehouse Mgr*
Brad Stone, *VP Bus Dvlpt*
EMP: 168
SQ FT: 100,000
SALES (est): 62.8MM **Privately Held**
WEB: www.dpharm.net
SIC: 2834 Mfg Pharmaceutical Preparations

(G-20568)
DIVERSIFIED METAL CRAFTERS INC
4 Carol Dr (02865-4402)
P.O. Box 97, Glendale (02826-0097)
PHONE..................................401 305-7700
Bernhard Nordin, *CEO*
Nancy Ronci, *Controller*
EMP: 26
SALES: 2.5MM **Privately Held**
SIC: 3469 Mfg Metal Stampings

(G-20569)
DURASTONE CORPORATION
150 Higginson Ave (02865-2705)
PHONE..................................401 723-7100
Carol Ann Discuillo, *President*
Joanne Ciccarilli, *Treasurer*
Joanne Discuillo, *Treasurer*
Mary Ann Discuillo, *Admin Sec*
EMP: 15
SALES (est): 2.1MM **Privately Held**
WEB: www.durastonecorporation.com
SIC: 3272 8742 Mfg Concrete Products Management Consulting Services

(G-20570)
DYNAMIC CONVERTING SYSTEMS
623 George Washington Hwy (02865-4245)
PHONE..................................401 333-4363
Richard McCally, *President*
EMP: 3
SALES (est): 323.1K **Privately Held**
WEB: www.dynamicconvertingsys.com
SIC: 3599 Mfg Industrial Machinery

(G-20571)
ELECTROCHEMICAL DEVICES INC (PA)
Also Called: E D I
29 Kennedy Blvd (02865-3617)
P.O. Box 31, Albion (02802-0031)
PHONE..................................401 333-6112
Frank Ansuini, *President*
John Olson, *Treasurer*
EMP: 3
SQ FT: 1,000
SALES (est): 310K **Privately Held**
WEB: www.edi-cp.com
SIC: 3823 Mfg Of Specialty Products For Corrosion Control

(G-20572)
EVERETT CHARLES TECH LLC
Also Called: Ostby Barton Division
6 Court Dr (02865-4203)
PHONE..................................401 739-7310
Bob Chartrand, *Branch Mgr*
EMP: 19
SALES (corp-wide): 451.7MM **Publicly Held**
WEB: www.ectinfo.com
SIC: 3825 Mfg Electrical Measuring Instruments
HQ: Everett Charles Technologies, Llc
14570 Meyer Canyon Dr # 100
Fontana CA 92336
909 625-5551

(G-20573)
EVERETT J PRESCOTT INC
Red Head Manufacturing
38 Albion Rd (02865-3707)
PHONE..................................401 333-8588
Denise Raymond, *Safety Mgr*
Jack Blade, *Branch Mgr*
EMP: 8
SALES (corp-wide): 104.6MM **Privately Held**
SIC: 3469 3494 Mfg Valves & Stamped & Pressed Metal Machine Parts
PA: Everett J. Prescott, Inc.
32 Prescott St Libby Libby Hill
Gardiner ME 04345
207 582-2006

(G-20574)
FINLAY EXT INGREDIENTS USA INC (DH)
Also Called: Autocrat Coffee
10 Blackstone Valley Pl (02865-1145)
PHONE..................................800 288-6272
Steve Olyha, *CEO*
Gez Williams, *Opers Dir*
Neil Willsher, *Opers Dir*
Ann Malinowski, *CFO*
Tamie Hutchins, *Human Res Dir*
▲ **EMP:** 70
SQ FT: 54,000
SALES (est): 30.2MM
SALES (corp-wide): 13.9B **Privately Held**
WEB: www.autocrat.com
SIC: 2095 5149 2087 Mfg Roasted Coffee Whol Groceries Mfg Flavor Extracts/Syrup
HQ: James Finlay International, Inc.
120 Corporate Dr
Beaver Dam WI
920 887-8146

(G-20575)
GENERAL CABLE INDUSTRIES INC
Also Called: Lincoln, RI Plant
3 Carol Dr (02865-4401)
PHONE..................................401 333-4848
Michael Brown, *Branch Mgr*
Christine Tinsley, *Executive*
EMP: 192
SQ FT: 200,000 **Privately Held**
WEB: www.generalcable.com
SIC: 3357 Nonferrous Wiredrawing/Insulating
HQ: General Cable Industries, Inc.
4 Tesseneer Dr
Highland Heights KY 41076

(G-20576)
GREYSTONE OF LINCOLN INC (PA)
Also Called: Induplate
7 Wellington Rd (02865-4411)
PHONE..................................401 333-0444
Everett H Fernald Jr, *Principal*
David Lippy, *Exec VP*
▲ **EMP:** 140
SQ FT: 75,000
SALES (est): 57.1MM **Privately Held**
SIC: 3451 3462 Mfg Screw Machine Products Mfg Iron/Steel Forgings

(G-20577)
KLITZNER INDUSTRIES INC
Also Called: H.K. Klitzner Company Division
26 Kirkbrae Dr (02865-1019)
PHONE..................................800 621-0161
Alan J Klitzner, *President*
Dean Klitzner, *Principal*
Henry Riccitelli, *Vice Pres*
Leta Klitzner, *Admin Sec*
▲ **EMP:** 75
SQ FT: 20,000
SALES (est): 10.3MM **Privately Held**
WEB: www.klitzner.com
SIC: 3911 3961 Mfg Precious Metal Jewelry Mfg Costume Jewelry

(G-20578)
LANCE INDUSTRIES INC (PA)
Also Called: Symmetry Products
55 Industrial Cir Ste 3 (02865-2606)
PHONE..................................401 365-6272
Stephen Lancia, *President*
▲ **EMP:** 100
SQ FT: 200,000
SALES (est): 16.4MM **Privately Held**
WEB: www.foamtech.com
SIC: 3086 Mfg Plastic Foam Products

(G-20579)
LINCOLN CREAMERY INC
276 Front St Frnt 1 (02865-2427)
PHONE..................................401 724-1050
Lisa Kesley, *President*
EMP: 12

SALES (est): 987.8K Privately Held
SIC: 2052 Mfg Cookies/Crackers

(G-20580)
LIVINGSTONE STUDIOS
85 Industrial Cir Ste 113 (02865-2600)
PHONE....401 475-1145
Justin Hawkins, *Principal*
EMP: 6 EST: 2010
SALES (est): 610.5K Privately Held
SIC: 3272 Mfg Concrete Products

(G-20581)
MANDEVILLE SIGNS INC
676 George Washington Hwy (02865-4229)
PHONE....401 334-9100
Thomas Mandeville, *President*
James E Mandeville, *Vice Pres*
Jeanne Mandeville, *Vice Pres*
EMP: 32 EST: 1917
SQ FT: 44,000
SALES (est): 4.7MM Privately Held
WEB: www.mandevillesign.com
SIC: 3993 Mfg Signs/Advertising Specialties

(G-20582)
MARVEL ABRASIVES PRODUCTS LLC
6 Carol Dr (02865-4402)
PHONE....800 621-0673
Lelsie J Branch, *President*
Barbara Branch, *Vice Pres*
Craig Pickell,
▲ EMP: 14
SALES (est): 1.5MM Privately Held
SIC: 3291 Mfg Abrasive Products

(G-20583)
MATERION TECHNICAL MTLS INC
5 Wellington Rd (02865-4411)
PHONE....401 333-1700
Al Lubrano, *President*
Robert Tavares, *Vice Pres*
M C Hasychak, *Treasurer*
Shawn Lefort, *Controller*
Stephen Desroches, *IT/INT Sup*
▲ EMP: 200
SQ FT: 125,000
SALES (est): 76.8MM
SALES (corp-wide): 1.2B Publicly Held
SIC: 3331 3339 3423 Primary Copper Producer Primary Nonferrous Metal Producer Mfg Hand/Edge Tools
PA: Materion Corporation
6070 Parkland Blvd Ste 1
Mayfield Heights OH 44124
216 486-4200

(G-20584)
MIX UP PRINTER
1060 Great Rd (02865-3832)
PHONE....401 334-4291
Kevin McPeak, *President*
John McPeak, *President*
EMP: 6
SALES (est): 440K Privately Held
SIC: 2759 Commercial Printing

(G-20585)
MJH CRAWFORD INDUSTRIES I
11 Browne Hill Ct (02865-2901)
PHONE....401 728-3443
Michael Crawford, *Principal*
EMP: 3 EST: 2010
SALES (est): 151.1K Privately Held
SIC: 3999 Mfg Misc Products

(G-20586)
MOO INC
Also Called: Moo.com
14 Blackstone Valley Pl (02865-1145)
PHONE....401 434-3561
Richard Moross, *President*
Brian Murphy, *COO*
Simon Cobby, *Vice Pres*
Cristina Hopkins, *Sales Mgr*
Sarah Gill, *Accounts Exec*
▲ EMP: 80
SQ FT: 18,000
SALES (est): 18.7MM Privately Held
SIC: 2759 Commercial Printing
PA: Moo Print Limited
2nd Floor, Farringdon Place
London EC1M

(G-20587)
MYCABINETSONLINE
24 Ballou Ave (02865-2807)
PHONE....401 722-3863
EMP: 4
SALES (est): 334K Privately Held
SIC: 2434 Mfg Wood Kitchen Cabinets

(G-20588)
NIANTIC SEAL INC
Also Called: Niantic Seal Nrtheast Rbr Pdts
17 Powder Hill Rd (02865-4407)
PHONE....401 334-6870
Robert Dirienzo, *President*
Pefer Divoll, *Vice Pres*
David Barrows, *Production*
Kevin Diaz, *Engineer*
Robert Rampone, *Engineer*
▲ EMP: 21 EST: 1963
SQ FT: 12,500
SALES (est): 7.3MM Privately Held
SIC: 3599 5085 Mfg Industrial Machinery Whol Industrial Supplies
PA: Insco Intermediate Holdings, Llc
17 Powder Hill Rd
Lincoln RI 02865

(G-20589)
PEARL COMET INC
16 Jason Dr (02865-4938)
PHONE....401 475-1309
Jerome Mattoni, *Branch Mgr*
EMP: 3
SALES (corp-wide): 750K Privately Held
SIC: 3911 Mfg Precious Metal Jewelry
PA: Pearl Comet Inc
184 Woonasquatucket Ave
North Providence RI
401 475-1309

(G-20590)
PHILIPPINE POT PARTNERS LLC
6 Princess Pine Rd (02865-4728)
PHONE....401 789-7372
Michael Sabatino,
Michael Horsfield,
EMP: 4
SALES (est): 282.6K Privately Held
SIC: 3269 7389 Mfg Pottery Products Business Serv Non-Commercial Site

(G-20591)
PHOTONIC MARKETING CORPORATION
22 Ducarl Dr (02865-1328)
PHONE....401 333-3538
H Lynn Lin, *President*
Jeffrey Lin, *Vice Pres*
Veronica Yu, *Vice Pres*
EMP: 6
SQ FT: 3,000
SALES: 3MM Privately Held
WEB: www.photonicmkt.com
SIC: 3678 Mfg Fiber Optic Cable & Components

(G-20592)
PRECISE PRODUCTS COMPANY
21 Lower Rd (02865-1825)
P.O. Box 25 (02865-0025)
PHONE....401 724-7190
William Alberg, *President*
Robert Alberg, *Engineer*
Robert T Alberg, *Treasurer*
EMP: 12
SQ FT: 6,000
SALES (est): 1.6MM Privately Held
SIC: 3315 3545 3851 3544 Mfg Steel Wire/Rltd Prdt Mfg Machine Tool Access Mfg Ophthalmic Goods Mfg Dies/Tools/Jigs/Fixt Mfg Metal Stampings

(G-20593)
PROTEIN PLUS PEANUT BUTTER CO
4 View St (02865-3542)
PHONE....401 996-5583
EMP: 3
SALES (est): 110.9K Privately Held
SIC: 2099 Mfg Food Preparations

(G-20594)
RHODY RUG INC
9 Powder Hill Rd (02865-4407)
P.O. Box 310, Cumberland (02864-0310)
PHONE....401 728-5903
Luis Agrela, *President*
Manny Martins, *Vice Pres*
Peter Lombardi, *Admin Sec*
EMP: 15
SQ FT: 50,000
SALES: 1.4MM Privately Held
WEB: www.tourblackstone.com
SIC: 2273 Mfg Carpets/Rugs

(G-20595)
RYCO TRIMMING INC
25 Carrington St (02865-1702)
PHONE....401 725-1779
Patricia Ryan, *President*
Donald Ryan, *Vice Pres*
▲ EMP: 15
SQ FT: 27,000
SALES (est): 1.1MM Privately Held
SIC: 2396 Mfg Auto/Apparel Trimming

(G-20596)
SCREENCRAFT TILEWORKS LLC
9 Powder Hill Rd (02865-4407)
PHONE....401 427-2816
Julie Champagne-Rouss, *Director*
Robert S Wolfskehl,
▲ EMP: 7
SALES (est): 973.9K Privately Held
SIC: 3999 Mfg Misc Products

(G-20597)
STACKBIN CORPORATION
29 Powder Hill Rd (02865-4424)
PHONE....401 333-1600
William A Shaw, *President*
Scott A Shaw, *Vice Pres*
Roy A Medeiros, *Treasurer*
Roy Mederios, *VP Finance*
Joe Laginhas, *Sales Mgr*
▼ EMP: 45 EST: 1931
SQ FT: 60,000
SALES: 1MM Privately Held
WEB: www.stackbin.com
SIC: 2599 3444 3443 Mfg Furniture/Fixtures Mfg Sheet Metalwork Mfg Fabricated Plate Wrk

(G-20598)
TANURY INDUSTRIES INC
6 New England Way (02865-4286)
PHONE....800 428-6213
Thomas Tanury, *Ch of Bd*
Michael Akkaoui, *President*
Joseph Akkaoui, *Vice Pres*
Martin Buckholtz, *Vice Pres*
Robert Corcoran, *Vice Pres*
EMP: 200 EST: 1948
SQ FT: 50,000
SALES (est): 30.7MM Privately Held
WEB: www.tanury.com
SIC: 3471 Plating/Polishing Service

(G-20599)
WILDTREE INC
15 Wellington Rd (02865-4411)
PHONE....401 732-1856
Leslie Montie, *CEO*
Frank Montie Jr, *President*
Judith L Montie, *Vice Pres*
Gina Thayer, *Vice Pres*
Michael Gilkenson, *Prdtn Mgr*
▲ EMP: 80 EST: 1994
SALES (est): 7MM Privately Held
WEB: www.wildtreeherbs.com
SIC: 2099 Mfg Food Preparations

(G-20600)
WORLDWIDE TOOLING LLC
1 Christopher Dr (02865-4946)
PHONE....401 334-9806
John Pereira,
▲ EMP: 10
SQ FT: 800
SALES: 1MM Privately Held
WEB: www.worldwidetooling.com
SIC: 3599 Mfg Industrial Machinery

(G-20601)
WYATT ENGINEERING LLC (PA)
6 Blackstone Valley Pl # 401 (02865-1162)
PHONE....401 334-1170
David C Wyatt, *Mng Member*
Robin Anderson,
Susan Wyatt,
▲ EMP: 8
SQ FT: 3,750
SALES (est): 1.6MM Privately Held
WEB: www.wyattflow.com
SIC: 3823 Mfg Process Control Instruments

(G-20602)
ZAMPINI INDUSTRIAL GROUP LLC
85 Industrial Cir # 2211 (02865-2645)
PHONE....401 305-7997
Lou Zampini Jr, *Mng Member*
EMP: 3
SALES: 1.2MM Privately Held
WEB: www.desouttertools.com
SIC: 3546 5251 5072 5085 Mfg Power-driven Handtool Ret Hardware Whol Hardware Whol Industrial Supplies Whol Industrial Equip

Little Compton
Newport County

(G-20603)
176 WILLOW AVENUE LLC
176 Willow Ave (02837-1525)
P.O. Box 136 (02837-0101)
PHONE....401 635-2329
Thomas Arkins,
EMP: 3
SALES: 60K Privately Held
SIC: 2329 Mfg Men's/Boy's Clothing

(G-20604)
CASE HARD
56 Indian Rd (02837-2111)
PHONE....401 635-8201
Greg Berdan, *CEO*
Norm Paasche, *President*
▲ EMP: 7
SALES (est): 557.5K Privately Held
SIC: 3089 Mfg Plastic Products

(G-20605)
JAMES L GALLAGHER INC
408 W Main Rd (02837-1119)
PHONE....508 758-3102
James L Gallagher, *President*
EMP: 13
SALES (est): 2.4MM Privately Held
SIC: 3552 Mfg Industrial Machinery

(G-20606)
MOONLITE GRAPHICS CO INC
175 W Main Rd (02837-1361)
PHONE....401 635-2962
William Boudreau, *President*
Theresa Boudreau, *Clerk*
EMP: 3
SQ FT: 14,000
SALES: 350K Privately Held
SIC: 2759 Commercial Printing

Manville
Providence County

(G-20607)
EASTERN DESIGN INC
70 New River Rd (02838-1712)
P.O. Box 104 (02838-0104)
PHONE....401 765-0558
Edward Kelleher, *President*
Donna Kelleher, *Vice Pres*
EMP: 9
SALES (est): 960K Privately Held
SIC: 2431 Mfg Millwork

(G-20608)
GLOBAL ENGINEERED MTLS CORP
200 Sayles Hill Rd (02838-1200)
PHONE....401 725-2100

Rachel Pacheco, *CEO*
EMP: 3
SALES (est): 220K **Privately Held**
SIC: 2241 Narrow Fabric Mill

(G-20609)
JOSEPH C LA FOND CO INC
340 Old River Rd (02838-1033)
P.O. Box 20 (02838-0020)
PHONE..................................401 769-3744
Dennis Lafond, *President*
Susan Buckless, *Corp Secy*
Micheal Lafond, *Vice Pres*
EMP: 10 **EST:** 1947
SQ FT: 9,800
SALES: 1MM **Privately Held**
SIC: 2231 Weaving Mill

(G-20610)
MICHAEL HEALY DESIGNS INC
Also Called: Healy Plaques
60 New River Rd (02838-1712)
P.O. Box 4 (02838-0004)
PHONE..................................401 597-5900
Michael F Healy, *President*
▲ **EMP:** 8
SQ FT: 20,000
SALES (est): 1.6MM **Privately Held**
WEB: www.tributeawards.com
SIC: 3366 3365 3999 3961 Copper Foundry Aluminum Foundry Mfg Misc Products Mfg Costume Jewelry Repair Services

Mapleville
Providence County

(G-20611)
BLACKSTONE VALLEY PRESTAIN
730 Broncos Hwy (02839-1214)
PHONE..................................401 568-9745
Frederick J Hawley, *President*
EMP: 5
SALES (est): 439.5K **Privately Held**
SIC: 2421 Sawmill/Planing Mill

(G-20612)
DANIELE INTERNATIONAL INC (PA)
1000 Danielle Dr (02839-1264)
P.O. Box 106, Pascoag (02859-0106)
PHONE..................................401 568-6228
Vlado Duckcevich, *CEO*
Stefano Dukcevich, *President*
Brandon Richards, *Export Mgr*
Anthony Vitale, *QC Mgr*
Rich St Pierre, *CFO*
◆ **EMP:** 112
SQ FT: 400,000
SALES (est): 101.9MM **Privately Held**
WEB: www.danielefoods.com
SIC: 2013 Manufacture Prepared Meats

(G-20613)
EDWOODS FIREWOOD & LOGGING
529 Cooper Hill Rd (02839-1131)
PHONE..................................401 568-6585
Ed Grenier, *Principal*
EMP: 3 **EST:** 2008
SALES (est): 189.4K **Privately Held**
SIC: 2411 Logging

(G-20614)
SANDBERG ENTERPRISES INC (PA)
Also Called: Sandberg Machine
806 Broncos Hwy (02839-1214)
P.O. Box 779, Chepachet (02814-0997)
PHONE..................................401 568-1602
Robert Sandberg Jr, *President*
Leah Sandberg, *Info Tech Mgr*
EMP: 28
SALES: 2MM **Privately Held**
SIC: 3599 Mfg Industrial Machinery

(G-20615)
STEDAGIO LLC
1000 Danielle Dr (02839-1264)
P.O. Box 129, Pascoag (02859-0129)
PHONE..................................401 568-6228
Stefano Dukcevich,
David Dukcevich,
Giovanna Dukcevich,
▲ **EMP:** 9
SALES (est): 770K **Privately Held**
SIC: 2099 Mfg Prepared Meats

Middletown
Newport County

(G-20616)
BAE SYSTEMS TECH SOL SRVC INC
76 Hammarlund Way Ste 3 (02842-5640)
PHONE..................................401 846-5500
James Zagranis, *Branch Mgr*
EMP: 40
SALES (corp-wide): 22.1B **Privately Held**
SIC: 3812 Mfg Search/Navigation Equipment
HQ: Bae Systems Technology Solutions & Services Inc.
520 Gaither Rd
Rockville MD 20850
703 847-5820

(G-20617)
CHEW PUBLISHING INC
190 E Main Rd Ste 3 (02842-4987)
PHONE..................................401 808-0648
EMP: 3
SALES (est): 50K **Privately Held**
SIC: 2741 Misc Publishing

(G-20618)
D & H INC
Also Called: Coddington Brewing Co
210 Coddington Hwy (02842-4884)
PHONE..................................401 847-6690
William Christy, *President*
Helen Christy, *Treasurer*
EMP: 9
SALES (est): 922.6K **Privately Held**
SIC: 2082 Mfg Malt Beverages

(G-20619)
GAINES TRUCKING INC
35 Roosters Way (02842-7951)
P.O. Box 4005 (02842-0005)
PHONE..................................401 862-2993
Manuel V Gaines, *President*
EMP: 3
SALES: 300K **Privately Held**
SIC: 3715 Mfg Truck Trailers

(G-20620)
HOOD SAILMAKERS INC (PA)
23 Johnny Cake Hill Rd (02842-5635)
PHONE..................................401 849-9400
John Woodhouse, *President*
John T Woodhouse, *President*
Rob Macmillan, *Vice Pres*
▲ **EMP:** 13 **EST:** 1950
SQ FT: 20,000
SALES (est): 1.3MM **Privately Held**
WEB: www.hood-sails.com
SIC: 2394 Mfg Canvas/Related Products

(G-20621)
IGITT INC
Also Called: New England Woodworking Co
210 Airport Access Rd (02842-7444)
PHONE..................................401 841-5544
William Nagle, *President*
EMP: 10
SQ FT: 6,000
SALES (est): 1.1MM **Privately Held**
WEB: www.newoodworking.com
SIC: 2431 Mfg Millwork

(G-20622)
KVH INDUSTRIES INC
75 Enterprise Ctr (02842)
PHONE..................................401 847-3327
Martin A Kits Van Heyningen, *CEO*
EMP: 200
SALES (corp-wide): 170.7MM **Publicly Held**
SIC: 3663 Mfg Radio/Tv Communication Equipment
PA: Kvh Industries, Inc.
50 Enterprise Ctr
Middletown RI 02842
401 847-3327

(G-20623)
KVH INDUSTRIES INC (PA)
50 Enterprise Ctr (02842-5279)
PHONE..................................401 847-3327
Martin K Van Heyningen, *CEO*
Brent Bruun, *COO*
Jennifer Baker, *Vice Pres*
Robert Kits, *Vice Pres*
Paul Boudreau, *Engineer*
◆ **EMP:** 165
SQ FT: 75,000
SALES: 170.7MM **Publicly Held**
WEB: www.kvh.com
SIC: 3663 3812 Mfg Mobile Communications Products & Digital Navigation Systems

(G-20624)
LMG RHODE ISLAND HOLDINGS INC
Also Called: Newport Daily News, The
272 Valley Rd (02842-5238)
P.O. Box 420, Newport (02840-0936)
PHONE..................................401 849-3300
Kirk Davis, *President*
Veronica Musch, *Graphic Designe*
▲ **EMP:** 100 **EST:** 1846
SALES (est): 10.3MM
SALES (corp-wide): 1.5B **Publicly Held**
WEB: www.newportri.com
SIC: 2711 Newspapers-Publishing/Printing
HQ: Local Media Group, Inc.
40 Mulberry St
Middletown NY 10940
845 341-1100

(G-20625)
LOCKHEED MARTIN GLOBAL INC
Also Called: Lockheed Martin Info. Tech
76 Hammarlund Way Ste 1 (02842-5640)
PHONE..................................401 849-3703
Ron Jennings, *Engineer*
EMP: 10 **Publicly Held**
SIC: 3721 Mfg Aircraft
HQ: Lockheed Martin Global, Inc.
497 Electronics Pkwy # 5
Liverpool NY 13088
315 456-2982

(G-20626)
MINUTE MAN PRESS
Also Called: Minuteman Press
687 W Main Rd (02842-6352)
PHONE..................................401 619-1650
Helen Andromalos, *Owner*
EMP: 3 **EST:** 2014
SALES (est): 267.9K **Privately Held**
SIC: 2752 Comm Prtg Litho

(G-20627)
NEWPORT LIFE MAGAZINE INC
272 Valley Rd 2 (02842-5238)
PHONE..................................401 841-0200
Lynne Tungett, *President*
Veronica Musch, *Graphic Designe*
EMP: 4
SALES (est): 356.5K **Privately Held**
WEB: www.newportlifemagazine.com
SIC: 2721 Periodicals-Publishing/Printing

(G-20628)
NEWPORT TOOL & DIE INC
1219 Aquidneck Ave (02842-7240)
PHONE..................................401 847-6711
Mark Nardelli, *President*
Salvatore Nardelli, *President*
Ron Alves, *Engineer*
EMP: 11
SQ FT: 7,000
SALES: 750K **Privately Held**
WEB: www.newporttool.com
SIC: 3544 3599 Mfg Dies/Tools/Jigs/Fixtures Mfg Industrial Machinery

(G-20629)
PAX INCORPORATED PRINTERS
687 W Main Rd (02842-6352)
PHONE..................................401 847-1157
Dan Hague, *Principal*
EMP: 3
SALES (est): 260K **Privately Held**
SIC: 2759 Commercial Printing

(G-20630)
QUICK FAB INC
307 Oliphant Ln Unit 8 (02842-4687)
PHONE..................................401 848-0055
Joseph Reynolds, *President*
Kevin Reynolds, *Vice Pres*
EMP: 5
SALES (est): 559.6K **Privately Held**
SIC: 3599 Machine Shop/Jobbing/Repair

(G-20631)
RESEARCH ENGINEERING & MFG INC
Also Called: Reminc
55 Hammarlund Way (02842-5696)
PHONE..................................401 841-8880
Laurie Mandly, *CEO*
John Reynolds, *Engineer*
EMP: 10
SALES (est): 1.7MM **Privately Held**
WEB: www.reminc.net
SIC: 3452 Mfg Bolts/Screws/Rivets

(G-20632)
SMITHS DETECTION INC
88 Silva Ln Ste 1 (02842-7628)
PHONE..................................401 848-7678
EMP: 15
SALES (corp-wide): 4.9B **Privately Held**
SIC: 7372 7371 Technology Development
HQ: Smiths Detection Inc.
2202 Lakeside Blvd
Edgewood MD 21040
410 510-9100

Narragansett
Washington County

(G-20633)
AMERICAN BOOKEND COMPANY LLC
207 S Pier Rd (02882-3512)
PHONE..................................401 932-2700
Jeffrey Richardson,
EMP: 4
SALES (est): 343.7K **Privately Held**
SIC: 3499 Mfg Misc Fabricated Metal Products

(G-20634)
ANACKO CORDAGE CO
102 Dean Knauss Dr (02882-1100)
PHONE..................................401 792-3936
Walter Anacko, *Partner*
▲ **EMP:** 4
SQ FT: 4,800
SALES (est): 388.4K **Privately Held**
SIC: 2298 Mfg Cordage/Twine

(G-20635)
CELESTIAL MONITORING CORP (HQ)
24 Celestial Dr Ste B (02882-1148)
P.O. Box 410, Wakefield (02880-0410)
PHONE..................................401 782-1045
Pierre Gouvin, *President*
Steve Pennington, *Regional Mgr*
Mike Switzer, *Regional Mgr*
Paul Thurlow, *Vice Pres*
EMP: 30
SQ FT: 3,000
SALES (est): 1.3MM
SALES (corp-wide): 2.9B **Privately Held**
SIC: 3823 1731 8711 Geotechnical And Structural Monitoring Services
PA: Keller Group Plc
5th Floor, 1 Sheldon Square
London W2 6T
207 616-7575

(G-20636)
CHAMPLIN WELDING INC
Also Called: Champlin Boat Works
556 Point Judith Rd (02882-4539)
PHONE..................................401 782-4099
Paul Champlin, *President*
Shawn Champlin, *Treasurer*
Ryan Champlin, *Admin Sec*
EMP: 3

▲ = Import ▼=Export
◆ =Import/Export

SALES (est): 260K Privately Held
SIC: 7692 1799 3444 Welding Repair Trade Contractor Mfg Sheet Metalwork

(G-20637)
DEWAL INDUSTRIES LLC
15 Ray Trainor Dr (02882-1105)
P.O. Box 372, Saunderstown (02874-0372)
PHONE..................................401 789-9736
Eric Walsh, *President*
Warren Diclemente, *Treasurer*
Cline Propst, *Supervisor*
▲ EMP: 150 EST: 1975
SQ FT: 64,000
SALES (est): 69.9MM
SALES (corp-wide): 879MM Publicly Held
WEB: www.dewal.com
SIC: 2672 3861 3069 3081 Manufacture Coat/Laminated Paper Photo Equip/Supplies Fabrcatd Rubber Prdt Unsupport Plstc Film
PA: Rogers Corporation
2225 W Chandler Blvd
Chandler AZ 85224
480 917-6000

(G-20638)
EARTEC COMPANY INC
145 Dean Knauss Dr (02882-1141)
PHONE..................................401 789-8700
John Hooper Jr, *President*
Paul Hooper, *Vice Pres*
Aaron Cassidy, *Opers Mgr*
Leigh Oconner, *Mktg Dir*
▲ EMP: 35
SALES (est): 4.1MM Privately Held
SIC: 3661 Manufactures Communication Headsets

(G-20639)
FABRI TEC ENGINEERING INC
25 Walts Way (02882-3438)
P.O. Box 5670, Wakefield (02880-5670)
PHONE..................................401 783-0051
Richard Berndt, *President*
Barbara Berndt, *Vice Pres*
EMP: 6
SQ FT: 3,000
SALES (est): 701.6K Privately Held
WEB: www.fabri-tecengineering.com
SIC: 3599 Mfg Industrial Machinery

(G-20640)
GLOBAL RFID SYSTEMS N AMER LLC
Also Called: Global ID Technologies
1004 Boston Neck Rd # 7 (02882-1765)
PHONE..................................401 783-3818
Dave Munch, *Opers Mgr*
John Larned, *Mng Member*
Jennifer McGovern, *Office Admin*
Richard Drumm, *Technical Staff*
Jennifer Hart, *Executive Asst*
EMP: 4
SALES: 950K Privately Held
SIC: 3953 3699 Mfg Marking Devices Mfg Electrical Equipment/Supplies

(G-20641)
ISLAND REFLECTIONS CORPORATION
83 Conanicus Rd (02882-2434)
PHONE..................................401 782-2744
Timothy Tibbetts, *President*
Deborah Tibbetts, *Vice Pres*
EMP: 3
SALES: 100K Privately Held
SIC: 3993 Mfg Signs/Advertising Specialties

(G-20642)
MIX MARKETING CORP
68 Old Pine Rd (02882-2422)
PHONE..................................401 954-6121
Barbiejo Fratus, *Principal*
EMP: 4 EST: 2011
SALES (est): 293.3K Privately Held
SIC: 3273 Mfg Ready-Mixed Concrete

(G-20643)
OCEAN STATE SHELLFISH COOP
20 Walts Way (02882-3438)
PHONE..................................401 789-2065
Graham Brawley, *Principal*
EMP: 9
SALES: 2.7MM Privately Held
SIC: 2092 0919 Mfg Fresh/Frozen Packaged Fish Marine Products Catching

(G-20644)
OPEN SRC PRJCT FR NTWK DT ACS
Also Called: OPENDAP
165 Dean Knauss Dr (02882-1172)
P.O. Box 112, Saunderstown (02874-0112)
PHONE..................................401 284-1304
Dr Peter Fox, *President*
James Gallagher, *Vice Pres*
Dan Holloway, *Treasurer*
EMP: 3
SALES: 586.5K Privately Held
WEB: www.opendap.org
SIC: 7372 Open Source Software Develeopement

(G-20645)
PIER ICE PLANT INC
132 Kingstown Rd (02882-3337)
PHONE..................................401 789-6090
Robert F Shumate, *President*
EMP: 5
SQ FT: 6,500
SALES (est): 250K Privately Held
SIC: 2097 Mfg Ice

(G-20646)
PORTA PHONE CO INC
Also Called: Porta Phones
145 Dean Knauss Dr (02882-1141)
P.O. Box 560 (02882-0560)
PHONE..................................401 789-8700
John Hooper Jr, *President*
Paul Hooper, *Treasurer*
Frank Terminesi, *Sales Staff*
Leigh Oconner, *Advt Staff*
Aaron Cassidy, *Manager*
▲ EMP: 35
SALES (est): 4.4MM Privately Held
WEB: www.portaphone.com
SIC: 3679 Mfg Electronic Components

(G-20647)
ROCKY BROOK ASSOCIATES INC
Also Called: Rba
155 Dean Knauss Dr (02882-1141)
P.O. Box 52, Wakefield (02880-0052)
PHONE..................................401 789-0259
Richard Sawyer, *President*
Barbara Sawyer, *Corp Secy*
▲ EMP: 6
SQ FT: 8,000
SALES (est): 921.4K Privately Held
SIC: 3599 Machine Shop

(G-20648)
SEA SIDE FUEL
55 State St (02882-5705)
PHONE..................................401 284-2636
Christopher D Roebuck, *President*
EMP: 4
SALES (est): 263K Privately Held
SIC: 2869 Ret Fuel Oil Dealer

(G-20649)
SHORESIDE ORGANICS LLC
65 State St (02882-5712)
PHONE..................................401 267-4473
EMP: 4
SALES (est): 277.6K Privately Held
SIC: 2873 Mfg Nitrogenous Fertilizers

(G-20650)
SOUTH COUNTY CHOPPERS
22 1st St (02882-5824)
PHONE..................................401 788-1000
John Tomasso, *Owner*
EMP: 3
SALES (est): 227.3K Privately Held
SIC: 3751 Mfg Motorcycles/Bicycles

(G-20651)
STEPHEN C DEMATRICK
201p Gravelly Hill Rd (02879-4707)
PHONE..................................401 789-4712
Stephen C Dematrick, *Principal*
EMP: 4
SALES (est): 411.8K Privately Held
SIC: 2431 Mfg Millwork

(G-20652)
TAP TECHNOLOGIES INC
23 Sachem Rd (02882-2305)
PHONE..................................860 333-7834
Anthony Curreri, *CEO*
Connor McGill, *CFO*
Antonio Melegari, *Mktg Dir*
EMP: 5
SALES: 128.9K Privately Held
SIC: 7372 Prepackaged Software Services

(G-20653)
THAYER WOOD PRODUCTS INC
100 Brook Farm Rd N (02879-2721)
PHONE..................................401 789-8825
Henry Thayer III, *President*
Paula H Thayer, *Admin Sec*
EMP: 3 EST: 2000
SALES (est): 220K Privately Held
SIC: 2491 Wood Preserving

Newport
Newport County

(G-20654)
AMERICAN BOAT BUILDERS
1 Washington St (02840-1513)
PHONE..................................401 236-2466
EMP: 23
SALES: 175.8K Privately Held
SIC: 3732 Boatbuilding/Repairing

(G-20655)
AMERICAN FOAM TECHNOLOGIES INC
221 3rd St Ste 101 (02840-1088)
PHONE..................................304 497-3000
William Palombo, *President*
▼ EMP: 20
SQ FT: 66,000
SALES (est): 4.9MM Privately Held
SIC: 2899 Mfg Chemical Preparations

(G-20656)
BEDJET LLC
217 Goddard Row (02840-6607)
PHONE..................................401 404-5250
Mark Aramli, *President*
▲ EMP: 5
SQ FT: 1,000
SALES (est): 656K Privately Held
SIC: 3634 Mfg Electric Housewares/Fans

(G-20657)
BERTHON USA INC
40 May St & The New Prt (02840)
PHONE..................................401 846-8404
Jennifer Stewart, *Principal*
EMP: 3
SALES (est): 96.7K Privately Held
SIC: 3732 5551 Boatbuilding/Repairing Ret Boats

(G-20658)
BUMPER BOATS INC
Also Called: Kiddie Bumbper Boats
9 Connell Hwy (02840-1516)
P.O. Box 739 (02840-0007)
PHONE..................................401 841-8200
Arthur Grover, *President*
Cathy Silvestri, *Corp Secy*
▲ EMP: 5
SQ FT: 24,000
SALES (est): 698.7K Privately Held
WEB: www.kiddiebumperboats.com
SIC: 3599 Mfg Amusement Rides

(G-20659)
C R SCOTT MARINE WDWKG CO
43 3rd St Fl 2 (02840-1937)
PHONE..................................401 849-0715
Christopher R Scott, *President*
EMP: 3
SQ FT: 3,000
SALES (est): 440K Privately Held
SIC: 3731 3732 Shipbuilding/Repairing Boatbuilding/Repairing

(G-20660)
COASTAL EXTREME BREWING CO LLC
Also Called: Newport Storm Brewery
293 Jt Connell Rd (02840)
PHONE..................................401 849-5232
Brent Ryan, *Mng Member*
Derek Luke,
▲ EMP: 5
SQ FT: 2,500
SALES (est): 647.3K Privately Held
WEB: www.newportstorm.com
SIC: 2082 Mfg Malt Beverages

(G-20661)
COLONIAL PRINTING INC
Also Called: PDQ Graphics
176 Broadway (02840-2747)
PHONE..................................401 367-6690
Josh Bainton, *Vice Pres*
EMP: 5
SALES (corp-wide): 4.8MM Privately Held
SIC: 2752 Lithographic Commercial Printing
PA: Colonial Printing, Inc.
333 Strawberry Field Rd # 11
Warwick RI 02886
401 691-3400

(G-20662)
DLA DOCUMENT SERVICES
47 Chandler St (02841-1718)
PHONE..................................401 841-6011
Trish Lovett, *Branch Mgr*
EMP: 5 Publicly Held
SIC: 2752 9711 Document Automation Services
HQ: Dla Document Services
5450 Carlisle Pike Bldg 9
Mechanicsburg PA 17050
717 605-2362

(G-20663)
DOWN WIND DOCKSIDE SVCS LLC
5 Merton Rd (02840-3624)
PHONE..................................401 619-1990
Frank Petersten, *Mng Member*
EMP: 6
SALES (est): 593.2K Privately Held
SIC: 3441 Structural Metal Fabrication

(G-20664)
EPPLEY LABORATORY INC
12 Sheffield Ave (02840-1671)
P.O. Box 419 (02840-0419)
PHONE..................................401 847-1020
Tom Kirk, *President*
George L Kirk, *Treasurer*
EMP: 15 EST: 1916
SQ FT: 20,000
SALES (est): 865.3K Privately Held
WEB: www.eppleylab.com
SIC: 3829 Mfg Measuring/Controlling Devices

(G-20665)
FELICIA WINKFIELD
2 Lowndes St (02840-3623)
PHONE..................................401 849-3029
Felicia Winkfield, *Executive*
EMP: 3 EST: 2018
SALES (est): 91.3K Privately Held
SIC: 2079 Mfg Edible Fats/Oils

(G-20666)
INTERNATIONAL YACHT RESTORATIO
Also Called: Iyrs
449 Thames St Unit 100 (02840-6751)
PHONE..................................401 846-2587
Ruth Taylor, *President*
Warren Barker, *Instructor*
Jill Levin, *Associate*
▲ EMP: 12 EST: 1993
SALES: 5.9MM Privately Held
WEB: www.iyrs.org
SIC: 3732 5551 3731 Boatbuilding/Repairing Ret Boats Shipbuilding/Repairing

(G-20667)
J H BREAKELL & COMPANY INC
132 Spring St (02840-6818)
PHONE..................................401 849-3522

GEOGRAPHIC

James Breakell, *President*
Joan Breakeall, *Vice Pres*
EMP: 10 **EST:** 1973
SALES (est): 630K **Privately Held**
WEB: www.breakell.com
SIC: 3914 3911 5961 Mfg Silver/Plated Ware Mfg Precious Mtl Jewelry Ret Mail-Order House

(G-20668)
JASPER AARON
Also Called: Jasper & Bailey Sail Makers
64 Halsey St Unit 11 (02840-1347)
P.O. Box 852 (02840-0852)
PHONE..................................401 847-8796
Aaron Jasper, *Owner*
EMP: 4
SALES (est): 200K **Privately Held**
WEB: www.jasperandbailey.com
SIC: 2394 Manufactures Sails

(G-20669)
JON BARRETT ASSOCIATES INC
555 Thames St (02840-6745)
P.O. Box 630 (02840-0946)
PHONE..................................401 846-8226
Jon Barrett, *President*
EMP: 8
SALES (est): 510K **Privately Held**
SIC: 3732 Boatbuilding/Repairing

(G-20670)
KINDERWAGON COMPANY
5 Gooseberry Rd (02840-4309)
PHONE..................................617 256-7599
Justin L Shull, *Owner*
▲ **EMP:** 6
SALES (est): 545.1K **Privately Held**
SIC: 2013 Mfg Prepared Meats

(G-20671)
LIRAKIS SAFETY HARNESS INC
18 Sheffield Ave (02840-1618)
PHONE..................................401 846-5356
W Stephen Lirakis, *President*
EMP: 5
SQ FT: 4,000
SALES (est): 260K **Privately Held**
SIC: 3199 Mfg Leather Goods

(G-20672)
METAL GUY LLC
1 Washington St (02840-1513)
PHONE..................................401 474-0234
Kevin Christensen,
EMP: 3
SALES: 75K **Privately Held**
SIC: 3441 Metal Fabrication

(G-20673)
NAIAD INFLATABLES NEWPORT INC
4 Thurston Ave (02840-1760)
P.O. Box 4153, Middletown (02842-0153)
PHONE..................................401 683-6700
Stephen Connett Sr, *President*
Mary Henriques, *Business Mgr*
Jennifer Arnold, *Marketing Mgr*
Donna Defusco, *Manager*
▲ **EMP:** 14
SQ FT: 6,000
SALES (est): 3.4MM **Privately Held**
WEB: www.naiadnewport.com
SIC: 3732 Boatbuilding/Repairing

(G-20674)
NARRAGANSETT SHIPWRIGHTS INC
1 Spring Wharf (02840-3459)
PHONE..................................401 846-3312
Michael McCaffrey, *President*
EMP: 3
SALES: 160K **Privately Held**
SIC: 3732 Wood Boat Repair & Building

(G-20675)
NORTH SAILS GROUP LLC
449 Thames St Unit 400 (02840-6750)
PHONE..................................401 849-7997
Caitlin Niemic, *Mng Member*
EMP: 90
SALES (est): 2.4MM **Privately Held**
SIC: 3949 5963 Mfg Sporting/Athletic Goods Direct Retail Sales

(G-20676)
RI WATERJET LLC
3 Long Lane Ct (02840-1520)
P.O. Box 221 (02840-0203)
PHONE..................................781 801-2500
Thomas Lemaire, *Mng Member*
EMP: 5 **EST:** 2016
SALES: 250K **Privately Held**
SIC: 3541 8711 Mfg Machine Tools-Cutting Engineering Services

(G-20677)
ROBERT A RANDALL
12 Barney St (02840-2918)
PHONE..................................401 847-3118
Peter E Randall, *President*
Daniel J Randall, *Vice Pres*
Elizabeth Kilmer, *Admin Sec*
EMP: 4 **EST:** 1962
SALES (est): 259.9K **Privately Held**
SIC: 3443 Mfg Fabricated Plate Work

(G-20678)
SALUTE SPIRITS LLC
52 Lee Ave Apt 1 (02840-8604)
PHONE..................................609 306-2258
Zachary Schulze,
EMP: 3
SALES: 60K **Privately Held**
SIC: 3993 Marketing And Graphic Designs

(G-20679)
SEA-BAND INTERNATIONAL INC
580 Thames St 440 (02840-6741)
PHONE..................................401 841-5900
Barry Jackson, *Branch Mgr*
EMP: 9 **Privately Held**
SIC: 2834 5122 Mfg & Whol Pharmaceuticals
PA: Sea-Band Limited
8 Hawley Road
Hinckley LEICS
145 563-9750

(G-20680)
SEVEN STAR INC
Also Called: Seven Star Marine Engineering
190 Admiral Kalbfus Rd (02840-1309)
PHONE..................................401 683-6222
Taylor K Ackman, *President*
EMP: 5
SQ FT: 3,200
SALES (est): 675.5K **Privately Held**
SIC: 3441 3599 7692 1799 Fabricated Structural Metal

(G-20681)
SHEGEAR INC
Also Called: Cgear Uniforms
128 Long Wharf Fl 2 (02840-2407)
P.O. Box 359 (02840-0306)
PHONE..................................401 619-0072
Carolyn Fletcher, *President*
EMP: 6
SQ FT: 2,000
SALES: 400K **Privately Held**
SIC: 3949 Mfg Sporting/Athletic Goods

(G-20682)
SOLID ACCESS TECHNOLOGIES LLC
6 Liberty St (02840-3221)
PHONE..................................978 463-0642
Tomas Havrda,
Jaroslav Belonoznik,
Jerome Ruzicka,
EMP: 4
SALES (est): 505.4K **Privately Held**
WEB: www.solidaccess.com
SIC: 3572 Mfg Computer Storage Devices

(G-20683)
SPARKMAN & STEPHENS LLC (PA)
26 Washington Sq Ste 3 (02840-2947)
PHONE..................................401 847-5449
John Reuter, *CEO*
Brooke Parish, *Chairman*
Jason Black, *COO*
EMP: 16
SALES (est): 1.8MM **Privately Held**
SIC: 3732 7389 Boatbuilding/Repairing Business Services

(G-20684)
SPINLOCK USA
11 Bowler Ln Unit A (02840-7705)
PHONE..................................401 619-5200
Ted Winston, *Marketing Mgr*
Emily Gaffney, *Marketing Staff*
James Turenne, *Marketing Staff*
Christopher Ross Hill, *Director*
▲ **EMP:** 5
SALES (est): 425K **Privately Held**
SIC: 3069 Mfg Fabricated Rubber Products

(G-20685)
STABAARTE INC
90 Bliss Rd Apt 1 (02840-5805)
PHONE..................................401 364-8633
Joern Liebelt, *President*
Nina Hildebrand, *Admin Sec*
Joshua Gutman, *Asst Sec*
▲ **EMP:** 3
SALES: 1MM
SALES (corp-wide): 2.3MM **Privately Held**
SIC: 2542 Mfg Partitions/Fixtures-Non-wood
PA: Stabaarte Gmbh
Kleinfischbach 6a
Wiehl 51674
226 271-2490

(G-20686)
THAMES GLASS INC
139 Old Beach Rd (02840-3358)
PHONE..................................401 846-0576
Matthew Buechner, *President*
Adrian Buechner, *Vice Pres*
EMP: 10 **EST:** 1981
SQ FT: 950
SALES (est): 1.2MM **Privately Held**
WEB: www.thamesglass.com
SIC: 3229 Mfg Hand Blown Glassware

(G-20687)
VENDOME GUIDE
Also Called: Western Managment Co
28 Pelham St (02840-3048)
P.O. Box 1461 (02840-0901)
PHONE..................................401 849-8025
Barclay Tim Warburton, *President*
EMP: 25
SALES (est): 1.4MM **Privately Held**
SIC: 2721 Periodicals-Publishing/Printing

(G-20688)
WITCHES ALMANAC
32 Halsey St (02840-1638)
P.O. Box 1292 (02840-0998)
PHONE..................................401 847-3388
EMP: 4
SALES (est): 136K **Privately Held**
SIC: 2711 Newspapers-Publishing/Printing

(G-20689)
YOFFA WOODWORKING
62 Halsey St Unit I (02840-1349)
PHONE..................................401 846-7659
Joseph Yoffa, *Principal*
EMP: 10
SALES (est): 610K **Privately Held**
SIC: 2431 Mfg Millwork

North Kingstown
Washington County

(G-20690)
ANCHOR BEND GLASSWORKS LLC (PA)
215 Shady Lea Rd Ste 100 (02852-7017)
PHONE..................................401 667-7338
Michael Richardson, *Principal*
EMP: 7
SALES (est): 570.3K **Privately Held**
SIC: 3229 Mfg Pressed/Blown Glass

(G-20691)
ANVIL INTERNATIONAL LLC
Anvil International Eps
160 Frenchtown Rd (02852-1759)
PHONE..................................401 886-3000
Carol Rancourt, *Sales Staff*
Rick Laviottle, *Branch Mgr*
EMP: 104 **Privately Held**
WEB: www.anvilint.com
SIC: 3498 Mfg Fabricated Pipe/Fittings
HQ: Anvil International, Llc
2 Holland Way
Exeter NH 03833
603 418-2800

(G-20692)
B E PUBLISHING
346 Smith St (02852-7723)
P.O. Box 8558, Warwick (02888-0598)
PHONE..................................401 294-2490
Michael Gecawich, *President*
EMP: 4
SALES (est): 432.5K **Privately Held**
SIC: 2741 Misc Publishing

(G-20693)
BEL AIR FINISHING SUPPLY CORP
101 Circuit Dr (02852-7439)
PHONE..................................401 667-7902
Steven Alviti, *President*
Gina Alviti, *Sales Staff*
▲ **EMP:** 4
SQ FT: 3,000
SALES (est): 535.9K **Privately Held**
WEB: www.belairfinishing.com
SIC: 3471 Plating/Polishing Service

(G-20694)
BSM PUMP CORP
Also Called: Brown & Sharpe Pumps
180 Frenchtown Rd (02852-1759)
PHONE..................................401 471-6350
Thomas Ruthman, *President*
Henry F Machado Jr, *General Mgr*
EMP: 23
SQ FT: 55,000
SALES (est): 4.6MM **Privately Held**
WEB: www.bsmpump.com
SIC: 3561 Mfg Pumps/Pumping Equipment

(G-20695)
CALLICO METALS INC
Also Called: Oster Pewter
512 Old Baptist Rd (02852-2532)
PHONE..................................401 398-8238
John E Baldwin, *President*
EMP: 7
SALES (est): 1.1MM **Privately Held**
WEB: www.osterpewter.com
SIC: 3356 Nonferrous Rolling/Drawing

(G-20696)
CLARKE INDUSTRIAL ENGINEERING (PA)
42 Whitecap Dr (02852-7445)
PHONE..................................401 667-7880
Kyle Daniels, *CEO*
Kyle Benson, *Principal*
Jeff Buck, *Vice Pres*
Coryn Degrands, *VP Opers*
Mark Kacer, *CFO*
EMP: 8
SALES (est): 2MM **Privately Held**
SIC: 3861 Mfg Photographic Equipment/Supplies

(G-20697)
COLONIAL CUTLERY INTL INC
Also Called: Colonial Knife Company
606 Ten Rod Rd (02852-4214)
P.O. Box 110, East Greenwich (02818-0110)
PHONE..................................401 737-0024
Kathryn M Paolantonio, *President*
Steven Paolantonio, *Opers Staff*
EMP: 143
SQ FT: 40,000
SALES: 12.5MM **Privately Held**
SIC: 3421 Mfg Cutlery

(G-20698)
COTO TECHNOLOGY INC
66 Whitecap Dr (02852-7445)
PHONE..................................401 943-2686
Jeffrey A Bentley, *President*
Larry Blackman, *CFO*
Mark A Chamberlin, *Director*
Robert R Dyson, *Director*
John H Fitzsimons, *Admin Sec*
EMP: 350

SALES (est): 57MM
SALES (corp-wide): 482MM **Privately Held**
SIC: 3625 Mfg Relays/Industrial Controls
PA: The Dyson-Kissner-Moran Corporation
2515 South Rd Ste 5
Poughkeepsie NY 12601
212 661-4600

(G-20699)
CRITICARE TECHNOLOGIES INC
125 Commerce Park Rd (02852-8420)
PHONE.....401 667-3837
Thomas Dietiker, *Director*
EMP: 20
SQ FT: 30,000
SALES (est): 894.7K **Privately Held**
SIC: 3845 Mfg Electromedical Equipment

(G-20700)
CUSTOM DESIGN INCORPORATED
370 Commerce Park Rd (02852-8419)
PHONE.....401 294-0200
Raul Dias Jr, *President*
Jesse Godin, *Prdtn Mgr*
John Barth, *Engineer*
Mike Milligan, *Engineer*
Dina Martino, *Controller*
EMP: 49 **EST:** 1976
SQ FT: 52,000
SALES (est): 13.7MM **Privately Held**
WEB: www.cdiri.com
SIC: 3089 2542 2541 Mfg Plastic Products Mfg Partitions/Fixtures-Nonwood Mfg Wood Partitions/Fixtures

(G-20701)
D MAC CONSULTING LLC (PA)
Also Called: American Chest Company
50 Reynolds St (02852-5820)
P.O. Box 113 (02852-0113)
PHONE.....401 500-3879
David McLoughlin,
EMP: 6
SALES: 1.2MM **Privately Held**
SIC: 2441 Mfg Wood Boxes/Shook

(G-20702)
DEVELOPMENT ASSOCIATES INC
300 Old Baptist Rd (02852-2598)
PHONE.....401 884-1350
Douglas Nannig, *President*
Paul Nannig, *Vice Pres*
Donna Gaumitz, *Technician*
▲ **EMP:** 17
SQ FT: 5,000
SALES (est): 2.5MM **Privately Held**
SIC: 3479 2851 2821 Coating/Engraving Service Mfg Paints/Allied Products Mfg Plastic Materials/Resins

(G-20703)
DURANT TOOL COMPANY INC
200 Circuit Dr (02852-7441)
PHONE.....401 781-7800
Edward W Bouclin, *President*
Ken Thomas, *Purch Agent*
▲ **EMP:** 20
SALES (est): 2MM **Privately Held**
WEB: www.durantco.com
SIC: 3542 3549 3545 Mfg Machine Tools-Forming Mfg Metalworking Machinery Mfg Machine Tool Accessories

(G-20704)
EDESIA INC
550 Romano Vineyard Way (02852-8429)
PHONE.....401 272-5521
Navyn Salem, *President*
Gary Therrien, *Warehouse Mgr*
Ludovino Rosario, *Maint Spvr*
Todd Paschoal, *Production*
Nicole Henretty, *Research*
▲ **EMP:** 70
SQ FT: 70,000
SALES: 22.9MM **Privately Held**
SIC: 2834 Mfg Pharmaceutical Preparations

(G-20705)
EDESIA ENTERPRISES LLC
550 Romano Vineyard Way (02852-8429)
PHONE.....401 272-5521
Navyn Salem, *Mng Member*
Jj Coughlin, *Manager*
John Bucci, *CIO*
Adeline Lescanne,
◆ **EMP:** 70
SQ FT: 70,000
SALES: 38MM **Privately Held**
SIC: 2834 Mfg Pharmaceutical Preparations

(G-20706)
EDESIA INDUSTRIES LLC
550 Romano Vineyard Way (02852-8429)
PHONE.....401 272-5521
Peter Craig, *Principal*
M Kasparian, *Exec Dir*
EMP: 86
SALES (est): 5.5MM **Privately Held**
SIC: 2099 5149 Mfg Food Preparations Whol Groceries

(G-20707)
ELECTRIC BOAT CORPORATION
Also Called: Quonset Point Facility
165 Dillabur Ave (02852-7542)
PHONE.....401 268-2410
John D Holmander, *Branch Mgr*
EMP: 91
SALES (corp-wide): 36.1B **Publicly Held**
SIC: 3731 8711 Shipbuilding/Repairing Engineering Services
HQ: Electric Boat Corporation
75 Eastern Point Rd
Groton CT 06340

(G-20708)
ELEMENT METAL ARTS
215 Shady Lea Rd (02852-7016)
P.O. Box 545, Newport (02840-0500)
PHONE.....631 896-9683
EMP: 3
SALES (est): 181.1K **Privately Held**
SIC: 2819 Industrial Inorganic Chemicals, Nec

(G-20709)
EMISSIVE ENERGY CORP
Also Called: Inforce
135 Circuit Dr (02852-7439)
PHONE.....401 294-2030
Robert Galli, *CEO*
Mark Lehman, *Vice Pres*
Peter Leon, *Vice Pres*
Matthew S Wolfe, *Vice Pres*
Al Jacobs, *CFO*
▲ **EMP:** 57
SQ FT: 50,000
SALES (est): 11.9MM **Privately Held**
WEB: www.inforce-mil.com
SIC: 3648 Manufactures Lighting Equipment

(G-20710)
FINE DESIGNS INC
Also Called: Sign-A-Rama
6855 Post Rd (02852-2127)
PHONE.....401 886-5000
Joseph Lomastro, *President*
EMP: 3
SALES (est): 311.7K **Privately Held**
SIC: 3993 Mfg Signs/Ad Specialties

(G-20711)
FIT N STITCH INC
486 Dry Bridge Rd (02852-5211)
PHONE.....401 294-3492
John Stanley Stroker, *President*
Lois Mary Stroker, *Corp Secy*
Jeffrey Stroker, *Vice Pres*
EMP: 3
SQ FT: 2,000
SALES: 150K **Privately Held**
SIC: 2394 Mfg Custom Yacht Canvas

(G-20712)
FRANK PASSARELLA INC
375 Earle Dr (02852-6216)
PHONE.....401 295-4943
Fran Passarella, *Principal*
EMP: 5
SALES (est): 529.5K **Privately Held**
SIC: 3432 Mfg Plumbing Fixture Fittings

(G-20713)
GOLDLINE CONTROLS INC (HQ)
61 Whitecap Dr (02852-7444)
PHONE.....401 583-1100
Gilbert Conover, *President*
Larry McLaughlin, *Engineer*
Douglas Pickard, *CFO*
Steve Pfaff, *Finance*
▲ **EMP:** 75
SQ FT: 43,000
SALES (est): 16.8MM
SALES (corp-wide): 542.1MM **Privately Held**
WEB: www.goldlinecontrols.com
SIC: 3822 Mfg Environmental Controls
PA: Hayward Industries, Inc.
620 Division St
Elizabeth NJ 07201
908 351-5400

(G-20714)
HAYWARD INDUSTRIES INC
61 Whitecap Dr (02852-7444)
PHONE.....401 583-1150
Laurie Dutra, *Buyer*
David Blaine, *Engineer*
Russell Buckley, *Engineer*
Andy Monson, *Engineer*
Nathaniel Nadow, *Engineer*
EMP: 5
SALES (corp-wide): 542.1MM **Privately Held**
SIC: 3949 Mfg Sporting/Athletic Goods
PA: Hayward Industries, Inc.
620 Division St
Elizabeth NJ 07201
908 351-5400

(G-20715)
HEXAGON HOLDINGS INC (DH)
250 Circuit Dr (02852-7441)
PHONE.....401 886-2000
Norbert Hanke, *President*
Morten Holum, *COO*
Mark Delaney, *CFO*
Collin A Webb, *Admin Sec*
▲ **EMP:** 3
SALES (est): 304.9MM
SALES (corp-wide): 4.1B **Privately Held**
WEB: www.hexagonholdings.com
SIC: 3823 3545 Mfg Process Control Instruments Mfg Machine Tool Accessories
HQ: Hexagon Metrology Ab
Lilla Bantorget 15
Stockholm
418 449-200

(G-20716)
HEXAGON METROLOGY INC (DH)
Also Called: Hexagon Mfg Intelligence
250 Circuit Dr (02852-7441)
PHONE.....401 886-2000
Angus Taylor, *President*
Mark Delaney, *CFO*
Collin Webb, *Admin Sec*
◆ **EMP:** 277
SQ FT: 120,000
SALES (est): 338.8MM
SALES (corp-wide): 4.1B **Privately Held**
WEB: www.hexagonmetrology.us
SIC: 3545 3823 Mfg Machine Tool Accessories Mfg Process Control Instruments
HQ: Hexagon Holdings, Inc.
250 Circuit Dr
North Kingstown RI 02852
401 886-2000

(G-20717)
HUTCHISON COMPANY INC
Also Called: Hutchison Company Advg Display
376 Dry Bridge Rd Ste J1 (02852-5239)
PHONE.....401 294-3503
Euan Hutchison, *President*
EMP: 10
SQ FT: 45,000
SALES (est): 3.4MM **Privately Held**
WEB: www.hutchco.com
SIC: 3861 3993 Mfg Photographic Equipment/Supplies Mfg Signs/Advertising Specialties

(G-20718)
INTERNATIONAL DIOXCIDE INC
Also Called: Dupont Water Technologies
40 Whitecap Dr (02852-7445)
PHONE.....401 295-8800
Arthur Dornbusch, *Vice Pres*
Peter Martin, *Vice Pres*
Tom Dwyer, *CFO*
Peter Rapin, *Treasurer*
▼ **EMP:** 25 **EST:** 1961
SQ FT: 2,500
SALES (est): 8.3MM
SALES (corp-wide): 7.9B **Privately Held**
WEB: www.idiclo2.com
SIC: 2812 2819 2899 Mfg Alkalies/Chlorine Mfg Industrial Inorganic Chemicals Mfg Chemical Preparations
HQ: Lanxess Corporation
111 Ridc Park West Dr
Pittsburgh PA 15275
800 526-9377

(G-20719)
KEARNEY-NATIONAL INC
Also Called: Coto Technology
66 Whitecap Dr (02852-7445)
PHONE.....401 943-2686
Robert R Dyson, *President*
Tanios Bouramia, *Production*
EMP: 24
SQ FT: 9,989
SALES (corp-wide): 482MM **Privately Held**
WEB: www.cotorelay.com
SIC: 3679 3677 3625 3621 Mfg Elec Components Mfg Elec Coil/Transfrmrs Mfg Relay/Indstl Control Mfg Motors/Generators Mfg Switchgear/Boards
HQ: Kearney-National Inc.
565 5th Ave Fl 4
New York NY 10017
212 661-4600

(G-20720)
KENNEDY INCORPORATED
21 Circuit Dr (02852-7435)
PHONE.....401 295-7800
Steve Kennedy, *President*
Steven M Kennedy, *President*
EMP: 18
SQ FT: 15,000
SALES (est): 6MM **Privately Held**
WEB: www.newportsterling.com
SIC: 3714 3911 3961 2395 Mfg Motor Vehicle Parts Mfg Precious Mtl Jewelry Mfg Costume Jewelry Pleating/Stitching Svcs

(G-20721)
KNIGHT OPTICAL (USA) LLC
1130 Ten Rod Rd Ste D102 (02852-4167)
PHONE.....401 521-7000
Susan A Keller, *Principal*
EMP: 3 **EST:** 2014
SALES (est): 365.8K **Privately Held**
SIC: 3827 Mfg Optical Instruments/Lenses

(G-20722)
LIFTBAG USA INC
6946 Post Rd N Kingstown (02852)
P.O. Box 2030 (02852-0655)
PHONE.....401 884-8801
Richard Fryburg, *President*
Judi Odonnell, *Marketing Staff*
▲ **EMP:** 15 **EST:** 1977
SALES (est): 2.9MM **Privately Held**
WEB: www.subsalve.com
SIC: 3089 2673 Mfg Plastic Products Mfg Bags-Plastic/Coated Paper

(G-20723)
LIGHTSHIP GROUP LLC (PA)
Also Called: Ask Services
606 Ten Rod Rd Unit 6 (02852-4240)
P.O. Box 1470 (02852-0632)
PHONE.....401 294-3341
Peter Starr, *Vice Pres*
Maryellen Shardow, *Controller*
Thomas Alexander, *Manager*
EMP: 20
SALES: 4.6MM **Privately Held**
WEB: www.lightshipgroup.com
SIC: 3444 5551 Mfg Sheet Metalwork Ret Boats

(G-20724)
LJM PACKAGING CO INC
330 Romano Vineyard Way (02852-8417)
PHONE.....401 295-2660
John A Pezza, *President*
EMP: 55
SQ FT: 56,000
SALES (est): 15.6MM **Privately Held**
WEB: www.ljmpackaging.com
SIC: 2653 2449 Mfg Corrugated/Solid Fiber Boxes Mfg Wood Containers

(G-20725)
LORIMER STUDIOS LLC
35 Brown St (02852-5035)
PHONE.....401 714-0014
David Elison, *Mng Member*
Chris Paulhus, *Manager*
EMP: 10
SALES (est): 997.4K **Privately Held**
SIC: 2521 Mfg Wood Office Furniture

(G-20726)
MARO DISPLAY INC
112 Dillabur Ave (02852-7512)
PHONE.....401 294-5551
Steven Di Censo, *President*
Michael Di Censo, *Vice Pres*
▲ **EMP:** 25
SQ FT: 250,000
SALES: 3.4MM **Privately Held**
WEB: www.marodisplay.com
SIC: 2542 Mfg Partitions/Fixtures-Non-wood

(G-20727)
MEISTER ABRASIVES USA INC
201 Circuit Dr (02852-7440)
PHONE.....401 294-4503
Thomas Meister, *President*
Bruce Northrup, *General Mgr*
Andy Miller, *Vice Pres*
Patrick Roberts, *Engineer*
Erin Ferrazza, *Admin Asst*
▲ **EMP:** 14
SQ FT: 15,000
SALES (est): 2.2MM
SALES (corp-wide): 355.8K **Privately Held**
SIC: 3291 5085 Mfg & Whol Abrasives
HQ: Meister Abrasives Ag
Industriestrasse 10
Andelfingen ZH 8450
523 042-200

(G-20728)
METAL COMPONENTS
250 Old Baptist Rd (02852-2515)
PHONE.....401 886-7979
Mike Evans, *Owner*
EMP: 5
SALES (est): 250K **Privately Held**
SIC: 3469 Mfg Metal Stampings

(G-20729)
MULTI-COLOR CORPORATION
311 Wilbert Way (02852-7321)
PHONE.....401 884-7100
EMP: 151
SALES (corp-wide): 1.7B **Privately Held**
SIC: 2759 Commercial Printing
PA: Multi-Color Corporation
4053 Clough Woods Dr
Batavia OH 45103
513 381-1480

(G-20730)
NOONEY CONTROLS CORPORATION (PA)
466 Dry Bridge Rd (02852-5211)
P.O. Box 375 (02852-0375)
PHONE.....401 294-6000
James Nooney, *President*
Lawrence Dionne, *Corp Secy*
Wayne Seekell, *Vice Pres*
Jason D Seekell, *Production*
Ken Valiquette, *Engineer*
▲ **EMP:** 24
SQ FT: 12,000
SALES (est): 4.9MM **Privately Held**
WEB: www.nooneycontrols.com
SIC: 3822 Mfg Environmental Controls

(G-20731)
NUNNERY ORTHTIC PROSTHETIC LLC
7408 Post Rd (02852-3217)
PHONE.....401 294-4210
Doug Wilson, *QC Mgr*
Michael Nunnery, *Mng Member*
Desiree Roberts, *Office Admin*
EMP: 4
SQ FT: 1,000
SALES: 350K **Privately Held**
WEB: www.nunneryoandp.com
SIC: 3842 Mfg Surgical Appliances/Supplies

(G-20732)
OUTSOURCE ELECTRONIC MFG
29 Linwood Dr (02852-2313)
PHONE.....401 615-0705
Marie Jackson, *Owner*
EMP: 7
SALES (est): 980.9K **Privately Held**
SIC: 3699 Mfg Electrical Equipment/Supplies

(G-20733)
POWER CHAIR RECYCLERS NENG LLC
6802 Post Rd (02852-2137)
PHONE.....401 294-4111
John Perrotti Jr, *CEO*
Andrew Celani, *Opers Mgr*
EMP: 4 **EST:** 2014
SALES (est): 424.6K **Privately Held**
SIC: 3842 Mfg Surgical Appliances/Supplies

(G-20734)
R & D TECHNOLOGIES INC
60 Romano Vineyard Way (02852-8424)
PHONE.....401 885-6400
Andrew Coutu, *CEO*
Justin Coutu, *President*
Cyndy Moniz, *President*
Debra Lamoureux, *Controller*
EMP: 18
SQ FT: 3,000
SALES: 3.9MM **Privately Held**
SIC: 3555 Mfg Printing Trades Machinery

(G-20735)
R J H PRINTING INC
Also Called: Printworld
6770 Post Rd (02852-1854)
PHONE.....401 885-6262
Raoul Holzinger, *President*
EMP: 6
SQ FT: 1,350
SALES (est): 630K **Privately Held**
WEB: www.printworldri.com
SIC: 2752 Offset Printers

(G-20736)
RELENTLESS INC
100 Davisville Pier Rd (02852-8011)
PHONE.....401 295-2585
Richard Goodwin, *President*
Glenn Goodwin, *Vice Pres*
EMP: 16 **EST:** 1987
SALES (est): 1.3MM **Privately Held**
SIC: 3731 Shipbuilding/Repairing

(G-20737)
RENAISSANCE SHEET METAL L
8 Fishing Cove Rd (02852-4011)
PHONE.....401 294-3703
Thomas Ucci, *Principal*
EMP: 4
SALES (est): 344.9K **Privately Held**
SIC: 3444 Mfg Sheet Metalwork

(G-20738)
SC TECHNOLOGIES INC
342 Compass Cir Unit A2 (02852-2618)
PHONE.....401 667-7370
William McCormick, *President*
▼ **EMP:** 20
SQ FT: 20,000
SALES (est): 3.9MM **Privately Held**
WEB: www.tiyoda-serec.com
SIC: 3589 Mfg Service Industry Machinery

(G-20739)
SEIFERT SYSTEMS INC
Also Called: Seifert Mtm Systems, Inc.
75 Circuit Dr (02852-7435)
PHONE.....401 294-6960
Paulo Macedo, *President*
Michael Seifert, *Vice Pres*
Brian Thomas, *Controller*
Andrew Liles, *Technical Staff*
Caitlyn Honeycutt, *Executive*
▲ **EMP:** 14
SQ FT: 16,000
SALES (est): 2.9MM
SALES (corp-wide): 212.8K **Privately Held**
WEB: www.seifertinc.com
SIC: 3443 Mfg Fabricated Plate Work
HQ: Seifert Systems Gmbh
Albert-Einstein-Str. 3
Gevelsberg 42477
233 255-1240

(G-20740)
SENESCO MARINE LLC
10 Macnaught St (02852-7414)
PHONE.....401 295-0373
Tom Johnson, *President*
Michael J Foster, *Vice Pres*
Gayle A Corrigan, *Mng Member*
▲ **EMP:** 300
SALES (est): 106.6MM **Privately Held**
SIC: 3731 Shipbuilding/Repairing
PA: Reinauer Transportation Companies, Llc
1983 Richmond Ter
Staten Island NY 10302

(G-20741)
SHORELINE BUS SOLUTIONS INC (DH)
275 Circuit Dr (02852-7440)
PHONE.....877 914-7856
D Gordon Strickland, *CEO*
Wright Ohrstrom, *President*
Jim Beatty, *Exec VP*
John Scarborough, *Exec VP*
John Valla, *CFO*
EMP: 10
SQ FT: 4,000
SALES (est): 16.3MM
SALES (corp-wide): 253.9MM **Privately Held**
SIC: 2759 Card Production
HQ: Gemalto Holding B.V.
Barbara Strozzilaan 382
Amsterdam
205 620-680

(G-20742)
STRUCTURAL STONE LLC
285 Smith St (02852-7730)
PHONE.....401 667-4969
Don Conte, *Sales Executive*
Angela Conte, *Mng Member*
▲ **EMP:** 15
SQ FT: 60,000
SALES (est): 2.3MM **Privately Held**
SIC: 3281 Mfg Cut Stone/Products

(G-20743)
SUBSALVE USA LLC
51 Circuit Dr (02852-7435)
P.O. Box 2030 (02852-0655)
PHONE.....401 884-8801
Richard Heath, *CEO*
Richard Fryburg, *Officer*
EMP: 18
SQ FT: 16,320
SALES (est): 1MM
SALES (corp-wide): 4.5MM **Privately Held**
SIC: 3089 2673 Mfg Plastic Products Mfg Bags-Plastic/Coated Paper
HQ: Performance Inflatables Co., Llc
7975 E Mcclain Dr Ste 201
Scottsdale AZ 85260
602 315-2391

(G-20744)
SUPFINA MACHINE CO INC
181 Circuit Dr (02852-7439)
PHONE.....401 294-6600
Andy Corsini, *President*
Florian Berger, *Principal*
Raphael Kusch, *Principal*
Stefan Mueller, *Prdtn Mgr*
Kevin McBride, *Buyer*
▲ **EMP:** 40
SQ FT: 35,000
SALES (est): 9.6MM
SALES (corp-wide): 533.7K **Privately Held**
WEB: www.supfina.com
SIC: 3541 Mfg Industrial Machinery
HQ: Supfina Grieshaber Gmbh & Co. Kg
Schmelzegrun 7
Wolfach 77709
783 486-60

(G-20745)
THERMO FISHER SCIENTIFIC INC
1130 Ten Rod Rd (02852-4161)
PHONE.....401 294-1234
Scott Chapin, *Manager*
EMP: 7
SALES (corp-wide): 24.3B **Publicly Held**
WEB: www.thermo.com
SIC: 3826 Mfg Analytical Instruments
PA: Thermo Fisher Scientific Inc.
168 3rd Ave
Waltham MA 02451
781 622-1000

(G-20746)
TRICO SPECIALTY FILMS LLC
310 Compass Cir (02852-2606)
PHONE.....401 294-7022
Ed Cote, *President*
Rick Cayer, *President*
Richard J Cayer, *Mng Member*
Theodore R Coburn,
EMP: 15
SQ FT: 40,000
SALES (est): 3.5MM **Privately Held**
WEB: www.tricoindustries.com
SIC: 3081 Mfg Unsupported Plastic Film/Sheet

(G-20747)
TRUSSCO INC
25 Bonneau Rd (02852-2612)
P.O. Box 839 (02852-0608)
PHONE.....401 295-0669
Richard Duckworth, *President*
Lorraine Duckworth, *Vice Pres*
EMP: 22
SQ FT: 20,200
SALES: 3MM **Privately Held**
WEB: www.trussus.com
SIC: 2439 7389 5211 Mfg Structural Wood Members Business Services Ret Lumber/Building Materials

(G-20748)
UNETIXS VASCULAR INC
125 Commerce Park Rd (02852-8420)
PHONE.....401 583-0089
Peter Moscovita, *President*
Joshua Mason, *Technology*
EMP: 45
SQ FT: 33,000
SALES (est): 9.6MM **Privately Held**
WEB: www.unetixs.com
SIC: 3841 Mfg Surgical/Medical Instruments
PA: Opto Circuits (India) Limited
Plot No 83, Electronic City,
Bengaluru KA 56010

(G-20749)
WELMOLD TOOL & DIE INC
40 Fairfield Dr (02852-1952)
PHONE.....401 738-0505
Sidney Steen, *President*
Barbara Steen, *Vice Pres*
Mike Thibaudeau, *Manager*
EMP: 6
SQ FT: 2,400
SALES (est): 330K **Privately Held**
SIC: 3544 Mfg Dies/Tools/Jigs/Fixtures

(G-20750)
ZUERNER DESIGN LLC
376 Dry Bridge Rd G3 (02852-5249)
PHONE.....401 324-9490
Peter Zuerner, *Principal*
EMP: 5
SALES (est): 426.8K **Privately Held**
SIC: 2511 Mfg Wood Household Furniture

North Providence
Providence County

(G-20751)
A & N JEWELRY COMPANY
1029 Charles St Ste 2 (02904-5076)
PHONE..........401 431-9500
Diane Elmekawy, *President*
Mark Elmekawy, *Treasurer*
EMP: 5
SQ FT: 1,100
SALES: 170K **Privately Held**
SIC: 3911 Ret Jewelry

(G-20752)
ANATONE JEWELRY CO INC
Also Called: Ocean State Creations
10 Mark Dr (02904-3330)
PHONE..........401 728-0490
Lillian Anatone, *President*
EMP: 50 **EST:** 1959
SQ FT: 50,000
SALES (est): 4.3MM **Privately Held**
WEB: www.oscjewelry.com
SIC: 3911 Mfg Precious Metal Jewelry

(G-20753)
APAC TOOL INC
49 Hurdis St (02904-4905)
PHONE..........401 724-6090
Anthony Squillacci Jr, *President*
Anthony Squillacci Sr, *COO*
EMP: 15 **EST:** 1966
SQ FT: 1,000
SALES (est): 2.2MM **Privately Held**
WEB: www.apactool.com
SIC: 3915 5944 Mfg Jewelers' Materials Ret Jewelry

(G-20754)
ARO-SAC INC
1 Warren Ave (02911-2495)
PHONE..........401 231-6655
Robert Montaquila, *President*
Madeline Montaquila, *Corp Secy*
EMP: 50 **EST:** 1935
SQ FT: 15,000
SALES (est): 6.8MM **Privately Held**
WEB: www.aro-sac.com
SIC: 3915 3469 Mfg Jewelers' Materials Mfg Metal Stampings

(G-20755)
DEA LLC
1861 Smith St (02911-1903)
PHONE..........401 349-3446
Nestor Xjupi, *Mng Member*
EMP: 4
SALES (est): 291.1K **Privately Held**
SIC: 3421 Mfg Cutlery

(G-20756)
DFI-EP LLC
Also Called: Dfi-Electroplating
50 Waterman Ave (02911-1004)
P.O. Box 113856 (02911-0056)
PHONE..........401 943-9900
Clifford Blanchard, *President*
Elizabeth B Rafferty, *Admin Sec*
EMP: 26 **EST:** 1952
SQ FT: 10,000
SALES (est): 3.2MM **Privately Held**
WEB: www.evansplating.com
SIC: 3471 Plating/Polishing Service

(G-20757)
DOUGLAS WINE & SPIRITS INC
1661 Mineral Spring Ave (02904-4003)
PHONE..........401 353-6400
Kathy Haronian, *President*
John Haronian, *Principal*
EMP: 10 **EST:** 1995
SQ FT: 4,000
SALES (est): 853.8K **Privately Held**
SIC: 2084 8741 Mfg Wines/Brandy/Spirits Management Services

(G-20758)
E&B PRINTING LLC
1375 Mineral Spring Ave # 5 (02904-4638)
PHONE..........401 353-5777
Brenda Pearson, *Mng Member*
EMP: 5 **EST:** 2013
SQ FT: 1,600
SALES (est): 599.2K **Privately Held**
SIC: 2752 Lithographic Commercial Printing

(G-20759)
EASTERN MANUFACTURING COMPANY
9 Humbert St (02911-2783)
PHONE..........401 231-8330
Anthony Salvatore Jr, *President*
Anthony Salvatore Sr, *Treasurer*
EMP: 15 **EST:** 1954
SQ FT: 18,000
SALES (est): 2.5MM **Privately Held**
SIC: 3469 Mfg Metal Stampings

(G-20760)
ETCHED IMAGE LLC
1800 Mineral Spring Ave # 101 (02904-3980)
PHONE..........401 225-6095
Daniel Belhumeur,
EMP: 3
SALES: 250K **Privately Held**
SIC: 3479 Etched Stone

(G-20761)
FORMATT PRINTING INC
1063 Mineral Spring Ave (02904-4172)
PHONE..........401 475-6666
Matthew Salisbury, *President*
EMP: 6
SALES (est): 715.5K **Privately Held**
SIC: 2752 Lithographic Commercial Printing

(G-20762)
G & A PLATING & POLISHING CO
94 Silver Spring St (02904-2525)
PHONE..........401 351-8693
Guy J Aglione, *President*
Albert V Aglione, *Vice Pres*
EMP: 24
SQ FT: 10,000
SALES (est): 2.2MM **Privately Held**
SIC: 3471 Plating/Polishing Service

(G-20763)
GRAPHIC APPLICATION TECH INC
Also Called: Aptech Graphics
60 Waterman Ave (02911-1004)
PHONE..........401 233-2100
Mark Mader, *President*
EMP: 6 **EST:** 1998
SQ FT: 6,000
SALES (est): 732.1K **Privately Held**
SIC: 2759 Commercial Printing

(G-20764)
HOPKINS PRESS
345 Woonasquatucket Ave (02911-2427)
PHONE..........401 231-9654
Gerald Pepe, *Owner*
EMP: 3 **EST:** 1940
SQ FT: 1,000
SALES (est): 160K **Privately Held**
SIC: 2759 2752 Commercial Printing Lithographic Commercial Printing

(G-20765)
INDUPLATE INC (PA)
Also Called: Greystone
1 Greystone Ave Ste 1 # 1 (02911-1082)
PHONE..........401 231-5770
John Maconi, *CEO*
Everett Fernald Jr, *President*
Susan Marie Piccolomini, *Principal*
David Lippy, *Vice Pres*
EMP: 100
SQ FT: 65,000
SALES (est): 25.7MM **Privately Held**
SIC: 3471 3398 Plating/Polishing Service Metal Heat Treating

(G-20766)
LANCE INDUSTRIES
1119 Douglas Ave (02904-5305)
PHONE..........401 654-5394
Rocco Lancia, *Principal*
Lance Wallnau, *Director*
EMP: 5
SALES (est): 545.5K **Privately Held**
SIC: 3999 Mfg Misc Products

(G-20767)
NEW ANNEX PLATING INC
9 Warren Ave (02911-2425)
PHONE..........401 349-0911
Robert Silverman, *President*
Barry Fishback, *Vice Pres*
▲ **EMP:** 15
SALES: 1.2MM **Privately Held**
SIC: 3471 Electroplating Of Metals Or Formed Products

(G-20768)
OCEAN ORTHOPEDIC SERVICES INC (PA)
872 Charles St (02904-5667)
PHONE..........401 725-5240
John A Murphy, *President*
EMP: 11
SQ FT: 1,600
SALES (est): 1MM **Privately Held**
SIC: 3842 Mfg Custom Orthopedic Appliances

(G-20769)
OUR PLACE - SHOP FOR MEN INC (PA)
Also Called: Our Place For Tuxedos
2044 Smith St (02911-1785)
PHONE..........401 231-2370
Victor Russo, *President*
EMP: 5
SQ FT: 5,500
SALES (est): 921K **Privately Held**
SIC: 2311 5699 Mfg Men's/Boy's Suits/Coats Ret Misc Apparel/Accessories

(G-20770)
PALMER INDUSTRIES INC
862r Charles St (02904-5643)
PHONE..........800 398-9676
Anthony Palmer, *President*
Anne Palmer, *Vice Pres*
▲ **EMP:** 16 **EST:** 1985
SALES (est): 953.9K **Privately Held**
SIC: 3431 8711 Mfg Metal Sanitary Ware Engineering Services

(G-20771)
PERRY BLACKBURNE INC
330 Woonasquatucket Ave (02911-2720)
PHONE..........401 231-7200
Edward Paul, *President*
Alisa Pease, *President*
Mark Rosenberg, *VP Sales*
◆ **EMP:** 35
SQ FT: 30,000
SALES (est): 4.5MM **Privately Held**
WEB: www.perryblackburne.com
SIC: 3089 3172 3961 3496 Mfg Plastic Products Mfg Personal Leather Gds Mfg Costume Jewelry Mfg Misc Fab Wire Prdts Mfg Iron/Steel Forgings

(G-20772)
PLATINUM RECOGNITION LLC (PA)
862 Charles St (02904-5669)
PHONE..........401 305-6700
Dinna Finnegan, *President*
EMP: 3
SALES (est): 314.2K **Privately Held**
SIC: 3479 5999 7336 Coating/Engraving Service Ret Misc Merchandise Commercial Art/Graphic Design

(G-20773)
PROVIDENCE CASTING INC
3 Warren Ave (02911-2425)
PHONE..........401 231-0860
Anthony Bizzacco, *President*
Robert Bizzacco, *Vice Pres*
David Bizzacco, *Treasurer*
EMP: 7 **EST:** 1957
SQ FT: 2,400
SALES (est): 810K **Privately Held**
WEB: www.providencecasting.com
SIC: 3369 Mfg Casting & Nonferrous Metals

(G-20774)
SERVICE TECH INC (PA)
1164 Douglas Ave (02904-5371)
PHONE..........401 353-3664
Andrew R Bilodeau, *President*
▲ **EMP:** 12
SQ FT: 22,000
SALES (est): 1.1MM **Privately Held**
WEB: www.servicetechinc.com
SIC: 3589 Mfg Service Industry Machinery

(G-20775)
YACHT CLUB BOTTLING WORKS INC
2239 Mineral Spring Ave (02911-1772)
PHONE..........401 231-9290
John Sgambato, *President*
EMP: 4 **EST:** 1915
SQ FT: 12,000
SALES: 100K **Privately Held**
SIC: 2086 Mfg Carbonated Beverages

North Scituate
Providence County

(G-20776)
CASTE GLASS
102 Pole Bridge Rd (02857-1103)
PHONE..........401 934-2959
Neal Drobnis, *Owner*
EMP: 3
SALES (est): 225.1K **Privately Held**
WEB: www.nealdrobnis.com
SIC: 3299 Mfg Nonmetallic Mineral Products

(G-20777)
FITZWATER ENGINEERING CORP
271 Plainfield Pike (02857-2028)
PHONE..........401 647-7600
Edward J Field, *President*
▼ **EMP:** 6 **EST:** 1979
SQ FT: 4,500
SALES: 600K **Privately Held**
WEB: www.fitzwaterengineering.com
SIC: 3599 Mfg Industrial Machinery

(G-20778)
GLAXOSMITHKLINE LLC
176 Snake Hill Rd (02857-3017)
PHONE..........401 934-2834
Steven Sette, *Branch Mgr*
EMP: 14
SALES (corp-wide): 40.6B **Privately Held**
WEB: www.delks.com
SIC: 2834 Mfg Pharmaceutical Preparations
HQ: Glaxosmithkline Llc
5 Crescent Dr
Philadelphia PA 19112
215 751-4000

(G-20779)
J-TECH AUTOMATION LLC
205 Sandy Brook Rd (02857-2842)
PHONE..........401 934-2435
Jonathan Gamble, *Mng Member*
Karen Gamble,
EMP: 4
SALES: 370K **Privately Held**
SIC: 3549 Designer And Manufacturer Of Robotic Machinery

(G-20780)
MARCIAS DOLLCLOTHES
965 Chopmist Hill Rd (02857-1043)
PHONE..........401 742-3654
Marcia Sharkey, *Principal*
EMP: 3
SALES (est): 183.4K **Privately Held**
SIC: 3942 Mfg Dolls/Stuffed Toys

GEOGRAPHIC

North Smithfield
Providence County

(G-20781)
AR-RO ENGINEERING COMPANY INC (PA)
16 Vincent Ave Ste 1 (02896-7599)
PHONE.................................401 766-6669
Jefferey D Cote, *President*
EMP: 6
SQ FT: 15,000
SALES (est): 914.6K **Privately Held**
SIC: 3544 3545 5085 Mfg Industrial Molds Dies & Machine Tool Accessories & Distributor Industrial Supplies

(G-20782)
ATLANTIC FOOTCARE INC
229 Quaker Hwy Apt 3 (02896-7648)
PHONE.................................401 568-4918
Charlie Sipes, *President*
Jane Carroll, *Vice Pres*
John Conroy,
Ken Mazer,
◆ **EMP:** 75
SQ FT: 41,000
SALES (est): 12.3MM **Privately Held**
SIC: 3842 Mfg Surgical Appliances/Supplies
PA: Af International, Inc.
24 Albion Rd Ste 210
Lincoln RI 02865
401 757-3908

(G-20783)
CAS ACQUISITION CO LLC
Also Called: Cas America
20 Providence Pike (02896-8046)
PHONE.................................401 884-8556
Joe Cannon,
Kenneth Beck,
Tracey Beck,
Gladys Cannon,
EMP: 18 **EST:** 2015
SALES (est): 116K **Privately Held**
SIC: 2431 5031 3999 Mfg Millwork Whol Lumber/Plywood/Millwork Mfg Misc Products

(G-20784)
COBRA PRECISION PRODUCTS INC
2131 Providence Pike (02896-9340)
PHONE.................................401 766-3333
David Mitchell, *President*
EMP: 5
SALES (est): 513.6K **Privately Held**
SIC: 3599 Mfg Industrial Machinery

(G-20785)
EUROPEAN CUSTOM CASEWORK INC
473 Saint Paul St (02896-6865)
PHONE.................................401 356-0400
Michael Prudhomme, *President*
Yvette Gladu, *Treasurer*
EMP: 5
SALES (est): 647.7K **Privately Held**
WEB: www.europeancustomcasework.com
SIC: 2434 Mfg Wood Kitchen Cabinets

(G-20786)
FRED F WALTZ CO INC
97 Industrial Dr (02896-8032)
P.O. Box 156, Slatersville (02876-0156)
PHONE.................................401 769-4900
Kimberley J Waltz, *President*
EMP: 14
SALES (est): 2.1MM **Privately Held**
SIC: 2677 5112 5942 5999 Mfg Envelopes Whol Stationery/Offc Sup Ret Books Ret Misc Merchandise

(G-20787)
GERARD R DAVIS LTD
521 Providence Pike (02896-9531)
P.O. Box 1424, Woonsocket (02895-0843)
PHONE.................................401 766-8760
Gerard R Davis Jr, *President*
EMP: 4
SQ FT: 2,000
SALES (est): 340K **Privately Held**
SIC: 2311 Mfg Men's/Boy's Suits/Coats

(G-20788)
KONNECO INTERNATIONAL LLC
34 Georgianna Ave (02896-7857)
P.O. Box 129, Slatersville (02876-0129)
PHONE.................................401 767-3690
Chris Koney, *Mng Member*
▼ **EMP:** 4
SALES: 200K **Privately Held**
SIC: 2821 5162 Mfg Plastic Materials/Resins Whol Plastic Materials/Shapes

(G-20789)
LKQ PRECIOUS METALS INC
Also Called: MST
800 Central St (02896-7631)
PHONE.................................401 762-0094
John Silvestri, *President*
EMP: 130 **EST:** 2009
SALES (est): 22.8MM
SALES (corp-wide): 11.8B **Publicly Held**
SIC: 2611 Pulp Mill
PA: Lkq Corporation
500 W Madison St Ste 2800
Chicago IL 60661
312 621-1950

(G-20790)
MATERIAL CONCRETE CORP
618 Greenville Rd (02896-9553)
PHONE.................................401 765-0204
Constance Pezza, *President*
Robert Pezza, *Vice Pres*
EMP: 15
SALES (est): 2.3MM **Privately Held**
SIC: 3273 Mfg Ready-Mixed Concrete

(G-20791)
NARRAGANSETT IMAGING USA LLC
51 Industrial Dr (02896-8032)
P.O. Box 278, Slatersville (02876-0278)
PHONE.................................401 762-3800
Frank Epps,
William Ulmschneider,
EMP: 35
SQ FT: 80,000
SALES (est): 7.3MM **Privately Held**
WEB: www.nimaging.com
SIC: 3679 3674 3671 Mfg Electronic Components Mfg Semiconductors/Related Devices Mfg Electron Tubes

(G-20792)
NATIONAL MARKER COMPANY
100 Providence Pike (02896-8046)
PHONE.................................401 762-9700
Michael Black, *President*
◆ **EMP:** 100
SQ FT: 40,800
SALES (est): 16.1MM **Privately Held**
SIC: 3993 Mfg Signs/Advertising Specialties

(G-20793)
NEW ENGLAND IMAGE & PRINT INC
585 Smithfield Rd (02896-7226)
PHONE.................................401 769-3708
Judith Beauchemin, *President*
EMP: 3 **EST:** 2007
SQ FT: 2,000
SALES: 80K **Privately Held**
SIC: 2752 7384 Lithographic Commercial Printing Photofinishing Laboratory

(G-20794)
POLYWORKS LLC
1 Tupperware Dr Ste 7 (02896-6815)
PHONE.................................401 769-0994
Richard Fox, *President*
EMP: 45
SALES (est): 8.4MM **Privately Held**
SIC: 3089 2821 Mfg Plastic Products Mfg Plstc Material/Resin

(G-20795)
R & R MACHINE INDUSTRIES INC
147 Industrial Dr (02896-8035)
P.O. Box 119, Slatersville (02876-0119)
PHONE.................................401 766-2505
Roland Legare, *President*
Chuck Picard-EXT, *General Mgr*
Elizabeth Legare, *Principal*
Renay Curran, *CFO*
Renay Curran-EXT, *CFO*
EMP: 14
SQ FT: 35,000
SALES (est): 3MM **Privately Held**
WEB: www.rrmachine.com
SIC: 3599 Mfg Industrial Machinery

(G-20796)
STONE SYSTEMS NEW ENGLAND LLC
9 Steel St (02896-8055)
PHONE.................................401 766-3603
Roberto Contreras, *President*
▲ **EMP:** 134
SALES (est): 12MM
SALES (corp-wide): 4MM **Privately Held**
SIC: 3281 1799 Mfg And Installs Stone Countertops
HQ: Stone Suppliers, Inc.
13124 Trinity Dr
Stafford TX

(G-20797)
STRANGE FAMOUS INC
2 Meadowbrook Dr (02896-6905)
PHONE.................................310 254-8974
Paul Landry, *President*
Hugo Lopez, *Merchandising*
EMP: 4
SALES: 200K **Privately Held**
SIC: 2782 Record Labels

Oakland
Providence County

(G-20798)
BURRILLVILLE TOWN OF INC
Also Called: Burrillville Waste Water
141 Clair River Dr (02858)
P.O. Box 71, Harrisville (02830-0071)
PHONE.................................401 568-6296
John E Martin, *Superintendent*
EMP: 8 **Privately Held**
SIC: 2899 Mfg Chemical Preparations
PA: Burrillville, Town Of Inc
105 Harrisville Main St
Harrisville RI 02830
401 568-9451

Pascoag
Providence County

(G-20799)
DANIELE INC
105 Davis Dr (02859-3507)
P.O. Box 106 (02859-0106)
PHONE.................................401 568-6228
Stefano Dukcevich, *President*
▲ **EMP:** 50
SALES (est): 13.3MM **Privately Held**
SIC: 2013 Mfg Prepared Meats

(G-20800)
DANIELE INTERNATIONAL INC
105 Davis Dr (02859-3507)
PHONE.................................401 568-6228
Stefano Dukcevich, *President*
EMP: 95
SALES (corp-wide): 101.9MM **Privately Held**
SIC: 2013 Mfg Prepared Meats
PA: Daniele International, Inc.
1000 Danielle Dr
Mapleville RI 02839
401 568-6228

(G-20801)
DANIELE INTERNATIONAL INC
180 Davis Dr (02859-3506)
PHONE.................................401 568-6228
Stefano Dukcevich, *President*
EMP: 245
SALES (corp-wide): 101.9MM **Privately Held**
SIC: 2013 Mfg Prepared Meats
PA: Daniele International, Inc.
1000 Danielle Dr
Mapleville RI 02839
401 568-6228

(G-20802)
LOCKHEED WINDOW CORP
925 S Main St (02859-3521)
P.O. Box 166 (02859-0166)
PHONE.................................401 568-3061
Jeffrey Kosiver, *President*
Michael Kosiver, *President*
Bob G Gregoire, *General Mgr*
Michele Marchand, *Project Mgr*
Kathleen Courtney, *Admin Asst*
▲ **EMP:** 100
SQ FT: 60,000
SALES (est): 40.6MM **Privately Held**
WEB: www.lockheedwindow.com
SIC: 3442 1751 1542 Mfg Metal Doors/Sash/Trim Carpentry Contractor Nonresidential Construction

(G-20803)
NEWS STAR INC
170 Pascoag Main St (02859-3101)
PHONE.................................401 567-7077
Xiang Da Zheng, *Principal*
EMP: 4
SALES (est): 197.1K **Privately Held**
SIC: 2711 Newspapers-Publishing/Printing

(G-20804)
SANDBERG ENTERPRISES INC
Also Called: Machine Shop
806 Broncos Hwy (02859)
PHONE.................................401 568-1602
Robert Sandberg, *President*
EMP: 20
SALES (corp-wide): 2MM **Privately Held**
SIC: 3599 Mfg Industrial Machinery
PA: Sandberg Enterprises, Inc.
806 Broncos Hwy
Mapleville RI 02839
401 568-1602

Pawtucket
Providence County

(G-20805)
ACCENT PLATING COMPANY INC
25 Esten Ave Unit 5 (02860-4826)
PHONE.................................401 722-6306
Robert Mancini, *President*
EMP: 20 **EST:** 1963
SQ FT: 15,000
SALES (est): 2.4MM **Privately Held**
SIC: 3471 Plating/Polishing Service

(G-20806)
ACCU-TOOL INC
Also Called: ATI
250 Esten Ave Unit 101 (02860-4827)
PHONE.................................401 725-5350
Robert Gonzenbach, *President*
EMP: 4 **EST:** 1971
SALES (est): 481.9K **Privately Held**
SIC: 3961 3911 Mfg Costume Jewelry Mfg Precious Metal Jewelry

(G-20807)
ADAMS PRINTING INC
Also Called: Ocean State Printers
545 Pawtucket Ave # 103 (02860-6046)
PHONE.................................401 722-9222
Peter Adams, *President*
EMP: 4
SQ FT: 3,500
SALES: 350K **Privately Held**
WEB: www.osprinters.com
SIC: 2752 7334 Commercial Printer

▲ = Import ▼=Export
◆ =Import/Export

(G-20808)
ADAMSDALE CONCRETE & PDTS CO
551 Weeden St (02860-1625)
P.O. Box 516 (02862-0516)
PHONE....401 722-6725
John Courtois, *President*
David Courtois, *Vice Pres*
Suzanne Courtois, *Treasurer*
Norman Courtois, *Shareholder*
EMP: 5
SQ FT: 3,200
SALES (est): 802.4K **Privately Held**
WEB: www.adamsdaleconcrete.com
SIC: 3273 Mfg Ready-Mixed Concrete

(G-20809)
AGAR MACHINING & WELDING INC
270 York Ave (02860-5826)
PHONE....401 724-2260
George Lanoie, *President*
Thomas Mc Gee, *Vice Pres*
EMP: 15
SQ FT: 10,000
SALES (est): 2.5MM **Privately Held**
SIC: 3599 Mfg Industrial Machinery

(G-20810)
AGELESS INNOVATION LLC (PA)
161 Exchange St Unit 2a (02860-2276)
PHONE....888 569-4255
Edward Fischer,
Thomas Canterino,
Andrew Jeas,
EMP: 4
SALES (est): 639.1K **Privately Held**
SIC: 3944 5092 Mfg Games/Toys Whol Toys/Hobby Goods

(G-20811)
AHLERS DESIGNS INC
Also Called: Ahlers Gifts.com
999 Main St Unit 707 (02860-7816)
PHONE....401 365-1010
Gail Ahlers, *President*
▲ **EMP:** 3
SQ FT: 1,700
SALES (est): 355.5K **Privately Held**
WEB: www.ahlersgifts.com
SIC: 3499 5944 3993 Mfg Misc Fabricated Metal Products Ret Jewelry Mfg Signs/Advertising Specialties

(G-20812)
ALLIANCE PAPER COMPANY INC
33 India St (02860-5521)
PHONE....508 324-9100
Richard G Jones, *President*
Jim Dykes, *Vice Pres*
▲ **EMP:** 10
SQ FT: 100,000
SALES (est): 2.5MM **Privately Held**
SIC: 2679 Mfg Converted Paper Products

(G-20813)
ARTISAN MILLWORK INC CABI
750 School St (02860-5748)
PHONE....401 721-5500
Peter D Spaulding, *Principal*
EMP: 4
SALES (est): 611.2K **Privately Held**
SIC: 2431 Mfg Millwork

(G-20814)
B & L PLASTICS INC
Also Called: Blow Molded Specialties
535 Prospect St (02860-6200)
PHONE....401 723-3000
Thomas Boyd, *President*
Avril Cook, *COO*
EMP: 30
SQ FT: 35,000
SALES: 5MM **Privately Held**
WEB: www.bmsplastics.com
SIC: 3089 Mfg Plastic Products

(G-20815)
B & M PLASTICS INC
511 York Ave (02861-3427)
PHONE....401 728-0404
Brian Regan, *President*
Manny Viera, *Vice Pres*
EMP: 4
SQ FT: 6,000
SALES: 650K **Privately Held**
SIC: 3559 3599 Mfg Metal Finishing Equipment For Plating

(G-20816)
BIO-DETEK INCORPORATED
Also Called: Zoll Medical
525 Narragansett Park Dr (02861-4352)
PHONE....401 729-1400
Michael Cole, *President*
Victor Faria, *Engineer*
Christopher Tupper, *Engineer*
Edna Rojas, *Info Tech Mgr*
Diane Chapman, *Executive*
▲ **EMP:** 175
SALES (est): 29MM **Privately Held**
WEB: www.bio-detek.com
SIC: 3845 Mfg Electromedical Equipment

(G-20817)
BLACKLEDGE INDUSTRIES LLC
Also Called: Maritox
255 Main St (02860-4064)
PHONE....401 270-6779
Scott Blackledge, *CEO*
EMP: 3
SALES (est): 179.5K **Privately Held**
SIC: 3999 Mfg Misc Products

(G-20818)
BLISS MANUFACTURING CO INC
50 Bacon St (02860-4535)
P.O. Box 3440 (02861-0900)
PHONE....401 729-1690
Francis Bliss Jr, *President*
Jane Bliss, *Vice Pres*
Rick Douglas, *Sales Staff*
Steve Loewenthal, *Webmaster*
Alan Hess, *Executive*
EMP: 48 **EST:** 1901
SQ FT: 300,000
SALES (est): 5.5MM **Privately Held**
WEB: www.blissmfg.com
SIC: 3961 3911 Mfg Costume Jewelry Mfg Precious Metal Jewelry

(G-20819)
CALA FRUIT DISTRIBUTORS INC
71 Dexter St (02860-1917)
PHONE....401 725-8189
Gerald Faella, *President*
EMP: 10 **EST:** 1947
SQ FT: 5,100
SALES (est): 967.6K **Privately Held**
SIC: 2033 Mfg Packaged Fruits

(G-20820)
CATANZARO FOOD PRODUCTS INC
203 Concord St Unit 457 (02860-3481)
PHONE....401 255-1700
Kristen J Catanzoro, *President*
EMP: 8
SQ FT: 2,200
SALES (est): 834K **Privately Held**
WEB: www.catanzarofoodproducts.com
SIC: 2052 2033 2051 Mfg Cookies/Crackers Mfg Canned Fruits/Vegetables Mfg Bread/Related Products

(G-20821)
CELLMARK INC
Also Called: Semper/Exeter Paper Company
402 Walcott St (02860-3247)
P.O. Box 7427, Cumberland (02864-0805)
PHONE....401 723-4200
Stephen Cavanaugh, *Branch Mgr*
EMP: 4
SALES (corp-wide): 2.9B **Privately Held**
SIC: 2621 Paper Mill
HQ: Cellmark, Inc.
88 Rowland Way Ste 300
Novato CA 94945
415 927-1700

(G-20822)
CHAUDHARY LLC
371 Benefit St (02861-1201)
PHONE....401 954-9695
Brij Chaundry, *Partner*
EMP: 6
SALES (est): 421.3K **Privately Held**
SIC: 2842 Mfg Polish/Sanitation Goods

(G-20823)
CINTAS CORPORATION NO 2
700 Narragansett Park Dr (02861-4326)
PHONE....401 723-7300
EMP: 7
SALES (corp-wide): 6.8B **Publicly Held**
SIC: 3842 Mfg Surgical Appliances/Supplies
HQ: Cintas Corporation No. 2
6800 Cintas Blvd
Mason OH 45040

(G-20824)
CONRAD-JARVIS CORP
217 Conant St (02860-1801)
P.O. Box 878 (02862-0878)
PHONE....401 722-8700
William T Jarvis, *President*
George Scoggins, *Treasurer*
Michele Scoggins, *Admin Sec*
▲ **EMP:** 90 **EST:** 1917
SQ FT: 120,000
SALES: 8.5MM **Privately Held**
SIC: 2241 Narrow Fabric Mill

(G-20825)
COOLEY INCORPORATED (HQ)
Also Called: Cooley Building Products
50 Esten Ave (02860-4840)
PHONE....401 724-9000
Daniel Dwight, *CEO*
Bryan Rose, *Vice Pres*
Stephen Siener, *Vice Pres*
Walter Kelley, *Purch Mgr*
Justin Silvia, *Technical Mgr*
◆ **EMP:** 125
SQ FT: 300,000
SALES (est): 105.7MM **Privately Held**
WEB: www.cooleygroup.com
SIC: 2295 3069 2262 Mfg Coated Fabrics Mfg Fabricated Rubber Products Manmade Fiber & Silk Finishing Plant
PA: Cooley Group Holdings, Inc.
50 Esten Ave
Pawtucket RI 02860
401 724-0510

(G-20826)
COVE METAL COMPANY INC (PA)
Also Called: Cove Textile Machinery Co
160 Grenville St (02860-4804)
P.O. Box 29, Providence (02901-0029)
PHONE....401 724-3500
Charles T Cove, *President*
EMP: 12 **EST:** 1955
SQ FT: 14,000
SALES (est): 1.5MM **Privately Held**
SIC: 3552 3549 Mfg Textile Machinery Mfg Metalworking Machinery

(G-20827)
CREATIVE CASTINGS INC
1090 Main St (02860-4979)
PHONE....401 724-1070
Ivan Rozowsky, *President*
Selwyn Katz, *Admin Sec*
EMP: 6
SQ FT: 5,000
SALES: 520K **Privately Held**
WEB: www.creativecastings.com
SIC: 3915 Operates As A Manufacturer Of Metal Castings For Jewelry

(G-20828)
CREATIVE FINDINGS LLC
270 Broadway (02860-2209)
P.O. Box 3606, Attleboro MA (02703-0059)
PHONE....401 274-5579
Leonard Rosenblatt,
Debbie Plant,
▲ **EMP:** 3
SALES (est): 419.9K **Privately Held**
WEB: www.creativefindings.com
SIC: 3911 Whol Jewelry/Precious Stones

(G-20829)
CRYSTAL HORD CORPORATION
33 York Ave Ste 45 (02860-6423)
PHONE....401 723-2989
Mark Thomas, *CEO*
▲ **EMP:** 43
SALES (est): 14.7MM **Privately Held**
WEB: www.hordcrystal.com
SIC: 3915 Mfg Jewelers' Materials Mfg Precious Metal Jewelry

(G-20830)
CRYSTAL STAMPING
51 Charlton Ave (02860-6211)
PHONE....401 724-5880
James Dimello, *President*
EMP: 5
SALES (est): 580.2K **Privately Held**
SIC: 3469 Mfg Metal Stampings

(G-20831)
CUSTOM SEAMLESS GUTTERS INC
260 Pawtucket Ave Frnt (02860-5159)
PHONE....401 726-3137
Daniel Daluz, *President*
EMP: 4
SQ FT: 5,000
SALES (est): 588.3K **Privately Held**
SIC: 3444 5039 5031 Mfg Downspouts & Whol Eavestroughing Parts & Supplies & Windows

(G-20832)
D & W TOOL FINDINGS INC
304 Cottage St (02860-2327)
PHONE....401 727-3030
Nisim Tzadok, *President*
EMP: 14 **EST:** 1945
SALES (est): 1.9MM **Privately Held**
SIC: 3495 3493 Mfg Wire Springs Mfg Steel Springs-Nonwire

(G-20833)
DAG MACHINE AND TOOL INC
92 Pleasant St 1 (02860-4017)
PHONE....401 724-0450
Fax: 401 724-0680
EMP: 4
SQ FT: 4,000
SALES (est): 320K **Privately Held**
SIC: 3599 Machine Shop

(G-20834)
DOMINION REBAR COMPANY
30 Lockbridge St (02860-1612)
PHONE....401 724-9200
Mark H Mainelli, *President*
John Pursche, *Treasurer*
Roy Jackson, *VP Sales*
EMP: 50
SQ FT: 10,000
SALES: 20MM **Privately Held**
SIC: 3449 3441 Mfg Misc Structural Metalwork Structural Metal Fabrication
PA: Aetna Bridge Company
100 Jefferson Blvd # 100
Warwick RI 02888
401 728-0400

(G-20835)
EAGLE SCREEN CO LLC
100 Dexter St Ste 1 (02860-1961)
PHONE....401 722-9315
Wayne Mallory, *General Mgr*
Ernest Mallory, *Mng Member*
EMP: 3 **EST:** 1965
SQ FT: 2,800
SALES: 300K **Privately Held**
SIC: 3442 Mfg Louvers Shutters & Similar Items

(G-20836)
ECOLOGICAL FIBERS INC
Also Called: Narragansett Coated Paper
730 York Ave (02861-2846)
P.O. Box 2203 (02861-0203)
PHONE....401 725-9700
Mary Rose Peloquin, *Buyer*
Ed Quill, *Manager*
EMP: 95
SQ FT: 140,000
SALES (corp-wide): 66.6MM **Privately Held**
SIC: 2672 Mfg Coated Paper
PA: Ecological Fibers, Inc.
40 Pioneer Dr
Lunenburg MA 01462
978 537-0003

(G-20837)
FARBER INDUSTRIAL FABRICATING
55 Moss St (02860-4543)
PHONE..................................401 725-2492
Ray Auger, *President*
Jane Auger, *Vice Pres*
Richard Nadeau, *Admin Sec*
EMP: 9
SQ FT: 9,000
SALES (est): 1.7MM **Privately Held**
SIC: 3441 Structural Metal Fabrication

(G-20838)
FASHIONS BY GARY INC
108 Tweed St (02861-1736)
PHONE..................................401 726-1453
Gary Weintraub, *President*
Judy Weintraub, *Manager*
▲ **EMP:** 12
SALES (est): 1.3MM **Privately Held**
SIC: 3915 Mfg Precious Metal Jewelry

(G-20839)
FIESTA JEWELRY CORPORATION
Also Called: F2nyc
250 East Ave (02860)
PHONE..................................212 564-6847
Carlos Hatch, *President*
EMP: 6
SALES (corp-wide): 1MM **Privately Held**
SIC: 3911 Mfg Precious Metal Jewelry
PA: Fiesta Jewelry Corporation
8 W 38th St Rm 801
New York NY 10018
212 564-6847

(G-20840)
FILTERS INC
593 Mineral Spring Ave (02860-3364)
PHONE..................................401 722-8999
EMP: 8
SALES (est): 119.5K **Privately Held**
SIC: 3231 1321 3569 Mfg Products-Purchased Glass Natural Gas Liquids Production Mfg General Industrial Machinery

(G-20841)
FRONTIER MANUFACTURING INC
Also Called: Lace Unlimited
245 Esten Ave (02860-4818)
P.O. Box 253, Narragansett (02882-0253)
PHONE..................................401 722-0852
Fax: 401 722-7136
EMP: 8
SQ FT: 3,500
SALES (est): 610K **Privately Held**
SIC: 2258 Lace/Warp Knit Fabric Mill

(G-20842)
GEM LABEL & TAPE COMPANY
65 Blackstone Ave # 6532 (02860-1068)
PHONE..................................401 724-1300
Jim Jalkin, *President*
Ann Foncellino, *President*
EMP: 10
SQ FT: 500
SALES (est): 1.1MM **Privately Held**
WEB: www.gemlabel.com
SIC: 2672 Whol Nondurable Goods

(G-20843)
GEO H FULLER AND SON COMPANY
Also Called: F F J
151 Exchange St (02860-2210)
P.O. Box 620 (02862-0620)
PHONE..................................401 722-6530
Fax: 401 723-1720
EMP: 50 **EST:** 1858
SQ FT: 25,000
SALES: 3.4MM **Privately Held**
WEB: www.fullerfindings.com
SIC: 3915 3911 Mfg Jewelers' Materials Mfg Precious Metal Jewelry

(G-20844)
GFXCO LLC
66 Stearns St (02861-1146)
PHONE..................................401 722-8888
Thomas Barber, *Principal*
EMP: 3 **EST:** 2017
SALES (est): 97.8K **Privately Held**
SIC: 3443 Mfg Fabricated Plate Work

(G-20845)
HASBRO INC (PA)
1027 Newport Ave (02861-2500)
P.O. Box 1059 (02862-1059)
PHONE..................................401 431-8697
Brian D Goldner, *Ch of Bd*
John A Frascotti, *President*
John Frascotti, *President*
Patricia Healey, *District Mgr*
Lisa Lukiewski, *Business Mgr*
▲ **EMP:** 2800
SQ FT: 343,000
SALES: 4.5B **Publicly Held**
WEB: www.hasbro.com
SIC: 3942 3069 3944 Mfg Dolls/Stuffed Toys Mfg Fabrcatd Rubber Prdt Mfg Games/Toys

(G-20846)
HASBRO INC
1011 Newport Ave (02861-2538)
PHONE..................................401 726-2090
Jane Ritson-Parsons, *Manager*
EMP: 11
SALES (corp-wide): 4.5B **Publicly Held**
SIC: 3944 Mfg Games/Toys
PA: Hasbro, Inc.
1027 Newport Ave
Pawtucket RI 02861
401 431-8697

(G-20847)
HASBRO INC
200 Narragansett Park Dr (02861-4342)
PHONE..................................401 431-8412
Rosanne Reddington, *Project Mgr*
Keeley Murphy, *Project Engr*
Paul Alexander, *VP Finance*
Kim Proulx, *Accountant*
Bob Kiely, *Human Res Dir*
EMP: 49
SALES (corp-wide): 4.5B **Publicly Held**
SIC: 3944 Mfg Games/Toys
PA: Hasbro, Inc.
1027 Newport Ave
Pawtucket RI 02861
401 431-8697

(G-20848)
HASBRO INTERNATIONAL INC (HQ)
1027 Newport Ave (02861-2500)
PHONE..................................401 431-8697
Brian Coldner, *President*
Nelson R Chaffee Corp, *Vice Pres*
Barry Nagler, *Vice Pres*
David D Hargreaves, *CFO*
EMP: 1000
SQ FT: 343,000
SALES (est): 499.9MM
SALES (corp-wide): 4.5B **Publicly Held**
SIC: 3944 Mfg Games/Toys
PA: Hasbro, Inc.
1027 Newport Ave
Pawtucket RI 02861
401 431-8697

(G-20849)
JOHN H COLLINS & SON CO
Dunnell Ln (02862)
P.O. Box 741 (02862-0741)
PHONE..................................401 722-0775
Louis G Provencal Jr, *President*
EMP: 5 **EST:** 1901
SQ FT: 1,800
SALES: 1MM **Privately Held**
SIC: 3412 Mfg Steel Drums

(G-20850)
JS PALLET CO INC
60 Lockbridge St (02860-1612)
P.O. Box 1907 (02862-1907)
PHONE..................................401 723-0223
Carlos Da Silva, *President*
Joseph Da Silva, *Principal*
▲ **EMP:** 46
SALES (est): 7.5MM **Privately Held**
WEB: www.jspalletinc.com
SIC: 2448 Mfg Wood Pallets/Skids

(G-20851)
KEY CONTAINER CORPORATION (PA)
21 Campbell St (02861-4005)
P.O. Box 2370 (02861-0370)
PHONE..................................401 723-2000
David Strauss, *President*
▲ **EMP:** 128
SQ FT: 150,000
SALES (est): 55.2MM **Privately Held**
WEB: www.keycontainercorp.com
SIC: 2653 Mfg Corrugated/Solid Fiber Boxes

(G-20852)
KITCHEN CENTER RI INC
121 Terrace Ave (02860-4640)
PHONE..................................401 640-6514
Paula Ruzzano, *President*
Dean Ruzzano, *Principal*
George Ruzzano, *Vice Pres*
EMP: 3
SALES (est): 270.6K **Privately Held**
SIC: 2434 Mfg Wood Kitchen Cabinets

(G-20853)
LASERVALL NORTH AMERICA LLC
Also Called: Lna Laser Technology
136 Newell Ave (02860-4922)
P.O. Box 998 (02862-0998)
PHONE..................................401 724-0076
Brianne Pereira, *Purchasing*
Rosie Spooner, *Controller*
Joshua M Gold, *Mng Member*
Daniel Gold,
Al Davis, *Technician*
EMP: 9
SQ FT: 32,000
SALES (est): 1.9MM **Privately Held**
WEB: www.laservall-usa.com
SIC: 3699 Mfg Electrical Equipment/Supplies

(G-20854)
LIFETIME BRANDS INC
999 Main St Unit 115 (02860-7816)
PHONE..................................401 333-2040
EMP: 4
SALES (corp-wide): 704.5MM **Publicly Held**
SIC: 3421 5023 5719 Mfg Cutlery Whol Homefurnishings
PA: Lifetime Brands, Inc.
1000 Stewart Ave
Garden City NY 11530
516 683-6000

(G-20855)
MAINLINE PAINT MFG CO
768 Main St (02860-3630)
PHONE..................................401 726-3650
Richard J Main, *President*
EMP: 5 **EST:** 1957
SQ FT: 10,000
SALES (est): 1MM **Privately Held**
SIC: 2851 5231 Mfg Paints

(G-20856)
MARR OFFICE EQUIPMENT INC
751 Main St (02860-3627)
P.O. Box 53 (02862-0053)
PHONE..................................401 725-5186
Raymond Marr, *President*
Michael Marr, *Vice Pres*
EMP: 4
SQ FT: 1,500
SALES: 150K **Privately Held**
SIC: 3577 7699 Mfg Computer Peripheral Equipment Repair Services

(G-20857)
MASON BOX COMPANY
517 Mineral Spring Ave (02860-3408)
PHONE..................................800 842-9526
Hugh D Mason, *President*
Ronnie Henry, *Cust Mgr*
▲ **EMP:** 50 **EST:** 1891
SQ FT: 96,000
SALES (est): 9.7MM **Privately Held**
WEB: www.masonbox.com
SIC: 2674 2671 2653 2652 Mfg Bags-Uncoated Paper Mfg Packaging Paper/Film Mfg Corrugated/Fiber Box Mfg Setup Paperboard Box

(G-20858)
MASTERCAST LTD
56 Barnes St (02860-4961)
PHONE..................................401 726-3100
David Katseff, *President*
EMP: 13
SQ FT: 6,500
SALES: 1MM **Privately Held**
SIC: 3089 3993 Casting Of Plastics & Mfg Advertising Specialties/Lucite Products

(G-20859)
MEL-CO-ED INC
381 Roosevelt Ave (02860-2145)
P.O. Box 1245 (02862-1245)
PHONE..................................401 724-2160
Randolph Sowa, *President*
▲ **EMP:** 35 **EST:** 1946
SQ FT: 40,000
SALES (est): 4.6MM **Privately Held**
WEB: www.melcoed.com
SIC: 3999 Mfg Misc Products

(G-20860)
MINUTEMAN PRESS OF PAWTUCKET
805 Central Ave (02861-2150)
PHONE..................................401 305-6644
Jeanne Salisbury, *Principal*
EMP: 4
SALES (est): 416.7K **Privately Held**
SIC: 2752 Comm Prtg Litho

(G-20861)
MOUNT TOM BOX CO INC
21 Campbell St (02861-4005)
PHONE..................................413 781-5300
Domenic Lapati, *Principal*
EMP: 3
SALES (est): 269.9K **Privately Held**
SIC: 2653 Mfg Corrugated/Solid Fiber Boxes

(G-20862)
MUHAMMAD CHOUDHRY
530 Broadway (02860-1289)
PHONE..................................401 726-1118
Mohommad Choudhry, *Owner*
EMP: 4 **EST:** 2010
SALES (est): 206.7K **Privately Held**
SIC: 3911 Mfg Precious Metal Jewelry

(G-20863)
NEPTCO INCORPORATED (HQ)
30 Hamlet St (02861-2827)
PHONE..................................401 722-5500
Guy Marini, *CEO*
Frank Conti, *Vice Pres*
Ken Feroldi, *Vice Pres*
Joel Gruhn, *Vice Pres*
Lois Kilsey, *Vice Pres*
◆ **EMP:** 95 **EST:** 1955
SQ FT: 50,000
SALES (est): 103.1MM
SALES (corp-wide): 281.3MM **Publicly Held**
WEB: www.neptco.com
SIC: 3496 3083 2672 Mfg Misc Fabricated Wire Products Mfg Laminated Plastic Plate/Sheet Mfg Coated/Laminated Paper
PA: Chase Corporation
295 University Ave
Westwood MA 02090
781 332-0700

(G-20864)
NESTOR TRAFFIC SYSTEMS INC (PA)
1080 Main St (02860-4847)
PHONE..................................401 714-7781
William Danzell, *Ch of Bd*
Nigel Hebborn, *President*
Mary Ann Branin, *Manager*
EMP: 30 **EST:** 1997
SQ FT: 20,000
SALES (est): 4.3MM **Privately Held**
SIC: 3669 8748 Mfg Communications Equipment Business Consulting Services

(G-20865)
NEW ENGLAND FILTER CO INC
560 Mineral Spring Ave 2-123 (02860-8612)
PHONE..................................401 722-8999

Ken Borino, *President*
EMP: 12
SQ FT: 3,000
SALES (est): 2.3MM **Privately Held**
SIC: 3585 Mfg Refrigeration/Heating Equipment

(G-20866)
NEW ENGLAND NEWSPAPERS INC
Also Called: Pawtucket Times, The
2 Dexter St Ste 2 # 2 (02860-2991)
P.O. Box 307 (02862-0307)
PHONE..................................401 722-4000
Michael Moses, *Manager*
EMP: 75
SALES (corp-wide): 4.2B **Privately Held**
SIC: 2711 Newspapers-Publishing/Printing
HQ: New England Newspapers, Inc.
75 S Church St Ste L1
Pittsfield MA 01201

(G-20867)
NEW ENGLAND OVERSEAS CORP
Also Called: N E O
358 Lowden St (02860-6052)
P.O. Box 16069, Rumford (02916-0698)
PHONE..................................401 722-3800
Andrew Davis Jencks, *President*
Stephen B Jencks, *Vice Pres*
Sara Lodge, *Director*
Suvia Siekman, *Director*
Benjamin Thurston, *Director*
▲ **EMP:** 16
SQ FT: 28,000
SALES: 2.9MM **Privately Held**
WEB: www.neo.com
SIC: 2298 Mfg Cordage/Twine

(G-20868)
NEW ENGLAND PAPER TUBE CO INC
200 Conant St (02860-1836)
P.O. Box 186 (02862-0186)
PHONE..................................401 725-2610
Kenneth W Douglas Jr, *President*
James Douglas, *Vice Pres*
EMP: 50 **EST:** 1907
SQ FT: 250,000
SALES (est): 1.6MM **Privately Held**
WEB: www.nepapertube.com
SIC: 2655 2675 Mfg Fiber Can/Drums Mfg Die-Cut Paper/Board

(G-20869)
NORTH EAST KNITTING INC
179 Conant St (02860-1801)
PHONE..................................401 727-0500
Rosalie Darosa, *President*
Michael Darosa, *General Mgr*
Alexander Darosa, *Vice Pres*
Eric Darosa, *Vice Pres*
Mike Darosa, *Vice Pres*
▲ **EMP:** 105
SQ FT: 120,000
SALES (est): 13.2MM **Privately Held**
WEB: www.nekinc.com
SIC: 2241 5949 Narrow Fabric Mill Ret Sewing Supplies/Fabrics

(G-20870)
OPTICAL POLYMERS LAB CORP
200 Weeden St (02860-1804)
PHONE..................................401 722-0710
Cynthia M Donadio, *President*
EMP: 10
SQ FT: 15,000
SALES (est): 1.2MM **Privately Held**
SIC: 2821 3369 Mfg Plastic Materials/Resins Nonferrous Metal Foundry

(G-20871)
ORGANIC STUDIO 13 LLC
110 Kenyon Ave Unit 13 (02861-1690)
PHONE..................................770 369-0756
Keidric Perry, *Principal*
Thaisha Demosthenes,
EMP: 4 **EST:** 2014
SALES (est): 75.4K **Privately Held**
SIC: 2086 Mfg Bottled/Canned Soft Drinks

(G-20872)
P & B FABRICS INC
45 Washington St Ste 47 (02860-3615)
PHONE..................................800 351-9087
Wendy Gay Bear, *CEO*
Edward P Odessa, *President*
David G Odessa, *COO*
▲ **EMP:** 17
SQ FT: 4,220
SALES: 6MM
SALES (corp-wide): 32MM **Privately Held**
WEB: www.pbtex.com
SIC: 2211 5131 Cotton Broadwoven Fabric Mill Whol Piece Goods/Notions
PA: General Fabrics Company
208 Clock Tower Sq
Portsmouth RI 02871
401 728-4200

(G-20873)
PALEO PRODUCTS LLC
Also Called: Paleonola
560 Mineral Spring Ave (02860-3363)
PHONE..................................401 305-3473
Dinos A Stamoulis, *Administration*
EMP: 7 **EST:** 2011
SALES (est): 549.3K **Privately Held**
SIC: 2064 Mfg Candy/Confectionery

(G-20874)
PARK PRINTERS
496 Power Rd (02860-1526)
PHONE..................................401 728-8650
Peter Sawaia, *President*
Mark Sawaia, *Vice Pres*
Mary Killian, *Treasurer*
Pat Sawaia, *Admin Sec*
EMP: 4
SQ FT: 3,164
SALES (est): 420.1K **Privately Held**
SIC: 2759 2752 Commercial Printing Lithographic Commercial Printing

(G-20875)
PAROLINE/WRIGHT DESIGN INC
89 Harris St (02861-1718)
PHONE..................................401 781-5300
Richard Wright, *President*
Richard Paroline, *Vice Pres*
EMP: 10
SQ FT: 3,500
SALES (est): 730K **Privately Held**
SIC: 3873 7389 3911 Design & Mfg Watchcases & Jewelry

(G-20876)
PAWTUCKET HOT MIX
25 Concord St (02860-3423)
PHONE..................................401 722-4488
Nick Hernandez, *Plant Mgr*
Pete Dickie, *Sales Staff*
EMP: 12
SALES (est): 2MM **Privately Held**
SIC: 3273 Mfg Ready-Mixed Concrete

(G-20877)
PBUTTRI LLC
Also Called: Hanks Protein Plus
160 Smithfield Ave Unit C (02860-8623)
PHONE..................................401 996-5583
Henry Capasso,
EMP: 4
SALES: 365K **Privately Held**
SIC: 2099 5099 Mfg Food Preparations Whol Durable Goods

(G-20878)
PEKO CREATIONS LTD
390 Pine St (02860-1833)
PHONE..................................401 722-6661
EMP: 15 **EST:** 1961
SQ FT: 5,000
SALES (est): 1.3MM **Privately Held**
SIC: 2389 Mfg Apparel/Accessories

(G-20879)
PHILIP MACHINE COMPANY INC
190 York Ave (02860-6449)
PHONE..................................401 353-7383
Kevin Vanier, *President*
Bob Young, *Prdtn Mgr*
Joshua Swanson, *Engineer*
Lee Sormanti, *Manager*
EMP: 16 **EST:** 1979
SQ FT: 15,000
SALES: 1.2MM **Privately Held**
WEB: www.philipmachine.com
SIC: 3312 3469 Wire Forms And Metal Stampings

(G-20880)
PIATEK MACHINE COMPANY INC
25 Monticello Rd (02861-3899)
PHONE..................................401 728-9930
Gail Piatek, *President*
EMP: 10 **EST:** 1940
SQ FT: 2,100
SALES (est): 1.5MM **Privately Held**
SIC: 3599 3541 Mfg Industrial Machinery Mfg Machine Tools-Cutting

(G-20881)
POLYMER SOLUTIONS INC
200 Weeden St (02860-1804)
P.O. Box 267, Jamestown (02835-0267)
PHONE..................................401 423-1638
Robert Miniutti, *President*
EMP: 3
SQ FT: 2,500
SALES (est): 500K **Privately Held**
WEB: www.laserprotection.com
SIC: 2821 3087 2865 Mfg Plastic Materials/Resins Custom Compounding-Purchased Resins Mfg Cyclic Crudes/Intermediates/Dyes

(G-20882)
POLYTECHNIC INC
110 Tweed St (02861-1736)
PHONE..................................401 724-3608
Mark E Amesbury, *President*
EMP: 3
SQ FT: 42,000
SALES (est): 228K **Privately Held**
SIC: 3471 6531 Plating/Polishing Service Real Estate Agent/Manager

(G-20883)
PRECISION PLSG ORNAMENTALS INC
601 Mineral Spring Ave # 2 (02860-3366)
PHONE..................................401 728-9994
Edward Audet, *President*
▲ **EMP:** 50
SQ FT: 12,000
SALES (est): 2.6MM **Privately Held**
SIC: 2842 3965 3471 Mfg Polish/Sanitation Goods Mfg Fasteners/Buttons Polishing Service

(G-20884)
PROFESSIONAL IMAGES INC
Also Called: Berry Manufacturing
274 Broadway (02860-2209)
PHONE..................................401 725-7000
Robert Campellone, *President*
EMP: 3
SQ FT: 4,000
SALES: 750K **Privately Held**
SIC: 2311 2337 Mfg Men's Uniforms & Custom Suits & Women's Uniforms

(G-20885)
PROVIDENCE BRAID COMPANY
358 Lowden St (02860-6093)
P.O. Box 6211, Providence (02940-6211)
PHONE..................................401 722-2120
Harrison Huntoon, *President*
Howard Huntoon Jr, *Vice Pres*
Burton Huntoon, *Manager*
EMP: 43
SQ FT: 115,000
SALES: 6MM **Privately Held**
SIC: 2241 Narrow Fabric Mill

(G-20886)
PROVIDENCE METALLIZING CO INC (PA)
51 Fairlawn Ave (02860-2579)
PHONE..................................401 722-5300
Richard Sugarman, *President*
Beverly Sugarman, *Vice Pres*
Charles Gadon, *Treasurer*
▲ **EMP:** 55
SQ FT: 300,000
SALES (est): 11MM **Privately Held**
WEB: www.provmet.com
SIC: 3471 3479 Plating/Polishing Service Coating/Engraving Service

(G-20887)
R & D MANUFACTURING COMPANY
60 Dunnell Ln (02860-5828)
PHONE..................................401 305-7662
Phillip Montalto, *CEO*
Diane Fontaine, *President*
EMP: 17
SQ FT: 30,000
SALES: 3.2MM **Privately Held**
SIC: 3961 5094 Mfg Costume Jewelry Whol Jewelry/Precious Stones

(G-20888)
RACECAR JEWELRY CO INC
19 Mendon Ave (02861-2335)
PHONE..................................401 475-5701
Daniel Grandi, *President*
Karan Taleghani, *General Mgr*
EMP: 8 **EST:** 1999
SALES: 800K **Privately Held**
WEB: www.racecarjewelry.com
SIC: 3911 5944 Mfg Precious Metal Jewelry Ret Jewelry

(G-20889)
RAG AND BONE BINDERY LTD
1088 Main St Frnt 1 (02860-4890)
PHONE..................................401 728-0762
Jason Thompson, *President*
Ilira Steinman, *Vice Pres*
EMP: 11
SQ FT: 10,000
SALES (est): 1.4MM **Privately Held**
WEB: www.ragandbonebindery.com
SIC: 2789 Bookbinding Studio

(G-20890)
RAND-WHITNEY CONTAINER LLC
Southeast Container
455 Narragansett Park Dr (02861-4321)
PHONE..................................401 729-7900
Scott Robertson, *Principal*
Jim Bauchiero, *Adv Dir*
EMP: 50 **Privately Held**
SIC: 2631 3412 2653 Paperboard Mill Mfg Metal Barrels/Pails Mfg Corrugated/Solid Fiber Boxes
HQ: Rand-Whitney Container Llc
1 Rand Whitney Way
Worcester MA 01607
508 890-7000

(G-20891)
RAYS NEWSPAPERS
9 Maplecrest Dr (02861-1539)
PHONE..................................401 728-1364
EMP: 3 **EST:** 2010
SALES (est): 158K **Privately Held**
SIC: 2711 Newspapers-Publishing/Printing

(G-20892)
RHODE ISLAND LIMB CO
59 Prospect St (02860-4482)
PHONE..................................401 475-3501
Jonathan Teoli, *Branch Mgr*
EMP: 3
SALES (corp-wide): 900K **Privately Held**
SIC: 3842 Mfg Surgical Appliances/Supplies
PA: Rhode Island Limb Co.
1559 Elmwood Ave
Cranston RI 02910
401 941-6230

(G-20893)
RIDCO CASTING CO
6 Beverage Hill Ave (02860-6202)
PHONE..................................401 724-0400
Stanley Cohen, *CEO*
Jeffrey A Cohen, *President*
EMP: 88 **EST:** 1955
SQ FT: 63,000
SALES (est): 18.8MM **Privately Held**
WEB: www.ridco.com
SIC: 3369 3364 Nonferrous Metal Foundry Mfg Nonferrous Die-Castings

(G-20894)
SAFE GUARD SIGNS
211 Weeden St (02860-1807)
PHONE..................................401 725-9090
Robert Chito, *Principal*
EMP: 40

SALES (est): 3.1MM **Privately Held**
SIC: 3993 Mfg Signs/Advertising Specialties

(G-20895)
SAGE ENVIROTECH DRLG SVCS INC
172 Armistice Blvd (02860-3281)
PHONE..................................401 723-9900
Richard Mandile, *President*
EMP: 4
SALES (est): 111.3K **Privately Held**
SIC: 1081 Metal Mining Services

(G-20896)
SARGEANT & WILBUR INC
20 Monticello Pl (02861-3500)
P.O. Box 1166 (02862-1166)
PHONE..................................401 726-0013
Michael F Wilbur, *President*
Marcia J Wilbur, *Treasurer*
Raymond Mc Mahon, *Admin Sec*
EMP: 18 **EST:** 1939
SQ FT: 18,700
SALES (est): 3.5MM **Privately Held**
WEB: www.sargeantandwilbur.com
SIC: 3567 Mfg Industrial Furnaces/Ovens

(G-20897)
SCARBOROUGH FAIRE INC (PA)
1151 Main St (02860-4800)
PHONE..................................401 724-4200
Kenneth G Bruce, *President*
Cecelia Bruce, *Vice Pres*
▲ **EMP:** 20
SQ FT: 11,000
SALES: 2.5MM **Privately Held**
SIC: 3089 5013 5531 7311 Mfg Whol & Ret Automotive Supplies & Parts Advertising Agencies

(G-20898)
SCHOFIELD PRINTING INC
211 Weeden St (02860-1807)
PHONE..................................401 728-6980
Robert Chito, *President*
EMP: 38
SQ FT: 32,000
SALES (est): 2MM **Privately Held**
SIC: 2759 3993 Commercial Printing Mfg Signs/Advertising Specialties

(G-20899)
SEABOARD FOLDING BOX CO INC
1 Campbell St (02860-4896)
PHONE..................................401 753-7778
EMP: 7
SALES (corp-wide): 11.2MM **Privately Held**
SIC: 2657 Manufactures Folding Paperboard Boxes
PA: Seaboard Folding Box Company, Inc.
100 Simplex Dr
Westminster MA 01473
978 342-8921

(G-20900)
STRETCH PRODUCTS CORP
392 Pine St (02860-1833)
P.O. Box 1676 (02862-1651)
PHONE..................................401 722-0400
David Sheibley, *President*
Abel Pereira, *Vice Pres*
EMP: 42
SQ FT: 85,000
SALES (est): 5.4MM **Privately Held**
WEB: www.stretchproducts.com
SIC: 2241 Narrow Fabric Mill

(G-20901)
SUMMIT MFG CORP
248 Pine St (02860-2932)
PHONE..................................401 723-6272
Paul Cotter, *President*
EMP: 6
SQ FT: 15,000
SALES (est): 1.1MM **Privately Held**
WEB: www.summitmt.com
SIC: 3599 Mfg Industrial Machinery

(G-20902)
TECHNIC INC
Also Called: Technic Inc Equipment Division
55 Maryland Ave (02860-6278)
PHONE..................................401 781-6100
Tony Guglielmo, *Exec VP*
EMP: 30
SALES (corp-wide): 125.5MM **Privately Held**
WEB: www.technic.com
SIC: 3559 Mfg Chemical Preparations
PA: Technic, Inc.
47 Molter St
Cranston RI 02910
401 781-6100

(G-20903)
TEKNOR APEX COMPANY (PA)
505 Central Ave (02861-1900)
P.O. Box 2290 (02861-0290)
PHONE..................................401 725-8000
Jonathan D Fain, *Ch of Bd*
Bill Murray, *Vice Pres*
Sachin Sakhalkar, *Vice Pres*
Craig White, *Vice Pres*
Andy Stone, *Project Mgr*
◆ **EMP:** 450
SQ FT: 500,000
SALES (est): 845.9MM **Privately Held**
WEB: www.teknorapex.com
SIC: 3087 3069 3052 2869 Custm Cmpnd Prchsd Resin Mfg Fabrcatd Rubber Prdt Mfg Rubr/Plstc Hose/Belt Mfg Industl Organic Chem

(G-20904)
TEKNOR COLOR COMPANY
Also Called: Teknor Apex Co
505 Central Ave (02861-1945)
PHONE..................................401 725-8000
Tom Lepozsky, *Manager*
EMP: 75
SALES (corp-wide): 845.9MM **Privately Held**
SIC: 2865 2851 Mfg Cyclic Crudes/Intermediates/Dyes Mfg Paints/Allied Products
HQ: Teknor Color Company
505 Central Ave
Pawtucket RI 02861

(G-20905)
TEKNOR PRFMCE ELASTOMERS INC
505 Central Ave (02861-1945)
PHONE..................................401 725-8000
Jonathan D Fain, *President*
James Morrison, *CFO*
EMP: 6
SALES (est): 632.5K
SALES (corp-wide): 845.9MM **Privately Held**
SIC: 3087 Custom Compounding-Purchased Resins
PA: Teknor Apex Company
505 Central Ave
Pawtucket RI 02861
401 725-8000

(G-20906)
TRACEY GEAR INC
Also Called: Tracey Gear & Precision Shaft
740 York Ave (02861-2846)
P.O. Box 2226 (02861-0226)
PHONE..................................401 725-3920
Terrence Tracey, *President*
Douglas Tracey, *Vice Pres*
Kevin Tracey, *CFO*
Terrence Tracet, *Shareholder*
EMP: 25
SQ FT: 20,000
SALES (est): 6.4MM **Privately Held**
WEB: www.traceygear.com
SIC: 3568 3429 Mfg Power Transmsn Equip Mfg Hardware

(G-20907)
TWENTIETH CENTURY CASTING
11 Webb St (02860-8224)
PHONE..................................401 728-6836
David Cooley, *Partner*
Mark Manougian, *Partner*
▲ **EMP:** 5
SALES (est): 385.7K **Privately Held**
WEB: www.fitnessconcepts4u.com
SIC: 3911 Mfg Precious Metal Jewelry

(G-20908)
VAN & COMPANY INC
547 Weeden St (02860-1625)
PHONE..................................401 722-9829
Albert P Van Herpe, *President*
Robert L Van Herpe, *Vice Pres*
▲ **EMP:** 13 **EST:** 1958
SQ FT: 22,500
SALES (est): 3.2MM **Privately Held**
WEB: www.vanandcompany.com
SIC: 3161 Manufacture Carrying Cases

(G-20909)
VELLANO CORPORATION
124 Reservoir Ave Unit 1 (02860-1660)
PHONE..................................401 434-1030
EMP: 4 **Privately Held**
SIC: 3494 Mfg Valves/Pipe Fittings

(G-20910)
VEMURI INTERNATIONAL LLC
Queen City Paper Co
402 Walcott St (02860-3247)
PHONE..................................401 723-4200
Brian Gordon, *Branch Mgr*
EMP: 5
SALES (corp-wide): 9.1MM **Privately Held**
WEB: www.queencitypaper.com
SIC: 2631 5111 Paperboard Mill Whol Printing/Writing Paper
PA: Vemuri International, Llc
10600 Evendale Dr
Cincinnati OH 45241
513 483-6300

(G-20911)
VISUAL CREATIONS INC
500 Narragansett Park Dr (02861-4325)
PHONE..................................401 588-5151
Jay Long, *President*
Douglas Robertson, *Exec VP*
Nathan Oliveira, *Project Mgr*
Matthew Petisce, *Project Mgr*
Kristie Belmont, *Senior Buyer*
▲ **EMP:** 225
SQ FT: 150,000
SALES: 29.1MM **Privately Held**
WEB: www.vci-displays.com
SIC: 2541 Mfg Wood Partitions/Fixtures

(G-20912)
WEEDEN STREET ASSOCIATES LLC
173 Weeden St (02860-1803)
PHONE..................................401 725-2610
Melvin Cournoyer, *President*
EMP: 21
SALES (est): 1.2MM **Privately Held**
SIC: 2621 2655 Paper Mill Mfg Fiber Can/Drums

Peace Dale
Washington County

(G-20913)
FORTERRA PIPE & PRECAST LLC
170 Fiore Industrial Dr (02879-2156)
PHONE..................................401 782-2600
Richard Williams, *Manager*
EMP: 15
SALES (corp-wide): 1.4B **Publicly Held**
SIC: 3272 Mfg Concrete Products
HQ: Forterra Pipe & Precast, Llc
511 E John Carpenter Fwy
Irving TX 75062
469 458-7973

(G-20914)
M & T MANUFACTURING CO
30 Hopkins Ln (02879-2163)
P.O. Box 3730 (02883-0393)
PHONE..................................401 789-0472
Burton Strom, *President*
Kevin Heartman, *Vice Pres*
EMP: 6
SQ FT: 4,400
SALES (est): 953.8K **Privately Held**
WEB: www.mtmfg.com
SIC: 2431 3714 Mfg Millwork Mfg Motor Vehicle Parts/Accessories

(G-20915)
PALISADES LTD
1080 Kingstown Rd (02879-8317)
P.O. Box 7 (02883-0007)
PHONE..................................401 789-0295
Gary Guarriello, *President*
Kevin Guarriello, *Admin Sec*
▲ **EMP:** 33
SQ FT: 125,000
SALES (est): 2.4MM **Privately Held**
SIC: 2261 2269 2262 Cotton Finishing Plant Finishing Plant Manmade Fiber & Silk Finishing Plant

Portsmouth
Newport County

(G-20916)
1947 LLC
208 Clock Tower Sq (02871-1397)
PHONE..................................401 293-5500
Bryan Boulis, *Vice Pres*
Edward Ricci,
Ben Galpen,
EMP: 3
SQ FT: 2,000
SALES: 10MM **Privately Held**
SIC: 2399 Mfg Fabricated Textile Products

(G-20917)
ARAMID RIGGING INC
14 Regatta Way Ste 3 (02871-6167)
PHONE..................................401 683-6966
J Alexander C Wadson, *President*
EMP: 9
SALES (est): 760K **Privately Held**
SIC: 3731 5551 Mfg Marine Rigging Ret Marine Rigging

(G-20918)
BIO HOLDINGS INC
45 Highpoint Ave Ste 3 (02871-8600)
PHONE..................................401 683-5400
Timothy P Burns, *President*
Peter Annunziato, *Engineer*
EMP: 11
SALES (est): 1MM **Privately Held**
WEB: www.bioprocesstechnologies.com
SIC: 3677 Mfg Electronic Coils/Transformers

(G-20919)
BIOPROCESSH2O LLC
45 Highpoint Ave (02871-8601)
PHONE..................................401 683-5400
Tim Burns, *Mng Member*
Diana Di Ruggeiro,
Dr John Haley,
Jeffrey Marshall,
Vijay Menon,
▼ **EMP:** 22
SQ FT: 50,000
SALES (est): 6.5MM
SALES (corp-wide): 14.3B **Publicly Held**
WEB: www.clarcor.com
SIC: 3569 8731 Mfg General Industrial Machinery Commercial Physical Research
HQ: Clarcor Inc.
840 Crescent Centre Dr # 600
Franklin TN 37067
615 771-3100

(G-20920)
BLACK DOG CORPORATION
Also Called: S & S Fabric Products
1 Maritime Dr Ste 3 (02871-6100)
PHONE..................................401 683-5858
Paul Di Martino, *President*
Victoria Di Martino, *Treasurer*
EMP: 22
SQ FT: 10,000
SALES (est): 2.8MM **Privately Held**
WEB: www.ssfabricproducts.com
SIC: 2394 2399 5961 Mfg Canvas/Related Prdts Mfg Fabrctd Textile Pdts

(G-20921)
BRAND & OPPENHEIMER CO INC (PA)
Also Called: Ocean State Innovations
208 Clock Tower Sq (02871-1397)
PHONE..................................401 293-5500

▲ = Import ▼=Export
◆ =Import/Export

Edward W Ricci, *CEO*
Bryan Boulis, *President*
Mark Hinch, *Vice Pres*
Lynn Decristofaro, *Controller*
Dana Albanese, *Accountant*
EMP: 66
SQ FT: 1,200
SALES (est): 20.3MM **Privately Held**
SIC: 2231 2211 2221 Wool Brdwv Fabric Mill Cotton Brdwv Fabric Mill

(G-20922)
EDUCATIONAL DIRECTIONS INC
156 Anthony Rd (02871-4815)
P.O. Box 768 (02871-0768)
PHONE..................................401 683-3523
Stephen Dicicco, *President*
Chris Arnold, *Treasurer*
EMP: 4
SQ FT: 2,400
SALES (est): 250K **Privately Held**
WEB: www.edu-directions.com
SIC: 2741 8748 Publishing Of News Letters And Business Consulting

(G-20923)
HODGES BADGE COMPANY INC (PA)
Also Called: Image Award Ribbons
1170 E Main Rd (02871-2333)
PHONE..................................401 682-2000
F James Hodges Jr, *Ch of Bd*
Frederick J Hodges III, *President*
Jane Sousa, *Vice Pres*
Sue Brescia, *Art Dir*
Sheila H Hodges, *Admin Sec*
▲ **EMP:** 160 **EST:** 1920
SQ FT: 45,000
SALES (est): 19.1MM **Privately Held**
WEB: www.hodgesbadge.com
SIC: 2396 3999 Mfg Auto/Apparel Trimming Mfg Misc Products

(G-20924)
HUNT BOATBUILDERS INC
1909 Alden Lndg (02871-6164)
PHONE..................................401 324-4205
Winn Willard, *President*
EMP: 6 **EST:** 1997
SQ FT: 12,000
SALES (est): 939K **Privately Held**
SIC: 3732 Boatbuilding/Repairing

(G-20925)
HUNT YACHTS LLC
1909 Alden Lndg (02871-6164)
PHONE..................................401 324-4201
Dave Goodman, *Principal*
Peter Van Lancker, *Principal*
Dan Cocuzzo, *Purch Mgr*
Marty Letts, *Sales Dir*
Lat Spinney, *Director*
◆ **EMP:** 55
SQ FT: 36,000
SALES (est): 7.5MM **Privately Held**
SIC: 3732 Boatbuilding/Repairing
PA: Scout Partners Llc
712 5th Ave Fl 47
New York NY

(G-20926)
JOURNAL ROMAN ARCHAEOLOGY LLC
Also Called: Jra
95 Peleg Rd (02871-3831)
PHONE..................................401 683-1955
John Humphrey, *President*
EMP: 3
SALES (est): 195.4K **Privately Held**
WEB: www.journalofromanarch.com
SIC: 2711 Newspapers-Publishing/Printing

(G-20927)
M D F POWDER COAT SYSTEMS LLC
207 Highpoint Ave Ste 300 (02871-1444)
P.O. Box 855 (02871-0855)
PHONE..................................401 683-7525
Michael Chapman,
▲ **EMP:** 16
SALES (est): 831K **Privately Held**
WEB: www.vulcan-mdf.com
SIC: 3479 Powder Coating

(G-20928)
MESCO CORPORATION
1676 E Main Rd Bay A (02871-2447)
P.O. Box 945 (02871-0919)
PHONE..................................401 683-2677
Bill Watson, *President*
EMP: 8
SALES (est): 2.1MM **Privately Held**
SIC: 3561 Mfg Pumps/Pumping Equipment

(G-20929)
MORRIS YACHTS LLC
1 Little Harbor Lndg # 1 (02871-6141)
PHONE..................................207 667-2499
Donald Dow, *Principal*
EMP: 6
SALES (est): 705.8K **Privately Held**
SIC: 3732 Boatbuilding/Repairing

(G-20930)
NEWPORT ELECTRIC CORPORATION
200 Highpoint Ave Ste B5 (02871-1356)
PHONE..................................401 293-0527
David Aaron McMullen, *President*
EMP: 14
SALES (est): 2.4MM **Privately Held**
SIC: 3699 1731 Mfg Electrical Equipment/Supplies Electrical Contractor

(G-20931)
NEXT EVENT CORPORATION
Also Called: National Embroidery
3390 E Main Rd Unit 1 (02871-4272)
PHONE..................................401 683-0070
Dale B Wood, *President*
EMP: 5
SQ FT: 5,000
SALES (est): 484.6K **Privately Held**
SIC: 2395 5947 Pleating/Stitching Svcs Ret Gifts/Novelties

(G-20932)
NIKOTRACK LLC
300 Highpoint Ave Ste 1b (02871-1445)
P.O. Box 855 (02871-0855)
PHONE..................................401 683-7525
Michael Chapman, *Mng Member*
Margaret Chapman,
Geoff Spiter,
▲ **EMP:** 8
SALES (est): 1MM **Privately Held**
SIC: 3535 Mfg Conveyors/Equipment

(G-20933)
NORTH SAILS GROUP LLC
Also Called: Cruising Direct Sails
1 Maritime Dr Ste 1 # 1 (02871-6100)
PHONE..................................401 683-7997
Chuck Allen, *Opers Staff*
Nick Dobvniak, *Sales Staff*
EMP: 5 **Privately Held**
WEB: www.northsails.com
SIC: 2394 Mfg Canvas/Related Products
HQ: North Sails Group, Llc
125 Old Gate Ln Ste 7
Milford CT 06460
203 874-7548

(G-20934)
NORTHEAST MANUFACTURING INC
300 Highpoint Ave Ste D (02871-1394)
PHONE..................................401 683-2075
Craig Lawson, *President*
Cherie Lawson, *Vice Pres*
EMP: 4
SQ FT: 7,000
SALES (est): 580.1K **Privately Held**
SIC: 3672 Mfg Circuit Boards

(G-20935)
OCEAN LINK INC
1 Maritime Dr Ste 10 (02871-6100)
PHONE..................................401 683-4434
Andy Cortvriend, *President*
Terri Cortvriend, *Principal*
EMP: 6
SALES (est): 924.5K **Privately Held**
WEB: www.oceanlinkinc.com
SIC: 3429 Mfg Hardware

(G-20936)
PELLA CORPORATION
Also Called: Pella Window Door
25 Narragansett Blvd (02871-5807)
PHONE..................................401 662-2621
EMP: 316
SALES (corp-wide): 1.7B **Privately Held**
SIC: 2431 Mfg Millwork
PA: Pella Corporation
102 Main St
Pella IA 50219
641 621-1000

(G-20937)
QUARTER MOON INCORPORATED (PA)
Also Called: Laserperformance North America
200 Highpoint Ave (02871-1443)
P.O. Box 1409, Norwalk CT (06856-1409)
PHONE..................................401 683-0400
David W Johns II, *President*
Stephen H Clark, *Chairman*
▲ **EMP:** 44
SQ FT: 40,000
SALES (est): 10.4MM **Privately Held**
WEB: www.teamvanguard.com
SIC: 3732 Boatbuilding/Repairing

(G-20938)
RAYTHEON COMPANY
1847 W Main Rd (02871-1087)
PHONE..................................401 847-8000
Bob Pulley, *Research*
Richard Harding, *Engineer*
Erik Item, *Engineer*
Mark Langelier, *Engineer*
Matthew Loo, *Engineer*
EMP: 100
SQ FT: 350,000
SALES (corp-wide): 27B **Publicly Held**
SIC: 3812 3679 3829 3625 Mfg Search/Navgatn Equip Mfg Elec Components Mfg Measure/Control Dvcs Mfg Relay/Indstl Control
PA: Raytheon Company
870 Winter St
Waltham MA 02451
781 522-3000

(G-20939)
RHODE NORTHSALES ISLAND INC
Also Called: North Sales Rhode Island
1 Maritime Dr Ste 1 # 1 (02871-6100)
PHONE..................................401 683-7997
Thomas Widden, *President*
Henry Little, *VP Finance*
EMP: 30
SQ FT: 14,000
SALES (est): 2MM **Privately Held**
SIC: 2394 3732 Mfg Canvas/Related Products Boatbuilding/Repairing

(G-20940)
TALARIA COMPANY LLC (PA)
Also Called: Hinckley Company, The
1 Lil Hrbr Landing Prt (02871)
PHONE..................................401 683-7100
Tim Shields, *General Mgr*
Jeanette Smith, *CFO*
Ralph Willerd, *Mng Member*
Ellen Kinley, *Officer*
▲ **EMP:** 14 **EST:** 1999
SALES (est): 209.7MM **Privately Held**
SIC: 3732 Boatbuilding/Repairing

(G-20941)
TALARIA COMPANY LLC
Also Called: Hinckley Co
1 Little Harbor Lndg # 1 (02871-6168)
PHONE..................................401 683-7280
Jim McManus, *President*
EMP: 205
SALES (corp-wide): 209.7MM **Privately Held**
SIC: 3732 Boatbuilding/Repairing
PA: The Talaria Company Llc
1 Lil Hrbr Landing Prt
Portsmouth RI 02871
401 683-7100

(G-20942)
VEMPLOYEE
47 Taylor Rd (02871-5430)
PHONE..................................888 471-1982
Paul Chiumento, *Principal*
Parul Batra, *Engineer*
EMP: 4
SALES (est): 82.9K **Privately Held**
SIC: 3296 Mfg Mineral Wool

Providence
Providence County

(G-20943)
A & F PLATING CO INC
45 River Ave (02908-5427)
P.O. Box 28081 (02908-0081)
PHONE..................................401 861-3597
Antonio Alfieri, *President*
EMP: 15
SQ FT: 15,000
SALES (est): 2.1MM **Privately Held**
SIC: 3471 Plating/Polishing Service

(G-20944)
A & H DUFFY POLISHING & FINSHG
175 Dupont Dr (02907-3105)
PHONE..................................401 785-9203
Michael D'Angelo, *President*
Christopher D'Angelo, *COO*
Christopher Dangelo, *COO*
Maria Keeny, *Accounting Dir*
Joseph D'Angelo, *Executive*
EMP: 70 **EST:** 1941
SQ FT: 10,000
SALES (est): 8MM **Privately Held**
SIC: 3471 Plating/Polishing Service

(G-20945)
ADMIRAL PACKAGING INC
10 Admiral St (02908-3203)
P.O. Box 6025 (02940-6025)
PHONE..................................401 274-5588
Herbert Allan, *Ch of Bd*
Harley Frank, *President*
John Wilbur, *CFO*
Anita Lussier, *Sales Staff*
Hutch Smith, *Sales Staff*
▲ **EMP:** 78
SQ FT: 200,000
SALES: 25.8MM **Privately Held**
WEB: www.admiralpkg.com
SIC: 2671 2673 5113 Mfg Packaging Paper/Film Mfg Plstc/Coat Paper Bag

(G-20946)
ADOLF MELLER COMPANY (PA)
Also Called: Meller Optics, Inc.
120 Corliss St (02904-2602)
P.O. Box 6001 (02940-6001)
PHONE..................................800 821-0180
David Lydon, *CEO*
Ted Turnquist, *Site Mgr*
Joanne Allen, *Purch Mgr*
Dale J Dejoy, *Sales Staff*
◆ **EMP:** 32 **EST:** 1946
SQ FT: 12,000
SALES: 15MM **Privately Held**
WEB: www.melleroptics.com
SIC: 3827 Mfg Optical Instruments/Lenses

(G-20947)
ADOLF MELLER COMPANY
Also Called: Meller Optics, Inc.
120 Corliss St (02904-2602)
PHONE..................................401 331-3838
EMP: 30
SALES (corp-wide): 15MM **Privately Held**
WEB: www.melleroptics.com
SIC: 3827 Mfg Optical Instruments/Lenses
PA: Adolf Meller Company
120 Corliss St
Providence RI 02904
800 821-0180

(G-20948)
AETNA MANUFACTURING COMPANY
Also Called: Aetna Jewelery Mfg
720 Harris Ave (02909-2423)
PHONE..................................401 751-3260
Frank Caliri, *President*
EMP: 8
SQ FT: 6,500

GEOGRAPHIC

SALES (est): 560K **Privately Held**
SIC: 3961 Mfg Costume Jewelry

(G-20949)
AGAPE DERMATOLOGY
49 Seekonk St Unit 3 (02906-5176)
PHONE..................................401 396-2227
Gina G La Prova, *Principal*
Paul A Mallari, *Principal*
EMP: 5 **EST:** 2013
SALES (est): 255.3K **Privately Held**
SIC: 2834 8011 Mfg Pharmaceutical Preparations Medical Doctor's Office

(G-20950)
ALLIED GROUP INC
333 Bucklin St (02907-1843)
PHONE..................................401 946-6100
Barbara Landry, *Manager*
EMP: 4
SALES (est): 511.6K
SALES (corp-wide): 24.8MM **Privately Held**
SIC: 2752 Lithographic Commercial Printing
PA: The Allied Group Inc
25 Amflex Dr
Cranston RI 02921
401 461-1700

(G-20951)
ALLOY HOLDINGS LLC
160 Niantic Ave (02907-3118)
PHONE..................................401 353-7500
Todd R Morvillo, *President*
Charles P Morvillo, *Vice Pres*
Marian Morvillo, *Admin Sec*
EMP: 25
SALES (est): 5.1MM **Privately Held**
WEB: www.morvilloandsons.com
SIC: 3496 3444 3315 Mfg Misc Fabricated Wire Products Mfg Sheet Metalwork Mfg Steel Wire/Related Products

(G-20952)
AMERICAN ACCESS CARE RI LLC
100 Highland Ave (02906-2740)
PHONE..................................401 277-9729
Patrick Johnson, *General Mgr*
EMP: 3
SALES (est): 380K **Privately Held**
SIC: 3841 Mfg Surgical/Medical Instruments

(G-20953)
ANDERA INC
15 Park Row W Ste 200 (02903-1115)
PHONE..................................401 621-7900
Charles Kroll, *CEO*
Ying Chen, *Senior VP*
Craig Wilke, *Senior VP*
Chris Burns, *CFO*
EMP: 57
SALES (est): 8.5MM
SALES (corp-wide): 421.9MM **Publicly Held**
WEB: www.andera.com
SIC: 7372 Prepackaged Software Services
PA: Bottomline Technologies (De), Inc.
325 Corporate Dr Ste 300
Portsmouth NH 03801
603 436-0700

(G-20954)
ANGELO DI MARIA INC
395 Admiral St (02908-2560)
P.O. Box 6106 (02940-6106)
PHONE..................................401 274-0100
John Scungio, *President*
Theresa Scungio, *Admin Sec*
EMP: 35 **EST:** 1928
SQ FT: 17,500
SALES (est): 4MM **Privately Held**
SIC: 3469 3915 Mfg Metal Stampings Mfg Jewelers' Materials

(G-20955)
ANSYS INC
235 Promenade St Rm 485 (02908-5761)
PHONE..................................401 455-1955
Wenliang Zhang, *Engineer*
Andy Farington, *Manager*
EMP: 6
SALES (corp-wide): 1.2B **Publicly Held**
WEB: www.ansys.com
SIC: 7372 Prepackaged Software Services
PA: Ansys, Inc.
2600 Ansys Dr
Canonsburg PA 15317
884 462-6797

(G-20956)
APPLITEK TECHNOLOGIES CORP
160 Georgia Ave (02905-4423)
PHONE..................................401 467-0007
Bruce Getchell, *President*
Nancy Getchell, *Vice Pres*
EMP: 9
SQ FT: 6,000
SALES (est): 1.1MM **Privately Held**
WEB: www.applitek-usa.com
SIC: 3549 Mfg Wire Processing Equipment

(G-20957)
ARMBRUST INTERNATIONAL LTD
735 Allens Ave (02905-5412)
PHONE..................................401 781-3300
Thomas J Baker, *CEO*
Erwin Pearl, *Ch of Bd*
Jim Roberts, *President*
Kerilyn Rodi, *Cust Svc Dir*
EMP: 125
SALES (est): 21MM **Privately Held**
WEB: www.armbrustintl.com
SIC: 3911 Mfg Precious Metal Jewelry

(G-20958)
ARTCRETE ENTERPRISES INC
53 Capitol View Ave (02908-1008)
PHONE..................................401 270-0700
Tracey Gardiner, *President*
EMP: 4
SALES: 200K **Privately Held**
SIC: 3272 Mfg Concrete Products

(G-20959)
ATAMIAN MANUFACTURING CORP
910 Plainfield St (02909-5451)
PHONE..................................800 286-9614
EMP: 20
SQ FT: 20,000
SALES (est): 2.5MM **Privately Held**
WEB: www.atamianmfg.com
SIC: 3911 3469 Mfg Metal Stampings Mfg Precious Metal Jewelry

(G-20960)
ATLAS ATM CORP
1106 N Main St (02904-5709)
PHONE..................................401 421-4183
Peter Porrazzo, *President*
Beatrice Porrazzo, *Admin Sec*
EMP: 15
SALES (est): 1.8MM **Privately Held**
WEB: www.atlasmusic.com
SIC: 3578 Mfg Calculating Equipment

(G-20961)
ATLAS FABRICATION INC
491 Silver Spring St (02904-1541)
PHONE..................................401 861-4911
Kenneth Beck, *President*
Andrew Patterson, *Vice Pres*
EMP: 3
SQ FT: 8,000
SALES (est): 524.8K **Privately Held**
WEB: www.scapefurniture.com
SIC: 2542 Manufactures Store Fixtures And Office Furniture

(G-20962)
ATOM ADHESIVES
226 S Main St (02903-7105)
PHONE..................................401 413-9902
EMP: 3
SALES (est): 123.2K **Privately Held**
SIC: 2891 Mfg Adhesives/Sealants

(G-20963)
AUDETTE GROUP LLC
144 Westminster St # 302 (02903-2216)
PHONE..................................401 667-5884
Roland Audette, *President*
EMP: 20
SQ FT: 3,600
SALES (est): 2.9MM **Privately Held**
SIC: 3449 Structural Steel And Miscellaneous Steel Fabrication And Eradication

(G-20964)
AUSTIN HARD CHROME
57 Sprague St (02907)
PHONE..................................401 421-0840
EMP: 3 **EST:** 2008
SALES (est): 190K **Privately Held**
SIC: 3471 Plating/Polishing Service

(G-20965)
AVCO CORPORATION (DH)
40 Westminster St (02903-2525)
PHONE..................................401 421-2800
Richard J Millman, *Principal*
▲ **EMP:** 139
SALES (est): 47.5MM
SALES (corp-wide): 13.9B **Publicly Held**
SIC: 3728 3724 Mfg Aircraft Parts/Equipment Mfg Aircraft Engines/Parts
HQ: Textron Lycoming Corp
40 Westminster St
Providence RI 02903
401 421-2800

(G-20966)
AWNING GUY LLC
182 Waterman St (02906-4015)
PHONE..................................401 787-0097
Nancy Prescott, *President*
EMP: 3
SALES (est): 387.6K **Privately Held**
SIC: 2394 Mfg Canvas/Related Products

(G-20967)
AZULITE INC
10 Davol Sq (02903-4754)
PHONE..................................916 801-8528
Adam Eltorai, *President*
Dan Gertrudes, *Vice Pres*
Steven Byler, *Marketing Staff*
EMP: 5
SALES (est): 198.4K **Privately Held**
SIC: 3845 Mfg Electromedical Equipment

(G-20968)
BEECHCRAFT DEFENSE CO LLC
40 Westminster St Fl 5 (02903-2525)
PHONE..................................401 457-2485
EMP: 3
SALES (est): 160.1K **Privately Held**
SIC: 3812 Mfg Search/Navigation Equipment

(G-20969)
BELL HELICOPTER KOREA INC
40 Westminster St (02903-2525)
PHONE..................................401 421-2800
John R Murphey, *Principal*
Felipe Gumucio, *Senior VP*
Glenn Isbell, *Vice Pres*
Barry Kohler, *Vice Pres*
Whitney Lessem, *Mfg Staff*
EMP: 4
SALES (est): 266.3K
SALES (corp-wide): 13.9B **Publicly Held**
SIC: 3721 Mfg Aircraft
PA: Textron Inc.
40 Westminster St
Providence RI 02903
401 421-2800

(G-20970)
BJORKLUND CORP
17 Freese St (02908-4054)
PHONE..................................401 944-6400
Paul Bjorklund, *Principal*
EMP: 3
SALES (est): 353.1K **Privately Held**
SIC: 2951 1771 Mfg Asphalt Mixtures/Blocks Concrete Contractor

(G-20971)
BOSTON PHOENIX INC (PA)
Also Called: 101.7 FM
1 Chestnut St Ste 1 # 1 (02903-4155)
PHONE..................................617 536-5390
Stephen M Mindich, *Principal*
EMP: 10
SQ FT: 19,500
SALES (est): 6.2MM **Privately Held**
WEB: www.worcesterphoenix.com
SIC: 2711 Newspapers-Publishing/Printing

(G-20972)
BRADFORD PRESS INC
91 Atwells Ave (02903-1050)
PHONE..................................401 621-7195
Rudolph Sigismondi, *President*
Pauline Sigismondi, *Vice Pres*
EMP: 8
SQ FT: 4,000
SALES (est): 867.6K **Privately Held**
SIC: 2759 2752 Commercial Printing Lithographic Commercial Printing

(G-20973)
BRADLEY GOODWIN PATTERN CO
216 Oxford St (02905-2041)
PHONE..................................401 461-5220
Robert H Goodwin, *President*
EMP: 12 **EST:** 1912
SQ FT: 15,000
SALES: 1.3MM **Privately Held**
SIC: 3544 3543 Mfg Dies/Tools/Jigs/Fixtures Mfg Industrial Patterns

(G-20974)
BREWERS SUPPLY GROUP INC
250 Niantic Ave (02907-3120)
PHONE..................................401 275-4920
Oscar A Cruz, *Principal*
Nick Sotelo, *Manager*
EMP: 3
SALES (corp-wide): 86.1MM **Privately Held**
SIC: 2082 Mfg Malt Beverages
HQ: Brewers Supply Group, Inc.
800 1st Ave W
Shakopee MN 55379

(G-20975)
BSG HANDCRAFT
250 Niantic Ave (02907-3120)
PHONE..................................508 636-5154
Gary Lee, *President*
▲ **EMP:** 24
SALES (est): 3.5MM **Privately Held**
SIC: 3585 Mfg Refrigeration/Heating Equipment

(G-20976)
BU INC
812 Charles St (02904-1362)
PHONE..................................401 831-2112
Byron Urizar, *President*
EMP: 10 **EST:** 2015
SALES (est): 172.6K **Privately Held**
SIC: 3911 Mfg Precious Metal Jewelry

(G-20977)
C & W CO INC
231 Georgia Ave (02905-4516)
PHONE..................................401 941-6311
Martin Chappell, *President*
EMP: 5 **EST:** 1920
SQ FT: 1,800
SALES (est): 572.5K **Privately Held**
WEB: www.ringstamp.com
SIC: 3469 3544 3089 Mfg Metal Stampings Mfg Dies/Tools/Jigs/Fixtures Mfg Plastic Products

(G-20978)
CAPCO PLASTICS INC (PA)
297 Dexter St (02907-2730)
P.O. Box 9591 (02940-9591)
PHONE..................................401 272-3833
Richard Capuano, *President*
Bob Arno, *Vice Pres*
EMP: 90 **EST:** 1978
SQ FT: 40,000
SALES (est): 14.9MM **Privately Held**
WEB: www.capcoplastics.com
SIC: 3089 Mfg Plastic Products

(G-20979)
CAPCO STEEL ERECTION COMPANY
33 Acorn St Unit 2 (02903-1094)
PHONE..................................401 383-9388
Michael Caparco Sr, *CEO*
Michael J Caparco Jr, *President*
David Michaels, *Principal*
John Casale, *VP Sales*
EMP: 18
SQ FT: 5,000

SALES (est): 10MM Privately Held
SIC: 3499 3312 Mfg Misc Fabricated Metal Products Blast Furnace-Steel Works

(G-20980)
CARROLL COATINGS COMPANY INC (PA)
150 Ernest St (02905-4604)
PHONE....401 781-4942
William Rooks, *President*
John Rooks, *Vice Pres*
EMP: 14
SQ FT: 5,800
SALES (est): 959.1K Privately Held
WEB: www.carrollcoatings.com
SIC: 2851 Mfg Paints/Allied Products

(G-20981)
CATHEDRAL ART METAL CO INC
Also Called: Camco Display & Screen Prtg
25 Manton Ave (02909-3349)
P.O. Box 6146 (02940-6146)
PHONE....401 273-7200
Leo Tracey, *President*
Julieanne Wade, *Treasurer*
◆ EMP: 45 EST: 1920
SQ FT: 93,300
SALES: 7.8MM Privately Held
WEB: www.cathedralartmetal.com
SIC: 3499 Mfg Misc Fabricated Metal Products

(G-20982)
CHEMICAL COATINGS CORP
35 Livingston St (02904-2726)
PHONE....401 331-9000
Barry Shepard, *President*
EMP: 11 EST: 1963
SQ FT: 19,000
SALES (est): 3.2MM
SALES (corp-wide): 51MM Privately Held
SIC: 2851 Mfg Water Base And Solvent Base Coating And Pigment Vispersions
HQ: Ecc Holdings, Inc.
35 Livingston St
Providence RI 02904
401 331-9000

(G-20983)
CHI FOODS LLC
79 10th St (02906-2919)
PHONE....310 309-1186
Minnie Luong, *CEO*
EMP: 6
SALES (est): 538.8K Privately Held
SIC: 2035 Mfg Pickles/Sauces/Dressing

(G-20984)
CLAYTON COMPANY INC
999 Chalkstone Ave (02908-4235)
PHONE....401 421-2978
Robert J Moretti, *President*
EMP: 5
SQ FT: 12,000
SALES (est): 449.6K Privately Held
SIC: 3961 Mfg Costume Jewelry Made Of Non-Precious Materials

(G-20985)
CLEAR CHOICE INC
40 Agnes St (02909-3418)
PHONE....401 421-5275
Jason Krikorian, *President*
George Lucas, *Treasurer*
EMP: 9
SALES (est): 1.2MM Privately Held
WEB: www.ccpkg.com
SIC: 2671 Plastic Film Coated Or Laminated For Packaging

(G-20986)
COCA-COLA REFRESHMENTS USA INC
95 Pleasant Valley Pkwy (02908-5603)
PHONE....401 331-1981
Tom Hunt, *Sales/Mktg Mgr*
EMP: 290
SQ FT: 20,000
SALES (corp-wide): 31.8B Publicly Held
WEB: www.cokecce.com
SIC: 2086 5149 Mfg Bottled/Canned Soft Drinks Whol Groceries
HQ: Coca-Cola Refreshments Usa, Inc.
2500 Windy Ridge Pkwy Se
Atlanta GA 30339
770 989-3000

(G-20987)
COLONY CASKET INC
50 Curtis St (02909-3316)
P.O. Box 19146, Johnston (02919-0146)
PHONE....401 831-7100
Thomas De Concilis, *President*
Madeline Leonardo, *CTO*
EMP: 5
SQ FT: 10,000
SALES (est): 479.5K Privately Held
SIC: 3995 Mfg Burial Caskets

(G-20988)
COMPOST PLANT L3C
Also Called: Compost Plant, The
21 Mount Hope Ave (02906-1626)
PHONE....401 644-6179
Leo Pollock, *Co-Owner*
Nat Harris, *Co-Owner*
EMP: 4
SALES (est): 229.4K Privately Held
SIC: 2873 4953 Mfg Nitrogenous Fertilizers Refuse System

(G-20989)
CONTECH MEDICAL INC
99 Hartford Ave (02909-3366)
PHONE....401 351-4890
Raymond A Byrnes, *CEO*
Frank Barrett, *President*
Christopher M Byrnes, *President*
Bob Di Petrillo, *Vice Pres*
Stephanie Lombari, *Purchasing*
EMP: 90
SQ FT: 110,000
SALES: 16MM Privately Held
WEB: www.contechmedicalusa.com
SIC: 3841 7389 4783 Mfg Surgical/Medical Instruments Business Services Packing/Crating Service

(G-20990)
CONTEMPO CARD CO INC (PA)
69 Tingley St Ste 1a (02903-1085)
PHONE....401 272-4210
Vark Markarian, *President*
Lynne A Markarian, *Vice Pres*
Lynne Markarian, *Vice Pres*
Ron Pezzullo, *Project Mgr*
Colleen Henry, *VP Sales*
▲ EMP: 53
SQ FT: 60,000
SALES (est): 7.1MM Privately Held
WEB: www.contempocard.com
SIC: 2653 2671 2631 Mfg Corrugated/Solid Fiber Boxes Mfg Packaging Paper/Film Paperboard Mill

(G-20991)
CUSTOM FLOW SOLUTIONS LLC
61 Dora St (02909-3015)
PHONE....401 487-2957
Hanaan Rosenthal, *Owner*
EMP: 3
SALES: 90K Privately Held
WEB: www.customflowsolutions.com
SIC: 2741 Misc Publishing

(G-20992)
DAILY HERALD BROWN INC
195 Angell St (02906-1207)
P.O. Box 2538 (02906-0538)
PHONE....401 351-3372
Sheralie Luthra, *President*
Dee Gill, *President*
Julia Kuwahara, *General Mgr*
Samuel Plotner, *General Mgr*
EMP: 3
SQ FT: 3,000
SALES: 204.2K Privately Held
SIC: 2711 2721 Newspapers-Publishing/Printing Periodicals-Publishing/Printing

(G-20993)
DANECRAFT INC (PA)
1 Baker St (02905-4416)
PHONE....401 941-7700
Victor Primavera III, *CEO*
Victor Primavera Jr, *Ch of Bd*
Robert Soltys, *President*
Gail Primavera Gesmondi, *Vice Pres*
Michelle Costa, *Controller*
▲ EMP: 100 EST: 1934
SQ FT: 100,000
SALES (est): 13.6MM Privately Held
WEB: www.danecraft.com
SIC: 3911 5944 3961 Mfg Precious Metal Jewelry Ret Jewelry Mfg Costume Jewelry

(G-20994)
DANECRAFT INC
Also Called: House of Primavera
1 Baker St (02905-4416)
PHONE....401 941-7700
Trice Clancy, *Manager*
EMP: 138
SALES (corp-wide): 13.6MM Privately Held
WEB: www.danecraft.com
SIC: 3911 Mfg Precious Metal Jewelry
PA: Danecraft, Inc.
1 Baker St
Providence RI 02905
401 941-7700

(G-20995)
DAVID GRAU
11 Dorrance St (02903-1734)
PHONE....401 831-0351
EMP: 3
SALES (est): 200K Privately Held
SIC: 3911 Mfg Jewelry Precious Metal

(G-20996)
DECOR CRAFT INC
Also Called: DCI
133 Mathewson St (02903-1854)
PHONE....401 621-2324
Roni Kabessa, *CEO*
▲ EMP: 34
SQ FT: 2,200
SALES (est): 6.5MM Privately Held
WEB: www.decorcraftinc.com
SIC: 3961 Mfg Costume Jewelry

(G-20997)
DMANIELLY EXPRESS
918 Atwells Ave (02909-3123)
PHONE....401 490-2900
Seraapio Inirio, *Administration*
EMP: 4
SALES (est): 260K Privately Held
SIC: 2741 Misc Publishing

(G-20998)
DRYVIT HOLDINGS INC (DH)
1 Energy Way (02903)
PHONE....401 822-4100
Peter Balint, *President*
Dennis M Dallman, *Treasurer*
Kenneth Nota, *Admin Sec*
◆ EMP: 4
SALES (est): 111.2MM
SALES (corp-wide): 5.5B Publicly Held
SIC: 2822 2899 Mfg Synthetic Rubber Mfg Chemical Preparations
HQ: Republic Powdered Metals, Inc.
2628 Pearl Rd
Medina OH 44256
330 225-3192

(G-20999)
E H BENZ CO INC
Also Called: Benz, Edwin H Co
73 Maplehurst Ave (02908-5324)
PHONE....401 331-5650
Ted Benz, *President*
EMP: 8
SQ FT: 9,800
SALES (est): 1.4MM Privately Held
SIC: 3823 7699 Mfg Industrial Instruments For Measurement Display & Control Of Process Variables & Mechanical Instrument Repair

(G-21000)
E SPHERE INC
255 Promenade St Apt 162 (02908-5768)
PHONE....401 270-7512
Deborah Dunning,
Michael Zimmer,
EMP: 10
SALES (est): 676.1K Privately Held
SIC: 7372 Prepackaged Software Services

(G-21001)
EAGLE TOOL INC
430 Kinsley Ave (02909-1092)
PHONE....401 421-5105
Edward Iannone, *President*
Frank Iannucci, *Corp Secy*
EMP: 18 EST: 1940
SQ FT: 40,000
SALES: 2.6MM Privately Held
WEB: www.eagletool.com
SIC: 3915 Mfg Jewelry Findings & Metal Stampings

(G-21002)
ECC HOLDINGS INC (HQ)
35 Livingston St (02904-2726)
P.O. Box 6161 (02940-6161)
PHONE....401 331-9000
Barry Shepard, *President*
◆ EMP: 38 EST: 1928
SQ FT: 19,000
SALES (est): 8MM
SALES (corp-wide): 51MM Privately Held
SIC: 2816 2865 Mfg Inorganic Pigments Mfg Cyclic Crudes/Intermediates/Dyes
PA: Organic Dyes And Pigments, Llc
1 Crownmark Dr
Lincoln RI 02865
401 434-3300

(G-21003)
EDGAR MODELIERS
95 Hathaway St Ste 37 (02907-3781)
PHONE....401 781-3506
Edgar Berrebbi, *President*
EMP: 20
SALES (est): 1.5MM Privately Held
SIC: 3911 Mfg Precious Metal Jewelry

(G-21004)
ELECTROLIZING INC
20 Houghton St (02904)
PHONE....401 861-5900
Kevin Burr, *General Mgr*
Kim Moniz, *General Mgr*
Greg Jiede, *Branch Mgr*
EMP: 38 Privately Held
SIC: 3471 5169 Plating/Polishing Service Whol Chemicals/Products
HQ: Electrolizing Inc
114 Simonds Ave
Dekalb IL
815 758-6657

(G-21005)
ELLIOTT SALES GROUP INC
Also Called: Elliott Group
111 Dupont Dr (02907-3105)
P.O. Box 6344 (02940-6344)
PHONE....401 944-0002
Elliott Brodsky, *President*
◆ EMP: 65
SQ FT: 110,000
SALES (est): 11MM Privately Held
WEB: www.elliottgroup-displays.com
SIC: 2541 2542 3993 Mfg Wood Partitions/Fixt Mfg Nonwd Partition/Fixt

(G-21006)
ENDIPREV USA LLC
10 Dorrance St Ste 700 (02903-2014)
PHONE....401 519-3600
Andre Ribeiro, *CEO*
EMP: 70
SALES (est): 2.3MM Privately Held
SIC: 3699 Mfg Electrical Equipment/Supplies

(G-21007)
EPIVAX INC
188 Valley St Ste 424 (02909-2468)
PHONE....401 272-2123
Daniel Adams, *Ch of Bd*
Anne S Degroot, *President*
William Martin, *Vice Pres*
Danielle Dupras, *Research*
Sarah Botelho, *Bookkeeper*
EMP: 15
SALES (est): 3.7MM Privately Held
WEB: www.epivax.com
SIC: 2836 8322 Mfg Non Diagnostic Biological Preparations Individual Or Family Social Srvcs

GEOGRAPHIC

(G-21008)
ESPOSITO JEWELRY INC
225 Dupont Dr Ste 1 (02907-3138)
P.O. Box 72777 (02907-0777)
PHONE..................................401 943-1900
Joseph F Esposito, *President*
EMP: 10
SQ FT: 80,000
SALES (est): 1.1MM **Privately Held**
WEB: www.espositojewelry.com
SIC: 3961 3911 Mfg Nonprecious Costume & Precious Metal Jewelry

(G-21009)
FACES TYPOGRAPHY INC
40 Rice St 1 (02907-2205)
PHONE..................................401 273-4455
Stephen Putnam, *President*
Arna Zucker, *Principal*
EMP: 6
SQ FT: 1,200
SALES (est): 600K **Privately Held**
WEB: www.facesimaging.com
SIC: 2791 Typesetting Service

(G-21010)
FAIRMONT SONS LLC (PA)
Also Called: AlphaGraphics
20 Westminster St (02903-2422)
PHONE..................................401 351-4000
John A Ryan,
EMP: 8
SALES (est): 920.5K **Privately Held**
SIC: 2752 Comm Prtg Litho

(G-21011)
FARMER WILLIES INC
Also Called: Willie's Superbrew
50 Terminal St Bldg (02906)
PHONE..................................401 441-2997
Nico Enriquez, *President*
Arnold Lau, *COO*
EMP: 3
SALES (est): 199.9K **Privately Held**
SIC: 2095 Mfg Roasted Coffee

(G-21012)
FASHION ACCENTS LLC (PA)
Also Called: Museum Collection
100 Nashua St (02904-1816)
PHONE..................................401 331-6626
James Coogan, *President*
Robert Allen, *Vice Pres*
Philip Shockman, *Vice Pres*
Walter Kuciuba, *Purchasing*
Chrissa Trimble, *Sales Staff*
▲ **EMP:** 27
SALES (est): 3.4MM **Privately Held**
WEB: www.fashionaccents.com
SIC: 3911 Mfg Precious Metal Jewelry

(G-21013)
FERGUSON PERFORATING COMPANY (DH)
130 Ernest St (02905-4602)
PHONE..................................401 941-8876
Charles Flack, *CEO*
▼ **EMP:** 100 **EST:** 1927
SQ FT: 68,000
SALES (est): 24.8MM
SALES (corp-wide): 11.5B **Publicly Held**
WEB: www.fergusonperf.com
SIC: 3469 3496 3444 Mfg Metal Stampings Mfg Misc Fab Wire Prdts Mfg Sheet Metalwork
HQ: Diamond Manufacturing Company
243 W Eigth St
Wyoming PA 18644
570 693-0300

(G-21014)
FOUNTAIN DISPENSERS CO INC
35 Greenwich St (02907-2534)
PHONE..................................401 461-8400
Francis Marceau, *Principal*
EMP: 3
SALES (est): 115.9K **Privately Held**
SIC: 2087 Mfg Flavor Extracts/Syrup

(G-21015)
FOXON COMPANY
235 W Park St (02908-4881)
P.O. Box 223, Tiverton (02878-0223)
PHONE..................................401 421-2386
EMP: 32
SQ FT: 28,000
SALES (est): 4.6MM **Privately Held**
SIC: 2679 2653 2759 2796 Mfg Converted Paper Prdt Mfg Corrugated/Fiber Box Commercial Printing Platemaking Services Mfg Packaging Paper/Film

(G-21016)
FRANK MORROW COMPANY
129 Baker St (02905-4504)
P.O. Box 25066 (02905-0596)
PHONE..................................401 941-3900
Gregg Morrow, *President*
▲ **EMP:** 10
SQ FT: 60,000
SALES (est): 1.3MM **Privately Held**
WEB: www.frankmorrow.com
SIC: 3469 Mfg Metal Stampings

(G-21017)
FRUEII
68 Dorrance St 177 (02903-2210)
PHONE..................................401 499-5887
Christian Dale, *Principal*
EMP: 4
SALES (est): 175.7K **Privately Held**
SIC: 2844 Mfg Soap And Cleansers

(G-21018)
FUEL CO
9 Hylestead St (02905-1519)
PHONE..................................401 467-8773
EMP: 3
SALES (est): 186.5K **Privately Held**
SIC: 2869 Mfg Industrial Organic Chemicals

(G-21019)
GA REL MANUFACTURING COMPANY
564 Manton Ave (02909-5031)
PHONE..................................401 331-5455
Gregory Lang, *Vice Pres*
Alicia Lang, *Treasurer*
Karen Lang Fusaro, *Admin Sec*
EMP: 20
SQ FT: 20,000
SALES (est): 1.9MM **Privately Held**
WEB: www.garel.com
SIC: 3479 3544 3999 3444 Coating/Engraving Svcs Mfg Dies/Tools/Jigs/Fixt Mfg Misc Products

(G-21020)
GASPEE PUBLISHING
22 Parsonage St (02903-4758)
PHONE..................................401 272-3668
Frank Mauran, *Owner*
EMP: 6
SALES (est): 563.4K **Privately Held**
SIC: 2741 Misc Publishing

(G-21021)
GRACO AWARDS MANUFACTURING INC
177 Georgia Ave (02905-4422)
P.O. Box 27, Tomball TX (77377-0027)
PHONE..................................281 255-2161
Tommy G Tucker, *President*
EMP: 50
SQ FT: 3,812
SALES (est): 3.6MM **Privately Held**
WEB: www.gracoind.com
SIC: 3999 2241 Mfg Misc Products Narrow Fabric Mill

(G-21022)
GRAPHENE COMPOSITES USA INC
177 N Main St (02903-1220)
PHONE..................................401 261-5811
Sandy Chen, *CEO*
Steven Devine, *Principal*
Carol Jarvest, *Principal*
Graham Laycock, *Principal*
John Pagliarini, *Principal*
EMP: 5
SALES (est): 216K **Privately Held**
SIC: 3624 Mfg Carbon/Graphite Products

(G-21023)
GRECO BROS INC
1 Greco Ln (02909-2622)
PHONE..................................401 421-9306
Ralph M Greco, *President*
David Greco, *Vice Pres*
EMP: 19 **EST:** 1945
SQ FT: 16,000
SALES (est): 4MM **Privately Held**
WEB: www.grecobrothers.com
SIC: 3559 Mfg Plating Equipment Such As Degreasers & Metal Finishing Equipment

(G-21024)
HADC
85 Whipple St (02908-3260)
PHONE..................................401 274-1870
Jeff Burley, *President*
▲ **EMP:** 4
SALES (est): 279.2K **Privately Held**
SIC: 3911 5094 Mfg Precious Metal Jewelry Whol Jewelry/Precious Stones

(G-21025)
HAMILTON TOOL INC
26 Turner St (02908-5322)
PHONE..................................401 421-8870
Bill Lannucci, *President*
Brian Richards, *Treasurer*
Paul Iannucci, *Admin Sec*
EMP: 20
SQ FT: 10,000 **Privately Held**
WEB: www.hamiltontoolinc.com
SIC: 3469 Mfg Metal Stampings

(G-21026)
HASBRO INC
1 Hasbro Pl (02903-1849)
PHONE..................................401 280-2127
Mike Iemma, *Vice Pres*
Joann Kunitz, *Engineer*
Joe Bradford, *Manager*
Stephanie Decorpo, *Manager*
Kristen Dziedzic, *Manager*
EMP: 19
SALES (corp-wide): 4.5B **Publicly Held**
SIC: 3944 Mfg Games/Toys
PA: Hasbro, Inc.
1027 Newport Ave
Pawtucket RI 02861
401 431-8697

(G-21027)
HEAVY METAL CORP
1 Park Row Ste 300 (02903-1246)
PHONE..................................401 944-2002
Jeremy V Moses, *President*
Jeremy Moses, *President*
EMP: 16 **EST:** 2013
SALES (est): 3.3MM **Privately Held**
SIC: 3449 Business Services At Non-Commercial Site

(G-21028)
HENRY A EVERS CORP INC
72 Oxford St (02905-4709)
PHONE..................................401 781-4767
Anthony J Diorio, *President*
EMP: 10 **EST:** 1898
SQ FT: 16,000
SALES (est): 740K **Privately Held**
WEB: www.henryaevers.com
SIC: 3953 Mfg Marking Devices

(G-21029)
HERFF JONES LLC
10 Temple St (02905)
P.O. Box 6400 (02940-6400)
PHONE..................................401 331-0888
Jane Byrne, *General Mgr*
EMP: 50
SALES (corp-wide): 1.1B **Privately Held**
WEB: www.herffjones.com
SIC: 3911 Mfg Precious Metal Jewelry
HQ: Herff Jones, Llc
4501 W 62nd St
Indianapolis IN 46268
800 419-5462

(G-21030)
HIGH PRFMCE COMPOSITES LTD
99 Power St (02906-1013)
PHONE..................................401 274-8560
Michael W Joukowsky, *President*
Madeleine Telfeyan, *Admin Sec*
EMP: 3 **EST:** 2010
SALES (est): 158.6K **Privately Held**
SIC: 3624 Carbon And Graphite Products

(G-21031)
HOOKFAST SPECIALTIES INC
63 Seymour St (02905-4716)
PHONE..................................401 781-4466
Dan Garriaran, *CEO*
Daniel Gorriaran, *President*
Michael Gorriaran, *Treasurer*
Steven Gorriaran, *Admin Sec*
EMP: 25 **EST:** 1926
SQ FT: 10,000
SALES (est): 2.6MM **Privately Held**
WEB: www.hookfast.com
SIC: 2399 Mfg Of Badges

(G-21032)
HUB-FEDERAL INC
Also Called: Hub & Federal Sign
135 Dean St (02903-1603)
P.O. Box 1 (02901-0001)
PHONE..................................401 421-3400
Frank R Benell Jr, *President*
William Benell, *Treasurer*
EMP: 12 **EST:** 1938
SQ FT: 10,000
SALES (est): 940.7K **Privately Held**
SIC: 3993 Mfg Signs/Advertising Specialties

(G-21033)
HUDSON TERMINAL CORP (PA)
Also Called: Hudson Liquid Asphalts
29 Terminal Rd (02905)
PHONE..................................401 274-2200
Tom Hudson, *CEO*
Francis J Obrien, *President*
Edward R Lodge Jr, *Senior VP*
▲ **EMP:** 13 **EST:** 1962
SQ FT: 60,000
SALES (est): 2.5MM **Privately Held**
SIC: 3531 Mfg Construction Machinery

(G-21034)
IDEAL PLATING & POLSG CO INC
175 Public St (02903-4915)
PHONE..................................401 455-1700
Arnold De Senna, *President*
EMP: 18 **EST:** 1956
SQ FT: 4,500
SALES (est): 2.2MM **Privately Held**
SIC: 3471 Plating/Polishing Service

(G-21035)
IMAGINATION PLAYGROUND LLC
292 Charles St (02904-2240)
PHONE..................................678 604-7466
Marc Hacker,
▲ **EMP:** 5
SALES (est): 569.4K **Privately Held**
SIC: 3949 Mfg Sporting/Athletic Goods

(G-21036)
IMPACTWEAR INTERNATIONAL LLLP
16 Elbow St (02903-4210)
PHONE..................................213 559-2454
Natasha Williams, *Principal*
EMP: 3 **EST:** 2016
SALES (est): 230.5K **Privately Held**
SIC: 3842 Mfg Surgical Appliances/Supplies

(G-21037)
INTERNATIONAL CHROMIUM PLTG CO
Also Called: Intrnatl Chromium Plating Co
2 Addison Pl (02909-2498)
PHONE..................................401 421-0205
Linda Fogarty, *President*
Jean Fogarty, *Principal*
Tim Fogarty, *Vice Pres*
Joseph Fogarty, *Admin Sec*
EMP: 9 **EST:** 1927
SQ FT: 15,000
SALES (est): 881.6K **Privately Held**
SIC: 3471 Electroplating Specializing In Industrial Chrome & Decorative Plating

(G-21038)
INTERNATIONAL ETCHING INC
7 Ninigret Ave (02907-3000)
PHONE..................................401 781-6800
Jonathan Zucchi, *President*
EMP: 12

SQ FT: 14,000
SALES (est): 1.9MM **Privately Held**
WEB: www.internationaletching.com
SIC: 3479 Coating/Engraving Service

(G-21039)
INTERNATIONAL INSIGNIA CORP
1280 Eddy St (02905-4534)
PHONE..................................401 784-0000
Robert K Reaburn, *President*
Debbie Jones, *Safety Mgr*
EMP: 60 **EST:** 1954
SQ FT: 25,000
SALES (est): 6.2MM **Privately Held**
WEB: www.internationalinsignia.com
SIC: 3999 Mfg Misc Products

(G-21040)
IRA GREEN INC
177 Georgia Ave (02905-4422)
PHONE..................................800 663-7487
Michael Mc Allister, *Ch of Bd*
Robert D Gilmartin, *Exec VP*
Jerry Kassner, *CFO*
Scott Gardner, *CIO*
Ed Doyle, *Info Tech Mgr*
▲ **EMP:** 211 **EST:** 1945
SQ FT: 80,000
SALES (est): 42MM **Privately Held**
WEB: www.iragreen.com
SIC: 3469 3999 5199 2395 Mfg Metal Stampings Mfg Misc Products Whol Nondurable Goods Pleating/Stitching Svcs

(G-21041)
J B FOLEY PRINTING COMPANY
1469 Broad St (02905-2834)
PHONE..................................401 467-3616
Thomas Giammatteo Jr, *President*
▲ **EMP:** 5 **EST:** 1901
SQ FT: 3,000
SALES (est): 650.8K **Privately Held**
WEB: www.jbfoley.com
SIC: 2752 2759 Offset Printing & Letterpress

(G-21042)
JCM DESIGN & DISPLAY INC
610 Manton Ave Ste 1 (02909-5633)
PHONE..................................401 781-0470
Joseph Martins, *President*
EMP: 41
SQ FT: 54,000
SALES (est): 6.6MM **Privately Held**
SIC: 2542 Mfg Partitions/Fixtures-Nonwood

(G-21043)
JENS & MARIE INC
2 Thomas St Ste 1 (02903-1354)
PHONE..................................401 475-9991
Jens Retlev, *CEO*
John Narkiewiz, *Vice Pres*
EMP: 6
SALES (est): 243.1K **Privately Held**
SIC: 2033 5142 Mfg Canned Fruits/Vegetables Whol Packaged Frozen Goods

(G-21044)
JEWEL CASE CORPORATION
110 Dupont Dr (02907-3181)
PHONE..................................401 943-1400
Therese Eisen, *President*
Ken Sabbagh, *Sales Staff*
Elisabeth D Slocum, *Admin Sec*
▲ **EMP:** 300 **EST:** 1950
SQ FT: 48,000
SALES (est): 38.8MM **Privately Held**
WEB: www.jewelcase.com
SIC: 3499 3172 2631 2671 Mfg Misc Fab Metal Prdts Mfg Personal Leather Gds Paperboard Mill Mfg Packaging Paper/Film

(G-21045)
JMS CASTING INC
183 Public St (02903-4915)
PHONE..................................401 453-5990
Jeannie Manni, *President*
Michael Stanley, *Vice Pres*
EMP: 6
SALES: 300K **Privately Held**
SIC: 3911 Whol Jewelry/Precious Stones

(G-21046)
JMT EPOXY
95 Hartford Ave Rear Bldg (02909-3326)
PHONE..................................401 331-9730
Joanne Gadwah, *Partner*
Thomas Gudavich, *Partner*
EMP: 3
SALES (est): 352.8K **Privately Held**
SIC: 3915 Mfg Jewelers' Materials

(G-21047)
KERB INC
Also Called: Dibs
301 Promenade St (02908-5720)
PHONE..................................401 491-9595
EMP: 80
SALES (est): 1.1MM **Privately Held**
SIC: 7372 Prepackaged Software Services

(G-21048)
L & M TORSION SPRING CO INC
22 Fisher St (02906-2626)
PHONE..................................401 231-5635
Anne F Lafauci, *President*
Carmino La Fauci, *General Mgr*
Kenny Lafauci, *Vice Pres*
EMP: 3 **EST:** 1961
SQ FT: 7,200
SALES: 310K **Privately Held**
SIC: 3915 Mfg Jewelers' Materials

(G-21049)
LASALLE DONUTS INC
251 Smith St (02908-4954)
PHONE..................................401 272-9773
Daniel Del Prete, *President*
EMP: 4
SALES (est): 229.9K **Privately Held**
SIC: 2051 Mfg Bread/Related Products

(G-21050)
LEES MANUFACTURING CO INC
160 Niantic Ave (02907-3118)
PHONE..................................401 275-2383
Charles P Morvillo, *President*
Vito P Torrisi, *COO*
Todd R Morvillo, *Vice Pres*
Sandy Norris, *CFO*
EMP: 50 **EST:** 1953
SQ FT: 15,000
SALES (est): 7.4MM **Privately Held**
WEB: www.leesmfg.com
SIC: 3915 Mfg Jewelers' Materials

(G-21051)
LEHIGH CEMENT COMPANY
55 Fields Point Dr (02905-5601)
PHONE..................................800 833-4157
EMP: 3
SALES (corp-wide): 356.1MM **Privately Held**
SIC: 3241 Mfg Hydraulic Cement
HQ: Lehigh Cement Company
313 Warren St
Glens Falls NY 12801
518 792-1137

(G-21052)
LEHIGH CEMENT COMPANY LLC
Municipal Whrf 25 Tremial Municipal Wharf (02905)
PHONE..................................401 467-6750
R P Mac Donnell, *Branch Mgr*
EMP: 4
SQ FT: 1,200
SALES (corp-wide): 20B **Privately Held**
WEB: www.lehighcement.com
SIC: 3273 Mfg Ready Mixed Concrete
HQ: Lehigh Cement Company Llc
300 E John Carpenter Fwy
Irving TX 75062
877 534-4442

(G-21053)
LEVITON MANUFACTURING CO INC
1 State St Ste 400 (02908-5035)
PHONE..................................401 273-4875
William Cheetham, *Branch Mgr*
EMP: 11
SALES (corp-wide): 1.4B **Privately Held**
WEB: www.leviton.com
SIC: 3643 Mfg Conductive Wiring Devices
PA: Leviton Manufacturing Co., Inc.
201 N Service Rd
Melville NY 11747
631 812-6000

(G-21054)
LMG RHODE ISLAND HOLDINGS INC (HQ)
119 Harris Ave (02902)
PHONE..................................585 598-0030
Garrett J Cummings,
EMP: 8
SALES (est): 51.5MM
SALES (corp-wide): 1.5B **Publicly Held**
SIC: 2711 Newspapers-Publishing/Printing
PA: Gannett Co., Inc.
7950 Jones Branch Dr
Mc Lean VA 22102
703 854-6000

(G-21055)
LOCKETT MEDICAL CORPORATION (PA)
3 Richmond Sq (02906-5175)
PHONE..................................401 421-6599
William Lockett, *President*
▲ **EMP:** 5
SALES (est): 456.5K **Privately Held**
SIC: 2834 Pharmaceutical Preparations

(G-21056)
LONG LIVE BEERWORKS INC
58 Hudson St (02909-1707)
PHONE..................................203 980-0121
Armando Dedona, *President*
EMP: 5
SALES (est): 139.9K **Privately Held**
SIC: 2082 Mfg Malt Beverages

(G-21057)
LORAC COMPANY INC
Also Called: Lorac Union Tool
97 Johnson St (02905-4518)
PHONE..................................401 781-3330
Richard Carroll, *President*
Steve Carroll, *Vice Pres*
EMP: 46 **EST:** 1944
SQ FT: 51,000
SALES (est): 7.8MM **Privately Held**
WEB: www.loracunion.com
SIC: 3915 3469 Mfg Jewelers' Materials Mfg Metal Stampings

(G-21058)
LRV PROPERTIES LLC
94 Ridge St (02909-1585)
P.O. Box 40803 (02940-0803)
PHONE..................................401 714-7001
Luis Vicioso, *CEO*
EMP: 3
SALES: 6.2MM **Privately Held**
SIC: 2298 6512 6519 6531 Mfg Cordage/Twine Nonresdentl Bldg Operatr Real Property Lessor Real Estate Agent/Mgr Computer Systems Design

(G-21059)
MAP OF MONTH
1 Richmond Sq Ste 150e (02906-5157)
P.O. Box 2484 (02906-0484)
PHONE..................................401 274-4288
Deborah L Newton, *Partner*
Jason Newton, *Partner*
EMP: 3
SALES (est): 200K **Privately Held**
WEB: www.mapofthemonth.com
SIC: 2741 Publisher

(G-21060)
MARION MFG CO
87 Corliss St (02904-2601)
PHONE..................................401 331-4343
Jorge Medeiros, *President*
Maria Teresa Medeiros, *President*
EMP: 14 **EST:** 1945
SQ FT: 6,000
SALES (est): 1.2MM **Privately Held**
SIC: 2391 5714 Mfg & Ret Custom Draperies

(G-21061)
MARS 2000 INC
Also Called: Mars Plastics
45 Troy St (02909-2816)
PHONE..................................401 421-5275
Karl J Krikorian, *President*
Claudette Soucy, *CFO*
▲ **EMP:** 850 **EST:** 1972
SQ FT: 120,000
SALES (est): 107.4MM **Privately Held**
WEB: www.marsplastics.com
SIC: 3089 Mfg Plastic Products

(G-21062)
MASS WEB PRINTING COMPANY INC
150 Chestnut St Ste 1 (02903-4649)
PHONE..................................508 832-5317
Bradley M Mindich, *President*
Stephen Mindich, *Treasurer*
Michael E Mooney, *Admin Sec*
EMP: 75 **EST:** 1982
SQ FT: 15,000
SALES (est): 7.5MM **Privately Held**
WEB: www.masswebprinting.com
SIC: 2732 2752 Book Printing Lithographic Commercial Printing

(G-21063)
MASTRO LIGHTING MFG CO INC (PA)
555 Elmwood Ave (02907-1810)
PHONE..................................401 467-7700
Albert A Mastrostefano, *President*
Vincent A Mastrostefano, *President*
Patricia Di Matteo, *Vice Pres*
Mary Mastrostefano, *Treasurer*
Donna Kane, *Admin Sec*
EMP: 4 **EST:** 1965
SQ FT: 10,000
SALES (est): 560.5K **Privately Held**
SIC: 3646 3645 Mfg Lighting Fixtures

(G-21064)
MCM TECHNOLOGIES INC
175 Dupont Dr (02907-3105)
PHONE..................................401 785-9204
Michael T D'Angelo, *President*
Ray Bert, *President*
Chris D'Angelo, *Vice Pres*
▲ **EMP:** 80
SQ FT: 12,000
SALES (est): 18.4MM **Privately Held**
WEB: www.mcmtechnologies.net
SIC: 3399 Mfg Primary Metal Products

(G-21065)
ME-92 OPERATIONS INC
10 Houghton St (02904-1014)
PHONE..................................401 831-9200
Kevin Burr, *General Mgr*
Nolan Hannan, *COO*
Jacob Meier, *COO*
Kim Moniz, *Human Res Mgr*
EMP: 45
SALES (est): 310.9K **Privately Held**
WEB: www.me-92operations.com
SIC: 3479 Coating/Engraving Service

(G-21066)
METALLURGICAL SOLUTIONS INC
85 Aldrich St (02905-1502)
PHONE..................................401 941-2100
John O'Meara, *President*
Gregory Dexter, *Treasurer*
EMP: 12
SQ FT: 17,000
SALES (est): 2MM **Privately Held**
WEB: www.met-sol.com
SIC: 3398 8711 Metal Heat Treating & Engineering Consulting Service

(G-21067)
MH STALLMAN COMPANY INC (PA)
292 Charles St (02904-2240)
PHONE..................................401 331-5129
Milton Stallman, *Ch of Bd*
James Stallman, *President*
Neil Pereira, *Prdtn Mgr*
Stephen Trembley, *Opers Staff*
Jay Lembree, *VP Sales*
▲ **EMP:** 40 **EST:** 1970
SQ FT: 4,000
SALES (est): 9MM **Privately Held**
WEB: www.mhsco.com
SIC: 3086 Mfg Plastic Foam Products

(G-21068)
MILLS COFFEE ROASTING CO
1058 Broad St (02905-1600)
PHONE....................................401 781-7860
Toll Free:....................................888 -
David Mills, *President*
Susan Mills, *Vice Pres*
▲ **EMP:** 13 **EST:** 1860
SQ FT: 20,000
SALES (est): 1.9MM **Privately Held**
WEB: www.millscoffee.com
SIC: 2095 5149 Mfg Roasted Coffee Whol Groceries

(G-21069)
MISTER SISTER
268 Wickenden St (02903-4424)
PHONE....................................401 421-6969
EMP: 6 **EST:** 2008
SALES (est): 250K **Privately Held**
SIC: 2253 Knit Outerwear Mill

(G-21070)
MONARCH METAL FINISHING CO INC
189 Georgia Ave (02905-4516)
PHONE....................................401 785-3200
Marc E Marandola, *President*
Sharon Volpe, *Admin Sec*
▲ **EMP:** 32
SQ FT: 15,000
SALES (est): 4.5MM **Privately Held**
WEB: www.monarchmetfin.com
SIC: 3471 Metal Plating & Polishing

(G-21071)
MOODY MACHINE PRODUCTS INC
141 Carolina Ave (02905-4418)
PHONE....................................401 941-5130
David A Franklin, *President*
Micheal J Franklin, *Treasurer*
Robert B Gates, *Admin Sec*
EMP: 9
SQ FT: 15,000
SALES: 1MM **Privately Held**
SIC: 3451 Mfg Screw Machine Products

(G-21072)
MORTON INTERNATIONAL LLC
144 Allens Ave (02903-4935)
PHONE....................................401 274-7258
William Colello, *Manager*
EMP: 5
SALES (corp-wide): 61B **Publicly Held**
WEB: www.mortonintl.com
SIC: 2891 Mfg Adhesives/Sealants
HQ: Morton International, Llc
400 Arcola Rd
Collegeville PA 19426
989 636-1000

(G-21073)
MYMETICS CORPORATION
150 Chestnut St (02903-4645)
PHONE....................................410 216-5345
EMP: 3
SALES (est): 171.2K **Privately Held**
SIC: 2834 Mfg Pharmaceutical Preparations

(G-21074)
MYRIAD INC
10 Eagle St Fl 5 (02908-5605)
P.O. Box 41041 (02940-1041)
PHONE....................................401 855-2000
EMP: 6
SQ FT: 9,000
SALES (est): 410K **Privately Held**
WEB: www.divotfixers.com
SIC: 3993 Exclusive Private Label Contract Manufacturer

(G-21075)
NARRAGASETT JEWELRY INC
Also Called: C & J Jewelry
100 Dupont Dr Ste 1 (02907-3102)
PHONE....................................401 944-2200
Gary Jacobsen, *CEO*
Robert Sirhal, *Exec VP*
Jeff Dangelo, *Vice Pres*
Esteban Molina, *Opers Staff*
Douglas Poirier, *CFO*
▼ **EMP:** 50
SQ FT: 40,000
SALES (est): 8.5MM **Privately Held**
WEB: www.candjjewelry.com
SIC: 3911 Mfg Costume Jewelry Mfg Precious Mtl Jewelry Mfg Pens/Mechncl Pencils

(G-21076)
NESTOR INC (PA)
42 Oriental St Fl 3 (02908-3238)
PHONE....................................401 274-5345
William B Danzell, *CEO*
Michael C James, *CEO*
Brian R Haskell, *Vice Pres*
Tadas A Eikinas, *CTO*
Brian M Milette,
EMP: 12
SQ FT: 12,700
SALES (est): 6.3MM **Privately Held**
WEB: www.nestor.com
SIC: 3669 7373 Mfg Communications Equip Computer Systems Design

(G-21077)
NICKEL CORPORAXION
836 Hope St (02906-3744)
PHONE....................................401 351-6555
Mohammed M Islam, *President*
EMP: 3
SALES (est): 243.1K **Privately Held**
SIC: 3356 Nonferrous Rolling/Drawing

(G-21078)
NORTHEASTERN IMPORTING CORP
483 Elmgrove Ave (02906-3471)
PHONE....................................401 276-0654
EMP: 5
SALES (est): 279K **Privately Held**
SIC: 3299 Mfg Nonmetallic Mineral Products

(G-21079)
NU-LUSTRE FINISHING CORP
1 Magnolia St (02909-2945)
PHONE....................................401 521-7800
Robert Mansour, *President*
Patricia Moran, *Treasurer*
EMP: 100
SQ FT: 12,500
SALES (est): 6.3MM **Privately Held**
SIC: 3471 3841 Plating/Polishing Service Mfg Surgical/Medical Instruments

(G-21080)
OBERLIN LLC
186 Union St (02903-3408)
PHONE....................................401 588-8755
EMP: 3
SALES (est): 122.8K **Privately Held**
SIC: 2752 Lithographic Commercial Printing

(G-21081)
OCEAN STATE BOOK BINDING INC
225 Dupont Dr (02907-3112)
PHONE....................................401 528-1172
Bruce Boyarsky, *President*
EMP: 10
SQ FT: 2,000
SALES (est): 1.5MM **Privately Held**
WEB: www.oceanstatebookbinding.com
SIC: 2789 Bookbinding/Related Work

(G-21082)
OFFICERS EQUIPMENT CO
177 Georgia Ave (02905-4422)
PHONE....................................703 221-1912
William Milona, *Vice Pres*
Margaret S Welch, *Admin Sec*
▲ **EMP:** 35 **EST:** 1946
SQ FT: 3,000
SALES (est): 2.5MM **Privately Held**
SIC: 3999 5137 Mfg Military Accessories

(G-21083)
OLIVER BARRETTE MILLWRIGHTS
6 Fox Pl (02903-1053)
P.O. Box 8143, Warwick (02888-0143)
PHONE....................................401 421-3750
EMP: 5 **EST:** 1926
SQ FT: 40,000
SALES (est): 573.4K **Privately Held**
SIC: 3599 1796 Machine Shop & Millwright Contractors

(G-21084)
OMO INC
Also Called: Allegra Print & Imaging
102 Waterman St Unit 2 (02906-1170)
PHONE....................................401 421-5160
Ted Stein, *President*
EMP: 6 **EST:** 1972
SALES (est): 806K **Privately Held**
WEB: www.omo.com
SIC: 2752 7334 Lithographic Commercial Printing Photocopying Services

(G-21085)
OPAL DATA TECHNOLOGY INC
1 Richmond Sq Ste 230e (02906-5141)
PHONE....................................401 435-0033
Peter Dicicco, *President*
EMP: 4
SALES (est): 370K **Privately Held**
SIC: 7372 Prepackaged Software Services

(G-21086)
OUTPOST JOURNAL
532 Kinsley Ave Unit 501 (02909-1000)
PHONE....................................401 569-1211
EMP: 4 **EST:** 2011
SALES (est): 172.6K **Privately Held**
SIC: 2711 Newspapers-Publishing/Printing

(G-21087)
PATRICK T CONLEY ATTY
Also Called: Saber Line Club
200 Allens Ave Ste 4 (02903-4943)
EMP: 3
SALES (corp-wide): 462K **Privately Held**
SIC: 2514 Mfg Metal Household Furniture
PA: Patrick T Conley Atty
1445 Wampanoag Trl # 203
Riverside RI 02915
401 273-1787

(G-21088)
PEAK PRINTING INC
Also Called: Minuteman Press
88 Orange St (02903-2856)
PHONE....................................401 351-0500
Karen Fraielli, *President*
EMP: 13
SALES (est): 1.7MM **Privately Held**
SIC: 2752 Comm Prtg Litho

(G-21089)
PERFECT PRINT LLC
195 Dupont Dr (02907-3105)
PHONE....................................401 347-2370
Jessica Aruda, *Manager*
EMP: 27
SALES (est): 2.9MM **Privately Held**
SIC: 2752 Lithographic Commercial Printing

(G-21090)
PLASTIC SERVICES ENTPS INC
Also Called: Genere Food
100 Niantic Ave Ste 104 (02907-3146)
PHONE....................................401 490-3811
Jose D Genere, *President*
Francis Genere, *Admin Sec*
▲ **EMP:** 10
SALES (est): 3.3MM **Privately Held**
WEB: www.plasticservicesenterprise.com
SIC: 2631 Paperboard Mill

(G-21091)
PLUMBERS OF RI
Also Called: Rooterman
10 Rosario Dr (02909-5402)
P.O. Box 121, North Scituate (02857-0121)
PHONE....................................401 919-0980
EMP: 3 **EST:** 2011
SQ FT: 1,000
SALES (est): 250K **Privately Held**
SIC: 3432 Mfg Plumbing Fixture Fittings

(G-21092)
PORTION MEAT ASSOCIATES INC
356 Valley St (02908-5666)
PHONE....................................401 421-2438
Henry Lantagne, *Vice Pres*
Garry Marshall, *Treasurer*
EMP: 16 **EST:** 1964
SQ FT: 20,000
SALES (est): 2.4MM **Privately Held**
SIC: 2013 5141 Mfg Prepared Meats Whol General Groceries

(G-21093)
PREMIUM POULTRY CO
850 Eddy St (02905-4810)
PHONE....................................401 467-3200
Chad Verdi, *President*
EMP: 30
SALES (est): 4.7MM **Privately Held**
SIC: 2015 Mfg Poultry

(G-21094)
PROMET MARINE SERVICE CORP
242 Allens Ave (02905-5002)
PHONE....................................401 467-3730
David Cohen, *President*
Joel Cohen, *Vice Pres*
▲ **EMP:** 50
SQ FT: 40,000
SALES (est): 6.9MM **Privately Held**
WEB: www.prometmarineservices.com
SIC: 3731 Ship/Repairing

(G-21095)
PROVIDENCE BUSINESS NEWS
400 Westminster St # 600 (02903-3222)
PHONE....................................401 273-2201
Roger Bergenheim, *President*
Mike Mello, *Editor*
Jim Hanrahan, *Accounts Mgr*
Tracy Hoyt, *Marketing Staff*
Donna Rofino, *Marketing Staff*
EMP: 30
SALES (est): 1.8MM **Privately Held**
WEB: www.pbn.com
SIC: 2711 Publisher Of A Weekly Business Newspaper

(G-21096)
PROVIDENCE JOURNAL COMPANY
75 Fountain St (02902-0004)
PHONE....................................401 277-7000
Howard G Sutton, *President*
Kevin Jarbeau, *President*
Sandra J Radcliffe, *Exec VP*
Thomas E Heslin, *Vice Pres*
Deb Hill, *Vice Pres*
▲ **EMP:** 445 **EST:** 1997
SQ FT: 100,000
SALES (est): 51.5MM
SALES (corp-wide): 1.5B **Publicly Held**
WEB: www.projo.com
SIC: 2711 Newspapers-Publishing/Printing
HQ: Rhode Lmg Island Holdings Inc
119 Harris Ave
Providence RI 02902
585 598-0030

(G-21097)
PROVIDENCE LABEL & TAG CO
315 Harris Ave (02909-1062)
PHONE....................................401 751-6677
Thomas H Moran, *President*
EMP: 12
SQ FT: 22,000
SALES (est): 1.3MM **Privately Held**
WEB: www.providencelabel.com
SIC: 2754 2672 Gravure Commercial Printing Mfg Coated/Laminated Paper

(G-21098)
PROVIDENCE MINT INC
1205 Westminster St (02909-1410)
PHONE....................................401 272-7760
Ronald J Medeiros, *President*
Anthony Dineo, *Vice Pres*
EMP: 30
SQ FT: 14,000
SALES (est): 3.4MM **Privately Held**
SIC: 3469 Metal Stamping

(G-21099)
PROVIDENCE SPILLPROOF CNTRS
60 Valley St Apt 4 (02909-7404)
P.O. Box 40672 (02940-0672)
PHONE....................................401 723-4900
Warren Eve, *Owner*
▲ **EMP:** 5

SALES: 500K **Privately Held**
WEB: www.kcup.com
SIC: 3086 Mfg Plastic Foam Products

(G-21100)
PROVIDENCE WELDING
101 Poe St (02905-4900)
PHONE..................................401 941-2700
Robert Cavanagh, *President*
Brian Lester, *Vice Pres*
EMP: 3
SQ FT: 1,400
SALES (est): 450K **Privately Held**
SIC: 3444 3446 7692 Mfg Sheet Metalwork Mfg Architectural Metalwork Welding Repair

(G-21101)
PYRAMID CASE CO INC
Also Called: Embassy Creations
122 Manton Ave (02909-3368)
PHONE..................................401 273-0643
Joseph Caruso, *President*
Richard Caruso, *Vice Pres*
Steve Hartley, *Opers Mgr*
Adrianna Canaan, *Admin Asst*
▲ **EMP:** 531
SQ FT: 333,000
SALES: 25MM **Privately Held**
SIC: 3827 Mfg Optical Instruments/Lenses

(G-21102)
QBM NEW YORK INC
30 Caroline St (02904)
P.O. Box 1330 (02901-1330)
PHONE..................................716 821-1475
EMP: 11
SALES (est): 650.8K **Privately Held**
SIC: 3496 Mfg Misc Fabricated Wire Products

(G-21103)
QUALITY SPRAYING STENCILING CO
175 Dupont Dr (02907-3105)
PHONE..................................401 861-2413
Christopher M D'Angelo, *President*
Ron Dellamorte, *Facilities Mgr*
EMP: 80
SQ FT: 20,000
SALES (est): 9.4MM **Privately Held**
WEB: www.qualityspray.com
SIC: 3479 Coating/Engraving Service

(G-21104)
QUINONEZ MYNOR
Also Called: Quinonez Enterprises
249 Admiral St (02908-2535)
PHONE..................................401 751-9292
EMP: 8
SALES (est): 600K **Privately Held**
SIC: 3911 Mfg Precious Metal Jewelry

(G-21105)
R I HEAT TREATING CO INC
81 Aldrich St (02905-1502)
PHONE..................................401 467-9200
Robert Emerson, *President*
Mary Emerson, *Vice Pres*
EMP: 5 **EST:** 1945
SQ FT: 8,000
SALES (est): 600K **Privately Held**
SIC: 3398 Metal Heat Treating

(G-21106)
REALTY PUBLISHING CENTER INC
572 Smith St (02908-4330)
PHONE..................................401 331-2505
Robert B Pruefer, *President*
Ann Pruefer, *Vice Pres*
EMP: 4
SALES: 350K **Privately Held**
SIC: 2752 Lithographic Commercial Printing

(G-21107)
REED ALLISON GROUP INC
Also Called: P & B Manufacturing
144 Wayland Ave Ste 1 (02906-4370)
PHONE..................................617 846-1237
Barry Cohen, *Ch of Bd*
Lawrence Cohen, *President*
Pauline Cohen, *Vice Pres*
Bill Metzger, *VP Sales*
▲ **EMP:** 80
SALES (est): 12.8MM **Privately Held**
SIC: 3961 3911 2542 3471 Mfg Costume Jewelry Mfg Precious Mtl Jewelry

(G-21108)
REGINE PRINTING CO INC
208 Laurel Hill Ave (02909-4517)
PHONE..................................401 943-3404
John V Regine, *President*
Jean Mantaian, *Sales Mgr*
EMP: 8
SQ FT: 6,000
SALES (est): 820K **Privately Held**
SIC: 2752 2759 Lithographic Commercial Printing Commercial Printing

(G-21109)
REVISION AUTOMOTIVE INC
275 Niantic Ave (02907-3121)
PHONE..................................401 944-4444
Gerald Carlson, *President*
EMP: 5
SALES: 1MM **Privately Held**
SIC: 3465 Mfr Automotive Stampings

(G-21110)
REVIVAL BREWING COMPANY
505 Atwood Ave (02903)
PHONE..................................401 372-7009
Owen Johnson, *CEO*
EMP: 12
SQ FT: 7,500
SALES (est): 753.7K **Privately Held**
SIC: 2082 5181 Mfg Malt Beverages Whol Beer/Ale

(G-21111)
RHODE ISLAND CHEMICAL CORP
754 Branch Ave (02904-2246)
P.O. Box 9122 (02940-9122)
PHONE..................................401 274-3905
John Tapis, *President*
Irma Tapis, *Vice Pres*
EMP: 12
SQ FT: 12,000
SALES (est): 2.1MM **Privately Held**
SIC: 2841 Mfg Synthetic Detergents

(G-21112)
RHODE ISLAND MONTHLY
717 Allens Ave Ste 105 (02905-5442)
PHONE..................................401 649-4800
John J Palumbo, *President*
EMP: 28
SQ FT: 8,000
SALES (est): 3.1MM **Privately Held**
WEB: www.projo.com
SIC: 2721 Periodicals-Publishing/Printing

(G-21113)
RHODE ISLAND PRECISION CO
25 Dorr St (02908-5310)
P.O. Box 19610, Johnston (02919-0610)
PHONE..................................401 421-6661
Keith Hartley, *President*
Deena Hartley, *Vice Pres*
EMP: 15
SQ FT: 1,000
SALES (est): 2MM **Privately Held**
SIC: 3451 Mfg Machine Products

(G-21114)
RHODE ISLAND PUBLICATIONS SOC
200 Allens Ave Ste 1 (02903-4943)
PHONE..................................401 273-1787
EMP: 4 **EST:** 2009
SALES (est): 191.2K **Privately Held**
SIC: 2741 Miscellaneous Publishing, Nsk

(G-21115)
RICHMOND GRAPHIC PRODUCTS INC
188 Progress Ave (02909-3848)
PHONE..................................401 233-2700
Hugh C Neville, *CEO*
Wendy Kraunelis, *President*
Frank Ragazzo, *Vice Pres*
Deloris A Griffee, *Treasurer*
Douglas A Giron, *Admin Sec*
EMP: 15
SQ FT: 25,000
SALES (est): 3.4MM **Privately Held**
WEB: www.richmond-graphic.com
SIC: 3552 Mfg Textile Machinery

(G-21116)
RJ MANSOUR INC
1 Magnolia St (02909-2945)
PHONE..................................401 521-7800
Robert Mansour, *President*
Cesar Vargas, *Vice Pres*
EMP: 50
SQ FT: 6,500
SALES (est): 4.9MM **Privately Held**
SIC: 3841 3999 Manufactures Medical And Religious Products

(G-21117)
ROLAND & WHYTOCK COMPANY
75 Oxford St Ste 202 (02905-4722)
PHONE..................................401 781-1234
William J Roland, *President*
Jeanne McConnelly, *CPA*
EMP: 20 **EST:** 1909
SQ FT: 12,500
SALES (est): 3.2MM **Privately Held**
WEB: www.rolandwhytock.com
SIC: 2499 3915 Mfg Tool Parts And Jewelers' Findings

(G-21118)
S & M ENAMELING CO INC
70 South St (02903-4747)
PHONE..................................401 272-0333
EMP: 3 **EST:** 1925
SQ FT: 1,500
SALES (est): 180K **Privately Held**
SIC: 3479 Enameling Of Metal Jewelry Parts

(G-21119)
SALVADORE TOOL & FINDINGS INC (PA)
Also Called: Fulford Findings
24 Althea St (02907-2802)
PHONE..................................401 331-6000
David Salvadore, *President*
Steven Salvadore, *CFO*
Amleto Salvadore, *Treasurer*
EMP: 25 **EST:** 1945
SQ FT: 55,000
SALES (est): 2.4MM **Privately Held**
WEB: www.salvadoretool.com
SIC: 3915 3961 3469 Mfg Jewelers' Materials Mfg Costume Jewelry Mfg Metal Stampings

(G-21120)
SCOPE DISPLAY & BOX CO INC
Also Called: Shapewood
421 Station St (02910-2934)
PHONE..................................401 467-3910
Steve Thifault, *Principal*
EMP: 3
SALES (corp-wide): 8.8MM **Privately Held**
WEB: www.scopedisplay.com
SIC: 2541 Mfg Wood Partitions/Fixtures
PA: Scope Display & Box Co., Inc.
1840 Cranston St
Cranston RI 02920
401 942-7150

(G-21121)
SHELFDIG LLC
150 Meeting St (02906-1348)
P.O. Box 2792 (02906-0973)
PHONE..................................617 299-6335
Michele Meek, *President*
EMP: 5
SALES (est): 188.8K **Privately Held**
SIC: 7372 7389 Prepackaged Software Services Business Services At Non-Commercial Site

(G-21122)
SIR SPEEDY
1 Charles St Unit 1 # 1 (02904-2229)
PHONE..................................401 232-2000
Robert Annaldo, *President*
Antonio Branco, *President*
Debbie Branco, *Vice Pres*
EMP: 3
SQ FT: 1,600
SALES (est): 447.7K **Privately Held**
SIC: 2752 7334 4822 Lithographic Commercial Printing Photocopying Services Telegraph Communications

(G-21123)
SITE RESOURCES LLC
1 Cedar St Ste 3 (02903-1023)
PHONE..................................401 295-4998
EMP: 5
SALES (est): 1.1MM
SALES (corp-wide): 4.2MM **Privately Held**
SIC: 3663 Radio And Tv Communications Equipment,Nsk
PA: H & N Holdings, Llc

Scottsdale AZ

(G-21124)
SPECTRUM COATINGS LABS INC
217 Chapman St (02905-4507)
PHONE..................................401 781-4847
Earl Faria, *President*
EMP: 12
SQ FT: 7,000
SALES (est): 1.3MM **Privately Held**
WEB: www.spectrumcoatings.com
SIC: 2851 Mfg Paints/Allied Products

(G-21125)
SPENCER PLATING COMPANY
77 Bucklin St (02907-2551)
PHONE..................................401 331-5923
Fax: 401 270-2511
EMP: 8 **EST:** 1952
SQ FT: 30,000
SALES (est): 612.4K
SALES (corp-wide): 4MM **Privately Held**
SIC: 3471 Polishing & Plating
PA: H E L Enterprise Inc
77 Bucklin St
Providence RI
401 331-6437

(G-21126)
SPROUTEL INC
60 Valley St Apt 29 (02909-7405)
PHONE..................................914 806-6514
Aaron Horowitz, *President*
Joel Schwartz, *CTO*
Brian Oley, *Software Dev*
EMP: 6
SQ FT: 1,100
SALES (est): 330K **Privately Held**
SIC: 3942 3944 8711 7371 Mfg Dolls/Stuffed Toys Mfg Games/Toys Engineering Services Computer Programming Svc

(G-21127)
STEARNS TOOL COMPANY INC
56 Sprague St (02907-2503)
PHONE..................................401 351-4765
Robert J Stearns, *President*
Robert J Stearns Jr, *Vice Pres*
Scott R Stearns, *Treasurer*
Dorothy Stearns, *Admin Sec*
EMP: 7 **EST:** 1973
SQ FT: 6,000
SALES (est): 995K **Privately Held**
WEB: www.stearnstool.com
SIC: 3544 3554 Mfg Dies/Tools/Jigs/Fixtures Mfg Paper Industrial Machinery

(G-21128)
STUDIO 4 RI LLC
122 Manton Ave Ste 1 (02909-3369)
PHONE..................................401 578-5419
Vincent Lafazia, *Principal*
Rikki Colacurcio, *Mng Member*
EMP: 3
SALES: 90K **Privately Held**
SIC: 2511 Mfg Wood Household Furniture

(G-21129)
STURBRIDGE ASSOCIATES III LLC (PA)
Also Called: M and J Supply
185 Union Ave (02909-3000)
PHONE..................................401 943-8600
Louis F Simonini PHD, *Partner*
Annette N Simonini, *Partner*
EMP: 3

SQ FT: 34,000
SALES (est): 5.7MM **Privately Held**
SIC: 3089 Mfg Plastic Products

(G-21130)
SWG PROMOTIONS LLC
6 Robin St (02908-5505)
PHONE..................................401 272-6050
Seamus Gately, *Principal*
EMP: 3
SALES (est): 248.2K **Privately Held**
SIC: 2759 Commercial Printing

(G-21131)
T M MORRIS PRODUCTIONS INC
11 Peck St (02903-2804)
PHONE..................................401 331-7780
Theresa M Morris, *President*
Jim De Luzio, *Principal*
EMP: 3
SALES (est): 258.1K **Privately Held**
SIC: 2791 7336 Type Setting & Mechanical Art Work & Layout And Design Work

(G-21132)
TECHNODIC INC
245 Carolina Ave (02905-4505)
PHONE..................................401 467-6660
Stephen Masso, *President*
Joe Dilorenzo, *General Mgr*
Steve Masso, *Vice Pres*
Robin Masso, *Sales Staff*
EMP: 20 **EST:** 1963
SQ FT: 6,000
SALES (est): 1.8MM **Privately Held**
WEB: www.technodic.com
SIC: 3471 Aluminum Anodizing

(G-21133)
TERCAT TOOL AND DIE CO INC
31 Delaine St (02909-2430)
P.O. Box 3375 (02909-0375)
PHONE..................................401 421-3371
Joseph Terino Jr, *President*
EMP: 70 **EST:** 1946
SQ FT: 35,000
SALES (est): 7.8MM **Privately Held**
WEB: www.tercat.com
SIC: 3469 3915 Mfg Metal Stampings Mfg Jewelers' Materials

(G-21134)
TEXTRON INC (PA)
40 Westminster St (02903-2525)
PHONE..................................401 421-2800
Scott C Donnelly, *Ch of Bd*
Manoj Achuthan, *General Mgr*
Gilbert Guthrie, *Counsel*
Julie G Duffy, *Exec VP*
E Robert Lupone, *Exec VP*
◆ **EMP:** 277
SALES: 13.9B **Publicly Held**
WEB: www.textron.com
SIC: 3721 3724 3728 3799 Mfg Aircraft Aircraft Engine/Parts & Aircraft Parts/Equipment

(G-21135)
TEXTRON LYCOMING CORP (HQ)
40 Westminster St (02903-2525)
PHONE..................................401 421-2800
Mike Kraft, *General Mgr*
Dave Dawes, *Vice Pres*
Steve Logue, *Vice Pres*
Gregg Shimp, *Vice Pres*
Judson Rupert, *Chief Engr*
◆ **EMP:** 45
SALES (est): 202MM
SALES (corp-wide): 13.9B **Publicly Held**
WEB: www.lycoming.textron.com
SIC: 3728 3724 Mfg Aircraft Parts/Equipment Mfg Aircraft Engines/Parts
PA: Textron Inc.
40 Westminster St
Providence RI 02903
401 421-2800

(G-21136)
TIARA ENTERPRISES INC
299 Carpenter St Unit 209 (02909-1435)
PHONE..................................401 521-2988
Andrea Porcaro, *President*
EMP: 4 **EST:** 1997
SALES (est): 403.5K **Privately Held**
WEB: www.tiaras.com
SIC: 2389 Mfg Apparel/Accessories

(G-21137)
TIVORSAN PHARMACEUTICALS INC
3 Davol Sq Ste A301 (02903-4762)
PHONE..................................410 419-2171
James E Connolly, *CEO*
Rachel Resnick, *Admin Asst*
EMP: 5
SALES (est): 475.5K **Privately Held**
SIC: 2836 Mfg Biological Products

(G-21138)
TIZRA
9 Catalpa Rd (02906-2614)
PHONE..................................401 935-5317
David G Durand, *Principal*
Carlos R Martinez, *Vice Pres*
EMP: 3
SALES (est): 145.4K **Privately Held**
SIC: 2741 Misc Publishing

(G-21139)
TME CO INC
315 Cole Ave (02906-4855)
PHONE..................................860 354-0686
Peter Orenski, *President*
Dan Gorriaran, *Vice Pres*
EMP: 28
SQ FT: 1,500
SALES (est): 1.8MM **Privately Held**
WEB: www.tmealf.com
SIC: 2399 3911 Mfg Fabricated Textile Products Mfg Precious Metal Jewelry

(G-21140)
TOWER MANUFACTURING CORP
25 Reservoir Ave (02907-3387)
PHONE..................................401 467-7550
Louis Shatkin, *Principal*
Drew Shatkin, *Vice Pres*
David Shatkin, *VP Mfg*
Rob Oliver, *QC Mgr*
Victor Aromin, *Engineer*
▲ **EMP:** 99 **EST:** 1946
SQ FT: 60,000
SALES (est): 16.1MM **Privately Held**
WEB: www.towermfg.com
SIC: 3643 Mfg Conductive Wiring Devices

(G-21141)
TRIMED MEDIA GROUP INC
235 Promenade St Rm 298 (02908-5761)
P.O. Box 245, Barrington (02806-0245)
PHONE..................................401 919-5165
Jack Spears, *President*
EMP: 17 **EST:** 2002
SALES: 2MM **Privately Held**
WEB: www.healthimaging.com
SIC: 2759 8742 Commercial Printing Management Consulting Services

(G-21142)
TWO HANDS INC
7 Ninigret Ave (02907-3023)
PHONE..................................401 785-2727
Linda Brunini, *President*
Jonathan Zucchi, *Vice Pres*
Paula Rodrigues, *Manager*
EMP: 28
SQ FT: 3,000
SALES: 2.5MM **Privately Held**
WEB: www.twohandsinc.com
SIC: 3961 Design Mfg & Distribution Of Costume Jewelry & Giftware

(G-21143)
UNITED STATES ASSOCIATES LLC
1205 Westminster St (02909-1410)
PHONE..................................401 272-7760
Bill Iannucci,
EMP: 25
SALES (est): 1.9MM **Privately Held**
SIC: 3469 Nonclassified Establishment

(G-21144)
UNIVERSAL PLATING CO INC
25 River Ave (02908-5427)
P.O. Box 28579 (02908-0579)
PHONE..................................401 861-3530
Edward A Johnson Sr, *President*
Edward A Johnson Jr, *Vice Pres*
EMP: 8
SALES: 360K **Privately Held**
SIC: 3471 Plating And Electroplating For Jewelry Trade

(G-21145)
UNIVERSAL SPECIALTY AWARDS
1205 Westminster St (02909-1410)
PHONE..................................401 272-7760
Paul Roderick, *Owner*
EMP: 17 **EST:** 2000
SALES (est): 837.6K **Privately Held**
SIC: 2399 Mfg Military Insignia & Police Badges

(G-21146)
VEGA FOOD INDUSTRIES INC
1 Financial Plz Fl 26 (02903-2403)
PHONE..................................401 942-0620
Steve Christofaro, *President*
Dennis Christofaro, *Vice Pres*
EMP: 16
SALES (est): 1.9MM **Privately Held**
SIC: 2035 Packer Of Hot Stuffed Peppers & Other Pickled Items

(G-21147)
VENDA RAVIOLI INC
Also Called: Costantino's Venda Ravioli
150 Royal Little Dr (02904-1860)
PHONE..................................401 421-9105
Alan Costantino, *Branch Mgr*
EMP: 50
SALES (corp-wide): 18.1MM **Privately Held**
SIC: 2098 Mfg Macaroni/Spaghetti
PA: Venda Ravioli Inc.
265 Atwells Ave Ste 1
Providence RI 02903
401 421-9105

(G-21148)
VENDA RAVIOLI INC (PA)
Also Called: Costantino's Venda Ravioli
265 Atwells Ave Ste 1 (02903-1584)
PHONE..................................401 421-9105
Alan Costantino, *President*
▲ **EMP:** 107
SALES (est): 18.1MM **Privately Held**
WEB: www.vendaravioli.com
SIC: 2098 Mfg Food Preparations

(G-21149)
VERVE INC
498 Pine St (02907-1361)
PHONE..................................401 351-6415
Deborah Schimberg, *President*
Kevin Neel, *Manager*
▲ **EMP:** 5
SALES (est): 736.6K **Privately Held**
SIC: 2067 3942 Mfg Chewing Gum Mfg Dolls/Stuffed Toys

(G-21150)
VETERANS ASSEMBLED ELEC LLC (PA)
Also Called: Vae
40 Fountain St Fl 8 (02903-1800)
PHONE..................................401 228-6165
John Shepard, *CEO*
Matthew Vargas, *COO*
Zachary Barrett, *Engineer*
Michael Videira, *CFO*
EMP: 9
SQ FT: 3,500
SALES: 3.7MM **Privately Held**
SIC: 3629 8711 3674 3679 Mfg Elec Indstl Equip Engineering Services Mfg Semiconductors/Dvcs

(G-21151)
VISITOR PRINTING CO
Also Called: Providence Visitor
1 Cathedral Sq (02903-3601)
PHONE..................................401 272-1010
Michael Brown, *Division Mgr*
Rick Snizek, *Principal*
EMP: 11
SALES (est): 520K **Privately Held**
SIC: 2711 Newspapers-Publishing/Printing

(G-21152)
WELLER E E CO INC/MCS FINSHG
253 Georgia Ave (02905-4516)
P.O. Box 25179 (02905-0597)
PHONE..................................401 461-4275
Louis Saritelli, *President*
▲ **EMP:** 35 **EST:** 1961
SQ FT: 15,000
SALES (est): 3.7MM **Privately Held**
SIC: 3131 3479 3965 2395 Mfg Footwear Cut Stock Coating/Engraving Svcs Mfg Fastener/Button/Pins Pleating/Stitching Svcs

(G-21153)
WENCO MOLDING INC
90 Narragansett Ave (02907-3358)
PHONE..................................401 781-2600
Paul Tocco, *President*
EMP: 4
SALES (est): 450K **Privately Held**
SIC: 3089 Injection Molding Of Plastics

(G-21154)
WESTWELL INDUSTRIES INC
Also Called: Surface Coatings Div
26 Plymouth St (02907-2918)
P.O. Box 27039 (02907-0595)
PHONE..................................401 467-2992
EMP: 14
SQ FT: 6,500
SALES: 1.1MM **Privately Held**
WEB: www.surfacecoatingsdivision.com
SIC: 3471 Plating/Polishing Service

(G-21155)
WHITEGATE INTERNATIONAL CORP
Also Called: Whitegate Features Syndicate
71 Faunce Dr (02906-4805)
PHONE..................................401 274-2149
Ed Isaac, *President*
Steve Corey, *Vice Pres*
EMP: 8
SALES (est): 246.7K **Privately Held**
WEB: www.whitegatefeatures.com
SIC: 2711 Newspapers-Publishing/Printing

(G-21156)
WOMEN & INFANTS HOSPITAL
Also Called: West Bay Printing
79 Plain St (02903-4800)
PHONE..................................401 453-7600
Matt Quin, *President*
Ray Salisbury, *Manager*
EMP: 3
SALES (est): 497.3K **Privately Held**
SIC: 2759 Commercial Printing

(G-21157)
WORLD TROPHIES COMPANY INC
275 Silver Spring St (02904-2555)
PHONE..................................401 272-5846
Toll Free:..866 -
Peter Evangelista, *President*
Jim Gorman, *VP Engrg*
Diane Bostic, *Office Mgr*
EMP: 20
SQ FT: 3,000
SALES (est): 3.5MM **Privately Held**
WEB: www.worldtrophies.com
SIC: 3499 Mfg Trophies & Awards

(G-21158)
YOUR HEAVEN LLC
172 Congdon St (02906-1458)
PHONE..................................401 273-7076
Stephen R Schwartz,
EMP: 5
SALES: 50K **Privately Held**
SIC: 3931 5099 7389 Mfg Musical Instruments Whol Durable Goods Business Services At Non-Commercial Site

(G-21159)
ZINGON LLC
100 Exchange St Unit 1207 (02903-2613)
PHONE..................................716 491-0000
Reginald Williams III, *President*
EMP: 5
SQ FT: 3,000
SALES: 1MM **Privately Held**
SIC: 7372 Prepackaged Software Services

Prudence Island
Bristol County

(G-21160)
ISLAND MOORING SUPPLIES LLC
68 John Oldham Rd (02872)
PHONE....................................401 447-5387
David B Homan,
David C Homan,
Sharon Homan,
EMP: 10
SALES (est): 847.4K **Privately Held**
SIC: 3089 Mfg Plastic Products

Richmond
Washington County

(G-21161)
FAMARS USA LLC
87 Kingstown Rd Unit C330 (02898-1101)
P.O. Box 1464, Coventry (02816-0028)
PHONE....................................401 397-5500
John A Glasson, *Administration*
EMP: 3
SALES (est): 196.8K **Privately Held**
SIC: 3421 3489 Mfg Cutlery Mfg Ordnance/Accessories

(G-21162)
RICHMOND SAND & STONE LLC
35 Stilson Rd (02898-1027)
PHONE....................................401 539-7770
Michael D'Ambra,
EMP: 15
SALES (est): 1.5MM **Privately Held**
SIC: 1442 Construction Sand/Gravel

Riverside
Providence County

(G-21163)
ALLSTATE DRILLING CO
Also Called: Geisser Industry
227 Wampanoag Trl (02915-2211)
PHONE....................................401 434-7458
George Geisser III, *President*
Linda Geisser, *Admin Sec*
EMP: 4
SQ FT: 1,000
SALES (est): 593.9K **Privately Held**
SIC: 1481 8734 Nonmetallic Mineral Services Testing Laboratory

(G-21164)
BILL LZTTE ARCHTCTURAL GL ALUM
400 Wampanoag Trl (02915-2210)
PHONE....................................401 383-9535
William Lizotte, *President*
Cathy Lizotte, *Treasurer*
EMP: 11
SALES: 1MM **Privately Held**
SIC: 3334 1793 Primary Aluminum Producer Glass/Glazing Contractor

(G-21165)
BRAIDED PRODUCTS COMPANY
9 Industrial Way (02915-5297)
PHONE....................................401 434-0300
Theodore Hale, *President*
EMP: 5 **EST:** 1933
SQ FT: 7,680
SALES (est): 520K **Privately Held**
WEB: www.braidedproducts.com
SIC: 2295 Mfg Coated Fabrics

(G-21166)
CENTURY SHEET METAL INC
19 Maple Ave (02915-5405)
PHONE....................................401 433-1380
Charles Patterson III, *President*
Pamel Paterson, *Vice Pres*
EMP: 7
SQ FT: 3,200
SALES: 250K **Privately Held**
SIC: 3444 1711 Mfg Of Custom-Made Sheet Metal Products & A Heating And Air Conditioning Contractor

(G-21167)
ELEGANT PUBLISHING INC
120 Amaral St Ste 3 (02915-2227)
P.O. Box 89, Barrington (02806-0089)
PHONE....................................401 245-9726
Paula Dacosta, *Manager*
Tracy Trouf, *Director*
EMP: 4
SALES (est): 348.3K **Privately Held**
SIC: 2741 Misc Publishing

(G-21168)
FULFORD MANUFACTURING COMPANY (PA)
65 Tripps Ln (02915-3013)
PHONE....................................401 431-2000
Anthony Hart, *President*
David Bainer, *Vice Pres*
EMP: 16 **EST:** 1889
SQ FT: 25,000
SALES (est): 2.2MM **Privately Held**
WEB: www.fulfordmfg.com
SIC: 3429 3432 3469 3961 Mfg Hardware Mfg Plumbing Fxtr Fittng Mfg Metal Stampings Mfg Costume Jewelry Mfg Jewelers' Materials

(G-21169)
GRACE ORMONDE MARRIAGE INC
Also Called: Grace Ormonde Wedding Style
120 Amaral St Ste 3 (02915-2227)
P.O. Box 89, Barrington (02806-0089)
PHONE....................................401 245-9726
Grace Ormond, *CEO*
Carolyn Carver, *Publisher*
Yanni Tzoumas, *Publisher*
Erica F Couto, *Editor*
Pamela Esche, *Marketing Staff*
EMP: 10
SALES (est): 680K **Privately Held**
SIC: 2721 7299 Periodicals-Publishing/Printing Misc Personal Services

(G-21170)
INSTANTRON CO INC
3712 Pawtucket Ave (02915-4314)
PHONE....................................401 433-6800
Harold C Mahler Jr, *President*
EMP: 3 **EST:** 1880
SQ FT: 4,950
SALES (est): 488.5K **Privately Held**
WEB: www.instantron.com
SIC: 3699 Mfg Electrical Equipment/Supplies

(G-21171)
K&M/NORDIC CO INC
5 Tripps Ln (02915-3013)
PHONE....................................401 431-5150
Bradford N Kindberg, *President*
▼ **EMP:** 32 **EST:** 1965
SQ FT: 32,000
SALES (est): 4.6MM **Privately Held**
SIC: 2759 Commercial Printing

(G-21172)
MICROWELD CO INC
Also Called: Robert Bagdasarian
285 Wampanoag Trl (02915-2284)
PHONE....................................401 438-5985
Robert Bagdasarian, *President*
EMP: 3 **EST:** 1961
SQ FT: 2,000
SALES (est): 347.4K **Privately Held**
SIC: 7692 3444 3398 Welding Repair Mfg Sheet Metalwork Metal Heat Treating

(G-21173)
MONO DIE CUTTING CO INC
7 Hemingway Dr (02915-2225)
PHONE....................................401 434-1274
Alfred T Morris Jr, *President*
EMP: 17 **EST:** 1943
SQ FT: 21,000
SALES (est): 2MM **Privately Held**
WEB: www.monodiecutting.com
SIC: 3544 2752 2675 Mfg Dies/Tools/Jigs/Fixtures Lithographic Commercial Printing Mfg Die-Cut Paper/Paperboard

(G-21174)
NORTHEAST BUFFINTON GROUP INC
75 Tripps Ln (02915-3013)
PHONE....................................401 434-1107
Leo Cesareo, *President*
Julia Cesareo, *Vice Pres*
EMP: 15
SQ FT: 36,000
SALES: 4MM **Privately Held**
SIC: 2657 Mfg Folding Paperboard Boxes

(G-21175)
QUANTIFACTS INC
100 Amaral St Ste 2 (02915-2226)
PHONE....................................401 421-8300
Jack Nichols, *President*
EMP: 7
SQ FT: 2,500
SALES (est): 834.5K **Privately Held**
WEB: www.quantifacts.com
SIC: 7372 5734 Prepackaged Software Services Ret Computers/Software

(G-21176)
TRANE US INC
10 Hemingway Dr (02915-2224)
PHONE....................................401 434-3146
Nick Sluet, *Branch Mgr*
EMP: 20 **Privately Held**
SIC: 3585 Mfg Refrigeration/Heating Equipment
HQ: Trane U.S. Inc.
3600 Pammel Creek Rd
La Crosse WI 54601
608 787-2000

(G-21177)
TUBODYNE COMPANY
4 Industrial Way (02915-5200)
PHONE....................................401 438-2540
Jeanie Juckett, *President*
Laurie Macleod, *CFO*
EMP: 6
SQ FT: 14,000
SALES (est): 1MM **Privately Held**
WEB: www.tubodyne.com
SIC: 3498 Mfg Steel Pipe/Tubes

(G-21178)
UMICORE PRECIOUS MTLS USA INC
300 Wampanoag Trl Ste A (02915-2200)
PHONE....................................401 450-0907
Keith Mason, *CEO*
EMP: 3
SQ FT: 1,500
SALES (est): 431K
SALES (corp-wide): 3.6B **Privately Held**
SIC: 3339 Primary Nonferrous Metal Producer
HQ: Umicore Precious Metals Canada Inc
451 Denison St
Markham ON L3R 1
905 475-9566

Rumford
Providence County

(G-21179)
ACCU-CARE SUPPLY INC
109 King Philip Rd (02916-3505)
PHONE....................................401 438-7110
Pravin Shah, *President*
Sheela Shah, *Vice Pres*
Barbara Bousquet, *Credit Mgr*
▲ **EMP:** 20
SQ FT: 1,000
SALES: 7.6MM **Privately Held**
SIC: 3589 5169 Mfg Service Industry Machinery Whol Chemicals/Products

(G-21180)
AMARAL CUSTOM FABRICATIONS INC
310 Bourne Ave Ste 5 (02916-3368)
PHONE....................................401 396-5663
EMP: 12
SALES (est): 1.8MM **Privately Held**
SIC: 3441 Structural Metal Fabrication

(G-21181)
C & S MACHINE CO INC
55 Pawtucket Ave Ste F (02916-2429)
PHONE....................................401 431-1830
Brian Crevier, *President*
EMP: 3
SQ FT: 9,000
SALES: 250K **Privately Held**
WEB: www.csmachineco.com
SIC: 3599 Mfg Industrial Machinery

(G-21182)
CHOICE PRINTING & PRODUCT LLC
150 Newport Ave (02916-2038)
PHONE....................................401 438-3838
Vijay Malhotra,
Mrinal Malhotra,
Vipin Malhotra,
EMP: 12
SALES (est): 910K **Privately Held**
SIC: 2752 5943 5112 Lithographic Commercial Printing Ret Stationery Whol Stationery/Office Supplies

(G-21183)
COLONIAL MILLS INC
77 Pawtucket Ave (02916-2422)
PHONE....................................401 724-6279
Don Scarlata, *CEO*
Steve Broman, *CFO*
▼ **EMP:** 90
SALES (est): 18.6MM **Privately Held**
WEB: www.colonialmills.com
SIC: 2273 Mfg Carpets/Rugs

(G-21184)
ENTERPRISE PRTG & PDTS CORP
150 Newport Ave (02916-2038)
PHONE....................................401 438-3838
Vijay Malhotra, *President*
EMP: 15
SQ FT: 8,000
SALES (est): 1.7MM **Privately Held**
SIC: 2752 Lithographic Commercial Printing

(G-21185)
GLORIA DUCHIN INC
201 Narragansett Park Dr (02916-1043)
P.O. Box 4860 (02916-0860)
PHONE....................................401 431-5016
Gloria Duchin, *CEO*
Robyn Smalletz, *President*
David Duchin, *Vice Chairman*
Theodore Smalletz, *CFO*
Richard Zacks, *Admin Sec*
▲ **EMP:** 70 **EST:** 1979
SQ FT: 40,000
SALES (est): 6MM **Privately Held**
SIC: 3999 3961 Mfg Misc Products Mfg Costume Jewelry

(G-21186)
HOMESTEAD BAKING CO
145 N Broadway (02916-2801)
PHONE....................................401 434-0551
Peter Vican, *President*
Jimmy Amaral, *Transptn Dir*
James Amaral, *Opers Mgr*
Tj Pascalides, *Opers Mgr*
Bob Canavan, *Plant Engr*
EMP: 95 **EST:** 1920
SQ FT: 40,000
SALES (est): 19.7MM **Privately Held**
WEB: www.homesteadbaking.com
SIC: 2051 Mfg Bread/Related Products

(G-21187)
INTERPLEX ENGINEERED PDTS INC
231 Ferris Ave (02916-1033)
PHONE....................................401 434-6543
Mark Erickson, *General Mgr*
EMP: 30 **Privately Held**

GEOGRAPHIC

WEB: www.metallogic.com
SIC: 3471 Plating/Polishing Service
HQ: Interplex Engineered Products, Inc.
54 Venus Way
Attleboro MA 02703
508 399-6810

(G-21188)
INTERPLEX INDUSTRIES INC (DH)
231 Ferris Ave (02916-1033)
PHONE....718 961-6212
Jack Seidler, *Ch of Bd*
Sanjiv Chhahira, *President*
Roman Herman, *Opers Staff*
Belinda Lin Zijun, *CFO*
Jose Galvao, *Manager*
▲ EMP: 10
SQ FT: 40,000
SALES (est): 135.7MM **Privately Held**
WEB: www.interplex.com
SIC: 3471 3825 3674 3469 Plating/Polishing Svcs Mfg Elec Measuring Instr Mfg Semiconductors/Dvcs Mfg Metal Stampings
HQ: Interplex Holdings Pte. Ltd.
298 Tiong Bahru Raod
Singapore 16873
626 400-33

(G-21189)
INTERPLEX INDUSTRIES INC
Also Called: Interplex Engineered Products
231 Ferris Ave (02916-1033)
PHONE....401 434-6543
Robert Hudson, *Branch Mgr*
EMP: 8 **Privately Held**
SIC: 3469 Mfg Metal Stampings
HQ: Interplex Industries, Inc.
231 Ferris Ave
Rumford RI 02916
718 961-6212

(G-21190)
INTERPLEX METAL LOGIC
231 Ferris Ave (02916-1033)
PHONE....401 434-6543
Steve Pucci, *President*
Jeff Parrish, *Engineer*
Dora Garcia, *Personnel Assit*
Susan Hart, *Products*
EMP: 3
SALES (est): 490.2K **Privately Held**
SIC: 3469 Mfg Metal Stampings
HQ: Interplex Industries, Inc.
231 Ferris Ave
Rumford RI 02916
718 961-6212

(G-21191)
INTERPLEX METALS RI INC
231 Ferris Ave (02916-1033)
PHONE....401 732-9999
John Robertson, *President*
Kauser Farooqi, *Vice Pres*
Kathy Litchfield, *Representative*
▲ EMP: 70
SQ FT: 16,000
SALES (est): 6.5MM **Privately Held**
SIC: 3471 Plating/Polishing Service
HQ: Nas Cp Corp.
1434 110th St Apt 4a
College Point NY 11356
718 961-6757

(G-21192)
LEXINGTON LIGHTING GROUP LLC
Also Called: Prismatrix Lighting
181 Narragansett Park Dr (02916-1052)
PHONE....860 564-4512
Steven Kaufman, *CEO*
Mike Durkay, *CFO*
EMP: 30 EST: 2013
SALES (est): 1.4MM **Privately Held**
SIC: 3646 3645 Mfg Commercial Lighting Fixtures Mfg Residential Lighting Fixtures

(G-21193)
PCL FIXTURES INC
275 Ferris Ave Unit A (02916-1047)
PHONE....401 334-4646
Donald Budnick, *President*
Joe Collins, *Vice Pres*
Alan Sill, *Prdtn Mgr*
▲ EMP: 7
SQ FT: 320,000
SALES (est): 247.7K **Privately Held**
SIC: 2542 Mfg Partitions/Fixtures-Nonwood

(G-21194)
QUALITY PRINTING SERVICES INC
103 Wilson Ave (02916-2841)
PHONE....401 434-4321
Kenneth G Kazarian, *President*
Joanne Mattera, *Vice Pres*
Debra Maio, *Treasurer*
EMP: 3
SALES: 500K **Privately Held**
SIC: 2759 Commercial Printing

(G-21195)
SHERWOOD BRANDS OF RI
275 Ferris Ave (02916-1033)
PHONE....401 726-4500
▲ EMP: 41
SALES (est): 5.1MM
SALES (corp-wide): 11MM **Privately Held**
SIC: 2052 2064 Mfg Cookies/Crackers Mfg Candy/Confectionery
PA: Sherwood Brands Inc.
9601 Blackwell Rd Ste 225
Rockville MD

(G-21196)
SIGNODE INDUSTRIAL GROUP LLC
Multi Wall Packaging
50 Taylor Dr (02916-1030)
PHONE....401 438-5203
Mike Landry, *Plant Mgr*
Donald Bullock, *Maint Spvr*
Neil Stubbs, *Sales Staff*
EMP: 70
SALES (corp-wide): 11.1B **Publicly Held**
SIC: 2631 2655 2621 Paperboard Mill Mfg Fiber Can/Drums Paper Mill
HQ: Signode Industrial Group Llc
3650 W Lake Ave
Glenview IL 60026
847 724-7500

(G-21197)
TEKNICOTE INC
10 New Rd Unit 4 (02916-2071)
PHONE....401 724-2230
Steve Dolan, *President*
Al Ducharme, *Vice Pres*
Jeffrey Nathan, *Vice Pres*
Luis Obispo, *Purchasing*
EMP: 100 EST: 1971
SQ FT: 85,000
SALES (est): 14.3MM **Privately Held**
WEB: www.teknicote.com
SIC: 3479 Coating/Engraving Service

(G-21198)
VILLAGE PRESS INC
Also Called: Omnicolor Printing
331 N Broadway (02916-3516)
PHONE....401 434-8130
John Nickson Jr, *President*
John Nickson Sr, *Vice Pres*
Noreen Tracey, *Office Mgr*
Mary Nickson, *Admin Sec*
EMP: 18
SALES (est): 3.3MM **Privately Held**
WEB: www.omnicolorprinting.com
SIC: 2752 Lithographic Commercial Printing

(G-21199)
WINKLER GROUP LTD (PA)
Also Called: Bernardo Manufacuring
54 Taylor Dr (02916-1030)
PHONE....401 272-2885
Traci Winkler Maceroni, *CEO*
Norma Winkler, *President*
Heidi Winkler Loomis, *CFO*
▲ EMP: 150 EST: 1963
SQ FT: 43,000
SALES (est): 20.2MM **Privately Held**
WEB: www.bernardomfg.com
SIC: 3961 Mfg Costume Jewelry

(G-21200)
WINKLER GROUP LTD
Bernardo Manufacturing
54 Taylor Dr (02916-1030)
PHONE....401 751-6120
Heidi Loomis, *CFO*
EMP: 40
SALES (corp-wide): 20.2MM **Privately Held**
SIC: 3961 Mfg Costume Jewelry
PA: Winkler Group, Ltd.
54 Taylor Dr
Rumford RI 02916
401 272-2885

Saunderstown
Washington County

(G-21201)
DRIVEWAYS BY R STANLEY INC
794 Slocum Rd (02874-1605)
PHONE....401 789-8600
Richard Stanley Jr, *President*
EMP: 8
SALES (est): 253.3K **Privately Held**
SIC: 2951 Mfg Asphalt Mixtures/Blocks

(G-21202)
JAVA WORX INTERNATIONAL LLC
Also Called: Java Skin Care
28 Bow Run (02874-2471)
PHONE....866 609-3258
Stephanie Additon, *CEO*
Denise Drouin, *COO*
Emily Johnson, *Vice Pres*
EMP: 7 EST: 2008
SQ FT: 1,200
SALES (est): 631.1K **Privately Held**
SIC: 2844 Mfg Toilet Preparations

Slatersville
Providence County

(G-21203)
COMTORGAGE CORPORATION
58 Industrial Dr (02876)
P.O. Box 1217 (02876-0896)
PHONE....401 765-0900
Pauline Brodeur, *President*
Walter Gradolf, *Regl Sales Mgr*
Mike Carrier, *Technology*
EMP: 20 EST: 1928
SQ FT: 6,000
SALES (est): 3.5MM **Privately Held**
WEB: www.comtorgage.com
SIC: 3545 Mfg Precision Gages

(G-21204)
DARTEX COATINGS INC
22 Steel St (02876)
PHONE....401 766-1500
Susan Watson, *President*
Patricia Tilden, *General Mgr*
Charles Jacques, *QC Mgr*
Ian Westaby, *Technical Mgr*
Dan Pezold, *VP Bus Dvlpt*
◆ EMP: 38
SALES (est): 10.6MM
SALES (corp-wide): 3.5B **Privately Held**
WEB: www.dartexcoatings.com
SIC: 2851 Mfg Paints/Allied Products
PA: Trelleborg Ab
Johan Kocksgatan 10
Trelleborg 231 4
410 670-00

(G-21205)
PRAXAIR DISTRIBUTION INC
21 Steel St (02876)
P.O. Box 67 (02876-0067)
PHONE....401 767-3450
Gary Bassett, *Branch Mgr*
EMP: 20 **Privately Held**
SIC: 2813 5084 5999 Mfg Industrial Gases Whol Industrial Equip
HQ: Praxair Distribution, Inc.
10 Riverview Dr
Danbury CT 06810
203 837-2000

(G-21206)
SILGAN DISPENSING SYSTEMS (DH)
110 Graham Dr (02876-1024)
PHONE....401 767-2400
Chris Flater, *VP Finance*
Kevin Clark,
EMP: 118 EST: 1957
SALES (est): 38.5MM
SALES (corp-wide): 4.4B **Publicly Held**
WEB: www.polytop.com
SIC: 3089 Mfg Plastic Products
HQ: Silgan Holdings Llc
4 Landmark Sq Ste 400
Stamford CT 06901
203 975-7110

Smithfield
Providence County

(G-21207)
ACTION CONVEYOR TECH INC
Also Called: Conveyor Installation
90 Douglas Pike Unit 1 (02917-2374)
PHONE....401 722-2300
Antonio Cipolla, *CEO*
Antonio Cipolla, *President*
EMP: 12 EST: 1996
SALES (est): 2.2MM **Privately Held**
SIC: 3535 Mfg Misc Fabricated Wire Products

(G-21208)
ALLMARK INTERNATIONAL INC
18 Industrial Dr (02917-1502)
P.O. Box 17385 (02917-0724)
PHONE....401 232-7080
Tracy Goyette, *President*
Michael Goyette, *Vice Pres*
EMP: 6
SQ FT: 12,000
SALES: 900K **Privately Held**
SIC: 3993 Manufactures Signs

(G-21209)
AMPLEON USA INC
310 Grge Wash Hwy Ste 500 (02917)
PHONE....401 830-5420
Roger Williams, *CEO*
Michael Richter, *Senior VP*
Frans Van Heesbeen, *Vice Pres*
Kevin Gao, *CFO*
Paul Possemato, *Sales Staff*
EMP: 20
SQ FT: 20,000
SALES: 1MM **Privately Held**
SIC: 3674 Mfg Semiconductors/Related Devices

(G-21210)
AUTOMATED INDUSTRIAL MCH INC
Also Called: Aim Joraco
347 Farnum Pike (02917-1205)
PHONE....401 232-1710
Andrew Lewis, *President*
▼ EMP: 12
SQ FT: 8,000
SALES: 2.5MM **Privately Held**
WEB: www.joraco.com
SIC: 3542 Mfg Machine Tools-Forming

(G-21211)
BACOU DALLOZ USA INC
900 Douglas Pike Ste 100 (02917-1879)
PHONE....401 757-2428
Vittoria Michael, *Principal*
EMP: 10
SALES (est): 1MM **Privately Held**
SIC: 3949 Mfg Sporting/Athletic Goods

(G-21212)
BACOU-DALLOZ SAFETY INC
900 Douglas Pike Ste 100 (02917-1879)
PHONE....401 232-1200
Mark Hampton, *President*
Jerry Mc Gurkin, *Vice Pres*
Olivier Touchais, *Treasurer*
Henri- Dominique Petit, *Director*
EMP: 6

SALES (est): 655.2K
SALES (corp-wide): 41.8B **Publicly Held**
WEB: www.posichek.com
SIC: 3842 Mfg Surgical Appliances/Supplies
HQ: Honeywell Safety Products Usa, Inc.
900 Douglas Pike
Smithfield RI 02917
800 430-5490

(G-21213)
BLACKHAWK MACHINE PRODUCTS INC
6 Industrial Dr (02917-1502)
P.O. Box 17250 (02917-0723)
PHONE..................................401 232-7563
Joseph A Cilento, *President*
Dorothy Cilento, *Shareholder*
Eugene Cilento, *Shareholder*
EMP: 35 **EST:** 1976
SQ FT: 18,500
SALES (est): 5.7MM **Privately Held**
WEB: www.blackhawk-machine.com
SIC: 3451 3663 Mfg Screw Machine Products Mfg Radio/Tv Communication Equipment

(G-21214)
BRANCH RIVER PLASTICS INC
15 Thurber Blvd (02917-1859)
PHONE..................................401 232-0270
Robert H Mayo, *President*
Lee Beausoleil, *Accounting Dir*
EMP: 40
SQ FT: 50,000
SALES (est): 7.1MM **Privately Held**
WEB: www.branchriver.com
SIC: 3086 2821 Mfg Plastic Foam Products Mfg Plastic Materials/Resins

(G-21215)
CHECK MATE SERVICE LINE LLC
375 Putnam Pike (02917-2443)
P.O. Box 41582, Providence (02940-1582)
PHONE..................................401 231-7296
Andrew Puleo, *Principal*
EMP: 5
SQ FT: 10,000
SALES (est): 463.6K **Privately Held**
SIC: 2782 Mfg Blankbooks/Binders

(G-21216)
COOL AIR CREATIONS INC
10 Business Park Dr (02917-1954)
PHONE..................................401 830-5780
David Campbell, *President*
Tom Bolio, *Sales Staff*
John Celona, *Manager*
Merry Peloquin, *Art Dir*
EMP: 20
SALES (est): 3.3MM **Privately Held**
WEB: www.morethantees.com
SIC: 2759 2395 Commercial Printing Pleating/Stitching Services

(G-21217)
D SIMPSON INC
Also Called: Ultra Precision Machining
13 Industrial Dr (02917-1516)
PHONE..................................401 232-3638
Donald Simpson, *President*
Linda Simpson, *Vice Pres*
EMP: 11 **EST:** 1978
SQ FT: 6,400
SALES (est): 1.6MM **Privately Held**
SIC: 3599 Precision Machine Shop

(G-21218)
DAVES MRKTPLACE SMTHFIELD INC
371 Putnam Pike Ste 590 (02917-2451)
PHONE..................................401 830-5650
David A Cesario, *President*
EMP: 8 **EST:** 2011
SALES (est): 897K **Privately Held**
SIC: 2449 Mfg Wood Containers

(G-21219)
DEGANIA SILICONE INC (PA)
Also Called: Degania Medical
14 Thurber Blvd (02917-1858)
PHONE..................................401 349-5373
Luis Weijers, *Vice Pres*
▲ **EMP:** 3
SALES (est): 635.5K **Privately Held**
SIC: 3841 Mfg Surgical/Medical Instruments

(G-21220)
DEJANA TRCK UTILITY EQP CO LLC
Also Called: Dejana Truck & Utility Eqp
9 Business Park Dr (02917-1955)
PHONE..................................401 231-9797
Andrew Dejana, *Branch Mgr*
EMP: 45
SQ FT: 24,650 **Publicly Held**
WEB: www.dejana.com
SIC: 3711 5013 3713 Mfg Motor Vehicle/Car Bodies Whol Auto Parts/Supplies Mfg Truck/Bus Bodies
HQ: Dejana Truck & Utility Equipment Company, Llc
490 Pulaski Rd
Kings Park NY 11754
631 544-9000

(G-21221)
DIOPTICS MEDICAL PRODUCTS INC
Also Called: Fgx International
500 Washington Hwy (02917-1926)
PHONE..................................805 781-3300
Anthony Dipaola, *President*
Steven Crellin, *Vice Pres*
Carol Johnson, *Vice Pres*
▲ **EMP:** 75
SQ FT: 8,000
SALES: 11.7MM
SALES (corp-wide): 1.4MM **Privately Held**
WEB: www.dioptics.com
SIC: 3851 Mfg Ophthalmic Goods
HQ: Fgx International Inc.
500 George Washington Hwy
Smithfield RI 02917
401 231-3800

(G-21222)
DYCEM CORPORATION (DH)
33 Appian Way (02917-1777)
PHONE..................................401 738-4420
Stewart Cantley, *President*
Kasey Scullion, *Analyst*
▲ **EMP:** 20
SALES (est): 1.6MM **Privately Held**
WEB: www.dycem.com
SIC: 2426 Hardwood Dimension/Floor Mill
HQ: Dycem Limited
Unit 2-4, Ashley Trading Estate
Bristol BS2 9
117 955-9921

(G-21223)
FERNANDES PRECAST COMPANY
356 Washington Hwy (02917-1921)
PHONE..................................401 349-4907
Jason Fernandes, *President*
EMP: 5
SALES (est): 657.2K **Privately Held**
SIC: 3272 Mfg Concrete Products

(G-21224)
FIBERGLASS FABRICATORS INC
Also Called: F F I
964 Douglas Pike (02917-1875)
P.O. Box 17068 (02917-0702)
PHONE..................................401 231-3552
Anthony J Capo, *President*
Adam Larocque, *Design Engr*
Steve Mooney, *Design Engr*
EMP: 20 **EST:** 1978
SQ FT: 23,000
SALES (est): 5.7MM **Privately Held**
WEB: www.fibfab.com
SIC: 3443 5999 Mfg Fabricated Plate Work Ret Misc Merchandise
PA: Opac Inc
964 Douglas Pike
Smithfield RI 02917
401 231-3552

(G-21225)
FINE LINE GRAPHICS INC
90 Douglas Pike Unit 4 (02917-2374)
PHONE..................................401 349-3300
Axel Kling, *Site Mgr*
EMP: 30 **Privately Held**
WEB: www.flgcorp.com
SIC: 2752 Lithographic Commercial Printing
PA: Fine Line Graphics, Inc.
90 Douglas Pike Unit 3
Smithfield RI 02917

(G-21226)
FINE LINE GRAPHICS INC (PA)
90 Douglas Pike Unit 3 (02917-2374)
P.O. Box 17370 (02917-0724)
PHONE..................................401 349-3300
James Toles, *President*
Daniel Kress, *Production*
Donna Covill-Webb, *Purch Mgr*
Ronald Beauregard, *Treasurer*
David McCabe, *Manager*
EMP: 50
SQ FT: 20,000
SALES (est): 25.9MM **Privately Held**
WEB: www.flgcorp.com
SIC: 3555 7336 Mfg Printing Trades Machinery Commercial Art/Graphic Design

(G-21227)
GEORGIA STONE INDUSTRIES INC (HQ)
Also Called: New England Stone Industries
15 Branch Pike (02917-1223)
PHONE..................................401 232-2040
Antonio Ramos, *CEO*
Ann Marie Ajami, *CFO*
Ann Marie Ramos, *CFO*
EMP: 8
SQ FT: 5,000
SALES (est): 4.7MM
SALES (corp-wide): 17.3MM **Privately Held**
SIC: 1411 Dimension Stone Quarry Mfg Cut Stone/Products
PA: New England Stone Industries, Inc.
15 Branch Pike
Smithfield RI 02917
401 232-2040

(G-21228)
GETCHELL & SON INC
950 Douglas Pike (02917-1875)
P.O. Box 17028 (02917-0701)
PHONE..................................401 231-3850
Donald O Jones, *President*
Ellen Szymanski, *Controller*
EMP: 19 **EST:** 1872
SQ FT: 17,400
SALES (est): 3MM **Privately Held**
WEB: www.getchell.com
SIC: 3441 Structural Metal Fabrication

(G-21229)
GRANT FOSTER GROUP L P
500 Washington Hwy (02917-1926)
PHONE..................................401 231-4077
Anne Reed, *Vice Pres*
Paul Tremblay, *Materials Mgr*
Mark Stigers, *Purchasing*
Brian Lagarto, *CFO*
Craig Scherit, *CFO*
▲ **EMP:** 11
SALES (est): 1.7MM **Privately Held**
SIC: 3911 5999 Mfg Precious Metal Jewelry Ret Misc Merchandise

(G-21230)
GROOV-PIN CORPORATION (PA)
331 Farnum Pike (02917-1205)
PHONE..................................770 251-5054
Scot A Jones, *President*
Jacqueline Beshar, *COO*
Jean Lemieux, *Production*
Edward Fox, *Controller*
Jim Shaffer, *Controller*
EMP: 60
SQ FT: 18,000
SALES (est): 18.7MM **Privately Held**
SIC: 3452 3429 3451 Mfg Bolts/Screws/Rivets Mfg Hardware Mfg Screw Machine Products

(G-21231)
HONEYWELL INTERNATIONAL INC
10 Thurber Blvd (02917-1858)
PHONE..................................401 757-2560
Jeff Brown, *Senior VP*
EMP: 147
SALES (corp-wide): 41.8B **Publicly Held**
SIC: 3724 Mfg Aircraft Engines/Parts
PA: Honeywell International Inc.
300 S Tryon St
Charlotte NC 28202
973 455-2000

(G-21232)
HONEYWELL SAFETY PDTS USA INC
10 Thurber Bouevard (02828)
PHONE..................................800 500-4739
Michael Francisco, *Branch Mgr*
EMP: 4
SALES (corp-wide): 41.8B **Publicly Held**
SIC: 3842 Mfg Surgical Appliances/Supplies
HQ: Honeywell Safety Products Usa, Inc.
900 Douglas Pike
Smithfield RI 02917
800 430-5490

(G-21233)
HONEYWELL SAFETY PRODUCTS USA
Also Called: Bacou-Dalloz Eye & Face Protec
10 Thurber Blvd (02917-1858)
PHONE..................................401 233-0333
Michael Vittoria, *Branch Mgr*
EMP: 19
SALES (corp-wide): 41.8B **Publicly Held**
WEB: www.posichek.com
SIC: 3851 3842 Mfg Ophthalmic Goods Mfg Surgical Appliances/Supplies
HQ: Honeywell Safety Products Usa, Inc.
900 Douglas Pike
Smithfield RI 02917
800 430-5490

(G-21234)
JORACO INC
Also Called: Toggle-Aire
347 Farnum Pike (02917-1205)
PHONE..................................401 232-1710
John A Orabone, *President*
James D Orabone, *Vice Pres*
EMP: 15 **EST:** 1947
SQ FT: 6,200
SALES (est): 1.3MM **Privately Held**
SIC: 3542 3599 Mfg Machine Tools-Forming Mfg Industrial Machinery

(G-21235)
LASER FARE INC (PA)
1 Industrial Dr S (02917-1515)
PHONE..................................401 231-4400
Clifford Brockmyre III, *Ch of Bd*
Thomas Beattie, *Engineer*
EMP: 70
SQ FT: 17,000
SALES (est): 7.1MM **Privately Held**
SIC: 3599 3542 3699 7692 Mfg Industrial Machinery Mfg Machine Tool-Forming Mfg Elec Mach/Equip/Supp Welding Repair

(G-21236)
LFI INC (PA)
1 Industrial Dr S (02917-1515)
PHONE..................................401 231-4400
Clifford Brockmyre III, *President*
Carolyn Faiola, *Mfg Mgr*
Dave Vigneau, *Safety Mgr*
Gimo Barrera, *Engineer*
Rory Berghammer, *Engineer*
EMP: 60
SALES (est): 9.3MM **Privately Held**
SIC: 3699 Mfg Electrical Equipment/Supplies

(G-21237)
MACHINEX COMPANY INC
350 Washington Hwy (02917-1921)
P.O. Box 345, Greenville (02828-0345)
PHONE..................................401 231-3230
Joan Gagnon, *President*
Mary Clark, *Treasurer*
EMP: 10
SQ FT: 1,000
SALES (est): 850K **Privately Held**
WEB: www.machinex.com
SIC: 3599 3451 Mfg Industrial Machinery Mfg Screw Machine Products

(G-21238)
MASBRO POLISHING COMPANY INC
5 Lori Ellen Dr (02917-2313)
PHONE..................................401 722-2227
Thomas Masso, *President*
Larry Masso, *Corp Secy*
EMP: 15 **EST:** 1952
SQ FT: 6,000
SALES (est): 1.5MM **Privately Held**
SIC: 3471 Contract Polishing & Finishing Of Metals

(G-21239)
MICHAELSON FLUID POWER INC
9 Rocky Hill Rd (02917-1319)
P.O. Box 291, Greenville (02828-0291)
PHONE..................................401 232-7070
Richard Codega, *President*
Paul Lopez, *Vice Pres*
EMP: 16
SQ FT: 5,000
SALES (est): 3.9MM **Privately Held**
WEB: www.micflu.com
SIC: 3594 Design & Mfg Hydraulic Power Units

(G-21240)
NEW ENGLAND COPPERWORKS
25 Maple Ave (02917-3643)
PHONE..................................401 232-9899
William Juaire, *President*
EMP: 4
SALES (est): 380K **Privately Held**
WEB: www.necopperworks.com
SIC: 3441 Mfg Metal Stampings

(G-21241)
NXP USA INC
310 Washington Hwy (02917-1958)
PHONE..................................401 830-5410
Erick Olsen, *Branch Mgr*
EMP: 7
SALES (corp-wide): 9.4B **Privately Held**
SIC: 3674 Mfg Semiconductors/Related Devices
HQ: Nxp Usa, Inc.
6501 W William Cannon Dr
Austin TX 78735
512 933-8214

(G-21242)
OPAC INC (PA)
964 Douglas Pike (02917-1875)
P.O. Box 17068 (02917-0702)
PHONE..................................401 231-3552
Anthony J Capo Sr, *President*
Kathleen E Capo, *Vice Pres*
EMP: 7
SQ FT: 23,000
SALES (est): 5.7MM **Privately Held**
SIC: 3089 5085 Mfg Plastic Products Whol Industrial Supplies

(G-21243)
ORION RET SVCS & FIXTURING INC
Also Called: Orion Red
270 Jenckes Hill Rd (02917-1953)
PHONE..................................401 334-5000
Kenneth S Musket, *President*
Tom Mackay, *Vice Pres*
Richard Worringham, *Project Mgr*
▲ **EMP:** 100
SQ FT: 60,000
SALES: 10MM **Privately Held**
WEB: www.orionretail.com
SIC: 2431 3993 2541 3646 Mfg Millwork Mfg Signs/Ad Specialties Mfg Wood Partitions/Fixt Mfg Coml Light Fixtures

(G-21244)
PRECISION TRNED CMPONENTS CORP
331 Farnum Pike (02917-1205)
PHONE..................................401 232-3377
Scot Jones, *President*
Virginia Weston, *QC Mgr*
EMP: 65 **EST:** 1946
SQ FT: 18,000
SALES (est): 11MM
SALES (corp-wide): 18.7MM **Privately Held**
WEB: www.groov-pin.com
SIC: 3451 3679 3678 3643 Mfg Screw Machine Prdts Mfg Elec Components Mfg Elec Connectors Mfg Conductive Wire Dvcs
PA: Groov-Pin Corporation
331 Farnum Pike
Smithfield RI 02917
770 251-5054

(G-21245)
QUALITY SCREW MACHINE PDTS INC
9 Industrial Dr S (02917-1515)
PHONE..................................401 231-8900
Alan Sparadeo, *President*
Francis Sparadeo, *Shareholder*
EMP: 11
SQ FT: 6,500
SALES (est): 980K **Privately Held**
SIC: 3451 Mfg Screw Machine Products

(G-21246)
RETROMEDIA INC
20 Cedar Swamp Rd Ste 8 (02917-2413)
PHONE..................................401 349-4640
Lou Leta, *Vice Pres*
EMP: 4
SALES (est): 194.8K **Privately Held**
SIC: 3577 Mfg Computer Peripheral Equipment

(G-21247)
RHODE ISLAND FRT SYRUP CO INC
250 Putnam Pike (02917-2702)
P.O. Box 17138 (02917-0722)
PHONE..................................401 231-0040
Christopher Stone, *President*
Walter Vigneau, *Admin Sec*
EMP: 11 **EST:** 1948
SQ FT: 5,000
SALES (est): 1.9MM **Privately Held**
SIC: 2087 Mfg Flavoring Syrups

(G-21248)
RI CARBIDE TOOL CO
Also Called: International Header
339 Farnum Pike (02917-1205)
PHONE..................................401 231-1020
John F Lombari, *President*
▲ **EMP:** 32 **EST:** 1959
SQ FT: 12,000
SALES (est): 5.4MM **Privately Held**
WEB: www.ricarbide.com
SIC: 3545 Mfg Machine Tools-Cutting

(G-21249)
RIVERDALE WINDOW AND DOOR CORP
2 Esmond St (02917-3018)
PHONE..................................401 231-6000
Kenneth Caito, *President*
Anthony Lisi, *Vice Pres*
EMP: 160
SALES (est): 17.7MM
SALES (corp-wide): 20.8MM **Privately Held**
WEB: www.riverdalewindow.com
SIC: 2431 Mfg Millwork
PA: Northeast Distributors, Inc.
21 Riverdale Ct
Warwick RI 02886
401 828-7145

(G-21250)
SPERIAN PROTECTION USA INC (DH)
Also Called: Honeywell Safety Products
900 Douglas Pike (02917-1879)
PHONE..................................401 232-1200
Mark Levy, *President*
Erik Loch, *CFO*
▲ **EMP:** 20
SALES: 398.1MM
SALES (corp-wide): 41.8B **Publicly Held**
SIC: 3851 3842 2311 7218 Manufactures Ophthalmic Goods Surgical Appliances Mens And Boys Suit And Coats Industrial Launderer
HQ: Honeywell Safety Products Usa, Inc.
2711 Centerville Rd
Wilmington DE 19808
302 636-5401

(G-21251)
UVEX DISTRIBUTION INC
900 Douglas Pike Ste 100 (02917-1879)
PHONE..................................401 232-1200
Rainer Winter, *Ch of Bd*
Mike Morefield, *President*
Klaus Wiedner, *President*
Walter Stepan, *Treasurer*
EMP: 10
SQ FT: 125,500
SALES (est): 933.4K
SALES (corp-wide): 2.6MM **Privately Held**
WEB: www.uvexsports.com
SIC: 3851 Mfg Ophthalmic Goods
PA: Uvex Sports Inc
45 Marian Ave
Narragansett RI 02882
401 464-8844

(G-21252)
UVEX SAFETY MANUFACTURING LTD
10 Thurber Blvd (02917-1858)
PHONE..................................401 232-1200
Herve Meillat, *President*
EMP: 200
SALES (est): 12.8MM
SALES (corp-wide): 41.8B **Publicly Held**
SIC: 3851 Mfg Ophthalmic Goods
HQ: Honeywell Safety Products Usa, Inc.
900 Douglas Pike
Smithfield RI 02917
800 430-5490

Tiverton
Newport County

(G-21253)
CAPEWAY YARNS INC
209 Horizon Dr (02878-1370)
P.O. Box 432, Portsmouth (02871-0432)
PHONE..................................401 624-1311
Tom Tracy, *President*
Alice Nasise, *Vice Pres*
EMP: 8
SQ FT: 15,000
SALES (est): 440K **Privately Held**
SIC: 2269 Finishing Plant

(G-21254)
CARON ALPINE TECHNOLOGIES INC
Also Called: Catek
164 Nanaquaket Rd (02878-4718)
P.O. Box 5111, Newport (02841-0101)
PHONE..................................401 624-8999
Jeffrey Caron, *President*
Rebecca Caron, *Vice Pres*
Paul Caron, *Treasurer*
▲ **EMP:** 4
SALES: 500K **Privately Held**
WEB: www.catek.com
SIC: 3949 Mfg Snowboards Bindings

(G-21255)
CASANNA DESIGNS
41 Charles Dr Unit 1 (02878-3748)
PHONE..................................401 835-4029
Carol Scavotto, *Owner*
EMP: 3
SALES (est): 214.7K **Privately Held**
SIC: 3691 Mfg Storage Batteries

(G-21256)
CUSTOM WOODTURNING
381 State Ave (02878-1064)
PHONE..................................401 625-5909
Thomas Duarte, *Partner*
Stephen Plaud, *Partner*
EMP: 3
SALES: 600K **Privately Held**
WEB: www.customwoodturning.net
SIC: 2499 Mfg Wood Products

(G-21257)
DUTCHMEN DENTAL LLC
1359 Main Rd (02878-4426)
PHONE..................................401 624-9177
Jon Paul Vanregenmorter, *Manager*
EMP: 8
SALES (est): 918K **Privately Held**
SIC: 3843 Mfg Dental Equipment/Supplies

(G-21258)
FARM COAST BREWERY LLC
241 Cornell Rd (02878-3221)
PHONE..................................401 816-5021
Ester Bishop, *Principal*
EMP: 4
SALES (est): 80.3K **Privately Held**
SIC: 2082 Mfg Malt Beverages

(G-21259)
GIVENS MARINE SURVIVAL SVC CO
550 Main Rd (02878-1350)
PHONE..................................617 441-5400
James William Gill, *Vice Pres*
Joanne Perrino, *Treasurer*
Frank Perrino, *Director*
◆ **EMP:** 10
SALES (est): 1.3MM **Privately Held**
WEB: www.givensliferafts.com
SIC: 3069 Mfg Life Rafts

(G-21260)
NORTHEAST MILLWORK CORP
500 Eagleville Rd (02878-3006)
PHONE..................................401 624-7744
Peter Corr, *Owner*
Karen Corr, *Vice Pres*
EMP: 4
SALES (est): 775.9K **Privately Held**
SIC: 2431 Mfg Millwork

(G-21261)
RELIABLE FUEL INCORPORATED
550 Fish Rd (02878-3762)
P.O. Box 283 (02878-0283)
PHONE..................................401 624-2903
Ed Giblin, *Principal*
EMP: 4
SALES (est): 243.5K **Privately Held**
SIC: 2869 Mfg Industrial Organic Chemicals

(G-21262)
SCANDIA MARINE INC
337 Nanaquaket Rd (02878-4719)
PHONE..................................401 625-5881
Herman Hinrichsen, *President*
EMP: 3
SALES (est): 248.8K **Privately Held**
SIC: 3731 Shipbuilding/Repairing

(G-21263)
STEPHEN PLAUD INC
381 State Ave (02878-1064)
PHONE..................................401 625-5909
Stephen Plaud, *President*
Jeffrey Jenkins, *Vice Pres*
Susan Plaud, *Treasurer*
▲ **EMP:** 18
SQ FT: 8,400
SALES (est): 1.4MM **Privately Held**
WEB: www.jenkinsplaud.com
SIC: 2511 Mfg Custom Wood Furniture

(G-21264)
STONEBRIDGE RESTAURANT INC
Also Called: Stone Bridge Restaurant
25 Russell Dr (02878-1627)
PHONE..................................401 625-5780
EMP: 25
SALES (est): 2MM **Privately Held**
SIC: 2099 Mfg Food Preparations

(G-21265)
STUR-DEE BOAT CO
1117 Bulgarmarsh Rd (02878-3324)
PHONE..................................401 624-9373
Ernest C Gavin, *Owner*
EMP: 3
SQ FT: 2,200
SALES (est): 232.3K **Privately Held**
SIC: 3732 Boatbuilding/Repairing

▲ = Import ▼=Export
◆ =Import/Export

(G-21266)
WHEELTRAK INC
3622 Main Rd (02878-4834)
PHONE.................................800 296-1326
David Belmore, *President*
Melissa Vertentes, *Treasurer*
Evan Acquaviva, *Director*
EMP: 21
SQ FT: 11,000
SALES: 17.5MM **Privately Held**
SIC: 3714 3559 5013 7549 Mfg Motor Vehicle Parts Mfg Misc Industry Mach Whol Auto Parts/Supplies Automotive Services

Wakefield
Washington County

(G-21267)
ATEC
214 High St (02879-3140)
PHONE.................................401 782-6950
Wes Cooper, *President*
EMP: 6
SQ FT: 3,072
SALES (est): 830K **Privately Held**
SIC: 3678 5065 3829 Mfg & Dist Electrical Connectors Assembles And Programs Electronic Testing Equip & Distributes Electronic Parts

(G-21268)
CRYSTAL STAMPING CORP
2984 Post Rd (02879-7557)
PHONE.................................401 724-5880
James Dimello, *President*
Jeffrey Dimello, *Vice Pres*
▲ **EMP:** 12
SQ FT: 16,000
SALES (est): 1.2MM **Privately Held**
SIC: 3469 Mfg Metal Stampings

(G-21269)
DON-MAY OF WAKEFIELD INC
Also Called: Printsource
128 Main St (02879-3567)
PHONE.................................401 789-9339
Mary Schortman, *President*
Lisa Edwards, *Vice Pres*
EMP: 6
SQ FT: 2,700
SALES (est): 970.1K **Privately Held**
SIC: 2752 Lithographic Commercial Printing

(G-21270)
F V SEA BREEZE LLC
28 Serenity Way (02879-2369)
PHONE.................................401 792-0188
Philip R Ruhle Sr,
Philip Ruhle Jr,
EMP: 4
SALES: 1MM **Privately Held**
SIC: 3732 Boatbuilding/Repairing

(G-21271)
HIRST FUEL LLC
83 Birchwood Dr (02879-8114)
PHONE.................................401 789-6376
EMP: 3
SALES (est): 212.1K **Privately Held**
SIC: 2869 Mfg Industrial Organic Chemicals

(G-21272)
HK CHAIN USA INC
1058 Kingstown Rd Unit 8 (02879-2487)
P.O. Box 411 (02880-0411)
PHONE.................................401 782-0402
Peter Velleco, *President*
▲ **EMP:** 3
SQ FT: 6,000
SALES (est): 440.1K **Privately Held**
SIC: 3496 Mfg Misc Fabricated Wire Products

(G-21273)
JONATHAN KNIGHT
Also Called: Superior Trawl
74 Table Rock Rd (02879-1825)
PHONE.................................401 263-3671
Jonathan Knight, *Owner*
EMP: 3 **EST:** 1996
SALES (est): 177.9K **Privately Held**
WEB: www.jonathanknight.com
SIC: 3949 2298 Mfg Sporting/Athletic Goods Mfg Cordage/Twine

(G-21274)
PRISM STREETLIGHTS INC
344 Main St (02879-7426)
PHONE.................................401 792-9900
Jeff Broadhead, *Exec Dir*
EMP: 4
SALES (est): 261.4K **Privately Held**
SIC: 3648 Mfg Lighting Equipment

(G-21275)
SEA STARR ANIMAL HEALTH
Also Called: Sea Pet
1305 Kingstown Rd B-7 (02879-2446)
PHONE.................................401 783-2185
Carder Starr, *Principal*
EMP: 3
SALES (est): 160K **Privately Held**
WEB: www.seapet.com
SIC: 2834 Whol Nondurable Goods

(G-21276)
SONS LIBERTY SPIRITS COMPANY
1425 Kingstown Rd (02879-8313)
PHONE.................................401 284-4006
Mike Reppucti, *Owner*
EMP: 8
SALES (est): 1MM **Privately Held**
SIC: 2082 Mfg Malt Beverages

(G-21277)
SOUTHERN RI NEWSPAPERS (HQ)
Also Called: Standard Times
187 Main St (02879-3504)
P.O. Box 232 (02880-0232)
PHONE.................................401 789-9744
Lori Hickey, *Treasurer*
Lory Hickey, *Controller*
EMP: 30
SQ FT: 8,000
SALES (est): 3.4MM
SALES (corp-wide): 693.9MM **Privately Held**
SIC: 2711 2791 Newspapers-Publishing/Printing Typesetting Services

(G-21278)
SPLENDID LOON STUDIO
726 Tuckertown Rd (02879-2730)
PHONE.................................401 789-7879
Barbara Briggs, *Partner*
Josiah B Briggs, *Partner*
Nina Briggs, *Partner*
EMP: 3
SALES: 100K **Privately Held**
SIC: 3999 Mfg Misc Products

(G-21279)
STEELE AND STEELE INC
682 Kingstown Rd (02879-3000)
PHONE.................................401 782-2278
Susan Steele, *President*
EMP: 4
SQ FT: 1,200
SALES (est): 249.4K **Privately Held**
SIC: 2752 Offset Printer

(G-21280)
SWEENORS CHOCOLATES INC (PA)
21 Charles St (02879-3621)
PHONE.................................401 783-4433
Brian Sweenor, *President*
Lisa Dunham, *Vice Pres*
EMP: 20 **EST:** 1935
SQ FT: 1,600
SALES (est): 2MM **Privately Held**
WEB: www.sweenorschocolates.com
SIC: 2064 5441 Mfg & Ret Candy

(G-21281)
THAYER INDUSTRIES INC
Also Called: Tug Hollow Firearms
100 Brook Farm Rd N (02879-2721)
PHONE.................................401 789-8825
Henry H Thayer IV, *President*
EMP: 3
SALES (est): 205.7K **Privately Held**
SIC: 3484 Mfg Small Arms

(G-21282)
YANKEE PRIDE FISHERIES INC
81 Point Ave (02879-6015)
PHONE.................................401 783-9647
Christopher Roebuck, *President*
EMP: 4
SALES (est): 231.6K **Privately Held**
SIC: 2092 Mfg Fresh/Frozen Packaged Fish

Warren
Bristol County

(G-21283)
ALL STAR ADHESIVE PRODUCTS
30 Cutler St Unit 201 (02885-2772)
P.O. Box 41281, Providence (02940-1281)
PHONE.................................401 247-1866
John Murphy, *President*
Michael Murphy, *Natl Sales Mgr*
Ann Murphy, *Account Dir*
EMP: 3
SALES (est): 410.6K **Privately Held**
WEB: www.allstaradhesives.com
SIC: 2891 Mfg Adhesives/Sealants

(G-21284)
AMT ACQUISITION INC
Also Called: Applied Machine Technology
5 Greenlawn Ave (02885-2810)
PHONE.................................401 247-1680
EMP: 15
SQ FT: 3,200
SALES (est): 2.8MM **Privately Held**
SIC: 3469 Mfg Custom Machine Parts

(G-21285)
ANCHORAGE INC
Also Called: Anchorage Inc-Dyer Boats
57 Miller St (02885-3118)
P.O. Box 403 (02885-0403)
PHONE.................................401 245-3300
Theodore F Jones, *President*
Anna V Jones, *Admin Sec*
▼ **EMP:** 10
SQ FT: 12,000
SALES (est): 1.3MM **Privately Held**
SIC: 3732 Boatbuilding/Repairing

(G-21286)
ASPECTS INC
245 Child St (02885-2748)
P.O. Box 408 (02885-0408)
PHONE.................................401 247-1854
Barry D Colvin, *President*
Trisha A Torres, *Vice Pres*
Trisha Torres, *Vice Pres*
EMP: 20
SQ FT: 14,320
SALES (est): 3.5MM **Privately Held**
WEB: www.birdfeeding.com
SIC: 3089 2449 3499 3829 Mfg Plastic Products Mfg Wood Containers Mfg Misc Fab Metal Prdts Mfg Measure/Control Dvcs

(G-21287)
AVTECH SOFTWARE INC (PA)
16 Cutler St (02885-2770)
PHONE.................................401 628-1600
Michael Sigourney, *President*
Anne Sigourney, *Finance*
Rick Grundy, *Manager*
Allie Wojtanowski, *Info Tech Mgr*
Margarita Medeiros, *Technology*
EMP: 21
SALES (est): 2.8MM **Privately Held**
WEB: www.pagerenterprise.com
SIC: 3822 7371 7372 Mfg Environmental Controls Custom Computer Programing Prepackaged Software Services

(G-21288)
BARRINGTON MANUFACTURING INC
Also Called: Bmi
8 Rockland Rd (02885-1442)
PHONE.................................401 245-1737
Thomas Louttit, *President*
Pamela R Brandvik, *Accounts Exec*
EMP: 12
SQ FT: 4,000
SALES (est): 1.2MM **Privately Held**
WEB: www.bmiri.com
SIC: 3961 Mfg Promotional Jewelry

(G-21289)
BLOUNT BOATS INC
461 Water St (02885-3929)
PHONE.................................401 245-8300
Marcia Blount, *President*
Julie Blount, *Exec VP*
Nancy Blount, *Admin Sec*
▲ **EMP:** 60 **EST:** 2003
SQ FT: 500,000
SALES (est): 11.9MM **Privately Held**
SIC: 3732 3731 3441 Boatbuilding/Repairing Shipbuilding/Repairing Structural Metal Fabrication

(G-21290)
BLOUNT FINE FOODS CORP
383-93 Water St (02885)
PHONE.................................401 245-8800
Todd Blount, *President*
Todd Brown, *Vice Pres*
Sean Gerbi, *Financial Analy*
EMP: 65
SALES (corp-wide): 80.7MM **Privately Held**
WEB: www.blountseafood.com
SIC: 2092 2038 Mfg Fresh/Froze Packaged Fish & Frozen Soup Canned/Cured Fish/Seafood
PA: Blount Fine Foods Corp.
630 Currant Rd
Fall River MA 02720
774 888-1300

(G-21291)
BRISTAL CUSHION & ACC LLC
6 Commercial Way (02885-1637)
PHONE.................................401 247-4499
Steve Starret,
EMP: 11
SALES (est): 1.1MM **Privately Held**
SIC: 2392 Mfg Household Furnishings

(G-21292)
BROWNLIE LAMAR DESIGN GROUP
Also Called: Altamira Lighting
79 Joyce St (02885-3209)
PHONE.................................401 714-9371
Michael Lamar, *President*
Gibb Brownlie, *Vice Pres*
EMP: 8
SQ FT: 7,500
SALES (est): 926.1K **Privately Held**
WEB: www.altamiralighting.com
SIC: 3641 3645 Mfg Electric Lamps Mfg Residential Lighting Fixtures

(G-21293)
CHARTER INDUSTRIES INC
Also Called: Newport Wire & Cable
329 Market St (02885-2637)
PHONE.................................401 245-0850
Arthur Cannon, *Owner*
EMP: 4
SQ FT: 4,574
SALES (est): 460.7K **Privately Held**
SIC: 3679 Mfg Electronic Components

(G-21294)
DAVID P CIOE
Also Called: D C Industrial Sales
59 Baker St (02885-3109)
P.O. Box 238, Barrington (02806-0238)
PHONE.................................401 247-0079
David P Cioe, *Owner*
EMP: 5
SQ FT: 5,000
SALES (est): 808.3K **Privately Held**
WEB: www.columbusfan.com
SIC: 3612 Mfg Transformers

(G-21295)
HOPE & MAIN
691 Main St (02885-4318)
PHONE.................................401 245-7400
Lisa Raiola, *President*
Marilyn Mathison, *Finance*
Luca Carnevale, *Exec Dir*
Ali Montagnon, *Director*
EMP: 8
SQ FT: 18,000

GEOGRAPHIC

SALES: 916.6K **Privately Held**
SIC: 3263 8748 Mfg Semivetreous China Tableware Business Consulting Services

(G-21296)
HWANG BISHOP DESIGNS LTD
30 Cutler St Unit 209 (02885-2744)
PHONE..................................401 245-9557
Felicia Hwang Bishop, *President*
▲ **EMP:** 3
SALES (est): 338.9K **Privately Held**
SIC: 2512 Mfg Upholstered Household Furniture

(G-21297)
LUCA
139 Water St (02885-3077)
PHONE..................................401 289-2251
Stephen Nelson, *Owner*
EMP: 5
SALES (est): 521.6K **Privately Held**
SIC: 2339 Mfg Women's/Misses' Outerwear

(G-21298)
MAGNETIC SEAL CORP
365 Market St (02885-2636)
P.O. Box 445 (02885-0445)
PHONE..................................401 247-2800
Richard Colby, *President*
Bruce S Place, *Vice Pres*
Paul Ryan, *Engineer*
Kailyn Charron, *Human Resources*
Chuck Nevola, *Marketing Staff*
EMP: 44
SQ FT: 20,000
SALES (est): 10.1MM **Privately Held**
WEB: www.magseal.com
SIC: 3728 3053 Mfg Aircraft Parts/Equipment Mfg Gaskets/Packing/Sealing Devices

(G-21299)
NITROTAP LTD
100 Child St (02885-3224)
PHONE..................................401 247-2141
Spencer Morris, *President*
Carl Blomgren, *Sales Staff*
EMP: 4
SQ FT: 15,000
SALES (est): 697.2K **Privately Held**
WEB: www.nitrotap.com
SIC: 3585 Mfg Wine Preserving Equipment

(G-21300)
NORTHEAST COATINGS INC
19 Hezekiah Dr (02885-1162)
PHONE..................................401 649-1552
Wayne Rebello, *Principal*
EMP: 4
SALES (est): 312.4K **Privately Held**
SIC: 3479 Coating/Engraving Service

(G-21301)
PEARSON COMPOSITES LLC
373 Market St (02885-2636)
PHONE..................................401 245-1200
Pat Burke, *Mng Member*
EMP: 10
SALES (est): 1.5MM **Privately Held**
WEB: www.pearsoncomposites.net
SIC: 3732 Boatbuilding/Repairing

(G-21302)
PLANET ECLIPSE LLC
130 Franklin St Bldg L4l5 (02885-3539)
PHONE..................................401 247-9061
Ian Parsons,
▲ **EMP:** 7
SALES (est): 505.6K
SALES (corp-wide): 13.9MM **Privately Held**
SIC: 3949 5091 Mfg/Whol Paintball Equip
HQ: Planet Eclipse Limited
Unit 14 Premier Park
Manchester
161 872-5572

(G-21303)
PROGRESSIVE DISPLAYS INC
Also Called: Displays For Less
605 Main St (02885-4316)
PHONE..................................401 245-2909
Tara K Thibaudeau, *President*
EMP: 25
SQ FT: 3,200
SALES (est): 2.5MM **Privately Held**
SIC: 3993 Signs & Advertising Specialities

(G-21304)
ROYAL DIVERSIFIED PRODUCTS
287 Market St (02885-2637)
P.O. Box 444 (02885-0444)
PHONE..................................401 245-6900
Roger E Ellin, *President*
Marjorie E Ellin, *Corp Secy*
Douglas Johnston, *CFO*
◆ **EMP:** 51 **EST:** 1946
SQ FT: 27,000
SALES (est): 7.9MM **Privately Held**
WEB: www.royalpins.com
SIC: 3544 3496 Mfg Dies/Tools/Jigs/Fixtures Mfg Misc Fabricated Wire Products

(G-21305)
SAFFRON GROUP INC (PA)
Also Called: East Bay Printing & Copying
601 Metacom Ave (02885-2829)
P.O. Box 49 (02885-0049)
PHONE..................................401 245-3725
Alan Albergaria, *President*
EMP: 5 **EST:** 1950
SQ FT: 3,100
SALES (est): 606.5K **Privately Held**
WEB: www.eastbayprinting.com
SIC: 2752 Lithographic Commercial Printing

(G-21306)
SAMSONITE COMPANY STORES LLC
95 Main St (02885-4301)
PHONE..................................401 245-2100
Steve Labao, *Manager*
EMP: 10
SALES (corp-wide): 177.9K **Privately Held**
WEB: www.samsonitecompanystores.com
SIC: 3161 5137 Mfg & Whol Luggage
HQ: Samsonite Company Stores, Llc
575 West St Ste 110
Mansfield MA 02048
508 851-1400

(G-21307)
SCOTTS DOORS AND WINDOWS
30 Cutler St Unit 227 (02885-2751)
PHONE..................................401 743-2083
Scott Mathison, *Owner*
EMP: 5
SALES (est): 270K **Privately Held**
SIC: 2431 Mfg Millwork

(G-21308)
TAP PRINTING INC
628 Metacom Ave Unit 6 (02885-2834)
PHONE..................................401 247-2188
Timothy A Pray, *President*
EMP: 3
SQ FT: 2,500
SALES (est): 487K **Privately Held**
SIC: 2752 Lithographic Commercial Printing

(G-21309)
TAYLOR BOX COMPANY
293 Child St (02885-1907)
P.O. Box 343 (02885-0343)
PHONE..................................401 245-5900
Daniel S Shedd, *President*
Dave Shedd, *Mfg Staff*
Pat Liddell, *CFO*
Taylor Box, *Bd of Directors*
Susan Leach Deblasio, *Admin Sec*
▲ **EMP:** 40
SQ FT: 55,000
SALES (est): 9.8MM **Privately Held**
WEB: www.taylorbox.com
SIC: 2652 Mfg Setup Paperboard Boxes

(G-21310)
TPI INC
Also Called: Tpi Composites
373 Market St Unit B (02885-2681)
P.O. Box 367 (02885-0367)
PHONE..................................401 247-4010
Steven Lockard, *CEO*
J P Aleskus Jr, *President*
Wayne Monie, *Principal*
Dan Shelton, *Vice Pres*
Brian Lucchesi, *Engineer*
▲ **EMP:** 100
SQ FT: 66,000
SALES (est): 21.6MM
SALES (corp-wide): 1B **Publicly Held**
WEB: www.tpicomposites.com
SIC: 3083 Mfg Laminated Plastic Plate/Sheet
PA: Tpi Composites, Inc.
8501 N Scottsdale Rd # 280
Scottsdale AZ 85253
480 305-8910

(G-21311)
TPI COMPOSITES INC
373 Market St (02885-2681)
PHONE..................................401 247-4010
EMP: 3
SALES (corp-wide): 1B **Publicly Held**
SIC: 3083 Mfg Laminated Plastic Plate/Sheet
PA: Tpi Composites, Inc.
8501 N Scottsdale Rd # 280
Scottsdale AZ 85253
480 305-8910

(G-21312)
VIENTEK LLC (PA)
373 Market St (02885-2681)
P.O. Box 367 (02885-0367)
PHONE..................................915 225-1309
Steve Lockard,
▲ **EMP:** 650
SALES (est): 47.9MM **Privately Held**
WEB: www.tpicomp.com
SIC: 3511 Mfg Turbines/Generator Sets

(G-21313)
WARREN CHAIR WORKS INC
30 Cutler St Unit 220 (02885-2751)
PHONE..................................401 247-0426
Robert Barrow, *President*
▲ **EMP:** 18
SQ FT: 30,000
SALES (est): 1MM **Privately Held**
WEB: www.warrenchairworks.com
SIC: 2511 Mfg Wooden Chairs

(G-21314)
WARREN RIVER BOATWORKS INC
66 Church St B (02885-3122)
P.O. Box 202 (02885-0202)
PHONE..................................401 245-6949
Paul Dennis, *President*
EMP: 3
SALES (est): 200K **Privately Held**
SIC: 3732 Marina Operation

(G-21315)
WATER STREET WOODWORKING
332 Water St Frnt (02885-3340)
PHONE..................................401 245-1921
Michael P Mongeon, *Owner*
EMP: 3
SALES: 170K **Privately Held**
SIC: 2431 2434 Mfg Millwork Mfg Wood Kitchen Cabinets

(G-21316)
WATERROWER INC
560 Metacom Ave (02885-2839)
PHONE..................................800 852-2210
Peter King, *Principal*
Gabriel Luis, *Opers Mgr*
Donald Ruest, *Prdtn Mgr*
Deb Arruda, *Executive*
▲ **EMP:** 51
SQ FT: 4,000
SALES (est): 7.7MM **Privately Held**
WEB: www.watercoach.com
SIC: 3949 Mfg Sporting/Athletic Goods
HQ: Waterrower (Uk) Ltd.
Unit 19 Acton Park Estate The Vale
London W3 7Q

Warwick
Kent County

(G-21317)
ACCURATE MOLDED PRODUCTS INC
Also Called: AMP
459 Warwick Industrial Dr (02886-2460)
PHONE..................................401 739-2400
Howard Devine Sr, *President*
Kay Duckworth, *Vice Pres*
EMP: 30
SQ FT: 30,000
SALES (est): 5.1MM **Privately Held**
WEB: www.accuratemolded.com
SIC: 3089 Mfg Plastic Products Mfg Dies/Tools/Jigs/Fixtures

(G-21318)
ADVANCED CHEMICAL COMPANY
105-131 Bellows St (02888)
PHONE..................................401 785-3434
Gerald A Smith, *President*
Jack Griffin, *Business Mgr*
Jonathan Crowell, *Vice Pres*
Michael W Floskis, *CFO*
Rozlynn Smith, *Human Res Mgr*
▲ **EMP:** 50
SQ FT: 24,000
SALES (est): 15.7MM **Privately Held**
WEB: www.advchem.com
SIC: 2899 3339 Mfg Chemical Preparations Primary Nonferrous Metal Producer

(G-21319)
AEQRX TECHNOLOGIES LTD
50 Minnesota Ave (02888-6033)
P.O. Box 8639 (02888-0599)
PHONE..................................401 463-8822
J Robert Dunn, *President*
John Appleton, *Director*
EMP: 3
SQ FT: 1,000
SALES (est): 386.3K **Privately Held**
WEB: www.aeqrx.com
SIC: 3589 Water Treatment Chemicals

(G-21320)
ALA CASTING CO INC
185 Jefferson Blvd (02888-3817)
PHONE..................................516 371-4350
EMP: 50
SQ FT: 15,000
SALES (est): 4.2MM **Privately Held**
WEB: www.alacasting.com
SIC: 3915 Mfg Jewelers' Materials

(G-21321)
ALBERT KEMPERLE INC
288 Lincoln Ave (02888-3030)
PHONE..................................401 826-5111
Albert Kemperle, *Principal*
EMP: 23
SALES (corp-wide): 163.8MM **Privately Held**
SIC: 3465 Mfg Automotive Stampings
PA: Albert Kemperle, Inc.
8400 New Horizons Blvd
Amityville NY 11701
631 841-1241

(G-21322)
AMMERAAL BELTECH INC
46 Warwick Industrial Dr (02886-2456)
PHONE..................................401 732-8131
Gary Williamson, *Manager*
David Belisle, *Manager*
EMP: 8
SALES (corp-wide): 242.1K **Privately Held**
WEB: www.ammeraalbeltechusa.com
SIC: 3496 Mfg Misc Fabricated Wire Products
HQ: Ammeraal Beltech, Inc.
7501 Saint Louis Ave
Skokie IL 60076
847 673-6720

(G-21323)
ANATOLIA CREATIONS
1692 Warwick Ave (02889-1531)
PHONE..................................401 737-4774

▲ = Import ▼=Export
◆ =Import/Export

Hernan Padilla, *Principal*
EMP: 4
SALES (est): 277.4K **Privately Held**
SIC: 3911 Mfg Precious Metal Jewelry

(G-21324)
ANTAYA INC
333 Strawbery F Rd 3 (02886)
PHONE..................................401 941-7050
Donald Antaya, *Ch of Bd*
Stephen C Antaya, *President*
John Pereira, *President*
Mary Antaya, *Treasurer*
▼ **EMP:** 50
SQ FT: 15,000
SALES: 4.8MM **Privately Held**
SIC: 3694 Mfg Automotive Electrical Equipment

(G-21325)
ANTAYA TECHNOLOGIES CORP
333 Strawberry Field Rd # 3 (02886-2459)
PHONE..................................401 921-3197
Jarod Scherer, *President*
Luis Gonzalez, *Project Mgr*
George Caduto, *CFO*
Kathy Flanagan, *Sales Staff*
▲ **EMP:** 225 **EST:** 1998
SQ FT: 25,000
SALES: 34MM **Privately Held**
WEB: www.antaya.com
SIC: 3694 Mfg Engine Electrical Equipment

(G-21326)
AQUAMOTION INC
88 Jefferson Blvd Ste C (02888-1000)
PHONE..................................401 785-3000
Han L Kuster, *President*
Mike Ferruccio, *Opers Mgr*
▲ **EMP:** 15
SALES (est): 2MM **Privately Held**
SIC: 3561 Mfg Pumps/Pumping Equipment

(G-21327)
ARTISTIC LABEL COMPANY INC
60 Gilbane St (02886-6996)
P.O. Box 20037, Cranston (02920-0941)
PHONE..................................401 737-0666
Ellen Kaplan, *President*
EMP: 5
SQ FT: 3,500
SALES (est): 657.6K **Privately Held**
SIC: 2752 Lithographic Commercial Printing

(G-21328)
ASTONISH RESULTS LP
300 Metro Center Blvd (02886-1710)
PHONE..................................401 921-6220
David Simas, *Principal*
EMP: 15
SALES (est): 2.7MM **Privately Held**
SIC: 3823 Mfg Process Control Instruments

(G-21329)
AT WALL COMPANY (HQ)
55 Service Ave (02886-1020)
PHONE..................................401 739-0740
Peter Frost, *President*
Caryn E Mitchell, *CFO*
▲ **EMP:** 45
SQ FT: 64,000
SALES (est): 5.6MM
SALES (corp-wide): 77.1MM **Privately Held**
SIC: 3351 Manufacturer Cold Drawn Tubing & Metal Stampings
PA: Atw Companies, Inc.
125 Metro Center Blvd # 3001
Warwick RI 02886
401 244-1002

(G-21330)
ATW COMPANIES INC (PA)
125 Metro Center Blvd # 3001
(02886-1768)
PHONE..................................401 244-1002
Frederick G Frost III, *Ch of Bd*
Peter C Frost, *President*
Duane Ottolini, *Vice Pres*
Caryn E Mitchell, *CFO*
Ceasar Abreu, *IT/INT Sup*
▲ **EMP:** 70 **EST:** 1886
SQ FT: 64,000
SALES (est): 77.1MM **Privately Held**
WEB: www.atwall.com
SIC: 3674 3498 Mfg Semiconductors/Related Devices Mfg Fabricated Pipe/Fittings

(G-21331)
BAKER COMMODITIES INC
Also Called: Corenco
4 Riverdale Ct (02886-0507)
PHONE..................................401 821-3003
Charlie Odonnell, *Manager*
EMP: 7
SALES (corp-wide): 153.6MM **Privately Held**
WEB: www.bakercommodities.com
SIC: 2077 Mfg Animal/Marine Fat/Oil
PA: Baker Commodities, Inc.
4020 Bandini Blvd
Vernon CA 90058
323 268-2801

(G-21332)
BARRINGTON PRINT & COPY LLC
Also Called: Barrington Printing
133 Central St Ste 1 (02886-1277)
PHONE..................................401 943-8300
Barry Couto, *Co-Owner*
Keith Couto, *Co-Owner*
Adam Couto, *Sales Mgr*
EMP: 26
SALES (est): 5.3MM **Privately Held**
WEB: www.barringtonprinting.com
SIC: 2752 Lithographic Commercial Printing

(G-21333)
BAYVIEW MARINE INC
781 Oakland Beach Ave (02889-9615)
PHONE..................................401 737-3111
Charles Greaves, *President*
EMP: 6 **EST:** 1965
SQ FT: 8,000
SALES (est): 618.1K **Privately Held**
SIC: 3599 3369 7699 Mfg Industrial Machinery Nonferrous Metal Foundry Repair Services

(G-21334)
BEACON COMMUNICATIONS INC (PA)
Also Called: Pennysaver, The
1944 Warwick Ave Ste W4 (02889-2448)
PHONE..................................401 732-3100
John Howell, *President*
Richard Fleischer, *General Mgr*
Lynne Taylor, *Credit Mgr*
Ethan Hartley, *Assoc Editor*
EMP: 30
SQ FT: 1,500
SALES (est): 2.7MM **Privately Held**
WEB: www.warwickonline.com
SIC: 2711 Newspapers-Publishing/Printing

(G-21335)
BEAR HYDRAULICS INC
45 Fullerton Rd (02886-1421)
PHONE..................................401 732-5832
Vincent Gambardella, *President*
Thomas Gambardella, *Treasurer*
Robert Gambardella, *Admin Sec*
EMP: 7
SQ FT: 1,200
SALES (est): 715.1K **Privately Held**
SIC: 3714 3699 Mfg Tire Demounters Bead Breakers & Centrifugal Extracting Equipment

(G-21336)
BIOMEDICAL STRUCTURES LLC
60 Commerce Dr (02886-2470)
PHONE..................................401 223-0990
Dean Tulumaris, *President*
Jim Jestude, *Opers Staff*
Harshad Paranjape, *Engineer*
Diane Baxster, *CFO*
▲ **EMP:** 37
SALES (est): 7.2MM **Privately Held**
SIC: 3841 Mfg Surgical/Medical Instruments
HQ: Ete Medical, Inc.
242 Humboldt Ct
Sunnyvale CA

(G-21337)
BRADA MANUFACTURING INC
46 Warwick Industrial Dr (02886-2456)
P.O. Box 7614 (02887-7614)
PHONE..................................401 739-3774
Michael W Hamilton, *President*
EMP: 30
SQ FT: 15,000
SALES (est): 4MM **Privately Held**
WEB: www.bradamfg.com
SIC: 3599 Mfg Industrial Machinery

(G-21338)
C R BARD INC
100 Crossings Blvd (02886-2850)
PHONE..................................401 825-8300
Paul Robinson, *Vice Pres*
Joseph Panniello, *Mfg Mgr*
Andy St Laurent, *Purch Agent*
Stephen A Eldridge, *Research*
Laurie McGlone, *Human Res Mgr*
EMP: 485
SALES (corp-wide): 15.9B **Publicly Held**
SIC: 3841 Mfg Surgical And Medical Instrument
HQ: C. R. Bard, Inc.
1 Becton Dr
Franklin Lakes NJ 07417
908 277-8000

(G-21339)
CARA INCORPORATED
333 Strawberry Field Rd # 2 (02886-2459)
PHONE..................................401 732-6535
Kenneth P O'Leary, *President*
Kathy O'Leary, *Vice Pres*
David Viens, *Purch Mgr*
Michael Damiani, *Treasurer*
Gary O'Leary, *VP Sales*
▲ **EMP:** 9
SQ FT: 23,000
SALES (est): 1.8MM **Privately Held**
SIC: 3069 Mfg Fabricated Rubber Products

(G-21340)
CARDI MATERIALS LLC (PA)
400 Lincoln Ave (02888-3049)
PHONE..................................401 739-8300
Antonio Cardi, *Mng Member*
Stephen A Cardi II,
EMP: 20
SQ FT: 20,000
SALES (est): 3.3MM **Privately Held**
SIC: 3272 Mfg Concrete Products

(G-21341)
CARE NEW ENGLAND HEALTH SYSTEM
CNE Printing Services
11 Knight St Bldg C10 (02886-1281)
PHONE..................................401 739-9255
Ernie Pascal, *Manager*
EMP: 6
SALES (corp-wide): 1.1B **Privately Held**
WEB: www.carene.org
SIC: 2741 Misc Publishing
PA: Care New England Health System Inc
45 Willard Ave
Providence RI 02905
401 453-7900

(G-21342)
CLEANBRANDS LLC
Also Called: Cleanrest
240 Bald Hill Rd (02886-1126)
PHONE..................................877 215-7378
Gary Goldberg,
▲ **EMP:** 10
SQ FT: 4,800
SALES (est): 1.4MM **Privately Held**
WEB: www.cleanrest.com
SIC: 2392 5021 Mfg Household Furnishings Whol Furniture

(G-21343)
COLONIAL PRINTING INC (PA)
333 Strawberry Field Rd # 11 (02886-2459)
PHONE..................................401 691-3400
Richard Herr, *President*
Josh Bainton, *Vice Pres*
Ken Menna, *Vice Pres*
Richard Pulie, *CFO*
EMP: 25 **EST:** 2017
SALES (est): 4.8MM **Privately Held**
SIC: 2752 Lithographic Commercial Printing

(G-21344)
CONFLUENT MEDICAL TECH INC
60 Commerce Dr (02886-2470)
PHONE..................................401 223-0990
Brian Adcock, *Officer*
EMP: 4 **Privately Held**
SIC: 3841 5047 Mfg Surgical/Medical Instruments Whol Medical/Hospital Equipment
PA: Confluent Medical Technologies, Inc.
47533 Westinghouse Dr
Fremont CA 94539

(G-21345)
CONLEY CASTING SUPPLY CORP (PA)
Also Called: Tekcast Industries RI
124 Maple St (02888-2188)
PHONE..................................401 461-4710
Arthur T Francis, *President*
▲ **EMP:** 30
SQ FT: 20,000
SALES (est): 4.7MM **Privately Held**
WEB: www.conleycasting.com
SIC: 3544 3559 2822 Mfg Dies/Tools/Jigs/Fixt Mfg Misc Industry Mach Mfg Synthetic Rubber

(G-21346)
COOLIANCE INC
60 Alhambra Rd Ste 1 (02886-1442)
PHONE..................................401 921-6500
Russell Hall, *President*
Robert F Mazzeo, *Vice Pres*
▲ **EMP:** 10
SALES (est): 1.6MM **Privately Held**
SIC: 3679 Mfg Thermal Electronic Components

(G-21347)
DAIKIN U S CORPORATION
10 Globe St (02886-4309)
PHONE..................................401 738-0261
D Tober, *Principal*
EMP: 4 **Privately Held**
SIC: 3087 Custom Compounding-Purchased Resins
HQ: Daikin U. S. Corporation
475 5th Ave Fl 21
New York NY 10017
212 340-7400

(G-21348)
DATA BINDING INC
10 New England Way (02886-6913)
PHONE..................................401 738-7901
Nicholas Picchione II, *President*
Michael Halperson, *Exec VP*
Ann O Picchione, *Asst Treas*
▲ **EMP:** 60 **EST:** 1945
SQ FT: 40,000
SALES (est): 7.7MM **Privately Held**
WEB: www.databinding.com
SIC: 2789 Bookbinding/Related Work
PA: Dome Enterprises Trust
10 New England Way
Warwick RI 02886

(G-21349)
DAVIDON INDUSTRIES INC
Also Called: Davidon Alloys
87 Dewey Ave (02886-2431)
PHONE..................................401 737-8380
Donald Dinuccio, *President*
Maria Toneva, *Sales Mgr*
Jorge Mendez, *Marketing Staff*
▲ **EMP:** 15
SQ FT: 4,000
SALES (est): 2.6MM **Privately Held**
WEB: www.davidonindustries.com
SIC: 3585 Mfg Refrigeration/Heating Equipment

GEOGRAPHIC

(G-21350)
DAVOL INC (DH)
100 Crossings Blvd (02886-2850)
P.O. Box 1210 (02887-1210)
PHONE..................................401 825-8300
B P Kelly, *President*
Andre St Laurent, *Purchasing*
Kristin Lynch, *Accounts Mgr*
Arlene M Andreozzi, *Representative*
▲ **EMP:** 22
SQ FT: 180,000
SALES (est): 6.3MM
SALES (corp-wide): 15.9B **Publicly Held**
WEB: www.perfixplug.com
SIC: 3841 Mfg Surgical/Medical Instruments

(G-21351)
DAYTON SUPERIOR CORPORATION
3970 Post Rd (02886-9235)
PHONE..................................401 885-1934
Claudette Harris, *Branch Mgr*
EMP: 40
SALES (corp-wide): 42.9B **Publicly Held**
SIC: 3315 Mfr Specialized Metal Accessories For Use In Concrete Construction
HQ: Dayton Superior Corporation
1125 Byers Rd
Miamisburg OH 45342
937 866-0711

(G-21352)
DITTMAR & MCNEIL CPA S INC
501 Centerville Rd # 103 (02886-4367)
PHONE..................................401 921-2600
Dunckan McNeil, *Vice Pres*
Randolph Dittmar,
EMP: 5
SQ FT: 1,200
SALES (est): 514K **Privately Held**
SIC: 2048 5191 8721 Mfg Prepared Feeds Whol Farm Supplies Accounting/Auditing/Bookkeeping

(G-21353)
DOME ENTERPRISES TRUST (PA)
10 New England Way (02886-6904)
P.O. Box 1220 (02887-1220)
PHONE..................................401 738-7900
Nicholas Picchione II, *Trustee*
EMP: 8
SQ FT: 40,000
SALES (est): 11.9MM **Privately Held**
SIC: 2789 Book Bindery

(G-21354)
DOME PUBLISHING COMPANY INC (HQ)
Also Called: Dome Industries
10 New England Way (02886-6913)
P.O. Box 1220 (02887-1220)
PHONE..................................401 738-7900
Michael Halperson, *President*
Ann O Picchione, *Vice Pres*
John S Renza Jr, *Treasurer*
Jeffrey Avanzino, *Sales Staff*
Denise Deschenes, *Admin Sec*
EMP: 35 **EST:** 1947
SQ FT: 50,000
SALES (est): 4.2MM **Privately Held**
SIC: 2789 Bookbinding/Related Work

(G-21355)
DROITCOUR COMPANY
28 Graystone St (02886-1384)
PHONE..................................401 737-4646
Mike Droitcour, *President*
Andrew Droitcour, *Vice Pres*
Joseph Walsh, *Foreman/Supr*
Eddy Jim, *Opers Staff*
Mike Davis, *Treasurer*
EMP: 80
SQ FT: 58,000
SALES (est): 15.6MM **Privately Held**
WEB: www.droitcour.com
SIC: 3451 Mfg Screw Machine Products

(G-21356)
DUR A FLEX MOTOR SPORTS
875 W Shore Rd (02889-2731)
PHONE..................................401 739-0202
Carl Gustafson, *Principal*
EMP: 3
SALES (est): 361.3K **Privately Held**
SIC: 3732 Boatbuilding/Repairing

(G-21357)
E G & G SEALOL EAGLE INC
Also Called: Dickson Eagle
33 Plan Way Bldg 5 (02886-1013)
PHONE..................................401 732-0333
Paul Grant, *General Mgr*
EMP: 17
SALES (est): 1.3MM **Privately Held**
SIC: 3053 Mfg Gaskets/Packing/Sealing Devices

(G-21358)
EAGLE AMERICA INC
33 Plan Way Bldg 5 (02886-1013)
PHONE..................................401 732-0333
Raymond F Grandchamp Jr, *President*
▲ **EMP:** 16
SALES (est): 3.9MM **Privately Held**
WEB: www.eagle-america.net
SIC: 3592 Mfg Carburetors/Pistons/Rings

(G-21359)
ELITE CUSTOM COMPOUNDING INC
303 Kilvert St (02886-1344)
PHONE..................................401 921-2136
EMP: 4
SALES (est): 153.6K **Privately Held**
SIC: 3087 Custom Compounding-Purchased Resins

(G-21360)
ENOW INC
133 Hallene Rd B2 (02886-2449)
PHONE..................................401 732-7080
Jeffrey Flath, *President*
Ellen Flath, *Admin Asst*
▲ **EMP:** 12
SALES (est): 1.2MM **Privately Held**
SIC: 3674 Mfg Semiconductors/Related Devices

(G-21361)
ETCO INCORPORATED (PA)
25 Bellows St (02888-1501)
PHONE..................................401 467-2400
David Dunn, *Ch of Bd*
Afshin Etebar, *President*
John Macaluso, *President*
Bob Etebar, *COO*
Andrew Coyle, *QC Mgr*
◆ **EMP:** 80 **EST:** 1947
SQ FT: 25,000
SALES (est): 24.8MM **Privately Held**
WEB: www.etco.com
SIC: 3469 3061 Mfg Metal Stampings Mfg Mechanical Rubber Goods

(G-21362)
EUROSOCKS NORTH AMERICA INC
300 Centerville Rd # 450 (02886-0200)
PHONE..................................401 739-6500
Alan Jacober, *President*
Sanford Altman, *Principal*
EMP: 3
SALES (est): 300K **Privately Held**
SIC: 2252 Market Athletic Socks

(G-21363)
FARSOUNDER INC
151 Lavan St (02888-1017)
PHONE..................................401 784-6700
Cheryl M Zimmerman, *President*
Evan Lapisky, *Engineer*
Heath Henley, *Software Engr*
EMP: 6
SQ FT: 3,000
SALES (est): 1MM **Privately Held**
WEB: www.farsounder.com
SIC: 3812 Mfg Search/Navigation Equipment

(G-21364)
FRANK SHATZ & CO
61 Dewey Ave Ste D (02886-2471)
PHONE..................................401 739-1822
Frank Shatz, *President*
Keith Leclair, *General Mgr*
Randy Shatz, *Vice Pres*
EMP: 23 **EST:** 1959
SQ FT: 20,000
SALES (est): 4MM **Privately Held**
WEB: www.frankshatzcompany.com
SIC: 2542 Mfg Partitions/Fixtures-Nonwood

(G-21365)
GEIB REFINING CORPORATION
399 Kilvert St (02886-1381)
PHONE..................................401 738-8560
Gladys Geib, *Ch of Bd*
Kenneth Wightman, *President*
James Geib, *Vice Pres*
Robert Slack, *Vice Pres*
Ron Steele, *Vice Pres*
EMP: 28
SQ FT: 15,000
SALES (est): 6.4MM **Privately Held**
SIC: 3339 Primary Nonferrous Metal Producer

(G-21366)
GEOTEC INC
89 Bellows St (02888-1503)
PHONE..................................401 228-7395
Thomas Jellison, *President*
Tammy Healey, *QC Mgr*
EMP: 21
SQ FT: 20,000
SALES: 2MM **Privately Held**
SIC: 3841 7389 8742 Mfg Surgical/Medical Instruments Business Services Management Consulting Services

(G-21367)
GEPP LLC
Also Called: Go East Promotions
83 Vermont Ave Bldg 3-4 (02888-3054)
PHONE..................................401 808-8004
Mark Mercurio, *President*
Brian Richards, *Vice Pres*
▲ **EMP:** 11 **EST:** 2011
SALES: 13MM **Privately Held**
SIC: 3993 Mfg Signs/Advertising Specialties

(G-21368)
GF HEALTH PRODUCTS INC
Also Called: Graham Field Bandage
33 Plan Way Bldg 2 (02886-1013)
PHONE..................................401 738-1500
Donna Carlin, *Office Mgr*
Linda Peterson, *Branch Mgr*
EMP: 20
SALES (corp-wide): 80.4MM **Privately Held**
SIC: 3842 Mfg Surgical Appliances/Supplies
PA: Gf Health Products, Inc.
1 Graham Field Way
Atlanta GA 30340
770 368-4700

(G-21369)
GLENN LLC
Also Called: Glenn, Inc.
300 Jefferson Blvd # 206 (02888-3860)
PHONE..................................800 521-0065
Tim Gooling, *President*
EMP: 7
SALES (est): 160.7K
SALES (corp-wide): 9.1MM **Privately Held**
SIC: 2911 Petroleum Refiner
HQ: Azelis Americas, Llc
262 Harbor Dr Fl 1
Stamford CT 06902
203 274-8691

(G-21370)
HERFF JONES LLC
Also Called: Herff Jones - Dieges & Clust
150 Herff Jones Way (02888-1332)
P.O. Box 6500, Providence (02940-6500)
PHONE..................................401 331-1240
Robert Potts, *Mng Member*
EMP: 10
SALES (corp-wide): 1.1B **Privately Held**
WEB: www.herffjones.com
SIC: 3911 Mfg Precious Metal Jewelry
HQ: Herff Jones, Llc
4501 W 62nd St
Indianapolis IN 46268
800 419-5462

(G-21371)
HONEYWELL INTERNATIONAL INC
65 Acceri Rd Ste 1 (02886)
PHONE..................................973 455-2000
Heidi Kuster, *Branch Mgr*
EMP: 3
SALES (corp-wide): 41.8B **Publicly Held**
WEB: www.honeywell.com
SIC: 3724 Mfg Aerospace Systems
PA: Honeywell International Inc.
300 S Tryon St
Charlotte NC 28202
973 455-2000

(G-21372)
HOPKINS HILL SAND & STONE LLC
400 Lincoln Ave (02888-3049)
PHONE..................................401 739-8300
Joseph Catelli, *Principal*
EMP: 6
SALES (est): 690.6K **Privately Held**
SIC: 1442 Construction Sand/Gravel

(G-21373)
HOT STUFF RI INC
70 Jefferson Blvd (02888-1056)
PHONE..................................401 781-7500
Harry Harootunian, *President*
EMP: 3
SALES (est): 220K **Privately Held**
SIC: 3581 Mfg Vending Machines

(G-21374)
IMAGE PRINTING & COPYING INC
33 Plan Way Bldg 7 (02886-1013)
PHONE..................................401 737-9311
Kevin Martin, *Principal*
Jim Tracey, *Sales Staff*
Bill Dier, *Manager*
Frank Freitas, *Representative*
Joan Newell, *Representative*
EMP: 17
SALES (est): 3.4MM **Privately Held**
WEB: www.imageprintingri.com
SIC: 2759 Commercial Printing

(G-21375)
IMPERIAL CERAMICS
1621 Warwick Ave (02889-1525)
PHONE..................................401 732-0500
Linda Seguin, *Owner*
EMP: 3
SALES: 180K **Privately Held**
SIC: 3999 Mfg Novelties Bric-A-Brac & Hobby Kits

(G-21376)
INTERNATIONAL TECHNOLOGIES INC
Also Called: River Point Station
115 Maple St (02888-2130)
PHONE..................................401 467-6907
Ronald Elsdoerfer, *CEO*
◆ **EMP:** 15
SQ FT: 10,000
SALES (est): 950K **Privately Held**
WEB: www.internationaltechnologies.com
SIC: 3629 Mfg Electrical Industrial Apparatus

(G-21377)
J P I INC
405 Kilvert St Ste E (02886-1375)
PHONE..................................401 737-7433
Daniel Leonard, *President*
EMP: 5
SQ FT: 1,800
SALES (est): 581K **Privately Held**
SIC: 3961 Mfg & Distributor Of Jewelry & Costume Novelties

(G-21378)
JADE MANUFACTURING COMPANY INC
132 Meadow St (02886-6909)
PHONE..................................401 737-2400
Donald Boyle, *President*
Chris Burch, *Vice Pres*
Steve Gruner, *Mfg Staff*
EMP: 20
SQ FT: 8,000

▲ = Import ▼=Export
◆ =Import/Export

SALES: 2MM Privately Held
SIC: 3599 Mfg Industrial Machinery

(G-21379)
JAY PACKAGING GROUP INC (PA)
100 Warwick Industrial Dr (02886-2486)
PHONE....401 244-1300
Richard Kelly, *President*
Fernando A Lemos, *CFO*
▲ EMP: 100
SQ FT: 180,000
SALES (est): 17.1MM Privately Held
SIC: 2752 3089 Lithographic Commercial Printing Mfg Plastic Products

(G-21380)
JOHN CRANE INC
75 Commerce Dr (02886-2429)
PHONE....401 463-8700
EMP: 71
SALES (corp-wide): 3.1B Privately Held
SIC: 3053 Mfg Gaskets
HQ: John Crane Inc.
227 W Monroe St Ste 1800
Chicago IL 60606
312 605-7800

(G-21381)
JOHN CRANE SEALOL INC (DH)
Also Called: Eagle Div
75 Commerce Dr 101 (02886-2429)
PHONE....401 732-0715
Michael Galluccio, *President*
D Mills, *Engineer*
Denis Rainville, *Engineer*
Paul Richards, *Mktg Dir*
Jesse Fordyce, *Executive*
▼ EMP: 200
SALES (est): 30.9MM
SALES (corp-wide): 3.1B Privately Held
WEB: www.johncranesealol.com
SIC: 3053 3492 3599 Mfg Gaskets Packing & Sealing Devices & Hydraulic & Pneumatic Aircraft Control Valves & Metal Bellows
HQ: John Crane Inc.
227 W Monroe St Ste 1800
Chicago IL 60606
312 605-7800

(G-21382)
KEARFLEX ENGINEERING COMPANY
66 Cypress St (02888-2119)
PHONE....401 781-4900
Thomas Kearney, *President*
Medeiros Lynn, *Purch Agent*
Keith Kearney, *Treasurer*
Norma Capron, *Controller*
EMP: 18
SALES: 3.4MM Privately Held
WEB: www.kearflex.com
SIC: 3812 3829 3625 Mfg Search/Navgatn Equip Mfg Measure/Control Dvcs Mfg Relay/Indstl Control

(G-21383)
KENNEY MANUFACTURING COMPANY (PA)
1000 Jefferson Blvd (02886-2200)
PHONE....401 739-2200
G D Kenney, *Ch of Bd*
Leslie M Kenney, *President*
Matt Fearon, *Purch Mgr*
Agnes Sarudi, *Buyer*
Roberto Perez, *Sales Mgr*
◆ EMP: 500 EST: 1914
SQ FT: 300,000
SALES (est): 91.2MM Privately Held
WEB: www.kenney.com
SIC: 3261 2511 3699 3499 Mfg Vetreous Plmbng Fxtr Mfg Wood Household Furn Mfg Elec Mach/Equip/Supp Mfg Misc Fab Metal Prdts Mfg Wood Partitions/Fixt

(G-21384)
LADY ANN CANDIES
Also Called: Fruit & Nut House
86 Warwick Industrial Dr # 1 (02886-2464)
PHONE....401 738-4321
John Burke, *Owner*
EMP: 30
SQ FT: 3,000
SALES (est): 3.5MM Privately Held
SIC: 2064 5441 5961 2066 Mfg Candy/Confectionery Ret Candy/Confectionery Ret Mail-Order House Mfg Chocolate/Cocoa Prdt

(G-21385)
LUMETTA INC
33 Minnesota Ave (02888-6010)
PHONE....401 691-3994
William Prichett, *Owner*
Pat Martin, *Controller*
Ian Prichett, *Sales Mgr*
EMP: 38
SQ FT: 36,000
SALES: 10MM Privately Held
SIC: 3646 Mfg Commercial Lighting Fixtures

(G-21386)
MALEY LASER PROCESSING INC
1280 Jefferson Blvd (02886-2501)
P.O. Box 81024 (02888-0931)
PHONE....401 732-8400
Kurt R Maley, *President*
EMP: 15
SQ FT: 44,000
SALES (est): 3.2MM Privately Held
WEB: www.maleylaser.com
SIC: 3699 3498 Mfg Electrical Equipment/Supplies Mfg Fabricated Pipe/Fittings

(G-21387)
MAROS PRODUCTS INCORPORATED
36 Bellair Ave Unit 4 (02886-2269)
PHONE....401 885-1788
Mark O Dermanouelian, *President*
EMP: 5 EST: 2011
SALES (est): 565.9K Privately Held
SIC: 3469 Mfg Metal Stampings

(G-21388)
MCLEOD OPTICAL COMPANY INC (PA)
50 Jefferson Park Rd (02888-1016)
P.O. Box 6045, Providence (02940-6045)
PHONE....401 467-3000
Scott McLeod, *President*
Diane Hague, *Cust Mgr*
Larry Wentworth, *Sales Staff*
Don Mattaboni, *Branch Mgr*
EMP: 50 EST: 1922
SQ FT: 12,900
SALES (est): 5.8MM Privately Held
SIC: 3851 5048 Ophthalmic Lens Grinding & Whol Ophthalmic Goods

(G-21389)
MILLARD WIRE COMPANY (PA)
Also Called: Millard Jewelry Division
449 Warwick Industrial Dr (02886-2460)
PHONE....401 737-9330
Daniel R La Croix Sr, *President*
Paul Gilgun, *Corp Secy*
Rich Daigneault, *Vice Pres*
Richard Daigneault, *Vice Pres*
Scott Hague, *Vice Pres*
▲ EMP: 60 EST: 1991
SQ FT: 110,000
SALES (est): 13.2MM Privately Held
WEB: www.millardwire.com
SIC: 3547 3351 Mfg Rolling Mill Machinery Copper Rolling/Drawing

(G-21390)
MILLARD WIRE COMPANY
Millard Wireland
259 Industrial Dr (02886)
PHONE....401 737-9330
Daniel R La Croix Sr, *Branch Mgr*
EMP: 3
SALES (est): 247.7K
SALES (corp-wide): 13.2MM Privately Held
WEB: www.millardwire.com
SIC: 3547 Mfg Rolling Mill Machinery
PA: Millard Wire Company
449 Warwick Industrial Dr
Warwick RI 02886
401 737-9330

(G-21391)
MILLER CORRUGATED BOX CO
289 Kilvert St (02886-1344)
P.O. Box 7229 (02887-7229)
PHONE....401 739-7020
Barry Miller, *President*
Paul Miller, *Vice Pres*
EMP: 20
SQ FT: 50,000
SALES (est): 3.4MM Privately Held
WEB: www.millerbox.net
SIC: 2653 Mfg Corrugated/Solid Fiber Boxes

(G-21392)
MODERN PLASTICS
380 Jefferson Blvd Ste A (02886-1356)
PHONE....401 732-0415
Rita Cesario, *Manager*
EMP: 5
SALES (est): 476.3K Privately Held
SIC: 2821 Mfg Plastic Products

(G-21393)
NATIONAL CHAIN COMPANY (PA)
55 Access Rd Ste 500 (02886-1000)
PHONE....401 732-3634
Steven Cipolla, *President*
Miguel Valdez, *General Mgr*
Ralph Cipolla, *Vice Pres*
Vincent Ferrante, *Vice Pres*
Al Wiesner, *Vice Pres*
▲ EMP: 99
SALES (est): 12.2MM Privately Held
WEB: www.natchain.com
SIC: 3911 Mfg Precious Metal Jewelry

(G-21394)
NATIONAL VELOUR CORPORATION
36 Bellair Ave (02886-2268)
PHONE....401 737-8300
Oscar Der Manouelian, *President*
▲ EMP: 25
SQ FT: 65,000
SALES (est): 3.6MM Privately Held
WEB: www.nationalvelour.com
SIC: 2299 Mfg Textile Goods

(G-21395)
NATUS MEDICAL INCORPORATED
200 Metro Center Blvd (02886-1779)
PHONE....401 732-5251
Michael Morawetz, *Vice Pres*
EMP: 6
SALES (est): 534.2K Privately Held
SIC: 3845 Mfg Electromedical Equipment

(G-21396)
NEW ENGLAND ORTHOPEDICS INC (PA)
220 Toll Gate Rd Ste A (02886-4418)
PHONE....401 739-9838
Joseph Infantolino, *President*
Susan Infantolino, *Vice Pres*
EMP: 7
SQ FT: 500
SALES (est): 626.5K Privately Held
WEB: www.brokernet-usa.com
SIC: 3842 Mfg Surgical Appliances/Supplies

(G-21397)
OCEAN DATA EQUIPMENT CORP
222 Metro Center Blvd (02886-1746)
PHONE....401 454-1810
EMP: 15
SALES (est): 916.4K Privately Held
SIC: 3829 Mfg Survey Equipment

(G-21398)
OLDCASTLE BUILDINGENVELOPE INC
333 Straw Field Rd 3 (02886)
PHONE....866 653-2278
Edwin B Hathaway, *Branch Mgr*
EMP: 6
SALES (corp-wide): 29.7B Privately Held
SIC: 3826 Mfg Analytical Instruments
HQ: Oldcastle Buildingenvelope, Inc.
5005 Lndn B Jnsn Fwy 10
Dallas TX 75244
214 273-3400

(G-21399)
ORACLE CORPORATION
20 Altieri Way (02886-1780)
PHONE....401 658-3900
EMP: 5
SALES (corp-wide): 39.5B Publicly Held
SIC: 7372 Prepackaged Software Services
PA: Oracle Corporation
500 Oracle Pkwy
Redwood City CA 94065
650 506-7000

(G-21400)
PAULEY CO
1924 Elmwood Ave (02888-2402)
P.O. Box 351, East Greenwich (02818-0351)
PHONE....401 467-2930
Alan Webber, *President*
Betsy Golden, *Vice Pres*
James Webber, *Vice Pres*
EMP: 10
SQ FT: 4,000
SALES: 125K Privately Held
SIC: 3961 Mfg Costume Jewelry

(G-21401)
PEASE & CURREN INCORPORATED
75 Pennsylvania Ave (02888-3028)
PHONE....401 738-6449
Francis H Curren III, *President*
Lisa Rowe,
EMP: 40 EST: 1916
SQ FT: 30,000
SALES (est): 8.3MM Privately Held
WEB: www.peaseandcurren.com
SIC: 3341 Secondary Nonferrous Metal Producer

(G-21402)
PEP CENTRAL INC
Also Called: Pentair Electronic Packaging
170 Commerce Dr (02886-2430)
PHONE....401 732-3770
Randall Hogan, *CEO*
▲ EMP: 4982 EST: 1981
SQ FT: 166,000
SALES (est): 228.8MM Privately Held
SIC: 3544 3469 7373 3496 Mfg Dies/Tools/Jigs/Fixt Mfg Metal Stampings Computer Systems Design Mfg Misc Fab Wire Prdts
HQ: Schroff, Inc.
170 Commerce Dr
Warwick RI 02886
763 204-7700

(G-21403)
PERRY PAVING
20 Keystone Dr (02889-8519)
PHONE....401 732-1730
Joe Perry, *Principal*
EMP: 5
SALES (est): 474.4K Privately Held
SIC: 2951 1611 Mfg Asphalt Mixtures/Blocks Highway/Street Construction

(G-21404)
PMC LIGHTING INC
100 Gilbane St (02886-6902)
PHONE....401 738-7266
Larry Crystal, *President*
Arthur Goldstein, *Vice Pres*
▲ EMP: 38
SQ FT: 28,000
SALES (est): 7.9MM Privately Held
SIC: 3646 Mfg Commercial Lighting Fixtures

(G-21405)
PRINTCRAFT INC
3076 Post Rd (02886-3166)
PHONE....401 739-0700
Stephen Schofield, *President*
EMP: 5 EST: 1954
SQ FT: 3,000

GEOGRAPHIC

SALES (est): 757K **Privately Held**
WEB: www.printcraftri.com
SIC: 2752 Lithographic Commercial Printing

(G-21406)
PROVIDENCE MACHINE AND TL WORK
126 Bellows St (02888-1504)
PHONE..................................401 751-1526
Don Nguyen, *Owner*
Rachel Nguyen, *Treasurer*
EMP: 6
SQ FT: 12,000
SALES (est): 798.6K **Privately Held**
SIC: 3599 Mfg Industrial Machinery

(G-21407)
PRUEFER METALWORKS INC
320 Elm St (02888-3123)
P.O. Box 8407 (02888-0597)
PHONE..................................401 785-4688
Fax: 401 785-4771
EMP: 18
SALES (est): 1.7MM **Privately Held**
WEB: www.pruefermetalworks.com
SIC: 3915 Metal Jewerly Findings

(G-21408)
QUICK FITTING INC
30 Plan Way (02886-1012)
P.O. Box 164, Tiverton (02878-0164)
PHONE..................................401 734-9500
David B Crompton, *President*
Frank Kosky, *Exec VP*
Michael Pappas, *Exec VP*
James Trice, *Vice Pres*
John Cronin, *Mfg Staff*
▲ **EMP:** 87
SALES (est): 18.1MM **Privately Held**
SIC: 3432 3643 Mfg Plumbing Fixture Fittings Mfg Conductive Wiring Devices

(G-21409)
RAMCO INC
205 Hallene Rd Unit 207 (02886-2452)
PHONE..................................401 739-4343
Peter F Holmes, *President*
William May, *Admin Sec*
EMP: 5
SALES (est): 681.1K **Privately Held**
WEB: www.tannewitz.com
SIC: 3961 Mfg Award And Recognition Jewelry

(G-21410)
RBC INDUSTRIES INC
80 Cypress St (02888-2119)
PHONE..................................401 941-3000
◆ **EMP:** 73 **EST:** 1976
SQ FT: 22,000
SALES (est): 24.1MM **Privately Held**
WEB: www.rbcepoxy.com
SIC: 2821 2822 5084 Plastics Materials Or Resins, Nec

(G-21411)
RENOVA LIGHTING SYSTEMS INC
36 Bellair Ave Unit 4 (02886-2269)
PHONE..................................800 635-6682
Rick Edwards, *President*
▲ **EMP:** 25
SQ FT: 20,000
SALES (est): 4.8MM **Privately Held**
WEB: www.renova.com
SIC: 3646 Mfg Commercial Lighting Fixtures

(G-21412)
RHODE ISLAND DRIVESHAFT SUP CO
Also Called: Rhode Island Driveshaft & Sup
3 Jefferson Blvd (02888-1032)
PHONE..................................401 941-0210
Toll Free:..888 -
Thomas Crosby Sr, *President*
Tom Crosby, *Vice Pres*
Olga Crosby, *Treasurer*
EMP: 3 **EST:** 1977
SQ FT: 2,000
SALES: 1MM **Privately Held**
SIC: 3714 7539 Mfg Motor Vehicle Parts/Accessories Automotive Repair

(G-21413)
RITEC INC
60 Alhambra Rd Ste 5 (02886-1442)
PHONE..................................401 738-3660
Mark McKenna, *CEO*
Bruce B Chick, *Ch of Bd*
Michael A Ragosta, *Vice Pres*
Gary Petersen, *Admin Sec*
EMP: 10
SQ FT: 2,800
SALES (est): 1.2MM **Privately Held**
WEB: www.ritecinc.com
SIC: 3699 Mfg Electronic Research Instruments

(G-21414)
RITRONICS INC
60 Alhambra Rd Ste 1 (02886-1442)
PHONE..................................401 732-8175
James T Hagan, *President*
Russell J Hall, *Vice Pres*
Robert F Nazzeo, *Treasurer*
EMP: 10
SALES (est): 1.7MM **Privately Held**
SIC: 3679 Mfg Electronic Components

(G-21415)
RJB MEAT PROCESSING
466 Atlantic Ave (02888-2637)
PHONE..................................401 781-5315
EMP: 3
SALES (est): 184.3K **Privately Held**
SIC: 2011 Meat Packing Plant

(G-21416)
ROMANO INVESTMENTS INC
333 Strawberry Field Rd # 11 (02886-2476)
PHONE..................................401 691-3400
Raymond G Menna, *President*
Kenneth Menna, *Vice Pres*
EMP: 40
SQ FT: 39,600
SALES (est): 6.3MM **Privately Held**
SIC: 2752 Lithographic Commercial Printing

(G-21417)
RONA INCORPORATED
70 Dewey Ave (02886-2432)
PHONE..................................401 737-4388
EMP: 6 **EST:** 1958
SALES (est): 706.4K **Privately Held**
SIC: 3364 Mfg Nonferrous Die Castings

(G-21418)
RUSCO STEEL COMPANY
25 Bleachery Ct (02886-1201)
P.O. Box 7630 (02887-7630)
PHONE..................................401 732-0548
Robert S Russell, *President*
EMP: 70
SALES (est): 12.2MM **Privately Held**
SIC: 3449 Mfg Misc Structural Metalwork

(G-21419)
S & P HEAT TREATING INC
Also Called: S & P Metallurgy Service
16a Dewey Ave (02886-2432)
PHONE..................................401 737-9272
Arvind Patel, *President*
Rajul Patel, *Vice Pres*
Michael Rapoza, *Plant Mgr*
EMP: 13
SQ FT: 6,000
SALES (est): 1.4MM **Privately Held**
WEB: www.spheattreating.com
SIC: 3398 Metal Heat Treating

(G-21420)
SANDSTROM CARBIDE PDTS CORP
140 Imera Ave (02886-1435)
PHONE..................................401 739-5220
Jon J Ash, *President*
Chris Ash, *Manager*
EMP: 10 **EST:** 1941
SQ FT: 4,800
SALES (est): 1.1MM **Privately Held**
SIC: 3599 Mfg Industrial Machinery

(G-21421)
SCHROFF INC (HQ)
Also Called: Pentair Electronic Packaging
170 Commerce Dr (02886-2430)
PHONE..................................763 204-7700
Beth Wozniak, *CEO*
Sara Zawoyski, *Vice Pres*
Mark Borin, *Treasurer*
Scott Richards, *Prgrmr*
Spencer Leslie, *Director*
▲ **EMP:** 260 **EST:** 1982
SQ FT: 100,000
SALES (est): 228.8MM **Privately Held**
SIC: 3469 7629 Mfg Metal Stampings Electrical Repair

(G-21422)
SCHROFF INC
170 Commerce Dr (02886-2430)
PHONE..................................401 535-4826
Brett Windrow, *Manager*
EMP: 100 **Privately Held**
SIC: 3469 Mfg Metal Stampings
HQ: Schroff, Inc.
170 Commerce Dr
Warwick RI 02886
763 204-7700

(G-21423)
SCW CORPORATION
Also Called: Day-O-Lite Fluorescent Fixs
126 Chestnut St (02888-2104)
PHONE..................................401 808-6849
Steve Weisman, *President*
Cheryl Weisman, *Vice Pres*
EMP: 34 **EST:** 1935
SQ FT: 30,000
SALES (est): 7.6MM **Privately Held**
WEB: www.dayolite.com
SIC: 3645 3646 Mfg Residential Lighting Fixtures Mfg Commercial Lighting Fixtures

(G-21424)
SERVICE PLUS PRESS INC
662 Warwick Ave (02888-2632)
PHONE..................................401 461-2929
John F Marotto Jr, *President*
Christopher Marotto, *Vice Pres*
Beverly Huges, *Admin Sec*
Donna Roles, *Admin Sec*
EMP: 3 **EST:** 1922
SQ FT: 15,000
SALES (est): 190K **Privately Held**
SIC: 2759 2752 Commercial Printing Lithographic Commercial Printing

(G-21425)
SGRI INC
1643 Warwick Ave Unit 164 (02889-1525)
PHONE..................................401 473-7320
Errol Graham, *Principal*
EMP: 3
SALES (est): 243.9K **Privately Held**
SIC: 3823 Mfg Process Control Instruments

(G-21426)
SMART TEXTILE PRODUCTS LLC
240 Bald Hill Rd (02886-1126)
PHONE..................................401 427-1374
Richard Kalhofer, *Vice Pres*
Gary Goldberg, *Opers Staff*
EMP: 4
SALES (est): 162.3K **Privately Held**
SIC: 2299 Mfg Textile Goods

(G-21427)
SONCO WORLDWIDE INC
450 Pavilion Ave (02888-6035)
PHONE..................................401 406-3761
Steve Greer, *CEO*
Bill King, *Principal*
EMP: 10
SALES (corp-wide): 60.3MM **Privately Held**
SIC: 3315 5039 2421 7359 Mfg Steel Wire/Rltd Prdt Whol Cnstn Materials Sawmill/Planing Mill Equipment Rental/Leasing Business Services
PA: Sonco Worldwide, Inc.
6500 Ammendale Rd
Beltsville MD 20705
240 487-2490

(G-21428)
SPECTRAL INC
50 Minnesota Ave Unit 1 (02888-6014)
P.O. Box 7111 (02887-7111)
PHONE..................................401 921-2690
Michael C Craig, *President*
Carolyn Picozzi, *Vice Pres*
EMP: 5
SQ FT: 10,000
SALES (est): 970.7K **Privately Held**
WEB: www.spectralchemical.com
SIC: 2841 Mfg Industrial Detergents

(G-21429)
STANDARD CHAIN CO
55 Access Rd Ste 500 (02886-1045)
P.O. Box 66, North Attleboro MA (02761-0066)
PHONE..................................508 695-6611
Gregory C Smith, *President*
EMP: 32
SQ FT: 22,000
SALES (est): 4.2MM **Privately Held**
SIC: 3496 Mfg Misc Fabricated Wire Products

(G-21430)
STATE-WIDE MLTIPLE LISTING SVC
100 Bignall St (02888-1005)
PHONE..................................401 785-3650
Gilbert Bricault, *President*
Susan Arnold, *Vice Pres*
Joyce Lafortune, *Executive Asst*
EMP: 9
SALES: 1.5MM
SALES (corp-wide): 3MM **Privately Held**
WEB: www.statewidemls.com
SIC: 2721 Real Estate Information Services
PA: Rhode Island Association Of Realtors, Inc
100 Bignall St
Warwick RI 02888
401 785-3650

(G-21431)
SUMMIT PRINTING LLC
Also Called: Minuteman Press
155 Jefferson Blvd Ste 3 (02888-3878)
PHONE..................................401 732-7848
Valerie Chanoux,
Karen Fraielli,
EMP: 3
SQ FT: 1,200
SALES (est): 493.1K **Privately Held**
WEB: www.mmpwarwick.com
SIC: 2752 Comm Prtg Litho

(G-21432)
SUPERMEDIA LLC
Also Called: Verizon
300 Jefferson Blvd # 201 (02888-3888)
PHONE..................................401 468-1500
Todd Sanislow, *Manager*
EMP: 50
SALES (corp-wide): 1.6B **Privately Held**
WEB: www.verizon.superpages.com
SIC: 2741 Telephone Directory Publishing
HQ: Supermedia Llc
2200 W Airfield Dr
Dfw Airport TX 75261
972 453-7000

(G-21433)
SWAROVSKI NORTH AMERICA LTD
400 Bald Hill Rd (02886-1617)
PHONE..................................401 732-0794
Gloria Quinn, *Exec Dir*
Phr Casey, *Analyst*
EMP: 7
SALES (corp-wide): 4.7B **Privately Held**
SIC: 3961 Mfg Costume Jewelry
HQ: Swarovski North America Limited
1 Kenney Dr
Cranston RI 02920
401 463-6400

(G-21434)
T TECH MACHINE INC
11 Knight St Bldg A (02886-1281)
PHONE..................................401 732-3590
Earl Tillinghast, *President*
John Ficorilli, *Vice Pres*
EMP: 15
SQ FT: 9,000
SALES (est): 2.6MM **Privately Held**
WEB: www.t-techmachine.com
SIC: 3599 Mfg Industrial Machinery

▲ = Import ▼=Export
◆ =Import/Export

(G-21435)
TAYLOR COMMUNICATIONS INC
2346 Post Rd Ste 101 (02886-2217)
PHONE....................................401 738-0257
EMP: 7
SALES (corp-wide): 3.4B **Privately Held**
SIC: 2759 Mfg Electronic Business Forms
HQ: Taylor Communications, Inc.
4205 S 96th St
Omaha NE 56003
402 898-6422

(G-21436)
UNIT TOOL CO
101 Venturi Ave Frnt 1 (02888-1582)
P.O. Box 8699 (02888-0595)
PHONE....................................401 781-2647
Roger Ferragamo, *President*
Joseph Ferragamo Jr, *Vice Pres*
EMP: 30 **EST:** 1959
SQ FT: 45,000
SALES (est): 4.1MM **Privately Held**
WEB: www.unittoolco.com
SIC: 3915 3961 Mfg Jewelers' Materials Mfg Costume Jewelry

(G-21437)
VINCENT METALS CORPORATION
33 Plan Way Bldg 3c (02886-1013)
PHONE....................................401 737-4167
Blake Vincent, *President*
Greg Anderson, *Engineer*
EMP: 4 **EST:** 2001
SALES (est): 626.4K **Privately Held**
SIC: 3429 Mfg Hardware

(G-21438)
VISHAY SPRAGUE INC
Also Called: Vishay Electrofilm
111 Gilbane St (02886-6901)
PHONE....................................401 738-9150
Gerald Paul, *President*
Robert A Freece, *Senior VP*
Sue Newman, *Purch Agent*
Richard N Grubb, *Treasurer*
William J Spires, *Admin Sec*
EMP: 1393
SQ FT: 240,000
SALES (est): 149.7MM
SALES (corp-wide): 3B **Publicly Held**
SIC: 3629 Mfg Electrical Industrial Apparatus
PA: Vishay Intertechnology, Inc.
63 Lancaster Ave
Malvern PA 19355
610 644-1300

(G-21439)
VOICESCRIPT TECHNOLOGIES
193 Crestwood Rd (02886-9436)
PHONE....................................401 524-2246
Andrew Levine, *CEO*
Bruce Hrovat, *President*
EMP: 20 **EST:** 2017
SALES (est): 421K **Privately Held**
SIC: 7372 Prepackaged Software

(G-21440)
VR INDUSTRIES INC
333 Strawberry Field Rd # 6 (02886-2459)
PHONE....................................401 732-6800
Brian Pestana, *President*
Wayne Sanita, *Mfg Mgr*
Alan Medeiros, *Manager*
Steven Nolan, *Director*
Stephen Gillissie, *Administration*
EMP: 35
SQ FT: 35,000
SALES: 7.5MM **Privately Held**
WEB: www.vrindustries.com
SIC: 3672 Mfg Printed Circuit Boards

(G-21441)
W L FULLER
7 Cypress St (02888-2124)
P.O. Box 8767 (02888-0767)
PHONE....................................401 467-2900
Gary Fuller, *President*
Lisa Fuller, *Vice Pres*
Deborah Fuller, *Admin Sec*
Diane Nobile, *Asst Sec*
EMP: 31 **EST:** 1930
SQ FT: 14,000
SALES (est): 4.1MM **Privately Held**
WEB: www.wlfuller.com
SIC: 3545 5085 Mfg Machine Tool Access Whol Industrial Supplies

(G-21442)
WAREHOUSE CABLES LLC
1303 Jefferson Blvd (02886-2531)
PHONE....................................401 737-5677
Peter L Hail,
▼ **EMP:** 4
SQ FT: 8,000
SALES (est): 464.6K **Privately Held**
SIC: 3577 5045 3644 5063 Mfg Computer Peripherals Whol Computer/Peripheral Mfg Nonconductv Wire Dvc Whol Electrical Equip

(G-21443)
WARWICK ICE CREAM COMPANY
743 Bald Hill Rd (02886-0713)
PHONE....................................401 821-8403
Gerard Bucci Jr, *President*
Thomas Bucci, *Vice Pres*
Antonette Bucci, *Admin Sec*
EMP: 22 **EST:** 1932
SQ FT: 25,000
SALES (est): 4.4MM **Privately Held**
WEB: www.warwickicecreamco.com
SIC: 2024 Mfg Ice Cream/Frozen Desert

(G-21444)
WEHR INDUSTRIES INC
Also Called: Pin-Line
14 Minnesota Ave (02888-6011)
PHONE....................................401 732-6565
W David Wehr, *President*
David A Wehr, *President*
Tracey Barker, *Credit Mgr*
▲ **EMP:** 20
SQ FT: 9,000
SALES (est): 1.6MM **Privately Held**
WEB: www.pinline.com
SIC: 3479 3961 3911 Coating/Engraving Service Mfg Costume Jewelry Mfg Precious Metal Jewelry

(G-21445)
WESTBAY WELDING & FABRICATION
Also Called: West Bay Welding & Fabrication
19 Locust Ave (02886-4732)
PHONE....................................401 737-2357
Andrew Quinn, *President*
EMP: 6
SALES (est): 640K **Privately Held**
SIC: 3441 Mfg Fabricated Structural Metal Products

(G-21446)
WHAT WOODWORKING
163 Reynolds Ave (02889-8735)
PHONE....................................617 429-2461
Paul Dooley, *Principal*
EMP: 4 **EST:** 2011
SALES (est): 301.6K **Privately Held**
SIC: 2431 Mfg Millwork

(G-21447)
WIESNER MANUFACTURING COMPANY
Also Called: Wiesner Chain
55 Access Rd Ste 700 (02886-1045)
PHONE....................................401 421-2406
Albert F Wiesner III, *President*
Al Wiesner, *Vice Pres*
EMP: 40 **EST:** 1890
SALES (est): 3.5MM **Privately Held**
SIC: 3911 3462 Mfg Precious Metal Jewelry Mfg Iron/Steel Forgings

(G-21448)
WINDMILL ASSOCIATES INC
Also Called: Atlantic Braiding Machinery
112 Knight St (02886-1225)
PHONE....................................401 732-4700
William Miller, *President*
Maureen Miller, *Admin Sec*
EMP: 6 **EST:** 1978
SQ FT: 7,900
SALES (est): 909.7K **Privately Held**
SIC: 3552 Mfg Textile Machinery

(G-21449)
WINTECH INTL CORP - NK
36 Bellair Ave (02886-2268)
PHONE....................................401 383-3307
Todd Manouelian, *President*
EMP: 7
SALES (est): 996.5K **Privately Held**
SIC: 2671 Mfg Packaging Paper/Film

(G-21450)
WINWHOLESALE INC
Also Called: Winsupply of Warwick
289 Kilvert St (02886-1344)
PHONE....................................401 732-1585
Tony Ruales, *Principal*
Brett Bouley, *Principal*
EMP: 6 **EST:** 1992
SALES (est): 107.5K **Privately Held**
SIC: 3463 Mfg Nonferrous Forgings

(G-21451)
WONDERLAND SMOKE SHOP INC
666 East Ave (02886-0736)
PHONE....................................401 823-3134
David Zuza, *President*
EMP: 4 **EST:** 1997
SALES (est): 555.5K **Privately Held**
SIC: 2131 5311 Mfg Chewing/Smoking Tobacco Department Store

West Greenwich
Kent County

(G-21452)
AMGEN INC
40 Technology Way Unit 1 (02817-1712)
PHONE....................................401 392-1200
Tom Byrne, *COO*
Ian Thompson, *Vice Pres*
Chris Genest, *Mfg Staff*
Randi Richert, *Mfg Staff*
Sam Guhan, *Research*
EMP: 100
SALES (corp-wide): 23.7B **Publicly Held**
WEB: www.amgen.com
SIC: 2836 8731 2834 Mfg Biological Products Commercial Physical Research Mfg Pharmaceutical Preparations
PA: Amgen Inc.
1 Amgen Center Dr
Thousand Oaks CA 91320
805 447-1000

(G-21453)
COLDSTASH INC
879 Hopkins Hill Rd (02817-2515)
PHONE....................................617 780-5603
EMP: 4 **EST:** 2014
SALES (est): 288.9K **Privately Held**
SIC: 3823 Mfg Process Control Instruments

(G-21454)
CONNEAUT INDUSTRIES INC
89 Hopkins Hill Rd (02817-1709)
P.O. Box 1425, Coventry (02816-0026)
PHONE....................................401 392-1110
Lancelot Banfield, *President*
John P Santos, *Principal*
Mario Diaz, *Prdtn Mgr*
Russell C Kibbe, *CFO*
Caryl Moore, *Manager*
▲ **EMP:** 55 **EST:** 1930
SQ FT: 50,000
SALES (est): 10.8MM **Privately Held**
WEB: www.conneaut.com
SIC: 2282 2241 2281 Throwing/Winding Mill Narrow Fabric Mill Yarn Spinning Mill

(G-21455)
CRANSTON PRINT WORKS COMPANY
Also Called: Cranston Trucking
25 Hopkins Hill Rd (02817-1707)
PHONE....................................401 397-2442
Mike Emmitt, *Manager*
EMP: 20
SALES (corp-wide): 147.3MM **Privately Held**
WEB: www.cpw.com
SIC: 2261 2262 Printer And Finisher Of Craft And Fashion Fabrics
PA: Cranston Print Works Company Inc
1381 Cranston St
Cranston RI 02920
401 943-4800

(G-21456)
IGT GLOBAL SOLUTIONS CORP
55 Technology Way (02817-1711)
PHONE....................................401 392-7025
Gillis Hill, *Principal*
EMP: 40
SALES (corp-wide): 4.8B **Privately Held**
SIC: 3575 7372 2752 Mfg Computer Terminals Prepackaged Software Services Lithographic Commercial Printing
HQ: Igt Global Solutions Corporation
10 Memorial Blvd
Providence RI 02903
401 392-1000

(G-21457)
IMMUNEX RHODE ISLAND CORP
40 Technology Way (02817-1700)
PHONE....................................401 392-1200
Fabrizio Bonanni, *President*
Nadia Meshkova, *Manager*
▲ **EMP:** 26
SALES (est): 8.2MM
SALES (corp-wide): 23.7B **Publicly Held**
SIC: 2834 Mfg Pharmaceutical Preparations
PA: Amgen Inc.
1 Amgen Center Dr
Thousand Oaks CA 91320
805 447-1000

(G-21458)
INTERLOTT TECHNOLOGIES INC
55 Technology Way (02817-1711)
PHONE....................................401 463-6392
EMP: 245
SQ FT: 52,000
SALES (est): 16.9MM **Publicly Held**
SIC: 3578 Mfg Calculating Equipment
HQ: Gtech Holdings Corporation
10 Memorial Blvd Ste 101
Providence RI 02903
401 392-1000

(G-21459)
JOHN CARLEVALE
Also Called: Tot-Lot Child Care Products
640 Weaver Hill Rd (02817-2261)
PHONE....................................401 392-1926
John Carlevale, *Owner*
EMP: 20
SALES (est): 739K **Privately Held**
SIC: 2731 5099 Books-Publishing/Printing Whol Durable Goods

(G-21460)
KMC INC
Also Called: K M C Bearings
20 Technology Way (02817-1710)
PHONE....................................401 392-1900
Fouad Zeidan, *President*
▼ **EMP:** 35
SQ FT: 30,000
SALES (est): 5.9MM **Privately Held**
WEB: www.kmcbearings.com
SIC: 3568 Mfg Power Transmission Equipment

(G-21461)
LEAVERS LACE CORPORATION (PA)
144 Mishnock Rd (02817-1669)
PHONE....................................401 397-5555
Mark Klauber, *President*
Gordon Klauber, *Vice Pres*
York Roberts, *Treasurer*
Deborah Ruzzo, *Manager*
▲ **EMP:** 12 **EST:** 1975
SQ FT: 12,000
SALES: 22MM **Privately Held**
WEB: www.leaverslace.com
SIC: 2258 Mfg Knit Lace

(G-21462)
PAGE MC LELLAN INC
136 Mishnock Rd (02817-1669)
PHONE....................................401 397-2795
Wayne J McLellan, *President*
Ron Pelletier, *Purch Mgr*
Dianne McLellan, *Manager*

GEOGRAPHIC

Diane McLellan, *Admin Sec*
EMP: 7
SALES: 700K **Privately Held**
WEB: www.mclellanpageinc.com
SIC: 3599 Mfg Industrial Machinery

(G-21463)
PORTER MACHINE INC
765 Victory Hwy Unit 1 (02817-2111)
P.O. Box 567, Coventry (02816-0010)
PHONE..................................401 397-8889
Earl Porter Jr, *President*
Larry F Fox, *Manager*
EMP: 28
SQ FT: 9,500
SALES: 2.8MM **Privately Held**
SIC: 3599 Machine Shop

(G-21464)
RATHBUNS SAWMILL INC
239 Plain Rd (02817-2035)
PHONE..................................401 397-3996
Gilbert Rathbun Jr, *Principal*
EMP: 3
SALES (est): 168K **Privately Held**
SIC: 2421 Sawmill/Planing Mill

(G-21465)
RHODE ISLAND DISTRG CO LLC
Also Called: C C Distributors
119 Hopkins Hill Rd (02817-1709)
PHONE..................................401 822-6400
Jason Birkett, *General Mgr*
Michele Danforth, *Buyer*
Michelle Meenagh, *Purchasing*
Keri Smith, *Human Res Mgr*
Juan Rosa, *Technology*
▲ **EMP:** 33
SALES (est): 5.8MM **Privately Held**
SIC: 2087 Mfg Flavor Extracts/Syrup

(G-21466)
TM CUSTOM
510 Victory Hwy (02817-2159)
PHONE..................................401 226-2173
EMP: 4 **EST:** 2016
SALES (est): 371.8K **Privately Held**
SIC: 2434 Mfg Wood Kitchen Cabinets

West Kingston
Washington County

(G-21467)
MODINE MANUFACTURING COMPANY
604 Liberty Ln (02892-1802)
P.O. Box 308 (02892-0308)
PHONE..................................401 792-1231
EMP: 75
SALES (corp-wide): 2.2B **Publicly Held**
WEB: www.modine.com
SIC: 3443 Mfg Fabricated Plate Work
PA: Modine Manufacturing Company Inc
1500 Dekoven Ave
Racine WI 53403
262 636-1200

(G-21468)
MRD WOODWORKING LLC
32 Frank Ave (02892)
PHONE..................................401 789-3933
Matthew Doyon,
EMP: 6
SQ FT: 4,550
SALES (est): 267.3K **Privately Held**
SIC: 2431 Mfg Millwork

(G-21469)
NEW ENGLAND WOOD PRODUCTS LLC
535 Liberty Ln (02892-1801)
PHONE..................................401 789-7474
Ryan Rathbun,
Kimberly Rathbun,
EMP: 8
SALES (est): 1.4MM **Privately Held**
SIC: 2499 Mfg Custom Wood Products

(G-21470)
RHODE ISLAND WIRING SERVICE
567 Liberty Ln (02892-1801)
P.O. Box 434 (02892-0434)
PHONE..................................401 789-1955
John H Pease, *President*
Patricia Pease, *Vice Pres*
Travis Pease, *Vice Pres*
EMP: 8
SQ FT: 24,000
SALES: 499K **Privately Held**
WEB: www.riwire.com
SIC: 3714 Mfg Motor Vehicle Parts & Accessories

(G-21471)
SCHNEIDER ELECTRIC IT CORP (DH)
Also Called: A P C M G E
132 Fairgrounds Rd (02892-1511)
PHONE..................................401 789-5735
David Johnson, *CEO*
Neil E Rasmussen, *Senior VP*
John Donovan, *Vice Pres*
Jean-Marc Lang, *Vice Pres*
Robert Murray, *Vice Pres*
◆ **EMP:** 900
SQ FT: 252,000
SALES (est): 1.3B
SALES (corp-wide): 177.9K **Privately Held**
WEB: www.apcc.com
SIC: 3629 3677 7372 Mfg Electrical Industrial Apparatus Mfg Electronic Coils/Transformers Prepackaged Software Services
HQ: Schneider Electric Industries Sas
35 Rue Joseph Monier
Rueil-Malmaison 92500
141 297-000

(G-21472)
SCHNEIDER ELECTRIC IT USA INC (DH)
132 Fairgrounds Rd (02892-1511)
PHONE..................................401 789-5735
Laurent Vernerey, *President*
Jay Owen, *Regional Mgr*
Matthew Andrews, *District Mgr*
Ronald Scaletta, *District Mgr*
Aaron Davis, *Vice Pres*
◆ **EMP:** 272
SALES (est): 167.4MM
SALES (corp-wide): 177.9K **Privately Held**
SIC: 3612 Mfg Transformers
HQ: Schneider Electric It Corporation
132 Fairgrounds Rd
West Kingston RI 02892
401 789-5735

(G-21473)
SOUTH COUNTY STEEL INC
192 Waites Corner Rd (02892-1422)
PHONE..................................401 789-5570
David Moultrop, *President*
David Moutrop, *President*
EMP: 6
SALES (est): 902.2K **Privately Held**
SIC: 3441 Structural Metal Fabrication

(G-21474)
USQUEPAUGH BAKING CO LLC
87 Old Usquepaugh Rd (02892-1961)
PHONE..................................401 782-6907
Meredith Westner, *Administration*
EMP: 5 **EST:** 2012
SALES (est): 168.1K **Privately Held**
SIC: 2051 Mfg Bread/Related Products

West Warwick
Kent County

(G-21475)
ABS PRINTING INC
173 Washington St (02893-5015)
PHONE..................................401 826-0870
Bruce Demoranville Jr, *President*
Melanie Demoranville, *Vice Pres*
EMP: 9
SQ FT: 12,000
SALES (est): 1.4MM **Privately Held**
WEB: www.mailsol.com
SIC: 2752 7331 Lithographic Commercial Printing Direct Mail Advertising Services

(G-21476)
ADVANCED INTERCONNECTIONS CORP
5 Energy Way (02893-2389)
PHONE..................................401 823-5200
Michael J Murphy, *President*
Ron Lambert, *Safety Mgr*
Sandra Manson, *Buyer*
Michelle Mottram, *Buyer*
Mark Leach, *Engineer*
EMP: 85 **EST:** 1982
SQ FT: 30,000
SALES (est): 16.4MM **Privately Held**
WEB: www.advintcorp.com
SIC: 3678 Mfg Electronic Connectors

(G-21477)
AMTROL INC (DH)
1400 Division Rd (02893-2300)
PHONE..................................401 884-6300
Geoff G Gilmore, *President*
Marcus A Rogier, *Treasurer*
Dale T Brinkman, *Admin Sec*
▲ **EMP:** 450
SQ FT: 270,000
SALES (est): 291.6MM
SALES (corp-wide): 3.7B **Publicly Held**
WEB: www.amtrol.com
SIC: 3443 3585 Manufacture Fabricated Plate Work Refrigeration/Heating Equip
HQ: New Amtrol Holdings, Inc.
1400 Division Rd
West Warwick RI 02893
614 438-3210

(G-21478)
AMTROL INTL INVESTMENTS INC (DH)
1400 Division Rd (02893-2300)
PHONE..................................401 884-6300
Larry T Guillemette, *President*
◆ **EMP:** 4
SALES (est): 378.2K
SALES (corp-wide): 3.7B **Publicly Held**
SIC: 3443 3585 Mfg Fabricated Plate Work Mfg Refrigeration/Heating Equipment
HQ: Amtrol Inc.
1400 Division Rd
West Warwick RI 02893
401 884-6300

(G-21479)
ASTRONOVA INC (PA)
600 E Greenwich Ave (02893-7526)
PHONE..................................401 828-4000
Gregory A Woods, *President*
Michael M Morawetz, *Vice Pres*
Michael J Natalizia, *Vice Pres*
Stephen M Petrarca, *Vice Pres*
Robert Phillips, *Buyer*
EMP: 277
SQ FT: 135,500
SALES: 136.6MM **Publicly Held**
WEB: www.astro-med.com
SIC: 3577 3829 Mfg Specialty Printers

(G-21480)
ASTRONOVA INC
Quick Label Systems
600 E Greenwich Ave (02893-7526)
PHONE..................................401 828-4000
Bryan Nadeau, *General Mgr*
Jacques Lemaire, *District Mgr*
Matthew Cook, *Vice Pres*
Elias G Deeb, *Vice Pres*
Roger Fontaine, *Vice Pres*
EMP: 250
SALES (corp-wide): 136.6MM **Publicly Held**
WEB: www.astro-med.com
SIC: 3577 3841 Mfg Printers Specializing In Bar Codes
PA: Astronova, Inc.
600 E Greenwich Ave
West Warwick RI 02893
401 828-4000

(G-21481)
AURORA FUEL COMPANY INC
191 Pulaski St (02893-5227)
PHONE..................................401 345-5996
Wayne Johnson, *Principal*
EMP: 5 **EST:** 2009
SALES (est): 759.6K **Privately Held**
SIC: 2869 Mfg Industrial Organic Chemicals

(G-21482)
AURORA FUEL COMPANY INC
92 Pond St (02893-5814)
PHONE..................................401 821-5996
Dwayne Johnson, *Owner*
EMP: 4
SALES (est): 297.3K **Privately Held**
SIC: 2869 Mfg Industrial Organic Chemicals

(G-21483)
BATTENFELD OF AMERICA INC
31 James P Murphy Ind Hwy (02893-2382)
PHONE..................................401 823-0700
Wolfgang Meyer, *Principal*
EMP: 3
SALES (est): 253.8K **Privately Held**
SIC: 2992 Mfg Lubricating Oils/Greases

(G-21484)
BESS HOME FASHIONS INC
155 Brookside Ave (02893-3800)
PHONE..................................401 828-0300
Michael Litner, *President*
Steven Burke, *CFO*
Debra Obrien, *Executive Asst*
◆ **EMP:** 13
SQ FT: 40,000
SALES (est): 1.9MM **Privately Held**
SIC: 2511 2392 Mfg Wood Household Furniture Mfg Household Furnishings
PA: Natco Home Fashions, Inc.
155 Brookside Ave Ste 3
West Warwick RI 02893

(G-21485)
BRADFORD SOAP MEXICO INC (HQ)
200 Providence St (02893-2511)
PHONE..................................401 821-2141
John Howland, *CEO*
▲ **EMP:** 21
SALES (est): 42.6MM **Privately Held**
SIC: 2841 Mfg Soap/Other Detergents

(G-21486)
CHASE MACHINE CO INC
324 Washington St (02893-5926)
PHONE..................................401 821-8879
Mike Sutila, *Vice Pres*
Diana Colombo, *Admin Asst*
▲ **EMP:** 35
SQ FT: 10,000
SALES (est): 6.3MM **Privately Held**
WEB: www.chasemachine.com
SIC: 3599 Mfg Custom Machinery

(G-21487)
COLLOIDAL SCIENCE SOLUTIONS
Also Called: Bioscience Beads Division
1454 Main St Ste 24 (02893-3883)
PHONE..................................401 826-3641
Richard B Cook, *President*
EMP: 3
SALES: 40K **Privately Held**
WEB: www.bioscience-beads.com
SIC: 2836 Mfg Chromatographic Beads For Biotechnology

(G-21488)
CPC PLASTICS INC
Also Called: Precision Assisted Plastics
770 Main St (02893-4442)
PHONE..................................401 828-0820
Toll Free:..888 -
EMP: 4
SQ FT: 4,500
SALES (est): 672.3K **Privately Held**
WEB: www.cpcplastics.com
SIC: 3089 Mfg Plastic Products

(G-21489)
CREATIVE BRONZE INC
21 Brayton St Unit 2 (02893-3659)
PHONE..................................401 823-7340
Joseph Izzi, *President*
Stephen Izzi, *Vice Pres*
EMP: 7
SQ FT: 21,000
SALES: 500K **Privately Held**
SIC: 3281 Mfg Cremation Urns

(G-21490)
DAWN INDUSTRIES INC
1300 Division Rd (02893-7556)
PHONE..................................401 884-8175
Steven J Ursillo Sr, *Principal*
EMP: 3
SALES (est): 167.6K **Privately Held**
SIC: 3999 Mfg Misc Products

(G-21491)
DRYVIT SYSTEMS INC (DH)
1 Energy Way (02893-2322)
PHONE..................................401 822-4100
Robert Michael Murphy, *President*
Larry Shipley, *Regional Mgr*
Dennis Dallman, *Vice Pres*
Justin Stockard, *Vice Pres*
Chander Patil, *Engineer*
◆ **EMP:** 80 **EST:** 1969
SQ FT: 33,000
SALES (est): 109MM
SALES (corp-wide): 5.5B **Publicly Held**
WEB: www.dryvitcompanystore.com
SIC: 2899 Mfg Chemical Preparations
HQ: Dryvit Holdings, Inc
1 Energy Way
Providence RI 02903
401 822-4100

(G-21492)
GLOBAL VALUE LIGHTING LLC (PA)
1350 Division Rd Ste 204 (02893-7554)
PHONE..................................401 535-4002
Ed Bednarcik, *CEO*
Jeff Epstein, *Ch Credit Ofcr*
EMP: 14
SQ FT: 2,745
SALES (est): 90MM **Privately Held**
SIC: 3641 Mfg Electric Lamps

(G-21493)
GUILL TOOL & ENGRG CO INC
10 Pike St (02893-3647)
PHONE..................................401 822-8186
Roger Guillemette, *CEO*
Glen Guillemette, *President*
Chuck Paull, *COO*
Diane Guillemette, *Vice Pres*
Richard Guillemette, *Vice Pres*
EMP: 55 **EST:** 1962
SQ FT: 30,000
SALES (est): 11.4MM **Privately Held**
WEB: www.guill.com
SIC: 3544 3494 3599 7692 Mfg Dies/Tools/Jigs/Fixt Mfg Valves/Pipe Fittings Mfg Industrial Machinery Welding Repair

(G-21494)
GUILL TOOL AND ENGRG CO INC
20 Pike St (02893-3600)
PHONE..................................401 828-7600
Charles Paul, *General Mgr*
Diane Guillemette, *Vice Pres*
Patti Martinson, *Data Proc Exec*
EMP: 4
SALES (est): 212.1K **Privately Held**
SIC: 3599 Mfg Industrial Machinery

(G-21495)
HILCO ATHLETIC & GRAPHICS INC
55 Greenhill St (02893-1516)
PHONE..................................401 822-1775
Jeffrey Hill, *President*
EMP: 10
SQ FT: 8,000
SALES (est): 1.5MM **Privately Held**
WEB: www.hilcoathletic.com
SIC: 2759 7389 2339 2329 Commercial Printing Business Services Mfg Women/Miss Outerwear Mfg Mens/Boys Clothing Thread Mill

(G-21496)
JEWELRY HOLDING CO INC
30 Fairview Ave (02893-4405)
PHONE..................................401 826-7934
John Michael Richardson, *President*
Charles Richardson, *Vice Pres*
EMP: 6
SALES: 70K **Privately Held**
SIC: 3961 Mfg Jewelry Made Of Non Precious Materials

(G-21497)
JOE MARTIN
Also Called: Martin Woodworks
3 Bridal Ave Unit 1 (02893-2901)
PHONE..................................401 823-1860
Joe Martin, *Owner*
EMP: 4
SALES (est): 270K **Privately Held**
SIC: 2434 2511 Mfg Wood Kitchen Cabinets Mfg Wood Household Furniture

(G-21498)
KENT COUNTY DAILY TIMES
Also Called: Free Times
1353 Main St (02893-3859)
PHONE..................................401 789-9744
David Dear, *Principal*
Louis Hockman, *Principal*
EMP: 20
SQ FT: 3,000
SALES (est): 842.4K **Privately Held**
WEB: www.ricentral.com
SIC: 2711 Newspapers-Publishing/Printing

(G-21499)
LEAVERS LACE CORPORATION
Also Called: Klauber Brothers
100 Pulaski St (02893-5356)
PHONE..................................401 828-8117
EMP: 13
SALES (corp-wide): 22MM **Privately Held**
SIC: 2258 Lace/Warp Knit Fabric Mill
PA: Leavers Lace Corporation
144 Mishnock Rd
West Greenwich RI 02817
401 397-5555

(G-21500)
NAGEL MACHINE COMPANY INC
27 Wightman St (02893-3425)
PHONE..................................401 827-8962
Dorothy Nagel, *President*
Ron Nagel, *Vice Pres*
EMP: 7 **EST:** 1999
SQ FT: 2,500
SALES (est): 1MM **Privately Held**
SIC: 3599 Machine Shop

(G-21501)
NATCO HOME FASHIONS INC
Corona Curtain Mfg
155 Brookside Ave (02893-3800)
PHONE..................................401 828-0300
Christine Bolton, *Branch Mgr*
EMP: 10 **Privately Held**
SIC: 2391 2221 Mfg Curtains/Draperies
PA: Natco Home Fashions, Inc.
155 Brookside Ave Ste 3
West Warwick RI 02893

(G-21502)
NATCO HOME FASHIONS INC
Soft Impressions
155 Brookside Ave (02893-3800)
PHONE..................................401 828-0300
Richard Russo, *Branch Mgr*
EMP: 10 **Privately Held**
SIC: 2391 2221 Mfg And Imports Curtains/Draperies Pillows Carpet Remnants
PA: Natco Home Fashions, Inc.
155 Brookside Ave Ste 3
West Warwick RI 02893

(G-21503)
NATCO HOME FASHIONS INC (PA)
Also Called: Best Home Fashions
155 Brookside Ave Ste 3 (02893-3865)
P.O. Box 190 (02893-0190)
PHONE..................................401 828-0300
Michael Litner, *Ch of Bd*
Robert T Galkin, *President*
Alan Ross, *Treasurer*
Mary Mazza, *Accounting Mgr*
Tan Vu, *Technology*
▲ **EMP:** 10
SALES (est): 54.5MM **Privately Held**
SIC: 2391 2221 Mfg Curtains/Draperies Manmade Broadwoven Fabric Mill

(G-21504)
NATCO PRODUCTS CORPORATION (PA)
155 Brookside Ave (02893-3800)
P.O. Box 190 (02893-0190)
PHONE..................................401 828-0300
Robert T Galkin, *Ch of Bd*
Warren B Galkin, *Vice Ch Bd*
Michael Litner, *President*
Paul Kawa, *COO*
Alan Ross, *Exec VP*
▲ **EMP:** 260
SALES (est): 184.7MM **Privately Held**
WEB: www.natcohome.com
SIC: 3996 2273 5023 Mfg Hard Floor Coverings Mfg Carpets/Rugs Whol Homefurnishings

(G-21505)
NEW AMTROL HOLDINGS INC (DH)
1400 Division Rd (02893-2323)
PHONE..................................614 438-3210
John P McConnell, *CEO*
EMP: 4 **EST:** 2013
SALES (est): 318.2MM
SALES (corp-wide): 3.7B **Publicly Held**
SIC: 3316 Manufacture Cold-Rolled Steel Shapes
HQ: Worthington Steel Of Michigan Inc
11700 Worthington Dr
Taylor MI 48180
734 374-3260

(G-21506)
ORIGINAL BRDFORD SOAP WRKS INC (HQ)
200 Providence St (02893-2508)
PHONE..................................401 821-2141
Stuart Benton, *President*
Chris Buckley, *Exec VP*
Jimmy Curran, *Exec VP*
Paul Russo, *Facilities Mgr*
Stephen Drown, *Controller*
◆ **EMP:** 300
SQ FT: 300,000
SALES: 70MM **Privately Held**
WEB: www.bradfordsoap.com
SIC: 2841 Mfg Soap/Other Detergents

(G-21507)
QUALITY FUEL
1086 Main St (02893-3745)
PHONE..................................401 822-9482
Anthony Zampa, *Principal*
EMP: 3
SALES (est): 176.5K **Privately Held**
SIC: 2869 Mfg Industrial Organic Chemicals

(G-21508)
RESPONSE TECHNOLOGIES LLC
1505 Main St Ste B (02893-2927)
PHONE..................................401 585-5918
David Pettey, *CEO*
Edmund Bard, *President*
EMP: 3
SALES (est): 310.6K **Privately Held**
SIC: 3089 Mfg Plastic Products

(G-21509)
SNOW FINDINGS COMPANY INC
14 Sheldon St (02893-1499)
PHONE..................................401 821-7712
Robert B Snow, *President*
EMP: 6 **EST:** 1951
SQ FT: 5,000
SALES: 600K **Privately Held**
SIC: 3911 Whol Jewelry/Precious Stones

(G-21510)
STANDARD MILL MACHINERY CORP
1370c Main St (02893-3815)
P.O. Box 1335 (02893-0701)
PHONE..................................401 822-7871
Arthur La Voie, *President*
David Austin, *Vice Pres*
EMP: 7
SQ FT: 15,000
SALES (est): 500K **Privately Held**
WEB: www.standardmill.com
SIC: 3552 Reconditions Textile Winders

(G-21511)
TOOLLAB INC
65 Manchester St (02893-5329)
PHONE..................................401 461-2110
Charles Melino, *President*
Charles Melino Jr, *Vice Pres*
▲ **EMP:** 8
SQ FT: 20,000
SALES: 6MM **Privately Held**
SIC: 3564 Mfg Blowers/Fans

(G-21512)
WEST WARWICK SCREW PRODUCTS CO
21 Factory St (02893-3708)
P.O. Box 310 (02893-0310)
PHONE..................................401 821-4729
Steven Materne, *President*
Carolyn R Materne, *Admin Sec*
EMP: 9 **EST:** 1945
SQ FT: 7,500
SALES: 990K **Privately Held**
SIC: 3451 Mfg Screw Machine Products

(G-21513)
WEST WARWICK WELDING INC
970 Main St (02893-3527)
PHONE..................................401 822-8200
Louis Campisani, *President*
Brandon Cardoza, *Sales Staff*
EMP: 15 **EST:** 1943
SQ FT: 26,000
SALES: 4MM **Privately Held**
WEB: www.pressurevessel.org
SIC: 3443 7692 Mfg Fabricated Plate Work Welding Repair

(G-21514)
WESTCOTT BAKING COMPANY INC
30 Newell St (02893-1825)
PHONE..................................401 821-8007
Michael Pinga, *President*
EMP: 10 **EST:** 1956
SQ FT: 12,000
SALES (est): 710K **Privately Held**
SIC: 2051 Mfg Bread/Related Products

Westerly
Washington County

(G-21515)
AMETEK SCP INC (HQ)
52 Airport Rd (02891-3402)
P.O. Box 2236 (02891-0920)
PHONE..................................401 596-6658
David Sapio, *CEO*
Timothy N Jones, *President*
Diana Dal PRA, *General Mgr*
Phillip Pilewski, *Program Mgr*
▲ **EMP:** 60
SQ FT: 30,000
SALES (est): 24.5MM
SALES (corp-wide): 4.8B **Publicly Held**
WEB: www.ametekscp.com
SIC: 3678 3496 3643 Mfg Electronic Connectors Mfg Misc Fabricated Wire Products Mfg Conductive Wiring Devices
PA: Ametek, Inc.
1100 Cassatt Rd
Berwyn PA 19312
610 647-2121

GEOGRAPHIC

(G-21516)
AQUARION WATER COMPANY
87 Margin St (02891-2118)
P.O. Box 2924 (02891-0932)
PHONE..................................401 596-2847
Whiff Peterson, *Branch Mgr*
EMP: 5
SALES (corp-wide): 8.4B **Publicly Held**
SIC: 2899 Mfg Chemical Preparations
HQ: Aquarion Water Company
835 Main St
Bridgeport CT 06604
800 732-9678

(G-21517)
ARCH PARENT INC
13 Airport Rd (02891-3401)
PHONE..................................401 388-9802
EMP: 4 **Privately Held**
SIC: 2752 Lithographic Commercial Printing
HQ: Arch Parent Inc.
9 W 57th St Fl 31
New York NY 10019
212 796-8500

(G-21518)
BRANDING COMPANY INC
5 C St (02891-2803)
PHONE..................................203 793-1923
Patrick E Muli Jr, *President*
Suzanne M Thompson, *Vice Pres*
EMP: 4
SALES (est): 526.5K **Privately Held**
SIC: 2759 8743 Commercial Printing Public Relations Services

(G-21519)
CM PUBLICATIONS INC
Also Called: Challenging Tms, Pzzl Plyrs Wk
6 Bayview Dr (02891-3202)
P.O. Box 1247 (02891-0900)
PHONE..................................401 596-9358
Arthur P Macauley, *President*
EMP: 3
SQ FT: 1,000
SALES: 500K **Privately Held**
SIC: 2721 2741 Periodicals-Publishing/Printing Misc Publishing

(G-21520)
COMSTOCK PRESS
58 Benson Ave (02891-5318)
PHONE..................................401 596-8719
Richard Aldrich, *Owner*
EMP: 4
SALES (est): 198K **Privately Held**
SIC: 2759 Commercial Printing

(G-21521)
CRAMIK ENTERPRISES INC
Also Called: Warwick Hanger Company
34 Canal St Ste 1 (02891-1573)
PHONE..................................401 596-8171
Michael K Ellery, *President*
▲ **EMP:** 30
SALES (est): 5.2MM **Privately Held**
WEB: www.cramik.com
SIC: 3432 Mfg Plumbing Fixture Fittings

(G-21522)
DARLINGTON FABRICS CORPORATION
36 Beach St (02891-2728)
P.O. Box 538 (02891-0538)
PHONE..................................401 596-2816
Dana Barlow, *President*
Steve Perry, *Vice Pres*
Laura Parzych, *Research*
Pete Johnson, *Engineer*
Carol Gross, *Natl Sales Mgr*
◆ **EMP:** 200
SALES (est): 21.6MM
SALES (corp-wide): 179.3MM **Privately Held**
SIC: 2221 Manmade Broadwoven Fabric Mill
PA: The Moore Company
36 Beach St
Westerly RI 02891
401 596-2816

(G-21523)
DONALD G LOCKARD
Also Called: Yankee Soldering Technology
11 Setting Sun Dr (02891-4114)
PHONE..................................401 965-3182
Donald Lockard, *Owner*
Maryann Garner, *Owner*
EMP: 3
SALES (est): 199.2K **Privately Held**
SIC: 3548 5084 Mfg Welding Apparatus Whol Industrial Equipment

(G-21524)
ERSA INC
83 Tom Harvey Rd (02891-3688)
PHONE..................................401 348-4000
Christopher J Andaloro, *President*
EMP: 40
SQ FT: 46,000
SALES (est): 14.9MM **Privately Held**
WEB: www.ersmith.com
SIC: 3599 8711 7629 Mfg Industrial Machinery Engineering Services Electrical Repair

(G-21525)
GRISWOLD TEXTILE PRINT INC
84 White Rock Rd (02891-1224)
P.O. Box 514 (02891-0514)
PHONE..................................401 596-2784
Linda Lockwood, *President*
Paul Bergendahl, *Vice Pres*
▲ **EMP:** 24
SQ FT: 15,000
SALES (est): 2.8MM **Privately Held**
SIC: 2759 Commercial Printing

(G-21526)
HAUSER FOODS INC
Also Called: Hauser Chocolatier
59 Tom Harvey Rd (02891-3685)
PHONE..................................401 596-8866
Rudolf Hauser Jr, *President*
Rudolf Hauser Sr, *Vice Pres*
Lucille Hauser, *Vice Pres*
Lori Bueno, *Sales Staff*
▲ **EMP:** 22
SQ FT: 4,000
SALES (est): 3.9MM **Privately Held**
WEB: www.hauserchocolatier.com
SIC: 2064 5441 Mfg & Ret Chocolate & Candies

(G-21527)
J J TRASKOS MFG INC
113 Canal St (02891-1540)
P.O. Box 1126 (02891-0903)
PHONE..................................401 348-2080
James Traskos, *President*
Kathleen Traskos, *Vice Pres*
EMP: 3
SQ FT: 2,500
SALES (est): 443K **Privately Held**
SIC: 3599 Mfg Industrial Machinery

(G-21528)
J MACK STUDIOS LLC
101 Cross St (02891-2407)
PHONE..................................401 932-8600
Kevin Adams, *Owner*
Mary Adams, *Co-Owner*
EMP: 6
SALES (est): 588K **Privately Held**
WEB: www.jmackstudios.com
SIC: 2759 Commercial Printing

(G-21529)
MARILU FOODS INC
3 Gilleo Dr (02891-3312)
PHONE..................................401 348-2858
Megan Kyan, *Principal*
EMP: 3
SALES (est): 217.5K **Privately Held**
SIC: 2099 Mfg Food Preparations

(G-21530)
MAXSON AUTOMATIC MACHINERY CO (PA)
Also Called: Mamco
70 Airport Rd (02891-3428)
PHONE..................................401 596-0162
Merton L Matthews, *Ch of Bd*
Joseph F Matthews, *President*
Michael J Terranova, *Vice Pres*
Eric Dumas, *Design Engr*
Robert Counts, *Controller*
EMP: 50 **EST:** 1932
SQ FT: 75,000
SALES (est): 13.6MM **Privately Held**
WEB: www.maxsonautomatic.com
SIC: 3554 3317 Mfg Paper Industrial Machinery Mfg Steel Pipe/Tubes

(G-21531)
MOORE COMPANY (PA)
36 Beach St (02891-2771)
P.O. Box 538 (02891-0538)
PHONE..................................401 596-2816
Dana Barlow, *President*
Alexandra Moore, *President*
Kevin Crompton, *Technical Mgr*
Janet Robidoux, *Treasurer*
Monica Coughlin, *Manager*
◆ **EMP:** 180 **EST:** 1909
SQ FT: 150,000
SALES (est): 179.3MM **Privately Held**
WEB: www.themooreco.com
SIC: 2258 2241 3069 3061 Lace/Knit Fabric Mill Narrow Fabric Mill Mfg Fabrcatd Rubber Prdt Mfg Mechanical Rubber Gd

(G-21532)
MOORE COMPANY
Fulflex
36 Beach St (02891-2771)
PHONE..................................401 596-2816
Jon Senior, *Manager*
EMP: 150
SALES (corp-wide): 179.3MM **Privately Held**
WEB: www.themooreco.com
SIC: 2258 2241 3069 3061 Lace/Knit Fabric Mill Narrow Fabric Mill Mfg Fabrcatd Rubber Prdt Mfg Mechanical Rubber Gd
PA: The Moore Company
36 Beach St
Westerly RI 02891
401 596-2816

(G-21533)
MOORE COMPANY
Darlington Fabrics
48 Canal St (02891-1539)
PHONE..................................401 596-0219
Peter Moore, *Branch Mgr*
EMP: 103
SALES (corp-wide): 179.3MM **Privately Held**
WEB: www.themooreco.com
SIC: 2258 Lace/Warp Knit Fabric Mill
PA: The Moore Company
36 Beach St
Westerly RI 02891
401 596-2816

(G-21534)
MOORE COMPANY
Darlington Fabrics
36 Beach St (02891-2771)
P.O. Box 539 (02891-0539)
PHONE..................................401 596-2816
Steven Perry, *Branch Mgr*
EMP: 230
SALES (corp-wide): 179.3MM **Privately Held**
WEB: www.themooreco.com
SIC: 2258 2211 Lace/Warp Knit Fabric Mill Cotton Broadwoven Fabric Mill
PA: The Moore Company
36 Beach St
Westerly RI 02891
401 596-2816

(G-21535)
NOODLE REVOLUTION
87 Oak St (02891-1736)
PHONE..................................401 596-9559
EMP: 6
SALES (est): 230.5K **Privately Held**
SIC: 2098 Mfg Macaroni/Spaghetti

(G-21536)
PRINTING PLUS
179 Main St (02891-2112)
PHONE..................................401 596-6970
Colin Donahue, *Owner*
EMP: 3
SALES (est): 291K **Privately Held**
SIC: 2752 Lithographic Commercial Printing

(G-21537)
RIVERVIEW SIGNS & GRAPHICS
17 Riverview Ave (02891-3220)
PHONE..................................401 596-7889
Nancy Socha, *Owner*
EMP: 4
SALES: 56K **Privately Held**
SIC: 3993 7389 Mfg Signs/Advertising Specialties Business Services

(G-21538)
ROBERT B EVANS INC
Also Called: Evans Welding & Construction
128 Oak St (02891-1715)
PHONE..................................401 596-2719
Robert B Evans Sr, *President*
EMP: 4
SALES (est): 326K **Privately Held**
SIC: 7692 1542 1521 3444 Welding Repair Nonresidential Cnstn Single-Family House Cnst

(G-21539)
ROL-FLO ENGINEERING INC
85a Tom Harvey Rd (02891-3691)
PHONE..................................401 596-0060
Randall Orlomoski, *President*
Richard Orlomoksi, *Vice Pres*
EMP: 20
SQ FT: 7,400
SALES (est): 2.6MM **Privately Held**
WEB: www.rolflo.com
SIC: 3544 3545 Mfg Dies/Tools/Jigs/Fixtures Mfg Machine Tool Accessories

(G-21540)
SCIENTIFIC ALLOYS INC
72 Old Hopkinton Rd (02891-1406)
P.O. Box 523 (02891-0523)
PHONE..................................401 596-4947
James F Rossi, *President*
EMP: 6
SQ FT: 2,000
SALES (est): 600K **Privately Held**
WEB: www.scientificalloys.com
SIC: 3312 3449 Mfg Misc Structural Metalwork Blast Furnace-Steel Works

(G-21541)
SOLID OAK INC
244 Post Rd Ste 102 (02891-2621)
P.O. Box 2194 (02891-0919)
PHONE..................................401 637-4855
Steven Lord, *President*
Chris Servidio, *Vice Pres*
▲ **EMP:** 4
SALES (est): 481.4K **Privately Held**
SIC: 2339 Mfg Women's/Misses' Outerwear

(G-21542)
TAPPED APPLE WINERY
37 High St (02891-1853)
PHONE..................................401 637-4946
EMP: 3
SALES (est): 104K **Privately Held**
SIC: 2084 Mfg Wines/Brandy/Spirits

(G-21543)
TMC RHODE ISLAND COMPANY INC
36 Beach St (02891-2728)
P.O. Box 538 (02891-0538)
PHONE..................................401 596-2816
Dana Barlow, *President*
EMP: 11
SALES (est): 974.4K
SALES (corp-wide): 179.3MM **Privately Held**
WEB: www.themooreco.com
SIC: 3069 Mfg Fabricated Rubber Products
PA: The Moore Company
36 Beach St
Westerly RI 02891
401 596-2816

▲ = Import ▼=Export
◆ =Import/Export

(G-21544)
TOM AND SALLYS HANDMADE CHOCO
59 Tom Harvey Rd (02891-3685)
PHONE..................................800 289-8783
Sally E Fegley, *President*
Thomas E Fegley, *Chairman*
EMP: 11
SQ FT: 11,000
SALES (est): 1.1MM **Privately Held**
WEB: www.tomandsallys.com
SIC: 2064 5145 5441 Mfg Candy/Confectionery Whol Confectionery Ret Candy/Confectionery

(G-21545)
TRANSFUSION BOAT WORKS INC
67a Tom Harvey Rd (02891-3617)
PHONE..................................401 348-5878
Robert Darling III, *Principal*
EMP: 3 **EST:** 2009
SALES (est): 280.2K **Privately Held**
SIC: 3732 Boatbuilding/Repairing

(G-21546)
US EXTRUDERS INC
87 Tom Harvey Rd (02891-3688)
PHONE..................................401 584-4710
Bill Kramer, *President*
Stephen Montalto, *Sales Staff*
Kevin Slusarz, *Technology*
EMP: 15
SALES (est): 2.7MM **Privately Held**
SIC: 3559 Mfg Misc Industry Machinery

Woonsocket
Providence County

(G-21547)
AIDANCE SKINCARE & TOPICAL SOL
184 Burnside Ave (02895-2114)
PHONE..................................401 432-7750
Andrew Warren, *Info Tech Dir*
David Goldsmith, *Business Dir*
▲ **EMP:** 18
SALES (est): 3.3MM **Privately Held**
SIC: 2844 Cosmetics Preparations

(G-21548)
ALFA INTERNATIONAL CORP
32 Mechanic Ave Ste 99 (02895-2050)
PHONE..................................401 765-0503
Rajab Aboubakr, *President*
Satimah Bakr, *Office Mgr*
EMP: 5
SQ FT: 19,000
SALES: 2MM **Privately Held**
WEB: www.AlfaAdhesives.com
SIC: 2891 Mfg Adhesives/Sealants

(G-21549)
ALFRED N GRAVEL
300 S Main St (02895-4258)
PHONE..................................401 765-4432
EMP: 3 **EST:** 2010
SALES (est): 140K **Privately Held**
SIC: 1442 Construction Sand/Gravel

(G-21550)
AXIS MACHINING INC
549 River St (02895-1819)
PHONE..................................401 766-9911
Paul Sufflotto, *President*
Bruce Macdermott, *Vice Pres*
EMP: 7
SQ FT: 3,000
SALES (est): 968K **Privately Held**
SIC: 3599 Machine Shop

(G-21551)
BLOUIN GENERAL WELDING & FABG
574 2nd Ave (02895-4147)
PHONE..................................401 762-4542
Peter Blouin, *President*
EMP: 4
SALES (est): 310K **Privately Held**
SIC: 3441 3599 7692 Structural Metal Fabrication Mfg Industrial Machinery Welding Repair

(G-21552)
BOUCKAERT INDUSTRIAL TEXTILES
235 Singleton St (02895-1832)
PHONE..................................401 769-5474
Max Brockle, *CEO*
Rob Dirienzo, *President*
Tom Bouckaert, *Vice Pres*
Keith Taylor, *Prdtn Mgr*
▲ **EMP:** 43
SQ FT: 60,000
SALES (est): 7.4MM **Privately Held**
WEB: www.bitfelt.com
SIC: 2231 Wool Broadwoven Fabric Mill

(G-21553)
BRANDYWINE MATERIALS LLC
308 E School St (02895-1318)
PHONE..................................781 281-2746
Edward Stein, *Principal*
EMP: 5
SALES (est): 787.6K **Privately Held**
SIC: 2891 Mfg Adhesives/Sealants

(G-21554)
BUDCO PRODUCTS CORP
60 Kindergarten St (02895-2919)
P.O. Box 923 (02895-0787)
PHONE..................................401 767-2590
Mark Weiss, *President*
EMP: 6 **EST:** 1961
SQ FT: 20,000
SALES (est): 718.6K **Privately Held**
WEB: www.budcoproducts.com
SIC: 3161 5941 Mfg Luggage Ret Sporting Goods/Bicycles

(G-21555)
CARPENTER POWDER PRODUCTS INC
500 Park East Dr (02895-6148)
PHONE..................................401 769-5600
Brian Tuttle, *Business Mgr*
Jerry Wayock, *Project Dir*
Philip E Jones, *Branch Mgr*
EMP: 12
SALES (corp-wide): 2.3B **Publicly Held**
SIC: 3339 Nonferrous Rolling/Drawing
HQ: Carpenter Powder Products Inc.
682 Mayer St
Bridgeville PA 15017
412 257-5103

(G-21556)
CNC INTERNATIONAL LTD PARTNR
20 Privilege St (02895-1239)
P.O. Box 3000 (02895-0862)
PHONE..................................401 769-6100
Bruce Moger, *Partner*
▼ **EMP:** 20 **EST:** 1967
SQ FT: 225,000
SALES (est): 3.9MM **Privately Held**
SIC: 2843 Mfg Specialty Chemicals

(G-21557)
DURALECTRA-CHN LLC
Also Called: Precision Coating
1 Shorr Ct (02895-2062)
PHONE..................................401 597-5000
Neil Tumienski, *Director*
Tim Cabot,
Laurie Tremblay, *Administration*
Robert D'Angelis,
Steven Schaepe,
EMP: 85
SALES (est): 6.5MM
SALES (corp-wide): 17.7MM **Privately Held**
SIC: 3471 Plating/Polishing Service
PA: Katahdin Industries, Inc.
51 Parmenter Rd
Hudson MA 01749
781 329-1420

(G-21558)
E A M T INC
Also Called: Textile Engineering & Mfg
841 Park East Dr (02895-6112)
P.O. Box 25 (02895-0779)
PHONE..................................401 762-1500
Steve Clarke, *President*
Jerry Moore, *VP Mfg*
▲ **EMP:** 22
SQ FT: 30,000
SALES (est): 5.1MM **Privately Held**
WEB: www.teamtextiles.com
SIC: 2297 2299 2221 Mfg Nonwoven Fabrics Mfg Textile Goods Manmade Broadwoven Fabric Mill

(G-21559)
EASTERN RESINS CORP
1174 River St (02895-1865)
PHONE..................................401 769-6700
David Viola, *President*
EMP: 37
SQ FT: 25,000
SALES (est): 2MM **Privately Held**
SIC: 2821 Mfg Plastic Materials/Resins

(G-21560)
EPOXYTECH INC
Also Called: Epoxyset
718 Park East Dr (02895-6159)
P.O. Box 1256 (02895-0826)
PHONE..................................401 726-4500
Sukirtee Patel, *President*
Kiran Patel, *Vice Pres*
Paven Patel, *Associate Dir*
EMP: 20 **EST:** 1998
SQ FT: 23,000
SALES: 5MM **Privately Held**
SIC: 2821 Mfg Plstc Material/Resin

(G-21561)
FAIRMOUNT FOUNDRY INC
25 2nd Ave (02895-5194)
PHONE..................................401 769-1585
James W De Witt, *President*
Gerald Dewitt, *Vice Pres*
Chris Dewitt, *VP Sales*
Jean De Witt, *Admin Sec*
EMP: 19
SQ FT: 30,000
SALES (est): 3.7MM **Privately Held**
WEB: www.fairmountfdry.com
SIC: 3321 Gray/Ductile Iron Foundry

(G-21562)
FINLAY EXT INGREDIENTS USA INC
1268 Park East Dr (02895-6183)
PHONE..................................401 769-5490
EMP: 7
SALES (corp-wide): 10.4B **Privately Held**
SIC: 2095 Mfg Roasted Coffee
HQ: Finlay Extracts & Ingredients Usa, Inc.
10 Blackstone Valley Pl
Lincoln RI 02865
800 288-6272

(G-21563)
FRANK B STRUZIK INC
129 Ballou St (02895-5108)
P.O. Box 985 (02895-0910)
PHONE..................................401 766-6880
Frank B Struzik, *President*
▲ **EMP:** 10 **EST:** 1956
SQ FT: 14,000
SALES (est): 991.1K **Privately Held**
SIC: 2298 Mfg Braided Cord & Twine

(G-21564)
FRIENDS FOUNDRY INC
416 Pond St (02895-1220)
PHONE..................................401 769-0160
Normand Vadenais, *President*
John Vadenais, *Vice Pres*
Paul Vadenais, *Admin Sec*
EMP: 10 **EST:** 1967
SQ FT: 12,000
SALES (est): 1MM **Privately Held**
SIC: 3365 Copper Foundry

(G-21565)
FRONTIER WELDING & FABRICATION
63 Transit St (02895-5859)
PHONE..................................401 769-0271
David Coutear, *President*
Timothy Natyniak, *Vice Pres*
EMP: 5 **EST:** 1954
SQ FT: 12,000
SALES (est): 830.9K **Privately Held**
SIC: 3441 1791 7692 Mfg Structural Steel Building Components & Structural Steel Erection

(G-21566)
GARY ELDRIDGE
Also Called: Alpine Kitchens
32 Mechanic Ave Ste 225 (02895-2052)
PHONE..................................401 769-0026
Gary Eldridge, *Owner*
EMP: 4
SALES (est): 328K **Privately Held**
WEB: www.garyeldridge.com
SIC: 2434 Mfg Wood Kitchen Cabinets

(G-21567)
HANNA INSTRUMENTS INC (PA)
584 Park East Dr (02895-6177)
PHONE..................................401 765-7500
Martino Nardo, *President*
Anna Maria Nardo, *Vice Pres*
Pamela Nardo, *Vice Pres*
Sara Morse, *Buyer*
Jason Lessard, *Engineer*
▲ **EMP:** 40
SQ FT: 26,000
SALES (est): 24.7MM **Privately Held**
WEB: www.hannainst.com
SIC: 3825 3845 3826 3823 Mfg Elec Measuring Instr Mfg Electromedical Equip Mfg Analytical Instr Mfg Process Cntrl Instr Mfg Industrial Gases

(G-21568)
HONEYWELL INTERNATIONAL INC
245 Railroad St (02895-3039)
PHONE..................................401 769-7274
David Marsh, *Manager*
EMP: 120
SALES (corp-wide): 41.8B **Publicly Held**
WEB: www.honeywell.com
SIC: 3829 Sensor Manufacturing
PA: Honeywell International Inc.
300 S Tryon St
Charlotte NC 28202
973 455-2000

(G-21569)
HONEYWELL INTERNATIONAL INC
245 Rlroad St Wnsocket Ri Woonsocket Ri (02895)
PHONE..................................401 762-6200
Denise Leclerc, *Branch Mgr*
EMP: 100
SALES (corp-wide): 41.8B **Publicly Held**
SIC: 3676 3769 Mfg Electronic Resistors & Space Vehicle Equipment
PA: Honeywell International Inc.
300 S Tryon St
Charlotte NC 28202
973 455-2000

(G-21570)
HONEYWELL INTERNATIONAL INC
245 Railroad St (02895-3039)
PHONE..................................401 769-7274
EMP: 46
SALES (corp-wide): 41.8B **Publicly Held**
SIC: 3823 Process Control Instruments
PA: Honeywell International Inc.
300 S Tryon St
Charlotte NC 28202
973 455-2000

(G-21571)
IMPREGLON INC
222 Goldstein Dr (02895-6174)
PHONE..................................401 766-3353
Henning J Claassen, *Principal*
Steven Muccino, *Plant Mgr*
EMP: 14
SALES (est): 2MM **Privately Held**
SIC: 3559 Mfg Misc Industry Machinery

(G-21572)
JCC RESIDUAL LTD
Also Called: Jeweled Cross
811 Park East Dr (02895-6112)
PHONE..................................508 699-4401
James S Brennan, *Ch of Bd*
James S Brennan II, *President*
Gary S Beyer, *Treasurer*
▲ **EMP:** 47
SQ FT: 20,000

SALES (est): 6.7MM Privately Held
WEB: www.jeweledcross.com
SIC: 3961 3911 Mfg Precious Mtl Jewelry Mfg Costume Jewelry

(G-21573)
LAMINATED PRODUCTS INC
32 Mechanic Ave Ste 204 (02895-2052)
P.O. Box 1349 (02895-0865)
PHONE..................................401 762-0711
Ernest Bibeault, *President*
EMP: 6
SQ FT: 8,000
SALES (est): 866.7K **Privately Held**
SIC: 2541 Mfg Wood Partitions/Fixtures

(G-21574)
MARS MANUFACTURING CO INC
32 Mechanic Ave Ste 100 (02895-2050)
PHONE..................................401 769-9663
Douglas Stets, *President*
Brian McDade, *Mfg Staff*
EMP: 6
SQ FT: 5,000
SALES: 400K **Privately Held**
WEB: www.marsmanufacturing.com
SIC: 3599 Mfg Industrial Machinery

(G-21575)
POLIFIL INC
1112 River St (02895-6901)
PHONE..................................401 767-2700
Robert A Lebeaux, *President*
Michael A Rosenthal, *Exec VP*
EMP: 22
SQ FT: 71,000
SALES (est): 2.4MM
SALES (corp-wide): 12.9MM **Privately Held**
SIC: 2821 Mfg Plastic Materials/Resins
PA: Ralco Industries, Inc.
1112 River St
Woonsocket RI 02895
401 765-1000

(G-21576)
POLYURETHANE MOLDING INDS INC
Also Called: P M I
100 Founders Dr (02895-6154)
PHONE..................................401 765-6700
William Ober, *President*
Susan Ober, *Vice Pres*
EMP: 23 **EST:** 1979
SQ FT: 30,000
SALES (est): 4.1MM **Privately Held**
WEB: www.pmirim.com
SIC: 3544 Mfg Plastic Products

(G-21577)
RALCO INDUSTRIES INC (PA)
Also Called: Plastics Group
1112 River St (02895-1861)
PHONE..................................401 765-1000
Robert Lebeaux, *President*
John McElreath, *General Mgr*
Matthew Maskell, *Vice Pres*
Michael Rosenthal, *Vice Pres*
Deb McGee, *Office Mgr*
EMP: 34 **EST:** 1978
SQ FT: 70,000
SALES (est): 12.9MM **Privately Held**
SIC: 2821 Mfg Plastic Materials/Resins

(G-21578)
RHODE ISLAND MEDIA GROUP
Also Called: Call, The
75 Main St (02895-4312)
P.O. Box A (02895-0992)
PHONE..................................401 762-3000
Barry Mechanic, *Principal*
EMP: 50
SALES (est): 2.4MM **Privately Held**
SIC: 2711 Newspapers-Publishing/Printing

(G-21579)
SPORTS SYSTEMS CUSTOM BAGS
44 Hazel St (02895-1228)
P.O. Box 1225 (02895-0826)
PHONE..................................401 767-3770
Marc Staelen, *President*
EMP: 100
SQ FT: 150,000
SALES (est): 10.1MM **Privately Held**
SIC: 2393 Mfg Sporting/Athletic Goods

(G-21580)
SPRINT SYSTEMS OF PHOTOGRAPHY
60 Kindergarten St (02895-2919)
PHONE..................................401 597-5790
Roy Zimmerman, *President*
EMP: 4
SQ FT: 7,500
SALES (est): 529.7K **Privately Held**
WEB: www.sprintsystems.com
SIC: 3861 Mfg Photographic Chemicals

(G-21581)
SUMMER INFANT INC (PA)
1275 Park East Dr (02895-6185)
PHONE..................................401 671-6550
Stuart Noyes, *CEO*
Dave Medeiros, *VP Engrg*
Mark Sousa, *Research*
Anthony Carbone, *Engineer*
James Erickson, *Project Engr*
▲ **EMP:** 100
SQ FT: 62,500
SALES: 173.6MM **Publicly Held**
WEB: www.summerinfant.com
SIC: 2514 2399 3842 3261 Mfg Juvenile Health Safety And Wellness Products

(G-21582)
SUMMER INFANT INC
1275 Park East Dr (02895-6185)
P.O. Box 829, Slatersville (02876-0899)
PHONE..................................401 671-6550
Jason Macari, *Branch Mgr*
EMP: 4
SALES (corp-wide): 173.6MM **Publicly Held**
SIC: 2514 2399 3842 3261 Mfg Metal Household Furn Mfg Fabrctd Textile Pdts Mfg Surgical Appliances Mfg Vetreous Plmbng Fxtr
PA: Summer Infant, Inc.
1275 Park East Dr
Woonsocket RI 02895
401 671-6550

(G-21583)
SUMMER INFANT (USA) INC
1275 Park East Dr (02895-6185)
PHONE..................................401 671-6551
William E Mote Jr, *CFO*
Ted Klowan, *Asst Treas*
▲ **EMP:** 183
SALES (est): 18.8MM
SALES (corp-wide): 173.6MM **Publicly Held**
SIC: 2399 Mfg Fabricated Textile Products
PA: Summer Infant, Inc.
1275 Park East Dr
Woonsocket RI 02895
401 671-6550

(G-21584)
SURPLUS SOLUTIONS LLC
2010 Diamond Hill Rd (02895-1542)
PHONE..................................401 526-0055
Joseph D'Alton, *President*
Sarita Capobianco, *President*
EMP: 12
SQ FT: 137,800
SALES (est): 2.2MM **Privately Held**
SIC: 3821 5047 5122 Mfg Lab Apparatus/Furn Whol Med/Hospital Equip Whol Drugs/Sundries

(G-21585)
TECHNIC INC
Also Called: Engineering Powders Division
300 Park East Dr (02895-6147)
PHONE..................................401 769-7000
Ana Contreras, *Buyer*
Peter Ribbans, *Engineer*
Keith Hammerschlag, *Engng Exec*
Gary Hemphill, *Finance*
EMP: 30
SALES (corp-wide): 125.5MM **Privately Held**
WEB: www.technic.com
SIC: 2899 3559 Mfg Chemical Preparations Mfg Misc Industry Machinery
PA: Technic, Inc.
47 Molter St
Cranston RI 02910
401 781-6100

(G-21586)
TEX FLOCK INC
200 Founders Dr (02895-6119)
PHONE..................................401 765-2340
Edward T Abramek Jr, *Ch of Bd*
▲ **EMP:** 35
SQ FT: 33,000
SALES (est): 7MM **Privately Held**
WEB: www.flocktex.com
SIC: 2262 2299 3086 2671 Manmade Fabric Fnshg Plt Mfg Textile Goods Mfg Plastic Foam Prdts Mfg Packaging Paper/Film Mfg Coated Fabrics

(G-21587)
TORY INC
481 2nd Ave (02895-4173)
P.O. Box 1416 (02895-0843)
PHONE..................................401 766-4502
Ronald E Lemieux, *President*
Cheryl A Lemieux, *Vice Pres*
Steven M Lemieux, *Treasurer*
Rachel Flood, *Admin Sec*
EMP: 5
SQ FT: 1,500
SALES (est): 808.1K **Privately Held**
WEB: www.toryinc.com
SIC: 3069 Mfr Rubber Office Supply Products

Wyoming
Washington County

(G-21588)
ASHAWAY CEMENT PRODUCTS INC
65 Stilson Rd (02898-1027)
P.O. Box 435, Ashaway (02804-0005)
PHONE..................................401 539-1010
Charles Di Pollino, *President*
Sheila Di Pollino, *Admin Sec*
Linda D Pollino, *Admin Sec*
EMP: 6 **EST:** 1945
SQ FT: 9,000
SALES: 900K **Privately Held**
SIC: 3272 Mfg Concrete Products

(G-21589)
MECHANICAL SPECIALTIES INC
Also Called: Ms Global
1143 Main St Pmb 782 (02898-1074)
PHONE..................................401 267-4410
Jeffrey C Blake, *President*
Carrie L Delia, *Vice Pres*
Arthur T Blake, *Director*
EMP: 3 **EST:** 2015
SALES (est): 184.4K **Privately Held**
SIC: 3545 Mfg Machine Tool Accessories

(G-21590)
RHODE ISLAND READY MIX LLC
35 Stilson Rd (02898-1027)
PHONE..................................401 539-8222
Michael V D'Ambra, *Mng Member*
Lisa D' Ambra, *Manager*
EMP: 15
SALES (est): 1.3MM **Privately Held**
SIC: 3273 Mfg Ready-Mixed Concrete

(G-21591)
VIBCO INC (PA)
75 Stilson Rd (02898-1027)
P.O. Box 8 (02898-0008)
PHONE..................................401 539-2392
Ted S Wadensten, *President*
Karl Wadensten, *President*
Aina E Wadensten, *Corp Secy*
Karl A Wadensten, *Vice Pres*
John Goodwin, *Materials Mgr*
▼ **EMP:** 75 **EST:** 1962
SQ FT: 52,000
SALES (est): 13.7MM **Privately Held**
WEB: www.vibco.com
SIC: 3531 Mfg Construction Machinery

VERMONT

Albany
Orleans County

(G-21592)
GOODRIDGE LUMBER
183 Bailey Hazen Rd E (05820)
P.O. Box 515 (05820-0515)
PHONE..................................802 755-6298
Colleen Goodrich, *President*
Doug Goodrich, *Vice Pres*
Mark Goodrich, *Vice Pres*
Brian Goodrich, *Admin Sec*
EMP: 6
SALES (est): 857K **Privately Held**
SIC: 2452 5211 Mfg Prefabricated Wood Buildings Ret Lumber/Building Materials

Alburg
Grand Isle County

(G-21593)
UV III SYSTEMS INC
59 Cedarvale Est (05440-9698)
PHONE..................................508 883-4881
Gordon B Knight, *President*
Loretta M Knight, *Vice Pres*
EMP: 10
SQ FT: 8,000
SALES (est): 1.4MM **Privately Held**
WEB: www.uv3.com
SIC: 3648 Mfg Lighting Equipment

Arlington
Bennington County

(G-21594)
ARLINGTON INDUSTRIES INC
Also Called: Quadra-Tek
2617 Vt Route 7a (05250-8882)
PHONE..................................802 375-6139
John N Haugsrud, *President*
Brenda Holton, *General Mgr*
Jason Underhill, *Engineer*
David Hazelton, *Project Engr*
EMP: 32 **EST:** 1968
SALES: 3.9MM **Privately Held**
WEB: www.quadra-tek.com
SIC: 3089 Mfg Plastic Products

(G-21595)
ART LICENSING INTL INC
6366 Vt Route 7a (05250-8427)
P.O. Box 2568, Manchester Center (05255-2568)
PHONE..................................802 362-3662
Jack Appelman, *Administration*
EMP: 11
SALES (est): 1.1MM **Privately Held**
SIC: 2741 Misc Publishing

(G-21596)
HBH PRESTAIN INC (PA)
1223 E Arlington Rd (05250-8620)
P.O. Box 1103 (05250-1103)
PHONE..................................802 375-9723
Frederick Hawley, *President*
Ed Hawley, *Vice Pres*
▲ **EMP:** 35
SQ FT: 20,000
SALES (est): 5.1MM **Privately Held**
WEB: www.hbhprestain.com
SIC: 2851 Mfg Paints/Allied Products

(G-21597)
MACK GROUP INC (PA)
608 Warm Brook Rd (05250-8570)
PHONE..................................802 375-2511
Donald S Kendall III, *President*
Melissa Holly, *Plant Mgr*
Tracie Jones, *Purchasing*
Jeff Worthington, *Engineer*
Holly Skea, *Controller*
◆ **EMP:** 400
SQ FT: 300,000
SALES (est): 432.8MM **Privately Held**
SIC: 3089 3577 6719 Mfg Plastic Products Mfg Computer Peripherals Holding Company

▲ = Import ▼=Export
◆ =Import/Export

(G-21598)
MACK MOLDING COMPANY INC (HQ)
608 Warm Brook Rd (05250-8570)
PHONE..................................802 375-2511
Donald S Kendall III, *President*
Jeff Somple, *President*
Jeffrey Somple, *President*
Chris Wartinger, *Business Mgr*
Randy Boduch, *Vice Pres*
◆ **EMP:** 250
SQ FT: 310,000
SALES (est): 262MM
SALES (corp-wide): 432.8MM **Privately Held**
WEB: www.mack.com
SIC: 3089 3577 Mfg Plastic Products Mfg Computer Peripheral Equipment
PA: Mack Group, Inc.
608 Warm Brook Rd
Arlington VT 05250
802 375-2511

(G-21599)
MACK MOLDING COMPANY INC
79 E Arlington Rd (05250-8609)
PHONE..................................802 375-0500
Bud Pagliccia, *Branch Mgr*
EMP: 175
SALES (corp-wide): 432.8MM **Privately Held**
WEB: www.mack.com
SIC: 3089 Mfg Plastic Products
HQ: Mack Molding Company, Inc.
608 Warm Brook Rd
Arlington VT 05250
802 375-2511

(G-21600)
SUGAR SHACK ON ROARING BRANCH
Rr Box 7a (05250)
P.O. Box 296 (05250-0296)
PHONE..................................802 375-6747
Richie Mears, *Owner*
Kim Hawley, *Engineer*
EMP: 3
SQ FT: 3,500
SALES (est): 215K **Privately Held**
WEB: www.sugarshackvt.com
SIC: 2099 5399 5947 Mfg Maple Syrup Country Store Craft Center

(G-21601)
TOOL FACTORY INC
3336 Sunderland Hill Rd (05250-4443)
P.O. Box 52, Milton DE (19968-0052)
PHONE..................................802 375-6549
Heather Chirtaa, *President*
Gordon Woodrow, *Corp Secy*
▲ **EMP:** 6 **EST:** 2000
SQ FT: 3,000
SALES (est): 583.9K **Privately Held**
WEB: www.toolfactory.com
SIC: 2741 Publishing Services

(G-21602)
WILD FARM MAPLE
670 Bentley Hill Rd (05250-8595)
PHONE..................................802 362-1656
Ann Clay, *Owner*
EMP: 3
SALES (est): 162.8K **Privately Held**
SIC: 2087 7389 Mfg Flavor Extracts/Syrup Business Services At Non-Commercial Site

Bakersfield
Franklin County

(G-21603)
POTTER FAMILY MAPLE
544 King Rd (05441-4401)
PHONE..................................802 578-0937
Dean Potter, *Principal*
EMP: 3
SALES (est): 151.7K **Privately Held**
SIC: 2099 Mfg Food Preparations

Barnet
Caledonia County

(G-21604)
GENUINE JAMAICAN
609 Barnet Center Rd (05821-9442)
PHONE..................................802 633-2676
Derrick Samuels, *Principal*
EMP: 3
SALES (est): 143.8K **Privately Held**
SIC: 2079 Mfg Edible Fats/Oils

(G-21605)
VERMONT MOLD & TOOL CORP
Also Called: Vermont Microtechnologies
4693 Garland Hl (05821-9504)
PHONE..................................802 633-2300
John Mullen, *CEO*
EMP: 8
SALES (est): 1.4MM **Privately Held**
SIC: 3544 3825 Mfg Dies/Tools/Jigs/Fixtures Mfg Electrical Measuring Instruments

(G-21606)
VMT LLC
477 W Main St (05821-9790)
PHONE..................................802 633-3900
Darlene J Cote, *Principal*
EMP: 6 **EST:** 2016
SALES (est): 577.7K **Privately Held**
SIC: 3544 Mfg Dies/Tools/Jigs/Fixtures

Barre
Washington County

(G-21607)
ACCURA PRINTING
80 East Rd (05641-5391)
P.O. Box 529, South Barre (05670-0529)
PHONE..................................802 476-4429
Garritt Bresett, *President*
Robin Parry, *Admin Sec*
EMP: 11
SQ FT: 6,000
SALES (est): 1.1MM **Privately Held**
WEB: www.accuraprinting.com
SIC: 2791 2752 Typesetting Services Lithographic Commercial Printing

(G-21608)
ASTERISK TYPOGRAPHICS INC
70 Smith St (05641-4076)
P.O. Box 664 (05641-0664)
PHONE..................................802 476-8399
Leslie Sanborn, *President*
Richard Lynch, *President*
EMP: 6
SALES (est): 341K **Privately Held**
SIC: 2791 Typesetting Services

(G-21609)
BETH MUELLER INC
Also Called: Beth Mueller Design
13 Pleasant St (05641-3454)
PHONE..................................802 476-3582
Beth Mueller, *President*
Philip Morris, *Vice Pres*
EMP: 7
SALES (est): 98K **Privately Held**
WEB: www.bethmueller.com
SIC: 3269 Mfg Pottery Products

(G-21610)
BUTTURA & SONS INC
Also Called: Buttura Gherardi Gran Artisans
109 Boynton St (05641-4905)
P.O. Box 606 (05641-0606)
PHONE..................................802 476-6646
Mark A Gherardi, *President*
Paige Lamthi, *Vice Pres*
Milton Todd, *Treasurer*
Micheal Calevro, *Sales Staff*
▲ **EMP:** 50
SALES (est): 5.9MM **Privately Held**
WEB: www.graniteartisans.com
SIC: 3281 Mfg Cut Stone/Products

(G-21611)
CARROLL CONCRETE CO
379 Granger Rd (05641-5368)
P.O. Box 1000, Newport NH (03773-1000)
PHONE..................................802 229-0191
Shaun Carroll, *Principal*
EMP: 3
SALES (est): 209.1K **Privately Held**
SIC: 3273 Mfg Ready-Mixed Concrete

(G-21612)
DELICATE DECADENCE LLC
15 Cottage St Ste 4 (05641-3764)
PHONE..................................802 479-7948
Timbleton Bolton, *President*
EMP: 4
SALES (est): 355.6K **Privately Held**
SIC: 2051 5812 Mfg Bread/Related Products Eating Place

(G-21613)
DESSUREAU MACHINES INC
53 Granite St (05641-4139)
P.O. Box 402 (05641-0402)
PHONE..................................802 476-4561
Mark C Dessureau, *President*
Arthur J Dessureau, *Principal*
EMP: 19
SQ FT: 15,000
SALES: 3MM **Privately Held**
WEB: www.dessureau.com
SIC: 3599 3291 Mfg Industrial Machinery Mfg Abrasive Products

(G-21614)
FAMILY MEMORIALS INC
36 Burnham St (05641-4708)
P.O. Box 383 (05641-0383)
PHONE..................................802 476-7831
Robert Couture, *President*
Armand Couture, *Vice Pres*
Mary Anne Couture, *Admin Sec*
EMP: 4 **EST:** 1938
SQ FT: 4,000
SALES (est): 375.1K **Privately Held**
WEB: www.family-memorials.ca
SIC: 3281 Mfg Cut Stone/Products

(G-21615)
FOLLENDERWERKS INC
30 Ayers St Apt 1 (05641-4394)
PHONE..................................802 362-0911
Teresa Birns, *CEO*
Ross Birns, *Vice Pres*
EMP: 3
SALES: 186K **Privately Held**
SIC: 2395 5699 Pleating/Stitching Services Ret Misc Apparel/Accessories

(G-21616)
GLOBAL VALUES VT LLC
Also Called: Northern Mosoleum
25 S Front St (05641-2530)
PHONE..................................802 476-8000
Anand Su Anandan, *Owner*
Anand Anandan, *Owner*
EMP: 40
SALES (est): 1.4MM **Privately Held**
SIC: 3281 Mfg Cut Stone/Products

(G-21617)
GLOUCESTER ASSOCIATES INC
Also Called: DMS Machining & Fabrication
10 Transport Dr 1 (05641-4937)
PHONE..................................802 479-1088
Byrom Atwood, *President*
Byron A Atwood, *COO*
Charles Atwood, *Vice Pres*
Richard Keefer, *Controller*
Diane Atwood, *Admin Sec*
EMP: 35
SQ FT: 60,000
SALES (est): 6.9MM **Privately Held**
SIC: 3599 3444 7692 Mfg Industrial Machinery Mfg Sheet Metalwork Welding Repair

(G-21618)
GRANITE INDUSTRIES VERMONT INC
Also Called: Giv
Vanneti Pl (05641)
P.O. Box 537 (05641-0537)
PHONE..................................800 451-3236
Jeffrey Martell, *President*
Forrest Rouelle, *Vice Pres*
◆ **EMP:** 52 **EST:** 1971
SQ FT: 47,000
SALES (est): 6.1MM
SALES (corp-wide): 2.1MM **Privately Held**
WEB: www.granitevermont.com
SIC: 3281 Mfg Cut Stone/Products
HQ: Polycor Stone Corporation
200 Georgia Marble Ln
Tate GA 30177

(G-21619)
HARDROCK GRANITE CO INC
95 Boynton St (05641-4903)
P.O. Box 446 (05641-0446)
PHONE..................................802 479-3606
Norbit Lapade, *President*
Fred Craig, *Vice Pres*
EMP: 4
SALES: 700K **Privately Held**
SIC: 3272 Mfg Of Cemetery Monuments

(G-21620)
HEART OF VERMONT INC
131 S Main St Ste 5 (05641-4814)
PHONE..................................802 476-3098
Reid Lawson, *President*
EMP: 3
SALES (est): 247.7K **Privately Held**
WEB: www.heartofvermont.com
SIC: 2392 Mfg Household Furnishings

(G-21621)
HERITAGE POST & BEAM
449 East Rd (05641-5388)
PHONE..................................802 223-6319
Albert Lewis, *Owner*
EMP: 11
SALES (est): 785.3K **Privately Held**
WEB: www.heritagepostandbeam.net
SIC: 3523 Mfg Farm Machinery/Equipment

(G-21622)
HILLSIDE SOLID SURFACES
Also Called: Hillside Stone Product
Gable Pl Ste 37 (05641)
P.O. Box 134 (05641-0134)
PHONE..................................802 479-2508
Randy Carbonneau, *President*
Sarah Summerville, *Vice Pres*
EMP: 10
SQ FT: 12,200
SALES (est): 1.2MM **Privately Held**
WEB: www.hillsidestone.com
SIC: 3281 Mfg Granite Cut & Shaped

(G-21623)
HILLSIDE STONE PRODUCTS INC
37 Gable Pl (05641-4137)
PHONE..................................802 479-2508
Sarah Somerville, *Vice Pres*
EMP: 14 **EST:** 1954
SALES (est): 1MM **Privately Held**
SIC: 2411 Logging

(G-21624)
HOULE BROS GRANITE CO INC
25 S Front St (05641-2530)
PHONE..................................802 476-6825
Charles J Houle, *President*
Roger Houle, *Vice Pres*
EMP: 20 **EST:** 1956
SQ FT: 32,537
SALES (est): 3.2MM **Privately Held**
WEB: www.houlebrothers.com
SIC: 1411 Dimension Stone

(G-21625)
INTERNATIONAL STONE PRODUCTS (PA)
21 Metro Way (05641-4478)
PHONE..................................802 476-6636
John Dernavich, *President*
Rodney Dernavich, *Vice Pres*
Paul Dernavich, *Treasurer*
Dorothy R Dernavich, *Admin Sec*
EMP: 75 **EST:** 1937
SQ FT: 100,000
SALES (est): 4.8MM **Privately Held**
SIC: 3281 1411 Mfg Cut Stone/Products Dimension Stone Quarry

GEOGRAPHIC

(G-21626)
JET SERVICE ENVELOPE CO INC (PA)
80 East Rd (05641-5391)
PHONE..................................802 229-9335
Jeffrey Blow, *President*
EMP: 13 **EST:** 1915
SQ FT: 14,000
SALES (est): 1.3MM **Privately Held**
WEB: www.jetservice-envelope.com
SIC: 2759 Commercial Printing

(G-21627)
L BROWN AND SONS PRINTING INC
14 Jefferson St 20 (05641-4249)
PHONE..................................802 476-3164
Lawrence Brown, *President*
Diane Brown, *Vice Pres*
EMP: 32
SQ FT: 22,000
SALES (est): 4.9MM **Privately Held**
WEB: www.lbrownandsonsprinting.com
SIC: 2752 7331 2791 2789 Commerical Printing Mailing Services Typesetting Bookbinding & Related Work

(G-21628)
LA PERLE & SONS GRANITE CO
140 Railroad St (05641-4527)
PHONE..................................802 476-6463
EMP: 6
SQ FT: 1,000
SALES (est): 70K **Privately Held**
SIC: 3281 Cut Stone And Stone Products

(G-21629)
MEMORIAL SANDBLAST INC
15 Blackwell St (05641-4052)
P.O. Box 582 (05641-0582)
PHONE..................................802 476-7086
John M Pelkey, *President*
Robert Pelkey, *Vice Pres*
Sharon Pelkey, *Treasurer*
Brynn Pelkey, *Admin Sec*
EMP: 8
SALES: 400K **Privately Held**
SIC: 3281 Mfg Cut Stone/Products

(G-21630)
MOSCOW MILLS INC
11 Averill St Apt 1 (05641-3813)
PHONE..................................802 253-2036
Anderson Leveille, *President*
EMP: 3
SALES (est): 312K **Privately Held**
SIC: 3499 Mfg Misc Fabricated Metal Products

(G-21631)
NORTHERN POWER SYSTEMS INC (HQ)
29 Pitman Rd Ste 1 (05641-8943)
P.O. Box 588 (05641-0588)
PHONE..................................802 461-2955
Ciel Cardwell, *CEO*
William F Leimkuhler, *Chairman*
Reinout G Oussoren, *Vice Pres*
◆ **EMP:** 71
SQ FT: 119,000
SALES (est): 24.7MM
SALES (corp-wide): 38.5MM **Privately Held**
SIC: 3511 3629 Mfg Turbines/Generator Sets Mfg Electrical Industrial Apparatus
PA: Northern Power Systems Corp.
29 Pitman Rd
Barre VT 05641
802 461-2955

(G-21632)
NORTHERN POWER SYSTEMS CORP (PA)
29 Pitman Rd (05641-8920)
P.O. Box 588 (05641-0588)
PHONE..................................802 461-2955
William F Leimkuhler, *Ch of Bd*
Ciel R Caldwell, *President*
Eric Larson, *Vice Pres*
William St Lawrence, *Vice Pres*
EMP: 34
SQ FT: 61,000
SALES: 38.5MM **Privately Held**
SIC: 3511 Wind Turbines

(G-21633)
OLD ROUTE TWO SPIRITS INC
69 Pitman Rd (05641-8920)
PHONE..................................802 424-4864
Ryan Dumperth, *President*
Adam Overbay, *Vice Pres*
Jennifer West, *Admin Sec*
EMP: 7
SALES (est): 309.3K **Privately Held**
SIC: 2085 Mfg Distilled/Blended Liquor

(G-21634)
PEERLESS GRANITE CO INC
35 S Front St (05641-2530)
P.O. Box 313 (05641-0313)
PHONE..................................802 476-3061
Bret Mugford, *President*
Jeffery Mugford, *Vice Pres*
Jan Belfield, *Manager*
EMP: 10
SQ FT: 1,000
SALES (est): 166.6K
SALES (corp-wide): 200K **Privately Held**
SIC: 3281 Mfg Cut Stone/Products
PA: M & W Polishing Inc
19 Smith St
Barre VT 05641
802 476-8340

(G-21635)
PELLETIER LUBE SERVICE
298 E Montpelier Rd (05641-8372)
PHONE..................................802 622-0725
EMP: 3
SALES (est): 262.4K **Privately Held**
SIC: 2992 Mfg Lubricating Oils/Greases

(G-21636)
PEPIN GRANITE COMPANY INC
58 Granite St (05641-4142)
P.O. Box 566 (05641-0566)
PHONE..................................802 476-6103
John Pepin, *President*
Scott Pepin, *Treasurer*
EMP: 22 **EST:** 1962
SALES (est): 2MM **Privately Held**
SIC: 3281 Mfg Cut Stone/Products

(G-21637)
REBTEK DIAMND BLADES BITS LLC
423 E Montpelier Rd (05641-8374)
PHONE..................................802 476-6520
Robert Browning,
▲ **EMP:** 3
SALES (est): 373.8K **Privately Held**
SIC: 3531 Mfg Construction Machinery

(G-21638)
S B E INC (PA)
Also Called: Sb Electronics
81 Parker Rd (05641-9106)
PHONE..................................802 476-4146
Edward Sawyer, *President*
Mark Browning, *Vice Pres*
Terry Hosking, *Research*
Michael Brueaker, *CTO*
◆ **EMP:** 23
SQ FT: 5,400
SALES: 5.1MM **Privately Held**
WEB: www.sbelectronics.com
SIC: 3629 3675 Mfg Electrical Industrial Apparatus Mfg Electronic Capacitors

(G-21639)
SPRUCE MOUNTIAN GRANITES INC
84 Pitman Rd (05641)
P.O. Box 427 (05641-0427)
PHONE..................................802 476-7474
Paul Bagalio II, *CEO*
Sherrel Whittemore,
EMP: 30 **EST:** 1999
SALES (est): 2.8MM **Privately Held**
SIC: 3281 Mfg Cut Stone/Products

(G-21640)
STEPHEN MCARTHUR
Also Called: Multicultural Media
Granger Rd (05641)
PHONE..................................802 839-0371
F Stephen McArthur, *Owner*
Stephen McArthur, *Owner*
EMP: 5
SQ FT: 4,000
SALES: 550K **Privately Held**
WEB: www.multiculturalmedia.com
SIC: 3652 7812 7389 5961 Manufacturing Production Distribution Mail Order And Consultation Of Cds And Videos Of Traditional Music Of Various Countries

(G-21641)
SWENSON GRANITE COMPANY LLC
Anderson-Friberg Division
54 Willey St (05641-2500)
P.O. Box 626 (05641-0626)
PHONE..................................802 476-7021
Robert Pope, *Mng Member*
EMP: 30
SALES (corp-wide): 2.1MM **Privately Held**
WEB: www.swensongranite.com
SIC: 3281 5999 Mfg Cut Stone/Products Ret Misc Merchandise
HQ: Swenson Granite Company Llc
369 N State St
Concord NH 03301
603 225-4322

(G-21642)
TA UPDATE INC (PA)
Also Called: Country Courier
47 N Main St Ste 200 (05641-4168)
PHONE..................................802 479-4040
Robert J Mitchell, *President*
R John Mitchell, *President*
EMP: 90
SQ FT: 18,000
SALES (est): 5.3MM **Privately Held**
WEB: www.timesargus.com
SIC: 2711 Newspapers-Publishing/Printing

(G-21643)
TROW & HOLDEN CO INC
45 S Main St Ste 57 (05641-4880)
P.O. Box 475 (05641-0475)
PHONE..................................802 476-7221
Norman Akley, *President*
Lauren Lamorte, *Vice Pres*
Jordan Keyes, *Marketing Staff*
EMP: 17
SQ FT: 22,000
SALES: 3.8MM **Privately Held**
WEB: www.trowandholden.com
SIC: 3559 3545 3398 Mfg Misc Industry Machinery Mfg Machine Tool Accessories Metal Heat Treating

(G-21644)
VERMONT STONE ART LLC
21 Metro Way Ste 1 (05641-4478)
PHONE..................................802 238-1498
EMP: 5
SALES (est): 289.9K **Privately Held**
SIC: 3281 Mfg Cut Stone/Products

(G-21645)
WORKSAFE TRAFFIC CTRL INDS INC (PA)
115 Industrial Ln (05641-5432)
PHONE..................................802 223-8948
Deborah Ricker, *President*
Debra Ricker, *President*
Lorena La Prade, *Vice Pres*
Steve Florucci, *Site Mgr*
Lorena Laprade, *Treasurer*
EMP: 10
SQ FT: 4,000
SALES (est): 1.6MM **Privately Held**
WEB: www.worksafetci.com
SIC: 3669 1611 5084 Mfg Communications Equipment Highway/Street Construction Whol Industrial Equipment

(G-21646)
WORLD PUBLICATIONS INC
Also Called: World, The
403 Us Route 302 (05641-2272)
PHONE..................................802 479-2582
Gary Hass, *Principal*
Deborah Phillips, *Vice Pres*
EMP: 23
SALES (est): 1.7MM **Privately Held**
WEB: www.vt-world.com
SIC: 2711 Newspapers-Publishing/Printing

Barton
Orleans County

(G-21647)
CHRONICLE INC
133 Water St (05822)
P.O. Box 660 (05822-0660)
PHONE..................................802 525-3531
Christopher Braithwaite, *President*
EMP: 24
SALES (est): 1.1MM **Privately Held**
WEB: www.bartonchronicle.com
SIC: 2711 Newspapers-Publishing/Printing

(G-21648)
CLASSIC SPORTING ENTERPRISES
214 Higgins Ln (05822-8648)
PHONE..................................802 525-3623
Bailey Wood, *President*
Barbara Wood, *Admin Sec*
EMP: 3
SQ FT: 1,000
SALES (est): 210K **Privately Held**
SIC: 3599 Precision Machine Shop

(G-21649)
DAVE AND JEFF LOGGING & FIREWD
84 May Farm Rd (05822-9483)
PHONE..................................802 355-0465
David B Poirier, *Principal*
EMP: 3
SALES (est): 154.2K **Privately Held**
SIC: 2411 Logging

Bellows Falls
Windham County

(G-21650)
CHROMA TECHNOLOGY CORP
10 Imtec Ln (05101-3119)
PHONE..................................802 428-2500
Paul Millman, *President*
Emily Kimball, *COO*
Willem Auer, *Vice Pres*
Kate Guerrina, *Vice Pres*
Mark Conca, *Mfg Staff*
▼ **EMP:** 107
SQ FT: 28,800
SALES: 38.3MM **Privately Held**
WEB: www.chroma.com
SIC: 3827 Mfg Optical Instruments/Lenses

(G-21651)
COOPERMAN FIFE & DRUM CO
1007 Route 121 (05101-4408)
PHONE..................................802 463-9750
Patsy C Ellis, *President*
Patricia Cooperman, *Corp Secy*
Patrick M Cooperman, *Vice Pres*
James Ellis, *Vice Pres*
EMP: 6 **EST:** 1960
SQ FT: 4,200
SALES (est): 782.3K **Privately Held**
WEB: www.cooperman.com
SIC: 3944 3931 Mfg Wood Toys Fifes & Drums

(G-21652)
NATUROPATCHES VERMONT INC
9 Spencer Dr (05101-3161)
PHONE..................................800 340-9083
Hurley Blakeney, *President*
EMP: 5
SQ FT: 50,000
SALES: 200K **Privately Held**
SIC: 2899 Mfg Chemical Preparations

(G-21653)
PJF TRUCKING AND LOGGING LLC
35 Schoolbus Depot Rd (05101-3154)
PHONE..................................802 463-3343
Paul J Furgat, *Principal*
EMP: 3
SALES (est): 392.3K **Privately Held**
SIC: 2411 Logging

▲ = Import ▼=Export
◆ =Import/Export

(G-21654)
SONNAX INDUSTRIES INC (PA)
1 Automatic Dr (05101-4000)
P.O. Box 440 (05101-0440)
PHONE..................................802 463-9722
Tommy A Harmon Jr, *President*
Robert Steinmetz, *President*
Marie S Wiese, *President*
Katherine Stahl, *Vice Pres*
Robert Moreau, *Technical Staff*
◆ **EMP:** 152
SALES (est): 53.9MM **Privately Held**
WEB: www.sonnax.com
SIC: 3714 Mfg Motor Vehicle Parts/Accessories

(G-21655)
VILLAGE PRINTER
5 Canal St (05101-1371)
P.O. Box 685 (05101-0685)
PHONE..................................802 463-9697
Norman Robertson, *Owner*
EMP: 3
SQ FT: 1,500
SALES: 220K **Privately Held**
SIC: 2752 Lithographic Commercial Printing

(G-21656)
WOODLAN TOOL AND MACHINE CO
9 Spencer Dr (05101-3161)
P.O. Box 7211, Portland ME (04112-7211)
PHONE..................................802 463-4597
Patrick Boylan, *President*
EMP: 45 **EST:** 1969
SQ FT: 27,000
SALES (est): 6.2MM **Privately Held**
SIC: 3599 3545 Mfg Industrial Machinery Mfg Machine Tool Accessories

Belmont
Rutland County

(G-21657)
CHESTERS CUSTOM WOODWORKING
1292 Frost Hill Rd (05730)
PHONE..................................802 259-3232
Mary Chester, *Principal*
EMP: 4 **EST:** 2008
SALES (est): 228.3K **Privately Held**
SIC: 2431 Mfg Millwork

Belvidere Center
Lamoille County

(G-21658)
BASIN TIMBER LLC
3721 Vt Route 109 (05442-9513)
PHONE..................................802 343-4694
John Stoddard, *Principal*
EMP: 3
SALES (est): 210.6K **Privately Held**
SIC: 2411 Logging

(G-21659)
GREEN MTN MAPLE SUG REF CO INC
204 Boarding House Hl Rd (05442-9627)
P.O. Box 82, Waterville (05492-0082)
PHONE..................................802 644-2625
Joseph Russo Jr, *President*
Robert B Chimilseski, *Admin Sec*
EMP: 23
SALES (est): 1.4MM **Privately Held**
SIC: 2099 Maple Sugar Production

(G-21660)
LEAVITT LOGGING LLC
4269 Vt Route 109 (05442-9508)
PHONE..................................802 644-1440
Kevin R Leavitt, *Administration*
EMP: 7 **EST:** 2015
SALES (est): 141.9K **Privately Held**
SIC: 2411 Logging

Bennington
Bennington County

(G-21661)
ABACUS AUTOMATION INC
264 Shields Dr (05201-8307)
PHONE..................................802 442-3662
Donald S Alvarado, *President*
Richard G Zens, *Vice Pres*
EMP: 30
SQ FT: 8,000
SALES: 5MM **Privately Held**
WEB: www.abacusautomation.com
SIC: 3599 3549 Mfg Industrial Machinery Mfg Metalworking Machinery

(G-21662)
ADVANCED FLEXIBLE COMPOSITES
452 Morse Rd (05201-1660)
PHONE..................................802 681-7121
EMP: 3 **EST:** 2016
SALES (est): 225.4K **Privately Held**
SIC: 3052 Mfg Rubber/Plastic Hose/Belting

(G-21663)
BENNINGTON ARMY AND NAVY INC
Also Called: Bennington Sports & Graphic
451 Main St 453 (05201-2141)
PHONE..................................802 447-0020
Thomas A Husser, *President*
Bernard J Husser, *Vice Pres*
Joyce M Husser, *Admin Sec*
EMP: 15 **EST:** 1978
SQ FT: 15,000
SALES: 1MM **Privately Held**
SIC: 2395 5651 5661 Pleating/Stitching Services Ret Family Clothing Ret Shoes

(G-21664)
BENNINGTON POTTERS INC (PA)
324 County St (05201-1902)
P.O. Box 199 (05201-0199)
PHONE..................................800 205-8033
Paul Silberman, *President*
Gloria Gil, *Principal*
Sheela Harden, *Vice Pres*
David Gil, *Treasurer*
▲ **EMP:** 50 **EST:** 1948
SQ FT: 30,000
SALES (est): 8.8MM **Privately Held**
WEB: www.benningtonpotters.com
SIC: 3269 5023 5812 Mfg Pottery Products Whol Homefurnishings Eating Place

(G-21665)
BENNINGTON SHRIFF GLC SLAR LLC
811 Us Route 7 S (05201-9388)
PHONE..................................802 233-3370
Luke Shullenberger,
EMP: 4
SALES (est): 163.3K **Privately Held**
SIC: 2711 Newspapers-Publishing/Printing

(G-21666)
CATAMOUNT GLASSWARE CO INC
309 County St (05201-1901)
PHONE..................................802 442-5438
Alan Karyo, *President*
Adam Volpi, *Vice Pres*
Irene Volpi, *Vice Pres*
▲ **EMP:** 25
SQ FT: 18,000
SALES (est): 3.7MM **Privately Held**
SIC: 3229 Mfg Pressed/Blown Glass

(G-21667)
CRAZY RUSSIAN GIRLS WHOLE
101 Main St (05201-2102)
PHONE..................................802 681-3983
EMP: 3
SALES (est): 165.6K **Privately Held**
SIC: 2053 Mfg Frozen Bakery Products

(G-21668)
EDGEWELL PER CARE BRANDS LLC
401 Gage St (05201-2515)
PHONE..................................802 442-5551
William G Wright, *Manager*
EMP: 322
SALES (corp-wide): 2.1B **Publicly Held**
WEB: www.eveready.com
SIC: 3421 Mfg Storage Batteries
HQ: Edgewell Personal Care Brands, Llc
6 Research Dr
Shelton CT 06484
203 944-5500

(G-21669)
ENERGIZER MANUFACTURING INC
401 Gage St (05201-2515)
PHONE..................................802 442-6301
EMP: 22
SALES (corp-wide): 2.4B **Publicly Held**
SIC: 3692 Mfg Primary Batteries
HQ: Energizer Manufacturing, Inc.
533 Maryville Univ Dr
Saint Louis MO 63141
314 985-2000

(G-21670)
FULCRUM DESIGN
107 Rutter Rd (05201-2651)
P.O. Box 104 (05201-0104)
PHONE..................................802 442-6441
Thomas Longton, *Owner*
EMP: 10
SALES (est): 558.6K **Privately Held**
WEB: www.fulcrumdc.com
SIC: 3577 Mfg Computer Peripheral Equipment

(G-21671)
GVH STUDIO INC
40 Pageant St (05201-1849)
PHONE..................................802 379-1135
Gregory Vanhouten, *President*
EMP: 5 **EST:** 2007
SALES: 600K **Privately Held**
SIC: 3577 2399 3993 Mfg Computer Peripheral Equipment Mfg Fabricated Textile Products Mfg Signs/Advertising Specialties

(G-21672)
HEX DESIGN INC (PA)
215 Benmont Ave (05201-1935)
PHONE..................................802 442-3309
Steve Golden, *President*
EMP: 5 **EST:** 1978
SQ FT: 14,000
SALES: 250K **Privately Held**
SIC: 2499 3499 Manufactures Wood And Brass Giftware

(G-21673)
INKSPOT PRESS
736 Main St (05201-2633)
PHONE..................................802 447-1768
Margaret Price, *President*
Michael Carver, *Principal*
EMP: 11
SQ FT: 9,000
SALES (est): 2.4MM **Privately Held**
SIC: 2752 Lithographic Commercial Printing

(G-21674)
JBM CARMEL LLC
14 Morse Rd (05201-1639)
PHONE..................................802 442-9110
Amanda Lewsey, *Project Mgr*
Jeffrey Thomayer,
Benny Danino,
Meir Shani,
EMP: 27
SQ FT: 42,000
SALES (est): 3MM **Privately Held**
SIC: 3479 Coating/Engraving Service

(G-21675)
JBM SHERMAN CARMEL INC
14 Morse Rd (05201-1639)
PHONE..................................802 442-5115
Jeffrey Thomayer, *President*
Benny Danino, *Principal*
Meir Shani, *Principal*
Lior Sherman, *Principal*
Christine Frazier, *Sales Staff*
▲ **EMP:** 45
SQ FT: 42,000
SALES (est): 10.5MM **Privately Held**
SIC: 3714 Mfg Motor Vehicle Parts/Accessories

(G-21676)
K & E PLASTICS INC
141 Morse Rd (05201-1661)
PHONE..................................802 375-0011
Eric Broderson, *President*
Lisa Kalbfliesh, *VP Opers*
Patricia Broderson, *Treasurer*
Kurt Broderson, *Admin Sec*
EMP: 24
SQ FT: 12,500
SALES: 3MM **Privately Held**
WEB: www.keplastics.com
SIC: 3089 Mfg Plastic Products

(G-21677)
K&H GROUP INC
Also Called: Vermont Container Div
473 Bowen Rd (05201-2757)
PHONE..................................802 442-5455
Charles Pious, *Manager*
EMP: 20
SALES (corp-wide): 121.1MM **Privately Held**
SIC: 2653 5113 Mfg Corrugated/Solid Fiber Boxes Whol Industrial/Service Paper
HQ: K&H Group, Inc.
330 Lake Osiris Rd
Walden NY 12586
845 778-3555

(G-21678)
KAMAN COMPOSITES - VERMONT INC
25 Performance Dr (05201-1947)
PHONE..................................802 442-9964
James C Larwood Jr, *President*
Alphonse J Lariviere Jr, *Division Pres*
Michael Lafleur, *Vice Pres*
Mark Schmitz, *Vice Pres*
James Sharkey, *Vice Pres*
◆ **EMP:** 188
SQ FT: 82,000
SALES (est): 29.1MM
SALES (corp-wide): 1.8B **Publicly Held**
WEB: www.vtcomposites.com
SIC: 3083 Mfg Laminated Plastic Plate/Sheet
HQ: Kaman Aerospace Group, Inc.
1332 Blue Hills Ave
Bloomfield CT 06002

(G-21679)
L & G FABRICATORS INC
137 Harwood Hill Rd (05201-1641)
P.O. Box 1016 (05201-1016)
PHONE..................................802 447-0965
Leo Gauthier, *President*
Mona Gauthier, *Vice Pres*
David McCutcheon, *Admin Sec*
EMP: 10 **EST:** 1979
SQ FT: 20,000
SALES (est): 1.5MM **Privately Held**
SIC: 3441 3433 Steel Fabrication & Mfg Wood & Coal Burning Stoves

(G-21680)
LAUZON MACHINE AND ENGRG INC
Also Called: Lauzon's Machine & Engineering
757 Main St (05201-2588)
P.O. Box 406 (05201-0406)
PHONE..................................802 442-3116
Steve Gallant, *President*
Eugene Lauzon, *Vice Pres*
Wanda Provensal, *Admin Sec*
EMP: 17 **EST:** 1957
SQ FT: 38,748
SALES (est): 2.2MM **Privately Held**
SIC: 3599 Mfg Industrial Machinery

(G-21681)
MAHAR EXCAVATING & LOGGING
592 Coleville Rd (05201-8879)
PHONE..................................802 442-2954

Michael Mahar, *Principal*
EMP: 8
SALES (est): 679.5K **Privately Held**
SIC: 2411 Logging

(G-21682)
MCCAINS VERMONT PRODUCTS INC
Also Called: Candy House Confections
1541 West Rd (05201-9630)
P.O. Box 380, Shaftsbury (05262-0380)
PHONE..................................802 447-2610
George McCain, *Principal*
Jill McCain, *Corp Secy*
EMP: 5
SALES (est): 361.2K **Privately Held**
WEB: www.vermontcandy.com
SIC: 2064 Ret Candy/Confectionery

(G-21683)
MCGILL AIRFLOW LLC
452 Harwood Hill Rd (05201-8807)
PHONE..................................802 442-1900
David McNelly, *Branch Mgr*
EMP: 50
SALES (corp-wide): 67.7MM **Privately Held**
WEB: www.mcgillairflow.com
SIC: 3444 Mfg Sheet Metalwork
HQ: Mcgill Airflow Llc
1 Mission Park
Groveport OH 43125
614 829-1200

(G-21684)
MONUMENT INDUSTRIES INC
159 Phyllis Ln (05201-1663)
P.O. Box 617 (05201-0617)
PHONE..................................802 442-8187
Lawrence W Amos, *President*
Jay L Whitten, *Vice Pres*
EMP: 22
SQ FT: 24,000
SALES: 1.8MM **Privately Held**
SIC: 2673 Mfg Bags-Plastic/Coated Paper

(G-21685)
MONUMENTAL ESTATES LLC
253 Fox Hill Rd (05201-2832)
P.O. Box 941 (05201-0941)
PHONE..................................802 442-7339
EMP: 5
SALES (est): 529.1K **Privately Held**
SIC: 3272 Mfg Concrete Products

(G-21686)
NORTH EASTERN PUBLISHING CO
Also Called: Bennington Banner
425 Main St (05201-2141)
PHONE..................................802 447-7567
JM Wall, *President*
Kathy Worth, *CFO*
James Mc Dougald, *Treasurer*
Evan Pringle, *Manager*
EMP: 30
SQ FT: 10,000
SALES (est): 1.4MM
SALES (corp-wide): 4.2B **Privately Held**
WEB: www.benningtonbanner.com
SIC: 2711 7313 Newspapers-Publishing/Printing Advertising Representative
HQ: New England Newspapers, Inc.
75 S Church St Ste L1
Pittsfield MA 01201

(G-21687)
NORTHSHIRE BREWERY INC
108 County St (05201-1807)
PHONE..................................802 681-0201
Christopher Mayne, *Principal*
EMP: 4 **EST:** 2010
SALES (est): 283.9K **Privately Held**
SIC: 2082 Drinking Place

(G-21688)
NSK STEERING SYSTEMS AMER INC
Also Called: Nssa, Bennington Plant
110 Shields Dr (05201-8309)
PHONE..................................802 442-5448
Michael Allan, *Plant Mgr*
Teresa Altman, *Engineer*
Mark Merrell, *Engineer*
Victor St Peter, *Engineer*
Stan Wilson, *Engineer*
EMP: 353 **Privately Held**
SIC: 3714 Mfg Motor Vehicle Parts/Accessories
HQ: Nsk Steering Systems America, Inc.
4200 Goss Rd
Ann Arbor MI 48105
734 913-7500

(G-21689)
PORTA-BRACE INC
160 Benmont Ave Ste 100 (05201-1889)
P.O. Box 246 (05201-0246)
PHONE..................................802 442-8171
Gregg Haythorn, *President*
Thomas S Stark, *Chairman*
Lee Loomis, *Purch Mgr*
Willis Hunt, *Sales Staff*
▲ **EMP:** 60 **EST:** 1974
SQ FT: 1,000
SALES (est): 9.7MM **Privately Held**
WEB: www.portabrace.com
SIC: 3161 Mfg Luggage

(G-21690)
R JOHN WRIGHT DOLLS INC
2402 West Rd (05201-9811)
PHONE..................................802 447-7072
R John Wright, *President*
Susan D Wright, *Vice Pres*
▲ **EMP:** 45
SQ FT: 6,000
SALES (est): 4.9MM **Privately Held**
WEB: www.rjohnwright.com
SIC: 3942 5945 Mfg Dolls/Stuffed Toys Ret Hobbies/Toys/Games

(G-21691)
SPERBER TOOL WORKS INC
75 Bowen Rd (05201-2759)
P.O. Box 439 (05201-0439)
PHONE..................................802 442-8839
Robert Sperber, *President*
EMP: 3
SQ FT: 6,000
SALES (est): 230K **Privately Held**
SIC: 3448 3546 Mfg Prefabricated Metal Buildings Mfg Power-Driven Handtools

Benson
Rutland County

(G-21692)
NORM BROWN LOGGING
240 Hulett Hill Rd (05743-9439)
PHONE..................................802 537-4474
Norman Brown, *Principal*
EMP: 4
SALES (est): 235.3K **Privately Held**
SIC: 2411 Logging

(G-21693)
ORWELL SAND & GRAVEL
1200 Park Hill Rd (05743-9894)
PHONE..................................802 345-6028
Bob Shaw, *Principal*
EMP: 3
SALES (est): 209.8K **Privately Held**
SIC: 1442 Construction Sand/Gravel

Bethel
Windsor County

(G-21694)
G W PLASTICS INC
Gw Silicones
239 Pleasant St (05032-9762)
PHONE..................................802 234-9941
Brenan Riehl, *CEO*
EMP: 5
SALES (corp-wide): 171.1MM **Privately Held**
SIC: 2822 Mfg Synthetic Rubber
PA: G W Plastics, Inc.
239 Pleasant St
Bethel VT 05032
802 234-9941

(G-21695)
G W PLASTICS INC (PA)
239 Pleasant St (05032-9762)
P.O. Box 56 (05032-0056)
PHONE..................................802 234-9941
Brenan Riehl, *President*
James Ford, *General Mgr*
John Lenahan, *Business Mgr*
Russell Roy, *Business Mgr*
Timothy Holmes, *Vice Pres*
▲ **EMP:** 410
SQ FT: 200,000
SALES (est): 171.1MM **Privately Held**
SIC: 3089 3544 Mfg Plastic Products Mfg Dies/Tools/Jigs/Fixtures

(G-21696)
MID-VT MOLDING LLC
768 S Main St (05032-4472)
P.O. Box 64 (05032-0064)
PHONE..................................802 234-9777
Don Lewis,
Jason Lewis,
Anissa Murray,
◆ **EMP:** 6
SQ FT: 3,000
SALES (est): 715K **Privately Held**
SIC: 3089 Mfg Plastic Products

Bondville
Bennington County

(G-21697)
CLOUD FOREST SOLUTIONS INC
4 Stoney Hill Rd (05340)
PHONE..................................802 353-2848
EMP: 3
SALES (est): 135K **Privately Held**
SIC: 7372 Prepackaged Software Services

Bradford
Orange County

(G-21698)
ABLAP INC
226 Industrial Dr (05033-9236)
PHONE..................................802 748-5900
Dwayne Salisbury, *President*
George Uhl, *Vice Pres*
Arcelina Salisbury, *Admin Sec*
EMP: 3 **EST:** 1974
SQ FT: 2,000
SALES (est): 339.3K **Privately Held**
WEB: www.ablap.com
SIC: 3915 Mfg Jewelers' Materials

(G-21699)
COHASA PUBLISHING INC
Also Called: Journal Opinion
Rr 5 (05033)
P.O. Box 378 (05033-0378)
PHONE..................................802 222-5281
Connie Sanville, *President*
EMP: 8
SALES (est): 353.1K **Privately Held**
SIC: 2711 Newspapers-Publishing/Printing

(G-21700)
GREENWOOD MILL INC
599 Goose Green Rd (05033-9742)
P.O. Box 1348, Lyndonville (05851-1348)
PHONE..................................802 626-0800
Bruno Couture, *CEO*
EMP: 10
SALES (est): 1.1MM **Privately Held**
SIC: 2421 Sawmill/Planing Mill

(G-21701)
ITS CLASSIFIED INC
900 S Main St (05033-8878)
P.O. Box 886 (05033-0886)
PHONE..................................802 222-5152
Peter Mallary, *President*
Frances Mallary, *Vice Pres*
EMP: 6
SALES (est): 270K **Privately Held**
WEB: www.itsclassified.com
SIC: 2711 Newspapers-Publishing/Printing

(G-21702)
JOURNAL OPINION INC
48 Main St (05033-9274)
P.O. Box 378 (05033-0378)
PHONE..................................802 222-5281
Robert F Huminski, *President*
EMP: 24
SALES (est): 1MM **Privately Held**
WEB: www.jonews.com
SIC: 2711 Newspapers-Publishing/Printing

(G-21703)
LONGTO TREE SERVICE
887 Mink Hl (05033-9316)
PHONE..................................802 274-9308
EMP: 3
SALES (est): 172.5K **Privately Held**
SIC: 2411 0783 0781 Logging Shrub/Tree Services Landscape Services

(G-21704)
NATURCOM ENTERPRISES LLC
203 Depot St (05033-9001)
P.O. Box 372 (05033-0372)
PHONE..................................802 222-4277
Paul Sachs, *Mng Member*
EMP: 4
SALES (est): 17.4K **Privately Held**
SIC: 2875 Mfg Fertilizers-Mix Only

(G-21705)
STEPHENS PRECISION INC
293 Industrial Dr (05033-9221)
PHONE..................................802 222-9600
Franklin Stephens, *President*
Ann Stephens, *Corp Secy*
EMP: 16
SQ FT: 8,000
SALES (est): 3.4MM **Privately Held**
WEB: www.stephensprecision.com
SIC: 3599 Mfg Industrial Machinery

(G-21706)
VILLAGE INDUSTRIAL POWER INC
330 Industrial Dr (05033-9306)
PHONE..................................802 522-8584
Felicity Lodge, *CEO*
Carl N Bielenberg, *Shareholder*
EMP: 10
SALES (est): 335.2K **Privately Held**
SIC: 3511 Mfg Turbines/Generator Sets

Brandon
Rutland County

(G-21707)
BLACK BEAR TREE SVC
3466 Franklin St (05733-9334)
PHONE..................................802 345-2815
Thad Poremski, *Owner*
EMP: 3
SALES (est): 257.8K **Privately Held**
SIC: 2411 Logging

(G-21708)
HAYES RECYCLED PALLETS
16 Maple St (05733-1004)
PHONE..................................802 247-4620
Ronald Hayes, *President*
Randy Hayes, *Vice Pres*
Ricky Hayes, *Vice Pres*
Carolyn Hayes, *Treasurer*
Lynn Hayes, *Admin Sec*
EMP: 22 **EST:** 1983
SQ FT: 10,000
SALES (est): 2.9MM **Privately Held**
SIC: 2448 Mfg Wood Pallets/Skids

(G-21709)
KENT NUTRITION GROUP INC
57 Alta Woods (05733-9703)
P.O. Box 189 (05733-0189)
PHONE..................................802 247-9599
David Bodette, *Manager*
EMP: 25
SALES (corp-wide): 449.1MM **Privately Held**
WEB: www.blueseal.com
SIC: 2048 Whol Farm Supplies

▲ = Import ▼=Export
◆ =Import/Export

HQ: Kent Nutrition Group, Inc.
1600 Oregon St
Muscatine IA 52761
866 647-1212

(G-21710)
NESHOBE RIVER WINERY
79 Stone Mill Dam Rd (05733-8945)
PHONE..................................802 247-8002
Robert Foley,
EMP: 3
SALES (est): 250.6K **Privately Held**
SIC: 2084 Mfg Wines/Brandy/Spirits

(G-21711)
NESHOBE WOOD PRODUCTS INC
56 Pearl St (05733-1022)
PHONE..................................802 247-3805
Ralph Ethier, *President*
Francine Ethier, *Owner*
EMP: 10
SALES (est): 1MM **Privately Held**
SIC: 2493 Mfg Reconstituted Wood Products

(G-21712)
NEW ENGLAND WOODCRAFT INC
481 North St (05733)
P.O. Box 165, Forest Dale (05745-0165)
PHONE..................................802 247-8211
Charles Thurston, *CEO*
Gary Marini, *President*
Peter Osborne, *Admin Sec*
◆ **EMP:** 130
SQ FT: 65,000
SALES: 35.7MM **Privately Held**
WEB: www.newoodcraft.com
SIC: 2512 2511 2531 2521 Mfg Uphls Household Furn Mfg Wood Household Furn Mfg Public Building Furn Mfg Wood Office Furn

(G-21713)
OLIVIAS CROUTONS COMPANY INC
Also Called: Olivia's Croutons.
2014 Frstdale Rd Brandon (05733)
P.O. Box 183, Forest Dale (05745-0183)
PHONE..................................802 465-8245
Francie Caccavo, *President*
David Caccavo, *Vice Pres*
EMP: 5
SQ FT: 36,000
SALES (est): 813.7K **Privately Held**
WEB: www.oliviascroutons.com
SIC: 2099 Mfg Food Preparations

(G-21714)
VERMONT SPECIALITY SLATE INC
855 North St (05733-8768)
P.O. Box 4 (05733-0004)
PHONE..................................802 247-6615
▼ **EMP:** 6
SALES (est): 810K **Privately Held**
WEB: www.vtslate.com
SIC: 3281 Mfg Slate Products

Brattleboro
Windham County

(G-21715)
ADAPTIVE FABRICATION LLC
22 Browne Ct Unit 117 (05301-4488)
PHONE..................................802 380-3376
Donald Meno,
EMP: 3 **EST:** 2016
SALES (est): 145.1K **Privately Held**
SIC: 3449 Mfg Misc Structural Metalwork

(G-21716)
AGAINST GRN GOURMET FOODS LLC
22 Browne Ct Unit 119 (05301-4428)
P.O. Box 225 (05302-0225)
PHONE..................................802 258-3838
Nancy Cain, *Mng Member*
EMP: 8
SALES (est): 1MM **Privately Held**
SIC: 2051 Mfg Bread/Related Products

(G-21717)
ALLARD LUMBER COMPANY (PA)
74 Glen Orne Dr (05301-9274)
PHONE..................................802 254-4939
Clifford Allard, *President*
Richard Holden, *Treasurer*
EMP: 37
SQ FT: 18,800
SALES (est): 4.9MM **Privately Held**
WEB: www.allardlumber.com
SIC: 2421 Sawmill/Planing Mill

(G-21718)
ASHE AMERICA INC
Also Called: Ashe Converting Equipment
23 Marlboro Rd (05301-9708)
PHONE..................................802 254-0200
John O M Godbold, *President*
James Godbold, *Vice Pres*
Guy Carrington, *Sales Staff*
Barbara M Godbold, *Admin Sec*
◆ **EMP:** 70
SQ FT: 1,000
SALES (est): 6.4MM **Privately Held**
WEB: www.asheconvertingequipment.com
SIC: 3554 5084 Mfg Paper Industrial Machinery Whol Industrial Equipment

(G-21719)
BLW LLC
Also Called: Window Quilt
22 Browne Ct Unit 105 (05301-4428)
PHONE..................................802 246-4500
Bryan Wittler,
EMP: 6
SQ FT: 10,000
SALES (est): 500K **Privately Held**
WEB: www.windowquilt.com
SIC: 2591 Ret Misc Homefurnishings

(G-21720)
BRATTLEBORO KILN DRY & MILLING
1103 Vernon St (05301-5104)
PHONE..................................802 254-4528
Dominic Cersosimo, *President*
Michael Elkins, *Vice Pres*
Richard Elkins, *Vice Pres*
Lawrin Crispe, *Admin Sec*
EMP: 50 **EST:** 1954
SQ FT: 300,000
SALES (est): 4.7MM **Privately Held**
SIC: 2421 2431 Sawmill/Planing Mill Mfg Millwork

(G-21721)
C E BRADELY LAB INC
Also Called: Oro
55 Bennett Dr (05301-5100)
P.O. Box 8238 (05304-8238)
PHONE..................................802 257-1122
Hisham Kanaan, *CEO*
Rashed Kanaan, *President*
Edward Rochford, *Vice Pres*
Robert Rowinski, *Vice Pres*
EMP: 55 **EST:** 1955
SQ FT: 80,000
SALES (est): 7MM
SALES (corp-wide): 12.6MM **Privately Held**
WEB: www.oro.com
SIC: 2851 2869 Mfg Paints/Allied Products Mfg Industrial Organic Chemicals
PA: C. E. Bradley Laboratories, Inc
56 Bennett Dr
Brattleboro VT 05301
802 257-1122

(G-21722)
C E BRADLEY LABORATORIES (PA)
Also Called: Flo-Matic
56 Bennett Dr (05301-5105)
P.O. Box 8238 (05304-8238)
PHONE..................................802 257-1122
Hisham R Kanaan, *Ch of Bd*
Rashed H Kanaan, *President*
Edward Rochford, *Vice Pres*
Robert Rowinski, *Vice Pres*
June Forrett, *Purchasing*
▲ **EMP:** 50
SALES (est): 12.6MM **Privately Held**
WEB: www.cebradley.com
SIC: 2851 2869 Mfg Paints/Allied Products Mfg Industrial Organic Chemicals

(G-21723)
CAVE MANUFACTURING INC
Also Called: Bradford Machine
22 Browne Ct Unit 104 (05301-5406)
PHONE..................................802 257-9253
Jim Hayssen, *President*
EMP: 30
SQ FT: 12,000
SALES (est): 5.2MM **Privately Held**
WEB: www.bradfordmachine.com
SIC: 3599 7692 Mfg Industrial Machinery Welding Repair

(G-21724)
CERSOSIMO LUMBER COMPANY INC (PA)
Also Called: Hardwick Dry Kilns
1103 Vernon St (05301-5110)
PHONE..................................802 254-4508
Michael A Cersosimo, *President*
Dominic A Butch, *Chairman*
John Caveney, *Vice Pres*
Jeffrey Hardy, *Vice Pres*
Phil Mann, *Opers Mgr*
◆ **EMP:** 150 **EST:** 1947
SALES: 46.8MM **Privately Held**
WEB: www.cersosimolumber.com
SIC: 2421 Sawmill/Planing Mill

(G-21725)
COUNTRY SHOP ROBB FMLY LTD
827 Ames Hill Rd (05301-4247)
PHONE..................................802 258-9087
Charles Robb Jr, *Principal*
Helen Robb, *Principal*
EMP: 3
SALES: 100K **Privately Held**
SIC: 2099 Mfg Food Preparations

(G-21726)
G S P COATINGS INC
101 John Seitz Dr (05301-3642)
PHONE..................................802 257-5858
Norman Schneeberger, *President*
David Henry, *Corp Secy*
David Sprague, *Vice Pres*
Brian Robinson, *Engineer*
Tim La Grant, *Data Proc Exec*
EMP: 15
SQ FT: 2,400
SALES (est): 1.6MM **Privately Held**
SIC: 3479 Coating/Engraving Service

(G-21727)
G S PRECISION INC (PA)
101 John Seitz Dr (05301-3642)
PHONE..................................802 257-5200
Norman A Schneeberger, *President*
David Sprague, *President*
Doug Kirker, *Plant Mgr*
Jerry Dubie, *Facilities Mgr*
Scott Jones, *Purch Mgr*
◆ **EMP:** 410 **EST:** 1958
SQ FT: 102,000
SALES (est): 121.9MM **Privately Held**
WEB: www.gsprecision.com
SIC: 3599 Mfg Industrial Machinery

(G-21728)
GARFLEX INC
Also Called: Fulflex
32 Justin Holden Dr (05301-7050)
PHONE..................................802 257-5256
Maria Teresa Santiago, *President*
Tara Castine, *Purchasing*
EMP: 100
SALES (corp-wide): 30MM **Privately Held**
WEB: www.themooreco.com
SIC: 2258 2241 3069 3061 Lace/Knit Fabric Mill Narrow Fabric Mill Mfg Fabricatd Rubber Prdt Mfg Mechanical Rubber Gd
PA: Garflex Inc
9594 Nw 41st St Ste 209
Doral FL 33178
305 436-8915

(G-21729)
GEORGE L MARTIN
Also Called: Wayside Fences
218 Main St (05301-2843)
P.O. Box 2201 (05303-2201)
PHONE..................................802 254-5838
George L Martin, *Owner*
EMP: 5
SALES (est): 450K **Privately Held**
SIC: 2499 3496 3446 Mfg Wood Products Mfg Misc Fabricated Wire Products Mfg Architectural Metalwork

(G-21730)
GRAFTON VILLAGE CHEESE CO LLC
400 Linden St (05301-4474)
P.O. Box 87, Grafton (05146-0087)
PHONE..................................802 843-2221
Wendy Brewer, *Sales Staff*
Kelly McNamara, *Sales Staff*
Elena Santogade, *Sales Staff*
Meri Spicer, *Marketing Staff*
Vince Razionale, *Director*
EMP: 35
SQ FT: 2,500
SALES (est): 348.2K
SALES (corp-wide): 1.1MM **Privately Held**
WEB: www.graftonvillagecheese.com
SIC: 2022 Mfg Cheese
PA: Windham Foundation
225 Townshend Rd
Grafton VT 05146
802 843-2211

(G-21731)
GREEN MOUNTAIN FRAGRANCES INC
Also Called: Scentastics
185 Meeting House Ln (05301-8982)
PHONE..................................802 490-2268
Pamela Wilcox, *President*
Kenneth Gilbert, *CFO*
▲ **EMP:** 3
SALES (est): 150K **Privately Held**
SIC: 2844 Mfg Toilet Preparations

(G-21732)
HONORA WINERY & VINEYARD INC
1950 Collins Rd (05301-9343)
P.O. Box 129, West Halifax (05358-0129)
PHONE..................................802 368-2930
Patricia Farrington, *President*
EMP: 4
SALES (est): 350.3K **Privately Held**
SIC: 2084 Mfg Wines/Brandy/Spirits

(G-21733)
HOWARD PRINTING INC
Also Called: New England Showcase
14 Noahs Ln (05301-4463)
P.O. Box 996 (05302-0996)
PHONE..................................802 254-3550
Gregory Howard, *President*
Donna McElligott, *Marketing Mgr*
Ben Briggs, *Graphic Designe*
EMP: 8
SALES (est): 1.4MM **Privately Held**
WEB: www.newenglandshowcase.com
SIC: 2752 Lithographic Commercial Printing

(G-21734)
IBRATTLEBORO
41 Cedar St (05301-5528)
PHONE..................................802 257-7475
EMP: 3
SALES (est): 105.9K **Privately Held**
SIC: 2711 Newspapers-Publishing/Printing

(G-21735)
JOUVE OF NORTH AMERICA INC (DH)
70 Landmark Hill Dr (05301-9102)
P.O. Box 1338 (05302-1338)
PHONE..................................802 254-6073
Emmanuel Benoit, *CEO*
EMP: 8
SALES (est): 7MM
SALES (corp-wide): 20.1MM **Privately Held**
SIC: 2721 Periodicals-Publishing/Printing

GEOGRAPHIC

HQ: Jouve
Voir Rubrique 16
Mayenne 53100
243 082-554

(G-21736)
LEADER DIST SYSTEMS INC
1566 Putney Rd (05301-9497)
P.O. Box 8285 (05304-8285)
PHONE....802 254-6093
John Leader, *President*
Shaun M Leary, *Vice Pres*
Jennifer Donovan, *Purch Mgr*
Roland Currier, *CFO*
William M McCarty, *Admin Sec*
EMP: 65
SALES (est): 10.4MM **Privately Held**
SIC: 2086 Mfg Bottled/Canned Soft Drinks

(G-21737)
LONG FALLS PAPERBOARD LLC
161 Wellington Rd (05301-7052)
PHONE....802 257-0365
Ben Rankin, *Mng Member*
▼ **EMP:** 104
SALES: 26MM **Privately Held**
SIC: 2631 Paperboard Mill

(G-21738)
MATTS MAPLE SYRUP
370 Higley Hill Rd (05301-7975)
PHONE....802 464-9788
David Matt, *Principal*
EMP: 6 **EST:** 2008
SALES (est): 426.3K **Privately Held**
SIC: 2099 Mfg Food Preparations

(G-21739)
NEW CHAPTER INC (HQ)
Also Called: New Charter Distribution
90 Technology Dr (05301-9180)
PHONE....800 543-7279
Larry Allgaier, *CEO*
Mark Gavin, *President*
Tom Newmark, *Chairman*
Ruth B Austin, *Vice Pres*
EMP: 105
SQ FT: 93,406
SALES (est): 37.5MM
SALES (corp-wide): 67.6B **Publicly Held**
WEB: www.new-chapter.com
SIC: 2834 Mfg Pharmaceutical Preparations
PA: The Procter & Gamble Company
1 Procter And Gamble Plz
Cincinnati OH 45202
513 983-1100

(G-21740)
NEW ENGLAND NEWSPAPERS INC
Also Called: Brattleboro Reformer
62 Black Mountain Rd (05301-9241)
P.O. Box 802 (05302-0802)
PHONE....802 254-2311
Edward Woods, *Branch Mgr*
EMP: 40
SALES (corp-wide): 4.2B **Privately Held**
WEB: www.berkshireeagle.com
SIC: 2711 Newspapers-Publishing/Printing
HQ: New England Newspapers, Inc.
75 S Church St Ste L1
Pittsfield MA 01201

(G-21741)
NUTRAGENESIS LLC
76 Highland St Ste 208 (05301-6489)
PHONE....802 257-5345
EMP: 5
SALES (est): 340K **Privately Held**
WEB: www.nutragenesisnutrition.com
SIC: 2023 Mfg Dry/Evaporated Dairy Products

(G-21742)
OMEGA OPTICAL INCORPORATED
Also Called: Omega Filters
21 Omega Dr (05301-4444)
PHONE....802 251-7300
Robert L Johnson Jr, *President*
Renee Levasseur, *Purch Agent*
Paul Jensen, *QA Dir*
Gary Carver, *Engineer*
Florin Grosu, *Engineer*
EMP: 82 **EST:** 1968
SQ FT: 32,000
SALES (est): 12.5MM **Privately Held**
WEB: www.omegafilters.com
SIC: 3827 Mfg Optical Instruments/Lenses

(G-21743)
PEPSI COLA BOTTLING CO
1566 Putney Rd (05301-9497)
P.O. Box 8285 (05304-8285)
PHONE....802 254-6093
John Leader, *Ch of Bd*
Shaun M Leary, *President*
EMP: 106
SALES (est): 11.1MM **Privately Held**
WEB: www.pepsibrattleboro.com
SIC: 2086 Mfg Bottled/Canned Soft Drinks

(G-21744)
PRISON LEGAL NEWS
35 Yorkshire Cir (05301-6189)
PHONE....802 257-1342
Susan Schwartzkopf, *Principal*
EMP: 3 **EST:** 2018
SALES (est): 105.9K **Privately Held**
SIC: 2711 Newspapers-Publishing/Printing

(G-21745)
PRO LINGUA ASSOCIATES INC
74 Cotton Mill Hl A315 (05301-8603)
PHONE....802 257-7779
Arthur A Burrows, *President*
Raymond Clark, *Vice Pres*
Elise C Burrows, *Treasurer*
Patrick R Moran, *Admin Sec*
EMP: 4
SALES: 325K **Privately Held**
WEB: www.prolinguaassociates.com
SIC: 2731 Books-Publishing/Printing

(G-21746)
PUTNEY PASTA COMPANY INC
28 Vernon St Ste 434 (05301-3668)
P.O. Box 445, Chester (05143-0445)
PHONE....802 257-4800
Carol S Berry, *President*
Jonathan H Altman, *Vice Pres*
EMP: 30
SQ FT: 42,000
SALES (est): 3.9MM **Privately Held**
WEB: www.putneypasta.com
SIC: 2038 2098 2035 Mfg Frozen Specialties Mfg Macaroni/Spaghetti Mfg Pickles/Sauces/Dressing

(G-21747)
STRATFORD PUBLISHING SERVICES
70 Landmark Hill Dr (05301-9102)
P.O. Box 1338 (05302-1338)
PHONE....802 254-6073
James E Bristol, *President*
EMP: 50
SQ FT: 8,000
SALES (est): 3.2MM **Privately Held**
SIC: 2731 2791 Books-Publishing/Printing Typesetting Services

(G-21748)
SWISS PRECISION TURNING INC
74 Cotton Mill Hl A108 (05301-7809)
PHONE....802 257-1935
Willy Buhlmann, *President*
EMP: 14
SQ FT: 3,200
SALES (est): 2.3MM **Privately Held**
SIC: 3599 Machine Job Shop

(G-21749)
TEXTECH INC
70 Landmark Hill Dr (05301-9102)
PHONE....802 254-6073
EMP: 3
SALES (est): 215.6K **Privately Held**
SIC: 2791 Typesetting, Nsk

(G-21750)
VERMONT CULINARY ISLANDS LLC
Also Called: Vermont Islands
22 Browne Ct Unit 115 (05301-4488)
PHONE....802 246-2277
Tom Meyer, *Mng Member*
EMP: 10
SALES (est): 1.1MM **Privately Held**
SIC: 2511 2599 Mfg Wood Household Furniture Mfg Furniture/Fixtures

(G-21751)
VERMONT INDEPENDENT MEDIA INC
Also Called: COMMONS, THE
139 Main St Rm 604 (05301-2871)
P.O. Box 1212 (05302-1212)
PHONE....802 246-6397
Barry Aleshnick, *President*
Jeffrey Potter, *Director*
Jane Noyes, *Admin Sec*
EMP: 6
SALES: 477.5K **Privately Held**
SIC: 2711 Newspapers-Publishing/Printing

(G-21752)
VERMONT ISLANDS CULINARY LLC
Also Called: Vermont Islands Kitchens Bars
22 Browne Ct Unit 115 (05301-4488)
PHONE....802 387-8591
Tom Meyer,
Nancy Meyer,
EMP: 10
SQ FT: 6,000
SALES (est): 840K **Privately Held**
SIC: 3639 Mfg Household Appliances

(G-21753)
VTFOLKUS
Also Called: Peacemedia Foundation
51 Main St Ste 1 (05301-3294)
PHONE....802 246-1410
Eric Reagan, *President*
Pamela Reagan, *Partner*
EMP: 3
SALES: 30K **Privately Held**
SIC: 2711 Newspapers-Publishing/Printing

(G-21754)
WASHBURN VAULT COMPANY INC
795 Meadowbrook Rd (05301-4402)
PHONE....802 254-9150
John Baldwin, *President*
Linda Baldwin, *Vice Pres*
Dorothy Baldwin, *Treasurer*
EMP: 8 **EST:** 1942
SQ FT: 3,435
SALES (est): 967.3K **Privately Held**
SIC: 3272 5032 Mfg Concrete Products Whol Brick/Stone Material

(G-21755)
ZEPHYR DESIGNS LTD
129 Main St (05301-3061)
PHONE....802 254-2788
Robert W Clements, *President*
John Clements, *Vice Pres*
EMP: 8 **EST:** 1972
SQ FT: 3,000
SALES: 480K **Privately Held**
SIC: 2499 5999 Mfg Wood Products Ret Misc Merchandise

(G-21756)
ZINN GRAPHICS INC
1012 Western Ave (05301-5113)
PHONE....802 254-6742
Rupert W Zinn, *President*
Honora F Zinn, *Treasurer*
EMP: 3
SQ FT: 1,500
SALES: 250K **Privately Held**
WEB: www.zinngraphics.com
SIC: 2752 4822 7334 7336 Offset Printing Facsimile And Copying Services & Film Prep

Bridgewater
Windsor County

(G-21757)
CHARLES SHACKLETON & MIRANDA T
Also Called: Shackletonthomas
The Mill Rte 4 (05034)
PHONE....802 672-5175
Charles R Shackleton, *President*
EMP: 23
SQ FT: 18,000
SALES (est): 2.5MM **Privately Held**
WEB: www.shackletonthomas.com
SIC: 2511 Mfg Wood Household Furniture

Bridgewater Corners
Windsor County

(G-21758)
LONG TRAIL BREWING COMPANY
5520 Us Route 4 (05035-9600)
PHONE....802 672-5011
Brian Walsh, *President*
Tim Fulham, *Corp Secy*
Ed York, *Exec VP*
Thomas A O'Grady, *CFO*
Marc Peluso, *Sales Staff*
▲ **EMP:** 100
SQ FT: 25,000
SALES (est): 17.6MM
SALES (corp-wide): 26.7MM **Privately Held**
SIC: 2082 Mfg Malt Beverages
PA: Fulham Investors Lp
593 Washington St
Wellesley MA 02482
781 235-2266

Bridport
Addison County

(G-21759)
RED NUN INSTRUMENT CORPORATION
1627 Middle Rd (05734-9549)
PHONE....802 758-6000
Lynn Boie, *President*
EMP: 4
SALES (est): 396.6K **Privately Held**
SIC: 3825 Mfg Measuring Equipment For Electronic & Electrical Circuits & Equipment

Bristol
Addison County

(G-21760)
A JOHNSON CO
995 S 116 Rd (05443-5076)
PHONE....802 453-4884
Kenneth D Johnson, *President*
David F Johnson, *Partner*
Carolyn J Sayre, *Partner*
William R Sayre, *Partner*
Rebecca James, *Senior Mgr*
◆ **EMP:** 55
SQ FT: 3,000
SALES (est): 8.5MM **Privately Held**
SIC: 2421 5031 5211 0851 Sawmill/Planing Mill Whol Lumber/Plywd/Millwk Ret Lumber/Building Mtrl Forestry Services Hdwd Dimension/Flr Mill

(G-21761)
AUTUMN HARP INC
61 Pine St (05443-1043)
P.O. Box 267 (05443-0267)
PHONE....802 453-4807
EMP: 3
SALES (est): 246.1K **Privately Held**
SIC: 2844 Mfg Toilet Preparations

(G-21762)
BROWNS CERTIFIED WELDING INC
275 S 116 Rd (05443-5090)
PHONE....802 453-3351
Craig W Brown, *President*
Kim Chamberlin, *Vice Pres*
EMP: 10
SQ FT: 8,000
SALES (est): 907.5K **Privately Held**
SIC: 3441 7692 Welding Repair And Steel Fabrication

▲ = Import ▼=Export
◆ =Import/Export

(G-21763)
CLAIRE LATHROP BAND MILL INC
Also Called: Lathrop Mill
44 South St (05443-1231)
PHONE..................................802 453-3606
James Lathrop, *President*
Jason Lathrop, *Vice Pres*
Justin Lathrop, *Treasurer*
Claire Lathrop, *Admin Sec*
EMP: 50
SQ FT: 32,000
SALES (est): 5.8MM **Privately Held**
SIC: 2421 Sawmill/Planing Mill

(G-21764)
LUNCH BUNDLES INC
202 Barnum Rd (05443-4412)
PHONE..................................802 272-3051
Steve Konczal, *CFO*
EMP: 4
SALES (est): 410.2K **Privately Held**
SIC: 2099 Mfg Food Preparations

Brookfield
Orange County

(G-21765)
T B LINCOLN LOGGING INC
64 Bakers Pond Rd (05036)
P.O. Box 121, Northfield Falls (05664-0121)
PHONE..................................802 276-3172
Thomas Lincoln, *President*
Gaye E Lincoln, *Admin Sec*
EMP: 3
SALES (est): 373.3K **Privately Held**
SIC: 2411 1629 Logging Contractor Land Clearing

Burlington
Chittenden County

(G-21766)
AMALGAMATED CULTURE WORK INC (PA)
Also Called: T Shirt Gallery
420 Pine St (05401-4779)
PHONE..................................800 272-2066
Wayne Turiansky, *President*
EMP: 6
SQ FT: 3,500
SALES (est): 21.9MM **Privately Held**
WEB: www.cultureworks.com
SIC: 2759 Commercial Printing

(G-21767)
ASIANA NOODLE SHOP
88 Church St (05401-4408)
PHONE..................................802 862-8828
San Kong, *Principal*
EMP: 4
SALES (est): 390.8K **Privately Held**
SIC: 2098 Eating Place

(G-21768)
AURORA NORTH SOFTWARE INC
29 Church St Ste 303 (05401-4433)
PHONE..................................802 540-2504
Christopher Ryan Kave, *President*
Chris Wood, *Engineer*
Sheehan Lake, *CTO*
Monica Mello, *Executive Asst*
EMP: 44
SALES (est): 287.1K **Privately Held**
SIC: 7372 Prepackaged Software Services

(G-21769)
BOGNER OF AMERICA INC (DH)
128 Lakeside Ave Ste 302 (05401-5190)
PHONE..................................802 861-6900
Willy Bogner, *President*
Peter Born, *President*
Constantine Brandstetter, *Exec VP*
Matthias Mack, *Exec VP*
▲ **EMP:** 30
SQ FT: 85,000
SALES (est): 2.3MM
SALES (corp-wide): 182.6MM **Privately Held**
WEB: www.bognerofamerica.com
SIC: 2339 2329 Mfg Women/Miss Outerwear Mfg Mens/Boys Clothing
HQ: Bogner Sport Gmbh & Co. Verwaltungs Kg
St.-Veit-Str. 4
Munchen 81673
894 360-60

(G-21770)
BURTON CORPORATION (PA)
Also Called: Riding Enhancement Designs
180 Queen City Park Rd (05401-5935)
P.O. Box 4449 (05406-4449)
PHONE..................................802 862-4500
Donna Carpenter, *CEO*
Mike Reesr, *CEO*
Jake Burton Carpenter, *Chairman*
Karen Drabkin, *COO*
Philippe Gouzes, *Senior VP*
◆ **EMP:** 332
SQ FT: 70,000
SALES (est): 188.4MM **Privately Held**
WEB: www.burton.com
SIC: 3949 Mfg Sporting/Athletic Goods

(G-21771)
BURTON CORPORATION
266 Queen City Park Rd (05401-5934)
PHONE..................................802 862-4500
EMP: 3
SALES (corp-wide): 188.4MM **Privately Held**
SIC: 3949 Mfg Sporting/Athletic Goods
PA: The Burton Corporation
180 Queen City Park Rd
Burlington VT 05401
802 862-4500

(G-21772)
CERES LLC (PA)
Also Called: Ceres Natural Remedies
190 College St (05401)
PHONE..................................833 237-3767
David Mickenberg,
EMP: 3
SALES (est): 902.8K **Privately Held**
SIC: 2834 Mfg Pharmaceutical Preparations

(G-21773)
CHURCH & MAPLE GLASS STUDIO
37 N Prospect St Apt 5 (05401-3377)
PHONE..................................802 863-3880
Wilbur L Shriner, *Owner*
EMP: 3
SQ FT: 2,600
SALES: 170K **Privately Held**
SIC: 3229 Blown Glass

(G-21774)
CITIZEN CIDER LLC
316 Pine St Ste 114 (05401-4740)
PHONE..................................802 448-3278
Justin Heilenbach, *Principal*
Cheray Macfarland, *Sales Staff*
EMP: 19
SALES (est): 3.9MM **Privately Held**
SIC: 2084 Mfg Wines/Brandy/Spirits

(G-21775)
CLEVERFOODIES INC
70 S Winooski Ave Ste 141 (05401-3898)
PHONE..................................888 938-7984
Warren Wison Jr, *Co-Founder*
Marc Gascon, *Co-Founder*
EMP: 5
SQ FT: 1,000
SALES: 1MM **Privately Held**
SIC: 2099 Mfg Food Preparations

(G-21776)
CORNELL ONLINE LLC
Also Called: April Cornell
131 Battery St (05401-5208)
PHONE..................................802 448-3281
April Cornell, *Mng Member*
EMP: 49
SALES (est): 2MM **Privately Held**
SIC: 2299 5137 Mfg Textile Goods Whol Women's/Child's Clothing

(G-21777)
CRICKET RADIO LLC
260 Battery St (05401-3201)
PHONE..................................802 825-8368
Elizabeth Archangeli,
EMP: 4 **EST:** 2011
SALES (est): 433K **Privately Held**
SIC: 2599 Mfg Furniture/Fixtures

(G-21778)
DA CAPO PUBLISHING INC
Also Called: Seven Days Newspaper
255 S Champlain St Ste 5 (05401-7703)
P.O. Box 1164 (05402-1164)
PHONE..................................802 864-5684
Paula Routly, *President*
Courtney Copp, *Editor*
Candace Page, *Editor*
Pamela Polston, *Vice Pres*
Lisa Matanle, *Project Mgr*
EMP: 33
SALES: 3MM **Privately Held**
WEB: www.sevendaysvt.com
SIC: 2711 Newspapers-Publishing/Printing

(G-21779)
DAILY RIDER LLC
1541 North Ave (05408-2429)
PHONE..................................802 497-1269
Mark Davidson, *Principal*
EMP: 5
SALES (est): 216.1K **Privately Held**
SIC: 2711 Newspapers-Publishing/Printing

(G-21780)
DESIGNED ESSENCE ENTERPRISE
Also Called: Designers' Circle
52 Church St Ste 2b (05401-4407)
PHONE..................................802 864-4238
David Sisco, *President*
Marjorie S Sisco, *Admin Sec*
EMP: 6
SALES (est): 630K **Privately Held**
WEB: www.vermontjeweler.com
SIC: 3911 5944 Ret Fine Jewelry And Also Provides Custom Work

(G-21781)
EMILY POST INSTITUTE INC
444 S Union St Ste 340 (05401-4995)
PHONE..................................802 860-1814
Allen Post, *President*
Peter Post, *Managing Dir*
Lucinda Senning, *Treasurer*
William Post, *Director*
Cindy Senning, *Director*
EMP: 5
SALES (est): 478.5K **Privately Held**
WEB: www.emilypost.com
SIC: 2731 Books-Publishing/Printing

(G-21782)
FLASHBAGS LLC
70 S Winooski Ave (05401-3898)
PHONE..................................802 999-8981
Liza Cowan, *Principal*
EMP: 4 **EST:** 2008
SALES (est): 281.7K **Privately Held**
SIC: 2673 Mfg Bags-Plastic/Coated Paper

(G-21783)
FOAM BREWERS
112 Lake St (05401-5284)
PHONE..................................802 399-2511
Robert Grim, *Principal*
EMP: 4 **EST:** 2015
SALES (est): 83K **Privately Held**
SIC: 2082 Mfg Malt Beverages

(G-21784)
FUEL ON LINE CORP
1127 North Ave Ste 27169 (05408-2757)
PHONE..................................888 475-2552
EMP: 32
SQ FT: 1,500
SALES (est): 916.4K **Privately Held**
SIC: 2741 Miscellaneous Publishing, Nsk

(G-21785)
GAMETHEORY INC
Also Called: Birnam Wood Games
266 Main St (05401-8322)
PHONE..................................802 779-2322
Marguerite Dibble, *Principal*
Matthew Brand, *Principal*
Michael Hopke, *Principal*
EMP: 4
SALES (est): 278.5K **Privately Held**
SIC: 7372 Prepackaged Software

(G-21786)
GANNETT CO INC
Also Called: Burlington Free Press
100 Bank St Ste 700 (05401-4946)
P.O. Box 10 (05402-0010)
PHONE..................................802 863-3441
John Curley, *CEO*
EMP: 76
SALES (corp-wide): 1.5B **Publicly Held**
SIC: 2711 Newspapers-Publishing/Printing
HQ: Gannett Media Corp.
7950 Jones Branch Dr
Mc Lean VA 22102
703 854-6000

(G-21787)
GIRAL LLC
1 Lawson Ln Ste 120 (05401-8445)
PHONE..................................802 238-7852
Mariasha Dombro Giral,
Ozzy Giral,
EMP: 3
SALES (est): 250K **Privately Held**
SIC: 2259 Knitting Mill

(G-21788)
HUNTINGTON GRAPHICS
168 Battery St Ste 2 (05401-5286)
P.O. Box 373 (05402-0373)
PHONE..................................802 660-3605
Jared Gange, *CEO*
EMP: 3
SQ FT: 400
SALES: 80K **Privately Held**
WEB: www.letsclimb.com
SIC: 2731 Books-Publishing/Printing

(G-21789)
INDEPENDENT BREWERS UNTD CORP (DH)
Also Called: Magic Hat Brewing Company
431 Pine St Ste G12 (05401-5093)
PHONE..................................802 862-6114
Martin R Kelly, *President*
Steve Hood, *Vice Pres*
Susan Dorey, *Admin Sec*
EMP: 13
SALES (est): 79.7MM **Privately Held**
SIC: 2082 2084 Mfg Malt Beverages Mfg Wines/Brandy/Spirits

(G-21790)
KIDS ON BLOCK - VERMONT INC
294 N Winooski Ave # 125 (05401-3680)
PHONE..................................802 860-3349
Deb W Lyons, *President*
Karen Newman, *Prgrmr*
EMP: 5
SALES: 223.4K **Privately Held**
WEB: www.kidsontheblockvermont.org
SIC: 3999 Mfg Misc Products

(G-21791)
KOSS INDUSTRIES INC
Also Called: Waterseed Wooden Bird Feeders
191 Loomis St (05401-3356)
PHONE..................................802 863-5004
Robert Koss, *President*
Diane Koss, *Vice Pres*
EMP: 3
SALES (est): 220K **Privately Held**
SIC: 2449 5031 5211 5961 Mfg/Whol/Ret/Mail-Order Wooden Bird Feeders/Baths

(G-21792)
LAKE CHAMPLAIN TRNSP CO
Lake Industries Div
King Street Dock (05401)
PHONE..................................802 660-3495
Raymond C Pecor Jr, *President*
EMP: 130
SALES (corp-wide): 15MM **Privately Held**
SIC: 3731 5947 Shipbuilding/Repairing Ret Gifts/Novelties

GEOGRAPHIC

PA: Lake Champlain Transportation Company
1 King St
Burlington VT 05401
802 864-9804

(G-21793)
LEARNING MATERIALS WORKSHOP
58 Henry St (05401-3329)
PHONE....802 862-0112
Karen Hewitt, *President*
Fred Lager, *Principal*
▲ **EMP:** 3
SQ FT: 1,800
SALES (est): 394.2K **Privately Held**
WEB: www.learningmaterialswork.com
SIC: 3944 5092 5945 5961 Mfg Games/Toys Whol Toys/Hobby Goods Ret Hobbies/Toys/Games Ret Mail-Order House School/Educational Svcs

(G-21794)
LIVING SYSTEMS INSTRUMENTATION
156 Battery St Ste 5 (05401-5276)
P.O. Box 1100, Saint Albans (05478-1100)
PHONE....802 863-5547
William Halpern, *President*
Rosalie G Osol, *Vice Pres*
George Coy, *Treasurer*
EMP: 4
SQ FT: 1,200
SALES: 478.5K **Privately Held**
WEB: www.livingsys.com
SIC: 3826 Mfg Analytical Instruments

(G-21795)
MCCLURE NEWSPAPERS INC
Also Called: Burlington Free Press
100 Bank St Ste 700 (05401-4946)
P.O. Box 10 (05402-0010)
PHONE....802 863-3441
James M Carey, *President*
Ryan Mercer, *Editor*
EMP: 220 **EST:** 1827
SQ FT: 80,000
SALES (est): 12.8MM
SALES (corp-wide): 1.5B **Publicly Held**
WEB: www.burlingtonfreepress.com
SIC: 2711 2796 2791 2752 Newspapers-Publish/Print Platemaking Services Typesetting Services Lithographic Coml Print
HQ: Gannett Satellite Information Network, Llc
7950 Jones Branch Dr
Mc Lean VA 22102
703 854-6000

(G-21796)
METALWORKS INC
205 Flynn Ave (05401-5302)
P.O. Box 4307 (05406-4307)
PHONE....802 863-0414
Michael Dowling, *President*
EMP: 6
SQ FT: 10,000
SALES (est): 949.1K **Privately Held**
SIC: 3446 7692 Mfg Architectural Metalwork Welding Repair

(G-21797)
MFI CORP
44 Lakeside Ave (05401-5242)
PHONE....802 658-6600
Steve Spittle, *President*
Louis Rotondo, *President*
EMP: 81
SALES (est): 12.4MM
SALES (corp-wide): 2.7B **Publicly Held**
WEB: www.mfii.com
SIC: 3589 Mfg Service Industry Machinery
PA: The Middleby Corporation
1400 Toastmaster Dr
Elgin IL 60120
847 741-3300

(G-21798)
MONUMENT VIEW APTS LP
100 Bank St Ste 400 (05401-0002)
PHONE....802 863-8424
Karen Allen, *Principal*
Janet Spitler, *Principal*
EMP: 3
SALES (est): 128.1K **Privately Held**
SIC: 3272 Mfg Concrete Products

(G-21799)
NOTABLI INC
209 College St Ste 3w (05401-8394)
PHONE....802 448-0810
Thomas O' Leary, *CEO*
EMP: 10
SQ FT: 35,000
SALES (est): 607K
SALES (corp-wide): 848.3K **Privately Held**
SIC: 7372 Prepackaged Software Services
PA: Parent Company Applications, Inc.
20 Hillside Cir
Essex Junction VT 05452
802 233-3612

(G-21800)
OGEE INC
1 Lawson Ln Ste 130 (05401-8445)
PHONE....802 540-8082
Mark Rice, *CEO*
Abbott Stark, *Managing Dir*
Alex Stark, *COO*
EMP: 3 **EST:** 2014
SQ FT: 150
SALES (est): 288.4K **Privately Held**
SIC: 2844 Mfg Toilet Preparations

(G-21801)
OXBOW CREATIVE LLC
47 Maple St Ste 332 (05401-5097)
PHONE....802 870-0354
Evan Deutsch, *Principal*
EMP: 12 **EST:** 2014
SALES (est): 1.8MM **Privately Held**
SIC: 2911 Petroleum Refiner

(G-21802)
PHAT THAI
100 North St Ste 1 (05401-5145)
PHONE....802 863-8827
Banh Thai, *Owner*
EMP: 3
SALES (est): 219.3K **Privately Held**
SIC: 2032 Mfg Canned Specialties

(G-21803)
PIEMATRIX INC
106 Main St (05401-8484)
PHONE....802 318-4891
Paul Dandurand, *CEO*
Chris Smith, *Administration*
EMP: 10
SALES (est): 830.7K **Privately Held**
SIC: 7372 Prepackaged Software Services

(G-21804)
QUEEN CITY PRINTERS INC
701 Pine St (05401-4941)
P.O. Box 756 (05402-0756)
PHONE....802 864-4566
Alan R Schillhammer, *President*
Margaret Kane, *Production*
EMP: 35 **EST:** 1951
SQ FT: 25,000
SALES (est): 6.5MM **Privately Held**
WEB: www.qcpinc.com
SIC: 2752 2791 2789 Lithographic Commercial Printing Typesetting Services Bookbinding/Related Work

(G-21805)
QUEEN CITY SOIL & STONE DBA
20 Ferguson Ave (05401-5313)
PHONE....802 318-2411
Chas Macmartin, *Principal*
EMP: 3
SALES (est): 282.1K **Privately Held**
SIC: 2875 Mfg Fertilizers-Mix Only

(G-21806)
RED CORP
180 Queen City Park Rd (05401-5935)
PHONE....802 862-4500
Laurent Potdevin, *President*
Emmett Manning, *Finance Mgr*
Connor Stewart, *Credit Staff*
Katie Wibben, *Sales Staff*
EMP: 100
SALES (est): 4.3MM
SALES (corp-wide): 188.4MM **Privately Held**
WEB: www.burton.com
SIC: 3949 Mfg Snowboard Accessories
PA: The Burton Corporation
180 Queen City Park Rd
Burlington VT 05401
802 862-4500

(G-21807)
RHINO FOODS INC (PA)
179 Queen City Park Rd (05401-5932)
PHONE....802 862-0252
Ted Castle, *President*
Anne Castle, *Vice Pres*
Anthony Buscarello, *Opers Mgr*
Rick Fadden, *Opers Mgr*
Wayne King, *Warehouse Mgr*
EMP: 130
SQ FT: 27,000
SALES (est): 26.2MM **Privately Held**
WEB: www.rhinofoods.com
SIC: 2045 2024 Mfg Prepared Flour Mixes/Doughs Mfg Ice Cream/Frozen Desert

(G-21808)
SEVENTH GENERATION INC (DH)
60 Lake St Ste 3n (05401-5307)
PHONE....802 658-3773
John Replogle, *President*
Maureen Usifer, *Corp Secy*
Sarah McLaren, *Manager*
Ashley Laporte, *Senior Mgr*
Patty McGrath, *Director*
▲ **EMP:** 146
SALES (est): 58.8MM
SALES (corp-wide): 56.5B **Privately Held**
SIC: 2676 5162 5169 5122 Manufactures Sanitary Paper Products Wholesales Plastic Mtrl/Shapes Wholesales Chemicals/Products
HQ: Unilever United States, Inc.
700 Sylvan Ave
Englewood Cliffs NJ 07632
201 735-9661

(G-21809)
SMITH & SALMON INC
Also Called: Sap
110 Summit St (05401-3928)
PHONE....802 578-8242
Charles Smith, *President*
EMP: 5 **EST:** 2016
SALES: 500K **Privately Held**
SIC: 2086 Mfg Bottled/Canned Soft Drinks

(G-21810)
SOCIAL SENTINEL INC
128 Lakeside Ave Ste 100 (05401-4936)
PHONE....800 628-0158
Gary Margolis, *CEO*
Rick Gibbs, *President*
Nicole Clegg, *Vice Pres*
Crystal Gallo, *Vice Pres*
Laurie Dupont, *Accountant*
EMP: 16 **EST:** 2015
SALES (est): 1.4MM **Privately Held**
SIC: 7372 Prepackaged Software Services

(G-21811)
SWITCHBACK BEERWORKS INC
Also Called: Switchback Brewing Co
160 Flynn Ave (05401-5400)
P.O. Box 4210 (05406-4210)
PHONE....802 651-4114
William Cherry, *President*
▲ **EMP:** 30
SALES (est): 241.5K **Privately Held**
SIC: 2082 Mfg Malt Beverages

(G-21812)
THINKMD INC
210 Colchester Ave (05405-0303)
PHONE....802 734-7993
Barry Finette, *Principal*
Nick Donowitz, *COO*
EMP: 3 **EST:** 2014
SALES (est): 116.1K **Privately Held**
SIC: 7372 7371 Prepackaged Software Services Custom Computer Programing

(G-21813)
TRI C TOOL & DIE
228 Elmwood Ave (05401-4233)
PHONE....802 864-7144
Fax: 802 862-3228
EMP: 3 **EST:** 1946
SALES: 100K **Privately Held**
SIC: 3544 Mfg Dies/Tools/Jigs/Fixtures

(G-21814)
URBAN MNSHINE NATURAL PDTS LLC
1 Mill St Ste 101 (05401-1542)
PHONE....802 862-6233
EMP: 4
SALES (est): 29.2K **Privately Held**
SIC: 2833 Medicinals And Botanicals, Nsk

(G-21815)
VERMONT FARM TABLE LLC (PA)
206 College St (05401-8305)
P.O. Box 130, Charlotte (05445-0130)
PHONE....888 425-8838
Dustin Glasscoe, *Mng Member*
EMP: 3
SALES: 768.2K **Privately Held**
SIC: 2519 3523 Mfg Household Furniture Mfg Farm Machinery/Equipment

(G-21816)
VERMONT PUB BREWRY BURLINGTON
144 College St (05401-8416)
PHONE....802 865-0500
Greg Noonan, *President*
Robert Beaupre, *Vice Pres*
Gregory Donlin, *Shareholder*
EMP: 60
SQ FT: 5,000
SALES: 1.8MM **Privately Held**
SIC: 2082 5813 5812 Mfg Malt Beverages Drinking Place Eating Place

(G-21817)
WILLIAM R RAAP
Also Called: Intervale Farm & Gardens
128 Intervale Rd (05401-2804)
PHONE....802 660-3508
William R Raap, *Partner*
EMP: 3
SALES (est): 364.2K **Privately Held**
SIC: 2875 Mfg Fertilizers-Mix Only

(G-21818)
YOUNG WRITERS PROJECT INC
47 Maple St Ste 216 (05401-4956)
PHONE....802 324-9537
John Canning, *Principal*
EMP: 15
SALES: 385K **Privately Held**
SIC: 2711 Newspapers-Publishing/Printing

Cabot
Washington County

(G-21819)
CABOT HILLS MAPLE LLC
979 Thistle Hill Rd (05647-9759)
P.O. Box 68 (05647-0068)
PHONE....802 426-3463
Marcia Maynard,
Kenneth Denton,
EMP: 4
SALES (est): 199.8K **Privately Held**
WEB: www.cabothillsmaple.com
SIC: 2099 Mfg Food Preparations

(G-21820)
RHAPSODY NATURAL FOODS INC
752 Danville Hill Rd (05647-4435)
PHONE....802 563-2172
Maria T Welters, *President*
Oliver J Welters, *Vice Pres*
Madelief Welters, *Admin Sec*
EMP: 4
SALES (est): 165K **Privately Held**
SIC: 2099 Mfg Food Preparations

▲ = Import ▼=Export
◆ =Import/Export

Calais
Washington County

(G-21821)
DAILY GARDENER
2930 Dugar Brook Rd (05648-7585)
P.O. Box 13 (05648-0013)
PHONE..................................802 223-7851
Peter Burke, *Principal*
EMP: 3
SALES (est): 141K **Privately Held**
SIC: 2711 Newspapers-Publishing/Printing

Cambridge
Chittenden County

(G-21822)
BOYDEN VALLEY WINERY LLC
64 Vt Route 104 (05444-9811)
PHONE..................................802 644-8151
David Boyden, *Mng Member*
EMP: 3
SALES (est): 310K **Privately Held**
WEB: www.boydenvalley.com
SIC: 2084 Mfg Wines/Brandy/Spirits

(G-21823)
DUELMARK AEROSPACE CORPORATION
96 John Putnam Memorial (05444-4470)
P.O. Box 62 (05444-0062)
PHONE..................................802 644-2603
Sewall B Rent Jr, *President*
Edward B French, *Admin Sec*
EMP: 5
SQ FT: 2,200
SALES (est): 490K **Privately Held**
SIC: 3643 5063 Mfg Conductive Wiring Devices Whol Electrical Equipment

Cambridgeport
Windham County

(G-21824)
MATRIXCHEM INC
3992 Route 121 (05141)
P.O. Box 2036, South Londonderry (05155-2036)
PHONE..................................347 727-6886
Doug Butler, *President*
EMP: 3
SQ FT: 2,500
SALES (est): 349.3K **Privately Held**
WEB: www.matrixchem.com
SIC: 2819 Mfg Industrial Inorganic Chemicals

Canaan
Essex County

(G-21825)
SQUEEGEE PRINTERS INC
4067 Vt Route 102 (05903-9718)
PHONE..................................802 266-3426
Patricia Beauregard, *CEO*
EMP: 5
SALES: 400K **Privately Held**
WEB: www.squeegeeprinters.com
SIC: 2759 2395 Commercial Printing Pleating/Stitching Services

(G-21826)
STEPHANE INKEL INC
1780 Vt Route 102 (05903-9737)
P.O. Box 111 (05903-0111)
PHONE..................................802 266-8878
Stephane Drobbins, *Principal*
EMP: 3
SALES (est): 237.4K **Privately Held**
SIC: 2411 Logging

Castleton
Rutland County

(G-21827)
BROWNS QUARRIED SLATE PDTS INC
2504 S Street Ext (05735-9359)
PHONE..................................802 468-2297
Charles W Brown, *Principal*
EMP: 4 **EST:** 2009
SALES (est): 307.9K **Privately Held**
SIC: 3281 Mfg Cut Stone/Products

(G-21828)
HUBBARDTON FORGE LLC
154 Route 30 S (05735-9521)
P.O. Box 827 (05735-0827)
PHONE..................................802 468-3090
Bob Dillon, *CEO*
◆ **EMP:** 225
SQ FT: 117,000
SALES (est): 51.6MM **Privately Held**
WEB: www.hubbardtonforge.com
SIC: 3645 5063 3446 Mfg Residential Lighting Fixtures Whol Electrical Equipment Mfg Architectural Metalwork

(G-21829)
MARY LEE HARRIS
825 Sand Hill Rd (05735-9243)
PHONE..................................802 468-5370
Mary Lee Harris, *Owner*
EMP: 5 **EST:** 1939
SALES (est): 232K **Privately Held**
SIC: 3142 Mfg House Slippers

(G-21830)
VERMONT MBL GRAN SLATE SPSTONE
1565 Main St (05735-4458)
PHONE..................................802 468-8800
Paul H Thompson, *Partner*
Lori M Thompson, *Partner*
▲ **EMP:** 8
SALES (est): 1.1MM **Privately Held**
SIC: 2541 Mfg Countertops

Center Rutland
Rutland County

(G-21831)
CARRIS REELS INC
Also Called: Carris Plastics
628 Us Business Rte (05736)
PHONE..................................802 773-9111
Mike Curn, *CEO*
Bill Carris, *President*
EMP: 14
SALES (est): 1.6MM **Privately Held**
WEB: www.carrisplastics.com
SIC: 2499 Mfg Wood Products
HQ: Carris Reels Inc
49 Main St
Proctor VT 05765
802 773-9111

Charlotte
Chittenden County

(G-21832)
CHARLOTTE NEWS
823 Ferry Rd (05445-9092)
P.O. Box 251 (05445-0251)
PHONE..................................802 425-4949
Janice Heilmann, *Principal*
EMP: 6
SALES: 97.2K **Privately Held**
SIC: 2711 Newspapers-Publishing/Printing

(G-21833)
DARLING BOATWORKS INC
821 Ferry Rd (05445-9092)
P.O. Box 32 (05445-0032)
PHONE..................................802 425-2004
George Darling, *President*
EMP: 7
SALES (est): 610.5K **Privately Held**
SIC: 3732 Boatbuilding/Repairing

(G-21834)
MIRAVIA LLC (PA)
236 Lucys Ln (05445-9068)
PHONE..................................802 425-6483
Bruce Wellman, *Mng Member*
Laura Lipton,
EMP: 3 **EST:** 2000
SALES: 400K **Privately Held**
SIC: 2731 8748 Books-Publishing/Printing Business Consulting Services

(G-21835)
VERMONT ECO FLOORS
3222 Greenbush Rd (05445-9311)
PHONE..................................802 425-7737
Michael Frost, *President*
EMP: 4
SALES (est): 285.3K **Privately Held**
SIC: 3531 Mfg Construction Machinery

(G-21836)
VERMONT OPTECHS INC
3195 Ethan Allen Hwy (05445)
P.O. Box 69 (05445-0069)
PHONE..................................802 425-2040
John Oren, *President*
EMP: 5
SALES: 600K **Privately Held**
WEB: www.scopeshop.com
SIC: 3826 Mfg Analytical Instruments

Chelsea
Orange County

(G-21837)
CALVIN JOHNSON
620 Vermont Rm 110 (05038)
P.O. Box 283 (05038-0283)
PHONE..................................802 685-3205
Calvin Johnson, *Owner*
EMP: 3
SALES (est): 208.9K **Privately Held**
SIC: 2411 Logging

(G-21838)
HEB MANUFACTURING COMPANY INC
67 Vt Rte 110 (05038-9078)
P.O. Box 188 (05038-0188)
PHONE..................................802 685-4821
Bonnie Kennedy, *President*
Howard R Parker, *Corp Secy*
Sharon Gallacher, *Traffic Mgr*
EMP: 45
SQ FT: 35,000
SALES (est): 8.2MM **Privately Held**
WEB: www.hebmfg.com
SIC: 3469 3315 Mfg Metal Stampings Mfg Steel Wire/Related Products

(G-21839)
LAWRENCE LYON
Also Called: Lyons Surface Plate Co
100 N Main St (05038)
P.O. Box 217 (05038-0217)
PHONE..................................802 685-7790
Lawrence Lyon, *Owner*
EMP: 3
SQ FT: 6,320
SALES (est): 159.8K **Privately Held**
SIC: 3471 Plating/Polishing Service

(G-21840)
VERMONT WIREFORM INC
Rr 110 (05038)
P.O. Box 248 (05038-0248)
PHONE..................................802 889-3200
Richard Colby, *President*
Karen Colby, *Admin Sec*
EMP: 15
SQ FT: 20,000
SALES (est): 2.9MM **Privately Held**
WEB: www.vermontwireform.com
SIC: 3496 Mfg Misc Fabricated Wire Products

Chester
Windsor County

(G-21841)
BONNIES BUNDLES DOLLS
250 North St (05143-8807)
PHONE..................................802 875-2114
Nora Watters, *Partner*
Lewis Watters, *Partner*
EMP: 6
SALES (est): 470K **Privately Held**
WEB: www.bonniesbundlesdolls.com
SIC: 3942 Custom Doll Manufacturer

(G-21842)
DREWS LLC (HQ)
Also Called: Drew's All Natural
926 Vermont Route 103 S (05143-8461)
PHONE..................................802 875-1184
Nancy Hadwen, *Purch Mgr*
Christian Thayer, *Research*
Laura Skibinski, *Finance*
Jessica Austin, *Supervisor*
David Hawk,
EMP: 29
SQ FT: 7,000
SALES (est): 6.1MM
SALES (corp-wide): 8.9MM **Privately Held**
WEB: www.drewsallnatural.com
SIC: 2035 2099 Manufactures Pickles/Sauces/Dressing Food Preparations
PA: Schlotterbeck & Foss, Llc
3 Ledgeview Dr
Westbrook ME 04092
207 772-4666

(G-21843)
HUME SPECIALTIES INC
Also Called: Green Mountain Greengo
291 Pleasant St (05143-9351)
P.O. Box 4329, Winston Salem NC (27115-4329)
PHONE..................................802 875-3117
Christine Hume, *President*
Dave Hume, *Vice Pres*
EMP: 22
SALES: 3MM **Privately Held**
WEB: www.greenmountaingringo.com
SIC: 2032 Mfg Mexican Hot Sauce & Tortilla Chips

(G-21844)
JULIAN MATERIALS LLC
3643 Vt Route 103 N (05143-9780)
PHONE..................................802 875-6564
EMP: 11
SALES (corp-wide): 3.8MM **Privately Held**
SIC: 1411 Dimension Stone Quarry
PA: Julian Materials, Llc
418 Meadow St
Fairfield CT

(G-21845)
MITCHS MAPLES SUGAR HOUSE
2440 Green Mountain Tpke (05143-8872)
PHONE..................................802 875-5240
EMP: 3
SALES (est): 168.9K **Privately Held**
SIC: 2099 Mfg Food Preparations

(G-21846)
NORTHEAST TIMBER EXCHANGE LLC (PA)
535 Cummings Rd (05143-8459)
PHONE..................................802 875-1037
Pete Durgin, *Manager*
EMP: 6
SALES (est): 456.5K **Privately Held**
SIC: 2421 Sawmill/Planing Mill

(G-21847)
P AND L TRUCKING
31 Toma Rd (05143)
P.O. Box 993 (05143-0993)
PHONE..................................802 875-2819
Palmer Goodrich II, *Owner*
Palmer H Goodrich II, *Owner*
EMP: 8

SALES (est): 660K Privately Held
SIC: 2411 4212 Logging Local Trucking Operator

(G-21848)
PAUL THOMAS
Also Called: Microcut Laser Designs
244 Main St (05143-9358)
PHONE....802 875-4004
Paul Thomas, *Owner*
EMP: 5
SALES (est): 260K Privately Held
SIC: 2759 3281 Commercial Printing Mfg Cut Stone/Products

(G-21849)
SEMYA CORP (PA)
Also Called: The Stone Depot
3643 Vt Route 103 N (05143-9780)
PHONE....802 875-6564
Gregg P Adamovich, *President*
EMP: 8
SALES (est): 3MM Privately Held
SIC: 1411 Dimension Stone Quarry

(G-21850)
STEPHEN J RUSSELL & CO
60 Atcherson Hollow Rd (05143-9340)
PHONE....802 869-2540
Stephen J Russell, *Owner*
Patricia Noble, *Vice Pres*
EMP: 3
SQ FT: 5,600
SALES: 600K Privately Held
WEB: www.russellorgan.com
SIC: 3931 Mfg Musical Instruments

(G-21851)
TELEGRAPH PUBLISHING LLC
3008 Popple Dungeon Rd (05143)
P.O. Box 221 (05143-0221)
PHONE....802 875-2703
EMP: 4
SALES (est): 65.7K Privately Held
SIC: 2741 Misc Publishing

(G-21852)
VERMONT FURN HARDWOODS INC
Also Called: Vermont Hardwoods
386 Depot St (05143-9342)
P.O. Box 769 (05143-0769)
PHONE....802 875-2550
David Waldmann, *President*
Rebecca Waldmann, *Vice Pres*
EMP: 14
SQ FT: 27,000
SALES (est): 1.5MM Privately Held
WEB: www.vermonthardwoods.com
SIC: 2431 Mfg Millwork

(G-21853)
VERMONT TS INC
354 Elm St (05143-9349)
P.O. Box 820 (05143-0820)
PHONE....802 875-2091
Robert Morgan, *President*
Margaret Morgan, *Treasurer*
EMP: 3
SQ FT: 6,500
SALES: 650K Privately Held
SIC: 2396 2395 5699 Mfg Auto/Apparel Trimming Pleating/Stitching Services Ret Misc Apparel/Accessories

Chittenden
Rutland County

(G-21854)
HAWLEYS FINE WOODWORK
1 River Rd (05737)
PHONE....802 483-2575
Scott Hawley, *Principal*
EMP: 4
SALES (est): 373.4K Privately Held
WEB: www.hawleysfinewoodworking.com
SIC: 2431 Mfg Millwork

Colchester
Chittenden County

(G-21855)
A C PERFORMANCE CENTER LTD
Also Called: AC Performance Ctr
306 Mallard Dr (05446-7015)
PHONE....802 862-6074
Andrew Costello, *President*
Carol Costello, *Vice Pres*
EMP: 5
SQ FT: 3,500
SALES (est): 563.6K Privately Held
WEB: www.acperformancecenter.com
SIC: 3714 5531 Manufactures And Rebuilds Motor Vehicle Engines And Retails Related Parts

(G-21856)
ALKEN INC
Also Called: Polhemus
40 Hercules Dr (05446-5835)
P.O. Box 560 (05446-0560)
PHONE....802 655-3159
Allan G Rodgers, *CEO*
Allan G Rodgers Jr, *President*
Francine Roy, *CFO*
David Wood, *CPA*
Keith Hanf, *Manager*
▲ EMP: 29
SQ FT: 18,000
SALES (est): 7MM Privately Held
WEB: www.polhemus.com
SIC: 3577 3829 Mfg Computer Peripheral Equipment Mfg Measuring/Controlling Devices

(G-21857)
BAKERS DOZEN INC
Also Called: Baker's Dozen Bakery
70 Roosevelt Hwy Ste 2 (05446-5934)
PHONE....802 879-4001
Mike Le Blanc, *President*
EMP: 12
SQ FT: 5,000
SALES (est): 1.2MM Privately Held
SIC: 2051 Mfg Bread/Related Products

(G-21858)
BLACK BEAUTY DRIVEWAY SEALING
60 Mercier Dr (05446-6808)
PHONE....802 860-7113
Richard Kirby, *Owner*
EMP: 6
SALES (est): 479.1K Privately Held
SIC: 2951 1611 Mfg Asphalt Mixtures/Blocks Highway/Street Construction

(G-21859)
CLOTH N CANVAS RECOVERY INC
354 Prim Rd (05446-8096)
PHONE....802 658-6826
Ernie Reuter, *President*
Betty Reuter, *Treasurer*
EMP: 3
SQ FT: 5,000
SALES (est): 250K Privately Held
WEB: www.clothncanvas.com
SIC: 2394 7641 5091 Mfg Canvas/Related Products Reupholstery/Furniture Repair Whol Sporting/Recreational Goods

(G-21860)
COCA-COLA BOTTLING COMPANY
733 Hercules Dr (05446-5842)
PHONE....802 654-3800
David La Rose, *Manager*
EMP: 100
SQ FT: 55,000 Privately Held
SIC: 2086 4226 Mfg Bottled/Canned Soft Drinks Special Warehouse/Storage
HQ: Coca-Cola Beverages Northeast, Inc.
1 Executive Park Dr # 330
Bedford NH 03110
603 627-7871

(G-21861)
DELLAMORE ENTERPRISES INC
Also Called: Dell'amore Pasta Sauce
948 Hercules Dr Ste 1 (05446-5926)
P.O. Box 974 (05446-0974)
PHONE....802 655-6264
Frank Dell'amore, *President*
Lorene Spagnuolo Dell'amore, *Vice Pres*
EMP: 7
SQ FT: 4,000
SALES (est): 540K Privately Held
WEB: www.dellamore.com
SIC: 2033 Mfg Canned Fruits/Vegetables

(G-21862)
ELUTION TECHNOLOGIES LLC
480 Hercules Dr Ste 1 (05446-5948)
PHONE....802 540-0296
Thom Grace, *CEO*
John G Leslie, *President*
EMP: 3
SALES (est): 259.4K Privately Held
SIC: 2836 1541 3826 Mfg Biological Products Industrial Building Construction Mfg Analytical Instruments

(G-21863)
EVERETT M WINDOVER INC
Also Called: Culligan Water Technologies
154 Brentwood Dr Unit 1 (05446-7989)
PHONE....802 865-0000
Everett M Windover, *President*
EMP: 29
SQ FT: 8,000
SALES: 3MM Privately Held
WEB: www.culligan4u.com
SIC: 2899 8734 Mfg Chemical Preparations Testing Laboratory

(G-21864)
HAYWARD TYLER INC (DH)
480 Roosevelt Hwy (05446-1594)
P.O. Box 680 (05446-0680)
PHONE....802 655-4444
Vince Conte, *President*
Jeffrey Belotti, *Business Mgr*
Bob Readie, *Safety Mgr*
Roger Degree, *Foreman/Supr*
Ed Flett, *Research*
▲ EMP: 75
SQ FT: 40,000
SALES (est): 15.4MM
SALES (corp-wide): 89.2MM Privately Held
WEB: www.haywardtyler.com
SIC: 3561 7699 3621 Mfg Pumps/Pumping Equipment Repair Services Mfg Motors/Generators

(G-21865)
HAZELETT STRIP-CASTING CORP
63 Brentwood Dr (05446-7795)
PHONE....802 951-6846
Thomas J Hill, *Branch Mgr*
EMP: 5 Privately Held
SIC: 3999 Mfg Misc Products
HQ: Hazelett Strip-Casting Corp
135 W Lakeshore Dr
Colchester VT 05446
802 863-6376

(G-21866)
IHEARTCOMMUNICATIONS INC
265 Hegeman Ave (05446-3174)
PHONE....802 655-0093
Pom Barney, *Branch Mgr*
EMP: 30 Publicly Held
SIC: 3663 7313 Mfg Radio/Tv Communication Equipment Advertising Representative
HQ: Iheartcommunications, Inc.
20880 Stone Oak Pkwy
San Antonio TX 78258
210 822-2828

(G-21867)
INDUSTRIAL SAFETY PRODUCTS LLC
195 Acorn Ln (05446-5815)
P.O. Box 501, Charlotte (05445-0501)
PHONE....802 338-9035
Timothy Ziter,
EMP: 3
SALES (est): 345.2K Privately Held
SIC: 3589 5046 Mfg /Whol Smoke Elimination Equipment

(G-21868)
ISOTECH NORTH AMERICA INC
Also Called: Specmatrix
158 Brentwood Dr Ste 4 (05446-7994)
PHONE....802 863-8050
Scott Sabourin, *President*
EMP: 5
SQ FT: 5,000
SALES (est): 858.6K Privately Held
WEB: www.isotechna.com
SIC: 3823 Mfg Process Control Instruments

(G-21869)
JEN COL INNOVATIONS LLC
Also Called: Em-Bolt
875 Roosevelt Hwy Ste 130 (05446-4460)
PHONE....802 448-3053
Tim Hardy, *Mng Member*
EMP: 3
SALES (est): 294.5K Privately Held
SIC: 3312 Blast Furnace-Steel Works

(G-21870)
KOFFEE KUP BAKERY INC (PA)
59 Rathe Rd Ste A (05446-4490)
PHONE....802 863-2696
Huburt Aubery, *President*
Ronald Roberge, *President*
Brian Carpentier, *Exec VP*
Andrew Matthews, *Vice Pres*
Carol Roberge, *Vice Pres*
EMP: 75
SQ FT: 50,000
SALES (est): 30.8MM Privately Held
WEB: www.koffeekupbakery.biz
SIC: 2051 5149 Mfg Bread/Related Products Whol Groceries

(G-21871)
LARCOLINE INC (PA)
Also Called: Minuteman Press
113 Acorn Ln Ste 2 (05446-5947)
PHONE....802 864-5440
Jon Cunningham, *President*
EMP: 12
SALES (est): 2MM Privately Held
WEB: www.joncunningham.com
SIC: 2752 Comm Prtg Litho

(G-21872)
LITTLE HOUSE BY ANDRE INC
69 Creek Farm Plz Ste 3 (05446-7266)
PHONE....802 878-8733
Nancy Plouffe, *President*
EMP: 3
SALES (est): 351.4K Privately Held
SIC: 3524 5211 Mfg Lawn/Garden Equipment Ret Lumber/Building Materials

(G-21873)
MAXI GREEN INC
Also Called: Rite Aid Pharmacy
1184 Prim Rd Ste 2 (05446-4449)
PHONE....802 657-3586
Kenneth Black, *CEO*
Jennifer Zorek, *Principal*
S Lowell M Podgurski, *Vice Pres*
Matthew Schroeder, *Treasurer*
Gerald Cardinale, *Admin Sec*
EMP: 5
SALES (est): 285.4K
SALES (corp-wide): 21.6B Publicly Held
SIC: 2836 Mfg Biological Products
PA: Rite Aid Corporation
30 Hunter Ln
Camp Hill PA 17011
717 761-2633

(G-21874)
OLIVES OIL
87 Waybury Rd (05446-6962)
PHONE....802 864-4908
Tracey Calista, *Principal*
EMP: 3
SALES (est): 157.6K Privately Held
SIC: 2079 Mfg Edible Fats/Oils

▲ = Import ▼=Export
◆ =Import/Export

(G-21875)
OMNI MEASUREMENT SYSTEMS INC
Also Called: Omni Medical Systems
808 Hercules Dr (05446-5839)
PHONE..................................802 497-2253
Mark Harvie, *President*
EMP: 40
SQ FT: 29,000
SALES (est): 7.4MM **Privately Held**
WEB: www.omnimedicalsys.com
SIC: 3612 3825 3699 Mfg Transformers Mfg Electrical Measuring Instruments Mfg Electrical Equipment/Supplies

(G-21876)
PBL INCORPORATED
Also Called: Ace Castings
158 Brentwood Dr Ste 2 (05446-7994)
PHONE..................................802 893-0111
Phillip R Lux, *President*
EMP: 12
SQ FT: 80,200
SALES (est): 1.6MM **Privately Held**
WEB: www.pblinc.com
SIC: 3911 3561 3841 Mfg Jewelry Industrial & Medical Parts

(G-21877)
RELIANCE STEEL INC (PA)
94 S Oak Cir (05446-5814)
PHONE..................................802 655-4810
Darin Gillies, *President*
EMP: 14
SQ FT: 18,000
SALES: 4.3MM **Privately Held**
WEB: www.reliancesteel.com
SIC: 3441 Structural Metal Fabrication

(G-21878)
RELIANCE STEEL VERMONT INC
94 S Oak Cir (05446-5814)
PHONE..................................802 655-4810
John M Wisener, *President*
Darin Gillies, *Vice Pres*
Becky Butler, *Bookkeeper*
EMP: 25
SQ FT: 12,000
SALES: 4.5MM **Privately Held**
WEB: www.reliancesteel.com
SIC: 3441 Structural Metal Fabrication
PA: Reliance Steel, Inc.
94 S Oak Cir
Colchester VT 05446

(G-21879)
RETTIG USA INC
948 Hercules Dr Ste 5 (05446-5926)
P.O. Box 1460, Williston (05495-1460)
PHONE..................................802 654-7500
Luc Cardinaels, *Principal*
▲ **EMP:** 9
SALES (est): 1.3MM **Privately Held**
SIC: 3567 Mfg Industrial Furnaces/Ovens

(G-21880)
STEPHEN A BURT
162 Jimmo Dr (05446-7957)
PHONE..................................802 893-0600
Stephen A Burt, *Owner*
EMP: 4
SALES (est): 289.4K **Privately Held**
SIC: 3495 Mfg Wire Springs

(G-21881)
THOMAS DRAKE
Also Called: Midtown Machine & Tool
46 Troy Ave (05446-3120)
PHONE..................................802 655-0990
Thomas Drake, *Owner*
EMP: 6
SQ FT: 6,200
SALES: 400K **Privately Held**
WEB: www.midtownmachine.com
SIC: 3542 7692 3544 Mfg Machine Tools-Forming Welding Repair Mfg Dies/Tools/Jigs/Fixtures

(G-21882)
TRANSMILLE CALIBRATION INC
158 Brentwood Dr Ste 4 (05446-7994)
PHONE..................................802 846-7582
Scott Sabourin, *President*
Amy Sabourin, *Treasurer*
EMP: 5
SALES (est): 398.9K **Privately Held**
SIC: 3825 Mfg Electrical Measuring Instruments

(G-21883)
TROY MINERALS CO
312 Village Dr (05446-7212)
P.O. Box 47 (05446-0047)
PHONE..................................802 878-5103
Michael Chmielewski, *Owner*
EMP: 9
SQ FT: 1,000
SALES (est): 1.1MM **Privately Held**
SIC: 1499 3281 Nonmetallic Mineral Mining Mfg Cut Stone/Products

(G-21884)
VERMONT AWARDS AND ENGRV INC
566 Hercules Dr (05446-5837)
P.O. Box 2332, South Burlington (05407-2332)
PHONE..................................802 862-3000
Margaret Swett, *President*
Steve Swett, *Corp Secy*
EMP: 6
SQ FT: 3,400
SALES (est): 839.3K **Privately Held**
WEB: www.vermontawards.com
SIC: 3499 7389 Mfg Misc Fabricated Metal Products Business Services

(G-21885)
VERMONT BASE WATERS LLC
156 Brentwood Dr (05446-7996)
PHONE..................................802 893-2131
Gene Beaudry,
EMP: 3
SALES (est): 377.2K **Privately Held**
WEB: www.vtsoda.com
SIC: 2023 Mfg Dry/Evaporated Dairy Products

(G-21886)
VERMONT NUT FREE CHOCLAT INC
146 Brentwood Dr (05446-7976)
PHONE..................................802 372-4654
Gail Elvidge, *President*
Mark T Elvidge, *Vice Pres*
EMP: 10 **EST:** 1998
SALES (est): 1.2MM **Privately Held**
SIC: 2066 5947 Mfg Chocolate/Cocoa Products Ret Gifts/Novelties

(G-21887)
VERMONT SPORTSWEAR EMBORIDERY
34 Princess Ann Dr (05446-6738)
PHONE..................................802 863-0237
Nancy L Japhet, *Partner*
Richard Japhet, *Partner*
EMP: 3
SALES (est): 133.1K **Privately Held**
SIC: 2395 Pleating/Stitching Services

(G-21888)
VERMONT THINSTONE ASSOC LLC
4211 Roosevelt Hwy (05446-7551)
PHONE..................................802 448-3000
Ronald Kingsbury, *Mng Member*
EMP: 6
SALES: 600K **Privately Held**
SIC: 3281 Mfg Cut Stone/Products

(G-21889)
VISIBLE ELECTROPHYSIOLOGY LLC
197 Moonlight Rdg (05446-7797)
P.O. Box 73, Winooski (05404-0073)
PHONE..................................802 847-4539
Peter Spector,
EMP: 10
SALES (est): 332.8K **Privately Held**
SIC: 7372 Prepackaged Software Services

Concord
Essex County

(G-21890)
CEYLON R MOREHOUSE LOGGING
617 Sawmill Rd (05824-9568)
PHONE..................................802 695-4660
EMP: 6
SALES (est): 444.3K **Privately Held**
SIC: 2411 Logging

Corinth
Orange County

(G-21891)
GREG MANNING LOGGING LLC
1388 Center Rd (05039-9550)
PHONE..................................802 439-6255
Greg Manning, *Principal*
EMP: 3
SALES (est): 234.5K **Privately Held**
SIC: 2411 Logging

Craftsbury
Orleans County

(G-21892)
DENTON AUTO INC
2200 Wild Branch Rd (05826-9641)
PHONE..................................802 586-2828
Michael Denton, *President*
Brenda Denton, *Admin Sec*
EMP: 3
SQ FT: 1,000
SALES (est): 374.7K **Privately Held**
WEB: www.dentonauto.com
SIC: 3711 Mfg Motor Vehicle/Car Bodies

Danby
Rutland County

(G-21893)
FULLER SAND & GRAVEL INC
9 N Main St (05739-9604)
P.O. Box 102 (05739-0102)
PHONE..................................802 293-5700
Thomas Fuller Jr, *President*
EMP: 6
SALES (est): 1.1MM **Privately Held**
SIC: 1442 Construction Sand/Gravel

(G-21894)
S WHITE FUEL STOP
1187 Us Route 7 (05739-9624)
PHONE..................................802 293-5804
EMP: 4
SALES (est): 369.7K **Privately Held**
SIC: 2869 Industrial Organic Chemicals, Nec

Danville
Caledonia County

(G-21895)
CHARLES CURTIS LLC
462 Hill St (05828-9660)
P.O. Box 13 (05828-0013)
PHONE..................................802 274-0060
Craig R Vance, *Mng Member*
EMP: 6
SQ FT: 4,000
SALES: 500K **Privately Held**
WEB: www.charlescurtis.com
SIC: 3272 1623 6512 Mfg Concrete Products Water/Sewer/Utility Construction Nonresidential Building Operator

(G-21896)
GREEN MOUNTAIN BLOCKS
316 Vance Rd (05828-9466)
PHONE..................................802 748-1341
Clifton Mueller, *Owner*
EMP: 6
SALES (est): 281K **Privately Held**
WEB: www.greenmountainblocks.com
SIC: 3944 Mfg Games/Toys

(G-21897)
MARC J RIENDEAU
676 Morrill Rd (05828)
PHONE..................................802 748-6252
Marc Riendeau, *Co-Owner*
EMP: 3
SALES (est): 235.7K **Privately Held**
SIC: 2411 Logging

(G-21898)
NORTHSTAR PUBLISHING LLC
Also Called: North Star Monthly, The
29 Hill St (05828-9703)
P.O. Box 319 (05828-0319)
PHONE..................................802 684-1056
Fredrick Hoffer, *Treasurer*
Justin Laveley,
EMP: 6
SQ FT: 500
SALES: 185K **Privately Held**
SIC: 2711 Newspapers-Publishing/Printing

Derby
Orleans County

(G-21899)
BARRUP FARMS INC
Also Called: Green Mountain Mulch
516 Lower Quarry Rd (05829)
P.O. Box 129 (05829-0129)
PHONE..................................802 334-2331
EMP: 35
SQ FT: 8,450
SALES (est): 5.1MM **Privately Held**
SIC: 2499 4213 Wood Products, Nec, Nsk

(G-21900)
JASON PATENAUDE EXCAVATING INC
311 Fortin Rd (05829-9695)
P.O. Box 597 (05829-0597)
PHONE..................................802 766-4567
Jason A Patenaude, *President*
EMP: 3 **EST:** 1999
SALES (est): 291K **Privately Held**
SIC: 3531 Mfg Construction Machinery

(G-21901)
LOUIS GARNEAU USA INC
3916 Us Route 5 (05829-9846)
P.O. Box 1460 (05829-5460)
PHONE..................................802 334-5885
Louis Garneau, *President*
Cassy Moulton, *Opers Staff*
Jennifer Gonnella, *Purch Agent*
Brandon Pray, *Technology*
Michele Reed, *Executive*
▲ **EMP:** 70
SQ FT: 11,000
SALES (est): 7.3MM
SALES (corp-wide): 79.6MM **Privately Held**
WEB: www.louisgarneau.us
SIC: 2339 2329 Mfg Women's/Misses' Outerwear Mfg Men's/Boy's Clothing
PA: Louis Garneau Sports Inc
30 Rue Des Grands-Lacs
Saint-Augustin-De-Desmaures QC G3A 2
418 878-4135

(G-21902)
NORTH COUNTRY ENGINEERING INC
106 John Taplin Rd (05829-9778)
PHONE..................................802 766-5396
Jean S Clark, *President*
Tammy Benoit, *Admin Sec*
EMP: 35 **EST:** 1963
SQ FT: 12,000
SALES: 1.9MM **Privately Held**
WEB: www.northcountryeng.com
SIC: 3599 6512 7692 Mfg Industrial Machinery Nonresidential Building Operator Welding Repair

GEOGRAPHIC

(G-21903)
NOTTINGHAM WOOD PRODUCTS
108 John Taplin Rd (05829-9778)
P.O. Box 915 (05829-0915)
PHONE..................................802 766-2791
David Labelle, *Owner*
EMP: 5
SQ FT: 2,200
SALES (est): 620.9K **Privately Held**
WEB: www.nottinghamwood.com
SIC: 2842 2499 Mfg Polish/Sanitation Goods Mfg Wood Products

(G-21904)
VERMONT HERITAGE SPRING WATER
3662 N Derby Rd (05829)
P.O. Box 74, Beebe Plain (05823-0074)
PHONE..................................802 334-2528
Danny Martin, *Owner*
EMP: 4
SQ FT: 3,500
SALES (est): 150K **Privately Held**
SIC: 2086 Bottle & Distribute Natural Spring Water

(G-21905)
VERMONT PIE AND PASTA CO
4278 Us Rte 5 (05829)
PHONE..................................802 334-7770
Gregory Bliss, *Owner*
EMP: 3
SALES (est): 16K **Privately Held**
SIC: 2099 Mfg Food Preparations

Derby Line
Orleans County

(G-21906)
TIVOLY INC
434 Baxter Ave (05830-8901)
PHONE..................................802 873-3106
Mark Tivoly, *President*
Avery Williams, *Purch Agent*
Rene Leblanc, *Engineer*
Noel Talagrand, *Director*
Jean Michele Tivoly, *Director*
▲ **EMP:** 150
SQ FT: 160,000
SALES (est): 45.1MM
SALES (corp-wide): 1.4MM **Privately Held**
WEB: www.tivolyinc.com
SIC: 3545 Mfg Machine Tool Accessories
HQ: Tivoly
266 Route Porte De Tarentaise
Tours-En-Savoie 73790
479 895-959

Dorset
Bennington County

(G-21907)
BRUCE WAITE LOGGING INC
88 Snow Rd (05251-9681)
PHONE..................................802 867-2213
Bruce Waite, *President*
Brett Waite, *Vice Pres*
EMP: 6
SALES: 1MM **Privately Held**
SIC: 2411 Logging

(G-21908)
J K ADAMS COMPANY INC
Also Called: Kitchen Store, The
1430 Route 30 (05251-9720)
PHONE..................................802 362-2303
Malcolm E Cooper Jr, *CEO*
John Rodrigues, *Vice Pres*
Jessi Kerner, *Store Mgr*
Deborah Minger, *Natl Sales Mgr*
Sharon Rishell, *Natl Sales Mgr*
▲ **EMP:** 40 **EST:** 1944
SQ FT: 45,000
SALES (est): 6.5MM **Privately Held**
WEB: www.jkadams.com
SIC: 2499 5719 Mfg Wood Products Ret Misc Homefurnishings

(G-21909)
TATES BUILDING & WOODWORKING
Also Called: Tate Woodworking
414 Scarlet Dr (05251)
P.O. Box 827 (05251-0827)
PHONE..................................802 867-4082
William K Tate III, *President*
Phyllis Tate, *Admin Sec*
EMP: 3 **EST:** 1989
SALES (est): 125K **Privately Held**
WEB: www.tatebuild.com
SIC: 2431 Mfg Millwork

East Arlington
Bennington County

(G-21910)
SPERRY VALVE INC
181 Barney Orchard Rd (05252-9750)
P.O. Box 266 (05252-0266)
PHONE..................................802 375-6703
Thomas Corcoran, *President*
EMP: 3
SQ FT: 2,800
SALES (est): 262.7K **Privately Held**
WEB: www.sperryvalve.com
SIC: 3511 3599 Mfg Turbines/Generator Sets Mfg Industrial Machinery

East Barre
Washington County

(G-21911)
JOES CUSTOM POLISHING
874 E Barre Rd (05649)
PHONE..................................802 479-9266
Gerard Perreault, *Owner*
▲ **EMP:** 5
SQ FT: 16,300
SALES (est): 383.2K **Privately Held**
WEB: www.joescustompolishing.com
SIC: 3281 Mfg Cut Stone/Products

(G-21912)
KINFOLK MEMORIALS INC
Lowery Rd (05649)
P.O. Box 236 (05649-0236)
PHONE..................................802 479-1423
Norman Fournier, *President*
EMP: 3
SALES: 500K **Privately Held**
SIC: 3272 5999 3281 Mfg Concrete Products Ret Misc Merchandise Mfg Cut Stone/Products

East Corinth
Orange County

(G-21913)
COBBLE MOUNTAIN INC
1051 Village Rd (05040-9708)
P.O. Box 237 (05040-0237)
PHONE..................................802 439-5232
Gordon Kittredge, *President*
Nancy Kittredge, *Vice Pres*
▲ **EMP:** 3
SQ FT: 4,000
SALES (est): 160K **Privately Held**
WEB: www.cobblemountain.com
SIC: 2399 2514 Mfg Fabricated Textile Products Mfg Metal Household Furniture

(G-21914)
MARTIN R L & W B INC
Also Called: Martin Quarry
8678 Vt Route 25 (05040-9751)
PHONE..................................802 439-5797
Roger L Martin, *President*
Kathrine Martin, *Vice Pres*
EMP: 5
SALES (est): 297.2K **Privately Held**
SIC: 1429 Crushed/Broken Stone

East Dorset
Bennington County

(G-21915)
PAD PRINT MACHINERY OF VERMONT
Also Called: Engineered Printing Solutions
201 Tennis Way (05253-9649)
PHONE..................................802 362-0844
Julian Joffe, *President*
Graciela Aguilar, *General Mgr*
Micky Wood, *Opers Staff*
Keith Carpenter, *Purch Mgr*
Adam Danaher, *Engineer*
▲ **EMP:** 60
SALES (est): 14.9MM **Privately Held**
WEB: www.padprintmachinery.com
SIC: 3541 Manufactures Machine Tools-Cutting
PA: Xaar Plc
316 Science Park Milton Road
Cambridge CAMBS CB4 0

(G-21916)
STAR WIND TURBINES LLC
95 Tesla Ln (05253-9801)
PHONE..................................802 779-8118
Jason Day,
▲ **EMP:** 3
SALES (est): 258.5K **Privately Held**
SIC: 3441 3621 Structural Metal Fabrication Mfg Motors/Generators

(G-21917)
SYKES HOLLOW INNOVATIONS LTD
Also Called: Pirit Heated Hose
315 Tennis Way (05253-9774)
PHONE..................................802 549-4671
William G Ferrone, *CEO*
Christopher Ferrone, *Admin Sec*
▲ **EMP:** 5
SQ FT: 1,400
SALES: 5MM **Privately Held**
SIC: 2821 Mfg Plastic Materials/Resins

(G-21918)
WOOD & SIGNS LTD
2036 Vermont Rte 7 (05253)
P.O. Box 29 (05253-0029)
PHONE..................................802 362-2386
Richard Farley, *Principal*
EMP: 4
SALES (est): 322.2K **Privately Held**
SIC: 2499 Mfg Wood Products

East Dummerston
Windham County

(G-21919)
GREEN MOUNTAIN SPINNERY INC
7 Brickyard Ln (05346-9752)
P.O. Box 568, Putney (05346-0568)
PHONE..................................802 387-4528
David Ritchie, *President*
Clare Wilson, *Vice Pres*
Elizabeth Mills, *Admin Sec*
EMP: 13
SQ FT: 2,200
SALES: 400K **Privately Held**
WEB: www.dosolutions.com
SIC: 2281 5949 Mfg Wool Yarn & Ret Yarn

East Ryegate
Caledonia County

(G-21920)
KIMBERLY-CLARK CORPORATION
352 Papermill Rd (05042-3008)
P.O. Box 95 (05042-0095)
PHONE..................................972 281-1200
Dick Marklein, *Manager*
EMP: 85
SALES (corp-wide): 18.4B **Publicly Held**
WEB: www.kimberly-clark.com
SIC: 2621 2676 Paper Mill Mfg Sanitary Paper Products
PA: Kimberly-Clark Corporation
351 Phelps Dr
Irving TX 75038
972 281-1200

Eden
Lamoille County

(G-21921)
TOM KNOWS SALSA LLC
445 White Rd (05652-9795)
P.O. Box 24 (05652-0024)
PHONE..................................802 793-5079
Devon H Williams, *Principal*
EMP: 3
SALES (est): 137.5K **Privately Held**
SIC: 2099 Mfg Food Preparations

Elmore
Lamoille County

(G-21922)
RUSTY D INC
442 Worcester Rdg (05661-4479)
PHONE..................................802 888-8838
Rusty Dewees, *President*
William Dewees, *Vice Pres*
Marilyn Dewees, *Treasurer*
EMP: 3
SALES (est): 207.7K **Privately Held**
SIC: 2411 Logging

Enosburg Falls
Franklin County

(G-21923)
COLD HOLLOW PRECISION INC
154 Butternut Hollow Rd (05450-5733)
P.O. Box 218 (05450-0218)
PHONE..................................802 933-5542
David Tryhorne, *President*
Matthew Tryhorne, *Vice Pres*
Sara Tryhorne, *Treasurer*
EMP: 9
SQ FT: 10,000
SALES (est): 800.5K **Privately Held**
SIC: 3469 Mfg Machine Parts

(G-21924)
COUNTY COURIER INC
342 Main St N (05450-5990)
P.O. Box 398 (05450-0398)
PHONE..................................802 933-4375
Ed Shamy, *CEO*
EMP: 11 **EST:** 1949
SALES (est): 642.1K **Privately Held**
SIC: 2711 Newspapers-Publishing/Printing

(G-21925)
MOUNTAIN VIEW SKIDS
5290 Boston Post Rd (05450-6125)
PHONE..................................802 933-2623
Jamie Larosa, *Manager*
EMP: 3
SALES (est): 308K **Privately Held**
SIC: 2448 Mfg Wood Pallets/Skids

(G-21926)
PLOUFFS MONUMENT CO INC
1087 Colton Rd (05450-5486)
PHONE..................................802 933-4346
Steve Plouff, *President*
Sharon Plouff, *Vice Pres*
EMP: 3
SALES: 200K **Privately Held**
SIC: 3272 5999 Mfg Concrete Products Ret Misc Merchandise

(G-21927)
SNOWSHOE POND MPLE SGRWRKS LLC
431 Barnes Rd (05450-5833)
PHONE..................................802 777-9676
George Saig, *Administration*

EMP: 3
SALES (est): 142.6K Privately Held
SIC: 3949 Mfg Sporting/Athletic Goods

Essex Junction
Chittenden County

(G-21928)
ALPA INCORPORATED
34 River Rd (05452-3808)
PHONE....802 662-8401
EMP: 4
SALES (est): 388.2K Privately Held
SIC: 3081 Mfg Unsupported Plastic Film/Sheet

(G-21929)
ASK-INTTAG LLC
1000 River St Bldg 966d (05452-4201)
P.O. Box 169 (05453-0169)
PHONE....802 288-7210
Thierry Burgess, *Mng Member*
▲ EMP: 20
SALES: 4.2MM Privately Held
SIC: 3699 Mfg Electrical Equipment/Supplies

(G-21930)
AUTUMN-HARP INC
26 Thompson Dr (05452-3405)
PHONE....802 857-4600
David Logan, *CEO*
Hillary Burrows, *President*
Michael Currier, *Production*
Garett Serke, *Project Engr*
Lisa Mosca, *Human Res Mgr*
▲ EMP: 200
SALES (est): 61.6MM Privately Held
WEB: www.autumnharp.com
SIC: 2844 Mfg Toilet Preparations

(G-21931)
BLACK FLANNEL BREWING CO LLC
21 Essex Way Ste 201 (05452-3385)
PHONE....802 488-0089
Chris Kesler,
Karen Bisbee,
Peter Edelmann,
Dan Sartwell,
EMP: 4
SALES (est): 116.1K Privately Held
SIC: 2082 Mfg Malt Beverages

(G-21932)
BROWNS RIVER BINDERY INC
Also Called: Browns Rver Rec Prsrvtion Svcs
1 Allen Martin Dr (05452-3403)
P.O. Box 8501, Essex (05451-8501)
PHONE....802 878-3335
Charles Remmey, *President*
Janet Remmey, *Corp Secy*
Marianne Holzer, *Vice Pres*
EMP: 24
SQ FT: 8,000
SALES (est): 2.2MM
SALES (corp-wide): 16.3MM Privately Held
WEB: www.brownsriver.com
SIC: 2789 Bookbinding & Paper Conservation
PA: Kofile Products, Inc.
6480 Enduro Dr
Washington MO 63090
636 239-0140

(G-21933)
BROWNS RIVER MAPLE
375 Browns River Rd (05452-2260)
PHONE....802 878-2880
Robert Lemire, *Owner*
EMP: 3
SALES (est): 178K Privately Held
SIC: 2099 Mfg Food Preparations

(G-21934)
BRUSO-HOLMES INC
34 Park St Ste 10 (05452-4420)
PHONE....802 878-8337
Dennis Bruso, *President*
Sandra Bruso, *Vice Pres*
EMP: 6
SQ FT: 3,600
SALES: 500K Privately Held
WEB: www.eastcoastprinters.com
SIC: 2759 Screen Printing

(G-21935)
CATAMOUNT NORTH CABINETRY LLC
Also Called: Simpson Cabinetry
15 Corporate Dr (05452-4434)
PHONE....802 264-9009
Andrew Cabrera, *Principal*
EMP: 10
SALES (est): 565.4K Privately Held
SIC: 2434 Mfg Wood Kitchen Cabinets

(G-21936)
CHARTER DEV & CONSULTING CORP
Also Called: Tony's Trains Exchange
57 River Rd Unit 1023 (05452-3842)
PHONE....802 878-5005
Anthony Parisi, *President*
Ed Furrer, *Manager*
EMP: 8
SQ FT: 2,500
SALES (est): 1.1MM Privately Held
WEB: www.dcctrains.com
SIC: 3629 Mfg Electrical Industrial Apparatus

(G-21937)
COOPER LIGHTING INC
Also Called: Cooper Controls
16 Perkins Dr (05452-3858)
PHONE....800 767-3674
Neil Scrimshire, *President*
EMP: 18
SQ FT: 15,000
SALES (est): 3.5MM Privately Held
WEB: www.pcilightingcontrols.com
SIC: 3648 3646 3643 3625 Mfg Lighting Equipment Mfg Coml Light Fixtures Mfg Conductive Wire Dvcs Mfg Relay/Indstl Control
HQ: Cooper Industries Unlimited Company
41 A B Drury Street
Dublin
-

(G-21938)
CRANK SHOP INC
23 Kellogg Rd (05452-2820)
PHONE....802 878-3615
Larry Audette, *President*
Debbie Tucker, *Admin Sec*
Paula Bean, *Administration*
EMP: 3
SALES (est): 1.8MM Privately Held
WEB: www.thecrankshopvt.com
SIC: 3799 Mfg Transportation Equipment

(G-21939)
DESIGN SIGNS INC
4 Andrew Dr (05452-2836)
P.O. Box 1246, Williston (05495-1246)
PHONE....802 872-9906
John Floyd, *President*
EMP: 3
SQ FT: 1,500
SALES: 400K Privately Held
WEB: www.designsignsvt.com
SIC: 3993 Mfg Signs/Advertising Specialties

(G-21940)
GALVION BALLISTICS LTD (PA)
7 Corporate Dr (05452-4434)
PHONE....802 879-7002
Jonathan Blanshay, *President*
Alex Hooper, *Vice Pres*
Eric Hounchell, *Vice Pres*
Linda Watson, *Vice Pres*
Oliver Pentenrieder, *Research*
▲ EMP: 160
SQ FT: 45,000
SALES (est): 59.1MM Privately Held
WEB: www.revisioneyewear.com
SIC: 3851 Mfg Ophthalmic Goods

(G-21941)
GLOBALFOUNDRIES US 2 LLC
Also Called: Global Foundries
1000 River St (05452-4201)
PHONE....408 462-4452
Tyler Tassin, *Manager*
Bill Wagner, *IT/INT Sup*
Kelly Smith, *Director*
Doug Duval, *Officer*
Steven Grasso,
EMP: 2700 Privately Held
SIC: 3674 Mfg Semiconductors/Related Devices
HQ: Globalfoundries U.S. 2 Llc
2070 Route 52
Hopewell Junction NY 12533
512 457-3900

(G-21942)
GORDINI USA INC (PA)
Also Called: Drop
67 Allen Martin Dr (05452)
P.O. Box 8440, Essex (05451-8440)
PHONE....802 879-5211
Philip Gellis, *President*
David Gellis, *President*
Kevin Holmes-Henry, *CFO*
▲ EMP: 45
SQ FT: 50,000
SALES (est): 5.6MM Privately Held
WEB: www.gordini.com
SIC: 3949 Mfg Sporting/Athletic Goods

(G-21943)
GS BLODGETT CORPORATION
19 Thompson Dr (05452-3408)
PHONE....802 871-3287
EMP: 5
SALES (corp-wide): 2.7B Publicly Held
SIC: 3631 Mfg Household Cooking Equipment
HQ: G.S. Blodgett Corporation
42 Allen Martin Dr
Essex Junction VT 05452
802 860-3700

(G-21944)
GS BLODGETT CORPORATION (HQ)
Also Called: Blodget Oven Company, The
42 Allen Martin Dr (05452-3400)
PHONE....802 860-3700
Selim A Bassoul, *President*
Mark Findel-Halpin, *President*
Timothy J Fitzgerald, *Vice Pres*
Jeff Herren, *Vice Pres*
Dan Coolbeth, *Opers Mgr*
◆ EMP: 150
SQ FT: 200,000
SALES (est): 51.9MM
SALES (corp-wide): 2.7B Publicly Held
SIC: 3631 3589 Mfg Household Cooking Equipment Mfg Service Industry Machinery
PA: The Middleby Corporation
1400 Toastmaster Dr
Elgin IL 60120
847 741-3300

(G-21945)
GS BLODGETT CORPORATION
Blodgett Combi
42 Allen Martin Dr (05452-3400)
PHONE....802 860-3700
Selim A Bassoul, *President*
Bridgett Blow, *Purch Mgr*
Larry Sweeney, *Manager*
EMP: 30
SALES (corp-wide): 2.7B Publicly Held
SIC: 3589 Mfg Service Industry Machinery
HQ: G.S. Blodgett Corporation
42 Allen Martin Dr
Essex Junction VT 05452
802 860-3700

(G-21946)
HAYLEY CUSTOM STAIR CO INC
19 Gauthier Dr (05452-2825)
PHONE....802 861-6400
Greg Shover, *President*
EMP: 4
SALES (est): 428.3K Privately Held
SIC: 2431 Mfg Millwork

(G-21947)
INFINEON TECH AMERICAS CORP
Also Called: Siemens Components
1000 River St (05452-4201)
PHONE....802 769-6824
Wolfram Malzsfeld, *Sales Mgr*
Oliver Kiehl, *Sales Mgr*
EMP: 40
SALES (corp-wide): 8.9B Privately Held
WEB: www.infineon-ncs.com
SIC: 3679 3674 Mfg Electronic Components Mfg Semiconductors/Related Devices
HQ: Infineon Technologies Americas Corp.
101 N Pacific Coast Hwy
El Segundo CA 90245
310 726-8000

(G-21948)
LAMELL LUMBER CORPORATION
82a Jericho Rd (05452-2799)
PHONE....802 878-2475
Ronald R Lamell Sr, *President*
Ronald R Lamell Jr, *Vice Pres*
Sheila Lamell, *Treasurer*
EMP: 32
SQ FT: 6,200
SALES (est): 5.1MM Privately Held
SIC: 2421 Sawmill/Planing Mill

(G-21949)
MEDIWARE/SYNERGY HUMAN & SOCIA
25 New England Dr (05452-2899)
PHONE....802 878-8514
Joe Sander, *President*
EMP: 80
SQ FT: 20,000
SALES: 18MM
SALES (corp-wide): 118.3MM Privately Held
WEB: www.synergysw.com
SIC: 7372 7371 Prepackaged Software Services Custom Computer Programing
HQ: Wellsky Human & Social Services Corporation
11700 Plaza America Dr
Reston VA 20190
703 674-5100

(G-21950)
MESSER LLC
Ibm Plant (05452)
PHONE....802 878-6339
EMP: 23
SALES (corp-wide): 1.4B Privately Held
SIC: 2813 Mfg Gases
HQ: Messer Llc
200 Somerset Corp Blvd # 7000
Bridgewater NJ 08807
908 464-8100

(G-21951)
MICRO WIRE TRANSM SYSTEMS INC
8 Ewing Pl (05452-2821)
PHONE....802 876-7901
Helena Liu, *Project Mgr*
Fred Kane, *Engineer*
Brendan Barden, *Director*
Hwang Chang-Soon, *Director*
EMP: 19
SALES (est): 4.1MM Privately Held
SIC: 3315 Mfg Steel Wire/Related Products

(G-21952)
NEW HRIZONS EMB SCREENPRINTING
5 Laurette Dr (05452-4007)
PHONE....802 651-9801
Anthony Neri, *Owner*
EMP: 4
SALES (est): 94.4K Privately Held
SIC: 2395 Pleating/Stitching Services

(G-21953)
PARENT CO APPLICATIONS INC (PA)
20 Hillside Cir (05452-3969)
PHONE....802 233-3612
Thomas O' Leary, *CEO*
Justin Martin, *COO*
Mike Dececco, *Chief Mktg Ofcr*
EMP: 10 EST: 2014
SALES (est): 848.3K Privately Held
SIC: 2759 Commercial Printing

GEOGRAPHIC

(G-21954)
PERFECT STORM SPORTS TECH LLC
Also Called: Dodgeskiboots
5b David Dr (05452-2805)
PHONE..................................802 662-2102
David Dodge, *Mng Member*
William Doble,
◆ **EMP:** 4
SQ FT: 2,500
SALES (est): 166.2K **Privately Held**
SIC: 3949 Mfg Sporting/Athletic Goods

(G-21955)
RAYMOND REYNOLDS WELDING
15 West St (05452-3549)
PHONE..................................802 879-4650
Raymond Reynolds, *Owner*
EMP: 3
SALES (est): 110K **Privately Held**
SIC: 7692 Welding Contractor

(G-21956)
REVISION BALLISTICS LTD
Also Called: Revision Military
7 Corporate Dr (05452-4434)
PHONE..................................802 879-7002
Jonathan Blanshay, *President*
Jonathan Wainer, *CFO*
Peter Erly, *Treasurer*
Gregory Macguire, *Admin Sec*
EMP: 34
SQ FT: 30,000
SALES (est): 4.8MM
SALES (corp-wide): 59.1MM **Privately Held**
SIC: 3842 Mfg Surgical Appliances/Supplies
PA: Revision Military Ltd.
7 Corporate Dr
Essex Junction VT 05452
802 879-7002

(G-21957)
REVISION MILITARY JV
7 Corporate Dr (05452-4434)
PHONE..................................802 879-7002
Gregory Maguire,
EMP: 302
SALES (est): 12.7MM **Privately Held**
SIC: 3842 Surgical Appliances And Supplies, Nsk

(G-21958)
SAMMEL SIGN COMPANY
20 Morse Dr Ste C (05452-2811)
PHONE..................................802 879-3360
Roger A Sammel, *President*
Roger Sammel, *President*
Kelly Sammel, *Vice Pres*
EMP: 3
SALES (est): 180K **Privately Held**
WEB: www.sammelsign.com
SIC: 3993 Mfg Signs/Advertising Specialties

(G-21959)
SEMIVATION
9 Oakwood Ln (05452-3327)
PHONE..................................802 878-5153
Mark Hakey, *Principal*
Peter Mitchell, *Principal*
EMP: 4
SALES (est): 197.7K **Privately Held**
SIC: 3674 Mfg Semiconductors/Related Devices

(G-21960)
SHEET METAL DESIGN
3 Corporate Dr (05452-4434)
PHONE..................................802 288-9700
Jim Carew, *Partner*
Reggie Swenor, *Partner*
EMP: 7
SALES (est): 899.5K **Privately Held**
WEB: www.sheetmetaldesign.com
SIC: 3444 Mfg Sheet Metalwork

(G-21961)
SIMPLY CUPCAKES
8 Pioneer St (05452-2930)
PHONE..................................802 871-5634
Heidi Danforth, *Principal*
EMP: 4
SALES (est): 238K **Privately Held**
SIC: 2051 Mfg Bread/Related Products

(G-21962)
TWIN STATE SIGNS INC
14 Gauthier Dr (05452-2825)
P.O. Box 8206, Essex (05451-8206)
PHONE..................................802 872-8949
Mary Denault, *President*
Raymond Denault, *Corp Secy*
EMP: 9
SALES (est): 1MM **Privately Held**
SIC: 3993 1799 7389 Mfg Signs/Ad Specialties Special Trade Contractor Business Services

(G-21963)
VERMONT SYSTEMS INC
12 Market Pl (05452-2939)
PHONE..................................802 879-6993
Randy Eckels, *CEO*
Kathy Messier, *Vice Pres*
Jan Plaza, *Asst Treas*
Lance Bapp, *Finance*
John Gretkowski, *Sales Mgr*
EMP: 87
SQ FT: 6,000
SALES: 21.2MM **Privately Held**
WEB: www.vermontsystems.com
SIC: 7372 7371 5045 Prepackaged Software Services Custom Computer Programing Whol Computers/Peripherals

(G-21964)
VERMONT TONER RECHARGE INC
12 Claire Dr (05452-4423)
PHONE..................................802 864-7637
Sheri Cushman, *President*
John Cushman, *Vice Pres*
EMP: 5
SQ FT: 3,000
SALES (est): 586K **Privately Held**
WEB: www.vermonttonerrecharge.com
SIC: 3955 Mfg Remanufactured Toner Cartridges For Laser Printers

Fair Haven
Rutland County

(G-21965)
BB METAL FABRICATION INC
653 River St (05743-1180)
PHONE..................................802 265-8375
Raymond W Beebe, *Principal*
EMP: 4
SALES (est): 246.1K **Privately Held**
SIC: 3499 Mfg Misc Fabricated Metal Products

(G-21966)
CAMARA SLATE PRODUCTS INC
963 S Main St (05743-4435)
P.O. Box 8 (05743-0008)
PHONE..................................802 265-3200
David Camara Jr, *President*
Shawn Camara, *Admin Sec*
▲ **EMP:** 23
SALES (est): 3.2MM **Privately Held**
WEB: www.camaraslate.com
SIC: 3281 Mfg Cut Stone And Stone Products

(G-21967)
PEDRO REESE
Also Called: Pedro Slate
1078 River St (05743-1189)
PHONE..................................802 265-3658
Reese Pedro, *Owner*
Gertrude Pedro, *Co-Owner*
EMP: 4
SALES (est): 497.5K **Privately Held**
WEB: www.pedroslate.com
SIC: 3281 Mfg Cut Stone/Products

(G-21968)
POULTNEY PALLET INC
10 Winham Ln (05743-9781)
PHONE..................................802 265-4444
Millie Winham, *President*
EMP: 4
SALES (est): 483.2K **Privately Held**
SIC: 2653 2441 Mfg Pallets/Shipping Crates

(G-21969)
SKYLINE CORPORATION
Vermont Division
875 S Main St (05743-1178)
PHONE..................................802 278-8222
Peter Heck, *Branch Mgr*
EMP: 120
SALES (corp-wide): 1.3B **Publicly Held**
WEB: www.skylinecorp.com
SIC: 2451 Ret Mobile Homes
PA: Skyline Champion Corporation
200 Nibco Pkwy Ste 200 # 200
Elkhart IN 46516
574 294-6521

(G-21970)
VERMONT STRUCTURAL SLATE CO (PA)
3 Prospect St (05743-1219)
PHONE..................................802 265-4933
Craig E Markcrow, *President*
W E Markcrow, *President*
Eloise Wemette, *Corp Secy*
Ralph Sheldon, *Plant Mgr*
Doug Sheldon, *Manager*
▼ **EMP:** 50 **EST:** 1866
SQ FT: 1,500
SALES (est): 10.3MM **Privately Held**
WEB: www.vermontstructuralslate.com
SIC: 3281 2952 Mfg Cut Stone/Products Mfg Asphalt Felts/Coatings

(G-21971)
VERMONT UNFADING GREEN SLATE (PA)
963 S Main St (05743-4435)
P.O. Box 8 (05743-0008)
PHONE..................................802 265-3200
David Camara Jr, *President*
David Camara Sr, *Vice Pres*
EMP: 19
SQ FT: 8,000
SALES (est): 3MM **Privately Held**
SIC: 3281 Mfg Slate

Fairfax
Chittenden County

(G-21972)
BARIATRIX NUTRITION CORP
308 Industrial Park Rd (05454-4414)
PHONE..................................802 527-2500
Thomas Egger, *President*
Rod Egger, *Vice Pres*
Mark Waldron, *Opers Mgr*
▲ **EMP:** 33
SQ FT: 30,000
SALES (est): 6.6MM
SALES (corp-wide): 13.2MM **Privately Held**
SIC: 2023 Mfg Dry/Evaporated Dairy Products
PA: Bariatrix Nutrition Inc
4905 Rue Fairway
Lachine QC H8T 1
514 633-7455

(G-21973)
BUYERS DIGEST PRESS INC
57 Yankee Park Rd (05454-5515)
P.O. Box 10, Burlington (05402-0010)
PHONE..................................802 893-4214
Jim Carey, *President*
Kevin Domingue, *Partner*
EMP: 60
SQ FT: 12,000
SALES (est): 4.5MM **Privately Held**
WEB: www.buyerdigest.com
SIC: 2752 Lithographic Commercial Printing

(G-21974)
DOMINION & GRIMM USA
164 Yankee Park Rd (05454-5448)
PHONE..................................802 524-9625
EMP: 6 **EST:** 2009
SALES (est): 497.7K **Privately Held**
SIC: 2099 Mfg Food Preparations

(G-21975)
GANNETT RIVER STATES PUBG CORP
Also Called: Buyers Digest
57 Yankee Park Rd (05454-5515)
PHONE..................................802 893-4214
Allen Messier, *Manager*
EMP: 60
SALES (corp-wide): 1.5B **Publicly Held**
SIC: 2711 Newspapers-Publishing/Printing
HQ: Gannett River States Publishing Corporation
7950 Jones Branch Dr
Mc Lean VA 22102
703 284-6000

(G-21976)
HARRISON REDI-MIX CORP
1803 Skunk Hill Rd (05454-5565)
P.O. Box 2098, Milton (05468-2098)
PHONE..................................802 849-6688
James Harrison, *President*
Janet Harrison, *Vice Pres*
EMP: 12
SALES (est): 1.7MM **Privately Held**
SIC: 3273 Mfg Ready-Mixed Concrete

(G-21977)
MED ASSOCIATES INC (PA)
166 Industrial Park Rd (05454-4452)
P.O. Box 319, Saint Albans (05478-0319)
PHONE..................................802 527-2343
Bridget Garibay, *President*
Jane Zurn, *Corp Secy*
Joaquin P Aja, *Vice Pres*
Ted Cantin, *Engineer*
Tony Audet, *Network Mgr*
EMP: 72
SQ FT: 20,000
SALES (est): 10.2MM **Privately Held**
WEB: www.med-associates.com
SIC: 3826 Mfg Analytical Instruments

(G-21978)
RUNAMOK MAPLE LLC
293 Fletcher Rd (05454-9768)
PHONE..................................802 849-7943
Eric Sorkin,
EMP: 5
SQ FT: 55,000
SALES (est): 122K **Privately Held**
SIC: 2099 5149 2087 2064 Mfg Food Preparations Whol Groceries Mfg Flavor Extracts Mfg Candy/Confectionery

(G-21979)
SERAC CORPORATION (HQ)
Arrwhead Indstl Bldg 110b (05454)
PHONE..................................802 527-9609
Alan P Gay, *President*
William Raap, *President*
Irwin Langer, *Vice Pres*
Cynthia Turcot, *Admin Sec*
▲ **EMP:** 10
SALES (est): 702.6K
SALES (corp-wide): 59.6MM **Privately Held**
SIC: 2452 3448 Mfg Greenhouses
PA: America's Gardening Resource, Inc.
128 Intervale Rd
Burlington VT 05401
802 660-3500

(G-21980)
VERMONT INDEXABLE TOOLING INC
331b Bryce Blvd (05454-5578)
PHONE..................................802 752-2002
Brian Matthews, *President*
Blease M Matthews, *Director*
EMP: 9
SQ FT: 10,000
SALES (est): 107K **Privately Held**
WEB: www.vermontindexable.com
SIC: 3599 1799 3441 Mfg Industrial Machinery Trade Contractor Structural Metal Fabrication

(G-21981)
YANKEE CORPORATION
125 Yankee Park Rd (05454-5547)
PHONE..................................802 527-0177
James E Bryce, *President*
James L Bryce, *Vice Pres*
EMP: 65 **EST:** 1980

▲ = Import ▼=Export
◆ =Import/Export

SQ FT: 20,000
SALES (est): 9.2MM **Privately Held**
WEB: www.yankeereamer.com
SIC: 3541 3545 Mfg Machine Tools-Cutting Mfg Machine Tool Accessories

Fairfield
Franklin County

(G-21982)
BRANON FAMILY MAPLE ORCHARDS
539 Branon Rd (05455-5672)
PHONE....................................802 827-3914
Thomas Branon, *Co-Owner*
Cecile Branon, *Co-Owner*
EMP: 8
SALES: 800K **Privately Held**
SIC: 2099 Mfg Food Preparations

(G-21983)
BRANON SHADY MAPLES INC
1097 North Rd (05455-5521)
PHONE....................................802 827-6605
Damian Branon, *President*
EMP: 5 **EST:** 2014
SALES (est): 354.6K **Privately Held**
SIC: 2099 Food Preparations, Nec, Nsk

(G-21984)
COLD CORNERS MAPLEWORKS LLC
2893 North Rd (05455-5647)
P.O. Box 3 (05455-0003)
PHONE....................................802 551-2270
Erin Howrigan,
Kyle Howrigan,
Sean Howrigan,
EMP: 4
SALES (est): 156.9K **Privately Held**
SIC: 2099 5149 Mfg Food Preparations Whol Groceries

(G-21985)
VERMONT SYRUP COMPANY LLC
406 Johnny Bull Hl (05455-5702)
PHONE....................................802 309-8861
Ben Howrigan, *Principal*
EMP: 3
SALES (est): 156.4K **Privately Held**
SIC: 2099 Mfg Food Preparations

Ferrisburg
Addison County

(G-21986)
GREEN MOUNTAIN HONEY FARMS
Also Called: Mailloux Vermont Cntry Farms
Rr 7 (05456)
PHONE....................................802 877-3396
Jeannette Mailloux, *President*
Justin McClay, *Corp Secy*
Paul Mailloux, *Vice Pres*
John Mailloux, *Treasurer*
EMP: 3
SALES (est): 185.7K **Privately Held**
SIC: 2099 0175 8748 Produce & Sell Honey Farm Stand Greenhouse Apple Orchard & Consulting

Ferrisburgh
Addison County

(G-21987)
BRICKYARD ENTERPRISES INC
239 Brickyard Rd (05456-9887)
PHONE....................................802 338-7267
Ann Poskas, *Principal*
EMP: 4
SALES (est): 369.3K **Privately Held**
SIC: 3842 Mfg Surgical Appliances/Supplies

(G-21988)
DOCK DOCTORS LLC
19 Little Otter Ln (05456-9651)
PHONE....................................802 877-6756
Chris Girard, *Sales Mgr*
Mike Savioli, *Sales Mgr*
Paige Kaleita, *Marketing Mgr*
Jeff Provost, *Mng Member*
Dan Provost, *Manager*
EMP: 35
SQ FT: 20,000
SALES (est): 5MM **Privately Held**
WEB: www.thedockdoctors.com
SIC: 2511 3999 4491 5088 Mfg Wood Household Furn Mfg Misc Products Marine Cargo Handler Whol Trans Equip Whol Sporting Goods/Supp

(G-21989)
MEADHAM INC
Also Called: MD Cosmetic Laser & Botox Ctr
34 Middlebrook Rd (05456-9623)
PHONE....................................802 878-1236
Henry Harris, *CEO*
Irina Leontieva, *President*
Erin Jewell, *Admin Sec*
EMP: 5
SALES (est): 930K **Privately Held**
WEB: www.mdlaserandbotox.com
SIC: 2834 Mfg Pharmaceutical Preparations

(G-21990)
VERMONT LVSTK SLGHTER PROC LLC
76 Depot Rd (05456-9692)
PHONE....................................802 877-3421
Carl W Cushing,
EMP: 10
SALES (est): 923.3K **Privately Held**
SIC: 2011 Meat Packing Plant

Florence
Rutland County

(G-21991)
OMYA INC
Also Called: Verpol Plant
206 Omya W Whipple (05744)
PHONE....................................802 459-3311
John Hock, *Principal*
EMP: 23
SALES (corp-wide): 4B **Privately Held**
WEB: www.omya-na.com
SIC: 2819 Mfg Industrial Inorganic Chemicals
HQ: Omya Inc.
9987 Carver Rd Ste 300
Blue Ash OH 45242
513 387-4600

(G-21992)
TROY MINERALS INC
Also Called: Florence Crushed Stone
180 Fire Hill Rd (05744)
PHONE....................................802 878-5103
Michael P Chmielewski, *President*
EMP: 3
SALES (est): 131.8K **Privately Held**
SIC: 1411 Dimension Stone Quarry

Forest Dale
Rutland County

(G-21993)
TUCEL INDUSTRIES INC
2014 Forest Dale Rd (05745)
PHONE....................................802 247-6824
John C Lewis Jr, *President*
Joanne Raleigh, *Vice Pres*
▲ **EMP:** 13 **EST:** 1970
SALES (est): 1.9MM **Privately Held**
WEB: www.tucel.com
SIC: 3991 Mfg Brooms/Brushes

Franklin
Franklin County

(G-21994)
GAYLORD WEST
1762 Rice Hill Rd (05457-9817)
PHONE....................................802 285-6438
Gaylord West, *Owner*
EMP: 3
SALES (est): 172.7K **Privately Held**
SIC: 2511 5099 5989 Mfg Wood Household Furniture Whol Durable Goods Ret Fuel Dealer

Glover
Orleans County

(G-21995)
VERMONT BIRCH SYRUP CO
440 Clark Rd (05839-9744)
PHONE....................................802 249-0574
Darrell Bussino, *Principal*
EMP: 3 **EST:** 2016
SALES (est): 155.9K **Privately Held**
SIC: 2099 Mfg Food Preparations

Grafton
Windham County

(G-21996)
SAMMARVAL CO LTD
661 Wright Orchard Rd (05146-9772)
PHONE....................................802 843-2637
Joseph G Valente, *President*
Wai Tung Ng, *Director*
Nanae Valente, *Director*
▲ **EMP:** 3 **EST:** 1982
SALES: 200K **Privately Held**
SIC: 3679 Mfg Electronic Components

Grand Isle
Grand Isle County

(G-21997)
BINDERY SOLUTIONS INC (PA)
225 W Shore Rd (05458-2101)
PHONE....................................802 372-3492
James Aloi, *President*
EMP: 3 **EST:** 1997
SALES: 18MM **Privately Held**
SIC: 3535 7389 Mfg Conveyors/Equipment

(G-21998)
I C HAUS CORP
Also Called: Ic-Haus
9 Dodge Ter (05458-4400)
PHONE....................................802 372-8340
Heiner Flocke, *President*
Manfred Herz, *Vice Pres*
Michael Walczack, *Vice Pres*
EMP: 5
SQ FT: 2,000
SALES (est): 270K **Privately Held**
WEB: www.ichaus.com
SIC: 3674 Distributors In Integrated Circuits

Graniteville
Washington County

(G-21999)
DUCHARME MACHINE SHOP INC
1668 Mcglynn Rd (05654-8100)
P.O. Box 6 (05654-0006)
PHONE....................................802 476-6575
Pierre Ducharme, *President*
Carmen Ducharme, *Admin Sec*
EMP: 4
SQ FT: 4,500
SALES (est): 496K **Privately Held**
SIC: 3599 1799 Mfg Industrial Machinery Trade Contractor

(G-22000)
NORTH EAST MATERIALS GROUP LLC
751 Graniteville Rd (05654-8024)
P.O. Box 231, Milton WA (98354-0231)
PHONE....................................802 479-7004
Joe Dimick, *Opers Mgr*
L P Hughes, *Mng Member*
Harry Hart,
Jonathan Hart,
EMP: 10
SALES (est): 809.4K **Privately Held**
SIC: 1499 Nonmetallic Mineral Mining

(G-22001)
ORDWAY ELECTRIC & MACHINE
1599 Carrier Rd (05654-4400)
PHONE....................................802 476-8011
Carroll E Ordway, *President*
Ned Ordway, *Treasurer*
EMP: 3
SQ FT: 3,200
SALES (est): 290K **Privately Held**
SIC: 3531 Mfg Cranes & Polishing Machines

(G-22002)
ROCK OF AGES CORPORATION
Also Called: Autumn Rose Quarry
558 Graniteville Rd (05654-8001)
P.O. Box 482, Barre (05641-0482)
PHONE....................................802 476-3119
EMP: 19
SALES (corp-wide): 2.1MM **Privately Held**
WEB: www.rockofages.com
SIC: 1411 3281 Dimension Stone, Nsk
HQ: Rock Of Ages Corporation
560 Graniteville Rd
Graniteville VT 05654
802 476-3115

Granville
Addison County

(G-22003)
GRANVILLE MANUFACTURING CO
45 Mill Rd Ofc Rte 100 (05747-9669)
P.O. Box 15 (05747-0015)
PHONE....................................802 767-4747
Jeffrey Fuller, *President*
Cindy Fuller, *Vice Pres*
Douglas Fuller, *Vice Pres*
Carol Fuller, *Treasurer*
EMP: 4
SQ FT: 20,000
SALES (est): 594.6K **Privately Held**
WEB: www.woodsiding.com
SIC: 2421 5211 2449 2439 Sawmill/Planing Mill Ret Lumber/Building Mtrl Mfg Wood Containers Mfg Structural Wd Member Hdwd Dimension/Flr Mill

Greensboro Bend
Orleans County

(G-22004)
HILL FARMSTEAD LLC
Also Called: Hill Farmstead Brewery
403 Hill Rd (05842-8813)
PHONE....................................802 533-7450
Shaun E Hill, *Mng Member*
EMP: 10
SALES (est): 1.7MM **Privately Held**
SIC: 2082 Mfg Malt Beverages

GEOGRAPHIC

Groton
Caledonia County

(G-22005)
GROTON TIMBERWORKS OF VERMONT
2126 Scott Hwy (05046-5617)
PHONE..................................802 584-4446
Nathan Puffer, *Owner*
EMP: 8
SALES: 500K **Privately Held**
SIC: 2452 Mfg Prefabricated Wood Buildings

Guildhall
Essex County

(G-22006)
NEWPORT SAND & GRAVEL CO INC
Also Called: Carroll Concrete Co
429 Breault Rd (05905-9752)
PHONE..................................802 328-3384
Shawn Carroll, *President*
EMP: 5
SALES (corp-wide): 44MM **Privately Held**
SIC: 3273 Mfg Ready-Mixed Concrete
PA: Newport Sand & Gravel Co., Inc.
8 Reeds Mill Rd
Newport NH 03773
603 298-0199

Guilford
Windham County

(G-22007)
KERBER SAW MILL
3550 Coolidge Hwy (05301-8625)
PHONE..................................802 257-0614
Peter Kerber, *Owner*
EMP: 6
SALES (est): 418K **Privately Held**
SIC: 2421 Sawmill

(G-22008)
WH PROPERTY SERVICE LLC
287 Locust Hill Rd (05301-8079)
PHONE..................................802 257-8566
Daniel Systo,
EMP: 12
SALES: 100K **Privately Held**
SIC: 2099 Mfg Food Preparations

Hardwick
Caledonia County

(G-22009)
AUTHENTIC LOG HOMES INC
1670 Craftsbury Rd (05843-9783)
PHONE..................................802 472-5096
Gary Darling, *President*
Julie Darling, *Vice Pres*
EMP: 5
SALES (est): 531.2K **Privately Held**
WEB: www.authenticloghomes.com
SIC: 2411 2452 Logging Mfg Prefabricated Wood Buildings

(G-22010)
CALEDONIA SPIRITS INC
46 Buffalo Mtn Commons Dr (05843)
P.O. Box 840, Montpelier (05601-0840)
PHONE..................................802 472-8000
Ryan Christiansen, *President*
Todd Hardie, *President*
EMP: 30 **EST:** 2010
SALES (est): 1.1MM **Privately Held**
SIC: 2085 Mfg Distilled/Blended Liquor

(G-22011)
FONTAINE LOGGING
62 Center Rd (05843-9886)
PHONE..................................802 472-6140
Lynette Fontaine, *Principal*
EMP: 3 **EST:** 2010
SALES (est): 251.8K **Privately Held**
SIC: 2411 Logging

(G-22012)
GREEN MOUNTAIN CBD INC
273 Kate Brook Rd (05843-9443)
PHONE..................................802 595-3258
Alejandro Bergad, *President*
EMP: 9
SALES (est): 3.3MM
SALES (corp-wide): 6.5MM **Privately Held**
SIC: 3999 Cannabis Products
PA: Skyview Naturals Pbc
180 Battery St Ste 250
Burlington VT 05401
802 495-0795

(G-22013)
HARDWICK GAZETTE PRINT SHOP
Also Called: Hardwick Gazette Newspaper
42 S Main St (05843-7067)
P.O. Box 367 (05843-0367)
PHONE..................................802 472-6521
Ross Connelly, *President*
Susan Jarzyna, *Vice Pres*
EMP: 7
SALES (est): 398.3K **Privately Held**
SIC: 2711 Newspapers-Publishing/Printing

(G-22014)
VERMONT SOY LLC
180 Junction Rd (05843)
P.O. Box 401 (05843-0401)
PHONE..................................802 472-8500
Andrew Meyer,
EMP: 9
SALES (est): 918.2K **Privately Held**
SIC: 2099 Mfg Food Preparations

Hartland
Windsor County

(G-22015)
DARWIN A LEWIS INC
Also Called: Lewis Bible Bindery
243 Densmore Hill Rd (05048-8105)
PHONE..................................802 457-4521
Darwin A Lewis, *President*
Karen Lewis, *Corp Secy*
Robert F Lewis Jr, *Vice Pres*
▲ **EMP:** 7
SQ FT: 30,000
SALES (est): 320K **Privately Held**
WEB: www.lewisbibles.com
SIC: 2789 Bookbinding/Related Work

(G-22016)
MARUS PRINTING
115 Merritt Rd (05048-9413)
P.O. Box 156 (05048-0156)
PHONE..................................802 436-2044
Robert Peeler, *Owner*
EMP: 4
SALES: 400K **Privately Held**
SIC: 2752 Commercial Offset Printing

(G-22017)
PRECISION CUTTER GRINDING INC
Also Called: Pcg Machine Shop
7 Ferry Rd (05048)
P.O. Box 248 (05048-0248)
PHONE..................................802 436-2039
Lee Hood, *President*
Todd Hood, *President*
EMP: 11
SALES (est): 1.6MM **Privately Held**
SIC: 3599 Mfg Industrial Machinery

(G-22018)
STEBENNES LOGGING
468 Route 12 (05048-8109)
PHONE..................................802 436-3250
Donald Stebenne, *Principal*
EMP: 3
SALES (est): 193.9K **Privately Held**
SIC: 2411 Logging

Highgate Center
Franklin County

(G-22019)
DUHAMEL FAMILY FARM LLC
107 Franklin Rd (05459-4167)
PHONE..................................802 868-4954
James Duhamel, *Mng Member*
Holly Duhamel, *Mng Member*
EMP: 8
SALES (est): 886.3K **Privately Held**
SIC: 2026 Manufactures Fluid Milk

(G-22020)
GREEN MOUNTAIN FOREST PRODUCTS
962 Morey Rd (05459)
P.O. Box 162 (05459-0162)
PHONE..................................802 868-2306
Brian Rowell, *President*
Rolande Fortin, *Corp Secy*
Willard Rowell Sr, *Vice Pres*
EMP: 15
SQ FT: 6,000
SALES (est): 1.2MM **Privately Held**
SIC: 2421 Mfg Wood Chips

Hinesburg
Chittenden County

(G-22021)
CLIFFORD LUMBER LLP
24 Gardner Cir (05461-9412)
P.O. Box 150 (05461-0150)
PHONE..................................802 482-2325
Lynn E Gardner, *Partner*
Peter Gardner, *Partner*
Marie Gardner, *General Ptnr*
EMP: 3
SQ FT: 22,000
SALES: 600K **Privately Held**
SIC: 2421 Sawmill/Planing Mill

(G-22022)
DOBLE ENGINEERING COMPANY
Also Called: Renewable NRG Systems
110 Riggs Rd (05461-4453)
PHONE..................................802 482-2255
EMP: 115
SALES (corp-wide): 571.4MM **Publicly Held**
SIC: 3829 3823 Mfg Process Control Instruments Mfg Measuring/Controlling Devices
HQ: Doble Engineering Company
85 Walnut St
Watertown MA 02472
617 926-4900

(G-22023)
ELEMENTAL DEVELOPMENT LLC
519 Sherman Hollow Rd (05461-3121)
PHONE..................................802 318-1041
EMP: 3
SALES (est): 253.7K **Privately Held**
SIC: 2819 Industrial Inorganic Chemicals, Nec

(G-22024)
FROST BEER WORKS LLC
171 Commerce St (05461-4482)
PHONE..................................949 945-4064
Joseph Tucker, *Director*
EMP: 10
SQ FT: 6,700
SALES (est): 380.5K **Privately Held**
SIC: 2082 Mfg Malt Beverages

(G-22025)
GIROUX BODY SHOP INC
10370 Route 116 (05461-9163)
PHONE..................................802 482-2162
Victor Giroux, *President*
Robert Giroux, *Treasurer*
Steve Giroux, *Treasurer*
David Giroux, *Admin Sec*
EMP: 10
SQ FT: 95,000
SALES (est): 1MM **Privately Held**
SIC: 7692 7532 Welding Repair Auto Body Repair/Painting

(G-22026)
GREEN MTN ORGANIC CRMRY LLC
10516 Route 116 Ste 100 (05461-8505)
PHONE..................................802 482-6455
Cheryl Devos,
EMP: 5
SALES (est): 600K **Privately Held**
SIC: 2026 Mfg Fluid Milk

(G-22027)
GREENRANGE FURNITURE COMPANY
Also Called: Cotswold Furniture Makers
2778 Shelburne Falls Rd (05461-9781)
PHONE..................................802 747-8564
James Ozanne, *President*
John Lomas, *Treasurer*
EMP: 7
SQ FT: 8,000
SALES (est): 841.5K **Privately Held**
WEB: www.cotswoldfurniture.com
SIC: 2511 Mfg Wood Household Furniture

(G-22028)
HINESBURG RECORD
327 Charlotte Rd (05461-9228)
P.O. Box 304 (05461-0304)
PHONE..................................802 482-2350
June Giroux, *Principal*
EMP: 10
SALES (est): 102.1K **Privately Held**
SIC: 2711 8699 Newspapers-Publishing/Printing Membership Organization

(G-22029)
NESTECH MACHINE SYSTEMS INC
223 Commerce St (05461)
P.O. Box 462 (05461-0462)
PHONE..................................802 482-4575
Steve Foldesi Jr, *President*
▼ **EMP:** 8
SQ FT: 28,000
SALES (est): 1.6MM **Privately Held**
WEB: www.nesms.com
SIC: 3565 Mfg Packaging Machinery

(G-22030)
SENIX CORPORATION
10516 Route 116 Ste 300 (05461-8505)
PHONE..................................802 489-7300
Doug Boehm, *President*
Patricia Ogilvie, *Admin Sec*
EMP: 14
SQ FT: 6,300
SALES (est): 2.5MM **Privately Held**
WEB: www.senix.com
SIC: 3823 Mfg Process Control Instruments

(G-22031)
UGLY DOG HUNTING CO
1067 Silver St (05461-9401)
PHONE..................................802 482-7054
Terald Wilson, *President*
EMP: 4
SALES (est): 380K **Privately Held**
WEB: www.ugly-dog.com
SIC: 2329 Direct Mail

(G-22032)
UPPER ACCESS INC
Also Called: Upper Access Book Publishers
87 Upper Access Rd (05461-4431)
PHONE..................................802 482-2988
Elizabeth Carlson, *President*
Stephen Carlson, *Vice Pres*
Kristen Lewis, *Admin Sec*
EMP: 4
SQ FT: 576
SALES: 1MM **Privately Held**
WEB: www.upperaccess.com
SIC: 2731 7372 Books-Publishing/Printing Prepackaged Software Services

▲ = Import ▼=Export
◆ =Import/Export

(G-22033)
VSC HOLDINGS INC
Also Called: Vermont Smoke and Cure
10516 Route 116 Ste 200 (05461-8505)
PHONE..................................802 482-4666
Cathy Berry, *Ch of Bd*
Christopher Bailey, *President*
Mark Davitt, *Vice Pres*
EMP: 54
SQ FT: 5,300
SALES (est): 8.7MM **Privately Held**
WEB: www.farmersdiner.com
SIC: 2013 Mfg Prepared Meats

Huntington
Chittenden County

(G-22034)
TAFTS MILK MAPLE FARM
1470 Taft Rd (05462-9780)
PHONE..................................802 434-2727
Bruce Taft, *Owner*
Mary Taft, *Co-Owner*
EMP: 3
SALES (est): 110K **Privately Held**
WEB: www.vtmaplesyrup.com
SIC: 2099 2064 2026 Mfg Food Preparations Mfg Candy/Confectionery Mfg Fluid Milk

Hyde Park
Lamoille County

(G-22035)
CUSTOM MTAL FABRICATORS VT LLC
327 Ferry St (05655-9540)
PHONE..................................802 888-0033
David Vilord, *Mng Member*
Lisa Vilord,
EMP: 7
SALES (est): 865.1K **Privately Held**
SIC: 3499 Structural Metal Fabrication

(G-22036)
LEHOUILLIER MAPLE ORCHARD
798 Sterling View Rd (05655-9021)
PHONE..................................802 888-6465
Rita Lehouillier, *Partner*
John Lehouillier, *Partner*
Richard Lehouillier, *Partner*
EMP: 3
SALES (est): 163.8K **Privately Held**
SIC: 2099 Maple Syrup Production

(G-22037)
LIGHT LOGIC INC
Also Called: House of Troy
902 Silver Ridge Rd (05655-9396)
PHONE..................................802 888-7984
Malcolm Tripp, *CEO*
William S Brown, *COO*
Jean S Maria, *Credit Mgr*
◆ **EMP:** 35
SQ FT: 32,000
SALES (est): 6.3MM **Privately Held**
SIC: 3645 Mfg Residential Lighting Fixtures

(G-22038)
SUTHERLAND WELLES LTD
123 Locke Ave (05655-5406)
P.O. Box 180, North Hyde Park (05665-0180)
PHONE..................................802 635-2700
Mary Goderwis, *CEO*
EMP: 4
SQ FT: 9,000
SALES (est): 595.5K **Privately Held**
SIC: 2851 5198 Mfg Paints/Allied Products Whol Paints/Varnishes

Hydeville
Rutland County

(G-22039)
CAM DVLPMENT MCRO CMPNENTS INC
84 Blissville Rd (05750)
P.O. Box 177 (05750-0177)
PHONE..................................802 265-3240
Stephen Corbett, *President*
Lawrence Corbett, *Vice Pres*
Derek Corbett, *Officer*
EMP: 10 **EST:** 1960
SQ FT: 6,500
SALES (est): 1.5MM **Privately Held**
WEB: www.camdevelopment.net
SIC: 3599 Mfg Industrial Machinery

Irasburg
Orleans County

(G-22040)
M PIETTE & SONS LUMBER INC
6 Seminole Ln (05845)
PHONE..................................802 754-8876
Louie Piette, *President*
Dennis Piette, *Vice Pres*
EMP: 11
SALES (est): 1.8MM **Privately Held**
SIC: 2421 5211 Saw Mill & Whol Lumber Mfg

Island Pond
Essex County

(G-22041)
STADION PUBLISHING CO INC
135 Fitzgerald Ave (05846)
P.O. Box 447 (05846-0447)
PHONE..................................802 723-6175
Tomas Kurzej, *President*
Krystyna J Kurzej, *Vice Pres*
▲ **EMP:** 3
SALES: 225K **Privately Held**
WEB: www.stadion.com
SIC: 2741 Misc Publishing

(G-22042)
SWEET TREE HOLDINGS 1 LLC
Also Called: Maple Guild
1 Sweet Tree Ln (05846)
P.O. Box 137 (05846-0137)
PHONE..................................802 723-6753
Michael Argyelan, *CFO*
EMP: 37
SALES (est): 5.1MM **Privately Held**
SIC: 2099 Mfg Food Preparations

Jacksonville
Windham County

(G-22043)
SPRAGUE & SON MAPLE
Rr 100 (05342)
P.O. Box 378 (05342-0378)
PHONE..................................802 368-2776
Martin Sprague, *Owner*
EMP: 3
SALES (est): 116.7K **Privately Held**
SIC: 2099 Mfg Food Preparations

Jay
Orleans County

(G-22044)
COUNTRY RIDERS SNOW MOBILE CLB
974 N Jay Rd (05859-9478)
PHONE..................................802 988-2255
Ernest Choquette, *President*
Robert Tetreault, *Vice Pres*
Cindy Vincent, *Treasurer*
Ann Jones, *Admin Sec*
EMP: 4
SALES: 134K **Privately Held**
SIC: 3799 Mfg Transportation Equipment

Jeffersonville
Lamoille County

(G-22045)
BACKCOUNTRY MAGAZINE
168 Main St (05464-2100)
P.O. Box 190 (05464-0190)
PHONE..................................802 644-6794
Jon Howard, *Partner*
EMP: 4
SALES (est): 323.4K **Privately Held**
WEB: www.backcountrymagazine.com
SIC: 2721 Periodicals-Publishing/Printing

(G-22046)
MOUNTAIN ROAD FARM
656 Vermont Route 108 S (05464-6550)
PHONE..................................802 644-5138
Robert Nuzzo, *Owner*
EMP: 3
SALES: 205.8K **Privately Held**
SIC: 2099 0191 Mfg Food Preparations General Crop Farm

(G-22047)
PUMPKIN HARBOR DESIGNS INC
950 N Cambridge Rd (05464-9881)
PHONE..................................802 644-6588
David Robins, *President*
Cheryl Page Robins, *Vice Pres*
EMP: 3
SALES: 210K **Privately Held**
WEB: www.pumpkinharbordesigns.com
SIC: 2395 2759 5949 Pleating/Stitching Services Commercial Printing Ret Sewing Supplies/Fabrics

Jericho
Chittenden County

(G-22048)
VERMONT MAPLE SUG MAKERS ASSOC
189 Vt Route 15 (05465-9642)
PHONE..................................802 763-7435
EMP: 3
SALES: 80.9K **Privately Held**
SIC: 2099 Management Services

Johnson
Lamoille County

(G-22049)
EMERY FLOOR INC
2938 Plot Rd (05656-5917)
PHONE..................................802 635-7652
Rick Emery, *President*
Marla Emery, *Vice Pres*
EMP: 3
SALES (est): 195.2K **Privately Held**
SIC: 2426 Hardwood Dimension/Floor Mill

(G-22050)
JOHNSON WOOLEN MILLS LLC
51 Lower Main St E (05656)
P.O. Box 612 (05656-0612)
PHONE..................................802 635-2271
Stacy Manosh,
Stacy B Manosh,
EMP: 35 **EST:** 1842
SQ FT: 30,000
SALES (est): 5.3MM **Privately Held**
WEB: www.johnsonwoolenmills.com
SIC: 2231 5651 2339 Wool Broadwoven Fabric Mill Ret Family Clothing Mfg Women's/Misses' Outerwear

(G-22051)
MANCHESTER LUMBER INC
66 River Rd E (05656-9521)
P.O. Box 304 (05656-0304)
PHONE..................................802 635-2315
Alan E Manchester, *President*
Carroll J Manchester, *Vice Pres*
EMP: 25
SALES: 4MM **Privately Held**
SIC: 2421 5031 Sawmill & Whol Hardwood Lumber

(G-22052)
VERMONT MAPLE SUGAR CO INC
Also Called: Butternut Mountain Farm
31 Main St (05656)
P.O. Box 381 (05656-0381)
PHONE..................................802 635-7483
Lucy Marvin, *Manager*
EMP: 90
SALES (corp-wide): 21.6MM **Privately Held**
SIC: 2099 Mfg Maple Syrup Products
PA: Sugar Vermont Maple Company Inc
37 Industrial Park Dr
Morrisville VT 05661
802 888-3491

Killington
Rutland County

(G-22053)
KILLINGTON LTD
Also Called: Killington Resort & Pico Mtn
4763 Killington Rd (05751-9746)
PHONE..................................802 422-3333
Allen Wilson, *President*
John D Cumming, *Principal*
Mike Solimano, *Vice Pres*
Tracy Taylor, *Vice Pres*
Merissa Sherman, *Buyer*
EMP: 59
SALES (est): 8.4MM **Privately Held**
SIC: 3949 7011 Mfg Sporting/Athletic Goods Hotel/Motel Operation

(G-22054)
KILLINGTON CABINETS
281 Rebecca Ln (05751-9311)
P.O. Box 910 (05751-0910)
PHONE..................................802 773-3960
EMP: 8
SALES (est): 1.1MM **Privately Held**
SIC: 2434 Mfg Wood Kitchen Cabinets

(G-22055)
OUTER LIMITS PUBLISHING LLC
Also Called: Mountain Times, The
5465 Rte 4 (05751)
P.O. Box 183 (05751-0183)
PHONE..................................802 422-2399
Polly Lynn, *Mng Member*
EMP: 10
SQ FT: 3,500
SALES (est): 346K **Privately Held**
SIC: 2711 8721 Newspapers-Publishing/Printing Accounting/Auditing/Bookkeeping

(G-22056)
SUN RAY TECHNOLOGIES INC
80 Weathervane Dr (05751-9689)
PHONE..................................802 422-8680
John Tracey, *President*
EMP: 5
SALES (est): 400K **Privately Held**
WEB: www.sunraytech.com
SIC: 3589 5063 Mfg Service Industry Machinery Whol Electrical Equipment

Londonderry
Windham County

(G-22057)
D LASSER CERAMICS
6405 Vt Route 100 (05148-9522)
PHONE..................................802 824-5383
Dan Lasser, *Owner*
Jayme Venne, *Manager*
EMP: 9
SALES: 750K **Privately Held**
WEB: www.lasserceramics.com
SIC: 3253 Mfg Ceramic Wall/Floor Tile

(G-22058)
WESTON ISLAND LOGGING INC
25 Johnson Hill Rd (05148-9606)
PHONE..................................802 824-3708
Jeffrey Yrsha, *President*
EMP: 6
SALES (est): 534.1K **Privately Held**
SIC: 2411 Logging

Lowell
Orleans County

(G-22059)
BONNEAUS VERMONT MAPLE
224 Buck Hill Rd (05847-9515)
P.O. Box 38 (05847-0038)
PHONE..................................802 744-2742
Douglas Bonneau, *Principal*
EMP: 4
SALES: 36K **Privately Held**
SIC: 2099 Mfg Food Preparations

Lower Waterford
Caledonia County

(G-22060)
BROOKLINE TEXTILES INC
Lower Waterford Rd (05848)
P.O. Box 15 (05848-0015)
PHONE..................................802 748-1933
EMP: 5
SALES (est): 558.6K **Privately Held**
WEB: www.brooklinetextiles.com
SIC: 2231 Mfg Upholstery Fabric

Ludlow
Windsor County

(G-22061)
BUILT RITE MANUFACTURING INC
750 E Hill Rd (05149-9621)
PHONE..................................802 228-7293
John R Smith, *President*
Jeremy Smith, *Vice Pres*
EMP: 10
SQ FT: 8,000
SALES (est): 2.1MM **Privately Held**
WEB: www.built-rite.com
SIC: 3531 Mfg Construction Machinery

(G-22062)
CHRISANDRAS INTERIORS INC
72 Pond St A (05149-1031)
PHONE..................................802 228-2075
Chrisandra Burgess, *President*
EMP: 7
SQ FT: 1,600
SALES (est): 724.3K **Privately Held**
WEB: www.chrisandras.com
SIC: 2391 5714 5949 Mfg Curtains/Drapery Ret Draperies/Upholstery Ret Sewing Supplies/Fbrc

(G-22063)
IMERYS TALC AMERICA INC
73 E Hill Rd (05149-9798)
PHONE..................................802 228-6400
EMP: 59
SALES (corp-wide): 2.9MM **Privately Held**
SIC: 3295 Mfg Minerals-Ground/Treated
HQ: Imerys Talc America, Inc.
1732 N 1st St Ste 450
San Jose CA 95112

(G-22064)
JELD-WEN INC
Jeld-Wen Doors
146 Pleasant St Ext (05149-9783)
P.O. Box 465 (05149-0465)
PHONE..................................802 228-2020
Joe Tinney, *Branch Mgr*
EMP: 100
SQ FT: 48,000 **Publicly Held**
WEB: www.jeld-wen.com
SIC: 2431 Mfg Millwork
HQ: Jeld-Wen, Inc.
2645 Silver Crescent Dr
Charlotte NC 28273
800 535-3936

(G-22065)
JOURNAL LLC (PA)
8 High St (05149-1008)
P.O. Box 228 (05149-0228)
PHONE..................................802 228-3600
Brandy Todt, *Editor*
Robert Miller,
EMP: 3
SALES (est): 456.5K **Privately Held**
SIC: 2711 Newspapers-Publishing/Printing

Lunenburg
Essex County

(G-22066)
AUNT SADIES INC
108 S Lunenburg Rd (05906)
PHONE..................................802 892-5267
Brian Schnetzer, *President*
Gary Briggs, *Treasurer*
EMP: 10 **EST:** 1998
SQ FT: 1,800
SALES (est): 1.2MM **Privately Held**
WEB: www.auntsadies.com
SIC: 3999 Mfg Misc Products

Lyndonville
Caledonia County

(G-22067)
CALKINS ROCK PRODUCTS INC
Also Called: Calkins Sand & Gravel
34 Calkins Dr (05851)
P.O. Box 82 (05851-0082)
PHONE..................................802 626-5755
Paul R Calkins, *President*
Kevin Calkins, *Vice Pres*
Rita Calkins, *Treasurer*
Karen Martell, *Admin Sec*
EMP: 8 **EST:** 1956
SQ FT: 8,200
SALES: 563.1K **Privately Held**
SIC: 1442 Mfg Sand And Gravel

(G-22068)
JENNE MACHINE LLC
180 Commercial Ln (05851-4518)
P.O. Box 158, Lyndon Center (05850-0158)
PHONE..................................802 626-1106
Larry Petreault, *President*
EMP: 15
SQ FT: 8,000
SALES: 735K **Privately Held**
SIC: 3599 Mfg Small Parts Machine Shop

(G-22069)
MARK HUNTER
Also Called: Leading Edge Tool Co,
315 Hill St (05851-8797)
P.O. Box 32 (05851-0032)
PHONE..................................802 626-8407
Mark Hunter, *Owner*
EMP: 5
SQ FT: 3,000
SALES (est): 476.7K **Privately Held**
WEB: www.markhunter.com
SIC: 3599 3545 Machine Shop

(G-22070)
NORTHEAST AGRICULTURAL SLS INC (PA)
Also Called: Burke Mountain Bird Seed
205 East St (05851)
PHONE..................................802 626-3351
James Choiniere, *President*
Francine Choiniere, *Vice Pres*
EMP: 10
SQ FT: 25,000
SALES (est): 4MM **Privately Held**
SIC: 2875 2879 0181 0711 Mfg Fertilizer Mfg Agricultural Chemcl Ornamental Nursery Soil Preparation Service

(G-22071)
NORTHERN STRIKE
Also Called: Chamberlain Release, Owner
842 Calendar Brook Rd (05851-4458)
PHONE..................................802 427-3201
Keith Chamberlain, *Principal*
EMP: 4
SALES (est): 153.2K **Privately Held**
SIC: 3949 Mfg Sporting/Athletic Goods

(G-22072)
PRECISION COMPOSITES VT LLC
630 Gilman Rd (05851-8311)
P.O. Box 134, Lyndon Center (05850-0134)
PHONE..................................802 626-5900
Timothy Nolan,
EMP: 12
SQ FT: 24,000
SALES (est): 2.6MM **Privately Held**
SIC: 2655 3089 Mfg Fiber Cans/Drums Mfg Plastic Products

(G-22073)
VERMONT AEROSPACE INDS LLC
966 Industrial Pkwy (05851)
P.O. Box 1148 (05851-1148)
PHONE..................................802 748-8705
Leonard M Levie, *President*
Larry Lyford, *COO*
EMP: 66
SQ FT: 40,000
SALES: 8MM **Privately Held**
SIC: 3599 Mfg Industrial Machinery

(G-22074)
VERMONT CUSTOM GAGE LLC
180 Commercial Ln (05851-4518)
P.O. Box 5, Swanton (05488-0005)
PHONE..................................802 868-0104
Monica Greene, *President*
EMP: 5 **EST:** 2014
SQ FT: 40,000
SALES (est): 697K **Privately Held**
SIC: 3545 Mfg Machine Tool Accessories

(G-22075)
VERMONT FLEXIBLE TUBING INC
75 Smiths Rd (05851)
PHONE..................................802 626-5723
EMP: 20 **EST:** 1950
SQ FT: 22,320
SALES (est): 2.9MM **Privately Held**
WEB: www.vermontflex.com
SIC: 3599 Mfg Flexible Metallic Tubing

(G-22076)
VERMONTS ORIGINAL LLC
Also Called: Bag Balm
91 Williams St (05851)
P.O. Box 145 (05851-0145)
PHONE..................................802 626-3610
James Kelly, *CEO*
EMP: 8
SALES (est): 1.5MM **Privately Held**
SIC: 2834 Mfg Pharmaceutical Preparations

Manchester
Bennington County

(G-22077)
J YEAGER INC (PA)
Also Called: Herend Store , The
4542 Main St (05254)
P.O. Box 1180 (05254-1180)
PHONE..................................802 362-0810
John Yeager, *President*
Brenda Yeager, *Admin Sec*
EMP: 5
SQ FT: 2,000
SALES (est): 1MM **Privately Held**
WEB: www.herendshopvt.com
SIC: 3264 Mfg Porcelain Electrical Supplies

(G-22078)
ORVIS COMPANY
4182 Main St (05254-4182)
PHONE..................................802 362-3750
▲ **EMP:** 17 **EST:** 2013
SALES (est): 1.7MM **Privately Held**
SIC: 3949 Mfg Sporting/Athletic Goods

(G-22079)
WHALE WATER SYSTEMS INC
Also Called: Mumster Engineering
91 Manchstr Vly Bldg E (05254)
PHONE..................................802 367-1091
Jennifer Stearnf, *Manager*
▲ **EMP:** 10
SALES (est): 920K **Privately Held**
SIC: 3561 Mfg Pumps/Pumping Equipment

Manchester Center
Bennington County

(G-22080)
BALANCE DESIGNS INC
Also Called: Vew Do Balance Boards
245 Airport Rd (05255)
PHONE..................................802 362-2893
Brew Moscarello, *President*
Janine Moscarello, *Admin Asst*
▲ **EMP:** 4
SQ FT: 2,000
SALES: 500K **Privately Held**
WEB: www.bongoboard.com
SIC: 3949 7336 Mfg Sporting/Athletic Goods Commercial Art/Graphic Design

(G-22081)
BATTENKILL COMMUNICATIONS LLP
Also Called: Brew Your Own
5515 Main St (05255-9482)
PHONE..................................802 362-3981
Bradford L Ring, *Partner*
Kathleen J Ring, *Partner*
EMP: 7
SQ FT: 1,000
SALES (est): 906K **Privately Held**
WEB: www.byo.com
SIC: 2721 Periodicals-Publishing/Printing

(G-22082)
DOMETIC UK BLIND SYSTEMS LTD
Also Called: Dometic US Blind Systems
91 Manchester Valley Rd (05255-8801)
PHONE..................................802 362-5258
EMP: 23
SALES (corp-wide): 1.9B **Privately Held**
SIC: 2591 Mfg Drapery Hardware/Blinds
HQ: Dometic Uk Blind Systems Ltd
Atlantic House
Chichester W SUSSEX PO20

(G-22083)
EDIBLE GREEN MOUNTAINS LLC
2584 Richville Rd (05255-9545)
P.O. Box 2607 (05255-2607)
PHONE..................................802 768-8356
Mary Blair, *Publisher*
EMP: 3
SALES (est): 149.9K **Privately Held**
SIC: 2721 Periodicals-Publishing/Printing

(G-22084)
EXPRESS COPY INC
275c Manchester Valley Rd (05255-8802)
P.O. Box 1341 (05255-1341)
PHONE..................................802 362-0501
Donald Reiser, *President*
Doris Reiser, *Vice Pres*
EMP: 9
SQ FT: 3,900
SALES: 930K **Privately Held**
SIC: 2752 Lithographic Commercial Printing

(G-22085)
FUDGE FACTORY INC
Also Called: Mother Myricks
4367 Main St (05255)
P.O. Box 1142 (05255-1142)
PHONE..................................888 669-7425
Jacqueline Baker, *President*
Ronald Mancini, *Vice Pres*
EMP: 16 **EST:** 1977
SQ FT: 2,500

SALES (est): 3.9MM Privately Held
WEB: www.mothermyricks.com
SIC: 2064 2051 5441 5461 Mfg Candy/Confectionery Mfg Bread/Related Prdts Ret Candy/Confectionery Retail Bakery Eating Place

(G-22086)
GRINGO KITCHENS LLC
Also Called: Gringo Jack's
5103 Main St (05255-9772)
PHONE.................................802 362-0836
Jack Gilbert, *Mng Member*
EMP: 12
SALES (est): 1.6MM Privately Held
SIC: 2096 2035 Mfg Potato Chips/Snacks Mfg Pickles/Sauces/Dressing

(G-22087)
HERSAM ACORN NEWSPAPERS LLC
Also Called: Vermont News Guide
Rr 7 (05255)
PHONE.................................802 362-3535
Dave Honan, *Branch Mgr*
EMP: 8
SALES (corp-wide): 5.3MM Privately Held
WEB: www.oshkoshinfo.com
SIC: 2711 Newspapers-Publishing/Printing
PA: Hersam Acorn Newspapers, Llc
16 Bailey Ave
Ridgefield CT
203 438-6000

(G-22088)
RENEWABLE FUELS VERMONT LLC
114 Cemetery St (05255-9701)
P.O. Box 1812 (05255-1812)
PHONE.................................802 362-1516
William Drunsic, *Mng Member*
Andrew Boutin,
EMP: 15 EST: 2015
SALES (est): 888.6K Privately Held
SIC: 2493 Mfg Reconstituted Wood Products

(G-22089)
RIHM MANAGEMENT INC
Also Called: Mountain Weavers
140 Powderhorn Rd (05255-9190)
PHONE.................................802 867-5325
David Rihm, *President*
Bonnie Rihm, *Vice Pres*
EMP: 8
SALES (est): 743.6K Privately Held
WEB: www.mountainweavers.com
SIC: 2392 2211 Mfg Household Furnishings Cotton Broadwoven Fabric Mill

(G-22090)
SMALL BATCH ORGANICS LLC
53b Manchester Valley Rd (05255-8801)
P.O. Box 1054 (05255-1054)
PHONE.................................802 367-1054
Lindsay Martin, *Mng Member*
Jack Desario, *Mng Member*
EMP: 10
SQ FT: 2,000
SALES: 3.5MM Privately Held
SIC: 2043 2064 Mfg Cereal Breakfast Food Mfg Candy/Confectionery

(G-22091)
THOMPSON PRINTING INC
Also Called: Inkspot Press of Manchester
4995 Main St (05255)
P.O. Box 1939 (05255-1939)
PHONE.................................802 362-1140
Michael Carver, *President*
Margaret Price, *Vice Pres*
EMP: 10
SALES (est): 1.5MM Privately Held
WEB: www.inkspotpress.com
SIC: 2752 7336 Lithographic Commercial Printing Commercial Art/Graphic Design

Marshfield
Washington County

(G-22092)
BLACKTHORNE FORGE LTD
3821 Us Route 2 (05658-7132)
PHONE.................................802 426-3369
Steven Bronstein, *President*
EMP: 3
SALES: 200K Privately Held
WEB: www.blackthorneforge.com
SIC: 3446 Sculptural Ironwork

(G-22093)
CARTER MACHINE INC
360 Pattys Xing (05658-7043)
PHONE.................................802 426-3501
Brian Carter, *President*
Thomas Carter, *Vice Pres*
EMP: 7
SQ FT: 5,500
SALES: 650K Privately Held
SIC: 3599 Machine Shop/Job Shop

(G-22094)
DENNIS DUCHARME
Also Called: Ducharme Logging
87 Bailey Pond Rd (05658-8041)
PHONE.................................802 426-3796
Dennis Ducharme, *Owner*
EMP: 3
SALES (est): 187.5K Privately Held
SIC: 2411 2426 2421 Logging Hardwood Dimension/Floor Mill Sawmill/Planing Mill

Middlebury
Addison County

(G-22095)
7 SOUTH SANDWICH COMPANY LLC
1396 Route 7 S Ste 4 (05753-2061)
PHONE.................................802 388-3354
Amy Sweet,
EMP: 8
SALES: 250K Privately Held
SIC: 2599 Mfg Furniture/Fixtures

(G-22096)
ADDISON COUNTY ASPHALT PDTS
34 Main St (05753-1416)
P.O. Box 534 (05753-0534)
PHONE.................................802 388-2338
Theo Lowell, *Owner*
EMP: 5
SALES (est): 249.2K Privately Held
SIC: 2951 Manufactures Asphalt Paving Mixtures

(G-22097)
ADDISON PRESS INC
Also Called: Addison Independent
58 Maple St (05753-1276)
P.O. Box 31 (05753-0031)
PHONE.................................802 388-4944
Angelo Lynn, *President*
Michael Giorgio, *Human Res Mgr*
Elisa Fitzgerald, *Advt Staff*
Sue Miller, *Graphic Designe*
Emma Cotton, *Internal Med*
EMP: 30 EST: 1946
SALES (est): 2.1MM Privately Held
WEB: www.addisonindependent.com
SIC: 2711 Newspapers-Publishing/Printing

(G-22098)
AGRI-MARK INC
Also Called: Agri-Mark Cabot
869 Exchange St (05753-1559)
PHONE.................................802 388-6731
Raymond Dyke, *Vice Pres*
Lori Jacoby, *QC Mgr*
David Brault, *Engineer*
David Hill, *Advt Staff*
Bernard Boudreau, *Manager*
EMP: 108
SALES (corp-wide): 382MM Privately Held
WEB: www.agrimark.net
SIC: 2026 2022 Mfg Fluid Milk Mfg Cheese
PA: Agri-Mark, Inc.
40 Shattuck Rd Ste 301
Andover MA 01810
978 552-5500

(G-22099)
APPALACHIAN GAP DISTILLERY INC
88 Mainelli Rd Ste 2 (05753-1453)
PHONE.................................802 989-7359
Lars Hubbard, *Principal*
EMP: 7
SALES (est): 626.3K Privately Held
SIC: 2085 Mfg Distilled/Blended Liquor

(G-22100)
AQUA VITEA LLC
Also Called: Aqua Vitea Kombucha
153 Pond Ln (05753-1190)
PHONE.................................802 453-8590
Christian Schider, *Sales Staff*
Jeff Weaber,
EMP: 3
SALES (est): 68.6K Privately Held
SIC: 2086 Mfg Bottled/Canned Soft Drinks

(G-22101)
BEES WRAP LLC
383 Exchange St (05753-1195)
P.O. Box 1016 (05753-5016)
PHONE.................................802 643-2132
Sarah Kaeck, *Mng Member*
EMP: 22
SQ FT: 6,000
SALES (est): 1.1MM Privately Held
SIC: 2429 5113 Special Product Sawmill Whol Industrial/Service Paper

(G-22102)
BIKE & SKI TOURING CTR OF NENG
Also Called: Bike Center, The
74 Main St (05753-1464)
PHONE.................................802 388-6666
David Tier, *President*
Justin Crocker, *Treasurer*
EMP: 3
SQ FT: 2,000
SALES: 360K Privately Held
WEB: www.bikecentermid.com
SIC: 3751 5941 Mfg Motorcycles/Bicycles Ret Sporting Goods/Bicycles

(G-22103)
BOYLE ENGINEERING
91 Court St (05753-1408)
PHONE.................................802 388-6966
Doria Boyle, *Owner*
EMP: 3
SALES (est): 219.3K Privately Held
SIC: 3599 Mfg Industrial Machinery

(G-22104)
BROWN NOVELTY CO INC
Also Called: Brown Wood Products
406 E Main St (05753-8685)
P.O. Box 13, East Middlebury (05740-0013)
PHONE.................................802 388-2502
John Brown, *President*
John M Brown, *Director*
EMP: 6
SQ FT: 26,000
SALES: 60K Privately Held
SIC: 2491 Wood Preserving

(G-22105)
BTL HOLDINGS LLC
Also Called: Beau Ties Limited of Vermont
69 Industrial Ave (05753-1129)
PHONE.................................917 596-3660
David Kramer,
EMP: 25
SALES (est): 1.3MM Privately Held
SIC: 2323 Mfg Men's/Boy's Neckwear

(G-22106)
CABOT CREAMERY
869 Exchange St (05753-1559)
PHONE.................................888 792-2268
Averill Earls, *Principal*
EMP: 5
SALES (est): 237.3K Privately Held
SIC: 2021 Mfg Creamery Butter

(G-22107)
CANOPY TIMBER ALTERNATIVES
30 Grist Mill Rd (05753-4478)
P.O. Box 463, East Middlebury (05740-0463)
PHONE.................................802 388-1548
John Anderson, *Principal*
EMP: 6 EST: 2007
SALES (est): 706.1K Privately Held
SIC: 2411 Logging

(G-22108)
CHAMPLAIN CONSTRUCTION CO INC
189 Birchard Park (05753-8818)
PHONE.................................802 388-2652
James Danyow, *President*
Larry Danyow, *Vice Pres*
John Danyow, *Admin Sec*
EMP: 11
SALES (est): 3MM Privately Held
SIC: 3531 1794 Mfg Construction Machinery Excavation Contractor

(G-22109)
DURASOL SYSTEMS INC
Durasol Awnings
38b Pond Ln (05753-1189)
PHONE.................................802 388-7309
Craig Dowden, *Manager*
EMP: 28
SALES (corp-wide): 31.1MM Privately Held
WEB: www.durasol.com
SIC: 3444 2394 Mfg Sheet Metalwork Mfg Canvas/Related Products
HQ: Durasol Systems, Inc.
445 Bellvale Rd
Chester NY 10918
845 610-1100

(G-22110)
FARADAY INC
5 Court St (05753-6014)
PHONE.................................800 442-1521
Robert Adler, *President*
EMP: 4 EST: 2012
SALES (est): 367.3K Privately Held
SIC: 7372 Prepackaged Software Services

(G-22111)
FULL SUN COMPANY
616 Exchange St Unit 2 (05753-1181)
PHONE.................................802 989-7011
Netaka White, *President*
David McManus, *Vice Pres*
EMP: 6
SQ FT: 8,000
SALES: 77K Privately Held
SIC: 2076 Oilseed Processor

(G-22112)
GEIGER OF AUSTRIA INC
38 Pond Ln (05753-2033)
P.O. Box 728 (05753-0728)
PHONE.................................802 388-3156
Hansjorg Geiger, *President*
Wolfgang Miska, *Exec VP*
EMP: 21 EST: 1980
SQ FT: 55,000
SALES (est): 3.8MM
SALES (corp-wide): 13MM Privately Held
SIC: 2339 Mfg Women's/Misses' Outerwear
PA: Geiger Gmbh
Fiecht Au 15
Vomp 6130
524 269-110

(G-22113)
JOSEPH P CARRARA & SONS INC
Also Called: JP Carrara & Sons
2464 Case St (05753-9190)
P.O. Box 1000 (05753-5000)
PHONE.................................802 388-6363
Paul J Carrara, *President*
EMP: 100

GEOGRAPHIC

SALES (corp-wide): 20.2MM Privately Held
SIC: 3273 3272 Mfg Ready-Mixed Concrete Mfg Concrete Products
PA: Joseph P. Carrara & Sons, Inc.
167 N Shrewsbury Rd
North Clarendon VT 05759
802 775-2301

(G-22114)
MAPLE LANDMARK INC
Also Called: Maple Landmark Woodcraft
1297 Exchange St (05753-1187)
PHONE..................................802 388-0627
Michael Rainville, *President*
John Gallagher, *Sales Mgr*
George Macedo, *Manager*
Jill Rainville, *Admin Sec*
EMP: 35
SQ FT: 15,000
SALES (est): 3.9MM Privately Held
WEB: www.maplelandmark.com
SIC: 3944 Mfg Games/Toys

(G-22115)
NEW MARKET PRESS INC
Also Called: Vermont Times Vox
16 Creek Rd Ste 5a (05753-1376)
P.O. Box 182, Elizabethtown NY (12932-0182)
PHONE..................................802 388-6397
Ed Coats, *President*
Nathaniel Winthrop, *Vice Pres*
EMP: 12
SALES (est): 614.4K Privately Held
SIC: 2711 Newspapers-Publishing/Printing

(G-22116)
NOPS METAL WORKS
1479 Route 7 S (05753-8803)
PHONE..................................802 382-9300
Louis Nop, *President*
EMP: 10
SALES (est): 501.9K Privately Held
SIC: 3441 Structural Metal Fabrication

(G-22117)
OSHEA MARY LYNN WEAVING STUDIO
2672 Weybridge Rd (05753-9513)
PHONE..................................802 545-2090
Mary Lynn Oshea, *Owner*
Jennifer Bruch, *Systems Mgr*
EMP: 5
SALES: 650K Privately Held
WEB: www.marylynnoshea.com
SIC: 2211 2221 5621 5131 Mfg Apparel & Outerwear Cotton Man-Made Fiber & Silk Ret Women's Apparel & Whol Woven Textiles Cotton Silk & Synthetic

(G-22118)
OTTER CREEK BREWING CO LLC
793 Exchange St (05753-1193)
PHONE..................................802 388-0727
Brian Walsh, *CEO*
▲ EMP: 32
SALES (est): 5.2MM
SALES (corp-wide): 26.7MM Privately Held
WEB: www.ottercreekbrewing.com
SIC: 2082 Drinking Place
PA: Fulham Investors Lp
593 Washington St
Wellesley MA 02482
781 235-2266

(G-22119)
VERMONT COUNTRY SOAP CORP
Also Called: Vermont Soap
183 Industrial Ave (05753-1621)
PHONE..................................802 388-4302
Larry Plesent, *President*
◆ EMP: 25
SQ FT: 9,200
SALES (est): 2.4MM Privately Held
WEB: www.vermontsoap.com
SIC: 2841 Mfg Soap/Other Detergents

(G-22120)
VERMONT HARD CIDER COMPANY LLC (HQ)
Also Called: Green Mountain Beverages
1321 Exchange St (05753-1477)
PHONE..................................802 388-0700
Benjamin Calvi, *General Mgr*
Michael Paquette, *Safety Mgr*
Michele Lalonde, *Accounting Mgr*
Bridget Hennessey, *Financial Analy*
Bridgett Blacklock, *Mktg Dir*
◆ EMP: 85
SQ FT: 62,500
SALES (est): 22.4MM Privately Held
SIC: 2085 Mfg Distilled/Blended Liquor

(G-22121)
VERMONT SWEET MAPLE INC
1197 Exchange St Ste 3 (05753-4463)
PHONE..................................802 398-2776
Paul Ralston, *Vice Pres*
EMP: 5
SALES (est): 245.9K Privately Held
SIC: 2499 Mfg Wood Products

Middlesex
Washington County

(G-22122)
MCCULLOUGH CRUSHING INC (PA)
548 Mccullough Hill Rd (05602-8488)
PHONE..................................802 223-5693
Frederick McCullough, *President*
Scott McCullough, *Vice Pres*
EMP: 35
SQ FT: 3,500
SALES (est): 4MM Privately Held
SIC: 1423 Gravel Crushing Sand And Stone

Middletown Springs
Rutland County

(G-22123)
CHRIS J SEAMANS
4370 Vermont Route 140 (05757-7608)
PHONE..................................802 287-9399
Chris J Seamans, *Principal*
EMP: 3
SALES (est): 151.2K Privately Held
SIC: 2411 Logging

Milton
Chittenden County

(G-22124)
ADVANCED MACHINE AND TL CO INC
Also Called: A M T
63b Gonyeau Rd (05468)
P.O. Box 802 (05468-0802)
PHONE..................................802 893-6322
Frank R Simms, *President*
Steven Carlin, *Admin Sec*
EMP: 15
SQ FT: 8,000
SALES (est): 2.5MM Privately Held
SIC: 3599 Mfg Industrial Machinery

(G-22125)
BOVES OF VERMONT INC
8 Catamount Dr (05468-3212)
PHONE..................................802 862-7235
Mark Bove, *President*
Richard Bove Jr, *Treasurer*
EMP: 3
SQ FT: 200
SALES (est): 435.3K Privately Held
WEB: www.boves.com
SIC: 2033 Mfg Canned Fruits/Vegetables

(G-22126)
DM INC
28 Industrial Dr (05468-3234)
PHONE..................................802 425-2119
Dennis Morey, *President*
Marie Perry, *Vice Pres*
EMP: 4
SALES (est): 381.2K Privately Held
SIC: 3089 Mfg Plastic Products

(G-22127)
FILCORP INDUSTRIES INC
63 Gonyeau Rd B (05468-3200)
P.O. Box 802 (05468-0802)
PHONE..................................802 893-1882
Frank Simms, *President*
William G Congleton, *Admin Sec*
EMP: 5
SQ FT: 4,000
SALES: 500K Privately Held
SIC: 3569 Mfg Carbon Canisters & Filters

(G-22128)
GARY F GIROME
Also Called: Girome, Gary F and Associates
25 Quarry Ln (05468-4016)
PHONE..................................802 893-7870
Gary F Girome, *Owner*
EMP: 5 EST: 1999
SALES (est): 291.2K Privately Held
SIC: 7372 Prepackaged Software Services

(G-22129)
GENFOOT AMERICA INC
33 Catamount Dr (05468-3236)
PHONE..................................802 893-4280
Richard G Cook, *CEO*
Norman Cook, *Exec VP*
Steven Cook, *Exec VP*
David Hallgren, *Vice Pres*
Irwin Kastner, *Vice Pres*
▲ EMP: 12
SQ FT: 75,000
SALES (est): 2.9MM
SALES (corp-wide): 1.3MM Privately Held
SIC: 3021 Mfg Rubber & Plastic Footwear
HQ: Genfoot America, Inc
1940 55e Av
Lachine QC
514 341-3950

(G-22130)
GRAY ROCK CONCRETE
54 W Milton Rd (05468-3299)
PHONE..................................802 379-5393
William Dailey,
EMP: 10 EST: 2013
SALES (est): 726.5K Privately Held
SIC: 3273 Mfg Ready-Mixed Concrete

(G-22131)
GREEN MOUNTAIN KNITTING INC
Also Called: Qmd Medical
28 Industrial Dr (05468-3234)
PHONE..................................800 361-1190
Jeffrey Abyoub, *President*
Calvert Kogan, *President*
Martin Kogan, *Vice Pres*
▲ EMP: 25
SQ FT: 20,000
SALES: 16MM Privately Held
WEB: www.greenmountainknitting.com
SIC: 2221 Manmade Broadwoven Fabric Mill

(G-22132)
LEAD CONVERSION PLUS
710 Everest Rd (05468-3880)
PHONE..................................802 497-1557
John Bean, *Principal*
EMP: 5
SALES (est): 338.8K Privately Held
SIC: 3356 Nonferrous Rolling/Drawing

(G-22133)
LIQUID MEASUREMENT SYSTEMS INC
Also Called: LMS
141 Morse Dr (05468)
P.O. Box 2070 (05468-2070)
PHONE..................................802 528-8100
George Lamphere, *President*
Martha Hanson, *Officer*
▼ EMP: 43
SQ FT: 22,000
SALES (est): 11MM Privately Held
WEB: www.liquidmeasurement.com
SIC: 3728 3812 Mfg Aircraft Parts/Equipment Mfg Search/Navigation Equipment

(G-22134)
MILTON VERMONT SHEET METAL INC
Also Called: Tri-Angle Metal Fab
103 Gonyeau Rd (05468-3296)
PHONE..................................802 893-1581
Yancy D Martell, *President*
Armand Auclair, *Purchasing*
Martin Martell, *CFO*
Marvin A Martell, *Shareholder*
Martin D Martell, *Admin Sec*
EMP: 64
SQ FT: 40,000
SALES (est): 11.5MM Privately Held
WEB: www.trianglereamer.com
SIC: 3599 3444 3441 1799 Mfg Industrial Machinery Mfg Sheet Metalwork Structural Metal Fabrctn Special Trade Contractor Welding Repair

(G-22135)
PBM NUTRITIONALS LLC (DH)
Also Called: Perrigo Nutritionals
147 Industrial Park Rd (05468)
PHONE..................................802 527-0521
Joseph C Papa, *CEO*
Svend Andersen, *President*
Jeff Needham, *President*
▲ EMP: 71
SQ FT: 218,600
SALES (est): 44.4MM Privately Held
WEB: www.pbmproducts.com
SIC: 2834 Mfg Pharmaceutical Preparations
HQ: Perrigo Company
515 Eastern Ave
Allegan MI 49010
269 673-8451

(G-22136)
PLASTIC MONOFIL CO LTD
28 Industrial Dr (05468-3234)
PHONE..................................802 893-1543
George Lavigne, *Manager*
EMP: 4
SALES (est): 107.6K Privately Held
SIC: 3089 Mfg Plastic Products

(G-22137)
RENEW ENERGY
7 Clapper Rd (05468-3204)
PHONE..................................802 891-6774
EMP: 3
SALES (est): 170K Privately Held
SIC: 3511 Mfg Turbines/Generator Sets

(G-22138)
RENNLINE INC
Also Called: Rennline Design
32 Catamount Dr (05468-3212)
PHONE..................................802 893-7366
Paul Jacques, *President*
Tom Rittenburg, *Vice Pres*
Jake Teffner, *Mfg Mgr*
Joe Desimone, *Manager*
▲ EMP: 3
SALES (est): 563.7K Privately Held
WEB: www.rennline.com
SIC: 3714 Designs Auto Accessories

(G-22139)
VERMONT CHRISTMAS COMPANY
Also Called: Bridge Building Images
24 Clapper Rd (05468-3216)
P.O. Box 1048, Burlington (05402-1048)
PHONE..................................802 893-1670
William Flynn, *President*
Andrew E Kelly, *Admin Sec*
▲ EMP: 8
SQ FT: 18,000
SALES (est): 596.4K Privately Held
WEB: www.bridgebuilding.com
SIC: 2754 2771 5961 3944 Gravure Coml Printing Mfg Greeting Cards

(G-22140)
VILLANTI & SONS PRINTERS INC
Also Called: Villanti Printers
15 Catamount Dr (05468-3236)
PHONE..................................802 864-0723
Jon Villanti, *CEO*
Matthew Noonan, *President*
Jay Anthony Villanti, *President*

▲ = Import ▼=Export
◆ =Import/Export

Jay Villanti, *Opers Mgr*
Darryl Moschelle, *Prdtn Mgr*
EMP: 60
SALES (est): 10.1MM **Privately Held**
WEB: www.villanti.com
SIC: 2752 7331 2789 2791 Lithographic Coml Print Direct Mail Ad Svcs Bookbinding/Related Work Typesetting Services

Montgomery Center
Franklin County

(G-22141)
BUMWRAPS INC (PA)
578 Vt Route 242 (05471-5106)
PHONE....................802 326-4080
Todd G Alix, *President*
Myra Alix, *Admin Sec*
▼ **EMP:** 9
SQ FT: 10,000
SALES (est): 1.2MM **Privately Held**
WEB: www.bumwraps.com
SIC: 2395 2759 Embroidery & Screen Printing

(G-22142)
GODFREYS SAWMILL LLC
926 Deep Gibou Rd (05471-2024)
PHONE....................802 326-4868
Luke Godfrey,
EMP: 3
SALES (est): 219.5K **Privately Held**
SIC: 2421 Sawmill/Planing Mill

(G-22143)
GORILLA BARS INC
Also Called: Garuka Bars
650 Fisher Rd (05471-5102)
PHONE....................802 309-4997
Mike Rosenberg, *Principal*
EMP: 7 **EST:** 2011
SALES (est): 668.1K **Privately Held**
SIC: 2064 Mfg Candy/Confectionery

Montpelier
Washington County

(G-22144)
ALLAVITA
27 State St (05602-3171)
PHONE....................802 225-6526
Christina Ebersole, *Owner*
EMP: 3
SALES (est): 196.9K **Privately Held**
SIC: 2079 Mfg Edible Fats/Oils

(G-22145)
ASC DUPLICATING INC
Also Called: Minuteman Press
407 Barre St 1 (05602-3629)
PHONE....................802 229-0660
Arthur S Clark, *President*
Jean Clark, *Corp Secy*
Kevin Clark, *Vice Pres*
EMP: 5
SQ FT: 1,500
SALES (est): 490K **Privately Held**
SIC: 2752 7334 4822 Lithographic Commercial Printing Photocopying Services Telegraph Communications

(G-22146)
CANADIAN AMERICAN RESOURCES
104 Main St (05602-3098)
PHONE....................802 223-2271
Dierdre Allen, *President*
EMP: 3
SALES (est): 155.8K **Privately Held**
SIC: 2023 Mfg Dry/Evaporated Dairy Products

(G-22147)
CAPITOL CUPCAKE COMPANY LLC
64 Meadowbrook Dr (05602-2012)
PHONE....................802 522-3576
Cynthia Golonka, *President*
EMP: 4 **EST:** 2013
SALES (est): 202.2K **Privately Held**
SIC: 2051 Mfg Bread/Related Products

(G-22148)
GREEN MOUNTAIN FLY WHEELER
550 Stewart Rd (05602-8317)
PHONE....................802 223-1595
Robert Felch, *Principal*
EMP: 3
SALES (est): 333.5K **Privately Held**
SIC: 3511 Mfg Turbines/Generator Sets

(G-22149)
HARMONIZED COOKERY
450 Sparrow Farm Rd (05602-9514)
PHONE....................802 598-9206
Lisa Mase, *Principal*
EMP: 3
SALES (est): 133.1K **Privately Held**
SIC: 2099 Mfg Food Preparations

(G-22150)
HYZER INDUSTRIES
108 Main St (05602-2906)
PHONE....................802 223-8277
Scott Kerner, *Principal*
EMP: 3
SALES (est): 225.3K **Privately Held**
SIC: 3999 Mfg Misc Products

(G-22151)
KERINS SIGN SERVICE
E Montpelier Rd Rr 2 (05602)
P.O. Box 1109 (05601-1109)
PHONE....................802 223-0357
John Kerin, *President*
EMP: 12
SALES (est): 990K **Privately Held**
SIC: 3993 7532 Mfg Signs/Advertising Specialties Auto Body Repair/Painting

(G-22152)
LARCOLINE INC
Also Called: Minuteman Vermont Print & Mail
7 Main St (05602-2870)
PHONE....................802 229-0660
Arthur S Clark, *Branch Mgr*
EMP: 3
SALES (corp-wide): 2MM **Privately Held**
SIC: 2752 Lithographic Commercial Printing
PA: Larcoline, Inc.
113 Acorn Ln Ste 2
Colchester VT 05446
802 864-5440

(G-22153)
LEAHY PRESS INC
Also Called: Northlight Studio Press
79 River St (05602-3757)
P.O. Box 428 (05601-0428)
PHONE....................802 223-2100
Ronald Kowalkowski, *President*
Steve Smead, *Vice Pres*
Mike Messier, *Technology*
EMP: 22 **EST:** 1969
SQ FT: 12,000
SALES (est): 3.7MM **Privately Held**
WEB: www.leahypress.com
SIC: 2752 2759 2677 Lithographic Commercial Printing Commercial Printing Mfg Envelopes

(G-22154)
MAPLE ON TAP
378 Mccullough Hill Rd (05602-8710)
PHONE....................802 498-4477
Cody Long, *President*
EMP: 6
SALES (est): 388.3K **Privately Held**
SIC: 2099 Mfg Food Preparations

(G-22155)
MONTPELIER GRANITE WORKS INC
43 Granite Shed Ln (05602-3677)
P.O. Box 9 (05601-0009)
PHONE....................802 223-2581
Michelle Parker, *President*
▼ **EMP:** 17
SQ FT: 8,400
SALES: 1.5MM **Privately Held**
SIC: 3281 Mfg Granite Memorials

(G-22156)
MORSE FARM INC
Also Called: Sugar Shack, The
1168 County Rd (05602-8135)
PHONE....................802 223-2740
Harry Morse Jr, *President*
Claude Stone, *Technology*
Elizabeth P Morse, *Admin Sec*
EMP: 5
SALES (est): 587.8K **Privately Held**
WEB: www.morsefarm.com
SIC: 2099 Mfg Food Preparations

(G-22157)
NATIONAL CLOTHES PIN CO INC
Also Called: National Klip
1 Granite St (05602-3658)
P.O. Box 427 (05601-0427)
PHONE....................802 223-7332
Jay Merrill, *President*
EMP: 3 **EST:** 1906
SQ FT: 15,000
SALES (est): 384.7K **Privately Held**
SIC: 2499 Mfg Wood Clothespins

(G-22158)
NUTRICOPIA INC
15 E State St Ste 1 (05602-3015)
PHONE....................808 832-2080
Arnold Jay Koss, *President*
Ron Koss, *Vice Pres*
EMP: 3
SQ FT: 1,500
SALES (est): 254.1K **Privately Held**
SIC: 2024 Mfg Ice Cream/Frozen Desert

(G-22159)
REAL GOOD TOYS INC
Also Called: Diamond Deans Dollhouse Co
22 Gallison Hill Rd # 1 (05602)
PHONE....................802 479-2217
James Abrams, *President*
Christine Abrams, *Vice Pres*
▲ **EMP:** 8
SQ FT: 25,000
SALES (est): 1.4MM **Privately Held**
WEB: www.realgoodtoys.com
SIC: 3944 Mfg Games/Toys

(G-22160)
RUSSIAN INFORMATION SERVICES
Also Called: Ris
88 Grandview Ter (05602-8440)
P.O. Box 567 (05601-0567)
PHONE....................802 223-4955
Paul Richardson, *President*
Stephanie Ratmeyer, *Treasurer*
Paul E Richardson, *Director*
EMP: 5
SALES (est): 33K **Privately Held**
WEB: www.rispubs.com
SIC: 2741 7929 Misc Publishing Entertainer/Entertainment Group

(G-22161)
SULLIVAN INDUSTRIES LLC
1 Deerfield Dr (05602-2126)
PHONE....................802 229-1909
Benjamin Sullivan,
EMP: 4
SALES (est): 240K **Privately Held**
SIC: 3999 Mfg Misc Products

(G-22162)
VERMONT COMPOST COMPANY INC
1996 Main St (05602-8523)
PHONE....................802 223-6049
Carl Hammer, *President*
EMP: 6
SALES (est): 1.1MM **Privately Held**
WEB: www.vermontcompost.com
SIC: 2875 Mfg Fertilizers-Mix Only

(G-22163)
VERMONT JOURNALISM TRUST LTD
Also Called: Vtdigger.org
97 State St Ste 1 (05602-3219)
PHONE....................802 225-6224
Christopher Kaufman Ilstrup, *COO*
Anne Galloway, *Director*
EMP: 12 **EST:** 2009
SALES: 1.4MM **Privately Held**
SIC: 2721 Periodicals-Publishing/Printing

(G-22164)
WHISTLEKICK LLC
2030 Jones Brook Rd (05602-8375)
PHONE....................802 225-6676
Jeremy Lesnika,
EMP: 10 **EST:** 2013
SALES (est): 723K **Privately Held**
SIC: 3949 Mfg Sporting/Athletic Goods

Morrisville
Lamoille County

(G-22165)
BROSSEAU FUELS LLC
2148 Cadys Falls Rd (05661-4430)
PHONE....................802 888-9209
James P Brosseau, *Principal*
EMP: 4 **EST:** 2007
SALES (est): 249.4K **Privately Held**
SIC: 2869 Mfg Industrial Organic Chemicals

(G-22166)
CONCEPT2 INC (PA)
105 Industrial Park Dr (05661-8532)
PHONE....................802 888-7971
Richard Dreissigacker, *President*
Peter Dreissigacker, *Vice Pres*
Linda Markin, *CFO*
Lisa Washburn, *Controller*
Lewis Franco, *Human Res Dir*
◆ **EMP:** 44
SQ FT: 52,000
SALES (est): 14.3MM **Privately Held**
WEB: www.concept2.com
SIC: 2499 3949 Mfg Wood Products Mfg Sporting/Athletic Goods

(G-22167)
GREAT BIG GRAPHICS INC (PA)
355 Industrial Park Dr (05661-7912)
PHONE....................802 888-5515
Nichole Gilbert, *President*
EMP: 5
SALES (est): 697.4K **Privately Held**
WEB: www.greatbiggraphics.net
SIC: 3993 Mfg Signs/Advertising Specialties

(G-22168)
GREEN MOUNTAIN DISTILLERS LLC
2919 Laporte Rd (05661-8310)
PHONE....................802 498-4848
Timothy Danahy, *Principal*
EMP: 5
SALES (est): 356.2K **Privately Held**
SIC: 2085 Mfg Distilled/Blended Liquor

(G-22169)
HEART QUALI HOME HEATI PRODU
Also Called: Hearthstone Stoves
317 Stafford Ave (05661-8695)
PHONE....................802 888-5232
David Kuhfahl, *President*
German Gomez Casuso, *Vice Pres*
▲ **EMP:** 61
SALES (est): 13.3MM
SALES (corp-wide): 181.8K **Privately Held**
WEB: www.hearthstonestoves.com
SIC: 3433 Mfg Heating Equipment-Non-electric
HQ: Industrias Hergom Sl
Barrio Borrancho (Antes Cl Mies Del Agua), S/N
Soto De La Marina 39110
942 587-000

(G-22170)
HOWARD P FAIRFIELD LLC
87 Old Creamery Rd B (05661-6152)
P.O. Box 640 (05661-0640)
PHONE....................802 888-2092
Nicole Terreri, *Manager*
EMP: 6
SALES (corp-wide): 1B **Publicly Held**
WEB: www.hpfairfield.com
SIC: 3531 Mfg Construction Machinery

HQ: Howard P. Fairfield, Llc
9 Green St
Skowhegan ME 04976
207 474-9836

(G-22171)
LOST NATION BREWING LLC
87 Old Creamery Rd (05661-6152)
PHONE..................................802 851-8041
Allen Van Anda,
James Griffith,
EMP: 12 **EST:** 2012
SALES (est): 1.4MM **Privately Held**
SIC: **2082** 5813 5812 Mfg Malt Beverages Drinking Place Eating Place

(G-22172)
MANUFACTURING SOLUTIONS INC
153 Stafford Ave (05661-8515)
PHONE..................................802 888-3289
Garrett Hirchak, *President*
Beth Salvis, *Vice Pres*
▲ **EMP:** 50
SALES (est): 7.2MM **Privately Held**
WEB: www.msivt.com
SIC: **3949** Mfg Sporting/Athletic Goods

(G-22173)
MILLERS WOOD WORKING
1967 Cote Hill Rd (05661-9156)
PHONE..................................802 730-9374
EMP: 4
SALES (est): 377.7K **Privately Held**
SIC: **2431** Mfg Millwork

(G-22174)
NA MANOSH INC
120 Northgate Plz Ste B (05661-8747)
PHONE..................................802 888-5722
Nick Manosh, *President*
Andrea Jones, *Admin Sec*
EMP: 36
SALES (est): 108.1K **Privately Held**
SIC: **1381** Oil/Gas Well Drilling

(G-22175)
NEWS AND CITIZEN INC
Also Called: Transcript, The
417 Brooklyn St (05661-8510)
PHONE..................................802 888-2212
Bradley Limoge, *President*
Kristen Braley, *Sales Executive*
EMP: 20
SQ FT: 5,000
SALES (est): 1.2MM **Privately Held**
WEB: www.newsandcitizen.com
SIC: **2711** Newspapers-Publishing/Printing

(G-22176)
S & A TROMBLEY CORPORATION
Also Called: Lwi Metalworks
76 Houle Ave (05661-8543)
PHONE..................................802 888-2394
Steve Trombley, *President*
Lois Trombley, *Vice Pres*
Andrea Trombley, *Treasurer*
EMP: 25
SALES: 1.1MM **Privately Held**
WEB: www.lwiweld.com
SIC: **3446** 3441 3499 3599 Mfg Architectural Mtlwrk Structural Metal Fabrctn Mfg Misc Fab Metal Prdts Mfg Industrial Machinery

(G-22177)
STERLING TECHNOLOGIES INC
320 Wilkins St (05661-6098)
P.O. Box 728 (05661-0728)
PHONE..................................802 888-4753
Jeffrey Walker, *President*
Michael Boudreau, *Vice Pres*
EMP: 7
SQ FT: 10,000
SALES (est): 1MM **Privately Held**
SIC: **3599** Mfg Industrial Machinery

(G-22178)
VERMONT MAPLE SUGAR CO INC (PA)
Also Called: Butternut Mountain Farm
37 Industrial Park Dr (05661-8533)
PHONE..................................802 888-3491
David Marvin, *President*
Lucy Marvin, *Vice Pres*
Julianna Savage, *Purchasing*
John Kingston, *CFO*
EMP: 40
SQ FT: 50,000
SALES (est): 21.6MM **Privately Held**
SIC: **2099** Mfg Food Preparations

(G-22179)
WASHBURN COMPANY INC
Also Called: Vermont Originals
320 Wilkins St (05661-6098)
PHONE..................................802 888-3032
Edward Washburn, *CEO*
Jane Washburn, *President*
▲ **EMP:** 20
SQ FT: 5,000
SALES: 1MM **Privately Held**
SIC: **2353** Mfg Hats/Caps/Millinery

(G-22180)
WHEEL HOUSE DESIGNS INC
559 Harrel St Apt A (05661-9056)
P.O. Box 295 (05661-0295)
PHONE..................................802 888-8552
Gail Wheel, *Owner*
EMP: 8
SALES (est): 808.3K **Privately Held**
SIC: **3999** 5199 Mfg Misc Products Whol Nondurable Goods

Mount Holly
Rutland County

(G-22181)
CROWLEY CHEESE INCORPORATED
14 Crowley Ln (05758-9656)
PHONE..................................802 259-2340
Neil Driscoll, *President*
EMP: 5 **EST:** 1882
SALES (est): 410K **Privately Held**
WEB: www.crowleycheese.com
SIC: **2022** Manufactures Cheese

(G-22182)
KEEN WOODWORKING
2817 Shunpike Rd (05758-9627)
PHONE..................................802 259-2963
Robert Keen, *Owner*
Lori Keen, *Co-Owner*
EMP: 5
SALES: 400K **Privately Held**
SIC: **2431** Mfg Millwork

N Chittenden
Rutland County

(G-22183)
MOUNTAIN CIDER LLC
99 West Rd (05763-9691)
PHONE..................................802 483-2270
William L Gormly, *Mng Member*
EMP: 3
SALES (est): 400K **Privately Held**
WEB: www.mountaincider.com
SIC: **2099** Mfg Food Preparations

New Haven
Addison County

(G-22184)
CHAMPLAIN PRECISION INC (PA)
235 Campground Rd (05472-1107)
PHONE..................................802 453-7225
Pete Whittemore, *President*
EMP: 5
SALES (est): 583.8K **Privately Held**
SIC: **3499** Mfg Misc Fabricated Metal Products

(G-22185)
LYNN YARRINGTON
Also Called: Yarrington Weaving Studio
602 Laffin Rd (05472-2032)
P.O. Box 3 (05472-0003)
PHONE..................................802 453-4221
Lynn Yarrington, *Owner*
EMP: 4
SALES (est): 285K **Privately Held**
WEB: www.michaelmode.com
SIC: **2399** Mfg Fabricated Textile Products

(G-22186)
PHOENIX FEEDS ORGANIX LLC
5482 Ethan Allen Hwy (05472-1113)
P.O. Box 36 (05472-0036)
PHONE..................................802 453-6684
David Santos, *President*
EMP: 50
SALES (est): 1.7MM **Privately Held**
SIC: **2048** Mfg Prepared Feeds

(G-22187)
STARK MOUNTAIN WOODWORKS CO
Also Called: Stark Mountain Woodworking Co
359 South St (05472-4064)
PHONE..................................802 453-5549
Walter Hellier, *President*
Louis Dupont, *Vice Pres*
EMP: 10
SALES: 1.1MM **Privately Held**
WEB: www.starkmountain.com
SIC: **2499** Mfg Millwork

Newfane
Windham County

(G-22188)
WILD WOOD ACRES ALPACAS INC
8 Wildwood Acres Rd (05345-9688)
PHONE..................................802 365-7053
Vikki Butynski, *Principal*
EMP: 3
SALES (est): 293.7K **Privately Held**
SIC: **2231** Wool Broadwoven Fabric Mill

(G-22189)
WRIGHT MAINTENANCE INC
151 Vt Route 30 (05345-9657)
PHONE..................................802 365-9253
Joe Wright, *President*
Priscilla Wright, *Admin Sec*
EMP: 3
SALES (est): 396.5K **Privately Held**
SIC: **2411** 1794 1629 4959 Logging Excavation Contractor Heavy Construction Sanitary Services Plumbing/Heat/Ac Contr

Newport
Orleans County

(G-22190)
BUMWRAPS INC
Also Called: Whisper Tree
158 Main St Ste 3 (05855-4417)
PHONE..................................802 326-4080
Nancy Fontaine, *Manager*
EMP: 4
SALES (corp-wide): 1.2MM **Privately Held**
WEB: www.bumwraps.com
SIC: **2395** 2759 Pleating/Stitching Services Commercial Printing
PA: Bumwraps Inc
578 Vt Route 242
Montgomery Center VT 05471
802 326-4080

(G-22191)
CALKINS SAND & GRAVEL INC
3258 Vt Route 14 N (05855-8604)
PHONE..................................802 334-8418
Criss Martel, *Manager*
EMP: 14
SALES (corp-wide): 2MM **Privately Held**
SIC: **1442** Construction Sand/Gravel
PA: Calkins Sand & Gravel, Inc.
Rr 5
Lyndonville VT 05851
802 626-5755

(G-22192)
CODET-NEWPORT CORPORATION (HQ)
Also Called: Big Bill
294 Crawford Rd (05855-9502)
PHONE..................................802 334-5811
Vincent Audet, *President*
Gilbert Audet, *President*
Robert H Audet, *Corp Secy*
Jessika Audet, *Vice Pres*
Stephen Audet, *Vice Pres*
▲ **EMP:** 10
SALES (est): 1.1MM
SALES (corp-wide): 29.7MM **Privately Held**
WEB: www.bigbill.com
SIC: **2326** 3021 Mfg Men's/Boy's Work Clothing Mfg Rubber/Plastic Footwear
PA: Codet Inc
49 Rue Maple
Coaticook QC J1A 1
819 849-4819

(G-22193)
COLUMBIA FOREST PRODUCTS INC
Indian Head Division
115 Columbia Way (05855-5496)
P.O. Box 605 (05855-0605)
PHONE..................................802 334-6711
Theodore N Jewett, *Vice Pres*
EMP: 400
SALES (corp-wide): 778.2MM **Privately Held**
WEB: www.columbiaveneer.com
SIC: **2435** 2426 Mfg Hardwood Veneer/Plywood Hardwood Dimension/Floor Mill
PA: Columbia Forest Products, Inc.
7900 Mccloud Rd Ste 200
Greensboro NC 27409
336 605-0429

(G-22194)
COLUMBIA FOREST PRODUCTS INC
324 Bluff Rd (05855-9531)
PHONE..................................802 334-3600
Gary Gillespie, *Vice Pres*
David Siciliano, *Purch Agent*
EMP: 235
SALES (corp-wide): 778.2MM **Privately Held**
WEB: www.columbiaveneer.com
SIC: **2435** Mfg Hardwood Veneer/Plywood
PA: Columbia Forest Products, Inc.
7900 Mccloud Rd Ste 200
Greensboro NC 27409
336 605-0429

(G-22195)
D40 GRAVEL LLP
71 Cliff St (05855-9433)
PHONE..................................802 673-5494
Anthony Moccia, *Partner*
EMP: 3
SALES (est): 96.7K **Privately Held**
SIC: **1442** Construction Sand/Gravel

(G-22196)
DAWN BRAINARD
Also Called: Memphremagog Press Printers
415 Union St (05855-5499)
PHONE..................................802 334-2780
Dawn Brainard, *Owner*
EMP: 4
SALES (est): 408.4K **Privately Held**
SIC: **2752** 2791 2759 Lithographic Commercial Printing Typesetting Services Commercial Printing

(G-22197)
FEED COMMODITIES INTL INC
758 S Yard Rd (05855-9869)
PHONE..................................802 334-2942
Ryan Abel, *Branch Mgr*
EMP: 4
SALES (corp-wide): 18.6MM **Privately Held**
SIC: **3523** 5191 Mfg Farm Machinery/Equip Whol Farm Supplies
HQ: Feed Commodities International, Inc.
47 Feed Mill Ln
Middlebury VT 05753
800 639-3191

▲ = Import ▼=Export
◆ =Import/Export

(G-22198)
GALVION BALLISTICS LTD
30 Industrial Dr Ste 10 (05855-9898)
PHONE....................................802 334-2774
Rudy Chase, *Manager*
EMP: 57
SALES (corp-wide): 59.1MM **Privately Held**
WEB: www.msanet.com
SIC: 3469 Mfg Metal Stampings
PA: Revision Military Ltd.
7 Corporate Dr
Essex Junction VT 05452
802 879-7002

(G-22199)
GALVION BALLISTICS LTD
30 Industrial Dr Ste 100 (05855-9898)
PHONE....................................802 334-2774
Jonathan Blanshay, *CEO*
EMP: 17
SALES (est): 2.6MM
SALES (corp-wide): 17.2MM **Privately Held**
SIC: 3851 Mfg Ophthalmic Goods
HQ: Galvion Ltd.
200 International Dr # 250
Portsmouth NH 03801
514 739-4444

(G-22200)
LONG MEADOW FARMS QUILTS
305 Union St Ste A (05855-5464)
PHONE....................................802 334-5532
Laurie D Salzmann, *Owner*
EMP: 3 **EST:** 1996
SQ FT: 625
SALES: 27K **Privately Held**
WEB: www.longmeadowfarms.com
SIC: 2395 Pleating/Stitching Services

(G-22201)
METAL-FLEX WELDED BELLOWS INC
149 Lakemont Rd (05855-9453)
PHONE....................................802 334-5550
Barrie W Hume, *President*
Matthew Campbell, *Engineer*
Dave Hunt, *Engineer*
Gwen Hume, *Admin Sec*
EMP: 36
SQ FT: 13,000
SALES: 4.5MM **Privately Held**
WEB: www.metalflexbellows.com
SIC: 3599 Mfg Industrial Machinery

(G-22202)
MICHAEL OLDEN
Also Called: Mr O'S Sporting Goods Store
1670 E Main St (05855-9465)
PHONE....................................802 334-5525
Michael Olden, *Owner*
EMP: 3
SQ FT: 3,200
SALES: 260K **Privately Held**
SIC: 3949 Mfg Sporting/Athletic Goods

(G-22203)
NEWPORT FURNITURE PARTS CORP
Also Called: Newport Rocking Chair Center
450 Main St (05855-5535)
PHONE....................................802 334-5428
Laurent Daigneault, *President*
David Laforce, *Treasurer*
▲ **EMP:** 75 **EST:** 1963
SQ FT: 100,000
SALES (est): 10.2MM **Privately Held**
WEB: www.nfpcorp.com
SIC: 2511 Mfg Wood Household Furniture

(G-22204)
NEWPORT SAND & GRAVEL CO INC
Also Called: Carroll Concrete Co
2014 Alderbrook Rd (05855-9006)
PHONE....................................802 334-2000
Shaun P Carroll Sr, *Manager*
EMP: 10
SALES (corp-wide): 44MM **Privately Held**
SIC: 3273 Mfg Ready-Mixed Concrete
PA: Newport Sand & Gravel Co., Inc.
8 Reeds Mill Rd
Newport NH 03773
603 298-0199

(G-22205)
QUIRION LUC (PA)
Also Called: Vermont Olde Tyme Kettle Corn
96 Western Ave (05855-8001)
PHONE....................................802 673-8386
Luc Quirion, *Owner*
Rhonda Quirion, *Co-Owner*
EMP: 3
SQ FT: 7,000
SALES: 1.2MM **Privately Held**
SIC: 2064 5145 5441 Mfg Candy/Confectionery Whol Confectionery Ret Candy/Confectionery

(G-22206)
VERMONTS NORTHLAND JOURNAL LLC
2180 Pine Hill Rd (05855-9398)
PHONE....................................802 334-5920
Scott A Wheeler, *Principal*
EMP: 3
SALES (est): 109.8K **Privately Held**
SIC: 2711 Newspapers-Publishing/Printing

Newport Center
Orleans County

(G-22207)
PAUL A MORSE
Also Called: Paul Morse Logging
553 Vt Route 100 (05857-9617)
PHONE....................................802 334-9160
Paul A Morse, *Owner*
EMP: 3
SALES (est): 264.4K **Privately Held**
SIC: 2411 Logging

(G-22208)
VERMONT CENTER WREATHS INC
Also Called: Makers Natural Green Wreaths
44 Kimberly Ln (05857-9432)
P.O. Box 38 (05857-0038)
PHONE....................................802 334-6432
Michael Sicard, *President*
Paulette Sicard, *Vice Pres*
EMP: 60 **EST:** 1988
SALES (est): 869.6K **Privately Held**
SIC: 3999 Mfg Misc Products

North Bennington
Bennington County

(G-22209)
BENNINGTON MICROTCHNLGY CENTER
441 Water St (05257-4420)
PHONE....................................802 442-8975
Henry Klin, *President*
EMP: 6
SQ FT: 12,000
SALES (est): 428K **Privately Held**
WEB: www.benningtonmicro.org
SIC: 7372 Prepackaged Software Services

(G-22210)
MOUNTAIN MOZZARELLA LLC
Also Called: Maple Brook Farm
441 Water St (05257-4420)
PHONE....................................802 440-9950
Johann Englert, *Principal*
Michael Scheps, *Mng Member*
EMP: 50
SALES (est): 7.8MM **Privately Held**
WEB: www.mountainmozzarella.com
SIC: 2022 Mfg Cheese

(G-22211)
NATIONAL HANGER COMPANY INC
Also Called: National Store Supply
276 Water St (05257-4437)
PHONE....................................800 426-4377
Michele Pilcher, *President*
Eric Erthein, *Vice Pres*
Elaine Clayton, *Human Res Mgr*
Sandy Cross, *Info Tech Mgr*
Mary Bennitt, *Officer*
◆ **EMP:** 92
SQ FT: 200,000
SALES (est): 18.4MM **Privately Held**
WEB: www.nationalstoresupply.com
SIC: 3089 Mfg Plastic Products

(G-22212)
POULIN GRAIN INC
Also Called: Whitman's Feed Store
1873 Vt Route 67 E (05257-8103)
PHONE....................................802 681-1605
Scott Birch, *Branch Mgr*
EMP: 20
SALES (corp-wide): 24.2MM **Privately Held**
SIC: 2048 Mfg Prepared Feeds
PA: Poulin Grain, Inc.
24 Railroad Sq
Newport VT 05855
802 334-6731

(G-22213)
STERLING GUN DRILLS INC
940 Water St (05257-9810)
P.O. Box 806 (05257-0806)
PHONE....................................802 442-3525
Thomas Hall, *President*
Doug Holley, *General Mgr*
John J Hall III, *Vice Pres*
William Hultberg, *Treasurer*
EMP: 13
SQ FT: 10,000
SALES (est): 1.2MM **Privately Held**
WEB: www.sterlinggundrills.com
SIC: 3545 Mfg Machine Tool Accessories

North Clarendon
Rutland County

(G-22214)
CHARLES E TUTTLE CO INC (DH)
Also Called: Tuttle Publishing
364 Innovation Dr (05759-9436)
PHONE....................................802 773-8930
Eric Oey, *President*
Terri Jadick, *Editor*
Michael Sargent, *Senior VP*
David Loseby, *Controller*
Christopher Johns, *Sales Staff*
▲ **EMP:** 35 **EST:** 1832
SQ FT: 72,000
SALES (est): 4.5MM **Privately Held**
WEB: www.tuttlepublishing.com
SIC: 2731 Books-Publishing/Printing

(G-22215)
ELLISON SURFACE TECH INC
106 Innovation Dr (05759-9386)
PHONE....................................802 775-9300
Kevin Mattson, *Manager*
EMP: 52 **Privately Held**
WEB: www.ellisonsurfacetech.com
SIC: 3479 Coating/Engraving Service
HQ: Ellison Surface Technologies, Inc.
8118 Corp Way Ste 201
Mason OH 45040
513 770-4922

(G-22216)
JOSEPH P CARRARA & SONS INC (PA)
167 N Shrewsbury Rd (05759-9507)
P.O. Box 60 (05759-0060)
PHONE....................................802 775-2301
Paul J Carrara, *President*
Robert Carrara, *Treasurer*
Christine M Carrara, *Admin Sec*
▲ **EMP:** 40 **EST:** 1935
SQ FT: 20,500
SALES (est): 20.2MM **Privately Held**
SIC: 3272 3273 1442 1771 Mfg Concrete Products Mfg Ready-Mixed Concrete Construction Sand/Gravel Concrete Contractor

(G-22217)
KALOW TECHNOLOGIES LLC
238 Innovation Dr (05759-9387)
PHONE....................................802 775-4633
Paul Van Huis, *President*
Jeff Bartell, *Vice Pres*
▲ **EMP:** 61
SQ FT: 57,000
SALES (est): 23.4MM **Privately Held**
WEB: www.kalowtech.com
SIC: 3569 Mfg General Industrial Machinery

(G-22218)
KINGDOM PELLETS LLC
1105 Route 7b Central (05759-9508)
PHONE....................................802 747-1093
Chris Brooks,
EMP: 21
SQ FT: 20,000
SALES (est): 803.5K **Privately Held**
SIC: 2499 Mfg Wood Products

(G-22219)
KNIGHT INDUSTRIES INC
Also Called: Knight Kitchens
20 Innovation Dr (05759-8802)
P.O. Box 66 (05759-0066)
PHONE....................................802 773-8777
George A Ritter Sr, *President*
Eric Ritter, *Vice Pres*
▼ **EMP:** 28
SQ FT: 36,000
SALES: 5MM **Privately Held**
WEB: www.knightkitchens.com
SIC: 2434 Mfg Wood Kitchen Cabinets

(G-22220)
MILL RIVER LUMBER LTD
2639 Middle Rd (05759-4413)
P.O. Box 100 (05759-0100)
PHONE....................................802 775-0032
Michael C Roberts, *President*
Frank Cecot, *Corp Secy*
Peter Buckley, *Vice Pres*
Fred Burnett, *Vice Pres*
Harry Robbins, *Vice Pres*
EMP: 55
SQ FT: 2,800
SALES: 8.5MM **Privately Held**
WEB: www.millriverlumber.com
SIC: 2421 5191 5261 5211 Sawmill/Planing Mill Whol Farm Supplies Ret Nursery/Garden Supp

(G-22221)
SUGARBAKERS MAPLE SYRUP
940 Middle Rd (05759-9435)
PHONE....................................802 773-7731
Edward Baker, *Principal*
EMP: 3
SALES (est): 169.3K **Privately Held**
SIC: 2099 Mfg Food Preparations

(G-22222)
VERMONT WOOD PELLET CO LLC
1105 Route 7b Central (05759-9508)
PHONE....................................802 747-1093
Jessica Wood, *Controller*
Chris Brooks,
EMP: 24
SALES (est): 3.5MM **Privately Held**
SIC: 2499 Mfg Wood Products

North Concord
Essex County

(G-22223)
WILLIAM CHADBURN
Also Called: Willson Road Woodworking
980 Willson Rd (05858-7009)
PHONE....................................802 695-8166
William Chadburn, *Owner*
EMP: 4
SALES (est): 240K **Privately Held**
SIC: 2431 2522 2521 2511 Mfg Millwork Mfg Nonwood Office Furn Mfg Wood Office Furn Mfg Wood Household Furn Mfg Wood Kitchen Cabinet

North Ferrisburgh
Addison County

(G-22224)
ADIRONDACK GUIDE BOAT
6821 Route 7 (05473-7005)
PHONE..................................802 425-3926
David Rosen, *CEO*
Randy Stewart, *Manager*
EMP: 5
SALES (est): 828.9K **Privately Held**
WEB: www.adirondack-guide-boat.com
SIC: 3732 Boatbuilding/Repairing

(G-22225)
BOWLES CORPORATION
445 Longpoint Rd (05473-7089)
PHONE..................................802 425-3447
David Bowles, *President*
Carol Bowles, *Vice Pres*
EMP: 12
SQ FT: 6,000
SALES (est): 3.1MM **Privately Held**
SIC: 3829 Mfg Measuring/Controlling Devices

(G-22226)
MARTIN CUSTOM BOAT WORKS LLC
Also Called: Adirondack Guide Boat
6821 Route 7 (05473-7005)
PHONE..................................802 318-7882
Justin Martin, *Mng Member*
Ian Martin,
EMP: 6
SQ FT: 3,200
SALES: 800K **Privately Held**
SIC: 3732 Boatbuilding/Repairing

(G-22227)
SMB LLC
239 Quaker St (05473-7099)
PHONE..................................802 425-2862
Larry Barnes, *Owner*
EMP: 7
SALES (est): 558.9K **Privately Held**
SIC: 3369 Nonferrous Metal Foundry

(G-22228)
STROMATEC INC
3050 Fuller Mt Rd (05473-4060)
PHONE..................................802 425-2700
Robert Davis, *President*
EMP: 5
SALES: 100K **Privately Held**
SIC: 3841 Mfg Surgical/Medical Instruments

North Hartland
Windsor County

(G-22229)
NORTH HARTLAND TOOL CORP
14 Evarts Rd (05052-9719)
P.O. Box 38 (05052-0038)
PHONE..................................802 295-3196
John M Mullen, *President*
Carol J Mullen, *Admin Sec*
EMP: 94 **EST:** 1957
SQ FT: 15,500
SALES (est): 43.9K **Privately Held**
SIC: 3544 Mfg Dies/Tools/Jigs/Fixtures

North Hero
Grand Isle County

(G-22230)
FIBERGLASS PLUS INC
2355 Us Route 2 (05474-9404)
PHONE..................................802 878-2066
Ron Pampineau, *President*
EMP: 3
SALES: 200K **Privately Held**
SIC: 3732 Boatbuilding/Repairing

(G-22231)
ISLANDER
Also Called: Northern Champlain Islander
2355 Us Route 2 (05474-9404)
P.O. Box 212, South Hero (05486-0212)
PHONE..................................802 372-5600
George Fowler, *President*
Elaine Fowler, *Vice Pres*
EMP: 4 **EST:** 1974
SALES (est): 241.1K **Privately Held**
SIC: 2711 Newspapers-Publishing/Printing

North Hyde Park
Lamoille County

(G-22232)
M B HEATH & SONS LUMBER INC
Also Called: Heath Lumber
6 Heath Rd (05665)
P.O. Box 72 (05665-0072)
PHONE..................................802 635-2538
Dennis Heath, *President*
EMP: 9
SALES (est): 1.3MM **Privately Held**
SIC: 2421 5211 Sawmill & Retail Lumber

(G-22233)
WAY OUT WAX INC
Also Called: Candle Cabin, The
76 Deer Run Ln (05665)
P.O. Box 175 (05665-0175)
PHONE..................................802 730-8069
James Rossiter, *President*
Dave Cacciamani, *Vice Pres*
Erin Kopacz, *Bookkeeper*
EMP: 15
SQ FT: 6,000
SALES (est): 2.1MM **Privately Held**
WEB: www.wayoutwax.com
SIC: 3999 Mfg Misc Products

North Pomfret
Windsor County

(G-22234)
A DAVID MOORE INC
6810 Pomfret Rd (05053-5017)
PHONE..................................802 457-3914
A David Moore, *President*
Susan Moore, *Corp Secy*
▲ **EMP:** 3
SALES: 85K **Privately Held**
SIC: 3931 Mfg Pipe Organs

(G-22235)
TRAFALGAR SQUARE FARM INC
Also Called: Green Mountain Book Bargains
388 Howe Hill Rd (05053)
P.O. Box 257 (05053-0257)
PHONE..................................802 457-1911
Caroline Robbins, *President*
Theodore Robbins, *Admin Sec*
▲ **EMP:** 14
SQ FT: 3,000
SALES (est): 1.8MM **Privately Held**
SIC: 2731 5192 Books-Publishing/Printing Whol Books/Newspapers

North Springfield
Windsor County

(G-22236)
IVEK CORP
10 Fairbanks Rd (05150-9743)
PHONE..................................802 886-2238
Mark N Tanny, *President*
John McDonald, *Director*
Michael F Hanley, *Admin Sec*
EMP: 75
SQ FT: 31,000
SALES (est): 38.6MM **Privately Held**
WEB: www.ivek.com
SIC: 3561 Mfg Pumps/Pumping Equipment

(G-22237)
JELD-WEN INC
Also Called: Jeld-Wen Doors
36 Precision Dr Ste 130 (05150-9706)
PHONE..................................802 886-1728
Mary Van Treese, *COO*
Peter Farmakis, *Exec VP*
Bob Merrill, *Exec VP*
Daniel Castillo, *Vice Pres*
James Hayes, *Vice Pres*
EMP: 121 **Publicly Held**
SIC: 2431 Mfg Millwork
HQ: Jeld-Wen, Inc.
2645 Silver Crescent Dr
Charlotte NC 28273
800 535-3936

(G-22238)
SPRINGFIELD PRINTING CORP
Also Called: Spc Marcom Studio
19 Precision Dr (05150-9778)
PHONE..................................802 886-2201
Mark Sanderson, *President*
Barbara J Sanderson, *Corp Secy*
Bruce Sanderson, *Vice Pres*
Jim Norman, *Opers Mgr*
Chris Cozi, *Manager*
EMP: 34 **EST:** 1878
SQ FT: 25,000
SALES: 4.6MM **Privately Held**
WEB: www.springfieldprinting.com
SIC: 2752 Lithographic Commercial Printing

(G-22239)
VERMONT PACKINGHOUSE LLC
25 Fairbanks Rd (05150-9743)
PHONE..................................802 886-8688
Dr Arion Thiboumery, *Managing Prtnr*
EMP: 15
SQ FT: 22,000
SALES: 720K **Privately Held**
SIC: 2011 5147 Meat Packing Plant Whol Meats/Products

North Troy
Orleans County

(G-22240)
APPALCHIAN ENGINEERED FLRG INC
105 Industrial Park Dr (05859)
PHONE..................................802 988-1073
Jean Leduc, *President*
Gordon Duplain, *Vice Pres*
EMP: 18
SQ FT: 26,000
SALES: 4.5MM
SALES (corp-wide): 19.2MM **Privately Held**
SIC: 2426 Hardwood Dimension/Floor Mill
PA: Planchers Des Appalaches Ltee
454 Rue De La Riviere
Cowansville QC J2K 3
450 266-3999

(G-22241)
NUTRA-BLEND LLC
53 E Main St (05859-9590)
PHONE..................................802 988-4474
Ashley Miller, *Branch Mgr*
EMP: 5
SALES (corp-wide): 6.8B **Privately Held**
SIC: 2048 Mfg Prepared Feeds
HQ: Nutra-Blend, L.L.C.
3200 2nd St
Neosho MO 64850
417 451-6111

(G-22242)
PROLENS INC
47 Main St (05859-9563)
PHONE..................................802 988-1018
Dominicque Alain, *President*
EMP: 7
SALES (corp-wide): 1.5MM **Privately Held**
SIC: 3851 Mfg Ophthalmic Goods
PA: Prolens Inc
28 Daniel Plummer Rd # 5
Goffstown NH 03045
603 487-1019

Northfield
Washington County

(G-22243)
HERITAGE JOINERY LTD
1688 Route 12 (05663-6512)
PHONE..................................802 485-6107
Richard Tintle, *President*
Barbara Murphy, *Admin Sec*
EMP: 5
SALES (est): 483.5K **Privately Held**
WEB: www.heritagejoinery.com
SIC: 2431 Mfg Millwork

(G-22244)
NATWORKS INC
454 S Main St (05663-5690)
PHONE..................................802 485-6818
Chris Bradley, *President*
Andrew Bothfield, *Vice Pres*
EMP: 10
SALES: 900K **Privately Held**
WEB: www.natworks-inc.com
SIC: 7372 7371 Prepackaged Software Services Custom Computer Programing

(G-22245)
VERMONT PROBIOTICA
162 Pine Hill Dr (05663-6505)
P.O. Box 136, East Montpelier (05651-0136)
PHONE..................................802 279-4998
Martin Smith, *Co-Owner*
Robert Connolly, *Co-Owner*
EMP: 4
SALES (est): 165.9K **Privately Held**
SIC: 2032 Mfg Canned Specialties

(G-22246)
WALLGOLDFINGER INC
706 Garvey Hill Rd (05663-6760)
PHONE..................................802 483-4200
John C Wall, *President*
Anne Gould, *Treasurer*
Gerry Gatch, *VP Sales*
Robin Palmer, *Comms Dir*
Mike Spencer, *Admin Sec*
EMP: 45
SALES (est): 8.1MM **Privately Held**
WEB: www.wallgoldfinger.com
SIC: 2431 Mfg Millwork

Norwich
Windsor County

(G-22247)
CORE VALUE SOFTWARE
316 Main St (05055-4428)
PHONE..................................802 473-3147
George Sandmann, *President*
EMP: 10
SALES (est): 749.6K **Privately Held**
SIC: 7372 Prepackaged Software Services

Orleans
Orleans County

(G-22248)
KIMTEK CORPORATION
326 Industrial Park Ln (05860-9423)
PHONE..................................802 754-9000
Kimball Johnson, *President*
EMP: 8
SQ FT: 4,000
SALES: 340K **Privately Held**
WEB: www.kimtekresearch.com
SIC: 3444 Mfg Sheet Metalwork

(G-22249)
LA FOE BRIAN
151 Tarbox Hill Rd (05860-9435)
PHONE..................................802 754-8837
Brian La Foe, *Owner*
EMP: 3
SALES: 1.7MM **Privately Held**
SIC: 2411 Logging Service

▲ = Import ▼=Export
◆ =Import/Export

(G-22250)
LAFOE LOGGING LLC
151 Tarbox Hill Rd (05860-9435)
PHONE..................................802 754-8837
Brian Lafoe, *Principal*
EMP: 6 **EST:** 2009
SALES (est): 472K **Privately Held**
SIC: 2411 Logging

(G-22251)
REGINALD J RIENDEAU
Also Called: Reg Riendeau Logging
109 River Rd (05860-9281)
PHONE..................................802 754-6003
Reginald J Riendeau, *Principal*
EMP: 4
SALES (est): 36K **Privately Held**
SIC: 2411 Logging

(G-22252)
VERMONT BEEF JERKY CO
348 Industrial Park Ln (05860-9423)
PHONE..................................802 754-9412
Wayne Leiberum, *Partner*
William Perkins, *Partner*
EMP: 22
SQ FT: 6,000
SALES (est): 1.5MM **Privately Held**
SIC: 2013 Manufactures Beef Jerkey

(G-22253)
VILLAGE OF ORLEANS
Also Called: Incoporated Villge of Orlean
1 Memorial Sq (05860-1215)
PHONE..................................802 754-8584
Shelia Martin, *Treasurer*
Marilyn Prue, *Office Mgr*
John Morley, *Manager*
EMP: 8
SALES: 729.7K **Privately Held**
SIC: 3679 Mfg Electronic Components

Orwell
Addison County

(G-22254)
DERRICK CLIFFORD LOGGING LLC
133 Raymond Hill Rd (05760-9626)
PHONE..................................802 948-2798
Derrick Clifford, *Principal*
EMP: 3
SALES (est): 252.6K **Privately Held**
SIC: 2411 Logging

(G-22255)
HUB CONSOLIDATED INC
690 Route 73 (05760-9625)
PHONE..................................802 948-2209
John Chiles, *President*
May Mantell, *Vice Pres*
▼ **EMP:** 5
SQ FT: 10,000
SALES (est): 496.1K **Privately Held**
WEB: www.johnchilesglass.com
SIC: 3559 Mfg Glass Melting And Heating Equipment Tool & Supplies

Pawlet
Rutland County

(G-22256)
CONIX SYSTEMS (PA)
441 W Tinmouth Rd (05761-9516)
PHONE..................................800 332-1899
Mike Charles, *CEO*
EMP: 3
SALES (est): 2.2MM **Privately Held**
WEB: www.conixsystems.com
SIC: 7372 Prepackaged Software Services

Perkinsville
Windsor County

(G-22257)
SAFE AND SECURE FOU A NJ NON
448 Henry Gould Rd (05151-9779)
PHONE..................................848 992-3623
Thomas Leach, *Principal*
EMP: 3
SALES (est): 329.4K **Privately Held**
SIC: 3714 Motor Vehicle Parts And Accessories

(G-22258)
SHEEHAN & SONS LUMBER
251 Stoughton Pond Rd (05151-9688)
PHONE..................................802 263-5545
Peter Sheehan, *Owner*
EMP: 7
SALES (est): 520K **Privately Held**
SIC: 2421 4212 Saw Mill/Trucking And Land Holding Company

(G-22259)
V P E INC
22 Kendricks Corner Rd (05151-9637)
PHONE..................................802 263-9474
Zachery Jewett, *President*
EMP: 5
SQ FT: 4,600
SALES (est): 603.1K **Privately Held**
SIC: 3599 Machine Shop

(G-22260)
VERMONT SOAPSTONE INC
248 Stoughton Pond Rd (05151-9695)
P.O. Box 268 (05151-0268)
PHONE..................................802 263-5577
Glenn Bowman, *Principal*
Joy Fletcher, *Admin Asst*
EMP: 15
SALES (est): 1.7MM **Privately Held**
SIC: 3281 Mfg Cut Stone/Products

(G-22261)
WILLIAMS & CO MINING INC
248 Stoughton Pond Rd (05151-9695)
PHONE..................................802 263-5404
Glenn Bowman, *President*
Gail Bowman, *Vice Pres*
EMP: 17
SQ FT: 6,000
SALES (est): 1.5MM **Privately Held**
WEB: www.vermontsoapstone.com
SIC: 3281 1499 Mfg Cut Stone/Products Nonmetallic Mineral Mining

Pittsfield
Rutland County

(G-22262)
COLTON ENTERPRISES INC
1697 Rte 100 (05762)
P.O. Box 688 (05762-0688)
PHONE..................................802 746-8033
Ray Colton, *President*
Lynda J Colton, *Treasurer*
EMP: 6
SALES (est): 859.2K **Privately Held**
WEB: www.coltonenterprises.com
SIC: 2421 Kiln Drying Of Firewood And Bark Mulch Grinding & Sales

Pittsford
Rutland County

(G-22263)
GIDDINGS MANUFACTURING CO INC
Also Called: Giddings Equipment
1448 Us Route 7 (05763-9266)
PHONE..................................802 483-2292
Robert Giddings, *President*
Rachael Giddings, *Vice Pres*
EMP: 6
SQ FT: 3,200
SALES: 1.3MM **Privately Held**
WEB: www.giddingsonline.com
SIC: 3444 5083 Mfg Sheet Metalwork Whol Farm/Garden Machinery

(G-22264)
MITCHELL TEES & SIGNS INC
41 Gloriosa Dr (05763-4413)
P.O. Box 38 (05763-0038)
PHONE..................................802 483-6866
Timothy Mitchell, *President*
EMP: 3
SALES (est): 411.6K **Privately Held**
SIC: 2759 Commercial Printing

(G-22265)
VERMONT VERDE ANTIQUE INTL
2561 Sugar Hollow Rd (05763-9891)
PHONE..................................802 767-4421
Dorando Cavallacci, *President*
Mike Solari, *General Mgr*
▲ **EMP:** 8
SALES (est): 810K **Privately Held**
WEB: www.pl8s.com
SIC: 1411 Quarry

Plainfield
Washington County

(G-22266)
CODLING BROTHERS LOGGING
1165 Maple Hill Rd (05667-9351)
PHONE..................................802 454-7177
EMP: 3
SALES (est): 376.8K **Privately Held**
SIC: 2411 Logging

(G-22267)
GRAND VIEW WINERY CO LLC
2039 Max Gray Rd (05667-9472)
PHONE..................................802 456-8810
Philip Tonks, *Mng Member*
EMP: 13
SQ FT: 2,000
SALES (est): 1.4MM **Privately Held**
WEB: www.grandviewwinery.com
SIC: 2084 Mfg Wines/Brandy/Spirits

(G-22268)
INTERNATIONAL INNOVATIONS INC
Also Called: Powerhearth
1127 Max Gray Rd (05667)
PHONE..................................802 454-7764
William Klein, *President*
Jack Humphries, *Vice Pres*
Chris Roy, *Shareholder*
Frank Shepherd, *Shareholder*
Milton Smith, *Shareholder*
EMP: 3
SQ FT: 12,000
SALES (est): 257.9K **Privately Held**
SIC: 3612 Mfg Transformers

(G-22269)
RAND KEVIN
656 Vermont Route 14 (05667-9464)
PHONE..................................802 454-1440
Kevin Rand, *Principal*
EMP: 3
SALES (est): 297.4K **Privately Held**
SIC: 3131 Noncommercial Research Organization

Poultney
Rutland County

(G-22270)
BRASS BUTTERFLY INC
Also Called: Decorative Window Ware
169 Main St (05764-1196)
P.O. Box 237 (05764-0237)
PHONE..................................802 287-9818
Joseph Debonis, *President*
Ann Debonis, *Vice Pres*
Frank Bowles, *CFO*
EMP: 4
SQ FT: 12,500
SALES (est): 471.7K **Privately Held**
WEB: www.brassbutterfly.com
SIC: 3231 3496 2591 2499 Mfg Glassware Wirecraft Products Decorative Wrought Iron Window Ware & Novelty Wood Products

(G-22271)
FIRST LIGHT TECHNOLOGIES INC
212 Ideal Way (05764-1052)
PHONE..................................802 287-4195
Kenneth Ell, *President*
Dan Ducharme, *Engineer*
John Ell, *Director*
Alexandra Kurtz, *Director*
Mark E Kurtz, *Director*
▲ **EMP:** 85
SQ FT: 25,000
SALES (est): 14.7MM **Privately Held**
WEB: www.firstlightusa.com
SIC: 3641 Mfg Electric Lamps

(G-22272)
JOHN WILEY & SONS INC
1966 Hillside Rd (05764-9252)
PHONE..................................802 287-4326
Michelle Blue, *Manager*
EMP: 65
SALES (corp-wide): 1.8B **Publicly Held**
WEB: www.wiley.com
SIC: 2731 Nonclassified Establishment
PA: John Wiley & Sons, Inc.
111 River St Ste 2000
Hoboken NJ 07030
201 748-6000

(G-22273)
MACRYAN INC
Also Called: Best Products
244 Lewis Rd (05764-9269)
PHONE..................................802 287-4788
Craig Fahan, *President*
Wendi Fahan, *Director*
EMP: 5
SQ FT: 1,200
SALES: 300K **Privately Held**
SIC: 3496 Mfg Misc Fabricated Wire Products

(G-22274)
QUARRY SLATE INDUSTRIES INC
Also Called: Briar Hill
325 Upper Rd (05764)
PHONE..................................802 287-9701
John Hill, *President*
Edward Valavyka, *Manager*
EMP: 88
SQ FT: 14,000
SALES (est): 13MM **Privately Held**
WEB: www.greenstoneslate.com
SIC: 2952 1411 Dimension Stone Quarry Mfg Asphalt Felts/Coatings

(G-22275)
R&B POWDER COATING LLC
60 Firehouse Ln (05764-1211)
P.O. Box 164 (05764-0164)
PHONE..................................802 287-2300
Robert Hughes,
EMP: 4
SALES (est): 449.4K **Privately Held**
SIC: 3479 Coating/Engraving Service

(G-22276)
RUPE SLATE CO
54 New Boston Rd (05764-9752)
PHONE..................................802 287-9692
Richard Rupe, *President*
ADM Nancy A Rute, *Admin Sec*
Michael C Rupe,
EMP: 7
SALES (est): 710K **Privately Held**
SIC: 3259 Mfg Structural Clay Products

(G-22277)
SOUTH POULTNEY SLATE
376 York St (05764-1023)
PHONE..................................802 287-9278
Frances Hayes, *Owner*
EMP: 7
SALES (est): 618.6K **Privately Held**
SIC: 1411 Dimension Stone Quarry

(G-22278)
TARAN BROS INC (PA)
Also Called: Red Slate Quarry
Rr 30 (05764)
PHONE..................................802 287-5853
Stephen M Taran, *President*
Barbara Taran, *Corp Secy*
Gretel Taran, *Corp Secy*
Joseph Taran, *Vice Pres*
EMP: 20 **EST:** 1930
SALES: 227K **Privately Held**
SIC: 1411 Dimension Slate Quarry

(G-22279)
TARAN BROS INC
Also Called: Fair Haven Slate
2522 Vermont Route 30 N (05764-9685)
PHONE..................................802 287-9308
Stephen Taran, *President*
EMP: 7
SALES (corp-wide): 227K **Privately Held**
SIC: 1411 Lmbrbldng Mtrls
PA: Taran Bros Inc
Rr 30
Poultney VT 05764
802 287-5853

(G-22280)
VERMONT SWEETWATER BOTTLING CO
2087 Hillside Rd (05764-9251)
PHONE..................................800 974-9877
Richard Munch, *President*
Robert Munch, *Vice Pres*
EMP: 4
SQ FT: 5,040
SALES: 150K **Privately Held**
WEB: www.vtsweetwater.com
SIC: 2086 5149 Mfg Bottled/Canned Soft Drinks Whol Groceries

Pownal
Bennington County

(G-22281)
GAMMELGARDEN CREAMERY
431 Quarry Hill Rd (05261-9615)
PHONE..................................802 823-5757
EMP: 4
SALES (est): 177.5K **Privately Held**
SIC: 2021 Mfg Creamery Butter

(G-22282)
N W P INC
Also Called: Northeast Wood Products
171 Church St (05261)
PHONE..................................802 442-4749
Robert L Kobelia, *President*
Robert Kobelia, *President*
Kristena Kobelia, *Treasurer*
EMP: 9
SALES (est): 750K **Privately Held**
SIC: 2421 5031 2426 Sawmill/Planing Mill Whol Lumber/Plywood/Millwork Hardwood Dimension/Floor Mill

Proctor
Rutland County

(G-22283)
CARRIS FINANCIAL CORP (PA)
49 Main St (05765-1178)
PHONE..................................802 773-9111
William Carris, *Ch of Bd*
Dave Ferraro, *President*
David Ferraro, *President*
Mike Hendricks, *General Mgr*
Alberto Aguilar, *Vice Pres*
▲ **EMP:** 15
SALES (est): 91.3MM **Privately Held**
SIC: 2499 3499 3089 2448 Mfg Wood Products Mfg Misc Fab Metal Prdts Mfg Plastic Products Mfg Wood Pallets/Skids Mfg Wood Household Furn

(G-22284)
CARRIS REELS INC (HQ)
Also Called: Carris Plastics
49 Main St (05765-1178)
PHONE..................................802 773-9111
Dave Ferraro, *President*
Alberto Aguilar, *Vice Pres*
Brian Connell, *Opers Staff*
David C Fitz-Gerald, *Treasurer*
David Fitz-Gerald, *VP Finance*
▲ **EMP:** 150 **EST:** 1951
SQ FT: 10,531
SALES (est): 61.2MM **Privately Held**
WEB: www.carris.com
SIC: 2499 3499 3089 2655 Mfg Wood Products Mfg Misc Fab Metal Prdts Mfg Plastic Products Mfg Fiber Can/Drums

(G-22285)
JOHNSON MARBLE AND GRANITE
61 Main St (05765-1178)
P.O. Box 645 (05765-0645)
PHONE..................................802 459-3303
Herbert Johnson Jr, *President*
Herb Johnson III, *Vice Pres*
Lisa Johnson, *Treasurer*
Patricia Johnson, *Admin Sec*
EMP: 5
SQ FT: 14,000
SALES (est): 549.6K **Privately Held**
WEB: www.johnsonmarbleandgranite.com
SIC: 3281 5947 Mfg Specialty Marble Giftware

(G-22286)
O M Y A INC
62 Main St (05765-1177)
PHONE..................................802 499-8131
EMP: 8
SALES (est): 626K **Privately Held**
SIC: 2819 Mfg Industrial Inorganic Chemicals

(G-22287)
OMYA INC
39 Main St (05765)
PHONE..................................802 459-3311
Patrick Gane, *Vice Pres*
Elizabeth Smith, *Purch Agent*
Mallory Ezequelle, *Engineer*
Dan Firliet, *Engineer*
Sami Korenius, *Engineer*
EMP: 15
SALES (corp-wide): 4B **Privately Held**
SIC: 2819 Mfg Industrial Inorganic Chemicals
HQ: Omya Inc.
9987 Carver Rd Ste 300
Blue Ash OH 45242
513 387-4600

Proctorsville
Windsor County

(G-22288)
GILCRIS ENTERPRISES INC
Also Called: Proctor Piper Log Homes
283 Peaceful Valley Rd (05153-9751)
PHONE..................................802 226-7764
Richard Gilcris, *President*
Wayne Gilcris, *Vice Pres*
EMP: 10
SQ FT: 30,000
SALES (est): 750K **Privately Held**
SIC: 2421 2452 Sawmill Log Home Contractor

Putney
Windham County

(G-22289)
H L HANDY COMPANY INC
Also Called: Vermonter, The
22 W Hill Rd (05346-8606)
P.O. Box 755 (05346-0755)
PHONE..................................802 387-4040
Carolyn Handy, *President*
David Handy, *Treasurer*
EMP: 6
SALES: 50K **Privately Held**
SIC: 2064 Mfg Candy/Confectionery

(G-22290)
PENELOPE WURR GLASS
719 W Hill Rd (05346-8986)
PHONE..................................802 387-5607
Penelope J Wilner, *Owner*
▲ **EMP:** 3
SALES: 80K **Privately Held**
WEB: www.penelopewurr.com
SIC: 3229 Mfg Pressed/Blown Glass

(G-22291)
PUTNEY MOUNTAIN WINERY
8 Bellows Falls Rd (05346-8681)
PHONE..................................802 387-5925
Charles Dodge, *Owner*
EMP: 6
SALES (est): 397.2K **Privately Held**
SIC: 2084 Mfg Wines/Brandy/Spirits

(G-22292)
SOUNDVIEW VERMONT HOLDINGS LLC
67 Kathan Meadow Rd (05346)
PHONE..................................802 387-5571
Matt Denton, *COO*
EMP: 136
SALES (est): 29MM
SALES (corp-wide): 2.9B **Privately Held**
SIC: 2621 Paper Mill
HQ: Marcal Manufacturing, Llc
1 Market St
Elmwood Park NJ 07407

(G-22293)
TOMS OF MAINE INC
148 Banning Rd (05346-8861)
PHONE..................................802 387-2393
Lucinda Alcorn, *Branch Mgr*
EMP: 136
SALES (corp-wide): 15.5B **Publicly Held**
WEB: www.tomsofmaine.com
SIC: 2844 Mfg Toilet Preparations
HQ: Tom's Of Maine, Inc.
2 Storer St Ste 302
Kennebunk ME 04043
207 985-2944

Quechee
Windsor County

(G-22294)
FAT HAT CLOTHING CO
1 Quechee Main St (05059-3052)
P.O. Box 863 (05059-0863)
PHONE..................................802 296-6646
Joan Ecker, *President*
Allen Malcolm, *Corp Secy*
EMP: 13
SQ FT: 9,000
SALES (est): 1.5MM **Privately Held**
WEB: www.fathat.com
SIC: 2339 2353 2329 Mfg Women's/Misses' Outerwear Mfg Hats/Caps/Millinery Mfg Men's/Boy's Clothing

(G-22295)
WHISPER HILLS
5573 Woodstock Rd (05059)
P.O. Box 11, Hartland Cors (05049-0011)
PHONE..................................802 296-7627
Randy Cysyk, *President*
EMP: 3
SALES (est): 301.3K **Privately Held**
SIC: 2841 Mfg Soap/Other Detergents

Randolph
Orange County

(G-22296)
AADCO MEDICAL INC
2279 Vt Route 66 (05060-4406)
P.O. Box 410 (05060-0410)
PHONE..................................802 728-3400
Robert Marchione, *President*
Andrew Curran, *Vice Pres*
Anthony Skidmore, *Vice Pres*
Darrel Lasell, *Project Mgr*
Mary Orticari, *Mfg Mgr*
▲ **EMP:** 64
SQ FT: 20,000
SALES (est): 13.6MM **Privately Held**
SIC: 3844 3842 5047 Mfg X-Ray Apparatus/Tubes Mfg Surgical Appliances/Supplies Whol Medical/Hospital Equipment

(G-22297)
HERALD OF RANDOLPH
30 Pleasant St (05060-1156)
P.O. Box 309 (05060-0309)
PHONE..................................802 728-3232
M D Drysdale, *Owner*
EMP: 15 **EST:** 1874
SALES (est): 735.2K **Privately Held**
WEB: www.rherald.com
SIC: 2711 Newspapers-Publishing/Printing

(G-22298)
LEDDYNAMICS INC
296 Beanville Rd (05060-9301)
P.O. Box 444 (05060-0444)
PHONE..................................802 728-4533
William McGrath, *President*
Dan Yasi, *Vice Pres*
Oliver Piluski, *Engineer*
Patrick Schlott, *Engineer*
Robert Sparadeo, *Info Tech Mgr*
◆ **EMP:** 75
SQ FT: 18,000
SALES (est): 16.6MM **Privately Held**
WEB: www.leddynamics.com
SIC: 3674 Mfg Semiconductors/Related Devices

(G-22299)
NEW ENGLAND PRECISION INC
281 Beanville Rd (05060-9300)
PHONE..................................800 293-4112
Bruce Uryase, *President*
Ed Merrill, *QC Mgr*
Joseph Holland, *CFO*
Doreen Audette, *CTO*
Harry Holland, *Admin Sec*
EMP: 75
SQ FT: 80,000
SALES: 36MM **Privately Held**
WEB: www.newenglandprecision.com
SIC: 3469 3364 3366 Mfg Metal Stampings Mfg Nonferrous Die-Castings Copper Foundry

(G-22300)
NEWPORT SAND & GRAVEL CO INC
Also Called: Carroll Concrete Co
37 Central St (05060-1003)
PHONE..................................802 728-5055
John Barnes, *Manager*
EMP: 5
SALES (corp-wide): 44MM **Privately Held**
SIC: 3273 Mfg Ready-Mixed Concrete
PA: Newport Sand & Gravel Co., Inc.
8 Reeds Mill Rd
Newport NH 03773
603 298-0199

(G-22301)
PORTER MUSIC BOX COMPANY INC
33 Sunset Hill Rd (05060-9288)
P.O. Box 424 (05060-0424)
PHONE..................................802 728-9694
Dwight Porter, *President*
Mary Porter, *Vice Pres*
▲ **EMP:** 7
SALES: 1.3MM **Privately Held**
WEB: www.portermusicbox.com
SIC: 3652 3999 Mfg Prerecorded Records/Tapes Mfg Misc Products

(G-22302)
RULE SIGNS
792 Bear Hill Rd (05060-9029)
PHONE..................................802 728-6030
Rob Niedleng, *Owner*
EMP: 3
SALES: 100K **Privately Held**
SIC: 3993 Mfg Signs/Advertising Specialties

(G-22303)
SPRAGUES DAIRY INC
13 Weston St Ste 1 (05060-1233)
PHONE.................................802 728-3863
Michael G Sprague, *President*
Douglas Sprague, *Treasurer*
EMP: 3 **EST:** 1946
SQ FT: 2,400
SALES (est): 750K **Privately Held**
SIC: 2026 Mfg Fluid Milk

(G-22304)
WOODS VERMONT SYRUP COMPANY
780 Hebard Rd (05060)
PHONE.................................802 565-0309
Albert Wood, *Mng Member*
EMP: 4 **EST:** 2015
SALES: 250K **Privately Held**
SIC: 2099 Mfg Food Preparations

Reading
Windsor County

(G-22305)
CORBIN & SON LOGGING INC
2334 Route 106 (05062-9786)
PHONE.................................802 484-3329
Russell Corbin, *Principal*
EMP: 3
SALES (est): 169.5K **Privately Held**
SIC: 2411 Logging

Richford
Franklin County

(G-22306)
HI-VUE MAPLES LLC
224 Stvens Mills Slide Rd (05476-9690)
PHONE.................................802 752-8888
Dale Smith, *Principal*
Jessica Boone, *Principal*
EMP: 5 **EST:** 1965
SALES: 60K **Privately Held**
SIC: 2099 0831 5149 7389 Mfg Food Preparations Forest Product Gathering Whol Groceries Bus Servs Non-Comcl Site

(G-22307)
KAYTEC INC
1 Memorial Dr (05476-7627)
PHONE.................................802 848-7010
Lionel Dubrofsky, *President*
Tami Dubrofsky, *Corp Secy*
Mitchell Coleman, *Vice Pres*
Dennis Jean, *Vice Pres*
EMP: 85
SQ FT: 77,000
SALES (est): 13.8MM
SALES (corp-wide): 537.7MM **Privately Held**
SIC: 3089 Mfg Plastic Products
PA: Kaycan Ltee
3075 Rte Transcanadienne
Pointe-Claire QC H9R 1
514 694-5855

(G-22308)
KENT NUTRITION GROUP INC
1 Webster St (05476-7624)
PHONE.................................802 848-7718
Paul Fleld, *Branch Mgr*
EMP: 55
SALES (corp-wide): 449.1MM **Privately Held**
WEB: www.blueseal.com
SIC: 2048 Mfg Prepared Feeds
HQ: Kent Nutrition Group, Inc.
1600 Oregon St
Muscatine IA 52761
866 647-1212

(G-22309)
MCALLISTER FUELS INC
5023 Corliss Rd (05476-1200)
PHONE.................................802 782-5293
Robert A McAllister, *Principal*
EMP: 3 **EST:** 2010
SALES (est): 224.5K **Privately Held**
SIC: 2869 Mfg Industrial Organic Chemicals

(G-22310)
STAIRS UNLIMITED INC
484 Hardwood Hill Rd (05476-9647)
P.O. Box 267 (05476-0267)
PHONE.................................802 848-7030
Larry Patterson, *President*
Michael Phillips, *Corp Secy*
EMP: 7
SQ FT: 23,000
SALES: 600K **Privately Held**
WEB: www.stairsunlimited.com
SIC: 3441 Manufactures Metal & Steel Products

Richmond
Chittenden County

(G-22311)
GREEN MTN GRN & BARREL LLC
17 Christmas Hill Rd (05477-9429)
PHONE.................................802 324-5838
Mac Broich, *Co-Owner*
Anthony Fletcher, *Co-Owner*
Joshua Waterhouse, *Co-Owner*
EMP: 3
SALES (est): 159.6K **Privately Held**
SIC: 2429 Special Product Sawmill

(G-22312)
HARRINGTONS IN VERMONT INC (PA)
Also Called: Harrington's of Vermont
210 Main Rd (05477)
P.O. Box 288 (05477-0288)
PHONE.................................802 434-7500
Peter Klinkenberg, *President*
Joyce Klinkenberg, *Corp Secy*
R B Klinkenberg, *Vice Pres*
EMP: 10
SQ FT: 5,000
SALES (est): 12.5MM **Privately Held**
WEB: www.hamvermont.com
SIC: 2013 5947 2053 2052 Mfg Prepared Meats Ret Gifts/Novelties Mfg Frozen Bakery Prdts

(G-22313)
Z M WEAPONS HIGH PERFORMANCE
Also Called: Airtight Ink
1958 Wes White Hl (05477-7766)
PHONE.................................802 777-8964
Allen Zitta, *Owner*
EMP: 8
SQ FT: 11,000
SALES (est): 410K **Privately Held**
SIC: 3484 Mfg Small Arms

Riverton
Washington County

(G-22314)
RIVERTON MEMORIAL INC
2074 Route 12 (05663)
PHONE.................................802 485-3371
Ernest Lavigne Jr, *President*
Arthur Miller, *Treasurer*
Jacqueline Miller, *Admin Sec*
EMP: 15
SALES (est): 1.5MM **Privately Held**
SIC: 3281 Mfg Monuments

Rochester
Windsor County

(G-22315)
ADVANCED ILLUMINATION INC
440 State Garage Rd (05767-9739)
P.O. Box 237 (05767-0237)
PHONE.................................802 767-3830
William Thrailkill, *CEO*
John Thrailkill, *President*
Mary Keenan-Haff, *CFO*
Michael Romano, *Manager*
Zygmunt Labejsza, *Director*
▲ **EMP:** 45
SQ FT: 12,000
SALES (est): 7.5MM **Privately Held**
WEB: www.advill.com
SIC: 3559 Mfg Misc Industry Machinery

(G-22316)
ARTISTIC WOODWORKS INC
606 Fiske Rd Unit 28 (05767-9208)
PHONE.................................802 767-3123
James Browne, *President*
Bruce McCarty, *Vice Pres*
EMP: 3
SALES: 200K **Privately Held**
WEB: www.gardenspiritsticks.com
SIC: 2431 3993 Mfg Millwork Mfg Signs/Advertising Specialties

(G-22317)
INNER TRADITIONS INTERNATIONAL (PA)
Also Called: Bera Company
1 Park St (05767)
P.O. Box 388 (05767-0388)
PHONE.................................802 767-3174
Ehud Sperling, *President*
Pat Harvey, *Vice Pres*
Diane Shepard, *Vice Pres*
Julius Sperling, *Vice Pres*
Rob Meadows, *Sales/Mktg Mgr*
▲ **EMP:** 33
SQ FT: 2,000
SALES (est): 2.9MM **Privately Held**
WEB: www.innertraditions.com
SIC: 2731 Book Publishers

(G-22318)
LCS CONTROLS INC
1678 Vt Route 100 S (05767)
P.O. Box 286 (05767-0286)
PHONE.................................802 767-3128
Thomas Allen, *President*
Donald Crickard, *Vice Pres*
John Allen, *Prdtn Mgr*
Lucia Perry, *Admin Sec*
EMP: 7
SQ FT: 7,500
SALES (est): 1.4MM **Privately Held**
SIC: 3663 Mfg Radio/Tv Communication Equipment

(G-22319)
NEW LIFE LOGGING
440 Clay Hill Rd (05767-9574)
PHONE.................................802 767-9142
Wm Harvey, *Principal*
EMP: 3
SALES (est): 238.2K **Privately Held**
SIC: 2411 Logging

(G-22320)
OATMEAL STUDIOS INC
Town Rd 35 (05767)
P.O. Box 410, Lenox Dale MA (01242-0410)
PHONE.................................802 967-8014
Joseph Massimino, *President*
Helene Lehrer Massimino, *Vice Pres*
▼ **EMP:** 17
SQ FT: 22,000
SALES (est): 1.6MM **Privately Held**
WEB: www.oatmealstudios.com
SIC: 2771 2678 7336 Mfg Greeting Cards

(G-22321)
WHEN WORDS COUNT PRESS LLC
1764 Marsh Brook Rd (05767-9733)
PHONE.................................802 767-4372
EMP: 12
SALES (est): 677.3K **Privately Held**
SIC: 2741 Misc Publishing

Rutland
Rutland County

(G-22322)
ACCORDANT ENERGY LLC
225 S Main St Ste 2 (05701-4791)
PHONE.................................802 772-7368
Lawrence M Clark Jr, *CEO*
Paula Calabrese, *Vice Pres*
Josh Mandell, *Manager*
EMP: 8
SALES (est): 989.8K **Privately Held**
SIC: 2869 Mfg Industrial Organic Chemicals

(G-22323)
AW PERKINS COMPANY
36 Curtis Ave (05701-4844)
P.O. Box 637 (05702-0637)
PHONE.................................802 773-3600
Thomas P Martin, *Owner*
Vicky Matteson, *Vice Pres*
Patricia Consolatti, *Treasurer*
Thomas Martin, *Director*
▲ **EMP:** 6
SALES (est): 822.7K **Privately Held**
SIC: 3255 Mfg Clay Refractories

(G-22324)
AWESOME GRAPHICS INC
77 Woodstock Ave (05701-3535)
PHONE.................................802 773-6143
Michael Napolitano, *Principal*
Tammy Napolitano, *Principal*
EMP: 5
SQ FT: 1,200
SALES (est): 608.7K **Privately Held**
WEB: www.awesomegraphics.com
SIC: 3993 Mfg Signs/Advertising Specialties

(G-22325)
BLAIR CAMPBELL
Also Called: Quicksplint Company
298 Us Route 4 E (05701-8845)
PHONE.................................802 773-7711
Blair Campbell, *Owner*
EMP: 3
SQ FT: 4,000
SALES (est): 220K **Privately Held**
WEB: www.blaircampbell.com
SIC: 3841 Mfg Plastic Splints

(G-22326)
BULLOCK & BLOCK LTD
Also Called: Beer King
57 Crescent St (05701-3128)
PHONE.................................802 773-3350
Roger R Block, *President*
EMP: 14
SALES (est): 1.4MM **Privately Held**
SIC: 2082 Mfg Malt Beverages

(G-22327)
CREATIVE MARKETING SERVICES
Also Called: Rutland Business Journal
27 Wales St (05701-4027)
P.O. Box 6064 (05702-6064)
PHONE.................................802 775-9500
Richard Rohe, *President*
Lillian Rohe, *Vice Pres*
EMP: 10
SQ FT: 1,543
SALES (est): 504.4K **Privately Held**
WEB: www.businessvermont.com
SIC: 2711 Newspapers-Publishing/Printing

(G-22328)
DAMASCUS WORLDWIDE INC
194 Seward Rd (05701-4973)
P.O. Box 706, Barre (05641-0706)
PHONE.................................802 775-6062
Lawrence Welton, *President*
Dave Derman, *Treasurer*
Jason Fisher, *Sales Mgr*
▲ **EMP:** 5 **EST:** 1975
SQ FT: 8,500
SALES (est): 828.4K **Privately Held**
WEB: www.slashguard.com
SIC: 3151 3949 Mfg Leather Gloves/Mittens Mfg Sporting/Athletic Goods

(G-22329)
DEERMONT CORPOPRATION
Also Called: Vermont Platting
113 S Main St (05701-4436)
PHONE.................................802 775-5759
Jim Ruth, *President*
▲ **EMP:** 6
SALES (est): 458.3K **Privately Held**
SIC: 3471 Plating/Polishing Service

(G-22330)
DR LUCYS LLC
1 Scale Ave Ste 14 (05701-4454)
PHONE....................................757 233-9495
Lucy Gibney, *CEO*
Paul Harrison, *CFO*
EMP: 45
SQ FT: 22,000
SALES (est): 9.4MM **Privately Held**
WEB: www.drlucys.com
SIC: 2052 Mfg Cookies/Crackers

(G-22331)
E & G GRAPHICS
2 Clover St (05701-4424)
PHONE....................................802 773-3111
Jerry Gorruso Jr, *Partner*
Leslie Eno Jr, *Partner*
EMP: 4 **EST:** 1977
SQ FT: 2,000
SALES (est): 380K **Privately Held**
SIC: 2752 Lithographic Commercial Printing

(G-22332)
EDWARD GROUP INC
Also Called: Quickprint of Rutland , The
194 Seward Rd (05701-4973)
P.O. Box 110 (05702-0110)
PHONE....................................802 775-1029
Mark Lawrence, *President*
Patricia Lawrence, *Vice Pres*
EMP: 10
SALES (est): 1.1MM **Privately Held**
SIC: 2752 Lithographic Commercial Printing

(G-22333)
ELLISON SURFACE TECH - W LLC
112 Quality Ln (05701-4745)
PHONE....................................802 773-4278
Robert Ellison, *Branch Mgr*
EMP: 5 **Privately Held**
SIC: 3479 Coating/Engraving Service
HQ: Ellison Surface Technologies - West, Llc
8093 Columbia Rd Ste 201
Mason OH 45040

(G-22334)
EMPORIUM
Also Called: Long Trail Glass Distributor
133 Strongs Ave (05701-4440)
PHONE....................................802 773-4478
James Stone, *President*
EMP: 5
SALES: 500K **Privately Held**
SIC: 3911 Mfg Precious Metal Jewelry

(G-22335)
GENERAL ELECTRIC COMPANY
210 Columbian Ave (05701-2799)
PHONE....................................802 775-9842
Doug Folsom, *Branch Mgr*
Tim Henderson, *Analyst*
EMP: 1400
SALES (corp-wide): 121.6B **Publicly Held**
SIC: 3724 3714 Mfg Aircraft Engines/Parts Mfg Motor Vehicle Parts/Accessories
PA: General Electric Company
5 Necco St
Boston MA 02210
617 443-3000

(G-22336)
GRAPHIC EDGE INC
Also Called: Keith's Sports Ltd II
155 Seward Rd (05701-4739)
P.O. Box 757 (05702-0757)
PHONE....................................802 855-8840
Pat Venteicher, *Branch Mgr*
EMP: 30
SALES (corp-wide): 45.2MM **Privately Held**
SIC: 2759 Commercial Printing
PA: The Graphic Edge Inc
743 E Us Highway 30
Carroll IA 51401
712 792-7777

(G-22337)
GREEN MOUNTAIN RECOGNITION
9 Grandview Ter (05701-3749)
PHONE....................................802 775-7063
Dale Patterson, *President*
EMP: 5
SQ FT: 13,000
SALES (est): 380.4K **Privately Held**
WEB: www.greenmr.com
SIC: 3993 Mfg Signs/Advertising Specialties

(G-22338)
HERALD ASSOCIATION INC
Also Called: Rutland Herald
27 Wales St (05701-4027)
P.O. Box 668 (05702-0668)
PHONE....................................802 747-6121
Robert J Mitchell, *President*
John Mitchell, *President*
Robert G Miller, *Vice Pres*
EMP: 130 **EST:** 1947
SALES (est): 8.6MM **Privately Held**
WEB: www.vermonttoday.com
SIC: 2711 2796 2791 2759 Newspapers-Publish/Print Platemaking Services Typesetting Services Commercial Printing

(G-22339)
INITIAL IDEAS INC (PA)
142 West St (05701-2860)
P.O. Box 186 (05702-0186)
PHONE....................................802 773-6310
Peter Louras, *President*
EMP: 13
SQ FT: 6,000
SALES (est): 957.8K **Privately Held**
SIC: 2395 Pleating/Stitching Services

(G-22340)
INITIAL IDEAS INC
378 Quality Ln (05701-4919)
PHONE....................................802 775-1685
Peter Louras, *Branch Mgr*
EMP: 3
SALES (corp-wide): 957.8K **Privately Held**
SIC: 2499 Mfg Wood Products
PA: Initial Ideas Inc
142 West St
Rutland VT 05701
802 773-6310

(G-22341)
ISOVOLTA INC
477 Windcrest Rd (05701)
PHONE....................................802 775-5528
Heinz Riedler, *President*
Johnnes Mensporss, *President*
John Roberts, *Plant Mgr*
Lawrence Bilodeau, *QC Mgr*
Jordi Casanas, *Treasurer*
▲ **EMP:** 35
SQ FT: 50,000
SALES (est): 10.1MM
SALES (corp-wide): 10.3MM **Privately Held**
WEB: www.ussamica.com
SIC: 3644 3295 Mfg Nonconductive Wiring Devices Mfg Minerals-Ground/Treated
HQ: Isovolta Ag
Iz No-Sud/StraBe 3, Objekt 1
Wr. Neudorf 2355
595 950-

(G-22342)
KEEBOWIL INC
126 Spruce St (05701-4420)
P.O. Box 237 (05702-0237)
PHONE....................................802 775-3572
Richard L Sharon, *Opers-Prdtn-Mfg*
EMP: 35
SALES (corp-wide): 39.7MM **Privately Held**
WEB: www.melanson.com
SIC: 3444 Sheet Metal Fabrication
PA: Keebowil, Inc.
353 West St
Keene NH 03431
603 352-4232

(G-22343)
LEADER EVAPORATORINC
Also Called: Grimm, G H Co
2 Pine St (05701-2855)
PHONE....................................802 775-5411
John Record, *President*
Gary Gaudette, *Principal*
Jean Guilmette, *Admin Sec*
EMP: 39 **EST:** 1890
SALES (est): 3.3MM
SALES (corp-wide): 13.1MM **Privately Held**
SIC: 3523 Mfg Farm Machinery/Equipment
PA: Leader Evaporator Co., Inc.
49 Jonergin Dr
Swanton VT 05488
802 868-5444

(G-22344)
LENCO INC
175 Quality Ln (05701-4995)
P.O. Box 979 (05702-0979)
PHONE....................................802 775-2505
Harold Leonard Jr, *President*
David Leonard, *Vice Pres*
Dorothea Leonard, *Treasurer*
▲ **EMP:** 20
SALES (est): 3MM **Privately Held**
WEB: www.lencom.net
SIC: 3827 Mfg Optical Instruments/Lenses

(G-22345)
MARIAH GROUP LLC
92 Park St (05701-5079)
PHONE....................................802 747-4000
Doug Babbitt, *Vice Pres*
EMP: 99
SALES (est): 6.7MM **Privately Held**
SIC: 2435 Hardwood Veneer And Plywood, Nsk

(G-22346)
NEW ENGLAND SMOKED SEAFOOD
Also Called: Noel Specialty Foods
46 Hazel St (05701-2618)
PHONE....................................802 773-4628
William S Noel, *President*
Kimberly Noel, *Admin Sec*
EMP: 3
SQ FT: 1,400
SALES (est): 392.3K **Privately Held**
SIC: 2013 5812 Mfg Prepared Meats Eating Place

(G-22347)
QUESTECH CORPORATION (PA)
Also Called: Questech Metals
92 Park St (05701-4710)
PHONE....................................802 773-1228
Barry Culkin, *President*
Gary Marmer, *Vice Pres*
Peter Schelle, *Vice Pres*
Jeff Douglass, *Opers Mgr*
Robert Bates, *Purch Mgr*
EMP: 20
SQ FT: 20,000
SALES (est): 15MM **Privately Held**
SIC: 3089 Mfg Plastic Products

(G-22348)
QUESTECH TILE LLC
92 Park St (05701-4710)
PHONE....................................802 773-1228
EMP: 3
SALES (est): 123.8K **Privately Held**
SIC: 3089 Mfg Plastic Products

(G-22349)
RUTLAND CITY BAND
129 Cannon Dr (05701-9376)
PHONE....................................802 775-5378
EMP: 4
SALES: 6.5K **Privately Held**
SIC: 2711 Newspapers-Publishing/Printing

(G-22350)
RUTLAND PLYWOOD CORP
92 Park St Ste 1 (05701-3856)
PHONE....................................802 747-4000
Jack Barrett, *CEO*
EMP: 4 **EST:** 2014
SALES (est): 350.5K **Privately Held**
SIC: 2435 Hardwood Veneer And Plywood, Nsk

(G-22351)
RUTLAND PRINTING CO INC
267 Lincoln Ave (05701-2407)
PHONE....................................802 775-1948
Salvatore Bellomo, *President*
Barbara Bellomo, *Admin Sec*
EMP: 6 **EST:** 1945
SQ FT: 4,000
SALES: 480K **Privately Held**
SIC: 2752 2759 Commercial Offset & Letterpress Printing

(G-22352)
SAMS GOOD NEWS
162 N Main St Ste 8 (05701-3024)
PHONE....................................802 773-4040
Samuel Gorrusso, *President*
EMP: 12
SALES (est): 685.4K **Privately Held**
WEB: www.samsgoodnews.com
SIC: 2711 Newspapers-Publishing/Printing

(G-22353)
SBFK INC
251 West St Unit A (05701-2851)
PHONE....................................802 297-7665
Robert Hausslein, *President*
EMP: 3
SALES (est): 181K **Privately Held**
SIC: 2099 Mfg Food Preparations

(G-22354)
STO CORP
251 Quality Ln (05701-4994)
PHONE....................................802 775-4117
Jeff Fay, *Warehouse Mgr*
Guy Auger, *Opers-Prdtn-Mfg*
EMP: 30
SALES (corp-wide): 398.1K **Privately Held**
SIC: 2899 2851 Mfg Chemical Preparations Mfg Paints/Allied Products
HQ: Sto Corp.
3800 Camp Creek Pkwy Sw 1400-120
Atlanta GA 30331
404 346-3666

(G-22355)
STRATABOND CO INC
92 Park St (05701-5079)
PHONE....................................802 747-4000
John M Barrett, *Manager*
EMP: 4
SALES (est): 416.4K **Privately Held**
SIC: 2435 Mfg Hardwood Veneer/Plywood

(G-22356)
TUTTLE LAW PRINT INC
Also Called: Tuttle Printing & Engraving
414 Quality Ln 453 (05701-4999)
P.O. Box 110 (05702-0110)
PHONE....................................802 773-9171
Deva M Bolgioni, *Ch of Bd*
Joanne M Cillo, *President*
Shirley Moody, *Sales Staff*
Thomas Brooks, *Technology*
R Joseph O'Rourke, *Admin Sec*
EMP: 62 **EST:** 1912
SQ FT: 34,000
SALES (est): 9.7MM **Privately Held**
WEB: www.tuttleprinting.com
SIC: 2752 2791 2759 Lithographic Coml Print Typesetting Services Commercial Printing

(G-22357)
UNILEVER BESTFOODS NORTH AMER
Also Called: Bouyea-Fassetts
69 Park St (05701-4708)
PHONE....................................802 775-4986
Phil Beudin, *Manager*
EMP: 8
SALES (corp-wide): 56.5B **Privately Held**
WEB: www.bestfoods.com
SIC: 2051 Mfg Bread/Related Products
HQ: Unilever Bestfoods North America
800 Sylvan Ave
Englewood Cliffs NJ 07632

(G-22358)
VERMONT ART STUDIO INC
175 Woodstock Ave (05701-3317)
PHONE....................................802 747-7446

Aaron Davis, *President*
EMP: 3
SQ FT: 5,000
SALES (est): 307.2K **Privately Held**
WEB: www.vermontartstudio.com
SIC: 2759 Screen Printing

(G-22359)
VERMONT CANVAS PRODUCTS
259 Woodstock Ave (05701)
PHONE..................................802 773-7311
Gail Dufresne, *Owner*
EMP: 5
SALES: 130K **Privately Held**
SIC: 2394 Mfg Canvas/Related Products

(G-22360)
VERMONT QUARRIES CORP
1591 Us Route 4 (05701-6605)
PHONE..................................802 775-1065
Fabrizio Ponzanelli, *President*
Vincenzo Maucchelli, *Treasurer*
Luca Mannolini, *Executive*
Melissa Dahlin, *Admin Asst*
◆ **EMP:** 18
SQ FT: 1,300
SALES (est): 6.4MM **Privately Held**
WEB: www.vermontquarries.com
SIC: 1411 5032 Dimension Stone Quarry Whol Brick/Stone Material

(G-22361)
WIRELESS FOR LESS
Also Called: the Installation Station
161 S Main St (05701-4439)
PHONE..................................802 786-0918
Matthew Maniaci, *Owner*
EMP: 4
SQ FT: 1,800
SALES: 105K **Privately Held**
SIC: 3663 Wireless Telecommunications And Peripheral Devices

Saint Albans
Franklin County

(G-22362)
14TH STAR BREWING LLC
133 N Main St Ste 7 (05478-1735)
PHONE..................................802 528-5988
Steven Gagner, *Mng Member*
EMP: 5 **EST:** 2014
SQ FT: 16,000
SALES (est): 519.3K **Privately Held**
SIC: 2082 Mfg Malt Beverages

(G-22363)
ALLTECH INC
90 Parah Dr (05478-2622)
PHONE..................................802 524-7460
EMP: 7
SALES (corp-wide): 1.5B **Privately Held**
SIC: 2869 Mfg Industl Organic Chem
PA: Alltech, Inc.
3031 Catnip Hill Rd
Nicholasville KY 40356
859 885-9613

(G-22364)
BARRY CALLEBAUT USA LLC
400 Industrial Park Rd (05478-1875)
PHONE..................................802 524-9711
Peter Totten, *Maint Spvr*
Carmen Hartmann, *Manager*
Anthony Loignon, *Manager*
Gary Ovitt, *Manager*
EMP: 58
SALES (corp-wide): 46.1MM **Privately Held**
SIC: 2066 Mfg Chocolate/Cocoa Products
HQ: Barry Callebaut U.S.A. Llc
600 W Chicago Ave Ste 860
Chicago IL 60654

(G-22365)
CO OP CREAMERY
140 Federal St (05478-2015)
PHONE..................................802 524-6581
EMP: 4 **EST:** 2001
SALES (est): 248.7K **Privately Held**
SIC: 2021 Mfg Creamery Butter

(G-22366)
COSMIC BAKERS OF VERMONT LLC
30 S Main St (05478-2202)
PHONE..................................802 524-0800
EMP: 10
SALES (est): 56.6K **Privately Held**
SIC: 2053 Mfg Frozen Bakery Products

(G-22367)
DRINKMAPLE
75 N Elm St (05478-2121)
PHONE..................................802 528-5279
Kathryn Weiler, *Director*
EMP: 3 **EST:** 2016
SALES (est): 232.4K **Privately Held**
SIC: 2099 Mfg Food Preparations

(G-22368)
EDGEWELL PER CARE BRANDS LLC
75 Swanton Rd (05478-2614)
PHONE..................................802 524-2151
Javad Mirtanah, *Opers-Prdtn-Mfg*
EMP: 181
SALES (corp-wide): 2.1B **Publicly Held**
WEB: www.eveready.com
SIC: 3421 Mfg Primary Batteries
HQ: Edgewell Personal Care Brands, Llc
6 Research Dr
Shelton CT 06484
203 944-5500

(G-22369)
J C IMAGE INC
88 Walnut St (05478-2145)
PHONE..................................802 527-1557
Jay Cummings, *President*
EMP: 9
SQ FT: 4,000
SALES (est): 730.2K **Privately Held**
WEB: www.jcimage.com
SIC: 2395 Pleating/Stitching Services

(G-22370)
JAMISON COMPUTER SERVICES
1624 Cline Rd (05478-3109)
P.O. Box 566, Saint Albans Bay (05481-0566)
PHONE..................................802 527-9758
Tom Jameison, *Owner*
EMP: 3
SALES (est): 247.1K **Privately Held**
SIC: 7372 Prepackaged Software Services

(G-22371)
L & B ASSOCIATES INC
1088 Cook Rd (05478-8074)
PHONE..................................802 868-5210
Ed Laberge, *Manager*
EMP: 6
SALES (corp-wide): 1.5MM **Privately Held**
SIC: 3498 5085 Mfg Fabricated Pipe/Fittings Whol Industrial Supplies
PA: L & B Associates, Inc.
1150 Tolland St
East Hartford CT 06108
860 528-0385

(G-22372)
MILTON INDEPENDENT INC
Also Called: Lynn Publishing Group
281 N Main St (05478-2503)
PHONE..................................802 893-2028
Emerson Lynn, *President*
EMP: 3
SALES (est): 195.2K **Privately Held**
SIC: 2711 Newspapers-Publishing/Printing

(G-22373)
MYLAN TECHNOLOGIES INC (DH)
110 Lake St (05478-2287)
PHONE..................................802 527-7792
Harry Korman, *President*
Matthew Erick, *Principal*
David Kennedy, *Vice Pres*
Brian Byala, *Treasurer*
William Coseo, *Info Tech Dir*
◆ **EMP:** 170 **EST:** 1992
SQ FT: 100,000
SALES (est): 45MM
SALES (corp-wide): 204.1K **Privately Held**
WEB: www.mylantech.com
SIC: 2834 2833 2675 2891 Mfg Pharmaceutical Preps Mfg Medicinal/Botanicals Mfg Die-Cut Paper/Board Mfg Adhesives/Sealants
HQ: Mylan Inc
1000 Mylan Blvd
Canonsburg PA 15317
724 514-1800

(G-22374)
MYLAN TECHNOLOGIES INC
700 Industrial Park Rd (05478-1889)
PHONE..................................802 527-7792
EMP: 8
SALES (corp-wide): 204.1K **Privately Held**
SIC: 2834 Mfg Pharmaceutical Preparations
HQ: Mylan Technologies, Inc.
110 Lake St
Saint Albans VT 05478
802 527-7792

(G-22375)
MYSTIC MOUNTAIN MAPLES LLC
77 Rock Island Rd (05478-3061)
PHONE..................................802 524-6163
Bret McCuin, *Partner*
EMP: 3 **EST:** 2014
SALES (est): 213.2K **Privately Held**
SIC: 2099 Mfg Food Preparations

(G-22376)
NORTHEAST AGGREGATE CORP
1881 Sheldon Rd (05478-8082)
PHONE..................................802 524-2627
Ivan Charbonneau, *President*
Ryan Charbonneau, *Vice Pres*
EMP: 5
SALES (est): 372.6K **Privately Held**
SIC: 1442 Construction Sand/Gravel

(G-22377)
QST INC
Also Called: Q S T
300 Industrial Park Rd (05478-1899)
PHONE..................................802 524-7704
Paul Burke, *Mfg Staff*
James E Morrison, *CFO*
▲ **EMP:** 37
SQ FT: 42,000
SALES (est): 6.9MM
SALES (corp-wide): 845.9MM **Privately Held**
SIC: 2821 5169 2822 Mfg Plstc Material/Resin Whol Chemicals/Products Mfg Synthetic Rubber
PA: Teknor Apex Company
505 Central Ave
Pawtucket RI 02861
401 725-8000

(G-22378)
SOLO CUP OPERATING CORPORATION
Hoffmaster Division
1521 Lower Newton Rd (05478)
PHONE..................................802 524-5966
EMP: 10
SQ FT: 485,000
SALES (corp-wide): 1.3B **Privately Held**
SIC: 2679 Mfg Converted Paper Products
HQ: Solo Cup Operating Corporation
300 Tr State Intl Ste 200
Lincolnshire IL 48854
847 444-5000

(G-22379)
ST ALBANS COOPERATIVE CRMRY
140 Federal St (05478-2000)
PHONE..................................802 524-9366
Ralph McNall, *President*
Michael Janson, *CFO*
Leon Berthiaume, *Exec Dir*
Bryan Davis, *Admin Sec*
EMP: 70
SQ FT: 2,000
SALES (est): 253.9MM **Privately Held**
WEB: www.stalbanscooperative.com
SIC: 2026 2023 Mfg Fluid Milk Mfg Dry/Evaporated Dairy Products

(G-22380)
SUPERIOR TCHNCAL CERAMICS CORP
600 Industrial Park Rd (05478-1877)
PHONE..................................802 527-7726
Richard Feeser, *President*
John Goodrich, *President*
Peter Hunter, *Principal*
James Ward, *Principal*
Brian Gold, *Corp Secy*
▲ **EMP:** 147 **EST:** 1978
SQ FT: 123,500
SALES (est): 31.7MM **Privately Held**
WEB: www.ceramic.net
SIC: 3644 3264 3724 3769 Mfg Nonconductv Wire Dvc Mfg Porcelain Elc Supply Mfg Aircraft Engine/Part
PA: Artemis Capital Partners
1150 Main St Ste 5
Concord MA 01742
617 830-1117

(G-22381)
TEKNOR APEX CO
300 Industrial Park Rd (05478-1899)
PHONE..................................802 524-7704
Paul Burke, *Vice Pres*
▼ **EMP:** 12 **EST:** 2011
SALES (est): 1.6MM **Privately Held**
SIC: 3089 Mfg Plastic Materials/Resins

(G-22382)
TRAVIS M BONNETT
Also Called: Vermont Made Scents
6 Rublee St (05478-1528)
PHONE..................................802 524-1890
Travis Bonnett, *Owner*
EMP: 12 **EST:** 1997
SQ FT: 1,700
SALES: 186K **Privately Held**
SIC: 3999 Mfg Candles

(G-22383)
TROY MICRO FIVE INC
79 Walnut St (05478-2144)
PHONE..................................802 524-0076
Gabriel Paquett, *Manager*
EMP: 9
SALES (corp-wide): 18.7MM **Privately Held**
WEB: www.oldmilltroy.com
SIC: 2833 Mfg Vitamins & Minerals
PA: Troy Micro Five, Inc.
53 E Main St
North Troy VT 05859
802 988-4474

(G-22384)
VERMONT PUBLISHING COMANY
Also Called: St Albans Messenger
281 N Main St (05478-2503)
P.O. Box 1250 (05478-1250)
PHONE..................................802 524-9771
Emerson Lynn, *President*
Lynne Fletcher, *Prdtn Mgr*
Jeremy Read, *Adv Dir*
EMP: 39 **EST:** 1861
SQ FT: 12,000
SALES (est): 2.7MM **Privately Held**
WEB: www.samessenger.com
SIC: 2711 2752 2741 Newspaper Publishing & Printing

(G-22385)
ZONEUP INC
2396 Highgate Rd (05478-9795)
PHONE..................................802 868-2300
Andrea Forrest, *President*
EMP: 3
SALES (est): 215.5K **Privately Held**
SIC: 3524 Mfg Lawn/Garden Equipment

Saint Johnsbury
Caledonia County

(G-22386)
BIMBO BAKERIES USA INC
1188 Memorial Dr (05819-9249)
PHONE..................................802 748-1389
Brenda Sargent, *Branch Mgr*
EMP: 4 **Privately Held**
WEB: www.gwbakeries.com
SIC: 2051 Mfg Bread/Related Products
HQ: Bimbo Bakeries Usa, Inc
255 Business Center Dr # 200
Horsham PA 19044
215 347-5500

(G-22387)
BLUE OX ENTERPRISE INC
Also Called: B O E
2085 New Boston Rd (05819-8797)
PHONE..................................802 274-4494
Pierre Fortin, *President*
Gary Hockerman, *Vice Pres*
EMP: 5
SALES (est): 417.3K **Privately Held**
WEB: www.blueoxequipment.com
SIC: 3531 Mfg Construction Machinery

(G-22388)
CALEDONIA INC (PA)
Also Called: Calco
2878 Vt Route 18 (05819-9714)
P.O. Box 631 (05819-0631)
PHONE..................................802 748-2319
Ken Wood, *President*
James Wilkins, *Vice Pres*
Betsy Forgin, *Admin Sec*
EMP: 12
SQ FT: 15,000
SALES: 1.1MM **Privately Held**
WEB: www.caledonia.com
SIC: 3272 Mfg Pre-Cast Concrete Products

(G-22389)
CALEDONIAN RECORD PUBG CO INC (PA)
Also Called: Caledonian-Record
190 Federal St (05819-5616)
P.O. Box 8 (05819-0008)
PHONE..................................802 748-8121
Mark Smith, *President*
Michael Gonyaw, *Adv Dir*
Rosie Chaloux, *Director*
EMP: 51
SQ FT: 8,000
SALES (est): 8.7MM **Privately Held**
WEB: www.caledonian-record.com
SIC: 2711 7375 Newspapers-Publishing/Printing Information Retrieval Services

(G-22390)
LYNDON WOODWORKING INC (PA)
Also Called: Lyndon Furniture
1135 Industrial Pkwy (05819)
P.O. Box 45, Lyndon (05849-0045)
PHONE..................................802 748-0100
David Allard, *President*
Judy Allard, *Vice Pres*
Ball Brian, *Vice Pres*
EMP: 50
SQ FT: 10,000
SALES (est): 10.3MM **Privately Held**
WEB: www.lyndon.com
SIC: 2511 2499 Mfg Wood Household Furniture Mfg Wood Products

(G-22391)
MAPLE GROVE FARMS VERMONT INC (HQ)
1052 Portland St (05819-2041)
PHONE..................................802 748-5141
David L Wenner, *President*
David H Burke, *Vice Pres*
Mark Bigelow, *Plant Mgr*
Robert C Cantwell, *Treasurer*
▲ **EMP:** 100 **EST:** 1915
SQ FT: 250,000
SALES (est): 13.3MM
SALES (corp-wide): 1.7B **Publicly Held**
WEB: www.maplegrove.com
SIC: 2099 2035 2045 2087 Mfg Food Preparations Mfg Pickles/Sauces Mfg Prepared Flour Mixes Mfg Flavor Extracts Mfg Candy/Confectionery
PA: B&G Foods, Inc.
4 Gatehall Dr Ste 110
Parsippany NJ 07054
973 401-6500

(G-22392)
NORTH EAST PRECISION INC
3606 Memorial Dr (05819-8777)
PHONE..................................802 748-1440
EMP: 57
SQ FT: 43,000
SALES (est): 10.8MM **Privately Held**
WEB: www.neprecision.net
SIC: 3599 Mfg Industrial Machinery

(G-22393)
NSA INDUSTRIES LLC (PA)
210 Pierce Rd (05819-8343)
P.O. Box 54, Lyndonville (05851-0054)
PHONE..................................802 748-5007
James Moroney, *CEO*
Ed Stanley, *Vice Pres*
James Meyers, *Prdtn Mgr*
Nicole Dewing, *Purch Mgr*
Shelley Newland, *Buyer*
▲ **EMP:** 162
SQ FT: 170,000
SALES (est): 42.8MM **Privately Held**
WEB: www.nsaindustries.com
SIC: 3444 1799 1796 Mfg Sheet Metal-work Trade Contractor Building Equipment Installation

(G-22394)
ROBILLARDS APPLE CRISP
184 Barker Ave (05819-2345)
PHONE..................................802 748-4451
EMP: 3
SALES (est): 301.3K **Privately Held**
SIC: 3571 Mfg Electronic Computers

(G-22395)
SILVER MOUNTAIN GRAPHICS INC
89 Maple St (05819-2273)
PHONE..................................802 748-1170
Judith Bourque, *President*
Kim Poach, *Partner*
EMP: 4
SQ FT: 3,000
SALES (est): 608.7K **Privately Held**
SIC: 2752 Lithographic Commercial Printing

(G-22396)
TJ MOLD AND TOOL COMPANY INC
61 Lewis Ct (05819-2679)
PHONE..................................802 748-1390
Todd A Colby, *President*
Joseph Peters, *Vice Pres*
Diane Colby, *Treasurer*
EMP: 5
SQ FT: 3,800
SALES (est): 618.9K **Privately Held**
SIC: 3599 3544 Mfg Industrial Machinery Mfg Dies/Tools/Jigs/Fixt

(G-22397)
WICOR AMERICAS INC (HQ)
1 Gordon Mills Way (05819-8925)
PHONE..................................802 751-3404
Jurg Brunner, *President*
Rob Begin, *General Mgr*
Bill Stimpson, *General Mgr*
Justin Crocker, *Engineer*
Bernie Brochu, *Project Engr*
◆ **EMP:** 18
SALES (est): 112.8MM
SALES (corp-wide): 365.5MM **Privately Held**
SIC: 3694 Mfg Engine Electrical Equipment
PA: Weidmann Holding Ag
Neue Jonastrasse 60
Rapperswil SG 8640
412 214-109

Salisbury
Addison County

(G-22398)
AQUA VITEA LLC
8 Shard Villa Rd (05769-9432)
PHONE..................................802 352-1049
Jeff Weaber,
EMP: 3
SALES (est): 276.4K **Privately Held**
SIC: 2087 Mfg Flavor Extracts/Syrup

(G-22399)
MERLE SCHLOFF
Also Called: Otter Creek Furniture
Prospect St (05769)
P.O. Box 125 (05769-0125)
PHONE..................................802 352-4246
Merle Schloff, *President*
EMP: 3
SQ FT: 6,000
SALES (est): 185.4K **Privately Held**
SIC: 2511 Mfg Wood Household Furniture

Sandgate
Bennington County

(G-22400)
FORTUNAS SAUSAGE CO LLC
Also Called: Fortuna's Italian Market
723 Stannard Rd (05250-9088)
P.O. Box 130, Arlington (05250-0130)
PHONE..................................802 375-0200
Patti Stannard, *Mng Member*
EMP: 5
SALES (est): 150.5K **Privately Held**
SIC: 2013 Mfg Prepared Meats

Saxtons River
Windham County

(G-22401)
OLD TIMERS TIMBER FRAMES
37 Westminster W Rd (05154)
PHONE..................................802 376-9529
Jason Robert Snell, *Owner*
EMP: 3
SALES (est): 211.2K **Privately Held**
SIC: 2439 7389 Mfg Structural Wood Members

Shaftsbury
Bennington County

(G-22402)
DAILEY PRECAST LLC
381 Airport Rd (05262-4409)
PHONE..................................802 442-4418
Noble Levefque, *Manager*
EMP: 5
SALES (corp-wide): 171.1MM **Privately Held**
SIC: 3273 Mfg Ready-Mixed Concrete
HQ: Dailey Precast, Llc
295 Airport Rd
Shaftsbury VT 05262
802 442-4418

(G-22403)
KCM OIL
2155 East Rd (05262-9794)
PHONE..................................802 447-7371
Michael Greene, *Principal*
EMP: 4 **EST:** 2016
SALES (est): 119.9K **Privately Held**
SIC: 1311 Crude Petroleum/Natural Gas Production

(G-22404)
LEO D BERNSTEIN & SONS INC
372 Vt Route 67 E (05262-9425)
PHONE..................................802 442-8029
Anthony Tripoli, *Branch Mgr*
EMP: 65
SALES (corp-wide): 19MM **Privately Held**
WEB: www.bernsteindisplay.com
SIC: 3999 2541 5046 7389 Mfg Display Forms Wooden Partitions Whol Commercial Equipment & Business Services
PA: Leo D. Bernstein & Sons Inc.
151 W 25th St Frnt 1
New York NY 10001
212 337-9578

(G-22405)
LEO D BERNSTEIN AND SONS INC
Also Called: Berstein Display
372 Vt Route 67 E (05262-9425)
PHONE..................................212 337-9578
Roger Friedman, *President*
Edmond Bernstein, *Corp Secy*
Michelle Bernstein, *COO*
◆ **EMP:** 145
SQ FT: 200,000
SALES (est): 12.4MM **Privately Held**
SIC: 3999 2295 Mfg Misc Products Mfg Coated Fabrics

(G-22406)
T & M ENTERPRISES INC
251 Church St (05262)
P.O. Box 410 (05262-0410)
PHONE..................................802 447-0601
Thomas T Paquin, *President*
Martha Paquin, *Corp Secy*
EMP: 9
SQ FT: 30,000
SALES (est): 1.6MM **Privately Held**
SIC: 3089 Mfg Plastic Products

(G-22407)
TOUCHFIGHT GAMES LLC
545 Twitchell Hill Rd (05262-9256)
PHONE..................................802 753-7360
Nathan Meunier, *Director*
EMP: 3
SALES: 10K **Privately Held**
SIC: 7372 7389 Prepackaged Software Services Business Services At Non-Commercial Site

Sharon
Windsor County

(G-22408)
G W PLASTICS INC
101 Commerce Park (05065)
PHONE..................................802 233-0319
Brenan Riehl, *Branch Mgr*
EMP: 5
SALES (corp-wide): 171.1MM **Privately Held**
SIC: 3089 Mfg Plastic Products
PA: G W Plastics, Inc.
239 Pleasant St
Bethel VT 05032
802 234-9941

(G-22409)
GENERAL ABRASIVES INC
Back River Rd (05065)
P.O. Box 9 (05065-0009)
PHONE..................................802 763-7264
Natascha Niffka, *President*
Natascha N Niffka, *President*
Jurgen Niffka, *Admin Sec*
Eric Janson, *Clerk*
▲ **EMP:** 10
SQ FT: 15,000
SALES (est): 1.2MM **Privately Held**
SIC: 3291 Mfg Abrasive Products

Shelburne
Chittenden County

(G-22410)
AMERICAN MEADOWS INC
Also Called: High Country Gardens
2438 Shelburne Rd (05482-6839)
PHONE..................................802 862-6560
Ethan Platt, *President*
Charlotte S Allen, *Vice Pres*
EMP: 18 **EST:** 1982

SQ FT: 6,000
SALES (est): 4.5MM **Privately Held**
WEB: www.americanmeadows.com
SIC: 2678 5621 Mfg Stationery Products

(G-22411)
ASCENSION TECHNOLOGY CORP
120 Graham Way Ste 130 (05482-7217)
P.O. Box 527, Burlington (05402-0527)
PHONE..................................802 893-6657
Ernest B Blood, *President*
Westley Ashe, *Engineer*
EMP: 50
SQ FT: 20,000
SALES (est): 800.8K **Privately Held**
WEB: www.ascension-tech.com
SIC: 3841 Mfg Of Surgical And Medical Instruments

(G-22412)
AUTISM SUPPORT DAILY
42 Oakhill Rd (05482-6732)
P.O. Box 4556, Burlington (05406-4556)
PHONE..................................802 985-8773
Lynn M George, *Principal*
EMP: 3
SALES (est): 144.1K **Privately Held**
SIC: 2711 Newspapers-Publishing/Printing

(G-22413)
BEEKEN/PARSONS INC
1611 Harbor Rd (05482-7697)
PHONE..................................802 985-2913
Bruce Beeken, *President*
EMP: 3
SQ FT: 6,500
SALES: 200K **Privately Held**
WEB: www.beekenparsons.com
SIC: 2511 5712 Mfg & Ret Wood Furniture

(G-22414)
BRETT LEWIS THREADS LTD
Also Called: BLT
118 Peeper Pond Ln (05482-6406)
PHONE..................................802 985-1166
Brett Lewis, *President*
Willmott Lewis Jr, *Bd of Directors*
Kathryne Lewis, *Admin Sec*
EMP: 5
SQ FT: 1,800
SALES: 400K **Privately Held**
SIC: 2395 Pleating/Stitching Services

(G-22415)
EATING WELL INC (HQ)
Also Called: Eatingwell Media Group
120 Graham Way Ste 100 (05482-7217)
PHONE..................................802 425-5700
Thomas P Witschi, *CEO*
Richard McCormick, *CFO*
James Van Fleteren, *Creative Dir*
EMP: 8
SALES (est): 2.8MM
SALES (corp-wide): 3.1B **Publicly Held**
WEB: www.eatingwell.com
SIC: 2721 Periodicals-Publishing/Printing
PA: Meredith Corporation
1716 Locust St
Des Moines IA 50309
515 284-3000

(G-22416)
EQUINOX PUBLISHING
987 Bay Rd (05482-7761)
PHONE..................................802 497-0276
Ellen L Clay, *Principal*
EMP: 4 **EST:** 2010
SALES (est): 234.1K **Privately Held**
SIC: 2741 Misc Publishing

(G-22417)
FORWARD INC
Also Called: 4frng
237 Morse Dr (05482-6423)
PHONE..................................802 585-1098
Jason Levinthal, *President*
EMP: 4
SALES (est): 120.7K **Privately Held**
SIC: 3949 7389 Mfg Sporting/Athletic Goods

(G-22418)
GSG INC
Also Called: Double Diamond Sportswear
3986 Harbor Rd (05482-7796)
PHONE..................................802 828-6221
Gary S Guggemos, *President*
Dorinda L Crowell, *Admin Sec*
▲ **EMP:** 5
SALES (est): 758.4K **Privately Held**
SIC: 2339 5136 Mfg Women's/Misses' Outerwear Whol Men's/Boy's Clothing

(G-22419)
HIBERNATION HOLDING CO INC
Also Called: Vermont Teddy Bear Company
6655 Shelburne Rd (05482-6500)
PHONE..................................802 985-3001
John Gilbert, *President*
Jason Baer, *Engineer*
EMP: 290
SALES (est): 15.4MM **Privately Held**
SIC: 3942 5961 Mfg Dolls/Stuffed Toys Ret Mail-Order House

(G-22420)
NPC PROCESSING INC
97 Executive Dr (05482-6476)
PHONE..................................802 660-0496
Daniel Desautels, *President*
Robert Desautels Jr, *Vice Pres*
Joyce Desautels, *Admin Sec*
EMP: 25
SALES (est): 5.4MM **Privately Held**
SIC: 2015 2011 2013 Poultry Processing Meat Packing Plant Mfg Prepared Meats

(G-22421)
PARKMATIC CAR PRKG SYSTEMS LLC
145 Pine Haven Shores Rd (05482-7703)
PHONE..................................802 495-0903
EMP: 3
SALES (est): 166.8K **Privately Held**
SIC: 3559 Mfg Misc Industry Machinery

(G-22422)
REEF TO RAINFOREST MEDIA LLC
140 Webster Rd (05482-7107)
P.O. Box 490 (05482-0490)
PHONE..................................802 985-9977
James Lawrence, *Principal*
EMP: 3
SALES (est): 266.3K **Privately Held**
SIC: 2721 Periodicals-Publishing/Printing

(G-22423)
RWO INC
251 Pinehurst Dr (05482-6882)
PHONE..................................802 497-1563
Randy Oglesby, *CEO*
EMP: 5
SALES (est): 601.6K **Privately Held**
SIC: 3577 Mfg Computer Peripheral Equipment

(G-22424)
SHELBURNE CORPORATION (PA)
6221 Shelburne Rd (05482-7147)
P.O. Box 158 (05482-0158)
PHONE..................................802 985-3321
Mark H Snelling, *President*
Ann Janda, *Director*
Andrew Snelling, *Admin Sec*
EMP: 14
SQ FT: 70,000
SALES (est): 1.8MM **Privately Held**
WEB: www.shelburnemuseum.org
SIC: 3469 Mfg Metal Stampings

(G-22425)
SPARK VT INC
6221 Shelburne Rd (05482-7147)
P.O. Box 158 (05482-0158)
PHONE..................................802 985-3321
▲ **EMP:** 11 **EST:** 1962
SQ FT: 73,000
SALES (est): 855.8K
SALES (corp-wide): 1.9MM **Privately Held**
WEB: www.mechwin.com
SIC: 3351 Copper Rolling/Drawing
PA: The Shelburne Corporation
6221 Shelburne Rd
Shelburne VT 05482
802 985-3321

(G-22426)
VERMONT TEDDY BEAR CO INC
Also Called: Pajama Gram Company
6655 Shelburne Rd (05482-6910)
P.O. Box 965 (05482-0965)
PHONE..................................802 985-1319
Bill Shouldice IV, *CEO*
John F Gilbert, *President*
Catherine Camardo, *COO*
Jason Baer, *Vice Pres*
Nic Deboulay, *Vice Pres*
▲ **EMP:** 140
SALES (est): 55.9MM **Privately Held**
SIC: 3942 5961 5699 Mfg Dolls/Stuffed Toys Ret Mail-Order House Ret Misc Apparel/Accessories

(G-22427)
WILD HART DISTILLERY
26 Sage Ct (05482-1100)
PHONE..................................802 489-5067
EMP: 4
SALES (est): 242K **Privately Held**
SIC: 2085 Mfg Distilled/Blended Liquor

Sheldon
Franklin County

(G-22428)
GRANT JOHN
Also Called: Grizzly Graphix
16 Sheldon Hts (05483-9754)
PHONE..................................802 933-4808
John Grant, *Principal*
EMP: 3
SALES (est): 202.8K **Privately Held**
SIC: 3861 Commercial Printing

(G-22429)
ROGER REED
351 Central St (05483-9663)
PHONE..................................802 933-2535
Roger Reed, *Principal*
EMP: 3
SALES (est): 160.5K **Privately Held**
SIC: 2062 7389 Cane Sugar Refining Business Services At Non-Commercial Site

Sheldon Springs
Franklin County

(G-22430)
WESTROCK CONVERTING COMPANY
369 Mill St (05485)
PHONE..................................802 933-7733
EMP: 3
SALES (corp-wide): 18.2B **Publicly Held**
SIC: 2631 Paperboard Mill
HQ: Westrock Converting, Llc
1000 Abernathy Rd Ste 125
Atlanta GA 30328
770 448-2193

(G-22431)
WESTROCK CP LLC
Also Called: Rock-Tenn Missisquoi Mill
369 Mill St (05485)
P.O. Box 98 (05485-0098)
PHONE..................................802 933-7733
Chris Ham-Ellis, *Branch Mgr*
EMP: 146
SALES (corp-wide): 18.2B **Publicly Held**
WEB: www.rocktenn.com
SIC: 2631 2611 Paperboard Mill Pulp Mill
HQ: Westrock Cp, Llc
1000 Abernathy Rd
Atlanta GA 30328

Shoreham
Addison County

(G-22432)
GOAMERICAGO BEVERAGES LLC
2139 Quiet Valley Rd (05770-9710)
PHONE..................................802 897-7700
Sivan Cotel, *COO*
Raj Bhakta,
EMP: 6
SALES (est): 105.9K **Privately Held**
SIC: 2085 Mfg Distilled/Blended Liquor
PA: Whistlepig, Llc
2139 Quiet Valley Rd
Shoreham VT 05770

(G-22433)
S M T GRAPHICS LLC
Also Called: Middlebury Print & Copy
260 Shacksboro Rd (05770-9587)
PHONE..................................802 897-5231
Sam Trudel, *President*
EMP: 5
SQ FT: 1,500
SALES (est): 430K **Privately Held**
SIC: 2752 7334 Offset Printing And Photocopying Services

(G-22434)
WHISTLEPIG LLC (PA)
2139 Quiet Valley Rd (05770-9710)
PHONE..................................802 897-7700
Raj Bhakta, *CEO*
Sivan Cotel, *COO*
EMP: 15
SALES (est): 3.5MM **Privately Held**
SIC: 2085 Mfg Distilled/Blended Liquor

South Burlington
Chittenden County

(G-22435)
AEROPARTS PLUS INC
12 Gregory Dr Ste 1 (05403-6058)
PHONE..................................802 489-5023
David Gregory, *President*
EMP: 3
SQ FT: 1,250
SALES: 125K **Privately Held**
SIC: 3724 5088 Mfg Aircraft Engines/Parts Whol Transportation Equipment

(G-22436)
ALEXANDRIA PRESS
Also Called: Alexandria Communications
11 Harbor Ridge Rd (05403-7880)
PHONE..................................802 497-0074
Michael Albertson, *Owner*
Skip Jorckel, *Publisher*
Rachel Sykes, *Publisher*
EMP: 5
SALES (est): 180K **Privately Held**
WEB: www.alexandria-press.com
SIC: 2731 Books-Publishing/Printing

(G-22437)
AVIATRON INC (US)
25 Customs Dr (05403-6067)
PHONE..................................802 865-9318
Ross Carpenter, *Vice Pres*
Stuart Monteith, *Purch Mgr*
Paul Charron, *Manager*
Todd Callender, *Exec Dir*
EMP: 17
SALES (est): 2.2MM **Privately Held**
WEB: www.aviatron.com
SIC: 3679 Mfg Electronic Components

(G-22438)
BIRNN CHOCOLATES VERMONT INC
102 Kimball Ave Ste 4 (05403-6800)
PHONE..................................802 860-1047
H Jeffrey Birnn, *President*
William M Birnn, *Vice Pres*
Melvin Fields, *Info Tech Mgr*
Christina Burbo, *Admin Asst*
▲ **EMP:** 18

GEOGRAPHIC

SQ FT: 18,000
SALES (est): 4.5MM **Privately Held**
WEB: www.birnn.com
SIC: 2066 5149 Mfg Chocolate/Cocoa Products Whol Groceries

(G-22439)
BOUTIN MCQUISTON INC (PA)
Also Called: Vermont Business Magazine
365 Dorset St (05403-6210)
PHONE..................................802 863-8038
John Boutin, *President*
Tim McQuiston, *Principal*
EMP: 16
SQ FT: 2,000
SALES: 752.1K **Privately Held**
WEB: www.vermontbiz.com
SIC: 2721 Periodicals-Publishing/Printing

(G-22440)
BURLINGTON PETROLEUM EQUIPMENT
32 San Remo Dr (05403-6310)
PHONE..................................802 864-5155
David Simendinger, *President*
EMP: 20
SALES (est): 1.5MM **Privately Held**
SIC: 3586 Mfg Measuring/Dispensing Pumps

(G-22441)
BURTON CORPORATION
Also Called: Burton Manufacturing Center
30 Technology Park Way (05403)
PHONE..................................802 652-3600
Israel Maynard, *Vice Pres*
Laurie Brunet, *Manager*
EMP: 100
SALES (corp-wide): 188.4MM **Privately Held**
WEB: www.burton.com
SIC: 3949 Mfg Snowboards
PA: The Burton Corporation
180 Queen City Park Rd
Burlington VT 05401
802 862-4500

(G-22442)
CENTRODYNE CORP OF AMERICA
75 Ethan Allen Dr (05403-5972)
PHONE..................................802 658-4715
Jack Steiner, *President*
Sheve Steiner, *Treasurer*
EMP: 4
SQ FT: 3,000
SALES (est): 482.8K **Privately Held**
WEB: www.centrodyne.com
SIC: 3825 Mfg Electrical Measuring Instruments
HQ: Centrodyne Inc
3485 Boul Thimens
Saint-Laurent QC H4R 1
514 331-8760

(G-22443)
CLARITY LABORATORIES INC
Also Called: Educational Assessment Svcs
20 Kimball Ave (05403-6840)
P.O. Box 66, Colchester (05446-0066)
PHONE..................................802 658-6321
James Pallmadge, *President*
James Tallmadge, *Psychologist*
EMP: 3
SALES: 140K **Privately Held**
SIC: 3841 Mfg Surgical/Medical Instruments

(G-22444)
CONSOLIDATED CONTAINER CO LLC
Also Called: Shelburne Plastics
8 Harbor View Rd (05403-7850)
PHONE..................................802 658-6588
Gene Torvend, *Branch Mgr*
EMP: 47
SALES (corp-wide): 14B **Publicly Held**
SIC: 3089 Mfg Plastic Products
HQ: Consolidated Container Company, Llc
2500 Windy Ridge Pkwy Se # 1400
Atlanta GA 30339
678 742-4600

(G-22445)
D G ROBERTSON INC
3016 Williston Rd (05403-6050)
P.O. Box 58, Williston (05495-0058)
PHONE..................................802 864-6027
Don Robertson, *President*
Patricia Robertson, *Admin Sec*
EMP: 6
SQ FT: 7,000
SALES (est): 680K **Privately Held**
SIC: 3272 Mfg Concrete Burial Vaults

(G-22446)
DIACO COMMUNICATION INC
Also Called: Sign-A-Rama
3073 Williston Rd (05403-6074)
PHONE..................................802 863-6233
Robert Diaco, *President*
Paula Tedford Diaco, *Treasurer*
EMP: 6
SQ FT: 3,000
SALES (est): 619.5K **Privately Held**
WEB: www.signaramavt.com
SIC: 3993 7389 Mfg Signs/Advertising Specialties Business Services

(G-22447)
DYNAPOWER COMPANY LLC (PA)
85 Meadowland Dr (05403-4401)
PHONE..................................802 860-7200
Peter Pollak, *CEO*
Adam M Knudsen, *President*
Benjamin Allen, *Engineer*
Bob Gladden, *VP Sales*
Steven Audy, *Sales Associate*
▲ **EMP:** 175 **EST:** 1963
SQ FT: 150,000
SALES (est): 35.6MM **Privately Held**
WEB: www.dynapower.com
SIC: 3677 3612 3625 3613 Mfg Elec Coil/Transfrmrs Mfg Transformers Mfg Relay/Indstl Control Mfg Switchgear/Boards

(G-22448)
HUMAN BIOMED INC
159 Crispin Dr (05403-4483)
PHONE..................................802 556-1394
Kyungsoo Lee, *CEO*
Sung Ryel Choi, *Chief Engr*
Taebeom Cho, *Development*
EMP: 3
SALES (est): 117.4K **Privately Held**
SIC: 3841 Mfg Surgical/Medical Instruments

(G-22449)
INTERGRATED CONTROL SYSTEMS
38 Eastwood Dr (05403-4403)
PHONE..................................802 658-6385
Tink Pelkey, *Principal*
EMP: 3 **EST:** 2009
SALES (est): 322.7K **Privately Held**
SIC: 3625 Mfg Relays/Industrial Controls

(G-22450)
ITECH DATA SERVICES INC
20 Kimball Ave Ste 303n (05403-6831)
PHONE..................................802 383-1500
Kishore Khandavalli, *President*
G William Meckert, *Treasurer*
EMP: 5
SALES (est): 216.8K **Privately Held**
SIC: 3679 Mfg Electronic Components

(G-22451)
JENSON ENTERPRISES LLC
Also Called: Treehouse Hardwoods & Mill Sp
1891 Williston Rd (05403-6021)
PHONE..................................802 497-3530
Carl Farnsworth, *Manager*
Lucas Jenson,
Karl Farnsworth,
EMP: 6
SALES (est): 910.7K **Privately Held**
SIC: 2541 5031 Mfg Wood Partitions/Fixtures Whol Lumber/Plywood/Millwork

(G-22452)
MACH 7 TECHNOLOGIES INC
120 Kimball Ave Ste 210 (05403-6837)
P.O. Box 586, Burlington (05402-0586)
PHONE..................................802 861-7745
Michael Jackman, *CEO*
John Memarian, *General Mgr*
Scott Rulapaugh, *Project Mgr*
Tony Palmer, *VP Engrg*
Shawn Bosley, *Engineer*
EMP: 13
SQ FT: 2,100
SALES (est): 1.7MM **Privately Held**
SIC: 7372 5045 Prepackaged Software Services Whol Computers/Peripherals
HQ: Mach7 Technologies Pte. Ltd.
28 Sin Ming Lane
Singapore 57397
622 242-10

(G-22453)
MAGIC HAT BREWING COMPANY & PE
5 Bartlett Bay Rd (05403-7727)
PHONE..................................802 658-2739
Alan Newman, *Ch of Bd*
Martin Kelly, *President*
▲ **EMP:** 70
SQ FT: 35,000
SALES (est): 9.5MM **Privately Held**
WEB: www.magichat.net
SIC: 2082 Drinking Place
HQ: Independent Brewers United Corporation
431 Pine St Ste G12
Burlington VT 05401
802 862-6114

(G-22454)
NATIONAL CHIMNEY SUPPLY
3 Green Tree Dr (05403-6025)
PHONE..................................802 861-2217
Darin Bibeau, *President*
Martin Fuller, *Treasurer*
Thomas G Dragon, *Admin Sec*
EMP: 88
SALES (est): 26.7MM **Privately Held**
WEB: www.nationalchimneyvt.com
SIC: 3317 Mfg Steel Pipe/Tubes

(G-22455)
OTHER PAPER
1340 Williston Rd Ste 201 (05403-6469)
P.O. Box 2032 (05407-2032)
PHONE..................................802 864-6670
George Chamberland, *Principal*
EMP: 5
SALES (est): 226.4K **Privately Held**
SIC: 2711 Newspapers-Publishing/Printing

(G-22456)
PAW PRINTS PRESS INC
Also Called: Paw Print Offset/Digital
12 Gregory Dr Ste 8 (05403-6058)
PHONE..................................802 865-2872
Thomas Brassard, *President*
Sharon Bessette, *Finance Mgr*
EMP: 6
SQ FT: 4,800
SALES: 800K **Privately Held**
WEB: www.paw-prints.com
SIC: 2759 2789 7331 Commercial Printing Bookbinding/Related Work Direct Mail Advertising Services

(G-22457)
PG ADAMS INC
1215 Airport Pkwy (05403-5805)
PHONE..................................802 862-8664
Paul G Adams, *President*
Ashley Adams, *Vice Pres*
Taja Hall, *Manager*
EMP: 13
SQ FT: 13,000
SALES (est): 2MM **Privately Held**
WEB: www.pgadams.com
SIC: 7692 3441 Welding Repair Structural Metal Fabrication

(G-22458)
PIONEER MOTORS AND DRIVES INC
30 Berard Dr Unit 6 (05403-5809)
PHONE..................................802 651-0114
Douglas Hoffman, *President*
Larisa Hoffman, *Treasurer*
Douglas A Hoffman, *Director*
Evan Hoffman, *Director*
Thea C Robson, *Admin Sec*
EMP: 21
SALES (est): 3.1MM **Privately Held**
WEB: www.pioneerdrives.com
SIC: 7694 Armature Rewinding

(G-22459)
PLASTIC TECHNOLOGIES MD INC
Also Called: Shelburne Plastics
8 Harbor Rd (05403)
PHONE..................................802 658-6588
Gene Torvend, *President*
John Mayer, *CFO*
EMP: 4
SALES (est): 254.8K **Privately Held**
SIC: 3085 Mfg Plastic Bottles

(G-22460)
PLASTIC TECHNOLOGIES NY LLC
Also Called: Shelborne Plastics
8 Harbor View Rd (05403-7850)
PHONE..................................802 658-6588
Gene Tovend, *President*
John Mayer, *CFO*
EMP: 3
SALES (est): 171.2K **Privately Held**
SIC: 3085 Mfg Plastic Bottles

(G-22461)
PPG INDUSTRIES INC
60 San Remo Dr (05403-6347)
PHONE..................................802 863-6387
John Currier, *Branch Mgr*
EMP: 3
SALES (corp-wide): 15.3B **Publicly Held**
SIC: 2851 Mfg Paints/Allied Products
PA: Ppg Industries, Inc.
1 Ppg Pl
Pittsburgh PA 15272
412 434-3131

(G-22462)
PROM SOFTWARE INC
150 Dorset St Ste 294 (05403-6256)
P.O. Box 4027, Burlington (05406-4027)
PHONE..................................802 862-7500
William Symmes, *President*
EMP: 10
SQ FT: 7,000
SALES (est): 1MM **Privately Held**
WEB: www.promsoft.com
SIC: 3679 7371 Mfg Electronic Components Custom Computer Programing

(G-22463)
R & W GIBSON CORP
Also Called: Kershner Sign
208 White St (05403-5940)
PHONE..................................802 864-4791
Wayne Gibson, *President*
Ruby Gibson, *Vice Pres*
Sara Gibson, *Vice Pres*
EMP: 4
SALES: 225K **Privately Held**
SIC: 3993 Mfg Signs/Advertising Specialties

(G-22464)
SARA SASSY INC
29 Myers Ct (05403-6410)
PHONE..................................802 864-4791
Sara Blanchard, *President*
Ruby Gibson, *Director*
EMP: 3
SALES: 200K **Privately Held**
SIC: 3993 Mfg Signs/Advertising Specialties

(G-22465)
SENTAR INC
Also Called: Selection Unlimited
102 Kimball Ave Ste 2 (05403-6800)
PHONE..................................802 861-6004
Ric Lashway, *President*
Derrick W Senior, *President*
Randal F Senior, *Treasurer*
▲ **EMP:** 39
SQ FT: 12,000
SALES (est): 9.1MM **Privately Held**
WEB: www.selectu.com
SIC: 2066 Mfg Chocolate/Cocoa Products

(G-22466)
SPRING FILL
1775 Williston Rd Ste 250 (05403-6491)
PHONE.................................802 846-5900
David Kline, *President*
EMP: 10
SALES (est): 900K **Privately Held**
WEB: www.spring-fill.com
SIC: 3086 Mfg Plastic Foam Products

(G-22467)
SRC LIQUIDATION COMPANY
20 Kimball Ave Ste 206 (05403-6805)
PHONE.................................802 862-9932
EMP: 3 **Publicly Held**
SIC: 2759 Commercial Printing
PA: Src Liquidation Company
600 Albany St
Dayton OH 45402
937 221-1000

(G-22468)
STEP AHEAD INNOVATIONS INC
Also Called: Mindstream
6 Green Tree Dr (05403-6025)
PHONE.................................802 233-0211
Brian Degen, *President*
James Clark, *Principal*
Giuseppe Detrucci, *Vice Pres*
EMP: 10
SALES (est): 948K **Privately Held**
SIC: 3823 Mfg Process Control Instruments

(G-22469)
SUNNY SKY PRODUCTS LLC
Also Called: Nectar Cappuccino Group
102 Kimball Ave Ste 1 (05403-6800)
P.O. Box 868, Milton (05468-0868)
PHONE.................................802 861-6004
EMP: 35
SALES (corp-wide): 24.1MM **Privately Held**
SIC: 2066 Manufatcures Chocolate/Cocoa Products
PA: Sunny Sky Products, Llc
11747 Windfern Rd Ste 100
Houston TX 77064
713 683-9399

(G-22470)
SUPER-TEMP WIRE & CABLE INC
104 Bowdoin St (05403-8021)
PHONE.................................802 655-4211
Randy Miller, *President*
Peter Kenny, *Vice Pres*
Ryan Lewis, *Production*
Jody Place, *Cust Mgr*
Erin Miller, *Manager*
EMP: 23
SQ FT: 10,000
SALES (est): 6.3MM **Privately Held**
WEB: www.super-temp.com
SIC: 3357 Nonferrous Wiredrawing/Insulating

(G-22471)
THE LANE PRESS INC
87 Meadowland Dr (05403-7605)
P.O. Box 130, Burlington (05402-0130)
PHONE.................................802 863-5555
Philip M Drumheller, *President*
Wayne Peterson, *Exec VP*
Mark Hershey, *Vice Pres*
Bob Morris, *Vice Pres*
Robert Morris, *Vice Pres*
▲ **EMP:** 200 **EST:** 1904
SQ FT: 225,000
SALES (est): 72.3MM **Privately Held**
WEB: www.lanepress.com
SIC: 2759 Commercial Printing

(G-22472)
TOP SHOP INC
87 Ethan Allen Dr (05403-5857)
P.O. Box 9493 (05407-9493)
PHONE.................................802 658-1351
Bruce Bouchard, *President*
Michelle Bouchard, *Admin Sec*
EMP: 10
SQ FT: 6,000
SALES (est): 1.9MM **Privately Held**
SIC: 2542 2541 Mfg Partitions/Fixtures-Nonwood Mfg Wood Partitions/Fixtures

(G-22473)
TRIDYNE PROCESS SYSTEMS INC
80 Allen Rd (05403-7801)
PHONE.................................802 863-6873
Suzette Wijetunga, *President*
EMP: 12
SALES (est): 2.1MM **Privately Held**
SIC: 3596 Mfg Scales/Balances-Nonlaboratory

(G-22474)
TWO GO DRYCLEANING INC
1233 Shelburne Rd Ste 190 (05403-7733)
PHONE.................................802 658-9469
William Obrien, *Principal*
EMP: 20
SALES (est): 781.8K **Privately Held**
SIC: 3582 Mfg Commercial Laundry Equipment

(G-22475)
VERMONT CUSTOM TOOL BOX INC
5 Ethan Allen Dr (05403-5849)
PHONE.................................802 863-9798
Robert M Shand, *President*
EMP: 4
SQ FT: 12,000
SALES (est): 380K **Privately Held**
SIC: 3469 Mfg Custom Tool Boxes

(G-22476)
VERMONT POWDER COATING SY
57 Commerce Ave Ste 5 (05403-4442)
PHONE.................................802 862-0061
Bob Shepard, *Principal*
EMP: 4
SALES (est): 474.9K **Privately Held**
SIC: 3399 Coating/Engraving Service

(G-22477)
VERMONT ROLLING PINS
68 East Ter (05403-6144)
PHONE.................................802 658-3733
Cyndi Freeman, *Principal*
EMP: 4
SALES (est): 233.8K **Privately Held**
SIC: 3452 Mfg Bolts/Screws/Rivets

(G-22478)
VERMONT WOMAN NEWSPAPER
4 Laurel Hill Dr Ste 5 (05403-7378)
P.O. Box 490, South Hero (05486-0490)
PHONE.................................802 861-6200
Jan Doerler, *Principal*
EMP: 5
SALES (est): 251.5K **Privately Held**
SIC: 2711 Newspapers-Publishing/Printing

(G-22479)
WORKS IN PROGRESS INC (PA)
20 Farrell St Ste 103 (05403-6567)
PHONE.................................802 658-3797
Larry Cain, *President*
Cara Cain V Pres-SEC, *Vice Pres*
EMP: 14
SQ FT: 2,400
SALES (est): 1.3MM **Privately Held**
WEB: www.worksinprog.com
SIC: 2741 Construction Report Publishing

South Hero
Grand Isle County

(G-22480)
CHAMPLAIN DISTILLERIES
139 E Shore Rd (05486-4911)
PHONE.................................802 378-5059
Donald Holly, *Principal*
EMP: 3
SALES (est): 129.9K **Privately Held**
SIC: 2085 Mfg Distilled/Blended Liquor

(G-22481)
PHOENIX WIRE INC
31 Tracy Rd (05486-4508)
P.O. Box 186 (05486-0186)
PHONE.................................802 372-4561
Horace W Corbin Jr, *President*
Thomas Parizo, *Vice Pres*
Sylvia Corbin, *Admin Sec*
EMP: 8
SQ FT: 10,000
SALES (est): 1.1MM **Privately Held**
WEB: www.phoenixwireinc.com
SIC: 3357 Mfg Microminiature Wire & Cable

(G-22482)
SNOW FARM WINERY
190 W Shore Rd (05486-4617)
PHONE.................................802 372-9463
David Lane,
EMP: 10
SALES: 300K **Privately Held**
WEB: www.snowfarm.com
SIC: 2084 Mfg Wines/Brandy/Spirits

(G-22483)
SOUTH HERO FIRE DISTRICT 4
28 Hill Rd (05486-4112)
PHONE.................................802 372-3088
James Robistow, *Principal*
Cynthia Spence, *Principal*
Richard Whittlesey, *Principal*
Guy Winch, *Principal*
Kenneth R Little, *Chairman*
EMP: 5
SALES (est): 172K **Privately Held**
SIC: 3589 Mfg Service Industry Machinery

South Londonderry
Windham County

(G-22484)
COBB LUMBER INC
1683 Springhill Rd (05155-9203)
PHONE.................................802 824-5228
William Cobb, *President*
EMP: 4
SALES: 1MM **Privately Held**
SIC: 2421 2411 Sawmill & Logging

(G-22485)
DERAND PRECISION
354 Mountain Rd (05155)
P.O. Box 428 (05155-0428)
PHONE.................................802 874-7161
John Nault, *President*
Helen Nault, *Exec Sec*
EMP: 8
SALES (est): 629.3K **Privately Held**
WEB: www.derandprecision.com
SIC: 3951 Mfg Pens/Mechanical Pencils

(G-22486)
GAFFCO BALLISTICS LLC
114 Horton Rd (05155-9221)
P.O. Box 2074 (05155-2074)
PHONE.................................802 824-9899
Tom Gaffney,
EMP: 4
SALES (est): 615K **Privately Held**
SIC: 3599 3842 Mfg Industrial Machinery Mfg Surgical Appliances/Supplies

(G-22487)
JAMAICA COTTAGE SHOP INC
170 Winhall Station Rd (05155-9235)
PHONE.................................802 297-3760
Domenic Mangano, *President*
Avery Fowler, *Sales Staff*
Nate Pollard, *Manager*
Mindy Fisher, *Associate*
EMP: 50
SALES (est): 3.7MM **Privately Held**
WEB: www.jamaicacottageshop.com
SIC: 2452 3272 Mfg Prefabricated Wood Buildings Mfg Concrete Products

(G-22488)
OMICHRON CORP
340 Melendy Hill Rd (05155)
PHONE.................................802 824-3136
Fergus Smith, *President*
Margaret Tooney, *Corp Secy*
David Arch, *Vice Pres*
Drake Smith, *Vice Pres*
EMP: 16 **EST:** 1971
SQ FT: 7,000
SALES (est): 1.9MM **Privately Held**
WEB: www.omichron.com
SIC: 3585 3821 Mfg Refrigeration/Heating Equipment Mfg Lab Apparatus/Furniture

South Pomfret
Windsor County

(G-22489)
WOOD DYNAMICS CORPORATION (PA)
4120 Pomfret Rd (05067)
P.O. Box 473, Woodstock (05091-0473)
PHONE.................................802 457-3970
Jesse B Nichols, *President*
Janice G Nichols, *Treasurer*
EMP: 5
SQ FT: 15,000
SALES (est): 456.5K **Privately Held**
SIC: 2499 3421 3531 3949 Mfg Decorative Wood & Woodwork & Cutlery

South Royalton
Windsor County

(G-22490)
DCI INC
324 Waterman Rd (05068-5116)
PHONE.................................802 763-7847
EMP: 15
SALES (corp-wide): 75.7MM **Privately Held**
SIC: 2421 2426 Sawmill/Planing Mill Hardwood Dimension/Floor Mill
PA: Dci, Inc.
265 S Main St
Lisbon NH 03585
603 838-6544

(G-22491)
ERIC LAWHITE CO
2907 Dairy Hill Rd (05068-4419)
PHONE.................................802 763-7670
Eric Lawhite, *Owner*
EMP: 4
SQ FT: 3,600
SALES: 200K **Privately Held**
SIC: 3841 8711 Mfg Surgical/Medical Instruments

(G-22492)
G W PLASTICS INC
272 Waterman Rd (05068-5115)
PHONE.................................802 763-2194
Ben Riehl, *President*
Jim Bennett, *Maintence Staff*
EMP: 100
SALES (corp-wide): 171.1MM **Privately Held**
WEB: www.gwtool.com
SIC: 3089 Mfg Plastic Products
PA: G W Plastics, Inc.
239 Pleasant St
Bethel VT 05032
802 234-9941

(G-22493)
SORO SYSTEMS INC
190 Chelsea St 9 (05068)
P.O. Box 601 (05068-0601)
PHONE.................................802 763-2248
Frank Pagliughi, *President*
EMP: 6
SALES (est): 650.3K **Privately Held**
SIC: 3695 Mfg Magnetic/Optical Recording Media

(G-22494)
VAN ALSTYNE FAMILY FARM INC
Also Called: Van Alstyne Farm and Mill
330 Walker Hill Rd (05068-9537)
PHONE.................................802 763-7036
Floyd Van Alstyne, *President*
EMP: 3
SALES (est): 175.8K **Privately Held**
WEB: www.vanalstynefamily.com
SIC: 2421 Sawmill/Planing Mill

GEOGRAPHIC

South Ryegate
Caledonia County

(G-22495)
CHIEF LOGGING & CNSTR INC
2494 Stone Rd (05069-8993)
PHONE..................................802 584-3868
Clark S Bogie, *President*
EMP: 13
SALES (est): 1.7MM **Privately Held**
SIC: 2411 Logging

(G-22496)
GANDIN BROTHERS INC
87 Stoneshed Rd (05069-4415)
P.O. Box 155 (05069-0155)
PHONE..................................802 584-3521
Gaylord J Gandin, *President*
Judith Gandin, *Admin Sec*
EMP: 14
SQ FT: 3,500
SALES (est): 1.3MM **Privately Held**
SIC: 3281 Mfg Cut Stone/Products

South Woodstock
Windsor County

(G-22497)
D & T SPINNING INC
608 Fletcher Hill Rd (05071-4635)
PHONE..................................802 228-2925
Harriet Dubin, *President*
Paul Dubin, *Treasurer*
Dorothy J Lundgren, *Admin Sec*
EMP: 58
SQ FT: 48,000
SALES (est): 3.2MM **Privately Held**
SIC: 2281 Yarn Spinning Mill

(G-22498)
KENDLE ENTERPRISES
Also Called: Kedron Sugar Makers
109 Kendle Rd (05071)
P.O. Box 111 (05071-0111)
PHONE..................................802 457-3015
Paul C Kendall, *President*
EMP: 10
SALES (est): 701.3K **Privately Held**
SIC: 2099 Mfg Maple Syrup

Springfield
Windsor County

(G-22499)
ARTISAN SURFACES INC
200 Clinton St (05156-3306)
P.O. Box 377 (05156-0377)
PHONE..................................802 885-8677
EMP: 26
SALES: 3.5MM **Privately Held**
SIC: 2541 Mfg Wood Partitions/Fixtures

(G-22500)
GEAR WORKS INC
76 Pearl St Ste 1 (05156-3040)
PHONE..................................802 885-5039
Don Shattuck, *President*
Debbie Leitgeb, *Vice Pres*
EMP: 30 **EST:** 1996
SQ FT: 2,200
SALES (est): 3.9MM **Privately Held**
SIC: 3541 Mfg Machine Tools-Cutting

(G-22501)
HANCOR INC
30 Precision Dr (05156)
PHONE..................................802 886-8403
Jason Sidel, *Manager*
EMP: 50
SALES (corp-wide): 1.3B **Publicly Held**
SIC: 3084 3088 3089 3444 Mfg Plastic Pipe Mfg Plstc Plumbing Fixtr Mfg Plastic Products Mfg Sheet Metalwork
HQ: Hancor, Inc.
4640 Trueman Blvd
Hilliard OH 43026
614 658-0050

(G-22502)
IMAGE TEK MFG INC
Also Called: Imagetek Manufacturing
280 Clinton St (05156-3308)
PHONE..................................802 885-6208
Michael Hathaway, *President*
John Holzinger, *Senior Buyer*
George Norfleet, *CFO*
Loreen Billings, *Treasurer*
EMP: 40
SQ FT: 33,000
SALES (est): 23.4MM **Privately Held**
WEB: www.pcmanufacturing.com
SIC: 3672 3679 3577 2679 Mfg Printed Circuit Brds Mfg Elec Components Mfg Computer Peripherals Mfg Converted Paper Prdt

(G-22503)
J & L METROLOGY INC
280 Clinton St (05156-3308)
PHONE..................................802 885-8291
Peter Klepp, *President*
Nathalie Klepp, *Vice Pres*
EMP: 25
SALES (est): 5.3MM **Privately Held**
SIC: 3827 Mfg Optical Instruments/Lenses

(G-22504)
KONRAD PREFAB LLC
260 Clinton St (05156-3308)
PHONE..................................802 885-6780
David Jaacks,
EMP: 3
SALES (est): 233.8K **Privately Held**
SIC: 3448 2542 8742 8711 Mfg Prefab Metal Bldgs Mfg Nonwd Partition/Fixt Mgmt Consulting Svcs Engineering Services

(G-22505)
LETTER BARN
128 Union St (05156-3147)
PHONE..................................802 885-5451
Edward Szad, *Owner*
EMP: 3
SALES (est): 100K **Privately Held**
SIC: 3993 Mfg Signs/Advertising Specialties

(G-22506)
LOVEJOY TOOL COMPANY INC
133 Main St (05156-3509)
P.O. Box 949 (05156-0949)
PHONE..................................802 885-2194
Douglas Priestley, *President*
Todd Priestley, *Vice Pres*
Warren Garfield, *Mfg Staff*
Renee Amsden, *Human Res Dir*
Nancy Lindsay, *Admin Sec*
EMP: 48 **EST:** 1917
SQ FT: 36,000
SALES (est): 8.6MM **Privately Held**
WEB: www.lovejoytool.com
SIC: 3545 Mfg Machine Tool Accessories

(G-22507)
MACDERMID INCORPORATED
260 Clinton St (05156-3308)
PHONE..................................802 885-8089
Michael Chilson, *Branch Mgr*
EMP: 15
SALES (corp-wide): 1.9B **Publicly Held**
WEB: www.macdermid.com
SIC: 3699 Mfg Electrical Equipment
HQ: Macdermid, Incorporated
245 Freight St
Waterbury CT 06702
203 575-5700

(G-22508)
PRECISION VALLEY FINISHING
135 Main St (05156-3509)
P.O. Box 480 (05156-0480)
PHONE..................................802 885-3150
Donald Davis, *Owner*
EMP: 6 **EST:** 1946
SQ FT: 2,000
SALES: 672K **Privately Held**
SIC: 3471 Plating/Polishing Service

(G-22509)
SPRINGFIELD REPORTER INC
151 Summer St (05156-3503)
PHONE..................................802 885-2246
Rodney Arnold, *President*
EMP: 3
SALES: 140K **Privately Held**
SIC: 2711 7313 Newspapers-Publishing/Printing Advertising Representative

(G-22510)
VERMONT BEER SHAPERS LTD
100 River St (05156-2930)
P.O. Box 45, Proctorsville (05153-0045)
PHONE..................................802 376-0889
Kelen Beardsley, *President*
Gabriel Streeter, *Vice Pres*
Trevor Billings, *Treasurer*
EMP: 3
SALES (est): 225.8K **Privately Held**
SIC: 2082 Mfg Malt Beverages

(G-22511)
VERMONT PRECISION MACHINE SVCS
Also Called: V P M S
280 Clinton St (05156-3308)
P.O. Box 10 (05156-0010)
PHONE..................................802 885-8291
William Otis, *President*
Paulette Otis, *Vice Pres*
EMP: 9
SQ FT: 15,000
SALES (est): 2MM **Privately Held**
WEB: www.jlmetrology.com
SIC: 3827 Mfg Optical Instruments/Lenses

(G-22512)
VERMONT STONEWORKS
100 River St (05156-2930)
P.O. Box 117, Chester (05143-0117)
PHONE..................................802 885-6535
Paul Thomas Jr, *Owner*
EMP: 4
SALES (est): 180K **Privately Held**
SIC: 3281 Mfg Cut Stone/Products

(G-22513)
WILLIS WOOD
Also Called: Wood Cider Mill
1482 Weathersfield Ctr Rd (05156-9648)
PHONE..................................802 263-5547
Willis Wood, *Owner*
EMP: 5
SALES: 50K **Privately Held**
WEB: www.woodscidermill.com
SIC: 2033 5499 0139 0175 Mfg Canned Fruits/Vegtbl Ret Misc Foods Field Crop Farm Fruit Tree Orchard Mfg Food Preparations

St George
Chittenden County

(G-22514)
VERMONT WARE INC
157 Barber Rd A (05495-8015)
PHONE..................................802 482-4426
Dale Dawson, *President*
Tyler Dawson, *Vice Pres*
Elizabeth Dawson, *Admin Sec*
EMP: 7
SQ FT: 36,000
SALES (est): 610K **Privately Held**
WEB: www.vermontware.com
SIC: 3524 3479 Manufactures Lawn Or Garden Tractors Or Equipment Also Specializing In Coating Of Metals Or Formed Products

Starksboro
Addison County

(G-22515)
ENERGY SMART BUILDING INC
Also Called: Foam Laminates of Vermont
22 Varney Hill Rd (05487-4417)
P.O. Box 100, Hinesburg (05461-0100)
PHONE..................................802 453-4438
James Giroux, *President*
Mark Driscoll, *Vice Pres*
EMP: 20
SALES (est): 2.6MM **Privately Held**
SIC: 2452 2439 7353 Mfg Prefabricated Wood Buildings Mfg Structural Wood Members Heavy Construction Equipment Rental

(G-22516)
MARU LTD DBA GREENLEAF METALS
1022 Mason Hl N (05487-7233)
PHONE..................................802 985-5200
Linda Snelling, *Exec Dir*
EMP: 3
SALES (est): 251K **Privately Held**
SIC: 3312 Blast Furnace-Steel Works

(G-22517)
STEVEN W WILLSEY
Also Called: Shaker Maple Farm
2047 Shaker Hill Rd (05487-7206)
PHONE..................................802 434-5353
Steve Willsey, *Owner*
Leah Willsey, *Co-Owner*
EMP: 3
SALES: 250K **Privately Held**
SIC: 2099 Mfg Food Preparations

Stockbridge
Windsor County

(G-22518)
ADVANCED ANIMATIONS
Also Called: Advanced Exhibits
534 Vt Route 107 (05772-6803)
P.O. Box 34 (05772-0034)
PHONE..................................802 746-8974
Peggy Toth, *President*
Robert Crean, *Vice Pres*
Thomas W Marquis, *Treasurer*
▲ **EMP:** 25
SQ FT: 48,000
SALES (est): 3.4MM **Privately Held**
WEB: www.advancedanimations.com
SIC: 3999 Mfg Misc Products

Stowe
Lamoille County

(G-22519)
ALCHEMY CANNING LTD
Also Called: Alchemist - Waterbury, The
100 Cottage Club Rd (05672-4139)
PHONE..................................802 244-7744
Jennifer Kimmich, *Director*
EMP: 24
SALES (est): 4.5MM **Privately Held**
SIC: 2082 Mfg Malt Beverages

(G-22520)
CAMBRIDGE PRECISION MACHINE CO
347 Baird Rd (05672-4210)
PHONE..................................802 253-9269
Richard Story, *President*
EMP: 5
SALES (est): 100K **Privately Held**
WEB: www.storylamps.com
SIC: 3599 Machine Shop Jobbing And Repair

(G-22521)
DALE E PERCY INC
269 Weeks Hill Rd (05672-5245)
PHONE..................................802 253-8503
Dana T Percy, *President*
Peter Percy, *Vice Pres*
Matt Percy, *Project Mgr*
Jessica Couture, *Administration*
EMP: 10
SQ FT: 15,000
SALES (est): 3.5MM **Privately Held**
WEB: www.dalepercyinc.com
SIC: 1442 1794 Construction Sand/Gravel Excavation Contractor

(G-22522)
KNEEBINDING INC
782 Mountain Rd (05672-4629)
P.O. Box 1416 (05672-1416)
PHONE..................................802 760-3026

John Springer-Miller, *Principal*
Steeve Walkerman, *CFO*
EMP: 5
SALES (est): 522.6K **Privately Held**
SIC: 2253 Knit Outerwear Mill

(G-22523)
LITTLE RIVER HOTGLASS STUDIO
Also Called: Little River Hot Glass Studio
593 Moscow Rd (05672-5113)
P.O. Box 1504 (05672-1504)
PHONE..................................802 253-0889
Michael Trimpol, *President*
EMP: 7
SQ FT: 1,500
SALES (est): 520K **Privately Held**
WEB: www.littleriverhotglass.com
SIC: 3229 5947 Mfg Pressed/Blown Glass Ret Gifts/Novelties

(G-22524)
MOSCOW MILLS INCORPORATED
435 Moscow Rd (05672)
PHONE..................................802 253-2036
Anderson Leveille, *President*
▲ **EMP:** 14
SQ FT: 18,000
SALES (est): 2.3MM **Privately Held**
SIC: 3679 Mfg Electronic Components

(G-22525)
X PRESS IN STOWE INC
73 Pond Ln (05672)
P.O. Box 1441 (05672-1441)
PHONE..................................802 253-9788
Douglas Nerber, *President*
EMP: 7
SQ FT: 2,500
SALES (est): 930.8K **Privately Held**
WEB: www.thexpressink.com
SIC: 2752 Offset Printing Shop

Strafford
Orange County

(G-22526)
EBWS LLC
Also Called: Strafford Organic Creamery
61 Rockbottom Rd (05072)
PHONE..................................802 765-4180
Earl Ransom,
EMP: 7 **EST:** 2001
SALES (est): 692.8K **Privately Held**
WEB: www.ebws.com
SIC: 2026 Mfg Fluid Milk

(G-22527)
GREEN MOUNTAIN RISK MGT INC
191 Kibling Hill Rd (05072-9770)
PHONE..................................802 763-7773
EMP: 6 **EST:** 2007
SALES (est): 463.9K **Privately Held**
SIC: 3482 Mfg Small Arms Ammunition

Sutton
Caledonia County

(G-22528)
PURE GOLD SUGARING LLC
20 Craig Pond Rd (05867-9611)
P.O. Box 3, West Burke (05871-0003)
PHONE..................................802 467-3921
Bud Smith, *Mng Member*
Douglas Solinsky, *Mng Member*
Kurt Solinsky, *Mng Member*
Janice Solinsky,
EMP: 4
SALES: 45K **Privately Held**
SIC: 2099 5149 Mfg Food Preparations Whol Groceries

Swanton
Franklin County

(G-22529)
ACCURATE RUBBER PRODUCTS INC
22 Lake St (05488-1339)
PHONE..................................802 868-3063
David J Reid, *President*
EMP: 5 **EST:** 1999
SALES: 200K **Privately Held**
SIC: 3069 Mfg Fabricated Rubber Products

(G-22530)
DEXTER PRODUCTS INC
716 Vt Route 78 (05488-8616)
P.O. Box 193 (05488-0193)
PHONE..................................802 868-7085
Ralph Dexter, *President*
Jennifer Dexter, *Vice Pres*
Stephens Dexter, *Vice Pres*
Florence Dexter, *Admin Sec*
EMP: 5
SQ FT: 2,400
SALES: 100K **Privately Held**
SIC: 3993 Mfg Signs/Advertising Specialties

(G-22531)
LEADER EVAPORATOR CO INC (PA)
Also Called: G.H. Grimm Company
49 Jonergin Dr (05488-1311)
PHONE..................................802 868-5444
Gary J Gaudette, *President*
Bruce Gillilan, *Vice Pres*
Adrianne McAllister, *Purch Agent*
David Marvin, *Treasurer*
Randy Gaudette, *Sales Mgr*
▲ **EMP:** 60 **EST:** 1888
SQ FT: 50,000
SALES (est): 13.1MM **Privately Held**
WEB: www.leaderevaporator.com
SIC: 3523 3556 3443 Mfg Farm Machinery/Equipment Mfg Food Products Machinery Mfg Fabricated Plate Work

(G-22532)
NEWPORT SAND & GRAVEL CO INC
1st St (05488)
P.O. Box 158 (05488-0158)
PHONE..................................802 868-4119
Bob Carrel, *Manager*
EMP: 9
SALES (corp-wide): 44MM **Privately Held**
SIC: 3273 Mfg Ready-Mixed Concrete
PA: Newport Sand & Gravel Co., Inc.
8 Reeds Mill Rd
Newport NH 03773
603 298-0199

(G-22533)
PLUMROSE USA INC
14 Jonergin Dr (05488-1312)
PHONE..................................802 868-7314
Dave Schanzer, *CEO*
Trisha Longway, *Manager*
EMP: 62 **Publicly Held**
SIC: 2013 Mfg Prepared Meats
HQ: Plumrose Usa, Inc.
1901 Butterfield Rd # 305
Downers Grove IL 60515

(G-22534)
POULIN GRAIN INC
24 Depot St (05488)
PHONE..................................802 868-3323
Krista Rowe, *Manager*
EMP: 16
SALES (corp-wide): 24.2MM **Privately Held**
WEB: www.poulingrain.com
SIC: 2048 5153 Mfg Prepared Feed & Feed Ingredients For Animals
PA: Poulin Grain, Inc.
24 Railroad Sq
Newport VT 05855
802 334-6731

(G-22535)
R R SPRINKLER INC
28 Canada St (05488-1335)
PHONE..................................802 868-2423
Robert C Rain, *President*
Ronald Rain, *Vice Pres*
Brenda Rain, *Admin Sec*
EMP: 3
SALES: 200K **Privately Held**
SIC: 3569 1711 Mfg General Industrial Machinery Plumbing/Heating/Air Cond Contractor

(G-22536)
RAYMOND GADUES INC
Also Called: Ray's Extrusion Dies Tubing Co
Rr 78 Box East (05488)
P.O. Box 385, Saint Albans (05478-0385)
PHONE..................................802 868-2033
Kevin R Gadue, *President*
Lori A Kennison, *Vice Pres*
EMP: 25
SQ FT: 22,500
SALES (est): 4.6MM **Privately Held**
WEB: www.raven-ind.com
SIC: 3544 3498 5051 Mfg Dies/Tools/Jigs/Fixtures Mfg Fabricated Pipe/Fittings Metals Service Center

(G-22537)
SWAN VALLEY CHEESE VERMONT LLC
11 Jonergin Dr (05488-1311)
PHONE..................................802 868-7181
Christopher Lotito,
▲ **EMP:** 30
SALES (est): 4.2MM **Privately Held**
SIC: 2022 Mfg Cheese

(G-22538)
VERMONT PRECISION TOOLS INC (PA)
Also Called: Vermont Gage
10 Precision Ln (05488-4447)
P.O. Box 182 (05488-0182)
PHONE..................................802 868-4246
Monica Greene, *Principal*
Mark Rocheleau, *Vice Pres*
Rob Green, *Opers Dir*
Paul Field, *Mfg Dir*
Tyler Greene, *Project Mgr*
▲ **EMP:** 125
SQ FT: 90,000
SALES (est): 25.2MM **Privately Held**
WEB: www.vermontgage.com
SIC: 3545 3823 Mfg Machine Tool Accessories Mfg Process Control Instruments

(G-22539)
VERMONT THREAD GAGE LLC
Also Called: Vermont Gage
10 Precision Ln (05488-4447)
P.O. Box 182 (05488-0182)
PHONE..................................802 868-4246
Monica Greene, *President*
EMP: 9
SALES (est): 1MM **Privately Held**
SIC: 3545 Mfg Machine Tool Accessories

Topsham
Orange County

(G-22540)
N NEWS LLC
4 Swamp Rd (05076-3035)
P.O. Box 275, East Corinth (05040-0275)
PHONE..................................802 439-6054
Robert Rinaldi Jr, *Partner*
Laurie Rinaldi,
EMP: 3
SALES: 220K **Privately Held**
WEB: www.n-news.com
SIC: 2721 Periodicals-Publishing/Printing

Townshend
Windham County

(G-22541)
CREST STUDIOS
Also Called: Robert Dugrenier Associates
1096 Vt Route 30 (05353-9725)
PHONE..................................802 365-4200
Robert Dugrenier, *Owner*
EMP: 12
SALES (est): 717.6K **Privately Held**
WEB: www.creststudios.com
SIC: 3229 Mfg Pressed/Blown Glass

Tunbridge
Orange County

(G-22542)
CUTTER & LOCKE INC (PA)
Also Called: Historical Publications
234 Monarch Hill Rd (05077-9626)
PHONE..................................802 889-3500
Kathryn Jorgenson, *President*
C Peter Jorgensen, *President*
EMP: 8
SALES (est): 300K **Privately Held**
WEB: www.civilwarnews.com
SIC: 2711 Newspapers-Publishing/Printing

(G-22543)
E I J INC
Also Called: Iron Horse Standing Seam Roofg
467 Vt Route 110 (05077-9703)
P.O. Box 165 (05077-0165)
PHONE..................................802 889-3432
John Kinnarney, *President*
Jennifer Bettis, *Treasurer*
EMP: 17
SQ FT: 3,600
SALES (est): 3MM **Privately Held**
SIC: 3442 Mfg Metal Doors/Sash/Trim

(G-22544)
UPPER PASS BEER CO LLC
37 Ordway Rd (05077-9560)
P.O. Box 244 (05077-0244)
PHONE..................................802 889-3421
Christopher Perry,
Andrew Puchalik,
Ivan Tomek,
EMP: 3
SQ FT: 200
SALES (est): 110.5K **Privately Held**
SIC: 2082 Mfg Malt Beverages

Underhill
Chittenden County

(G-22545)
ABBA FUELS INC
1018 Vt Route 15 (05489-9337)
P.O. Box 5212, Essex Junction (05453-5212)
PHONE..................................802 878-8095
Kevin Whitten, *Principal*
EMP: 7 **EST:** 2009
SALES (est): 763K **Privately Held**
SIC: 2869 Mfg Industrial Organic Chemicals

(G-22546)
BURGESS SUGARHOUSE LLC
251 Irish Settlement Rd (05489-9775)
PHONE..................................802 899-5228
William Laporte, *Principal*
EMP: 3
SALES (est): 237.5K **Privately Held**
SIC: 2099 Mfg Food Preparations

(G-22547)
FIRST STEP PRINT SHOP LLC
22 Park St (05489-9602)
P.O. Box 311 (05489-0311)
PHONE..................................802 899-2708
Mary A Martelle, *Owner*
Robert Martelle, *Mng Member*
Mary Martelle, *Mng Member*
EMP: 7

SALES: 300K **Privately Held**
SIC: 2752 5112 7334 Lithographic Commercial Printing Whol Stationery/Office Supplies Photocopying Services

(G-22548)
GREEN MOUNTAIN CHIPPING INC (PA)
Rr 15 (05489)
P.O. Box 360 (05489-0360)
PHONE..................................802 899-1239
David Villeneuve, *President*
Brenda Villeneuve, *Corp Secy*
EMP: 3
SQ FT: 720
SALES (est): 654K **Privately Held**
SIC: 2411 1629 Logging & Land Clearing Contractor

(G-22549)
VERMONT SKI SAFETY EQUIPMENT
Also Called: VSR Video
1 Sand Hill Rd (05489-9353)
P.O. Box 85, Underhill Center (05490-0085)
PHONE..................................802 899-4738
Carl Ettlinger, *President*
EMP: 3
SALES: 650K **Privately Held**
WEB: www.vermontskisafety.com
SIC: 3949 8742 Mfg Safety Equipment For Skis

(G-22550)
VIRIDIS DIAGNOSTICS INC
6 Depot St (05489-9623)
PHONE..................................802 316-0894
Matthew Gombrich, *CEO*
EMP: 3
SALES (est): 156.6K **Privately Held**
SIC: 2835 In Vitro Diagnostics

(G-22551)
WALKERS VT PURE MPLE SYRUP LLC
75 Sand Hill Rd (05489-9353)
PHONE..................................802 899-3088
Craig G Walker, *Principal*
EMP: 3
SALES (est): 210.1K **Privately Held**
SIC: 2099 Mfg Food Preparations

Vergennes
Addison County

(G-22552)
BF GOODRICH AERSPCE AIRCRFT IN
100 Panton Rd (05491-1008)
PHONE..................................802 877-2911
David Gitlin, *President*
EMP: 3
SALES (est): 103K **Privately Held**
SIC: 3812 3721 Mfg Search/Navigation Equipment Mfg Aircraft

(G-22553)
GOODRICH CORPORATION
Also Called: UTC Aerospace
100 Panton Rd (05491-1008)
P.O. Box 3023, Troy OH (45373-7323)
PHONE..................................802 877-4000
Christian Bradley, *Purch Agent*
Jacques Dupuis, *Engineer*
Scott Durkee, *Engineer*
Dale Tucker, *Engineer*
Jessica Wieman, *Engineer*
EMP: 34
SALES (corp-wide): 66.5B **Publicly Held**
SIC: 3728 Mfg Aircraft Parts/Equipment
HQ: Goodrich Corporation
2730 W Tyvola Rd 4
Charlotte NC 28217
704 423-7000

(G-22554)
NECSEL INTLLCTUAL PROPERTY INC
Also Called: Necsel Ip
101 Panton Rd Ste 1 (05491-1073)
PHONE..................................802 877-6432
Joel Melnick, *Branch Mgr*
EMP: 20 **Privately Held**
SIC: 3679 Mfg Electronic Components
HQ: Necsel Intellectual Property, Inc.
801 Ames Ave
Milpitas CA 95035

(G-22555)
PRECISION PRINT AND COPY INC
12 Main St Ste 1 (05491-8670)
PHONE..................................802 877-3711
James Lutton, *President*
Alan Mayer, *Treasurer*
Allan Mayer, *Treasurer*
EMP: 3
SQ FT: 3,600
SALES: 377.2K **Privately Held**
SIC: 2752 5111 5699 Lithographic Commercial Printing Whol Printing/Writing Paper Ret Misc Apparel/Accessories

(G-22556)
SIMMONDS PRECISION PDTS INC (DH)
Also Called: Goodrich Corporation
100 Panton Rd (05491-1008)
PHONE..................................802 877-4000
Justin Robert Keppy, *CEO*
Paul V Cappiello, *Vice Pres*
Dave Crowne, *Engineer*
Christine Sinkewicz, *Engineer*
Brian Syverson, *Engineer*
EMP: 650
SQ FT: 211,000
SALES (est): 134.3MM
SALES (corp-wide): 66.5B **Publicly Held**
SIC: 3829 3694 3724 3728 Mfg Measure/Control Dvcs Mfg Engine Elec Equip Mfg Aircraft Engine/Part Mfg Aircraft Parts/Equip
HQ: Goodrich Corporation
2730 W Tyvola Rd 4
Charlotte NC 28217
704 423-7000

(G-22557)
VENDITUOLI LIMITED COMPANY
44 W Main St (05491-1061)
PHONE..................................802 535-4319
Tyler Vendituoli, *Principal*
EMP: 3
SALES (est): 197.8K **Privately Held**
SIC: 3441 8999 Structural Metal Fabrication Services-Misc

Vershire
Orange County

(G-22558)
CHRIS CLARK
1848 Parker Rd (05079-9502)
PHONE..................................802 356-0044
Chris Clark, *Principal*
EMP: 4
SALES (est): 360.3K **Privately Held**
SIC: 2411 Logging

Waitsfield
Washington County

(G-22559)
AGRI-MARK INC
Also Called: Cabot Creamery
193 Home Farm Way (05673-7512)
PHONE..................................802 496-1200
Mark Graupman, *Branch Mgr*
EMP: 91
SALES (corp-wide): 382MM **Privately Held**
SIC: 2026 2022 Mfg Fluid Milk Mfg Cheese
PA: Agri-Mark, Inc.
40 Shattuck Rd Ste 301
Andover MA 01810
978 552-5500

(G-22560)
BAKED BEADS INC
6973 Main St (05673-6023)
PHONE..................................802 496-2440
David R Cohen, *President*
Robin Cohen, *Admin Sec*
▲ **EMP:** 18
SQ FT: 2,000
SALES: 1MM **Privately Held**
WEB: www.bakedbeads.com
SIC: 3961 5094 Mfg Costume Jewelry And Wholesale Costume Jewelry

(G-22561)
BERING TECHNOLOGY INC
5086 Main St (05673-6156)
PHONE..................................408 364-6500
Leung C Lok, *CEO*
EMP: 49
SALES: 900K **Privately Held**
SIC: 3589 Mfg Service Industry Machinery

(G-22562)
CABOT CREAMERY COOPERATIVE INC
193 Home Farm Way (05673-7512)
PHONE..................................978 552-5500
Ed Townley, *CEO*
Jeff Saforek, *COO*
Charlotte Green, *Vice Pres*
Mark Graupman, *CFO*
Suzanne Hedding, *Human Res Mgr*
EMP: 300 **EST:** 1919
SALES (est): 94.3MM
SALES (corp-wide): 382MM **Privately Held**
WEB: www.seriouslysharp.com
SIC: 2022 5143 5451 Mfg Cheese Whol Dairy Products Ret Dairy Products
PA: Agri-Mark, Inc.
40 Shattuck Rd Ste 301
Andover MA 01810
978 552-5500

(G-22563)
CHOOSECO LLC
49 Fiddlers Grn (05673-6009)
P.O. Box 46 (05673-0046)
PHONE..................................802 496-2595
R A Montgomery,
Shannon Gilligan,
▲ **EMP:** 5
SQ FT: 2,100
SALES (est): 676.5K **Privately Held**
WEB: www.chooseco.com
SIC: 2731 Books-Publishing/Printing

(G-22564)
DISCOVERY MAP INTL INC
Also Called: Destination Map Only In WA
5197 Main St Unit 8 (05673-7239)
P.O. Box 726 (05673-0726)
PHONE..................................802 316-4060
Peter Hans, *President*
Laura Potter, *Production*
Barbara Murphy, *Admin Sec*
EMP: 4
SALES (est): 329.8K **Privately Held**
SIC: 2741 6794 Misc Publishing

(G-22565)
EASTERN SYSTEMS INC (PA)
Also Called: Eastern Systems Group
5197 Main St Unit 4 (05673-7239)
P.O. Box 55 (05673-0055)
PHONE..................................802 496-1000
L James Leyton, *Ch of Bd*
Josephine A Leyton, *President*
EMP: 4 **EST:** 1959
SQ FT: 2,500
SALES (est): 742.6K **Privately Held**
WEB: www.goeastern.com
SIC: 2759 5943 Commercial Printing Ret Stationery

(G-22566)
ELEMENT MARKETING
80 Pinebrook Rd (05673-6180)
PHONE..................................802 448-4252
EMP: 7
SALES (est): 914K **Privately Held**
SIC: 2819 Industrial Inorganic Chemicals, Nec

(G-22567)
MAD RIVER MEDIA
House Fuller (05673)
P.O. Box 762 (05673-0762)
PHONE..................................802 496-9173
Ed Dooley, *President*
EMP: 3
SALES (est): 303.3K **Privately Held**
WEB: www.madrivermedia.com
SIC: 3695 Mfg Magnetic/Optical Recording Media

(G-22568)
RESOURCE ENGINEERING INC
Also Called: Qualitytrainingportal.com
80 Mobus Rd (05673-4410)
P.O. Box 449 (05673-0449)
PHONE..................................802 496-5888
Ray Mikulak, *President*
EMP: 5
SQ FT: 1,200
SALES: 410K **Privately Held**
WEB: www.qualitytrainingportal.com
SIC: 7372 Prepackaged Software Services

(G-22569)
VALLEY REPORTER INC
5222 Main St Ste 2 (05673-4445)
P.O. Box 119 (05673-0119)
PHONE..................................802 496-3607
Patricia Clark, *President*
Lisa Loomis, *Editor*
EMP: 8
SALES: 255K **Privately Held**
WEB: www.valleyreporter.com
SIC: 2711 Weekly Tabloid Newspaper

(G-22570)
VT ADIRONDACK
1358 German Flats Rd (05673-7274)
PHONE..................................802 496-9271
EMP: 3
SALES (est): 141.2K **Privately Held**
SIC: 2512 Mfg Upholstered Household Furniture

(G-22571)
WINTERSTEIGER INC
Also Called: Grindrite
3489 Main St (05673-6273)
P.O. Box 1240 (05673-1240)
PHONE..................................802 496-6166
Stan Woliner, *Manager*
EMP: 5
SALES (corp-wide): 267.9K **Privately Held**
WEB: www.wintersteiger.com
SIC: 3531 Mfg Construction Machinery
HQ: Wintersteiger, Inc.
4705 W Amelia Earhart Dr
Salt Lake City UT 84116
801 355-6550

(G-22572)
WOOD & WOOD INC
Also Called: Wood & Wood Sign Systems
98 Carroll Rd (05673-4408)
PHONE..................................802 496-3000
Richard Potter, *President*
EMP: 8
SALES (est): 1.2MM **Privately Held**
WEB: www.woodandwoodsigns.com
SIC: 2499 3952 3993 Mfg Wood Products Mfg Lead Pencils/Art Goods Mfg Signs/Advertising Specialties

Wallingford
Rutland County

(G-22573)
AMES COMPANIES INC
82 Creek Rd (05773)
P.O. Box 249 (05773-0249)
PHONE..................................802 446-2601
EMP: 102
SALES (corp-wide): 2.2B **Publicly Held**
WEB: www.ames.com
SIC: 3423 Mfg Garden Tool Handles
HQ: The Ames Companies Inc
465 Railroad Ave
Camp Hill PA 17011
717 737-1500

(G-22574)
SHELBURNE LIMESTONE CORP
4792 Us Route 7 S (05773-9538)
PHONE..................................802 446-2045
Chris Carl, *Manager*
EMP: 6
SALES (corp-wide): 22.2MM **Privately Held**
SIC: 1422 Crushed/Broken Limestone
PA: Shelburne Limestone Corp
1949 Main St
Colchester VT 05446
802 878-2656

(G-22575)
VERMONT FORGINGS INC
41 Cook Dr (05773-9403)
PHONE..................................802 446-3900
Kevin Mulholland, *President*
Michelle Mulholland, *Vice Pres*
EMP: 5
SALES: 175K **Privately Held**
WEB: www.vermontforgings.com
SIC: 3462 Mfg Iron/Steel Forgings

Wardsboro
Windham County

(G-22576)
E&M LOGGING & LAND CLEARING LL
338 Mill Rd (05355-9757)
PHONE..................................802 896-6091
Everett Bills, *Principal*
EMP: 3 **EST:** 2008
SALES (est): 296.2K **Privately Held**
SIC: 2411 Logging

Warren
Washington County

(G-22577)
MAD RIVER DISTILLERS
156 Cold Springs Farm Rd (05674-9453)
PHONE..................................802 496-6973
Alex Hilton, *President*
▲ **EMP:** 7
SALES (est): 703.1K **Privately Held**
SIC: 2085 Mfg Distilled/Blended Liquor

(G-22578)
R H TRAVERS COMPANY
Also Called: Free Aire
200 Burnt Mountain Rd (05674-9660)
PHONE..................................802 496-5205
Richard Travers, *President*
Constance Colman, *Vice Pres*
EMP: 3
SALES: 150K **Privately Held**
WEB: www.freeaire.com
SIC: 3822 7623 Mfg Environmental Controls Refrigeration Service/Repair

(G-22579)
VACUTHERM INC
2535 Airport Rd (05674-9842)
P.O. Box 650, Waitsfield (05673-0650)
PHONE..................................802 496-4241
James Parker, *President*
Brian Kingsbury, *Engineer*
Ralph Moxness, *Treasurer*
EMP: 3
SQ FT: 11,000
SALES (est): 660.5K **Privately Held**
WEB: www.vacutherm.com
SIC: 3559 Mfg Lumber Kilns

Washington
Orange County

(G-22580)
ROMULUS CRAFT
8495 Vt Route 110 (05675-7711)
PHONE..................................802 685-3869
Iikuzi Teraki, *Partner*
Jeanne Bisson, *Partner*
Iikuzi Teraki, *Partner*
EMP: 3
SQ FT: 5,620
SALES (est): 176.6K **Privately Held**
WEB: www.romuluscraft.com
SIC: 3269 5719 Mfg Pottery Products Ret Misc Homefurnishings

(G-22581)
VERMONT MAPLE DIRECT
233 Emery Rd (05675-2008)
PHONE..................................802 793-3326
Mike Collins, *Principal*
EMP: 3
SALES (est): 211.9K **Privately Held**
SIC: 2099 Mfg Food Preparations

Waterbury
Washington County

(G-22582)
DARTMOUTH JOURNAL SERVICES INC
5 Pilgrim Park Rd Ste 5 # 5 (05676-1735)
PHONE..................................802 244-1457
Garry Kittredge, *President*
Allison Leathery, *Production*
EMP: 25
SALES (est): 3.8MM
SALES (corp-wide): 536.1MM **Privately Held**
WEB: www.dartmouthjournals.com
SIC: 2721 Periodicals-Publishing/Printing
HQ: The Sheridan Group Inc
450 Fame Ave
Hanover PA 17331
717 632-3535

(G-22583)
ION SCIENCE LLC
162 S Main St (05676-1520)
PHONE..................................802 244-5153
Sam Holson, *Executive*
EMP: 7
SALES (est): 645.8K **Privately Held**
SIC: 3829 Mfg Measuring/Controlling Devices

(G-22584)
NEUDORFER INC
Also Called: Neudorfer Tables
183 Crossett Hl (05676-9408)
P.O. Box 501 (05676-0501)
PHONE..................................802 244-5338
Robert Neudorfer, *President*
Kathy Dean, *Vice Pres*
Joshua Neudorfer, *Admin Sec*
EMP: 10
SALES (est): 1.4MM **Privately Held**
WEB: www.neudorfer.com
SIC: 2521 Mfg Wood Office Furniture

(G-22585)
SUNJAS ORIENTAL FOODS INC
40 Foundry St Ste 1a (05676-1554)
PHONE..................................802 244-7644
Sunja Yi Hayden, *President*
David Hayden, *Vice Pres*
EMP: 8
SQ FT: 2,500
SALES: 800K **Privately Held**
SIC: 2032 Mfg Oriental Specialty Food Items

(G-22586)
T S S INC
Also Called: Super Thin Saws
80 Commercial Dr Ste 5 (05676-8957)
PHONE..................................802 244-8101
John Schultz, *President*
Robert D Bisbee, *Vice Pres*
Roland D Strom, *Vice Pres*
EMP: 21
SQ FT: 10,000
SALES (est): 3.9MM **Privately Held**
WEB: www.sts-locates.com
SIC: 3425 7699 Mfg Saw Blades/Handsaws Repair Services

(G-22587)
URSA MAJOR LLC
1 Stowe St (05676-1820)
PHONE..................................802 560-7116
Emily Doyle,
EMP: 4 **EST:** 2016
SALES (est): 519.1K **Privately Held**
SIC: 2844 Mfg Toilet Preparations

(G-22588)
VERMONT HAND CRAFTERS INC
Also Called: Vermont Handcrafters
855 Bolton Vly Access Rd (05676-9136)
P.O. Box 1184, Williston (05495-1184)
PHONE..................................802 434-5044
Meta Strick, *President*
Margaret Bonham, *Principal*
EMP: 5
SALES: 169.3K **Privately Held**
WEB: www.vermonthandcrafters.com
SIC: 3944 5945 Mfg Games/Toys Ret Hobbies/Toys/Games

(G-22589)
WORKWISE LLC
121 S Pinnacle Ridge Rd (05676-4430)
PHONE..................................802 881-8178
Kristin Kassis,
Linda Wade,
EMP: 20
SALES (est): 1MM **Privately Held**
SIC: 7372 Prepackaged Software Services

Waterbury Center
Washington County

(G-22590)
BUY MONTHLY PUBLISHING INC
2687 Waterbury-Stowe Rd (05677-7141)
PHONE..................................802 244-6620
EMP: 7
SQ FT: 3,000
SALES: 700K **Privately Held**
WEB: www.buymonthlypublishing.com
SIC: 2752 Lithographic Job Printing

(G-22591)
GRENIERS GARDEN & BAKERY
1413 Guptil Rd (05677-7001)
PHONE..................................802 244-8057
Joan Grenier, *Owner*
Roger Grenier Jr, *Co-Owner*
EMP: 6
SALES (est): 240K **Privately Held**
SIC: 2051 Mfg Bread/Related Products

(G-22592)
STATICWORX INC
4706 Waterbury-Stowe Rd (05677-8315)
P.O. Box 248 (05677-0248)
PHONE..................................617 923-2000
David H Long, *President*
Terri A Long, *Treasurer*
▲ **EMP:** 5
SALES (est): 1.1MM **Privately Held**
WEB: www.staticworx.com
SIC: 3089 Mfg Plastic Products

(G-22593)
VERMONT MAPLE SUG MAKERS ASSOC
248 Maggies Way (05677-8043)
PHONE..................................802 498-7767
Arnold Piper, *Exec Dir*
EMP: 3 **EST:** 2014
SALES (est): 168.4K **Privately Held**
SIC: 2099 Mfg Food Preparations

(G-22594)
ZIEMKE GLASS BLOWING STUDIO
3033 Rte 100 N (05677)
P.O. Box 327 (05677-0327)
PHONE..................................802 244-6126
Glenn Ziemke, *Owner*
EMP: 4
SALES (est): 276.8K **Privately Held**
SIC: 3229 Mfg Pressed/Blown Glass

Waterville
Lamoille County

(G-22595)
LARAWAY MOUNTAIN MAPLE
1959 Codding Hollow Rd (05492-9664)
PHONE..................................802 644-5433
Cheryl Dark, *Owner*
EMP: 4
SALES: 6K **Privately Held**
SIC: 2099 Mfg Food Preparations

Websterville
Washington County

(G-22596)
ADAMS GRANITE COMPANY INC
58 Pitman Rd (05678)
P.O. Box 126, Barre (05641-0126)
PHONE..................................802 476-5281
Kerry Zorzi, *President*
Carole Cecchini, *Vice Pres*
Matt Dion, *Director*
Michael Ornitz, *Administration*
◆ **EMP:** 60
SQ FT: 70,000
SALES (est): 8.2MM **Privately Held**
WEB: www.adamsgranite.com
SIC: 3281 1411 Mfg Cut Stone/Products Dimension Stone Quarry

(G-22597)
HIGHLAND SUGARWORKS INC
49 Parker Rd (05678)
P.O. Box 58 (05678-0058)
PHONE..................................802 479-1747
James E Macisaac, *President*
Deborah L Frimodig, *Corp Secy*
▲ **EMP:** 12
SQ FT: 20,000
SALES (est): 1.9MM **Privately Held**
WEB: www.highlandsugarworks.com
SIC: 2099 5149 Mfg Food Preparations Whol Groceries

(G-22598)
VERMONT CREAMERY LLC
40 Pitman Rd (05678)
P.O. Box 95 (05678-0095)
PHONE..................................802 479-9371
Adeline Druart, *President*
Matthew Reese, *Controller*
Frank Michael Muoz, *Marketing Staff*
Allison Hooper,
▲ **EMP:** 29
SALES (est): 6.4MM
SALES (corp-wide): 6.8B **Privately Held**
WEB: www.vtbutterandcheeseco.com
SIC: 2022 Mfg Cheese
PA: Land O'lakes, Inc.
4001 Lexington Ave N
Arden Hills MN 55126
651 375-2222

Wells
Rutland County

(G-22599)
GRANNY BLOSSOM SPECIALTY
Also Called: Granny Blossom's
425 Vt Route 30 (05774)
PHONE..................................802 645-0507
Robert Kopp, *President*
Doris Kopp, *Treasurer*
EMP: 5
SQ FT: 4,000
SALES: 3.5MM **Privately Held**
WEB: www.grannyblossomsspecialty-foods.com
SIC: 2099 5149 Mfg Food Preparations Whol Groceries

Wells River
Orange County

(G-22600)
BREAD & CHOCOLATE INC
Also Called: Moose Mountain Food Co.
1538 Industrial Park (05081-9806)
P.O. Box 692 (05081-0692)
PHONE..................................802 429-2920
Jonathan Rutstein, *President*
Fran Rutstein, *Corp Secy*
Wolf Gang Leibmann, *Exec VP*
▲ **EMP:** 8
SQ FT: 9,600
SALES (est): 1MM **Privately Held**
WEB: www.burnhamandmills.com
SIC: 2099 5499 Mfg And Retails Gourmet Foods

(G-22601)
GREEN MOUNTAIN MONOGRAM INC
Also Called: Top Dead Center Apparel
14 Creamery St (05081)
P.O. Box 753 (05081-0753)
PHONE..................................802 757-2553
Gene R Eastman, *President*
EMP: 15
SALES (est): 1.3MM **Privately Held**
WEB: www.topdead.com
SIC: 2395 Pleating/Stitching Services

(G-22602)
ROWDEN BROS CORPORATION
Also Called: Robco Steel Fabricators
416 Ryegate Rd (05081-8942)
PHONE..................................802 757-2807
Robert D Rowden, *President*
William T Rowden, *Vice Pres*
EMP: 5
SALES: 950K **Privately Held**
SIC: 3441 Structural Metal Fabrication

(G-22603)
SILLY COW FARMS LLC
293 Industrial Park Rd (05081)
P.O. Box 692 (05081-0692)
PHONE..................................802 429-2920
William Burnham, *Mng Member*
EMP: 20 **EST:** 2015
SALES: 3.5MM **Privately Held**
SIC: 2066 Mfg Chocolate/Cocoa Products

West Burke
Caledonia County

(G-22604)
A & J GRINDING SERVICE
42 A Frame Dr (05871-8995)
PHONE..................................802 467-3038
Tony Amodeo, *Owner*
EMP: 3
SALES: 225K **Privately Held**
SIC: 3421 Mfg Cutlery

West Dover
Windham County

(G-22605)
BACHAR SAMAWI INNOVATIONS LLC (PA)
266a Handle Rd (05356)
PHONE..................................802 464-0440
Bachar Samawi, *CEO*
EMP: 3
SALES (est): 198.6K **Privately Held**
SIC: 3829 3949 5961 Mfg Measuring/Controlling Devices Mfg Sporting/Athletic Goods Ret Mail-Order House

(G-22606)
BROWN COUNTRY SERVICES LLC
131 Route 100 (05356)
P.O. Box 127 (05356-0127)
PHONE..................................802 464-5200
Robert Fisher Esq, *Administration*
EMP: 6
SALES (est): 635.8K **Privately Held**
SIC: 2842 Mfg Polish/Sanitation Goods

West Glover
Orleans County

(G-22607)
GIBSON PEGGY DAY
Also Called: Northeast Kingdom Balsam
2492 Parker Rd (05875-9666)
PHONE..................................802 525-3034
Peggy Day Gibson, *Owner*
EMP: 13
SQ FT: 1,800
SALES (est): 823.7K **Privately Held**
SIC: 3999 Mfg Misc Products

West Halifax
Windham County

(G-22608)
VITRI FORMS INC
675 Thomashill Rd (05358)
PHONE..................................802 254-5235
Heather Nelson, *President*
Kaleb Sherman, *Engineer*
EMP: 4
SQ FT: 1,500
SALES: 400K **Privately Held**
WEB: www.vitriforms.com
SIC: 3229 Mfg Blown Glass Products

West Marlboro
Windham County

(G-22609)
VERMONT DISTILLERS INC
7627 Route 9 E (05363-9519)
PHONE..................................802 464-2003
Edward C Metcalfe Jr, *Principal*
EMP: 6
SALES (est): 488.2K **Privately Held**
SIC: 2085 Mfg Distilled/Blended Liquor

West Newbury
Orange County

(G-22610)
ARK OF SAFETY
Also Called: Green Maountain Yogurt
265 French Rd (05085)
P.O. Box 95 (05085-0095)
PHONE..................................802 429-2537
Dianne Wyatt, *Mng Member*
Sharon Jones,
EMP: 5
SALES: 25K **Privately Held**
SIC: 2841 Mfg Soap/Other Detergents

West Pawlet
Rutland County

(G-22611)
J N G HADEKA SLATE FLOORING
773 Briar Hill Rd (05775-9664)
PHONE..................................802 265-3351
Gary Hadeka, *President*
John Hadeka, *Vice Pres*
Anne Hadeka, *Treasurer*
EMP: 8 **EST:** 1984
SALES (est): 778.1K **Privately Held**
SIC: 3281 Mfg Cut Stone/Products

(G-22612)
NEWMONT SLATE CO INC (PA)
720 Vt Route 149 (05775-9792)
PHONE..................................802 645-0203
John M Williams, *President*
David Bean, *Vice Pres*
EMP: 26
SQ FT: 24,000
SALES (est): 6.4MM **Privately Held**
WEB: www.neslate.com
SIC: 3281 2952 Mfg Cut Stone/Products Mfg Asphalt Felts/Coatings

(G-22613)
VITRIESSE GLASS STUDIO
1258 Betts Bridge Rd (05775-8803)
PHONE..................................802 645-9800
Lucy Berghaimni, *Owner*
EMP: 3
SALES (est): 140K **Privately Held**
WEB: www.vitriesse.com
SIC: 3231 Mfg Products-Purchased Glass

West Rupert
Bennington County

(G-22614)
AUTHENTIC DESIGNS INC
Also Called: Bast Road Collection
154 Mill Rd (05776-9716)
PHONE..................................802 394-7715
Daniel Krauss, *President*
▼ **EMP:** 10
SALES (est): 890K **Privately Held**
SIC: 3645 3646 Mfg Residential Lighting Fixtures Mfg Commercial Lighting Fixtures

West Rutland
Rutland County

(G-22615)
GREEN MOUNTAIN AWNING INC
36 Marble St (05777)
P.O. Box 929 (05777-0929)
PHONE..................................802 438-2951
Robert Pearo Sr, *President*
Robert Pearo Jr, *Vice Pres*
EMP: 6 **EST:** 1935
SALES: 312K **Privately Held**
WEB: www.greenmountainawning.com
SIC: 2394 3444 Mfg Canvas & Aluminum Awnings

(G-22616)
H HIRSCHMANN LTD
Also Called: HIRSCHMANN WINDOWS AND DOORS
467 Sheldon Ave (05777-9394)
PHONE..................................802 438-4447
Rolf Hirschmann, *President*
Ursula Hirschmann, *Treasurer*
▲ **EMP:** 12
SALES: 3MM **Privately Held**
WEB: www.eurollscreen.com
SIC: 2431 5211 5031 Mfg Millwork Ret Lumber/Building Mtrl Whol Lumber/Plywd/Millwk

(G-22617)
JACK RUSSELL
Also Called: Russell Optics
186 Marble St (05777-4413)
P.O. Box 5 (05777-0005)
PHONE..................................802 438-5213
Jack Russell, *Owner*
EMP: 3
SQ FT: 6,000
SALES: 380K **Privately Held**
WEB: www.opticalflats.com
SIC: 3827 3229 Mfg Optical Instruments/Lenses Mfg Pressed/Blown Glass

(G-22618)
MCCORMACKS MACHINE CO INC
Also Called: Clarendon Harwood Bowls
5383 Walker Mt Rd (05777)
P.O. Box 30 (05777-0030)
PHONE..................................802 438-2345
Edward B McCormack, *President*
Mark Mc Cormack, *Vice Pres*
EMP: 6 **EST:** 1956
SALES: 148.9K **Privately Held**
SIC: 3559 3553 3599 3541 Mfg Misc Industry Mach Mfg Woodworking Mach Mfg Industrial Machinery Mfg Machine Tool-Cutting

(G-22619)
MENARD MANUFACTURING
162 Misty Mdws (05777-9843)
PHONE..................................802 438-5173
Arthur Menard, *Owner*
EMP: 4
SALES: 125K **Privately Held**
SIC: 3599 Mfg Industrial Machinery

(G-22620)
VERMONT JUVENILE FURN MFG INC
Also Called: Pet Gear
192 Sheldon Ave (05777-9615)
P.O. Box 99 (05777-0099)
PHONE..................................802 438-2231
Scott Jakubowski, *Vice Pres*
Chris Jakubowski, *Vice Pres*
Todd Jakubowski, *Exec Sec*
▲ **EMP:** 12 **EST:** 1934
SQ FT: 86,000
SALES (est): 4.3MM **Privately Held**
WEB: www.petgearinc.com
SIC: 3999 Mfg Pet Products

West Topsham
Orange County

(G-22621)
BLACKLIGHTNING PUBLISHING INC
252 Riddle Pond Rd (05086-8901)
PHONE..................................802 439-6462
Walter V Jeffries, *President*
Jessica Dion, *Treasurer*
EMP: 6
SALES (est): 306.1K **Privately Held**
WEB: www.bltserve.com
SIC: 2731 Publisher

(G-22622)
LIMLAWS PULPWOOD INC
Also Called: Limo Chipping and Land Query
261 Vt Route 25 (05086-9741)
PHONE..................................802 439-3503
Bruce E Limlaw, *President*
Ruth Limlaw, *Admin Sec*
EMP: 15
SQ FT: 500
SALES (est): 3MM **Privately Held**
SIC: 2631 Paperboard Mill

(G-22623)
OTTERMAN LOGGING & EXCAVATING
11 Branch Road Pvt (05086-9601)
PHONE..................................802 439-5714
Steve Otterman, *President*
EMP: 6
SALES (est): 520K **Privately Held**
SIC: 2411 Logging

(G-22624)
SUGAR MOUNTAIN FARM LLC
252 Riddle Pond Rd (05086-8901)
PHONE..................................802 439-6462
Amy Swingle, *Cust Mgr*
Walter Jeffries, *Mng Member*
EMP: 5
SQ FT: 1,200
SALES (est): 353.4K **Privately Held**
SIC: 2013 Mfg Prepared Meats

West Townshend
Windham County

(G-22625)
AMP TIMBER HARVESTING INC
449 Cross Rd (05359-9622)
P.O. Box 1104 (05359-1104)
PHONE..................................802 874-7260
William Parker, *President*
Dennis Allard, *Corp Secy*
EMP: 3
SALES (est): 393K **Privately Held**
SIC: 2411 Logging

▲ = Import ▼=Export
◆ =Import/Export

Westfield
Orleans County

(G-22626)
BACKUS DISTILLERY LLC
379 Kennison Rd (05874-9754)
P.O. Box 92 (05874-0092)
PHONE....802 999-2255
Luke Backus, *Administration*
EMP: 3
SALES (est): 131.5K **Privately Held**
SIC: 2085 Mfg Distilled/Blended Liquor

(G-22627)
ROZELLE INC
4260 Loop Rd (05874-9729)
P.O. Box 70 (05874-0070)
PHONE....802 744-2270
Marielle Demuth, *President*
Gene Besaw, *Principal*
Marcia Rozelle, *Exec VP*
EMP: 27 **EST:** 1968
SQ FT: 22,000
SALES (est): 5.4MM **Privately Held**
WEB: www.rozelle.com
SIC: 2844 Mfg Toilet Preparations

Westford
Chittenden County

(G-22628)
G SCATCHARD LTD
Also Called: G Scatchard Lamps
958 Vt Route 128 15 (05494)
P.O. Box 71, Underhill (05489-0071)
PHONE....802 899-2181
George Scatchard, *President*
EMP: 3
SALES: 190K **Privately Held**
WEB: www.gslamps.com
SIC: 3645 5023 5719 Mfg Residentl Light Fixt Whol Homefurnishings

(G-22629)
TOM STEBBINS DBA KITE ENE
745 Woods Hollow Rd (05494-9771)
PHONE....802 878-9650
Susan Stebbins, *Principal*
EMP: 3 **EST:** 2009
SALES (est): 178.2K **Privately Held**
SIC: 3944 Mfg Games/Toys

Westminster
Windham County

(G-22630)
GREEN MOUNTAIN GAZEBO
237 Kimball Hill Rd (05158)
P.O. Box 80, Saxtons River (05154-0080)
PHONE....802 869-1212
Dennis Gilkenson, *Owner*
EMP: 8
SALES (est): 600K **Privately Held**
WEB: www.greenmountaingazebo.com
SIC: 2542 Mfg Gazebos

(G-22631)
UNITED PUETT STARTING GATE
7668 Us Route 5 Ste B (05158-4405)
PHONE....802 463-3440
Michael Costello, *President*
Eileen Costello, *Corp Secy*
Noel Cassidy, *Vice Pres*
EMP: 3
SALES: 1MM **Privately Held**
SIC: 3441 Structural Metal Fabrication

(G-22632)
WOODSTONE COMPANY INC (PA)
17 Morse Brook Rd (05158)
PHONE....802 722-9217
H Jay Eshelman III, *President*
Tony Elliott, *Principal*
J Barton Elliott Jr, *Treasurer*
George Nostrand, *Admin Sec*
EMP: 15
SALES (est): 5.3MM **Privately Held**
WEB: www.woodstone.com
SIC: 2431 Mfg Millwork

Westminster Station
Windham County

(G-22633)
BURTCO INC
185 Rte 123 (05159)
P.O. Box 40 (05159-0040)
PHONE....802 722-3358
Stanton N Scott, *President*
George W Nostrand, *Admin Sec*
EMP: 10
SQ FT: 25,000
SALES: 1.4MM **Privately Held**
WEB: www.burtcoinc.com
SIC: 2911 3443 3446 Petroleum Refiner Mfg Fabricated Plate Work Mfg Architectural Metalwork

Westminster W
Windham County

(G-22634)
HORIZON MANUFACTURING & DESIGN
56 Burnett Rd (05346-8927)
PHONE....802 384-3715
Richard W Crocker, *President*
EMP: 3 **EST:** 2014
SALES (est): 237K **Privately Held**
SIC: 3599 Mfg Industrial Machinery

White River Junction
Windsor County

(G-22635)
BLUE MOON FOODS INC
Also Called: Blue Moon Sorbet
568 N Main St Ste 1 (05001-7222)
P.O. Box 874, Quechee (05059-0874)
PHONE....802 295-1165
John Donaldson, *President*
Pamela Frantz, *Vice Pres*
EMP: 7
SQ FT: 600
SALES: 300K **Privately Held**
WEB: www.bluemoonsorbet.com
SIC: 2024 Mfg Frozen Dessert

(G-22636)
CHELSEA GREEN PUBLISHING CO
85 N Main St Ste 120 (05001-7135)
P.O. Box 428 (05001-0428)
PHONE....802 295-6300
Margaret Baldwin Jr, *President*
Ian Baldwin, *Vice Pres*
▲ **EMP:** 20
SQ FT: 1,800
SALES (est): 3.5MM **Privately Held**
WEB: www.chelseagreen.com
SIC: 2731 Books-Publishing/Printing

(G-22637)
CONCEPTS ETI INC
217 Billings Farm Rd (05001-9486)
PHONE....802 296-2321
David Japikse, *CEO*
Harold A Keiling, *President*
Daniel V Hinch, *Vice Pres*
Harold Keiling, *Vice Pres*
Peter Weitzman, *Vice Pres*
▲ **EMP:** 100 **EST:** 2015
SQ FT: 20,000
SALES (est): 824.1K **Privately Held**
WEB: www.conceptseti.com
SIC: 7372 Prepackaged Software Services

(G-22638)
CONCEPTS NREC LLC (PA)
217 Billings Farm Rd (05001-9486)
PHONE....802 296-2321
David Japikse, *CEO*
Shawna O'Neal, *Administration*
Ryan Morrison, *Technician*
EMP: 60
SALES (est): 1.9MM **Privately Held**
SIC: 7372 Prepackaged Software Services

(G-22639)
IBEX OUTDOOR CLOTHING LLC
132 Ballardvale Dr (05001-7008)
PHONE....802 359-4239
Ted Manning, *CEO*
Tina Bourgeois,
John Fernsell,
▲ **EMP:** 25
SQ FT: 7,000
SALES (est): 2.7MM
SALES (corp-wide): 67.3MM **Privately Held**
WEB: www.ibexwear.com
SIC: 2321 Mfg Men's/Boy's Furnishings
PA: North Castle Partners, L.L.C.
183 E Putnam Ave
Greenwich CT 06830
203 485-0216

(G-22640)
JERICHO WOODWORKING
3221 Jericho St (05001-9308)
PHONE....802 295-9399
Steven Sass, *Owner*
EMP: 4
SALES (est): 329.5K **Privately Held**
SIC: 2431 2434 Mfg Millwork Mfg Wood Kitchen Cabinets

(G-22641)
JUNCTION FRAME SHOP INC
55 S Main St (05001-7097)
PHONE....802 296-2121
Mark Estes, *President*
Dianne Estes, *Vice Pres*
EMP: 4
SALES: 350K **Privately Held**
WEB: www.junctionframeshop.com
SIC: 2499 7699 Mfg Wood Products Repair Services

(G-22642)
RICHARD AKERBOOM
Also Called: Sylvan Software
85 N Main St Ste 245 (05001-7174)
P.O. Box 566, Norwich (05055-0566)
PHONE....802 291-6116
Richard Akerboom, *Owner*
EMP: 3
SALES (est): 140K **Privately Held**
SIC: 7372 Prepackaged Software Services

(G-22643)
TOWN OF HARTFORD
Also Called: Fire Dept
812 Va Cutoff Rd (05001-9777)
PHONE....802 295-9425
Steven Locke, *Chief*
EMP: 30 **Privately Held**
SIC: 3711 Mfg Motor Vehicle/Car Bodies
PA: Town Of Hartford
171 Bridge St
White River Junction VT 05001
802 295-9353

(G-22644)
WORLD CUISINE CONCEPTS LLC
Also Called: A Taste Afrcas - World Cuisine
43 Pine St (05001-7031)
P.O. Box 241, Hartford (05047-0241)
PHONE....603 676-8591
Damaris Hall,
EMP: 5
SALES (est): 287.8K **Privately Held**
SIC: 2099 Mfg Food Preparations

Whiting
Addison County

(G-22645)
TATAS NATURAL ALCHEMY LLC (PA)
Also Called: Tata Harper Skincare
1135 Wooster Rd (05778-9727)
PHONE....802 462-3814
Pav Volkert, *Creative Dir*
Graciela Guzman,
Henry Harper,
Blake Perlman,
▲ **EMP:** 50
SQ FT: 2,000
SALES (est): 25.5MM **Privately Held**
SIC: 2844 Mfg Toilet Preparations

(G-22646)
TATAS NATURAL ALCHEMY LLC
Also Called: Tata Harper Labratory
1136 Wooster Rd (05778-9712)
PHONE....802 462-3958
Ferro Tamera, *Vice Pres*
Jon Faris, *Research*
Graciela Guzman, *Mng Member*
EMP: 96
SALES (corp-wide): 25.5MM **Privately Held**
SIC: 2844 Mfg Toilet Preparations
PA: Tata's Natural Alchemy, Llc
1135 Wooster Rd
Whiting VT 05778
802 462-3814

Whitingham
Windham County

(G-22647)
SAWYER BENTWOOD INC
247 Maple Dr (05361-9749)
PHONE....802 368-2357
George Campo, *President*
EMP: 25 **EST:** 1801
SQ FT: 10,000
SALES (est): 3.5MM **Privately Held**
WEB: www.sawyerbentwood.com
SIC: 2511 Mfg Wood Household Furniture Parts Specializing In Hardwood Bending

Wilder
Windsor County

(G-22648)
STAVE PUZZLES INCORPORATED
163 Olcott Dr (05088)
P.O. Box 329, Norwich (05055-0329)
PHONE....802 295-5200
Steve Richardson, *President*
Martha Richardson, *Treasurer*
EMP: 20
SQ FT: 3,500
SALES (est): 3.1MM **Privately Held**
WEB: www.stavepuzzles.com
SIC: 3944 Mfg Wooden Jigsaw Puzzles

Williamstown
Orange County

(G-22649)
AMERICAN RURAL FIRE APPARATUS
Also Called: Vermont Fire Technologies
154 Industry St (05679-9317)
P.O. Box 154 (05679-0154)
PHONE....802 433-1554
James Pinard, *Vice Pres*
Earl Everhart, *Vice Pres*
EMP: 7
SQ FT: 6,000
SALES (est): 941K **Privately Held**
SIC: 3711 3569 Mfg Motor Vehicle/Car Bodies Mfg General Industrial Machinery

(G-22650)
PROGRESSIVE PLASTICS INC
Also Called: P P I
85 Industry St (05679-9819)
P.O. Box 435 (05679-0435)
PHONE....802 433-1563
Hank Buermann, *President*
▲ **EMP:** 37
SQ FT: 12,000
SALES (est): 8.4MM **Privately Held**
SIC: 3089 Mfg Plastic Products

GEOGRAPHIC

(G-22651)
STILLWATER GRAPHICS INC
71 Depot St (05679-9126)
PHONE....802 433-9898
John Rhodes, *President*
Dana Laplant, *Vice Pres*
EMP: 13 **EST:** 1994
SQ FT: 6,000
SALES (est): 1.2MM **Privately Held**
SIC: 2752 7336 2791 Lithographic Commercial Printing Commercial Art/Graphic Design Typesetting Services

Williston
Chittenden County

(G-22652)
4382412 CANADA INC
Also Called: Illumination Devices
310 Hurricane Ln Unit 3 (05495-2082)
PHONE....802 225-5911
Josh Niebling, *CEO*
EMP: 5
SALES (est): 876.7K **Privately Held**
SIC: 3674 Mfg Semiconductors/Related Devices

(G-22653)
89 NORTH INC
20 Winter Sport Ln # 135 (05495-8146)
PHONE....802 881-0302
Paul Millman, *CEO*
Henry Schek, *Managing Dir*
Mark Laplante, *Engineer*
Sam Stats, *Engineer*
Carl Padula, *CFO*
EMP: 9
SQ FT: 2,700
SALES (est): 1.5MM **Privately Held**
SIC: 3827 Mfg Optical Instruments/Lenses

(G-22654)
ALLEARTH RENEWABLES INC
94 Harvest Ln (05495-8997)
PHONE....802 872-9600
David Blittersdorf, *President*
Dar Gibson, *Opers Staff*
Phillip Pouech, *Opers Staff*
Jim Becker, *Purch Mgr*
Paul Gustafson, *Technical Mgr*
EMP: 43 **EST:** 2005
SALES (est): 20MM **Privately Held**
SIC: 3674 5211 Mfg Semiconductors/Related Devices Ret Lumber/Building Materials

(G-22655)
ASTENJOHNSON INC
Also Called: Johnson Filaments
192 Industrial Ave (05495-9820)
PHONE....802 658-2040
Jeff Bouffard, *Sales Staff*
Teresa Renaud, *Manager*
John Paugh, *Maintence Staff*
EMP: 70
SALES (corp-wide): 542.1MM **Privately Held**
SIC: 3089 3496 3081 2221 Mfg Plastic Products Mfg Misc Fab Wire Prdts Mfg Unsupport Plstc Film Manmad Brdwv Fabric Mill
PA: Astenjohnson, Inc.
4399 Corporate Rd
North Charleston SC 29405
843 747-7800

(G-22656)
ATC GROUP SERVICES LLC
171 Commerce St (05495-7836)
P.O. Box 1486 (05495-1486)
PHONE....802 862-1980
Thomas Broydo, *Branch Mgr*
EMP: 8 **Privately Held**
SIC: 3292 Mfg Asbestos Products
HQ: Atc Group Services Llc
5750 Johnston St Ste 400
Lafayette LA 70503
337 234-8777

(G-22657)
BAKER COMMODITIES INC
354 Avenue B (05495-7149)
PHONE....802 658-0721
David King, *Manager*
EMP: 7
SALES (corp-wide): 153.6MM **Privately Held**
WEB: www.bakercommodities.com
SIC: 2077 Rendering Plant & Transfer Station
PA: Baker Commodities, Inc.
4020 Bandini Blvd
Vernon CA 90058
323 268-2801

(G-22658)
BUSINESS FINANCIAL PUBG LLC
380 Hurricane Ln Ste 202 (05495-2085)
PHONE....802 865-9886
Ian Wyatt, *Principal*
EMP: 12
SALES (est): 456.4K **Privately Held**
SIC: 2741 Misc Publishing

(G-22659)
CHAMPLAIN CHOCOLATE COMPANY
Also Called: Lake Champlain Chocolates
290 Boyer Cir (05495-8931)
PHONE....802 864-1808
EMP: 4
SALES (corp-wide): 20.1MM **Privately Held**
SIC: 2066 Mfg Chocolate/Cocoa Products
PA: Champlain Chocolate Company Inc
750 Pine St
Burlington VT 05401
802 864-1808

(G-22660)
CHITTENDEN ENVIRONMENTAL
8195 Williston Rd (05495-5289)
PHONE....802 578-0194
Ronnie Finney, *COO*
EMP: 3 **EST:** 2014
SALES (est): 253.7K **Privately Held**
SIC: 2611 7389 Pulp Mill

(G-22661)
DEALERPOLICY LLC
2300 St George Rd (05495-7433)
PHONE....802 655-9000
Travis Fitzgerald, *CEO*
Jeffrey Mongeon, *President*
Ryan Fitzgerald, *VP Business*
Kurt Liebegott, *CFO*
Chris Wells, *Director*
EMP: 6 **EST:** 2015
SALES: 1MM **Privately Held**
SIC: 7372 Prepackaged Software Services

(G-22662)
DIGITAL PRESS PRINTERS LLC
Also Called: Print Tech
128 Commerce St (05495-8126)
PHONE....802 863-5579
Susan Ghobadi,
Benjamin Ghobadi,
EMP: 15
SQ FT: 6,000
SALES (est): 1.8MM **Privately Held**
SIC: 2752 7334 Commercial Lithographic Printing & Photocopying & Duplicating Services

(G-22663)
DURASOL SYSTEMS INC
Also Called: Otter Creek Awning
19 Echo Pl (05495-9374)
PHONE....802 864-3009
Toll Free:....888 -
Todd Warren, *President*
EMP: 20
SALES (corp-wide): 31.1MM **Privately Held**
WEB: www.durasol.com
SIC: 2394 5999 Mfg Canvas/Related Products Ret Misc Merchandise
HQ: Durasol Systems, Inc.
445 Bellvale Rd
Chester NY 10918
845 610-1100

(G-22664)
ENGINEERED MONOFILAMENTS CORP
21 Commerce St (05495-9731)
PHONE....802 863-6823
F Richard Cramton, *President*
Michel Allen, *General Mgr*
Mitch Allen, *General Mgr*
EMP: 5
SQ FT: 5,000
SALES (est): 681K **Privately Held**
WEB: www.engmono.com
SIC: 3089 Mfg Plastic Products

(G-22665)
ESSEX MANUFACTURING CO
301 Avenue D Ste 15 (05495-7905)
P.O. Box 556, Summerfield FL (34492-0556)
PHONE....802 864-4584
Robert Loiselle, *Owner*
EMP: 6
SQ FT: 3,000
SALES (est): 43.8K **Privately Held**
SIC: 3569 Mfg Industrial Filters

(G-22666)
G W LUMBER & MILLWORK INC (PA)
1860 Williston Rd Ste 3 (05495)
PHONE....802 860-7370
Gerald Wilcox, *President*
Robert Guy, *Vice Pres*
Maryse Wilcox, *Admin Sec*
EMP: 6
SQ FT: 15,000
SALES (est): 915.3K **Privately Held**
SIC: 2426 Hardwood Dimension/Floor Mill

(G-22667)
GARLIC PRESS INC
Also Called: Pop Color
237 Commerce St Ste 102 (05495-7157)
PHONE....802 864-0670
Michael Swaidner, *President*
Carol Mac Donald, *Vice Pres*
EMP: 11
SQ FT: 2,200
SALES: 906.3K **Privately Held**
WEB: www.nehomes.com
SIC: 2741 7336 Magazine Pre-Press Production & Graphic Design

(G-22668)
GARLIC PRESS INC
237 Commerce St (05495-7157)
PHONE....802 864-0670
Michael Swaidner, *President*
EMP: 4
SALES (est): 199K **Privately Held**
SIC: 2741 Misc Publishing

(G-22669)
GDS MANUFACTURING COMPANY
Also Called: Kemtuff
32 Boyer Cir (05495-8932)
P.O. Box 663 (05495-0663)
PHONE....802 862-7610
Gary Riggs, *President*
Tim Wissell, *Vice Pres*
EMP: 7
SQ FT: 16,000
SALES (est): 932.4K **Privately Held**
WEB: www.kemtuff.com
SIC: 3479 Coating/Engraving Service

(G-22670)
GENERAL DYNAMICS-OTS INC
Also Called: Gd-Ots Williston
326 Ibm Rd Bldg 862 (05495-7999)
PHONE....802 662-7000
Steve Elgin, *Manager*
EMP: 9
SALES (corp-wide): 36.1B **Publicly Held**
WEB: www.gdatp.com
SIC: 3728 7382 3812 Mfg Aircraft Parts/Equipment Security Systems Services Mfg Search/Navigation Equipment
HQ: General Dynamics Ots (California), Inc.
11399 16th Ct N Ste 200
Saint Petersburg FL 33716
727 578-8100

(G-22671)
GORDONS WINDOW DECOR INC (PA)
Also Called: Gordons Window Decor Centl V T
8 Leroy Rd (05495-8965)
PHONE....802 655-7777
Gordon Clements, *President*
Brian Werneke, *Vice Pres*
EMP: 12
SQ FT: 7,000
SALES (est): 1.9MM **Privately Held**
WEB: www.sheerblinds.com
SIC: 2591 2211 5023 2391 Mfg Drape Hardware/Blind Cotton Brdwv Fabric Mill

(G-22672)
GREEN MOUNTAIN COMPOST
1042 Redmond Rd (05495-7729)
PHONE....802 660-4949
Adam Sherman, *Project Mgr*
Dan Goosen, *Manager*
Holly Taylor, *Manager*
Kit Terkins, *Exec Dir*
EMP: 6
SALES (est): 1MM **Privately Held**
SIC: 2879 2875 Mfg Agricultural Chemicals & Composts

(G-22673)
GREEN MOUNTAIN VISTA INC
223 Avenue D 10 (05495-7139)
P.O. Box 950 (05495-0950)
PHONE....802 862-0159
Susan Bender, *President*
Ian Bender, *Vice Pres*
▲ **EMP:** 5
SALES (est): 490K **Privately Held**
WEB: www.gmvista.com
SIC: 2599 5023 Mfg Furniture/Fixtures Whol Homefurnishings

(G-22674)
HONEYWELL INTERNATIONAL INC
203 Cornerstone Dr (05495-4035)
PHONE....877 841-2840
Scott Bellows, *Manager*
EMP: 7
SALES (corp-wide): 41.8B **Publicly Held**
WEB: www.honeywellrefrigerants.com
SIC: 3724 Mfg Aircraft Engines/Parts
PA: Honeywell International Inc.
300 S Tryon St
Charlotte NC 28202
973 455-2000

(G-22675)
KELLEY BROS NEW ENGLAND LLC
87 Holly Ct (05495-7247)
PHONE....802 865-5133
Randy Kruger, *Manager*
EMP: 10
SALES (corp-wide): 43.1MM **Privately Held**
SIC: 2431 Mfg Millwork
HQ: Kelley Bros. Of New England, Llc
17 Hampshire Dr Ste 20
Hudson NH 03051
603 881-5559

(G-22676)
KESTREL HEALTH INFORMATION INC
206 Commerce St (05495-7152)
P.O. Box 189, Hinesburg (05461-0189)
PHONE....802 482-4000
Jeanne Cunningham, *President*
Brian Duerr, *Treasurer*
EMP: 3
SALES (est): 279.7K **Privately Held**
SIC: 2721 Periodicals-Publishing/Printing

(G-22677)
KLA CORPORATION
57 Day Ln 20 (05495-4420)
PHONE....802 318-9100
EMP: 16
SALES (corp-wide): 4.5B **Publicly Held**
SIC: 3827 Mfg Semiconductors/Related Devices

▲ = Import ▼=Export
◆ =Import/Export

PA: Kla Corporation
1 Technology Dr
Milpitas CA 95035
408 875-3000

(G-22678)
KP BUILDING PRODUCTS INC
402 Boyer Cir (05495-8924)
PHONE..........866 850-4447
Lionel Dubrofsky, *President*
Tami Dubrofsky, *Admin Sec*
EMP: 11
SALES (est): 3.6MM
SALES (corp-wide): 537.7MM **Privately Held**
SIC: 3089 5033 Mfg Plastic Products Whol Roofing/Siding/Insulation
HQ: Kaycan Ltd.
402 Boyer Cir
Williston VT 05495
802 865-0114

(G-22679)
LLC COCHRAN COUSINS
Also Called: Slopeside Syrup
170 Boyer Cir Ste 20 (05495-9561)
PHONE..........802 222-0440
Douglas Brown,
EMP: 4
SALES (est): 312.3K **Privately Held**
SIC: 2099 Mfg Food Preparations

(G-22680)
LORD CORPORATION (DH)
Also Called: Lord Microstrain
459 Hurricane Ln Ste 102 (05495-7824)
PHONE..........802 862-6629
Steven Arms, *President*
Christopher Townsend, *Vice Pres*
Lisa Cassell Arms, *Treasurer*
EMP: 62
SQ FT: 30,000
SALES (est): 11.8MM
SALES (corp-wide): 14.3B **Publicly Held**
WEB: www.microstrain.com
SIC: 3823 3841 Mfg Process Control Instruments Mfg Surgical/Medical Instruments
HQ: Lord Corporation
111 Lord Dr
Cary NC 27511
919 468-5979

(G-22681)
MICROSTRAIN INC
459 Hurricane Ln Ste 102 (05495-7824)
PHONE..........802 862-6629
Steven Arms, *President*
Lisa Cassell-Arms, *Treasurer*
Chris Townsend, *Admin Sec*
EMP: 17 **EST:** 1994
SALES (est): 2.1MM **Privately Held**
SIC: 3829 Mfg Measuring/Controlling Devices

(G-22682)
MILL PUBLISHING INC
Also Called: Business People Vermont
237 Commerce St Ste 202 (05495-7157)
P.O. Box 953 (05495-0953)
PHONE..........802 862-4109
EMP: 6
SALES (est): 600.9K **Privately Held**
WEB: www.businesspeoplevermont.com
SIC: 2721 8611 Periodicals

(G-22683)
MOBILE SEMICONDUCTOR CORP
237 Commerce St (05495-7157)
PHONE..........802 399-2449
EMP: 3
SALES (est): 196.5K **Privately Held**
SIC: 3674 Mfg Semiconductors/Related Devices

(G-22684)
NAEPAC
338 Commerce St Unit 10 (05495-7835)
PHONE..........802 497-3654
John J Collins Esq, *Partner*
EMP: 4
SALES (est): 346.3K **Privately Held**
SIC: 3565 Mfg Packaging Machinery

(G-22685)
NEHP INC
1193 S Brownell Rd Ste 35 (05495-7416)
PHONE..........802 652-1444
Adam Tarr, *CEO*
Russ Walton, *President*
Michael St Louis, *Vice Pres*
Joe Mastro, *Engineer*
Ryan Rzepka, *Design Engr*
EMP: 55 **EST:** 2000
SQ FT: 15,000
SALES (est): 10.7MM **Privately Held**
WEB: www.nehp.com
SIC: 3674 Mfg Semiconductors/Related Devices

(G-22686)
NOCO ENERGY CORP
Also Called: Noco Lubricants
461 Avenue D (05495-7853)
PHONE..........802 864-6626
Rob Gaborault, *Manager*
EMP: 8 **Privately Held**
WEB: www.noco.com
SIC: 2992 Whol Petroleum Products
HQ: Noco Energy Corp.
2440 Sheridan Dr Ste 202
Tonawanda NY 14150
716 833-6626

(G-22687)
RAJ COMMUNICATIONS LTD
Also Called: Ladd Research Industries
83 Holly Ct (05495-7247)
PHONE..........802 658-4961
JD Arnott, *President*
John Arnott, *Chairman*
Rita Arnott, *Vice Pres*
EMP: 19
SQ FT: 5,000
SALES: 3.8MM **Privately Held**
WEB: www.laddresearch.com
SIC: 3826 5049 3845 3841 Mfg Analytical Instr Whol Professional Equip Mfg Electromedical Equip Mfg Surgical/Med Instr Mfg Lab Apparatus/Furn

(G-22688)
RETTIG USA INC
Also Called: Myson
45 Krupp Dr (05495-8911)
P.O. Box 1460 (05495-1460)
PHONE..........802 654-7500
Raymond E Farley, *President*
▲ **EMP:** 11
SQ FT: 17,500
SALES (est): 3.5MM
SALES (corp-wide): 1B **Privately Held**
WEB: www.mysoninc.com
SIC: 3567 Mfg Industrial Furnaces/Ovens
HQ: Rettig Icc B.V.
Australielaan 6
Maastricht-Airport 6199

(G-22689)
SATHORN CORPORATION
581 Industrial Ave (05495-7129)
PHONE..........802 860-2121
Bertran Blazy, *President*
Mott James, *General Mgr*
Ernie Oldenburgh, *General Mgr*
Kim Jensen, *Office Mgr*
Brian Matthews, *Office Mgr*
EMP: 20
SALES (est): 3.5MM **Privately Held**
SIC: 3728 Mfg Aircraft Parts/Equipment

(G-22690)
SB SIGNS INC
466 Shunpike Rd (05495-9585)
PHONE..........802 879-7969
Steve Boutin, *Owner*
EMP: 3
SALES (est): 336.1K **Privately Held**
SIC: 3993 Mfg Signs/Advertising Specialties

(G-22691)
SIMMEDTEC LLC
309 Highlands Dr (05495-2141)
PHONE..........802 872-5968
Stephen Bell,
Martin Lewinter,
Markus Meyer,
Bradley Palmer,
EMP: 4
SALES (est): 214.8K **Privately Held**
SIC: 3841 Mfg Surgical/Medical Instruments

(G-22692)
SIMPLEX TIME RECORDER LLC
310 Hurricane Ln Unit 2 (05495-2082)
PHONE..........802 879-6149
Todd Buffum, *Branch Mgr*
EMP: 53 **Privately Held**
WEB: www.comtec-alaska.com
SIC: 3579 Electrical Contractor
HQ: Simplex Time Recorder Llc
50 Technology Dr
Westminster MA 01441

(G-22693)
STATIC & DYNAMIC TECH INC
Also Called: Timbernest
289 Leroy Rd (05495-8991)
PHONE..........802 859-0238
Fax: 802 862-2444
EMP: 4
SQ FT: 23,000
SALES: 1MM **Privately Held**
SIC: 2511 Mfg Wood Household Furniture

(G-22694)
SUBATOMIC DIGITAL LLC
151 Blair Park Rd (05495-7435)
PHONE..........802 857-4864
Alexander Lintott, *CEO*
EMP: 26
SQ FT: 15,000
SALES (est): 1.2MM **Privately Held**
SIC: 2621 Paper Mill

(G-22695)
TSL SNOWSHOES LLC
73 Armand Ln (05495-8915)
P.O. Box 962 (05495-0962)
PHONE..........802 660-8232
Tedd McGuinnes,
▲ **EMP:** 3
SALES (est): 304.2K **Privately Held**
SIC: 3949 Mfg Sporting/Athletic Goods

(G-22696)
VERMONT PLASTICS SPECIALTIES
209 Blair Park Rd (05495-7434)
P.O. Box 483 (05495-0483)
PHONE..........802 879-0072
Richard Dolliver, *President*
EMP: 8 **EST:** 1976
SQ FT: 15,000
SALES (est): 1.1MM **Privately Held**
WEB: www.vermontplastics.com
SIC: 3089 Mfg Plastic Products

(G-22697)
WASHBURN BOAT & AUTO BODY
4989 Williston Rd (05495-5312)
PHONE..........802 863-1383
Christopher Washburn, *Owner*
EMP: 5
SQ FT: 5,000
SALES (est): 360K **Privately Held**
WEB: www.washburnsautobody.com
SIC: 3732 7532 Boatbuilding/Repairing Auto Body Repair/Painting

(G-22698)
WERE TOPS INC
90 Adams Dr Ste 10 (05495-9779)
PHONE..........802 660-8677
EMP: 5
SALES (est): 450K **Privately Held**
SIC: 2541 Counter Top Construction

(G-22699)
WILLISTON PUBG PROMOTIONS LLC
Also Called: Vermont Maturity
300 Cornerstone Dr # 330 (05495-4012)
P.O. Box 1158 (05495-1158)
PHONE..........802 872-9000
Paul Apfelbaum,
EMP: 14
SQ FT: 4,000
SALES (est): 1.5MM **Privately Held**
SIC: 2741 Misc Publishing

Wilmington
Windham County

(G-22700)
CASK & KILN KITCHEN LLC
228 Stowe Hill Rd (05363-9784)
P.O. Box 295 (05363-0295)
PHONE..........802 464-2275
Vincent Gubin, *Principal*
EMP: 4
SALES (est): 451.6K **Privately Held**
SIC: 3559 Mfg Misc Industry Machinery

(G-22701)
INTELLIHOME OF VERMONT L L C
18 Coldbrook Rd (05363-9624)
P.O. Box 851 (05363-0851)
PHONE..........802 464-2499
Douglas Swanson, *Principal*
EMP: 10
SALES (est): 804.6K **Privately Held**
SIC: 3644 Mfg Nonconductive Wiring Devices

(G-22702)
JOHN MC LEOD LTD (PA)
111 W Main St (05363)
P.O. Box 338 (05363-0338)
PHONE..........802 464-8175
John McLeod, *President*
EMP: 20
SQ FT: 13,500
SALES (est): 1.6MM **Privately Held**
WEB: www.vermontbowl.com
SIC: 2499 Mfg Wood Products

(G-22703)
MAPLE LEAF MALT & BREWING
3 N Main St (05363)
PHONE..........802 464-9900
EMP: 9
SALES (est): 578K **Privately Held**
SIC: 2082 Mfg Malt Beverages

(G-22704)
MOOSEHEAD CEDAR LOG HOMES
225 Vermont 9 (05363)
P.O. Box 633 (05363-0633)
PHONE..........802 464-7609
Skip Holton, *Owner*
EMP: 3
SALES (est): 195.9K **Privately Held**
SIC: 2452 Mfg Prefabricated Wood Buildings

(G-22705)
VERMONT MEDIA CORP
Also Called: Deerfield Valley News
797 Vt Route 100 N (05363-7919)
P.O. Box 310, West Dover (05356-0310)
PHONE..........802 464-5757
Randy Capitani, *President*
Vicki Capitani, *Vice Pres*
EMP: 11
SALES (est): 633.8K **Privately Held**
WEB: www.dvalnews.com
SIC: 2711 Newspapers-Publishing/Printing

Windsor
Windsor County

(G-22706)
CHARRON WOOD PRODUCTS INC
28 River St Ste 8 (05089-1436)
P.O. Box 552 (05089-0552)
PHONE..........802 369-0166
Andy Charron, *President*
EMP: 5 **EST:** 1989
SALES (est): 642.2K **Privately Held**
SIC: 2426 Mfg Wood Furniture

(G-22707)
EASTWIND LAPIDARY INC
Also Called: Eastwind Diamond Abrasives
61 Main St (05089-1316)
P.O. Box 302 (05089-0302)
PHONE..........802 674-5427

Douglas Klein, *President*
Lisa Barney, *Admin Sec*
▲ **EMP:** 5
SQ FT: 12,000
SALES (est): 250K **Privately Held**
WEB: www.eastwindabrasive.com
SIC: 3915 5094 3291 Mfg Jewelers' Materials Whol Jewelry/Precs Stone Mfg Abrasive Products

(G-22708)
FELLOWS CORPORATION
7 Everett Ln (05089-1444)
PHONE..................................802 674-6500
Gregory Goldman, *CEO*
David L Goldman, *Ch of Bd*
Mark Swift, *President*
Donald Paulson, *Admin Sec*
EMP: 200 **EST:** 1896
SQ FT: 372,000
SALES (est): 23.5MM **Privately Held**
SIC: 3541 5084 Mfg Machine Tools-Cutting Whol Industrial Equipment

(G-22709)
GREEN MOUNTAIN SMOKEHOUSE
341 Us Route 5 S (05089-9493)
P.O. Box 104, Reading (05062-0104)
PHONE..................................802 674-6653
Jake Henne, *Owner*
EMP: 4 **EST:** 2001
SALES (est): 544.7K **Privately Held**
SIC: 3556 Ret Meat/Fish

(G-22710)
JAM FUEL LLC
5087 Us Route 5 N 1 (05089-9709)
PHONE..................................802 345-6118
Joshua Marcell, *Owner*
EMP: 5
SALES (est): 363.7K **Privately Held**
SIC: 2869 Mfg Industrial Organic Chemicals

(G-22711)
LEBANON SCREW PRODUCTS INC
39 Park Rd (05089-4401)
P.O. Box 379, Hartland (05048-0379)
PHONE..................................802 674-6347
David L Teffner, *President*
Susan Teffner, *Principal*
EMP: 10
SALES: 1.4MM **Privately Held**
WEB: www.lsp-vt.com
SIC: 3451 Mfg Screw Machine Products

(G-22712)
MBBC VERMONT LLC
Also Called: Harpoon Brewery
336 Ruth Carney Dr (05089-9419)
PHONE..................................802 674-5491
Rich Doyle, *CEO*
Dan Kenary, *President*
EMP: 69
SQ FT: 10,000
SALES (est): 8.8MM
SALES (corp-wide): 35.4MM **Privately Held**
WEB: www.harpoonbrewery.com
SIC: 2082 5921 Mfg Malt Beverages Ret Alcoholic Beverages
PA: Mass. Bay Brewing Company, Inc.
306 Northern Ave
Boston MA 02210
617 574-9551

(G-22713)
PURCHASING & INVENTORY CONS
Also Called: P I C
1706 Brook Rd (05089-9314)
PHONE..................................802 674-2620
Francis Hurlburt, *President*
Gloria Hurlburt, *Vice Pres*
EMP: 12
SQ FT: 9,500
SALES (est): 900K **Privately Held**
SIC: 3672 7379 Mfg Printed Circuit Boards & Computer Consulting

(G-22714)
SIMON PEARCE US INC (PA)
Also Called: Simon Pearce Glass and Pottery
109 Park Rd (05089-4440)
PHONE..................................802 674-6280
Clayton Adams, *CEO*
James Murray, *Vice Pres*
Jerod Rockwell, *Site Mgr*
Matthew McFarland, *Production*
Eric Danieli, *QC Mgr*
◆ **EMP:** 164 **EST:** 1981
SQ FT: 81,000
SALES (est): 64.2MM **Privately Held**
WEB: www.simonpearce.com
SIC: 3269 5719 5812 5949 Eating Place

(G-22715)
SIMON PEARCE US INC
Also Called: Simon Pearce PA
109 Park Rd (05089-4440)
P.O. Box 1 (05089-0001)
PHONE..................................802 674-6280
Cora Blake, *Opers Staff*
Jay Benson, *Sales Mgr*
Annmarie Nobile, *Accounts Mgr*
Neil Cockwill, *Marketing Staff*
Meghan Mahoney, *Marketing Staff*
EMP: 60
SALES (corp-wide): 64.2MM **Privately Held**
WEB: www.simonpearce.com
SIC: 3229 Mfg Household Furnishings
PA: Simon Pearce U.S., Inc.
109 Park Rd
Windsor VT 05089
802 674-6280

Winooski
Chittenden County

(G-22716)
AUTOTECH INC
246 Main St (05404-1328)
PHONE..................................802 497-2482
Robert Wetmore, *President*
EMP: 5
SQ FT: 152
SALES: 450K **Privately Held**
SIC: 3714 Mfg Motor Vehicle Parts/Accessories

(G-22717)
BIOTEK INSTRUMENTS INC (HQ)
100 Tigan St (05404-1356)
P.O. Box 998 (05404-0998)
PHONE..................................802 655-4040
Briar Alpert, *President*
Jamie Alpert, *Admin Sec*
▲ **EMP:** 71
SQ FT: 30,600
SALES (est): 30.1MM
SALES (corp-wide): 5.1B **Publicly Held**
WEB: www.biotek.com
SIC: 3826 3841 Mfg Analytical Instruments Mfg Surgical/Medical Instruments
PA: Agilent Technologies, Inc.
5301 Stevens Creek Blvd
Santa Clara CA 95051
408 345-8886

(G-22718)
CHESTER BROTHERS
Also Called: Turmax Printing Services
146 W Canal St (05404-2109)
PHONE..................................802 655-4159
Chester Brothers, *President*
EMP: 5
SQ FT: 900
SALES (est): 484.6K **Privately Held**
SIC: 2752 Lithographic Commercial Printing

(G-22719)
COLBURNTREAT LLC
Also Called: Stellar Steam
276 E Allen St Ste 5 (05404-1570)
PHONE..................................802 654-8603
Michael G Colburn, *President*
Mary Esther Treat, *Exec VP*
▲ **EMP:** 15
SQ FT: 5,000
SALES (est): 1.9MM **Privately Held**
WEB: www.colburntreat.com
SIC: 3589 Mfg Service Industry Machinery

(G-22720)
CREATIVE LABELS VERMONT INC
Also Called: C L O V
11 Tigan St (05404-1327)
P.O. Box 9342, South Burlington (05407-9342)
PHONE..................................802 655-7654
Dwane L Wall, *President*
Frederic TW Wall, *Corp Secy*
Kiana Donegan, *Purch Agent*
Ryan Lucia, *Manager*
Bryan Brosseau, *Supervisor*
EMP: 26 **EST:** 1969
SQ FT: 15,000
SALES (est): 4.5MM **Privately Held**
WEB: www.clov.com
SIC: 2754 Gravure Commercial Printing

(G-22721)
LIONHEART TECHNOLOGIES INC (PA)
Also Called: Bio-Tek Instruments
100 Tigan St (05404-1356)
P.O. Box 998 (05404-0998)
PHONE..................................802 655-4040
Briar L Alpert, *President*
Valentina McLaughlin, *COO*
Adam Alpert, *Vice Pres*
Klaus Deutscher, *CFO*
Brian Struhammer, *Software Engr*
EMP: 160
SALES (est): 41K **Privately Held**
SIC: 3845 Mfg Electromedical Equipment

(G-22722)
M2 INC
170 Franklin St (05404-1401)
P.O. Box 386 (05404-0386)
PHONE..................................802 655-2364
Michael Moran, *President*
Jane Moran, *Vice Pres*
EMP: 5
SALES: 1.5MM **Privately Held**
WEB: www.m2intl.com
SIC: 3466 Design & Engineering Mechanical Closure Systems Mfg

(G-22723)
SEMIPROBE INC
276 E Allen St (05404-1570)
PHONE..................................802 860-7000
Dennis Place, *President*
EMP: 3
SQ FT: 2,500
SALES (est): 545.8K **Privately Held**
SIC: 3674 Mfg Semiconductors/Related Devices

(G-22724)
SPORTS PRODUCTS INCORPORATED
1 East St (05404-2023)
PHONE..................................802 655-2620
EMP: 6
SALES (est): 306.2K **Privately Held**
SIC: 3949 Mfg Sporting/Athletic Goods

(G-22725)
SYNAPSE IC LLC
50 Main St Unit 157 (05404-2309)
P.O. Box 157 (05404-0157)
PHONE..................................802 881-4028
Christian Fayomi, *Manager*
EMP: 3
SALES (est): 196.9K **Privately Held**
SIC: 3825 Mfg Electrical Measuring Instruments

(G-22726)
TWINCRAFT INC (PA)
Also Called: Twincraft Soap
2 Tigan St (05404-1326)
PHONE..................................802 655-2200
Peter Asch, *President*
Richard Asch, *Vice Pres*
Joe Braun, *Vice Pres*
Micheal Ly, *CFO*
Jim Howard, *VP Sales*
▲ **EMP:** 176
SALES (est): 42.7MM **Privately Held**
WEB: www.twincraft.com
SIC: 2841 7389 Mfg Soap/Other Detergents

(G-22727)
VERMONT FURNITURE DESIGNS INC
4 Tigan St (05404-1326)
P.O. Box 4533, Burlington (05406-4533)
PHONE..................................802 655-6568
Arthur Weitzenfeld, *President*
Sherry Smith, *Vice Pres*
Shirley Adams, *Admin Sec*
EMP: 30
SQ FT: 35,000
SALES (est): 4MM **Privately Held**
WEB: www.vermontfurnituredesign.com
SIC: 2511 Mfg Wood Household Furniture

(G-22728)
WINOOSKI PRESS LLC
10 Stevens St (05404-1323)
PHONE..................................802 655-1611
Richard Bonneau,
Janet Bonneau,
EMP: 3
SQ FT: 1,500
SALES (est): 240K **Privately Held**
SIC: 2752 2759 Offset Printing

Wolcott
Lamoille County

(G-22729)
CASPIAN ARMS LTD
75 Cal Foster Dr (05680-4476)
P.O. Box 465, Hardwick (05843-0465)
PHONE..................................802 472-6454
Patricia Foster, *President*
EMP: 5
SQ FT: 7,000
SALES: 1MM **Privately Held**
SIC: 3484 Mfg Small Arms

(G-22730)
FOSTER INDUSTRIES INC
75 Cal Foster Dr (05680-4476)
PHONE..................................802 472-6147
Patricia Foster, *President*
Amy Sayers, *Vice Pres*
EMP: 20
SQ FT: 7,000
SALES: 1MM **Privately Held**
WEB: www.caspianarms.com
SIC: 3484 Manufactures Competetive Pistol Components

(G-22731)
MIKE LOWELL LOGGING & WOOD
678 Brook Rd (05680-4296)
PHONE..................................802 279-6993
Michael Lowell, *Principal*
EMP: 3
SALES (est): 149.8K **Privately Held**
SIC: 2411 Logging

(G-22732)
STEVENS KILN DRYING LLC
289 Marsh Rd (05680-4022)
PHONE..................................802 472-5013
Robert Stevens, *Principal*
EMP: 3 **EST:** 2008
SALES (est): 253.6K **Privately Held**
SIC: 3559 Mfg Misc Industry Machinery

(G-22733)
TOWN & COUNTRY SHEDS
2175 N Wolcott Rd (05680-3047)
PHONE..................................802 888-7012
Glen Burkholder, *Partner*
Glen Bukholder, *Partner*
Calvin Nolt, *Partner*
Clinton Nolt, *Partner*
Nelson Steiner, *Partner*
EMP: 5
SALES (est): 300K **Privately Held**
SIC: 2542 5039 Mfg Partitions/Fixtures-Nonwood Whol Construction Materials

Woodbury
Washington County

(G-22734)
THOMPSON FAMILY ENTERPRISES
Also Called: Woodbury Golf Course
2280 E Hill Rd (05681)
P.O. Box 231 (05681-0231)
PHONE..................................802 456-7421
Lenora Thompson, *President*
Kurt Thompson, *Corp Secy*
Jason Thompson, *Vice Pres*
EMP: 4
SALES: 240K **Privately Held**
SIC: 2411 7999 Logging Amusement/Recreation Services

Woodstock
Windsor County

(G-22735)
ANYTHING PRINTED LLC
414 Woodstock Rd (05091)
PHONE..................................802 457-3414
Horst Dresler, *Mng Member*
EMP: 3
SQ FT: 1,000
SALES (est): 381.8K **Privately Held**
WEB: www.anythingprinted.net
SIC: 2752 3993 7389 Lithographic Commercial Printing Mfg Signs/Advertising Specialties Business Services

(G-22736)
BATTILANA & ASSOCIATES
6 Swain St (05091-1347)
PHONE..................................802 457-3375
William Battilana, *Owner*
EMP: 5
SALES (est): 430.6K **Privately Held**
SIC: 3571 4813 Mfg Electronic Computers/Telephone Communications

(G-22737)
BIKE TRACK INC
19 Central St Ste D (05091-1005)
P.O. Box 235 (05091-0235)
PHONE..................................802 457-3275
Timothy Callaghan, *President*
Max Wunderlich, *Vice Pres*
Nancy Hoblin, *Office Mgr*
Carol Weingeist, *Admin Sec*
EMP: 3
SQ FT: 900
SALES: 3MM **Privately Held**
WEB: www.biketrack.com
SIC: 3089 Mfg Plastic Products

(G-22738)
LONGHILL PARTNERS INC (PA)
Also Called: Antoinette Leonard Associates
4 Sunset Farms (05091-1155)
P.O. Box 237 (05091-0237)
PHONE..................................802 457-4000
Stuart M Matlins, *President*
Amy Wilson, *President*
Emily Wichland, *Vice Pres*
Jenny Buono, *Marketing Staff*
Antoinette Leonard Matlins, *Director*
▲ **EMP:** 26
SQ FT: 4,000
SALES (est): 2.3MM **Privately Held**
WEB: www.jewishlights.com
SIC: 2731 Books-Publishing/Printing

(G-22739)
SUGARBUSH FARM INC
591 Sugarbush Farm Rd (05091-8089)
PHONE..................................802 457-1757
Elizabeth Betsy Luce, *President*
Jeffery M Luce, *Vice Pres*
Lawerence Luce, *Treasurer*
Keery McNally, *Admin Sec*
EMP: 7 **EST:** 1944
SQ FT: 8,000
SALES: 2.1MM **Privately Held**
WEB: www.sugarbushfarm.com
SIC: 2099 2022 5961 Mfg Food Preparations Mfg Cheese Ret Mail-Order House

(G-22740)
VERMONT FLANNEL CO
Also Called: Ad Art America
13 Elm St (05091-1010)
P.O. Box 220, East Barre (05649-0220)
PHONE..................................802 457-4111
Mark Baker, *Branch Mgr*
EMP: 3 **Privately Held**
WEB: www.vermontflannel.com
SIC: 2759 Commercial Printing
PA: The Vermont Flannel Co
128 Mill St
East Barre VT 05649

(G-22741)
WILD APPLE GRAPHICS LTD
2513 W Woodstock Rd (05091-3211)
PHONE..................................802 457-3003
John Chester, *President*
Laurie Chester, *Vice Pres*
Shannon Kenison, *Controller*
Sarah Donington, *Sales Staff*
Clair Hunt, *Sales Staff*
EMP: 40
SQ FT: 16,000
SALES (est): 4.7MM **Privately Held**
WEB: www.wildapple.com
SIC: 2741 Commercial Art/Graphic Design

(G-22742)
WOODSTOCK GRNOLA TRAIL MIX LLC
112 Pomfret Rd (05091-4433)
P.O. Box 771 (05091-0771)
PHONE..................................802 457-3149
EMP: 3 **EST:** 2009
SALES (est): 199K **Privately Held**
SIC: 3273 Mfg Ready-Mixed Concrete

Worcester
Washington County

(G-22743)
QUANTUM CORPORATION LLC
46 Worcester Village Rd (05682-9685)
PHONE..................................802 505-5088
Lilliam Weisbart, *Principal*
EMP: 4
SALES (est): 333.4K **Privately Held**
SIC: 3572 Mfg Computer Storage Devices

SIC INDEX

Standard Industrial Classification Alphabetical Index

S I C

SIC INDEX

Standard Industrial Classification Numerical Index

SIC NO PRODUCT

2951 Paving Mixtures & Blocks
2952 Asphalt Felts & Coatings
2992 Lubricating Oils & Greases
2999 Products Of Petroleum & Coal, NEC

30 rubber and miscellaneous plastics products

3011 Tires & Inner Tubes
3021 Rubber & Plastic Footwear
3052 Rubber & Plastic Hose & Belting
3053 Gaskets, Packing & Sealing Devices
3061 Molded, Extruded & Lathe-Cut Rubber Mechanical Goods
3069 Fabricated Rubber Prdts, NEC
3081 Plastic Unsupported Sheet & Film
3082 Plastic Unsupported Profile Shapes
3083 Plastic Laminated Plate & Sheet
3084 Plastic Pipe
3085 Plastic Bottles
3086 Plastic Foam Prdts
3087 Custom Compounding Of Purchased Plastic Resins
3088 Plastic Plumbing Fixtures
3089 Plastic Prdts

31 leather and leather products

3111 Leather Tanning & Finishing
3131 Boot & Shoe Cut Stock & Findings
3142 House Slippers
3143 Men's Footwear, Exc Athletic
3144 Women's Footwear, Exc Athletic
3149 Footwear, NEC
3151 Leather Gloves & Mittens
3161 Luggage
3171 Handbags & Purses
3172 Personal Leather Goods
3199 Leather Goods, NEC

32 stone, clay, glass, and concrete products

3211 Flat Glass
3221 Glass Containers
3229 Pressed & Blown Glassware, NEC
3231 Glass Prdts Made Of Purchased Glass
3241 Cement, Hydraulic
3251 Brick & Structural Clay Tile
3253 Ceramic Tile
3255 Clay Refractories
3259 Structural Clay Prdts, NEC
3261 China Plumbing Fixtures & Fittings
3262 China, Table & Kitchen Articles
3263 Earthenware, Whiteware, Table & Kitchen Articles
3264 Porcelain Electrical Splys
3269 Pottery Prdts, NEC
3271 Concrete Block & Brick
3272 Concrete Prdts
3273 Ready-Mixed Concrete
3274 Lime
3275 Gypsum Prdts
3281 Cut Stone Prdts
3291 Abrasive Prdts
3292 Asbestos products
3295 Minerals & Earths: Ground Or Treated
3296 Mineral Wool
3297 Nonclay Refractories
3299 Nonmetallic Mineral Prdts, NEC

33 primary metal industries

3312 Blast Furnaces, Coke Ovens, Steel & Rolling Mills
3313 Electrometallurgical Prdts
3315 Steel Wire Drawing & Nails & Spikes
3316 Cold Rolled Steel Sheet, Strip & Bars
3317 Steel Pipe & Tubes
3321 Gray Iron Foundries
3322 Malleable Iron Foundries
3324 Steel Investment Foundries
3325 Steel Foundries, NEC
3331 Primary Smelting & Refining Of Copper
3334 Primary Production Of Aluminum
3339 Primary Nonferrous Metals, NEC
3341 Secondary Smelting & Refining Of Nonferrous Metals
3351 Rolling, Drawing & Extruding Of Copper
3353 Aluminum Sheet, Plate & Foil
3354 Aluminum Extruded Prdts
3355 Aluminum Rolling & Drawing, NEC
3356 Rolling, Drawing-Extruding Of Nonferrous Metals
3357 Nonferrous Wire Drawing
3363 Aluminum Die Castings
3364 Nonferrous Die Castings, Exc Aluminum
3365 Aluminum Foundries
3366 Copper Foundries
3369 Nonferrous Foundries: Castings, NEC
3398 Metal Heat Treating

SIC NO PRODUCT

3399 Primary Metal Prdts, NEC

34 fabricated metal products, except machinery and transportation equipment

3411 Metal Cans
3412 Metal Barrels, Drums, Kegs & Pails
3421 Cutlery
3423 Hand & Edge Tools
3425 Hand Saws & Saw Blades
3429 Hardware, NEC
3431 Enameled Iron & Metal Sanitary Ware
3432 Plumbing Fixture Fittings & Trim, Brass
3433 Heating Eqpt
3441 Fabricated Structural Steel
3442 Metal Doors, Sash, Frames, Molding & Trim
3443 Fabricated Plate Work
3444 Sheet Metal Work
3446 Architectural & Ornamental Metal Work
3448 Prefabricated Metal Buildings & Cmpnts
3449 Misc Structural Metal Work
3451 Screw Machine Prdts
3452 Bolts, Nuts, Screws, Rivets & Washers
3462 Iron & Steel Forgings
3463 Nonferrous Forgings
3465 Automotive Stampings
3466 Crowns & Closures
3469 Metal Stampings, NEC
3471 Electroplating, Plating, Polishing, Anodizing & Coloring
3479 Coating & Engraving, NEC
3482 Small Arms Ammunition
3483 Ammunition, Large
3484 Small Arms
3489 Ordnance & Access, NEC
3491 Industrial Valves
3492 Fluid Power Valves & Hose Fittings
3493 Steel Springs, Except Wire
3494 Valves & Pipe Fittings, NEC
3495 Wire Springs
3496 Misc Fabricated Wire Prdts
3497 Metal Foil & Leaf
3498 Fabricated Pipe & Pipe Fittings
3499 Fabricated Metal Prdts, NEC

35 industrial and commercial machinery and computer equipment

3511 Steam, Gas & Hydraulic Turbines & Engines
3519 Internal Combustion Engines, NEC
3523 Farm Machinery & Eqpt
3524 Garden, Lawn Tractors & Eqpt
3531 Construction Machinery & Eqpt
3532 Mining Machinery & Eqpt
3533 Oil Field Machinery & Eqpt
3534 Elevators & Moving Stairways
3535 Conveyors & Eqpt
3536 Hoists, Cranes & Monorails
3537 Indl Trucks, Tractors, Trailers & Stackers
3541 Machine Tools: Cutting
3542 Machine Tools: Forming
3543 Industrial Patterns
3544 Dies, Tools, Jigs, Fixtures & Indl Molds
3545 Machine Tool Access
3546 Power Hand Tools
3547 Rolling Mill Machinery & Eqpt
3548 Welding Apparatus
3549 Metalworking Machinery, NEC
3552 Textile Machinery
3553 Woodworking Machinery
3554 Paper Inds Machinery
3555 Printing Trades Machinery & Eqpt
3556 Food Prdts Machinery
3559 Special Ind Machinery, NEC
3561 Pumps & Pumping Eqpt
3562 Ball & Roller Bearings
3563 Air & Gas Compressors
3564 Blowers & Fans
3565 Packaging Machinery
3566 Speed Changers, Drives & Gears
3567 Indl Process Furnaces & Ovens
3568 Mechanical Power Transmission Eqpt, NEC
3569 Indl Machinery & Eqpt, NEC
3571 Electronic Computers
3572 Computer Storage Devices
3575 Computer Terminals
3577 Computer Peripheral Eqpt, NEC
3578 Calculating & Accounting Eqpt
3579 Office Machines, NEC
3581 Automatic Vending Machines
3582 Commercial Laundry, Dry Clean & Pressing Mchs
3585 Air Conditioning & Heating Eqpt
3586 Measuring & Dispensing Pumps

SIC NO PRODUCT

3589 Service Ind Machines, NEC
3592 Carburetors, Pistons, Rings & Valves
3593 Fluid Power Cylinders & Actuators
3594 Fluid Power Pumps & Motors
3596 Scales & Balances, Exc Laboratory
3599 Machinery & Eqpt, Indl & Commercial, NEC

36 electronic and other electrical equipment and components, except computer

3612 Power, Distribution & Specialty Transformers
3613 Switchgear & Switchboard Apparatus
3621 Motors & Generators
3624 Carbon & Graphite Prdts
3625 Relays & Indl Controls
3629 Electrical Indl Apparatus, NEC
3631 Household Cooking Eqpt
3632 Household Refrigerators & Freezers
3633 Household Laundry Eqpt
3634 Electric Household Appliances
3635 Household Vacuum Cleaners
3639 Household Appliances, NEC
3641 Electric Lamps
3643 Current-Carrying Wiring Devices
3644 Noncurrent-Carrying Wiring Devices
3645 Residential Lighting Fixtures
3646 Commercial, Indl & Institutional Lighting Fixtures
3647 Vehicular Lighting Eqpt
3648 Lighting Eqpt, NEC
3651 Household Audio & Video Eqpt
3652 Phonograph Records & Magnetic Tape
3661 Telephone & Telegraph Apparatus
3663 Radio & T V Communications, Systs & Eqpt, Broadcast/Studio
3669 Communications Eqpt, NEC
3671 Radio & T V Receiving Electron Tubes
3672 Printed Circuit Boards
3674 Semiconductors
3675 Electronic Capacitors
3676 Electronic Resistors
3677 Electronic Coils & Transformers
3678 Electronic Connectors
3679 Electronic Components, NEC
3691 Storage Batteries
3692 Primary Batteries: Dry & Wet
3694 Electrical Eqpt For Internal Combustion Engines
3695 Recording Media
3699 Electrical Machinery, Eqpt & Splys, NEC

37 transportation equipment

3711 Motor Vehicles & Car Bodies
3713 Truck & Bus Bodies
3714 Motor Vehicle Parts & Access
3715 Truck Trailers
3721 Aircraft
3724 Aircraft Engines & Engine Parts
3728 Aircraft Parts & Eqpt, NEC
3731 Shipbuilding & Repairing
3732 Boat Building & Repairing
3743 Railroad Eqpt
3751 Motorcycles, Bicycles & Parts
3761 Guided Missiles & Space Vehicles
3764 Guided Missile/Space Vehicle Propulsion Units & parts
3769 Guided Missile/Space Vehicle Parts & Eqpt, NEC
3792 Travel Trailers & Campers
3795 Tanks & Tank Components
3799 Transportation Eqpt, NEC

38 measuring, analyzing and controlling instruments; photographic, medical an

3812 Search, Detection, Navigation & Guidance Systs & Instrs
3821 Laboratory Apparatus & Furniture
3822 Automatic Temperature Controls
3823 Indl Instruments For Meas, Display & Control
3824 Fluid Meters & Counters
3825 Instrs For Measuring & Testing Electricity
3826 Analytical Instruments
3827 Optical Instruments
3829 Measuring & Controlling Devices, NEC
3841 Surgical & Medical Instrs & Apparatus
3842 Orthopedic, Prosthetic & Surgical Appliances/Splys
3843 Dental Eqpt & Splys
3844 X-ray Apparatus & Tubes
3845 Electromedical & Electrotherapeutic Apparatus
3851 Ophthalmic Goods
3861 Photographic Eqpt & Splys
3873 Watch & Clock Devices & Parts

39 miscellaneous manufacturing industries

3911 Jewelry: Precious Metal
3914 Silverware, Plated & Stainless Steel Ware

SIC NO PRODUCT

3915 Jewelers Findings & Lapidary Work
3931 Musical Instruments
3942 Dolls & Stuffed Toys
3944 Games, Toys & Children's Vehicles
3949 Sporting & Athletic Goods, NEC
3951 Pens & Mechanical Pencils
3952 Lead Pencils, Crayons & Artist's Mtrls
3953 Marking Devices

SIC NO PRODUCT

3955 Carbon Paper & Inked Ribbons
3961 Costume Jewelry & Novelties
3965 Fasteners, Buttons, Needles & Pins
3991 Brooms & Brushes
3993 Signs & Advertising Displays
3995 Burial Caskets
3996 Linoleum & Hard Surface Floor Coverings, NEC
3999 Manufacturing Industries, NEC

SIC NO PRODUCT

73 business services

7372 Prepackaged Software

76 miscellaneous repair services

7692 Welding Repair

7694 Armature Rewinding Shops

S
I
C

SIC SECTION

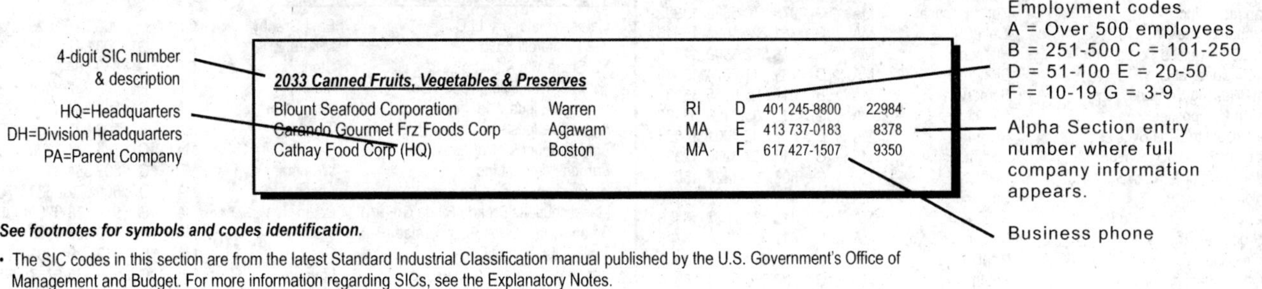

See footnotes for symbols and codes identification.

- The SIC codes in this section are from the latest Standard Industrial Classification manual published by the U.S. Government's Office of Management and Budget. For more information regarding SICs, see the Explanatory Notes.
- Companies may be listed under multiple classifications.

10 METAL MINING

1011 Iron Ores

	CITY	ST	EMP	PHONE	ENTRY #
Farrel Corporation **(DH)**	Ansonia	CT	D	203 736-5500	15

1021 Copper Ores

	CITY	ST	EMP	PHONE	ENTRY #
Baobab Asset Management LLC	Greenwich	CT	G	203 340-5700	1597
Quantum Discoveries Inc	Boston	MA	G	857 272-9998	8803

1041 Gold Ores

	CITY	ST	EMP	PHONE	ENTRY #
Lion Gold Mining Llc	Malden	MA	G	617 785-2345	12577
US Gold and Diamond Exch LLC **(PA)**	Derry	NH	G	603 300-8888	18001

1061 Ferroalloy Ores, Except Vanadium

	CITY	ST	EMP	PHONE	ENTRY #
Africa China Mining Corp	Braintree	MA	G	617 921-5500	8985

1081 Metal Mining Svcs

	CITY	ST	EMP	PHONE	ENTRY #
Liberty Mtals Min Holdings LLC **(PA)**	Boston	MA	G	617 654-4374	8664
Metal Suppliers Online LLC	Hampstead	NH	G	603 329-0101	18244
Sage Envirotech Drlg Svcs Inc	Pawtucket	RI	G	401 723-9900	20895

1099 Metal Ores, NEC

	CITY	ST	EMP	PHONE	ENTRY #
Tronox Limited	Stamford	CT	G	203 705-3800	4351
Wenstrom Metalworks	Whitefield	ME	G	207 215-0651	7219

12 COAL MINING

1221 Bituminous Coal & Lignite: Surface Mining

	CITY	ST	EMP	PHONE	ENTRY #
Rhino Energy Holdings LLC	Greenwich	CT	A	203 862-7000	1642

1222 Bituminous Coal: Underground Mining

	CITY	ST	EMP	PHONE	ENTRY #
Rhino Energy Holdings LLC	Greenwich	CT	A	203 862-7000	1642

1241 Coal Mining Svcs

	CITY	ST	EMP	PHONE	ENTRY #
Buchanan Minerals LLC **(DH)**	Wilton	CT	D	304 392-1000	5281
Coronado Group LLC **(PA)**	Wilton	CT	G	203 761-1291	5284
Tronox LLC **(PA)**	Stamford	CT	E	203 705-3800	4352
New Hampshire Boring Inc	Brockton	MA	F	508 584-8201	9169

13 OIL AND GAS EXTRACTION

1311 Crude Petroleum & Natural Gas

	CITY	ST	EMP	PHONE	ENTRY #
Alternate Energy Futures	Danbury	CT	G	917 745-7097	870
CCI Robinsons Bend LLC	Stamford	CT	G	203 564-8571	4160
Dietze & Associates LLC	Wilton	CT	F	203 762-3500	5288
El Paso Prod Oil Gas Texas LP	Hartford	CT	F	860 293-1990	1819
Fpr Pinedale LLC	Stamford	CT	G	203 542-6000	4196
Merrill Oil LLC	Woodbridge	CT	G	203 387-1130	5472
Outpost Exploration LLC	Wilton	CT	G	203 762-7206	5297
Promise Propane	Newington	CT	G	860 685-0676	2894
River Valley Oil Service LLC	Portland	CT	G	860 342-5670	3574
South Bend Ethanol LLC	Stamford	CT	E	203 326-8132	4325
Bradley Oil Company	Rehoboth	MA	G	508 336-4400	14746
Exxonmobil Oil Corporation	Randolph	MA	G	781 963-7252	14679
Hess Corporation	West Bridgewater	MA	F	508 580-6530	16441
Landfil Gas Prodcrs of Plnvlle	Plainville	MA	G	508 695-3252	14525
MRC Global (us) Inc	Bellingham	MA	E	508 966-3205	8051
Poweroptions Inc	Boston	MA	G	617 737-8480	8788
Speedway LLC	Saugus	MA	D	781 233-5491	14999
Speedway LLC	Auburndale	MA	G	617 244-4601	7870
Spotliteusa LLC	Sturbridge	MA	G	508 347-2627	15649
MRC Global (us) Inc	South Portland	ME	F	207 767-3861	7033
Revision Heat LLC	Windham	ME	F	207 221-5677	7247
Liberty Enrgy Utilities NH Corp **(DH)**	Londonderry	NH	D	905 287-2061	18713
Speedway LLC	Derry	NH	F	603 434-9702	17996
Speedway LLC	Chichester	NH	D	603 798-3154	17830
Your Oil Tools LLC	Hooksett	NH	G	701 645-8665	18361
Speedway LLC	Cranston	RI	G	401 941-4740	20288
Kcm Oil	Shaftsbury	VT	G	802 447-7371	22403

1321 Natural Gas Liquids

	CITY	ST	EMP	PHONE	ENTRY #
Sea Land Energy Maine Inc	Windham	ME	G	207 892-3284	7250
Inov8v Energy LLC	Canaan	NH	G	603 632-7333	17779
Keene Gas Corporation	Keene	NH	F	603 352-4134	18510
Filters Inc	Pawtucket	RI	G	401 722-8999	20840

1381 Drilling Oil & Gas Wells

	CITY	ST	EMP	PHONE	ENTRY #
Coleman Drilling & Blasting	Voluntown	CT	G	860 376-3813	4690
Eows Midland Inc	Stamford	CT	E	203 358-5705	4194
Louis E Allyn Sons Inc	Norfolk	CT	G	860 542-5741	2958
Mercuria Energy Trading Inc	Greenwich	CT	G	203 413-3355	1630
Millbrae Energy LLC **(PA)**	Greenwich	CT	F	203 742-2800	1631
Marks Wells & Pumps Inc	Bellingham	MA	G	508 528-1741	8046
Soil Exploration Corp **(PA)**	Leominster	MA	G	978 840-0391	12187
High Pine Well Drilling Inc	Buxton	ME	G	207 929-4122	5857
Pine State Drilling Inc	Athens	ME	G	207 654-2771	5543
Jeff Cummings Services LLC	Warner	NH	G	603 456-3706	19927
NA Manosh Inc	Morrisville	VT	E	802 888-5722	22174

1382 Oil & Gas Field Exploration Svcs

	CITY	ST	EMP	PHONE	ENTRY #
El Paso Prod Oil Gas Texas LP	Hartford	CT	F	860 293-1990	1819
Geosonics Inc	Cheshire	CT	F	203 271-2504	735
Maine Power Express LLC	Greenwich	CT	G	203 661-0055	1628
Vab Inc	Plainville	CT	G	860 793-0246	3523
Als Oil Service	Shrewsbury	MA	G	508 853-2539	15099
Greener 3000 LLC	Boston	MA	G	781 589-5777	8579
Nuvera Fuel Cells LLC	Billerica	MA	D	617 245-7500	8269
Quantum Discoveries Inc	Boston	MA	G	857 272-9998	8803
Schlumberger Technology Corp	Cambridge	MA	C	617 768-2000	9645
SIVS Oil Inc	North Dartmouth	MA	G	508 951-0528	13925
Stroud International Ltd	Marblehead	MA	G	781 631-8806	12695
Hunting Dearborn Inc	Fryeburg	ME	C	207 935-2171	6099
D F Richard Inc	Dover	NH	D	603 742-2020	18017
Energy Today Inc	Manchester	NH	G	603 425-8933	18816
Dionne & Sons Piping Dynamics	Coventry	RI	G	401 821-9266	20145

1389 Oil & Gas Field Svcs, NEC

	CITY	ST	EMP	PHONE	ENTRY #
Ace Servicing Co Inc	Orange	CT	G	203 795-1400	3356
Acuren Inspection Inc **(HQ)**	Danbury	CT	A	203 702-8740	867
Acuren Inspection Inc	Greenwich	CT	D	203 869-6734	1592
Alliance Energy LLC	New Haven	CT	G	203 933-2511	2655
Alterio Tractor Pulling LLC	Oxford	CT	G	203 305-9812	3390
Buon Appetito From Italy LLC	New London	CT	G	860 437-3668	2767
Cameron International Corp	Glastonbury	CT	F	860 633-0277	1543
Connectcut Shreline Developers	Clinton	CT	G	860 669-4424	781
Eastern Connecticut	Willimantic	CT	F	860 423-1972	5263
GE Oil & Gas Esp Inc	Redding	CT	E	405 670-1431	3647
J & M Plumbing & Cnstr LLC	Norwich	CT	F	860 319-3082	3284
Kafa Group LLC	Bridgeport	CT	G	475 275-0090	438
Loanworks Servicing LLC	Shelton	CT	G	203 402-7304	3829
My Slide Lines LLC	Norwalk	CT	G	203 324-1642	3202
Palmieri Industries Inc	Bridgeport	CT	D	203 384-6020	462
Rockwood Service Corporation **(PA)**	Greenwich	CT	G	203 869-6734	1645
Sigma Tankers Inc	Norwalk	CT	F	203 662-2600	3244
Tri State Maintenance Svcs LLC	North Haven	CT	F	203 691-1343	3064
W M G and Sons Inc	Bristol	CT	G	860 584-0143	623
Weatherford International LLC	Wallingford	CT	E	203 294-0190	4828
Acheson Company LLC	Williamsburg	MA	G	413 268-0246	16946
Baker Hghes Olfld Oprtions LLC	Walpole	MA	C	508 668-0400	15989

	CITY	ST	EMP	PHONE	ENTRY #
Biszko Contracting Corp	Fall River	MA	E	508 679-0518	10668
Cleanbasins Inc	North Billerica	MA	G	978 670-5838	13802
Commtank Cares Inc	Wakefield	MA	G	781 224-1021	15946
Consoldted Utlities Corporaion	Hudson	MA	G	978 562-3500	11765
Cyn Oil Corporation	Stoughton	MA	D	781 341-8074	15585
Home Heating Services Corp	Somerville	MA	E	617 625-8255	15183
Kenyon Composites	Gloucester	MA	G	617 803-3198	11195
Liberty Construction Svcs LLC	Roxbury	MA	D	617 602-4001	14874
Maple Road Service Station	Longmeadow	MA	G	413 567-6233	12336
Modern Tractor & Truck Service	Seekonk	MA	G	508 761-4425	15029
Msr Utility	Dunstable	MA	G	978 649-0002	10390
North End Oil Service Co Inc	Springfield	MA	G	413 734-7057	15493
Old Ironsides Energy LLC	Boston	MA	F	617 366-2030	8745
On-Site Analysis Inc	Marlborough	MA	E	508 460-7778	12802
RCO Renovations Inc	South Walpole	MA	G	508 668-5524	15320
Schlumberger Technology Corp	Cambridge	MA	C	617 768-2000	9645
Sea-Land Envmtl Svcs Inc	Medfield	MA	G	508 359-1085	12919
Sensing Systems Corporation	Dartmouth	MA	F	508 992-0872	10276
Test Rep Associates Inc	Westford	MA	G	978 692-8000	16797
W & G Gas Services LLC	Roslindale	MA	G	617 327-2515	14844
Acuren Inspection Inc	Auburn	ME	F	207 786-7884	5546
Cameron International Corp	Limerick	ME	F	207 793-2289	6333
Copp Excavating Inc	Durham	ME	F	207 926-4988	5970
Dysarts	Hermon	ME	G	207 947-8649	6185
Orono Spectral Solutions Inc	Hermon	ME	G	866 269-8007	6192
Weymouths Inc	Clinton	ME	G	207 426-3211	5917
Wireless Construction Inc	Standish	ME	E	207 642-5751	7064
Daniel Johnston & Co Inc	Hancock	NH	G	603 525-9330	18284
Doggie Passport	Manchester	NH	G	603 315-8243	18812
Hamco Tank Systems LLC	Mason	NH	G	603 878-0585	18968
Maillet Construction	Mason	NH	G	603 582-2810	18969
Sorby & Son Heating	Jaffrey	NH	G	603 532-7214	18477
Dig Rite Company Inc	Cranston	RI	G	401 862-5895	20211

14 MINING AND QUARRYING OF NONMETALLIC MINERALS, EXCEPT FUELS

1411 Dimension Stone

	CITY	ST	EMP	PHONE	ENTRY #
Academy Marble & Granite LLC **(PA)**	Bethel	CT	G	203 791-2956	126
Armetta LLC	Middletown	CT	E	860 788-2369	2172
Coccomo Brothers Drilling LLC	Berlin	CT	F	860 828-1632	81
Connecticut Stone Supplies Inc **(PA)**	Milford	CT	D	203 882-1000	2270
Infinity Stone Inc	Waterbury	CT	F	203 575-9484	4888
LH Gault & Son Incorporated	Westport	CT	D	203 227-5181	5209
Stony Creek Quarry Corporation	Branford	CT	G	203 483-3904	353
West Hartford Stone Mulch LLC	West Hartford	CT	G	860 461-7616	5103
Fletcher Granite LLC **(DH)**	Westford	MA	G	978 692-1312	16767
Le Masurier Granite Quarry	North Chelmsford	MA	G	978 251-3841	13900
Precision Stone Works Inc	Shrewsbury	MA	G	774 261-4420	15129
Southcoast Stoneworks Inc	Westport	MA	F	774 319-5200	16848
Sudbury Granite & Marble Inc **(PA)**	Hopedale	MA	E	508 478-3976	11684
Williams Stone Co Inc	East Otis	MA	E	413 269-4544	10504
World Stone	Everett	MA	G	617 293-4373	10634
Old York Quarry Inc	York	ME	G	603 772-6061	7315
Flat Rock Tile and Stone	Claremont	NH	G	603 542-0678	17850
Swenson Granite Company LLC **(DH)**	Concord	NH	E	603 225-4322	17933
Georgia Stone Industries Inc **(HQ)**	Smithfield	RI	G	401 232-2040	21227
Adams Granite Company Inc	Websterville	VT	D	802 476-5281	22596
Houle Bros Granite Co Inc	Barre	VT	E	802 476-6825	21624
International Stone Products **(PA)**	Barre	VT	D	802 476-6636	21625
Julian Materials LLC	Chester	VT	F	802 875-6564	21844
Quarry Slate Industries Inc	Poultney	VT	D	802 287-9701	22274
Rock of Ages Corporation	Graniteville	VT	F	802 476-3119	22002
Semya Corp **(PA)**	Chester	VT	G	802 875-6564	21849
South Poultney Slate	Poultney	VT	G	802 287-9278	22277
Taran Bros Inc **(PA)**	Poultney	VT	E	802 287-5853	22278
Taran Bros Inc	Poultney	VT	G	802 287-9308	22279
Troy Minerals Inc	Florence	VT	G	802 878-5103	21992
Vermont Quarries Corp	Rutland	VT	F	802 775-1065	22360
Vermont Verde Antique Intl	Pittsford	VT	G	802 767-4421	22265

1422 Crushed & Broken Limestone

	CITY	ST	EMP	PHONE	ENTRY #
Allyndale Corporation	East Canaan	CT	F	860 824-7959	1111
Specialty Minerals Inc	Canaan	CT	C	860 824-5435	690
Trap Rock Quarry	Southbury	CT	G	203 263-2195	4035
S Lane John & Son Incorporated	Oxford	MA	F	508 987-3959	14273
Dragon Products Company LLC	Thomaston	ME	C	207 594-5555	7083
Dragon Products Company LLC **(DH)**	South Portland	ME	E	207 774-6355	7022
Conklin Limestone Company	Lincoln	RI	G	401 334-2330	20565
Shelburne Limestone Corp	Wallingford	VT	G	802 446-2045	22574

1423 Crushed & Broken Granite

	CITY	ST	EMP	PHONE	ENTRY #
Skyline Quarry	Stafford Springs	CT	E	860 875-3580	4115
Stone Company	Pittsfield	MA	G	413 442-1447	14510
Tables of Stone **(PA)**	Merrimack	NH	G	603 424-7577	19035
McCullough Crushing Inc **(PA)**	Middlesex	VT	E	802 223-5693	22122

1429 Crushed & Broken Stone, NEC

	CITY	ST	EMP	PHONE	ENTRY #
Galasso Materials LLC	East Granby	CT	C	860 527-1825	1128
Joe Passarelli & Co	Milford	CT	G	203 877-1434	2304
Nu-Stone Mfg & Distrg LLC	Sterling	CT	G	860 564-6555	4370
York Hill Trap Rock Quarry Co	Meriden	CT	F	203 237-8421	2152
Aggregate Inds - Northeast Reg	Wrentham	MA	E	508 384-3161	17513
Aggregate Inds - Northeast Reg	Taunton	MA	F	508 821-9508	15720
Aggregate Inds - Northeast Reg	Saugus	MA	G	781 941-7200	14975
Bardon Trimount Inc	Wrentham	MA	G	508 384-3161	17516
Isp Freetown Fine Chem Inc	Assonet	MA	D	508 672-0634	7681
Massachusetts Broken Stone Co **(PA)**	Berlin	MA	G	978 838-9999	8091
S Lane John & Son Incorporated **(PA)**	Westfield	MA	F	413 568-8986	16725
Tonlino & Sons LLC	Otis	MA	G	413 329-8083	14250
Concord Sand and Gravel Inc	Loudon	NH	G	603 435-6787	18747
K & B Rock Crushing LLC	Auburn	NH	G	603 622-1188	17612
Marcou Construction Company	Dunbarton	NH	G	603 774-6511	18073
Scallops Mineral & Shell Empor	Portsmouth	NH	G	603 431-7658	19617
Martin R L & W B Inc	East Corinth	VT	G	802 439-5797	21914

1442 Construction Sand & Gravel

	CITY	ST	EMP	PHONE	ENTRY #
B & C Sand & Gravel Company	Bridgeport	CT	G	203 335-6640	379
Bethel Sand & Gravel Co	Bethel	CT	G	203 743-4469	132
Brooklyn Sand & Gravel LLC	Danielson	CT	G	860 779-3980	1012
Dan Beard Inc	Shelton	CT	F	203 924-4346	3794
Dens Sand & Gravel	Lebanon	CT	G	860 642-6478	1934
Dunning Sand & Gravel Company	Farmington	CT	F	860 677-1616	1478
Galasso Materials LLC	East Granby	CT	C	860 527-1825	1128
Geer Construction Co Inc	Jewett City	CT	G	860 376-5321	1912
John Hychko	Waterbury	CT	G	203 757-3458	4893
Kacerguis Farms Inc	Bethlehem	CT	G	203 405-1202	197
Kobyluck Sand and Gravel Inc	Waterford	CT	F	860 444-9600	4988
Laurelbrook Ntral Rsources LLC	East Canaan	CT	F	860 824-5843	1113
Pine Ridge Gravel LLC	East Haddam	CT	G	860 873-2500	1152
Rawson Development Inc	Putnam	CT	F	860 928-4536	3629
Skyline Quarry	Stafford Springs	CT	E	860 875-3580	4115
Sterling Sand and Gravel LLC	Sterling	CT	G	860 774-3985	4373
Tilcon Connecticut Inc	Newington	CT	G	860 756-8016	2907
Tronox LLC **(PA)**	Stamford	CT	E	203 705-3800	4352
Turning Stone Sand & Grav LLC	Enfield	CT	G	413 519-1560	1388
West Hartford Stone Mulch LLC	West Hartford	CT	G	860 461-7616	5103
Wfs Earth Materialsi LLC	Branford	CT	G	203 488-2055	361
Aggregate Inds - Northeast Reg	Ashland	MA	E	508 881-1430	7655
B R S Inc	Bridgewater	MA	E	508 697-5448	9061
Baxter Sand & Gravel Inc	Chicopee	MA	E	413 536-3370	9999
Benevento Asphalt Corp	Wilmington	MA	F	978 658-5300	16982
Benevento Sand & Stone Corp	Wilmington	MA	F	978 658-4762	16983
Berkshire Concrete Corp **(HQ)**	Pittsfield	MA	C	413 443-4734	14456
Boston Sand & Gravel Company **(PA)**	Boston	MA	E	617 227-9000	8440
Brox Industries Inc **(PA)**	Dracut	MA	D	978 454-9105	10355
Construction Source MGT LLC	Raynham	MA	G	508 484-5100	14707
Dedham Recycled Gravel Inc	Dedham	MA	F	781 329-1044	10287
FT Smith Trckg & Excvtg Inc	North Brookfield	MA	G	508 867-0400	13880
Gravel Public House	Wrentham	MA	G	508 384-0888	17522
Greylock Sand & Gravel LLC	Adams	MA	G	413 441-4967	7411
Indian River Sand LLC	Quincy	MA	G	413 977-0646	14634
J G Maclellan Con Co Inc **(PA)**	Lowell	MA	D	978 458-1223	12385
Lakeside Management Corp	Plainville	MA	E	508 695-3252	14524
Lorusso Corp **(PA)**	Plainville	MA	E	508 668-6520	14527
Lower Cape Sand and Gravel Inc	Eastham	MA	G	508 255-2839	10550
New England Gravel Haulers	Rehoboth	MA	G	508 922-4518	14754
New England Sand & Gravel Co	Framingham	MA	F	508 877-2460	10987
Ossipee Aggregates Corporation **(HQ)**	Boston	MA	G	617 227-9000	8762
Pitcherville Sand and Gravel	Burlington	MA	G	781 365-1721	9320
Rosenfeld Concrete Corp **(HQ)**	Hopedale	MA	E	508 473-7200	11682
S Lane John & Son Incorporated **(PA)**	Westfield	MA	F	413 568-8986	16725
S M Lorusso & Sons Inc **(PA)**	Walpole	MA	E	508 668-2600	16010
S M Lorusso & Sons Inc	Boston	MA	E	617 323-6380	8830
S M Lorusso & Sons Inc	Wrentham	MA	G	508 384-3587	17528
Salgado Sand & Gravel Inc	South Dartmouth	MA	G	774 202-2626	15243
Sanger Equipment and Mfg	Conway	MA	G	413 625-8304	10166
Scapin Sand & Gravel Inc	Russell	MA	G	413 568-0091	14878
Southeastern Sand and Grav Inc	Kingston	MA	G	781 413-6884	11964
Varney Bros Sand & Gravel Inc	Bellingham	MA	E	508 966-1313	8062
Wakefield Investments Inc	Lunenburg	MA	D	978 582-0261	12486
We Love Construction	Ipswich	MA	G	978 239-1308	11938
A & G Dirtworks Inc	Howland	ME	G	207 290-5054	6213
A&M Sand & Gravel LLC	Winterport	ME	G	207 223-4189	7275
Caleb Churchill	Somerville	ME	G	207 215-7949	6998
Dayton Sand & Gravel Inc	Dayton	ME	D	207 499-2306	5944
Dragon Products Company LLC	Thomaston	ME	C	207 594-5555	7083
Dragon Products Company LLC **(DH)**	South Portland	ME	E	207 774-6355	7022
Dwight R Mills Inc	Porter	ME	G	207 625-3965	6602
Earl W Gerrish & Sons Inc	Brownville	ME	F	207 965-2171	5826
F R Carroll Inc	Limerick	ME	E	207 793-8615	6334
Gravel Doctor Midcoast Maine	Bristol	ME	G	207 633-1099	5812
Hermon Sand & Gravel LLC	Hermon	ME	G	207 848-5977	6189

	CITY	ST	EMP	PHONE	ENTRY #
J and L Sand	Lyman	ME	G	207 499-2545	6390
Jerome Martin Paul	North Sullivan	ME	G	207 422-3965	6513
K W Aggregates	Denmark	ME	G	207 452-8888	5950
McQuade Tidd Industries	Houlton	ME	D	207 532-2675	6207
Ouellette Sand & Gravel Inc	South China	ME	G	207 445-4131	7006
Penobscot Sand Grav Stone LLC	Milford	ME	G	207 827-2829	6437
Pine Tree Gravel Inc	Hampden	ME	G	207 862-4983	6168
Portland Sand & Gravel Inc	Cumberland Center	ME	G	207 829-2196	5931
A B Excavating Inc	Lancaster	NH	E	603 788-5110	18596
Big Foote Crushing LLC	Weare	NH	G	603 345-0695	19932
Brook Hollow Sand & Gravel	Bedford	NH	G	603 231-0238	17634
Chick Trucking Inc	Newmarket	NH	G	603 659-3566	19331
Cloutier Sand & Gravel	Stark	NH	G	603 636-1100	19859
Concord Sand and Gravel Inc	Loudon	NH	G	603 435-6787	18747
Gorham Sand & Gravel	Gorham	NH	E	603 466-2291	18212
Granite State Concrete Co Inc	Milford	NH	E	603 673-3327	19057
Gravel Hill Partners LLC	Hanover	NH	G	603 277-9074	18288
Hampton Sand and Gravel	Hampton	NH	G	603 601-2275	18264
Jimtown Sand and Gravel Inc	Berlin	NH	G	603 752-4622	17698
Lane Construction Corporation	East Swanzey	NH	G	603 352-2006	18093
Litchfield Sand & Gravel	Londonderry	NH	G	603 424-6515	18715
Malcolm Bradsher Co Inc	Epping	NH	G	603 679-3888	18101
Michie Corporation	Henniker	NH	D	603 428-7426	18307
Mitchell Sand & Gravel LLC	Winchester	NH	G	603 357-0881	19993
Nashua Sand & Gravel LLC	Hudson	NH	G	603 459-8662	18419
Northeast Sand & Gravel	Amherst	NH	G	603 213-6133	17579
Northeast Sand and Gravel LLC	New Ipswich	NH	G	603 305-9429	19307
Pitcherville Sand & Grav Corp	Greenville	NH	G	603 878-0035	18226
Smith River Sand & Gravel LLC	Danbury	NH	G	603 768-3330	17965
Strong H J G Bros Grav Corp	New Boston	NH	G	603 487-5551	19298
Tilcon Arthur Whitcomb Inc **(HQ)**	North Swanzey	NH	F	603 352-0101	19393
Alfred N Gravel	Woonsocket	RI	G	401 765-4432	21549
Gravel Electric Inc	Harrisville	RI	G	401 265-6041	20479
Hopkins Hill Sand & Stone LLC	Warwick	RI	G	401 739-8300	21372
Richmond Sand & Stone LLC	Richmond	RI	F	401 539-7770	21162
Calkins Rock Products Inc	Lyndonville	VT	G	802 626-5755	22067
Calkins Sand & Gravel Inc	Newport	VT	F	802 334-8418	22191
D40 Gravel LLP	Newport	VT	G	802 673-5494	22195
Dale E Percy Inc	Stowe	VT	F	802 253-8503	22521
Fuller Sand & Gravel Inc	Danby	VT	G	802 293-5700	21893
Joseph P Carrara & Sons Inc **(PA)**	North Clarendon	VT	E	802 775-2301	22216
Northeast Aggregate Corp	Saint Albans	VT	G	802 524-2627	22376
Orwell Sand & Gravel	Benson	VT	G	802 345-6028	21693

1446 Industrial Sand

	CITY	ST	EMP	PHONE	ENTRY #
Unimin Lime Corporation **(DH)**	New Canaan	CT	F	203 966-8880	2619

1455 Kaolin & Ball Clay

	CITY	ST	EMP	PHONE	ENTRY #
Sandballz International LLC	Storrs Mansfield	CT	G	860 465-9628	4386
Imerys Kaolin Inc	South Portland	ME	G	207 741-2118	7030
Imerys Usa Inc	Skowhegan	ME	C	207 238-9267	6977

1459 Clay, Ceramic & Refractory Minerals, NEC

	CITY	ST	EMP	PHONE	ENTRY #
Vanderbilt Minerals LLC **(HQ)**	Norwalk	CT	E	203 295-2140	3266
Lumacera Innovative Mtls Inc	Pepperell	MA	G	978 302-6475	14442
Sheffield Pottery Inc	Sheffield	MA	E	413 229-7700	15065

1474 Potash, Soda & Borate Minerals

	CITY	ST	EMP	PHONE	ENTRY #
American Natural Soda Ash Corp **(PA)**	Westport	CT	E	203 226-9056	5181

1481 Nonmetallic Minerals Svcs, Except Fuels

	CITY	ST	EMP	PHONE	ENTRY #
New England Boring Contractors	Glastonbury	CT	F	860 633-4649	1566
All American Deleading Inc	Hingham	MA	G	781 953-1673	11490
Carr-Dee Corp	Medford	MA	F	781 391-4500	12925
Rowe Contracting Co	Melrose	MA	G	781 620-0052	12991
Soil Exploration Corp **(PA)**	Leominster	MA	G	978 840-0391	12187
Ensio Resources Inc	Bow	NH	G	603 224-0221	17712
Allstate Drilling Co	Riverside	RI	G	401 434-7458	21163

1499 Miscellaneous Nonmetallic Mining

	CITY	ST	EMP	PHONE	ENTRY #
Galasso Materials LLC	East Granby	CT	C	860 527-1825	1128
Brox Industries Inc **(PA)**	Dracut	MA	D	978 454-9105	10355
Mkl Stone LLC	Everett	MA	G	781 844-9811	10622
Sterling Peat Inc	Sterling	MA	G	978 422-8294	15547
Sun Gro Horticulture Dist Inc	Agawam	MA	E	800 732-8667	7455
Dodlin Hill Stone Company LLC	Oakland	ME	G	207 465-6463	6532
North East Materials Group LLC	Graniteville	VT	F	802 479-7004	22000
Troy Minerals Co	Colchester	VT	G	802 878-5103	21883
Williams & Co Mining Inc	Perkinsville	VT	F	802 263-5404	22261

20 FOOD AND KINDRED PRODUCTS

2011 Meat Packing Plants

	CITY	ST	EMP	PHONE	ENTRY #
E & J Andrychowski Farms	Windham	CT	G	860 423-4124	5311
Grote & Weigel Inc **(PA)**	Bloomfield	CT	E	860 242-8528	221
Manchester Packing Company Inc	Manchester	CT	D	860 646-5000	2024
Martin Rosols Inc	New Britain	CT	E	860 223-2707	2551
Maurices Country Meat Mkt LLC	Canterbury	CT	G	860 546-9588	694
A Arena & Sons Inc	Hopkinton	MA	G	508 435-3673	11685
Boston Lamb & Veal Co Inc	Boston	MA	D	617 442-3644	8433
Chicopee Provision Company Inc	Chicopee	MA	E	413 594-4765	10009
Crocetti-Oakdale Packing Inc **(PA)**	East Bridgewater	MA	E	508 587-0035	10410
Demakes Enterprises Inc	Lynn	MA	C	781 586-0212	12500
Hass Bros Inc	Rehoboth	MA	G	508 336-9323	14750
Kayem Foods Inc **(PA)**	Chelsea	MA	B	781 933-3115	9957
Mutual Beef Co Inc	Boston	MA	F	617 442-3238	8717
Robbins Beef Co Inc	Boston	MA	F	617 269-1826	8824
Smithfield Direct LLC	Springfield	MA	B	413 781-5620	15505
Smithfield Foods Inc	Springfield	MA	A	413 781-5620	15506
Bubiers Meats	Greene	ME	G	207 946-7761	6148
Castonguay Meats Inc	Livermore	ME	G	207 897-4989	6373
Pig + Poet Restaurant	Camden	ME	G	207 236-3391	5869
West Gardiner Beef Inc	West Gardiner	ME	G	207 724-3378	7173
Lincoln Packing Co	Cranston	RI	E	401 943-0878	20255
Rjb Meat Processing	Warwick	RI	G	401 781-5315	21415
Npc Processing Inc	Shelburne	VT	E	802 660-0496	22420
Vermont Lvstk Slghter Proc LLC	Ferrisburgh	VT	F	802 877-3421	21990
Vermont Packinghouse LLC	North Springfield	VT	F	802 886-8688	22239

2013 Sausages & Meat Prdts

	CITY	ST	EMP	PHONE	ENTRY #
Baltasar & Sons Inc	Naugatuck	CT	G	203 723-0425	2462
Capitol Sausage & Provs Inc	Hartford	CT	G	860 527-5510	1811
Custom Food Pdts Holdings LLC	Greenwich	CT	D	310 637-0900	1605
Deyulio Sausage Company LLC	Bridgeport	CT	F	203 348-1863	406
Grote & Weigel Inc **(PA)**	Bloomfield	CT	E	860 242-8528	221
Hummel Bros Inc	New Haven	CT	D	203 787-4113	2697
Janik Sausage Co Inc	Enfield	CT	G	860 749-4661	1367
Lamberti Packing Company	New Haven	CT	G	203 562-0436	2705
Longhini LLC	New Haven	CT	E	212 219-1230	2707
Manchester Packing Company Inc	Manchester	CT	D	860 646-5000	2024
Martin Rosols Inc	New Britain	CT	E	860 223-2707	2551
Maurices Country Meat Mkt LLC	Canterbury	CT	G	860 546-9588	694
Mister BS Jerky Co	Meriden	CT	G	203 631-2758	2110
Alden Acoreana Realty Trust **(PA)**	Fall River	MA	G	508 678-2098	10652
Amazon Fruit Corp	Ludlow	MA	G	774 244-2820	12453
Boston Lamb & Veal Co Inc	Boston	MA	D	617 442-3644	8433
Carando Gourmet Foods Corp **(PA)**	Agawam	MA	E	413 737-0183	7426
Chair City Meats Inc	Gardner	MA	F	978 630-1050	11108
Chicopee Provision Company Inc	Chicopee	MA	E	413 594-4765	10009
Crocetti-Oakdale Packing Inc **(PA)**	East Bridgewater	MA	E	508 587-0035	10410
Crocetti-Oakdale Packing Inc	Brockton	MA	E	508 941-0458	9135
Demakes Enterprises Inc **(PA)**	Lynn	MA	C	781 417-1100	12499
Demakes Enterprises Inc	Lynn	MA	C	781 586-0212	12500
Diluigis Inc	Danvers	MA	D	978 750-9900	10213
Gaspars Sausage Co Inc	North Dartmouth	MA	E	508 998-2012	13920
Genoa Sausage Co Inc	Woburn	MA	D	781 933-3115	17190
Hilltown Pork Inc	Granville	MA	F	413 357-6661	11230
Home Market Foods Inc **(PA)**	Norwood	MA	C	781 948-1500	14157
Hopps Company	Quincy	MA	G	617 481-1379	14632
Kayem Foods Inc **(PA)**	Chelsea	MA	B	781 933-3115	9957
Kraft Heinz Foods Company	Woburn	MA	C	781 933-2800	17212
Lisbon Sausage Co Inc	New Bedford	MA	F	508 993-7645	13408
Marias Food Products Inc	Medford	MA	G	781 396-4110	12940
Massachusetts Importing Co	Medford	MA	G	781 395-1210	12942
Mellos North End Mfg Co Inc	Fall River	MA	G	508 673-2320	10729
Miranda Brothers Inc	Fall River	MA	G	508 672-0982	10735
New Bedford Salchicharia Inc **(PA)**	New Bedford	MA	G	508 992-6257	13420
Newport Jerky Company	Carver	MA	G	347 913-6882	9805
Old Neighborhood Foods	Lynn	MA	G	781 595-1557	12531
Pig Rock Sausages LLC	Milton	MA	G	617 851-9422	13198
Smithfield Direct LLC	Springfield	MA	B	413 781-5620	15505
Waniewski Farms Inc	Feeding Hills	MA	F	413 786-1182	10805
Whip City Jerky LLC	Westfield	MA	G	413 568-2050	16749
Wohrles Foods Inc **(PA)**	Pittsfield	MA	E	413 442-1518	14513
Angostura International Ltd	Auburn	ME	G	207 786-3200	5551
Brava Enterprises LLC	Lewiston	ME	G	207 241-2420	6277
Noon Family Sheep Farm	Springvale	ME	G	207 324-3733	7055
Butcher Block Inc	Claremont	NH	E	800 258-4304	17837
Garfields Smokehouse Inc	Meriden	NH	G	603 469-3225	18983
Green Mountain Marinades	Bristol	NH	G	802 434-3731	17766
Heidi Jos LLC	Derry	NH	G	603 774-5375	17982
Msn Corporation	Manchester	NH	D	603 623-3528	18879
Central Falls Provision Co	Central Falls	RI	G	401 725-7020	20112
Daniele Inc	Pascoag	RI	E	401 568-6228	20799
Daniele International Inc	Pascoag	RI	D	401 568-6228	20800
Daniele International Inc	Pascoag	RI	C	401 568-6228	20801
Daniele International Inc **(PA)**	Mapleville	RI	C	401 568-6228	20612
Kinderwagon Company	Newport	RI	G	617 256-7599	20670
Lincoln Packing Co	Cranston	RI	E	401 943-0878	20255
Marcello Sausage Co	Cranston	RI	F	401 275-1952	20259
Newport Creamery LLC	Cranston	RI	B	401 946-4000	20268
Portion Meat Associates Inc	Providence	RI	F	401 421-2438	21092

	CITY	ST	EMP	PHONE	ENTRY #
Rhode Island Provision Co Inc	Johnston	RI	F	401 831-0815	20537
T O Nam Sausage	Cranston	RI	G	401 941-9620	20298
Whitestone Provision Sup Corp **(PA)**	Barrington	RI	G	401 245-1346	20057
Fortunas Sausage Co LLC	Sandgate	VT	G	802 375-0200	22400
Harringtons In Vermont Inc **(PA)**	Richmond	VT	F	802 434-7500	22312
New England Smoked Seafood	Rutland	VT	G	802 773-4628	22346
Npc Processing Inc	Shelburne	VT	E	802 660-0496	22420
Plumrose Usa Inc	Swanton	VT	D	802 868-7314	22533
Sugar Mountain Farm LLC	West Topsham	VT	G	802 439-6462	22624
Vermont Beef Jerky Co	Orleans	VT	E	802 754-9412	22252
VSC Holdings Inc	Hinesburg	VT	D	802 482-4666	22033

2015 Poultry Slaughtering, Dressing & Processing

	CITY	ST	EMP	PHONE	ENTRY #
Chris & Zack LLC	Orange	CT	G	203 298-0742	3361
Phoenix Poultry Corporation	Enfield	CT	E	413 732-1433	1374
Waybest Foods Inc	South Windsor	CT	G	860 289-7948	4020
Gerard Farms Inc	Framingham	MA	G	781 858-1013	10959
Puritan Food Co Inc	Boston	MA	E	617 269-5650	8800
Suffield Poultry Inc	Springfield	MA	G	413 737-8392	15510
Advancepierre Foods Inc	Portland	ME	E	207 541-2800	6610
Barber Foods **(DH)**	Portland	ME	E	207 482-5500	6619
Barber Foods	Portland	ME	E	207 772-1934	6620
Pete and Gerrys Organics LLC	Monroe	NH	E	603 638-2827	19091
Taylor Egg Products Inc	Madbury	NH	E	603 742-1050	18761
Premium Poultry Co	Providence	RI	E	401 467-3200	21093
Saugy Inc	Cranston	RI	G	401 640-1879	20283
Npc Processing Inc	Shelburne	VT	E	802 660-0496	22420

2021 Butter

	CITY	ST	EMP	PHONE	ENTRY #
Grass Roots Creamery	Granby	CT	G	860 653-6303	1589
Redding Creamery LLC	Redding	CT	G	203 938-2766	3651
Square Creamery LLC	Bethel	CT	G	203 456-3490	180
Agri-Mark Inc	West Springfield	MA	D	413 732-4168	16506
Captain Bonneys Creamery	Rochester	MA	G	774 218-3586	14784
Maple Valley Creamery	Hadley	MA	G	413 588-4881	11310
Seafood Hut and Creamery	Acushnet	MA	G	508 993-9355	7406
Casco Bay Butter Company LLC	Portland	ME	G	207 712-9148	6632
Kates Homemade Butter Inc	Kennebunkport	ME	G	207 934-5134	6246
SBwinsor Creamery LLC	Johnston	RI	G	401 231-5113	20541
Cabot Creamery	Middlebury	VT	G	888 792-2268	22106
Co Op Creamery	Saint Albans	VT	G	802 524-6581	22365
Gammelgarden Creamery	Pownal	VT	G	802 823-5757	22281

2022 Cheese

	CITY	ST	EMP	PHONE	ENTRY #
Chris & Zack LLC	Orange	CT	G	203 298-0742	3361
Elm City Cheese Company Inc	Hamden	CT	F	203 865-5768	1746
Mozzicato Fmly Investments LLC	Wethersfield	CT	G	860 296-0426	5259
Ndr Liuzzi Inc	Hamden	CT	E	203 287-8477	1774
Orange Cheese Company	Orange	CT	G	917 603-4378	3377
Red Apple Cheese LLC **(PA)**	Watertown	CT	G	203 755-5579	5021
Agri-Mark Inc	Hingham	MA	G	781 740-0090	11489
Agri-Mark Inc **(PA)**	Andover	MA	D	978 552-5500	7535
Emga Foods LLC	Peabody	MA	G	978 532-0000	14333
Extra Virgin Foods Inc	Watertown	MA	G	617 407-9161	16285
HP Hood LLC **(PA)**	Lynnfield	MA	C	617 887-8441	12549
Julima Cheese Inc	Baldwinville	MA	G	978 939-8800	7944
Kraft Heinz Foods Company	Woburn	MA	C	781 933-2800	17212
Martins Cheese Co Inc	Westport	MA	G	508 636-2357	16843
Mondelez Global LLC	Hanover	MA	G	781 878-0103	11348
Tribe Mediterranean Foods Inc	Taunton	MA	D	774 961-0000	15791
Crooked Face Creamery LLC	Norridgewock	ME	G	207 858-5096	6496
Pine Land Farm Cheese Factory	New Gloucester	ME	G	207 688-6400	6470
State Maine Cheese Company LLC	Hope	ME	G	207 236-8895	6201
York Hill Farm	New Sharon	ME	G	207 778-9741	6479
Garfields Smokehouse Inc	Meriden	NH	G	603 469-3225	18983
Agri-Mark Inc	Middlebury	VT	C	802 388-6731	22098
Agri-Mark Inc	Waitsfield	VT	D	802 496-1200	22559
Cabot Creamery Cooperative Inc	Waitsfield	VT	B	978 552-5500	22562
Crowley Cheese Incorporated	Mount Holly	VT	G	802 259-2340	22181
Grafton Village Cheese Co LLC	Brattleboro	VT	E	802 843-2221	21730
Mountain Mozzarella LLC	North Bennington	VT	E	802 440-9950	22210
Sugarbush Farm Inc	Woodstock	VT	G	802 457-1757	22739
Swan Valley Cheese Vermont LLC	Swanton	VT	E	802 868-7181	22537
Vermont Creamery LLC	Websterville	VT	E	802 479-9371	22598

2023 Milk, Condensed & Evaporated

	CITY	ST	EMP	PHONE	ENTRY #
Kohler Mix Specialties LLC	Newington	CT	C	860 666-1511	2876
Natures First Inc **(PA)**	Orange	CT	G	203 795-8400	3374
Nestle Usa Inc	Pomfret Center	CT	C	860 928-0082	3558
Ajinomoto Cambrooke Inc **(DH)**	Ayer	MA	E	508 782-2300	7906
Breed Nutrition Inc	Rehoboth	MA	G	508 840-3888	14747
Dmi Nutraceuticals Inc	Bedford	MA	G	617 999-7219	7971
Meganutra Inc **(PA)**	Norwood	MA	G	781 762-9600	14177
Nestle Usa Inc	Wilmington	MA	C	978 988-2030	17028
Partylite Inc **(HQ)**	Plymouth	MA	D	203 661-1926	14572
Prescientpharma LLC	Canton	MA	G	617 955-0490	9772
Salarius Pharmaceuticals Inc **(PA)**	Boston	MA	E	617 874-1821	8832
Human Body Recon Company	Nottingham	NH	G	603 895-2920	19415
Naked Nutrient By Deseo LLC	Derry	NH	G	646 809-4943	17989
Bariatrix Nutrition Corp	Fairfax	VT	E	802 527-2500	21972
Canadian American Resources	Montpelier	VT	G	802 223-2271	22146
Nutragenesis LLC	Brattleboro	VT	G	802 257-5345	21741
St Albans Cooperative Crmry	Saint Albans	VT	D	802 524-9366	22379
Vermont Base Waters LLC	Colchester	VT	G	802 893-2131	21885

2024 Ice Cream

	CITY	ST	EMP	PHONE	ENTRY #
Abbydabby	West Hartford	CT	G	860 586-8832	5051
B-Sweet LLC	Monroe	CT	G	203 452-0499	2393
Ben & Jerrys Homemade Inc	Newington	CT	G	203 488-9666	2848
Bucks Spumoni Company Inc	Milford	CT	F	203 874-2007	2257
Chip In A Bottle LLC	New Haven	CT	G	203 460-0665	2676
Conopco Inc	Trumbull	CT	E	708 606-0540	4620
Dari-Farms Ice Cream Co Inc	Tolland	CT	F	860 872-8313	4544
Gelato Giuliana LLC	New Haven	CT	G	203 772-0607	2690
Greg Robbins and Associates	Branford	CT	G	888 699-8876	321
HP Hood LLC	Suffield	CT	C	860 623-4435	4463
J Foster Ice Cream	Simsbury	CT	G	860 651-1499	3907
Kan Pak LLC	Southbury	CT	G	203 933-6631	4029
Longfords Ice Cream Ltd	Stamford	CT	F	914 935-9469	4239
Poppys LLC	Hartford	CT	F	860 778-9044	1860
Pralines Inc	Wallingford	CT	F	203 284-8847	4786
Pralines of Plainville	Plainville	CT	G	860 410-1151	3512
Rbf Frozen Desserts LLC	West Hartford	CT	F	516 474-6488	5092
Reeds Inc	Norwalk	CT	E	203 890-0557	3228
Rich Products Corporation	New Britain	CT	B	860 827-8000	2572
Ritas of Milford	Milford	CT	F	203 301-4490	2353
Royal Ice Cream Company Inc **(PA)**	Manchester	CT	F	860 649-5358	2043
Salem Vly Farms Ice Cream Inc	Salem	CT	G	860 859-2980	3739
Thomas J Lipton Inc	Trumbull	CT	A	206 381-3500	4635
Berry Twist	Boston	MA	G	857 362-7455	8402
Bruce Luong DBA Pure Froyo	Lowell	MA	G	978 996-7800	12357
Captain Dustys Ice Cream	Salem	MA	G	978 744-0777	14901
County Street Ice Cream Corp	Somerset	MA	G	508 674-3357	15143
Dads	Charlton	MA	G	508 248-9774	9848
Gone Troppo Inc **(PA)**	Brookline	MA	G	617 739-7995	9201
HP Hood LLC **(PA)**	Lynnfield	MA	C	617 887-8441	12549
Ice Effects	Rockland	MA	G	781 871-7070	14807
Ice Treat Inc	Chelsea	MA	G	617 889-0300	9954
Incredible Foods Inc	Boston	MA	E	617 491-6600	8614
J P Licks Homemade Ice Cream	Dedham	MA	G	781 329-9100	10294
Masonry & More Inc	Framingham	MA	G	508 740-8537	10981
Mixx Frozen Yogurt Inc **(PA)**	Allston	MA	F	617 782-6499	7470
Philip RS Sorbets	Winchester	MA	F	781 721-6330	17095
Puleos Dairy	Salem	MA	G	978 590-7611	14937
Puritan Ice Cream Co of Boston	Boston	MA	G	617 524-3580	8801
Puritan Icecream Inc	Roslindale	MA	G	617 524-7500	14842
Rainbow Shack	Adams	MA	G	413 743-4031	7414
Richardsons Ice Cream	Reading	MA	G	781 944-9121	14740
Richies King Slush Mfg Co Inc	Everett	MA	F	800 287-5874	10627
Russos Inc	Saugus	MA	F	781 233-1737	14995
Slush Connection Inc	North Easton	MA	G	508 230-3788	13952
Snows Nice Cream Co Inc	Greenfield	MA	G	413 774-7438	11277
Spadafora Slush Co	Malden	MA	G	617 548-5870	12597
Giffords Dairy Inc	Skowhegan	ME	E	207 474-9821	6975
Gorgeous Gelato LLC	Portland	ME	G	207 699-4309	6666
HP Hood LLC	Portland	ME	D	207 774-9861	6672
Mount Desert Island Ice Cream	Bar Harbor	ME	G	207 460-5515	5666
Protein Holdings Inc **(PA)**	Portland	ME	F	207 771-0965	6717
Round Top Ice Cream Inc	Damariscotta	ME	E	207 563-5307	5939
Stephen E Witham	Gray	ME	G	207 657-3410	6142
Woolwich Ice Cream Inc	Woolwich	ME	G	207 442-8830	7291
Big Dipper	Somersworth	NH	E	603 742-7075	19829
Kellerhaus Inc	Laconia	NH	E	603 366-4466	18569
Morano Gelato Inc	Hanover	NH	G	603 643-4233	18295
Soda Shoppe of Franklin	Franklin	NH	F	603 934-0100	18164
Sunshine Scoops LLC	Manchester	NH	G	603 668-0992	18770
Walpole Creamery Ltd	Walpole	NH	G	603 445-5700	19926
A Baileys LLC	Barrington	RI	G	401 252-6002	20042
Ice Cream Machine Co	Cumberland	RI	F	401 333-5053	20327
Newport Creamery LLC	Cranston	RI	B	401 946-4000	20268
SA Feole Masonry Svcs Inc	Cranston	RI	G	401 273-2766	20282
Warwick Ice Cream Company	Warwick	RI	E	401 821-8403	21443
Blue Moon Foods Inc	White River Junction	VT	G	802 295-1165	22635
Nutricopia Inc	Montpelier	VT	G	808 832-2080	22158
Rhino Foods Inc **(PA)**	Burlington	VT	C	802 862-0252	21807

2026 Milk

	CITY	ST	EMP	PHONE	ENTRY #
Guida-Seibert Dairy Company **(PA)**	New Britain	CT	C	860 224-2404	2537
HP Hood LLC	Newtown	CT	B	203 304-9151	2925
Kohler Mix Specialties LLC	Newington	CT	C	860 666-1511	2876
Peachwave of Watertown	Watertown	CT	G	203 942-4949	5015
R & D Services LLC	Southington	CT	G	860 628-5205	4072
Swizzles of Greenwhich	Cos Cob	CT	G	917 662-0080	830

	CITY	ST	EMP	PHONE	ENTRY #
Willard J Stearns & Sons Inc	Storrs Mansfield	CT	E	860 423-9289	4387
Agri-Mark Inc **(PA)**	Andover	MA	D	978 552-5500	7535
Agri-Mark Inc	West Springfield	MA	D	413 732-4168	16506
Dahlicious Holdings LLC	Leominster	MA	F	978 401-2103	12131
Dahlicious LLC	Leominster	MA	E	505 200-0396	12132
Frozen Cups LLC	Lawrence	MA	G	978 918-1872	12026
Garelick Farms LLC **(DH)**	Franklin	MA	A	508 528-9000	11049
Garelick Farms LLC	Haverhill	MA	F	781 599-1300	11438
Garelick Farms LLC	Franklin	MA	C	508 528-9000	11050
HP Hood LLC	Agawam	MA	C	413 786-2178	7431
HP Hood LLC	Feeding Hills	MA	B	413 789-8194	10800
HP Hood LLC	Peabody	MA	F	978 535-3385	14342
HP Hood LLC **(PA)**	Lynnfield	MA	C	617 887-8441	12549
Johnsons Food Products Corp	Boston	MA	F	617 265-3400	8637
Lets Yo Yogurt	East Longmeadow	MA	G	413 525-4002	10482
Pinkberry	Cambridge	MA	G	617 547-0573	9611
Pioneer Vly Milk Mktg Coop Inc	Greenfield	MA	G	413 772-2332	11272
Postdoc Ventures LLC	Cambridge	MA	G	617 492-3555	9613
Puleos Dairy	Salem	MA	G	978 590-7611	14937
Tribe Mediterranean Foods Inc	Taunton	MA	D	774 961-0000	15791
Tutti Frutti	North Attleboro	MA	G	508 695-7795	13785
Yoway LLC	Brookline	MA	G	617 505-5158	9225
Yoway LLC **(PA)**	Worcester	MA	G	508 459-0611	17512
Houlton Farms Dairy Inc **(PA)**	Houlton	ME	F	207 532-3170	6206
HP Hood LLC	Portland	ME	D	207 774-9861	6672
Protein Holdings Inc **(PA)**	Portland	ME	F	207 771-0965	6717
Main Street Cheese LLC	Hancock	NH	G	603 525-3300	18285
A B Munroe Dairy Inc	East Providence	RI	D	401 438-4450	20384
Agri-Mark Inc	Middlebury	VT	C	802 388-6731	22098
Agri-Mark Inc	Waitsfield	VT	D	802 496-1200	22559
Duhamel Family Farm LLC	Highgate Center	VT	G	802 868-4954	22019
Ebws LLC	Strafford	VT	G	802 765-4180	22526
Green Mtn Organic Crmry LLC	Hinesburg	VT	G	802 482-6455	22026
Spragues Dairy Inc	Randolph	VT	G	802 728-3863	22303
St Albans Cooperative Crmry	Saint Albans	VT	D	802 524-9366	22379
Tafts Milk Maple Farm	Huntington	VT	G	802 434-2727	22034

2032 Canned Specialties

	CITY	ST	EMP	PHONE	ENTRY #
A S Fine Foods	Stamford	CT	D	203 322-3899	4124
Cushs Homegrown LLC	Old Lyme	CT	G	860 739-7373	3318
Foundry Foods Inc	Norwalk	CT	G	314 982-3204	3154
Louis Rodriguz	New Haven	CT	G	203 777-6937	2708
Shenondah Vly Specialty Foods	Stamford	CT	G	203 348-0402	4315
Au Soleil	Boston	MA	G	617 535-6040	8386
Drews LLC	Woburn	MA	G	781 935-6045	17170
Garan Enterprises Inc	Chicopee	MA	F	413 594-4991	10027
Kettle Cuisine LLC **(PA)**	Lynn	MA	C	617 409-1100	12519
Lolas Italian Harvest LLC	Natick	MA	G	508 651-0524	13265
New England Country Foods LLC	Cambridge	MA	G	617 682-3650	9580
R Walters Foods	Danvers	MA	D	978 646-8950	10249
Stonewall Kitchen LLC **(PA)**	York	ME	C	207 351-2713	7316
494 Amherst St LLC	Nashua	NH	G	470 430-4608	19102
Great Soups Inc	Bristol	RI	F	401 253-3200	20082
Rachels Table LLC	Greenville	RI	G	401 949-5333	20472
Hume Specialties Inc	Chester	VT	E	802 875-3117	21843
Phat Thai	Burlington	VT	G	802 863-8827	21802
Sunjas Oriental Foods Inc	Waterbury	VT	G	802 244-7644	22585
Vermont Probiotica	Northfield	VT	G	802 279-4998	22245

2033 Canned Fruits, Vegetables & Preserves

	CITY	ST	EMP	PHONE	ENTRY #
Conopco Inc	Trumbull	CT	E	708 606-0540	4620
Cosmos Food Products Inc	West Haven	CT	E	800 942-6766	5114
Country Pure Foods Inc	Ellington	CT	C	330 753-2293	1331
Fruitbud Juice LLC	Danbury	CT	E	203 790-8200	923
Guida-Seibert Dairy Company **(PA)**	New Britain	CT	C	860 224-2404	2537
Onofrios Ultimate Foods Inc	New Haven	CT	F	203 469-4014	2721
Ragozzino Foods Inc **(PA)**	Meriden	CT	F	203 238-2553	2123
Sabatino North America LLC **(PA)**	West Haven	CT	E	718 328-4120	5144
Sweet Country Roads LLC	Colchester	CT	G	860 537-0069	811
Thomas J Lipton Inc	Trumbull	CT	A	206 381-3500	4635
Winding Drive Corporation	Woodbury	CT	G	203 263-6961	5491
Clives Jams LLC	Everett	MA	G	617 294-9766	10606
Company of Coca-Cola Bottling	Northampton	MA	D	413 586-8450	14000
Decas Cranberry Co Inc **(PA)**	Carver	MA	G	508 866-8506	9803
Gebelein Group Inc	Hyde Park	MA	F	617 361-6611	11867
Graystone Limited LLC **(PA)**	North Easton	MA	G	855 356-1027	13946
Howard Foods Inc **(PA)**	Danvers	MA	G	978 774-6207	10224
HP Hood LLC	Agawam	MA	C	413 786-2178	7431
Jam & Jelly Chatham	West Chatham	MA	G	508 945-3052	16474
Kens Foods Inc **(PA)**	Marlborough	MA	B	508 229-1100	12782
Marias Food Products Inc	Medford	MA	G	781 396-4110	12940
National Grape Coop Assn Inc	Concord	MA	G	978 371-1000	10145
Ocean Spray (europe) Ltd	Middleboro	MA	F	508 946-1000	13071
Ocean Spray Cranberries Inc **(PA)**	Middleboro	MA	B	508 946-1000	13072
Ocean Spray Cranberries Inc	Middleboro	MA	C	508 947-4940	13073
Ocean Spray Cranberries Inc	South Carver	MA	G	508 866-5306	15235
Ocean Spray International Inc **(HQ)**	Middleboro	MA	D	508 946-1000	13074
Ocean Spray Intl Svcs Inc **(HQ)**	Lakeville	MA	E	508 946-1000	11977
Odwalla Inc	Brookline	MA	E	336 877-1634	9213
RE Kimball & Co Inc	Amesbury	MA	G	978 388-1826	7505
Spinelli Ravioli Mfg Co Inc	Boston	MA	E	617 567-1992	8859
Tropicana Products Inc	Taunton	MA	E	508 821-2056	15792
Welch Foods Inc A Cooperative **(HQ)**	Concord	MA	B	978 371-1000	10160
Welch Foods Inc A Cooperative	Concord	MA	C	978 371-3762	10161
B&G Foods Inc	Portland	ME	C	207 772-8341	6616
Cherryfield Foods Inc **(DH)**	Cherryfield	ME	D	207 546-7573	5902
Denny Mikes cue Stuff Inc **(PA)**	Westbrook	ME	G	207 591-5084	7187
Farm Truck Institute	Dresden	ME	G	207 400-2242	5966
Jarden LLC	East Wilton	ME	C	207 645-2574	5987
Jasper Wyman & Son	Cherryfield	ME	E	207 546-3381	5903
Jasper Wyman & Son	Deblois	ME	E	207 638-2201	5946
Jasper Wyman & Son	Milbridge	ME	G	207 546-2311	6434
Jasper Wyman & Son	Cherryfield	ME	E	207 546-3381	5904
Jasper Wyman & Son **(PA)**	Milbridge	ME	G	207 546-3800	6433
Maine Wild Blueberry Company **(DH)**	Machias	ME	D	207 255-8364	6392
Maine Wild Blueberry Company	Machias	ME	D	207 255-8364	6393
McCain Foods Usa Inc	Easton	ME	B	207 488-2561	5991
Oyster Creek Mushrooms Company	Damariscotta	ME	G	207 563-1076	5938
Pembertons Food Inc	Gray	ME	G	207 657-6446	6141
Sisters Salsa Inc	Blue Hill	ME	G	207 374-2170	5774
Stonewall Kitchen LLC **(PA)**	York	ME	C	207 351-2713	7316
Todds Originals LLC	Glenburn	ME	G	844 328-7257	6108
Old Dutch Mustard Co Inc	Greenville	NH	D	516 466-0522	18229
Stonewall Kitchen LLC	North Conway	NH	D	603 356-3342	19379
Cala Fruit Distributors Inc	Pawtucket	RI	F	401 725-8189	20819
Catanzaro Food Products Inc	Pawtucket	RI	G	401 255-1700	20820
Jens & Marie Inc	Providence	RI	G	401 475-9991	21043
Boves of Vermont Inc	Milton	VT	G	802 862-7235	22125
Dellamore Enterprises Inc	Colchester	VT	G	802 655-6264	21861
Willis Wood	Springfield	VT	G	802 263-5547	22513

2034 Dried Fruits, Vegetables & Soup

	CITY	ST	EMP	PHONE	ENTRY #
Conopco Inc	Trumbull	CT	E	708 606-0540	4620
Thomas J Lipton Inc	Trumbull	CT	A	206 381-3500	4635
American Nut & Chocolate Inc	Boston	MA	G	617 427-1510	8362
Arcade Industries Inc	Auburn	MA	F	508 832-6300	7826
Decas Cranberry Products Inc	Carver	MA	E	508 866-8506	9804
Ocean Spray Cranberries Inc **(PA)**	Middleboro	MA	B	508 946-1000	13072
Ocean Spray International Inc **(HQ)**	Middleboro	MA	D	508 946-1000	13074
Ocean Spray Intl Svcs Inc **(HQ)**	Lakeville	MA	E	508 946-1000	11977
Good To-Go LLC	Kittery	ME	F	207 451-9060	6256
Maine Wild Blueberry Company	Machias	ME	D	207 255-8364	6393
Peeled Inc	Cumberland	RI	F	212 706-2001	20338

2035 Pickled Fruits, Vegetables, Sauces & Dressings

	CITY	ST	EMP	PHONE	ENTRY #
Da Silva Klanko Ltd	Waterbury	CT	G	203 756-4932	4863
JKL Specialty Foods Inc	Stamford	CT	F	203 541-3990	4230
Kerry R Wood	Westport	CT	G	203 221-7780	5205
Newmans Own Inc **(PA)**	Westport	CT	E	203 222-0136	5218
Onofrios Ultimate Foods Inc	New Haven	CT	F	203 469-4014	2721
Thomas J Lipton Inc	Trumbull	CT	A	206 381-3500	4635
Albert Capone **(PA)**	Somerville	MA	G	617 629-2296	15151
Alexs Ugly Sauce LLC	Roslindale	MA	G	617 300-0180	14837
Four In One LLC	Chelmsford	MA	D	978 250-0751	9900
Howard Foods Inc **(PA)**	Danvers	MA	G	978 774-6207	10224
Kettle Cuisine LLC **(PA)**	Lynn	MA	C	617 409-1100	12519
Pearlco of Boston Inc	Canton	MA	E	781 821-1010	9766
Plenus Group Inc	Lowell	MA	E	978 970-3832	12422
RE Kimball & Co Inc	Amesbury	MA	G	978 388-1826	7505
Real Pickles Coperative Inc	Greenfield	MA	E	413 774-2600	11273
Star Pickling Corp	Swansea	MA	F	508 672-8535	15716
Mike Maine Pickle	Easton	ME	G	207 488-6881	5993
Morses Sauerkraut	Waldoboro	ME	F	207 832-5569	7135
Rayes Mustard Mill	Eastport	ME	G	207 853-4451	5996
Schlotterbeck & Foss LLC **(PA)**	Westbrook	ME	E	207 772-4666	7206
Stanchfield Farms	Milo	ME	G	207 943-2133	6448
Stonewall Kitchen LLC **(PA)**	York	ME	C	207 351-2713	7316
World Harbors Inc	Auburn	ME	E	207 786-3200	5601
Old Dutch Mustard Co Inc	Greenville	NH	D	516 466-0522	18229
CHI Foods LLC	Providence	RI	G	310 309-1186	20983
Great Soups Inc	Bristol	RI	F	401 253-3200	20082
Vega Food Industries Inc	Providence	RI	F	401 942-0620	21146
Drews LLC **(HQ)**	Chester	VT	E	802 875-1184	21842
Gringo Kitchens LLC	Manchester Center	VT	F	802 362-0836	22086
Maple Grove Farms Vermont Inc **(HQ)**	Saint Johnsbury	VT	D	802 748-5141	22391
Putney Pasta Company Inc	Brattleboro	VT	E	802 257-4800	21746

2037 Frozen Fruits, Juices & Vegetables

	CITY	ST	EMP	PHONE	ENTRY #
Conopco Inc	Trumbull	CT	D	203 381-3557	4621
Fruitbud Juice LLC	Danbury	CT	E	203 790-8200	923
Fruta Juice Bar LLC	Bridgeport	CT	G	203 690-9168	416
Quality Kitchen Corp Delaware	Danbury	CT	G	203 744-2000	977
Santorini Breeze LLC	Branford	CT	G	203 640-3431	344
Bevovations LLC **(PA)**	Leominster	MA	F	978 227-5469	12118

	CITY	ST	EMP	PHONE	ENTRY #
Local Juice Inc	Hyannis	MA	G	508 813-9282	11846
Ocean Spray Cranberries Inc	Middleboro	MA	C	508 947-4940	13073
Ocean Spray Cranberries Inc **(PA)**	Middleboro	MA	B	508 946-1000	13072
Ocean Spray International Inc **(HQ)**	Middleboro	MA	D	508 946-1000	13074
Ocean Spray Intl Svcs Inc **(HQ)**	Lakeville	MA	E	508 946-1000	11977
Tropicana Products Inc	Taunton	MA	E	508 821-2056	15792
Welch Foods Inc A Cooperative **(HQ)**	Concord	MA	B	978 371-1000	10160
Allens Blueberry Freezer Inc **(PA)**	Ellsworth	ME	E	207 667-5561	6013
G M Allen & Son Inc	Orland	ME	G	207 469-7060	6549
Jasper Wyman & Son **(PA)**	Milbridge	ME	G	207 546-3800	6433
Jasper Wyman & Son	Milbridge	ME	G	207 546-2311	6434
Maine Wild Blueberry Company **(DH)**	Machias	ME	D	207 255-8364	6392
Maine Wild Blueberry Company	Machias	ME	D	207 255-8364	6393
McCain Foods Usa Inc	Easton	ME	B	207 488-2561	5991
McCain Foods Usa Inc	Easton	ME	A	207 488-2561	5992
Merrill Blueberry Farms Inc	Hancock	ME	F	207 667-2541	6170
Penobscot McCrum LLC	Belfast	ME	C	207 338-4360	5696
Purbeck Isle Inc **(PA)**	Augusta	ME	E	207 623-5119	5617

2038 Frozen Specialties

	CITY	ST	EMP	PHONE	ENTRY #
Just Breakfast & Things	Lisbon	CT	G	860 376-4040	1943
Kohler Mix Specialties LLC	Newington	CT	C	860 666-1511	2876
Orange Cheese Company	Orange	CT	G	917 603-4378	3377
Ragozzino Foods Inc **(PA)**	Meriden	CT	F	203 238-2553	2123
Villarina Pasta & Fine Foods **(PA)**	Danbury	CT	G	203 917-4463	1004
Blount Fine Foods Corp **(PA)**	Fall River	MA	C	774 888-1300	10669
Chinamerica Food Manufacture	Boston	MA	F	617 426-1818	8469
Mama Rosies Co Inc	Boston	MA	E	617 242-4300	8680
Marias Food Products Inc	Medford	MA	G	781 396-4110	12940
Nestle	Taunton	MA	G	508 828-3954	15768
Paramount South Boston	Boston	MA	G	617 269-9999	8765
Plenus Group Inc	Lowell	MA	E	978 970-3832	12422
Stuffed Foods LLC	Wilmington	MA	E	978 203-0370	17049
Uno Foods Inc	Brockton	MA	E	508 580-1561	9185
Waterwood Corporation	Westfield	MA	E	413 572-1010	16740
Bafs Inc **(PA)**	Bangor	ME	F	207 942-5226	5630
Barber Foods	Portland	ME	E	207 772-1934	6620
Maine Meal LLC	Skowhegan	ME	G	207 779-4185	6980
McCain Foods Usa Inc	Easton	ME	B	207 488-2561	5991
Orono House of Pizza	Orono	ME	G	207 866-5505	6557
Slacktide Cafe LLC	Arundel	ME	G	207 467-3822	5535
Take 2 Dough Productions Inc	Sanford	ME	F	207 490-6502	6893
Wise-Acre Inc	Blue Hill	ME	G	207 374-5400	5775
Bobby OS Foods LLC	Salem	NH	G	603 458-2502	19714
A B Munroe Dairy Inc	East Providence	RI	D	401 438-4450	20384
Blount Fine Foods Corp	Warren	RI	D	401 245-8800	21290
Putney Pasta Company Inc	Brattleboro	VT	E	802 257-4800	21746

2041 Flour, Grain Milling

	CITY	ST	EMP	PHONE	ENTRY #
Channel Alloys	Norwalk	CT	G	203 975-1404	3123
Michele Schiano Di Cola Inc	Wallingford	CT	G	203 265-5301	4773
Pelletier Millwrights LLC	Danielson	CT	G	860 564-8936	1016
Ardent Mills LLC	Ayer	MA	E	978 772-6337	7911
Bay State Milling Company **(PA)**	Quincy	MA	E	617 328-4423	14614
Biena LLC	Boston	MA	G	617 202-5210	8407
KPM Analytics Inc **(PA)**	Milford	MA	G	774 462-6700	13122
Pillsbury Company LLC	Chelsea	MA	D	617 884-9800	9964
Seaboard Flour LLC **(PA)**	Boston	MA	G	917 928-6040	8842
Itllbe LLC	Scarborough	ME	G	207 730-7301	6927
Management Controls LLC	Auburn	ME	G	207 753-6844	5579
Pro Dough Inc	Manchester	NH	F	603 623-6844	18906

2043 Cereal Breakfast Foods

	CITY	ST	EMP	PHONE	ENTRY #
Garden of Light Inc	East Hartford	CT	D	860 895-6622	1197
Kellogg Company	Newington	CT	A	860 665-9920	2875
Munk Pack Inc	Greenwich	CT	F	203 769-5005	1632
Barbaras Bakery Inc **(DH)**	Marlborough	MA	E	800 343-0590	12725
Kraft Heinz Foods Company	Mansfield	MA	D	508 763-3311	12640
Old Creamery Grocery Store	Cummington	MA	G	413 634-5560	10173
Weetabix Company Inc	Sterling	MA	G	978 422-2905	15549
Wild Blue Yonder Foods	Marblehead	MA	G	978 532-3400	12696
Small Batch Organics LLC	Manchester Center	VT	F	802 367-1054	22090

2044 Rice Milling

	CITY	ST	EMP	PHONE	ENTRY #
Saw Mill Site Farm	Greenfield	MA	G	413 665-3005	11274

2045 Flour, Blended & Prepared

	CITY	ST	EMP	PHONE	ENTRY #
Watson LLC **(DH)**	West Haven	CT	B	203 932-3000	5149
Concord Foods LLC	Brockton	MA	C	508 580-1700	9131
Dough Connection Corporation	Woburn	MA	G	877 693-6844	17169
Wilevco Inc	Billerica	MA	F	978 667-0400	8310
Bouchard Family Farm Products	Fort Kent	ME	G	207 834-3237	6058
Ever Better Eating Inc	Pittsfield	NH	D	603 435-5119	19499
Pollys Pancake Parlor	Sugar Hill	NH	G	603 823-5575	19878
Maple Grove Farms Vermont Inc **(HQ)**	Saint Johnsbury	VT	D	802 748-5141	22391
Rhino Foods Inc **(PA)**	Burlington	VT	C	802 862-0252	21807

2046 Wet Corn Milling

	CITY	ST	EMP	PHONE	ENTRY #
Tate Lyle Ingrdnts Amricas LLC	Westborough	MA	G	508 366-8322	16654
Tate Lyle Ingrdnts Amricas LLC	Houlton	ME	E	207 532-9523	6211
Western Polymer Corporation	Fort Fairfield	ME	E	207 472-1250	6057

2047 Dog & Cat Food

	CITY	ST	EMP	PHONE	ENTRY #
A L C Inovators Inc	Milford	CT	G	203 877-8526	2232
Blue Buffalo Company Ltd **(DH)**	Wilton	CT	B	203 762-9751	5279
Bravo LLC **(PA)**	Manchester	CT	F	866 922-9222	1988
Bravo LLC	Vernon	CT	E	860 896-1899	4664
Fine Pets LLC	Greenwich	CT	G	203 833-1517	1611
2 Dogs Treats LLC	Dorchester	MA	G	617 286-4844	10339
Channel Fish Co Inc	Boston	MA	D	617 569-3200	8467
Mars Incorporated	Bellingham	MA	G	508 966-0022	8047
Polka Dog Designs LLC **(PA)**	Boston	MA	F	617 338-5155	8784
Wellpet LLC **(PA)**	Tewksbury	MA	D	877 869-2971	15848
Pure Pup Love Inc	Scarborough	ME	G	207 588-8111	6936
Kent Nutrition Group Inc	Londonderry	NH	F	603 437-3400	18708
Tbd Brands LLC	Exeter	NH	G	603 775-7772	18133
Wholistic Pet Organics LLC	Bedford	NH	G	603 472-8300	17667

2048 Prepared Feeds For Animals & Fowls

	CITY	ST	EMP	PHONE	ENTRY #
A L C Inovators Inc	Milford	CT	G	203 877-8526	2232
ALC Sales Company LLC **(PA)**	Milford	CT	G	203 877-8526	2239
Blue Buffalo Pet Products Inc **(HQ)**	Wilton	CT	E	203 762-9751	5280
Earth Animal Ventures Inc	Stamford	CT	G	717 271-6393	4190
HJ Baker & Bro LLC **(PA)**	Shelton	CT	E	203 682-9200	3812
Source Inc **(PA)**	North Branford	CT	G	203 488-6400	2977
Channel Fish Co Inc	Boston	MA	D	617 569-3200	8467
CMS Enterprise Inc	New Bedford	MA	G	508 995-2372	13371
Designing Health Inc	East Longmeadow	MA	E	661 257-1705	10472
Euroduna Americas Inc	Plymouth	MA	G	508 888-2710	14556
Finicky Pet Food Inc	New Bedford	MA	E	508 991-8448	13386
N2bm Nutrition Inc	Salisbury	MA	G	978 241-2851	14954
Q A S	Boston	MA	G	617 345-3000	8802
Savory Creations International	Lynn	MA	F	650 638-1024	12537
Smartpak Equine LLC **(DH)**	Plymouth	MA	D	774 773-1100	14583
Tropicana Products Inc	Taunton	MA	E	508 821-2056	15792
Kent Nutrition Group Inc	Augusta	ME	F	207 622-1530	5611
Kent Nutrition Group Inc	Windham	ME	G	207 892-9411	7239
Lucerne Farms	Fort Fairfield	ME	E	207 488-2520	6056
Northern Tack	Calais	ME	G	207 217-7584	5865
Offshore Marine Outfitters	York	ME	G	207 363-8862	7314
Source Inc	Brunswick	ME	G	207 729-1107	5845
Kent Nutrition Group Inc	Londonderry	NH	F	603 437-3400	18708
Trividia Mfg Solutions **(DH)**	Lancaster	NH	C	603 788-2848	18606
Trividia Mfg Solutions	Lancaster	NH	G	603 788-4952	18607
Wholistic Pet Organics LLC	Bedford	NH	G	603 472-8300	17667
Dittmar & McNeil CPA S Inc	Warwick	RI	G	401 921-2600	21352
Kent Nutrition Group Inc	Richford	VT	D	802 848-7718	22308
Kent Nutrition Group Inc	Brandon	VT	E	802 247-9599	21709
Nutra-Blend LLC	North Troy	VT	G	802 988-4474	22241
Phoenix Feeds Organix LLC	New Haven	VT	E	802 453-6684	22186
Poulin Grain Inc	North Bennington	VT	E	802 681-1605	22212
Poulin Grain Inc	Swanton	VT	F	802 868-3323	22534

2051 Bread, Bakery Prdts Exc Cookies & Crackers

	CITY	ST	EMP	PHONE	ENTRY #
Amodios Inc **(PA)**	Waterbury	CT	F	203 573-1229	4843
Artisan Bread & Products LLC	Norwalk	CT	G	914 843-4401	3103
Atticus Bakery LLC	New Haven	CT	C	203 562-9007	2661
Bagel Boys Inc **(PA)**	Glastonbury	CT	F	860 657-4400	1539
Beans Inc	Watertown	CT	G	860 945-9234	4999
Beldotti Bakeries	Stamford	CT	F	203 348-9029	4148
Better Baking By Beth	Torrington	CT	G	860 482-4706	4564
Big Purple Cupcake LLC	Branford	CT	G	203 483-8738	297
Bimbo Bakeries Usa Inc	Orange	CT	D	203 932-1000	3360
Bimbo Bakeries Usa Inc	Portland	CT	E	860 691-1180	3564
Boston Model Bakery	New Haven	CT	E	203 562-9491	2671
Bricins Inc	Torrington	CT	F	860 482-0250	4567
Daybrake Donuts Inc	Bridgeport	CT	F	203 368-4962	401
Dl Distributors LLC	West Haven	CT	G	203 931-1724	5117
Donut Stop	Shelton	CT	G	203 924-7133	3797
Freihofer Charles Baking Co	Naugatuck	CT	G	203 729-4545	2474
Gracie Maes Kitchen LLC	Griswold	CT	G	860 885-8250	1663
Hardcore Sweet Cupcakes LLC	Waterbury	CT	G	203 808-5547	4882
Hartford Cpl Co-Op Inc	Hartford	CT	C	860 296-5636	1833
Haylons Market LLC	Niantic	CT	G	860 739-9509	2951
I and U LLC	Waterbury	CT	G	860 803-1491	4886
Izzi BS Allergy Free LLC	Norwalk	CT	G	203 810-4378	3177
Katona Bakery LLC	Fairfield	CT	E	203 337-5349	1440
Krafty Kakes Inc	Wallingford	CT	G	203 284-0299	4762
Lupis Inc	New Haven	CT	E	203 562-9491	2710
Massconn Distribute Cpl	South Windsor	CT	D	860 882-0717	3992
Milite Bakery	Waterbury	CT	G	203 753-9451	4916
Northeast Foods Inc	Dayville	CT	D	860 779-1117	1049
Pastry Shop	Meriden	CT	G	203 238-0483	2115

	CITY	ST	EMP	PHONE	ENTRY #
Pops Donuts	Milford	CT	G	203 876-1210	2335
Red Rose Desserts	Colchester	CT	G	860 603-2670	807
Riverside Baking Company LLC	Fairfield	CT	G	203 451-0331	1452
Spinella Bakery	Waterbury	CT	F	203 753-9451	4959
Stonehouse Fine Cakes	Meriden	CT	F	203 235-5091	2134
Take Cake LLC	Guilford	CT	G	203 453-1896	1722
Thadieo LLC	Southington	CT	G	860 621-4500	4084
Watson LLC **(DH)**	West Haven	CT	B	203 932-3000	5149
Whole German Breads LLC	New Haven	CT	G	203 507-0663	2754
Wildflour Cupcakes Sweets LLC	Seymour	CT	G	203 828-6576	3768
3 Little Figs LLC	Somerville	MA	G	617 623-3447	15150
Alves Baking Co	Fall River	MA	G	508 673-8003	10654
Arnold Bakeries	Bass River	MA	G	508 398-6588	7953
Arts International Wholesale	Raynham	MA	G	508 822-7181	14705
Athans Inc	Brighton	MA	F	617 783-0313	9095
Bagel Boy Inc	Lawrence	MA	D	978 682-8646	11998
Bakery To Go Inc	Boston	MA	G	617 482-1015	8388
Bbu Inc	Chicopee	MA	E	413 593-2700	10000
Berkshire Mtn Bky Pizza Cafe	Pittsfield	MA	G	413 464-9394	14458
Bernardinos Bakery Inc **(PA)**	Chicopee	MA	D	413 592-1944	10001
Beth Veneto	Quincy	MA	G	617 472-4729	14615
Bimbo Bakeries Usa Inc	Middleboro	MA	F	508 923-1023	13055
Bimbo Bakeries Usa Inc	Medford	MA	F	781 306-0221	12922
Bimbo Bakeries Usa Inc	Wilbraham	MA	G	413 543-5328	16933
Bollywood Delights Inc	Southborough	MA	G	508 740-1908	15350
Boston Bagel Inc	Hyde Park	MA	E	617 364-6900	11863
Boston Baking Inc	Boston	MA	E	617 364-6900	8421
Budiproducts	Boston	MA	G	617 470-3086	8448
Buttergirl Baking Co	Lexington	MA	G	857 891-6625	12210
Buzzworthy Baking LLC	Concord	MA	G	978 254-5910	10119
C Q P Bakery	Lawrence	MA	E	978 557-5626	12000
Cakewalk Bakers LLC	Boston	MA	G	617 903-4352	8454
Cohens United Baking Inc	Worcester	MA	G	508 754-0232	17357
Concord Teacakes Etcetera Inc	Concord	MA	F	978 369-7644	10123
Concord Teacakes Etcetera Inc **(PA)**	Concord	MA	E	978 369-2409	10124
Cupcake Town	Mansfield	MA	G	774 284-4667	12625
Duva Distributors Inc	Shrewsbury	MA	E	508 841-8182	15109
Elie Baking Corporation	Brockton	MA	F	508 584-4890	9143
Forge Baking Company Inc	Arlington	MA	G	617 764-5365	7627
Frozen Batters Inc	North Andover	MA	D	508 683-1414	13706
G H Bent Company	Milton	MA	E	617 322-9287	13192
George Weston Bakeries	Pittsfield	MA	G	413 443-6095	14473
Ginsco Inc	Fall River	MA	F	508 677-4767	10703
Ginsco Inc **(PA)**	Fall River	MA	F	508 677-4767	10704
Ginsco Inc	North Dartmouth	MA	F	508 990-3350	13921
Gold Medal Bakery Inc **(PA)**	Fall River	MA	B	508 674-5766	10705
Hole In One	Eastham	MA	E	508 255-5359	10549
Iggys Bread Ltd	Watertown	MA	E	617 491-7600	16291
Iggys Bread Ltd **(PA)**	Cambridge	MA	D	617 491-7600	9512
Jacquelines Wholesale Bky Inc	Salem	MA	D	978 744-8600	14923
Jean Charles Blondine	Roxbury	MA	G	857 247-9369	14873
Jumbo Donuts	Uxbridge	MA	F	508 278-9977	15922
Junes Place	Medway	MA	G	508 533-5037	12964
Korner Bagel Partnership	Seekonk	MA	E	508 336-5204	15025
Little Delights Bakery	Lowell	MA	G	978 455-0040	12396
Lorenzos Bakery LLC	New Bedford	MA	G	508 287-9974	13411
Margies Sweet Surrender	Hull	MA	G	781 925-2271	11828
Mercolino Bakery	Longmeadow	MA	G	413 733-9595	12337
Meyers Gluten Free Baking LLC	Beverly	MA	G	978 381-9629	8152
Middle East Bakery Inc **(PA)**	Lawrence	MA	D	978 688-2221	12057
Montiones Biscotti **(PA)**	Norton	MA	F	508 285-7004	14083
Morais Marizete	Marlborough	MA	G	508 460-8200	12795
Mrs Macks Bakery Inc	Worcester	MA	G	508 753-0610	17426
Multigrains Inc	Lawrence	MA	C	978 691-6100	12060
Murray Biscuit Company LLC	Canton	MA	G	781 760-0220	9758
N B Baking Co	New Bedford	MA	G	508 992-5413	13419
Nantucket Bake Shop Inc	Nantucket	MA	G	508 228-2797	13228
New Brand Sebsatians LLC	Boston	MA	G	617 624-7999	8729
Newly Weds Foods Inc	Watertown	MA	D	617 926-7600	16303
Old San Juan Bakery Inc	Holyoke	MA	F	413 534-5555	11646
Pain DAvignon II Inc	Hyannis	MA	E	508 771-9771	11853
Piantedosi Baking Co	Malden	MA	G	781 321-3400	12589
Piantedosi Baking Co Inc **(PA)**	Malden	MA	C	781 321-3400	12590
Pin Hsiao & Associates LLC	Milford	MA	D	206 818-0155	13138
Pipe Dream Cupcakes LLC	North Andover	MA	G	978 397-6470	13724
Pittsfield Rye Bakery Inc	Pittsfield	MA	E	413 443-9141	14501
SMH Fine Foods Inc	Hyde Park	MA	G	617 364-1772	11879
Spinelli Ravioli Mfg Co Inc	Boston	MA	E	617 567-1992	8859
Sun Ray Bakery	Beverly	MA	G	978 922-1941	8184
Superior Baking Co Inc	Brockton	MA	E	508 586-6601	9180
Superior Cake Products Inc	Southbridge	MA	D	508 764-3276	15406
Sweet Creations	Wakefield	MA	E	781 246-0836	15979
Table Talk Pies Inc **(PA)**	Worcester	MA	D	508 438-1556	17485
Traditional Breads Inc	Lynn	MA	E	781 598-4451	12544
Tripoli Bakery Inc	Lawrence	MA	E	978 682-7754	12078
Yuen Ho Bakery Inc	Boston	MA	G	617 426-8320	8939
B&G Foods Inc	Portland	ME	C	207 772-8341	6616
Betty Reez Whoopiez	Freeport	ME	G	207 865-1735	6072
Bimbo Bakeries Usa Inc	Scarborough	ME	G	207 883-5252	6911
C J Cranam Inc	Oxford	ME	E	207 739-1016	6564
Cakes For All Seasons LLC	Biddeford	ME	G	207 432-9192	5724
Dicks Baking	Milo	ME	G	207 284-3779	6445
Freihofer Baking Co	Bangor	ME	G	207 947-2387	5646
Holy Donut	Scarborough	ME	G	207 303-0137	6924
Italian Bakery Products Co	Lewiston	ME	F	207 782-8312	6293
Kennebunkport Pie Company LLC	Kennebunkport	ME	G	207 205-4466	6247
Labrees Inc	Old Town	ME	B	207 827-6121	6543
Lepage Bakeries Park St LLC	Lewiston	ME	D	207 783-9161	6298
Lepage Bakeries Park St LLC	Auburn	ME	E	207 783-9161	5576
Lepage Bakeries Park St LLC **(HQ)**	Auburn	ME	E	207 783-9161	5577
Limerick Dough Boy	Limerick	ME	G	207 793-4145	6336
Little Gottage Baking	Sanford	ME	G	207 432-2930	6880
Little Notch Bakery	Southwest Harbor	ME	G	207 244-4043	7048
Mathews Bakery Inc	Portland	ME	E	207 773-9647	6693
Moonbat City Baking Co LLC	Belfast	ME	G	207 323-4955	5695
Out Sweet Tooth Cupcakes	South Portland	ME	G	207 272-4363	7035
Stiletto Cupcakes	Lisbon	ME	G	207 212-9788	6365
Tm and Tm Inc	Livermore Falls	ME	F	207 897-3442	6382
A Sweet As Sugar Life-Cupcakes	Londonderry	NH	G	603 591-8957	18669
Barbara Brownie LLC	Hampton	NH	G	603 601-2886	18257
Bimbo Bakeries Usa Inc	Hooksett	NH	E	603 626-7405	18343
Bimbo Bakeries Usa Inc	Lebanon	NH	F	603 448-4227	18615
Cupcake Rowe LLC	Milford	NH	G	603 673-0489	19054
Fredericks Pastries **(PA)**	Amherst	NH	G	603 882-7725	17563
Gone Baking LLC	Bedford	NH	G	603 305-6026	17643
Happy Bird Baking Company LLC	Peterborough	NH	G	603 759-0714	19471
Harveys Bakeries	Dover	NH	G	603 749-5149	18027
Koffee Kup Bakery Inc	Bow	NH	G	603 225-6149	17720
Lafayette Distributors Cpl Inc	Hampton	NH	E	603 430-9405	18266
Lepage Bakeries Park St LLC	Belmont	NH	F	603 524-9104	17677
Lepage Bakeries Park St LLC	Hudson	NH	E	603 880-4446	18410
ME and Ollies	Portsmouth	NH	G	603 319-1561	19592
Small Bites Cupcakes	Laconia	NH	G	603 387-6333	18586
Souhegan Management Corp	Manchester	NH	E	603 898-8868	18927
White Mountain Cupcakery LLC	North Conway	NH	G	603 730-5140	19381
Withrow Inc	Salem	NH	E	603 898-8868	19779
Calise & Sons Bakery Inc **(PA)**	Lincoln	RI	C	401 334-3444	20560
Catanzaro Food Products Inc	Pawtucket	RI	G	401 255-1700	20820
Cavanagh Company	Greenville	RI	E	401 949-4000	20464
Frostbite Cupcakes	Chepachet	RI	G	508 801-6706	20134
Homestead Baking Co	Rumford	RI	D	401 434-0551	21186
Jojoscupcakes LLC	Coventry	RI	G	401 297-4900	20151
La Casona Restaurant Inc	Central Falls	RI	G	401 727-0002	20118
Lasalle Donuts Inc	Providence	RI	G	401 272-9773	21049
Usquepaugh Baking Co LLC	West Kingston	RI	G	401 782-6907	21474
Westcott Baking Company Inc	West Warwick	RI	F	401 821-8007	21514
Against Grn Gourmet Foods LLC	Brattleboro	VT	G	802 258-3838	21716
Bakers Dozen Inc	Colchester	VT	F	802 879-4001	21857
Bimbo Bakeries Usa Inc	Saint Johnsbury	VT	G	802 748-1389	22386
Capitol Cupcake Company LLC	Montpelier	VT	G	802 522-3576	22147
Delicate Decadence LLC	Barre	VT	G	802 479-7948	21612
Fudge Factory Inc	Manchester Center	VT	F	888 669-7425	22085
Greniers Garden & Bakery	Waterbury Center	VT	G	802 244-8057	22591
Harringtons In Vermont Inc **(PA)**	Richmond	VT	F	802 434-7500	22312
Koffee Kup Bakery Inc **(PA)**	Colchester	VT	D	802 863-2696	21870
Simply Cupcakes	Essex Junction	VT	G	802 871-5634	21961
Unilever Bestfoods North Amer	Rutland	VT	G	802 775-4986	22357

2052 Cookies & Crackers

	CITY	ST	EMP	PHONE	ENTRY #
Beldotti Bakeries	Stamford	CT	F	203 348-9029	4148
Bimbo Bakeries Usa Inc	Orange	CT	D	203 932-1000	3360
Bob The Baker LLC	Brookfield	CT	F	203 775-1032	635
Cherise Cpl LLC	Meriden	CT	G	203 238-3482	2085
Foundry Foods Inc	Norwalk	CT	G	314 982-3204	3154
Harsha Inc	Waterford	CT	G	860 439-1466	4985
R & K Cookies LLC	Cromwell	CT	G	860 613-2893	858
Barbaras Bakery Inc **(DH)**	Marlborough	MA	E	800 343-0590	12725
Boston Chipyard The Inc	Boston	MA	F	617 742-9537	8428
Concord Teacakes Etcetera Inc	Concord	MA	F	978 369-7644	10123
G H Bent Company	Milton	MA	E	617 322-9287	13192
Ho Toy Noodles Inc **(PA)**	Stoughton	MA	F	617 426-0247	15596
Julie Cecchini	Southwick	MA	F	413 562-2042	15414
Keebler Company	Franklin	MA	D	508 520-7223	11060
Murray Biscuit Company LLC	Canton	MA	G	781 760-0220	9758
Nantucket Bake Shop Inc	Nantucket	MA	G	508 228-2797	13228
New England Prtzel Popcorn Inc	Lawrence	MA	G	978 687-0342	12064
Peggy Lawton Kitchens Inc	East Walpole	MA	E	508 668-1215	10528
Sharrocks English Bakery Inc	New Bedford	MA	G	508 997-5710	13450
Snyders-Lance Inc	Hyannis	MA	G	508 771-1872	11858
Sweet Creations	Wakefield	MA	E	781 246-0836	15979
Venus Wafers Inc	Hingham	MA	E	781 740-1002	11514
Chase S Daily LLC	Belfast	ME	G	207 338-0555	5687
Daddys Private Stock LLC	Canaan	ME	G	207 399-7154	5872
Maine Crisp Company LLC **(PA)**	Waterville	ME	G	207 213-9296	7158

	CITY	ST	EMP	PHONE	ENTRY #
Moms Organic Munchies	Freeport	ME	G	207 869-4078	6084
Twisted	Bangor	ME	G	207 942-9530	5661
Wild Cow Creamery LLC	Bangor	ME	G	207 907-0301	5664
Homefree LLC	Windham	NH	E	603 898-0172	20008
Catanzaro Food Products Inc	Pawtucket	RI	G	401 255-1700	20820
Lincoln Creamery Inc	Lincoln	RI	F	401 724-1050	20579
Sherwood Brands of RI	Rumford	RI	E	401 726-4500	21195
Dr Lucys LLC	Rutland	VT	E	757 233-9495	22330
Harringtons In Vermont Inc **(PA)**	Richmond	VT	F	802 434-7500	22312

2053 Frozen Bakery Prdts

	CITY	ST	EMP	PHONE	ENTRY #
Cooper Marketing Group Inc	Danbury	CT	G	203 797-9386	893
Rich Products Corporation	New Britain	CT	A	866 737-8884	2570
Rich Products Corporation	New Britain	CT	A	800 356-7094	2571
Something Sweet Inc **(PA)**	New Haven	CT	E	203 603-9766	2738
Aristocrat Products Inc	Upton	MA	G	508 529-3471	15904
Bimbo Bakeries Usa Inc	Rehoboth	MA	C	508 336-7735	14745
Diannes Fine Desserts Inc **(PA)**	Newburyport	MA	C	978 463-3832	13482
Diannes Fine Desserts Inc	Newburyport	MA	C	978 463-3881	13483
New England Country Pies LLC	Lynn	MA	F	781 596-0176	12528
Peppercorn Food Service Inc	Marblehead	MA	E	781 639-6035	12690
Somerville Office	Somerville	MA	G	617 776-0738	15217
Stone House Farm Inc	West Boxford	MA	G	978 352-2323	16408
C J Cranam Inc	Oxford	ME	E	207 739-1016	6564
Ocean State Cpl Inc	East Providence	RI	C	401 431-0153	20438
Cosmic Bakers of Vermont LLC	Saint Albans	VT	F	802 524-0800	22366
Crazy Russian Girls Whole	Bennington	VT	G	802 681-3983	21667
Harringtons In Vermont Inc **(PA)**	Richmond	VT	F	802 434-7500	22312

2061 Sugar, Cane

	CITY	ST	EMP	PHONE	ENTRY #
New England Sugars LLC	Worcester	MA	G	508 792-3801	17433

2062 Sugar, Cane Refining

	CITY	ST	EMP	PHONE	ENTRY #
Jenkins Sugar Group Inc	Norwalk	CT	F	203 853-3000	3181
Roger Reed	Sheldon	VT	G	802 933-2535	22429

2064 Candy & Confectionery Prdts

	CITY	ST	EMP	PHONE	ENTRY #
Lollipop Kids LLC	Redding	CT	G	203 664-1799	3649
Mantrose-Haeuser Co Inc **(HQ)**	Westport	CT	E	203 454-1800	5212
Pez Candy Inc **(HQ)**	Orange	CT	D	203 795-0531	3379
Pez Manufacturing Corp	Orange	CT	D	203 795-0531	3380
Reeds Inc	Norwalk	CT	E	203 890-0557	3228
Sonias Chocolaterie Inc	Ridgefield	CT	F	203 438-5965	3685
Thompson Brands LLC	Meriden	CT	D	203 235-2541	2141
Thompson Candy Company	Meriden	CT	D	203 235-2541	2142
Yummyearth LLC **(PA)**	Stamford	CT	G	203 276-1259	4363
Attleboro Pancakes Inc	Attleboro	MA	G	508 399-8189	7707
Barbaras Bakery Inc **(DH)**	Marlborough	MA	E	800 343-0590	12725
Bb Walpole Liquidation NH Inc	Boston	MA	G	617 303-0113	8394
Belgiums Chocolate Source Inc	Milton	MA	G	781 283-5787	13190
Ben & Bills Chocolate Emporium	Falmouth	MA	F	508 548-7878	10787
Ben & Blls Chclat Emporium Inc **(PA)**	Northampton	MA	F	413 584-5695	13997
Boston Pretzel Bakery Inc	Boston	MA	F	617 522-9494	8438
Cambridge Brands Mfg Inc	Cambridge	MA	C	617 491-2500	9425
Dante Confection	North Billerica	MA	G	978 262-2242	13806
Dorothy Coxs Candies Inc	Wareham	MA	E	774 678-0654	16245
Eaton Farm Confectioners Inc	Worcester	MA	G	508 865-5235	17369
F B Washburn Candy Corporation	Brockton	MA	E	508 588-0820	9145
Furlongs Cottage Candies	Norwood	MA	F	781 762-4124	14154
Hebert Retail LLC	Shrewsbury	MA	D	508 845-8051	15116
Hilliards House Candy Inc **(PA)**	North Easton	MA	D	508 238-6231	13947
Hilltop Candies	Brockton	MA	G	508 583-0895	9154
McCrea Capital Advisors Inc	Hyde Park	MA	G	617 276-3388	11874
Melville Candy Corporation	Randolph	MA	E	800 638-8063	14690
Mini Pops Inc	Sharon	MA	G	781 436-5864	15053
Nafp Inc	Methuen	MA	D	978 682-1855	13038
Nichols Candies Inc	Gloucester	MA	F	978 283-9850	11197
Phillips Candy House Inc	Boston	MA	E	617 282-2090	8778
Russos Inc	Saugus	MA	F	781 233-1737	14995
Salems Old Fshoned Candies Inc	Salem	MA	F	978 744-3242	14941
Samarc Inc	Boston	MA	G	617 924-3884	8837
Seven Sweets Inc	Marblehead	MA	F	781 631-0303	12693
Silver Sweet Products Co	Lawrence	MA	G	978 688-0474	12074
Stage Stop Candy Ltd Inc	Dennis Port	MA	G	508 394-1791	10315
Strawbrry Hl Grnd Delights LLC	Waltham	MA	G	617 319-3557	16202
Sweethearts Candy Co LLC	Revere	MA	B	781 485-4500	14776
Winfreys Olde English Fdge Inc **(PA)**	Rowley	MA	F	978 948-7448	14868
Bixby & Co LLC	Rockland	ME	G	207 691-1778	6785
Gartland Distributors LLC	Biddeford	ME	G	207 282-9456	5736
Harbor Candy Shop Inc	Ogunquit	ME	E	207 646-8078	6537
Len Libbys Inc	Scarborough	ME	E	207 883-4897	6931
Bavarian Chocolate Haus Inc	North Conway	NH	G	603 356-2663	19372
Bb Walpole Liquidation NH Inc	Walpole	NH	G	603 756-2882	19915
Bb Walpole Liquidation NH Inc **(PA)**	Walpole	NH	D	603 756-3701	19916
Bens Sugar Shack	Temple	NH	G	603 924-3177	19896
Fredericks Pastries **(PA)**	Amherst	NH	G	603 882-7725	17563
Granite State Candy Shoppe LLC **(PA)**	Concord	NH	F	603 225-2591	17903
Grist For Mill LLC	Bristol	NH	F	603 744-0405	17767
Kellerhaus Inc	Laconia	NH	E	603 366-4466	18569
Maple Nut Kitchen LLC	Keene	NH	G	603 354-3219	18514
Original Gourmet Food Co LLC	Salem	NH	G	603 894-1200	19759
Pollys Pancake Parlor	Sugar Hill	NH	G	603 823-5575	19878
B Fresh	Greenville	RI	G	401 349-0001	20463
Hauser Foods Inc	Westerly	RI	E	401 596-8866	21526
Lady Ann Candies	Warwick	RI	E	401 738-4321	21384
Paleo Products LLC	Pawtucket	RI	G	401 305-3473	20873
Sherwood Brands of RI	Rumford	RI	E	401 726-4500	21195
Sweenors Chocolates Inc **(PA)**	Wakefield	RI	E	401 783-4433	21280
Tom and Sallys Handmade Choco	Westerly	RI	F	800 289-8783	21544
Fudge Factory Inc	Manchester Center	VT	F	888 669-7425	22085
Gorilla Bars Inc	Montgomery Center	VT	G	802 309-4997	22143
H L Handy Company Inc	Putney	VT	G	802 387-4040	22289
Maple Grove Farms Vermont Inc **(HQ)**	Saint Johnsbury	VT	D	802 748-5141	22391
McCains Vermont Products Inc	Bennington	VT	G	802 447-2610	21682
Quirion Luc **(PA)**	Newport	VT	G	802 673-8386	22205
Runamok Maple LLC	Fairfax	VT	G	802 849-7943	21978
Small Batch Organics LLC	Manchester Center	VT	F	802 367-1054	22090
Tafts Milk Maple Farm	Huntington	VT	G	802 434-2727	22034

2066 Chocolate & Cocoa Prdts

	CITY	ST	EMP	PHONE	ENTRY #
Chip In A Bottle LLC	New Haven	CT	G	203 460-0665	2676
CSC Cocoa LLC	New Canaan	CT	G	203 846-5611	2596
Divine Treasure	Manchester	CT	G	860 643-2552	2001
Mantrose-Haeuser Co Inc **(HQ)**	Westport	CT	E	203 454-1800	5212
Nel Group LLC	Windsor	CT	F	860 683-0190	5350
Thompson Brands LLC	Meriden	CT	D	203 235-2541	2141
Bb Walpole Liquidation NH Inc	Cambridge	MA	E	617 491-4340	9406
Beacon Hill Chocolates	Boston	MA	G	617 725-1900	8395
Cambridge Brands Mfg Inc	Cambridge	MA	C	617 491-2500	9425
Cape Cod Sweets LLC	Pocasset	MA	F	508 564-5840	14594
Chilmark Chocolates Inc	Chilmark	MA	F	508 645-3013	10072
Chocolate Therapy	Framingham	MA	F	508 875-1571	10933
Dark Matter Chocolate LLC	Cambridge	MA	G	303 718-3835	9451
Dorothy Coxs Candies Inc	Wareham	MA	E	774 678-0654	16245
Godiva Chocolatier Inc	Braintree	MA	F	781 843-0466	9011
Gowell Candy Shop Inc	Brockton	MA	G	508 583-2521	9152
Green Mountain Chocolate Co **(PA)**	Hopedale	MA	G	508 473-9060	11673
Heavenly Chocolate	Northampton	MA	E	413 586-0038	14008
Hilliards House Candy Inc **(PA)**	North Easton	MA	D	508 238-6231	13947
Levaggis Candies	South Weymouth	MA	G	781 335-1231	15321
Phillips Candy House Inc	Boston	MA	E	617 282-2090	8778
Russos Inc	Saugus	MA	F	781 233-1737	14995
Samarc Inc	Boston	MA	G	617 924-3884	8837
Sweethearts Candy Co LLC	Revere	MA	B	781 485-4500	14776
Sweethearts Three Inc	Sharon	MA	G	781 784-5193	15058
Tru Chocolate Inc	Haverhill	MA	G	855 878-2462	11479
Whitmore Family Entps LLC	Somerville	MA	F	617 623-0804	15232
Winfreys Olde English Fdge Inc **(PA)**	Rowley	MA	F	978 948-7448	14868
Bixby & Co LLC	Rockland	ME	G	207 691-1778	6785
Harbor Candy Shop Inc	Ogunquit	ME	E	207 646-8078	6537
La Creme Chocolat Inc	Standish	ME	G	443 841-2458	7062
Nibmor Inc	Biddeford	ME	G	207 502-7540	5752
Lindt & Sprungli (usa) Inc **(HQ)**	Stratham	NH	C	603 778-8100	19871
Lady Ann Candies	Warwick	RI	E	401 738-4321	21384
Barry Callebaut USA LLC	Saint Albans	VT	D	802 524-9711	22364
Birnn Chocolates Vermont Inc	South Burlington	VT	F	802 860-1047	22438
Champlain Chocolate Company	Williston	VT	G	802 864-1808	22659
Sentar Inc	South Burlington	VT	E	802 861-6004	22465
Silly Cow Farms LLC	Wells River	VT	E	802 429-2920	22603
Sunny Sky Products LLC	South Burlington	VT	E	802 861-6004	22469
Vermont Nut Free Choclat Inc	Colchester	VT	F	802 372-4654	21886

2067 Chewing Gum

	CITY	ST	EMP	PHONE	ENTRY #
Verve Inc	Providence	RI	G	401 351-6415	21149

2068 Salted & Roasted Nuts & Seeds

	CITY	ST	EMP	PHONE	ENTRY #
40parklane LLC	Maynard	MA	F	978 369-2940	12893
American Nut & Chocolate Inc	Boston	MA	G	617 427-1510	8362
Arcade Industries Inc	Auburn	MA	F	508 832-6300	7826
Leavitt Corporation **(HQ)**	Everett	MA	C	617 389-2600	10616
Superior Nut Company Inc	Cambridge	MA	E	800 251-6060	9665
Peeled Inc	Cumberland	RI	F	212 706-2001	20338

2075 Soybean Oil Mills

	CITY	ST	EMP	PHONE	ENTRY #
Feldhaus Consulting LLC	Belmont	MA	G	603 276-0508	8073
Protein Products Inc	North Andover	MA	G	508 954-6020	13727
South River Miso Co Inc	Conway	MA	G	413 369-4057	10167

2076 Vegetable Oil Mills

	CITY	ST	EMP	PHONE	ENTRY #
Baker Commodities Inc	North Billerica	MA	D	978 454-8811	13795
Full Sun Company	Middlebury	VT	G	802 989-7011	22111

2077 Animal, Marine Fats & Oils

	CITY	ST	EMP	PHONE	ENTRY #
Baker Commodities Inc	North Billerica	MA	D	978 454-8811	13795
Marine Bioproducts	Quincy	MA	G	617 847-1426	14638
Western Mass Rendering Co Inc	Southwick	MA	E	413 569-6265	15420
Baker Commodities Inc	Vassalboro	ME	G	207 622-3505	7124
Baker Commodities Inc	Warwick	RI	G	401 821-3003	21331
Baker Commodities Inc	Williston	VT	G	802 658-0721	22657

2079 Shortening, Oils & Margarine

	CITY	ST	EMP	PHONE	ENTRY #
New Canaan Olive Oil LLC	Stamford	CT	G	845 240-3294	4255
Olive Capizzano Oils & Vinegar	Pawcatuck	CT	G	860 495-2187	3439
Olive Chiappetta Oil LLC	Stamford	CT	G	203 223-3655	4268
Olive Nutmeg Oil	New Milford	CT	G	860 354-7300	2821
Olive Oils and Balsamics LLC	Rocky Hill	CT	G	860 563-0105	3726
Olive Sabor Oil Co	Somers	CT	G	860 922-7483	3919
Shoreline Vine	Madison	CT	G	203 779-5331	1976
Andaluna Enterprises Inc	West Newbury	MA	G	617 335-3204	16489
Baker Commodities Inc	North Billerica	MA	D	978 454-8811	13795
Bogaris Corporation	Brookline	MA	G	617 505-6696	9196
Branch Olive Oil Company LLC	Peabody	MA	G	781 775-8788	14317
Cape Ann Olive Oil Company	Gloucester	MA	G	978 281-1061	11170
Catania-Spagna Corporation	Ayer	MA	E	978 772-7900	7914
Extra Virgin Foods Inc	Watertown	MA	G	617 407-9161	16285
Little Shop of Olive Oils Inc	Medway	MA	G	508 533-5522	12965
New England Olive Oil Company	Concord	MA	G	978 610-6776	10146
Olive Mannys Oil Inc	Wilbraham	MA	G	413 233-2532	16942
Olive Newburyport Oil	Newburyport	MA	G	978 462-7700	13519
Olive Northampton Oil Co	Northampton	MA	G	413 537-7357	14014
Omega Olive Oil Inc	Kingston	MA	G	781 585-3179	11962
Tre Olive LLC	East Longmeadow	MA	G	617 680-0096	10499
Fiore Artisan Olive Oils	Bangor	ME	G	207 801-8549	5644
Lakonia Greek Products LLC	Biddeford	ME	G	207 282-4002	5742
Olive Fiore Oils & Vinegars	Rockland	ME	G	207 596-0276	6807
Olive Wildrose Oil	South Berwick	ME	G	603 767-0597	7003
American Enrgy Indpendence LLC	Pittsfield	NH	G	603 228-3611	19498
North Conway Olive Oil Company	North Conway	NH	G	603 307-1066	19377
Olive Lakonian Oil LLC	Manchester	NH	G	603 264-5025	18894
Felicia Winkfield	Newport	RI	G	401 849-3029	20665
Allavita	Montpelier	VT	G	802 225-6526	22144
Genuine Jamaican	Barnet	VT	G	802 633-2676	21604
Olives Oil	Colchester	VT	G	802 864-4908	21874

2082 Malt Beverages

	CITY	ST	EMP	PHONE	ENTRY #
Alvarium Beer Company LLC	New Britain	CT	G	860 306-3857	2508
Bear Hands Brewing Company	Central Village	CT	G	860 576-5374	705
Beerd Brewing Co LLC	Stonington	CT	F	585 771-7428	4375
Breakaway Brew Haus LLC	Bolton	CT	G	860 647-9811	275
Brook Broad Brewing LLC	East Windsor	CT	F	860 623-1000	1280
Cold Brew Coffee Company LLC	Cheshire	CT	G	860 250-4410	723
Diageo Investment Corporation	Norwalk	CT	F	203 229-2100	3137
East Rock Brewing Company LLC	New Haven	CT	G	203 530-3484	2684
Easton Brewing Company LLC	Easton	CT	G	203 921-7263	1317
Front Porch Brewing	Wallingford	CT	G	203 679-1096	4747
Guinness America Inc	Norwalk	CT	G	203 229-2100	3165
Hamden Brewing Company LLC	Shelton	CT	G	203 247-4677	3807
Kent Falls Brewing Company	Kent	CT	G	860 398-9645	1923
New England Brewing Co LLC	Woodbridge	CT	G	203 387-2222	5473
Nutmeg Brewing Rest Group LLC	Shelton	CT	E	203 256-2337	3843
Outer Light Brewing Co LLC	Groton	CT	G	475 201-9972	1681
Southport Brewing Co	Milford	CT	E	203 874-2337	2365
Stetson Brewing Co Inc	Manchester	CT	G	860 643-0257	2053
Swagnificent Ent LLC	Bridgeport	CT	G	203 449-0124	498
Thomas Hooker Brewing Co LLC	Bloomfield	CT	E	860 242-3111	266
3cross Brewing Company	Worcester	MA	F	508 615-8195	17328
861 Corp	Boston	MA	G	617 268-8855	8330
A&S Brewing Collaborative LLC	Boston	MA	G	617 368-5000	8333
American Craft Brewery LLC **(DH)**	Boston	MA	G	617 368-5000	8359
Amherst Brewing Co Inc	Amherst	MA	E	413 253-4400	7511
Atlas Distributing Inc	Auburn	MA	C	508 791-6221	7828
Barrel House Z LLC	Weymouth	MA	G	339 207-7888	16885
Basement LLC	Worcester	MA	G	508 762-9080	17345
Bent Water Brewing Co	Lynn	MA	G	781 780-9948	12492
Berkshire Brewing Company Inc **(PA)**	South Deerfield	MA	F	413 665-6600	15246
Boston Beer Company Inc	Boston	MA	F	617 368-5080	8422
Boston Beer Company Inc **(PA)**	Boston	MA	B	617 368-5000	8423
Boston Beer Corporation **(DH)**	Boston	MA	C	617 368-5000	8424
Brewmasters Brewing Svcs LLC	Williamsburg	MA	G	413 268-2199	16947
British Beer Company Inc	Westford	MA	E	978 577-6034	16758
Buzzards Bay Brewing Inc	Westport	MA	G	508 636-2288	16836
Cambridge Brewing Co Inc	Cambridge	MA	E	617 494-1994	9426
Cape Ann Brewing Company Inc	Gloucester	MA	F	978 281-4782	11169
Cape Cod Beer Inc	Barnstable	MA	F	508 790-4200	7947
Castle Island Brewing Co LLC	Norwood	MA	E	781 951-2029	14140
Cisco Brewers Inc	Nantucket	MA	E	508 325-5929	13222
Cody Brewing Company	Amesbury	MA	G	978 387-4329	7482
Common Crossing Inc	Berkley	MA	G	508 822-8225	8084
Craft Beer Guild Distrg VT LLC **(PA)**	Kingston	MA	E	781 585-5165	11956
Crue Brew Brewery LLC	Raynham	MA	G	508 272-6090	14708
Deja Brew Inc	Shrewsbury	MA	G	508 842-8991	15107
Dorchester Beer Holdings LLC	Boston	MA	G	617 869-7092	8508
Downeast Cider House LLC	Boston	MA	G	857 301-8881	8509
Endurance Brewing Company LLC	Boston	MA	G	617 725-0256	8525
Essex County Brewing Co LLC	Peabody	MA	G	978 587-2254	14334
Independent Fermentations	Plymouth	MA	G	508 789-9940	14561
John Harvards Brewhouse Llc	Framingham	MA	D	508 875-2337	10974
Lamplighter Brewing Co LLC	Cambridge	MA	G	207 650-3325	9531
Life Force Beverages LLC	Boston	MA	G	551 265-9482	8665
Lord Hobo Brewing Company LLC	Woburn	MA	F	781 281-0809	17218
Mass Bay Brewing Company Inc **(PA)**	Boston	MA	C	617 574-9551	8682
Massachusetts Bev Aliance LLC	Bellingham	MA	F	617 701-6238	8048
Mayflower Brewing Company LLC	Plymouth	MA	E	508 746-2674	14562
Medusa Brewing Company Inc	Hudson	MA	G	978 310-1933	11791
Mercury Brewing & Dist Co	Ipswich	MA	F	978 356-3329	11930
Paragraph 11 LLC	Woburn	MA	G	781 281-1143	17254
Pioneer Brewing Company LLC	Fiskdale	MA	G	508 347-7500	10808
Redemption Rock Brewery Co	Worcester	MA	G	978 660-5526	17454
Riverwalk Brewing	Newburyport	MA	F	978 499-2337	13530
Slesar Bros Brewing Co Inc	Hingham	MA	E	781 749-2337	11511
Slesar Bros Brewing Co Inc	Salem	MA	E	978 745-2337	14943
Sullivan Apple Cider	Saugus	MA	G	781 233-7090	15000
Sunday River Brewing Co Inc	Boston	MA	D	207 824-4253	8869
Tri Town Discount Liquors	Canton	MA	G	781 828-8393	9790
Wachusett Brewing Company Inc	Westminster	MA	D	978 874-9965	16820
Allagash Brewing Company	Portland	ME	D	207 878-5385	6611
Ashleigh Inc **(PA)**	Kennebunk	ME	E	207 967-4311	6228
Belfast Bay Brewing Company	Belfast	ME	G	866 338-5722	5686
Maine Beer Company LLC	Freeport	ME	F	207 221-5711	6082
One Eye Open Brewing Co LLC	Portland	ME	G	207 536-4176	6706
Salisbury Cove Associates Inc	Bar Harbor	ME	E	207 288-2337	5669
Sebago Brewing Co **(PA)**	Gorham	ME	E	207 856-2537	6129
Sebago Brewing Co	Gorham	ME	E	207 856-2537	6130
Shipyard Brewing Ltd Lblty Co	Portland	ME	E	207 761-0807	6726
York Harbor Brewing Company	Kittery	ME	G	207 703-8060	6260
7th Settlement Brewery LLC	Dover	NH	E	603 534-5292	18002
Big Daddy Brews LLC	East Kingston	NH	G	603 569-5647	18084
Capitol Distributors Inc	Concord	NH	G	603 224-3348	17890
Craft Brew Alliance Inc	Portsmouth	NH	D	603 430-8600	19555
Great Rhythm Brewing Co LLC	Portsmouth	NH	G	603 300-8588	19569
Hobbs Tavern & Brewing Co LLC	West Ossipee	NH	E	603 539-2000	19966
Incredibrew Inc	Nashua	NH	G	603 891-2477	19187
Neighborhood Beer Company Inc	Stratham	NH	G	603 418-7124	19875
Oddball Brewing Co	Pembroke	NH	G	603 210-5654	19461
White Birch Brewing LLC	Nashua	NH	F	603 402-4444	19286
Brewers Supply Group Inc	Providence	RI	G	401 275-4920	20974
Coastal Extreme Brewing Co LLC	Newport	RI	G	401 849-5232	20660
D & H Inc	Middletown	RI	G	401 847-6690	20618
Farm Coast Brewery LLC	Tiverton	RI	G	401 816-5021	21258
Linesider Brewing Company LLC	East Greenwich	RI	F	401 398-7700	20371
Long Live Beerworks Inc	Providence	RI	G	203 980-0121	21056
Revival Brewing Company	Providence	RI	F	401 372-7009	21110
Sons Liberty Spirits Company	Wakefield	RI	G	401 284-4006	21276
14th Star Brewing LLC	Saint Albans	VT	G	802 528-5988	22362
Alchemy Canning Ltd	Stowe	VT	E	802 244-7744	22519
Black Flannel Brewing Co LLC	Essex Junction	VT	G	802 488-0089	21931
Bullock & Block Ltd	Rutland	VT	F	802 773-3350	22326
Foam Brewers	Burlington	VT	G	802 399-2511	21783
Frost Beer Works LLC	Hinesburg	VT	F	949 945-4064	22024
Hill Farmstead LLC	Greensboro Bend	VT	F	802 533-7450	22004
Independent Brewers Untd Corp **(DH)**	Burlington	VT	F	802 862-6114	21789
Long Trail Brewing Company	Bridgewater Corners	VT	D	802 672-5011	21758
Lost Nation Brewing LLC	Morrisville	VT	F	802 851-8041	22171
Magic Hat Brewing Company & Pe	South Burlington	VT	D	802 658-2739	22453
Maple Leaf Malt & Brewing	Wilmington	VT	G	802 464-9900	22703
Mbbc Vermont LLC	Windsor	VT	D	802 674-5491	22712
Northshire Brewery Inc	Bennington	VT	G	802 681-0201	21687
Otter Creek Brewing Co LLC	Middlebury	VT	E	802 388-0727	22118
Switchback Beerworks Inc	Burlington	VT	E	802 651-4114	21811
Upper Pass Beer Co LLC	Tunbridge	VT	G	802 889-3421	22544
Vermont Beer Shapers Ltd	Springfield	VT	G	802 376-0889	22510
Vermont Pub Brewry Burlington	Burlington	VT	D	802 865-0500	21816

2083 Malt

	CITY	ST	EMP	PHONE	ENTRY #
Blue Ox Malthouse LLC	Lisbon Falls	ME	G	207 649-0018	6367

2084 Wine & Brandy

	CITY	ST	EMP	PHONE	ENTRY #
Arrigoni Winery	Portland	CT	G	860 342-1999	3562
Brooke Taylor Winery LLC **(PA)**	Woodstock	CT	G	860 974-1263	5495
Cocchia Norwalk Grape Co	Norwalk	CT	F	203 855-7911	3127
Connecticut Valley Winery LLC	New Hartford	CT	G	860 489-9463	2633
Crush Club LLC	Wallingford	CT	G	203 626-9545	4729
Diageo Americas Inc	Norwalk	CT	G	203 229-2100	3135
Diageo Americas Supply Inc	Norwalk	CT	G	203 229-2100	3136
Diageo North America Inc **(HQ)**	Norwalk	CT	A	203 229-2100	3138

Employee Codes: A=Over 500 employees, B=251-500
C=101-250, D=51-100 E=20-50, F=10-19, G=3-9

	CITY	ST	EMP	PHONE	ENTRY #
Diageo PLC	Norwalk	CT	D	203 229-2100	3139
Edwards Wines LLC	North Stonington	CT	G	860 535-0202	3073
His Vineyard Inc	Bethel	CT	G	203 790-1600	159
Land of Nod Winery LLC	East Canaan	CT	G	860 824-5225	1112
Miranda Vineyard LLC	Goshen	CT	G	860 491-9906	1586
Paradise Hlls Vnyrd Winery LLC	Wallingford	CT	G	203 284-0123	4782
Pozzi Fmly Wine & Spirits LLC	Stamford	CT	G	646 422-9134	4289
Preston Ridge Vineyard LLC	Preston	CT	G	860 383-4278	3582
Sharpe Hill Vineyard Inc	Pomfret	CT	E	860 974-3549	3554
Stonington Vineyards Inc	Stonington	CT	G	860 535-1222	4378
Strawberry Ridge Vineyard Inc	Cornwall Bridge	CT	G	860 868-0730	821
Sunset Hill Vineyard	Lyme	CT	G	860 598-9427	1956
Three Suns Ltd	Hartford	CT	G	860 233-7658	1880
UST LLC **(HQ)**	Stamford	CT	G	203 817-3000	4355
1634 Meadery	Ipswich	MA	G	508 517-4058	11899
21st Century Foods Inc	Boston	MA	G	617 522-7595	8327
59 Beecher Street LLC	Southbridge	MA	G	631 734-6200	15373
Archer Roose Inc	Boston	MA	G	646 283-4152	8373
Balderdash Cellars	Pittsfield	MA	G	413 464-4629	14455
Boston Winery LLC	Dorchester	MA	G	617 265-9463	10341
Cape Cod Winery	East Falmouth	MA	F	508 457-5592	10438
Clos De La Tech	East Falmouth	MA	G	508 648-2505	10439
Constellation Brands Inc	Quincy	MA	G	617 249-5082	14619
E & J Gallo Winery	Wakefield	MA	E	781 213-5050	15951
Eno Massachusetts	Stoughton	MA	G	781 297-7331	15587
Grove Street Enterprises Inc	Richmond	MA	F	413 698-3301	14780
Hardwickvmeyard & Winery	Hardwick	MA	G	413 967-7763	11372
Hirsch Retail Store Inc	Acton	MA	G	978 621-4634	7360
Holden Wine & Spirits Inc	Holden	MA	G	508 829-6632	11544
Kwik Mart	Pittsfield	MA	G	413 464-7902	14479
Longmeadow Package Store Inc	Longmeadow	MA	G	413 567-3201	12335
Marthas Seastreak Vineyard LLC	New Bedford	MA	G	617 896-0293	13416
Mount Warner Vineyards LLC	Hadley	MA	G	413 531-4046	11311
Nashoba Valley Spirits Limited	Bolton	MA	E	978 779-5521	8321
Nemerever Vineyards LLC	Chestnut Hill	MA	G	617 320-6994	9989
Oak Barrel Imports LLC	Beverly	MA	G	617 286-2524	8162
Phoenix Vintners LLC	Ipswich	MA	F	877 340-9869	11934
Plymouth Bay Winery	Plymouth	MA	G	508 746-2100	14575
Pony Shack Cider Company	Boxborough	MA	G	781 367-4060	8967
Queen Bee Vineyard Inc	Monson	MA	G	413 267-9329	13210
Red Oak Winnery LLC	Saugus	MA	G	781 558-1702	14994
Terroir Wines LLC	Westborough	MA	G	508 329-1626	16655
University Wine Shop Inc	Cambridge	MA	G	617 547-4258	9686
West County Winery	Colrain	MA	G	413 624-3481	10106
Bartlett Maine Estate Winery	Gouldsboro	ME	G	207 546-2408	6135
Cellar Door Winery **(PA)**	Lincolnville	ME	G	207 763-4478	6361
Maine Craft Distilling LLC	Portland	ME	G	207 798-2528	6685
Mr Boston Brands LLC **(HQ)**	Lewiston	ME	E	207 783-1433	6308
Winterport Winery Inc	Winterport	ME	G	207 223-4500	7278
Executive Wine & Spirits Inc	Manchester	NH	E	603 647-8048	18820
Flag Hill Distillery LLC	Lee	NH	G	603 659-2949	18643
Flag Hill Winery & Vinyrd LLC	Lee	NH	G	603 659-2949	18644
Hermit Woods Inc	Meredith	NH	G	603 253-7968	18974
Moonlight Meadery LLC	Londonderry	NH	F	603 216-2162	18724
Vintners Cellar Winery	North Conway	NH	G	603 356-9463	19380
Vision Wine & Spirits LLC	Manchester	NH	F	781 278-2000	18953
Douglas Wine & Spirits Inc	North Providence	RI	F	401 353-6400	20757
Nickle Creek Vineyard LLC	Foster	RI	G	401 369-3694	20458
Tapped Apple Winery	Westerly	RI	G	401 637-4946	21542
Boyden Valley Winery LLC	Cambridge	VT	G	802 644-8151	21822
Citizen Cider LLC	Burlington	VT	F	802 448-3278	21774
Grand View Winery Co LLC	Plainfield	VT	F	802 456-8810	22267
Honora Winery & Vineyard Inc	Brattleboro	VT	G	802 368-2930	21732
Independent Brewers Untd Corp **(DH)**	Burlington	VT	F	802 862-6114	21789
Neshobe River Winery	Brandon	VT	G	802 247-8002	21710
Putney Mountain Winery	Putney	VT	G	802 387-5925	22291
Snow Farm Winery	South Hero	VT	F	802 372-9463	22482

2085 Liquors, Distilled, Rectified & Blended

	CITY	ST	EMP	PHONE	ENTRY #
American Distilling Inc	Marlborough	CT	G	860 267-4444	2063
American Distilling Inc **(PA)**	East Hampton	CT	D	860 267-4444	1156
Asylum Distillery	Southport	CT	G	203 209-0146	4093
Cylinder Vodka Inc	Stamford	CT	G	203 979-0792	4182
Diageo North America Inc **(HQ)**	Norwalk	CT	A	203 229-2100	3138
Diageo PLC	Norwalk	CT	D	203 229-2100	3139
Hartford Flavor Company LLC	Hartford	CT	G	860 604-9767	1834
Millbrook Distillery LLC	Cos Cob	CT	G	203 637-2231	828
Mine Hill Distillery	Roxbury	CT	G	860 210-1872	3736
Modern Distillery Age	Norwalk	CT	G	203 971-8710	3200
Waypoint Distillery	Bloomfield	CT	G	860 519-5390	271
Westford Hill Distillers LLC	Ashford	CT	G	860 429-0464	29
Berkshire Mountain Distlrs Inc	Great Barrington	MA	G	413 229-0219	11234
Bradford Distillery LLC **(PA)**	Scituate	MA	G	781 378-2491	15006
Bradford Distillery LLC	Hingham	MA	G	781 385-7145	11494
Bully Boy Distillers	Roxbury	MA	G	617 442-6000	14870
Deacon Giles Inc	Salem	MA	G	781 883-8256	14905
Downeast Cider House LLC	Boston	MA	G	857 301-8881	8509
Mad River Distillers	Boston	MA	G	617 262-1990	8679
Pirate Dog Brand LLC	Salem	MA	G	978 745-4786	14935
Powerhouse Botanic Distillery	Newbury	MA	G	978 930-8281	13464
Privateer International LLC	Ipswich	MA	F	978 356-0477	11935
Ryan & Wood Distillery	Gloucester	MA	G	978 281-2282	11208
Short Path Distillery Inc	Arlington	MA	G	857 417-2396	7639
Short Path Distillery Inc	Everett	MA	G	617 830-7954	10631
Silver Bear Distillery LLC	Dalton	MA	G	413 242-4892	10185
Stirrings LLC	Fall River	MA	E	508 324-9800	10764
Backwash Brew Holdings LLC	Brewer	ME	F	207 659-2300	5794
Doom Forest Distillery LLC	Pittston	ME	G	207 462-1990	6592
Maine Distilleries LLC	Freeport	ME	G	207 865-4828	6083
Mr Boston Brands LLC **(HQ)**	Lewiston	ME	E	207 783-1433	6308
New England Distilling Co	Portland	ME	G	207 878-9759	6701
Sebago Lake Distillery LLC	Gardiner	ME	G	207 557-0557	6105
Sea Hagg Distillery	Hampton	NH	G	603 380-4022	18271
Smoky Quartz Distillery LLC	Seabrook	NH	G	603 601-0342	19819
Tall Ship Distillery LLC	Dover	NH	G	603 842-0098	18057
White Mountain Distillery LLC	Manchester	NH	G	603 391-1306	18955
Appalachian Gap Distillery Inc	Middlebury	VT	G	802 989-7359	22099
Backus Distillery LLC	Westfield	VT	G	802 999-2255	22626
Caledonia Spirits Inc	Hardwick	VT	E	802 472-8000	22010
Champlain Distilleries	South Hero	VT	G	802 378-5059	22480
Goamericago Beverages LLC	Shoreham	VT	G	802 897-7700	22432
Green Mountain Distillers LLC	Morrisville	VT	G	802 498-4848	22168
Mad River Distillers	Warren	VT	G	802 496-6973	22577
Old Route Two Spirits Inc	Barre	VT	G	802 424-4864	21633
Vermont Distillers Inc	West Marlboro	VT	G	802 464-2003	22609
Vermont Hard Cider Company LLC **(HQ)**	Middlebury	VT	D	802 388-0700	22120
Whistlepig LLC **(PA)**	Shoreham	VT	F	802 897-7700	22434
Wild Hart Distillery	Shelburne	VT	G	802 489-5067	22427

2086 Soft Drinks

	CITY	ST	EMP	PHONE	ENTRY #
Als Beverage Company Inc	East Windsor	CT	E	860 627-7003	1276
Averys Beverage LLC	New Britain	CT	G	860 224-0830	2511
B & E Juices Inc	Bridgeport	CT	E	203 333-1802	380
Bombadils Spirit Shop Inc	Mansfield Center	CT	G	860 423-9661	2062
Castle Beverages Inc	Ansonia	CT	G	203 732-0883	8
Cell Nique	Weston	CT	G	888 417-9343	5170
Coca-Cola Company	Waterford	CT	G	860 443-2816	4983
Company of Coca-Cola Bottling	East Hartford	CT	D	860 569-0037	1183
Company of Coca-Cola Bottling	Stamford	CT	D	203 905-3900	4169
Crystal Rock Holdings Inc **(HQ)**	Watertown	CT	E	860 945-0661	5005
Danone Holdings Inc	Stamford	CT	A	203 229-7000	4184
Foundry Foods Inc	Norwalk	CT	G	314 982-3204	3154
Foxon Park Beverages Inc	East Haven	CT	G	203 467-7874	1250
Harvest Hill Holdings LLC **(PA)**	Stamford	CT	F	203 914-1620	4211
Light Rock Spring Water Co	Danbury	CT	F	203 743-2251	948
New England Beverages LLC	Branford	CT	G	203 208-4517	332
Newmans Own Inc **(PA)**	Westport	CT	E	203 222-0136	5218
Niagara Bottling LLC	Bloomfield	CT	G	909 226-7353	245
Pepsi-Cola Btlg of Wrcster Inc	Dayville	CT	E	860 774-4007	1050
Pepsi-Cola Metro Btlg Co Inc	Stratford	CT	B	203 375-2484	4439
Pepsi-Cola Metro Btlg Co Inc	Uncasville	CT	E	860 848-1231	4648
Pepsi-Cola Metro Btlg Co Inc	North Haven	CT	C	203 234-9014	3050
Pepsi-Cola Metro Btlg Co Inc	Windsor	CT	C	860 688-6281	5353
Pepsico	New Haven	CT	F	203 974-8912	2723
Red Bull LLC	Bloomfield	CT	G	860 519-1018	255
Reeds Inc	Norwalk	CT	E	203 890-0557	3228
Sigg Switzerland (usa) Inc	Stamford	CT	G	203 321-1232	4317
Simply Originals LLC	Norwalk	CT	G	203 273-3523	3247
Sweet Leaf Tea Company **(DH)**	Stamford	CT	F	203 863-0263	4338
Adams Redemption Center	Adams	MA	G	413 743-7691	7408
Adonai Spring Water Inc	Randolph	MA	G	844 273-7672	14669
Better Bottling Solutions LLC	Newton	MA	G	219 308-5616	13567
Coca Cola Btlg Co of Cape Cod	Sandwich	MA	D	508 888-0001	14964
Coca-Cola Bottling Company	Sandwich	MA	D	508 888-0001	14965
Coca-Cola Bottling Company	Lowell	MA	D	978 459-9378	12360
Coca-Cola Refreshments USA Inc	Northampton	MA	D	413 586-8450	13999
Coca-Cola Refreshments USA Inc	Greenfield	MA	C	413 772-2617	11255
Company of Coca-Cola Bottling	Waltham	MA	E	781 672-8624	16073
Company of Coca-Cola Bottling	Waltham	MA	G	617 622-5400	16074
Company of Coca-Cola Bottling	Westborough	MA	E	508 836-5200	16606
Company of Coca-Cola Bottling	Greenfield	MA	E	413 448-8296	11257
Company of Coca-Cola Bottling	Needham Heights	MA	D	781 449-4300	13322
Company of Coca-Cola Bottling	Northampton	MA	D	413 586-8450	14000
Enterade USA	Norwood	MA	F	781 352-5450	14149
Epic Enterprises Inc	Ayer	MA	D	978 772-2340	7919
Everybody Water LLC	Cohasset	MA	G	855 374-6539	10098
Flavrz Beverage Corporation	Gloucester	MA	G	978 879-4567	11182
Ginseng Up Corporation **(PA)**	Worcester	MA	G	508 799-6178	17383
Goodbev Inc	Lynn	MA	G	617 545-5240	12514
Katalyst Kombucha LLC	Greenfield	MA	G	413 773-9700	11265
Keurig Dr Pepper Inc	Canton	MA	D	781 575-4033	9750
Keurig Dr Pepper Inc **(PA)**	Burlington	MA	D	781 418-7000	9292
Keurig Green Mountain Inc	Burlington	MA	D	781 246-3466	9293
Market Square Beverage Co Inc	Lynn	MA	G	781 593-2150	12525

	CITY	ST	EMP	PHONE	ENTRY #
Mocktail Beverages Inc	Wenham	MA	G	855 662-5824	16403
Nixie Sparkling Water LLC	Chatham	MA	G	617 784-8671	9861
Northeast Hot-Fill Co-Op Inc	Ayer	MA	E	978 772-2338	7930
Pepsi	Randolph	MA	G	781 986-5249	14692
Pepsi Bottling Group Inc	Ayer	MA	G	978 772-2340	7933
Pepsi-Cola Btlg of Wrcster Inc **(PA)**	Holden	MA	D	508 829-6551	11549
Pepsico	Foxboro	MA	G	508 216-1681	10897
Pepsico Inc	Boylston	MA	G	508 869-1000	8982
Pepsico Inc	Randolph	MA	C	781 767-6622	14693
Pocahontas Spring Water Co **(PA)**	Middleton	MA	G	978 774-2690	13098
Polar Corp **(PA)**	Worcester	MA	A	508 753-6383	17443
Refresco Beverages US Inc	East Freetown	MA	G	508 763-3515	10458
Spring Water Associates USA	Watertown	MA	G	978 371-0138	16318
Tropicana Products Inc	Taunton	MA	E	508 821-2056	15792
Veryfine Products Inc **(DH)**	Littleton	MA	D	978 486-0812	12325
Wise Mouth Inc	North Attleboro	MA	G	508 345-2559	13786
Coca-Cola Bottling Company	Bangor	ME	D	207 942-5546	5637
Coca-Cola Bottling Company	South Portland	ME	C	207 773-5505	7020
Coca-Cola Bottling Company	Presque Isle	ME	E	207 764-4481	6756
Crystal Spring Water Co Inc **(PA)**	Auburn	ME	F	207 782-1521	5558
Dr Pepper Bottling Co Portland	Portland	ME	G	207 773-4258	6654
Farmington Coca Cola Btlg Dstr	Farmington	ME	E	207 778-4733	6047
G C Management Corp **(PA)**	Southwest Harbor	ME	G	207 244-5363	7047
Maine Pure	Fryeburg	ME	G	207 256-8111	6100
Maine Soft Drink Association	South Portland	ME	D	207 773-5505	7032
Pepsi Cola Bottling Aroostook	Presque Isle	ME	E	207 760-3000	6769
Pepsi-Cola Metro Btlg Co Inc	Augusta	ME	D	207 623-1313	5616
Pepsi-Cola Metro Btlg Co Inc	Hampden	ME	D	207 973-2217	6167
Pepsi-Cola Metro Btlg Co Inc	Auburn	ME	C	207 784-5791	5588
Pepsi-Cola Metro Btlg Co Inc	Portland	ME	C	207 773-4258	6707
Roopers Redemption & Bev Ctr	Lewiston	ME	F	207 782-1482	6319
Cg Roxane LLC	Moultonborough	NH	E	603 476-8844	19095
Coca-Cola Bottling Company	Manchester	NH	D	603 623-6033	18800
Coca-Cola Bottling Company	Seabrook	NH	E	603 926-0404	19796
Coca-Cola Bottling Company	Londonderry	NH	D	603 437-3530	18685
Coca-Cola Bottling Company	Belmont	NH	D	603 267-8834	17672
Discount Beverages Plus Cig	Center Conway	NH	G	603 356-8844	17794
North Country Hard Cider LLC	Rollinsford	NH	G	603 834-9915	19694
Pepsi-Cola Metro Btlg Co Inc	Manchester	NH	D	603 625-5764	18899
Surry Licensing LLC	Keene	NH	G	603 354-7000	18532
Thomas H Conner	Newfields	NH	G	603 778-0322	19320
Coca-Cola Refreshments USA Inc	Providence	RI	B	401 331-1981	20986
L & B Beverage Inc	East Providence	RI	G	401 434-9991	20427
Organic Studio 13 LLC	Pawtucket	RI	G	770 369-0756	20871
Pepsi-Cola Metro Btlg Co Inc	Cranston	RI	D	401 468-3221	20270
Pepsi-Cola Metro Btlg Co Inc	Cranston	RI	C	401 468-3300	20271
Yacht Club Bottling Works Inc	North Providence	RI	G	401 231-9290	20775
Aqua Vitea LLC	Middlebury	VT	G	802 453-8590	22100
Coca-Cola Bottling Company	Colchester	VT	D	802 654-3800	21860
Leader Dist Systems Inc	Brattleboro	VT	D	802 254-6093	21736
Pepsi Cola Bottling Co	Brattleboro	VT	C	802 254-6093	21743
Smith & Salmon Inc	Burlington	VT	G	802 578-8242	21809
Vermont Heritage Spring Water	Derby	VT	G	802 334-2528	21904
Vermont Sweetwater Bottling Co	Poultney	VT	G	800 974-9877	22280

2087 Flavoring Extracts & Syrups

	CITY	ST	EMP	PHONE	ENTRY #
America Extract Corporation	East Hampton	CT	F	860 267-4444	1155
American Distilling Inc	Marlborough	CT	G	860 267-4444	2063
American Distilling Inc **(PA)**	East Hampton	CT	D	860 267-4444	1156
Brookside Flvors Ingrdents LLC **(HQ)**	Stamford	CT	D	203 595-4520	4152
Carrubba Incorporated	Milford	CT	D	203 878-0605	2262
Charles Boggini Company LLC	Coventry	CT	G	860 742-2652	832
Flavrz Organic Beverages LLC	Darien	CT	G	203 716-8082	1026
Focus Now Solutions LLC	Fairfield	CT	G	203 247-9038	1432
Herbasway Laboratories LLC	Wallingford	CT	E	203 269-6991	4750
Jmf Group LLC	East Windsor	CT	D	860 627-7003	1288
Osf Flavors Inc **(PA)**	Windsor	CT	F	860 298-8350	5352
Scitech International LLC	Stamford	CT	G	203 967-8502	4311
Target Flavors Inc	Brookfield	CT	F	203 775-4727	659
Watson LLC **(DH)**	West Haven	CT	B	203 932-3000	5149
Brady Enterprises Inc **(PA)**	East Weymouth	MA	D	781 682-6280	10538
Coca-Cola Refreshments USA Inc	Northampton	MA	D	413 586-8450	13999
Company of Coca-Cola Bottling	Needham Heights	MA	D	781 449-4300	13322
Diageo North America Inc	Mansfield	MA	G	508 324-9800	12628
Drink Maple Inc	Sudbury	MA	G	978 610-6408	15656
Filtered By Forest LLC	Lynn	MA	G	978 590-3203	12508
Keurig Dr Pepper Inc **(PA)**	Burlington	MA	D	781 418-7000	9292
Mrp Trading Innovations LLC	Beverly	MA	F	978 762-3900	8157
Northice	Plymouth	MA	F	781 985-5225	14569
Ocean Cliff Corporation	New Bedford	MA	G	508 990-7900	13432
Powell and Mahoney LLC	Salem	MA	G	978 745-4332	14936
Stirrings LLC	Fall River	MA	E	508 324-9800	10764
Walter Scott	Lexington	MA	G	781 862-4893	12284
B&G Foods Inc	Portland	ME	C	207 772-8341	6616
FMC Corporation	Rockland	ME	C	207 594-3200	6795
Luces Pure Maple Syrup	Anson	ME	G	207 696-3732	5525
Schlotterbeck & Foss LLC **(PA)**	Westbrook	ME	E	207 772-4666	7206
Sunrise Foods Incorporated	Brentwood	NH	F	603 772-4420	17760
Finlay EXT Ingredients USA Inc **(DH)**	Lincoln	RI	D	800 288-6272	20574
Fountain Dispensers Co Inc	Providence	RI	G	401 461-8400	21014
Rhode Island Distrg Co LLC	West Greenwich	RI	E	401 822-6400	21465
Rhode Island Frt Syrup Co Inc	Smithfield	RI	F	401 231-0040	21247
Aqua Vitea LLC	Salisbury	VT	G	802 352-1049	22398
Maple Grove Farms Vermont Inc **(HQ)**	Saint Johnsbury	VT	D	802 748-5141	22391
Runamok Maple LLC	Fairfax	VT	G	802 849-7943	21978
Wild Farm Maple	Arlington	VT	G	802 362-1656	21602

2091 Fish & Seafoods, Canned & Cured

	CITY	ST	EMP	PHONE	ENTRY #
Greenport Foods LLC	Westport	CT	F	203 221-2673	5199
Boston Smoked Fish Company LLC	Boston	MA	G	617 819-5476	8442
Christhopher Dinatale	Marshfield	MA	G	781 834-4248	12857
Ditusa Corporation	Gloucester	MA	E	978 335-5259	11178
Gortons Inc **(DH)**	Gloucester	MA	B	978 283-3000	11189
IQF Custom Packing LLC	Fall River	MA	G	508 646-0400	10715
Kneeland Bros Inc	Rowley	MA	F	978 948-3919	14855
Spence & Co Ltd	Brockton	MA	E	508 427-5577	9177
Cherry Point Products Inc	Milbridge	ME	D	207 546-0930	6431
Ducktrap River of Maine LLC	Belfast	ME	C	207 338-6280	5688
Ecohouse LLC	Bremen	ME	G	207 529-2700	5791
L Ray Packing Company	Milbridge	ME	G	207 546-2355	6435
Looks Gourmet Food Co Inc **(HQ)**	Whiting	ME	E	207 259-3341	7221
Wild Ocean Aquaculture LLC	Portland	ME	G	207 458-6288	6745

2092 Fish & Seafoods, Fresh & Frozen

	CITY	ST	EMP	PHONE	ENTRY #
Coastal Seafoods Inc **(PA)**	Fairfield	CT	F	203 431-0453	1421
Rich Products Corporation	New Britain	CT	C	609 589-3049	2573
Saugatuck Kitchens LLC	Stratford	CT	G	203 334-1099	4442
Seafood Gourmet Inc	Wolcott	CT	F	203 272-1544	5456
Big G Seafood Inc	New Bedford	MA	G	508 994-5113	13361
Blount Fine Foods Corp **(PA)**	Fall River	MA	C	774 888-1300	10669
Bluemoon Oyster Co Lcc	Duxbury	MA	G	781 585-6000	10393
Bonamar Corp	Newton	MA	F	617 965-3400	13571
Channel Fish Co Inc	Boston	MA	D	617 569-3200	8467
Cold Atlantic Seafood Inc	New Bedford	MA	G	508 996-3352	13373
Georges Bank LLC	Boston	MA	F	617 423-3474	8560
Gortons Inc **(DH)**	Gloucester	MA	B	978 283-3000	11189
High Liner Foods USA Inc	Peabody	MA	C	978 977-5305	14341
Higson Inc	Fall River	MA	G	508 678-4970	10714
Hunts Seafood Inc	Salisbury	MA	G	978 255-2636	14951
Jordan Bros Seafood Co Inc	Boston	MA	F	508 583-9797	8638
Kyler Seafood Inc	New Bedford	MA	D	508 984-5150	13406
M F Fley Incrprtd-New Bdford	New Bedford	MA	E	508 997-0773	13413
North Coast Sea-Foods Corp **(PA)**	Boston	MA	C	617 345-4400	8740
North Coast Sea-Foods Corp	New Bedford	MA	E	508 997-0766	13428
Northern Pelagic Group LLC	New Bedford	MA	E	508 979-1171	13430
Ocean Crest Seafood Inc	Gloucester	MA	F	978 281-0232	11198
Ocean Crest Seafoods Inc **(PA)**	Gloucester	MA	E	978 281-0232	11199
Raw Sea Foods Inc	Fall River	MA	C	508 673-0111	10753
Sea Watch International Ltd	New Bedford	MA	D	508 984-1406	13449
Spence & Co Ltd	Brockton	MA	E	508 427-5577	9177
Zeus Packing Inc	Gloucester	MA	E	978 281-6900	11221
Bayley Quality Seafood Inc	Scarborough	ME	G	207 883-4581	6909
Bristol Seafood LLC	Portland	ME	D	207 761-4251	6627
Central Maine Cold Storage	Bucksport	ME	G	419 215-7955	5854
Danny Boy Fisheries Inc	North Yarmouth	ME	G	207 829-6622	6516
Ducktrap River of Maine LLC	Belfast	ME	C	207 338-6280	5688
Harmons Clam Cakes	Portland	ME	G	207 967-4100	6669
Maine Coast Nordic	Machiasport	ME	F	207 255-6714	6398
Maine Seafood Ventures LLC	Saco	ME	G	207 303-0165	6853
North Atlantic Inc	Portland	ME	G	207 774-6025	6704
Sea & Reef Aquaculture LLC	Franklin	ME	G	207 422-2422	6069
Shucks Maine Lobster LLC	Richmond	ME	F	207 737-4800	6783
Ocean Premier Seafood Inc	Manchester	NH	G	603 206-4787	18892
Blount Fine Foods Corp	Warren	RI	D	401 245-8800	21290
Galilean Seafood Inc	Bristol	RI	D	401 253-3030	20081
Ocean State Shellfish Coop	Narragansett	RI	G	401 789-2065	20643
Yankee Pride Fisheries Inc	Wakefield	RI	G	401 783-9647	21282

2095 Coffee

	CITY	ST	EMP	PHONE	ENTRY #
Als Beverage Company Inc	East Windsor	CT	E	860 627-7003	1276
B & B Ventures Ltd Lblty Co	Branford	CT	E	203 481-1700	294
Fjb America LLC	Westport	CT	G	203 682-2424	5194
Foundry Foods Inc	Norwalk	CT	G	314 982-3204	3154
Oasis Coffee Corp	Norwalk	CT	E	203 847-0554	3210
Omar Coffee Company	Newington	CT	E	860 667-8889	2888
Riseandshine Corporation **(PA)**	Stamford	CT	F	917 599-7541	4302
Saccuzzo Company Inc	Newington	CT	G	860 665-1101	2900
Tm Ward Co of Connecticut LLC	Norwalk	CT	G	203 866-9203	3257
Atomic Cafe **(PA)**	Salem	MA	F	978 910-0489	14895
Batian Peak Coffee	Lowell	MA	G	978 663-2305	12351
Birds & Beans LLC	South Dartmouth	MA	G	857 233-2722	15236
George Howell Coffee Co LLC	Acton	MA	F	978 635-9033	7358
Jnp Coffee LLC	Shrewsbury	MA	G	858 518-7437	15120
Kraft Heinz Foods Company	Woburn	MA	C	781 933-2800	17212

	CITY	ST	EMP	PHONE	ENTRY #
Mojo Cold Brewed Coffee Inc	Beverly	MA	G	617 877-2997	8156
New England Partnership Inc	Norwood	MA	C	800 225-3537	14182
Reily Foods Company	Malden	MA	G	504 524-6131	12593
Carpe Diem Coffee Roasting Co	North Berwick	ME	G	207 676-2233	6505
Kerry Inc	Portland	ME	E	207 775-7060	6677
Red 23 Holdings Inc	Portsmouth	NH	F	603 433-3011	19613
Vera Roasting Company	Portsmouth	NH	G	603 969-7970	19628
Farmer Willies Inc	Providence	RI	G	401 441-2997	21011
Finlay EXT Ingredients USA Inc **(DH)**	Lincoln	RI	D	800 288-6272	20574
Finlay EXT Ingredients USA Inc	Woonsocket	RI	G	401 769-5490	21562
Mills Coffee Roasting Co	Providence	RI	F	401 781-7860	21068

2096 Potato Chips & Similar Prdts

	CITY	ST	EMP	PHONE	ENTRY #
Frito-Lay North America Inc	Dayville	CT	A	860 412-1000	1045
Mediterranean Snack Fd Co LLC	Stamford	CT	F	973 402-2644	4248
Severance Foods Inc	Hartford	CT	E	860 724-7063	1868
U T Z	North Franklin	CT	G	860 383-4266	2992
3 Potato 4 LLC	Salem	MA	G	978 744-0948	14888
Barbaras Bakery Inc **(DH)**	Marlborough	MA	E	800 343-0590	12725
Denny S Sweet Onion Rings	Lynn	MA	G	781 598-5317	12501
Frito-Lay North America Inc	Wilmington	MA	C	978 657-8344	17002
Frito-Lay North America Inc	Braintree	MA	F	781 348-1500	9008
New England Prtzel Popcorn Inc	Lawrence	MA	G	978 687-0342	12064
Plant Snacks LLC	Needham	MA	G	617 480-6265	13308
Regco Corporation	Haverhill	MA	E	978 521-4370	11468
Sacar Enterprises LLC	Amesbury	MA	G	978 834-6494	7506
Stacys Pita Chip Company Inc	Randolph	MA	D	781 961-2800	14698
Utz Quality Foods Inc	Fitchburg	MA	E	978 342-6038	10860
Smith & Assoc	Scarborough	ME	G	866 299-6487	6940
Vintage Maine Kitchen LLC	Freeport	ME	G	207 317-2536	6088
Micheles Sweet Shoppe LLC	Londonderry	NH	G	603 425-2946	18722
Gringo Kitchens LLC	Manchester Center	VT	F	802 362-0836	22086

2097 Ice

	CITY	ST	EMP	PHONE	ENTRY #
Dee Zee Ice LLC	Southington	CT	F	860 276-3500	4046
Leonard F Brooks **(PA)**	Bridgeport	CT	G	203 335-4934	445
Olde Burnside Brewing Co LLC	East Hartford	CT	G	860 528-2200	1208
Twenty Five Commerce Inc	Norwalk	CT	G	203 866-0540	3263
Vaporizer LLC	Moosup	CT	E	860 564-7225	2429
American Dry Ice Corporation **(PA)**	Palmer	MA	F	413 283-9906	14279
Brewster Ice Co	Brewster	MA	G	508 896-3593	9052
Cape Pond Ice Company **(PA)**	Gloucester	MA	E	978 283-0174	11172
Cape Pond Ice Company	Lawrence	MA	G	978 688-2300	12002
Cape Pond Ice Company	Peabody	MA	G	978 531-4853	14320
Crystal Ice Co Inc	New Bedford	MA	F	508 997-7522	13375
Eastern Ice Company Inc	Fall River	MA	E	508 672-1800	10685
Got Ice LLC	Nantucket	MA	G	508 228-1156	13225
JP Lillis Enterprises Inc **(PA)**	Sandwich	MA	F	508 888-8394	14970
Leominster Ice Company Inc	Leominster	MA	G	978 537-5322	12162
Getchell Bros Inc	Sanford	ME	E	207 490-0809	6877
Natural Rocks Spring Water Ice	Eliot	ME	G	207 451-2110	6009
Taggart Ice Inc	Nashua	NH	F	603 888-4630	19270
East Bay Ice Co Inc	East Providence	RI	G	401 434-7485	20408
Pier Ice Plant Inc	Narragansett	RI	G	401 789-6090	20645

2098 Macaroni, Spaghetti & Noodles

	CITY	ST	EMP	PHONE	ENTRY #
Carlas Pasta Inc	South Windsor	CT	C	860 436-4042	3949
Conopco Inc	Trumbull	CT	E	708 606-0540	4620
Mecha Noodle Bar	New Haven	CT	G	203 691-9671	2711
Oasis Coffee Corp	Norwalk	CT	E	203 847-0554	3210
Roodle Rice & Noodle Bar	Wallingford	CT	G	203 269-9899	4800
Thomas J Lipton Inc	Trumbull	CT	A	206 381-3500	4635
Villarina Pasta & Fine Foods **(PA)**	Danbury	CT	G	203 917-4463	1004
Albert Capone **(PA)**	Somerville	MA	G	617 629-2296	15151
Chinese Spaghetti Factory	Boston	MA	G	617 542-0224	8470
Chinese Spaghetti Factory Inc	Boston	MA	F	617 445-7714	8471
Ho Toy Noodles Inc **(PA)**	Stoughton	MA	F	617 426-0247	15596
L & L Noodle Inc	Chelsea	MA	G	617 889-6888	9958
Noodle Lab LLC	Chelsea	MA	G	617 717-4370	9961
O C M Inc	Fall River	MA	F	508 675-7711	10742
Spinelli Ravioli Mfg Co Inc	Boston	MA	E	617 567-1992	8859
Thai Noodle Bar	Quincy	MA	G	617 689-8847	14661
United Foods Incorporated **(PA)**	Boston	MA	G	617 482-9879	8898
Zenna Noodle Bar	Brookline	MA	G	781 883-8624	9226
Bubble Mneia Dssert Noodle Bar	Portland	ME	G	207 773-9559	6628
Umami Noodle	Bangor	ME	F	207 947-9991	5662
Noodle Revolution	Westerly	RI	G	401 596-9559	21535
Pasta Patch Inc	East Greenwich	RI	F	401 884-1234	20376
Venda Ravioli Inc	Providence	RI	E	401 421-9105	21147
Venda Ravioli Inc **(PA)**	Providence	RI	C	401 421-9105	21148
Asiana Noodle Shop	Burlington	VT	G	802 862-8828	21767
Putney Pasta Company Inc	Brattleboro	VT	E	802 257-4800	21746

2099 Food Preparations, NEC

	CITY	ST	EMP	PHONE	ENTRY #
Amodios Inc **(PA)**	Waterbury	CT	F	203 573-1229	4843
Balsam Woods Farm	Stafford Springs	CT	G	860 265-1800	4106
Brothers & Sons Sugar House	Torrington	CT	G	860 489-2719	4569
Burnside Supermarket LLC	East Hartford	CT	G	860 291-9965	1178
Carriage House Companies Inc	Manchester	CT	B	860 647-1909	1992
Conopco Inc	Trumbull	CT	E	708 606-0540	4620
Durantes Pasta Inc	West Haven	CT	G	203 387-5560	5118
Entrees Made Easy	Monroe	CT	G	203 261-5777	2402
Fine Food Services Inc	Groton	CT	E	860 445-5276	1676
Frescobene Foods LLC	Fairfield	CT	G	203 610-4688	1433
Global Palate Foods LLC	Westport	CT	G	203 543-3028	5198
Guasa Salsa Vzla	Norwalk	CT	G	203 981-7011	3164
Herbasway Laboratories LLC	Wallingford	CT	E	203 269-6991	4750
Hummel Bros Inc	New Haven	CT	D	203 787-4113	2697
Ikigai Foods LLC	Shelton	CT	G	203 954-8083	3816
Kerry R Wood	Westport	CT	G	203 221-7780	5205
Kohler Mix Specialties LLC	Newington	CT	C	860 666-1511	2876
Lesser Evil	Danbury	CT	G	203 529-3555	946
Loaves & Fishes Ministries	Hartford	CT	G	860 524-1730	1840
Malta Food Pantry Inc	Hartford	CT	G	860 725-0944	1842
Maple Craft Foods LLC	Sandy Hook	CT	G	203 913-7066	3744
Mastriani Gourmet Food LLC	Bridgeport	CT	G	203 368-9556	448
Nuovo Pasta Productions Ltd	Stratford	CT	C	203 380-4090	4437
Old Castle Foods LLC	Newtown	CT	G	203 426-1344	2932
Paridise Foods LLC	Milford	CT	G	203 283-3903	2331
Peanut Butter and Jelly	Stamford	CT	G	203 504-2280	4280
Podunk Popcorn	South Windsor	CT	G	860 648-9565	4002
Premiere Packg Partners LLC	Waterbury	CT	E	203 694-0003	4944
RC Bigelow Inc **(PA)**	Fairfield	CT	C	888 244-3569	1451
Rivers Edge Sugar House	Ashford	CT	G	860 429-1510	27
Source Inc **(PA)**	North Branford	CT	G	203 488-6400	2977
Sovipe Food Distributors LLC	Danbury	CT	G	203 648-2781	995
Supreme Storm Services LLC	Southington	CT	G	860 201-0642	4083
Thomas J Lipton Inc	Trumbull	CT	A	206 381-3500	4635
Uncle Wileys Inc	Fairfield	CT	F	203 256-9313	1458
Unilever Ascc AG	Shelton	CT	B	203 381-2482	3884
Vinegar Syndrome LLC	Bridgeport	CT	G	212 722-9755	504
Vita Pasta Inc	Old Saybrook	CT	G	860 395-1452	3355
21st Century Foods Inc	Boston	MA	G	617 522-7595	8327
A Lot Bakery Products Inc	Boston	MA	G	617 561-1122	8332
A To Z Foods Inc	Arlington	MA	G	781 413-0221	7621
Albert Capone **(PA)**	Somerville	MA	G	617 629-2296	15151
Alexis Foods Inc **(PA)**	Holden	MA	G	508 829-9111	11541
Alexis Foods Inc	Littleton	MA	G	978 952-6777	12290
Avon Food Company LLC	Stoughton	MA	F	781 341-4981	15582
Beyond Shaker LLC	Woburn	MA	G	617 461-6608	17131
Blitz Foods LLC	Boston	MA	G	617 243-7446	8414
Boston Salads and Provs Inc	Boston	MA	E	617 307-6340	8439
Boyajian Inc	Canton	MA	F	781 828-9966	9718
Brady Enterprises Inc **(PA)**	East Weymouth	MA	D	781 682-6280	10538
Brady Enterprises Inc	Weymouth	MA	F	781 337-7057	16886
Breakwater Foods LLC	Lynn	MA	G	617 335-6475	12493
Brozzian LLC	Whitinsville	MA	G	774 280-9338	16911
Chang Shing Tofu Inc	Cambridge	MA	G	617 868-8878	9436
Chef Creations LLC	Lynn	MA	D	407 228-0069	12497
Cherrybrook Kitchen LLC	Burlington	MA	G	781 272-0400	9248
Chinamerica Food Manufacture	Boston	MA	F	617 426-1818	8469
Choice Foods	Bellingham	MA	G	508 332-2442	8034
City Fresh Foods Inc	Roxbury	MA	D	617 606-7123	14871
City Fresh Foods Inc	Roxbury	MA	D	617 606-7123	14872
Cocomama Foods Inc	Boston	MA	G	978 621-2126	8479
Concord Foods LLC	Brockton	MA	C	508 580-1700	9131
Cuizina Foods Company	Lynn	MA	E	425 486-7000	12498
Custom Seasonings Inc	Gloucester	MA	E	978 762-6300	11176
Double Diamond Sugar House	Dover	MA	G	508 479-4950	10350
Dough Connection Corporation	Woburn	MA	G	877 693-6844	17169
Dufresnes Sugar House	Williamsburg	MA	G	413 268-7509	16950
Durkee-Mower Inc	Lynn	MA	E	781 593-8007	12503
Fedhal Foods Inc	Worcester	MA	G	508 595-9178	17374
Fogg Flavor Labs LLC	West Newbury	MA	G	978 808-1732	16491
Franklin Area Survival Center	Turners Falls	MA	F	413 863-9549	15877
Freeda S Foods LLC	Stoneham	MA	G	781 662-6474	15564
Fuel For Fire Inc	Natick	MA	F	508 975-4573	13256
Gillians Foods Inc	Salem	MA	E	781 586-0086	14915
Good Wives Inc	Lynn	MA	G	781 596-0070	12513
Goose Valley Natural Foods LLC	Boston	MA	G	617 914-0126	8574
Greencore Oars LLC	Brockton	MA	D	508 586-8418	9153
Gustare Oils & Vinegars **(PA)**	Chatham	MA	G	508 945-4505	9859
Hans Kissle Company LLC	Haverhill	MA	C	978 556-4500	11440
Harbar LLC	Canton	MA	C	781 828-0848	9735
Holiday Farm Inc	Dalton	MA	G	413 684-0444	10178
International Food Products	Norwood	MA	G	781 769-6666	14166
Island Desserts LLC	Walpole	MA	D	508 660-2200	15995
Jbnj Foods Incorporated	Hanson	MA	G	781 293-0912	11364
Josephs Gourmet Pasta Company	Haverhill	MA	B	978 521-1718	11443
Kayjay Foods Inc	East Templeton	MA	G	978 833-0728	10519
Km Foods Inc	Waltham	MA	G	781 894-7616	16138
Leavitt Corporation **(HQ)**	Everett	MA	C	617 389-2600	10616
Lillys Gastronomia Italian	Everett	MA	F	617 387-9666	10617

	CITY	ST	EMP	PHONE	ENTRY #
Local Tortilla LLC	Hadley	MA	G	413 387-7140	11309
Longrun LLC	Belmont	MA	G	617 758-8674	8077
Mange LLC	Somerville	MA	G	917 880-2104	15194
Mary Ann Caproni	North Adams	MA	G	413 663-7330	13679
Nasoya Foods Inc	Ayer	MA	D	978 772-6880	7927
Nasoya Foods Usa LLC	Ayer	MA	C	978 772-6880	7928
Navarrete Foods Inc	Charlestown	MA	G	508 735-7319	9839
New England Prtzel Popcorn Inc	Lawrence	MA	G	978 687-0342	12064
Newly Weds Foods Inc	Watertown	MA	D	617 926-7600	16303
Nolas Fresh Foods LLC	Roslindale	MA	G	617 283-2644	14840
Palaka Corp	Peabody	MA	G	978 531-6252	14359
Pasta Bene Inc	Brockton	MA	F	508 583-1515	9170
Pauls Sugar House	Haydenville	MA	G	413 268-3544	11487
Precision Pasta Dies Inc	Hyannis	MA	G	978 866-7720	11854
Pride India Inc **(PA)**	Brighton	MA	F	617 202-9659	9105
Puratos Corporation	Norwood	MA	G	781 688-8560	14190
Reily Foods Company	Malden	MA	G	504 524-6131	12593
Richelieu Foods Inc **(DH)**	Braintree	MA	E	781 786-6800	9034
Severances Sugarhouse	Northfield	MA	F	413 498-2032	14066
Shire City Herbals Inc	Pittsfield	MA	F	413 344-4740	14508
Sidekim LLC	Lynn	MA	E	781 595-3663	12539
Sonnys Pizza Inc	Saugus	MA	F	617 381-1900	14998
Soulas Homemade Salsa LLC	Boxford	MA	G	978 314-7735	8978
Sun Country Foods Inc **(HQ)**	Norwood	MA	E	855 824-7645	14202
Sunopta Ingredients Inc	Bedford	MA	G	781 276-5100	8012
Superior Nut Company Inc	Cambridge	MA	E	800 251-6060	9665
Tea Forte Inc	Maynard	MA	E	978 369-7777	12904
Tekkware Inc	Gloucester	MA	G	603 380-4257	11215
Tribe Mediterranean Foods Inc	Taunton	MA	D	774 961-0000	15791
True Words Tortillas Inc	Orleans	MA	G	508 255-3338	14243
United Citrus Products Co	Taunton	MA	G	800 229-7300	15794
Uno Foods Inc **(DH)**	Boston	MA	F	617 323-9200	8900
Vinegar Hill LLC	Saugus	MA	G	781 233-3190	15001
Vivido Natural LLC	Newton	MA	F	617 630-0131	13653
Walter Scott	Lexington	MA	G	781 862-4893	12284
Yankee Trader Seafood Ltd	Pembroke	MA	F	781 829-4350	14434
Allagash Maple Products Inc	Skowhegan	ME	G	207 431-1481	6967
Barney & Co California LLC	Cape Elizabeth	ME	G	559 442-1752	5874
Cherry Point Products Inc	Milbridge	ME	D	207 546-0930	6431
Galaxie Salsa Co	Buxton	ME	G	207 939-3392	5856
Jackson Sgrhuse Vgtable Stands	Oxford	ME	G	207 539-4613	6568
Jims Salad Co	Unity	ME	G	207 948-2613	7116
Lukas Foods Inc	Biddeford	ME	E	207 284-7052	5744
Maine Medicinals Inc	Dresden	ME	G	207 737-8717	5967
Mainely Maple LLC	Norridgewock	ME	G	207 634-3073	6498
Modernist Pantry LLC	Eliot	ME	G	207 200-3817	6008
Montecito Roadhouse Inc	Westbrook	ME	G	207 856-6811	7197
R & N Inc	Unity	ME	G	207 948-2613	7118
Reginaspices	Portland	ME	G	207 632-5544	6721
Schlotterbeck & Foss LLC **(PA)**	Westbrook	ME	E	207 772-4666	7206
Spring Break Maple & Honey	Smyrna Mills	ME	G	207 757-7373	6995
Srods LLC	Norway	ME	F	207 743-6194	6525
Strawberry Hill Farms LLC	Skowhegan	ME	G	207 474-5262	6987
Tortilleria Pachanga	Portland	ME	G	207 797-9700	6742
Tyler R Hews	Caribou	ME	G	207 272-9273	5891
Vervain Mill	Portland	ME	G	207 774-5744	6744
Zen Bear Honey Tea LLC	Bath	ME	G	207 449-1553	5682
Discerning Palate LLC **(PA)**	Meredith	NH	G	603 279-8600	18973
Forgotten Traditions LLC	Tilton	NH	G	603 344-2231	19905
Four Saps Sugar Shack Corp	Lyndeborough	NH	G	603 858-5159	18758
Gourmet Oils and Vinegars Neng	Center Barnstead	NH	G	603 269-2271	17789
Hannah International Foods Inc	Seabrook	NH	D	603 474-5805	19803
J H Faddens & Sons	North Woodstock	NH	G	603 745-2406	19398
Little Acre Gourmet Foods	Dover	NH	G	603 749-7227	18035
Manna Mix	Newport	NH	G	213 519-0719	19350
Maple Guys LLC	Wilton	NH	G	603 654-2415	19982
Maple Heights Farm	Northfield	NH	G	603 286-7942	19406
Msn Corporation	Manchester	NH	D	603 623-3528	18879
Old Dutch Mustard Co Inc	Greenville	NH	D	516 466-0522	18229
Pollys Pancake Parlor	Sugar Hill	NH	G	603 823-5575	19878
Popzup LLC	Dover	NH	G	978 502-1737	18046
Riverside Specialty Foods Inc	Seabrook	NH	G	603 474-5805	19813
Stump City Cider	Rochester	NH	G	603 234-6288	19688
Sunnyside Maples	Canterbury	NH	G	603 848-7091	17786
Sunnyside Maples Inc	Gilmanton	NH	G	603 783-9961	18194
Terracotta Pasta Co **(PA)**	Dover	NH	G	603 749-2288	18059
White Oak Farms	Sandown	NH	G	603 887-2233	19789
Woodards Sugar House LLC	Surry	NH	G	603 358-3321	19883
Cocofuel	Cranston	RI	G	401 209-8099	20198
Edesia Industries LLC	North Kingstown	RI	D	401 272-5521	20706
Marilu Foods Inc	Westerly	RI	G	401 348-2858	21529
Pbuttri LLC	Pawtucket	RI	G	401 996-5583	20877
Protein Plus Peanut Butter Co	Lincoln	RI	G	401 996-5583	20593
Stedagio LLC	Mapleville	RI	G	401 568-6228	20615
Stonebridge Restaurant Inc	Tiverton	RI	E	401 625-5780	21264
Top Shell LLC	Central Falls	RI	F	401 726-7890	20127
Wildtree Inc	Lincoln	RI	D	401 732-1856	20599
Bonneaus Vermont Maple	Lowell	VT	G	802 744-2742	22059
Branon Family Maple Orchards	Fairfield	VT	G	802 827-3914	21982
Branon Shady Maples Inc	Fairfield	VT	G	802 827-6605	21983
Bread & Chocolate Inc	Wells River	VT	G	802 429-2920	22600
Browns River Maple	Essex Junction	VT	G	802 878-2880	21933
Burgess Sugarhouse LLC	Underhill	VT	G	802 899-5228	22546
Cabot Hills Maple LLC	Cabot	VT	G	802 426-3463	21819
Cleverfoodies Inc	Burlington	VT	G	888 938-7984	21775
Cold Corners Mapleworks LLC	Fairfield	VT	G	802 551-2270	21984
Country Shop Robb Fmly Ltd	Brattleboro	VT	G	802 258-9087	21725
Dominion & Grimm USA	Fairfax	VT	G	802 524-9625	21974
Drews LLC **(HQ)**	Chester	VT	E	802 875-1184	21842
Drinkmaple	Saint Albans	VT	G	802 528-5279	22367
Granny Blossom Specialty	Wells	VT	G	802 645-0507	22599
Green Mountain Honey Farms	Ferrisburg	VT	G	802 877-3396	21986
Green Mtn Maple Sug Ref Co Inc	Belvidere Center	VT	E	802 644-2625	21659
Harmonized Cookery	Montpelier	VT	G	802 598-9206	22149
Hi-Vue Maples LLC	Richford	VT	G	802 752-8888	22306
Highland Sugarworks Inc	Websterville	VT	F	802 479-1747	22597
Kendle Enterprises	South Woodstock	VT	F	802 457-3015	22498
Laraway Mountain Maple	Waterville	VT	G	802 644-5433	22595
Lehouillier Maple Orchard	Hyde Park	VT	G	802 888-6465	22036
LLC Cochran Cousins	Williston	VT	G	802 222-0440	22679
Lunch Bundles Inc	Bristol	VT	G	802 272-3051	21764
Maple Grove Farms Vermont Inc **(HQ)**	Saint Johnsbury	VT	D	802 748-5141	22391
Maple On Tap	Montpelier	VT	G	802 498-4477	22154
Matts Maple Syrup	Brattleboro	VT	G	802 464-9788	21738
Mitchs Maples Sugar House	Chester	VT	G	802 875-5240	21845
Morse Farm Inc	Montpelier	VT	G	802 223-2740	22156
Mountain Cider LLC	N Chittenden	VT	G	802 483-2270	22183
Mountain Road Farm	Jeffersonville	VT	G	802 644-5138	22046
Mystic Mountain Maples LLC	Saint Albans	VT	G	802 524-6163	22375
Olivias Croutons Company Inc	Brandon	VT	G	802 465-8245	21713
Potter Family Maple	Bakersfield	VT	G	802 578-0937	21603
Pure Gold Sugaring LLC	Sutton	VT	G	802 467-3921	22528
Rhapsody Natural Foods Inc	Cabot	VT	G	802 563-2172	21820
Runamok Maple LLC	Fairfax	VT	G	802 849-7943	21978
Sbfk Inc	Rutland	VT	G	802 297-7665	22353
Sprague & Son Maple	Jacksonville	VT	G	802 368-2776	22043
Steven W Willsey	Starksboro	VT	G	802 434-5353	22517
Sugar Shack On Roaring Branch	Arlington	VT	G	802 375-6747	21600
Sugarbakers Maple Syrup	North Clarendon	VT	G	802 773-7731	22221
Sugarbush Farm Inc	Woodstock	VT	G	802 457-1757	22739
Sweet Tree Holdings 1 LLC	Island Pond	VT	E	802 723-6753	22042
Tafts Milk Maple Farm	Huntington	VT	G	802 434-2727	22034
Tom Knows Salsa LLC	Eden	VT	G	802 793-5079	21921
Vermont Birch Syrup Co	Glover	VT	G	802 249-0574	21995
Vermont Maple Direct	Washington	VT	G	802 793-3326	22581
Vermont Maple Sug Makers Assoc	Waterbury Center	VT	G	802 498-7767	22593
Vermont Maple Sug Makers Assoc	Jericho	VT	G	802 763-7435	22048
Vermont Maple Sugar Co Inc **(PA)**	Morrisville	VT	E	802 888-3491	22178
Vermont Maple Sugar Co Inc	Johnson	VT	D	802 635-7483	22052
Vermont Pie and Pasta Co	Derby	VT	G	802 334-7770	21905
Vermont Soy LLC	Hardwick	VT	G	802 472-8500	22014
Vermont Syrup Company LLC	Fairfield	VT	G	802 309-8861	21985
Walkers VT Pure Mple Syrup LLC	Underhill	VT	G	802 899-3088	22551
Wh Property Service LLC	Guilford	VT	F	802 257-8566	22008
Willis Wood	Springfield	VT	G	802 263-5547	22513
Woods Vermont Syrup Company	Randolph	VT	G	802 565-0309	22304
World Cuisine Concepts LLC	White River Junction	VT	G	603 676-8591	22644

21 TOBACCO PRODUCTS

2121 Cigars

	CITY	ST	EMP	PHONE	ENTRY #
F D Grave & Son Inc	North Haven	CT	G	203 239-9394	3026
Foundation Cigar Company LLC	Windsor	CT	F	203 738-9377	5334

2131 Tobacco, Chewing & Snuff

	CITY	ST	EMP	PHONE	ENTRY #
Nordic American Smokeless Inc	Danbury	CT	F	203 207-9977	961
Nuway Tobacco Company	South Windsor	CT	D	860 289-6414	3996
Smokey Mountain Chew Inc **(PA)**	Darien	CT	G	203 656-1088	1032
US Smokeless Tobacco Co LLC	Stamford	CT	D	203 661-1100	4354
UST LLC **(HQ)**	Stamford	CT	G	203 817-3000	4355
Wonderland Smoke Shop Inc	Warwick	RI	G	401 823-3134	21451

2141 Tobacco Stemming & Redrying

	CITY	ST	EMP	PHONE	ENTRY #
UST	Greenwich	CT	F	203 661-1100	1659

22 TEXTILE MILL PRODUCTS

2211 Cotton, Woven Fabric

	CITY	ST	EMP	PHONE	ENTRY #
American Woolen Company Inc	Stafford Springs	CT	G	860 684-2766	4105
Arnitex LLC	Cos Cob	CT	G	203 869-1406	822
Custom Marine Canvas LLC	Groton	CT	G	860 572-9547	1669
Dimension-Polyant Inc	Putnam	CT	E	860 928-8300	3610
Dominics Decorating Inc	Norwalk	CT	G	203 838-1827	3141

	CITY	ST	EMP	PHONE	ENTRY #
North Sails Group LLC **(DH)**	Milford	CT	D	203 874-7548	2323
138 Barrows Street Realty Inc	Norton	MA	D	508 285-2904	14069
A Lyons & Company Inc	Manchester	MA	F	978 526-4244	12601
All American Embroidery Inc	Wilmington	MA	G	978 657-0414	16970
Bass River Marine Canvas LLC	South Dennis	MA	G	781 856-5145	15265
Brand & Oppenheimer Co Inc	Bedford	MA	E	781 271-0000	7965
Cesyl Mills Inc	Millbury	MA	D	508 865-6129	13159
CM Bedding Group Inc	Fall River	MA	F	508 673-1001	10676
Contract Decor Intl Inc	Brockton	MA	D	508 587-7000	9132
Dawn Auger	Brockton	MA	G	508 587-0363	9137
E W Winship Ltd Inc	Nantucket	MA	G	508 228-1908	13223
Gingham Ventures LLC **(PA)**	Boston	MA	G	617 206-1197	8564
Green Solar LLC	Springfield	MA	G	413 552-4114	15473
Kings Draperies Inc	Brockton	MA	G	508 230-0055	9159
Kravet Inc	Boston	MA	G	617 428-0370	8655
Lifecanvas Technologies Inc	Cambridge	MA	G	404 274-1953	9536
Marjorie Royer Interiors Inc	Middleton	MA	G	978 774-0533	13095
New England Worldwide Export	Quincy	MA	G	617 472-0251	14642
Parrot The & Bird Emporium	Feeding Hills	MA	G	413 569-5555	10803
Salt Marsh Canvas	Newbury	MA	G	978 462-0070	13465
Staceys Shade Shop Inc **(PA)**	Lynn	MA	G	781 595-0097	12540
Stacis Stitches LLC	Scituate	MA	G	781 206-7478	15015
Stevens Linen Associates Inc	Dudley	MA	D	508 943-0813	10387
Textile Waste Supply LLC	Boston	MA	E	617 241-8100	8880
Alfreds Upholstering & Custom	Alfred	ME	F	207 536-5565	5514
C B P Corp **(PA)**	Arundel	ME	F	207 985-9767	5529
Center Harbor Sails LLC	Brooklin	ME	G	207 359-2003	5818
Insulsafe Textiles Inc	Lewiston	ME	E	207 782-7011	6292
Maine Heritage Weavers	Monmouth	ME	F	207 933-2605	6449
Maine Woolens LLC	Brunswick	ME	E	207 725-7900	5841
Brand & Oppenheimer Co Inc **(PA)**	Portsmouth	RI	D	401 293-5500	20921
Kinder Industries Inc	Bristol	RI	F	401 253-7076	20087
Moore Company	Westerly	RI	C	401 596-2816	21534
P & B Fabrics Inc	Pawtucket	RI	F	800 351-9087	20872
Gordons Window Decor Inc **(PA)**	Williston	VT	F	802 655-7777	22671
Oshea Mary Lynn Weaving Studio	Middlebury	VT	G	802 545-2090	22117
Rihm Management Inc	Manchester Center	VT	G	802 867-5325	22089

2221 Silk & Man-Made Fiber

	CITY	ST	EMP	PHONE	ENTRY #
Cap-Tech Products Inc	Wethersfield	CT	F	860 490-5078	5243
Claremont Sales Corporation	Durham	CT	E	860 349-4499	1089
Deer Creek Fabrics Inc	Stamford	CT	G	203 964-0922	4188
Deitsch Plastic Company Inc	West Haven	CT	D	203 934-6601	5115
Dimension-Polyant Inc	Putnam	CT	E	860 928-8300	3610
Furs By Prezioso Ltd	Hamden	CT	G	203 230-2930	1750
G Thomas and Sons Inc	North Grosvenordale	CT	G	860 935-5174	2995
Nextec Applications Inc **(PA)**	Greenwich	CT	G	203 661-1484	1634
Noreaster Yachts Inc	Milford	CT	G	203 877-4339	2322
Peristere LLC	Manchester	CT	G	860 783-5301	2038
Sally Conant	Orange	CT	F	203 878-3005	3383
Second Lac Inc **(PA)**	Norwalk	CT	G	203 321-1221	3239
Swift Textile Metalizing LLC **(PA)**	Bloomfield	CT	D	860 243-1122	265
138 Barrows Street Realty Inc	Norton	MA	D	508 285-2904	14069
Anglo Silver Liner Co	Webster	MA	F	508 943-1440	16339
Astenjohnson Inc	Springfield	MA	C	413 733-6603	15448
Avcarb LLC	Lowell	MA	D	978 452-8961	12347
Brand & Oppenheimer Co Inc	Bedford	MA	E	781 271-0000	7965
Dawson Forte LLP	Westwood	MA	G	781 467-0170	16864
Deco Interior Finishes Inc	New Bedford	MA	G	508 994-9436	13378
E W Winship Ltd Inc	Nantucket	MA	G	508 228-1908	13223
Harodite Industries Inc **(PA)**	Taunton	MA	D	508 824-6961	15757
Kravet Inc	Boston	MA	G	617 428-0370	8655
Larsdale Inc **(PA)**	Ipswich	MA	D	978 356-9995	11928
Phoenix Trading Co Inc **(PA)**	Framingham	MA	G	617 794-8368	10994
Pwh Corporation	Haverhill	MA	E	978 373-9111	11463
Rosscommon Quilts Inc	Dorchester	MA	G	617 436-5848	10348
Sam Kasten Handweaver LLC	Lenox	MA	G	413 637-8900	12103
Sanderson-Macleod Incorporated	Palmer	MA	C	413 283-3481	14295
Steele Canvas Basket Corp	Chelsea	MA	E	800 541-8929	9970
US Bedding Inc	Fall River	MA	F	508 678-6988	10777
Whitecap Composites Inc	Peabody	MA	G	978 278-5718	14382
Auburn Manufacturing Inc **(PA)**	Mechanic Falls	ME	E	207 345-8271	6418
Duvaltex (us) Inc **(DH)**	Guilford	ME	C	207 873-3331	6157
Tex-Tech Industries Inc	North Monmouth	ME	C	207 933-4404	6512
Tex-Tech Industries Inc **(PA)**	Portland	ME	C	207 756-8606	6738
Albany International Corp **(PA)**	Rochester	NH	D	603 330-5850	19655
Albany International Corp	Rochester	NH	G	603 330-5993	19656
Amatex Corporation	Laconia	NH	E	603 524-2552	18556
Booth Felt Co Inc	Dover	NH	G	603 330-3334	18009
Cramer Fabrics Inc	Dover	NH	E	603 742-3838	18016
Duro-Fiber Co Inc	Hudson	NH	F	603 881-4200	18387
Pro Design & Manufacturing	Newton	NH	G	603 819-4131	19367
Saint-Gobain Abrasives Inc	Milford	NH	B	603 673-7560	19074
Warwick Mills Inc **(PA)**	New Ipswich	NH	C	603 291-1000	19311
Brand & Oppenheimer Co Inc **(PA)**	Portsmouth	RI	D	401 293-5500	20921
Crww Specialty Composites Inc	Hope Valley	RI	F	401 539-8555	20483
Darlington Fabrics Corporation	Westerly	RI	C	401 596-2816	21522
E A M T Inc	Woonsocket	RI	E	401 762-1500	21558
Natco Home Fashions Inc	West Warwick	RI	F	401 828-0300	21501
Natco Home Fashions Inc	West Warwick	RI	F	401 828-0300	21502
Natco Home Fashions Inc **(PA)**	West Warwick	RI	F	401 828-0300	21503
Nfa Corp	Cumberland	RI	B	401 333-8990	20333
Rosco Laboratories Inc	Central Falls	RI	G	401 725-6765	20124
Astenjohnson Inc	Williston	VT	D	802 658-2040	22655
Green Mountain Knitting Inc	Milton	VT	E	800 361-1190	22131
Oshea Mary Lynn Weaving Studio	Middlebury	VT	G	802 545-2090	22117

2231 Wool, Woven Fabric

	CITY	ST	EMP	PHONE	ENTRY #
Chas W House & Sons Inc	Unionville	CT	D	860 673-2518	4654
Dominics Decorating Inc	Norwalk	CT	G	203 838-1827	3141
138 Barrows Street Realty Inc	Norton	MA	D	508 285-2904	14069
E W Winship Ltd Inc	Nantucket	MA	G	508 228-1908	13223
Joseph Lotuff Sr	Ware	MA	E	413 967-5964	16234
Kravet Inc	Boston	MA	G	617 428-0370	8655
National Nonwovens Inc **(PA)**	Easthampton	MA	D	413 527-3445	10568
National Nonwovens Inc	Easthampton	MA	E	413 527-3445	10570
New England Fleece Company	Fall River	MA	G	508 678-5550	10738
Richmond Textiles Inc	South Grafton	MA	F	508 839-6600	15298
Swan Finishing Company Inc **(PA)**	Fall River	MA	C	508 674-4611	10767
Atlantic Blanket Company Inc	Northport	ME	E	207 338-9691	6520
Ramblers Way Farm Inc	Kennebunk	ME	E	888 793-9665	6240
Ramblers Way Farm Inc	Portland	ME	G	207 699-4600	6720
Robinson Manufacturing Co **(PA)**	Oxford	ME	F	207 539-4481	6572
U S Felt Company Inc	Sanford	ME	E	207 324-0063	6895
Custom Banner & Graphics LLC	Rochester	NH	G	603 332-2067	19666
Ramblers Way Farm Inc	Portsmouth	NH	G	603 319-5141	19612
Bouckaert Industrial Textiles	Woonsocket	RI	E	401 769-5474	21552
Brand & Oppenheimer Co Inc **(PA)**	Portsmouth	RI	D	401 293-5500	20921
Joseph C La Fond Co Inc	Manville	RI	F	401 769-3744	20609
Brookline Textiles Inc	Lower Waterford	VT	G	802 748-1933	22060
Johnson Woolen Mills LLC	Johnson	VT	E	802 635-2271	22050
Wild Wood Acres Alpacas Inc	Newfane	VT	G	802 365-7053	22188

2241 Fabric Mills, Cotton, Wool, Silk & Man-Made

	CITY	ST	EMP	PHONE	ENTRY #
Brockway Ferry Corporation **(PA)**	Essex	CT	G	860 767-8231	1394
H-O Products Corporation	Winsted	CT	E	860 379-9875	5412
National Ribbon LLC	Coventry	CT	G	860 742-6966	836
138 Barrows Street Realty Inc	Norton	MA	D	508 285-2904	14069
American Biltrite Inc **(PA)**	Wellesley	MA	G	781 237-6655	16359
Avila Textiles Inc	North Dighton	MA	G	508 828-5882	13929
Chase Corporation	Randolph	MA	E	781 963-2600	14673
Dial Fabrics Co Inc	Taunton	MA	E	508 822-5333	15742
E W Winship Ltd Inc	Nantucket	MA	G	508 228-1908	13223
Fringe Factory	New Bedford	MA	G	508 992-7563	13389
Gta-Nht Inc **(HQ)**	Rockland	MA	C	781 331-5900	14804
Julius Koch USA Inc	Mattapoisett	MA	D	508 995-9565	12887
Massasoit/Tackband Inc	Chicopee	MA	E	413 593-6731	10041
MM Reif Ltd	Boston	MA	D	617 442-9500	8708
Nutex Industries Inc	New Bedford	MA	E	508 993-2501	13431
Pepperell Braiding Company Inc **(PA)**	Pepperell	MA	E	978 433-2133	14444
Revolution Composites LLC	Norwood	MA	G	781 255-1111	14196
RI Knitting Co Inc	Taunton	MA	E	508 822-5333	15780
Sam Kasten Handweaver LLC	Lenox	MA	G	413 637-8900	12103
Tweave LLC	Fall River	MA	E	508 285-6701	10774
United Stretch Design Corp	Hudson	MA	E	978 562-7781	11824
Vulplex Incorporated	New Bedford	MA	E	508 996-6787	13458
Auburn Manufacturing Inc **(PA)**	Mechanic Falls	ME	E	207 345-8271	6418
Bell Manufacturing Co	Lewiston	ME	D	207 784-2961	6276
Sml Inc	Lewiston	ME	E	207 784-2961	6324
Spectrum Marketing Dbalogo Loc	Manchester	NH	G	603 644-4800	18928
Velcro Inc **(HQ)**	Manchester	NH	A	603 669-4880	18948
Velcro USA Inc **(DH)**	Manchester	NH	A	603 669-4880	18949
Conneaut Industries Inc	West Greenwich	RI	D	401 392-1110	21454
Conrad-Jarvis Corp	Pawtucket	RI	D	401 722-8700	20824
Global Engineered Mtls Corp	Manville	RI	G	401 725-2100	20608
Graco Awards Manufacturing Inc	Providence	RI	E	281 255-2161	21021
K & W Webbing Company Inc	Central Falls	RI	F	401 725-4441	20117
Leedon Webbing Co Inc	Central Falls	RI	E	401 722-1043	20119
Moore Company **(PA)**	Westerly	RI	C	401 596-2816	21531
Moore Company	Westerly	RI	C	401 596-2816	21532
Murdock Webbing Company Inc **(PA)**	Central Falls	RI	C	401 724-3000	20121
Nfa Corp	Cumberland	RI	B	401 333-8947	20331
Nfa Corp	Cumberland	RI	E	401 333-8990	20332
Nfa Corp	Cumberland	RI	B	401 333-8990	20334
North East Knitting Inc	Pawtucket	RI	C	401 727-0500	20869
Providence Braid Company	Pawtucket	RI	E	401 722-2120	20885
Stretch Products Corp	Pawtucket	RI	E	401 722-0400	20900
Texcel Industries Inc	Cumberland	RI	E	401 727-2113	20348
Garflex Inc	Brattleboro	VT	D	802 257-5256	21728

2251 Hosiery, Women's Full & Knee Length

	CITY	ST	EMP	PHONE	ENTRY #
Footsox Inc	Gloucester	MA	G	800 338-0833	11183

2252 Hosiery, Except Women's

	CITY	ST	EMP	PHONE	ENTRY #
Shock Sock Inc LLC	Farmington	CT	G	860 680-7252	1512
Soldier Socks	Stamford	CT	G	203 832-2005	4324
Tommy LLC Sock It	Windsor	CT	G	860 688-2019	5375
Lost Sock Corporation	North Reading	MA	G	978 664-0730	13986
Mvk Silt Sock	Rowley	MA	G	978 204-9483	14860
Socks For Siberia Inc	Brookfield	MA	G	774 200-1617	9192
Sock Shack	Portland	ME	G	207 805-1348	6731
Secret Sock Society	Franconia	NH	G	603 443-3208	18154
Eurosocks North America Inc	Warwick	RI	G	401 739-6500	21362

2253 Knit Outerwear Mills

	CITY	ST	EMP	PHONE	ENTRY #
Kielo America Inc	Ridgefield	CT	G	203 431-3999	3671
Ahead LLC	New Bedford	MA	B	508 985-9898	13354
Alps Sportswear Mfg Co Inc	Natick	MA	E	978 685-5159	13233
Douglas DK Company Incorporate	Longmeadow	MA	G	413 567-8572	12332
Egyptian Cotton Tshirts LLC	Burlington	MA	G	781 272-7922	9261
Evergreen Enterprises Inc	Berkley	MA	G	508 823-2377	8086
Legends & Heroes	Sudbury	MA	E	617 571-6990	15662
New England Shirt Co LLC	Fall River	MA	G	508 672-2223	10739
Northeast Knitting Mills Inc **(PA)**	Fall River	MA	E	508 678-7553	10741
Pvh Corp	Wrentham	MA	F	508 384-0070	17527
River Falls Manufacturing Co	Fall River	MA	D	508 646-2900	10759
Russell Brands LLC	Holyoke	MA	G	413 735-1400	11653
Tamboo Bistro	Brockton	MA	G	508 584-8585	9181
Babtech Inc	Rockland	ME	G	207 594-7106	6784
Hanesbrands Inc	Merrimack	NH	F	603 424-6737	19006
Mountain Corporation	Marlborough	NH	D	603 876-3630	18963
Mountain Corporation **(PA)**	Keene	NH	C	603 355-2272	18517
Red Fish-Blue Fish Dye Works	Somersworth	NH	F	603 692-3900	19846
Shirt Out of Luck LLC	Salem	NH	G	603 898-9002	19767
Mister Sister	Providence	RI	G	401 421-6969	21069
Kneebinding Inc	Stowe	VT	G	802 760-3026	22522

2254 Knit Underwear Mills

	CITY	ST	EMP	PHONE	ENTRY #
Blvd Graphix	Limestone	ME	G	207 325-2583	6339

2257 Circular Knit Fabric Mills

	CITY	ST	EMP	PHONE	ENTRY #
Swift Textile Metalizing LLC **(PA)**	Bloomfield	CT	D	860 243-1122	265
Draper Knitting Company Inc	Canton	MA	E	781 828-0029	9728
Nfa Corp	Cumberland	RI	B	401 333-8990	20334

2258 Lace & Warp Knit Fabric Mills

	CITY	ST	EMP	PHONE	ENTRY #
Novelty Textile Mills LLC	Waterford	CT	G	860 774-5000	4990
Charbert Inc	Chestnut Hill	MA	C	401 364-7751	9984
Frontier Manufacturing Inc	Pawtucket	RI	G	401 722-0852	20841
Leavers Lace Corporation **(PA)**	West Greenwich	RI	F	401 397-5555	21461
Leavers Lace Corporation	West Warwick	RI	F	401 828-8117	21499
Maguire Lace & Warping Inc	Coventry	RI	G	401 821-1290	20154
Midland Co Inc	Coventry	RI	G	401 397-4425	20156
Moore Company **(PA)**	Westerly	RI	C	401 596-2816	21531
Moore Company	Westerly	RI	C	401 596-2816	21532
Moore Company	Westerly	RI	C	401 596-0219	21533
Moore Company	Westerly	RI	C	401 596-2816	21534
Garflex Inc	Brattleboro	VT	D	802 257-5256	21728

2259 Knitting Mills, NEC

	CITY	ST	EMP	PHONE	ENTRY #
Stevens Linen Associates Inc	Dudley	MA	D	508 943-0813	10387
Giral LLC	Burlington	VT	G	802 238-7852	21787

2261 Cotton Fabric Finishers

	CITY	ST	EMP	PHONE	ENTRY #
To Give Is Better	Bristol	CT	G	860 261-5443	618
Ultimate Ink LLC	Wilton	CT	G	203 762-0602	5309
Action Apparel Inc **(PA)**	Stoneham	MA	F	781 224-0777	15552
Brand & Oppenheimer Co Inc	Bedford	MA	E	781 271-0000	7965
Dasein Inc	Winchester	MA	G	781 756-0380	17086
Emco Services Inc	Fall River	MA	G	508 674-5504	10688
Gonco Inc **(PA)**	Sandwich	MA	G	508 833-3900	14968
Hendrickson Advertising Inc	Sterling	MA	G	978 422-8087	15539
Lawrence Textile Inc	Lawrence	MA	G	978 689-4355	12047
Majilite Corporation	Dracut	MA	D	978 441-6800	10363
Middlesex Research Mfg Co Inc	Hudson	MA	E	978 562-3697	11793
Pacific Printing Inc	Northampton	MA	G	413 585-5700	14016
Silver Screen Design Inc	Greenfield	MA	F	413 773-1692	11275
Starensier Inc **(PA)**	Byfield	MA	F	978 462-7311	9365
Swan Finishing Company Inc **(PA)**	Fall River	MA	C	508 674-4611	10767
Tls International LLC	Needham	MA	G	781 449-4454	13315
Tyca Corporation **(PA)**	Clinton	MA	E	978 612-0002	10094
Gemini Firfield Screenprinting	Keene	NH	G	603 357-3847	18505
Life Is Good Wholesale Inc	Hudson	NH	D	603 594-6100	18412
Liquid Blue Inc	Derry	NH	D	401 333-6200	17987
Screen Printed Special TS	Manchester	NH	G	603 622-2901	18919
Cranston Print Works Company **(PA)**	Cranston	RI	E	401 943-4800	20202
Cranston Print Works Company	Cranston	RI	E	800 525-0595	20203
Cranston Print Works Company	West Greenwich	RI	E	401 397-2442	21455
Dee Kay Designs Inc **(PA)**	Hope Valley	RI	D	401 539-2400	20484
Palisades Ltd	Peace Dale	RI	E	401 789-0295	20915

2262 Silk & Man-Made Fabric Finishers

	CITY	ST	EMP	PHONE	ENTRY #
Nextec Applications Inc **(PA)**	Greenwich	CT	G	203 661-1484	1634
Tees & More LLC	Hartford	CT	G	860 244-2224	1876
Yankee Screen Printing	Derby	CT	G	203 924-9926	1085
Fosters Promotional Goods	Marblehead	MA	F	781 631-3824	12683
Gloucester Graphics Inc **(PA)**	Gloucester	MA	F	978 281-4500	11188
Majilite Manufacturing Inc	Dracut	MA	D	978 441-6800	10364
Pacific Printing Inc	Northampton	MA	G	413 585-5700	14016
Repro Craft Inc	Chicopee	MA	G	413 533-4937	10057
Serigraphics Unlimited	Rowley	MA	G	978 356-4896	14866
Starensier Inc **(PA)**	Byfield	MA	F	978 462-7311	9365
Stevens Linen Associates Inc	Dudley	MA	D	508 943-0813	10387
Swan Finishing Company Inc **(PA)**	Fall River	MA	C	508 674-4611	10767
T-Shirts N Jeans Inc	Danvers	MA	G	781 279-4220	10260
Auburn Manufacturing Inc	Mechanic Falls	ME	E	207 345-8271	6417
Auburn Manufacturing Inc **(PA)**	Mechanic Falls	ME	E	207 345-8271	6418
Commercial Screenprint EMB Inc	Bangor	ME	G	207 942-2862	5639
Better Life LLC	Manchester	NH	G	603 647-0077	18787
First Impressions Embroidery	Hooksett	NH	G	603 606-1400	18350
Hammar & Sons Inc	Pelham	NH	E	603 635-2292	19434
Jembow Inc	Bow	NH	G	603 774-6055	17717
My-T-Man Screen Printing Inc	Manchester	NH	F	603 622-7740	18881
Cooley Incorporated **(HQ)**	Pawtucket	RI	C	401 724-9000	20825
Cranston Print Works Company **(PA)**	Cranston	RI	E	401 943-4800	20202
Cranston Print Works Company	Cranston	RI	E	800 525-0595	20203
Cranston Print Works Company	West Greenwich	RI	E	401 397-2442	21455
Kenyon Industries Inc	Kenyon	RI	B	401 364-7761	20548
Palisades Ltd	Peace Dale	RI	E	401 789-0295	20915
Tex Flock Inc	Woonsocket	RI	E	401 765-2340	21586

2269 Textile Finishers, NEC

	CITY	ST	EMP	PHONE	ENTRY #
Brookwood Laminating Inc	Wauregan	CT	D	860 774-5001	5038
Gorilla Graphics Inc	Middletown	CT	F	860 704-8208	2187
Grand Embroidery Inc	Oxford	CT	F	203 888-7484	3406
Sterling Name Tape Company	Winsted	CT	G	860 379-5142	5426
Berkshire Corporation **(HQ)**	Great Barrington	MA	E	413 528-2602	11233
Brittany Global Tech Corp	New Bedford	MA	D	508 999-3281	13365
Conntext Labels	Great Barrington	MA	G	413 528-3303	11237
Nova Idea Inc	Woburn	MA	G	781 281-2183	17246
Screenco Printing Inc	Newburyport	MA	G	978 465-1211	13533
Stevens Linen Associates Inc	Dudley	MA	D	508 943-0813	10387
Web Industries Inc **(PA)**	Marlborough	MA	G	508 898-2988	12848
Albany Engnered Composites Inc	Rochester	NH	D	603 330-5851	19651
Albany Engnered Composites Inc	Rochester	NH	F	603 330-5993	19652
Albany Engnered Composites Inc	Rochester	NH	E	603 330-5800	19653
Albany Engnered Composites Inc **(HQ)**	Rochester	NH	C	603 330-5800	19654
Custom Banner & Graphics LLC	Rochester	NH	G	603 332-2067	19666
Capeway Yarns Inc	Tiverton	RI	G	401 624-1311	21253
Dee Kay Designs Inc **(PA)**	Hope Valley	RI	D	401 539-2400	20484
Kenyon Industries Inc	Kenyon	RI	B	401 364-7761	20548
Palisades Ltd	Peace Dale	RI	E	401 789-0295	20915

2273 Carpets & Rugs

	CITY	ST	EMP	PHONE	ENTRY #
Aj Mfg	Thompson	CT	G	860 963-7622	4530
American Veteran Textile LLC	Ansonia	CT	G	203 583-0576	6
Apricot Home LLC	Greenwich	CT	G	203 552-1791	1593
Holland & Sherry Inc **(PA)**	Norwalk	CT	F	212 628-1950	3169
Mohawk Industries Inc	Danbury	CT	C	203 739-0260	956
Mohawk Industries Inc	Torrington	CT	G	706 629-7721	4588
New Haven Companies Inc	East Haven	CT	F	203 469-6421	1257
Rugsalecom LLC	West Hartford	CT	G	860 756-0959	5094
Bentley Mills Inc	Boston	MA	G	617 439-0405	8401
Cape Cod Braided Rug Co Inc	Marstons Mills	MA	F	508 432-3133	12872
Cape Cod Drmats of Distinction	Hyannis	MA	E	508 790-0070	11836
Delaware Valley Corp	Tewksbury	MA	E	978 459-6932	15814
ICP Construction Inc	Andover	MA	G	508 829-0035	7557
Julie Industries Inc **(PA)**	Andover	MA	G	978 276-0820	7560
Medallion Gallery Inc	Boston	MA	G	617 236-8283	8692
Merida LLC	Fall River	MA	E	508 675-6572	10731
Mohawk Industries Inc	Walpole	MA	C	508 660-8935	16003
Sam Kasten Handweaver LLC	Lenox	MA	G	413 637-8900	12103
Stevens Linen Associates Inc	Dudley	MA	D	508 943-0813	10387
TMI Industries Inc	Palmer	MA	E	413 283-9021	14297
Weymouth Braided Rug Co Inc	North Oxford	MA	G	508 987-8525	13976
Flemish Master Weavers Inc	Sanford	ME	E	207 324-6600	6876
Colonial Mills Inc	Rumford	RI	D	401 724-6279	21183
East Providence Mohawks	East Providence	RI	G	401 829-1411	20409
Natco Products Corporation **(PA)**	West Warwick	RI	B	401 828-0300	21504
Rhody Rug Inc	Lincoln	RI	F	401 728-5903	20594
Robin Industries Inc	Bristol	RI	D	401 253-8350	20101

2281 Yarn Spinning Mills

	CITY	ST	EMP	PHONE	ENTRY #
Buffalo Industrial Fabrics Inc	Wilton	CT	G	203 553-9400	5282

SIC

Employee Codes: A=Over 500 employees, B=251-500
C=101-250, D=51-100 E=20-50, F=10-19, G=3-9

	CITY	ST	EMP	PHONE	ENTRY #
Robertson-Chase Fibers LLC	North Billerica	MA	F	978 453-2837	13862
S & D Spinning Mill Inc	Millbury	MA	E	508 865-2267	13175
St Regis Sportswear Ltd	North Andover	MA	G	518 725-6767	13729
Family Yarns Inc	Etna	ME	G	207 269-3852	6025
Jagger Brothers	Springvale	ME	E	207 324-5622	7053
Worsted Spinning Neng LLC	Springvale	ME	G	207 324-5622	7056
Harrisville Designs Inc **(PA)**	Harrisville	NH	G	603 827-3333	18302
Conneaut Industries Inc	West Greenwich	RI	D	401 392-1110	21454
D & T Spinning Inc	South Woodstock	VT	D	802 228-2925	22497
Green Mountain Spinnery Inc	East Dummerston	VT	F	802 387-4528	21919

2282 Yarn Texturizing, Throwing, Twisting & Winding Mills

	CITY	ST	EMP	PHONE	ENTRY #
Archerdx Inc	Beverly	MA	D	978 232-3570	8101
New England Water Jet Cutting	New Bedford	MA	G	508 993-9235	13425
Windle Industries Inc	Sutton	MA	F	508 865-5773	15696
Conneaut Industries Inc	West Greenwich	RI	D	401 392-1110	21454

2284 Thread Mills

	CITY	ST	EMP	PHONE	ENTRY #
J Arnold Mittleman	Middletown	CT	E	860 346-6562	2192
Dhm Thread Corporation	Fall River	MA	F	508 672-0032	10682
Erich Husemoller Import & Expo	Easthampton	MA	G	413 585-9855	10563
New Bedford Thread Co Inc	Fairhaven	MA	E	508 996-8584	10644
Pacific Printing Inc	Northampton	MA	G	413 585-5700	14016
Hilco Athletic & Graphics Inc	West Warwick	RI	F	401 822-1775	21495

2295 Fabrics Coated Not Rubberized

	CITY	ST	EMP	PHONE	ENTRY #
Advanced Def Slutions Tech LLC	Bloomfield	CT	G	860 243-1122	199
Au New Haven LLC	New Haven	CT	C	203 468-0342	2662
Brookwood Laminating Inc	Wauregan	CT	D	860 774-5001	5038
Deitsch Plastic Company Inc	West Haven	CT	D	203 934-6601	5115
Nextec Applications Inc **(PA)**	Greenwich	CT	G	203 661-1484	1634
Park Advnced Cmposite Mtls Inc	Waterbury	CT	D	203 755-1344	4936
Second Lac Inc **(PA)**	Norwalk	CT	G	203 321-1221	3239
Swift Textile Metalizing LLC **(PA)**	Bloomfield	CT	D	860 243-1122	265
Trelleborg Ctd Systems US Inc	New Haven	CT	C	203 468-0342	2747
Allied Resin Technologies LLC	Leominster	MA	G	978 401-2267	12112
Bennett Goding & Cooper Inc	Waltham	MA	G	978 682-8868	16046
Bradford Coatings Inc	Lowell	MA	D	978 459-4100	12354
Clark Hammerbeam Corporation	Dedham	MA	E	781 461-1946	10283
Coaters Inc	New Bedford	MA	E	508 996-5700	13372
Custom Metal Fabrication	Leeds	MA	G	413 584-8200	12098
Dela Incorporated **(PA)**	Haverhill	MA	E	978 372-7783	11424
Flame Laminating Corporation **(PA)**	North Andover	MA	F	978 725-9527	13705
Foamtech LLC	Fitchburg	MA	F	978 343-4022	10827
Gta-Nht Inc **(HQ)**	Rockland	MA	C	781 331-5900	14804
Haartz Corporation **(PA)**	Acton	MA	B	978 264-2600	7359
Hardwick Laminators Inc	Gilbertville	MA	G	413 477-6600	11154
Industrial Polymers & Chem Inc **(PA)**	Shrewsbury	MA	E	508 845-6112	15117
Ipac Fabrics Inc	Shrewsbury	MA	G	508 845-6112	15119
Laminating Coating Tech Inc	Monson	MA	D	413 267-4808	13208
Majilite Corporation	Dracut	MA	D	978 441-6800	10363
Middlesex Research Mfg Co Inc	Hudson	MA	E	978 562-3697	11793
Miles Kedex Co Inc	Westminster	MA	E	978 874-1403	16810
Pascale Industries Inc	Fall River	MA	E	508 673-3307	10745
Polar Focus Inc	South Deerfield	MA	G	413 665-2044	15253
Shawmut LLC **(PA)**	West Bridgewater	MA	C	508 588-3300	16453
Sika Sarnafil Inc **(HQ)**	Canton	MA	C	781 828-5400	9780
Starensier Inc **(PA)**	Byfield	MA	F	978 462-7311	9365
Teknor Apex Elastomers Inc	Leominster	MA	D	978 466-5344	12193
Tpi Industries LLC	West Bridgewater	MA	G	508 588-3300	16460
Vulplex Incorporated	New Bedford	MA	E	508 996-6787	13458
Whitecap Composites Inc	Peabody	MA	G	978 278-5718	14382
Auburn Manufacturing Inc **(PA)**	Mechanic Falls	ME	E	207 345-8271	6418
Junora Ltd	Biddeford	ME	G	207 284-4900	5741
Jaeger Usa Inc	Rochester	NH	F	603 332-5816	19674
Regal Sleeving & Tubing LLC	Somersworth	NH	E	603 659-5555	19847
Textiles Coated Incorporated	Manchester	NH	C	603 296-2221	18940
Textiles Coated Incorporated **(PA)**	Londonderry	NH	D	603 296-2221	18741
Wf Holdings Inc **(PA)**	Nashua	NH	G	603 888-5443	19285
Worthen Industries Inc	Nashua	NH	F	603 886-0973	19289
Braided Products Company	Riverside	RI	G	401 434-0300	21165
Bruin Plastics Co Inc	Glendale	RI	E	401 568-3081	20459
Cooley Incorporated **(HQ)**	Pawtucket	RI	C	401 724-9000	20825
Cooley Incorporated	Cranston	RI	E	401 721-6374	20200
Kenyon Industries Inc	Kenyon	RI	B	401 364-7761	20548
Tex Flock Inc	Woonsocket	RI	E	401 765-2340	21586
Leo D Bernstein and Sons Inc	Shaftsbury	VT	C	212 337-9578	22405

2296 Tire Cord & Fabric

	CITY	ST	EMP	PHONE	ENTRY #
United Abrasives Inc **(PA)**	North Windham	CT	B	860 456-7131	3084
Alvin Johnson	East Longmeadow	MA	G	413 525-6334	10465

2297 Fabrics, Nonwoven

	CITY	ST	EMP	PHONE	ENTRY #
Lydall Inc **(PA)**	Manchester	CT	E	860 646-1233	2021
Lydall Thermal Acoustical Inc	Manchester	CT	G	860 646-1233	2022
New England Nonwovens LLC	West Haven	CT	F	203 891-0851	5137
Suominen US Holding Inc **(HQ)**	East Windsor	CT	F	860 386-8001	1306
Swift Textile Metalizing LLC **(PA)**	Bloomfield	CT	D	860 243-1122	265
Windsor Locks Nonwovens Inc **(DH)**	East Windsor	CT	E	860 292-5600	1311
Xamax Industries Inc	Seymour	CT	E	203 888-7200	3769
Delaware Valley Corp	Tewksbury	MA	E	978 459-6932	15814
Draper Knitting Company Inc	Canton	MA	E	781 828-0029	9728
Georgia-Pacific LLC	Leominster	MA	C	978 537-4701	12144
Hollingsworth & Vose Company **(PA)**	East Walpole	MA	C	508 850-2000	10524
National Nonwovens Inc **(PA)**	Easthampton	MA	D	413 527-3445	10568
National Nonwovens Inc	Easthampton	MA	E	413 527-3445	10570
Neenah Technical Materials	Pittsfield	MA	G	413 684-7488	14494
Nonwovens Inc	North Chelmsford	MA	F	978 251-8612	13905
Pwh Corporation	Haverhill	MA	E	978 373-9111	11463
Vulplex Incorporated	New Bedford	MA	E	508 996-6787	13458
Insulsafe Textiles Inc	Lewiston	ME	E	207 782-7011	6292
Scotia Company	Lewiston	ME	G	207 782-3824	6321
Booth Felt Co Inc	Dover	NH	G	603 330-3334	18009
Cramer Fabrics Inc	Dover	NH	E	603 742-3838	18016
Northeastern Nonwovens Inc	Rochester	NH	E	603 332-5900	19680
Rontex America Inc	Amherst	NH	E	603 883-5076	17586
E A M T Inc	Woonsocket	RI	E	401 762-1500	21558

2298 Cordage & Twine

	CITY	ST	EMP	PHONE	ENTRY #
Brownell & Company Inc **(PA)**	Moodus	CT	F	860 873-8625	2423
Detotec North America Inc	Moosup	CT	G	860 230-0078	2425
Detotec North America Inc	Sterling	CT	G	860 564-1012	4366
International Cordage East Ltd	Colchester	CT	D	860 873-5000	804
Loos & Co Inc **(PA)**	Pomfret	CT	B	860 928-7981	3552
Nca Inc	Abington	CT	G	860 974-2310	1
Woodstock Line Co	Putnam	CT	F	860 928-6557	3641
Artcraft Braid Co LLC	Hudson	MA	E	401 831-9077	11757
Dhm Thread Corporation	Fall River	MA	F	508 672-0032	10682
Heinrich LLC	Waltham	MA	G	781 891-9591	16125
I & I Sling Inc	Norwood	MA	D	781 575-0600	14159
Its A Corker	Winchester	MA	G	781 729-9630	17089
John E Ruggles & Co	New Bedford	MA	G	508 992-9766	13400
Julius Koch USA Inc	Mattapoisett	MA	D	508 995-9565	12887
Link Enterprises Corp	Northampton	MA	G	413 585-9869	14010
Pepperell Braiding Company Inc **(PA)**	Pepperell	MA	E	978 433-2133	14444
Photonic Systems Inc	Billerica	MA	F	978 670-4990	8275
Tauten Inc	Beverly	MA	G	978 961-3272	8186
Teufelberger Fiber Rope Corp	Fall River	MA	C	508 678-8200	10772
Advanced Indus Solutions Inc	Waldoboro	ME	E	207 832-0569	7129
Auburn Manufacturing Inc **(PA)**	Mechanic Falls	ME	E	207 345-8271	6418
David Bird LLC	Waldoboro	ME	F	207 832-0569	7132
Highliner Rope Co LLC	Saint George	ME	G	207 372-6300	6869
Orion Ropeworks Inc **(PA)**	Winslow	ME	E	207 877-2224	7273
Rope Co LLC	Spruce Head	ME	G	207 838-4358	7057
Sterling Rope Company Inc	Biddeford	ME	G	207 885-0033	5765
Yale Cordage Inc	Saco	ME	D	207 282-3396	6863
Calling All Cargo LLC	Dover	NH	F	603 740-1900	18011
Marmon Utility	Milford	NH	G	603 249-1302	19068
Two In One Manufacturing Inc	Nashua	NH	E	603 595-8212	19276
Anacko Cordage Co	Narragansett	RI	G	401 792-3936	20634
Ashaway Line & Twine Mfg Co	Ashaway	RI	D	401 377-2221	20031
Frank B Struzik Inc	Woonsocket	RI	F	401 766-6880	21563
Jonathan Knight	Wakefield	RI	G	401 263-3671	21273
Lrv Properties LLC	Providence	RI	G	401 714-7001	21058
New England Overseas Corp	Pawtucket	RI	F	401 722-3800	20867

2299 Textile Goods, NEC

	CITY	ST	EMP	PHONE	ENTRY #
A & P Coat Apron & Lin Sup Inc	Hartford	CT	D	914 840-3200	1799
Advanced Linen Group	Milford	CT	F	203 877-3896	2236
New Haven Companies Inc	East Haven	CT	F	203 469-6421	1257
Dek Tillett Ltd	Sheffield	MA	G	413 229-8764	15059
FTC Enterprise Inc	East Bridgewater	MA	F	508 378-2799	10413
Full Circle Padding Inc	Norton	MA	F	508 285-2500	14077
Gilbride Enterprises LLC	Lowell	MA	G	978 452-0878	12375
Joan Fabrics LLC	Lowell	MA	G	978 454-3777	12386
Lenis Inc	Canton	MA	G	781 401-3273	9752
National Nonwovens Inc	Easthampton	MA	E	413 527-3445	10569
Polartec LLC **(PA)**	Andover	MA	A	978 659-5109	7585
Spectro Coating Corp	Leominster	MA	E	978 534-6191	12188
Spectro Coating Corp **(PA)**	Leominster	MA	D	978 534-1800	12189
Strickland K Wheelock	Uxbridge	MA	G	508 265-2896	15930
United Industrial Tex Pdts Inc **(PA)**	West Springfield	MA	E	413 737-0095	16559
United Industrial Tex Pdts Inc	West Springfield	MA	G	413 737-0095	16560
Windle Industries Inc	Sutton	MA	F	508 865-5773	15696
Best Felts Inc	Thomaston	ME	F	207 596-0566	7081
Fiber Materials Inc **(HQ)**	Biddeford	ME	E	207 282-5911	5733
Globeco Maine LLC	Scarborough	ME	G	207 809-2671	6921
Hair Studio At Lafayette	Kennebunk	ME	G	207 604-5005	6235
Kws Inc	Waldoboro	ME	G	207 832-5095	7133
Maine Balsam Fir Prodcts	West Paris	ME	F	207 674-5090	7176
Roxanne L Tardie	Ashland	ME	G	207 540-4945	5540
Sea Bags LLC **(PA)**	Portland	ME	E	207 780-0744	6724
True Guilford Inc	Guilford	ME	G	207 876-3331	6162

	CITY	ST	EMP	PHONE	ENTRY #
American Bacon Boston Felt Inc	Rochester	NH	E	603 332-7000	19658
Booth Felt Co Inc	Dover	NH	G	603 330-3334	18009
Carbon Felt Inc	Claremont	NH	F	603 542-0202	17840
Jackson Bond Enterprises LLC	Dover	NH	G	603 742-2350	18032
S M Services Inc	Nashua	NH	G	603 883-3381	19256
Specialty Textile Products LLC	Dover	NH	F	603 330-3334	18053
Textiles Coated Incorporated **(PA)**	Londonderry	NH	D	603 296-2221	18741
E A M T Inc	Woonsocket	RI	E	401 762-1500	21558
National Velour Corporation	Warwick	RI	E	401 737-8300	21394
Smart Textile Products LLC	Warwick	RI	G	401 427-1374	21426
Tex Flock Inc	Woonsocket	RI	E	401 765-2340	21586
Cornell Online LLC	Burlington	VT	E	802 448-3281	21776

23 APPAREL AND OTHER FINISHED PRODUCTS MADE FROM FABRICS AND SIMILAR MATERIAL

2311 Men's & Boys' Suits, Coats & Overcoats

	CITY	ST	EMP	PHONE	ENTRY #
Bayer Clothing Group Inc **(PA)**	Greenwich	CT	D	203 661-4140	1599
Corinth Acquisition Corp **(PA)**	Stamford	CT	G	203 504-6260	4174
Sassone Labwear LLC	Bridgeport	CT	G	860 666-4484	485
Charles River Apparel Inc	Sharon	MA	D	781 793-5300	15047
Ja Apparel Corp	New Bedford	MA	G	580 990-4580	13399
Joseph Abboud Mfg Corp **(DH)**	New Bedford	MA	B	508 999-1301	13401
Joseph Abboud Mfg Corp	New Bedford	MA	G	508 961-1726	13402
Neptune Garment Company	Boston	MA	D	617 482-3980	8722
Southwick Clothing LLC **(HQ)**	Haverhill	MA	C	800 634-5312	11472
Sterlingwear of Boston Inc	Boston	MA	C	617 567-6465	8866
Sterlingwear of Boston Inc **(PA)**	Boston	MA	D	617 567-2100	8865
Woolrich Inc	Boston	MA	G	857 263-7554	8932
Creative Apparel Assoc LLC	Dover Foxcroft	ME	E	207 564-0235	5960
Tom James Company	Hampton	NH	F	603 601-6944	18274
Gerard R Davis Ltd	North Smithfield	RI	G	401 766-8760	20787
Our Place - Shop For Men Inc **(PA)**	North Providence	RI	G	401 231-2370	20769
Professional Images Inc	Pawtucket	RI	G	401 725-7000	20884
Sperian Protection Usa Inc **(DH)**	Smithfield	RI	E	401 232-1200	21250

2321 Men's & Boys' Shirts

	CITY	ST	EMP	PHONE	ENTRY #
MB Sport LLC **(PA)**	New Canaan	CT	F	203 966-1985	2605
16sur20 Management LLC	Lenox	MA	F	413 637-5061	12099
Acme Merchandise and AP Inc	Gloucester	MA	E	978 282-4800	11158
Kathy Clark	Natick	MA	G	508 655-3666	13263
New Balance Athletics Inc **(HQ)**	Boston	MA	B	617 783-4000	8727
Pickwick	Scituate	MA	G	781 545-0884	15010
Pvh Corp	Wrentham	MA	F	508 384-0070	17527
Pvh Corp	Chatham	MA	G	508 945-4063	9863
Shop Therapy Imports	Provincetown	MA	G	508 487-8970	14609
Imeldas Fabrics & Designs	New Sharon	ME	G	207 778-0665	6476
Mountain Tops Custom T-Shirts **(PA)**	Arundel	ME	G	207 985-1919	5534
Timberland LLC **(HQ)**	Stratham	NH	B	603 772-9500	19876
Halbro America Inc	East Providence	RI	G	401 438-2727	20418
Ibex Outdoor Clothing LLC	White River Junction	VT	E	802 359-4239	22639

2322 Men's & Boys' Underwear & Nightwear

	CITY	ST	EMP	PHONE	ENTRY #
L L Bean Inc	Brunswick	ME	B	207 725-0300	5840

2323 Men's & Boys' Neckwear

	CITY	ST	EMP	PHONE	ENTRY #
Xmi Corporation	Greenwich	CT	G	800 838-0424	1662
Foster-Miller Inc	Devens	MA	D	781 684-4000	10320
Grande Brothers Inc	West Roxbury	MA	G	617 323-6169	16496
New York Accessory Group Inc	Bristol	RI	D	401 245-6096	20095
Btl Holdings LLC	Middlebury	VT	E	917 596-3660	22105

2325 Men's & Boys' Separate Trousers & Casual Slacks

	CITY	ST	EMP	PHONE	ENTRY #
Bayer Clothing Group Inc **(PA)**	Greenwich	CT	D	203 661-4140	1599
16sur20 Management LLC	Lenox	MA	F	413 637-5061	12099
American Power Source Inc **(PA)**	Fall River	MA	C	508 672-8847	10657
Guess Inc	Braintree	MA	E	781 843-3147	9014
Southwick Clothing LLC **(HQ)**	Haverhill	MA	C	800 634-5312	11472
Timberland LLC **(HQ)**	Stratham	NH	B	603 772-9500	19876

2326 Men's & Boys' Work Clothing

	CITY	ST	EMP	PHONE	ENTRY #
A Gerber Corp	Stamford	CT	G	203 918-1913	4123
Cintas Corporation	Cheshire	CT	F	203 272-2036	722
G&K Services LLC	Hartford	CT	G	860 856-4400	1823
Sassone Labwear LLC	Bridgeport	CT	G	860 666-4484	485
Sewn In America Inc **(PA)**	Ridgefield	CT	D	203 438-9149	3683
Ideal Bias Binding Corp	Marion	MA	G	508 748-2712	12698
Madewell Manufacturing Co Inc	New Bedford	MA	G	508 997-0768	13414
Outlast Uniform Corporation	Chelsea	MA	G	617 889-0510	9962
Salk Company Inc	Allston	MA	E	617 782-4030	7474
Theatre Stricken Apparel LLC	Bellingham	MA	G	978 325-2335	8060
Tyca Corporation **(PA)**	Clinton	MA	E	978 612-0002	10094
W D C Holdings Inc	Attleboro	MA	D	508 699-4412	7806
Ad M Holdings LLC	Trenton	ME	F	207 667-9696	7096
Cintas Corporation	Bangor	ME	G	207 307-2448	5636

	CITY	ST	EMP	PHONE	ENTRY #
Izzy Industries Inc	Pembroke	NH	F	603 219-0596	19458
Labonville Inc	Gorham	NH	E	603 752-3221	18214
Nitefighter International	Silver Lake	NH	G	603 367-4741	19824
Codet-Newport Corporation **(HQ)**	Newport	VT	F	802 334-5811	22192

2329 Men's & Boys' Clothing, NEC

	CITY	ST	EMP	PHONE	ENTRY #
Custom Sportswear Mfg	Wolcott	CT	G	203 879-4420	5437
Cycling Sports Group Inc **(HQ)**	Wilton	CT	D	608 268-8916	5286
Del Arbour LLC	Milford	CT	F	203 882-8501	2274
Everest Isles LLC	Wallingford	CT	G	203 561-5128	4739
Gg Sportswear Inc	Hartford	CT	E	860 296-4441	1825
Gima LLC	Hartford	CT	E	860 296-4441	1826
Nomis Enterprises	Wallingford	CT	G	631 821-3120	4778
Tribal Wear	Riverside	CT	G	203 637-7884	3691
Turq LLC	Riverside	CT	G	203 344-1257	3692
16sur20 Management LLC	Lenox	MA	F	413 637-5061	12099
Collegiate Uniforms Inc	Medford	MA	G	781 219-4952	12927
Companystuffcom Inc	Ipswich	MA	G	978 282-1525	11913
Custom Crafted Enterprises	North Attleboro	MA	G	508 695-2878	13754
Custom Sports Sleeves LLC	Leominster	MA	G	508 344-9749	12129
Fieldston Clothes Inc **(HQ)**	Fall River	MA	G	508 646-2900	10700
Golden Fleece Mfg Group LLC **(HQ)**	Haverhill	MA	B	978 686-3833	11439
Griffin Manufacturing Co Inc	Fall River	MA	C	508 677-0048	10707
Kellsport Industries Inc	Fall River	MA	E	508 646-0855	10719
M & M Garment Manufacturing	Everett	MA	F	617 389-7787	10620
Madewell Manufacturing Co Inc	New Bedford	MA	G	508 997-0768	13414
New Balance Athletics Inc **(HQ)**	Boston	MA	B	617 783-4000	8727
Niche Inc	New Bedford	MA	E	508 990-4202	13427
Perfect Curve Inc **(PA)**	Boston	MA	G	617 224-1600	8774
Pop Tops Company Inc	South Easton	MA	E	508 580-2580	15286
Precision Sportswear Inc	Fall River	MA	E	508 674-3034	10748
Reebok International Ltd **(HQ)**	Boston	MA	B	781 401-5000	8816
Robert H Thoms	Cambridge	MA	G	617 876-0662	9637
Saucony Inc **(DH)**	Waltham	MA	C	617 824-6000	16191
Tracksmith Corporation	Boston	MA	F	781 235-0037	8891
Tyca Corporation **(PA)**	Clinton	MA	E	978 612-0002	10094
Vf Outdoor Inc	Natick	MA	F	508 651-7676	13286
Creative Apparel Assoc LLC **(HQ)**	Belmont	ME	E	207 342-2814	5702
Alcor-Usa Llc	Alton	NH	G	603 398-1564	17544
Chuck Roast Equipment Inc **(PA)**	Conway	NH	E	603 447-5492	17951
Dartmouth Undying Inc	Hanover	NH	G	603 643-2143	18287
H R P Products Inc	Farmington	NH	F	603 330-3757	18142
Legacy Global Sports LP	Portsmouth	NH	G	603 373-7262	19585
Nitefighter International	Silver Lake	NH	G	603 367-4741	19824
Richardson Mfg Co Inc	Silver Lake	NH	G	603 367-9018	19825
Timberland LLC **(HQ)**	Stratham	NH	B	603 772-9500	19876
Waterwear Inc	Wilton	NH	E	603 654-5344	19991
176 Willow Avenue LLC	Little Compton	RI	G	401 635-2329	20603
Hilco Athletic & Graphics Inc	West Warwick	RI	F	401 822-1775	21495
Bogner of America Inc **(DH)**	Burlington	VT	E	802 861-6900	21769
Fat Hat Clothing Co	Quechee	VT	F	802 296-6646	22294
Louis Garneau USA Inc	Derby	VT	D	802 334-5885	21901
Ugly Dog Hunting Co	Hinesburg	VT	G	802 482-7054	22031

2331 Women's & Misses' Blouses

	CITY	ST	EMP	PHONE	ENTRY #
Fyc Apparel Group LLC	East Haven	CT	E	203 466-6525	1252
Fyc Apparel Group LLC **(PA)**	Branford	CT	D	203 481-2420	319
A Personal Touch Inc **(PA)**	Hanson	MA	G	781 447-0467	11360
Acme Merchandise and AP Inc	Gloucester	MA	E	978 282-4800	11158
American Power Source Inc **(PA)**	Fall River	MA	C	508 672-8847	10657
Contemporary Apparel Inc	Mansfield	MA	G	508 339-3523	12619
Counterwerks Inc	Bellingham	MA	G	508 553-9600	8035
LJL Enterprises Inc	Peabody	MA	G	781 639-2714	14353
Pvh Corp	Wrentham	MA	F	508 384-0070	17527
Shop Therapy Imports	Provincetown	MA	G	508 487-8970	14609
Imeldas Fabrics & Designs	New Sharon	ME	G	207 778-0665	6476

2335 Women's & Misses' Dresses

	CITY	ST	EMP	PHONE	ENTRY #
Fyc Apparel Group LLC **(PA)**	Branford	CT	D	203 481-2420	319
Chic LLC	Pembroke	MA	G	781 312-7800	14395
Fall River Apparel Inc	Fall River	MA	G	508 677-1975	10694
Kathy Clark	Natick	MA	G	508 655-3666	13263
LJL Enterprises Inc	Peabody	MA	G	781 639-2714	14353

2337 Women's & Misses' Suits, Coats & Skirts

	CITY	ST	EMP	PHONE	ENTRY #
Bayer Clothing Group Inc **(PA)**	Greenwich	CT	D	203 661-4140	1599
Fyc Apparel Group LLC **(PA)**	Branford	CT	D	203 481-2420	319
MB Sport LLC **(PA)**	New Canaan	CT	F	203 966-1985	2605
Nine West Holdings Inc	Clinton	CT	G	860 669-3799	791
A Personal Touch Inc **(PA)**	Hanson	MA	G	781 447-0467	11360
Collegiate Uniforms Inc	Medford	MA	G	781 219-4952	12927
LJL Enterprises Inc	Peabody	MA	G	781 639-2714	14353
Sara Campbell Ltd **(PA)**	Boston	MA	F	617 423-3134	8838
Sterlingwear of Boston Inc **(PA)**	Boston	MA	D	617 567-2100	8865
Sterlingwear of Boston Inc	Boston	MA	C	617 567-6465	8866
Nancy Lawrence	Portland	ME	G	207 774-7276	6697

	CITY	ST	EMP	PHONE	ENTRY #
Nitefighter International	Silver Lake	NH	G	603 367-4741	19824
Professional Images Inc	Pawtucket	RI	G	401 725-7000	20884

2339 Women's & Misses' Outerwear, NEC

	CITY	ST	EMP	PHONE	ENTRY #
Custom Sportswear Mfg	Wolcott	CT	G	203 879-4420	5437
Del Arbour LLC	Milford	CT	F	203 882-8501	2274
Gg Sportswear Inc	Hartford	CT	E	860 296-4441	1825
Teta Activewear By Custom	Wolcott	CT	G	203 879-4420	5461
Tribal Wear	Riverside	CT	G	203 637-7884	3691
A Personal Touch Inc **(PA)**	Hanson	MA	G	781 447-0467	11360
Accurate Services Inc	Fall River	MA	E	508 674-5773	10650
Charles River Apparel Inc	Sharon	MA	D	781 793-5300	15047
Cloak & Dagger Creations	Littleton	MA	G	978 486-4414	12296
Collegiate Uniforms Inc	Medford	MA	G	781 219-4952	12927
Custom Crafted Enterprises	North Attleboro	MA	G	508 695-2878	13754
Dek Tillett Ltd	Sheffield	MA	G	413 229-8764	15059
Fashions Inc **(PA)**	Boston	MA	G	617 338-0163	8538
Fieldston Clothes Inc **(HQ)**	Fall River	MA	G	508 646-2900	10700
Griffin Manufacturing Co Inc	Fall River	MA	C	508 677-0048	10707
Ideal Bias Binding Corp	Marion	MA	G	508 748-2712	12698
Kathy Clark	Natick	MA	G	508 655-3666	13263
Kellsport Industries Inc	Fall River	MA	E	508 646-0855	10719
LJL Enterprises Inc	Peabody	MA	G	781 639-2714	14353
M & M Garment Manufacturing	Everett	MA	F	617 389-7787	10620
Madewell Manufacturing Co Inc	New Bedford	MA	G	508 997-0768	13414
New Balance Athletics Inc **(HQ)**	Boston	MA	B	617 783-4000	8727
Northeast Knitting Mills Inc **(PA)**	Fall River	MA	E	508 678-7553	10741
Pashi Inc	Everett	MA	G	617 304-2742	10624
Pellys Sports	Indian Orchard	MA	G	413 301-0889	11893
Perfect Curve Inc **(PA)**	Boston	MA	G	617 224-1600	8774
Pop Tops Company Inc	South Easton	MA	E	508 580-2580	15286
Reebok International Ltd **(HQ)**	Boston	MA	B	781 401-5000	8816
Salt Wellfleet	Wellfleet	MA	G	508 237-4415	16402
Saucony Inc **(DH)**	Waltham	MA	C	617 824-6000	16191
Tango Seaport	Boston	MA	G	857 277-1191	8873
Therese Rose Manufacturing	Brockton	MA	G	508 586-5812	9183
Tracksmith Corporation	Boston	MA	F	781 235-0037	8891
Tyca Corporation **(PA)**	Clinton	MA	E	978 612-0002	10094
Creative Apparel Assoc LLC **(HQ)**	Belmont	ME	E	207 342-2814	5702
Two Islands Corporation	Orland	ME	G	207 469-3600	6551
Chuck Roast Equipment Inc **(PA)**	Conway	NH	E	603 447-5492	17951
Legacy Global Sports LP	Portsmouth	NH	G	603 373-7262	19585
Lululemon USA Inc	Portsmouth	NH	G	603 431-0871	19591
Mat Game Set	Lyme	NH	G	603 277-9763	18755
Nitefighter International	Silver Lake	NH	G	603 367-4741	19824
Richardson Mfg Co Inc	Silver Lake	NH	G	603 367-9018	19825
Waterwear Inc	Wilton	NH	E	603 654-5344	19991
Hilco Athletic & Graphics Inc	West Warwick	RI	F	401 822-1775	21495
Luca	Warren	RI	G	401 289-2251	21297
Solid Oak Inc	Westerly	RI	G	401 637-4855	21541
St John	Cranston	RI	G	401 944-0159	20290
Bogner of America Inc **(DH)**	Burlington	VT	E	802 861-6900	21769
Fat Hat Clothing Co	Quechee	VT	F	802 296-6646	22294
Geiger of Austria Inc	Middlebury	VT	E	802 388-3156	22112
Gsg Inc	Shelburne	VT	G	802 828-6221	22418
Johnson Woolen Mills LLC	Johnson	VT	E	802 635-2271	22050
Louis Garneau USA Inc	Derby	VT	D	802 334-5885	21901

2341 Women's, Misses' & Children's Underwear & Nightwear

	CITY	ST	EMP	PHONE	ENTRY #
LJL Enterprises Inc	Peabody	MA	G	781 639-2714	14353
L L Bean Inc	Brunswick	ME	B	207 725-0300	5840

2342 Brassieres, Girdles & Garments

	CITY	ST	EMP	PHONE	ENTRY #
Fastech Inc	Canton	MA	E	781 964-3010	9732
Valmont Inc	Ludlow	MA	F	413 583-8351	12478

2353 Hats, Caps & Millinery

	CITY	ST	EMP	PHONE	ENTRY #
Indigo Coast Inc	Kent	CT	G	860 592-0088	1922
New England Cap Company	Seymour	CT	F	203 736-6184	3758
Athletic Emblem & Lettering Co	Springfield	MA	F	413 734-0415	15449
Joseph A Owen Jr	Littleton	MA	G	978 486-3318	12310
Therese Rose Manufacturing	Brockton	MA	G	508 586-5812	9183
Whole Earth Hat Co Inc	Fall River	MA	F	508 672-7033	10783
DVE Manufacturing Inc	Lewiston	ME	E	207 783-9895	6284
Nes Embroidery Inc	Tilton	NH	F	603 293-4664	19908
New York Accessory Group Inc	Bristol	RI	D	401 245-6096	20095
Fat Hat Clothing Co	Quechee	VT	F	802 296-6646	22294
Washburn Company Inc	Morrisville	VT	E	802 888-3032	22179

2361 Children's & Infants' Dresses & Blouses

	CITY	ST	EMP	PHONE	ENTRY #
Agawam Novelty Company Inc	Agawam	MA	G	413 536-0471	7418
Ideal Bias Binding Corp	Marion	MA	G	508 748-2712	12698

2369 Girls' & Infants' Outerwear, NEC

	CITY	ST	EMP	PHONE	ENTRY #
One Kid LLC **(PA)**	Westport	CT	G	203 254-9978	5219
Accurate Services Inc	Fall River	MA	E	508 674-5773	10650
Charles River Apparel Inc	Sharon	MA	D	781 793-5300	15047
E-I-E-I-o Incorporated	Fall River	MA	G	508 324-9311	10684
Precision Sportswear Inc	Fall River	MA	E	508 674-3034	10748
Shop Therapy Imports	Provincetown	MA	G	508 487-8970	14609
Imeldas Fabrics & Designs	New Sharon	ME	G	207 778-0665	6476
Richardson Mfg Co Inc	Silver Lake	NH	G	603 367-9018	19825

2371 Fur Goods

	CITY	ST	EMP	PHONE	ENTRY #
Varpro Inc	Westport	CT	E	203 227-6876	5236
Surell Accessories Inc	Troy	NH	F	603 242-7784	19914

2381 Dress & Work Gloves

	CITY	ST	EMP	PHONE	ENTRY #
Acushnet Company **(DH)**	Fairhaven	MA	A	508 979-2000	10635
Cold River Stitching LLC	Fryeburg	ME	G	207 515-0039	6096

2384 Robes & Dressing Gowns

	CITY	ST	EMP	PHONE	ENTRY #
Graduation Solutions LLC	Greenwich	CT	E	914 934-5991	1617
L L Bean Inc	Brunswick	ME	B	207 725-0300	5840

2385 Waterproof Outerwear

	CITY	ST	EMP	PHONE	ENTRY #
Gonco Inc **(PA)**	Sandwich	MA	G	508 833-3900	14968
Ideal Bias Binding Corp	Marion	MA	G	508 748-2712	12698
Mr Idea Inc	Attleboro	MA	E	508 222-0155	7770
Neptune Garment Company	Boston	MA	D	617 482-3980	8722
Sterlingwear of Boston Inc **(PA)**	Boston	MA	D	617 567-2100	8865
Sterlingwear of Boston Inc	Boston	MA	C	617 567-6465	8866
Wristies Inc	Lowell	MA	G	978 937-9500	12449
Log House Designs Inc **(PA)**	Chatham	NH	E	603 694-3373	17822

2386 Leather & Sheep Lined Clothing

	CITY	ST	EMP	PHONE	ENTRY #
L & J Leathers Manufacturing	Revere	MA	G	781 289-6466	14770
Leprechaun Sheepskin Company	Charlemont	MA	G	413 339-4355	9820
S & S Computer Imaging Inc	Holyoke	MA	G	413 536-0117	11655
U S Made Co Inc	Danvers	MA	E	978 777-8383	10269
Vanson Leathers Inc	Fall River	MA	D	508 678-2000	10778
Surell Accessories Inc	Troy	NH	F	603 242-7784	19914
Timberland LLC **(HQ)**	Stratham	NH	B	603 772-9500	19876
Bren Corporation	Johnston	RI	E	401 943-8200	20501

2387 Apparel Belts

	CITY	ST	EMP	PHONE	ENTRY #
Dooney & Bourke Inc **(PA)**	Norwalk	CT	E	203 853-7515	3142
Cape Cod Manufacturing	Mashpee	MA	G	508 477-1188	12878
Chaucer Accessories Inc	Haverhill	MA	F	978 373-1566	11416
Contemporary Apparel Inc	Mansfield	MA	G	508 339-3523	12619
Dick Muller Designer/Craftsman	Shelburne Falls	MA	G	413 625-0016	15068
Mackenzie Couture ACC Inc	Lynnfield	MA	G	781 334-2805	12552
Surtan Manufacturing Co	South Yarmouth	MA	G	508 394-4099	15334

2389 Apparel & Accessories, NEC

	CITY	ST	EMP	PHONE	ENTRY #
De Muerte Usa LLC	Hartford	CT	G	860 331-7085	1817
Malabar Bay LLC	Stamford	CT	G	203 359-9714	4243
Matrix Apparel Group LLC	New Fairfield	CT	G	203 740-7837	2625
Ricco Vishnu	Bridgeport	CT	G	203 449-0124	482
Style and Grace LLC	Westport	CT	G	917 751-2043	5232
Bravo Maslow LLC	Quincy	MA	G	912 580-0044	14618
Chaucer Accessories Inc	Haverhill	MA	F	978 373-1566	11416
Costume Works Inc	Somerville	MA	F	617 623-7510	15167
Dynasty Production	Boston	MA	G	617 361-5297	8513
Gava Group Inc	Hanover	MA	G	781 878-9889	11338
Image Factory	Pocasset	MA	G	508 295-3876	14598
Marblehead Weather Gmts LLC	Marblehead	MA	G	781 639-1060	12688
Savvy On Main	Orleans	MA	G	508 255-5076	14241
Theological Threads Inc	Beverly	MA	G	978 927-7031	8190
Vampfangs / 321fx Studios LLC	Beverly	MA	G	781 799-5048	8194
CM Almy & Son Inc	Pittsfield	ME	C	207 487-3232	6589
Masquerade	Salem	NH	F	603 275-0717	19749
New York Accessory Group Inc	Bristol	RI	D	401 245-6096	20095
Peko Creations Ltd	Pawtucket	RI	F	401 722-6661	20878
Tiara Enterprises Inc	Providence	RI	G	401 521-2988	21136

2391 Curtains & Draperies

	CITY	ST	EMP	PHONE	ENTRY #
Byron Lord Inc	Old Lyme	CT	G	203 287-9881	3315
Decorator Services Inc	Bridgeport	CT	E	203 384-8144	402
Dominics Decorating Inc	Norwalk	CT	G	203 838-1827	3141
R L Fisher Inc	Hartford	CT	D	860 951-8110	1865
Tetrault & Sons Inc	Stafford Springs	CT	G	860 872-9187	4117
Thomas W Raftery Inc	Hartford	CT	E	860 278-9870	1879
Threads of Evidence LLC	Shelton	CT	G	203 929-5209	3879
Yard Stick Decore	Bridgeport	CT	F	203 330-0360	508
A L Ellis Inc	Fall River	MA	D	508 672-4799	10649
Angies Work Room Inc	Attleboro	MA	F	508 761-5636	7705
Bloom & Company Inc	Watertown	MA	F	617 923-1526	16273
Craft Interiors	Malden	MA	G	781 321-8695	12566
Curtain Manufacturers Plus	Fall River	MA	E	508 675-8680	10681
Davids Drapery	Braintree	MA	G	781 849-9499	8999
Dra-Cor Industries Inc	Brockton	MA	E	508 580-3770	9140

	CITY	ST	EMP	PHONE	ENTRY #
Drape It Inc	Waltham	MA	F	781 209-1912	16091
Fall River Apparel Inc	Fall River	MA	G	508 677-1975	10694
Huot Enterprises Inc	Ludlow	MA	G	413 589-7422	12468
Ksg Enterprises Inc	Peabody	MA	F	978 977-7357	14349
Mohawk Shade & Blind Co Inc	Cambridge	MA	G	617 868-6000	9568
Quest Drape	Woburn	MA	G	781 859-0300	17278
Reliable Fabrics Inc	Everett	MA	E	617 387-5321	10626
Sam Kasten Handweaver LLC	Lenox	MA	G	413 637-8900	12103
Sams Drapery Workroom Inc	Hyde Park	MA	F	617 364-9440	11878
Staceys Shade Shop Inc **(PA)**	Lynn	MA	G	781 595-0097	12540
United Curtain Co Inc **(PA)**	Avon	MA	F	508 588-4100	7900
Dirigo Stitching Inc	Skowhegan	ME	E	207 474-8421	6972
Salo Bay Trading Co	Biddeford	ME	G	207 283-4732	5762
J & R Langley Co Inc	Manchester	NH	F	603 622-9653	18847
Perfect Fit Industries LLC	Allenstown	NH	G	603 485-7161	17540
Marion Mfg Co	Providence	RI	F	401 331-4343	21060
Natco Home Fashions Inc	West Warwick	RI	F	401 828-0300	21501
Natco Home Fashions Inc	West Warwick	RI	F	401 828-0300	21502
Natco Home Fashions Inc **(PA)**	West Warwick	RI	F	401 828-0300	21503
Chrisandras Interiors Inc	Ludlow	VT	G	802 228-2075	22062
Gordons Window Decor Inc **(PA)**	Williston	VT	F	802 655-7777	22671

2392 House furnishings: Textile

	CITY	ST	EMP	PHONE	ENTRY #
Dominics Decorating Inc	Norwalk	CT	G	203 838-1827	3141
Hills Point Industries LLC **(PA)**	Westport	CT	G	917 515-8650	5200
Latex Foam International LLC **(HQ)**	Shelton	CT	D	203 924-0700	3825
Patricia Spratt For Home LLC	Old Lyme	CT	F	860 434-9291	3326
R L Fisher Inc	Hartford	CT	D	860 951-8110	1865
Sammi Sleeping Systems LLC	New Haven	CT	G	203 684-3131	2734
Thomas W Raftery Inc	Hartford	CT	E	860 278-9870	1879
7 Waves Inc	Braintree	MA	G	781 519-9389	8984
Agawam Novelty Company Inc	Agawam	MA	G	413 536-0471	7418
Almont Company Inc	East Weymouth	MA	E	617 269-8244	10534
Beantown Bedding LLC	Hingham	MA	F	781 608-9915	11493
Berkshire Corporation **(HQ)**	Great Barrington	MA	E	413 528-2602	11233
Brian Summer	Shelburne Falls	MA	G	413 625-9990	15066
Butler Home Products LLC **(DH)**	Hudson	MA	F	508 597-8000	11761
Century-Ty Wood Mfg Inc	Holliston	MA	D	508 429-4011	11563
Craft Interiors	Malden	MA	G	781 321-8695	12566
Fall River Apparel Inc	Fall River	MA	G	508 677-1975	10694
Klear-Vu Corporation **(PA)**	Fall River	MA	D	508 674-5723	10721
Ksg Enterprises Inc	Peabody	MA	F	978 977-7357	14349
PDk Worldwide Entps Inc **(PA)**	Fall River	MA	E	508 676-2155	10746
Stevens Linen Associates Inc	Dudley	MA	D	508 943-0813	10387
Therapedic of New England LLC	Brockton	MA	G	508 559-9944	9182
Unwrapped Inc	Lowell	MA	D	978 441-0242	12443
Dirigo Stitching Inc	Skowhegan	ME	E	207 474-8421	6972
Lulla Smith	Camden	ME	G	207 230-0832	5867
Maine Balsam Fir Prodcts	West Paris	ME	F	207 674-5090	7176
North Country Comforters	Great Pond	ME	G	207 584-2196	6145
Rsv Management	Machias	ME	G	207 255-8608	6394
Two Rivers Pet Products Inc	Turner	ME	E	207 225-3965	7112
Boston Billows Inc	Nashua	NH	G	603 598-1200	19129
Lucci Corp	Peterborough	NH	F	603 567-4301	19475
Masquerade	Salem	NH	F	603 275-0717	19749
Perfect Fit Industries LLC	Allenstown	NH	G	603 485-7161	17540
Bess Home Fashions Inc	West Warwick	RI	F	401 828-0300	21484
Bristal Cushion & ACC LLC	Warren	RI	F	401 247-4499	21291
Bristol Cushions Inc	Bristol	RI	F	401 247-4499	20065
Cleanbrands LLC	Warwick	RI	F	877 215-7378	21342
Moore Company	Westerly	RI	C	401 596-2816	21532
Garflex Inc	Brattleboro	VT	D	802 257-5256	21728
Heart of Vermont Inc	Barre	VT	G	802 476-3098	21620
Rihm Management Inc	Manchester Center	VT	G	802 867-5325	22089

2393 Textile Bags

	CITY	ST	EMP	PHONE	ENTRY #
Dayton Bag & Burlap Co	East Granby	CT	G	860 653-8191	1125
Dow Cover Company Incorporated	New Haven	CT	D	203 469-5394	2683
Smiling Dog	Middletown	CT	G	860 344-0707	2223
Uninsred Alttude Cnnection Inc	Brooklyn	CT	G	860 333-1461	673
CB Sports Inc	Malden	MA	G	781 322-0307	12564
Clarkie Industries	North Attleboro	MA	F	508 404-0202	13753
Fall River Apparel Inc	Fall River	MA	G	508 677-1975	10694
Fleming Industries Inc	Chicopee	MA	D	413 593-3300	10026
Hosokawa Micron International	Northborough	MA	F	508 655-1123	14037
MM Reif Ltd	Boston	MA	D	617 442-9500	8708
Pacheco Gear Inc	East Freetown	MA	G	508 763-5709	10456
Sorenson Sewing Inc	Hyde Park	MA	G	617 333-6955	11880
Steele Canvas Basket Corp	Chelsea	MA	E	800 541-8929	9970
Under Cover Inc	New Bedford	MA	F	508 997-7600	13456
United Industrial Tex Pdts Inc **(PA)**	West Springfield	MA	E	413 737-0095	16559
United Industrial Tex Pdts Inc	West Springfield	MA	G	413 737-0095	16560
Unwrapped Inc	Lowell	MA	D	978 441-0242	12443
Byer Manufacturing Company	Orono	ME	E	207 866-2171	6552
C B P Corp **(PA)**	Arundel	ME	F	207 985-9767	5529
Lapoint Industries Inc **(PA)**	Auburn	ME	D	207 777-3100	5575
Nancy Lawrence	Portland	ME	G	207 774-7276	6697
Baileyworks Inc	Newmarket	NH	G	603 292-6485	19330
Curator	Walpole	NH	G	603 756-3888	19919
Enviro-Tote Inc	Londonderry	NH	E	603 647-7171	18696
J B A Products	Effingham	NH	G	603 539-5034	18095
Absorbent Specialty Pdts LLC	Cumberland	RI	F	401 722-1177	20312
Sports Systems Custom Bags	Woonsocket	RI	D	401 767-3770	21579

2394 Canvas Prdts

	CITY	ST	EMP	PHONE	ENTRY #
Ace Sailmakers	East Lyme	CT	G	860 739-5999	1268
B and G Enterprise LLC **(PA)**	New Haven	CT	G	203 562-7232	2663
Commercial Sewing Inc	Torrington	CT	C	860 482-5509	4571
Custom Covers	Clinton	CT	G	860 669-4169	784
Custom Marine Canvas LLC	Groton	CT	G	860 572-9547	1669
Dimension-Polyant Inc	Putnam	CT	E	860 928-8300	3610
Farrar Sails Inc	New London	CT	G	860 447-0382	2772
Fitzgerald-Norwalk Awning Co	Norwalk	CT	G	203 847-5858	3153
Genvario Awning Co	Norwalk	CT	G	203 847-5858	3161
Kappa Sails LLC	Gales Ferry	CT	G	860 399-8899	1527
Liberty Services LLC	Westbrook	CT	G	860 399-0077	5159
Mbm Sales	Norwalk	CT	F	203 866-3674	3193
New Haven Companies Inc	East Haven	CT	F	203 469-6421	1257
North Sails Group LLC **(DH)**	Milford	CT	D	203 874-7548	2323
Seafarer Canvas **(PA)**	Norwalk	CT	F	203 853-2624	3237
Second Lac Inc **(PA)**	Norwalk	CT	G	203 321-1221	3239
Shelterlogic Corp **(HQ)**	Watertown	CT	C	860 945-6442	5023
Slogic Holding Corp **(PA)**	New Canaan	CT	G	203 966-2800	2614
State Awning Company	Hartford	CT	G	860 246-2575	1872
Tetrault & Sons Inc	Stafford Springs	CT	G	860 872-9187	4117
Toff Industry Inc	Milldale	CT	G	860 378-0532	2388
Topside Canvas Upholstery	Westbrook	CT	G	860 399-4845	5164
Watertown Canvas and Awng LLC	Oakville	CT	G	860 274-0933	3305
Canvas Link Inc	Westborough	MA	G	508 366-3323	16600
Canvasmith	Fairhaven	MA	G	207 379-2121	10641
Cape Cod Sailmakers Inc	Cataumet	MA	G	508 563-3080	9810
Cheyne Awning & Sign Co	Pittsfield	MA	G	413 442-4742	14464
Columbia ASC Inc	Lawrence	MA	F	978 683-2205	12012
Cramaro Tarpaulin Systems Inc	Northborough	MA	G	508 393-3062	14031
Da Costa Awnings & Canvas Spc	Taunton	MA	G	508 822-4944	15739
Dartmouth Awning Co Inc	Westport	MA	G	508 636-6838	16838
Downs Sails	Danvers	MA	G	978 750-8140	10214
Doyle Sailmakers Inc **(PA)**	Salem	MA	E	978 740-5950	14907
Doyle Sailmakers Inc	South Dartmouth	MA	G	508 992-6322	15238
Expansion Opportunities Inc	Northborough	MA	E	508 303-8200	14033
Federal Specialties Inc	West Springfield	MA	G	413 782-6900	16520
Harding Sails Inc	Marion	MA	F	508 748-0334	12697
Harry Miller Co Inc	Boston	MA	E	617 427-2300	8589
Harry Miller Co LLC **(PA)**	Boston	MA	E	617 427-2300	8590
Katherine McAloon	Gloucester	MA	G	978 525-2223	11194
Leisure Time Canvas	West Springfield	MA	G	413 785-5500	16528
Lyman Conrad **(PA)**	South Hadley	MA	E	413 538-8200	15306
Maple Leaf Cpitl Ventures Corp **(PA)**	Medford	MA	G	781 569-6311	12939
MM Reif Ltd	Boston	MA	D	617 442-9500	8708
Moderne Rug Inc	Fitchburg	MA	G	978 343-3210	10840
Oakum Bay Sail Co	Marblehead	MA	G	781 631-8983	12689
Olsen Marine	Dennis	MA	G	508 385-2180	10308
Peaks Tarps	Clinton	MA	G	978 365-5555	10088
Pioneer Consolidated Corp	North Oxford	MA	E	508 987-8438	13973
R H M Group Inc	Beverly	MA	G	978 745-4710	8169
Readys Window Products Inc	Tewksbury	MA	G	978 851-3963	15832
Signs By J Inc	Boston	MA	G	617 825-9855	8845
Sperry Sails Inc	Marion	MA	G	508 748-2581	12705
Sperry Tents Inc	Marion	MA	G	508 748-1792	12706
Steele & Rowe Inc	North Dartmouth	MA	G	508 993-6413	13927
Steele Canvas Basket Corp	Chelsea	MA	E	800 541-8929	9970
Sunsetter Products Ltd Partnr	Malden	MA	D	781 321-9600	12598
Tent Connection Inc	Northbridge	MA	G	508 234-8746	14062
Tim Gratuski	Leominster	MA	G	978 466-9000	12195
United Industrial Tex Pdts Inc **(PA)**	West Springfield	MA	E	413 737-0095	16559
United Industrial Tex Pdts Inc	West Springfield	MA	G	413 737-0095	16560
William Blanchard Co Inc	Wakefield	MA	F	781 245-8050	15985
Zmetra Clarspan Structures LLC	Webster	MA	G	508 943-0940	16355
Byer Manufacturing Company	Orono	ME	E	207 866-2171	6552
C B P Corp **(PA)**	Arundel	ME	F	207 985-9767	5529
Canvasworks Inc	Kennebunk	ME	G	207 985-2419	6230
Center Harbor Sails LLC	Brooklin	ME	G	207 359-2003	5818
Collabric	Veazie	ME	F	207 945-5095	7126
Custom Canvas & Upholstery LLC	Lewiston	ME	F	207 241-8518	6281
E S Bohndell & Co Inc	Rockport	ME	G	207 236-3549	6821
Fortune Inc **(PA)**	Portland	ME	F	207 878-5760	6663
Leavitt & Parris Inc	Portland	ME	F	207 797-0100	6679
Lewiston-Auburn Tent & Awng Co	Lewiston	ME	G	207 784-7353	6301
Maine Sailing Partners LLC	Harpswell	ME	G	207 865-0850	6173
McDonald Duvall Design Inc	Rockland	ME	G	207 596-7940	6805
Nancy Lawrence	Portland	ME	G	207 774-7276	6697
Nathaniel S Wilson Sailmaker	East Boothbay	ME	G	207 633-5071	5978
Nilsen Canvas Products	Portland	ME	G	207 797-4863	6703
Pope Sails and Rigging Inc	Rockland	ME	G	207 596-7293	6808

SIC

	CITY	ST	EMP	PHONE	ENTRY #
Seth Hetherington	South Harpswell	ME	G	207 833-5400	7008
American Canvas Company LLC	Kingston	NH	G	603 642-6665	18539
Anson Sailmakers Inc	Greenland	NH	G	603 431-6676	18220
Enviro-Tote Inc	Londonderry	NH	E	603 647-7171	18696
Image Awnings Inc	Wolfeboro	NH	G	603 569-6680	20020
Just Right Awnings & Signs	Dover	NH	G	603 740-8416	18033
Peter Marques	Conway	NH	G	603 447-2344	17957
Yarra Design & Fabrication LLC	Bow	NH	F	603 224-6880	17736
Awning Guy LLC	Providence	RI	G	401 787-0097	20966
Black Dog Corporation	Portsmouth	RI	E	401 683-5858	20920
Corrados Canvas & Cushions Inc	Bristol	RI	G	401 253-5511	20070
Doyle Sailmakers Inc	East Greenwich	RI	F	401 884-4227	20361
Doyle Sails	East Greenwich	RI	G	401 884-4227	20362
Fit N Stitch Inc	North Kingstown	RI	G	401 294-3492	20711
Hood Sailmakers Inc **(PA)**	Middletown	RI	F	401 849-9400	20620
Jasper Aaron	Newport	RI	G	401 847-8796	20668
Kinder Industries Inc	Bristol	RI	F	401 253-7076	20087
L F Pease Co	East Providence	RI	F	401 438-2850	20428
North Sails Group LLC	Portsmouth	RI	G	401 683-7997	20933
Rhode Northsales Island Inc	Portsmouth	RI	E	401 683-7997	20939
Stupell Industries Ltd Inc	Johnston	RI	F	401 831-5640	20543
Thurston Sails Inc	Bristol	RI	F	401 254-0970	20105
Cloth N Canvas Recovery Inc	Colchester	VT	G	802 658-6826	21859
Durasol Systems Inc	Williston	VT	E	802 864-3009	22663
Durasol Systems Inc	Middlebury	VT	E	802 388-7309	22109
Green Mountain Awning Inc	West Rutland	VT	G	802 438-2951	22615
Vermont Canvas Products	Rutland	VT	G	802 773-7311	22359

2395 Pleating & Stitching For The Trade

	CITY	ST	EMP	PHONE	ENTRY #
American Stitch & Print Inc	North Haven	CT	G	203 239-5383	3006
Baa Creations	Ledyard	CT	G	860 464-1339	1939
Bruce Park Sports EMB LLC	Norwalk	CT	G	203 853-4488	3115
Expert Embroidery	Wallingford	CT	F	203 269-9675	4741
Gg Sportswear Inc	Hartford	CT	E	860 296-4441	1825
Grand Embroidery Inc	Oxford	CT	F	203 888-7484	3406
Guidera Marketing Services	Pawcatuck	CT	E	860 599-8880	3436
Initial Step Monogramming	West Hartford	CT	G	860 665-0542	5078
J & D Embroidering Co	Baltic	CT	G	860 822-9777	50
Mad Sportswear LLC	West Haven	CT	G	203 932-4868	5133
Monogramit LLC	Brooklyn	CT	G	860 779-0694	671
R F H Company Inc	Norwalk	CT	F	203 853-2863	3226
Rainbow Graphics Inc	Manchester	CT	G	860 646-8997	2042
Robert Audette **(PA)**	Cheshire	CT	G	203 872-3119	760
Rss Enterprises LLC	Derby	CT	G	203 736-6220	1078
Shirt Graphix	Wallingford	CT	G	203 294-1656	4805
Stitchers Hideaway LLC	Manchester	CT	G	860 268-4741	2054
Tee-It-Up LLC	Wallingford	CT	G	203 949-9455	4816
TSS & A Inc	Prospect	CT	F	800 633-3536	3599
Zuse Inc	Guilford	CT	F	203 458-3295	1725
290 Industrial Stitching Inc	South Barre	MA	G	978 355-0271	15234
Abra-Cadabra Promotional AP	Lakeville	MA	G	508 821-2002	11970
All American Embroidery Inc	Wilmington	MA	G	978 657-0414	16970
All City Screen Printing Inc	Wakefield	MA	G	781 665-0000	15940
Apparel 2000 LLC	Rockland	MA	G	781 740-6204	14790
Athletic Emblem & Lettering Co	Springfield	MA	F	413 734-0415	15449
Avon Cstm EMB & Screenprinting	Avon	MA	F	781 341-4663	7878
Callenstitch LLC	Concord	MA	E	978 369-9080	10120
Camelot Enterprises Inc **(PA)**	Stoughton	MA	F	781 341-9100	15583
Coastal Image Inc	Harwich	MA	G	508 430-7870	11391
Copy Caps	Wellfleet	MA	G	508 349-1300	16401
Corporate Image Apparel Inc	Fall River	MA	E	508 676-3099	10680
Custom Stitch	Wilmington	MA	G	978 988-1344	16991
E S Sports Corporation	Holyoke	MA	D	413 534-5634	11623
Elegant Stitches Inc	Pittsfield	MA	G	413 447-9452	14469
Embroider-Ism LLC	Centerville	MA	G	508 375-6461	9814
Embroidery Clinic LLC	Braintree	MA	G	781 843-5293	9004
Embroidery Loft	Methuen	MA	G	978 681-1155	13020
Embroidery Place	Shrewsbury	MA	G	508 842-5311	15110
ESP Solutions Services LLC	Taunton	MA	E	508 285-0017	15749
Fosters Promotional Goods	Marblehead	MA	F	781 631-3824	12683
G & G Silk Screening	Plymouth	MA	G	508 830-1075	14559
Gemini Screenprinting & EMB Co	Brockton	MA	G	508 586-8223	9149
Gonco Inc **(PA)**	Sandwich	MA	G	508 833-3900	14968
Great Threads	Belchertown	MA	G	413 323-9402	8024
Haiti Projects Inc	Hanover	MA	C	978 969-1064	11341
Imperial Monogram Company Inc	West Roxbury	MA	G	617 323-0100	16497
Inter-All Corporation	Granby	MA	E	413 467-7181	11228
Jph Graphics LLC	Salem	MA	G	978 744-7873	14926
Lisa Signs Inc	Woburn	MA	G	781 935-1821	17215
Marcott Designs	Attleboro	MA	G	508 226-2680	7762
Matouk Textile Works Inc	Fall River	MA	E	508 997-3444	10728
Nixon Company Inc	Indian Orchard	MA	E	413 543-3701	11890
Olde Village Monogramming Inc	Great Barrington	MA	G	413 528-3904	11244
Pop Tops Company Inc	South Easton	MA	E	508 580-2580	15286
Premier Services Inc	Weymouth	MA	G	781 335-9305	16898
Pro Am Enterprises Inc	Melrose	MA	G	781 662-8888	12989
Sew What Embroidery	Dalton	MA	G	413 684-0672	10184
Silver Screen Design Inc	Greenfield	MA	F	413 773-1692	11275
Threadhead Inc	Hyannis	MA	F	508 778-6516	11859
Tri-Star Sportswear Inc	Worcester	MA	G	508 799-4117	17490
Universal Screening Studio Inc	Everett	MA	G	617 387-1832	10633
B & B Embroidery Inc	Oakland	ME	G	207 465-2846	6529
BBH Apparrel	Boothbay Harbor	ME	F	207 633-0601	5783
Black Bear Graphics	Kingfield	ME	G	207 265-4593	6252
Commercial Screenprint EMB Inc	Bangor	ME	G	207 942-2862	5639
Creative Embroidery LLC	Auburn	ME	G	207 777-6300	5556
D R Designs Inc	Manchester	ME	G	207 622-3303	6409
Maine Coast Marketing	Portland	ME	G	207 781-9801	6684
Michael V Morin	Sanford	ME	G	207 459-1200	6883
Perfect Stitch Emroidery Inc	South Paris	ME	G	207 743-2830	7016
T Henri Inc	Southwest Harbor	ME	G	207 244-7787	7051
Woodland Studios Inc	Ellsworth	ME	F	207 667-3286	6024
Better Life LLC	Manchester	NH	G	603 647-0077	18787
Creative Threads LLC	Gorham	NH	G	603 466-2752	18211
Embrodery By Evrything Per LLC	Littleton	NH	G	603 444-0130	18658
Evergreen Embroidery	Campton	NH	F	603 726-4271	17776
First Impressions Embroidery	Hooksett	NH	G	603 606-1400	18350
Martin D Marguerite	Londonderry	NH	G	603 421-9654	18718
Nes Embroidery Inc	Tilton	NH	F	603 293-4664	19908
New England Embroidery Company	Conway	NH	G	603 447-3878	17956
Quilted Threads LLC	Henniker	NH	G	603 428-6622	18311
Say It In Stitches Inc	Concord	NH	G	603 224-6470	17927
Silver Graphics	Manchester	NH	G	603 669-6955	18924
Stitch This	Dunbarton	NH	G	603 774-0736	18074
Stitches By Kayo Inc	Londonderry	NH	G	603 965-0158	18739
Top Stitch Embroidery Inc	Lebanon	NH	G	603 448-2931	18639
U S Artistic Embroidery Inc	Hampton	NH	G	603 929-0505	18276
Classic Embroidery Co	East Providence	RI	E	401 434-9632	20397
Cool Air Creations Inc	Smithfield	RI	E	401 830-5780	21216
GA Rel Manufacturing Company	Providence	RI	E	401 331-5455	21019
Ira Green Inc	Providence	RI	C	800 663-7487	21040
Kennedy Incorporated	North Kingstown	RI	F	401 295-7800	20720
Next Event Corporation	Portsmouth	RI	G	401 683-0070	20931
Sewrite Mfg Inc	Cumberland	RI	G	401 334-3868	20342
Stitchs Custom Embroidery LLC	Johnston	RI	G	401 943-5900	20542
Weller E E Co Inc/MCS Finshg	Providence	RI	E	401 461-4275	21152
Bennington Army and Navy Inc	Bennington	VT	F	802 447-0020	21663
Brett Lewis Threads Ltd	Shelburne	VT	G	802 985-1166	22414
Bumwraps Inc **(PA)**	Montgomery Center	VT	G	802 326-4080	22141
Bumwraps Inc	Newport	VT	G	802 326-4080	22190
Follenderwerks Inc	Barre	VT	G	802 362-0911	21615
Green Mountain Monogram Inc	Wells River	VT	F	802 757-2553	22601
Initial Ideas Inc **(PA)**	Rutland	VT	F	802 773-6310	22339
J C Image Inc	Saint Albans	VT	G	802 527-1557	22369
Long Meadow Farms Quilts	Newport	VT	G	802 334-5532	22200
New Hrizons EMB Screenprinting	Essex Junction	VT	G	802 651-9801	21952
Pumpkin Harbor Designs Inc	Jeffersonville	VT	G	802 644-6588	22047
Squeegee Printers Inc	Canaan	VT	G	802 266-3426	21825
Vermont Sportswear Emboridery	Colchester	VT	G	802 863-0237	21887
Vermont TS Inc	Chester	VT	G	802 875-2091	21853

2396 Automotive Trimmings, Apparel Findings, Related Prdts

	CITY	ST	EMP	PHONE	ENTRY #
Ace Finishing Co LLC	Bristol	CT	G	860 582-4600	513
Advanced Graphics Inc	Stratford	CT	E	203 378-0471	4388
Allied Printing Services Inc **(PA)**	Manchester	CT	B	860 643-1101	1984
Bennettsville Holdings LLC	Hebron	CT	D	860 444-9400	1895
Byron Lord Inc	Old Lyme	CT	G	203 287-9881	3315
Charles Clay Ltd	New Canaan	CT	G	203 662-0125	2593
Concordia Ltd	North Branford	CT	G	203 483-0221	2960
Hi-Tech Fabricating Inc	Cheshire	CT	E	203 284-0894	737
J & D Embroidering Co	Baltic	CT	G	860 822-9777	50
Jornik Man Corp	Stamford	CT	F	203 969-0500	4232
Kinamor Incorporated	Wallingford	CT	E	203 269-0380	4760
Quality Name Plate Inc	East Glastonbury	CT	D	860 633-9495	1114
R F H Company Inc	Norwalk	CT	F	203 853-2863	3226
Rainbow Graphics Inc	Manchester	CT	G	860 646-8997	2042
Sam & Ty LLC **(PA)**	Norwalk	CT	G	212 840-1871	3236
Second Lac Inc **(PA)**	Norwalk	CT	G	203 321-1221	3239
Zuse Inc	Guilford	CT	F	203 458-3295	1725
Advanced Print Technology Inc	Fitchburg	MA	G	978 342-0093	10809
Agawam Novelty Company Inc	Agawam	MA	G	413 536-0471	7418
Argosy Publishing Inc **(PA)**	Newton	MA	E	617 527-9999	13562
Brand & Oppenheimer Co Inc	Bedford	MA	E	781 271-0000	7965
E S Sports Corporation	Holyoke	MA	D	413 534-5634	11623
E V Yeuell Inc	Woburn	MA	E	781 933-2984	17171
ESP Solutions Services LLC	Taunton	MA	E	508 285-0017	15749
First Print Inc	Winchester	MA	F	781 729-7714	17087
Fleming Industries Inc	Chicopee	MA	D	413 593-3300	10026
Gemini Screenprinting & EMB Co	Brockton	MA	G	508 586-8223	9149
Ghp Media Inc	North Adams	MA	D	413 663-3771	13675
Gloucester Graphics Inc **(PA)**	Gloucester	MA	F	978 281-4500	11188
Imprinted Sportswear Inc	West Springfield	MA	G	413 732-5271	16525
Industrial Lbling Systems Corp	Tyngsboro	MA	E	978 649-7004	15890
Jph Graphics LLC	Salem	MA	G	978 744-7873	14926

	CITY	ST	EMP	PHONE	ENTRY #
Light Metal Platers LLC	Waltham	MA	E	781 899-8855	16145
Marcott Designs	Attleboro	MA	G	508 226-2680	7762
Nrz Companies Inc	Worcester	MA	G	508 856-7237	17435
Pro Am Enterprises Inc	Melrose	MA	G	781 662-8888	12989
Serigraphics Unlimited	Rowley	MA	G	978 356-4896	14866
Silver Screen Design Inc	Greenfield	MA	F	413 773-1692	11275
Specialty Manufacturing Inc	Amesbury	MA	E	978 388-1601	7509
Sundance Screenprints	Gloucester	MA	G	978 281-6006	11213
Sunset Engravers	Methuen	MA	G	978 687-1111	13045
Swan Dyeing and Printing Corp	Fall River	MA	D	508 674-4611	10766
Theatre Stricken Apparel LLC	Bellingham	MA	G	978 325-2335	8060
Universal Screening Studio Inc	Everett	MA	G	617 387-1832	10633
Atlantic Sportswear Inc	Portland	ME	E	207 797-5028	6612
Black Bear Graphics	Kingfield	ME	G	207 265-4593	6252
DVE Manufacturing Inc	Lewiston	ME	E	207 783-9895	6284
Liberty Graphics Inc	Liberty	ME	E	207 589-4596	6331
Lynne Bailey	York	ME	G	207 363-7999	7310
Robert Gaynor	Bar Harbor	ME	G	207 288-4398	5668
Liquid Blue Inc	Derry	NH	D	401 333-6200	17987
Mountain Corporation	Marlborough	NH	D	603 876-3630	18963
Mrp Manufacturing LLC	Pittsfield	NH	G	603 435-5337	19503
Printed Matter Inc	Newfields	NH	E	603 778-2990	19318
Rapid Finishing Corp	Nashua	NH	E	603 889-4234	19244
Say It In Stitches Inc	Concord	NH	G	603 224-6470	17927
Vantastic Inc	Laconia	NH	G	603 524-1419	18591
Fuller Box Co Inc	Central Falls	RI	D	401 725-4300	20113
Hodges Badge Company Inc **(PA)**	Portsmouth	RI	C	401 682-2000	20923
Ryco Trimming Inc	Lincoln	RI	F	401 725-1779	20595
Vermont TS Inc	Chester	VT	G	802 875-2091	21853

2397 Schiffli Machine Embroideries

	CITY	ST	EMP	PHONE	ENTRY #
Inter-All Corporation	Granby	MA	E	413 467-7181	11228

2399 Fabricated Textile Prdts, NEC

	CITY	ST	EMP	PHONE	ENTRY #
Airborne Industries Inc	Branford	CT	F	203 315-0200	286
Banner Works	Oakville	CT	G	203 597-9999	3297
Cap-Tech Products Inc	Wethersfield	CT	F	860 490-5078	5243
Kemper Manufacturing Corp	West Haven	CT	E	203 934-1600	5128
Nomis Enterprises	Wallingford	CT	G	631 821-3120	4778
On Time Screen Printing & Embr	Derby	CT	F	203 874-4581	1076
Power Cover Usa LLC	Waterbury	CT	G	203 755-2687	4942
Puppy Hugger	Greenwich	CT	G	203 661-4858	1639
Accent Banner LLC	Medford	MA	F	781 391-7300	12920
Athletic Emblem & Lettering Co	Springfield	MA	F	413 734-0415	15449
Bannerama Instant Signs Inc	Weston	MA	G	781 899-4744	16822
Brewer Banner Designs	New Bedford	MA	G	508 996-6006	13364
Cyr Sign & Banner Company	Medford	MA	G	781 395-7297	12928
Equinature LLC	Northbridge	MA	G	774 217-8057	14055
Faverco Inc	Boston	MA	G	617 247-1440	8540
Flag & Gift Store Ltd	Seekonk	MA	G	508 675-6400	15022
Flagraphics Inc	Somerville	MA	E	617 776-7549	15172
Lane Printing Co Inc	Holbrook	MA	F	781 767-4450	11529
Mackenzie Couture ACC Inc	Lynnfield	MA	G	781 334-2805	12552
Mass Sign & Decal Inc	Rockland	MA	G	781 878-7446	14812
Niche Inc	New Bedford	MA	E	508 990-4202	13427
Nixon Company Inc	Indian Orchard	MA	E	413 543-3701	11890
Ouellette Industries Inc	Attleboro Falls	MA	G	508 695-0964	7816
Pb & J Discoveries LLC	Newton	MA	G	617 903-7253	13624
US Flag Manufacturing Inc	Cohasset	MA	G	781 383-6607	10103
VH Blackinton & Co Inc	Attleboro Falls	MA	C	508 699-4436	7818
Allen Manufacturing Inc	Lewiston	ME	E	207 333-3385	6273
Bailey Sign Inc	Westbrook	ME	E	207 774-2843	7181
Carrot Signs	Brunswick	ME	G	207 725-0769	5834
Albany International Corp **(PA)**	Rochester	NH	D	603 330-5850	19655
Arlington Sample Book Co Inc **(PA)**	Sunapee	NH	G	603 763-9082	19879
Custom Banner & Graphics LLC	Rochester	NH	G	603 332-2067	19666
Flag-Works Over America LLC	Concord	NH	G	603 225-2530	17902
Lupine Inc	Center Conway	NH	D	603 356-7371	17801
1947 LLC	Portsmouth	RI	G	401 293-5500	20916
Black Dog Corporation	Portsmouth	RI	E	401 683-5858	20920
Hookfast Specialties Inc	Providence	RI	E	401 781-4466	21031
Josef Creations Inc **(PA)**	Chepachet	RI	E	401 421-4198	20135
Summer Infant Inc **(PA)**	Woonsocket	RI	D	401 671-6550	21581
Summer Infant Inc	Woonsocket	RI	G	401 671-6550	21582
Summer Infant (usa) Inc	Woonsocket	RI	C	401 671-6551	21583
Tme Co Inc	Providence	RI	E	860 354-0686	21139
Universal Specialty Awards	Providence	RI	F	401 272-7760	21145
Vogue Industries Ltd Partnr	Central Falls	RI	E	401 722-0900	20128
Cobble Mountain Inc	East Corinth	VT	G	802 439-5232	21913
Gvh Studio Inc	Bennington	VT	G	802 379-1135	21671
Lynn Yarrington	New Haven	VT	G	802 453-4221	22185

24 LUMBER AND WOOD PRODUCTS, EXCEPT FURNITURE

2411 Logging

	CITY	ST	EMP	PHONE	ENTRY #
B&B Logging LLC	Higganum	CT	G	860 982-2425	1900
Brad Kettle	Canterbury	CT	G	860 546-9929	692
Bryan Heavens Logging & Firewo	Harwinton	CT	G	860 485-1712	1887
C & C Logging	Windsor	CT	G	860 683-0071	5323
Clover Hill Forest LLC	Cornwall	CT	G	860 672-0394	819
Cold River Logging LLC	North Windham	CT	G	860 334-9506	3080
Industrial Forrest Products LL	Greenwich	CT	G	203 863-9486	1622
James Callahan	Ridgefield	CT	G	914 641-2852	3670
James M Munch	Sherman	CT	G	802 353-3114	3894
Limb-It-Less Logging LLC	Essex	CT	G	860 227-0987	1403
Tr Landworks LLC	East Hartland	CT	G	860 402-6177	1240
Wayne Horn	New Hartford	CT	G	860 491-3315	2649
Witkowsky John	North Branford	CT	G	203 483-0152	2985
Anderson Logging and Lumber	Westminster	MA	G	978 874-2751	16802
Brightman Corp	Assonet	MA	E	508 644-2620	7678
Ezequelle Logging Inc	Sandisfield	MA	G	413 258-0265	14960
Fisher Logging	Northfield	MA	G	413 498-2615	14063
Forward Enterprises Inc	Oakham	MA	G	508 882-0265	14212
George A Vollans	Nantucket	MA	G	508 257-6241	13224
Gmo Threshold Logging II LLC	Boston	MA	G	617 330-7500	8569
Gmo Threshold Logging LLC	Boston	MA	G	617 330-7500	8570
Gmo Thrshold Tmber Hldings LLC	Boston	MA	G	617 330-7500	8571
Godin Land Clearing	Spencer	MA	G	508 885-9666	15431
Honey Hill Farm	Millers Falls	MA	G	413 659-3141	13180
Lashway Logging Inc	Williamsburg	MA	F	413 268-3600	16952
Lenox Lumber Co	Pittsfield	MA	F	413 637-2744	14484
Mike Orzel Logging	Northampton	MA	G	413 320-3367	14013
Norton Land Clearing and Log	Ayer	MA	G	978 391-4029	7931
OConnell Logging LLC	Hudson	MA	G	978 568-9740	11796
Paul R Hicks	Charlemont	MA	G	413 625-2623	9822
Roberts Brothers Lumber Co	Ashfield	MA	E	413 628-3333	7654
Select Logging	Ashby	MA	G	978 386-6861	7648
Thomas J Doane	Orange	MA	G	978 821-2361	14229
Tim Meiklejohn Logging	Clarksburg	MA	G	413 652-1223	10076
Tim Robinson Logging	Barre	MA	F	978 355-4287	7951
Tree Co Inc	South Dennis	MA	G	508 432-7529	15267
A S & C B Gould & Sons Inc	Cornville	ME	E	207 474-3930	5926
Alan Stevens	Sidney	ME	G	207 547-3840	6961
Albert M M Johnston IV	Hermon	ME	G	207 848-2561	6181
Ambrose G McCarthy Jr	Skowhegan	ME	E	207 474-8837	6968
Anderson Family Tree Farm Inc	Crystal	ME	G	207 463-2843	5928
Andrew Irish Logging	Peru	ME	F	207 562-8839	6583
Ashley & Harmon Logging Inc	East Machias	ME	F	207 259-2043	5982
B & R Bartlett Enterprises	Amity	ME	F	207 448-7060	5522
Barrette Outdoor Living Inc	Biddeford	ME	E	800 866-8101	5721
Ben Jordan Logging LLC	Millinocket	ME	G	207 694-2011	6439
Ben Savage Logging Inc	Sebec	ME	G	207 735-6699	6955
Bernard Ginn and Sons Inc	Winterport	ME	G	207 234-2187	7276
Berry Logging/R A Berry & Sons	Norridgewock	ME	G	207 634-4808	6495
Bolduc Brothers Log & Shipg	Lisbon Falls	ME	G	207 353-5990	6368
BP Logging	Saint Francis	ME	G	207 398-4457	6866
Brochu Logging Inc	Benton	ME	G	207 453-2982	5704
Brook Wiles Logging Inc	Allagash	ME	G	207 398-4105	5518
Bruce C Smith Logging	Machiasport	ME	G	207 255-3259	6397
C T L Land Management Inc	Washington	ME	G	207 845-2841	7149
CB Logging	New Canada	ME	G	207 231-4952	6462
Chapman & Wheeler Inc	Bethel	ME	G	207 824-2224	5714
Charles Lane Inc	Sherman Mills	ME	G	207 365-4606	6960
Chipping & Logging	Porter	ME	G	207 625-4056	6601
Chopper One Inc	Eagle Lake	ME	G	207 444-5476	5973
Clinton G Bradbury Inc	Rumford	ME	G	207 562-8014	6833
Colin Bartlett & Sons Inc	Amity	ME	E	207 532-2214	5523
Corey Madden Logging Inc	Greenbush	ME	G	207 827-1632	6146
Cranes Contract Cutting Inc	Lamoine	ME	G	207 667-9008	6263
D F Moody LLC	Cornville	ME	G	207 474-6029	5927
D M G Enterprises	Edmunds Twp	ME	G	207 726-4603	6005
Dana Hardy	Dyer Brook	ME	G	207 757-8445	5972
Daniel L Dunnells Logging Inc	Parsonsfield	ME	G	207 793-2901	6574
Darrel L Tibbetts	Livermore	ME	G	207 897-4932	6374
Darrell C McGuire & Sons Inc	Houlton	ME	F	207 532-0511	6205
Day Bros	Oxford	ME	G	207 743-0508	6565
Dennis Frigon	Caratunk	ME	F	207 672-4076	5881
Ducas Logging Inc	Wallagrass	ME	G	207 834-5506	7138
E J Carrier Inc	Jackman	ME	D	207 668-4457	6216
Edward Bernard Inc	West Enfield	ME	F	207 732-3987	7170
Ellen McLaughlin	Medway	ME	E	207 746-3398	6424
Farmington Chipping Enterprise	Farmington	ME	G	207 778-4888	6046
Fogg Lumbering Inc	Lowell	ME	G	207 732-4087	6385
Forest Chester Products Inc	Lincoln	ME	E	207 794-2303	6353
G J Logging	Mapleton	ME	G	207 764-3826	6412
G R Logging Inc	Van Buren	ME	G	207 868-2692	7120
Gammon Milam	Rumford	ME	G	207 364-2889	6834

SIC

	CITY	ST	EMP	PHONE	ENTRY #
Gary Green Trucking Logging	Turner	ME	G	207 225-3433	7107
Gary M Pomeroy Logging Inc	Hermon	ME	F	207 848-3171	6187
Gca Logging Inc	Avon	ME	G	207 639-3941	5623
Gerard Poulin & Sons Logging	Readfield	ME	F	207 246-3537	6777
Glenn S Viles & Sons Inc	North Anson	ME	G	207 635-2493	6502
Gloria J Gordon Logging	Strong	ME	G	207 684-4462	7071
Guimond Logging	Fort Kent	ME	G	207 834-6329	6060
H Arthur York Logging Inc **(PA)**	Medway	ME	E	207 746-5883	6425
H Arthur York Logging Inc	Medway	ME	G	207 746-5912	6426
Hanington Bros Inc	Macwahoc Plt	ME	E	207 765-2681	6399
Hanington Timberlands	Reed Plt	ME	F	207 456-7003	6779
Harold C Moore II	South Paris	ME	G	207 595-5683	7011
Hartland Inc	Rockport	ME	G	207 785-4350	6823
Hellgren Logging LLC	Temple	ME	G	207 778-0401	7079
Herbert C Haynes Inc **(PA)**	Winn	ME	E	207 736-3412	7264
Herbert C Haynes Inc	Hermon	ME	G	207 848-5930	6188
Herbert L Hardy and Son Inc	Smyrna Mills	ME	G	207 757-8550	6992
Hickey Logging	West Gardiner	ME	G	207 724-3648	7172
Highland Logging Inc	Wallagrass	ME	G	207 436-1113	7139
Humphrey Mh & Sons Inc	Parsonsfield	ME	F	207 625-4965	6575
J & M Logging Inc	Sidney	ME	F	207 622-6353	6962
J & S Logging	Rangeley	ME	G	207 864-5617	6772
J C Logging Inc	Lincoln	ME	G	207 794-4349	6354
J Voisine & Son Logging Inc	Fort Kent	ME	G	207 436-0932	6061
Jackman Lumber Inc	Skowhegan	ME	G	207 858-0321	6979
Jackman Lumber Inc **(PA)**	Jackman	ME	E	207 668-4407	6217
Jacob Burdin Logging	Sebec	ME	G	207 564-3384	6957
James H Carville	Lisbon Falls	ME	G	207 353-2625	6370
James M Dunn	Hebron	ME	G	207 212-2963	6180
Jmk Logging LLC	Mapleton	ME	G	207 227-2964	6413
John Khiel III Log Chpping Inc	Denmark	ME	E	207 452-2157	5949
Johnny H Castonguay	Livermore	ME	G	207 897-5945	6375
Jordan Family Chipping Inc	Kezar Falls	ME	G	207 625-8890	6249
Jordan Millworks Inc	Lincoln	ME	G	207 794-6178	6356
Jordan Tree Harvesters Inc **(PA)**	Kezar Falls	ME	G	207 625-4378	6250
K B Logging Inc	Smyrna Mills	ME	F	207 757-8818	6993
K M Morin Logging Inc	Clinton	ME	G	207 399-8835	5915
L E Taylor and Sons Inc	Porter	ME	G	207 625-4056	6603
Lakewood Logging Inc	Madison	ME	G	207 431-4052	6405
Leslie W Robertson	Newry	ME	G	207 824-2764	6491
Luce Dirt Excavation	Union	ME	G	207 785-3478	7114
M B Eastman Logging Inc	Parsonsfield	ME	G	207 625-8020	6576
Madden Timberlands Inc	Old Town	ME	E	207 827-0112	6544
Madtown Logging LLC	Madawaska	ME	G	207 728-6260	6400
Maine Custom Woodlands LLC	Durham	ME	F	207 353-9020	5971
Mainely Trees Inc	Strong	ME	G	207 684-3301	7073
Martin Forest Products	Caribou	ME	G	207 498-6723	5887
Mc Crossins Logging Inc	Cardville	ME	G	207 826-2225	5883
McCafferty Logging LLC	Buckfield	ME	G	207 212-8600	5852
MJB Logging Inc	Fort Kent	ME	G	207 231-1376	6062
Mk Logging	Frenchville	ME	G	207 436-1809	6091
Morris Logging	Fort Kent	ME	G	207 834-6210	6064
Nadeau Logging Inc	Fort Kent	ME	F	207 834-6338	6065
Nicols Brothers Inc	Rumford	ME	E	207 364-7032	6840
Nicols Brothers Logging Inc	Mexico	ME	F	207 364-8685	6428
Norman White Inc	Shapleigh	ME	G	207 636-1636	6958
North Shore Logging Inc	Saint Francis	ME	G	207 398-4173	6867
Olson S Logging LLC	Canaan	ME	G	207 474-8835	5873
Paul H Warren Forest Products	Smithfield	ME	G	207 362-3681	6990
Paul N Foulkes Inc	Williamsburg Twp	ME	G	207 965-9481	7223
Pelletier & Pelletier	Fort Kent	ME	E	207 834-2296	6066
PFC Logging Inc	Danforth	ME	G	207 448-7998	5942
Premium Log Yards Inc **(PA)**	Rumford	ME	F	207 364-7500	6842
Pride Manufacturing Co LLC **(PA)**	Burnham	ME	C	207 487-3322	5855
Pride Manufacturing Co LLC	Guilford	ME	F	207 876-2719	6159
R A Thomas Logging Inc	Guilford	ME	G	207 876-2722	6161
R B Logging Inc	Saint Francis	ME	G	207 398-3176	6868
R H Wales & Son Inc	Fryeburg	ME	G	207 925-1363	6102
R&R Logging Forest Management	Addison	ME	G	207 483-4612	5510
Regan S Pingree	Phillips	ME	F	207 639-5706	6586
Reginold D Ricker	Newburgh	ME	G	207 234-4811	6480
Rich Logging	Mexico	ME	G	207 357-7863	6429
Richard A Tibbetts	Oxford	ME	G	207 539-5073	6571
Rickie D Osgood Sr	Greenwood	ME	G	207 674-3529	6155
Robert Babb & Sons	Windham	ME	G	207 892-9692	7248
Robert Daigle & Sons Inc	New Canada	ME	G	207 834-3676	6463
Robert W Carr & Sons Inc	Limington	ME	G	207 637-2885	6348
Robert W Libby	Porter	ME	G	207 625-8285	6604
Roland H Tyler Logging Inc	Dixfield	ME	G	207 562-7282	5958
Roland Levesque	Fort Kent	ME	G	207 834-6244	6067
Ron Ledger Son Logging	Amity	ME	G	207 532-2423	5524
Roussel Logging Inc	Madawaska	ME	G	207 728-3250	6401
S&S Excavation and Logging LLC	Auburn	ME	G	207 312-5590	5597
Solifor Timberlands Inc	Old Town	ME	G	207 827-7195	6547
Stephen F Madden	Cardville	ME	F	207 827-5737	5884
Swh Inc	Linneus	ME	G	207 538-6666	6363
Syl Ver Logging Inc	Allagash	ME	G	207 398-3158	5520
T Raymond Forest Products Inc	Lee	ME	E	207 738-2313	6266
T Roy Inc	St John Plt	ME	G	207 834-6385	7059
T&R Flagg Log Sons & Daughters	Livermore	ME	G	207 897-5212	6377
Tdf Incorporated	Howland	ME	G	207 631-4325	6214
Teresa Burgess	Bangor	ME	G	207 848-5697	5659
Terrence L Hayford	Hartford	ME	G	207 357-0142	6178
Theriault Jr Peter Inc	Danforth	ME	G	207 446-9441	5943
Thompson Timber Harvesting	Washburn	ME	G	207 227-6290	7147
Thompson Trucking Inc	Lincoln	ME	E	207 794-6101	6360
Tide Mill Enterprises	Edmunds Twp	ME	G	207 733-4425	6006
Tough End Logging Corp	Perham	ME	G	207 455-8016	6582
Tr Dillon Logging Inc	Madison	ME	F	207 696-8137	6407
Tracy J Morrison	Harmony	ME	G	207 683-2371	6172
Travis Worster	Carroll Plt	ME	G	207 738-3792	5894
Trees Ltd A Partnr Consisting	Sidney	ME	G	207 547-3168	6965
Troy Voisine Logging Inc	Chester	ME	G	207 794-6301	5906
Trp Logging	East Machias	ME	G	207 263-6425	5984
TW Clark Pulp & Logging LLC	Newport	ME	G	207 368-4766	6487
Up North Corp Inc	Fort Kent	ME	E	207 834-6178	6068
Voisine & Son Logging Inc	Chester	ME	G	207 794-3336	5907
WA Logging LLC	Hodgdon	ME	G	207 694-2921	6195
Wayne Peters Phill	Mattawamkeag	ME	G	207 736-4191	6416
Western Maine Timberlands	Fryeburg	ME	F	207 925-1138	6103
Wheeler Hill Logging Inc	Phillips	ME	G	207 639-2391	6587
Whitcombs Forest Harvesting	Newburgh	ME	G	207 234-2351	6481
Willard S Hanington & Son Inc	Reed Plt	ME	E	207 456-7511	6780
William A Day Jr & Sons Inc	Porter	ME	E	207 625-8181	6607
William B Sparrow Jr	Pittston	ME	G	207 582-5731	6593
Yankee Hardwoods LLC	Sanford	ME	G	207 459-7779	6897
3d Logging Co Inc	Berlin	NH	F	603 915-3020	17690
A B Excavating Inc	Lancaster	NH	E	603 788-5110	18596
Adam Burtt Tree and Log LLC	Center Barnstead	NH	G	603 269-2019	17787
Adam E Mock and Son Logging An	Webster	NH	G	603 648-2444	19943
B Hall & Sons Logging Inc	Errol	NH	G	603 482-7741	18108
B P Logging	Stewartstown	NH	G	603 237-4131	19860
Bliss Logging	Meredith	NH	G	603 279-5674	18971
Bolstridge Logging LLC	New Durham	NH	G	603 859-8241	19300
Bunnell Rocky Log & Forest Mgt	Monroe	NH	G	603 638-4983	19089
Butch Eaton Logging & Trucki	East Wakefield	NH	G	603 522-3894	18094
C W Mock Logging	Bradford	NH	G	603 938-6096	17740
CCM Logging Land Clearing LLC	New London	NH	G	603 387-1853	19314
Chuck Rose Inc	Contoocook	NH	F	603 746-2311	17942
Cmd Logging	Center Barnstead	NH	G	603 986-5055	17788
Copp Logging LLC	Fremont	NH	G	603 479-4828	18175
Dale E Crawford	Sanbornville	NH	G	603 473-2738	19782
Dans Logging & Construction	Colebrook	NH	G	603 237-4040	17867
David R Burl	Goffstown	NH	G	603 235-2661	18199
DH Hardwick & Sons Inc	Bennington	NH	E	603 588-6618	17688
Fadden Chipping & Logging Inc	Center Conway	NH	F	603 939-2462	17797
Forrest P Hicks II	Jefferson	NH	G	603 586-9819	18483
Fred C Weld Inc	Cornish	NH	G	603 675-6147	17960
G M L of NH Inc	Colebrook	NH	G	603 237-5231	17868
G&S Logging	Colebrook	NH	G	603 237-4929	17869
Gagne & Sons Logging Co LLC	Dummer	NH	G	603 449-2255	18070
Garland Lumber Company Inc	Center Conway	NH	E	603 356-5636	17798
Garland Transportation Corp	Center Conway	NH	G	603 356-5636	17799
Garrett G Gilpatric	Bristol	NH	G	603 744-3286	17765
Gilles Champagne	Colebrook	NH	G	603 237-5272	17870
Haffordlogging	Hillsboro	NH	G	603 478-0142	18313
HB Logging LLC	Monroe	NH	G	603 638-4983	19090
High Tech Harvesting LLC	Loudon	NH	G	603 229-0750	18748
Huntington Logging	Piermont	NH	G	603 272-9322	19492
J R Logging Inc	Colebrook	NH	G	603 237-8010	17872
Jason S Landry	Loudon	NH	G	603 783-1154	18749
John C Whyte	Salisbury	NH	G	603 530-1168	19781
Jon Strong Low Impact Log LLC	New Boston	NH	G	603 487-5298	19293
Kel Log Inc **(PA)**	Milan	NH	E	603 752-2000	19040
Kel Log Inc	Gorham	NH	E	603 752-2000	18213
Lance Williams & Son Logging &	Center Tuftonboro	NH	G	603 569-3349	17808
Laurence Sharpe	Alexandria	NH	G	603 744-8175	17537
Lemire R & Sons LLC	Antrim	NH	G	603 588-3718	17595
Lessard & Sons Logging Inc	Berlin	NH	G	603 752-5767	17699
Magoon Logging LLC	Loudon	NH	G	603 435-9918	18750
Margaret Quint Logging	Conway	NH	G	603 447-3957	17955
Mark Welch	Walpole	NH	G	603 835-6347	19923
Monadnock Land Clearing	Greenville	NH	G	603 878-2803	18227
Moose Mountain Logging Inc	Tamworth	NH	G	603 491-3667	19893
Nadeau Logging	Lyndeborough	NH	G	603 654-2594	18759
On The Ball Cutnhaul	Laconia	NH	G	603 851-3283	18578
Ossipee Mountain Land Co LLC	Tamworth	NH	E	603 323-7677	19894
Pat Gagne Logging	Dummer	NH	G	603 449-2479	18071
Peter Pierce	Belmont	NH	G	603 524-8312	17679
Phils Tree Service and Log	Keene	NH	G	603 352-0202	18521
Pine River Logging	Effingham	NH	G	603 833-1340	18096
R L Cook Timber Harvesting	Winchester	NH	G	603 239-6424	19994
Rancloes Logging LLC	Stewartstown	NH	G	603 237-4474	19863
Richard Dupuis Logging Inc	Groveton	NH	G	603 636-2986	18234

	CITY	ST	EMP	PHONE	ENTRY #
Roy E Amey	Pittsburg	NH	G	603 538-6913	19495
SDS Logging Inc	Jefferson	NH	G	603 586-7098	18486
Stacey Thompson	Orford	NH	G	603 353-9700	19421
Steve Leighton	Barnstead	NH	G	603 664-2378	17617
Stockley Trucking Inc	Landaff	NH	G	603 838-2860	18609
Swr & Son Logging	Stewartstown	NH	G	603 237-4158	19864
Th Logging	North Haverhill	NH	G	603 787-6235	19390
Thibodeau Logging & Excav LLC	Wolfeboro	NH	G	603 953-5983	20026
Treeline Timber	Jefferson	NH	G	603 586-7725	18487
W Craig Washburn	Colebrook	NH	G	603 237-8403	17877
Walter Buckwold Logging	Orange	NH	G	603 523-9626	19419
Warick Management Company Inc	Pittsburg	NH	G	603 538-7112	19496
Welog Inc	Colebrook	NH	F	603 237-8277	17878
Edwoods Firewood & Logging	Mapleville	RI	G	401 568-6585	20613
J Tefft Logging & Firewoo	Hope Valley	RI	G	401 539-9838	20485
James Thompson Native Lumber	Hopkinton	RI	F	401 377-2837	20487
Mark Goodwin Wooden Bowls	Foster	RI	G	866 478-4065	20457
Miller Firewood & Logging Inc	Exeter	RI	G	401 539-7707	20452
AMP Timber Harvesting Inc	West Townshend	VT	G	802 874-7260	22625
Authentic Log Homes Inc	Hardwick	VT	G	802 472-5096	22009
Basin Timber LLC	Belvidere Center	VT	G	802 343-4694	21658
Black Bear Tree Svc	Brandon	VT	G	802 345-2815	21707
Bruce Waite Logging Inc	Dorset	VT	G	802 867-2213	21907
Calvin Johnson	Chelsea	VT	G	802 685-3205	21837
Canopy Timber Alternatives	Middlebury	VT	G	802 388-1548	22107
Ceylon R Morehouse Logging	Concord	VT	G	802 695-4660	21890
Chief Logging & Cnstr Inc	South Ryegate	VT	F	802 584-3868	22495
Chris Clark	Vershire	VT	G	802 356-0044	22558
Chris J Seamans	Middletown Springs	VT	G	802 287-9399	22123
Cobb Lumber Inc	South Londonderry	VT	G	802 824-5228	22484
Codling Brothers Logging	Plainfield	VT	G	802 454-7177	22266
Corbin & Son Logging Inc	Reading	VT	G	802 484-3329	22305
Dave and Jeff Logging & Firewd	Barton	VT	G	802 355-0465	21649
Dennis Ducharme	Marshfield	VT	G	802 426-3796	22094
Derrick Clifford Logging LLC	Orwell	VT	G	802 948-2798	22254
E&M Logging & Land Clearing LL	Wardsboro	VT	G	802 896-6091	22576
Fontaine Logging	Hardwick	VT	G	802 472-6140	22011
Green Mountain Chipping Inc **(PA)**	Underhill	VT	G	802 899-1239	22548
Greg Manning Logging LLC	Corinth	VT	G	802 439-6255	21891
Hillside Stone Products Inc	Barre	VT	F	802 479-2508	21623
La Foe Brian	Orleans	VT	G	802 754-8837	22249
Lafoe Logging LLC	Orleans	VT	G	802 754-8837	22250
Leavitt Logging LLC	Belvidere Center	VT	G	802 644-1440	21660
Longto Tree Service	Bradford	VT	G	802 274-9308	21703
Mahar Excavating & Logging	Bennington	VT	G	802 442-2954	21681
Marc J Riendeau	Danville	VT	G	802 748-6252	21897
Mike Lowell Logging & Wood	Wolcott	VT	G	802 279-6993	22731
New Life Logging	Rochester	VT	G	802 767-9142	22319
Norm Brown Logging	Benson	VT	G	802 537-4474	21692
Otterman Logging & Excavating	West Topsham	VT	G	802 439-5714	22623
P and L Trucking	Chester	VT	G	802 875-2819	21847
Paul A Morse	Newport Center	VT	G	802 334-9160	22207
Pjf Trucking and Logging LLC	Bellows Falls	VT	G	802 463-3343	21653
Reginald J Riendeau	Orleans	VT	G	802 754-6003	22251
Rusty D Inc	Elmore	VT	G	802 888-8838	21922
Stebennes Logging	Hartland	VT	G	802 436-3250	22018
Stephane Inkel Inc	Canaan	VT	G	802 266-8878	21826
T B Lincoln Logging Inc	Brookfield	VT	G	802 276-3172	21765
Thompson Family Enterprises	Woodbury	VT	G	802 456-7421	22734
Weston Island Logging Inc	Londonderry	VT	G	802 824-3708	22058
Wright Maintenance Inc	Newfane	VT	G	802 365-9253	22189

2421 Saw & Planing Mills

	CITY	ST	EMP	PHONE	ENTRY #
Biomass Energy LLC	Weatogue	CT	E	540 872-3300	5041
Burell Bros Inc	Hampton	CT	G	860 455-9681	1796
Cedar Swamp Log & Lumber	Woodstock	CT	G	860 974-2344	5496
Charles Pike & Sons	Hampton	CT	G	860 455-9968	1797
Dalla Corte Lumber	Stafford Springs	CT	G	860 875-9480	4108
Decks R US	New Britain	CT	G	860 505-0726	2527
E R Hinman & Sons Inc	Burlington	CT	G	860 673-9170	677
Ensign-Bckford Rnwble Enrgies	Simsbury	CT	E	860 843-2000	3902
Eylward Timber Co	Wallingford	CT	G	203 265-4276	4742
Interstate + Lakeland Lbr Corp	Greenwich	CT	F	203 531-8050	1623
John J Pawloski Lumber Inc	Bethel	CT	G	203 794-0737	165
Jordan Saw Mill L L C	Sterling	CT	F	860 774-0247	4367
Moores Sawmill Inc	Bloomfield	CT	G	860 242-3003	244
Ppk Inc	Branford	CT	G	203 376-9180	338
Scotland Hardwoods LLC	Scotland	CT	E	860 423-1233	3747
Sigfridson Wood Products LLC	Brooklyn	CT	G	860 774-2075	672
Stuart Hardwood Corp	New Haven	CT	G	203 376-0036	2740
Tallon Lumber Inc	Canaan	CT	E	860 824-0733	691
Tronox Incorporated **(DH)**	Stamford	CT	C	203 705-3800	4350
Walker Industries LLC	Ashford	CT	G	860 455-3554	28
Bannish Lumber Inc	Chester	MA	F	413 354-2279	9980
Cersosimo Lumber Company Inc	Hardwick	MA	F	413 477-6258	11373
Chocorua Valley Lumber Company	Bellingham	MA	F	508 883-6878	8033
Cns Outdoor Technologies LLC	Greenfield	MA	F	413 475-3840	11254
Cook Forest Products Inc	Upton	MA	E	508 634-3300	15906
Environmental Improvements **(PA)**	Abington	MA	G	781 857-2375	7324
Georgia-Pacific LLC	Norwood	MA	G	781 440-3600	14155
Gingras Lumber Inc	Ashley Falls	MA	G	413 229-2182	7674
Gsoutfitting	Greenfield	MA	G	413 773-0247	11263
Heyes Forest Products Inc	Orange	MA	G	978 544-8801	14217
Heyoka Solutions LLC	Falmouth	MA	G	866 389-8578	10790
Jarvenpaa & Sons	Westminster	MA	G	978 874-2231	16807
Joseph K Delano Sawmill Inc	North Dartmouth	MA	G	508 994-8752	13923
Lashway Logging Inc	Williamsburg	MA	F	413 268-3600	16952
Lenox Lumber Co	Pittsfield	MA	F	413 637-2744	14484
Leon M Fiske Company Inc	Greenfield	MA	G	413 772-6833	11268
Northeast Building Products	Marlborough	MA	G	508 786-5600	12798
Rex Lumber Company **(PA)**	Acton	MA	D	800 343-0567	7378
Roberts Brothers Lumber Co	Ashfield	MA	E	413 628-3333	7654
Saw Mill Brook LLC	Newton	MA	G	617 332-5793	13632
Sawmill Brook Farm	Bridgewater	MA	G	508 697-7847	9087
Sawmill Park	Southwick	MA	G	413 569-3393	15417
Shedworks Inc	Palmer	MA	G	413 284-1600	14296
Theodore Wolf Inc	East Falmouth	MA	G	508 457-0667	10450
Turn Key Lumber Inc	Lunenburg	MA	E	978 798-1370	12484
West Wearham Pine	East Freetown	MA	G	508 763-4108	10463
Wood St Wood Co	Middleboro	MA	G	508 947-6886	13082
A W Chaffee **(PA)**	Oakland	ME	G	207 465-3234	6528
A W Chaffee	Clinton	ME	E	207 426-8588	5912
Bear Hill Lumber Co	Hollis Center	ME	F	207 929-5225	6198
Carrier Chipping Inc	Skowhegan	ME	F	207 858-4277	6971
Cousineau Wood Products ME LLC	North Anson	ME	F	207 635-4445	6500
Cousins Sawmill	Windsor	ME	G	207 445-2467	7263
Daaquam Lumber Maine Inc **(HQ)**	Masardis	ME	C	207 435-6401	6415
Dimension Lumber	Peru	ME	G	207 897-9973	6585
Forest Chester Products Inc	Lincoln	ME	E	207 794-2303	6353
Fulghum Fibres Inc	Baileyville	ME	E	207 427-6560	5625
Georgia-Pacific LLC	Baileyville	ME	G	207 427-4077	5626
Gerrity Company Incorporated	Leeds	ME	E	207 933-2804	6269
Gillis Lumber Inc	Danforth	ME	G	207 448-2218	5941
Great Brook Lumber Inc	Lebanon	ME	G	207 457-1063	6265
Hotham & Sons Lumber Inc	New Gloucester	ME	G	207 926-4231	6467
Irving Woodlands LLC	Dixfield	ME	C	207 562-4400	5957
Irving Woodlands LLC **(HQ)**	St John Plt	ME	E	207 834-5767	7058
Jackman Lumber Inc **(PA)**	Jackman	ME	E	207 668-4407	6217
Jordan Family Chipping Inc	Kezar Falls	ME	G	207 625-8890	6249
K B Logging Inc	Smyrna Mills	ME	F	207 757-8818	6993
K L Mason & Sons Inc	North Turner	ME	G	207 224-7628	6515
Limington Lumber Company	East Baldwin	ME	E	207 625-3286	5974
Linkletter and Sons Inc	Athens	ME	E	207 654-2301	5541
Lmj Enterprises LLC **(PA)**	Lincoln	ME	G	207 794-3489	6358
Lovell Lumber Co Inc	Lovell	ME	E	207 925-6455	6384
Maine Cedar Specialty Products	Ludlow	ME	G	207 532-4034	6387
Maine Post & Beam LLC	North Yarmouth	ME	G	207 751-6793	6518
Maine Woods Company LLC	Portage	ME	G	207 435-4393	6598
Melvin L Yoder	Corinna	ME	G	207 278-3539	5922
Moose River Lumber Company Inc	Moose River	ME	D	207 668-4426	6453
N C Hunt Inc	Damariscotta	ME	E	207 563-8503	5937
Oxford Timber Inc	Oxford	ME	F	207 539-9656	6570
Palletone of Maine Inc	Livermore Falls	ME	C	207 897-5711	6380
Phinney Lumber Co	Gorham	ME	E	207 839-3336	6124
Pleasant River Lumber Company **(PA)**	Dover Foxcroft	ME	D	207 564-8520	5964
Portable Sawmill	Eddington	ME	G	207 843-7216	5998
Price Companies Inc	West Paris	ME	E	207 674-3663	7177
Prl Hancock LLC	Hancock	ME	E	207 564-8520	6171
R & R Lumber Company Inc	Carmel	ME	G	207 848-3726	5893
R H Wales & Son Inc	Fryeburg	ME	G	207 925-1363	6102
Red Mill	Casco	ME	G	207 655-7520	5895
Repose Fire Logs LLC	Sebago	ME	G	207 595-8035	6954
Robbins Lumber Inc	Searsmont	ME	C	207 342-5221	6945
Robert W Libby	Porter	ME	G	207 625-8285	6604
Sebasticook Lumber LLC	Saint Albans	ME	G	207 660-1360	6865
Tukey Brothers Inc	Belgrade	ME	F	207 465-3570	5700
Usaccess Inc	New Portland	ME	G	207 541-9421	6475
Whitefield Dry Kiln Inc	Whitefield	ME	G	207 549-5470	7220
Wood-Mizer Holdings Inc	Chesterville	ME	F	207 645-2072	5909
Yates Lumber Inc	Lee	ME	F	207 738-2331	6267
Breezy Hill Lumber Co	Barnstead	NH	F	603 496-8870	17615
Cellar Crafts	Mont Vernon	NH	G	603 673-3615	19092
Cersosimo Lumber Company Inc	Rumney	NH	E	603 786-9482	19695
Chester Forest Products Inc	Chester	NH	G	603 887-4123	17823
Contoocook River Lumber Inc	Henniker	NH	E	603 428-3636	18303
Cousineau Lumber Inc	Henniker	NH	G	603 428-7155	18304
Daves Sitework and Sawmill	Fitzwilliam	NH	G	603 313-0787	18148
Durgin and Crowell Lbr Co Inc	New London	NH	C	603 763-2860	19315
F C Hammond & Son Lbr Co Inc	Canaan	NH	F	603 523-4353	17778
Goss Lumber Co Inc	Henniker	NH	G	603 428-3363	18305
Granite State Forest Products	Henniker	NH	G	603 428-7890	18306
Harold Estey Lumber Inc	Londonderry	NH	G	603 432-5184	18701
Homegrown Lumber	Center Conway	NH	G	603 447-3800	17800
Josselyns Sawmill Inc	Jefferson	NH	G	603 586-4507	18485

Employee Codes: A=Over 500 employees, B=251-500
C=101-250, D=51-100 E=20-50, F=10-19, G=3-9

	CITY	ST	EMP	PHONE	ENTRY #
King Forest Industries Inc **(PA)**	Wentworth	NH	D	603 764-5711	19946
Madison Lumber Mill Inc	Madison	NH	D	603 539-4145	18764
Ossipee Chipping Inc	Center Ossipee	NH	G	603 539-5097	17805
Outdoor Enhancements LLC	Laconia	NH	G	603 524-8090	18580
Patenaude Lumber Company Inc	Henniker	NH	E	603 428-3224	18310
Perras Lumber Co Inc	Groveton	NH	E	603 636-1830	18232
Precision Lumber Inc	Wentworth	NH	D	603 764-9450	19947
R L Balla Inc	South Acworth	NH	F	603 835-6529	19854
Tommila Brothers Inc	Fitzwilliam	NH	F	603 242-7774	18153
Wilkins Lumber Co Inc	Milford	NH	G	603 673-2545	19082
Blackstone Valley Prestain	Mapleville	RI	G	401 568-9745	20611
James Thompson Native Lumber	Hopkinton	RI	F	401 377-2837	20487
Rathbuns Sawmill Inc	West Greenwich	RI	G	401 397-3996	21464
Sonco Worldwide Inc	Warwick	RI	F	401 406-3761	21427
A Johnson Co	Bristol	VT	D	802 453-4884	21760
Allard Lumber Company **(PA)**	Brattleboro	VT	E	802 254-4939	21717
Brattleboro Kiln Dry & Milling	Brattleboro	VT	E	802 254-4528	21720
Carris Reels Inc **(HQ)**	Proctor	VT	C	802 773-9111	22284
Cersosimo Lumber Company Inc **(PA)**	Brattleboro	VT	C	802 254-4508	21724
Claire Lathrop Band Mill Inc	Bristol	VT	E	802 453-3606	21763
Clifford Lumber LLP	Hinesburg	VT	G	802 482-2325	22021
Cobb Lumber Inc	South Londonderry	VT	G	802 824-5228	22484
Colton Enterprises Inc	Pittsfield	VT	G	802 746-8033	22262
Dci Inc	South Royalton	VT	F	802 763-7847	22490
Dennis Ducharme	Marshfield	VT	G	802 426-3796	22094
Gilcris Enterprises Inc	Proctorsville	VT	F	802 226-7764	22288
Godfreys Sawmill LLC	Montgomery Center	VT	G	802 326-4868	22142
Granville Manufacturing Co	Granville	VT	G	802 767-4747	22003
Green Mountain Forest Products	Highgate Center	VT	F	802 868-2306	22020
Greenwood Mill Inc	Bradford	VT	F	802 626-0800	21700
Kerber Saw Mill	Guilford	VT	G	802 257-0614	22007
Lamell Lumber Corporation	Essex Junction	VT	E	802 878-2475	21948
M B Heath & Sons Lumber Inc	North Hyde Park	VT	G	802 635-2538	22232
M Piette & Sons Lumber Inc	Irasburg	VT	F	802 754-8876	22040
Manchester Lumber Inc	Johnson	VT	E	802 635-2315	22051
Mill River Lumber Ltd	North Clarendon	VT	D	802 775-0032	22220
N W P Inc	Pownal	VT	G	802 442-4749	22282
Northeast Timber Exchange LLC **(PA)**	Chester	VT	G	802 875-1037	21846
Sheehan & Sons Lumber	Perkinsville	VT	G	802 263-5545	22258
Van Alstyne Family Farm Inc	South Royalton	VT	G	802 763-7036	22494

2426 Hardwood Dimension & Flooring Mills

	CITY	ST	EMP	PHONE	ENTRY #
Ben Barretts LLC	Thompson	CT	G	860 928-9373	4532
Conway Hardwood Products LLC	Gaylordsville	CT	E	860 355-4030	1530
E R Hinman & Sons Inc	Burlington	CT	G	860 673-9170	677
Kellogg Hardwoods Inc	Bethel	CT	G	203 797-1992	166
Stake Company LLC	East Windsor	CT	G	860 623-2700	1305
Tallon Lumber Inc	Canaan	CT	E	860 824-0733	691
Wilson Woodworks Inc	Windsor	CT	F	860 870-2500	5379
Architectural Timber Mllwk Inc	Hadley	MA	F	413 586-3045	11305
Bannish Lumber Inc	Chester	MA	F	413 354-2279	9980
Canner Incorporated	West Groton	MA	F	978 448-3063	16479
Hydronics Manufacturing Inc	North Billerica	MA	G	978 528-4335	13825
L S Hardwood Floor	Dorchester	MA	G	617 288-0339	10346
Lawson Hemphill Inc	Swansea	MA	G	508 679-5364	15706
Mr Sandless Central Mass	Worcester	MA	G	508 864-6517	17425
Oak Gallery Inc **(PA)**	Littleton	MA	G	978 486-9846	12314
Pine and Baker Mfg Inc	Tewksbury	MA	F	978 851-1215	15825
Roberts Brothers Lumber Co	Ashfield	MA	E	413 628-3333	7654
South Shore Wood Pellets Inc	Holbrook	MA	G	781 986-7797	11538
Stiles & Hart Brick Company	Bridgewater	MA	E	508 697-6928	9088
Universal Hardwood Flooring	Boston	MA	G	617 783-2307	8899
Bear Paw Lumber Corp **(PA)**	Fryeburg	ME	F	207 935-3052	6095
Blue Hill Cabinet & Woodwork	Blue Hill	ME	G	207 374-2260	5770
Columbia Forest Products Inc	Presque Isle	ME	C	207 760-3800	6757
Elkins & Co Inc	Boothbay	ME	F	207 633-0109	5777
Ernest R Palmer Lumber Co Inc	Sangerville	ME	G	207 876-2725	6899
K B Logging Inc	Smyrna Mills	ME	F	207 757-8818	6993
Kelly Lumber Sales Inc	Old Town	ME	F	207 435-4950	6542
Lovell Lumber Co Inc	Lovell	ME	E	207 925-6455	6384
Moosewood Millworks LLC	Ashland	ME	F	207 435-4950	5537
Pride Manufacturing Co LLC	Guilford	ME	F	207 876-2719	6159
Turning Acquisitions LLC	Buckfield	ME	E	207 336-2400	5853
Vic Firth Company	Newport	ME	G	207 368-4358	6488
Vic Firth Manufacturing Inc	Newport	ME	C	207 368-4358	6489
Precision Lumber Inc	Wentworth	NH	D	603 764-9450	19947
Robes Dana Wood Craftsmen **(PA)**	Hanover	NH	G	603 643-9355	18296
Scott L Northcott	Walpole	NH	G	603 756-4204	19924
Swift River Wood Products	Chocorua	NH	G	603 323-3317	17832
Tommila Brothers Inc	Fitzwilliam	NH	F	603 242-7774	18153
Dycem Corporation **(DH)**	Smithfield	RI	E	401 738-4420	21222
F & S Wood Products	Jamestown	RI	G	401 423-1048	20490
A Johnson Co	Bristol	VT	D	802 453-4884	21760
Appalachian Engineered Flrg Inc	North Troy	VT	F	802 988-1073	22240
Charron Wood Products Inc	Windsor	VT	G	802 369-0166	22706
Columbia Forest Products Inc	Newport	VT	B	802 334-6711	22193
Dci Inc	South Royalton	VT	F	802 763-7847	22490
Dennis Ducharme	Marshfield	VT	G	802 426-3796	22094
Emery Floor Inc	Johnson	VT	G	802 635-7652	22049
G W Lumber & Millwork Inc **(PA)**	Williston	VT	G	802 860-7370	22666
Granville Manufacturing Co	Granville	VT	G	802 767-4747	22003
N W P Inc	Pownal	VT	G	802 442-4749	22282

2429 Special Prdt Sawmills, NEC

	CITY	ST	EMP	PHONE	ENTRY #
Bonito Manufacturing Inc	North Haven	CT	D	203 234-8786	3011
Bees Wrap LLC	Middlebury	VT	E	802 643-2132	22101
Green Mtn Grn & Barrel LLC	Richmond	VT	G	802 324-5838	22311

2431 Millwork

	CITY	ST	EMP	PHONE	ENTRY #
77 Mattatuck Heights LLC	Waterbury	CT	E	203 597-9338	4834
Alvarado Custom Cabinetry LLC	Norwalk	CT	F	203 831-0181	3099
American Overhead Ret Div Inc	Middletown	CT	G	860 876-4552	2171
Anderson Stair & Railing	North Haven	CT	F	203 288-0117	3008
Arbon Equipment Corporation	Bloomfield	CT	G	410 796-5902	202
Atlantic Woodcraft Inc	Enfield	CT	F	860 749-4887	1347
Axels Custom Woodworking LLC	Greenwich	CT	G	203 869-1317	1595
B H Davis Co	Thompson	CT	G	860 923-2771	4531
Bergan Architectural Wdwkg Inc	Middletown	CT	E	860 346-0869	2177
Birkett Woodworking LLC	Morris	CT	G	860 361-9142	2431
Breakfast Woodworks Inc	Guilford	CT	G	203 458-8888	1694
Byrne Woodworking Inc	Bridgeport	CT	G	203 953-3205	393
C J S Millwork Inc	Stamford	CT	F	203 708-0080	4153
Clancy Woodworking LLC	Sherman	CT	G	860 355-3655	3893
Colonial Wood Products Inc	West Haven	CT	F	203 932-9003	5112
Colonial Woodworking Inc	Norwalk	CT	F	203 866-5844	3128
Connecticut Carpentry LLC	Meriden	CT	E	203 639-8585	2088
Connecticut Millwork Inc	Vernon	CT	G	860 875-2860	4665
Conway Hardwood Products LLC	Gaylordsville	CT	E	860 355-4030	1530
CT Woodworking LLC	North Franklin	CT	G	860 884-9586	2988
Curtiss Woodworking Inc	Prospect	CT	F	203 527-9305	3586
Custom Design Woodworks LLC	Old Lyme	CT	G	860 434-0515	3319
Dalbergia LLC **(PA)**	Tolland	CT	G	860 870-2500	4543
Dante Ltd	Jewett City	CT	G	860 376-0204	1911
Deschenes & Cooper Architectur	Pawcatuck	CT	G	860 599-2481	3434
Dlz Architectural Mill Work	Hartford	CT	G	860 883-7562	1818
East Coast Stairs Co Inc	South Windsor	CT	G	860 528-7096	3960
Fagan Design & Fabrication	West Haven	CT	G	203 937-1874	5122
Fairfield County Millwork	Bethany	CT	F	203 393-9751	120
Fairfield Woodworks LLC	Stratford	CT	F	203 380-9842	4411
Ferraro Custom Woodwork LLC	Milford	CT	G	203 876-1280	2289
G M F Woodworking LLC	Norwalk	CT	G	203 788-8979	3155
Griffin Green	Bethlehem	CT	G	203 266-5727	195
H & S Woodworks L T D	New Milford	CT	G	914 391-3926	2805
Indars Stairs LLC	Lebanon	CT	G	860 208-3826	1935
Industrial Sales Corp **(PA)**	Westport	CT	F	203 227-5988	5202
Industrial Wood Product Co	Shelton	CT	G	203 735-2374	3817
Jacobsen Woodworking Co Inc	Greenwich	CT	G	203 531-9050	1624
Jakes Jr Lawrence	Pomfret Center	CT	E	860 974-3744	3555
James J Licari **(PA)**	Bridgeport	CT	G	203 333-5000	434
John M Kriskey Carpentry	Greenwich	CT	G	203 531-0194	1625
Johnson Millwork Inc	East Hampton	CT	G	860 267-4693	1161
KB Custom Stair Builders Inc	North Haven	CT	G	203 234-0836	3037
Kingsland Co	Norfolk	CT	G	860 542-6981	2957
Legacy Woodworking LLC	Meriden	CT	G	203 440-9710	2099
Legere Group Ltd	Avon	CT	C	860 674-0392	37
Leos Kitchen & Stair Corp	New Britain	CT	G	860 225-7363	2548
Lingard Cabinet Co LLC	Manchester	CT	G	860 647-9886	2019
Luckey LLC	New Haven	CT	F	203 285-3819	2709
Maddog LLC	Milford	CT	G	203 878-0147	2312
Madigan Millwork Inc	Unionville	CT	G	860 673-7601	4658
Mars Architectural Millwork	Bridgeport	CT	G	203 579-2632	447
Maurer & Shepherd Joyners	Glastonbury	CT	F	860 633-2383	1563
Millwork Shop LLC	Torrington	CT	G	860 489-8848	4587
Modern Woodcrafts LLC	Plainville	CT	D	860 677-7371	3508
Naugatuck Stair Company Inc	Naugatuck	CT	F	203 729-7134	2488
New England Cabinet Co Inc	New Britain	CT	F	860 747-9995	2555
New England Fine Woodworking	Chester	CT	G	860 526-5799	773
New England Joinery Works Inc	Essex	CT	G	860 767-3377	1404
New England Stair Company Inc	Shelton	CT	E	203 924-0606	3838
New England Standard Corp	Milford	CT	G	203 876-7733	2320
Niantic Awning Company	Niantic	CT	G	860 739-0161	2954
Nichols Woodworking LLC **(PA)**	Washington Depot	CT	G	860 350-4223	4833
Northeast Stair Company LLC	Tolland	CT	G	860 875-3358	4551
Orion Manufacturing LLC	Mystic	CT	G	860 572-2921	2447
Paco Assensio Woodworking LLC	Norwalk	CT	G	203 536-2608	3213
Petrunti Design & Wdwkg LLC	West Hartford	CT	G	860 953-5332	5090
Porta Door Co	Seymour	CT	E	203 888-6191	3761
Precision Woodcraft Inc	Canton	CT	G	860 693-3641	698
Prescott Cabinet Co	Pawcatuck	CT	G	860 495-0176	3441
Quality Stairs Inc	Bridgeport	CT	E	203 367-8390	477
R Woodworking Larson Inc	Manchester	CT	E	860 646-7904	2041
Red Barn Woodworkers	Winsted	CT	G	860 379-3158	5420
Ridgefield Overhead Door LLC	Ridgefield	CT	G	203 431-3667	3679
River Mill Co	Clinton	CT	F	860 669-5915	794

	CITY	ST	EMP	PHONE	ENTRY #
Robert L Lovallo	Stamford	CT	G	203 324-6655	4304
Roman Woodworking	New Britain	CT	G	860 490-5989	2574
Saxony Wood Products Inc	Greenwich	CT	G	203 869-3717	1647
Schuco USA Lllp **(HQ)**	Newington	CT	D	860 666-0505	2901
Soja Woodworking LLC	Higganum	CT	G	860 345-3909	1906
Stately Stair Co Inc	Waterbury	CT	E	203 575-1966	4960
Summit Stair Co Inc	Bethel	CT	F	203 778-2251	181
Swanhart Woodworking	New Fairfield	CT	G	203 746-1184	2628
Tl Woodworking	Hamden	CT	G	203 787-9661	1788
Torrington Lumber Company	Torrington	CT	G	860 482-3529	4605
V & V Woodworking LLC	Bethel	CT	G	203 740-9494	188
Walston Inc	Guilford	CT	G	203 453-5929	1724
Wesconn Stairs Inc	Danbury	CT	G	203 792-7367	1008
West Hrtford Stirs Cbinets Inc	Newington	CT	D	860 953-9151	2912
Wezenski Woodworking	Branford	CT	G	203 488-3255	360
White Dog Woodworking LLC	Torrington	CT	G	860 482-3776	4607
Winchester Woodworks LLC	Winsted	CT	G	860 379-9875	5431
Woodwork Specialties Inc	Bristol	CT	G	860 583-4848	627
Woodworkers Club LLC	Norwalk	CT	G	203 847-9663	3273
Woodworking Plus LLC	Bethany	CT	G	203 393-1967	125
York Millwork LLC	Old Greenwich	CT	G	203 698-3460	3314
Zavarella Woodworking Inc	Newington	CT	G	860 666-6969	2913
A & P Woodworking Inc	Boston	MA	G	617 569-4664	8331
Abbas Shahrestanaki	Norwood	MA	G	617 548-0986	14116
Ackles Steel & Iron Company	Waltham	MA	F	781 893-6818	16022
Advanced Trimwright Inc	East Taunton	MA	E	508 822-7745	10509
Advanced Woodworking Technolog	Lowell	MA	G	978 937-1400	12340
AKa McHlngelo Strbuilder LLC	North Easton	MA	C	508 238-9054	13940
Al Woodworking	Rutland	MA	G	508 886-2883	14879
Allen Woodworking LLC	Bellingham	MA	G	617 306-6479	8029
Andersen Corporation	Fall River	MA	G	508 235-0300	10659
Architectural Elements Inc	Boxboro	MA	G	978 263-2482	8951
Architectural Openings Inc	Somerville	MA	F	617 776-9223	15155
Architectural Timber Mllwk Inc	Hadley	MA	F	413 586-3045	11305
Atlantis Woodworking Inc	Salem	MA	G	978 745-5312	14894
Bancroft Custom Woodworks	Williamstown	MA	G	413 738-7001	16954
Baranowski Woodworking Co Inc	East Bridgewater	MA	G	508 690-1515	10407
Bay State Partition & Fix Co	Boston	MA	G	617 782-1113	8393
Berger Corporation	Orleans	MA	G	508 255-3267	14230
Blue Anchor Woodworks Inc	Marblehead	MA	G	781 631-2390	12677
Boston Sash & Millwork Inc	North Dighton	MA	F	508 880-8808	13930
Boston Turning Works	Watertown	MA	G	617 924-4747	16275
Botelho Wood Working	Fall River	MA	G	774 240-7235	10671
Brendan C Kinnane Inc	Fall River	MA	G	508 679-8479	10672
Brockway-Smith Company	West Hatfield	MA	D	413 247-9674	16482
Brogans Custom Woodworking	Westminster	MA	G	978 502-8013	16803
Builders Supply of Cape Cod	Sandwich	MA	G	508 888-0444	14963
Bwi of MA LLC	Leominster	MA	G	978 534-4065	12122
Caliper Woodworking Corp	Malden	MA	E	781 322-9760	12563
Cape Cod Cupola Co Inc	North Dartmouth	MA	G	508 994-2119	13916
Chebli Architectural Woodwork	Waltham	MA	G	781 642-0733	16066
Chilmark Archtctural Wdwkg LLC	Worcester	MA	F	508 856-9200	17355
Choice Woodworking Inc	North Reading	MA	G	978 207-0289	13980
Contemporary Cabinet Designs	Norwood	MA	G	781 769-7979	14143
Continental Woodcraft Inc **(PA)**	Worcester	MA	E	508 581-9560	17359
Craig F Bradford	Northampton	MA	G	413 586-4500	14003
Custom Woodworking LLC	Hubbardston	MA	G	978 928-3366	11743
D A Mfg Co LLC	Winchendon	MA	G	978 297-1059	17072
Dbi Woodworks Inc	Avon	MA	G	781 739-2060	7885
DH Custom Woodworks	Sharon	MA	G	781 784-5951	15049
Dixon Bros Millwork Inc	Abington	MA	G	781 261-9962	7323
East Coast Interiors Inc	North Dartmouth	MA	F	508 995-4200	13919
Ebano Woodworks Inc	Lawrence	MA	G	978 879-7206	12021
Everett Custom Woodworking	Hopkinton	MA	G	508 435-7675	11712
Forester Moulding & Lumber	Leominster	MA	F	978 840-3100	12140
General Woodworking Inc **(PA)**	Lowell	MA	F	978 458-6625	12373
George Dawe	Amesbury	MA	G	978 388-5565	7486
Georgia-Pacific LLC	Norwood	MA	G	781 440-3600	14155
Glenns Gardening & Woodworking	Boston	MA	G	617 548-7977	8566
Hawkes & Huberdeau Woodworking	Amesbury	MA	G	978 388-7747	7489
Horner Millwork Corp	Pembroke	MA	E	781 826-7770	14408
J B Sash & Door Company Inc	Chelsea	MA	E	617 884-8940	9955
J P Moriarty & Co Inc	Somerville	MA	G	617 628-3000	15187
Jain America Foods Inc	Chicopee	MA	E	413 593-8883	10035
Jan Woodworks Renovation	Westfield	MA	G	413 563-2534	16691
JC Clocks Company Inc	North Dartmouth	MA	E	508 998-8442	13922
Johncarlo Woodworking Inc	Westfield	MA	F	413 562-4002	16695
Joinery Shop Inc	Charlestown	MA	G	617 242-4718	9838
K Int L Woodworking	Norwood	MA	G	781 440-0512	14168
Kabinet Korner Inc	Malden	MA	E	781 324-9600	12574
Keiver Willard-Lumber Corp	Newburyport	MA	D	978 462-7193	13503
Kenyon Woodworking Inc	Jamaica Plain	MA	F	617 524-6883	11945
Kevin Cradock Woodworking Inc	Hyde Park	MA	G	617 524-2405	11872
Kevins Woodworks LLC	Fall River	MA	G	508 989-8692	10720
Laird Woodworking Inc	Rochdale	MA	G	508 892-8877	14782
Leveillee Archtctral Mllwk Inc	Spencer	MA	F	508 885-9731	15432
Lloyds Woodworking Inc	Hudson	MA	G	978 562-9007	11787
Louis Richards	Webster	MA	G	508 671-9017	16348
Marie Deprofio	Waltham	MA	G	781 894-9793	16147
Mark Gauvin	Mattapoisett	MA	G	508 758-2324	12888
Mark Richey Wdwkg & Design Inc	Newburyport	MA	D	978 499-3800	13510
Meridian Custom Woodworking In	Brockton	MA	G	508 587-4400	9165
Michael Humphries Woodworking	Northfield	MA	G	413 498-2187	14065
Miller H C Wood Working Inc	Holliston	MA	G	508 429-4220	11586
Mitton Millworks	Andover	MA	G	978 475-7761	7573
Modern Heritage LLC	Rowley	MA	G	781 913-8261	14859
Moore Woodworking Inc	Nantucket	MA	G	508 364-7338	13227
Munro Woodworking	Bellingham	MA	G	508 966-2654	8052
Nelson & Power Inc	Woburn	MA	G	781 933-0679	17238
New England Custom Wood Wkg	New Bedford	MA	G	508 991-8038	13422
New England Shrlines Companies	Pembroke	MA	F	781 826-0140	14418
Olde Bostonian	Boston	MA	G	617 282-9300	8746
P A W Inc	Ludlow	MA	G	413 589-0399	12474
Pomeroy & Co Inc	Charlestown	MA	E	617 241-0234	9841
Precision Woodworking	Quincy	MA	G	617 479-7604	14647
R P Woodworking Inc	North Oxford	MA	G	508 987-3722	13974
Ran Woodworking	Charlton	MA	G	508 248-4818	9855
Rex Lumber Company **(PA)**	Acton	MA	D	800 343-0567	7378
Rgc Millwork Incorporated	Lowell	MA	G	978 275-9529	12427
Richard Cantwell Woodworking	New Bedford	MA	G	508 984-7921	13445
Richard Pg Millwork Co Inc	Cummaquid	MA	G	508 776-2433	10172
Rjd Woodworking LLC	Fairhaven	MA	G	508 984-4315	10646
Ronald F Birrell	Becket	MA	G	413 219-6729	7954
Sb Development Corp	Acton	MA	G	978 263-2744	7384
Shaw Woodworking Inc	Pocasset	MA	G	508 563-1242	14601
Shawn Roberts Woodworking	Gilbertville	MA	G	413 477-0060	11155
Silva Woodworking	Westport	MA	G	508 636-0059	16846
South Shore Millwork Inc	Norton	MA	D	508 226-5500	14090
Southcoast Woodworking Inc	Mattapoisett	MA	G	508 758-3184	12890
Southeastern Millwork Co Inc	Sagamore Beach	MA	F	508 888-6038	14887
Southeastern Millwork Co Inc	Bourne	MA	F	508 888-6038	8949
Specialty Wholesale Sup Corp	Gardner	MA	E	978 632-1472	11128
Stokes Woodworking Co Inc **(PA)**	Hudson	MA	G	508 481-0414	11820
Thl-Nortek Investors LLC **(PA)**	Boston	MA	D	617 227-1050	8882
Toby Leary Fine Wdwkg Inc	Hyannis	MA	F	508 957-2281	11860
Top Notch Mill Work	Bourne	MA	G	508 432-4976	8950
Tradern Fine Woodworking Inc	Newton	MA	G	617 393-3733	13644
Trellis Structures Inc	East Templeton	MA	F	888 285-4624	10521
Triple Crown Cbnets Mllwk Corp	Sandwich	MA	G	508 833-6500	14974
Valiant Industries Inc	Amesbury	MA	E	978 388-3792	7510
VCA Inc	Northampton	MA	E	413 587-2750	14025
Vintage Millwork Corporation	Dracut	MA	G	978 957-1400	10370
Walter A Furman Co Inc	Fall River	MA	D	508 674-7751	10782
Watson Brothers Inc	Middleton	MA	F	978 774-7677	13106
Wayland Millwork Corporation	Marlborough	MA	F	508 485-4172	12847
Wesco Building & Design Inc	Stoneham	MA	E	781 279-0490	15572
Wescor Ltd	Boston	MA	G	617 731-3963	8921
Wescor Ltd **(PA)**	Stoneham	MA	F	781 279-0490	15573
Westek Architectural Wdwkg Inc	Westfield	MA	F	413 562-6363	16741
Westminster Millwork Corp	Fitchburg	MA	F	978 665-9200	10862
Wide Angle Marketing Inc	Hubbardston	MA	E	978 928-5400	11747
Widham Wood Corporation	Woburn	MA	G	781 932-8572	17320
Windham Wood Interiors Inc	Woburn	MA	G	781 932-8572	17321
Winer Woodworking	Plainville	MA	G	508 695-5871	14538
Woodcraft Designers Bldrs LLC	Canton	MA	G	508 584-4200	9796
Woodsmiths Inc	Fall River	MA	G	508 548-8343	10784
Wright Archtectural Mllwk Corp	Northampton	MA	E	413 586-3528	14027
Ziggy Woodworking	East Weymouth	MA	G	781 335-5218	10547
Alfreds Upholstering & Custom	Alfred	ME	F	207 536-5565	5514
Bass Cabinetry and Mllwk LLC	Greene	ME	G	207 754-0087	6147
Blevins Company	Edgecomb	ME	G	207 882-6396	5999
Blue Hill Cabinet & Woodwork	Blue Hill	ME	G	207 374-2260	5770
Coastal Woodworking Inc	Nobleboro	ME	E	207 563-1072	6492
Downeast Woodworks	Freeport	ME	G	207 781-4800	6076
East Coast Woodworking Inc	Brunswick	ME	G	207 442-0025	5835
F A Wilnauer Woodwork Inc	South Berwick	ME	G	207 384-4824	7002
Fernwood Inc **(PA)**	Cape Neddick	ME	G	207 363-7891	5879
Georgia-Pacific LLC	Baileyville	ME	G	207 427-4077	5626
Hill Tim Fine Woodworking	Gorham	ME	G	207 854-1387	6114
JC Millwork Inc	Mount Vernon	ME	G	207 293-4204	6459
John Costin Studio	Kennebunk	ME	G	207 985-7221	6237
Jordan Millworks Inc	Lincoln	ME	G	207 794-6178	6356
Kelley Bros New England LLC	Westbrook	ME	G	207 517-4100	7192
L M C Light Iron Inc	Limerick	ME	F	207 793-9957	6335
Little Harbor Window Co Inc	Berwick	ME	E	207 698-1332	5710
Lovett & Hall Woodworks	Gray	ME	G	207 650-5139	6140
Mathews Brothers Company **(PA)**	Belfast	ME	C	207 338-3360	5693
Morrison Millwork and Str Fixs	Windham	ME	G	207 892-9418	7242
New England Woodworks	Springvale	ME	G	207 324-6343	7054
Owen Gray & Son	Brewer	ME	G	207 989-3575	5800
P M Kelly Inc	Ashland	ME	F	207 435-6654	5539
Pickens Woodworking	Topsham	ME	G	207 725-8955	7092
Pond Cove Millwork Inc	Saco	ME	E	207 773-6819	6855
Quarter Point Woodworking LLC **(PA)**	New Gloucester	ME	G	207 926-1032	6471

Employee Codes: A=Over 500 employees, B=251-500
C=101-250, D=51-100 E=20-50, F=10-19, G=3-9

	CITY	ST	EMP	PHONE	ENTRY #
Quarter Point Woodworking LLC	Windham	ME	G	207 892-7022	7245
Saco Bay Millwork Co	Buxton	ME	F	207 929-8400	5860
Sunrise Home Inc	Scarborough	ME	G	207 839-8801	6941
Topsham Woodworking LLC	Topsham	ME	G	207 751-1032	7095
Traditional Wood Works Inc	Berwick	ME	G	207 676-9668	5713
Unique Spiral Stairs Inc	Albion	ME	G	207 437-2415	5513
West Minot Millwork Inc	West Minot	ME	G	207 966-3200	7175
Windham Millwork Inc	Windham	ME	D	207 892-3238	7260
American Custom Design Wdwkg	Tilton	NH	G	603 286-3239	19903
Anthony Galluzzo Corp	Londonderry	NH	E	603 432-2681	18676
AP Dley Cstm Laminating Corp	Windham	NH	E	603 437-6666	20000
Beech River Mill	Center Ossipee	NH	G	603 539-2636	17802
Boulia-Gorrell Lumber Co Inc	Laconia	NH	F	603 524-1300	18560
Boyce Highlands Furn Co Inc	Concord	NH	E	603 753-1042	17885
Chester Braley	Epsom	NH	G	239 841-0019	18105
Cogworks Ltd	Antrim	NH	G	603 588-3333	17594
Colonial Woodworking Inc	Bradford	NH	F	603 938-5131	17741
Complete Cvrage Wodpriming LLC	Allenstown	NH	G	603 485-1122	17538
Cox Woodworking Inc	Westmoreland	NH	G	603 399-7704	19970
Crossknots Woodworking	Stewartstown	NH	G	603 237-8392	19861
Depot Millworks	Littleton	NH	G	603 444-1656	18657
Dodge Woodworking LLC	East Kingston	NH	G	603 642-6188	18086
Donald A Jhnson Fine Wdwkg LLC	Intervale	NH	G	603 356-9080	18454
Dunn Woodworks	Chesterfield	NH	G	603 363-4180	17828
Fairview Millwork Inc	Seabrook	NH	G	603 929-4449	19800
Forest Manufacturing Corp	Auburn	NH	F	603 647-6991	17609
Hampshire Hardwoods LLC	Laconia	NH	G	603 434-1144	18565
Herrick Mill Work Inc	Contoocook	NH	E	603 746-5092	17945
Index Packaging Inc	Milton	NH	C	603 350-0018	19086
Jewell Woodworks LLC	Nottingham	NH	G	603 679-8025	19416
John J Marr	Conway	NH	F	603 939-2698	17954
Keller Products Incorporated	Bow	NH	E	603 224-5502	17719
Kelley Bros New England LLC	Nashua	NH	G	603 748-0274	19193
Kelley Bros New England LLC **(HQ)**	Hudson	NH	F	603 881-5559	18406
Kimballs Lumber Center LLC **(PA)**	Wolfeboro	NH	G	603 569-2477	20021
Kindelan Woodworking	Derry	NH	G	603 434-3253	17985
King & Co Architectural Wdwkg	Marlborough	NH	G	603 876-4900	18961
KSD Custom Wood Products Inc	Boscawen	NH	E	603 796-2951	17704
Littleton Millwork Inc	Littleton	NH	E	603 444-2677	18662
Mill City Leather Works	Manchester	NH	G	603 935-9974	18874
Millwork Masters Ltd **(PA)**	Keene	NH	F	603 358-3038	18515
Newfound Wood Works Inc **(PA)**	Bristol	NH	G	603 744-6872	17768
NH Woodworks LLC	Milford	NH	G	603 361-4727	19071
Norteast Woodworking Inc	Raymond	NH	G	603 895-4271	19641
Pasture Hill Millwork LLC	Rochester	NH	G	603 335-4175	19681
Port-O-Lite Company Inc	West Swanzey	NH	F	603 352-3205	19967
Procraft Corporation	New Boston	NH	F	603 487-2080	19296
Roland J Soucy Company LLC	Pelham	NH	G	603 635-3265	19445
Salmon Falls Woodworks LLC	Dover	NH	F	603 740-6060	18051
Thibco Inc	Manchester	NH	E	603 623-3011	18941
Tommila Brothers Inc	Fitzwilliam	NH	F	603 242-7774	18153
Traditional Woodworking LLC	Piermont	NH	G	603 272-9324	19493
Wards Woodworking Inc	Kingston	NH	G	603 642-7300	18548
Wood Works	Portsmouth	NH	G	603 436-3805	19632
Woodstone Company Inc	North Walpole	NH	E	603 445-2449	19397
Woodworks Architectural Mllwk	Londonderry	NH	E	603 432-4050	18746
Yankee Craftsman Inc	Auburn	NH	G	603 483-5900	17614
Yankee Shutter Co	New Boston	NH	G	603 487-2400	19299
Artisan Millwork Inc Cabi	Pawtucket	RI	G	401 721-5500	20813
Beasley Woodworks LLC	Charlestown	RI	G	401 529-5099	20130
Brouillette Realty LLC	Barrington	RI	G	401 499-4867	20043
Cas Acquisition Co LLC	North Smithfield	RI	F	401 884-8556	20783
Cloos Woodworking Inc	Johnston	RI	G	401 528-8629	20504
Design Fabricators Inc	Cranston	RI	E	401 944-5294	20209
East Coast Laminiating Company	Cumberland	RI	G	401 729-0097	20319
Eastern Design Inc	Manville	RI	G	401 765-0558	20607
Grinnell Cabinet Makers Inc	Cranston	RI	E	401 781-1080	20236
Hardwood Design Inc	Exeter	RI	E	401 294-2235	20450
Igitt Inc	Middletown	RI	F	401 841-5544	20621
Imperia Corporation	Barrington	RI	E	508 894-3000	20046
Interior Wdwkg Solutions Inc	Cranston	RI	G	401 261-6329	20240
L F Pease Co	East Providence	RI	F	401 438-2850	20428
M & T Manufacturing Co	Peace Dale	RI	G	401 789-0472	20914
Millwork One Inc	Cranston	RI	D	401 738-6990	20263
Mrd Woodworking LLC	West Kingston	RI	G	401 789-3933	21468
Northeast Millwork Corp	Tiverton	RI	G	401 624-7744	21260
Orion Ret Svcs & Fixturing Inc	Smithfield	RI	D	401 334-5000	21243
Pella Corporation	Portsmouth	RI	B	401 662-2621	20936
Pella Corporation	Barrington	RI	B	401 247-0309	20051
Riverdale Window and Door Corp	Smithfield	RI	C	401 231-6000	21249
Scotts Doors and Windows	Warren	RI	G	401 743-2083	21307
Stephen C Dematrick	Narragansett	RI	G	401 789-4712	20651
Water Street Woodworking	Warren	RI	G	401 245-1921	21315
What Woodworking	Warwick	RI	G	617 429-2461	21446
Wood St Woodworkers	Bristol	RI	G	401 253-8257	20111
Yoffa Woodworking	Newport	RI	F	401 846-7659	20689
Artistic Woodworks Inc	Rochester	VT	G	802 767-3123	22316
Brattleboro Kiln Dry & Milling	Brattleboro	VT	E	802 254-4528	21720
Chesters Custom Woodworking	Belmont	VT	G	802 259-3232	21657
H Hirschmann Ltd	West Rutland	VT	F	802 438-4447	22616
Hawleys Fine Woodwork	Chittenden	VT	G	802 483-2575	21854
Hayley Custom Stair Co Inc	Essex Junction	VT	G	802 861-6400	21946
Heritage Joinery Ltd	Northfield	VT	G	802 485-6107	22243
Jeld-Wen Inc	Ludlow	VT	D	802 228-2020	22064
Jeld-Wen Inc	North Springfield	VT	C	802 886-1728	22237
Jericho Woodworking	White River Junction	VT	G	802 295-9399	22640
Keen Woodworking	Mount Holly	VT	G	802 259-2963	22182
Kelley Bros New England LLC	Williston	VT	F	802 865-5133	22675
Millers Wood Working	Morrisville	VT	G	802 730-9374	22173
Tates Building & Woodworking	Dorset	VT	G	802 867-4082	21909
Vermont Furn Hardwoods Inc	Chester	VT	F	802 875-2550	21852
Wallgoldfinger Inc	Northfield	VT	E	802 483-4200	22246
William Chadburn	North Concord	VT	G	802 695-8166	22223
Woodstone Company Inc **(PA)**	Westminster	VT	F	802 722-9217	22632

2434 Wood Kitchen Cabinets

	CITY	ST	EMP	PHONE	ENTRY #
A S J Specialties LLC	Wallingford	CT	G	203 284-8650	4692
American Refacing Cstm Cab LLC	Manchester	CT	G	860 647-0868	1986
Bailey Avenue Kitchens	Ridgefield	CT	G	203 438-4868	3656
Belmont Corporation	Bristol	CT	E	860 589-5700	532
Bergan Architectural Wdwkg Inc	Middletown	CT	E	860 346-0869	2177
Bonito Manufacturing Inc	North Haven	CT	D	203 234-8786	3011
BP Countertop Design Co LLC	Derby	CT	G	203 732-1620	1069
C J Brand & Son	Mystic	CT	G	860 536-9266	2435
Cabinet Harward Specialti	West Hartford	CT	G	860 231-1192	5056
Cabinet Resources Ct Inc	Canton	CT	G	860 352-2030	696
Chris Cross LLC	Stratford	CT	G	203 386-8426	4404
Christopoulos Designs Inc	Bridgeport	CT	F	203 576-1110	397
Connecticut Solid Surface LLC	Plainville	CT	E	860 410-9800	3477
Conway Hardwood Products LLC	Gaylordsville	CT	E	860 355-4030	1530
Custom Furniture & Design LLC	Litchfield	CT	F	860 567-3519	1947
Custom Interiors	Winchester Center	CT	G	860 738-8754	5310
Cyr Woodworking Inc	Newington	CT	G	860 232-1991	2858
Dante Ltd	Jewett City	CT	G	860 376-0204	1911
Domestic Kitchens Inc	Fairfield	CT	E	203 368-1651	1427
East Hartford Lamination Co	Glastonbury	CT	G	860 633-4637	1547
Forest Remodeling	Somers	CT	G	413 222-7953	3918
Greenhaven Cabinetry & Millwor	Stonington	CT	G	860 535-1106	4376
Gridiron Capital LLC **(PA)**	New Canaan	CT	D	203 972-1100	2599
H & B Woodworking Co	Plainville	CT	G	860 793-6991	3495
Hanford Cabinet & Wdwkg Co	Old Saybrook	CT	G	860 388-5055	3337
Heartwood Cabinetry	Marlborough	CT	G	860 295-0304	2065
Homewood Cabinet Co Inc	Pawcatuck	CT	G	860 599-2441	3437
Hope Kit Cbinets Stone Sup LLC **(PA)**	Bridgeport	CT	G	203 610-6147	427
Industrial Wood Product Co	Shelton	CT	G	203 735-2374	3817
John June Custom Cabinetry LLC	Bridgeport	CT	G	203 334-1720	436
John M Kriskey Carpentry	Greenwich	CT	G	203 531-0194	1625
Kingswood Kitchens Co Inc	Danbury	CT	D	203 792-8700	945
Kitchen Cab Resurfacing LLC	Bridgeport	CT	F	203 334-2857	441
Kitchen Kraftsmen	Windsor	CT	G	860 616-1240	5343
Knb Design LLC	New Haven	CT	G	203 777-6661	2701
Legere Group Ltd	Avon	CT	C	860 674-0392	37
Leos Kitchen & Stair Corp	New Britain	CT	G	860 225-7363	2548
Luchon Cabinet Woodwork	Stafford Springs	CT	G	860 684-5037	4112
Martin Cabinet Inc **(PA)**	Plainville	CT	E	860 747-5769	3505
Martin Cabinet Inc	Bristol	CT	D	860 747-5769	579
N Excellence Wood Inc	Higganum	CT	G	860 345-2050	1904
New England Kitchen Design Ctr	Monroe	CT	G	203 268-2626	2411
Northeast Cabinet Design	Ridgefield	CT	G	203 438-1709	3674
P L Woodworking	Sherman	CT	G	860 354-6855	3895
Peacock Cabinetry	Norwalk	CT	G	203 862-9333	3216
Porta Door Co	Seymour	CT	E	203 888-6191	3761
Prescott Cabinet Co	Pawcatuck	CT	G	860 495-0176	3441
Quality Woodworks LLC	Ansonia	CT	G	203 736-9200	22
Rj Cabinetry LLC	Westport	CT	G	203 515-8401	5226
Robert L Lovallo	Stamford	CT	G	203 324-6655	4304
Sebastian Kitchen Cabinets	Norwalk	CT	G	203 853-4411	3238
Song Bath LLC	New Canaan	CT	G	800 353-0313	2615
Specialty Shop Inc	Manchester	CT	G	860 647-1477	2050
Sterling Custom Cabinetry LLC	Bridgeport	CT	G	203 335-5151	495
West Hrtford Stirs Cbinets Inc	Newington	CT	D	860 953-9151	2912
West Mont Group	West Haven	CT	G	203 931-1033	5150
28 Kitchen Cabinet LLC	Auburn	MA	G	774 321-6099	7820
About-Face Kitchens Inc	Peabody	MA	G	978 532-0212	14305
Alcides D Fortes D/B/A Custom	East Bridgewater	MA	G	508 378-7815	10405
Ancom Custom Cabinets	Ayer	MA	G	978 456-7780	7908
Anthony Manufacturing Co Inc	Medford	MA	F	781 396-1400	12921
Architectural Kitchens Inc	Wellesley	MA	G	781 239-9750	16360
Ashland Cabinet Corp	Southborough	MA	G	508 303-8100	15343
Avon Cabinet Company	Avon	MA	G	508 587-9122	7877
B & G Cabinet	Newburyport	MA	F	978 465-6455	13471
Builders Choice Kitchen & Bath	Southwick	MA	G	413 569-9802	15412
Cabinet House LLC	Norwell	MA	G	781 424-2259	14099
Cabinet Warehouse LLC **(PA)**	Marlborough	MA	G	508 281-2077	12732

	CITY	ST	EMP	PHONE	ENTRY #
Camio Custom Cabinetry Inc	Canton	MA	F	781 562-1573	9720
Classic Kitchen Design Inc	Hyannis	MA	F	508 775-3075	11837
Classic Woodworks Inc	Cataumet	MA	G	508 563-9922	9811
Clever Green Cabinets LLC	Waltham	MA	G	508 963-6776	16070
Coastal N Counters Inc	Mashpee	MA	F	508 539-3500	12879
Colonial Village Refinishing	Hingham	MA	G	781 740-8844	11496
Cope & Scribe Incorporated	West Brookfield	MA	G	508 410-7100	16467
Counter Productions Inc	Brockton	MA	F	508 587-0416	9133
Counterra LLC	Canton	MA	F	781 821-2100	9723
Craig F Bradford	Northampton	MA	G	413 586-4500	14003
Creative Kitchen & Bath Inc	Mashpee	MA	G	508 477-3347	12880
Cronin Cabinet Marine LLP	Charlton	MA	G	508 248-7026	9847
Custom Ktchens By Chmpagne Inc	Franklin	MA	E	508 528-7919	11034
Detail Woodworking Ltd	Billerica	MA	G	617 323-8100	8236
Diakosmisis Corporation	Somerville	MA	G	617 776-7714	15169
Dixon Bros Millwork Inc	Abington	MA	G	781 261-9962	7323
Dracut Kitchen & Bath	Dracut	MA	G	978 453-3869	10359
Eastern Cabinet Shop Inc	Boston	MA	G	617 361-7575	8517
European Cabinet Design Inc	Norwood	MA	G	781 769-7100	14151
Fallon Fine Cabinetry	Needham Heights	MA	F	781 453-6988	13331
Furniture Design Services Inc	Peabody	MA	F	978 531-3250	14335
Glenwood Kitchens USA	Framingham	MA	G	508 875-1180	10960
Hamlin Cabinets Corp	Norfolk	MA	G	508 384-8371	13662
Heartwood Cabinetmakers LLC	Uxbridge	MA	G	508 634-2004	15918
Holland Woodworking Inc	Marlborough	MA	G	508 481-2990	12768
Ideal Kitchens of Palmer **(PA)**	Chicopee	MA	G	413 532-2253	10030
Ipswich Cabinetry Inc	Ipswich	MA	G	978 356-1123	11922
J & M Cabinet Shop Inc	Walpole	MA	F	508 660-6660	15996
J Dana Design Inc	Hardwick	MA	G	413 477-6844	11374
JC Clocks Company Inc	North Dartmouth	MA	E	508 998-8442	13922
Jim Lovejoy Cabinetmaker	Sheffield	MA	G	413 229-9008	15061
Joe Batson	Lawrence	MA	G	978 689-0072	12041
Joel Cassidy	Medway	MA	G	508 533-5887	12963
JS International Inc	Fall River	MA	E	508 675-4722	10718
Kitchens & Bath of Norwood	Norwood	MA	G	781 255-1448	14171
Kitchens R US Inc	East Bridgewater	MA	G	508 378-7474	10415
Kochman Reidt & Haigh Inc	Stoughton	MA	E	781 573-1500	15601
Landmark Finish Inc	Andover	MA	G	978 470-2040	7564
Macdonald Cabinet &	South Easton	MA	G	508 346-3221	15285
Mascaros Woodcraft Co Inc **(PA)**	Chicopee	MA	G	413 594-4255	10040
Mass Cabinets Inc	Methuen	MA	E	978 738-0600	13034
Mediterranean Custom Cabinets	West Bridgewater	MA	G	508 588-5498	16445
Metropolitan Cab Distrs Corp	Natick	MA	G	508 651-8950	13267
Metropolitan Cab Distrs Corp **(PA)**	Norwood	MA	G	781 949-8900	14178
Milford Woodworking Company	Milford	MA	F	508 473-2335	13128
Miller H C Wood Working Inc	Holliston	MA	G	508 429-4220	11586
Modern Woodworks Co	Foxboro	MA	G	508 543-9830	10892
Munro Woodworking	Bellingham	MA	G	508 966-2654	8052
Ne Choice Cabinet	Wakefield	MA	G	781 245-3800	15964
Norfolk Factory Direct Kitchen	Braintree	MA	G	781 848-5333	9027
Northast Cab Cntrtop Dstrs Inc	Braintree	MA	G	617 296-2100	9028
Pridemaxx Fine Wood Cabinetry	Walpole	MA	G	508 527-8700	16007
R F Mc Manus Company Inc	Charlestown	MA	F	617 241-8081	9842
Rgc Millwork Incorporated	Lowell	MA	G	978 275-9529	12427
Richards Dean Custom Wdwkg	Essex	MA	G	978 768-7104	10597
Rosario Cabinets Inc	Dedham	MA	G	781 329-0639	10296
Scandia Kitchens Inc	Bellingham	MA	E	508 966-0300	8058
Shadowbrook Custom Cabinetry	Williamstown	MA	G	413 664-9590	16960
Star Kitchen Cabinets Inc	Avon	MA	G	508 510-3123	7897
Stokes Woodworking Co Inc **(PA)**	Hudson	MA	G	508 481-0414	11820
Superior Kitchen Designs Inc	Gardner	MA	E	978 632-5072	11130
Taylor Made Cabinets LLC	Leominster	MA	G	978 840-0100	12192
Triple Crown Cbnets Mllwk Corp	Sandwich	MA	G	508 833-6500	14974
Vanity World Inc	Canton	MA	G	508 668-1800	9792
Vartanian Custom Cabinets	Palmer	MA	F	413 283-3438	14300
Watson Brothers Inc	Middleton	MA	F	978 774-7677	13106
Winfield Woodworking Inc	Holliston	MA	G	508 429-4320	11614
Atlantic Wood & Cabinet Works	Scarborough	ME	F	207 885-0767	6905
Bench Dogs	Washington	ME	G	207 845-2084	7148
Black Cove Cabinetry	Scarborough	ME	F	207 883-8901	6912
Kennebec Cabinetry Inc	Bath	ME	F	207 442-0813	5678
Kennebec Company	Bath	ME	E	207 443-2131	5679
Lauzon Gilles	Biddeford	ME	G	207 286-0600	5743
Lawrence Parson	Brownfield	ME	G	207 935-3737	5825
Mike Guillemette & Sons	Lyman	ME	G	207 324-6221	6391
Naheks Inc	Hermon	ME	G	207 848-7770	6191
Northport LLC	East Waterboro	ME	G	207 247-7600	5985
Ridgetop Cabinetry	Boothbay Harbor	ME	G	207 563-8249	5786
Topsham Woodworking LLC	Topsham	ME	G	207 751-1032	7095
Town and Country Cabinets Inc	Gorham	ME	G	207 839-2709	6131
Trico Millworks Inc	Limington	ME	E	207 637-2711	6351
West Minot Millwork Inc	West Minot	ME	G	207 966-3200	7175
Advanced Custom Cabinets Inc	Brentwood	NH	E	603 772-6211	17743
Cabinet Masters Inc	Derry	NH	G	603 425-6428	17975
Cabinets For Less LLC	Manchester	NH	G	603 935-7551	18794
Counter Pro Inc	Manchester	NH	F	603 647-2444	18807
Crown Point Cabinetry Corp	Claremont	NH	D	603 542-1273	17845
Crown Point Realty Corp Inc	Claremont	NH	D	603 543-1208	17846
Custom Woodworking Brentwood	Chester	NH	G	603 887-6766	17824
Evergreen Cabinetry LLC	Milton	NH	G	603 833-6881	19085
Exeter Cabinet Company Inc	Exeter	NH	G	603 778-8113	18120
Jensen Cabinet Co	Milford	NH	G	603 554-8363	19067
Kimballs Lumber Center LLC **(PA)**	Wolfeboro	NH	G	603 569-2477	20021
King & Co Architectural Wdwkg	Marlborough	NH	G	603 876-4900	18961
Mark Allen Cabinetry LLC	Amherst	NH	G	603 491-7570	17573
Mark Allen Cabinetry LLC **(PA)**	Brookline	NH	G	603 321-3163	17772
Northeast Cabinet Designs LLC	Hampstead	NH	G	603 329-3465	18246
Northeast Woodworking Products	Raymond	NH	G	603 895-4271	19642
Nutfield Cabinetry LLC	Derry	NH	G	603 498-6252	17992
Oakwood Cabinetry	Concord	NH	G	603 927-4713	17920
Plaistow Cabinet Co Inc	Plaistow	NH	F	603 382-1098	19520
Purewood Cabinetry	Newton	NH	G	603 378-2001	19368
Taylor & Stevens Cabinetry	Pelham	NH	G	603 880-2022	19449
Vermont Custom Wood Products	North Walpole	NH	F	802 463-9930	19396
Walpole Cabinetry	Walpole	NH	F	603 826-4100	19925
Ws Dennison Cabinets Inc	Pembroke	NH	G	603 224-8434	19464
Young Furniture Mfg Inc	Bow	NH	E	603 224-8830	17737
Cabinet Assembly Systems Corp	East Greenwich	RI	F	401 884-8556	20355
European Custom Casework Inc	North Smithfield	RI	G	401 356-0400	20785
Gary Eldridge	Woonsocket	RI	G	401 769-0026	21566
Hardwood Design Inc	Exeter	RI	E	401 294-2235	20450
Imperia Corporation	Barrington	RI	E	508 894-3000	20046
Joe Martin	West Warwick	RI	G	401 823-1860	21497
Kitchen Center RI Inc	Pawtucket	RI	G	401 640-6514	20852
Mycabinetsonline	Lincoln	RI	G	401 722-3863	20587
Riley Kitchen & Bath Co Inc	Bristol	RI	G	401 253-2205	20100
Tm Custom	West Greenwich	RI	G	401 226-2173	21466
Water Street Woodworking	Warren	RI	G	401 245-1921	21315
Catamount North Cabinetry LLC	Essex Junction	VT	F	802 264-9009	21935
Jericho Woodworking	White River Junction	VT	G	802 295-9399	22640
Killington Cabinets	Killington	VT	G	802 773-3960	22054
Knight Industries Inc	North Clarendon	VT	E	802 773-8777	22219
William Chadburn	North Concord	VT	G	802 695-8166	22223

2435 Hardwood Veneer & Plywood

	CITY	ST	EMP	PHONE	ENTRY #
Bergan Architectural Wdwkg Inc	Middletown	CT	E	860 346-0869	2177
Thomas Bernhard Building Sys	Southport	CT	E	203 925-0414	4102
Bear Paw Lumber Corp **(PA)**	Fryeburg	ME	F	207 935-3052	6095
Columbia Forest Products Inc	Presque Isle	ME	C	207 760-3800	6757
Herrick Mill Work Inc	Contoocook	NH	E	603 746-5092	17945
Columbia Forest Products Inc	Newport	VT	B	802 334-6711	22193
Columbia Forest Products Inc	Newport	VT	C	802 334-3600	22194
Mariah Group LLC	Rutland	VT	D	802 747-4000	22345
Rutland Plywood Corp	Rutland	VT	G	802 747-4000	22350
Stratabond Co Inc	Rutland	VT	G	802 747-4000	22355

2439 Structural Wood Members, NEC

	CITY	ST	EMP	PHONE	ENTRY #
Country Carpenters Inc	Hebron	CT	G	860 228-2276	1896
Eastern Company **(PA)**	Naugatuck	CT	E	203 729-2255	2471
Thomas Bernhard Building Sys	Southport	CT	E	203 925-0414	4102
Timber Frame Barn Conversions	Windsor	CT	G	860 219-0519	5373
Truss Manufacturing Inc	Newington	CT	F	860 665-0000	2908
Universal Component Corp	East Haven	CT	E	203 481-8787	1267
Architectural Timber Mllwk Inc	Hadley	MA	F	413 586-3045	11305
Caliper Woodworking Corp	Malden	MA	E	781 322-9760	12563
Nu-Truss Inc	Westfield	MA	F	413 562-3861	16708
Perkins Brothers Corp	Stoughton	MA	E	781 858-3031	15615
Reliable Truss & Components In	Mansfield	MA	G	508 339-8020	12655
Truss Engineering Corporation	Indian Orchard	MA	E	413 543-1298	11898
Aroostook Trusses Inc	Presque Isle	ME	E	207 768-5817	6754
Soyaz	Fairfield	ME	E	207 453-4911	6029
Truss Worthy Truss	Hodgdon	ME	G	207 532-3200	6194
Atlantic Prefab Inc **(PA)**	Wilton	NH	G	603 668-2648	19975
Benson Woodworking Company Inc	Walpole	NH	D	603 756-3600	19917
Saxon Manufacturing Inc	Salem	NH	F	603 898-2499	19765
Southworth Timber Frames Inc	Lancaster	NH	G	603 788-2619	18605
Specialty Truss Inc	Nashua	NH	G	603 886-5523	19263
Trussco Inc	North Kingstown	RI	E	401 295-0669	20747
Energy Smart Building Inc	Starksboro	VT	E	802 453-4438	22515
Granville Manufacturing Co	Granville	VT	G	802 767-4747	22003
Old Timers Timber Frames	Saxtons River	VT	G	802 376-9529	22401

2441 Wood Boxes

	CITY	ST	EMP	PHONE	ENTRY #
Champlin-Packrite Inc	Manchester	CT	E	860 951-9217	1993
Coastal Pallet Corporation	Bridgeport	CT	E	203 333-1892	398
Colonial Wood Products Inc	West Haven	CT	F	203 932-9003	5112
Merrill Industries Inc	Ellington	CT	E	860 871-1888	1336
St Pierre Box and Lumber Co	Canton	CT	G	860 413-9813	699
Vermont Pallet & Skid Shop	Norwich	CT	G	860 822-6949	3292
W R Hartigan & Son Inc	Burlington	CT	G	860 673-9203	682
Westwood Products Inc	Winsted	CT	F	860 379-9401	5428
Atlas Box and Crating Co Inc **(PA)**	Sutton	MA	C	508 865-1155	15679
D A Mfg Co LLC	Winchendon	MA	G	978 297-1059	17072
Kelley Wood Products Inc	Fitchburg	MA	F	978 345-7531	10830

	CITY	ST	EMP	PHONE	ENTRY #
Nefab Packaging North East LLC	Bellingham	MA	F	800 258-4692	8053
Unified2 Globl Packg Group LLC	Sutton	MA	A	508 865-1155	15694
Barton Corporation Salisbury	Seabrook	NH	G	603 760-2669	19793
E B Frye & Son Inc	Wilton	NH	G	603 654-6581	19979
Granite State Forest Products	Henniker	NH	G	603 428-7890	18306
Herrick Mill Work Inc	Contoocook	NH	E	603 746-5092	17945
Index Packaging Inc	Milton	NH	C	603 350-0018	19086
J H Dunning Corporation	North Walpole	NH	E	603 445-5591	19394
Manning Brothers Wood Products	Northfield	NH	G	603 286-4896	19405
D Mac Consulting LLC **(PA)**	North Kingstown	RI	G	401 500-3879	20701
Greene Industries Inc	East Greenwich	RI	G	401 884-7530	20369
Poultney Pallet Inc	Fair Haven	VT	G	802 265-4444	21968

2448 Wood Pallets & Skids

	CITY	ST	EMP	PHONE	ENTRY #
Acm Warehouse & Distribution	North Haven	CT	G	203 239-9557	3001
Better Pallets Inc	Branford	CT	G	203 230-9549	296
Central Pallet & Box	New Britain	CT	F	860 224-4416	2520
Coastal Pallet Corporation	Bridgeport	CT	E	203 333-1892	398
FCA LLC	Norwalk	CT	G	203 857-0825	3151
Global Pallet Solutions LLC	New Britain	CT	G	860 826-5000	2535
Guy Ravenelle	Central Village	CT	G	860 564-3200	706
HI-Tech Packaging Inc	Stratford	CT	E	203 378-2700	4420
Industrial Pallet LLC	Eastford	CT	E	860 974-0093	1313
J J Box Co Inc	Bridgeport	CT	G	203 367-1211	432
Pallet Guys LLC	North Haven	CT	G	203 691-6716	3048
Pallet Inc LLC	Westport	CT	G	203 227-8148	5222
R & R Pallet Corp	Cheshire	CT	F	203 272-2784	755
Southern Conn Pallet Co Inc	Wallingford	CT	G	203 265-1313	4808
St Pierre Box and Lumber Co	Canton	CT	G	860 413-9813	699
Tcc Multi Kargo	Norwalk	CT	G	203 803-1462	3255
Toy Pallet	Ellington	CT	G	860 803-9838	1342
Vermont Pallet & Skid Shop	Norwich	CT	G	860 822-6949	3292
Westwood Products Inc	Winsted	CT	F	860 379-9401	5428
A1 Pallets Inc	Berlin	MA	G	978 838-2720	8090
ABS Pallet	Hopedale	MA	G	508 246-1041	11668
Atlas Box and Crating Co Inc **(PA)**	Sutton	MA	C	508 865-1155	15679
B&D Pallet Bldg & Indus Sup	Westfield	MA	F	413 568-9624	16670
Beverly Pallet Company Inc	Ipswich	MA	G	978 356-1121	11905
Briggs Lumber Products	Rutland	MA	F	508 886-2054	14880
Briggs Lumber Products	Gardner	MA	G	978 630-4207	11106
Conway Pallet Inc	Williamsburg	MA	F	413 268-3343	16949
Custom Pallets Inc	Brookfield	MA	G	508 867-2411	9189
Deadwood Pallets	Bellingham	MA	G	774 214-8628	8037
Fruit Basket World Division	Everett	MA	E	617 389-8989	10611
Groton Pallet Incorporated	Groton	MA	G	978 448-5651	11290
Industrial Pallet LLC	Princeton	MA	G	860 234-0962	14605
Jbm Service Inc	Templeton	MA	D	978 939-8004	15803
Kelley Wood Products Inc	Fitchburg	MA	F	978 345-7531	10830
Lelanite Corporation	Oxford	MA	G	508 987-1771	14266
Lelanite Corporation **(PA)**	Webster	MA	E	508 987-2637	16346
Lenox Lumber Co	Pittsfield	MA	F	413 637-2744	14484
Lignetics New England Inc	Palmer	MA	G	413 284-1050	14288
Lohnes Pallet	Hanover	MA	G	781 878-6801	11345
Nefab Packaging North East LLC	Bellingham	MA	F	800 258-4692	8053
New England Pallets Skids Inc	Ludlow	MA	F	413 583-6628	12473
Pallets Recreated	Fitchburg	MA	G	978 345-5936	10848
Peco Pallet	Brighton	MA	G	845 642-2780	9104
Progress Pallet Inc	Middleboro	MA	E	508 923-1930	13076
Slowinski Wood Products	Colrain	MA	G	413 624-3415	10105
Springfield Pallet Inc	Indian Orchard	MA	G	413 593-0044	11896
Timothy Sills	Rockland	MA	G	781 635-8193	14830
Unified2 Globl Packg Group LLC	Sutton	MA	A	508 865-1155	15694
Wackerbarth Box Mfg Co	Granville	MA	F	413 357-8816	11231
Wood Products Unlimited Inc	Methuen	MA	G	978 687-7449	13048
B & T Pallet Recycling Inc	Lewiston	ME	G	207 784-9048	6275
Edgar Clark & Sons Pallet Inc	Mount Vernon	ME	G	207 685-3888	6458
Gerrity Company Incorporated	Leeds	ME	E	207 933-2804	6269
Ifco Systems Us LLC	Scarborough	ME	E	207 883-0244	6926
Isaacson Lumber Co Inc	Livermore Falls	ME	G	207 897-2115	6378
Levesque Farm Pallets	Van Buren	ME	G	207 868-3905	7122
Mason Pallet Inc	Livermore Falls	ME	G	207 897-6270	6379
Nevells Pallet Inc	Sidney	ME	G	207 547-4605	6963
Palletone of Maine Inc	Livermore Falls	ME	C	207 897-5711	6380
Barlow Wood Products	Milford	NH	G	603 673-2642	19048
Global Pallet & Packaging LLC	Seabrook	NH	G	603 969-6660	19801
Hills Pallet Company	Somersworth	NH	G	603 988-8624	19840
Lignetics New England Inc	Jaffrey	NH	F	603 532-4666	18471
Lignetics New England Inc	Jaffrey	NH	E	603 532-4666	18472
Perras Pallet LLC	Lancaster	NH	G	603 631-1169	18604
Atlas Barrell & Pallet Inc	Harrisville	RI	D	401 568-2900	20477
Greene Industries Inc	East Greenwich	RI	G	401 884-7530	20369
Js Pallet Co Inc	Pawtucket	RI	E	401 723-0223	20850
Carris Financial Corp **(PA)**	Proctor	VT	F	802 773-9111	22283
Carris Reels Inc **(HQ)**	Proctor	VT	C	802 773-9111	22284
Hayes Recycled Pallets	Brandon	VT	E	802 247-4620	21708
Mountain View Skids	Enosburg Falls	VT	G	802 933-2623	21925

2449 Wood Containers, NEC

	CITY	ST	EMP	PHONE	ENTRY #
Champlin-Packrite Inc	Manchester	CT	E	860 951-9217	1993
Pith Products LLC	Ashford	CT	F	860 487-4859	26
St Pierre Box and Lumber Co	Canton	CT	G	860 413-9813	699
Vermont Pallet & Skid Shop	Norwich	CT	G	860 822-6949	3292
Westwood Products Inc	Winsted	CT	F	860 379-9401	5428
Woodfree Crating Systems Inc	Waterbury	CT	F	203 759-1799	4979
Abbott-Action Inc	Canton	MA	E	781 702-5710	9710
Brattleworks Company Inc	Gardner	MA	G	978 410-5078	11105
Dartmouth Feeders & Traps Inc	South Dartmouth	MA	G	774 202-6594	15237
Hardigg Industries Inc	Northampton	MA	G	413 665-2163	14007
Nefab Packaging North East LLC	Bellingham	MA	F	800 258-4692	8053
Central Maine Crate Inc	Oakland	ME	G	207 873-5880	6531
E G W Bradbury Enterprises	Bridgewater	ME	F	207 429-8141	5805
Brentwood Box Company Inc	Raymond	NH	G	603 895-0829	19637
Index Packaging Inc	Milton	NH	C	603 350-0018	19086
Old Dublin Road Inc	Peterborough	NH	D	603 924-3861	19482
Aspects Inc	Warren	RI	E	401 247-1854	21286
Daves Mrktplace Smthfield Inc	Smithfield	RI	G	401 830-5650	21218
Ljm Packaging Co Inc	North Kingstown	RI	D	401 295-2660	20724
Granville Manufacturing Co	Granville	VT	G	802 767-4747	22003
Koss Industries Inc	Burlington	VT	G	802 863-5004	21791

2451 Mobile Homes

	CITY	ST	EMP	PHONE	ENTRY #
Old Coach Home Sales	Sterling	CT	E	860 774-1379	4371
Crown Properties & HM Sls LLC	North Hampton	NH	G	603 964-2005	19382
Hilltop Cooperative	Raymond	NH	G	603 895-6476	19638
Topek LLC	Grantham	NH	F	603 863-2400	18217
Skyline Corporation	Fair Haven	VT	C	802 278-8222	21969

2452 Prefabricated Wood Buildings & Cmpnts

	CITY	ST	EMP	PHONE	ENTRY #
American Prefab Wood Pdts Co	Bloomfield	CT	G	860 242-5468	200
Bond-Bilt Garages Inc	Wallingford	CT	G	203 269-3375	4711
Carefree Building Co Inc **(PA)**	Colchester	CT	F	860 267-7600	800
Country Carpenters Inc	Hebron	CT	G	860 228-2276	1896
Country Log Homes Inc	Goshen	CT	F	413 229-8084	1582
Post & Beam Homes Inc	East Hampton	CT	G	860 267-2060	1163
Trigila Construction Inc	Berlin	CT	E	860 828-8444	115
Walpole Woodworkers Inc	Ridgefield	CT	E	508 668-2800	3689
Walpole Woodworkers Inc	Westport	CT	G	203 255-9010	5237
Architectural Timber Mllwk Inc	Hadley	MA	F	413 586-3045	11305
Chapins Wood Products Inc **(PA)**	Halifax	MA	G	781 294-0758	11316
Fox Modular Homes Inc	Lee	MA	F	413 243-1950	12092
Habitat Post & Beam Inc	South Deerfield	MA	E	413 665-4006	15250
Home Kore Mfg Co Mass Inc	Lakeville	MA	G	508 947-0000	11976
Jarica Inc	Woburn	MA	F	781 935-1907	17210
Jobart Inc **(PA)**	Methuen	MA	F	978 689-4414	13029
Marvic Inc	Auburn	MA	E	508 798-2600	7842
Modulease Corporation	North Attleboro	MA	G	508 695-4145	13766
Walpole Woodworkers Inc	Wilmington	MA	F	978 658-3373	17064
Walpole Woodworkers Inc	East Falmouth	MA	F	508 540-0300	10451
Walpole Woodworkers Inc	Norwell	MA	G	781 681-9099	14114
Katahdin Forest Products Co **(PA)**	Oakfield	ME	D	800 845-4533	6527
Kbs Building Systems Inc	South Paris	ME	G	207 739-2222	7012
Leland Boggs II	Warren	ME	G	207 273-2610	7143
Modular Fun I Inc	South Paris	ME	C	207 739-2400	7014
Moose Creek Home Center Inc	Turner	ME	G	207 224-7497	7109
Moosehead Country Log Homes	Greenville	ME	E	207 695-3730	6153
Moosehead Wood Components Inc	Greenville Junction	ME	F	207 695-3730	6154
New England Bldg Solutions LLC	Scarborough	ME	G	603 323-0012	6934
Schiavi Homes LLC	Oxford	ME	E	207 539-9600	6573
Walpole Woodworkers Inc	Detroit	ME	E	207 368-4302	5954
Walpole Woodworkers Inc	Chester	ME	E	207 794-2248	5908
Wlhc Inc **(PA)**	Houlton	ME	G	207 532-6531	6212
AG Structures LLC	Salisbury	NH	G	603 648-2987	19780
Benson Woodworking Company Inc	Walpole	NH	D	603 756-3600	19917
Coventry Log Homes	Woodsville	NH	E	603 747-8177	20030
Granite State Log Homes Inc **(PA)**	Campton	NH	F	603 536-4949	17777
L & M Sheds LLC	Epping	NH	G	603 679-5243	18100
Log Cabin Bldg Co & Sawmill	Lancaster	NH	G	603 788-3036	18601
Monadnock Log Home Svcs LLC	Jaffrey	NH	F	603 876-4800	18474
New England Homes Inc	Dover	NH	D	603 436-8830	18038
Post Woodworking Inc	Danville	NH	E	603 382-4951	17969
Reeds Ferry Small Buildings	Hudson	NH	D	603 883-1362	18434
Southworth Timber Frames Inc	Lancaster	NH	G	603 788-2619	18605
Timberpeg East Inc **(PA)**	Claremont	NH	E	603 542-7762	17862
Tucker Mountain Homes Inc	Meredith	NH	G	603 279-4320	18981
Wallace Building Products Corp	Danbury	NH	E	603 768-5402	17966
WH Silverstein Inc	Claremont	NH	E	603 542-5418	17864
Yankee Barn Homes Inc	Claremont	NH	D	603 863-4545	17865
Authentic Log Homes Inc	Hardwick	VT	G	802 472-5096	22009
Energy Smart Building Inc	Starksboro	VT	E	802 453-4438	22515
Gilcris Enterprises Inc	Proctorsville	VT	F	802 226-7764	22288
Goodridge Lumber	Albany	VT	G	802 755-6298	21592
Groton Timberworks of Vermont	Groton	VT	G	802 584-4446	22005
Jamaica Cottage Shop Inc	South Londonderry	VT	E	802 297-3760	22487

	CITY	ST	EMP	PHONE	ENTRY #
Moosehead Cedar Log Homes	Wilmington	VT	G	802 464-7609	22704
Serac Corporation **(HQ)**	Fairfax	VT	F	802 527-9609	21979

2491 Wood Preserving

	CITY	ST	EMP	PHONE	ENTRY #
Amerifix LLC	West Haven	CT	G	203 931-7290	5108
Country Carpenters Inc	Hebron	CT	G	860 228-2276	1896
Techno Mtal Post Watertown LLC	Waterbury	CT	G	203 755-6403	4961
Bestway of New England Inc	South Lancaster	MA	F	978 368-7667	15316
Forest Economic Advisors LLC	Littleton	MA	G	978 496-6336	12306
Midway United Limited	Needham Heights	MA	B	781 400-1742	13338
Northeast Treaters Inc **(PA)**	Belchertown	MA	E	413 323-7811	8026
Wood Mill LLC	Lawrence	MA	G	978 683-2901	12085
Integrity Composites LLC	Biddeford	ME	F	207 571-0743	5740
Maine Wood Treaters Inc	Mechanic Falls	ME	E	207 345-8411	6421
Millwork City Internet Svcs	York	ME	G	207 370-5020	7313
Oxford Timber Inc	Oxford	ME	F	207 539-9656	6570
University of Maine System	Orono	ME	F	207 581-2843	6559
Thayer Wood Products Inc	Narragansett	RI	G	401 789-8825	20653
Brown Novelty Co Inc	Middlebury	VT	G	802 388-2502	22104

2493 Reconstituted Wood Prdts

	CITY	ST	EMP	PHONE	ENTRY #
Biofibers Capital Group LLC	Ashford	CT	G	203 561-6133	25
Central Marble & Granite LLC	Ansonia	CT	G	203 734-4644	9
Panolam Industries Intl Inc **(PA)**	Shelton	CT	E	203 925-1556	3849
Stepping Stones MBL & Gran LLC **(PA)**	Norwalk	CT	G	203 854-0552	3251
Bnz Materials Inc	North Billerica	MA	E	978 663-3401	13796
Colonial Marble Co Inc	Everett	MA	G	617 389-1130	10608
Designer Board Specialties	Braintree	MA	G	781 794-9413	9000
Speedboard Usa Inc	Newburyport	MA	G	978 462-2700	13534
Huber Engineered Woods LLC	Easton	ME	D	207 488-6700	5989
Panolam Industries Intl Inc	Auburn	ME	E	207 784-9111	5586
Saunders At Locke Mills LLC	Greenwood	ME	F	207 875-2853	6156
Souhegan Wood Products Inc	Wilton	NH	F	603 654-2311	19988
Neshobe Wood Products Inc	Brandon	VT	F	802 247-3805	21711
Renewable Fuels Vermont LLC	Manchester Center	VT	F	802 362-1516	22088

2499 Wood Prdts, NEC

	CITY	ST	EMP	PHONE	ENTRY #
Acme United Corporation **(PA)**	Fairfield	CT	C	203 254-6060	1412
Alpine Management Group LLC	Westport	CT	G	954 531-1692	5180
C N C Router Technologies	Danbury	CT	G	203 744-6651	883
Carris Reels Connecticut Inc	Enfield	CT	D	860 749-8308	1348
Clint S Custom Woodworkin	Jewett City	CT	G	860 887-1476	1910
Company of Craftsmen	Mystic	CT	G	860 536-4189	2436
Connecticut Sign Service LLC	Essex	CT	G	860 767-7446	1395
Dante Ltd	Jewett City	CT	G	860 376-0204	1911
Desjardins Woodworking Inc	Goshen	CT	G	860 491-9972	1583
Diy Awards LLC **(PA)**	Stamford	CT	G	800 810-1216	4189
Dundorf Designs USA Inc	Salem	CT	G	860 859-2955	3738
Elm City Manufacturing LLC	North Haven	CT	F	203 248-1969	3024
Essex Wood Products Inc	Colchester	CT	E	860 537-3451	802
Fagan Design & Fabrication	West Haven	CT	G	203 937-1874	5122
Finishing Solutions LLC	Colchester	CT	G	860 705-8231	803
Freezer Hill Mulch Company LLC	Bethany	CT	G	203 758-3725	121
John M Kriskey Carpentry	Greenwich	CT	G	203 531-0194	1625
Kensington Glass and Frmng Co	Berlin	CT	G	860 828-9428	91
Legere Group Ltd	Avon	CT	C	860 674-0392	37
Mulch Ferris Products LLC	Danbury	CT	G	203 790-1155	957
New England Joinery Works Inc	Essex	CT	G	860 767-3377	1404
New England Tile & Stone Inc	Stamford	CT	F	914 481-4488	4256
Pleasant Valley Fence Co Inc	Pleasant Valley	CT	F	860 379-0088	3546
Regional Stairs LLC	East Hartford	CT	G	860 290-1242	1217
Rockwell Art & Framing LLC **(PA)**	Wilton	CT	G	203 762-8311	5302
Saint Josephs Wood Pdts LLC	New Haven	CT	G	203 787-5746	2732
Strouts Woodworking	Broad Brook	CT	G	860 623-8445	630
Sweet Peet North America Inc	Litchfield	CT	G	860 361-6444	1953
Vacca Architectural Woodworkin	Pawcatuck	CT	G	860 599-3677	3443
W R Hartigan & Son Inc	Burlington	CT	G	860 673-9203	682
Walpole Woodworkers Inc	Ridgefield	CT	E	508 668-2800	3689
Walpole Woodworkers Inc	Westport	CT	G	203 255-9010	5237
Alfred J Cavallaro Inc	Andover	MA	G	978 475-2466	7536
April Twenty One Corporation	Billerica	MA	G	978 667-8472	8213
Assonet Industries Inc	Assonet	MA	G	508 644-5001	7677
Blank Industries Inc	Hudson	MA	F	855 887-3123	11759
Boston Turning Works	Watertown	MA	G	617 924-4747	16275
Boston Wood Art	Natick	MA	G	508 353-4129	13240
Brattleworks Company Inc	Gardner	MA	G	978 410-5078	11105
Butler Architectural Wdwkg Inc	New Bedford	MA	F	508 985-9980	13368
Cape Cod Fence Co	South Yarmouth	MA	F	508 398-2293	15326
Cook Forest Products Inc	Upton	MA	E	508 634-3300	15906
Cork Technologies LLC	Lawrence	MA	G	978 687-9500	12013
Eagle Woodworking Inc	Lawrence	MA	F	978 681-6194	12019
Flagraphics Inc	Somerville	MA	E	617 776-7549	15172
Frame Center of Norwood Inc **(PA)**	Hyannis	MA	G	781 762-2535	11841
Granite Brook LLC	Weston	MA	G	781 788-9700	16826
Holland Woodworking	Southampton	MA	G	413 527-6588	15339
Hollingsworth & Vose Company **(PA)**	East Walpole	MA	C	508 850-2000	10524
J Carvalho LLC	New Bedford	MA	G	774 206-1435	13398
Joe Batson	Lawrence	MA	G	978 689-0072	12041
Jones & Vining Incorporated **(PA)**	Brockton	MA	E	508 232-7470	9158
Lashway Logging Inc	Williamsburg	MA	F	413 268-3600	16952
Lyn-Lad Group Ltd **(PA)**	Lynn	MA	F	781 598-6010	12523
Malden Intl Designs Inc	Middleboro	MA	D	508 946-2270	13067
Mark Gauvin	Mattapoisett	MA	G	508 758-2324	12888
Mass Sign & Decal Inc	Rockland	MA	G	781 878-7446	14812
Michael Humphries Wdwkg Inc	Northfield	MA	G	413 498-0018	14064
New England Fencewrights Inc	New Bedford	MA	G	508 999-3337	13423
North Bridge Woodworking	Pepperell	MA	G	978 433-0148	14443
Oborain	Montague	MA	G	413 376-8854	13212
OBs Woodcrafts Inc	Swansea	MA	F	508 679-0480	15711
Paul White Woodcarving	East Sandwich	MA	G	508 888-1394	10507
Petermans Boards and Bowls Inc	Gill	MA	E	413 863-2116	11157
Pine and Baker Mfg Inc	Tewksbury	MA	F	978 851-1215	15825
Pine Baker Inc	Tewksbury	MA	G	978 851-1215	15826
Pobco Inc	Worcester	MA	E	508 791-6376	17442
Pridecraft Inc	North Andover	MA	G	978 685-2831	13726
Psg Framing Inc	Somerville	MA	F	617 261-1817	15206
RD Contractors Inc	North Billerica	MA	F	978 667-6545	13859
Scott Grusby LLC	Newton	MA	G	617 538-9112	13633
South Shore Millwork Inc	Norton	MA	D	508 226-5500	14090
T J Bark Mulch Inc	Southwick	MA	F	413 569-2400	15418
Walpole Woodworkers Inc	East Falmouth	MA	F	508 540-0300	10451
Walpole Woodworkers Inc	Norwell	MA	G	781 681-9099	14114
Walpole Woodworkers Inc	Wilmington	MA	F	978 658-3373	17064
Watson Brothers Inc	Middleton	MA	F	978 774-7677	13106
Wescor Ltd	Woburn	MA	G	781 938-8686	17318
William Crosby	Concord	MA	G	978 371-1111	10162
Wood & Wood Inc	Greenfield	MA	E	413 772-0889	11284
Wood Decor Inc	Pembroke	MA	G	781 826-4954	14433
A-Po-G Inc	Portland	ME	G	207 774-7606	6608
Clark Island Boat Works	South Thomaston	ME	G	207 594-4112	7045
Coastal Woodworking Inc	Nobleboro	ME	E	207 563-1072	6492
Finest Kind	Dayton	ME	G	207 499-7176	5945
Frontier Forge Inc	Kingfield	ME	E	207 265-2151	6253
Frost Cedar Products Inc	North Anson	ME	G	207 566-5912	6501
Hardwood Products Company LP	Guilford	ME	B	207 876-3311	6158
Jsi Store Fixtures Inc **(PA)**	Milo	ME	C	207 943-5203	6446
Kangas Inc	North Anson	ME	G	207 635-3745	6503
Katahdin Forest Products Co **(PA)**	Oakfield	ME	D	800 845-4533	6527
La Valley Wood Inc	Van Buren	ME	F	207 316-6263	7121
Lignetics of Maine	Strong	ME	G	207 684-3457	7072
Lucerne Farms	Fort Fairfield	ME	E	207 488-2520	6056
Maine Heritage Timber LLC	Millinocket	ME	E	207 723-9200	6442
Maine Pursuit LLC	Whitefield	ME	G	207 549-7972	7217
Maine Turnpike Authority	Cumberland Center	ME	F	207 829-4531	5929
Maine Woods Pellet Company LLC	Athens	ME	E	207 654-2237	5542
New England Outerwear	Lewiston	ME	G	207 240-3069	6311
Peavey Manufacturing Company	Eddington	ME	E	207 843-7861	5997
Picture Frame Inc	Topsham	ME	G	207 729-7765	7093
Pierce Point Laser	Westbrook	ME	G	207 854-0133	7201
S P Holt Corporation	Orono	ME	G	207 866-4867	6558
Saco Manufacturing & Wdwkg	Saco	ME	G	207 284-6613	6857
Scott Docks Inc	Bridgton	ME	G	207 647-3824	5811
Strong Wood Products Inc	Temple	ME	F	207 778-4063	7080
Turning Acquisitions LLC	Buckfield	ME	E	207 336-2400	5853
Walpole Woodworkers Inc	Detroit	ME	E	207 368-4302	5954
Walpole Woodworkers Inc	Chester	ME	E	207 794-2248	5908
Woodex Bearing Company Inc	Georgetown	ME	E	207 371-2210	6107
Woodshop Cupolas Inc	Trenton	ME	G	207 667-6331	7104
Anthony Galluzzo Corp	Londonderry	NH	E	603 432-2681	18676
Barlow Architectural Mllwk LLC	Hampstead	NH	E	603 329-6026	18237
Chasco Inc	Portsmouth	NH	F	603 436-2141	19552
Gemini Signs & Design Ltd	Conway	NH	G	603 447-3336	17952
Herbert Mosher	Nashua	NH	G	603 882-4357	19177
Herrick Mill Work Inc	Contoocook	NH	E	603 746-5092	17945
Ingerson Transportation	Jefferson	NH	G	603 586-4335	18484
Inkberry	Marlborough	NH	G	603 876-4880	18960
Jensen Cabinet Co	Milford	NH	G	603 554-8363	19067
Kings Cornr Woodturning Wdwkg	Weare	NH	G	603 529-0063	19937
Mike Sequore	Marlborough	NH	G	603 876-4634	18962
Moneysworth & Best USA Inc	Ashland	NH	E	603 968-3301	17600
Peg Kearsarge Co Inc	Bartlett	NH	G	603 374-2341	17627
Riley Mountain Products Inc	Antrim	NH	F	603 588-7234	17597
Rochester Shoe Tree Co Inc **(PA)**	Ashland	NH	D	603 968-3301	17601
Seymour Woodworking	Epping	NH	G	603 679-2055	18102
Souhegan Wood Products Inc	Wilton	NH	F	603 654-2311	19988
Vigilant Incoporated	Dover	NH	E	603 285-0400	18065
We Cork Enterprises Inc	Exeter	NH	G	603 778-8558	18138
Wood Visions Inc	Hudson	NH	G	603 595-9663	18453
Cedar Craft Fence Co	Coventry	RI	G	401 397-7765	20141
Custom Woodturning	Tiverton	RI	G	401 625-5909	21256
Moore Company	Westerly	RI	C	401 596-2816	21532
New England Wood Products LLC	West Kingston	RI	G	401 789-7474	21469
Roland & Whytock Company	Providence	RI	E	401 781-1234	21117
Stupell Industries Ltd Inc	Johnston	RI	F	401 831-5640	20543

	CITY	ST	EMP	PHONE	ENTRY #
Barrup Farms Inc	Derby	VT	E	802 334-2331	21899
Brass Butterfly Inc	Poultney	VT	G	802 287-9818	22270
Carris Financial Corp **(PA)**	Proctor	VT	F	802 773-9111	22283
Carris Reels Inc **(HQ)**	Proctor	VT	C	802 773-9111	22284
Carris Reels Inc	Center Rutland	VT	F	802 773-9111	21831
Concept2 Inc **(PA)**	Morrisville	VT	E	802 888-7971	22166
Garflex Inc	Brattleboro	VT	D	802 257-5256	21728
George L Martin	Brattleboro	VT	G	802 254-5838	21729
Hex Design Inc **(PA)**	Bennington	VT	G	802 442-3309	21672
Initial Ideas Inc	Rutland	VT	G	802 775-1685	22340
J K Adams Company Inc	Dorset	VT	E	802 362-2303	21908
John Mc Leod Ltd **(PA)**	Wilmington	VT	E	802 464-8175	22702
Junction Frame Shop Inc	White River Junction	VT	G	802 296-2121	22641
Kingdom Pellets LLC	North Clarendon	VT	E	802 747-1093	22218
Lyndon Woodworking Inc **(PA)**	Saint Johnsbury	VT	E	802 748-0100	22390
National Clothes Pin Co Inc	Montpelier	VT	G	802 223-7332	22157
Nottingham Wood Products	Derby	VT	G	802 766-2791	21903
Stark Mountain Woodworks Co	New Haven	VT	F	802 453-5549	22187
Vermont Sweet Maple Inc	Middlebury	VT	G	802 398-2776	22121
Vermont Wood Pellet Co LLC	North Clarendon	VT	E	802 747-1093	22222
Wood & Signs Ltd	East Dorset	VT	G	802 362-2386	21918
Wood & Wood Inc	Waitsfield	VT	G	802 496-3000	22572
Wood Dynamics Corporation **(PA)**	South Pomfret	VT	G	802 457-3970	22489
Zephyr Designs Ltd	Brattleboro	VT	G	802 254-2788	21755

25 FURNITURE AND FIXTURES

2511 Wood Household Furniture

	CITY	ST	EMP	PHONE	ENTRY #
American Wood Products	North Haven	CT	G	203 248-4433	3007
Andre Furniture Industries	South Windsor	CT	G	860 528-8826	3938
Baldwin Lawn Furniture LLC	Middletown	CT	F	860 347-1306	2176
Bonito Manufacturing Inc	North Haven	CT	D	203 234-8786	3011
Carefree Building Co Inc **(PA)**	Colchester	CT	F	860 267-7600	800
CB Seating Etc LLC **(PA)**	Norwalk	CT	G	203 359-3880	3120
Cherner Chair Company LLC	Ridgefield	CT	G	203 894-4702	3662
Christopoulos Designs Inc	Bridgeport	CT	F	203 576-1110	397
Connecticut Solid Surface LLC	Plainville	CT	E	860 410-9800	3477
Custom Furniture & Design LLC	Litchfield	CT	F	860 567-3519	1947
Ethan Allen Interiors Inc **(PA)**	Danbury	CT	C	203 743-8000	914
Industrial Wood Product Co	Shelton	CT	G	203 735-2374	3817
Lookout Solutions LLC	Norwalk	CT	G	203 750-0307	3187
Madigan Millwork Inc	Unionville	CT	G	860 673-7601	4658
Nap Brothers Parlor Frame Inc	Glastonbury	CT	F	860 633-9998	1565
Oomph LLC	New Canaan	CT	G	203 216-9848	2612
Parish Associates Inc	Fairfield	CT	G	203 335-4100	1448
Salamander Designs Ltd	Bloomfield	CT	E	860 761-9500	262
Tudor House Furniture Co Inc	Hamden	CT	E	203 288-8451	1792
USA Wood Incorporated	Meriden	CT	G	203 238-4285	2147
Walpole Woodworkers Inc	Westport	CT	G	203 255-9010	5237
Walpole Woodworkers Inc	Ridgefield	CT	E	508 668-2800	3689
Western Conn Craftsmen LLC	New Fairfield	CT	G	203 312-8167	2631
Woodworkers Heaven Inc	Bridgeport	CT	F	203 333-2778	506
Abcrosby & Company Inc	Ashburnham	MA	G	978 827-6064	7643
Acton Woodworks Inc	Acton	MA	G	978 263-0222	7335
Bellecraft Woodworking Inc	Winchendon	MA	E	978 297-2672	17071
Bostoncounters LLC	Woburn	MA	G	781 281-1622	17138
Cedar Chest Inc	Northampton	MA	F	413 584-3860	13998
Charles Webb Inc **(PA)**	Woburn	MA	E	781 569-0444	17143
Connors Design Ltd	Marlborough	MA	G	508 481-1930	12739
Country Bed Shop Inc	Ashby	MA	G	978 386-7550	7646
Countryside Woodcraft	Russell	MA	F	413 862-3276	14877
Cove Woodworking Inc	Gloucester	MA	G	978 704-9773	11175
Craig F Bradford	Northampton	MA	G	413 586-4500	14003
Custom Ktchens By Chmpagne Inc	Franklin	MA	E	508 528-7919	11034
Custom Woods Designs M Marion	Hampden	MA	G	413 566-8230	11320
Damark Woodcraft Inc	Haverhill	MA	G	978 373-6670	11422
David Lefort	Halifax	MA	E	781 826-9033	11317
Drive-O-Rama Inc	Dennis Port	MA	D	508 394-0028	10312
Eustis Enterprises Inc	Cambridge	MA	G	978 827-3103	9474
Fabrizio Corporation	Medford	MA	E	781 396-1400	12933
Field Pendleton	Jefferson	MA	G	508 829-2470	11953
Fine Line Woodworking Inc	Boxboro	MA	G	978 263-4322	8952
Fox Brothers Furniture Studio	Newburyport	MA	G	978 462-7726	13491
Klein Design Inc	Gloucester	MA	G	978 281-5276	11196
M1 Project LLC	Boston	MA	G	617 906-6032	8676
Modu Form Inc **(PA)**	Fitchburg	MA	D	978 345-7942	10841
Peter Galbert	Roslindale	MA	G	978 660-5580	14841
Pridecraft Inc	North Andover	MA	G	978 685-2831	13726
R H Le Mieur Corp	Templeton	MA	F	978 939-8741	15804
Ralph Curcio Co Inc	Gardner	MA	G	978 632-1120	11124
Robert Kowalski	Spencer	MA	G	508 885-5392	15435
Royal Furniture Mfg Co Inc	Gardner	MA	G	978 632-1301	11125
Saloom Furniture Co Inc	Winchendon	MA	D	978 297-1901	17082
Sincere Specialty Fabrication	Chelsea	MA	G	781 974-9580	9967
SIT Inc	Quincy	MA	G	617 479-7796	14656
Standard Chair Gardner Inc	Gardner	MA	D	978 632-1301	11129
Thos Moser Cabinetmakers Inc	Boston	MA	G	617 224-1245	8883
Van Benten Joseph Furn Makers	Chestnut Hill	MA	G	617 738-6575	9994
VCA Inc	Northampton	MA	E	413 587-2750	14025
Walpole Woodworkers Inc	Wilmington	MA	F	978 658-3373	17064
Walpole Woodworkers Inc	East Falmouth	MA	F	508 540-0300	10451
Walpole Woodworkers Inc	Norwell	MA	G	781 681-9099	14114
Winning Solutions Inc	Manchester	MA	G	978 525-2813	12609
Wood Geek Inc	New Bedford	MA	G	508 858-5282	13459
Woodforms Inc	Foxboro	MA	G	508 543-9417	10909
Burger-Roy Inc	Madison	ME	D	207 696-3978	6404
Byer Manufacturing Company	Orono	ME	E	207 866-2171	6552
Cedarworks of Maine Inc **(PA)**	Rockport	ME	E	207 596-1010	6817
Healthy Homeworks	Portland	ME	G	207 415-4245	6670
Huston & Company Wood Design	Arundel	ME	G	207 967-2345	5532
Imagineering Inc	Rockland	ME	E	207 596-6483	6798
Jackson Caldwell	Oxford	ME	G	207 539-2325	6567
Jim Brown	Lincolnville	ME	F	207 789-5188	6362
Mayville House	Bethel	ME	G	207 824-6545	5715
Mystic Woodworks	Warren	ME	G	207 273-3937	7145
Premium Log Yards Inc **(PA)**	Rumford	ME	F	207 364-7500	6842
Richardson-Allen Inc	Biddeford	ME	F	207 284-8402	5761
Shed Happens Inc **(PA)**	Portland	ME	G	207 892-3636	6725
Thos Moser Cabinetmakers Inc **(PA)**	Auburn	ME	D	207 753-9834	5599
Thos Moser Cabinetmakers Inc	Freeport	ME	G	207 865-4519	6087
Town and Country Cabinets Inc	Gorham	ME	G	207 839-2709	6131
Townsend Cabinet Makers Inc	Limington	ME	G	207 793-7086	6350
Tracy Joseph Woodworks	Mount Desert	ME	G	207 244-0004	6457
Walpole Woodworkers Inc	Detroit	ME	E	207 368-4302	5954
Walpole Woodworkers Inc	Chester	ME	E	207 794-2248	5908
Waterworks	Bangor	ME	F	207 941-8306	5663
Wooden Things Inc	Gray	ME	G	207 712-4654	6144
Anthony Galluzzo Corp	Londonderry	NH	E	603 432-2681	18676
Chatham Furn Reproductions	South Hampton	NH	E	603 394-0089	19855
Cherry Pond Designs Inc	Jefferson	NH	F	603 586-7795	18482
Janice Miller	Manchester	NH	G	603 629-9995	18848
Kimballs Lumber Center LLC **(PA)**	Wolfeboro	NH	G	603 569-2477	20021
L & M Sheds LLC	Epping	NH	G	603 679-5243	18100
Maynard & Maynard Furn Makers	South Acworth	NH	G	603 835-2969	19853
Michael Perra Inc	Manchester	NH	F	603 644-2110	18871
Swift River Wood Products	Chocorua	NH	G	603 323-3317	17832
Vermont Custom Wood Products	North Walpole	NH	F	802 463-9930	19396
Whitney Bros Co	Keene	NH	E	603 352-2610	18534
Bess Home Fashions Inc	West Warwick	RI	F	401 828-0300	21484
Cedar Craft Fence Co	Coventry	RI	G	401 397-7765	20141
Joe Martin	West Warwick	RI	G	401 823-1860	21497
Kenney Manufacturing Company **(PA)**	Warwick	RI	B	401 739-2200	21383
Stephen Plaud Inc	Tiverton	RI	F	401 625-5909	21263
Studio 4 RI LLC	Providence	RI	G	401 578-5419	21128
Two Saints Inc	Cranston	RI	F	401 490-5500	20306
Warren Chair Works Inc	Warren	RI	F	401 247-0426	21313
Zuerner Design LLC	North Kingstown	RI	G	401 324-9490	20750
Beeken/Parsons Inc	Shelburne	VT	G	802 985-2913	22413
Carris Financial Corp **(PA)**	Proctor	VT	F	802 773-9111	22283
Charles Shackleton & Miranda T	Bridgewater	VT	E	802 672-5175	21757
Dock Doctors LLC	Ferrisburgh	VT	E	802 877-6756	21988
Gaylord West	Franklin	VT	G	802 285-6438	21994
Greenrange Furniture Company	Hinesburg	VT	G	802 747-8564	22027
Lyndon Woodworking Inc **(PA)**	Saint Johnsbury	VT	E	802 748-0100	22390
Merle Schloff	Salisbury	VT	G	802 352-4246	22399
New England Woodcraft Inc	Brandon	VT	C	802 247-8211	21712
Newport Furniture Parts Corp	Newport	VT	D	802 334-5428	22203
Sawyer Bentwood Inc	Whitingham	VT	E	802 368-2357	22647
Static & Dynamic Tech Inc	Williston	VT	G	802 859-0238	22693
Vermont Culinary Islands LLC	Brattleboro	VT	F	802 246-2277	21750
Vermont Furniture Designs Inc	Winooski	VT	E	802 655-6568	22727
William Chadburn	North Concord	VT	G	802 695-8166	22223

2512 Wood Household Furniture, Upholstered

	CITY	ST	EMP	PHONE	ENTRY #
Cerrito Furniture Inds Inc	Branford	CT	F	203 481-2580	304
Clark Manner Marguarite	New London	CT	G	860 444-7679	2769
Ethan Allen Interiors Inc **(PA)**	Danbury	CT	C	203 743-8000	914
Tudor House Furniture Co Inc	Hamden	CT	E	203 288-8451	1792
1817 Shoppe Inc **(PA)**	Sturbridge	MA	G	508 347-2241	15636
Alliance Upholstery Inc	Springfield	MA	G	413 731-7857	15444
Barclay Furniture Associates	Holyoke	MA	G	413 536-8084	11617
Charles Webb Inc **(PA)**	Woburn	MA	E	781 569-0444	17143
David Lefort	Halifax	MA	E	781 826-9033	11317
Huot Enterprises Inc	Ludlow	MA	G	413 589-7422	12468
Jerrys Custom Upholstery	Bridgewater	MA	G	508 697-2183	9078
Twin Cy Upholstering & Mat Co	Braintree	MA	F	781 843-1780	9044
Alfreds Upholstering & Custom	Alfred	ME	F	207 536-5565	5514
Custom Canvas & Upholstery LLC	Lewiston	ME	F	207 241-8518	6281
Jackson Caldwell	Oxford	ME	G	207 539-2325	6567
Hwang Bishop Designs Ltd	Warren	RI	G	401 245-9557	21296
New England Woodcraft Inc	Brandon	VT	C	802 247-8211	21712
VT Adirondack	Waitsfield	VT	G	802 496-9271	22570

2514 Metal Household Furniture

	CITY	ST	EMP	PHONE	ENTRY #
Advanced Prototype Development	Southbury	CT	G	203 267-1262	4022
CT Acquisitions LLC	Wallingford	CT	E	888 441-0537	4730
Durham Manufacturing Company **(PA)**	Durham	CT	D	860 349-3427	1090
Modern Objects Inc	Norwalk	CT	G	203 378-5785	3201
Salamander Designs Ltd	Bloomfield	CT	E	860 761-9500	262
Stonewall Kitchen LLC	South Windsor	CT	C	860 648-9215	4015
Allegheny River Group Inc	Milford	MA	E	508 634-0181	13107
Bostoncounters LLC	Woburn	MA	G	781 281-1622	17138
Coastal N Counters Inc	Mashpee	MA	F	508 539-3500	12879
Graney John F Metal Design LLC	Sheffield	MA	G	413 528-6744	15060
Leggett & Platt Incorporated	Oxford	MA	E	508 987-8706	14265
M J Industries Inc	Georgetown	MA	E	978 352-6190	11145
Raredon Resources Inc	Florence	MA	F	413 586-0941	10868
Sincere Specialty Fabrication	Chelsea	MA	G	781 974-9580	9967
GKS Service Company Inc	Candia	NH	G	603 483-2122	17784
Winnepesaukee Forge Inc	Meredith	NH	G	603 279-5492	18982
Patrick T Conley Atty	Providence	RI	G	-	21087
Summer Infant Inc **(PA)**	Woonsocket	RI	D	401 671-6550	21581
Summer Infant Inc	Woonsocket	RI	G	401 671-6550	21582
Cobble Mountain Inc	East Corinth	VT	G	802 439-5232	21913

2515 Mattresses & Bedsprings

	CITY	ST	EMP	PHONE	ENTRY #
A&S Innersprings Usa LLC	Windsor	CT	G	860 298-0401	5313
Blue Bell Mattress Company LLC	East Windsor	CT	C	860 292-6372	1278
J J Concrete Foundations	Bethel	CT	G	203 798-8310	164
Ramdial Parts and Services LLC	Hartford	CT	G	860 296-5175	1866
Restopedic Inc	Bethany	CT	G	203 393-1520	124
Saatva Inc	Westport	CT	E	877 672-2882	5228
Subinas USA LLC	Windsor	CT	F	860 298-0401	5370
Symbol Mattress of New England	Dayville	CT	B	860 779-3112	1053
Vijon Studios Inc	Old Saybrook	CT	G	860 399-7440	3353
Ecin Industries Inc	Fall River	MA	E	508 675-6920	10686
Gardner Mattress Corporation **(PA)**	Salem	MA	F	978 744-1810	14914
Kendall Productions	Cambridge	MA	G	617 661-0402	9525
Leggett & Platt Incorporated	Oxford	MA	E	508 987-8706	14265
Leggett & Platt Incorporated	Woburn	MA	B	336 956-5000	17213
Mockingbird Studios Inc	Mansfield	MA	G	508 339-6755	12646
Spring Air Ohio LLC	Chelsea	MA	E	617 884-0041	9968
Ssb Manufacturing Company	Agawam	MA	C	413 789-4410	7452
Steel Panel Foundations LLC	West Springfield	MA	G	413 439-0218	16552
Therapedic of New England LLC	Brockton	MA	G	508 559-9944	9182
Twin Cy Upholstering & Mat Co	Braintree	MA	F	781 843-1780	9044
US Bedding Inc	Fall River	MA	F	508 678-6988	10777
Vital Wood Products Inc	Fall River	MA	F	508 673-7976	10780
World Sleep Products Inc	North Billerica	MA	D	978 667-6648	13879
Daly Bros Bedding Co Inc	Biddeford	ME	G	207 282-9583	5727
Portland Mattress Makers Inc **(PA)**	Biddeford	ME	F	207 772-2276	5756
Bourdons Institutional Sls Inc	Claremont	NH	E	603 542-8709	17836
Massage Chairs For Less	Nashua	NH	G	603 882-7580	19205

2517 Wood T V, Radio, Phono & Sewing Cabinets

	CITY	ST	EMP	PHONE	ENTRY #
Belmont Corporation	Bristol	CT	E	860 589-5700	532
Christopoulos Designs Inc	Bridgeport	CT	F	203 576-1110	397
Custom Ktchens By Chmpagne Inc	Franklin	MA	E	508 528-7919	11034
Frame My Tvcom LLC	Haverhill	MA	G	978 912-7200	11435
Hilltop Wood Crafts	Auburn	MA	G	508 754-3915	7838
Superior Kitchen Designs Inc	Gardner	MA	E	978 632-5072	11130
VCA Inc	Northampton	MA	E	413 587-2750	14025
Crown Point Realty Corp Inc	Claremont	NH	D	603 543-1208	17846

2519 Household Furniture, NEC

	CITY	ST	EMP	PHONE	ENTRY #
New Age Motorsports LLC	Monroe	CT	G	203 268-1999	2410
Oomph LLC	New Canaan	CT	G	203 216-9848	2612
Ace Result LLC	Norwood	MA	G	612 559-3838	14118
CJ Sprong & Co Inc	Williamsburg	MA	G	413 628-4410	16948
Northeastern Rustic Furni	Smyrna Mills	ME	G	207 757-8300	6994
Yogibo LLC **(PA)**	Nashua	NH	E	603 595-0207	19291
Vermont Farm Table LLC **(PA)**	Burlington	VT	G	888 425-8838	21815

2521 Wood Office Furniture

	CITY	ST	EMP	PHONE	ENTRY #
Belmont Corporation	Bristol	CT	E	860 589-5700	532
Bergan Architectural Wdwkg Inc	Middletown	CT	E	860 346-0869	2177
Bloomfield Wood & Melamine Inc	Bloomfield	CT	F	860 243-3226	211
Bold Wood Interiors LLC	New Haven	CT	F	203 907-4077	2670
Clay Furniture Industries Inc	Manchester	CT	F	860 643-7580	1995
Conco Wood Working Inc	West Haven	CT	G	203 934-9665	5113
Cyr Woodworking Inc	Newington	CT	G	860 232-1991	2858
G Woodcraft	Norwalk	CT	G	203 846-4168	3156
Gregory Woodworks LLC	Bethel	CT	G	203 794-0726	157
Knoll Inc	Old Saybrook	CT	E	860 395-2093	3341
Lesro Industries Inc	Bloomfield	CT	D	800 275-7545	240
Neiss Corp	Vernon	CT	F	860 872-8528	4671
Salamander Designs Ltd	Bloomfield	CT	E	860 761-9500	262
Statham Woodwork	Norwalk	CT	G	203 831-0629	3250
Cano Corporation **(PA)**	Fitchburg	MA	E	978 342-0953	10818
Charles Webb Inc **(PA)**	Woburn	MA	E	781 569-0444	17143
Contemporary Cabinet Designs	Norwood	MA	G	781 769-7979	14143
Custom Office Furn Boston Inc	Woburn	MA	F	781 933-9970	17158
Desco Industries Inc	Canton	MA	E	781 821-8370	9726
F W Lombard Company **(PA)**	Winchendon	MA	E	978 827-5333	17075
Fox Brothers Furniture Studio	Newburyport	MA	G	978 462-7726	13491
Gill Metal Fab Inc	Brockton	MA	E	508 580-4445	9151
JC Clocks Company Inc	North Dartmouth	MA	E	508 998-8442	13922
Knoll Inc	Boston	MA	E	617 695-0220	8653
McKearney Associates Inc **(PA)**	Boston	MA	G	617 269-7600	8691
Modern Woodworks Co	Foxboro	MA	G	508 543-9830	10892
Modu Form Inc **(PA)**	Fitchburg	MA	D	978 345-7942	10841
Modu Form Inc	Fitchburg	MA	G	978 345-7942	10842
NS Converters LLC	Sudbury	MA	G	508 628-1501	15664
Source International Corp	Sutton	MA	E	508 842-5555	15692
Wright Line LLC **(HQ)**	Worcester	MA	C	508 852-4300	17510
Cabinet Assembly Systems Corp	East Greenwich	RI	F	401 884-8556	20355
Imperia Corporation	Barrington	RI	E	508 894-3000	20046
Lorimer Studios LLC	North Kingstown	RI	F	401 714-0014	20725
Neudorfer Inc	Waterbury	VT	F	802 244-5338	22584
New England Woodcraft Inc	Brandon	VT	C	802 247-8211	21712
William Chadburn	North Concord	VT	G	802 695-8166	22223

2522 Office Furniture, Except Wood

	CITY	ST	EMP	PHONE	ENTRY #
Bonito Manufacturing Inc	North Haven	CT	D	203 234-8786	3011
Conco Wood Working Inc	West Haven	CT	G	203 934-9665	5113
Durham Manufacturing Company **(PA)**	Durham	CT	D	860 349-3427	1090
Nutmeg Architectural Wdwrk Inc	Stamford	CT	E	203 325-4434	4264
One and Co Inc	Norwich	CT	F	860 892-5180	3288
Peristere LLC	Manchester	CT	G	860 783-5301	2038
Sabon Industries Inc	Fairfield	CT	G	203 255-8880	1453
Static Safe Products Company	Cornwall Bridge	CT	F	203 937-6391	820
Affordable Intr Systems Inc **(DH)**	Leominster	MA	D	978 562-7500	12108
Ais Group Holdings LLC **(PA)**	Hudson	MA	G	978 562-7500	11753
Ais Holdings Corp **(DH)**	Leominster	MA	G	978 562-7500	12110
Cano Corporation **(PA)**	Fitchburg	MA	E	978 342-0953	10818
Custom Office Furn Boston Inc	Woburn	MA	F	781 933-9970	17158
Desco Industries Inc	Canton	MA	E	781 821-8370	9726
Flex-Rest Inc	Worcester	MA	G	508 797-4046	17376
Krueger International Inc	Boston	MA	G	617 542-4043	8656
L D G Corporation	East Weymouth	MA	G	781 337-7155	10545
Modu Form Inc	Fitchburg	MA	G	978 345-7942	10842
Modu Form Inc **(PA)**	Fitchburg	MA	D	978 345-7942	10841
Production Basics Inc	Billerica	MA	E	617 926-8100	8278
Source International Corp	Sutton	MA	E	508 842-5555	15692
Wright Line LLC **(HQ)**	Worcester	MA	C	508 852-4300	17510
Mkind Inc	Manchester	NH	G	603 493-6882	18877
Nouveau Interiors LLC	Manchester	NH	G	603 398-1732	18889
SIS-USA Inc	Londonderry	NH	F	603 432-4495	18736
William Chadburn	North Concord	VT	G	802 695-8166	22223

2531 Public Building & Related Furniture

	CITY	ST	EMP	PHONE	ENTRY #
Clarios	Ledyard	CT	D	860 886-9021	1940
Clarios	Meriden	CT	D	678 297-4040	2086
Halls Rental Service LLC	North Branford	CT	G	203 488-0383	2966
Johnson Controls Inc	Rocky Hill	CT	G	860 571-3300	3720
Torrington Distributors Inc **(PA)**	Torrington	CT	E	860 482-4464	4604
Accudyne Machine Tool Inc	Bellingham	MA	G	508 966-3110	8027
B/E Aerospace Inc	Rockport	MA	G	978 546-1331	14834
Columbia Manufacturing Inc	Westfield	MA	D	413 562-3664	16679
Gallivan Company Inc	Foxboro	MA	G	508 543-5233	10883
Johnson Controls Inc	Boston	MA	D	617 992-2073	8636
Modu Form Inc	Fitchburg	MA	G	978 345-7942	10842
Modu Form Inc **(PA)**	Fitchburg	MA	D	978 345-7942	10841
New England Scenic LLC	Canton	MA	G	781 562-1792	9762
Production Basics Inc	Billerica	MA	E	617 926-8100	8278
Ry KY Inc	Wellesley	MA	G	781 235-4581	16385
VCA Inc	Northampton	MA	E	413 587-2750	14025
Clarios	Portland	ME	G	603 222-2400	6638
Hussey Corporation **(PA)**	North Berwick	ME	C	207 676-2271	6506
Hussey Seating Company	North Berwick	ME	B	207 676-2271	6507
B/E Aerospace Inc	Hampton	NH	G	603 926-5700	18256
Clarios	Manchester	NH	G	603 222-2400	18799
Dci Inc **(PA)**	Lisbon	NH	D	603 838-6544	18648
Lucci Corp	Peterborough	NH	F	603 567-4301	19475
Nhrpa	Concord	NH	G	603 340-5583	17919
Whitney Bros Co	Keene	NH	E	603 352-2610	18534
New England Woodcraft Inc	Brandon	VT	C	802 247-8211	21712

2541 Wood, Office & Store Fixtures

	CITY	ST	EMP	PHONE	ENTRY #
A S J Specialties LLC	Wallingford	CT	G	203 284-8650	4692
Ace Cabinet Company	New Britain	CT	G	860 225-6111	2502
BP Countertop Design Co LLC	Derby	CT	G	203 732-1620	1069
C Mather Company Inc	South Windsor	CT	G	860 528-5667	3946
Creative Dimensions Inc	Cheshire	CT	E	203 250-6500	725
Custom Crft Ktchns By Rizio BR	Monroe	CT	F	203 268-0271	2400
East Hartford Lamination Co	Glastonbury	CT	G	860 633-4637	1547

Employee Codes: A=Over 500 employees, B=251-500
C=101-250, D=51-100 E=20-50, F=10-19, G=3-9

	CITY	ST	EMP	PHONE	ENTRY #
Formatron Ltd	Farmington	CT	F	860 676-0227	1482
Gregory Woodworks LLC	Bethel	CT	G	203 794-0726	157
John M Kriskey Carpentry	Greenwich	CT	G	203 531-0194	1625
Leos Kitchen & Stair Corp	New Britain	CT	G	860 225-7363	2548
Lingard Cabinet Co LLC	Manchester	CT	G	860 647-9886	2019
Modern Woodcrafts LLC	Plainville	CT	D	860 677-7371	3508
New England Cabinet Co Inc	New Britain	CT	F	860 747-9995	2555
One and Co Inc	Norwich	CT	F	860 892-5180	3288
Premier Mfg Group Inc	Shelton	CT	D	203 924-6617	3863
Pro Counters New England LLC	Ansonia	CT	G	203 347-8663	21
Robert L Lovallo	Stamford	CT	G	203 324-6655	4304
Specialty Shop Inc	Manchester	CT	G	860 647-1477	2050
W R Hartigan & Son Inc	Burlington	CT	G	860 673-9203	682
American Custom Displays	Hanover	MA	G	781 829-0585	11326
Anthony Manufacturing Co Inc	Medford	MA	F	781 396-1400	12921
Armco Woodworking & Display	Worcester	MA	G	508 831-0990	17342
B&B Micro Manufacturing Inc	Adams	MA	E	413 281-9431	7410
Baranowski Woodworking Co Inc	East Bridgewater	MA	G	508 690-1515	10407
Blue Barn Inc	Gardner	MA	F	617 894-6987	11104
Boston Fabrications	Attleboro	MA	F	781 762-9185	7713
Cano Corporation **(PA)**	Fitchburg	MA	E	978 342-0953	10818
Carriage Hse Developments LLC	Winchester	MA	G	339 221-4253	17085
CN Custom Cabinets Inc	Townsend	MA	G	978 300-5531	15870
Continental Woodcraft Inc **(PA)**	Worcester	MA	E	508 581-9560	17359
Csl Building Group LLC **(PA)**	Lee	MA	G	616 669-6692	12091
Custom Ktchens By Chmpagne Inc	Franklin	MA	E	508 528-7919	11034
Diakosmisis Corporation	Somerville	MA	G	617 776-7714	15169
Dorie Enterprises Inc	Attleboro	MA	G	508 761-7588	7728
Eagle Woodworking Inc	Lawrence	MA	F	978 681-6194	12019
Franklin Fixtures Inc **(PA)**	West Wareham	MA	E	508 291-1475	16573
General Woodworking Inc **(PA)**	Lowell	MA	F	978 458-6625	12373
Jarica Inc	Woburn	MA	F	781 935-1907	17210
Jules A Gourdeau Inc	Beverly	MA	G	978 922-0102	8144
Kenyon Woodworking Inc	Jamaica Plain	MA	F	617 524-6883	11945
Kochman Reidt & Haigh Inc	Stoughton	MA	E	781 573-1500	15601
Metropolitan Cab Distrs Corp	Natick	MA	G	508 651-8950	13267
Metropolitan Cab Distrs Corp **(PA)**	Norwood	MA	G	781 949-8900	14178
Norwood Woodworking Inc	Norwood	MA	G	781 762-8367	14185
Padco Inc	Worcester	MA	F	508 753-8486	17438
Pbd Productions LLC	Hopedale	MA	F	508 482-9300	11679
Phillips Enterprises Inc	Northampton	MA	F	413 586-5860	14018
Rau Brothers Inc	Winchendon	MA	G	978 297-1381	17080
Twd Inc	Bridgewater	MA	E	508 279-2650	9091
Valiant Industries Inc	Amesbury	MA	E	978 388-3792	7510
Van Stry Design Inc	Malden	MA	E	781 388-9998	12600
Ware Rite Distributors Inc	East Bridgewater	MA	D	508 690-2145	10422
Wilsonart Intl Holdings LLC	North Reading	MA	E	978 664-5230	13994
Bangor Millwork & Supply Inc	Portland	ME	F	207 878-8548	6618
E G W Bradbury Enterprises	Bridgewater	ME	F	207 429-8141	5805
F A Wilnauer Woodwork Inc	South Berwick	ME	G	207 384-4824	7002
John Costin Studio	Kennebunk	ME	G	207 985-7221	6237
Jsi Store Fixtures Inc **(PA)**	Milo	ME	C	207 943-5203	6446
K & D Millworks Inc	Windham	ME	E	207 892-5188	7238
Maine Barrel & Display Company	Lewiston	ME	E	207 784-6700	6303
Portland Stone Works Inc	Portland	ME	F	207 878-6832	6713
Tozier Group Inc	Falmouth	ME	E	207 838-7939	6035
Advanced Custom Cabinets Inc	Brentwood	NH	E	603 772-6211	17743
Counter Tech Inc	Keene	NH	G	603 352-1882	18498
Daniel Preston	Hudson	NH	G	603 579-0525	18383
Excalibur Shelving Systems Inc	Contoocook	NH	E	603 746-6200	17944
Herrick Mill Work Inc	Contoocook	NH	E	603 746-5092	17945
J H Dunning Corporation	North Walpole	NH	E	603 445-5591	19394
Just Counters	Goffstown	NH	G	603 627-2027	18205
Yankee Craftsman Inc	Auburn	NH	G	603 483-5900	17614
Cole Cabinet Co Inc	Cranston	RI	F	401 467-4343	20199
Custom Design Incorporated	North Kingstown	RI	E	401 294-0200	20700
Elliott Sales Group Inc	Providence	RI	D	401 944-0002	21005
Elmwood Countertop Inc	Cranston	RI	G	401 785-1677	20216
Herrick & White Ltd	Cumberland	RI	D	401 658-0440	20324
Kenney Manufacturing Company **(PA)**	Warwick	RI	B	401 739-2200	21383
Laminated Products Inc	Woonsocket	RI	G	401 762-0711	21573
Orion Ret Svcs & Fixturing Inc	Smithfield	RI	D	401 334-5000	21243
Plastics Plus Inc	Cumberland	RI	E	401 727-1447	20339
R B L Holdings Inc	Coventry	RI	F	401 821-2200	20163
Scope Display & Box Co Inc	Providence	RI	G	401 467-3910	21120
Scope Display & Box Co Inc **(PA)**	Cranston	RI	D	401 942-7150	20284
Visual Creations Inc	Pawtucket	RI	C	401 588-5151	20911
Artisan Surfaces Inc	Springfield	VT	E	802 885-8677	22499
Jenson Enterprises LLC	South Burlington	VT	G	802 497-3530	22451
Leo D Bernstein & Sons Inc	Shaftsbury	VT	D	802 442-8029	22404
Top Shop Inc	South Burlington	VT	F	802 658-1351	22472
Vermont MBL Gran Slate Spstone	Castleton	VT	G	802 468-8800	21830
Were Tops Inc	Williston	VT	G	802 660-8677	22698

2542 Partitions & Fixtures, Except Wood

	CITY	ST	EMP	PHONE	ENTRY #
American Stonecrafters Inc	Wallingford	CT	G	203 514-9725	4698
Ardent Inc **(PA)**	East Hartford	CT	E	860 528-6000	1173
Bethel Mail Service	Bethel	CT	F	203 730-1399	130
Bull Metal Products Inc	Middletown	CT	E	860 346-9691	2180
C Mather Company Inc	South Windsor	CT	G	860 528-5667	3946
Di-Cor Industries Inc	Bristol	CT	F	860 585-5583	549
Displaycraft Inc	Plainville	CT	E	860 747-9110	3481
Durham Manufacturing Company **(PA)**	Durham	CT	D	860 349-3427	1090
In Store Experience Inc	Westport	CT	E	203 221-4777	5201
Mitchell-Bate Company	Waterbury	CT	E	203 233-0862	4918
Platt-Labonia of N Haven Inc	North Haven	CT	D	203 239-5681	3052
Boston Retail Products Inc **(PA)**	Medford	MA	C	781 395-7417	12923
Buckley Co Inc	Scituate	MA	G	781 545-7975	15007
Cano Corporation **(PA)**	Fitchburg	MA	E	978 342-0953	10818
Central Mass Installations	West Boylston	MA	G	508 612-3092	16412
Continental Woodcraft Inc **(PA)**	Worcester	MA	E	508 581-9560	17359
Fx Group	Oxford	MA	G	508 987-1366	14262
JH Smith Co Inc **(PA)**	Greenfield	MA	F	413 772-0191	11264
New England Wire Products Inc **(PA)**	Leominster	MA	C	800 254-9473	12171
Phillips Enterprises Inc	Northampton	MA	F	413 586-5860	14018
Present Arms Inc	Indian Orchard	MA	G	413 575-4656	11894
Rack Attack USA LLP	Framingham	MA	G	508 665-4361	10998
Rogers Cabinets	Norwood	MA	G	781 762-5700	14197
Stanley Vidmar	Holliston	MA	G	610 797-6600	11605
Top Shelf Installations	Bridgewater	MA	G	508 697-1550	9090
Wood & Wood Inc	Greenfield	MA	E	413 772-0889	11284
E G W Bradbury Enterprises	Bridgewater	ME	F	207 429-8141	5805
Jsi Store Fixtures Inc **(PA)**	Milo	ME	C	207 943-5203	6446
Maine Wood & Design LLC	York	ME	F	207 363-5270	7312
Stainless Fdsrvice Eqp Mfg Inc	Limestone	ME	F	207 227-7747	6344
Starc Systems Inc	Brunswick	ME	G	844 596-1784	5846
Alco Construction Inc	Hudson	NH	G	603 305-8493	18372
Borroughs Corporation	Raymond	NH	G	603 895-3991	19636
Ronnie Marvin Enterprises	Littleton	NH	G	603 444-5017	18664
Atlas Fabrication Inc	Providence	RI	G	401 861-4911	20961
Custom Design Incorporated	North Kingstown	RI	E	401 294-0200	20700
Elliott Sales Group Inc	Providence	RI	D	401 944-0002	21005
Frank Shatz & Co	Warwick	RI	E	401 739-1822	21364
Herrick & White Ltd	Cumberland	RI	D	401 658-0440	20324
JCM Design & Display Inc	Providence	RI	E	401 781-0470	21042
Maro Display Inc	North Kingstown	RI	E	401 294-5551	20726
PCL Fixtures Inc	Rumford	RI	G	401 334-4646	21193
Reed Allison Group Inc	Providence	RI	D	617 846-1237	21107
Scope Display & Box Co Inc **(PA)**	Cranston	RI	D	401 942-7150	20284
Stabaarte Inc	Newport	RI	G	401 364-8633	20685
Green Mountain Gazebo	Westminster	VT	G	802 869-1212	22630
Konrad Prefab LLC	Springfield	VT	G	802 885-6780	22504
Top Shop Inc	South Burlington	VT	F	802 658-1351	22472
Town & Country Sheds	Wolcott	VT	G	802 888-7012	22733

2591 Drapery Hardware, Window Blinds & Shades

	CITY	ST	EMP	PHONE	ENTRY #
Ahlstrom-Munksjo Nonwovens LLC **(DH)**	Windsor Locks	CT	B	860 654-8300	5382
Arrow Window Shade Mfg Co	Wethersfield	CT	G	860 956-3570	5240
Arrow Window Shade Mfg Co Mrdn	Wethersfield	CT	F	860 563-4035	5241
Ben Baena & Son	Bridgeport	CT	G	203 334-8568	382
Decorator Services Inc	Bridgeport	CT	E	203 384-8144	402
Kilcourse Specialty Products	New Milford	CT	G	860 210-2075	2810
Niantic Awning Company	Niantic	CT	G	860 739-0161	2954
Porter Preston Inc	Waterbury	CT	E	203 753-1113	4941
Rollease Acmeda Inc **(PA)**	Stamford	CT	D	203 964-1573	4305
Roto-Frank of America Inc	Chester	CT	C	860 526-4996	775
Thomas W Raftery Inc	Hartford	CT	E	860 278-9870	1879
Beverly Shade Shoppe	Beverly	MA	G	978 922-0374	8110
Cdi LLC A Valley Forge Co	Brockton	MA	C	508 587-7000	9128
Craft Interiors	Malden	MA	G	781 321-8695	12566
High Grade Shade & Screen Co	Lynn	MA	F	781 592-5027	12516
Kings Draperies Inc	Brockton	MA	G	508 230-0055	9159
Landmark Window Fashions Inc	Holbrook	MA	E	781 767-3535	11528
Lundys Company Inc	Lynn	MA	F	781 595-8639	12522
Marjorie Royer Interiors Inc	Middleton	MA	G	978 774-0533	13095
Mohawk Shade & Blind Co Inc	Cambridge	MA	G	617 868-6000	9568
New England Blinds	Sterling	MA	G	508 868-5399	15542
New England Drapery Assoc Inc	Woburn	MA	G	781 944-7536	17241
Reliable Shade & Screen Co	Somerville	MA	G	617 776-9538	15209
Shade Adams & Screen Co	Framingham	MA	G	617 244-2188	11004
Staceys Shade Shop Inc **(PA)**	Lynn	MA	G	781 595-0097	12540
Taunton Venetian Blind Inc	Taunton	MA	G	508 822-7548	15789
TLC Vision (usa) Corporation	Peabody	MA	E	978 531-4114	14378
Custom Window Decorators	Lewiston	ME	G	207 784-4113	6282
Vertical Dreams	Nashua	NH	G	603 943-7571	19282
Winnepesaukee Forge Inc	Meredith	NH	G	603 279-5492	18982
Bristol Cushions Inc	Bristol	RI	F	401 247-4499	20065
Decorators Sewing Shoppe Inc	Johnston	RI	G	401 453-3500	20507
Kenney Manufacturing Company **(PA)**	Warwick	RI	B	401 739-2200	21383
L F Pease Co	East Providence	RI	F	401 438-2850	20428
Blw LLC	Brattleboro	VT	G	802 246-4500	21719
Brass Butterfly Inc	Poultney	VT	G	802 287-9818	22270
Dometic Uk Blind Systems Ltd	Manchester Center	VT	E	802 362-5258	22082
Gordons Window Decor Inc **(PA)**	Williston	VT	F	802 655-7777	22671

2599 Furniture & Fixtures, NEC

	CITY	ST	EMP	PHONE	ENTRY #
Curtiss Woodworking Inc	Prospect	CT	F	203 527-9305	3586
General Seating Solutions LLC	South Windsor	CT	F	860 242-3307	3971
Liberty Garage Inc	Danbury	CT	G	203 778-0222	947
River Mill Co	Clinton	CT	F	860 669-5915	794
Triple Play Sports	Watertown	CT	F	860 417-2877	5030
Westmount Group LLC	West Haven	CT	G	203 931-1033	5151
42 Design Fab Studio Inc	Indian Orchard	MA	G	413 203-4948	11882
Cove Woodworking Inc	Gloucester	MA	G	978 704-9773	11175
General Woodworking Inc **(PA)**	Lowell	MA	F	978 458-6625	12373
General Woodworking Inc	Lowell	MA	E	978 251-4070	12374
Hendrick Manufacturing Corp **(PA)**	Salem	MA	F	781 631-4400	14919
Hostar Mar Trnspt Systems Inc	Wareham	MA	E	508 295-2900	16250
JS International Inc	Fall River	MA	E	508 675-4722	10718
Metzys Taqueria LLC	Newburyport	MA	G	978 992-1451	13512
October Company Inc **(PA)**	Easthampton	MA	C	413 527-9380	10572
R W Hatfield Company Inc **(PA)**	Haverhill	MA	E	978 521-2600	11466
Sampco Inc **(PA)**	Pittsfield	MA	C	413 442-4043	14507
Stanley Industrial & Auto LLC	Holliston	MA	B	508 429-1350	11604
B and R Modern Hand Tool Inc	Portland	ME	G	207 773-6706	6615
Bunzl Maine	Portland	ME	G	207 772-9825	6629
Chase S Daily LLC	Belfast	ME	G	207 338-0555	5687
Higgins Fabrication LLC	Bangor	ME	G	719 930-6437	5650
Quarry Tap Room LLC	Hallowell	ME	G	207 213-6173	6164
Coast To Coast Ff & E Installa	Greenland	NH	F	603 433-0164	18222
Holmris US Inc	Manchester	NH	G	603 232-3490	18836
Storage Concepts	Berlin	NH	G	603 752-1111	17701
Wingate Sales Associates LLC	Stratham	NH	G	603 303-7189	19877
Kingston Krafts	Cranston	RI	G	401 272-0292	20248
Stackbin Corporation	Lincoln	RI	E	401 333-1600	20597
7 South Sandwich Company LLC	Middlebury	VT	G	802 388-3354	22095
Cricket Radio LLC	Burlington	VT	G	802 825-8368	21777
Green Mountain Vista Inc	Williston	VT	G	802 862-0159	22673
Vermont Culinary Islands LLC	Brattleboro	VT	F	802 246-2277	21750

26 PAPER AND ALLIED PRODUCTS

2611 Pulp Mills

	CITY	ST	EMP	PHONE	ENTRY #
Cellmark Pulp & Paper Inc	Norwalk	CT	F	203 299-5050	3122
Eldorado Usa Inc	Branford	CT	G	203 208-2282	312
International Paper - 16 Inc **(HQ)**	Stamford	CT	G	203 329-8544	4227
American Paper Recycling Corp **(PA)**	Mansfield	MA	E	800 422-3220	12613
Georgia-Pacific LLC	Norwood	MA	G	781 440-3600	14155
Melt Cognition	Bedford	MA	G	781 275-6400	7990
Tomra Mass LLC	New Bedford	MA	E	203 395-3484	13455
County of Lincoln	Wiscasset	ME	G	207 882-5276	7284
Georgia-Pacific LLC	Baileyville	ME	G	207 427-4077	5626
ND Otm LLC	Old Town	ME	C	207 401-2879	6545
ND Paper Inc	Rumford	ME	G	207 364-4521	6838
Robbins Lumber Inc	Searsmont	ME	C	207 342-5221	6945
Woodland Pulp LLC **(PA)**	Baileyville	ME	B	207 427-3311	5627
Petrofiber Corporation **(PA)**	Hopkinton	NH	G	603 627-0416	18364
Lkq Precious Metals Inc	North Smithfield	RI	C	401 762-0094	20789
Chittenden Environmental	Williston	VT	G	802 578-0194	22660
Westrock Cp LLC	Sheldon Springs	VT	C	802 933-7733	22431

2621 Paper Mills

	CITY	ST	EMP	PHONE	ENTRY #
Ahlstrom Windsor Locks LLC	Windsor Locks	CT	F	860 654-8629	5381
Ahlstrom-Munksjo USA Inc **(HQ)**	Windsor Locks	CT	F	860 654-8300	5383
American Banknote Corporation **(PA)**	Stamford	CT	G	203 941-4090	4135
Brant Industries Inc **(PA)**	Greenwich	CT	F	203 661-3344	1601
Bristol Adult Resource Ctr Inc	Bristol	CT	E	860 583-8721	536
D K Schulman	New Preston	CT	G	860 868-4300	2834
Doubletree	Bristol	CT	F	860 589-7766	550
Dunn Paper Holdings Inc	East Hartford	CT	D	860 289-7496	1188
International Paper - 16 Inc **(HQ)**	Stamford	CT	G	203 329-8544	4227
International Paper Company	Putnam	CT	C	860 928-7901	3616
Kimberly-Clark Corporation	New Milford	CT	A	860 210-1602	2811
Kimberly-Clark Corporation	Stratford	CT	C	973 986-8454	4427
LP Hometown Pizza LLC	Bristol	CT	G	860 589-1208	577
Mafcote International Inc **(HQ)**	Norwalk	CT	F	203 644-1200	3189
Norcell Inc **(DH)**	Shelton	CT	F	203 254-5292	3841
Resolute FP US Inc	Southport	CT	B	203 292-6560	4097
Royal Consumer Products LLC **(HQ)**	Norwalk	CT	E	203 847-8500	3234
Sheaffer Pen Corp	Shelton	CT	B	203 783-2894	3869
Thomas Design Group LLC	Stamford	CT	G	203 588-1910	4345
Up With Paper	Guilford	CT	G	203 453-3300	1723
UST LLC **(HQ)**	Stamford	CT	G	203 817-3000	4355
Xamax Industries Inc	Seymour	CT	E	203 888-7200	3769
Yale University	New Haven	CT	G	203 432-2424	2760
Yale University	New Haven	CT	G	203 432-7494	2762
Agricltral Resources Mass Dept	Attleboro	MA	G	774 331-2818	7702
Ahlstrom-Munksjo Paper Inc	Leominster	MA	F	978 342-1080	12109
Birch Point Paper Products Inc	Fitchburg	MA	E	978 422-1447	10811
Boston Paper Board Corp	Boston	MA	E	617 666-1154	8436
Bristol Bay LLC	Salem	MA	G	978 744-4272	14898
Bristol Myers Squibb	Cambridge	MA	G	781 209-2309	9423
Bristol Place Inc	Attleboro	MA	G	508 226-2300	7714
Corona Films Inc	West Townsend	MA	G	978 597-6444	16566
Crane & Co Inc	Pittsfield	MA	F	413 684-6856	14466
Crane & Co Inc **(HQ)**	Boston	MA	C	617 648-3799	8487
Crane & Co Inc	Pittsfield	MA	C	413 684-2600	14467
Crane & Co Inc	North Adams	MA	C	413 664-4321	13672
Crane & Co Inc	Dalton	MA	G	413 684-2600	10176
Crane & Co Inc	Dalton	MA	C	413 684-2600	10177
Crane Stationery LLC	North Adams	MA	A	413 664-2256	13673
Creative Celebrations	Danvers	MA	F	978 774-7737	10208
Dennecrepe Corporation	Gardner	MA	D	978 630-8669	11112
Erving Industries Inc **(PA)**	Erving	MA	C	413 422-2700	10589
Erving Paper Mills Inc	Erving	MA	C	413 422-2700	10590
Fortifiber Corporation	Attleboro	MA	E	508 222-3500	7738
Georgia-Pacific LLC	Norwood	MA	G	781 440-3600	14155
Georgia-Pacific LLC	Leominster	MA	C	978 537-4701	12144
H & C Sales Inc	Stoughton	MA	G	781 344-6445	15595
Hollingsworth & Vose Company **(PA)**	East Walpole	MA	C	508 850-2000	10524
Horizon Sales	Bolton	MA	G	978 779-0487	8320
Imperial Bag and Paper	Franklin	MA	G	508 541-7220	11055
Irving Consumer Products Inc	Burlington	MA	F	781 273-3222	9286
Kadant Inc **(PA)**	Westford	MA	B	978 776-2000	16774
Kanzaki Specialty Papers Inc **(DH)**	Ware	MA	C	413 967-6204	16235
Kimberly-Clark Corporation	Franklin	MA	G	508 520-1355	11062
L & P Paper Inc	Charlton	MA	D	508 248-3265	9853
Lenmarine Inc	Somerset	MA	F	508 678-1234	15146
McNairn Packaging Inc **(PA)**	Westfield	MA	D	413 568-1989	16699
Neenah Technical Materials Inc **(HQ)**	Dalton	MA	F	678 518-3343	10180
Neenah Technical Materials Inc	Pittsfield	MA	C	413 684-7874	14495
Onyx Specialty Papers Inc	South Lee	MA	C	413 243-1231	15319
Packaging Specialties Inc	Newburyport	MA	D	978 462-1300	13520
Pacothane Technologies **(PA)**	Winchester	MA	E	781 729-0927	17094
Pacothane Technologies	Woburn	MA	E	781 756-3163	17253
Pagell Corporation	Holliston	MA	E	508 429-2998	11594
Red Sun Press Inc	Jamaica Plain	MA	F	617 524-6822	11949
Seaman Paper Company Mass Inc **(PA)**	Gardner	MA	E	978 632-1513	11126
Seaman Paper Company Mass Inc	Orange	MA	G	978 544-2455	14228
Seaman Paper Company Mass Inc	Baldwinville	MA	D	978 939-5356	7945
Sonoco Products Company	Holyoke	MA	D	413 536-4546	11658
Tropical Smoothie of Bristol	Dartmouth	MA	G	508 636-1424	10278
Veterans Affairs US Dept	Fall River	MA	G	774 240-6764	10779
Cascades Auburn Fiber Inc	Auburn	ME	E	207 753-5300	5552
Domtar Paper Company LLC	Baileyville	ME	A	207 427-6400	5624
Georgia-Pacific LLC	Old Town	ME	B	207 827-7711	6538
Georgia-Pacific LLC	Baileyville	ME	G	207 427-4077	5626
Huhtamaki Inc	Waterville	ME	B	207 873-3351	7157
International Paper Company	Auburn	ME	C	207 784-4051	5572
L L Bean Inc	Freeport	ME	A	207 552-2000	6081
ND Paper LLC	Rumford	ME	A	207 364-4521	6839
Presumpscot Water Power Co	Westbrook	ME	G	207 856-4000	7204
Sappi North America Inc	Skowhegan	ME	G	207 858-4201	6985
Sappi North America Inc	Westbrook	ME	B	207 856-4000	7205
Sappi North America Inc	Skowhegan	ME	A	207 238-3000	6986
Sappi North America Inc	South Portland	ME	D	207 854-7000	7039
Twin Rivers Paper Company Corp	Madawaska	ME	A	207 523-2350	6402
Twin Rivers Paper Company LLC	South Portland	ME	D	207 523-2350	7043
Twin Rivers Paper Company LLC **(PA)**	Madawaska	ME	E	207 728-3321	6403
Verso Paper Holding LLC	Jay	ME	A	207 897-3431	6222
APC Paper Company Inc **(PA)**	Claremont	NH	D	603 542-0411	17835
Arlington Sample Book Co Inc **(PA)**	Sunapee	NH	G	603 763-9082	19879
Crane Security Tech Inc	Nashua	NH	E	603 881-1860	19139
Eagle Copy Center	Windham	NH	G	603 225-3713	20004
Enco Container Services Inc	Plaistow	NH	G	603 382-8481	19511
Ges Control Systems Inc	Dover	NH	G	905 336-5517	18023
Innovative Paper Tech LLC	Tilton	NH	D	603 286-4891	19906
Monadnock Paper Mills Inc **(PA)**	Bennington	NH	C	603 588-3311	17689
Cellmark Inc	Pawtucket	RI	G	401 723-4200	20821
Friends Historic Bristol Inc	Bristol	RI	G	401 451-2735	20079
Signode Industrial Group LLC	Rumford	RI	D	401 438-5203	21196
Weeden Street Associates LLC	Pawtucket	RI	E	401 725-2610	20912
Kimberly-Clark Corporation	East Ryegate	VT	D	972 281-1200	21920
Soundview Vermont Holdings LLC	Putney	VT	C	802 387-5571	22292
Subatomic Digital LLC	Williston	VT	E	802 857-4864	22694

2631 Paperboard Mills

	CITY	ST	EMP	PHONE	ENTRY #
Action Packaging Systems Inc **(PA)**	Ellington	CT	G	860 222-9510	1325
B-P Products Inc	Hamden	CT	E	203 288-0200	1733
Connecticut Container Corp **(PA)**	North Haven	CT	C	203 248-2161	3018
Fluted Partition Inc **(PA)**	Bridgeport	CT	C	203 368-2548	414
Graphic Packaging Intl LLC	Litchfield	CT	G	860 567-4196	1949
Keystone Paper & Box Co Inc	South Windsor	CT	D	860 291-0027	3988
Lydall Inc **(PA)**	Manchester	CT	E	860 646-1233	2021
Metsa Board Americas Corp	Norwalk	CT	D	203 229-0037	3196
Millen Industries Inc **(PA)**	Norwalk	CT	G	203 847-8500	3198
Pact Inc	Waterbury	CT	F	203 759-1799	4934
Paper Alliance LLC	Branford	CT	G	203 315-3116	334

	CITY	ST	EMP	PHONE	ENTRY #
Rice Packaging Inc	Ellington	CT	D	860 870-7057	1338
Risha Rishi LLC	Middletown	CT	G	860 346-7645	2219
Russell Partition Co Inc	North Haven	CT	G	203 239-5749	3059
Schrafel Paperboard Converting	West Haven	CT	E	203 931-1700	5145
Westrock Cp LLC	Uncasville	CT	C	860 848-1500	4651
Baird & Bartlett Coi NC	West Bridgewater	MA	G	508 588-9400	16431
Caraustar Industries Inc	Fitchburg	MA	D	978 665-2632	10819
Core Concepts Inc	Franklin	MA	E	508 528-0070	11032
Danvers Industrial Packg Corp	Beverly	MA	E	978 777-0020	8124
G3 Incorporated **(PA)**	Lowell	MA	E	978 805-5001	12372
Georgia-Pacific LLC	Norwood	MA	G	781 440-3600	14155
Georgia-Pacific LLC	Leominster	MA	C	978 537-4701	12144
Graphic Arts Finishers Inc	Newton	MA	E	617 241-9292	13597
Hampden Papers Inc **(PA)**	Holyoke	MA	D	413 536-1000	11630
Lamitech	Rockland	MA	F	781 878-7708	14811
Miles Kedex Co Inc	Westminster	MA	E	978 874-1403	16810
Millstone Med Outsourcing LLC **(PA)**	Fall River	MA	C	508 679-8384	10733
Neenah Northeast LLC **(HQ)**	West Springfield	MA	C	413 533-0699	16534
New-Indy Cntinerboard Hold LLC **(HQ)**	Foxboro	MA	C	508 384-4230	10894
Njf Packaging Enterprise	Osterville	MA	G	508 428-1255	14249
Northeast Document Conservatio	Andover	MA	E	978 470-1010	7577
Quality Carton Converting LLC	Haverhill	MA	F	978 556-5008	11464
Rand-Whitney Container Board L	Worcester	MA	D	860 848-1900	17449
Rand-Whitney Container LLC **(DH)**	Worcester	MA	C	508 890-7000	17450
Rand-Whitney Group LLC **(HQ)**	Worcester	MA	C	508 791-2301	17452
Sonoco Products Company	Holyoke	MA	D	413 536-4546	11658
Sonoco Products Company	Holyoke	MA	E	413 493-1298	11659
Westrock Cp LLC	Mansfield	MA	E	508 337-0400	12672
Westrock Cp LLC	Mansfield	MA	C	770 448-2193	12671
Westrock Mwv LLC	Springfield	MA	A	413 736-7211	15527
Westrock Rkt Company	Springfield	MA	G	413 543-7300	15528
Wood Products Unlimited Inc	Methuen	MA	G	978 687-7449	13048
Georgia-Pacific LLC	Baileyville	ME	G	207 427-4077	5626
RTS Packaging LLC	Scarborough	ME	D	207 883-8921	6938
Sonoco Products Company	Pittsfield	ME	E	207 487-3206	6591
Environmental Packg Tech Inc	Plaistow	NH	G	603 378-0340	19515
Graphic Packaging Intl LLC	Concord	NH	C	603 230-5100	17904
Graphic Packaging Intl LLC	Concord	NH	E	603 230-5486	17905
Graphic Packaging Intl LLC	Concord	NH	D	603 230-5100	17906
Graphic Packaging Intl LLC	Concord	NH	D	603 224-2333	17907
Contempo Card Co Inc **(PA)**	Providence	RI	D	401 272-4210	20990
Jewel Case Corporation	Providence	RI	B	401 943-1400	21044
Nfa Corp	Cumberland	RI	E	401 333-8990	20332
Plastic Services Entps Inc	Providence	RI	F	401 490-3811	21090
Rand-Whitney Container LLC	Pawtucket	RI	E	401 729-7900	20890
Signode Industrial Group LLC	Rumford	RI	D	401 438-5203	21196
Vemuri International LLC	Pawtucket	RI	G	401 723-4200	20910
Limlaws Pulpwood Inc	West Topsham	VT	F	802 439-3503	22622
Long Falls Paperboard LLC	Brattleboro	VT	C	802 257-0365	21737
Westrock Converting Company	Sheldon Springs	VT	G	802 933-7733	22430
Westrock Cp LLC	Sheldon Springs	VT	C	802 933-7733	22431

2652 Set-Up Paperboard Boxes

	CITY	ST	EMP	PHONE	ENTRY #
Agi-Shorewood Group Us LLC	Stamford	CT	A	203 324-4839	4132
Millen Industries Inc **(PA)**	Norwalk	CT	G	203 847-8500	3198
Rice Packaging Inc	Ellington	CT	D	860 870-7057	1338
Rondo America Incorporated	Naugatuck	CT	C	203 723-5831	2494
Egoh Packaging Inc	Marlborough	MA	E	508 460-6683	12752
Friend Box Company Inc	Danvers	MA	D	978 774-0240	10218
Packaging Specialties Inc	Newburyport	MA	D	978 462-1300	13520
Quality Packaging & Graphics	Westfield	MA	G	413 568-1923	16722
Specialty Packaging Inc	Indian Orchard	MA	G	413 543-1814	11895
UNI-Pac Inc	Holyoke	MA	D	413 534-5284	11662
Westrock Cp LLC	Mansfield	MA	C	770 448-2193	12671
Westrock Rkt Company	Springfield	MA	G	413 543-7300	15528
Volk Packaging Corporation	Biddeford	ME	D	207 282-6151	5768
C & O Box & Printing Company	Hooksett	NH	G	508 881-1760	18345
Graphic Packaging Intl LLC	Concord	NH	D	603 230-5100	17906
Graphic Packaging Intl LLC	Concord	NH	C	603 230-5100	17904
Fuller Box Co Inc	Central Falls	RI	D	401 725-4300	20113
Hope Buffinton Packaging Inc	Central Falls	RI	E	401 725-3646	20115
Mason Box Company	Pawtucket	RI	E	800 842-9526	20857
Numaco Packaging LLC	East Providence	RI	F	401 438-4952	20436
Taylor Box Company	Warren	RI	E	401 245-5900	21309

2653 Corrugated & Solid Fiber Boxes

	CITY	ST	EMP	PHONE	ENTRY #
AP Disposition LLC	Norwich	CT	D	860 889-1344	3276
Cascades Holding US Inc	Newtown	CT	D	203 426-5871	2918
Champlin-Packrite Inc	Manchester	CT	E	860 951-9217	1993
Colonial Corrugated Pdts Inc	Waterbury	CT	E	203 597-1707	4860
Common Sense Engineered Pdts	Beacon Falls	CT	G	203 888-8695	56
Connecticut Container Corp **(PA)**	North Haven	CT	C	203 248-2161	3018
Corr/Dis Incorporated	Norwalk	CT	G	203 838-6075	3132
Danbury Square Box Company	Danbury	CT	E	203 744-4611	899
Fluted Partition Inc	Bridgeport	CT	F	203 334-3500	415
Fluted Partition Inc **(PA)**	Bridgeport	CT	C	203 368-2548	414
General Packaging Products Inc	Norwalk	CT	G	203 846-1340	3160
HI-Tech Packaging Inc	Stratford	CT	E	203 378-2700	4420
Holm Corrugated Container Inc	Southington	CT	E	860 628-5559	4058
Jackson Corrugated Cont Corp	Essex	CT	E	860 767-3373	1399
Kapstone Paper and Packg Corp	Putnam	CT	G	860 928-2211	3619
Knapp Container Inc	Beacon Falls	CT	G	203 888-0511	59
Merrill Industries Inc	Ellington	CT	E	860 871-1888	1336
Merrill Industries LLC	Ellington	CT	E	860 871-1888	1337
Nutmeg Container Corporation **(HQ)**	Putnam	CT	D	860 963-6727	3622
R & R Corrugated Container Inc	Bristol	CT	D	860 584-1194	601
Rand-Whitney Group LLC	Newtown	CT	D	203 426-5871	2934
Rice Packaging Inc	Ellington	CT	D	860 870-7057	1338
Russell Partition Co Inc	North Haven	CT	G	203 239-5749	3059
Skyline Exhibits & Graphics	Middletown	CT	F	860 635-2400	2222
Westrock Rkt Company	Bethel	CT	F	203 739-0318	193
Windham Container Corporation	Putnam	CT	E	860 928-7934	3640
Abbott-Action Inc **(PA)**	Attleboro	MA	E	401 722-2100	7699
Atlas Box and Crating Co Inc **(PA)**	Sutton	MA	C	508 865-1155	15679
Buy Boxescom LLC	Boston	MA	G	617 305-7865	8451
Commonwealth Packaging Corp	Chicopee	MA	D	413 593-1482	10015
Corrugated Packaging Inc	Fitchburg	MA	F	978 342-6076	10821
Corrugated Stitcher Service	Berkley	MA	G	508 823-2844	8085
Craft Corrugated Box Inc	New Bedford	MA	F	508 998-2115	13374
E Ink Corporation	Billerica	MA	D	617 499-6000	8242
Friend Box Company Inc	Danvers	MA	D	978 774-0240	10218
Horn Corporation **(PA)**	Lancaster	MA	E	800 832-7020	11984
Ideal Box Company	Lawrence	MA	G	978 683-2802	12037
Interstate Cont Lowell LLC **(DH)**	Lowell	MA	D	978 458-4555	12383
Kerrigan Paper Products Inc	Haverhill	MA	G	978 374-4797	11445
Kraft Group LLC **(PA)**	Foxboro	MA	C	508 384-4230	10890
Massachusetts Container Corp	Marlborough	MA	C	508 481-1100	12793
Mount Tom Box Company Inc	West Springfield	MA	E	413 781-5300	16531
New England Business Svc Inc **(HQ)**	Groton	MA	D	978 448-6111	11291
New England Wooden Ware Corp **(PA)**	Gardner	MA	E	978 632-3600	11122
Newcorr Packaging Inc	Northborough	MA	D	508 393-9256	14040
Packaging Corporation America	Chelmsford	MA	E	978 256-4586	9920
Packaging Corporation America	Northampton	MA	D	413 584-6132	14017
Packaging Corporation America	Westfield	MA	G	413 562-0610	16710
Phillips Packaging	Palmer	MA	G	413 289-1070	14292
Rand-Whitney Container LLC **(DH)**	Worcester	MA	C	508 890-7000	17450
Rand-Whitney Container LLC	Worcester	MA	G	774 420-2425	17451
Rand-Whitney Group LLC **(HQ)**	Worcester	MA	C	508 791-2301	17452
Romanow Inc **(PA)**	Westwood	MA	C	781 320-9200	16874
Romanow Packaging LLC	Westwood	MA	C	781 320-8309	16875
Triple P Packg & Ppr Pdts Inc	Brockton	MA	D	508 588-0444	9184
Unified2 Globl Packg Group LLC	Sutton	MA	A	508 865-1155	15694
Westrock - Southern Cont LLC	Boston	MA	F	978 772-5050	8924
Westrock Container LLC	Springfield	MA	D	413 733-2211	15525
Westrock Cp LLC	Wakefield	MA	D	781 245-8600	15984
Westrock Cp LLC	Mansfield	MA	C	770 448-2193	12671
Westrock Cp LLC	Springfield	MA	C	413 543-2311	15526
Westrock Rkt Company	Springfield	MA	G	413 543-7300	15528
Wood Products Unlimited Inc	Methuen	MA	G	978 687-7449	13048
RTS Packaging LLC	Scarborough	ME	D	207 883-8921	6938
Volk Packaging Corporation	Biddeford	ME	D	207 282-6151	5768
Aegis Holdings LLC	Milford	NH	E	603 673-8900	19042
Environmental Science Tech Inc	Plaistow	NH	F	603 378-0809	19516
Mills Industries Inc	Laconia	NH	F	603 528-4217	18576
Rand-Whitney Container LLC	Dover	NH	C	603 822-7300	18049
Total Packaging Concepts Inc	Derry	NH	F	603 432-4651	18000
Contempo Card Co Inc **(PA)**	Providence	RI	D	401 272-4210	20990
Custom & Miller Box Company	East Providence	RI	E	401 431-9007	20401
Elmco/Mpc Tool Company LLC **(PA)**	Bristol	RI	G	401 253-3611	20076
Foxon Company	Providence	RI	E	401 421-2386	21015
Fuller Box Co Inc	Central Falls	RI	D	401 725-4300	20113
Hope-Bffnton Pckging Group LLC	Central Falls	RI	F	401 725-3646	20116
Key Container Corporation **(PA)**	Pawtucket	RI	C	401 723-2000	20851
Ljm Packaging Co Inc	North Kingstown	RI	D	401 295-2660	20724
Mason Box Company	Pawtucket	RI	E	800 842-9526	20857
Miller Corrugated Box Co	Warwick	RI	E	401 739-7020	21391
Mount Tom Box Co Inc	Pawtucket	RI	G	413 781-5300	20861
Packaging Company LLC **(PA)**	Johnston	RI	D	401 943-5040	20527
Rand-Whitney Container LLC	Pawtucket	RI	E	401 729-7900	20890
K&H Group Inc	Bennington	VT	E	802 442-5455	21677
Poultney Pallet Inc	Fair Haven	VT	G	802 265-4444	21968

2655 Fiber Cans, Tubes & Drums

	CITY	ST	EMP	PHONE	ENTRY #
Greif Inc	Windsor Locks	CT	D	740 549-6000	5394
Barrday Corporation **(HQ)**	Millbury	MA	D	508 581-2100	13156
CA J&L Enterprises Inc	Canton	MA	E	781 963-6666	9719
Caraustar Industries Inc	Chicopee	MA	D	413 593-9700	10006
Echo Industries Inc	Orange	MA	E	978 544-7000	14215
Globe Composite Solutions LLC	Stoughton	MA	E	781 871-3700	15593
Merrimac Spool and Reel Co Inc	Haverhill	MA	E	978 372-7777	11453
Ox Paper Tube and Core Inc	Holliston	MA	F	508 879-1141	11593
Sonoco Products Company	Holyoke	MA	E	413 493-1298	11659
Lapoint Industries Inc **(PA)**	Auburn	ME	D	207 777-3100	5575
R F Consulting LLC **(PA)**	Freeport	ME	G	207 233-8846	6085

	CITY	ST	EMP	PHONE	ENTRY #
Sonoco Products Company	Pittsfield	ME	E	207 487-3206	6591
Enco Industries Inc	Plaistow	NH	F	603 382-8481	19512
Environmental Container Svcs	Plaistow	NH	G	603 382-8481	19514
Hard Core Spral Tube Wnders In	Brentwood	NH	G	603 775-0230	17751
New England Paper Tube Co Inc	Pawtucket	RI	E	401 725-2610	20868
Signode Industrial Group LLC	Rumford	RI	D	401 438-5203	21196
Txv Aerospace Composites LLC	Bristol	RI	E	425 785-0883	20108
Weeden Street Associates LLC	Pawtucket	RI	E	401 725-2610	20912
Carris Reels Inc **(HQ)**	Proctor	VT	C	802 773-9111	22284
Precision Composites VT LLC	Lyndonville	VT	F	802 626-5900	22072

2656 Sanitary Food Containers

	CITY	ST	EMP	PHONE	ENTRY #
Dixie Consumer Products LLC	Leominster	MA	G	978 537-4701	12133
Menchies Frozen Yogurt	Hingham	MA	F	781 740-1245	11504

2657 Folding Paperboard Boxes

	CITY	ST	EMP	PHONE	ENTRY #
Agi-Shorewood Group Us LLC	Stamford	CT	A	203 324-4839	4132
B-P Products Inc	Hamden	CT	E	203 288-0200	1733
Clondalkin Pharma & Healthcare	Portland	CT	E	860 342-1987	3565
Curtis Corporation A Del Corp	Sandy Hook	CT	C	203 426-5861	3742
Curtis Packaging Corporation	Sandy Hook	CT	C	203 426-5861	3743
Keystone Paper & Box Co Inc	South Windsor	CT	D	860 291-0027	3988
Rice Packaging Inc	Ellington	CT	D	860 870-7057	1338
Accutech Packaging Inc	Foxboro	MA	D	508 543-3800	10873
Americraft Carton Inc	Lowell	MA	C	978 459-9328	12343
Boutwell Owens & Co Inc **(PA)**	Fitchburg	MA	C	978 343-3067	10813
Dusobox Co Inc	Haverhill	MA	E	978 372-7192	11426
Fuller Box Co Inc **(PA)**	North Attleboro	MA	D	508 695-2525	13756
Gooby Industries Corp	Methuen	MA	C	978 689-0100	13024
Harvard Folding Box Co Inc	Lawrence	MA	G	978 683-2802	12030
Hub Folding Box Company Inc	Mansfield	MA	B	508 339-0005	12636
Packaging Specialties Inc	Newburyport	MA	D	978 462-1300	13520
Pioneer Packaging Inc **(PA)**	Chicopee	MA	D	413 378-6930	10050
Rand-Whitney Group LLC **(HQ)**	Worcester	MA	C	508 791-2301	17452
Standard Box Company Inc	Chelsea	MA	G	617 884-2345	9969
Stephen Gould Corporation	Tewksbury	MA	E	978 851-2500	15838
UNI-Pac Inc	Holyoke	MA	D	413 534-5284	11662
RTS Packaging LLC	Scarborough	ME	D	207 883-8921	6938
Volk Packaging Corporation	Biddeford	ME	D	207 282-6151	5768
Autajon Packg - Boston Corp	Nashua	NH	D	603 595-0700	19118
Graphic Packaging Intl LLC	Concord	NH	D	603 224-2333	17907
Graphic Packaging Intl LLC	Concord	NH	C	603 230-5100	17904
Kimark Specialty Box Company	Manchester	NH	E	603 668-1336	18855
Foxon Company	Providence	RI	E	401 421-2386	21015
Northeast Buffinton Group Inc	Riverside	RI	F	401 434-1107	21174
Numaco Packaging LLC	East Providence	RI	F	401 438-4952	20436
Seaboard Folding Box Co Inc	Pawtucket	RI	G	401 753-7778	20899

2671 Paper Coating & Laminating for Packaging

	CITY	ST	EMP	PHONE	ENTRY #
Agi-Shorewood Group Us LLC	Stamford	CT	A	203 324-4839	4132
Amgraph Packaging Inc	Baltic	CT	C	860 822-2000	48
Ansel Label and Packaging Corp	Trumbull	CT	E	203 452-0311	4612
Atlas Agi Holdings LLC	Greenwich	CT	A	203 622-9138	1594
Bollore Inc	Dayville	CT	D	860 774-2930	1039
CCL Label Inc	Shelton	CT	C	203 926-1253	3786
Flagship Converters Inc	Danbury	CT	D	203 792-0034	920
Fluted Partition Inc **(PA)**	Bridgeport	CT	C	203 368-2548	414
General Packaging Products Inc	Norwalk	CT	G	203 846-1340	3160
Identification Products Corp	Bridgeport	CT	F	203 334-5969	429
Knox Enterprises Inc **(PA)**	Westport	CT	G	203 226-6408	5206
Koster Keunen LLC **(PA)**	Watertown	CT	F	860 945-3333	5013
Miami Wabash Paper LLC **(HQ)**	Norwalk	CT	E	203 847-8500	3197
Mid State Assembly & Packg Inc	Meriden	CT	G	203 634-8740	2107
Packaging and Crating Tech LLC	Waterbury	CT	G	203 759-1799	4933
Paxxus Inc	Bloomfield	CT	E	860 242-0663	250
Polymer Films Inc	West Haven	CT	E	203 932-3000	5142
Polymeric Converting LLC	Enfield	CT	E	860 623-1335	1375
Quality Name Plate Inc	East Glastonbury	CT	D	860 633-9495	1114
Rol-Vac Limited Partnership	Dayville	CT	F	860 928-9929	1052
Sealed Air Corporation	Danbury	CT	C	203 791-3648	988
Sonoco Prtective Solutions Inc	Putnam	CT	E	860 928-7795	3634
Stora Enso N Amercn Sls Inc **(HQ)**	Stamford	CT	G	203 541-5178	4334
Tht Inc	Westport	CT	G	203 226-6408	5235
Windham Container Corporation	Putnam	CT	E	860 928-7934	3640
Accu Packaging Inc	Wilmington	MA	G	978 447-5590	16964
Adhesive Packaging Spc Inc **(DH)**	Peabody	MA	E	800 222-1117	14307
Allen-Bailey Tag & Label Inc	Whitinsville	MA	E	585 538-2324	16910
Ampac Packaging LLC	Westfield	MA	G	413 572-2658	16665
Boutwell Owens & Co Inc **(PA)**	Fitchburg	MA	C	978 343-3067	10813
CCL Label Inc **(HQ)**	Framingham	MA	D	508 872-4511	10932
Coveris Advanced Coatings	West Springfield	MA	E	413 539-5547	16513
E V Yeuell Inc	Woburn	MA	E	781 933-2984	17171
Fortifiber Corporation	Attleboro	MA	E	508 222-3500	7738
Free-Flow Packaging Intl Inc	Auburn	MA	E	508 832-5369	7835
Gta-Nht Inc **(HQ)**	Rockland	MA	C	781 331-5900	14804
Hampden Papers Inc **(PA)**	Holyoke	MA	D	413 536-1000	11630
Healthy Life Snack Inc	Canton	MA	G	781 575-6744	9738
Ideal Tape Co Inc	Lowell	MA	D	978 458-6833	12381
Industrial Lbling Systems Corp	Tyngsboro	MA	E	978 649-7004	15890
Jmd Manufacturing Inc	Framingham	MA	G	508 620-6563	10972
K & K Thermoforming Inc	Southbridge	MA	E	508 764-7700	15390
Millstone Med Outsourcing LLC **(PA)**	Fall River	MA	C	508 679-8384	10733
Novacel Inc **(DH)**	Palmer	MA	E	413 283-3468	14289
OK Durable Packaging Inc	Marlborough	MA	F	508 303-8067	12800
Opsec Security Inc	Boston	MA	F	617 226-3000	8756
Ovtene Inc	Marion	MA	E	617 852-4828	12701
Package Printing Company Inc	West Springfield	MA	E	413 736-2748	16539
Packaging Devices Inc **(PA)**	Teaticket	MA	F	508 548-0224	15802
Pioneer Packaging Inc **(PA)**	Chicopee	MA	D	413 378-6930	10050
Polyfiber LLC	Attleboro	MA	E	508 222-3500	7779
Prolamina Corporation	Westfield	MA	G	413 562-2315	16718
Reid Graphics Inc	Andover	MA	D	978 474-1930	7598
Sealed Air Corp	Ayer	MA	G	508 521-5694	7936
Sealed Air Corporation	Holyoke	MA	D	413 534-0231	11656
Suddekor LLC	East Longmeadow	MA	E	413 525-4070	10495
Vangy Tool Company Inc	Worcester	MA	G	508 754-2669	17498
Walter Drake Inc **(PA)**	Holyoke	MA	G	413 536-5463	11666
Web Industries Inc **(PA)**	Marlborough	MA	G	508 898-2988	12848
Westrock Cp LLC	Mansfield	MA	C	770 448-2193	12671
Westrock Mwv LLC	Springfield	MA	A	413 736-7211	15527
Huhtamaki Inc	Lewiston	ME	E	207 795-6000	6290
Kullson Holding Company Inc	Lewiston	ME	E	207 783-3442	6296
Penta-Tech Coated Products LLC **(PA)**	Hampden	ME	F	207 862-3105	6166
Verso Paper Holding LLC	Jay	ME	A	207 897-3431	6222
Verso Paper Holding LLC	Jay	ME	A	207 897-3431	6223
J-Pac LLC **(HQ)**	Somersworth	NH	D	603 692-9955	19842
Label Tech Inc	Somersworth	NH	C	603 692-2005	19843
Pak 2000 Inc	Lancaster	NH	D	603 569-3700	18603
Roymal Inc	Newport	NH	E	603 863-2410	19357
Admiral Packaging Inc	Providence	RI	D	401 274-5588	20945
Allied Group Inc **(PA)**	Cranston	RI	C	401 461-1700	20177
Clear Choice Inc	Providence	RI	G	401 421-5275	20985
Contempo Card Co Inc **(PA)**	Providence	RI	D	401 272-4210	20990
Foxon Company	Providence	RI	E	401 421-2386	21015
Jewel Case Corporation	Providence	RI	B	401 943-1400	21044
Mason Box Company	Pawtucket	RI	E	800 842-9526	20857
Morris Transparent Box Co	East Providence	RI	E	401 438-6116	20433
Nelipak Corporation **(PA)**	Cranston	RI	D	401 946-2699	20267
Packaging Company LLC **(PA)**	Johnston	RI	D	401 943-5040	20527
Tex Flock Inc	Woonsocket	RI	E	401 765-2340	21586
Wheeler Avenue LLC	Cranston	RI	G	401 714-0996	20311
Wintech Intl Corp - Nk	Warwick	RI	G	401 383-3307	21449

2672 Paper Coating & Laminating, Exc for Packaging

	CITY	ST	EMP	PHONE	ENTRY #
Beiersdorf Inc	Norwalk	CT	B	203 854-8000	3110
Beiersdorf North America Inc **(DH)**	Wilton	CT	F	203 563-5800	5277
Comengs Inc	Danbury	CT	G	203 792-7306	889
Design Label Manufacturing Inc **(PA)**	Old Lyme	CT	E	860 739-6266	3321
H-O Products Corporation	Winsted	CT	E	860 379-9875	5412
Illinois Tool Works Inc	Manchester	CT	C	860 646-8153	2011
Lgl Group Inc	Greenwich	CT	G	407 298-2000	1626
Markal Finishing Co Inc	Bridgeport	CT	E	203 384-8219	446
Neato Products LLC	Milford	CT	G	203 466-5170	2318
Robinson Tape & Label Inc	Branford	CT	E	203 481-5581	342
Scapa Holdings Inc **(HQ)**	Windsor	CT	B	860 688-8000	5360
Securemark Decal Corp	Trumbull	CT	F	773 622-6815	4632
Specialty Printing LLC **(PA)**	East Windsor	CT	D	860 623-8870	1303
The E J Davis Company	North Haven	CT	E	203 239-5391	3063
3M Company	Haverhill	MA	G	978 420-0001	11403
Accucon Inc	Leominster	MA	G	978 840-0337	12106
Allen-Bailey Tag & Label Inc	Whitinsville	MA	E	585 538-2324	16910
American Biltrite Inc **(PA)**	Wellesley	MA	G	781 237-6655	16359
AR Metallizing Ltd	Franklin	MA	D	508 541-7700	11024
Arclin Surfaces - E Longmeadow	East Longmeadow	MA	F	678 781-5341	10467
Avery Dennison Corporation	Fitchburg	MA	C	978 353-2100	10810
Avery Dennison Corporation	Westborough	MA	C	508 948-3500	16591
Avery Dennison Corporation	Framingham	MA	C	508 988-8200	10923
Computr Imprntble Lbl Systms	Burlington	MA	F	877 512-8763	9252
Fortifiber Corporation	Attleboro	MA	E	508 222-3500	7738
Gta-Nht Inc **(HQ)**	Rockland	MA	C	781 331-5900	14804
Hampden Papers Inc **(PA)**	Holyoke	MA	D	413 536-1000	11630
Hazen Paper Company **(PA)**	Holyoke	MA	C	413 538-8204	11631
Ideal Tape Co Inc	Lowell	MA	D	978 458-6833	12381
Industrial Lbling Systems Corp	Tyngsboro	MA	E	978 649-7004	15890
Infinity Tapes LLC	Lawrence	MA	E	978 686-0632	12038
Jaybird & Mais Inc	Lawrence	MA	E	978 686-8659	12040
Keena Corporation	Newton	MA	G	617 928-3493	13608
Lion Labels Inc	South Easton	MA	E	508 230-8211	15284
M & M Label Co Inc	Malden	MA	G	781 321-2737	12579
New England Ultimate Finishing	Holyoke	MA	E	413 532-7777	11644
Pacon Corporation	Framingham	MA	E	508 370-0780	10992
Precision Tape & Label Co Inc	Uxbridge	MA	F	508 278-7700	15929
Regal Press Incorporated **(PA)**	Norwood	MA	C	781 769-3900	14192
Shawsheen Rubber Co Inc	Andover	MA	D	978 470-1760	7604

	CITY	ST	EMP	PHONE	ENTRY #
Springfield Label Tape Co Inc	Springfield	MA	E	413 733-6634	15509
Suddekor LLC **(DH)**	Agawam	MA	E	413 821-9000	7453
Tekni-Plex Inc	Ashland	MA	F	508 881-2440	7671
Visual Magnetics Ltd	Mendon	MA	E	508 381-2400	12997
Visual Magnetics Ltd Partnr	Mendon	MA	F	508 381-2400	12998
Panolam Industries Intl Inc	Auburn	ME	E	207 784-9111	5586
Quick Print Color Center	Saco	ME	G	207 282-6480	6856
R & W Engraving Inc	Biddeford	ME	G	207 286-3020	5760
Sappi North America Inc	Skowhegan	ME	A	207 238-3000	6986
Sappi North America Inc	South Portland	ME	D	207 854-7000	7039
Verso Paper Holding LLC	Jay	ME	A	207 897-3431	6222
Avery Dennison Corporation	Belmont	NH	E	603 217-4144	17670
Colormark Inc	Nashua	NH	F	603 595-2244	19137
Contract Mfg Tech LLC	Dover	NH	G	603 692-4488	18014
Electronic Imaging Mtls Inc	Keene	NH	E	603 357-1459	18501
Gardoc Inc **(DH)**	Milford	NH	F	603 673-6400	19056
Label Tech Inc	Somersworth	NH	C	603 692-2005	19843
Nashua Corporation	Merrimack	NH	B	603 880-1110	19015
Spear Group Holdings	Milford	NH	E	603 673-6400	19078
W S Packaging	Wilton	NH	C	603 654-6131	19990
Dewal Industries LLC	Narragansett	RI	C	401 789-9736	20637
Ecological Fibers Inc	Pawtucket	RI	D	401 725-9700	20836
Gem Label & Tape Company	Pawtucket	RI	F	401 724-1300	20842
Neptco Incorporated **(HQ)**	Pawtucket	RI	D	401 722-5500	20863
Providence Label & Tag Co	Providence	RI	F	401 751-6677	21097
Te Connectivity Corporation	East Providence	RI	E	401 432-8200	20446
Trans-Tex LLC	Cranston	RI	E	401 331-8483	20304

2673 Bags: Plastics, Laminated & Coated

	CITY	ST	EMP	PHONE	ENTRY #
Amgraph Packaging Inc	Baltic	CT	C	860 822-2000	48
Re-Style Your Closets LLC	Simsbury	CT	G	860 658-9450	3910
Safety Bags Inc	Shelton	CT	G	203 242-0727	3867
Ace-Lon Corporation	Malden	MA	E	781 322-7121	12556
Armin Innovative Products Inc	Dighton	MA	E	508 822-4629	10335
Cold River Mining Inc	Greenfield	MA	G	413 219-3315	11256
Convanta Holliston	Holliston	MA	G	508 429-9750	11564
Crown Poly Inc	Norton	MA	G	781 883-4979	14075
Eastern Packaging Inc	Lawrence	MA	D	978 685-7723	12020
Extrafresh LLC	Longmeadow	MA	G	413 567-8995	12333
Hi-De Liners Inc	Orange	MA	E	978 544-7801	14218
Inteplast Engineered Films Inc	Westborough	MA	D	508 366-8884	16626
Jannel Manufacturing Inc	Holbrook	MA	E	781 767-0666	11527
Laddawn Inc **(HQ)**	Devens	MA	D	800 446-3639	10322
Mettler Packaging LLC	Raynham	MA	G	508 738-2201	14719
Pakpro Inc	Andover	MA	G	978 474-5018	7580
R & P Plastics LLC	Winchendon	MA	G	978 297-1115	17079
Maine Cleaners Supply Inc	North Yarmouth	ME	G	207 657-3166	6517
Northeast Packaging Co **(PA)**	Presque Isle	ME	E	207 764-6271	6763
Northeast Packaging Co	Caribou	ME	G	207 496-3141	5888
Pak 2000 Inc	Lancaster	NH	D	603 569-3700	18603
Tufpak Inc	Ossipee	NH	E	603 539-4126	19424
Admiral Packaging Inc	Providence	RI	D	401 274-5588	20945
Liftbag Usa Inc	North Kingstown	RI	F	401 884-8801	20722
Subsalve USA LLC	North Kingstown	RI	F	401 884-8801	20743
Flashbags LLC	Burlington	VT	G	802 999-8981	21782
Monument Industries Inc	Bennington	VT	E	802 442-8187	21684

2674 Bags: Uncoated Paper & Multiwall

	CITY	ST	EMP	PHONE	ENTRY #
Accurate Services Inc	Fall River	MA	E	508 674-5773	10650
Accutech Packaging Inc	Foxboro	MA	D	508 543-3800	10873
Maine Potato Growers Inc	Caribou	ME	E	207 764-3131	5886
Northeast Packaging Co **(PA)**	Presque Isle	ME	E	207 764-6271	6763
Sappi North America Inc	Skowhegan	ME	A	207 238-3000	6986
Sappi North America Inc	South Portland	ME	D	207 854-7000	7039
Pak 2000 Inc	Lancaster	NH	D	603 569-3700	18603
Mason Box Company	Pawtucket	RI	E	800 842-9526	20857

2675 Die-Cut Paper & Board

	CITY	ST	EMP	PHONE	ENTRY #
American CT Rng Bnder Index &	Washington	CT	F	860 868-7900	4830
B-P Products Inc	Hamden	CT	E	203 288-0200	1733
C & T Print Finishing Inc	South Windsor	CT	F	860 282-0616	3945
Liftline Capital LLC	Old Saybrook	CT	F	860 395-0150	3342
Makino Inc	New Britain	CT	F	860 223-0236	2549
Walker Products Incorporated	Glastonbury	CT	F	860 659-3781	1581
Agawam Novelty Company Inc	Agawam	MA	G	413 536-0471	7418
Ames Safety Envelope Company **(DH)**	Somerville	MA	D	617 684-1000	15154
B & K Enterprises Inc	Ashland	MA	G	508 881-1168	7656
Eastern Index Inc	Lynn	MA	F	781 581-1100	12505
Elbe-Cesco Inc	Fall River	MA	D	508 676-8531	10687
Fuller Box Co Inc **(PA)**	North Attleboro	MA	D	508 695-2525	13756
H Loeb Corporation	New Bedford	MA	E	508 996-3745	13392
Merrimac Spool and Reel Co Inc	Haverhill	MA	E	978 372-7777	11453
Neci LLC	Canton	MA	E	781 828-4883	9761
New England Ultimate Finishing	Holyoke	MA	E	413 532-7777	11644
New England Water Jet Cutting	New Bedford	MA	G	508 993-9235	13425
Union Bookbinding Company Inc **(PA)**	Fall River	MA	E	508 676-8580	10775
Yankee Printing Group Inc	South Hadley	MA	E	413 532-9513	15313
Zenith Die Cutting Inc	Framingham	MA	G	508 877-8811	11018
Custom Die Cut Inc	Windham	NH	G	603 437-3090	20003
Fife Packaging LLC	Penacook	NH	E	603 753-2669	19465
Stencils Online LLC	Franklin	NH	G	603 934-5034	18165
Stentech Inc **(HQ)**	Derry	NH	F	603 505-4470	17998
Stentech Photo Stencil LLC	Derry	NH	F	719 287-7934	17999
American Ring Co Inc **(PA)**	East Providence	RI	E	401 438-9060	20385
Mono Die Cutting Co Inc	Riverside	RI	F	401 434-1274	21173
New England Paper Tube Co Inc	Pawtucket	RI	E	401 725-2610	20868
Mylan Technologies Inc **(DH)**	Saint Albans	VT	C	802 527-7792	22373

2676 Sanitary Paper Prdts

	CITY	ST	EMP	PHONE	ENTRY #
Alfa Nobel LLC	Milford	CT	G	203 876-2823	2241
Capricorn Investors II LP	Greenwich	CT	A	203 861-6600	1602
Dunn Paper LLC	East Hartford	CT	D	860 466-4141	1189
Edgewell Per Care Brands LLC **(HQ)**	Shelton	CT	B	203 944-5500	3799
Kimberly-Clark Corporation	New Milford	CT	A	860 210-1602	2811
Kimberly-Clark Corporation	Stratford	CT	C	973 986-8454	4427
Playtex Products LLC **(HQ)**	Shelton	CT	D	203 944-5500	3856
Soundview Paper Mills LLC **(DH)**	Greenwich	CT	G	201 796-4000	1652
American Disposables Inc	Hardwick	MA	E	413 967-6201	11371
Bumboosa LLC	Mashpee	MA	G	508 539-1373	12876
Erving Industries Inc **(PA)**	Erving	MA	C	413 422-2700	10589
Essity	Palmer	MA	D	413 289-1221	14287
Irving Tissue Corporation	Burlington	MA	G	781 273-3222	9287
Kimberly-Clark Corporation	Franklin	MA	G	508 520-1355	11062
W2w Partners LLC	Duxbury	MA	G	781 424-7824	10404
Maine Cleaners Supply Inc	North Yarmouth	ME	G	207 657-3166	6517
Milo Chip LLC	Milo	ME	G	207 943-2682	6447
Passifora Personal Products	Nashua	NH	G	603 809-6762	19227
Sumner Printing Inc	Somersworth	NH	E	603 692-7424	19849
Johnson & Johnson	Foster	RI	D	401 647-1493	20456
Kimberly-Clark Corporation	East Ryegate	VT	D	972 281-1200	21920
Seventh Generation Inc **(DH)**	Burlington	VT	C	802 658-3773	21808

2677 Envelopes

	CITY	ST	EMP	PHONE	ENTRY #
Cenveo Inc	Stamford	CT	A	203 595-3000	4161
Cenveo Enterprises Inc **(PA)**	Stamford	CT	G	203 595-3000	4162
Cenveo Worldwide Limited **(DH)**	Stamford	CT	F	203 595-3000	4163
Cwl Enterprises Inc **(HQ)**	Stamford	CT	G	303 790-8023	4181
Accutech Packaging Inc	Foxboro	MA	D	508 543-3800	10873
American Prtg & Envelope Inc	Auburn	MA	E	508 832-6100	7825
Classic Envelope Inc	East Douglas	MA	D	508 731-6747	10425
Jannel Manufacturing Inc	Holbrook	MA	E	781 767-0666	11527
Sheppard Envelope Company Inc	Auburn	MA	E	508 791-5588	7849
Westrock Mwv LLC	Springfield	MA	A	413 736-7211	15527
Worcester Envelope Company	Auburn	MA	C	508 832-5394	7853
Tufpak Inc	Ossipee	NH	E	603 539-4126	19424
Fred F Waltz Co Inc	North Smithfield	RI	F	401 769-4900	20786
Leahy Press Inc	Montpelier	VT	E	802 223-2100	22153

2678 Stationery Prdts

	CITY	ST	EMP	PHONE	ENTRY #
American CT Rng Bnder Index &	Washington	CT	F	860 868-7900	4830
Classic Images Inc	Bloomfield	CT	G	860 243-8365	214
Panagrafix Inc	West Haven	CT	E	203 691-5529	5139
Pulp Paper Products Inc	Torrington	CT	G	860 806-0143	4594
Avery Dennison Corporation	Westborough	MA	C	508 948-3500	16591
Bouncepad North America Inc	Charlestown	MA	F	617 804-0110	9827
Eureka Lab Book Inc	Holyoke	MA	F	413 534-5671	11625
Great Northern Industries Inc **(PA)**	Boston	MA	C	617 262-4314	8578
Hd Merrimack	Lawrence	MA	G	978 681-9969	12032
Viabella Holdings LLC	Wareham	MA	F	800 688-9998	16257
Jak Designs LLC	Kennebunk	ME	E	330 689-6849	6236
Jak Designs LLC **(PA)**	Kennebunkport	ME	F	207 204-0396	6245
William Arthur Inc	West Kennebunk	ME	C	413 684-2600	7174
Paper Packaging and Panache	Bristol	RI	G	401 253-2273	20097
American Meadows Inc	Shelburne	VT	F	802 862-6560	22410
Oatmeal Studios Inc	Rochester	VT	F	802 967-8014	22320

2679 Converted Paper Prdts, NEC

	CITY	ST	EMP	PHONE	ENTRY #
Ambiance Painting LLC	Norwalk	CT	F	203 354-8689	3100
B-P Products Inc	Hamden	CT	E	203 288-0200	1733
Cenveo Inc	Stamford	CT	A	203 595-3000	4161
Cenveo Enterprises Inc **(PA)**	Stamford	CT	G	203 595-3000	4162
Cenveo Worldwide Limited **(DH)**	Stamford	CT	F	203 595-3000	4163
Cwl Enterprises Inc **(HQ)**	Stamford	CT	G	303 790-8023	4181
Eagle Tissue LLC	South Windsor	CT	F	860 282-2535	3959
Flexo Label Solutions LLC	Deep River	CT	G	860 243-9300	1060
Harrison Enterprise LLC	Bridgeport	CT	G	914 665-8348	423
Honey Cell Inc **(PA)**	Bridgeport	CT	G	203 925-1818	426
Knox Industries Inc	Westport	CT	C	203 226-6408	5207
Mercantile Development Inc	Shelton	CT	E	203 922-8880	3832
Pactiv Corporation	North Haven	CT	E	203 288-7722	3047
Rand-Whitney Recycling LLC	Montville	CT	D	860 848-1900	2422
Royal Consumer Products LLC **(HQ)**	Norwalk	CT	E	203 847-8500	3234
Schrafel Paperboard Converting	West Haven	CT	E	203 931-1700	5145

	CITY	ST	EMP	PHONE	ENTRY #
Specialty Printing LLC **(PA)**	East Windsor	CT	D	860 623-8870	1303
Surys Inc	Trumbull	CT	C	203 333-5503	4633
Tudor Converted Products Inc **(PA)**	Newtown	CT	E	203 304-1875	2946
Valley Container Inc	Bridgeport	CT	E	203 368-6546	503
3M Company	Haverhill	MA	B	978 659-9000	11402
3M Company	Methuen	MA	B	978 659-9000	13007
Allen-Bailey Tag & Label Inc	Whitinsville	MA	E	585 538-2324	16910
BBC Printing and Products Inc	Waltham	MA	G	781 647-4646	16042
Canson Inc	South Hadley	MA	D	413 538-9250	15300
D B S Industries Inc	Haverhill	MA	D	978 373-4748	11421
Dennecrepe Corporation	Gardner	MA	D	978 630-8669	11112
Dion Label Printing Inc	Westfield	MA	D	413 568-3713	16680
Ecological Fibers Inc **(PA)**	Lunenburg	MA	C	978 537-0003	12481
Erolls Inc	Orange	MA	F	978 544-0100	14216
Expressive Design Group Inc	Holyoke	MA	E	413 315-6296	11626
Garlock Prtg & Converting Corp	Gardner	MA	C	978 630-1028	11116
Garlock Prtg & Converting Corp **(PA)**	Gardner	MA	D	978 630-1028	11117
Graphics Source Co	Southampton	MA	F	413 543-0700	15338
Johnston Dandy Company	Holyoke	MA	F	413 315-4596	11635
Masterwork	Woburn	MA	G	781 995-3354	17224
Mbw Incorporated	Orange	MA	C	978 544-6462	14221
Neci LLC	Canton	MA	E	781 828-4883	9761
Nouveau Packaging LLC	Raynham	MA	G	508 880-0300	14722
RPM Technologies Inc	Ludlow	MA	G	413 583-3385	12477
Screenprint/Dow Inc	Wilmington	MA	D	978 657-7290	17043
Seaman Paper Warehouse	Gardner	MA	E	978 632-5524	11127
Smyth Companies LLC	Wilmington	MA	G	800 776-1201	17045
Sullivan Paper Company Inc **(PA)**	West Springfield	MA	C	413 827-7030	16554
Tls Printing LLC	Townsend	MA	F	508 234-2344	15874
Universal Tag Inc	Dudley	MA	E	508 949-2411	10388
W G Fry Corp	Florence	MA	E	413 747-2551	10870
Westrock - Southern Cont LLC	Boston	MA	F	978 772-5050	8924
Lamtec Inc	Portland	ME	G	207 774-6560	6678
Sappi North America Inc	Skowhegan	ME	A	207 238-3000	6986
Sappi North America Inc	South Portland	ME	D	207 854-7000	7039
Computype Inc	Concord	NH	F	603 225-5500	17894
Flexogrphic Print Slutions LLC	Bedford	NH	G	603 570-6339	17641
Len-Tex Corp	North Walpole	NH	C	603 445-2342	19395
Nashua Corporation	Merrimack	NH	B	603 880-1110	19015
Swing Labels Inc	Jaffrey	NH	G	978 425-0855	18478
Absorbent Specialty Pdts LLC	Cumberland	RI	F	401 722-1177	20312
Alliance Paper Company Inc	Pawtucket	RI	F	508 324-9100	20812
Arkwright Advanced Coating Inc	Fiskeville	RI	C	401 821-1000	20454
Dasko Identification Products	East Providence	RI	F	401 435-6500	20403
Foxon Company	Providence	RI	E	401 421-2386	21015
Image Tek Mfg Inc	Springfield	VT	E	802 885-6208	22502
Solo Cup Operating Corporation	Saint Albans	VT	F	802 524-5966	22378

27 PRINTING, PUBLISHING, AND ALLIED INDUSTRIES

2711 Newspapers: Publishing & Printing

	CITY	ST	EMP	PHONE	ENTRY #
200 Mill Plain Road LLC	Fairfield	CT	G	203 254-0113	1411
21st Century Fox America Inc	Wilton	CT	G	203 563-6600	5273
8 Times LLC	Westport	CT	G	203 227-7575	5177
Advisor	North Haven	CT	F	203 239-4121	3002
Alm Media LLC	Hartford	CT	E	860 527-7900	1805
American-Republican Inc **(PA)**	Waterbury	CT	D	203 574-3636	4842
American-Republican Inc	Torrington	CT	C	860 496-9301	4559
Bargain News Free Classified A	Stratford	CT	D	203 377-3000	4395
Bristol Press	Torrington	CT	D	860 584-0501	4568
Browser Daily	Winsted	CT	G	860 469-5534	5406
Cantata Media LLC	Norwalk	CT	F	203 951-9885	3118
Capital Cities Communications	New Haven	CT	G	203 784-8800	2673
Car Buyers Market	Trumbull	CT	E	516 482-0292	4618
Catholic Transcript Inc	Bloomfield	CT	F	860 286-2828	213
CCC Media LLC	New Britain	CT	G	860 225-4601	2518
Central Conn Cmmunications LLC	New Britain	CT	D	860 225-4601	2519
Chase Media Group	Newtown	CT	F	914 962-3871	2919
Chromatic Press US Inc	West Hartford	CT	G	860 796-7667	5059
Chronicle Printing Company	Willimantic	CT	D	860 423-8466	5262
Citizen News	New Fairfield	CT	G	203 746-4669	2623
Comunidade News	Danbury	CT	G	203 730-0175	891
Conn Daily Campus	Storrs Mansfield	CT	G	860 486-3407	4384
Connecticut Newspapers Inc	Stamford	CT	G	203 964-2200	4172
Courant Specialty Products Inc	Hartford	CT	E	860 241-3795	1816
Cromwell Chronicle	Rocky Hill	CT	G	860 257-8715	3705
Daily Fare LLC	Bethel	CT	G	203 743-7300	141
Daily Impressions LLC	Hamden	CT	G	203 508-5305	1743
Daily Mart	Rocky Hill	CT	G	860 529-5210	3707
Day Publishing Company **(HQ)**	New London	CT	B	860 701-4200	2770
Disco Chick	Middletown	CT	G	860 788-6203	2183
Efitzgerald Publishing LLC	West Hartford	CT	G	860 904-7250	5067
Freshiana LLC	Greenwich	CT	G	800 301-8071	1616
Gamut Publishing	Hartford	CT	E	860 296-6128	1824
Gatehouse Media LLC	Norwich	CT	C	860 886-0106	3280
Gatehouse Media Conn Holdings	Norwich	CT	E	860 887-9211	3281
Glastonbury Citizen Inc	Glastonbury	CT	E	860 633-4691	1555
GPA	Plainville	CT	G	860 410-0624	3494
Green Manor Corporation **(PA)**	Manchester	CT	B	860 643-8111	2007
Greenwich Gofer	Old Greenwich	CT	G	203 637-8425	3309
Greenwich Sentinel	Greenwich	CT	G	203 883-1430	1619
Greenwich Time	Stamford	CT	G	203 253-2922	4203
Hamden Journal LLC	Hamden	CT	G	203 668-6307	1754
Hamiltonbookcom LLC	Falls Village	CT	G	860 824-0275	1463
Hamlethub LLC	Ridgefield	CT	G	203 431-6400	3667
Hartford Courant Company	Avon	CT	G	860 678-1330	35
Hartford Courant Company	West Hartford	CT	F	860 560-3747	5074
Hartford Courant Company LLC **(HQ)**	Hartford	CT	A	860 241-6200	1831
Hartford Courant Company LLC	Hartford	CT	F	860 525-5555	1832
Hartford Monthly Meeting	West Hartford	CT	G	860 232-3631	5076
Hearst Corporation	New Canaan	CT	E	203 438-6544	2600
Hearst Corporation	Shelton	CT	G	203 926-2080	3811
Hearst Corporation	Norwalk	CT	E	203 625-4445	3167
Hersam Acorn Cmnty Pubg LLC	Trumbull	CT	F	203 261-2548	4624
Hersam Acorn Cmnty Pubg LLC **(HQ)**	Ridgefield	CT	F	203 438-6544	3668
Hersam Publishing Company	New Canaan	CT	B	203 966-9541	2601
Hillside Capital Inc De Corp **(HQ)**	Stamford	CT	F	203 618-0202	4217
Hispanic Communications LLC	Stamford	CT	G	203 674-6793	4218
Hispanic Communications LLC	New Haven	CT	G	203 624-8007	2696
India Weekly Co	Cheshire	CT	G	203 699-8419	739
Inquiring News	Bloomfield	CT	G	860 983-7587	226
Jewish Leader Newspaper	New London	CT	G	860 442-7395	2774
Jj Portland News LLC	Middletown	CT	G	860 342-1432	2194
Journal Publishing Company Inc	Manchester	CT	A	860 646-0500	2014
Lakeville Journal Company LLC **(PA)**	Lakeville	CT	D	860 435-9873	1931
Life Publications	West Hartford	CT	E	860 953-0444	5083
Local Media Group Inc	New Milford	CT	G	860 354-2273	2813
Los Angles Tmes Cmmnctions LLC	Stamford	CT	C	203 965-6434	4240
M&G Berman Inc	Wilton	CT	G	203 834-8754	5293
Meade Daily Group LLC	Westbrook	CT	G	860 399-7342	5160
Medianews Group Inc	Norwalk	CT	F	203 333-0161	3195
Middlbury Bee-Intelligencer-Ct	Middlebury	CT	G	203 577-6800	2156
Minuteman Newspaper **(PA)**	Westport	CT	E	203 226-8877	5214
Mkrs Corporation	Wilton	CT	G	203 762-2662	5294
Morris Communications Co LLC	Guilford	CT	D	203 458-4500	1712
My Citizens News	Waterbury	CT	G	203 729-2228	4919
New Haven Register LLC	New Haven	CT	A	203 789-5200	2716
New Mass Media Inc	Hartford	CT	E	860 241-3617	1852
News 12 Connecticut	Norwalk	CT	E	203 849-1321	3208
News Times	Danbury	CT	G	203 744-5100	960
Newspaper Space Buyers	Norwalk	CT	G	203 967-6452	3209
Newtown Sports Group	Newtown	CT	G	508 341-1238	2931
Northeast Minority News Inc	Hartford	CT	G	860 249-6065	1853
Northend Agents LLC	Hartford	CT	G	860 244-2445	1854
NRG Connecticut LLC	Hartford	CT	E	860 231-2424	1855
Orange Democrat	Orange	CT	G	203 298-4575	3378
Our Town Crier	Westport	CT	G	203 400-5000	5220
Peaceful Daily Inc	Guilford	CT	G	203 909-2961	1714
Prime Publishers Inc	Watertown	CT	G	860 274-6721	5018
Printed Communications	South Windsor	CT	G	860 436-9619	4005
Quinnipiac Valley Times	Hamden	CT	G	203 675-9483	1778
Record-Journal Newspaper **(PA)**	Meriden	CT	C	203 235-1661	2124
Record-Journal Newspaper	Mystic	CT	G	860 536-9577	2450
Reminder Broadcaster	Vernon	CT	D	860 875-3366	4672
Rhode Island Beverage Journal	Hamden	CT	G	203 288-3375	1780
Ritch Herald & Linda	Greenwich	CT	G	203 661-8634	1643
Rmi Inc	Vernon Rockville	CT	C	860 875-3366	4681
Second Wind Media Limited	New Haven	CT	F	203 781-3480	2736
Shore Publishing LLC	Madison	CT	E	203 245-1877	1975
Southington Citizen	Meriden	CT	G	860 620-5960	2132
Stella Press LLC	Greenwich	CT	G	203 661-2735	1653
Suburban Voices Publishing LLC	West Haven	CT	G	203 934-6397	5146
Swedish News Inc	Norwalk	CT	G	203 299-0380	3253
The Bee Publishing Company **(PA)**	Newtown	CT	E	203 426-8036	2943
The Bee Publishing Company	Newtown	CT	G	203 426-0178	2944
Thomson Reuters US LLC **(DH)**	Stamford	CT	E	203 539-8000	4346
Times Community News Group	New London	CT	G	860 437-1150	2783
TLC Media LLC	Hamden	CT	G	203 980-1361	1789
Town Tribune LLC	New Fairfield	CT	G	203 648-6085	2629
Track180 LLC	New Haven	CT	G	203 605-3540	2745
Tradewinds	Beacon Falls	CT	G	203 723-6966	65
Tradewinds	Stamford	CT	G	203 324-2994	4348
Tribuna Newspaper LLC	Danbury	CT	G	203 730-0457	1001
True Publishing Company	Wallingford	CT	F	203 272-5316	4823
Valley Independent Sentinel	Ansonia	CT	G	203 446-2335	24
Valley Publishing Company Inc	Derby	CT	F	203 735-6696	1081
Villager Newspapers	Putnam	CT	G	860 928-1818	3639
Westerly Sun	Pawcatuck	CT	G	401 348-1000	3445
Wicks Business Information LLC **(PA)**	Shelton	CT	F	203 334-2002	3889
Yale Daily News Publishing Co	New Haven	CT	G	203 432-2400	2757
Yale University	New Haven	CT	G	203 432-2880	2758
Yankee Pennysaver Inc	Brookfield	CT	E	203 775-9122	667
2 Cool Promos	Westborough	MA	G	508 351-9700	16583
Ack 60 Main LLC	Nantucket	MA	G	508 228-1398	13217

	CITY	ST	EMP	PHONE	ENTRY #
Ack Surf School LLC	Nantucket	MA	G	508 325-2589	13218
Advocate Newspapers **(PA)**	Everett	MA	G	617 387-2200	10601
Alberto Vasallo Jr	Boston	MA	F	617 522-5060	8350
Amherst College Public Affairs	Amherst	MA	F	413 542-2321	7512
Anchor	Fall River	MA	G	508 675-7151	10658
Andover Publishing Company	North Andover	MA	E	978 475-7000	13690
Antique Homes Magazine	East Douglas	MA	G	508 476-7271	10424
Arion Jrnl of Hmnties Classics	Boston	MA	G	617 353-6480	8375
Athol Press Inc	Athol	MA	E	978 249-3535	7684
Bagdon Advertising Inc	Westborough	MA	F	508 366-5500	16592
Baikar Association Inc **(PA)**	Watertown	MA	F	617 924-4420	16271
Barnstable Patriot Newsppr Inc	Hyannis	MA	F	508 771-1427	11835
Berkshire Totes For Tots Inc	Pittsfield	MA	G	413 442-7048	14461
Beverly Citizen	Beverly	MA	G	978 927-2777	8108
Bh Media Inc **(HQ)**	Braintree	MA	D	617 426-3000	8990
Boston Business Journal Inc	Boston	MA	E	617 330-1000	8426
Boston Chinese News Inc	Cambridge	MA	G	617 354-4154	9417
Boston Globe LLC	Boston	MA	A	617 929-2684	8431
Boston Irish Reporter	Dorchester	MA	F	617 436-1222	10340
Boston Neighborhood News Inc	Boston	MA	G	617 436-1222	8435
Braintree Forum & Observer	Braintree	MA	G	781 843-2937	8991
Brazilian Times	Somerville	MA	G	617 625-5559	15161
Bridge Publishing LLC	Osterville	MA	G	508 681-8914	14246
Brookline T A B	Needham Heights	MA	G	617 566-3585	13321
Bulletin Newspapers Inc	Hyde Park	MA	G	617 361-1406	11864
Bulletin Newspapers Inc **(PA)**	Hyde Park	MA	F	617 361-8400	11865
Bureau of National Affairs Inc	Marshfield	MA	F	781 843-9422	12856
Burlington Union	Lexington	MA	G	781 229-0918	12209
Business West	Springfield	MA	G	413 781-8600	15457
C Newspaper Inc	Ipswich	MA	G	978 412-1800	11908
Canton Citizen Inc	Canton	MA	F	781 821-4418	9721
Canton Journal	Needham	MA	G	781 828-0006	13295
Caribe Cmmnctions Publications	Boston	MA	F	617 522-5060	8459
Carlisle Communications Inc	Carlisle	MA	G	978 369-7921	9797
Changs Publishing Company	Boston	MA	G	617 542-1230	8466
Charlestown Bridge	Charlestown	MA	G	617 241-8500	9829
Chicopee Register Newspaper	Chicopee	MA	G	413 592-3599	10010
Chicopee Tribune	Chicopee	MA	G	413 552-3775	10011
Christian Science Pubg Soc **(PA)**	Boston	MA	B	617 450-2000	8473
Circulation	Fall River	MA	G	508 676-2526	10674
Colonial Times Publishing	Lexington	MA	F	781 274-9997	12212
Community Newspaper	Framingham	MA	G	508 339-8977	10935
Community Newspaper Company	Auburn	MA	D	508 721-5600	7832
Community Newspaper Inc	Marblehead	MA	G	781 639-4800	12679
Creative Publishing Corp Amer **(PA)**	Peabody	MA	E	978 532-5880	14326
Cricket Press Inc	Manchester	MA	F	978 526-7131	12604
Daily Catch	Brookline	MA	G	617 734-2700	9199
Daily General Counsel Pllc	Brookline	MA	G	617 721-4342	9200
Daily Hampshire Gazette	Easthampton	MA	G	413 527-4000	10558
Daily News Tribune	Needham Heights	MA	G	781 329-5008	13327
Daily Paper	Hyannis	MA	G	508 790-8800	11839
Daily Stroll LLC	Brighton	MA	G	678 770-4531	9097
Daily Woburn Times Inc **(PA)**	Woburn	MA	D	781 933-3700	17162
Daily Woburn Times Inc	Wilmington	MA	G	978 658-2346	16993
Daily Woburn Times Inc	Reading	MA	E	781 944-2200	14733
Danvers Herald	Danvers	MA	G	978 774-0505	10212
Demosthenes Greek-AM Demo	Somerville	MA	G	617 628-7766	15168
Dig Media Group Inc	Boston	MA	G	617 418-9075	8504
Dinner Daily LLC	Westford	MA	G	978 392-5887	16764
Diocesan Press Inc	Fall River	MA	G	508 675-3857	10683
Dispatch	Marshfield	MA	G	781 837-8700	12859
Dispatch News	Lowell	MA	G	978 458-7100	12368
Dolan LLC	Boston	MA	G	617 451-7300	8507
Doncar Inc	Concord	MA	E	978 371-2442	10129
Dow Jones & Company Inc	Chicopee	MA	E	413 598-4000	10020
Dow Jones & Company Inc	Chicopee	MA	E	212 416-3858	10021
Driggin Sandra DBA Extra Extra	Quincy	MA	E	617 773-6996	14620
Duxbury Clipper Inc	Duxbury	MA	F	781 934-2811	10396
Eagle-Tribune Publishing Co **(DH)**	North Andover	MA	C	978 946-2000	13698
Eagle-Tribune Publishing Co	Haverhill	MA	E	978 374-0321	11430
Eagle-Tribune Publishing Co	North Andover	MA	D	978 946-2000	13699
Eagle-Tribune Publishing Co	Gloucester	MA	E	978 282-0077	11179
East Boston Times Inc	Boston	MA	E	617 567-9600	8515
East Coast Publications Inc **(PA)**	Norwell	MA	E	781 878-4540	14102
Eastern Mddlsex Press Pblctons **(PA)**	Malden	MA	E	781 321-8000	12569
Easton Journal	Milford	MA	G	508 230-7964	13113
Edic Bi Weekly	Boston	MA	G	617 918-5406	8518
Enterprise Newsmedia LLC **(HQ)**	Quincy	MA	G	585 598-0030	14623
Enterprise Newsmedia LLC	Norwood	MA	F	781 769-5535	14150
Enterprise Publications **(PA)**	Falmouth	MA	E	508 548-4700	10789
Enterprise Publications	West Falmouth	MA	G	508 457-9180	16478
Enterprise Publishing Co LLC	Fall River	MA	A	585 598-0030	10689
Epoch Times Boston-Chinese	Cambridge	MA	G	617 968-8019	9470
Ethnic Publishers Inc	Boston	MA	G	617 227-8929	8528
Everest Herald Ltd Partnership	Watertown	MA	G	617 744-0620	16283
Families and Wealth LLC	Newton	MA	G	617 558-5800	13592
Framingham Source	Framingham	MA	G	508 315-7176	10947
Free Press	Florence	MA	E	413 585-1533	10867
Gardner News Incorporated	Gardner	MA	E	978 632-8000	11114
Gatehouse Media LLC	Norwell	MA	E	781 829-9305	14103
Gatehouse Media LLC	Concord	MA	G	978 263-4736	10130
Gatehouse Media LLC	Fall River	MA	C	508 676-8211	10701
Gatehouse Media LLC	Taunton	MA	E	508 880-9000	15752
Gatehouse Media Mass I Inc	Beverly	MA	E	781 233-2040	8134
Gatehouse Media Mass I Inc **(HQ)**	Beverly	MA	A	585 598-0030	8135
Gatehouse Media Mass I Inc	Framingham	MA	C	508 626-4412	10948
Gatehouse Media Mass I Inc	Randolph	MA	C	781 235-4000	14683
Gatehouse Media Mass I Inc	Wareham	MA	E	508 295-1190	16247
Gatehouse Media Mass I Inc	Marlborough	MA	F	508 626-3859	12758
Gatehouse Media Mass I Inc	Concord	MA	D	978 667-2156	10131
Gatehouse Media Mass I Inc	Milford	MA	F	508 634-7522	13118
Gatehouse Media Mass I Inc	Somerville	MA	G	617 629-3381	15176
Gatehouse Media Mass I Inc	Lexington	MA	G	781 861-9110	12227
Gatehouse Media Mass I Inc	Beverly	MA	G	781 639-4800	8136
Gatehouse Media Mass I Inc	Weymouth	MA	G	781 682-4850	16889
Gatehouse Media Mass I Inc	Chelmsford	MA	E	978 256-7196	9902
Gazette Publications Inc	Boston	MA	G	617 524-2626	8555
Grafton News Holdings LLC	Worcester	MA	G	508 839-2259	17385
Great Oak Publications Inc	North Reading	MA	F	978 664-4761	13983
Greylock Press LLC	Peabody	MA	G	978 530-1740	14337
Groton Herald Inc	Groton	MA	G	978 448-6061	11289
Hairenik Association Inc	Watertown	MA	F	617 926-3974	16289
Hanson Whitman Express	Hanson	MA	G	781 293-0420	11363
Harbus News Corporation	Boston	MA	G	617 495-6528	8588
Harvard Crimson Inc	Cambridge	MA	G	617 576-6600	9502
Harvard Press	Harvard	MA	G	978 456-3700	11377
Harwich Oracle	Orleans	MA	E	508 247-3200	14234
Hearst Communications Inc	Worcester	MA	C	508 793-9100	17389
Holbrook Sun Inc	Randolph	MA	F	781 767-4000	14684
Hollan Publishing Inc	Manchester	MA	G	978 704-9342	12605
Hopkington Independent	Westborough	MA	G	508 435-5188	16624
Hopkinton Crier	Framingham	MA	G	508 626-3939	10963
Hyora Publications Inc	Chatham	MA	F	508 430-2700	9860
I Make News	Newton	MA	G	617 864-4400	13603
Independant Newspaper Group	Revere	MA	E	781 485-0588	14767
Independent News	Shelburne Falls	MA	G	413 522-5046	15071
Independent Newspaper Group	Revere	MA	E	781 485-0588	14768
Infotrak National Data Service	Needham	MA	F	781 276-1711	13301
Inquirer and Mirror Inc	Nantucket	MA	F	508 228-0001	13226
Ipswich Chronicle	Ipswich	MA	G	978 356-5141	11923
Jamaica Plain Porchfest Inc	Boston	MA	G	617 320-6230	8625
Jewish Advocate Pubg Corp	Boston	MA	F	617 523-6232	8629
Jewish Journal	Salem	MA	F	978 745-4111	14925
Jornal Dos Sports LLC	Melrose	MA	G	857 888-9186	12983
Journal Computing In Higher	Amherst	MA	G	413 549-5150	7516
Journal Infectious Diseases	Boston	MA	G	617 367-1848	8639
Journal of Commerce Inc	Boston	MA	G	617 439-7099	8640
Journal of Interdiscplinary	Lexington	MA	G	781 862-4089	12233
Journal Register Company	Fall River	MA	F	508 678-3844	10717
JTL Falcon Title Examiner	Haverhill	MA	G	978 377-0223	11444
Khmerpost USA LLC	Lowell	MA	G	978 677-7163	12388
Lancaster Times Inc	Concord	MA	G	978 368-3393	10137
Lawyers Weekly LLC **(PA)**	Boston	MA	C	617 451-7300	8660
Leader Publishing Co Inc	Everett	MA	G	617 387-4570	10615
Leominster Champion	Leominster	MA	G	978 534-6006	12161
Limestone Communications **(PA)**	Great Barrington	MA	E	413 528-5380	11241
Lisa Jo Rudy	Falmouth	MA	G	508 540-7293	10795
Local Media Group Inc	Hyannis	MA	B	508 775-1200	11847
Local Media Group Inc	New Bedford	MA	B	508 997-7411	13409
Local Media Group Inc	New Bedford	MA	G	508 947-1760	13410
Loop Weekly	Methuen	MA	G	978 683-8800	13033
Lowell Sun Publishing Company **(DH)**	Lowell	MA	E	978 459-1300	12399
Lujean Printing Co Inc	Cotuit	MA	F	508 428-8700	10170
M A D Signs	Wareham	MA	G	508 273-7887	16252
Marborough Enterprise	Marlborough	MA	G	508 485-5200	12790
Mariner Ablngton Edition	Marshfield	MA	G	781 878-4489	12862
Marthas Vineyard Times	Vineyard Haven	MA	F	508 693-6100	15933
Martins News Shop	Boston	MA	G	617 267-1334	8681
Massachstts Med Dvcs Jurnl LLC	Boston	MA	G	617 358-5631	8683
Massachusetts Institute Tech	Cambridge	MA	E	617 253-1541	9545
Massachusetts Institute Tech	Cambridge	MA	G	617 253-7183	9548
Medford Transcript	Medford	MA	G	781 396-1982	12943
Medianews Group Inc	Fitchburg	MA	D	978 343-6911	10835
Melrose Free Press Inc	Beverly	MA	D	781 665-4000	8150
Metro Boston LLC	Boston	MA	E	617 210-7905	8701
Middlesex News	Framingham	MA	G	508 626-3800	10985
Milton Times Inc	Milton	MA	G	617 696-7758	13196
Montague Reporter Incorporated	Turners Falls	MA	G	413 863-8666	15883
Moquin and Daley PA	Boston	MA	G	617 536-0606	8711
Nantucket Chronicle LLC	Siasconset	MA	G	508 257-6683	15141
Ne Media Group Inc **(PA)**	Boston	MA	D	617 929-2000	8721
New England Business Media LLC **(PA)**	Worcester	MA	E	508 755-8004	17429
New England Newspapers Inc **(DH)**	Pittsfield	MA	C	413 447-7311	14496
New England Runner	Norwell	MA	G	781 987-1730	14108

	CITY	ST	EMP	PHONE	ENTRY #
Newspapers of Massachusetts	Greenfield	MA	B	978 544-2118	11270
North Shore Jewish Press Ltd	Salem	MA	F	978 745-4111	14932
Nrt Inc	Medway	MA	F	508 533-4588	12968
On The Beat Inc	Cambridge	MA	G	617 491-8878	9598
Ottaway Newspapers	Hyannis	MA	G	508 775-1200	11852
Patriot-News Co	Boston	MA	G	617 345-0971	8769
Pinestream Communications Inc	Weston	MA	G	781 893-6836	16829
Pittsfield Gazette Inc	Pittsfield	MA	G	413 443-2010	14499
President Fllows Hrvard Cllege	Boston	MA	G	617 783-7888	8792
Profile News	West Roxbury	MA	G	617 325-1515	16501
Quincy Sun Publishing Co Inc	Quincy	MA	F	617 471-3100	14652
Reminder Publications	East Longmeadow	MA	E	413 525-3947	10491
Republican Company **(HQ)**	Springfield	MA	A	413 788-1000	15502
Retail Sales Inc	Randolph	MA	G	781 963-8169	14696
Revere Independent	Revere	MA	E	781 485-0588	14775
Robert Weiss Associates Inc	Boston	MA	G	617 561-4000	8825
Rosscommon Quilts Inc	Dorchester	MA	G	617 436-5848	10348
S & S Publications Inc	Hull	MA	G	781 925-9266	11830
Saugus Advertiser	Beverly	MA	G	781 233-2040	8174
Shewstone Publishing LLC	Arlington	MA	G	781 648-1251	7638
Shrewsbury Chronicle	Framingham	MA	G	508 842-8787	11005
Sing Tao Newspapers NY Ltd	Boston	MA	E	617 426-9642	8848
Sippican Week	Marion	MA	G	774 553-5250	12704
Somerville News	Somerville	MA	G	617 666-4010	15216
South Boston Today	Boston	MA	G	617 268-4032	8856
Starting Treatment Effctvly	Boston	MA	G	857 544-8051	8863
State House News	Waban	MA	G	617 969-9175	15939
Stonebridge Press Inc **(PA)**	Southbridge	MA	E	508 764-4325	15405
Streak Media LLC	Boston	MA	G	617 242-9460	8868
Suburban News Dealers LLC	Carver	MA	G	508 962-9807	9808
Suburban Publishing Corp	Peabody	MA	F	978 818-6300	14373
Summer Ink Inc	Brookline	MA	G	617 714-0263	9220
Susan M Rexford Title Examiner	Ashburnham	MA	G	978 827-3015	7645
Target Marketing Group Inc	Rehoboth	MA	G	508 252-6575	14761
Taunton MA	Taunton	MA	G	774 226-0681	15788
Technology Organization Inc	Somerville	MA	G	617 623-4488	15222
Tinytown Gazette **(PA)**	Cohasset	MA	G	781 383-9115	10102
Town Common Inc	Rowley	MA	F	978 948-8696	14867
Town Crier Publications Inc	Upton	MA	F	508 529-7791	15911
Tri Town Transcript	Danvers	MA	G	978 887-4146	10266
Trustees of Tufts College	Medford	MA	E	617 628-5000	12951
Turley Publications Inc **(PA)**	Palmer	MA	C	800 824-6548	14298
Turley Publications Inc	Ware	MA	G	413 967-3505	16239
Turley Publications Inc	Barre	MA	G	978 355-4000	7952
United Communications Corp	Attleboro	MA	C	508 222-7000	7804
University Massachusetts Inc	Amherst	MA	G	413 545-2682	7529
University of Massachusetts	Amherst	MA	D	413 545-3500	7530
Valley Advocate	Northampton	MA	G	413 584-0003	14024
Village Netmedia Inc	Winthrop	MA	G	617 846-3700	17101
Vineyard Gazette LLC **(PA)**	Edgartown	MA	E	508 627-4311	10588
Vocero Hispano Newspaper Inc	Southbridge	MA	G	508 792-1942	15408
Wakefield Item Co	Wakefield	MA	E	781 245-0080	15983
Wall Street Journal	Chicopee	MA	G	800 369-5663	10068
Walpole Times Inc	Framingham	MA	F	508 668-0243	11013
Wanderer Communications Inc	Mattapoisett	MA	G	508 758-9055	12892
West Springfield Record Inc	West Springfield	MA	G	413 736-1587	16563
Westfield News Group LLC	Westfield	MA	E	413 562-4181	16745
Westfield News Publishing Inc **(DH)**	Westfield	MA	E	413 562-4181	16746
Weymouth News	Randolph	MA	G	781 337-1944	14702
Worcester Publishing	Worcester	MA	G	508 749-3166	17506
Worcester Sun LLC	Holden	MA	G	774 364-0553	11552
Worcester Tlegram Gazette Corp **(HQ)**	Worcester	MA	B	508 793-9100	17507
Worcester Tlegram Gazette Corp	Worcester	MA	E	978 368-0176	17508
Worcester Tlegram Gazette Corp	Southbridge	MA	F	508 764-2519	15409
World Journal Chinese Daily	Boston	MA	G	617 542-1230	8937
World News Firm Inc	Weymouth	MA	G	781 335-0113	16904
Yankee Shopper	Webster	MA	F	508 943-8784	16354
Yoga For Daily Living	Groton	MA	G	978 448-3751	11297
Advertiser-Democrat	Norway	ME	G	207 743-7011	6521
Bangor Publishing Company **(PA)**	Bangor	ME	C	207 990-8000	5632
Bangor Publishing Company	Belfast	ME	G	207 338-3034	5685
Bangor Publishing Company	Ellsworth	ME	G	207 667-9393	6014
Beacon Press Inc	Biddeford	ME	E	207 282-1535	5722
Blethen Maine Newspapers Inc	Portland	ME	G	207 791-6650	6624
Bridgton News Corp	Bridgton	ME	F	207 647-2851	5806
Brunswick Publishing LLC	Brunswick	ME	D	207 729-3311	5833
Camden Herald	Rockland	ME	G	207 236-8511	6786
Central Maine Morning Sentinel	Waterville	ME	G	207 873-3341	7153
Central Maine Online	Waterville	ME	G	207 872-2985	7154
Chases Daily LLC	Freedom	ME	G	207 930-0464	6070
Citizen Printers Incorporated	Albany Twp	ME	G	207 824-2444	5512
Coffee News USA Inc **(PA)**	Bangor	ME	G	207 941-0860	5638
Community Advertiser	Farmingdale	ME	G	207 582-8486	6038
Current Publishing LLC	Falmouth	ME	E	207 854-2577	6030
Ellsworth American Inc	Ellsworth	ME	D	207 667-2576	6018
Fiddlehead Focus	Fort Kent	ME	G	207 316-2243	6059
Forecaster Publishing Inc	South Portland	ME	F	207 781-3661	7027
Franklin Group	Farmington	ME	E	207 778-2075	6048
Free Press Inc	Rockland	ME	E	207 594-4408	6796
Gorham Growl	Gorham	ME	G	207 839-4795	6112
James Newspapers Inc **(PA)**	Norway	ME	E	207 743-7011	6523
Katahdin Regional Dev Corp	Millinocket	ME	G	207 447-6913	6441
Kirkland Newspaper Inc	Farmington	ME	F	207 778-2075	6051
Lewiston Daily Sun **(PA)**	Lewiston	ME	C	207 784-3555	6299
Lewiston Daily Sun	Lewiston	ME	G	207 784-5411	6300
Lewiston Daily Sun	Rumford	ME	G	207 364-8728	6837
Lincoln County Publishing Co	Newcastle	ME	E	207 563-3171	6483
Lincoln News	Lincoln	ME	F	207 794-6532	6357
Maine Antique Digest Inc	Waldoboro	ME	E	207 832-7534	7134
Maine Nwsppers In Educatn Fund	Portland	ME	G	207 791-6650	6688
Maine-OK Enterprises Inc	Boothbay Harbor	ME	E	207 633-4620	5784
Mainely Newspapers Inc	Biddeford	ME	F	207 282-4337	5746
Mount Desert Islander	Bar Harbor	ME	G	207 288-0556	5667
Mtm Oldco Inc **(PA)**	Portland	ME	B	207 791-6650	6696
Nandu Press	South Portland	ME	G	207 767-3144	7034
New England Business Media LLC	Portland	ME	F	207 761-8379	6700
Northeast Publishing Company **(HQ)**	Presque Isle	ME	D	207 764-4471	6764
Northeast Publishing Company	Houlton	ME	G	207 532-2281	6208
Northeast Publishing Company	Presque Isle	ME	G	207 768-5431	6766
Northeast Publishing Company	Dover Foxcroft	ME	G	207 564-8355	5961
Northwoods Publications LLC	West Enfield	ME	F	207 732-4880	7171
Original Irregular	Kingfield	ME	G	207 265-2773	6254
Otis Gazette	Allagash	ME	G	207 398-9001	5519
Penobscot Bay Press Inc **(PA)**	Stonington	ME	F	207 367-2200	7070
Penobscot Bay Press Inc	Blue Hill	ME	G	207 374-2341	5772
Penobscot Times Inc	Old Town	ME	G	207 827-4451	6546
Quoddy Tides Inc	Eastport	ME	G	207 853-4806	5995
RH Rosenfield Co	Sanford	ME	E	207 324-1798	6889
Rolling Thunder Press Inc	Newport	ME	G	207 368-2028	6486
Salty Dog Gallery	Southwest Harbor	ME	G	207 244-5918	7050
Seattle Times Company	Augusta	ME	C	207 623-3811	5619
Shoreline Publications	Wells	ME	F	207 646-8448	7165
SMA Inc	Yarmouth	ME	F	207 846-4112	7300
Sunrise Guide LLC	Portland	ME	F	207 221-3450	6735
Times Record Main Ofc	Brunswick	ME	G	207 729-3311	5849
Town Line	South China	ME	G	207 445-2234	7007
Tree Enterprises	Parsonsfield	ME	G	207 233-6479	6577
Turner Publishing Inc	Turner	ME	F	207 225-2076	7111
Twin City Times	Gorham	ME	G	207 795-5017	6134
Two Old Broads	Machias	ME	G	207 255-6561	6396
University of Maine System	Orono	ME	D	207 581-1273	6560
Upstairs	Falmouth	ME	G	207 799-2217	6036
Village Netmedia Inc **(PA)**	Rockland	ME	E	207 594-4401	6813
Village Netmedia Inc	Rockland	ME	E	207 594-4401	6814
Village Netmedia Inc	Belfast	ME	G	207 338-3333	5698
York County Coast Star Inc	Kennebunk	ME	F	207 985-5901	6243
Berlin Daily Sun	Berlin	NH	G	603 752-5858	17692
Caledonian Record Pubg Co Inc	Littleton	NH	G	603 444-7141	18656
Cardinal Communications Inc	Plaistow	NH	G	603 382-4800	19510
Carriage Towne News	Kingston	NH	G	603 642-4499	18541
Concord Monitor	Contoocook	NH	G	603 224-5301	17943
Constrction Summary of NH Main	Manchester	NH	G	603 627-8856	18804
Country News Club Inc	North Conway	NH	E	603 356-2999	19376
Daily Fantasy Spt Rankings LLC	Dover	NH	G	609 273-8408	18018
Daily Portsmouth	Portsmouth	NH	G	603 767-1395	19556
Dartmouth Inc	Hanover	NH	E	603 646-2600	18286
Eagle Publications Inc	Claremont	NH	E	603 543-3100	17849
Eagle-Tribune Publishing Co	Derry	NH	D	603 437-7000	17978
Eoutreach Solutions LLC	Manchester	NH	F	603 410-5000	18817
Fosters Daily Dmcrat Fstrs Sun	Portsmouth	NH	G	603 431-4888	19565
George J Foster Co Inc	Rochester	NH	G	603 332-2200	19670
Granite Quill Publishers	Hillsborough	NH	G	603 464-3388	18316
Great Bay Gazette	Exeter	NH	G	603 793-2620	18123
Greater Manchester Sports	Manchester	NH	G	603 627-3892	18830
Hippopress LLC **(PA)**	Manchester	NH	E	603 625-1855	18834
Independent Rowing News Inc	Hanover	NH	G	603 448-5090	18293
Jordan Associates	Pittsburg	NH	F	603 246-8998	19494
Keene Publishing Corporation	Keene	NH	D	603 352-1234	18511
Lakes Region News Club Inc	Laconia	NH	G	603 527-9299	18572
Local Media Group Inc	Portsmouth	NH	C	603 436-1800	19587
Mason Grapevine LLC	Mason	NH	G	603 878-4272	18970
McLean Communications LLC	Manchester	NH	D	603 624-1442	18869
Mount Washington Vly Mtn Ear	Lancaster	NH	G	603 447-6336	18602
Neighborhood News	Manchester	NH	E	603 206-7800	18882
New Boston Bulletin	New Boston	NH	G	603 487-5200	19294
New Hampshirecom	Manchester	NH	G	603 314-0447	18885
News & Sentinel Inc	Colebrook	NH	F	603 237-5501	17874
Newspapers New England Inc **(PA)**	Concord	NH	G	603 224-5301	17917
Newspapers of New Hampshire **(HQ)**	Concord	NH	C	603 224-5301	17918
Newspapers of New Hampshire	Peterborough	NH	F	603 924-7172	19481
Ogden Newspapers NH LLC	Nashua	NH	G	603 882-2741	19222
Panoramic Publishing Group LLC	Wolfeboro Falls	NH	F	603 569-5257	20028
Pennysaver	Plymouth	NH	G	603 536-3160	19530
Queen City Examiner	Manchester	NH	G	603 289-6835	18907

S I C

Employee Codes: A=Over 500 employees, B=251-500
C=101-250, D=51-100 E=20-50, F=10-19, G=3-9

	CITY	ST	EMP	PHONE	ENTRY #
Salmon Press LLC **(PA)**	Meredith	NH	F	603 279-4516	18978
Salmon Press LLC	Rochester	NH	E	603 332-2300	19686
Seacoast Shearwater Dev LLC	Portsmouth	NH	G	603 427-0000	19618
Shakour Publishers Inc	Keene	NH	E	603 352-5250	18524
State Military Reservation	Concord	NH	G	603 225-1230	17931
Stateline Review	Salem	NH	G	603 898-2554	19770
Suncook Valley Sun Inc	Pittsfield	NH	G	603 435-6291	19505
Telegraph Publishing Company **(HQ)**	Nashua	NH	C	603 594-6472	19271
Tolles Communications Corp	Manchester	NH	G	603 627-9500	18942
Union Leader Corporation **(PA)**	Manchester	NH	B	603 668-4321	18944
Weirs Publishing Company Inc	Laconia	NH	F	888 308-8463	18593
Beacon Communications Inc **(PA)**	Warwick	RI	E	401 732-3100	21334
Boston Phoenix Inc **(PA)**	Providence	RI	F	617 536-5390	20971
Breeze Publications Inc	Lincoln	RI	E	401 334-9555	20559
Bristol Phoenix	Bristol	RI	D	401 253-6000	20066
Corvus Publishing LLC	Barrington	RI	G	401 595-8937	20045
Daily Herald Brown Inc	Providence	RI	G	401 351-3372	20992
Fishermens Daily Catch LLC	Bristol	RI	G	401 252-1190	20078
International Journal of Arts	Cumberland	RI	G	401 333-1804	20329
Island News Enterprise	Jamestown	RI	G	401 423-3200	20491
Journal Roman Archaeology LLC	Portsmouth	RI	G	401 683-1955	20926
Kent County Daily Times	West Warwick	RI	E	401 789-9744	21498
Lmg Rhode Island Holdings Inc	Middletown	RI	D	401 849-3300	20624
Lmg Rhode Island Holdings Inc **(HQ)**	Providence	RI	G	585 598-0030	21054
Manisses Inc	Block Island	RI	G	401 466-2222	20058
New England Newspapers Inc	Pawtucket	RI	D	401 722-4000	20866
News Star Inc	Pascoag	RI	G	401 567-7077	20803
Outpost Journal	Providence	RI	G	401 569-1211	21086
Phoenix-Times Publishing Co	Bristol	RI	D	401 253-6000	20098
Providence Business News	Providence	RI	E	401 273-2201	21095
Providence Journal Company	Providence	RI	B	401 277-7000	21096
Rays Newspapers	Pawtucket	RI	G	401 728-1364	20891
Real Estate Journal of RI Inc	Johnston	RI	G	401 831-7778	20534
Rhode Island Media Group	Woonsocket	RI	E	401 762-3000	21578
Smithfied Times	Greenville	RI	G	401 232-9600	20475
Southern RI Newspapers **(HQ)**	Wakefield	RI	E	401 789-9744	21277
Stevens Publishing Inc	Coventry	RI	F	401 821-2216	20165
Visitor Printing Co	Providence	RI	F	401 272-1010	21151
Whitegate International Corp	Providence	RI	G	401 274-2149	21155
Witches Almanac	Newport	RI	G	401 847-3388	20688
Addison Press Inc	Middlebury	VT	E	802 388-4944	22097
Autism Support Daily	Shelburne	VT	G	802 985-8773	22412
Bennington Shriff GLC Slar LLC	Bennington	VT	G	802 233-3370	21665
Caledonian Record Pubg Co Inc **(PA)**	Saint Johnsbury	VT	D	802 748-8121	22389
Charlotte News	Charlotte	VT	G	802 425-4949	21832
Chronicle Inc	Barton	VT	E	802 525-3531	21647
Cohasa Publishing Inc	Bradford	VT	G	802 222-5281	21699
County Courier Inc	Enosburg Falls	VT	F	802 933-4375	21924
Creative Marketing Services	Rutland	VT	F	802 775-9500	22327
Cutter & Locke Inc **(PA)**	Tunbridge	VT	G	802 889-3500	22542
Da Capo Publishing Inc	Burlington	VT	E	802 864-5684	21778
Daily Gardener	Calais	VT	G	802 223-7851	21821
Daily Rider LLC	Burlington	VT	G	802 497-1269	21779
Gannett Co Inc	Burlington	VT	D	802 863-3441	21786
Gannett River States Pubg Corp	Fairfax	VT	D	802 893-4214	21975
Hardwick Gazette Print Shop	Hardwick	VT	G	802 472-6521	22013
Herald Association Inc	Rutland	VT	C	802 747-6121	22338
Herald of Randolph	Randolph	VT	F	802 728-3232	22297
Hersam Acorn Newspapers LLC	Manchester Center	VT	G	802 362-3535	22087
Hinesburg Record	Hinesburg	VT	F	802 482-2350	22028
Ibrattleboro	Brattleboro	VT	G	802 257-7475	21734
Islander	North Hero	VT	G	802 372-5600	22231
Its Classified Inc	Bradford	VT	G	802 222-5152	21701
Journal LLC **(PA)**	Ludlow	VT	G	802 228-3600	22065
Journal Opinion Inc	Bradford	VT	E	802 222-5281	21702
McClure Newspapers Inc	Burlington	VT	C	802 863-3441	21795
Milton Independent Inc	Saint Albans	VT	G	802 893-2028	22372
New England Newspapers Inc	Brattleboro	VT	E	802 254-2311	21740
New Market Press Inc	Middlebury	VT	F	802 388-6397	22115
News and Citizen Inc	Morrisville	VT	E	802 888-2212	22175
North Eastern Publishing Co	Bennington	VT	E	802 447-7567	21686
Northstar Publishing LLC	Danville	VT	G	802 684-1056	21898
Other Paper	South Burlington	VT	G	802 864-6670	22455
Outer Limits Publishing LLC	Killington	VT	F	802 422-2399	22055
Prison Legal News	Brattleboro	VT	G	802 257-1342	21744
Rutland City Band	Rutland	VT	G	802 775-5378	22349
Sams Good News	Rutland	VT	F	802 773-4040	22352
Springfield Reporter Inc	Springfield	VT	G	802 885-2246	22509
Ta Update Inc **(PA)**	Barre	VT	D	802 479-4040	21642
Valley Reporter Inc	Waitsfield	VT	G	802 496-3607	22569
Vermont Independent Media Inc	Brattleboro	VT	G	802 246-6397	21751
Vermont Media Corp	Wilmington	VT	F	802 464-5757	22705
Vermont Publishing Comany	Saint Albans	VT	E	802 524-9771	22384
Vermont Woman Newspaper	South Burlington	VT	G	802 861-6200	22478
Vermonts Northland Journal LLC	Newport	VT	G	802 334-5920	22206
Vtfolkus	Brattleboro	VT	G	802 246-1410	21753
World Publications Inc	Barre	VT	E	802 479-2582	21646
Young Writers Project Inc	Burlington	VT	F	802 324-9537	21818

2721 Periodicals: Publishing & Printing

	CITY	ST	EMP	PHONE	ENTRY #
Aapi	Monroe	CT	G	203 268-2450	2389
Access Intelligence	Norwalk	CT	G	203 854-6730	3096
Advantage Communications LLC	New Canaan	CT	E	203 966-8390	2592
Air Age Inc	Wilton	CT	E	203 431-9000	5274
Airtime Publishing Inc	Westport	CT	E	203 454-4773	5179
American Library Association	Middletown	CT	E	860 347-6933	2170
Bargain News Free Classified A	Stratford	CT	D	203 377-3000	4395
Baxter Bros Inc	Greenwich	CT	G	203 637-4559	1598
Bay Tact Corporation	Woodstock Valley	CT	E	860 315-7372	5503
Belvoir Media Group LLC	Norwalk	CT	G	203 857-3128	3111
Beverage Publications Inc	Hamden	CT	G	203 288-3375	1735
Bff Holdings Inc **(HQ)**	Old Saybrook	CT	C	860 510-0100	3328
Bottom Line Inc **(PA)**	Stamford	CT	D	203 973-5900	4151
Business Journals Inc **(PA)**	Norwalk	CT	D	203 853-6015	3117
Chief Executive Group LLC **(PA)**	Stamford	CT	F	785 832-0303	4164
Chief Executive Group LP **(PA)**	Stamford	CT	E	203 930-2700	4165
Comicana Inc	Stamford	CT	G	203 968-0748	4168
Commerce Connect Media Inc	Westport	CT	A	800 547-7377	5184
Corporate Connecticut Mag LLC	Wethersfield	CT	G	860 257-0500	5246
Domino Media Group Inc	Westport	CT	E	877 223-7844	5188
Donnin Publishing Inc	Guilford	CT	G	203 453-8866	1702
Douglas Moss	Norwalk	CT	G	203 854-5559	3144
Dulce Domum LLC	Norwalk	CT	E	203 227-1400	3145
Fairfield County Look	Greenwich	CT	G	203 869-0077	1610
Gamut Publishing	Hartford	CT	E	860 296-6128	1824
Granta USA Ltd	Danbury	CT	F	440 207-6051	928
Ida Publishing Co Inc	Greenwich	CT	G	203 661-9090	1621
Imani Magazine/Fmi	West Haven	CT	G	203 809-2565	5126
Informa Business Media Inc	Stamford	CT	D	203 358-9900	4223
Informa Business Media Inc	Stamford	CT	C	203 358-9900	4224
Information Today Inc	Wilton	CT	F	203 761-1466	5291
International Mktg Strategies	Stamford	CT	F	203 406-0106	4226
Interstate Tax Corporation	Norwalk	CT	G	203 854-0704	3176
Karger S Publishers Inc	Unionville	CT	G	860 675-7834	4657
L M T Communications Inc	Newtown	CT	F	203 426-4568	2927
Legal Affairs Inc	Hamden	CT	G	203 865-2520	1767
Liturgical Publications Inc	New Canaan	CT	F	203 966-6470	2603
Living Magazine	Milford	CT	G	203 283-5290	2310
Maplegate Media Group Inc	Danbury	CT	E	203 826-7557	952
Mason Medical Communications	Westport	CT	G	203 227-9252	5213
Media Ventures Inc	Norwalk	CT	E	203 852-6570	3194
Moffly Publications Inc	Westport	CT	F	203 222-0600	5215
Moffly Publications Inc **(PA)**	Westport	CT	E	203 222-0600	5216
Motorcyclists Post	Shelton	CT	G	203 929-9409	3835
National Shooting Sports Found	Newtown	CT	E	203 426-1320	2929
Natural Nutmeg LLC	Avon	CT	G	860 206-9500	38
Penny Marketing Ltd Partnr **(PA)**	Norwalk	CT	E	203 866-6688	3217
Penny Press Inc **(PA)**	Norwalk	CT	C	203 866-6688	3218
Penny Press Inc	Milford	CT	E	203 866-6688	2332
Penny Publications LLC **(PA)**	Norwalk	CT	D	203 866-6688	3219
Ppc Books Ltd	Westport	CT	G	203 226-6644	5224
Premier Graphics LLC	Stratford	CT	D	800 414-1624	4440
Quad/Graphics Inc	North Haven	CT	A	203 288-2468	3057
R G L Inc	East Granby	CT	E	860 653-7254	1142
Racing Times	Wallingford	CT	E	203 298-2899	4793
Red 7 Media LLC **(HQ)**	Norwalk	CT	E	203 853-2474	3227
Relocation Information Svc Inc	Norwalk	CT	E	203 855-1234	3229
Relx Inc	Norwalk	CT	A	203 840-4800	3230
S Karger Publishers Inc	Unionville	CT	G	860 675-7834	4661
Scholastic Library Pubg Inc **(HQ)**	Danbury	CT	A	203 797-3500	986
Sixfurlongs LLC	Fairfield	CT	G	203 255-8553	1456
Soundings Publications LLC	Essex	CT	E	860 767-8227	1406
Steed Read Horsemans Classifie	Salem	CT	G	860 859-0770	3740
Sumner Communications Inc	Bethel	CT	E	203 748-2050	182
Tam Communications Inc	Norwalk	CT	E	203 425-8777	3254
Taunton Inc	Newtown	CT	A	203 426-8171	2941
Taunton Press Inc	Newtown	CT	B	203 426-8171	2942
This Old House Ventures LLC	Stamford	CT	E	475 209-8665	4344
Timer Digest Publishing Inc	Greenwich	CT	G	203 629-2589	1655
Ubm LLC	Darien	CT	G	203 662-6501	1035
Venu Magazine LLC	Fairfield	CT	G	203 259-2075	1460
Westchester Forge Inc	New Canaan	CT	G	914 584-2429	2621
Wicks Business Information LLC **(PA)**	Shelton	CT	F	203 334-2002	3889
Windhover Information Inc **(DH)**	Norwalk	CT	E	203 838-4401	3272
Wire Journal Inc	Madison	CT	E	203 453-2777	1979
Yale Alumni Publications Inc	New Haven	CT	G	203 432-0645	2756
Zackin Publications Inc	Oxford	CT	E	203 262-4670	3431
73 75 Magazine Street LLC	Allston	MA	G	617 787-1913	7459
Advanstar Communications Inc	Burlington	MA	E	339 298-4200	9229
American Academy Arts Sciences	Cambridge	MA	G	617 491-2600	9387
American Mteorological Soc Inc **(PA)**	Boston	MA	D	617 227-2425	8361
Anderson Publishing Inc	Nantucket	MA	G	508 228-3866	13219
Art New England Magazine	Boston	MA	G	617 259-1040	8376
Atc Information Inc	Boston	MA	G	617 723-7030	8378

	CITY	ST	EMP	PHONE	ENTRY #
Atlantic Printing Co Inc	Medfield	MA	F	781 449-2700	12909
Boston Critic Inc	Cambridge	MA	G	617 324-1360	9418
Boston Design Guide Inc	Sudbury	MA	F	978 443-9886	15654
Brumberg Publications Inc	Brookline	MA	F	617 734-1979	9198
Cabot Heritage Corp	Salem	MA	E	978 745-5532	14900
Cambridge Fund Raising Assoc	Medfield	MA	G	508 359-0019	12911
Cape Cod Life LLC	Mashpee	MA	F	508 419-7381	12877
Carnegie Communications LLC	Westford	MA	E	978 692-5092	16760
Carnegie Dartlet LLC **(PA)**	Westford	MA	G	978 692-5092	16761
Cell Press Inc	Cambridge	MA	D	617 397-2800	9433
Chevalier Associates Inc	Sutton	MA	G	508 770-0092	15680
Christian Science Pubg Soc **(PA)**	Boston	MA	B	617 450-2000	8473
Cmio Magazine Publications	Newton	MA	G	617 851-6671	13580
Community of Jesus Inc **(PA)**	Orleans	MA	D	508 255-1094	14232
Contact Quarterly	Northampton	MA	G	413 586-1181	14001
Country Standard Time	Newton	MA	E	617 969-0331	13582
Crane Data LLC	Westborough	MA	F	508 439-4419	16610
Cxo Media Inc **(DH)**	Framingham	MA	C	508 766-5696	10938
Davis Corp of Worcester Inc **(PA)**	Worcester	MA	E	508 754-7201	17363
Davis Publications Inc	Worcester	MA	E	508 754-7201	17364
Dental Kaleidoscope Magazine	Canton	MA	G	781 821-8898	9724
Diacritech Inc	Boston	MA	F	617 236-7500	8502
Dow Jones & Company Inc	Chicopee	MA	E	413 598-4000	10020
Dunfey Publishing Company Inc	Jamaica Plain	MA	G	617 522-3267	11943
Early American Industries Assn	South Dartmouth	MA	G	508 439-2215	15239
East Coast Publications Inc **(PA)**	Norwell	MA	E	781 878-4540	14102
Ebsco Publishing Inc **(HQ)**	Ipswich	MA	A	978 356-6500	11917
Enterprise Publications **(PA)**	Falmouth	MA	E	508 548-4700	10789
Fine Magazine	Woburn	MA	E	617 721-7372	17180
First Magazine LLC	Waban	MA	G	617 965-0504	15936
Forced Exposure Inc	Arlington	MA	E	781 321-0320	7626
Gasworld Publishing LLC	Lexington	MA	G	781 862-0624	12225
Griffin Publishing Co Inc	Duxbury	MA	F	781 829-4700	10398
Guncanco Ltd	Georgetown	MA	G	978 352-3320	11143
H O Zimman Inc	Lynn	MA	F	781 598-9230	12515
Harvard Bus Schl Pubg Corp **(HQ)**	Brighton	MA	C	617 783-7400	9100
Harvard Crimson Inc	Cambridge	MA	G	617 576-6600	9502
Harvard Lampoon Inc	Cambridge	MA	E	617 495-7801	9503
Harvard Magazine Inc	Cambridge	MA	E	617 495-5746	9504
Healthcare Publishing Inc	Natick	MA	G	508 655-4489	13260
Horizon House Publications Inc **(PA)**	Norwood	MA	D	781 769-9750	14158
Horn Book Inc	Boston	MA	F	617 278-0225	8601
Hot Stepz Magazine	Dorchester	MA	G	617 959-6403	10343
Hotrod Hotline	North Adams	MA	G	208 562-0470	13676
Hunter Associates Inc	Saugus	MA	E	781 233-9100	14986
Idg **(HQ)**	Boston	MA	G	508 875-5000	8613
Idg Communications Inc **(HQ)**	Framingham	MA	C	508 872-8200	10965
Idg Communications Inc	Framingham	MA	F	508 766-5300	10966
Idg Corporate Services Group	Framingham	MA	F	508 875-5000	10967
Information Gatekeepers Inc	Winchester	MA	G	617 782-5033	17088
Institute For Scial Cltral Cmm	Dedham	MA	G	508 548-9063	10293
International Data Group Inc **(PA)**	Boston	MA	F	508 875-5000	8618
International Data Group Inc	Framingham	MA	E	508 766-5632	10970
International Data Group Inc	Framingham	MA	F	508 935-4719	10971
J Magazine Inc	Brookline	MA	G	617 515-1822	9205
Journal Computing In Higher	Amherst	MA	G	413 549-5150	7516
Journal of Bone Jint Srgery In	Needham	MA	E	781 449-9780	13302
Just Publications Inc	Brookline	MA	G	617 739-5878	9207
Laurin Publishing Co Inc **(PA)**	Pittsfield	MA	D	413 499-0514	14482
Liberty Publishing Inc	Beverly	MA	E	978 777-8200	8148
Magazine Columbiano	Revere	MA	G	617 365-3182	14772
Management Roundtable Inc	Newton	MA	G	781 891-8080	13612
Massachusetts Institute Tech	Cambridge	MA	D	617 253-5646	9546
Massachusetts Institute Tech	Cambridge	MA	D	617 253-1000	9547
Massachusetts Medical Society **(PA)**	Waltham	MA	B	781 893-4610	16148
Massachusetts Medical Society	Boston	MA	E	617 734-9800	8685
Massachusetts Review Inc	Amherst	MA	E	413 545-2689	7518
McKnight Management Co Inc **(PA)**	Falmouth	MA	G	508 540-5051	10796
Medical Publishing Assoc	Boston	MA	G	617 530-6222	8694
Meredith Corporation	Springfield	MA	G	413 733-4040	15488
Metro Corp	Boston	MA	E	617 262-9700	8702
Municipal Market Analytics Inc **(PA)**	Concord	MA	F	978 287-0014	10143
Myrin Institute Inc	Great Barrington	MA	F	413 528-4422	11242
National Braille Press Inc	Boston	MA	D	617 425-2400	8720
Network World Inc	Framingham	MA	C	800 622-1108	10986
New Beverage Publications Inc	Boston	MA	G	617 598-1900	8728
New England Bride Inc	Lynnfield	MA	F	781 334-6093	12553
New England Business Media LLC **(PA)**	Worcester	MA	E	508 755-8004	17429
New England Home	Boston	MA	G	617 938-3991	8731
New England RE Bulltin	Swansea	MA	F	508 675-8884	15710
New Generation Research Inc	Boston	MA	F	617 573-9550	8734
Northast Prformer Publications	Somerville	MA	G	617 627-9200	15202
Northeast Outdoors Inc	Paxton	MA	F	508 752-8762	14302
Now Publishers Inc	Norwell	MA	G	781 871-0245	14109
Open Studios Press Inc	Boston	MA	G	617 778-5265	8751
Out & About Magazine	Springfield	MA	G	413 783-6704	15496
Page Same Publishing Inc	Littleton	MA	G	978 486-4684	12317

	CITY	ST	EMP	PHONE	ENTRY #
Pagio Inc	Worcester	MA	G	508 756-5006	17439
Paraclete Press Inc	Brewster	MA	G	508 255-4685	9056
Penwell	Sturbridge	MA	G	508 347-8245	15645
Prime National Publishing Corp	Weston	MA	F	781 899-2702	16830
Provincetown Arts Press Inc **(PA)**	Provincetown	MA	G	508 487-3167	14608
Quarterly Review of Wines	Quincy	MA	E	781 721-0525	14650
Quarterly Update	North Falmouth	MA	G	508 540-0848	13953
Questex Brazil LLC	Framingham	MA	G	617 219-8300	10997
Quinlan Publishing Co Inc **(PA)**	Boston	MA	G	617 439-0076	8805
Regional Spt Media Group LLC	Rockland	MA	G	781 871-9271	14821
Relx Inc	Newton	MA	D	617 558-4925	13629
Rhee Gold Company	Norton	MA	F	508 285-6650	14086
RMS Media Group Inc	Andover	MA	E	978 623-8020	7600
Robb Curtco Media LLC	Acton	MA	E	978 264-7500	7380
Rosenoff Reports Inc	Somerville	MA	G	617 628-7783	15213
Seak Inc **(PA)**	Falmouth	MA	G	508 548-7023	10797
Seamans Media Inc	Milton	MA	G	617 773-9955	13200
Smarter Travel Media LLC	Boston	MA	C	617 886-5555	8850
Society For Marine Mammalogy	Yarmouth Port	MA	G	508 744-2276	17531
Standard Publishing Corp **(PA)**	Boston	MA	F	617 457-0600	8861
Steelfish Media LLC	Beverly	MA	G	312 730-8016	8182
Stellar Medical Publications	Plymouth	MA	G	508 732-6767	14585
Stysil Enterprises Ltd	Marshfield	MA	G	781 834-7279	12870
Suburban Publishing Corp	Peabody	MA	F	978 818-6300	14373
Suburban Shopper Inc	Canton	MA	G	781 821-2590	9788
Synchrgnix Info Strategies Inc	Cambridge	MA	G	302 892-4800	9670
Technology Review Inc	Cambridge	MA	E	617 475-8000	9677
Telco Communications Inc	Seekonk	MA	E	508 336-6633	15041
The Orion Society Inc	Great Barrington	MA	F	413 528-4422	11248
Town of North Reading	North Reading	MA	E	978 664-6027	13992
Trailjournals LLC	Newburyport	MA	G	978 358-7536	13542
Travel Medicine Inc	Northampton	MA	G	413 584-0381	14023
Trustees of Boston University	Brookline	MA	F	617 353-3081	9223
Turley Publications Inc	Ware	MA	G	413 967-3505	16239
Vdc Research Group Inc **(PA)**	Natick	MA	E	508 653-9000	13284
Ve Interactive LLC	Boston	MA	G	857 284-7000	8905
Verifacts	Weymouth	MA	G	781 337-1717	16903
Village Netmedia Inc	Winthrop	MA	G	617 846-3700	17101
Werner Publishing Corporation	Braintree	MA	D	310 820-1500	9049
Weston Medical Publishing LLC	Weston	MA	G	781 899-2702	16834
Wilmington Compliance Week	Boston	MA	E	888 519-9200	8929
Young Authors Foundation Inc	Newton	MA	G	617 964-6800	13655
Audio File Publications Inc	Portland	ME	G	207 774-7563	6614
Beloit Ptry Jrnl Fundation Inc	Gorham	ME	G	207 522-1303	6110
Casco Bay Sbstnce Abuse Rsrces	Portland	ME	F	207 773-7993	6634
Compass Publications Inc	Deer Isle	ME	G	207 348-1057	5947
Cremark Inc	Portland	ME	G	207 874-7720	6644
D E Enterprise Inc	Rockport	ME	D	207 594-9544	6818
Down East Enterprise Inc	Rockport	ME	E	207 594-9544	6820
Dream Spirit Publishers	Arundel	ME	G	207 283-0667	5531
Flavor Unlimited Inc	Freeport	ME	G	207 865-4432	6078
Informtion Consulting Svcs Inc	Rockland	ME	E	207 596-7783	6799
Maine Antique Digest Inc	Waldoboro	ME	E	207 832-7534	7134
Maine Bats Hrbors Publications	Camden	ME	G	207 594-8622	5868
Navigator Publishing LLC	Portland	ME	E	207 822-4350	6698
Port Cy Lf Communications Inc	Cumberland Foreside	ME	G	207 781-4644	5932
Portland Monthly Inc	Portland	ME	G	207 775-4339	6711
Soyatech Inc	Bar Harbor	ME	G	207 288-4969	5670
Taproot	Portland	ME	G	802 472-1617	6737
Trueline Publishing LLC	Portland	ME	E	207 510-4099	6743
United Publications Inc	Yarmouth	ME	E	207 846-0600	7303
Wild Fibers Magazine	Rockland	ME	G	207 594-9455	6815
Woodenboat Publications Inc	Brooklin	ME	E	207 359-4651	5822
Center For Northern Woodlands	Lyme	NH	G	802 439-6292	18753
Common Sense Marketing	Sunapee	NH	G	603 763-2441	19880
Connell Communications Inc	Keene	NH	E	603 924-7271	18496
Echo Communications Inc	New London	NH	E	603 526-6006	19316
Harrison Publishing House Inc	Littleton	NH	E	603 444-0820	18661
Helmers Publishing Inc	Dublin	NH	F	603 563-1631	18068
Laser Group Publishing Inc	Manchester	NH	F	603 880-8909	18861
Paine Publishing LLC	Durham	NH	G	603 682-0735	18079
Pennwell Corporation	Nashua	NH	C	603 891-9425	19228
Pennwell Corporation	Nashua	NH	C	603 891-0123	19229
Reid Publication Inc	Portsmouth	NH	G	603 433-2200	19614
Relx Inc	Salem	NH	E	603 898-9664	19762
Relx Inc	Portsmouth	NH	D	603 431-7894	19615
Simon & Schuster Inc	Peterborough	NH	E	603 924-7209	19488
Village West Publishing Inc	Laconia	NH	F	603 528-4285	18592
Yankee Publishing Incorporated **(PA)**	Dublin	NH	E	603 563-8111	18069
CM Publications Inc	Westerly	RI	G	401 596-9358	21519
Daily Herald Brown Inc	Providence	RI	G	401 351-3372	20992
Grace Ormonde Marriage Inc	Riverside	RI	F	401 245-9726	21169
Homeland Company	East Greenwich	RI	G	401 884-2427	20370
La Bella Bride Magazine	Coventry	RI	G	401 397-5795	20152
Metro Inc **(PA)**	Cranston	RI	E	401 461-2200	20262
Newport Life Magazine Inc	Middletown	RI	G	401 841-0200	20627

Employee Codes: A=Over 500 employees, B=251-500
C=101-250, D=51-100 E=20-50, F=10-19, G=3-9

	CITY	ST	EMP	PHONE	ENTRY #
Ocean Side Publications	East Providence	RI	G	401 331-8426	20437
Rhode Island Monthly	Providence	RI	E	401 649-4800	21112
Richardson Landscaping Corp	Jamestown	RI	G	401 423-1505	20494
State-Wide Mltiple Listing Svc	Warwick	RI	G	401 785-3650	21430
Vendome Guide	Newport	RI	E	401 849-8025	20687
Backcountry Magazine	Jeffersonville	VT	G	802 644-6794	22045
Battenkill Communications LLP	Manchester Center	VT	G	802 362-3981	22081
Boutin McQuiston Inc **(PA)**	South Burlington	VT	F	802 863-8038	22439
Dartmouth Journal Services Inc	Waterbury	VT	E	802 244-1457	22582
Eating Well Inc **(HQ)**	Shelburne	VT	G	802 425-5700	22415
Edible Green Mountains LLC	Manchester Center	VT	G	802 768-8356	22083
Jouve of North America Inc **(DH)**	Brattleboro	VT	G	802 254-6073	21735
Kestrel Health Information Inc	Williston	VT	G	802 482-4000	22676
Mill Publishing Inc	Williston	VT	G	802 862-4109	22682
N News LLC	Topsham	VT	G	802 439-6054	22540
Reef To Rainforest Media LLC	Shelburne	VT	G	802 985-9977	22422
Vermont Journalism Trust Ltd	Montpelier	VT	F	802 225-6224	22163

2731 Books: Publishing & Printing

	CITY	ST	EMP	PHONE	ENTRY #
Air Age Inc	Wilton	CT	E	203 431-9000	5274
Bay Tact Corporation	Woodstock Valley	CT	E	860 315-7372	5503
Begell House Inc	Danbury	CT	F	203 456-6161	878
Belvoir Publications Inc **(PA)**	Norwalk	CT	E	203 857-3100	3112
Bff Holdings Inc **(HQ)**	Old Saybrook	CT	C	860 510-0100	3328
Birdtrack Press	New Haven	CT	G	203 389-7789	2669
Bunting & Lyon Inc	Cheshire	CT	G	203 272-4623	718
Burns Walton	Branford	CT	G	203 422-5222	300
Calculator Training	New Milford	CT	G	860 355-8255	2789
Carala Ventures Ltd	Stratford	CT	E	800 483-6449	4402
Comicana Inc	Stamford	CT	G	203 968-0748	4168
Connecticut Law Book Co Inc	Guilford	CT	F	203 458-8000	1698
Connecticut Parent Magazine	Branford	CT	F	203 483-1700	306
Cortina Learning Intl Inc **(PA)**	Wilton	CT	F	800 245-2145	5285
Creative Media Applications	Weston	CT	F	203 226-0544	5171
Early Advantage LLC	Fairfield	CT	F	203 259-6480	1428
Eye Ear It LLC	Woodbury	CT	F	203 487-8949	5487
Forecast International Inc	Newtown	CT	D	203 426-0800	2922
Gamut Publishing	Hartford	CT	E	860 296-6128	1824
Graphics Press LLC	Cheshire	CT	G	203 272-9187	736
Industrial Press Inc	Norwalk	CT	F	212 889-6330	3172
Information Today Inc	Wilton	CT	F	203 761-1466	5291
Kieffer Associates Inc	Stamford	CT	G	203 323-3437	4235
Kirchoff Wohlberg Inc	Madison	CT	F	212 644-2020	1967
Life Study Fllwship Foundation	Darien	CT	E	203 655-1436	1028
McBooks Press Inc	Guilford	CT	G	607 272-2114	1710
Millbrook Press Inc	Brookfield	CT	E	203 740-2220	652
Peninsula Publishing	Westport	CT	G	203 292-5621	5223
Ppc Books Ltd	Westport	CT	G	203 226-6644	5224
R G L Inc	East Granby	CT	E	860 653-7254	1142
Rocket Books Inc	Easton	CT	G	203 372-1818	1323
S Karger Publishers Inc	Unionville	CT	G	860 675-7834	4661
Sasc LLC **(PA)**	Greenwich	CT	G	203 846-2274	1646
Scholastic Library Pubg Inc **(HQ)**	Danbury	CT	A	203 797-3500	986
Stamler Publishing Company	Branford	CT	G	203 488-9808	351
Summer Street Press LLC	Stamford	CT	F	203 978-0098	4335
Tantor Media Incorporated	Old Saybrook	CT	C	860 395-1155	3351
Taunton Inc	Newtown	CT	A	203 426-8171	2941
Ubm LLC	Darien	CT	G	203 662-6501	1035
Vital Health Publishing Inc	Ridgefield	CT	G	203 438-3229	3688
Wesleyan University	Middletown	CT	G	860 685-2980	2230
Windhover Information Inc **(DH)**	Norwalk	CT	E	203 838-4401	3272
Yale Daily News Publishing Co	New Haven	CT	G	203 432-2400	2757
Ziga Media LLC	Darien	CT	G	203 656-0076	1037
Zp Couture LLC	North Haven	CT	G	888 697-7239	3070
Acom Publishing Inc	Monson	MA	G	413 267-4999	13202
Anglo-Saxon Federation of Amer	Merrimac	MA	G	978 346-9311	13000
Anti-Phishing Wkg Group Inc	Cambridge	MA	G	404 434-7282	9390
Argosy Publishing Inc **(PA)**	Newton	MA	E	617 527-9999	13562
Artech House Inc **(HQ)**	Norwood	MA	F	781 769-9750	14134
Aspect Inc	Brookline	MA	G	617 713-2813	9194
Atlantic Printing Co Inc	Medfield	MA	F	781 449-2700	12909
Baikar Association Inc **(PA)**	Watertown	MA	F	617 924-4420	16271
Bedford Freeman & Worth	Boston	MA	D	617 426-7440	8398
Berkshire Publishing Group LLC	Great Barrington	MA	F	413 528-0206	11235
Black Ice Publishers	Southborough	MA	G	508 481-0910	15347
Borderlines Foundation	Brookline	MA	G	617 365-9438	9197
Brill Usa Inc	Boston	MA	F	617 263-2323	8445
Brillacademic Publishers Inc	Boston	MA	G	617 742-5277	8446
Brown Publishing Network Inc **(PA)**	Charlestown	MA	E	781 547-7600	9828
Candlewick Press Inc	Somerville	MA	D	617 661-3330	15164
Career Press Inc **(PA)**	Newburyport	MA	E	201 848-0310	13477
Cengage Learning Inc **(PA)**	Boston	MA	D	617 289-7918	8462
Cengage Lrng Holdings II Inc **(PA)**	Boston	MA	E	617 289-7700	8463
Channing Bete Company Inc **(PA)**	South Deerfield	MA	B	413 665-7611	15247
Charlesbridge Publishing Inc **(PA)**	Watertown	MA	E	617 926-0329	16276
Christopher-Gordon Publishing	Foxboro	MA	F	781 762-5577	10879
Circlet Press Inc	Cambridge	MA	G	617 864-0663	9438

	CITY	ST	EMP	PHONE	ENTRY #
Clp Pb LLC	Boston	MA	C	617 252-5213	8478
Community of Jesus Inc **(PA)**	Orleans	MA	D	508 255-1094	14232
Council On Intl Pub Affirs Inc **(PA)**	Northampton	MA	G	212 972-9878	14002
Courier Communications LLC **(HQ)**	North Chelmsford	MA	F	978 251-6000	13887
Courier New Media Inc **(DH)**	North Chelmsford	MA	E	978 251-3945	13890
Crawford Chandler Agency Inc	Monterey	MA	G	413 528-3035	13213
Credo Reference Limited	Boston	MA	F	617 292-6100	8489
Curriculum Associates LLC	Boston	MA	G	978 313-1331	8492
Curriculum Associates LLC	Littleton	MA	E	978 313-1276	12298
Curriculum Associates LLC **(PA)**	North Billerica	MA	B	978 667-8000	13805
Da Capo Press	Boston	MA	E	617 252-5200	8494
Dahlstrom & Company Inc	Holliston	MA	G	508 429-3367	11566
Daughters of St Paul Inc	Billerica	MA	G	617 522-2566	8235
David R Godine Publisher Inc **(PA)**	Boston	MA	G	617 451-9600	8497
Davis Corp of Worcester Inc **(PA)**	Worcester	MA	E	508 754-7201	17363
Diacritech Inc	Boston	MA	F	617 236-7500	8502
Eastgate Systems Inc	Watertown	MA	G	617 924-9044	16280
Ebsco Publishing Inc **(HQ)**	Ipswich	MA	A	978 356-6500	11917
Edward Elgar Publishing Inc	Northampton	MA	G	413 584-5551	14005
Eric Carle LLC	Northampton	MA	G	413 586-2046	14006
Exact Change	Cambridge	MA	G	617 492-5405	9475
Fair Winds Press and Quiver	Beverly	MA	G	978 282-9590	8130
Freeman Bedford	Boston	MA	C	617 399-4000	8554
Greenwood Publishing Group LLC **(DH)**	Boston	MA	E	617 351-5000	8581
Gwb Corporation	Andover	MA	G	508 896-9486	7554
Hachette Book Group Inc	Boston	MA	D	617 227-0730	8586
Hachette Book Group Inc	Boston	MA	G	617 227-0730	8587
Hackett Publishing Company	Cambridge	MA	F	617 497-6303	9499
Harvard Bus Schl Pubg Corp **(HQ)**	Brighton	MA	C	617 783-7400	9100
Hendrickson Publishers LLC	Peabody	MA	F	978 532-6546	14339
Hendrickson Publishers Inc	Peabody	MA	G	800 358-3111	14340
Higginson Book Company	Salem	MA	G	978 745-7170	14921
HM Publishing Corp	Boston	MA	A	617 251-5000	8598
Hmh Publishers LLC **(DH)**	Boston	MA	G	617 351-5000	8599
Holy Cross Orthodox Press	Brookline	MA	G	800 245-0599	9203
Horizon House Publications Inc **(PA)**	Norwood	MA	D	781 769-9750	14158
Houghton Mifflin LLC	Boston	MA	E	617 351-5000	8602
Houghton Mifflin Co Intl Inc	Boston	MA	G	617 351-5000	8603
Houghton Mifflin Harcourt	Boston	MA	F	617 351-5000	8604
Houghton Mifflin Harcourt **(HQ)**	Boston	MA	F	617 351-5000	8605
Houghton Mifflin Harcourt Co **(PA)**	Boston	MA	B	617 351-5000	8606
Houghton Mifflin Harcourt Pubg **(HQ)**	Boston	MA	A	617 351-5000	8607
Houghton Mifflin Holdings Inc **(PA)**	Boston	MA	G	617 351-5000	8608
Human Resource Dev Press **(PA)**	Pelham	MA	E	413 253-3488	14388
Idg Communications Inc **(HQ)**	Framingham	MA	C	508 872-8200	10965
Idg Paper Services	Framingham	MA	E	508 875-5000	10968
Information Gatekeepers Inc	Winchester	MA	G	617 782-5033	17088
International Press of Boston	Somerville	MA	G	617 623-3016	15184
Jones & Bartlett Learning LLC **(PA)**	Burlington	MA	C	978 443-5000	9289
Kidsbooks LLC	Boston	MA	G	617 425-0300	8648
Lama Yeshe Wisdom Archive Inc	Lincoln	MA	F	781 259-4466	12286
Macmillan Publishing Group LLC	Boston	MA	D	646 307-5617	8677
Maitri Learning LLC	Westhampton	MA	G	413 529-2868	16801
Massachsetts Prosecutors Guide	Milton	MA	G	617 696-6729	13195
Massachusetts Institute Tech	Cambridge	MA	D	617 253-1000	9547
Memoirs Unlimited Inc	Beverly	MA	G	978 985-3206	8151
Meno Publishing Inc	Needham Heights	MA	G	781 209-2665	13336
Merriam-Webster Incorporated **(DH)**	Springfield	MA	C	413 734-3134	15489
Microtraining Assoc Inc	Hanover	MA	G	781 982-8984	11347
Nahas Selim	Newton	MA	G	617 595-8808	13616
National Braille Press Inc	Boston	MA	D	617 425-2400	8720
Nicholas Brealey Pubg Inc	Boston	MA	G	617 523-3801	8737
North River Press Pubg Corp	Great Barrington	MA	F	413 528-0034	11243
Nsight Inc	Andover	MA	E	781 273-6300	7579
O E M Health Information Inc	Beverly	MA	G	978 921-7300	8161
Old Salt Box Publishing & Dist	Danvers	MA	G	978 750-8090	10244
OReilly Media Inc	Boston	MA	C	617 354-5800	8758
Oriental Research Partners	Framingham	MA	G	781 642-1216	10990
Page Street Publishing Company	Salem	MA	F	978 594-8758	14934
Pagoda Group LLC	Brookline	MA	G	617 833-3137	9214
Paraclete Press Inc **(HQ)**	Brewster	MA	E	508 255-4685	9055
Paraclete Press Inc	Brewster	MA	G	508 255-4685	9056
Pearson Education Inc	Bedford	MA	G	781 687-8800	7999
Pearson Education Inc	Boston	MA	E	617 848-6000	8770
Pearson Education Holdings Inc	Boston	MA	D	617 671-2000	8771
Pedipress Inc	Amherst	MA	G	413 549-3918	7521
Pioneer Vly Eductl Press Inc	Northampton	MA	F	413 727-3573	14019
Planet Small Communications	Lawrence	MA	G	978 794-2201	12071
Porter Sargent Publishers Inc	Westford	MA	G	617 922-0076	16785
President Fllows Hrvard Cllege	Cambridge	MA	D	617 495-9897	9616
Publishing Solutions Group Inc	Woburn	MA	F	617 274-9001	17272
Quarto Pubg Group USA Inc	Beverly	MA	E	978 282-9590	8166
Quayside Publishing Group	Beverly	MA	G	978 282-9590	8167
Quinlan Publishing Co Inc **(PA)**	Boston	MA	G	617 439-0076	8805
Redwheel/Weiser LLC **(PA)**	Newburyport	MA	G	978 465-0504	13527
Robert Bentley Inc	Cambridge	MA	E	617 547-4170	9636
Robert Murphy	Salem	MA	E	978 745-7170	14938

	CITY	ST	EMP	PHONE	ENTRY #
Salem House Press	Salem	MA	E	978 578-9238	14940
School Specialty Inc	Cambridge	MA	D	617 547-6706	9647
School Yourself Inc	Brookline	MA	G	516 729-7478	9219
Short Courses	Marblehead	MA	G	781 631-1178	12694
Silver Leaf Books LLC	Holliston	MA	E	781 799-6609	11602
Sinauer Associates Inc	Sunderland	MA	E	413 549-4300	15676
Singing River Publications	Brighton	MA	G	218 365-3498	9106
Society For Marine Mammalogy	Yarmouth Port	MA	G	508 744-2276	17531
Spinner Publications Inc	New Bedford	MA	G	508 994-4564	13451
Sproutman Publications	Great Barrington	MA	G	413 528-5200	11247
Stevenson Learning Skills Inc	Holliston	MA	G	774 233-0457	11607
Storey Publishing LLC **(HQ)**	North Adams	MA	E	413 346-2100	13685
Sundance/Newbridge LLC **(HQ)**	Marlborough	MA	G	800 343-8204	12831
Tapestry Press Ltd	Littleton	MA	G	978 486-0200	12324
Technologies/Typography	Merrimac	MA	G	978 346-4867	13006
Textcafe	Natick	MA	G	508 654-8520	13281
Unitarian Universalist Assn	Boston	MA	E	617 742-2110	8897
Victory Productions Inc	Worcester	MA	E	508 755-0051	17500
Vineyard Gazette LLC **(PA)**	Edgartown	MA	E	508 627-4311	10588
Walter De Gruyter Inc	Boston	MA	G	857 284-7073	8915
Wellesley Information Svcs LLC **(HQ)**	Dedham	MA	D	781 407-0360	10301
Wild Apples Inc	Harvard	MA	G	978 456-9616	11385
Willett Institute of Finance	Reading	MA	G	617 247-3030	14744
Wisdom Publications Inc **(PA)**	Somerville	MA	G	617 776-7416	15233
Wristies Inc	Lowell	MA	G	978 937-9500	12449
Xam Online Inc **(PA)**	Cambridge	MA	G	781 662-9268	9707
Zachary Shuster Hrmswoth Agncy	Boston	MA	G	617 262-2400	8940
Alice James Poetry Coop Inc	Farmington	ME	G	207 778-7071	6040
Child Safety Solutions Inc	Rockland	ME	G	207 226-3870	6789
D E Enterprise Inc	Rockport	ME	D	207 594-9544	6818
Garmin International Inc	Yarmouth	ME	C	800 561-5105	7294
Herb Allure Inc	Amherst	ME	G	207 584-3550	5521
Invision Inc	Brunswick	ME	G	207 725-7123	5839
J Weston Walch Publisher	Portland	ME	E	207 772-2846	6676
Mathematics Problem Solving LLC	Portland	ME	G	207 772-2846	6692
Memoir Network	Lisbon	ME	G	207 353-5454	6364
North Country Press	Unity	ME	G	207 948-2208	7117
Penobscot Bay Press Inc **(PA)**	Stonington	ME	F	207 367-2200	7070
Tilbury House Publishers	Thomaston	ME	G	800 582-1899	7089
Wayside Publishing	Freeport	ME	F	888 302-2519	6089
Avocus Publishing Inc	Gilsum	NH	G	603 357-0236	18195
Blue Tree LLC	Portsmouth	NH	G	603 436-0831	19545
Cafe Refugee Inc	Claremont	NH	G	603 499-7415	17838
Carrington International LLC	Candia	NH	G	603 867-8957	17780
David R Godine Publisher Inc	Jaffrey	NH	G	603 532-4100	18460
Earth Sky + Water LLC	Wilton	NH	G	603 654-7649	19980
Elan Publishing Company Inc	Moultonborough	NH	E	603 253-6002	19096
Enfield Publishing & Dist Co	Enfield	NH	G	603 632-7377	18098
Fishing Hot Spots Inc	Nashua	NH	G	715 365-5555	19158
Greenwood Publishing Group LLC	Portsmouth	NH	E	603 431-7894	19570
Helmers Publishing Inc	Dublin	NH	E	603 563-1631	18068
Houghton Mifflin Harcourt Co	Portsmouth	NH	G	630 467-7000	19576
Kensington Group Incorporated	Hampton Falls	NH	F	603 926-6742	18283
Loreto Publications Inc	Fitzwilliam	NH	G	603 239-6671	18150
Mann Publishing Incorporated	Rollinsford	NH	F	603 601-0325	19693
Peter E Randall Publisher LLC	Portsmouth	NH	G	603 431-5667	19607
Secret Guide To Computers	Manchester	NH	G	603 666-6644	18920
Simon & Schuster Inc	Peterborough	NH	E	603 924-7209	19488
Stenhouse Publishers	Portsmouth	NH	F	207 253-1600	19623
Stillpoint International Inc	Peterborough	NH	G	603 756-9281	19490
TMC Books LLC	Conway	NH	G	603 447-5589	17959
Travelbrains Inc	Bedford	NH	G	603 471-0127	17665
John Carlevale	West Greenwich	RI	E	401 392-1926	21459
Metro Inc **(PA)**	Cranston	RI	E	401 461-2200	20262
Ocean Side Publications	East Providence	RI	G	401 331-8426	20437
Rhode Island Family Guide	Barrington	RI	G	401 247-0850	20053
Alexandria Press	South Burlington	VT	G	802 497-0074	22436
Blacklightning Publishing Inc	West Topsham	VT	G	802 439-6462	22621
Charles E Tuttle Co Inc **(DH)**	North Clarendon	VT	E	802 773-8930	22214
Chelsea Green Publishing Co	White River Junction	VT	E	802 295-6300	22636
Chooseco LLC	Waitsfield	VT	G	802 496-2595	22563
Emily Post Institute Inc	Burlington	VT	G	802 860-1814	21781
Huntington Graphics	Burlington	VT	G	802 660-3605	21788
Inner Traditions International **(PA)**	Rochester	VT	E	802 767-3174	22317
John Wiley & Sons Inc	Poultney	VT	D	802 287-4326	22272
Longhill Partners Inc **(PA)**	Woodstock	VT	E	802 457-4000	22738
Miravia LLC **(PA)**	Charlotte	VT	G	802 425-6483	21834
Pro Lingua Associates Inc	Brattleboro	VT	G	802 257-7779	21745
Stratford Publishing Services	Brattleboro	VT	E	802 254-6073	21747
Trafalgar Square Farm Inc	North Pomfret	VT	F	802 457-1911	22235
Upper Access Inc	Hinesburg	VT	G	802 482-2988	22032

2732 Book Printing, Not Publishing

	CITY	ST	EMP	PHONE	ENTRY #
Ppc Books Ltd	Westport	CT	G	203 226-6644	5224
R R Donnelley & Sons Company	Manchester	CT	F	860 649-5570	2040
Baikar Association Inc **(PA)**	Watertown	MA	F	617 924-4420	16271
Book-Mart Press Inc	North Chelmsford	MA	D	978 251-6000	13886
Channing Bete Company Inc **(PA)**	South Deerfield	MA	B	413 665-7611	15247
Courier Companies Inc **(PA)**	North Chelmsford	MA	E	978 251-6000	13888
Courier Intl Holdings LLC	North Chelmsford	MA	G	978 251-6000	13889
Courier New Media Inc **(DH)**	North Chelmsford	MA	E	978 251-3945	13890
Dunn & Co Inc	Clinton	MA	C	978 368-8505	10080
Graphic Arts Repair	Braintree	MA	G	781 843-7954	9012
Lexington Press Inc	Lexington	MA	G	781 862-8900	12238
Lsc Communications Inc	North Chelmsford	MA	D	978 251-6000	13902
Red Sun Press Inc	Jamaica Plain	MA	F	617 524-6822	11949
Center Point Inc	Knox	ME	E	207 568-3717	6262
J Weston Walch Publisher	Portland	ME	E	207 772-2846	6676
Kensington Group Incorporated	Hampton Falls	NH	F	603 926-6742	18283
Mass Web Printing Company Inc	Providence	RI	D	508 832-5317	21062

2741 Misc Publishing

	CITY	ST	EMP	PHONE	ENTRY #
American Trade Fairs Org	Westport	CT	G	203 221-0114	5182
Arcat Inc	Fairfield	CT	G	203 929-9444	1414
Audubon Copy Shppe of Firfield	Bridgeport	CT	G	203 259-4311	378
Bay Tact Corporation	Woodstock Valley	CT	E	860 315-7372	5503
Beardsley Publishing Corp	Woodbury	CT	G	203 263-0888	5483
Bertram Sirkin	West Hartford	CT	G	860 656-7446	5055
Betx LLC	New Hartford	CT	G	860 459-1681	2632
Bff Holdings Inc **(HQ)**	Old Saybrook	CT	C	860 510-0100	3328
Broadcastmed Inc	Farmington	CT	E	860 953-2900	1470
Burns Walton	Branford	CT	G	203 422-5222	300
Business Journals Inc **(PA)**	Norwalk	CT	D	203 853-6015	3117
Campus Yellow Pages LLC	West Hartford	CT	G	860 523-9909	5057
Chicken Soup For Soul LLC	Cos Cob	CT	E	203 861-4000	823
Chicken Soup For Soul Entrmt I **(HQ)**	Cos Cob	CT	G	855 398-0443	824
Chief Executive Group LLC **(PA)**	Stamford	CT	F	785 832-0303	4164
Childrens Health Market Inc	Wilton	CT	G	203 762-2938	5283
Connectcut Hspnic Yellow Pages	Hartford	CT	F	860 560-8713	1815
Connelly 3 Pubg Group Inc	Clinton	CT	G	860 664-4988	782
Custom Publishing Design Group	Rocky Hill	CT	F	860 513-1213	3706
Debrasong Publishing LLC	Lyme	CT	G	413 204-4682	1954
Executive Greetings Inc **(HQ)**	New Hartford	CT	B	860 379-9911	2636
Freedom Press	Pawcatuck	CT	G	860 599-5390	3435
Gcn Publishing Inc	Norwalk	CT	F	203 665-6211	3158
Harbor Publications Inc	Madison	CT	G	203 245-8009	1962
Hearst Corporation	New Canaan	CT	E	203 438-6544	2600
Hersam Publishing Company	New Canaan	CT	B	203 966-9541	2601
Historical Art Prints	Southbury	CT	G	203 262-6680	4027
Hollow Frost Publishers	Woodstock	CT	G	860 974-2081	5497
Insight Media LLC	Norwalk	CT	G	203 831-8464	3174
Life Study Fllwship Foundation	Darien	CT	E	203 655-1436	1028
Liturgical Publications Inc	New Canaan	CT	F	203 966-6470	2603
Media Ventures Inc	Norwalk	CT	E	203 852-6570	3194
Militarylife Publishing LLC	Shelton	CT	G	203 402-7234	3834
Mr Boltons Music Inc	Westport	CT	G	646 578-8081	5217
Nancy Larson Publishers Inc	Old Lyme	CT	E	860 434-0800	3325
National Shooting Sports Found	Newtown	CT	E	203 426-1320	2929
Nelson & Miller Associates	Stamford	CT	G	203 356-9694	4253
Newsbank Inc	New Canaan	CT	G	203 966-1100	2611
Penny Publications LLC	Milford	CT	E	203 866-6688	2333
Pixels 2 Press LLC	Norwalk	CT	G	203 642-3740	3221
Portfolio Arts Group Ltd	Norwalk	CT	F	203 661-2400	3222
Publishing Dimensions LLC	Weston	CT	G	203 856-7716	5173
Publishing Directions LLC	Avon	CT	G	860 673-7650	42
Qmdi Press	North Franklin	CT	G	860 642-8074	2991
R G L Inc	East Granby	CT	E	860 653-7254	1142
Rand Media Co LLC	Westport	CT	G	203 226-8727	5225
Rare Reminder Incorporated	Rocky Hill	CT	E	860 563-9386	3728
Relocation Information Svc Inc	Norwalk	CT	E	203 855-1234	3229
Sandvik Pubg Interactive Inc **(PA)**	Danbury	CT	F	203 205-0188	981
Senior Network Inc	Stamford	CT	E	203 969-2700	4314
Shiller and Company Inc	Wilton	CT	D	203 210-5208	5303
Shop Smart Central Inc	Newtown	CT	G	914 962-3871	2936
Shoppers-Turnpike Corporation	Putnam	CT	F	860 928-3040	3632
Stamford Capital Group Inc **(PA)**	Stamford	CT	A	800 977-7837	4329
Stamler Publishing Company	Branford	CT	G	203 488-9808	351
Step Saver Inc	Southington	CT	E	860 621-6751	4082
Tam Communications Inc	Norwalk	CT	E	203 425-8777	3254
Teed Off Publishing Inc	Greenwich	CT	G	561 266-0872	1654
The Merrill Anderson Co Inc	Stratford	CT	F	203 377-4996	4453
Thomson Reuters Corporation	East Haven	CT	F	203 466-5055	1265
Times Publishing LLC	Middlefield	CT	G	860 349-8532	2167
Topaz Enterprise Sand Pubg	Norwalk	CT	G	203 449-1903	3259
Ubm LLC	Darien	CT	G	203 662-6501	1035
Universe Publishing Co LLC	Milford	CT	G	203 283-5201	2378
University Hlth Pubg Group LLC	Bethel	CT	G	203 791-0101	187
US Games Systems Inc	Stamford	CT	E	203 353-8400	4353
Valley Press Inc	Simsbury	CT	E	860 651-4700	3914
Wizard Too LLC	Westport	CT	G	203 984-7180	5238
Ziga Media LLC	Darien	CT	G	203 656-0076	1037
A Bismark Company	Fall River	MA	G	508 675-2002	10648
Accounting Web	Woburn	MA	D	978 331-1243	17106
Ad-A-Day Company Inc	Taunton	MA	E	508 824-8676	15719

	CITY	ST	EMP	PHONE	ENTRY #
Advisor Perspectives Inc	Woburn	MA	D	781 376-0050	17113
All Set Press LLC	Malden	MA	G	781 397-1993	12557
American Journal Trnsp	Plymouth	MA	G	508 927-4183	14542
Anthroposophic Press Inc	Great Barrington	MA	F	212 414-2275	11232
Artquick Corp	Wayland	MA	G	508 358-4864	16333
Assoction For Grvstone Studies	Greenfield	MA	F	413 772-0836	11251
Atlantic Printing Co Inc	Medfield	MA	F	781 449-2700	12909
Axon Communications Inc	Braintree	MA	G	781 849-6700	8988
B V T V Inc	Marstons Mills	MA	G	508 737-7754	12871
Bergquist Family Entps Inc	Needham Heights	MA	G	781 449-9196	13318
Bigfoot Seo Strategies	Marblehead	MA	G	617 448-4848	12676
Black Ice Publishers	Southborough	MA	G	508 481-0910	15347
Boston Sports Journal LLC	Medway	MA	G	617 306-0166	12957
Boxcar Media LLC	North Adams	MA	E	413 663-3384	13670
Broude International Editions	Williamstown	MA	G	413 458-8131	16956
Brown Publishing Network Inc **(PA)**	Charlestown	MA	E	781 547-7600	9828
Buzzafricocom	Lynn	MA	G	617 903-0152	12494
Caldwell Cmmnications Advisors	Boston	MA	G	617 425-7318	8455
Cambridge Brickhouse Inc	Lawrence	MA	G	978 725-8001	12001
Charlesbridge Publishing Inc **(PA)**	Watertown	MA	E	617 926-0329	16276
Circadian Information	Stoneham	MA	F	781 439-6326	15557
Clearesult Consulting Inc	Westborough	MA	G	508 836-9500	16603
Communication Ink Inc	Peabody	MA	F	978 977-4595	14324
Corporate Press	Norwood	MA	F	781 769-6656	14146
Crain Communications Inc	Boston	MA	G	617 357-9090	8486
Creative Success Alliance Corp	Rockland	MA	E	781 878-7114	14796
Crimson Press	Stoneham	MA	G	781 914-3111	15558
Crossed Genres	Framingham	MA	G	617 335-2101	10937
Culver Company LLC	Salisbury	MA	F	978 463-1700	14949
Curriculum Associates LLC **(PA)**	North Billerica	MA	B	978 667-8000	13805
D B S Industries Inc	Haverhill	MA	D	978 373-4748	11421
Daily Juice Press LLC	Cohasset	MA	G	781 261-6099	10097
Datanyze Inc **(DH)**	Waltham	MA	E	415 237-3434	16080
Destrail	Cambridge	MA	G	818 687-7037	9453
Diacritech Inc	Boston	MA	F	617 236-7500	8502
Driggin Sandra DBA Extra Extra	Quincy	MA	E	617 773-6996	14620
E H Publishing Inc **(PA)**	Framingham	MA	E	508 663-1500	10943
Early American Industries Assn	South Dartmouth	MA	G	508 439-2215	15239
Eastern Woods Music Publishing	Sandwich	MA	G	508 238-3270	14967
Ebsco Publishing Inc **(HQ)**	Ipswich	MA	A	978 356-6500	11917
Edgewater Marine Inds LLC	New Bedford	MA	E	508 992-6555	13383
Eglean Inc	Boston	MA	G	617 229-5863	8520
Electronic Publishing Services	Charlestown	MA	G	508 544-1254	9833
Elsevier Inc	Cambridge	MA	D	781 663-5200	9464
Envie Company Inc	Stoughton	MA	G	866 700-6410	15588
Fluent Technologies Inc	Woburn	MA	F	781 939-0900	17183
Fourth Street Press Inc	Beverly	MA	G	978 232-9251	8133
Frg Publications	West Springfield	MA	F	413 734-3411	16522
Gatco Inc	Hyannis	MA	F	508 815-4910	11842
Gatehouse Media LLC	Fall River	MA	C	508 676-8211	10701
Gems Publishing Usa Inc	Framingham	MA	G	508 872-0066	10949
George Publishing Company	Pembroke	MA	G	781 826-4996	14406
Global Enterprises Inc	Attleboro	MA	G	508 399-8270	7742
Global Prints Inc	Hyde Park	MA	G	800 578-4278	11868
Good Tern Press Inc	Boston	MA	G	508 277-5500	8573
Greatheart Inc	Andover	MA	G	978 475-8732	7553
Groupglobalnet Corp	Boston	MA	G	857 212-4012	8583
Gtxcel Inc	Southborough	MA	F	508 804-3092	15358
Guiding Channels Co	Worcester	MA	G	508 853-0781	17387
Harvard Bus Schl Pubg Corp **(HQ)**	Brighton	MA	C	617 783-7400	9100
Hmh Supplemental Publishers	Boston	MA	G	407 345-2000	8600
Ian Marie Inc	Newburyport	MA	E	978 463-6742	13499
Idg Paper Services	Framingham	MA	E	508 875-5000	10968
Image Software Services Inc	Shirley	MA	E	978 425-3600	15087
Image Source International Inc	Pocasset	MA	E	508 801-9252	14599
Information Gatekeepers Inc	Winchester	MA	G	617 782-5033	17088
Ink Inc Publishing Service	Cambridge	MA	G	617 576-6740	9516
Innovative Publishing Co LLC	Edgartown	MA	F	267 266-8876	10585
Interntonal Science Foundation	Somerville	MA	G	703 869-1853	15185
Jf Griffin Publishing LLC	Williamstown	MA	G	413 458-4800	16957
Kidpub Press LLC	North Attleboro	MA	G	617 407-2337	13761
Lab Publications LLC	Swampscott	MA	G	781 598-9779	15698
Larson Worldwide Inc	Norwell	MA	G	781 659-2115	14105
Laurin Publishing Co Inc **(PA)**	Pittsfield	MA	D	413 499-0514	14482
Legacy Publishing Group Inc	Clinton	MA	E	800 322-3866	10083
Lets Go Inc	Cambridge	MA	A	617 495-9659	9534
Liberty Publishing Inc	Beverly	MA	E	978 777-8200	8148
Lighthouse Publications **(PA)**	Hyannis	MA	G	508 534-9291	11845
LPI Printing and Graphic Inc	Stoneham	MA	E	781 438-5400	15566
Massachusetts Institute Tech	Cambridge	MA	E	617 253-1541	9545
Massinvestor Incorporated	Arlington	MA	G	617 620-4606	7629
Mbo Advertising Services	Marshfield	MA	G	781 837-5897	12863
Medical Arts Press Inc	Framingham	MA	G	508 253-5000	10982
Megatech Corporation	Tewksbury	MA	F	978 937-9600	15822
Meno Publishing Inc	Needham Heights	MA	G	781 209-2665	13336
Mercury Learning and Info LLC	Duxbury	MA	G	781 934-0500	10400
Merriam-Webster Incorporated **(DH)**	Springfield	MA	C	413 734-3134	15489
Microtraining Assoc Inc	Hanover	MA	G	781 982-8984	11347
Mom Central	Chestnut Hill	MA	G	617 332-6819	9988
MSP Digital Marketing	Allston	MA	G	617 868-5778	7471
Mundos Crazy Music Pubg Corp	Stoneham	MA	G	781 438-1704	15568
Myjove Corporation	Cambridge	MA	D	617 945-9051	9572
Mystockplancom Inc	Brookline	MA	F	617 734-1979	9211
Norris Enterprises Inc	Hanover	MA	G	781 982-8158	11349
Northeastern Publishing Co	Holliston	MA	G	508 429-5588	11591
Nrt Inc	Medway	MA	F	508 533-4588	12968
O E M Health Information Inc	Beverly	MA	G	978 921-7300	8161
OBrien Publications Inc	Cohasset	MA	G	781 378-2126	10101
Online Moderation Inc	Dover	MA	G	617 686-7737	10352
OReilly Media Inc	Boston	MA	C	617 354-5800	8758
P Straker Ltd	South Dartmouth	MA	G	508 996-4804	15241
Patricia Seybold Group Inc	Brighton	MA	F	617 742-5200	9103
Pearson Education Inc	Boston	MA	E	617 848-6000	8770
Performer Publications Inc	Somerville	MA	G	617 627-9200	15204
Porter Sargent Publishers Inc	Westford	MA	G	617 922-0076	16785
Preferred Publications Inc	Wilmington	MA	G	978 697-4180	17039
President Fllows Hrvard Cllege	Cambridge	MA	D	617 495-9897	9616
Press Ganey	Lexington	MA	G	800 232-8032	12254
Press-It LLC	Woburn	MA	G	781 935-0035	17269
PRI Financial Publishing	Holliston	MA	G	508 429-5949	11597
Promax Supply LLC	Melrose	MA	F	781 620-1602	12990
Pure Cold Press	Brookline	MA	G	617 487-8948	9216
Quality Solutions Inc **(PA)**	Newburyport	MA	E	978 465-7755	13525
Quayside Publishing Group	Beverly	MA	G	978 282-9590	8167
Quinlan Publishing Co Inc **(PA)**	Boston	MA	G	617 439-0076	8805
Racemaker Press	Boston	MA	G	617 391-0911	8807
Real Data Corp	Boston	MA	G	603 669-3822	8812
Relx Inc	Cambridge	MA	D	781 663-5200	9629
Reminder Publications	East Longmeadow	MA	E	413 525-3947	10491
Rheinwerk Publishing Inc	Quincy	MA	F	781 228-5070	14654
Rockport Custom Publishing LLC	Beverly	MA	G	978 522-4316	8172
Roundtown Inc	Cambridge	MA	G	415 425-6891	9639
Russell Group	Arlington	MA	G	781 648-0302	7636
S & S Publications Inc	Hull	MA	G	781 925-9266	11830
Safari Books Online LLC	Boston	MA	G	617 426-8600	8831
Sandcastle Publishing LLC	South Dennis	MA	G	508 398-3100	15266
Santorella Publication Ltd **(PA)**	Danvers	MA	G	978 750-0566	10254
Sap Professional Journal **(PA)**	Dedham	MA	D	781 407-0360	10297
Scarlet Ltr Press Gallery LLC	Salem	MA	G	978 741-1850	14942
Scholastic Corporation	Allston	MA	G	617 924-3846	7475
School Specialty Inc	Cambridge	MA	D	617 547-6706	9647
Simply Media Inc	Lincoln	MA	E	781 259-8029	12289
Singing River Publications	Brighton	MA	G	218 365-3498	9106
Sky Publishing Corporation	Cambridge	MA	E	617 864-7360	9652
Smaall Beer Press	Easthampton	MA	G	413 203-1636	10579
Smpretty Inc	Wayland	MA	G	508 358-1639	16336
Southern Berkshire Shoppers Gu	Great Barrington	MA	F	413 528-0095	11246
Spectrum Press Inc	Canton	MA	G	781 828-5050	9786
Spidle Corp	Waltham	MA	G	617 448-7386	16199
SRC Publishing Inc	Auburn	MA	G	508 749-3212	7850
Steves Publication Svc	Webster	MA	G	508 671-9192	16351
Supermedia LLC	Braintree	MA	B	781 849-7670	9040
TCI America Inc	Seekonk	MA	E	508 336-6633	15039
Then & Now Publishing	Scituate	MA	F	781 378-2013	15016
Thryv Inc	Waltham	MA	E	972 453-7000	16215
Trustees of Boston College	Chestnut Hill	MA	F	617 552-2844	9993
Turley Publications Inc	Feeding Hills	MA	F	413 786-7747	10804
Turley Publications Inc **(PA)**	Palmer	MA	C	800 824-6548	14298
University Massachusetts Inc	Amherst	MA	F	413 545-2217	7528
University of Massachusetts	Amherst	MA	D	413 545-3500	7530
Vegan Publishers LLC	Danvers	MA	G	857 364-4344	10271
Veritas Medicine Inc	Cambridge	MA	F	617 234-1500	9695
Visitor Guide Publishing Inc	Newton	MA	G	617 542-5283	13650
Web Closeout	Springfield	MA	E	413 222-8302	15524
Westwood Press	Framingham	MA	E	781 433-8354	11015
White Knight Studio	Grafton	MA	G	781 799-0569	11226
Wiscasset Music Publishing Co	Cambridge	MA	G	617 492-5720	9702
World Publications Inc	North Dighton	MA	G	508 880-5555	13938
Xos Technologies Inc **(HQ)**	Wilmington	MA	E	978 447-5220	17070
Zlink Inc	Maynard	MA	G	978 309-3628	12907
Zoom Information LLC **(HQ)**	Waltham	MA	D	781 693-7500	16227
A & D Print Shop	Presque Isle	ME	G	207 764-2662	6751
Allagash Guide Inc	Norridgewock	ME	G	207 634-3748	6494
Almanac Publishing Co	Lewiston	ME	G	207 755-2000	6274
Bolinda Publishing Inc	Jackson	ME	G	207 722-3185	6218
Center Point Inc	Knox	ME	E	207 568-3717	6262
Central Street Corporation	Bangor	ME	F	207 947-8049	5635
Darby Pop LLC	Cape Elizabeth	ME	G	207 799-4202	5875
Direct Display Publishing Inc	Bath	ME	G	207 443-4800	5676
Downeast Networking Services	Portland	ME	G	772 485-4304	6653
Dramatic Dffrence Publications	Farmington	ME	G	207 778-9696	6044
Eat Drink Lucky	Cape Elizabeth	ME	G	207 450-9060	5876
Eztousecom Directories	Bangor	ME	G	207 974-3171	5643
Garmin International Inc	Yarmouth	ME	C	800 561-5105	7294

	CITY	ST	EMP	PHONE	ENTRY #
Macleay Interactive Design Inc	Rome	ME	G	207 495-2208	6828
Maine Authors Publishing	Thomaston	ME	G	207 594-0090	7087
National Poetry Foundation	Orono	ME	G	207 581-3814	6556
Noah Publications	Brooklin	ME	G	207 359-2131	5821
Original Irregular	Kingfield	ME	G	207 265-2773	6254
S3 Digital Publishing Inc	Lisbon Falls	ME	G	207 351-8006	6372
Scorebuilders	Scarborough	ME	G	207 885-0304	6939
Sellers Publishing Inc	South Portland	ME	E	207 772-6833	7040
SMA Inc	Yarmouth	ME	F	207 846-4112	7300
Soyatech Inc	Bar Harbor	ME	G	207 288-4969	5670
Supermedia LLC	South Portland	ME	B	207 828-6100	7041
Taylor Bryson Inc	Saco	ME	G	207 838-0961	6859
Town of Gorham **(PA)**	Gorham	ME	E	207 222-1610	6132
Town of Gorham	Gorham	ME	G	207 839-5555	6133
Valentine & Company Inc	Westbrook	ME	G	207 774-4769	7212
Writing Company	Portland	ME	G	207 370-8078	6746
Backporch Publishing	Keene	NH	G	603 357-8761	18494
Battle Road Press	Peterborough	NH	G	603 924-7600	19467
Bauhan Publishing	Peterborough	NH	G	603 567-4430	19468
Carlisle Publications	Manchester	NH	G	603 622-4056	18796
Carus Publishing	Peterborough	NH	G	603 924-7209	19466
Clark Publishing	Portsmouth	NH	G	603 431-1238	19553
Connectcut Rver Vly Yllow Pges	Lebanon	NH	G	603 727-4700	18619
Connell Communications Inc	Keene	NH	E	603 924-7271	18496
Constrction Summary of NH Main	Manchester	NH	G	603 627-8856	18804
Doolittles Print Serve Inc	Claremont	NH	G	603 543-0700	17848
Fishing Hot Spots Inc	Nashua	NH	G	715 365-5555	19158
Hawthorn Creative Group LLC	Portsmouth	NH	E	603 610-0533	19574
Helmers Publishing Inc	Dublin	NH	E	603 563-1631	18068
Kennedy Information LLC	Keene	NH	E	603 357-8100	18512
Kensington Group Incorporated	Hampton Falls	NH	F	603 926-6742	18283
Lbry Inc	Manchester	NH	G	267 210-4292	18863
Leopard Snow Publishing LLC	Dover	NH	G	603 742-7714	18034
Live Wire Marketing Corp	Manchester	NH	G	603 969-8771	18865
Mac Observer Inc	Durham	NH	G	603 868-2030	18077
Nutfield Publishing LLC	Londonderry	NH	G	603 537-2760	18730
Ocean Publishing	Rye	NH	G	603 812-5557	19700
Our Town Publishing Inc	Center Barnstead	NH	G	603 776-2500	17790
Paramount Publishing Inc/	Bedford	NH	G	603 472-3528	17659
Proffe Publishing	Wilton	NH	G	603 654-1070	19984
Sign Express LLC	Manchester	NH	G	603 606-1279	18922
Sophia Institute	Manchester	NH	G	603 641-9344	18926
Square Spot Publishing LLC	Manchester	NH	G	603 625-6003	18929
Stamp News Publishing Inc	Merrimack	NH	G	603 424-7556	19034
Starcrafts Publishing LLC	Epping	NH	G	603 734-5303	18103
Steerforth Press LLC	Hanover	NH	G	603 643-4787	18298
Textnology Corp	Nashua	NH	F	603 465-8398	19273
Tmax Publishing LLC	Salem	NH	G	603 505-7693	19772
Top Kayaker Geo Odyssey Llc	Center Ossipee	NH	G	603 651-1036	17806
Virtual Publishing LLC	Manchester	NH	F	603 627-9500	18952
Ymaa Publication Center Inc	Wolfeboro	NH	G	603 569-7988	20027
Alert Solutions Inc	Cranston	RI	F	401 427-2100	20174
B E Publishing	North Kingstown	RI	G	401 294-2490	20692
Care New England Health System	Warwick	RI	G	401 739-9255	21341
Cars Realty LLC	Johnston	RI	G	401 231-1389	20502
Chew Publishing Inc	Middletown	RI	G	401 808-0648	20617
CM Publications Inc	Westerly	RI	G	401 596-9358	21519
Copy Print Company	Cranston	RI	G	401 228-3900	20201
Custom Flow Solutions LLC	Providence	RI	G	401 487-2957	20991
DManielly Express	Providence	RI	G	401 490-2900	20997
Educational Directions Inc	Portsmouth	RI	G	401 683-3523	20922
Elegant Publishing Inc	Riverside	RI	G	401 245-9726	21167
Gaspee Publishing	Providence	RI	G	401 272-3668	21020
Guia Commercial Portugues Inc	East Providence	RI	G	401 438-1740	20417
Map of Month	Providence	RI	G	401 274-4288	21059
Rhode Island Publications Soc	Providence	RI	G	401 273-1787	21114
Stevens Publishing Inc	Coventry	RI	F	401 821-2216	20165
Supermedia LLC	Warwick	RI	E	401 468-1500	21432
Tizra	Providence	RI	G	401 935-5317	21138
Art Licensing Intl Inc	Arlington	VT	F	802 362-3662	21595
Business Financial Pubg LLC	Williston	VT	F	802 865-9886	22658
Discovery Map Intl Inc	Waitsfield	VT	G	802 316-4060	22564
Equinox Publishing	Shelburne	VT	G	802 497-0276	22416
Fuel On Line Corp	Burlington	VT	E	888 475-2552	21784
Garlic Press Inc	Williston	VT	F	802 864-0670	22667
Garlic Press Inc	Williston	VT	G	802 864-0670	22668
Russian Information Services	Montpelier	VT	G	802 223-4955	22160
Stadion Publishing Co Inc	Island Pond	VT	G	802 723-6175	22041
Telegraph Publishing LLC	Chester	VT	G	802 875-2703	21851
Tool Factory Inc	Arlington	VT	G	802 375-6549	21601
Vermont Publishing Comany	Saint Albans	VT	E	802 524-9771	22384
When Words Count Press LLC	Rochester	VT	F	802 767-4372	22321
Wild Apple Graphics Ltd	Woodstock	VT	E	802 457-3003	22741
Williston Pubg Promotions LLC	Williston	VT	F	802 872-9000	22699
Works In Progress Inc **(PA)**	South Burlington	VT	F	802 658-3797	22479

2752 Commercial Printing: Lithographic

	CITY	ST	EMP	PHONE	ENTRY #
A B C Printing Inc	East Haven	CT	F	203 468-1245	1241
Abbott Printing Company Inc	Hamden	CT	G	203 562-5562	1729
Academy Printing Service	Kensington	CT	G	860 828-5549	1916
Acme Press Inc	Milford	CT	G	203 334-8221	2235
Adkins Printing Company	New Britain	CT	E	800 228-9745	2506
Alliance Graphics Inc	Newington	CT	F	860 666-7992	2840
Allied Printing Services Inc **(PA)**	Manchester	CT	B	860 643-1101	1984
AlphaGraphics LLC	Hamden	CT	G	203 230-0018	1731
American Banknote Corporation **(PA)**	Stamford	CT	G	203 941-4090	4135
American-Republican Inc **(PA)**	Waterbury	CT	D	203 574-3636	4842
Amgraph Packaging Inc	Baltic	CT	C	860 822-2000	48
Ampco Publishing & Prtg Corp	Stamford	CT	G	203 325-1509	4137
Anderson Publishing LLC	Southington	CT	G	860 621-2192	4038
Appels Printing & Mailing Bur	Hartford	CT	F	860 522-8189	1806
Arcat Inc	Fairfield	CT	G	203 929-9444	1414
Arch Parent Inc	Willimantic	CT	G	860 336-4856	5261
Audubon Copy Shppe of Firfield	Bridgeport	CT	G	203 259-4311	378
Barile Printers LLC	New Britain	CT	G	860 224-0127	2513
BCT Reporting LLC	Plainville	CT	G	860 302-1876	3469
Bethel Printing & Graphics	Bethel	CT	G	203 748-7034	131
Bizcard Xpress LLC	Higganum	CT	G	860 324-6840	1901
Brescias Printing Services Inc	East Hartford	CT	G	860 528-4254	1177
Brian Berlepsch	North Branford	CT	G	203 484-9799	2959
Briarwood Printing Company Inc	Plainville	CT	F	860 747-6805	3470
Brody Printing Company Inc	Bridgeport	CT	F	203 384-9313	391
Business Cards Tomorrow Inc	Naugatuck	CT	G	203 723-5858	2464
Byrne Group Inc	Waterbury	CT	G	203 573-0100	4852
Cadmus	Stamford	CT	G	203 595-3000	4154
Cannelli Printing Co Inc	West Haven	CT	G	203 932-1719	5110
Capitol Printing Co Inc	Hartford	CT	G	860 522-1547	1810
Chase Graphics Inc	Putnam	CT	F	860 315-9006	3605
Child Evngelism Fellowship Inc	Wolcott	CT	E	203 879-2154	5434
Clanol Systems Inc	Old Greenwich	CT	G	203 637-9909	3306
Colonial Printers of Windsor	Windsor Locks	CT	G	860 627-5433	5389
Copy Stop Inc	Hamden	CT	G	203 288-6401	1738
Craftsmen Printing Group Inc	Stamford	CT	G	203 327-2817	4175
Cricket Press Inc	West Hartford	CT	G	860 521-9279	5063
Custom Printing & Copy Inc **(PA)**	Enfield	CT	F	860 290-6890	1354
Data Management Incorporated	Unionville	CT	E	860 677-8586	4655
Data-Graphics Inc	Newington	CT	D	860 667-0435	2859
Derosa Printing Company Inc	Manchester	CT	F	860 646-1698	2000
Design Idea Printing	Ellington	CT	G	860 896-0103	1332
Docuprint & Imaging Inc	New Haven	CT	G	203 776-6000	2682
E R Hitchcock Company	New Britain	CT	E	860 229-2024	2529
East Coast Packaging LLC **(PA)**	Farmington	CT	G	860 675-8500	1479
East Longmeadow Business Svcs	Enfield	CT	G	413 525-6111	1355
Easy Graphics Inc	Greenwich	CT	G	203 622-0001	1609
Eccles-Lehman Inc	Easton	CT	G	203 268-0605	1318
Economy Printing & Copy Center **(PA)**	Danbury	CT	G	203 792-5610	906
Economy Printing & Copy Center	Ridgefield	CT	G	203 438-7401	3666
Ellington Printery Inc	Ellington	CT	G	860 875-3310	1334
Elm Press Incorporated	Terryville	CT	E	860 583-3600	4477
Empire Printing Systems LLC	Glastonbury	CT	G	860 633-3333	1549
Executive Office Services Inc	Bridgeport	CT	E	203 373-1333	411
Executive Press Inc	Plainville	CT	G	860 793-0060	3487
Executive Printing Darien LLC	Darien	CT	G	203 655-4691	1023
Falcon Press	Enfield	CT	G	860 763-2293	1362
Financial Prtg Solutions LLC	Preston	CT	G	860 886-9931	3580
Fine Print New England Inc	Newington	CT	G	860 953-0660	2863
Flow Resources Inc **(HQ)**	Newington	CT	E	860 666-1200	2864
Franklin Print Shoppe Inc	Torrington	CT	G	860 496-9516	4578
FSNB Enterprises Inc	Monroe	CT	G	203 254-1947	2403
Fulcrum Promotions & Printing	Bridgeport	CT	G	203 909-6362	417
G & R Enterprises Incorporated	Hartford	CT	G	860 549-6120	1822
Garrett Printing & Graphics	Bristol	CT	G	860 589-6710	567
Gateway Digital Inc	Norwalk	CT	F	203 853-4929	3157
Ghp Media Inc **(PA)**	West Haven	CT	C	203 479-7500	5124
Goodcopy Printing Center Inc	New Haven	CT	E	203 624-0194	2691
Goulet Enterprises Inc	Pleasant Valley	CT	F	860 379-0793	3546
Graphic Image Inc	Milford	CT	E	203 877-8787	2293
Gulemo Inc	Willimantic	CT	G	860 456-1151	5265
Hamden Press Inc	Hamden	CT	G	203 624-0554	1756
Hartford Business Supply Inc	Hartford	CT	E	860 233-2138	1830
Harty Press Inc	New Haven	CT	D	203 562-5112	2695
Hat Trick Graphics LLC	Danbury	CT	G	203 748-1128	930
Herff Jones LLC	Bethlehem	CT	G	203 266-7170	196
High Ridge Copy Inc	Stamford	CT	F	203 329-1889	4216
Holly Press Inc	Norwalk	CT	G	203 846-1720	3170
Ideal Printing Co Inc	New Haven	CT	G	203 777-7626	2698
Image Ink Inc	Newington	CT	G	860 665-9792	2871
Imperial Grphic Cmmnctions Inc	Milford	CT	E	203 650-3478	2301
Impression Point Inc	Stamford	CT	F	203 353-8800	4221
Inform Inc	Shelton	CT	G	203 924-9929	3818
Integrity Graphics Inc	Simsbury	CT	D	800 343-1248	3906
J & T Printing LLC	Wethersfield	CT	G	860 529-4628	5250
Jerrys Printing & Graphics LLC	Bridgeport	CT	G	203 384-0015	435

S I C

	CITY	ST	EMP	PHONE	ENTRY #
JMS Graphics Inc	Middlebury	CT	G	203 598-7555	2155
Joseph Merritt & Company Inc	Danbury	CT	G	203 743-6734	940
JS McCarthy Co Inc	Stamford	CT	E	203 355-7600	4233
Jupiter Communications LLC	West Haven	CT	F	475 238-7082	5127
Kool Ink LLC	Bloomfield	CT	F	860 242-0303	238
Kramer Printing Company Inc	West Haven	CT	F	203 933-5416	5129
L P Macadams Company Inc	Bridgeport	CT	D	203 366-3647	442
Liberty Screen Print Co LLC	Beacon Falls	CT	F	203 632-5449	60
Lighthouse Printing LLC	Old Saybrook	CT	G	860 388-2677	3343
Lithographics Inc	Farmington	CT	D	860 678-1660	1491
Macdermid Incorporated **(HQ)**	Waterbury	CT	C	203 575-5700	4900
Magnani Press Incorporated	Hartford	CT	G	860 236-2802	1841
Maple Print Services Inc	Jewett City	CT	G	860 381-5470	1915
Marketing Sltons Unlimited LLC	West Hartford	CT	E	860 523-0670	5085
Massachusetts Envelope Co Inc	Hartford	CT	E	860 727-9100	1845
Master Engrv & Printery Inc **(PA)**	Waterbury	CT	G	203 723-2779	4911
Material Promotions Inc	Waterbury	CT	G	203 757-8900	4912
Matthews Printing Co	Wallingford	CT	F	203 265-0363	4770
Max Productions LLC	Norwalk	CT	G	203 838-2795	3191
Melega Inc	Stamford	CT	G	203 961-8703	4249
Middletown Printing Co Inc	Middletown	CT	F	860 347-5700	2206
Minute Man Press	Hamden	CT	G	203 891-6251	1772
Minuteman Press	Wethersfield	CT	G	860 529-4628	5258
Minuteman Press of Bristol	Bristol	CT	G	860 589-1100	582
Minuteman Press of Danbury	Danbury	CT	G	203 743-6755	955
Muir Envelope Plus Inc	Newington	CT	F	860 953-6847	2884
Napp Printing Plate Dist Inc	Waterbury	CT	G	203 575-5727	4921
Naugatuck Vly Photo Engrv Inc	Waterbury	CT	G	203 756-7345	4924
New Fairfield Press Inc	New Fairfield	CT	F	203 746-2700	2626
New Haven Register LLC	New Haven	CT	A	203 789-5200	2716
New London Printing Co LLC	New London	CT	G	860 701-9171	2775
Oddo Print Shop Inc	Torrington	CT	G	860 489-6585	4590
One Source Print and Promo LLC	Cromwell	CT	G	860 635-3257	857
Optamark CT LLC	Stamford	CT	G	203 325-1180	4270
P & M Investments LLC	Enfield	CT	G	860 745-3600	1373
P & S Printing LLC	Stamford	CT	G	203 327-9818	4275
P C I Group	Stamford	CT	F	203 327-0410	4276
Paladin Commercial Prtrs LLC	Newington	CT	E	860 953-4900	2890
Palmisano Printing LLC	Bristol	CT	G	860 582-6883	590
Paul Dewitt	Danbury	CT	F	203 792-5610	965
Paw Print Pantry LLC **(PA)**	East Lyme	CT	G	860 447-8442	1271
Paw Print Pantry LLC	Niantic	CT	G	860 447-8442	2956
Phoenix Press Inc	New Haven	CT	E	203 865-5555	2726
Pinpoint Promotions & Prtg LLC	West Haven	CT	F	203 301-4273	5141
Play-It Productions Inc	Colchester	CT	F	212 695-6530	805
Prentis Printing Solutions Inc	Meriden	CT	G	203 634-1266	2117
Print House LLC	Glastonbury	CT	G	860 652-0803	1573
Print Master LLC	Torrington	CT	G	860 482-8152	4593
Print Shop of Wolcott LLC	Wolcott	CT	G	203 879-3353	5453
Professional Graphics Inc	Norwalk	CT	F	203 846-4291	3225
Pronto Printer of Newington	Newington	CT	G	860 666-2245	2895
Prospect Printing LLC	Prospect	CT	F	203 758-6007	3594
Prosperous Printing LLC	Wilton	CT	G	203 834-1962	5300
Protopac Inc	Watertown	CT	G	860 274-6796	5020
Pyne-Davidson Company	Hartford	CT	E	860 522-9106	1862
Qg Printing II Corp	Enfield	CT	A	860 741-0150	1378
Quad/Graphics Inc	North Haven	CT	A	203 288-2468	3057
Quality Printers Inc	New London	CT	G	860 443-2800	2778
R R Donnelley & Sons Company	Manchester	CT	F	860 649-5570	2040
R R Donnelley & Sons Company	Avon	CT	E	860 773-6140	43
Rare Reminder Incorporated	Rocky Hill	CT	E	860 563-9386	3728
Ready4 Print LLC	Bridgeport	CT	G	203 345-0376	480
Record-Journal Newspaper **(PA)**	Meriden	CT	C	203 235-1661	2124
Rf Printing LLC	Wallingford	CT	G	203 265-9939	4797
Rm Printing	Plantsville	CT	G	860 621-0498	3538
Rmi Inc	Vernon Rockville	CT	C	860 875-3366	4681
Rollins Printing Incorporated	Hamden	CT	G	203 248-3200	1781
Ronald Bottino	Bristol	CT	G	860 585-9505	608
S and Z Graphics LLC	Milford	CT	G	203 783-9675	2358
Sabar Graphics LLC **(PA)**	East Haven	CT	G	203 467-3016	1260
Sazacks Inc	Manchester	CT	G	860 647-8367	2045
Screen Tek Printing Co Inc	Hamden	CT	G	203 248-6248	1782
Sir Speedy Printing	Middlebury	CT	E	203 346-0716	2158
Smoke & Print Universe	Bridgeport	CT	G	203 540-5151	493
Southbury Printing Centre Inc	Southbury	CT	G	203 264-0102	4033
Specialty Printing LLC	East Windsor	CT	F	860 654-1850	1302
Spectrum Press	Milford	CT	F	203 878-9090	2368
Speed Printing & Graphics Inc	Stamford	CT	G	203 324-4000	4328
Step Saver Inc	Southington	CT	E	860 621-6751	4082
Streamline Press	North Branford	CT	G	203 484-9799	2978
Streamline Press LLC	North Branford	CT	G	203 484-9799	2979
Success Printing & Mailing Inc	Norwalk	CT	F	203 847-1112	3252
System Intgrtion Cnsulting LLC	Shelton	CT	G	203 926-9599	3876
Team Destination Inc	Meriden	CT	G	203 235-6000	2138
Technique Printers Inc	Clinton	CT	G	860 669-2516	795
Thelemic Printshop	Plainfield	CT	G	860 383-4014	3458
Toto LLC	New Haven	CT	F	203 776-6000	2744
Transmonde USa Inc	North Branford	CT	D	203 484-1528	2982
Trumbull Printing Inc	Trumbull	CT	C	203 261-2548	4636
Turnstone Inc	Greenwich	CT	F	203 625-0000	1658
Typeisright	Moosup	CT	G	860 564-0537	2428
US Games Systems Inc	Stamford	CT	E	203 353-8400	4353
Value Print Incorporated	Wallingford	CT	F	203 265-1371	4826
Vernon Printing Co Inc	Vernon Rockville	CT	G	860 872-1826	4688
Westrock Commercial LLC	Stamford	CT	G	203 595-3130	4359
Wethersfield Offset Inc	Rocky Hill	CT	G	860 721-8236	3734
Wethersfield Printing Co Inc	Rocky Hill	CT	F	860 721-8236	3735
Wild Rver Cstm Screen Prtg LLC	Newtown	CT	G	203 426-1500	2948
Williams Printing Group LLC	North Windham	CT	G	860 423-8779	3085
Woodway Print Inc	Stamford	CT	G	203 323-6423	4361
Yankee Screen Printing	Derby	CT	G	203 924-9926	1085
Youngs Communications Inc	Middletown	CT	F	860 347-8567	2231
Ziga Media LLC	Darien	CT	G	203 656-0076	1037
AA Global Printing Inc	Newton	MA	G	617 527-7629	13552
Abby Printing Co Inc	Easthampton	MA	G	413 536-5269	10551
Accent Printing Inc	North Billerica	MA	G	781 487-9300	13788
Accucon Inc	Leominster	MA	G	978 840-0337	12106
Ad Print	Medway	MA	G	508 533-7411	12952
Adams Specialty & Printing Co	Adams	MA	G	413 743-9101	7409
Adg Printing Incorporated	North Billerica	MA	G	978 667-9285	13790
Adidas Printing Inc	Ipswich	MA	F	978 851-6337	11900
Advanced Print Solutions Inc **(PA)**	Sharon	MA	G	508 655-8434	15045
Advantage Media & Marketing	Framingham	MA	G	508 875-0011	10918
Aldam Press Inc	Pittsfield	MA	G	413 443-2800	14450
Alden Hauk Inc	Woburn	MA	F	781 281-0154	17115
Aleksandr S Yaskovich	Taunton	MA	G	508 822-7267	15722
Allegra Network LLC	Franklin	MA	G	508 528-5339	11021
Allegra Print & Imaging	Mansfield	MA	G	508 339-3555	12612
American Copy Print	Norwood	MA	G	781 769-9077	14128
American Prtg & Envelope Inc	Auburn	MA	E	508 832-6100	7825
Andrew T Johnson Company Inc **(PA)**	Boston	MA	E	617 742-1610	8366
Apb Enterprises Inc	Marlborough	MA	G	508 481-0966	12715
Apex Press Inc	Westborough	MA	F	508 366-1110	16589
Arch Parent Inc	West Springfield	MA	G	413 504-1433	16508
Arlington Swifty Printing Inc	Arlington	MA	G	781 646-8700	7623
Artco Offset Inc	Canton	MA	D	781 830-7900	9716
Artcraft Co Inc	North Attleboro	MA	D	508 695-4042	13746
Arvest Press Inc	Waltham	MA	G	781 894-4844	16038
Atlantic Printing Co Inc	Medfield	MA	F	781 449-2700	12909
Atlas Press Worcester Inc	West Boylston	MA	G	508 835-9440	16409
Aucoins Press Inc	Spencer	MA	G	508 885-0800	15425
Austin Print	Concord	MA	G	978 369-8591	10115
B N M Printing & Promotion	Boston	MA	G	617 464-1120	8387
Bassett & Cassidy Inc	Lowell	MA	G	978 452-9595	12350
Bassette Printers LLC	Belchertown	MA	D	413 781-7140	8022
Bateman & Slade Inc	Stoneham	MA	G	617 423-5556	15556
BBC Printing and Products Inc	Waltham	MA	G	781 647-4646	16042
BBCg LLC	Norwood	MA	G	617 796-8800	14137
Becks Printing Co	North Adams	MA	G	413 664-7411	13668
Belmont Printing Company	Belmont	MA	E	617 484-0833	8066
Bh Media Inc **(HQ)**	Braintree	MA	D	617 426-3000	8990
Biz Tek Printing and Mktg LLC	Ware	MA	G	508 248-3377	16230
Blake Press Inc	Boston	MA	G	617 742-8700	8412
Blanchard Press Inc	Winchester	MA	F	617 426-6690	17084
Bolton Printing Co	Bolton	MA	G	978 365-4844	8317
Bond Printing Company Inc	Hanover	MA	G	781 871-3990	11329
Boston Business Printing Inc	Boston	MA	F	617 482-7955	8427
Boston Ltigation Solutions LLC	Boston	MA	F	617 933-9780	8434
Boutwell Owens & Co Inc **(PA)**	Fitchburg	MA	C	978 343-3067	10813
Bradford & Bigelow Inc	Newburyport	MA	C	978 904-3112	13474
Brady Business Forms Inc	Lowell	MA	G	978 458-2585	12355
Braintree Printing Inc	Braintree	MA	E	781 848-5300	8992
Bridgewater Prtg Copy Ctr LLC	Bridgewater	MA	G	508 697-5227	9065
Brookline Print Center	Waltham	MA	G	617 926-0300	16052
Bruno Diduca	Waltham	MA	G	781 894-5300	16053
Budget Printing Concord LLC	Concord	MA	G	978 369-4630	10118
Business Cards Overnight Inc	Lawrence	MA	G	978 974-9271	11999
Cab Screen Printing	North Attleboro	MA	G	508 695-8421	13751
Calendar Press Inc	Peabody	MA	E	978 531-1860	14319
Cambridge Printing Co Inc	Cambridge	MA	G	617 547-0270	9427
Canalside Printing	Monument Beach	MA	G	508 759-4141	13214
Capeway Printing & Copy Center	Rockland	MA	G	781 878-1600	14795
Castle Complements Printing Co	Chelmsford	MA	G	978 250-9122	9886
Cdl Print Mail LLC	Gardner	MA	G	978 410-5148	11107
Central Printing & Supply	Haverhill	MA	G	781 322-1220	11415
Chaco Inc	Norwood	MA	G	781 769-5557	14141
Chisholm and Hunt Printers Inc	Gloucester	MA	G	978 283-0318	11173
Choice Graphics Inc	Rowley	MA	G	978 948-2789	14851
Cimpress USA Incorporated **(DH)**	Waltham	MA	B	866 614-8002	16067
Citius Printing & Graphics LLC	Waltham	MA	G	781 547-5550	16068
CJ Corrado & Sons Inc	Sharon	MA	G	508 655-8434	15048
Classic Envelope Inc	East Douglas	MA	D	508 731-6747	10425
Co Press	Ludlow	MA	G	413 525-6686	12459
Colonial Lithograph Inc	Attleboro	MA	F	508 222-1832	7722

	CITY	ST	EMP	PHONE	ENTRY #
Color Images Inc	Methuen	MA	G	978 688-4994	13015
Congruity 360 LLC	Fall River	MA	D	508 689-9516	10679
Connolly Printing LLC	Woburn	MA	G	781 932-8885	17149
Coprico Inc	Chelsea	MA	G	617 889-0520	9951
Corporate Press	Norwood	MA	F	781 769-6656	14146
Country Press Inc	Lakeville	MA	F	508 947-4485	11975
Courier Printing Inc	Pittsfield	MA	G	413 442-3242	14465
Creative Imprints Inc	Norton	MA	E	508 285-7650	14074
Creative Ink	Salem	MA	G	978 741-2244	14903
Crest Printing Co Inc	Melrose	MA	G	617 889-1171	12980
Cricket Press Inc	Manchester	MA	F	978 526-7131	12604
Crockergraphics Inc	Needham Heights	MA	G	781 444-7020	13324
D & L Associates Inc	Needham Heights	MA	G	781 400-5068	13326
D B S Industries Inc	Haverhill	MA	D	978 373-4748	11421
D S Graphics Inc **(PA)**	Lowell	MA	C	978 970-1359	12365
D&P Media For Print Inc	Methuen	MA	G	978 685-2210	13017
D-Lew Inc	Southborough	MA	G	508 481-7709	15353
Da Rosas	Oak Bluffs	MA	F	508 693-0110	14210
Daily Printing Inc	Beverly	MA	G	978 927-4630	8123
Data Print Inc	Woburn	MA	F	781 935-3350	17164
Davis Enterprises Inc	Dedham	MA	G	781 461-8444	10286
Davol/Taunton Printing Inc	Taunton	MA	F	508 824-4305	15741
Ddfhklt Inc	West Springfield	MA	F	413 733-7441	16515
Defiance Graphics Corp	Rowley	MA	F	978 948-2789	14852
Descal Inc	Waltham	MA	G	781 736-9400	16085
Design Copy Printers Inc	Salem	MA	G	978 741-2244	14906
Desk Top Graphics Inc **(HQ)**	Peabody	MA	E	617 832-1927	14330
Devincentis Press Inc	Malden	MA	F	781 605-3796	12567
Digipress Inc **(PA)**	Peabody	MA	C	617 832-1927	14331
Digital Graphics Inc	North Billerica	MA	E	781 270-3670	13809
Dion Label Printing Inc	Westfield	MA	D	413 568-3713	16680
Dmr Print Inc **(PA)**	Concord	MA	E	617 876-3688	10128
Dns Inc	Charlton	MA	F	508 248-5901	9849
Documents On Demand Inc	Worcester	MA	F	508 793-0956	17366
Docuserve Inc	Marlborough	MA	E	508 786-5820	12749
Donnelley Financial LLC	Wilmington	MA	F	978 251-4000	16995
DSA Printing & Publishing Inc	Chelmsford	MA	G	978 256-3900	9893
Duggan Associates Inc	Framingham	MA	G	508 879-3277	10942
E D Abbott Company Inc	Boston	MA	F	617 267-5550	8514
E V Yeuell Inc	Woburn	MA	E	781 933-2984	17171
East Coast Printing Inc	Hingham	MA	G	781 331-5635	11498
Eastern Etching and Mfg Co	Chicopee	MA	E	413 594-6601	10022
Eco2 Office Inc	Milford	MA	G	508 478-8511	13114
Economy Coupon & Printing Inc	Peabody	MA	G	781 279-8555	14332
Elbonais Incorporated	Framingham	MA	G	508 626-2318	10945
Emco/Fgs LLC	Braintree	MA	D	617 389-0076	9005
Enon Copy Inc **(PA)**	Beverly	MA	F	978 927-8757	8128
Essex Ruling & Printing Co	Methuen	MA	G	978 682-2457	13021
Excella Graphics	Malden	MA	G	781 763-7768	12571
Fall River Modern Printing Co	Fall River	MA	F	508 673-9421	10697
Farrar Press Inc	Paxton	MA	G	508 799-9874	14301
Fasprint Inc **(PA)**	Brockton	MA	F	508 588-9961	9146
Fenway Cmmunications Group Inc	Boston	MA	E	617 226-1900	8542
Flagship Press Inc	North Andover	MA	C	978 975-3100	13704
Fleming & Son Corp	Somerville	MA	F	617 623-3047	15173
Footprint Pwr Acquisitions LLC	Salem	MA	G	978 740-8411	14912
Foster Carroll Inc	Hopkinton	MA	G	508 497-0068	11715
Fowler Printing and Graphics	Randolph	MA	F	781 986-8900	14682
Freedom Digital Printing LLC	Ashland	MA	F	508 881-6940	7660
Full Line Graphics Inc	Taunton	MA	G	508 238-1914	15750
G B Enterprises	Amherst	MA	G	413 210-4658	7515
Gangi Printing Inc	Somerville	MA	F	617 776-6071	15175
Gatehouse Media LLC	Lexington	MA	G	781 275-7204	12226
Gateway Printing	Wareham	MA	G	508 295-0505	16248
Gazette Printing Co Inc	Easthampton	MA	F	413 527-7700	10564
Generation Four Inc	Waltham	MA	G	781 899-3180	16119
Ggs Custom Metals Inc	South Hadley	MA	F	413 315-4344	15303
Ghp Media Inc	North Adams	MA	D	413 663-3771	13675
Gmf Engineering Inc	Saugus	MA	G	781 233-0315	14983
Golden Manet Press Inc	Quincy	MA	G	617 773-2423	14629
Granite Print LLC	Quincy	MA	G	617 479-5777	14630
Graphic Developments Inc	Hanover	MA	E	781 878-2222	11340
Graphic Excellence LLC	Springfield	MA	G	413 733-6691	15471
Graphix Plus Inc	Fall River	MA	F	508 677-2122	10706
Green Summer	Everett	MA	G	617 387-0120	10612
Greentree Marketing Inc	Framingham	MA	F	508 877-2581	10961
Grenier Print Shop Inc	Boston	MA	G	617 522-2225	8582
Guy T Piro & Sons	Somerville	MA	G	617 776-2840	15180
Hadley Printing Company Inc	Holyoke	MA	E	413 536-8517	11629
Harborside Printing Co Inc	Newburyport	MA	F	978 462-2026	13495
Harper Bros Printing Inc	North Billerica	MA	G	978 667-9459	13823
Harry B Harding & Son Inc	Whitman	MA	G	781 447-3941	16924
Harvard Instant Printing	Waltham	MA	G	781 893-2622	16124
Henry N Sawyer Co Inc	Boston	MA	F	617 242-4610	8594
Heritage Press Inc	Sandwich	MA	G	508 888-2111	14969
High-Speed Process Prtg Corp	Lawrence	MA	F	978 683-2766	12035
Hitchcock Press Inc	Holyoke	MA	F	413 538-8811	11632

	CITY	ST	EMP	PHONE	ENTRY #
I B A Inc	Millbury	MA	G	508 865-2507	13167
Imperial Image Inc	North Chelmsford	MA	F	978 251-0420	13897
Impress Systems Inc	Chelmsford	MA	G	978 441-2022	9906
Impressions Plus Inc	Quincy	MA	F	617 479-5777	14633
Imprint Boston Inc	Dorchester	MA	G	857 251-9383	10344
Imprint Marketing	Natick	MA	G	508 315-3433	13261
Infinite Graphic Solutions	Woburn	MA	G	781 938-6333	17201
Ingleside Corporation	Wrentham	MA	G	774 847-9386	17523
Ingleside Corporation	Norwood	MA	G	781 769-6656	14161
Ink Etcetera Corporation	Acton	MA	G	978 263-1555	7364
Inkstone Inc	Brockton	MA	E	508 587-5200	9155
Instant Offset Press Inc	Hyannis	MA	F	508 790-1100	11843
J & R Graphics Inc	Hanover	MA	F	781 871-7577	11343
J C Enterprises Inc	Ashland	MA	G	508 881-7228	7662
J Joy Associates Inc	Rockland	MA	G	781 871-1569	14810
J R V Smita Company LLC	Canton	MA	G	781 828-6490	9747
J T Gardner Inc	Auburn	MA	G	508 832-2036	7839
J T Gardner Inc	Westborough	MA	G	508 366-2679	16628
J T Gardner Inc	Worcester	MA	G	508 751-6600	17396
J T Gardner Inc **(PA)**	Westborough	MA	E	800 540-4993	16627
Jam Plastics Inc	Leominster	MA	E	978 537-2570	12156
Jen Ren Corporation	West Boylston	MA	G	508 835-3331	16419
Jet Press	Milford	MA	G	508 478-1814	13121
Jodys Quick Print	Middleton	MA	G	978 777-6114	13092
John Latka & Co Inc	Westfield	MA	G	413 562-4374	16694
John P Pow Company Inc	Boston	MA	E	617 269-6040	8635
Jordan Enterprises Inc	Marlborough	MA	F	508 481-2948	12781
Jotas Corporation	Burlington	MA	G	781 273-1155	9290
Kapson Printing Service Inc	Dorchester	MA	G	617 265-2543	10345
Keating Communication Group	Canton	MA	G	781 828-9030	9749
Kenco Printing	Lowell	MA	G	781 391-9500	12387
Kerrin Graphics & Printing	Dudley	MA	G	508 765-1339	10379
Kervick Family Foundation Inc	Worcester	MA	G	508 853-4500	17399
King Printing Company Inc	Lowell	MA	D	978 458-2345	12390
Kirkwood Holdings Inc **(PA)**	Wilmington	MA	C	978 658-4200	17012
Kondelin Associates Inc **(HQ)**	Peabody	MA	F	978 281-3663	14348
Kwik Print Inc	Great Barrington	MA	F	413 528-2885	11240
Lamb Printing Company Inc	North Adams	MA	G	413 662-2495	13678
Lane Printing Co Inc	Holbrook	MA	F	781 767-4450	11529
Laplume & Sons Printing Inc	Lawrence	MA	E	978 683-1009	12045
Lexington Graphics	Lexington	MA	F	781 863-9510	12237
Lexington Press Inc	Lexington	MA	G	781 862-8900	12238
Liberty Printing Co Inc	Brockton	MA	G	508 586-6810	9162
Lincoln Press Co Inc	Fall River	MA	E	508 673-3241	10723
Linmel Associates Inc	Marlborough	MA	F	508 481-6699	12787
Lion Labels Inc	South Easton	MA	E	508 230-8211	15284
Litho-Craft Inc	Winchester	MA	F	781 729-1789	17091
LPI Printing and Graphic Inc	Stoneham	MA	E	781 438-5400	15566
Lujean Printing Co Inc	Cotuit	MA	F	508 428-8700	10170
M & C Press Inc	Cambridge	MA	F	617 354-2584	9541
M & M Printing Rush Service	East Douglas	MA	G	508 476-4495	10429
Mackinnon Printing Co Inc	Acton	MA	G	978 263-8435	7371
Mallard Printing Inc	Fall River	MA	F	508 675-5733	10724
Mansir Printing LLC	Holyoke	MA	F	413 536-4250	11636
Map Printing Inc	Fall River	MA	G	508 676-5177	10725
Marbuo Inc	North Dartmouth	MA	G	508 994-7700	13924
Marcus Company Inc	Holyoke	MA	E	413 534-3303	11637
Maroney Associates Inc	Holbrook	MA	G	781 767-3970	11530
Mass Printing & Forms Inc	North Reading	MA	G	781 396-1970	13987
Massachusetts Repro Ltd	Boston	MA	F	617 227-2237	8686
Master Printing & Signs	Somerville	MA	G	617 623-8270	15196
Maximus	Lowell	MA	G	978 728-8000	12404
May Graphics & Printing Inc	Westford	MA	G	978 392-1302	16779
Mbf Printing	Holliston	MA	G	774 233-0337	11583
MBI Graphics & Printing Corp	Southbridge	MA	F	508 765-0658	15394
Mc Kinnon Printing Co Inc	Revere	MA	G	781 592-3677	14773
McClelland Press Inc **(PA)**	Williamstown	MA	F	413 663-5750	16958
McDermott Pallotta Inc	Watertown	MA	G	617 924-2318	16300
McGirr Graphics Incorporated	Plymouth	MA	G	508 747-6400	14563
McGirr Graphics Incorporated	Plymouth	MA	E	508 747-6400	14564
Medi - Print Inc **(PA)**	Malden	MA	E	781 324-4455	12582
Medi - Print Inc	Boston	MA	G	617 566-7594	8693
Medianews Group Inc	Fitchburg	MA	D	978 343-6911	10835
Merrill Corporation	Boston	MA	E	617 535-1500	8698
Merrill Graphics Incorporated	Braintree	MA	G	781 843-0666	9026
Miano Printing Services Inc	Holliston	MA	F	617 935-2830	11585
Michael M Almeida	Taunton	MA	G	508 823-4957	15765
Miles Press Inc	Auburn	MA	F	508 752-6430	7843
Milk Street Press Inc	Boston	MA	F	617 742-7900	8706
Millennium Press Inc	Agawam	MA	E	413 821-0028	7440
Millennium Printing Corp	Weymouth	MA	G	781 337-0002	16893
Mina Custom Print	Cambridge	MA	G	617 520-4797	9561
Minute Man Airfield	Stow	MA	F	978 897-3933	15633
Minuteman Governance Inc	Hopkinton	MA	G	508 837-3004	11729
Minuteman Implant Club Inc	Natick	MA	G	413 549-4108	13269
Minuteman Press	Hyde Park	MA	G	617 361-7400	11875
Minuteman Press	Centerville	MA	G	508 775-9890	9817

Employee Codes: A=Over 500 employees, B=251-500
C=101-250, D=51-100 E=20-50, F=10-19, G=3-9

	CITY	ST	EMP	PHONE	ENTRY #
Minuteman Press	Newburyport	MA	G	978 465-2242	13515
Minuteman Press	Fall River	MA	G	508 673-1407	10734
Minuteman Press	Fitchburg	MA	G	978 345-0818	10839
Minuteman Press	Seekonk	MA	G	508 336-3050	15028
Minuteman Press	Hyannis	MA	G	508 778-0220	11850
Minuteman Press Intl Inc	Newton	MA	G	617 244-7001	13615
Minuteman Press Worcester Inc	Worcester	MA	G	508 757-5450	17420
Minuteman Printing Corp	Concord	MA	F	978 369-2808	10141
Modus Media Inc	Waltham	MA	E	781 663-5000	16153
Monaghan Printing Company	Fairhaven	MA	F	508 991-8087	10643
Mrf Enterprises Inc	Seekonk	MA	G	508 336-3050	15030
My Print and Copy LLC	Beverly	MA	G	978 232-3552	8158
Mystic Parker Printing Inc	Malden	MA	G	781 321-4948	12583
Neenah Technical Materials Inc **(HQ)**	Dalton	MA	F	678 518-3343	10180
Neenah Technical Materials Inc	Pittsfield	MA	C	413 684-7874	14495
New Valence Robotics Corp	Boston	MA	G	857 529-6397	8735
Newprint Offset Inc	Lexington	MA	F	781 891-6002	12250
Newspapers of Massachusetts	Greenfield	MA	B	978 544-2118	11270
Nexus Print Group Inc	Milton	MA	G	617 429-9666	13197
North End Press Inc	Boston	MA	G	617 227-8929	8741
North River Graphics Inc	Pembroke	MA	G	781 826-6866	14420
North Shore Printing Inc	North Reading	MA	G	978 664-2609	13988
Northern Graphics Inc	Middleton	MA	F	978 646-9925	13097
Office Management Systems	Stoughton	MA	G	617 921-2966	15612
Officers Wives Club	Bedford	MA	G	781 274-8079	7998
On Site Printing & Copying	Needham Heights	MA	G	781 449-1871	13341
Online Print Resources	Winthrop	MA	G	617 539-3961	17100
Optamark LLC **(PA)**	North Attleboro	MA	G	508 643-1017	13770
Ouimette Printing Inc	West Springfield	MA	G	413 736-5926	16538
Owl Stamp Company Inc	Lowell	MA	G	978 452-4541	12418
Ozzie Printing Inc	Woburn	MA	G	978 657-9400	17252
Pace Associates Inc	Wellesley	MA	G	781 433-0639	16379
Palomar Printing	West Boylston	MA	G	508 856-7237	16425
Paper Plus Inc	West Springfield	MA	G	413 785-1363	16540
Parker Press Inc	Malden	MA	G	781 321-4948	12588
Partnership Resources	Chelmsford	MA	G	978 256-0499	9922
Patriot Customs Incorporated	Southbridge	MA	G	508 764-7342	15399
Photographic Corp New England	Concord	MA	G	978 369-3002	10150
Picken Printing Inc	North Chelmsford	MA	E	978 251-0730	13907
Pioneer Valley Printing Co	West Springfield	MA	G	413 739-2855	16544
PIP Foundation Inc	Framingham	MA	E	508 757-0103	10995
PIP Itsa Inc	Beverly	MA	G	978 927-5717	8165
Pleasant Printing Co	Attleboro	MA	F	508 222-3366	7778
PMS Printing Inc **(PA)**	East Longmeadow	MA	G	860 563-1676	10486
Poets Corner Press Inc	Nantucket	MA	G	508 228-1051	13230
Postal Instant Press **(PA)**	East Longmeadow	MA	G	413 525-4044	10487
Potters Printing Inc	Fall River	MA	G	617 547-3161	10747
Powder Horn Press Inc **(PA)**	Plymouth	MA	G	508 746-8777	14576
Power Graphics Printing	Tewksbury	MA	G	978 851-8988	15827
President Press Inc	Quincy	MA	F	617 773-1235	14648
Pressed For Time Printing Inc	Boston	MA	G	617 267-4113	8793
Pressroom Incorporated	Gloucester	MA	E	978 283-5562	11204
Pretty Instant LLC	Boston	MA	G	888 551-6765	8794
Print All of Boston Inc	Boston	MA	G	617 361-7400	8796
Print Buyers International LLC	Chestnut Hill	MA	G	617 730-5951	9991
Print Management Systems Inc	Woburn	MA	F	781 944-1041	17270
Print Resource	Westborough	MA	G	508 433-4660	16644
Print Synergy Solutions LLC	Brockton	MA	F	508 587-5200	9172
Print Works Inc	Hopkinton	MA	G	508 589-4626	11734
Printing & Graphic Services	Billerica	MA	G	978 667-6950	8277
Printing Place Inc	Melrose	MA	G	781 272-7209	12988
Printing Services Inc	Natick	MA	G	508 655-2535	13275
Printing Solutions Inc	Westford	MA	F	978 392-9903	16786
Printsake Inc	Mashpee	MA	G	508 419-7393	12882
Puffer International Inc	Westfield	MA	G	413 562-9100	16719
Pynchon Press Co Inc	Chicopee	MA	G	413 315-8798	10054
Pyramid Printing and Advg Inc	Weymouth	MA	E	781 337-7609	16899
Qg LLC	Taunton	MA	B	508 828-4400	15776
Qg Printing Corp	Leominster	MA	C	978 534-8351	12179
Quad/Graphics Inc	Leominster	MA	A	860 741-0150	12180
Quad/Graphics Inc	Taunton	MA	B	508 692-3100	15777
Quad/Graphics Inc	Woburn	MA	C	781 231-7200	17275
Quad/Graphics Inc	Weymouth	MA	A	781 917-1601	16900
Quad/Graphics Inc	East Longmeadow	MA	C	413 525-8552	10490
Quality Envelope & Printing Co	Middleboro	MA	G	508 947-8878	13077
Quality Printing Company Inc	Pittsfield	MA	D	413 442-4166	14504
Quick Print Ltd Inc	Chelmsford	MA	G	978 256-1822	9924
R & H Communications Inc **(PA)**	Waltham	MA	F	781 893-6221	16181
R E K Management Inc	West Harwich	MA	G	508 775-3005	16481
R R Donnelley & Sons Company	Hyde Park	MA	B	617 360-2000	11877
Ralph Traynham	Billerica	MA	G	978 667-0977	8282
Ramsbottom Printing Inc	Fall River	MA	D	508 730-2220	10752
REA-Craft Press Incorporated	Foxboro	MA	F	508 543-8710	10899
Red Spot Printing	Waltham	MA	G	781 894-2211	16186
Red Sun Press Inc	Jamaica Plain	MA	F	617 524-6822	11949
Regal Press Incorporated **(PA)**	Norwood	MA	C	781 769-3900	14192
Reid Graphics Inc	Andover	MA	D	978 474-1930	7598

	CITY	ST	EMP	PHONE	ENTRY #
Rgp Corp	Milford	MA	G	508 478-8511	13141
Rhode Island Mktg & Prtg Inc	Attleboro	MA	G	401 351-4000	7786
Rickenbacker Resources Inc	Andover	MA	G	978 475-4520	7599
Rivkind Associates Inc **(PA)**	South Easton	MA	F	781 269-2415	15291
Rj Printing LLC	Boston	MA	G	617 523-7656	8822
Robert Murphy	Salem	MA	E	978 745-7170	14938
Roberts & Sons Printing Inc	Springfield	MA	G	413 283-9356	15503
Rogers Printing Co Inc	Leominster	MA	E	978 537-9791	12184
S A N Inc **(PA)**	Lawrence	MA	G	978 686-3875	12073
Scorpian Printing	Framingham	MA	E	617 319-6114	11003
Screenco Printing Inc	Newburyport	MA	G	978 465-1211	13533
Seventy Nine N Main St Prtg	Andover	MA	G	978 475-4945	7603
Shafiis Inc **(PA)**	East Longmeadow	MA	E	413 224-2100	10492
Shawmut Advertising Inc **(PA)**	Danvers	MA	E	978 762-7500	10255
Shawmut Printing	Danvers	MA	F	978 762-7500	10256
Shear Color Printing Inc	Woburn	MA	E	781 376-9607	17293
Sherman Printing Co Inc	Canton	MA	E	781 828-8855	9778
Shrewsbury National Press	Shrewsbury	MA	G	508 756-7502	15132
Sierra Press Inc	Waltham	MA	G	617 923-4150	16194
Signal Graphics 225	Quincy	MA	G	617 472-1700	14655
Sir Speedy Inc	North Attleboro	MA	G	508 643-1016	13780
Skyline Productions	Cherry Valley	MA	G	508 326-4982	9977
Somerville Quick Print Inc	Cambridge	MA	G	617 492-5343	9656
Son Co Inc	Bellingham	MA	G	508 966-2970	8059
South Shore Custom Prints	Pembroke	MA	G	781 293-8300	14427
Spectrum Litho Inc	Canton	MA	G	781 575-0700	9785
Standard Modern Company	New Bedford	MA	G	774 425-3537	13452
Star Litho Inc	Weymouth	MA	E	781 340-9401	16901
Star Printing Corp	Taunton	MA	E	508 583-9046	15787
Starburst Prtg & Graphics Inc	Holliston	MA	F	508 893-0900	11606
State-Line Graphics Inc	Everett	MA	F	617 389-1200	10632
Strange Planet Printing	Brockton	MA	G	508 857-1816	9179
Studio 24 Graphix & Prtg Inc	Mattapan	MA	G	617 296-2058	12884
Studley Press Inc	Dalton	MA	E	413 684-0441	10187
Summit Forms	Worcester	MA	G	508 853-6838	17483
Summit Press Inc **(PA)**	Chelsea	MA	F	617 889-3991	9972
Superlative Printing Inc	Stoughton	MA	F	781 341-9000	15624
Tantar Corp	North Attleboro	MA	G	508 643-1017	13783
Task Printing Inc	Newton	MA	G	617 332-4414	13643
Taylor Communications Inc	Avon	MA	F	508 584-0102	7898
TCI Press Inc	Seekonk	MA	E	508 336-6633	15040
Technical Publications Inc	Waltham	MA	F	781 899-0263	16206
Techprint Inc	Lawrence	MA	D	978 975-1245	12077
Ted Best	Hyde Park	MA	G	617 361-7258	11881
Thermal Printing Solutions	Hudson	MA	G	978 562-1329	11822
Thomas B Fullen	Leominster	MA	G	978 534-5255	12194
Thompsons Printing Inc	Orleans	MA	F	508 255-0099	14242
Thriftco Speedi-Print Center	Peabody	MA	G	978 531-5546	14377
Tisbury Printer Inc	Vineyard Haven	MA	F	508 693-4222	15935
Titus & Bean Graphics Inc	Kingston	MA	F	781 585-1355	11965
Trademark Print Inc	Pembroke	MA	G	781 829-0209	14429
Transamerica Printing Corp	Natick	MA	G	781 821-6166	13283
Travers Printing Inc	Gardner	MA	E	978 632-0530	11131
Tri Star Printing & Graphics	Somerville	MA	G	617 666-4480	15225
Trinity Press Inc	North Dartmouth	MA	G	508 998-1072	13928
Tshb Inc	Newburyport	MA	E	978 465-8950	13543
Universal Business Forms Inc	Worcester	MA	G	508 852-5520	17495
Universal Tag Inc	Dudley	MA	E	508 949-2411	10388
Universal Wilde Inc	Holliston	MA	C	508 429-5515	11611
Universal Wilde Inc	Rockland	MA	C	781 251-2700	14832
Universal Wilde Inc **(PA)**	Westwood	MA	C	781 251-2700	16880
Universal Wilde Inc	Westwood	MA	C	978 658-0800	16881
Valley Printing Company	Cherry Valley	MA	G	508 892-9818	9978
Van-Go Graphics	Grafton	MA	F	508 865-7300	11225
Versatile Printing	Burlington	MA	G	781 221-2112	9352
Victoria H Bradshaw	New Bedford	MA	G	508 992-1702	13457
Vogel Printing Company Inc	Lawrence	MA	G	978 682-6828	12082
W S Walcott Inc	Orleans	MA	G	508 240-0882	14244
Wakefield Item Co	Wakefield	MA	E	781 245-0080	15983
Walpole Print Works Inc	Walpole	MA	G	508 668-0247	16017
Waterfront Printing Company	Boston	MA	F	617 345-9711	8917
Watson Printing Co Inc	Wellesley	MA	G	781 237-1336	16393
We Print Today LLC	Kingston	MA	F	781 585-6021	11966
Webb-Mason Inc	Burlington	MA	G	781 272-5530	9356
Webster Printing Company Inc **(PA)**	Hanson	MA	E	781 447-5484	11370
Western Mass Copying Prtg Inc	West Springfield	MA	G	413 734-2679	16565
Westfield News Publishing Inc **(DH)**	Westfield	MA	E	413 562-4181	16746
Westrex International Inc	Boston	MA	F	617 254-1200	8923
Wilkscraft Inc	Beverly	MA	F	978 922-1855	8197
Windsor Press Inc	Wellesley	MA	G	781 235-0265	16394
Winkir Instant Printing Inc	South Yarmouth	MA	G	508 398-9748	15335
Xpression Prints	Franklin	MA	G	401 413-6930	11099
Yankee Printing Group Inc	South Hadley	MA	E	413 532-9513	15313
Ziprint Centers Inc	Randolph	MA	G	781 963-2250	14703
Albisons Printing Inc	Augusta	ME	G	207 622-1941	5603
Alliance Printers LLC	Brunswick	ME	F	207 504-8200	5828
Armstrong Family Inds Inc	Hermon	ME	E	207 848-7300	6183

	CITY	ST	EMP	PHONE	ENTRY #
Atlantic Coastal Printing Inc	Biddeford	ME	G	207 284-4328	5719
Bromar	Skowhegan	ME	G	207 474-3784	6970
Brown Fox Printing Inc **(PA)**	Scarborough	ME	G	207 883-9525	6913
Bruce A Pettengill	Leeds	ME	G	207 933-2578	6268
Brunswick Instant Printing Inc	Brunswick	ME	G	207 729-6854	5832
Calais Press Inc	Calais	ME	G	207 454-8613	5864
Camden Printing Inc	Rockland	ME	G	207 236-4112	6787
Cardinal Printing Co Inc	Denmark	ME	G	207 452-2931	5948
Central Street Corporation	Bangor	ME	F	207 947-8049	5635
Charlie Horse Screen Printing/	Arundel	ME	G	207 985-3293	5530
Checksforlesscom	Portland	ME	G	800 245-5775	6636
Cmyk Print Services	Scarborough	ME	G	207 228-3838	6914
Computech Inc	Auburn	ME	G	207 777-7468	5554
Curry Printing & Copy Center	Portland	ME	F	207 772-5897	6645
Cybercopy Inc	Portland	ME	G	207 775-2679	6646
Dale Rand Printing Inc	Portland	ME	G	207 773-8198	6647
Davic Inc	Portland	ME	F	207 774-0093	6649
Donald McIntire	Farmington	ME	G	207 778-3581	6043
Downeast Graphics & Prtg Inc	Ellsworth	ME	F	207 667-5582	6016
E I Printing Co	Portland	ME	F	207 797-4838	6656
Evergreen Custom Printing Inc	Auburn	ME	G	207 782-2327	5563
Everlasting Images Inc	Cape Neddick	ME	G	207 351-3277	5878
Fast Forms Printing & Paper	Hermon	ME	G	207 941-8383	6186
Fine Print Booksellers	Kennebunkport	ME	G	207 967-9989	6244
First Choice Printing Inc	Lisbon Falls	ME	G	207 353-8006	6369
Furbush Roberts Prtg Co Inc	Bangor	ME	G	207 945-9409	5647
Harbor Print Shop	Boothbay	ME	G	207 633-4176	5778
Hoy Printing Corp	Biddeford	ME	G	207 284-5531	5739
Infinite Imaging Inc	York	ME	E	207 363-4402	7309
J A Black Company	Belfast	ME	G	207 338-4040	5691
Jiffy Print Inc	Bangor	ME	G	207 947-4490	5652
Johnson Printing & Graphics	Eliot	ME	G	207 439-2567	6007
JS McCarthy Co Inc **(PA)**	Augusta	ME	D	207 622-6241	5609
L H Thompson Inc	Brewer	ME	F	207 989-3280	5797
Laura Marr Productions LLC	Westbrook	ME	G	207 856-9700	7194
Letter Systems Inc **(PA)**	Augusta	ME	C	207 622-7126	5613
Lincoln County Publishing Co	Newcastle	ME	E	207 563-3171	6483
Marks Printing House Inc	Belfast	ME	G	207 338-5460	5692
Mpx	Portland	ME	E	207 774-6116	6695
Nemi Publishing Inc	Farmington	ME	E	207 778-4801	6052
Northeast Publishing Company	Dover Foxcroft	ME	G	207 564-8355	5961
Northern Printers Inc	Presque Isle	ME	G	207 769-1231	6767
Onesource Printing	Lewiston	ME	G	207 784-1538	6313
Park Street Press Inc	South Paris	ME	G	207 743-7702	7015
Partners Printing Inc	South Portland	ME	G	207 773-0439	7036
Penmor Lithographers Inc	Lewiston	ME	E	207 784-1341	6316
Port Printing Solutions Inc	South Portland	ME	G	207 741-5200	7037
Prints Charming Printers Inc	Boothbay	ME	G	207 633-6663	5780
Pyramid Checks & Printing	Portland	ME	D	207 878-9832	6718
Quick Print Color Center	Saco	ME	G	207 282-6480	6856
R & W Engraving Inc	Biddeford	ME	G	207 286-3020	5760
R N Haskins Printing Inc	Sidney	ME	F	207 465-2155	6964
Regal Press Inc	Ellsworth	ME	G	207 667-5227	6021
RH Rosenfield Co	Sanford	ME	E	207 324-1798	6889
Sunrise Printing & Graphics	Windham	ME	G	207 892-3534	7255
Supplies Unlimited	Damariscotta	ME	G	207 563-7010	5940
Tall Oak Printing LLC	Wells	ME	G	207 251-4138	7166
Time4printing Inc	Windham	ME	G	207 838-1496	7257
Vc Print	Caribou	ME	G	207 492-1919	5892
Waterfront Graphics & Prtg LLC	South Portland	ME	G	207 799-3519	7044
Allegra Print & Imaging	Bedford	NH	G	603 622-3821	17630
Alpha Graph Printshop	Nashua	NH	F	603 595-1444	19111
AlphaGraphics Pntshp of Future	Manchester	NH	G	603 645-0002	18778
American Printing Inc	Amherst	NH	F	603 880-0277	17550
Ariel Instant Printing	Keene	NH	G	603 352-3663	18492
Baker Graphics Inc	Manchester	NH	G	603 625-5427	18784
Bam Lab LLC	Somersworth	NH	G	603 973-9388	19828
Bank & Business Forms Inc	Keene	NH	G	603 357-0567	18495
Barn Door Screen Printers	Conway	NH	G	603 447-5369	17950
Blacksmith Prtg & Copy Ctr LLC	Wolfeboro	NH	G	603 569-6300	20015
Blanchard Printing	Nashua	NH	G	603 891-1505	19127
Bob Bean Company Inc	Londonderry	NH	G	603 818-4390	18680
Boles Enterprises Inc	Manchester	NH	G	603 622-4282	18789
Bridge & Byron Inc	Concord	NH	G	603 225-5221	17887
Brn Corporation	Campton	NH	G	603 726-3800	17775
C & O Box & Printing Company	Hooksett	NH	G	508 881-1760	18345
Capitol Copy Inc	Concord	NH	G	603 226-2679	17889
Concord Litho Group Inc **(PA)**	Concord	NH	C	603 224-1202	17895
Curry Copy Center of Keene	Keene	NH	G	603 352-9542	18499
D M Printing Service Inc	Hudson	NH	G	603 883-1897	18382
Digital Printer Service	Gilford	NH	G	860 395-7942	18186
Dr Biron Incorporated **(PA)**	Manchester	NH	F	603 622-5222	18813
E Print Inc	Hudson	NH	G	603 594-0009	18388
Eagle Copy Center	Windham	NH	G	603 225-3713	20004
Eagle Publications Inc	Claremont	NH	E	603 543-3100	17849
Echo Communications Inc	New London	NH	E	603 526-6006	19316
Evans Printing Co	Bow	NH	G	603 856-8238	17713
Frugal Printer Inc	Salem	NH	F	603 894-6333	19737
Gemgraphics Inc	Keene	NH	G	603 352-7112	18504
Graphic Consumer Services Inc	Candia	NH	G	603 483-5355	17785
Harrison Publishing House Inc	Littleton	NH	E	603 444-0820	18661
Hurley Ink LLC	Manchester	NH	G	603 645-0002	18840
Independent Color Press LLC	Rochester	NH	G	603 539-5959	19672
Infinite Imaging Inc **(PA)**	Portsmouth	NH	E	603 436-3030	19578
Insty-Prints of Bedford Inc	Bedford	NH	G	603 622-3821	17646
Itnh Inc	Manchester	NH	F	603 669-6900	18845
Jeba Graphics LLC	Jaffrey	NH	G	603 532-7726	18468
Just Rewards Inc	Lebanon	NH	G	603 448-6800	18626
Kase Printing Inc	Hudson	NH	E	603 883-9223	18405
Kelley Solutions Inc	Portsmouth	NH	G	603 431-3881	19583
Kensington Group Incorporated	Hampton Falls	NH	F	603 926-6742	18283
Keystone Press LLC	Manchester	NH	F	603 622-5222	18768
Letterman Press LLC	West Lebanon	NH	G	603 543-0500	19956
Lew A Cummings Co Inc	Hooksett	NH	C	603 625-6901	18352
Liberty Press Inc	Manchester	NH	G	603 641-1991	18864
Loral Press Inc	Atkinson	NH	G	603 362-5549	17605
Mg Print and Promotions	Dover	NH	G	603 343-2534	18037
Minuteman Press Intl Inc	Nashua	NH	G	603 718-1439	19208
Miss Print	Meredith	NH	G	603 279-5939	18975
Murroneys Printing Inc	Manchester	NH	G	603 623-4677	18880
New England Printing Corp	Portsmouth	NH	F	603 431-0142	19599
North East Printing McHy Inc	Seabrook	NH	G	603 474-7455	19811
P2k Printing LLC	North Conway	NH	G	603 356-2010	19378
Papergraphics Print & Copy	Merrimack	NH	F	603 880-1835	19019
Paul Revere Press Inc	Newton	NH	G	781 289-4031	19366
Print Factory Inc	Nashua	NH	G	603 880-4519	19239
Printers Square Inc	Manchester	NH	F	603 623-0802	18905
Printfusion LLC	Swanzey	NH	G	603 283-0007	19888
Proforma Piper Printing	Tilton	NH	G	603 934-5055	19909
Puritan Press Inc **(PA)**	Hollis	NH	E	603 889-4500	18339
Quality Press Inc	Concord	NH	G	603 889-7211	17925
R C Brayshaw & Co Inc **(PA)**	Warner	NH	E	603 456-3101	19929
Rainville Printing Entps Inc	Pembroke	NH	G	603 485-3422	19463
Ram Printing Incorporated **(PA)**	East Hampstead	NH	E	603 382-7045	18082
Ram Printing Incorporated	East Hampstead	NH	G	603 382-3400	18083
RB Graphics Inc	Hooksett	NH	G	603 624-4025	18358
S & Q Printers Inc	Wilton	NH	G	603 654-2888	19987
Sant Bani Press Inc	Manchester	NH	F	603 286-3114	18915
Savron Graphics Inc **(PA)**	Jaffrey	NH	G	603 532-7726	18476
Savron Graphics Inc	Peterborough	NH	G	603 924-7088	19487
Shaughnessy Seagull Inc	Portsmouth	NH	G	603 433-4680	19620
Sheridan NH	Hanover	NH	G	603 643-2220	18297
Sir Speedy	Manchester	NH	G	603 625-6868	18925
Smith & Town Printers LLC	Berlin	NH	G	603 752-2150	17700
Southport Management Group LLC	Portsmouth	NH	G	603 433-4664	19621
Spirit Advisory LLC	Portsmouth	NH	G	603 433-4664	19622
Sterling Business Corp	Peterborough	NH	G	603 924-9401	19489
Sumner Fancy	Windham	NH	G	603 893-3081	20011
Sumner Printing Inc	Somersworth	NH	E	603 692-7424	19849
Teddys Tees Inc	Concord	NH	G	603 226-2762	17935
Thh Associates LLC	North Woodstock	NH	F	603 536-3600	19399
Town & Country Reprographics	Concord	NH	F	603 225-9521	17936
Txc Inc	Salem	NH	F	603 893-4999	19773
Underground Press	Freedom	NH	G	603 323-2022	18171
Upper Valley Press Inc	North Haverhill	NH	D	603 787-7000	19391
Ventricom Wireless Tech	Concord	NH	G	603 226-0025	17938
Walnut Bottom Inc	Concord	NH	G	603 224-6606	17939
Water Street Printing LLC	Nashua	NH	F	603 595-1444	19284
Wharf Industries Printing Inc	Windham	NH	F	603 421-2566	20014
Whitman Communications Inc	Lebanon	NH	E	603 448-2600	18641
Winnisquam Printing Inc	Laconia	NH	G	603 524-2803	18595
136 Express Printing Inc	Bristol	RI	G	401 253-0136	20059
A & H Composition and Prtg Inc	East Providence	RI	G	401 438-1200	20383
ABS Printing Inc	West Warwick	RI	G	401 826-0870	21475
Adams Printing Inc	Pawtucket	RI	G	401 722-9222	20807
Allegra Print & Imaging	East Greenwich	RI	G	401 884-9280	20352
Allied Group Inc	Providence	RI	G	401 946-6100	20950
Arch Parent Inc	Westerly	RI	G	401 388-9802	21517
Artistic Label Company Inc	Warwick	RI	G	401 737-0666	21327
B & M Printing Inc	Cumberland	RI	G	401 334-3190	20314
Barrington Print & Copy LLC	Warwick	RI	E	401 943-8300	21332
Bradford Press Inc	Providence	RI	G	401 621-7195	20972
Camirob Corp	East Providence	RI	E	401 435-4477	20394
Choice Printing & Product LLC	Rumford	RI	F	401 438-3838	21182
Colonial Printing Inc **(PA)**	Warwick	RI	E	401 691-3400	21343
Colonial Printing Inc	Newport	RI	G	401 367-6690	20661
Copy Print Company	Cranston	RI	G	401 228-3900	20201
Crosstown Press Inc	Cranston	RI	F	401 941-4061	20205
Dla Document Services	Newport	RI	G	401 841-6011	20662
Don-May of Wakefield Inc	Wakefield	RI	G	401 789-9339	21269
E&B Printing LLC	North Providence	RI	G	401 353-5777	20758
Enterprise Prtg & Pdts Corp	Rumford	RI	F	401 438-3838	21184
Fairmont Sons LLC **(PA)**	Providence	RI	G	401 351-4000	21010
Fine Line Graphics Inc	Smithfield	RI	E	401 349-3300	21225

	CITY	ST	EMP	PHONE	ENTRY #
Formatt Printing Inc	North Providence	RI	G	401 475-6666	20761
Hopkins Press	North Providence	RI	G	401 231-9654	20764
I Copy	Kingston	RI	G	401 788-8277	20550
Igt Global Solutions Corp	West Greenwich	RI	E	401 392-7025	21456
J B Foley Printing Company	Providence	RI	G	401 467-3616	21041
Jay Packaging Group Inc **(PA)**	Warwick	RI	D	401 244-1300	21379
Key Graphics Inc	Kingston	RI	G	401 826-2425	20551
Lewis Graphics Inc	Cranston	RI	G	401 943-8300	20253
Louis Press Inc	Johnston	RI	G	401 351-9229	20519
Mass Web Printing Company Inc	Providence	RI	D	508 832-5317	21062
Meridian Printing Inc	East Greenwich	RI	D	401 885-4882	20373
Minute Man Press	Middletown	RI	G	401 619-1650	20626
Minuteman Press of Johnston	Johnston	RI	G	401 944-0667	20522
Minuteman Press of Pawtucket	Pawtucket	RI	G	401 305-6644	20860
Mono Die Cutting Co Inc	Riverside	RI	F	401 434-1274	21173
Narragansett Bus Forms Inc	East Providence	RI	E	401 331-2000	20434
New England Image & Print Inc	North Smithfield	RI	G	401 769-3708	20793
Oberlin LLC	Providence	RI	G	401 588-8755	21080
Omo Inc	Providence	RI	G	401 421-5160	21084
Park Printers	Pawtucket	RI	G	401 728-8650	20874
Peak Printing Inc	Providence	RI	F	401 351-0500	21088
Perfect Print LLC	Providence	RI	E	401 347-2370	21089
Print Shops Inc	East Greenwich	RI	F	401 885-1226	20377
Printcraft Inc	Warwick	RI	G	401 739-0700	21405
Printing Plus	Westerly	RI	G	401 596-6970	21536
R J H Printing Inc	North Kingstown	RI	G	401 885-6262	20735
Realty Publishing Center Inc	Providence	RI	G	401 331-2505	21106
Regine Printing Co Inc	Providence	RI	G	401 943-3404	21108
Romano Investments Inc	Warwick	RI	E	401 691-3400	21416
Saffron Group Inc **(PA)**	Warren	RI	G	401 245-3725	21305
Service Plus Press Inc	Warwick	RI	G	401 461-2929	21424
Signature Printing Inc	East Providence	RI	D	401 438-1200	20444
Sir Speedy	Providence	RI	G	401 232-2000	21122
Sir Speedy Printing Inc	Cranston	RI	F	401 781-5650	20286
Steele and Steele Inc	Wakefield	RI	G	401 782-2278	21279
Summit Printing LLC	Warwick	RI	G	401 732-7848	21431
Tap Printing Inc	Warren	RI	G	401 247-2188	21308
Tiffany Printing Company	Coventry	RI	G	401 828-5514	20168
Village Press Inc	Rumford	RI	F	401 434-8130	21198
Warwick Group Inc	Bristol	RI	F	401 438-9451	20109
Accura Printing	Barre	VT	F	802 476-4429	21607
Anything Printed LLC	Woodstock	VT	G	802 457-3414	22735
ASC Duplicating Inc	Montpelier	VT	G	802 229-0660	22145
Buy Monthly Publishing Inc	Waterbury Center	VT	G	802 244-6620	22590
Buyers Digest Press Inc	Fairfax	VT	D	802 893-4214	21973
Chester Brothers	Winooski	VT	G	802 655-4159	22718
Dawn Brainard	Newport	VT	G	802 334-2780	22196
Digital Press Printers LLC	Williston	VT	F	802 863-5579	22662
E & G Graphics	Rutland	VT	G	802 773-3111	22331
Edward Group Inc	Rutland	VT	F	802 775-1029	22332
Express Copy Inc	Manchester Center	VT	G	802 362-0501	22084
First Step Print Shop LLC	Underhill	VT	G	802 899-2708	22547
Howard Printing Inc	Brattleboro	VT	G	802 254-3550	21733
Inkspot Press	Bennington	VT	F	802 447-1768	21673
L Brown and Sons Printing Inc	Barre	VT	E	802 476-3164	21627
Larcoline Inc **(PA)**	Colchester	VT	F	802 864-5440	21871
Larcoline Inc	Montpelier	VT	G	802 229-0660	22152
Leahy Press Inc	Montpelier	VT	E	802 223-2100	22153
Marus Printing	Hartland	VT	G	802 436-2044	22016
McClure Newspapers Inc	Burlington	VT	C	802 863-3441	21795
Precision Print and Copy Inc	Vergennes	VT	G	802 877-3711	22555
Queen City Printers Inc	Burlington	VT	E	802 864-4566	21804
Rutland Printing Co Inc	Rutland	VT	G	802 775-1948	22351
S M T Graphics LLC	Shoreham	VT	G	802 897-5231	22433
Silver Mountain Graphics Inc	Saint Johnsbury	VT	G	802 748-1170	22395
Springfield Printing Corp	North Springfield	VT	E	802 886-2201	22238
Stillwater Graphics Inc	Williamstown	VT	F	802 433-9898	22651
Thompson Printing Inc	Manchester Center	VT	F	802 362-1140	22091
Tuttle Law Print Inc	Rutland	VT	D	802 773-9171	22356
Vermont Publishing Comany	Saint Albans	VT	E	802 524-9771	22384
Village Printer	Bellows Falls	VT	G	802 463-9697	21655
Villanti & Sons Printers Inc	Milton	VT	D	802 864-0723	22140
Winooski Press LLC	Winooski	VT	G	802 655-1611	22728
X Press In Stowe Inc	Stowe	VT	G	802 253-9788	22525
Zinn Graphics Inc	Brattleboro	VT	G	802 254-6742	21756

2754 Commercial Printing: Gravure

	CITY	ST	EMP	PHONE	ENTRY #
Brook & Whittle Limited **(HQ)**	Guilford	CT	C	203 483-5602	1695
Ideas Inc	Milford	CT	G	203 878-9686	2299
Massachusetts Envelope Co Inc	Hartford	CT	E	860 727-9100	1845
Naugatuck Vly Photo Engrv Inc	Waterbury	CT	G	203 756-7345	4924
Quad/Graphics Inc	North Haven	CT	A	203 288-2468	3057
R R Donnelley & Sons Company	Manchester	CT	F	860 649-5570	2040
Rubber Labels USA LLC	Milford	CT	G	203 713-8059	2357
Schmitt Realty Holdings Inc	Branford	CT	E	203 488-3252	346
Trade Labels Inc	Mystic	CT	G	860 535-4828	2454
D B S Industries Inc	Haverhill	MA	D	978 373-4748	11421
Giannetti Mfg Services Inc	South Hadley	MA	G	413 532-9736	15304
Jon Goodman	Williamsburg	MA	G	413 586-9650	16951
Laplume & Sons Printing Inc	Lawrence	MA	E	978 683-1009	12045
Leap Year Publishing LLC	North Andover	MA	F	978 688-9900	13717
Minike Card Care	Worcester	MA	G	508 853-4490	17419
Peel People LLC	Attleboro	MA	G	773 255-9886	7775
Shear Color Printing Inc	Woburn	MA	E	781 376-9607	17293
Stat Products Inc	Ashland	MA	E	508 881-8022	7670
Redden Publishing Co LLC	Rockport	ME	G	207 236-0767	6825
Label Tech Inc	Somersworth	NH	C	603 692-2005	19843
Capitol Stationery Company	Cranston	RI	G	401 943-5333	20194
Providence Label & Tag Co	Providence	RI	F	401 751-6677	21097
Creative Labels Vermont Inc	Winooski	VT	E	802 655-7654	22720
Vermont Christmas Company	Milton	VT	G	802 893-1670	22139

2759 Commercial Printing

	CITY	ST	EMP	PHONE	ENTRY #
Accent Screenprinting	Wallingford	CT	G	203 284-8601	4693
Acme Typesetting Service Co	West Hartford	CT	G	860 953-1470	5052
Ad Label Inc	Brooklyn	CT	G	860 779-0513	669
Advanced Graphics Inc	Stratford	CT	E	203 378-0471	4388
Allied Printing Services Inc **(PA)**	Manchester	CT	B	860 643-1101	1984
American Banknote Corporation **(PA)**	Stamford	CT	G	203 941-4090	4135
American Silk Screening LLC	Berlin	CT	G	860 828-5486	71
American Stitch & Print Inc	North Haven	CT	G	203 239-5383	3006
Amgraph Packaging Inc	Baltic	CT	C	860 822-2000	48
Ansel Label and Packaging Corp	Trumbull	CT	E	203 452-0311	4612
AZ Copy Center Inc	Southington	CT	G	860 621-7325	4040
B T S Graphics LLC	Oakville	CT	G	860 274-6422	3296
B-P Products Inc	Hamden	CT	E	203 288-0200	1733
Bardell Printing Corp	East Haven	CT	G	203 469-2441	1242
Baron Technology Inc	Trumbull	CT	E	203 452-0515	4614
Bayard Inc **(DH)**	New London	CT	E	860 437-3012	2765
Biz Wiz Print & Copy Ctr LLC **(PA)**	Rocky Hill	CT	G	860 721-0040	3704
Bl Printing Shop	Bridgeport	CT	G	203 334-7779	383
Bread and Wine Publishing LLC	Manchester	CT	G	860 649-3109	1989
Cannelli Printing Co Inc	West Haven	CT	G	203 932-1719	5110
CCL Industries Corporation **(DH)**	Shelton	CT	D	203 926-1253	3785
CCL Label Inc	Shelton	CT	C	203 926-1253	3786
CCL Label (delaware) Inc **(DH)**	Shelton	CT	G	203 926-1253	3787
Christopher Condors	Norwalk	CT	G	203 852-8181	3124
Clanol Systems Inc	Old Greenwich	CT	G	203 637-9909	3306
Classic Label Inc	Woodbridge	CT	G	203 389-3535	5466
Colonial Printers of Windsor	Windsor Locks	CT	G	860 627-5433	5389
Colorgraphix LLC	Oxford	CT	G	203 264-5212	3397
Concordia Ltd	North Branford	CT	G	203 483-0221	2960
Creative Envelope Inc	Putnam	CT	G	860 963-1231	3609
Custom Tees Plus	New Haven	CT	E	203 752-1071	2681
Custom TS n More LLC	Ridgefield	CT	G	203 438-1592	3665
Design Label Manufacturing Inc **(PA)**	Old Lyme	CT	E	860 739-6266	3321
Diversified Printing Solutions	Danbury	CT	G	203 826-7198	902
Doctor Stuff LLC	Wallingford	CT	G	203 785-8475	4735
Dst Output East LLC **(DH)**	South Windsor	CT	E	816 221-1234	3957
E & A Enterprises Inc	Wallingford	CT	E	203 250-8050	4736
Eastwood Printing Inc	Wethersfield	CT	F	860 529-6673	5248
Eccles-Lehman Inc	Easton	CT	G	203 268-0605	1318
ECI Screen Print Inc	Watertown	CT	F	860 283-9849	5008
Elm Press Incorporated	Terryville	CT	E	860 583-3600	4477
Envelopes & More Inc	Newington	CT	F	860 286-7570	2862
Ever Ready Press	Ansonia	CT	G	203 734-5157	14
Executive Greetings Inc **(HQ)**	New Hartford	CT	B	860 379-9911	2636
Executive Office Services Inc	Bridgeport	CT	E	203 373-1333	411
Falcon Press	Enfield	CT	G	860 763-2293	1362
Frank Printing Co R	Wallingford	CT	G	203 265-6152	4746
G & R Enterprises Incorporated	Hartford	CT	G	860 549-6120	1822
Gateway Digital Inc	Norwalk	CT	F	203 853-4929	3157
Hartford Toner & Cartridge Inc **(PA)**	Broad Brook	CT	G	860 292-1280	629
Hat Trick Graphics LLC	Danbury	CT	G	203 748-1128	930
Hw Graphics	Windsor	CT	G	860 278-2338	5339
Ideal Printing Co Inc	New Haven	CT	G	203 777-7626	2698
Ideas Inc	Milford	CT	G	203 878-9686	2299
Identification Products Corp	Bridgeport	CT	F	203 334-5969	429
Image One Prtg & Graphics Inc	Monroe	CT	G	203 459-1880	2404
Imperial Grphic Cmmnctions Inc	Milford	CT	E	203 650-3478	2301
Integrated Print Solutions Inc	Bridgeport	CT	F	203 330-0200	431
International Comm Svcs Inc	Guilford	CT	G	401 580-8888	1706
Iovino Bros Sporting Goods	Danbury	CT	G	203 790-5966	934
Jb Muze Enterprises	New Milford	CT	G	860 355-5949	2807
JMS Graphics Inc	Middlebury	CT	G	203 598-7555	2155
Joyce Printers Inc	Woodbridge	CT	G	203 389-4452	5469
Keno Graphic Services Inc	Shelton	CT	E	203 925-7722	3822
Kool Ink LLC	Bloomfield	CT	F	860 242-0303	238
Kramer Printing Company Inc	West Haven	CT	F	203 933-5416	5129
L P Macadams Company Inc	Bridgeport	CT	D	203 366-3647	442
L R K Communications Inc	Fairfield	CT	G	203 372-1456	1441
Liberty Screen Print Co LLC	Beacon Falls	CT	F	203 632-5449	60
Logo Sportswear Inc	Wallingford	CT	G	203 678-4700	4767
Lorenco Industries Inc	Bethel	CT	F	203 743-6962	169

	CITY	ST	EMP	PHONE	ENTRY #
Lrp Conferences LLC	Trumbull	CT	E	203 663-0100	4627
Mad Sportswear LLC	West Haven	CT	G	203 932-4868	5133
Master Engrv & Printery Inc **(PA)**	Waterbury	CT	G	203 723-2779	4911
Matthews Printing Co	Wallingford	CT	F	203 265-0363	4770
McWeeney Marketing Group Inc	Orange	CT	G	203 891-8100	3373
Merrill Corporation	Hartford	CT	D	860 249-7220	1846
Mickey Herbst	Fairfield	CT	G	203 993-5879	1444
Mlk Business Forms Inc	New Haven	CT	F	203 624-6304	2712
Moonlight Media LLC	Haddam	CT	G	860 345-3595	1727
Muir Envelope Plus Inc	Newington	CT	F	860 953-6847	2884
Multiprints Inc	Meriden	CT	F	203 235-4409	2111
New England Printing LLC	Enfield	CT	G	860 745-3600	1372
New Fairfield Press Inc	New Fairfield	CT	F	203 746-2700	2626
Novel Tees Screen Prtg EMB LLC	Manchester	CT	F	860 643-6008	2026
Novel-Tees Unlimited LLC	Manchester	CT	G	860 643-6008	2027
Omega Engineering Inc **(HQ)**	Norwalk	CT	C	203 359-1660	3211
On Time Screen Printing & Embr	Derby	CT	F	203 874-4581	1076
Patriot Envelope LLC	Wethersfield	CT	G	860 529-1553	5260
Paul Dewitt	Danbury	CT	F	203 792-5610	965
Platt Brothers Realty II LLC	New Haven	CT	G	203 562-5112	2727
Popcorn Movie Poster Co LLC	East Hartford	CT	F	860 610-0000	1211
Practical Automation Inc **(HQ)**	Milford	CT	D	203 882-5640	2336
Prime Resources Corp	Bridgeport	CT	B	203 331-9100	474
Print & Post Services	Bridgeport	CT	G	203 336-0055	475
Print Shop of Wolcott LLC	Wolcott	CT	G	203 879-3353	5453
Print Source Ltd	Milford	CT	G	203 876-1822	2341
Privateer Ltd	Old Saybrook	CT	F	860 526-1837	3349
Production Decorating Co Inc	Waterbury	CT	E	203 574-2975	4946
Psd Inc	East Haven	CT	G	860 305-6346	1259
Quality Name Plate Inc	East Glastonbury	CT	D	860 633-9495	1114
R & B Apparel Plus LLC	Groton	CT	G	860 333-1757	1685
R R Donnelley & Sons Company	Manchester	CT	F	860 649-5570	2040
R R Donnelley & Sons Company	Avon	CT	E	860 773-6140	43
Rainbow Graphics Inc	Manchester	CT	G	860 646-8997	2042
Robert Audette **(PA)**	Cheshire	CT	G	203 872-3119	760
Roto-Die Company Inc	East Windsor	CT	F	860 292-7030	1300
Saybrook Press Incorporated	Guilford	CT	F	203 458-3637	1717
Schmitt Realty Holdings Inc **(PA)**	Guilford	CT	D	203 453-4334	1718
Schmitt Realty Holdings Inc	Guilford	CT	G	203 453-4334	1719
Sheila P Patrick	Waterbury	CT	G	203 575-1716	4956
Shirt Graphix	Wallingford	CT	G	203 294-1656	4805
Signs Now LLC	Newington	CT	G	860 667-8339	2903
Silkscreen Plus LLC	Wolcott	CT	G	203 879-0345	5460
Silvermine Press Inc	Norwalk	CT	G	203 847-4368	3246
Special Events Screen Prtg LLC	East Haven	CT	G	203 468-5453	1263
Specialty Printing LLC **(PA)**	East Windsor	CT	D	860 623-8870	1303
Speed Printing & Graphics Inc	Stamford	CT	G	203 324-4000	4328
Sportees LLC	Waterford	CT	G	860 440-3922	4994
Surys Inc	Trumbull	CT	C	203 333-5503	4633
Tee-It-Up LLC	Wallingford	CT	G	203 949-9455	4816
Tees Plus	Bridgeport	CT	F	800 782-8337	499
Tex Elm Inc	East Haddam	CT	F	860 873-9715	1153
Therma-Scan Inc	Vernon Rockville	CT	G	860 872-9770	4684
Varsity Imprints	Milford	CT	G	203 354-4371	2379
Vision Designs LLC	Brookfield	CT	F	203 778-9898	664
Visual Impact LLC	Danbury	CT	G	203 790-9650	1005
Wallingford Prtg Bus Forms Inc	Branford	CT	F	203 481-1911	359
Wink Ink LLC	Somers	CT	G	860 202-8709	3922
Yankee Screen Printing	Derby	CT	G	203 924-9926	1085
508tees Screenprinting	Acushnet	MA	G	508 717-3835	7396
Abby Printing Co Inc	Easthampton	MA	G	413 536-5269	10551
Accela Graphics Neng Inc	Westborough	MA	G	508 366-5999	16586
Ad Plus Inc	Boston	MA	G	617 859-3128	8340
Ad-A-Day Company Inc	Taunton	MA	E	508 824-8676	15719
ADI Print Solutions Inc	Chelsea	MA	G	508 230-7024	9943
Advanced Graphics Inc	Norwood	MA	G	781 551-0550	14121
Advanced Imaging Inc	Wilmington	MA	E	978 658-7776	16966
Agawam Novelty Company Inc	Agawam	MA	G	413 536-0471	7418
Albert Basse Associates Inc	Stoughton	MA	E	781 344-3555	15577
All American Embroidery Inc	Wilmington	MA	G	978 657-0414	16970
All City Screen Printing Inc	Wakefield	MA	G	781 665-0000	15940
Alltec Laser Technology	Southbridge	MA	F	508 765-6666	15375
Alternative Screen Printing	Topsfield	MA	F	978 887-9927	15853
Apex Press Inc	Westborough	MA	F	508 366-1110	16589
Appalachian Press	Westfield	MA	G	413 568-2621	16666
Applied Graphics Inc	Amesbury	MA	E	978 241-5300	7478
Archimedia Solutions Group LLC **(PA)**	Danvers	MA	G	978 774-5400	10195
Art Shirt Co	Somerville	MA	G	617 625-2636	15157
Art Swiss Corporation	New Bedford	MA	F	508 999-3281	13359
Aucoins Press Inc	Spencer	MA	G	508 885-0800	15425
Aucoins Printing	Spencer	MA	G	508 885-3595	15426
Avon Cstm EMB & Screenprinting	Avon	MA	F	781 341-4663	7878
Barney Rabin Company Inc	Marblehead	MA	F	781 639-0593	12675
Basement Designs Inc	Oak Bluffs	MA	G	508 693-4442	14209
Bay State Envelope Inc **(PA)**	Mansfield	MA	E	508 337-8900	12614
Bayview Graphics	North Weymouth	MA	G	781 878-3340	13996
BBC Printing and Products Inc	Waltham	MA	G	781 647-4646	16042
Belmont Printing Company	Belmont	MA	E	617 484-0833	8066
Billard Corporation	Sandwich	MA	G	508 888-4964	14961
Black and White Printing	Stow	MA	G	401 265-7811	15631
Blake Press Inc	Boston	MA	G	617 742-8700	8412
Bltees	Palmer	MA	G	413 289-0050	14281
Boostercom	Auburndale	MA	G	855 631-6850	7857
Boston Tag and Label Inc	Waltham	MA	G	781 893-9080	16050
Boutwell Owens & Co Inc **(PA)**	Fitchburg	MA	C	978 343-3067	10813
Brady Business Forms Inc	Lowell	MA	G	978 458-2585	12355
Business Cards Overnight Inc	Lawrence	MA	G	978 974-9271	11999
Business Resources Inc	Westborough	MA	F	508 433-4600	16596
Byd Corp	Everett	MA	G	617 394-0799	10605
Cambridge Printing Co Inc	Cambridge	MA	G	617 547-0270	9427
Campaignsthatwincom LLC	Worcester	MA	G	508 667-6365	17353
Causeway Graphics	Framingham	MA	G	508 309-6592	10931
CCL Label Inc **(HQ)**	Framingham	MA	D	508 872-4511	10932
Classic Envelope Inc	East Douglas	MA	D	508 731-6747	10425
Classic Letter Press Inc	South Yarmouth	MA	G	508 221-7496	15328
Coatings Adhesives Inks	Georgetown	MA	E	978 352-7273	11140
Colonial Key & Engraving	Salem	MA	G	978 745-8237	14902
Comdec Incorporated	Newburyport	MA	E	978 462-3399	13478
Corporate Image Apparel Inc	Fall River	MA	E	508 676-3099	10680
Courier Printing Inc	Pittsfield	MA	G	413 442-3242	14465
Crane Currency Us LLC	Boston	MA	G	617 648-3710	8488
Crest Printing Co Inc	Melrose	MA	G	617 889-1171	12980
Custom Quality Silk Screen	Rockland	MA	G	781 878-0760	14797
D & H Print Management Ltd	Pembroke	MA	G	781 829-0209	14396
Data Associates Business Trust	Waltham	MA	E	781 890-0110	16079
Davol/Taunton Printing Inc	Taunton	MA	F	508 824-4305	15741
Defiance Graphics Corp	Rowley	MA	F	978 948-2789	14852
Design Mark Industries Inc	Wareham	MA	D	800 451-3275	16244
Designs By Lainie	Lynn	MA	G	781 592-2126	12502
Desk Top Graphics Inc **(HQ)**	Peabody	MA	E	617 832-1927	14330
Desk Top Solutions Inc	Waltham	MA	F	781 890-7500	16086
Diehl Graphics Co	Winchendon	MA	G	978 297-1598	17074
Digital Graphics Inc	North Billerica	MA	E	781 270-3670	13809
Diversity Studio Inc	Littleton	MA	G	978 250-5553	12303
Docuprint Express Ltd	West Bridgewater	MA	G	508 895-9090	16437
Docuserve Inc	Marlborough	MA	E	508 786-5820	12749
DSA Printing & Publishing Inc	Chelmsford	MA	G	978 256-3900	9893
Duckhill River Corp	Wilmington	MA	G	978 657-6186	16997
Eastern Etching and Mfg Co	Chicopee	MA	E	413 594-6601	10022
Economy Coupon & Printing Inc	Peabody	MA	G	781 279-8555	14332
Elbe-Cesco Inc	Fall River	MA	D	508 676-8531	10687
Elbonais Incorporated	Framingham	MA	G	508 626-2318	10945
Elegant Stitches Inc	Pittsfield	MA	G	413 447-9452	14469
Elite	Watertown	MA	G	617 407-9300	16281
Em Screen Systems Inc	Millbury	MA	G	508 865-9995	13163
Excel Graphix	Norwood	MA	G	781 642-6736	14152
Fall River Modern Printing Co	Fall River	MA	F	508 673-9421	10697
Fast Mailing	Randolph	MA	G	617 605-8693	14680
Faux Designs	Auburndale	MA	F	617 965-0142	7861
Fedex Office & Print Svcs Inc	Chelmsford	MA	G	978 275-0574	9898
Financial Graphic Services Inc	Braintree	MA	F	617 389-0076	9007
First Impression Printing Inc	Stoughton	MA	G	781 344-8855	15592
Fit America Inc	Southborough	MA	G	309 839-1695	15357
Fluidform Inc	Acton	MA	G	978 287-4698	7356
Formlabs Inc **(PA)**	Somerville	MA	B	617 932-5227	15174
Four Seasons Trattoria Inc	South Yarmouth	MA	G	508 760-6600	15329
G & G Silk Screening	Plymouth	MA	G	508 830-1075	14559
G B Enterprises	Amherst	MA	G	413 210-4658	7515
Garlock Prtg & Converting Corp	Gardner	MA	C	978 630-1028	11116
Garlock Prtg & Converting Corp **(PA)**	Gardner	MA	D	978 630-1028	11117
Gatehouse Media Mass I Inc	Sharon	MA	C	781 487-7200	15050
Gazette Printing Co Inc	Easthampton	MA	F	413 527-7700	10564
George R King	Raynham	MA	G	508 821-3826	14715
Gerard F Scalley	Woburn	MA	G	781 933-3009	17192
Ghp Media Inc	North Adams	MA	D	413 663-3771	13675
Gloucester Graphics Inc **(PA)**	Gloucester	MA	F	978 281-4500	11188
Golden Manet Press Inc	Quincy	MA	G	617 773-2423	14629
Green Summer	Everett	MA	G	617 387-0120	10612
Guertin Graphics & Awards Inc	Worcester	MA	F	508 754-0200	17386
Hadley Printing Company Inc	Holyoke	MA	E	413 536-8517	11629
Hannaford & Dumas Corporation	Woburn	MA	E	781 503-0100	17195
Hendrickson Advertising Inc	Sterling	MA	G	978 422-8087	15539
Hercules Press	Boston	MA	G	617 323-1950	8596
Highland Press of Athol Inc	Athol	MA	G	978 249-6588	7687
Hillside Press	Melrose	MA	G	617 742-1922	12982
Hitchcock Press Inc	Holyoke	MA	F	413 538-8811	11632
Hot Plates Company	Ashland	MA	G	508 429-1445	7661
Howarth Specialty Company	Westport	MA	G	508 674-8950	16841
I N I Screen Printing	New Bedford	MA	G	774 206-1341	13396
Image Factory	Pocasset	MA	G	508 295-3876	14598
Image Resolutions Inc	Norwell	MA	G	781 659-0900	14104
Image Software Services Inc	Shirley	MA	E	978 425-3600	15087
Imaging Data Corporation	Clinton	MA	G	978 365-9353	10081
Imperial Image Inc	North Chelmsford	MA	F	978 251-0420	13897

	CITY	ST	EMP	PHONE	ENTRY #
Independant Newspaper Group	Revere	MA	E	781 485-0588	14767
Industrial Etching Inc	East Longmeadow	MA	F	413 525-4110	10479
Inkify LLC	Walpole	MA	G	617 304-6642	15994
Inovar Packaging Group LLC	Newburyport	MA	E	978 463-4004	13501
Instant Offset Press Inc	Hyannis	MA	F	508 790-1100	11843
Integrity Graphics LLC	Randolph	MA	G	339 987-5533	14688
International Laser Systems	Holyoke	MA	G	413 533-4372	11634
Interticketcom Inc **(PA)**	Bedford	MA	G	781 275-5724	7984
Intouch Labels and Packg Inc	Lowell	MA	G	800 370-2693	12384
Itg Group Inc	Medway	MA	G	508 645-4994	12962
J & S Business Products Inc	Ayer	MA	G	877 425-4049	7922
Jackiestees	Beverly	MA	G	617 799-8404	8143
John Brown US LLC	Boston	MA	F	617 449-4354	8632
John Karl Dietrich & Assoc	Cambridge	MA	F	617 868-4140	9521
Journal of Antq & Collectibles	Sturbridge	MA	F	508 347-1960	15639
Kirkwood Holdings Inc **(PA)**	Wilmington	MA	C	978 658-4200	17012
Kondelin Associates Inc **(HQ)**	Peabody	MA	F	978 281-3663	14348
Kreate & Print Inc	Norwood	MA	G	781 255-0505	14172
Kwik Kopy Printing	Beverly	MA	G	978 232-3552	8146
L & J of New England Inc	Worcester	MA	E	508 756-8080	17403
L & J Screen Printers Inc	Worcester	MA	G	508 791-7320	17404
La Semana Newspaper	Boston	MA	G	617 427-6212	8658
Label Haus Inc	Danvers	MA	G	978 777-1773	10230
Labelprint America Inc	Newburyport	MA	E	978 463-4004	13506
Lamb Printing Company Inc	North Adams	MA	G	413 662-2495	13678
Laplume & Sons Printing Inc	Lawrence	MA	E	978 683-1009	12045
Lasercraze	North Andover	MA	E	978 689-7700	13716
Leap Year Publishing LLC	North Andover	MA	F	978 688-9900	13717
Lennys Screen Printing	Braintree	MA	G	781 267-5977	9022
Letterpress Services Inc	West Springfield	MA	G	413 732-0399	16529
Liberated Images Inc	Peabody	MA	G	978 532-1880	14352
Liberty Printing Co Inc	Brockton	MA	G	508 586-6810	9162
Lincoln Press Co Inc	Fall River	MA	E	508 673-3241	10723
Lisa Signs Inc	Woburn	MA	G	781 935-1821	17215
Lopesdzine	West Bridgewater	MA	G	508 857-0121	16443
Ludlow Printing and Copy Ctr	Ludlow	MA	G	413 583-5220	12472
Lujean Printing Co Inc	Cotuit	MA	F	508 428-8700	10170
M & R Screen Printing Inc	New Bedford	MA	E	508 996-0419	13412
M Squared Lasers Inc	Cambridge	MA	G	408 667-0553	9542
Madison Group Inc	Revere	MA	G	781 853-0029	14771
Marcott Designs	Attleboro	MA	G	508 226-2680	7762
Massachusetts Envelope Co Inc **(PA)**	Somerville	MA	E	617 623-8000	15195
Mc Kinnon Printing Co Inc	Revere	MA	G	781 592-3677	14773
McGirr Graphics Incorporated	Plymouth	MA	E	508 747-6400	14564
Medi - Print Inc	Boston	MA	G	617 566-7594	8693
Medianews Group Inc	Devens	MA	D	978 772-0777	10325
Merrill Corporation	Boston	MA	E	617 535-1500	8698
Minuteman Press	Fitchburg	MA	G	978 345-0818	10839
Moonlight Ltd	Brockton	MA	G	508 584-0094	9168
Morgan Enterprises Inc	Worcester	MA	G	985 377-3216	17424
Nano Ops Inc	Needham	MA	G	617 543-2921	13306
New England Business Svc Inc **(HQ)**	Groton	MA	D	978 448-6111	11291
New Tek Design Group Inc	West Boylston	MA	F	508 835-4544	16423
Nfi LLC	New Bedford	MA	E	508 998-9021	13426
Nitor Corp	Southwick	MA	G	413 998-0510	15416
Norman Ellis	Auburn	MA	G	508 853-5833	7845
Northeast Printing & Graphics	Plymouth	MA	G	508 746-8689	14568
Northern Graphics Inc	Middleton	MA	F	978 646-9925	13097
Northpoint Printing Svcs Inc	Waltham	MA	F	781 895-1900	16161
Nova Idea Inc	Woburn	MA	G	781 281-2183	17246
Offset Prep Inc	Quincy	MA	G	617 472-7887	14643
Old School Apparel	Saugus	MA	G	781 231-0753	14993
On Site Printing & Copying	Needham Heights	MA	G	781 449-1871	13341
One Off Apparel Inc	West Boylston	MA	G	508 835-8883	16424
Optamark LLC **(PA)**	North Attleboro	MA	G	508 643-1017	13770
Optimum Sportswear Inc	Lawrence	MA	G	978 689-2290	12069
Pacific Printing Inc	Northampton	MA	G	413 585-5700	14016
Package Printing Company Inc	West Springfield	MA	E	413 736-2748	16539
Papers & Presents	Wellesley Hills	MA	G	781 235-1079	16399
Paul H Murphy & Co Inc	Quincy	MA	F	617 472-7707	14645
Peter Young Company	Watertown	MA	G	617 923-1101	16306
Pictex Corporation	Boston	MA	G	617 375-5801	8779
PIP Itsa Inc	Beverly	MA	G	978 927-5717	8165
Poputees Co	Blackstone	MA	G	401 497-6512	8314
Power Graphics Printing	Tewksbury	MA	G	978 851-8988	15827
Precision Images Inc	North Dighton	MA	G	508 824-6200	13934
Primary Graphics Corporation	Taunton	MA	F	781 575-0411	15773
Print Management Systems Inc	Woburn	MA	F	781 944-1041	17270
Print Shop	Williamstown	MA	G	413 458-6039	16959
Printpro Silkscreen & EMB	Haverhill	MA	F	978 556-1695	11461
Professional Lithography Inc	South Hadley	MA	E	413 532-9473	15309
Proforma Printing & Promotion	Milton	MA	G	617 464-1120	13199
Pros Choice Inc	Agawam	MA	F	413 583-3435	7448
Puffer International Inc	Westfield	MA	G	413 527-1069	16720
Qrsts LLC	Somerville	MA	G	617 625-3335	15208
Quad/Graphics Inc	East Longmeadow	MA	C	413 525-8552	10490
Quality Envelope & Printing Co	Middleboro	MA	G	508 947-8878	13077
Quick Stop Printing	Worcester	MA	G	508 797-4788	17448
R R Donnelley & Sons Company	Boston	MA	D	617 345-4300	8806
Red Mill Graphics Incorporated	Chelmsford	MA	F	978 251-4081	9926
Regal Press Incorporated **(PA)**	Norwood	MA	C	781 769-3900	14192
Reid Graphics Inc	Andover	MA	D	978 474-1930	7598
Rgp Corp	Milford	MA	G	508 478-8511	13141
Roberts & Sons Printing Inc	Springfield	MA	G	413 283-9356	15503
Royal Label Co Inc	Boston	MA	F	617 825-6050	8828
S & S Computer Imaging Inc	Holyoke	MA	G	413 536-0117	11655
Sallyharrold Inc	Dennis	MA	G	508 258-0253	10310
Sanchez Octavio Storage	Worcester	MA	G	508 853-3309	17468
Scrimshaw Screenprinting	New Bedford	MA	G	508 617-7498	13447
Shrewsbury National Press	Shrewsbury	MA	G	508 756-7502	15132
Silver Screen Design Inc	Greenfield	MA	F	413 773-1692	11275
Simply Designs & Printing	Northbridge	MA	G	508 234-3424	14061
Smudge Ink Incorporated	Charlestown	MA	G	617 242-8228	9844
Specialty Manufacturing Inc	Amesbury	MA	E	978 388-1601	7509
Specialty Prtrs F Bush Son Co	Plympton	MA	G	781 585-9444	14593
Steves Sports	West Springfield	MA	G	413 746-1696	16553
Super Sport Screen Printing	Malden	MA	G	781 397-8166	12599
Taylor Communications Inc	Avon	MA	F	508 584-0102	7898
Techprint Inc	Lawrence	MA	D	978 975-1245	12077
Ted Best	Hyde Park	MA	G	617 361-7258	11881
Teesmile Inc	Burlington	MA	G	781 325-8587	9343
Tekni-Plex Inc	Ashland	MA	F	508 881-2440	7671
Thomas B Fullen	Leominster	MA	G	978 534-5255	12194
Three Jakes	Plymouth	MA	G	781 706-6886	14588
Three Twins Productions Inc	Watertown	MA	F	617 926-0377	16323
Tomandtim Enterprises LLC	Northborough	MA	G	508 380-5550	14051
Triad Designs	Groton	MA	G	978 952-0136	11296
Union Bookbinding Company Inc **(PA)**	Fall River	MA	E	508 676-8580	10775
University of Massachusetts	Amherst	MA	F	413 545-2718	7531
Van-Go Graphics	Grafton	MA	F	508 865-7300	11225
Viridis3d LLC	Woburn	MA	G	781 305-4961	17313
Washington ABC Imaging Inc	Boston	MA	D	857 753-4241	8916
Watertown Printers Inc	Somerville	MA	G	781 893-9400	15230
West Park Stamping Co Inc	Attleboro	MA	G	508 399-7488	7809
Whaling City Graphics Inc	Acushnet	MA	G	508 998-3511	7407
White Dog Printing Inc	Gardner	MA	G	978 630-1091	11133
Wholesale Printing Inc	Woburn	MA	F	781 937-3357	17319
Wish Designs Inc **(PA)**	Lawrence	MA	F	978 566-1232	12084
Wtd Inc **(PA)**	Wilmington	MA	D	978 658-8200	17068
Yankee Printing Group Inc	South Hadley	MA	E	413 532-9513	15313
Yblank	Cambridge	MA	G	857 544-9991	9708
Action Screen Printing	Lewiston	ME	G	207 795-7786	6272
Adept Screen Prtg & Graphics	Lisbon Falls	ME	G	207 353-6094	6366
Albisons Printing Inc	Augusta	ME	G	207 622-1941	5603
Andys Silkscreen	Bingham	ME	G	207 672-3302	5769
Armstrong Family Inds Inc	Hermon	ME	E	207 848-7300	6183
Artforms **(PA)**	Brunswick	ME	E	800 828-8518	5829
Atlantic Sportswear Inc	Portland	ME	E	207 797-5028	6612
Bell Manufacturing Co	Lewiston	ME	D	207 784-2961	6276
Black Bear Graphics	Kingfield	ME	G	207 265-4593	6252
Black Bear Graphics Inc	Farmington	ME	G	207 778-9715	6041
Black Dog Screen Printing	Clinton	ME	G	207 426-9041	5913
Blue Sky Inc	Portland	ME	G	207 772-0073	6625
Brady Screenprint Inc	Biddeford	ME	G	207 284-8531	5723
Bruce A Pettengill	Leeds	ME	G	207 933-2578	6268
Coastal T Shirts Inc	Auburn	ME	G	207 784-4184	5553
Computech Inc	Auburn	ME	G	207 777-7468	5554
Creative Digital Imaging	Bangor	ME	E	207 973-0500	5640
Csg Inc	Yarmouth	ME	G	207 846-9567	7293
D R Designs Inc	Manchester	ME	G	207 622-3303	6409
Designtex Group Inc	Portland	ME	E	207 774-2689	6650
Downeast Graphics & Prtg Inc	Ellsworth	ME	F	207 667-5582	6016
East Shore Production	Portland	ME	G	207 775-5353	6657
Erin Murphy	Windham	ME	G	928 525-2056	7232
Evergreen Custom Printing Inc	Auburn	ME	G	207 782-2327	5563
Full Court Press	Westbrook	ME	F	207 464-0002	7189
Gossamer Press	Old Town	ME	G	207 827-9881	6539
Graphic Explosion Inc	Lewiston	ME	G	207 576-3210	6289
Guy Little Press Inc **(PA)**	Auburn	ME	G	207 795-0650	5570
Harbor Print Shop	Boothbay	ME	G	207 633-4176	5778
Identity Group Holdings Corp	Brunswick	ME	E	207 510-6800	5837
Island Approaches Inc	Sunset	ME	F	207 348-2459	7075
J A Black Company	Belfast	ME	G	207 338-4040	5691
J Weston Walch Publisher	Portland	ME	E	207 772-2846	6676
James Newspapers Inc	Rumford	ME	G	207 364-7893	6836
JS McCarthy Co Inc **(PA)**	Augusta	ME	D	207 622-6241	5609
Liberty Graphics Inc	Liberty	ME	E	207 589-4596	6331
Lts Inc	Portland	ME	E	207 774-1104	6680
Maine Poly Aquisition Corp	Greene	ME	E	207 946-7000	6150
Northeast Publishing Company	Presque Isle	ME	F	207 764-4471	6765
Northeast Publishing Company	Dover Foxcroft	ME	G	207 564-8355	5961
Omni Press Inc	Portland	ME	G	207 780-6664	6705
Park Street Press Inc	South Paris	ME	G	207 743-7702	7015
Penobscot Bay Press Inc **(PA)**	Stonington	ME	F	207 367-2200	7070

	CITY	ST	EMP	PHONE	ENTRY #
Port City Graphics Inc	Gorham	ME	G	207 450-6299	6127
Precision Direct Inc	Portland	ME	G	207 321-3677	6715
Printgraphics of Maine Inc	Portland	ME	G	207 347-5700	6716
Quick Print Color Center	Saco	ME	G	207 282-6480	6856
Seastreet Graphics	Thomaston	ME	G	207 594-1915	7088
Shoreline Publications	Wells	ME	F	207 646-8448	7165
Sunrise Printing & Graphics	Windham	ME	G	207 892-3534	7255
Tranquilitees	Augusta	ME	G	207 441-8058	5622
Trems Inc	Rockland	ME	G	207 596-6989	6812
W S Emerson Company Inc **(PA)**	Brewer	ME	E	207 989-3410	5803
Waterfront Graphics & Prtg LLC	South Portland	ME	G	207 799-3519	7044
Woodland Studios Inc	Ellsworth	ME	F	207 667-3286	6024
Xpress of Maine **(PA)**	Portland	ME	G	207 775-2444	6747
Xtreme Screen & Sportswear LLC	Westbrook	ME	G	207 857-9200	7215
603 Screenprinting LLC	Salem	NH	G	603 505-7693	19702
Acara Holdings LLC	Concord	NH	F	603 434-3175	17879
All Seasons Printing & Awards	Pelham	NH	G	603 881-7106	19427
Amherst Label Inc	Milford	NH	E	603 673-7849	19047
AMI Graphics Inc **(PA)**	Strafford	NH	D	603 664-7174	19865
Argyle Associates Inc	Concord	NH	E	603 226-4300	17883
Bank & Business Forms Inc	Keene	NH	G	603 357-0567	18495
Bovie Screen Process Prtg Inc	Bow	NH	E	603 224-0651	17708
C & O Box & Printing Company	Hooksett	NH	G	508 881-1760	18345
C K Productions Inc	Pelham	NH	E	603 893-5069	19429
Camera Works Inc	Londonderry	NH	G	603 898-7175	18683
Capitol Copy Inc	Concord	NH	G	603 226-2679	17889
CB Ventures LLC	Concord	NH	F	603 434-3175	17891
Computype Inc	Concord	NH	F	603 225-5500	17894
Custom Die Cut Inc	Windham	NH	G	603 437-3090	20003
D M Printing Service Inc	Hudson	NH	G	603 883-1897	18382
Digital Ink Printing LLC	Somersworth	NH	G	603 692-6002	19835
Doolittles Print Serve Inc	Claremont	NH	G	603 543-0700	17848
Eagle Copy Center	Windham	NH	G	603 225-3713	20004
Electronic Imaging Mtls Inc	Keene	NH	E	603 357-1459	18501
Electronics For Imaging Inc	Londonderry	NH	F	603 279-4635	18695
Embrodery By Evrything Per LLC	Littleton	NH	G	603 444-0130	18658
Evans Printing Co	Bow	NH	G	603 856-8238	17713
Fedex Office & Print Svcs Inc	West Lebanon	NH	G	603 298-5891	19951
Flex-Print-Labels	Hampton	NH	E	603 929-3088	18263
Forward Merch LLC	Dover	NH	G	603 742-4377	18022
Gus & Ruby Letterpress LLC	Portsmouth	NH	G	603 319-1717	19571
Jembow Inc	Bow	NH	G	603 774-6055	17717
Lamprey River Screen Print	Newmarket	NH	G	603 659-9959	19336
Left-Tees Designs Bayou LLC	Derry	NH	F	603 437-6630	17986
Letterman Press LLC	West Lebanon	NH	G	603 543-0500	19956
Liebl Printing Co	Colebrook	NH	G	603 237-8650	17873
Life Is Good **(PA)**	Hudson	NH	D	603 594-6100	18411
Loudon Screen Printing Inc	Epsom	NH	G	603 736-9420	18106
Megaprint Inc	Holderness	NH	F	603 536-2900	18323
Mg Print and Promotions	Dover	NH	G	603 343-2534	18037
Nishi Enterprises Inc	Dover	NH	G	603 749-0113	18040
Northeast Silk Screen Inc	Nashua	NH	G	603 883-6933	19220
Northstar Direct LLC	Manchester	NH	F	603 627-3334	18888
Paul Revere Press Inc	Newton	NH	G	781 289-4031	19366
Phoenix Screen Printing	Nashua	NH	F	603 578-9599	19233
Piches Ski Shop Inc	Belmont	NH	F	603 524-4413	17680
Powerplay Management LLC	Portsmouth	NH	E	603 436-3030	19609
Printed Matter Inc	Newfields	NH	E	603 778-2990	19318
Puritan Press Inc **(PA)**	Hollis	NH	E	603 889-4500	18339
RB Graphics Inc	Hooksett	NH	G	603 624-4025	18358
Red Brick Clothing Co	Hudson	NH	G	603 882-4100	18433
Red Fish-Blue Fish Dye Works	Somersworth	NH	F	603 692-3900	19846
Relyco Sales Inc	Dover	NH	E	603 742-0999	18050
Rgm Enterprises Inc	Manchester	NH	G	603 644-3336	18911
Savvy Workshop	Manchester	NH	G	603 792-0080	18916
Say It In Stitches Inc	Concord	NH	G	603 224-6470	17927
Screen Gems Inc	Seabrook	NH	F	603 474-5353	19815
Seacoast Screen Printing	Newmarket	NH	G	603 758-6398	19341
Sherwin Dodge Printers Inc	Littleton	NH	F	603 444-6552	18666
Silver Direct Inc	Swanzey	NH	G	603 355-8855	19889
Smith & Town Printers LLC	Berlin	NH	G	603 752-2150	17700
Spear Group Holdings	Milford	NH	E	603 673-6400	19078
Spear USA Inc	Milford	NH	G	513 459-1100	19079
Spectrum Marketing Dbalogo Loc	Manchester	NH	G	603 644-4800	18928
Suleys Soccer Center	Manchester	NH	G	603 668-7227	18931
Sumner Fancy	Windham	NH	G	603 893-3081	20011
Sumner Printing Inc	Somersworth	NH	E	603 692-7424	19849
Swaffield Enterprises Inc	Wolfeboro	NH	G	603 569-3017	20025
T K O Printing Inc	Rochester	NH	G	603 332-0511	19689
Talient Action Group	Manchester	NH	E	603 703-0795	18935
Telegraph Publishing Company **(HQ)**	Nashua	NH	C	603 594-6472	19271
TI Sports Sales Inc	Windham	NH	G	603 577-1931	20012
Tylergraphics Inc	Laconia	NH	G	603 524-6625	18590
U S Product Labels Inc	Salem	NH	G	603 894-6020	19774
Vantastic Inc	Laconia	NH	G	603 524-1419	18591
Venture Print Unlimited Inc	Plymouth	NH	F	603 536-2410	19531
Allied Group Inc **(PA)**	Cranston	RI	C	401 461-1700	20177
American Trophy & Supply Co	East Providence	RI	G	401 438-3060	20386
Bradford Press Inc	Providence	RI	G	401 621-7195	20972
Branding Company Inc	Westerly	RI	G	203 793-1923	21518
Classic Embroidery Co	East Providence	RI	E	401 434-9632	20397
Comstock Press	Westerly	RI	G	401 596-8719	21520
Cool Air Creations Inc	Smithfield	RI	E	401 830-5780	21216
Davis Press	Bristol	RI	G	401 624-9331	20072
Digital Printing Concepts Inc	East Providence	RI	G	401 431-2110	20407
Foxon Company	Providence	RI	E	401 421-2386	21015
Graphic Application Tech Inc	North Providence	RI	G	401 233-2100	20763
Graphic Ink Incorporated	East Providence	RI	F	401 431-5081	20415
Griswold Textile Print Inc	Westerly	RI	E	401 596-2784	21525
Hilco Athletic & Graphics Inc	West Warwick	RI	F	401 822-1775	21495
Hopkins Press	North Providence	RI	G	401 231-9654	20764
Image Printing & Copying Inc	Warwick	RI	F	401 737-9311	21374
J B Foley Printing Company	Providence	RI	G	401 467-3616	21041
J Mack Studios LLC	Westerly	RI	G	401 932-8600	21528
K&M/Nordic Co Inc	Riverside	RI	E	401 431-5150	21171
Lighthouse Publications	Bristol	RI	G	401 396-9888	20090
Mix Up Printer	Lincoln	RI	G	401 334-4291	20584
Moo Inc	Lincoln	RI	D	401 434-3561	20586
Moonlite Graphics Co Inc	Little Compton	RI	G	401 635-2962	20606
Multi-Color Corporation	North Kingstown	RI	C	401 884-7100	20729
N-M Letters Inc	Barrington	RI	G	401 245-5565	20048
National Cthlic Bthics Ctr Inc	Barrington	RI	G	401 289-0680	20049
Park Printers	Pawtucket	RI	G	401 728-8650	20874
Pax Incorporated Printers	Middletown	RI	G	401 847-1157	20629
Proprint Inc	Johnston	RI	F	401 944-3855	20531
Quality Printing Services Inc	Rumford	RI	G	401 434-4321	21194
Regine Printing Co Inc	Providence	RI	G	401 943-3404	21108
Rlcp Inc	Barrington	RI	E	401 461-6560	20054
Schofield Printing Inc	Pawtucket	RI	E	401 728-6980	20898
Service Plus Press Inc	Warwick	RI	G	401 461-2929	21424
Shoreline Bus Solutions Inc **(DH)**	North Kingstown	RI	F	877 914-7856	20741
Swg Promotions LLC	Providence	RI	G	401 272-6050	21130
Taylor Communications Inc	Warwick	RI	G	401 738-0257	21435
Trimed Media Group Inc	Providence	RI	F	401 919-5165	21141
Warwick Group Inc	Bristol	RI	F	401 438-9451	20109
Women & Infants Hospital	Providence	RI	G	401 453-7600	21156
Amalgamated Culture Work Inc **(PA)**	Burlington	VT	G	800 272-2066	21766
Bruso-Holmes Inc	Essex Junction	VT	G	802 878-8337	21934
Bumwraps Inc **(PA)**	Montgomery Center	VT	G	802 326-4080	22141
Bumwraps Inc	Newport	VT	G	802 326-4080	22190
Dawn Brainard	Newport	VT	G	802 334-2780	22196
Eastern Systems Inc **(PA)**	Waitsfield	VT	G	802 496-1000	22565
Graphic Edge Inc	Rutland	VT	E	802 855-8840	22336
Herald Association Inc	Rutland	VT	C	802 747-6121	22338
Jet Service Envelope Co Inc **(PA)**	Barre	VT	F	802 229-9335	21626
Leahy Press Inc	Montpelier	VT	E	802 223-2100	22153
Mitchell Tees & Signs Inc	Pittsford	VT	G	802 483-6866	22264
Parent Co Applications Inc **(PA)**	Essex Junction	VT	F	802 233-3612	21953
Paul Thomas	Chester	VT	G	802 875-4004	21848
Paw Prints Press Inc	South Burlington	VT	G	802 865-2872	22456
Pumpkin Harbor Designs Inc	Jeffersonville	VT	G	802 644-6588	22047
Rutland Printing Co Inc	Rutland	VT	G	802 775-1948	22351
Squeegee Printers Inc	Canaan	VT	G	802 266-3426	21825
SRC Liquidation Company	South Burlington	VT	G	802 862-9932	22467
The Lane Press Inc	South Burlington	VT	C	802 863-5555	22471
Tuttle Law Print Inc	Rutland	VT	D	802 773-9171	22356
Vermont Art Studio Inc	Rutland	VT	G	802 747-7446	22358
Vermont Flannel Co	Woodstock	VT	G	802 457-4111	22740
Winooski Press LLC	Winooski	VT	G	802 655-1611	22728

2761 Manifold Business Forms

	CITY	ST	EMP	PHONE	ENTRY #
Mlk Business Forms Inc	New Haven	CT	F	203 624-6304	2712
Taylor Communications Inc	East Hartford	CT	F	860 290-6851	1227
Wallingford Prtg Bus Forms Inc	Branford	CT	F	203 481-1911	359
American Health Resources Inc	North Easton	MA	G	508 588-7700	13941
Belmont Printing Company	Belmont	MA	E	617 484-0833	8066
BFI Print Communications Inc **(PA)**	Boston	MA	D	781 447-1199	8405
D B S Industries Inc	Haverhill	MA	D	978 373-4748	11421
Regal Press Incorporated **(PA)**	Norwood	MA	C	781 769-3900	14192
Stat Products Inc	Ashland	MA	E	508 881-8022	7670
Taylor Communications Inc	Avon	MA	F	508 584-0102	7898
Taylor Communications Inc	Braintree	MA	F	781 843-0250	9043
Wolters Kluwer Fincl Svcs Inc	Waltham	MA	B	978 263-1212	16224
J A Black Company	Belfast	ME	G	207 338-4040	5691
Bank & Business Forms Inc	Keene	NH	G	603 357-0567	18495
Allied Group Inc **(PA)**	Cranston	RI	C	401 461-1700	20177

2771 Greeting Card Publishing

	CITY	ST	EMP	PHONE	ENTRY #
Caspari Inc **(PA)**	Seymour	CT	F	203 888-1100	3750
Joy Carole Creations Inc	Danbury	CT	G	203 794-1401	942
Smiling Dog	Middletown	CT	G	860 344-0707	2223
Caspi Cards and Art	Newton	MA	G	617 964-8888	13574
Expressive Design Group Inc	Holyoke	MA	E	413 315-6296	11626
Fein Things	Centerville	MA	G	508 778-5200	9815

SIC

	CITY	ST	EMP	PHONE	ENTRY #
Good Cause Greetings Inc	Wilbraham	MA	G	413 543-1515	16938
New England Business Svc Inc **(HQ)**	Groton	MA	D	978 448-6111	11291
Viabella Holdings LLC	Wareham	MA	F	800 688-9998	16257
Borealis Press Inc	Blue Hill	ME	G	207 370-6020	5771
In Your Own Words LLC	Greene	ME	G	207 946-5049	6149
Patricks Inc	Bangor	ME	G	207 990-9303	5657
Renaissance Greeting Cards Inc	Sanford	ME	C	207 324-4153	6888
William Arthur Inc	West Kennebunk	ME	C	413 684-2600	7174
Be Youneeq LLC	Raymond	NH	G	603 244-3933	19635
Gloria Jean Photography	Pembroke	NH	G	603 485-7176	19457
Pen & Inc	Bow	NH	G	603 225-7522	17726
Oatmeal Studios Inc	Rochester	VT	F	802 967-8014	22320
Vermont Christmas Company	Milton	VT	G	802 893-1670	22139

2782 Blankbooks & Looseleaf Binders

	CITY	ST	EMP	PHONE	ENTRY #
American CT Rng Bnder Index &	Washington	CT	F	860 868-7900	4830
Data Management Incorporated	Unionville	CT	E	860 677-8586	4655
Grannys Got It	Wolcott	CT	G	203 879-0042	5443
Mbsw Inc	West Hartford	CT	D	860 243-0303	5086
Scrapbook Clubhouse	Westbrook	CT	F	860 399-4443	5162
Yolanda Dubose Records and	West Haven	CT	F	203 823-6699	5153
Atlantic Bookbinders Inc	South Lancaster	MA	G	978 365-4524	15315
Deluxe Corporation	Townsend	MA	C	978 597-8715	15871
Elbe-Cesco Inc	Fall River	MA	D	508 676-8531	10687
Eureka Lab Book Inc	Holyoke	MA	F	413 534-5671	11625
Laser Laser Inc	West Roxbury	MA	G	617 615-2292	16498
Nettwerk Music Group LLC	Cambridge	MA	G	617 497-8200	9576
Quality Loose Leaf Co	South Hadley	MA	G	413 534-5891	15310
Union Bookbinding Company Inc **(PA)**	Fall River	MA	E	508 676-8580	10775
Union Bookbinding II LLC	Fall River	MA	E	508 676-8580	10776
W G Fry Corp	Florence	MA	E	413 747-2551	10870
Fabricate LLC	Bar Harbor	ME	G	207 288-5113	5665
Bank & Business Forms Inc	Keene	NH	G	603 357-0567	18495
Rosencrntz Gldnstern Banknotes	Wilton	NH	F	603 654-6160	19986
Scrappin Soul Sisters	Concord	NH	G	603 717-7136	17928
Allied Group Inc **(PA)**	Cranston	RI	C	401 461-1700	20177
Check Mate Service Line LLC	Smithfield	RI	G	401 231-7296	21215
Jackson Bookbinding Co Inc	Greenville	RI	F	401 231-0800	20469
Strange Famous Inc	North Smithfield	RI	G	310 254-8974	20797

2789 Bookbinding

	CITY	ST	EMP	PHONE	ENTRY #
Adkins Printing Company	New Britain	CT	E	800 228-9745	2506
Allied Printing Services Inc **(PA)**	Manchester	CT	B	860 643-1101	1984
Book Automation Inc	New Milford	CT	G	860 354-7900	2788
Connecticut Valley Bindery	New Britain	CT	E	860 229-7637	2521
E R Hitchcock Company	New Britain	CT	E	860 229-2024	2529
Eccles-Lehman Inc	Easton	CT	G	203 268-0605	1318
Elm Press Incorporated	Terryville	CT	E	860 583-3600	4477
Falcon Press	Enfield	CT	G	860 763-2293	1362
G & R Enterprises Incorporated	Hartford	CT	G	860 549-6120	1822
Imperial Grphic Cmmnctions Inc	Milford	CT	E	203 650-3478	2301
Jerrys Printing & Graphics LLC	Bridgeport	CT	G	203 384-0015	435
Joseph Merritt & Company Inc	Danbury	CT	G	203 743-6734	940
Kool Ink LLC	Bloomfield	CT	F	860 242-0303	238
Master Engrv & Printery Inc **(PA)**	Waterbury	CT	G	203 723-2779	4911
Palmisano Printing LLC	Bristol	CT	G	860 582-6883	590
Paul Dewitt	Danbury	CT	F	203 792-5610	965
Phoenix Press Inc	New Haven	CT	E	203 865-5555	2726
Prosperous Printing LLC	Wilton	CT	G	203 834-1962	5300
Saybrook Press Incorporated	Guilford	CT	F	203 458-3637	1717
Step Saver Inc	Southington	CT	E	860 621-6751	4082
STP Bindery Services Inc	East Hartford	CT	E	860 528-1430	1223
Vernon Printing Co Inc	Vernon Rockville	CT	G	860 872-1826	4688
Acme Bookbinding Company Inc	Charlestown	MA	D	617 242-1100	9823
Alliance Book Mfg Co Inc	Pembroke	MA	G	781 294-0802	14390
American Prtg & Envelope Inc	Auburn	MA	E	508 832-6100	7825
Andrew T Johnson Company Inc **(PA)**	Boston	MA	E	617 742-1610	8366
Apb Enterprises Inc	Marlborough	MA	G	508 481-0966	12715
Atlantic Bookbinders Inc	South Lancaster	MA	G	978 365-4524	15315
Belmont Printing Company	Belmont	MA	E	617 484-0833	8066
Bill Martel	Somerville	MA	G	617 776-1040	15158
Bridgeport Nat Bindery Inc	Agawam	MA	D	413 789-1981	7425
Business Cards Overnight Inc	Lawrence	MA	G	978 974-9271	11999
Chaco Inc	Norwood	MA	G	781 769-5557	14141
Color Images Inc	Methuen	MA	G	978 688-4994	13015
Coprico Inc	Chelsea	MA	G	617 889-0520	9951
D & L Associates Inc	Needham Heights	MA	G	781 400-5068	13326
D S Graphics Inc **(PA)**	Lowell	MA	C	978 970-1359	12365
Ddfhklt Inc	West Springfield	MA	F	413 733-7441	16515
Dmr Print Inc **(PA)**	Concord	MA	E	617 876-3688	10128
Elbonais Incorporated	Framingham	MA	G	508 626-2318	10945
Flagship Press Inc	North Andover	MA	C	978 975-3100	13704
Generation Four Inc	Waltham	MA	G	781 899-3180	16119
Ghp Media Inc	North Adams	MA	D	413 663-3771	13675
Graphic Fllfillment Finshg Inc	Holbrook	MA	G	781 727-8845	11525
Green Dragon Bindery Inc	Shrewsbury	MA	G	508 842-8250	15115
Hf Group LLC	Charlestown	MA	G	617 242-1100	9836
J C Enterprises Inc	Ashland	MA	G	508 881-7228	7662
J T Gardner Inc **(PA)**	Westborough	MA	E	800 540-4993	16627
J T Gardner Inc	Worcester	MA	G	508 751-6600	17396
Keating Communication Group	Canton	MA	G	781 828-9030	9749
Kirkwood Holdings Inc **(PA)**	Wilmington	MA	C	978 658-4200	17012
Laplume & Sons Printing Inc	Lawrence	MA	E	978 683-1009	12045
Linmel Associates Inc	Marlborough	MA	F	508 481-6699	12787
LPI Printing and Graphic Inc	Stoneham	MA	E	781 438-5400	15566
Marcus Company Inc	Holyoke	MA	E	413 534-3303	11637
Massachusetts Repro Ltd	Boston	MA	F	617 227-2237	8686
McDermott Pallotta Inc	Watertown	MA	G	617 924-2318	16300
Miles Press Inc	Auburn	MA	F	508 752-6430	7843
Minuteman Press	Newburyport	MA	G	978 465-2242	13515
Minuteman Press	Fitchburg	MA	G	978 345-0818	10839
Minuteman Printing Corp	Concord	MA	F	978 369-2808	10141
Modus Media Inc	Waltham	MA	E	781 663-5000	16153
Nabs Inc	Waltham	MA	F	781 899-7719	16154
Northeast Document Conservatio	Andover	MA	E	978 470-1010	7577
Northern Graphics Inc	Middleton	MA	F	978 646-9925	13097
Picken Printing Inc	North Chelmsford	MA	E	978 251-0730	13907
PIP Itsa Inc	Beverly	MA	G	978 927-5717	8165
Power Graphics Printing	Tewksbury	MA	G	978 851-8988	15827
Praxis Bookbinding	Easthampton	MA	G	413 527-7275	10576
Printing Place Inc	Melrose	MA	G	781 272-7209	12988
Professional Lithography Inc	South Hadley	MA	E	413 532-9473	15309
Pyramid Printing and Advg Inc	Weymouth	MA	E	781 337-7609	16899
R & H Communications Inc **(PA)**	Waltham	MA	F	781 893-6221	16181
Robert Murphy	Salem	MA	E	978 745-7170	14938
Rogers Printing Co Inc	Leominster	MA	E	978 537-9791	12184
S A N Inc **(PA)**	Lawrence	MA	G	978 686-3875	12073
Sherman Printing Co Inc	Canton	MA	E	781 828-8855	9778
Superior Bindery Inc	Braintree	MA	C	781 303-0022	9039
Talin Bookbindery	Yarmouth Port	MA	G	508 362-8144	17532
Ted Best	Hyde Park	MA	G	617 361-7258	11881
Three Ring Binders	Somerville	MA	G	617 354-4084	15223
Town Bookbindery Inc	East Freetown	MA	E	508 763-2713	10461
Universal Wilde Inc	Westwood	MA	C	978 658-0800	16881
W G Fry Corp	Florence	MA	E	413 747-2551	10870
We Print Today LLC	Kingston	MA	F	781 585-6021	11966
Yankee Printing Group Inc	South Hadley	MA	E	413 532-9513	15313
Bruce A Pettengill	Leeds	ME	G	207 933-2578	6268
Davic Inc	Portland	ME	F	207 774-0093	6649
JS McCarthy Co Inc **(PA)**	Augusta	ME	D	207 622-6241	5609
Penmor Lithographers Inc	Lewiston	ME	E	207 784-1341	6316
Quick Print Color Center	Saco	ME	G	207 282-6480	6856
R & W Engraving Inc	Biddeford	ME	G	207 286-3020	5760
Xpress of Maine **(PA)**	Portland	ME	G	207 775-2444	6747
Capitol Copy Inc	Concord	NH	G	603 226-2679	17889
Channelbind International Corp **(PA)**	Concord	NH	E	864 579-7072	17892
Custom Die Cut Inc	Windham	NH	G	603 437-3090	20003
Letterman Press LLC	West Lebanon	NH	G	603 543-0500	19956
New England Printing Corp	Portsmouth	NH	F	603 431-0142	19599
New Hampshire Bindery Inc	Bow	NH	F	603 224-0441	17723
Optimum Bindery Svcs of Neng	Nashua	NH	E	603 886-3889	19224
RB Graphics Inc	Hooksett	NH	G	603 624-4025	18358
Visual Inspection Products	Hampton	NH	G	603 929-4414	18279
Walnut Bottom Inc	Concord	NH	G	603 224-6606	17939
A & H Composition and Prtg Inc	East Providence	RI	G	401 438-1200	20383
Data Binding Inc	Warwick	RI	D	401 738-7901	21348
Dome Enterprises Trust **(PA)**	Warwick	RI	G	401 738-7900	21353
Dome Publishing Company Inc **(HQ)**	Warwick	RI	E	401 738-7900	21354
Jackson Bookbinding Co Inc	Greenville	RI	F	401 231-0800	20469
Ocean State Book Binding Inc	Providence	RI	F	401 528-1172	21081
Rag and Bone Bindery Ltd	Pawtucket	RI	F	401 728-0762	20889
Warwick Group Inc	Bristol	RI	F	401 438-9451	20109
Browns River Bindery Inc	Essex Junction	VT	E	802 878-3335	21932
Darwin A Lewis Inc	Hartland	VT	G	802 457-4521	22015
L Brown and Sons Printing Inc	Barre	VT	E	802 476-3164	21627
Paw Prints Press Inc	South Burlington	VT	G	802 865-2872	22456
Queen City Printers Inc	Burlington	VT	E	802 864-4566	21804
Villanti & Sons Printers Inc	Milton	VT	D	802 864-0723	22140

2791 Typesetting

	CITY	ST	EMP	PHONE	ENTRY #
Acme Typesetting Service Co	West Hartford	CT	G	860 953-1470	5052
Allied Printing Services Inc **(PA)**	Manchester	CT	B	860 643-1101	1984
Appels Printing & Mailing Bur	Hartford	CT	F	860 522-8189	1806
Birdtrack Press	New Haven	CT	G	203 389-7789	2669
Brescias Printing Services Inc	East Hartford	CT	G	860 528-4254	1177
Copy Stop Inc	Hamden	CT	G	203 288-6401	1738
E R Hitchcock Company	New Britain	CT	E	860 229-2024	2529
Eccles-Lehman Inc	Easton	CT	G	203 268-0605	1318
Elm Press Incorporated	Terryville	CT	E	860 583-3600	4477
Executive Office Services Inc	Bridgeport	CT	E	203 373-1333	411
Franklin Print Shoppe Inc	Torrington	CT	G	860 496-9516	4578
G & R Enterprises Incorporated	Hartford	CT	G	860 549-6120	1822
Gateway Digital Inc	Norwalk	CT	F	203 853-4929	3157
Jerrys Printing & Graphics LLC	Bridgeport	CT	G	203 384-0015	435

	CITY	ST	EMP	PHONE	ENTRY #
Jupiter Communications LLC	West Haven	CT	F	475 238-7082	5127
Kool Ink LLC	Bloomfield	CT	F	860 242-0303	238
Magnani Press Incorporated	Hartford	CT	G	860 236-2802	1841
Master Engrv & Printery Inc **(PA)**	Waterbury	CT	G	203 723-2779	4911
Oddo Print Shop Inc	Torrington	CT	G	860 489-6585	4590
Palmisano Printing LLC	Bristol	CT	G	860 582-6883	590
Paul Dewitt	Danbury	CT	F	203 792-5610	965
Phoenix Press Inc	New Haven	CT	E	203 865-5555	2726
Professional Graphics Inc	Norwalk	CT	F	203 846-4291	3225
Prosperous Printing LLC	Wilton	CT	G	203 834-1962	5300
Saybrook Press Incorporated	Guilford	CT	F	203 458-3637	1717
Step Saver Inc	Southington	CT	E	860 621-6751	4082
Vernon Printing Co Inc	Vernon Rockville	CT	G	860 872-1826	4688
Westchester Pubg Svcs LLC **(PA)**	Danbury	CT	G	203 791-0080	1009
Westchster Bk/Rnsford Type Inc	Danbury	CT	C	203 791-0080	1010
Abby Printing Co Inc	Easthampton	MA	G	413 536-5269	10551
American Prtg & Envelope Inc	Auburn	MA	E	508 832-6100	7825
Andrew T Johnson Company Inc **(PA)**	Boston	MA	E	617 742-1610	8366
Apb Enterprises Inc	Marlborough	MA	G	508 481-0966	12715
Argosy Publishing Inc **(PA)**	Newton	MA	E	617 527-9999	13562
Belmont Printing Company	Belmont	MA	E	617 484-0833	8066
Business Cards Overnight Inc	Lawrence	MA	G	978 974-9271	11999
Chaco Inc	Norwood	MA	G	781 769-5557	14141
Color Images Inc	Methuen	MA	G	978 688-4994	13015
Coprico Inc	Chelsea	MA	G	617 889-0520	9951
Crane Composition Inc	East Sandwich	MA	G	774 338-5183	10506
Creative Publishing Corp Amer **(PA)**	Peabody	MA	E	978 532-5880	14326
Crockergraphics Inc	Needham Heights	MA	G	781 444-7020	13324
Cxo Media Inc **(DH)**	Framingham	MA	C	508 766-5696	10938
D & L Associates Inc	Needham Heights	MA	G	781 400-5068	13326
D B S Industries Inc	Haverhill	MA	D	978 373-4748	11421
D S Graphics Inc **(PA)**	Lowell	MA	C	978 970-1359	12365
Desk Top Graphics Inc **(HQ)**	Peabody	MA	E	617 832-1927	14330
Dmr Print Inc **(PA)**	Concord	MA	E	617 876-3688	10128
Elbonais Incorporated	Framingham	MA	G	508 626-2318	10945
Electronic Distribution Corp	Chicopee	MA	G	413 536-3400	10023
Fasprint Inc **(PA)**	Brockton	MA	F	508 588-9961	9146
Flagship Press Inc	North Andover	MA	C	978 975-3100	13704
Generation Four Inc	Waltham	MA	G	781 899-3180	16119
Ghp Media Inc	North Adams	MA	D	413 663-3771	13675
Harvard Instant Printing	Waltham	MA	G	781 893-2622	16124
J C Enterprises Inc	Ashland	MA	G	508 881-7228	7662
J T Gardner Inc	Worcester	MA	G	508 751-6600	17396
J T Gardner Inc **(PA)**	Westborough	MA	E	800 540-4993	16627
John Karl Dietrich & Assoc	Cambridge	MA	F	617 868-4140	9521
Keating Communication Group	Canton	MA	G	781 828-9030	9749
Kirkwood Holdings Inc **(PA)**	Wilmington	MA	C	978 658-4200	17012
Laplume & Sons Printing Inc	Lawrence	MA	E	978 683-1009	12045
Linmel Associates Inc	Marlborough	MA	F	508 481-6699	12787
LPI Printing and Graphic Inc	Stoneham	MA	E	781 438-5400	15566
Marcus Company Inc	Holyoke	MA	E	413 534-3303	11637
Massachusetts Repro Ltd	Boston	MA	F	617 227-2237	8686
McDermott Pallotta Inc	Watertown	MA	G	617 924-2318	16300
Merrill Graphics Incorporated	Braintree	MA	G	781 843-0666	9026
Michael M Almeida	Taunton	MA	G	508 823-4957	15765
Minuteman Press	Newburyport	MA	G	978 465-2242	13515
Minuteman Press	Fitchburg	MA	G	978 345-0818	10839
Modern Graphics Inc	Quincy	MA	F	781 331-5000	14640
Newspapers of Massachusetts	Greenfield	MA	B	978 544-2118	11270
Northern Graphics Inc	Middleton	MA	F	978 646-9925	13097
Picken Printing Inc	North Chelmsford	MA	E	978 251-0730	13907
PIP Itsa Inc	Beverly	MA	G	978 927-5717	8165
Postal Instant Press **(PA)**	East Longmeadow	MA	G	413 525-4044	10487
Printing Place Inc	Melrose	MA	G	781 272-7209	12988
Professional Lithography Inc	South Hadley	MA	E	413 532-9473	15309
Publishers Design & Prod Svcs	Sagamore Beach	MA	F	508 833-8300	14886
Pyramid Printing and Advg Inc	Weymouth	MA	E	781 337-7609	16899
R & H Communications Inc **(PA)**	Waltham	MA	F	781 893-6221	16181
Ramsbottom Printing Inc	Fall River	MA	D	508 730-2220	10752
Red Sun Press Inc	Jamaica Plain	MA	F	617 524-6822	11949
Reminder Publications	East Longmeadow	MA	E	413 525-3947	10491
Rgp Corp	Milford	MA	G	508 478-8511	13141
Rogers Printing Co Inc	Leominster	MA	E	978 537-9791	12184
S A N Inc **(PA)**	Lawrence	MA	G	978 686-3875	12073
Serigraphics Unlimited	Rowley	MA	G	978 356-4896	14866
Sherman Printing Co Inc	Canton	MA	E	781 828-8855	9778
Southern Berkshire Shoppers Gu	Great Barrington	MA	F	413 528-0095	11246
Technologies/Typography	Merrimac	MA	G	978 346-4867	13006
Ted Best	Hyde Park	MA	G	617 361-7258	11881
Teletypesetting Company Inc	Boston	MA	F	617 542-6220	8877
Universal Wilde Inc	Westwood	MA	C	978 658-0800	16881
Weston Corporation	Hingham	MA	F	781 749-0936	11516
Yankee Printing Group Inc	South Hadley	MA	E	413 532-9513	15313
Bruce A Pettengill	Leeds	ME	G	207 933-2578	6268
Davic Inc	Portland	ME	F	207 774-0093	6649
J A Black Company	Belfast	ME	G	207 338-4040	5691
JS McCarthy Co Inc **(PA)**	Augusta	ME	D	207 622-6241	5609
Laserwords Maine	Lewiston	ME	E	207 782-9595	6297
Marks Printing House Inc	Belfast	ME	G	207 338-5460	5692
Quick Print Color Center	Saco	ME	G	207 282-6480	6856
R & W Engraving Inc	Biddeford	ME	G	207 286-3020	5760
Alpha Design & Composition	Pittsfield	NH	G	603 435-8592	19497
Echo Communications Inc	New London	NH	E	603 526-6006	19316
Flash Card Inc	Manchester	NH	G	603 625-0803	18823
Graphic Consumer Services Inc	Candia	NH	G	603 483-5355	17785
Kensington Group Incorporated	Hampton Falls	NH	F	603 926-6742	18283
Letterman Press LLC	West Lebanon	NH	G	603 543-0500	19956
New England Printing Corp	Portsmouth	NH	F	603 431-0142	19599
Print Factory Inc	Nashua	NH	G	603 880-4519	19239
Puritan Press Inc **(PA)**	Hollis	NH	E	603 889-4500	18339
Ram Printing Incorporated **(PA)**	East Hampstead	NH	E	603 382-7045	18082
Scansmart LLC	Manchester	NH	G	603 664-7773	18917
Smith & Town Printers LLC	Berlin	NH	G	603 752-2150	17700
Southport Management Group LLC	Portsmouth	NH	G	603 433-4664	19621
Whitman Communications Inc	Lebanon	NH	E	603 448-2600	18641
A & H Composition and Prtg Inc	East Providence	RI	G	401 438-1200	20383
Allegra Print & Imaging	East Greenwich	RI	G	401 884-9280	20352
Copy Print Company	Cranston	RI	G	401 228-3900	20201
Creative Digital Inc	Cranston	RI	G	401 942-0771	20204
Faces Typography Inc	Providence	RI	G	401 273-4455	21009
Southern RI Newspapers **(HQ)**	Wakefield	RI	E	401 789-9744	21277
T M Morris Productions Inc	Providence	RI	G	401 331-7780	21131
Warwick Group Inc	Bristol	RI	F	401 438-9451	20109
Accura Printing	Barre	VT	F	802 476-4429	21607
Asterisk Typographics Inc	Barre	VT	G	802 476-8399	21608
Dawn Brainard	Newport	VT	G	802 334-2780	22196
Herald Association Inc	Rutland	VT	C	802 747-6121	22338
L Brown and Sons Printing Inc	Barre	VT	E	802 476-3164	21627
McClure Newspapers Inc	Burlington	VT	C	802 863-3441	21795
Queen City Printers Inc	Burlington	VT	E	802 864-4566	21804
Stillwater Graphics Inc	Williamstown	VT	F	802 433-9898	22651
Stratford Publishing Services	Brattleboro	VT	E	802 254-6073	21747
Textech Inc	Brattleboro	VT	G	802 254-6073	21749
Tuttle Law Print Inc	Rutland	VT	D	802 773-9171	22356
Villanti & Sons Printers Inc	Milton	VT	D	802 864-0723	22140

2796 Platemaking & Related Svcs

	CITY	ST	EMP	PHONE	ENTRY #
Baron Technology Inc	Trumbull	CT	E	203 452-0515	4614
Eccles-Lehman Inc	Easton	CT	G	203 268-0605	1318
Endo Graphics Inc	Danbury	CT	G	203 778-1557	910
Four Color Ink LLC	Old Saybrook	CT	G	860 395-5471	3335
Gateway Digital Inc	Norwalk	CT	F	203 853-4929	3157
Ghp Media Inc **(PA)**	West Haven	CT	C	203 479-7500	5124
Paul Dewitt	Danbury	CT	F	203 792-5610	965
Schmitt Realty Holdings Inc	Darien	CT	G	203 662-6661	1031
Schmitt Realty Holdings Inc	Branford	CT	E	203 488-3252	346
Schrader Bellows	Enfield	CT	E	860 749-2215	1380
Success Printing & Mailing Inc	Norwalk	CT	F	203 847-1112	3252
Urg Graphics Inc **(PA)**	Stafford Springs	CT	E	860 928-0835	4121
Belmont Printing Company	Belmont	MA	E	617 484-0833	8066
Chemi-Graphic Inc	Ludlow	MA	E	413 589-0151	12458
Csw Inc **(PA)**	Ludlow	MA	C	413 589-1311	12461
Desk Top Graphics Inc **(HQ)**	Peabody	MA	E	617 832-1927	14330
Ezra J Leboff Co Inc	Brighton	MA	G	617 783-4200	9098
Flex-O-Graphic Prtg Plate Inc	Worcester	MA	E	508 752-8100	17375
Ghp Media Inc	North Adams	MA	D	413 663-3771	13675
Gillies W Technologies LLC	Worcester	MA	G	508 852-2502	17382
Hot Plates Company	Ashland	MA	G	508 429-1445	7661
ID Graphics Group Inc	South Easton	MA	E	508 238-8500	15279
J C Enterprises Inc	Ashland	MA	G	508 881-7228	7662
J T Gardner Inc **(PA)**	Westborough	MA	E	800 540-4993	16627
J T Gardner Inc	Worcester	MA	G	508 751-6600	17396
Linmel Associates Inc	Marlborough	MA	F	508 481-6699	12787
Minuteman Press	Fitchburg	MA	G	978 345-0818	10839
Prima Products	Forestdale	MA	G	508 553-8875	10872
Pure Imaging	Woburn	MA	G	781 537-6992	17273
Rogers Printing Co Inc	Leominster	MA	E	978 537-9791	12184
Rotation Dynamics Corporation	Marlborough	MA	F	508 481-0900	12822
Southern Berkshire Shoppers Gu	Great Barrington	MA	F	413 528-0095	11246
Desk Top Graphics Inc	Portland	ME	G	207 828-0041	6651
Concord Photo Engraving Co	Concord	NH	F	603 225-3681	17896
New England Printing Corp	Portsmouth	NH	F	603 431-0142	19599
Foxon Company	Providence	RI	E	401 421-2386	21015
Herald Association Inc	Rutland	VT	C	802 747-6121	22338
McClure Newspapers Inc	Burlington	VT	C	802 863-3441	21795

28 CHEMICALS AND ALLIED PRODUCTS

2812 Alkalies & Chlorine

	CITY	ST	EMP	PHONE	ENTRY #
Genesis Alkali LLC	Stamford	CT	D	215 299-6773	4198
Kuehne New Haven LLC	New Haven	CT	E	203 508-6703	2703
Driscolls Restaurant	Mansfield	MA	F	508 261-1574	12629
International Dioxcide Inc	North Kingstown	RI	E	401 295-8800	20718

2813 Industrial Gases

	CITY	ST	EMP	PHONE	ENTRY #
A Helium Plus Balloons LLC	Wethersfield	CT	G	860 833-1761	5239
Airgas Usa LLC	Naugatuck	CT	G	203 729-2159	2459
Aldlab Chemicals LLC	North Haven	CT	G	203 589-4934	3005
Helium Plus Inc	Newtown	CT	G	203 304-1880	2923
Hydrogen Highway LLC	North Branford	CT	G	203 871-1000	2968
New England Ortho Neuro LLC	Hamden	CT	G	203 200-7228	1776
Praxair Inc	Wallingford	CT	E	203 793-1200	4787
Praxair Inc	Naugatuck	CT	E	203 720-2477	2491
Praxair Inc	Suffield	CT	D	860 292-5400	4466
Praxair Inc **(HQ)**	Danbury	CT	B	203 837-2000	971
Praxair Distribution Inc	Durham	CT	E	860 349-0305	1093
Praxair Distribution Inc **(DH)**	Danbury	CT	F	203 837-2000	972
Praxair Distribution Inc	Danbury	CT	F	203 837-2162	973
Air Products and Chemicals Inc	Hopkinton	MA	E	508 435-3428	11688
Airgas Usa LLC	Billerica	MA	E	978 439-1344	8207
Boc Gases	Boston	MA	G	617 878-2090	8418
Boc Gasses At Mit	Cambridge	MA	G	617 374-9992	9413
Electrochem Inc	Woburn	MA	F	781 938-5300	17175
Hydro-Test Products Inc	Stow	MA	F	978 897-4647	15632
Hydrogen Energy California LLC	Concord	MA	E	978 287-9529	10134
Linde Gas North America LLC	Marlborough	MA	F	508 229-8118	12786
M J Gordon Company Inc	Pittsfield	MA	G	413 448-6066	14487
Messer LLC	Attleboro	MA	E	508 236-0222	7767
Messer LLC	Bellingham	MA	F	508 966-3148	8050
Messer LLC	Stoughton	MA	F	781 341-4575	15607
Neon Goose	Hull	MA	G	781 925-5118	11829
Praxair Distribution Inc	Auburn	MA	E	203 837-2000	7848
Safe Hydrogen LLC	Lexington	MA	G	781 861-7016	12261
Safe Hydrogen LLC	Lexington	MA	G	781 861-7252	12262
Shield Packaging Co Inc	Dudley	MA	D	508 949-0900	10384
Verde LLC	Quincy	MA	G	617 955-2402	14666
Weldship Industries Inc	Westborough	MA	G	508 898-0100	16658
Edwards Ltd	Kittery	ME	G	207 439-2400	6255
Matheson Tri-Gas Inc	Westbrook	ME	F	207 775-0515	7195
Messer LLC	Kittery	ME	E	207 475-3102	6257
Neon Pipe	Corinth	ME	G	207 285-7420	5924
Airgas Usa LLC	East Greenwich	RI	G	401 884-0201	20351
Hanna Instruments Inc **(PA)**	Woonsocket	RI	E	401 765-7500	21567
Praxair Distribution Inc	Slatersville	RI	E	401 767-3450	21205
Messer LLC	Essex Junction	VT	E	802 878-6339	21950

2816 Inorganic Pigments

	CITY	ST	EMP	PHONE	ENTRY #
Magneli Materials LLC	New Canaan	CT	G	203 644-8560	2604
Clariant Plas Coatings USA LLC	Holden	MA	D	508 829-6321	11543
Color Change Technology Inc	North Andover	MA	G	978 377-0050	13695
F & D Plastics Inc **(PA)**	Leominster	MA	E	978 668-5140	12136
Hudson Color Concentrates LLC	Leominster	MA	D	978 537-3538	12153
O A Both Corporation	Ashland	MA	G	508 881-4100	7666
Okchem Inc	Cambridge	MA	G	978 992-1811	9597
Atlantic Hardchrome Ltd	Wilton	ME	E	207 645-4300	7224
Dalegip America Inc	Searsport	ME	E	207 323-1880	6950
Engelhard Corp Scales	Eastport	ME	G	207 853-2501	5994
Ecc Holdings Inc **(HQ)**	Providence	RI	E	401 331-9000	21002

2819 Indl Inorganic Chemicals, NEC

	CITY	ST	EMP	PHONE	ENTRY #
Carbide Solutions LLC	Windsor	CT	G	860 515-8665	5324
Carbide Technology Inc	Southington	CT	G	860 621-8981	4043
Carbtrol Corporation	Stratford	CT	E	203 337-4340	4403
CCL Industries Corporation **(DH)**	Shelton	CT	D	203 926-1253	3785
Chromatics Inc	Bethel	CT	F	203 743-6868	137
Designing Element	Norwalk	CT	G	203 849-3076	3134
Element One LLC	Norwalk	CT	G	203 344-1553	3149
Elements LLC	West Hartford	CT	G	860 231-8011	5069
Fitness Elemnet	New Britain	CT	G	860 670-2855	2534
Greek Elements LLC	New Canaan	CT	G	203 594-2022	2598
H Krevit and Company Inc	New Haven	CT	E	203 772-3350	2694
Innophase Corp	Westbrook	CT	G	860 399-2269	5156
Joshua LLC **(PA)**	New Haven	CT	E	203 624-0080	2699
Kwant Elements Intl LLC	Cos Cob	CT	G	203 625-5553	827
Meb Enterprises Inc	Meriden	CT	G	203 599-0273	2102
Metamorphic Materials Inc	Winsted	CT	F	860 738-8638	5417
New Haven Chlor-Alkali LLC	New Haven	CT	D	203 772-3350	2714
Perennial Elements LLC	Mystic	CT	G	860 536-8593	2448
Solidification Pdts Intl Inc	Northford	CT	G	203 484-9494	3092
Solidification Products Intl	Northford	CT	F	203 484-9494	3093
Specialty Minerals Inc	Canaan	CT	C	860 824-5435	690
Tiger-Sul Products LLC	Shelton	CT	E	251 202-3850	3880
Tronox Incorporated **(DH)**	Stamford	CT	C	203 705-3800	4350
Vanderbilt Chemicals LLC **(HQ)**	Norwalk	CT	D	203 295-2141	3265
Vanderbilt Chemicals LLC	Bethel	CT	E	203 744-3900	189
A W Chesterton Company	Groveland	MA	B	781 438-7000	11299
Alphamed Incorporated	Wrentham	MA	G	774 571-9415	17514
Americanbio Inc	Canton	MA	E	508 655-4336	9713
Benchmark Carbide	Springfield	MA	G	800 523-8570	15451
Bruker Detection Corporation	Billerica	MA	F	978 663-3660	8225
Cabot Corporation **(PA)**	Boston	MA	C	617 345-0100	8452
Cabot Corporation	Haverhill	MA	C	978 556-8400	11413
Concept Chemicals Inc	Hingham	MA	F	781 740-0711	11497
Cutting Edge Carbide Tech Inc	Leominster	MA	G	888 210-9670	12130
Distinct Element	Mattapan	MA	G	617 322-3979	12883
Div Cabot Road LLC	Medford	MA	F	781 396-3122	12931
Dow Chemical Company	Marlborough	MA	E	508 229-7676	12750
E I Du Pont De Nemours & Co	North Billerica	MA	E	978 663-7113	13811
Element Brainerd LLC	Allston	MA	G	617 487-8114	7465
Element LLC	West Dennis	MA	G	508 394-3032	16475
Element Precision LLC	Southbridge	MA	G	774 318-1777	15381
Elements East LLC	Franklin	MA	G	508 528-1902	11040
Fiberlock Technologies Inc	Andover	MA	F	978 623-9987	7548
Four Elements Salon & Spa	Westport	MA	G	508 672-3111	16839
Gcp Applied Technologies Inc **(PA)**	Cambridge	MA	B	617 876-1400	9486
Hgi Incorporated	Amesbury	MA	G	978 388-2808	7490
Holland Company Inc	Adams	MA	E	413 743-1292	7413
Instrumentation Laboratory Co **(DH)**	Bedford	MA	A	781 861-0710	7982
Jordi Labs LLC	Mansfield	MA	E	508 719-8543	12639
Magellan Diagnostics Inc **(HQ)**	Chelmsford	MA	D	978 250-7000	9915
MD Stetson Company Inc	Randolph	MA	E	781 986-6161	14689
Menon Laboratories Inc	Somerville	MA	G	339 224-2787	15198
Metallium Inc	Watertown	MA	G	508 728-9074	16301
Metalor USA Refining Corp **(DH)**	North Attleboro	MA	C	508 699-8800	13764
Mindful Elements LLC	Shrewsbury	MA	G	508 845-2833	15123
Nyacol Nano Technologies Inc	Ashland	MA	E	508 881-2220	7665
Omnova Solutions Inc	Fitchburg	MA	E	978 342-5831	10845
Peroxygen Systems Inc	Lowell	MA	G	248 835-9026	12420
Qsa Global Inc **(HQ)**	Burlington	MA	D	781 272-2000	9325
Rohm Haas Electronic Mtls LLC **(DH)**	Marlborough	MA	A	508 481-7950	12820
S & T Global Inc	Woburn	MA	F	781 376-1774	17287
Saint-Gobain Ceramics Plas Inc	Worcester	MA	G	508 795-5000	17466
Sharp Tool Co Inc	Hudson	MA	E	978 568-9292	11816
Strem Chemicals Incorporated	Newburyport	MA	D	978 499-1600	13537
Sud-Chemie Protech Inc	Needham Heights	MA	E	781 444-5188	13345
Thermal Fluids Inc	South Easton	MA	G	508 238-9660	15293
Transene Company Inc	Danvers	MA	F	978 777-7860	10265
Trelleborg Offshore Boston Inc	Randolph	MA	D	774 719-1400	14699
Twin Rivers Tech Holdings Inc	Quincy	MA	C	617 472-9200	14662
Twin Rivers Tech Mfg Corp	Quincy	MA	G	888 929-8780	14664
Union Etchants International	Danvers	MA	G	978 777-7860	10270
Veolia NA Regeneration Srvcs **(DH)**	Boston	MA	G	312 552-2800	8906
W R Grace & Co	Lexington	MA	B	617 876-1400	12283
Element All Stars	Lewiston	ME	G	207 576-6931	6286
Elemental Energies	Wells	ME	G	207 641-5070	7162
Gac Chemical Corporation **(PA)**	Searsport	ME	D	207 548-2525	6951
General Alum New England Corp	Searsport	ME	D	207 548-2525	6952
JM Huber Corporation	Easton	ME	C	207 488-2051	5990
Monahan Associates	Portland	ME	G	207 771-0900	6694
Plasmine Technology Inc	Portland	ME	G	207 797-5009	6710
Specialty Minerals Inc	Jay	ME	F	207 897-4492	6221
All Natures Elements	Fremont	NH	G	603 427-3535	18173
Arzol Corp	Keene	NH	G	603 352-5242	18493
Chemtrade Chemicals US LLC	Hampton	NH	F	603 926-0191	18261
Element Hanover - Lebanon	Lebanon	NH	G	603 646-8108	18621
Hampshire Chemical Corp **(DH)**	Nashua	NH	E	603 888-2320	19176
Medical Isotopes Inc	Pelham	NH	G	603 635-2255	19439
Pure Element	Derry	NH	G	603 235-4373	17995
Saint-Gobain Ceramics Plas Inc	Milford	NH	D	603 673-5831	19075
Z-Tech LLC	Bow	NH	E	603 228-1305	17738
Cal Chemical Corporation	Coventry	RI	E	401 821-0320	20140
Element Metal Arts	North Kingstown	RI	G	631 896-9683	20708
International Dioxcide Inc	North Kingstown	RI	E	401 295-8800	20718
Prosys Finishing Tech Inc	Cranston	RI	G	401 781-1011	20275
Element Marketing	Waitsfield	VT	G	802 448-4252	22566
Elemental Development LLC	Hinesburg	VT	G	802 318-1041	22023
Matrixchem Inc	Cambridgeport	VT	G	347 727-6886	21824
O M Y A Inc	Proctor	VT	G	802 499-8131	22286
Omya Inc	Florence	VT	E	802 459-3311	21991
Omya Inc	Proctor	VT	F	802 459-3311	22287

2821 Plastics, Mtrls & Nonvulcanizable Elastomers

	CITY	ST	EMP	PHONE	ENTRY #
Allnex USA Inc	Wallingford	CT	D	203 269-4481	4695
Allread Products Co LLC	Terryville	CT	F	860 589-3566	4474
Anapo Plastics Corp	Farmington	CT	G	860 874-8174	1465
Axel Plastics RES Labs Inc	Monroe	CT	E	718 672-8300	2392
Bakelite N Sumitomo Amer Inc **(DH)**	Manchester	CT	D	860 645-3851	1987
C Mather Company Inc	South Windsor	CT	G	860 528-5667	3946
Chessco Industries Inc **(PA)**	Westport	CT	E	203 255-2804	5183
Enflo Corporation **(PA)**	Bristol	CT	E	860 589-0014	556
Engineered Polymers Inds Inc	Cheshire	CT	G	203 272-2233	730
Fimor North America Inc **(HQ)**	Cheshire	CT	E	203 272-3219	733
Forum Plastics LLC	Waterbury	CT	E	203 754-0777	4875
Henkel of America Inc **(HQ)**	Rocky Hill	CT	B	860 571-5100	3715
Henkel US Operations Corp **(DH)**	Rocky Hill	CT	B	860 571-5100	3716
Hexcel Corporation **(PA)**	Stamford	CT	E	203 969-0666	4213
Lanxess Solutions US Inc **(DH)**	Shelton	CT	E	203 573-2000	3824

	CITY	ST	EMP	PHONE	ENTRY #
Neu Spclty Engineered Mtls LLC	North Haven	CT	F	203 239-9629	3043
Osterman & Company Inc **(PA)**	Cheshire	CT	D	203 272-2233	751
Osterman & Company Inc	Cheshire	CT	E	203 272-2233	752
Oxford Industries Conn Inc	New Britain	CT	E	860 225-3700	2559
Oxford Performance Mtls Inc	South Windsor	CT	E	860 698-9300	3997
Oxpekk Performance Mtls Inc	South Windsor	CT	F	860 698-9300	3998
Pinnacle Polymers LLC	Ridgefield	CT	G	203 313-4116	3677
Polar Industries Inc **(PA)**	Prospect	CT	E	203 758-6651	3592
Polymer Resources Ltd **(PA)**	Farmington	CT	D	203 324-3737	1507
Polyone Corporation	Stamford	CT	G	203 327-6010	4288
Precision Dip Coating LLC	Waterbury	CT	G	203 805-4564	4943
Presidium USA Inc	Stamford	CT	G	203 674-9374	4291
Ravago Americas LLC	Wilton	CT	E	203 855-6000	5301
Resinall Corp **(DH)**	Stamford	CT	F	203 329-7100	4298
Roehm America LLC	Wallingford	CT	E	203 269-4481	4798
SMS Machine Inc	East Berlin	CT	G	860 829-0813	1108
Sonoco Prtective Solutions Inc	Putnam	CT	E	860 928-7795	3634
Spartech LLC	Stamford	CT	C	203 327-6010	4327
Thornton and Company Inc	Southington	CT	F	860 628-6771	4086
Total Ptrchemicals Ref USA Inc	Stratford	CT	E	203 375-0668	4454
Trinseo LLC	Gales Ferry	CT	E	860 447-7298	1528
Tyne Plastics LLC **(PA)**	Burlington	CT	G	860 673-7100	681
W S Polymers	Trumbull	CT	G	203 268-1557	4643
Aaron Industries Corp	Leominster	MA	E	978 534-6135	12105
Accurate Plastics Inc	East Falmouth	MA	E	508 457-9097	10434
Acushnet Rubber Company Inc	New Bedford	MA	B	508 998-4000	13352
Alden and Broden Corporation	Westford	MA	G	603 882-0330	16752
Ameramesh Technologies Inc	Fall River	MA	G	508 324-9977	10655
Andrew Roberts Inc	Natick	MA	G	508 653-6412	13235
Argotec LLC **(HQ)**	Greenfield	MA	C	413 772-2564	11250
Atoll-Bio USA Inc	Gloucester	MA	F	978 281-4595	11162
Bagge Inc	Holliston	MA	G	508 429-8080	11558
Barrday Corporation **(HQ)**	Millbury	MA	D	508 581-2100	13156
Bi-Qem Inc	Florence	MA	G	413 584-2472	10864
Cambridge Polymer Group Inc	Boston	MA	F	617 629-4400	8456
CDF Corporation **(PA)**	Plymouth	MA	D	508 747-5858	14550
Chase Corp	Bridgewater	MA	F	508 819-4200	9066
Chemiplastica Inc	Florence	MA	E	413 584-2472	10865
Cold Chain Technologies Inc **(PA)**	Franklin	MA	D	508 429-1395	11030
Dj Microlaminates Inc	Sudbury	MA	G	978 261-3188	15655
Dow Chemical Company	Marlborough	MA	E	508 229-7676	12750
DSM Coating Resins Inc	Wilmington	MA	C	800 458-0014	16996
Eastern Packaging Inc	Lawrence	MA	D	978 685-7723	12020
Enginred Syntactic Systems LLC	Attleboro	MA	G	508 226-3907	7733
Entec Polymers	Sutton	MA	G	508 865-2001	15682
Eps Polymer Distribution Inc	Shrewsbury	MA	G	508 925-5932	15111
Ernest Johnson	Marlborough	MA	G	508 259-6727	12753
Fraivillig Technologies Co	Boston	MA	G	512 784-5698	8551
Gare Incorporated	Haverhill	MA	E	978 373-9131	11437
Gxt Green Inc	Billerica	MA	E	978 735-4367	8253
Image Polymers Company **(DH)**	Wakefield	MA	G	978 296-0194	15955
Indusol Inc	Sutton	MA	E	508 865-9516	15683
Ineos Melamines LLC	Springfield	MA	E	413 730-3811	15478
Ineos Nova Lcc	Winchendon	MA	G	978 297-2265	17077
Interpolymer Corporation **(DH)**	Canton	MA	E	781 828-7120	9745
Isp Freetown Fine Chem Inc	Assonet	MA	D	508 672-0634	7681
Jarica Inc	Woburn	MA	F	781 935-1907	17210
Kickemuit Industries LLC	Somerset	MA	G	508 675-0594	15145
Kpt Company Inc	Malden	MA	G	978 558-4009	12575
L H C Inc **(PA)**	Lynn	MA	E	781 592-6444	12520
Macgregor Bay Corporation	Belchertown	MA	E	413 283-8747	8025
Manufacturing Service Corp	Millbury	MA	G	508 865-2550	13169
Modern Dispersions Inc **(PA)**	Leominster	MA	D	978 534-3370	12168
Novolac Epoxy Technologies Inc **(PA)**	Harwich	MA	G	508 385-5598	11396
Omnova Solutions Inc	Fitchburg	MA	E	978 342-5831	10845
Origyn Inc	Boston	MA	G	781 888-8834	8759
P & K Custom Acrylics Inc	Malden	MA	G	781 388-2601	12585
Pepperell International	Pepperell	MA	G	508 878-7987	14445
Plaskolite LLC	Sheffield	MA	C	800 628-5084	15062
Plaskolite LLC	Sheffield	MA	C	800 628-5084	15063
Plaskolite Massachusetts LLC	Sheffield	MA	C	413 229-8711	15064
Plastic Design Inc	North Chelmsford	MA	E	978 251-4830	13908
Poly-Mark Corp	Clinton	MA	G	978 368-1300	10090
Polyone Corporation	Littleton	MA	E	978 772-0764	12319
Reinforced Structures For Elec	Worcester	MA	E	508 754-5316	17457
RES-Tech Corporation **(HQ)**	Hudson	MA	E	978 567-1000	11811
Resource Colors LLC	Leominster	MA	F	978 537-3700	12182
S&E Specialty Polymers LLC	Lunenburg	MA	D	978 537-8261	12483
Sabic US Holdings LP	Pittsfield	MA	A	413 448-7110	14506
Saint-Gobain Ceramics Plas Inc	Northborough	MA	B	508 351-7754	14046
Saint-Gobain Prfmce Plas Corp	Taunton	MA	C	508 823-7701	15783
Solutia Inc	Springfield	MA	A	413 788-6911	15507
Steel Products Corporation **(PA)**	Rochdale	MA	G	508 892-4770	14783
Styletech Company	Leominster	MA	G	978 537-0711	12190
Swm	Greenfield	MA	F	413 772-2564	11278
Swm International	Greenfield	MA	G	413 774-3772	11279
TAC Life Systems LLC	Walpole	MA	G	617 719-8797	16013
Tapecoat Company	Westwood	MA	G	781 332-0700	16879
Titeflex Corporation	Springfield	MA	E	413 781-0008	15517
Tpe Solutions Inc **(PA)**	Shirley	MA	G	978 425-3033	15096
Unicore LLC	Palmer	MA	E	413 284-9995	14299
Ware Rite Distributors Inc	East Bridgewater	MA	D	508 690-2145	10422
Wilsonart Intl Holdings LLC	North Reading	MA	E	978 664-5230	13994
Bosal Foam and Fiber **(PA)**	Limerick	ME	E	207 793-2245	6332
Cyro Industry	Sanford	ME	G	207 324-6000	6873
G & G Products LLC	Kennebunk	ME	E	207 985-9100	6234
Panolam Industries Intl Inc	Auburn	ME	E	207 784-9111	5586
Roehm America LLC	Sanford	ME	C	207 324-6000	6891
Rynel Inc **(DH)**	Wiscasset	ME	D	207 882-0200	7287
Aeroplas Corp International	Hollis	NH	G	603 465-7300	18324
AP Extrusion Inc	Salem	NH	F	603 890-1086	19708
Avilite Corp	Merrimack	NH	G	603 626-4388	18988
Core Elastomers	Portsmouth	NH	G	603 319-6912	19554
Dalau Incorporated	Merrimack	NH	G	603 670-1031	18997
Faber Family Associates Lpa **(PA)**	Salem	NH	G	603 681-0484	19728
Faber Industries LLC **(HQ)**	Salem	NH	F	603 681-0484	19729
Freudenberg-Nok General Partnr	Northfield	NH	E	603 286-1600	19402
Freudenberg-Nok General Partnr	Northfield	NH	D	603 286-1600	19401
Global Plastics LLC **(HQ)**	Manchester	NH	F	603 782-2835	18828
Itaconix Corporation	Stratham	NH	F	603 775-4400	19869
Keller Products Incorporated	Bow	NH	E	603 224-5502	17719
Metzger/Mcguire Inc	Bow	NH	E	603 224-6122	17722
MTI Polyexe Corporation	Brentwood	NH	F	603 778-1449	17752
New Hampshire Plastics LLC	Manchester	NH	D	603 669-8523	18884
Nylon Corporation America Inc	Manchester	NH	D	603 627-5150	18890
Nyltech North America	Manchester	NH	G	603 627-5150	18891
Omni Metals Company Inc	Somersworth	NH	E	603 692-6664	19845
Plan Tech Inc	Loudon	NH	E	603 783-4767	18752
Polyexe Corporation	Brentwood	NH	E	603 778-1143	17754
Polymer Technologies LLC	Nashua	NH	G	603 883-4002	19235
Saint-Gobain Prfmce Plas Corp	Merrimack	NH	C	603 424-9000	19027
Scandia Plastics Inc	Plaistow	NH	E	603 382-6533	19523
Textiles Coated Incorporated	Manchester	NH	C	603 296-2221	18940
Textiles Coated Incorporated **(PA)**	Londonderry	NH	D	603 296-2221	18741
Universal Systems USA Inc	Manchester	NH	F	603 222-9070	18947
Applied Plastics Tech Inc	Bristol	RI	E	401 253-0200	20062
Branch River Plastics Inc	Smithfield	RI	E	401 232-0270	21214
Coastal Plastics Inc	Hope Valley	RI	E	401 539-2446	20482
Development Associates Inc	North Kingstown	RI	F	401 884-1350	20702
Eastern Resins Corp	Woonsocket	RI	E	401 769-6700	21559
Epoxytech Inc	Woonsocket	RI	E	401 726-4500	21560
Konneco International LLC	North Smithfield	RI	G	401 767-3690	20788
Modern Plastics	Warwick	RI	G	401 732-0415	21392
Moore Company **(PA)**	Westerly	RI	C	401 596-2816	21531
Optical Polymers Lab Corp	Pawtucket	RI	F	401 722-0710	20870
Polifil Inc	Woonsocket	RI	E	401 767-2700	21575
Polyfoam Corporation	Cranston	RI	G	401 781-3220	20272
Polymer Solutions Inc	Pawtucket	RI	G	401 423-1638	20881
Polyworks LLC	North Smithfield	RI	E	401 769-0994	20794
Ralco Industries Inc **(PA)**	Woonsocket	RI	E	401 765-1000	21577
Rbc Industries Inc	Warwick	RI	D	401 941-3000	21410
Teknor Apex Company **(PA)**	Pawtucket	RI	B	401 725-8000	20903
QST Inc	Saint Albans	VT	E	802 524-7704	22377
Sykes Hollow Innovations Ltd	East Dorset	VT	G	802 549-4671	21917

2822 Synthetic Rubber (Vulcanizable Elastomers)

	CITY	ST	EMP	PHONE	ENTRY #
Aardvark Polymers	Woodstock	CT	G	609 483-1013	5493
FMI Chemical Inc	Bloomfield	CT	F	860 243-3222	219
Heaters Inc	Niantic	CT	G	860 739-5477	2952
Si Group USA (usaa) LLC **(DH)**	Danbury	CT	C	203 702-6140	989
Specialty Polymers Inc	Waterbury	CT	G	203 575-5727	4958
Advanced Frp Systems Inc	Weymouth	MA	G	508 927-6915	16883
Allcoat Technology Inc	Wilmington	MA	E	978 988-0880	16971
American Prfmce Polymers LLC	Manchester	MA	G	603 237-8001	12603
Covestro LLC	South Deerfield	MA	D	412 777-2000	15248
Heveatex Corporation	Fall River	MA	F	508 675-0181	10713
Cri-Sil LLC	Biddeford	ME	E	207 283-6422	5726
Southworth Intl Group Inc **(PA)**	Falmouth	ME	D	207 878-0700	6033
Contitech Thermopol LLC	Somersworth	NH	G	603 692-6300	19832
Contitech Thermopol LLC	Rochester	NH	D	603 692-6300	19665
Contitech Thermopol LLC **(HQ)**	Somersworth	NH	G	603 692-6300	19833
Diversified Decorating Sales	Jaffrey	NH	G	603 532-4557	18461
Ipotec LLC	Exeter	NH	G	603 778-2882	18124
Conley Casting Supply Corp **(PA)**	Warwick	RI	E	401 461-4710	21345
Dryvit Holdings Inc **(DH)**	Providence	RI	G	401 822-4100	20998
Rbc Industries Inc	Warwick	RI	D	401 941-3000	21410
G W Plastics Inc	Bethel	VT	G	802 234-9941	21694
QST Inc	Saint Albans	VT	E	802 524-7704	22377

2823 Cellulosic Man-Made Fibers

	CITY	ST	EMP	PHONE	ENTRY #
Global Materials Inc	Lowell	MA	E	978 322-1900	12376
Casco Bay Fibers	Freeport	ME	G	207 869-5429	6073
Conform Gissing Intl LLC	Auburn	ME	C	207 784-1118	5555
Detroit Technologies Inc	Auburn	ME	A	207 784-1118	5560

SIC

2824 Synthetic Organic Fibers, Exc Cellulosic

	CITY	ST	EMP	PHONE	ENTRY #
Fairfield Processing Corp **(PA)**	Danbury	CT	C	203 744-2090	918
Proteus Industries Inc	Gloucester	MA	G	978 281-9545	11205
Casco Bay Fibers	Freeport	ME	G	207 869-5429	6073
Conform Gissing Intl LLC	Auburn	ME	C	207 784-1118	5555
Detroit Technologies Inc	Auburn	ME	A	207 784-1118	5560

2833 Medicinal Chemicals & Botanical Prdts

	CITY	ST	EMP	PHONE	ENTRY #
American Distilling Inc	Marlborough	CT	G	860 267-4444	2063
American Distilling Inc **(PA)**	East Hampton	CT	D	860 267-4444	1156
Biomed Health Inc	Glastonbury	CT	F	860 657-2258	1540
Candlewood Stars Inc	Danbury	CT	G	203 994-8826	885
Effihealth LLC	Stamford	CT	G	888 435-3108	4192
Henkel of America Inc **(HQ)**	Rocky Hill	CT	B	860 571-5100	3715
Henkel US Operations Corp **(DH)**	Rocky Hill	CT	B	860 571-5100	3716
Mantrose-Haeuser Co Inc **(HQ)**	Westport	CT	E	203 454-1800	5212
Modern Nutrition & Biotech	Ridgefield	CT	G	203 244-5830	3672
Nzymsys Inc	Manchester	CT	G	877 729-4190	2028
Watson LLC **(DH)**	West Haven	CT	B	203 932-3000	5149
Yale University	New Haven	CT	G	203 432-6320	2761
Albany Molecular Research Inc	Waltham	MA	F	781 672-4530	16027
Anexis LLC	Beverly	MA	G	978 921-6293	8100
Cequr Corporation	Marlborough	MA	E	508 486-0010	12737
Corden Pharma Intl Inc	Braintree	MA	G	781 305-3332	8996
Country Life LLC	Norwell	MA	G	781 659-1321	14101
Designing Health Inc	East Longmeadow	MA	E	661 257-1705	10472
Flo Chemical Corp	Ashburnham	MA	G	978 827-5101	7644
Fulcrum Thrptics Scrities Corp	Cambridge	MA	G	617 651-8851	9483
GE Healthcare Inc **(DH)**	Marlborough	MA	B	800 526-3593	12759
Ionic Pharmaceuticals LLC	Brookline	MA	G	978 509-4980	9204
Johnson Matthey Phrm Mtls Inc	North Andover	MA	E	978 784-5000	13713
Microbiotix Inc	Worcester	MA	E	508 757-2800	17416
Moderna LLC **(HQ)**	Cambridge	MA	G	617 714-6500	9565
Naturex-Dbs LLC	Sagamore	MA	G	774 247-0022	14884
Nitto Denko Avecia Inc **(DH)**	Milford	MA	C	508 532-2500	13131
Nova Biomedical Corporation **(PA)**	Waltham	MA	A	781 894-0800	16162
Nova Biomedical Corporation	Billerica	MA	F	781 894-0800	8268
Resilience Therapeutics Inc	Duxbury	MA	G	617 780-2375	10401
Tetraphase Pharmaceuticals Inc **(PA)**	Watertown	MA	D	617 715-3600	16321
U S Fluids Inc	East Longmeadow	MA	G	413 525-0660	10500
W R Grace & Co	Lexington	MA	B	617 876-1400	12283
Yuma Therapeutics Corporaiton	Cambridge	MA	G	617 953-4618	9709
Biodesign International Inc	Saco	ME	E	207 283-6500	6843
Global Biotechnologies Inc	Scarborough	ME	G	800 755-8420	6920
Indian Meadow Herbals LLC	Eastbrook	ME	G	207 565-3010	5988
Medical Isotopes Inc	Pelham	NH	G	603 635-2255	19439
Ticked Off Inc	Dover	NH	G	603 742-0925	18061
Airgas Usa LLC	East Greenwich	RI	G	401 884-0201	20351
Mylan Technologies Inc **(DH)**	Saint Albans	VT	C	802 527-7792	22373
Troy Micro Five Inc	Saint Albans	VT	G	802 524-0076	22383
Urban Mnshine Natural Pdts LLC	Burlington	VT	G	802 862-6233	21814

2834 Pharmaceuticals

	CITY	ST	EMP	PHONE	ENTRY #
A & S Pharmaceutical Corp	Bridgeport	CT	E	203 368-2538	364
Achillion Pharmaceuticals Inc	New Haven	CT	D	203 624-7000	2652
Actimus Inc	Cromwell	CT	D	617 438-9968	843
Aeromics Inc	Branford	CT	G	216 772-1004	285
Alexion Pharma LLC **(HQ)**	New Haven	CT	E	203 272-2596	2653
Aplicare Products LLC **(HQ)**	Meriden	CT	C	203 630-0500	2077
Arvinas Inc **(PA)**	New Haven	CT	F	203 535-1456	2658
Avara Pharmaceutical Svcs Inc **(HQ)**	Norwalk	CT	E	203 918-1659	3109
Beta Pharma Inc	Shelton	CT	F	203 315-5062	3780
Biohaven Pharmaceuticals Inc	New Haven	CT	D	203 404-0410	2666
Biohaven Phrm Holdg Co Ltd	New Haven	CT	E	203 404-0410	2667
Biomed Health Inc	Glastonbury	CT	F	860 657-2258	1540
Bioxcel Therapeutics Inc	New Haven	CT	F	475 238-6837	2668
Boehringer Ingelheim Corp **(DH)**	Ridgefield	CT	A	203 798-9988	3657
Boehringer Ingelheim Pharma **(DH)**	Ridgefield	CT	A	203 798-9988	3658
Boehringer Ingelheim USA Corp **(DH)**	Ridgefield	CT	C	203 798-9988	3659
Boehrnger Ingelheim Roxane Inc	Ridgefield	CT	E	203 798-5555	3660
Brookfeld Mdcl/Srgical Sup Inc	Brookfield	CT	F	203 775-0862	636
Cara Therapeutics Inc	Stamford	CT	E	203 406-3700	4155
Cardinal Health 414 LLC	East Hartford	CT	G	860 291-9135	1179
Cardioxyl Pharmaceuticals Inc	Wallingford	CT	G	919 869-8586	4715
Carigent Therapeutics Inc	New Haven	CT	G	203 887-2873	2675
Chemin Pharma LLC	Woodbridge	CT	G	203 208-2811	5465
Condomdepot Co	Plainville	CT	G	860 747-1338	3475
Evotec (us) Inc	Branford	CT	E	650 228-1400	314
Foster Delivery Science Inc **(DH)**	Putnam	CT	F	860 928-4102	3614
Foster Delivery Science Inc	Putnam	CT	F	860 630-4515	3615
Frederick Purdue Company Inc **(PA)**	Stamford	CT	B	203 588-8000	4197
Frequency Therapeutics Inc	Farmington	CT	E	978 436-0704	1484
Gaia Chemical Corporation	Gaylordsville	CT	G	860 355-2730	1531
Glaxosmithkline LLC	Southbury	CT	E	203 232-5145	4026
Henry Thayer Company	Easton	CT	G	203 226-0940	1319
Hoffmann-La Roche Inc	Branford	CT	A	203 871-2303	323
Humphreys Pharmacal Inc	East Hampton	CT	F	860 267-8710	1159
Infirst Healthcare Inc	Westport	CT	G	203 222-1300	5203
Innoteq Inc **(PA)**	Stratford	CT	E	203 659-4444	4424
Iterum Therapeutics Inc	Old Saybrook	CT	G	860 391-8349	3339
J & J Precision Eyelet Inc	Thomaston	CT	D	860 283-8243	4505
Kinderma LLC	Glastonbury	CT	G	860 796-5503	1562
Kolltan Pharmaceuticals Inc **(HQ)**	New Haven	CT	E	203 773-3000	2702
Koster Keunen LLC **(PA)**	Watertown	CT	F	860 945-3333	5013
Lipid Genomics Inc	Farmington	CT	G	443 465-3495	1490
Loxo Oncology Inc **(HQ)**	Stamford	CT	E	203 653-3880	4241
MD Solarsciences Corporation	Stamford	CT	F	203 857-0095	4247
Micro Source Discovery Systems	Gaylordsville	CT	G	860 350-8078	1532
Neurohydrate LLC	Bridgeport	CT	G	203 799-7900	455
New England Drmtlgcal Soc Bret	New Haven	CT	G	203 432-0092	2713
New Haven Naturopathic Center	New Haven	CT	G	203 387-8661	2715
New Leaf Pharmaceutical	Newtown	CT	F	203 270-4167	2930
Northstar Biosciences LLC	Guilford	CT	G	203 689-5399	1713
Oncoarendi Therapeutics LLC	Madison	CT	G	609 571-0306	1971
Perosphere Inc	Danbury	CT	F	203 885-1111	966
PF Laboratories Inc **(HQ)**	Stamford	CT	C	973 256-3100	4283
Pfizer Inc	New Haven	CT	G	203 401-0100	2724
Pfizer Inc	Groton	CT	C	860 441-4100	1684
Pgxhealthholding Inc **(PA)**	New Haven	CT	C	203 786-3400	2725
Pharmaceutical RES Assoc Inc **(HQ)**	Stamford	CT	G	203 588-8000	4284
Pharmavite Corp	Simsbury	CT	G	860 651-1885	3909
PRA Holdings Inc	Stamford	CT	G	203 853-0123	4290
Pre -Clinical Safety Inc	East Lyme	CT	G	860 739-9797	1272
Protein Sciences Corporation **(HQ)**	Meriden	CT	D	203 686-0800	2119
Purdue Pharma LP	Stamford	CT	G	203 588-8000	4293
Purdue Pharma LP **(PA)**	Stamford	CT	B	203 588-8000	4294
Purdue Pharma Manufacturing LP	Stamford	CT	E	252 265-1924	4295
Quality Care Drg/Cntrbrook LLC	Centerbrook	CT	G	860 767-0206	702
Renetx Bio Inc	New Haven	CT	G	203 444-6642	2731
Rx Analytic Inc	Ridgefield	CT	G	203 733-0837	3681
Sca Pharmaceuticals LLC	Windsor	CT	G	501 312-2800	5359
SDA Laboratories Inc	Greenwich	CT	G	203 861-0005	1648
Sheffield Pharmaceuticals LLC	Norwich	CT	F	860 442-4451	3290
Shire Rgenerative Medicine Inc **(DH)**	Westport	CT	G	877 422-4463	5231
Shore Therapeutics Inc	Stamford	CT	G	646 562-1243	4316
Sinol Usa Inc	Newtown	CT	F	203 470-7404	2937
Skyline Vet Pharma Inc	Groton	CT	G	860 625-0424	1686
Systamedic Inc	Groton	CT	G	860 912-6101	1687
Syzygy Halthcare Solutions LLC	Wilton	CT	G	203 226-4449	5307
Tower Laboratories Ltd	Clinton	CT	E	860 669-7078	796
Tower Laboratories Ltd **(PA)**	Centerbrook	CT	D	860 767-2127	704
Trevi Therapeutics Inc	New Haven	CT	F	203 304-2499	2748
AA Pharmaceuticals Inc	Woburn	MA	G	617 935-1241	17103
Aastrom Biosciences Inc	Cambridge	MA	G	617 761-8642	9368
Abbott	Westford	MA	F	978 577-3467	16750
Abbott Laboratories	Worcester	MA	A	508 849-2500	17331
Abbvie Inc	Worcester	MA	E	508 849-2500	17332
Abbvie Inc	Cambridge	MA	G	617 335-7640	9369
Abpro Corporation	Woburn	MA	E	617 225-0808	17105
Abtelum Biomedical Inc	Westwood	MA	G	781 367-1696	16856
Acceleron Pharma Inc **(PA)**	Cambridge	MA	C	617 649-9200	9370
Acer Therapeutics Inc **(PA)**	Newton	MA	G	844 902-6100	13553
Acusphere Inc	Cambridge	MA	G	617 577-8800	9372
Acusphere Inc **(PA)**	Lexington	MA	D	617 648-8800	12201
Adolor Corporation	Lexington	MA	D	781 860-8660	12202
Aegerion Pharmaceuticals Inc **(HQ)**	Cambridge	MA	F	877 764-3131	9375
Agentus Therapeutics Inc **(HQ)**	Lexington	MA	G	701 674-4400	12203
Agios Pharmaceuticals Inc **(PA)**	Cambridge	MA	C	617 649-8600	9377
Aileron Therapeutics Inc	Watertown	MA	E	774 444-0704	16265
Akcea Therapeutics Inc **(HQ)**	Boston	MA	D	617 207-0202	8347
Akebia Therapeutics Inc **(PA)**	Cambridge	MA	D	617 871-2098	9379
Akston Biosciences Corporation	Beverly	MA	G	978 969-3381	8097
Albireo Pharma Inc	Boston	MA	G	857 415-4774	8351
Albireo Pharma Inc **(PA)**	Boston	MA	E	857 254-5555	8352
Aldeyra Therapeutics Inc **(PA)**	Lexington	MA	G	781 761-4904	12206
Alexion Pharmaceuticals Inc **(PA)**	Boston	MA	C	475 230-2596	8353
Alinea Pharmaceuticals Inc	Cambridge	MA	G	617 500-7867	9381
Alkalol Company	Boston	MA	G	617 304-3668	8357
Alkermes Inc **(HQ)**	Waltham	MA	B	781 609-6000	16029
Alkermes Cntrlled Therapeutics	Waltham	MA	D	877 706-0510	16030
Allena Labs	Sudbury	MA	G	617 467-4577	15652
Allena Pharmaceuticals Inc **(PA)**	Newton	MA	E	617 467-4577	13558
Allergan Sales LLC	Fall River	MA	G	508 324-1481	10653
Alnara Pharmaceuticals Inc	Cambridge	MA	F	617 349-3690	9382
Alnylam Pharmaceuticals Inc	Cambridge	MA	F	617 551-8200	9383
Alnylam Pharmaceuticals Inc **(PA)**	Cambridge	MA	C	617 551-8200	9384
Alnylam US Inc	Cambridge	MA	E	617 551-8200	9385
Alopexx Pharmaceuticals LLC	Concord	MA	F	617 945-2510	10108
Alseres Pharmaceuticals Inc	Auburndale	MA	G	508 497-2360	7855
Alzheon Inc	Framingham	MA	G	508 861-7709	10919
Amag Pharmaceuticals Inc **(PA)**	Waltham	MA	B	617 498-3300	16032
Amorsa Therapeutics Inc	Southborough	MA	G	508 571-8240	15342
Amplicea Therapeutics Inc	Worcester	MA	G	617 515-6755	17337

	CITY	ST	EMP	PHONE	ENTRY #
Amri Burlington Inc **(DH)**	Burlington	MA	E	781 270-7900	9233
Annovation Biopharma Inc	Wayland	MA	G	617 724-0343	16332
Anterion Therapeutics Inc	Salem	MA	G	617 240-0324	14892
Apellis Pharmaceuticals Inc **(PA)**	Waltham	MA	E	617 977-5700	16034
Appetites	Barnstable	MA	G	508 362-3623	7946
Aprea (us) Inc	Boston	MA	G	857 239-9072	8370
Aprea Therapeutics Inc	Boston	MA	F	617 463-9385	8371
Aratana Therapeutics Inc	Boston	MA	G	617 425-9226	8372
Armstrong Pharmaceuticals Inc **(HQ)**	West Roxbury	MA	D	617 323-7404	16493
Armstrong Pharmaceuticals Inc	Canton	MA	E	617 323-7404	9715
Arqule Inc **(PA)**	Burlington	MA	E	781 994-0300	9234
Atlantic Animal Health Inc	Revere	MA	G	781 289-9600	14763
Avedro Inc **(HQ)**	Waltham	MA	D	781 768-3400	16040
Aveo Pharmaceuticals Inc	Cambridge	MA	F	617 299-5000	9398
Aveo Pharmaceuticals Inc **(PA)**	Cambridge	MA	F	617 588-1960	9399
Aveo Securities Corporation	Cambridge	MA	G	617 588-1960	9400
Aveta Biomics Inc	Bedford	MA	G	339 927-5994	7960
Avrobio Inc **(PA)**	Cambridge	MA	E	617 914-8420	9401
Azurity Pharmaceuticals **(PA)**	Woburn	MA	F	855 379-0382	17125
Barbaras Bakery Inc **(DH)**	Marlborough	MA	E	800 343-0590	12725
Baxalta US Inc	Cambridge	MA	F	312 656-8021	9405
Beigene Usa Inc **(HQ)**	Cambridge	MA	G	781 801-1887	9407
Benu Biopharma Inc	Sudbury	MA	G	508 208-5634	15653
Berg LLC **(PA)**	Framingham	MA	D	617 588-0083	10927
Berkshire Sterile Mfg Inc	Lee	MA	F	413 243-0330	12088
Biogen Inc **(PA)**	Cambridge	MA	B	617 679-2000	9409
Biopharma of Cape Cod Inc	Cotuit	MA	G	508 428-5823	10168
Bioverativ Inc **(DH)**	Waltham	MA	D	781 663-4400	16048
Bluefin Biomedicine Inc	Beverly	MA	E	978 712-8105	8112
Blueprint Medicines Corp **(PA)**	Cambridge	MA	C	617 374-7580	9412
Boaopharma Inc	Natick	MA	G	508 315-8080	13239
Boston Biomedical Pharma Inc	Cambridge	MA	G	617 674-6800	9416
Boston Biopharma LLC	Weston	MA	G	617 780-9300	16823
Boston Oncology LLC	Cambridge	MA	G	857 209-5052	9420
Bristol-Myers Squibb Company	Billerica	MA	E	978 667-9532	8220
Bryan Oncor Inc	Somerville	MA	G	617 957-9858	15162
Bwt Pharma & Biotech Inc	Marlborough	MA	E	508 485-4291	12731
Cadrus Therapeutics Inc	Worcester	MA	G	508 344-9719	17352
Cardurion Pharmaceuticals Inc	Cambridge	MA	G	617 863-8088	9428
Carrick Pharmaceuticals Inc	Somerville	MA	G	617 623-0525	15165
Casma Therapeutics Inc	Cambridge	MA	F	857 777-4248	9429
Catabasis Pharmaceuticals Inc	Cambridge	MA	E	617 349-1971	9430
Cedilla Therapeutics Inc	Cambridge	MA	F	617 581-9333	9431
Celgene Avilomics Research Inc	Cambridge	MA	F	857 706-1311	9432
Celgene Corporation	Amesbury	MA	G	857 225-2309	7481
Celyad Inc	Boston	MA	G	857 990-6900	8461
Censa Pharmaceuticals Inc **(PA)**	Wellesley Hills	MA	F	617 225-7700	16396
Central Admxture Phrm Svcs Inc	Woburn	MA	E	781 376-0032	17142
Centrexion Therapeutics Corp	Boston	MA	F	617 837-6911	8464
Cerevance Inc **(PA)**	Boston	MA	G	408 220-5722	8465
Chiasma Inc	Needham	MA	F	617 928-5300	13296
Cielo Therapeutics Inc	Hopkinton	MA	G	617 649-2005	11696
Citra Labs LLC	Braintree	MA	E	781 848-9386	8994
Civitas Therapeutics Inc	Chelsea	MA	D	617 884-3004	9949
Clementia Pharmaceuticals USA	Auburndale	MA	G	857 226-5588	7858
Clio Designs Incorporated	Needham	MA	F	781 449-9500	13297
Cnh Technologies Inc	Woburn	MA	G	781 933-0362	17145
Coley Pharmaceutical Group Inc	Wellesley	MA	C	781 431-9000	16366
Collagen Medical LLC	Belmont	MA	G	857 928-8817	8070
Collegium Pharmaceutical Inc	Stoughton	MA	C	781 713-3699	15584
Colucid Pharmaceuticals Inc	Cambridge	MA	G	857 285-6495	9439
Concert Pharmaceuticals Inc **(PA)**	Lexington	MA	D	781 860-0045	12213
Conseal International Inc	Norwood	MA	G	781 278-0010	14142
Constlltion Phrmaceuticals Inc	Cambridge	MA	D	617 714-0555	9441
Continuus Pharmaceutical	Woburn	MA	G	781 281-0099	17152
Corbus Pharmaceuticals Inc	Norwood	MA	G	617 963-1000	14144
Corbus Phrmctcals Holdings Inc **(PA)**	Norwood	MA	E	617 963-0100	14145
Corden Pharma Intl Inc	Braintree	MA	G	781 305-3332	8996
Cordenpharma	Cambridge	MA	G	617 401-2828	9443
Courage Therapeutics Inc	Newton	MA	G	617 216-9921	13583
Cristcot LLC	Concord	MA	G	978 212-6380	10126
Cubist Pharmaceuticals LLC	Lexington	MA	D	781 860-8660	12216
Cue Biopharma Inc **(PA)**	Cambridge	MA	E	617 949-2680	9446
Curagen Corporation **(HQ)**	Needham Heights	MA	F	908 200-7500	13325
Curirx Inc	Wilmington	MA	G	978 658-2962	16990
Cutanea Life Sciences Inc	Woburn	MA	E	484 568-0100	17160
Cutispharma Inc	Wilmington	MA	F	800 461-7449	16992
Cyclerion Therapeutics Inc **(PA)**	Cambridge	MA	G	857 327-8778	9447
Cyta Therapeutics Inc	Woburn	MA	G	617 947-1416	17161
Cytosol Laboratories Inc	Braintree	MA	F	781 848-9386	8998
Decco	Westborough	MA	G	508 329-1391	16613
Deciphera Pharmaceuticals LLC	Waltham	MA	G	781 209-6400	16081
Deciphera Pharmaceuticals Inc **(PA)**	Waltham	MA	E	781 209-6400	16082
Dicerna Pharmaceuticals Inc	Lexington	MA	E	617 621-8097	12219
Djd Enterprises LLC	Cambridge	MA	G	617 803-6875	9455
Dusa Pharmaceuticals Inc **(DH)**	Wilmington	MA	D	978 657-7500	16998
Dyax Corp	Lexington	MA	C	617 349-0200	12221
Eip Pharma Inc	Cambridge	MA	G	617 945-9146	9459
Eisai Inc	Cambridge	MA	E	978 837-4616	9460
Elan Pharma	Cambridge	MA	G	415 885-6780	9461
Eli Lilly and Company	Hopkinton	MA	F	508 435-8326	11702
Eli Lilly and Company	Cambridge	MA	G	317 209-6287	9462
EMD Serono Inc	Billerica	MA	G	781 982-9000	8244
EMD Serono Inc	Burlington	MA	G	978 715-1804	9265
EMD Serono Inc **(DH)**	Rockland	MA	A	781 982-9000	14799
EMD Serono Inc	Quincy	MA	G	781 261-7500	14621
EMD Serono Biotech Center Inc	Billerica	MA	D	978 294-1100	8245
EMD Serono Biotech Center Inc **(HQ)**	Rockland	MA	D	800 283-8088	14800
EMD Serono Biotech Center Inc	Quincy	MA	E	978 294-1100	14622
EMD Serono Holding Inc	Rockland	MA	E	781 982-9000	14801
EMD Serono Research Inst Inc **(HQ)**	Rockland	MA	E	781 982-9000	14802
Enanta Pharmaceuticals Inc	Watertown	MA	D	617 607-0800	16282
Enlivity Corporation	Newton	MA	G	617 964-5237	13589
Entasis Thrputics Holdings Inc **(PA)**	Waltham	MA	G	781 810-0120	16099
Epirus Biopharmaceuticals Inc **(PA)**	Foxboro	MA	E	617 600-3497	10882
Epizyme Inc	Cambridge	MA	C	617 229-5872	9469
Epoxy Technology Inc **(PA)**	Billerica	MA	E	978 667-3805	8248
Erytech Pharma Inc	Cambridge	MA	G	360 320-3325	9472
Eusa Pharma (us) LLC	Burlington	MA	F	617 584-8012	9270
Exarca Pharmaceuticals LLC	Lexington	MA	G	617 620-2776	12223
Exemplar Laboratories LLC	Fall River	MA	G	508 676-6726	10692
Exemplar Pharma LLC	Fall River	MA	G	508 676-6726	10693
Eyegate Pharmaceuticals Inc **(PA)**	Waltham	MA	F	781 788-9043	16105
Eyemax LLC	Weston	MA	G	781 424-9281	16825
FDA Group LLC	North Grafton	MA	F	413 330-7476	13960
Flexion Therapeutics Inc **(PA)**	Burlington	MA	E	781 305-7777	9275
Fog Pharmaceuticals Inc	Cambridge	MA	G	617 945-9510	9480
Fog Pharmaceuticals Inc	Cambridge	MA	G	781 929-9187	9481
For Astellas Institute **(HQ)**	Marlborough	MA	E	508 756-1212	12755
Fortress Biotech Inc	Waltham	MA	F	781 652-4500	16109
Frequency Therapeutics Inc **(PA)**	Woburn	MA	F	866 389-1970	17187
Fresenius Kabi Compounding LLC	Canton	MA	E	224 358-1150	9733
Fresenius Usa Inc	Marlborough	MA	E	508 460-1150	12757
Front Run Organx Inc	Ipswich	MA	G	978 356-7133	11921
Fulcrum Therapeutics Inc	Cambridge	MA	D	617 651-8851	9482
Genocea Biosciences Inc	Cambridge	MA	D	617 876-8191	9488
Gentest Corporation	Woburn	MA	E	781 935-5115	17191
Genzyme Corporation	Framingham	MA	C	508 271-2642	10951
Genzyme Corporation	Framingham	MA	D	617 252-7500	10952
Genzyme Corporation	Framingham	MA	E	508 370-9690	10953
Genzyme Corporation	Allston	MA	D	617 252-7500	7466
Genzyme Corporation	Northborough	MA	D	508 351-2699	14034
Genzyme Corporation	Westborough	MA	C	508 351-2600	16620
Genzyme Corporation	Framingham	MA	D	508 872-8400	10954
Genzyme Corporation	Cambridge	MA	C	508 872-8400	9491
Genzyme Corporation	Cambridge	MA	C	617 252-7500	9492
Genzyme Corporation	Cambridge	MA	B	617 494-8484	9493
Genzyme Corporation	Westborough	MA	E	508 898-9001	16621
Genzyme Corporation	Framingham	MA	C	508 872-8400	10955
Genzyme Corporation	Framingham	MA	C	508 872-8400	10956
Genzyme Corporation	Framingham	MA	C	508 872-8400	10957
Genzyme Corporation	Framingham	MA	C	508 872-8400	10958
Genzyme Corporation **(DH)**	Cambridge	MA	A	617 252-7500	9489
Genzyme Corporation	Cambridge	MA	D	508 271-2919	9490
Genzyme Corporation	Boston	MA	C	617 779-3100	8559
Genzyme Securities Corporation	Cambridge	MA	G	617 252-7500	9494
Glaxosmithkline LLC	Braintree	MA	E	617 828-9028	9010
Glaxosmithkline LLC	Topsfield	MA	E	978 853-6490	15860
Global Lf Scnces Sltons USA LL	Westborough	MA	G	508 475-2000	16622
Glsynthesis Inc	Worcester	MA	E	508 754-6700	17384
Group Artic Inc	Braintree	MA	E	781 848-2174	9013
Gsk Innovations	East Walpole	MA	G	508 566-5212	10523
Harbour Biomed	Cambridge	MA	F	617 682-3679	9500
Idenix Pharmaceuticals Inc **(HQ)**	Cambridge	MA	E	617 995-9800	9510
Idenix Pharmaceuticals Inc	Cambridge	MA	D	617 876-5883	9511
IL Pharma Inc	Cambridge	MA	G	617 355-6910	9513
Imabiotech Corp	Billerica	MA	G	978 362-1825	8256
Immunogen Inc **(PA)**	Waltham	MA	C	781 895-0600	16130
Immunogen Securities Corp	Waltham	MA	E	617 995-2500	16131
Infinity Pharmaceuticals Inc **(PA)**	Cambridge	MA	D	617 453-1000	9515
Innovation Pharmaceuticals Inc **(PA)**	Beverly	MA	G	978 921-4125	8141
Inozyme Pharma Inc **(PA)**	Boston	MA	F	857 330-4340	8617
Ipsen Bioscience Inc	Cambridge	MA	E	617 679-8500	9519
Ironwood Pharmaceuticals Inc **(PA)**	Boston	MA	C	617 621-7722	8622
Johnson Matthey Phrm Mtls Inc **(DH)**	Devens	MA	C	978 784-5000	10321
Johnson Matthey Phrm Mtls Inc	North Andover	MA	E	978 784-5000	13713
Juniper Pharmaceuticals Inc **(DH)**	Boston	MA	E	617 639-1500	8644
Kadmon Corporation LLC	Cambridge	MA	G	724 778-6125	9523
Kala Pharmaceuticals Inc	Watertown	MA	E	781 996-5252	16293
Kalvista Pharmaceuticals Inc **(PA)**	Cambridge	MA	F	857 999-0075	9524
Karuna Therapeutics Inc	Boston	MA	F	857 449-2244	8647
Karyopharm Therapeutics Inc **(PA)**	Newton	MA	C	617 658-0600	13606
Keryx Biopharmaceuticals Inc **(HQ)**	Cambridge	MA	D	617 871-2098	9526
Kintai Therapeutics Inc	Cambridge	MA	E	617 409-7395	9527

Employee Codes: A=Over 500 employees, B=251-500
C=101-250, D=51-100 E=20-50, F=10-19, G=3-9

	CITY	ST	EMP	PHONE	ENTRY #
Kyon Pharma Inc	Boston	MA	G	617 567-2436	8657
Lantheus Holdings Inc **(PA)**	North Billerica	MA	E	978 671-8001	13831
Lantheus Medical Imaging Inc **(HQ)**	North Billerica	MA	B	800 362-2668	13832
Lantheus MI Intermediate Inc	North Billerica	MA	A	978 671-8001	13833
Leap Therapeutics Inc **(PA)**	Cambridge	MA	E	617 714-0360	9533
Lipomed Inc	Cambridge	MA	G	617 577-7222	9537
Lloyd Labs	Wakefield	MA	G	781 224-0083	15957
Longray Inc	Lexington	MA	G	781 862-5137	12240
Ludlow Corporation **(DH)**	Mansfield	MA	G	508 261-8000	12643
Lutronic USA	Billerica	MA	G	888 588-7644	8263
Luxuriance Biopharma Inc	Concord	MA	G	617 817-6679	10139
Lyne Laboratories Inc	Brockton	MA	D	508 583-8700	9163
Magenta Therapeutics Inc	Cambridge	MA	D	857 242-0170	9543
Makscientific LLC	Burlington	MA	G	781 365-0958	9300
Matrivax Research & Dev Corp	Boston	MA	G	617 385-7640	8688
MBL International Corporation **(DH)**	Woburn	MA	F	781 939-6964	17225
Medical Asthtics Assoc Neng PC	Acton	MA	G	978 263-5376	7374
Merck Group	Bedford	MA	G	781 858-3284	7991
Merck Research Laboratories	Boston	MA	F	617 992-2000	8696
Merck Sharp & Dohme Corp	Lexington	MA	C	781 860-8660	12243
Merck Sharp & Dohme Corp	Boston	MA	G	617 992-2074	8697
Merrimack Pharmaceuticals Inc	Cambridge	MA	D	617 441-1000	9551
Mersana Therapeutics Inc **(PA)**	Cambridge	MA	D	617 498-0020	9552
Metastat Inc **(PA)**	Boston	MA	G	617 531-6500	8700
Microbot Medical Inc **(PA)**	Hingham	MA	G	781 875-3605	11505
Millennium Pharmaceuticals Inc	Cambridge	MA	C	617 679-7000	9556
Millennium Pharmaceuticals Inc	Cambridge	MA	D	617 679-7000	9557
Millennium Pharmaceuticals Inc	Cambridge	MA	C	617 679-7000	9558
Millennium Pharmaceuticals Inc	Cambridge	MA	F	617 679-7000	9559
Millennium Pharmaceuticals Inc	Cambridge	MA	C	617 679-7000	9560
Minerva Neurosciences Inc **(PA)**	Waltham	MA	F	617 600-7373	16151
Moderna Inc **(PA)**	Cambridge	MA	E	617 714-6500	9564
Moderna LLC **(HQ)**	Cambridge	MA	G	617 714-6500	9565
Moderna Therapeutics Inc	Cambridge	MA	E	617 714-6500	9566
Momenta Pharmaceuticals Inc **(PA)**	Cambridge	MA	B	617 491-9700	9569
Nanofuse Biologics LLC	Malden	MA	F	978 232-3990	12584
Navitor Pharmaceuticals Inc	Cambridge	MA	F	857 285-4300	9575
Nemucore Med Innovations Inc	Wellesley	MA	G	617 943-9983	16375
Neovii Biotech Na Inc	Lexington	MA	F	781 966-3830	12247
Neuform Pharmaceuticals	Auburndale	MA	G	617 559-9822	7865
Neuro Phage Phrmaceuticals Inc	Cambridge	MA	F	617 941-7004	9578
Neurobo Pharmaceuticals Inc **(PA)**	Boston	MA	F	617 313-7331	8724
Neurobo Therapeutics Inc	Boston	MA	F	617 313-7331	8725
Neurogastrx Incorporated	Woburn	MA	G	781 730-4006	17240
New England Compounding Phrm	Boston	MA	E	800 994-6322	8730
New England Peptide Inc	Gardner	MA	E	978 630-0020	11121
New England Pet Distr Ctr LLC	Woburn	MA	G	781 937-3600	17242
Nextcea Inc	Woburn	MA	G	800 225-1645	17245
Nimbus Lakshmi Inc	Cambridge	MA	G	857 999-2009	9583
Nirogyone Therapeutics LLC	Northborough	MA	G	508 439-2197	14041
Nocion Therapeutics Inc	Waltham	MA	G	781 812-6176	16160
Novartis Corporation	Cambridge	MA	G	617 871-3594	9586
Novartis Corporation	Cambridge	MA	G	617 871-8000	9587
Novartis Corporation	Cambridge	MA	D	617 871-8000	9588
Novartis Inst For Biomedical R	Cambridge	MA	E	617 871-7523	9589
Novartis Inst For Biomedical R **(HQ)**	Cambridge	MA	E	617 871-8000	9590
Novartis Vccnes Dagnostics Inc	Cambridge	MA	A	617 871-7000	9591
Novartis Vccnes Dagnostics Inc	Cambridge	MA	D	617 871-7000	9592
Novelion Therapeutics Inc	Cambridge	MA	F	877 764-3131	9593
Noxxon Pharma Inc	Weston	MA	G	617 232-0638	16828
Nuvelution Pharma Inc	Pembroke	MA	G	781 924-1148	14421
Nypro Finpack Clinton	Clinton	MA	F	978 368-6021	10085
Oasis Pharmaceuticals LLC	Lexington	MA	G	781 752-6094	12251
Ocular Therapeutix Inc **(PA)**	Bedford	MA	E	781 357-4000	7997
Olaf Pharmaceutical Inc	Worcester	MA	G	508 755-3570	17436
Oncomed Phrm Svcs MA Inc	Waltham	MA	G	781 209-5470	16166
Padlock Therapeutics Inc	Cambridge	MA	G	978 381-9601	9604
Palleon Pharma Inc	Waltham	MA	G	857 285-5904	16170
Paloma Pharmaceuticals Inc	Jamaica Plain	MA	F	617 407-6314	11947
Paratek Pharmaceuticals Inc **(PA)**	Boston	MA	G	617 807-6600	8766
Parexel International LLC	Billerica	MA	F	978 313-3435	8272
Partner Therapeutics Inc **(PA)**	Lexington	MA	G	781 727-4259	12253
Pathfinder Cell Therapy Inc	Cambridge	MA	G	617 245-0289	9607
Pear Tree Pharmaceuticals Inc	Auburndale	MA	G	617 500-3871	7867
Pfizer Inc	Westford	MA	G	978 799-8657	16784
Pfizer Inc	Andover	MA	C	978 247-1000	7581
Pharma Compliance Group LLC	Hampden	MA	G	508 377-4561	11323
Pharma Interface Analysis LLC	Groton	MA	G	978 448-6137	11294
Pharma Launcher LLC	Watertown	MA	G	508 812-0850	16307
Pharma Models LLC	Newton	MA	G	617 630-1729	13625
Pharma Models LLC	Marlborough	MA	G	617 306-2281	12806
Pharmaceutical Strtgs Stfng LL	Stoneham	MA	D	781 835-2300	15570
Pharmahealth Specialty/Lon	Fairhaven	MA	F	508 998-8000	10645
Pharmalucence Inc **(HQ)**	Billerica	MA	D	781 275-7120	8273
Pharmate Inc	Cambridge	MA	G	617 800-5804	9610
Phio Pharmaceuticals Corp **(PA)**	Marlborough	MA	F	508 767-3681	12807
Phio Pharmaceuticals Corp	Worcester	MA	G	508 767-3861	17440

	CITY	ST	EMP	PHONE	ENTRY #
Phosphorex Incorporated	Hopkinton	MA	F	508 435-9100	11732
Pioneer Instnl Solutions	Boston	MA	G	617 723-2277	8780
Polycarbon Industries Inc	Devens	MA	G	978 772-2111	10330
Polycarbon Industries Inc **(DH)**	Newburyport	MA	D	978 462-5555	13521
Pp Manufacturing Corporation	Framingham	MA	F	508 766-2700	10996
Praecis Pharmaceuticals Inc	Waltham	MA	D	781 795-4100	16176
Praktikatalyst Pharma LLC	Pittsfield	MA	G	413 442-1857	14502
Prismic Pharmaceuticals Inc	Holden	MA	G	971 506-6415	11550
Promedior Inc	Lexington	MA	F	781 538-4200	12255
Proteostasis Therapeutics Inc	Boston	MA	D	617 225-0096	8798
Ptc As LLC	Lynnfield	MA	G	339 440-5818	12555
Ptc Therapeutics Gt Inc	Cambridge	MA	G	781 799-9179	9619
Pulmatrix Inc **(PA)**	Lexington	MA	E	781 357-2333	12256
Pulmatrix Operating Co Inc	Lexington	MA	G	781 357-2333	12257
Qpharmetra LLC **(PA)**	Andover	MA	F	978 655-1943	7589
Quantum Designs LLC **(PA)**	Cambridge	MA	G	617 491-6600	9621
Ra Pharmaceuticals Inc	Cambridge	MA	E	617 401-4060	9624
Radius Health Inc **(PA)**	Waltham	MA	D	617 551-4000	16183
Red Oak Sourcing LLC	Foxborough	MA	D	401 742-0701	10913
Reform Biologics LLC	Woburn	MA	F	617 871-2101	17282
Rentschler Biopharma Inc	Milford	MA	G	508 282-5800	13140
Restorbio Inc	Boston	MA	E	857 315-5521	8818
Revere Pharmaceuticals Inc	Arlington	MA	G	781 718-9033	7635
Rhenovia Incorporated	Cambridge	MA	G	310 382-4079	9632
Rhythm Pharmaceuticals Inc	Boston	MA	E	857 264-4280	8820
Riptide Synthetics Inc	Cambridge	MA	G	617 945-8832	9634
Safecor Health LLC	Woburn	MA	D	781 933-8780	17288
Sage Therapeutics Inc **(PA)**	Cambridge	MA	D	617 299-8380	9640
Sangstat Medical LLC	Cambridge	MA	B	510 789-4300	9642
Sanofi Genzyme	Framingham	MA	E	508 871-5871	11001
Sanofi US Services Inc	Cambridge	MA	E	617 562-4555	9643
Sanova Bioscience Inc	Acton	MA	G	978 429-8079	7383
Santhera Pharmaceuticals usa	Burlington	MA	G	781 552-5145	9333
Santhera Phrmceuticals USA Inc	Charlestown	MA	G	617 886-5161	9843
Sarepta Therapeutics Inc **(PA)**	Cambridge	MA	B	617 274-4000	9644
Scholar Rock Holding Corp **(PA)**	Cambridge	MA	G	857 259-3860	9646
Scpharmaceuticals Inc	Burlington	MA	E	617 517-0730	9335
Sefacor Inc	Somerville	MA	G	617 471-0176	15214
Selecta Biosciences Inc **(PA)**	Watertown	MA	E	617 923-1400	16314
Selvita Inc	Boston	MA	G	857 998-4075	8843
Senopsys LLC	Woburn	MA	G	781 935-7450	17292
Sentien Biotechnologies Inc	Lexington	MA	G	781 361-9031	12265
Serono Inc	Rockland	MA	F	781 681-2137	14824
Serono Laboratories Inc	Rockland	MA	D	781 681-2288	14825
Sfj Pharma	Pembroke	MA	G	781 924-1148	14426
Shire Inc **(HQ)**	Lexington	MA	C	781 482-9222	12267
Shire Humn Gntic Therapies Inc	Waltham	MA	G	781 862-1561	16192
Shire Humn Gntic Therapies Inc	Cambridge	MA	G	617 349-0200	9649
Shire Humn Gntic Therapies Inc **(HQ)**	Lexington	MA	C	617 349-0200	12268
Shire Humn Gntic Therapies Inc	Lexington	MA	G	617 349-0200	12269
Shire Humn Gntic Therapies Inc	North Reading	MA	F	781 482-0883	13989
Shire Inc **(HQ)**	Lexington	MA	E	781 274-1248	12270
Shire Pharmaceuticals LLC	Lexington	MA	G	617 349-0200	12271
Shire Pharmaceuticals LLC	Cambridge	MA	G	617 588-8800	9650
Shire US Inc **(DH)**	Lexington	MA	A	781 482-9222	12272
Shire Viropharma Incorporated **(DH)**	Lexington	MA	E	610 458-7300	12273
Shire-NPS Pharmaceuticals Inc **(DH)**	Lexington	MA	A	617 349-0200	12274
Sigilon Therapeutics Inc	Cambridge	MA	E	617 336-7540	9651
Sobi Inc	Waltham	MA	E	610 228-2040	16196
Sojournix Inc	Waltham	MA	G	781 864-1111	16198
Soleo Health Inc	Canton	MA	G	781 298-3427	9782
Spero Therapeutics Inc **(PA)**	Cambridge	MA	E	857 242-1600	9658
Splice Therapeutics Inc	West Roxbury	MA	G	914 804-4136	16503
Spring Bnk Pharmaceuticals Inc **(PA)**	Hopkinton	MA	E	508 473-5993	11738
Sq Innovation Inc	Burlington	MA	G	617 500-0121	9339
St Jude Medical LLC	Wilmington	MA	E	978 657-6519	17047
Stallrgenes Greer Holdings Inc	Cambridge	MA	E	617 588-4900	9660
Summit Therapeutics Inc	Cambridge	MA	G	617 225-4455	9662
Sunovion Pharmaceuticals Inc **(DH)**	Marlborough	MA	A	508 481-6700	12832
Suzhou-Chem Inc	Wellesley	MA	G	781 433-8618	16388
Syndax Pharmaceuticals Inc **(PA)**	Waltham	MA	F	781 419-1400	16204
Syndax Securities Corporation	Waltham	MA	G	781 472-2985	16205
Syner-G Pharma Consulting LLC	Southborough	MA	G	508 460-9700	15368
Synertide Pharmaceuticals Inc	Wellesley	MA	G	801 671-1329	16389
Synlogic Inc **(PA)**	Cambridge	MA	E	617 401-9975	9671
Synostics Inc	Weston	MA	G	781 248-5699	16832
Syros Pharmaceuticals Inc **(PA)**	Cambridge	MA	D	617 744-1340	9672
Takeda Building 35 5	Cambridge	MA	G	617 444-4352	9673
Takeda Pharmaceuticals	Cambridge	MA	F	617 441-6930	9674
Takeda Pharmaceuticals USA Inc	Duxbury	MA	G	781 837-1528	10403
Takeda Pharmaceuticals USA Inc **(HQ)**	Lexington	MA	A	617 349-0200	12277
Takeda Pharmaceuticals USA Inc	Cambridge	MA	E	617 444-1348	9675
Taris Biomedical LLC	Lexington	MA	E	781 676-7750	12278
Tarpon Biosystems Inc	Marlborough	MA	G	978 979-4222	12835
Tarveda Therapeutics Inc	Watertown	MA	E	617 923-4100	16320
Tesaro Inc **(HQ)**	Waltham	MA	C	339 970-0900	16210
Tesaro Securities Corporation	Waltham	MA	A	339 970-0900	16211

	CITY	ST	EMP	PHONE	ENTRY #
Tetraphase Pharmaceuticals Inc **(PA)**	Watertown	MA	D	617 715-3600	16321
Teva Pharmaceuticals	Cambridge	MA	G	617 252-6586	9680
Theragenics Corporation	North Billerica	MA	G	978 528-4307	13872
Thrombolytic Science LLC	Cambridge	MA	G	617 661-1107	9681
Tolerx Inc	Cambridge	MA	D	617 354-8100	9682
Ultragenyx Pharmaceutical Inc	Cambridge	MA	G	617 949-4010	9685
Unicus Pharmaceuticals LLC	Taunton	MA	E	508 659-7002	15793
UNUM Therapeutics Inc	Cambridge	MA	D	617 945-5576	9687
Uptite Company Inc	Haverhill	MA	G	978 377-0451	11483
Vapco Inc	Lawrence	MA	G	978 975-0302	12081
Vectura Incorporated	Southborough	MA	G	508 573-5700	15370
Verastem Inc **(PA)**	Needham	MA	D	781 292-4200	13316
Vertex Pharmaceuticals Inc	Boston	MA	F	617 201-4171	8908
Vertex Pharmaceuticals Inc **(PA)**	Boston	MA	B	617 341-6100	8909
Viacell Inc **(DH)**	Waltham	MA	E	617 914-3400	16219
Viamet Phrmctcals Holdings LLC	Foxboro	MA	E	919 467-8539	10908
Vietaz Inc	Dorchester	MA	G	617 322-1933	10349
Viropharma Biologics Inc	Lexington	MA	G	610 458-7300	12282
Visionaid Inc	Wareham	MA	E	508 295-3300	16258
Visterra Inc	Waltham	MA	E	617 498-1070	16221
W F Young Incorporated **(PA)**	East Longmeadow	MA	E	800 628-9653	10503
Wellfleet Pharmaceuticals Inc	Boston	MA	G	617 767-6264	8920
West St Intrmdate Hldings Corp **(PA)**	Waltham	MA	F	781 434-5051	16223
Wilex Inc	Cambridge	MA	F	617 492-3900	9701
Wilmington Partners LP	Wilmington	MA	C	978 658-6111	17067
Wyeth Pharmaceuticals LLC	Andover	MA	B	978 475-9214	7619
Xenetic Biosciences Inc	Framingham	MA	G	781 778-7720	11017
Zafgen Inc	Boston	MA	E	617 622-4003	8941
Ziopharm Oncology Inc	Charlestown	MA	G	617 259-1970	9845
Biodesign International Inc	Saco	ME	E	207 283-6500	6843
Biotech Source Inc **(PA)**	Windham	ME	G	207 894-5690	7230
Clearh2o	Portland	ME	F	207 221-0039	6639
Dermalogix Partners Inc	Scarborough	ME	E	207 883-4103	6916
Global Biotechnologies Inc	Scarborough	ME	G	800 755-8420	6920
Holland Drug Inc	Farmington	ME	G	207 778-5419	6050
Idexx Laboratories Inc **(PA)**	Westbrook	ME	A	207 556-0300	7191
Jfm No 3 Corp	Auburn	ME	E	207 782-2726	5573
M Drug LLC	Brewer	ME	G	207 973-9444	5798
Mad Gabs Inc	Yarmouth	ME	G	207 854-1679	7298
Maine Biotechnology Svcs Inc	Portland	ME	E	207 797-5454	6683
Naturally Maine	Biddeford	ME	G	207 423-6443	5751
Pondera Pharmaceuticals Inc	Pownal	ME	G	207 688-4494	6750
Abbott Laboratories	Nashua	NH	A	603 891-3380	19103
Bentley Pharmaceuticals Inc **(HQ)**	Exeter	NH	F	603 658-6100	18113
Biosan Laboratories Inc	Derry	NH	E	603 437-0861	17972
Cellgenix USA	Portsmouth	NH	G	603 373-0408	19550
Chemcage US LLC	East Kingston	NH	G	617 504-9548	18085
Critical Prcess Filtration Inc **(PA)**	Nashua	NH	E	603 595-0140	19140
Icad Inc **(PA)**	Nashua	NH	C	603 882-5200	19181
Lonza Biologics Inc	Portsmouth	NH	F	603 610-4696	19588
Lonza Biologics Inc **(DH)**	Portsmouth	NH	B	603 610-4500	19589
Lyophilization Svcs Neng Inc **(PA)**	Manchester	NH	F	603 626-5763	18866
Max Pharmaceutical LLC	Bedford	NH	G	603 472-2813	17653
Msm Protein Technologies Inc	East Kingston	NH	F	617 504-9548	18088
Novo Nordisk US Bio Prod Inc	West Lebanon	NH	C	603 298-3169	19958
Seachange Therapeutics Inc	Merrimack	NH	G	603 424-6009	19028
Statim Pharmaceuticals Inc	Moultonborough	NH	G	650 305-0657	19098
Stealth Biologics LLC	Lebanon	NH	G	603 643-5134	18637
Susie BZ Natural Lip Balm	Weare	NH	G	603 529-7083	19940
Tender Corporation **(PA)**	Littleton	NH	D	603 444-5464	18667
Trimaran Pharma Inc	Nashua	NH	G	508 577-7110	19275
Trividia Mfg Solutions **(DH)**	Lancaster	NH	C	603 788-2848	18606
Trividia Mfg Solutions	Lancaster	NH	G	603 788-4952	18607
Uptite Co Inc	Salem	NH	G	603 401-3856	19776
Agape Dermatology	Providence	RI	G	401 396-2227	20949
Amgen Inc	West Greenwich	RI	D	401 392-1200	21452
Calista Therapeutics Inc	Lincoln	RI	G	401 345-5979	20561
Denison Pharmaceuticals LLC	Lincoln	RI	C	401 723-5500	20567
Edesia Inc	North Kingstown	RI	D	401 272-5521	20704
Edesia Enterprises LLC	North Kingstown	RI	D	401 272-5521	20705
Glaxosmithkline LLC	North Scituate	RI	F	401 934-2834	20778
Immunex Rhode Island Corp	West Greenwich	RI	E	401 392-1200	21457
Lockett Medical Corporation **(PA)**	Providence	RI	G	401 421-6599	21055
Mymetics Corporation	Providence	RI	G	410 216-5345	21073
Phe Investments LLC	Johnston	RI	D	401 289-2900	20529
Rhodes Pharmaceuticals LP	Coventry	RI	F	401 262-9200	20164
Sea Starr Animal Health	Wakefield	RI	G	401 783-2185	21275
Sea-Band International Inc	Newport	RI	G	401 841-5900	20679
Techtrak LLC	Coventry	RI	G	401 397-3983	20166
Tedor Pharma Inc	Cumberland	RI	E	401 658-5219	20346
Ceres LLC **(PA)**	Burlington	VT	G	833 237-3767	21772
Meadham Inc	Ferrisburgh	VT	G	802 878-1236	21989
Mylan Technologies Inc **(DH)**	Saint Albans	VT	C	802 527-7792	22373
Mylan Technologies Inc	Saint Albans	VT	G	802 527-7792	22374
New Chapter Inc **(HQ)**	Brattleboro	VT	C	800 543-7279	21739
PBM Nutritionals LLC **(DH)**	Milton	VT	D	802 527-0521	22135
Vermonts Original LLC	Lyndonville	VT	G	802 626-3610	22076

2835 Diagnostic Substances

	CITY	ST	EMP	PHONE	ENTRY #
Bioarray Genetics Inc	Farmington	CT	G	508 577-0205	1468
Branford Open Mri & Diagnostic	Branford	CT	G	203 481-7800	299
Cardinal Health 414 LLC	East Hartford	CT	G	860 291-9135	1179
Charles River Laboratories Inc	Storrs	CT	E	860 429-7261	4381
Lam Therapeutics Inc	Guilford	CT	F	203 458-7100	1707
Veterinary Medical Associates	Canton	CT	G	860 693-0214	700
Abclonal-Neo Inc	Woburn	MA	F	617 412-1176	17104
Abpro Corporation	Woburn	MA	E	617 225-0808	17105
Akrivis Technologies LLC	Cambridge	MA	G	617 233-4097	9380
Aldatu Biosciences Inc	Watertown	MA	G	978 705-1036	16266
Alere US Holdings LLC	Waltham	MA	G	781 647-3900	16028
Amag Pharmaceuticals Inc **(PA)**	Waltham	MA	B	617 498-3300	16032
Amasa Technologies Inc	Andover	MA	G	617 899-8223	7537
Asimov Inc	Cambridge	MA	E	425 750-4182	9395
Associates of Cape Cod Inc **(PA)**	East Falmouth	MA	D	508 540-3444	10435
Axis-Shield Poc As	Norton	MA	E	508 285-4870	14071
Bionostics Inc	Devens	MA	D	978 772-7070	10319
Bluejay Diagnostics Inc	Acton	MA	G	978 631-0152	7345
Catalyst Medical LLC	Belmont	MA	G	857 928-8817	8068
Cellanyx Diagnostics LLC	Beverly	MA	G	571 212-9991	8114
Cellay LLC	Cambridge	MA	F	617 995-1307	9434
Confer Health Inc	Charlestown	MA	G	617 433-8810	9830
Creatics LLC	Braintree	MA	F	781 843-2202	8997
Daktari Diagnostics Inc	Cambridge	MA	F	617 336-3299	9449
Detectogen Inc	Westborough	MA	G	508 330-1709	16615
Endogen Inc	Woburn	MA	D	617 225-0055	17177
Genzyme Corporation	Framingham	MA	G	508 271-3631	10950
Genzyme Corporation **(DH)**	Cambridge	MA	A	617 252-7500	9489
Genzyme Corporation	Cambridge	MA	D	508 271-2919	9490
Genzyme Corporation	Natick	MA	C	617 768-9292	13258
Genzyme Corporation	Waltham	MA	D	781 487-5728	16120
Genzyme Corporation	Boston	MA	C	617 779-3100	8559
Glycozym Usa Inc	Beverly	MA	G	425 985-2556	8137
Hypoxyprobe Inc	Burlington	MA	G	781 272-6888	9283
Instrumentation Laboratory Co **(DH)**	Bedford	MA	A	781 861-0710	7982
Jane Diagnostics Inc	Brookline	MA	G	617 651-2295	9206
Lantheus Holdings Inc **(PA)**	North Billerica	MA	E	978 671-8001	13831
Moderna LLC **(HQ)**	Cambridge	MA	G	617 714-6500	9565
Nanobiosym Inc	Cambridge	MA	E	781 391-7979	9574
Nanobiosym Inc	Medford	MA	F	781 391-7979	12944
New England Immunology Assoc	Lexington	MA	G	781 863-5774	12249
Ninth Sense Inc	Boston	MA	G	617 835-4472	8738
Northern Berkshire Pregnancy	North Adams	MA	G	413 346-4291	13684
Oxford Immunotec Inc **(DH)**	Marlborough	MA	D	508 481-4648	12804
Petnet Solutions Inc	Woburn	MA	G	865 218-2000	17261
Phoenix Diagnostics Inc	Natick	MA	F	508 655-8310	13272
Pierce Biotechnology Inc	Woburn	MA	E	781 622-1000	17264
Preceding Inc	Natick	MA	G	617 953-6173	13273
Qsa Global Inc **(HQ)**	Burlington	MA	D	781 272-2000	9325
Qteros LLC	Amherst	MA	G	413 531-6884	7523
Quidel Corporation	Beverly	MA	G	866 800-5458	8168
Regenocell Therapeutics Inc	Natick	MA	G	508 651-1598	13277
Reservoir Genomics Inc	Cambridge	MA	G	412 304-5063	9631
Rootpath Genomics	Cambridge	MA	G	857 209-1060	9638
Rootpath Genomics Inc	Boston	MA	G	501 258-0969	8827
Sangstat Medical LLC	Cambridge	MA	B	510 789-4300	9642
Sano LLC	Wellesley	MA	G	617 290-3348	16386
Sbh Diagnostics Inc	Natick	MA	G	508 545-0333	13278
Seracare Life Sciences Inc **(DH)**	Milford	MA	C	508 244-6400	13143
T2 Biosystems Inc **(PA)**	Lexington	MA	C	781 761-4646	12276
Telome Inc	Waltham	MA	G	617 383-7565	16209
Therastat LLC	Weston	MA	G	781 373-1865	16833
Third Wave Technologies Inc **(HQ)**	Marlborough	MA	E	608 273-8933	12836
Thorne Diagnostics Inc	Beverly	MA	G	978 299-1727	8191
USA Renewable LLC	Newton	MA	G	617 319-7237	13645
Werfen USA LLC	Bedford	MA	C	781 861-0710	8020
Abbott Dgnstics Scrborough Inc **(DH)**	Scarborough	ME	D	207 730-5750	6901
Alere Inc	Scarborough	ME	G	207 730-5714	6903
Bioprocessing Inc	Portland	ME	F	207 457-0025	6623
Cape Technologies LLC	South Portland	ME	G	207 741-2995	7018
Capricorn Products LLC	Portland	ME	E	207 321-0014	6630
Idexx Distribution Inc	Westbrook	ME	D	207 556-0637	7190
Immucell Corporation **(PA)**	Portland	ME	E	207 878-2770	6673
Maine Biotechnology Svcs Inc	Portland	ME	E	207 797-5454	6683
O E M Concepts **(HQ)**	Saco	ME	G	207 283-6500	6854
Solidphase Inc	Portland	ME	G	207 797-0211	6732
Sun Diagnostics LLC	New Gloucester	ME	G	207 926-1125	6472
Virostat Inc	Westbrook	ME	G	207 856-6620	7213
C&S Chmcal Sprtons Sensors LLC	Pembroke	NH	G	603 491-9511	19456
Viridis Diagnostics Inc	Underhill	VT	G	802 316-0894	22550

2836 Biological Prdts, Exc Diagnostic Substances

	CITY	ST	EMP	PHONE	ENTRY #
Axiomx Inc	Branford	CT	E	203 208-1034	293
Charles River Laboratories Inc	Voluntown	CT	E	860 376-1240	4689
Charles River Laboratories Inc	Norwich	CT	E	860 889-1389	3277

	CITY	ST	EMP	PHONE	ENTRY #
Charles River Laboratories Inc	Storrs	CT	E	860 429-7261	4381
Coopersurgical Inc	Guilford	CT	E	203 453-1700	1699
Evotec (us) Inc	Branford	CT	E	650 228-1400	314
Genx International Inc **(PA)**	Guilford	CT	E	203 453-1700	1705
Oncosynergy Inc	Greenwich	CT	G	617 755-9156	1636
Phoenixsongs Biologicals Inc	Branford	CT	G	203 433-4329	337
Plasma Coatings Inc	Waterbury	CT	G	203 598-3100	4939
Plasma Technology Incorporated	South Windsor	CT	E	860 282-0659	4001
Protein Sciences Corporation **(HQ)**	Meriden	CT	D	203 686-0800	2119
Vegware Us Inc	Danielson	CT	G	860 779-7970	1020
Westchester Pet Vaccines	Colchester	CT	G	860 267-4554	812
3dm Inc	Cambridge	MA	G	617 875-6204	9367
Acceleron Pharma Inc **(PA)**	Cambridge	MA	C	617 649-9200	9370
ACS Division Biochemical Tech	Boston	MA	F	617 216-6144	8338
Agenus Inc **(PA)**	Lexington	MA	C	781 674-4400	12204
Akebia Therapeutics Inc **(PA)**	Cambridge	MA	D	617 871-2098	9379
Allena Pharmaceuticals Inc **(PA)**	Newton	MA	E	617 467-4577	13558
Ambergen Inc **(PA)**	Watertown	MA	F	617 923-9990	16268
Amgen Inc	Cambridge	MA	E	617 444-5000	9388
Aqua Bio Compliance Corp	Worcester	MA	G	508 798-2966	17341
Ariad Pharmaceuticals Inc	Cambridge	MA	B	617 494-0400	9392
Beverly Qiagen Inc	Beverly	MA	D	978 927-7027	8109
Bioanalytix Inc	Cambridge	MA	G	857 829-3200	9408
Biogen Inc **(PA)**	Cambridge	MA	B	617 679-2000	9409
Biogen MA Inc **(HQ)**	Cambridge	MA	C	617 679-2000	9410
Biohelix Corporation	Beverly	MA	F	978 927-5056	8111
Bittid LLC	Winchester	MA	G	781 570-2077	17083
Boston Biochem Inc	Cambridge	MA	G	617 241-7072	9415
Capralogics Inc	Gilbertville	MA	G	413 477-6866	11153
Cellaria Biosciences LLC	Boxford	MA	G	617 981-4208	8974
Curevac Inc	Boston	MA	G	617 694-1537	8490
Curis Inc **(PA)**	Lexington	MA	E	617 503-6500	12217
Cytocure LLC	Beverly	MA	G	978 232-1243	8122
Diagnosys LLC **(PA)**	Lowell	MA	E	978 458-1600	12367
Dicerna Pharmaceuticals Inc	Lexington	MA	E	617 621-8097	12219
Diversified Biotech Inc	Dedham	MA	F	781 326-6709	10288
Editas Medicine Inc	Cambridge	MA	D	617 401-9000	9458
Elicio Therapeutics Inc	Cambridge	MA	G	617 945-2077	9463
Endogen Inc	Woburn	MA	D	617 225-0055	17177
Excelimmune Inc	Beverly	MA	G	617 262-8055	8129
Excelimmune Inc **(PA)**	Lexington	MA	G	781 262-8055	12224
Extend Biosciences Inc	Newton	MA	G	732 599-8580	13591
Fresenius Usa Inc	Marlborough	MA	E	508 460-1150	12757
Genocea Biosciences Inc	Cambridge	MA	D	617 876-8191	9488
Genzyme Corporation **(DH)**	Cambridge	MA	A	617 252-7500	9489
Ginkgo Bioworks Inc	Boston	MA	C	814 422-5362	8565
Global Lf Scnces Sltons USA LL	Marlborough	MA	D	508 480-9235	12761
Heka Instruments Incorporated	Holliston	MA	G	516 882-1155	11576
Helixbind Inc	Marlborough	MA	F	508 460-1028	12767
Hockey12com	Billerica	MA	G	781 910-2877	8254
Hooke Laboratories Inc	Lawrence	MA	D	617 475-5114	12036
Intellia Therapeutics Inc **(PA)**	Cambridge	MA	D	857 285-6200	9517
Jounce Therapeutics Inc **(PA)**	Cambridge	MA	D	857 259-3840	9522
Joyn Bio LLC	Boston	MA	E	978 549-3723	8641
Kaleido Biosciences Inc **(PA)**	Lexington	MA	D	617 674-9000	12234
Kbioscience LLC	Beverly	MA	G	978 232-9430	8145
Kiniksa Pharmaceuticals Corp	Lexington	MA	G	781 431-9100	12236
Koan Biotherapeutics Inc	Waban	MA	G	617 968-7882	15937
Lariat Biosciences Inc	Chelsea	MA	G	603 244-9657	9960
Launchworks LLC	Beverly	MA	E	978 338-3045	8147
Logicbio Therapeutics Inc	Cambridge	MA	E	617 230-0399	9540
Massbiologics	Boston	MA	C	617 474-3000	8687
Microbot Medical Inc **(PA)**	Hingham	MA	G	781 875-3605	11505
Moderna Inc **(PA)**	Cambridge	MA	E	617 714-6500	9564
Moderna LLC **(HQ)**	Cambridge	MA	G	617 714-6500	9565
Nashoba Valley Extract LLC	Stow	MA	G	978 201-5245	15634
New England Immunology Assoc	Lexington	MA	G	781 863-5774	12249
Organogenesis Inc **(HQ)**	Canton	MA	B	781 575-0775	9764
Pathfire Inc	Needham Heights	MA	G	972 581-2000	13343
Pierce Biotechnology Inc	Woburn	MA	E	781 622-1000	17264
Plasma Giken Limited Company	Webster	MA	G	508 640-7708	16349
Primmbiotech Inc	West Roxbury	MA	G	617 308-8135	16500
Program LLC	Marlborough	MA	G	781 281-0751	12810
Project Plasma Holdings Corp **(DH)**	Milford	MA	G	508 244-6400	13139
Puretech Health LLC **(PA)**	Boston	MA	D	617 482-2333	8799
Repligen Corporation **(PA)**	Waltham	MA	B	781 250-0111	16187
Replimune Group Inc	Woburn	MA	D	781 995-2443	17283
Revo Biologics Inc	Spencer	MA	E	508 370-5451	15434
Revo Biologics Inc **(DH)**	Framingham	MA	D	508 620-9700	11000
Rowley Biochemical Institute	Danvers	MA	G	978 739-4883	10253
Scholar Rock Holding Corp **(PA)**	Cambridge	MA	G	857 259-3860	9646
Science Serum LLC	Norton	MA	G	508 369-7733	14088
Solid Biosciences Inc **(PA)**	Cambridge	MA	D	617 337-4680	9655
Sports Insights Inc	Beverly	MA	G	877 838-2853	8179
Star Vaccine Inc	Newton	MA	G	617 584-5483	13640
Takeda Vaccines Inc	Cambridge	MA	G	970 672-4918	9676
Tetragenetics Inc	Arlington	MA	F	617 500-7471	7641
Twentyfrst Cntury Bchmcals Inc	Marlborough	MA	E	508 303-8222	12839
Vaccine Technologies Inc **(PA)**	Wellesley	MA	G	781 489-3388	16391
Variation Btechnologies US Inc	Cambridge	MA	E	617 830-3031	9688
Vbi Vaccines	Cambridge	MA	G	617 714-3451	9689
Vbi Vaccines Inc	Cambridge	MA	G	617 830-3031	9690
Vericel Corporation	Cambridge	MA	G	857 600-8191	9692
Vericel Corporation **(PA)**	Cambridge	MA	C	800 556-0311	9693
Vivagene Biotech Inc	Quincy	MA	G	617 302-4398	14667
Voyager Therapeutics Inc **(PA)**	Cambridge	MA	D	857 259-5340	9698
X4 Pharmaceuticals Inc **(PA)**	Cambridge	MA	F	857 529-8300	9706
Gulf of Maine Inc	Pembroke	ME	G	207 726-4620	6580
Hightech Extracts LLC	Biddeford	ME	G	207 590-3251	5738
Lobster Rx	Orono	ME	G	207 949-2028	6555
Lohmann Animal Health Intl Inc	Winslow	ME	C	207 873-3989	7270
Lonza Rockland Inc	Rockland	ME	D	207 594-3400	6802
McWilliams Inc	North Berwick	ME	G	207 676-7639	6509
Northeast Laboratory Svcs Inc **(PA)**	Winslow	ME	D	207 873-7711	7272
Opco Inc	Edgecomb	ME	G	207 882-6783	6003
Solidphase Inc	Portland	ME	G	207 797-0211	6732
Special Diversified Opp Inc	Windham	ME	E	207 856-6151	7254
Aurora Biosystems LLC	Portsmouth	NH	G	603 766-1947	19540
Avitide Inc	Lebanon	NH	E	603 965-2100	18613
Lyophilization Svcs Neng Inc **(PA)**	Manchester	NH	F	603 626-5763	18866
Lyophilization Svcs Neng Inc	Bedford	NH	E	603 668-5763	17651
Lyophilization Svcs Neng Inc	Bedford	NH	F	603 626-9559	17652
Amgen Inc	West Greenwich	RI	D	401 392-1200	21452
Colloidal Science Solutions	West Warwick	RI	G	401 826-3641	21487
Epivax Inc	Providence	RI	F	401 272-2123	21007
Tivorsan Pharmaceuticals Inc	Providence	RI	G	410 419-2171	21137
Elution Technologies LLC	Colchester	VT	G	802 540-0296	21862
Maxi Green Inc	Colchester	VT	G	802 657-3586	21873

2841 Soap & Detergents

	CITY	ST	EMP	PHONE	ENTRY #
Amodex Products Inc	Bridgeport	CT	E	203 335-1255	375
Beiersdorf Inc	Norwalk	CT	B	203 854-8000	3110
Beiersdorf North America Inc **(DH)**	Wilton	CT	F	203 563-5800	5277
Du-Lite Corporation	Middletown	CT	G	860 347-2505	2184
Henkel Consumer Goods Inc **(DH)**	Stamford	CT	A	475 210-0230	4212
Integrity Industries Inc	New Fairfield	CT	G	203 312-9788	2624
Pharmacal Research Labs Inc	Waterbury	CT	E	203 755-4908	4937
Simoniz Usa Inc **(PA)**	Bolton	CT	C	860 646-0172	278
Unilever Ascc AG	Shelton	CT	B	203 381-2482	3884
Unilever Home and Per Care NA	Trumbull	CT	D	203 502-0086	4637
United States Chemical Corp	Plantsville	CT	G	860 621-6831	3544
Alpha Chemical Services Inc	Stoughton	MA	E	781 344-8688	15579
Blendco Systems LLC	Holyoke	MA	E	800 537-7797	11619
Buckeye International Inc	East Weymouth	MA	G	617 827-2137	10539
Christeyns Laundry Tech LLC	East Bridgewater	MA	F	617 203-2169	10409
Commonwealth Liquids LLC	Fall River	MA	G	508 676-9355	10677
Commonwlth Soap Toiletries Inc **(PA)**	Fall River	MA	D	508 676-9355	10678
Crazy Foam International LLC	Newton	MA	G	781 985-5048	13584
Dr Bessette Naturals	Ware	MA	G	413 277-6188	16232
Dynasol Industries Inc	Canton	MA	F	781 821-8888	9729
Ecolab Inc	Norwood	MA	D	781 688-2100	14147
Ecolab Inc	Wilmington	MA	F	978 658-2423	17000
I2biomed Inc	Concord	MA	G	857 259-4410	10135
James Austin Company	Ludlow	MA	E	413 589-1600	12469
Just Soap	Ashfield	MA	G	413 625-6990	7653
MD Stetson Company Inc	Randolph	MA	E	781 986-6161	14689
Spectrowax Corporation **(PA)**	Canton	MA	D	617 543-0400	9784
Starchem Inc **(PA)**	Ware	MA	G	413 967-8700	16237
Starchem Inc	Dudley	MA	G	508 943-2337	10386
Synthetic Labs Inc	Dracut	MA	F	978 957-2919	10368
Trans-Mate LLC	North Billerica	MA	E	800 867-9274	13873
Ruby Moon LLC	Casco	ME	G	207 200-3242	5897
Chem Quest Inc	Hampton	NH	G	207 856-2993	18260
Deborah Ludington	Greenland	NH	G	603 766-1651	18223
J R Liggett Ltd Inc	Cornish	NH	G	603 675-2055	17961
Bradford Soap Mexico Inc **(HQ)**	West Warwick	RI	E	401 821-2141	21485
Original Brdford Soap Wrks Inc **(HQ)**	West Warwick	RI	B	401 821-2141	21506
Rhode Island Chemical Corp	Providence	RI	F	401 274-3905	21111
Spectral Inc	Warwick	RI	G	401 921-2690	21428
Ark of Safety	West Newbury	VT	G	802 429-2537	22610
Twincraft Inc **(PA)**	Winooski	VT	C	802 655-2200	22726
Vermont Country Soap Corp	Middlebury	VT	E	802 388-4302	22119
Whisper Hills	Quechee	VT	G	802 296-7627	22295

2842 Spec Cleaning, Polishing & Sanitation Preparations

	CITY	ST	EMP	PHONE	ENTRY #
Amodex Products Inc	Bridgeport	CT	E	203 335-1255	375
Armored Autogroup Parent Inc **(DH)**	Danbury	CT	G	203 205-2900	875
Citra Solv LLC	Ridgefield	CT	G	203 778-0881	3663
Cloverdale Inc	West Cornwall	CT	G	860 672-0216	5046
Comanche Clean Energy Corp	Stamford	CT	G	203 326-4570	4167
Edsan Chemical Company Inc	New Haven	CT	C	203 624-3123	2685
Great Lakes Chemical Corp **(DH)**	Shelton	CT	E	203 573-2000	3806
Griffith Company	Bridgeport	CT	G	203 333-5557	422
Grill Daddy Brush Company	Old Greenwich	CT	E	888 840-7552	3310

	CITY	ST	EMP	PHONE	ENTRY #
Hydrochemical Techniques Inc	Hartford	CT	G	860 527-6350	1836
Korner Kare	Goshen	CT	G	860 491-3731	1584
Koster Keunen LLC **(PA)**	Watertown	CT	F	860 945-3333	5013
Lanxess Solutions US Inc **(DH)**	Shelton	CT	E	203 573-2000	3824
Macdermid Incorporated **(HQ)**	Waterbury	CT	C	203 575-5700	4900
Micro Care Corporation **(PA)**	New Britain	CT	F	860 827-0626	2554
Nature Plus Inc	Stratford	CT	G	203 380-0316	4432
NC Brands LP	Norwalk	CT	D	203 295-2300	3204
Nci Holdings Inc **(PA)**	Norwalk	CT	E	203 295-2300	3205
Odd Jobs Handyman Service LLC	Woodbridge	CT	G	203 397-5275	5474
Roebic Laboratories Inc **(PA)**	Orange	CT	G	203 795-1283	3382
Simoniz Usa Inc **(PA)**	Bolton	CT	C	860 646-0172	278
Woods End Inc	Weston	CT	G	203 226-6303	5176
3M Company	Haverhill	MA	G	978 420-0001	11403
Alpha Chemical Services Inc	Stoughton	MA	E	781 344-8688	15579
Blendco Systems LLC	Holyoke	MA	E	800 537-7797	11619
Brady Enterprises Inc **(PA)**	East Weymouth	MA	D	781 682-6280	10538
Buckeye International Inc	East Weymouth	MA	G	617 827-2137	10539
Cape Cod Polish Company Inc	Gloucester	MA	G	800 682-4246	11171
Cape Cod Polish Company Inc	Dennis	MA	G	508 385-5099	10306
Chemco Corporation	Lawrence	MA	E	978 687-9000	12006
Clint Sales & Manufacturing	Beverly	MA	G	978 927-3010	8118
Concept Chemicals Inc	Hingham	MA	F	781 740-0711	11497
Connoisseurs Products Corp **(PA)**	Woburn	MA	D	800 851-5333	17148
D J Bass Inc	New Bedford	MA	G	508 678-4499	13376
Dmar Environmental LLC	Clinton	MA	G	508 331-1884	10079
Dynasol Industries Inc	Canton	MA	F	781 821-8888	9729
Elliott Auto Supply Co Inc	Ayer	MA	G	978 772-9882	7918
Head 2 Toe	Reading	MA	F	781 944-0286	14736
HI Tunes	Whately	MA	F	435 962-0405	16906
Lamco Chemical Company Inc	Chelsea	MA	G	617 884-8470	9959
Maranatha Industries Inc **(PA)**	Wakefield	MA	F	781 245-0038	15960
MD Stetson Company Inc	Randolph	MA	E	781 986-6161	14689
Perma Incorporated	Bedford	MA	F	978 667-5161	8000
Porex Cleanroom Products Inc	Chicopee	MA	D	800 628-8606	10052
Powerwash Co	Raynham	MA	G	508 823-9274	14726
Protech Associates Inc	Newburyport	MA	G	978 462-1241	13524
R G J Associates Inc	Sudbury	MA	G	978 443-7642	15667
Rectorseal Corporation	Fall River	MA	G	508 673-7561	10755
Roger A Reed Inc	Reading	MA	E	781 944-4640	14741
Savin Products Company Inc	Randolph	MA	F	781 961-2743	14697
Shield Packaging Co Inc	Dudley	MA	D	508 949-0900	10384
Spectrowax Corporation **(PA)**	Canton	MA	D	617 543-0400	9784
Tbs Technologies LLC	Holliston	MA	G	508 429-3111	11608
Uls of New England LLC	Lawrence	MA	D	978 683-7390	12079
Union Specialties Inc	Newburyport	MA	E	978 465-1717	13546
Winfield Brooks Company Inc	Woburn	MA	F	781 933-5300	17323
Wonder Tablitz Corporation	Walpole	MA	G	508 660-0011	16018
Allens Environmental Svcs Inc	Presque Isle	ME	G	207 764-9336	6752
Cml Services Inc	Westbrook	ME	G	207 772-5032	7184
Global Biotechnologies Inc	Scarborough	ME	G	800 755-8420	6920
GM Specialties Inc	Scarborough	ME	G	207 883-8300	6922
Kicteam Inc	Auburn	ME	E	207 514-7030	5574
Maine Cleaners Supply Inc	North Yarmouth	ME	G	207 657-3166	6517
Aqua Tite Innovative Solutions	Hampton	NH	G	603 431-5555	18254
Booth Felt Co Inc	Dover	NH	G	603 330-3334	18009
Chem Quest Inc	Hampton	NH	G	207 856-2993	18260
Hampshire Chemical Corp **(DH)**	Nashua	NH	E	603 888-2320	19176
House of Laurila	Hopkinton	NH	G	603 224-8123	18363
Peg Kearsarge Co Inc	Bartlett	NH	G	603 374-2341	17627
Rochester Shoe Tree Co Inc **(PA)**	Ashland	NH	D	603 968-3301	17601
Roll Tide of Nh LLC	Nashua	NH	G	603 417-2498	19255
Absorbent Specialty Pdts LLC	Cumberland	RI	F	401 722-1177	20312
Chaudhary LLC	Pawtucket	RI	G	401 954-9695	20822
Precision Plsg Ornamentals Inc	Pawtucket	RI	E	401 728-9994	20883
Brown Country Services LLC	West Dover	VT	G	802 464-5200	22606
Nottingham Wood Products	Derby	VT	G	802 766-2791	21903

2843 Surface Active & Finishing Agents, Sulfonated Oils

	CITY	ST	EMP	PHONE	ENTRY #
Henkel of America Inc **(HQ)**	Rocky Hill	CT	B	860 571-5100	3715
Henkel US Operations Corp **(DH)**	Rocky Hill	CT	B	860 571-5100	3716
Lanxess Solutions US Inc **(DH)**	Shelton	CT	E	203 573-2000	3824
Solidification Pdts Intl Inc	Northford	CT	G	203 484-9494	3092
Unimetal Surface Finishing LLC **(PA)**	Thomaston	CT	E	860 283-0271	4524
Isp Freetown Fine Chem Inc	Assonet	MA	D	508 672-0634	7681
Union Specialties Inc	Newburyport	MA	E	978 465-1717	13546
Henkel Corporation	Seabrook	NH	C	508 230-1100	19804
Peg Kearsarge Co Inc	Bartlett	NH	G	603 374-2341	17627
CNc International Ltd Partnr	Woonsocket	RI	E	401 769-6100	21556

2844 Perfumes, Cosmetics & Toilet Preparations

	CITY	ST	EMP	PHONE	ENTRY #
Albea Thomaston Inc	Thomaston	CT	B	860 283-2000	4497
American Distilling Inc	Marlborough	CT	G	860 267-4444	2063
American Distilling Inc **(PA)**	East Hampton	CT	D	860 267-4444	1156
Amodex Products Inc	Bridgeport	CT	E	203 335-1255	375
Bedoukian Research Inc **(PA)**	Danbury	CT	E	203 830-4000	877
Beiersdorf Inc **(DH)**	Wilton	CT	G	203 563-5800	5276
Beiersdorf Inc	Norwalk	CT	B	203 854-8000	3110
Beiersdorf North America Inc **(DH)**	Wilton	CT	F	203 563-5800	5277
Blessed Creek	Suffield	CT	G	860 416-3692	4460
Browne Hansen LLC	Wallingford	CT	G	203 269-0557	4714
Bunsen Rush Laboratories Inc	Woodbridge	CT	G	203 397-0820	5463
Carrubba Incorporated	Milford	CT	D	203 878-0605	2262
Casaro Labs Ltd	Stamford	CT	G	203 353-8500	4156
CCL Industries Corporation **(DH)**	Shelton	CT	D	203 926-1253	3785
Chemessence Inc	New Milford	CT	G	860 355-4108	2792
Connectcut Crnial Fcial Imgery	Manchester	CT	G	860 643-2940	1996
Conopco Inc	Clinton	CT	B	860 669-8601	783
Continental Fragrances Ltd	Stamford	CT	F	800 542-5903	4173
Durol Laboratories LLC	West Haven	CT	F	866 611-9694	5119
Ecometics Inc	Norwalk	CT	E	203 853-7856	3148
Edgewell Per Care Brands LLC **(HQ)**	Shelton	CT	B	203 944-5500	3799
Gillette Company	Bethel	CT	G	203 796-4000	155
Golden Sun Inc	Stamford	CT	F	800 575-7960	4200
Harjani Hitesh	Waterford	CT	G	860 913-6032	4984
High Ridge Brands Co **(HQ)**	Stamford	CT	D	203 674-8080	4215
Innarah Inc	Stratford	CT	G	203 873-0015	4423
Jolen Cream Bleach Corp	Fairfield	CT	F	203 259-8779	1439
Judith Jackson Inc	Old Greenwich	CT	G	203 698-3011	3311
Kims Nail Corporation	Stratford	CT	G	203 380-8608	4428
Lady Anne Cosmetics Inc	Trumbull	CT	G	203 372-6972	4626
Milbar Labs Inc	East Haven	CT	F	203 467-1577	1255
Miyoshi America Inc **(HQ)**	Dayville	CT	D	860 779-3990	1046
Miyoshi America Inc	Dayville	CT	F	860 779-3990	1047
Miyoshi America Inc	Dayville	CT	G	860 779-3990	1048
Parfums De Coeur Ltd **(PA)**	Stamford	CT	E	203 655-8807	4277
Playtex Products LLC **(HQ)**	Shelton	CT	D	203 944-5500	3856
Rjtb Group LLC	Greenwich	CT	G	203 531-7216	1644
Russell Organics LLC	Wallingford	CT	G	203 285-6633	4803
Sheffield Pharmaceuticals LLC **(PA)**	New London	CT	C	860 442-4451	2779
T N Dickinson Company	East Hampton	CT	F	860 267-2279	1166
Unilever Home and Per Care NA	Trumbull	CT	D	203 502-0086	4637
Unilever Hpc USA	Trumbull	CT	G	203 381-3311	4638
Unilever Trumbull RES Svcs Inc **(HQ)**	Trumbull	CT	G	203 502-0086	4639
Bumboosa LLC	Mashpee	MA	G	508 539-1373	12876
Commonwlth Soap Toiletries Inc **(PA)**	Fall River	MA	D	508 676-9355	10678
Concept Chemicals Inc	Hingham	MA	F	781 740-0711	11497
Conopco Inc	Foxboro	MA	F	508 543-6767	10880
Dentovations Inc	Boston	MA	F	617 737-1199	8499
Elemental Scents LLC	Auburndale	MA	G	617 504-2559	7860
Elizabeth Arden Inc	Wrentham	MA	G	508 384-9018	17519
Elma & Sana LLC	Littleton	MA	G	617 529-4532	12304
European Cubicles LLC	Boston	MA	G	617 681-6700	8529
Gillette Company	Boston	MA	D	617 268-1363	8562
Gillette Company	Andover	MA	A	781 662-9600	7552
Gillette Company **(HQ)**	Boston	MA	A	617 421-7000	8561
Harrison Specialty Co Inc **(PA)**	Canton	MA	E	781 828-8180	9736
Harrison Specialty Co Inc	Canton	MA	E	781 828-8180	9737
LAvant Garde Inc	Newburyport	MA	G	805 522-0045	13508
Novagenesis	Sharon	MA	E	781 784-1149	15054
Oraceutical LLC	Lee	MA	E	413 243-6634	12094
Peninsula Skincare Labs Inc	Boston	MA	G	650 339-4299	8773
Pride India Inc **(PA)**	Brighton	MA	F	617 202-9659	9105
Prostrong Inc	Pembroke	MA	G	781 829-0000	14422
Rare Beauty Brands Inc	Norwood	MA	D	888 243-0646	14191
Rougeluxe Apothecary Inc	Oak Bluffs	MA	G	508 696-0900	14211
Somersets Usa LLC	Arlington	MA	G	617 803-6833	7640
St Cyr Inc	Worcester	MA	E	508 752-2222	17478
Tropical Products Inc	Salem	MA	E	978 740-5665	14947
Brickell Brands LLC	Portland	ME	E	877 598-0060	6626
Fabula Nebulae LLC	Holden	ME	G	917 545-9049	6197
Procter & Gamble Company	Auburn	ME	C	207 753-4000	5593
Toms of Maine Inc	Kennebunk	ME	C	207 985-2944	6241
Toms of Maine Inc **(HQ)**	Kennebunk	ME	D	207 985-2944	6242
Toms of Maine Inc	Sanford	ME	C	207 985-2944	6894
Cabot Hill Naturals Inc	Lancaster	NH	F	800 747-4372	18598
Chuckles Inc	Manchester	NH	E	603 669-4228	18798
Fizz Time	Salem	NH	F	603 870-0000	19734
J R Liggett Ltd Inc	Cornish	NH	G	603 675-2055	17961
Just Naturals & Company LLC	Bedford	NH	G	603 471-0944	17647
Kanu Inc	Londonderry	NH	G	603 437-6311	18706
Maybrook Inc	Salem	NH	F	603 898-0811	19750
Riverview Labs Inc	Bow	NH	G	603 715-2759	17729
Trividia Mfg Solutions **(DH)**	Lancaster	NH	C	603 788-2848	18606
Trividia Mfg Solutions	Lancaster	NH	G	603 788-4952	18607
WS Badger Company Inc	Gilsum	NH	E	603 357-2958	18196
Aidance Skincare & Topical Sol	Woonsocket	RI	F	401 432-7750	21547
Frueii	Providence	RI	G	401 499-5887	21017
Java Worx International LLC	Saunderstown	RI	G	866 609-3258	21202
Toscana European Day Spa	Cumberland	RI	G	401 658-5277	20349
Autumn Harp Inc	Bristol	VT	G	802 453-4807	21761
Autumn-Harp Inc	Essex Junction	VT	C	802 857-4600	21930
Green Mountain Fragrances Inc	Brattleboro	VT	G	802 490-2268	21731
Ogee Inc	Burlington	VT	G	802 540-8082	21800

	CITY	ST	EMP	PHONE	ENTRY #
Rozelle Inc	Westfield	VT	E	802 744-2270	22627
Tatas Natural Alchemy LLC **(PA)**	Whiting	VT	E	802 462-3814	22645
Tatas Natural Alchemy LLC	Whiting	VT	D	802 462-3958	22646
Toms of Maine Inc	Putney	VT	C	802 387-2393	22293
Ursa Major LLC	Waterbury	VT	G	802 560-7116	22587

2851 Paints, Varnishes, Lacquers, Enamels

	CITY	ST	EMP	PHONE	ENTRY #
A G C Incorporated **(PA)**	Meriden	CT	C	203 235-3361	2072
Albert Kemperle Inc	Hartford	CT	F	860 727-0933	1804
Brico LLC	Bloomfield	CT	G	860 242-7068	212
Chromalloy Component Svcs Inc	Windsor	CT	C	860 688-7798	5325
Clean Up Group	Meriden	CT	G	203 668-8323	2087
Colonial Coatings Inc	Milford	CT	E	203 783-9933	2265
Dumond Chemicals Inc	Milford	CT	G	609 655-7700	2277
Element 119 LLC	Thomaston	CT	F	860 358-0119	4503
Five Star Products Inc	Shelton	CT	E	203 336-7900	3802
FMI Paint & Chemical Inc	East Hartford	CT	F	860 218-2210	1196
Fougera Pharmaceuticals Inc	Wallingford	CT	D	203 265-2086	4745
Greenmaker Industries Conn LLC	West Hartford	CT	F	860 761-2830	5072
Handyscape LLC	Southington	CT	G	860 318-1067	4056
J + J Branford Inc **(PA)**	Branford	CT	G	203 488-5637	327
Jet Process Corporation	North Haven	CT	G	203 985-6000	3035
M & D Coatings LLC	Stratford	CT	G	203 380-9466	4430
Mantrose-Haeuser Co Inc **(HQ)**	Westport	CT	E	203 454-1800	5212
Materials Proc Dev Group LLC	Wallingford	CT	G	203 269-6617	4769
Merrifield Paint Company Inc	Rocky Hill	CT	G	860 529-1583	3723
Minteq International Inc	Canaan	CT	C	860 824-5435	689
PPG Industries Inc	Norwalk	CT	G	203 750-9553	3223
PPG Industries Inc	New Haven	CT	G	203 562-5173	2728
PPG Industries Inc	Danbury	CT	G	203 744-4977	969
PPG Industries Inc	Hartford	CT	G	860 522-9544	1861
Tcg Green Technologies Inc	Sharon	CT	F	860 364-4694	3770
A I C Inc **(PA)**	Georgetown	MA	E	978 352-4510	11135
A W Chesterton Company **(PA)**	Groveland	MA	E	781 438-7000	11298
Acton Research Corporation	Acton	MA	E	941 556-2601	7334
Bemis Associates Inc **(PA)**	Shirley	MA	C	978 425-6761	15081
Bemis Associates Inc	Shirley	MA	C	978 425-6761	15082
Benjamin Moore & Co	Milford	MA	D	508 473-8900	13108
C F Jameson & Co Inc	Newburyport	MA	F	978 462-4097	13476
C L Hauthaway & Sons Corp	Lynn	MA	E	781 592-6444	12495
Camger Coatings Systems Inc	Norfolk	MA	E	508 528-5787	13659
Cast Coat Inc	West Bridgewater	MA	G	508 587-4502	16433
CCS Marine Inc	West Bridgewater	MA	G	508 587-8877	16434
Chase Speciality Coating	Westwood	MA	F	781 332-0700	16863
CJ Shaughnessy Crane Svc Inc	Avon	MA	G	781 924-1168	7883
Clark Paint & Varnish Company	West Springfield	MA	G	413 733-3554	16512
Coveris Advanced Coatings	West Springfield	MA	E	413 539-5547	16513
Creative Stone Systems Inc	Buzzards Bay	MA	F	866 608-7625	9360
Dampney Company Inc	Everett	MA	E	617 389-2805	10609
Desco Industries Inc	Canton	MA	E	781 821-8370	9726
DSM Coating Resins Inc	Wilmington	MA	C	800 458-0014	16996
Durant Prfmce Coatings Inc	Revere	MA	F	781 289-1400	14765
Duromar Inc	Pembroke	MA	G	781 826-2525	14401
E Paint Company	East Falmouth	MA	F	508 540-4412	10441
F & D Plastics Inc **(PA)**	Leominster	MA	E	978 668-5140	12136
Franklin Paint Company Inc	Franklin	MA	E	800 486-0304	11047
Gare Incorporated	Haverhill	MA	E	978 373-9131	11437
Highland Labs Inc	Holliston	MA	E	508 429-2918	11577
ICP Construction Inc **(HQ)**	Andover	MA	C	978 623-9980	7556
Innovative Chem Pdts Group LLC	Boston	MA	F	800 393-5250	8616
Katahdin Industries Inc **(PA)**	Hudson	MA	E	781 329-1420	11781
Kirby George Jr Paint Co Inc	New Bedford	MA	G	508 997-9008	13405
L H C Inc **(PA)**	Lynn	MA	E	781 592-6444	12520
Mantrose-Haeuser Co Inc	Attleboro	MA	D	203 454-1800	7761
Microplasmic Corporation	Peabody	MA	G	978 548-9762	14355
Mr Plow	Natick	MA	G	508 207-8999	13270
Norfolk Corporation	Marshfield	MA	F	781 319-0400	12864
Novolac Epoxy Technologies Inc **(PA)**	Harwich	MA	G	508 385-5598	11396
Old Fashion Milk Paint Co Inc	Groton	MA	G	978 448-6336	11292
Perma Incorporated	Bedford	MA	F	978 667-5161	8000
PPG Industries Inc	Boston	MA	E	617 268-4111	8789
Procoat Products Inc	Holbrook	MA	G	781 767-2270	11536
Raymond Agler	Gloucester	MA	G	978 281-5048	11206
RPM Wood Finishes Group Inc	Westfield	MA	F	413 562-9655	16724
Rustoleum Attleboro Plant	Attleboro	MA	G	508 222-3710	7791
Stainless Steel Coatings Inc	Lancaster	MA	F	978 365-9828	11985
Steel Products Corporation **(PA)**	Rochdale	MA	G	508 892-4770	14783
TH Glennon Co Inc	Salisbury	MA	E	978 465-7222	14957
Tnemec East Inc	Wilmington	MA	E	978 988-9500	17056
Union Specialties Inc	Newburyport	MA	E	978 465-1717	13546
Warren Environmental Inc **(PA)**	Middleboro	MA	G	508 947-8539	13081
Waterlac Coating Inc	Lowell	MA	G	573 885-2506	12448
Winfield Brooks Company Inc	Woburn	MA	F	781 933-5300	17323
Chilton Paint Co Inc ME	Freeport	ME	G	207 865-4443	6074
Fisher LLC **(PA)**	Rockland	ME	F	207 701-4200	6793
H P Fairfield LLC	Scarborough	ME	G	207 885-4895	6923
Howard P Fairfield LLC	Scarborough	ME	G	207 885-4895	6925
Urethane Solutions LLC	Saco	ME	G	207 284-5400	6861
Foundation Armor LLC	Nashua	NH	F	866 306-0246	19163
H F Staples & Co Inc	Merrimack	NH	G	603 889-8600	19005
Hampshire Chemical Corp **(DH)**	Nashua	NH	E	603 888-2320	19176
Kretetek Industries LLC	Hudson	NH	F	603 402-3073	18408
Roymal Inc	Newport	NH	E	603 863-2410	19357
White Mountain Plowing	Farmington	NH	G	603 817-0913	18146
American-International TI Inds	Cranston	RI	G	401 942-7855	20180
Carroll Coatings Company Inc **(PA)**	Providence	RI	F	401 781-4942	20980
Chemical Coatings Corp	Providence	RI	F	401 331-9000	20982
Dartex Coatings Inc	Slatersville	RI	E	401 766-1500	21204
Development Associates Inc	North Kingstown	RI	F	401 884-1350	20702
Fri Resins Holding Company	Cranston	RI	F	401 946-5564	20228
General Polymer Inc	Central Falls	RI	G	401 723-6660	20114
Mainline Paint Mfg Co	Pawtucket	RI	G	401 726-3650	20855
Northern Industries Inc **(PA)**	Coventry	RI	G	401 769-4305	20160
Pg Imtech of Californ	East Providence	RI	G	401 521-2490	20441
Spectrum Coatings Labs Inc	Providence	RI	F	401 781-4847	21124
Teknor Color Company	Pawtucket	RI	D	401 725-8000	20904
C E Bradely Lab Inc	Brattleboro	VT	D	802 257-1122	21721
C E Bradley Laboratories **(PA)**	Brattleboro	VT	E	802 257-1122	21722
Hbh Prestain Inc **(PA)**	Arlington	VT	E	802 375-9723	21596
PPG Industries Inc	South Burlington	VT	G	802 863-6387	22461
Sto Corp	Rutland	VT	E	802 775-4117	22354
Sutherland Welles Ltd	Hyde Park	VT	G	802 635-2700	22038

2861 Gum & Wood Chemicals

	CITY	ST	EMP	PHONE	ENTRY #
Sychron Inc	Newington	CT	G	860 953-8157	2905

2865 Cyclic-Crudes, Intermediates, Dyes & Org Pigments

	CITY	ST	EMP	PHONE	ENTRY #
Bioenergy International LLC	Quincy	MA	D	617 657-5200	14616
Creative Stone Systems Inc	Buzzards Bay	MA	F	866 608-7625	9360
Primary Colors Inc	North Grafton	MA	E	508 839-3202	13964
Rowley Biochemical Institute	Danvers	MA	G	978 739-4883	10253
Solvent Kleene Inc	Peabody	MA	F	978 531-2279	14370
U S Synthetics Corp	Fitchburg	MA	G	978 345-0176	10858
Walrus Enterprises LLC	Northampton	MA	G	413 387-4387	14026
Clariant Plas Coatings USA LLC	Lewiston	ME	E	207 784-0733	6280
Ecc Holdings Inc **(HQ)**	Providence	RI	E	401 331-9000	21002
Polymer Solutions Inc	Pawtucket	RI	G	401 423-1638	20881
Teknor Color Company	Pawtucket	RI	D	401 725-8000	20904

2869 Industrial Organic Chemicals, NEC

	CITY	ST	EMP	PHONE	ENTRY #
Advanced Fuel Co LLC	North Franklin	CT	G	860 642-4817	2986
Ai Divestitures Inc	Waterbury	CT	G	203 575-5727	4837
Alternative Fuel & Energy LLC	Colchester	CT	G	860 537-5345	798
Anthony s Fuel	Shelton	CT	G	203 513-7400	3776
Bedoukian Research Inc **(PA)**	Danbury	CT	E	203 830-4000	877
Bestway Food and Fuel	Waterford	CT	G	860 447-0729	4981
Brian Safa	Cheshire	CT	G	203 271-3499	716
Carrubba Incorporated	Milford	CT	D	203 878-0605	2262
Cobal-USA Altrnative Fuels LLC	Ansonia	CT	G	203 751-1974	10
Crossroads Deli & Fuel LLC	Falls Village	CT	G	860 824-8474	1462
CTS Services LLC	Shelton	CT	G	203 268-5865	3791
Deep River Fuel Terminals LLC	Portland	CT	G	860 342-4619	3566
Dragonlab LLC	Rocky Hill	CT	G	860 436-9221	3708
Dymax Corporation	Torrington	CT	G	860 626-7006	4575
Dymax Materials Inc **(HQ)**	Torrington	CT	G	860 482-1010	4576
Dymax Oligomers & Coatings	Torrington	CT	F	860 626-7006	4577
E&S Automotive Operations LLC	Bridgeport	CT	G	203 332-4555	409
Element Solutions Inc	Waterbury	CT	E	203 575-5850	4870
Extra Fuel	Bridgeport	CT	G	203 330-0613	412
Falls Fuel LLC	Bethel	CT	G	203 744-3835	153
Firehouse Discount Oil LLC **(PA)**	Unionville	CT	G	860 404-1827	4656
Fuel First	Ansonia	CT	G	203 735-5097	16
Fuel For Humanity Inc	Westport	CT	G	203 255-5913	5196
Fuel Lab	Farmington	CT	G	860 677-4987	1485
Galaxy Fuel LLC	Milford	CT	G	203 878-8173	2292
Greenleaf Bfuels New Haven LLC	New Haven	CT	F	203 672-9028	2692
H Krevit and Company Inc	New Haven	CT	E	203 772-3350	2694
Hajan LLC	New Britain	CT	G	860 223-2005	2538
Hampford Research Inc **(PA)**	Stratford	CT	E	203 375-1137	4417
Henkel of America Inc **(HQ)**	Rocky Hill	CT	B	860 571-5100	3715
Hitbro Realty LLC	Canaan	CT	G	860 824-1370	687
Houston Macdermid Inc	Waterbury	CT	G	203 575-5700	4885
Husky Fuel	Oxford	CT	G	203 783-0783	3408
Lanxess Solutions US Inc **(DH)**	Shelton	CT	E	203 573-2000	3824
Macdermid Anion Inc	Waterbury	CT	G	203 575-5700	4904
Macdermid Brazil Inc	Waterbury	CT	G	203 575-5700	4905
Macdermid South America Inc	Waterbury	CT	G	203 575-5700	4908
Macdermid South Atlantic Inc	Waterbury	CT	G	203 575-5700	4909
Miller Fuel LLC	Burlington	CT	G	860 675-6121	679
Nalas Engineering Services	Norwich	CT	D	860 861-3691	3286
New England Fuels & Energy LLC	Terryville	CT	G	860 585-5917	4487
Power Fuels LLC	Cheshire	CT	G	203 699-0099	754
Priced Right Fuel LLC	Norwalk	CT	G	203 856-7031	3224
Pucks Putters & Fuel LLC	Milford	CT	F	203 877-5457	2343

	CITY	ST	EMP	PHONE	ENTRY #
Pucks Putters & Fuel LLC **(PA)**	Shelton	CT	G	203 494-3952	3864
RSA Corp	Danbury	CT	E	203 790-8100	980
Sanco Energy	Fairfield	CT	F	203 259-5914	1454
Si Group USA (usaa) LLC **(DH)**	Danbury	CT	C	203 702-6140	989
Si Group USA Hldings Usha Corp **(HQ)**	Danbury	CT	E	203 702-6140	990
Superior Fuel Co	Bridgeport	CT	G	203 337-1213	497
Ultra Food and Fuel	New Britain	CT	G	860 223-2005	2587
Vanderbilt Chemicals LLC **(HQ)**	Norwalk	CT	D	203 295-2141	3265
Vanderbilt Chemicals LLC	Bethel	CT	E	203 744-3900	189
Victory Fuel LLC	Terryville	CT	G	860 585-0532	4496
Waste Resource Recovery Inc **(PA)**	Lebanon	CT	G	860 287-3332	1938
Waste To Green Fuel LLC	Bridgeport	CT	G	203 536-5855	505
XCEL Fuel	Branford	CT	G	203 481-4510	363
Yale University	New Haven	CT	G	203 432-3916	2759
Alcresta Therapeutics Inc	Newton	MA	E	617 431-3600	13557
All Seasonal Fuel Inc	Dedham	MA	G	781 329-7800	10279
Amal Fuel Inc	Chelmsford	MA	G	978 934-9704	9870
Avantgarde Molecular LLC	Maynard	MA	G	617 549-2238	12895
Belco Fuel Company Inc	Pembroke	MA	G	781 331-6521	14393
Bio Energy Inc	Boston	MA	G	617 822-1220	8409
Bio-Catalytic Enterprises Inc	Springfield	MA	E	413 739-9148	15454
C5bio	Cambridge	MA	G	617 955-4626	9424
Cambridge Isotope Labs Inc **(DH)**	Tewksbury	MA	D	978 749-8000	15810
Cannan Fuels	Mansfield	MA	G	508 339-3317	12616
Chapman Fuel	Lowell	MA	G	978 452-9656	12358
Coelho Fuel Inc	Lowell	MA	G	978 458-8252	12361
Commonwealth Biofuel	Newburyport	MA	G	978 881-0478	13479
Commonwealth Fuel Corp	Waltham	MA	G	617 884-5444	16071
Continuus Pharmaceuticals Inc	Woburn	MA	F	781 281-0226	17153
Dems Fuel Inc	Chelmsford	MA	G	978 660-0018	9892
Dodge Company Inc **(PA)**	Billerica	MA	G	800 443-6343	8237
E J White Fuel	Rockland	MA	G	781 878-0802	14798
Epoxy Technology Inc **(PA)**	Billerica	MA	E	978 667-3805	8248
Felicia Oil Co Inc	Gloucester	MA	G	978 283-3808	11181
Fisher Scientific Intl LLC **(HQ)**	Waltham	MA	C	781 622-1000	16107
Fuel America	Brighton	MA	G	617 782-0999	9099
Fuel First Elm Inc	West Springfield	MA	G	413 732-5732	16523
Fuel Gym LLC	Wakefield	MA	G	781 315-8001	15953
Fuel Magazine	Hatfield	MA	G	413 247-5579	11400
Fuel Source Inc	Norwood	MA	G	781 469-8449	14153
Fuel Training Studio LLC	Newburyport	MA	G	617 694-5489	13492
Giner Life Sciences Inc	Auburndale	MA	G	781 529-0576	7863
Girouard Tool Corp	Leominster	MA	G	978 534-4147	12147
Glixx Laboratories Inc	Hopkinton	MA	G	781 333-5348	11716
H I Five Renewables	Merrimac	MA	G	978 384-8032	13001
Homeland Fuels Company LLC	Canton	MA	F	781 737-1892	9739
Inversant Inc	Boston	MA	F	617 423-0331	8620
Isp Freetown Fine Chem Inc	Assonet	MA	D	508 672-0634	7681
James Devaney Fuel Co	Dedham	MA	G	781 326-7608	10295
Kalion Inc	Milton	MA	G	617 698-2113	13193
Khoury Fuel Inc	Melrose	MA	G	781 251-0993	12984
Kinetic Fuel LLC	Walpole	MA	G	508 668-8278	15997
Lawrence Fuel Inc	Lawrence	MA	G	978 984-5255	12046
Liquiglide Inc	Cambridge	MA	E	617 901-0700	9538
Lisha & Nirali Fuel LLC	Middleton	MA	G	908 433-6504	13094
McCarthy Bros Fuel Co Inc	West Brookfield	MA	G	508 867-5515	16471
Miami Heat Discount Fuel	Fairhaven	MA	G	508 991-2875	10642
MK Fuel Inc	Brimfield	MA	G	413 245-7507	9110
Myriant Lake Providence Inc	Quincy	MA	E	617 657-5200	14641
Northeast Biodiesel LLC	Greenfield	MA	G	413 772-8891	11271
Novogy Inc	Cambridge	MA	F	617 674-5800	9594
Nutrasweet Company	Waltham	MA	E	706 303-5600	16163
Nutrasweet Company	Waltham	MA	E	706 303-5600	16164
Parallel Products of Neng **(DH)**	New Bedford	MA	G	508 884-5100	13435
Paul M Depalma Fuel LLC	Weymouth	MA	G	781 812-0156	16896
Perley Burrill Fuel	Lynnfield	MA	G	781 593-9292	12554
Polar Fuel Inc	Foxboro	MA	G	508 543-5200	10898
Polnox Corporation	Lowell	MA	G	978 735-4438	12423
Powersure Fuel Rcndtioning LLC	Andover	MA	G	978 886-2476	7587
Pttgc Innovation America Corp **(HQ)**	Woburn	MA	E	617 657-5234	17271
Pure Energy Corporation **(PA)**	Burlington	MA	F	201 843-8100	9324
Purposeenergy Inc **(PA)**	Woburn	MA	G	617 202-9156	17274
Rachad Fuel Inc	Burlington	MA	G	781 273-0292	9328
Rohm Haas Electronic Mtls LLC	Marlborough	MA	E	978 689-1503	12821
Rohm Haas Electronic Mtls LLC **(DH)**	Marlborough	MA	A	508 481-7950	12820
S & E Fuels Inc	Taunton	MA	G	617 407-9977	15782
S & M Fuels Inc	Plymouth	MA	G	508 746-1495	14581
Sea Fuels Marine	New Bedford	MA	G	508 992-2323	13448
Sherborn Market Inc	Wellesley	MA	G	781 489-5006	16387
Stabilizing Technologies LLC	Hubbardston	MA	G	978 928-4142	11746
State Fuel	Winchester	MA	G	781 438-5557	17097
Stateline Fuel	Seekonk	MA	G	508 336-0665	15038
Strem Chemicals Incorporated	Newburyport	MA	D	978 499-1600	13537
Swampscott Fuel Inc	Swampscott	MA	G	781 592-1065	15700
Swampscott Fuel Inc	Westwood	MA	G	781 251-0993	16877
Szr Fuel LLC	Tyngsboro	MA	G	978 649-2409	15901
TK&k Services LLC	Beverly	MA	C	770 844-8710	8192
Twin Rivers Tech Ltd Partnr	Quincy	MA	D	617 472-9200	14663
Unlimited Fuel Heating Inc	Foxboro	MA	G	508 543-1043	10907
US Biofuels Inc	Boston	MA	F	706 291-4829	8902
Waltham Fuel	Chelsea	MA	G	617 364-2890	9974
Westwood Youth Softball Inc	Westwood	MA	G	781 762-5185	16882
World Asset Management LLC	Boston	MA	F	617 889-7300	8935
World Energy Biox Biofuels LLC **(PA)**	Boston	MA	F	617 889-7300	8936
Yield10 Bioscience Inc **(PA)**	Woburn	MA	D	617 583-1700	17326
Ysnc Fuel Inc	Brockton	MA	G	508 436-2716	9188
Bbi Enzymes USA Ltd	Portland	ME	G	608 709-5270	6621
D & J Fuels LLC	Wells	ME	G	207 646-5561	7161
FMC Corporation	Rockland	ME	C	207 594-3200	6795
Grenier Fuels LLC	Saco	ME	G	207 602-1400	6848
Hometown Fuel DBA Hometo	Limestone	ME	G	207 325-4411	6341
Inland Technologies	Portland	ME	G	207 761-6951	6674
J S Wholesale Fuels	Manchester	ME	G	207 622-4332	6410
Jessicas Discount Fuel	Pownal	ME	G	207 310-1966	6749
John Seavey Acadia Fuel	Trenton	ME	G	207 664-6050	7099
Land & Sea Fuel	Lubec	ME	G	207 733-0005	6386
Legu Tool and Mold LLC	Sanford	ME	G	207 850-1450	6879
M A Haskell & Sons LLC	China	ME	F	207 993-2265	5910
MA Haskell Fuel Co LLC	China	ME	G	207 993-2265	5911
Maine Bio-Fuel Inc	Portland	ME	F	207 878-3001	6682
Milford Fuel	Milford	ME	G	207 827-2701	6436
Offshore Fuel	Gouldsboro	ME	G	207 963-7068	6137
R H Foster Inc	Van Buren	ME	G	207 868-2983	7123
Stored Solar J&We LLC	Jonesboro	ME	E	207 434-6500	6225
Yoc	York	ME	G	207 363-9322	7318
A F Fuels	Brookline	NH	G	603 672-7010	17769
Alternative Fuel Systems E LLC	Dunbarton	NH	G	603 231-1942	18072
Americ An Novelty Inc	Seabrook	NH	G	401 785-9850	19792
Energex Pellet Fuel Inc	West Lebanon	NH	G	603 298-7007	19950
Favorite Fuels LLC	Hampton Falls	NH	G	603 967-4889	18282
Hampshire Chemical Corp **(DH)**	Nashua	NH	E	603 888-2320	19176
Howards Fuel Co Inc	Manchester	NH	G	603 635-9955	18837
L R Fuel Systems	Gilmanton	NH	G	603 848-3835	18193
Medical Isotopes Inc	Pelham	NH	G	603 635-2255	19439
Nas Fuels LLC	Rye	NH	G	603 964-6967	19699
Racing Mart Fuels LLC	Nashua	NH	G	508 878-7664	19243
Z-Tech LLC	Bow	NH	E	603 228-1305	17738
Aurora Fuel Company Inc	West Warwick	RI	G	401 345-5996	21481
Aurora Fuel Company Inc	West Warwick	RI	G	401 821-5996	21482
Bi Medical LLC	Coventry	RI	G	866 246-3301	20139
Cal Chemical Corporation	Coventry	RI	E	401 821-0320	20140
Epoxies Inc	Cranston	RI	F	401 946-5564	20219
Fri Resins Holding Company	Cranston	RI	F	401 946-5564	20228
Fuel Co	Providence	RI	G	401 467-8773	21018
Hirst Fuel LLC	Wakefield	RI	G	401 789-6376	21271
Quality Fuel	West Warwick	RI	G	401 822-9482	21507
Reliable Fuel Incorporated	Tiverton	RI	G	401 624-2903	21261
Sea Side Fuel	Narragansett	RI	G	401 284-2636	20648
Teknor Apex Company **(PA)**	Pawtucket	RI	B	401 725-8000	20903
Abba Fuels Inc	Underhill	VT	G	802 878-8095	22545
Accordant Energy LLC	Rutland	VT	G	802 772-7368	22322
Alltech Inc	Saint Albans	VT	G	802 524-7460	22363
Brosseau Fuels LLC	Morrisville	VT	G	802 888-9209	22165
C E Bradely Lab Inc	Brattleboro	VT	D	802 257-1122	21721
C E Bradley Laboratories **(PA)**	Brattleboro	VT	E	802 257-1122	21722
Jam Fuel LLC	Windsor	VT	G	802 345-6118	22710
McAllister Fuels Inc	Richford	VT	G	802 782-5293	22309
S White Fuel Stop	Danby	VT	G	802 293-5804	21894

2873 Nitrogenous Fertilizers

	CITY	ST	EMP	PHONE	ENTRY #
Bobbex Inc	Monroe	CT	G	800 792-4449	2396
Agrium Advanced Tech US Inc	Sterling	MA	G	978 422-3331	15532
Allstar Foundation For Urea Cy	Wilmington	MA	G	978 658-5319	16972
Inspire Hope Foundtn For Urea	Braintree	MA	G	781 817-6664	9020
Ocean Crest Seafoods Inc **(PA)**	Gloucester	MA	E	978 281-0232	11199
Gac Chemical Corporation **(PA)**	Searsport	ME	D	207 548-2525	6951
Living Acres LLC	New Sharon	ME	G	207 778-2390	6478
Northeast Agricultural Sls Inc	Detroit	ME	G	207 487-6273	5952
Ocean Organics Corp	Waldoboro	ME	E	207 832-4305	7136
Scotts Company LLC	Medway	ME	F	207 746-9033	6427
Purely Organic Products LLC	Portsmouth	NH	G	212 826-9150	19610
Compost Plant L3c	Providence	RI	G	401 644-6179	20988
Shoreside Organics LLC	Narragansett	RI	G	401 267-4473	20649

2874 Phosphatic Fertilizers

	CITY	ST	EMP	PHONE	ENTRY #
Atlantic Laboratories Inc	Waldoboro	ME	G	207 832-5376	7131

2875 Fertilizers, Mixing Only

	CITY	ST	EMP	PHONE	ENTRY #
Collins Compost	Enfield	CT	G	860 749-3416	1350
Curbside Compost LLC	Ridgefield	CT	G	914 646-6890	3664
Grillo Services LLC	Milford	CT	E	203 877-5070	2294
New Milford Farms Inc	New Milford	CT	F	860 210-0250	2818
Scotts Company LLC	Lebanon	CT	D	860 642-7591	1937
360 Recycling LLC	Westfield	MA	F	413 562-0193	16659

	CITY	ST	EMP	PHONE	ENTRY #
Black Earth Compost LLC	Gloucester	MA	F	262 227-1067	11166
Garden World Inc	Saugus	MA	G	781 233-9510	14982
Infinite Compost	Hyde Park	MA	G	617 922-6419	11870
Martins Farm Recycling	Greenfield	MA	G	413 774-5631	11269
Massachusetts Natural Fert Inc	Westminster	MA	G	978 874-0744	16808
North Shore Compost LLC	Lynn	MA	G	781 581-3489	12529
Ocean Crest Seafoods Inc **(PA)**	Gloucester	MA	E	978 281-0232	11199
Offbeet Composting Llc	Lowell	MA	G	603 568-2756	12415
Sun Gro Holdings Inc	Agawam	MA	A	413 786-4343	7454
Sun Gro Horticulture Dist Inc	Agawam	MA	E	800 732-8667	7455
Wecare Environmental LLC	Marlborough	MA	G	508 480-9922	12849
Envirem Organics Ltd	Unity	ME	G	207 948-4500	7115
Ideal Compost Company	Peterborough	NH	G	603 924-5050	19474
Rx Green Solutions LLC	Manchester	NH	F	603 769-3450	18913
Green Mountain Compost	Williston	VT	G	802 660-4949	22672
Naturcom Enterprises LLC	Bradford	VT	G	802 222-4277	21704
Northeast Agricultural Sls Inc **(PA)**	Lyndonville	VT	F	802 626-3351	22070
Queen City Soil & Stone DBA	Burlington	VT	G	802 318-2411	21805
Vermont Compost Company Inc	Montpelier	VT	G	802 223-6049	22162
William R Raap	Burlington	VT	G	802 660-3508	21817

2879 Pesticides & Agricultural Chemicals, NEC

	CITY	ST	EMP	PHONE	ENTRY #
Andrews Arboriculture LLC	Naugatuck	CT	G	203 565-8570	2460
Bedoukian Research Inc **(PA)**	Danbury	CT	E	203 830-4000	877
Chemtura Receivables LLC	Waterbury	CT	G	203 573-3327	4856
Healthy Harvest Inc	Madison	CT	G	203 245-3786	1963
Lanxess Solutions US Inc	Naugatuck	CT	D	203 723-2237	2483
Macdermid AG Solutions Inc	Waterbury	CT	F	203 575-5727	4903
P2 Science Inc	Woodbridge	CT	G	203 821-7457	5475
Tick Box Technology Corp	Norwalk	CT	G	203 852-7171	3256
Wilt Pruf Products Inc	Essex	CT	G	860 767-7033	1408
Able Pest Control Service	Brockton	MA	G	508 559-7987	9114
Lynwood Laboratories Inc	Needham	MA	G	781 449-6776	13304
Monsanto Company	Cambridge	MA	D	617 551-7200	9570
Munters Moisture Control Svcs	Amesbury	MA	G	978 388-4900	7499
Shield Packaging Co Inc	Dudley	MA	D	508 949-0900	10384
Thermacell Repellents Inc	Bedford	MA	E	781 541-6900	8016
Coast Maine Organic Pdts Inc **(PA)**	Portland	ME	F	207 879-0002	6640
Holy Terra Products Inc	Yarmouth	ME	G	207 846-4170	7295
Northern Turf Prfessionals Inc	Brunswick	ME	G	207 522-8598	5843
Pine State Pest Solutions Inc	Auburn	ME	G	207 795-1100	5590
Snug	Portland	ME	G	207 772-6839	6730
Sunrise Composting	Addison	ME	G	207 483-4081	5511
Bio-Concept Laboratories Inc	Salem	NH	E	603 437-4990	19713
Boston Fog LLC	Belmont	NH	G	888 846-4145	17671
Tender Corporation **(PA)**	Littleton	NH	D	603 444-5464	18667
Green Mountain Compost	Williston	VT	G	802 660-4949	22672
Northeast Agricultural Sls Inc **(PA)**	Lyndonville	VT	F	802 626-3351	22070

2891 Adhesives & Sealants

	CITY	ST	EMP	PHONE	ENTRY #
Advanced Adhesive Systems Inc	Newington	CT	E	860 953-4100	2838
Apcm Manufacturing LLC	Plainfield	CT	G	860 564-7817	3448
Babcock & King Incorporated **(PA)**	Fairfield	CT	G	203 336-7989	1415
Chessco Industries Inc **(PA)**	Westport	CT	E	203 255-2804	5183
Converting McHy Adhesives LLC	Newington	CT	G	860 561-0226	2856
Ctech Adhesives	New Hartford	CT	G	860 482-5947	2634
Cunningham Tech LLC **(PA)**	New Hartford	CT	G	860 738-8759	2635
Edison Coatings Inc	Plainville	CT	F	860 747-2220	3484
Ensign-Bickford Industries Inc	Weatogue	CT	C	860 843-2000	5042
Five Star Products Inc	Shelton	CT	E	203 336-7900	3802
Grafted Coatings Inc	Stratford	CT	F	203 377-9979	4416
Henkel Loctite Corporation **(DH)**	Rocky Hill	CT	E	860 571-5100	3714
Henkel of America Inc **(HQ)**	Rocky Hill	CT	B	860 571-5100	3715
Henkel US Operations Corp **(DH)**	Rocky Hill	CT	B	860 571-5100	3716
Hexcel Corporation **(PA)**	Stamford	CT	E	203 969-0666	4213
Incure Inc	New Britain	CT	G	860 748-2979	2540
Metamorphic Materials Inc	Winsted	CT	F	860 738-8638	5417
Panacol-Usa Inc	Torrington	CT	F	860 738-7449	4592
Permatex Inc **(PA)**	Hartford	CT	E	860 543-7500	1856
S & S Sealcoating LLC	Wallingford	CT	G	203 284-0054	4804
Sealpro LLC	East Hartford	CT	G	860 289-0804	1219
Shurtape Specialty Coating LLC **(DH)**	New Hartford	CT	E	860 738-2600	2648
Smarter Sealants LLC	East Hartford	CT	G	860 218-2210	1221
Vanderbilt Chemicals LLC	Bethel	CT	E	203 744-3900	189
Xg Industries LLC	Stratford	CT	F	475 282-4643	4459
3M Company	Rockland	MA	F	781 871-1400	14788
3M Company	Haverhill	MA	G	978 420-0001	11403
A W Chesterton Company **(PA)**	Groveland	MA	E	781 438-7000	11298
Acton Research Corporation	Acton	MA	E	941 556-2601	7334
Adhesive Applications Inc	Easthampton	MA	G	413 527-7120	10552
Adhesive Applications Inc	Easthampton	MA	E	413 527-7120	10553
Aerospace Adhsive Bonding Tech	Chicopee	MA	G	413 315-9349	9997
Allcoat Technology Inc	Wilmington	MA	E	978 988-0880	16971
Allied Sealant Inc	Chelmsford	MA	G	978 254-7117	9869
American Adhesive Coatings LLC **(PA)**	Lawrence	MA	E	978 688-7400	11992
Anchor-Seal Inc	Gloucester	MA	G	978 515-6004	11159
AP Plastics LLC	Peabody	MA	G	800 222-1117	14313
Arcor Epoxy Inc	Harwich	MA	F	508 385-5598	11388
Bacon Industries Inc	Wrentham	MA	F	508 384-0780	17515
Bemis Associates Inc **(PA)**	Shirley	MA	C	978 425-6761	15081
Bemis Associates Inc	Shirley	MA	C	978 425-6761	15082
Bostik Inc	Middleton	MA	C	978 777-0100	13085
C L Hauthaway & Sons Corp	Lynn	MA	E	781 592-6444	12495
Clint Sales & Manufacturing	Beverly	MA	G	978 927-3010	8118
Coatings Adhesives Inks	Georgetown	MA	E	978 352-7273	11140
Creative Materials Inc	Ayer	MA	F	978 391-4700	7916
Diemat Inc	Byfield	MA	F	978 499-0900	9362
Dorn Equipment Corp	Melrose	MA	F	781 662-9300	12981
Elite Adhesives LLC	Haverhill	MA	G	978 852-8269	11431
Emseal Joint Systems Ltd	Westborough	MA	E	508 836-0280	16617
Epoxy Technology Inc **(PA)**	Billerica	MA	E	978 667-3805	8248
Falmer	Lynn	MA	G	781 593-0088	12507
FDM Adhesives LLC	Haverhill	MA	G	978 423-3553	11433
Flexcon Company Inc **(PA)**	Spencer	MA	A	508 885-8200	15429
Functional Coatings LLC	Newburyport	MA	D	978 462-0746	13493
Granger Lynch Corp	Millbury	MA	E	508 756-6244	13165
Hero Coatings Inc	Newburyport	MA	G	978 462-0746	13497
Illinois Tool Works Inc	Danvers	MA	E	978 777-1100	10225
Illinois Tool Works Inc	Rockland	MA	D	781 878-7015	14808
Indusol Inc	Sutton	MA	E	508 865-9516	15683
Innovative Chem Pdts Group LLC **(PA)**	Andover	MA	E	978 623-9980	7558
ITW Devcon Inc	Danvers	MA	E	978 777-1100	10227
ITW Plymers Salants N Amer Inc	Rockland	MA	E	781 681-0418	14809
JP Sealcoating Inc	Norton	MA	G	508 954-3510	14080
Key Polymer Holdings LLC	Lawrence	MA	E	978 683-9411	12043
L H C Inc **(PA)**	Lynn	MA	E	781 592-6444	12520
Mace Adhesives Coatings Co Inc	Dudley	MA	E	508 943-9052	10380
Middlesex Research Mfg Co Inc	Hudson	MA	E	978 562-3697	11793
Mussel Bound LLC	Brewster	MA	G	774 212-5488	9054
Ngac LLC	Burlington	MA	E	781 258-0008	9309
Nova Sports Usa Inc	Milford	MA	F	508 473-6540	13133
Olympic Adhesives Inc **(PA)**	Norwood	MA	E	800 829-1871	14186
Parker-Hannifin Corporation	Woburn	MA	B	781 935-4850	17257
Rectorseal Corporation	Fall River	MA	G	508 673-7561	10755
Resin Designs LLC **(HQ)**	Woburn	MA	E	781 935-3133	17284
Rogers Corporation	Kingston	MA	G	508 746-3311	11963
Saint-Gobain Abrasives Inc **(DH)**	Worcester	MA	A	508 795-5000	17464
Saint-Gobain Corporation	Northborough	MA	E	508 351-7112	14047
Stahl (usa) Inc **(DH)**	Peabody	MA	E	978 968-1382	14372
Standard Rubber Products Inc	Hanover	MA	E	781 878-2626	11353
Synthetic Surfaces Inc	Lynn	MA	F	781 593-0860	12542
Techfilm Services Inc	Peabody	MA	G	978 531-3300	14375
Transene Company Inc	Danvers	MA	F	978 777-7860	10265
Tulco Inc	Ayer	MA	G	978 772-4412	7941
Tyco Adhesives	Franklin	MA	G	508 918-1600	11094
Union Specialties Inc	Newburyport	MA	E	978 465-1717	13546
Winfield Brooks Company Inc	Woburn	MA	F	781 933-5300	17323
Xl Adhesives North LLC	Fall River	MA	G	508 675-0528	10786
Enterprise Castings LLC	Lewiston	ME	G	207 782-5511	6288
Exact Dispensing Systems	Newcastle	ME	G	207 563-2299	6482
Gripwet Inc	South Portland	ME	G	207 239-0486	7029
Piping Specialties Inc	Portland	ME	F	207 878-3955	6708
Absolute Rstrtion Slant Sltons	Bow	NH	G	603 518-5864	17706
Adhesive Engineering & Supply	Seabrook	NH	G	603 895-4028	19790
Adhesive Innovations LLC	Dover	NH	G	877 589-0544	18003
Adhesive Technologies Inc **(PA)**	Hampton	NH	E	603 926-1616	18252
Aqua Tite Innovative Solutions	Hampton	NH	G	603 431-5555	18254
Bond Adhesives & Coatings Corp	Seabrook	NH	G	603 474-3811	19795
Dichtomatik Americas LP	Manchester	NH	G	603 628-7030	18809
Hampshire Chemical Corp **(DH)**	Nashua	NH	E	603 888-2320	19176
Henkel Locktite	Seabrook	NH	G	603 474-5541	19805
Ipn Industries Inc	Londonderry	NH	G	603 623-8626	18705
Mereco Technologies Group Inc **(HQ)**	Londonderry	NH	E	401 822-9300	18720
Polymer Technologies LLC	Nashua	NH	G	603 883-4002	19235
Protavic America Inc	Londonderry	NH	G	603 623-8624	18733
Royal Adhesives & Sealants LLC	Raymond	NH	G	860 788-3380	19644
Schul International Co Inc	Hudson	NH	G	603 889-6872	18367
Schul International Co LLC	Pelham	NH	F	603 889-6872	19446
Trellborg Pipe Sals Mlford Inc **(DH)**	Milford	NH	C	800 626-2180	19080
Wf Holdings Inc **(PA)**	Nashua	NH	G	603 888-5443	19285
Worthen Industries Inc **(HQ)**	Nashua	NH	D	603 888-5443	19288
Worthen Industries Inc	Nashua	NH	F	603 886-0973	19289
Alfa International Corp	Woonsocket	RI	G	401 765-0503	21548
All Star Adhesive Products	Warren	RI	G	401 247-1866	21283
Atom Adhesives	Providence	RI	G	401 413-9902	20962
Brandywine Materials LLC	Woonsocket	RI	G	781 281-2746	21553
Epoxies Inc	Cranston	RI	F	401 946-5564	20219
Fri Resins Holding Company	Cranston	RI	F	401 946-5564	20228
Gurit (usa) Inc	Bristol	RI	E	401 396-5008	20083
Jmt Epoxy	Cranston	RI	G	401 331-9730	20245
Morton International LLC	Providence	RI	G	401 274-7258	21072
Mylan Technologies Inc **(DH)**	Saint Albans	VT	C	802 527-7792	22373

2892 Explosives

	CITY	ST	EMP	PHONE	ENTRY #
Austin Powder Company	Sterling	CT	E	860 564-5466	4365
Dyno Nobel Inc	Simsbury	CT	C	860 843-2000	3900
Ensign-Bickford Arospc Def Co **(HQ)**	Simsbury	CT	B	860 843-2289	3903
Ensign-Bickford Company **(HQ)**	Simsbury	CT	G	860 843-2001	3904
Ensign-Bickford Industries Inc	Weatogue	CT	C	860 843-2000	5042
Ensign-Bickford Industries Inc	Simsbury	CT	E	860 658-4411	3905
Maxam Initiation Systems LLC	Sterling	CT	F	860 774-3507	4368
Maxam North America Inc	Sterling	CT	G	860 774-2333	4369
Ensign-Bickford Industries Inc	Waltham	MA	G	781 693-1870	16098

2893 Printing Ink

	CITY	ST	EMP	PHONE	ENTRY #
Hubergroup Usa Inc	Windsor	CT	F	860 687-1617	5338
Superior Printing Ink Co Inc	Hamden	CT	E	203 281-1921	1786
A I C Inc **(PA)**	Georgetown	MA	E	978 352-4510	11135
Actega North America Inc	Shrewsbury	MA	G	508 845-6600	15097
Brian Leopold	Carver	MA	G	508 465-0345	9802
Coatings Adhesives Inks	Georgetown	MA	E	978 352-7273	11140
Flint Group US LLC	Rockland	MA	F	781 763-0600	14803
Fry Company J M	Canton	MA	G	781 575-1520	9734
Gem Gravure Co Inc **(PA)**	Hanover	MA	D	781 878-0456	11339
Gotham Ink of New England Inc	Marlborough	MA	G	508 485-7911	12762
Keystone Printing Ink Co	Norwood	MA	G	781 762-6974	14170
RPM Wood Finishes Group Inc	Westfield	MA	F	413 562-9655	16724
Superior Printing Ink Co Inc	Marlborough	MA	E	508 481-8250	12833
Universal Color Corp Inc	Wilmington	MA	F	978 658-2300	17061
Graphic Utilities Incorporated	Limestone	ME	F	207 370-9178	6340
Ink Mill Corp	Belmont	NH	F	603 217-4144	17674
Wikoff Color Corporation	Hudson	NH	F	603 864-6456	18452

2895 Carbon Black

	CITY	ST	EMP	PHONE	ENTRY #
Cabot Corporation **(PA)**	Boston	MA	C	617 345-0100	8452
Cabot Corporation	Billerica	MA	E	978 671-4000	8230
Cabot Corporation	Haverhill	MA	C	978 556-8400	11413

2899 Chemical Preparations, NEC

	CITY	ST	EMP	PHONE	ENTRY #
Alent USA Holding Inc	Waterbury	CT	B	203 575-5727	4839
All Power Manufacturing Co **(HQ)**	Oxford	CT	C	562 802-2640	3389
Armored Autogroup Parent Inc **(DH)**	Danbury	CT	G	203 205-2900	875
Bic Consumer Products Mfg Co	Milford	CT	C	203 783-2000	2254
Bic Corporation **(HQ)**	Shelton	CT	A	203 783-2000	3782
Bic USA Inc **(DH)**	Shelton	CT	C	203 783-2000	3783
Brand-Nu Laboratories Inc **(PA)**	Meriden	CT	E	203 235-7989	2080
Caap Co Inc	Milford	CT	E	203 877-0375	2258
Chemotex Protective Coatings **(PA)**	Durham	CT	F	860 349-0144	1088
Chessco Industries Inc **(PA)**	Westport	CT	E	203 255-2804	5183
Command Chemical Corporation	Fairfield	CT	G	203 319-1857	1422
Concrete Supplement Co	Litchfield	CT	G	860 567-5556	1946
Cytec Industries Inc	Stamford	CT	D	203 321-2200	4183
Element Solutions Inc	Waterbury	CT	E	203 575-5850	4870
Five Star Products Inc	Shelton	CT	E	203 336-7900	3802
Flottec International Sls Corp	Westport	CT	G	973 588-4717	5195
Gillette Company	Bethel	CT	G	203 796-4000	155
Globe Environmental Corp	Branford	CT	F	203 481-5586	320
Gotham Chemical Company Inc	Norwalk	CT	D	203 854-6644	3163
Great Lakes Chemical Corp **(DH)**	Shelton	CT	E	203 573-2000	3806
Henkel of America Inc **(HQ)**	Rocky Hill	CT	B	860 571-5100	3715
Henkel US Operations Corp **(DH)**	Rocky Hill	CT	B	860 571-5100	3716
Intersurface Dynamics Inc	Bethel	CT	F	203 778-9995	161
Inventec Prfmce Chem USA LLC	Deep River	CT	E	860 526-8300	1063
Kuehne New Haven LLC	New Haven	CT	E	203 508-6703	2703
Lanxess Solutions US Inc **(DH)**	Shelton	CT	E	203 573-2000	3824
Lonza Wood Protection	Norwalk	CT	G	203 229-2900	3186
Lydall Inc **(PA)**	Manchester	CT	E	860 646-1233	2021
Macdermid Incorporated	Waterbury	CT	E	203 575-5700	4901
Macdermid Incorporated **(HQ)**	Waterbury	CT	C	203 575-5700	4900
Macdermid Acumen Inc	Waterbury	CT	G	203 575-5700	4902
Macdermid Enthone Inc **(HQ)**	West Haven	CT	C	203 934-8611	5132
Macdermid Overseas Asia Ltd **(HQ)**	Waterbury	CT	G	203 575-5799	4906
Macdermid Printing Solutions	Waterbury	CT	G	203 575-5727	4907
OMI International Corporation	West Haven	CT	G	203 575-5727	5138
Perfect Infinity Inc	Milford	CT	G	203 906-0442	2334
Permatex Inc **(PA)**	Hartford	CT	E	860 543-7500	1856
Prestone Products Corporation	Danbury	CT	E	203 731-7880	975
Purification Technologies LLC **(DH)**	Chester	CT	F	860 526-7801	774
REM Chemicals Inc **(PA)**	Southington	CT	F	860 621-6755	4074
Suez Wts Services Usa Inc	East Hartford	CT	E	860 291-9660	1225
Three Kings Products LLC	Watertown	CT	G	860 945-5294	5028
United States Chemical Corp	Plantsville	CT	G	860 621-6831	3544
W Canning Inc	Waterbury	CT	G	203 575-5727	4971
A W Chesterton Company	Groveland	MA	B	781 438-7000	11299
Adaptive Surface Tech Inc	Cambridge	MA	G	617 360-7080	9373
Airy Technology Inc	Stoughton	MA	G	781 341-1850	15576
Alden Medical LLC **(PA)**	West Springfield	MA	G	413 747-9717	16507
Amastan Technologies Inc	North Andover	MA	F	978 258-1645	13689
American Ink & Oil Corporation	Norwood	MA	G	781 762-0026	14129
Arrakis Therapeutics Inc	Waltham	MA	G	617 913-0348	16037
Ashland LLC	Assonet	MA	E	508 235-7164	7676
Aspen Aerogels Inc **(PA)**	Northborough	MA	C	508 691-1111	14029
Aspen Products Group Inc	Marlborough	MA	G	508 481-5058	12722
Assayquant Technologies Inc	Marlborough	MA	G	774 278-3302	12723
Avtec Industries Inc	Wellesley	MA	G	978 562-2300	16362
Baker Petrolite LLC	Braintree	MA	C	781 849-9699	8989
Barclay Water Management Inc	Newton	MA	D	617 926-3400	13565
Bay State Galvanizing Inc	Everett	MA	F	617 389-0671	10604
Biosolve Company	Dracut	MA	G	781 482-7900	10354
Blank Industries Inc	Hudson	MA	F	855 887-3123	11759
Bolger & OHearn Inc	Fall River	MA	E	508 676-1518	10670
Cabot Corporation	Billerica	MA	E	978 671-4000	8230
Cabot Specialty Chemicals Inc **(HQ)**	Boston	MA	G	617 345-0100	8453
Camco Manufacturing Inc	Leominster	MA	F	978 537-6777	12123
Charm Sciences Inc **(PA)**	Lawrence	MA	C	978 687-9200	12005
Chase Corporation	Randolph	MA	E	781 963-2600	14673
Cold Chain Technologies Inc **(PA)**	Franklin	MA	D	508 429-1395	11030
Conseal International Inc	Norwood	MA	G	781 278-0010	14142
Creative Materials Inc	Ayer	MA	F	978 391-4700	7916
Cristy Corporation	Fitchburg	MA	F	978 343-4330	10822
Dropwise Technologies Corp	Cambridge	MA	G	617 945-5180	9457
Duraflow LLC	Tewksbury	MA	F	978 851-7439	15815
Eagle Fire Safety Inc	Chelmsford	MA	G	978 256-3777	9894
Ecochlor Inc	Maynard	MA	G	978 298-1463	12898
Emco Services Inc	Fall River	MA	G	508 674-5504	10688
Gcp Applied Technologies Inc **(PA)**	Cambridge	MA	B	617 876-1400	9486
Gillette Company	Andover	MA	A	781 662-9600	7552
Gillette Company **(HQ)**	Boston	MA	A	617 421-7000	8561
Grate Products LLC	Westport	MA	G	800 649-6140	16840
Holland Company Inc	Adams	MA	E	413 743-1292	7413
Jakes Mint Chew LLC	Danvers	MA	G	978 304-0528	10228
Katahdin Industries Inc **(PA)**	Hudson	MA	E	781 329-1420	11781
Kayaku Advanced Materials Inc **(PA)**	Westborough	MA	E	617 965-5511	16629
Kayaku Advanced Materials Inc	Newton	MA	F	617 965-5511	13607
Key Polymer Corporation	Lawrence	MA	E	978 683-9411	12042
King Fisher Co Inc	Lowell	MA	E	978 596-0214	12389
Lubrizol Global Management	Wilmington	MA	D	978 642-5051	17019
Luster-On Products Inc	Springfield	MA	F	413 739-2541	15486
Maranatha Industries Inc **(PA)**	Wakefield	MA	F	781 245-0038	15960
MD Chemicals LLC	Holliston	MA	G	508 314-9664	11584
MD Stetson Company Inc	Randolph	MA	E	781 986-6161	14689
Mexichem Spcalty Compounds Inc **(HQ)**	Leominster	MA	C	978 537-8071	12166
Morgan Advanced Ceramics Inc	New Bedford	MA	C	508 995-1725	13418
Quality Incense	Cambridge	MA	G	339 224-0655	9620
Rectorseal Corporation	Fall River	MA	G	508 673-7561	10755
Ro 59 Inc	Stoughton	MA	G	781 341-1222	15618
Rousselot Peabody Inc	Peabody	MA	F	978 573-3700	14366
Salt Woods LLC	Watertown	MA	G	617 744-9401	16313
Solenis LLC	Chicopee	MA	E	413 536-6426	10061
Terecon Corp **(PA)**	Worcester	MA	G	508 791-1875	17487
Terraverdae Bioworks Inc	Beverly	MA	G	978 712-0220	8189
Tli Group Ltd	Carver	MA	F	508 866-9825	9809
Town of Burlington	Burlington	MA	G	781 270-1680	9349
Transene Company Inc	Danvers	MA	F	978 777-7860	10265
Westford Chemical Corporation	Westford	MA	G	978 392-0689	16800
Yankee Candle Company Inc **(DH)**	South Deerfield	MA	C	413 665-8306	15260
Yankee Holding Corp **(DH)**	South Deerfield	MA	G	413 665-8306	15262
Ycc Holdings LLC	South Deerfield	MA	A	413 665-8306	15263
Carrier Wldg & Fabrication LLC	Wilton	ME	G	207 645-3100	7225
Chute Chemical Agency	Houlton	ME	G	207 532-4370	6204
Enterprise Castings LLC	Lewiston	ME	G	207 782-5511	6288
FMC Corporation	Rockland	ME	C	207 594-3200	6795
Foam Pro Inc	Bangor	ME	G	207 212-9657	5645
New England Salt Co LLC	Bangor	ME	G	207 262-9779	5656
Ouellette Sand & Gravel Inc	South China	ME	G	207 445-4131	7006
Paine Products Inc	Auburn	ME	F	207 782-0931	5585
Albany International Corp **(PA)**	Rochester	NH	D	603 330-5850	19655
Americ An Novelty Inc	Seabrook	NH	G	401 785-9850	19792
Atlas Pyrovision Entertainment **(PA)**	Jaffrey	NH	E	603 532-8324	18457
CIM Industries Inc	Peterborough	NH	F	603 924-9481	19469
Continental Braze Supply LLC	Rochester	NH	G	603 948-1016	19664
D C Speeney Sons Pyrotechnics	Jaffrey	NH	G	603 532-9323	18458
Dispersion Services LLC	Nashua	NH	G	603 577-9520	19146
Diversified Enterprises-ADT	Claremont	NH	G	603 543-0038	17847
Hampshire Chemical Corp **(DH)**	Nashua	NH	E	603 888-2320	19176
Onsite Drug Testing Neng	Concord	NH	G	603 226-3858	17921
Performance Chemicals LLC	Franklin	NH	F	603 228-1200	18163
Advanced Chemical Company	Warwick	RI	E	401 785-3434	21318
American Foam Technologies Inc	Newport	RI	E	304 497-3000	20655
Aquarion Water Company	Westerly	RI	G	401 596-2847	21516
Aspen Aerogels Inc	East Providence	RI	F	401 432-2612	20388
Aspen Aerogels RI LLC	East Providence	RI	F	401 432-2612	20389
Atlantic Water Management	Coventry	RI	G	401 397-8200	20137
Bardon Industries Inc	East Greenwich	RI	F	401 884-1814	20353
Burrillville Town of Inc	Oakland	RI	G	401 568-6296	20798
Cranston Print Works Company **(PA)**	Cranston	RI	E	401 943-4800	20202

S I C

Employee Codes: A=Over 500 employees, B=251-500 C=101-250, D=51-100 E=20-50, F=10-19, G=3-9

	CITY	ST	EMP	PHONE	ENTRY #
Dryvit Holdings Inc **(DH)**	Providence	RI	G	401 822-4100	20998
Dryvit Systems Inc **(DH)**	West Warwick	RI	D	401 822-4100	21491
International Dioxcide Inc	North Kingstown	RI	E	401 295-8800	20718
Northern Industries Inc **(PA)**	Coventry	RI	G	401 769-4305	20160
Technic Inc **(PA)**	Cranston	RI	C	401 781-6100	20301
Technic Inc	Woonsocket	RI	E	401 769-7000	21585
Everett M Windover Inc	Colchester	VT	E	802 865-0000	21863
Naturopatches Vermont Inc	Bellows Falls	VT	G	800 340-9083	21652
Sto Corp	Rutland	VT	E	802 775-4117	22354

29 PETROLEUM REFINING AND RELATED INDUSTRIES

2911 Petroleum Refining

	CITY	ST	EMP	PHONE	ENTRY #
Armored Autogroup Parent Inc **(DH)**	Danbury	CT	G	203 205-2900	875
CCI Corpus Christi LLC	Stamford	CT	G	203 564-8100	4158
Chessco Industries Inc **(PA)**	Westport	CT	E	203 255-2804	5183
Du-Lite Corporation	Middletown	CT	G	860 347-2505	2184
Koster Keunen Inc	Watertown	CT	G	860 945-3333	5012
Koster Keunen Mfg Inc	Watertown	CT	D	860 945-3333	5014
Lanxess Solutions US Inc **(DH)**	Shelton	CT	E	203 573-2000	3824
Leclaire Fuel Oil LLC	Shelton	CT	G	203 922-1512	3827
Purification Technologies LLC **(DH)**	Chester	CT	F	860 526-7801	774
STP Products Manufacturing Co **(DH)**	Danbury	CT	F	203 205-2900	997
US Chemicals Inc	New Canaan	CT	G	203 655-8878	2620
269 Walpole Street LLC	Norwood	MA	G	781 762-1128	14115
Blue Rhino of Ne	Springfield	MA	G	413 781-3694	15455
Dal-Trac Oil Company	Attleboro	MA	G	508 222-3935	7726
Exxonmobil Oil Corporation	Randolph	MA	G	781 963-7252	14679
Exxonmobil Pipeline Company	Springfield	MA	G	413 736-1881	15470
Greener 3000 LLC	Boston	MA	G	781 589-5777	8579
Homeland Fuels Company LLC	Canton	MA	F	781 737-1892	9739
Isp Freetown Fine Chem Inc	Assonet	MA	D	508 672-0634	7681
Solvent Kleene Inc	Peabody	MA	F	978 531-2279	14370
Thibault Fuel Oil	Springfield	MA	G	413 782-9577	15512
CN Brown Company	Windham	ME	G	207 892-5955	7231
Kenoco Inc	Farmingdale	ME	G	207 620-7260	6039
Koch Industries Inc	South Portland	ME	F	207 767-2161	7031
Maine Bio-Fuel Inc	Portland	ME	F	207 878-3001	6682
Paul E Wentworth	Vassalboro	ME	G	207 923-3547	7125
Ultron LLC	Waldoboro	ME	G	207 832-4502	7137
Baycorp Holdings Ltd **(PA)**	Portsmouth	NH	F	603 294-4850	19542
Prima America Corporation	Groveton	NH	E	603 631-5407	18233
Smartfuel America LLC	Seabrook	NH	G	603 474-5005	19818
Ultramar Inc	Lancaster	NH	F	603 788-2771	18608
White Mountain Biodiesel LLC	Littleton	NH	G	603 444-0335	18668
Glenn LLC	Warwick	RI	G	800 521-0065	21369
Burtco Inc	Westminster Station	VT	F	802 722-3358	22633
Oxbow Creative LLC	Burlington	VT	F	802 870-0354	21801

2951 Paving Mixtures & Blocks

	CITY	ST	EMP	PHONE	ENTRY #
A-1 Asphalt Paving	Rocky Hill	CT	G	860 436-6085	3700
AEN Asphalt Inc	Bozrah	CT	G	860 885-0500	279
All States Asphalt Inc	Dayville	CT	G	860 774-7550	1038
Betkoski Brothers LLC	Beacon Falls	CT	G	203 723-8262	55
E B Asphalt & Landscaping LLC	Norwich	CT	F	860 639-1921	3279
L Suzio Asphalt Co Inc	Meriden	CT	F	203 237-8421	2098
O & G Industries Inc	Stamford	CT	E	203 977-1618	4265
O & G Industries Inc	New Milford	CT	D	860 354-4438	2820
O & G Industries Inc	Bridgeport	CT	E	203 366-4586	459
T D I Enterprises LLC	Meriden	CT	G	203 630-1268	2136
Tilcon Connecticut Inc	Portland	CT	G	860 342-6157	3577
Wescon Corp of Conn	Pawcatuck	CT	G	860 599-2500	3444
Westchester Industries Inc	Greenwich	CT	F	203 661-0055	1661
Aggregate Inds - Northeast Reg	Raynham	MA	G	508 822-7120	14704
Aggregate Inds - Northeast Reg	Saugus	MA	G	781 941-7200	14975
Aggregate Inds - Northeast Reg	Wrentham	MA	E	508 384-3161	17513
Aggregate Inds - Northeast Reg	Ashland	MA	E	508 881-1430	7655
Brox Industries Inc **(PA)**	Dracut	MA	D	978 454-9105	10355
Fletcher Granite LLC **(DH)**	Westford	MA	G	978 692-1312	16767
Granger Lynch Corp	Millbury	MA	E	508 756-6244	13165
Heffron Asphalt Corp **(PA)**	North Reading	MA	G	781 935-1455	13984
Jr & Sons Construction	Westport	MA	G	508 326-7884	16842
Kdo LLC	Taunton	MA	G	508 802-1347	15761
Kol-Tar Inc	Abington	MA	G	781 871-0883	7326
Lorusso Corp **(PA)**	Plainville	MA	E	508 668-6520	14527
Massachusetts Broken Stone Co **(PA)**	Berlin	MA	G	978 838-9999	8091
Massachusetts Broken Stone Co	Holden	MA	F	508 829-5353	11547
New England Emulsions Corp	Holliston	MA	G	508 429-5550	11590
Norfolk Asphalt Company Inc	Plainville	MA	E	508 668-3100	14531
Oxford Asphalt Inc	Oxford	MA	G	508 987-0321	14271
Rochester Bituminous Products	West Wareham	MA	G	508 295-8001	16576
Sealcoating	Worcester	MA	G	508 926-8080	17470
Ted Ondrick Company LLC **(PA)**	Chicopee	MA	F	413 592-2565	10064
Trew Corp **(PA)**	Sunderland	MA	G	413 665-4051	15677
Trew Corp	Deerfield	MA	F	413 773-9798	10304
A & W Paving & Sealcoating	South Paris	ME	G	207 743-6615	7009
Dayton Sand & Gravel Inc	Dayton	ME	D	207 499-2306	5944
Down E Emulsions Ltd Lblty Co	Bangor	ME	G	207 947-8624	5641
F R Carroll Inc	Limerick	ME	E	207 793-8615	6334
Mattingly Products Company	North Anson	ME	E	207 635-2719	6504
McBreairty Ransford	Woodland	ME	G	207 498-3182	7288
Morin Brothers	Fort Kent	ME	G	207 834-5361	6063
Trombley Industries Inc	Limestone	ME	G	207 328-4503	6345
Asphalt Recovery Tech LLC	Brentwood	NH	G	603 778-1449	17744
M & L Asphalt Services LLC	Swanzey	NH	G	603 355-1230	19884
Recycled Asp Shingle Tech LLC	Brentwood	NH	G	603 778-1449	17757
Bjorklund Corp	Providence	RI	G	401 944-6400	20970
Cruz Construction Company Inc	Cumberland	RI	F	401 727-3770	20316
Driveways By R Stanley Inc	Saunderstown	RI	G	401 789-8600	21201
Hudson Liquid Asphalts Inc **(PA)**	Cranston	RI	D	401 274-2200	20238
JH Lynch & Sons Inc	East Providence	RI	C	401 434-7100	20422
Pavement Warehouse	Greenville	RI	G	401 233-3200	20471
Perry Paving	Warwick	RI	G	401 732-1730	21403
Addison County Asphalt Pdts	Middlebury	VT	G	802 388-2338	22096
Black Beauty Driveway Sealing	Colchester	VT	G	802 860-7113	21858

2952 Asphalt Felts & Coatings

	CITY	ST	EMP	PHONE	ENTRY #
Bella Casa Roofing LLC	Stamford	CT	G	475 619-0393	4149
Neyra Industries Inc	South Windsor	CT	G	860 289-4359	3995
Qba Inc	Woodstock	CT	G	860 963-9438	5500
Westfort Construction Corp	Hamden	CT	G	860 833-7970	1795
Driveway Medics LLC	Seekonk	MA	G	508 761-6921	15021
Duro-Last Inc	Ludlow	MA	E	413 631-0050	12463
Johns Manville Corporation	West Boylston	MA	C	774 261-8500	16420
Kol-Tar Inc	Abington	MA	G	781 871-0883	7326
Omg Inc **(DH)**	Agawam	MA	B	413 789-0252	7443
Sarnafil Services Inc	Canton	MA	C	781 828-5400	9775
Sika Sarnafil Inc	Canton	MA	G	800 451-2502	9781
Newmont Slate Co Inc **(PA)**	West Pawlet	VT	E	802 645-0203	22612
Quarry Slate Industries Inc	Poultney	VT	D	802 287-9701	22274
Vermont Structural Slate Co **(PA)**	Fair Haven	VT	E	802 265-4933	21970

2992 Lubricating Oils & Greases

	CITY	ST	EMP	PHONE	ENTRY #
Artech Packaging LLC	Bethel	CT	G	845 858-8558	128
Axel Plastics RES Labs Inc	Monroe	CT	E	718 672-8300	2392
Castrol Industrial N Amer Inc	Putnam	CT	G	860 928-5100	3603
CCL Industries Corporation **(DH)**	Shelton	CT	D	203 926-1253	3785
Chessco Industries Inc **(PA)**	Westport	CT	E	203 255-2804	5183
Fuchs Lubricants Co	East Haven	CT	E	203 469-2336	1251
Macdermid Incorporated **(HQ)**	Waterbury	CT	C	203 575-5700	4900
Permatex Inc **(PA)**	Hartford	CT	E	860 543-7500	1856
Price-Driscoll Corporation	Waterford	CT	G	860 442-3575	4991
Safe Harbour Products Inc	Norwalk	CT	G	203 295-8377	3235
A W Chesterton Company **(PA)**	Groveland	MA	E	781 438-7000	11298
A W Chesterton Company	Groveland	MA	B	781 438-7000	11299
Alvin Products Inc	Everett	MA	G	978 975-4580	10602
BP Lubricants USA Inc	Worcester	MA	G	508 791-3201	17351
Change Logic	Newton Upper Falls	MA	F	617 274-8661	13657
Circuit Systems Inc **(PA)**	Westfield	MA	F	413 562-5019	16678
Homeland Fuels Company LLC	Canton	MA	F	781 737-1892	9739
J G Performance Inc	Abington	MA	G	781 871-1404	7325
M J Gordon Company Inc	Pittsfield	MA	G	413 448-6066	14487
O & E High-Tech Corporation	Medford	MA	G	617 497-1108	12945
Ro 59 Inc	Stoughton	MA	G	781 341-1222	15618
Sally Seaver	Burlington	MA	G	833 322-8483	9332
Winfield Brooks Company Inc	Woburn	MA	F	781 933-5300	17323
Ed Sanders	Lancaster	NH	G	603 788-3626	18600
Kluber Lubric North Amercia LP	Londonderry	NH	G	603 647-4104	18709
Kluber Lubrication N Amer LP	Londonderry	NH	G	800 447-2238	18710
Kluber Lubrication NA LP **(DH)**	Londonderry	NH	D	603 647-4104	18711
Battenfeld of America Inc	West Warwick	RI	G	401 823-0700	21483
Noco Energy Corp	Williston	VT	G	802 864-6626	22686
Pelletier Lube Service	Barre	VT	G	802 622-0725	21635

2999 Products Of Petroleum & Coal, NEC

	CITY	ST	EMP	PHONE	ENTRY #
Koster Keunen LLC **(PA)**	Watertown	CT	F	860 945-3333	5013
Rain Cii Carbon LLC	Stamford	CT	F	203 406-0535	4297
Trans-Mate LLC	North Billerica	MA	E	800 867-9274	13873
Speedy Petroleum Inc	Cranston	RI	G	401 781-3350	20289

30 RUBBER AND MISCELLANEOUS PLASTICS PRODUCTS

3011 Tires & Inner Tubes

	CITY	ST	EMP	PHONE	ENTRY #
Ace Tire & Auto Center Inc	Ridgefield	CT	F	203 438-4042	3654
Town Fair Tire Centers Inc	Manchester	CT	F	860 646-2807	2056
Cochin Rubbers Intl LLC **(PA)**	Mansfield	MA	G	877 289-0364	12618
Cri Rubber LLC **(HQ)**	Hopkinton	MA	G	508 657-8488	11698
Gpx International Tire Corp **(PA)**	Foxboro	MA	E	781 321-3910	10885
Larkin Motors LLC	Bridgewater	MA	G	508 807-1333	9082
Main Industrial Tires Ltd **(PA)**	Wakefield	MA	F	713 676-0251	15958
Maine Rubber International	Wakefield	MA	C	877 648-1949	15959
Maxam Tire North America Inc	Danvers	MA	G	844 629-2662	10235

	CITY	ST	EMP	PHONE	ENTRY #
Sullivan Manufacturing Company	Norwell	MA	E	781 982-1550	14112

3021 Rubber & Plastic Footwear

	CITY	ST	EMP	PHONE	ENTRY #
Biltrite Corporation	Chelsea	MA	E	617 884-3124	9945
Black Diamond Group Inc	Woburn	MA	F	781 932-4173	17133
Dance Paws LLC	Cambridge	MA	G	617 945-3044	9450
Klone Lab LLC	Newburyport	MA	G	978 378-3434	13505
Macneill Engineering Co Inc	Westborough	MA	E	508 481-8830	16633
New Balance Athletics Inc **(HQ)**	Boston	MA	B	617 783-4000	8727
New Balance Athletics Inc	Lawrence	MA	B	978 685-8400	12063
New Balance Licensing LLC	Brighton	MA	G	800 343-4648	9102
Nike Inc	Lee	MA	E	413 243-1861	12093
Nike Inc	Burlington	MA	F	781 564-9929	9310
Twin Leather Co Inc	West Bridgewater	MA	G	508 583-3485	16461
Vans Inc	Burlington	MA	G	781 229-7700	9351
32 North Corporation	Biddeford	ME	G	207 284-5010	5716
Dyeables Inc	Farmington	ME	G	207 778-9871	6045
New Balance Athletics Inc	Skowhegan	ME	B	207 474-2042	6983
New Balance Athletics Inc	Norridgewock	ME	B	207 634-3033	6499
Genfoot America Inc	Littleton	NH	D	603 575-5114	18660
Paclantic Inc	Claremont	NH	G	603 542-8600	17858
Simply Footwear Utah LLC	Concord	NH	G	603 715-2259	17930
Codet-Newport Corporation **(HQ)**	Newport	VT	F	802 334-5811	22192
Genfoot America Inc	Milton	VT	F	802 893-4280	22129

3052 Rubber & Plastic Hose & Belting

	CITY	ST	EMP	PHONE	ENTRY #
Kongsberg Actuation **(HQ)**	Suffield	CT	G	860 668-1285	4464
Ram Belting Company Inc	New Britain	CT	G	860 438-7029	2568
Rubco Products Company	Torrington	CT	G	860 496-1178	4597
Diversified Industrial Sup LLC	Charlestown	MA	F	800 244-3647	9831
Dresco Belting Co Inc	East Weymouth	MA	G	781 335-1350	10541
Flexaust Company Inc	Newburyport	MA	G	978 465-0445	13489
Flexaust Inc	Amesbury	MA	G	978 388-1005	7485
Guardair Corporation	Chicopee	MA	E	413 594-4400	10028
Samar Co Inc	Stoughton	MA	D	781 297-7264	15620
Seven Mist LLC	Amherst	MA	G	413 210-7255	7525
Techflex Enterprises Inc	Chicopee	MA	G	413 592-2800	10063
Titeflex Commercial Inc	Springfield	MA	F	413 739-5631	15515
Titeflex Corporation **(HQ)**	Springfield	MA	B	413 739-5631	15516
Contitech Thermopol LLC	Somersworth	NH	G	603 692-6300	19832
Contitech Thermopol LLC	Rochester	NH	D	603 692-6300	19665
Contitech Thermopol LLC **(HQ)**	Somersworth	NH	G	603 692-6300	19833
Teknor Apex Company **(PA)**	Pawtucket	RI	B	401 725-8000	20903
Advanced Flexible Composites	Bennington	VT	G	802 681-7121	21662

3053 Gaskets, Packing & Sealing Devices

	CITY	ST	EMP	PHONE	ENTRY #
A G C Incorporated **(PA)**	Meriden	CT	C	203 235-3361	2072
American Seal and Engrg Co Inc **(DH)**	Orange	CT	E	203 789-8819	3358
Ametek Inc	Wallingford	CT	C	203 265-6731	4699
Auburn Manufacturing Company	Middletown	CT	E	860 346-6677	2173
Beacon Group Inc **(PA)**	Newington	CT	C	860 594-5200	2846
Chas W House & Sons Inc	Unionville	CT	D	860 673-2518	4654
Corru Seals Inc	Wallingford	CT	F	203 284-0319	4728
Derby Cellular Products Inc	Shelton	CT	C	203 735-4661	3795
EMR Global Inc	East Hartford	CT	G	203 452-8166	1192
H-O Products Corporation	Winsted	CT	E	860 379-9875	5412
Lydall Inc **(PA)**	Manchester	CT	E	860 646-1233	2021
Parker-Hannifin Corporation	North Haven	CT	D	203 239-3341	3049
Rubber Supplies Company Inc	Derby	CT	G	203 736-9995	1079
SKF USA Inc	Winsted	CT	E	860 379-8511	5423
Spirol International Corp **(HQ)**	Danielson	CT	C	860 774-8571	1018
Standard Washer & Mat Inc	Manchester	CT	E	860 643-5125	2051
Vanguard Products Corporation	Danbury	CT	D	203 744-7265	1003
A W Chesterton Company **(PA)**	Groveland	MA	E	781 438-7000	11298
A W Chesterton Company	Groveland	MA	B	781 438-7000	11299
Acushnet Rubber Company Inc	New Bedford	MA	B	508 998-4000	13352
Atlantic Rubber Company Inc	Littleton	MA	F	800 882-3666	12294
B G Peck Company Inc	Lawrence	MA	E	978 686-4181	11997
Barbour Plastics Inc **(HQ)**	Brockton	MA	E	508 583-8200	9125
Boston Atlantic Corp	Worcester	MA	F	508 754-4076	17350
Coorstek Inc	Worcester	MA	B	774 317-2600	17360
D V Die Cutting Inc	Danvers	MA	E	978 777-0300	10210
Eastern Industrial Products	Pembroke	MA	F	781 826-9511	14403
Emseal Joint Systems Ltd	Westborough	MA	E	508 836-0280	16617
Hollingsworth & Vose Company **(PA)**	East Walpole	MA	C	508 850-2000	10524
I G Marston Company	Holbrook	MA	F	781 767-2894	11526
Interstate Gasket Company Inc	Sutton	MA	F	508 234-5500	15684
New England Die Cutting Inc	Methuen	MA	E	978 374-0789	13039
Northeast Equipment Inc	Fall River	MA	E	508 324-0083	10740
Parker-Hannifin Corporation	Woburn	MA	B	781 939-4278	17255
Parker-Hannifin Corporation	Woburn	MA	G	781 935-4850	17256
Parker-Hannifin Corporation	Woburn	MA	B	781 935-4850	17257
Precision Assemblies	Malden	MA	G	781 324-9054	12591
Saint-Gobain Prfmce Plas Corp	Worcester	MA	E	508 852-3072	17467
Schott North America Inc	Southbridge	MA	D	508 765-7450	15402
Twin Leather Co Inc	West Bridgewater	MA	G	508 583-3485	16461
Vellumoid Inc	Worcester	MA	E	508 853-2500	17499
Web Die Cutters Etc Inc	Agawam	MA	F	413 552-3100	7456
Worcester Indus Rbr Sup Co Inc	Holden	MA	G	508 853-2332	11551
Xtreme Seal LLC	Hingham	MA	G	508 933-1894	11519
Zd USA Holdings Inc **(PA)**	New Bedford	MA	C	508 998-4000	13460
Woodex Bearing Company Inc	Georgetown	ME	E	207 371-2210	6107
Amatex Corporation	Laconia	NH	E	603 524-2552	18556
Booth Felt Co Inc	Dover	NH	G	603 330-3334	18009
Cooper Products Inc	Laconia	NH	E	603 524-3367	18563
Dichtomatik Americas LP	Manchester	NH	G	603 628-7030	18809
Felton Inc	Londonderry	NH	D	603 425-0200	18697
Ferrotec (usa) Corporation **(HQ)**	Bedford	NH	D	603 472-6800	17640
Freudenberg-Nok General Partnr	Northfield	NH	D	603 286-1600	19401
Freudenberg-Nok General Partnr	Bristol	NH	C	603 934-7800	17763
Freudenberg-Nok General Partnr	Bristol	NH	B	603 744-0371	17764
Freudenberg-Nok General Partnr	Ashland	NH	C	603 968-7187	17599
Freudenberg-Nok General Partnr	Northfield	NH	E	603 286-1600	19402
New England Braiding Co Inc	Manchester	NH	F	603 669-1987	18883
Trellborg Pipe Sals Mlford Inc **(DH)**	Milford	NH	C	800 626-2180	19080
Trellborg Pipe Sals Mlford Inc	Milford	NH	G	603 673-8680	19081
E G & G Sealol Eagle Inc	Warwick	RI	F	401 732-0333	21357
Jade Engineered Plastics Inc	Bristol	RI	D	401 253-4440	20085
John Crane Inc	Warwick	RI	D	401 463-8700	21380
John Crane Sealol Inc **(DH)**	Warwick	RI	C	401 732-0715	21381
Magnetic Seal Corp	Warren	RI	E	401 247-2800	21298

3061 Molded, Extruded & Lathe-Cut Rubber Mechanical Goods

	CITY	ST	EMP	PHONE	ENTRY #
Acmt Inc	Manchester	CT	D	860 645-0592	1982
Applied Rubber & Plastics Inc	Windsor	CT	F	860 987-9018	5321
Jem Manufacturing Inc	Wallingford	CT	G	203 250-9404	4759
Vanguard Products Corporation	Danbury	CT	D	203 744-7265	1003
Acushnet Rubber Company Inc	New Bedford	MA	B	508 998-4000	13352
Chardan Ltd	Attleboro	MA	G	508 992-0854	7718
Device Technologies Inc	Southborough	MA	E	508 229-2000	15354
Hutchinson Arospc & Indust Inc **(DH)**	Hopkinton	MA	B	508 417-7000	11718
Jefferson Rubber Works Inc	Worcester	MA	D	508 791-3600	17397
Pocasset Machine Corporation	Pocasset	MA	E	508 563-5572	14600
Saint-Gobain Prfmce Plas Corp	Worcester	MA	E	508 852-3072	17467
Jones & Vining Incorporated	Lewiston	ME	E	207 784-3547	6295
Brn Corporation	Campton	NH	G	603 726-3800	17775
Cooper Products Inc	Laconia	NH	E	603 524-3367	18563
Extrusion Alternatives Inc	Portsmouth	NH	F	603 430-9600	19562
Freudenberg-Nok General Partnr	Northfield	NH	E	603 286-1600	19402
Etco Incorporated **(PA)**	Warwick	RI	D	401 467-2400	21361
Moore Company **(PA)**	Westerly	RI	C	401 596-2816	21531
Moore Company	Westerly	RI	C	401 596-2816	21532
Garflex Inc	Brattleboro	VT	D	802 257-5256	21728

3069 Fabricated Rubber Prdts, NEC

	CITY	ST	EMP	PHONE	ENTRY #
American Roller Company LLC	Middlebury	CT	F	203 598-3100	2154
Anchor Rubber Products LLC	Newington	CT	G	860 667-2628	2843
Auburn Manufacturing Company	Middletown	CT	E	860 346-6677	2173
Bite Tech Inc	Norwalk	CT	E	203 987-6898	3114
Cooper Crouse-Hinds LLC	Windsor	CT	D	860 683-4300	5327
Gordon Rubber and Pkg Co Inc	Derby	CT	E	203 735-7441	1072
Griswold LLC	Moosup	CT	D	860 564-3321	2426
H-O Products Corporation	Winsted	CT	E	860 379-9875	5412
Hutchinson Precision Ss Inc	Danielson	CT	C	860 779-0300	1013
IR Industries Inc	Bethel	CT	F	203 790-8273	162
Ktt Enterprises LLC	Hamden	CT	G	203 288-7883	1765
Latex Foam International LLC **(HQ)**	Shelton	CT	D	203 924-0700	3825
Latex Foam Intl Holdings Inc **(PA)**	Shelton	CT	C	203 924-0700	3826
Lord & Hodge Inc	Middletown	CT	F	860 632-7006	2201
Mayborn Usa Inc	Stamford	CT	F	781 269-7490	4245
Meridian Operations LLC	Plainfield	CT	F	860 564-8811	3454
Midsun Specialty Products Inc	Berlin	CT	E	860 378-0111	96
Nauta Roll Corporation	East Hampton	CT	G	860 267-2027	1162
New England Foam Products LLC **(PA)**	Hartford	CT	E	860 524-0121	1851
Playtex Products LLC **(HQ)**	Shelton	CT	D	203 944-5500	3856
Reilly Foam Corp	Bloomfield	CT	E	860 243-8200	256
Rogers Corporation	Woodstock	CT	C	860 928-3622	5501
Standard Washer & Mat Inc	Manchester	CT	E	860 643-5125	2051
Tellus Technology Inc **(PA)**	Darien	CT	G	646 265-7960	1033
Universal Foam Products LLC	Bloomfield	CT	F	860 216-3015	270
Advent Medical Products Inc	Lincoln	MA	E	781 272-2813	12285
Allan Ponn	Stoneham	MA	G	781 438-4338	15553
American Biltrite Inc **(PA)**	Wellesley	MA	G	781 237-6655	16359
Apothecary Products LLC	North Attleboro	MA	E	508 695-0727	13745
Avon Custom Mixing Svcs Inc	Holbrook	MA	E	781 767-0511	11521
Bandera Acquisition LLC **(DH)**	Foxborough	MA	C	480 553-6400	10911
Biltrite Corporation	Chelsea	MA	E	617 884-3124	9945
C H Yates Rubber Corp	Fall River	MA	G	508 674-3378	10673
Cape Cod Drmats of Distinction	Hyannis	MA	E	508 790-0070	11836
Cataki International Inc	Wareham	MA	E	508 295-9630	16243
Certainteed Corporation	Natick	MA	G	508 655-9731	13244
Chase Corporation	Randolph	MA	E	781 963-2600	14673
Cri-Tech Inc	Hanover	MA	E	781 826-5600	11333
David A Payne	Brockton	MA	G	508 588-7500	9136

SIC

	CITY	ST	EMP	PHONE	ENTRY #
Dorel Juvenile Group Inc	Foxboro	MA	D	800 544-1108	10881
Fastcast Consortium Inc	Worcester	MA	C	508 853-4500	17373
Gs Rubber Industries LLC	Fall River	MA	F	508 672-0742	10708
Haartz Corporation **(PA)**	Acton	MA	B	978 264-2600	7359
Heveatex Corporation	Fall River	MA	F	508 675-0181	10713
Hytex Industries Inc	Randolph	MA	E	781 963-4400	14686
Interstate Mat Corporation	South Easton	MA	G	508 238-0116	15282
Jefferson Rubber Works Inc	Worcester	MA	D	508 791-3600	17397
Kevin Lyman Roofing Co	Bridgewater	MA	G	508 697-8244	9081
L&E Floorcovering	Hopedale	MA	G	508 473-0723	11675
New England Business Svc Inc **(HQ)**	Groton	MA	D	978 448-6111	11291
Patten Machine Inc	Hudson	MA	F	978 562-9847	11801
Plymouth Rubber Company LLC	Canton	MA	E	781 828-0220	9768
Plymouth Rubber Europa SA	Canton	MA	F	781 828-0220	9769
Polyneer Inc	New Bedford	MA	E	508 998-5225	13440
Ponn Machine Cutting Co	Woburn	MA	F	781 937-3373	17267
Renco Corporation **(PA)**	Manchester	MA	G	978 526-8494	12606
Rubber Right Rollers Inc	Chelsea	MA	F	617 466-1447	9965
Rubberright Rollers Inc	Everett	MA	G	617 387-6060	10629
Saint-Gobain Prfmce Plas Corp	Worcester	MA	E	508 852-3072	17467
Simons Stamps Inc	Turners Falls	MA	F	413 863-6800	15885
SRC Medical Inc	Hanover	MA	D	781 826-9100	11352
Standard Rubber Products Inc	Hanover	MA	E	781 878-2626	11353
Tc Design Works Inc	Beverly	MA	G	978 768-0034	8187
Tempron Products Corp	Milford	MA	G	508 473-5880	13147
Tillotson Corporation **(PA)**	Seekonk	MA	F	781 402-1731	15042
Vibram Corporation **(DH)**	North Brookfield	MA	C	508 867-6494	13883
Vibram Corporation **(HQ)**	Concord	MA	E	978 318-0000	10159
Worthen Industries Inc	Clinton	MA	E	978 365-6345	10095
Bosal Foam and Fiber **(PA)**	Limerick	ME	E	207 793-2245	6332
Expanded Rubber Products Inc	Kennebunk	ME	G	207 985-4141	6233
Expanded Rubber Products Inc **(PA)**	Sanford	ME	E	207 324-8226	6875
Hants White LLC	Mars Hill	ME	G	207 429-9786	6414
Maine Industrial P & R Corp	Newcastle	ME	G	207 563-5532	6484
Dhf LLC	Brentwood	NH	G	603 778-2440	17748
Diacom Corporation	Amherst	NH	D	603 880-1900	17557
Humphreys Industrial Pdts Inc	Rochester	NH	D	603 692-5005	19671
Hutchinson Sealing Systems Inc	Newfields	NH	C	603 772-3771	19317
Kingswood Sales Inc	Sanbornville	NH	G	603 522-6636	19783
Nora Systems Inc **(DH)**	Salem	NH	D	603 894-1021	19755
Nordson Medical (nh) Inc **(HQ)**	Salem	NH	C	603 327-0600	19756
Schaeferrolls Inc	Farmington	NH	E	603 335-1786	18144
Stowe Woodward LLC	Concord	NH	E	603 224-6300	17932
Cara Incorporated	Warwick	RI	G	401 732-6535	21339
Cooley Incorporated **(HQ)**	Pawtucket	RI	C	401 724-9000	20825
Dewal Industries LLC	Narragansett	RI	C	401 789-9736	20637
Fuller Box Co Inc	Central Falls	RI	D	401 725-4300	20113
Givens Marine Survival Svc Co	Tiverton	RI	F	617 441-5400	21259
Hasbro Inc **(PA)**	Pawtucket	RI	A	401 431-8697	20845
Hl Tech Profiles Inc	Ashaway	RI	E	401 377-2040	20037
Iselann Moss Industries Inc	Cranston	RI	F	401 463-5950	20242
Moore Company **(PA)**	Westerly	RI	C	401 596-2816	21531
Moore Company	Westerly	RI	C	401 596-2816	21532
Rihani Plastics Inc	Cranston	RI	F	401 942-7393	20280
Spinlock USA	Newport	RI	G	401 619-5200	20684
Teknor Apex Company **(PA)**	Pawtucket	RI	B	401 725-8000	20903
TMC Rhode Island Company Inc	Westerly	RI	F	401 596-2816	21543
Tory Inc	Woonsocket	RI	G	401 766-4502	21587
Wright Industrial Products Co	Cumberland	RI	G	508 695-3924	20350
Accurate Rubber Products Inc	Swanton	VT	G	802 868-3063	22529
Garflex Inc	Brattleboro	VT	D	802 257-5256	21728

3081 Plastic Unsupported Sheet & Film

	CITY	ST	EMP	PHONE	ENTRY #
American Polyfilm Inc **(PA)**	Branford	CT	G	203 483-9797	289
Apogee Corporation **(PA)**	Putnam	CT	D	860 963-1976	3601
Apogee Corporation	Cromwell	CT	D	860 632-3550	846
Atlas Metallizing Inc	New Britain	CT	F	860 827-9777	2510
Brushfoil LLC	Guilford	CT	F	203 453-7403	1696
Clopay Corporation	North Haven	CT	C	203 230-9116	3015
Engineering Services & Pdts Co **(PA)**	South Windsor	CT	D	860 528-1119	3965
Ensign-Bickford Industries Inc	Weatogue	CT	C	860 843-2000	5042
Filmx Technologies	Dayville	CT	G	860 779-3403	1044
Flagship Converters Inc	Danbury	CT	D	203 792-0034	920
Grimco Inc	New Britain	CT	G	800 542-9941	2536
Orafol Americas Inc	Avon	CT	C	860 676-7100	41
Plastic Factory LLC	Bridgeport	CT	G	203 908-3468	470
Polymer Films Inc	West Haven	CT	E	203 932-3000	5142
Rowland Technologies Inc	Wallingford	CT	D	203 269-9500	4801
Spartech LLC	Stamford	CT	C	203 327-6010	4327
Str Holdings Inc **(PA)**	Enfield	CT	F	860 272-4235	1386
Superior Plas Extrusion Co Inc	Cromwell	CT	G	860 234-1864	861
Superior Plas Extrusion Co Inc **(PA)**	Putnam	CT	E	860 963-1976	3636
Abcorp NA Inc	Boston	MA	B	617 325-9600	8335
Applied Nnstrctred Sltions LLC	Billerica	MA	E	978 670-6959	8211
Argotec LLC **(HQ)**	Greenfield	MA	C	413 772-2564	11250
Arlin Mfg Co Inc	Lowell	MA	F	978 454-9165	12345
Atlantic Poly Inc	Norwood	MA	F	781 769-4260	14136
Avery Dennison Corporation	Westborough	MA	C	508 948-3500	16591
Berry Global Films LLC	Danvers	MA	C	978 532-2000	10202
Brightec Inc	Natick	MA	G	508 647-9710	13241
Cabot Corporation **(PA)**	Boston	MA	C	617 345-0100	8452
Cabot Corporation	Haverhill	MA	C	978 556-8400	11413
CDF Corporation **(PA)**	Plymouth	MA	D	508 747-5858	14550
Charter Nex Films Inc	Turners Falls	MA	G	413 863-3171	15875
Chase Corporation	Randolph	MA	E	781 963-2600	14673
Coorstek Inc	Worcester	MA	B	774 317-2600	17360
Covestro LLC	South Deerfield	MA	D	412 777-2000	15248
Danafilms Corp	Westborough	MA	G	508 366-8884	16612
Dielectrics Inc **(HQ)**	Chicopee	MA	E	413 594-8111	10019
Eastern Etching and Mfg Co	Chicopee	MA	E	413 594-6601	10022
Entegris Inc **(PA)**	Billerica	MA	A	978 436-6500	8246
Epv Plastics Corporation	Oxford	MA	G	508 987-2595	14259
Flexcon Company Inc **(PA)**	Spencer	MA	A	508 885-8200	15429
Glad Products Company	Braintree	MA	G	781 848-6272	9009
Gregory Manufacturing Inc	Holyoke	MA	D	413 536-5432	11628
Guardian Indus Pdts Inc Mass	Norfolk	MA	G	508 384-0060	13660
Hartwell Assoicates	Cambridge	MA	G	617 686-7571	9501
Hudson Poly Bag Inc	Hudson	MA	F	978 562-7566	11776
Hytex Industries Inc	Randolph	MA	E	781 963-4400	14686
Inteplast Group Corporation	North Dighton	MA	F	508 880-7640	13932
JP Plastics Inc	Bridgewater	MA	G	508 697-4202	9080
K2w LLC	Waltham	MA	G	617 818-2613	16136
Laddawn Inc **(HQ)**	Devens	MA	D	800 446-3639	10322
Micron Plastics Inc	Ayer	MA	F	978 772-6900	7926
New England Extrusion Inc	Turners Falls	MA	C	413 863-3171	15884
New England Plastics Corp **(PA)**	Woburn	MA	E	781 933-6004	17243
New England Plastics Corp	New Bedford	MA	E	508 995-7334	13424
Nordic Shield Plastic Corp	Oxford	MA	G	508 987-5361	14270
Packaging Products Corporation **(PA)**	New Bedford	MA	F	508 997-5150	13434
Polyvinyl Films Inc	Sutton	MA	D	508 865-3558	15690
Sika Sarnafil Inc **(HQ)**	Canton	MA	C	781 828-5400	9780
Specialized Plastics Inc	Hudson	MA	E	978 562-9314	11819
Swm International	Greenfield	MA	G	413 774-3772	11279
Tekni-Plex Inc	Ashland	MA	F	508 881-2440	7671
Tel Epion Inc	Billerica	MA	E	978 436-2300	8302
Walter Drake Inc **(PA)**	Holyoke	MA	G	413 536-5463	11666
Ward Process Inc	Holliston	MA	D	508 429-1165	11613
Wbc Extrusion Products Inc **(HQ)**	Haverhill	MA	E	978 469-0668	11485
Zatec LLC	North Dighton	MA	E	508 880-3388	13939
Shrinkfast Marketing	Newport	NH	D	603 863-7719	19358
Textiles Coated Incorporated **(PA)**	Londonderry	NH	D	603 296-2221	18741
Dewal Industries LLC	Narragansett	RI	C	401 789-9736	20637
Nelipak Corporation **(PA)**	Cranston	RI	D	401 946-2699	20267
Teknor Apex Company **(PA)**	Pawtucket	RI	B	401 725-8000	20903
Trico Specialty Films LLC	North Kingstown	RI	F	401 294-7022	20746
Alpa Incorporated	Essex Junction	VT	G	802 662-8401	21928
Astenjohnson Inc	Williston	VT	D	802 658-2040	22655

3082 Plastic Unsupported Profile Shapes

	CITY	ST	EMP	PHONE	ENTRY #
Cebal Americas **(PA)**	Norwalk	CT	G	203 845-6356	3121
East Coast Precision Mfg LLC	Killingworth	CT	G	978 887-5920	1926
Plastic Factory LLC	Bridgeport	CT	G	203 908-3468	470
Polymedex Discovery Group Inc **(PA)**	Putnam	CT	F	860 928-4102	3627
Putnam Plastics Corporation	Dayville	CT	C	860 774-1559	1051
Web Industries Hartford Inc **(HQ)**	Dayville	CT	E	860 779-3197	1055
Argos Corporation	Taunton	MA	F	508 828-5900	15726
Coorstek Inc	Worcester	MA	B	774 317-2600	17360
Insultab Inc	Woburn	MA	D	781 935-0800	17203
Kilder Corporation	North Billerica	MA	E	978 663-8800	13830
Plasti-Graphics Inc	Lynn	MA	G	781 599-7766	12533
Saint-Gobain Abrasives Inc **(DH)**	Worcester	MA	A	508 795-5000	17464
Samar Co Inc	Stoughton	MA	D	781 297-7264	15620
Seymour Associates Inc	Hudson	MA	G	978 562-1373	11815
David Michaud	Winthrop	ME	G	207 377-8037	7280
Nordson Medical (nh) Inc **(HQ)**	Salem	NH	C	603 327-0600	19756
Teleflex Incorporated	Jaffrey	NH	E	603 532-7706	18479
Tfx Medical Incorporated	Jaffrey	NH	B	603 532-7706	18480
Hitachi Cable America Inc	Ashaway	RI	C	401 315-5100	20038

3083 Plastic Laminated Plate & Sheet

	CITY	ST	EMP	PHONE	ENTRY #
Alcat Incorporated	Milford	CT	E	203 878-0648	2240
Aptar Inc	Torrington	CT	G	860 489-6249	4562
Beckson Manufacturing Inc **(PA)**	Bridgeport	CT	E	203 366-3644	381
CT Composites & Marine Svc LLC	South Windsor	CT	G	860 282-0100	3955
Diba Industries Inc **(HQ)**	Danbury	CT	C	203 744-0773	901
Hicks and Otis Prints Inc	Norwalk	CT	E	203 846-2087	3168
New Precision Technology LLC	Madison	CT	G	800 243-4565	1969
Panolam Industries Inc **(HQ)**	Shelton	CT	E	203 925-1556	3848
Pioneer Plastics Corporation **(HQ)**	Shelton	CT	D	203 925-1556	3853
Polymedex Discovery Group Inc **(PA)**	Putnam	CT	F	860 928-4102	3627
Quality Name Plate Inc	East Glastonbury	CT	D	860 633-9495	1114
The E J Davis Company	North Haven	CT	E	203 239-5391	3063
3M Company	Chelmsford	MA	C	978 256-3911	9865
Bixby International Corp	Newburyport	MA	D	978 462-4100	13473

	CITY	ST	EMP	PHONE	ENTRY #
Fort Hill Sign Products Inc	Hopedale	MA	G	781 321-4320	11672
General Woodworking Inc **(PA)**	Lowell	MA	F	978 458-6625	12373
Geonautics Manufacturing Inc	Newburyport	MA	E	978 462-7161	13494
H Loeb Corporation	New Bedford	MA	E	508 996-3745	13392
High Speed Routing LLC	Haverhill	MA	G	603 527-8027	11441
Insultab Inc	Woburn	MA	D	781 935-0800	17203
M M Newman Corporation	Marblehead	MA	F	781 631-7100	12687
October Company Inc	Easthampton	MA	E	413 529-0718	10573
Pilgrim Badge & Label Corp	Brockton	MA	D	508 436-6300	9171
Samar Co Inc	Stoughton	MA	D	781 297-7264	15620
United Plastic Fabricating Inc **(PA)**	North Andover	MA	D	978 975-4520	13734
Advanced Building Products Inc	Sanford	ME	F	207 490-2306	6870
Panolam Industries Intl Inc	Auburn	ME	E	207 784-9111	5586
Pioneer Plastics Corporation	Auburn	ME	C	207 784-9111	5591
Pioneer Plastics Corporation	Auburn	ME	B	207 784-9111	5592
York Manufacturing Inc	Sanford	ME	F	207 324-1300	6898
American Marine Products Inc	Charlestown	NH	E	954 782-1400	17810
Kalwall Corporation **(PA)**	Manchester	NH	B	603 627-3861	18854
Nordson Medical (nh) Inc **(HQ)**	Salem	NH	C	603 327-0600	19756
Plasti-Clip Corporation	Milford	NH	F	603 672-1166	19072
Riley Mountain Products Inc	Antrim	NH	F	603 588-7234	17597
Scandia Plastics Inc	Plaistow	NH	E	603 382-6533	19523
Spaulding Composites Inc **(PA)**	Rochester	NH	D	603 332-0555	19687
Teleflex Incorporated	Jaffrey	NH	E	603 532-7706	18479
Tfx Medical Incorporated	Jaffrey	NH	B	603 532-7706	18480
Nelipak Corporation **(PA)**	Cranston	RI	D	401 946-2699	20267
Neptco Incorporated **(HQ)**	Pawtucket	RI	D	401 722-5500	20863
Tpi Inc	Warren	RI	D	401 247-4010	21310
Tpi Composites Inc	Warren	RI	G	401 247-4010	21311
Kaman Composites - Vermont Inc	Bennington	VT	C	802 442-9964	21678

3084 Plastic Pipe

	CITY	ST	EMP	PHONE	ENTRY #
Advanced Drainage Systems Inc	Rocky Hill	CT	E	860 529-8188	3701
Monarch Plastic LLC	Granby	CT	F	860 653-2000	1590
Virginia Industries Inc **(PA)**	Rocky Hill	CT	G	860 571-3600	3733
Advanced Drainage Systems Inc	Ludlow	MA	E	413 589-0515	12452
Applied Nnstrctred Sltions LLC	Billerica	MA	E	978 670-6959	8211
Asahi/America Inc **(HQ)**	Lawrence	MA	C	781 321-5409	11995
Asahi/America Inc	Lawrence	MA	G	800 343-3618	11996
Brand Dielectrics Inc	Taunton	MA	G	508 828-1200	15734
Cabot Corporation **(PA)**	Boston	MA	C	617 345-0100	8452
Cabot Corporation	Haverhill	MA	C	978 556-8400	11413
Fiberspar Spoolable Products **(PA)**	West Wareham	MA	E	508 291-9000	16572
Orion Enterprises Inc **(HQ)**	North Andover	MA	C	913 342-1653	13722
Orion Fittings Inc	North Andover	MA	G	978 689-6150	13723
Contech Engnered Solutions LLC	Scarborough	ME	E	207 885-9830	6915
Hancor Inc	Springfield	VT	E	802 886-8403	22501

3085 Plastic Bottles

	CITY	ST	EMP	PHONE	ENTRY #
Ansa Company Inc	Norwalk	CT	F	203 687-1664	3101
Green Egg Design LLC	Hartford	CT	G	860 541-5411	1828
Mayborn Usa Inc	Stamford	CT	F	781 269-7490	4245
Packaging Concepts Assoc LLC	Torrington	CT	G	860 489-0480	4591
Silgan Holdings Inc **(PA)**	Stamford	CT	C	203 975-7110	4321
Camco Manufacturing Inc	Leominster	MA	F	978 537-6777	12123
Maine Container LLC	Poland	ME	E	603 888-1315	6594
Quality Containers of Neng	Yarmouth	ME	G	207 846-5420	7299
Carr Management Inc **(PA)**	Nashua	NH	F	603 888-1315	19131
Devtech Pet Inc **(PA)**	Amherst	NH	E	603 889-8311	17556
Foxx Life Sciences LLC	Salem	NH	F	603 890-3699	19736
Plastic Industries Inc **(HQ)**	Nashua	NH	D	603 888-1315	19234
Preforms Plus	Nashua	NH	G	603 889-8311	19101
Plastic Technologies MD Inc	South Burlington	VT	G	802 658-6588	22459
Plastic Technologies NY LLC	South Burlington	VT	G	802 658-6588	22460

3086 Plastic Foam Prdts

	CITY	ST	EMP	PHONE	ENTRY #
Ansonia Plastics LLC	Ansonia	CT	D	203 736-5200	7
Claremont Sales Corporation	Durham	CT	E	860 349-4499	1089
Covit America Inc	Watertown	CT	B	860 274-6791	5004
Duz Manufacturing Inc	Milford	CT	G	203 874-1032	2278
Fc Meyer Packaging LLC **(HQ)**	Norwalk	CT	D	203 847-8500	3150
Foam Plastics New England Inc	Waterbury	CT	G	203 758-6651	4874
General Packaging Products Inc	Norwalk	CT	G	203 846-1340	3160
Gilman Corporation	Gilman	CT	E	860 887-7080	1534
H-O Products Corporation	Winsted	CT	E	860 379-9875	5412
Hhc LLC	Manchester	CT	E	860 456-0677	2008
HI-Tech Packaging Inc	Stratford	CT	E	203 378-2700	4420
Hopp Companies Inc	Newtown	CT	F	800 889-8425	2924
Hydrofera LLC	Manchester	CT	D	860 456-0677	2010
Madison Polymeric Engrg Inc	Branford	CT	E	203 488-4554	330
Merrill Industries Inc	Ellington	CT	E	860 871-1888	1336
New England Foam Products LLC **(PA)**	Hartford	CT	E	860 524-0121	1851
Paxxus Inc	Bloomfield	CT	E	860 242-0663	250
Plastic Forming Company Inc **(PA)**	Woodbridge	CT	E	203 397-1338	5476
Preferred Foam Products Inc	Clinton	CT	G	860 669-3626	793
Reilly Foam Corp	Bloomfield	CT	E	860 243-8200	256
Sealed Air Corporation	Danbury	CT	C	203 791-3648	988
Sonoco Prtective Solutions Inc	Putnam	CT	E	860 928-7795	3634
Sprayfoampolymerscom LLC	Wilton	CT	G	800 853-1577	5304
Universal Foam Products LLC	Bloomfield	CT	F	860 216-3015	270
Vibrascience Inc	Branford	CT	G	203 483-6113	356
Architects of Packaging Inc	Westfield	MA	G	413 568-3187	16667
Ashworth International Inc	Fall River	MA	G	508 674-4693	10664
Bbmc Inc	Hancock	MA	F	413 443-3333	11324
Concrete Block Insulating Syst	West Brookfield	MA	E	508 867-4241	16466
Danvers Industrial Packg Corp	Beverly	MA	E	978 777-0020	8124
Desco Industries Inc	Canton	MA	E	781 821-8370	9726
Flexcon Industrial LLC **(HQ)**	Spencer	MA	E	210 798-1900	15430
Foam Concepts Inc	Uxbridge	MA	E	508 278-7255	15917
Fuller Box Co Inc **(PA)**	North Attleboro	MA	D	508 695-2525	13756
Future Foam Inc	Mansfield	MA	F	508 339-0354	12633
Geonautics Manufacturing Inc	Newburyport	MA	E	978 462-7161	13494
Georgia-Pacific LLC	Leominster	MA	C	978 537-4701	12144
Horn Corporation **(PA)**	Lancaster	MA	E	800 832-7020	11984
Imanova Packaging	Leominster	MA	D	978 537-8534	12154
Innocor Foam Technical	Newburyport	MA	F	978 462-5400	13500
Insulation Technology Inc	Bridgewater	MA	G	508 697-6926	9077
Jeffco Fibres Inc **(PA)**	Webster	MA	C	508 943-0440	16345
Lelanite Corporation **(PA)**	Webster	MA	E	508 987-2637	16346
Liberty Packaging Co Inc	Braintree	MA	G	781 849-3355	9023
Osaap America LLC	Chelmsford	MA	G	877 652-7227	9919
Packaging Products Corporation **(PA)**	New Bedford	MA	F	508 997-5150	13434
Polyfoam Corp	Northbridge	MA	D	508 234-6323	14058
Rogers Foam Automotive Corp	Somerville	MA	F	617 623-3010	15211
Rogers Foam Corporation **(PA)**	Somerville	MA	B	617 623-3010	15212
Sealed Air Corporation	Holyoke	MA	D	413 534-0231	11656
Splash Shield Inc	Woburn	MA	G	781 935-8844	17300
Trelleborg Offshore Boston Inc	Randolph	MA	D	774 719-1400	14699
Trexel Inc	Wilmington	MA	E	781 932-0202	17059
Ufp Technologies Inc **(PA)**	Newburyport	MA	E	978 352-2200	13544
Ufp Technologies Inc	Haverhill	MA	F	978 352-2200	11480
Waddington North America Inc	Chelmsford	MA	C	978 256-6551	9941
Ward Process Inc	Holliston	MA	D	508 429-1165	11613
Wood Products Unlimited Inc	Methuen	MA	G	978 687-7449	13048
Carlisle Construction Mtls LLC	Portland	ME	C	888 746-1114	6631
Deepwater Buoyancy Inc	Biddeford	ME	F	207 468-2565	5728
Der-Tex Corporation	Saco	ME	E	207 284-5931	6846
Enefco International Inc **(PA)**	Auburn	ME	D	207 514-7218	5561
Johns Manville Corporation	Saco	ME	E	207 283-8000	6850
Rynel Inc **(DH)**	Wiscasset	ME	D	207 882-0200	7287
Index Packaging Inc	Milton	NH	C	603 350-0018	19086
Langer Associates Inc	Manchester	NH	E	603 626-4388	18859
Robert A Collins	Fremont	NH	G	603 895-2345	18180
Wayne Manufacturing Inds LLC	Brentwood	NH	E	978 416-0899	17761
Branch River Plastics Inc	Smithfield	RI	E	401 232-0270	21214
Lance Industries Inc **(PA)**	Lincoln	RI	D	401 365-6272	20578
MH Stallman Company Inc **(PA)**	Providence	RI	E	401 331-5129	21067
Providence Spillproof Cntrs	Providence	RI	G	401 723-4900	21099
Tex Flock Inc	Woonsocket	RI	E	401 765-2340	21586
Spring Fill	South Burlington	VT	F	802 846-5900	22466

3087 Custom Compounding Of Purchased Plastic Resins

	CITY	ST	EMP	PHONE	ENTRY #
Electric Cable Compounds Inc	Naugatuck	CT	D	203 723-2590	2472
Foster Corporation **(HQ)**	Putnam	CT	D	860 928-4102	3613
Neu Spclty Engineered Mtls LLC	North Haven	CT	F	203 239-9629	3043
Performance Compounding Inc	Pawcatuck	CT	G	860 599-5616	3440
Pioneer Plastics Corporation **(HQ)**	Shelton	CT	D	203 925-1556	3853
Clariant Plas Coatings USA LLC	Holden	MA	D	508 829-6321	11543
Mexichem Spcalty Compounds Inc **(HQ)**	Leominster	MA	C	978 537-8071	12166
Shield Packaging Co Inc	Dudley	MA	D	508 949-0900	10384
Neal Specialty Compounding LLC	Lewiston	ME	D	207 777-1122	6309
Pioneer Plastics Corporation	Auburn	ME	B	207 784-9111	5592
New Hampshire Stamping Co Inc	Goffstown	NH	E	603 641-1234	18206
Visual Polymer Tech LLC	Bedford	NH	F	603 488-5064	17666
Daikin U S Corporation	Warwick	RI	G	401 738-0261	21347
Elite Custom Compounding Inc	Warwick	RI	G	401 921-2136	21359
Polymer Solutions Inc	Pawtucket	RI	G	401 423-1638	20881
Teknor Apex Company **(PA)**	Pawtucket	RI	B	401 725-8000	20903
Teknor Prfmce Elastomers Inc	Pawtucket	RI	G	401 725-8000	20905

3088 Plastic Plumbing Fixtures

	CITY	ST	EMP	PHONE	ENTRY #
Neoperl Inc	Waterbury	CT	D	203 756-8891	4926
New Resources Group Inc	Bridgeport	CT	G	203 366-1000	457
Syn-Mar Products Inc	Ellington	CT	F	860 872-8505	1341
Trumbull Recreation Supply Co	Willington	CT	G	860 429-6604	5271
Roma Marble Inc	Ludlow	MA	E	413 583-5017	12476
Toto USA Holdings Inc	Boston	MA	G	617 227-1321	8888
Eco Services LLC	Durham	NH	G	603 682-0963	18076
Water Structures LLC	Seabrook	NH	G	603 474-0615	19822
Hancor Inc	Springfield	VT	E	802 886-8403	22501

3089 Plastic Prdts

	CITY	ST	EMP	PHONE	ENTRY #
AA & B Co	West Haven	CT	G	203 933-9110	5107
Aba-PGT Inc **(PA)**	Manchester	CT	C	860 649-4591	1980

	CITY	ST	EMP	PHONE	ENTRY #
Aba-PGT Inc	Vernon Rockville	CT	G	860 872-2058	4677
Able Coil and Electronics Co	Bolton	CT	E	860 646-5686	273
Accumold Technologies Inc	Bridgeport	CT	G	203 384-9256	366
Accurate Mold Company Inc	Cromwell	CT	G	860 301-1988	842
Ace Technical Plastics Inc	Hartford	CT	G	860 278-2444	1801
Advance Mold & Mfg Inc	Manchester	CT	C	860 432-5887	1983
Advance Mold Mfg Inc	Ellington	CT	G	860 783-5024	1326
Aero-Med Molding Technologies **(PA)**	Ansonia	CT	F	203 735-2331	4
All-Time Manufacturing Co Inc	Montville	CT	F	860 848-9258	2421
Althor Products LLC	Windsor Locks	CT	G	860 386-6700	5385
American Molded Products Inc	Bridgeport	CT	F	203 333-0183	374
American Plastic Products Inc	Waterbury	CT	C	203 596-2410	4841
Anderson David C & Assoc LLC **(PA)**	Enfield	CT	F	860 749-7547	1346
Apex Machine Tool Company Inc	Cheshire	CT	D	860 677-2884	711
Aptargroup Inc	Stratford	CT	B	203 377-8100	4391
Architectural Supplements LLC	Waterbury	CT	F	203 591-5505	4845
Armor Box Company LLC	Bloomfield	CT	G	860 242-9981	203
Asti Company Inc	Torrington	CT	G	860 482-2675	4563
Atlas Hobbing and Tool Co Inc	Vernon Rockville	CT	F	860 870-9226	4678
Awm LLC	Windsor Locks	CT	D	860 386-1000	5386
Balfor Industries Inc	Oxford	CT	F	203 828-6473	3391
Bennice Molding Co	Meriden	CT	G	203 440-2543	2079
Better Molded Products Inc **(PA)**	Bristol	CT	C	860 589-0066	534
Betz Tool Company Inc	Milford	CT	G	203 878-1187	2253
Bey-Low Molds	Torrington	CT	G	860 482-6561	4565
Bidwell Industrial Group Inc **(PA)**	Middletown	CT	E	860 346-9283	2178
Bprex Halthcare Brookville Inc	Waterbury	CT	C	203 754-4141	4851
Brighton & Hove Mold Ltd	Oxford	CT	G	203 264-3013	3392
C Cowles & Company **(PA)**	North Haven	CT	D	203 865-3117	3012
Canevari Plastics Inc	Milford	CT	G	203 878-4319	2260
Carpin Manufacturing Inc	Waterbury	CT	D	203 574-2556	4854
CKS Packaging Inc	Naugatuck	CT	D	203 729-0716	2466
Clearly Clean Products LLC **(PA)**	South Windsor	CT	F	860 646-1040	3950
Coating Design Group Inc	Stratford	CT	E	203 878-3663	4405
Colts Plastics Company Inc	Dayville	CT	C	860 774-2277	1042
Connecticut Laminating Co Inc	New Haven	CT	D	203 787-2184	2677
Connecticut Tool Co Inc	Putnam	CT	E	860 928-0565	3606
Cool-It LLC	Wallingford	CT	G	203 284-4848	4727
Cowles Products Company Inc	North Haven	CT	D	203 865-3110	3022
Crown Molding Etc LLC	Hamden	CT	G	203 287-9424	1739
Cultec Inc	Brookfield	CT	F	203 775-4416	639
Davis-Standard LLC **(HQ)**	Pawcatuck	CT	B	860 599-1010	3432
Design Engineering Inc	Torrington	CT	G	860 482-4120	4574
Dfs In-Home Services	Danbury	CT	G	845 405-6464	900
Doss Corporation	Wethersfield	CT	G	860 721-7384	5247
Dymotek Corporation	Somers	CT	G	800 788-1984	3916
Dymotek Corporation	Ellington	CT	E	860 875-2868	1333
East Branch Engrg & Mfg Inc	New Milford	CT	F	860 355-9661	2798
Edco Industries Inc	Bridgeport	CT	F	203 333-8982	410
Empire Tool LLC	Derby	CT	G	203 735-7467	1071
Ensign-Bickford Industries Inc	Simsbury	CT	E	860 658-4411	3905
Ensinger Prcsion Cmponents Inc	Putnam	CT	D	860 928-7911	3611
Entegris Inc	Danbury	CT	B	800 766-2681	912
F F Screw Products Inc	Southington	CT	E	860 621-4567	4049
Farrel Corporation **(DH)**	Ansonia	CT	D	203 736-5500	15
Fiberglass Engr & Design Co	Wallingford	CT	G	203 265-1644	4743
Fimor North America Inc **(HQ)**	Cheshire	CT	E	203 272-3219	733
Flagship Converters Inc	Danbury	CT	D	203 792-0034	920
Fluoropolymer Resources LLC **(PA)**	East Hartford	CT	G	860 423-7622	1195
Form-All Plastics Corporation	Meriden	CT	G	203 634-1137	2093
Fsm Plasticoid Mfg Inc	East Windsor	CT	F	860 623-1361	1284
GP Industries	Taftville	CT	G	860 859-9938	4470
Hawk Integrated Plastics LLC	Columbia	CT	F	860 337-0310	818
Hexcel Corporation **(PA)**	Stamford	CT	E	203 969-0666	4213
Hosokawa Micron Intl Inc	Berlin	CT	E	860 828-0541	89
Idemia Identity & SEC USA LLC	Rocky Hill	CT	G	860 529-2559	3717
Idex Health & Science LLC	Bristol	CT	C	860 314-2880	570
Illinois Tool Works Inc	Lakeville	CT	E	860 435-2574	1930
Injectech Engineering LLC **(PA)**	New Hartford	CT	G	860 379-9781	2641
Inline Plastics Corp **(PA)**	Shelton	CT	C	203 924-5933	3819
J&L Plastic Molding LLC	Wallingford	CT	G	203 265-6237	4758
Jarden Corporation	Oxford	CT	G	203 264-9717	3410
Jarden LLC	Norwalk	CT	E	203 845-5300	3179
Jor Services LLC	New Canaan	CT	G	203 594-7774	2602
K-Tec LLC	Thomaston	CT	G	860 283-8875	4507
Kensco Inc **(PA)**	Ansonia	CT	F	203 734-8827	20
Kinamor Incorporated	Wallingford	CT	E	203 269-0380	4760
Lacey Manufacturing Co LLC	Bridgeport	CT	B	203 336-7427	443
Lawrence Holdings Inc **(PA)**	Wallingford	CT	F	203 949-1600	4764
Lehvoss North America LLC	Pawcatuck	CT	F	860 495-2046	3438
Lingol Corporation	Wallingford	CT	F	203 265-3608	4766
Little Bits Manufacturing Inc	North Grosvenordale	CT	G	860 923-2772	2998
Lorex Plastics Co Inc	Norwalk	CT	G	203 286-0020	3188
Manchester Molding and Mfg Co	Manchester	CT	E	860 643-2141	2023
Marlborough Plastics Inc	Marlborough	CT	G	860 295-9124	2066
Mbsw Inc	West Hartford	CT	D	860 243-0303	5086
Mdm Products LLC	Milford	CT	F	203 877-7070	2314
Meriden Precision Plastics LLC	Meriden	CT	G	203 235-3261	2105
Merritt Extruder Corp	Hamden	CT	E	203 230-8100	1770
Mohawk Tool and Die Mfg Co Inc	Bridgeport	CT	F	203 367-2181	452
Mold Threads Inc	Branford	CT	G	203 483-1420	331
Molding Technologies LLC	Old Saybrook	CT	G	860 395-3230	3345
Monarch Plastic LLC	Granby	CT	F	860 653-2000	1590
MPS Plastics Incorporated	Marlborough	CT	E	860 295-1161	2067
Nevamar Company LLC **(HQ)**	Shelton	CT	B	203 925-1556	3837
Newhart Plastics Inc	Milford	CT	G	203 877-5367	2321
Orbit Design LLC	Meriden	CT	F	203 393-0171	2114
Packaging and Crating Tech LLC	Waterbury	CT	G	203 759-1799	4933
Panolam Industries Inc **(HQ)**	Shelton	CT	E	203 925-1556	3848
Panolam Industries Intl Inc **(PA)**	Shelton	CT	E	203 925-1556	3849
Paragon Products Inc	Old Saybrook	CT	G	860 388-1363	3346
Park-PMC Liquidation Corp	Putnam	CT	E	860 928-0401	3626
Pel Associates LLC **(PA)**	Groton	CT	G	860 446-9921	1683
Plastic Design Intl Inc **(PA)**	Middletown	CT	E	860 632-2001	2210
Plastic Forming Company Inc **(PA)**	Woodbridge	CT	E	203 397-1338	5476
Plastic Molding Technology	Seymour	CT	G	203 881-1811	3760
Plastic Solutions LLC	Bethlehem	CT	G	203 266-5675	198
Plasticoid Manufacturing Inc	East Windsor	CT	E	860 623-1361	1298
Plastics and Concepts Conn Inc	Glastonbury	CT	F	860 657-9655	1572
Polymer Engineered Pdts Inc **(PA)**	Stamford	CT	D	203 324-3737	4287
Polymeric Converting LLC	Enfield	CT	E	860 623-1335	1375
Polymold Corp	Cheshire	CT	F	203 272-2622	753
Polytronics Corporation	Windsor	CT	G	860 683-2442	5355
Precision Engineered Pdts LLC	Wallingford	CT	E	203 265-3299	4789
Precision Plastic Fab	Brookfield	CT	G	203 775-7047	657
Precision Plastic Products Inc	Portland	CT	F	860 342-2233	3571
Prospect Products Incorporated	Newington	CT	E	860 666-0323	2896
Prototype Plastic Mold Co Inc	Middletown	CT	E	860 632-2800	2214
Pucuda Inc	Madison	CT	F	860 526-8004	1972
Quatum Inc	Hartford	CT	G	860 666-3464	1864
Quest Plastics Inc	Torrington	CT	F	860 489-1404	4595
RES-Tech Corporation	Berlin	CT	D	860 828-1504	107
Rogers Manufacturing Company	Rockfall	CT	D	860 346-8648	3699
Savetime Corporation	Bridgeport	CT	F	203 382-2991	486
Scan Tool & Mold Inc	Trumbull	CT	E	203 459-4950	4631
Schaeffler Aerospace USA Corp **(DH)**	Danbury	CT	B	203 744-2211	984
Select Plastics LLC	Norwalk	CT	G	203 866-3767	3240
Selectives LLC	Thomaston	CT	G	860 585-1956	4514
Shaeffer Plastic Mfg Corp	Colchester	CT	G	860 537-5524	808
Siemon Company **(PA)**	Watertown	CT	A	860 945-4200	5024
Siftex Equipment Company	South Windsor	CT	E	860 289-8779	4009
Signs Unlimited Inc	Derby	CT	G	203 734-7446	1080
Silgan Holdings Inc **(PA)**	Stamford	CT	C	203 975-7110	4321
Silgan Plastics LLC	Deep River	CT	C	860 526-6300	1066
Somerset Plastics Company	Middletown	CT	E	860 635-1601	2224
Southpack LLC	New Britain	CT	E	860 224-2242	2577
Spartech LLC	Stamford	CT	C	203 327-6010	4327
Standard Washer & Mat Inc	Manchester	CT	E	860 643-5125	2051
Stelray Plastic Products Inc	Ansonia	CT	E	203 735-2331	23
Super Seal Corp	Stratford	CT	F	203 378-5015	4451
Swpc Plastics LLC	Deep River	CT	C	860 526-3200	1067
Technical Industries Inc **(PA)**	Torrington	CT	D	860 489-2160	4600
Technology Plastics LLC	Terryville	CT	F	806 583-1590	4493
Tops Manufacturing Co Inc **(PA)**	Darien	CT	G	203 655-9367	1034
Trento Group LLC	East Windsor	CT	G	860 623-1361	1308
TWC Trans World Consulting	Windsor Locks	CT	G	860 668-5108	5402
United Plastics Technologies	New Britain	CT	F	860 224-1110	2588
Upc LLC	Meriden	CT	G	877 466-1137	2146
Vanguard Plastics Corporation	Southington	CT	E	860 628-4736	4089
Vision Technical Molding	Manchester	CT	G	860 783-5050	2057
Watertown Plastics Inc	Watertown	CT	E	860 274-7535	5035
Wepco Plastics Inc	Middlefield	CT	E	860 349-3407	2168
Wilkinson Tool & Die Co	North Stonington	CT	G	860 599-5821	3077
3dfortify Inc	Boston	MA	G	978 399-4075	8329
A & J Industries LLC	Uxbridge	MA	F	508 278-4531	15912
A A Plastic & Met Fabricators	Danvers	MA	G	978 777-0367	10188
A Schulman Custom Compounding	Worcester	MA	C	508 756-0002	17330
Absolute Haitian Corporation **(PA)**	Worcester	MA	F	508 459-5372	17333
Accellent Holdings Corp	Wilmington	MA	A	978 570-6900	16962
Accutech Packaging Inc	Foxboro	MA	D	508 543-3800	10873
Accutech Packaging Inc	Mansfield	MA	F	508 543-3800	12610
Ace Moulding Co Inc	Monson	MA	G	413 267-4875	13201
Advance Plastics Inc	Oxford	MA	G	508 987-7235	14252
Advanced Prototypes & Molding	Leominster	MA	G	978 534-0584	12107
Agi Polymatrix LLC **(HQ)**	Pittsfield	MA	D	413 499-3550	14449
Air-Tite Holders Inc	North Adams	MA	F	413 664-2730	13667
Albright Technologies Inc	Leominster	MA	F	978 466-5870	12111
Aline Systems Inc	Marblehead	MA	G	781 990-1462	12673
Alsco Industries Inc	Sturbridge	MA	D	508 347-1199	15637
Alumi-Nex Mold Inc	Webster	MA	F	508 949-2200	16338
Amaray Plastics	Pittsfield	MA	F	413 499-3550	14451
Americad Technology Corporat	Norwood	MA	E	781 551-8220	14126
American Marketing & Sales	Leominster	MA	G	978 514-8929	12113

	CITY	ST	EMP	PHONE	ENTRY #
American Molding Corporation	Leominster	MA	G	978 534-0009	12114
Andrew Rolden PC	Ayer	MA	G	978 391-4655	7909
Apex Resource Technologies Inc	Pittsfield	MA	D	413 442-1414	14452
Apothecary Products LLC	North Attleboro	MA	E	508 695-0727	13745
Applied Plastic Technology Inc	Worcester	MA	E	508 752-5924	17340
Armstrong Mold Corporation	Hingham	MA	G	781 749-3207	11492
Asahi/America Inc **(HQ)**	Lawrence	MA	C	781 321-5409	11995
Atco Plastics Inc	Plainville	MA	D	508 695-3573	14515
Atlantic Auto & Trck Parts LLC	Peabody	MA	G	978 535-6777	14314
Atom Marketing Inc **(PA)**	Hanover	MA	G	781 982-9930	11327
Axygen Bioscience Inc	Tewksbury	MA	A	978 442-2200	15808
Bacon Industries Inc	Wrentham	MA	F	508 384-0780	17515
Bandera Acquisition LLC **(DH)**	Foxborough	MA	C	480 553-6400	10911
Benoit & Company	Palmer	MA	G	413 283-8348	14280
Berry Global Inc	Franklin	MA	C	508 918-1715	11026
Berry Global Inc	Easthampton	MA	C	812 424-2904	10555
Berry Global Inc	Nantucket	MA	G	508 325-0004	13221
Berry Plastics Corp	Easthampton	MA	F	413 529-2183	10556
Berry Plastics Corporation	Easthampton	MA	G	413 527-1250	10557
Bertoldo Inc	Wakefield	MA	G	781 324-9145	15944
Big Dog Disposal Inc	Seekonk	MA	G	508 695-9539	15019
Big Rock Oyster Company Inc	Harwich	MA	G	774 408-7951	11389
Billy Hill Tubs LLC	Sterling	MA	G	978 422-8800	15536
Biomedical Polymers Inc	Sterling	MA	D	978 632-2555	15537
Bixby International Corp	Newburyport	MA	D	978 462-4100	13473
Black Diamond Mfg & Engrg Inc	Georgetown	MA	F	978 352-6716	11137
Brenmar Molding Inc	Fitchburg	MA	G	978 343-3198	10814
Broadstone Industries	Lowell	MA	G	978 691-2790	12356
Budgetcard Inc	Attleboro Falls	MA	F	508 695-8762	7811
Built-Rite Tool and Die Inc **(PA)**	Lancaster	MA	E	978 368-7250	11982
Bway Corporation	Leominster	MA	F	978 537-4911	12121
C & C Lamination	Chicopee	MA	G	413 594-6910	10004
C & C Thermoforming Inc	Palmer	MA	G	413 289-1900	14282
Cado Manufacturing Inc	Fitchburg	MA	F	978 343-2989	10816
Cardinal Comb & Brush Mfg Corp	Leominster	MA	E	978 537-6330	12125
Castle Plastics Inc	Leominster	MA	G	978 534-6220	12126
CDF Corporation **(PA)**	Plymouth	MA	D	508 747-5858	14550
Chatham Plastic Ventures Inc	Brockton	MA	E	518 392-5761	9130
Clean Products LLC	Fall River	MA	G	508 676-9355	10675
Cmt Materials Inc	Attleboro	MA	F	508 226-3901	7721
Consolidated Cont Holdings LLC	Marlborough	MA	F	508 485-2109	12740
Consolidated Container Co LLC	Franklin	MA	B	508 520-8800	11031
Cool Gear International LLC	Plymouth	MA	D	508 830-3440	14551
Cordmaster Engineering Co Inc	North Adams	MA	E	413 664-9371	13671
Covalnce Spcalty Adhesives LLC	Franklin	MA	C	812 424-2904	11033
Creative Extrusion & Tech Inc	Brockton	MA	E	508 587-2290	9134
Crisci Tool and Die Inc	Leominster	MA	E	978 537-4102	12128
Dan-Kar Plastics Products	Woburn	MA	G	781 935-9221	17163
Dela Incorporated **(PA)**	Haverhill	MA	E	978 372-7783	11424
Design Mark Industries Inc	Wareham	MA	D	800 451-3275	16244
Di-MO Manufacturing Inc	Middleboro	MA	G	508 947-2200	13062
Diamond Windows Doors Mfg Inc	Boston	MA	E	617 282-1688	8503
Donahue Industries Inc	Shrewsbury	MA	E	508 845-6501	15108
Dorel Juvenile Group Inc	Foxboro	MA	D	800 544-1108	10881
Double A Plastics Co Inc	Monson	MA	G	413 267-4403	13206
Dupont Packaging Inc	Holyoke	MA	F	413 552-0048	11622
E F Inc	Gardner	MA	F	978 630-3800	11113
Elkay Plastics	Woburn	MA	G	781 932-9800	17176
Elm Industries Inc	West Springfield	MA	E	413 734-7762	16518
Enginred Plas Sltons Group Inc	Norwood	MA	G	781 762-3913	14148
Entegris Inc	Bedford	MA	E	978 436-6575	7975
Entegris Inc **(PA)**	Billerica	MA	A	978 436-6500	8246
Ezra J Leboff Co Inc	Brighton	MA	G	617 783-4200	9098
F & D Plastics Inc **(PA)**	Leominster	MA	E	978 668-5140	12136
F & M Tool & Plastics Inc	Leominster	MA	D	978 840-1897	12138
Fall River Tool & Die Co Inc	Fall River	MA	F	508 674-4621	10699
Fiberglass Building Pdts Inc	Halifax	MA	G	847 650-3045	11318
Fibertec Inc	Bridgewater	MA	D	508 697-5100	9073
Final Forge LLC	Plymouth	MA	G	857 244-0764	14557
First Plastics Corp	Leominster	MA	F	978 537-0367	12139
Flagraphics Inc	Somerville	MA	E	617 776-7549	15172
Fort Hill Sign Products Inc	Hopedale	MA	G	781 321-4320	11672
Fraen Corporation **(PA)**	Reading	MA	C	781 205-5300	14734
Fusion Optix Inc	Woburn	MA	E	781 995-0805	17189
G and W Precision	South Deerfield	MA	G	413 397-3361	15249
G and W Precision Inc	Whately	MA	G	413 665-0983	16905
G&F Medical Inc	Fiskdale	MA	E	978 560-2622	10806
G&F Precision Molding Inc **(PA)**	Fiskdale	MA	D	508 347-9132	10807
Girouard Tool & Die Inc	Leominster	MA	G	978 534-4147	12146
Glass Molders Pottery Pla	Milford	MA	G	508 634-2932	13119
Globe Composite Solutions Ltd	Stoughton	MA	D	781 871-3700	15594
Governor Supply Co	Lancaster	MA	G	978 870-6888	11983
Grainpro Inc **(PA)**	Concord	MA	G	978 371-7118	10133
Great Northern Industries Inc **(PA)**	Boston	MA	C	617 262-4314	8578
Gregory Manufacturing Inc	Holyoke	MA	D	413 536-5432	11628
Gregstrom Corporation	Woburn	MA	D	781 935-6600	17194
Grove Products Inc	Leominster	MA	F	978 534-5188	12148
Handyaid Co	Feeding Hills	MA	G	413 786-9865	10799
Harpoon Productions	Cohasset	MA	G	781 383-0500	10099
Hillside Plastics Inc	Turners Falls	MA	C	413 863-2222	15879
Home Pdts Intl - N Amer Inc	Leominster	MA	C	978 534-6536	12152
Howland Tool & Machine Ltd	East Freetown	MA	G	508 763-8472	10452
Hutchison Co Advg Display	Whitinsville	MA	G	508 234-4681	16913
Hytex Industries Inc	Randolph	MA	E	781 963-4400	14686
I G Marston Company	Holbrook	MA	F	781 767-2894	11526
ID Graphics Group Inc	South Easton	MA	E	508 238-8500	15279
Idemia America Corp **(DH)**	Billerica	MA	B	978 215-2400	8255
Illinois Tool Works Inc	Raynham	MA	D	508 821-9828	14716
Illinois Tool Works Inc	Westminster	MA	C	978 874-0151	16805
Incase Inc	Holden	MA	G	508 478-6500	11545
Industrial Production Supplies	Attleboro	MA	F	508 226-1776	7749
Injected Solutions Inc	Lanesborough	MA	F	413 499-5800	11987
Innovative Mold Solutions Inc	Leominster	MA	E	978 840-1503	12155
Innovative Tooling Company Inc	Lenox	MA	F	413 637-1031	12101
Jam Plastics Inc	Leominster	MA	E	978 537-2570	12156
Jewelry Creations	Norton	MA	G	508 285-4230	14079
JMS Manufacturing Inc	Taunton	MA	F	508 675-1141	15760
John F Wielock	Dudley	MA	G	508 943-5366	10378
Jumbo Plastics Inc	Leominster	MA	F	978 537-7835	12157
K & C Industries Inc	Franklin	MA	F	508 520-4600	11059
K and C Plastics Inc	Leominster	MA	E	978 537-0605	12158
Knobby Krafters Inc	Attleboro	MA	E	508 222-7272	7757
Korolath of New England Inc **(HQ)**	Woburn	MA	G	781 933-6004	17211
Korolath of New England Inc	Hudson	MA	F	978 562-7366	11783
Krest Products Corp	Leominster	MA	E	978 537-1244	12159
Lacerta Group Inc	Mansfield	MA	G	508 339-3312	12641
Lacerta Group Inc **(PA)**	Mansfield	MA	D	508 339-3312	12642
Lakewood Industries Inc	Pittsfield	MA	D	413 499-3550	14480
Lamson and Goodnow LLC	Shelburne Falls	MA	E	413 625-0201	15073
Lansen Mold Co Inc	Hancock	MA	F	413 443-5328	11325
Larkin Motors LLC	Bridgewater	MA	G	508 807-1333	9082
LD Plastics Inc	Brockton	MA	E	508 584-7651	9161
Leaktite Corporation **(PA)**	Leominster	MA	D	978 537-8000	12160
Little Kids Inc	Seekonk	MA	E	401 454-7600	15026
Lyman Conrad **(PA)**	South Hadley	MA	E	413 538-8200	15306
M & A Plastics Inc	Dracut	MA	G	978 319-9930	10362
Mack Prototype Inc	Gardner	MA	E	978 632-3700	11119
Macneill Engineering Co Inc	Westborough	MA	E	508 481-8830	16633
Magnus Molding Inc	Pittsfield	MA	E	413 443-1192	14488
Mair-Mac Machine Company Inc	Brockton	MA	F	508 895-9001	9164
Mar-Lee Companies Inc	Fitchburg	MA	G	978 343-9600	10833
Mascon Inc	Woburn	MA	E	781 938-5800	17223
Matallurgical Perspectives	Wilbraham	MA	G	413 596-4283	16940
Mauser Packg Solutions Holdg	Leominster	MA	C	978 728-5000	12165
Mayfield Plastics Inc	Sutton	MA	E	508 865-8150	15687
Mayhew Basque Plastics LLC	Westminster	MA	F	978 537-5219	16809
Midstate Mold & Engineering	Franklin	MA	F	508 520-0011	11066
Milacron Marketing Company LLC	Rowley	MA	E	978 238-7100	14858
Mill Valley Molding Inc	West Hatfield	MA	D	413 247-9313	16483
Mill Valley Molding LLC	West Hatfield	MA	G	413 247-9313	16484
Millennium Plastics Inc	Groveland	MA	F	978 372-4822	11302
MJW Mass Inc	Winchester	MA	D	781 721-0332	17092
Modern Mold & Tool Inc **(PA)**	Pittsfield	MA	E	413 443-1192	14491
Moldmaster Engineering Inc	Pittsfield	MA	E	413 442-5793	14492
Mtd Micro Molding Inc	Charlton	MA	E	508 248-0111	9854
Multifab Plastics Inc	Dorchester	MA	F	617 287-1411	10347
Mysdispensers Inc	Roslindale	MA	G	617 327-1124	14839
N P Medical Inc	Clinton	MA	E	978 365-9721	10084
National Vinyl LLC	Chicopee	MA	E	413 420-0548	10049
Naugler Mold & Engineering	Beverly	MA	F	978 922-5634	8159
Netco Extruded Plastics Inc	Hudson	MA	E	978 562-3485	11795
Neu-Tool Design Inc	Wilmington	MA	E	978 658-5881	17029
Nevron Plastics Inc	Saugus	MA	F	781 233-1310	14991
New England Business Svc Inc **(HQ)**	Groton	MA	D	978 448-6111	11291
New England Plastics Corp	New Bedford	MA	E	508 995-7334	13424
New England Plastics Corp **(PA)**	Woburn	MA	E	781 933-6004	17243
Newell Brands Inc	East Longmeadow	MA	B	413 526-5150	10484
North/Win Ltd	Leominster	MA	G	978 537-5518	12172
Northeast Plastics Inc	Wakefield	MA	F	781 245-5512	15965
Northern Products Inc	Leominster	MA	F	978 840-3383	12173
Northern Tool Mfg Co Inc	Springfield	MA	F	413 732-5549	15494
Ntp/Republic Clear Thru Corp	Holyoke	MA	E	413 493-6800	11645
Nypro Inc	Devens	MA	G	978 784-2006	10328
Nypro Inc **(HQ)**	Clinton	MA	A	978 365-8100	10086
Onebin	Boston	MA	G	617 851-6402	8748
Orbit Plastics Corp	Danvers	MA	E	978 465-5300	10245
Orion Enterprises Inc **(HQ)**	North Andover	MA	C	913 342-1653	13722
Parallel Products of Neng **(DH)**	New Bedford	MA	G	508 884-5100	13435
Pen Ro Mold and Tool Inc	Pittsfield	MA	E	413 499-0464	14498
Pep Industries LLC	Attleboro	MA	A	508 226-5600	7776
Pepperell Braiding Company Inc **(PA)**	Pepperell	MA	E	978 433-2133	14444
Pexco LLC	Athol	MA	C	978 249-5343	7692
Phadean Engineering Co Inc	Shrewsbury	MA	G	888 204-0900	15128
Phillips-Medisize LLC	Clinton	MA	G	978 365-1262	10089

	CITY	ST	EMP	PHONE	ENTRY #
Pilgrim Innovative Plas LLC	Plymouth	MA	F	508 732-0297	14573
Pioneer Packaging Inc **(PA)**	Chicopee	MA	D	413 378-6930	10050
Pittsfield Plastics Engrg Inc	Pittsfield	MA	D	413 442-0067	14500
Placon Corporation	West Springfield	MA	C	413 785-1553	16546
Plastic Assembly Corporation	Ayer	MA	F	978 772-4725	7934
Plastic Concepts Inc	North Billerica	MA	E	978 663-7996	13856
Plastic Distrs Fabricators Inc	Haverhill	MA	E	978 374-0300	11459
Plastic Fabricators Corp	Woburn	MA	G	781 933-6007	17266
Plastic Molding Mfg Inc **(PA)**	Hudson	MA	D	978 567-1000	11802
Plastic Monofil Co Ltd	Medway	MA	F	732 629-7701	12969
Plastican Inc	Leominster	MA	A	978 728-5000	12176
Pobco Inc	Worcester	MA	E	508 791-6376	17442
Poly-Cel Inc	Marlborough	MA	F	508 229-8310	12809
Polymer Corporation	Palmer	MA	E	413 267-5524	14293
Polymer Corporation **(HQ)**	Rockland	MA	D	781 871-4606	14819
Portuamerica Inc	Ludlow	MA	G	413 589-0095	12475
Pourer Fedora LLC	Boston	MA	G	617 267-0333	8786
Precision Dynamics Corporation	Burlington	MA	D	888 202-3684	9321
Precision Dynamics Corporation	Billerica	MA	D	800 528-8005	8276
Precision Engineered Pdts LLC **(DH)**	Attleboro	MA	G	508 226-5600	7782
Precision Plastics Inc	Wilmington	MA	G	978 658-5345	17038
Pro Pel Plastech Inc	South Deerfield	MA	G	413 665-2282	15254
Pro Pel Plastech Inc **(PA)**	South Deerfield	MA	E	413 665-3379	15255
QEP Co Inc	Clinton	MA	G	978 368-8991	10091
Radius Pipesystems Corp	Boston	MA	G	857 263-7161	8808
Raitto Engineering & Mfg Inc	Wheelwright	MA	G	413 477-6637	16908
REc Manufacturing Corp	Hopedale	MA	E	508 634-7999	11681
Reeves Coinc	Attleboro	MA	E	508 222-2877	7785
RES-Tech Corporation **(HQ)**	Hudson	MA	E	978 567-1000	11811
Restech Plastic Molding LLC **(DH)**	Hudson	MA	F	978 567-1000	11812
Saint-Gobain Prfmce Plas Corp	Worcester	MA	E	508 852-3072	17467
Schaller Corporation	Franklin	MA	G	508 655-9171	11078
Seabury Splash Inc	Plymouth	MA	E	508 830-3440	14582
Selectech Inc	Avon	MA	G	508 583-3200	7896
Shelpak Plastics Inc	Middleton	MA	G	781 305-3937	13101
Sinicon Plastics Inc	Dalton	MA	E	413 684-5290	10186
Slideways Inc	Worcester	MA	E	508 854-0799	17475
SMC Ltd	Devens	MA	D	978 422-6800	10333
Sonicron Systems Corporation	Westfield	MA	E	413 562-5218	16731
Sonolite Plastics Corporation	Gloucester	MA	F	978 281-0662	11211
Sparrow Engineering	East Brookfield	MA	G	508 867-3984	10423
Spectrum Plastics Group	Athol	MA	G	978 249-5343	7694
SRC Medical Inc	Hanover	MA	D	781 826-9100	11352
Stergis Aluminum Products Corp	Attleboro	MA	E	508 455-0661	7795
Sterling Manufacturing Co Inc	Lancaster	MA	E	978 368-8733	11986
Streamline Plastics Co Inc	East Longmeadow	MA	E	718 401-4000	10494
Strong Electric	Tewksbury	MA	G	855 709-0701	15840
Stuart Allyn Co Inc	Pittsfield	MA	G	413 443-7306	14511
Super Brush LLC	Springfield	MA	D	413 543-1442	15511
Swaponz Inc	Natick	MA	G	508 650-4456	13280
Terracon Corporation	Franklin	MA	F	508 429-9950	11085
Texas Dip Molding Coating Inc **(PA)**	Medway	MA	G	508 533-6101	12971
Thermo-Fab Corporation	Shirley	MA	E	978 425-2311	15094
Toner Plastics Inc	East Longmeadow	MA	E	413 789-1300	10498
Trans Form Plastics Corp	Danvers	MA	E	978 777-1440	10264
Trexel Inc	Wilmington	MA	E	781 932-0202	17059
Tuftane Extrusion Tech Inc	Fall River	MA	F	978 921-8200	10773
Tyca Corporation **(PA)**	Clinton	MA	E	978 612-0002	10094
United Comb & Novelty Corp **(PA)**	Leominster	MA	D	978 537-2096	12196
United Plastic Fabricating Inc **(PA)**	North Andover	MA	D	978 975-4520	13734
Universal Plastics Corporation **(PA)**	Holyoke	MA	D	413 592-4791	11664
Universal Tipping Co Inc	Pembroke	MA	G	781 826-5135	14431
W M Gulliksen Mfg Co Inc **(PA)**	South Weymouth	MA	E	617 323-5750	15323
W R H Industries Ltd	Fall River	MA	G	508 674-2444	10781
Wachusett Molding LLC	Auburn	MA	G	508 459-0477	7852
Waddington Group Inc	Chelmsford	MA	F	201 610-6728	9940
Waddington North America Inc	Chelmsford	MA	C	978 256-6551	9941
Walter Drake Inc **(PA)**	Holyoke	MA	G	413 536-5463	11666
Web Converting Inc	Framingham	MA	G	508 879-4442	11014
Web Industries Inc **(PA)**	Marlborough	MA	G	508 898-2988	12848
Whitewater Plastics Inc	West Hatfield	MA	G	413 237-5032	16488
Wood Products Unlimited Inc	Methuen	MA	G	978 687-7449	13048
Worthen Industries Inc	Clinton	MA	E	978 365-6345	10095
Xponent Global Inc	Hudson	MA	E	978 562-3485	11827
C-O Bella Rouge At Belissino	South Portland	ME	G	207 318-5214	7017
Clark Island Boat Works	South Thomaston	ME	G	207 594-4112	7045
Composimold	Manchester	ME	G	888 281-2674	6408
Conform Gissing Intl LLC	Auburn	ME	C	207 784-1118	5555
Consolidated Container Co LLC	Portland	ME	F	207 772-7468	6642
Cpk Manufacturing LLC	Augusta	ME	E	207 622-6229	5606
Creative Canvas	Boothbay	ME	G	207 633-2056	5776
Detroit Technologies Inc	Auburn	ME	A	207 784-1118	5560
Dynamic Urethanes Inc	Gray	ME	G	207 657-3770	6138
Ecoshel Inc **(PA)**	Ashland	ME	G	207 274-3508	5536
G & G Products LLC	Kennebunk	ME	E	207 985-9100	6234
G Pro Industrial Services	Biddeford	ME	G	207 766-1671	5735
Genplex Inc	Skowhegan	ME	G	207 474-3500	6974
Hiperfax Inc	Presque Isle	ME	G	207 764-4319	6759
Jarden LLC	East Wilton	ME	C	207 645-2574	5987
Jones & Vining Incorporated	Lewiston	ME	E	207 784-3547	6295
Kw Boats **(DH)**	Augusta	ME	G	207 622-6229	5612
Maine Manufacturing LLC	Sanford	ME	D	207 324-1754	6881
Maine Mold & Machine Inc	Hartford	ME	G	207 388-2732	6177
Mathews Brothers Company **(PA)**	Belfast	ME	C	207 338-3360	5693
Molding Tooling and Design	Biddeford	ME	F	207 247-4077	5750
Molds Plus Inc	Lewiston	ME	G	207 795-0000	6307
Panolam Surface Systems	Auburn	ME	G	203 925-1556	5587
Plas-Tech Inc	Gorham	ME	G	207 854-8324	6125
R&V Industries Inc	Sanford	ME	D	207 324-5200	6887
Thermoformed Plastics Neng LLC	Biddeford	ME	F	207 286-1775	5766
Tri-Star Molding	Lewiston	ME	G	207 783-5820	6326
Villeroy & Boch Usa Inc	Kittery	ME	F	207 439-6440	6259
Advantage Mold Inc	Londonderry	NH	G	603 647-6678	18672
Advantage Plastic Products Inc	Concord	NH	E	603 227-9540	17880
Albany International Corp **(PA)**	Rochester	NH	D	603 330-5850	19655
Ambix Manufacturing Inc	Albany	NH	F	603 452-5247	17535
Bayhead Products Corporation	Dover	NH	E	603 742-3000	18008
Burbak Companies	Wilton	NH	D	603 654-2291	19976
Century Robotics LLC	Bedford	NH	G	603 540-2576	17635
Coastal Inflatables LLC	Newmarket	NH	G	603 490-7606	19332
Comstock Industries Inc	Meredith	NH	E	603 279-7045	18972
Concept Tool and Design Inc	Goffstown	NH	G	603 622-0216	18198
Consolidated Container Co LLC	Londonderry	NH	E	603 329-6747	18687
Consolidated Container Co LLC	Londonderry	NH	E	603 624-6055	18688
Deflex Innovations Inc	Berlin	NH	G	603 215-6738	17695
Detroit Forming Inc	Hudson	NH	G	603 598-2767	18385
Dunn Industries Inc	Manchester	NH	E	603 666-4800	18814
Faber Polivol LLC **(DH)**	Salem	NH	G	603 681-0484	19730
Fbn Plastics Inc	Salem	NH	F	603 894-4326	19732
Flexi-Door Corporation	Epping	NH	G	603 679-2286	18099
G & G Tool & Die Corp	Goffstown	NH	G	603 625-9744	18201
Genfoot America Inc	Littleton	NH	D	603 575-5114	18660
Gl Plastek LLC	Wolfeboro	NH	B	603 569-5100	20017
Gl Plastek Ltd Partnership	Wolfeboro	NH	B	603 569-5100	20018
Global Laminates	Portsmouth	NH	G	603 373-8081	19567
Granite State Plastics Inc	Hudson	NH	E	603 669-6715	18393
Hcp Packaging Usa Inc	Hinsdale	NH	C	603 256-3141	18320
Hy-Ten Die & Development Corp	Milford	NH	E	603 673-1611	19065
Ifg Industries LLC **(DH)**	Salem	NH	G	603 681-0484	19742
Inofab-Nnovation Infabrication	Belmont	NH	G	603 491-2946	17675
Insulfab Plastics Inc	Franklin	NH	F	603 934-2770	18158
Janco Inc **(PA)**	Rollinsford	NH	D	603 742-0043	19691
Kalwall Corporation **(PA)**	Manchester	NH	B	603 627-3861	18854
Kalwall Corporation	Bow	NH	D	603 224-6881	17718
Mills Industries Inc	Laconia	NH	F	603 528-4217	18576
Moldpro Inc	Swanzey	NH	E	603 357-2523	19885
Mrp Manufacturing LLC	Pittsfield	NH	G	603 435-5337	19503
Mrpc Northeast LLC	Hudson	NH	E	603 880-3616	18417
New England Signs & Awngs LLC	Hudson	NH	G	603 235-7205	18420
North American Plastics Ltd	Manchester	NH	E	603 644-1660	18887
Paclantic Inc	Claremont	NH	G	603 542-8600	17858
Pbs Plastics Inc	Barrington	NH	F	603 868-1717	17620
Pelham Plastics Inc	Pelham	NH	D	603 886-7226	19440
Plan Tech Inc	Loudon	NH	E	603 783-4767	18752
Plastic Techniques Inc	Goffstown	NH	E	603 622-5570	18209
Plp Composite Technologies	Fitzwilliam	NH	E	603 585-9100	18152
Poly-Ject Inc	Amherst	NH	E	603 882-6570	17581
Precision Letter Corporation	Manchester	NH	F	603 625-9625	18904
Precision Tool & Molding LLC	Derry	NH	D	603 437-6685	17994
Presby Plastics Inc	Whitefield	NH	E	603 837-3826	19972
Proto Part Inc	Hudson	NH	F	603 883-6531	18429
PSI Molded Plastics NH Inc	Wolfeboro	NH	D	603 569-5100	20024
R H Murphy Co Inc	Amherst	NH	G	603 889-2255	17583
Rapid Mold Evolution	Milford	NH	G	603 673-1027	19073
Resin Systems Corporation	Amherst	NH	D	603 673-1234	17584
Scarzello & Assocs Inc	Amherst	NH	G	603 673-7746	17548
Separett-Usa	Barrington	NH	G	603 682-0963	17623
Summit Packaging Systems Inc **(PA)**	Manchester	NH	B	603 669-5410	18932
Tech Nh Inc **(PA)**	Merrimack	NH	D	603 424-4404	19036
W K Hillquist Inc	Hudson	NH	E	603 595-7790	18451
Welch Fluorocarbon Inc	Dover	NH	E	603 742-0164	18067
Accurate Molded Products Inc	Warwick	RI	E	401 739-2400	21317
Anco Tool & Die Co Inc	East Providence	RI	F	401 438-5860	20387
Aspects Inc	Warren	RI	E	401 247-1854	21286
B & L Plastics Inc	Pawtucket	RI	E	401 723-3000	20814
Bates Plastics Inc	Cranston	RI	E	401 781-7711	20188
Berry Global Inc	Bristol	RI	C	401 254-0600	20064
C & W Co Inc	Providence	RI	G	401 941-6311	20977
Capco Plastics Inc **(PA)**	Providence	RI	D	401 272-3833	20978
Case Hard	Little Compton	RI	G	401 635-8201	20604
Chem-Tainer Industries Inc	Cranston	RI	D	401 467-2750	20196
Clear Carbon & Components Inc	Bristol	RI	F	401 254-5085	20068
Covalnce Spcalty Adhesives LLC	Bristol	RI	C	401 253-2595	20071
CPC Plastics Inc	West Warwick	RI	G	401 828-0820	21488

	CITY	ST	EMP	PHONE	ENTRY #
Custom Design Incorporated	North Kingstown	RI	E	401 294-0200	20700
East Coast Laminiating Company	Cumberland	RI	G	401 729-0097	20319
Edward F Briggs Disposal Inc	East Greenwich	RI	G	401 294-6391	20365
Eli Engineering Co Inc	Coventry	RI	G	401 822-1494	20146
Fielding Manufacturing Inc	Cranston	RI	E	401 461-0400	20226
Island Mooring Supplies LLC	Prudence Island	RI	F	401 447-5387	21160
Jade Engineered Plastics Inc	Bristol	RI	D	401 253-4440	20085
Jay Packaging Group Inc **(PA)**	Warwick	RI	D	401 244-1300	21379
Liftbag Usa Inc	North Kingstown	RI	F	401 884-8801	20722
Mars 2000 Inc	Providence	RI	A	401 421-5275	21061
Mastercast Ltd	Pawtucket	RI	F	401 726-3100	20858
Matrix I LLC	East Providence	RI	D	401 434-3040	20431
Mearthane Products Corporation **(PA)**	Cranston	RI	C	401 946-4400	20260
Morris Transparent Box Co	East Providence	RI	E	401 438-6116	20433
Opac Inc **(PA)**	Smithfield	RI	G	401 231-3552	21242
Perry Blackburne Inc	North Providence	RI	E	401 231-7200	20771
Polyworks LLC	North Smithfield	RI	E	401 769-0994	20794
R B L Holdings Inc	Coventry	RI	F	401 821-2200	20163
Response Technologies LLC	West Warwick	RI	G	401 585-5918	21508
Saint-Gobain Prfmce Plas Corp	Bristol	RI	C	401 253-2000	20102
Scarborough Faire Inc **(PA)**	Pawtucket	RI	E	401 724-4200	20897
Silgan Dispensing Systems **(DH)**	Slatersville	RI	C	401 767-2400	21206
Sturbridge Associates III LLC **(PA)**	Providence	RI	G	401 943-8600	21129
Subsalve USA LLC	North Kingstown	RI	F	401 884-8801	20743
Total Plastics Resources LLC	Cranston	RI	E	401 463-3090	20303
Tri-Mack Plastics Mfg Corp	Bristol	RI	D	401 253-2140	20107
Wenco Molding Inc	Providence	RI	G	401 781-2600	21153
Arlington Industries Inc	Arlington	VT	E	802 375-6139	21594
Astenjohnson Inc	Williston	VT	D	802 658-2040	22655
Bike Track Inc	Woodstock	VT	G	802 457-3275	22737
Carris Financial Corp **(PA)**	Proctor	VT	F	802 773-9111	22283
Carris Reels Inc **(HQ)**	Proctor	VT	C	802 773-9111	22284
Consolidated Container Co LLC	South Burlington	VT	E	802 658-6588	22444
Dm Inc	Milton	VT	G	802 425-2119	22126
Engineered Monofilaments Corp	Williston	VT	G	802 863-6823	22664
G W Plastics Inc **(PA)**	Bethel	VT	B	802 234-9941	21695
G W Plastics Inc	South Royalton	VT	D	802 763-2194	22492
G W Plastics Inc	Sharon	VT	G	802 233-0319	22408
Hancor Inc	Springfield	VT	E	802 886-8403	22501
K & E Plastics Inc	Bennington	VT	E	802 375-0011	21676
Kaytec Inc	Richford	VT	D	802 848-7010	22307
Kp Building Products Inc	Williston	VT	F	866 850-4447	22678
Mack Group Inc **(PA)**	Arlington	VT	B	802 375-2511	21597
Mack Molding Company Inc **(HQ)**	Arlington	VT	C	802 375-2511	21598
Mack Molding Company Inc	Arlington	VT	C	802 375-0500	21599
Mid-VT Molding LLC	Bethel	VT	G	802 234-9777	21696
National Hanger Company Inc	North Bennington	VT	D	800 426-4377	22211
Plastic Monofil Co Ltd	Milton	VT	G	802 893-1543	22136
Precision Composites VT LLC	Lyndonville	VT	F	802 626-5900	22072
Progressive Plastics Inc	Williamstown	VT	E	802 433-1563	22650
Questech Corporation **(PA)**	Rutland	VT	E	802 773-1228	22347
Questech Tile LLC	Rutland	VT	G	802 773-1228	22348
Staticworx Inc	Waterbury Center	VT	G	617 923-2000	22592
T & M Enterprises Inc	Shaftsbury	VT	G	802 447-0601	22406
Teknor Apex Co	Saint Albans	VT	F	802 524-7704	22381
Vermont Plastics Specialties	Williston	VT	G	802 879-0072	22696

31 LEATHER AND LEATHER PRODUCTS

3111 Leather Tanning & Finishing

	CITY	ST	EMP	PHONE	ENTRY #
Cuero Operating	Westport	CT	G	203 253-8651	5187
MGI usa Inc	Danbury	CT	G	203 312-1200	954
Patricia Poke	New Milford	CT	G	860 354-4193	2823
Veto Pro Pac LLC	Norwalk	CT	G	203 847-0297	3267
Alliance Leather Finishing	Peabody	MA	F	978 531-6771	14309
Barbour Plastics Inc **(HQ)**	Brockton	MA	E	508 583-8200	9125
Broleco Inc **(PA)**	North Andover	MA	G	978 689-3200	13693
Hawtan Leathers LLC	Newburyport	MA	C	978 465-3791	13496
Malik Embossing Corp	Salem	MA	G	978 745-6060	14928
Shrut & Asch Leather Co Inc	Woburn	MA	G	781 460-2288	17294
Twin Leather Co Inc	West Bridgewater	MA	G	508 583-3485	16461
Brettunsvillagecom	Lewiston	ME	F	207 782-7863	6278
Tasman Industries Inc	Hartland	ME	E	207 938-4491	6179

3131 Boot & Shoe Cut Stock & Findings

	CITY	ST	EMP	PHONE	ENTRY #
Catskill Gran Countertops Inc	Newington	CT	F	860 667-1555	2852
Middle Quarter Animal Hospital	Woodbury	CT	G	203 263-4772	5489
Rand Whitney	New Milford	CT	G	860 354-6063	2825
Top Source Inc	Waterbury	CT	G	203 753-6490	4964
Adra Rand	Acton	MA	G	978 274-2652	7336
Barbour Corporation **(PA)**	Brockton	MA	C	508 583-8200	9124
Barbour Plastics Inc **(HQ)**	Brockton	MA	E	508 583-8200	9125
Counter Culture	Saugus	MA	G	781 439-9810	14979
Counteredge LLC	Waltham	MA	F	781 891-0050	16078
Furnished Quarters LLC	Cambridge	MA	D	212 367-9400	9484
Gaynor Minden Inc	Lawrence	MA	G	212 929-0087	12027
Healthquarters Inc	Beverly	MA	G	978 922-4490	8139
Ingersoll-Rand Company	Marlborough	MA	G	508 573-1524	12776
International Sole & Lea Corp	South Easton	MA	F	508 588-0905	15281
Jones & Vining Incorporated **(PA)**	Brockton	MA	E	508 232-7470	9158
L Hewitt Rand	North Adams	MA	G	413 664-8171	13677
Leisure Manufacturing	Haverhill	MA	F	978 373-3831	11448
Macneill Engineering Co Inc	Westborough	MA	E	508 481-8830	16633
McManus E Vq Gp LLC	Woburn	MA	G	781 935-2483	17226
Montello Heel Mfg Inc	Brockton	MA	E	508 586-0603	9167
North American Chemical Co	Lawrence	MA	G	978 687-9500	12066
Quarter LLC	Boston	MA	G	617 848-1249	8804
Quarter Line Drssge Unlmted	Georgetown	MA	G	978 476-6554	11149
Quarter Productions	Amesbury	MA	G	774 217-8073	7503
Rand Barthel Treasurer	Mendon	MA	G	508 473-3305	12994
Rand Corporation	Boston	MA	G	617 338-2059	8809
Rand Grantwriting	Jamaica Plain	MA	G	617 524-5367	11948
Rhine Inc	Weston	MA	G	781 710-7121	16831
Sx Industries Inc **(PA)**	Stoughton	MA	E	781 828-7111	15625
Twin Leather Co Inc	West Bridgewater	MA	G	508 583-3485	16461
Vibram Corporation **(HQ)**	Concord	MA	E	978 318-0000	10159
Enefco International Inc **(PA)**	Auburn	ME	D	207 514-7218	5561
Jones & Vining Incorporated	Lewiston	ME	E	207 784-3547	6295
Lunder Manufacturing Inc	Saco	ME	E	207 284-5961	6851
Cohos Counters LLC	Lancaster	NH	G	603 788-4928	18599
Weller E E Co Inc/MCS Finshg	Providence	RI	E	401 461-4275	21152
Rand Kevin	Plainfield	VT	G	802 454-1440	22269

3142 House Slippers

	CITY	ST	EMP	PHONE	ENTRY #
Mary Lee Harris	Castleton	VT	G	802 468-5370	21829

3143 Men's Footwear, Exc Athletic

	CITY	ST	EMP	PHONE	ENTRY #
B H Shoe Holdings Inc **(HQ)**	Greenwich	CT	E	203 661-2424	1596
Fisher Footwear LLC	Greenwich	CT	F	203 302-2800	1612
HH Brown Shoe Company Inc **(DH)**	Greenwich	CT	E	203 661-2424	1620
Mbf Holdings LLC	Greenwich	CT	F	203 302-2812	1629
Vcs Group LLC	Greenwich	CT	G	203 413-6500	1660
Alden Shoe Company Inc	Middleboro	MA	C	508 947-3926	13050
C & J Clark America Inc **(DH)**	Waltham	MA	B	617 964-1222	16054
C & J Clark Latin America	Waltham	MA	F	617 243-4100	16055
Pvh Corp	Wrentham	MA	F	508 384-0070	17527
Reebok International Ltd **(HQ)**	Boston	MA	B	781 401-5000	8816
Saucony Inc **(DH)**	Waltham	MA	C	617 824-6000	16191
Surtan Manufacturing Co	South Yarmouth	MA	G	508 394-4099	15334
Falcon Performance Ftwr LLC	Auburn	ME	D	207 784-9186	5564
Footwear Specialties Inc	Biddeford	ME	F	207 284-5003	5734
Globe Footwear LLC	Auburn	ME	E	207 784-9186	5568
L L Bean Inc	Brunswick	ME	B	207 725-0300	5840
New Balance Athletics Inc	Norridgewock	ME	B	207 634-3033	6499
Rancourt & Co Shoecrafters Inc	Lewiston	ME	D	207 782-1577	6318
Peter Limmer & Sons Inc	Intervale	NH	G	603 356-5378	18455
Timberland LLC **(HQ)**	Stratham	NH	B	603 772-9500	19876

3144 Women's Footwear, Exc Athletic

	CITY	ST	EMP	PHONE	ENTRY #
Aj Casey LLC	Norwalk	CT	G	203 226-5961	3098
Cecelia New York LLC	Darien	CT	G	917 392-4536	1021
Dooney & Bourke Inc **(PA)**	Norwalk	CT	E	203 853-7515	3142
Fisher Footwear LLC	Greenwich	CT	F	203 302-2800	1612
Fisher Sigerson Morrison LLC	Greenwich	CT	E	203 302-2800	1613
HH Brown Shoe Company Inc **(DH)**	Greenwich	CT	E	203 661-2424	1620
Cardinal Shoe Corporation	Lawrence	MA	E	978 686-9706	12003
Modern Shoe Company LLC	Hyde Park	MA	F	617 333-7470	11876
Reebok International Ltd **(HQ)**	Boston	MA	B	781 401-5000	8816
Saucony Inc **(DH)**	Waltham	MA	C	617 824-6000	16191
Surtan Manufacturing Co	South Yarmouth	MA	G	508 394-4099	15334
Footwear Specialties Inc	Biddeford	ME	F	207 284-5003	5734
L L Bean Inc	Brunswick	ME	B	207 725-0300	5840
New Balance Athletics Inc	Norridgewock	ME	B	207 634-3033	6499
Colby Footwear Inc	Somersworth	NH	C	603 332-2283	19830
Peter Limmer & Sons Inc	Intervale	NH	G	603 356-5378	18455
Timberland LLC **(HQ)**	Stratham	NH	B	603 772-9500	19876

3149 Footwear, NEC

	CITY	ST	EMP	PHONE	ENTRY #
Acushnet Company **(DH)**	Fairhaven	MA	A	508 979-2000	10635
Arrow Moccasin Company	Hudson	MA	G	978 562-7870	11756
Barry Manufacturing Co Inc	Lynn	MA	E	781 598-1055	12491
New Balance Athletics Inc	Lawrence	MA	B	978 685-8400	12063
Reebok International Ltd **(HQ)**	Boston	MA	B	781 401-5000	8816
Saucony Inc **(DH)**	Waltham	MA	C	617 824-6000	16191
Tommy Hilfiger Footwear Inc	Lexington	MA	E	617 824-6000	12279
Callaway Golf Ball Oprtons Inc	Richmond	ME	C	207 737-4324	6781
New Balance Athletics Inc	Norridgewock	ME	B	207 634-3033	6499
New Balance Athletics Inc	Skowhegan	ME	B	207 474-2042	6983

3151 Leather Gloves & Mittens

	CITY	ST	EMP	PHONE	ENTRY #
Damascus Worldwide Inc	Rutland	VT	G	802 775-6062	22328

3161 Luggage

	CITY	ST	EMP	PHONE	ENTRY #
2 Girl A Trunk	Wilton	CT	G	203 762-0360	5272
Armor Box Company LLC	Bloomfield	CT	G	860 242-9981	203
Calzone Ltd **(PA)**	Bridgeport	CT	E	203 367-5766	394
Case Concepts Intl LLC **(PA)**	Stamford	CT	F	203 883-8602	4157
Commercial Sewing Inc	Torrington	CT	C	860 482-5509	4571
Dooney & Bourke Inc **(PA)**	Norwalk	CT	E	203 853-7515	3142
Fabrique Ltd	Branford	CT	F	203 481-5400	315
Leatherby	Weatogue	CT	G	860 658-6166	5043
Marc Johnson	Danielson	CT	G	860 774-3315	1015
A T S Cases Inc	Northborough	MA	G	508 393-9110	14028
Baby Briefcase LLC	Milton	MA	G	617 696-7668	13189
Brahmin Leather Works LLC	Fairhaven	MA	G	509 994-4000	10638
Case Technology Inc	Ipswich	MA	G	978 356-6011	11910
Currys Leather Shop Inc	Randolph	MA	F	781 963-0679	14675
David King & Co Inc	Boston	MA	G	617 482-6950	8496
Hartmann Incorporated	Mansfield	MA	D	508 851-1400	12634
Hl Operating LLC **(DH)**	Mansfield	MA	E	508 851-1400	12635
L & J Leathers Manufacturing	Revere	MA	G	781 289-6466	14770
Overtone Labs Inc	Lawrence	MA	G	978 682-1257	12070
Pelican Products Inc	East Longmeadow	MA	G	413 525-3990	10485
Sherwood Trunks	Amherst	MA	G	413 687-3167	7526
Specialty Packaging Inc	Indian Orchard	MA	G	413 543-1814	11895
Ten West Trunk Shows	Beverly	MA	G	508 755-7547	8188
Union Bookbinding Company Inc **(PA)**	Fall River	MA	E	508 676-8580	10775
Byer Manufacturing Company	Orono	ME	E	207 866-2171	6552
C B P Corp **(PA)**	Arundel	ME	F	207 985-9767	5529
L L Bean Inc	Brunswick	ME	B	207 725-0300	5840
Nancy Lawrence	Portland	ME	G	207 774-7276	6697
Sea Bags Inc	Freeport	ME	G	207 939-3679	6086
Baileyworks Inc	Newmarket	NH	G	603 292-6485	19330
Code Briefcase	New Boston	NH	G	603 487-2381	19292
Monkey-Trunks	Tamworth	NH	G	603 367-4427	19892
Budco Products Corp	Woonsocket	RI	G	401 767-2590	21554
Samsonite Company Stores LLC	Warren	RI	F	401 245-2100	21306
Van & Company Inc	Pawtucket	RI	F	401 722-9829	20908
Porta-Brace Inc	Bennington	VT	D	802 442-8171	21689

3171 Handbags & Purses

	CITY	ST	EMP	PHONE	ENTRY #
Coach Inc	Trumbull	CT	F	203 372-0208	4619
Dooney & Bourke Inc **(PA)**	Norwalk	CT	E	203 853-7515	3142
Leatherby	Weatogue	CT	G	860 658-6166	5043
Bagrout Inc	Ware	MA	G	413 949-0743	16229
Brahmin Leather Works LLC	Fairhaven	MA	G	509 994-4000	10638
Dick Muller Designer/Craftsman	Shelburne Falls	MA	G	413 625-0016	15068
Surtan Manufacturing Co	South Yarmouth	MA	G	508 394-4099	15334
Tapestry Inc	Boston	MA	G	617 723-1777	8874
Vera Bradley Designs Inc	Braintree	MA	G	781 794-9860	9047
W D C Holdings Inc	Attleboro	MA	D	508 699-4412	7806
Nancy Lawrence	Portland	ME	G	207 774-7276	6697
Bren Corporation	Johnston	RI	E	401 943-8200	20501

3172 Personal Leather Goods

	CITY	ST	EMP	PHONE	ENTRY #
Boccelli	Uncasville	CT	G	860 862-9300	4646
Brockway Ferry Corporation **(PA)**	Essex	CT	G	860 767-8231	1394
Dooney & Bourke Inc **(PA)**	Norwalk	CT	E	203 853-7515	3142
Ecoflik LLC	Old Lyme	CT	G	860 460-4419	3322
Leatherby	Weatogue	CT	G	860 658-6166	5043
Mayan Corporation	Norwalk	CT	F	203 854-4711	3192
Putu LLC	New Canaan	CT	G	203 594-9700	2613
Waterbury Leatherworks Co	Waterbury	CT	F	203 755-7789	4972
Alliance Leather Finishing	Peabody	MA	F	978 531-6771	14309
Brahmin Leather Works LLC	Fairhaven	MA	G	509 994-4000	10638
Charles Thomae & Son Inc	Attleboro	MA	E	508 222-0785	7719
Currys Leather Shop Inc	Randolph	MA	F	781 963-0679	14675
Dick Muller Designer/Craftsman	Shelburne Falls	MA	G	413 625-0016	15068
Fuller Box Co Inc **(PA)**	North Attleboro	MA	D	508 695-2525	13756
Hague Textiles Inc	Fall River	MA	E	508 678-7556	10711
Hl Operating LLC **(DH)**	Mansfield	MA	E	508 851-1400	12635
Miles Kedex Co Inc	Westminster	MA	E	978 874-1403	16810
Montello Heel Mfg Inc	Brockton	MA	E	508 586-0603	9167
Niche Inc	New Bedford	MA	E	508 990-4202	13427
Strong Group Inc **(PA)**	Gloucester	MA	E	978 281-3300	11212
Surtan Manufacturing Co	South Yarmouth	MA	G	508 394-4099	15334
Valkyrie Company Inc **(PA)**	Worcester	MA	D	508 756-3633	17496
Valkyrie Company Inc	Worcester	MA	D	508 756-3633	17497
Maineline Industries Inc	Lewiston	ME	G	207 782-6622	6304
Perfect Fit	Corinna	ME	F	207 278-3333	5923
Appalachian Stitching Co LLC **(PA)**	Littleton	NH	E	603 444-4422	18654
Bren Corporation	Johnston	RI	E	401 943-8200	20501
Jewel Case Corporation	Providence	RI	B	401 943-1400	21044
Numaco Packaging LLC	East Providence	RI	F	401 438-4952	20436
Perry Blackburne Inc	North Providence	RI	E	401 231-7200	20771

3199 Leather Goods, NEC

	CITY	ST	EMP	PHONE	ENTRY #
A X M S Inc	Woodbury	CT	G	203 263-5046	5480
Brockway Ferry Corporation **(PA)**	Essex	CT	G	860 767-8231	1394
The Smith Worthington Sad Co	Hartford	CT	G	860 527-9117	1878
Craftmens Corner	Springfield	MA	G	413 782-3783	15462
Currys Leather Shop Inc	Randolph	MA	F	781 963-0679	14675
Hague Textiles Inc **(PA)**	Fall River	MA	G	508 678-7556	10710
Hague Textiles Inc	Fall River	MA	E	508 678-7556	10711
Kerr Leathers Inc	Salem	MA	E	978 852-0660	14927
Niche Inc	New Bedford	MA	E	508 990-4202	13427
Safariland LLC	Dalton	MA	D	413 684-3104	10183
Strong Group Inc **(PA)**	Gloucester	MA	E	978 281-3300	11212
Tapestry Inc	Lee	MA	F	413 243-4897	12096
Venlo Company	Pembroke	MA	G	781 826-0485	14432
Westfield Whip Mfg Co	Westfield	MA	F	413 568-8244	16748
Gallery Leather Co Inc	Trenton	ME	E	207 667-9474	7098
Justleathercom	Wells	ME	G	207 641-8313	7163
Maineline Industries Inc	Lewiston	ME	G	207 782-6622	6304
Perfect Fit	Corinna	ME	F	207 278-3333	5923
Safe Approach Inc	Poland	ME	F	207 345-9900	6597
Jaeger Usa Inc	Rochester	NH	F	603 332-5816	19674
Mitch Rosen Extraordinary Gunl	Manchester	NH	F	603 647-2971	18876
Page Belting Company Inc	Boscawen	NH	E	603 796-2463	17705
Bellows Inc	Forestdale	RI	G	401 766-5331	20455
Lirakis Safety Harness Inc	Newport	RI	G	401 846-5356	20671

32 STONE, CLAY, GLASS, AND CONCRETE PRODUCTS

3211 Flat Glass

	CITY	ST	EMP	PHONE	ENTRY #
Insulpane Connecticut Inc	Hamden	CT	D	800 922-3248	1761
All Pro Tint	New Bedford	MA	G	508 992-8468	13355
Contract Glass Service Inc	Billerica	MA	E	978 262-1323	8233
Custom Glass and Alum Co Inc	Tewksbury	MA	G	978 640-5800	15813
LTI Smart Glass Inc	Pittsfield	MA	D	413 637-5001	14486
Nantucket Glass & Mirror Inc	Nantucket	MA	G	508 228-3713	13229
Protective Armored Systems Inc	Lee	MA	E	413 637-1060	12095
Shaw Glass Holdings LLC	South Easton	MA	C	508 238-0112	15292
Thermal Seal Insulating GL Inc	Uxbridge	MA	F	508 278-4243	15931
American Tinter	Windham	NH	G	603 458-6379	19999
Erie Scientific LLC **(DH)**	Portsmouth	NH	B	603 430-6859	19560
Green Mountain Glass LLC	Charlestown	NH	G	603 826-4660	17815
Guild Optical Associates Inc	Amherst	NH	F	603 889-6247	17567
Renaissance Glassworks Inc	Nashua	NH	G	603 882-1779	19249
Robert Cairns Company LLC	Plaistow	NH	G	603 382-0044	19522
Jmh Industries Inc	East Providence	RI	G	401 438-2500	20423

3221 Glass Containers

	CITY	ST	EMP	PHONE	ENTRY #
Emhart Glass Manufacturing Inc **(DH)**	Windsor	CT	E	860 298-7340	5332
Matthew Fisel ND	Guilford	CT	G	203 453-0122	1709
Calyx Containers LLC	Allston	MA	E	617 249-6870	7461
Glass By Petze	Osterville	MA	F	508 428-0971	14248
Saint-Gobain Corporation	Northborough	MA	E	508 351-7112	14047
Yankee Glass Blower Inc	Carlisle	MA	G	978 369-7545	9801
Jarden LLC	East Wilton	ME	C	207 645-2574	5987
Erie Scientific LLC **(DH)**	Portsmouth	NH	B	603 430-6859	19560

3229 Pressed & Blown Glassware, NEC

	CITY	ST	EMP	PHONE	ENTRY #
Bovano Industries Incorporated	Cheshire	CT	F	203 272-3208	715
Fiberoptics Technology Inc	Pomfret	CT	D	860 928-0443	3551
Flabeg Technical Glass US Corp	Naugatuck	CT	E	203 729-5227	2473
Fluid Coating Technology Inc	Putnam	CT	G	860 963-2505	3612
G Schoepferinc	Cheshire	CT	F	203 250-7794	734
Incjet Inc	Norwich	CT	F	860 823-3090	3283
Liberty Glass and Met Inds Inc	North Grosvenordale	CT	E	860 923-3623	2997
Magic Industries Inc	Bozrah	CT	F	860 949-8380	281
Medelco Inc	Bridgeport	CT	G	203 275-8070	449
Nufern	East Granby	CT	D	860 408-5000	1137
O E M Controls Inc **(PA)**	Shelton	CT	C	203 929-8431	3845
Periodic Tableware LLC	Shelton	CT	F	310 428-4250	3850
Pioneer Optics Company Inc	Bloomfield	CT	F	860 286-0071	251
Schaeffler Aerospace USA Corp	Winsted	CT	D	860 379-7558	5421
Simon Pearce US Inc	Greenwich	CT	G	203 861-0780	1650
Tops Manufacturing Co Inc **(PA)**	Darien	CT	G	203 655-9367	1034
Vitro Technology Ltd	Milford	CT	G	203 783-9566	2380
Whalley Glass Company **(PA)**	Derby	CT	D	203 735-9388	1083
Woolworks Ltd	Putnam	CT	G	860 963-1228	3642
Apogent Technologies Inc	Waltham	MA	A	781 622-1300	16035
Atlas Global Ltg Solutions Inc **(PA)**	Boston	MA	G	617 304-3264	8384
Beon Home Inc	North Easton	MA	G	617 600-8329	13944
Brook Heath Studio	Heath	MA	G	413 337-5736	11488
Diamond USA Inc **(HQ)**	North Billerica	MA	E	978 256-6544	13807
Ed Branson	Ashfield	MA	G	413 625-2933	7649
Fritz Glass	Dennis Port	MA	G	508 394-0441	10313
Fused Fiberoptics LLC	Southbridge	MA	F	508 765-1652	15383
G Finkenbeiner Inc	Waltham	MA	G	781 899-3138	16117
Glass Dimension Inc	Essex	MA	E	978 768-7984	10593
Hosokawa Alpine American Inc	Northborough	MA	F	508 655-1123	14036

	CITY	ST	EMP	PHONE	ENTRY #
Ipg Photonics Corporation **(PA)**	Oxford	MA	B	508 373-1100	14263
Josh Smpson Cntemporary GL Inc	Shelburne Falls	MA	F	413 625-6145	15072
Mini-Systems Inc	Plainville	MA	E	508 695-2000	14528
Mp Optical Communications Inc **(PA)**	Harvard	MA	G	978 456-7728	11382
Myriad Fiber Imaging Tech Inc	Dudley	MA	F	508 949-3000	10382
Omni Glass Inc	North Billerica	MA	G	978 667-6664	13850
Pegasus Glassworks Inc	Sturbridge	MA	F	508 347-5656	15644
Pgc Acquisition LLC	Reading	MA	F	508 888-2344	14738
Schott North America Inc	Southbridge	MA	C	508 765-3300	15400
Schott North America Inc	Southbridge	MA	D	508 765-9744	15401
Simon Pearce US Inc	Boston	MA	G	617 450-8388	8847
Simple Syrup Glass Studio LLC	Needham	MA	G	781 444-8275	13311
Sound Seal Holdings Inc **(HQ)**	Agawam	MA	G	413 789-1770	7451
Stiles & Hart Brick Company	Bridgewater	MA	E	508 697-6928	9088
Sydenstricker Galleries Inc **(PA)**	Brewster	MA	F	508 385-3272	9058
T & T Machine Products Inc	Rockland	MA	F	781 878-3861	14829
Vaillancourt Folk Art Inc	Sutton	MA	E	508 476-3601	15695
Ward Process Inc	Holliston	MA	D	508 429-1165	11613
Yankee Glass Blower Inc	Carlisle	MA	G	978 369-7545	9801
Young & Constantin N River GL **(PA)**	Shelburne Falls	MA	G	413 625-6422	15076
Corning Incorporated	Kennebunk	ME	D	207 985-3111	6231
McDonald Stain Glass Ltd	Boothbay Harbor	ME	G	207 633-4815	5785
Pams Wreaths	Harpswell	ME	G	207 751-7234	6174
Avian Technologies LLC	New London	NH	G	603 526-2420	19313
Corning Incorporated	Keene	NH	C	603 357-7662	18497
Erie Scientific LLC **(DH)**	Portsmouth	NH	B	603 430-6859	19560
Herrmann Pepi Crystal Inc	Gilford	NH	G	603 528-1020	18188
M & M Glass Blowing Co Inc	Nashua	NH	G	603 598-8195	19202
New Hampshire Optical Sys Inc	Nashua	NH	G	603 391-2909	19215
Robert Cairns Company LLC	Plaistow	NH	G	603 382-0044	19522
Anchor Bend Glassworks LLC **(PA)**	North Kingstown	RI	G	401 667-7338	20690
Brantner and Associates Inc	Ashaway	RI	G	401 326-9368	20032
Saint-Gobain Prfmce Plas Corp	Bristol	RI	C	401 253-2000	20102
Te Connctvity Phenix Optix Inc	Ashaway	RI	E	401 637-4600	20041
Thames Glass Inc	Newport	RI	F	401 846-0576	20686
Catamount Glassware Co Inc	Bennington	VT	E	802 442-5438	21666
Church & Maple Glass Studio	Burlington	VT	G	802 863-3880	21773
Crest Studios	Townshend	VT	F	802 365-4200	22541
Jack Russell	West Rutland	VT	G	802 438-5213	22617
Little River Hotglass Studio	Stowe	VT	G	802 253-0889	22523
Penelope Wurr Glass	Putney	VT	G	802 387-5607	22290
Simon Pearce US Inc	Windsor	VT	D	802 674-6280	22715
Vitri Forms Inc	West Halifax	VT	G	802 254-5235	22608
Ziemke Glass Blowing Studio	Waterbury Center	VT	G	802 244-6126	22594

3231 Glass Prdts Made Of Purchased Glass

	CITY	ST	EMP	PHONE	ENTRY #
Baron Technology Inc	Trumbull	CT	E	203 452-0515	4614
Bovano Industries Incorporated	Cheshire	CT	F	203 272-3208	715
Flabeg Technical Glass US Corp	Naugatuck	CT	E	203 729-5227	2473
Glass Industries America LLC	Wallingford	CT	F	203 269-6700	4749
Periodic Tableware LLC	Shelton	CT	F	310 428-4250	3850
Vijon Studios Inc	Old Saybrook	CT	G	860 399-7440	3354
Acton Research Corporation	Acton	MA	E	941 556-2601	7334
AMS Glass Bead Cabinets	Hampden	MA	E	413 566-0037	11319
Artigiano Stained Glass	Newton	MA	G	617 244-0141	13563
Canner Incorporated	West Groton	MA	F	978 448-3063	16479
Designer Stained Glass	Acushnet	MA	G	508 763-3255	7401
Diamond Windows Doors Mfg Inc	Boston	MA	E	617 282-1688	8503
Fibertec Inc	Bridgewater	MA	D	508 697-5100	9073
Glass By Petze	Osterville	MA	F	508 428-0971	14248
Glass Dimension Inc	Essex	MA	E	978 768-7984	10593
Guarducci Stained GL Studios	Great Barrington	MA	G	413 528-6287	11239
Hardric Laboratories Inc	North Chelmsford	MA	E	978 251-1702	13895
Idex Health & Science LLC	Middleboro	MA	C	774 213-0200	13064
LTI Smart Glass Inc	Pittsfield	MA	D	413 637-5001	14486
Mini-Systems Inc	Plainville	MA	E	508 695-2000	14528
Modern Mfg Inc Worcester	Worcester	MA	E	508 791-7151	17421
New England Stained Glass	North Attleboro	MA	G	508 699-6965	13769
Omni Glass Inc	North Billerica	MA	G	978 667-6664	13850
Patriot Armored Systems LLC	Lenox Dale	MA	E	413 637-1060	12104
Prestige Custom Mirror & Glass	Waltham	MA	F	781 647-0878	16177
Printguard Inc	Millbury	MA	F	508 890-8822	13173
Protective Armored Systems Inc	Lee	MA	E	413 637-1060	12095
Sidney Hutter Glass & Light	Auburndale	MA	G	617 630-1929	7869
T J Holmes Co Inc	Chartley	MA	E	508 222-1723	9858
Brass Foundry	West Rockport	ME	G	207 236-3200	7178
McDonald Stain Glass Ltd	Boothbay Harbor	ME	G	207 633-4815	5785
Sigco LLC	Westbrook	ME	E	207 775-2676	7207
Sigco LLC **(DH)**	Westbrook	ME	C	207 775-2676	7208
American Crystal Works	North Conway	NH	G	603 356-7879	19371
American Marine Products Inc	Charlestown	NH	E	954 782-1400	17810
Baker Salmon Christopher	Antrim	NH	G	603 588-4000	17592
Dan Dailey Inc	Kensington	NH	F	603 778-2303	18536
Daniel Wheeler	Gilford	NH	G	603 528-6363	18184
Erie Scientific LLC **(DH)**	Portsmouth	NH	B	603 430-6859	19560
Glass Pro Inc	Brentwood	NH	G	603 436-2882	17750
Kheops International Inc **(PA)**	Stewartstown	NH	E	603 237-8188	19862

	CITY	ST	EMP	PHONE	ENTRY #
Renaissance Glassworks Inc	Nashua	NH	G	603 882-1779	19249
Ultimate Glass Services LLC	Kingston	NH	G	603 642-3375	18547
Filters Inc	Pawtucket	RI	G	401 722-8999	20840
Jmh Industries Inc	East Providence	RI	G	401 438-2500	20423
Swarovski North America Ltd **(DH)**	Cranston	RI	A	401 463-6400	20295
Swarovski US Holding Limited **(HQ)**	Cranston	RI	G	401 463-6400	20296
Brass Butterfly Inc	Poultney	VT	G	802 287-9818	22270
Vitriesse Glass Studio	West Pawlet	VT	G	802 645-9800	22613

3241 Cement, Hydraulic

	CITY	ST	EMP	PHONE	ENTRY #
Beard Concrete Co Derby Inc	Derby	CT	F	203 735-4641	1068
Lafarge North America Inc	New Haven	CT	G	203 468-6068	2704
McInnis USA Inc	Stamford	CT	E	203 890-9950	4246
Andrews Holdings Inc	Ayer	MA	F	978 772-4444	7910
Dragon Products Company LLC **(DH)**	South Portland	ME	E	207 774-6355	7022
Dragon Products Company LLC	Thomaston	ME	C	207 594-5555	7083
Conproco Corp	Bow	NH	G	603 743-5800	17710
Lehigh Cement Company	Providence	RI	G	800 833-4157	21051

3251 Brick & Structural Clay Tile

	CITY	ST	EMP	PHONE	ENTRY #
K & G Corp	Manchester	CT	F	860 643-1133	2015
Redland Brick Inc	South Windsor	CT	C	860 528-1311	4007
Hi-Way Concrete Pdts Co Inc	Wareham	MA	E	508 295-0834	16249
Morgan Advanced Ceramics Inc	New Bedford	MA	C	508 995-1725	13418
Redi-Mix Services Incorporated	Taunton	MA	G	508 823-0771	15778
Stiles & Hart Brick Company	Bridgewater	MA	E	508 697-6928	9088
Rjf - Morin Brick LLC	Auburn	ME	D	207 784-9375	5595
Ventech Industries Inc	Eliot	ME	G	207 439-0069	6012
Morgan Advanced Ceramics Inc	Hudson	NH	E	603 598-9122	18416

3253 Ceramic Tile

	CITY	ST	EMP	PHONE	ENTRY #
Mohawk Industries Inc	Danbury	CT	C	203 739-0260	956
Quemere International LLC	Middletown	CT	G	914 934-8366	2215
Figulo Corporation	Boston	MA	G	617 269-0807	8543
Fit America Inc	Southborough	MA	G	309 839-1695	15357
Ventech Industries Inc	Eliot	ME	G	207 439-0069	6012
Wiseman & Spaulding Designs	Hampden	ME	E	207 862-3513	6169
Besheer Studios	Bedford	NH	G	603 472-5288	17632
Cabinets For Less LLC	Manchester	NH	G	603 935-7551	18794
D Lasser Ceramics	Londonderry	VT	G	802 824-5383	22057

3255 Clay Refractories

	CITY	ST	EMP	PHONE	ENTRY #
Bonsal American Inc	Canaan	CT	E	860 824-7733	685
Harbisonwalker Intl Inc	West Haven	CT	G	203 934-7960	5125
Redland Brick Inc	South Windsor	CT	C	860 528-1311	4007
Aspell Saggers LLC	North Attleboro	MA	G	508 216-3264	13748
Bnz Materials Inc	North Billerica	MA	E	978 663-3401	13796
LMI Liquidation Corporation	Lynn	MA	G	781 593-2561	12521
Lynn Products Co	Lynn	MA	E	781 593-2500	12524
Contact Inc	Edgecomb	ME	G	207 882-6116	6001
Zampell Refractories Inc	Auburn	ME	E	207 786-2400	5602
Conproco Corp **(PA)**	Somersworth	NH	F	603 743-5800	19831
AW Perkins Company	Rutland	VT	G	802 773-3600	22323

3259 Structural Clay Prdts, NEC

	CITY	ST	EMP	PHONE	ENTRY #
Eljen Corporation	East Hartford	CT	E	860 610-0426	1191
North American Supaflu Systems	Scarborough	ME	F	207 883-1155	6935
Z-Flex (us) Inc	Bedford	NH	E	603 669-5136	17668
Rupe Slate Co	Poultney	VT	G	802 287-9692	22276

3261 China Plumbing Fixtures & Fittings

	CITY	ST	EMP	PHONE	ENTRY #
Syn-Mar Products Inc	Ellington	CT	F	860 872-8505	1341
Water Works	Danbury	CT	G	203 546-6000	1007
Clivus Multrum Inc	Lawrence	MA	G	978 725-5591	12010
Clivus New England Inc	Lawrence	MA	G	978 794-9400	12011
Kenney Manufacturing Company **(PA)**	Warwick	RI	B	401 739-2200	21383
Summer Infant Inc **(PA)**	Woonsocket	RI	D	401 671-6550	21581
Summer Infant Inc	Woonsocket	RI	G	401 671-6550	21582

3262 China, Table & Kitchen Articles

	CITY	ST	EMP	PHONE	ENTRY #
International Event Products	Stoughton	MA	G	781 341-0929	15598
Wainwright USA LLC	Great Barrington	MA	G	413 717-4211	11249
Butternuts Good Dishes Inc	Wolfeboro	NH	G	603 569-6869	20016

3263 Earthenware, Whiteware, Table & Kitchen Articles

	CITY	ST	EMP	PHONE	ENTRY #
Express Cntertops Kit Flrg LLC	Orange	CT	G	203 283-4909	3365
JH Smith Co Inc **(PA)**	Greenfield	MA	F	413 772-0191	11264
Waddington North America Inc	Chelmsford	MA	C	978 256-6551	9941
Hope & Main	Warren	RI	G	401 245-7400	21295

3264 Porcelain Electrical Splys

	CITY	ST	EMP	PHONE	ENTRY #
Coorstek Inc	East Granby	CT	E	860 653-8071	1124
Newco Condenser Inc	Shelton	CT	G	475 882-4000	3839
Accumet Engineering Corp	Hudson	MA	E	978 568-8311	11750
Ceramics Grinding Co Inc	Maynard	MA	G	978 461-5935	12897

	CITY	ST	EMP	PHONE	ENTRY #
Coorstek Inc	Worcester	MA	B	774 317-2600	17360
Idex Health & Science LLC	Middleboro	MA	C	774 213-0200	13064
Ceramco Inc	Center Conway	NH	E	603 447-2090	17793
Coorstek Inc	Milford	NH	D	603 673-7560	19052
J Yeager Inc **(PA)**	Manchester	VT	G	802 362-0810	22077
Superior Tchncal Ceramics Corp	Saint Albans	VT	C	802 527-7726	22380

3269 Pottery Prdts, NEC

	CITY	ST	EMP	PHONE	ENTRY #
Company of Craftsmen	Mystic	CT	G	860 536-4189	2436
Tonmar LLC	Pomfret Center	CT	G	860 974-3714	3559
Bodycote Imt Inc **(DH)**	Andover	MA	D	978 470-0876	7542
Central Garden & Pet Company	Taunton	MA	E	508 884-5426	15735
Conversation Concepts LLC	Fitchburg	MA	F	978 342-1414	10820
Gare Incorporated	Haverhill	MA	E	978 373-9131	11437
Jill Rosenwald Ceramic Design	Boston	MA	G	617 422-0787	8630
Mudpie Potters	Leverett	MA	E	413 548-3939	12198
Potting Shed Inc	Concord	MA	G	617 899-6290	10151
Saint-Gobain Corporation	Northborough	MA	E	508 351-7112	14047
Scargo Stoneware Pottery	Dennis	MA	G	508 385-3894	10311
Sheffield Pottery Inc	Sheffield	MA	E	413 229-7700	15065
Vaillancourt Folk Art Inc	Sutton	MA	E	508 476-3601	15695
ZB Ceramic	Chicopee	MA	G	413 512-0879	10070
Chris Davis Stoneware Pottery	York	ME	G	207 363-7561	7306
Darmariscotta Pottery Inc	Damariscotta	ME	G	207 563-8843	5935
Georgetown Pottery	Georgetown	ME	G	207 371-2801	6106
Hendersons Redware	Bangor	ME	G	207 942-9013	5649
Rackliffe Pottery Inc	Blue Hill	ME	G	207 374-2297	5773
Sylvia Wyler Pottery Inc **(PA)**	Brunswick	ME	G	207 729-1321	5848
Ah Nelsen Associates LLC	Kingston	NH	G	603 716-6687	18538
Clayground	East Greenwich	RI	G	401 884-4888	20358
Philippine Pot Partners LLC	Lincoln	RI	G	401 789-7372	20590
Bennington Potters Inc **(PA)**	Bennington	VT	E	800 205-8033	21664
Beth Mueller Inc	Barre	VT	G	802 476-3582	21609
Romulus Craft	Washington	VT	G	802 685-3869	22580
Simon Pearce US Inc **(PA)**	Windsor	VT	C	802 674-6280	22714

3271 Concrete Block & Brick

	CITY	ST	EMP	PHONE	ENTRY #
Connecticut Concrete Form Inc	Farmington	CT	F	860 674-1314	1474
Kobyluck Ready-Mix Inc	Waterford	CT	F	860 444-9604	4987
Messiah Development LLC	Bridgeport	CT	G	203 368-2405	450
New Milford Block & Supply	New Milford	CT	F	860 355-1101	2816
Westbrook Con Block Co Inc	Westbrook	CT	E	860 399-6201	5166
Adolf Jandris & Sons Inc	Gardner	MA	E	978 632-0089	11102
Greener Group LLC	Lowell	MA	D	978 441-3900	12378
Hi-Way Concrete Pdts Co Inc	Wareham	MA	E	508 295-0834	16249
Ideal Concrete Block Co **(PA)**	Westford	MA	E	978 692-3076	16773
J & O Construction Inc	Brockton	MA	G	508 586-4900	9157
Johns Building Supply Co Inc	Pittsfield	MA	F	413 442-7846	14478
Kingston Block Co Inc	Kingston	MA	G	781 585-6400	11960
Oldcastle Apg Northeast Inc	Holbrook	MA	D	781 506-9473	11535
P & M Brick & Block Inc	Watertown	MA	G	617 924-6020	16304
R Ducharme Inc	Chicopee	MA	G	413 534-4516	10055
State Road Cement Block Co	North Dartmouth	MA	G	508 993-9473	13926
Stiles & Hart Brick Company	Bridgewater	MA	E	508 697-6928	9088
Vynorius Prestress Inc	Salisbury	MA	F	978 462-7765	14959
Gagne & Son Con Blocks Inc	Auburn	ME	G	207 495-3313	5566
Rjf - Morin Brick LLC	Auburn	ME	D	207 784-9375	5595
Gorham Brick & Block Inc	Berlin	NH	G	603 752-3631	17696
Tilcon Arthur Whitcomb Inc **(HQ)**	North Swanzey	NH	F	603 352-0101	19393
Anchor Concrete	Cranston	RI	E	401 942-4800	20182
Anthony Corrado Inc	Lincoln	RI	G	401 723-7600	20556
Ferreira Concrete Forms Inc	East Providence	RI	F	401 639-0931	20413

3272 Concrete Prdts

	CITY	ST	EMP	PHONE	ENTRY #
Advanced Drainage Systems Inc	Rocky Hill	CT	E	860 529-8188	3701
Arrow Concrete Products Inc **(PA)**	Granby	CT	E	860 653-5063	1588
Atlantic Pipe Corporation	Plainville	CT	D	860 747-5557	3466
Blakeslee Prestress Inc **(PA)**	Branford	CT	B	203 315-7090	298
Bonsal American Inc	Canaan	CT	G	860 824-7733	684
Bonsal American Inc	Canaan	CT	E	860 824-7733	685
Bridgeport Burial Vault Co	Stratford	CT	G	203 375-7375	4399
Concrete Products	North Windham	CT	G	860 423-4144	3081
Connecticut Precast Corp	Monroe	CT	E	203 268-8688	2398
Dalton Enterprises Inc **(PA)**	Cheshire	CT	D	203 272-3221	726
David Shuck	Old Lyme	CT	G	860 434-8562	3320
Dawn Enterprises LLC	Manchester	CT	G	860 646-8200	1999
Direct Sales LLC **(PA)**	Fairfield	CT	G	203 371-2373	1426
Eastern Precast Company Inc	Brookfield	CT	E	203 775-0230	643
Elm-Cap Industries Inc	West Hartford	CT	E	860 953-1060	5070
Essex Concrete Products Inc	Essex	CT	F	860 767-1768	1396
Forterra Pipe & Precast LLC	Wauregan	CT	F	860 564-9000	5039
J B Concrete Products Inc	Putnam	CT	G	860 928-9365	3617
Jolley Precast Inc	Danielson	CT	E	860 774-9066	1014
M & M Precast Corp	Danbury	CT	F	203 743-5559	951
Mono Crete Step Co of CT LLC	Bethel	CT	F	203 748-8419	172
New Milford Block & Supply	New Milford	CT	F	860 355-1101	2816
Nteco Inc	Darien	CT	E	203 656-1154	1030
Oldcastle Infrastructure Inc	Avon	CT	E	860 673-3291	40
Pauls Marble Depot LLC	Stamford	CT	F	203 978-0669	4279
Platt Brothers & Company **(PA)**	Waterbury	CT	D	203 753-4194	4940
Stone Image Custom Concrete	Suffield	CT	G	860 668-2434	4468
Superior Concrete Products LLC	Portland	CT	G	860 342-0186	3576
Techno Mtal Post Watertown LLC	Waterbury	CT	G	203 755-6403	4961
West Hartford Stone Mulch LLC	West Hartford	CT	G	860 461-7616	5103
WJ Kettleworks LLC	Stratford	CT	G	203 377-5000	4458
Acme Precast Co Inc	West Falmouth	MA	E	508 548-9607	16477
Acme-Shorey Precast Co Inc **(PA)**	Harwich	MA	F	508 432-0530	11386
Acme-Shorey Precast Co Inc	South Yarmouth	MA	E	508 430-0956	15324
Amazing Glaze	Norton	MA	G	508 285-7234	14070
Benson Enterprises Inc	North Easton	MA	F	508 583-5401	13943
Bonsal American Inc	Millbury	MA	G	508 791-6366	13157
Bonsal American Inc	Oxford	MA	E	508 987-8188	14254
Bonsal American Inc	Lee	MA	E	413 243-0053	12090
Byrne Sand & Gravel Co Inc	Middleboro	MA	F	508 947-0724	13058
Cement Well Concrete Products	Palmer	MA	G	413 283-8450	14284
Concrete Pdts of Londonderry	Wilmington	MA	G	978 658-2645	16988
Concretebenchmolds LLC	Framingham	MA	G	800 242-1809	10936
County Concrete Corp **(PA)**	Dalton	MA	E	413 499-3359	10175
DAngelo Burial Vaults	Franklin	MA	G	508 528-0385	11036
David Sevigny Inc	Winchendon	MA	G	978 297-2775	17073
Derek Ciccone	East Douglas	MA	G	508 476-2105	10426
Diversitech Corporation	Taunton	MA	G	800 699-0453	15744
Environmental Improvements **(PA)**	Abington	MA	G	781 857-2375	7324
Essex Column Corp	Georgetown	MA	F	978 352-7670	11141
Fireslate 2 Inc	East Wareham	MA	F	508 273-0047	10530
Flagg Palmer Precast Inc	Oxford	MA	G	508 987-3400	14261
Fletcher Granite LLC **(DH)**	Westford	MA	G	978 692-1312	16767
Forterra Pipe & Precast LLC	Ashland	MA	A	508 881-2000	7659
Green Burial Massachusetts	Gill	MA	G	413 863-4634	11156
Hardy Doric Inc	Chelmsford	MA	G	978 250-1113	9903
J & D Associates Corp	Milford	MA	G	508 478-9770	13120
J and R Pre Cast Inc	Berkley	MA	F	508 822-3311	8087
Keating Wilbert Vault Company	Wilbraham	MA	F	413 543-1226	16939
Kellogg Bros Inc	Southwick	MA	G	413 569-6029	15415
Kingston Block Co Inc	Kingston	MA	G	781 585-6400	11960
L & L Concrete Products Inc	Oxford	MA	F	508 987-8175	14264
Lorusso Corp **(PA)**	Plainville	MA	E	508 668-6520	14527
Means Pre-Cast Co Inc	Braintree	MA	G	781 843-1909	9025
Montachsett Tcci Burial Vaults	Leominster	MA	G	978 537-6190	12169
Monument Street Entps LLC	Concord	MA	G	781 820-1888	10142
Nantucket Pavers Inc	Rehoboth	MA	F	508 336-5800	14753
National Con Tnks / Frguard JV	Concord	MA	F	978 505-5533	10144
Northeast Building Supply LLC	Hanson	MA	G	781 294-0400	11367
Oldcastle Apg Northeast Inc	Holbrook	MA	D	781 506-9473	11535
Oldcastle Infrastructure Inc	Rehoboth	MA	D	508 336-7600	14756
Oldcastle Infrastructure Inc	Littleton	MA	E	978 486-9600	12315
Oldcastle Precast Inc	Rehoboth	MA	E	508 867-8312	14757
Paul Young Precast Company	Bellingham	MA	G	508 966-4333	8056
Pavestone LLC	Middleboro	MA	D	508 947-6001	13075
Pine Tree Concrete Products	Millville	MA	G	508 883-7072	13187
Popular Precast Products	Bellingham	MA	G	508 966-4622	8057
Portland Stone Ware Co Inc **(PA)**	Dracut	MA	E	978 459-7272	10367
Precast Specialties Corp	Abington	MA	E	781 878-7220	7328
Precast Vault Co Inc	North Dighton	MA	G	508 252-4886	13933
Precast Vault Co Inc **(PA)**	Braintree	MA	G	508 252-4886	9031
Quintal Burial Vaults	Dighton	MA	F	508 669-5717	10338
Ray Scituate Precast Con Corp	Marshfield	MA	E	781 837-1747	12866
Sani Tank Inc	Leominster	MA	G	978 537-9784	12186
Schofield Concrete Forms Inc	Melrose	MA	G	781 662-0796	12992
Scituate Concrete Pipe Corp	Scituate	MA	E	781 545-0564	15013
Shea Concrete Products Inc **(PA)**	Amesbury	MA	E	978 658-2645	7507
Shea Concrete Products Inc	Amesbury	MA	E	978 388-1509	7508
Stone Soup Concrete	Easthampton	MA	G	413 203-5600	10580
Strafello Precast Inc	East Taunton	MA	F	774 501-2628	10518
Strescon of New England	Burlington	MA	G	781 221-2153	9342
TFC Enterprises LLC	Westborough	MA	G	866 996-2701	16656
Turn Key Lumber Inc	Lunenburg	MA	E	978 798-1370	12484
Umaco Inc	Lowell	MA	G	978 453-8881	12441
Unistress Corp	Pittsfield	MA	B	413 499-1441	14512
Wachusett Precast Inc	Sterling	MA	G	978 422-3311	15548
Watertown Engineering Corp	Whitman	MA	E	781 857-2555	16929
Wiggin Means Precast Co Inc	Pocasset	MA	G	508 564-6776	14603
Wiggin Precast Corp	Pocasset	MA	F	508 564-6776	14604
Williams Stone Co Inc	East Otis	MA	E	413 269-4544	10504
American Concrete Inds Inc **(PA)**	Auburn	ME	E	207 947-8334	5550
American Concrete Inds Inc	Bangor	ME	D	207 947-8334	5629
Aroostacast Inc	Presque Isle	ME	F	207 764-0077	6753
Elm Street Vault Inc	Biddeford	ME	G	207 284-4855	5731
Ferraiolo Construction Inc	Rockland	ME	E	207 582-6162	6792
Frederick Wieninger Monuments	Milbridge	ME	G	207 546-2356	6432
Gagne & Son Con Blocks Inc	Auburn	ME	G	207 495-3313	5566
Greenstone Precast	New Gloucester	ME	G	207 926-5704	6466
H W Dunn & Son Inc	Ellsworth	ME	G	207 667-8121	6019
Lunaform LLC	North Sullivan	ME	G	207 422-3306	6514

	CITY	ST	EMP	PHONE	ENTRY #
M G A Cast Stone Inc	Oxford	ME	E	207 926-5993	6569
Mattingly Products Company	North Anson	ME	E	207 635-2719	6504
Nicmar Industries	Alfred	ME	E	207 324-6571	5516
Richard Genest Inc	Sanford	ME	F	207 324-7215	6890
Sandelin Foundation Inc	Topsham	ME	F	207 725-7004	7094
Trombley Industries Inc	Limestone	ME	G	207 328-4503	6345
Wilbert Swans Vault Co	Westbrook	ME	E	207 854-5324	7214
Andrew J Foss Company Inc	Farmington	NH	F	603 755-2515	18139
Arthurs Memorials Inc	Center Conway	NH	G	603 356-5398	17791
Concrete Systems Inc	Londonderry	NH	F	603 432-1840	18686
Concrete Systems Inc	Hudson	NH	D	603 886-5472	18380
Conproco Corp	Bow	NH	G	603 743-5800	17710
Conproco Corp **(PA)**	Somersworth	NH	F	603 743-5800	19831
E-Z Crete LLC	Keene	NH	G	603 313-6462	18500
E-Z Crete LLC	Harrisville	NH	G	603 313-6462	18301
East Coast Concrete Pdts LLC	Amherst	NH	G	603 883-3042	17558
Eldorado Stone	Rochester	NH	G	617 947-6722	19669
Michie Corporation	Henniker	NH	D	603 428-7426	18307
N H Central Concrete Corp	Henniker	NH	F	603 428-7900	18308
New England Vlts Monuments LLC	Milan	NH	G	603 449-2165	19041
Newstress Inc	Epsom	NH	E	603 736-9000	18107
Northern Design Precast Inc	Loudon	NH	E	603 783-8989	18751
Quikrete Companies LLC	Brentwood	NH	E	603 778-2123	17756
Sabbow and Co Inc	Littleton	NH	F	603 444-6724	18665
Syphers Monument DBA Affordabl	Seabrook	NH	G	603 468-3033	19821
Tuff Crete Corporation	South Hampton	NH	G	603 485-1969	19857
William N Lamarre Con Pdts Inc	Greenville	NH	F	603 878-1340	18230
Anchor Concrete	Cranston	RI	E	401 942-4800	20182
Artcrete Enterprises Inc	Providence	RI	G	401 270-0700	20958
Ashaway Cement Products Inc	Wyoming	RI	G	401 539-1010	21588
Cardi Materials LLC **(PA)**	Warwick	RI	E	401 739-8300	21340
Durastone Corporation	Lincoln	RI	F	401 723-7100	20569
Fernandes Precast Company	Smithfield	RI	G	401 349-4907	21223
Forterra Pipe & Precast LLC	Peace Dale	RI	F	401 782-2600	20913
Livingstone Studios	Lincoln	RI	G	401 475-1145	20580
New Canaan Stone Service LLC	Johnston	RI	G	401 829-8293	20525
R B L Holdings Inc	Coventry	RI	F	401 821-2200	20163
Caledonia Inc **(PA)**	Saint Johnsbury	VT	F	802 748-2319	22388
Charles Curtis LLC	Danville	VT	G	802 274-0060	21895
D G Robertson Inc	South Burlington	VT	G	802 864-6027	22445
Hardrock Granite Co Inc	Barre	VT	G	802 479-3606	21619
Jamaica Cottage Shop Inc	South Londonderry	VT	E	802 297-3760	22487
Joseph P Carrara & Sons Inc **(PA)**	North Clarendon	VT	E	802 775-2301	22216
Joseph P Carrara & Sons Inc	Middlebury	VT	D	802 388-6363	22113
Kinfolk Memorials Inc	East Barre	VT	G	802 479-1423	21912
Monument View Apts LP	Burlington	VT	G	802 863-8424	21798
Monumental Estates LLC	Bennington	VT	G	802 442-7339	21685
Plouffs Monument Co Inc	Enosburg Falls	VT	G	802 933-4346	21926
Washburn Vault Company Inc	Brattleboro	VT	G	802 254-9150	21754

3273 Ready-Mixed Concrete

	CITY	ST	EMP	PHONE	ENTRY #
Aiudi Concrete Inc	Westbrook	CT	G	860 399-9289	5155
Armed & Ready Alarm System	Waterbury	CT	F	203 596-0327	4846
B&R Sand and Gravel	Gales Ferry	CT	G	860 464-5099	1525
Barnes Concrete Co Inc	Putnam	CT	E	860 928-7242	3602
Beard Concrete Co Derby Inc **(PA)**	Milford	CT	G	203 874-2533	2252
Bonsal American Inc	Canaan	CT	E	860 824-7733	685
Builders Concrete East LLC	North Windham	CT	E	860 456-4111	3079
Century Acquisition	Canaan	CT	G	518 758-7229	686
Enfield Transit Mix Inc	Enfield	CT	F	860 763-0864	1357
Essex Concrete Products Inc	Essex	CT	F	860 767-1768	1396
Federici Brands LLC	Wilton	CT	F	203 762-7667	5289
Five Star Products Inc	Shelton	CT	E	203 336-7900	3802
Mohican Valley Concrete Corp	Fairfield	CT	E	203 254-7133	1446
Mohican Vly Sand & Grav Corp	Fairfield	CT	F	203 254-7133	1447
O & G Industries Inc	Bridgeport	CT	E	203 366-4586	459
O & G Industries Inc	Danbury	CT	E	203 748-5694	963
Pick & Mix Corp	West Hartford	CT	G	860 521-1521	5091
Sega Ready Mix Incorporated **(PA)**	New Milford	CT	F	860 354-3969	2827
Sega Ready Mix Incorporated	Waterbury	CT	G	203 465-1052	4953
Sterling Materials LLC	Branford	CT	G	203 315-6619	352
The L Suzio Concrete Co Inc **(PA)**	Meriden	CT	E	203 237-8421	2140
Tilcon Connecticut Inc	Portland	CT	G	860 342-1096	3578
Windham Sand and Stone Inc	Manchester	CT	D	860 643-5578	2060
Aggregate Inds - Northeast Reg	Waltham	MA	F	781 893-7562	16026
Aggregate Inds - Northeast Reg	Stoughton	MA	G	781 344-1100	15574
Aggregate Inds - Northeast Reg	South Dennis	MA	G	508 398-8865	15264
Aggregate Inds - Northeast Reg	Watertown	MA	G	617 924-8550	16264
Aggregate Inds - Northeast Reg	Dennis	MA	G	508 398-8865	10305
Aggregate Inds - Northeast Reg	Saugus	MA	G	781 941-7200	14975
Aggregate Industries	Lunenburg	MA	E	978 582-0261	12480
Aggregate Industries - Mwr Inc	Saugus	MA	E	781 941-7200	14976
Aggregate Industries - Mwr Inc	Saugus	MA	D	781 231-3400	14977
Aggregate Industries - Mwr Inc	East Weymouth	MA	E	781 337-2304	10533
Aggregate Industries - Mwr Inc	Stoughton	MA	E	781 344-1100	15575
Aggregate Industries - Mwr Inc	Shrewsbury	MA	G	508 754-4709	15098
Aggregate Industries - Mwr Inc	Saugus	MA	E	781 941-3108	14978
Attleboro Sand & Gravel Corp	Attleboro	MA	G	508 222-2870	7708
Banas Sand & Gravel Co Inc	Ludlow	MA	F	413 583-8321	12456
Berkshire Concrete Corp **(HQ)**	Pittsfield	MA	C	413 443-4734	14456
Bill Willard Inc	Springfield	MA	G	413 584-1054	15453
Bonded Concrete Inc	Ashley Falls	MA	G	413 229-2075	7672
Boro Sand & Stone Corp **(PA)**	North Attleboro	MA	E	508 699-2911	13750
Boro Sand & Stone Corp	South Easton	MA	G	508 238-7222	15271
Boston Sand & Gravel Company **(PA)**	Boston	MA	E	617 227-9000	8440
Boston Sand & Gravel Company	Charlestown	MA	C	617 242-5540	9826
Boston Sand & Gravel Company	Sandwich	MA	F	508 888-8002	14962
Boucher Con Foundation Sups	Middleboro	MA	G	508 947-4279	13056
Cape Cod Ready Mix Inc	Orleans	MA	E	508 255-4600	14231
Cemex Materials LLC	Westfield	MA	E	413 562-3647	16677
Chicopee Foundations Inc **(PA)**	Chicopee	MA	E	413 536-3370	10007
Chicopee Foundations Inc	Chicopee	MA	E	413 594-4700	10008
Concrete & Mortar Packg LLC	Milford	MA	G	508 473-1799	13111
Crh Americas Inc	Leominster	MA	G	978 840-1176	12127
Cs-Ma LLC	Wilbraham	MA	E	413 733-6631	16934
Dauphinais & Son Inc	North Grafton	MA	G	508 839-9258	13959
Dauphinais & Son Inc	Wilbraham	MA	F	413 596-3964	16935
Dmjl Consulting LLC	Methuen	MA	F	978 989-0790	13018
Fall River Ready-Mix Con LLC	Fall River	MA	G	508 675-7540	10698
Falmouth Ready Mix Inc	East Falmouth	MA	F	508 548-6100	10443
Fuccillo Ready Mix Inc	East Falmouth	MA	F	508 540-2821	10444
GP Aggregate Corp	Gloucester	MA	G	978 283-5318	11190
Graziano Redi-Mix Inc	Bridgewater	MA	E	508 697-8350	9074
Hyde Park Concrete Inc	Hyde Park	MA	G	617 364-5485	11869
J G Maclellan Con Co Inc **(PA)**	Lowell	MA	D	978 458-1223	12385
L & S Industries Inc **(PA)**	New Bedford	MA	E	508 995-4654	13407
L & S Industries Inc	Acushnet	MA	E	508 998-7900	7403
McCabe Sand & Gravel Co Inc	Taunton	MA	E	508 823-0771	15764
Mix	Vineyard Haven	MA	G	508 693-8240	15934
Mix and Company Ltd	Wellesley	MA	F	781 235-0028	16373
Morse Ready Mix LLC	Plainville	MA	E	508 809-4644	14529
Morse Sand & Gravel Corp	Attleboro	MA	E	508 809-4644	7769
Preferred Concrete Corp	East Freetown	MA	F	508 763-5500	10457
Ragged Hill Incorporated	East Templeton	MA	E	978 939-5712	10520
Ready 4	Cambridge	MA	G	857 233-5455	9627
Redi-Mix Services Incorporated	Taunton	MA	G	508 823-0771	15778
Rosenfeld Concrete Corp **(HQ)**	Hopedale	MA	E	508 473-7200	11682
Rowley Ready Mix Inc	Rowley	MA	F	978 948-2544	14864
Southern Redi-Mix Corporation	Marshfield	MA	E	781 837-5353	12869
Sterling Concrete Corp	Sterling	MA	F	978 422-8282	15546
Varney Bros Sand & Gravel Inc	Bellingham	MA	E	508 966-1313	8062
Vita-Crete Inc	Milford	MA	G	508 473-1799	13151
Wakefield Investments Inc	Lunenburg	MA	D	978 582-0261	12486
Wbmx Mix 985 Tweeter Cntr	Mansfield	MA	G	508 339-1296	12670
Westfield Concrete Inc	Westfield	MA	E	413 562-4814	16742
Westfield Ready-Mix Inc	Chicopee	MA	E	413 594-4700	10069
County Concrete & Cnstr Co	Columbia Falls	ME	E	207 483-4409	5919
Dayton Sand & Gravel Inc	Dayton	ME	D	207 499-2306	5944
Dragon Products Company Inc	Portland	ME	F	207 879-2328	6655
Dragon Products Company LLC **(DH)**	South Portland	ME	E	207 774-6355	7022
Dragon Products Company LLC	Thomaston	ME	C	207 594-5555	7083
F R Carroll Inc	Limerick	ME	E	207 793-8615	6334
Haley Construction Inc	Farmington	ME	G	207 778-9990	6049
Lees Concrete Inc	Bangor	ME	G	207 974-4936	5653
Mattingly Products Company	North Anson	ME	E	207 635-2719	6504
R A Cummings Inc	Auburn	ME	E	207 777-7100	5594
R Pepin & Sons Inc	Sanford	ME	E	207 324-6125	6886
Scanmix Inc	Lewiston	ME	G	207 782-1885	6320
Trombley Industries Inc	Limestone	ME	G	207 328-4503	6345
Trombley Redi-Mix Inc **(PA)**	Presque Isle	ME	G	207 551-3770	6770
Aggregate Industries - Mwr Inc	Portsmouth	NH	E	603 427-1137	19533
Aggregate Industries - Mwr Inc	Raymond	NH	F	603 243-3554	19633
Alvin J Coleman & Son Inc	Albany	NH	E	603 447-3056	17534
Boston Sand & Gravel Company	Rochester	NH	C	603 330-3999	19662
Carroll Concrete Co Inc	Newport	NH	F	603 863-1765	19343
Coleman Concrete Inc	Albany	NH	E	603 447-5936	17536
Granite State Concrete Co Inc	Milford	NH	E	603 673-3327	19057
In The Mix	Nashua	NH	G	603 557-2078	19186
LE Weed & Son LLC **(PA)**	Newport	NH	F	603 863-1540	19349
Michie Corporation	Henniker	NH	D	603 428-7426	18307
Newport Concrete Block Co	Newport	NH	F	603 863-1540	19351
Newport Sand & Gravel Co Inc **(PA)**	Newport	NH	F	603 298-0199	19352
Newport Sand & Gravel Co Inc	Peterborough	NH	G	603 924-1999	19480
Newport Sand & Gravel Co Inc	Charlestown	NH	G	603 826-4444	17817
Oldcastle Materials Inc	Manchester	NH	G	603 669-2373	18893
Redimix Companies Inc **(DH)**	Belmont	NH	E	603 524-4434	17682
Seacoast Redimix Concrete LLC **(PA)**	Dover	NH	F	603 742-4441	18052
Tilcon Arthur Whitcomb Inc **(HQ)**	North Swanzey	NH	F	603 352-0101	19393
Torromeo Industries Inc	Kingston	NH	E	603 642-5564	18546
Adamsdale Concrete & Pdts Co	Pawtucket	RI	G	401 722-6725	20808
Consolidated Concrete Corp **(PA)**	East Providence	RI	G	401 438-4700	20399
Consolidated Concrete Corp	Coventry	RI	G	401 828-4700	20143
Greenville Ready Mix Inc	Ashaway	RI	G	401 539-2333	20035
Heritage Concrete Corp	Exeter	RI	F	401 294-1524	20451

	CITY	ST	EMP	PHONE	ENTRY #
Lehigh Cement Company LLC	Providence	RI	G	401 467-6750	21052
Material Concrete Corp	North Smithfield	RI	F	401 765-0204	20790
Mix Marketing Corp	Narragansett	RI	G	401 954-6121	20642
Pawtucket Hot Mix	Pawtucket	RI	F	401 722-4488	20876
Rhode Island Ready Mix LLC	Wyoming	RI	F	401 539-8222	21590
Carroll Concrete Co	Barre	VT	G	802 229-0191	21611
Dailey Precast LLC	Shaftsbury	VT	G	802 442-4418	22402
Gray Rock Concrete	Milton	VT	F	802 379-5393	22130
Harrison Redi-Mix Corp	Fairfax	VT	F	802 849-6688	21976
Joseph P Carrara & Sons Inc	Middlebury	VT	D	802 388-6363	22113
Joseph P Carrara & Sons Inc **(PA)**	North Clarendon	VT	E	802 775-2301	22216
Newport Sand & Gravel Co Inc	Swanton	VT	G	802 868-4119	22532
Newport Sand & Gravel Co Inc	Randolph	VT	G	802 728-5055	22300
Newport Sand & Gravel Co Inc	Guildhall	VT	G	802 328-3384	22006
Newport Sand & Gravel Co Inc	Newport	VT	F	802 334-2000	22204
Woodstock Grnola Trail Mix LLC	Woodstock	VT	G	802 457-3149	22742

3274 Lime

	CITY	ST	EMP	PHONE	ENTRY #
Bonsal American Inc	Lee	MA	E	413 243-0053	12090
Dragon Products Company LLC **(DH)**	South Portland	ME	E	207 774-6355	7022

3275 Gypsum Prdts

	CITY	ST	EMP	PHONE	ENTRY #
Proudfoot Company Inc	Monroe	CT	F	203 459-0031	2416
Georgia-Pacific LLC	Norwood	MA	G	781 440-3600	14155
County Concrete & Cnstr Co	Columbia Falls	ME	E	207 483-4409	5919
Georgia-Pacific LLC	Newington	NH	C	603 433-8000	19322

3281 Cut Stone Prdts

	CITY	ST	EMP	PHONE	ENTRY #
American Stonecrafters Inc	Wallingford	CT	G	203 514-9725	4698
Architectural Stone Group LLC	Bridgeport	CT	G	203 494-5451	377
Central Marble & Granite LLC	Ansonia	CT	G	203 734-4644	9
Connecticut Solid Surface LLC	Plainville	CT	E	860 410-9800	3477
Connecticut Stone Supplies Inc **(PA)**	Milford	CT	D	203 882-1000	2270
Creative Stone LLC	East Haven	CT	F	203 624-1882	1246
Dan Beard Inc	Shelton	CT	F	203 924-4346	3794
Eastern Marble & Granite LLC	Milford	CT	F	203 882-8221	2280
French River Mtls Thompson LLC	North Grosvenordale	CT	G	860 450-9574	2994
Granite & Kitchen Studio LLC	South Windsor	CT	G	860 290-4444	3975
Granite LLC	Newington	CT	G	860 586-8132	2868
Granitech LLC	Plantsville	CT	G	860 620-1733	3532
Interntonal MBL Gran Entps Inc	Hartford	CT	G	860 296-0741	1838
Kenneth Lynch & Sons Inc	Oxford	CT	G	203 762-8363	3411
La Pietra Thinstone Veneer	Brookfield	CT	G	203 775-6162	650
Mark Dzidzk	Plainville	CT	E	860 793-2767	3504
New England Gran Cabinets LLC	West Hartford	CT	G	860 310-2981	5087
New England Materials LLC	Monroe	CT	G	203 261-5500	2412
O & G Industries Inc	Beacon Falls	CT	F	203 729-4529	64
Paul H Gesswein & Company Inc	Old Saybrook	CT	G	860 388-0652	3348
Pistritto Marble Imports Inc	Hartford	CT	G	860 296-5263	1857
Skyline Quarry	Stafford Springs	CT	E	860 875-3580	4115
Stone Workshop LLC	Bridgeport	CT	G	203 362-1144	496
Stoneage LLC	Shelton	CT	G	203 926-1133	3874
Surface Plate Co	Glastonbury	CT	G	860 652-8905	1578
Tri LLC	Stamford	CT	G	203 353-8418	4349
270 University Ave LLC	Westwood	MA	G	781 407-0836	16855
Aldrich Marble & Granite Co	Norwood	MA	E	781 762-6111	14124
All Granite & Marble Inc II	Charlton	MA	G	508 434-0611	9846
Atlantic MBL & Gran Group Inc	East Falmouth	MA	G	508 540-9770	10436
B R S Inc	Bridgewater	MA	E	508 697-5448	9061
Bates Bros Seam Face Gran Co	East Weymouth	MA	F	781 337-1150	10537
Bonsal American Inc	Lee	MA	E	413 243-0053	12090
Cassa Floor Design Inc	Shrewsbury	MA	F	508 845-0600	15106
Colonial Landscape Corp	Groton	MA	G	978 448-3329	11287
Continental Stone MBL Gran Inc	Sterling	MA	E	978 422-8700	15538
Counterra LLC	Canton	MA	F	781 821-2100	9723
David P Deveney Memorial Co	Medford	MA	G	781 396-7772	12929
Deveney & White Inc	Boston	MA	G	617 288-3080	8501
Divine Stoneworks LLC	Ashland	MA	G	774 221-6006	7657
E W Sykes General Contractors	Athol	MA	F	978 249-7655	7686
Earthworks Granite & Marble	Braintree	MA	G	781 356-3544	9002
East Coast Marble & Gran Corp	Lynn	MA	G	781 760-0207	12504
Escountertops LLC	West Springfield	MA	G	413 732-8128	16519
Fletcher Granite LLC **(DH)**	Westford	MA	G	978 692-1312	16767
Foxrock Granite LLC	Quincy	MA	G	617 249-8015	14626
Hi-Way Concrete Pdts Co Inc	Wareham	MA	E	508 295-0834	16249
International Stone Inc	Woburn	MA	D	781 937-3300	17206
Ital Marble Co Inc	Lynn	MA	F	781 595-4859	12517
Louis W Mian Inc **(PA)**	Boston	MA	E	617 241-7900	8672
Mackenzie Vault Inc	East Longmeadow	MA	F	413 525-8827	10483
Majestic Marble & Granite Inc	Canton	MA	G	781 830-1020	9755
McC Materials Inc	North Adams	MA	G	860 309-9491	13680
Mkl Stone LLC	Everett	MA	G	781 844-9811	10622
Nickerson Stonecrafters of Cao	Orleans	MA	G	508 255-8600	14238
Phillip Ippolito	Seekonk	MA	F	508 336-9616	15033
Progressive Marble Fabrication	Randolph	MA	G	781 963-6029	14694
Quarry Brothers Incorporated	Rehoboth	MA	G	508 252-9922	14758
Quintal Burial Vaults	Dighton	MA	F	508 669-5717	10338
Ricciardi Marble and Granite	Hyannis	MA	G	508 790-2734	11855
Roma Stone	Harwich	MA	G	508 430-1200	11397
S M Lorusso & Sons Inc	East Weymouth	MA	E	781 337-6770	10546
Santo C De Spirt Marble & Gran	Agawam	MA	G	413 786-7073	7450
Steven Tedesco	Danvers	MA	G	978 777-4070	10258
Stone Decor Galleria Inc	Woburn	MA	G	781 937-9377	17302
Stone Design Marble & Gran Co	South Weymouth	MA	G	781 331-3000	15322
Stone Surfaces Inc	Woburn	MA	F	781 270-4600	17303
United Marble Fabricators Inc	Watertown	MA	G	617 926-6226	16328
Vanity World Inc	Canton	MA	G	508 668-1800	9792
W C Canniff & Sons Inc **(PA)**	Boston	MA	G	617 323-3690	8914
W C Canniff & Sons Inc	Roslindale	MA	F	617 323-3690	14845
Williams Stone Co Inc	East Otis	MA	E	413 269-4544	10504
Dragon Products Company LLC **(DH)**	South Portland	ME	E	207 774-6355	7022
Flagstone Inc	Mapleton	ME	G	207 227-5883	6411
Morning Star Marble & Gran Inc	Topsham	ME	F	207 725-7309	7091
Sheldon Slate Products Co Inc	Monson	ME	F	207 997-3615	6452
Trombley Industries Inc	Limestone	ME	G	207 328-4503	6345
Arens Stoneworks Inc	Greenland	NH	F	603 436-8000	18221
Barre Tile Inc	Lebanon	NH	F	802 476-0912	18614
Conproco Corp	Bow	NH	G	603 743-5800	17710
Galleria Stone	Merrimack	NH	G	603 424-2884	19001
High Standard Inc	Jaffrey	NH	G	603 532-8000	18466
Ripano Stoneworks Ltd	Nashua	NH	E	603 886-6655	19254
Stone Vault Co	Newport	NH	G	603 863-2720	19359
Swenson Granite Company LLC **(DH)**	Concord	NH	E	603 225-4322	17933
Creative Bronze Inc	West Warwick	RI	G	401 823-7340	21489
Stone Systems New England LLC	North Smithfield	RI	C	401 766-3603	20796
Structural Stone LLC	North Kingstown	RI	F	401 667-4969	20742
Adams Granite Company Inc	Websterville	VT	D	802 476-5281	22596
Browns Quarried Slate Pdts Inc	Castleton	VT	G	802 468-2297	21827
Buttura & Sons Inc	Barre	VT	E	802 476-6646	21610
Camara Slate Products Inc	Fair Haven	VT	E	802 265-3200	21966
Family Memorials Inc	Barre	VT	G	802 476-7831	21614
Gandin Brothers Inc	South Ryegate	VT	F	802 584-3521	22496
Global Values VT LLC	Barre	VT	E	802 476-8000	21616
Granite Industries Vermont Inc	Barre	VT	D	800 451-3236	21618
Hillside Solid Surfaces	Barre	VT	F	802 479-2508	21622
International Stone Products **(PA)**	Barre	VT	D	802 476-6636	21625
J N G Hadeka Slate Flooring	West Pawlet	VT	G	802 265-3351	22611
Joes Custom Polishing	East Barre	VT	G	802 479-9266	21911
Johnson Marble and Granite	Proctor	VT	G	802 459-3303	22285
Kinfolk Memorials Inc	East Barre	VT	G	802 479-1423	21912
La Perle & Sons Granite Co	Barre	VT	G	802 476-6463	21628
Memorial Sandblast Inc	Barre	VT	G	802 476-7086	21629
Montpelier Granite Works Inc	Montpelier	VT	F	802 223-2581	22155
Newmont Slate Co Inc **(PA)**	West Pawlet	VT	E	802 645-0203	22612
Paul Thomas	Chester	VT	G	802 875-4004	21848
Pedro Reese	Fair Haven	VT	G	802 265-3658	21967
Peerless Granite Co Inc	Barre	VT	F	802 476-3061	21634
Pepin Granite Company Inc	Barre	VT	E	802 476-6103	21636
Riverton Memorial Inc	Riverton	VT	F	802 485-3371	22314
Rock of Ages Corporation	Graniteville	VT	F	802 476-3119	22002
Spruce Mountian Granites Inc	Barre	VT	E	802 476-7474	21639
Swenson Granite Company LLC	Barre	VT	E	802 476-7021	21641
Troy Minerals Co	Colchester	VT	G	802 878-5103	21883
Vermont Soapstone Inc	Perkinsville	VT	F	802 263-5577	22260
Vermont Speciality Slate Inc	Brandon	VT	G	802 247-6615	21714
Vermont Stone Art LLC	Barre	VT	G	802 238-1498	21644
Vermont Stoneworks	Springfield	VT	G	802 885-6535	22512
Vermont Structural Slate Co **(PA)**	Fair Haven	VT	E	802 265-4933	21970
Vermont Thinstone Assoc LLC	Colchester	VT	G	802 448-3000	21888
Vermont Unfading Green Slate **(PA)**	Fair Haven	VT	F	802 265-3200	21971
Williams & Co Mining Inc	Perkinsville	VT	F	802 263-5404	22261

3291 Abrasive Prdts

	CITY	ST	EMP	PHONE	ENTRY #
Ahlstrom-Munksjo Nonwovens LLC **(DH)**	Windsor Locks	CT	B	860 654-8300	5382
Avery Abrasives Inc	Trumbull	CT	E	203 372-3513	4613
Chessco Industries Inc **(PA)**	Westport	CT	E	203 255-2804	5183
Magcor Inc	Monroe	CT	G	203 445-0302	2408
Precision Dip Coating LLC	Waterbury	CT	G	203 805-4564	4943
Pressure Blast Mfg Co Inc	South Windsor	CT	F	800 722-5278	4004
Tcg Green Technologies Inc	Sharon	CT	F	860 364-4694	3770
Triatic Incorporated	West Hartford	CT	F	860 236-2298	5099
United Abrasives Inc **(PA)**	North Windham	CT	B	860 456-7131	3084
3M Company	Haverhill	MA	G	978 420-0001	11403
Chas G Allen Realty LLC	Barre	MA	D	978 355-2911	7950
Diamond Plated Technology Inc	Taunton	MA	G	508 823-2711	15743
Ewm Corp **(PA)**	Middleton	MA	G	978 774-1191	13088
Micro Abrasives Corporation	Westfield	MA	E	413 562-3641	16704
Mosher Company Inc	Chicopee	MA	F	413 598-8341	10047
New England Abrasives	Holliston	MA	G	508 893-9540	11589
Olsen & Silk Abrasives	Salem	MA	G	978 744-4720	14933
Prematech LLC	Worcester	MA	E	508 791-9549	17445
Rex Cut Products Incorporated	Fall River	MA	D	508 678-1985	10757
Saint-Gobain Abrasives Inc **(DH)**	Worcester	MA	A	508 795-5000	17464

	CITY	ST	EMP	PHONE	ENTRY #
Saint-Gobain Ceramics Plas Inc	Worcester	MA	D	508 795-5000	17465
Techno Bloc	North Brookfield	MA	G	774 449-8400	13882
Textile Buff & Wheel Co Inc	Boston	MA	E	617 241-8100	8879
True Grit Abrasive Inc	Westport	MA	F	508 636-2008	16849
Vogel Capital Inc **(HQ)**	Marlborough	MA	E	508 481-5944	12846
Washington Mills Ceramic Corp **(DH)**	North Grafton	MA	B	508 839-6511	13967
Washington Mills N Grafton Inc **(HQ)**	North Grafton	MA	D	508 839-6511	13968
Westfield Grinding Wheel Co	Westfield	MA	E	413 568-8634	16744
Best Machine Inc	Fremont	NH	G	603 895-4018	18174
Hones LLC	Hanover	NH	G	603 643-4223	18289
Johnson Abrasives Co Inc	Jaffrey	NH	E	603 532-4434	18469
Peg Kearsarge Co Inc	Bartlett	NH	G	603 374-2341	17627
RP Abrasives & Machine Inc	Rochester	NH	F	603 335-2132	19685
ACS Industries Inc **(PA)**	Lincoln	RI	E	401 769-4700	20552
Bates Abrasive Products Inc	Lincoln	RI	E	773 586-8700	20558
Joseph A Thomas Ltd	Bristol	RI	F	401 253-1330	20086
Marvel Abrasives Products LLC	Lincoln	RI	F	800 621-0673	20582
Meister Abrasives Usa Inc	North Kingstown	RI	F	401 294-4503	20727
Rhode Island Centerless Inc	Johnston	RI	F	401 942-0403	20536
Dessureau Machines Inc	Barre	VT	F	802 476-4561	21613
Eastwind Lapidary Inc	Windsor	VT	G	802 674-5427	22707
General Abrasives Inc	Sharon	VT	F	802 763-7264	22409

3292 Asbestos products

	CITY	ST	EMP	PHONE	ENTRY #
Zero Hazard LLC	Farmington	CT	G	860 561-9879	1524
Atc Group Services LLC	Williston	VT	G	802 862-1980	22656

3295 Minerals & Earths: Ground Or Treated

	CITY	ST	EMP	PHONE	ENTRY #
Miyoshi America Inc	Dayville	CT	F	860 779-3990	1047
Miyoshi America Inc	Dayville	CT	G	860 779-3990	1048
Polstal Corporation	Wilton	CT	G	203 849-7788	5299
Micro-Mech Inc	Ipswich	MA	E	978 356-2966	11931
P J Albert Inc	Fitchburg	MA	E	978 345-7828	10847
Whittemore Company Inc	Lawrence	MA	E	978 681-8833	12083
Chemrock Corporation	Thomaston	ME	G	207 594-8225	7082
FMC Corporation	Rockland	ME	C	207 594-3200	6795
Imerys Talc America Inc	Ludlow	VT	D	802 228-6400	22063
Isovolta Inc	Rutland	VT	E	802 775-5528	22341

3296 Mineral Wool

	CITY	ST	EMP	PHONE	ENTRY #
Ecologic Energy Solutions LLC	Stamford	CT	E	203 889-0505	4191
Installed Building Pdts Inc	Stamford	CT	G	203 889-0505	4225
Leek Building Products Inc	Norwalk	CT	E	203 853-3883	3185
The E J Davis Company	North Haven	CT	E	203 239-5391	3063
Bnz Materials Inc	North Billerica	MA	E	978 663-3401	13796
Composite Engineering Inc	Concord	MA	G	978 371-3132	10122
Eckel Industries Inc **(PA)**	Ayer	MA	F	978 772-0840	7917
Ward Process Inc	Holliston	MA	D	508 429-1165	11613
Colonial Green Products LLC	Sanford	ME	G	207 614-6660	6872
Johns Manville Corporation	Lewiston	ME	E	207 784-0123	6294
Booth Felt Co Inc	Dover	NH	G	603 330-3334	18009
Colonial Green Products LLC **(PA)**	Rindge	NH	F	603 532-7005	19648
Duxbury Composite Products	Fitzwilliam	NH	E	603 585-9100	18149
Vemployee	Portsmouth	RI	G	888 471-1982	20942

3297 Nonclay Refractories

	CITY	ST	EMP	PHONE	ENTRY #
Joshua LLC **(PA)**	New Haven	CT	E	203 624-0080	2699
Specialty Minerals Inc	Canaan	CT	C	860 824-5435	690
Bay State Crucible Co	Taunton	MA	E	508 824-5121	15732
Coleman Manufacturing Co Inc	Everett	MA	G	617 389-0380	10607
LMI Liquidation Corporation	Lynn	MA	G	781 593-2561	12521
Osram Sylvania Inc **(HQ)**	Wilmington	MA	A	978 570-3000	17036
Saint-Gobain Abrasives Inc **(DH)**	Worcester	MA	A	508 795-5000	17464
Saint-Gobain Ceramics Plas Inc	Northampton	MA	F	413 586-8167	14020
Infab Refractories Inc	Lewiston	ME	G	207 783-2075	6291
Newport Sand & Gravel Co Inc **(PA)**	Newport	NH	F	603 298-0199	19352

3299 Nonmetallic Mineral Prdts, NEC

	CITY	ST	EMP	PHONE	ENTRY #
AK Stucco LLC	New Britain	CT	G	860 832-9589	2507
Luckey LLC	New Haven	CT	F	203 285-3819	2709
Tim Prentice	West Cornwall	CT	G	860 672-6728	5047
U S Stucco LLC	Newington	CT	G	860 667-1935	2909
George Guertin Trophy Inc	Auburn	MA	G	508 832-4001	7836
Helmick & Schechter Inc	Newton	MA	G	617 332-2433	13600
Hergon Design Inc	Revere	MA	G	781 286-0663	14766
International Crmic Engrg Corp **(PA)**	Worcester	MA	E	508 853-4700	17394
Katahdin Hill Co	Lexington	MA	G	781 862-7566	12235
Nixon Company Inc	Indian Orchard	MA	E	413 543-3701	11890
S & S Statuary	Peabody	MA	G	978 535-5837	14368
Sincere Specialty Fabrication	Chelsea	MA	G	781 974-9580	9967
Wee Forest Folk Inc	Carlisle	MA	E	978 369-0286	9800
Ceramco Inc	Center Conway	NH	E	603 447-2090	17793
Jonathan Clowes Sculpture	Walpole	NH	G	603 835-6441	19922
Lightblocks Inc	Salem	NH	E	603 889-1115	19747
Saphikon Inc	Milford	NH	D	603 672-7221	19077
Caste Glass	North Scituate	RI	G	401 934-2959	20776
Northeastern Importing Corp	Providence	RI	G	401 276-0654	21078

33 PRIMARY METAL INDUSTRIES

3312 Blast Furnaces, Coke Ovens, Steel & Rolling Mills

	CITY	ST	EMP	PHONE	ENTRY #
American Standard Company	Southington	CT	E	860 628-9643	4037
Applied Diamond Coatings LLC	Durham	CT	G	860 349-3133	1086
ATI Flat Rlled Pdts Hldngs LLC	Waterbury	CT	F	203 756-7414	4847
Ball & Roller Bearing Co LLC	New Milford	CT	F	860 355-4161	2787
Boudreaus Welding Co Inc	Dayville	CT	E	860 774-2771	1040
Bushwick Metals LLC	Meriden	CT	G	203 630-2459	2081
Ccr Products LLC	West Hartford	CT	E	860 953-0499	5058
CMI Specialty Products Inc	Bristol	CT	F	860 585-0409	542
Everything 2 Wheels LLC	New Britain	CT	G	860 225-2453	2532
Gerdau Ameristeel US Inc	Plainville	CT	G	860 351-9029	3493
Industrial Flame Cutting Inc	Beacon Falls	CT	G	203 723-4897	58
J J Ryan Corporation	Plantsville	CT	C	860 628-0393	3534
Jo Vek Tool and Die Mfg Co	Waterbury	CT	G	203 755-1884	4892
Kimchuk Incorporated **(PA)**	Danbury	CT	F	203 790-7800	943
Microdyne Technologies	Plainville	CT	G	860 747-9473	3507
Mott Corporation	Farmington	CT	C	800 289-6688	1494
National Integrated Inds Inc **(PA)**	Farmington	CT	C	860 677-7995	1495
Nucor Steel Connecticut Inc	Wallingford	CT	C	203 265-0615	4780
Pequonnock Ironworks Inc	Bridgeport	CT	F	203 336-2178	465
Portland Slitting Co Inc	Portland	CT	G	860 342-1500	3570
Redifoils LLC	Portland	CT	F	860 342-1500	3573
Sandvik Wire and Htg Tech Corp	Bethel	CT	D	203 744-1440	177
Scp Management LLC	New Hartford	CT	E	860 738-2600	2647
Thermo Conductor Services Inc	Prospect	CT	G	203 758-6611	3598
Tms International LLC	Greenwich	CT	G	203 629-8383	1656
Ulbrich Stainless Steels	Wallingford	CT	C	203 269-2507	4824
Ulbrich Stnless Stels Spcial M **(PA)**	North Haven	CT	D	203 239-4481	3067
Waterbury Rolling Mills Inc	Waterbury	CT	D	203 597-5000	4973
Yankee Steel Service LLC	Wolcott	CT	G	203 879-5707	5462
A & G Manufacturing Co Inc	Lynn	MA	G	781 581-1892	12487
A & R Machining Tool & Die	New Bedford	MA	G	508 985-0916	13346
Ackles Steel & Iron Company	Waltham	MA	F	781 893-6818	16022
Armor Holdings Protech Div	Pittsfield	MA	G	413 445-4000	14454
Barker Steel LLC	Westfield	MA	E	413 568-7803	16671
Biasin Enterprises Inc	Lee	MA	G	413 243-0885	12089
Central Steel Rule Die Inc	Worcester	MA	G	508 853-2663	17354
Concentric Fabrication LLC	Middleboro	MA	F	508 672-4098	13059
Cutlass Marine Inc	East Weymouth	MA	G	781 740-1260	10540
Dakota Systems Inc	Dracut	MA	D	978 275-0600	10356
Draper Metals	West Bridgewater	MA	G	508 584-4617	16439
Henrys Railings	Boston	MA	G	617 333-0535	8595
Hillman Enterprises **(PA)**	Attleboro	MA	G	508 761-6967	7747
Ludlow Tool Co	Agawam	MA	G	413 786-6415	7439
Mark Dykeman	Tewksbury	MA	G	978 691-1100	15821
Martells Metal Works	Attleboro	MA	G	508 226-0136	7764
Natale Co Safetycare LL	Woburn	MA	G	781 933-7205	17237
Ne Stainless Steel Fab	Weymouth	MA	G	781 335-0121	16895
Primetals Technologies USA LLC	Worcester	MA	F	508 755-6111	17447
Rivinius & Sons Inc	Woburn	MA	F	781 933-5620	17285
Rudison Routhier Engrg Co	West Hatfield	MA	G	413 247-9341	16485
Vito Wheel Music More	Revere	MA	G	781 241-9476	14777
Vortex Inc	Peabody	MA	D	978 535-8721	14381
Chase Associates Inc	Edgecomb	ME	G	207 882-7526	6000
Millincket Fabrication Mch Inc **(PA)**	Millinocket	ME	E	207 723-9733	6443
Avilite Corp	Merrimack	NH	G	603 626-4388	18988
Cnc Design & Counsulting LLC	Kingston	NH	G	603 686-5437	18542
Harding Metals Inc	Northwood	NH	E	603 942-5573	19412
New Hampshire Stamping Co Inc	Goffstown	NH	E	603 641-1234	18206
New Hmpshire Ball Bearings Inc	Laconia	NH	B	603 524-0004	18577
RSI Metal Fabrication LLC	East Kingston	NH	G	603 382-8367	18091
Shookus Special Tools Inc	Raymond	NH	F	603 895-1200	19645
Stamping Technologies Inc	Laconia	NH	F	603 524-5958	18588
ACS Industries Inc **(PA)**	Lincoln	RI	E	401 769-4700	20552
Capco Steel Erection Company	Providence	RI	F	401 383-9388	20979
Ldc Inc	East Providence	RI	F	401 861-4667	20429
Philip Machine Company Inc	Pawtucket	RI	F	401 353-7383	20879
Scientific Alloys Inc	Westerly	RI	G	401 596-4947	21540
Jen Col Innovations LLC	Colchester	VT	G	802 448-3053	21869
Maru Ltd DBA Greenleaf Metals	Starksboro	VT	G	802 985-5200	22516

3313 Electrometallurgical Prdts

	CITY	ST	EMP	PHONE	ENTRY #
Alent USA Holding Inc	Waterbury	CT	B	203 575-5727	4839
Fit America Inc	Southborough	MA	G	309 839-1695	15357
H C Starck Inc **(HQ)**	Newton	MA	C	617 630-5800	13598
Purecoat International LLC	Belmont	MA	E	561 844-0100	8079

3315 Steel Wire Drawing & Nails & Spikes

	CITY	ST	EMP	PHONE	ENTRY #
Accel Intl Holdings Inc	Meriden	CT	E	203 237-2700	2073
Ametek Inc	Wallingford	CT	C	203 265-6731	4699
Bridgeport Insulated Wire Co **(PA)**	Bridgeport	CT	E	203 333-3191	388
City Data Cable Co	Stamford	CT	G	203 327-7917	4166

	CITY	ST	EMP	PHONE	ENTRY #
Custom House LLC	East Haddam	CT	F	860 873-1259	1150
Federal Prison Industries	Danbury	CT	F	203 743-6471	919
Hamden Metal Service Company	Hamden	CT	F	203 281-1522	1755
Housatonic Wire Co	Seymour	CT	F	203 888-9670	3752
International Pipe & Stl Corp	North Branford	CT	F	203 481-7102	2969
Lee Spring Company LLC	Bristol	CT	E	860 584-0991	576
Lex Products LLC **(PA)**	Shelton	CT	C	203 363-3738	3828
Loos & Co Inc	Pomfret	CT	F	860 928-6681	3553
Loos & Co Inc **(PA)**	Pomfret	CT	B	860 928-7981	3552
Marmon Utility LLC	Seymour	CT	E	203 881-5358	3755
Nutmeg Wire	Baltic	CT	F	860 822-8616	51
Polstal Corporation	Wilton	CT	G	203 849-7788	5299
Radcliff Wire Inc	Bristol	CT	E	312 876-1754	602
Rscc Wire & Cable LLC **(DH)**	East Granby	CT	B	860 653-8300	1143
S A Candelora Enterprises	North Branford	CT	F	203 484-2863	2975
Sandvik Wire and Htg Tech Corp	Bethel	CT	D	203 744-1440	177
Siri Manufacturing Company	Danielson	CT	E	860 236-5901	1017
Specialty Cable Corp	Wallingford	CT	D	203 265-7126	4809
Tool Logistics II	Norwalk	CT	F	203 855-9754	3258
Wiremold Company **(DH)**	West Hartford	CT	A	860 233-6251	5104
Wiretek Inc	Bloomfield	CT	F	860 242-9473	272
Accellent Holdings Corp	Wilmington	MA	A	978 570-6900	16962
Alliance Cable Corp	Taunton	MA	E	508 824-5896	15724
Belden Inc	Leominster	MA	E	978 537-8911	12117
Bergeron Machine Inc	Westford	MA	F	978 577-6235	16756
Brookfield Wire Company Inc **(HQ)**	West Brookfield	MA	E	508 867-6474	16465
Electroweave Inc	Worcester	MA	G	508 752-8932	17371
Frank L Reed Inc	Wilbraham	MA	E	413 596-3861	16937
General Wire Products Inc	Worcester	MA	E	508 752-8260	17381
Graham Whitehead & Manger Co **(PA)**	Topsfield	MA	G	203 922-9225	15861
Hampden Fence Supply Inc	Agawam	MA	F	413 786-4390	7430
Hancock Marine Inc	Fall River	MA	G	508 678-0301	10712
Heat Trace Products LLC	Leominster	MA	E	978 534-2810	12151
James Cable LLC **(PA)**	Braintree	MA	E	781 356-8701	9021
James Monroe Wire & Cable Corp **(PA)**	South Lancaster	MA	D	978 368-0131	15318
Lanoco Specialty Wire Pdts Inc	Sutton	MA	F	508 865-1500	15686
Larsdale Inc **(PA)**	Ipswich	MA	D	978 356-9995	11928
Leoni Wire Inc	Chicopee	MA	D	413 593-6618	10038
Master-Halco Inc	West Bridgewater	MA	E	508 583-7474	16444
Mersen USA Ep Corp **(DH)**	Newburyport	MA	D	805 351-8400	13511
Profiles Incorporated	Palmer	MA	E	413 283-7790	14294
Prysmian Cbles Systems USA LLC	North Dighton	MA	G	508 822-5444	13936
Quirk Wire Co Inc	West Brookfield	MA	E	508 867-3155	16473
S&S Industries Inc **(PA)**	Stoughton	MA	F	914 885-1500	15619
Sanderson-Macleod Incorporated	Palmer	MA	C	413 283-3481	14295
Stafford Wire Specialty Inc	Worcester	MA	G	508 799-6124	17480
Sumo Steel Corp	Beverly	MA	G	978 927-4950	8183
Sundial Wire LLC	Florence	MA	G	413 582-6909	10869
Temp-Flex LLC	South Grafton	MA	D	508 839-3120	15299
Acme Staple Company Inc	Franklin	NH	F	603 934-2320	18155
D L S Detailing	New Ipswich	NH	G	603 878-2554	19303
King Manufacturing Co Inc	Jaffrey	NH	F	603 532-6455	18470
ACS Industries Inc **(PA)**	Lincoln	RI	E	401 769-4700	20552
Alloy Holdings LLC	Providence	RI	E	401 353-7500	20951
Altenloh Brinck & Co US Inc	Bristol	RI	G	401 253-8600	20061
Dayton Superior Corporation	Warwick	RI	E	401 885-1934	21351
Precise Products Company	Lincoln	RI	F	401 724-7190	20592
Sonco Worldwide Inc	Warwick	RI	F	401 406-3761	21427
Heb Manufacturing Company Inc	Chelsea	VT	E	802 685-4821	21838
Micro Wire Transm Systems Inc	Essex Junction	VT	F	802 876-7901	21951

3316 Cold Rolled Steel Sheet, Strip & Bars

	CITY	ST	EMP	PHONE	ENTRY #
Channel Alloys	Norwalk	CT	G	203 975-1404	3123
Deringer-Ney Inc **(PA)**	Bloomfield	CT	C	860 242-2281	217
Eastern Company **(PA)**	Naugatuck	CT	E	203 729-2255	2471
Feroleto Steel Company Inc **(DH)**	Bridgeport	CT	D	203 366-3263	413
North East Fasteners Corp	Terryville	CT	E	860 589-3242	4488
Paradigm Manchester Inc	Manchester	CT	C	860 649-2888	2032
Sandvik Wire and Htg Tech Corp **(DH)**	Bethel	CT	D	203 744-1440	178
Sandvik Wire and Htg Tech Corp	Bethel	CT	D	203 744-1440	177
Shepard Steel Co Inc	Newington	CT	E	860 525-4446	2902
Theis Precision Steel USA Inc **(HQ)**	Bristol	CT	C	860 589-5511	616
Ulbrich Stainless Steels	Wallingford	CT	C	203 269-2507	4824
Ulbrich Stnless Stels Spcial M **(PA)**	North Haven	CT	D	203 239-4481	3067
Fall River Mfg Co Inc	Fall River	MA	D	508 675-1125	10696
Frank L Reed Inc	Wilbraham	MA	E	413 596-3861	16937
Premier Roll & Tool Inc	North Attleboro	MA	G	508 695-2551	13774
Tri Cast Inc **(PA)**	Somersworth	NH	F	603 692-2480	19851
New Amtrol Holdings Inc **(DH)**	West Warwick	RI	G	614 438-3210	21505

3317 Steel Pipe & Tubes

	CITY	ST	EMP	PHONE	ENTRY #
Gordon Corporation	Southington	CT	D	860 628-4775	4055
Litchfield International Inc	Litchfield	CT	G	860 567-8824	1951
3M Company	Chelmsford	MA	C	978 256-3911	9865
A1a Steel LLC	East Falmouth	MA	G	774 763-2503	10432
Accellent Holdings Corp	Wilmington	MA	A	978 570-6900	16962
New Can Holdings Inc **(PA)**	Holbrook	MA	G	781 767-1650	11534
Thermatron Engineering Inc	Methuen	MA	E	978 687-8844	13046
Wyman-Gordon Company **(DH)**	North Grafton	MA	B	508 839-8252	13969
Contech Engnered Solutions LLC	Scarborough	ME	E	207 885-9830	6915
Anvil International LLC **(HQ)**	Exeter	NH	E	603 418-2800	18110
Unique Mechanical Services Inc	Bow	NH	G	603 856-0057	17735
Maxson Automatic Machinery Co **(PA)**	Westerly	RI	E	401 596-0162	21530
National Chimney Supply	South Burlington	VT	D	802 861-2217	22454

3321 Gray Iron Foundries

	CITY	ST	EMP	PHONE	ENTRY #
Bingham & Taylor Corp **(HQ)**	Rocky Hill	CT	G	540 825-8334	3703
Taylor & Fenn Company	Windsor	CT	D	860 219-9393	5372
Virginia Industries Inc **(PA)**	Rocky Hill	CT	G	860 571-3600	3733
Ej Usa Inc	Brockton	MA	F	508 586-3130	9142
G & W Foundry Corp	Millbury	MA	E	508 581-8719	13164
Henry Perkins Company	Bridgewater	MA	F	508 697-6978	9076
Kadant Inc **(PA)**	Westford	MA	B	978 776-2000	16774
Neenah Foundry Company	Stoughton	MA	G	781 344-1711	15610
Whitman Castings Inc **(PA)**	Whitman	MA	E	781 447-4417	16930
Millincket Fabrication Mch Inc **(PA)**	Millinocket	ME	E	207 723-9733	6443
Anvil International LLC **(HQ)**	Exeter	NH	E	603 418-2800	18110
Nashua Foundries Inc	Nashua	NH	E	603 882-4811	19213
Cumberland Foundry Co Inc	Cumberland	RI	E	401 658-3300	20317
Fairmount Foundry Inc	Woonsocket	RI	F	401 769-1585	21561

3322 Malleable Iron Foundries

	CITY	ST	EMP	PHONE	ENTRY #
G & W Foundry Corp	Millbury	MA	E	508 581-8719	13164
Rodney Hunt-Fontaine Inc **(DH)**	Orange	MA	C	978 544-2511	14227

3324 Steel Investment Foundries

	CITY	ST	EMP	PHONE	ENTRY #
Doncasters Inc	Groton	CT	D	860 446-4803	1670
Doncasters US Hldings 2018 Inc	Groton	CT	F	860 677-1376	1672
Dundee Holding Inc **(DH)**	Farmington	CT	G	860 677-1376	1477
Hexcel Corporation	South Windsor	CT	D	925 520-3232	3979
Howmet Castings & Services Inc	Winsted	CT	B	860 379-3314	5413
Howmet Corporation	Branford	CT	B	203 481-3451	325
Integra-Cast Inc	New Britain	CT	D	860 225-7600	2541
Jl Aerotech Inc	South Windsor	CT	G	860 248-8628	3985
Miller Castings Inc	North Franklin	CT	C	860 822-9991	2989
Sturm Ruger & Company Inc **(PA)**	Southport	CT	B	203 259-7843	4099
Tps Acquisition LLC **(PA)**	Waterbury	CT	G	860 589-5511	4965
A Young Casting	Attleboro	MA	F	508 222-8188	7697
Consoldted Precision Pdts Corp	Braintree	MA	C	781 848-3333	8995
Kervick Family Foundation Inc	Worcester	MA	G	508 853-4500	17399
Parts Tool and Die Inc	Agawam	MA	E	413 821-9718	7445
Tecomet Inc	Wilmington	MA	D	978 642-2400	17051
Wyman-Gordon Company **(DH)**	North Grafton	MA	B	508 839-8252	13969
New England Castings LLC	Standish	ME	E	207 642-3029	7063
Hitchiner Manufacturing Co Inc **(PA)**	Milford	NH	A	603 673-1100	19060
Hitchiner Manufacturing Co Inc	Milford	NH	D	603 673-1100	19061
Hitchiner Manufacturing Co Inc	Milford	NH	C	603 732-1935	19062
Hitchiner Manufacturing Co Inc	Milford	NH	B	603 673-1100	19063
PCC Structurals Groton	Franklin	NH	G	603 286-4301	18162
Sturm Ruger & Company Inc	Newport	NH	B	603 865-2424	19361
Sturm Ruger & Company Inc	Newport	NH	C	603 863-3300	19362
Tidland Corporation	Keene	NH	D	603 352-1696	18533
Leemar Casting Company Inc	Johnston	RI	G	401 276-2844	20517

3325 Steel Foundries, NEC

	CITY	ST	EMP	PHONE	ENTRY #
Frank Roth Co Inc	Stratford	CT	D	203 377-2155	4413
Polstal Corporation	Wilton	CT	G	203 849-7788	5299
Silicone Casting Technologies	Middletown	CT	G	860 347-5227	2221
D W Clark Inc **(PA)**	East Bridgewater	MA	E	508 378-4014	10411
Doncasters Inc	Springfield	MA	D	413 785-1801	15467
Trident Alloys Inc	Springfield	MA	E	413 737-1477	15518
Wollaston Alloys Inc	Braintree	MA	C	781 848-3333	9051

3331 Primary Smelting & Refining Of Copper

	CITY	ST	EMP	PHONE	ENTRY #
Ametek Inc	Wallingford	CT	C	203 265-6731	4699
Browns Greens	Brooksville	ME	G	207 326-4636	5824
Materion Technical Mtls Inc	Lincoln	RI	C	401 333-1700	20583

3334 Primary Production Of Aluminum

	CITY	ST	EMP	PHONE	ENTRY #
All Steel LLC	Ellington	CT	G	860 871-6023	1328
Arconic Inc	Winsted	CT	G	860 379-3314	5404
Wilson Partitions Inc	Stamford	CT	F	203 316-8033	4360
Gear/Tronics Inc	North Billerica	MA	E	781 933-1400	13819
Putnam Rf Machining LLC	Manchester	NH	G	603 623-0700	18769
Bill Lztte Archtctural GL Alum	Riverside	RI	F	401 383-9535	21164

3339 Primary Nonferrous Metals, NEC

	CITY	ST	EMP	PHONE	ENTRY #
Alent USA Holding Inc	Waterbury	CT	B	203 575-5727	4839
Aztec Industries LLC	Middletown	CT	E	860 343-1960	2175
Bal International Inc	Stamford	CT	E	203 359-6775	4147
Northeastern Metals Corp	Stamford	CT	G	203 348-8088	4261
Reliable Silver Corporation	Naugatuck	CT	F	203 574-7732	2493
Ulbrich Stainless Steels	Wallingford	CT	C	203 269-2507	4824

	CITY	ST	EMP	PHONE	ENTRY #
Cabot Corporation **(PA)**	Boston	MA	C	617 345-0100	8452
Cabot Corporation	Haverhill	MA	C	978 556-8400	11413
Global Advanced Metals USA Inc **(PA)**	Wellesley Hills	MA	D	781 996-7300	16397
H C Starck Inc **(HQ)**	Newton	MA	C	617 630-5800	13598
Hallmark Sweet/Ekru Inc	Attleboro	MA	C	508 226-9600	7745
J T Inman Co Inc	Attleboro Falls	MA	E	508 226-0080	7814
J-A Industries Incorporated	North Easton	MA	G	508 297-1648	13948
Metalor Technologies USA Corp **(DH)**	North Attleboro	MA	C	508 699-8800	13763
Metalor USA Refining Corp **(DH)**	North Attleboro	MA	C	508 699-8800	13764
Spindle City Precious Metals	Somerset	MA	G	508 567-1597	15148
Colt Refining Inc **(PA)**	Merrimack	NH	E	603 429-9966	18993
Harding Metals Inc	Northwood	NH	E	603 942-5573	19412
Advanced Chemical Company	Warwick	RI	E	401 785-3434	21318
Carpenter Powder Products Inc	Woonsocket	RI	F	401 769-5600	21555
Geib Refining Corporation	Warwick	RI	E	401 738-8560	21365
Materion Technical Mtls Inc	Lincoln	RI	C	401 333-1700	20583
Umicore Precious Mtls USA Inc	Riverside	RI	G	401 450-0907	21178

3341 Secondary Smelting & Refining Of Nonferrous Metals

	CITY	ST	EMP	PHONE	ENTRY #
5n Plus Wisconsin Inc	Trumbull	CT	F	203 384-0331	4610
Alent USA Holding Inc	Waterbury	CT	B	203 575-5727	4839
Paradigm Manchester Inc	Manchester	CT	C	860 649-2888	2032
Surf Metal Co Inc	Stratford	CT	G	203 375-2211	4452
Ulbrich Stnless Stels Spcial M **(PA)**	North Haven	CT	D	203 239-4481	3067
Utitec Inc **(HQ)**	Watertown	CT	D	860 945-0605	5032
Viking Platinum LLC	Waterbury	CT	F	203 574-7979	4969
Connell Limited Partnership **(PA)**	Boston	MA	F	617 737-2700	8481
Greene Lyon Group Inc	Amesbury	MA	G	617 290-2276	7488
Metalor Technologies USA Corp **(DH)**	North Attleboro	MA	C	508 699-8800	13763
Metalor USA Refining Corp **(DH)**	North Attleboro	MA	C	508 699-8800	13764
Polymetallurgical LLC	North Attleboro	MA	E	508 695-9312	13773
Precious Alloy Refining LLC	Stoughton	MA	G	774 296-5000	15616
Precious Metals Reclaiming Svc **(PA)**	Canton	MA	G	781 326-3442	9771
Colt Refining Inc **(PA)**	Merrimack	NH	E	603 429-9966	18993
Harding Metals Inc	Northwood	NH	E	603 942-5573	19412
N Kamenske & Co Inc	Nashua	NH	G	603 888-1007	19211
Sturm Ruger & Company Inc	Newport	NH	C	603 863-3300	19362
Gannon & Scott Inc	Cranston	RI	D	401 463-5550	20229
Kelley Metal Corp	East Providence	RI	F	401 434-8795	20426
Morgan Mill Metals LLC	Johnston	RI	F	401 270-9944	20524
Pease & Curren Incorporated	Warwick	RI	E	401 738-6449	21401

3351 Rolling, Drawing & Extruding Of Copper

	CITY	ST	EMP	PHONE	ENTRY #
Alloy Metals Inc **(PA)**	Wallingford	CT	F	203 774-3270	4696
Global Brass & Copper LLC **(PA)**	Waterbury	CT	G	203 597-5000	4879
Miller Company	Meriden	CT	E	203 235-4474	2108
Specialty Wire & Cord Sets	Hamden	CT	F	203 498-2932	1785
Waterbury Rolling Mills Inc	Waterbury	CT	D	203 597-5000	4973
Aimtek Inc **(PA)**	Auburn	MA	E	508 832-5035	7823
Data Guide Cable Corporation	Gardner	MA	D	978 632-0900	11111
Ems Engnred Mtls Solutions LLC **(DH)**	Attleboro	MA	C	508 342-2100	7732
Frank L Reed Inc	Wilbraham	MA	E	413 596-3861	16937
Leoni Wire Inc	Chicopee	MA	D	413 593-6618	10038
McIntire Brass Works Inc	Somerville	MA	G	617 547-1819	15197
Pep Industries LLC	Attleboro	MA	A	508 226-5600	7776
Precision Engineered Pdts LLC **(DH)**	Attleboro	MA	G	508 226-5600	7782
Sanderson-Macleod Incorporated	Palmer	MA	C	413 283-3481	14295
Thermatron Engineering Inc	Methuen	MA	E	978 687-8844	13046
Advanced Building Products Inc	Sanford	ME	F	207 490-2306	6870
York Manufacturing Inc	Sanford	ME	F	207 324-1300	6898
Aetna Insulated Wire LLC	Milford	NH	C	757 460-3381	19043
AT Wall Company **(HQ)**	Warwick	RI	E	401 739-0740	21329
House of Stainless Inc	Cranston	RI	E	800 556-3470	20237
Millard Wire Company **(PA)**	Warwick	RI	D	401 737-9330	21389
Spark Vt Inc	Shelburne	VT	F	802 985-3321	22425

3353 Aluminum Sheet, Plate & Foil

	CITY	ST	EMP	PHONE	ENTRY #
CMI Specialty Products Inc	Bristol	CT	F	860 585-0409	542
Berkshire Screen	Pittsfield	MA	G	413 212-8360	14460
Cutlass Marine Inc	East Weymouth	MA	G	781 740-1260	10540
Sunset Engravers	Methuen	MA	G	978 687-1111	13045
GA Rel Manufacturing Company	Providence	RI	E	401 331-5455	21019

3354 Aluminum Extruded Prdts

	CITY	ST	EMP	PHONE	ENTRY #
Narragansett Screw Co	Winsted	CT	F	860 379-4059	5418
Unique Extrusions Incorporated	Cromwell	CT	E	860 632-1314	862
Atrenne Cmpt Solutions LLC **(DH)**	Brockton	MA	B	508 588-6110	9121
Atrenne Cmpt Solutions LLC	Brockton	MA	G	508 588-6110	9122
Cycle-TEC	Bellingham	MA	G	508 966-0066	8036
Mair-Mac Machine Company Inc	Brockton	MA	F	508 895-9001	9164
Mestek Inc **(PA)**	Westfield	MA	E	470 898-4533	16700
Silver City Aluminum Corp	Taunton	MA	D	508 824-8631	15785
Wakefeld Thermal Solutions Inc **(HQ)**	Pelham	NH	C	603 635-2800	19454

3355 Aluminum Rolling & Drawing, NEC

	CITY	ST	EMP	PHONE	ENTRY #
Acme Monaco Corporation **(PA)**	New Britain	CT	C	860 224-1349	2503
Alpha-Core Inc	Shelton	CT	E	203 954-0050	3773
Echo Industries Inc	Orange	MA	E	978 544-7000	14215
Joseph Freedman Co Inc **(PA)**	Springfield	MA	D	888 677-7818	15481
Joseph Freedman Co Inc	Springfield	MA	E	413 781-4444	15482
Ocean Marine Fabricating	New Bedford	MA	G	508 999-5554	13433

3356 Rolling, Drawing-Extruding Of Nonferrous Metals

	CITY	ST	EMP	PHONE	ENTRY #
Aerospace Metals Inc	Hartford	CT	C	860 522-3123	1803
Alent USA Holding Inc	Waterbury	CT	B	203 575-5727	4839
Doncasters Inc	Groton	CT	D	860 446-4803	1670
Doncasters Inc **(HQ)**	Groton	CT	D	860 449-1603	1671
Magnesium Interactive LLC	Westport	CT	G	917 609-1306	5211
Norilsk Nickel USA Inc	Ridgefield	CT	G	203 730-0676	3673
Platt Brothers & Company **(PA)**	Waterbury	CT	D	203 753-4194	4940
Titanium Industries Inc	Tolland	CT	G	860 870-3939	4554
Titanium Metals Corporation	East Windsor	CT	F	860 627-7051	1307
Torrey S Crane Company	Plantsville	CT	E	860 628-4778	3543
Ulbrich Stainless Steels	Wallingford	CT	C	203 269-2507	4824
Ulbrich Stnless Stels Spcial M **(PA)**	North Haven	CT	D	203 239-4481	3067
United Stts Sgn & Fbrction	Trumbull	CT	E	203 601-1000	4640
Waterbury Rolling Mills Inc	Waterbury	CT	D	203 597-5000	4973
Comtran Cable LLC	Attleboro	MA	C	508 399-7004	7724
Dan-Kar Plastics Products	Woburn	MA	G	781 935-9221	17163
Echo Industries Inc	Orange	MA	E	978 544-7000	14215
EF Leach & Company	Attleboro	MA	B	508 643-3309	7731
Garner Leach Inc	North Attleboro	MA	D	508 695-9395	13757
Garner Leach Inc	Attleboro	MA	E	508 226-5660	7739
H C Starck Inc **(HQ)**	Newton	MA	C	617 630-5800	13598
Rmi Titanium Company LLC	Burlington	MA	F	781 272-5967	9330
Sx Industries Inc **(PA)**	Stoughton	MA	E	781 828-7111	15625
Tien Vo Corp	Weymouth	MA	G	781 340-7245	16902
Titanium Advisors	Franklin	MA	G	508 528-3120	11092
Elmet Technologies LLC	Lewiston	ME	C	207 333-6100	6287
Jarden LLC	East Wilton	ME	C	207 645-2574	5987
Dgf Indstrial Innvations Group	Gilford	NH	F	603 528-6591	18185
Hair Designs By Debbie Tin	Sandown	NH	G	603 887-0643	19784
If I Only Had A Nickel	Concord	NH	G	603 225-3972	17910
Microspec Corporation	Peterborough	NH	E	603 924-4300	19477
1st Casting Company	Johnston	RI	F	401 272-0750	20495
American Iron & Metal USA Inc **(HQ)**	Cranston	RI	E	401 463-5605	20178
Callico Metals Inc	North Kingstown	RI	G	401 398-8238	20695
Nickel Corporaxion	Providence	RI	G	401 351-6555	21077
Tin Man Fabrication Inc	Coventry	RI	G	401 822-4509	20169
Lead Conversion Plus	Milton	VT	G	802 497-1557	22132

3357 Nonferrous Wire Drawing

	CITY	ST	EMP	PHONE	ENTRY #
A J R Inc	Bridgeport	CT	F	203 384-0400	365
Algonquin Industries Inc **(HQ)**	Guilford	CT	D	203 453-4348	1692
Alpha-Core Inc	Shelton	CT	E	203 954-0050	3773
Altek Electronics Inc	Torrington	CT	C	860 482-7626	4558
American Alloy Wire Corp	Newtown	CT	G	203 426-3133	2914
American Imex Corporation	Monroe	CT	G	203 261-5200	2391
American Wire Corporation	Newtown	CT	F	203 426-3133	2915
Autac Incorporated **(PA)**	Branford	CT	G	203 481-3444	291
Bridgeport Insulated Wire Co **(PA)**	Bridgeport	CT	E	203 333-3191	388
Bridgeport Insulated Wire Co	Stratford	CT	E	203 375-9579	4401
Bridgeport Magnetics Group Inc	Shelton	CT	E	203 954-0050	3784
Cable Technology Inc	Willington	CT	E	860 429-7889	5270
Ensign-Bickford Industries Inc	Weatogue	CT	C	860 843-2000	5042
Fiberoptics Technology Inc **(PA)**	Pomfret	CT	C	860 928-0443	3550
General Cable Industries Inc	Willimantic	CT	C	860 456-8000	5264
Hamden Metal Service Company	Hamden	CT	F	203 281-1522	1755
Insulated Wire Inc	Bethel	CT	F	203 791-1999	160
Loos & Co Inc **(PA)**	Pomfret	CT	B	860 928-7981	3552
Luvata Waterbury Inc	Waterbury	CT	D	203 753-5215	4899
Marmon Utility LLC	Seymour	CT	E	203 881-5358	3755
Multi-Cable Corp	Bristol	CT	F	860 589-9035	585
Ofs Fitel LLC	Avon	CT	B	860 678-0371	39
Omerin Usa Inc	Meriden	CT	E	475 343-3450	2113
Ortronics Inc **(DH)**	New London	CT	D	860 445-3900	2776
Ortronics Inc	West Hartford	CT	G	877 295-3472	5088
Platt Brothers & Company **(PA)**	Waterbury	CT	D	203 753-4194	4940
Radcliff Wire Inc	Bristol	CT	E	312 876-1754	602
REA Magnet Wire Company Inc	Guilford	CT	D	203 738-6100	1716
Rscc Wire & Cable LLC **(DH)**	East Granby	CT	B	860 653-8300	1143
Sandvik Wire and Htg Tech Corp	Bethel	CT	D	203 744-1440	177
Sandvik Wire and Htg Tech Corp **(DH)**	Bethel	CT	D	203 744-1440	178
Siemon Company **(PA)**	Watertown	CT	A	860 945-4200	5024
Specialty Cable Corp	Wallingford	CT	D	203 265-7126	4809
Times Fiber Communications Inc **(HQ)**	Wallingford	CT	D	203 265-8500	4818
Times Microwave Systems Inc **(HQ)**	Wallingford	CT	B	203 949-8400	4819
Volpe Cable Corporation	Branford	CT	C	203 623-1818	357
Wiretek Inc	Bloomfield	CT	F	860 242-9473	272
ABB Installation Products Inc	Hopkinton	MA	C	508 435-0101	11686
Afc Cable Systems Inc	New Bedford	MA	C	508 998-8277	13353
Alliance Cable Corp	Taunton	MA	E	508 824-5896	15724
America Cable Assemblies Inc **(PA)**	Palmer	MA	G	413 283-2515	14278

	CITY	ST	EMP	PHONE	ENTRY #
Anomet Products Inc	Shrewsbury	MA	E	508 842-0174	15102
Belden Inc	Worcester	MA	C	508 754-4858	17347
Belden Inc	Peabody	MA	C	978 573-0908	14315
Belden Inc	Leominster	MA	E	978 537-8911	12117
Brookfield Wire Company Inc **(HQ)**	West Brookfield	MA	E	508 867-6474	16465
Caton Connector Corp	Kingston	MA	E	781 585-4315	11955
Chase Corporation	Randolph	MA	E	781 963-2600	14673
Cooper Interconnect Inc	Chelsea	MA	D	617 389-7080	9950
Data Guide Cable Corporation	Gardner	MA	D	978 632-0900	11111
Draka Fibre Technology	Taunton	MA	G	508 822-0246	15745
Dynawave Cable Incorporated	Haverhill	MA	G	978 469-9448	11428
Eis Wire & Cable Inc	South Hadley	MA	D	413 536-0152	15302
Electroweave Inc	Worcester	MA	G	508 752-8932	17371
Gavitt Wire and Cable Co Inc	West Brookfield	MA	D	508 867-6476	16469
General Airmotive Pwr Pdts LLC	Fall River	MA	G	508 674-6400	10702
General Wire Products Inc	Worcester	MA	E	508 752-8260	17381
Hueson Corp	South Grafton	MA	F	508 234-6372	15297
Inter-Connection Tech Inc	Lawrence	MA	F	978 975-7510	12039
James Monroe Wire & Cable Corp **(PA)**	South Lancaster	MA	D	978 368-0131	15318
Judd Wire Inc **(DH)**	Turners Falls	MA	B	413 863-9402	15880
L-Com Inc **(DH)**	North Andover	MA	D	978 682-6936	13715
Linden Photonics Inc	Westford	MA	G	978 392-7985	16776
Madison Cable Corporation	Worcester	MA	C	508 752-2884	17410
Mercury Wire Products Inc	Spencer	MA	C	508 885-6363	15433
Milford Manufacturing Svcs LLC	Hopedale	MA	D	508 478-8544	11678
Mor-Wire & Cable Inc	Lowell	MA	F	978 453-1782	12413
Ofs Brightwave LLC	Sturbridge	MA	G	508 347-2261	15641
Ofs Fitel LLC	Sturbridge	MA	E	508 347-2261	15642
Prysmian Cbles Systems USA LLC	North Dighton	MA	C	508 822-5444	13935
Prysmian Cbles Systems USA LLC	Taunton	MA	G	508 822-0246	15775
Quabbin Wire & Cable Co Inc **(PA)**	Ware	MA	D	413 967-6281	16236
Quirk Wire Co Inc	West Brookfield	MA	E	508 867-3155	16473
Saint-Gobain Prfmce Plas Corp	Worcester	MA	E	508 852-3072	17467
Segue Manufacturing Svcs LLC	Lowell	MA	D	978 970-1200	12432
Tech-Etch Inc	Fall River	MA	D	508 675-5757	10770
Temp-Flex LLC	South Grafton	MA	D	508 839-3120	15299
Tricab (usa) Inc	Worcester	MA	E	508 421-4680	17491
United Wire & Cable Corp **(PA)**	Worcester	MA	G	508 757-3872	17494
V-Tron Electronics Corp	Attleboro	MA	D	508 761-9100	7805
Eldur Corporation	Bangor	ME	E	207 942-6592	5642
Maine Fiber Company LLC	Portland	ME	G	207 699-4550	6686
Transparent Audio Inc	Saco	ME	E	207 284-1100	6860
Aetna Insulated Wire LLC	Milford	NH	C	757 460-3381	19043
AFL Telecommunications LLC	Belmont	NH	E	603 528-7780	17669
Amphenol Corporation	Nashua	NH	B	603 879-3000	19114
Amphenol Printed Circuits Inc	Nashua	NH	A	603 324-4500	19115
Burton Wire & Cable Inc	Hooksett	NH	F	603 624-2427	18344
Cable Assemblies Inc	Amherst	NH	F	603 889-4090	17553
Elektrisola Incorporated **(PA)**	Boscawen	NH	C	603 796-2114	17703
Enterasys Networks Inc **(HQ)**	Salem	NH	D	603 952-5000	19725
Fiberoptic Resale Corp	Nashua	NH	G	603 496-1258	19157
General Cable Industries Inc	Manchester	NH	C	603 668-1620	18825
Hitachi Cable America Inc	Manchester	NH	C	603 669-4347	18835
Marmon Aerospace & Defense LLC	Manchester	NH	D	603 622-3500	18867
Marmon Utility LLC **(DH)**	Milford	NH	C	603 673-2040	19069
Marmon Utility LLC	Amherst	NH	G	603 673-2040	17574
Microspec Corporation	Peterborough	NH	E	603 924-4300	19477
MJM Holdings Inc **(PA)**	Lisbon	NH	G	603 838-6624	18649
New England Wire Tech Corp **(HQ)**	Lisbon	NH	B	603 838-6624	18650
Optical Fiber Systems Inc	New Ipswich	NH	G	603 291-0345	19309
Retcomp Inc	New Boston	NH	E	603 487-5010	19297
Rscc Wire & Cable LLC	Manchester	NH	D	603 622-3500	18912
Stonewall Cable Inc	Rumney	NH	D	603 536-1601	19698
Subcom Cable Systems LLC	Newington	NH	B	603 436-6100	19327
Teledyne Instruments Inc	Portsmouth	NH	C	603 474-5571	19624
Electro Standards Lab Inc	Cranston	RI	D	401 946-1390	20215
General Cable Industries Inc	Lincoln	RI	C	401 333-4848	20575
Okonite Company	Cumberland	RI	D	401 333-3500	20336
Providence Cable Corporation	Johnston	RI	F	401 632-7650	20532
Phoenix Wire Inc	South Hero	VT	G	802 372-4561	22481
Super-Temp Wire & Cable Inc	South Burlington	VT	E	802 655-4211	22470

3363 Aluminum Die Castings

	CITY	ST	EMP	PHONE	ENTRY #
Advanced Prcsion Castings Corp	Milford	CT	G	203 736-9452	2237
Arrow Diversified Tooling Inc	Ellington	CT	E	860 872-9072	1329
Custom Metal Crafters Inc	Newington	CT	D	860 953-4210	2857
Atlas Brass & Aluminum Co	Westfield	MA	G	413 732-4604	16668
Atlas Founders Inc	Agawam	MA	F	413 786-4210	7420
Bulcast LLC	Chestnut Hill	MA	G	617 901-6836	9983
Diecast Connections Co Inc	Plymouth	MA	C	413 592-8444	14552
Kingston Aluminum Foundry Inc	Kingston	MA	G	781 585-6631	11959
Mascon Inc	Woburn	MA	E	781 938-5800	17223
Meteor Globl Mfg Solutions Inc	Monson	MA	G	617 733-6506	13209
Mystic Valley Foundry Inc	Somerville	MA	G	617 547-1819	15201
Pace Industries LLC	North Billerica	MA	C	978 667-8400	13852
Connectcut Prcsion Cstings Inc	Claremont	NH	G	603 542-3373	17843
Diamond Casting and Mch Co Inc	Hollis	NH	E	603 465-2263	18330
Hebert Manufacturing Company **(PA)**	Laconia	NH	D	603 524-2065	18567
Hitchiner Manufacturing Co Inc	Milford	NH	D	603 673-1100	19061
Hitchiner Manufacturing Co Inc	Milford	NH	B	603 673-1100	19063
Wyman-Gordon Company	Franklin	NH	E	603 934-6630	18169

3364 Nonferrous Die Castings, Exc Aluminum

	CITY	ST	EMP	PHONE	ENTRY #
Custom Metal Crafters Inc	Newington	CT	D	860 953-4210	2857
Integra-Cast Inc	New Britain	CT	D	860 225-7600	2541
Narragansett Screw Co	Winsted	CT	F	860 379-4059	5418
PCC Structurals Groton **(DH)**	Groton	CT	C	860 405-3700	1682
Atlas Founders Inc	Agawam	MA	F	413 786-4210	7420
Fall River Tool & Die Co Inc	Fall River	MA	F	508 674-4621	10699
Industrial Foundry Corporation	Uxbridge	MA	G	508 278-5523	15920
Kingston Aluminum Foundry Inc	Kingston	MA	G	781 585-6631	11959
Medalco Metals Inc **(PA)**	South Hadley	MA	F	413 586-6010	15307
Meteor Globl Mfg Solutions Inc	Monson	MA	G	617 733-6506	13209
Pace Industries LLC	North Billerica	MA	C	978 667-8400	13852
Diamond Casting and Mch Co Inc	Hollis	NH	E	603 465-2263	18330
Hebert Manufacturing Company **(PA)**	Laconia	NH	D	603 524-2065	18567
Watts Regulator Co	Franklin	NH	A	603 934-5110	18166
Fielding Manufacturing Inc	Cranston	RI	E	401 461-0400	20226
Fielding Mfg Zinc Diecasting	Cranston	RI	D	401 461-0400	20227
Miniature Casting Corporation	Cranston	RI	F	401 463-5090	20264
Ridco Casting Co	Pawtucket	RI	D	401 724-0400	20893
Rona Incorporated	Warwick	RI	G	401 737-4388	21417
Rvs & Co	Johnston	RI	F	401 231-8200	20539
New England Precision Inc	Randolph	VT	D	800 293-4112	22299

3365 Aluminum Foundries

	CITY	ST	EMP	PHONE	ENTRY #
Accu-Mill Technologies LLC	Plainville	CT	G	860 747-3921	3462
Aerocess Inc	Berlin	CT	F	860 357-2451	67
Dwyer Aluminum Mast Company	North Branford	CT	F	203 484-0419	2962
Integra-Cast Inc	New Britain	CT	D	860 225-7600	2541
Us-Malabar Company Inc	Weston	CT	G	203 226-1773	5174
Amesbury Foundry Co	Amesbury	MA	G	978 388-0830	7477
Arcam Cad To Metal Inc	Woburn	MA	F	781 281-1718	17121
Bulcast LLC	Chestnut Hill	MA	G	617 901-6836	9983
Burlington Foundry Co Inc	Burlington	MA	G	781 272-1182	9242
Consoldted Precision Pdts Corp	Braintree	MA	C	781 848-3333	8995
Half-Time Ventures Inc	Carlisle	MA	G	978 369-2907	9798
Industrial Biomedical Sensors	Waltham	MA	F	781 891-4201	16132
Industrial Foundry Corporation	Uxbridge	MA	G	508 278-5523	15920
Kingston Aluminum Foundry Inc	Kingston	MA	G	781 585-6631	11959
Marlborough Foundry Inc	Marlborough	MA	E	508 485-2848	12791
Mystic Valley Foundry Inc	Somerville	MA	G	617 547-1819	15201
Pace Industries LLC	North Billerica	MA	C	978 667-8400	13852
Parts Tool and Die Inc	Agawam	MA	E	413 821-9718	7445
Prue Foundry Inc	Dennis	MA	G	508 385-3011	10309
Supreme Brass & Alum Castings	West Springfield	MA	G	413 737-4433	16555
Taunton Aluminum Foundry Inc	Berkley	MA	G	508 822-4141	8089
Tecomet Inc	Wilmington	MA	D	978 642-2400	17051
Bronze Craft Corporation	Nashua	NH	D	603 883-7747	19130
Diamond Casting and Mch Co Inc	Hollis	NH	E	603 465-2263	18330
Granite State Casting	Mason	NH	G	603 878-2759	18967
Nu-Cast Inc	Londonderry	NH	C	603 432-1600	18729
Patriot Foundry & Castings LLC	Franklin	NH	F	603 934-3919	18161
UNI-Cast LLC	Londonderry	NH	C	603 625-5761	18742
UPS Scs Pratt & Whitney	Londonderry	NH	G	860 565-0353	18744
Friends Foundry Inc	Woonsocket	RI	F	401 769-0160	21564
Michael Healy Designs Inc	Manville	RI	G	401 597-5900	20610

3366 Copper Foundries

	CITY	ST	EMP	PHONE	ENTRY #
American Sleeve Bearing LLC	Stafford Springs	CT	E	860 684-8060	4104
Mystic River Foundry LLC	Mystic	CT	G	860 536-7634	2445
Spirol International Corp **(HQ)**	Danielson	CT	C	860 774-8571	1018
Alloy Castings Co Inc	East Bridgewater	MA	F	508 378-2541	10406
Amesbury Foundry Co	Amesbury	MA	G	978 388-0830	7477
Atlas Brass & Aluminum Co	Westfield	MA	G	413 732-4604	16668
D W Clark Inc **(PA)**	East Bridgewater	MA	E	508 378-4014	10411
Flex O Fold North America Inc	Marblehead	MA	F	781 631-3190	12682
Kt Acquisition LLC	Worcester	MA	D	508 853-4500	17402
Mystic Valley Foundry Inc	Somerville	MA	G	617 547-1819	15201
Palmer Foundry Inc	Palmer	MA	D	413 283-2976	14291
Sincere Specialty Fabrication	Chelsea	MA	G	781 974-9580	9967
Supreme Brass & Alum Castings	West Springfield	MA	G	413 737-4433	16555
Taunton Aluminum Foundry Inc	Berkley	MA	G	508 822-4141	8089
Western Bronze Inc	West Springfield	MA	F	413 737-1319	16564
Bronze Craft Corporation	Nashua	NH	D	603 883-7747	19130
Granite State Casting	Mason	NH	G	603 878-2759	18967
Hebert Foundry & Machine Inc	Laconia	NH	E	603 524-2065	18566
New Hmpshire Ball Bearings Inc	Laconia	NH	B	603 524-0004	18577
Quality Babbitting Services	East Kingston	NH	G	603 642-7147	18090
Michael Healy Designs Inc	Manville	RI	G	401 597-5900	20610
Paul King Foundry Inc	Johnston	RI	G	401 231-3120	20528
New England Precision Inc	Randolph	VT	D	800 293-4112	22299

3369 Nonferrous Foundries: Castings, NEC

	CITY	ST	EMP	PHONE	ENTRY #
B H S Industries Ltd	Wallingford	CT	G	203 284-9764	4708
Carrier Manufacturing Inc	New Britain	CT	G	860 223-2264	2517
Consoldted Inds Acqsition Corp	Cheshire	CT	D	203 272-5371	724
Custom Metal Crafters Inc	Newington	CT	D	860 953-4210	2857
Doncasters Inc	Groton	CT	D	860 446-4803	1670
Sycast Inc	Hartford	CT	G	860 308-2122	1875
Tighitco Inc	Berlin	CT	C	860 828-0298	112
Winchester Products Inc	Winsted	CT	G	860 379-8590	5430
Yankee Casting Co Inc	Enfield	CT	D	860 749-6171	1392
Accent On Industrial Metal Inc	Springfield	MA	F	413 785-1654	15439
Castechnologies Inc	Attleboro	MA	F	508 222-2915	7716
D W Clark Inc **(PA)**	East Bridgewater	MA	E	508 378-4014	10411
Dupliform Casting Co	Marlborough	MA	G	508 485-9333	12751
Edson Corporation	Taunton	MA	G	508 822-0100	15747
Gary Kellner	Westwood	MA	G	781 329-0404	16866
Glines Rhodes Inc	Brewster	MA	G	508 385-8828	9053
Kervick Family Foundation Inc	Worcester	MA	G	508 853-4500	17399
Langstrom Metals Inc	North Grafton	MA	G	508 839-5224	13962
Mack Prototype Inc	Gardner	MA	E	978 632-3700	11119
Merrimac Vly Alum Brass Fndry	Amesbury	MA	G	978 388-0830	7495
MPingo Multi Casting	Springfield	MA	G	413 241-2500	15491
Oerlikon Blzers Cating USA Inc	Agawam	MA	E	413 786-9380	7442
Pace Industries LLC	North Billerica	MA	C	978 667-8400	13852
Parts Tool and Die Inc	Agawam	MA	E	413 821-9718	7445
Tecomet Inc	Wilmington	MA	D	978 642-2400	17051
Trident Alloys Inc	Springfield	MA	E	413 737-1477	15518
Whitman Castings Inc **(PA)**	Whitman	MA	E	781 447-4417	16930
Wollaston Alloys Inc	Braintree	MA	C	781 848-3333	9051
Hawk Motors Inc	York	ME	G	207 363-4716	7308
Al CU Met Inc	Londonderry	NH	E	603 432-6220	18674
Bomar Inc	Charlestown	NH	D	603 826-5781	17811
Diamond Casting and Mch Co Inc	Hollis	NH	E	603 465-2263	18330
Graphicast Inc	Jaffrey	NH	E	603 532-4481	18465
PCC Structurals Groton	Northfield	NH	C	603 286-4301	19407
Bayview Marine Inc	Warwick	RI	G	401 737-3111	21333
Component Technologies Corpora	Barrington	RI	G	401 965-2699	20044
Fielding Manufacturing Inc	Cranston	RI	E	401 461-0400	20226
Optical Polymers Lab Corp	Pawtucket	RI	F	401 722-0710	20870
Osram Sylvania Inc	Central Falls	RI	B	401 723-1378	20122
Providence Casting Inc	North Providence	RI	G	401 231-0860	20773
Ridco Casting Co	Pawtucket	RI	D	401 724-0400	20893
Stevells Jewelry Inc	Cranston	RI	G	401 521-1930	20292
Smb LLC	North Ferrisburgh	VT	G	802 425-2862	22227

3398 Metal Heat Treating

	CITY	ST	EMP	PHONE	ENTRY #
A G C Incorporated **(PA)**	Meriden	CT	C	203 235-3361	2072
Accurate Brazing Corporation	Manchester	CT	F	860 432-1840	1981
Advance Heat Treating Co	Bridgeport	CT	G	203 380-8898	368
American Heat Treating Inc	Monroe	CT	E	203 268-1750	2390
Amk Welding Inc **(HQ)**	South Windsor	CT	E	860 289-5634	3937
Anderson Specialty Company	West Hartford	CT	G	860 953-6630	5053
Aqua Blasting Corp	Bloomfield	CT	F	860 242-8855	201
Beehive Heat Treating Svcs Inc	Fairfield	CT	G	203 866-1635	1416
Bodycote Thermal Proc Inc	Berlin	CT	E	860 225-7691	76
Bodycote Thermal Proc Inc	South Windsor	CT	E	860 282-1371	3944
Eastern Metal Treating Inc	Enfield	CT	F	860 763-4311	1356
General Heat Treating Co	Waterbury	CT	G	203 755-5441	4878
Hydro Honing Laboratories Inc **(PA)**	East Hartford	CT	E	860 289-4328	1200
Johnstone Company Inc	North Haven	CT	E	203 239-5834	3036
Metal Improvement Company LLC	Middletown	CT	E	860 635-9994	2204
Metal Improvement Company LLC	New Britain	CT	E	860 224-9148	2552
Metal Improvement Company LLC	Windsor	CT	E	860 688-6201	5349
Metal Improvement Company LLC	East Windsor	CT	D	860 523-9901	1295
Nelson Heat Treating Co Inc	Waterbury	CT	F	203 754-0670	4925
New Britain Heat Treating Corp	Enfield	CT	F	860 223-0684	1371
O W Heat Treat Inc	South Glastonbury	CT	G	860 430-6709	3924
P&G Metal Components Corp	Bloomfield	CT	F	860 243-2220	248
Paradigm Manchester Inc	Manchester	CT	C	860 649-2888	2032
Peening Technologies Eqp LLC	East Hartford	CT	E	860 289-4328	1209
Sousa Corp	Newington	CT	F	860 523-9090	2904
Specialty Steel Treating Inc	East Granby	CT	E	860 653-0061	1145
Bodycote Imt Inc **(DH)**	Andover	MA	D	978 470-0876	7542
Bodycote Thermal Proc Inc	Ipswich	MA	E	978 356-3818	11906
Bodycote Thermal Proc Inc	Worcester	MA	E	508 754-1724	17349
Fireball Heat Treating Co Inc	Attleboro	MA	G	508 222-2617	7737
Hardline Heat Treating Inc	Southbridge	MA	E	508 764-6669	15384
Heatbath Corporation **(HQ)**	Indian Orchard	MA	E	413 452-2000	11887
Hy-Temp Inc	Attleboro	MA	F	508 222-6626	7748
Industrial Heat Treating Inc	North Quincy	MA	E	617 328-1010	13977
Materials Development Corp	Andover	MA	F	781 391-0400	7568
Metal Improvement Company LLC	Wakefield	MA	F	781 246-3848	15961
Metal Improvement Company LLC	Wilmington	MA	E	978 658-0032	17023
Metal Processing Co Inc	Tyngsboro	MA	G	978 649-1289	15896
Norking Company Inc	Attleboro	MA	E	508 222-3100	7773
Northeast Metals Tech LLC	Rowley	MA	G	978 948-2633	14861
S M Engineering Co Inc	North Attleboro	MA	F	508 699-4484	13778
Thermal Technic Inc	Newburyport	MA	G	978 270-5674	13540
United-County Industries Corp	Millbury	MA	E	508 865-5885	13179
Enterprise Castings LLC	Lewiston	ME	G	207 782-5511	6288
Accurate Brazing Corporation **(HQ)**	Goffstown	NH	E	603 945-3750	18197
Bodycote Thermal Proc Inc	Laconia	NH	E	603 524-7886	18559
Brazecom Industries LLC	Weare	NH	G	603 529-2080	19933
Brazen Innovations Inc	Marlow	NH	G	603 446-7919	18966
Ionbond LLC	Portsmouth	NH	E	603 610-4460	19580
Mushield Company Inc	Londonderry	NH	E	603 666-4433	18726
Smiths Tblar Systms-Lconia Inc	Laconia	NH	B	603 524-2064	18587
Tsi Group Inc **(DH)**	Hampton	NH	E	603 964-0296	18275
Turbocam Energy Solutions LLC	Dover	NH	E	603 905-0200	18063
Induplate Inc **(PA)**	North Providence	RI	D	401 231-5770	20765
Metallurgical Solutions Inc	Providence	RI	F	401 941-2100	21066
Microweld Co Inc	Riverside	RI	G	401 438-5985	21172
R I Heat Treating Co Inc	Providence	RI	G	401 467-9200	21105
S & P Heat Treating Inc	Warwick	RI	F	401 737-9272	21419
Spectrum Thermal Proc LLC	Cranston	RI	F	401 808-6249	20287
Trow & Holden Co Inc	Barre	VT	F	802 476-7221	21643

3399 Primary Metal Prdts, NEC

	CITY	ST	EMP	PHONE	ENTRY #
Abbott Ball Company	West Hartford	CT	D	860 236-5901	5050
Alinabal Inc **(HQ)**	Milford	CT	C	203 877-3241	2242
Alinabal Holdings Corporation **(PA)**	Milford	CT	B	203 877-3241	2243
Allied Sinterings Incorporated	Danbury	CT	E	203 743-7502	869
Allread Products Co LLC	Terryville	CT	F	860 589-3566	4474
Ametek Inc	Wallingford	CT	C	203 265-6731	4699
Ball Supply Corporation	Avon	CT	G	860 673-3364	32
Ccr Products LLC	West Hartford	CT	E	860 953-0499	5058
Centritec Seals LLC	East Hartford	CT	G	860 594-7183	1181
Conn Engineering Assoc Corp	Sandy Hook	CT	F	203 426-4733	3741
Hartford Technologies Inc	Rocky Hill	CT	E	860 571-3602	3712
Lisa Lee Creations Inc	New Haven	CT	G	203 479-4462	2706
Norwalk Powdered Metals Inc	Stratford	CT	D	203 338-8000	4435
Schaeffler Aerospace USA Corp	Winsted	CT	D	860 379-7558	5421
Schaeffler Aerospace USA Corp **(DH)**	Danbury	CT	B	203 744-2211	984
Timber-Top Inc	Watertown	CT	G	860 274-6706	5029
Trd Specialties Inc	Pine Meadow	CT	G	860 738-4505	3446
Bay State Surface Technologies	Auburn	MA	F	508 832-5035	7829
Metal Housings Enclosures	Hudson	MA	G	978 567-3324	11792
Rmi Titanium Company LLC	Burlington	MA	F	781 272-5967	9330
Sem-Tec Inc	Worcester	MA	E	508 798-8551	17471
Browns Greens	Brooksville	ME	G	207 326-4636	5824
Maine Pursuit LLC	Whitefield	ME	G	207 549-7972	7217
Mgi Inc	Hermon	ME	G	207 817-3280	6190
Sabian Ltd	Houlton	ME	G	506 272-2199	6210
Eastern Metals Inc	Londonderry	NH	G	603 818-8639	18693
Omni Technologies Corp	Brentwood	NH	G	603 679-2211	17753
Powdered Metal Technology Corp	Nashua	NH	F	617 642-4135	19236
MCM Technologies Inc	Providence	RI	D	401 785-9204	21064
Stanley Fastening Systems LP **(HQ)**	East Greenwich	RI	D	401 884-2500	20381
Vermont Powder Coating Sy	South Burlington	VT	G	802 862-0061	22476

34 FABRICATED METAL PRODUCTS, EXCEPT MACHINERY AND TRANSPORTATION EQUIPMENT

3411 Metal Cans

	CITY	ST	EMP	PHONE	ENTRY #
CCL Industries Corporation **(DH)**	Shelton	CT	D	203 926-1253	3785
CCL Label Inc	Shelton	CT	C	203 926-1253	3786
Silgan Containers Corporation	Stamford	CT	F	203 975-7110	4320
Silgan Holdings Inc **(PA)**	Stamford	CT	C	203 975-7110	4321
CCL Label Inc **(HQ)**	Framingham	MA	D	508 872-4511	10932
Leaktite Corporation **(PA)**	Leominster	MA	D	978 537-8000	12160
MIW Corp	Fall River	MA	E	508 672-4029	10736
Tin Can Alley	Provincetown	MA	G	508 487-1648	14610
Tin Can Sally	Eliot	ME	G	207 651-6188	6011
Tincanpally LLC	Belfast	ME	G	732 485-5636	5697
Van Dorn and Curtiss	Claremont	NH	G	603 542-3081	17863

3412 Metal Barrels, Drums, Kegs & Pails

	CITY	ST	EMP	PHONE	ENTRY #
Architectural Supplements LLC	Waterbury	CT	F	203 591-5505	4845
Champlin-Packrite Inc	Manchester	CT	E	860 951-9217	1993
Connecticut Container Corp **(PA)**	North Haven	CT	C	203 248-2161	3018
Mobile Mini Inc	Suffield	CT	E	860 668-1888	4465
3 M N Corp	Brockton	MA	G	508 586-4471	9112
Clarks Steel Drum Company	Medford	MA	G	781 396-1109	12926
Cold Chain Technologies Inc **(PA)**	Franklin	MA	D	508 429-1395	11030
Mass Engineering & Tank Inc	Middleboro	MA	E	508 947-8669	13068
Roche Bros Barrel & Drum Co	Lowell	MA	E	978 454-9135	12428
Roche Manufacturing Inc	Lowell	MA	F	978 454-9135	12429
Index Packaging Inc	Milton	NH	C	603 350-0018	19086
Modern Metal Solutions LLC	Hudson	NH	G	603 402-3022	18415
Van Leer Jodi	Hanover	NH	G	603 643-3034	18300
John H Collins & Son Co	Pawtucket	RI	G	401 722-0775	20849
Rand-Whitney Container LLC	Pawtucket	RI	E	401 729-7900	20890

S
I
C

3421 Cutlery

	CITY	ST	EMP	PHONE	ENTRY #
Acme United Corporation **(PA)**	Fairfield	CT	C	203 254-6060	1412
Baingan LLC	Shelton	CT	G	203 924-2626	3778
Bic Corporation **(HQ)**	Shelton	CT	A	203 783-2000	3782
Bic USA Inc **(DH)**	Shelton	CT	C	203 783-2000	3783
Edgewell Per Care Brands LLC	Milford	CT	D	203 882-2300	2282
Edgewell Per Care Brands LLC **(HQ)**	Shelton	CT	B	203 944-5500	3799
Edgewell Personal Care Company	Milford	CT	E	203 882-2308	2283
Gillette Company	Bethel	CT	G	203 796-4000	155
Goong	East Hartford	CT	G	860 216-3041	1198
Laylas Falafel	Stamford	CT	G	203 685-2830	4236
Mexi-Grill LLC	Waterbury	CT	G	203 574-2127	4914
Schick Manufacturing Inc **(HQ)**	Milford	CT	D	203 882-2100	2360
Dexter-Russell Inc	Southbridge	MA	C	800 343-6042	15380
Donahue Industries Inc	Shrewsbury	MA	E	508 845-6501	15108
El Paissa Butchershop	Boston	MA	G	617 567-0493	8521
Exotic Foods	Milford	MA	G	508 422-9540	13117
Georgia-Pacific LLC	Leominster	MA	C	978 537-4701	12144
Gillette Company **(HQ)**	Boston	MA	A	617 421-7000	8561
Gillette Company	Andover	MA	A	781 662-9600	7552
Greenfield Silver Inc **(PA)**	Greenfield	MA	D	413 774-2774	11262
Hyde Group Inc **(PA)**	Southbridge	MA	C	800 872-4933	15385
JH Smith Co Inc **(PA)**	Greenfield	MA	F	413 772-0191	11264
Khalsa Jot	Millis	MA	G	508 376-6206	13185
Lacucina Express	Hampden	MA	G	413 566-8015	11321
Lamson and Goodnow LLC	Shelburne Falls	MA	E	413 625-0201	15073
Lamson and Goodnow Mfg Co	Shelburne Falls	MA	E	413 625-6311	15074
Longcap Lamson Products LLC	Westfield	MA	F	413 642-8135	16697
Mandes Inc	Stoughton	MA	G	781 344-6915	15604
R Murphy Company Inc	Ayer	MA	F	978 772-3481	7935
Countryside Butchers	Biddeford	ME	G	207 282-2882	5725
Pedro Oharas	Lewiston	ME	G	207 783-6200	6315
Colonial Cutlery Intl Inc	North Kingstown	RI	C	401 737-0024	20697
DEA LLC	North Providence	RI	G	401 349-3446	20755
Famars USA LLC	Richmond	RI	G	401 397-5500	21161
Lifetime Brands Inc	Pawtucket	RI	G	401 333-2040	20854
Pacos Tacos Mobile Mex LLC	Cranston	RI	G	401 793-0515	20269
Perry Blackburne Inc	North Providence	RI	E	401 231-7200	20771
A & J Grinding Service	West Burke	VT	G	802 467-3038	22604
Edgewell Per Care Brands LLC	Bennington	VT	B	802 442-5551	21668
Edgewell Per Care Brands LLC	Saint Albans	VT	C	802 524-2151	22368
Wood Dynamics Corporation **(PA)**	South Pomfret	VT	G	802 457-3970	22489

3423 Hand & Edge Tools

	CITY	ST	EMP	PHONE	ENTRY #
A Line Design Inc	Wallingford	CT	G	203 294-0080	4691
Ampol Tool Inc	West Haven	CT	G	203 932-3161	5109
An Designs Inc	Torrington	CT	G	860 618-0183	4560
Atlantic Woodcraft Inc	Enfield	CT	F	860 749-4887	1347
Bessette Holdings Inc	East Hartford	CT	E	860 289-6000	1176
Brimatco Corporation	Cheshire	CT	G	203 272-0044	717
Cambridge Specialty Co Inc	Berlin	CT	D	860 828-3579	80
Conquip Systems LLC	Chester	CT	G	860 526-7883	770
Crrc LLC	Cromwell	CT	D	860 635-2200	852
E-Z Tools Inc	Norwalk	CT	G	203 838-2102	3146
Fletcher-Terry Company LLC **(PA)**	East Berlin	CT	D	860 828-3400	1102
Integrity Manufacturing LLC	Farmington	CT	G	860 678-1599	1487
J J Ryan Corporation	Plantsville	CT	C	860 628-0393	3534
Kell-Strom Tool Co Inc **(PA)**	Wethersfield	CT	E	860 529-6851	5253
Kell-Strom Tool Intl Inc	Wethersfield	CT	E	860 529-6851	5254
Lewmar Inc **(DH)**	Guilford	CT	E	203 458-6200	1708
Ngraver Company	Bozrah	CT	G	860 823-1533	283
Power-Dyne LLC	Middletown	CT	E	860 346-9283	2211
Rostra Tool Company	Branford	CT	E	203 488-8665	343
Skillcraft Machine Tool Co	South Windsor	CT	F	860 953-1246	4010
Southwire Company LLC	Stamford	CT	F	203 324-0067	4326
Stanley Black & Decker Inc	Farmington	CT	F	860 225-5111	1514
Stanley Black & Decker Inc **(PA)**	New Britain	CT	C	860 225-5111	2580
Stanley Black & Decker Inc	New Britain	CT	E	860 225-5111	2583
Sterling Jewelers Inc	Manchester	CT	G	860 644-7207	2052
Tiger Enterprises Inc	Plantsville	CT	E	860 621-9155	3542
Tool 2000	Southington	CT	G	860 620-0020	4087
Toolmax Designing Tooling Inc	Tolland	CT	G	860 871-7265	4555
Triple Clover Products LLC	New Canaan	CT	G	475 558-9503	2618
Trumpf Inc **(DH)**	Farmington	CT	B	860 255-6000	1517
Trumpf Inc	Farmington	CT	B	860 255-6000	1518
Trumpf Inc	Plainville	CT	B	860 255-6000	3522
Ullman Devices Corporation	Ridgefield	CT	D	203 438-6577	3687
Unger Enterprises LLC	Bridgeport	CT	C	203 366-4884	500
Uniprise International Inc	Terryville	CT	E	860 589-7262	4495
Arbortech Tools USA Corp	Norwell	MA	G	866 517-7869	14094
Art For A Cause LLC	East Weymouth	MA	E	248 645-3966	10536
Arthur H Gaebel Inc	Boxborough	MA	G	978 263-4401	8958
Camelot Tools LLC	Holden	MA	G	508 981-7443	11542
Dexter-Russell Inc	Southbridge	MA	C	800 343-6042	15380
Earths Elements Inc	Bridgewater	MA	G	508 697-2277	9072
Echo Industries Inc	Orange	MA	E	978 544-7000	14215
Feteria Tool & Findings	Attleboro	MA	G	508 222-7788	7734
Fine Edge Tool Company Inc	Attleboro	MA	G	508 222-7511	7736
Foster-Miller Inc	Devens	MA	D	781 684-4000	10320
Great Neck Saw Mfrs Inc	Millbury	MA	E	508 865-4482	13166
Greenfield Silver Inc **(PA)**	Greenfield	MA	D	413 774-2774	11262
Hot Tools Inc	Marblehead	MA	F	781 639-1000	12686
Hyde Group Inc **(PA)**	Southbridge	MA	C	800 872-4933	15385
Hyde Tools	Southbridge	MA	G	508 764-4344	15386
Interstate Specialty Pdts Inc	Sutton	MA	E	800 984-1811	15685
Irwin Industrial Tool Company	East Longmeadow	MA	A	413 525-3961	10480
JH Smith Co Inc **(PA)**	Greenfield	MA	F	413 772-0191	11264
Killoran Contracting Inc	Milton	MA	G	617 298-5248	13194
Lamson and Goodnow LLC	Shelburne Falls	MA	E	413 625-0201	15073
Lamson and Goodnow Mfg Co	Shelburne Falls	MA	E	413 625-6311	15074
Lowell Corporation	West Boylston	MA	E	508 835-2900	16421
LS Starrett Company **(PA)**	Athol	MA	A	978 249-3551	7689
Ludlow Tool	Agawam	MA	F	413 786-6360	7438
Lund Precision Products Inc	Hyannis	MA	G	617 413-0236	11848
M M Newman Corporation	Marblehead	MA	F	781 631-7100	12687
Mayhew Steel Products Inc **(PA)**	Turners Falls	MA	E	413 625-6351	15881
Peterson and Nash Inc	Norwell	MA	E	781 826-9085	14111
Pilgrim Badge & Label Corp	Brockton	MA	D	508 436-6300	9171
Quality Die Cutting Inc **(PA)**	Haverhill	MA	F	978 374-8027	11465
Quickpoint Corporation	Concord	MA	G	978 371-3267	10154
R Murphy Company Inc	Ayer	MA	F	978 772-3481	7935
Riverdale Mills Corporation	Northbridge	MA	C	508 234-8715	14060
Rugg Manufacturing Company Inc	Leominster	MA	F	413 773-5471	12185
Safe T Cut Inc	Monson	MA	F	413 267-9984	13211
Seekonk Manufacturing Co Inc	Seekonk	MA	E	508 761-8284	15036
Silpro Llc **(PA)**	Ayer	MA	E	978 772-4444	7939
Skew Products Incorporated	West Bridgewater	MA	E	508 580-5800	16454
Stiebel Eltron Inc	Holyoke	MA	G	413 535-1734	11661
US Discount Products LLC	West Bridgewater	MA	G	877 841-5782	16462
Wrentham Tool Group LLC	Bellingham	MA	D	508 966-2332	8064
Anthony Automotive	Gardiner	ME	G	207 582-7105	6104
David Michaud	Winthrop	ME	G	207 377-8037	7280
Irwin Industrial Tool Company	Gorham	ME	C	207 856-6111	6115
Lie-Nielsen Toolworks Inc	Warren	ME	D	800 327-2520	7144
Peavey Manufacturing Company	Eddington	ME	E	207 843-7861	5997
R2b Inc	Portland	ME	F	207 797-0019	6719
Xuron Corp	Saco	ME	E	207 283-1401	6862
Chadwick & Trefethen Inc	Portsmouth	NH	F	603 436-2568	19551
Pavelok	Bow	NH	G	603 225-7283	17725
Swansons Die Co Inc	Manchester	NH	E	603 623-3832	18934
Trellborg Pipe Sals Milford Inc **(DH)**	Milford	NH	C	800 626-2180	19080
Tucker Mountain Homes Inc	Meredith	NH	G	603 279-4320	18981
Joseph A Thomas Ltd	Bristol	RI	F	401 253-1330	20086
Materion Technical Mtls Inc	Lincoln	RI	C	401 333-1700	20583
Ames Companies Inc	Wallingford	VT	C	802 446-2601	22573

3425 Hand Saws & Saw Blades

	CITY	ST	EMP	PHONE	ENTRY #
Blackstone Industries LLC	Bethel	CT	D	203 792-8622	133
DArcy Saw LLC	Windsor Locks	CT	G	800 569-1264	5390
Specialty Saw Inc	Simsbury	CT	E	860 658-4419	3912
LS Starrett Company **(PA)**	Athol	MA	A	978 249-3551	7689
Lie-Nielsen Toolworks Inc	Warren	ME	D	800 327-2520	7144
Malco Saw Co Inc	Cranston	RI	G	401 942-7380	20258
T S S Inc	Waterbury	VT	E	802 244-8101	22586

3429 Hardware, NEC

	CITY	ST	EMP	PHONE	ENTRY #
Ador Inc	Bristol	CT	G	860 583-2367	515
Air-Lock Incorporated	Milford	CT	E	203 878-4691	2238
Assa Inc **(HQ)**	New Haven	CT	B	203 624-5225	2659
Assa Inc	New Haven	CT	G	800 235-7482	2660
Assa Abloy Accss & Edrss Hrdwr	Berlin	CT	B	860 225-7411	73
Beckson Manufacturing Inc **(PA)**	Bridgeport	CT	E	203 366-3644	381
Bourdon Forge Co Inc	Middletown	CT	C	860 632-2740	2179
Brookfield Industries Inc	Thomaston	CT	E	860 283-6211	4500
C Sherman Johnson Company	East Haddam	CT	F	860 873-8697	1149
Colonial Bronze Company	Torrington	CT	D	860 489-9233	4570
Composite McHining Experts LLC	North Haven	CT	G	203 624-0664	3017
Connecticut Greenstar Inc	Fairfield	CT	G	203 368-1522	1423
Connecticut Trade Company Inc	Fairfield	CT	G	203 368-0398	1424
Corbin Russwin	New Haven	CT	G	860 225-7411	2679
Cornell-Carr Co Inc	Monroe	CT	E	203 261-2529	2399
Crrc LLC	Cromwell	CT	D	860 635-2200	852
D & B Tool Co LLC	Milford	CT	G	203 878-6026	2272
D & M Screw Machine Pdts LLC	Plainville	CT	G	860 410-9781	3479
Dwyer Aluminum Mast Company	North Branford	CT	F	203 484-0419	2962
Eastern Company **(PA)**	Naugatuck	CT	E	203 729-2255	2471
Engineered Inserts & Systems **(PA)**	Milford	CT	F	203 301-3334	2285
Fsb Inc	Berlin	CT	F	203 404-4700	86
GK Mechanical Systems LLC	Brookfield	CT	G	203 775-4970	644
Halls Edge Inc	Stamford	CT	G	203 653-2281	4204
Hartford Aircraft Products	Bloomfield	CT	E	860 242-8228	223
Hicks and Otis Prints Inc	Norwalk	CT	E	203 846-2087	3168
Horton Brasses Inc	Cromwell	CT	G	860 635-4400	855

	CITY	ST	EMP	PHONE	ENTRY #
Industrial Shipg Entps MGT LLC	Stamford	CT	G	203 504-5800	4222
James Ippolito & Co Conn Inc	Bridgeport	CT	E	203 366-3840	433
James L Howard and Company Inc	Bloomfield	CT	E	860 242-3581	228
Kell-Strom Tool Co Inc **(PA)**	Wethersfield	CT	E	860 529-6851	5253
Kell-Strom Tool Intl Inc	Wethersfield	CT	E	860 529-6851	5254
Lab Security Systems Corp	Bristol	CT	E	860 589-6037	575
Lassy Tools Inc	Plainville	CT	G	860 747-2748	3500
Lewmar Inc **(DH)**	Guilford	CT	E	203 458-6200	1708
Mc Kinney Products Company	Berlin	CT	C	800 346-7707	95
Morning Star Tool LLC	Milford	CT	G	203 878-6026	2316
Norse Inc	Torrington	CT	G	860 482-1532	4589
Oslo Switch Inc	Cheshire	CT	E	203 272-2794	750
Outland Engineering Inc	Milford	CT	F	800 797-3709	2329
Paneloc Corporation	Farmington	CT	E	860 677-6711	1505
Panza Woodwork & Supply LLC	West Haven	CT	G	203 934-3430	5140
Paradigm Manchester Inc	Manchester	CT	C	860 649-2888	2032
Pemko Manufacturing Co	New Haven	CT	G	901 365-2160	2722
Perry Technology Corporation	New Hartford	CT	D	860 738-2525	2644
Pro-Lock USA LLC	Monroe	CT	G	203 382-3428	2414
Roller Bearing Co Amer Inc	Middlebury	CT	E	203 758-8272	2157
Sargent Manufacturing Company	New Haven	CT	A	203 562-2151	2735
Specialty Products Mfg LLC	Southington	CT	G	860 621-6969	4081
Stanley Black & Decker Inc **(PA)**	New Britain	CT	C	860 225-5111	2580
Stanley Black & Decker Inc	New Britain	CT	D	860 225-5111	2581
Stanley Black & Decker Inc	New Britain	CT	E	860 225-5111	2583
Stanley Black & Decker Inc	New Britain	CT	C	860 225-5111	2582
Stanley Industrial & Auto LLC	New Britain	CT	E	800 800-8005	2585
Tiger Enterprises Inc	Plantsville	CT	E	860 621-9155	3542
Unger Industrial LLC	Bridgeport	CT	G	203 336-3344	501
Vector Engineering Inc	Mystic	CT	F	860 572-0422	2455
Walz & Krenzer Inc **(PA)**	Oxford	CT	F	203 267-5712	3429
Wind Corporation	Newtown	CT	E	203 778-1001	2949
Wtm Company	Thomaston	CT	G	860 283-5871	4528
Yale Security Inc	Berlin	CT	B	865 986-7511	117
York Street Studio Inc	New Milford	CT	G	203 266-9000	2833
Zephyr Lock LLC	Newtown	CT	F	866 937-4971	2950
A N C Tool and Manufacturing	Worcester	MA	G	508 757-0224	17329
Acorn Manufacturing Co Inc	Mansfield	MA	E	508 339-4500	12611
AMS Glass Bead Cabinets	Hampden	MA	E	413 566-0037	11319
Anderson Components Corp	Malden	MA	F	781 324-0350	12558
Atlantic RES Mktg Systems Inc	West Bridgewater	MA	F	508 584-7816	16429
Atrenne Cmpt Solutions LLC **(DH)**	Brockton	MA	B	508 588-6110	9121
Boston Garage	Hanover	MA	F	339 788-9580	11330
Craft Inc	Attleboro	MA	E	508 761-7917	7725
Delaware Valley Corp	Tewksbury	MA	E	978 459-6932	15814
Device Technologies Inc	Southborough	MA	E	508 229-2000	15354
Dorel Juvenile Group Inc	Foxboro	MA	D	800 544-1108	10881
Dormakaba USA Inc	Randolph	MA	E	781 963-0182	14676
Eastern Cast Hardware Co Inc	West Springfield	MA	G	413 733-7690	16517
G S Davidson Co Inc	North Reading	MA	G	617 389-4000	13982
Grant Larkin	Richmond	MA	G	413 698-2599	14779
Hancock Marine Inc	Fall River	MA	G	508 678-0301	10712
Hostar Mar Trnspt Systems Inc	Wareham	MA	E	508 295-2900	16250
Inner-Tite Corp	Holden	MA	D	508 829-6361	11546
Ketcham Supply Co Inc	New Bedford	MA	F	508 997-4787	13403
Ketcham Traps	New Bedford	MA	G	508 997-4787	13404
Kingslide USA Inc	Andover	MA	G	978 475-0120	7562
Lighthouse Woodworks LLC	Boston	MA	G	781 223-4302	8666
McStowe Engineering & Met Pdts	East Bridgewater	MA	F	508 378-7400	10417
Molly Merchandising Unlimited	Holden	MA	G	508 829-2544	11548
Newstamp Lighting Corp	North Easton	MA	F	508 238-7073	13949
Peerless Handcuff Co Inc	West Springfield	MA	G	413 732-2156	16541
Qc Industries Inc **(PA)**	Mansfield	MA	D	781 344-1000	12653
Relcor Inc	East Sandwich	MA	G	561 844-8335	10508
Renovators Supply Inc	Millers Falls	MA	E	413 423-3300	13181
Rj Marine Industries	Oxford	MA	G	508 248-9933	14272
Rolls-Royce Marine North Amer **(DH)**	Walpole	MA	C	508 668-9610	16009
Schlage Lock Company LLC	Canton	MA	E	781 828-6655	9776
Submarine Research Labs	Hingham	MA	G	781 749-0900	11512
Taunton Stove Company Inc	North Dighton	MA	E	508 823-0786	13937
Turning Point Industry FL	Pembroke	MA	G	239 340-1942	14430
Universal Hinge Corp **(PA)**	Westminster	MA	F	603 935-9848	16819
Vaughan W C Co Ltd Inc	Braintree	MA	G	781 848-0308	9046
W J Roberts Co Inc	Saugus	MA	E	781 233-8176	15002
Williamsburg Blacksmiths Inc	Williamsburg	MA	G	413 268-7341	16953
Xcerra Corporation **(HQ)**	Norwood	MA	C	781 461-1000	14206
Edgar Clark & Son Inc	Readfield	ME	G	207 685-4568	6776
Island Lobster Supply	Vinalhaven	ME	G	207 863-4807	7128
Knight Underwater Bearing Llc	Cape Neddick	ME	G	207 251-0001	5880
Paul E Luke Inc	East Boothbay	ME	G	207 633-4971	5979
Richard Fisher	Prospect Harbor	ME	G	207 963-7184	6771
T Henri Inc	Southwest Harbor	ME	G	207 244-7787	7051
Albany Safran Composites LLC **(HQ)**	Rochester	NH	E	603 330-5800	19657
Anvil International LLC **(HQ)**	Exeter	NH	E	603 418-2800	18110
Bomar Inc	Charlestown	NH	D	603 826-5781	17811
Bronze Craft Corporation	Nashua	NH	D	603 883-7747	19130
Cascaded Purchase Holdings Inc **(PA)**	Claremont	NH	C	603 448-1090	17841

	CITY	ST	EMP	PHONE	ENTRY #
Elemental Innovation Inc	Newton	NH	F	603 259-4400	19365
Mitee-Bite Products LLC	Center Ossipee	NH	F	603 539-4538	17804
Mrp Manufacturing LLC	Pittsfield	NH	G	603 435-5337	19503
Nantucket Beadboard Co Inc	Rochester	NH	F	603 330-3338	19679
Pompanette LLC **(PA)**	Charlestown	NH	D	717 569-2300	17819
United Mch & Tl Design Co Inc	Fremont	NH	E	603 642-3601	18181
Universal Hinge Corp	Manchester	NH	G	603 935-9848	18946
Fulford Manufacturing Company **(PA)**	Riverside	RI	F	401 431-2000	21168
Gripnail Corporation	East Providence	RI	E	401 431-1791	20416
Groov-Pin Corporation **(PA)**	Smithfield	RI	D	770 251-5054	21230
Hindley Manufacturing Co Inc	Cumberland	RI	D	401 722-2550	20325
Ocean Link Inc	Portsmouth	RI	G	401 683-4434	20935
Tracey Gear Inc	Pawtucket	RI	E	401 725-3920	20906
Vincent Metals Corporation	Warwick	RI	G	401 737-4167	21437

3431 Enameled Iron & Metal Sanitary Ware

	CITY	ST	EMP	PHONE	ENTRY #
Kensco Inc **(PA)**	Ansonia	CT	F	203 734-8827	20
Acushnet International Inc **(DH)**	Fairhaven	MA	C	508 979-2000	10637
Designer Sinks & Faucets	Hanover	MA	G	781 924-1768	11335
Palmer Industries Inc	North Providence	RI	F	800 398-9676	20770

3432 Plumbing Fixture Fittings & Trim, Brass

	CITY	ST	EMP	PHONE	ENTRY #
Bead Industries Inc **(PA)**	Milford	CT	E	203 301-0270	2251
Colonial Bronze Company	Torrington	CT	D	860 489-9233	4570
F W Webb Company	New Haven	CT	F	203 865-6124	2688
Fitzgerald & Wood Inc	Branford	CT	G	203 488-2553	316
Macristy Industries Inc **(PA)**	Newington	CT	C	860 225-4637	2879
Mc Guire Manufacturing Co Inc	Cheshire	CT	D	203 699-1801	744
Neoperl Inc	Waterbury	CT	D	203 756-8891	4926
Plastic Assembly Systems LLC	Bethany	CT	F	203 393-0639	123
The Keeney Manufacturing Co **(PA)**	Newington	CT	C	603 239-6371	2906
Boston Atmtc Sprnklr Fbrcation	Rockland	MA	G	781 681-5122	14794
Idex Health & Science LLC	Middleboro	MA	C	774 213-0200	13064
Lash Lamour	Boston	MA	G	617 247-1871	8659
Orion Enterprises Inc **(HQ)**	North Andover	MA	C	913 342-1653	13722
P A G Industries Inc	North Chelmsford	MA	F	978 265-5610	13906
Renovators Supply Inc	Millers Falls	MA	E	413 423-3300	13181
Symmons Industries Inc **(PA)**	Braintree	MA	C	781 848-2250	9041
Turning Point Industry FL	Pembroke	MA	G	239 340-1942	14430
Viola Associates Inc	Hyannis	MA	F	508 771-3457	11861
Eos Design LLC **(PA)**	Westbrook	ME	G	740 392-3642	7188
The Keeney Manufacturing Co	Winchester	NH	C	603 239-6371	19996
Cramik Enterprises Inc	Westerly	RI	E	401 596-8171	21521
Frank Passarella Inc	North Kingstown	RI	G	401 295-4943	20712
Fulford Manufacturing Company **(PA)**	Riverside	RI	F	401 431-2000	21168
Plumbers of RI	Providence	RI	G	401 919-0980	21091
Quick Fitting Inc	Warwick	RI	D	401 734-9500	21408

3433 Heating Eqpt

	CITY	ST	EMP	PHONE	ENTRY #
Allgreenit LLC	Bristol	CT	G	860 516-4948	517
Carlin Combustion Tech Inc	North Haven	CT	G	413 525-7700	3013
Carlin Combustion Tech Inc **(HQ)**	North Haven	CT	D	203 680-9401	3014
CP Solar Thermal LLC	Bristol	CT	G	860 877-2238	544
Dp2 LLC Head	Darien	CT	F	203 655-0747	1022
Fives N Amercn Combustn Inc	East Lyme	CT	G	860 739-3466	1270
Fives N Amercn Combustn Inc	Southington	CT	E	216 271-6000	4051
Hamworthy Peabody Combustn Inc **(DH)**	Shelton	CT	E	203 922-1199	3808
Hi-Temp Products Corp	Danbury	CT	G	203 744-3025	931
Jad LLC	South Windsor	CT	E	860 289-1551	3983
John Zink Company LLC	Shelton	CT	D	203 925-0380	3821
Kerigans Fuel Inc	Bridgeport	CT	G	203 334-3646	439
Lewis R Martino	Oxford	CT	G	203 463-4430	3412
Macristy Industries Inc **(PA)**	Newington	CT	C	860 225-4637	2879
McIntire Company **(HQ)**	Bristol	CT	F	860 585-8559	580
Omega Engineering Inc **(HQ)**	Norwalk	CT	C	203 359-1660	3211
Optical Energy Technologies	Stamford	CT	G	203 357-0626	4272
Preferred Utilities Mfg Corp **(HQ)**	Danbury	CT	D	203 743-6741	974
Pumc Holding Corporation **(PA)**	Danbury	CT	E	203 743-6741	976
Schindler Combustion LLC	Fairfield	CT	G	203 371-5068	1455
Zeeco Inc	Plainville	CT	G	860 479-0999	3524
AAA Radiator	Melrose	MA	G	781 662-7203	12973
Advanced Burner Solutions Corp	Medway	MA	G	508 400-3289	12953
Babcock Power Inc **(PA)**	Lynnfield	MA	G	978 646-3300	12545
Creative Hydronics Intl Inc	Sagamore Beach	MA	G	508 524-3535	14885
Cunniff Corp **(PA)**	East Falmouth	MA	G	508 540-6232	10440
H B Smith Company Inc	Westfield	MA	E	413 568-3148	16687
Heatmaker Parts & Service	Reading	MA	G	617 930-0036	14737
Integrated Clean Tech Inc	Pittsfield	MA	G	413 281-2555	14477
Mainline Energy Systems Inc	Northbridge	MA	G	860 429-9663	14057
Marios Oil Corp	Everett	MA	G	617 202-8259	10621
Maxon Corporation	Acton	MA	G	978 795-1285	7373
Mestek Inc	Westfield	MA	B	413 568-9571	16702
Neutrasafe Corporation	Stoughton	MA	G	781 616-3951	15611
New England Solar Hot Wtr Inc	Pembroke	MA	G	781 536-8633	14419
Real Goods Solar Inc	New Bedford	MA	C	508 992-1416	13444
Riley Power Inc	Worcester	MA	C	508 852-7100	17459
Riley Power Inc	Marlborough	MA	C	508 852-7100	12817

	CITY	ST	EMP	PHONE	ENTRY #
Runtal North America Inc	Haverhill	MA	E	800 526-2621	11469
Spire Solar Inc	Bedford	MA	C	781 275-6000	8009
Stiebel Eltron Inc	Holyoke	MA	G	413 535-1734	11661
Sunborne Energy Technologies	Cambridge	MA	G	617 234-7000	9663
Sundrum Solar Inc	Northborough	MA	G	508 740-6256	14049
Sunfield Solar	Spencer	MA	G	508 885-3300	15437
Taco Inc	Fall River	MA	D	508 675-7300	10769
Thermal Circuits Inc	Salem	MA	C	978 745-1162	14945
Thermo Products	Wilbraham	MA	G	413 279-1980	16943
Trinity Heating & Air Inc	West Wareham	MA	D	508 291-0007	16577
Tunstall Corporation **(PA)**	Chicopee	MA	E	413 594-8695	10065
Warm Water Sales Group	Longmeadow	MA	G	413 567-0750	12338
American Solartechnics LLC	Stockton Springs	ME	G	207 548-1122	7068
Antoine Mechanical Inc	Jay	ME	G	207 897-4100	6219
GS Inc	Rockland	ME	G	207 593-7730	6797
Jotul North America Inc	Gorham	ME	D	207 797-5912	6116
Mestek Inc	Clinton	ME	C	207 426-2351	5916
Onix Corporation	Caribou	ME	E	866 290-5362	5889
Bbt North America Corporation	Londonderry	NH	G	603 552-1100	18679
Bradford White Corp	Rochester	NH	G	603 332-0116	19663
Efficiency Plus	Center Ossipee	NH	G	603 539-8125	17803
Granite 3 LLC	Temple	NH	G	603 566-0339	19897
Osram Sylvania Inc	Exeter	NH	D	603 772-4331	18127
R Filion Manufacturing Inc	Newport	NH	F	603 865-1893	19355
Taco Inc **(PA)**	Cranston	RI	B	401 942-8000	20299
Heart Quali Home Heati Produ	Morrisville	VT	D	802 888-5232	22169
L & G Fabricators Inc	Bennington	VT	F	802 447-0965	21679

3441 Fabricated Structural Steel

	CITY	ST	EMP	PHONE	ENTRY #
Accutron Inc	Windsor	CT	C	860 683-8300	5315
Acquisitions Controlled Svcs	Stamford	CT	G	203 327-6364	4129
All Panel Systems LLC	Branford	CT	D	203 208-3142	288
All Phase Steel Works LLC	New Haven	CT	D	203 375-8881	2654
Alloy Welding & Mfg Co Inc	Bristol	CT	F	860 582-3638	518
Anco Engineering Inc	Shelton	CT	D	203 925-9235	3775
Andert Inc	Eastford	CT	G	860 974-3893	1312
Ansonia Stl Fabrication Co Inc	Beacon Falls	CT	E	203 888-4509	53
Applied Laser Solutions Inc	Danbury	CT	G	203 739-0179	873
ARC Dynamics Inc	Rocky Hill	CT	G	860 563-1006	3702
Atlantic Eqp Installers Inc	Wallingford	CT	E	203 284-0402	4705
Atlantic Fabricating Co Inc	South Windsor	CT	F	860 291-9882	3940
Atlas Metal Works LLC	South Windsor	CT	F	860 282-1030	3941
Bri Metal Works Inc	Bridgeport	CT	G	203 368-1649	386
Carpin Manufacturing Inc	Waterbury	CT	D	203 574-2556	4854
Central Construction Inds LLC	Putnam	CT	E	860 963-8902	3604
Cirillo Manufacturing Group	East Haven	CT	G	203 484-5010	1244
Coastal Steel Corporation	Waterford	CT	E	860 443-4073	4982
Colonial Iron Shop Inc	Enfield	CT	G	860 763-0659	1351
Connecticut Iron Works Inc	Greenwich	CT	G	203 869-0657	1603
Delany & Long Ltd	Greenwich	CT	G	203 532-0010	1606
Di-Cor Industries Inc	Bristol	CT	F	860 585-5583	549
Division 5 LLC	Stafford Springs	CT	G	860 752-4127	4109
Eagle Manufacturing Co Inc	Colchester	CT	F	860 537-3759	801
East Windsor Metal Fabg Inc	South Windsor	CT	F	860 528-7107	3961
Eastern Inc	New Canaan	CT	G	203 563-9535	2597
Enginering Components Pdts LLC	Plainville	CT	G	860 747-6222	3486
ES Metal Fabrications Inc	Terryville	CT	F	860 585-6067	4478
Gulf Manufacturing Inc	Rocky Hill	CT	E	860 529-8601	3710
HRF Fastener Systems Inc	Bristol	CT	E	860 589-0750	569
Iron Craft Fabricating LLC	North Grosvenordale	CT	G	860 923-9869	2996
Kinamor Incorporated	Wallingford	CT	E	203 269-0380	4760
Lemac Iron Works Inc	West Hartford	CT	G	860 232-7380	5081
LH Gault & Son Incorporated	Westport	CT	D	203 227-5181	5209
Magna Steel Sales Inc	Beacon Falls	CT	F	203 888-0300	62
Mayarc Industries Inc	Ellington	CT	G	860 871-1872	1335
Mobile Mini Inc	Suffield	CT	E	860 668-1888	4465
Mtj Manufacturing Inc	Bridgeport	CT	G	203 334-4939	454
Mystic Stainless & Alum Inc	Mystic	CT	G	860 536-2236	2446
Ovl Manufacturing Inc LLC	Berlin	CT	G	860 829-0271	100
Pcx Aerostructures LLC	Newington	CT	E	860 666-2471	2892
Pisani Steel Fabrication Inc	Naugatuck	CT	G	203 720-0679	2490
Platt & Labonia Company LLC	North Haven	CT	E	800 505-9099	3051
Qsr Steel Corporation LLC	Hartford	CT	E	860 548-0248	1863
Reliable Welding & Speed LLC	Enfield	CT	G	860 749-3977	1379
Romco Contractors Inc	Bloomfield	CT	F	860 243-8872	257
Rwt Corporation	Madison	CT	E	203 245-2731	1973
Shepard Steel Co Inc **(PA)**	Hartford	CT	D	860 525-4446	1869
Shepard Steel Co Inc	Newington	CT	E	860 525-4446	2902
Stamford Iron & Stl Works Inc	Stamford	CT	F	203 324-6751	4331
State Welding & Fabg Inc	Wallingford	CT	G	203 294-4071	4813
Steeltech Building Pdts Inc	South Windsor	CT	D	860 290-8930	4014
Stratford Steel LLC	Stratford	CT	E	203 612-7350	4449
Swift Innovations LLC	Mystic	CT	G	860 572-8322	2452
T Keefe and Sons	Guilford	CT	G	203 457-0267	1721
Thomas La Ganga	Torrington	CT	G	860 489-0920	4601
Tinsley GROup-Ps&w Inc **(HQ)**	Milford	CT	D	919 742-5832	2376
Total Fab LLC	East Haven	CT	F	475 238-8176	1266
United Steel Inc	East Hartford	CT	C	860 289-2323	1232
Varnum Enterprises LLC	Bethel	CT	F	203 743-4443	190
Vernier Metal Fabricating Inc	Seymour	CT	D	203 881-3133	3767
Viking Enterprises Inc	Waterford	CT	G	860 440-0728	4995
Yankee Metals LLC	Bridgeport	CT	G	203 612-7470	507
2l Inc	Hudson	MA	F	978 567-8867	11748
3-D Welding Inc	Attleboro	MA	F	508 222-2500	7695
A G Industries Inc	North Attleboro	MA	G	508 695-4219	13741
Accufab Iron Works Inc	Goshen	MA	F	413 268-7133	11222
All Star Fabrication Inc	Ipswich	MA	G	978 887-7617	11901
All Steel Fabricating Inc	North Grafton	MA	E	508 839-4471	13958
Allied Fabrication Inc	North Billerica	MA	G	978 667-5901	13791
American Metalcraft Co	East Weymouth	MA	G	781 331-8588	10535
Atlantic Steel Fabricators Inc	Wilmington	MA	G	978 657-8292	16976
Auciello Iron Works Inc **(PA)**	Hudson	MA	E	978 568-8382	11758
Barker Steel LLC	South Deerfield	MA	E	413 665-2381	15245
Barker Steel LLC	Westfield	MA	E	413 568-7803	16671
Bay Steel Co Inc **(PA)**	Halifax	MA	G	781 294-8308	11315
Bellingham Metal Works LLC	Franklin	MA	G	617 519-5958	11025
Berkshire Bridge & Iron Co Inc	Dalton	MA	F	413 684-3182	10174
Blue Atlantic Fabricators LLC	Boston	MA	F	617 874-8503	8415
Boston Forging & Welding Corp	Boston	MA	G	617 567-2300	8430
Boston Steel Fabricators Inc	Holbrook	MA	G	781 767-1540	11522
Brayton Wilson Cole Corp	Hingham	MA	G	781 803-6624	11495
Butler Metal Fabricators Inc	Indian Orchard	MA	G	413 306-5762	11885
Capone Iron Corporation	Rowley	MA	E	978 948-8000	14848
Carl Fisher Co Inc	Springfield	MA	E	413 736-3661	15458
Composite Modules	Attleboro	MA	D	508 226-6969	7723
Custom Steel Fabrication Corp	Middleton	MA	G	978 774-4555	13087
D Clement Inc	Dunstable	MA	G	978 649-3263	10389
D Cronins Welding Service	Lawrence	MA	G	978 664-4488	12014
Danvers Engineering Co Inc	Danvers	MA	G	978 774-7501	10211
Dean Paige Welding Inc	Baldwinville	MA	G	978 939-8187	7943
Diamond Ironworks Inc	Lawrence	MA	E	978 794-4640	12017
Diamond Stl & Fabrication LLC	Wakefield	MA	G	781 245-3255	15950
Digital Alloys Incorporated	Burlington	MA	F	617 557-3432	9256
Dublin Steel Corporation	Palmer	MA	E	413 289-1218	14286
E T Duval & Son Inc	Leominster	MA	G	978 537-7596	12134
East Coast Fabrications	West Wareham	MA	G	508 295-1982	16569
Eastern Metal Industries Inc	Saugus	MA	F	781 231-5220	14980
Emseal Joint Systems Ltd	Westborough	MA	E	508 836-0280	16617
Environmental Improvements **(PA)**	Abington	MA	G	781 857-2375	7324
Ernest Johnson	Marlborough	MA	G	508 259-6727	12753
Fall River Boiler & Welding Co	Fall River	MA	G	508 677-4479	10695
First Fabricators Co Inc	Ipswich	MA	G	978 356-2901	11919
Fitchburg Welding Co Inc	Westminster	MA	E	978 874-2911	16804
Flametech Steels Inc	Lawrence	MA	G	978 686-9518	12024
General Steel Products Co Inc	Lexington	MA	F	617 387-5400	12228
Gill Metal Fab Inc	Brockton	MA	E	508 580-4445	9151
Industrial Metal Pdts Co Inc	Sharon	MA	D	781 762-3330	15052
Industrial Stl Boiler Svcs Inc	Chicopee	MA	E	413 532-7788	10032
International Stone Inc	Woburn	MA	D	781 937-3300	17206
Ironman Inc	Mansfield	MA	G	989 386-8975	12638
Jeff Schiff	Chelsea	MA	G	617 887-0202	9956
Jlp Services Inc	Rutland	MA	G	508 667-5498	14882
Kent Fabrications Inc	Pembroke	MA	G	339 244-4533	14413
Kw Steel Structures LLC	Walpole	MA	G	857 342-7838	15998
L & J Enterprises Inc	Malden	MA	G	781 233-1966	12576
Lally Column Corp	Stoughton	MA	G	508 828-5997	15602
Mass Metalworks LLC	Medway	MA	G	508 533-7500	12966
Mbs Fabrication Inc **(PA)**	Southbridge	MA	F	508 765-0900	15395
Metal Solutions LLC	Millbury	MA	G	774 276-0096	13171
Metrick Manufacturing Co Inc	Woburn	MA	G	781 935-1331	17228
Mill City Iron Fabricators	Dracut	MA	F	978 957-6833	10366
Moseley Corporation	Franklin	MA	E	508 520-4004	11068
Nevron Plastics Inc	Saugus	MA	F	781 233-1310	14991
New England Bridge Products	Lynn	MA	G	781 592-2444	12527
New England Welding Inc	Avon	MA	F	508 580-2024	7891
North American Steel Corp	Peabody	MA	G	978 535-7587	14357
North Shore Steel Co Inc **(PA)**	Lynn	MA	E	781 598-1645	12530
O W Landergren Inc	Pittsfield	MA	E	413 442-5632	14497
Package Steel Systems Inc	Sutton	MA	E	508 865-5871	15689
Payne Engrg Fabrication Co Inc	Canton	MA	E	781 828-9046	9765
PEC Detailing Co Inc	Walpole	MA	G	508 660-8954	16006
Quality Laser Inc	Woburn	MA	G	617 479-7374	17276
R I Baker Co Inc **(PA)**	Clarksburg	MA	E	413 663-3791	10075
R Moody Machine & Fabrication	Deerfield	MA	G	413 773-3329	10303
Ranor Inc	Westminster	MA	D	978 874-0591	16812
Rayco Inc	Amesbury	MA	G	978 388-1039	7504
Rens Welding & Fabricating	Taunton	MA	F	508 828-1702	15779
Republic Iron Works Inc	Chicopee	MA	G	413 594-8819	10058
Robert Russell Co Inc	Rehoboth	MA	G	508 226-4140	14760
Rodney Hunt-Fontaine Inc **(DH)**	Orange	MA	C	978 544-2511	14227
Sajawi Corporation	Littleton	MA	E	978 486-9050	12323
Scannell Boiler Works Inc	Lowell	MA	F	978 454-5629	12431
Schiff Archtectural Detail LLC	Chelsea	MA	G	617 846-6437	9966

	CITY	ST	EMP	PHONE	ENTRY #
Service Oriented Sales Inc	Shrewsbury	MA	G	508 845-3330	15131
Shawmut Metal Products Inc	Swansea	MA	E	508 379-0803	15715
Smj Metal Co Inc	Northampton	MA	E	413 586-3535	14021
Sousa Bros & Demayo Inc	Attleboro Falls	MA	E	508 695-6800	7817
Southstern Mtal Fbricators Inc	Rockland	MA	E	781 878-1505	14826
Spector Metal Products Co Inc	Holbrook	MA	F	781 767-5600	11539
Standex International Corp	North Billerica	MA	D	978 667-2771	13869
Starkweather Engineering Inc	Tewksbury	MA	F	978 858-3700	15837
Steel Connections Inc	Franklin	MA	G	508 958-5129	11082
Steel-Fab Inc	Fitchburg	MA	E	978 345-1112	10857
Stoughton Steel Company Inc	Hanover	MA	E	781 826-6496	11354
Taco Inc	Fall River	MA	D	508 675-7300	10769
Techprecision Corporation **(PA)**	Westminster	MA	G	978 874-0591	16815
Tuckerman Stl Fabricators Inc	Boston	MA	D	617 569-8373	8892
Uniweld Inc	Georgetown	MA	G	978 352-8008	11152
Village Forge Inc	Boston	MA	F	617 361-2591	8911
Web Industries Inc **(PA)**	Marlborough	MA	G	508 898-2988	12848
Welfab Inc	North Billerica	MA	E	978 667-0180	13876
Westwood Systems Inc	Canton	MA	F	781 821-1117	9795
Advanced Resources & Construct	Kingfield	ME	E	207 265-2646	6251
Belanger Welding & Fabrication	New Gloucester	ME	G	207 657-5558	6464
Brass Foundry	West Rockport	ME	G	207 236-3200	7178
Casco Bay Steel Structures Inc	South Portland	ME	F	207 780-6722	7019
Cianbro Fbrcation Coating Corp	Pittsfield	ME	C	207 487-3311	6588
Cives Corporation	Augusta	ME	C	207 622-6141	5605
Clark Metal Fabrication Inc	Turner	ME	G	207 330-6322	7106
Contech Engnered Solutions LLC	Scarborough	ME	E	207 885-9830	6915
Design Fab Inc	Auburn	ME	G	207 786-2446	5559
Floyd Baker Metal Fabrication	Oakland	ME	G	207 465-9346	6533
Fournier Steel Fabrication	West Bath	ME	G	207 443-6404	7169
Franke Associates Inc	South Paris	ME	G	207 743-6654	7010
Glover Company Inc	Rockport	ME	F	207 236-8644	6822
Harmac Rebar & Steel Corp	Fryeburg	ME	E	207 935-3531	6098
Howies Wldg & Fabrication Inc	Jay	ME	G	207 645-2581	6220
James A McBrady Inc	Scarborough	ME	E	207 883-4176	6928
Jf Hutchinson Co	New Gloucester	ME	F	207 926-3676	6468
Jr Robert Austin	Sanford	ME	G	207 490-1500	6878
Kantahdin Welding	Patten	ME	G	207 528-2924	6578
Knowlton Machine Company	Gorham	ME	E	207 854-8471	6117
L M C Light Iron Inc	Limerick	ME	F	207 793-9957	6335
Maine Fabricators Inc	Gorham	ME	G	207 839-8555	6119
McCann Fabrication	New Gloucester	ME	E	207 926-4118	6469
ME Tomacelli Inc	Boothbay	ME	G	207 633-7553	5779
Metal Magic Inc	Trenton	ME	G	207 667-8519	7100
Mid State Sheet Metal & Wldg	Monmouth	ME	G	207 933-5603	6450
Newport Indus Fabrication Inc	Newport	ME	E	207 368-4344	6485
North ATL Cstm Fabrication Inc	Westbrook	ME	G	207 839-8410	7199
North E Wldg & Fabrication Inc	Auburn	ME	E	207 786-2446	5583
Prescott Metal **(PA)**	Biddeford	ME	E	207 283-0115	5759
Pro-Vac Inc	Alfred	ME	G	207 324-1846	5517
Ramsays Welding & Machine Inc	Lincoln	ME	F	207 794-8839	6359
Rbw Inc	Windham	ME	F	207 786-2446	7246
Robert Mitchell Co Inc **(DH)**	Portland	ME	E	207 797-6771	6722
Senior Operations LLC	Lewiston	ME	D	207 784-2338	6322
Seth Hetherington	South Harpswell	ME	G	207 833-5400	7008
Steel-Pro Inc	Rockland	ME	E	207 596-0061	6810
Thermal Fab Inc	New Gloucester	ME	G	207 926-5212	6473
Velux America LLC	Wells	ME	D	207 216-4500	7167
Wahlcometroflex Inc	Lewiston	ME	B	207 784-2338	6327
William Smith Enterprises Inc	Sidney	ME	G	207 549-3103	6966
Ace Welding Co Inc	Merrimack	NH	E	603 424-9936	18984
Alpine Machine Co Inc	Berlin	NH	F	603 752-1441	17691
American Steel Fabricators Inc	Greenfield	NH	E	603 547-6311	18218
Apollo Steel LLC	Jaffrey	NH	G	603 532-1156	18456
Canam Bridges US Inc	Claremont	NH	E	603 542-5202	17839
Charles Leonard Steel Svcs LLC	Concord	NH	F	603 225-0211	17893
Charles Smith Steel LLC	Boscawen	NH	G	603 753-9844	17702
Cross Machine Inc	Berlin	NH	F	603 752-6111	17694
Custom Welding & Fabrications	West Nottingham	NH	F	603 942-5170	19964
East Coast Metal Works Co Inc	Kingston	NH	G	603 642-9600	18543
Fronek Anchor Darling Entp	Laconia	NH	F	603 528-1931	18564
Fwm Inc	Hudson	NH	E	603 578-3366	18391
Gilchrist Metal Fabg Co Inc **(PA)**	Hudson	NH	E	603 889-2600	18392
Granite State Plasma Cutting	Portsmouth	NH	E	603 536-4415	19568
Greenfield Industries Inc	Amherst	NH	G	603 883-6423	17565
New Hampshire Stl Erectors Inc	Goffstown	NH	E	603 668-3464	18207
New Hmpshire Stl Fbrcators Inc	Goffstown	NH	E	603 668-3464	18208
Novel Iron Works Inc	Greenland	NH	C	603 436-7950	18224
Powerfab Inc	Merrimack	NH	G	603 424-3900	19023
Protective Technologies Svcs	North Hampton	NH	G	603 964-9421	19387
Quality Components Rp	Pelham	NH	G	603 864-8196	19443
Quality Fabricators LLC	Barrington	NH	G	603 905-9012	17621
Radius Mfg & Fabrication Inc	Weare	NH	G	603 529-0801	19939
Smiths Tblar Systms-Lconia Inc	Laconia	NH	B	603 524-2064	18587
Steel Elements Intl LLC	Hudson	NH	G	603 466-2500	18442
Summit Metal Fabricators Inc	Plaistow	NH	D	603 328-2211	19525
Superior Steel Fabricators Inc	Brookline	NH	F	603 673-7509	17773
Tri-State Iron Works Inc	Concord	NH	E	603 228-0020	17937
Valley Welding & Fabg Inc	Hollis	NH	E	603 465-3266	18340
Viking Wldg & Fabrication LLC	Kensington	NH	G	603 394-7887	18537
Winchester Precision Tech Ltd	Winchester	NH	F	603 239-6326	19997
Amaral Custom Fabrications Inc	Rumford	RI	F	401 396-5663	21180
Blouin General Welding & Fabg	Woonsocket	RI	G	401 762-4542	21551
Blount Boats Inc	Warren	RI	D	401 245-8300	21289
Custom Iron Works Inc	Coventry	RI	F	401 826-3310	20144
Desnoyers Enterprises Inc	Harrisville	RI	G	800 922-4445	20478
Dominion Rebar Company	Pawtucket	RI	E	401 724-9200	20834
Down Wind Dockside Svcs LLC	Newport	RI	G	401 619-1990	20663
Farber Industrial Fabricating	Pawtucket	RI	G	401 725-2492	20837
Frontier Welding & Fabrication	Woonsocket	RI	G	401 769-0271	21565
Getchell & Son Inc	Smithfield	RI	F	401 231-3850	21228
Luthers Repair Shop Inc	Bristol	RI	F	401 253-5550	20091
Metal Guy LLC	Newport	RI	G	401 474-0234	20672
New England Copperworks	Smithfield	RI	G	401 232-9899	21240
Seven Star Inc	Newport	RI	G	401 683-6222	20680
South County Steel Inc	West Kingston	RI	G	401 789-5570	21473
Westbay Welding & Fabrication	Warwick	RI	G	401 737-2357	21445
Browns Certified Welding Inc	Bristol	VT	F	802 453-3351	21762
L & G Fabricators Inc	Bennington	VT	F	802 447-0965	21679
Milton Vermont Sheet Metal Inc	Milton	VT	D	802 893-1581	22134
Nops Metal Works	Middlebury	VT	F	802 382-9300	22116
PG Adams Inc	South Burlington	VT	F	802 862-8664	22457
Reliance Steel Inc **(PA)**	Colchester	VT	F	802 655-4810	21877
Reliance Steel Vermont Inc	Colchester	VT	E	802 655-4810	21878
Rowden Bros Corporation	Wells River	VT	G	802 757-2807	22602
S & A Trombley Corporation	Morrisville	VT	E	802 888-2394	22176
Stairs Unlimited Inc	Richford	VT	G	802 848-7030	22310
Star Wind Turbines LLC	East Dorset	VT	G	802 779-8118	21916
United Puett Starting Gate	Westminster	VT	G	802 463-3440	22631
Vendituoli Limited Company	Vergennes	VT	G	802 535-4319	22557
Vermont Indexable Tooling Inc	Fairfax	VT	G	802 752-2002	21980

3442 Metal Doors, Sash, Frames, Molding & Trim

	CITY	ST	EMP	PHONE	ENTRY #
Advanced Window Systems LLC	Cromwell	CT	F	800 841-6544	844
All-Time Manufacturing Co Inc	Montville	CT	F	860 848-9258	2421
American Overhead Ret Div Inc	Middletown	CT	G	860 876-4552	2171
Arcadia Architectural Pdts Inc	Stamford	CT	E	203 316-8000	4142
Carey Automatic Door LLC	Southbury	CT	G	203 267-4278	4024
Ckh Industries Inc	Wethersfield	CT	D	860 563-2999	5244
Connecticut Screen Works Inc	Wallingford	CT	G	203 269-4499	4726
Cornell-Carr Co Inc	Monroe	CT	E	203 261-2529	2399
Cusson Sash Company	Glastonbury	CT	G	860 659-0354	1546
Girardin Moulding Inc	Windsor Locks	CT	F	860 623-4486	5393
Gordon Corporation	Southington	CT	D	860 628-4775	4055
K H Cornell International Inc	New Haven	CT	G	203 392-3660	2700
Ld Assoc LLC	Monroe	CT	G	203 452-9393	2406
Lee Brown Co LLC	Riverton	CT	F	860 379-4706	3695
Legere Group Ltd	Avon	CT	C	860 674-0392	37
Liberty Glass and Met Inds Inc	North Grosvenordale	CT	E	860 923-3623	2997
Odorox Iaq Inc	Stamford	CT	G	203 541-5577	4266
Shutters & Sails LLC	Mystic	CT	G	860 331-1510	2451
Aerc Removals LLC	North Attleboro	MA	G	774 218-4212	13743
Architectural Glazing Systems	Avon	MA	E	508 588-4845	7876
Aroyan Inc	Abington	MA	G	781 421-3107	7320
Assa Abloy Entrance Sys US Inc	Auburn	MA	E	508 368-2600	7827
Brunswick Enclosure Company	North Billerica	MA	G	978 670-1124	13799
Centco Architectural Metals	East Bridgewater	MA	F	508 456-1888	10408
Coastal Industries Inc	Haverhill	MA	E	978 373-1543	11418
Diamond Windows Doors Mfg Inc	Boston	MA	E	617 282-1688	8503
ER Lewin Inc	Wrentham	MA	E	508 384-0363	17520
Far Industries Inc	Assonet	MA	F	508 644-3122	7679
Hampton Door Company Inc	Westfield	MA	G	413 568-5730	16688
Harvey Industries Inc	Woburn	MA	E	781 935-7990	17197
High Grade Shade & Screen Co	Lynn	MA	F	781 592-5027	12516
Logan Grate Inc	Everett	MA	G	617 569-5280	10619
Modern Mfg Inc Worcester	Worcester	MA	E	508 791-7151	17421
National Service Systems Inc	Stoughton	MA	G	781 344-6504	15609
National Store Fronts Co Inc	Avon	MA	E	508 584-8880	7890
Orange Shutter Studios	West Springfield	MA	G	413 544-8403	16537
Philipp Manufacturing Co Inc	Easthampton	MA	D	413 527-4444	10575
Pjs To Your Door LLC	Newbury	MA	G	978 462-0699	13463
Portal Inc	Avon	MA	E	800 966-3030	7892
Reliable Shade & Screen Co	Somerville	MA	G	617 776-9538	15209
Shutters R US	Newbury	MA	G	978 376-0201	13466
Stergis Aluminum Products Corp	Attleboro	MA	E	508 455-0661	7795
Universal Window and Door LLC	Marlborough	MA	D	508 481-2850	12840
Watertown Engineering Corp	Whitman	MA	E	781 857-2555	16929
West Side Metal Door Corp	Ludlow	MA	F	413 589-0945	12479
William Connell LLC	Dover	MA	G	508 785-1292	10353
Ron-Bet Company Inc	Kittery	ME	G	207 439-5868	6258
Win-Pressor LLC	Unity	ME	G	207 948-4800	7119
Beacon Sales Acquisition Inc	Salem	NH	G	207 797-7950	19712
Harvey Industries Inc	Manchester	NH	B	603 622-4232	18832

	CITY	ST	EMP	PHONE	ENTRY #
Paclantic Inc	Claremont	NH	G	603 542-8600	17858
Roland J Soucy Company LLC	Pelham	NH	G	603 635-3265	19445
Eagle Screen Co LLC	Pawtucket	RI	G	401 722-9315	20835
Lockheed Window Corp	Pascoag	RI	D	401 568-3061	20802
Visco Products Inc	Johnston	RI	G	401 831-1665	20547
E I J Inc	Tunbridge	VT	F	802 889-3432	22543

3443 Fabricated Plate Work

	CITY	ST	EMP	PHONE	ENTRY #
All Phase Dumpsters LLC	Bethel	CT	G	203 778-9104	127
Angel Fuel LLC	Waterbury	CT	G	203 597-8759	4844
C Cowles & Company **(PA)**	North Haven	CT	D	203 865-3117	3012
Containment Solutions Inc	Simsbury	CT	C	860 651-4371	3898
CT Dumpster LLC	Milford	CT	G	203 521-0779	2271
CTI Industries Inc **(HQ)**	Orange	CT	E	203 795-0070	3362
Hi-Tech Fabricating Inc	Cheshire	CT	E	203 284-0894	737
ITT Standard	Windsor	CT	G	860 683-2144	5340
JFd Tube & Coil Products Inc	Hamden	CT	E	203 288-6941	1763
Johnstone Company Inc	North Haven	CT	E	203 239-5834	3036
L & L Mechanical LLC	Goshen	CT	F	860 491-4007	1585
Linvar LLC	Rocky Hill	CT	G	860 951-3818	3721
Mastercraft Tool and Mch Co	Southington	CT	F	860 628-5551	4064
Matias Importing & Distrg Corp	Newington	CT	G	860 666-5544	2880
Mimforms LLC	Norwalk	CT	G	800 445-1245	3199
Mitchell-Bate Company	Waterbury	CT	E	203 233-0862	4918
Mp Systems Inc	East Granby	CT	F	860 687-3460	1134
New Haven Sheet Metal Co	New Haven	CT	G	203 468-0341	2717
Pioneer Capital Corp	Windsor	CT	G	860 683-2005	5354
Porobond Products LLC	Hamden	CT	F	203 234-7747	1777
PSI Plus Inc	East Hampton	CT	F	860 267-6667	1164
Safe-T-Tank Corp	Meriden	CT	G	203 237-6320	2129
Same Day Dumpsters LLC	New Haven	CT	G	203 676-1219	2733
SMR Metal Technology	South Windsor	CT	G	860 291-8259	4011
Tesco Resources Inc	Waterbury	CT	G	203 754-3900	4962
Thermaxx LLC **(PA)**	West Haven	CT	G	203 672-1021	5148
United Steel Inc	East Hartford	CT	C	860 289-2323	1232
Vitta Corporation	Bethel	CT	E	203 790-8155	192
Vulcan Industries Inc	Windsor	CT	C	860 683-2005	5377
Walz & Krenzer Inc	Oxford	CT	G	203 267-5712	3430
Whitcraft LLC **(PA)**	Eastford	CT	C	860 974-0786	1315
Whitcraft Scrborough/Tempe LLC **(HQ)**	Eastford	CT	C	860 974-0786	1316
1 Call Does It All and Then	South Deerfield	MA	G	413 584-5381	15244
Advanced Materials Processing	Lowell	MA	G	978 251-3060	12339
Alfa Laval Inc	Newburyport	MA	E	978 465-5777	13468
All In One Dumpster Service	Millbury	MA	G	508 735-8979	13155
All Metal Fabricators Inc	Acton	MA	F	978 263-3904	7337
All Steel Fabricating Inc	North Grafton	MA	E	508 839-4471	13958
Alloy Fabricators of Neng	Randolph	MA	F	781 986-6400	14670
Alvin Johnson	East Longmeadow	MA	G	413 525-6334	10465
Atlantic Industrial Models LLC	Essex	MA	E	978 768-7686	10591
Babcock Power Capital Corp **(HQ)**	Danvers	MA	F	978 646-3300	10200
Babcock Power Inc **(PA)**	Lynnfield	MA	G	978 646-3300	12545
Babcock Power Inc Research Ctr	Worcester	MA	G	508 792-4800	17344
Bath Systems Massachusetts Inc	West Bridgewater	MA	F	508 521-2700	16432
BE Peterson Inc	Avon	MA	D	508 436-7900	7879
Big Dog Disposal Inc	Seekonk	MA	G	508 695-9539	15019
Boston Steel & Mfg Co	Haverhill	MA	E	781 324-3000	11409
Cape Cod Cupola Co Inc	North Dartmouth	MA	G	508 994-2119	13916
Connell Limited Partnership **(PA)**	Boston	MA	F	617 737-2700	8481
Contech Engnered Solutions LLC	Woburn	MA	F	781 932-4201	17150
Contech Engnered Solutions LLC	Palmer	MA	E	413 283-7611	14285
Cotter Corporation	Danvers	MA	E	978 774-6777	10207
Credit Card Supplies Corp	Marlborough	MA	F	508 485-4230	12743
Dustin W Ciampa	Haverhill	MA	G	603 571-4325	11427
Fall River Boiler & Welding Co	Fall River	MA	G	508 677-4479	10695
Fiba Technologies Inc **(PA)**	Littleton	MA	C	508 887-7100	12305
Flexcon Industries Inc	Randolph	MA	C	781 986-2424	14681
Franklin County Fabricators	Greenfield	MA	G	413 774-3518	11261
Geo Knight & Co Inc	Brockton	MA	E	508 588-0186	9150
Gill Metal Fab Inc	Brockton	MA	E	508 580-4445	9151
Green Brothers Fabricating	Taunton	MA	E	508 880-3608	15756
Gregory Engineering Corp	Marlborough	MA	F	508 481-0480	12765
H & H Engineering Co Inc	Methuen	MA	F	978 682-0567	13025
Haulaway Dumpster Disposal	Rockland	MA	G	781 871-1234	14806
Heat Exchanger Products Corp	Hingham	MA	G	781 749-0220	11499
Heat Fab Inc	Turners Falls	MA	D	413 863-2242	15878
Helfrich Bros Boiler Works Inc	Lawrence	MA	E	978 975-2464	12033
Helfrich Construction Svcs LLC	Lawrence	MA	E	978 683-7244	12034
Herb Chambers Brookline Inc	Brookline	MA	C	617 278-3920	9202
Industrial Stl Boiler Svcs Inc	Chicopee	MA	E	413 532-7788	10032
Kables and Konnector Services	Maynard	MA	G	978 897-4852	12899
Larson Tool & Stamping Company	Attleboro	MA	D	508 222-0897	7758
Lytron Incorporated	Woburn	MA	G	781 933-7300	17220
Mair-Mac Machine Company Inc	Brockton	MA	F	508 895-9001	9164
Mass Engineering & Tank Inc	Middleboro	MA	E	508 947-8669	13068
Mass Tank Sales Corp	Middleboro	MA	E	508 947-8826	13069
McNamara Fabricating Co Inc	West Boylston	MA	F	774 243-7425	16422
Merchants Fabrication Inc **(PA)**	Southbridge	MA	G	508 784-6700	15396
Mersen USA Ep Corp **(DH)**	Newburyport	MA	D	805 351-8400	13511
Mr Dumpster	Boston	MA	G	781 233-3006	8715
Northbridge Companies	Burlington	MA	F	781 272-2424	9311
Riley Power Inc	Marlborough	MA	C	508 852-7100	12817
Riley Power Inc	Worcester	MA	C	508 852-7100	17459
Scannell Boiler Works Inc	Lowell	MA	F	978 454-5629	12431
Sharon Vacuum Co Inc	Brockton	MA	F	508 588-2323	9173
SPX Corporation	Norwood	MA	F	704 752-4400	14201
Steel-Fab Inc	Fitchburg	MA	E	978 345-1112	10857
Taco Inc	Fall River	MA	D	508 675-7300	10769
Therma-Flow Inc	Watertown	MA	E	617 924-3877	16322
Thermatron Engineering Inc	Methuen	MA	E	978 687-8844	13046
Triangle Engineering Inc	Hanover	MA	F	781 878-1500	11356
United Metal Fabricators Inc	Worcester	MA	F	508 754-1800	17493
Usmdumpsters	Middleboro	MA	G	774 218-2822	13080
Vent-Rite Valve Corp **(PA)**	Randolph	MA	E	781 986-2000	14701
Waste Water Evaporators Inc	Wilmington	MA	G	978 256-3259	17065
Weil McLain	Marlborough	MA	G	508 485-8050	12850
Wind Tunnel Heating & AC LLC	Peabody	MA	G	978 977-7783	14386
Bear Pond Dumpster LLC	Turner	ME	G	207 224-0337	7105
Chester H Chapman	Porter	ME	G	207 625-3349	6600
Contech Engnered Solutions LLC	Scarborough	ME	E	207 885-9830	6915
Knowlton Machine Company	Gorham	ME	E	207 854-8471	6117
Millincket Fabrication Mch Inc **(PA)**	Millinocket	ME	E	207 723-9733	6443
Onix Corporation	Caribou	ME	E	866 290-5362	5889
Steel-Pro Inc	Rockland	ME	E	207 596-0061	6810
Westmor Industries LLC	Brewer	ME	E	207 989-0100	5804
William Smith Enterprises Inc	Sidney	ME	G	207 549-3103	6966
Aqua Systems Inc **(PA)**	Hampton Falls	NH	G	603 778-8796	18281
Bio Green	Portsmouth	NH	G	603 570-6159	19544
Boston Environmental LLC	Portsmouth	NH	F	603 334-1000	19546
Core Assemblies Inc	Gilford	NH	F	603 293-0270	18183
Custom Welding & Fabrications	West Nottingham	NH	F	603 942-5170	19964
Fluid Eqp Solutions Neng LLC	Exeter	NH	G	855 337-6633	18121
Gilchrist Metal Fabg Co Inc **(PA)**	Hudson	NH	E	603 889-2600	18392
Greenfield Industries Inc	Amherst	NH	G	603 883-6423	17565
John J Marr	Conway	NH	F	603 939-2698	17954
Laars Heating Systems Company	Rochester	NH	C	603 335-6300	19677
Ne Dumpster	Nashua	NH	G	603 438-6402	19214
Recycling Mechanical Neng LLC	Allenstown	NH	F	603 268-8028	17541
Skmr Construction LLC	Alton	NH	G	603 520-0117	17547
Tracs Chillers LLC	Ossipee	NH	G	603 707-2241	19423
Tsi Group Inc **(DH)**	Hampton	NH	E	603 964-0296	18275
Valley Welding & Fabg Inc	Hollis	NH	E	603 465-3266	18340
Vette Thermal Solutions LLC	Pelham	NH	D	603 635-2800	19453
Amtrol Inc **(DH)**	West Warwick	RI	B	401 884-6300	21477
Amtrol Intl Investments Inc **(DH)**	West Warwick	RI	G	401 884-6300	21478
Fiberglass Fabricators Inc	Smithfield	RI	E	401 231-3552	21224
Gfxco LLC	Pawtucket	RI	G	401 722-8888	20844
Hl Tech Mch & Fabrication LLC	Ashaway	RI	E	866 972-2077	20036
Modine Manufacturing Company	West Kingston	RI	D	401 792-1231	21467
Robert A Randall	Newport	RI	G	401 847-3118	20677
Seifert Systems Inc	North Kingstown	RI	F	401 294-6960	20739
Stackbin Corporation	Lincoln	RI	E	401 333-1600	20597
Taco Inc **(PA)**	Cranston	RI	B	401 942-8000	20299
West Warwick Welding Inc	West Warwick	RI	F	401 822-8200	21513
Burtco Inc	Westminster Station	VT	F	802 722-3358	22633
Leader Evaporator Co Inc **(PA)**	Swanton	VT	D	802 868-5444	22531

3444 Sheet Metal Work

	CITY	ST	EMP	PHONE	ENTRY #
A B & F Sheet Metal	Cheshire	CT	G	203 272-9340	707
A G C Incorporated **(PA)**	Meriden	CT	C	203 235-3361	2072
Advanced Sheetmetal Assoc LLC	Middlefield	CT	E	860 349-1644	2161
Advantage Sheet Metal Mfg LLC	Naugatuck	CT	E	203 720-0929	2457
Aerocor Inc	East Windsor	CT	F	860 281-9274	1275
American Cladding Technologies	East Granby	CT	G	860 413-3098	1116
American Performance Pdts LLC	Wallingford	CT	G	203 269-4468	4697
Anco Engineering Inc	Shelton	CT	D	203 925-9235	3775
Ansonia Stl Fabrication Co Inc	Beacon Falls	CT	E	203 888-4509	53
Atlas Industrial Services LLC	Branford	CT	E	203 315-4538	290
Axis Laser	Wallingford	CT	G	203 284-9455	4707
B L C Investments Inc	Milford	CT	G	203 877-1888	2249
Bantam Sheet Metal	Bantam	CT	G	860 567-9690	52
Brittany Company Inc	Wallingford	CT	G	203 269-7859	4712
Bull Metal Products Inc	Middletown	CT	E	860 346-9691	2180
Carlson Sheet Metal	New Milford	CT	G	860 354-4660	2791
Chapco Inc **(PA)**	Chester	CT	D	860 526-9535	769
Clemson Sheet Metal LLC	Vernon Rockville	CT	G	860 871-9369	4680
Connecticut Fabricating Co Inc	Milford	CT	G	203 878-3465	2268
Croteau Development Group Inc	Stafford Springs	CT	G	860 684-3605	4107
Custom & Precision Pdts Inc	Hamden	CT	G	203 281-0818	1740
Dasco Welded Products Inc	Waterbury	CT	F	203 754-9353	4864
Ductco LLC	Bloomfield	CT	E	860 243-0350	218
Dyco Industries Inc	South Windsor	CT	E	860 289-4957	3958
East Windsor Metal Fabg Inc	South Windsor	CT	F	860 528-7107	3961
Farrell Prcsion Mtalcraft Corp	New Milford	CT	E	860 355-2651	2799
Fonda Fabricating & Welding Co	Plainville	CT	G	860 793-0601	3489

	CITY	ST	EMP	PHONE	ENTRY #
General Sheet Metal Works Inc	Bridgeport	CT	F	203 333-6111	419
Hamden Sheet Metal Inc	Hamden	CT	G	203 776-1472	1757
Hi-Tech Fabricating Inc	Cheshire	CT	E	203 284-0894	737
Highway Safety Corp **(PA)**	Glastonbury	CT	D	860 659-4330	1558
Hispanic Enterprises Inc	Bridgeport	CT	E	203 588-9334	425
Illinois Tool Works Inc	Naugatuck	CT	E	203 720-1676	2479
J M Sheet Metal LLC	Plainville	CT	G	860 747-5537	3498
J OConnor LLC	Newington	CT	F	860 665-7702	2873
Jared Manufacturing Co Inc	Norwalk	CT	F	203 846-1732	3180
Jgs Properties LLC	Stratford	CT	E	203 378-7508	4425
Jhs Restoration Inc	South Windsor	CT	F	860 757-3870	3984
Jones Metal Products Co Inc	South Windsor	CT	G	860 289-8023	3986
Labco Welding Inc	Middletown	CT	G	860 632-2625	2200
Lee Manufacturing Inc	Wallingford	CT	D	203 284-0466	4765
Leek Building Products Inc	Norwalk	CT	E	203 853-3883	3185
Lyon Manufacturing LLC	Milford	CT	G	203 876-7386	2311
M Cubed Technologies Inc **(HQ)**	Newtown	CT	E	203 304-2940	2928
Manufacturers Service Co Inc	Woodbridge	CT	G	203 389-9595	5471
McMullin Manufacturing Corp	Brookfield	CT	E	203 740-3360	651
Midget Louver Company Inc	Milford	CT	G	203 783-1444	2315
Mrnd LLC	Enfield	CT	G	860 749-0256	1370
Niantic Awning Company	Niantic	CT	G	860 739-0161	2954
Northeast Panel Co LLC	Farmington	CT	G	860 678-9078	1501
Ovl Manufacturing Inc LLC	Berlin	CT	G	860 829-0271	100
Paradigm Manchester Inc	Manchester	CT	D	860 646-4048	2029
Paradigm Manchester Inc	Manchester	CT	C	860 646-4048	2030
Paradigm Manchester Inc	Manchester	CT	C	860 649-2888	2032
Paradigm Manchester Inc	Manchester	CT	G	860 646-4048	2033
Post Mortem Services LLC	Farmington	CT	G	860 675-1103	1508
Progressive Sheetmetal LLC	South Windsor	CT	E	860 436-9884	4006
Quality Sheet Metal Inc	Naugatuck	CT	F	203 729-2244	2492
R & D Precision Inc	Wallingford	CT	F	203 284-3396	4792
R W E Inc	Putnam	CT	E	860 974-1101	3628
R-D Mfg Inc	East Lyme	CT	F	860 739-3986	1273
Rader Industries Inc	Bridgeport	CT	G	203 334-6739	478
Reliable Welding & Speed LLC	Enfield	CT	G	860 749-3977	1379
Seconn Automation Solutions	Waterford	CT	F	860 442-4325	4992
Seconn Fabrication LLC	Waterford	CT	D	860 443-0000	4993
Shoreline Metal Services LLC	East Haven	CT	G	203 466-7372	1261
Sound Manufacturing Inc	Old Saybrook	CT	D	860 388-4466	3350
Stauffer Sheet Metal LLC	Windsor	CT	G	860 623-0518	5369
Suraci Corp	New Haven	CT	D	203 624-1345	2741
Target Custom Manufacturing Co	Old Saybrook	CT	G	860 388-5848	3352
Tech-Air Incorporated	Uncasville	CT	E	860 848-1287	4649
Tetrault & Sons Inc	Stafford Springs	CT	G	860 872-9187	4117
Thomas La Ganga	Torrington	CT	G	860 489-0920	4601
Trumpf Photonics Inc	Farmington	CT	G	860 255-6000	1519
U-Sealusa LLC	Newington	CT	D	860 667-0911	2910
United Steel Inc	East Hartford	CT	C	860 289-2323	1232
United Stts Sgn & Fbrction	Trumbull	CT	E	203 601-1000	4640
Vernier Metal Fabricating Inc	Seymour	CT	D	203 881-3133	3767
Vulcan Industries Inc	Windsor	CT	C	860 683-2005	5377
Wendon Technologies Inc	Stamford	CT	D	203 348-6271	4358
Whitcraft LLC **(PA)**	Eastford	CT	C	860 974-0786	1315
Whitcraft Scrborough/Tempe LLC **(HQ)**	Eastford	CT	C	860 974-0786	1316
White Welding Company Inc	Waterbury	CT	G	203 753-1197	4978
Yost Manufacturing & Supply	Waterford	CT	F	860 447-9678	4996
A & D Metal Inc	Westfield	MA	F	413 485-7505	16662
A & M Welding Fabrication Inc	East Weymouth	MA	G	781 335-9548	10532
A A A Sheet Metal Inc	Hanson	MA	G	781 523-1227	11359
A G Miller Company Inc	Springfield	MA	E	413 732-9297	15438
Absolute Sheet Metal	Billerica	MA	E	978 667-0236	8204
Accufab Inc	Waltham	MA	G	781 894-5737	16021
Advanced Air Systems Inc	Abington	MA	F	781 878-5733	7319
Advanced Metal Systems Corp	Holliston	MA	G	508 429-0480	11556
Aero Manufacturing Corp	Beverly	MA	D	978 720-1000	8096
Aerospace Fabricators Inc	Waltham	MA	G	781 899-4535	16025
Agwey Metal Designs Inc	Plymouth	MA	G	508 747-1037	14541
All Metal Fabricators Inc	Acton	MA	F	978 263-3904	7337
Allstate Hood & Duct Inc	Westfield	MA	F	413 568-4663	16664
American Sheet Metal LLC	Salisbury	MA	E	978 578-8360	14948
Apahouser Inc	Marlborough	MA	E	508 786-0309	12714
Arcam Cad To Metal Inc	Woburn	MA	F	781 281-1718	17121
Auciello Iron Works Inc **(PA)**	Hudson	MA	E	978 568-8382	11758
AW Airflo Industries Inc	Newburyport	MA	E	978 465-6260	13470
B&J Sheet Metal	Hyde Park	MA	G	617 590-2295	11862
Bedard Sheet Metal Company	Westfield	MA	G	413 572-3774	16672
Better Maintenance Sheet Metal	Rowley	MA	G	978 948-7067	14846
Bomco Inc	Gloucester	MA	C	978 283-9000	11167
Boston Forging & Welding Corp	Boston	MA	G	617 567-2300	8430
Brideau Shtmtl & Fabrication	Leominster	MA	F	978 537-3372	12119
Brouillette Hvac & Shtmtl Inc	East Taunton	MA	G	508 822-4800	10511
Bryant Sheet Metal & Cnstr	Hanover	MA	G	781 826-4113	11331
C S H Industries Inc	Plymouth	MA	E	508 747-1990	14547
Cambridgeport	Randolph	MA	G	781 302-3347	14672
Cambridgeport Air Systems Inc	Georgetown	MA	C	978 465-8481	11139
Carl Fisher Co Inc	Springfield	MA	E	413 736-3661	15458

	CITY	ST	EMP	PHONE	ENTRY #
Central Vacuum Cleaners **(PA)**	Methuen	MA	F	978 682-5294	13013
Central Vacuum Cleaners	Lawrence	MA	G	978 682-5295	12004
Ceric Fabrication Co Inc	Ayer	MA	E	978 772-9034	7915
Chicopee Welding & Tool Inc	Charlemont	MA	F	413 598-8215	9819
Churchill Corporation	Melrose	MA	E	781 665-4700	12978
Clark & Sons Seamless Gutter	Chicopee	MA	G	413 732-3934	10014
Columbia ASC Inc	Lawrence	MA	F	978 683-2205	12012
Computron Metal Products Inc	Whitman	MA	F	781 447-2265	16921
Connell Limited Partnership **(PA)**	Boston	MA	F	617 737-2700	8481
Crocker Architectural Shtmtl	North Oxford	MA	E	508 987-9900	13970
Crosby Machine Company Inc	West Brookfield	MA	G	508 867-3121	16468
Ctr Enterprises	Haverhill	MA	G	978 794-2093	11420
Cunniff Corp **(PA)**	East Falmouth	MA	G	508 540-6232	10440
D J Fabricators Inc	Ipswich	MA	F	978 356-0228	11914
Daves Sheet Metal Inc	Dracut	MA	G	978 454-3144	10357
Dimark Incorporated	Whitman	MA	E	781 447-7990	16923
Doranco Inc	Attleboro	MA	G	508 236-0290	7727
Dosco Sheet Metal and Mfg	Millbury	MA	G	508 865-9998	13162
Duc-Pac Corporation	East Longmeadow	MA	E	413 525-3302	10474
E T Duval & Son Inc	Leominster	MA	G	978 537-7596	12134
Eckel Industries Inc **(PA)**	Ayer	MA	F	978 772-0840	7917
Electrnic Shtmtal Crftsmen Inc	Stoughton	MA	E	781 341-3260	15586
Essex Engineering Inc	Lynn	MA	E	781 595-2114	12506
Eugene F Delfino Company Inc	Chelmsford	MA	G	978 221-6496	9897
Excell Solutions Inc	North Billerica	MA	G	978 663-6100	13813
Expansion Opportunities Inc	Northborough	MA	E	508 303-8200	14033
Fabco Mfg Inc	Hudson	MA	E	978 568-8519	11773
Fabtron Corporation	Waltham	MA	E	781 891-4430	16106
Far Industries Inc	Assonet	MA	F	508 644-3122	7679
First Quality Metal Products	Plympton	MA	G	781 585-5820	14591
Francer Industries Inc	East Weymouth	MA	E	781 337-2882	10542
Franklin Sheet Metal Works Inc	Franklin	MA	G	508 528-3600	11048
G T R Manufacturing Corp	Brockton	MA	D	508 588-3240	9148
Gerald F Dalton & Sons Inc	North Easton	MA	G	508 238-5374	13945
Gill Metal Fab Inc	Brockton	MA	E	508 580-4445	9151
Green Brothers Fabricating	Taunton	MA	E	508 880-3608	15756
Harrington Air Systems LLC	Watertown	MA	E	781 341-1999	16290
Heat Fab Inc	Turners Falls	MA	D	413 863-2242	15878
Helfrich Bros Boiler Works Inc	Lawrence	MA	E	978 975-2464	12033
Herfco Inc	Shirley	MA	E	978 772-4758	15086
Hi-Tech Metals Inc	Bellingham	MA	D	508 966-0332	8040
High Grade Shade & Screen Co	Lynn	MA	F	781 592-5027	12516
Hoodco Systems Inc	Tewksbury	MA	F	978 851-7473	15818
Horizon Sheet Metal Inc	Springfield	MA	D	413 734-6966	15477
Howard Products Incorporated	Worcester	MA	F	508 757-2440	17390
Ideas Inc	Lowell	MA	G	978 453-6864	12382
Industrial Metal Pdts Co Inc	Sharon	MA	D	781 762-3330	15052
Integrated Dynamic Metals Corp	Marlborough	MA	F	508 624-7271	12777
J & B Metal Products Company	Saugus	MA	G	781 233-7506	14988
Jay Engineering Corp	Chelmsford	MA	F	978 250-0115	9907
Kennedy Sheet Metal Inc	East Weymouth	MA	E	781 331-7764	10543
Kent Pearce	East Wareham	MA	G	508 295-3791	10531
Kevin Bonney	Pembroke	MA	G	781 826-6439	14414
Kleeberg Sheet Metal Inc	Ludlow	MA	D	413 589-1854	12470
L & L Race Cars	Tyngsboro	MA	G	978 420-7852	15892
Lamb & Ritchie Company Inc	Saugus	MA	E	781 941-2700	14990
Lectro Engineering Inc	Waltham	MA	F	781 891-9640	16144
Lehi Sheet Metal Corporation	Westborough	MA	E	508 366-8550	16632
Lyman Conrad **(PA)**	South Hadley	MA	E	413 538-8200	15306
Lyman Sheet Metal Co Inc	Southampton	MA	G	413 527-0848	15340
Malone Brothers Inc	Swansea	MA	G	508 379-3662	15708
Manufacturing Tech Group Inc	Westfield	MA	D	413 562-4337	16698
Marblehead Engineering	Essex	MA	F	978 432-1386	10595
Mc Garvin Engineering Co	Lowell	MA	F	978 454-2741	12405
Mestek Inc	Westfield	MA	B	413 568-9571	16702
Metal Men	Chicopee	MA	F	413 533-0513	10045
Metal Solutions LLC	Millbury	MA	G	774 276-0096	13171
Metal Tronics Inc	Georgetown	MA	E	978 659-6960	11146
Metalcrafters Inc	Methuen	MA	E	978 683-7097	13036
Metfab Engineering Inc	Attleboro Falls	MA	E	508 695-1007	7815
Minuteman Seamless Gutters	Hudson	MA	F	978 562-1744	11794
MLS Sheet Metal LLC	Bedford	MA	F	781 275-2265	7992
Modern Sheetmetal Inc	Worcester	MA	G	508 798-6665	17422
Moseley Corporation	Franklin	MA	E	508 520-4004	11068
Mr Gutter Inc	Holyoke	MA	G	413 536-7451	11640
New England Fab Mtls Inc	Leominster	MA	E	978 466-7823	12170
New England Laser Inc	Peabody	MA	G	978 587-3914	14356
New England Metalform Inc	Plainville	MA	E	508 695-9340	14530
New England Sheets LLC **(PA)**	Devens	MA	F	978 487-2500	10326
New-Com Metal Products Corp	Randolph	MA	E	781 767-7520	14691
Newstamp Lighting Corp	North Easton	MA	F	508 238-7073	13949
Norwood Sheet Metal Corp	Norwood	MA	F	781 762-0720	14184
Noyes Sheet Metal	Milford	MA	F	508 482-9302	13134
Omg Inc **(DH)**	Agawam	MA	B	413 789-0252	7443
On The Spot	West Bridgewater	MA	G	508 583-6070	16448
P G L Industries Inc	Swansea	MA	E	508 679-8845	15712
P M S Manufactured Pdts Inc	Gloucester	MA	F	978 281-2600	11200

S I C

	CITY	ST	EMP	PHONE	ENTRY #
Parker-Hannifin Corporation	Woburn	MA	B	781 935-4850	17257
Payne Engrg Fabrication Co Inc	Canton	MA	E	781 828-9046	9765
Peri Formwork Systems Inc	Boston	MA	G	857 524-5182	8775
Phoenix Sheet Metal	South Dartmouth	MA	G	508 994-4046	15242
Plymouth Awning Co	Plymouth	MA	G	508 746-3740	14574
Polaris Sheet Metal Inc	Gloucester	MA	G	978 281-5644	11203
Precise Industries Inc	Lowell	MA	E	978 453-8490	12424
Precision Engineering Inc	Uxbridge	MA	E	508 278-5700	15928
Precision Industrial Metals	Hudson	MA	G	978 562-1800	11807
Prima North America Inc	Chicopee	MA	G	413 598-5200	10053
Profab Metal Products Inc	Lynn	MA	E	781 599-8500	12535
Quality Air Metals Inc	Holbrook	MA	E	781 986-9967	11537
Quality Metal Craft Inc	Quincy	MA	G	617 479-7374	14649
Quincy Steel & Welding Co Inc	Quincy	MA	G	617 472-1180	14651
R G M Metals Inc	Hudson	MA	G	978 562-9773	11810
R I Baker Co Inc **(PA)**	Clarksburg	MA	E	413 663-3791	10075
R K Solutions Inc	Agawam	MA	G	413 351-1401	7449
R R Leduc Corp	Holyoke	MA	E	413 536-4329	11649
Railings Unlimited	Fall River	MA	G	508 679-5678	10751
Ralph Seaver	Cherry Valley	MA	G	508 892-9486	9976
Rhode Island Sheet Metal	Rehoboth	MA	G	508 557-1140	14759
Ricks Sheet Metal Inc	Fall River	MA	G	774 488-9576	10758
Riverside Sheet Metal & Contg	Medford	MA	F	781 396-0070	12946
Roar Industries Inc	Holliston	MA	F	508 429-5952	11599
Roberts Enterprises Inc	Brookfield	MA	F	508 867-7640	9191
Roland Gatchell	Georgetown	MA	G	978 352-6132	11150
Roland Teiner Company Inc	Everett	MA	F	617 387-7800	10628
S T White Concrete Forms	Abington	MA	G	781 982-9116	7329
Salem Metal Inc	Middleton	MA	E	978 774-2100	13100
Southbridge Shtmtl Works Inc	Sturbridge	MA	E	508 347-7800	15647
Standex International Corp	North Billerica	MA	D	978 667-2771	13869
Sx Industries Inc **(PA)**	Stoughton	MA	E	781 828-7111	15625
Tamer Industries Inc	Somerset	MA	D	508 677-0900	15149
Taunton Stove Company Inc	North Dighton	MA	E	508 823-0786	13937
Taunton Venetian Blind Inc	Taunton	MA	G	508 822-7548	15789
Tech Fab Inc	South Hadley	MA	E	413 532-9022	15311
Tech-Etch Inc	Fall River	MA	D	508 675-5757	10770
Techni-Products Inc	East Longmeadow	MA	E	413 525-6321	10497
Technical Metal Fabricators	Mendon	MA	F	508 473-2223	12996
Tecomet Inc **(PA)**	Wilmington	MA	C	978 642-2400	17052
Teltron Engineering Inc	Foxboro	MA	F	508 543-6600	10906
Thermo Craft Engineering Corp	Lynn	MA	E	781 599-4023	12543
Thl-Nortek Investors LLC **(PA)**	Boston	MA	D	617 227-1050	8882
Todrin Industries Inc	Lakeville	MA	F	508 946-3600	11979
Trijay Inc	Westford	MA	G	978 692-6104	16798
United Metal Fabricators Inc	Worcester	MA	F	508 754-1800	17493
US Sheetmetal Inc	West Bridgewater	MA	G	508 427-0500	16463
Vortex Inc	Peabody	MA	D	978 535-8721	14381
Waynes Sheet Metal Inc	Rehoboth	MA	G	508 431-8057	14762
Weiss Sheet Metal Inc	Avon	MA	E	508 583-8300	7901
Welch Welding and Trck Eqp Inc	North Chelmsford	MA	E	978 251-8726	13913
Weld Rite	Jamaica Plain	MA	G	617 524-9747	11951
Welding Craftsmen Co Inc	South Easton	MA	F	508 230-7878	15295
Welfab Inc	North Billerica	MA	E	978 667-0180	13876
Wireway/Husky Corp	Sterling	MA	E	978 422-6716	15550
Wrobel Engineering Co Inc	Avon	MA	D	508 586-8338	7903
XYZ Sheet Metal Inc	Abington	MA	F	781 878-1419	7332
Yogapipe Inc	Rockland	MA	G	844 964-2747	14833
Architectural Skylight Co Inc	Waterboro	ME	E	207 247-6747	7150
Belanger Sheet Metal Inc	Skowhegan	ME	G	207 474-8990	6969
Bob Walker Inc	Standish	ME	F	207 642-2083	7060
Collins Sheet Metal Inc	Berwick	ME	F	207 384-4428	5708
Contech Engnered Solutions LLC	Scarborough	ME	E	207 885-9830	6915
Down East Shtmtl & Certif Wldg	Brewer	ME	G	207 989-3443	5795
DSM Metal Fabrication Inc	Biddeford	ME	E	207 282-6740	5729
Eagle Industries Inc	Hollis Center	ME	E	207 929-3700	6199
Ekto Manufacturing Corp	Sanford	ME	E	207 324-4427	6874
Futureguard Building Pdts Inc **(PA)**	Auburn	ME	D	800 858-5818	5565
Gagne & Son Con Blocks Inc	Auburn	ME	G	207 495-3313	5566
Gutter Wholesalers Inc	Raymond	ME	G	207 655-7407	6773
Knowlton Machine Company	Gorham	ME	E	207 854-8471	6117
MC Faulkner & Sons Inc	Buxton	ME	F	207 929-4545	5858
North E Wldg & Fabrication Inc	Auburn	ME	E	207 786-2446	5583
Prescott Metal **(PA)**	Biddeford	ME	E	207 283-0115	5759
Ridlons Metal Shop	Casco	ME	G	207 655-7997	5896
S & D Sheet Metal Inc	Auburn	ME	G	207 777-7338	5596
Sweeney Ridge	Edgecomb	ME	G	207 482-0499	6004
Thompson & Anderson Inc	Westbrook	ME	G	207 854-2905	7210
Tri Star Sheet Metal Company	Turner	ME	F	207 225-2043	7110
Tylers Sheet Metal Shop Inc	Buxton	ME	G	207 929-6912	5862
William Smith Enterprises Inc	Sidney	ME	G	207 549-3103	6966
Zekes Sheet Metal	Scarborough	ME	G	207 883-3877	6943
Advance Concrete Form Inc	Manchester	NH	G	603 669-4496	18771
Albert Landry	Nashua	NH	G	603 883-1919	19108
April Metalworks	Hudson	NH	G	603 883-1510	18374
Atlantic Air Products Mfg LLC	Bow	NH	F	603 410-3900	17707
Barett and Gould Inc	Hillsborough	NH	F	603 464-6400	18314
Custom Welding & Fabrications	West Nottingham	NH	F	603 942-5170	19964
D D G Fabrication	Nashua	NH	G	603 883-9292	19142
Dgf Indstrial Innvations Group	Gilford	NH	F	603 528-6591	18185
Dm Semiconductor Company Inc	Salem	NH	G	603 898-7750	19722
East Coast Metal Works Co Inc	Kingston	NH	G	603 642-9600	18543
Evs New Hampshire Inc	Keene	NH	D	603 352-3000	18502
Garvin Industries Inc	Auburn	NH	G	603 647-5410	17610
Gerlach Sheet Metal	Manchester	NH	G	603 782-6136	18827
Gilchrist Metal Fabg Co Inc **(PA)**	Hudson	NH	E	603 889-2600	18392
Greenfield Industries Inc	Amherst	NH	G	603 883-6423	17565
H&H Custom Metal Fabg Inc	Plaistow	NH	G	603 382-2818	19518
H&M Metals LLC	Amherst	NH	D	603 889-8320	17568
Hd Supply Construction Supply	West Lebanon	NH	G	603 298-6072	19952
Hi-Tech Fabricators Inc	Milford	NH	F	603 672-3766	19059
Inofab LLC	Pittsfield	NH	G	603 435-5082	19501
Jsp Fabrication Inc	Charlestown	NH	G	603 826-3868	17816
Keebowil Inc **(PA)**	Keene	NH	D	603 352-4232	18509
LAD Welding & Fabrication	Concord	NH	F	603 228-6617	17911
Macy Industries Inc	Hooksett	NH	E	603 623-5568	18353
Martin Intl Enclosures LLC	Seabrook	NH	E	603 474-2626	19809
McNally Industries Inc	Wilton	NH	G	603 654-5361	19983
Metal Works Inc	Londonderry	NH	D	603 332-9323	18721
Nashua Fabrication Co Inc	Hudson	NH	F	603 889-2181	18418
New Hampshire Precision Met **(PA)**	Londonderry	NH	E	603 668-6777	18727
Nhp Stratham Inc	Londonderry	NH	E	603 668-6777	18728
Noise Reduction Products Inc	Langdon	NH	G	603 835-6400	18611
Omni Metals Company Inc	Somersworth	NH	E	603 692-6664	19845
Poole Sheet Metal & Wldg Inc	Brentwood	NH	G	603 679-3860	17755
Profile Metal Forming Inc **(HQ)**	Newmarket	NH	E	603 659-8323	19337
Progressive Manufacturing Inc	West Lebanon	NH	F	603 298-5778	19960
Prototek Shtmtal Fbrcation LLC **(PA)**	Contoocook	NH	D	603 746-2001	17947
Ran/All Metal Technology Inc	Hooksett	NH	G	603 668-1907	18357
Rapid Group	Nashua	NH	F	603 821-7300	19245
Rapid Manufacturing Group LLC	Nashua	NH	B	603 402-4020	19246
Rapid Sheet Metal LLC	Nashua	NH	D	603 821-5300	19247
S & H Precision Mfg Co Inc **(PA)**	Newmarket	NH	E	603 659-8323	19339
Sparton Technology Corp	Hudson	NH	D	603 880-3692	18439
Spiral Air Manufacturing Inc	Derry	NH	G	603 624-6647	17997
Standard Machine & Arms	Contoocook	NH	G	603 746-3562	17949
Superior Sheet Metal LLC	Hudson	NH	F	603 577-8620	18443
Sweeney Metal Fabricators Inc	Nashua	NH	F	603 881-8720	19268
Technical Machine Components	Hudson	NH	F	603 880-0444	18445
Tnd Inc	Pelham	NH	G	603 595-4795	19451
Total Air Supply Inc	Nashua	NH	E	603 889-0100	19274
Tri C Manufacturing Inc	East Kingston	NH	G	603 642-8448	18092
Triangle Sheet Metal Inc	Meredith	NH	G	603 393-6770	18980
Tsi Group Inc **(DH)**	Hampton	NH	E	603 964-0296	18275
Upcycle Solutions Inc	Londonderry	NH	G	603 609-6843	18743
Valley Welding & Fabg Inc	Hollis	NH	E	603 465-3266	18340
Ward Fabrication Inc	Sandown	NH	G	603 382-9700	19788
Will-Mor Manufacturing Inc	Seabrook	NH	D	603 474-8971	19823
Alloy Holdings LLC	Providence	RI	E	401 353-7500	20951
Century Sheet Metal Inc	Riverside	RI	G	401 433-1380	21166
Champlin Welding Inc	Narragansett	RI	G	401 782-4099	20636
Custom Seamless Gutters Inc	Pawtucket	RI	G	401 726-3137	20831
Ferguson Perforating Company **(DH)**	Providence	RI	D	401 941-8876	21013
Frank J Newman & Son Inc	Johnston	RI	G	401 231-0550	20511
GA Rel Manufacturing Company	Providence	RI	E	401 331-5455	21019
L F Pease Co	East Providence	RI	F	401 438-2850	20428
Lightship Group LLC **(PA)**	North Kingstown	RI	E	401 294-3341	20723
Microweld Co Inc	Riverside	RI	G	401 438-5985	21172
Morris & Broms LLC	Cranston	RI	F	401 781-3134	20265
Providence Welding	Providence	RI	G	401 941-2700	21100
Renaissance Sheet Metal L	North Kingstown	RI	G	401 294-3703	20737
Rhode Island Ventilating Co	Cumberland	RI	F	401 723-8920	20341
Robert B Evans Inc	Westerly	RI	G	401 596-2719	21538
Stackbin Corporation	Lincoln	RI	E	401 333-1600	20597
Durasol Systems Inc	Middlebury	VT	E	802 388-7309	22109
Giddings Manufacturing Co Inc	Pittsford	VT	G	802 483-2292	22263
Gloucester Associates Inc	Barre	VT	E	802 479-1088	21617
Green Mountain Awning Inc	West Rutland	VT	G	802 438-2951	22615
Hancor Inc	Springfield	VT	E	802 886-8403	22501
Keebowil Inc	Rutland	VT	E	802 775-3572	22342
Kimtek Corporation	Orleans	VT	G	802 754-9000	22248
McGill Airflow LLC	Bennington	VT	E	802 442-1900	21683
Milton Vermont Sheet Metal Inc	Milton	VT	D	802 893-1581	22134
Nsa Industries LLC **(PA)**	Saint Johnsbury	VT	C	802 748-5007	22393
Sheet Metal Design	Essex Junction	VT	G	802 288-9700	21960

3446 Architectural & Ornamental Metal Work

	CITY	ST	EMP	PHONE	ENTRY #
Artistic Iron Works LLC	Norwalk	CT	G	203 838-9200	3104
Boudreaus Welding Co Inc	Dayville	CT	E	860 774-2771	1040
Burdon Enterprises LLC	Higganum	CT	G	860 345-4882	1902
Company of Craftsmen	Mystic	CT	G	860 536-4189	2436
Connecticut Iron Works Inc	Greenwich	CT	G	203 869-0657	1603
Dyco Industries Inc	South Windsor	CT	E	860 289-4957	3958
East Windsor Metal Fabg Inc	South Windsor	CT	F	860 528-7107	3961

	CITY	ST	EMP	PHONE	ENTRY #
Eastern Metal Works Inc	Milford	CT	E	203 878-6995	2281
Edelman Metalworks Inc	Newtown	CT	G	203 744-7331	2920
F & L Iron Work Inc	New Haven	CT	G	203 777-0751	2687
Goodyfab Llc	North Branford	CT	G	203 927-3059	2964
Ida International Inc	Derby	CT	E	203 736-9249	1074
Imperial Metalworks LLC	Stamford	CT	G	203 791-8567	4220
International Pipe & Stl Corp	North Branford	CT	F	203 481-7102	2969
Jozef Custom Ironworks Inc	Bridgeport	CT	F	203 384-6363	437
Kammetal Inc **(PA)**	Naugatuck	CT	E	718 722-9991	2482
Kenneth Lynch & Sons Inc	Oxford	CT	G	203 762-8363	3411
Leed - Himmel Industries Inc	Hamden	CT	D	203 288-8484	1766
Leek Building Products Inc	Norwalk	CT	E	203 853-3883	3185
Loyal Fence Company LLC	Rockfall	CT	G	203 530-7046	3698
Lpg Metal Crafts LLC	Plainville	CT	G	860 982-3573	3502
Luckey LLC	New Haven	CT	F	203 285-3819	2709
Magic Industries Inc	Bozrah	CT	F	860 949-8380	281
Mono Crete Step Co of CT LLC	Bethel	CT	F	203 748-8419	172
Naugatuck Stair Company Inc	Naugatuck	CT	F	203 729-7134	2488
Patwil LLC	Bristol	CT	G	860 589-9085	593
Pequonnock Ironworks Inc	Bridgeport	CT	F	203 336-2178	465
Quality Stairs Inc	Bridgeport	CT	E	203 367-8390	477
S M Churyk Iron Works Inc	New Milford	CT	G	860 355-1777	2826
Shepard Steel Co Inc **(PA)**	Hartford	CT	D	860 525-4446	1869
Shepard Steel Co Inc	Newington	CT	E	860 525-4446	2902
Sorge Industries Inc	Shelton	CT	G	203 924-8900	3872
Southington Metal Fabg Co	Southington	CT	F	860 621-0149	4079
Stamford Forge & Metal Cft Inc	Stamford	CT	G	203 348-8290	4330
Stately Stair Co Inc	Waterbury	CT	E	203 575-1966	4960
Susan Martovich	Oxford	CT	G	203 881-1848	3426
T Woodward Stair Building LLC	North Branford	CT	G	860 664-0515	2980
United Steel Inc	East Hartford	CT	C	860 289-2323	1232
Advantcraft Inc	Upton	MA	G	508 498-4644	15903
Biasin Enterprises Inc	Lee	MA	G	413 243-0885	12089
Boston Blacksmith Inc	Boston	MA	G	617 364-1499	8425
Boston Forging & Welding Corp	Boston	MA	G	617 567-2300	8430
Boston Retail Products Inc **(PA)**	Medford	MA	C	781 395-7417	12923
Boston Steel Fabricators Inc	Holbrook	MA	G	781 767-1540	11522
Brayton Wilson Cole Corp	Hingham	MA	G	781 803-6624	11495
Cassidy Bros Forge Inc	Rowley	MA	E	978 948-7303	14849
Clayton LLC	Woburn	MA	E	617 250-8500	17144
Colonial Blacksmith	Sandwich	MA	G	508 420-5326	14966
Colonial Ornamental Iron Works	Peabody	MA	G	978 531-1474	14323
Concentric Fabrication LLC	Somerset	MA	G	774 955-5692	15142
Concentric Fabrication LLC	Middleboro	MA	F	508 672-4098	13059
D Cronins Welding Service	Lawrence	MA	G	978 664-4488	12014
DC Scaffold Inc	West Bridgewater	MA	F	508 580-5100	16436
DCB Welding and Fabrication	Lowell	MA	G	978 587-3883	12366
Deangelis Iron Work Inc	South Easton	MA	E	508 238-4310	15276
Eckel Industries Inc **(PA)**	Ayer	MA	F	978 772-0840	7917
Flagraphics Inc	Somerville	MA	E	617 776-7549	15172
G&E Steel Fabricators Inc	Salem	MA	F	978 741-0391	14913
Graney John F Metal Design LLC	Sheffield	MA	G	413 528-6744	15060
Green Brothers Fabricating	Taunton	MA	E	508 880-3608	15756
Impact Protection Systems Inc	Centerville	MA	G	508 737-8850	9816
Jeff Schiff	Chelsea	MA	G	617 887-0202	9956
John Carter Fire Escape Svcs	Boston	MA	G	617 990-7387	8633
Kamrowski Refinishing Co Inc	Framingham	MA	F	508 877-0367	10975
Larkin Iron Works Inc	Hyde Park	MA	G	617 333-9710	11873
Make Architectural Metalworking	West Wareham	MA	F	508 273-7603	16575
Marios Welding	Fall River	MA	G	508 646-1038	10727
Mass Sign & Decal Inc	Rockland	MA	G	781 878-7446	14812
Mestek Inc	Westfield	MA	G	413 568-9571	16703
Mezzanine Safeti Gates Inc	Essex	MA	G	978 768-3000	10596
N S R Metal Works	Plymouth	MA	G	508 732-0190	14567
Needham Certified Welding Corp	Needham Heights	MA	G	781 444-7470	13340
Ninos Ironworks	Everett	MA	G	617 389-6603	10623
Norfolk Iron Works Inc	Uxbridge	MA	G	508 482-9162	15926
Pbd Productions LLC	Hopedale	MA	F	508 482-9300	11679
Period Lighting Fixtures Inc	Clarksburg	MA	F	413 664-7141	10074
Railings Unlimited	Fall River	MA	G	508 679-5678	10751
Rens Welding & Fabricating	Taunton	MA	F	508 828-1702	15779
Rolls-Royce Marine North Amer **(DH)**	Walpole	MA	C	508 668-9610	16009
Ryan Iron Works Inc	Raynham	MA	E	508 821-2058	14729
Santini Brothers Ir Works Inc	Medford	MA	F	781 396-1450	12947
Somerville Ornamental Ir Works	Somerville	MA	G	617 666-8872	15218
Southeast Railing Co Inc	Canton	MA	F	781 828-7088	9783
Southstern Mtal Fbricators Inc	Rockland	MA	E	781 878-1505	14826
Stonybrook Fine Arts LLC	Jamaica Plain	MA	G	617 799-3644	11950
Sunsetter Products Ltd Partnr	Malden	MA	D	781 321-9600	12598
Ultra Elec Ocean Systems Inc	Braintree	MA	D	781 848-3400	9045
Village Forge Inc	Boston	MA	F	617 361-2591	8911
W and D Enterprise Inc	Millville	MA	G	508 883-4811	13188
Watertown Ironworks Inc	Woburn	MA	F	781 491-0229	17316
Welch Welding and Trck Eqp Inc	North Chelmsford	MA	E	978 251-8726	13913
Weld Rite	Jamaica Plain	MA	G	617 524-9747	11951
B & T Millworks	Gorham	ME	G	207 591-5740	6109
Bradbury Mtn Metalworks LLC	Pownal	ME	G	207 688-5009	6748

	CITY	ST	EMP	PHONE	ENTRY #
Cives Corporation	Augusta	ME	C	207 622-6141	5605
Clark Metal Fabrication Inc	Turner	ME	G	207 330-6322	7106
Sigco LLC **(DH)**	Westbrook	ME	C	207 775-2676	7208
Sigco LLC	Westbrook	ME	E	207 775-2676	7207
Asca Inc **(PA)**	Portsmouth	NH	E	603 433-6700	19539
Custom Welding & Fabrications	West Nottingham	NH	F	603 942-5170	19964
Flag-Works Over America LLC	Concord	NH	G	603 225-2530	17902
Greenfield Industries Inc	Amherst	NH	G	603 883-6423	17565
Mfb Holdings LLC	Dover	NH	E	603 742-0104	18036
Morris and Butler	North Hampton	NH	D	603 918-0355	19385
New Hampshire Stl Erectors Inc	Goffstown	NH	E	603 668-3464	18207
Plp Composite Technologies	Fitzwilliam	NH	E	603 585-9100	18152
Superior Steel Fabricators Inc	Brookline	NH	F	603 673-7509	17773
Upnovr Inc	Pelham	NH	E	603 625-8639	19452
Custom Iron Works Inc	Coventry	RI	F	401 826-3310	20144
Providence Welding	Providence	RI	G	401 941-2700	21100
Railing Pro Inc	Hope Valley	RI	G	401 539-7998	20486
Blackthorne Forge Ltd	Marshfield	VT	G	802 426-3369	22092
Burtco Inc	Westminster Station	VT	F	802 722-3358	22633
George L Martin	Brattleboro	VT	G	802 254-5838	21729
Hubbardton Forge LLC	Castleton	VT	C	802 468-3090	21828
Metalworks Inc	Burlington	VT	G	802 863-0414	21796
S & A Trombley Corporation	Morrisville	VT	E	802 888-2394	22176

3448 Prefabricated Metal Buildings & Cmpnts

	CITY	ST	EMP	PHONE	ENTRY #
Connecticut Screen Works Inc	Wallingford	CT	G	203 269-4499	4726
Illinois Tool Works Inc	Waterbury	CT	C	203 574-2119	4887
LLC Glass House	Pomfret Center	CT	G	860 974-1665	3556
Mdm Products LLC	Milford	CT	F	203 877-7070	2314
Mobile Mini Inc	Suffield	CT	E	860 668-1888	4465
Morin Corporation **(DH)**	Bristol	CT	D	860 584-0900	584
Niantic Awning Company	Niantic	CT	G	860 739-0161	2954
Readydock Inc	Avon	CT	G	860 523-9980	44
Rwt Corporation	Madison	CT	E	203 245-2731	1973
Shelters of America LLC	Woodbridge	CT	G	203 397-1037	5479
Star Steel Structures Inc	Somers	CT	G	860 763-5681	3920
Walpole Woodworkers Inc	Ridgefield	CT	E	508 668-2800	3689
Cmsr Services LLC	Auburn	MA	G	774 210-2513	7831
Custom Machine LLC	Woburn	MA	F	781 935-4940	17157
Gordon Industries Inc **(PA)**	Boston	MA	E	857 401-1114	8575
Green Brothers Fabricating	Taunton	MA	E	508 880-3608	15756
High Grade Shade & Screen Co	Lynn	MA	F	781 592-5027	12516
Isun International Group LLC	West Boylston	MA	G	508 835-9000	16418
Jf2 LLC	Holliston	MA	D	508 429-1022	11581
Membrane Structure Solutions	Hingham	MA	E	908 520-0112	11503
Mobile Mini Inc	Salisbury	MA	E	866 344-4092	14953
Mobile Mini Inc	West Bridgewater	MA	F	508 427-5395	16446
Morton Buildings Inc	Westfield	MA	F	413 562-7028	16706
Package Industries Inc	Sutton	MA	E	508 865-5871	15688
Space Building Corp	Lakeville	MA	E	508 947-7277	11978
The Cricket System Inc	Newburyport	MA	G	617 905-1420	13539
Walpole Woodworkers Inc	Wilmington	MA	F	978 658-3373	17064
Walpole Woodworkers Inc	East Falmouth	MA	F	508 540-0300	10451
Walpole Woodworkers Inc	Norwell	MA	G	781 681-9099	14114
Ekto Manufacturing Corp	Sanford	ME	E	207 324-4427	6874
Great Northern Docks Inc **(PA)**	Naples	ME	G	207 693-3770	6461
Maine Micro Furnace Inc	Portland	ME	G	207 329-9207	6687
Rubb Inc	Sanford	ME	D	207 324-2877	6892
Sturdibuilt Storage Bldgs LLC	Smyrna Mills	ME	G	207 757-7877	6996
Walpole Woodworkers Inc	Detroit	ME	E	207 368-4302	5954
Walpole Woodworkers Inc	Chester	ME	E	207 794-2248	5908
Concrete Systems Inc	Hudson	NH	D	603 886-5472	18380
Concrete Systems Inc	Londonderry	NH	F	603 432-1840	18686
Dyer S Docking Systems Corp	West Nottingham	NH	F	603 942-5122	19965
Inofab LLC	Pittsfield	NH	G	603 435-5082	19501
Rimol Greenhouse Systems Inc	Hooksett	NH	F	603 629-9004	18359
L F Pease Co	East Providence	RI	F	401 438-2850	20428
Konrad Prefab LLC	Springfield	VT	G	802 885-6780	22504
Serac Corporation **(HQ)**	Fairfax	VT	F	802 527-9609	21979
Sperber Tool Works Inc	Bennington	VT	G	802 442-8839	21691

3449 Misc Structural Metal Work

	CITY	ST	EMP	PHONE	ENTRY #
Barker Steel LLC	South Windsor	CT	E	860 282-1860	3943
C & S Engineering Inc	Meriden	CT	E	203 235-5727	2082
Cem Group LLC **(DH)**	Burlington	CT	F	860 675-5000	675
Eastern Metal Works Inc	Milford	CT	E	203 878-6995	2281
Met Tech Inc	Fairfield	CT	G	203 254-9319	1443
Nucor Steel Connecticut Inc	Wallingford	CT	C	203 265-0615	4780
Shamrock Sheet Metal	Colchester	CT	G	860 537-4282	809
Simpson Strong-Tie Company Inc	Enfield	CT	F	860 741-8923	1385
Applied Light Manufacturing	Holyoke	MA	F	413 552-3600	11616
Artisan Industries Inc	Stoughton	MA	D	781 893-6800	15581
Barker Steel LLC	Westfield	MA	E	413 568-7803	16671
Bay Steel Co Inc	Bridgewater	MA	F	508 697-7083	9062
Bay Steel Co Inc **(PA)**	Halifax	MA	G	781 294-8308	11315
Building Envelope Systems LLC	Plainville	MA	D	508 381-0429	14516
Cdp Manufacturing LLC	Brockton	MA	F	508 588-6400	9129

	CITY	ST	EMP	PHONE	ENTRY #
Marblehead Engineering	Essex	MA	F	978 432-1386	10595
Mill City Iron Fabricators	Dracut	MA	F	978 957-6833	10366
Rebars & Mesh Inc	Haverhill	MA	E	978 374-2244	11467
Santini Brothers Ir Works Inc	Medford	MA	F	781 396-1450	12947
Barker Steel LLC	Scarborough	ME	G	207 883-3444	6907
Interrotech	New Sharon	ME	G	207 778-4907	6477
Metaphor Bronze Tileworks LLC	Morrill	ME	G	207 342-2597	6455
Ingenven Flrplymer Slutions LL	Hampton	NH	G	603 601-0877	18265
Newbama Steel Inc	East Kingston	NH	G	603 382-2261	18089
Ward Fabrication Inc	Sandown	NH	G	603 382-9700	19788
Audette Group LLC	Providence	RI	E	401 667-5884	20963
Cuivre & Co LLC	East Greenwich	RI	G	401 965-4569	20359
Dominion Rebar Company	Pawtucket	RI	E	401 724-9200	20834
Heavy Metal Corp	Providence	RI	F	401 944-2002	21027
Rusco Steel Company	Warwick	RI	D	401 732-0548	21418
Scientific Alloys Inc	Westerly	RI	G	401 596-4947	21540
Adaptive Fabrication LLC	Brattleboro	VT	G	802 380-3376	21715

3451 Screw Machine Prdts

	CITY	ST	EMP	PHONE	ENTRY #
Alinabal Inc	Kensington	CT	F	860 828-9933	1917
Atp Industries LLC **(PA)**	Plainville	CT	F	860 479-5007	3467
Automatic Machine Products	Middletown	CT	G	860 346-7064	2174
B&T Screw Machine Co Inc	Bristol	CT	F	860 314-4410	524
Bar Work Manufacturing Co Inc	Waterbury	CT	F	203 753-4103	4848
Biedermann Mfg Inds Inc	Thomaston	CT	E	860 283-8268	4499
Bobken Automatics Inc	Waterbury	CT	G	203 757-5525	4850
Brass City Technologies LLC **(PA)**	Naugatuck	CT	G	203 723-7021	2463
C & A Machine Co Inc	Newington	CT	E	860 667-0605	2851
Cadcom Inc	Milford	CT	F	203 877-0640	2259
Caine Machining Inc	Winsted	CT	G	860 738-1619	5407
Cole S Crew Machine Products	North Haven	CT	E	203 723-1418	3016
Creed-Monarch Inc	New Britain	CT	B	860 225-7884	2524
Curtis Products LLC	Bristol	CT	F	203 754-4155	546
D & M Screw Machine Pdts LLC	Plainville	CT	G	860 410-9781	3479
Dacruz Manufacturing Inc	Bristol	CT	E	860 584-5315	547
David Derewianka	Manchester	CT	G	860 649-1983	1998
Day Fred A Co LLC	Bristol	CT	G	860 589-0531	548
Day Machine Systems Inc	New Britain	CT	F	860 229-3440	2526
Deco Products Inc	East Hartford	CT	G	860 528-4304	1185
Devon Precision Industries Inc	Wolcott	CT	D	203 879-1437	5438
Don S Screw Machine Pdts LLC	Thomaston	CT	G	860 283-6448	4501
Duda and Goodwin Inc	Woodbury	CT	F	203 263-4353	5486
Durco Manufacturing Co Inc	Waterbury	CT	G	203 575-0446	4865
E P M Co Inc	Bristol	CT	G	860 589-3233	552
Electro-Tech Inc	Cheshire	CT	E	203 271-1976	729
F F Screw Products Inc	Southington	CT	E	860 621-4567	4049
Fleetwood Industries Inc	Plainville	CT	G	860 747-6750	3488
Forestville Machine Co Inc	Plainville	CT	E	860 747-6000	3490
G M T Manufacturing Co Inc	Plantsville	CT	G	860 628-6757	3531
Garmac Screw Machine Inc	Naugatuck	CT	F	203 723-6911	2475
Horst Engrg De Mexico LLC	East Hartford	CT	E	860 289-8209	1199
J & R Projects	Waterbury	CT	G	203 879-2347	4890
J J Ryan Corporation	Plantsville	CT	C	860 628-0393	3534
James Wright Precision Pdts	Putnam	CT	F	860 928-7756	3618
Jay Sons Screw Mch Pdts Inc	Milldale	CT	F	860 621-0141	2384
Jeskey LLC	North Haven	CT	E	203 772-6675	3034
Kamatics Corporation **(DH)**	Bloomfield	CT	E	860 243-9704	235
Kemby Manufacturing	Terryville	CT	G	860 582-2850	4483
Leipold Inc	Windsor	CT	E	860 298-9791	5344
Mackson Mfg Co Inc	Bristol	CT	F	860 589-4035	578
Mailly Manufacturing Company	Wolcott	CT	G	203 879-1445	5448
Manufacturers Associates Inc	West Haven	CT	E	203 931-4344	5134
Mario Precision Products	Prospect	CT	G	203 758-3101	3589
Matthew Warren Inc	Seymour	CT	G	203 888-2133	3756
Microbest Inc	Waterbury	CT	C	203 597-0355	4915
OEM Sources LLC	Milford	CT	G	203 283-5415	2325
Olson Brothers Company	Plainville	CT	F	860 747-6844	3510
P-A-R Precision Inc	Wolcott	CT	E	860 491-4181	5451
Palladin Precision Pdts Inc	Waterbury	CT	E	203 574-0246	4935
Petron Automation Inc	Watertown	CT	E	860 274-9091	5016
Precision Methods Incorporated	Wolcott	CT	F	203 879-1429	5452
Prime Engneered Components Inc	Watertown	CT	G	860 274-6773	5017
Prime Screw Machine Pdts Inc **(PA)**	Watertown	CT	D	860 274-6773	5019
Pro-Manufactured Products Inc	Plainfield	CT	G	860 564-2197	3455
Quality Automatics Inc **(PA)**	Oakville	CT	E	860 945-4795	3300
Raypax Manufacturing Co Inc	Waterbury	CT	G	203 758-7416	4949
Rgd Technologies Corp	Bristol	CT	D	860 589-0756	605
Royal Screw Machine Pdts Co	Bristol	CT	E	860 845-8920	611
S & M Swiss Products Inc	Thomaston	CT	G	860 283-4020	4513
Selectcom Mfg Co Inc	Wolcott	CT	G	203 879-9900	5458
Sga Components Group LLC	Prospect	CT	G	203 758-3702	3596
Sheldon Precision LLC	Waterbury	CT	G	203 758-4441	4957
Sheldon Precision LLC	Prospect	CT	E	203 758-4441	3597
Space Swiss Manufacturing Inc	Litchfield	CT	F	860 567-4341	1952
Specialty Products Mfg LLC	Southington	CT	G	860 621-6969	4081
Sperry Automatics Co Inc	Naugatuck	CT	E	203 729-4589	2497
Sun Corp	Morris	CT	G	860 567-0817	2432
Supreme-Lake Mfg Inc	Plantsville	CT	D	860 621-8911	3541
T & J Screw Machine Pdts LLC	Oakville	CT	G	860 417-3801	3303
Thomastn-Mdtown Screw Mch Pdts	Thomaston	CT	F	860 283-9796	4520
Thomaston Industries Inc	Thomaston	CT	F	860 283-4358	4521
Tomz Corporation	Berlin	CT	C	860 829-0670	113
Tri-Star Industries Inc	Berlin	CT	E	860 828-7570	114
Tryon Manufacturing Company	Shelton	CT	G	203 929-0464	3883
Tyler Automatics Incorporated	Thomaston	CT	E	860 283-5878	4523
Ville Swiss Automatics Inc	Waterbury	CT	F	203 756-2825	4970
Waterbury Screw Machine	Waterbury	CT	G	203 756-8084	4974
Waterbury Screw Mch Pdts Co	Waterbury	CT	E	203 756-8084	4975
Waterbury Swiss Automatics	Waterbury	CT	E	203 573-8584	4976
Whiteledge Inc	Manchester	CT	G	860 647-1883	2058
Wincor Inc	Bristol	CT	G	860 589-5530	626
Winslow Manufacturing Inc	Wallingford	CT	F	203 269-1977	4829
Wold Tool Engineering Inc	Brooklyn	CT	G	860 564-8338	674
Alpha Grainger Mfg Inc	Franklin	MA	C	508 520-4005	11022
Amkor Industrial Products Inc	Worcester	MA	E	508 799-4970	17336
Atc Screw Machine Inc	Haverhill	MA	F	781 939-0725	11406
Athol Screw Machine Products	Orange	MA	G	978 249-8072	14213
Automatic Machine Pdts Sls Co	Taunton	MA	D	508 822-4226	15728
Automatic Machine Products Co	Taunton	MA	E	508 822-4226	15729
Berkmatics Inc	North Adams	MA	F	413 664-6152	13669
Boston Centerless Inc	Avon	MA	E	508 587-3500	7881
Bourgeois Machine Co	Middleton	MA	G	978 774-6240	13086
Burlington Machine Inc	Wilmington	MA	F	978 284-6525	16985
Condon Mfg Co Inc	Springfield	MA	F	413 543-1250	15461
Device Technologies Inc	Southborough	MA	E	508 229-2000	15354
E F Inc	Gardner	MA	F	978 630-3800	11113
FC Phillips Inc	Stoughton	MA	E	781 344-9400	15591
Fisk Industries Inc	Attleboro Falls	MA	G	508 695-3661	7813
Fraen Corporation **(PA)**	Reading	MA	C	781 205-5300	14734
Fraen Machining Corporation **(PA)**	Woburn	MA	D	781 205-5400	17186
Geonautics Manufacturing Inc	Newburyport	MA	E	978 462-7161	13494
Jacobs Precision Corp	Avon	MA	G	508 588-2121	7888
Labombard Machine	Methuen	MA	G	978 688-7773	13032
Louis C Morin Company Inc	North Billerica	MA	F	978 670-1222	13836
Lutco Bearings Inc	Worcester	MA	D	508 756-6296	17408
Mansfield Machinery Co Inc	Mansfield	MA	F	508 339-7973	12644
Marver Med Inc	Stoughton	MA	F	781 341-9372	15605
Mgb Us Inc	Franklin	MA	F	774 415-0060	11064
Munsey Screw Machine Products	North Billerica	MA	G	978 667-4053	13848
North Easton Companies Inc	North Easton	MA	G	774 259-0172	13950
North Easton Machine Co Inc	North Easton	MA	F	508 238-6219	13951
R Hueter Co	Beverly	MA	G	978 927-3482	8170
Reliable Screw Mch Pdts Inc	Peabody	MA	G	978 531-0520	14364
Rosellis Machine & Mfg Co	Westfield	MA	F	413 562-4317	16723
San-Tron Inc **(PA)**	Ipswich	MA	D	978 356-1585	11936
Screwtron Engineering Inc	Ashland	MA	G	508 881-1370	7669
Specialized Turning Inc	Peabody	MA	E	978 977-0444	14371
Sterling Machine Company Inc	Lynn	MA	E	781 593-3000	12541
Swissturn/Usa Inc	Oxford	MA	D	508 987-6211	14274
United Screw Machine Products	Millbury	MA	G	508 865-7295	13178
Yankee Hill Machine Co Inc	Easthampton	MA	D	413 584-1400	10583
Arundel Machine Tool Co	Arundel	ME	D	207 985-8555	5528
David Michaud	Winthrop	ME	G	207 377-8037	7280
Newberry Enterprise	Windham	ME	G	207 892-8596	7244
Barco Manufacturing Inc	Tilton	NH	E	603 286-3324	19904
Bay State Swiss CAM Design	Alton	NH	G	603 859-7552	17545
D & E Screw Machine Pdts Inc	Colebrook	NH	F	508 658-7344	17866
Green Mountain Metals of VT	Claremont	NH	F	603 542-0005	17852
Intelitek Inc	Derry	NH	E	800 221-2763	17983
J T Manufacturing Corporation	Pelham	NH	E	603 821-5720	19436
Jtc Precision Swiss Inc	Manchester	NH	G	603 935-9830	18853
Liberty Research Co Inc **(PA)**	Rochester	NH	F	603 332-2730	19678
Link Metal Corporation	Wolfeboro	NH	G	603 569-5085	20022
New Hampshire Machine Products	Exeter	NH	G	603 772-4404	18125
Omni Components Corp **(PA)**	Hudson	NH	D	603 882-4467	18422
Parker & Harper Companies Inc **(PA)**	Raymond	NH	D	603 895-4761	19643
Precision Components Inc	Peterborough	NH	G	603 924-3597	19484
Blackhawk Machine Products Inc	Smithfield	RI	E	401 232-7563	21213
Droitcour Company	Warwick	RI	D	401 737-4646	21355
Esmond Manufacturing Company	Cranston	RI	G	401 942-9103	20220
Fasano Corp	Cranston	RI	G	401 785-9646	20224
Greystone of Lincoln Inc **(PA)**	Lincoln	RI	C	401 333-0444	20576
Groov-Pin Corporation **(PA)**	Smithfield	RI	D	770 251-5054	21230
M F Engineering Company Inc	Bristol	RI	F	401 253-6163	20092
Machinex Company Inc	Smithfield	RI	F	401 231-3230	21237
Moody Machine Products Inc	Providence	RI	G	401 941-5130	21071
Precision Trned Cmponents Corp	Smithfield	RI	D	401 232-3377	21244
Quality Screw Machine Pdts Inc	Smithfield	RI	F	401 231-8900	21245
Rhode Island Precision Co	Providence	RI	F	401 421-6661	21113
Swissline Precision LLC	Cumberland	RI	D	401 333-8888	20343
West Warwick Screw Products Co	West Warwick	RI	G	401 821-4729	21512
Lebanon Screw Products Inc	Windsor	VT	F	802 674-6347	22711

3452 Bolts, Nuts, Screws, Rivets & Washers

	CITY	ST	EMP	PHONE	ENTRY #
Aerotech Fasteners Inc	Putnam	CT	F	860 928-6300	3600
Ametek Inc	Wallingford	CT	C	203 265-6731	4699
Atp Industries LLC **(PA)**	Plainville	CT	F	860 479-5007	3467
Bead Industries Inc **(PA)**	Milford	CT	E	203 301-0270	2251
Cast Global Manufacturing Corp	Oxford	CT	F	203 828-6147	3393
Click Bond Inc	Watertown	CT	E	860 274-5435	5003
Contorq Components LLC	New Britain	CT	F	860 225-3366	2523
Crescent Mnfacturing Operating	Burlington	CT	E	860 673-1921	676
Deringer-Ney Inc **(PA)**	Bloomfield	CT	C	860 242-2281	217
Eastern Company **(PA)**	Naugatuck	CT	E	203 729-2255	2471
Edson Manufacturing Inc	Wolcott	CT	F	203 879-1411	5441
Hessel Industries Inc	Derby	CT	G	203 736-2317	1073
Holo-Krome USA	Wallingford	CT	E	800 879-6205	4754
Horberg Industries Inc	Bridgeport	CT	F	203 334-9444	428
Horst Engrg De Mexico LLC	East Hartford	CT	E	860 289-8209	1199
Howard Engineering LLC	Naugatuck	CT	E	203 729-5213	2478
Industrial Prssure Washers LLC	Wethersfield	CT	G	860 608-6153	5249
L & M Manufacturing Co Inc	New Hartford	CT	E	860 379-2751	2642
Lab Security Systems Corp	Bristol	CT	E	860 589-6037	575
Luis Pressure Washer	Waterbury	CT	G	203 706-7399	4898
Matthew Warren Inc	Seymour	CT	G	203 888-2133	3756
McMellon Bros Incorporated	Stratford	CT	E	203 375-5685	4431
Metalform Acquisition LLC **(PA)**	New Britain	CT	E	860 224-2630	2553
Miniature Nut & Screw Corp	Newington	CT	G	860 953-4490	2883
Narragansett Screw Co	Winsted	CT	F	860 379-4059	5418
Nelson Stud Welding Inc	Farmington	CT	G	800 635-9353	1497
North East Fasteners Corp	Terryville	CT	E	860 589-3242	4488
Nucap US Inc **(DH)**	Wolcott	CT	E	203 879-1423	5450
Progressive Stamping Co De Inc	Farmington	CT	E	248 299-7100	1509
Rbc Prcision Pdts - Bremen Inc **(DH)**	Oxford	CT	E	203 267-7001	3422
Spirol International Corp **(HQ)**	Danielson	CT	C	860 774-8571	1018
Spirol Intl Holdg Corp **(PA)**	Danielson	CT	C	860 774-8571	1019
Stanley Black & Decker Inc **(PA)**	New Britain	CT	C	860 225-5111	2580
Thread Rolling Inc	East Hartford	CT	F	860 528-1515	1229
Triem Industries LLC	Terryville	CT	E	203 888-1212	4494
United Thread Rolling LLC	East Hartford	CT	G	860 290-9349	1239
Universal Thread Grinding Co	Fairfield	CT	F	203 336-1849	1459
Wilson Anchor Bolt Sleeve	Derby	CT	G	203 516-5260	1084
A1 Screw Machine Products Inc	Chicopee	MA	F	413 594-8939	9995
Alcoa Global Fasteners Inc	Stoughton	MA	E	412 553-4545	15578
American Bolt & Nut Co Inc	Chelsea	MA	G	617 884-3331	9944
Astron Inc **(PA)**	Pepperell	MA	E	978 433-9500	14436
Century-Ty Wood Mfg Inc	Holliston	MA	D	508 429-4011	11563
Chen Hsi Pin	Randolph	MA	G	781 986-7900	14674
Corner Washers Inc	Allston	MA	G	617 370-0350	7462
Crystal Engineering Co Inc	Newburyport	MA	E	978 465-7007	13480
Donahue Industries Inc	Shrewsbury	MA	E	508 845-6501	15108
Fall River Mfg Co Inc	Fall River	MA	D	508 675-1125	10696
Fisk Industries Inc	Attleboro Falls	MA	G	508 695-3661	7813
Gaynor Industries Corporation	Wilmington	MA	G	978 658-5500	17003
J I Morris Company	Southbridge	MA	G	508 764-4394	15388
Northeast Metal Co	Indian Orchard	MA	G	413 568-1981	11891
Omg Inc **(DH)**	Agawam	MA	B	413 789-0252	7443
Pin Stop	Raynham	MA	G	508 824-1886	14725
Q Pin2s Billiards	West Springfield	MA	G	413 285-7971	16550
Reed & Prince Mfg Corp	Leominster	MA	E	978 466-6903	12181
Reeves Coinc	Attleboro	MA	E	508 222-2877	7785
Rivet Direct Inc	Acton	MA	G	866 474-8387	7379
Robbins Manufacturing Co Inc	Fall River	MA	E	508 675-2555	10760
Send Pymets To Washer Wizzards	Springfield	MA	G	413 733-2739	15504
Standard Lock Washer & Mfg Co	Worcester	MA	E	508 757-4508	17481
Stanlok Corporation	Worcester	MA	E	508 757-4508	17482
Stillwater Fasteners LLC	East Freetown	MA	E	508 763-8044	10460
Merrimack Manufacturing Co	Bridgton	ME	G	207 647-3566	5809
Haydon Kerk Mtion Slutions Inc	Milford	NH	D	603 465-7227	19058
Neat As A Pin	Bedford	NH	G	603 627-3504	17628
On Pins & Needles	Manchester	NH	G	603 625-6573	18895
Allesco Industries Inc **(PA)**	Cranston	RI	C	401 943-0680	20176
Bobby Pins	Cranston	RI	G	401 461-3400	20191
Eastern Screw Company	Cranston	RI	C	401 943-0680	20214
Gripnail Corporation	East Providence	RI	E	401 431-1791	20416
Groov-Pin Corporation **(PA)**	Smithfield	RI	D	770 251-5054	21230
Hindley Manufacturing Co Inc	Cumberland	RI	D	401 722-2550	20325
MLS Screw Machine Corp	East Providence	RI	G	401 435-3850	20432
Research Engineering & Mfg Inc	Middletown	RI	F	401 841-8880	20631
Vermont Rolling Pins	South Burlington	VT	G	802 658-3733	22477

3462 Iron & Steel Forgings

	CITY	ST	EMP	PHONE	ENTRY #
Bourdon Forge Co Inc	Middletown	CT	C	860 632-2740	2179
Bristol Instrument Gears Inc	Bristol	CT	F	860 583-1395	537
Carlton Forge Works	Moodus	CT	E	860 873-9730	2424
Consoldted Inds Acqsition Corp	Cheshire	CT	D	203 272-5371	724
Cunningham Industries Inc	Stamford	CT	G	203 324-2942	4180
East Shore Wire Rope	East Haven	CT	G	203 469-5204	1247
Flange Lock LLC	Greenwich	CT	G	203 861-9400	1614
Geneve Holdings Inc **(PA)**	Stamford	CT	G	203 358-8000	4199
J J Ryan Corporation	Plantsville	CT	C	860 628-0393	3534
OEM Sources LLC	Milford	CT	G	203 283-5415	2325
Paradigm Manchester Inc	Manchester	CT	C	860 649-2888	2032
Perry Technology Corporation	New Hartford	CT	D	860 738-2525	2644
Roller Bearing Co Amer Inc	Middlebury	CT	E	203 758-8272	2157
Secondaries Inc	Wolcott	CT	G	203 879-4633	5457
United Gear & Machine Co Inc	Suffield	CT	F	860 623-6618	4469
Acorn Manufacturing Co Inc	Mansfield	MA	E	508 339-4500	12611
American Earth Anchors Inc	Franklin	MA	G	508 520-8511	11023
Boulevard Machine & Gear Inc	Springfield	MA	E	413 788-6466	15456
Doncasters Inc	Springfield	MA	D	413 785-1801	15467
Engineered Pressure Systems Inc	Haverhill	MA	F	978 469-8280	11432
Incident Control Systems LLC	New Bedford	MA	G	508 984-8820	13397
Kervick Family Foundation Inc	Worcester	MA	G	508 853-4500	17399
Lampin Corporation **(PA)**	Uxbridge	MA	E	508 278-2422	15923
Paradigm Prcision Holdings LLC	Malden	MA	F	781 321-0480	12587
St Pierre Manufacturing Corp	Worcester	MA	E	508 853-8010	17479
US Tsubaki Automotive LLC	Westfield	MA	F	413 593-1100	16738
US Tsubaki Automotive LLC **(DH)**	Chicopee	MA	C	413 593-1100	10067
Wyman-Gordon Company **(DH)**	North Grafton	MA	B	508 839-8252	13969
Wyman-Gordon Company	Worcester	MA	D	508 839-8253	17511
Ball and Chain Forge	Portland	ME	G	207 878-2217	6617
Jackman Equipment	Norridgewock	ME	G	207 858-0690	6497
ME Industries	Biddeford	ME	G	207 286-2030	5749
Tem Inc	Buxton	ME	E	207 929-8700	5861
J C B Leasing Inc	Weare	NH	D	603 529-7974	19934
New Hampshire Forge Inc	Keene	NH	E	603 357-5692	18520
Turbocam Atmted Prod Systems I **(HQ)**	Barrington	NH	E	603 905-0220	17626
Turbocam Automated Production	Dover	NH	G	603 905-0240	18062
Greystone of Lincoln Inc **(PA)**	Lincoln	RI	C	401 333-0444	20576
Perry Blackburne Inc	North Providence	RI	E	401 231-7200	20771
Wiesner Manufacturing Company	Warwick	RI	E	401 421-2406	21447
Vermont Forgings Inc	Wallingford	VT	G	802 446-3900	22575

3463 Nonferrous Forgings

	CITY	ST	EMP	PHONE	ENTRY #
Charles A Richardson Inc	Mansfield	MA	F	508 339-8600	12617
Flange Inc	Fitchburg	MA	G	978 343-9200	10826
GE Steam Power Inc	Feeding Hills	MA	G	860 688-1911	10798
Kervick Family Foundation Inc	Worcester	MA	G	508 853-4500	17399
Sullivan JW	Bedford	MA	G	781 275-5818	8011
Wyman-Gordon Company	Worcester	MA	D	508 839-8253	17511
Wyman-Gordon Company **(DH)**	North Grafton	MA	B	508 839-8252	13969
Tem Inc	Buxton	ME	E	207 929-8700	5861
Smiths Tblar Systms-Lconia Inc	Laconia	NH	B	603 524-2064	18587
Winwholesale Inc	Warwick	RI	G	401 732-1585	21450

3465 Automotive Stampings

	CITY	ST	EMP	PHONE	ENTRY #
3M Company	Meriden	CT	D	203 237-5541	2069
C Cowles & Company **(PA)**	North Haven	CT	D	203 865-3117	3012
Distinctive Steering Wheels	Watertown	CT	G	860 274-9087	5007
Inertia Dynamics Inc	New Hartford	CT	F	860 379-1252	2640
Progressive Stamping Co De Inc	Farmington	CT	E	248 299-7100	1509
Subimods LLC	Bloomfield	CT	G	860 291-0015	264
Auto Body Supplies and Paint	Worcester	MA	G	508 791-4111	17343
Energy Release LLC	Hudson	MA	G	978 466-9700	11771
Great Barrington Auto Sup Inc	Great Barrington	MA	G	413 528-0838	11238
Illinois Tool Works Inc	Westminster	MA	C	978 874-0151	16805
Acton Custom Enterprises	Holderness	NH	G	603 279-0241	18322
Albert Kemperle Inc	Warwick	RI	E	401 826-5111	21321
Revision Automotive Inc	Providence	RI	G	401 944-4444	21109

3466 Crowns & Closures

	CITY	ST	EMP	PHONE	ENTRY #
Eyelet Design Inc	Waterbury	CT	D	203 754-4141	4872
Orca Inc	New Britain	CT	E	860 223-4180	2558
Dental Studios of Western Mass	South Hadley	MA	G	413 787-9920	15301
Kinex Cappers LLC **(PA)**	Amherst	NH	F	603 883-2400	17571
M2 Inc	Winooski	VT	G	802 655-2364	22722

3469 Metal Stampings, NEC

	CITY	ST	EMP	PHONE	ENTRY #
A & D Components Inc	Bristol	CT	G	860 582-9541	509
A G Russell Company Inc	Hartford	CT	G	860 247-9093	1800
Acme Monaco Corporation **(PA)**	New Britain	CT	C	860 224-1349	2503
Addamo Manufacturing Inc	Newington	CT	G	860 667-2601	2837
Alfro Custom Manufacturing Co	Southbury	CT	G	203 264-6246	4023
Alinabal Inc **(HQ)**	Milford	CT	C	203 877-3241	2242
Alinabal Holdings Corporation **(PA)**	Milford	CT	B	203 877-3241	2243
Alto Products Corp Al	Plainville	CT	E	860 747-2736	3465
American Standard Company	Southington	CT	E	860 628-9643	4037
Anderson Manufacturing Company	Woodbury	CT	G	203 263-2318	5481
Arcade Technology LLC	Bridgeport	CT	E	203 366-3871	376
Arrow Manufacturing Company	Bristol	CT	E	860 589-3900	520
Astro Industries Inc	Berlin	CT	G	860 828-6304	74
Atlantic Precision Spring Inc	Bristol	CT	E	860 583-1864	522
Atlas Stamping & Mfg Corp	Newington	CT	E	860 757-3233	2844
B & G Forming Technology Inc	Meriden	CT	G	203 235-2169	2078

	CITY	ST	EMP	PHONE	ENTRY #
Barlow Metal Stamping Inc	Bristol	CT	E	860 583-1387	525
Barnes Group Inc	Bristol	CT	D	860 582-9581	527
Barnes Group Inc	Farmington	CT	G	860 298-7740	1467
Barnes Group Inc **(PA)**	Bristol	CT	B	860 583-7070	526
Bearicuda Inc	Litchfield	CT	G	860 361-6860	1945
Ben Art Manufacturing Co Inc	Prospect	CT	G	203 758-4435	3583
Bessette Holdings Inc	East Hartford	CT	E	860 289-6000	1176
Beta Shim Co	Shelton	CT	E	203 926-1150	3781
Birotech Inc	Stamford	CT	G	203 968-5080	4150
Blase Manufacturing Company **(PA)**	Stratford	CT	D	203 375-5646	4397
Bml Tool & Mfg Corp	Monroe	CT	D	203 880-9485	2395
Bracone Metal Spinning Inc	Southington	CT	E	860 628-5927	4041
Bridgeport Tl & Stamping Corp	Bridgeport	CT	E	203 336-2501	390
Bristol Tool & Die Company	Bristol	CT	E	860 582-2577	539
C F D Engineering Company **(PA)**	Prospect	CT	E	203 758-4148	3584
Carpin Manufacturing Inc	Waterbury	CT	D	203 574-2556	4854
Century Spring Mfg Co Inc	Bristol	CT	E	860 582-3344	540
Cgl Inc	Watertown	CT	F	860 945-6166	5002
Cheshire Manufacturing Co Inc	Cheshire	CT	G	203 272-3586	721
Cly-Del Manufacturing Company	Waterbury	CT	C	203 574-2100	4859
Companion Industries Inc	Southington	CT	D	860 628-0504	4045
Component Engineers Inc	Wallingford	CT	D	203 269-0557	4723
Connecticut Spring Stmping Corp	Farmington	CT	B	860 677-1341	1473
Consulting Engrg Dev Svcs Inc	Oxford	CT	D	203 828-6528	3398
Cowles Stamping Inc	North Haven	CT	E	203 865-3117	3023
Demsey Manufacturing Co Inc	Watertown	CT	E	860 274-6209	5006
Deringer-Ney Inc **(PA)**	Bloomfield	CT	C	860 242-2281	217
Di-El Tool & Manufacturing	Meriden	CT	G	203 235-2169	2091
Durham Manufacturing Company **(PA)**	Durham	CT	D	860 349-3427	1090
Dynamic Manufacturing Company	Bristol	CT	G	860 589-2751	551
Empire Industries Inc	Manchester	CT	E	860 647-1431	2005
Excel Spring & Stamping LLC	Bristol	CT	G	860 585-1495	559
Eyelet Crafters Inc	Waterbury	CT	D	203 757-9221	4871
Eyelet Design Inc	Waterbury	CT	D	203 754-4141	4872
Eyelet Tech LLC	Wolcott	CT	E	203 879-5306	5442
Eyelet Toolmakers Inc	Watertown	CT	E	860 274-5423	5009
Fabor Fourslide Inc	Waterbury	CT	G	203 753-4380	4873
Ferre Form Metal Products	Oakville	CT	F	860 274-3280	3298
Forrest Machine Inc	Berlin	CT	D	860 563-1796	84
Four Star Manufacturing Co	Bristol	CT	E	860 583-1614	563
Fourslide Spring Stamping Inc	Bristol	CT	E	860 583-1688	564
Gem Manufacturing Co Inc **(PA)**	Waterbury	CT	D	203 574-1466	4877
Gemco Manufacturing Co Inc	Southington	CT	E	860 628-5529	4052
Globe Tool & Met Stampg Co Inc	Southington	CT	E	860 621-6807	4054
Government Surplus Sales Inc	Hartford	CT	G	860 247-7787	1827
H&T Waterbury Inc	Waterbury	CT	C	203 574-2240	4880
Hessel Industries Inc	Derby	CT	G	203 736-2317	1073
Hexcel Corporation **(PA)**	Stamford	CT	E	203 969-0666	4213
Hi-Tech Fabricating Inc	Cheshire	CT	E	203 284-0894	737
Hob Industries Inc	Wolcott	CT	E	203 879-3028	5444
Hobson and Motzer Incorporated **(PA)**	Durham	CT	C	860 349-1756	1092
Howard Engineering LLC	Naugatuck	CT	E	203 729-5213	2478
Hoyt Manufacturing Co Inc	Southington	CT	G	860 628-2050	4059
Hurley Manufacturing Company	New Hartford	CT	E	860 379-8506	2638
Hylie Products Incorporated	Cheshire	CT	F	203 439-8786	738
Illinois Tool Works Inc	Naugatuck	CT	E	203 720-1676	2479
Illinois Tool Works Inc	Waterbury	CT	C	203 574-2119	4887
Insulpane Connecticut Inc	Hamden	CT	D	800 922-3248	1761
ITW Drawform Inc	Waterbury	CT	E	203 574-3200	4889
J & J Precision Eyelet Inc	Thomaston	CT	D	860 283-8243	4505
Jo Vek Tool and Die Mfg Co	Waterbury	CT	G	203 755-1884	4892
Joma Incorporated	Waterbury	CT	E	203 759-0848	4894
Joval Machine Co Inc	Yalesville	CT	E	203 284-0082	5505
Lawrence Holdings Inc **(PA)**	Wallingford	CT	F	203 949-1600	4764
Leelynd Corp	Waterbury	CT	G	203 753-9137	4897
Lyons Tool and Die Company	Meriden	CT	E	203 238-2689	2100
Marion Manufacturing Company	Cheshire	CT	E	203 272-5376	743
Mastercraft Tool and Mch Co	Southington	CT	F	860 628-5551	4064
McM Stamping Corporation	Danbury	CT	E	203 792-3080	953
McMullin Manufacturing Corp	Brookfield	CT	E	203 740-3360	651
Meriden Manufacturing Inc	Meriden	CT	D	203 237-7481	2104
Metalform Acquisition LLC **(PA)**	New Britain	CT	E	860 224-2630	2553
Metallon Inc	Thomaston	CT	E	860 283-8265	4509
Midconn Precision Mfg LLC	Bristol	CT	G	860 584-1340	581
MJM Marga LLC	Naugatuck	CT	G	203 729-0600	2485
Mohawk Manufacturing Company	Middletown	CT	F	860 632-2345	2207
National Die Company	Wolcott	CT	G	203 879-1408	5449
National Spring & Stamping Inc	Thomaston	CT	E	860 283-0203	4510
New Hartford Industrial Park	New Hartford	CT	E	860 379-8506	2643
No Butts Bin Company Inc	Madison	CT	G	203 245-5924	1970
Nucap US Inc **(DH)**	Wolcott	CT	E	203 879-1423	5450
OEM Sources LLC	Milford	CT	G	203 283-5415	2325
Okay Industries Inc	Berlin	CT	G	860 225-8707	99
Oscar Jobs	Bristol	CT	G	860 583-7834	588
Owen Tool and Mfg Co Inc	Southington	CT	G	860 628-6540	4070
P&G Metal Components Corp	Bloomfield	CT	F	860 243-2220	248
Paradigm Prcision Holdings LLC	Manchester	CT	G	860 649-2888	2034
Patriot Manufacturing LLC	Bristol	CT	G	860 506-2213	591
Platt Brothers & Company **(PA)**	Waterbury	CT	D	203 753-4194	4940
Pr-Mx Holdings Company LLC **(HQ)**	Shelton	CT	F	203 925-0012	3857
Pratt-Read Corporation **(PA)**	Branford	CT	F	860 625-3620	339
Precision Resource Inc **(PA)**	Shelton	CT	C	203 925-0012	3859
Preferred Tool & Die Inc **(PA)**	Shelton	CT	D	203 925-8525	3861
Pressure Blast Mfg Co Inc	South Windsor	CT	F	800 722-5278	4004
Preyco Mfg Co Inc	Waterbury	CT	G	203 574-4545	4945
Prospect Machine Products Inc	Prospect	CT	E	203 758-4448	3593
R A Tool Co	Milford	CT	G	203 877-2998	2346
Richards Metal Products Inc	Wolcott	CT	F	203 879-2555	5454
Rowley Spring & Stamping Corp	Bristol	CT	C	860 582-8175	610
RTC Mfg Co Inc	Watertown	CT	G	800 888-3701	5022
Satellite Aerospace Inc	Manchester	CT	E	860 643-2771	2044
Schaeffler Aerospace USA Corp **(DH)**	Danbury	CT	B	203 744-2211	984
Semco Tool Manufacturing Co	Naugatuck	CT	G	203 723-7411	2495
Siemon Company **(PA)**	Watertown	CT	A	860 945-4200	5024
Solla Eyelet Products Inc	Watertown	CT	E	860 274-5729	5026
Sonchief Electrics Inc	Winsted	CT	G	860 379-2741	5424
Southington Tool & Mfg Corp	Plantsville	CT	E	860 276-0021	3540
Spartan Aerospace LLC	Manchester	CT	D	860 533-7500	2049
Spirol International Corp **(HQ)**	Danielson	CT	C	860 774-8571	1018
Spirol Intl Holdg Corp **(PA)**	Danielson	CT	C	860 774-8571	1019
Stevens Company Incorporated	Thomaston	CT	D	860 283-8201	4515
Stewart Efi LLC **(PA)**	Thomaston	CT	C	860 283-8213	4516
Stewart Efi LLC	Thomaston	CT	E	860 283-2523	4517
Stewart Efi Connecticut LLC	Thomaston	CT	C	860 283-8213	4518
Taco Fasteners Inc	Plainville	CT	F	860 747-5597	3518
Target Custom Manufacturing Co	Old Saybrook	CT	G	860 388-5848	3352
Telke Tool & Die Mfg Co	Kensington	CT	G	860 828-9955	1921
Tiger Enterprises Inc	Plantsville	CT	E	860 621-9155	3542
Tops Manufacturing Co Inc **(PA)**	Darien	CT	G	203 655-9367	1034
Truelove & Maclean Inc	Watertown	CT	C	860 274-9600	5031
Tyger Tool Inc	Stratford	CT	F	203 375-4344	4455
Utitec Inc **(HQ)**	Watertown	CT	D	860 945-0605	5032
Utitec Holdings Inc **(PA)**	Watertown	CT	G	860 945-0601	5033
Washer Tech Inc	Meriden	CT	G	203 886-0054	2149
Wces Inc	Waterbury	CT	F	203 573-1325	4977
Weimann Brothers Mfg Co	Derby	CT	F	203 735-3311	1082
West Shore Metals LLC	Enfield	CT	G	860 749-8013	1390
A F Murphy Die & Mch Co Inc	Quincy	MA	G	617 328-3820	14612
A Luongo & Sons Incorporated	Bridgewater	MA	G	508 226-0788	9059
Aero Manufacturing Corp	Beverly	MA	D	978 720-1000	8096
Amkor Industrial Products Inc	Worcester	MA	E	508 799-4970	17336
Astron Inc **(PA)**	Pepperell	MA	E	978 433-9500	14436
Atlee Corp	Tewksbury	MA	G	978 681-1003	15807
Atrenne Cmpt Solutions LLC **(DH)**	Brockton	MA	B	508 588-6110	9121
Automatic Specialties Inc	Marlborough	MA	E	508 481-2370	12724
B & R Metal Products Inc	Lynn	MA	G	781 593-0888	12490
B G Peck Company Inc	Lawrence	MA	E	978 686-4181	11997
Barber Elc Enclosures Mfg Inc	North Attleboro	MA	E	508 699-4872	13749
Berkshire Mnufactured Pdts Inc	Newburyport	MA	C	978 462-8161	13472
Bnz Materials Inc	North Billerica	MA	E	978 663-3401	13796
Brodeur Machine Company Bus Tr	New Bedford	MA	D	508 995-2662	13367
Bruce Barrowclough	Beverly	MA	G	978 524-0022	8113
C & M Tool and Mfg Inc	Waltham	MA	G	781 899-1709	16058
Carlstrom Pressed Metal Co Inc	Westborough	MA	E	508 366-4472	16601
Century-Ty Wood Mfg Inc	Holliston	MA	D	508 429-4011	11563
Charles A Richardson Inc	Mansfield	MA	F	508 339-8600	12617
Collt Mfg Inc	Millis	MA	E	508 376-2525	13183
Craft Inc	Attleboro	MA	E	508 761-7917	7725
Crystal Engineering Co Inc	Newburyport	MA	E	978 465-7007	13480
Cunningham Machine Co Inc	Chelmsford	MA	G	978 256-7541	9890
Dakin Road Investments Inc	Littleton	MA	F	978 443-4020	12299
Deltran Inc	Attleboro Falls	MA	E	508 699-7506	7812
Echo Industries Inc	Orange	MA	E	978 544-7000	14215
Elite Metal Fabricators Inc	Ludlow	MA	G	413 547-2588	12464
Enjet Aero Malden LLC	Malden	MA	D	781 321-0366	12570
Excel Tool & Die Co Inc	Quincy	MA	G	617 472-0473	14624
Far Industries Inc	Assonet	MA	F	508 644-3122	7679
Fine Edge Tool Company Inc	Attleboro	MA	G	508 222-7511	7736
Fraen Corporation **(PA)**	Reading	MA	C	781 205-5300	14734
Fraen Corporation	Woburn	MA	E	781 937-8825	17185
Gardner Tool & Stamping Co	Gardner	MA	G	978 632-0823	11115
GJM Manufacturing Inc	Attleboro	MA	G	508 222-9322	7741
Green Brothers Fabricating	Taunton	MA	E	508 880-3608	15756
Hd Bennett Machine Co Inc	North Brookfield	MA	G	508 867-0154	13881
Hi-Tech Inc	Attleboro	MA	F	401 454-4086	7746
Impulse Packaging Inc	Rockport	MA	E	401 434-5588	14836
Intellgent Office Intriors LLC	Wilmington	MA	G	978 808-7884	17006
International Metal Pdts Inc	Chicopee	MA	E	413 532-2411	10033
Interplex Etch Logic LLC	Attleboro	MA	E	508 399-6810	7751
JAS F Mullen Co Inc	Merrimac	MA	G	978 346-0045	13003
Killeen Machine and Tl Co Inc	Worcester	MA	D	508 754-1714	17400
Larson Tool & Stamping Company	Attleboro	MA	D	508 222-0897	7758
Lee Tool Co Inc	Ludlow	MA	F	413 583-8750	12471
Lovallo Metalspinning	Cheshire	MA	G	413 743-3947	9979

	CITY	ST	EMP	PHONE	ENTRY#
Manufctrers Pattern Fndry Corp	Springfield	MA	G	413 732-8117	15487
Matrix Metal Products Inc	Attleboro	MA	F	508 226-2374	7765
Micrometals Tech Corp	Worcester	MA	F	508 792-1615	17417
New Can Company Inc **(HQ)**	Holbrook	MA	E	781 767-1650	11533
New England Metalform Inc	Plainville	MA	E	508 695-9340	14530
Norking Company Inc	Attleboro	MA	E	508 222-3100	7773
Norpin Mfg Co Inc	Wilbraham	MA	F	413 599-1628	16941
O W Landergren Inc	Pittsfield	MA	E	413 442-5632	14497
P M S Manufactured Pdts Inc	Gloucester	MA	F	978 281-2600	11200
Paramount Tool LLC	Fall River	MA	E	508 672-0844	10744
Pep Industries LLC	Attleboro	MA	A	508 226-5600	7776
Peter Forg Manufacturing Co	Somerville	MA	F	617 625-0337	15205
Pocasset Machine Corporation	Pocasset	MA	E	508 563-5572	14600
Precision Engineered Pdts LLC **(DH)**	Attleboro	MA	G	508 226-5600	7782
Quinn Manufacturing Inc	Danvers	MA	G	978 524-0310	10248
R H Cheney Inc	Attleboro	MA	F	508 222-7300	7783
Rock Bottom Stone Factory Outl	Milford	MA	G	508 634-9300	13142
Roland Teiner Company Inc	Everett	MA	F	617 387-7800	10628
Samtan Engineering Corp	Malden	MA	E	781 322-7880	12594
Schultz Co Inc	Westfield	MA	G	413 568-1592	16729
Shawmut Engineering Co	Walpole	MA	F	508 850-9500	16011
Skg Associates Inc	Dedham	MA	G	781 878-7250	10298
Sp Machine Inc	Hudson	MA	E	978 562-2019	11818
Springfield Spring Corporation **(PA)**	East Longmeadow	MA	E	413 525-6837	10493
Standex International Corp	North Billerica	MA	D	978 667-2771	13869
Stay Sharp Tool Company Inc	North Attleboro	MA	G	508 699-6990	13782
Tech Fab Inc	South Hadley	MA	E	413 532-9022	15311
Tech-Etch Inc **(PA)**	Plymouth	MA	B	508 747-0300	14587
Tech-Etch Inc	Fall River	MA	D	508 675-5757	10770
Techncal Hrdfcing McHining Inc	Attleboro	MA	F	508 223-2900	7801
Technical Enterprises Inc	Bridgewater	MA	G	781 603-9402	9089
Thermo-Fab Corporation	Shirley	MA	E	978 425-2311	15094
Thomson National Press Company **(PA)**	Franklin	MA	G	508 528-2000	11091
Timco Corporation	Stoughton	MA	E	781 821-1041	15626
True Machine Co Inc	Swansea	MA	G	508 379-0329	15718
Uneco Manufacturing Inc	Chicopee	MA	E	413 594-2700	10066
United Tool & Machine Corp	Wilmington	MA	E	978 658-5500	17060
Universal Tool Co Inc	Springfield	MA	E	413 732-4807	15520
Unlimited Manufacturing Svc	Lowell	MA	G	978 835-4915	12442
Valentine Tool & Stamping Inc	Norton	MA	F	508 285-6911	14091
Westwood Mills Corp	Hingham	MA	F	781 335-4466	11517
Whitman Tool and Die Co Inc	Whitman	MA	E	781 447-0421	16932
Worcester Manufacturing Inc	Worcester	MA	E	508 756-0301	17505
ZF Active Safety & Elec US LLC	Westminster	MA	E	978 874-0151	16821
Historic Map Works	Portland	ME	G	207 756-5215	6671
Howard Tool Company	Bangor	ME	E	207 942-1203	5651
Maine Toolroom Inc	Scarborough	ME	G	207 883-2455	6933
Northeast Tool & Die Co Inc	Norway	ME	G	207 743-7273	6524
Numberall Stamp & Tool Co	Sangerville	ME	F	207 876-3541	6900
Tuff Parts Inc	South Portland	ME	G	207 767-1063	7042
Alan T Seeler Inc	New Hampton	NH	F	603 744-3736	19301
Ameriforge Group Inc	Newport	NH	E	603 863-1270	19342
Barett and Gould Inc	Hillsborough	NH	F	603 464-6400	18314
Cobra Precision Machining Corp	Hooksett	NH	G	603 434-8424	18347
Costello/April Design Inc	Dover	NH	E	603 749-6755	18015
Design Standards Corp	Charlestown	NH	D	603 826-7744	17813
Feature Products Ltd	Goffstown	NH	G	603 669-0800	18200
Jorgensen Tool & Stamping Inc	Belmont	NH	E	603 524-5813	17676
Laird Technologies Inc	Manchester	NH	F	603 627-7877	18858
Mushield Company Inc	Londonderry	NH	E	603 666-4433	18726
New England Industries Inc	Lebanon	NH	E	603 448-5330	18633
New Hampshire Stamping Co Inc	Goffstown	NH	E	603 641-1234	18206
Northeast Metal Spinning Inc	Atkinson	NH	G	603 898-2232	17606
Pioneer Metal Products Inc	Sandown	NH	G	978 372-2100	19787
Powerbox (usa) Inc	Bedford	NH	G	303 439-7211	17660
Robert A Collins	Fremont	NH	G	603 895-2345	18180
Samson Manufacturing Corp	Keene	NH	E	603 355 3903	18523
Stamping Technologies Inc	Laconia	NH	F	603 524-5958	18588
State Pattern Works	Hudson	NH	G	603 882-0701	18440
Sunset Tool Inc	Keene	NH	E	603 355-2246	18531
United Tool & Stamping Co Inc	Alstead	NH	G	603 352-2585	17543
Wilton Pressed Metals	Newport	NH	G	603 863-1488	19364
Amt Acquisition Inc	Warren	RI	F	401 247-1680	21284
Angelo Di Maria Inc	Providence	RI	E	401 274-0100	20954
Aro-Sac Inc	North Providence	RI	E	401 231-6655	20754
Artic Tool & Engrg Co LLC	Greenville	RI	F	401 785-2210	20461
Atamian Manufacturing Corp	Providence	RI	E	800 286-9614	20959
C & W Co Inc	Providence	RI	G	401 941-6311	20977
C Sjoberg & Son Inc	Cranston	RI	F	401 461-8220	20192
Crest Manufacturing Company	Lincoln	RI	E	401 333-1350	20566
Crystal Stamping	Pawtucket	RI	G	401 724-5880	20830
Crystal Stamping Corp	Wakefield	RI	F	401 724-5880	21268
Demaich Industries Inc	Johnston	RI	F	401 944-3576	20508
Diversified Metal Crafters Inc	Lincoln	RI	E	401 305-7700	20568
Eastern Manufacturing Company	North Providence	RI	F	401 231-8330	20759
Etco Incorporated **(PA)**	Warwick	RI	D	401 467-2400	21361
Evans Capacitor Company	East Providence	RI	E	401 435-3555	20411
Evans Findings Company Inc	East Providence	RI	E	401 434-5600	20412
Everett J Prescott Inc	Lincoln	RI	G	401 333-8588	20573
Faco Metal Products Inc	Cranston	RI	F	401 943-7127	20223
Ferguson Perforating Company **(DH)**	Providence	RI	D	401 941-8876	21013
Frank Morrow Company	Providence	RI	F	401 941-3900	21016
Fulford Manufacturing Company **(PA)**	Riverside	RI	F	401 431-2000	21168
Hamilton Tool Inc	Providence	RI	E	401 421-8870	21025
HI Tech Mch & Fabrication LLC	Ashaway	RI	E	866 972-2077	20036
Interplex Industries Inc	Rumford	RI	G	401 434-6543	21189
Interplex Industries Inc **(DH)**	Rumford	RI	F	718 961-6212	21188
Interplex Metal Logic	Rumford	RI	G	401 434-6543	21190
Ira Green Inc	Providence	RI	C	800 663-7487	21040
Jackson Bookbinding Co Inc	Greenville	RI	F	401 231-0800	20469
Lorac Company Inc	Providence	RI	E	401 781-3330	21057
Maros Products Incorporated	Warwick	RI	G	401 885-1788	21387
Masiello Enterprises Inc	Coventry	RI	E	401 826-1883	20155
Metal Components	North Kingstown	RI	G	401 886-7979	20728
Morris & Broms LLC	Cranston	RI	F	401 781-3134	20265
Pep Central Inc	Warwick	RI	A	401 732-3770	21402
Philip Machine Company Inc	Pawtucket	RI	F	401 353-7383	20879
Precise Products Company	Lincoln	RI	F	401 724-7190	20592
Production Machine Sales & Svc	Cranston	RI	F	401 461-6830	20274
Providence Mint Inc	Providence	RI	E	401 272-7760	21098
R & D Tl Engrg Four-Slide Prod	Cranston	RI	G	401 942-9710	20276
Salvadore Tool & Findings Inc **(PA)**	Providence	RI	E	401 331-6000	21119
Samic Mfg Company	Johnston	RI	G	401 421-2400	20540
Schroff Inc **(HQ)**	Warwick	RI	B	763 204-7700	21421
Schroff Inc	Warwick	RI	D	401 535-4826	21422
Tercat Tool and Die Co Inc	Providence	RI	D	401 421-3371	21133
United States Associates LLC	Providence	RI	E	401 272-7760	21143
Cold Hollow Precision Inc	Enosburg Falls	VT	G	802 933-5542	21923
Galvion Ballistics Ltd	Newport	VT	D	802 334-2774	22198
Heb Manufacturing Company Inc	Chelsea	VT	E	802 685-4821	21838
New England Precision Inc	Randolph	VT	D	800 293-4112	22299
Shelburne Corporation **(PA)**	Shelburne	VT	F	802 985-3321	22424
Vermont Custom Tool Box Inc	South Burlington	VT	G	802 863-9798	22475

3471 Electroplating, Plating, Polishing, Anodizing & Coloring

	CITY	ST	EMP	PHONE	ENTRY#
A & A Products and Services	Windsor	CT	G	860 683-0879	5312
A&R Plating Services LLC	Oakville	CT	G	860 274-9562	3295
A-1 Chrome and Polishing Corp	Newington	CT	F	860 666-4593	2836
Accurate Burring Company	Plainville	CT	F	860 747-8640	3463
Allied Metal Finishing L L C	South Windsor	CT	G	860 290-8865	3934
Alpha Plating and Finishing Co	Plainville	CT	F	860 747-5002	3464
Aluminum Finishing Company Inc	Bridgeport	CT	E	203 333-1690	371
American Electro Products Inc	Waterbury	CT	C	203 756-7051	4840
Anodic Incorporated	Stevenson	CT	F	203 268-9966	4374
Anomatic Corporation	Naugatuck	CT	G	203 720-2367	2461
Aqua Blasting Corp	Bloomfield	CT	F	860 242-8855	201
B & P Plating Equipment LLC	Bristol	CT	F	860 589-5799	523
Baron & Young Co Inc	Bristol	CT	G	860 589-3235	529
Bass Plating Company	Bloomfield	CT	E	860 243-2557	207
Broad Peak Manufacturing LLC	Wallingford	CT	E	203 678-4664	4713
C & S Engineering Inc	Meriden	CT	E	203 235-5727	2082
Chemical-Electric Corporation	Danbury	CT	G	203 743-5131	888
Chromalloy Component Svcs Inc	Shelton	CT	G	203 924-1666	3789
Colonial Coatings Inc	Milford	CT	E	203 783-9933	2265
Component Technologies Inc **(PA)**	Newington	CT	E	860 667-1065	2855
Connecticut Anodizing Finshg	Bridgeport	CT	E	203 367-1765	400
CRC Chrome Corporation	Meriden	CT	F	203 630-1008	2090
Custom Chrome Plating	Wallingford	CT	G	203 265-5667	4731
D D M Metal Finishing Co Inc	Tolland	CT	G	860 872-4683	4542
Danbury Metal Finishing Inc	Danbury	CT	G	203 748-5044	897
Deburr Co	Plantsville	CT	E	860 621-6634	3529
Deburring House Inc	East Berlin	CT	E	860 828-0889	1098
E & J Parts Cleaning Inc	Waterbury	CT	F	203 757-1716	4866
Etherington Brothers Inc	Bristol	CT	G	860 585-5624	557
Eyelet Crafters Inc	Waterbury	CT	D	203 757-9221	4871
Gybenorth Industries LLC	Milford	CT	F	203 876-9876	2295
Halco Inc	Waterbury	CT	D	203 575-9450	4881
Har-Conn Chrome Company **(PA)**	West Hartford	CT	D	860 236-6801	5073
HI-Tech Polishing Inc	Newington	CT	F	860 665-1399	2870
Hitech Chrome Pltg & Polsg Lc	North Windham	CT	G	860 456-8070	3082
J H Metal Finishing Inc **(PA)**	New Britain	CT	G	860 223-6412	2545
J M Compounds Inc	Meriden	CT	G	203 376-9854	2095
Jarvis Precision Polishing	Bristol	CT	F	860 589-5822	572
K & K Black Oxide LLC	New Britain	CT	G	860 223-1805	2546
Lake Grinding Company	Bridgeport	CT	G	203 336-3767	444
Light Metals Coloring Co Inc	Southington	CT	D	860 621-0145	4062
M & Z Engineering Inc	Torrington	CT	G	860 496-0282	4585
Marsam Metal Finishing Co	New Britain	CT	E	860 826-5489	2550
Mirror Polishing & Pltg Co Inc	Waterbury	CT	E	203 574-5400	4917
National Chromium Company Inc	Putnam	CT	F	860 928-7965	3620
National Integrated Inds Inc **(PA)**	Farmington	CT	C	860 677-7995	1495
National Integrated Inds Inc	Waterbury	CT	D	203 756-7051	4922
New England Chrome Plating	East Hartford	CT	G	860 528-7176	1206
Niro Companies LLC	Berlin	CT	G	860 982-5645	98

	CITY	ST	EMP	PHONE	ENTRY #
Nylo Metal Finishing LLC	Waterbury	CT	G	203 574-5477	4930
P&G Metal Components Corp	Bloomfield	CT	F	860 243-2220	248
Plainville Electro Plating Co	Hartford	CT	G	860 525-5328	1858
Plainville Plating Company Inc	Plainville	CT	D	860 747-1624	3511
Plasma Technology Incorporated	South Windsor	CT	E	860 282-0659	4001
Praxair Inc **(HQ)**	Danbury	CT	B	203 837-2000	971
Precision Deburring Inc	Bristol	CT	G	860 583-4662	596
Precision Finishing Svcs Inc	Windsor	CT	E	860 882-1073	5356
Prestige Metal Finishing LLC	Woodstock Valley	CT	G	860 974-1999	5504
Preventative Maintenance Corp	Poquonock	CT	F	860 683-1180	3560
Quality Rolling Deburring Inc	Thomaston	CT	D	860 283-0271	4511
R J Brass Inc	Plainville	CT	F	860 793-2336	3513
Rader Industries Inc	Bridgeport	CT	G	203 334-6739	478
Rayco Inc	New Britain	CT	G	860 357-4693	2569
Rayco Metal Finishing Inc	Middletown	CT	F	860 347-7434	2217
Reliable Plating & Polsg Co	Bridgeport	CT	E	203 366-5261	481
Scotts Metal Finishing LLC	Bristol	CT	F	860 589-3778	612
Seaboard Metal Finishing Co	New Britain	CT	E	203 933-1603	2576
Seidel Inc	Waterbury	CT	D	203 757-7349	4954
Seidel Inc	Waterbury	CT	D	203 757-7349	4955
Sifco Applied Srfc Cncepts LLC	East Windsor	CT	G	860 623-6006	1301
Silversmith Inc	Greenwich	CT	G	203 869-4244	1649
Smart Polishing	Stamford	CT	G	203 559-1541	4322
SMS Machine Inc	East Berlin	CT	G	860 829-0813	1108
Sousa Corp	Newington	CT	F	860 523-9090	2904
Spec Plating Inc	Bridgeport	CT	F	203 366-3638	494
Summit Corporation of America	Thomaston	CT	D	860 283-4391	4519
Superior Plating Company	Southport	CT	D	203 255-1501	4100
Superior Technology Corp **(PA)**	Southport	CT	C	203 255-1501	4101
Suraci Metal Finishing LLC	New Haven	CT	E	203 624-1345	2742
Technical Metal Finishing Inc	Wallingford	CT	E	203 284-7825	4815
Unimetal Surface Finishing LLC	Naugatuck	CT	E	203 729-8244	2498
United States Fire Arms Mfg Co	Hartford	CT	E	860 296-7441	1883
Usc Technologies LLC	Stratford	CT	G	203 378-9622	4456
Whyco Finishing Tech LLC	Thomaston	CT	E	860 283-5826	4527
Absolute Metal Finishing Inc	Norwood	MA	E	781 551-8235	14117
Accumet Engineering Corp	Hudson	MA	E	978 568-8311	11750
Accurate Metal Finishing Corp	Randolph	MA	E	781 963-7300	14668
Ace Metal Finishing Inc	Lawrence	MA	E	978 683-2082	11989
Acton Metal Processing Corp	Waltham	MA	E	781 893-5890	16023
Aerospace Support Inc	Agawam	MA	G	413 789-3103	7417
Alternate Finishing Inc	Hudson	MA	G	978 567-9205	11754
American Metal Polishing	Shrewsbury	MA	G	978 726-7752	15100
Anomet Products Inc	Shrewsbury	MA	E	508 842-0174	15102
Aotco Metal Finishing Inc	Billerica	MA	E	781 275-0880	8210
Apmar Usa Inc	Springfield	MA	G	413 781-5261	15446
Arborway Metal Finishing Inc	Rockland	MA	F	781 982-0137	14792
Automated Finishing Co Inc	Attleboro	MA	E	508 222-6262	7710
B & J Manufacturing Corp	Taunton	MA	D	508 822-1990	15730
Bay State Galvanizing Inc	Everett	MA	F	617 389-0671	10604
Bay State Plating Inc	Holyoke	MA	G	413 533-6927	11618
Berkshire Mnufactured Pdts Inc	Newburyport	MA	C	978 462-8161	13472
Black Oxide Co Inc	Worcester	MA	G	508 757-0340	17348
Bob Bergeron	Georgetown	MA	G	978 352-7615	11138
Bradford Finshg Powdr Coat Inc	Haverhill	MA	G	978 469-9965	11410
Central Metal Finishing Inc	North Andover	MA	C	978 291-0500	13694
CIL Electroplating Inc **(PA)**	Lawrence	MA	C	978 683-2082	12007
CIL Electroplating Inc	Lawrence	MA	D	978 683-2082	12008
Cil Inc	Lawrence	MA	D	978 685-8300	12009
Circle Metal Finishing Inc	Methuen	MA	G	978 682-4297	13014
Coating Systems Inc	Lowell	MA	D	978 937-3712	12359
D & S Plating Co Inc	Holyoke	MA	F	413 533-7771	11621
Dav-Tech Plating Inc	Marlborough	MA	E	508 485-8472	12747
Dds Services Ltd	Pembroke	MA	G	781 837-3997	14398
Electropolishing Systems Inc	Plymouth	MA	E	508 830-1717	14554
Electrostat	Randolph	MA	G	781 885-2135	14678
F M Callahan and Son Inc	Malden	MA	D	781 324-5101	12572
Federal Metal Finishing Inc	Boston	MA	E	617 242-3371	8541
Five Star Plating LLC	Lawrence	MA	E	978 655-4081	12023
Fountain Plating Company Inc	West Springfield	MA	D	413 781-4651	16521
General Metal Finishing LLC	Attleboro	MA	D	508 222-9683	7740
H Larosee and Sons Inc	Westborough	MA	E	978 562-9417	16623
H O Wire Co Inc	West Boylston	MA	F	508 243-7177	16416
Hi-Tech Plating Inc	Everett	MA	F	617 389-3400	10613
Indepenent Plating Co	Worcester	MA	E	508 756-0301	17391
Interplex Engineered Pdts Inc **(DH)**	Attleboro	MA	D	508 399-6810	7750
J & B Metal Finishing	Westminster	MA	G	978 874-5944	16806
J Crosier Mold Polishing	Florida	MA	G	413 663-6262	10871
Katahdin Industries Inc **(PA)**	Hudson	MA	E	781 329-1420	11781
L & J of New England Inc	Worcester	MA	E	508 756-8080	17403
Light Metal Platers LLC	Waltham	MA	E	781 899-8855	16145
Lsa Cleanpart LLC	Southbridge	MA	G	508 765-4848	15393
Maclellan Co	Waltham	MA	G	781 891-5462	16146
Millennium Plating Company Inc	Lowell	MA	G	978 454-0526	12412
Mueller Corporation	East Bridgewater	MA	C	508 456-4500	10418
N-Tek Inc	Lawrence	MA	G	978 687-4010	12061
New England Electropolishing	Fall River	MA	E	508 672-6616	10737
New Method Plating Co Inc	Worcester	MA	E	508 754-2671	17434
Nu Chrome Corp	Seekonk	MA	F	508 557-1418	15032
Ouellette Industries Inc	Attleboro Falls	MA	G	508 695-0964	7816
Paul McNamara	Bridgewater	MA	F	508 245-5654	9086
Pep Industries LLC	Attleboro	MA	A	508 226-5600	7776
Pioneer Valley Plating Co	South Hadley	MA	G	413 535-1424	15308
Plating For Electronics Inc	Waltham	MA	E	781 893-2368	16175
Plating Technology Inc	New Bedford	MA	E	508 996-4006	13439
Poly Plating Inc	Chicopee	MA	F	413 593-5477	10051
Poly-Metal Finishing Inc	Springfield	MA	D	413 781-4535	15498
Precision Engineered Pdts LLC **(DH)**	Attleboro	MA	G	508 226-5600	7782
Purecoat North LLC	Belmont	MA	D	617 489-2750	8080
Qc Industries Inc **(PA)**	Mansfield	MA	D	781 344-1000	12653
R L Barry Inc	Attleboro	MA	F	508 226-3350	7784
Reliable Electro Plating Inc	Chartley	MA	G	508 222-0620	9857
Reliable Plating Co Inc	Worcester	MA	G	508 755-9434	17458
River Street Metal Finishing	Braintree	MA	G	781 843-9351	9035
Rsj LLC	North Attleboro	MA	G	508 695-5555	13777
South Shore Dstless Blastg LLC	Plymouth	MA	G	508 789-4575	14584
South Shore Plating Co Inc	Quincy	MA	G	617 773-8064	14657
Spec-Elec Plating Corp	Sturbridge	MA	G	508 347-7255	15648
Specialized Coating Services	North Billerica	MA	G	978 362-0346	13866
Specialized Plating Inc	Haverhill	MA	E	978 373-8030	11473
Spencer Metal Finishing Inc **(PA)**	Brookfield	MA	F	508 885-6477	9193
Sweet Metal Finishing Inc	Attleboro	MA	E	508 226-4359	7799
T & T Anodizing Inc	Lowell	MA	E	978 454-9631	12435
T & T Anodizing Incorporated	Lowell	MA	F	978 454-9631	12436
T D F Metal Finishing Co Inc	Danvers	MA	F	978 223-4292	10259
Tdf Metal Finishing Co Inc	Danvers	MA	G	978 223-4292	10261
Transene Company Inc	Danvers	MA	F	978 777-7860	10265
Valentine Plating Company Inc	West Springfield	MA	E	413 732-0009	16561
Valley Plating Inc 8-1-80	Springfield	MA	D	413 788-7375	15521
Westfield Electroplating Co **(PA)**	Westfield	MA	C	413 568-3716	16743
Whitman Company Inc	Whitman	MA	E	781 447-2422	16931
Worcester Manufacturing Inc	Worcester	MA	E	508 756-0301	17505
Cobra Powder Coating	Lyman	ME	G	207 391-3060	6388
Controlled Chaos	Portland	ME	G	802 274-5321	6643
Jarden LLC	East Wilton	ME	C	207 645-2574	5987
Mbw Tractor Sales LLC	Berwick	ME	F	207 384-2001	5711
Silvex Incorporated	Westbrook	ME	D	207 761-0392	7209
Southern Maine Industries Corp	Windham	ME	E	207 856-7391	7253
Turbine Specialists LLC	Brewer	ME	F	207 947-9327	5802
Aero-Dynamics Inc	Seabrook	NH	E	603 474-2547	19791
Bomar Inc	Charlestown	NH	D	603 826-5781	17811
Dyna Roll Inc	Seabrook	NH	G	603 474-2547	19799
Finishield Corp	Londonderry	NH	E	603 641-2164	18699
J & E Specialty Inc	Dover	NH	G	603 742-6357	18031
Jmd Industries Inc	Hudson	NH	E	603 882-3198	18404
Medina Plating Corp	Londonderry	NH	E	330 725-4155	18719
Northeast Custom Chrome Nashua	Nashua	NH	G	603 566-6165	19218
Peg Kearsarge Co Inc	Bartlett	NH	G	603 374-2341	17627
A & F Plating Co Inc	Providence	RI	F	401 861-3597	20943
A & H Duffy Polishing & Finshg	Providence	RI	D	401 785-9203	20944
A-1 Polishing Co	Johnston	RI	G	401 751-8944	20496
Accent Plating Company Inc	Pawtucket	RI	E	401 722-6306	20805
ADI Polishing Inc	Cranston	RI	G	401 942-3955	20172
American Ring Co Inc	Cranston	RI	E	401 467-4480	20179
American Ring Co Inc **(PA)**	East Providence	RI	E	401 438-9060	20385
Anton Enterprises Inc	Cranston	RI	F	401 781-3120	20183
Austin Hard Chrome	Providence	RI	G	401 421-0840	20964
Bel Air Finishing Supply Corp	North Kingstown	RI	G	401 667-7902	20693
Chemart Company **(PA)**	Lincoln	RI	D	401 333-9200	20563
DFI-Ep LLC	North Providence	RI	E	401 943-9900	20756
Dura Kote Technology Ltd	Johnston	RI	F	401 331-6460	20509
Duralectra-Chn LLC	Woonsocket	RI	D	401 597-5000	21557
Electrolizing Inc	Providence	RI	E	401 861-5900	21004
G & A Plating & Polishing Co	North Providence	RI	E	401 351-8693	20762
G Tanury Plating Co Inc	Johnston	RI	D	401 232-2330	20514
General Plating Inc	Johnston	RI	G	401 421-0219	20515
Ideal Plating & Polsg Co Inc	Providence	RI	F	401 455-1700	21034
Induplate Inc **(PA)**	North Providence	RI	D	401 231-5770	20765
International Chromium Pltg Co	Providence	RI	G	401 421-0205	21037
Interplex Engineered Pdts Inc	Rumford	RI	E	401 434-6543	21187
Interplex Industries Inc **(DH)**	Rumford	RI	F	718 961-6212	21188
Interplex Metals Ri Inc	Rumford	RI	D	401 732-9999	21191
Jet Electro-Finishing Co Inc	Barrington	RI	G	401 728-5809	20047
Jrb Associates Inc	Cranston	RI	E	401 351-8693	20247
Masbro Polishing Company Inc	Smithfield	RI	F	401 722-2227	21238
Monarch Metal Finishing Co Inc	Providence	RI	E	401 785-3200	21070
New Annex Plating Inc	North Providence	RI	F	401 349-0911	20767
Nu-Lustre Finishing Corp	Providence	RI	D	401 521-7800	21079
Polytechnic Inc	Pawtucket	RI	G	401 724-3608	20882
Precision Plsg Ornamentals Inc	Pawtucket	RI	E	401 728-9994	20883
Providence Metallizing Co Inc **(PA)**	Pawtucket	RI	D	401 722-5300	20886
R & R Polishing Co Inc	Cranston	RI	G	401 831-6335	20277
Reed Allison Group Inc	Providence	RI	D	617 846-1237	21107
Roberts Polishing Co	Johnston	RI	G	401 946-8922	20538

	CITY	ST	EMP	PHONE	ENTRY #
Spencer Plating Company	Providence	RI	G	401 331-5923	21125
Tanury Industries Inc	Lincoln	RI	C	800 428-6213	20598
Technodic Inc	Providence	RI	E	401 467-6660	21132
Time Plating Incorporated	Cranston	RI	G	401 943-3020	20302
Unique Plating Co	Johnston	RI	G	401 943-7366	20545
United Plating Inc	Cranston	RI	D	401 461-5857	20307
Universal Plating Co Inc	Providence	RI	G	401 861-3530	21144
Westwell Industries Inc	Providence	RI	F	401 467-2992	21154
Deermont Corpopration	Rutland	VT	G	802 775-5759	22329
Lawrence Lyon	Chelsea	VT	G	802 685-7790	21839
Precision Valley Finishing	Springfield	VT	G	802 885-3150	22508

3479 Coating & Engraving, NEC

	CITY	ST	EMP	PHONE	ENTRY #
Advanced Graphics Inc	Stratford	CT	E	203 378-0471	4388
American Metallizing	South Windsor	CT	G	860 289-1677	3936
American Roller Company LLC	Middlebury	CT	F	203 598-3100	2154
American Rubber Stamp Company	Cheshire	CT	G	203 755-1135	710
Ann S Davis	Lebanon	CT	F	860 642-7228	1932
Baron & Young Co Inc	Bristol	CT	G	860 589-3235	529
Cametoid Technologies Inc	Manchester	CT	F	860 646-4667	1991
Central Connecticut Coating	East Hartford	CT	F	860 528-8281	1180
Chem-Tron Pntg Pwdr Cating Inc	Danbury	CT	G	203 743-5131	887
Clear & Colored Coatings LLC **(PA)**	Wolcott	CT	G	203 879-1379	5435
Colonial Coatings Inc	Milford	CT	E	203 783-9933	2265
Competitive Edge Coatings LLC	South Windsor	CT	G	860 882-0762	3952
Conard Corporation	Glastonbury	CT	E	860 659-0591	1544
Connecticut Plasma Tech LLC	South Windsor	CT	F	860 289-5500	3953
Covalent Coating Tech LLC	East Hartford	CT	G	860 214-6452	1184
Donwell Company	Manchester	CT	E	860 649-5374	2002
Engineered Coatings Inc	Litchfield	CT	E	860 567-5556	1948
F J Weidner Inc	East Haven	CT	G	203 469-4202	1249
Farrell Prcsion Mtalcraft Corp	New Milford	CT	E	860 355-2651	2799
Fonda Fabricating & Welding Co	Plainville	CT	G	860 793-0601	3489
Gybenorth Industries LLC	Milford	CT	F	203 876-9876	2295
Halco Inc	Waterbury	CT	D	203 575-9450	4881
Hartford Industrial Finshg Co	Bloomfield	CT	G	860 243-2040	224
High Grade Finishing Co LLC	Enfield	CT	G	860 749-8883	1364
Highway Safety Corp **(PA)**	Glastonbury	CT	D	860 659-4330	1558
Identification Products Corp	Bridgeport	CT	F	203 334-5969	429
Imperial Metal Finishing Inc	Stratford	CT	G	203 377-1229	4422
Integrity Cylinder Sales LLC	East Hampton	CT	G	860 267-6667	1160
Jet Process Corporation	North Haven	CT	G	203 985-6000	3035
Jonmandy Corporation	Torrington	CT	G	860 482-2354	4583
K & G Corp	Manchester	CT	F	860 643-1133	2015
Marjan Inc	Waterbury	CT	F	203 573-1742	4910
Materion Lrge Area Catings LLC **(DH)**	Windsor	CT	D	216 486-4200	5347
Metallizing Service Co Inc **(PA)**	Hartford	CT	E	860 953-1144	1848
Metamorphic Materials Inc	Winsted	CT	F	860 738-8638	5417
Mitchell-Bate Company	Waterbury	CT	E	203 233-0862	4918
Modern Metal Finishing Inc	Oxford	CT	F	203 267-1510	3414
Paint & Powder Works LLC	New Britain	CT	F	860 225-2019	2560
Pauway Corp	Wallingford	CT	F	203 265-3939	4783
Plas-TEC Coatings Inc	South Windsor	CT	F	860 289-6029	4000
Plastonics Inc	Hartford	CT	E	860 249-5455	1859
Praxair Inc **(HQ)**	Danbury	CT	B	203 837-2000	971
Praxair Surface Tech Inc	Manchester	CT	D	860 646-0700	2039
Pti Industries Inc **(HQ)**	Enfield	CT	E	800 318-8438	1376
Robert Audette **(PA)**	Cheshire	CT	G	203 872-3119	760
Shoreline Coatings LLC	North Branford	CT	G	203 213-3471	2976
Silversmith Inc	Greenwich	CT	G	203 869-4244	1649
Summit Corporation of America	Thomaston	CT	D	860 283-4391	4519
Tim Poloski	Vernon Rockville	CT	G	860 508-6566	4685
Vitek Research Corporation	Naugatuck	CT	F	203 735-1813	2500
A S A P Engravers	Whitinsville	MA	G	508 234-6974	16909
Acralube Inc	Westfield	MA	G	413 562-5019	16663
Actnano Inc **(PA)**	Boston	MA	F	857 333-8631	8339
Amex Inc	Boston	MA	E	617 569-5630	8364
Anjen Finishing	Marlborough	MA	G	508 251-1532	12713
Applied Graphics Inc	Amesbury	MA	E	978 241-5300	7478
Applied Plastics Co Inc	Norwood	MA	E	781 762-1881	14133
Ariston Engraving & Machine Co	Woburn	MA	G	781 935-2328	17122
Automated Finishing Co Inc	Attleboro	MA	E	508 222-6262	7710
Bay State Galvanizing Inc	Everett	MA	F	617 389-0671	10604
Bemis Associates Inc **(PA)**	Shirley	MA	C	978 425-6761	15081
Berkshire Custom Coating Inc	Pittsfield	MA	E	413 442-3757	14457
Bertoldo Inc	Wakefield	MA	G	781 324-9145	15944
Carey Brothers Inc	Harwich Port	MA	E	508 222-7234	11399
Cast Coat Inc	West Bridgewater	MA	G	508 587-4502	16433
Central Coating Tech Inc	West Boylston	MA	D	508 835-6225	16411
Central Mass Powdr Coating Inc	Clinton	MA	G	978 365-1700	10077
Chase Corp Inc	Westwood	MA	G	781 332-0700	16860
Chase Corporation **(PA)**	Westwood	MA	G	781 332-0700	16861
Chase Corporation	Oxford	MA	F	508 731-2710	14256
Chase Corporation	Westwood	MA	F	781 329-3259	16862
Chemi-Graphic Inc	Ludlow	MA	E	413 589-0151	12458
Churchill Coatings Corporation	South Yarmouth	MA	G	508 394-6573	15327
Cil Inc	Lawrence	MA	D	978 685-8300	12009
Coating Application Tech	Woburn	MA	F	781 491-0699	17146
Coatings and Coverings	Harwich	MA	G	774 237-0882	11392
Collt Mfg Inc	Millis	MA	E	508 376-2525	13183
Custom Coatings	Hyannis	MA	G	508 771-8830	11838
DSM Coating Resins Inc	Wilmington	MA	C	800 458-0014	16996
Duncan Galvanizing Corporation	Everett	MA	D	617 389-8440	10610
E V Yeuell Inc	Woburn	MA	E	781 933-2984	17171
East Coast Plastics Inc	Framingham	MA	G	508 429-8080	10944
Eastern Etching and Mfg Co	Chicopee	MA	E	413 594-6601	10022
Elenel Industries Inc **(PA)**	Milford	MA	E	508 478-2025	13115
Epoxalot Jewelry	North Attleboro	MA	G	508 699-0767	13755
Falmer Associates Inc	Salem	MA	G	978 745-4000	14911
Feeleys Company Inc	Quincy	MA	G	617 773-1711	14625
Focal Point Technologies	Plymouth	MA	G	508 830-9716	14558
Fort Hill Sign Products Inc	Hopedale	MA	G	781 321-4320	11672
Framingham Engraving Co	Framingham	MA	G	508 877-7867	10946
G T R Finishing Corporation	Brockton	MA	E	508 588-3240	9147
Gvd Corporation **(PA)**	Cambridge	MA	F	617 661-0060	9498
Indepenent Plating Co	Worcester	MA	E	508 756-0301	17391
Industrial Etching Inc	East Longmeadow	MA	F	413 525-4110	10479
Innovative Coatings Inc	Medway	MA	F	508 533-6101	12961
Jack Hodgdon	Attleboro	MA	G	508 223-9990	7754
Jet Coating Co	Boylston	MA	G	508 869-2158	8981
Jet Tech Inc	Lynn	MA	F	781 599-8685	12518
Joseph Nachado	Assonet	MA	G	508 644-3404	7682
Jr Chemical Coatings LLC	Harwich	MA	G	508 896-3383	11394
L & J of New England Inc	Worcester	MA	E	508 756-8080	17403
Light Metal Platers LLC	Waltham	MA	E	781 899-8855	16145
Manning Way Cpitl Partners LLC	Bellingham	MA	E	508 966-4800	8044
Mass Coating Corp	East Walpole	MA	G	347 325-0001	10526
Modern Marking Products Inc	Bridgewater	MA	G	508 697-6066	9085
N2 Biomedical LLC	Bedford	MA	E	781 275-6001	7993
New England Etching Co Inc	Holyoke	MA	E	413 532-9482	11643
New England Indus Coatings	Worcester	MA	G	508 754-1066	17430
North East Indus Coatings Inc	Ipswich	MA	G	978 356-1200	11932
Northeast Stamp & Engraving	Milford	MA	G	508 473-5818	13132
Pace Industries LLC	North Billerica	MA	C	978 667-8400	13852
Paratronix Inc	Westborough	MA	F	508 222-8979	16642
Photofabrication Engrg Inc **(HQ)**	Milford	MA	E	508 478-2025	13137
Pike Powder Coating LLC	Allston	MA	G	617 779-7311	7473
Poly-Metal Finishing Inc	Springfield	MA	D	413 781-4535	15498
Polymetallurgical LLC	North Attleboro	MA	E	508 695-9312	13773
Powder Pro Powder Coating Inc	New Bedford	MA	G	508 991-5999	13441
Precision Coating Co Inc **(HQ)**	Hudson	MA	D	781 329-1420	11805
Precision Coating Co Inc	Hudson	MA	E	978 562-7561	11806
Reid Graphics Inc	Andover	MA	D	978 474-1930	7598
RPM Wood Finishes Group Inc	Westfield	MA	F	413 562-9655	16724
Spencer Industrial Painting	Spencer	MA	G	508 885-5406	15436
Spencer Metal Finishing Inc **(PA)**	Brookfield	MA	F	508 885-6477	9193
Spray Maine Inc	Newburyport	MA	F	207 384-2273	13535
Sunset Engravers	Methuen	MA	G	978 687-1111	13045
Tech-Etch Inc **(PA)**	Plymouth	MA	B	508 747-0300	14587
Thermoceramix Inc	Boston	MA	G	978 425-0404	8881
Titus Engraving & Stonesetting	Plainville	MA	E	508 695-6842	14536
Unerectors Inc	Boston	MA	F	617 436-8333	8894
United Technical Coating Inc	Haverhill	MA	G	978 521-2779	11482
V&S Taunton Galvanizing LLC	Taunton	MA	E	508 828-9499	15796
Vw Quality Coating	Norton	MA	F	617 963-6503	14092
Westfield Electroplating Co **(PA)**	Westfield	MA	C	413 568-3716	16743
Westside Finishing Co Inc	Holyoke	MA	E	413 533-4909	11667
Worcester Manufacturing Inc	Worcester	MA	E	508 756-0301	17505
Xtalic Corporation	Marlborough	MA	E	508 485-9730	12854
Cianbro Fbrcation Coating Corp	Pittsfield	ME	C	207 487-3311	6588
Epifanes North America Inc	Thomaston	ME	G	207 354-0804	7084
Futureguard Building Pdts Inc **(PA)**	Auburn	ME	D	800 858-5818	5565
Jarden LLC	East Wilton	ME	C	207 645-2574	5987
Northeast Coating Tech Inc	Kennebunk	ME	E	207 985-3232	6239
Performance Products Painting	Auburn	ME	E	207 783-4222	5589
Praxair Surface Tech Inc	Biddeford	ME	D	207 282-3787	5757
Superior Wldg Fabrication Inc	Ellsworth	ME	F	207 664-2121	6022
Advanced Polymerics Inc	Salem	NH	G	603 328-8177	19704
Atkinson Thin Film Systems	Hampstead	NH	G	603 329-7322	18236
Ckm Coatings	Brentwood	NH	G	603 642-5728	17747
Defense Manufacturers Inc	Somersworth	NH	G	603 332-4186	19834
Good Hues Custom Powdr Coating	Derry	NH	G	603 434-8034	17980
Granite State Finishing Inc	Nashua	NH	G	603 880-4130	19171
Omni Metals Company Inc	Somersworth	NH	E	603 692-6664	19845
Parker-Hannifin Corporation	Hudson	NH	C	603 880-4807	18425
Pf Pro Fnshg Silkscreening Inc	Hampstead	NH	G	603 329-8344	18248
Rapid Finishing Corp	Nashua	NH	E	603 889-4234	19244
American Trophy & Supply Co	East Providence	RI	G	401 438-3060	20386
Chemart Company	Lincoln	RI	E	401 333-9200	20562
Chemart Company **(PA)**	Lincoln	RI	D	401 333-9200	20563
Development Associates Inc	North Kingstown	RI	F	401 884-1350	20702
Difruscia Industries Inc	Cranston	RI	E	401 943-9900	20210
Etched Image LLC	North Providence	RI	G	401 225-6095	20760
GA Rel Manufacturing Company	Providence	RI	E	401 331-5455	21019

S I C

	CITY	ST	EMP	PHONE	ENTRY #
Industrial & Commercial Finshg	Johnston	RI	G	401 942-4680	20516
International Etching Inc	Providence	RI	F	401 781-6800	21038
M D F Powder Coat Systems LLC	Portsmouth	RI	F	401 683-7525	20927
Me-92 Operations Inc	Providence	RI	E	401 831-9200	21065
Metal Spraying Co Inc	Central Falls	RI	G	401 725-2722	20120
Northeast Coatings Inc	Warren	RI	G	401 649-1552	21300
Platinum Recognition LLC **(PA)**	North Providence	RI	G	401 305-6700	20772
PM Colors Inc	Johnston	RI	G	401 521-7280	20530
Providence Metallizing Co Inc **(PA)**	Pawtucket	RI	D	401 722-5300	20886
Quality Spraying Stenciling Co	Providence	RI	D	401 861-2413	21103
S & M Enameling Co Inc	Providence	RI	G	401 272-0333	21118
Teknicote Inc	Rumford	RI	D	401 724-2230	21197
Wehr Industries Inc	Warwick	RI	E	401 732-6565	21444
Weller E E Co Inc/MCS Finshg	Providence	RI	E	401 461-4275	21152
Ellison Surface Tech - W LLC	Rutland	VT	G	802 773-4278	22333
Ellison Surface Tech Inc	North Clarendon	VT	D	802 775-9300	22215
G S P Coatings Inc	Brattleboro	VT	F	802 257-5858	21726
Gds Manufacturing Company	Williston	VT	G	802 862-7610	22669
JBM Carmel LLC	Bennington	VT	E	802 442-9110	21674
R&B Powder Coating LLC	Poultney	VT	G	802 287-2300	22275
Vermont Ware Inc	St George	VT	G	802 482-4426	22514

3482 Small Arms Ammunition

	CITY	ST	EMP	PHONE	ENTRY #
General Dynamics Ordnance	Avon	CT	F	860 404-0162	34
Illinois Tool Works Inc	Waterbury	CT	C	203 574-2119	4887
Jkb Daira Inc **(PA)**	Norwalk	CT	G	203 642-4824	3182
Shell Shock Technologies Llc	Westport	CT	G	203 557-3256	5230
American Outdoor Brands Corp **(PA)**	Springfield	MA	A	800 331-0852	15445
Executive Force Protection LLC	Cambridge	MA	F	617 470-9230	9476
Ammo and Bullet Manufacturing	Arundel	ME	G	978 807-7681	5527
Green Mountain Risk MGT LLC	Dover	NH	F	802 683-8586	18024
Green Mtn Rifle Barrel Co Inc	Conway	NH	F	603 447-1095	17953
Green Mountain Risk MGT Inc	Strafford	VT	G	802 763-7773	22527

3483 Ammunition, Large

	CITY	ST	EMP	PHONE	ENTRY #
Ensign-Bickford Industries Inc	Simsbury	CT	E	860 658-4411	3905
Cadillac Gage Textron Inc **(HQ)**	Wilmington	MA	G	978 657-5111	16986
Chamberlain Manufacturing Corp	New Bedford	MA	B	508 996-5621	13370
Textron Systems Corporation **(DH)**	Wilmington	MA	E	978 657-5111	17054
Gun F X Tactical Development **(PA)**	Portland	ME	G	207 797-8200	6667

3484 Small Arms

	CITY	ST	EMP	PHONE	ENTRY #
Colt Defense LLC **(HQ)**	West Hartford	CT	B	860 232-4489	5060
Colts Manufacturing Co LLC **(DH)**	West Hartford	CT	C	860 236-6311	5061
Continental Machine Tl Co Inc	New Britain	CT	D	860 223-2896	2522
Deburring House Inc	East Berlin	CT	E	860 828-0889	1098
Dewey J Manufacturing Company	Oxford	CT	G	203 264-3064	3399
Gunworks International L L C	Old Saybrook	CT	G	860 388-4591	3336
Jkb Daira Inc **(PA)**	Norwalk	CT	G	203 642-4824	3182
Kinetic Development Group LLC	Seymour	CT	G	203 888-4321	3754
Maverick Arms Inc	North Haven	CT	G	203 230-5300	3038
Mike Sadlak	Coventry	CT	G	860 742-0227	835
Mossberg Corporation **(PA)**	North Haven	CT	G	203 230-5300	3042
New Designz Inc	Cheshire	CT	F	860 384-1809	747
O F Mossberg & Sons Inc **(HQ)**	North Haven	CT	C	203 230-5300	3045
Scott Olson Enterprises LLC	Torrington	CT	G	860 482-4391	4598
Stag Arms LLC	New Britain	CT	G	860 229-9994	2578
Stag Arms LLC	New Britain	CT	G	860 229-9994	2579
Sturm Ruger & Company Inc **(PA)**	Southport	CT	B	203 259-7843	4099
United States Fire Arms Mfg Co	Hartford	CT	E	860 296-7441	1883
US Firearms Manufacturing Co	Hartford	CT	G	860 296-7441	1884
Wilson Arms Company	Branford	CT	F	203 488-7297	362
Accudyne Machine Tool Inc	Bellingham	MA	G	508 966-3110	8027
Caliber Company **(PA)**	Westfield	MA	F	413 642-4260	16676
Davinci Arms LLC	Ludlow	MA	G	413 583-4327	12462
Kahr Arms Inc	Worcester	MA	E	508 635-1414	17398
Present Arms Inc	Indian Orchard	MA	G	413 575-4656	11894
Saeilo USA Inc	Worcester	MA	E	508 795-3919	17463
Savage Arms Inc **(DH)**	Westfield	MA	C	413 642-4135	16726
Savage Sports Corporation **(HQ)**	Westfield	MA	F	413 568-7001	16728
Thompson/Center Arms Co Inc **(HQ)**	Springfield	MA	E	800 331-0852	15513
American Outdoor Brands Sls Co	Houlton	ME	D	207 532-7966	6202
Windham Weaponry Inc	Windham	ME	D	207 893-2223	7261
Brigade Tactical Corp	Manchester	NH	G	603 682-7063	18790
Green Mtn Rifle Barrel Co Inc	Conway	NH	F	603 447-1095	17953
Grip Pod Systems Intl LLC	Dover	NH	G	239 233-3694	18025
Q LLC	Portsmouth	NH	G	603 294-0047	19611
Sig Sauer Inc	Exeter	NH	D	603 610-3000	18132
Sig Sauer Inc **(DH)**	Newington	NH	C	603 610-3000	19325
Sturm Ruger & Company Inc	Newport	NH	A	603 863-2000	19360
Sturm Ruger & Company Inc	Newport	NH	B	603 865-2424	19361
Sturm Ruger & Company Inc	Newport	NH	C	603 863-3300	19362
Tandem Kross LLC	Weare	NH	G	603 369-7060	19941
Thompson/Center Arms Co Inc	Rochester	NH	F	603 332-2394	19690
Thayer Industries Inc	Wakefield	RI	G	401 789-8825	21281
Caspian Arms Ltd	Wolcott	VT	G	802 472-6454	22729
Foster Industries Inc	Wolcott	VT	E	802 472-6147	22730
Z M Weapons High Performance	Richmond	VT	G	802 777-8964	22313

3489 Ordnance & Access, NEC

	CITY	ST	EMP	PHONE	ENTRY #
Ensign-Bickford Industries Inc	Simsbury	CT	E	860 658-4411	3905
Kaman Aerospace Corporation	Middletown	CT	C	860 632-1000	2195
Tek Arms Inc	Hebron	CT	G	860 748-6289	1898
United States Fire Arms Mfg Co	Hartford	CT	E	860 296-7441	1883
Entwistle Company **(HQ)**	Hudson	MA	C	508 481-4000	11772
Troy Industries Inc	West Springfield	MA	D	413 788-4288	16556
Combat Weapons Development LLC	Manchester	NH	G	603 978-0244	18801
Famars USA LLC	Richmond	RI	G	401 397-5500	21161

3491 Industrial Valves

	CITY	ST	EMP	PHONE	ENTRY #
BNL Industries Inc	Vernon	CT	E	860 870-6222	4663
Contemporary Products LLC	Middletown	CT	E	860 346-9283	2182
Conval Inc	Enfield	CT	C	860 749-0761	1353
Cr-TEC Engineering Inc	Madison	CT	G	203 318-9500	1957
Fisher Controls Intl LLC	North Stonington	CT	C	860 599-1140	3075
Kip Inc	Farmington	CT	C	860 677-0272	1488
Logic Seal LLC	Plainville	CT	G	203 598-3400	3501
Oventrop Corp	East Granby	CT	E	860 413-9173	1139
Parker-Hannifin Corporation	New Britain	CT	C	860 827-2300	2561
Peter Paul Electronics Co Inc	New Britain	CT	C	860 229-4884	2562
Rostra Vernatherm LLC	Bristol	CT	E	860 582-6776	609
Ruby Automation LLC **(HQ)**	Bloomfield	CT	C	860 687-5000	258
Ruby Industrial Tech LLC **(PA)**	Bloomfield	CT	D	860 687-5000	260
Saf Industries LLC	Meriden	CT	E	203 729-4900	2127
Universal Building Contrls Inc	Meriden	CT	F	203 235-1530	2145
Asahi/America Inc **(HQ)**	Lawrence	MA	C	781 321-5409	11995
Circor International Inc **(PA)**	Burlington	MA	B	781 270-1200	9250
Clark Solutions	Hudson	MA	F	978 568-3400	11763
Conant Controls Inc	Woburn	MA	F	781 395-2240	17147
Condon Mfg Co Inc	Springfield	MA	F	413 543-1250	15461
Crosby Valve & Gage Intl Inc	Mansfield	MA	D	508 384-3121	12624
CRS Steam Inc	Gardner	MA	G	978 630-2308	11110
Diebolt & Company	East Longmeadow	MA	F	860 434-2222	10473
Emerson Automation Solutions	Mansfield	MA	D	508 594-4356	12630
Emerson Automation Solutions	Mansfield	MA	D	508 594-4410	12631
Fr Flow Ctrl Vlves US Bdco Inc **(PA)**	Ipswich	MA	D	978 744-5690	11920
Mks Instruments Inc **(PA)**	Andover	MA	B	978 645-5500	7574
Mks Instruments Inc	Andover	MA	E	978 645-5500	7575
Mks Msc Inc	Wilmington	MA	A	978 284-4000	17025
Mostmed Inc	Salem	MA	G	978 740-0400	14931
Mueller Water Products Inc	Middleboro	MA	F	508 923-2870	13070
Pentair Valves & Contrls US LP	Mansfield	MA	C	508 594-4410	12651
Rodney Hunt-Fontaine Inc **(DH)**	Orange	MA	C	978 544-2511	14227
Ruggles-Klingemann Mfg Co **(PA)**	Beverly	MA	F	978 232-8300	8173
Tyco International MGT Co LLC	Mansfield	MA	G	508 261-6200	12667
Vent-Rite Valve Corp **(PA)**	Randolph	MA	E	781 986-2000	14701
Watts Regulator Co **(HQ)**	North Andover	MA	C	978 689-6000	13737
Watts Regulator Co	North Andover	MA	A	978 688-1811	13738
Watts Water Technologies Inc **(PA)**	North Andover	MA	C	978 688-1811	13739
McGuire & Co Inc	Falmouth	ME	G	207 797-3323	6032
Broen-Lab Inc	Bedford	NH	F	205 956-9444	17633
Cobra Precision Machining Corp	Hooksett	NH	G	603 434-8424	18347
Parker-Hannifin Corporation	Hollis	NH	E	973 575-4844	18337
Quality Controls Inc	Northfield	NH	E	603 286-3321	19408
Ruggles-Klingemann Mfg Co	Seabrook	NH	G	603 474-8500	19814
Watts Regulator Co	Franklin	NH	A	603 934-5110	18166
Watts Water Technologies Inc	Franklin	NH	D	603 934-1369	18167
Watts Water Technologies Inc	Franklin	NH	E	603 934-1367	18168

3492 Fluid Power Valves & Hose Fittings

	CITY	ST	EMP	PHONE	ENTRY #
American Metal Masters LLC	Plantsville	CT	G	860 621-6911	3526
Atp Industries LLC **(PA)**	Plainville	CT	F	860 479-5007	3467
Clarcor Eng MBL Solutions LLC **(DH)**	East Hartford	CT	D	860 920-4200	1182
Crane Aerospace Inc **(DH)**	Stamford	CT	C	203 363-7300	4176
Crane Co **(PA)**	Stamford	CT	D	203 363-7300	4177
Crane Controls Inc **(DH)**	Stamford	CT	G	203 363-7300	4178
Crane Intl Holdings Inc **(HQ)**	Stamford	CT	G	203 363-7300	4179
Enfield Technologies LLC	Shelton	CT	F	203 375-3100	3801
Fluid Dynamics LLC **(PA)**	Manchester	CT	G	860 791-6325	2006
Funkhouser Industrial Products	East Granby	CT	G	860 653-1972	1127
Navtec Rigging Solutions Inc	Clinton	CT	E	203 458-3163	790
Norgren Inc	Farmington	CT	C	860 677-0272	1500
Parker-Hannifin Corporation	New Britain	CT	C	860 827-2300	2561
Ruby Fluid Power LLC **(HQ)**	Bloomfield	CT	E	860 243-7100	259
Saf Industries LLC	Meriden	CT	E	203 729-4900	2127
Stanadyne Intrmdate Hldngs LLC **(HQ)**	Windsor	CT	C	860 525-0821	5367
Conant Controls Inc	Woburn	MA	F	781 395-2240	17147
Controls For Automation Inc	Taunton	MA	E	508 802-6005	15738
Guardair Corporation	Chicopee	MA	E	413 594-4400	10028
Hosetech Plus More Inc	Ludlow	MA	G	413 385-0035	12467
Landry Enterprises Inc	Franklin	MA	G	508 528-9122	11063
Op USA Inc	Acton	MA	G	978 658-5135	7376
Portland Valve LLC **(HQ)**	Warren	MA	E	704 289-6511	16261
Portland Valve LLC	Warren	MA	G	978 284-4000	16262

	CITY	ST	EMP	PHONE	ENTRY #
Wgi Inc	Southwick	MA	C	413 569-9444	15421
Ballistic Fluid Technologies **(PA)**	Lyndeborough	NH	G	603 654-3065	18757
Parker-Hannifin Corporation	Hollis	NH	C	603 595-1500	18336
Parker-Hannifin Corporation	Hollis	NH	E	973 575-4844	18337
Quality Controls Inc	Northfield	NH	E	603 286-3321	19408
John Crane Sealol Inc **(DH)**	Warwick	RI	C	401 732-0715	21381

3493 Steel Springs, Except Wire

	CITY	ST	EMP	PHONE	ENTRY #
Acme Monaco Corporation **(PA)**	New Britain	CT	C	860 224-1349	2503
American Specialty Co Inc	Shelton	CT	F	203 929-5324	3774
Arrow Manufacturing Company	Bristol	CT	E	860 589-3900	520
Atlantic Precision Spring Inc	Bristol	CT	E	860 583-1864	522
Century Spring Mfg Co Inc	Bristol	CT	E	860 582-3344	540
Connectcut Spring Stmping Corp	Farmington	CT	B	860 677-1341	1473
Dayon Manufacturing Inc	Farmington	CT	E	860 677-8561	1476
Dynamic Manufacturing Company	Bristol	CT	G	860 589-2751	551
Excel Spring & Stamping LLC	Bristol	CT	G	860 585-1495	559
Fourslide Spring Stamping Inc	Bristol	CT	E	860 583-1688	564
Hurley Manufacturing Company	New Hartford	CT	E	860 379-8506	2638
Lee Spring Company LLC	Bristol	CT	E	860 584-0991	576
Matthew Warren Inc	Southington	CT	D	860 621-7358	4065
Newcomb Spring Corp	Southington	CT	E	860 621-0111	4067
Oscar Jobs	Bristol	CT	G	860 583-7834	588
Rowley Spring & Stamping Corp	Bristol	CT	C	860 582-8175	610
Spring Computerized Inds LLC	Harwinton	CT	G	860 605-9206	1893
Tollman Spring Company Inc	Bristol	CT	G	860 583-4856	619
Triple A Spring Ltd Partnr	Bristol	CT	E	860 589-3231	620
Bay State Spring Corp	Jefferson	MA	G	508 829-5702	11952
Leggett & Platt Incorporated	Oxford	MA	E	508 987-8706	14265
Minuteman Spring Company Inc	Millbury	MA	G	508 299-6100	13172
Solid Earth Technologies Inc	Amherst	NH	G	603 882-5319	17588
D & W Tool Findings Inc	Pawtucket	RI	F	401 727-3030	20832

3494 Valves & Pipe Fittings, NEC

	CITY	ST	EMP	PHONE	ENTRY #
Carten Controls Inc	Cheshire	CT	F	203 699-2100	719
Crane Co **(PA)**	Stamford	CT	D	203 363-7300	4177
Enfield Technologies LLC	Shelton	CT	F	203 375-3100	3801
Fisher Controls Intl LLC	North Stonington	CT	C	860 599-1140	3075
Houston Weber Systems Inc	Branford	CT	G	203 481-0115	324
Hydrolevel Company	North Haven	CT	F	203 776-0473	3030
Hytek Plumbing and Heating LLC	Preston	CT	G	860 389-1122	3581
Idex Health & Science LLC	Bristol	CT	C	860 314-2880	570
Saf Industries LLC	Meriden	CT	E	203 729-4900	2127
Automatic Machine Pdts Sls Co	Taunton	MA	D	508 822-4226	15728
Axenics Inc **(PA)**	Middleton	MA	E	978 774-9393	13084
Conant Controls Inc	Woburn	MA	F	781 395-2240	17147
Economou Plumbing & Heating	Dracut	MA	G	978 957-6953	10360
Geneisis Sprinkler Systems	Osterville	MA	G	508 428-1842	14247
Larad Equipment Corp	Hopedale	MA	G	508 473-2700	11676
Maxon Corporation	Acton	MA	G	978 795-1285	7373
Mks Instruments Inc **(PA)**	Andover	MA	B	978 645-5500	7574
Mks Instruments Inc	Andover	MA	E	978 645-5500	7575
Mks Msc Inc	Wilmington	MA	A	978 284-4000	17025
Newstamp Lighting Corp	North Easton	MA	F	508 238-7073	13949
Portland Valve LLC **(HQ)**	Warren	MA	E	704 289-6511	16261
Rodney Hunt-Fontaine Inc **(DH)**	Orange	MA	C	978 544-2511	14227
Scully Signal Company **(PA)**	Wilmington	MA	C	617 692-8600	17044
Sem-Tec Inc	Worcester	MA	E	508 798-8551	17471
Sloan Valve Company	Andover	MA	C	617 796-9001	7607
Swiss Precision Products Inc **(DH)**	North Oxford	MA	E	508 987-8003	13975
Symmons Industries Inc **(PA)**	Braintree	MA	C	781 848-2250	9041
Symmons Industries Inc	Braintree	MA	G	781 664-5236	9042
Taco Inc	Fall River	MA	D	508 675-7300	10769
Takasago Electric Inc	Westborough	MA	G	508 983-1434	16653
Victaulic Company	Mansfield	MA	G	508 406-3220	12668
Watts Regulator Co **(HQ)**	North Andover	MA	C	978 689-6000	13737
Watts Water Technologies Inc **(PA)**	North Andover	MA	C	978 688-1811	13739
Flue Gas Solutions Inc	Windham	ME	G	207 893-1510	7234
Acme Sales	Londonderry	NH	G	603 434-8826	18670
Alan T Seeler Inc	New Hampton	NH	F	603 744-3736	19301
Anvil International LLC **(HQ)**	Exeter	NH	E	603 418-2800	18110
Fronek Anchor Darling Entp	Laconia	NH	F	603 528-1931	18564
Jmsc Enterprises Inc	Seabrook	NH	G	603 468-1010	19808
Mem-Co Fittings Inc	Hampstead	NH	G	603 329-9633	18243
Parker & Harper Companies Inc **(PA)**	Raymond	NH	D	603 895-4761	19643
Quality Controls Inc	Northfield	NH	E	603 286-3321	19408
Everett J Prescott Inc	Lincoln	RI	G	401 333-8588	20573
Guill Tool & Engrg Co Inc	West Warwick	RI	D	401 822-8186	21493
Vellano Corporation	Pawtucket	RI	G	401 434-1030	20909

3495 Wire Springs

	CITY	ST	EMP	PHONE	ENTRY #
A & A Manufacturing Co Inc	North Haven	CT	E	262 786-1500	3000
Atlantic Precision Spring Inc	Bristol	CT	E	860 583-1864	522
Barnes Group Inc	Farmington	CT	G	860 298-7740	1467
Barnes Group Inc **(PA)**	Bristol	CT	B	860 583-7070	526
Barnes Group Inc	Bristol	CT	D	860 582-9581	527
Century Spring Mfg Co Inc	Bristol	CT	E	860 582-3344	540
Connectcut Spring Stmping Corp	Farmington	CT	B	860 677-1341	1473
Dayon Manufacturing Inc	Farmington	CT	E	860 677-8561	1476
DR Templeman Company	Plainville	CT	F	860 747-2709	3482
Excel Spring & Stamping LLC	Bristol	CT	G	860 585-1495	559
Fourslide Spring Stamping Inc	Bristol	CT	E	860 583-1688	564
Gemco Manufacturing Co Inc	Southington	CT	E	860 628-5529	4052
Lee Spring Company LLC	Bristol	CT	E	860 584-0991	576
Matthew Warren Inc	Southington	CT	D	860 621-7358	4065
National Spring & Stamping Inc	Thomaston	CT	E	860 283-0203	4510
Newcomb Spring Corp	Southington	CT	E	860 621-0111	4067
Newcomb Springs Connecticut	Southington	CT	E	860 621-0111	4068
Oscar Jobs	Bristol	CT	G	860 583-7834	588
Plymouth Spring Company Inc	Bristol	CT	D	860 584-0594	595
Rowley Spring & Stamping Corp	Bristol	CT	C	860 582-8175	610
Southington Tool & Mfg Corp	Plantsville	CT	E	860 276-0021	3540
Spring Computerized Inds LLC	Harwinton	CT	G	860 605-9206	1893
Springfield Spring Corporation	Bristol	CT	F	860 584-6560	614
Thomas Spring Co of Connenicut	Milford	CT	G	203 874-7030	2375
Ulbrich of Georgia Inc	North Haven	CT	G	203 239-4481	3066
Bay State Spring Corp	Jefferson	MA	G	508 829-5702	11952
Catalyst/Spring I Ltd Partner	Chelsea	MA	E	617 884-9410	9947
Device Technologies Inc	Southborough	MA	E	508 229-2000	15354
Leggett & Platt Incorporated	Oxford	MA	E	508 987-8706	14265
Pdi International Inc	Lowell	MA	G	978 446-0840	12419
Spring Manufacturing Corp	Tewksbury	MA	F	978 658-7396	15836
Springfield Spring Corporation **(PA)**	East Longmeadow	MA	E	413 525-6837	10493
Stratosphere Inc	York	ME	D	207 351-8011	7317
D & W Tool Findings Inc	Pawtucket	RI	F	401 727-3030	20832
Stephen A Burt	Colchester	VT	G	802 893-0600	21880

3496 Misc Fabricated Wire Prdts

	CITY	ST	EMP	PHONE	ENTRY #
Acme Monaco Corporation **(PA)**	New Britain	CT	C	860 224-1349	2503
Acme Wire Products Co Inc	Mystic	CT	E	860 572-0511	2433
Amtec Corporation	Plainfield	CT	E	860 230-0006	3447
Apco Products	Centerbrook	CT	E	860 767-2108	701
Armored Shield Technologies	Redding	CT	F	714 848-5796	3646
Arrow Manufacturing Company	Bristol	CT	E	860 589-3900	520
Bes Cu Inc	Bristol	CT	G	860 582-8660	533
Bridgeport Insulated Wire Co **(PA)**	Bridgeport	CT	E	203 333-3191	388
Bridgeport Insulated Wire Co	Stratford	CT	E	203 375-9579	4401
C O Jelliff Corporation **(PA)**	Southport	CT	D	203 259-1615	4094
ERA Wire Inc	West Haven	CT	F	203 933-0480	5121
Excel Spring & Stamping LLC	Bristol	CT	G	860 585-1495	559
Gemco Manufacturing Co Inc	Southington	CT	E	860 628-5529	4052
General Cable Industries Inc	Willimantic	CT	C	860 456-8000	5264
Habasit Abt Inc	Middletown	CT	C	860 632-2211	2188
Habasit America Inc	Middletown	CT	D	860 632-2211	2189
Hessel Industries Inc	Derby	CT	G	203 736-2317	1073
International Pipe & Stl Corp	North Branford	CT	F	203 481-7102	2969
Knox Enterprises Inc **(PA)**	Westport	CT	G	203 226-6408	5206
Meyer Wire & Cable Company LLC	Hamden	CT	E	203 281-0817	1771
Netsource Inc **(PA)**	Manchester	CT	D	860 649-6000	2025
Novo Precision LLC	Bristol	CT	E	860 583-0517	587
Nucor Steel Connecticut Inc	Wallingford	CT	C	203 265-0615	4780
Pauls Wire Rope & Sling Inc	Branford	CT	F	203 481-3469	335
Protopac Inc	Watertown	CT	G	860 274-6796	5020
Radcliff Wire Inc	Bristol	CT	E	312 876-1754	602
Redco Audio Inc	Stratford	CT	F	203 502-7600	4441
Rowley Spring & Stamping Corp	Bristol	CT	C	860 582-8175	610
Tiger Enterprises Inc	Plantsville	CT	E	860 621-9155	3542
U-Tech Wire Rope & Supply LLC	North Haven	CT	G	203 865-8885	3065
Ultimate Wireforms Inc	Bristol	CT	D	860 582-9111	621
Wiremold Company **(DH)**	West Hartford	CT	A	860 233-6251	5104
Alvin Johnson	East Longmeadow	MA	G	413 525-6334	10465
Atlee Delaware Incorporated	Melrose	MA	F	978 681-1003	12975
Automatic Specialties Inc	Marlborough	MA	E	508 481-2370	12724
Axiom Wire and Cable	Attleboro	MA	G	508 498-8899	7711
Briscon Electric Mfg Corp	Auburn	MA	F	508 832-3481	7830
Citiworks Corp	Attleboro	MA	F	508 761-7400	7720
Custom Convyrs Fabrication Inc	North Oxford	MA	F	508 922-0283	13971
Den Technologies Corp	Boylston	MA	E	401 263-7579	8979
Dolan-Jenner Industries Inc	Boxborough	MA	E	978 263-1400	8961
Electro-Prep Inc	Wareham	MA	F	508 291-2880	16246
Frank L Reed Inc	Wilbraham	MA	E	413 596-3861	16937
General Wire Products Inc	Worcester	MA	E	508 752-8260	17381
Innovive LLC	Billerica	MA	G	617 500-1691	8257
International Metal Pdts Inc	Chicopee	MA	E	413 532-2411	10033
Johnston Dandy Company	Holyoke	MA	F	413 315-4596	11635
Ketcham Supply Co Inc	New Bedford	MA	F	508 997-4787	13403
Lanoco Specialty Wire Pdts Inc	Sutton	MA	F	508 865-1500	15686
Merchants Metals LLC	Chicopee	MA	F	413 562-9981	10044
Micro Wire Products Inc	Brockton	MA	E	508 584-0200	9166
New England Wire Products Inc **(PA)**	Leominster	MA	C	800 254-9473	12171
New England Wirecloth Co LLC	Fitchburg	MA	G	978 343-4998	10844
O/K Machinery Corporation	Marlborough	MA	E	508 303-8286	12799
Polymetallurgical LLC	North Attleboro	MA	E	508 695-9312	13773
Profiles Incorporated	Palmer	MA	E	413 283-7790	14294

S I C

	CITY	ST	EMP	PHONE	ENTRY #
Quirk Wire Co Inc	West Brookfield	MA	E	508 867-3155	16473
Riverdale Mills Corporation	Northbridge	MA	C	508 234-8715	14060
S&S Industries Inc **(PA)**	Stoughton	MA	F	914 885-1500	15619
Saint-Gobain Prfmce Plas Corp	Worcester	MA	E	508 852-3072	17467
St Pierre Manufacturing Corp	Worcester	MA	E	508 853-8010	17479
US Tsubaki Automotive LLC	Westfield	MA	F	413 593-1100	16738
US Tsubaki Automotive LLC **(DH)**	Chicopee	MA	C	413 593-1100	10067
Viamed Corp	South Easton	MA	F	508 238-0220	15294
W D C Holdings Inc	Attleboro	MA	D	508 699-4412	7806
Whitney & Son Inc	Fitchburg	MA	E	978 343-6353	10863
Winchester Interconnect Corp	Franklin	MA	F	978 717-2543	11098
Wireway/Husky Corp	Sterling	MA	E	978 422-6716	15550
Worcester Manufacturing Inc	Worcester	MA	E	508 756-0301	17505
Wright G F Steel & Wire Co	Worcester	MA	E	508 363-2718	17509
Bartletts Bench and Wire Inc **(PA)**	Friendship	ME	G	207 354-0138	6092
Downeast Fishing Gear Inc	Trenton	ME	E	207 667-3131	7097
Downeast Wire Trap Company	Jonesboro	ME	G	207 434-5791	6224
Eaton Trap Co Inc	Woolwich	ME	G	207 443-3617	7289
Ftc Inc **(PA)**	Friendship	ME	E	207 354-2545	6093
Maine Cleaners Supply Inc	North Yarmouth	ME	G	207 657-3166	6517
Scott-Lynn Mfg	Auburn	ME	G	207 784-3372	5598
Albany International Corp **(PA)**	Rochester	NH	D	603 330-5850	19655
Amphenol Corporation	Nashua	NH	B	603 879-3000	19114
Centroid Wire and Cable LLC	Bow	NH	G	603 227-0900	17709
Continental Cable LLC	Hinsdale	NH	D	800 229-5131	18319
Elektrisola Incorporated **(PA)**	Boscawen	NH	C	603 796-2114	17703
Felton Inc	Londonderry	NH	D	603 425-0200	18697
General Cable Industries Inc	Manchester	NH	C	603 668-1620	18825
Guidewire Technologies Inc	Salem	NH	E	603 894-4399	19740
Hale Brothers Inc	Seabrook	NH	G	603 474-2511	19802
Plasti-Clip Corporation	Milford	NH	F	603 672-1166	19072
Wire Belt Company of America **(PA)**	Londonderry	NH	D	603 644-2500	18745
ACS Industries Inc **(PA)**	Lincoln	RI	E	401 769-4700	20552
Alloy Holdings LLC	Providence	RI	E	401 353-7500	20951
Ametek Scp Inc **(HQ)**	Westerly	RI	D	401 596-6658	21515
Ammeraal Beltech Inc	Warwick	RI	G	401 732-8131	21322
Electro Standards Lab Inc	Cranston	RI	D	401 946-1390	20215
Ferguson Perforating Company **(DH)**	Providence	RI	D	401 941-8876	21013
Hindley Manufacturing Co Inc	Cumberland	RI	D	401 722-2550	20325
HK Chain Usa Inc	Wakefield	RI	G	401 782-0402	21272
LDB Tool and Findings Inc	Cranston	RI	G	401 944-6000	20252
Neptco Incorporated **(HQ)**	Pawtucket	RI	D	401 722-5500	20863
Pep Central Inc	Warwick	RI	A	401 732-3770	21402
Perry Blackburne Inc	North Providence	RI	E	401 231-7200	20771
Qbm New York Inc	Providence	RI	F	716 821-1475	21102
Royal Diversified Products	Warren	RI	D	401 245-6900	21304
Standard Chain Co	Warwick	RI	E	508 695-6611	21429
Astenjohnson Inc	Williston	VT	D	802 658-2040	22655
Brass Butterfly Inc	Poultney	VT	G	802 287-9818	22270
George L Martin	Brattleboro	VT	G	802 254-5838	21729
Macryan Inc	Poultney	VT	G	802 287-4788	22273
Vermont Wireform Inc	Chelsea	VT	F	802 889-3200	21840

3497 Metal Foil & Leaf

	CITY	ST	EMP	PHONE	ENTRY #
Dexmet Corporation	Wallingford	CT	D	203 294-4440	4734
Foilmark Inc	Bloomfield	CT	F	860 243-0343	220
PPG Industries Inc	Wallingford	CT	D	203 294-4440	4785
Avery Dennison Corporation	Westborough	MA	C	508 948-3500	16591
Foilmark Inc **(HQ)**	Newburyport	MA	D	978 225-8200	13490
Hazen Paper Company **(PA)**	Holyoke	MA	C	413 538-8204	11631

3498 Fabricated Pipe & Pipe Fittings

	CITY	ST	EMP	PHONE	ENTRY #
Carli Farm & Equipment LLC	Salem	CT	G	860 908-3227	3737
Clear Water Manufacturing Corp **(PA)**	Wethersfield	CT	G	860 372-4907	5245
Creative Rack Solutions Inc	Waterbury	CT	G	203 755-2102	4861
Diba Industries Inc **(HQ)**	Danbury	CT	C	203 744-0773	901
EA Patten Co LLC	Manchester	CT	D	860 649-2851	2004
Farmington Mtal Fbrication LLC	Bristol	CT	G	860 404-7415	561
Harry Thommen Company	Bridgeport	CT	G	203 333-3637	424
JFd Tube & Coil Products Inc	Hamden	CT	E	203 288-6941	1763
L&P Aerospace Acquisition LLC	Middletown	CT	D	860 635-8811	2199
Long Island Pipe Supply Inc	Windsor	CT	G	860 688-1780	5345
Macristy Industries Inc **(PA)**	Newington	CT	C	860 225-4637	2879
Optinova Americas Inc	Danbury	CT	G	203 743-0908	964
Plastics and Concepts Conn Inc	Glastonbury	CT	F	860 657-9655	1572
Spencer Turbine Company **(HQ)**	Windsor	CT	C	860 688-8361	5363
Vas Integrated LLC	Berlin	CT	G	860 748-4058	116
Bergen Pipe Supports Inc **(HQ)**	Woburn	MA	E	781 935-9550	17130
Fiberspar Linepipe LLC	New Bedford	MA	G	281 854-2636	13385
L & R Manufacturing Co Inc	Worcester	MA	F	508 853-0562	17405
Lawrence Metal Forming Corp	Peabody	MA	F	978 535-1200	14351
Paterson Group Inc	Woburn	MA	C	781 935-7036	17258
Triangle Engineering Inc	Hanover	MA	F	781 878-1500	11356
Virginia Stainless	Taunton	MA	G	508 880-5498	15797
Virginia Stainless Div	Cambridge	MA	G	508 823-1747	9697
Worcester Manufacturing Inc	Worcester	MA	E	508 756-0301	17505
Wardwell Piping Inc	Windham	ME	F	207 892-0034	7259
Anvil International LLC **(HQ)**	Exeter	NH	E	603 418-2800	18110
Long Island Pipe Supply NH Inc	Salem	NH	F	603 685-3200	19748
Micro Bends Corp	Peterborough	NH	G	603 924-0022	19476
Micro Weld Fabtec Corp	Windham	NH	G	603 234-6531	20009
New England Small Tube Corp	Litchfield	NH	D	603 429-1600	18652
Queen City Sounds Inc	Manchester	NH	G	603 668-4306	18908
Smiths Tblar Systms-Lconia Inc	Laconia	NH	B	603 524-2064	18587
Trellborg Pipe Sals Mlford Inc **(DH)**	Milford	NH	C	800 626-2180	19080
Anvil International LLC	North Kingstown	RI	C	401 886-3000	20691
ATW Companies Inc **(PA)**	Warwick	RI	D	401 244-1002	21330
Maley Laser Processing Inc	Warwick	RI	F	401 732-8400	21386
Osram Sylvania Inc	Central Falls	RI	B	401 723-1378	20122
Tubodyne Company	Riverside	RI	G	401 438-2540	21177
L & B Associates Inc	Saint Albans	VT	G	802 868-5210	22371
Raymond Gadues Inc	Swanton	VT	E	802 868-2033	22536

3499 Fabricated Metal Prdts, NEC

	CITY	ST	EMP	PHONE	ENTRY #
Airpot Corporation	Norwalk	CT	E	800 848-7681	3097
Aptargroup Inc	Stratford	CT	B	203 377-8100	4391
Beta Shim Co	Shelton	CT	E	203 926-1150	3781
Concord Industries Inc	Norwalk	CT	E	203 750-6060	3131
Dcg-Pmi Inc	Bethel	CT	E	203 743-5525	142
Farmington Engineering Inc	North Haven	CT	G	800 428-7584	3027
Greco Industries Inc	Bethel	CT	G	203 798-7804	156
H G Steinmetz Machine Works	Bethel	CT	F	203 794-1880	158
Independent Metalworx Inc	Ansonia	CT	G	203 520-4089	19
J OConnor LLC	Newington	CT	F	860 665-7702	2873
K-Tech International	Torrington	CT	E	860 489-9399	4584
M & B Enterprise LLC	Derby	CT	F	203 298-9781	1075
Nel Group LLC	Windsor	CT	F	860 683-0190	5350
Oxford General Industries Inc	Prospect	CT	F	203 758-4467	3590
Performance Connection Systems	Meriden	CT	G	203 868-5517	2116
Royal Welding LLC	Hartford	CT	G	860 232-5255	1867
Specialty Metals and Fab	Naugatuck	CT	G	203 509-5028	2496
Spirol International Corp **(HQ)**	Danielson	CT	C	860 774-8571	1018
Spirol Intl Holdg Corp **(PA)**	Danielson	CT	C	860 774-8571	1019
Torqmaster Inc	Stamford	CT	E	203 326-5945	4347
Yarde Metals Inc **(HQ)**	Southington	CT	B	860 406-6061	4092
A B Metal Fabricators	Lakeville	MA	G	508 947-5577	11969
Alliance Sheet Metal	Avon	MA	G	508 587-0314	7875
Alloy Fabricators of Neng	Randolph	MA	F	781 986-6400	14670
Aster Enterprises Inc	Acton	MA	G	978 264-0499	7343
B & J Manufacturing Corp	Taunton	MA	D	508 822-1990	15730
Benjamin Martin Corp	Dedham	MA	F	781 326-8311	10281
Bete Fog Nozzle Inc **(PA)**	Greenfield	MA	C	413 772-0846	11252
Bolger Products	Barre	MA	G	978 355-2226	7949
Boston America Corp	Woburn	MA	F	781 933-3535	17135
Capstan Atlantic	Wrentham	MA	C	508 384-3100	17517
Compass Company	Acton	MA	G	978 635-0303	7348
Conference Medal & Trophy Co	Buzzards Bay	MA	F	508 563-3600	9359
Dans Machine	Easthampton	MA	G	413 529-9635	10559
George Guertin Trophy Inc	Auburn	MA	G	508 832-4001	7836
Hampden Fence Supply Inc	Agawam	MA	F	413 786-4390	7430
Idemia America Corp **(DH)**	Billerica	MA	B	978 215-2400	8255
Jaco Inc	Franklin	MA	C	508 553-1000	11056
JH Smith Co Inc **(PA)**	Greenfield	MA	F	413 772-0191	11264
Lockheed Martin Sippican Inc **(HQ)**	Marion	MA	B	508 748-3399	12699
Malden Intl Designs Inc	Middleboro	MA	D	508 946-2270	13067
Noyes Sheet Metal	Milford	MA	F	508 482-9302	13134
October Company Inc **(PA)**	Easthampton	MA	C	413 527-9380	10572
October Company Inc	Easthampton	MA	E	413 529-0718	10573
Patriot Coatings Inc	Hudson	MA	G	978 567-9006	11800
Payne Engrg Fabrication Co Inc	Canton	MA	E	781 828-9046	9765
Plansee USA LLC **(DH)**	Franklin	MA	D	508 553-3800	11071
Pleasant Street Designs Inc	Methuen	MA	G	978 682-3910	13042
Production Basics Inc	Billerica	MA	E	617 926-8100	8278
Robert Emmet Company Inc	New Bedford	MA	G	508 997-2651	13446
Sabr Enterprises LLC	Acton	MA	G	978 264-0499	7382
Spoontiques Inc	Stoughton	MA	D	781 344-9530	15622
St Pierre Manufacturing Corp	Worcester	MA	E	508 853-8010	17479
V & G Iron Works Inc	Tewksbury	MA	F	978 851-9191	15846
Veloxint Corporation	Framingham	MA	E	774 777-3369	11010
VH Blackinton & Co Inc	Attleboro Falls	MA	C	508 699-4436	7818
Viking Corporation	Mansfield	MA	G	508 594-1800	12669
William McCaskie Inc	Westport	MA	G	508 636-8845	16852
Cynthia Carroll Pallian	Wells	ME	G	207 646-1600	7160
Elmet Technologies LLC	Lewiston	ME	C	207 333-6100	6287
Minuteman Metal LLC	Wilton	ME	G	207 217-8908	7226
Saunders Mfg Co Inc **(PA)**	Readfield	ME	D	207 685-9860	6778
Harmony Metal Products North	Portsmouth	NH	E	603 536-6012	19573
Holase Incorporated	Portsmouth	NH	G	603 397-0038	19575
Locked In Steel	Hudson	NH	G	603 233-8299	18365
Spraying Systems Co	Merrimack	NH	E	603 517-1854	19033
Spraying Systems Co	Bedford	NH	F	603 471-0505	17664
Summit Packaging Systems Inc **(PA)**	Manchester	NH	B	603 669-5410	18932
Three Night Delivery Inc	Pelham	NH	G	603 595-6230	19450
Ahlers Designs Inc	Pawtucket	RI	G	401 365-1010	20811

	CITY	ST	EMP	PHONE	ENTRY #
American Bookend Company LLC	Narragansett	RI	G	401 932-2700	20633
American Trophy & Supply Co	East Providence	RI	G	401 438-3060	20386
Artvac Corporation	Lincoln	RI	E	401 333-6120	20557
Aspects Inc	Warren	RI	E	401 247-1854	21286
Barlow Designs Inc	East Providence	RI	G	401 438-7925	20390
Capco Steel Erection Company	Providence	RI	F	401 383-9388	20979
Case Future Corporation Inc	Johnston	RI	E	401 944-0402	20503
Cathedral Art Metal Co Inc	Providence	RI	E	401 273-7200	20981
Fulford Manufacturing Company **(PA)**	Riverside	RI	F	401 431-2000	21168
Jewel Case Corporation	Providence	RI	B	401 943-1400	21044
Josef Creations Inc **(PA)**	Chepachet	RI	E	401 421-4198	20135
Kenney Manufacturing Company **(PA)**	Warwick	RI	B	401 739-2200	21383
Whetstone Workshop LLC	East Providence	RI	G	401 368-7410	20449
World Trophies Company Inc	Providence	RI	E	401 272-5846	21157
Bb Metal Fabrication Inc	Fair Haven	VT	G	802 265-8375	21965
Carris Financial Corp **(PA)**	Proctor	VT	F	802 773-9111	22283
Carris Reels Inc **(HQ)**	Proctor	VT	C	802 773-9111	22284
Champlain Precision Inc **(PA)**	New Haven	VT	G	802 453-7225	22184
Custom Mtal Fabricators VT LLC	Hyde Park	VT	G	802 888-0033	22035
Hex Design Inc **(PA)**	Bennington	VT	G	802 442-3309	21672
Moscow Mills Inc	Barre	VT	G	802 253-2036	21630
S & A Trombley Corporation	Morrisville	VT	E	802 888-2394	22176
Vermont Awards and Engrv Inc	Colchester	VT	G	802 862-3000	21884

35 INDUSTRIAL AND COMMERCIAL MACHINERY AND COMPUTER EQUIPMENT

3511 Steam, Gas & Hydraulic Turbines & Engines

	CITY	ST	EMP	PHONE	ENTRY #
American Metal Masters LLC	Plantsville	CT	G	860 621-6911	3526
Asea Brown Boveri Inc **(DH)**	Norwalk	CT	G	203 750-2200	3105
Becon Incorporated **(PA)**	Bloomfield	CT	D	860 243-1428	208
Blastech Overhaul & Repair	Bloomfield	CT	F	860 243-8811	210
Doncasters Inc **(HQ)**	Groton	CT	D	860 449-1603	1671
GE Engine Svcs UNC Holdg I Inc	New Haven	CT	G	518 380-0767	2689
GE Transportation Parts LLC	Fairfield	CT	G	816 650-6171	1435
Pequot	Bridgeport	CT	G	800 620-1492	466
Pw Power Systems LLC **(HQ)**	Glastonbury	CT	D	860 368-5900	1576
Aeronautica Windpower LLC	Plymouth	MA	E	508 732-8945	14539
Altaeros Energies Inc	Somerville	MA	G	617 908-8464	15153
Camar Corp	Northborough	MA	F	508 845-9263	14030
Ethosenergy Tc Inc	Chicopee	MA	C	413 593-0500	10024
Ethosenergy Tc Inc **(DH)**	Chicopee	MA	C	802 257-2721	10025
Ethosenergy Tc Inc	Leominster	MA	F	978 353-3089	12135
Free Flow Power Corporation	Boston	MA	E	978 283-2822	8553
GE Energy Parts Intl LLC **(HQ)**	Boston	MA	G	617 443-3000	8557
General Electric Company **(PA)**	Boston	MA	A	617 443-3000	8558
General Electric Company	Westborough	MA	F	508 870-5200	16619
Jet Industries Inc	Agawam	MA	E	413 786-2010	7435
Kingston Wind Independence LLC	East Weymouth	MA	G	781 871-8200	10544
Knm Holdings LLC	Marlborough	MA	G	508 229-1400	12783
LKM Industries Inc	Woburn	MA	D	781 935-9210	17216
Mavel Americas Inc	Boston	MA	G	617 242-2204	8689
Northast Renewable Enrgy Group	Boston	MA	G	617 878-2063	8742
Orsted North America Inc	Boston	MA	G	857 284-1430	8760
Pivotal Aero Wind Turbines Inc	Weymouth	MA	G	781 803-2982	16897
Riley Power Inc	Marlborough	MA	C	508 852-7100	12817
Trireme Manufacturing Co Inc	Topsfield	MA	E	978 887-2132	15867
Windstream Enrgy Solutions LLC	Woburn	MA	G	781 333-5450	17322
Flexor Energy Company	Orono	ME	G	207 866-3527	6554
General Electric Company	Bangor	ME	B	207 941-2500	5648
Machining Innovations Inc	Oakland	ME	G	207 465-2500	6534
Peregrine Turbine Tech LLC	Wiscasset	ME	F	207 687-8333	7286
Pika Energy Inc	Westbrook	ME	F	207 887-9105	7202
PJ Schwalbenberg & Assoc	Cushing	ME	G	207 354-0700	5934
Steam Turbine Services	North Yarmouth	ME	G	207 272-8664	6519
Energy Resources Group Inc **(PA)**	Farmington	NH	E	603 335-2535	18141
Flexenergy Inc	Portsmouth	NH	D	603 430-7000	19563
Flexenergy Holdings LLC **(PA)**	Portsmouth	NH	D	603 430-7000	19564
Malagar Group LLC	Stratham	NH	G	603 778-1372	19873
Steam Turbine 4 U	Hudson	NH	G	603 465-8881	18441
Airgas Usa LLC	East Greenwich	RI	G	401 884-0201	20351
Vientek LLC **(PA)**	Warren	RI	A	915 225-1309	21312
Green Mountain Fly Wheeler	Montpelier	VT	G	802 223-1595	22148
Northern Power Systems Inc **(HQ)**	Barre	VT	D	802 461-2955	21631
Northern Power Systems Corp **(PA)**	Barre	VT	E	802 461-2955	21632
Renew Energy	Milton	VT	G	802 891-6774	22137
Sperry Valve Inc	East Arlington	VT	G	802 375-6703	21910
Village Industrial Power Inc	Bradford	VT	F	802 522-8584	21706

3519 Internal Combustion Engines, NEC

	CITY	ST	EMP	PHONE	ENTRY #
American Unmanned Systems LLC	Stamford	CT	G	203 406-7611	4136
Bell Power Systems LLC	Essex	CT	D	860 767-7502	1393
CAM Group LLC	Manchester	CT	F	860 646-2378	1990
Jacobs Vehicle Systems Inc	Bloomfield	CT	B	860 243-5222	227
Kco Numet Inc	Orange	CT	F	203 375-4995	3367
Liquidpiston Inc	Bloomfield	CT	F	860 838-2677	241
Smith Hill of Delaware Inc	Essex	CT	E	860 767-7502	1405
Andy Collazzo	Danvers	MA	G	978 539-8962	10194
Cummins Inc	Springfield	MA	G	413 737-2659	15464
Cummins Northeast LLC	Dedham	MA	G	781 329-1750	10285
Growth I M33 L P	Boston	MA	E	617 877-0046	8584
Salem Preferred Partners LLC **(PA)**	Boston	MA	C	540 389-3922	8833
Westerbeke Corporation **(PA)**	Taunton	MA	E	508 977-4273	15799
Westerbeke Corporation	Avon	MA	E	508 823-7677	7902
Casco Bay Diesel LLC	Portland	ME	G	207 878-9377	6633
Melton Sales and Service Inc	Hallowell	ME	F	207 623-8895	6163
Vitaminsea LLC	Buxton	ME	G	207 671-0955	5863
Davis Village Solutions LLC	New Ipswich	NH	G	603 878-3662	19304

3523 Farm Machinery & Eqpt

	CITY	ST	EMP	PHONE	ENTRY #
Comex Machinery	Bridgeport	CT	G	203 334-2196	399
Engineering Services & Pdts Co **(PA)**	South Windsor	CT	D	860 528-1119	3965
Hayden Manufacturing Co Inc	West Wareham	MA	G	508 295-0497	16574
Oesco Inc	Conway	MA	E	413 369-4335	10164
Pressure Techniques Intl Corp	Haverhill	MA	G	978 686-2211	11460
Rf Biocidics Inc	Boston	MA	G	617 419-1800	8819
Scituate Caseworks Inc	Scituate	MA	G	781 534-4167	15012
US Discount Products LLC	West Bridgewater	MA	G	877 841-5782	16462
Dale A Thomas and Sons Inc	Brooks	ME	G	207 722-3505	5823
Harold Haines Inc	Presque Isle	ME	F	207 762-1411	6758
Hubbard Rake Co	Jonesport	ME	G	207 497-5949	6226
Innovasea Systems Inc	Morrill	ME	G	207 322-3219	6454
Maine Blueberry Equipment Co	Columbia	ME	G	207 483-4156	5918
Ocean Farm Technologies Inc	Morrill	ME	G	207 322-4322	6456
AGCO Corporation	Charlestown	NH	G	603 826-4664	17809
American Calan Inc	Northwood	NH	G	603 942-7711	19410
CPM Acquisition Corp	Merrimack	NH	E	319 232-8444	18994
CPM Acquisition Corp	Merrimack	NH	E	603 423-6300	18995
Hutchinson Machine	Atkinson	NH	G	603 329-9545	17604
Larchmont Engineering Inc	Manchester	NH	G	603 622-8825	18860
Siteone Landscape Supply LLC	Londonderry	NH	G	603 425-2572	18737
Spray Foam Distrs Neng Inc	Woodstock	NH	E	603 745-3911	20029
Coastal Aquacultural Supply	Cranston	RI	G	401 467-9370	20197
Grassroots of New England	Cumberland	RI	G	401 333-1963	20323
Feed Commodities Intl Inc	Newport	VT	G	802 334-2942	22197
Heritage Post & Beam	Barre	VT	F	802 223-6319	21621
Leader Evaporator Co Inc **(PA)**	Swanton	VT	D	802 868-5444	22531
Leader Evaporatorinc	Rutland	VT	E	802 775-5411	22343
Vermont Farm Table LLC **(PA)**	Burlington	VT	G	888 425-8838	21815

3524 Garden, Lawn Tractors & Eqpt

	CITY	ST	EMP	PHONE	ENTRY #
Greenscape of Clinton LLC	Clinton	CT	G	860 669-1880	787
Woodland Power Products Inc	West Haven	CT	E	888 531-7253	5152
Armatron International Inc **(PA)**	Malden	MA	D	781 321-2300	12559
Lps Enterprises Inc	East Freetown	MA	E	508 763-3830	10455
R I Baker Co Inc **(PA)**	Clarksburg	MA	E	413 663-3791	10075
Douglas Dynamics LLC	Rockland	ME	C	207 701-4200	6790
Eastman Industries **(PA)**	Portland	ME	E	207 878-5353	6658
Eschdale Lawn & Grdn Pdts LLC	Smyrna Mills	ME	G	207 757-7268	6991
Genest Landscape Masonry	Windham	ME	G	207 892-3778	7235
Machining Innovations Inc	Oakland	ME	G	207 465-2500	6534
Maine Barrel & Display Company	Lewiston	ME	E	207 784-6700	6303
Oldcastle Lawn & Garden Inc	Poland	ME	E	207 998-5580	6595
North Country Tractor Inc	Dover	NH	F	603 742-5488	18041
Little House By Andre Inc	Colchester	VT	G	802 878-8733	21872
Vermont Ware Inc	St George	VT	G	802 482-4426	22514
Zoneup Inc	Saint Albans	VT	G	802 868-2300	22385

3531 Construction Machinery & Eqpt

	CITY	ST	EMP	PHONE	ENTRY #
A & K Railroad Materials Inc	Hamden	CT	G	203 495-8790	1728
Bagela Usa LLC	Shelton	CT	G	203 944-0525	3777
Bay Crane Service Conn Inc	North Haven	CT	G	203 785-8000	3010
Calvin Brown	Gales Ferry	CT	G	860 536-6178	1526
Capewell Aerial Systems LLC **(PA)**	South Windsor	CT	D	860 610-0700	3947
Conair Corporation	Torrington	CT	D	800 492-7464	4572
Daves Paving and Construction	Prospect	CT	G	203 753-4992	3587
Dp Marine LLC	Riverside	CT	G	917 705-7435	3690
Ezflow Limited Partnership **(DH)**	Old Saybrook	CT	E	860 577-7064	3334
H Barber & Sons Inc	Naugatuck	CT	E	203 729-9000	2476
Indeco North America Inc	Milford	CT	E	203 713-1030	2302
LH Gault & Son Incorporated	Westport	CT	D	203 227-5181	5209
Maretron LLP	Plainville	CT	F	602 861-1707	3503
Metal Plus LLC	Winsted	CT	G	860 379-1327	5416
Michele Schiano Di Cola Inc	Wallingford	CT	G	203 265-5301	4773
Naiad Dynamics Us Inc **(HQ)**	Shelton	CT	E	203 929-6355	3836
Numa Tool Company **(PA)**	Thompson	CT	D	860 923-9551	4537
Rawson Manufacturing Inc **(PA)**	Putnam	CT	F	860 928-4458	3630
Show Motion Inc	Milford	CT	E	203 866-1866	2362
Spray Foam Outlets LLC	Norwalk	CT	E	631 291-9355	3249
Steelwrist Inc	Berlin	CT	G	225 936-1111	111
Terex Corporation **(PA)**	Westport	CT	F	203 222-7170	5233
Terex Utilities Inc	Hartford	CT	G	860 436-3700	1877
Tinsley GROup-Ps&w Inc **(HQ)**	Milford	CT	D	919 742-5832	2376

	CITY	ST	EMP	PHONE	ENTRY #
Town of Wilton	Wilton	CT	G	203 563-0152	5308
Ace Torwel Inc **(HQ)**	Framingham	MA	F	888 878-0898	10916
Altec Northeast LLC	Sterling	MA	F	508 320-9041	15533
American Crane and Hoist Corp	Boston	MA	C	617 482-8383	8360
Bertram & Leithner Inc	Lowell	MA	G	978 459-7474	12353
Bonsal American Inc	Oxford	MA	E	508 987-8188	14254
Boston and Maine Corporation **(HQ)**	North Billerica	MA	C	978 663-1130	13797
Caya Construction Co	Northbridge	MA	G	508 234-5082	14054
Ecochlor Inc	Acton	MA	G	978 263-5478	7352
Gckm Machines	Newton	MA	G	617 584-6266	13594
Ghm Industries Inc **(PA)**	Charlton	MA	F	508 248-3941	9850
Hancock Marine Inc	Fall River	MA	G	508 678-0301	10712
Hercules Slr (us) Inc **(PA)**	New Bedford	MA	F	508 993-0010	13394
Hydroid Inc **(PA)**	Pocasset	MA	C	508 563-6565	14596
Industrial Stl Boiler Svcs Inc	Chicopee	MA	E	413 532-7788	10032
JP Obelisk Inc	Bridgewater	MA	G	508 942-6248	9079
Leading Edge Attachments Inc **(PA)**	Jefferson	MA	G	508 829-4855	11954
Lewicki & Sons Excavating Inc	Plainville	MA	G	508 695-0122	14526
Louie and Teds Blacktop Inc	Swansea	MA	F	508 678-4948	15707
Metal Solutions LLC	Millbury	MA	G	774 276-0096	13171
Omg Inc	Agawam	MA	C	413 786-0516	7444
Omg Inc **(DH)**	Agawam	MA	B	413 789-0252	7443
PJ Keating Company	Acushnet	MA	G	508 992-3542	7405
Prazi USA Inc	Plymouth	MA	G	508 747-1490	14577
Rockland Equipment Company LLC	Rockland	MA	F	781 871-4400	14822
Rugg Manufacturing Company Inc	Leominster	MA	F	413 773-5471	12185
Santa Rosa Lead Products LLC	Holliston	MA	F	508 893-6021	11600
Sea Sciences Inc	Arlington	MA	G	781 643-1600	7637
Shemin Nurseries Inc	Lexington	MA	F	781 861-1111	12266
Statiflo International Ltd	Pittsfield	MA	G	413 684-9911	14509
Stoughton Steel Company Inc	Hanover	MA	E	781 826-6496	11354
Straightline Excavation Corp	Tewksbury	MA	G	978 858-0800	15839
Town of Brimfield	Brimfield	MA	G	413 245-4103	9111
US Discount Products LLC	West Bridgewater	MA	G	877 841-5782	16462
Valente Backhoe Service LLC	Shrewsbury	MA	G	508 754-7013	15134
Vulcan Company Inc **(PA)**	Hingham	MA	D	781 337-5970	11515
Williams Sign Erection Inc	Wilmington	MA	G	978 658-3787	17066
Advanced Concepts & Engrg LLC	Dexter	ME	G	207 270-3025	5955
County Concrete & Cnstr Co	Columbia Falls	ME	E	207 483-4409	5919
Douglas Dynamics LLC	Rockland	ME	C	207 701-4200	6790
Evergreen Landscaping Inc	Berwick	ME	G	207 451-5007	5709
Howard P Fairfield LLC **(DH)**	Skowhegan	ME	E	207 474-9836	6976
Kennebec Marine Company	Scarborough	ME	G	207 773-0392	6929
Kevin Call	Levant	ME	G	207 884-7786	6271
Maine Dock & Dredge LLC	Woolwich	ME	G	207 660-5577	7290
Marine Hydraulic Engrg Co **(PA)**	Rockland	ME	G	207 594-9525	6803
North E Wldg & Fabrication Inc	Auburn	ME	E	207 786-2446	5583
Portage Lkers Snwmbile CLB Inc	Portage	ME	F	207 415-0506	6599
Somatex Inc	Detroit	ME	E	207 487-6141	5953
Admix Inc	Londonderry	NH	E	603 627-2340	18671
Advanced Concrete Tech Inc-NH	Greenland	NH	G	603 431-5661	18219
All American Walls and Pavers	Concord	NH	G	603 219-0822	17882
Bolstridge Logging LLC	New Durham	NH	G	603 859-8241	19300
Davis Village Solutions LLC	New Ipswich	NH	G	603 878-3662	19304
J C B Leasing Inc	Weare	NH	D	603 529-7974	19934
J J Plank Corporation	Farmington	NH	G	920 733-4479	18143
Max Roads LLC	Raymond	NH	G	603 895-5200	19640
Tel -Tuk Enterprises LLC	Belmont	NH	G	603 267-1966	17685
Trellborg Pipe Sals Mlford Inc **(DH)**	Milford	NH	C	800 626-2180	19080
Tri-State Mfg Solutions LLC	Nottingham	NH	G	508 769-2891	19417
Dig Rite Company Inc	Cranston	RI	G	401 862-5895	20211
Hudson Terminal Corp **(PA)**	Providence	RI	F	401 274-2200	21033
Hudson Terminal Corp	Cranston	RI	G	401 941-0500	20239
Vibco Inc **(PA)**	Wyoming	RI	D	401 539-2392	21591
Blue Ox Enterprise Inc	Saint Johnsbury	VT	G	802 274-4494	22387
Built Rite Manufacturing Inc	Ludlow	VT	F	802 228-7293	22061
Champlain Construction Co Inc	Middlebury	VT	F	802 388-2652	22108
Howard P Fairfield LLC	Morrisville	VT	G	802 888-2092	22170
Jason Patenaude Excavating Inc	Derby	VT	G	802 766-4567	21900
Ordway Electric & Machine	Graniteville	VT	G	802 476-8011	22001
Rebtek Diamnd Blades Bits LLC	Barre	VT	G	802 476-6520	21637
Vermont Eco Floors	Charlotte	VT	G	802 425-7737	21835
Wintersteiger Inc	Waitsfield	VT	G	802 496-6166	22571
Wood Dynamics Corporation **(PA)**	South Pomfret	VT	G	802 457-3970	22489

3532 Mining Machinery & Eqpt

	CITY	ST	EMP	PHONE	ENTRY #
Numa Tool Company **(PA)**	Thompson	CT	D	860 923-9551	4537
P2 Science Inc	Woodbridge	CT	G	203 821-7457	5475
Powerscreen Connecticut Inc	South Windsor	CT	F	860 627-6596	4003
Terex Usa LLC **(HQ)**	Westport	CT	B	203 222-7170	5234
Eldred Wheeler Company	Hanover	MA	G	781 924-5067	11336
Northeast Pellets LLC	Ashland	ME	F	207 435-6230	5538
R S Pidacks Inc	Livermore	ME	G	207 897-4622	6376
Oldenburg Group Inc	Claremont	NH	C	603 542-9548	17856
Oldenburg Group Incorporated	Claremont	NH	E	603 542-9548	17857
Joseph A Thomas Ltd	Bristol	RI	F	401 253-1330	20086

3533 Oil Field Machinery & Eqpt

	CITY	ST	EMP	PHONE	ENTRY #
Numa Tool Company **(PA)**	Thompson	CT	D	860 923-9551	4537
Oil Purification Systems Inc	Waterbury	CT	F	203 346-1800	4932
General Electric Company **(PA)**	Boston	MA	A	617 443-3000	8558
Kyle Equipment Co Inc	Sterling	MA	G	978 422-8448	15541
Rmi Titanium Company LLC	Burlington	MA	F	781 272-5967	9330
S Kyle Equipment Llc	Sterling	MA	G	978 422-8448	15543
Deepwater Buoyancy Inc	Biddeford	ME	F	207 468-2565	5728
Shannon Drilling	Machias	ME	G	207 255-6149	6395
Northeast Drill Supply	Greenville	NH	G	603 878-0998	18228

3534 Elevators & Moving Stairways

	CITY	ST	EMP	PHONE	ENTRY #
Ascend Elevator Inc	Bloomfield	CT	C	215 703-0358	205
International Elevator Corp	Cos Cob	CT	G	203 302-1023	826
K-Tech International	Torrington	CT	E	860 489-9399	4584
Otis Elevator Company **(HQ)**	Farmington	CT	B	860 674-3000	1503
Otis Elevator Company	Farmington	CT	G	860 290-3318	1504
United Technologies Corp	East Granby	CT	F	860 292-3270	1146
United Technologies Corp **(PA)**	Farmington	CT	B	860 728-7000	1522
Bay State Elevator Company Inc **(PA)**	Agawam	MA	E	413 786-7000	7421
Draper Metal Fabrication Inc	Holbrook	MA	G	781 961-3146	11524
Eab Testing Inc	Salem	MA	G	978 548-7626	14908
Hamilton Elevator Interiors	Saugus	MA	F	781 233-9540	14984
Armanni Usa Inc	Windham	ME	G	207 893-0557	7229

3535 Conveyors & Eqpt

	CITY	ST	EMP	PHONE	ENTRY #
Affordable Conveyors Svcs LLC	Bristol	CT	F	860 582-1800	516
Alvest (usa) Inc **(HQ)**	Windsor	CT	E	860 602-3400	5320
CT Conveyor LLC	Bristol	CT	G	860 637-2926	545
Goldslager Conveyor Company	Hamden	CT	G	203 795-9886	1751
International Robotics Inc	Stamford	CT	F	914 630-1060	4228
National Conveyors Company Inc	East Granby	CT	E	860 653-0374	1135
Production Equipment Company	Meriden	CT	E	800 758-5697	2118
R & I Manufacturing Co	Terryville	CT	F	860 589-6364	4489
Roller Bearing Co Amer Inc	Middlebury	CT	E	203 758-8272	2157
Unimation	Bethel	CT	G	203 792-3412	186
Walker Magnetics Group Inc **(HQ)**	Windsor	CT	E	508 853-3232	5378
Z-Loda Systems Inc	Stamford	CT	G	203 359-2991	4364
Acorn Overhead Door	Quincy	MA	G	508 378-0441	14613
AMA Engineering Smartmove	Westport	MA	F	508 636-7740	16835
Anaconda Usa Inc	Natick	MA	F	800 285-5721	13234
Ascend Robotics LLC	Cambridge	MA	F	978 451-0170	9393
Ashworth Bros Inc **(PA)**	Fall River	MA	G	508 674-4693	10663
Barrett Technology Inc	Cambridge	MA	G	617 252-9000	9402
Belt Technologies Inc **(PA)**	Agawam	MA	E	413 786-9922	7422
Chelsea Industries Inc **(HQ)**	Newton	MA	G	617 232-6060	13578
Conveytrex LLC	Swansea	MA	G	508 812-4333	15704
Conviber Inc	Oxford	MA	G	724 274-6300	14257
Dg Marshall Associates Inc	Webster	MA	E	508 943-2394	16341
JR Grady Company LLC	North Chelmsford	MA	G	978 458-3662	13898
Kleenline LLC	Newburyport	MA	D	978 463-0827	13504
Luck Industrial Sales Inc	Watertown	MA	G	617 924-0728	16296
Magnemotion Inc	Devens	MA	D	978 757-9100	10323
Northeast Equipment Design Inc	Hingham	MA	E	781 740-0007	11508
Omtec Corp	Marlborough	MA	F	508 481-3322	12801
Precision Handling Devices **(PA)**	Westport	MA	F	508 679-5282	16845
Safe Conveyor Incorporated	Swansea	MA	G	774 688-9109	15714
Softbank Robotics America Inc	Boston	MA	E	617 986-6700	8851
TEC Engineering Corp	Oxford	MA	F	508 987-0231	14275
Eltec Industries Inc **(PA)**	Freeport	ME	G	207 541-9085	6077
Maine Barrel & Display Company	Lewiston	ME	E	207 784-6700	6303
Maine Conveyor Inc **(PA)**	Gorham	ME	G	207 854-5661	6118
Fabworx Solutions Inc	Concord	NH	G	603 224-9679	17901
Plastic Techniques Inc	Goffstown	NH	E	603 622-5570	18209
Action Conveyor Tech Inc	Smithfield	RI	F	401 722-2300	21207
Bmco Industries Inc	East Greenwich	RI	G	401 781-6884	20354
Nikotrack LLC	Portsmouth	RI	G	401 683-7525	20932
Orbetron LLC	Cumberland	RI	G	651 983-2872	20337
Bindery Solutions Inc **(PA)**	Grand Isle	VT	G	802 372-3492	21997

3536 Hoists, Cranes & Monorails

	CITY	ST	EMP	PHONE	ENTRY #
Production Equipment Company	Meriden	CT	E	800 758-5697	2118
Altec Northeast LLC	Sterling	MA	F	508 320-9041	15533
American Crane and Hoist Corp	Boston	MA	C	617 482-8383	8360
Capco Crane & Hoist Inc	Rowley	MA	E	978 948-2998	14847
Dearborn Crane and Engrg Co	Woburn	MA	G	781 897-4100	17166
Konecranes Inc	Chelmsford	MA	F	978 256-5525	9910
New England Crane Inc	Tyngsboro	MA	G	207 782-7353	15897
St Pierre Manufacturing Corp	Worcester	MA	E	508 853-8010	17479
Central Maine Crane Inc	Oakland	ME	G	207 465-2229	6530
Somatex Inc	Detroit	ME	E	207 487-6141	5953
Thermopol Inc	Somersworth	NH	F	603 692-6300	19850

3537 Indl Trucks, Tractors, Trailers & Stackers

	CITY	ST	EMP	PHONE	ENTRY #
Dri-Air Industries Inc	East Windsor	CT	E	860 627-5110	1282
Macton Corporation	Oxford	CT	D	203 267-1500	3413

	CITY	ST	EMP	PHONE	ENTRY #
New Haven Companies Inc	East Haven	CT	F	203 469-6421	1257
Power Cover Usa LLC	Waterbury	CT	G	203 755-2687	4942
Terex Corporation **(PA)**	Westport	CT	F	203 222-7170	5233
Truth Trckg Expedited Svcs LLC	Hartford	CT	G	860 306-5630	1882
Ada Fabricators Inc	Wilmington	MA	E	978 262-9900	16965
Brownell Boat Stands Inc	Mattapoisett	MA	F	508 758-3671	12885
Crown Equipment Corporation	Woburn	MA	D	781 933-3366	17155
Entwistle Company **(HQ)**	Hudson	MA	C	508 481-4000	11772
Greenwood Emrgncy Vehicles LLC **(HQ)**	North Attleboro	MA	D	508 695-7138	13758
Hostar Mar Trnspt Systems Inc	Wareham	MA	E	508 295-2900	16250
Ite LLC	Brockton	MA	E	508 313-5600	9156
Precision Handling Devices **(PA)**	Westport	MA	F	508 679-5282	16845
Stedt Hydraulic Crane Corp	Westborough	MA	F	508 366-9151	16651
Steele Canvas Basket Corp	Chelsea	MA	E	800 541-8929	9970
Truck Buyer Inc	Springfield	MA	G	413 273-9993	15519
WB Engineering Inc	Norton	MA	E	508 952-4000	14093
Crown Equipment Corporation	Westbrook	ME	E	207 773-5890	7185
North Country Tractor Inc	Sanford	ME	F	207 324-5646	6884
Paul E Wentworth	Vassalboro	ME	G	207 923-3547	7125
Southworth Intl Group Inc **(PA)**	Falmouth	ME	D	207 878-0700	6033
Southworth Products Corp **(HQ)**	Falmouth	ME	E	207 878-0700	6034
WB Engineering Inc **(HQ)**	Falmouth	ME	E	207 878-0700	6037
Davis Village Solutions LLC	New Ipswich	NH	G	603 878-3662	19304
Hawkes Motorsports LLC	Goffstown	NH	G	603 660-9864	18204

3541 Machine Tools: Cutting

	CITY	ST	EMP	PHONE	ENTRY #
Atp Industries LLC **(PA)**	Plainville	CT	F	860 479-5007	3467
B & L Tool and Machine Company	Plainville	CT	G	860 747-2721	3468
Bernell Tool & Mfg Co	Waterbury	CT	G	203 756-4405	4849
Book Automation Inc	New Milford	CT	G	860 354-7900	2788
Branson Ultrasonics Corp **(DH)**	Danbury	CT	B	203 796-0400	882
C V Tool Company Inc **(PA)**	Southington	CT	E	978 353-7901	4042
Ceda Company Inc	Newington	CT	G	860 666-1593	2853
Charter Oak Automation LLC	Wallingford	CT	G	203 562-0699	4716
Connecticut Tool & Cutter Co	Bristol	CT	E	860 314-1740	543
Denco Counter-Bore LLC	Southington	CT	G	860 276-0782	4047
Edac Technologies LLC	East Windsor	CT	F	860 789-2511	1283
Edac Technologies LLC **(HQ)**	Cheshire	CT	C	203 806-2090	728
Emhart Teknologies LLC	Danbury	CT	E	203 790-5000	908
Enginering Components Pdts LLC	Plainville	CT	G	860 747-6222	3486
Finishers Technology Corp	East Berlin	CT	F	860 829-1000	1101
Fletcher-Terry Company LLC **(PA)**	East Berlin	CT	D	860 828-3400	1102
Gary Tool Company	Stratford	CT	G	203 377-3077	4414
Gmn Usa LLC	Bristol	CT	F	800 686-1679	568
Hata Hi-Tech Machining LLC	Ansonia	CT	E	203 333-9139	18
JL Lucas Machinery Co Inc	Waterbury	CT	F	203 597-1300	4891
L C M Tool Co	Waterbury	CT	G	203 757-1575	4896
Laser Tool Company Inc	Thomaston	CT	F	860 283-8284	4508
Magcor Inc	Monroe	CT	G	203 445-0302	2408
Marena Industries Inc	East Hartford	CT	F	860 528-9701	1205
Max-Tek LLC	Wallingford	CT	F	860 372-4900	4771
Microbest Inc	Waterbury	CT	C	203 597-0355	4915
Mid-State Manufacturing Inc	Milldale	CT	F	860 621-6855	2386
Moon Cutter Co Inc	Hamden	CT	E	203 288-9249	1773
Moore Tool Company Inc **(HQ)**	Bridgeport	CT	D	203 366-3224	453
National Screw Manufacturing	East Haven	CT	F	203 469-7109	1256
Nemtec Inc	Cheshire	CT	G	203 272-0788	746
New England Die Co Inc	Waterbury	CT	F	203 574-5140	4927
New England Plasma Dev Corp	Putnam	CT	F	860 928-6561	3621
New England Tooling Inc	Killingworth	CT	F	800 866-5105	1928
Nowak Products Inc	Newington	CT	G	860 666-9685	2887
P-A-R Precision Inc	Wolcott	CT	E	860 491-4181	5451
Pmt Group Inc **(PA)**	Bridgeport	CT	C	203 367-8675	471
Precision Deburring Inc	Bristol	CT	G	860 583-4662	596
Producto Corporation **(HQ)**	Bridgeport	CT	F	203 366-3224	476
Ramdy Corporation	Oakville	CT	E	860 274-3713	3301
Ready Tool Company **(HQ)**	West Hartford	CT	E	860 524-7811	5093
Relx Inc	Windsor	CT	G	860 219-0733	5358
Sadlak Industries LLC	Coventry	CT	E	860 742-0227	838
Secondary Operations Inc	Hamden	CT	F	203 288-8241	1783
Sonitek Corporation	Milford	CT	E	203 878-9321	2364
Sperry Automatics Co Inc	Naugatuck	CT	E	203 729-4589	2497
Syman Machine LLC	Plainville	CT	G	860 747-8337	3517
Tetco Inc	Plainville	CT	F	860 747-1280	3519
Turbine Controls Inc **(PA)**	Bloomfield	CT	D	860 242-0448	269
United Tool and Die Company **(PA)**	West Hartford	CT	C	860 246-6531	5102
US Avionics Inc / Superabr	South Windsor	CT	G	860 528-1114	4019
Viking Tool Company	Shelton	CT	E	203 929-1457	3885
Watertown Jig Bore Service Inc	Watertown	CT	F	860 274-5898	5034
A N C Tool and Manufacturing	Worcester	MA	G	508 757-0224	17329
Accutech Machine Inc	Danvers	MA	F	978 922-7271	10192
Acp Waterjet Inc	Woburn	MA	E	800 951-5127	17108
Amherst Machine Co	Amherst	MA	F	413 549-4551	7513
B & D Precision Inc	Stoneham	MA	G	781 438-8644	15555
Babin Machine Inc	Brockton	MA	G	508 588-9189	9123
C and M Micro-Tool Inc	South Easton	MA	E	508 230-3535	15272
Central MA Waterjet Inc	Millbury	MA	G	508 769-4308	13158
Chas G Allen Realty LLC	Barre	MA	D	978 355-2911	7950
Component Sources Intl	Westborough	MA	F	508 986-2300	16607
Desktop Metal Inc **(PA)**	Burlington	MA	C	978 224-1244	9254
Dexter Innvative Solutions LLC	Orange	MA	G	978 544-2751	14214
Donahue Industries Inc	Shrewsbury	MA	E	508 845-6501	15108
E H Metalcraft Company Inc	West Bridgewater	MA	G	508 580-0870	16440
E T Duval & Son Inc	Leominster	MA	G	978 537-7596	12134
F W Derbyshire Inc	Blackstone	MA	G	508 883-2385	8312
Flow Grinding Corp **(PA)**	Woburn	MA	G	781 933-5300	17182
Frank E Lashua Inc **(PA)**	Worcester	MA	G	508 552-0023	17379
Hendrick Manufacturing Corp **(PA)**	Salem	MA	F	781 631-4400	14919
Iniram Precision Mch Tl LLC	Middleton	MA	G	978 854-3037	13089
Intech Inc	Acton	MA	E	978 263-2210	7366
J-T Machine Co Inc	East Douglas	MA	E	508 476-1508	10427
Kinefac Corporation	Worcester	MA	D	508 754-6901	17401
Leavitt Machine Co	Orange	MA	G	978 544-3872	14220
Leo Coons Jr	Acushnet	MA	G	508 995-3300	7404
Mardon Manufacturing Company	Rowley	MA	G	978 948-7040	14856
Merit Machine Manufacturing	Fitchburg	MA	F	978 342-7677	10836
Mini-Broach Machine Co Inc	Ashby	MA	G	978 386-7959	7647
Mrse	West Brookfield	MA	F	508 867-5083	16472
N E M T R LLC	Shutesbury	MA	G	413 259-1444	15140
Newtron Inc	Auburndale	MA	G	617 969-1100	7866
Nova Analytics Corporation	Beverly	MA	G	781 897-1208	8160
PCC Specialty Products Inc	Auburn	MA	D	508 753-6530	7847
Peterson and Nash Inc	Norwell	MA	E	781 826-9085	14111
Phoenix Inc	Seekonk	MA	E	508 399-7100	15034
Precision Pcb Products Inc	Whitman	MA	G	508 966-9484	16926
President Fllows Hrvard Cllege	Cambridge	MA	G	617 495-2020	9615
Production Tool & Grinding	Athol	MA	F	978 544-8206	7693
Prof Tool Grind Inc	South Easton	MA	E	508 230-3535	15289
Professional Tl Grinding Inc **(PA)**	South Easton	MA	E	508 230-3535	15290
Ramco Machine LLC	Rowley	MA	E	978 948-3778	14863
Sharp Grinding Co Inc	West Springfield	MA	G	413 737-8808	16551
Swift-Cut Automation Usa Inc	Plymouth	MA	G	888 572-1160	14586
Toolmex Indus Solutions Inc **(PA)**	Northborough	MA	D	508 653-5110	14052
True Machine Co Inc	Swansea	MA	G	508 379-0329	15718
Uva Lidkoping Inc	Milford	MA	G	508 634-4301	13150
Ark Plasma	Alfred	ME	G	207 332-6999	5515
Coastal Industrial Distrs	Saco	ME	F	207 286-3319	6845
Helical Solutions LLC	Gorham	ME	G	866 543-5422	6113
J D Paulsen	Bridgton	ME	G	207 647-5679	5808
Nanospire Inc	Buxton	ME	G	207 929-6226	5859
OBrien Consolidated Inds	Lewiston	ME	F	207 783-8543	6312
Speed Mat Inc	Biddeford	ME	G	207 294-4358	5764
Thomas Enterprises Inc	Searsmont	ME	G	207 342-5001	6946
Valmet Inc	Winthrop	ME	F	207 377-6909	7283
Airmar Technology Corp **(PA)**	Milford	NH	B	603 673-9570	19044
Ametek Precitech Inc **(HQ)**	Keene	NH	D	603 357-2510	18491
Centricut Manufacturing LLC	West Lebanon	NH	E	603 298-6191	19948
Cnc North Inc	Claremont	NH	G	603 542-3361	17842
Elmo Motion Control Inc	Nashua	NH	F	603 821-9979	19149
Express Assemblyproducts LLC	Amherst	NH	F	603 424-5590	17561
Fremont Machine & Tool Co Inc	Fremont	NH	G	603 895-9445	18176
Gary Blake Car Buffs	Exeter	NH	G	603 778-0563	18122
Hyertherm Inc	West Lebanon	NH	F	603 643-3441	19953
Hypertherm Inc **(PA)**	Hanover	NH	A	603 643-3441	18290
Hypertherm Inc	Hanover	NH	F	603 643-3441	18291
Hypertherm Inc	Hanover	NH	G	603 643-3441	18292
Jarvis Company Inc **(PA)**	Rochester	NH	D	603 332-9000	19675
Terex Usa LLC	Newton	NH	D	603 382-0556	19370
Thermacut Inc	Claremont	NH	E	603 543-0585	17861
Thermal Dynamics Corporation **(DH)**	West Lebanon	NH	B	603 298-5711	19963
Trellborg Pipe Sals Mlford Inc **(DH)**	Milford	NH	C	800 626-2180	19080
Williams & Hussey Mch Co Inc	Amherst	NH	F	603 732-0219	17591
J & J Machining	Coventry	RI	G	401 397-2782	20149
LDB Tool and Findings Inc	Cranston	RI	G	401 944 6000	20252
Malco Saw Co Inc	Cranston	RI	G	401 942-7380	20258
Piatek Machine Company Inc	Pawtucket	RI	F	401 728-9930	20880
RI Waterjet LLC	Newport	RI	G	781 801-2500	20676
Supfina Machine Co Inc	North Kingstown	RI	E	401 294-6600	20744
Swissline Precision Mfg Inc	Cumberland	RI	D	401 333-8888	20344
Fellows Corporation	Windsor	VT	C	802 674-6500	22708
Gear Works Inc	Springfield	VT	E	802 885-5039	22500
McCormacks Machine Co Inc	West Rutland	VT	G	802 438-2345	22618
Pad Print Machinery of Vermont	East Dorset	VT	D	802 362-0844	21915
Yankee Corporation	Fairfax	VT	D	802 527-0177	21981

3542 Machine Tools: Forming

	CITY	ST	EMP	PHONE	ENTRY #
A G Russell Company Inc	Hartford	CT	G	860 247-9093	1800
Accubend LLC	Plantsville	CT	G	860 378-0303	3525
Ace Finishing Co LLC	Bristol	CT	G	860 582-4600	513
Advanced Machine Services LLC **(PA)**	Waterbury	CT	G	203 888-6600	4836
American Actuator Corporation	Redding	CT	F	203 324-6334	3645
Arrow Diversified Tooling Inc	Ellington	CT	E	860 872-9072	1329
Cole S Crew Machine Products	North Haven	CT	E	203 723-1418	3016
Deringer-Ney Inc **(PA)**	Bloomfield	CT	C	860 242-2281	217

S I C

	CITY	ST	EMP	PHONE	ENTRY #
Eyelet Tech LLC	Wolcott	CT	E	203 879-5306	5442
Fenn LLC	East Berlin	CT	E	860 259-6600	1100
Grant Manufacturing & Mch Co	Bridgeport	CT	E	203 366-4557	421
J D & Associates	Canterbury	CT	G	860 546-2112	693
Joshua LLC **(PA)**	New Haven	CT	E	203 624-0080	2699
L M Gill Welding and Mfr LLC **(PA)**	Manchester	CT	F	860 647-9931	2017
L R Brown Manufacturing Co	Wallingford	CT	G	203 265-5639	4763
Lou-Jan Tool & Die Inc	Cheshire	CT	F	203 272-3536	742
Merritt Extruder Corp	Hamden	CT	E	203 230-8100	1770
OEM Sources LLC	Milford	CT	G	203 283-5415	2325
Okay Industries Inc	Berlin	CT	G	860 225-8707	99
Oxford General Industries Inc	Prospect	CT	F	203 758-4467	3590
Proiron LLC	West Haven	CT	G	203 934-7967	5143
Raymon Tool LLC	Hamden	CT	F	203 248-2199	1779
Richard Dahlen	Bristol	CT	G	860 584-8226	606
Riveting Systems USA LLC	Bridgeport	CT	G	203 366-4557	483
Sandviks Inc **(PA)**	Danbury	CT	G	866 984-0188	982
Sirois Tool Company Inc **(PA)**	Berlin	CT	D	860 828-5327	109
Trumpf Inc **(DH)**	Farmington	CT	B	860 255-6000	1517
Trumpf Inc	Plainville	CT	B	860 255-6000	3522
Trumpf Inc	Farmington	CT	B	860 255-6000	1518
Vital Stretch LLC	Norwalk	CT	G	203 847-4477	3268
Ab-Wey Machine & Die Co Inc	Pembroke	MA	F	781 294-8031	14389
Alcoa Global Fasteners Inc	Stoughton	MA	E	412 553-4545	15578
Altra Industrial Motion Corp **(PA)**	Braintree	MA	B	781 917-0600	8986
Armadillo Noise Vibration LLC	Acushnet	MA	G	774 992-7156	7399
ATI Flowform Products LLC	Billerica	MA	E	978 667-0202	8215
Babin Machine Inc	Brockton	MA	G	508 588-9189	9123
Diecast Manufacturer **(PA)**	North Billerica	MA	G	978 667-6784	13808
Form Roll Die Corp	Worcester	MA	F	508 755-5302	17378
Form Roll Die Corp **(PA)**	Worcester	MA	E	508 755-2010	17377
Hpm LLC	Bellingham	MA	G	508 958-5565	8041
Kinefac Corporation	Worcester	MA	D	508 754-6901	17401
Kt Acquisition LLC	Worcester	MA	D	508 853-4500	17402
Mestek Inc **(PA)**	Westfield	MA	E	470 898-4533	16700
Niagara Cutter Athol Inc	Athol	MA	E	978 249-2788	7691
PCC Specialty Products Inc	Auburn	MA	D	508 753-6530	7847
Roche Tool & Die	Marlborough	MA	G	508 485-6460	12818
Simsak Machine & Tool Co Inc	Southbridge	MA	G	508 764-4958	15404
Sonolite Plastics Corporation	Gloucester	MA	F	978 281-0662	11211
Thermocermet	Pepperell	MA	G	978 425-0404	14446
Thomson National Press Company **(PA)**	Franklin	MA	G	508 528-2000	11091
Valentine Tool & Stamping Inc	Norton	MA	F	508 285-6911	14091
Warner Electric	Braintree	MA	G	781 917-0600	9048
Westfield Tool & Die Inc	Westfield	MA	F	413 562-2393	16747
Whitman Castings Inc **(PA)**	Whitman	MA	E	781 447-4417	16930
Greenerd Press & Mch Co LLC **(PA)**	Nashua	NH	E	603 889-4101	19172
Nbr Diamond Tool Corp	South Hampton	NH	G	603 394-2113	19856
Praxair Surface Tech Inc	Concord	NH	D	603 224-9585	17924
Solidscape Inc	Merrimack	NH	E	603 424-0590	19030
Tafa Incorporated **(DH)**	Concord	NH	E	603 224-9585	17934
Unitec Engineering Inc	Windham	NH	F	978 764-0553	20013
Automated Industrial Mch Inc	Smithfield	RI	F	401 232-1710	21210
Durant Tool Company Inc	North Kingstown	RI	E	401 781-7800	20703
Gasbarre Products Inc	Cranston	RI	F	401 467-5200	20230
Joraco Inc	Smithfield	RI	F	401 232-1710	21234
Laser Fare Inc **(PA)**	Smithfield	RI	D	401 231-4400	21235
Meloni Tool Co Inc	Johnston	RI	G	401 272-6513	20521
Samic Mfg Company	Johnston	RI	G	401 421-2400	20540
Thomas Drake	Colchester	VT	G	802 655-0990	21881

3543 Industrial Patterns

	CITY	ST	EMP	PHONE	ENTRY #
Arrow Diversified Tooling Inc	Ellington	CT	E	860 872-9072	1329
Case Patterns Inc	Groton	CT	G	860 445-6722	1665
Fitchburg Pattern and Model Co	Fitchburg	MA	G	978 342-0770	10825
Manufctrers Pattern Fndry Corp	Springfield	MA	G	413 732-8117	15487
Roehr Tool Corp	Leominster	MA	F	978 562-4488	12183
S Ralph Cross and Sons Inc	Sutton	MA	E	508 865-8112	15691
Waiteco Machine Inc	Ayer	MA	G	978 772-5535	7942
Kestrel Tooling Company	Topsham	ME	G	207 721-0609	7090
Bomar Inc	Charlestown	NH	D	603 826-5781	17811
Bradley Goodwin Pattern Co	Providence	RI	F	401 461-5220	20973
Clear Carbon & Components Inc	Bristol	RI	F	401 254-5085	20068
Eagle Pattern & Casting Co	Cranston	RI	G	401 943-7154	20213

3544 Dies, Tools, Jigs, Fixtures & Indl Molds

	CITY	ST	EMP	PHONE	ENTRY #
Aba-PGT Inc **(PA)**	Manchester	CT	C	860 649-4591	1980
Accurate Tool & Die Inc	Stamford	CT	E	203 967-1200	4127
Acson Tool Company	Bridgeport	CT	F	203 334-8050	367
Advance Mold & Mfg Inc	Manchester	CT	C	860 432-5887	1983
Alinabal Inc **(HQ)**	Milford	CT	C	203 877-3241	2242
All Five Tool Co Inc	Berlin	CT	E	860 583-1693	69
American Molded Products Inc	Bridgeport	CT	F	203 333-0183	374
American Precision Mold Inc	East Hampton	CT	G	860 267-1356	1157
Anderson Tool Company Inc	New Haven	CT	G	203 777-4153	2657
Apex Machine Tool Company Inc	Cheshire	CT	D	860 677-2884	711
Arcade Technology LLC	Bridgeport	CT	E	203 366-3871	376
Arrow Diversified Tooling Inc	Ellington	CT	E	860 872-9072	1329
Astro Industries Inc	Berlin	CT	G	860 828-6304	74
Atlas Stamping & Mfg Corp	Newington	CT	E	860 757-3233	2844
B & D Machine Inc	Tolland	CT	F	860 871-9226	4539
B & L Tool and Machine Company	Plainville	CT	G	860 747-2721	3468
B & P Plating Equipment LLC	Bristol	CT	F	860 589-5799	523
B-P Products Inc	Hamden	CT	E	203 288-0200	1733
Bessette Holdings Inc	East Hartford	CT	E	860 289-6000	1176
Better Molded Products Inc **(PA)**	Bristol	CT	C	860 589-0066	534
Betz Tool Company Inc	Milford	CT	G	203 878-1187	2253
Bml Tool & Mfg Corp	Monroe	CT	D	203 880-9485	2395
Bremser Technologies Inc	Stratford	CT	F	203 378-8486	4398
Bridgeport Tl & Stamping Corp	Bridgeport	CT	E	203 336-2501	390
Bristol Tool & Die Company	Bristol	CT	E	860 582-2577	539
C V Tool Company Inc **(PA)**	Southington	CT	E	978 353-7901	4042
Cambridge Specialty Co Inc	Berlin	CT	D	860 828-3579	80
Candlewood Tool & Machine Shop	Gaylordsville	CT	F	860 355-1892	1529
Carnegie Tool Inc	Norwalk	CT	F	203 866-0744	3119
Century Tool Co Inc	Thompson	CT	F	860 923-9523	4533
Cgl Inc	Watertown	CT	F	860 945-6166	5002
Charles J Angelo Mfg Group LLC	Manchester	CT	F	860 646-2378	1994
Classic Tool & Mfg Inc	Waterbury	CT	G	203 755-6313	4857
Connecticut Tool Co Inc	Putnam	CT	E	860 928-0565	3606
D & M Tool Company Inc	West Hartford	CT	G	860 236-6037	5064
Diecraft Compacting Tool Inc	Wolcott	CT	G	203 879-3019	5439
E & E Tool & Manufacturing Co	Winsted	CT	F	860 738-8577	5409
E and S Gage Inc	Tolland	CT	F	860 872-5917	4546
F J Weidner Inc	East Haven	CT	G	203 469-4202	1249
Fad Tool Company LLC	Bristol	CT	E	860 582-7890	560
Ferron Mold and Tool LLC	Dayville	CT	G	860 774-5555	1043
Foilmark Inc	Bloomfield	CT	F	860 243-0343	220
G P Tool Co Inc	Danbury	CT	F	203 744-0310	924
Gary Tool Company	Stratford	CT	G	203 377-3077	4414
Globe Tool & Met Stampg Co Inc	Southington	CT	E	860 621-6807	4054
Gordon Rubber and Pkg Co Inc	Derby	CT	E	203 735-7441	1072
Hartford Gauge Co	West Hartford	CT	G	860 233-9619	5075
Heise Industries Inc	East Berlin	CT	D	860 828-6538	1103
Herman Schmidt Precision Workh	South Windsor	CT	G	860 289-3347	3977
Highland Manufacturing Inc	Manchester	CT	E	860 646-5142	2009
Hobson and Motzer Incorporated **(PA)**	Durham	CT	C	860 349-1756	1092
J & L Tool Company Inc	Wallingford	CT	E	203 265-6237	4757
J F Tool Inc	Rockfall	CT	G	860 349-3063	3697
Jovek Tool and Die	Bristol	CT	G	860 261-5020	573
Kovacs Machine and Tool Co	Wallingford	CT	E	203 269-4949	4761
Lassy Tools Inc	Plainville	CT	G	860 747-2748	3500
Laurel Tool & Manufacturing	Norwich	CT	G	860 889-5354	3285
Lawrence Holdings Inc **(PA)**	Wallingford	CT	F	203 949-1600	4764
Lou-Jan Tool & Die Inc	Cheshire	CT	F	203 272-3536	742
Lyons Tool and Die Company	Meriden	CT	E	203 238-2689	2100
M & R Manufacturing Inc	Newington	CT	G	860 666-5066	2878
Manchester Molding and Mfg Co	Manchester	CT	E	860 643-2141	2023
Marc Tool & Die Inc	Prospect	CT	G	203 758-5933	3588
Mastercraft Tool and Mch Co	Southington	CT	F	860 628-5551	4064
Michaud Tool Co Inc	Terryville	CT	G	860 582-6785	4486
Mid-State Manufacturing Inc	Milldale	CT	F	860 621-6855	2386
Mohawk Tool and Die Mfg Co Inc	Bridgeport	CT	F	203 367-2181	452
Mold Threads Inc	Branford	CT	G	203 483-1420	331
Moldvision LLC	Thompson	CT	G	860 315-1025	4536
Moore Tool Company Inc **(HQ)**	Bridgeport	CT	D	203 366-3224	453
My Tool Company Inc	Waterbury	CT	G	203 755-2333	4920
Northeast Carbide Inc	Southington	CT	F	860 628-2515	4069
Noujaim Tool Co Inc	Waterbury	CT	E	203 753-4441	4929
Omni Mold Systems LLC	Lisbon	CT	G	888 666-4755	1944
Oxford General Industries Inc	Prospect	CT	F	203 758-4467	3590
P&G Metal Components Corp	Bloomfield	CT	F	860 243-2220	248
Paragon Tool Company Inc	Manchester	CT	G	860 647-9935	2035
Patriot Manufacturing LLC	Bristol	CT	G	860 506-2213	591
Plainville Machine & Tl Co Inc	Bristol	CT	F	860 589-5595	594
Plastic Design Intl Inc **(PA)**	Middletown	CT	E	860 632-2001	2210
Pmt Group Inc **(PA)**	Bridgeport	CT	C	203 367-8675	471
Precision Punch + Tooling Corp **(PA)**	Berlin	CT	D	860 229-9902	103
Preferred Tool & Die Inc **(PA)**	Shelton	CT	D	203 925-8525	3861
Producto Corporation **(HQ)**	Bridgeport	CT	F	203 366-3224	476
Proman Inc	New Britain	CT	G	860 827-8778	2566
Prototype Plastic Mold Co Inc	Middletown	CT	E	860 632-2800	2214
Quality Wire Edm Inc	Bristol	CT	G	860 583-9867	600
R A Tool Co	Milford	CT	G	203 877-2998	2346
R&R Tool & Die LLC	East Windsor	CT	G	860 627-9197	1299
Ramar-Hall Inc	Middlefield	CT	E	860 349-1081	2165
Ray Machine Corporation	Terryville	CT	E	860 582-8202	4490
Reliable Tool & Die Inc	Milford	CT	E	203 877-3264	2348
Reno Machine Company Inc	Newington	CT	D	860 666-5641	2898
Reynolds Carbide Die Co Inc	Thomaston	CT	E	860 283-8246	4512
Richards Machine Tool Co Inc	Newington	CT	F	860 436-2938	2899
Rintec Corporation	Oakville	CT	F	860 274-3697	3302
Roto-Die Company Inc	East Windsor	CT	F	860 292-7030	1300
Royal Machine and Tool Corp	Berlin	CT	E	860 828-6555	108

	CITY	ST	EMP	PHONE	ENTRY #
Sandur Tool Co	Waterbury	CT	G	203 753-0004	4952
Scan Tool & Mold Inc	Trumbull	CT	E	203 459-4950	4631
Schmidt Tool Manufacturing	Milford	CT	G	203 877-8149	2361
Sirois Tool Company Inc **(PA)**	Berlin	CT	D	860 828-5327	109
Skico Manufacturing Co LLC	Hamden	CT	G	203 230-1305	1784
Skillcraft Machine Tool Co	South Windsor	CT	F	860 953-1246	4010
Somers Manufacturing Inc	Bristol	CT	G	860 314-1075	613
Somerset Plastics Company	Middletown	CT	E	860 635-1601	2224
Spartan Aerospace LLC	Manchester	CT	D	860 533-7500	2049
Steel Rule Die Corp America	Milldale	CT	G	860 621-5284	2387
Straton Industries Inc	Stratford	CT	D	203 375-4488	4450
Taco Fasteners Inc	Plainville	CT	F	860 747-5597	3518
Telke Tool & Die Mfg Co	Kensington	CT	G	860 828-9955	1921
Tmf Incorporated	Southbury	CT	G	203 267-7364	4034
Total Concept Tool Inc	Branford	CT	G	203 483-1130	355
Trueline Corporation	Waterbury	CT	G	203 757-0344	4968
Upper Valley Mold LLC	Torrington	CT	G	860 489-8282	4606
Victor Tool Co Inc	Meriden	CT	G	203 634-8113	2148
Watertown Jig Bore Service Inc	Watertown	CT	F	860 274-5898	5034
Watertown Plastics Inc	Watertown	CT	E	860 274-7535	5035
Weimann Brothers Mfg Co	Derby	CT	F	203 735-3311	1082
Wepco Plastics Inc	Middlefield	CT	E	860 349-3407	2168
Wess Tool & Die Company Inc	Meriden	CT	G	203 237-5277	2150
West-Conn Tool and Die Inc	Shelton	CT	F	203 538-5081	3888
Wilkinson Tool & Die Co	North Stonington	CT	G	860 599-5821	3077
Winthrop Tool LLC	Essex	CT	G	860 526-9079	1409
A & M Tool & Die Company Inc	Southbridge	MA	E	508 764-3241	15374
A Luongo & Sons Incorporated	Bridgewater	MA	G	508 226-0788	9059
Abco Tool & Die Inc	Hyannis	MA	E	508 771-3225	11832
Accudie Inc	Worcester	MA	G	508 756-8482	17334
Accutech Packaging Inc	Foxboro	MA	D	508 543-3800	10873
Adt/Diversity Inc	Attleboro	MA	G	508 222-9601	7701
Advanced Mfg Tech Inc	Spencer	MA	G	508 885-0249	15424
Advanced Prototypes & Molding	Leominster	MA	G	978 534-0584	12107
Alsco Industries Inc	Sturbridge	MA	D	508 347-1199	15637
Alumi-Nex Mold Inc	Webster	MA	F	508 949-2200	16338
Amherst Machine Co	Amherst	MA	F	413 549-4551	7513
Anderson Power Products Inc **(HQ)**	Sterling	MA	D	978 422-3600	15535
Apple Steel Rule Die Co Inc	Springfield	MA	E	414 353-2444	15447
Atco Plastics Inc	Plainville	MA	D	508 695-3573	14515
B & D Precision Inc	Stoneham	MA	G	781 438-8644	15555
Banner Mold & Die Co Inc	Leominster	MA	E	978 534-6558	12116
Barnard Die Inc	Wakefield	MA	F	781 246-3117	15942
Bay State Cast Products Inc	Springfield	MA	G	413 736-1028	15450
Berkshire Mnufactured Pdts Inc	Newburyport	MA	C	978 462-8161	13472
Bermer Precision Products LLC	Southbridge	MA	G	508 764-2521	15376
Bermer Tool & Die Inc	Southbridge	MA	E	508 764-2521	15377
Big 3 Precision Products Inc	Holliston	MA	F	508 429-4774	11559
Boniface Tool & Die Inc	Dudley	MA	E	508 764-3248	10373
Brenmar Molding Inc	Fitchburg	MA	G	978 343-3198	10814
Btd Precision Inc	Chicopee	MA	F	413 594-2783	10002
Built-Rite Tool and Die Inc	Leominster	MA	F	978 751-8432	12120
Built-Rite Tool and Die Inc	Lancaster	MA	F	978 365-3867	11981
C & M Tool and Die LLC	Waltham	MA	G	781 893-1880	16057
Cado Products Inc	Fitchburg	MA	E	978 343-2989	10817
Columbia ASC Inc	Lawrence	MA	F	978 683-2205	12012
Connell Limited Partnership **(PA)**	Boston	MA	F	617 737-2700	8481
Cr Technology Inc	Methuen	MA	G	978 681-5305	13016
Crisci Tool and Die Inc	Leominster	MA	E	978 537-4102	12128
Csw Inc **(PA)**	Ludlow	MA	C	413 589-1311	12461
Cycle Engineering Inc	Ware	MA	G	413 967-3818	16231
D V Die Cutting Inc	Danvers	MA	E	978 777-0300	10210
De Mari Pasta Dies USA Inc	Dracut	MA	G	978 454-4099	10358
Diecutting Tooling Svcs Inc **(PA)**	Chicopee	MA	F	413 331-3500	10018
Ditech	Byfield	MA	G	978 463-0665	9363
F & M Tool & Die Co Inc	Leominster	MA	E	978 537-0290	12137
Fall River Tool & Die Co Inc	Fall River	MA	F	508 674-4621	10699
Fiore Machine Inc	Indian Orchard	MA	G	413 543-5767	11886
Fit America Inc	Southborough	MA	G	309 839-1695	15357
Foilmark Inc **(HQ)**	Newburyport	MA	D	978 225-8200	13490
Fort Hill Sign Products Inc	Hopedale	MA	G	781 321-4320	11672
G&F Precision Molding Inc **(PA)**	Fiskdale	MA	D	508 347-9132	10807
Gare Incorporated	Haverhill	MA	E	978 373-9131	11437
Geonautics Manufacturing Inc	Newburyport	MA	E	978 462-7161	13494
Girouard Tool & Die Inc	Leominster	MA	G	978 534-4147	12146
Harris Tool & Die Company Inc	Fitchburg	MA	G	978 479-1842	10828
Harrys Mold & Machine Inc	Bridgewater	MA	G	508 697-6432	9075
Hi-Tech Mold & Tool Inc	Pittsfield	MA	C	413 443-9184	14476
Hoppe Technologies Inc	Chicopee	MA	D	413 592-9213	10029
Ideal Industries Inc	Sterling	MA	C	978 422-3600	15540
Innovative Tooling Company Inc	Lenox	MA	F	413 637-1031	12101
Interstate Design Company Inc	Agawam	MA	F	413 786-7730	7432
Interstate Manufacturing Co	Agawam	MA	G	413 789-8674	7433
J I Morris Company	Southbridge	MA	G	508 764-4394	15388
J-K Tool Co Inc	Agawam	MA	E	413 789-0613	7434
Jaquith Caibide Corp	Ipswich	MA	G	978 356-7770	11924
Jls Tool & Die Inc	Middleton	MA	G	978 304-3111	13091
Lakewood Industries Inc	Pittsfield	MA	D	413 499-3550	14480
Lansen Mold Co Inc	Hancock	MA	F	413 443-5328	11325
Lolli Company Inc	Leominster	MA	E	978 537-8343	12163
Lsa Cleanpart LLC	Southbridge	MA	G	508 765-4848	15393
M & H Engineering Co Inc	Danvers	MA	E	978 777-1222	10234
Mack Prototype Inc	Gardner	MA	E	978 632-3700	11119
Magnus Molding Inc	Pittsfield	MA	E	413 443-1192	14488
Mar-Lee Companies Inc	Fitchburg	MA	D	978 348-1291	10834
Mayhew Basque Plastics LLC	Westminster	MA	F	978 537-5219	16809
Micon Die Corporation	West Springfield	MA	G	413 478-5029	16530
Micron Products Inc	Fitchburg	MA	C	978 345-5000	10837
Millennium Die Group Inc	Three Rivers	MA	E	413 283-3500	15851
Modern Mold & Tool Inc **(PA)**	Pittsfield	MA	E	413 443-1192	14491
Mold Makers Inc	West Bridgewater	MA	G	508 588-4212	16447
Moldmaster Engineering Inc	Pittsfield	MA	E	413 442-5793	14492
Neu-Tool Design Inc	Wilmington	MA	E	978 658-5881	17029
Northeast Plastics Inc	Wakefield	MA	F	781 245-5512	15965
Nypromold Inc **(PA)**	Clinton	MA	D	978 365-4547	10087
Orchard Tool Die Inc	Indian Orchard	MA	G	413 433-1233	11892
Packaging Devices Inc **(PA)**	Teaticket	MA	F	508 548-0224	15802
PCC Specialty Products Inc	Auburn	MA	D	508 753-6530	7847
Pearl Die Cutting & Finishing	Woburn	MA	F	781 721-6900	17259
Pen Ro Mold and Tool Inc	Pittsfield	MA	E	413 499-0464	14498
Pilgrim Tool & Die Inc	Worcester	MA	G	508 753-0190	17441
Pittsfield Plastics Engrg Inc	Pittsfield	MA	D	413 442-0067	14500
Premier Roll & Tool Inc	North Attleboro	MA	G	508 695-2551	13774
Pyramid Mold Inc	Pittsfield	MA	G	413 442-6198	14503
Quality Die Cutting Inc **(PA)**	Haverhill	MA	F	978 374-8027	11465
Raitto Engineering & Mfg Inc	Wheelwright	MA	G	413 477-6637	16908
Raynham Tool & Die Inc	Raynham	MA	G	508 822-4489	14728
Roche Tool & Die	Marlborough	MA	G	508 485-6460	12818
S Ralph Cross and Sons Inc	Sutton	MA	E	508 865-8112	15691
Samtan Engineering Corp	Malden	MA	E	781 322-7880	12594
Sancliff Inc	Worcester	MA	F	508 795-0747	17469
Simsak Machine & Tool Co Inc	Southbridge	MA	G	508 764-4958	15404
Skg Associates Inc	Dedham	MA	G	781 878-7250	10298
Sonicron Systems Corporation	Westfield	MA	E	413 562-5218	16731
Stuart Allyn Co Inc	Pittsfield	MA	G	413 443-7306	14511
Superior Die & Stamping Inc	Attleboro	MA	G	774 203-3674	7797
Tech Ridge Inc	Chelmsford	MA	E	978 256-5741	9935
Thomson National Press Company **(PA)**	Franklin	MA	G	508 528-2000	11091
Ultraclad Corporation	Newburyport	MA	G	978 358-7945	13545
Uneco Manufacturing Inc	Chicopee	MA	E	413 594-2700	10066
United Tool & Machine Corp	Wilmington	MA	E	978 658-5500	17060
Vector Tool & Die Corporation	Westfield	MA	G	413 562-1616	16739
Volpe Tool & Die Incorporated	Franklin	MA	G	508 528-8103	11095
W M Gulliksen Mfg Co Inc **(PA)**	South Weymouth	MA	E	617 323-5750	15323
Westfield Tool & Die Inc	Westfield	MA	F	413 562-2393	16747
Whip City Tool & Die Corp	Southwick	MA	E	413 569-5528	15423
Whitewater LLC	West Hatfield	MA	G	413 237-5032	16487
Whitman Tool and Die Co Inc	Whitman	MA	E	781 447-0421	16932
WR Sharples Co Inc	North Attleboro	MA	E	508 695-5656	13787
Allied Endeavers Inc	Waldoboro	ME	G	207 832-0511	7130
Kennebec Technologies	Augusta	ME	D	207 626-0188	5610
Larry Balchen	Jonesport	ME	G	207 497-5621	6227
Maine Mold & Machine Inc	Hartford	ME	G	207 388-2732	6177
Northeast Tool & Die Co Inc	Norway	ME	G	207 743-7273	6524
OBrien Consolidated Inds	Lewiston	ME	F	207 783-8543	6312
Aluminum Castings Inc	Wilton	NH	G	603 654-9695	19974
Atlantic Microtool	Salem	NH	G	603 898-3212	19710
Atlantic Sports International	Langdon	NH	G	603 835-6948	18610
Berube Tool & Die Inc	Plaistow	NH	G	603 382-2224	19509
Bocra Industries Inc	Seabrook	NH	E	603 474-3598	19794
Complex Mold & Machine	Plymouth	NH	G	603 536-1221	19528
Comstock Industries Inc	Meredith	NH	E	603 279-7045	18972
Costa Precision Mfg Corp **(PA)**	Claremont	NH	E	603 542-5229	17844
Cotc Machine	Milford	NH	G	603 673-0211	19053
Freudenberg-Nok General Partnr	Ashland	NH	C	603 968-7187	17599
Hamilton Precision LLC	Belmont	NH	G	603 524-7622	17673
Hy-Ten Die & Development Corp	Milford	NH	E	603 673-1611	19065
Jamestown Industries Inc	Northfield	NH	G	603 286-3301	19403
Jr Frank Bolton	Weare	NH	G	603 529-3633	19936
Kimark Specialty Box Company	Manchester	NH	E	603 668-1336	18855
Moldpro Inc	Swanzey	NH	E	603 357-2523	19885
Mrpc Northeast LLC	Hudson	NH	E	603 880-3616	18417
New England Industries Inc	Lebanon	NH	E	603 448-5330	18633
North East Cutting Die Corp	Dover	NH	E	603 436-8952	18042
Precision Depaneling Mchs LLC	Fremont	NH	F	540 248-1381	18178
Robert Nixon	Wilton	NH	G	603 654-2285	19985
RTD Technologies Inc	Somersworth	NH	G	603 692-5978	19848
Stamping Technologies Inc	Laconia	NH	F	603 524-5958	18588
Sunset Tool Inc	Keene	NH	E	603 355-2246	18531
Swansons Die Co Inc	Manchester	NH	E	603 623-3832	18934
Temco Tool Company Inc	Manchester	NH	E	603 622-6989	18938
W H M Industries Inc	Charlestown	NH	G	603 835-6015	17820
Whelen Engineering Co	Charlestown	NH	E	860 526-9504	17821
Ar-Ro Engineering Company Inc **(PA)**	North Smithfield	RI	G	401 766-6669	20781

Employee Codes: A=Over 500 employees, B=251-500
C=101-250, D=51-100 E=20-50, F=10-19, G=3-9

	CITY	ST	EMP	PHONE	ENTRY #
Bradley Goodwin Pattern Co	Providence	RI	F	401 461-5220	20973
C & W Co Inc	Providence	RI	G	401 941-6311	20977
Choklit Mold Ltd	Lincoln	RI	G	401 725-7377	20564
Clear Carbon & Components Inc	Bristol	RI	F	401 254-5085	20068
Conley Casting Supply Corp **(PA)**	Warwick	RI	E	401 461-4710	21345
Fielding Manufacturing Inc	Cranston	RI	E	401 461-0400	20226
Formex Inc	East Greenwich	RI	E	401 885-9800	20368
GA Rel Manufacturing Company	Providence	RI	E	401 331-5455	21019
Guill Tool & Engrg Co Inc	West Warwick	RI	D	401 822-8186	21493
Jackson Bookbinding Co Inc	Greenville	RI	F	401 231-0800	20469
Ldc Inc	East Providence	RI	F	401 861-4667	20429
Matrix I LLC	East Providence	RI	D	401 434-3040	20431
Mono Die Cutting Co Inc	Riverside	RI	F	401 434-1274	21173
Mtd Inc	Coventry	RI	G	401 397-5460	20158
Newport Tool & Die Inc	Middletown	RI	F	401 847-6711	20628
Pep Central Inc	Warwick	RI	A	401 732-3770	21402
Polyurethane Molding Inds Inc	Woonsocket	RI	E	401 765-6700	21576
Precise Products Company	Lincoln	RI	F	401 724-7190	20592
Richard D Johnson & Son Inc	Ashaway	RI	G	401 377-4312	20040
Rol-Flo Engineering Inc	Westerly	RI	E	401 596-0060	21539
Royal Diversified Products	Warren	RI	D	401 245-6900	21304
Stearns Tool Company Inc	Providence	RI	G	401 351-4765	21127
Tri-Bro Tool Company	Cranston	RI	F	401 781-6323	20305
Welmold Tool & Die Inc	North Kingstown	RI	G	401 738-0505	20749
G W Plastics Inc **(PA)**	Bethel	VT	B	802 234-9941	21695
North Hartland Tool Corp	North Hartland	VT	D	802 295-3196	22229
Raymond Gadues Inc	Swanton	VT	E	802 868-2033	22536
Thomas Drake	Colchester	VT	G	802 655-0990	21881
Tj Mold and Tool Company Inc	Saint Johnsbury	VT	G	802 748-1390	22396
Tri C Tool & Die	Burlington	VT	G	802 864-7144	21813
Vermont Mold & Tool Corp	Barnet	VT	G	802 633-2300	21605
Vmt LLC	Barnet	VT	G	802 633-3900	21606

3545 Machine Tool Access

	CITY	ST	EMP	PHONE	ENTRY #
Accu-Rite Tool & Mfg Co	Tolland	CT	F	860 688-4844	4538
Advanced Torque Products LLC	Newington	CT	G	860 828-1523	2839
Aircraft Forged Tool Company	Rockfall	CT	G	860 347-3778	3696
AKO Inc	Windsor	CT	E	860 298-9765	5317
Alden Corporation	Wolcott	CT	D	203 879-8830	5432
Alden Tool Company Inc	Berlin	CT	E	860 828-3556	68
All Five Tool Co Inc	Berlin	CT	E	860 583-1693	69
American Grippers Inc	Trumbull	CT	E	203 459-8345	4611
Apex Machine Tool Company Inc	Cheshire	CT	D	860 677-2884	711
Blue Chip Tool	Tolland	CT	G	860 875-7999	4540
Brass City Technologies LLC **(PA)**	Naugatuck	CT	G	203 723-7021	2463
Byron Lord Inc	Old Lyme	CT	G	203 287-9881	3315
Center Broach & Machine Co	Meriden	CT	G	203 235-6329	2084
Century Tool and Design Inc	Milldale	CT	F	860 621-6748	2383
Coastal Group Inc	Killingworth	CT	G	860 452-4148	1925
Comex Machinery	Bridgeport	CT	G	203 334-2196	399
D & M Tool Company Inc	West Hartford	CT	G	860 236-6037	5064
Danjon Manufacturing Corp	Cheshire	CT	F	203 272-7258	727
Drill Rite Carbide Tool Co	Terryville	CT	G	860 583-3200	4476
E and S Gage Inc	Tolland	CT	F	860 872-5917	4546
Eastern Broach Inc	Plainville	CT	F	860 828-4800	3483
Edmunds Manufacturing Company **(PA)**	Farmington	CT	D	860 677-2813	1480
Edrive Actuators Inc	Newington	CT	G	860 953-0588	2861
Ewald Instruments Corp	Bristol	CT	F	860 491-9042	558
Fletcher-Terry Company LLC **(PA)**	East Berlin	CT	D	860 828-3400	1102
Guhring Inc	Bloomfield	CT	C	860 216-5948	222
H & B Tool & Engineering Co	South Windsor	CT	E	860 528-9341	3976
Hart Tool & Engineering	Oxford	CT	G	203 264-9776	3407
Hartford Gauge Co	West Hartford	CT	G	860 233-9619	5075
Hermann Schmidt Company Inc	South Windsor	CT	F	860 289-3347	3978
Hgh Industries LLC	South Windsor	CT	G	860 644-1150	3980
Highland Manufacturing Inc	Manchester	CT	E	860 646-5142	2009
Integral Industries Inc	Newington	CT	F	860 953-0686	2872
J F Tool Inc	Rockfall	CT	G	860 349-3063	3697
J J Industries Conn Inc	Southington	CT	F	860 628-4655	4060
James J Scott LLC	Rocky Hill	CT	G	860 571-9200	3719
Jet Tool & Cutter Mfg Inc	Southington	CT	E	860 621-5381	4061
Johnson Gage Company	Bloomfield	CT	E	860 242-5541	229
Kinetic Tool Co Inc	East Windsor	CT	F	860 627-5882	1292
LLC Dow Gage	Berlin	CT	E	860 828-5327	92
Lord & Hodge Inc	Middletown	CT	F	860 632-7006	2201
Lyons Tool and Die Company	Meriden	CT	E	203 238-2689	2100
M & M Carbide Inc	Southington	CT	G	860 628-2002	4063
M & R Manufacturing Inc	Newington	CT	G	860 666-5066	2878
M T S Tool LLC	Oakville	CT	G	860 945-0875	3299
Marena Industries Inc	East Hartford	CT	F	860 528-9701	1205
Meadow Manufacturing Inc	Kensington	CT	F	860 357-3785	1919
Meyer Gage Co Inc	South Windsor	CT	F	860 528-6526	3993
Micro Insert Inc	Milldale	CT	G	860 621-5789	2385
Mid-State Manufacturing Inc	Milldale	CT	F	860 621-6855	2386
Miracle Instruments Co	Lebanon	CT	F	860 642-7745	1936
Moon Cutter Co Inc	Hamden	CT	E	203 288-9249	1773
Moore Tool Company Inc **(HQ)**	Bridgeport	CT	D	203 366-3224	453
Mrh Tool LLC	Milford	CT	G	203 878-3359	2317
Nelson Apostle Inc	Hartford	CT	G	860 953-4633	1850
O S Walker Company Inc **(DH)**	Windsor	CT	D	508 853-3232	5351
Paradigm Prcision Holdings LLC	East Berlin	CT	D	860 829-3663	1105
Perry Technology Corporation	New Hartford	CT	D	860 738-2525	2644
Pine Meadow Machine Co Inc	Windsor Locks	CT	G	860 623-4494	5398
Pmt Group Inc **(PA)**	Bridgeport	CT	C	203 367-8675	471
Powerhold Inc	Middlefield	CT	E	860 349-1044	2163
Precision Punch + Tooling Corp	Berlin	CT	G	860 225-4159	104
Preferred Tool & Die Inc	Shelton	CT	E	203 925-8525	3862
Preferred Utilities Mfg Corp **(HQ)**	Danbury	CT	D	203 743-6741	974
Producto Corporation **(HQ)**	Bridgeport	CT	F	203 366-3224	476
Q Alpha Inc	Colchester	CT	E	860 357-7340	806
R&R Tool & Die LLC	East Windsor	CT	G	860 627-9197	1299
Ray Machine Corporation	Terryville	CT	E	860 582-8202	4490
Royal Machine and Tool Corp	Berlin	CT	E	860 828-6555	108
Sirois Tool Company Inc **(PA)**	Berlin	CT	D	860 828-5327	109
Sjm Properties Inc	Ellington	CT	G	860 979-0060	1340
Skico Manufacturing Co LLC	Hamden	CT	G	203 230-1305	1784
Southwick & Meister Inc	Meriden	CT	C	203 237-0000	2133
Space Electronics LLC	Berlin	CT	E	860 829-0001	110
Swanson Tool Manufacturing Inc	West Hartford	CT	E	860 953-1641	5097
Tool The Somma Company	Waterbury	CT	E	203 753-2114	4963
Trueline Corporation	Waterbury	CT	G	203 757-0344	4968
Universal Precision Mfg	Trumbull	CT	G	203 374-9809	4641
Victor Tool Co Inc	Meriden	CT	G	203 634-8113	2148
Viking Tool Company	Shelton	CT	E	203 929-1457	3885
Walker Magnetics Group Inc **(HQ)**	Windsor	CT	E	508 853-3232	5378
White Hills Tool	Monroe	CT	G	203 590-3143	2420
Zero Check LLC	Thomaston	CT	G	860 283-5629	4529
Ade Technologies Inc **(HQ)**	Westwood	MA	D	781 467-3500	16857
American Saw & Mfg Company Inc	East Longmeadow	MA	D	413 525-3961	10466
Arborjet Inc	Woburn	MA	E	781 935-9070	17120
Armset LLC	Middleton	MA	G	978 774-0035	13083
Automec Inc	Waltham	MA	E	781 893-3403	16039
Bay State Scale & Systems Inc	Burlington	MA	G	781 993-9035	9239
Ben Franklin Design Mfg Co Inc	Agawam	MA	F	413 786-4220	7423
Berkshire Precision Tool LLC	Pittsfield	MA	E	413 499-3875	14459
Bruce Diamond Corporation	Attleboro	MA	E	508 222-3755	7715
Columbia ASC Inc	Lawrence	MA	F	978 683-2205	12012
Coorstek Inc	Worcester	MA	B	774 317-2600	17360
Custom Carbide Corp	Springfield	MA	F	413 732-7470	15466
Cutting Edge Carbide Tech Inc	Leominster	MA	G	888 210-9670	12130
D & R Products Co Inc	Hudson	MA	E	978 562-4137	11767
Dff Corp	Agawam	MA	C	413 786-8880	7427
Dienes Corporation	Spencer	MA	E	508 885-6301	15428
Dmt Export Inc	Marlborough	MA	E	508 481-5944	12748
Double E Company LLC **(PA)**	West Bridgewater	MA	C	508 588-8099	16438
Drc Precision Machining Co	Stoneham	MA	G	781 438-4500	15560
Dynisco Instruments LLC **(HQ)**	Franklin	MA	C	508 541-9400	11037
Ely Tool Inc	Springfield	MA	E	413 732-2347	15469
Ephesian Arms Inc	Fall River	MA	G	508 674-7030	10690
Esco Technologies Inc	Holliston	MA	E	508 429-4441	11570
Form Roll Die Corp **(PA)**	Worcester	MA	E	508 755-2010	17377
Giltron Inc	North Dighton	MA	G	508 359-4310	13931
Great Neck Saw Mfrs Inc	Millbury	MA	E	508 865-4482	13166
Harvard Manufacturing Inc	Shirley	MA	G	978 425-5375	15085
Hoppe Technologies Inc	Chicopee	MA	D	413 592-9213	10029
Hugard Inc	Westborough	MA	G	508 986-2300	16625
Hutchinson Arospc & Indust Inc	Hopkinton	MA	C	508 417-7000	11719
Industrial Cutting Tools Inc	Westfield	MA	G	413 562-2996	16689
J I Morris Company	Southbridge	MA	G	508 764-4394	15388
Joma Diamond Tool Company	East Longmeadow	MA	F	413 525-0760	10481
Kennametal Inc	Greenfield	MA	B	802 626-3331	11267
Keo Milling Cutters LLC	Athol	MA	B	800 523-5233	7688
L Hardy Company Inc **(PA)**	Worcester	MA	F	508 757-3480	17406
Lapointe Hudson Broach Co Inc	Hudson	MA	E	978 562-7943	11784
Leavitt Machine Co	Orange	MA	G	978 544-3872	14220
Lee Tool Co Inc	Ludlow	MA	F	413 583-8750	12471
LS Starrett Company **(PA)**	Athol	MA	A	978 249-3551	7689
LS Starrett Company	Athol	MA	G	978 249-3551	7690
Magwen Diamond Pdts Inc	Yarmouth Port	MA	G	508 375-9152	17530
Michael Brisebois	Easthampton	MA	F	413 527-9590	10567
Microcut Inc	Plymouth	MA	G	781 582-8090	14566
Mk Services Corp	Middleton	MA	E	978 777-2196	13096
Ned Acquisition Corp	Worcester	MA	E	508 798-8546	17427
New England Broach Co Inc	Whately	MA	F	413 665-7064	16907
New England Carbide Inc	Topsfield	MA	F	978 887-0313	15863
Niagara Cutter Athol Inc	Athol	MA	E	978 249-2788	7691
Nortek Inc	West Springfield	MA	E	413 781-4777	16535
North East Form Engineering	Lowell	MA	G	978 454-5290	12414
PCC Specialty Products Inc	Auburn	MA	D	508 753-6530	7847
Pedros Inc	Haverhill	MA	G	978 657-7101	11458
Picture Frame Products Inc	Arlington	MA	G	781 648-7719	7634
Pilot Precision Properties LLC	South Deerfield	MA	G	413 350-5200	15252
Poly-Tech Diamond Co Inc	North Attleboro	MA	F	508 695-3561	13772
Prism Products LLC	Lynn	MA	G	781 581-1740	12534

	CITY	ST	EMP	PHONE	ENTRY #
Quabbin Inc	Orange	MA	F	978 544-3872	14223
Rajessa LLC	East Falmouth	MA	F	508 540-4420	10447
Razor Tool Inc	Woburn	MA	G	781 654-1582	17281
Reed Machinery Inc **(PA)**	Worcester	MA	F	508 595-9090	17456
Richards Micro-Tool LLC	Plymouth	MA	E	508 746-6900	14580
Safe T Cut Inc	Monson	MA	F	413 267-9984	13211
Saint-Gobain Abrasives Inc **(DH)**	Worcester	MA	A	508 795-5000	17464
Simonds Industries Intl	Fitchburg	MA	E	978 424-0100	10853
Simonds Saw LLC **(PA)**	Fitchburg	MA	E	978 424-0100	10856
Standex International Corp	Wakefield	MA	G	978 538-0808	15977
Tektron Inc	Topsfield	MA	F	978 887-0091	15866
Thomas Machine Works Inc	Newburyport	MA	G	978 462-7182	13541
Tnco Inc	New Bedford	MA	D	781 447-6661	13454
Tool Technology Inc	Middleton	MA	E	978 777-5006	13104
Toolmex Indus Solutions Inc **(PA)**	Northborough	MA	D	508 653-5110	14052
Tri State Precision Inc	Northfield	MA	G	413 498-2961	14068
Trilap Company Inc	Lowell	MA	G	978 453-2205	12439
US Cutting Chain Mfg Co Inc	Brockton	MA	G	508 588-0322	9186
Van Wal Machine Inc	Bellingham	MA	F	508 966-0733	8061
Vogel Capital Inc **(HQ)**	Marlborough	MA	E	508 481-5944	12846
Vogform Tool & Die Co Inc	West Springfield	MA	F	413 737-6947	16562
Vulcan Company Inc **(PA)**	Hingham	MA	D	781 337-5970	11515
Wellman Engineering Inc	Belmont	MA	G	617 484-8338	8082
Wells Tool Company	Greenfield	MA	F	413 773-3465	11283
Enercon **(PA)**	Gray	ME	C	207 657-7000	6139
Irwin Industrial Tool Company	Gorham	ME	C	207 856-6111	6115
Maine Scale LLC	Auburn	ME	F	207 777-9500	5578
Mestek Inc	Clinton	ME	C	207 426-2351	5916
Michael Good Designs Inc	Rockport	ME	F	207 236-9619	6824
Mid State Machine Products **(PA)**	Winslow	ME	C	207 873-6136	7271
Peavey Manufacturing Company	Eddington	ME	E	207 843-7861	5997
Xuron Corp	Saco	ME	E	207 283-1401	6862
Ametek Precitech Inc **(HQ)**	Keene	NH	D	603 357-2510	18491
Bocra Industries Inc	Seabrook	NH	E	603 474-3598	19794
Boudrieau Tool & Die Inc	Rindge	NH	G	603 899-5795	19647
Cobra Precision Machining Corp	Hooksett	NH	G	603 434-8424	18347
Cutting Tool Technologies Inc	Wilton	NH	G	603 654-2550	19977
Diamondsharp Corporation	Walpole	NH	G	603 445-2224	19920
Jarvis Cutting Tools Inc	Rochester	NH	D	603 332-9000	19676
Onvio LLC	Salem	NH	G	603 685-0404	19757
R & J Tool Inc **(PA)**	Laconia	NH	G	603 366-4925	18581
Russell Precision	Laconia	NH	G	603 524-3772	18584
Swisset Tool Company Inc	Belmont	NH	G	603 524-0082	17684
Team Solutions Machining Inc	Hampstead	NH	G	978 420-2389	18250
Tel -Tuk Enterprises LLC	Belmont	NH	G	603 267-1966	17685
Will-Mor Manufacturing Inc	Seabrook	NH	D	603 474-8971	19823
Ar-Ro Engineering Company Inc **(PA)**	North Smithfield	RI	G	401 766-6669	20781
Comtorgage Corporation	Slatersville	RI	E	401 765-0900	21203
Durant Tool Company Inc	North Kingstown	RI	E	401 781-7800	20703
Estate Agency Inc	Cranston	RI	G	401 946-5380	20222
Fielding Mfg Zinc Diecasting	Cranston	RI	D	401 461-0400	20227
Hexagon Holdings Inc **(DH)**	North Kingstown	RI	G	401 886-2000	20715
Hexagon Metrology Inc **(DH)**	North Kingstown	RI	B	401 886-2000	20716
Mechanical Specialties Inc	Wyoming	RI	G	401 267-4410	21589
Mouldcam Inc	Bristol	RI	G	401 396-5522	20094
Numaco Packaging LLC	East Providence	RI	F	401 438-4952	20436
Precise Products Company	Lincoln	RI	F	401 724-7190	20592
R & D Tl Engrg Four-Slide Prod	Cranston	RI	G	401 942-9710	20276
RI Carbide Tool Co	Smithfield	RI	E	401 231-1020	21248
Rol-Flo Engineering Inc	Westerly	RI	E	401 596-0060	21539
W L Fuller	Warwick	RI	E	401 467-2900	21441
Wei Inc **(PA)**	Cranston	RI	E	401 781-3904	20309
Lovejoy Tool Company Inc	Springfield	VT	E	802 885-2194	22506
Mark Hunter	Lyndonville	VT	G	802 626-8407	22069
Sterling Gun Drills Inc	North Bennington	VT	F	802 442-3525	22213
Tivoly Inc	Derby Line	VT	C	802 873-3106	21906
Trow & Holden Co Inc	Barre	VT	F	802 476-7221	21643
Vermont Custom Gage LLC	Lyndonville	VT	G	802 868-0104	22074
Vermont Precision Tools Inc **(PA)**	Swanton	VT	C	802 868-4246	22538
Vermont Thread Gage LLC	Swanton	VT	G	802 868-4246	22539
Woodlan Tool and Machine Co	Bellows Falls	VT	E	802 463-4597	21656
Yankee Corporation	Fairfax	VT	D	802 527-0177	21981

3546 Power Hand Tools

	CITY	ST	EMP	PHONE	ENTRY #
Air Tool Sales & Service Co **(PA)**	Unionville	CT	G	860 673-2714	4652
Alden Corporation	Wolcott	CT	D	203 879-8830	5432
Amro Tool Co	Watertown	CT	G	860 274-9766	4998
Apex Machine Tool Company Inc	Cheshire	CT	D	860 677-2884	711
Black & Decker (us) Inc	Wethersfield	CT	G	860 563-5800	5242
Black & Decker (us) Inc	New Britain	CT	G	860 225-5111	2514
Black & Decker (us) Inc **(HQ)**	New Britain	CT	G	860 225-5111	2515
Blackstone Industries LLC	Bethel	CT	D	203 792-8622	133
DArcy Saw LLC	Windsor Locks	CT	G	800 569-1264	5390
Frasal Tool Co Inc	Newington	CT	F	860 666-3524	2865
HRF Fastener Systems Inc	Bristol	CT	E	860 589-0750	569
Ridge View Associates Inc	Milford	CT	D	203 878-8560	2351
Slater Hill Tool LLC	Putnam	CT	G	860 963-0415	3633
Stanley Black & Decker Inc **(PA)**	New Britain	CT	C	860 225-5111	2580
Stanley Black & Decker Inc	New Britain	CT	E	860 225-5111	2583
Stihl Incorporated	Oxford	CT	E	203 929-8488	3425
Trumpf Inc	Plainville	CT	B	860 255-6000	3522
Trumpf Inc **(DH)**	Farmington	CT	B	860 255-6000	1517
Trumpf Inc	Farmington	CT	B	860 255-6000	1518
Universal Precision Mfg	Trumbull	CT	G	203 374-9809	4641
Aube Precision Tool Co Inc	Ludlow	MA	G	413 589-9048	12454
Black & Decker (us) Inc	East Longmeadow	MA	G	413 526-5150	10468
Black & Decker (us) Inc	Westwood	MA	G	781 329-3407	16858
Guardair Corporation	Chicopee	MA	E	413 594-4400	10028
Simonds Incorporated	Southbridge	MA	F	508 764-3235	15403
Vulcan Company Inc **(PA)**	Hingham	MA	D	781 337-5970	11515
Adhesive Technologies Inc **(PA)**	Hampton	NH	E	603 926-1616	18252
Black & Decker Corporation	North Conway	NH	G	603 356-7595	19373
Burndy LLC	Littleton	NH	C	603 444-6781	18655
Pneutek Inc	Hudson	NH	F	603 595-0302	18427
Malco Saw Co Inc	Cranston	RI	G	401 942-7380	20258
Textron Inc **(PA)**	Providence	RI	B	401 421-2800	21134
Zampini Industrial Group LLC	Lincoln	RI	G	401 305-7997	20602
Sperber Tool Works Inc	Bennington	VT	G	802 442-8839	21691

3547 Rolling Mill Machinery & Eqpt

	CITY	ST	EMP	PHONE	ENTRY #
Adam Z Golas **(PA)**	New Britain	CT	G	860 224-7178	2504
Ulbrich Stainless Steels	Wallingford	CT	C	203 269-2507	4824
Idex Mpt Inc **(HQ)**	Westwood	MA	D	630 530-3333	16869
Kinefac Corporation	Worcester	MA	D	508 754-6901	17401
N Ferrara Inc	Somerset	MA	F	508 679-2440	15147
Dicks Baking	Milo	ME	G	207 284-3779	6445
CPM Acquisition Corp	Merrimack	NH	E	319 232-8444	18994
CPM Acquisition Corp	Merrimack	NH	E	603 423-6300	18995
Winchester Precision Tech Ltd	Winchester	NH	F	603 239-6326	19997
Millard Wire Company **(PA)**	Warwick	RI	D	401 737-9330	21389
Millard Wire Company	Warwick	RI	G	401 737-9330	21390

3548 Welding Apparatus

	CITY	ST	EMP	PHONE	ENTRY #
Air-Vac Engineering Co Inc **(PA)**	Seymour	CT	E	203 888-9900	3748
Branson Ultrasonics Corp **(DH)**	Danbury	CT	B	203 796-0400	882
Cadi Co Inc **(PA)**	Naugatuck	CT	E	203 729-1111	2465
Industrial Prssure Washers LLC	Wethersfield	CT	G	860 608-6153	5249
L & P Gate Company Inc	Hartford	CT	G	860 296-8009	1839
Magnatech LLC	East Granby	CT	D	860 653-2573	1131
Nelson Stud Welding Inc	Farmington	CT	G	800 635-9353	1497
Praxair Surface Tech Inc	Manchester	CT	D	860 646-0700	2039
Quality Welding Service LLC	Portland	CT	G	860 342-7202	3572
Sonics & Materials Inc **(PA)**	Newtown	CT	D	203 270-4600	2938
Sonitek Corporation	Milford	CT	E	203 878-9321	2364
Systems and Tech Intl Inc	Tolland	CT	G	860 871-0401	4553
AGM Industries Inc	Brockton	MA	E	508 587-3900	9117
Hydro-Test Products Inc	Stow	MA	F	978 897-4647	15632
Kamweld Technologies Inc	Norwood	MA	F	781 762-6922	14169
Kent Pearce	East Wareham	MA	G	508 295-3791	10531
Lincoln Electric Holdings Inc	Uxbridge	MA	B	508 366-7070	15925
Mitchell Machine Incorporated **(PA)**	Springfield	MA	E	413 739-9693	15490
Power Systems Integrity Inc	Northborough	MA	G	508 393-1655	14045
Precision Electronics Corp	Marshfield	MA	F	781 834-6677	12865
Triad Inc	Plainville	MA	G	508 695-2247	14537
Weld Engineering Co Inc	Shrewsbury	MA	E	508 842-2224	15137
Contact Inc	Edgecomb	ME	G	207 882-6116	6001
Centricut Manufacturing LLC	West Lebanon	NH	E	603 298-6191	19948
Contract Fusion Inc	East Providence	RI	E	401 438-1298	20400
Donald G Lockard	Westerly	RI	G	401 965-3182	21523
Miller Electric Mfg LLC	Coventry	RI	G	401 828-0087	20157
Nordson Efd LLC **(HQ)**	East Providence	RI	C	401 431-7000	20435

3549 Metalworking Machinery, NEC

	CITY	ST	EMP	PHONE	ENTRY #
Adamczyk Enterprises Inc	Enfield	CT	G	860 745-9830	1345
Alpha-Core Inc	Shelton	CT	E	203 954-0050	3773
C & G Precisions Products Inc	Wolcott	CT	G	203 879-6989	5433
Charter Oak Automation LLC	Wallingford	CT	G	203 562-0699	4716
Clear Automation LLC	Southington	CT	E	860 621-2955	4044
Fletcher-Terry Company LLC **(PA)**	East Berlin	CT	D	860 828-3400	1102
Foilmark Inc	Bloomfield	CT	F	860 243-0343	220
Hall Machine Systems Inc **(HQ)**	North Branford	CT	G	203 481-4275	2965
Herrick & Cowell Company Inc	Hamden	CT	G	203 288-2578	1759
Jovil Universal LLC	Danbury	CT	E	203 792-6700	941
L M Gill Welding and Mfr LLC **(PA)**	Manchester	CT	F	860 647-9931	2017
Merritt Extruder Corp	Hamden	CT	E	203 230-8100	1770
MGS Manufacturing Inc	North Branford	CT	G	203 481-4275	2970
P/A Industries Inc **(PA)**	Bloomfield	CT	E	860 243-8306	249
Te Connectivity Corporation	Stafford Springs	CT	C	860 684-8000	4116
Tmf Incorporated	Southbury	CT	G	203 267-7364	4034
True Position Mfg LLC	South Windsor	CT	G	860 291-2987	4017
Tyger Tool Inc	Stratford	CT	F	203 375-4344	4455
Vangor Engineering Corporation	Oxford	CT	G	203 267-4377	3428
Automec Inc	Waltham	MA	E	781 893-3403	16039
Broomfield Laboratories Inc	Bolton	MA	E	978 779-6600	8318

	CITY	ST	EMP	PHONE	ENTRY #
Classic Engineering LLC	Gloucester	MA	G	978 526-9003	11174
Entwistle Company **(HQ)**	Hudson	MA	C	508 481-4000	11772
Flir Unmnned Grund Systems Inc **(DH)**	Chelmsford	MA	D	978 769-9333	9899
Foilmark Inc **(HQ)**	Newburyport	MA	D	978 225-8200	13490
Gear/Tronics Industries Inc	North Billerica	MA	D	781 933-1400	13820
Gorman Machine Corp	Middleboro	MA	E	508 923-9462	13063
Kamrowski Metal Refinishing	Boston	MA	G	508 877-0367	8646
Ktron Inc	Marlborough	MA	E	508 229-0919	12784
Lawrence Sigler	Princeton	MA	G	978 464-2027	14606
Mestek Inc **(PA)**	Westfield	MA	E	470 898-4533	16700
Mestek Inc	Westfield	MA	B	413 568-9571	16702
Micro Electronics Inc	Seekonk	MA	F	508 761-9161	15027
Milara Inc	Milford	MA	D	508 533-5322	13127
NC Converting Inc	Seekonk	MA	G	508 336-6510	15031
New England Water Jet Cutting	New Bedford	MA	G	508 993-9235	13425
Op USA Inc	Acton	MA	G	978 658-5135	7376
Quiet Logistics	Devens	MA	F	978 391-4439	10331
S & H Engineering Inc	Chelmsford	MA	E	978 256-7231	9929
Sandys Machine	Tewksbury	MA	G	978 970-1800	15834
Seymour Associates Inc	Hudson	MA	G	978 562-1373	11815
Shanklin Research Corporation	Ayer	MA	G	978 772-2090	7938
Symbotic LLC	Wilmington	MA	G	978 284-2800	17050
Assembly Specialists Inc	Manchester	NH	F	603 624-9563	18780
High Speed Technologies Inc	Bow	NH	E	603 483-0333	17716
Precision Depaneling Mchs LLC	Fremont	NH	F	540 248-1381	18178
Sawtech Scientific Inc	Bow	NH	G	603 228-1811	17731
Standex International Corp **(PA)**	Salem	NH	E	603 893-9701	19769
Applitek Technologies Corp	Providence	RI	G	401 467-0007	20956
Cove Metal Company Inc **(PA)**	Pawtucket	RI	F	401 724-3500	20826
Durant Tool Company Inc	North Kingstown	RI	E	401 781-7800	20703
Gasbarre Products Inc	Cranston	RI	F	401 467-5200	20230
J-Tech Automation LLC	North Scituate	RI	G	401 934-2435	20779
Abacus Automation Inc	Bennington	VT	E	802 442-3662	21661

3552 Textile Machinery

	CITY	ST	EMP	PHONE	ENTRY #
Advanced Machine Services LLC **(PA)**	Waterbury	CT	G	203 888-6600	4836
Reynolds Carbide Die Co Inc	Thomaston	CT	E	860 283-8246	4512
Screen-Tech Inc	Torrington	CT	G	860 496-8016	4599
Sonic Corp	Stratford	CT	F	203 375-0063	4448
Ultramatic West	Hamden	CT	G	203 745-4688	1793
Accellent Holdings Corp	Wilmington	MA	A	978 570-6900	16962
Gemini Screenprinting & EMB Co	Brockton	MA	G	508 586-8223	9149
Holyoke Machine Company **(PA)**	Holyoke	MA	E	413 534-5612	11633
Jaf Corporation	Webster	MA	G	508 943-8519	16344
Lamb Knitting Machine Corp	Chicopee	MA	G	413 592-2501	10037
Micrex Corporation	Walpole	MA	F	508 660-1900	16002
Olde Village Monogramming Inc	Great Barrington	MA	G	413 528-3904	11244
Romax Inc	Hudson	MA	G	502 327-8555	11813
J D Paulsen	Bridgton	ME	G	207 647-5679	5808
Macomber Looms	York	ME	G	207 363-2808	7311
Maine Stitching Spc LLC	Skowhegan	ME	F	207 812-5207	6981
Orion Ropeworks LLC	Winslow	ME	D	207 877-2224	7274
All Seasons	Nashua	NH	G	603 560-7777	19109
Ametek Precitech Inc **(HQ)**	Keene	NH	D	603 357-2510	18491
Harrisville Designs Inc **(PA)**	Harrisville	NH	G	603 827-3333	18302
Cove Metal Company Inc **(PA)**	Pawtucket	RI	F	401 724-3500	20826
James L Gallagher Inc	Little Compton	RI	F	508 758-3102	20605
Maguire Lace & Warping Inc	Coventry	RI	G	401 821-1290	20154
Reed Gowdey Company	Central Falls	RI	G	401 723-6114	20123
Richmond Graphic Products Inc	Providence	RI	F	401 233-2700	21115
Standard Mill Machinery Corp	West Warwick	RI	G	401 822-7871	21510
Stolberger Incorporated	Central Falls	RI	E	401 724-8800	20126
Texcel Inc	Cumberland	RI	F	401 727-2113	20347
Windmill Associates Inc	Warwick	RI	G	401 732-4700	21448

3553 Woodworking Machinery

	CITY	ST	EMP	PHONE	ENTRY #
United Abrasives Inc **(PA)**	North Windham	CT	B	860 456-7131	3084
Walsh Claim Services	North Branford	CT	G	203 481-0680	2983
A & A Architectural Wdwkg Inc	Westfield	MA	G	413 568-9914	16661
Boston Wood Art	Natick	MA	G	508 353-4129	13240
Enchanted World Boxes Inc	Cambridge	MA	G	617 492-6941	9466
Goodspeed Machine Company	Winchendon	MA	G	978 297-0296	17076
Heyes Forest Products Inc	Orange	MA	G	978 544-8801	14217
Lawrence Sigler	Princeton	MA	G	978 464-2027	14606
Simonds International LLC	Fitchburg	MA	G	978 424-0327	10854
Simonds International LLC **(HQ)**	Fitchburg	MA	B	978 424-0100	10855
Woodworking Machinery Services	North Billerica	MA	G	978 663-8488	13878
Downeast Machine & Engrg Inc	Mechanic Falls	ME	F	207 345-8111	6419
Machinery Service Co Inc	Wiscasset	ME	G	207 882-6788	7285
Maxym Technologies Inc	Biddeford	ME	G	207 283-8601	5747
Vacuum Pressing Systems Inc	Brunswick	ME	G	207 725-0935	5850
W A Mitchell Inc	Farmington	ME	G	207 778-5212	6054
HMC Corporation **(PA)**	Hopkinton	NH	E	603 746-3399	18362
Homestead Kitchen Centre LLC	Kingston	NH	G	603 642-8022	18544
Sawtech Scientific Inc	Bow	NH	G	603 228-1811	17731
Williams & Hussey Mch Co Inc	Amherst	NH	F	603 732-0219	17591
McCormacks Machine Co Inc	West Rutland	VT	G	802 438-2345	22618

3554 Paper Inds Machinery

	CITY	ST	EMP	PHONE	ENTRY #
Andritz Shw Inc	Torrington	CT	E	860 496-8888	4561
Bar-Plate Manufacturing Co	Hamden	CT	F	203 397-0033	1734
Sonic Corp	Stratford	CT	F	203 375-0063	4448
Zatorski Coating Company Inc	East Hampton	CT	F	860 267-9889	1168
Barton Rice Corporation	Oxford	MA	G	508 966-2194	14253
Butler Automatic Inc **(PA)**	Middleboro	MA	D	508 923-0544	13057
Functional Coatings LLC	Newburyport	MA	D	978 462-0746	13493
Garlock Prtg & Converting Corp **(PA)**	Gardner	MA	D	978 630-1028	11117
GL&v USA Inc	Lenox	MA	C	413 637-2424	12100
Holyoke Machine Company **(PA)**	Holyoke	MA	E	413 534-5612	11633
Jen-Coat Inc **(DH)**	Westfield	MA	C	413 875-9855	16693
Johnston Dandy Company	Holyoke	MA	F	413 315-4596	11635
Kadant Inc	Auburn	MA	C	508 791-8171	7840
Kadant Inc **(PA)**	Westford	MA	B	978 776-2000	16774
Kadant Inc	Auburn	MA	C	508 791-8171	7841
Magnat-Fairview LLC	Chicopee	MA	F	413 593-5742	10039
Metso Usa Inc **(HQ)**	Boston	MA	G	617 369-7850	8703
Micrex Corporation	Walpole	MA	F	508 660-1900	16002
Mitchell Machine Incorporated **(PA)**	Springfield	MA	E	413 739-9693	15490
Montague Industries Inc	Turners Falls	MA	E	413 863-4301	15882
Rudison Routhier Engrg Co	West Hatfield	MA	G	413 247-9341	16485
Snyder Machine Co Inc	Saugus	MA	F	781 233-2080	14997
Tecnau Inc **(DH)**	Billerica	MA	E	978 608-0356	8301
Thomson National Press Company **(PA)**	Franklin	MA	G	508 528-2000	11091
Webco Engineering Inc	Southborough	MA	F	508 303-0500	15372
Johnston Dandy Company **(PA)**	Lincoln	ME	E	207 794-6571	6355
Southworth Intl Group Inc **(PA)**	Falmouth	ME	D	207 878-0700	6033
Valmet Inc	Biddeford	ME	C	207 282-1521	5767
Bfmc LLC	Berlin	NH	E	603 752-4550	17693
GL&v USA Inc **(HQ)**	Nashua	NH	B	603 882-2711	19168
GL&v USA Inc	Nashua	NH	D	603 882-2711	19169
J J Plank Corporation	Farmington	NH	G	920 733-4479	18143
Spectex LLC	Dover	NH	F	603 330-3334	18054
Tidland Corporation	Keene	NH	D	603 352-1696	18533
Valmet Inc **(HQ)**	Nashua	NH	G	603 882-2711	19278
Maxson Automatic Machinery Co **(PA)**	Westerly	RI	E	401 596-0162	21530
Press Tech Company Inc	Ashaway	RI	G	401 377-4800	20039
Stearns Tool Company Inc	Providence	RI	G	401 351-4765	21127
Ashe America Inc	Brattleboro	VT	D	802 254-0200	21718

3555 Printing Trades Machinery & Eqpt

	CITY	ST	EMP	PHONE	ENTRY #
Arico Engineering Inc	North Franklin	CT	G	860 642-7040	2987
Asml Us LLC	Wilton	CT	A	203 761-4000	5275
I Q Technology LLC	Enfield	CT	F	860 749-7255	1365
Interpro LLC	Deep River	CT	F	860 526-5869	1062
J-Teck Usa Inc	Danbury	CT	G	203 791-2121	938
Santec Corporation	Milford	CT	F	203 878-1379	2359
Verico Technology LLC **(HQ)**	Enfield	CT	E	800 492-7286	1389
2l Inc	Hudson	MA	F	978 567-8867	11748
Alden and Broden Corporation	Westford	MA	G	603 882-0330	16752
Armstrong Machine Co Inc	Beverly	MA	F	978 232-9466	8102
Art Swiss Corporation	New Bedford	MA	F	508 999-3281	13359
Aurora Imaging Technology Inc	Wellesley	MA	G	617 522-6900	16361
Blade Tech Systems Inc	Plymouth	MA	G	508 830-9506	14545
Butler Automatic Inc **(PA)**	Middleboro	MA	D	508 923-0544	13057
Ecrm Incorporated **(PA)**	North Andover	MA	D	800 537-3276	13700
Gem Gravure Co Inc **(PA)**	Hanover	MA	D	781 878-0456	11339
Gillies W Technologies LLC	Worcester	MA	G	508 852-2502	17382
Honorcraft LLC	Stoughton	MA	E	781 341-0410	15597
Hosokawa Micron International	Northborough	MA	F	508 655-1123	14037
Inkbit LLC	Medford	MA	G	617 433-8842	12936
Integrated Web Finishing Syst	Avon	MA	E	508 580-5809	7887
Jaf Corporation	Webster	MA	G	508 943-8519	16344
Jet Graphics LLC	Avon	MA	E	508 580-5809	7889
Jnj Industries Inc	Franklin	MA	E	508 553-0529	11058
Milara Inc	Milford	MA	D	508 533-5322	13127
Nes Worldwide Inc	Westfield	MA	E	413 485-5038	16707
Net Vantage Point Inc	Lexington	MA	G	781 860-9158	12248
Rotation Dynamics Corporation	Marlborough	MA	F	508 481-0900	12822
Rudison Routhier Engrg Co	West Hatfield	MA	G	413 247-9341	16485
Signature Engrv Systems Inc	Holyoke	MA	E	413 533-7500	11657
Teca-Print USA Corp	Winchester	MA	F	781 369-1084	17098
Tooling Research Inc **(PA)**	Walpole	MA	F	508 668-1950	16014
Transition Automation Inc	North Billerica	MA	F	978 670-5500	13874
Verico Technology LLC	South Hadley	MA	C	413 539-9111	15312
Westcon Mfg Inc	Brunswick	ME	E	207 725-5537	5851
Cc1 Inc	Portsmouth	NH	E	603 319-2000	19548
Electronics For Imaging Inc	West Lebanon	NH	B	603 279-6800	19949
G P 2 Technologies Inc	Bow	NH	G	603 226-0336	17714
Manroland Goss Web Systems AMR **(DH)**	Durham	NH	B	603 750-6600	18078
Presstek Overseas Corp **(DH)**	Nashua	NH	G	603 595-7000	19238
Prodways	Merrimack	NH	G	763 568-7966	19024
Verico Technology LLC	Nashua	NH	C	603 402-7573	19281
Austrian Machine Corp	Cranston	RI	F	401 946-4090	20184

	CITY	ST	EMP	PHONE	ENTRY #
Dasko Identification Products	East Providence	RI	F	401 435-6500	20403
Eagle Industries Inc	Ashaway	RI	E	401 596-8111	20033
Fine Line Graphics Inc **(PA)**	Smithfield	RI	E	401 349-3300	21226
Imprint Inc	Greenville	RI	G	401 949-1177	20468
Press Tech Company Inc	Ashaway	RI	G	401 377-4800	20039
R & D Technologies Inc	North Kingstown	RI	F	401 885-6400	20734
Richard Chiovitti	Greenville	RI	G	401 949-1177	20474

3556 Food Prdts Machinery

	CITY	ST	EMP	PHONE	ENTRY #
A & I Concentrate LLC	Shelton	CT	F	203 447-1938	3771
Amt Micropure Inc	Weston	CT	G	203 226-7938	5168
Bakery Engineering/Winkler Inc	Shelton	CT	F	203 929-8630	3779
Cimbali Usa Inc	Fairfield	CT	G	203 254-6046	1418
Conair Corporation	Torrington	CT	D	800 492-7464	4572
EMI Inc	Clinton	CT	G	860 669-1199	786
Jarvis Products Corporation **(HQ)**	Middletown	CT	F	860 347-7271	2193
Penco Corporation	Middletown	CT	C	860 347-7271	2209
Pro Scientific Inc	Oxford	CT	F	203 267-4600	3420
Q-Jet DSI Inc	North Haven	CT	G	203 230-4700	3056
Sonic Corp	Stratford	CT	F	203 375-0063	4448
Sun Farm Corporation	Milford	CT	G	203 882-8000	2372
Taylor Coml Foodservice Inc	Farmington	CT	A	336 245-6400	1515
Treif USA Inc	Shelton	CT	F	203 929-9930	3881
Ventures LLC DOT Com LLC	Vernon	CT	G	203 930-8972	4676
Alfa Laval Inc	Newburyport	MA	E	978 465-5777	13468
Baker Parts Inc	New Bedford	MA	G	508 636-3121	13360
Bematek Systems Inc	Salem	MA	G	978 744-5816	14897
C H Babb Co Inc	Raynham	MA	E	508 977-0600	14706
Electrolyzer Corp	West Newbury	MA	G	978 363-5349	16490
Grandten Distilling LLC	Boston	MA	G	617 269-0497	8577
Gruenewald Mfg Co Inc	Danvers	MA	F	978 777-0200	10219
Jimsan Enterprises Inc	West Bridgewater	MA	G	508 587-3666	16442
Maxant Industries Inc	Devens	MA	F	978 772-0576	10324
Oesco Inc	Conway	MA	E	413 369-4335	10164
Pearce Processing Systems	Gloucester	MA	G	978 283-3800	11202
Sharp Services Inc	Saugus	MA	G	781 854-3334	14996
Somerset Industries Inc	Lowell	MA	E	978 667-3355	12433
Stonybrook Water Company LLC	Manchester	MA	G	978 865-9899	12607
Westport Envmtl Systems LP	Westport	MA	D	508 636-8811	16851
Wilevco Inc	Billerica	MA	F	978 667-0400	8310
Adjacent Bakery LLC	Scarborough	ME	G	207 252-6722	6902
Acana Northeast Inc	Pembroke	NH	F	800 922-2629	19455
Admix Inc	Londonderry	NH	E	603 627-2340	18671
Aquaback Technologies Inc	Salem	NH	F	978 863-1000	19709
Burlodge USA Inc	Litchfield	NH	F	336 776-1010	18651
Cooking Solutions Group Inc **(HQ)**	Salem	NH	G	603 893-9701	19719
Distillery Network Inc	Manchester	NH	G	603 997-6786	18810
L E Jackson Coropration	North Haverhill	NH	G	603 787-6036	19389
Superior Ice Cream Eqp LLC	Bow	NH	F	603 225-4207	17732
Superior Novelty Equipment	Bow	NH	G	603 225-4207	17733
Univex Corporation	Salem	NH	D	603 893-6191	19775
Green Mountain Smokehouse	Windsor	VT	G	802 674-6653	22709
Leader Evaporator Co Inc **(PA)**	Swanton	VT	D	802 868-5444	22531

3559 Special Ind Machinery, NEC

	CITY	ST	EMP	PHONE	ENTRY #
B & A Design Inc	Vernon Rockville	CT	G	860 871-0134	4679
Bausch Advanced Tech Inc **(PA)**	Clinton	CT	E	860 669-7380	779
Berkshire Photonics LLC	Washington Depot	CT	G	860 868-0412	4832
Davis-Standard Holdings Inc **(PA)**	Pawcatuck	CT	B	860 599-1010	3433
Day Machine Systems Inc	New Britain	CT	F	860 229-3440	2526
Edward Segal Inc	Thomaston	CT	E	860 283-5821	4502
Emhart Glass Inc **(DH)**	Windsor	CT	D	860 298-7340	5331
Emhart Teknologies LLC	Danbury	CT	G	877 364-2781	907
Evans Cooling Systems Inc **(PA)**	Suffield	CT	G	860 668-1114	4462
Farrel Corporation **(DH)**	Ansonia	CT	D	203 736-5500	15
Gerber Technology LLC **(HQ)**	Tolland	CT	B	860 871-8082	4549
Jet Process Corporation	North Haven	CT	G	203 985-6000	3035
Johnstone Company Inc	North Haven	CT	E	203 239-5834	3036
Lamor USA Corporation	Shelton	CT	G	203 888-7700	3823
Lyman Products Corporation **(PA)**	Middletown	CT	D	860 632-2020	2202
Lyman Products Corporation	Middletown	CT	E	860 632-2020	2203
Lynch Corp	Greenwich	CT	G	203 452-3007	1627
M I R Inc	Beacon Falls	CT	F	203 888-2541	61
Medelco Inc	Bridgeport	CT	G	203 275-8070	449
Media One LLC	Hamden	CT	E	203 745-5825	1769
Merritt Extruder Corp	Hamden	CT	E	203 230-8100	1770
Omega Engineering Inc	Norwalk	CT	D	714 540-4914	3212
Prospect Products Incorporated	Newington	CT	E	860 666-0323	2896
Puritan Industries Inc	Collinsville	CT	E	860 693-0791	816
PYC Deborring LLC F/K/A C &	Berlin	CT	G	860 828-6806	106
Quest Plastics Inc	Torrington	CT	F	860 489-1404	4595
Saf Industries LLC	Meriden	CT	E	203 729-4900	2127
Single Load LLC	Bridgeport	CT	G	860 944-7507	492
Snapwire Innovations LLC	Cheshire	CT	G	203 806-4773	763
Startech Environmental Corp **(PA)**	Wilton	CT	F	203 762-2499	5305
Toppan Photomasks Inc	Brookfield	CT	E	203 775-9001	661
Walker Magnetics Group Inc **(HQ)**	Windsor	CT	E	508 853-3232	5378
Windham Automated Machines Inc	South Windham	CT	F	860 208-5297	3929
Wittmann Battenfeld Inc **(DH)**	Torrington	CT	D	860 496-9603	4608
A & D Tool Co	Indian Orchard	MA	G	413 543-3166	11883
A B Engineering & Co	Oxford	MA	G	508 987-0318	14251
Accudyne Machine Tool Inc	Bellingham	MA	G	508 966-3110	8027
American & Schoen Machinery Co	Beverly	MA	E	978 524-0168	8098
Artisan Industries Inc	Stoughton	MA	D	781 893-6800	15581
Atlas Machine Tool Inc	Gloucester	MA	G	508 284-3542	11161
Automotive Mach Shop Sup	West Bridgewater	MA	G	508 586-6706	16430
Axcelis Technologies Inc **(PA)**	Beverly	MA	C	978 787-4000	8106
Bay State Plating Inc	Holyoke	MA	G	413 533-6927	11618
Bisco Environmental Inc	Danvers	MA	E	508 738-5100	10203
Black Oxide Co Inc	Worcester	MA	G	508 757-0340	17348
Boston Process Tech Inc	Peabody	MA	F	978 854-5579	14316
Brick Kiln Place LLC	Medford	MA	G	781 826-6027	12924
Brooks Automation Inc **(PA)**	Chelmsford	MA	B	978 262-2400	9880
Brooks Automation Inc	Chelmsford	MA	B	978 262-2795	9879
Btu International Inc **(HQ)**	North Billerica	MA	C	978 667-4111	13800
Capesym Inc	Natick	MA	G	508 653-7100	13242
Castaldo Products Mfg Co Inc	Franklin	MA	G	508 520-1666	11027
Celeros Inc	Newton	MA	E	248 478-2800	13576
Cipem USA Inc	Melrose	MA	G	347 642-1106	12979
Cotter Brothers Corporation	Danvers	MA	E	978 777-5001	10206
Cotuit Works	Cotuit	MA	G	508 428-3971	10169
Crosby Machine Company Inc	West Brookfield	MA	G	508 867-3121	16468
Csi Mfg Inc	Westborough	MA	E	508 986-2300	16611
Degreasing Devices Co	Southbridge	MA	G	508 765-0045	15379
DH Industries USA Inc	Burlington	MA	G	781 229-5814	9255
Edmund Carr	Braintree	MA	G	781 817-5616	9003
EMD Millipore Corporation **(DH)**	Burlington	MA	A	781 533-6000	9262
Farmer Brown Service Inc	Acton	MA	G	978 897-7550	7355
Gloucester Engineering Co Inc **(DH)**	Gloucester	MA	D	978 281-1800	11186
Gloucester Engineering Co Inc	Gloucester	MA	G	978 515-7008	11187
Gt Advanced Technologies	Danvers	MA	D	508 954-8249	10220
Healthstar Inc	Braintree	MA	E	781 428-3696	9017
Herb Con Machine Company Inc	Saugus	MA	G	781 233-2755	14985
Highland Labs Inc	Holliston	MA	E	508 429-2918	11577
Hosokawa Micron International	Northborough	MA	F	508 655-1123	14037
Innopad Inc	Newton	MA	G	978 253-4204	13605
Jgp Enterprises Inc	Andover	MA	E	978 691-2737	7559
Lacerta Group Inc	Mansfield	MA	G	508 339-3312	12641
Lacerta Group Inc **(PA)**	Mansfield	MA	D	508 339-3312	12642
Lambient Technologies LLC	Cambridge	MA	G	857 242-3963	9530
M E Baker Company **(PA)**	Framingham	MA	F	508 620-5304	10979
Mason Industries Inc	Marlborough	MA	G	508 485-8494	12792
Maxant Industries Inc	Devens	MA	F	978 772-0576	10324
Mediatek USA Inc	Woburn	MA	D	781 503-8000	17227
Microfluidics Intl Corp	Westwood	MA	E	617 969-5452	16873
Millers Petroleum Systems Inc	Pittsfield	MA	G	413 499-2134	14490
Mitchell Machine Incorporated **(PA)**	Springfield	MA	E	413 739-9693	15490
New England Alpaca Fiber Pool	Westport	MA	G	508 672-6032	16844
North American Auto Equipment	Plainville	MA	G	866 607-4022	14532
Northeast Data Destruction LLC	Mansfield	MA	G	800 783-6766	12650
Nypro Inc **(HQ)**	Clinton	MA	A	978 365-8100	10086
Oasys Water Inc	Foxboro	MA	E	617 963-0450	10895
OK Engineering Inc	Hudson	MA	G	978 562-1010	11797
Once Upon A Kiln	Bellingham	MA	G	508 657-1739	8055
Onyx Spectrum Technology	Lawrence	MA	G	978 686-7000	12068
Overlook Industries Inc	Easthampton	MA	F	413 527-4344	10574
Purecoat International LLC	Belmont	MA	E	561 844-0100	8079
Ranger Automation Systems Inc	Millbury	MA	E	508 842-6500	13174
Rapid Micro Biosystems Inc **(PA)**	Lowell	MA	D	978 349-3200	12425
Reifenhauser Incorporated	Danvers	MA	G	847 669-9972	10252
Reliable	Winchendon	MA	G	978 230-2689	17081
Rocheleau Tool and Die Co Inc	Fitchburg	MA	D	978 345-1723	10851
Roger Tool and Die Company Inc	Worcester	MA	G	508 853-3757	17460
Safety-Kleen Systems Inc	Marlborough	MA	F	508 481-3116	12823
Saint-Gobain Abrasives Inc **(DH)**	Worcester	MA	A	508 795-5000	17464
Sancliff Inc	Worcester	MA	F	508 795-0747	17469
Sonicron Systems Corporation	Westfield	MA	E	413 562-5218	16731
Sturtevant Inc **(PA)**	Hanover	MA	E	781 829-6501	11355
Synchroneuron Inc	Duxbury	MA	G	617 538-5688	10402
TEC Engineering Corp	Oxford	MA	F	508 987-0231	14275
Tecomet Inc	Woburn	MA	D	781 782-6400	17305
Thermoplastics Co Inc	Worcester	MA	E	508 754-4668	17488
Topsall Machine Tool Co Inc	Worcester	MA	G	508 755-0332	17489
Ultrasonic Systems Inc	Haverhill	MA	E	978 521-0095	11481
Universal Pharma Tech LLC	North Andover	MA	F	978 975-7216	13735
User-Friendly Recycling LLC	Stoughton	MA	G	781 269-5021	15627
Uspack Inc	Leominster	MA	E	978 466-9700	12197
Uspack Inc	Hudson	MA	E	978 562-8522	11825
Vacuum Barrier Corporation	Woburn	MA	E	781 933-3570	17310
Varian Semicdtr Eqp Assoc Inc	Newburyport	MA	C	978 463-1500	13548
Waste Mgmt Inc	Springfield	MA	E	413 747-9294	15523
Whitney & Son Inc	Fitchburg	MA	E	978 343-6353	10863
Willigent Corporation	Auburndale	MA	G	617 663-5707	7873
Witricity Corporation **(PA)**	Watertown	MA	F	617 926-2700	16331

S
I
C

	CITY	ST	EMP	PHONE	ENTRY #
Arcast Inc	Oxford	ME	G	207 539-9638	6563
Brass Foundry	West Rockport	ME	G	207 236-3200	7178
Eltec Industries Inc **(PA)**	Freeport	ME	G	207 541-9085	6077
Lanco Assembly Systems Inc **(PA)**	Westbrook	ME	D	207 773-2060	7193
Mid Cape Restoration	Hollis Center	ME	F	207 929-4759	6200
Northeast Time Trak Systems	Westbrook	ME	G	207 774-2336	7200
Torrefaction Tech USA LLC	Portland	ME	G	207 775-2464	6741
Admix Inc	Londonderry	NH	E	603 627-2340	18671
Bc Nichols Machine LLC	Hampton	NH	G	603 926-2333	18258
CET Technology LLC	Windham	NH	F	603 894-6100	20001
Fab Braze Corp **(PA)**	Nashua	NH	G	781 893-6777	19153
Hycon Inc	Manchester	NH	G	603 644-1414	18841
Ishigaki USA Ltd	Portsmouth	NH	F	603 433-3334	19581
Land and Sea Inc	Concord	NH	D	603 226-3966	17912
Micro-Precision Inc **(PA)**	Sunapee	NH	E	603 763-2394	19882
Mountain Firewood Kiln	Littleton	NH	G	603 444-6954	18663
MTS Associates Londonderry LLC	Londonderry	NH	G	603 425-2562	18725
Mushield Company Inc	Londonderry	NH	E	603 666-4433	18726
Pica Mfg Solutions Inc	Derry	NH	E	603 845-3258	17993
Province Kiln Dried Firewood	Belmont	NH	G	603 524-4447	17681
Semigen Inc	Londonderry	NH	E	603 624-8311	18735
White Mountain Imaging	Concord	NH	F	603 228-2630	17940
B & M Plastics Inc	Pawtucket	RI	G	401 728-0404	20815
Conley Casting Supply Corp **(PA)**	Warwick	RI	E	401 461-4710	21345
Danglers Inc	Johnston	RI	G	401 274-7742	20506
Environmental Ctrl Systems Inc	East Providence	RI	F	401 437-8612	20410
Fueling Services LLC	Johnston	RI	F	401 764-0711	20513
Greco Bros Inc	Providence	RI	F	401 421-9306	21023
Impreglon Inc	Woonsocket	RI	F	401 766-3353	21571
Technic Inc	Pawtucket	RI	E	401 781-6100	20902
Technic Inc **(PA)**	Cranston	RI	C	401 781-6100	20301
Technic Inc	Woonsocket	RI	E	401 769-7000	21585
US Extruders Inc	Westerly	RI	F	401 584-4710	21546
Wheeltrak Inc	Tiverton	RI	E	800 296-1326	21266
Advanced Illumination Inc	Rochester	VT	E	802 767-3830	22315
Cask & Kiln Kitchen LLC	Wilmington	VT	G	802 464-2275	22700
Hub Consolidated Inc	Orwell	VT	G	802 948-2209	22255
McCormacks Machine Co Inc	West Rutland	VT	G	802 438-2345	22618
Parkmatic Car Prkg Systems LLC	Shelburne	VT	G	802 495-0903	22421
Stevens Kiln Drying LLC	Wolcott	VT	G	802 472-5013	22732
Trow & Holden Co Inc	Barre	VT	F	802 476-7221	21643
Vacutherm Inc	Warren	VT	G	802 496-4241	22579

3561 Pumps & Pumping Eqpt

	CITY	ST	EMP	PHONE	ENTRY #
Beckson Manufacturing Inc **(PA)**	Bridgeport	CT	E	203 366-3644	381
Bjm Pumps LLC	Old Saybrook	CT	E	860 399-5937	3329
Dpc Quality Pump Service	Milford	CT	G	203 874-6877	2276
Flowserve Corporation	Milford	CT	E	203 877-4252	2290
Foleys Pump Service Inc	Danbury	CT	E	203 792-2236	921
Hamworthy Peabody Combustn Inc **(DH)**	Shelton	CT	E	203 922-1199	3808
ITT Water & Wastewater USA Inc **(HQ)**	Shelton	CT	D	262 548-8181	3820
Marsars Water Rescue Systems	Shelton	CT	G	203 924-7315	3831
Omega Engineering Inc	Norwalk	CT	D	714 540-4914	3212
Phillips Pump LLC	Bridgeport	CT	F	203 576-6688	469
Preferred Utilities Mfg Corp **(HQ)**	Danbury	CT	D	203 743-6741	974
Proflow Inc	North Haven	CT	E	203 230-4700	3055
Sonic Corp	Stratford	CT	F	203 375-0063	4448
Sulzer Pump Solutions US Inc **(PA)**	Meriden	CT	E	203 238-2700	2135
Talcott Mountain Engineering	Simsbury	CT	F	860 651-3141	3913
Xylem Water Solutions USA Inc	Shelton	CT	E	203 450-3715	3891
A W Chesterton Company	Groveland	MA	B	781 438-7000	11299
BEE International Inc	South Easton	MA	E	508 238-5558	15270
Boc Group Inc	Wilmington	MA	G	978 658-5410	16984
Brooks Automation Inc	Chelmsford	MA	B	978 262-2795	9879
Circor Naval Solutions LLC **(HQ)**	Warren	MA	D	413 436-7711	16260
Clark Solutions	Hudson	MA	F	978 568-3400	11763
Essential Life Solutions Ltd	Stoughton	MA	G	781 341-7240	15589
Flow Control LLC	Beverly	MA	E	978 281-0440	8131
Flowserve US Inc	Lawrence	MA	C	978 682-5248	12025
Fortis LLC	Northbridge	MA	G	617 600-4178	14056
Harvard Clinical Tech Inc	Natick	MA	E	508 655-2000	13259
Infutronix LLC	Natick	MA	G	508 650-2007	13262
Iwaki America Incorporated **(HQ)**	Holliston	MA	D	508 429-1440	11579
Iwaki Pumps Inc **(DH)**	Holliston	MA	E	508 429-1440	11580
Marlow Watson Inc **(HQ)**	Wilmington	MA	E	800 282-8823	17020
Mass Vac Inc	North Billerica	MA	E	978 667-2393	13839
Netzsch USA Holdings Inc **(PA)**	Burlington	MA	G	781 272-5353	9308
Northeast Equipment Inc	Fall River	MA	E	508 324-0083	10740
Rectorseal	Fall River	MA	G	508 673-7561	10754
Taco Inc	Fall River	MA	D	508 675-7300	10769
Tark Inc	Billerica	MA	F	978 663-8074	8300
Thermo Orion Inc **(HQ)**	Chelmsford	MA	E	800 225-1480	9937
TNT Manufacturing LLC	Westfield	MA	G	413 562-0690	16735
Vaccon Company Inc	Medway	MA	E	508 359-7200	12972
Xylem Water Solutions USA Inc	Woburn	MA	G	781 935-6515	17325
Martin Carmichael	Cardville	ME	F	207 827-2858	5882
Stevens Electric Pump Service	Monmouth	ME	G	207 933-2143	6451
Brailsford & Company Inc	Antrim	NH	E	603 588-2880	17593
Larchmont Engineering Inc	Manchester	NH	G	603 622-8825	18860
Pfeiffer Vacuum Inc **(DH)**	Nashua	NH	E	603 578-6500	19231
Solar-Stream LLC	Temple	NH	G	603 878-0066	19899
Airgas Usa LLC	East Greenwich	RI	G	401 884-0201	20351
Aquamotion Inc	Warwick	RI	F	401 785-3000	21326
Bosworth Company	East Providence	RI	F	401 438-1110	20392
Boydco Inc **(PA)**	East Providence	RI	F	401 438-6900	20393
Bsm Pump Corp	North Kingstown	RI	E	401 471-6350	20694
Mesco Corporation	Portsmouth	RI	G	401 683-2677	20928
Taco Inc **(PA)**	Cranston	RI	B	401 942-8000	20299
Hayward Tyler Inc **(DH)**	Colchester	VT	D	802 655-4444	21864
Ivek Corp	North Springfield	VT	D	802 886-2238	22236
PBL Incorporated	Colchester	VT	F	802 893-0111	21876
Whale Water Systems Inc	Manchester	VT	F	802 367-1091	22079

3562 Ball & Roller Bearings

	CITY	ST	EMP	PHONE	ENTRY #
Abek LLC	Bristol	CT	F	860 314-3905	510
Ball & Roller Bearing Co LLC	New Milford	CT	F	860 355-4161	2787
Buswell Manufacturing Co Inc	Bridgeport	CT	F	203 334-6069	392
C & S Engineering Inc	Meriden	CT	E	203 235-5727	2082
Del-Tron Precision Inc	Bethel	CT	E	203 778-2727	143
Fag Bearings LLC **(DH)**	Danbury	CT	D	203 790-5474	916
FAg Holding Corporation **(DH)**	Danbury	CT	F	203 790-5474	917
Gwilliam Company Inc	New Milford	CT	F	860 354-2884	2804
Hartford Technologies Inc	Rocky Hill	CT	E	860 571-3602	3712
K A F Manufacturing Co Inc	Stamford	CT	E	203 324-3012	4234
Kamatics Corporation	Bloomfield	CT	G	860 243-7230	236
Kamatics Corporation **(DH)**	Bloomfield	CT	E	860 243-9704	235
Rbc Bearings Incorporated **(PA)**	Oxford	CT	B	203 267-7001	3421
Rbc Linear Precision Pdts Inc	Fairfield	CT	G	203 255-1511	1450
Roller Bearing Co Amer Inc **(HQ)**	Oxford	CT	C	203 267-7001	3423
Roller Bearing Co Amer Inc	Oxford	CT	E	203 267-7001	3424
Schaeffler Aerospace USA Corp **(DH)**	Danbury	CT	B	203 744-2211	984
Schaeffler Aerospace USA Corp	Winsted	CT	D	860 379-7558	5421
Schaeffler Group USA Inc	Danbury	CT	B	203 790-5474	985
SKF Specialty Balls	Winsted	CT	G	860 379-8511	5422
SKF USA Inc	Winsted	CT	E	860 379-8511	5423
Timken Company	Glastonbury	CT	F	860 652-4630	1579
Virginia Industries Inc **(PA)**	Rocky Hill	CT	G	860 571-3600	3733
Vulcan Industries Inc	East Longmeadow	MA	G	413 525-8846	10502
Mpb Corporation **(HQ)**	Keene	NH	A	603 352-0310	18518
Mpb Corporation	Lebanon	NH	B	603 448-3000	18630
Mpb Corporation	Lebanon	NH	B	603 448-3000	18631
New Hmpshire Ball Bearings Inc **(DH)**	Peterborough	NH	B	603 924-3311	19478
New Hmpshire Ball Bearings Inc	Laconia	NH	B	603 524-0004	18577
New Hmpshire Ball Bearings Inc	Peterborough	NH	E	603 924-3311	19479
Timken Company	Lebanon	NH	A	603 443-5281	18638
Caster Crative Photography LLC	Charlestown	RI	G	401 364-3545	20131

3563 Air & Gas Compressors

	CITY	ST	EMP	PHONE	ENTRY #
Afcon Products Inc	Bethany	CT	F	203 393-9301	118
Bauer Compressors Inc	Monroe	CT	G	203 445-9514	2394
Comvac Systems Inc	Enfield	CT	G	860 265-3658	1352
Norwalk Compreseer Company	Stratford	CT	E	203 386-1234	4433
Norwalk Compressor Inc	Stratford	CT	G	203 386-1234	4434
P&G Metal Components Corp	Bloomfield	CT	F	860 243-2220	248
Standard Pneumatic Products	Newtown	CT	G	203 270-1400	2939
Stylair LLC	Plainville	CT	F	860 747-4588	3515
Air Energy Group LLC	South Easton	MA	E	508 230-9445	15269
Anver Corporation	Hudson	MA	D	978 568-0221	11755
Artisan Industries Inc	Stoughton	MA	D	781 893-6800	15581
Atlas Copco Compressors LLC	Westfield	MA	E	518 765-3344	16669
Atlas Copco Compressors LLC	West Springfield	MA	F	413 493-7290	16510
Brooks Automation Inc	Chelmsford	MA	B	978 262-2795	9879
Brooks Automation Inc **(PA)**	Chelmsford	MA	B	978 262-2400	9880
Ebara Technologies Inc	Newburyport	MA	G	978 465-1983	13485
Edwards Vacuum LLC	Chelmsford	MA	G	978 262-7565	9896
Guardair Corporation	Chicopee	MA	E	413 594-4400	10028
Lex-Aire Products Inc	North Billerica	MA	G	978 663-7202	13835
Mass Vac Inc	North Billerica	MA	E	978 667-2393	13839
Millibar Inc	Hopkinton	MA	F	508 488-9870	11728
Oscomp Systems Inc **(PA)**	Boston	MA	G	617 418-4640	8761
Ruwac Inc	Holyoke	MA	F	413 532-4030	11654
Teletrak Envmtl Systems Inc **(PA)**	Webster	MA	G	508 949-2430	16352
V Power Equipment LLC	Wareham	MA	F	508 273-7596	16256
Vaccon Company Inc	Medway	MA	E	508 359-7200	12972
Vacuum Technology Associates	Hingham	MA	D	781 740-8600	11513
General Electric Company	Bangor	ME	B	207 941-2500	5648
Compressor Energy Services LLC	Bedford	NH	G	603 491-2200	17636
Dr Guilbeault Air Comprsr LLC	Hudson	NH	E	603 598-0891	18386
Nexvac Inc **(PA)**	Sandown	NH	F	603 887-0015	19786
Praxair Surface Tech Inc	Concord	NH	D	603 224-9585	17924
Tafa Incorporated **(DH)**	Concord	NH	E	603 224-9585	17934

3564 Blowers & Fans

	CITY	ST	EMP	PHONE	ENTRY #
Adk Pressure Equipment Corp **(DH)**	Bristol	CT	G	860 585-0050	514

	CITY	ST	EMP	PHONE	ENTRY #
Anderson Technologies Inc	Killingworth	CT	G	860 663-2100	1924
Clean Air Group Inc	Fairfield	CT	E	203 335-3700	1420
Guardian Envmtl Tech Inc	New Milford	CT	F	860 350-2200	2802
Kennedy Gustafson and Cole Inc	Berlin	CT	E	860 828-2594	90
Lydall Inc **(PA)**	Manchester	CT	E	860 646-1233	2021
McIntire Company **(HQ)**	Bristol	CT	F	860 585-8559	580
Mechancal Engnered Systems LLC	New Canaan	CT	G	203 400-4658	2606
Nidec America Corporation	East Granby	CT	F	860 653-2144	1136
Novaerus US Inc **(PA)**	Stamford	CT	F	813 304-2468	4262
Nq Industries Inc	Rocky Hill	CT	G	860 258-3466	3725
Planet Technologies Inc	Ridgefield	CT	F	800 255-3749	3678
Spencer Turbine Company **(HQ)**	Windsor	CT	C	860 688-8361	5363
Stylair LLC	Plainville	CT	F	860 747-4588	3515
Treadwell Corporation	Thomaston	CT	E	860 283-7600	4522
7ac Technologies Inc	Beverly	MA	F	781 574-1348	8094
APA LLC	Canton	MA	E	781 986-5900	9714
Gremarco Industries Inc	West Brookfield	MA	F	508 867-5244	16470
Headwaters Inc	Marblehead	MA	G	781 715-6404	12685
Heat Fab Inc	Turners Falls	MA	D	413 863-2242	15878
Hendrick Manufacturing Corp **(PA)**	Salem	MA	F	781 631-4400	14919
Impolit Envmtl Ctrl Corp	Beverly	MA	E	978 927-4619	8140
K S E Inc	Sunderland	MA	F	413 549-5506	15675
Koch Separation Solutions Inc **(DH)**	Wilmington	MA	C	978 694-7000	17013
Munters Corporation **(DH)**	Amesbury	MA	C	978 241-1100	7498
Nauset Engineer Equipment	Mansfield	MA	G	508 339-2662	12648
Northern Air Inc	Raynham	MA	G	508 823-4900	14721
Pall Northborough **(DH)**	Northborough	MA	G	978 263-9888	14043
Parker-Hannifin Corporation	Haverhill	MA	C	978 858-0505	11457
Pioneer Consolidated Corp	North Oxford	MA	E	508 987-8438	13973
Riley Power Inc	Marlborough	MA	C	508 852-7100	12817
Spruce Environmental Tech Inc **(PA)**	Haverhill	MA	D	978 521-0901	11475
Vacuum Technology Inc	Gloucester	MA	G	510 333-6562	11216
Weld Engineering Co Inc	Shrewsbury	MA	E	508 842-2224	15137
Westport Envmtl Systems LP	Westport	MA	D	508 636-8811	16851
Air Control Industries Inc	Windsor	ME	G	207 445-2518	7262
Airex Corporation	Hudson	NH	E	603 821-3065	18371
Brailsford & Company Inc	Antrim	NH	E	603 588-2880	17593
Creative Filtration Systems	Tamworth	NH	F	603 323-2000	19891
Electrocraft New Hampshire Inc **(DH)**	Dover	NH	E	603 742-3330	18021
Measured Air Performance LLC	Manchester	NH	G	603 606-8350	18870
Pollution Research & Dev Corp **(PA)**	Newport	NH	F	603 863-7553	19353
Toollab Inc	West Warwick	RI	G	401 461-2110	21511

3565 Packaging Machinery

	CITY	ST	EMP	PHONE	ENTRY #
B & B Equipment LLC	Portland	CT	G	860 342-5773	3563
Beardsworth Group Inc	Thomaston	CT	G	860 283-4014	4498
Gtrpet Smf LLC	Cos Cob	CT	G	203 661-1229	825
Integrated Packg Systems Inc	East Windsor	CT	G	860 623-2623	1287
Millwood Inc	North Haven	CT	F	203 248-7902	3041
OEM Sources LLC	Milford	CT	G	203 283-5415	2325
Packard Inc	Prospect	CT	E	203 758-6219	3591
PDC International Corp **(PA)**	Norwalk	CT	D	203 853-1516	3215
Sanford Redmond Inc	Stamford	CT	G	203 351-9800	4309
Staban Engineering Corp	Wallingford	CT	F	203 294-1997	4812
Standard-Knapp Inc	Portland	CT	D	860 342-1100	3575
A & M Tool & Die Company Inc	Southbridge	MA	E	508 764-3241	15374
Accutech Packaging Inc	Foxboro	MA	D	508 543-3800	10873
Alepack LLC	Mashpee	MA	G	508 274-5792	12874
Butler Automatic Inc **(PA)**	Middleboro	MA	D	508 923-0544	13057
Econocorp Inc	Randolph	MA	E	781 986-7500	14677
Energy Sciences Inc	Wilmington	MA	E	978 694-9000	17001
Epic Technologies Inc	Woburn	MA	F	781 932-7870	17178
Hydration Labs Incorporated	Charlestown	MA	G	617 333-8191	9837
Illinois Tool Works Inc	Hopkinton	MA	E	508 520-0083	11721
JCB Inc	North Grafton	MA	G	508 839-5550	13961
Maruho Htsujyo Innovations Inc **(PA)**	Norwell	MA	F	617 653-1617	14107
Mrsi Systems LLC	North Billerica	MA	E	978 667-9449	13847
Nova Packaging Systems Inc	Leominster	MA	D	978 537-8534	12174
O/K Machinery Corporation	Marlborough	MA	E	508 303-8286	12799
Ohlson Packaging LLC **(DH)**	Taunton	MA	F	508 977-0004	15770
Package Machinery Company Inc	Holyoke	MA	G	413 315-3801	11648
Packaging Devices Inc **(PA)**	Teaticket	MA	F	508 548-0224	15802
Picture Frame Products Inc	Arlington	MA	G	781 648-7719	7634
Shanklin Corporation **(HQ)**	Ayer	MA	C	978 487-2204	7937
Sperry Product Innovation Inc	Bedford	MA	F	781 271-1400	8008
Tooling Research Inc **(PA)**	Walpole	MA	F	508 668-1950	16014
Eami Inc	Biddeford	ME	F	207 283-3001	5730
Oizero9 Inc	Sanford	ME	F	207 324-3582	6885
Paul Israelson	Biddeford	ME	G	512 574-4737	5754
Wrabacon Inc	Oakland	ME	F	207 465-2068	6536
Zajac LLC	Saco	ME	E	207 286-9100	6864
Computype Inc	Concord	NH	F	603 225-5500	17894
Flex-Print-Labels	Hampton	NH	E	603 929-3088	18263
Folder-Glr Techl Svs Grp LLC	Pelham	NH	G	603 635-7400	19433
George Gordon Associates Inc	Merrimack	NH	F	603 424-5204	19002
ID Technology LLC	Nashua	NH	G	603 598-1553	19182
Njm Packaging LLC **(HQ)**	Lebanon	NH	F	603 448-0300	18634
Ss & G LLC	Pelham	NH	G	603 635-7400	19448
Te Connectivity Corporation	East Providence	RI	E	401 432-8200	20446
Naepac	Williston	VT	G	802 497-3654	22684
Nestech Machine Systems Inc	Hinesburg	VT	G	802 482-4575	22029

3566 Speed Changers, Drives & Gears

	CITY	ST	EMP	PHONE	ENTRY #
Carlyle Johnson Machine Co LLC **(PA)**	Bolton	CT	E	860 643-1531	276
Control Concepts Inc **(PA)**	Putnam	CT	F	860 928-6551	3608
Cunningham Industries Inc	Stamford	CT	G	203 324-2942	4180
Roller Bearing Co Amer Inc	Middlebury	CT	E	203 758-8272	2157
So and Sew Plushies	Meriden	CT	G	860 916-2918	2131
Bendon Gear & Machine Inc	Rockland	MA	E	781 878-8100	14793
Commercial Gear Sprocket Inc	East Walpole	MA	F	508 668-1073	10522
Control Resources Inc	Littleton	MA	E	978 486-4160	12297
Custom Machine & Tool Co Inc	Hanover	MA	F	781 924-1003	11334
Gear/Tronics Industries Inc	North Billerica	MA	D	781 933-1400	13820
Gefran Inc **(DH)**	North Andover	MA	E	781 729-5249	13707
Harmonic Drive LLC **(HQ)**	Peabody	MA	D	978 532-1800	14338
Hersey Clutch Co	Orleans	MA	F	508 255-2533	14235
Lampin Corporation **(PA)**	Uxbridge	MA	E	508 278-2422	15923
Lenze Americas Corporation **(DH)**	Uxbridge	MA	D	508 278-9100	15924
Martin Sprocket & Gear Inc	Milford	MA	G	508 634-3990	13125
Maxon Precision Motors Inc **(HQ)**	Taunton	MA	E	508 677-0520	15763
Std Precision Gear & Instr Inc	West Bridgewater	MA	E	508 580-0035	16457
Allard Nazarian Group Inc **(PA)**	Manchester	NH	C	603 668-1900	18774
Electrocraft New Hampshire Inc **(DH)**	Dover	NH	E	603 742-3330	18021
Onvio Servo LLC	Salem	NH	E	603 685-0404	19758

3567 Indl Process Furnaces & Ovens

	CITY	ST	EMP	PHONE	ENTRY #
Birk Manufacturing Inc	East Lyme	CT	D	800 531-2070	1269
Catelectric Corp **(PA)**	Groton	CT	G	860 912-0800	1667
David Weisman LLC	Stamford	CT	G	203 322-9978	4187
Dri-Air Industries Inc	East Windsor	CT	E	860 627-5110	1282
Duralite Incorporated	Riverton	CT	F	860 379-3113	3694
Earth Engineered Systems	Derby	CT	G	203 231-4614	1070
Envax Products Inc	Oxford	CT	G	203 264-8181	3400
Furnace Source LLC	Terryville	CT	F	860 582-4201	4479
Hamworthy Peabody Combustn Inc **(DH)**	Shelton	CT	E	203 922-1199	3808
HI Heat Company Inc	South Windsor	CT	G	860 528-9315	3981
Industrial Heater Corp	Cheshire	CT	D	203 250-0500	740
Jad LLC	South Windsor	CT	E	860 289-1551	3983
Manufacturers Coml Fin LLC	West Hartford	CT	E	860 242-6287	5084
Modean Industries Inc	Easton	CT	G	203 371-6625	1321
Noble Fire Brick Company Inc **(PA)**	East Windsor	CT	G	860 623-9256	1297
Preferred Utilities Mfg Corp **(HQ)**	Danbury	CT	D	203 743-6741	974
Sandvik Wire and Htg Tech Corp	Bethel	CT	D	203 744-1440	177
Sshc Inc	Westbrook	CT	F	860 399-5434	5163
Warmup Inc	Danbury	CT	F	203 791-0072	1006
Avs Incorporated	Ayer	MA	D	978 772-0710	7912
Calorique LLC	West Wareham	MA	F	508 291-2000	16567
Dalton Electric Heating Co Inc	Ipswich	MA	E	978 356-9844	11915
Dielectric Products	Watertown	MA	G	617 924-5688	16278
Duc-Pac Corporation	East Longmeadow	MA	E	413 525-3302	10474
East Coast Induction Inc	Brockton	MA	F	508 587-2800	9141
Giltron Inc	North Dighton	MA	G	508 359-4310	13931
H B Smith Company Inc	Westfield	MA	E	413 568-3148	16687
I V I Corp	Pembroke	MA	F	781 826-3195	14410
Infinity	Worcester	MA	G	508 753-1981	17392
Radio Frequency Company Inc	Millis	MA	E	508 376-9555	13186
Reheat Co Inc	Danvers	MA	F	978 777-4441	10251
Runtal North America Inc	Haverhill	MA	E	800 526-2621	11469
S M Engineering Co Inc	North Attleboro	MA	F	508 699-4484	13778
Sentry Company	Foxboro	MA	G	508 543-5391	10904
Tevtech LLC	North Billerica	MA	F	978 667-4557	13871
Arcast Inc	Oxford	ME	G	207 539-9638	6562
Onix Corporation	Caribou	ME	E	866 290-5362	5889
Valmet Inc	Biddeford	ME	C	207 282-1521	5767
Vulcan Electric Company **(PA)**	Porter	ME	D	207 625-3231	6605
Centorr/Vacuum Industries LLC **(PA)**	Nashua	NH	E	603 595-7233	19132
CVI Group Inc **(PA)**	Nashua	NH	G	603 595-7233	19100
Ebner Furnaces	Londonderry	NH	G	603 552-3806	18694
Gtat Corporation	Nashua	NH	G	603 883-5200	19173
Gtat Corporation **(HQ)**	Hudson	NH	C	603 883-5200	18396
Hollis Line Machine Co Inc **(PA)**	Hollis	NH	E	603 465-2251	18332
Infra Red Technology Inc	Laconia	NH	G	603 524-1177	18568
Materials Research Frncs Inc	Allenstown	NH	F	603 485-2394	17539
Mellen Company Inc **(PA)**	Concord	NH	E	603 228-2929	17914
Sahara Heaters Mfg Co	Nashua	NH	G	603 888-7351	19257
Gasbarre Products Inc	Cranston	RI	F	401 467-5200	20230
Sargeant & Wilbur Inc	Pawtucket	RI	F	401 726-0013	20896
Rettig USA Inc	Colchester	VT	G	802 654-7500	21879
Rettig USA Inc	Williston	VT	F	802 654-7500	22688

3568 Mechanical Power Transmission Eqpt, NEC

	CITY	ST	EMP	PHONE	ENTRY #
A Papish Incorporated **(PA)**	Danbury	CT	E	203 744-0323	863
American Collars Couplings Inc	Winsted	CT	F	860 379-7043	5403
American Sleeve Bearing LLC	Stafford Springs	CT	E	860 684-8060	4104

SIC

Employee Codes: A=Over 500 employees, B=251-500
C=101-250, D=51-100 E=20-50, F=10-19, G=3-9

	CITY	ST	EMP	PHONE	ENTRY #
Ball & Roller Bearing Co LLC	New Milford	CT	F	860 355-4161	2787
Bead Industries Inc **(PA)**	Milford	CT	E	203 301-0270	2251
Carlyle Johnson Machine Co LLC **(PA)**	Bolton	CT	E	860 643-1531	276
Converter Consultants LLC	Naugatuck	CT	G	203 729-1031	2469
Del-Tron Precision Inc	Bethel	CT	E	203 778-2727	143
Gwilliam Company Inc	New Milford	CT	F	860 354-2884	2804
Helander Products Inc	Clinton	CT	F	860 669-7953	788
Inertia Dynamics LLC	New Hartford	CT	C	860 379-1252	2639
Kasheta Power Equipment	South Windsor	CT	G	860 528-8421	3987
Perry Technology Corporation	New Hartford	CT	D	860 738-2525	2644
Rollease Acmeda Inc **(PA)**	Stamford	CT	D	203 964-1573	4305
Roller Bearing Co Amer Inc	Middlebury	CT	E	203 758-8272	2157
Virginia Industries Inc **(PA)**	Rocky Hill	CT	G	860 571-3600	3733
Altra Industrial Motion Corp **(PA)**	Braintree	MA	B	781 917-0600	8986
Belt Technologies Inc **(PA)**	Agawam	MA	E	413 786-9922	7422
Curtis Universal Joint Co Inc	Springfield	MA	E	413 737-0281	15465
Custom Machine & Tool Co Inc	Hanover	MA	F	781 924-1003	11334
Datel Inc	Mansfield	MA	E	508 964-5131	12627
Double E Company LLC **(PA)**	West Bridgewater	MA	C	508 588-8099	16438
Emseal Joint Systems Ltd	Westborough	MA	E	508 836-0280	16617
Hersey Clutch Co	Orleans	MA	F	508 255-2533	14235
Lampin Corporation **(PA)**	Uxbridge	MA	E	508 278-2422	15923
Lovejoy Curtis LLC	Springfield	MA	E	413 737-0281	15485
Magnetic Technologies Ltd	Oxford	MA	F	508 987-3303	14268
Martin Sprocket & Gear Inc	Milford	MA	G	508 634-3990	13125
Mass-Flex Research Inc	Medford	MA	F	781 391-3640	12941
Naugler Co Inc	Newburyport	MA	G	978 463-9199	13517
Renbrandt Inc	Gloucester	MA	F	617 445-8910	11207
Savage Companies	Westborough	MA	G	508 616-8772	16646
Stafford Manufacturing Corp	Wilmington	MA	E	978 657-8000	17048
Stafford Manufacturing Corp	Norfolk	MA	G	978 657-8000	13664
US Bronze Foundry & Mch Inc	Hanover	MA	G	781 871-1420	11358
US Tsubaki Automotive LLC	Westfield	MA	F	413 593-1100	16738
US Tsubaki Automotive LLC **(DH)**	Chicopee	MA	C	413 593-1100	10067
US Tsubaki Power Transm LLC	Holyoke	MA	C	413 536-1576	11665
Warner Electric	Braintree	MA	G	781 917-0600	9048
Wgi Inc	Southwick	MA	C	413 569-9444	15421
Mikes and Sons	Presque Isle	ME	G	207 762-6310	6762
Montalvo Corporation	Gorham	ME	E	207 856-2501	6122
Woodex Bearing Company Inc	Georgetown	ME	E	207 371-2210	6107
Ametek Precitech Inc **(HQ)**	Keene	NH	D	603 357-2510	18491
Ferrotec (usa) Corporation **(HQ)**	Bedford	NH	D	603 472-6800	17640
Mpb Corporation	Lebanon	NH	B	603 448-3000	18630
Nelson Air Corporation	Milford	NH	G	603 673-3908	19070
Quik Loc Inc	Lincoln	NH	G	603 745-7008	18647
Tidland Corporation	Keene	NH	D	603 352-1696	18533
Kmc Inc	West Greenwich	RI	E	401 392-1900	21460
Tracey Gear Inc	Pawtucket	RI	E	401 725-3920	20906
Whittet-Higgins Company	Central Falls	RI	E	401 728-0700	20129

3569 Indl Machinery & Eqpt, NEC

	CITY	ST	EMP	PHONE	ENTRY #
3M Purification Inc **(HQ)**	Meriden	CT	B	203 237-5541	2070
A F M Engineering Corp	Brooklyn	CT	G	860 774-7518	668
Alstom Power Co	Windsor	CT	F	860 688-1911	5318
Applied Porous Tech Inc	Tariffville	CT	F	860 408-9793	4472
Arthur G Russell Company Inc	Bristol	CT	D	860 583-4109	521
Automation Inc	West Hartford	CT	F	860 236-5991	5054
Cable Management LLC	Meriden	CT	E	860 670-1890	2083
Environmantal Systems Cor	Hartford	CT	F	860 953-5167	1820
Fire Technology Inc	Southington	CT	G	860 276-2181	4050
Hamilton Standard Space	Windsor Locks	CT	E	860 654-6000	5396
Isopur Fluid Technologies Inc	North Stonington	CT	F	860 599-1872	3076
M P Robinson Production	Redding	CT	E	203 938-1336	3650
Mid State Assembly & Packg Inc	Meriden	CT	G	203 634-8740	2107
Mott Corporation **(PA)**	Farmington	CT	G	860 793-6333	1493
Naiad Dynamics Us Inc **(HQ)**	Shelton	CT	E	203 929-6355	3836
National Filter Media Corp	Wallingford	CT	E	203 741-2225	4777
North Haven Eqp & Lsg LLC	Orange	CT	G	203 795-9494	3375
Packard Inc	Prospect	CT	E	203 758-6219	3591
Pallflex Products Company	Putnam	CT	E	860 928-7761	3625
Praxair Inc **(HQ)**	Danbury	CT	B	203 837-2000	971
Proton Energy Systems Inc	Wallingford	CT	D	203 678-2000	4790
Qsonica LLC	Newtown	CT	G	203 426-0101	2933
Red Barn Innovations	Prospect	CT	G	203 393-0778	3595
Richard Dudgeon Inc	Waterbury	CT	G	203 336-4459	4950
Rondo America Incorporated	Naugatuck	CT	C	203 723-5831	2494
Schaefer Machine Company Inc	Deep River	CT	G	860 526-4000	1065
Sonics & Materials Inc **(PA)**	Newtown	CT	D	203 270-4600	2938
Tinny Corporation	Middletown	CT	E	860 854-6121	2228
900 Industries Inc	Sutton	MA	G	508 865-9600	15678
Angstrom Advanced Inc	Stoughton	MA	D	781 519-4765	15580
Armstrong Machine Co Inc	Beverly	MA	F	978 232-9466	8102
Avenger Inc	Ipswich	MA	F	978 356-7311	11904
Azelis Americas LLC	Leominster	MA	G	212 915-8178	12115
Babcock Power Inc **(PA)**	Lynnfield	MA	G	978 646-3300	12545
Balyo Inc	Woburn	MA	E	781 281-7957	17126
Barrett Technology LLC	Newton	MA	E	617 252-9000	13566
East Coast Filter Inc	Wrentham	MA	G	716 649-2326	17518
East Coast Filter Corp	Blackstone	MA	G	508 883-7744	8311
Evoqua Water Technologies LLC	Tewksbury	MA	E	978 863-4600	15817
Filter-Kleen Manufacturing Co	Westford	MA	F	978 692-5137	16766
Filtrex Corp	Attleboro	MA	G	508 226-7711	7735
Flexhead Industries Inc	Holliston	MA	F	508 893-9596	11571
Foster-Miller Inc	Devens	MA	D	781 684-4000	10320
Franklin Robotics Inc	North Billerica	MA	G	617 513-7666	13816
General Electric Company	Harwich	MA	C	617 444-8777	11393
Hostar Mar Trnspt Systems Inc	Wareham	MA	E	508 295-2900	16250
Hydro-Test Products Inc	Stow	MA	F	978 897-4647	15632
Illinois Tool Works Inc	Hopkinton	MA	E	508 520-0083	11721
Irobot Corporation **(PA)**	Bedford	MA	B	781 430-3000	7985
Isp Freetown Fine Chem Inc	Assonet	MA	D	508 672-0634	7681
King Fisher Co Inc	Lowell	MA	E	978 596-0214	12389
Koch Separation Solutions Inc **(DH)**	Wilmington	MA	C	978 694-7000	17013
Leavitt Machine Co	Orange	MA	G	978 544-3872	14220
Location Lube Inc	West Yarmouth	MA	G	508 888-5000	16579
Lubrite LLC	Hanover	MA	G	781 871-1420	11346
McIntire Brass Works Inc	Somerville	MA	G	617 547-1819	15197
Mestek Inc	Westfield	MA	D	413 564-5530	16701
Methods 3d Inc	Sudbury	MA	F	978 443-5388	15663
Multex Automation Corporation	Boston	MA	G	617 347-7278	8716
Munters Corporation **(DH)**	Amesbury	MA	C	978 241-1100	7498
New England Gen-Connect LLC	Hingham	MA	G	617 571-6884	11507
Op USA Inc	Acton	MA	G	978 658-5135	7376
Pall Corporation	Westborough	MA	B	508 871-5394	16641
Parker-Hannifin Corporation	Haverhill	MA	C	978 858-0505	11457
Peak Scientific Instruments	North Billerica	MA	E	978 262-1384	13854
Persimmon Technologies Corp	Wakefield	MA	F	781 587-0677	15968
Plating Supplies Intl Inc	Agawam	MA	G	413 786-2020	7446
Polytech Filtration Systems	Hudson	MA	F	978 562-7700	11804
Portuamerica Inc	Ludlow	MA	G	413 589-0095	12475
Precision Feeding Systems Inc	East Longmeadow	MA	G	413 525-9200	10488
Righthand Robotics Inc	Somerville	MA	G	617 501-0085	15210
Riley Power Inc	Marlborough	MA	C	508 852-7100	12817
Ryan Tool Co Inc	Taunton	MA	G	508 822-6576	15781
Rypos Inc **(PA)**	Franklin	MA	E	508 429-4552	11077
St Equipment and Tech LLC	Needham	MA	G	781 972-2300	13312
Thermal Dynamix Inc	Westfield	MA	G	413 562-1266	16734
Town of Westminster	Westminster	MA	E	978 874-2313	16816
Tyco Fire Products LP	Avon	MA	G	508 583-8447	7899
Ultra Filtronics Ltd	Randolph	MA	G	781 961-4775	14700
Vivaproducts Inc	Littleton	MA	F	978 952-6868	12327
Wollaston Foundry	Taunton	MA	G	508 884-3400	15800
Albarrie Technical Fabrics Inc	Auburn	ME	G	207 786-0424	5549
Comnav Engineering Inc	Portland	ME	E	207 221-8524	6641
Eltec Industries Inc **(PA)**	Freeport	ME	G	207 541-9085	6077
Environmental Energy & Finance	Newry	ME	F	978 807-0027	6490
Lapoint Industries Inc **(PA)**	Auburn	ME	D	207 777-3100	5575
National Filter Media Corp	Winthrop	ME	F	207 377-2626	7281
National Filter Media Corp	Winthrop	ME	D	207 377-2626	7282
Northast Emrgncy Apparatus LLC	Auburn	ME	F	207 753-0080	5584
Oizero9 Inc	Sanford	ME	F	207 324-3582	6885
United Fbrcnts Strainrite Corp **(HQ)**	Auburn	ME	D	207 376-1600	5600
Wrabacon Inc	Oakland	ME	F	207 465-2068	6536
Devprotek Inc	Hollis	NH	G	603 577-5557	18329
Equipois LLC	Manchester	NH	G	603 668-1900	18818
Fire Protection Team LLC	Hooksett	NH	G	603 641-2550	18349
Innovative Products & Eqp Inc	Hudson	NH	E	603 246-5858	18399
Interconnect Technology Inc	Hudson	NH	F	603 883-3116	18402
JP Sercel Associates Inc	Manchester	NH	D	603 595-7048	18852
M & A Advnced Design Cnstr Inc **(PA)**	Hampstead	NH	G	603 329-9515	18242
Micronics Filtration LLC **(HQ)**	Portsmouth	NH	C	603 433-1299	19596
Mikrolar Inc	Hampton	NH	G	603 617-2508	18267
Mobilerobots Inc	Amherst	NH	E	603 881-7960	17576
PSI Water Systems Inc **(PA)**	Hooksett	NH	E	603 624-5110	18356
R F Hunter Co Inc	Dover	NH	G	603 742-9565	18048
Rob Geoffroy	Londonderry	NH	G	603 425-2517	18734
Schleuniger Inc **(DH)**	Manchester	NH	E	603 627-4860	18918
ACS Industries Inc **(PA)**	Lincoln	RI	E	401 769-4700	20552
Airgas Usa LLC	East Greenwich	RI	G	401 884-0201	20351
Alert Fire Protection Inc	Cranston	RI	G	401 261-8836	20173
Bioprocessh2o LLC	Portsmouth	RI	E	401 683-5400	20919
Filters Inc	Pawtucket	RI	G	401 722-8999	20840
LDB Tool and Findings Inc	Cranston	RI	G	401 944-6000	20252
American Rural Fire Apparatus	Williamstown	VT	G	802 433-1554	22649
Essex Manufacturing Co	Williston	VT	G	802 864-4584	22665
Filcorp Industries Inc	Milton	VT	G	802 893-1882	22127
Kalow Technologies LLC	North Clarendon	VT	D	802 775-4633	22217
R R Sprinkler Inc	Swanton	VT	G	802 868-2423	22535

3571 Electronic Computers

	CITY	ST	EMP	PHONE	ENTRY #
American Railway Technologies	East Hartford	CT	G	860 291-1170	1172
Black Rock Tech Group LLC	Bridgeport	CT	F	203 916-7200	384
Cyclone Microsystems Inc	Hamden	CT	E	203 786-5536	1741
Frontier Vision Tech Inc	Rocky Hill	CT	E	860 953-0240	3709

	CITY	ST	EMP	PHONE	ENTRY #
Glacier Computer LLC **(PA)**	New Milford	CT	G	860 355-7552	2800
Hg Tech LLC	Naugatuck	CT	G	203 632-5946	2477
Interactive Marketing Corp	North Haven	CT	G	203 248-5324	3032
Kimchuk Incorporated	Danbury	CT	C	203 798-0799	944
Modern Electronic Fax & Cmpt	Fairfield	CT	G	203 292-6520	1445
Oracle America Inc	Stamford	CT	D	203 703-3000	4273
Abaco Systems Technology Corp	Billerica	MA	E	256 382-8115	8202
Acbel (usa) Polytech Inc	Hopkinton	MA	G	508 625-1768	11687
Advanced Electronic Design Inc	Attleboro Falls	MA	F	508 699-0249	7810
Biscom Inc	Westford	MA	D	978 250-1800	16757
Bull Data Systems Inc **(DH)**	Chelmsford	MA	G	978 294-6000	9882
Bull Hn Info Systems Inc	Chelmsford	MA	G	978 256-1033	9883
Cape Setups LLC	West Barnstable	MA	G	508 375-6444	16405
Comark LLC **(PA)**	Milford	MA	D	508 359-8161	13110
Embedded Now Inc	Holliston	MA	G	508 246-8196	11569
General Dynamics Mission	Dedham	MA	B	781 410-9635	10291
General Dynamics Mission	Taunton	MA	A	508 880-4000	15754
HP Inc	Littleton	MA	A	650 857-1501	12307
HP Inc	Littleton	MA	D	800 222-5547	12308
Industrial Biomedical Sensors	Waltham	MA	F	781 891-4201	16132
Kinetic Systems Inc	Boston	MA	E	617 522-8700	8649
Mack Technologies Inc **(HQ)**	Westford	MA	C	978 392-5500	16777
Onset Computer Corporation	Bourne	MA	C	508 759-9500	8948
Oram Corporate Advisors	Newton	MA	G	617 701-7430	13622
Power Systems Integrity Inc	Northborough	MA	G	508 393-1655	14045
Rhythm Rhyme Results LLC	Cambridge	MA	G	617 674-7524	9633
Scidyne	Pembroke	MA	F	781 293-3059	14425
Sie Computing Solutions Inc	Brockton	MA	D	508 588-6110	9174
Thinkflood Inc	Needham	MA	G	617 299-2000	13314
Veloxity One LLC	North Chelmsford	MA	G	855 844-5060	13912
Win Enterprises Inc	North Andover	MA	E	978 688-2000	13740
Cad Management Resources Inc	New Gloucester	ME	G	207 221-2911	6465
Ron Lavallee	Belgrade	ME	G	248 705-3231	5699
Alacron Inc	Nashua	NH	F	603 891-2750	19107
Citadel Computer Corporation	Amherst	NH	G	603 672-5500	17554
Dell Inc	Nashua	NH	C	603 579-9630	19143
Dutile Glines & Higgins Inc	Hooksett	NH	F	603 622-0452	18348
Elite Manufacturing Svcs Corp	Salem	NH	F	978 688-6150	19724
Ezenia Inc **(PA)**	Salem	NH	F	603 589-7600	19727
Glacier Computer LLC	Amherst	NH	F	603 882-1560	17564
Grolen Communications Inc	Manchester	NH	G	603 645-0101	18831
Lexington Data Incorporated	Rindge	NH	G	603 899-5673	19650
Marspec-Abernaqui-America	North Hampton	NH	G	603 964-4063	19384
Monarch International Inc	Amherst	NH	E	603 883-3390	17577
Robert Veinot	Merrimack	NH	G	603 424-1799	19025
Wagz Inc **(PA)**	Portsmouth	NH	F	603 570-6015	19630
Taco Electronic Solutions Inc	Cranston	RI	G	401 942-8000	20300
Battilana & Associates	Woodstock	VT	G	802 457-3375	22736
Robillards Apple Crisp	Saint Johnsbury	VT	G	802 748-4451	22394

3572 Computer Storage Devices

	CITY	ST	EMP	PHONE	ENTRY #
EMC Corporation	Fairfield	CT	D	203 418-4500	1429
Emc7 LLC	Fairfield	CT	G	203 429-4355	1430
Kaman Aerospace Corporation	Middletown	CT	C	860 632-1000	2195
Mini LLC	Naugatuck	CT	G	203 464-5495	2484
Pexagon Technology Inc	Branford	CT	E	203 458-3364	336
Quantum Bpower Southington LLC	Southington	CT	G	860 201-0621	4071
Quantum Circuits Inc	New Haven	CT	F	203 891-6216	2729
Systematics Inc	Rocky Hill	CT	F	860 721-0706	3729
Acbel (usa) Polytech Inc	Hopkinton	MA	G	508 625-1768	11687
Cambex Corporation	Southborough	MA	G	508 217-4508	15352
Cambex Corporation **(PA)**	Westborough	MA	F	508 983-1200	16598
Em &M Builders LLC	Hopkinton	MA	G	508 497-3446	11703
EMC Corporation	Hopkinton	MA	D	508 249-5883	11704
EMC Corporation	Southborough	MA	G	508 382-7556	15356
EMC Corporation	Hopkinton	MA	E	508 346-2900	11705
EMC Corporation **(HQ)**	Hopkinton	MA	B	508 435-1000	11706
EMC Corporation	Bellingham	MA	G	508 613-2022	8038
EMC Corporation	Newton	MA	C	617 618-3400	13587
EMC Corporation	Hopkinton	MA	F	508 435-0369	11707
EMC Corporation	Hopkinton	MA	F	800 445-2588	11708
EMC Corporation	Franklin	MA	D	508 435-1000	11041
EMC Corporation	Franklin	MA	D	508 528-2546	11042
EMC Corporation	Milford	MA	B	508 634-2774	13116
EMC Corporation	Franklin	MA	D	866 438-3622	11043
EMC Corporation	Franklin	MA	D	800 275-8777	11044
EMC Global Holdings Company	Hopkinton	MA	G	508 544-2852	11709
EMC International Holdings Inc **(DH)**	Hopkinton	MA	G	508 435-1000	11710
EMC Investment Corporation	Hopkinton	MA	G	508 435-1000	11711
Fidelis EMC	North Andover	MA	G	978 655-3390	13703
Interactive Media Corp	Millis	MA	E	508 376-4245	13184
Kaminario Inc **(PA)**	Needham Heights	MA	E	877 982-2555	13335
Paul Parrino	East Walpole	MA	G	508 668-2936	10527
Persistor Instruments Inc	Marstons Mills	MA	G	508 420-1600	12873
Primearray Systems Inc	Burlington	MA	G	978 455-9488	9322
Raid Inc	Andover	MA	E	978 683-6444	7591
Seagate Technology LLC	Shrewsbury	MA	C	508 770-3111	15130
Sepaton Inc	Marlborough	MA	D	508 490-7900	12824
Sudbury Systems Inc	Bedford	MA	E	800 876-8888	8010
Unicom Engineering Inc **(HQ)**	Canton	MA	B	781 332-1000	9791
Winchester Systems Inc **(PA)**	Littleton	MA	E	781 265-0200	12328
Zerious Electronic Pubg Corp	Beverly	MA	G	978 922-4990	8201
Blue Dawg Pwr Wash Southern NH	Hampstead	NH	G	603 498-9473	18238
Boulder Technologies LLC	Dover	NH	G	603 740-8402	18010
Memtec Corporation	Salem	NH	E	603 893-8080	19751
Visit WEI	Salem	NH	G	603 893-0900	19777
Solid Access Technologies LLC	Newport	RI	G	978 463-0642	20682
Quantum Corporation LLC	Worcester	VT	G	802 505-5088	22743

3575 Computer Terminals

	CITY	ST	EMP	PHONE	ENTRY #
Omega Engineering Inc **(HQ)**	Norwalk	CT	C	203 359-1660	3211
Precision Electronic Assembly	Monroe	CT	F	203 452-1839	2413
Actuality Systems Inc	Arlington	MA	G	617 325-9230	7622
C S I Keyboards Inc	Peabody	MA	E	978 532-8181	14318
Cortron Inc	Lowell	MA	E	978 975-5445	12362
Igt Global Solutions Corp	Braintree	MA	F	781 849-5642	9019
Imaging Solutions & More	Chicopee	MA	G	413 331-4100	10031
New England Keyboard Inc	Fitchburg	MA	E	978 345-8332	10843
Verizon Communications Inc	Natick	MA	F	508 647-4008	13285
American Business Service	Lee	NH	G	603 659-2912	18642
Assured Computing Technologies	Bedford	NH	G	603 627-8728	17631
Hyndsight Vision Systems Inc	Peterborough	NH	G	603 924-1334	19473
Igt Global Solutions Corp	West Greenwich	RI	E	401 392-7025	21456

3577 Computer Peripheral Eqpt, NEC

	CITY	ST	EMP	PHONE	ENTRY #
Alinabal Holdings Corporation **(PA)**	Milford	CT	B	203 877-3241	2243
Braxton Manufacturing Co Inc	Watertown	CT	C	860 274-6781	5000
Cadesk Company LLC **(PA)**	Trumbull	CT	G	203 268-8083	4617
Cisco Systems Inc	Norwalk	CT	E	203 229-2300	3125
Cisco Systems Inc	Farmington	CT	A	860 284-5500	1472
Computer Express LLC	Berlin	CT	F	860 829-1310	82
Contek International Corp	New Canaan	CT	G	203 972-3406	2594
Contek International Corp	New Canaan	CT	F	203 972-7330	2595
Cyclone Pcie Systems LLC	Hamden	CT	G	203 786-5536	1742
Data Technology Inc	Tolland	CT	E	860 871-8082	4545
Dictaphone Corporation **(HQ)**	Stratford	CT	C	203 381-7000	4409
Ebeam Film LLC	Shelton	CT	F	203 926-0100	3798
Ellipson Data LLC	Westport	CT	G	203 227-5520	5190
Eye Ear It LLC	Woodbury	CT	F	203 487-8949	5487
Frontier Vision Tech Inc	Rocky Hill	CT	E	860 953-0240	3709
Gerber Scientific LLC **(PA)**	Tolland	CT	C	860 871-8082	4548
Hint Peripherals Corp	Meriden	CT	G	203 634-4468	2094
Macdermid Incorporated **(HQ)**	Waterbury	CT	C	203 575-5700	4900
Magnetec Corporation	Wallingford	CT	D	203 949-9933	4768
Measurement Systems Inc	Wallingford	CT	E	203 949-3500	4772
Morse Watchmans Inc	Oxford	CT	E	203 264-1108	3415
Mumm Engineering Inc	Monroe	CT	G	203 445-9777	2409
O E M Controls Inc **(PA)**	Shelton	CT	C	203 929-8431	3845
Omega Engineering Inc **(HQ)**	Norwalk	CT	C	203 359-1660	3211
Ortronics Inc **(DH)**	New London	CT	D	860 445-3900	2776
Ortronics Inc	West Hartford	CT	G	877 295-3472	5088
Ortronics Legrand	Ivoryton	CT	G	860 767-3515	1908
Red Rocket Site 2	Centerbrook	CT	G	860 581-8019	703
Resavue Inc	Orange	CT	F	203 878-0944	3381
Scan-Optics LLC	Manchester	CT	D	860 645-7878	2046
Spectrum Virtual LLC	Cheshire	CT	G	203 303-7540	765
Syferlock Technology Corp	Shelton	CT	G	203 292-5441	3875
Transact Technologies Inc **(PA)**	Hamden	CT	C	203 859-6800	1791
Verico Technology LLC **(HQ)**	Enfield	CT	E	800 492-7286	1389
Xerox Corporation **(HQ)**	Norwalk	CT	B	203 968-3000	3274
Xijet Corp	New Haven	CT	F	203 397-2800	2755
Yellowfin Holdings Inc	Ellington	CT	E	866 341-0979	1344
3M Touch Systems Inc **(HQ)**	Methuen	MA	B	978 659-9000	13008
3M Touch Systems Inc	Methuen	MA	B	978 659-9000	13009
3M Touch Systems Inc	Westborough	MA	C	508 871-1840	16584
Abariscan Inc	Newburyport	MA	G	978 462-0284	13467
Adaptive Optics Associates Inc **(DH)**	Devens	MA	D	978 757 9600	10317
Aereo Inc	Hopedale	MA	E	617 861-8287	11669
Apem Inc **(HQ)**	Haverhill	MA	E	978 372-1602	11404
Bidirectional Display Inc	Acton	MA	G	617 599-8282	7344
Bull Data Systems Inc **(DH)**	Chelmsford	MA	G	978 294-6000	9882
Bull Hn Info Systems Inc	Chelmsford	MA	G	978 256-1033	9883
C S I Keyboards Inc	Peabody	MA	E	978 532-8181	14318
Camiant Inc	Marlborough	MA	D	508 486-9996	12733
Circle Twelve Inc	Framingham	MA	G	508 620-5360	10934
Cisco Systems Inc	Scituate	MA	G	978 936-1246	15008
Cisco Systems Inc	Boxborough	MA	A	408 526-4000	8960
Corero Network Security Inc	Marlborough	MA	E	978 212-1500	12741
Cortron Inc	Lowell	MA	E	978 975-5445	12362
Csp Inc **(PA)**	Lowell	MA	D	978 954-5038	12364
Data Translation Inc **(PA)**	Norton	MA	D	508 481-3700	14076
Decitek Corp	Westborough	MA	G	508 366-1011	16614
Di An Enterprises Inc	Chestnut Hill	MA	F	617 469-0819	9986
Divya Marigowda	Lexington	MA	G	781 863-5189	12220

	CITY	ST	EMP	PHONE	ENTRY #
EMC Corporation	Southborough	MA	G	508 382-7556	15356
EMC Corporation **(HQ)**	Hopkinton	MA	B	508 435-1000	11706
EMC International Holdings Inc **(DH)**	Hopkinton	MA	G	508 435-1000	11710
Encore Images Inc	Marblehead	MA	F	781 631-4568	12681
Eyedeal Scanning LLC	Needham	MA	G	617 519-8696	13299
Fujifilm Rcrding Media USA Inc **(DH)**	Bedford	MA	D	781 271-4400	7979
G4s Technology Software	Chelmsford	MA	D	781 457-0700	9901
Gforce Grafix Corporation	Leominster	MA	G	978 840-4401	12145
Grandstream Networks Inc **(PA)**	Boston	MA	E	617 566-9300	8576
Grey Force Cooling	Rochester	MA	G	508 441-1753	14787
Humanscale Corporation	Boston	MA	F	617 338-0077	8611
Imaging Data Corporation	Clinton	MA	G	978 365-9353	10081
Imaging Solutions & More	Chicopee	MA	G	413 331-4100	10031
INTEL Network Systems Inc **(HQ)**	Hudson	MA	C	978 553-4000	11778
Intellitech International Inc	Hudson	MA	F	978 212-7200	11779
Inteset Technologies LLC	Hanover	MA	G	781 826-1560	11342
Iva Corporation	Sudbury	MA	G	978 443-5800	15661
Kamel Peripherals Inc **(PA)**	Hopkinton	MA	E	508 435-7771	11724
Kemp Technologies Inc	Rochdale	MA	G	631 418-8407	14781
Kentron Technologies Inc	Wilmington	MA	E	978 988-9100	17011
L-Com Inc **(DH)**	North Andover	MA	D	978 682-6936	13715
M8trix Tech LLC	Canton	MA	G	617 925-7030	9753
Mack Technologies Inc **(HQ)**	Westford	MA	C	978 392-5500	16777
Macraigor Systems LLC **(PA)**	Brookline	MA	G	617 264-4459	9208
Madison Cable Corporation	Worcester	MA	C	508 752-2884	17410
Metroblity Optical Systems Inc	North Billerica	MA	D	781 255-5300	13843
Milford Manufacturing Svcs LLC	Hopedale	MA	D	508 478-8544	11678
Mimoco Inc	Needham Heights	MA	F	617 783-1100	13339
Mobile Monitor Tech LLC	Newton Centre	MA	G	617 965-5057	13656
MTI Unified Communications LLC	South Yarmouth	MA	G	774 352-1110	15331
Multi Touch Surface Inc	Somerville	MA	E	408 634-9224	15200
Nemonix Engineering Inc	Bolton	MA	G	508 393-7700	8322
Network Equipment Tech Inc **(DH)**	Westford	MA	E	510 713-7300	16780
New England Technology Group	Cambridge	MA	F	617 864-5551	9581
Newcastle Systems Inc	Haverhill	MA	E	781 935-3450	11455
Onset Computer Corporation	Bourne	MA	C	508 759-9500	8948
Parallel Systems Corp	Georgetown	MA	F	978 352-7100	11148
Pison Technology Inc	Brookline	MA	G	540 394-0998	9215
Power Systems Integrity Inc	Northborough	MA	G	508 393-1655	14045
Precision Handling Devices **(PA)**	Westport	MA	F	508 679-5282	16845
Project Resources Inc	Wareham	MA	F	508 295-7444	16254
Psjl Corporation **(PA)**	Billerica	MA	D	978 313-2500	8279
Pt Plus At Whitney Field	Leominster	MA	G	978 534-5922	12178
Rapiscan Systems Inc	Andover	MA	G	866 430-1913	7592
Riverbed Technology Inc	Cambridge	MA	G	617 250-5300	9635
Rsa Security LLC **(DH)**	Bedford	MA	A	781 515-5000	8007
Sap America Inc	Burlington	MA	E	781 852-3000	9334
Servomotive Corporation	Westborough	MA	G	508 726-9222	16648
Silicon Micro Display Inc	Newton	MA	G	617 433-7630	13638
Sky Computers Inc	Chelmsford	MA	F	978 250-2420	9933
Smart Modular Technologies Inc	Tewksbury	MA	G	978 221-3513	15835
Sunny Young LLC	Boston	MA	E	917 667-0528	8870
Teledyne Dgital Imaging US Inc **(HQ)**	Billerica	MA	E	978 670-2000	8303
Terarecon Inc	Acton	MA	D	978 274-0461	7390
Vitec Industries Inc	Gloucester	MA	G	978 282-7700	11217
Vivid Engineering	Shrewsbury	MA	G	508 842-0165	15136
Voxel8 Inc	Somerville	MA	F	916 396-3714	15229
Whitewood Encrytion	Boston	MA	G	617 419-1800	8926
Williams Lea Boston	Boston	MA	G	617 371-2300	8928
Winchester Systems Inc **(PA)**	Littleton	MA	E	781 265-0200	12328
Wright Line LLC **(HQ)**	Worcester	MA	C	508 852-4300	17510
Zoom Telephonics Inc **(PA)**	Boston	MA	E	617 423-1072	8944
Protech Digital Services LLC	Poland	ME	G	207 899-9237	6596
Allen Datagraph Systems Inc	Salem	NH	E	603 216-6344	19705
Allied Telesis Inc	Portsmouth	NH	G	603 334-6058	19534
Bantry Components Inc	Manchester	NH	E	603 668-3210	18785
Dasan Zhone Solutions Inc	Portsmouth	NH	E	510 777-7000	19557
Document Archives Imaging LLC	Manchester	NH	G	603 656-5209	18811
Dutile Glines & Higgins Inc	Hooksett	NH	F	603 622-0452	18348
Enterasys Networks Inc **(HQ)**	Salem	NH	D	603 952-5000	19725
Extech Instruments Corporation	Nashua	NH	D	887 439-8324	19152
Fujifilm Dimatix Inc	Lebanon	NH	C	603 443-5300	18623
Kaycee Group	Londonderry	NH	G	603 505-5754	18707
Memtec Corporation	Salem	NH	E	603 893-8080	19751
Nel-Tech Labs Incorporated	Derry	NH	F	603 425-1096	17990
Omron Microscan Systems Inc	Nashua	NH	G	603 598-8400	19223
Psjl Corporation	Exeter	NH	D	978 313-2550	18129
Seamark International LLC	Nashua	NH	F	603 546-0100	19258
Simpliprotected LLC	Auburn	NH	G	603 669-7465	17613
Syntegratech Incorporated	Bow	NH	G	603 225-4008	17734
Unarco Material Handling Inc	Exeter	NH	E	603 772-2070	18134
Astronova Inc **(PA)**	West Warwick	RI	B	401 828-4000	21479
Astronova Inc	West Warwick	RI	C	401 828-4000	21480
Electro Standards Lab Inc	Cranston	RI	D	401 946-1390	20215
Marr Office Equipment Inc	Pawtucket	RI	G	401 725-5186	20856
Retromedia Inc	Smithfield	RI	G	401 349-4640	21246
Warehouse Cables LLC	Warwick	RI	G	401 737-5677	21442
Alken Inc	Colchester	VT	E	802 655-3159	21856
Fulcrum Design	Bennington	VT	F	802 442-6441	21670
Gvh Studio Inc	Bennington	VT	G	802 379-1135	21671
Image Tek Mfg Inc	Springfield	VT	E	802 885-6208	22502
Mack Group Inc **(PA)**	Arlington	VT	B	802 375-2511	21597
Mack Molding Company Inc **(HQ)**	Arlington	VT	C	802 375-2511	21598
Rwo Inc	Shelburne	VT	G	802 497-1563	22423

3578 Calculating & Accounting Eqpt

	CITY	ST	EMP	PHONE	ENTRY #
Blackwold Inc	Chester	CT	D	860 526-0800	768
Hopp Companies Inc	Newtown	CT	F	800 889-8425	2924
Marinero Express 809 East	Stamford	CT	G	203 487-0636	4244
AAA Atm Services	Amesbury	MA	G	603 841-5615	7476
Arck Enterprises Inc	Danvers	MA	G	978 777-9166	10196
Atlantic Atm LLC	Ipswich	MA	G	978 356-4051	11903
Danversbank	South Hamilton	MA	G	978 468-2243	15314
Idemia America Corp **(DH)**	Billerica	MA	B	978 215-2400	8255
NCR Corporation	Newton	MA	C	617 558-2000	13617
Crane Payment Solutions Inc **(HQ)**	Bedford	NH	E	603 685-6999	17637
Atlas Atm Corp	Providence	RI	F	401 421-4183	20960
Interlott Technologies Inc	West Greenwich	RI	C	401 463-6392	21458
Plastics Plus Inc	Cumberland	RI	E	401 727-1447	20339

3579 Office Machines, NEC

	CITY	ST	EMP	PHONE	ENTRY #
Accu-Time Systems Inc **(DH)**	Ellington	CT	E	860 870-5000	1324
Acme United Corporation **(PA)**	Fairfield	CT	C	203 254-6060	1412
Agissar Corporation	Stratford	CT	D	203 375-8662	4389
Bell and Howell LLC	Deep River	CT	E	860 526-9561	1058
Bidwell Industrial Group Inc **(PA)**	Middletown	CT	E	860 346-9283	2178
Dictaphone Corporation **(HQ)**	Stratford	CT	C	203 381-7000	4409
Energy Saving Products and Sls	Burlington	CT	E	860 675-6443	678
Hasler Inc	Shelton	CT	G	203 301-3400	3810
Its New England Inc	Wallingford	CT	G	203 265-8100	4756
Neopost USA Inc **(DH)**	Milford	CT	C	203 301-3400	2319
Pitney Bowes Inc **(PA)**	Stamford	CT	A	203 356-5000	4285
Pitney Bowes Inc	Stamford	CT	E	203 356-5000	4286
Pitney Bowes Inc	Shelton	CT	E	203 922-4000	3854
Pitney Bowes Inc	Shelton	CT	E	203 356-5000	3855
Pyramid Time Systems LLC	Meriden	CT	E	203 238-0550	2120
Stanley Fastening Systems LP	New Britain	CT	G	860 225-5111	2584
Xerox Corporation **(HQ)**	Norwalk	CT	B	203 968-3000	3274
Accu-Time Systems Inc	Boston	MA	G	860 870-5000	8336
AM Technologies Inc	Watertown	MA	G	617 926-7920	16267
Bio Defense Corporation	Boston	MA	F	617 778-1800	8408
C P Bourg Inc **(PA)**	New Bedford	MA	D	508 998-2171	13369
Chauncey Wings Sons Inc	Greenfield	MA	G	413 772-6611	11253
Str Grinnell GP Holding LLC	Westminster	MA	E	978 731-2500	16814
Sudbury Systems Inc	Bedford	MA	E	800 876-8888	8010
Pitney Bowes Inc	Portland	ME	E	207 773-2345	6709
Acme Staple Company Inc	Franklin	NH	F	603 934-2320	18155
Pitney Bowes Inc	Keene	NH	E	603 352-7766	18522
Pitney Bowes Inc	East Providence	RI	E	401 435-8500	20442
Stanley Fastening Systems LP **(HQ)**	East Greenwich	RI	D	401 884-2500	20381
Simplex Time Recorder LLC	Williston	VT	D	802 879-6149	22692

3581 Automatic Vending Machines

	CITY	ST	EMP	PHONE	ENTRY #
Blackwold Inc	Chester	CT	D	860 526-0800	768
Eastern Company	Chester	CT	D	860 526-0800	772
Waterside Vending LLC	Westbrook	CT	G	860 399-6039	5165
Century Food Service Inc	Acushnet	MA	F	508 995-3221	7400
Interntonal Totalizing Systems **(PA)**	Bedford	MA	E	978 521-8867	7983
Diamond Music Co	Pelham	NH	G	603 635-2083	19431
Hot Stuff RI Inc	Warwick	RI	G	401 781-7500	21373

3582 Commercial Laundry, Dry Clean & Pressing Mchs

	CITY	ST	EMP	PHONE	ENTRY #
Edro Corporation	East Berlin	CT	E	860 828-0311	1099
Naugatuck Recovery Inc **(HQ)**	Naugatuck	CT	E	203 723-1122	2487
Rema Dri-Vac Corp	Norwalk	CT	F	203 847-2464	3231
Sumal Enterprises LLC	Watertown	CT	G	860 945-3337	5027
American Dryer Corporation	Fall River	MA	C	508 678-9000	10656
Jason Santelli Enterprises LLC	Jamaica Plain	MA	G	617 942-2205	11944
Two Go Drycleaning Inc	South Burlington	VT	E	802 658-9469	22474

3585 Air Conditioning & Heating Eqpt

	CITY	ST	EMP	PHONE	ENTRY #
All Phase Htg Coolg Contr LLC	East Haddam	CT	G	860 873-9680	1147
Alvest (usa) Inc **(HQ)**	Windsor	CT	E	860 602-3400	5320
Carrier Corporation	Farmington	CT	G	860 728-7000	1471
Comfortable Environments	Milford	CT	G	203 876-2140	2266
Croteau Development Group Inc	Stafford Springs	CT	G	860 684-3605	4107
Dasco Supply LLC	Stamford	CT	G	203 388-0095	4185
Demartino Fixture Co Inc	Wallingford	CT	E	203 269-3971	4733
Dp2 LLC Head	Darien	CT	F	203 655-0747	1022
Four Seasons Cooler Eqp LLC	Woodbury	CT	G	203 263-0705	5488
Mechancal Engnered Systems LLC	New Canaan	CT	G	203 400-4658	2606
Nanocap Technologies LLC **(PA)**	Hartford	CT	G	860 521-9743	1849
Novy International Inc	Danbury	CT	G	203 743-7720	962

	CITY	ST	EMP	PHONE	ENTRY #
Snowathome LLC	Terryville	CT	G	860 584-2991	4491
Tld Ace Corporation	Windsor	CT	B	860 602-3300	5374
Trane Inc	Norwalk	CT	D	203 866-7115	3261
Trane Inc	New Haven	CT	D	860 437-6208	2746
Trane US Inc	New London	CT	D	860 437-6208	2784
Trane US Inc	Farmington	CT	D	860 470-3901	1516
Trane US Inc	Hartford	CT	G	860 541-1721	1881
United Technologies Corp	East Hartford	CT	C	860 565-7622	1234
United Technologies Corp	Essex	CT	B	860 767-9592	1407
United Technologies Corp **(PA)**	Farmington	CT	B	860 728-7000	1522
Vector Controls LLC **(PA)**	Bethel	CT	F	203 749-0883	191
Wine Well Chiller Comp Inc	Milford	CT	G	203 878-2465	2382
7ac Technologies Inc	Beverly	MA	F	781 574-1348	8094
Ad Hoc Energy LLC	Millis	MA	G	508 507-8005	13182
Aipco Inc	Taunton	MA	E	508 823-7003	15721
Air-Mart Heating & Cooling LLC	Lowell	MA	G	603 821-1416	12342
Airxchange Inc	Rockland	MA	D	781 871-4816	14789
Alpha Instruments Inc	Acton	MA	G	978 264-2966	7339
Aspen Compressor LLC	Marlborough	MA	E	508 281-5322	12721
Backer Hotwatt Inc	Danvers	MA	G	978 777-0000	10201
Bluezone Products Inc	Woburn	MA	G	781 937-0202	17134
Broadstone Industries	Lowell	MA	G	978 691-2790	12356
Cambridgeport Air Systems Inc	Georgetown	MA	C	978 465-8481	11139
Cunniff Corp **(PA)**	East Falmouth	MA	G	508 540-6232	10440
Duc-Pac Corporation	East Longmeadow	MA	E	413 525-3302	10474
Engineered Assembly & Services	Marshfield	MA	G	781 834-9085	12860
Harris Envmtl Systems Inc	Andover	MA	D	978 470-8600	7555
Heat-Flo Inc	Uxbridge	MA	G	508 278-2400	15919
Hoshizaki America Inc	Marlborough	MA	C	508 251-7060	12774
Ilios Inc	Waltham	MA	G	781 466-6481	16128
Koda Industries Indiana LLC	Waltham	MA	D	781 891-3066	16140
Larchmont Engineering Inc	Chelmsford	MA	G	978 250-1177	9912
Lennox Roofing Inc	Abington	MA	G	508 328-5780	7327
LMI Liquidation Corporation	Lynn	MA	G	781 593-2561	12521
Massachusetts Control Ctr Inc	Tyngsboro	MA	G	978 649-1128	15895
Mestek Inc **(PA)**	Westfield	MA	E	470 898-4533	16700
Mestek Inc	Westfield	MA	D	413 564-5530	16701
Munters Corporation	Amesbury	MA	E	978 241-1100	7496
Munters Corporation	Amesbury	MA	F	978 388-2666	7497
Munters Corporation **(DH)**	Amesbury	MA	C	978 241-1100	7498
Munters USA Inc	Amesbury	MA	A	978 241-1100	7500
Northeast Twr Svc	Uxbridge	MA	G	508 533-1620	15927
Process Cooling Systems Inc	Leominster	MA	E	978 537-1996	12177
Refco Manufacturing Us Inc	Springfield	MA	G	413 746-3094	15500
Snow Economics Inc	Natick	MA	G	508 655-3232	13279
Tecogen Inc **(PA)**	Waltham	MA	E	781 622-1120	16207
Tecomet Inc	Woburn	MA	D	781 782-6400	17305
Thermal Circuits Inc	Salem	MA	C	978 745-1162	14945
Thermoceramix Inc	Boston	MA	G	978 425-0404	8881
Thl-Nortek Investors LLC **(PA)**	Boston	MA	D	617 227-1050	8882
Total Temp Inc	Middleboro	MA	G	508 947-8628	13078
Trane Inc	Wilmington	MA	D	978 737-3900	17057
Beer Saver USA	Kennebunk	ME	F	207 299-2826	6229
Fisher Engineering	Rockland	ME	C	207 701-4200	6794
Maine Market Refrigeration LLC **(PA)**	Fayette	ME	E	207 685-3504	6055
Mestek Inc	Clinton	ME	C	207 426-2351	5916
Nyle Systems LLC	Brewer	ME	E	207 989-4335	5799
Pool Environments Inc	Gorham	ME	F	207 839-8225	6126
Trane US Inc	Westbrook	ME	E	207 773-0637	7211
Ventech Industries Inc	Eliot	ME	G	207 439-0069	6012
Filtrine Manufacturing Co Inc **(PA)**	Keene	NH	D	603 352-5500	18503
Jmd Duct Fabrication LLC	Weare	NH	G	603 235-9314	19935
Larchmont Engineering Inc	Manchester	NH	G	603 622-8825	18860
Lyme Green Heat	Lyme	NH	G	603 359-8837	18754
Snomatic Controls & Engrg Inc	Lyme	NH	G	603 795-2900	18756
Standex International Corp **(PA)**	Salem	NH	E	603 893-9701	19769
Amtrol Inc **(DH)**	West Warwick	RI	B	401 884-6300	21477
Amtrol Intl Investments Inc **(DH)**	West Warwick	RI	G	401 884-6300	21478
Bsg Handcraft	Providence	RI	E	508 636-5154	20975
Davidon Industries Inc	Warwick	RI	F	401 737-8380	21349
New England Filter Co Inc	Pawtucket	RI	F	401 722-8999	20865
Nitrotap Ltd	Warren	RI	G	401 247-2141	21299
Trane US Inc	Riverside	RI	E	401 434-3146	21176
Omichron Corp	South Londonderry	VT	F	802 824-3136	22488

3586 Measuring & Dispensing Pumps

	CITY	ST	EMP	PHONE	ENTRY #
Proflow Inc	North Haven	CT	E	203 230-4700	3055
Fishman Corporation	Hopkinton	MA	F	508 435-2115	11713
Harvard Clinical Tech Inc	Natick	MA	E	508 655-2000	13259
Liquid Metronics Incorporated	Acton	MA	C	978 263-9800	7369
Sensing Systems Corporation	Dartmouth	MA	F	508 992-0872	10276
Seal 1 LLC	Brownville	ME	G	207 965-8860	5827
Nordson Efd LLC **(HQ)**	East Providence	RI	C	401 431-7000	20435
Burlington Petroleum Equipment	South Burlington	VT	E	802 864-5155	22440

3589 Service Ind Machines, NEC

	CITY	ST	EMP	PHONE	ENTRY #
3M Purification Inc **(HQ)**	Meriden	CT	B	203 237-5541	2070
Affordable Water Trtmnt	Mansfield Center	CT	G	860 423-3147	2061
Alliance Water Treatment Co	Stamford	CT	G	203 323-9968	4133
Aqualogic Inc	North Haven	CT	E	203 248-8959	3009
Atlas Filtri North America LLC	Wallingford	CT	F	203 284-0080	4706
Best Management Products Inc	East Haddam	CT	G	860 434-0277	1148
Brasco Technologies LLC	Northford	CT	G	203 484-4291	3086
Crane Co **(PA)**	Stamford	CT	D	203 363-7300	4177
Creative Mobile Systems Inc	Manchester	CT	G	860 649-6272	1997
Crystal Rock Holdings Inc **(HQ)**	Watertown	CT	E	860 945-0661	5005
D P Engineering Inc	Madison	CT	G	203 421-7965	1959
Ecosystem Consulting Svc Inc	Coventry	CT	G	860 742-0744	833
Evoqua Water Technologies LLC	South Windsor	CT	E	860 528-6512	3968
Guardian Envmtl Tech Inc	New Milford	CT	F	860 350-2200	2802
H Krevit and Company Inc	New Haven	CT	E	203 772-3350	2694
Hydro Service & Supplies Inc	Middletown	CT	G	203 265-3995	2190
Jfj Services LLC	Old Saybrook	CT	G	860 395-1922	3340
Kx Technologies LLC **(DH)**	West Haven	CT	F	203 799-9000	5130
New Milford Commission	New Milford	CT	F	860 354-3758	2817
Safe Water	Seymour	CT	G	203 732-4806	3764
Shaws Pump Company Inc	Ellington	CT	G	860 872-6891	1339
Spencer Turbine Company **(HQ)**	Windsor	CT	C	860 688-8361	5363
Suez Wts Services Usa Inc	East Hartford	CT	E	860 291-9660	1225
Town of Montville	Uncasville	CT	F	860 848-3830	4650
Town of Vernon	Vernon	CT	F	860 870-3545	4675
Town of Vernon	Vernon Rockville	CT	G	860 870-3699	4686
Abbey Water Treatment Inc	Sudbury	MA	G	978 443-5001	15650
Aertec	Andover	MA	G	978 475-6385	7533
Alexander Moles	Taunton	MA	G	508 823-8864	15723
American Water Systems LLC	Canton	MA	D	781 830-9722	9712
Applied Water Management Inc	Fall River	MA	G	508 675-5755	10660
Auto-Chlor System NY Cy Inc	Foxboro	MA	E	508 543-6767	10876
Bay State Espresso	Haverhill	MA	G	978 686-5049	11408
C E D Corp	Duxbury	MA	G	781 834-9312	10395
Central Vacuum Cleaners **(PA)**	Methuen	MA	F	978 682-5294	13013
Central Vacuum Cleaners	Lawrence	MA	G	978 682-5295	12004
Change Water Labs Inc	Cambridge	MA	G	917 292-5160	9437
Cleanbasins Inc	North Billerica	MA	G	978 670-5838	13802
Continental Metal Pdts Co Inc	Woburn	MA	E	781 935-4400	17151
Crane Mdsg Systems Inc	Dedham	MA	F	781 501-5800	10284
Den Mar Corporation	North Dartmouth	MA	F	508 999-3295	13918
Diamond Water Systems Inc	Chicopee	MA	E	413 536-8186	10017
Duraflow LLC	Tewksbury	MA	F	978 851-7439	15815
Edwards Vacuums Inc	Tewksbury	MA	G	978 753-3647	15816
Emco Engineering Inc	Canton	MA	G	508 314-8305	9730
Emerging Cpd Trtmnt Techngy	Burlington	MA	G	617 886-7400	9266
Evoqua Water Technologies LLC	Tewksbury	MA	E	978 863-4600	15817
Evoqua Water Technologies LLC	Lowell	MA	C	978 934-9349	12370
F R Mahony Associates	Townsend	MA	E	978 597-0703	15872
Filtered Air Systems Inc	Woburn	MA	G	781 491-0508	17179
Flodesign Sonics Inc	Wilbraham	MA	E	413 596-5900	16936
Hydro Quip Inc **(PA)**	Seekonk	MA	G	508 399-5771	15024
Hydrotech Services Inc	North Attleboro	MA	F	508 699-5977	13759
Keller Products Inc	North Chelmsford	MA	F	978 264-1911	13899
Kerfoot Technologies Inc	Mashpee	MA	F	508 539-3002	12881
KLA Systems Inc	Assonet	MA	G	508 359-7361	7683
Krofta Technologies LLC **(DH)**	Dalton	MA	G	413 236-5634	10179
L T Technologies	East Bridgewater	MA	G	508 456-0315	10416
M E Baker Company **(PA)**	Framingham	MA	F	508 620-5304	10979
Merrimack Valley Water Assn	Lawrence	MA	G	978 975-1800	12051
Metro Group Inc	Woburn	MA	F	781 932-9911	17229
Motion Technology Inc	Northborough	MA	E	508 460-9800	14039
National Water Main Clg Co	Canton	MA	E	617 361-5533	9760
North Amrcn Fltration Mass Inc	Walpole	MA	F	508 660-9016	16005
Omni-Trol Industries Inc	Revere	MA	F	781 284-8000	14774
Parts Per Million Inc	Cotuit	MA	G	508 479-5438	10171
Pequod Inc	New Bedford	MA	G	508 858-5123	13437
Present Arms Inc	Indian Orchard	MA	G	413 575-4656	11894
Pumping Systems Inc	Braintree	MA	G	508 588-6868	9033
RPM Technologies Inc	Ludlow	MA	G	413 583-3385	12477
Safve Inc	Scituate	MA	G	781 545-3546	15011
Spilldam Environmental Inc	Brockton	MA	F	508 583-7850	9178
Thermo Wave Technologies LLC	Danvers	MA	G	800 733-9615	10263
Town of Uxbridge	Uxbridge	MA	G	508 278-2887	15932
Under Pressure LLC	Lakeville	MA	G	508 641-0421	11980
Untha Shredding Tech Amer Inc	Newburyport	MA	G	978 465-0083	13547
Uvtech Systems Inc	Sudbury	MA	G	978 440-7282	15670
Wayland Sudbury Septage	Wayland	MA	G	508 358-7328	16337
Wetech	Dedham	MA	G	781 320-8646	10302
Woodard & Curran Inc	Provincetown	MA	G	508 487-5474	14611
Zero Discharge	Chicopee	MA	G	413 593-5470	10071
Fuji Clean Usa LLC	Brunswick	ME	G	207 406-2927	5836
J & M Enterprises Inc	Fairfield	ME	G	207 968-2729	6027
Maintenance Tech Inc	Portland	ME	G	207 797-7233	6691
Micronetixx Technologies LLC	Lewiston	ME	G	207 786-2000	6306
Salibas Rug & Upholstery Clrs	Bangor	ME	G	207 947-8876	5658
Septitech Inc	Lewiston	ME	F	207 333-6940	6323
Williams Partners Ltd	East Boothbay	ME	G	207 633-3111	5981

	CITY	ST	EMP	PHONE	ENTRY #
Yvons Valvoline Express Care	Lewiston	ME	G	207 777-3600	6328
Advanced Radon Mitigation Inc	Hooksett	NH	G	603 644-1207	18341
Aquawave of New England LLC	Portsmouth	NH	F	603 431-8975	19538
Dreamtech Water Solutions LLC	Nashua	NH	G	603 513-7829	19147
Filtrine Manufacturing Co Inc **(PA)**	Keene	NH	D	603 352-5500	18503
Global Filtration Systems	Wolfeboro	NH	G	603 651-8777	20019
GS Blodgett Corporation	Bow	NH	B	603 225-5688	17715
Hubscrub Co Inc	Manchester	NH	G	603 624-4243	18839
Itaconix LLC	Stratham	NH	G	603 775-4400	19870
Pentair Rsdntial Fltration LLC	Dover	NH	F	603 749-1610	18045
Pitco Frialator Inc **(HQ)**	Bow	NH	B	603 225-6684	17727
Pitco Frialator Inc	Pembroke	NH	E	603 225-6684	19462
Pitco Frialator Inc	Concord	NH	G	603 225-6684	17923
Richard Arikian	Nashua	NH	G	603 881-5427	19253
Accu-Care Supply Inc	Rumford	RI	E	401 438-7110	21179
Aeqrx Technologies Ltd	Warwick	RI	G	401 463-8822	21319
Benson Neptune Inc **(HQ)**	Coventry	RI	E	401 821-7140	20138
Enpure Process Systems Inc	Cranston	RI	G	401 447-3976	20218
Landa Pressure Washers of RI	Cranston	RI	G	401 463-8303	20250
SC Technologies Inc	North Kingstown	RI	E	401 667-7370	20738
Service Tech Inc **(PA)**	North Providence	RI	F	401 353-3664	20774
Siemens Industry Inc	Cranston	RI	E	401 942-2121	20285
Vacuum Processing Systems LLC	East Greenwich	RI	G	401 397-8578	20382
Westfall Manufacturing Co	Bristol	RI	F	401 253-3799	20110
Bering Technology Inc	Waitsfield	VT	E	408 364-6500	22561
Colburntreat LLC	Winooski	VT	F	802 654-8603	22719
GS Blodgett Corporation	Essex Junction	VT	E	802 860-3700	21945
GS Blodgett Corporation **(HQ)**	Essex Junction	VT	C	802 860-3700	21944
Industrial Safety Products LLC	Colchester	VT	G	802 338-9035	21867
Mfi Corp	Burlington	VT	D	802 658-6600	21797
South Hero Fire District 4	South Hero	VT	G	802 372-3088	22483
Sun Ray Technologies Inc	Killington	VT	G	802 422-8680	22056

3592 Carburetors, Pistons, Rings & Valves

	CITY	ST	EMP	PHONE	ENTRY #
Carten Controls Inc	Cheshire	CT	F	203 699-2100	719
James J Scott LLC	Rocky Hill	CT	G	860 571-9200	3719
Nutek Aerospace Corp	New Milford	CT	G	860 355-3169	2819
Saf Industries LLC	Meriden	CT	E	203 729-4900	2127
Schwing Bioset Technologies	Danbury	CT	E	203 744-2100	987
Amkor Industrial Products Inc	Worcester	MA	E	508 799-4970	17336
Conant Controls Inc	Woburn	MA	F	781 395-2240	17147
Neles USA Inc	Worcester	MA	G	508 852-0200	17428
Neles USA Inc **(DH)**	Shrewsbury	MA	C	508 852-0200	15125
Neles USA Inc	Shrewsbury	MA	G	508 852-0200	15126
Neles USA Inc	Shrewsbury	MA	F	508 852-0200	15127
Universal Carburetor Inc	Norwood	MA	G	781 762-3771	14204
Aqua Phoenix Limited	Coventry	RI	G	401 821-2732	20136
Eagle America Inc	Warwick	RI	F	401 732-0333	21358

3593 Fluid Power Cylinders & Actuators

	CITY	ST	EMP	PHONE	ENTRY #
Airpot Corporation	Norwalk	CT	E	800 848-7681	3097
Durant Machine Inc **(PA)**	Mystic	CT	G	860 536-7698	2438
Hydraulic Solutions of Ne	Winslow	ME	G	207 859-9955	7269
Wedgerock	Limerick	ME	G	207 793-2289	6338
Parker & Harper Companies Inc **(PA)**	Raymond	NH	D	603 895-4761	19643
Quality Controls Inc	Northfield	NH	E	603 286-3321	19408
Watts Regulator Co	Franklin	NH	A	603 934-5110	18166

3594 Fluid Power Pumps & Motors

	CITY	ST	EMP	PHONE	ENTRY #
Crane Co **(PA)**	Stamford	CT	D	203 363-7300	4177
Hamilton Sundstrand Corp **(HQ)**	Windsor Locks	CT	A	860 654-6000	5397
Navtec Rigging Solutions Inc	Clinton	CT	E	203 458-3163	790
Reidville Hydraulics & Mfg Inc	Torrington	CT	E	860 496-1133	4596
Dike Corporation **(PA)**	Lawrence	MA	G	978 208-7046	12018
Hostar Mar Trnspt Systems Inc	Wareham	MA	E	508 295-2900	16250
Kerfoot Technologies Inc	Mashpee	MA	F	508 539-3002	12881
Parker Hannifin Corpora	Merrimac	MA	G	978 346-0578	13005
Stedt Hydraulic Crane Corp	Westborough	MA	F	508 366-9151	16651
ECB Motor Company Inc	Lyman	ME	G	508 717-5441	6389
Parker-Hannifin Corporation	Portsmouth	NH	G	603 433-6400	19605
Michaelson Fluid Power Inc	Smithfield	RI	F	401 232-7070	21239

3596 Scales & Balances, Exc Laboratory

	CITY	ST	EMP	PHONE	ENTRY #
Reliable Scales & Systems LLC	Bristol	CT	G	860 380-0600	604
Bay State Scale & Systems Inc	Burlington	MA	G	781 993-9035	9239
C & C Scale Co Inc	Lakeville	MA	G	508 947-0001	11974
Highland Labs Inc	Holliston	MA	E	508 429-2918	11577
M & M Scale Company Inc	Malden	MA	F	781 321-2737	12580
Mettler-Toledo Intl Inc	Newton	MA	G	800 472-4646	13614
New Bedford Scale Co Inc	New Bedford	MA	G	508 997-6730	13421
Setra Systems Inc	Boxboro	MA	F	978 263-1400	8954
Thomas Higgins	Billerica	MA	G	978 930-0573	8306
Public Scales	Lewiston	ME	F	207 784-9466	6317
Ocean State Scale Balance LLC	Coventry	RI	G	401 340-6622	20162
Orbetron LLC	Cumberland	RI	G	651 983-2872	20337
Tridyne Process Systems Inc	South Burlington	VT	F	802 863-6873	22473

3599 Machinery & Eqpt, Indl & Commercial, NEC

	CITY	ST	EMP	PHONE	ENTRY #
A & M Auto Machine Inc	Meriden	CT	G	203 237-3502	2071
A C T Manufacturing LLC	South Windsor	CT	G	860 289-8837	3930
A D Grinding	Plainville	CT	F	860 747-6630	3460
A Hardiman Machine Co Inc	East Windsor	CT	G	860 623-8133	1274
Abstract Tool Inc	Deep River	CT	F	860 526-4635	1056
Accupaulo Holding Corporation **(PA)**	Bristol	CT	E	860 666-5621	511
Accurate Threaded Products Co	Bristol	CT	E	860 666-5621	512
Accurate Tool & Die Inc	Stamford	CT	E	203 967-1200	4127
Accutrol LLC	Danbury	CT	E	203 445-9991	866
Acucut Inc	Southington	CT	E	860 793-7012	4036
Addamo Manufacturing Inc	Newington	CT	G	860 667-2601	2837
Advance Development & Mfg	Guilford	CT	F	203 453-4325	1691
Advanced Machine Technology	Ellington	CT	G	860 872-2664	1327
Aeroswiss LLC	Meriden	CT	F	203 634-4545	2074
AJ Tuck Company	Brookfield	CT	E	203 775-1234	633
Albert E Erickson Co	Stratford	CT	F	203 386-8931	4390
Allen Precision LLC	Windsor Locks	CT	G	860 370-9881	5384
Allied Machining Co Inc	Newington	CT	G	860 665-1228	2841
Altek Electronics Inc	Torrington	CT	C	860 482-7626	4558
Alto Products Corp Al	Plainville	CT	E	860 747-2736	3465
AM Manufacturing LLC	Glastonbury	CT	G	860 573-1987	1537
American Fnshg Specialists Inc	Bridgeport	CT	G	203 367-0663	372
American Machining Tech Inc	Portland	CT	G	860 342-0005	3561
American Metal Masters LLC	Plantsville	CT	G	860 621-6911	3526
American Metallizing	South Windsor	CT	G	860 289-1677	3936
American Precision Mfg LLC	Ansonia	CT	E	203 734-1800	5
American Specialty Pdts LLC	Vernon	CT	G	860 871-2279	4662
American Tool & Mfg Corp	Newington	CT	F	860 666-2255	2842
Andy Rakowicz	Berlin	CT	G	860 828-1620	72
Apex Tool & Cutter Co Inc	Beacon Falls	CT	G	203 888-8970	54
APS Robotics & Integration LLC	Deep River	CT	G	860 526-1040	1057
Arcade Technology LLC	Bridgeport	CT	E	203 366-3871	376
ASAP Machine Sp & Fabrication	Plainfield	CT	G	860 564-4114	3450
Astro Aircom LLC	Bloomfield	CT	G	860 688-3320	206
Atlas Precision Mfg LLC	South Windsor	CT	E	860 290-9114	3942
Automatic Machine Products	Middletown	CT	G	860 346-7064	2174
B & A Company Inc	Milford	CT	E	203 876-7527	2248
B & F Machine Co Inc	New Britain	CT	D	860 225-6349	2512
B & R Machine Works Inc	Bethel	CT	G	203 798-0595	129
Balding Precision Inc	Milford	CT	G	203 878-9135	2250
Barlo Manufacturing	Branford	CT	G	203 481-3426	295
Barnes Technical Products LLC	New Haven	CT	G	203 931-8852	2664
Barre Precision Products Inc	Bolton	CT	G	860 647-1913	274
Bay State Machine Inc	Plainfield	CT	G	860 230-0054	3452
Bmi Cad Services Inc	Simsbury	CT	F	860 658-0808	3897
Boman Precision Tech Inc	Milford	CT	G	203 415-8350	2256
Bomar Machine LLC	Berlin	CT	G	860 505-7299	77
Bracone Metal Spinning Inc	Southington	CT	E	860 628-5927	4041
Braemar Machine Co	Bristol	CT	G	860 585-1903	535
Bristol Tool & Die Company	Bristol	CT	E	860 582-2577	539
British Precision Inc	Glastonbury	CT	E	860 633-3343	1541
Broadstripes LLC	New Haven	CT	G	203 350-9824	2672
Bryt Manufacturing	New Britain	CT	G	860 224-4772	2516
Budney Overhaul & Repair Ltd	Berlin	CT	C	860 828-0585	79
Budrad Engineering Co LLC	Monroe	CT	G	203 452-7310	2397
Burke Precision Machine Co Inc	East Granby	CT	G	860 408-1394	1119
Buswell Manufacturing Co Inc	Bridgeport	CT	F	203 334-6069	392
C & A Machine Co Inc	Newington	CT	E	860 667-0605	2851
C & W Manufacturing Co Inc	Glastonbury	CT	E	860 633-4631	1542
C V Tool Company Inc **(PA)**	Southington	CT	E	978 353-7901	4042
C-B Manufacturing & Tool Co	Terryville	CT	G	860 583-5402	4475
Cad CAM Machine LLC	Plainville	CT	G	860 410-9788	3471
Candlewood Machine Pdts LLC	New Milford	CT	G	860 350-2211	2790
Candlewood Tool & Machine Shop	Gaylordsville	CT	F	860 355-1892	1529
Capital Design & Engrg Inc	Danbury	CT	G	203 798-6027	886
Capitol Machine Inc Preci	Plainville	CT	G	860 410-0758	3472
Carl Associates Inc	South Windsor	CT	G	860 749-7620	3948
Carnegie Tool Inc	Norwalk	CT	F	203 866-0744	3119
Cavtech Industries	Waterbury	CT	G	203 437-8764	4855
Central Connecticut Sls & Mfg	Newington	CT	G	860 667-1411	2854
Cgl Inc	Watertown	CT	F	860 945-6166	5002
Chapco Inc **(PA)**	Chester	CT	D	860 526-9535	769
Cirillo Manufacturing Group	East Haven	CT	G	203 484-5010	1244
Compucision LLC	New Milford	CT	G	860 355-9790	2794
Con-Tec Inc	Naugatuck	CT	F	203 723-8942	2467
Connecticut Coining Inc	Bethel	CT	D	203 743-3861	138
Connecticut Hone Incorporated	Plainville	CT	G	860 747-3884	3476
Connecticut Machine & Welding	Stratford	CT	E	203 502-2605	4406
Connecticut Mch Tooling & Cast	Milford	CT	F	203 874-8300	2269
Consulting Engrg Dev Svcs Inc	Oxford	CT	D	203 828-6528	3398
Continental Machine Tl Co Inc	New Britain	CT	D	860 223-2896	2522
Continuity Engine Inc	New Haven	CT	G	866 631-5556	2678
Couturier Ino	Meriden	CT	G	203 238-4555	2089
Crystal Tool and Machine Co	Vernon	CT	G	860 870-7431	4666
D & L Engineering Company	Stratford	CT	G	203 375-5856	4408
D F & B Precision Mfg Inc	New Milford	CT	G	860 354-5663	2796

	CITY	ST	EMP	PHONE	ENTRY #
Darly Custom Technology Inc	Windsor	CT	F	860 298-7966	5328
Dawid Manufacturing Inc	Ansonia	CT	G	203 734-1800	12
Delltech Inc	Milford	CT	G	203 878-8266	2275
Dickson Product Development	Norwalk	CT	G	203 846-2128	3140
Draher Machine Company	Wolcott	CT	G	203 753-0179	5440
Dso Manufacturing Company Inc	New Britain	CT	E	860 224-2641	2528
Dundee Holding Inc **(DH)**	Farmington	CT	G	860 677-1376	1477
Durbin Machine Inc	Portland	CT	G	860 342-1602	3567
Durol Company	Hamden	CT	F	203 288-3383	1744
Durstin Machine & Mfg	Harwinton	CT	G	860 485-1257	1888
Dynamic Bldg Enrgy Sltions LLC **(PA)**	North Stonington	CT	F	860 599-1872	3072
E O Manufacturing Company Inc	West Haven	CT	E	203 932-5981	5120
E-B Manufacturing Company Inc	Middletown	CT	E	860 632-8563	2185
EA Patten Co LLC	Manchester	CT	D	860 649-2851	2004
East Coast Metal Hose Inc	Naugatuck	CT	G	203 723-7459	2470
El Mar Inc	West Hartford	CT	G	860 729-7232	5068
Empco Inc **(PA)**	Bristol	CT	G	860 589-3233	555
Esteem Manufacturing Corp	South Windsor	CT	E	860 282-9964	3966
Excello Tool Engrg & Mfg Co	Milford	CT	E	203 878-4073	2287
Experimental Prototype Pdts Co	South Windsor	CT	F	860 289-4948	3969
Expressway Lube Centers	Danbury	CT	F	203 744-2511	915
Faille Precision Machining	Baltic	CT	G	860 822-1964	49
Fairchild Auto-Mated Parts Inc	Winsted	CT	E	860 379-2725	5411
Filter Fab Inc	Somers	CT	G	860 749-6381	3917
Fisher Mfg Systems Inc **(PA)**	Wallingford	CT	F	203 269-3846	4744
Focus Technologies Inc	Berlin	CT	G	860 829-8998	83
Forrati Manufacturing & Tl LLC	Plantsville	CT	G	860 426-1105	3530
Frank Roth Co Inc	Stratford	CT	D	203 377-2155	4413
Frasal Tool Co Inc	Newington	CT	F	860 666-3524	2865
Fryer Corporation	Oxford	CT	G	203 888-9944	3402
G & M Tool Company	Seymour	CT	G	203 888-9354	3751
G F Grinding Tool Mfg Co Inc	Waterbury	CT	G	203 757-6244	4876
Gen-El-Mec Associates Inc	Oxford	CT	E	203 828-6566	3403
General Machine Company Inc	Southington	CT	F	860 426-9295	4053
Genovese Manufacturing Co	Terryville	CT	F	860 582-9944	4481
Golik Machine Co	South Windsor	CT	G	860 610-0095	3974
Grace Machine Company LLC	Berlin	CT	F	860 828-8789	87
Graham Tool and Machine LLC	Terryville	CT	G	860 585-1261	4482
Gregor Technologies LLC	Torrington	CT	E	860 482-2569	4580
Griswold Machine & Fabrication	Jewett City	CT	G	860 376-9891	1913
Gulf Manufacturing Inc	Rocky Hill	CT	E	860 529-8601	3710
H & B Tool & Engineering Co	South Windsor	CT	E	860 528-9341	3976
H & W Machine LLC	Berlin	CT	G	860 828-7679	88
H G Steinmetz Machine Works	Bethel	CT	F	203 794-1880	158
Harwest Holdings One Inc	South Windham	CT	E	860 423-8334	3925
Herrick & Cowell Company Inc	Hamden	CT	G	203 288-2578	1759
Hfo Chicago LLC	Windsor	CT	G	860 285-0709	5337
High Tech Precision Mfg L L C	Southington	CT	G	860 621-7242	4057
Houston Weber Systems Inc	Branford	CT	G	203 481-0115	324
Hygrade Precision Tech Inc	Plainville	CT	E	860 747-5773	3496
Integra-Cast Inc	New Britain	CT	D	860 225-7600	2541
Integral Technologies Inc **(DH)**	Enfield	CT	G	860 741-2281	1366
Interface Devices Incorporated	Milford	CT	G	203 878-4648	2303
Intrasonics Inc	Thomaston	CT	G	860 283-8040	4504
J & G Machining Company Inc	Winsted	CT	G	860 379-7038	5414
J & L Machine Co Inc	Manchester	CT	E	860 649-3539	2013
Jam Company	Darien	CT	G	203 655-3260	1027
Jan Manufacturing Inc	Wolcott	CT	G	203 879-0580	5445
Jared Manufacturing Co Inc	Norwalk	CT	F	203 846-1732	3180
Jaw Precision Machining LLC	Stonington	CT	G	860 535-0615	4377
Jeff Manufacturing Co Inc	Torrington	CT	F	860 482-8845	4582
JEM Precision Grinding Inc	Glastonbury	CT	G	860 633-0152	1560
Jensen Machine Co	Newington	CT	G	860 666-5438	2874
Jerome Ridel	West Granby	CT	G	860 379-1774	5049
Joe Valentine Machine Company	Stamford	CT	G	203 356-9776	4231
Joseph J McFadden Jr	New Milford	CT	G	860 354-6794	2808
Jovan Machine Co Inc	Wolcott	CT	G	203 879-2855	5446
JV Precision Machine Co	Seymour	CT	E	203 888-0748	3753
K & E Auto Machine L L C	Naugatuck	CT	G	203 723-7189	2481
K & K Precision Manufacturing	East Berlin	CT	G	860 828-7681	1104
Karas Engineering Co Inc	New Milford	CT	G	860 355-3153	2809
Kbj Manufacturing Inc	Bristol	CT	G	860 585-7257	574
Kell-Strom Tool Co Inc **(PA)**	Wethersfield	CT	E	860 529-6851	5253
Kell-Strom Tool Intl Inc	Wethersfield	CT	E	860 529-6851	5254
Kenneth Leroux	Bloomfield	CT	G	860 769-9800	237
Keyway Inc	Wethersfield	CT	G	860 571-9181	5255
Kovacs Machine and Tool Co	Wallingford	CT	E	203 269-4949	4761
Kovil Manufacturing LLC	Cheshire	CT	G	203 699-9425	741
L R Brown Manufacturing Co	Wallingford	CT	G	203 265-5639	4763
Labco Welding Inc	Middletown	CT	G	860 632-2625	2200
Larco Machines Co Inc	Bolton	CT	G	860 647-9769	277
Larrys Auto Machine LLC	Groton	CT	G	860 449-9112	1679
Lincoln Precision Machine Inc	Thompson	CT	G	860 923-9358	4535
Loric Tool Inc	North Grosvenordale	CT	F	860 928-0171	2999
Lynn Welding Co Inc	Newington	CT	F	860 667-4400	2877
M & B Automotive Machine Shop	Stamford	CT	G	203 348-6134	4242
M & Z Engineering Inc	Torrington	CT	G	860 496-0282	4585
M Cubed Technologies Inc	Monroe	CT	E	203 452-2333	2407
M Cubed Technologies Inc **(HQ)**	Newtown	CT	E	203 304-2940	2928
M T D Corporation	Trumbull	CT	F	203 261-3721	4628
M-Fab LLC	Torrington	CT	G	860 496-0055	4586
Macala Tool Inc	Enfield	CT	G	860 763-2580	1369
Mackenzie Mch & Mar Works Inc	East Haven	CT	G	203 777-3479	1254
Magna Standard Mfg Co Inc	Milford	CT	G	203 874-0444	2313
Manchester Tl & Design ADP LLC	Hartford	CT	G	860 296-6541	1843
Marc Bouley	Willimantic	CT	G	860 450-1713	5267
Marenna Amusements LLC	Orange	CT	F	203 623-4386	3372
Master Tool & Machine Inc	Plainville	CT	G	860 747-2581	3506
Mega Manufacturing LLC	Newington	CT	G	860 666-5555	2881
Mepp Tool Co Inc	Glastonbury	CT	G	860 289-8230	1564
Merritt Machine Company	Wethersfield	CT	G	860 257-4484	5257
Metal Industries Inc	Hartford	CT	G	860 296-6228	1847
Metalpro Inc	Old Saybrook	CT	E	860 388-1811	3344
Michaud Tool Co Inc	Terryville	CT	G	860 582-6785	4486
Micro Precision LLC	South Windham	CT	E	860 423-4575	3926
Mid-State Manufacturing Inc	Milldale	CT	F	860 621-6855	2386
Mikco Manufacturing Inc	Wallingford	CT	F	203 269-2250	4776
Mill Machine Tool & Die Co	Southington	CT	G	860 628-6700	4066
Mill Manufacturing Inc	Bridgeport	CT	G	203 367-9572	451
Millturn Manufacturing Co	North Haven	CT	G	203 248-1602	3040
Mj Tool & Manufacturing Inc	Simsbury	CT	G	860 352-2688	3908
Mkb Machine & Tool Mfg	Berlin	CT	G	860 828-5728	97
Mrh Tool LLC	Milford	CT	G	203 878-3359	2317
Mtr Precision Machining Inc	Pomfret Center	CT	G	860 928-9440	3557
My Tool Company Inc	Waterbury	CT	G	203 755-2333	4920
Myco Tool & Manufacturing Inc	Vernon	CT	G	860 875-7340	4670
Naiad Dynamics Us Inc **(HQ)**	Shelton	CT	E	203 929-6355	3836
Natures View Inc	Waterbury	CT	G	800 506-5307	4923
Nerjan Development Company	Stamford	CT	G	203 325-3228	4254
New England Cnc Inc	Hamden	CT	F	203 288-8241	1775
New England Grinding and MA	Bridgeport	CT	G	203 333-1885	456
New England Tool & Automtn Inc	New Britain	CT	G	860 827-9389	2556
New England Traveling Wire LLC	New Britain	CT	G	860 223-6297	2557
New Horizon Machine Co Inc	Stamford	CT	G	203 316-9355	4257
New Machine Products LLC	Danbury	CT	G	203 790-5520	959
Niantic Tool Inc	Niantic	CT	G	860 739-2182	2955
Nolan Industries Inc	New Haven	CT	G	203 865-8160	2720
Northeast Quality Services LLC	Cromwell	CT	E	860 632-7242	856
Northwest Connecticut Mfg Co	Colebrook	CT	G	860 379-1553	813
Noujaim Tool Co Inc	Waterbury	CT	E	203 753-4441	4929
Nova Machining LLC	Unionville	CT	G	860 675-8131	4660
Oakville Quality Products LLC	Waterbury	CT	F	203 757-5525	4931
P&P Tool & Die Corp	Milford	CT	G	203 874-2571	2330
Pal Corporation	Newington	CT	G	860 666-9211	2889
Pal Technologies LLC	West Hartford	CT	G	860 953-1984	5089
Par Manufacturing Inc	Farmington	CT	G	860 677-1797	1506
Paramount Machine Company Inc	Manchester	CT	E	860 643-5549	2036
Parason Machine Inc	Deep River	CT	F	860 526-3565	1064
Peter Tasi	Derby	CT	G	203 732-6540	1077
Phoenix Machine Inc	Seymour	CT	G	203 888-1135	3759
Pilot Machine Designers Inc	Norwalk	CT	G	203 866-2227	3220
Pine Meadow Machine Co Inc	Windsor Locks	CT	G	860 623-4494	5398
Pinto Manufacturing Llc	Glastonbury	CT	G	860 659-9543	1571
Pioneer Precision Products **(PA)**	Berlin	CT	F	860 828-5838	101
Poplar Tool & Mfg Co Inc	Bridgeport	CT	G	203 333-4369	472
Precision Grinding Company	New Britain	CT	F	860 229-9652	2565
Precision Machine and Gears	North Franklin	CT	G	860 822-6993	2990
Precision Manufacturing LLC	Bethel	CT	G	203 790-4663	175
Precision Tool & Components	Milford	CT	G	203 874-9215	2339
Precision Wire Cutting	Harwinton	CT	G	860 485-1494	1892
Preferred Manufacturing Co	North Haven	CT	G	203 239-0727	3054
Prestige Tool Mfg LLC	Milford	CT	G	203 874-0360	2340
Pro Tool and Design Inc	Berlin	CT	F	860 828-4667	105
Projects Inc	Glastonbury	CT	C	860 633-4615	1574
Proman Inc	New Britain	CT	G	860 827-8778	2566
Pulver Precision LLC	Enfield	CT	G	860 763-0763	1377
Pw Precision Machine LLC	Higganum	CT	G	203 889-8615	1905
Quality Machine Inc	New Milford	CT	G	860 354-6794	2824
Quality Wire Edm Inc	Bristol	CT	G	860 583-9867	600
Quick Machine Services LLC	Meriden	CT	G	203 634-8822	2121
Quick Turn Machine Company Inc	Windsor Locks	CT	F	860 623-2569	5399
R E F Machine Company Inc	Middlefield	CT	G	860 349-9344	2164
R K Machine Company LLC	New Britain	CT	G	860 224-7545	2567
R L Turick Co Inc	New Hartford	CT	G	860 693-2230	2646
Rand Machine & Fabrication Co	Cheshire	CT	F	203 272-1352	756
Rand Sheaves & Pulleys LLC	Cheshire	CT	G	203 272-1352	757
Rapidex	Windsor	CT	G	860 285-8818	5357
Rayflex Company Inc	Bridgeport	CT	G	203 336-2173	479
Raym-Co Inc	Farmington	CT	E	860 678-8292	1510
Reed & Stefanow Machine Tl Co	Bristol	CT	F	860 583-7834	603
Reidville Hydraulics & Mfg Inc	Torrington	CT	E	860 496-1133	4596
Renchel Tool Inc	Putnam	CT	F	860 315-9017	3631
Reno Machine Company Inc	Newington	CT	D	860 666-5641	2898

	CITY	ST	EMP	PHONE	ENTRY #
Richard Dahlen	Bristol	CT	G	860 584-8226	606
Richards Machine Tool Co Inc	Newington	CT	F	860 436-2938	2899
Riff Company Inc	Cheshire	CT	G	203 272-4899	759
RK Manufacturing Corp Conn	Danbury	CT	D	203 797-8700	979
Ross Mfg & Design LLC	Milford	CT	F	203 878-0187	2356
RWK Tool Inc	Cromwell	CT	E	860 635-0116	860
S S Fabrications Inc	Eastford	CT	G	860 974-1910	1314
Salamon Industries LLC	New Britain	CT	G	860 612-8420	2575
Schmidt Tool Manufacturing	Milford	CT	G	203 877-8149	2361
Secondaries Inc	Wolcott	CT	G	203 879-4633	5457
Secondary Operations Inc	Hamden	CT	F	203 288-8241	1783
Senior Operations LLC	Enfield	CT	D	860 741-2546	1383
Setma Inc	New Milford	CT	G	409 833-9797	2828
Sharpac LLC	Bridgeport	CT	G	203 384-0568	488
Simsbury Precision Products	Simsbury	CT	G	860 658-6909	3911
Simson Products Co Inc	Wallingford	CT	F	203 265-9882	4807
Sirois Tool Company Inc **(PA)**	Berlin	CT	D	860 828-5327	109
Skico Manufacturing Co LLC	Hamden	CT	G	203 230-1305	1784
Skytech Machining Inc	Stratford	CT	G	203 378-9994	4446
Slater Hill Tool LLC	Putnam	CT	G	860 963-0415	3633
Sneham Manufacturing Inc	Stratford	CT	G	203 610-6669	4447
Soldream Spcial Process - Wldg	Tolland	CT	G	860 858-5247	4552
Somers Manufacturing Inc	Bristol	CT	G	860 314-1075	613
Space Tool & Machine Co Inc	South Windsor	CT	G	860 290-8599	4013
Spargo Machine Products Inc	Terryville	CT	F	860 583-3925	4492
Specialty Components Inc **(PA)**	Wallingford	CT	G	203 284-9112	4810
Spectrum Machine & Design LLC	Windsor Locks	CT	G	860 386-6490	5400
Ssi Manufacturing Tech Corp	Bristol	CT	E	860 589-8004	615
Stacy B Goff	East Windsor	CT	G	860 623-2547	1304
Standard Bellows Co **(PA)**	Windsor Locks	CT	E	860 623-2307	5401
Sterling Engineering Corp	Pleasant Valley	CT	C	860 379-3366	3547
Sterling Precision Machining	Sterling	CT	F	860 564-4043	4372
Stevens Manufacturing Co Inc	Milford	CT	E	203 878-2328	2369
Stickler Machine Company LLC	East Hampton	CT	G	860 267-8246	1165
Straton Industries Inc	Stratford	CT	D	203 375-4488	4450
Sum Machine & Tool Co Inc	Coventry	CT	G	860 742-6827	840
Summit Screw Machine Corp	Milford	CT	G	203 693-2727	2371
T & J Manufacturing LLP	Middletown	CT	E	860 632-8655	2226
T G Industries Inc	Meriden	CT	F	203 235-3239	2137
T L S Design & Manufacturing	New London	CT	G	860 439-1414	2781
T M Industries Inc	East Berlin	CT	D	860 828-0344	1109
Target Machines Inc	Burlington	CT	G	860 675-1539	680
TET Mfg Co Inc	Middlefield	CT	E	860 349-1004	2166
Thavenet Machine Company Inc	Pawcatuck	CT	G	860 599-4495	3442
Thermatool Corp **(HQ)**	East Haven	CT	D	203 468-4100	1264
Tier One LLC	Newtown	CT	D	203 426-3030	2945
Timna Manufacturing Inc	Wallingford	CT	G	203 265-4656	4821
Tolland Machine Company LLC	Vernon	CT	G	860 872-4863	4674
Tool Logistics II	Norwalk	CT	F	203 855-9754	3258
Top Flight Machine Tool LLC	Plainville	CT	G	860 747-4726	3520
Total Concept Tool Inc	Branford	CT	G	203 483-1130	355
Total Parts Services LLC	Woodbury	CT	G	203 263-5619	5490
TP Cycle & Engineering Inc	Danbury	CT	E	203 744-4960	1000
Transportation Conn Dept	Portland	CT	G	860 342-5996	3579
Tri Mar Manufacturing Compan	Southington	CT	F	860 628-4791	4088
Triumph Manufacturing Co Inc	Middletown	CT	F	860 635-8811	2229
Tropax Precision Manufacturing	Danbury	CT	F	203 794-0733	1002
Unas Grinding Corporation	East Hartford	CT	E	860 289-1538	1231
Uniprise International Inc	Terryville	CT	E	860 589-7262	4495
United Gear & Machine Co Inc	Suffield	CT	F	860 623-6618	4469
Venture Tool and Manufacturing	East Hampton	CT	G	860 267-9647	1167
Verzatec Inc	Southington	CT	G	860 628-0511	4090
Vn Machine Co	Newington	CT	G	860 666-8797	2911
Vortex Manufacturing	Somers	CT	G	860 749-9769	3921
Voyteks Inc	East Windsor	CT	G	860 967-6558	1309
Wallingford Industries Inc	Branford	CT	F	203 481-0359	358
Wauregan Machine Shop	Wauregan	CT	G	860 774-0686	5040
Wdss Corporation	Norwalk	CT	F	203 854-5930	3269
Weld-All Inc	Southington	CT	F	860 621-3156	4091
Wendon Company Inc	Stamford	CT	F	203 348-6272	4357
Wentworth Manufacturing LLC **(PA)**	South Windham	CT	E	860 423-4575	3928
Westminster Tool Inc	Plainfield	CT	E	860 564-6966	3459
Westport Precision LLC	Stratford	CT	D	203 378-2175	4457
Willson Manufacturing of Conn	Manchester	CT	G	860 643-8182	2059
Winthrop Tool LLC	Essex	CT	G	860 526-9079	1409
Wire Tech LLC	Watertown	CT	G	860 945-9473	5036
Xuare LLC	Norwich	CT	G	860 383-8863	3293
17 Chestnut Inc	Georgetown	MA	G	800 897-3117	11134
325 Silver Street Inc	Agawam	MA	E	413 789-1800	7415
A & A Industries Inc	Peabody	MA	E	978 977-9660	14304
A & D Tool Co	Indian Orchard	MA	G	413 543-3166	11883
A & G Centerless Grinding Inc	Woburn	MA	F	781 281-0007	17102
A B & D Machining Inc	Waltham	MA	G	781 891-4120	16019
A B T Machine Co	Holliston	MA	G	508 429-4355	11554
A D & G Enterprises Inc	Franklin	MA	G	508 528-0232	11019
A1 Screw Machine Products Inc	Chicopee	MA	F	413 594-8939	9995
Ab-Wey Machine & Die Co Inc	Pembroke	MA	F	781 294-8031	14389

	CITY	ST	EMP	PHONE	ENTRY #
Absolute Manufacturing Inc	Pepperell	MA	G	978 433-0760	14435
Accudynamics LLC	Lakeville	MA	D	508 946-4545	11971
Accudyne Machine Tool Inc	Bellingham	MA	G	508 966-3110	8027
Accumet Engineering Inc	Westford	MA	E	978 692-6180	16751
Accurate Tool & Machine Inc	Lakeville	MA	G	508 946-3414	11972
Accurounds Inc	Avon	MA	D	508 587-3500	7874
Ace Precision Inc	Agawam	MA	F	413 789-7536	7416
Acme United Corporation	Marlborough	MA	G	508 481-5944	12709
Advance Machine & Tool Inc	Pittsfield	MA	F	413 499-4900	14448
Advance Machine Co Inc	Stow	MA	G	978 897-5808	15630
Advanced Engineering Corp	Danvers	MA	F	978 777-7147	10193
Agis Inc	Plymouth	MA	G	508 591-8400	14540
AJ Precision Inc	Agawam	MA	G	413 568-9099	7419
Algonquin Industries Inc **(PA)**	Bellingham	MA	D	508 966-4600	8028
Allied Machined Products Corp	Auburn	MA	D	508 756-4290	7824
Allpage Inc	New Bedford	MA	G	508 995-6614	13357
Alpine Precision LLC	North Billerica	MA	F	978 667-6333	13792
Alvin Johnson	East Longmeadow	MA	G	413 525-6334	10465
Ambur Machine Co Inc	Northbridge	MA	G	508 234-6341	14053
American Machine Co	Westborough	MA	G	508 366-9634	16588
American SCrew & Barrels Inc	Gardner	MA	F	978 630-1300	11103
Amic Inc	Attleboro	MA	G	508 222-5300	7704
AMS Grinding Co Inc	Brockton	MA	G	508 588-2283	9119
Andover Medical Dev Group	Lawrence	MA	G	978 685-0838	11993
Andys Machine Inc	Middleboro	MA	E	508 947-1192	13052
Antron Engineering & Mch Co	Bellingham	MA	D	508 966-2803	8030
Anver Corporation	Hudson	MA	D	978 568-0221	11755
Apogee Machining Services Inc	Salem	MA	G	978 740-4689	14893
Applied Precision Technology	Attleboro	MA	F	508 226-8700	7706
Arbo Machine Co Inc	Rockland	MA	G	781 871-3449	14791
Arland Tool & Mfg Inc **(PA)**	Sturbridge	MA	D	508 347-3368	15638
Arland Tool & Mfg Inc	West Brookfield	MA	F	508 867-3085	16464
Arm Centerless Grinding	Georgetown	MA	G	978 352-2410	11136
Arrow Machine LLC	Belchertown	MA	G	413 323-7280	8021
Arts Ipswich	Ipswich	MA	G	978 356-5335	11902
Arwood Machine Corporation	Newburyport	MA	D	978 463-3777	13469
Assabet Machine Corp	Boxborough	MA	E	978 562-7992	8959
Atlantic Tool Company	Weymouth	MA	G	781 331-5550	16884
Aube Precision Tool Co Inc	Ludlow	MA	G	413 589-9048	12454
Auto Industrial Machine Inc	Danvers	MA	F	978 777-3772	10199
Awl Assoc	Warren	MA	G	413 436-9600	16259
Axis Cnc Incorporated	Ware	MA	F	413 967-6803	16228
Axis Technologies Inc	Lowell	MA	E	978 275-9908	12348
B & C Tooling Company Inc	Whitman	MA	G	781 447-5292	16920
B & R Machine Inc	Ludlow	MA	E	413 589-0246	12455
B-C-D Metal Products Inc	Malden	MA	E	781 397-9922	12561
Ball Slides Inc	Medfield	MA	G	508 359-4348	12910
Banacek Invstgtons Srch Recove	Sharon	MA	G	781 784-1400	15046
Banks White Poliaris Co Inc	Halifax	MA	G	781 293-3033	11314
Bartley Machine & Mfg Co Inc	Amesbury	MA	E	978 388-0085	7479
Bass Precision Products	Beverly	MA	G	978 922-3608	8107
Bbb & Machine Inc	Wareham	MA	G	508 273-0050	16240
Bees Manufacturing LLC	Needham	MA	G	781 400-1280	13292
Belmar Company	Woburn	MA	G	781 935-2233	17129
Benco Precision Machining Inc	Gloucester	MA	G	978 281-2055	11165
Bendon Gear & Machine Inc	Rockland	MA	E	781 878-8100	14793
Berkshire Group Ltd	Westfield	MA	G	413 562-7200	16673
Berkshire Mnufactured Pdts Inc	Newburyport	MA	C	978 462-8161	13472
Bigwood Corporation	Mashpee	MA	G	508 477-2220	12875
Black Diamond Drill Grinders	Shrewsbury	MA	F	978 465-3799	15104
Boniface Tool & Die Inc	Dudley	MA	E	508 764-3248	10373
Borg Design Inc	Hudson	MA	F	978 562-1559	11760
Bossonnet Inc	Westborough	MA	G	508 986-2308	16594
Boston Centerless Inc	Avon	MA	E	508 587-3500	7881
Boston Machine Inc	Chelmsford	MA	G	978 458-7722	9877
Boulevard Machine & Gear Inc	Springfield	MA	E	413 788-6466	15456
Bourgeois Machine Co	Middleton	MA	G	978 774-6240	13086
Boynton Machine Company Inc	Waltham	MA	E	781 899-9900	16051
Brenmar Molding Inc	Fitchburg	MA	G	978 343-3198	10814
Brennan Machine Co Inc	Hanson	MA	E	781 293-3997	11361
Brodeur Machine Company Inc	New Bedford	MA	E	508 995-2662	13366
Brook Pond Machining Inc	Westfield	MA	G	413 562-7411	16675
Brooks Associates Inc **(PA)**	Norwell	MA	G	781 871-3400	14098
Brooks Precision Machining	Chelmsford	MA	F	978 256-7477	9881
Brothers Machining Corp	Norton	MA	G	508 286-9136	14072
Burr Industries Inc	Danvers	MA	G	978 774-2527	10205
C & C Fabricating Inc	Ipswich	MA	F	978 356-9980	11907
C & C Machine Inc	Tyngsboro	MA	E	978 649-0285	15887
C & C Metals Engineering Inc	West Boylston	MA	E	508 835-9011	16410
C & G Machine Tool Co Inc	Granby	MA	F	413 467-9556	11227
C M G Precision	Ludlow	MA	G	413 547-8124	12457
C V Tool Company Inc	Fitchburg	MA	F	978 353-7901	10815
C-R Machine Co Inc **(PA)**	Billerica	MA	D	978 663-3989	8229
Cad Tech Machine Incorporated	Westford	MA	G	978 692-0677	16759
CAM Engineering Inc	Townsend	MA	G	978 300-5073	15869
Camara Metalworks	Westport	MA	G	508 636-7822	16837
Cape Cod Cupola Co Inc	North Dartmouth	MA	G	508 994-2119	13916

	CITY	ST	EMP	PHONE	ENTRY #
Capeway Welding Inc	Plymouth	MA	F	508 747-6666	14549
Carbide Specialities	Waltham	MA	G	781 899-1300	16061
Castle Machine Co	Ipswich	MA	G	978 356-2151	11911
Center Manufacturing Corp	Ipswich	MA	G	978 356-8420	11912
Centerline Technologies LLC	Hudson	MA	F	978 568-1330	11762
Charles McCann	Pittsfield	MA	G	413 442-3922	14463
Chas G Allen Realty LLC	Barre	MA	D	978 355-2911	7950
City Machine Corporation	Holyoke	MA	E	413 538-9766	11620
Clarkworks Machine	Westford	MA	G	978 692-2556	16762
Clematis Machine & Fixture Co	Waltham	MA	F	781 894-0777	16069
Cliflex Bellows Corporation	Boston	MA	E	617 268-5774	8477
Cnc Specialties Inc	Monson	MA	F	413 267-5051	13204
CNE Machine Company	Walpole	MA	G	508 668-4110	15991
Cogent Engineering Inc	Peabody	MA	G	978 977-3310	14321
Colcord Machine Co Inc	Hopedale	MA	F	508 634-8840	11670
Collins Manufacturing Inc	Essex	MA	F	978 768-2553	10592
Colonial Machine Company	Peabody	MA	G	781 233-0026	14322
Commercial Machine Inc	Ludlow	MA	G	413 583-3670	12460
Concept Machining Inc	North Billerica	MA	G	978 663-4999	13803
Concept Tooling Inc	Worcester	MA	G	508 754-6466	17358
Conti Precision Tool Co Inc	Gardner	MA	G	978 632-6224	11109
Continental Machine Pdts Inc	Boston	MA	G	617 567-7396	8482
Contract Engineering Inc	Beverly	MA	E	978 921-0501	8120
Cotter Machine Co Inc **(PA)**	West Wareham	MA	F	508 291-7400	16568
Cranberry Country Machine & Tl	Middleboro	MA	G	508 923-1107	13060
Cunningham Engineering Inc	Danvers	MA	F	978 774-4169	10209
Cunningham Machine Co Inc	Chelmsford	MA	G	978 256-7541	9890
Custom Arospc Components LLC	Woburn	MA	D	781 935-4940	17156
Custom Plastics Machining Inc	Woburn	MA	G	781 937-9700	17159
D & D Precision Machine Co Inc	Middleboro	MA	E	508 946-8010	13061
D F Carter Co Inc	Peabody	MA	F	978 977-0444	14328
D S Greene Co Inc	Wakefield	MA	G	781 245-2644	15947
Daily Grind	Bridgewater	MA	G	508 279-9952	9070
Dale Engineering & Son Inc	Bedford	MA	F	781 541-6055	7969
Dalton Manufacturing Company	Amesbury	MA	F	978 388-2227	7483
Danvers Engineering Co Inc	Danvers	MA	G	978 774-7501	10211
David Gilbert	Framingham	MA	G	508 879-1507	10940
David Packard Company Inc	Oxford	MA	G	508 987-2998	14258
Davin Machining and Welding Co	Chelsea	MA	G	617 884-8933	9952
Debco Machine Inc	Natick	MA	F	508 655-4469	13250
Decker Machine Works Inc	Greenfield	MA	E	413 628-3300	11259
Denault Inc	North Adams	MA	G	413 664-6771	13674
Dimark Precision Machining	Pembroke	MA	F	781 447-7990	14399
Diversified Machining Inc	Hudson	MA	G	978 562-2213	11768
DJM Precision Machining	Beverly	MA	G	978 922-0407	8127
Dougherty Tool Company Inc	Southborough	MA	G	508 485-5566	15355
E & D Manufacturing	Fitchburg	MA	G	978 345-0183	10824
E&D Machining Inc	North Billerica	MA	G	978 667-4848	13812
East Coast Fabrication Inc	New Bedford	MA	G	508 990-7918	13381
Eastern Machine & Design Corp	Hanson	MA	F	781 293-6391	11362
Eastern Mass Machined Products	Salisbury	MA	F	978 462-9301	14950
Eastern Precision Machining Co **(PA)**	Ipswich	MA	G	978 356-2372	11916
Eastern Tool Corporation	Medford	MA	F	781 395-1472	12932
Easthampton Machine & Tool Inc	Easthampton	MA	G	413 527-8770	10561
Easthampton Precision Mfg Inc	Easthampton	MA	G	413 527-1650	10562
Enos Engineering LLC	Acton	MA	G	978 654-6522	7353
Entwistle Company **(HQ)**	Hudson	MA	C	508 481-4000	11772
Essex Bay Engineering Inc	Ipswich	MA	G	978 412-9600	11918
Essex Engineering Inc	Lynn	MA	E	781 595-2114	12506
Euro Precision Inc	Ashley Falls	MA	G	413 229-0004	7673
Ev Rite Tool Inc	Westfield	MA	G	413 568-1433	16683
Evans Industries Inc	Topsfield	MA	E	978 887-8561	15858
Evans Machine Co Inc	Brockton	MA	E	508 584-8085	9144
Eyesaver International Inc	Hanover	MA	D	781 829-0808	11337
F H Peterson Machine Corp	Stoughton	MA	D	781 341-4930	15590
F L C Machined Products Co	Rowley	MA	G	978 948-7525	14853
Fairview Machine Company Inc	Topsfield	MA	E	978 887-2141	15859
Falcon Precision Machine Co	Ludlow	MA	G	413 583-2117	12465
Fitz Machine Inc	Wakefield	MA	F	781 245-5966	15952
Form Centerless Grinding Inc	Franklin	MA	F	508 520-0900	11046
Form Roll Die Corp	Worcester	MA	F	508 755-5302	17378
Friday Engineering Inc	Woburn	MA	G	781 932-8686	17188
G & H Manufacturing Inc	Westfield	MA	G	413 562-2035	16684
G & L Tool Corp	Agawam	MA	F	413 786-2535	7429
Galaxie Labs Inc	Burlington	MA	G	781 272-3750	9278
Gallant Machine Works Inc	Shrewsbury	MA	F	508 799-2919	15114
Gardner Tool & Stamping Co	Gardner	MA	G	978 632-0823	11115
Gary Hullihen	Monson	MA	G	413 283-2383	13207
Gaskin Manufacturing Corp	Plainville	MA	F	508 695-8949	14519
Gdjr Machining Incorporated	Leominster	MA	G	978 365-3568	12143
General Machine Inc	Holyoke	MA	G	413 533-5744	11627
General Products & Gear Corp	Rowley	MA	G	978 948-8146	14854
Geometric Engineering Co	Georgetown	MA	G	978 352-4651	11142
GF Machining Solutions LLC	Holliston	MA	G	508 474-1100	11573
Gill Metal Fab Inc	Brockton	MA	E	508 580-4445	9151
Grassetti Sales Associates	Springfield	MA	G	413 737-2283	15472
Graycer Screw Products Co Inc	Bellingham	MA	E	508 966-1810	8039
Gustafson Machine	Gloucester	MA	G	978 281-2012	11191
H & R Machine Co Inc	Adams	MA	G	413 743-5610	7412
H & S Machine Company Inc	Lawrence	MA	F	978 686-2321	12029
H & S Tool and Engineering Inc	Fall River	MA	E	508 672-6509	10709
H & T Specialty Co Inc	Waltham	MA	F	781 893-3866	16123
H E Moore Corp **(PA)**	Norfolk	MA	G	617 268-1262	13661
H E Moore Corp	Boston	MA	G	617 268-1262	8585
H G Cockrill Corp	Holliston	MA	G	508 429-2005	11574
H H Arnold Co Inc	Rockland	MA	E	781 878-0346	14805
Hadley Propeller Inc	Hadley	MA	G	413 585-0500	11306
Hannah Engineering Inc	Danvers	MA	E	978 777-5892	10221
Harrys Machined Parts	Northborough	MA	G	508 366-1455	14035
Harvard Products Inc	Harvard	MA	F	978 772-0309	11378
Heron Machine & Engrg Inc	Ludlow	MA	G	413 547-6308	12466
High Tech Machinists Inc	Chelmsford	MA	E	978 256-1600	9904
Hillside Engineering Inc	Danvers	MA	G	978 762-6640	10222
Hollis Industries Inc	Holliston	MA	E	508 429-4328	11578
Holyoke Machine Company **(PA)**	Holyoke	MA	E	413 534-5612	11633
Honematic Machine Corporation	Boylston	MA	E	508 869-2131	8980
Howestemco Inc	Franklin	MA	D	508 528-6500	11053
HT Machine Co Inc	Webster	MA	F	508 949-1105	16343
IBC Advanced Alloys Inc-Belac	Wilmington	MA	G	978 284-8900	17004
Ideal Engineering Co Inc	Bellingham	MA	G	508 966-2324	8042
Ideal Instrument Co Inc	Canton	MA	F	781 828-0881	9741
Innovative Tooling Company Inc	Lenox	MA	F	413 637-1031	12101
Intech Inc	Acton	MA	E	978 263-2210	7366
Intellicut Inc	Middleton	MA	G	617 417-5236	13090
Ital-Tech Machined Pdts LLC	Groveland	MA	F	978 373-6773	11301
J & L Welding & Machine Co	Gloucester	MA	E	978 283-3388	11193
J & R Plastics	Acushnet	MA	G	508 995-0893	7402
J F Kessler Inc	Canton	MA	G	781 828-0134	9746
J G Machine Co Inc	Wilmington	MA	G	978 447-5279	17008
J P Precision Machine Co	Chicopee	MA	G	413 592-8191	10034
J T Machine Co Inc	East Douglas	MA	E	508 476-1508	10427
J W Machining Inc	Hudson	MA	F	978 562-5611	11780
J&J Machine Company Inc	Marlborough	MA	F	508 481-8166	12780
Jack Dilling	Hubbardston	MA	G	978 928-4002	11745
James E Cofran	Stoughton	MA	G	781 341-0897	15599
James F Mullen Co Inc	Merrimac	MA	D	978 346-0045	13002
Jamlab Enterprises	Methuen	MA	G	978 688-8750	13028
Jem Precision Technologies	Fall River	MA	G	508 672-0666	10716
Jesko Tool & Knife	Indian Orchard	MA	G	413 543-1520	11888
Jet Machined Products LLC	East Bridgewater	MA	F	508 378-3200	10414
Jeto Engineering Inc	Essex	MA	F	978 768-6472	10594
JG Manufacturing Corp	North Andover	MA	G	978 681-8400	13712
JJT Engineering Inc	Wilmington	MA	G	978 657-4137	17010
Jmc Asset Holdings Inc	Hanson	MA	G	781 447-9264	11365
John A Kachagian	North Billerica	MA	G	978 663-8511	13829
John Covey	Peabody	MA	F	978 535-4681	14346
JR Higgins Associates LLC	Acton	MA	E	978 266-1200	7367
Jrk Precision Machine	Agawam	MA	G	413 789-7200	7436
K & R Machine Co Corp	Westfield	MA	G	413 568-9335	16696
K & W Machine Works	Springfield	MA	G	413 543-3329	15483
K M T Machining	Upton	MA	G	508 529-6953	15907
K W Bristol Co Inc	North Attleboro	MA	G	508 699-4742	13760
Kad Machine Inc	Chicopee	MA	G	413 538-8684	10036
Kc Precision Machining LLC	Ipswich	MA	E	978 356-8900	11926
Kensol-Franklin Inc	Franklin	MA	G	508 528-2000	11061
Keystone Precision & Engrg	Pepperell	MA	E	978 433-8484	14440
Kingston Manufacturing Co Inc	Kingston	MA	G	781 585-4476	11961
Kms Machine Works Inc	Taunton	MA	F	508 822-3151	15762
Knight Machine & Tool Co Inc	South Hadley	MA	F	413 532-2507	15305
Kodiak Machining Co Inc	Ipswich	MA	F	978 356-9876	11927
L & M Machine Inc	Everett	MA	E	617 294-0378	10614
Lake Manufacturing Co Inc	Newburyport	MA	F	978 465-1617	13507
Lander Inc	Pittsfield	MA	F	413 448-8734	14481
Lanford Manufacturing Corp	Lawrence	MA	E	978 557-0240	12044
Laser Process Mfg Inc	Peabody	MA	F	978 531-6003	14350
Lavallee Machinery Inc	Southbridge	MA	G	508 764-2896	15391
Lavelle Machine & Tool Co Inc	Westford	MA	E	978 692-8825	16775
Lawrence Crankshaft Inc	Haverhill	MA	G	978 372-0504	11447
Lawrence Sigler	Princeton	MA	G	978 464-2027	14606
Lecam Machine Inc	Easton	MA	G	508 588-2300	10584
Legacy Machine & Mfg LLC	Amesbury	MA	G	978 388-0956	7493
Lennartz Enterprises LLC	North Billerica	MA	F	978 663-6100	13834
Lentros Engineering Inc	Ashland	MA	E	508 881-1160	7664
Leo Coons Jr	Acushnet	MA	G	508 995-3300	7404
Lincoln Precision Machining Co	North Grafton	MA	E	508 839-2175	13963
Lincoln Tool & Machine Corp	Hudson	MA	E	508 485-2940	11786
Line Bore Industries Inc	Oxford	MA	F	508 987-6509	14267
Little Enterprises Inc	Ipswich	MA	D	978 356-7422	11929
M & H Engineering Co Inc	Danvers	MA	E	978 777-1222	10234
M & K Engineering Inc	Woburn	MA	E	781 933-1760	17221
M C Machine Co Inc	Hopedale	MA	G	508 473-3642	11677
M R D Design & Manufacturing	Indian Orchard	MA	G	413 543-2012	11889
M-Tech	Tyngsboro	MA	G	978 649-4563	15894
MA Mfg LLC	Fitchburg	MA	E	978 400-9991	10832

	CITY	ST	EMP	PHONE	ENTRY #
Macdiarmid Machine Corp	Newburyport	MA	F	978 465-3546	13509
Mach Machine Inc	Hudson	MA	F	978 274-5700	11788
Machine Incorporated	Stoughton	MA	E	781 297-3700	15603
Machine Technology Inc	Beverly	MA	F	978 927-1900	8149
Machining For Electronics Inc	Hudson	MA	G	978 562-7554	11789
Mackenzie Machine & Design Inc	Pembroke	MA	F	339 933-8157	14416
Magnat-Fairview LLC	Chicopee	MA	F	413 593-5742	10039
Malden Centerless Grinding Co	Malden	MA	G	781 324-7991	12581
Manufacturing Service Corp	Millbury	MA	G	508 865-2550	13169
Manutech Industries	Pittsfield	MA	G	413 447-7794	14489
Maplewood Machine Co Inc	Fall River	MA	F	508 673-6710	10726
Marchand Machine Works Inc	Bellingham	MA	G	508 883-4040	8045
Markforged Inc **(PA)**	Watertown	MA	C	866 496-1805	16298
Markforged Inc	Billerica	MA	E	617 666-1935	8264
Markforged Inc	Watertown	MA	D	617 666-1935	16299
Marox Corporation	Holyoke	MA	F	413 536-1300	11638
Marver Med Inc	Stoughton	MA	F	781 341-9372	15605
Mass Automation Corporation	Bourne	MA	G	508 759-0770	8947
Mass Machine Inc	Walpole	MA	F	781 467-3550	16000
Massachusetts Machine Works	Walpole	MA	F	781 467-3550	16001
Mechanical Drv Components Inc	Chicopee	MA	G	413 535-2000	10042
Medical Cmpnent Spcialists Inc	Bellingham	MA	E	508 966-0992	8049
Menton Machine Co Inc	Hanson	MA	G	781 293-8394	11366
Merchant Machine Inc	Fall River	MA	G	508 672-1991	10730
Meridian Industrial Group LLC	Holyoke	MA	E	413 538-9880	11639
Merit Machine Manufacturing	Fitchburg	MA	F	978 342-7677	10836
Merrimac Tool Company Inc **(PA)**	Amesbury	MA	F	978 388-7159	7494
Metal Fish LLC	North Chelmsford	MA	G	978 930-0637	13904
Metalsmiths Inc	Boston	MA	G	617 265-4040	8699
Mica-Tron Products Corp	Holbrook	MA	G	781 767-2163	11531
Michael Monteiro	Marlborough	MA	G	508 481-1881	12794
Micro Machine & Electronics	Leominster	MA	G	978 466-9350	12167
Micro Tech Mfg Inc	Worcester	MA	F	508 752-5212	17415
Microwave Cmpnents Specialists	North Billerica	MA	F	978 667-1215	13845
Midas Technology Inc	Woburn	MA	E	781 938-0069	17232
Mikes Machine Co Inc	South Yarmouth	MA	G	508 619-3168	15330
Mikes Precision Machine Inc	North Billerica	MA	G	978 667-9793	13846
Millrite Machine Inc	Westfield	MA	E	413 562-9212	16705
Mj Machine Inc	Bridgewater	MA	G	508 697-5329	9084
Monks Manufacturing Co Inc	Wilmington	MA	E	978 657-8282	17026
Montague Industries Inc	Turners Falls	MA	E	413 863-4301	15882
Morrison Berkshire Inc	North Adams	MA	E	413 663-6501	13682
Morton & Company Inc	Wilmington	MA	E	978 657-7726	17027
Mountain View Machine	Southampton	MA	G	413 527-6837	15341
Myriad Engineering Co Inc	North Oxford	MA	F	508 731-6416	13972
Nadco International Inc	Holbrook	MA	G	781 767-1797	11532
Nash Mfg & Grinding Svcs	Springfield	MA	F	413 301-5416	15492
Nason Machine Company	East Douglas	MA	G	508 865-3545	10430
Nat Chiavettione Inc	Swansea	MA	G	508 336-4142	15709
New England Eagle Machine Inc	Westminster	MA	G	978 874-0017	16811
New England Water Jet Cutting	New Bedford	MA	G	508 993-9235	13425
Newjen Corp	Charlemont	MA	G	413 543-4888	9821
Noremac Manufacturing Corp	Westborough	MA	E	508 879-7514	16639
Norgaard Machine Inc	Feeding Hills	MA	G	413 789-1291	10802
Northampton Machine Co Inc	Easthampton	MA	E	413 529-2530	10571
Northeast E D M Inc	Newburyport	MA	G	978 462-4663	13518
Northeast Manufacturing Co Inc	Stoneham	MA	E	781 438-3022	15569
Nuforj LLC	Springfield	MA	F	413 530-0349	15495
Numeric Inc	West Springfield	MA	F	413 732-6544	16536
O W Landergren Inc	Pittsfield	MA	E	413 442-5632	14497
Oliver Welding & Fabricating	Ipswich	MA	G	978 356-4488	11933
Olympic Engineering Service	Haverhill	MA	G	978 373-2789	11456
Olympic Systems Corporation	Winchester	MA	E	781 721-2740	17093
Omni Manufacturing Co Inc	Westfield	MA	G	413 568-6175	16709
Opteon Corporation	Cambridge	MA	G	617 520-6658	9601
Optim Inc	Southbridge	MA	G	508 765-5879	15397
P & R Machines	Blackstone	MA	G	508 883-8727	8313
P T P Machining Inc	North Billerica	MA	G	800 872-3400	13851
Paragon Mfg Inc	Westfield	MA	F	413 562-7202	16711
Paramount Tool LLC	Fall River	MA	E	508 672-0844	10744
Parkway Manufacturing Co Inc	West Bridgewater	MA	G	508 559-6686	16449
Patten Machine Inc	Hudson	MA	F	978 562-9847	11801
Payne Engrg Fabrication Co Inc	Canton	MA	E	781 828-9046	9765
Pearson Machine Company LLC	Stoughton	MA	G	781 341-9416	15614
Peerless Precision Inc	Westfield	MA	E	413 562-2359	16712
Pegasus Inc	Holliston	MA	G	508 429-2461	11596
Performance Tool Inc	Westfield	MA	G	413 568-6643	16713
Pfr Machine Co	Westfield	MA	G	413 568-7603	16714
Phillips Precision Inc	Boylston	MA	F	508 869-3344	8983
Pierce Machine Co Inc **(PA)**	Dalton	MA	E	413 684-0056	10181
Pioneer Precision Grinding	West Springfield	MA	F	413 739-3371	16543
Pocasset Machine Corporation	Pocasset	MA	E	508 563-5572	14600
Poplar Hill Machine Inc	Conway	MA	F	413 369-4252	10165
Porogen Corporation **(DH)**	Woburn	MA	E	781 491-0807	17268
Portance Corp	Fitchburg	MA	F	978 400-9991	10849
Portland Valve LLC **(HQ)**	Warren	MA	E	704 289-6511	16261
Prattville Machine & Tl Co Inc	Peabody	MA	D	978 538-5229	14363

	CITY	ST	EMP	PHONE	ENTRY #
Precise Turning and Mfg	Agawam	MA	G	413 562-0052	7447
Precision Assemblies	Malden	MA	G	781 324-9054	12591
Precision Engineered Pdts LLC	Franklin	MA	G	508 528-6500	11072
Precision Machine & Gear Inc	West Boylston	MA	G	508 835-7888	16427
Precision Machinists Co Inc	Franklin	MA	F	508 528-2325	11073
Precision Technologies Inc	Tyngsboro	MA	E	978 649-8715	15900
Prematechnoligies LLC	Worcester	MA	E	508 791-9549	17446
Pro Tech Machine Inc	Brookfield	MA	G	508 867-7994	9190
Pro Tool & Machine	West Springfield	MA	G	413 732-8940	16548
Production Honing Inc	Westfield	MA	G	413 568-9238	16716
Prototype Services Inc	Hopedale	MA	G	508 478-8887	11680
Psjl Corporation **(PA)**	Billerica	MA	D	978 313-2500	8279
Pv Engineering & Mfg Inc	Salisbury	MA	E	978 465-1221	14955
Q6 Integration Inc	Northbridge	MA	G	508 266-0638	14059
Quabbin Inc	Orange	MA	F	978 544-3872	14223
Quabbin Inc	Royalston	MA	G	978 249-8891	14876
Quality Machining Co Inc	Westfield	MA	G	413 562-0389	16721
Queen Screw & Mfg Inc	Waltham	MA	D	781 894-8110	16180
Quick Manufacturing Co	Danvers	MA	G	978 750-4202	10247
R & M Precision Machine	Fall River	MA	G	508 678-2488	10750
R B Machine Co Inc	Plymouth	MA	G	508 830-0567	14578
R H Spencer Company	Byfield	MA	G	978 463-0433	9364
R I Baker Co Inc **(PA)**	Clarksburg	MA	E	413 663-3791	10075
R L Barry Inc	Attleboro	MA	F	508 226-3350	7784
R L Hachey Company	Waltham	MA	G	781 891-4237	16182
R M Machine LLC	Chicopee	MA	G	413 331-0576	10056
Ranor Inc	Westminster	MA	D	978 874-0591	16812
Raynham Tool & Die Inc	Raynham	MA	G	508 822-4489	14728
Ree Machine Works Inc	North Billerica	MA	G	978 663-9105	13861
Regional Industries Inc	Danvers	MA	E	978 750-8787	10250
Reklaw Machine Inc	North Attleboro	MA	G	508 699-9255	13775
Rer Machine Co	Charlton	MA	G	508 248-3029	9856
Richard Gilbert	Pembroke	MA	G	508 337-8774	14424
Richards Design Inc	East Falmouth	MA	G	508 540-4420	10448
Riverside Engineering Co Inc	Peabody	MA	G	978 531-1556	14365
Riverview Machine Company Inc	Holyoke	MA	F	413 533-5366	11652
Robert J Moran Inc	Littleton	MA	G	978 486-4718	12322
Roberts Machine and Engrg	Bolton	MA	G	978 779-5039	8323
Roberts Machine Shop Inc	Beverly	MA	G	978 927-6111	8171
Roberts Prototype Machining	North Chelmsford	MA	G	978 251-4200	13909
Rock Valley Tool LLC	Easthampton	MA	E	413 527-2350	10577
Rogers General Machining Inc	Chicopee	MA	F	413 532-4673	10059
Roland Le Gare	Blackstone	MA	G	508 883-2869	8315
Roland Teiner Company Inc	Everett	MA	F	617 387-7800	10628
Rolls-Royce Marine North Amer **(DH)**	Walpole	MA	C	508 668-9610	16009
Russard Inc	Rockland	MA	F	781 986-4545	14823
Ryan Tool Co Inc	Taunton	MA	G	508 822-6576	15781
Ryszard A Kokosinski	Dudley	MA	E	508 943-2700	10383
S & F Machine Co Inc	Haverhill	MA	F	978 374-1552	11470
S & R Tool & Die Inc	Hanson	MA	F	781 447-8446	11368
S & S Machine and Welding Inc	Savoy	MA	G	413 743-5714	15003
S & S Machine Company Inc	Marshfield	MA	G	781 319-9882	12867
S & T Precision Plate Cutting	Whitman	MA	G	781 447-1084	16928
S K Machine Co Inc	Fairhaven	MA	G	508 993-6387	10647
S M B Machine Co	Rowley	MA	G	978 948-7624	14865
S W Keats Company	Reading	MA	G	781 935-4282	14742
Saeilo Inc	Worcester	MA	E	508 799-9809	17462
Saliga Machine Co Inc	Hudson	MA	E	978 562-7959	11814
Samtan Engineering Corp	Malden	MA	E	781 322-7880	12594
Scientific Instrument Facility	Boston	MA	F	617 353-5056	8840
Semco Machine Corp	Plainville	MA	E	508 384-8303	14535
Senior Operations LLC	Sharon	MA	C	781 784-1400	15056
Sharp Manufacturing Inc	West Bridgewater	MA	G	508 583-4080	16452
Shattuck Prcsion Machining Inc	Westford	MA	G	978 392-0848	16792
Sigler Machine Co	Sterling	MA	F	978 422-7868	15544
Simfer Precision Machine Co	Billerica	MA	G	978 667-1138	8294
Sisson Engineering Corp	Northfield	MA	E	413 498-2840	14067
Smart Manufacturing	West Bridgewater	MA	G	508 219-0327	16455
SMI Ma Inc	Worcester	MA	E	508 799-9809	17476
Snyder Machine Co Inc	Saugus	MA	F	781 233-2080	14997
South Shore Manufacturing Inc	Scituate	MA	F	781 447-9264	15014
Southbridge Tool & Mfg Inc	Dudley	MA	E	508 764-6819	10385
Sp Machine Inc	Hudson	MA	E	978 562-2019	11818
Specialty Manufacturing Inc	Amesbury	MA	E	978 388-1601	7509
Springdale Machine & Gear Co	Holyoke	MA	G	413 536-2976	11660
Standex International Corp	North Billerica	MA	D	978 667-2771	13869
Standley Brothers Mch Co Inc	Beverly	MA	E	978 927-0278	8180
Sterling Machine Company Inc	Lynn	MA	E	781 593-3000	12541
Sterling Precision Inc	Clinton	MA	F	978 365-4999	10093
Suburban Machine	Westford	MA	G	978 392-9100	16794
Swiss Concept Inc	Waltham	MA	G	781 894-1281	16203
Swiss Precision Products Inc **(DH)**	North Oxford	MA	E	508 987-8003	13975
T G G Inc	Middleton	MA	E	978 777-5010	13103
T O C Finishing Corp	Somerville	MA	F	617 623-3310	15221
Talon Engineering	Newburyport	MA	G	978 465-5571	13538
Target Machine Inc	Ipswich	MA	G	978 356-7373	11937
Tattersall Machining Inc	Upton	MA	F	508 529-2300	15910

	CITY	ST	EMP	PHONE	ENTRY #
Taunton Stove Company Inc	North Dighton	MA	E	508 823-0786	13937
Tdr Co Inc	Attleboro	MA	G	508 226-1221	7800
Tech Ridge Inc	Chelmsford	MA	E	978 256-5741	9935
Techncal Hrdfcing McHining Inc	Attleboro	MA	F	508 223-2900	7801
Techni-Products Inc	East Longmeadow	MA	E	413 525-6321	10497
Technical Enterprises Inc	Bridgewater	MA	G	781 603-9402	9089
Techprecision Corporation **(PA)**	Westminster	MA	G	978 874-0591	16815
Tecomet Inc	Woburn	MA	D	781 782-6400	17305
Tektron Inc	Topsfield	MA	F	978 887-0091	15866
Teletrak Envmtl Systems Inc **(PA)**	Webster	MA	G	508 949-2430	16352
Thermo Craft Engineering Corp	Lynn	MA	E	781 599-4023	12543
Thorn Industries Inc	Springfield	MA	F	413 737-2464	15514
Titeflex Commercial Inc	Springfield	MA	F	413 739-5631	15515
Titeflex Corporation **(HQ)**	Springfield	MA	B	413 739-5631	15516
Tmh Machining & Welding Corp	West Bridgewater	MA	F	508 580-6899	16459
Tova Industries Inc	Southwick	MA	F	413 569-5688	15419
Tri-Star Machine Inc	Methuen	MA	G	978 683-2600	13047
Trikinetics Inc	Waltham	MA	G	781 891-6110	16217
Trilap Company Inc	Lowell	MA	G	978 453-2205	12439
Triple S Machine Inc	Danvers	MA	G	978 774-0354	10267
Trivak Inc	Lowell	MA	E	978 453-7123	12440
True Precision Inc	West Springfield	MA	F	413 788-4226	16557
True Precision Industries Inc	West Springfield	MA	F	413 788-4226	16558
True Technology	Georgetown	MA	G	978 352-8701	11151
Truex Machine Co Inc	Hanover	MA	G	781 826-6875	11357
Tucker Engineering Inc	Peabody	MA	E	978 532-5900	14380
Turn Wright Machine Work	West Dennis	MA	G	508 394-0724	16476
Twin City Machining Inc	Westminster	MA	G	978 874-1940	16817
Unimacts Global LLC **(PA)**	Lexington	MA	E	410 415-6070	12280
Union Machine Company Lynn Inc **(PA)**	Groveland	MA	E	978 521-5100	11304
United Glass To Metal Sealing	Lawrence	MA	F	978 327-5880	12080
United Metal Fabricators Inc	Worcester	MA	F	508 754-1800	17493
United Tool & Machine Corp	Wilmington	MA	E	978 658-5500	17060
Universal Machine & Design	Fitchburg	MA	G	978 343-4688	10859
Valco Precision Machine Inc	Brockton	MA	G	508 559-9009	9187
Vangy Tool Company Inc	Worcester	MA	G	508 754-2669	17498
Vertex Tool & Die Co	East Freetown	MA	G	508 763-4749	10462
Vibration & Shock Tech LLC	Beverly	MA	G	781 281-0721	8195
Villa Machine Associates Inc	Dedham	MA	F	781 326-5969	10300
Vinyl Technologies Inc	Fitchburg	MA	E	978 342-9800	10861
Vision Machining Inc	West Hatfield	MA	G	413 247-5678	16486
Volo Aero Mro Inc	East Longmeadow	MA	G	413 525-7211	10501
W B Machine Inc	Haverhill	MA	G	978 372-5396	11484
W G Machine Works Inc	Bellingham	MA	G	508 883-4903	8063
W J Roberts Co Inc	Saugus	MA	E	781 233-8176	15002
W P Moore Co Inc	Norwell	MA	G	781 878-9566	14113
Walker Machine	New Braintree	MA	G	508 867-8097	13461
Whalley Precision Inc	Southwick	MA	F	413 569-1400	15422
Williams Machine	Norwood	MA	G	781 762-1342	14205
Woodman Precision Engineering	Peabody	MA	F	978 538-9544	14387
WS Anderson Associates Inc	Auburn	MA	E	508 832-5550	7854
Wyz Machine Co Inc	Agawam	MA	F	413 786-6816	7457
Zipwall LLC **(PA)**	Arlington	MA	G	781 648-8808	7642
Zoiray Technologies Inc	Boston	MA	G	617 358-6003	8942
Zolikon Inc	Methuen	MA	G	978 689-4789	13049
Albion Manufacturing	Winslow	ME	G	207 873-5633	7265
Alexanders Welding & Mch Inc	Greenfield Twp	ME	G	207 827-3300	6152
Archer Machine	Limington	ME	G	207 637-3396	6346
Arundel Machine Tool Co	Arundel	ME	D	207 985-8555	5528
Brackett Machine Inc	Westbrook	ME	E	207 854-9789	7182
Burroughs Machine Tool Pdts	Charleston	ME	G	207 745-5558	5899
C&C Machine Shop Inc	Ellsworth	ME	G	207 667-6910	6015
CAM Mfg Inc	Presque Isle	ME	G	207 764-4199	6755
Chester H Chapman	Porter	ME	G	207 625-3349	6600
Christy Machine Company	South Berwick	ME	G	207 748-1092	7001
Clarks Machine Shop	Clinton	ME	G	207 426-8977	5914
Cox Machine	Searsmont	ME	G	207 342-2267	6944
D & G Machine Products Inc	Westbrook	ME	D	207 854-1500	7186
Dearborn Bortec Inc	Fryeburg	ME	F	207 935-2502	6097
Dewitt Machine & Fabrication	Medford	ME	G	207 732-3530	6422
Down East Inc	Bridgton	ME	F	207 647-5443	5807
Elco Inc **(PA)**	Lewiston	ME	G	207 784-3996	6285
Elmet Technologies LLC	Lewiston	ME	C	207 333-6100	6287
Eltec Industries Inc **(PA)**	Freeport	ME	G	207 541-9085	6077
Freeport Manufacturing Company	Freeport	ME	G	207 865-9340	6079
Grover Gundrilling LLC	Oxford	ME	E	207 743-7051	6566
Hunting Dearborn Inc	Fryeburg	ME	C	207 935-2171	6099
Innovtive McHning Slutions Inc	Norway	ME	G	207 515-2033	6522
J & M Machining Inc	Skowhegan	ME	F	207 474-7300	6978
J B J Machine Company Inc	North Berwick	ME	G	207 676-3380	6508
J D Paulsen	Bridgton	ME	G	207 647-5679	5808
Jr Robert Austin	Sanford	ME	G	207 490-1500	6878
Justin Jordan	New Portland	ME	G	207 628-4123	6474
Kennebec Marine Company	Scarborough	ME	G	207 773-0392	6929
Kennebec Technologies	Augusta	ME	D	207 626-0188	5610
Kenniston Machines	Rockland	ME	G	207 594-7810	6801
Knowlton Machine Company	Gorham	ME	E	207 854-8471	6117

	CITY	ST	EMP	PHONE	ENTRY #
Knox Machine Co Inc	Warren	ME	D	207 273-2296	7142
Lank Machining Co LLC	Arundel	ME	G	207 286-9549	5533
Larry Balchen	Jonesport	ME	G	207 497-5621	6227
Leightons Custom Machining	Stetson	ME	G	207 296-2601	7065
Limerick Machine Company Inc	Limerick	ME	E	207 793-2288	6337
Machinery Service Co Inc	Wiscasset	ME	G	207 882-6788	7285
Machining Innovations Inc	Oakland	ME	G	207 465-2500	6534
Maine Fabricators Inc	Gorham	ME	G	207 839-8555	6119
Maine Machine Products Company	South Paris	ME	C	207 743-6344	7013
Maine Parts & Machine Inc	Portland	ME	E	207 797-0024	6689
Maine Tool & Machine LLC	Lisbon Falls	ME	G	207 725-0038	6371
Marshall Specialty Grinding	Chelsea	ME	G	207 623-3700	5901
Masters Machine Company Inc	Round Pond	ME	C	207 529-5191	6830
McAllister Machine Inc	Biddeford	ME	E	207 282-8655	5748
McKenney Machine & Tool Co	Corinna	ME	F	207 278-7091	5921
ME Tomacelli Inc	Boothbay	ME	G	207 633-7553	5779
Melton Sales and Service Inc	Hallowell	ME	F	207 623-8895	6163
Metal Specialties Inc	Auburn	ME	F	207 786-4268	5580
Mid State Machine Products **(PA)**	Winslow	ME	C	207 873-6136	7271
Millincket Fabrication Mch Inc **(PA)**	Millinocket	ME	E	207 723-9733	6443
Montalvo Corporation	Gorham	ME	E	207 856-2501	6122
Mountain Machine Works	Auburn	ME	E	207 783-6680	5582
Nikel Precision Group LLC	Biddeford	ME	D	207 282-6080	5753
North Country Wind Bells Inc	Round Pond	ME	F	207 677-2224	6831
Northeast Doran Inc	Skowhegan	ME	G	207 474-2000	6984
Northwest Precision Inc	Rumford	ME	G	207 364-7597	6841
OBrien Consolidated Inds	Lewiston	ME	F	207 783-8543	6312
Odat Machine Inc	Gorham	ME	E	207 854-2455	6123
Oizero9 Inc	Sanford	ME	F	207 324-3582	6885
Precision Screw Mch Pdts Inc	Biddeford	ME	E	207 283-0121	5758
Ramsays Welding & Machine Inc	Lincoln	ME	F	207 794-8839	6359
Rich Technology International	Scarborough	ME	G	207 883-7424	6937
Robert Timmons Jr	Windham	ME	G	207 892-3366	7249
Sebago Converted Products Inc	Windham	ME	G	207 892-0576	7251
Soleras Advanced Coatings Ltd **(PA)**	Biddeford	ME	E	207 282-5699	5763
Specialty Products Company	Whitefield	ME	F	207 549-7232	7218
T R & H Inc	Norway	ME	G	207 743-8981	6526
Technical Sales & Svc of Neng	Greene	ME	F	207 946-5506	6151
TK Machining Inc	Waterboro	ME	F	207 247-3114	7152
Tube Hollows International	Windham	ME	E	844 721-8823	7258
W S Bessett Inc	Sanford	ME	F	207 324-9232	6896
Yankee Machine Inc	Casco	ME	E	207 627-4277	5898
Abtech Inc	Fitzwilliam	NH	E	603 585-7106	18147
Ace Machine Inc	East Hampstead	NH	F	603 329-6716	18080
Adax Machine Co Inc	Hudson	NH	E	603 598-6777	18369
Advanced Cnc Machine Inc	Manchester	NH	F	603 625-6631	18772
Aeration Technologies Inc	Londonderry	NH	G	603 434-3539	18673
Aeroweld Inc	Laconia	NH	F	603 524-8121	18553
Aka Tool Inc	Laconia	NH	G	603 524-1868	18554
Allard Nazarian Group Inc **(PA)**	Manchester	NH	C	603 668-1900	18774
Alpine Machine Co Inc	Berlin	NH	F	603 752-1441	17691
Als Precision Machining LLC	Hooksett	NH	G	603 647-1075	18342
Aluminum Castings Inc	Wilton	NH	G	603 654-9695	19974
Ameriforge Group Inc	Newport	NH	E	603 863-1270	19342
AMG-Awetis Mfg Group Corp	Gilford	NH	F	603 286-1645	18182
Anvil Machine Co	Pelham	NH	F	603 635-9009	19425
Applied Tool & Design LLC	Madbury	NH	G	603 740-2954	18760
Artemas Industries Inc	Farmington	NH	G	603 755-9777	18140
Barco Manufacturing Inc	Tilton	NH	E	603 286-3324	19904
Baron Machine Company Inc	Laconia	NH	D	603 524-6800	18557
Beaumac Company Inc	Epsom	NH	F	603 736-9321	18104
Belisle Machine Works Inc	Manchester	NH	G	603 669-8902	18786
Best Machine Inc	Fremont	NH	G	603 895-4018	18174
Bfmc LLC	Berlin	NH	E	603 752-4550	17693
Boucher Company Inc	North Conway	NH	G	603 356-6455	19374
Bradford Machine Inc	Bradford	NH	G	603 938-2355	17739
Brians Machine Shop LLC	Concord	NH	G	603 224-4333	17886
Burbak Companies	Wilton	NH	D	603 654-2291	19976
Burns Machine LLC	Laconia	NH	E	603 524-4080	18561
C & M Machine Products Inc	Hudson	NH	D	603 594-8100	18378
C-V Machine Company LLC	North Conway	NH	G	603 356-5189	19375
Carr Tool Co Inc	Londonderry	NH	F	603 669-0177	18684
Chamberlain Machine LLC	Walpole	NH	E	603 756-2560	19918
Cnc Design & Counsulting LLC	Kingston	NH	G	603 686-5437	18542
Collins Precision Machining	Nashua	NH	G	603 882-2474	19135
Comstock Industries Inc	Meredith	NH	E	603 279-7045	18972
Controlled Fluidics LLC	Milford	NH	F	603 673-4323	19051
Corbeil Enterprises Inc	Bristol	NH	F	603 744-2867	17762
Corcoran Machine Co	Charlestown	NH	G	603 445-5258	17812
Core Assemblies Inc	Gilford	NH	F	603 293-0270	18183
Costa Precision Mfg Corp **(PA)**	Claremont	NH	E	603 542-5229	17844
Cph Program & Machine Tool Des	Nashua	NH	F	603 716-3849	19138
Crucial Cmponent Machining LLC	Concord	NH	G	603 223-0012	17897
Cz Machine Inc	East Hampstead	NH	G	603 382-4259	18081
D M F Machine Co Inc	Londonderry	NH	G	603 434-4945	18691
Davis Village Solutions LLC	New Ipswich	NH	G	603 878-3662	19304
Dennis Thompson	Hudson	NH	G	603 595-6813	18384

	CITY	ST	EMP	PHONE	ENTRY #
Dennis Trudel	Pelham	NH	G	603 635-7208	19430
Dgf Indstrial Innvations Group	Gilford	NH	F	603 528-6591	18185
Diamond Casting and Mch Co Inc	Hollis	NH	E	603 465-2263	18330
Dmr Industries Inc	Rochester	NH	G	603 335-0325	19668
Elpakco Inc	Ashland	NH	G	603 968-9950	17598
Emm Precision Inc	Center Conway	NH	F	603 356-8892	17796
Endicott Custom Machine LLC	Newport	NH	G	603 865-1323	19346
Entech Manufacturing LLC	Franklin	NH	G	603 934-1288	18157
Eptam Plastics Ltd **(PA)**	Northfield	NH	D	603 286-8009	19400
Erimar System Integration	Candia	NH	G	603 483-4000	17782
Ermel Precision Machining Inc	Brookline	NH	G	603 673-7336	17770
Erwin Precision Inc	Manchester	NH	G	603 623-2333	18819
Fab Braze Corp **(PA)**	Nashua	NH	G	781 893-6777	19153
Fall Machine Company LLC	Somersworth	NH	D	603 750-7100	19837
Frank Wiggins **(PA)**	Guild	NH	G	603 863-3151	18235
Frank Wiggins	Newport	NH	G	603 863-1537	19347
Fuller Machine Co Inc	Alstead	NH	F	603 835-6559	17542
Fwm Inc	Hudson	NH	E	603 578-3366	18391
G & A Machine Inc	Salem	NH	F	603 894-6965	19738
Gentle Machine Co LLC	Jaffrey	NH	G	603 532-9363	18464
GKN Aerospace New England Inc	Charlestown	NH	D	603 542-5135	17814
GS Precision Inc-Keene Div	Keene	NH	D	603 355-1166	18506
Gutermann Inc	Newmarket	NH	G	603 200-0340	19334
Hagan Design and Machine Inc	Newmarket	NH	G	603 292-1101	19335
Hawk Quality Products Inc	Derry	NH	F	603 432-3319	17981
Hibernian Machine Tool Service	New Ipswich	NH	G	603 878-1917	19305
Hicks Machine Inc	Walpole	NH	E	603 756-3671	19921
Highland Tool Co Inc	Nashua	NH	F	603 882-6907	19178
Hillsgrove Machine Inc	Alton	NH	F	603 776-5090	17546
HM Machine LLC	Dover	NH	G	603 948-1178	18028
HM Machine LLC	Dover	NH	G	603 617-3450	18029
Hollis Line Machine Co Inc	Milford	NH	E	603 465-2251	19064
Hollis Line Machine Co Inc **(PA)**	Hollis	NH	E	603 465-2251	18332
Howard Precision Inc	Gilford	NH	F	603 293-8012	18189
Hurley Precision Machining LLC	Seabrook	NH	F	603 474-1879	19806
Hutchinson Machine	Atkinson	NH	G	603 329-9545	17604
Innovative Machine & Sup Inc	Winchester	NH	F	603 239-8082	19992
Insource Design & Mfg Tech LLC	Merrimack	NH	G	603 718-8228	19007
Intec Automation Inc	Rochester	NH	F	603 332-7733	19673
Integrated Design & Mfg LLC	Somersworth	NH	G	603 692-5563	19841
Interstate Manufacturing Assoc	Sunapee	NH	G	603 863-4855	19881
J & D Machine	Manchester	NH	G	603 624-9717	18846
J W Precision Company Inc	Barrington	NH	G	603 868-6574	17619
Jet-Co Precision Machining	Hudson	NH	G	603 882-7958	18403
Jorgensen Tool & Stamping Inc	Belmont	NH	E	603 524-5813	17676
JR Poirier Tool & Machine Co	Amherst	NH	F	603 882-9279	17570
K6 Manufacturing Inc	Nashua	NH	G	603 888-4669	19192
Karl Gschwind Machineworks LLC	Derry	NH	F	603 434-4211	17984
Kav Machine Company Inc	East Kingston	NH	G	603 642-5251	18087
Lake Machine Co Inc	Claremont	NH	F	603 542-8884	17853
Latva Machine Inc	Newport	NH	E	603 863-5155	19348
Leonard Philbrick Inc	Pelham	NH	G	603 635-3500	19438
Levasseur Precision Inc	Gilford	NH	G	603 524-6766	18190
Liberty Machine LLC	Barnstead	NH	G	603 435-6613	17616
Lighthouse Manufacturing LLC	Portsmouth	NH	E	978 532-5999	19586
Linear & Metric Co	Londonderry	NH	E	603 432-1700	18714
M J C Machine Inc	Nashua	NH	F	603 889-0300	19203
Machine Craft Company Inc	Concord	NH	F	603 225-0958	17913
Machined Integrations LLC	Merrimack	NH	G	603 420-8871	19013
Maclean Precision Mch Co Inc	Madison	NH	E	603 367-9011	18763
McBey John	Franklin	NH	G	603 934-2858	18160
Micro Tech Production Mch Co	Londonderry	NH	F	603 434-1743	18723
Micromatics Machine Co Inc	Hollis	NH	F	603 889-2115	18334
Mikros Manufacturing Inc	Claremont	NH	E	603 690-2020	17855
Millennium Precision LLC	Manchester	NH	G	603 644-1555	18875
Monadnock Grinding LLC	Fitzwilliam	NH	G	603 585-7275	18151
New England Innovations Corp	Dover	NH	F	603 742-6247	18039
NH Rapid Machining LLC	Nashua	NH	G	603 821-5200	19217
North East Cutting Die Corp	Dover	NH	E	603 436-8952	18042
P & D Machine Inc	Nashua	NH	G	603 883-1814	19226
P & M Tool & Die Inc	Northwood	NH	G	603 942-5636	19413
Pell Engineering and Mfg	Pelham	NH	F	603 598-6855	19441
Peterboro Tool Company Inc	Peterborough	NH	F	603 924-3034	19483
Photomachining Inc	Pelham	NH	F	603 882-9944	19442
Pj Diversified Machining Inc	Merrimack	NH	G	603 459-8655	19022
Plastech Machining Fabrication	Bow	NH	F	603 228-7601	17728
Play To Win Inc	Manchester	NH	G	603 669-6770	18901
Precision Model-Fab Inc	Nashua	NH	G	603 883-6680	19237
Pro Axis Machining	Nashua	NH	G	603 595-1616	19240
Pro Star Prcsion Machining LLC	Londonderry	NH	G	603 518-8570	18732
Pro-Cut Cnc Machine Inc	Hooksett	NH	G	603 623-5533	18355
Progeo Group Inc	Tilton	NH	G	603 286-1942	19910
Ptp Machining	Hudson	NH	G	603 204-5446	18430
Quality Machine Inc	Plaistow	NH	F	603 382-2334	19521
R & K Machine	Laconia	NH	G	603 528-0221	18582
R D S Machine Inc **(PA)**	Newport	NH	E	603 863-4131	19354
RDS Machine LLC	Newport	NH	G	603 863-4131	19356
Robinson Precision Tools Corp	Hudson	NH	F	603 889-1625	18436
Roland H Ripley & Son Inc	Portsmouth	NH	G	603 436-1926	19616
Rowe Machine Co	Hampton	NH	F	603 926-0029	18270
S & S Machine LLC	Amherst	NH	F	603 204-5542	17587
Saber Machine Design Corp	Salem	NH	G	603 870-8190	19764
Sarro Manufacturing Inc	Newton	NH	G	603 378-9161	19369
Sawtech Scientific Inc	Bow	NH	G	603 228-1811	17731
Seacoast Machine Company LLC	Newmarket	NH	G	603 659-3404	19340
Seneca Machine	Farmington	NH	G	603 755-8900	18145
Skytrans Mfg LLC	Contoocook	NH	F	802 230-7783	17948
Sparton Technology Corp	Hudson	NH	D	603 880-3692	18439
Standard Machine & Arms	Contoocook	NH	G	603 746-3562	17949
Star Machine Inc	Nashua	NH	G	603 882-1423	19267
Stingray Manufacturing LLC	Brentwood	NH	G	603 642-8987	17759
Stone Machine Co Inc	Chester	NH	F	603 887-4287	17826
Strafford Machine Inc	Strafford	NH	G	603 664-9758	19866
Sunset Tool Inc	Keene	NH	E	603 355-2246	18531
Technical Machine Components	Hudson	NH	F	603 880-0444	18445
Tee Enterprises	Conway	NH	F	603 447-5662	17958
Teleflex Incorporated	Jaffrey	NH	E	603 532-7706	18479
Tfx Medical Incorporated	Jaffrey	NH	B	603 532-7706	18480
Thayer Machine Shop	Hanover	NH	G	603 646-3261	18299
Tool Specialties Mfg Co LLC	Milton	NH	G	603 652-9346	19088
Tsi Group Inc **(DH)**	Hampton	NH	E	603 964-0296	18275
Turbocam Inc	Barrington	NH	G	603 905-0200	17624
Turbocam Inc **(PA)**	Barrington	NH	C	603 905-0200	17625
Unistar Corporation	Tamworth	NH	G	603 323-9327	19895
Vck Best Machining LLC	Nashua	NH	F	603 880-8858	19280
Vertal US Inc	Madbury	NH	G	603 490-1711	18762
Vier Eck Machine and Tool Inc	Freedom	NH	G	603 860-1616	18172
Water Works Supply Corp	Chester	NH	G	781 322-1238	17827
Wdw Machine Inc	Hampstead	NH	G	603 329-9604	18251
Werner Precision Machine Corp	Laconia	NH	G	603 524-0570	18594
Winchester Precision Tech Ltd	Winchester	NH	F	603 239-6326	19997
Ydc Precision Machine Inc	Franklin	NH	G	603 934-6200	18170
Agar Machining & Welding Inc	Pawtucket	RI	F	401 724-2260	20809
American Tool Company	Lincoln	RI	E	401 333-0111	20554
Artic Tool & Engrg Co LLC	Greenville	RI	F	401 785-2210	20461
Axis Machining Inc	Woonsocket	RI	G	401 766-9911	21550
B & M Plastics Inc	Pawtucket	RI	G	401 728-0404	20815
Bayview Marine Inc	Warwick	RI	G	401 737-3111	21333
Blouin General Welding & Fabg	Woonsocket	RI	G	401 762-4542	21551
Brada Manufacturing Inc	Warwick	RI	E	401 739-3774	21337
Bumper Boats Inc	Newport	RI	G	401 841-8200	20658
C & S Machine Co Inc	Rumford	RI	G	401 431-1830	21181
Chase Machine Co Inc	West Warwick	RI	E	401 821-8879	21486
Clement Machine Tool Co Inc	East Providence	RI	G	401 438-7248	20398
Cobra Precision Products Inc	North Smithfield	RI	G	401 766-3333	20784
Colonial Machine & Tool Co Inc	Coventry	RI	E	401 826-1883	20142
Contract Fusion Inc	East Providence	RI	E	401 438-1298	20400
D & B Machining Inc	Cumberland	RI	E	401 726-2347	20318
D Simpson Inc	Smithfield	RI	F	401 232-3638	21217
Dag Machine and Tool Inc	Pawtucket	RI	G	401 724-0450	20833
Dean Machine Incorporated	Cranston	RI	E	401 919-5100	20208
Demaich Industries Inc	Johnston	RI	F	401 944-3576	20508
Dynamic Converting Systems	Lincoln	RI	G	401 333-4363	20570
E & M Enterprises Inc	Johnston	RI	F	401 274-7405	20510
East Bay Manufacturers Inc	Bristol	RI	F	401 254-2960	20073
Ersa Inc	Westerly	RI	E	401 348-4000	21524
Estate Agency Inc **(PA)**	Cranston	RI	G	401 942-0700	20221
Fabri TEC Engineering Inc	Narragansett	RI	G	401 783-0051	20639
Fitzwater Engineering Corp	North Scituate	RI	G	401 647-7600	20777
Fred Ricci Tool Co Inc	Johnston	RI	F	401 464-9911	20512
Grind	Cranston	RI	G	401 223-1212	20235
Guill Tool & Engrg Co Inc	West Warwick	RI	D	401 822-8186	21493
Guill Tool and Engrg Co Inc	West Warwick	RI	G	401 828-7600	21494
Hawkins Machine Company Inc	Coventry	RI	F	401 828-1424	20148
HB Precision Products	Greenville	RI	F	401 767-4340	20467
Hitachi Cable America Inc	Ashaway	RI	C	401 315-5100	20038
HMC Holding Corporation **(PA)**	Bristol	RI	G	401 253-5501	20084
J J Traskos Mfg Inc	Westerly	RI	G	401 348-2080	21527
Jade Manufacturing Company Inc	Warwick	RI	E	401 737-2400	21378
John Crane Sealol Inc **(DH)**	Warwick	RI	C	401 732-0715	21381
Joraco Inc	Smithfield	RI	F	401 232-1710	21234
Laser Fare Inc **(PA)**	Smithfield	RI	D	401 231-4400	21235
Lavigne Manufacturing Inc	Cranston	RI	C	401 490-4627	20251
Little Rhody Machine Repair	Coventry	RI	F	401 828-1919	20153
Machinex Company Inc	Smithfield	RI	F	401 231-3230	21237
Mars Manufacturing Co Inc	Woonsocket	RI	G	401 769-9663	21574
Methods & Machining Svcs Inc	Cranston	RI	G	401 942-5700	20261
Mgb Machine Inc	Bristol	RI	G	401 253-0055	20093
Munroe Tool Co Inc	Coventry	RI	G	401 826-1040	20159
Nagel Machine Company Inc	West Warwick	RI	G	401 827-8962	21500
Newport Tool & Die Inc	Middletown	RI	F	401 847-6711	20628
Niantic Seal Inc	Lincoln	RI	E	401 334-6870	20588
Oliver Barrette Millwrights	Providence	RI	G	401 421-3750	21083
Page Mc Lellan Inc	West Greenwich	RI	G	401 397-2795	21462

	CITY	ST	EMP	PHONE	ENTRY #
Piatek Machine Company Inc	Pawtucket	RI	F	401 728-9930	20880
Porter Machine Inc	West Greenwich	RI	E	401 397-8889	21463
Providence Machine and Tl Work	Warwick	RI	G	401 751-1526	21406
Quick Fab Inc	Middletown	RI	G	401 848-0055	20630
R & R Machine Industries Inc	North Smithfield	RI	F	401 766-2505	20795
Rocky Brook Associates Inc	Narragansett	RI	G	401 789-0259	20647
Rosco Manufacturing Llc	Central Falls	RI	E	401 228-0120	20125
Sandberg Enterprises Inc	Pascoag	RI	E	401 568-1602	20804
Sandberg Enterprises Inc **(PA)**	Mapleville	RI	E	401 568-1602	20614
Sandstrom Carbide Pdts Corp	Warwick	RI	F	401 739-5220	21420
Seven Star Inc	Newport	RI	G	401 683-6222	20680
Summit Mfg Corp	Pawtucket	RI	G	401 723-6272	20901
Swissline Products Inc	Cumberland	RI	D	401 333-8888	20345
T Tech Machine Inc	Warwick	RI	F	401 732-3590	21434
Thomas Engineering	Coventry	RI	G	401 822-1235	20167
Worldwide Tooling LLC	Lincoln	RI	F	401 334-9806	20600
Abacus Automation Inc	Bennington	VT	E	802 442-3662	21661
Advanced Machine and Tl Co Inc	Milton	VT	F	802 893-6322	22124
Boyle Engineering	Middlebury	VT	G	802 388-6966	22103
CAM Dvlpment McRo Cmpnents Inc	Hydeville	VT	F	802 265-3240	22039
Cambridge Precision Machine Co	Stowe	VT	G	802 253-9269	22520
Carter Machine Inc	Marshfield	VT	G	802 426-3501	22093
Cave Manufacturing Inc	Brattleboro	VT	E	802 257-9253	21723
Classic Sporting Enterprises	Barton	VT	G	802 525-3623	21648
Dessureau Machines Inc	Barre	VT	F	802 476-4561	21613
Ducharme Machine Shop Inc	Graniteville	VT	G	802 476-6575	21999
G S Precision Inc **(PA)**	Brattleboro	VT	B	802 257-5200	21727
Gaffco Ballistics LLC	South Londonderry	VT	G	802 824-9899	22486
Gloucester Associates Inc	Barre	VT	E	802 479-1088	21617
Horizon Manufacturing & Design	Westminster W	VT	G	802 384-3715	22634
Jenne Machine LLC	Lyndonville	VT	F	802 626-1106	22068
Lauzon Machine and Engrg Inc	Bennington	VT	F	802 442-3116	21680
Mark Hunter	Lyndonville	VT	G	802 626-8407	22069
McCormacks Machine Co Inc	West Rutland	VT	G	802 438-2345	22618
Menard Manufacturing	West Rutland	VT	G	802 438-5173	22619
Metal-Flex Welded Bellows Inc	Newport	VT	E	802 334-5550	22201
Milton Vermont Sheet Metal Inc	Milton	VT	D	802 893-1581	22134
North Country Engineering Inc	Derby	VT	E	802 766-5396	21902
North East Precision Inc	Saint Johnsbury	VT	D	802 748-1440	22392
Precision Cutter Grinding Inc	Hartland	VT	F	802 436-2039	22017
S & A Trombley Corporation	Morrisville	VT	E	802 888-2394	22176
Sperry Valve Inc	East Arlington	VT	G	802 375-6703	21910
Stephens Precision Inc	Bradford	VT	F	802 222-9600	21705
Sterling Technologies Inc	Morrisville	VT	G	802 888-4753	22177
Swiss Precision Turning Inc	Brattleboro	VT	F	802 257-1935	21748
Tj Mold and Tool Company Inc	Saint Johnsbury	VT	G	802 748-1390	22396
V P E Inc	Perkinsville	VT	G	802 263-9474	22259
Vermont Aerospace Inds LLC	Lyndonville	VT	D	802 748-8705	22073
Vermont Flexible Tubing Inc	Lyndonville	VT	E	802 626-5723	22075
Vermont Indexable Tooling Inc	Fairfax	VT	G	802 752-2002	21980
Woodlan Tool and Machine Co	Bellows Falls	VT	E	802 463-4597	21656

36 ELECTRONIC AND OTHER ELECTRICAL EQUIPMENT AND COMPONENTS, EXCEPT COMPUTER

3612 Power, Distribution & Specialty Transformers

	CITY	ST	EMP	PHONE	ENTRY #
71 Pickett District Road LLC	New Milford	CT	G	860 350-5964	2786
ABB Enterprise Software Inc	Windsor	CT	D	860 285-0183	5314
ABB Enterprise Software Inc	Stamford	CT	F	203 329-8771	4125
ABB Inc	Danbury	CT	D	203 790-8588	865
Able Coil and Electronics Co	Bolton	CT	E	860 646-5686	273
Alpha-Core Inc	Shelton	CT	E	203 954-0050	3773
Asea Brown Boveri Inc **(DH)**	Norwalk	CT	G	203 750-2200	3105
Bicron Electronics Company **(PA)**	Torrington	CT	D	860 482-2524	4566
Bridgeport Magnetics Group Inc	Shelton	CT	E	203 954-0050	3784
Carling Technologies Inc **(PA)**	Plainville	CT	C	860 793-9281	3473
Emsc LLC	Stamford	CT	G	203 268-5101	4193
Neeltran Inc	New Milford	CT	C	860 350-5964	2815
Power Trans Co Inc	Oxford	CT	G	203 881-0314	3419
Superior Elc Holdg Group LLC **(HQ)**	Plainville	CT	E	860 582-9561	3516
Transformer Technology Inc	Durham	CT	F	860 349-1061	1095
Universal Voltronics Corp	Brookfield	CT	E	203 740-8555	662
Atrex Energy Inc **(PA)**	Walpole	MA	E	781 461-8251	15988
BP Fly Corporation **(PA)**	Tyngsboro	MA	E	978 649-9114	15886
Cgit Westboro Inc	Westborough	MA	C	508 836-4000	16602
Dsk Engineering and Technology	Waltham	MA	G	413 289-6485	16092
Ethosenergy Tc Inc **(DH)**	Chicopee	MA	C	802 257-2721	10025
GEC Durham Industries Inc **(PA)**	New Bedford	MA	E	508 995-2636	13390
General Electric Company	Westborough	MA	F	508 870-5200	16619
International Coil Inc	South Easton	MA	E	508 580-8515	15280
Kasalis Inc	Burlington	MA	E	781 273-6200	9291
Magnetika East Ltd	Marlborough	MA	F	508 485-7555	12789
McElroy Electronics Corp	Shirley	MA	F	978 425-4055	15089
Murata Pwr Sltons Portland LLC	Westborough	MA	G	508 339-3000	16638
Phoenix Electric Corp	Canton	MA	E	781 821-0200	9767
Precision Electronics Corp	Marshfield	MA	F	781 834-6677	12865
Schneider Electric Usa Inc **(DH)**	Boston	MA	A	978 975-9600	8839
Schneider Electric Usa Inc	Foxboro	MA	G	508 549-3385	10903
Total Recoil Magnetics Inc	Holliston	MA	F	508 429-9600	11609
Trans Mag Corp	Lowell	MA	G	978 458-1487	12438
Brookfield Power Neng LLC	Millinocket	ME	G	207 723-4341	6440
Winkumpaugh Line Construction	Ellsworth	ME	G	207 667-2962	6023
Airex LLC	Somersworth	NH	E	603 841-2040	19827
Century Magnetics Intl	Franklin	NH	F	603 934-4931	18156
Laconia Magnetics Inc	Laconia	NH	E	603 528-2766	18570
Moveras LLC	Salem	NH	E	603 685-0404	19753
National Meter Industries Inc	Bedford	NH	G	603 669-5790	17656
Pne Energy Supply LLC	Manchester	NH	G	603 413-6602	18902
Regional Mfg Specialists Inc	Concord	NH	D	800 805-8991	17926
Russound/Fmp Inc	Newmarket	NH	C	603 659-5170	19338
Semper FI Power Supply Inc	Manchester	NH	F	603 656-9729	18921
Spray Foam Distrs Neng Inc	Woodstock	NH	E	603 745-3911	20029
Vishay Hirel Systems LLC	Dover	NH	D	603 742-4375	18066
Wall Industries Inc	Exeter	NH	E	603 778-2300	18137
David P Cioe	Warren	RI	G	401 247-0079	21294
Formex Inc	East Greenwich	RI	E	401 885-9800	20368
Schneider Electric It USA Inc **(DH)**	West Kingston	RI	B	401 789-5735	21472
Dynapower Company LLC **(PA)**	South Burlington	VT	C	802 860-7200	22447
International Innovations Inc	Plainfield	VT	G	802 454-7764	22268
Omni Measurement Systems Inc	Colchester	VT	E	802 497-2253	21875

3613 Switchgear & Switchboard Apparatus

	CITY	ST	EMP	PHONE	ENTRY #
ABB Enterprise Software Inc	Plainville	CT	A	860 747-7111	3461
ABB Finance (usa) Inc	Norwalk	CT	G	919 856-2360	3095
Accutron Inc	Windsor	CT	C	860 683-8300	5315
Allied Controls Inc	Stamford	CT	F	860 628-8443	4134
Asea Brown Boveri Inc **(DH)**	Norwalk	CT	G	203 750-2200	3105
B & A Design Inc	Vernon Rockville	CT	G	860 871-0134	4679
Bass Products LLC	Bristol	CT	G	860 585-7923	530
Capitol Electronics Inc	Bethel	CT	F	203 744-3300	135
Carling Technologies Inc **(PA)**	Plainville	CT	C	860 793-9281	3473
Connecticut Valley Inds LLC	Old Saybrook	CT	G	860 388-0822	3332
Control Concepts Inc **(PA)**	Putnam	CT	F	860 928-6551	3608
Corotec Corp	Farmington	CT	F	860 678-0038	1475
Dow Div of UTC	Windsor	CT	G	860 683-7340	5329
EC Holdings Inc	Norwalk	CT	G	203 846-1651	3147
Ensign-Bickford Industries Inc	Simsbury	CT	E	860 658-4411	3905
Faria Beede Instruments Inc	North Stonington	CT	C	860 848-9271	3074
GE Grid Solutions LLC	Windsor	CT	G	425 250-2695	5335
Gems Sensors Inc **(HQ)**	Plainville	CT	B	860 747-3000	3491
General Electro Components	Glastonbury	CT	G	860 659-3573	1554
Industrial Cnnctons Sltons LLC	Plainville	CT	E	860 747-7677	3497
Kilo Ampere Switch Corporation	Milford	CT	G	203 877-5994	2307
La Chance Controls	Portland	CT	G	860 342-2212	3569
Lex Products LLC **(PA)**	Shelton	CT	C	203 363-3738	3828
Madison Company **(PA)**	Branford	CT	E	203 488-4477	329
MH Rhodes Cramer LLC	South Windsor	CT	G	860 291-8402	3994
Newco Condenser Inc	Shelton	CT	G	475 882-4000	3839
Omega Engineering Inc	Norwalk	CT	D	714 540-4914	3212
Oslo Switch Inc	Cheshire	CT	E	203 272-2794	750
Precision Graphics Inc	East Berlin	CT	E	860 828-6561	1106
Quality Name Plate Inc	East Glastonbury	CT	D	860 633-9495	1114
Reactel Inc	New Haven	CT	G	203 773-0135	2730
Satin American Corporation	Shelton	CT	E	203 929-6363	3868
Siemon Company **(PA)**	Watertown	CT	A	860 945-4200	5024
Skyko International LLC **(PA)**	Woodstock	CT	G	860 928-5170	5502
Ayan Electric Inc	Lowell	MA	G	978 256-6306	12349
C & K Components LLC **(PA)**	Waltham	MA	D	617 969-3700	16056
Cgit Westboro Inc	Westborough	MA	C	508 836-4000	16602
Coghlin Companies Inc **(PA)**	Westborough	MA	C	508 753-2354	16604
Columbia Electrical Contrs Inc	Westborough	MA	C	508 366-8297	16605
Comtech PST Corp	Topsfield	MA	F	978 887-5754	15854
Control 7 Inc	Bridgewater	MA	E	508 697-3197	9068
Cordmaster Engineering Co Inc	North Adams	MA	E	413 664-9371	13671
Dike Corporation **(PA)**	Lawrence	MA	G	978 208-7046	12018
Doranco Inc	Attleboro	MA	G	508 236-0290	7727
Easy Access Distribution Inc	Burlington	MA	G	781 893-3999	9260
Eaton Corporation	Franklin	MA	E	508 520-2444	11039
Electro Switch Corp	Weymouth	MA	C	781 607-3306	16887
McStowe Engineering & Met Pdts	East Bridgewater	MA	F	508 378-7400	10417
Mettler-Toledo Thornton Inc	Billerica	MA	D	978 262-0210	8266
Microtek Inc	Chicopee	MA	C	413 593-1025	10046
Pancon Corporation **(PA)**	East Taunton	MA	D	781 297-6000	10517
Power Systems Integrity Inc	Northborough	MA	G	508 393-1655	14045
Project Resources Inc	Wareham	MA	F	508 295-7444	16254
Russelectric Inc **(DH)**	Hingham	MA	C	781 749-6000	11509
Schneider Electric Usa Inc	Lynn	MA	C	781 571-9677	12538
Schneider Electric Usa Inc **(DH)**	Boston	MA	A	978 975-9600	8839
Schneider Electric Usa Inc	Foxboro	MA	G	508 549-3385	10903
Teknikor Automtn & Contrls Inc	Fall River	MA	F	508 679-9474	10771
Tektron Inc	Topsfield	MA	F	978 887-0091	15866
Texas Instruments Incorporated	Attleboro	MA	E	508 236-3800	7802
Total Power International Inc	Lowell	MA	F	978 453-7272	12437

SIC

	CITY	ST	EMP	PHONE	ENTRY #
Viacomcbs Inc	Framingham	MA	E	508 620-3342	11011
Vicor Corporation **(PA)**	Andover	MA	B	978 470-2900	7616
Whitmor Company Inc **(PA)**	Revere	MA	F	781 284-8000	14778
General Electric Company	Auburn	ME	B	207 786-5100	5567
Huber Engineered Woods LLC	Easton	ME	D	207 488-6700	5989
Bittware Inc **(DH)**	Concord	NH	E	603 226-0404	17884
Electrcal Instllations Inc Eii	Moultonborough	NH	E	603 253-4525	19097
Hoyt Elec Instr Works Inc	Concord	NH	D	603 753-6321	17909
Hycon Inc	Manchester	NH	G	603 644-1414	18841
Interconnect Technology Inc	Hudson	NH	F	603 883-3116	18402
Provencal Manufacturing Inc **(PA)**	Newfields	NH	G	603 772-6716	19319
Kearney-National Inc	North Kingstown	RI	E	401 943-2686	20719
SE Mass Devlopment LLC	East Providence	RI	G	401 434-3329	20443
Wei Inc **(PA)**	Cranston	RI	E	401 781-3904	20309
Wei Inc	Cranston	RI	F	401 781-3904	20310
Dynapower Company LLC **(PA)**	South Burlington	VT	C	802 860-7200	22447

3621 Motors & Generators

	CITY	ST	EMP	PHONE	ENTRY #
A-1 Machining Co	New Britain	CT	D	860 223-6420	2501
Ac/DC Industrial Electric LLC	Yantic	CT	G	860 886-2232	5506
Afcon Products Inc	Bethany	CT	F	203 393-9301	118
AKO Inc	Windsor	CT	E	860 298-9765	5317
Alstom Renewable US LLC	Windsor	CT	G	860 688-1911	5319
Autac Incorporated	Branford	CT	F	203 481-3444	292
Coils Plus Inc	Wolcott	CT	E	203 879-0755	5436
Cramer Company	South Windsor	CT	G	860 291-8402	3954
Drs Naval Power Systems Inc	Bridgeport	CT	B	203 366-5211	407
Drs Naval Power Systems Inc	Bridgeport	CT	E	203 366-5211	408
Energyblox Inc	Hamden	CT	G	203 230-3000	1748
Fuelcell Energy Inc	Torrington	CT	E	860 496-1111	4579
GE Steam Power Inc **(HQ)**	Windsor	CT	A	866 257-8664	5336
Generators On Demand LLC	Old Lyme	CT	F	860 662-4090	3323
Hamilton Sundstrand Corp **(HQ)**	Windsor Locks	CT	A	860 654-6000	5397
Hydrotec Inc	Oxford	CT	G	203 264-6700	3409
Ktcr Holding	Westport	CT	G	203 227-4115	5208
Polaris Management Inc	Easton	CT	G	203 261-6399	1322
Power Strategies LLC	Fairfield	CT	G	203 254-9926	1449
Rowley Spring & Stamping Corp	Bristol	CT	C	860 582-8175	610
Sandvik Wire and Htg Tech Corp	Bethel	CT	D	203 744-1440	177
Technipower Systems Inc **(HQ)**	Brookfield	CT	G	203 748-7001	660
Tritex Corporation	Waterbury	CT	C	203 756-7441	4967
Ward Leonard CT LLC **(DH)**	Thomaston	CT	C	860 283-5801	4525
Ward Leonard CT LLC	Thomaston	CT	D	860 283-2294	4526
ACS Group Inc	Everett	MA	F	617 381-0822	10600
Ad Hoc Energy LLC	Millis	MA	G	508 507-8005	13182
American Superconductor Corp **(PA)**	Ayer	MA	C	978 842-3000	7907
Ametek Inc	Wilmington	MA	D	978 988-4101	16973
Ametek Arizona Instrument LLC	Middleboro	MA	C	508 946-6200	13051
Andrus Power Solutions Inc	Lee	MA	F	413 243-0043	12087
Atlantic Power GP Inc	Boston	MA	G	617 977-2400	8382
Atlantic Pwr Enrgy Svcs US LLC	Dedham	MA	G	617 977-2400	10280
Aurora Wind Project LLC	Andover	MA	E	978 409-9712	7538
Creative Motion Technology	North Reading	MA	G	978 664-6218	13981
Dkd Solutions Inc	Worcester	MA	G	508 762-9114	17365
Dzi	Easthampton	MA	F	413 527-4500	10560
Electra Dyne Company Inc	Plymouth	MA	G	508 746-3270	14553
Electro Switch Corp	Weymouth	MA	C	781 607-3306	16887
Epropelled Inc **(PA)**	Lowell	MA	G	978 703-1350	12369
First Wind Holdings Inc	Boston	MA	F	617 960-2888	8547
Fraen Mechatronics LLC	Reading	MA	G	781 439-5934	14735
Hamilton Ferris Co Inc	Bourne	MA	G	508 743-9901	8946
Horlick Company Inc	Randolph	MA	G	781 963-0090	14685
Hy9 Corporation	Foxboro	MA	G	508 698-1040	10886
L3 Technologies Inc	Northampton	MA	A	413 586-2330	14009
Maxon Precision Motors Inc **(HQ)**	Taunton	MA	E	508 677-0520	15763
Mt Tom Generating Company LLC	Holyoke	MA	D	413 536-9586	11642
New England Gen-Connect LLC	Hingham	MA	G	617 571-6884	11507
Peak Scientific Inc **(DH)**	North Billerica	MA	E	866 647-1649	13853
Power Equipment Co Inc **(PA)**	Attleboro	MA	E	508 226-3410	7781
Precision Electronics Corp	Marshfield	MA	F	781 834-6677	12865
Raymond Thibault	Walpole	MA	G	508 281-5500	16008
Regen Power Systems LLC	Orange	MA	G	203 328-3045	14225
Sevcon Usa Inc	Southborough	MA	F	508 281-5500	15366
Spruce Mountain Wind LLC	Quincy	MA	G	617 890-0600	14658
Steven Sprott	Whitinsville	MA	G	774 276-6534	16918
Superior Power Systems	Attleboro	MA	G	508 226-3400	7798
Superpedestrian Inc	Cambridge	MA	G	617 945-1892	9666
Topsall Machine Tool Co Inc	Worcester	MA	G	508 755-0332	17489
Toshiba International Corp	Burlington	MA	G	781 273-9000	9348
Viking Industrial Products	Marlborough	MA	E	508 481-4600	12845
Bear Swamp Power Company LLC	Millinocket	ME	F	207 723-4341	6438
Raven Technology LLC	Brunswick	ME	F	207 729-7904	5844
Antrim Wind Energy LLC	Portsmouth	NH	G	603 570-4842	19537
Ashland Electric Products Inc	Rochester	NH	E	603 335-1100	19659
Data Electronic Devices Inc	Salem	NH	C	603 893-2047	19720
Dmi Technology Corp **(PA)**	Dover	NH	F	603 742-3330	18019
Electrocraft Inc **(HQ)**	Stratham	NH	E	855 697-7966	19867
Electrocraft New Hampshire Inc **(DH)**	Dover	NH	E	603 742-3330	18021
Generator Power Solutions Neng	Nashua	NH	G	603 577-1766	19166
Groton Wind LLC	Rumney	NH	G	603 786-2862	19696
Ion Physics Corp	Fremont	NH	G	603 895-5100	18177
Peaked Wind Power LLC	Portsmouth	NH	G	603 570-4842	19606
Sjm Etronics LLC	Londonderry	NH	G	603 512-3821	18738
Sumake North America LLC	Amherst	NH	G	603 402-2924	17589
Synchro Stars Sst	Nashua	NH	G	603 493-4762	19269
Teledyne Instruments Inc	Portsmouth	NH	C	603 474-5571	19624
Wall Industries Inc	Exeter	NH	E	603 778-2300	18137
Kearney-National Inc	North Kingstown	RI	E	401 943-2686	20719
Powerdyne International Inc	Cranston	RI	G	401 739-3300	20273
Wei Inc **(PA)**	Cranston	RI	E	401 781-3904	20309
Hayward Tyler Inc **(DH)**	Colchester	VT	D	802 655-4444	21864
Star Wind Turbines LLC	East Dorset	VT	G	802 779-8118	21916

3624 Carbon & Graphite Prdts

	CITY	ST	EMP	PHONE	ENTRY #
Carbon Products Inc	Somersville	CT	G	860 749-0614	3923
Graphite Die Mold Inc	Durham	CT	G	860 349-4444	1091
Hexcel Corporation **(PA)**	Stamford	CT	E	203 969-0666	4213
Joshua LLC **(PA)**	New Haven	CT	E	203 624-0080	2699
Minteq International Inc	Canaan	CT	C	860 824-5435	689
Rain Carbon Inc **(HQ)**	Stamford	CT	G	203 406-0535	4296
Across Usa Inc	Everett	MA	G	617 678-0350	10599
Advanced Diamond Solutions Inc	Cambridge	MA	G	617 291-3497	9374
Applied Nnstrctred Sltions LLC	Billerica	MA	E	978 670-6959	8211
Carbon Composites Inc	Leominster	MA	F	978 840-0707	12124
Electrodes Incorporated	Worcester	MA	G	508 757-2295	17370
Geonautics Manufacturing Inc	Newburyport	MA	E	978 462-7161	13494
Hyperion Catalysis Intl Inc **(PA)**	Cambridge	MA	E	617 354-9678	9509
N12 Technologies Inc	Foxboro	MA	G	857 259-6622	10893
Nanolab Inc	Waltham	MA	G	781 609-2722	16156
Nextchar LLC	Amherst	MA	G	877 582-1825	7520
2d Material Technologies LLC	New London	NH	G	603 763-4791	19312
Clear Carbon & Components Inc	Bristol	RI	F	401 254-5085	20068
Composite Energy Tech Inc	Bristol	RI	E	401 253-2670	20069
Graphene Composites Usa Inc	Providence	RI	G	401 261-5811	21022
High Prfmce Composites Ltd	Providence	RI	G	401 274-8560	21030

3625 Relays & Indl Controls

	CITY	ST	EMP	PHONE	ENTRY #
ABB Enterprise Software Inc	Danbury	CT	E	203 798-6210	864
Advanced Micro Controls Inc	Terryville	CT	E	860 585-1254	4473
Airflo Instrument Company	Glastonbury	CT	G	860 633-9455	1536
Alinabal Inc **(HQ)**	Milford	CT	C	203 877-3241	2242
Allied Controls Inc	Stamford	CT	F	860 628-8443	4134
Altek Company	Torrington	CT	C	860 482-7626	4557
Altek Electronics Inc	Torrington	CT	C	860 482-7626	4558
Asea Brown Boveri Inc **(DH)**	Norwalk	CT	G	203 750-2200	3105
Ashcroft Inc **(DH)**	Stratford	CT	B	203 378-8281	4392
Belimo Aircontrols (usa) Inc **(HQ)**	Danbury	CT	C	800 543-9038	879
Belimo Customization USA Inc	Danbury	CT	G	203 791-9915	881
Carlyle Johnson Machine Co LLC **(PA)**	Bolton	CT	E	860 643-1531	276
CET Inc	Milford	CT	G	203 882-8057	2263
Clarktron Products Inc	Fairfield	CT	G	203 333-6517	1419
Component Concepts Inc	West Hartford	CT	G	860 523-4066	5062
Computer Components Inc	East Granby	CT	F	860 653-9909	1123
Conntrol International Inc	Putnam	CT	F	860 928-0567	3607
Control Concepts Inc **(PA)**	Putnam	CT	F	860 928-6551	3608
Delta Elevator Service Corp **(DH)**	Canton	CT	E	860 676-6152	697
Devar Inc	Bridgeport	CT	E	203 368-6751	405
Digatron Power Electronics Inc	Shelton	CT	E	203 446-8000	3796
Dynamic Bldg Enrgy Sltions LLC **(PA)**	North Stonington	CT	F	860 599-1872	3072
E-Z Switch Manufacturing Inc	Milford	CT	F	203 874-7766	2279
Everlast Products LLC	Cheshire	CT	G	203 250-7111	731
Ewald Instruments Corp	Bristol	CT	F	860 491-9042	558
Gems Sensors Inc **(HQ)**	Plainville	CT	B	860 747-3000	3491
General Electric Company	Bridgeport	CT	D	203 396-1572	418
General Electro Components	Glastonbury	CT	G	860 659-3573	1554
Gordon Products Incorporated	Brookfield	CT	E	203 775-4501	646
Hamilton Sundstrand Corp **(HQ)**	Windsor Locks	CT	A	860 654-6000	5397
Idevices LLC	Avon	CT	E	860 352-5252	36
Independence Park	Madison	CT	G	203 421-9396	1965
Inertia Dynamics LLC	New Hartford	CT	C	860 379-1252	2639
Kc Crafts LLC	Plantsville	CT	G	860 426-9797	3535
Kimchuk Incorporated **(PA)**	Danbury	CT	F	203 790-7800	943
Linemaster Switch Corporation	Woodstock	CT	C	860 630-4920	5498
Measurement Systems Inc	Wallingford	CT	E	203 949-3500	4772
Micromod Automtn & Contrls LLC	Wallingford	CT	E	585 321-9200	4775
Minarik Corporation	Bloomfield	CT	C	860 687-5000	243
Naiad Dynamics Us Inc **(HQ)**	Shelton	CT	E	203 929-6355	3836
New Haven Companies Inc	East Haven	CT	F	203 469-6421	1257
O E M Controls Inc **(PA)**	Shelton	CT	C	203 929-8431	3845
P-Q Controls Inc **(PA)**	Bristol	CT	E	860 583-6994	589
P/A Industries Inc **(PA)**	Bloomfield	CT	E	860 243-8306	249
Park Distributories Inc **(PA)**	Bridgeport	CT	G	203 579-2140	463
Park Distributories Inc	Bridgeport	CT	F	203 366-7200	464
Quality Name Plate Inc	East Glastonbury	CT	D	860 633-9495	1114

	CITY	ST	EMP	PHONE	ENTRY #
Sound Construction & Engrg Co	Bloomfield	CT	E	860 242-2109	263
T & T Automation Inc	Windsor	CT	F	860 683-8788	5371
Thomas Products Ltd	Southington	CT	E	860 621-9101	4085
United Electric Controls Co	Milford	CT	D	203 877-2795	2377
Ward Leonard CT LLC **(DH)**	Thomaston	CT	C	860 283-5801	4525
AC General Inc	Hudson	MA	G	978 568-8229	11749
Advanced Control Systems Corp	Canton	MA	G	781 829-9228	9711
Airloc Corporation	Franklin	MA	G	508 528-0022	11020
Altra Industrial Motion Corp **(PA)**	Braintree	MA	B	781 917-0600	8986
Amphenol Pcd Inc	Peabody	MA	G	978 921-1531	14310
Amphenol Pcd Inc **(HQ)**	Beverly	MA	D	978 921-1531	8099
Asahi/America Inc **(HQ)**	Lawrence	MA	C	781 321-5409	11995
Backseat Gorilla Applications	Wilmington	MA	G	978 658-6161	16980
Barry Industries Inc	Attleboro	MA	D	508 226-3350	7712
Bell Rubber	Abington	MA	G	781 400-7262	7321
Ben Franklin Design Mfg Co Inc	Agawam	MA	F	413 786-4220	7423
Control Resources Inc	Littleton	MA	E	978 486-4160	12297
Control Technology Corporation **(PA)**	Hopkinton	MA	E	508 435-9596	11697
Contronautics Incorporated	Hudson	MA	G	978 568-8883	11766
Cordmaster Engineering Co Inc	North Adams	MA	E	413 664-9371	13671
Delta Magnetics and Controls	Holbrook	MA	F	781 963-2544	11523
Dolan-Jenner Industries Inc	Boxborough	MA	E	978 263-1400	8961
Dynisco Instruments LLC **(HQ)**	Franklin	MA	C	508 541-9400	11037
Electro Switch Corp	Weymouth	MA	C	781 607-3306	16887
Ewing Controls Inc	Greenfield	MA	F	413 774-7500	11260
Filtech Inc	Boston	MA	G	617 227-1133	8545
Fluigent Inc	Lowell	MA	G	978 934-5283	12371
GE Infrastructure Sensing LLC **(DH)**	Billerica	MA	A	978 437-1000	8249
Gefran Inc **(DH)**	North Andover	MA	E	781 729-5249	13707
General Dynamics Def	Pittsfield	MA	A	413 494-1110	14471
High Voltage Engineering Corp	Wakefield	MA	F	781 224-1001	15954
Horlick Company Inc	Randolph	MA	G	781 963-0090	14685
Hydroid Inc **(PA)**	Pocasset	MA	C	508 563-6565	14596
Ics Corp	Tyngsboro	MA	G	978 362-0057	15889
Intelligent Platforms LLC	Hadley	MA	G	413 586-7884	11308
Invetech Inc	Boxborough	MA	D	508 475-3400	8964
ITT Corporation	Woburn	MA	F	781 932-5665	17207
Iwaki America Incorporated **(HQ)**	Holliston	MA	D	508 429-1440	11579
Jena Piezosystem Inc	Hopedale	MA	G	508 634-6688	11674
Jnc Rebuilders Inc	Ipswich	MA	G	978 356-2996	11925
Keene Bradford Esq PC	Lynnfield	MA	G	781 246-4545	12551
Kenneth Crosby Co Inc	Hopkinton	MA	F	508 497-0048	11725
Kidde-Fenwal Inc **(HQ)**	Ashland	MA	A	508 881-2000	7663
L3 Technologies Inc	Northampton	MA	A	413 586-2330	14009
Lynx System Developers Inc	Haverhill	MA	E	978 556-9780	11451
Magnetic Technologies Ltd	Oxford	MA	F	508 987-3303	14268
Manufctring Resource Group Inc	Norwood	MA	C	781 440-9700	14176
Massa Products Corporation	Hingham	MA	D	781 749-3120	11501
Maxon Precision Motors Inc **(HQ)**	Taunton	MA	E	508 677-0520	15763
Murata Power Solutions Inc **(DH)**	Westborough	MA	C	508 339-3000	16637
Omni Control Technology Inc	Whitinsville	MA	E	508 234-9121	16917
Performance Motion Devices Inc	Westford	MA	E	978 266-1210	16783
Potomac Electric Corp	Boston	MA	E	617 364-0400	8785
Product Resources LLC	Newburyport	MA	E	978 524-8500	13523
Radar Technology Inc	Newburyport	MA	E	978 463-6064	13526
Recall Services Healthwatch	Concord	MA	G	978 369-7253	10155
Rexa Inc	West Bridgewater	MA	D	508 584-1199	16451
Rockwell Automation Inc	Chelmsford	MA	C	978 441-9500	9928
Rockwell Automation Inc	Marlborough	MA	D	508 357-8400	12819
Safe Process Systems Inc	Norton	MA	G	508 285-5109	14087
Schneider Electric Usa Inc **(DH)**	Boston	MA	A	978 975-9600	8839
Schneider Electric Usa Inc	Foxboro	MA	G	508 549-3385	10903
Scully Signal Company **(PA)**	Wilmington	MA	C	617 692-8600	17044
Sensata Technologies Ind Inc **(DH)**	Attleboro	MA	G	508 236-3800	7793
Setra Systems Inc	Boxboro	MA	F	978 263-1400	8954
Sick Inc **(DH)**	Stoughton	MA	F	781 302-2500	15621
SL Montevideo Technology Inc	Billerica	MA	E	978 667-5100	8296
Suns International LLC	Chelmsford	MA	G	978 349-2329	9934
Teknikor Automtn & Contrls Inc	Fall River	MA	F	508 679-9474	10771
Tektron Inc	Topsfield	MA	F	978 887 0091	15866
Texas Instruments Incorporated	Attleboro	MA	E	508 236-3800	7802
Tomkins Corporation	Franklin	MA	E	508 528-2000	11093
Viking Industrial Products	Marlborough	MA	E	508 481-4600	12845
Wabash Technologies Inc **(DH)**	Attleboro	MA	D	260 355-4100	7808
Waja Associates Inc	Franklin	MA	F	508 543-6050	11096
Warner Electric	Braintree	MA	G	781 917-0600	9048
Wilmington Research & Dev Corp	Newburyport	MA	G	978 499-0100	13549
Electrnic Mobility Contrls LLC	Augusta	ME	F	207 512-8009	5607
Elscott Manufacturing LLC **(PA)**	Gouldsboro	ME	D	207 422-6747	6136
Illinois Tool Works Inc	Mechanic Falls	ME	E	207 998-5140	6420
McGuire & Co Inc	Falmouth	ME	G	207 797-3323	6032
Montalvo Corporation	Gorham	ME	E	207 856-2501	6122
P-Q Controls Inc	Dover Foxcroft	ME	G	207 564-7141	5962
Richmond Contract Mfg	Bowdoinham	ME	E	207 737-4385	5790
Southworth Intl Group Inc **(PA)**	Falmouth	ME	D	207 878-0700	6033
Anaren Ceramics Inc	Salem	NH	D	603 898-2883	19706
Antrim Controls & Systems	Bennington	NH	G	603 588-6297	17687
Beckwood Services Inc	Plaistow	NH	D	603 382-3840	19508
C-R Control Systems Inc	Lebanon	NH	G	603 727-9149	18617
Dmi Technology Corp **(PA)**	Dover	NH	F	603 742-3330	18019
Electrocraft Inc **(HQ)**	Stratham	NH	E	855 697-7966	19867
Electrocraft New Hampshire Inc **(DH)**	Dover	NH	E	603 742-3330	18021
Hampshire Controls Corporation	Dover	NH	F	603 749-9424	18026
Hollis Controls Inc **(PA)**	Nashua	NH	G	603 595-2482	19179
Ie Chemical Systems Inc	Nashua	NH	F	603 888-4777	19183
Kusa LLC	Salem	NH	G	603 912-5325	19745
L3harris Technologies Inc	Nashua	NH	E	603 689-1450	19196
Mercury Systems Inc	Hudson	NH	G	203 792-7474	18366
Coto Technology Inc	North Kingstown	RI	B	401 943-2686	20698
Kearflex Engineering Company	Warwick	RI	F	401 781-4900	21382
Kearney-National Inc	North Kingstown	RI	E	401 943-2686	20719
Raytheon Company	Portsmouth	RI	D	401 847-8000	20938
Regent Controls Inc	Greenville	RI	F	203 732-6200	20473
Wei Inc **(PA)**	Cranston	RI	E	401 781-3904	20309
Wei Inc	Cranston	RI	F	401 781-3904	20310
Cooper Lighting Inc	Essex Junction	VT	F	800 767-3674	21937
Dynapower Company LLC **(PA)**	South Burlington	VT	C	802 860-7200	22447
Intergrated Control Systems	South Burlington	VT	G	802 658-6385	22449

3629 Electrical Indl Apparatus, NEC

	CITY	ST	EMP	PHONE	ENTRY #
Acceleron Inc	East Granby	CT	E	860 651-9333	1115
Advanced Sonics LLC	Oxford	CT	G	203 266-4440	3387
B S T Systems Inc	Plainfield	CT	D	860 564-4078	3451
Charge Solutions Inc	Milford	CT	G	203 871-7282	2264
Crystal Tool LLC	Old Saybrook	CT	G	860 510-0113	3333
Digatron Power Electronics Inc	Shelton	CT	E	203 446-8000	3796
GE Enrgy Pwr Cnversion USA Inc	Fairfield	CT	G	203 373-2211	1434
High Voltage Outsourcing LLC	Danbury	CT	G	203 456-3101	932
Parmaco LLC	Glastonbury	CT	G	860 573-7118	1570
Pressure Blast Mfg Co Inc	South Windsor	CT	F	800 722-5278	4004
3M Company	Chelmsford	MA	C	978 256-3911	9865
Acumentrics Rups LLC	Walpole	MA	E	617 932-7877	15987
Alpha Innovation Inc	Marblehead	MA	G	978 744-1100	12674
Asco Power Technologies LP	Marlborough	MA	G	508 624-0466	12720
Assurance Technology Corp	Chelmsford	MA	D	978 250-8060	9875
Atrex Energy Inc **(PA)**	Walpole	MA	E	781 461-8251	15988
Ballard Unmanned Systems Inc	Southborough	MA	F	508 687-4970	15344
Bel Power Inc	Westborough	MA	D	508 870-9775	16593
Cipem USA Inc	Melrose	MA	G	347 642-1106	12979
Desco Industries Inc	Canton	MA	E	781 821-8370	9725
Desco Industries Inc	Canton	MA	E	781 821-8370	9726
Helix Power Corporation	Somerville	MA	G	781 718-7282	15182
Murata Power Solutions Inc **(DH)**	Westborough	MA	C	508 339-3000	16637
Phoenix Electric Corp	Canton	MA	E	781 821-0200	9767
Solectria Renewables LLC	Lawrence	MA	C	978 683-9700	12076
Southwest Asian Incorporated	Worcester	MA	G	508 753-7126	17477
Superconductivity Inc **(HQ)**	Ayer	MA	D	608 831-5773	7940
Thermo Fisher Scientific Inc	Wilmington	MA	D	978 275-0800	17055
Thermo Fisher Scientific Inc **(PA)**	Waltham	MA	C	781 622-1000	16213
Thinklite LLC	Natick	MA	G	617 500-6689	13282
Vicor Corporation	Andover	MA	F	978 470-2900	7617
Wafer LLC	Danvers	MA	G	978 304-3821	10272
Williamson Neng Elc Mtr Svc	Chelsea	MA	G	617 884-9200	9975
Zexen Technology LLC	Shrewsbury	MA	G	508 786-9928	15138
AVX Tantalum Corporation	Biddeford	ME	C	207 282-5111	5720
Illinois Tool Works Inc	Mechanic Falls	ME	E	207 998-5140	6420
Sterling Power Usa LLC	Eliot	ME	G	207 226-3500	6010
Aak Power Supply Corporation	Plaistow	NH	F	603 382-2222	19506
Desco Industries Inc	Rochester	NH	G	603 332-0717	19667
El-Op US Inc	Merrimack	NH	B	603 889-2500	18998
Elecyr Corporation	Portsmouth	NH	G	617 905-6800	19558
Hollis Controls Inc **(PA)**	Nashua	NH	G	603 595-2482	19179
KMC Systems Inc	Merrimack	NH	D	866 742-0442	19010
Kollsman Inc **(DH)**	Merrimack	NH	A	603 889-2500	19011
Milpower Source Inc	Belmont	NH	D	603 267-8865	17678
Pyromate Inc	Peterborough	NH	G	603 924-4251	19485
Thomas Instruments Inc	Spofford	NH	G	603 363-4500	19858
Vicor Corporation	Manchester	NH	F	603 623-3222	18951
Warner Power Conversion LLC	Warner	NH	C	603 456-3111	19931
International Technologies Inc	Warwick	RI	F	401 467-6907	21376
Schneider Electric It Corp **(DH)**	West Kingston	RI	A	401 789-5735	21471
Veterans Assembled Elec LLC **(PA)**	Providence	RI	G	401 228-6165	21150
Vishay Sprague Inc	Warwick	RI	A	401 738-9150	21438
Charter Dev & Consulting Corp	Essex Junction	VT	G	802 878-5005	21936
Northern Power Systems Inc **(HQ)**	Barre	VT	D	802 461-2955	21631
S B E Inc **(PA)**	Barre	VT	E	802 476-4146	21638

3631 Household Cooking Eqpt

	CITY	ST	EMP	PHONE	ENTRY #
Conair Corporation **(PA)**	Stamford	CT	B	203 351-9000	4171
Kenyon International Inc	Clinton	CT	E	860 664-4906	789
Vigiroda Enterprises Inc	Trumbull	CT	G	203 268-6117	4642
General Electric Company **(PA)**	Boston	MA	A	617 443-3000	8558
Kettlepizza LLC	North Andover	MA	G	888 205-1931	13714
Taunton Stove Company Inc	North Dighton	MA	E	508 823-0786	13937

	CITY	ST	EMP	PHONE	ENTRY #
Cooking Solutions Group Inc **(HQ)**	Salem	NH	G	603 893-9701	19719
GS Blodgett Corporation	Essex Junction	VT	G	802 871-3287	21943
GS Blodgett Corporation **(HQ)**	Essex Junction	VT	C	802 860-3700	21944

3632 Household Refrigerators & Freezers

	CITY	ST	EMP	PHONE	ENTRY #
Medelco Inc	Bridgeport	CT	G	203 275-8070	449
General Electric Company	Westborough	MA	F	508 870-5200	16619
General Electric Company **(PA)**	Boston	MA	A	617 443-3000	8558
Raytheon Sutheast Asia Systems **(HQ)**	Billerica	MA	E	978 470-5000	8289
Gbo Inc	Portland	ME	G	207 772-0302	6665

3633 Household Laundry Eqpt

	CITY	ST	EMP	PHONE	ENTRY #
Instinctive Works LLC	Westport	CT	G	203 434-8094	5204
Easy Way Dry Cleaners Inc	Woburn	MA	G	781 933-1473	17173

3634 Electric Household Appliances

	CITY	ST	EMP	PHONE	ENTRY #
Betlan Corporation	Newtown	CT	F	203 270-7898	2916
Bkmfg Corp	Winsted	CT	E	860 738-2200	5405
Black & Decker (us) Inc	New Britain	CT	G	860 225-5111	2514
Black & Decker (us) Inc **(HQ)**	New Britain	CT	G	860 225-5111	2515
Conair Corporation	Torrington	CT	D	800 492-7464	4572
Conair Corporation **(PA)**	Stamford	CT	B	203 351-9000	4171
Crrc LLC	Cromwell	CT	D	860 635-2200	852
Dampits LLC	Wilton	CT	G	203 210-7946	5287
Jarden LLC	Norwalk	CT	E	203 845-5300	3179
Mayborn Usa Inc	Stamford	CT	F	781 269-7490	4245
McIntire Company **(HQ)**	Bristol	CT	F	860 585-8559	580
Casa Antigua	Lynn	MA	G	781 584-8240	12496
Convectronics Inc	Haverhill	MA	F	978 374-7714	11419
Ecovent Corp	Charlestown	MA	F	620 983-6863	9832
Gillette Company **(HQ)**	Boston	MA	A	617 421-7000	8561
Gillette De Mexico Inc	Boston	MA	A	617 421-7000	8563
Headwaters Inc	Marblehead	MA	G	781 715-6404	12685
Mestek Inc **(PA)**	Westfield	MA	E	470 898-4533	16700
Mrs Mitchells Kitchen Inc	Holyoke	MA	G	413 322-8816	11641
Qci Inc	Seekonk	MA	F	508 399-8983	15035
Reach Distribution Inc	Boston	MA	G	617 542-6466	8811
Sharon Associates	Sharon	MA	G	781 784-2455	15057
Spruce Environmental Tech Inc **(PA)**	Haverhill	MA	D	978 521-0901	11475
Thl-Nortek Investors LLC **(PA)**	Boston	MA	D	617 227-1050	8882
Vaughn Thermal Corporation	Salisbury	MA	E	978 462-6683	14958
1911 Office LLC	Keene	NH	G	603 352-2448	18488
Celios Corporation	Portsmouth	NH	G	978 877-2044	19549
Eichenauer Inc	Newport	NH	E	603 863-1454	19345
Infinite Creative Entps Inc	Seabrook	NH	G	603 910-5000	19807
Sahara Heaters Mfg Co	Nashua	NH	G	603 888-7351	19257
Bedjet LLC	Newport	RI	G	401 404-5250	20656

3635 Household Vacuum Cleaners

	CITY	ST	EMP	PHONE	ENTRY #
Central Vacuum Cleaners	Lawrence	MA	G	978 682-5295	12004
Headwaters Inc	Marblehead	MA	G	781 715-6404	12685
Static Solutions Inc **(PA)**	Marlborough	MA	F	508 480-0700	12830

3639 Household Appliances, NEC

	CITY	ST	EMP	PHONE	ENTRY #
Clarke Distribution Corp	Norwalk	CT	G	203 838-9385	3126
Conair Corporation **(PA)**	Stamford	CT	B	203 351-9000	4171
Eemax Inc **(DH)**	Waterbury	CT	D	203 267-7890	4867
Alco Technology	Fall River	MA	G	508 678-7449	10651
Dan-Ray Machine Co Inc	Haverhill	MA	G	978 374-7611	11423
Euro-Pro Holdco LLC	Needham Heights	MA	D	617 243-0235	13330
Maciel John	Maynard	MA	G	978 897-5865	12901
Sharkninja Operating LLC **(HQ)**	Needham	MA	E	617 243-0235	13310
Superior Manufacturing Corp	Fall River	MA	G	508 677-0100	10765
Therma-Flow Inc	Watertown	MA	E	617 924-3877	16322
Vaughn Thermal Corporation	Salisbury	MA	E	978 462-6683	14958
W S Bessett Inc	Sanford	ME	F	207 324-9232	6896
Vermont Islands Culinary LLC	Brattleboro	VT	F	802 387-8591	21752

3641 Electric Lamps

	CITY	ST	EMP	PHONE	ENTRY #
Lcd Lighting Inc	Orange	CT	C	203 799-7877	3370
Light Sources Inc **(PA)**	Orange	CT	C	203 799-7877	3371
Revolution Lighting **(HQ)**	Stamford	CT	G	203 504-1111	4299
Revolution Lighting Tech Inc **(PA)**	Stamford	CT	C	203 504-1111	4300
Southern Neng Ultraviolet Inc	Branford	CT	G	203 483-5810	350
Triton Thalassic Tech Inc **(PA)**	Ridgefield	CT	G	203 438-0633	3686
Whelen Engineering Company Inc **(PA)**	Chester	CT	B	860 526-9504	777
Acera Inc	Beverly	MA	G	978 998-4281	8095
Dolan-Jenner Industries Inc	Boxborough	MA	E	978 263-1400	8961
General Electric Company	Westborough	MA	F	508 870-5200	16619
International Light Tech Inc	Peabody	MA	E	978 818-6180	14343
Osram Sylvania Inc	Wilmington	MA	B	978 750-3900	17037
Osram Sylvania Inc	Beverly	MA	C	978 750-1529	8163
Osram Sylvania Inc **(HQ)**	Wilmington	MA	A	978 570-3000	17036
Partylite Inc **(HQ)**	Plymouth	MA	D	203 661-1926	14572
Philips Holding USA Inc **(HQ)**	Andover	MA	C	978 687-1501	7582
Traxon Technologies	Wilmington	MA	F	201 508-1570	17058
Luminescent Systems Inc	Lebanon	NH	C	603 643-7766	18629
Osram Sylvania Inc	Exeter	NH	D	603 772-4331	18127
Osram Sylvania Inc	Exeter	NH	C	603 669-5350	18128
Osram Sylvania Inc	Hillsborough	NH	B	603 464-7235	18317
Brownlie Lamar Design Group	Warren	RI	G	401 714-9371	21292
Global Value Lighting LLC **(PA)**	West Warwick	RI	F	401 535-4002	21492
Osram Sylvania Inc	Central Falls	RI	B	401 723-1378	20122
First Light Technologies Inc	Poultney	VT	D	802 287-4195	22271

3643 Current-Carrying Wiring Devices

	CITY	ST	EMP	PHONE	ENTRY #
ABB Enterprise Software Inc	Plainville	CT	A	860 747-7111	3461
Allied Controls Inc	Stamford	CT	F	860 628-8443	4134
American Specialty Pdts LLC	Vernon	CT	G	860 871-2279	4662
Amphenol Corporation	Stamford	CT	D	203 327-7300	4138
Amphenol Corporation **(PA)**	Wallingford	CT	D	203 265-8900	4700
Amphenol Nexus Technologies	Stamford	CT	D	203 327-7300	4139
Bead Industries Inc **(PA)**	Milford	CT	E	203 301-0270	2251
Burndy LLC	Bethel	CT	D	203 792-1115	134
Carling Technologies Inc **(PA)**	Plainville	CT	C	860 793-9281	3473
Deringer-Ney Inc **(PA)**	Bloomfield	CT	C	860 242-2281	217
Dicon Connections Inc	North Branford	CT	E	203 481-8080	2961
East Coast Lightning Eqp Inc	Winsted	CT	E	860 379-9072	5410
Eaton Aerospace LLC	Bethel	CT	E	203 796-6000	150
Eaton Corporation	Bethel	CT	E	203 796-6000	151
Ek-Ris Cable Company Inc	New Britain	CT	E	860 223-4327	2530
Everlast Products LLC	Cheshire	CT	G	203 250-7111	731
Faria Beede Instruments Inc	North Stonington	CT	C	860 848-9271	3074
Gold Line Connector Inc **(PA)**	Redding	CT	E	203 938-2588	3648
Gordon Products Incorporated	Brookfield	CT	E	203 775-4501	646
Hubbell Incorporated	Newtown	CT	E	203 426-2555	2926
Hubbell Incorporated Delaware	Shelton	CT	C	475 882-4800	3814
Hubbell Incorporated Delaware **(HQ)**	Shelton	CT	D	475 882-4000	3815
Hubbell Wiring Device	Milford	CT	F	203 882-4800	2297
Legrand Holding Inc **(DH)**	West Hartford	CT	E	860 233-6251	5080
Lex Products LLC **(PA)**	Shelton	CT	C	203 363-3738	3828
Northast Lghtning Prtction LLC	Bloomfield	CT	F	860 243-0010	246
Old Cambridge Products Corp	Bloomfield	CT	G	860 243-1761	247
Old Ni Incorporated	Stamford	CT	G	203 327-7300	4267
Oslo Switch Inc	Cheshire	CT	E	203 272-2794	750
Ripley Tools LLC **(PA)**	Cromwell	CT	E	860 635-2200	859
Siemon Company **(PA)**	Watertown	CT	A	860 945-4200	5024
Siemon Company	Watertown	CT	E	860 945-4218	5025
Southport Products LLC	Winsted	CT	G	860 379-0761	5425
Spectrum Associates Inc	Milford	CT	F	203 878-4618	2367
Thomas Products Ltd	Southington	CT	E	860 621-9101	4085
Times Wire and Cable Company **(HQ)**	Wallingford	CT	G	203 949-8400	4820
United Electric Controls Co	Milford	CT	D	203 877-2795	2377
Wiremold Company **(DH)**	West Hartford	CT	A	860 233-6251	5104
World Cord Sets Inc	Enfield	CT	G	860 763-2100	1391
Anderson Power Products Inc **(HQ)**	Sterling	MA	D	978 422-3600	15535
Anomet Products Inc	Shrewsbury	MA	E	508 842-0174	15102
Ark-Les Connectors Corporation	East Taunton	MA	F	781 297-6324	10510
Artisan Industries Inc	Stoughton	MA	D	781 893-6800	15581
Atlee Delaware Incorporated	Melrose	MA	F	978 681-1003	12975
Baystate Lightning Protection	Bridgewater	MA	G	508 697-7727	9063
C & K Components LLC **(PA)**	Waltham	MA	D	617 969-3700	16056
C S I Keyboards Inc	Peabody	MA	E	978 532-8181	14318
Caton Connector Corp	Kingston	MA	E	781 585-4315	11955
Checon Corporation **(PA)**	North Attleboro	MA	C	508 643-0940	13752
Component Sources Intl	Westborough	MA	F	508 986-2300	16607
Cooper Interconnect Inc	Chelsea	MA	D	617 389-7080	9950
Cordmaster Engineering Co Inc	North Adams	MA	E	413 664-9371	13671
Data Guide Cable Corporation	Gardner	MA	D	978 632-0900	11111
Dorn Equipment Corp	Melrose	MA	F	781 662-9300	12981
Dynawave Incorporated	Haverhill	MA	D	978 469-0555	11429
Electro Switch Corp	Weymouth	MA	C	781 607-3306	16887
Electro-Term Inc	Springfield	MA	D	413 734-6469	15468
Electroweave Inc	Worcester	MA	G	508 752-8932	17371
Exstar	Stoneham	MA	F	339 293-9334	15563
First Electronics Corporation	Dorchester	MA	D	617 288-2430	10342
General Electric Company	Newton	MA	C	617 608-6008	13595
General Wire Products Inc	Worcester	MA	E	508 752-8260	17381
Goremote	Wrentham	MA	G	508 384-0139	17521
Ideal Industries Inc	Sterling	MA	C	978 422-3600	15540
Intersense Incorporated	Billerica	MA	E	781 541-6330	8258
Kidde-Fenwal Inc **(HQ)**	Ashland	MA	A	508 881-2000	7663
Konnext Inc	Hudson	MA	G	978 567-0800	11782
Madison Cable Corporation	Worcester	MA	C	508 752-2884	17410
Membrane-Switchescom	Lynn	MA	G	508 277-2892	12526
Mini-Systems Inc	Plainville	MA	E	508 695-2000	14528
Opalala Inc	Fall River	MA	F	508 646-0950	10743
Osram Sylvania Inc **(HQ)**	Wilmington	MA	A	978 570-3000	17036
Pep Industries LLC	Attleboro	MA	A	508 226-5600	7776
Phoenix Electric Corp	Canton	MA	E	781 821-0200	9767
Precision Engineered Pdts LLC **(DH)**	Attleboro	MA	G	508 226-5600	7782
Quabbin Wire & Cable Co Inc **(PA)**	Ware	MA	D	413 967-6281	16236
San Francisco Market	Lynn	MA	G	781 780-3731	12536

	CITY	ST	EMP	PHONE	ENTRY #
San-Tron Inc **(PA)**	Ipswich	MA	D	978 356-1585	11936
Schneider Electric Usa Inc **(DH)**	Boston	MA	A	978 975-9600	8839
Schneider Electric Usa Inc	Foxboro	MA	G	508 549-3385	10903
Schott North America Inc	Southbridge	MA	D	508 765-7450	15402
Segue Manufacturing Svcs LLC	Lowell	MA	D	978 970-1200	12432
Steger Power Connection Inc	Fall River	MA	F	508 646-0950	10763
T & T Machine Products Inc	Rockland	MA	F	781 878-3861	14829
Te Connectivity Corporation	Worcester	MA	B	717 592-4299	17486
Teradyne Inc **(PA)**	North Reading	MA	B	978 370-2700	13990
Teradyne Inc	Woburn	MA	C	978 370-2700	17306
Texas Instruments Incorporated	Attleboro	MA	E	508 236-3800	7802
Tru Technologies Inc	Peabody	MA	C	978 532-0775	14379
Umech Technologies LLC	Watertown	MA	G	617 923-2942	16326
W J Roberts Co Inc	Saugus	MA	E	781 233-8176	15002
Winchster Interconnect Rf Corp **(HQ)**	Peabody	MA	D	978 532-0775	14385
Bcr Technology Center	Scarborough	ME	G	207 885-9700	6910
Corningware Corelle & More	Freeport	ME	G	207 865-3942	6075
General Electric Company	Auburn	ME	B	207 786-5100	5567
Amphenol Corporation	Nashua	NH	B	603 879-3000	19114
Burndy Americas Inc **(HQ)**	Manchester	NH	G	603 647-5000	18791
Burndy Americas Intl Holdg LLC	Manchester	NH	A	603 647-5000	18792
Burndy LLC	Londonderry	NH	C	603 647-5000	18681
Burndy LLC	Lincoln	NH	C	603 745-8114	18645
Burndy LLC	Londonderry	NH	C	603 647-5119	18682
Burndy LLC	Lincoln	NH	G	603 745-8114	18646
Burndy LLC **(DH)**	Manchester	NH	B	603 647-5000	18793
Burndy LLC	Littleton	NH	C	603 444-6781	18655
Fci Electrical-Brundy Products	Littleton	NH	G	603 444-6781	18659
Hubbell Incorporated	Londonderry	NH	D	800 346-4175	18703
Hubbell Incorporated	Manchester	NH	C	603 647-5000	18838
Inside Track Cabling Inc	Hudson	NH	E	603 886-8013	18400
Jr Hinds Const Serv	Tilton	NH	G	603 496-2344	19907
O Brien D G Inc	Seabrook	NH	F	603 474-5571	19812
Osram Sylvania Inc	Exeter	NH	D	603 772-4331	18127
Parker & Harper Companies Inc **(PA)**	Raymond	NH	D	603 895-4761	19643
Q A Technology Company Inc	Hampton	NH	D	603 926-1193	18269
Spire Technology Solutions LLC	Nashua	NH	F	603 594-0005	19264
Teledyne Instruments Inc	Portsmouth	NH	C	603 474-5571	19624
Ametek Scp Inc **(HQ)**	Westerly	RI	D	401 596-6658	21515
Kirk Electronics & Plastic	Cranston	RI	G	401 467-8585	20249
Leviton Manufacturing Co Inc	Providence	RI	F	401 273-4875	21053
Precision Trned Cmponents Corp	Smithfield	RI	D	401 232-3377	21244
Quick Fitting Inc	Warwick	RI	D	401 734-9500	21408
Tower Manufacturing Corp	Providence	RI	D	401 467-7550	21140
Cooper Lighting Inc	Essex Junction	VT	F	800 767-3674	21937
Duelmark Aerospace Corporation	Cambridge	VT	G	802 644-2603	21823

3644 Noncurrent-Carrying Wiring Devices

	CITY	ST	EMP	PHONE	ENTRY #
Arcade Technology LLC	Bridgeport	CT	E	203 366-3871	376
Bridgeport Fittings LLC	Stratford	CT	C	203 377-5944	4400
Chase Corporation	Woodbridge	CT	F	203 285-1244	5464
Family Raceway LLC	Vernon	CT	G	860 896-0171	4667
Rhode Island Raceway LLC	Quaker Hill	CT	G	860 701-0192	3643
Roaming Raceway and RR LLC	Suffield	CT	G	413 531-3390	4467
Stamford RPM Raceway LLC	Stamford	CT	G	203 323-7223	4333
Wiremold Company	West Hartford	CT	F	860 263-3115	5105
Wiremold Company **(DH)**	West Hartford	CT	A	860 233-6251	5104
Wiremold Legrand Co Centerex	West Hartford	CT	E	877 295-3472	5106
8 Raceway Drive LLC	Nantucket	MA	G	508 325-0040	13216
Chase Corp Inc	Westwood	MA	G	781 332-0700	16860
Chase Corporation **(PA)**	Westwood	MA	G	781 332-0700	16861
Chase Corporation	Oxford	MA	F	508 731-2710	14256
Chase Corporation	Westwood	MA	F	781 329-3259	16862
Chase Corporation	Randolph	MA	E	781 963-2600	14673
Coolcomposites Inc	Jamaica Plain	MA	G	510 717-9125	11942
Ezra J Leboff Co Inc	Brighton	MA	G	617 783-4200	9098
H Loeb Corporation	New Bedford	MA	E	508 996-3745	13392
Matkim Industries Inc	Oxford	MA	E	508 987-3599	14269
McStowe Engineering & Met Pdts	East Bridgewater	MA	F	508 378-7400	10417
Reinforced Structures For Elec	Worcester	MA	E	508 754-5316	17457
Signal Communications Corp	Woburn	MA	E	781 933-0998	17295
Speedboard Usa Inc	Newburyport	MA	G	978 462-2700	13534
Transene Company Inc	Danvers	MA	F	978 777-7860	10265
Baker Company Inc **(PA)**	Sanford	ME	C	207 324-8773	6871
Continental Cable LLC	Hinsdale	NH	D	800 229-5131	18319
Warehouse Cables LLC	Warwick	RI	G	401 737-5677	21442
Intellihome of Vermont L L C	Wilmington	VT	F	802 464-2499	22701
Isovolta Inc	Rutland	VT	E	802 775-5528	22341
Superior Tchncal Ceramics Corp	Saint Albans	VT	C	802 527-7726	22380

3645 Residential Lighting Fixtures

	CITY	ST	EMP	PHONE	ENTRY #
3t Lighting Inc	Brookfield	CT	G	203 775-1805	631
E-Lite Technologies Inc	Trumbull	CT	F	203 371-2070	4623
Gs Thermal Solutions Inc	Danbury	CT	G	475 289-4625	929
Keeling Company Inc	Old Lyme	CT	G	860 349-0916	3324
Light Fantastic Realty Inc	West Haven	CT	C	203 934-3441	5131
Light Sources Inc	Milford	CT	C	203 799-7877	2309
Premier Mfg Group Inc	Shelton	CT	D	203 924-6617	3863
Seesmart Inc	Stamford	CT	E	203 504-1111	4312
Washington Copper Works Inc	Washington	CT	G	860 868-7637	4831
Atlantic Lighting Inc	Fall River	MA	E	508 678-5411	10665
Blanche P Field LLC	Boston	MA	E	617 423-0714	8413
Genlyte Group Incorporated	Andover	MA	A	781 418-7900	7550
Genlyte Thomas Group LLC	Andover	MA	C	978 659-3732	7551
Genlyte Thomas Group LLC	Burlington	MA	C	781 418-7900	9279
Global Light Co LLC	Cambridge	MA	G	617 620-2084	9495
Janna Ugone & Associates Inc	Easthampton	MA	F	413 527-5530	10566
Newstamp Lighting Corp	North Easton	MA	F	508 238-7073	13949
Norwell Mfg Co Inc	East Taunton	MA	E	508 822-2831	10516
Period Lighting Fixtures Inc	Clarksburg	MA	F	413 664-7141	10074
Renovators Supply Inc	Millers Falls	MA	E	413 423-3300	13181
Sandwich Lantern	Sandwich	MA	G	508 833-0515	14973
Telefluent Communications Inc	Northborough	MA	F	508 393-0005	14050
Lighting Solutions Inc	Falmouth	ME	G	207 772-2738	6031
Collins Lighting & Assoc LLC	Salem	NH	G	603 893-1106	19717
Creative Ltg Designs Decor LLC	Lebanon	NH	G	603 448-2066	18620
Gates Moore Lighting	Hillsborough	NH	G	203 847-3231	18315
Visible Light Inc	Hampton	NH	G	603 926-6049	18277
Brownlie Lamar Design Group	Warren	RI	G	401 714-9371	21292
Lexington Lighting Group LLC	Rumford	RI	E	860 564-4512	21192
Mastro Lighting Mfg Co Inc **(PA)**	Providence	RI	G	401 467-7700	21063
SCW Corporation	Warwick	RI	E	401 808-6849	21423
Authentic Designs Inc	West Rupert	VT	F	802 394-7715	22614
G Scatchard Ltd	Westford	VT	G	802 899-2181	22628
Hubbardton Forge LLC	Castleton	VT	C	802 468-3090	21828
Light Logic Inc	Hyde Park	VT	E	802 888-7984	22037

3646 Commercial, Indl & Institutional Lighting Fixtures

	CITY	ST	EMP	PHONE	ENTRY #
3t Lighting Inc	Brookfield	CT	G	203 775-1805	631
C Cowles & Company **(PA)**	North Haven	CT	D	203 865-3117	3012
Green Ray Led Intl LLC **(PA)**	Greenwich	CT	G	203 485-1435	1618
Innovative ARC Tubes Corp	Bridgeport	CT	E	203 333-1031	430
Lcd Lighting Inc	Orange	CT	C	203 799-7877	3370
Lighting Edge Inc	Essex	CT	G	860 767-8968	1402
Newco Lighting Inc **(HQ)**	Shelton	CT	G	475 882-4000	3840
Nutron Manufacturing Inc	Norwich	CT	E	860 887-4550	3287
Pathway Lighting Products Inc	Old Saybrook	CT	D	860 388-6881	3347
Pegasus Capital Advisors LP **(PA)**	Stamford	CT	E	203 869-4400	4282
Prolume Inc	Monroe	CT	G	203 268-7778	2415
Seesmart Inc	Stamford	CT	E	203 504-1111	4312
Sylvan R Shemitz Designs LLC	West Haven	CT	C	203 934-3441	5147
The L C Doane Company **(PA)**	Ivoryton	CT	F	860 767-8295	1909
Tri-State Led Inc	Greenwich	CT	F	203 813-3791	1657
Whelen Engineering Company Inc	Chester	CT	F	860 526-9504	778
Whelen Engineering Company Inc **(PA)**	Chester	CT	B	860 526-9504	777
American Lighting Fixture Corp	Framingham	MA	C	508 824-1970	10920
Architectural Star Ltg LLC	Fall River	MA	F	508 678-1900	10662
Asd Lighting Corp	Canton	MA	F	781 739-3977	9717
Asd-Lighting Corp	Norwood	MA	G	781 739-3977	14135
Atlantic Lighting Inc	Fall River	MA	E	508 678-5411	10665
Cdiled LLC	Palmer	MA	G	413 530-2921	14283
Dion Signs and Service Inc	New Bedford	MA	F	401 724-4459	13379
Genlyte Group Incorporated	Andover	MA	A	781 418-7900	7550
Genlyte Thomas Group LLC	Burlington	MA	C	781 418-7900	9279
Genlyte Thomas Group LLC	Andover	MA	C	978 659-3732	7551
International Light Tech Inc	Peabody	MA	E	978 818-6180	14343
Janna Ugone & Associates Inc	Easthampton	MA	F	413 527-5530	10566
Jlc Tech LLC	Pembroke	MA	E	781 826-8162	14412
Light Engines LLC	Sturbridge	MA	G	508 347-3647	15640
Litecontrol Corporation	Plympton	MA	C	781 294-0100	14592
Loto Lighting LLc	Somerville	MA	G	617 776-3115	15191
Lumenpulse Lighting Corp	Boston	MA	E	617 307-5700	8673
Mg2 Technologies LLC	Danvers	MA	G	978 739-1068	10241
Newstamp Lighting Corp	North Easton	MA	F	508 238-7073	13949
O C White Company	Thorndike	MA	E	413 289-1751	15850
Osram Sylvania Inc **(HQ)**	Wilmington	MA	A	978 570-3000	17036
Renovators Supply Inc	Millers Falls	MA	E	413 423-3300	13181
Rpt Holdings LLC	Middleton	MA	E	877 997-3674	13099
Signify North America Corp	Fall River	MA	B	508 679-8131	10761
Signify North America Corp	Burlington	MA	B	617 423-9999	9337
Spec Lines	Wakefield	MA	G	781 245-0044	15976
Spectrum Lighting Inc	Fall River	MA	D	508 678-2303	10762
Lighting Solutions Inc	Falmouth	ME	G	207 772-2738	6031
Affinity Led Light LLC	Dover	NH	G	978 378-5338	18004
Plastic Techniques Inc	Goffstown	NH	E	603 622-5570	18209
Signify North America Corp	Manchester	NH	C	603 645-6061	18923
Lexington Lighting Group LLC	Rumford	RI	E	860 564-4512	21192
Lumetta Inc	Warwick	RI	E	401 691-3994	21385
Mastro Lighting Mfg Co Inc **(PA)**	Providence	RI	G	401 467-7700	21063
Orion Ret Svcs & Fixturing Inc	Smithfield	RI	D	401 334-5000	21243
PMC Lighting Inc	Warwick	RI	E	401 738-7266	21404
Renova Lighting Systems Inc	Warwick	RI	E	800 635-6682	21411
SCW Corporation	Warwick	RI	E	401 808-6849	21423
Authentic Designs Inc	West Rupert	VT	F	802 394-7715	22614

	CITY	ST	EMP	PHONE	ENTRY #
Cooper Lighting Inc	Essex Junction	VT	F	800 767-3674	21937

3647 Vehicular Lighting Eqpt

	CITY	ST	EMP	PHONE	ENTRY #
Cornell-Carr Co Inc	Monroe	CT	E	203 261-2529	2399
Light Fantastic Realty Inc	West Haven	CT	C	203 934-3441	5131
Ridge View Associates Inc	Milford	CT	D	203 878-8560	2351
The L C Doane Company **(PA)**	Ivoryton	CT	F	860 767-8295	1909
Whelen Engineering Company Inc **(PA)**	Chester	CT	B	860 526-9504	777
B/E Aerospace Inc	Rockport	MA	G	978 546-1331	14834
Cape Strobe Emergency Lighting	Harwich	MA	G	508 776-0911	11390
Hightechspeed LLC	Groveland	MA	G	978 600-8222	11300
Osram Sylvania Inc **(HQ)**	Wilmington	MA	A	978 570-3000	17036
B/E Aerospace Inc	Hampton	NH	G	603 926-5700	18256

3648 Lighting Eqpt, NEC

	CITY	ST	EMP	PHONE	ENTRY #
Airflo Instrument Company	Glastonbury	CT	G	860 633-9455	1536
Aquacomfort Solutions LLC	Cheshire	CT	G	407 831-1941	712
Astralite Inc	Brookfield	CT	G	203 775-0172	634
Connecticut Valley Inds LLC	Old Saybrook	CT	G	860 388-0822	3332
Cooper Crouse-Hinds LLC	Windsor	CT	D	860 683-4300	5327
Dave Ross	Brookfield	CT	G	203 775-4327	640
Eaton Electric Holdings LLC	Windsor	CT	F	860 683-4300	5330
Elc Acquisition Corporation	Bethel	CT	G	203 743-4059	152
Electrix LLC	New Haven	CT	D	203 776-5577	2686
Fidelux Lighting LLC **(HQ)**	Hartford	CT	F	860 436-5000	1821
Incure Inc	New Britain	CT	G	860 748-2979	2540
Integro LLC	New Britain	CT	E	860 832-8960	2542
Macris Industries Inc	Mystic	CT	G	860 514-7003	2441
Malco Inc	Terryville	CT	F	860 584-0446	4485
Moonlighting LLC	Brookfield	CT	G	203 740-8964	653
Pathway Lighting Products Inc	Old Saybrook	CT	D	860 388-6881	3347
Pegasus Capital Advisors LP **(PA)**	Stamford	CT	E	203 869-4400	4282
Pennsylvania Globe Gaslight Co	North Branford	CT	E	203 484-7749	2971
Point Lighting Corporation	Bloomfield	CT	E	860 243-0600	253
Rsl Fiber Systems LLC	East Hartford	CT	F	860 282-4930	1218
Sensor Switch Inc **(DH)**	New Haven	CT	E	203 265-2842	2737
Solais Lighting Inc	Stamford	CT	F	203 683-6222	4323
Sorenson Lighted Controls Inc **(PA)**	West Hartford	CT	D	860 527-3092	5095
Studio Steel Inc	New Preston	CT	G	860 868-7305	2835
Whelen Engineering Company Inc **(PA)**	Chester	CT	B	860 526-9504	777
York Street Studio Inc	New Milford	CT	G	203 266-9000	2833
Acton Research Corporation	Acton	MA	E	941 556-2601	7334
Bloom Boss LLC	Natick	MA	G	774 777-5208	13238
Brite-Strike Technologies Inc	Duxbury	MA	F	781 585-3525	10394
Current Ltg Employeeco LLC	Boston	MA	A	216 266-2906	8491
Cyalume Technologies Inc **(DH)**	West Springfield	MA	C	888 451-4885	16514
Dolan-Jenner Industries Inc	Boxborough	MA	E	978 263-1400	8961
Dorel Juvenile Group Inc	Foxboro	MA	D	800 544-1108	10881
Eclipse Mfg Inc	Ware	MA	E	920 457-2311	16233
Excelitas Tech Holdg Corp	Waltham	MA	F	781 522-5914	16102
Excelitas Tech Holdings LLC **(PA)**	Waltham	MA	F	781 522-5900	16103
Excelitas Technologies Corp **(DH)**	Waltham	MA	E	781 522-5910	16104
Genlyte Group Incorporated	Andover	MA	A	781 418-7900	7550
Genlyte Thomas Group LLC	Andover	MA	C	978 659-3732	7551
Genlyte Thomas Group LLC	Burlington	MA	C	781 418-7900	9279
Nauset Lantern Shop	Orleans	MA	G	508 255-1009	14236
Nedap Inc	Burlington	MA	F	844 876-3327	9305
Northast Green Enrgy Group Inc	Merrimac	MA	G	978 478-8425	13004
Northern Outdoor Lighting	Westford	MA	G	978 987-9845	16782
Pelican Products Inc	South Deerfield	MA	E	413 665-2163	15251
Period Lighting Fixtures Inc	Clarksburg	MA	F	413 664-7141	10074
Reflek Corp	Fall River	MA	G	508 603-6807	10756
Solarone Solutions Inc **(PA)**	Needham Heights	MA	F	339 225-4530	13344
Sunrise Technologies LLC	Raynham	MA	F	508 884-9732	14731
Taklite LLC	Norfolk	MA	G	508 298-8331	13666
TW Lighting Incorporated **(PA)**	Wellesley	MA	G	617 830-6755	16390
Xenon Corporation **(PA)**	Wilmington	MA	E	978 661-9033	17069
Heritage Lanterns	Windham	ME	F	207 893-1134	7236
Gates Moore Lighting	Hillsborough	NH	G	203 847-3231	18315
Grabber Construction Pdts Inc	Windham	NH	F	603 890-0455	20007
John J Marr	Conway	NH	F	603 939-2698	17954
Luminescent Systems Inc	Lebanon	NH	C	603 643-7766	18629
Tanorama Suntanning Center	Dover	NH	G	603 742-1600	18058
Visible Light Inc	Hampton	NH	G	603 926-6049	18278
Atomic Led Inc	Greenville	RI	G	401 265-0222	20462
Emissive Energy Corp	North Kingstown	RI	D	401 294-2030	20709
Prism Streetlights Inc	Wakefield	RI	G	401 792-9900	21274
Cooper Lighting Inc	Essex Junction	VT	F	800 767-3674	21937
Uv III Systems Inc	Alburg	VT	F	508 883-4881	21593

3651 Household Audio & Video Eqpt

	CITY	ST	EMP	PHONE	ENTRY #
Audioworks Inc	Milford	CT	G	203 876-1133	2247
Color Film Media Group LLC **(PA)**	Norwalk	CT	G	203 202-2929	3129
Harman Becker Automotive Syste	Stamford	CT	G	203 328-3501	4205
Harman Consumer Inc	Stamford	CT	G	203 328-3500	4206
Harman International Inds Inc **(DH)**	Stamford	CT	B	203 328-3500	4207
Harman International Inds Inc	Stamford	CT	G	203 328-3500	4208
Harman International Inds Inc	Stamford	CT	C	203 328-3500	4209
Harman KG Holding LLC **(DH)**	Stamford	CT	F	203 328-3500	4210
Impact Sales & Marketing LLC	West Hartford	CT	G	860 523-5366	5077
Insight Plus Technology LLC	Bristol	CT	G	860 930-4763	571
Ki Inc	Orange	CT	E	203 641-5492	3368
Krell Industries LLC	Orange	CT	F	203 298-4000	3369
Microphase Corporation	Shelton	CT	E	203 866-8000	3833
Omnicron Electronics	Putnam	CT	G	860 928-0377	3623
PMC Technologies LLC	Weston	CT	G	203 222-0000	5172
Proxtalkercom LLC **(PA)**	Waterbury	CT	G	203 721-6074	4947
Redco Audio Inc	Stratford	CT	F	203 502-7600	4441
Source Loudspeakers	South Windsor	CT	G	860 918-3088	4012
Telefunken USA LLC	South Windsor	CT	F	860 882-5919	4016
Viola Audio Laboratories Inc	New Haven	CT	G	203 772-0435	2752
Whelen Engineering Company Inc **(PA)**	Chester	CT	B	860 526-9504	777
Xintekidel Inc	Stamford	CT	G	203 348-9229	4362
Acoustic Magic Inc	Sudbury	MA	G	978 440-9384	15651
Aerial Acoustics Corporation	Wilmington	MA	F	978 988-1600	16968
Alto Technologies Corporation **(PA)**	Sterling	MA	F	978 422-9071	15534
Aquabotix Technology Corp	Fall River	MA	E	508 676-1000	10661
Artel Video Systems Corp	Westford	MA	E	978 263-5775	16755
Bose Corporation **(PA)**	Framingham	MA	A	508 879-7330	10928
Bose Corporation	Framingham	MA	E	508 766-1265	10929
Cambridge Soundworks Inc	Westwood	MA	G	781 329-2777	16859
Cambridge Soundworks Inc	Hanover	MA	G	781 829-8818	11332
Courtsmart Digital Systems Inc	North Chelmsford	MA	E	978 251-3300	13891
Cue Inc	South Easton	MA	F	617 591-9500	15275
Doranco Inc	Attleboro	MA	G	508 236-0290	7727
Fargo Ta LLC	Boston	MA	E	617 345-0066	8537
Fishman Transducers Inc	Andover	MA	D	978 988-9199	7549
Genelec Inc	Natick	MA	F	508 652-0900	13257
Headwaters Inc	Marblehead	MA	G	781 715-6404	12685
Hevc Advance LLC	Boston	MA	F	617 367-4802	8597
Industrial Video & Ctrl Co LLC	Newton	MA	E	617 467-3059	13604
Inter-Ego Systems Inc **(PA)**	Hatfield	MA	F	516 576-9052	11401
Loud Technologies Inc	Whitinsville	MA	C	508 234-6158	16916
Lyfeshot LLC	Acton	MA	G	978 451-4662	7370
Mini-Systems Inc **(PA)**	North Attleboro	MA	C	508 695-1420	13765
Outlaw Audio LLC	Norton	MA	F	508 286-4110	14085
Pine and Baker Mfg Inc	Tewksbury	MA	F	978 851-1215	15825
Polycom Inc	Andover	MA	E	978 292-5000	7586
Premium Sund Slutions Amer LLC **(PA)**	Wakefield	MA	F	781 968-5511	15972
Rf Venue Inc	Ashland	MA	G	800 795-0817	7668
Savant Systems LLC **(PA)**	Hyannis	MA	D	508 683-2500	11857
Taft Sound	Sutton	MA	G	508 476-2662	15693
Technomad Associates LLC	South Deerfield	MA	G	413 665-6704	15257
Technomad Associates LLC **(PA)**	South Deerfield	MA	G	413 665-6704	15258
Venmill Industries Inc	Oxford	MA	E	508 363-0410	14276
Vesper Technologies Inc	Boston	MA	F	617 315-9144	8910
Viking Industrial Products	Marlborough	MA	E	508 481-4600	12845
Volicon Inc	Burlington	MA	D	781 221-7400	9355
Yamaha Unfied Cmmnications Inc **(HQ)**	Sudbury	MA	D	978 610-4040	15674
Connectivity Works Inc	Holden	ME	G	207 843-0854	6196
Transparent Audio Inc	Saco	ME	E	207 284-1100	6860
Basis Audio Inc	Hollis	NH	G	603 889-4776	18326
Cc1 Inc	Portsmouth	NH	E	603 319-2000	19548
Gentex Corporation	Manchester	NH	C	603 657-1200	18826
Nel-Tech Labs Incorporated	Derry	NH	F	603 425-1096	17990
Russound/Fmp Inc	Newmarket	NH	C	603 659-5170	19338
Videology Imging Solutions Inc **(PA)**	Greenville	RI	E	401 949-5332	20476

3652 Phonograph Records & Magnetic Tape

	CITY	ST	EMP	PHONE	ENTRY #
Bff Holdings Inc **(HQ)**	Old Saybrook	CT	C	860 510-0100	3328
Mosaic Records Inc	Stamford	CT	G	203 327-7111	4252
Dj Wholesale Club Inc	Tyngsboro	MA	G	978 649-2525	15888
Fleetwood Multi-Media Inc	Lynn	MA	F	781 599-2400	12509
Harvey Bravman	Roslindale	MA	G	617 323-9969	14838
Image Software Services Inc	Shirley	MA	E	978 425-3600	15087
Gateway Mastering Studios Inc	Portland	ME	F	207 828-9400	6664
Porter Music Box Company Inc	Randolph	VT	G	802 728-9694	22301
Stephen McArthur	Barre	VT	G	802 839-0371	21640

3661 Telephone & Telegraph Apparatus

	CITY	ST	EMP	PHONE	ENTRY #
Ahead Communications Systems	Naugatuck	CT	D	203 720-0227	2458
Amphenol Corporation **(PA)**	Wallingford	CT	D	203 265-8900	4700
Arris Technology Inc	Wallingford	CT	F	678 473-8493	4704
Canoga Perkins Corporation	Seymour	CT	G	203 888-7914	3749
Carrier Access - Trin Networks	Brookfield	CT	G	203 778-8222	637
Communication Networks LLC	Danbury	CT	E	203 796-5300	890
Dac Systems Inc	Shelton	CT	F	203 924-7000	3793
Elot Inc **(PA)**	Old Greenwich	CT	G	203 388-1808	3308
Fibre Optic Plus Inc	South Windsor	CT	F	860 646-3581	3970
Freedom Technologies LLC	Glastonbury	CT	G	860 633-0452	1552
General Datacomm Inc **(HQ)**	Oxford	CT	E	203 729-0271	3404
General Datacomm Inds Inc **(PA)**	Oxford	CT	E	203 729-0271	3405
Hubbell Premise Wiring Inc	Mystic	CT	F	860 535-8326	2439
IPC Systems Inc	Old Saybrook	CT	F	203 339-7000	3338

	CITY	ST	EMP	PHONE	ENTRY #
IPC Systems Inc	Fairfield	CT	C	860 271-4100	1437
K-Tech International	Torrington	CT	E	860 489-9399	4584
Microphase Corporation	Shelton	CT	E	203 866-8000	3833
Nutmeg Utility Products Inc **(PA)**	Cheshire	CT	E	203 250-8802	748
Opticonx Inc	Putnam	CT	E	888 748-6855	3624
Pitney Bowes Inc **(PA)**	Stamford	CT	A	203 356-5000	4285
Pitney Bowes Inc	Shelton	CT	E	203 356-5000	3855
Radio Frequency Systems Inc **(DH)**	Meriden	CT	E	203 630-3311	2122
Ruckus Wireless Inc	Wallingford	CT	E	203 303-6400	4802
Sound Control Technologies	Norwalk	CT	G	203 854-5701	3248
Tango Modem LLC	Madison	CT	G	203 421-2245	1978
Total Communications Inc **(PA)**	East Hartford	CT	D	860 282-9999	1230
United Photonics LLC	Vernon Rockville	CT	G	617 752-2073	4687
Adva Optical Networking North	Chelmsford	MA	C	978 674-6800	9867
Allston-Brighton Tab	Somerville	MA	G	617 629-3387	15152
Artel Video Systems Corp	Westford	MA	E	978 263-5775	16755
Avaya Inc	Billerica	MA	C	908 953-6000	8216
Avvio Networks Inc	Bedford	MA	G	781 271-0002	7961
Biscom Inc	Westford	MA	D	978 250-1800	16757
Cambridge Electronics Laborato	Somerville	MA	G	617 629-2805	15163
Coriant America Inc **(HQ)**	Chelmsford	MA	C	978 250-2900	9888
Eas Holdings LLC **(DH)**	Needham Heights	MA	G	781 449-3056	13329
Em4 Inc **(DH)**	Bedford	MA	E	781 275-7501	7972
Fiberon Technologies Inc **(PA)**	Westborough	MA	F	508 616-9500	16618
Fibertech Networks LLC	Boxborough	MA	G	978 264-6000	8962
Genband US LLC	Billerica	MA	G	972 521-5800	8251
General Dynmics Mssion Systems	Taunton	MA	G	508 880-4000	15755
Global Connector Tech Ltd	Lawrence	MA	F	978 208-1618	12028
Gn Audio USA Inc **(DH)**	Lowell	MA	B	800 826-4656	12377
Gsr Global Corporation	Billerica	MA	G	781 687-9191	8252
Idg Woit Modem	Lexington	MA	G	781 861-6541	12231
Interntonal Micro Photonix Inc	North Andover	MA	G	978 685-3800	13710
Interntonal Totalizing Systems **(PA)**	Bedford	MA	E	978 521-8867	7983
LTS Group Holdings LLC **(HQ)**	Boxborough	MA	F	978 264-6001	8965
Modem Srismitha	West Roxbury	MA	G	617 323-0080	16499
Opus Telecom Inc	Framingham	MA	E	508 875-4444	10989
Photon Bounce	Roxbury	MA	G	617 708-1231	14875
Photonex Corporation	Maynard	MA	C	978 723-2200	12903
Photonic Systems Inc	Carlisle	MA	G	978 369-0729	9799
Ruckus Wireless Inc	Westborough	MA	E	508 870-1184	16645
Ruckus Wireless Inc	Lowell	MA	D	978 614-2900	12430
Sandy Bay Machine Inc	Gloucester	MA	E	978 546-1331	11209
Seaborn Management Inc	Beverly	MA	F	978 377-8366	8175
Seaborn Networks Holdings LLC **(PA)**	Beverly	MA	F	978 471-3171	8176
Signal Communications Corp	Woburn	MA	E	781 933-0998	17295
T S X Products Corporation	Westwood	MA	G	781 769-1800	16878
Vbrick Systems Inc	Canton	MA	G	203 265-0044	9793
Vxi Corporation	Lowell	MA	E	603 742-2888	12447
Xphotonics LLC	Littleton	MA	G	978 952-2568	12329
Zoom Telephonics Inc **(PA)**	Boston	MA	E	617 423-1072	8944
SPX Corporation	Raymond	ME	E	207 655-8525	6775
Amphenol Corporation	Nashua	NH	B	603 879-3000	19114
At Comm Corp	Manchester	NH	F	603 624-4424	18783
Deborah Frost	Bedford	NH	F	603 882-3100	17638
Exacom Inc	Concord	NH	E	603 228-0706	17900
Extreme Networks Inc	Salem	NH	F	603 952-5000	19726
Ezenia Inc **(PA)**	Salem	NH	F	603 589-7600	19727
H&L Instruments LLC	North Hampton	NH	F	603 964-1818	19383
Holase Incorporated	Portsmouth	NH	G	603 397-0038	19575
Maverick Photonics LLC	Manchester	NH	G	603 540-4434	18868
Nel-Tech Labs Incorporated	Derry	NH	F	603 425-1096	17990
Northeast Innovations Inc	Pembroke	NH	F	603 226-4000	19460
Pagepro Wireless	Dover	NH	G	603 749-5600	18044
Ripley Odm LLC	Laconia	NH	G	603 524-8350	18583
Sensear Inc	Nashua	NH	G	603 589-4072	19260
Subcom LLC	Newington	NH	D	603 436-6100	19326
Uraseal Inc	Dover	NH	F	603 749-1004	18064
Eartec Company Inc	Narragansett	RI	E	401 789-8700	20638
Electro Standards Lab Inc	Cranston	RI	D	401 946-1390	20215
Okonite Company	Cumberland	RI	D	401 333-3500	20336
Ramtel Corporation	Johnston	RI	F	401 231-3340	20533

3663 Radio & T V Communications, Systs & Eqpt, Broadcast/Studio

	CITY	ST	EMP	PHONE	ENTRY #
Advanced Receiver Research	Harwinton	CT	G	860 485-0310	1886
Ashcroft Inc **(DH)**	Stratford	CT	B	203 378-8281	4392
Axerra Networks Inc	Woodbury	CT	G	203 906-3570	5482
Commscope Technologies LLC	Prospect	CT	F	203 699-4100	3585
Comsat Inc	Southbury	CT	F	203 264-4091	4025
Cuescript Inc	Stratford	CT	G	203 763-4030	4407
Fenton Corp	Westport	CT	F	203 221-2788	5191
Frontier Vision Tech Inc	Rocky Hill	CT	E	860 953-0240	3709
Gold Line Connector Inc **(PA)**	Redding	CT	E	203 938-2588	3648
Jk Antennas Inc	Brookfield	CT	G	845 228-8700	649
Mango Dsp Inc	Norwalk	CT	E	203 857-4008	3190
Media Links Inc	Windsor	CT	F	860 206-9163	5348
Merl Inc	Meriden	CT	G	203 237-8811	2106
Microphase Corporation	Shelton	CT	E	203 866-8000	3833
Microtech Inc	Cheshire	CT	D	203 272-3234	745
Newtec America Inc	Stamford	CT	F	203 323-0042	4258
Radio Frequency Systems Inc **(DH)**	Meriden	CT	E	203 630-3311	2122
RFS Americas	Meriden	CT	G	203 630-3311	2125
Scinetx LLC	Stamford	CT	G	203 355-3676	4310
Sonitor Technologies Inc	Greenwich	CT	G	727 466-4557	1651
Video Automation Systems Inc	New Fairfield	CT	G	203 312-0152	2630
Wagz Inc	Stamford	CT	G	203 553-9336	4356
Xintekidel Inc	Stamford	CT	G	203 348-9229	4362
Accelerated Media Tech Inc	Auburn	MA	E	508 459-0300	7821
Adaptive Networks Inc	Needham	MA	F	781 444-4170	13291
Antenna Research Assoc Inc	Pembroke	MA	E	781 829-4740	14391
Arris Technology Inc	Lowell	MA	F	978 614-2900	12346
Artel Video Systems Corp	Westford	MA	E	978 263-5775	16755
Asco Power Technologies LP	Marlborough	MA	G	508 624-0466	12720
Assurance Technology Corp	Chelmsford	MA	D	978 250-8060	9875
AT&T Inc	Norwell	MA	G	781 878-8169	14095
Atc Ponderosa B-I LLC	Boston	MA	G	617 375-7500	8379
Atc Ponderosa K LLC	Boston	MA	G	617 375-7500	8380
Auriga Measurement Systems	Chelmsford	MA	E	978 452-7700	9876
Auriga Measurement Systems **(PA)**	Wayland	MA	G	978 452-7700	16334
Axiom Microdevices Inc	Woburn	MA	G	781 376-3000	17124
Big Pond Wireless LLC	North Reading	MA	G	781 593-2321	13979
Burk Technology Inc	Littleton	MA	E	978 486-0086	12295
Casa Systems Inc **(PA)**	Andover	MA	C	978 688-6706	7544
Cellassist LLC **(PA)**	Springfield	MA	G	413 559-1256	15459
Comtech PST Corp	Topsfield	MA	F	978 887-5754	15854
Copley Controls Corporation **(DH)**	Canton	MA	B	781 828-8090	9722
Courtsmart Digital Systems Inc	North Chelmsford	MA	E	978 251-3300	13891
CPI Radant Tech Div Inc	Clinton	MA	F	978 562-3866	10078
David Clark Company Inc **(PA)**	Worcester	MA	C	508 756-6216	17362
Diamond Antenna Microwave Corp	Littleton	MA	D	978 486-0039	12300
Digital Image Fidelity LLC	Whitman	MA	G	508 577-8496	16922
E Z Telecom	Chelsea	MA	G	617 466-0826	9953
Easy Locate LLC	Arlington	MA	G	617 216-3654	7624
Ei-Envrnmental Integration LLC	Shelburne Falls	MA	G	413 219-9547	15070
Fractal Antenna Systems Inc	Bedford	MA	F	781 290-5308	7977
G5 Scientific LLC	Burlington	MA	G	781 272-7877	9277
GE Infrastructure Sensing LLC **(DH)**	Billerica	MA	A	978 437-1000	8249
General Airmotive Pwr Pdts LLC	Fall River	MA	G	508 674-6400	10702
General Dynamics	Taunton	MA	D	508 880-4521	15753
Global Tower Holdings LLC	Boston	MA	G	617 375-7500	8568
Homeland Security Wireless Inc	Falmouth	MA	G	508 299-1404	10792
Hxi LLC	Harvard	MA	F	978 772-7774	11379
Infinite Electronics Intl Inc	North Billerica	MA	G	978 459-8800	13827
L3 Essco Inc	Ayer	MA	D	978 568-5100	7923
L3 Secrity Dtction Systems Inc	Haverhill	MA	F	781 939-3800	11446
L3 Technologies Inc	Burlington	MA	C	781 270-2100	9295
L3harris Technologies Inc	Chelmsford	MA	B	978 905-3500	9911
Linx Consulting LLC	Webster	MA	F	508 461-6333	16347
Loud Technologies Inc	Whitinsville	MA	C	508 234-6158	16916
Macom Technology Solutions Inc	Lowell	MA	G	978 656-2500	12402
Macom Technology Solutions Inc **(HQ)**	Lowell	MA	B	978 656-2500	12403
Magcap Engineering LLC	Canton	MA	F	781 821-2300	9754
Megapulse Incorporated	Bedford	MA	E	781 538-5299	7989
Microwave Engineering Corp	North Andover	MA	D	978 685-2776	13718
Microwave Video Systems LLC	Melrose	MA	G	781 665-6600	12985
Millennial Net Inc	Lexington	MA	E	978 569-1921	12244
Mlc Services LLC	Holliston	MA	G	781 366-1132	11587
Moble Internet Access Inc	Pembroke	MA	G	978 273-2390	14417
Motorola Mobility LLC	Marlborough	MA	D	847 523-5000	12796
Motorola Solutions Inc	Mansfield	MA	G	508 261-4502	12647
Newedge Signal Solutions LLC	Ayer	MA	G	978 425-5400	7929
Notch Inc	Cambridge	MA	G	203 258-9141	9585
Novelsat Inc	Newton	MA	F	617 658-1419	13621
Parece JP Company	Melrose	MA	G	781 662-8640	12987
Pnderosa K Atc Acquisition Inc	Boston	MA	G	617 375-7500	8782
Qualcomm Incorporated	Concord	MA	D	978 318-0650	10153
Radio Engineering Assoc Inc	Townsend	MA	G	978 597-0010	15873
Raytheon Company **(PA)**	Waltham	MA	B	781 522-3000	16184
Raytheon Company	Marlborough	MA	E	310 647-9438	12813
Raytheon Company	North Billerica	MA	G	978 313-0201	13858
Raytheon Sutheast Asia Systems **(HQ)**	Billerica	MA	E	978 470-5000	8289
Renaissnce Elec Cmmnctions LLC **(PA)**	Harvard	MA	E	978 772-7774	11383
Rennaissance Electronic Corp	Harvard	MA	E	978 772-7774	11384
Seachange International Inc **(PA)**	Acton	MA	C	978 897-0100	7385
Smiths Interconnect Inc	South Deerfield	MA	E	413 665-0965	15256
Southwest Asian Incorporated	Worcester	MA	G	508 753-7126	17477
Submarine Research Labs	Hingham	MA	G	781 749-0900	11512
Sunu Inc	Cambridge	MA	G	617 980-9807	9664
Technical Communications Corp **(PA)**	Concord	MA	E	978 287-5100	10158
Unadilla Antennas Mfgco	North Andover	MA	G	978 975-2711	13733
Unisite LLC	Boston	MA	G	781 926-7135	8896
Verizon Communications Inc	Natick	MA	F	508 647-4008	13285
Viasat Inc	Marlborough	MA	F	508 229-6500	12844
Victor Microwave Inc	Wakefield	MA	F	781 245-4472	15982
Vox Communications Group LLC	Wellesley	MA	D	781 239-8018	16392

	CITY	ST	EMP	PHONE	ENTRY #
Worldwide Antenna Systems LLC	Kingston	MA	G	781 275-1147	11968
Zeevee Inc	Littleton	MA	E	978 467-1395	12330
Alaris Usa LLC	Windham	ME	F	207 517-5304	7228
Maine Radio	Scarborough	ME	F	207 883-2929	6932
Mwave Industries LLC	Windham	ME	G	207 892-0011	7243
Nautel Maine Inc	Bangor	ME	C	207 947-8200	5654
SPX Corporation	Raymond	ME	C	207 655-8100	6774
Warner Graphics Inc	Camden	ME	G	207 236-2065	5871
Aerosat Avionics LLC	Amherst	NH	D	603 943-8680	17549
Airlinx Communications Inc	New Ipswich	NH	F	603 878-1926	19302
Alltraxx LLC	Portsmouth	NH	G	603 610-7179	19535
Aqyr Technologies Inc	Nashua	NH	E	603 402-6099	19116
Audio Accessories Inc	Marlow	NH	E	603 446-3335	18965
Communction Cmpnent Flters Inc **(PA)**	Seabrook	NH	G	603 294-4685	19797
County Communications	Kensington	NH	G	603 394-7070	18535
Custom Manufacturing Svcs Inc	Nashua	NH	E	603 883-1355	19141
Edge Velocity Corporation	Salem	NH	G	603 912-5618	19723
Haigh-Farr Inc	Bedford	NH	F	603 644-6170	17644
Iheartcommunications Inc	Portsmouth	NH	D	603 436-7300	19577
Insource Design & Mfg Tech LLC	Merrimack	NH	G	603 718-8228	19007
Laird Technologies Inc	Manchester	NH	F	603 627-7877	18858
Metz Communication Corporation	Laconia	NH	G	603 528-2590	18575
Nhrc LLC	Pembroke	NH	F	603 485-2248	19459
Qesidyne Inc	Hudson	NH	G	603 883-3116	18431
Research In Motion Rf Inc **(HQ)**	Nashua	NH	E	603 598-8880	19250
Richard Townsend	Barrington	NH	G	603 664-5987	17622
Rymsa Micro Communications **(PA)**	Merrimack	NH	E	603 429-0800	19026
Syntech Microwave Inc	Hudson	NH	G	603 880-9767	18444
Tensor Communications Systems	Bradford	NH	G	603 938-5206	17742
Blackhawk Machine Products Inc	Smithfield	RI	E	401 232-7563	21213
Hysen Technologies Inc **(PA)**	Cumberland	RI	F	401 312-6500	20326
Kvh Industries Inc	Middletown	RI	C	401 847-3327	20622
Kvh Industries Inc **(PA)**	Middletown	RI	C	401 847-3327	20623
Pcs Metro	East Providence	RI	G	401 574-6105	20440
Site Resources LLC	Providence	RI	G	401 295-4998	21123
Iheartcommunications Inc	Colchester	VT	E	802 655-0093	21866
Lcs Controls Inc	Rochester	VT	G	802 767-3128	22318
Wireless For Less	Rutland	VT	G	802 786-0918	22361

3669 Communications Eqpt, NEC

	CITY	ST	EMP	PHONE	ENTRY #
Alarm One	North Haven	CT	G	203 239-1714	3004
Aquatic Sensor Netwrk Tech LLC	Storrs Mansfield	CT	F	860 429-4303	4383
Endoto Corp	East Hartford	CT	G	860 289-8033	1193
Essential Trading Systems Corp	Marlborough	CT	F	860 295-8100	2064
Farmington River Holdings LLC	Hamden	CT	G	203 777-2130	1749
Gac Inc	Glastonbury	CT	G	860 633-1768	1553
Lumentum Operations LLC	Bloomfield	CT	G	408 546-5483	242
Nutmeg Utility Products Inc **(PA)**	Cheshire	CT	E	203 250-8802	748
Onsite Services Inc	Clinton	CT	F	860 669-3988	792
Q-Lane Turnstiles LLC	Sandy Hook	CT	F	860 410-1801	3745
T-S Display Systems Inc	Stamford	CT	G	203 964-0575	4340
Trans-Tek Inc	Ellington	CT	E	860 872-8351	1343
United Technologies Corp	Farmington	CT	B	954 485-6501	1523
United Technologies Corp **(PA)**	Farmington	CT	B	860 728-7000	1522
UTC Fire SEC Americas Corp Inc	Newtown	CT	C	203 426-1180	2947
Voice Express Corp	Fairfield	CT	G	203 221-7799	1461
Alarmsafe Inc	Chelmsford	MA	E	978 658-6717	9868
ARINC Incorporated	Lexington	MA	D	781 863-0711	12207
Avacea	Everett	MA	G	617 294-0261	10603
Bellofatto Electrical	Revere	MA	G	781 284-4164	14764
Bridgesat Inc	Boston	MA	G	617 419-1800	8444
Cambrdge Sund MGT Holdings LLC **(DH)**	Waltham	MA	G	781 547-7100	16059
Convergent Networks Inc	Boston	MA	D	978 262-0231	8483
Coredge Networks Inc	Boston	MA	D	617 267-5205	8484
Courtsmart Digital Systems Inc	North Chelmsford	MA	E	978 251-3300	13891
Eas Holdings LLC **(DH)**	Needham Heights	MA	G	781 449-3056	13329
Electro-Mechanical Tech Co	Hudson	MA	G	978 562-7898	11770
Fall Prevention Alarms Inc	Southbridge	MA	G	508 765-5050	15382
General Dynamics Mission	Needham Heights	MA	A	954 846-3000	13334
General Dynmics Mssion Systems	Pittsfield	MA	A	413 494-1110	14472
Housing Devices Inc	Medford	MA	F	781 395-5200	12935
I F Engineering Corp	Dudley	MA	E	860 935-0280	10377
IBC Communications Inc	North Chelmsford	MA	G	978 455-9692	13896
Image Stream Medical Inc	Littleton	MA	D	978 486-8494	12309
Irrigation Automtn Systms Inc	Whitinsville	MA	G	800 549-4551	16915
Keltron Corporation **(HQ)**	Waltham	MA	E	781 894-8710	16137
Kidde-Fenwal Inc **(HQ)**	Ashland	MA	A	508 881-2000	7663
King Fisher Co Inc	Lowell	MA	E	978 596-0214	12389
L W Bills Co	Georgetown	MA	E	978 352-6660	11144
L3 Technologies Inc	Ayer	MA	C	978 784-1999	7925
L3 Technologies Inc	Burlington	MA	C	781 270-2100	9295
Lifeline Systems Company **(DH)**	Framingham	MA	A	508 988-1000	10977
Lifeline Systems Company	Framingham	MA	C	508 988-3000	10978
Multec Communications	Rockland	MA	G	781 294-4992	14817
Philips Hlthcare Infrmtics Inc	Framingham	MA	F	508 988-1000	10993
Protectowire Co Inc	Pembroke	MA	E	781 826-3878	14423
Scoreboard Enterprises Inc	Mansfield	MA	G	508 339-8113	12657
Segue Manufacturing Svcs LLC	Lowell	MA	D	978 970-1200	12432
Shufro Security Company Inc	Newton	MA	G	617 244-3355	13637
Signal Communications Corp	Woburn	MA	E	781 933-0998	17295
Simplex Time Recorder Co **(DH)**	Westminster	MA	C	978 731-2500	16813
Space Age Electronics Inc **(PA)**	Sterling	MA	E	800 486-1723	15545
Space Age Electronics Inc	Templeton	MA	E	978 652-5421	15805
Starry Inc	Boston	MA	F	617 861-8300	8862
Tyco International MGT Co LLC	Mansfield	MA	G	508 261-6200	12667
UTC Fire SEC Americas Corp Inc	Framingham	MA	G	508 620-4773	11009
Vivox Inc **(DH)**	Framingham	MA	E	508 650-3571	11012
Voltree Power Inc	Canton	MA	G	781 858-4939	9794
Xtralis Inc	Avon	MA	E	800 229-4434	7904
Lifeline Systems Company	Lewiston	ME	C	207 777-8827	6302
Alltraxx LLC	Portsmouth	NH	G	603 610-7179	19535
As Liquidation I Company Inc **(PA)**	Amherst	NH	D	603 879-0205	17552
Astronics Aerosat Corporation	Manchester	NH	D	603 879-0205	18782
Custom Manufacturing Svcs Inc	Nashua	NH	E	603 883-1355	19141
Fireye Inc **(DH)**	Derry	NH	C	603 432-4100	17979
Lifeline Systems Company	Lebanon	NH	G	603 653-1610	18627
Navico Inc	Merrimack	NH	E	603 324-2042	19016
Nel-Tech Labs Incorporated	Derry	NH	F	603 425-1096	17990
Nextmove Technologies LLC	Hollis	NH	G	603 654-1280	18335
Saltwhistle Technology LLC	Chester	NH	G	603 887-3161	17825
Nestor Inc **(PA)**	Providence	RI	F	401 274-5345	21076
Nestor Traffic Systems Inc **(PA)**	Pawtucket	RI	E	401 714-7781	20864
Worksafe Traffic Ctrl Inds Inc **(PA)**	Barre	VT	F	802 223-8948	21645

3671 Radio & T V Receiving Electron Tubes

	CITY	ST	EMP	PHONE	ENTRY #
Conklin-Sherman Company Incthe	Beacon Falls	CT	G	203 881-0190	57
Connecticut Coining Inc	Bethel	CT	D	203 743-3861	138
Whelen Engineering Company Inc **(PA)**	Chester	CT	B	860 526-9504	777
Adaptas Solutions **(PA)**	Palmer	MA	D	413 284-9975	14277
Bridge 12 Technologies Inc	Framingham	MA	G	617 674-2766	10930
Communications & Pwr Inds LLC	Beverly	MA	B	978 922-6000	8119
Fil-Tech Inc	Boston	MA	G	617 227-1133	8544
Filtech Inc	Boston	MA	G	617 227-1133	8545
Jem Electronics Inc	Franklin	MA	C	508 520-3105	11057
Photonis Scientific Inc **(DH)**	Sturbridge	MA	D	508 347-4000	15646
Remtec Incorporated **(PA)**	Norwood	MA	E	781 762-9191	14194
Osram Sylvania Inc	Exeter	NH	D	603 772-4331	18127
Narragansett Imaging Usa LLC	North Smithfield	RI	E	401 762-3800	20791

3672 Printed Circuit Boards

	CITY	ST	EMP	PHONE	ENTRY #
AB Electronics Inc	Brookfield	CT	E	203 740-2793	632
Accutron Inc	Windsor	CT	C	860 683-8300	5315
Advanced Product Solutions LLC	Hamden	CT	G	203 745-4225	1730
Altek Electronics Inc	Torrington	CT	C	860 482-7626	4558
American Backplane Inc	Morris	CT	E	860 567-2360	2430
Apct-Ct Inc	Wallingford	CT	G	203 284-1215	4702
Apct-Wallingford Inc	Wallingford	CT	E	203 269-3311	4703
Carlton Industries Corp	Hamden	CT	E	203 288-5605	1736
Custom Design Service Corp	Danbury	CT	G	203 748-1105	895
Cyclone Microsystems Inc	Hamden	CT	E	203 786-5536	1741
Eastern Company	Clinton	CT	E	860 669-2233	785
Electronic Spc Conn Inc	Hamden	CT	E	203 288-1707	1745
Enhanced Mfg Solutions LLC	Branford	CT	F	203 488-5796	313
Microboard Processing Inc	Seymour	CT	C	203 881-4300	3757
Northeast Circuit Tech LLC	Glastonbury	CT	G	860 633-1967	1567
Power Trans Co Inc	Oxford	CT	G	203 881-0314	3419
Precise Circuit Company Inc	Shelton	CT	E	203 924-2512	3858
Te Connectivity Corporation	Stafford Springs	CT	C	860 684-8000	4116
Technical Manufacturing Corp	Durham	CT	E	860 349-1735	1094
Tek Industries Inc	Vernon	CT	E	860 870-0001	4673
Ttm Printed Circuit Group Inc	Stafford Springs	CT	C	860 684-8000	4118
Ttm Technologies Inc	Stafford Springs	CT	B	860 684-5881	4119
Ttm Technologies Inc	Stafford Springs	CT	D	860 684-8000	4120
Accusemble Electronics Inc	North Billerica	MA	F	978 584-0072	13789
Aerospace Semiconductor Inc	Lawrence	MA	F	978 688-1299	11990
An Electronic Instrumentation	Methuen	MA	D	978 208-4555	13011
Azores Corp **(DH)**	Wilmington	MA	F	978 253-6200	16977
Barry Industries Inc	Attleboro	MA	D	508 226-3350	7712
Bitflow Inc	Woburn	MA	F	781 932-2900	17132
Case Assembly Solutions Inc	South Easton	MA	E	508 238-5665	15273
Chase Corporation **(PA)**	Westwood	MA	G	781 332-0700	16861
Chase Corporation	Oxford	MA	F	508 731-2710	14256
Chase Corporation	Westwood	MA	F	781 329-3259	16862
Circuit Technology Center Inc	Haverhill	MA	E	978 374-5000	11417
Cooper Interconnect Inc	Chelsea	MA	D	617 389-7080	9950
Creative Exchange Inc	Chelmsford	MA	G	978 863-9955	9889
Custom Computer Systems Inc	Northborough	MA	G	508 393-8899	14032
Darrell Wheaton	Taunton	MA	G	508 824-1669	15740
Dilla St Corp	Milford	MA	G	508 478-3419	13112
East West Boston LLC	Boston	MA	D	617 598-3000	8516
Epec LLC **(PA)**	New Bedford	MA	D	508 995-5171	13384
Frain & Associates Inc	Assonet	MA	G	508 644-3424	7680
G3 Incorporated **(PA)**	Lowell	MA	E	978 805-5001	12372
Imi Inc	Haverhill	MA	E	978 373-9190	11442

	CITY	ST	EMP	PHONE	ENTRY #
J & J Technologies Inc	Wareham	MA	D	508 291-3803	16251
Jnj Industries Inc	Franklin	MA	E	508 553-0529	11058
L-Tronics Inc	Waltham	MA	G	781 893-6672	16142
L-Tronics Inc	Waltham	MA	E	781 893-6672	16143
Lockheed Martin Sippican Inc **(HQ)**	Marion	MA	B	508 748-3399	12699
M C Test Service Inc	North Billerica	MA	F	781 218-7550	13837
Mc Assembly International LLC	North Billerica	MA	B	781 729-1073	13840
Measurement Computing Corp **(HQ)**	Norton	MA	D	508 946-5100	14081
Mercury Systems Inc **(PA)**	Andover	MA	C	978 256-1300	7570
Mfg Electronics Inc	North Billerica	MA	G	978 671-5490	13844
Micron Corporation	Norwood	MA	E	781 769-5771	14179
Milford Manufacturing Svcs LLC	Hopedale	MA	D	508 478-8544	11678
Mini-Systems Inc **(PA)**	North Attleboro	MA	C	508 695-1420	13765
Murata Power Solutions Inc **(DH)**	Westborough	MA	C	508 339-3000	16637
New Age Ems Inc	Attleboro	MA	E	508 226-6090	7772
Parlex	Methuen	MA	F	978 946-2500	13041
Pcb Connect Inc	Sharon	MA	G	781 806-5670	15055
Photo Tool Engineering Inc	Lowell	MA	E	978 805-5000	12421
Ping Electronics Inc	Bedford	MA	G	781 275-4731	8001
Ppi/Time Zero Inc	Norwood	MA	E	508 226-6090	14188
Ppi/Time Zero Inc	Springfield	MA	G	781 881-2400	15499
Precision Circuit Corporation	Taunton	MA	G	508 479-8843	15772
Prodrive Technologies Inc	Canton	MA	G	617 475-1617	9773
Proxy Manufacturing Inc	Methuen	MA	E	978 687-3138	13044
Rbd Electronics Inc **(PA)**	Dalton	MA	F	413 442-1111	10182
Remtec Incorporated	Norwood	MA	G	781 762-5732	14193
Starflex Inc	Lowell	MA	F	978 937-3889	12434
Sunburst Electronic Manufactur **(PA)**	West Bridgewater	MA	D	508 580-1881	16458
Tech-Etch Inc **(PA)**	Plymouth	MA	B	508 747-0300	14587
Technical Services Inc	Raynham	MA	G	781 389-8342	14732
Techtrade Inc	Needham	MA	F	781-724-7878	13313
Tronica Circuits Inc	Haverhill	MA	G	978 372-7224	11478
Whitman Products Company Inc	Haverhill	MA	E	978 975-0502	11486
Worthington Assembly Inc	South Deerfield	MA	F	413 397-8265	15259
Zolin Technologies Inc	Lawrence	MA	F	978 794-4300	12086
Alternative Manufacturing Inc	Winthrop	ME	D	207 377-9377	7279
David Saunders Inc	South Portland	ME	E	207 228-1888	7021
Elscott Manufacturing LLC **(PA)**	Gouldsboro	ME	D	207 422-6747	6136
Enercon **(PA)**	Gray	ME	C	207 657-7000	6139
Enercon	Auburn	ME	E	207 657-7001	5562
Marja Corporation	Sanford	ME	F	207 324-2994	6882
Sanmina Corporation	Augusta	ME	D	207 623-6511	5618
Aci - Pcb Inc	Laconia	NH	G	603 528-7711	18551
Advanced Circuit Technolo	Nashua	NH	F	603 880-6000	19104
Amphenol Corporation	Nashua	NH	B	603 879-3000	19113
Amphenol Printed Circuits Inc	Nashua	NH	A	603 324-4500	19115
Anaren Ceramics Inc	Salem	NH	D	603 898-2883	19706
Benchmark Electronics Inc	Nashua	NH	B	603 879-7000	19126
Celestica LLC	Merrimack	NH	A	603 657-3000	18991
Circuit Connect Inc	Nashua	NH	E	603 880-7447	19133
Circuit Express Inc	Derry	NH	G	603 537-9392	17976
Circuit Technology Inc	Merrimack	NH	D	603 424-2200	18992
Cirtronics Corporation	Milford	NH	C	603 249-9190	19049
Cogent Mfg Solutions LLC	Atkinson	NH	G	603 898-3212	17603
Colonial Electronic Mfrs Inc	Nashua	NH	E	603 881-8244	19136
Core Assemblies Inc	Gilford	NH	F	603 293-0270	18183
Custom Manufacturing Svcs Inc	Nashua	NH	E	603 883-1355	19141
Data Electronic Devices Inc	Salem	NH	C	603 893-2047	19720
Electronics Aid Inc	Marlborough	NH	G	603 876-4161	18959
Electropac Co Inc	Concord	NH	E	603 622-3711	17899
Eltek USA Inc	Manchester	NH	G	603 421-0020	18815
Ema Services Inc	Amherst	NH	E	978 251-4044	17559
Finite Surface Mount Tech LLC	Merrimack	NH	G	603 423-0300	19000
Flex Technology Incorporated	Londonderry	NH	E	603 883-1500	18700
Gorilla Circuits	Nashua	NH	F	603 864-0283	19170
Guardian Technologies Inc	Nashua	NH	G	603 594-0430	19174
Hadco Corporation **(HQ)**	Salem	NH	B	603 421-3400	19741
Insulectro	Londonderry	NH	E	603 629-4403	18704
Manufacturing Services Group	Amherst	NH	F	603 883-1022	17572
Mass Design Inc **(PA)**	Nashua	NH	D	603 886-6460	19204
Mercury Systems Inc	Hudson	NH	C	603 883-2900	18414
Merrimack Micro LLC	Merrimack	NH	G	603 809-4183	19014
Metz Electronics Corp	Gilford	NH	E	603 524-8806	18191
Nashua Circuits Inc	Nashua	NH	E	603 882-1773	19212
Ncab Group Usa Inc **(PA)**	Hampstead	NH	E	603 329-4551	18245
Net Results In Cad Inc	Amherst	NH	G	603 249-9995	17578
Pd & E Electronics LLC	North Hampton	NH	G	603 964-3165	19386
Pica Mfg Solutions Inc	Derry	NH	E	603 845-3258	17993
Precision Placement Mchs Inc **(PA)**	Fremont	NH	F	603 895-5112	18179
Princeton Technology Corp	Hudson	NH	D	603 595-1987	18428
Qesidyne Inc	Hudson	NH	G	603 883-3116	18431
Retcomp Inc	New Boston	NH	E	603 487-5010	19297
Sanmina Corporation	Manchester	NH	C	603 621-1800	18914
Sonic Manufacturing Co Inc	Hudson	NH	E	603 882-1020	18438
Sparton Beckwood LLC	Plaistow	NH	D	603 382-3840	19524
Stellar Manufacturing Inc	Salem	NH	E	978 241-9537	19771
Test Msrment Instrmntation Inc	Nashua	NH	G	603 882-8610	19272
Two In One Manufacturing Inc	Nashua	NH	E	603 595-8212	19276
Valhalla Circuits Corp	Weare	NH	G	603 854-3300	19942
Varitron Technologies USA Inc	Hudson	NH	E	603 577-8855	18450
Wessmark NH LLC	Plaistow	NH	G	603 974-2932	19527
Willis & Pham LLC	Salem	NH	G	603 893-6029	19778
Ism Capital Corporation Ltd	East Providence	RI	G	401 454-8519	20421
Northeast Manufacturing Inc	Portsmouth	RI	G	401 683-2075	20934
Vr Industries Inc	Warwick	RI	E	401 732-6800	21440
Image Tek Mfg Inc	Springfield	VT	E	802 885-6208	22502
Purchasing & Inventory Cons	Windsor	VT	F	802 674-2620	22713

3674 Semiconductors

	CITY	ST	EMP	PHONE	ENTRY #
AG Semiconductor Services LLC	Stamford	CT	E	203 322-5300	4131
Alacrity Semiconductors Inc	Branford	CT	G	475 325-8435	287
Asct LLC	Durham	CT	G	860 349-1121	1087
Carten-Fujikin Incorporated	Cheshire	CT	G	203 699-2134	720
Convergent Solutions LLC	Westport	CT	G	203 293-3534	5186
Doosan Fuel Cell America Inc **(HQ)**	South Windsor	CT	C	860 727-2200	3956
Edal Industries Inc	East Haven	CT	E	203 467-2591	1248
Emosyn America Inc	Danbury	CT	E	203 794-1100	909
Entegris Prof Solutions Inc **(HQ)**	Danbury	CT	C	203 794-1100	913
Fiber Mountain Inc	Cheshire	CT	E	203 806-4040	732
Fidelux Lighting LLC **(HQ)**	Hartford	CT	F	860 436-5000	1821
Fuelcell Energy Inc	Torrington	CT	E	860 496-1111	4579
Gordon Products Incorporated	Brookfield	CT	E	203 775-4501	646
Hi-Rel Group LLC	Essex	CT	G	860 767-9031	1397
Hi-Rel Products LLC	Essex	CT	E	860 767-9031	1398
LLC Dow Gage	Berlin	CT	E	860 828-5327	93
Micro-Probe Incorporated	Southbury	CT	G	203 267-6446	4031
Microphase Corporation	Shelton	CT	E	203 866-8000	3833
Newco Condenser Inc	Shelton	CT	G	475 882-4000	3839
Opel Connecticut Solar LLC	Shelton	CT	E	203 612-2366	3847
Oracle America Inc	Stamford	CT	D	203 703-3000	4273
Pequot	Bridgeport	CT	G	800 620-1492	466
Photronics Inc **(PA)**	Brookfield	CT	B	203 775-9000	654
Photronics Texas Inc	Brookfield	CT	G	203 546-3039	655
Photronics Texas I LLC	Brookfield	CT	G	203 775-9000	656
Radeco of Ct Inc	Plainfield	CT	F	860 564-1220	3456
Ray Green Corp	Greenwich	CT	F	707 544-2662	1640
Revolution Lighting **(HQ)**	Stamford	CT	G	203 504-1111	4299
Revolution Lighting Tech Inc **(PA)**	Stamford	CT	C	203 504-1111	4300
Saphlux Inc	Branford	CT	G	475 221-8981	345
Servers Storage Networking LLC	Norwalk	CT	G	203 433-0808	3241
Silicon Catalyst LLC	Ridgefield	CT	G	203 240-0499	3684
Strain Measurement Devices Inc	Wallingford	CT	E	203 294-5800	4814
United Electric Controls Co	Milford	CT	D	203 877-2795	2377
Vishay Americas Inc **(HQ)**	Shelton	CT	B	203 452-5648	3886
1366 Technologies Inc	Bedford	MA	F	781 861-1611	7955
ABB Enterprise Software Inc	Boston	MA	G	617 574-1130	8334
Acacia Communications Inc **(PA)**	Maynard	MA	C	978 938-4896	12894
Accuprobe Corporation	Salem	MA	E	978 745-7878	14889
Aceinna Inc	Andover	MA	E	978 965-3200	7532
Addilat Inc **(PA)**	Woburn	MA	G	781 258-9963	17109
Advance Data Technology Inc	Topsfield	MA	F	978 801-4376	15852
Advanced Micro Devices Inc	Boxborough	MA	C	978 795-2500	8956
Aeroflex / Metelics Inc	Lowell	MA	G	603 641-3800	12341
Aerospace Semiconductor Inc	Lawrence	MA	F	978 688-1299	11990
Aetruim Incorporated	Billerica	MA	E	651 773-4200	8205
Albion Beams Inc	Manchester	MA	G	978 526-4406	12602
Allegro Microsystems LLC	Marlborough	MA	C	508 853-5000	12711
American Power Devices Inc	Lynn	MA	E	781 592-6090	12489
American Superconductor Corp **(PA)**	Ayer	MA	C	978 842-3000	7907
Ametek Inc	New Bedford	MA	G	508 998-4335	13358
Amicus Hlthcare Lving Ctrs LLC	North Chelmsford	MA	E	978 934-0000	13884
Amkor Technology Inc	Stoneham	MA	G	781 438-7800	15554
AMS Qi Inc	Cambridge	MA	G	617 797-4709	9389
Analog Devices Inc **(PA)**	Norwood	MA	A	781 329-4700	14130
Analog Devices Intl Inc **(HQ)**	Norwood	MA	F	781 329-4700	14131
Apeak Inc	Auburndale	MA	G	617 964-1709	7856
API Electronics Inc	Marlborough	MA	E	508 485 6350	12716
API Technologies Corp **(PA)**	Marlborough	MA	C	855 294-3800	12717
API Technologies Corporation	Marlborough	MA	D	508 485-0336	12718
Apple Mill Holding Company Inc	Pembroke	MA	F	781 826-9706	14392
Applied Materials	Gloucester	MA	G	978 282-2917	11160
Applied Materials Inc	Boxborough	MA	E	978 795-8000	8957
Applied Nanofemto Tech LLC	Lowell	MA	G	978 761-4293	12344
Ardeo Systems Inc	Haverhill	MA	G	978 373-4680	11405
Arm Inc	Waltham	MA	G	978 264-7300	16036
Arradiance LLC	Littleton	MA	F	508 202-0593	12293
Ase (us) Inc	Woburn	MA	G	781 305-5900	17123
Asm Nexx Inc	Billerica	MA	E	978 436-4600	8214
Atlas Devices LLC	Boston	MA	G	617 415-1657	8383
Aware Inc **(PA)**	Bedford	MA	D	781 276-4000	7962
Bae Systems Info & Elec Sys	Lexington	MA	B	603 885-4321	12208
Bidirectional Display Inc	Acton	MA	G	617 599-8282	7344
Black Earth Technologies Inc	Dighton	MA	G	508 397-1335	10336
Boston Process Tech Inc	Peabody	MA	F	978 854-5579	14316

	CITY	ST	EMP	PHONE	ENTRY #
Broadcom Corporation	Andover	MA	D	978 719-1300	7543
Cambridge Electronics Inc	Belmont	MA	G	617 710-7013	8067
Cavium Inc	Marlborough	MA	F	508 357-4111	12736
Celeno Communications	Belmont	MA	G	617 500-3683	8069
Ceramic Process Systems	Taunton	MA	G	508 222-0614	15736
Charge Analytics LLC	Boxford	MA	G	978 201-7952	8975
Component Hndng Inspctn Pckn	Peabody	MA	G	978 535-3997	14325
Composite Modules	Attleboro	MA	D	508 226-6969	7723
Contour Semiconductor Inc	North Billerica	MA	F	978 670-4100	13804
Control Resources Inc	Littleton	MA	E	978 486-4160	12297
CPS Technologies Corp	Norton	MA	C	508 222-0614	14073
Custom Mmic Design Svcs Inc	Chelmsford	MA	E	978 467-4290	9891
Desert Harvest Solar Farm LLC	Peabody	MA	G	978 531-2222	14329
Digital Lumens Incorporated	Boston	MA	E	617 723-1200	8505
Dolan-Jenner Industries Inc	Boxborough	MA	E	978 263-1400	8961
Dover Microsystems Inc	Waltham	MA	G	781 577-0300	16090
Drs Development LLC	Rochester	MA	G	774 271-0533	14785
Druck LLC **(HQ)**	Billerica	MA	C	978 437-1000	8238
Eastwind Communications Inc	Hyannis	MA	F	508 862-8600	11840
Electronic Products Inds Inc	Newburyport	MA	E	978 462-8101	13486
Elpakco Inc **(PA)**	Westford	MA	E	978 392-0400	16765
Encite LLC	Burlington	MA	G	781 750-8241	9267
Entegris Inc **(PA)**	Billerica	MA	A	978 436-6500	8246
Eos Photonics Inc	Cambridge	MA	G	617 945-9137	9468
Epi II Inc	Newburyport	MA	D	978 462-1514	13487
Eta Devices Inc	Cambridge	MA	E	617 577-8300	9473
Excelitas Technologies Corp **(DH)**	Waltham	MA	E	781 522-5910	16104
Flir Systems-Boston Inc **(HQ)**	North Billerica	MA	B	978 901-8000	13815
Forward Photonics LLC	Woburn	MA	F	617 767-3519	17184
Freebird Semiconductor Corp	Haverhill	MA	G	617 955-7152	11436
GE Infrastructure Sensing LLC **(DH)**	Billerica	MA	A	978 437-1000	8249
Graphenea Inc	Cambridge	MA	F	415 568-6243	9497
Gt Advanced Technologies Inc	Salem	MA	G	978 498-4294	14916
Guardion Inc	Burlington	MA	G	603 769-7265	9280
HCC Aegis Inc **(DH)**	New Bedford	MA	E	508 998-3141	13393
Heila Technologies Inc	Somerville	MA	G	954 829-4839	15181
Hittite Microwave LLC **(HQ)**	Chelmsford	MA	C	978 250-3343	9905
Huber + Shner Platis Photonics	Bedford	MA	F	781 275-5080	7981
Ii-VI Photonics (us) Inc **(HQ)**	Woburn	MA	E	781 938-1222	17200
Immedia Semiconductor Inc	North Reading	MA	F	978 296-4950	13985
Infineon Tech Americas Corp	Tewksbury	MA	G	978 640-3893	15819
Innovion Corporation	Wilmington	MA	G	978 267-4064	17005
Intel Massachusetts Inc	Hudson	MA	A	978 553-4000	11777
Ipg Photonics Corporation **(PA)**	Oxford	MA	B	508 373-1100	14263
Iqe Kc LLC	Taunton	MA	D	508 824-6696	15759
Isilon Systems LLC	Hopkinton	MA	G	206 315-7500	11723
Iwaki Pumps Inc **(DH)**	Holliston	MA	E	508 429-1440	11580
Ixys Intgrted Circuits Div LLC	Beverly	MA	D	978 524-6700	8142
Kcb Solutions LLC	Shirley	MA	F	978 425-0400	15088
Kita Usa Inc	Attleboro	MA	G	774 331-2265	7756
Kopin Corporation **(PA)**	Westborough	MA	C	508 870-5959	16630
Kopin Display Corporation **(PA)**	Westborough	MA	G	508 870-5959	16631
L T X International Inc	Norwood	MA	D	781 461-1000	14173
Lattice Semiconductor Corp	Burlington	MA	G	781 229-5819	9296
Lightmatter Inc	Boston	MA	E	857 244-0460	8667
Linear Technology LLC	North Chelmsford	MA	G	978 656-4750	13901
Macom Metelics LLC	Lowell	MA	D	978 656-2500	12400
Macom Tech Sltons Holdings Inc **(PA)**	Lowell	MA	C	978 656-2500	12401
Massachusetts Bay Tech Inc	Stoughton	MA	F	781 344-8809	15606
Maxim Integrated Products Inc	North Chelmsford	MA	A	978 934-7600	13903
Mediatek USA Inc	Woburn	MA	D	781 503-8000	17227
Mellanox Technologies Inc	Chelmsford	MA	G	978 439-5400	9916
Memsic Inc **(HQ)**	Andover	MA	G	978 738-0900	7569
Merrick Services	Millbury	MA	G	508 802-3751	13170
Metelics Corp	Lowell	MA	C	408 737-8197	12408
Micro Magnetics Inc	Fall River	MA	F	508 672-4489	10732
Microchip Technology Inc	Westborough	MA	C	774 760-0087	16634
Microscale Inc	Woburn	MA	G	781 995-2245	17230
Microsemi Corp- Massachusetts	Lowell	MA	D	978 442-5600	12409
Microsemi Corp- Massachusetts	Lawrence	MA	G	978 794-1666	12052
Microsemi Corp- Massachusetts	Lawrence	MA	B	978 620-2600	12053
Microsemi Corp-Colorado	Lawrence	MA	D	480 941-6300	12054
Microsemi Corporation	Lawrence	MA	D	781 665-1071	12055
Microsemi Corporation	Lowell	MA	D	978 442-5637	12410
Microsemi Corporation	Tewksbury	MA	G	978 232-3793	15823
Microsemi Corporation	Beverly	MA	G	978 232-0040	8154
Microsemi Nes Inc	Lawrence	MA	C	978 794-1666	12056
Micross Express	Woburn	MA	G	781 938-0866	17231
Microtronic Inc	Edgartown	MA	E	508 627-8951	10587
Mini-Systems Inc **(PA)**	North Attleboro	MA	C	508 695-1420	13765
Mini-Systems Inc	Plainville	MA	E	508 695-2000	14528
Murata Power Solutions Inc **(DH)**	Westborough	MA	C	508 339-3000	16637
Nano-Audio	Wellesley	MA	G	781 416-5096	16374
Nantero Inc	Woburn	MA	E	781 932-5338	17236
Nissin Ion Equipment Usa Inc	North Billerica	MA	F	978 362-2590	13849
North East Silicon Tech Inc	New Bedford	MA	D	508 999-2001	13429
Onset Computer Corporation	Bourne	MA	C	508 759-9500	8948
Optek Systems Inc	Groton	MA	G	978 448-9376	11293
Optomistic Products Inc	Leominster	MA	F	207 865-9181	12175
Overseas Project Advancement	West Newbury	MA	F	978 255-1816	16492
Performance Motion Devices Inc	Westford	MA	E	978 266-1210	16783
Philips Advanced Metrology Sys	Billerica	MA	G	508 647-8400	8274
Philips Holding USA Inc **(HQ)**	Andover	MA	C	978 687-1501	7582
Photronix Inc	Burlington	MA	G	781 221-0442	9319
Piconics Inc	Tyngsboro	MA	E	978 649-7501	15899
Precision Pcb Inc **(PA)**	Whitman	MA	G	781 447-6285	16925
Precision Sensing Devices Inc	Medfield	MA	G	508 359-2833	12917
Precisive LLC	Methuen	MA	G	781 850-4469	13043
Qbit Semiconductor Ltd	Littleton	MA	G	351 205-0005	12321
Qualcomm Incorporated	Andover	MA	B	858 587-1121	7590
Qualcomm Incorporated	Boxborough	MA	B	858 587-1121	8968
Quantance Inc **(PA)**	Woburn	MA	E	650 293-3300	17277
R F Integration Inc **(PA)**	North Billerica	MA	F	978 654-6770	13857
Radio Act Corporation	Brookline	MA	G	617 731-6542	9218
Raysolution LLC	Andover	MA	G	765 714-0645	7593
Raytheon Company	Quincy	MA	B	781 522-3000	14653
Raytheon Sutheast Asia Systems **(HQ)**	Billerica	MA	E	978 470-5000	8289
Realtime Dx Inc	Lexington	MA	G	508 479-9818	12259
Reinforced Structures For Elec	Worcester	MA	E	508 754-5316	17457
Renesas Electronics Amer Inc	Concord	MA	A	978 805-6900	10156
Rf1 Holding Company **(PA)**	Marlborough	MA	F	855 294-3800	12816
Rochester Electronics LLC **(PA)**	Newburyport	MA	C	978 462-9332	13531
Rochester Electronics LLC	Newburyport	MA	G	978 462-1248	13532
SA Photonics Inc	Lexington	MA	G	781 861-1430	12260
Sand 9 Inc	Cambridge	MA	E	617 358-0957	9641
Seminex Corporation	Peabody	MA	G	978 326-7700	14369
Semitech Solutions Inc	Acton	MA	G	978 589-3850	7386
Sevcon Inc **(HQ)**	Southborough	MA	E	508 281-5500	15365
Sheaumann Laser Inc	Marlborough	MA	G	508 970-0600	12825
Si Tech Inc	Topsfield	MA	G	978 887-3550	15865
Signet Products Corporation	North Attleboro	MA	G	650 592-3575	13779
Silex Microsystems Inc	Boston	MA	F	617 834-7197	8846
Silicon Transistor Corporation	Chelmsford	MA	D	978 256-3321	9932
Sionyx LLC **(PA)**	Beverly	MA	F	978 922-0684	8178
Skyworks Solutions Inc **(PA)**	Woburn	MA	A	781 376-3000	17297
Skyworks Solutions Inc	Andover	MA	C	978 327-6850	7606
Skyworks Solutions Inc	Woburn	MA	B	781 935-5150	17298
Soitec Usa Inc **(HQ)**	Gloucester	MA	F	978 531-2222	11210
Solect Energy Development LLC	Hopkinton	MA	G	508 250-8358	11736
Solect Energy Development LLC	Hopkinton	MA	F	508 598-3511	11737
Somerville Science and Tech	Somerville	MA	G	617 628-3150	15219
Sparta Kefalas Organics LLC	East Bridgewater	MA	G	978 810-5300	10420
Spectris Inc **(HQ)**	Westborough	MA	F	508 768-6400	16650
Spero Devices Inc	Acton	MA	G	978 849-8000	7388
Spire Corporation **(PA)**	Billerica	MA	B	978 584-3958	8297
Sst Components Inc **(PA)**	Billerica	MA	E	978 670-7300	8298
Stellar Industries Corp	Millbury	MA	E	508 865-1668	13177
Sunrise Systems Elec Co Inc **(PA)**	Pembroke	MA	G	781 826-9706	14428
Tego Inc	Waltham	MA	G	781 547-5680	16208
Tel Epion Inc	Billerica	MA	E	978 436-2300	8302
Telco Systems Inc **(HQ)**	Mansfield	MA	E	508 339-1516	12662
Teradyne Inc **(PA)**	North Reading	MA	B	978 370-2700	13990
Tessolar Inc	Woburn	MA	G	508 479-9818	17308
Texas Instruments Incorporated	Attleboro	MA	E	508 236-3800	7802
That Corporation **(PA)**	Milford	MA	E	508 478-9200	13148
Thought One LLC	North Andover	MA	G	408 623-3278	13730
Tier 7 Communications	Shirley	MA	G	978 425-9543	15095
Transene Company Inc	Danvers	MA	F	978 777-7860	10265
Twin Creeks Technologies Inc	Danvers	MA	E	978 777-0846	10268
Union Miniere	Boston	MA	E	617 960-5900	8895
Vacuum Plus Manufacturing Inc	Chelmsford	MA	F	978 441-3100	9939
Vanguard Solar Inc	Sudbury	MA	G	508 361-1463	15671
Verrillon Inc	North Grafton	MA	E	508 890-7100	13966
Vitalsensors Technologies LLC	Newton	MA	F	978 635-0450	13652
Vsea Inc	Gloucester	MA	E	978 282-2000	11218
Xcerra Corporation	Norwood	MA	E	781 461-1000	14208
Xp Power LLC	Gloucester	MA	D	978 282-0620	11220
Yankee Electrical Mfg Co	Wilbraham	MA	G	413 596-8256	16945
Fairchild Energy LLC	South Portland	ME	G	207 775-8100	7023
Fairchild Semiconductor Corp **(DH)**	South Portland	ME	B	207 775-8100	7024
Fairchild Semiconductor Corp	South Portland	ME	C	207 775-8100	7025
Fairchild Semiconductor W Corp	South Portland	ME	G	207 775-8100	7026
Ron Lavallee	Belgrade	ME	G	248 705-3231	5699
Vulcan Flex Circuit Corp	Porter	ME	D	603 883-1500	6606
4power LLC	Salem	NH	G	617 299-0068	19701
Advanced Consulting	Nashua	NH	G	603 882-5529	19099
Allegro Microsystems Inc	Manchester	NH	G	508 853-5000	18776
Allegro Microsystems LLC **(HQ)**	Manchester	NH	B	603 626-2300	18777
Ardent Concepts Inc	Hampton	NH	G	603 474-1760	18255
Bantry Components Inc	Manchester	NH	E	603 668-3210	18785
Be Semiconductor Inds USA Inc **(HQ)**	Salem	NH	E	603 626-4700	19711
Boxford Designs LLC	Derry	NH	G	603 216-2399	17973
Corfin Industries LLC	Manchester	NH	D	603 893-9900	18805
Cubic Wafer Inc	Merrimack	NH	G	603 546-0600	18996

	CITY	ST	EMP	PHONE	ENTRY #
Cxe Equipment Services LLC	Seabrook	NH	G	603 437-2477	19798
Cyclones Arena	Hudson	NH	F	603 880-4424	18381
Dale Vishay Electronics LLC	Hollis	NH	D	603 881-7799	18328
Distillation Tech Pdts LLC	Manchester	NH	G	603 935-7070	18766
Dutile Glines & Higgins Inc	Hooksett	NH	F	603 622-0452	18348
Eigenlight Corporation	Newmarket	NH	E	603 692-9200	19333
Eyepvideo Systems LLC	Danville	NH	G	603 382-2547	17968
Finetech	Amherst	NH	G	603 627-8989	17562
Gosolar NH LLC	Barrington	NH	E	603 948-1189	17618
Gpd Optoelectronics Corp	Salem	NH	E	603 894-6865	19739
Gt Advanced Cz LLC	Merrimack	NH	G	603 883-5200	19004
Gt Advanced Technologies Inc **(PA)**	Hudson	NH	C	603 883-5200	18394
Gt Advanced Technologies Ltd	Hudson	NH	G	603 883-5200	18395
Gtat Corporation	Nashua	NH	G	603 883-5200	19173
Gtat Corporation **(HQ)**	Hudson	NH	C	603 883-5200	18396
Impellimax Inc	Nashua	NH	F	603 886-9569	19185
Macom Tech Sltons Holdings Inc	Londonderry	NH	D	603 641-3800	18716
Masimo Semiconductor Inc	Hudson	NH	E	603 595-8900	18413
Melexis Inc	Nashua	NH	E	603 223-2362	19206
Micro-Precision Tech Inc	Salem	NH	E	603 893-7600	19752
Microsemi Corporation	Manchester	NH	C	978 232-3793	18873
Paragon Electronic Systems	Manchester	NH	F	603 645-7630	18898
Pd & E Electronics LLC	North Hampton	NH	G	603 964-3165	19386
Qmagiq LLC	Nashua	NH	G	603 821-3092	19242
Rob Geoffroy	Londonderry	NH	G	603 425-2517	18734
Saint-Gobain Glass Corporation	Milford	NH	F	603 673-7560	19076
Semikron Inc **(HQ)**	Hudson	NH	E	603 883-8102	18437
Signalquest LLC	Lebanon	NH	E	603 448-6266	18635
Silicon Sense Inc	Nashua	NH	G	603 891-4248	19261
Sparton Beckwood LLC	Plaistow	NH	D	603 382-3840	19524
Texas Instruments Incorporated	Manchester	NH	F	603 222-8500	18939
Texas Instruments Incorporated	Merrimack	NH	C	603 429-6079	19037
True North Networks LLC	Swanzey	NH	E	603 624-6777	19890
Two In One Manufacturing Inc	Nashua	NH	E	603 595-8212	19276
Unitrode Corporation **(HQ)**	Manchester	NH	B	603 222-8500	18945
Xilinx Inc	Nashua	NH	F	603 891-1096	19290
Ampleon USA Inc	Smithfield	RI	E	401 830-5420	21209
ATW Companies Inc **(PA)**	Warwick	RI	D	401 244-1002	21330
Cherry Semiconductor Corp	East Greenwich	RI	G	401 885-3600	20356
Enow Inc	Warwick	RI	F	401 732-7080	21360
Interplex Industries Inc **(DH)**	Rumford	RI	F	718 961-6212	21188
Lrv Properties LLC	Providence	RI	G	401 714-7001	21058
Narragansett Imaging Usa LLC	North Smithfield	RI	E	401 762-3800	20791
Numark International Inc	Cumberland	RI	F	954 761-7550	20335
Nxp Usa Inc	Smithfield	RI	G	401 830-5410	21241
Powerdocks LLC	Bristol	RI	G	401 253-3103	20099
Semicndctor Cmpnnts Inds of RI **(DH)**	East Greenwich	RI	A	401 885-3600	20379
Veterans Assembled Elec LLC **(PA)**	Providence	RI	G	401 228-6165	21150
Wei Inc **(PA)**	Cranston	RI	E	401 781-3904	20309
4382412 Canada Inc	Williston	VT	G	802 225-5911	22652
Allearth Renewables Inc	Williston	VT	E	802 872-9600	22654
Globalfoundries US 2 LLC	Essex Junction	VT	A	408 462-4452	21941
I C Haus Corp	Grand Isle	VT	G	802 372-8340	21998
Infineon Tech Americas Corp	Essex Junction	VT	E	802 769-6824	21947
Leddynamics Inc	Randolph	VT	D	802 728-4533	22298
Mobile Semiconductor Corp	Williston	VT	G	802 399-2449	22683
Nehp Inc	Williston	VT	D	802 652-1444	22685
Semiprobe Inc	Winooski	VT	G	802 860-7000	22723
Semivation	Essex Junction	VT	G	802 878-5153	21959

3675 Electronic Capacitors

	CITY	ST	EMP	PHONE	ENTRY #
Electronic Film Capacitors	Waterbury	CT	E	203 755-5629	4869
Newco Condenser Inc	Shelton	CT	G	475 882-4000	3839
Fortiming Corporation	Marlborough	MA	G	508 281-5980	12756
Philips Medical Systems Hsg **(PA)**	Andover	MA	E	978 687-1501	7583
Steinerfilm Inc	Williamstown	MA	C	413 458-9525	16961
Tdl Inc	Canton	MA	E	781 828-3366	9789
AVX Tantalum Corporation	Biddeford	ME	C	207 282-5111	5720
Standex International Corp **(PA)**	Salem	NH	E	603 893-9701	19769
Polyrack North America Corp	Cumberland	RI	G	401 770-1500	20340
S B E Inc **(PA)**	Barre	VT	E	802 476-4146	21638

3676 Electronic Resistors

	CITY	ST	EMP	PHONE	ENTRY #
Able Coil and Electronics Co	Bolton	CT	E	860 646-5686	273
Prime Technology LLC	North Branford	CT	C	203 481-5721	2974
Vishay Americas Inc **(HQ)**	Shelton	CT	B	203 452-5648	3886
Isotek Corporation	Swansea	MA	G	508 673-2900	15705
Mini-Systems Inc **(PA)**	North Attleboro	MA	C	508 695-1420	13765
Mini-Systems Inc	Attleboro	MA	D	508 695-0203	7768
Mini-Systems Inc	Plainville	MA	E	508 695-2000	14528
Philips Medical Systems Hsg **(PA)**	Andover	MA	E	978 687-1501	7583
Phoenix Electric Corp	Canton	MA	E	781 821-0200	9767
Sensata Technologies Ind Inc **(DH)**	Attleboro	MA	G	508 236-3800	7793
Wabash Technologies Inc **(DH)**	Attleboro	MA	D	260 355-4100	7808
Bantry Components Inc	Manchester	NH	E	603 668-3210	18785
Rcd Components LLC **(HQ)**	Manchester	NH	D	603 666-4627	18909
Two In One Manufacturing Inc	Nashua	NH	E	603 595-8212	19276

	CITY	ST	EMP	PHONE	ENTRY #
Cx Thin Films LLC	Cranston	RI	F	401 461-5500	20207
Honeywell International Inc	Woonsocket	RI	D	401 762-6200	21569

3677 Electronic Coils & Transformers

	CITY	ST	EMP	PHONE	ENTRY #
3M Purification Inc	Stafford Springs	CT	C	860 684-8628	4103
71 Pickett District Road LLC	New Milford	CT	G	860 350-5964	2786
Able Coil and Electronics Co	Bolton	CT	E	860 646-5686	273
Aer Control Systems LLC	North Haven	CT	G	203 772-4700	3003
Alpha Magnetics & Coils Inc	Torrington	CT	G	860 496-0122	4556
Bicron Electronics Company **(PA)**	Torrington	CT	D	860 482-2524	4566
Cable Technology Inc	Willington	CT	E	860 429-7889	5270
Classic Coil Company Inc	Bristol	CT	D	860 583-7600	541
Coils Plus Inc	Wolcott	CT	E	203 879-0755	5436
Future Manufacturing Inc	Bristol	CT	E	860 584-0685	565
Henkel Loctite Corporation **(DH)**	Rocky Hill	CT	E	860 571-5100	3714
JB Filtration LLC	Essex	CT	G	860 333-7962	1400
Microphase Corporation	Shelton	CT	E	203 866-8000	3833
Microtech Inc	Cheshire	CT	D	203 272-3234	745
Neeltran Inc	New Milford	CT	C	860 350-5964	2815
New England Filter Company Inc **(PA)**	Greenwich	CT	G	203 531-0500	1633
Omnicron Electronics	Putnam	CT	G	860 928-0377	3623
Purfx Inc	Westbrook	CT	G	860 399-4045	5161
Qtran Inc	Milford	CT	E	203 367-8777	2344
Quality Coils Incorporated **(PA)**	Bristol	CT	C	860 584-0927	598
Americansub	Dudley	MA	E	508 949-2320	10372
Atrex Energy Inc **(PA)**	Walpole	MA	E	781 461-8251	15988
ATW Electronics Inc	Charlestown	MA	F	617 304-3579	9824
Currier Engineering	Needham	MA	G	781 449-7706	13298
Degreasing Devices Co	Southbridge	MA	G	508 765-0045	15379
Excelitas Technologies Corp	Salem	MA	C	800 775-6786	14910
M V Mason Elec Inc	Walpole	MA	G	508 668-6200	15999
Magcap Engineering LLC	Canton	MA	F	781 821-2300	9754
Microwave Components Inc	Dracut	MA	F	978 453-6016	10365
Microwave Engineering Corp	North Andover	MA	D	978 685-2776	13718
Modular Air Filtration Systems	Raynham	MA	E	508 823-4900	14720
MV Mason Electronics Inc	Walpole	MA	G	508 668-6200	16004
Orbital Biosciences LLC **(PA)**	Topsfield	MA	G	978 887-5077	15864
Precision Electronics Corp	Marshfield	MA	F	781 834-6677	12865
Transcon Technologies Inc	Westfield	MA	E	413 562-7684	16736
Chemrock Corporation	Thomaston	ME	G	207 594-8225	7082
Porvair Filtration Group Inc	Caribou	ME	G	207 493-3027	5890
Design Consultants Associates	Hampstead	NH	F	603 329-4541	18239
GE Energy Management Svcs Inc	Somersworth	NH	C	603 692-2100	19838
Jmk Inc	Amherst	NH	E	603 886-4100	17569
Laconia Magnetics Inc	Laconia	NH	E	603 528-2766	18570
Ladesco Inc	Manchester	NH	C	603 623-3772	18857
Pd & E Electronics LLC	North Hampton	NH	G	603 964-3165	19386
Rcd Components LLC **(HQ)**	Manchester	NH	D	603 666-4627	18909
Rme Filters Inc	Amherst	NH	F	603 595-4573	17585
Technicoil LLC	Ossipee	NH	F	603 569-3100	19422
Vishay Hirel Systems LLC	Dover	NH	D	603 742-4375	18066
Bio Holdings Inc	Portsmouth	RI	F	401 683-5400	20918
Crest Manufacturing Company	Lincoln	RI	E	401 333-1350	20566
Kearney-National Inc	North Kingstown	RI	E	401 943-2686	20719
Schneider Electric It Corp **(DH)**	West Kingston	RI	A	401 789-5735	21471
Dynapower Company LLC **(PA)**	South Burlington	VT	C	802 860-7200	22447

3678 Electronic Connectors

	CITY	ST	EMP	PHONE	ENTRY #
Amphenol Corporation	Danbury	CT	C	203 743-9272	871
Amphenol Corporation **(PA)**	Wallingford	CT	D	203 265-8900	4700
Amphenol Corporation	Hamden	CT	D	203 287-2272	1732
Amphenol International Ltd **(HQ)**	Wallingford	CT	G	203 265-8900	4701
Bead Industries Inc **(PA)**	Milford	CT	E	203 301-0270	2251
Burndy LLC	Bethel	CT	D	203 792-1115	134
Component Concepts Inc	West Hartford	CT	G	860 523-4066	5062
Electro-Tech Inc	Cheshire	CT	E	203 271-1976	729
Hubbell Incorporated **(PA)**	Shelton	CT	D	475 882-4000	3813
Microtech Inc	Cheshire	CT	D	203 272-3234	745
Phoenix Company of Chicago Inc **(PA)**	Naugatuck	CT	D	630 595-2300	2489
Radiall Usa Inc	Wallingford	CT	C	203 776-2813	4794
RC Connectors LLC	Weatogue	CT	G	860 413-2196	5044
Surface Mount Devices LLC	Stamford	CT	G	203 322-8290	4336
Times Microwave Systems Inc **(HQ)**	Wallingford	CT	B	203 949-8400	4819
Winchester Interconnect Corp **(HQ)**	Norwalk	CT	E	203 741-5400	3271
Amphenol Alden Products Co **(HQ)**	Brockton	MA	C	508 427-7000	9118
Anderson Power Products Inc **(HQ)**	Sterling	MA	D	978 422-3600	15535
Atlee Delaware Incorporated	Melrose	MA	F	978 681-1003	12975
C & K Components LLC **(PA)**	Waltham	MA	D	617 969-3700	16056
Component Sources Intl	Westborough	MA	F	508 986-2300	16607
Cristek Interconnects Inc	Lowell	MA	G	978 735-2161	12363
Delta Electronics Mfg Corp	Beverly	MA	C	978 927-1060	8125
Electro-Term Inc	Springfield	MA	D	413 734-6469	15468
Elpakco Inc **(PA)**	Westford	MA	E	978 392-0400	16765
Global Interconnect Inc	Pocasset	MA	D	508 563-6306	14595
Ideal Industries Inc	Sterling	MA	C	978 422-3600	15540
Ksaria Corporation **(PA)**	Methuen	MA	D	866 457-2742	13030
L-Com Inc **(DH)**	North Andover	MA	D	978 682-6936	13715

	CITY	ST	EMP	PHONE	ENTRY #
Microwave Engineering Corp	North Andover	MA	D	978 685-2776	13718
Nabson Inc	Taunton	MA	G	617 323-1101	15767
Paricon Technologies Corp	Taunton	MA	F	508 823-0876	15771
Reinforced Structures For Elec	Worcester	MA	E	508 754-5316	17457
San-Tron Inc **(PA)**	Ipswich	MA	D	978 356-1585	11936
Te Connectivity Corporation	Norwood	MA	B	781 278-5273	14203
Te Connectivity Corporation	Worcester	MA	B	717 592-4299	17486
Texas Instruments Incorporated	Attleboro	MA	E	508 236-3800	7802
Trego Inc	Wareham	MA	G	508 291-3816	16255
Tru Technologies Inc	Peabody	MA	C	978 532-0775	14379
Winchester Interconnect Corp	Peabody	MA	D	978 532-0775	14383
Winchester Interconnect Corp	Peabody	MA	D	978 532-0775	14384
Winchester Interconnect Corp	Franklin	MA	F	978 717-2543	11098
Winchster Interconnect Rf Corp **(HQ)**	Peabody	MA	D	978 532-0775	14385
Wotech Associates	Woburn	MA	G	781 935-3787	17324
Xybol Interlynks Inc	Ipswich	MA	F	978 356-0750	11939
Alpha Technologies Group Inc	Pelham	NH	B	603 635-2800	19428
Amphenol Corporation	Nashua	NH	B	603 879-3000	19114
Amphenol Printed Circuits Inc	Nashua	NH	A	603 324-4500	19115
Burndy LLC	Littleton	NH	C	603 444-6781	18655
Electronics Aid Inc	Marlborough	NH	G	603 876-4161	18959
Hubbell Incorporated	Manchester	NH	C	603 647-5000	18838
Incon Inc	Hudson	NH	E	603 595-0550	18398
Q A Technology Company Inc	Hampton	NH	D	603 926-1193	18269
Special Hermetic Products	Wilton	NH	E	603 654-2002	19989
Teledyne Instruments Inc	Portsmouth	NH	C	603 474-5571	19624
Wavelink LLC	Manchester	NH	F	603 606-7489	18954
Xma Corporation	Manchester	NH	E	603 222-2256	18958
Advanced Interconnections Corp	West Warwick	RI	D	401 823-5200	21476
Ametek Scp Inc **(HQ)**	Westerly	RI	D	401 596-6658	21515
Atec	Wakefield	RI	G	401 782-6950	21267
Photonic Marketing Corporation	Lincoln	RI	G	401 333-3538	20591
Precision Trned Cmponents Corp	Smithfield	RI	D	401 232-3377	21244

3679 Electronic Components, NEC

	CITY	ST	EMP	PHONE	ENTRY #
71 Pickett District Road LLC	New Milford	CT	G	860 350-5964	2786
AB Electronics Inc	Brookfield	CT	E	203 740-2793	632
Able Coil and Electronics Co	Bolton	CT	E	860 646-5686	273
Alpha-Core Inc	Shelton	CT	E	203 954-0050	3773
Arccos Golf LLC	Stamford	CT	E	844 692-7226	4143
Ashcroft Inc **(DH)**	Stratford	CT	B	203 378-8281	4392
Bead Industries Inc **(PA)**	Milford	CT	E	203 301-0270	2251
Bicron Electronics Company **(PA)**	Torrington	CT	D	860 482-2524	4566
Bridgeport Magnetics Group Inc	Shelton	CT	E	203 954-0050	3784
Cable Electronics Inc	Hartford	CT	G	860 953-0300	1809
Component Concepts Inc	West Hartford	CT	G	860 523-4066	5062
Crystal Fairfield Tech LLC	New Milford	CT	F	860 354-2111	2795
Data Signal Corporation	Milford	CT	E	203 882-5393	2273
Dsaencore LLC **(PA)**	Brookfield	CT	D	203 740-4200	642
Eaton Aerospace LLC	Bethel	CT	E	203 796-6000	150
Ebl Products Inc	East Hartford	CT	F	860 290-3737	1190
Edal Industries Inc	East Haven	CT	E	203 467-2591	1248
Electro-Tech Inc	Cheshire	CT	E	203 271-1976	729
Electronic Connection Corp	Waterbury	CT	E	860 243-3356	4868
Ens Microwave LLC	Danbury	CT	G	203 794-7940	911
General Electro Components	Glastonbury	CT	G	860 659-3573	1554
Goodrich Corporation	Danbury	CT	B	505 345-9031	926
Hartford Electric Sup Co Inc	Rocky Hill	CT	F	860 760-4887	3711
Imperial Elctrnic Assembly Inc	Brookfield	CT	D	203 740-8425	647
Insys Micro Inc	Norwalk	CT	G	917 566-5045	3175
Kbc Electronics Inc	Milford	CT	F	203 298-9654	2306
Linemaster Switch Corporation	Plainfield	CT	G	860 564-7713	3453
Lq Mechatronics Inc	Branford	CT	G	203 433-4430	328
Microtech Inc	Cheshire	CT	D	203 272-3234	745
Neeltran Inc	New Milford	CT	C	860 350-5964	2815
Northeast Electronics Corp	Milford	CT	D	203 878-3511	2324
Osda Contract Services Inc	Milford	CT	E	203 878-2155	2327
Osda Inc	Milford	CT	G	203 878-2155	2328
Park Distributories Inc	Bridgeport	CT	F	203 366-7200	464
Power Controls Inc	Wallingford	CT	F	203 284-0235	4784
Power Trans Co Inc	Oxford	CT	G	203 881-0314	3419
Precision Electronic Assembly	Monroe	CT	F	203 452-1839	2413
Preferred PDT & Mktg Group LLC	Shelton	CT	G	203 567-0221	3860
Prime Technology LLC	North Branford	CT	C	203 481-5721	2974
Protronix Inc	Wallingford	CT	F	203 269-5858	4791
Qtran Inc	Milford	CT	E	203 367-8777	2344
Rel-Tech Electronics Inc	Milford	CT	D	203 877-8770	2347
Robert Warren LLC **(PA)**	Westport	CT	E	203 247-3347	5227
Sean Mecesery	Cos Cob	CT	G	203 869-2277	829
Siemon Company **(PA)**	Watertown	CT	A	860 945-4200	5024
Surface Mount Devices LLC	Stamford	CT	G	203 322-8290	4336
Sysdyne Technologies LLC	Stamford	CT	F	203 327-3649	4339
Technical Manufacturing Corp	Durham	CT	E	860 349-1735	1094
Tgs Cables	Meriden	CT	G	203 668-6568	2139
Times Microwave Systems Inc **(HQ)**	Wallingford	CT	B	203 949-8400	4819
Topex Inc	Danbury	CT	F	203 748-5918	999
Tornik Inc	Rocky Hill	CT	C	860 282-6081	3731
Transformer Technology Inc	Durham	CT	F	860 349-1061	1095
Tri Source Inc	Shelton	CT	F	203 924-7030	3882
Tritex Corporation	Waterbury	CT	C	203 756-7441	4967
USA Circuits LLC	Sandy Hook	CT	G	203 364-1378	3746
Validus DC Systems LLC	Brookfield	CT	F	203 448-3600	663
Verotec Inc	North Haven	CT	G	603 821-9921	3068
Accellent Holdings Corp	Wilmington	MA	A	978 570-6900	16962
Acon Inc	South Easton	MA	F	508 230-8022	15268
Acumentrics Rups LLC	Walpole	MA	E	617 932-7877	15987
Advanced Electronic Controls	West Springfield	MA	G	413 736-3625	16505
Allston Power LLC	Brighton	MA	F	617 562-4054	9093
Americansub	Dudley	MA	E	508 949-2320	10372
Apem Inc **(HQ)**	Haverhill	MA	E	978 372-1602	11404
API Technologies Corporation	Marlborough	MA	D	508 485-0336	12718
API Technologies Corporation	Marlborough	MA	D	508 251-6400	12719
Audio Video Designs	Nantucket	MA	G	508 325-9989	13220
Aved Electronics LLC	North Billerica	MA	D	978 453-6393	13794
Bae Systems Info & Elec Sys	Lexington	MA	B	603 885-4321	12208
Beta Dyne Inc	Bridgewater	MA	F	508 697-1993	9064
Biophysical Devices Inc	Somerville	MA	G	617 629-0304	15159
C & K Components LLC **(PA)**	Waltham	MA	D	617 969-3700	16056
Carlo Gavazzi Incorporated	Brockton	MA	G	508 588-6110	9126
Case Assembly Solutions Inc	South Easton	MA	E	508 238-5665	15273
Ceramic To Metal Seals Inc	Melrose	MA	F	781 665-5002	12977
Chassis Engineering LLC	Rowley	MA	F	978 948-0826	14850
Cmt Filters Inc	Marlborough	MA	E	508 258-6400	12738
Cooper Interconnect Inc	Chelsea	MA	D	617 389-7080	9950
Copley Controls Corporation **(DH)**	Canton	MA	B	781 828-8090	9722
Courtsmart Digital Systems Inc	North Chelmsford	MA	E	978 251-3300	13891
Cullinan Manufacturing Inc	Topsfield	MA	E	978 465-1110	15855
Cuming Microwave Corporation **(HQ)**	Avon	MA	D	508 521-6700	7884
Currier Engineering	Needham	MA	G	781 449-7706	13298
Datacon Inc	Burlington	MA	E	781 273-5800	9253
Datel Inc	Mansfield	MA	E	508 964-5131	12627
Delta Electronics Mfg Corp	Beverly	MA	C	978 927-1060	8125
Desco Electronics Inc	Plainville	MA	F	508 643-1950	14517
Design Mark Industries Inc	Wareham	MA	D	800 451-3275	16244
Designers Metalcraft	East Bridgewater	MA	G	508 378-0404	10412
Diamond Rf LLC	Littleton	MA	G	978 486-0039	12301
Dl Technology LLC	Haverhill	MA	F	978 374-6451	11425
Drs Power Technology Inc	Fitchburg	MA	C	978 343-9719	10823
Dsk Engineering and Technology	Waltham	MA	G	413 289-6485	16092
Dss Circuits Inc	Worcester	MA	G	508 852-8061	17367
Dynawave Cable Incorporated	Haverhill	MA	G	978 469-9448	11428
Dynawave Incorporated	Haverhill	MA	D	978 469-0555	11429
East West Boston LLC	Boston	MA	D	617 598-3000	8516
Electronic Assemblies Mfg Inc	Methuen	MA	E	978 374-6840	13019
Embr Labs Inc	Charlestown	MA	G	413 218-0629	9834
Esmail Riyaz	Andover	MA	G	978 689-3837	7547
Etc Components Usa Inc	Worcester	MA	G	508 353-7075	17372
Excelitas Technologies Corp	Salem	MA	C	800 775-6786	14910
Excelitas Technologies Corp **(DH)**	Waltham	MA	E	781 522-5910	16104
First Electronics Corporation	Dorchester	MA	D	617 288-2430	10342
Flintec Inc	Hudson	MA	E	978 562-4548	11774
Fraen Corporation **(PA)**	Reading	MA	C	781 205-5300	14734
General Manufacturing Corp	North Billerica	MA	E	978 667-5514	13822
Global Interconnect Inc	Pocasset	MA	D	508 563-6306	14595
Graytron Inc	Ashfield	MA	G	413 625-2456	7651
H & T Specialty Co Inc	Waltham	MA	F	781 893-3866	16123
Harvard Scientific Corporation	Cambridge	MA	F	617 876-5033	9505
Hdm Systems Corporation	Brighton	MA	F	617 562-4054	9101
Herley Industries Inc	Woburn	MA	C	781 729-9450	17199
High Voltage Engineering Corp	Wakefield	MA	F	781 224-1001	15954
Hottinger Bldwin Msrements Inc **(DH)**	Marlborough	MA	D	508 624-4500	12775
Hxi LLC	Harvard	MA	F	978 772-7774	11379
Intellisense Software Corp	Lynnfield	MA	E	781 933-8098	12550
Interface Prcsion Bnchwrks Inc	Orange	MA	G	978 544-8866	14219
K V A Electronics	Billerica	MA	G	978 262-2264	8260
Kennetron Inc	East Taunton	MA	G	508 828-9363	10515
Kernco Inc	Danvers	MA	F	978 777-1956	10229
Keystone Precision Inc	Pepperell	MA	G	978 433-8484	14441
Ksaria Corporation **(PA)**	Methuen	MA	D	866 457-2742	13030
L3 Technologies Inc	Burlington	MA	C	781 270-2100	9295
Liberty Engineering Inc	Newton	MA	E	617 965-6644	13609
M & G Metal Inc	Clarksburg	MA	G	413 664-4057	10073
Macom Technology Solutions Inc	Lowell	MA	G	978 656-2500	12402
Macom Technology Solutions Inc **(HQ)**	Lowell	MA	B	978 656-2500	12403
Magnetic Sciences Inc	Acton	MA	G	978 266-9355	7372
Massa Products Corporation	Hingham	MA	D	781 749-3120	11501
Massmicro LLC	Canton	MA	F	781 828-6110	9756
Massmicroelectronics LLC	Canton	MA	F	781 828-6110	9757
Matthew Associates Inc	Waban	MA	G	617 965-6126	15938
Meehan Electronics Corporation	North Adams	MA	F	413 664-9371	13681
Metal Processing Co Inc	Tyngsboro	MA	G	978 649-1289	15896
Metalogic Industries LLC	Dudley	MA	F	508 461-6787	10381
Micrometal Technologies Inc **(PA)**	Newburyport	MA	F	978 462-3600	13513
Microsorb Technologies Inc	Franklin	MA	G	401 767-2269	11065

	CITY	ST	EMP	PHONE	ENTRY #
Microtek Inc	Chicopee	MA	C	413 593-1025	10046
Microwave Cmpnents Systems Inc	Westborough	MA	F	508 466-8400	16636
Microwave Development Labs Inc	Needham Heights	MA	D	781 292-6600	13337
Microwave Engineering Corp	North Andover	MA	D	978 685-2776	13718
Midas Technology Inc	Woburn	MA	E	781 938-0069	17232
Minarik Corporation	Franklin	MA	G	781 329-2700	11067
Mioe Inc	Andover	MA	G	978 494-9460	7572
Mornsun America LLC	Milford	MA	G	978 293-3923	13129
Mti-Milliren Technologies Inc	Newburyport	MA	E	978 465-6064	13516
Murata Power Solutions Inc **(DH)**	Westborough	MA	C	508 339-3000	16637
Musical Playground	Centerville	MA	G	508 778-6679	9818
N&N Manufacturing Inc **(PA)**	Topsfield	MA	F	978 465-1110	15862
Nanosemi Inc	Waltham	MA	E	781 472-2832	16157
New England Cm Inc	Franklin	MA	G	508 541-1307	11069
Noeveon Inc	Wilmington	MA	G	978 642-5004	17031
Orion Industries Incorporated	Ayer	MA	E	978 772-0020	7932
Paricon Technologies Corp	Taunton	MA	F	508 823-0876	15771
Parisi Associates LLC	Chelmsford	MA	F	978 667-8700	9921
Photonis Scientific Inc **(DH)**	Sturbridge	MA	D	508 347-4000	15646
Piezo Systems Inc	Woburn	MA	G	781 933-4850	17265
Polyonics Corporation	Newburyport	MA	F	978 462-3600	13522
Port Electronics Corporation	Lawrence	MA	F	800 253-8510	12072
Power Guide Marketing Inc **(PA)**	Worcester	MA	G	508 853-7357	17444
Protek Power North America Inc	Hudson	MA	G	978 567-9615	11808
Quartzite Processing Inc	Malden	MA	F	781 322-3611	12592
Raytheon Arabian Systems Co	Billerica	MA	G	978 858-4547	8283
Raytheon European MGT Systems	Billerica	MA	G	978 858-4547	8284
Raytheon Intl Support Co	Billerica	MA	G	978 858-4547	8285
Raytheon Korean Support Co	Billerica	MA	F	978 858-4547	8286
Raytheon Middle E Systems Co	Billerica	MA	G	978 858-4547	8287
Raytheon Radar Ltd	Billerica	MA	G	978 858-4547	8288
Raytheon Tchnical ADM Svcs Ltd	Billerica	MA	G	978 858-4547	8290
REA Associates Inc	North Billerica	MA	G	209 521-2727	13860
Rife Mltplwave Oscillators LLC	Brewster	MA	G	508 737-8468	9057
Schott North America Inc	Southbridge	MA	D	508 765-7450	15402
Sensata Technologies Inc **(HQ)**	Attleboro	MA	A	508 236-3800	7792
Sensata Technologies Mass Inc **(DH)**	Attleboro	MA	D	508 236-3800	7794
Sie Computing Solutions Inc	Brockton	MA	D	508 588-6110	9174
Sinclair Manufacturing Co LLC	Norton	MA	D	508 222-7440	14089
Skyworks Solutions Inc	Woburn	MA	B	781 935-5150	17298
Smiths Intrcnnect Americas Inc	Hudson	MA	C	978 568-0451	11817
Socomec Inc **(DH)**	Watertown	MA	F	617 245-0447	16317
SRI Hermetics Inc	Haverhill	MA	G	508 321-1023	11476
Star Engineering Inc	North Attleboro	MA	E	508 316-1492	13781
Starboard Exchange Inc	Beverly	MA	G	978 810-5577	8181
Sunburst Electronic Manufactur **(PA)**	West Bridgewater	MA	D	508 580-1881	16458
Synqor Holdings LLC	Boxborough	MA	D	978 849-0600	8970
Synqor Inc **(PA)**	Boxborough	MA	C	978 849-0600	8971
Texas Instruments Incorporated	Attleboro	MA	E	508 236-3800	7802
That Corporation **(PA)**	Milford	MA	E	508 478-9200	13148
Theodores	Taunton	MA	G	508 409-1421	15790
Thorndike Corporation	East Bridgewater	MA	F	508 378-9797	10421
Toshiba America Electronic	Marlborough	MA	G	508 481-0034	12837
Tru Technologies Inc	Peabody	MA	C	978 532-0775	14379
V-Tron Electronics Corp	Attleboro	MA	D	508 761-9100	7805
Vicor Corporation **(PA)**	Andover	MA	B	978 470-2900	7616
Victor Microwave Inc	Wakefield	MA	F	781 245-4472	15982
Voltree Power Inc	Canton	MA	G	781 858-4939	9794
Wasik Associates Inc	Dracut	MA	F	978 454-9787	10371
Wurszt Inc	Wilbraham	MA	G	413 599-4900	16944
Advance Electronic Concepts	Portland	ME	G	207 797-9825	6609
Artel Inc	Westbrook	ME	E	207 854-0860	7180
Chip Component Electronx	Limington	ME	G	207 510-7608	6347
Micronetixx Microwave LLC	Lewiston	ME	F	207 786-2000	6305
603 Manufacturing LLC	Hudson	NH	G	603 578-9876	18368
Aavid Corporation	Laconia	NH	A	603 528-3400	18549
Accelerator Systems Inc	Atkinson	NH	G	603 898-6010	17602
Additive Circuits Inc	Laconia	NH	G	603 366-1578	18552
Advanced Design & Mfg Inc	Portsmouth	NH	E	603 430-7573	19532
American Power Design Inc	Windham	NH	F	603 894-4446	19998
Amphenol Printed Circuits Inc	Nashua	NH	A	603 324-4500	19115
Anaren Ceramics Inc	Salem	NH	D	603 898-2883	19706
Asia Direct LLC	Plaistow	NH	B	603 382-9485	19507
Atc Power Systems Inc	Merrimack	NH	E	603 429-0391	18985
Bae Systems Info & Elec Sys	Hudson	NH	A	603 885-4321	18376
Bae Systems Info & Elec Sys	Merrimack	NH	B	603 885-4321	18990
Cobham Exeter Inc	Exeter	NH	B	603 775-5200	18117
Custom Manufacturing Svcs Inc	Nashua	NH	E	603 883-1355	19141
Data Electronic Devices Inc	Salem	NH	C	603 893-2047	19720
Electronics Aid Inc	Marlborough	NH	G	603 876-4161	18959
Ferrite Microwave Tech LLC	Nashua	NH	E	603 881-5234	19156
Finite Surface Mount Tech LLC	Merrimack	NH	G	603 423-0300	19000
Frontier Design Group LLC	Lebanon	NH	G	603 448-6283	18622
Gill Design Inc	Windham	NH	G	603 890-1237	20006
Hammamatsu Corporation	Hudson	NH	G	603 883-3888	18397
Janco Electronics Inc	Rollinsford	NH	D	603 742-1581	19692
Long Range LLC	Franklin	NH	G	603 934-3009	18159

	CITY	ST	EMP	PHONE	ENTRY #
Metz Electronics Corp	Gilford	NH	E	603 524-8806	18191
Micro Metal Components Inc	Deerfield	NH	G	603 463-5986	17970
Microfab Inc	Manchester	NH	G	603 621-9522	18872
Miltronics Mfg Svcs Inc	Keene	NH	F	603 352-3333	18516
Monzite Corporation **(HQ)**	Nashua	NH	F	617 429-7050	19209
Odhner Holographics	Amherst	NH	G	603 673-8651	17580
Pd & E Electronics LLC	North Hampton	NH	G	603 964-3165	19386
Pgc Wire & Cable LLC	Hudson	NH	F	603 821-7300	18426
Phoenix Resources	Goshen	NH	G	603 863-9096	18215
Princeton Technology Corp	Hudson	NH	D	603 595-1987	18428
Provencal Manufacturing Inc **(PA)**	Newfields	NH	G	603 772-6716	19319
Remcon-North Corporation	Meredith	NH	D	603 279-7091	18977
Rf Logic LLC **(PA)**	Hudson	NH	E	603 578-9876	18435
RH Laboratories Inc	Nashua	NH	E	603 459-5900	19252
Rob Geoffroy	Londonderry	NH	G	603 425-2517	18734
Scott Electronics Inc **(PA)**	Salem	NH	D	603 893-2845	19766
Semiconductor Circuits Inc **(PA)**	Atkinson	NH	F	603 893-2330	17607
Sonesys LLC	Merrimack	NH	F	603 423-9000	19031
Special Hermetic Products	Wilton	NH	E	603 654-2002	19989
Stellar Manufacturing Inc	Salem	NH	E	978 241-9537	19771
Velocity Manufacturing Inc	Exeter	NH	E	603 773-2386	18136
Versatile Subcontracting LLC	Northfield	NH	G	603 286-8081	19409
Vette Thermal Solutions LLC **(HQ)**	Portsmouth	NH	F	603 635-2800	19629
W5 Circuits LLC	North Hampton	NH	G	603 964-6780	19388
Andon Electronics Corporation	Lincoln	RI	E	401 333-0388	20555
Charter Industries Inc	Warren	RI	G	401 245-0850	21293
Cooliance Inc	Warwick	RI	F	401 921-6500	21346
Federal Electronics Inc	Cranston	RI	D	401 944-6200	20225
IDS Highway Safety Inc	Cumberland	RI	G	401 333-0740	20328
Kearney-National Inc	North Kingstown	RI	E	401 943-2686	20719
Narragansett Imaging Usa LLC	North Smithfield	RI	E	401 762-3800	20791
Porta Phone Co Inc	Narragansett	RI	E	401 789-8700	20646
Precision Trned Cmponents Corp	Smithfield	RI	D	401 232-3377	21244
Raytheon Company	Portsmouth	RI	D	401 847-8000	20938
Ritronics Inc	Warwick	RI	F	401 732-8175	21414
Staffall Inc	Cranston	RI	E	401 461-5554	20291
Veterans Assembled Elec LLC **(PA)**	Providence	RI	G	401 228-6165	21150
Aviatron Inc (us)	South Burlington	VT	F	802 865-9318	22437
Image Tek Mfg Inc	Springfield	VT	E	802 885-6208	22502
Infineon Tech Americas Corp	Essex Junction	VT	E	802 769-6824	21947
Itech Data Services Inc	South Burlington	VT	G	802 383-1500	22450
Moscow Mills Incorporated	Stowe	VT	F	802 253-2036	22524
Necsel Intllctual Property Inc	Vergennes	VT	E	802 877-6432	22554
Prom Software Inc	South Burlington	VT	F	802 862-7500	22462
Sammarval Co Ltd	Grafton	VT	G	802 843-2637	21996
Village of Orleans	Orleans	VT	G	802 754-8584	22253

3691 Storage Batteries

	CITY	ST	EMP	PHONE	ENTRY #
B S T Systems Inc	Plainfield	CT	D	860 564-4078	3451
Clarios	Meriden	CT	D	678 297-4040	2086
Duracell Company **(HQ)**	Bethel	CT	E	203 796-4000	144
Duracell Company	Bethel	CT	A	203 796-4000	145
Duracell Manufacturing Inc	Bethel	CT	G	203 796-4000	146
Duracell US Holding LLC **(HQ)**	Bethel	CT	F	203 796-4000	148
Evercel Inc **(PA)**	Stamford	CT	D	781 741-8800	4195
Hbl America Inc **(HQ)**	Rocky Hill	CT	G	860 257-9800	3713
Nofet LLC	New Haven	CT	F	203 848-9064	2719
Saft America Inc	North Haven	CT	E	203 234-8333	3061
24m Technologies Inc	Cambridge	MA	G	617 553-1012	9366
A123 Systems LLC	Waltham	MA	C	617 778-5700	16020
Advanced Battery Systems Inc	Halifax	MA	G	508 378-2284	11313
American Battery Company LLC	Norwood	MA	G	781 440-0325	14127
Battery Resourcers LLC	Worcester	MA	G	206 948-6325	17346
Boston-Power Inc **(PA)**	Westborough	MA	D	508 366-0885	16595
Fastcap Systems Corporation	Boston	MA	F	857 239-7500	8539
Integer Holdings Corporation	Canton	MA	C	781 830-5800	9744
L3 Technologies Inc	Foxboro	MA	G	617 895-6841	10891
Lionano Inc	Woburn	MA	G	607 216-8156	17214
Mega-Power Inc	Newton	MA	G	800 982-4339	13613
Power Solutions LLC **(PA)**	Swansea	MA	F	800 876-9373	15713
Rolls Battery of New England	Salem	MA	G	978 745-3333	14939
Solidenergy Systems LLC	Woburn	MA	E	617 972-3412	17299
Thermacell Corporation	Bedford	MA	F	816 510-9428	8015
Titan Advnced Enrgy Sltons Inc	Salem	MA	F	561 654-5558	14946
Tracer Technologies Inc	Somerville	MA	E	617 776-6410	15224
Xilectric Inc	Fall River	MA	G	617 312-5678	10785
Tim Kat Inc	Lewiston	ME	G	207 784-9675	6325
Casanna Designs	Tiverton	RI	G	401 835-4029	21255
Eaglepicher Technologies LLC	East Greenwich	RI	F	401 471-6580	20363
Ener-Tek International Inc	East Greenwich	RI	C	401 471-6580	20366

3692 Primary Batteries: Dry & Wet

	CITY	ST	EMP	PHONE	ENTRY #
B S T Systems Inc	Plainfield	CT	D	860 564-4078	3451
Duracell Manufacturing LLC	Bethel	CT	C	203 796-4000	147
Vitec Production Solutions Inc **(HQ)**	Shelton	CT	D	203 929-1100	3887
Electrochem Solutions Inc	Raynham	MA	C	781 575-0800	14714
Integer Holdings Corporation	Canton	MA	C	781 830-5800	9744

	CITY	ST	EMP	PHONE	ENTRY #
Ener-Tek International Inc	East Greenwich	RI	C	401 471-6580	20366
Energizer Manufacturing Inc	Bennington	VT	E	802 442-6301	21669

3694 Electrical Eqpt For Internal Combustion Engines

	CITY	ST	EMP	PHONE	ENTRY #
All Tech Auto/Truck Electric	Danbury	CT	G	203 790-8990	868
Beede Electrical Instr Co Inc	North Stonington	CT	C	603 753-6362	3071
Merl Inc	Meriden	CT	G	203 237-8811	2106
Simmonds Precision Pdts Inc	Danbury	CT	E	203 797-5000	994
West End Auto Parts	North Branford	CT	G	203 453-9009	2984
Blackburn Energy Inc	Amesbury	MA	G	800 342-9194	7480
Jnc Rebuilders Inc	Ipswich	MA	G	978 356-2996	11925
Liquidsky Technologies Inc **(PA)**	Norwood	MA	F	857 389-9893	14175
Mobile Specialties	Lawrence	MA	G	978 416-0107	12059
Pellion Technologies Inc	Arlington	MA	E	617 547-3191	7632
Tanyx Measurements Inc	Billerica	MA	E	978 671-0183	8299
Taylor Rental Center	East Longmeadow	MA	G	413 525-2576	10496
Veoneer Roadscape Auto Inc	Lowell	MA	G	978 656-2500	12444
Veoneer Roadscape Auto Inc **(DH)**	Lowell	MA	G	978 656-2500	12445
Veoneer Us Inc	Lowell	MA	C	978 674-6500	12446
Gauss Corporation	Scarborough	ME	F	207 883-4121	6918
Electrocraft New Hampshire Inc **(DH)**	Dover	NH	E	603 742-3330	18021
Ev Launchpad LLC	Portsmouth	NH	F	603 828-2919	19561
Hubbell Incorporated	Manchester	NH	C	603 647-5000	18838
Kinne Electric Service Company	Manchester	NH	G	603 622-0441	18856
Rickss Motorsport Electrics	Hampstead	NH	G	603 329-9901	18249
Antaya Inc	Warwick	RI	E	401 941-7050	21324
Antaya Technologies Corp	Warwick	RI	C	401 921-3197	21325
Simmonds Precision Pdts Inc **(DH)**	Vergennes	VT	A	802 877-4000	22556
Wicor Americas Inc **(HQ)**	Saint Johnsbury	VT	F	802 751-3404	22397

3695 Recording Media

	CITY	ST	EMP	PHONE	ENTRY #
20/20 Software Inc	Stamford	CT	G	203 316-5500	4122
BEI Holdings Inc	Wallingford	CT	F	203 741-9300	4709
Cogz Systems LLC	Woodbury	CT	F	203 263-7882	5484
Dataquest Korea Inc	Stamford	CT	G	239 561-4862	4186
Dictaphone Corporation **(HQ)**	Stratford	CT	C	203 381-7000	4409
Adaptive Optics Associates Inc **(DH)**	Devens	MA	D	978 757-9600	10317
C2c Systems Inc	Westborough	MA	F	508 870-2205	16597
ER Enterprises LLC	Newton	MA	G	617 296-9140	13590
Flexible Information Systems	Needham Heights	MA	G	781 326-9977	13333
Go2 Media Inc	Boston	MA	F	617 457-7870	8572
Information Server Co	Sudbury	MA	G	978 443-1871	15658
Intellisense Software Corp	Lynnfield	MA	E	781 933-8098	12550
Media Scope International Inc	North Attleboro	MA	G	508 643-2988	13762
Qsr International Americas Inc	Burlington	MA	G	617 607-5112	9326
Queues Enforth Development Inc	Stoneham	MA	F	781 870-1100	15571
Sony Dadc	Cambridge	MA	G	617 714-5776	9657
E Crane Computing Inc	Concord	NH	G	603 226-4041	17898
Mad River Media	Waitsfield	VT	G	802 496-9173	22567
Soro Systems Inc	South Royalton	VT	G	802 763-2248	22493

3699 Electrical Machinery, Eqpt & Splys, NEC

	CITY	ST	EMP	PHONE	ENTRY #
Advanced Photonics Intl Inc	Fairfield	CT	G	203 259-0437	1413
Aeroturn LLC	Oxford	CT	G	203 262-8309	3388
Alent Inc	Waterbury	CT	D	203 575-5727	4838
Alent USA Holding Inc	Waterbury	CT	B	203 575-5727	4839
Assa Inc **(HQ)**	New Haven	CT	B	203 624-5225	2659
Bevin Bros Manufacturing Co	East Hampton	CT	E	860 267-4431	1158
Branson Ultrasonics Corp **(DH)**	Danbury	CT	B	203 796-0400	882
Brookfield Industries Inc	Thomaston	CT	E	860 283-6211	4500
Cadence Ct Inc	Suffield	CT	D	860 370-9780	4461
Carey Manufacturing Co Inc **(PA)**	Cromwell	CT	E	860 829-1803	850
Carey Manufacturing Co Inc	Cromwell	CT	E	860 829-1803	851
Coherent Inc	Bloomfield	CT	E	860 243-9557	215
Coherent-Deos LLC	Bloomfield	CT	C	860 243-9557	216
Command Corporation	East Granby	CT	F	800 851-6012	1122
DC & D Inc	Broad Brook	CT	G	860 623-2941	628
Donali Systems Integration Inc	Guilford	CT	G	860 715-5432	1701
E-J Electric T & D LLC	Wallingford	CT	D	203 626-9625	4737
Eagle Electric Service LLC	Bethlehem	CT	F	860 868-9898	194
Eastern Electric Cnstr Co	Harwinton	CT	G	860 485-1100	1889
Eastside Electric Inc	Harwinton	CT	F	860 485-0700	1890
Electro Mech Specialists LLC	Bozrah	CT	G	860 887-2613	280
Electrodes Incorporated	Milford	CT	E	203 878-7400	2284
Evse Llc	Enfield	CT	G	860 745-2433	1361
Fuelcell Energy Inc	Torrington	CT	E	860 496-1111	4579
Hubbell Incorporated **(PA)**	Shelton	CT	D	475 882-4000	3813
Iemct	Milford	CT	G	203 683-4382	2300
Insight Plus Technology LLC	Bristol	CT	G	860 930-4763	571
Integral Technologies Inc **(DH)**	Enfield	CT	G	860 741-2281	1366
Jamieson Laser LLC	Litchfield	CT	G	860 482-3375	1950
Jared Manufacturing Co Inc	Norwalk	CT	F	203 846-1732	3180
Magnatech LLC	East Granby	CT	D	860 653-2573	1131
Miracle Instruments Co	Lebanon	CT	F	860 642-7745	1936
Morse Watchmans Inc	Oxford	CT	E	203 264-1108	3415
Naugatuck Elec Indus Sup LLC	Naugatuck	CT	G	203 723-1082	2486
New Line USA Inc	Coventry	CT	G	860 498-0347	837
Newco Condenser Inc	Shelton	CT	G	475 882-4000	3839
Presco Incorporated	Woodbridge	CT	F	203 397-8722	5477
Rinco Ultrasonics USA Inc	Danbury	CT	G	203 744-4500	978
Security Systems Inc	Middletown	CT	G	800 833-3211	2220
Stanley Black & Decker Inc	New Britain	CT	C	860 225-5111	2582
Stanley Black & Decker Inc **(PA)**	New Britain	CT	C	860 225-5111	2580
Total Register Inc	New Milford	CT	F	860 210-0465	2831
Trine Access Technology Inc	Bethel	CT	F	203 730-1756	185
Ultra Clean Equipment Inc	Clinton	CT	G	860 669-1354	797
United Technologies Corp	Farmington	CT	B	954 485-6501	1523
United Technologies Corp	East Hartford	CT	B	860 610-7000	1237
United Technologies Corp **(PA)**	Farmington	CT	B	860 728-7000	1522
Varnum Enterprises LLC	Bethel	CT	F	203 743-4443	190
World Cord Sets Inc	Enfield	CT	G	860 763-2100	1391
Abisee Inc	Acton	MA	F	978 637-2900	7333
Accutronics Inc	Chelmsford	MA	E	978 250-9144	9866
AES Corporation	Peabody	MA	D	978 535-7310	14308
All Security Co Inc	New Bedford	MA	F	508 993-4271	13356
Arcam Cad To Metal Inc	Woburn	MA	F	781 281-1718	17121
Armatron International Inc **(PA)**	Malden	MA	D	781 321-2300	12559
Asco Power Technologies LP	Marlborough	MA	G	508 624-0466	12720
Assa Abloy Entrance Sys US Inc	Auburn	MA	E	508 368-2600	7827
Azz Inc	Medway	MA	E	774 854-0700	12956
Beon Home Inc	North Easton	MA	G	617 600-8329	13944
Branson Ultrasonics Corp	North Billerica	MA	E	978 262-9040	13798
Cc-Teknologies Inc	Brockton	MA	G	508 444-8810	9127
Cogniscent Inc	Weston	MA	F	508 863-0069	16824
Compu-Gard Inc	Swansea	MA	E	508 679-8845	15703
Convergent - Photonics LLC	Chicopee	MA	D	413 598-5200	10016
Cordmaster Engineering Co Inc	North Adams	MA	E	413 664-9371	13671
Cortron Inc	Lowell	MA	E	978 975-5445	12362
Degreasing Devices Co	Southbridge	MA	G	508 765-0045	15379
Diamond Solar Group LLC	Topsfield	MA	E	978 808-9288	15856
Diamond-Roltran LLC	Littleton	MA	F	978 486-0039	12302
Digital Vdeo Cmmunications Inc	Woburn	MA	G	781 932-6882	17168
Distribution & Control Product	Malden	MA	G	781 324-0070	12568
Dogwatch Inc **(PA)**	Natick	MA	F	508 650-0600	13252
Dorel Juvenile Group Inc	Foxboro	MA	D	800 544-1108	10881
Eikon Corporation	Andover	MA	G	978 662-5200	7546
Ekeys4 Cars	North Andover	MA	G	978 655-3135	13701
Electrical Safety Products LLC	Woburn	MA	G	781 249-5007	17174
Exatel Visual Systems Inc	Burlington	MA	F	781 221-7400	9273
Excel Dryer Inc	East Longmeadow	MA	E	413 525-4531	10475
Excel Technology Inc **(HQ)**	Bedford	MA	D	781 266-5700	7976
GE Infrastructure Sensing LLC **(DH)**	Billerica	MA	A	978 437-1000	8249
Giner Elx Inc	Auburndale	MA	F	781 392-0300	7862
Green Brothers Fabricating	Taunton	MA	E	508 880-3608	15756
Grove Labs Inc	Somerville	MA	F	703 608-8178	15179
Hardric Laboratories Inc	North Chelmsford	MA	E	978 251-1702	13895
Headwaters Inc	Marblehead	MA	G	781 715-6404	12685
Hutchinson Arospc & Indust Inc	Hopkinton	MA	E	508 417-7000	11720
Inner-Tite Corp	Holden	MA	D	508 829-6361	11546
Interntnal Br-Tech Sltions Inc **(PA)**	Springfield	MA	F	413 739-2271	15480
Ion Track Instruments LLC	Wilmington	MA	D	978 658-3767	17007
Ipg Photonics Corporation **(PA)**	Oxford	MA	B	508 373-1100	14263
Ipg Photonics Corporation	Marlborough	MA	F	508 229-2130	12778
Ipg Photonics Corporation	Marlborough	MA	F	508 506-2812	12779
Iradion Laser Inc	Uxbridge	MA	G	401 762-5100	15921
Jlg Technologies LLC	Southborough	MA	G	508 424-2338	15362
Lightspeed Mfg Co LLC	Haverhill	MA	F	978 521-7676	11449
Litron LLC	Agawam	MA	D	413 789-0700	7437
Living Power Systems Inc	Cambridge	MA	G	617 496-8328	9539
Lumina Power Inc	Haverhill	MA	E	978 241-8260	11450
Magiq Technologies Inc **(PA)**	Somerville	MA	F	617 661-8300	15192
Markarian Electric LLC	Watertown	MA	G	617 393-9700	16297
Matec Instrument Companies Inc **(PA)**	Northborough	MA	E	508 393-0155	14038
Mc10 Inc	Lexington	MA	E	617 234-4448	12242
McLane Research Labs Inc **(PA)**	East Falmouth	MA	G	508 495-4000	10445
Meddevice Concepts LLC	Edgartown	MA	G	617 834-7420	10586
Mettler-Toledo Process Analyti	Billerica	MA	D	781 301-8800	8265
Nextek Inc	Westford	MA	E	978 577-6214	16781
Nhv America Inc	Methuen	MA	F	978 682-4900	13040
North Andover Flight Academy	North Andover	MA	G	978 689-7600	13720
Novanta Corporation **(HQ)**	Bedford	MA	B	781 266-5700	7995
Novanta Inc **(PA)**	Bedford	MA	C	781 266-5700	7996
Optowares Incorporated	Woburn	MA	F	781 427-7106	17251
Ov Loop Inc	Danvers	MA	E	781 640-2234	10246
Photonwares Corporation **(PA)**	Woburn	MA	G	781 935-1200	17263
Polar Controls Inc	Shirley	MA	G	978 425-2233	15092
Polytec Inc	Hudson	MA	F	508 417-1040	11803
Precision Dynamics Corporation	Burlington	MA	D	888 202-3684	9321
Precision Dynamics Corporation	Billerica	MA	D	800 528-8005	8276
Product Resources LLC	Newburyport	MA	E	978 524-8500	13523
Raysecur Inc **(PA)**	Cambridge	MA	G	844 729-7328	9626
Rofin-Baasel Inc **(DH)**	Devens	MA	E	978 635-9100	10332
Sancliff Inc	Worcester	MA	F	508 795-0747	17469
Schneider Automation Inc	Andover	MA	D	978 975-9600	7602

	CITY	ST	EMP	PHONE	ENTRY #
Security Devices Intl Inc	Wakefield	MA	G	905 582-6402	15975
Seica Inc **(PA)**	Haverhill	MA	G	603 890-6002	11471
Siemens Industry Inc	Canton	MA	D	781 364-1000	9779
Sluggo-Ox Corporation	Franklin	MA	G	508 726-8221	11081
Socomec Inc **(DH)**	Watertown	MA	F	617 245-0447	16317
Sonosystems N Schunk Amer Corp **(DH)**	Wilmington	MA	E	978 658-9400	17046
Spirig Advanced Tech Incies	Springfield	MA	G	413 788-6191	15508
Static Clean International	North Billerica	MA	F	781 229-7799	13870
Stellar Industries Corp	Millbury	MA	E	508 865-1668	13177
Stoneridge Inc	Canton	MA	B	781 830-0340	9787
T H Grogan & Associates Inc	Acton	MA	F	978 266-9548	7389
Tel Epion Inc	Billerica	MA	E	978 436-2300	8302
Teledyne Instruments Inc	North Falmouth	MA	E	508 548-2077	13957
Teradiode Inc	Wilmington	MA	D	978 988-1040	17053
Terrasonics LLC	Westford	MA	G	978 692-3274	16796
Thermal Circuits Inc	Salem	MA	C	978 745-1162	14945
Tyco Safety Products Us Inc	Westminster	MA	E	800 435-3192	16818
Urolaze Inc	Wellesley Hills	MA	G	413 374-5006	16400
Urquhart Family LLC	Gardner	MA	G	978 632-3600	11132
Videoiq Inc	Somerville	MA	E	781 222-3069	15228
W J Roberts Co Inc	Saugus	MA	E	781 233-8176	15002
Whyte Electric LLC	Braintree	MA	G	781 348-6239	9050
Zero Balla	Lowell	MA	G	978 735-2015	12451
Design Architectural Heating	Lewiston	ME	F	207 784-0309	6283
Eami Inc	Biddeford	ME	F	207 283-3001	5730
Electrotech Inc	Rockland	ME	F	207 596-0556	6791
Enercon **(PA)**	Gray	ME	C	207 657-7000	6139
Kritzer Industries Inc	Scarborough	ME	F	207 883-4141	6930
Waughs Mountainview Elec	Mexico	ME	F	207 545-2421	6430
Albert Langin	Pelham	NH	G	603 635-3560	19426
Alert Products	Keene	NH	G	603 357-3331	18490
Associated Training Svcs LLC	Brentwood	NH	G	603 772-9002	17745
Auger Electric LLC	Rochester	NH	G	603 335-5633	19661
Auto Electric Service LLC	Brentwood	NH	G	603 642-5990	17746
Beckwood Services Inc	Plaistow	NH	D	603 382-3840	19508
Brailsford & Company Inc	Antrim	NH	E	603 588-2880	17593
Burns Industries Incorporated	Hollis	NH	G	603 881-8336	18327
Davco	Danbury	NH	G	603 768-3517	17963
Dual Control Inc	Londonderry	NH	G	603 627-4114	18692
Electronics Aid Inc	Marlborough	NH	G	603 876-4161	18959
Energetic Baltic MI	Enfield	NH	G	603 252-0804	18097
Faro Technologies Inc	Hudson	NH	G	603 893-6200	18390
I R Sources Inc	Brookline	NH	G	603 672-0582	17771
Ipg Photonics Corporation	Nashua	NH	E	603 518-3200	19191
JP Sercel Associates Inc	Manchester	NH	D	603 595-7048	18852
Laser Advantage LLC	Nashua	NH	F	603 886-9464	19197
Laser Light Engines Inc	Salem	NH	F	603 952-4550	19746
Laser Projection Technologies	Londonderry	NH	E	603 421-0209	18712
On Board Solutions LLC	Portsmouth	NH	F	603 373-6500	19603
Orion Entrance Control Inc	Laconia	NH	E	603 527-4187	18579
Prophotonix Limited **(PA)**	Salem	NH	E	603 893-8778	19761
Spinnaker Contract Mfg Inc	Tilton	NH	D	603 286-4366	19912
Teledyne Instruments Inc	Portsmouth	NH	C	603 474-5571	19624
Thermal Arc Inc	West Lebanon	NH	D	800 462-2782	19962
Warner Power Acquisition LLC **(HQ)**	Warner	NH	C	603 456-3111	19930
Wilcox Industries Corp **(PA)**	Newington	NH	C	603 431-1331	19329
Bear Hydraulics Inc	Warwick	RI	G	401 732-5832	21335
Endiprev Usa LLC	Providence	RI	D	401 519-3600	21006
Global Rfid Systems N Amer LLC	Narragansett	RI	G	401 783-3818	20640
Instantron Co Inc	Riverside	RI	G	401 433-6800	21170
Kenney Manufacturing Company **(PA)**	Warwick	RI	B	401 739-2200	21383
Laser Fare Inc **(PA)**	Smithfield	RI	D	401 231-4400	21235
Laservall North America LLC	Pawtucket	RI	G	401 724-0076	20853
Lfi Inc **(PA)**	Smithfield	RI	D	401 231-4400	21236
Maley Laser Processing Inc	Warwick	RI	F	401 732-8400	21386
Newport Electric Corporation	Portsmouth	RI	F	401 293-0527	20930
Nordson Efd LLC **(HQ)**	East Providence	RI	C	401 431-7000	20435
Outsource Electronic Mfg	North Kingstown	RI	G	401 615-0705	20732
Ritec Inc	Warwick	RI	F	401 738-3660	21413
Stanley Black & Decker Inc	East Greenwich	RI	C	401 471-4280	20380
Ask-Inttag LLC	Essex Junction	VT	E	802 288-7210	21929
Macdermid Incorporated	Springfield	VT	F	802 885-8089	22507
Omni Measurement Systems Inc	Colchester	VT	E	802 497-2253	21875

37 TRANSPORTATION EQUIPMENT

3711 Motor Vehicles & Car Bodies

	CITY	ST	EMP	PHONE	ENTRY #
Abair Manufacturing Company	Waterbury	CT	F	203 757-0112	4835
American Vehicles Sales LLC	Yantic	CT	G	860 886-0327	5507
CD Racing Products	Oxford	CT	G	203 264-7822	3395
Chassis Dynamics Inc	Oxford	CT	G	203 262-6272	3396
Markow Race Cars	South Windsor	CT	G	860 610-0776	3991
Oshkosh Corporation	East Granby	CT	F	860 653-5548	1138
Special Vhcl Developments Inc	Cheshire	CT	G	203 272-7928	764
Structured Solutions II LLC	New Canaan	CT	G	203 972-5717	2616
Triple D Transportation Inc	Bloomfield	CT	G	860 243-5057	267
Universal Body & Eqp Co LLC	Oakville	CT	F	860 274-7541	3304
Ally Automotive Inc	Newton	MA	G	734 604-2257	13559
Atlantic Turtle Top Inc	South Grafton	MA	G	508 839-1711	15296
Cabot Coach Builders Inc **(PA)**	Haverhill	MA	E	978 374-4530	11412
Cadillac Gage Textron Inc **(HQ)**	Wilmington	MA	G	978 657-5111	16986
Christphrs Emrgncy Eqptmnt &	Chelmsford	MA	G	978 265-8363	9887
Fire Emergency Maint Co LLC	Lynnfield	MA	G	781 334-3100	12548
Flexcar	Cambridge	MA	G	617 995-4231	9479
Greenwood Emrgncy Vehicles LLC **(HQ)**	North Attleboro	MA	D	508 695-7138	13758
L3 Essco Inc	Ayer	MA	D	978 568-5100	7923
Lenco Industries Inc	Pittsfield	MA	D	413 443-7359	14483
Mirak Building Trust	Arlington	MA	G	781 643-8000	7631
Mitchell Differential Inc	Shrewsbury	MA	G	508 755-3790	15124
Oshkosh Corporation	Burlington	MA	C	800 392-9921	9315
Prfrred Lancaster Partners LLC	Boston	MA	C	717 299-0782	8795
Tremcar USA	Haverhill	MA	F	978 556-5330	11477
Tube Chassis Designz	Hanson	MA	G	781 293-5005	11369
Wgi Inc	Southwick	MA	C	413 569-9444	15421
Autotronics LLC **(PA)**	Frenchville	ME	G	207 543-6262	6090
Douglas Dynamics LLC	Rockland	ME	C	207 701-4200	6790
Epping Volunteer Fire District	Columbia Falls	ME	F	207 483-2036	5920
Loring Industries LLC	Limestone	ME	G	207 328-7005	6342
Messer Truck Equipment **(PA)**	Westbrook	ME	E	207 854-9751	7196
Rod Jakes Shop LLC	Bridgton	ME	G	207 595-0677	5810
Costello/April Design Inc	Dover	NH	E	603 749-6755	18015
Larry Dingee	Cornish	NH	G	603 542-9682	17962
Needham Electric Supply LLC	Wolfeboro	NH	G	603 569-0643	20023
Patsys Bus Sales and Service	Concord	NH	F	603 226-2222	17922
Dejana Trck Utility Eqp Co LLC	Smithfield	RI	E	401 231-9797	21220
American Rural Fire Apparatus	Williamstown	VT	G	802 433-1554	22649
Denton Auto Inc	Craftsbury	VT	G	802 586-2828	21892
Town of Hartford	White River Junction	VT	E	802 295-9425	22643

3713 Truck & Bus Bodies

	CITY	ST	EMP	PHONE	ENTRY #
Lo Stocco Motors	Danbury	CT	G	203 797-9618	949
Rj 15 Inc	Bristol	CT	F	860 585-0111	607
Sure Industries Inc	East Hartford	CT	G	860 289-2522	1226
Universal Body & Eqp Co LLC	Oakville	CT	F	860 274-7541	3304
Altec Northeast LLC	Sterling	MA	F	508 320-9041	15533
Bart Truck Equipment LLC	West Springfield	MA	G	413 737-2766	16511
Boston Trailer Manufacturing	Walpole	MA	E	508 668-2242	15990
Commonwlth Ventr Funding Group **(PA)**	Waltham	MA	F	781 684-0095	16072
Cotta Truck Equipment	Bridgewater	MA	G	508 269-1960	9069
Curtis Industries LLC **(PA)**	West Boylston	MA	F	508 853-2200	16413
James A Kiley Company	Somerville	MA	E	617 776-0344	15188
Mark D Skiest	Shrewsbury	MA	G	508 754-0639	15122
Middlesex Truck & Auto Bdy Inc	Boston	MA	E	617 442-3000	8705
New England Wheels Inc **(PA)**	Billerica	MA	E	978 663-9724	8267
Tom Berkowitz Trucking Inc **(PA)**	Whitinsville	MA	E	508 234-2920	16919
F3 Mfg Inc	Waterville	ME	F	207 692-7178	7155
Messer Truck Equipment **(PA)**	Westbrook	ME	E	207 854-9751	7196
Larry Dingee	Cornish	NH	G	603 542-9682	17962
Nashua Fabrication Co Inc	Hudson	NH	F	603 889-2181	18418
Dejana Trck Utility Eqp Co LLC	Smithfield	RI	E	401 231-9797	21220
Utility Systems Inc	Johnston	RI	F	401 351-6681	20546

3714 Motor Vehicle Parts & Access

	CITY	ST	EMP	PHONE	ENTRY #
Airpot Corporation	Norwalk	CT	E	800 848-7681	3097
Alinabal Inc **(HQ)**	Milford	CT	C	203 877-3241	2242
Alinabal Holdings Corporation **(PA)**	Milford	CT	B	203 877-3241	2243
All Tech Auto/Truck Electric	Danbury	CT	G	203 790-8990	868
Armored Autogroup Inc **(DH)**	Danbury	CT	D	203 205-2900	874
Armored Autogroup Sales Inc	Danbury	CT	C	203 205-2900	876
Beacon Group Inc **(PA)**	Newington	CT	C	860 594-5200	2846
Callaway Cars Inc	Old Lyme	CT	F	860 434-9002	3316
Callaway Companies Inc **(PA)**	Old Lyme	CT	F	860 434-9002	3317
Cambridge Specialty Co Inc	Berlin	CT	D	860 828-3579	80
Casco Products Corporation **(HQ)**	Bridgeport	CT	F	203 922-3200	396
Cheshire Manufacturing Co Inc	Cheshire	CT	G	203 272-3586	721
Clarcor Eng MBL Solutions LLC **(DH)**	East Hartford	CT	D	860 920-4200	1182
Clarios	Meriden	CT	D	678 297-4040	2086
Clayton Offroad Manufacturer	East Haven	CT	G	475 238-8251	1245
Competition Engineering Inc	Guilford	CT	C	203 453-5200	1697
Continental Machine Tl Co Inc	New Britain	CT	D	860 223-2896	2522
Defeo Manufacturing Inc	Brookfield	CT	E	203 775-0254	641
Dynamic Racing Transm LLC	North Branford	CT	G	203 315-0138	2963
Expressway Lube Centers	Danbury	CT	F	203 744-2511	915
Fram Group Operations LLC	Danbury	CT	E	203 830-7800	922
Global Steering Systems LLC **(PA)**	Watertown	CT	C	860 945-5400	5011
International Automobile Entps **(PA)**	New Britain	CT	F	860 224-0253	2543
International Automobile Entps	New Britain	CT	F	860 224-0253	2544
Jk Motorsports	Fairfield	CT	G	203 255-9120	1438
Jobin Machine Inc	West Hartford	CT	E	860 953-1631	5079
JPsexton LLC	Windsor	CT	G	860 748-2048	5342
King of Covers Inc **(PA)**	Winsted	CT	G	860 379-2427	5415
Lac Landscaping LLC	Milford	CT	F	203 807-1067	2308
Lee Company **(PA)**	Westbrook	CT	A	860 399-6281	5157
Lewmar Inc **(DH)**	Guilford	CT	E	203 458-6200	1708

	CITY	ST	EMP	PHONE	ENTRY #
Lydall Inc **(PA)**	Manchester	CT	E	860 646-1233	2021
Moroso Performance Pdts Inc **(PA)**	Guilford	CT	C	203 453-6571	1711
Nathan Airchime Inc	South Windham	CT	G	860 423-4575	3927
Nickson Industries Inc	Plainville	CT	E	860 747-1671	3509
Nucap US Inc **(DH)**	Wolcott	CT	E	203 879-1423	5450
Phillips Fuel Systems	Bridgeport	CT	G	203 908-3323	468
Platt-Labonia of N Haven Inc	North Haven	CT	D	203 239-5681	3052
Pratt & Whitney Engine Svcs	Middletown	CT	B	860 344-4000	2212
S Camerota & Sons Inc	North Haven	CT	G	203 782-0360	3060
Southington Transm Auto Repr	Southington	CT	G	860 329-0381	4080
Spectrum Brands Inc	Danbury	CT	G	203 205-2900	996
Stanadyne Intrmdate Hldngs LLC **(HQ)**	Windsor	CT	C	860 525-0821	5367
Stanadyne LLC **(DH)**	Windsor	CT	A	860 525-0821	5368
Thule Inc **(DH)**	Seymour	CT	C	203 881-9600	3765
Thule Holding Inc **(DH)**	Seymour	CT	F	203 881-9600	3766
Tru Hitch Inc	Pleasant Valley	CT	F	860 379-7772	3548
Turbine Technologies Inc **(PA)**	Farmington	CT	D	860 678-1642	1521
Vulcan Industries Inc	Windsor	CT	C	860 683-2005	5377
Westfalia Inc	Bristol	CT	E	860 314-2920	624
Araces Incorporated	Pittsfield	MA	G	413 499-9997	14453
Armatron International Inc **(PA)**	Malden	MA	D	781 321-2300	12559
Blendco Systems LLC	Holyoke	MA	E	800 537-7797	11619
Blue Magic Inc	Marblehead	MA	G	781 639-8428	12678
Bm Undercar Warehouse	Chelsea	MA	G	516 736-0476	9946
Boston Steel & Mfg Co	Haverhill	MA	E	781 324-3000	11409
Cadillac Gage Textron Inc **(HQ)**	Wilmington	MA	G	978 657-5111	16986
Capeway Bearing & Machine Inc	Plymouth	MA	G	508 747-2800	14548
Clearmotion Inc	Wilmington	MA	G	617 313-0822	16987
Clearmotion Inc **(PA)**	Billerica	MA	F	617 313-0822	8231
Creative Services	East Longmeadow	MA	G	413 525-4993	10470
Curtis Industries LLC **(PA)**	West Boylston	MA	F	508 853-2200	16413
Davico Inc	New Bedford	MA	F	508 998-1150	13377
Dynex/Rivett Inc	Ashland	MA	G	508 881-5110	7658
General Electric Company	Lynn	MA	D	781 598-7303	12511
Geoorbital Inc	Somerville	MA	F	617 651-1102	15178
Gtb Innovative Solutions Inc	Westfield	MA	F	413 733-0146	16685
H&H Propeller Shop Inc **(PA)**	Salem	MA	E	978 744-3806	14918
Hewlett Packard HP Autonomy So	Southborough	MA	D	508 476-0000	15360
Hi-Tech Inc	Attleboro	MA	F	401 454-4086	7746
High Voltage Engineering Corp	Wakefield	MA	F	781 224-1001	15954
Hutchinson Arospc & Indust Inc **(DH)**	Hopkinton	MA	B	508 417-7000	11718
Jnc Rebuilders Inc	Ipswich	MA	G	978 356-2996	11925
King Kalipers Inc	Peabody	MA	E	978 977-4994	14347
Lfr Chassis Inc	Shrewsbury	MA	G	508 425-3117	15121
Magmotor Technologies Inc	Worcester	MA	F	508 835-4305	17411
Naugler Co Inc	Newburyport	MA	G	978 463-9199	13517
North Shore Laboratories Corp	Peabody	MA	F	978 531-5954	14358
Peter Thrasher	North Attleboro	MA	G	-	13771
Ryca Inc	Tewksbury	MA	G	978 851-3265	15833
Sevcon Inc **(HQ)**	Southborough	MA	E	508 281-5500	15365
Stoneridge Inc	Canton	MA	B	781 830-0340	9787
Thermokinetics	Dracut	MA	F	978 459-6073	10369
Tremco Products Inc	Billerica	MA	G	781 275-7692	8307
Tubular Automotive & Engrg	Rockland	MA	G	781 878-9875	14831
V Power Equipment LLC	Wareham	MA	F	508 273-7596	16256
Xl Hybrids Inc **(PA)**	Brighton	MA	E	617 718-0329	9108
Crescent Industries Company	Auburn	ME	G	207 777-3500	5557
Distance Racing Products	Fairfield	ME	G	207 453-2644	6026
Electrnic Mobility Contrls LLC	Augusta	ME	F	207 512-8009	5607
Irish Inc **(PA)**	Turner	ME	G	207 224-7605	7108
Marketing Worldwide Corp **(PA)**	Rockland	ME	G	631 444-8090	6804
Nichols Portland LLC **(PA)**	Portland	ME	B	207 774-6121	6702
Somic America Inc	Brewer	ME	D	207 989-1759	5801
Allard Nazarian Group Inc	Manchester	NH	F	603 314-0017	18775
Eco Touch Inc	Somersworth	NH	G	603 319-1762	19836
Freudenberg-Nok General Partnr	Northfield	NH	D	603 286-1600	19401
Freudenberg-Nok General Partnr	Northfield	NH	E	603 286-1600	19402
General Electric Company	Hooksett	NH	A	603 666-8300	18351
General Kinetics LLC	Bedford	NH	G	603 627-8547	17642
Jon Shafts & Stuff	Manchester	NH	G	603 518-5033	18851
Larry Dingee	Cornish	NH	G	603 542-9682	17962
Morin Engine Services LLC	Nashua	NH	G	603 880-3009	19210
Osram Sylvania Inc	Hillsborough	NH	B	603 464-7235	18317
S Camerota & Sons Inc	Bow	NH	G	603 228-9343	17730
Bear Hydraulics Inc	Warwick	RI	G	401 732-5832	21335
Kennedy Incorporated	North Kingstown	RI	F	401 295-7800	20720
M & T Manufacturing Co	Peace Dale	RI	G	401 789-0472	20914
Rhode Island Driveshaft Sup Co	Warwick	RI	G	401 941-0210	21412
Rhode Island Wiring Service	West Kingston	RI	G	401 789-1955	21470
Wheeltrak Inc	Tiverton	RI	E	800 296-1326	21266
A C Performance Center Ltd	Colchester	VT	G	802 862-6074	21855
Autotech Inc	Winooski	VT	G	802 497-2482	22716
General Electric Company	Rutland	VT	A	802 775-9842	22335
JBM Sherman Carmel Inc	Bennington	VT	E	802 442-5115	21675
NSK Steering Systems Amer Inc	Bennington	VT	B	802 442-5448	21688
Rennline Inc	Milton	VT	G	802 893-7366	22138
Safe and Secure Fou A NJ Non	Perkinsville	VT	G	848 992-3623	22257

	CITY	ST	EMP	PHONE	ENTRY #
Sonnax Industries Inc **(PA)**	Bellows Falls	VT	C	802 463-9722	21654

3715 Truck Trailers

	CITY	ST	EMP	PHONE	ENTRY #
Kensington Welding & Trlr Co	Kensington	CT	G	860 828-3564	1918
Mark Karotkin	Hartford	CT	G	860 202-7821	1844
Miller Professional Trans Svc	Vernon	CT	G	860 871-6818	4669
Webbers Truck Service Inc	East Windsor	CT	F	860 623-4554	1310
Boston Trailer Manufacturing	Walpole	MA	E	508 668-2242	15990
Butlers Rv Services Corp	Oxford	MA	G	508 987-0234	14255
Lins Propane Trucks Corp	Dighton	MA	F	508 669-6665	10337
U-Haul Co of Massachusetts	Walpole	MA	F	508 668-2242	16015
Alcom LLC **(PA)**	Winslow	ME	E	207 861-9800	7266
On The Road Inc	Warren	ME	E	207 273-3780	7146
Pelletier Manufacturing Inc	Millinocket	ME	F	207 723-6500	6444
Granite State Cover and Canvas	Plaistow	NH	F	603 382-5462	19517
Proline Products LLC	Milton	NH	G	603 652-7337	19087
Ricks Truck & Trailer Repair	Hillsborough	NH	G	603 464-3636	18318
Scott G Reed Truck Svcs Inc	Claremont	NH	F	603 542-5032	17860
Gaines Trucking Inc	Middletown	RI	G	401 862-2993	20619

3721 Aircraft

	CITY	ST	EMP	PHONE	ENTRY #
Amco Precision Tools Inc **(PA)**	Berlin	CT	E	860 828-5640	70
Aquiline Drones LLC	Hartford	CT	F	860 361-7958	1807
Avolon Aerospace New York Inc	Stamford	CT	G	203 663-5490	4146
Edac Nd Inc	Glastonbury	CT	D	860 633-9474	1548
Embraer Executive Jet Svcs LLC	Windsor Locks	CT	G	860 804-4600	5392
Gulfstream Aerospace Corp	New Milford	CT	G	860 210-1469	2803
Gulfstream Aerospace Corp	East Granby	CT	G	912 965-3000	1129
Hartford Jet Center LLC	Hartford	CT	G	860 548-9334	1835
Kaman Aerospace Corporation **(DH)**	Bloomfield	CT	A	860 242-4461	230
Kaman Aerospace Corporation	Bloomfield	CT	E	860 242-4461	231
Kaman Aerospace Corporation	Bloomfield	CT	D	860 242-4461	232
Kaman Aerospace Group Inc **(HQ)**	Bloomfield	CT	F	860 243-7100	233
Kaman Corporation **(PA)**	Bloomfield	CT	D	860 243-7100	234
MB Aerospace	East Granby	CT	G	860 653-0569	1133
New England Airfoil Pdts Inc	Farmington	CT	E	860 677-1376	1498
Santoto LLC	Danbury	CT	G	203 984-2540	983
Sikorsky Aircraft Corporation	Bridgeport	CT	B	203 384-7532	490
Sikorsky Aircraft Corporation	Shelton	CT	A	203 386-7861	3871
Sikorsky Aircraft Corporation	North Haven	CT	F	516 228-2000	3062
Sikorsky Aircraft Corporation	Bridgeport	CT	C	203 386-4000	491
Sikorsky Aircraft Corporation **(HQ)**	Stratford	CT	A	203 386-4000	4444
Sikorsky Aircraft Corporation	Farmington	CT	E	610 644-4430	1513
Sikorsky Export Corporation	Stratford	CT	B	203 386-4000	4445
Stonegate Capital Group	Hartford	CT	G	860 899-1181	1873
Straton Industries Inc	Stratford	CT	D	203 375-4488	4450
Target Marketing Assoc Inc	Rocky Hill	CT	G	860 571-7294	3730
Textron Aviation Inc	Oxford	CT	A	203 262-9366	3427
United Technologies Corp **(PA)**	Farmington	CT	B	860 728-7000	1522
Aerovironment Inc	Burlington	MA	E	805 520-8350	9230
Ambrose D Cedrone Lodge 1069	Newton	MA	G	617 460-4664	13561
American Drone Solutions LLC	West Bridgewater	MA	E	413 306-9427	16428
Arise Air Inc	Plympton	MA	E	888 359-2747	14590
Ascent Aerosystems LLC	Tewksbury	MA	G	330 554-6334	15806
Attleboro Scholarship Co	Attleboro	MA	G	508 226-4414	7709
Aurora Flight Sciences Corp	Cambridge	MA	F	617 500-4800	9397
Boeing Company	Concord	MA	A	978 369-9522	10117
Boston Executive Helicopters	Norwood	MA	G	781 603-6186	14138
C & H Air Inc	Plymouth	MA	G	508 746-5511	14546
D Cedrone Inc	Framingham	MA	G	508 405-4260	10939
Echelon Industries Corporation	Westfield	MA	E	413 562-6659	16681
Goodrich Corporation	Westford	MA	F	978 303-6700	16770
Greensight Agronomics Inc	Boston	MA	G	617 633-4919	8580
Gulfstream Aerospace Corp	Westfield	MA	E	413 562-5866	16686
Infotrends Research Group	Weymouth	MA	E	781 616-2100	16891
Legion Flying Club Inc	Granby	MA	G	413 467-7844	11229
Liquiglide Inc	Cambridge	MA	E	617 901-0700	9538
Plane Fantasy	Chestnut Hill	MA	G	617 734-4950	9990
Raytheon Sutheast Asia Systems **(HQ)**	Billerica	MA	E	978 470-5000	8289
Spike Aerospace Inc	Boston	MA	F	617 338-1400	8858
Terrafugia Inc	Woburn	MA	F	781 491-0812	17307
Vhp Flight Systems LLC	Southborough	MA	G	508 229-2615	15371
Wingbrace LLC	Hingham	MA	G	617 480-8737	11518
Sonic Blue Aerospace Inc	Portland	ME	G	207 776-2471	6733
Lagasse & Lewis LLC	Plaistow	NH	G	603 382-5898	19519
Mercury Systems Inc	Hudson	NH	G	203 792-7474	18366
Uav - America Inc	Nottingham	NH	G	603 389-6364	19418
Bell Helicopter Korea Inc	Providence	RI	G	401 421-2800	20969
Lockheed Martin Global Inc	Middletown	RI	F	401 849-3703	20625
Textron Inc **(PA)**	Providence	RI	B	401 421-2800	21134
BF Goodrich Aerspce Aircrft In	Vergennes	VT	G	802 877-2911	22552

3724 Aircraft Engines & Engine Parts

	CITY	ST	EMP	PHONE	ENTRY #
A-1 Machining Co	New Britain	CT	D	860 223-6420	2501
Absolute Precision Co	Southbury	CT	G	203 767-9066	4021
Accupaulo Holding Corporation **(PA)**	Bristol	CT	E	860 666-5621	511
Acmt Inc	Manchester	CT	D	860 645-0592	1982

	CITY	ST	EMP	PHONE	ENTRY #
Aero Component Services LLC	East Hartford	CT	G	860 291-0417	1171
AGC Acquisition LLC	Meriden	CT	C	203 639-7125	2075
Alloy Specialties Incorporated	Manchester	CT	E	860 646-4587	1985
American Design & Mfg Inc	South Windsor	CT	E	860 282-2719	3935
American Unmanned Systems LLC	Stamford	CT	G	203 406-7611	4136
ATI Ladish Machining Inc **(DH)**	East Hartford	CT	D	860 688-3688	1174
ATI Ladish Machining Inc	South Windsor	CT	D	860 688-3688	3939
ATI Ladish Machining Inc	East Hartford	CT	D	860 688-3688	1175
Barnes Group Inc **(PA)**	Bristol	CT	B	860 583-7070	526
Barnes Group Inc	Windsor	CT	A	860 298-7740	5322
Barnes Group Inc	Bristol	CT	A	513 759-3503	528
Beacon Group Inc **(PA)**	Newington	CT	C	860 594-5200	2846
Birken Manufacturing Company	Bloomfield	CT	D	860 242-2211	209
Birotech Inc	Stamford	CT	G	203 968-5080	4150
Bolducs Machine Works Inc	North Windham	CT	G	860 455-1232	3078
Cambridge Specialty Co Inc	Berlin	CT	D	860 828-3579	80
CBS Manufacturing Company	East Granby	CT	E	860 653-8100	1120
Chromalloy Component Svcs Inc	Windsor	CT	C	860 688-7798	5325
Chromalloy Gas Turbine LLC	Windsor	CT	D	860 688-7798	5326
Columbia Manufacturing Inc	Columbia	CT	D	860 228-2259	817
D & M Tool Company Inc	West Hartford	CT	G	860 236-6037	5064
Deburring House Inc	East Berlin	CT	E	860 828-0889	1098
Demusz Mfg Co Inc	East Hartford	CT	E	860 528-9845	1186
Drt Aerospace LLC	Meriden	CT	E	203 781-8020	2092
Dynamic Controls Hs Inc	Windsor Locks	CT	G	860 654-6000	5391
Edac Technologies LLC	East Windsor	CT	F	860 789-2511	1283
Edac Technologies LLC **(HQ)**	Cheshire	CT	C	203 806-2090	728
Electro-Methods Inc **(PA)**	South Windsor	CT	C	860 289-8661	3962
Electro-Methods Inc	South Windsor	CT	D	860 289-8661	3963
Engine Alliance LLC	Glastonbury	CT	B	860 565-2239	1550
Ethosenergy Component Repr LLC	Wallingford	CT	E	203 949-8144	4738
Evans Cooling Systems Inc **(PA)**	Suffield	CT	G	860 668-1114	4462
First Aviation Services Inc **(PA)**	Westport	CT	G	203 291-3300	5192
First Equity Group Inc **(PA)**	Westport	CT	F	203 291-7700	5193
Fredericks Jf Aero LLC	Farmington	CT	D	860 677-2646	1483
GKN Aerospace Newington LLC	Newington	CT	G	800 667-8502	2866
GKN Aerospace Newington LLC **(DH)**	Newington	CT	C	860 667-8502	2867
GKN Arspace Svcs Strctures LLC	Cromwell	CT	C	860 613-0236	853
Global Trbine Cmpnent Tech LLC	South Windsor	CT	E	860 528-4722	3973
Honeywell International Inc	Northford	CT	D	203 484-7161	3087
Honeywell International Inc	Northford	CT	B	203 484-7161	3088
Honeywell International Inc	Northford	CT	B	203 484-6202	3089
Honeywell International Inc	North Branford	CT	A	203 484-7161	2967
Honeywell International Inc	Northford	CT	E	203 484-7161	3090
Horst Engrg De Mexico LLC	East Hartford	CT	E	860 289-8209	1199
Hsb Aircraft Components LLC	New Britain	CT	F	860 505-7349	2539
I & J Machine Tool Company	Milford	CT	F	203 877-5376	2298
Iae International Aero Engs AG	East Hartford	CT	C	860 565-1773	1201
International Aero Engines LLC	East Hartford	CT	E	860 565-5515	1203
Intlaero Beta Corp	East Hartford	CT	G	317 821-2000	1204
Kaman Aerospace Corporation	Bloomfield	CT	D	860 242-4461	232
Kaman Aerospace Group Inc **(HQ)**	Bloomfield	CT	F	860 243-7100	233
Kamatics Corporation **(DH)**	Bloomfield	CT	E	860 243-9704	235
Lighthouse International LLC	South Windsor	CT	E	860 528-4722	3990
Morning Star Tool LLC	Milford	CT	G	203 878-6026	2316
Msj Investments Inc	Stafford Springs	CT	F	860 684-9956	4113
N & B Manufacturing Co Inc	Newington	CT	G	860 667-3204	2885
New England Airfoil Pdts Inc	Farmington	CT	E	860 677-1376	1498
Numet Machining Techniques LLC	Orange	CT	E	203 375-4995	3376
Pdq Inc **(PA)**	Rocky Hill	CT	E	860 529-9051	3727
Pinnacle Aerospace Mfg LLC	Greenwich	CT	F	203 258-3398	1637
Point Machine Company	Berlin	CT	E	860 828-6901	102
Polar Corporation	New Britain	CT	E	860 223-7891	2564
Pratt & Whitney Company Inc **(HQ)**	East Hartford	CT	C	860 565-4321	1212
Pratt & Whitney Eng Svcs Inc	East Hartford	CT	C	860 610-2631	1213
Pratt & Whitney Engine Svcs	North Haven	CT	B	203 934-2806	3053
Pratt & Whitney Engine Svcs	East Hartford	CT	E	860 565-4321	1214
Pratt & Whitney Engine Svcs	Middletown	CT	B	860 344-4000	2212
Pratt & Whitney Services Inc	East Hartford	CT	E	860 565-5489	1215
Precision Speed Mfg LLC	Middletown	CT	E	860 635-8811	2213
Saar Corporation	Farmington	CT	F	860 674-9440	1511
Schaefer Rolls Inc	Wolcott	CT	G	203 910-0224	5455
Sikorsky Aircraft Corporation	Stratford	CT	A	203 386-4000	4443
Simmonds Precision Pdts Inc	Danbury	CT	E	203 797-5000	994
Soto Holdings Inc	New Haven	CT	E	203 781-8020	2739
Spartan Aerospace LLC	Manchester	CT	D	860 533-7500	2049
Specialty Tool Company USA LLC	Milford	CT	F	203 874-2009	2366
Tdy Industries LLC	New Britain	CT	G	860 259-6346	2586
Timken Arospc Drv Systems LLC	Manchester	CT	C	860 649-0000	2055
Triumph Eng Ctrl Systems LLC	West Hartford	CT	A	860 236-0651	5100
Turbine Kinetics Inc	Glastonbury	CT	F	860 633-8520	1580
Turbine Technologies Inc **(PA)**	Farmington	CT	D	860 678-1642	1521
United Technologies Corp **(PA)**	Farmington	CT	B	860 728-7000	1522
United Technologies Corp	East Hartford	CT	G	860 565-4321	1233
United Technologies Corp	South Windsor	CT	B	860 727-2200	4018
United Technologies Corp	East Hartford	CT	D	860 565-4321	1235
United Technologies Corp	East Hartford	CT	G	860 565-4321	1236
United Tool and Die Company **(PA)**	West Hartford	CT	C	860 246-6531	5102
Wentworth Manufacturing LLC	New Britain	CT	G	860 205-6437	2589
Westbrook Products LLC	New Britain	CT	G	860 205-6437	2590
Winslow Automatics Inc	New Britain	CT	D	860 225-6321	2591
325 Silver Street Inc	Agawam	MA	E	413 789-1800	7415
Actronics Incorporated	Waltham	MA	F	781 890-7030	16024
Aero - Bond Corp	Springfield	MA	F	413 734-2224	15441
Aero Turbine Components Inc	Worcester	MA	G	508 755-2121	17335
Ametek Arospc Pwr Holdings Inc **(HQ)**	Wilmington	MA	C	978 988-4771	16974
Curtil North America LLC	Pittsfield	MA	G	661 294-0030	14468
Enjet Aero Danvers LLC **(HQ)**	Danvers	MA	E	978 777-1980	10216
Fountain Plating Company Inc	West Springfield	MA	D	413 781-4651	16521
GE Aviation	Lynn	MA	E	513 552-3272	12510
General Electric Company	Lynn	MA	D	781 598-7303	12511
General Electric Company	Lynn	MA	A	781 594-0100	12512
General Electric Company **(PA)**	Boston	MA	A	617 443-3000	8558
General Electric Company	Westborough	MA	F	508 870-5200	16619
Goodrich Corporation	Westford	MA	A	978 303-6700	16771
Honeywell International Inc	Canton	MA	A	781 298-2700	9740
Honeywell International Inc	Southborough	MA	C	508 490-7100	15361
Honeywell Robert Warner	Newburyport	MA	G	978 358-8080	13498
Hutchinson Arospc & Indust Inc **(DH)**	Hopkinton	MA	B	508 417-7000	11718
Jet Industries Inc	Agawam	MA	E	413 786-2010	7435
LKM Industries Inc	Woburn	MA	D	781 935-9210	17216
Magellan Arospc Haverhill Inc	Haverhill	MA	C	978 774-6000	11452
Materials Development Corp	Andover	MA	F	781 391-0400	7568
Mer+ge	Chestnut Hill	MA	G	512 665-2266	9987
Palmer Manufacturing Co Llc **(DH)**	Malden	MA	C	781 321-0480	12586
Palmer Manufacturing Co LLC	Peabody	MA	G	781 321-0480	14360
Paradigm Prcision Holdings LLC	Peabody	MA	F	978 278-7100	14361
Parker-Hannifin Corporation	Devens	MA	C	978 784-1200	10329
Precision Components Group	West Springfield	MA	G	413 333-4184	16547
Sterling Machine Company Inc	Lynn	MA	E	781 593-3000	12541
Tell Tool Inc	Westfield	MA	D	413 568-1671	16732
Tell Tool Acquisition Inc **(HQ)**	Westfield	MA	G	413 568-1671	16733
Union Machine Company Lynn Inc **(PA)**	Groveland	MA	E	978 521-5100	11304
United Technologies Corp	Taunton	MA	B	508 942-8883	15795
Van Pelt Capital Precision Inc	Easthampton	MA	F	413 527-1204	10582
Wgi Inc	Southwick	MA	C	413 569-9444	15421
C&L Engine Solutions LLC	Bangor	ME	G	307 217-6050	5634
Honeywell International Inc	Yarmouth	ME	A	207 846-3350	7296
Pratt & Whitney Engine Svcs	North Berwick	ME	B	207 676-4100	6510
Tem Inc	Buxton	ME	E	207 929-8700	5861
Aeroweld Inc	Laconia	NH	F	603 524-8121	18553
General Electric Company	Hooksett	NH	A	603 666-8300	18351
GKN Aerospace New England Inc	Charlestown	NH	D	603 542-5135	17814
Northeast Fuel Systems LLC	Merrimack	NH	G	603 365-4103	19017
Pratt & Whitney	Londonderry	NH	G	800 742-5877	18731
Titeflex Corporation	Laconia	NH	F	603 524-2064	18589
Avco Corporation **(DH)**	Providence	RI	C	401 421-2800	20965
Honeywell International Inc	Smithfield	RI	C	401 757-2560	21231
Honeywell International Inc	Warwick	RI	G	973 455-2000	21371
Textron Inc **(PA)**	Providence	RI	B	401 421-2800	21134
Textron Lycoming Corp **(HQ)**	Providence	RI	E	401 421-2800	21135
Aeroparts Plus Inc	South Burlington	VT	G	802 489-5023	22435
General Electric Company	Rutland	VT	A	802 775-9842	22335
Honeywell International Inc	Williston	VT	G	877 841-2840	22674
Simmonds Precision Pdts Inc **(DH)**	Vergennes	VT	A	802 877-4000	22556
Superior Tchncal Ceramics Corp	Saint Albans	VT	C	802 527-7726	22380

3728 Aircraft Parts & Eqpt, NEC

	CITY	ST	EMP	PHONE	ENTRY #
A G C Incorporated **(PA)**	Meriden	CT	C	203 235-3361	2072
A-1 Machining Co	New Britain	CT	D	860 223-6420	2501
Acmt Inc	Manchester	CT	D	860 645-0592	1982
Advanced Def Slutions Tech LLC	Bloomfield	CT	G	860 243-1122	199
Aero Gear Incorporated	Windsor	CT	C	860 688-0888	5316
Aero Tube Technologies LLC	South Windsor	CT	E	860 289-2520	3932
Aerocision LLC	Chester	CT	D	860 526-9700	767
Air-Lock Incorporated	Milford	CT	E	203 878-4691	2238
Airborne Industries Inc	Branford	CT	F	203 315-0200	286
Alexis Aerospace Inds LLC	Canton	CT	G	860 516-4602	695
Alinabal Inc **(HQ)**	Milford	CT	C	203 877-3241	2242
All Power Manufacturing Co **(HQ)**	Oxford	CT	C	562 802-2640	3389
Anderson Manufacturing Company	Woodbury	CT	G	203 263-2318	5481
Arrow Diversified Tooling Inc	Ellington	CT	E	860 872-9072	1329
Athens Industries Inc	Plantsville	CT	G	860 621-8957	3527
Avalon Advanced Tech Repr Inc	East Windsor	CT	E	860 254-5442	1277
B&N Aerospace Inc	Newington	CT	E	860 665-0134	2845
B/E Aerospace Inc	Stratford	CT	G	203 380-5000	4394
Beacon Industries Inc	Newington	CT	C	860 594-5200	2847
Birken Manufacturing Company	Bloomfield	CT	D	860 242-2211	209
Brandstrom Instruments Inc	Ridgefield	CT	E	203 544-9341	3661
Bryka Skystocks LLC	Newington	CT	G	845 507-8200	2850
Budney Aerospace Inc	Berlin	CT	D	860 828-0585	78
C & W Manufacturing Co Inc	Glastonbury	CT	E	860 633-4631	1542
C V Tool Company Inc **(PA)**	Southington	CT	E	978 353-7901	4042
Cambridge Specialty Co Inc	Berlin	CT	D	860 828-3579	80

	CITY	ST	EMP	PHONE	ENTRY #
CBS Manufacturing Company	East Granby	CT	E	860 653-8100	1120
Connecticut Advanced Products	Glastonbury	CT	G	860 659-2260	1545
Connecticut Tool & Mfg Co LLC	Plainville	CT	D	860 846-0800	3478
Continental Machine Tl Co Inc	New Britain	CT	D	860 223-2896	2522
Crane Aerospace Inc **(DH)**	Stamford	CT	C	203 363-7300	4176
Crane Co **(PA)**	Stamford	CT	D	203 363-7300	4177
Dell Acquisition LLC	Plainville	CT	E	860 677-8545	3480
Delta-Ray Industries Inc	Bridgeport	CT	F	203 367-9903	404
Doncasters Inc **(HQ)**	Groton	CT	D	860 449-1603	1671
Drt Aerospace LLC	Winsted	CT	F	860 379-0783	5408
Dynamic Flight Systems	Monroe	CT	G	203 449-7211	2401
Edac Nd Inc	Glastonbury	CT	D	860 633-9474	1548
Edac Technologies LLC	Newington	CT	C	860 667-2134	2860
Electro-Methods Inc **(PA)**	South Windsor	CT	C	860 289-8661	3962
Enjet Aero New Britain LLC	New Britain	CT	C	860 356-0330	2531
Evoaero Inc	South Windsor	CT	D	860 289-2520	3967
Faille Precision Machining	Baltic	CT	G	860 822-1964	49
First Aviation Services Inc **(PA)**	Westport	CT	G	203 291-3300	5192
Flanagan Brothers Inc	Glastonbury	CT	G	860 633-3558	1551
Flight Enhancements Corp	Oxford	CT	G	912 257-0440	3401
Flight Support Inc	North Haven	CT	E	203 562-1415	3028
Forrest Machine Inc	Berlin	CT	D	860 563-1796	84
Gelder Aerospace LLC	Shelton	CT	G	203 283-9524	3804
GKN Aerospace Newington LLC **(DH)**	Newington	CT	C	860 667-8502	2867
Global Trbine Cmpnent Tech LLC	South Windsor	CT	E	860 528-4722	3973
Glyne Manufacturing Co Inc	Stratford	CT	F	203 375-4495	4415
Goodrich Corporation	Danbury	CT	B	203 797-5000	927
H & B Tool & Engineering Co	South Windsor	CT	E	860 528-9341	3976
Hamilton Standard Space	Windsor Locks	CT	E	860 654-6000	5396
Hamilton Sundstrand Corp **(HQ)**	Windsor Locks	CT	A	860 654-6000	5397
Hexcel Corporation **(PA)**	Stamford	CT	E	203 969-0666	4213
Hexcel Pottsville Corporation	Stamford	CT	G	203 969-0666	4214
I & J Machine Tool Company	Milford	CT	F	203 877-5376	2298
Isr (ntllgnce Srvllance Reconn	Danbury	CT	G	203 797-5000	936
Ithaco Space Systems Inc	Danbury	CT	D	607 272-7640	937
Jarvis Airfoil Inc	Portland	CT	D	860 342-5000	3568
Jobin Machine Inc	West Hartford	CT	E	860 953-1631	5079
Jonal Labs Logistics LLC	Meriden	CT	G	203 634-4444	2097
Kaman Aerospace Corporation	Bloomfield	CT	D	860 242-4461	232
Kaman Aerospace Corporation **(DH)**	Bloomfield	CT	A	860 242-4461	230
Kaman Aerospace Corporation	Bloomfield	CT	E	860 242-4461	231
Kaman Aerospace Group Inc **(HQ)**	Bloomfield	CT	F	860 243-7100	233
Kaman Corporation **(PA)**	Bloomfield	CT	D	860 243-7100	234
Kamatics Corporation **(DH)**	Bloomfield	CT	E	860 243-9704	235
L M Gill Welding and Mfr LLC	Manchester	CT	E	860 647-9931	2018
Leading Edge Concepts Inc	Bethel	CT	G	203 797-1200	168
Lee Company **(PA)**	Westbrook	CT	A	860 399-6281	5157
LM Gill Welding & Mfg LLC	Manchester	CT	E	860 647-9931	2020
McMellon Bros Incorporated	Stratford	CT	E	203 375-5685	4431
Metallon Inc	Thomaston	CT	E	860 283-8265	4509
Morning Star Tool LLC	Milford	CT	G	203 878-6026	2316
Mtm Corporation	Andover	CT	G	860 742-9600	3
Naiad Dynamics Us Inc **(HQ)**	Shelton	CT	E	203 929-6355	3836
Nelson Tool & Machine Co Inc	Bristol	CT	G	860 589-8004	586
Overhaul Support Services LLC	East Granby	CT	G	860 653-1980	1140
Overhaul Support Services LLC **(PA)**	East Granby	CT	E	860 264-2101	1141
Paradigm Manchester Inc **(DH)**	Manchester	CT	B	860 646-4048	2031
Paradigm Manchester Inc	Manchester	CT	D	860 646-4048	2029
Paradigm Manchester Inc	Manchester	CT	C	860 646-4048	2030
Paragon Tool Company Inc	Manchester	CT	G	860 647-9935	2035
Pas Technologies Inc	Manchester	CT	E	860 649-2727	2037
Pcx Aerostructures LLC **(PA)**	Newington	CT	C	860 666-2471	2893
Perry Technology Corporation	New Hartford	CT	D	860 738-2525	2644
Polamer Precision Inc	New Britain	CT	C	860 259-6200	2563
Polar Corporation	New Britain	CT	E	860 223-7891	2564
Pratt & Whitney Engine Svcs	Middletown	CT	B	860 344-4000	2212
Precision Aerospace Inc	Seymour	CT	E	203 888-3022	3762
Precision Metals and Plastics	Winsted	CT	G	860 238-4320	5419
Precision Speed Mfg LLC	Middletown	CT	E	860 635-8811	2213
Ramar-Hall Inc	Middlefield	CT	E	860 349-1081	2165
Richard Manufacturing Co Inc	Milford	CT	E	203 874-3617	2350
Rotair Aerospace Corporation	Bridgeport	CT	E	203 576-6545	484
Rotating Composite Tech LLC	Kensington	CT	G	860 829-6809	1920
Saf Industries LLC **(HQ)**	Meriden	CT	E	203 729-4900	2128
Saf Industries LLC	Meriden	CT	E	203 729-4900	2127
Saklax Manufacturing Company	Bloomfield	CT	G	860 242-2538	261
Satellite Tool & Mch Co Inc	South Windsor	CT	E	860 290-8558	4008
Senior Operations LLC	Enfield	CT	D	860 741-2546	1382
Simmonds Precision Pdts Inc	Danbury	CT	E	203 797-5000	994
Sky Mfg Company	Cheshire	CT	G	203 439-7016	762
Straton Industries Inc	Stratford	CT	D	203 375-4488	4450
Susan Martovich	Oxford	CT	G	203 881-1848	3426
Tachwa Enterprises Inc	Hamden	CT	G	203 691-5772	1787
Thompson Aerospace LLC	Bristol	CT	F	860 516-0472	617
Timken Arospc Drv Systems LLC	Manchester	CT	C	860 649-0000	2055
Triumph Actuation Systems - Co **(HQ)**	Windsor	CT	D	860 687-5412	5376
Triumph Eng Ctrl Systems LLC	West Hartford	CT	A	860 236-0651	5100

	CITY	ST	EMP	PHONE	ENTRY #
Triumph Group Inc	Bloomfield	CT	G	860 726-9378	268
United Avionics Inc	Naugatuck	CT	E	203 723-1404	2499
United Technologies Corp	East Hartford	CT	D	860 557-3333	1238
Valley Tool and Mfg LLC **(HQ)**	Orange	CT	D	203 799-8800	3386
W and G Machine Company Inc	Hamden	CT	E	203 288-8772	1794
W&R Manufacturing Inc	Milford	CT	G	203 877-5955	2381
Whitcraft LLC **(PA)**	Eastford	CT	C	860 974-0786	1315
Whitcraft Scrborough/Tempe LLC **(HQ)**	Eastford	CT	C	860 974-0786	1316
325 Silver Street Inc	Agawam	MA	E	413 789-1800	7415
Actronics Incorporated	Waltham	MA	F	781 890-7030	16024
Advanced Aerostructures Inc **(PA)**	Chicopee	MA	G	413 315-9284	9996
Aerobond Composites LLC	Springfield	MA	E	413 734-2224	15442
B & E Tool Company Inc	Southwick	MA	D	413 569-5585	15411
B/E Aerospace Inc	Rockport	MA	G	978 546-1331	14834
Boniface Tool & Die Inc	Dudley	MA	E	508 764-3248	10373
Demars	Amesbury	MA	G	978 388-2349	7484
Drt Aerospace LLC	Agawam	MA	E	413 789-1800	7428
General Airmotive Pwr Pdts LLC	Fall River	MA	G	508 674-6400	10702
Goodrich Corporation	Peabody	MA	C	978 532-2350	14336
Goodrich Corporation	Westford	MA	A	978 303-6700	16771
Ground Support Products Corp	Pembroke	MA	G	860 491-3348	14407
Hardric Laboratories Inc	North Chelmsford	MA	E	978 251-1702	13895
Jet Industries Inc	Agawam	MA	E	413 786-2010	7435
MSC Manufacturing Inc	Rockland	MA	G	781 888-8587	14816
Newmind Robotics LLC	North Andover	MA	G	239 322-2997	13719
Opalala Inc	Fall River	MA	F	508 646-0950	10743
Parker-Hannifin Corporation	Devens	MA	C	978 784-1200	10329
Parts Tool and Die Inc	Agawam	MA	E	413 821-9718	7445
Precision Components Group	West Springfield	MA	G	413 333-4184	16547
Pressue Techniques	North Andover	MA	G	978 686-2211	13725
Raytheon Company	Marlborough	MA	C	508 490-1000	12814
Rodney Hunt-Fontaine Inc **(DH)**	Orange	MA	C	978 544-2511	14227
Sibco LLC	Franklin	MA	G	508 520-2040	11079
Steger Power Connection Inc	Fall River	MA	F	508 646-0950	10763
Union Machine Company Lynn Inc **(PA)**	Groveland	MA	E	978 521-5100	11304
Wyman-Gordon Company **(DH)**	North Grafton	MA	B	508 839-8252	13969
C & L Aviation Group **(PA)**	Bangor	ME	E	207 217-6050	5633
Elmet Technologies LLC	Lewiston	ME	C	207 333-6100	6287
General Dynamics-Ots Inc	Saco	ME	E	207 283-3611	6847
Granite Mountain Inds LLC	South Portland	ME	G	978 369-0014	7028
Whitcraft Scrborough/Tempe LLC	Scarborough	ME	C	763 780-0060	6942
Albany Safran Composites LLC **(HQ)**	Rochester	NH	E	603 330-5800	19657
Atco-Aircraft Technical Co	Newington	NH	G	603 433-0081	19321
B/E Aerospace Inc	Hampton	NH	G	603 926-5700	18256
Bae Systems Info & Elec Sys	Merrimack	NH	B	603 885-4321	18990
Bae Systems Info & Elec Sys	Nashua	NH	G	603 885-3770	19124
Brazonics Inc **(DH)**	Hampton	NH	D	603 758-6237	18259
Continental Cable LLC	Hinsdale	NH	D	800 229-5131	18319
Exothermics Inc	Amherst	NH	F	603 821-5660	17560
General Electric Company	Hooksett	NH	A	603 666-8300	18351
Insource Design & Mfg Tech LLC	Merrimack	NH	G	603 718-8228	19007
Integrated Deicing Svcs LLC **(DH)**	Manchester	NH	B	603 647-1717	18843
Integrated Deicing Svcs LLC	Manchester	NH	C	603 647-1717	18844
Lakes Region Tubular Pdts Inc	Laconia	NH	E	603 528-2838	18573
Lanair Research & Development	Portsmouth	NH	G	603 433-6134	19584
Matrix Aerospace Corp	Claremont	NH	D	603 542-0191	17854
Screw-Matic Corporation **(PA)**	Seabrook	NH	E	978 356-6200	19816
Screw-Matic Corporation	Laconia	NH	F	603 293-8850	18585
Sierra Nevada Corporation	Bedford	NH	B	775 331-0222	17663
Avco Corporation **(DH)**	Providence	RI	C	401 421-2800	20965
Magnetic Seal Corp	Warren	RI	E	401 247-2800	21298
Textron Inc **(PA)**	Providence	RI	B	401 421-2800	21134
Textron Lycoming Corp **(HQ)**	Providence	RI	E	401 421-2800	21135
General Dynamics-Ots Inc	Williston	VT	G	802 662-7000	22670
Goodrich Corporation	Vergennes	VT	E	802 877-4000	22553
Liquid Measurement Systems Inc	Milton	VT	E	802 528-8100	22133
Sathorn Corporation	Williston	VT	E	802 860-2121	22689
Simmonds Precision Pdts Inc **(DH)**	Vergennes	VT	A	802 877-4000	22556

3731 Shipbuilding & Repairing

	CITY	ST	EMP	PHONE	ENTRY #
Bridgeport Boatwork Inc **(PA)**	Bridgeport	CT	G	860 536-9651	387
Connecticut Diesel and Marine	Milford	CT	G	203 481-1010	2267
Dorado Tankers Pool Inc	Norwalk	CT	E	203 662-2600	3143
Electric Boat Corporation	Groton	CT	D	860 433-0503	1673
Electric Boat Corporation	Groton	CT	D	860 433-3000	1674
Electric Boat Corporation **(HQ)**	Groton	CT	A	860 433-3000	1675
Exocetus Autonomous Systems	Wallingford	CT	G	860 512-7260	4740
LM Gill Welding & Mfg LLC	Manchester	CT	E	860 647-9931	2020
Naiad Dynamics Us Inc **(HQ)**	Shelton	CT	E	203 929-6355	3836
Navtec Rigging Solutions Inc	Clinton	CT	E	203 458-3163	790
Ocean Rigging LLC	Bridgeport	CT	G	800 624-2101	460
Thames Shipyard & Repair Co	New London	CT	D	860 442-5349	2782
Timbercraft LLC	New Milford	CT	G	860 355-5538	2829
Boston Ship Repair LLC	Boston	MA	C	617 330-5045	8441
Cape Cod Sailmakers Inc	Cataumet	MA	G	508 563-3080	9810
Deep Sea Systems Intl Inc	Cataumet	MA	G	508 540-6732	9812
F L Tripp & Sons Inc	Westport Point	MA	E	508 636-4058	16854

	CITY	ST	EMP	PHONE	ENTRY #
General Dynamics Corporation	Hinsdale	MA	E	413 494-3137	11520
Hydroid LLC	Pocasset	MA	E	508 563-6565	14597
Irobot Corporation **(PA)**	Bedford	MA	B	781 430-3000	7985
Ksaria Service Corporation	Methuen	MA	E	978 933-0000	13031
Luscombe Ave Waiting Room	Woods Hole	MA	F	508 299-8051	17327
Northeast Ship Repair Inc **(PA)**	Boston	MA	C	617 330-5045	8743
Ocean Tug & Barge Engrg Corp	Milford	MA	G	508 473-0545	13135
American Lighthouse Foundation	Owls Head	ME	G	207 594-4174	6561
Bath Iron Works Corporation **(HQ)**	Bath	ME	B	207 443-3311	5674
Bath Iron Works Corporation	Brunswick	ME	D	207 442-1266	5830
General Dynamics Corporation	Bath	ME	E	207 442-3245	5677
Maloney Marine Rigging Inc	West Southport	ME	G	207 633-6788	7179
Robinson-Greaves Marine Pntg	Wells	ME	G	207 313-6132	7164
Rockland Marine Corporation	Rockland	ME	E	207 594-7860	6809
Supervisor of Shipbuilding	Bath	ME	G	207 442-2520	5681
Washburn & Doughty Assoc Inc	East Boothbay	ME	D	207 633-6517	5980
Yankee Marina Inc	Yarmouth	ME	E	207 846-9120	7304
Portsmouth Naval Shipyard	Portsmouth	NH	G	207 438-1000	19608
United States Dept of Navy	Portsmouth	NH	A	207 438-2714	19627
Aramid Rigging Inc	Portsmouth	RI	G	401 683-6966	20917
Blount Boats Inc	Warren	RI	D	401 245-8300	21289
C R Scott Marine Wdwkg Co	Newport	RI	G	401 849-0715	20659
Electric Boat Corporation	North Kingstown	RI	D	401 268-2410	20707
Fv Misty Blue LLC	Bristol	RI	G	609 884-3000	20080
International Yacht Restoratio	Newport	RI	F	401 846-2587	20666
Northrup & Gibson Entps LLC	Jamestown	RI	G	401 423-2152	20493
Promet Marine Service Corp	Providence	RI	E	401 467-3730	21094
Relentless Inc	North Kingstown	RI	F	401 295-2585	20736
Scandia Marine Inc	Tiverton	RI	G	401 625-5881	21262
Senesco Marine LLC	North Kingstown	RI	B	401 295-0373	20740
Lake Champlain Trnsp Co	Burlington	VT	C	802 660-3495	21792

3732 Boat Building & Repairing

	CITY	ST	EMP	PHONE	ENTRY #
Chester Boatworks	Deep River	CT	G	860 526-2227	1059
Dutch Wharf Boat Yard & Marina	Branford	CT	F	203 488-9000	310
Hbi Boat LLC	Groton	CT	G	860 536-7776	1677
Jennings Yacht Services	Mystic	CT	G	860 625-1368	2440
Kiwanis Fndtion Middletown Inc	Middletown	CT	G	860 638-8135	2198
McClave Philbrick & Giblin	Mystic	CT	G	860 572-7710	2443
New England Fiberglass Repair **(PA)**	Norwalk	CT	G	203 866-1690	3207
Vespoli Usa Inc	New Haven	CT	E	203 773-0311	2751
Vintage Boat Restorations LLC	Bristol	CT	G	860 582-0774	622
A To Z Boatworks Inc	Scituate	MA	G	781 545-6632	15004
Beetle Inc	Wareham	MA	G	508 295-8585	16241
Boston Boatworks LLC	Charlestown	MA	E	617 561-9111	9825
Boston Family Boat Building	Jamaica Plain	MA	G	617 522-5366	11941
Cape Cod Shipbuilding Co	Wareham	MA	F	508 295-3550	16242
Charr Custom Boat Company	Yarmouth Port	MA	G	508 375-0028	17529
Composite Engineering Inc	Concord	MA	G	978 371-3132	10122
Cooper Eldred Boat Builders	Falmouth	MA	G	508 540-7130	10788
Cutlass Marine Inc	East Weymouth	MA	G	781 740-1260	10540
CW Hood Yachts Inc	Marblehead	MA	F	781 631-0192	12680
Danalevi Corp	Belchertown	MA	G	413 626-8120	8023
E M Crosby Boat Works	West Barnstable	MA	G	508 362-7100	16406
Fiberglas Fabrications	Orleans	MA	G	508 255-9409	14233
Fortier Boats Inc	Somerset	MA	G	508 673-5253	15144
Hazard Marine A Div Ltd Inds	Webster	MA	G	508 943-7531	16342
Heritage Wharf Company LLC	Dartmouth	MA	G	508 990-1011	10275
Howard Boats LLC	Barnstable	MA	G	508 362-6859	7948
Inriver Tank & Boat Inc	Concord	MA	G	978 287-9534	10136
Intercept Boat Corp	Pembroke	MA	G	781 294-8100	14411
Karls Boat Shop Inc	Harwich	MA	F	508 432-4488	11395
Knd Machine Co	Rehoboth	MA	G	508 336-5509	14752
Marshall Marine Corp	South Dartmouth	MA	F	508 994-0414	15240
Newbury Port Meritown Society	Amesbury	MA	G	978 834-0050	7501
Pease Boat Works & Marine Rlwy	Chatham	MA	G	508 945-7800	9862
Peinert Boatworks Inc	Mattapoisett	MA	G	508 758-3020	12889
Pleasant Bay Boat Spar Co LLC	Orleans	MA	G	508 240-0058	14240
Sandy Point Boat Works LLC	Carver	MA	G	508 878-8057	9807
Scotia Boat Builders	Abington	MA	G	781 871-2120	7331
Sperry Sails Inc	Marion	MA	G	508 748-2581	12705
Still Water Design Inc	Chelsea	MA	G	617 308-5820	9971
Wenaumet Bluffs Boat Works Inc	Pocasset	MA	G	888 224-9942	14602
Whitecap Composites Inc	Peabody	MA	G	978 278-5718	14382
William Clements	North Billerica	MA	G	978 663-3103	13877
Winninghoff Boats Inc	Rowley	MA	F	978 948-2314	14869
Alley Road LLC	Boothbay Harbor	ME	E	207 633-3171	5781
Atlantic Boat Company	Brooklin	ME	E	207 664-2900	5813
B Marine Corp	Boothbay Harbor	ME	F	207 633-3171	5782
Belmont Boatworks LLC	Belmont	ME	F	207 342-2885	5701
Benjamin River Marine Inc	Brooklin	ME	G	207 359-2244	5814
Billings Diesel & Marine Svc	Stonington	ME	E	207 367-2328	7069
Blevins Company	Edgecomb	ME	G	207 882-6396	5999
Bridges Point Boat Yard Inc	Brooklin	ME	G	207 359-2713	5815
Brion Rieff Boatbuilder Inc	Brooklin	ME	G	207 359-4455	5816
Brooklin Boat Yard Inc **(PA)**	Brooklin	ME	D	207 359-2236	5817
C B Boatworks Inc	Peru	ME	G	207 562-8849	6584
C W Paine Yacht Design Inc	Camden	ME	G	207 236-2166	5866
Carpenters Boat Shop Inc	Pemaquid	ME	G	207 677-2614	6579
Clark Island Boat Works	South Thomaston	ME	G	207 594-4112	7045
Classic Boat Shop Inc	Bernard	ME	G	207 244-3374	5706
Custom Composite Technologies	Bath	ME	G	207 442-7007	5675
D N Hylan Associates Inc	Brooklin	ME	G	207 359-9807	5819
Dana Robes Boat Builders	Round Pond	ME	G	207 529-2433	6829
Danas Boat Shop	Westport Island	ME	G	207 882-7205	7216
Dark Harbor Boatyard Corp	Islesboro	ME	F	207 734-2246	6215
Downeast Boats & Composites	Penobscot	ME	G	207 326-9400	6581
Edgecomb Boat Works	Edgecomb	ME	G	207 882-5038	6002
Ellis Boat Co Inc	Southwest Harbor	ME	F	207 244-9221	7046
Eric Dow Boatbuilder	Brooklin	ME	G	207 359-2277	5820
Farrins Boat Shop	Walpole	ME	G	207 563-5510	7140
Flowers Boat Works Inc	Walpole	ME	G	207 563-7404	7141
French Webb & Co Inc	Belfast	ME	F	207 338-6706	5689
General Marine Inc	Biddeford	ME	G	207 284-7517	5737
H & H Marine Inc	Steuben	ME	F	207 546-7477	7067
Hodgdon Shipbuilding LLC	Damariscotta	ME	G	207 563-7033	5936
Hodgdon Shipbuilding LLC **(HQ)**	East Boothbay	ME	F	207 633-4194	5976
Hodgdon Yachts Inc	Richmond	ME	G	207 737-2802	6782
Hodgdon Yachts Inc **(PA)**	East Boothbay	ME	C	207 737-2802	5977
Hollands Boat Shop Inc	Belfast	ME	G	207 338-3155	5690
J O Brown & Son Inc	North Haven	ME	G	207 867-4621	6511
James H Rich Boatyard	Bernard	ME	G	207 244-3208	5707
Johansons Boatworks	Rockland	ME	F	207 596-7060	6800
Johns Bay Boat Co	South Bristol	ME	G	207 644-8261	7005
Johnson Otdoors Watercraft Inc **(HQ)**	Old Town	ME	E	207 827-5513	6541
Johnsons Boatyard Inc	Long Island	ME	G	207 766-3319	6383
Libbys Boat Shop	Beals	ME	G	207 497-5487	5684
Lyman Morse Boatbuilding Inc **(PA)**	Thomaston	ME	D	207 354-6904	7085
Lyman Morse Boatbuilding Inc	Thomaston	ME	D	207 354-6904	7086
Maine Cat Co Inc	Bremen	ME	F	207 529-6500	5792
Malcolm L Pettegrow Inc	Southwest Harbor	ME	F	207 244-3514	7049
Morris Yacht Inc **(PA)**	Bass Harbor	ME	E	207 667-6235	5672
North End Composites LLC	Rockland	ME	C	207 594-8427	6806
Northwood Canoe Co	Atkinson	ME	G	207 564-3667	5544
Otis Enterprises Marine Corp	Searsport	ME	G	207 548-6362	6953
Padebco Custom Boats Inc	Round Pond	ME	G	207 529-5106	6832
Portland Pudgy Inc	Portland	ME	G	207 761-2428	6712
Rockport Marine Inc	Rockport	ME	E	207 236-9651	6826
Spb LLC	Augusta	ME	G	207 620-7998	5620
Stuart Marine Corp Inc	Rockland	ME	G	207 594-5515	6811
SW Boatworks	Lamoine	ME	G	207 667-7427	6264
Talaria Company LLC	Southwest Harbor	ME	C	207 244-5572	7052
Talaria Company LLC	Trenton	ME	C	207 667-1891	7102
Washburn & Doughty Assoc Inc	East Boothbay	ME	D	207 633-6517	5980
Webbers Cove Boat Yard Inc	East Blue Hill	ME	G	207 374-2841	5975
Wesley Lash	Friendship	ME	G	207 832-7807	6094
Wesmac Custom Boats Inc **(PA)**	Surry	ME	F	207 667-4822	7077
Wesmac Custom Boats Inc	Surry	ME	G	207 667-4822	7078
Wild Duck Boat Works LLC	Harpswell	ME	G	207 837-2920	6175
York Marine Inc	Rockland	ME	G	207 596-7400	6816
American Marine Products Inc	Charlestown	NH	E	954 782-1400	17810
Chisletts Boating & Design LLC	Dover	NH	F	603 755-6815	18013
Eastern Boats Inc	Milton	NH	E	603 652-9213	19084
Hampton North Fisheries Inc	Nottingham	NH	G	603 463-5874	19414
Juliet Marine Systems Inc	Portsmouth	NH	G	603 319-8412	19582
New England Nautical LLC	Portsmouth	NH	G	603 601-3166	19598
Special Projects Group LLC	Gilford	NH	G	603 391-9700	18192
Viking Wldg & Fabrication LLC	Kensington	NH	G	603 394-7887	18537
Alden Yachts Corporation	Bristol	RI	D	401 683-4200	20060
American Boat Builders	Newport	RI	E	401 236-2466	20654
Anchorage Inc	Warren	RI	F	401 245-3300	21285
Aquidneck Cstm Composites Inc	Bristol	RI	G	401 254-6911	20063
Berthon Usa Inc	Newport	RI	G	401 846-8404	20657
Blount Boats Inc	Warren	RI	D	401 245-8300	21289
Bristol Cushions Inc	Bristol	RI	F	401 247-4499	20065
C & C Fiberglass Components	Bristol	RI	F	401 254-4342	20067
C R Scott Marine Wdwkg Co	Newport	RI	G	401 849-0715	20659
Chem-Tainer Industries Inc	Cranston	RI	D	401 467-2750	20196
Clark Boat-Yard	Jamestown	RI	G	401 423-3625	20488
Dur A Flex Motor Sports	Warwick	RI	G	401 739-0202	21356
East Passage Boatwrights Inc	Bristol	RI	G	401 253-5535	20074
Element Industries Inc	Bristol	RI	F	401 253-8802	20075
Eric Goetz Custom Sailboats	Bristol	RI	E	401 253-2670	20077
F V Sea Breeze LLC	Wakefield	RI	G	401 792-0188	21270
Hunt Boatbuilders Inc	Portsmouth	RI	G	401 324-4205	20924
Hunt Yachts LLC	Portsmouth	RI	D	401 324-4201	20925
International Yacht Restoratio	Newport	RI	F	401 846-2587	20666
Jamestown Boat Yard Inc	Jamestown	RI	E	401 423-0600	20492
Jon Barrett Associates Inc	Newport	RI	G	401 846-8226	20669
Lenmarine Inc **(PA)**	Bristol	RI	E	401 253-2200	20089
Midland Co Inc	Coventry	RI	G	401 397-4425	20156
Morris Yachts LLC	Portsmouth	RI	G	207 667-2499	20929
Naiad Inflatables Newport Inc	Newport	RI	F	401 683-6700	20673
Narragansett Shipwrights Inc	Newport	RI	G	401 846-3312	20674

	CITY	ST	EMP	PHONE	ENTRY #
Outerlmits Offshore Powerboats	Bristol	RI	F	401 253-7300	20096
Pearson Composites LLC	Warren	RI	F	401 245-1200	21301
Quarter Moon Incorporated **(PA)**	Portsmouth	RI	E	401 683-0400	20937
Rhode Northsales Island Inc	Portsmouth	RI	E	401 683-7997	20939
Shannon Boat Company Inc	Bristol	RI	E	401 253-2441	20103
Sparkman & Stephens LLC **(PA)**	Newport	RI	F	401 847-5449	20683
Stur-Dee Boat Co	Tiverton	RI	G	401 624-9373	21265
Talaria Company LLC **(PA)**	Portsmouth	RI	F	401 683-7100	20940
Talaria Company LLC	Portsmouth	RI	C	401 683-7280	20941
Transfusion Boat Works Inc	Westerly	RI	G	401 348-5878	21545
Warren River Boatworks Inc	Warren	RI	G	401 245-6949	21314
Adirondack Guide Boat	North Ferrisburgh	VT	G	802 425-3926	22224
Darling Boatworks Inc	Charlotte	VT	G	802 425-2004	21833
Fiberglass Plus Inc	North Hero	VT	G	802 878-2066	22230
Martin Custom Boat Works LLC	North Ferrisburgh	VT	G	802 318-7882	22226
Washburn Boat & Auto Body	Williston	VT	G	802 863-1383	22697

3743 Railroad Eqpt

	CITY	ST	EMP	PHONE	ENTRY #
James L Howard and Company Inc	Bloomfield	CT	E	860 242-3581	228
L T A Group Inc	South Windsor	CT	E	860 291-9911	3989
Transit Systems Inc	Plainville	CT	G	860 747-3669	3521
Winchester Industries Inc	Winsted	CT	G	860 379-5336	5429
Winslow Automatics Inc	New Britain	CT	D	860 225-6321	2591
Bombardier Services Corp	Boston	MA	G	617 464-0323	8419
Crrc MA Corporation	Springfield	MA	G	617 415-7190	15463
Motive Power	Boston	MA	G	857 350-3765	8713
N A Railrunner Inc	Lincoln	MA	G	781 860-7245	12288
Rl Controls LLC	Woburn	MA	E	781 932-3349	17286
Rtr Technologies Inc **(PA)**	Stockbridge	MA	F	413 298-0025	15551
Okonite Company	Cumberland	RI	D	401 333-3500	20336

3751 Motorcycles, Bicycles & Parts

	CITY	ST	EMP	PHONE	ENTRY #
Avalanche Downhill Racing Inc	Colchester	CT	G	860 537-4306	799
Cat LLC	Hartford	CT	G	860 953-1807	1812
Cycling Sports Group Inc **(HQ)**	Wilton	CT	D	608 268-8916	5286
Frank Roth Co Inc	Stratford	CT	D	203 377-2155	4413
Tri State Choppers LLC	New Milford	CT	G	860 210-1854	2832
Crimsonbikes LLC	Cambridge	MA	E	617 958-1727	9445
Italian Choppers LLC	Southbridge	MA	G	508 648-6816	15387
Lifestyle Hq LLC	Amherst	MA	G	310 741-8489	7517
Niche Inc	New Bedford	MA	E	508 990-4202	13427
Parlee Cycles Inc	Beverly	MA	G	978 998-4880	8164
Seven Cycles Inc	Watertown	MA	E	617 923-7774	16315
Superpedestrian Inc	Cambridge	MA	G	617 945-1892	9666
Heli Modified Inc	Cornish	ME	F	207 625-4642	5925
Rave Brothers LLC	South Portland	ME	G	207 773-7727	7038
JCP Trading Inc	Manchester	NH	G	603 232-0967	18849
Moto Tassinari Inc	West Lebanon	NH	F	603 298-6646	19957
Motorway Engineering Inc	Manchester	NH	F	603 668-6315	18878
Segway Inc **(DH)**	Bedford	NH	C	603 222-6000	17662
South County Choppers	Narragansett	RI	G	401 788-1000	20650
Bike & Ski Touring Ctr of Neng	Middlebury	VT	G	802 388-6666	22102

3761 Guided Missiles & Space Vehicles

	CITY	ST	EMP	PHONE	ENTRY #
Singularity Space Systems LLC	Granby	CT	G	860 713-3626	1591
Electron Solutions Inc	Lexington	MA	F	781 674-2440	12222
Raytheon Company	Tewksbury	MA	C	978 858-5000	15829
Raytheon Company **(PA)**	Waltham	MA	B	781 522-3000	16184
Raytheon Company	Marlborough	MA	E	310 647-9438	12813
Raytheon Company	North Billerica	MA	G	978 313-0201	13858
Raytheon Lgstics Spport Trning **(HQ)**	Bedford	MA	F	310 647-9438	8005
Blushift Aerospace Inc	Brunswick	ME	G	207 619-1703	5831

3764 Guided Missile/Space Vehicle Propulsion Units & parts

	CITY	ST	EMP	PHONE	ENTRY #
Wormtown Atomic Propulsion	Waltham	MA	G	781 487-7777	16225
Blushift Aerospace Inc	Brunswick	ME	G	207 619-1703	5831
Exothermics Inc	Amherst	NH	F	603 821-5660	17560

3769 Guided Missile/Space Vehicle Parts & Eqpt, NEC

	CITY	ST	EMP	PHONE	ENTRY #
Accupaulo Holding Corporation **(PA)**	Bristol	CT	E	860 666-5621	511
Aerocess Inc	Berlin	CT	F	860 357-2451	67
Braxton Manufacturing Co Inc	Watertown	CT	C	860 274-6781	5000
Edac Technologies LLC	East Windsor	CT	F	860 789-2511	1283
Edac Technologies LLC **(HQ)**	Cheshire	CT	C	203 806-2090	728
Kaman Aerospace Group Inc **(HQ)**	Bloomfield	CT	F	860 243-7100	233
Meriden Manufacturing Inc	Meriden	CT	D	203 237-7481	2104
Ramar-Hall Inc	Middlefield	CT	E	860 349-1081	2165
Spartan Aerospace LLC	Manchester	CT	D	860 533-7500	2049
Sterling Engineering Corp	Pleasant Valley	CT	C	860 379-3366	3547
United Tool and Die Company **(PA)**	West Hartford	CT	C	860 246-6531	5102
325 Silver Street Inc	Agawam	MA	E	413 789-1800	7415
Cliflex Bellows Corporation	Boston	MA	E	617 268-5774	8477
Entwistle Company **(HQ)**	Hudson	MA	C	508 481-4000	11772
Geonautics Manufacturing Inc	Newburyport	MA	E	978 462-7161	13494
L3 Technologies Inc	Burlington	MA	C	781 270-2100	9295
Massmicro LLC	Canton	MA	F	781 828-6110	9756
Raytheon Company	Tewksbury	MA	C	978 858-5000	15829
Raytheon International Inc **(PA)**	Waltham	MA	G	781 522-3000	16185
Tell Tool Inc	Westfield	MA	D	413 568-1671	16732
Tell Tool Acquisition Inc **(HQ)**	Westfield	MA	G	413 568-1671	16733
Wgi Inc	Southwick	MA	C	413 569-9444	15421
Elmet Technologies LLC	Lewiston	ME	C	207 333-6100	6287
Fiber Materials Inc **(HQ)**	Biddeford	ME	E	207 282-5911	5733
Honeywell International Inc	Woonsocket	RI	D	401 762-6200	21569
Masiello Enterprises Inc	Coventry	RI	E	401 826-1883	20155
Swissline Products Inc	Cumberland	RI	D	401 333-8888	20345
Superior Tchncal Ceramics Corp	Saint Albans	VT	C	802 527-7726	22380

3792 Travel Trailers & Campers

	CITY	ST	EMP	PHONE	ENTRY #
Fiberglass Engr & Design Co	Wallingford	CT	G	203 265-1644	4743
Keystone Rv Company	Bridgeport	CT	C	203 367-9847	440
Thule Holding Inc **(DH)**	Seymour	CT	F	203 881-9600	3766
Boston Trailer Manufacturing	Walpole	MA	E	508 668-2242	15990
American Keder Inc **(PA)**	Rindge	NH	G	603 899-3233	19646
Bear Country Powersports LLC	Errol	NH	G	603 482-3370	18109
Line-X Merrimack Valley LLC	Bow	NH	G	603 224-7792	17721

3795 Tanks & Tank Components

	CITY	ST	EMP	PHONE	ENTRY #
New England Airfoil Pdts Inc	Farmington	CT	E	860 677-1376	1498
Shawnee Chemical	Redding	CT	G	203 938-3003	3652
General Dynamics Def	Pittsfield	MA	A	413 494-1110	14471
Natgun Corporation **(HQ)**	Wakefield	MA	C	781 224-5180	15963
Negm Electric LLC	Somersworth	NH	G	603 692-4806	19844

3799 Transportation Eqpt, NEC

	CITY	ST	EMP	PHONE	ENTRY #
On Track Karting Inc **(PA)**	Wallingford	CT	F	203 626-0464	4781
Serafin Sulky Co	Stafford Springs	CT	G	860 684-2986	4114
Brownell Boat Trailers Inc	Fairhaven	MA	G	508 996-3110	10639
Brownell Trailers LLC	Fairhaven	MA	F	508 996-3110	10640
Dolly Plow Inc	Pembroke	MA	G	781 293-9828	14400
Hostar Mar Trnspt Systems Inc	Wareham	MA	E	508 295-2900	16250
Moseley Corporation	Franklin	MA	E	508 520-4004	11068
Places To Go LLC	New Bedford	MA	G	774 202-7756	13438
Steele Canvas Basket Corp	Chelsea	MA	E	800 541-8929	9970
Wright Trailers Inc	Seekonk	MA	F	508 336-8530	15044
Alfred St Germain	Hiram	ME	E	207 925-1135	6193
E M K Inc	Skowhegan	ME	F	207 474-2666	6973
Eimskip USA Inc	Portland	ME	G	207 221-5268	6660
M & C Powersports	Leeds	ME	G	207 713-3128	6270
Davis Village Solutions LLC	New Ipswich	NH	G	603 878-3662	19304
Proline Products LLC	Milton	NH	G	603 652-7337	19087
Rokon International Inc	Rochester	NH	F	603 335-3200	19684
Moody Investments LLC	Exeter	RI	G	401 423-0121	20453
Textron Inc **(PA)**	Providence	RI	B	401 421-2800	21134
Country Riders Snow Mobile CLB	Jay	VT	G	802 988-2255	22044
Crank Shop Inc	Essex Junction	VT	G	802 878-3615	21938

38 MEASURING, ANALYZING AND CONTROLLING INSTRUMENTS; PHOTOGRAPHIC, MEDICAL AN

3812 Search, Detection, Navigation & Guidance Systs & Instrs

	CITY	ST	EMP	PHONE	ENTRY #
Accuturn Mfg Co LLC	South Windsor	CT	F	860 289-6355	3931
Airflo Instrument Company	Glastonbury	CT	G	860 633-9455	1536
Ais Global Holdings LLC	Cheshire	CT	A	203 250-3500	709
Amius Partners LLC	New Haven	CT	G	203 526-5926	2656
Atlantic Inertial Systems Inc **(DH)**	Cheshire	CT	B	203 250-3500	713
Atlantic Inertial Systems Inc	Cheshire	CT	A	203 250-3500	714
Beacon Group Inc **(PA)**	Newington	CT	C	860 594-5200	2846
Boeing Company	East Windsor	CT	G	860 627-9393	1279
Brandstrom Instruments Inc	Ridgefield	CT	E	203 544-9341	3661
Carl Perry	Middletown	CT	G	860 834-4459	2181
Chromalloy Component Svcs Inc	Windsor	CT	C	860 688-7798	5325
Connecticut Analytical Corp	Bethany	CT	F	203 393-9666	119
Drs Naval Power Systems Inc	Danbury	CT	B	203 798-3000	904
Dynamic Controls Hs Inc	Windsor Locks	CT	G	860 654-6000	5391
Eaton Aerospace LLC	Bethel	CT	E	203 796-6000	150
Edac Nd Inc	Glastonbury	CT	D	860 633-9474	1548
Electro-Methods Inc **(PA)**	South Windsor	CT	C	860 289-8661	3962
Exocetus Autonomous Systems	Wallingford	CT	G	860 512-7260	4740
Gems Sensors Inc **(HQ)**	Plainville	CT	B	860 747-3000	3491
Hard-Core Self Defense	Shelton	CT	G	203 231-2344	3809
Hartford Aircraft Products	Bloomfield	CT	E	860 242-8228	223
Hermtech Inc	East Windsor	CT	G	860 758-7528	1285
Higgs Energy LLC	Norwich	CT	G	860 213-5561	3282
Kaman Corporation	Middletown	CT	C	860 632-1000	2196
Kaman Precision Products Inc	Middletown	CT	E	860 632-1000	2197
Ladrdefense LLC	Plantsville	CT	G	860 637-8488	3536
Lee Company **(PA)**	Westbrook	CT	A	860 399-6281	5157
Meriden Electronics Corp	Meriden	CT	G	203 237-8811	2103
Meriden Manufacturing Inc	Meriden	CT	D	203 237-7481	2104
Msj Investments Inc	Stafford Springs	CT	F	860 684-9956	4113
Mtu Aero Engines N Amer Inc	Rocky Hill	CT	G	860 258-9700	3724

	CITY	ST	EMP	PHONE	ENTRY #
Northmen Defense LLC	Oakdale	CT	G	860 908-9308	3294
Northrop Grumman Corporation	East Hartford	CT	D	860 282-4461	1207
Passur Aerospace Inc **(PA)**	Stamford	CT	E	203 622-4086	4278
Polar Corporation	New Britain	CT	E	860 223-7891	2564
Raytheon Company	Mystic	CT	E	860 446-4900	2449
Saf Industries LLC **(HQ)**	Meriden	CT	E	203 729-4900	2128
Sensor Switch Inc **(DH)**	New Haven	CT	E	203 265-2842	2737
Sextant Btsllc	Killingworth	CT	G	203 500-3245	1929
Spectrogram Corporation	Madison	CT	G	203 245-2433	1977
Sperian Protectn Instrumentatn	Middletown	CT	C	860 344-1079	2225
Thayermahan Inc	Groton	CT	E	860 785-9994	1688
Triumph Eng Ctrl Systems LLC	West Hartford	CT	F	860 236-0651	5101
Triumph Eng Ctrl Systems LLC	West Hartford	CT	A	860 236-0651	5100
United States Dept of Navy	Groton	CT	G	860 694-3524	1689
AC Navigation LLC	Medfield	MA	G	508 359-5903	12908
Accusonic Technologies **(DH)**	New Bedford	MA	F	508 495-6600	13348
Adcole Corporation **(HQ)**	Marlborough	MA	C	508 485-9100	12710
Advanced ID Detection LLC	Medway	MA	G	617 544-8030	12954
Aero Surveillance Inc	North Andover	MA	G	978 691-5832	13688
Agilynx Inc	Billerica	MA	G	617 314-6463	8206
Alakai Technologies Corp	Hopkinton	MA	G	774 248-4964	11689
Altair Avionics Corporation	Norwood	MA	E	781 762-8600	14125
Americas Best Defense	Shrewsbury	MA	G	774 745-5809	15101
Ametek Inc	Wilmington	MA	D	978 988-4101	16973
Ametek Arospc Pwr Holdings Inc **(HQ)**	Wilmington	MA	C	978 988-4771	16974
Analogic Corporation **(HQ)**	Peabody	MA	A	978 326-4000	14311
Antenna Associates Inc	Brockton	MA	E	508 583-3241	9120
API Technologies Corporation	Marlborough	MA	D	508 251-6400	12719
Asymmetrical Defense LLC	Townsend	MA	G	978 597-6078	15868
Atk Space Systems Inc	Hopkinton	MA	G	508 497-9457	11692
Auriga Measurement Systems **(PA)**	Wayland	MA	G	978 452-7700	16334
Bae Systems Info & Elec Sys	Burlington	MA	D	781 273-3388	9238
Bae Systems Tech Sol Srvc Inc	Sagamore	MA	G	508 833-9562	14883
Bounce Imaging Inc	Allston	MA	F	716 310-8281	7460
Chris Martin **(PA)**	Avon	MA	G	508 580-0069	7882
Cooper Interconnect Inc	Chelsea	MA	D	617 389-7080	9950
Cormiers Self Defense Aca	Holliston	MA	G	508 596-7326	11565
Craig AAR	North Andover	MA	G	978 691-0024	13696
Creighton Kayla	Whitinsville	MA	G	508 612-0685	16912
Defense Integration	Brockton	MA	G	617 515-2470	9138
Defense Support Solutions LLC	Lawrence	MA	G	978 989-9460	12016
E S Ritchie & Sons Inc	Pembroke	MA	E	781 826-5131	14402
Edgeone LLC	West Wareham	MA	G	508 291-0960	16570
Edgeone LLC	West Wareham	MA	D	508 291-0057	16571
Emergent Biodefense Ops	Canton	MA	G	718 302-3000	9731
Entwistle Company **(HQ)**	Hudson	MA	C	508 481-4000	11772
Flir Systems-Boston Inc **(HQ)**	North Billerica	MA	B	978 901-8000	13815
Foster-Miller Inc	Devens	MA	D	781 684-4000	10320
General Dynamics Corporation	Pittsfield	MA	G	413 494-2313	14470
General Dynamics Def	Pittsfield	MA	A	413 494-1110	14471
General Dynamics Mission Syste	Quincy	MA	D	617 715-7000	14628
General Dynmics Mssion Systems	Pittsfield	MA	A	413 494-1110	14472
GM Merc Inc	Hopkinton	MA	G	508 878-1305	11717
Hxi LLC	Harvard	MA	F	978 772-7774	11379
Hydroid Inc **(PA)**	Pocasset	MA	C	508 563-6565	14596
J W Fishers Mfg Inc	East Taunton	MA	F	508 822-7330	10514
L3 Technologies Inc	Ayer	MA	F	978 462-2400	7924
L3 Technologies Inc	Northampton	MA	A	413 586-2330	14009
L3 Technologies Inc	Burlington	MA	C	781 270-2100	9295
L3harris Technologies Inc	Bellingham	MA	D	508 966-9500	8043
L3harris Technologies Inc	Bedford	MA	D	781 538-4148	7987
Laser Labs Inc	Pembroke	MA	G	781 826-4138	14415
Lockheed Martin Corp - Boston	Burlington	MA	E	781 565-1100	9298
Lockheed Martin Corporation	Chelmsford	MA	C	978 256-4113	9913
Lockheed Martin Corporation	Chelmsford	MA	A	978 256-4113	9914
Lockheed Martin Corporation	Marlborough	MA	B	508 460-0086	12788
Lockheed Martin Corporation	Lexington	MA	G	781 862-6222	12239
Lockheed Martin Corporation	Pittsfield	MA	B	413 236-3400	14485
Lockheed Martin Services LLC	Lowell	MA	E	978 275-9730	12397
Lockheed Martin Sippican Inc **(HQ)**	Marion	MA	B	508 748-3399	12699
Lockheed Martin Sippican Inc	Marion	MA	E	774 553-6282	12700
Lowell Digisonde Intl LLC	Lowell	MA	G	978 735-4752	12398
Magcap Engineering LLC	Canton	MA	F	781 821-2300	9754
Magnetic Sciences Inc	Acton	MA	G	978 266-9355	7372
Massa Products Corporation	Hingham	MA	D	781 749-3120	11501
Megapulse Incorporated	Bedford	MA	E	781 538-5299	7989
Megawave Corporation	Worcester	MA	G	978 615-7200	17412
Mettler-Toledo Thornton Inc	Billerica	MA	D	978 262-0210	8266
Modeltronix	Upton	MA	G	508 529-3567	15909
MSI Transducers Corp	Littleton	MA	F	978 486-0404	12313
Navionics Inc	Wareham	MA	E	508 291-6000	16253
Northrop Grumman Corporation	Devens	MA	G	978 772-0352	10327
Northrop Grumman Systems Corp	Andover	MA	G	978 247-7812	7578
Parts Tool and Die Inc	Agawam	MA	E	413 821-9718	7445
Perspecta Svcs & Solutions Inc **(DH)**	Waltham	MA	E	781 684-4000	16173
Photonis Scientific Inc **(DH)**	Sturbridge	MA	D	508 347-4000	15646
Polaris Contract Mfg Inc	Marion	MA	B	508 748-3399	12702
Princeton Security Tech Inc **(HQ)**	Franklin	MA	G	609 924-7310	11074
Princton Gamma-Tech Instrs Inc	Franklin	MA	F	609 924-7310	11075
Prosensing Inc	Amherst	MA	F	413 549-4402	7522
Qualtre Inc **(HQ)**	Sudbury	MA	E	508 658-8360	15666
Radar Technology Inc	Newburyport	MA	E	978 463-6064	13526
Radenna LLC	Westford	MA	G	781 248-8826	16787
Raytheon Company	Andover	MA	C	978 470-5000	7594
Raytheon Company **(PA)**	Waltham	MA	B	781 522-3000	16184
Raytheon Company	Marlborough	MA	B	978 440-1000	12812
Raytheon Company	Andover	MA	D	781 522-3000	7595
Raytheon Company	Pittsfield	MA	G	413 494-8042	14505
Raytheon Company	Tewksbury	MA	F	978 858-5000	15828
Raytheon Company	Chelmsford	MA	C	978 256-6054	9925
Raytheon Company	Framingham	MA	C	508 877-5231	10999
Raytheon Company	Marlborough	MA	E	310 647-9438	12813
Raytheon Company	Lexington	MA	G	781 862-6800	12258
Raytheon Company	Woburn	MA	C	781 933-1863	17279
Raytheon Company	Woburn	MA	C	339 645-6000	17280
Raytheon Company	Tewksbury	MA	C	978 858-5000	15829
Raytheon Company	Marlborough	MA	C	508 490-1000	12814
Raytheon Company	Andover	MA	D	978 470-6922	7596
Raytheon Company	Tewksbury	MA	C	978 858-4700	15830
Raytheon Company	North Billerica	MA	G	978 313-0201	13858
Raytheon International Inc **(PA)**	Waltham	MA	G	781 522-3000	16185
Raytheon Italy Liaison Company	Andover	MA	D	978 684-5300	7597
Raytheon Sutheast Asia Systems **(HQ)**	Billerica	MA	E	978 470-5000	8289
Raytheon Systems Support Co **(HQ)**	Tewksbury	MA	G	978 851-2134	15831
Rigaku Analytical Devices Inc	Wilmington	MA	E	781 328-1024	17041
Roche Engineering LLC	East Freetown	MA	G	508 287-1964	10459
Sensarray Infrared Corporation	Medford	MA	G	781 306-0338	12948
Sensedriver Technologies LLC	Malden	MA	G	978 232-3990	12595
Sensomotoric Instruments Inc	Boston	MA	G	617 557-0010	8844
Sensormatic Electronics LLC	Lexington	MA	C	781 466-6660	12264
Sippi/GSM Subma Antenn Joint V	Marion	MA	G	774 553-6218	12703
Smiths Detection LLC	Andover	MA	C	510 449-4197	7610
Spike Aerospace Inc	Boston	MA	F	617 338-1400	8858
Symetrica Inc	Westford	MA	F	508 718-5610	16795
Techlaw Inc	North Chelmsford	MA	G	617 918-8612	13911
Teledyne Benthos Inc **(HQ)**	North Falmouth	MA	C	508 563-1000	13954
Teledyne Instruments Inc	North Falmouth	MA	F	508 563-1000	13955
Thin Line Defense LLC	Webster	MA	G	774 696-5285	16353
Trimble Inc	Marlborough	MA	G	508 381-5800	12838
Tru Technologies Inc	Peabody	MA	C	978 532-0775	14379
Ursa Navigation Solutions Inc	North Billerica	MA	G	781 538-5299	13875
Vacuum Barrier Corporation	Woburn	MA	E	781 933-3570	17310
Vaisala Inc	Woburn	MA	G	508 574-1163	17311
Wavesense Inc	Somerville	MA	G	917 488-9677	15231
Where Inc	Boston	MA	D	617 502-3100	8925
Bae Systems Tech Sol Srvc Inc	Bath	ME	G	207 449-3577	5673
General Dynamics-Ots Inc	Saco	ME	E	207 283-3611	6847
Hunting Dearborn Inc	Fryeburg	ME	C	207 935-2171	6099
Inreach Inc	Yarmouth	ME	G	207 846-7104	7297
Lockheed Martin Corporation	Bath	ME	E	207 442-1112	5680
Self Defense Innovations Inc	Orland	ME	G	207 991-1641	6550
Aero Defense International LLC	Manchester	NH	G	603 644-0305	18773
Allard Nazarian Group Inc **(PA)**	Manchester	NH	C	603 668-1900	18774
Allard Nazarian Group Inc	Manchester	NH	F	603 314-0017	18775
American Ir Solutions LLC	Hudson	NH	G	662 626-2477	18373
ARC Technology Solutions LLC	Nashua	NH	E	603 883-3027	19117
Bae Systems Elctronic Solution	Nashua	NH	F	603 885-3653	19120
Bae Systems Info & Elec Sys **(DH)**	Nashua	NH	B	603 885-4321	19121
Bae Systems Info & Elec Sys	Nashua	NH	B	603 885-4321	19122
Bae Systems Info & Elec Sys	Merrimack	NH	B	603 885-4321	18989
Bae Systems Info & Elec Sys	Nashua	NH	C	603 885-3653	19123
Bae Systems Info & Elec Sys	Londonderry	NH	G	603 647-5367	18678
Bae Systems Info & Elec Sys	Hudson	NH	A	603 885-4321	18376
Bae Systems Info & Elec Sys	Nashua	NH	G	603 885-3770	19124
C-R Control Systems Inc	Lebanon	NH	G	603 727-9149	18617
C3i Inc	Exeter	NH	E	603 929-9989	18115
Cobham	Exeter	NH	G	603 418-9786	18116
Contintential Microwave	Exeter	NH	G	603 775-5200	18118
Custom Manufacturing Svcs Inc	Nashua	NH	E	603 883-1355	19141
El-Op US Inc	Merrimack	NH	B	603 889-2500	18998
Fireye Inc **(DH)**	Derry	NH	C	603 432-4100	17979
Flir Maritime Us Inc	Nashua	NH	E	603 324-7900	19160
Flir Systems Inc	Nashua	NH	G	866 636-4487	19162
Klein Marine Systems Inc	Salem	NH	D	603 893-6131	19744
KMC Systems Inc	Merrimack	NH	D	866 742-0442	19010
Kollsman Inc **(DH)**	Merrimack	NH	A	603 889-2500	19011
L3harris Technologies Inc	Nashua	NH	E	603 689-1450	19195
Lewis and Saunders	Laconia	NH	G	603 528-1871	18574
Lockheed Martin Corporation	Merrimack	NH	F	603 885-5295	19012
Lockheed Martin Corporation	Nashua	NH	B	603 885-4321	19199
Lockheed Martin Corporation	Nashua	NH	A	603 885-4321	19200
Memtec Corporation	Salem	NH	E	603 893-8080	19751
Mevatec Corp	Nashua	NH	F	603 885-4321	19207
Micro-Precision Inc **(PA)**	Sunapee	NH	E	603 763-2394	19882

	CITY	ST	EMP	PHONE	ENTRY #
Online Defense Products LLC	Hudson	NH	G	603 845-3211	18423
Patriot Cyber Defense LLC	Rochester	NH	G	603 231-7000	19682
Qesidyne Inc	Hudson	NH	G	603 883-3116	18431
Raytheon Company	Pelham	NH	E	603 635-6800	19444
Research In Motion Rf Inc **(HQ)**	Nashua	NH	E	603 598-8880	19250
Resurrection Defense LLC	Winchester	NH	G	603 313-1040	19995
Sealite Usa LLC	Tilton	NH	F	603 737-1310	19911
Seapoint Sensors Inc	Exeter	NH	G	603 642-4921	18131
Sequa Corporation	Merrimack	NH	G	603 889-2500	19029
Sierra Nevada Corporation	Bedford	NH	B	775 331-0222	17663
Skeyetrac LLC	Salem	NH	F	603 898-8000	19768
Advanced Self Defense	Chepachet	RI	G	401 486-8135	20132
Bae Systems Tech Sol Srvc Inc	Middletown	RI	E	401 846-5500	20616
Beechcraft Defense Co LLC	Providence	RI	G	401 457-2485	20968
Farsounder Inc	Warwick	RI	G	401 784-6700	21363
Kearflex Engineering Company	Warwick	RI	F	401 781-4900	21382
Kvh Industries Inc **(PA)**	Middletown	RI	C	401 847-3327	20623
November Defense LLC	Coventry	RI	G	401 662-7902	20161
Raytheon Company	Portsmouth	RI	D	401 847-8000	20938
Syqwest Inc	Cranston	RI	E	401 432-7129	20297
Wei Inc **(PA)**	Cranston	RI	E	401 781-3904	20309
BF Goodrich Aerspce Aircrft In	Vergennes	VT	G	802 877-2911	22552
General Dynamics-Ots Inc	Williston	VT	G	802 662-7000	22670
Liquid Measurement Systems Inc	Milton	VT	E	802 528-8100	22133

3821 Laboratory Apparatus & Furniture

	CITY	ST	EMP	PHONE	ENTRY #
Bioclinica Inc	New London	CT	G	860 701-0082	2766
CFM Test & Balance Corp	Bethel	CT	G	203 778-1900	136
Dragonlab LLC	Rocky Hill	CT	G	860 436-9221	3708
Environics Inc	Tolland	CT	E	860 872-1111	4547
Eppendorf Inc **(DH)**	Enfield	CT	B	732 287-1200	1358
Eppendorf Holding Inc **(DH)**	Enfield	CT	E	860 253-3417	1359
Fmp Products	Greenwich	CT	G	203 422-0686	1615
Idex Health & Science LLC	Bristol	CT	C	860 314-2880	570
Mark V Laboratory Inc	East Granby	CT	G	860 653-7201	1132
Mayborn Usa Inc	Stamford	CT	F	781 269-7490	4245
Novamont North America Inc	Shelton	CT	F	203 744-8801	3842
Origio Midatlantic Devices Inc	Trumbull	CT	E	856 762-2000	4629
Proteowise Inc	Branford	CT	G	203 430-4187	340
Tomtec Inc	Hamden	CT	D	203 281-6790	1790
Aja International Inc	Scituate	MA	E	781 545-7365	15005
Andrew Alliance Usa Inc	Waltham	MA	G	617 797-9071	16033
Apogent Technologies Inc	Waltham	MA	A	781 622-1300	16035
Blacktrace Inc	Norwell	MA	G	617 848-1211	14097
Bluecatbio MA Inc	Concord	MA	G	978 405-2533	10116
Bnz Materials Inc	North Billerica	MA	E	978 663-3401	13796
Charles Supper Company Inc	Natick	MA	G	508 655-4610	13245
Dan-Kar Plastics Products	Woburn	MA	G	781 935-9221	17163
Davinci Biomedical RES Pdts	South Lancaster	MA	G	978 368-3477	15317
Digilab Inc	Hopkinton	MA	D	508 305-2410	11700
Eckert Ziegler Radiopharma Inc **(PA)**	Hopkinton	MA	G	508 497-0060	11701
Exeter Analytical Inc **(PA)**	North Chelmsford	MA	F	978 251-1411	13894
Fisher Scientific Intl LLC **(HQ)**	Waltham	MA	C	781 622-1000	16107
Hamilton Storage Tech Inc	Franklin	MA	G	508 544-7000	11052
Harvard Bioscience Inc **(PA)**	Holliston	MA	C	508 893-8999	11575
Idex Health & Science LLC	Middleboro	MA	C	774 213-0200	13064
Inert Corporation	Amesbury	MA	E	978 462-4415	7492
Infors USA Inc	Weymouth	MA	G	781 335-3108	16890
Inphotonics Inc	Norwood	MA	F	781 440-0202	14162
Instron Applications Lab	Norwood	MA	G	800 564-8378	14164
Jeio Tech Inc	Billerica	MA	G	781 376-0700	8259
Kinetic Systems Inc	Boston	MA	E	617 522-8700	8649
Lab Frnture Instlltons Sls Inc	Middleton	MA	F	978 646-0600	13093
Labminds Inc	Somerville	MA	G	844 956-8327	15189
Labtech Inc **(PA)**	Hopkinton	MA	G	508 435-5500	11726
Lc Technology Solutions Inc	Salisbury	MA	G	978 255-1620	14952
M/K Systems Inc	Peabody	MA	G	978 857-9228	14354
Mettler-Toledo Intl Inc	Newton	MA	G	800 472-4646	13614
Microcal LLC	Northampton	MA	G	413 586-7720	14012
Microfluidics Intl Corp	Westwood	MA	E	617 969-5452	16873
Nexcelom Bioscience LLC	Lawrence	MA	E	978 327-5340	12065
Oligo Factory Inc	Holliston	MA	G	508 275-3561	11592
Openclinica LLC	Waltham	MA	E	617 621-8585	16167
Pall Northborough **(DH)**	Northborough	MA	G	978 263-9888	14043
Parallel Systems Corp	Georgetown	MA	F	978 352-7100	11148
Perkinelmer Hlth Sciences Inc **(DH)**	Waltham	MA	C	781 663-6900	16172
Pharmask Inc	Medfield	MA	G	508 359-6700	12916
Pharyx Inc	Woburn	MA	G	617 792-0524	17262
Pinpoint Laser Systems Inc	Peabody	MA	E	978 532-8001	14362
Primevigilance Inc	Waltham	MA	G	781 703-5540	16178
R D Webb Co Inc	Natick	MA	G	508 650-0110	13276
Setra Systems Inc	Boxboro	MA	F	978 263-1400	8954
Spectris Inc **(HQ)**	Westborough	MA	F	508 768-6400	16650
Stem Solutions LLC	Wakefield	MA	G	617 826-6111	15978
Troemner	North Andover	MA	G	978 655-3377	13732
Unity Scientific LLC	Milford	MA	E	203 740-2999	13149
Vacuum Technology Inc	Gloucester	MA	G	510 333-6562	11216
Wright Line LLC **(HQ)**	Worcester	MA	C	508 852-4300	17510
Xylem Inc	Beverly	MA	E	978 778-1010	8200
Advanced Concepts & Engrg LLC	Dexter	ME	G	207 270-3025	5955
Baker Company Inc **(PA)**	Sanford	ME	C	207 324-8773	6871
Emerson Apparatus Company	Gorham	ME	F	207 856-0055	6111
Maine Mlclar Qulty Contrls Inc	Saco	ME	E	207 885-1072	6852
Colonial Medical Supply Co Inc	Windham	NH	G	603 328-5130	20002
Erie Scientific LLC **(DH)**	Portsmouth	NH	B	603 430-6859	19560
Kimball Physics Inc	Wilton	NH	E	603 878-1616	19981
Materials Research Frncs Inc	Allenstown	NH	F	603 485-2394	17539
Mellen Company Inc	Webster	NH	G	603 648-2121	19944
Owl Separation Systems LLC	Newington	NH	E	603 559-9297	19323
Rochester USA	Rochester	NH	G	603 332-0717	19683
Thermo Neslab LLC	Newington	NH	C	603 436-9444	19328
Surplus Solutions LLC	Woonsocket	RI	F	401 526-0055	21584
Omichron Corp	South Londonderry	VT	F	802 824-3136	22488
Raj Communications Ltd	Williston	VT	F	802 658-4961	22687

3822 Automatic Temperature Controls

	CITY	ST	EMP	PHONE	ENTRY #
Alloy Engineering Co Inc **(PA)**	Bridgeport	CT	E	203 366-5253	369
Belimo Aircontrols (usa) Inc **(HQ)**	Danbury	CT	C	800 543-9038	879
Belimo Automation AG	Danbury	CT	F	203 749-3319	880
Belimo Customization USA Inc	Danbury	CT	G	203 791-9915	881
Center For Discovery	Southport	CT	E	203 955-1381	4095
Clarios	Meriden	CT	D	678 297-4040	2086
Emme Controls LLC	Bristol	CT	G	503 793-3792	553
Emme E2ms LLC	Bristol	CT	F	860 845-8810	554
Food Atmtn - Svc Tchniques Inc **(PA)**	Stratford	CT	C	203 377-4414	4412
Graywolf Sensing Solutions LLC **(PA)**	Shelton	CT	G	203 402-0477	3805
Grove Systems Inc	Deep River	CT	G	860 663-2555	1061
Hamilton Standard Space	Windsor Locks	CT	E	860 654-6000	5396
Hamilton Sundstrand Corp **(HQ)**	Windsor Locks	CT	A	860 654-6000	5397
J & B Service Company LLC	Bethel	CT	G	203 743-9357	163
Johnson Controls Inc	Windsor	CT	C	860 688-7151	5341
Mission Allergy Inc	Hawleyville	CT	G	203 364-1570	1894
Omega Engineering Inc	Norwalk	CT	D	714 540-4914	3212
Rich Plastic Products Inc	Meriden	CT	G	203 235-4241	2126
Tek-Air Systems Inc	Monroe	CT	E	203 791-1400	2418
Universal Building Contrls Inc	Meriden	CT	F	203 235-1530	2145
Whitman Controls LLC	Bristol	CT	F	800 233-4401	625
7ac Technologies Inc	Beverly	MA	F	781 574-1348	8094
Bbhs Thermal Solutions Corp	Malden	MA	G	781 718-2352	12562
Bluezone Products Inc	Woburn	MA	G	781 937-0202	17134
Burnell Controls Inc	Danvers	MA	G	978 646-9992	10204
Clarios	Lynnfield	MA	C	781 213-3463	12547
Control Resources Inc	Littleton	MA	E	978 486-4160	12297
Contronautics Incorporated	Hudson	MA	G	978 568-8883	11766
Demandq Inc	Watertown	MA	G	617 401-2165	16277
Engineered Assembly & Services	Marshfield	MA	G	781 834-9085	12860
Falmouth Products Inc	East Falmouth	MA	G	508 548-6686	10442
Honeywell International Inc	Danvers	MA	D	978 774-3007	10223
Irrigation Automtn Systms Inc	Whitinsville	MA	G	800 549-4551	16915
Johnson Controls Inc	Wrentham	MA	E	508 384-0018	17524
Kidde-Fenwal Inc **(HQ)**	Ashland	MA	A	508 881-2000	7663
Lee Electric Inc	Danvers	MA	C	978 777-0070	10231
Massachusetts Clean Energy Ctr	Boston	MA	E	617 315-9355	8684
Mestek Inc	Westfield	MA	B	413 568-9571	16702
Mettler-Toledo Process Analyti	Billerica	MA	D	781 301-8800	8265
Molecular Health Inc	Boston	MA	E	832 482-3898	8709
Munters Corporation **(DH)**	Amesbury	MA	C	978 241-1100	7498
Mv3 LLC	Buzzards Bay	MA	G	617 658-4420	9361
Nanmac Corp	Holliston	MA	E	508 872-4811	11588
Pardi Mfg Inc	West Boylston	MA	G	508 835-7887	16426
Product Resources LLC	Newburyport	MA	E	978 524-8500	13523
Save Energy Systems Inc	Westborough	MA	G	617 564-4442	16647
Sensitech Inc **(DH)**	Beverly	MA	D	978 927-7033	8177
Siebe Inc **(DH)**	Foxboro	MA	G	508 549-6768	10905
Siemens Industry Inc	Worcester	MA	D	508 849-6519	17473
Sigma Systems Corp	Mansfield	MA	E	781 688-2354	12658
Spirig Advanced Tech Incies	Springfield	MA	G	413 788-6191	15508
Ssidm Inc	Rockland	MA	G	781 871-7677	14827
Static Solutions Inc **(PA)**	Marlborough	MA	F	508 480-0700	12830
Static Technologies Corp	Rockland	MA	F	781 871-8962	14828
Sud-Chemie Protech Inc	Needham Heights	MA	E	781 444-5188	13345
Tac Inc **(DH)**	Andover	MA	C	978 470-0555	7613
Senior Operations LLC	Lewiston	ME	D	207 784-2338	6322
Wahlcometroflex Inc	Lewiston	ME	B	207 784-2338	6327
Degree Controls Inc **(PA)**	Milford	NH	E	603 672-8900	19055
Dijitized Communications Inc	Middleton	NH	G	603 473-2144	19039
Ene Systems of Nh Inc	Bow	NH	G	603 856-0330	17711
Granite 3 LLC	Temple	NH	G	603 566-0339	19897
Hampshire Controls Corporation	Dover	NH	F	603 749-9424	18026
Hansa Consult North Amer LLC	Portsmouth	NH	F	603 422-8833	19572
Lyco Enterprises Inc	Nashua	NH	G	603 888-2640	19201
RMA Manufacturing LLC	West Swanzey	NH	E	603 352-0053	19968
Turmoil Inc	West Swanzey	NH	E	603 352-0053	19969
Xavier Corporation	Manchester	NH	G	603 668-8892	18956

	CITY	ST	EMP	PHONE	ENTRY #
Avtech Software Inc **(PA)**	Warren	RI	E	401 628-1600	21287
Energy MGT & Ctrl Svcs Inc	Cranston	RI	F	401 946-1440	20217
Goldline Controls Inc **(HQ)**	North Kingstown	RI	D	401 583-1100	20713
Nooney Controls Corporation **(PA)**	North Kingstown	RI	E	401 294-6000	20730
Taco Inc **(PA)**	Cranston	RI	B	401 942-8000	20299
R H Travers Company	Warren	VT	G	802 496-5205	22578

3823 Indl Instruments For Meas, Display & Control

	CITY	ST	EMP	PHONE	ENTRY #
AKO Inc	Windsor	CT	E	860 298-9765	5317
Alloy Engineering Co Inc **(PA)**	Bridgeport	CT	E	203 366-5253	369
Ametek Inc	Wallingford	CT	C	203 265-6731	4699
Appleton Grp LLC	East Granby	CT	E	860 653-1603	1117
Ashcroft Inc **(DH)**	Stratford	CT	B	203 378-8281	4392
Bristol Inc **(HQ)**	Watertown	CT	B	860 945-2200	5001
Buck Scientific Inc	Norwalk	CT	D	203 853-9444	3116
C F D Engineering Company	Waterbury	CT	F	203 754-2807	4853
Cidra Chemical Management Inc **(HQ)**	Wallingford	CT	D	203 265-0035	4717
Cidra Corporate Services Inc	Wallingford	CT	D	203 265-0035	4718
Cidra Corporation	Wallingford	CT	D	203 265-0035	4719
Cidra Mineral Processing Inc	Wallingford	CT	D	203 265-0035	4720
Cidra Oilsands Inc **(HQ)**	Wallingford	CT	G	203 265-0035	4721
Clinton Instrument Company	Clinton	CT	E	860 669-7548	780
Danaher Tool Group	Wallingford	CT	F	203 284-7000	4732
Devar Inc	Bridgeport	CT	E	203 368-6751	405
Diba Industries Inc **(HQ)**	Danbury	CT	C	203 744-0773	901
Differential Pressure Plus	Branford	CT	G	203 481-2545	309
Drs Naval Power Systems Inc	Danbury	CT	B	203 798-3000	905
Environics Inc	Tolland	CT	E	860 872-1111	4547
Faria Beede Instruments Inc	North Stonington	CT	C	860 848-9271	3074
Fleet Management LLC	Enfield	CT	G	800 722-6654	1363
Food Atmtn - Svc Tchniques Inc **(PA)**	Stratford	CT	C	203 377-4414	4412
GE Steam Power Inc **(HQ)**	Windsor	CT	A	866 257-8664	5336
Gordon Engineering Corp	Brookfield	CT	F	203 775-4501	645
H & B Tool & Engineering Co	South Windsor	CT	E	860 528-9341	3976
Hamilton Sundstrand Corp **(HQ)**	Windsor Locks	CT	A	860 654-6000	5397
Haydon Kerk Mtion Slutions Inc	Waterbury	CT	C	203 756-7441	4883
Idex Health & Science LLC	Bristol	CT	C	860 314-2880	570
Innovative Components LLC	Plantsville	CT	G	860 621-7220	3533
Jad LLC	South Windsor	CT	E	860 289-1551	3983
Johnson Gage Company	Bloomfield	CT	E	860 242-5541	229
Kaman Aerospace Corporation	Middletown	CT	C	860 632-1000	2195
Kapcom LLC	East Haven	CT	G	203 891-5112	1253
Laticrete Supercap LLC	Bethany	CT	G	203 393-4558	122
Lee Company **(PA)**	Westbrook	CT	A	860 399-6281	5157
Lee Company	Essex	CT	C	860 399-6281	1401
Lee Company	Westbrook	CT	E	860 399-6281	5158
Louis Electric Co Inc	Wolcott	CT	G	203 879-5483	5447
Lq Mechatronics Inc	Branford	CT	G	203 433-4430	328
Madison Company **(PA)**	Branford	CT	E	203 488-4477	329
Micromod Automation & Controls	Wallingford	CT	F	585 321-9209	4774
Minteq International Inc	Canaan	CT	C	860 824-5435	689
Moeller Instrument Company Inc	Ivoryton	CT	E	800 243-9310	1907
National Magnetic Sensors Inc	Plantsville	CT	G	860 621-6816	3537
Omega Engineering Inc **(HQ)**	Norwalk	CT	C	203 359-1660	3211
Omega Engineering Inc	Stamford	CT	G	203 359-7922	4269
Orange Research Inc	Milford	CT	D	203 877-5657	2326
PMC Engineering LLC	Danbury	CT	E	203 792-8686	968
Precision Sensors Inc	Milford	CT	E	203 877-2795	2338
Prime Technology LLC	North Branford	CT	C	203 481-5721	2974
Proflow Inc	North Haven	CT	E	203 230-4700	3055
Projects Inc	Glastonbury	CT	C	860 633-4615	1574
Quad/Graphics Inc	North Haven	CT	A	203 288-2468	3057
RA Smythe LLC	Middletown	CT	G	860 398-5764	2216
Singularity Space Systems LLC	Granby	CT	G	860 713-3626	1591
Solar Generations LLC	Guilford	CT	G	203 453-3920	1720
Sperian Protectn Instrumentatn	Middletown	CT	C	860 344-1079	2225
Tek-Air Systems Inc	Monroe	CT	E	203 791-1400	2418
United Electric Controls Co	Milford	CT	D	203 877-2795	2377
Veeder-Root Company **(HQ)**	Weatogue	CT	D	860 651-2700	5045
Vertiv Corporation	Wallingford	CT	F	203 294-6020	4827
Wentworth Laboratories Inc	Brookfield	CT	G	203 775-9311	666
Accusonic Technologies **(DH)**	New Bedford	MA	F	508 495-6600	13348
Aci Technology Inc	Woburn	MA	F	781 937-9888	17107
Adcole Corporation **(HQ)**	Marlborough	MA	C	508 485-9100	12710
Advanced Control Systems Corp	Canton	MA	G	781 829-9228	9711
Advanced Thermal Solutions Inc **(PA)**	Norwood	MA	E	781 769-2800	14123
Agency Systems Group	Sterling	MA	G	978 422-8479	15531
Airflow Direction Inc	Newbury	MA	G	978 462-9995	13462
Ametek Arizona Instrument LLC	Middleboro	MA	C	508 946-6200	13051
Amphenol Advanced Sensors	Billerica	MA	G	978 294-8300	8209
Applewood Controls Inc	Littleton	MA	G	978 486-9220	12292
Aqua Solutions Inc	Middleboro	MA	G	508 947-5777	13053
Assembly Guidance Systems Inc	Chelmsford	MA	F	978 244-1166	9874
Atlantic Metalcraft Co	Middleboro	MA	G	781 447-9900	13054
Auburn International Inc	Beverly	MA	F	978 777-2460	8104
Auburn Systems LLC	Beverly	MA	G	978 777-2460	8105
B C Ames Incorporated	Framingham	MA	G	781 893-0095	10924
Bae Systems Info & Elec Sys	Lexington	MA	B	603 885-4321	12208
Bedrock Automtn Platforms Inc	Mansfield	MA	G	781 821-0280	12615
Bel Legacy Corporation	Boston	MA	C	508 923-5000	8400
Big Belly Solar Inc	Needham Heights	MA	E	888 820-0300	13319
Brooks Automation Inc **(PA)**	Chelmsford	MA	B	978 262-2400	9880
Btu Overseas Ltd **(DH)**	North Billerica	MA	G	978 667-4111	13801
Cape Cod Wind Wther Indicators	Harwich Port	MA	G	508 432-9475	11398
CDI Meters Inc	Woburn	MA	G	508 867-3178	17141
Chemtrac Systems	Groton	MA	G	978 448-0061	11286
Cimetrics Inc	Boston	MA	D	617 350-7550	8475
City of Chicopee	Chicopee	MA	G	413 594-1870	10013
Cognex Corporation **(PA)**	Natick	MA	B	508 650-3000	13246
Cognex Corporation	Natick	MA	G	508 650-3044	13247
Cognex International Inc **(HQ)**	Natick	MA	F	508 650-3000	13249
Cybertools Inc	Boston	MA	G	978 772-9200	8493
D 2 Incorporated	Bourne	MA	G	508 329-2046	8945
Data Industrial Corporation	Mattapoisett	MA	E	508 758-6390	12886
Dias Infrared Corp	West Boylston	MA	G	845 987-8152	16414
Dolan-Jenner Industries Inc	Boxborough	MA	E	978 263-1400	8961
Druck LLC **(HQ)**	Billerica	MA	C	978 437-1000	8238
Dynisco Instruments LLC **(HQ)**	Franklin	MA	C	508 541-9400	11037
Dynisco Parent Inc	Billerica	MA	E	978 667-5301	8241
E Gs Gauging Incorporated	Wilmington	MA	G	978 663-2300	16999
Ecochlor Inc	Maynard	MA	G	978 298-1463	12898
Edgetech Instruments Inc	Hudson	MA	F	508 263-5900	11769
Emerson Electric Co	Mansfield	MA	G	774 266-4136	12632
Emerson Process Management	Lawrence	MA	C	978 689-2800	12022
Entegris Inc	Billerica	MA	F	978 436-6500	8247
Evoqua Water Technologies LLC	Tewksbury	MA	E	978 863-4600	15817
Finesse Solutions Inc	Newburyport	MA	G	978 255-1296	13488
Flir Systems-Boston Inc **(HQ)**	North Billerica	MA	B	978 901-8000	13815
GE Infrastructure Sensing LLC **(DH)**	Billerica	MA	A	978 437-1000	8249
GE Panametrics Inc	Billerica	MA	G	978 670-6454	8250
Gefran Isi Inc	North Andover	MA	E	781 729-0842	13708
Global Fire Products Inc	Boston	MA	G	617 750-1125	8567
Got Interface	Waltham	MA	F	781 547-5700	16121
Hamilton Storage Tech Inc **(DH)**	Franklin	MA	E	508 544-7000	11051
High Voltage Maintenance Corp	Walpole	MA	F	508 668-9205	15993
Honeywell Data Instruments Inc	Acton	MA	B	978 264-9550	7361
Impolit Envmtl Ctrl Corp	Beverly	MA	E	978 927-4619	8140
Industrial Biomedical Sensors	Waltham	MA	F	781 891-4201	16132
Infolibria Inc	Waltham	MA	D	781 392-2200	16134
Instrument & Valve Services Co	Shrewsbury	MA	G	508 842-7000	15118
Instrumentation & Control Tech	Waltham	MA	F	781 273-5052	16135
Invensense Inc **(PA)**	Boston	MA	F	857 268-4400	8619
Invensys Systems Argentina	Foxboro	MA	E	508 543-8750	10889
Invetech Inc	Boxborough	MA	D	508 475-3400	8964
Iwaki America Incorporated **(HQ)**	Holliston	MA	D	508 429-1440	11579
Jowa Usa Inc	Littleton	MA	E	978 486-9800	12311
Kadant Fibergen Inc **(HQ)**	Bedford	MA	F	781 275-3600	7986
Kidde-Fenwal Inc **(HQ)**	Ashland	MA	A	508 881-2000	7663
KPM Analytics North Amer Corp **(PA)**	Milford	MA	E	508 473-9901	13123
Liquid Metronics Incorporated	Acton	MA	C	978 263-9800	7369
LS Starrett Company **(PA)**	Athol	MA	A	978 249-3551	7689
Lynn Products Co	Lynn	MA	E	781 593-2500	12524
M & K Industries Inc	Leominster	MA	E	978 514-9850	12164
Magmotor Technologies Inc	Worcester	MA	F	508 835-4305	17411
Massmicro LLC	Canton	MA	F	781 828-6110	9756
Mettler-Toledo Intl Inc	Newton	MA	G	800 472-4646	13614
Mettler-Toledo Thornton Inc	Billerica	MA	D	978 262-0210	8266
Michell Instruments Inc	Rowley	MA	G	978 484-0005	14857
Mija Industries Inc	Rockland	MA	E	781 871-5629	14814
Mj Research Inc **(HQ)**	Waltham	MA	C	510 724-7000	16152
Mks Instruments Inc **(PA)**	Andover	MA	B	978 645-5500	7574
Mks Instruments Inc	Wilmington	MA	C	978 284-4000	17024
Mks Instruments Inc	Andover	MA	E	978 645-5500	7575
Mks Instruments Inc	Andover	MA	E	978 738-3721	7576
Mks Instruments Inc	Methuen	MA	D	978 682-3512	13037
Mks Instruments Inc	Lawrence	MA	C	978 975-2350	12058
Mks Msc Inc	Wilmington	MA	A	978 284-4000	17025
National Resource MGT Inc **(PA)**	Canton	MA	E	781 828-8877	9759
Netzsch Instruments N Amer LLC **(DH)**	Burlington	MA	E	781 272-5353	9307
Norcross Corporation	Newton	MA	G	617 969-7020	13620
Nova Instruments Corporation **(PA)**	Woburn	MA	G	781 897-1200	17247
Onset Computer Corporation	Bourne	MA	C	508 759-9500	8948
Patriot Worldwide Inc	Holliston	MA	G	800 786-4669	11595
Performance Motion Devices Inç	Westford	MA	E	978 266-1210	16783
Phoenix Electric Corp	Canton	MA	E	781 821-0200	9767
Pid Analyzers LLC	Sandwich	MA	F	774 413-5281	14972
Precision Digital Corporation	Hopkinton	MA	E	508 655-7300	11733
Richards Arklay S Co Inc	Newton	MA	E	617 527-4385	13630
Rigaku Analytical Devices Inc	Wilmington	MA	E	781 328-1024	17041
Rosemount Inc	Mansfield	MA	G	508 261-2928	12656
Schneider Elc Systems USA Inc	Foxboro	MA	F	508 543-8750	10901
Schneider Elc Systems USA Inc	Foxboro	MA	F	508 543-8750	10902
Schneider Electric Usa Inc **(DH)**	Boston	MA	A	978 975-9600	8839
Schneider Electric Usa Inc	Foxboro	MA	G	508 549-3385	10903

SIC

Employee Codes: A=Over 500 employees, B=251-500
C=101-250, D=51-100 E=20-50, F=10-19, G=3-9

	CITY	ST	EMP	PHONE	ENTRY #
Scully Signal Company **(PA)**	Wilmington	MA	C	617 692-8600	17044
Sensitech Inc **(DH)**	Beverly	MA	D	978 927-7033	8177
Set Americas Inc	Easthampton	MA	G	413 203-6130	10578
Setra Systems Inc	Boxboro	MA	F	978 263-1400	8954
Shawmut Advertising Inc **(PA)**	Danvers	MA	E	978 762-7500	10255
Signalfire Telemetry Inc	Marlborough	MA	G	978 212-2868	12826
Technlogy Dev Cllaborative LLC	Woburn	MA	G	781 933-6116	17304
Tecomet Inc	Woburn	MA	D	781 782-6400	17305
Teknikor Automtn & Contrls Inc	Fall River	MA	F	508 679-9474	10771
Temp-Pro Incorporated	Northampton	MA	E	413 584-3165	14022
Temptronic Corporation **(HQ)**	Mansfield	MA	D	781 688-2300	12664
Test Evolution Corporation	Hopkinton	MA	G	508 377-5757	11740
Thermedetec Inc	Waltham	MA	A	508 520-0430	16212
Thermo Envmtl Instrs LLC **(HQ)**	Franklin	MA	C	508 520-0430	11086
Thermo Fisher Scientific Inc **(PA)**	Waltham	MA	C	781 622-1000	16213
Thermo Fisher Scientific Inc	Wilmington	MA	D	978 275-0800	17055
Thermo Optek Corporation	Franklin	MA	A	508 553-5100	11088
Thermo Orion Inc **(HQ)**	Chelmsford	MA	E	800 225-1480	9937
Thermo Process Instruments LP	Franklin	MA	C	508 553-6913	11089
Thermonics Inc	Mansfield	MA	G	408 542-5900	12665
Tte Laboratories Inc	Hopkinton	MA	F	800 242-6022	11741
United Electric Controls Co	Watertown	MA	D	617 926-1000	16327
Verify LLC	Cambridge	MA	F	513 285-7258	9694
Verionix Inc	North Andover	MA	G	978 682-5671	13736
Walker Magnetics Group Inc	Worcester	MA	F	774 670-1423	17503
Water Analytics Inc	Andover	MA	F	978 749-9949	7618
Watertech International	Woburn	MA	G	781 592-8224	17315
Williamson Corporation	Concord	MA	E	978 369-9607	10163
Wilmington Research & Dev Corp	Newburyport	MA	G	978 499-0100	13549
Wintriss Controls Group LLC	Acton	MA	E	978 268-2700	7394
X Sonix	Boxborough	MA	G	978 266-2106	8972
AEC Engineering	Freeport	ME	F	207 865-4190	6071
Contact Inc	Edgecomb	ME	G	207 882-6116	6001
David Saunders Inc	South Portland	ME	E	207 228-1888	7021
Digitry Company Inc **(PA)**	Portland	ME	G	207 774-0300	6652
George Baggett	Union	ME	G	207 785-5442	7113
Montalvo Corporation	Gorham	ME	E	207 856-2501	6122
Aqua Specialties	Northwood	NH	G	603 942-5671	19411
Bantry Components Inc	Manchester	NH	E	603 668-3210	18785
Datapaq Inc	Derry	NH	E	603 537-2680	17977
Dutile Glines & Higgins Inc	Hooksett	NH	F	603 622-0452	18348
Ellab Inc	Nashua	NH	G	603 417-3363	19148
Extech Instruments Corporation	Nashua	NH	D	887 439-8324	19152
Fluke Electronics Corporation	Salem	NH	G	603 537-2680	19735
Industrial Marine Elec Inc	Manchester	NH	F	603 434-2309	18842
Jewell Instruments LLC **(PA)**	Manchester	NH	C	603 669-5121	18850
L3harris Technologies Inc	Nashua	NH	E	603 689-1450	19195
Madgetech Inc **(PA)**	Warner	NH	E	603 456-2011	19928
Memtec Corporation	Salem	NH	E	603 893-8080	19751
Monarch International Inc	Amherst	NH	E	603 883-3390	17577
Nelson Robotics Corp	Concord	NH	G	603 856-7421	17915
Neo Markets Inc	Portsmouth	NH	F	603 766-8716	19597
Optris Ir Sensing LLC	Portsmouth	NH	G	603 766-6060	19604
Paper Thermometer Co Inc	Manchester	NH	G	603 547-2034	18897
Parker-Hannifin Corporation	Hollis	NH	C	603 595-1500	18336
Pneucleus Technologies LLC	Hollis	NH	G	603 921-5300	18338
Praecis Inc	West Lebanon	NH	G	603 277-9288	19959
Qesidyne Inc	Hudson	NH	G	603 883-3116	18431
Teledyne Instruments Inc	Hampton	NH	D	603 474-5571	18273
Unarco Material Handling Inc	Exeter	NH	E	603 772-2070	18134
Valde Systems Inc	Brookline	NH	G	603 577-1728	17774
Wilcom Inc	Belmont	NH	E	603 524-2622	17686
Airgas Usa LLC	East Greenwich	RI	G	401 884-0201	20351
Astonish Results LP	Warwick	RI	F	401 921-6220	21328
Celestial Monitoring Corp **(HQ)**	Narragansett	RI	E	401 782-1045	20635
Coldstash Inc	West Greenwich	RI	G	617 780-5603	21453
Crest Manufacturing Company	Lincoln	RI	E	401 333-1350	20566
E H Benz Co Inc	Providence	RI	G	401 331-5650	20999
Electrochemical Devices Inc **(PA)**	Lincoln	RI	G	401 333-6112	20571
Hanna Instruments Inc **(PA)**	Woonsocket	RI	E	401 765-7500	21567
Hexagon Holdings Inc **(DH)**	North Kingstown	RI	G	401 886-2000	20715
Hexagon Metrology Inc **(DH)**	North Kingstown	RI	B	401 886-2000	20716
Honeywell International Inc	Woonsocket	RI	E	401 769-7274	21570
Northern RI Conservation Dst	Johnston	RI	G	401 934-0840	20526
Orbetron LLC	Cumberland	RI	G	651 983-2872	20337
Sgri Inc	Warwick	RI	G	401 473-7320	21425
Systematics Inc	Bristol	RI	G	401 253-0050	20104
Wyatt Engineering LLC **(PA)**	Lincoln	RI	G	401 334-1170	20601
Doble Engineering Company	Hinesburg	VT	C	802 482-2255	22022
Isotech North America Inc	Colchester	VT	G	802 863-8050	21868
Lord Corporation **(DH)**	Williston	VT	D	802 862-6629	22680
Senix Corporation	Hinesburg	VT	F	802 489-7300	22030
Step Ahead Innovations Inc	South Burlington	VT	F	802 233-0211	22468
Vermont Precision Tools Inc **(PA)**	Swanton	VT	C	802 868-4246	22538

3824 Fluid Meters & Counters

	CITY	ST	EMP	PHONE	ENTRY #
Alinabal Holdings Corporation **(PA)**	Milford	CT	B	203 877-3241	2243
Bidwell Industrial Group Inc **(PA)**	Middletown	CT	E	860 346-9283	2178
Denominator Company Inc	Woodbury	CT	F	203 263-3210	5485
Faria Beede Instruments Inc	North Stonington	CT	C	860 848-9271	3074
Gems Sensors Inc **(HQ)**	Plainville	CT	B	860 747-3000	3491
Habco Industries LLC	Glastonbury	CT	E	860 682-6800	1556
Kongsberg Dgtal Simulation Inc	Groton	CT	F	860 405-2300	1678
Lq Mechatronics Inc	Branford	CT	G	203 433-4430	328
Veeder-Root Company **(HQ)**	Weatogue	CT	D	860 651-2700	5045
Aclara Technologies LLC	Wellesley	MA	E	781 694-3300	16357
Ametek Arizona Instrument LLC	Middleboro	MA	C	508 946-6200	13051
Block Mems LLC	Southborough	MA	F	508 251-3100	15349
Connexus Manufacturing LLC	Hudson	MA	G	978 568-1831	11764
Data Industrial Corporation	Mattapoisett	MA	E	508 758-6390	12886
Dff Corp	Agawam	MA	C	413 786-8880	7427
Druck LLC **(HQ)**	Billerica	MA	C	978 437-1000	8238
High Voltage Engineering Corp	Wakefield	MA	F	781 224-1001	15954
Schleifring North America LLC	Chelmsford	MA	F	978 677-2500	9930
Setra Systems Inc	Boxboro	MA	F	978 263-1400	8954
Verify LLC	Cambridge	MA	F	513 285-7258	9694
Cei Flowmaster Products LLC	Hudson	NH	G	603 880-0094	18379
Digital Devices Inc	Wilton	NH	G	603 654-6240	19978
Monarch International Inc	Amherst	NH	E	603 883-3390	17577
Unarco Material Handling Inc	Exeter	NH	E	603 772-2070	18134
Orbetron LLC	Cumberland	RI	G	651 983-2872	20337

3825 Instrs For Measuring & Testing Electricity

	CITY	ST	EMP	PHONE	ENTRY #
AKO Inc	Windsor	CT	E	860 298-9765	5317
All-Test Pro LLC **(PA)**	Old Saybrook	CT	F	860 399-4222	3327
Altek Electronics Inc	Torrington	CT	C	860 482-7626	4558
ARS Products LLC	Plainfield	CT	E	860 564-0208	3449
Ashcroft Inc	Stratford	CT	E	203 378-8281	4393
Clinton Instrument Company	Clinton	CT	E	860 669-7548	780
Dictaphone Corporation **(HQ)**	Stratford	CT	C	203 381-7000	4409
Digatron Power Electronics Inc	Shelton	CT	E	203 446-8000	3796
Energy Tech LLC	Haddam	CT	G	860 345-3993	1726
Faria Beede Instruments Inc	North Stonington	CT	C	860 848-9271	3074
Fitzhugh Electrical Corp	Guilford	CT	G	203 453-3171	1704
Forte Rts Inc	Ledyard	CT	G	860 464-5221	1941
General Electric Company	Norwalk	CT	D	518 385-7164	3159
Gold Line Connector Inc **(PA)**	Redding	CT	E	203 938-2588	3648
Habco Industries LLC	Glastonbury	CT	E	860 682-6800	1556
International Contact Tech	Southbury	CT	E	203 264-5757	4028
Nutmeg Utility Products Inc **(PA)**	Cheshire	CT	E	203 250-8802	748
Omega Engineering Inc	Norwalk	CT	D	714 540-4914	3212
Oslo Switch Inc	Cheshire	CT	E	203 272-2794	750
Prime Technology LLC	North Branford	CT	C	203 481-5721	2974
Solar Data Systems Inc	Bethel	CT	F	203 702-7189	179
Space Electronics LLC	Berlin	CT	E	860 829-0001	110
Test Logic Inc	Middletown	CT	F	860 347-8378	2227
Trans-Tek Inc	Ellington	CT	E	860 872-8351	1343
Uses Mfg Inc	Quaker Hill	CT	G	860 443-8737	3644
Wentworth Laboratories Inc **(PA)**	Brookfield	CT	D	203 775-0448	665
Wentworth Laboratories Inc	Brookfield	CT	G	203 775-9311	666
Aclara Technologies LLC	Wellesley	MA	E	781 694-3300	16357
Advanced Mechanical Tech Inc **(PA)**	Watertown	MA	E	617 923-4174	16263
Aetruim Incorporated	Billerica	MA	E	651 773-4200	8205
Agilent Technologies Inc	Andover	MA	A	978 794-3664	7534
Agilent Technologies Inc	Chicopee	MA	F	413 593-2900	9998
Agilent Technologies Inc	Lexington	MA	C	781 861-7200	12205
Ametek Inc	Wilmington	MA	D	978 988-4101	16973
Ametek Arizona Instrument LLC	Middleboro	MA	C	508 946-6200	13051
Analog Devices Intl Inc **(HQ)**	Norwood	MA	F	781 329-4700	14131
Analogic Corporation **(HQ)**	Peabody	MA	A	978 326-4000	14311
Analogic Corporation	Peabody	MA	F	978 977-3000	14312
Analysis Tech Inc	Wakefield	MA	G	781 224-1223	15941
Anova Data Inc	Westford	MA	G	978 577-6600	16753
Auriga Measurement Systems **(PA)**	Wayland	MA	G	978 452-7700	16334
Axiam Inc **(PA)**	Gloucester	MA	G	978 281-3550	11163
B C Ames Incorporated	Framingham	MA	G	781 893-0095	10924
Barbour Stockwell Inc	Woburn	MA	E	781 933-5200	17127
Bose Corporation	Framingham	MA	E	508 766-1265	10929
Brewer Electric & Utilities In	South Yarmouth	MA	E	508 771-2040	15325
Cape Cod Wind Wther Indicators	Harwich Port	MA	G	508 432-9475	11398
Connected Automotive	South Easton	MA	E	508 238-5855	15274
Context Labs Inc	Cambridge	MA	E	617 902-0932	9442
CTS Valpey Corporation **(HQ)**	Hopkinton	MA	E	508 435-6831	11699
Desco Industries Inc	Canton	MA	E	781 821-8370	9726
Doble Engineering Company **(HQ)**	Watertown	MA	F	617 926-4900	16279
Durridge Company Inc	Billerica	MA	F	978 667-9556	8239
Dynisco Instruments LLC **(HQ)**	Franklin	MA	C	508 541-9400	11037
Electro-Fix Inc	Plainville	MA	E	508 695-0228	14518
EMC Test Design LLC	Newton	MA	F	508 292-1833	13588
Engement Company Inc	Topsfield	MA	G	978 561-3008	15857
Etec Inc	West Roxbury	MA	E	617 477-4308	16495
Fishman Transducers Inc	Andover	MA	D	978 988-9199	7549
Flintec Inc	Hudson	MA	E	978 562-4548	11774
Fulcrum9 Systems Inc	Acton	MA	G	978 549-3868	7357

	CITY	ST	EMP	PHONE	ENTRY #
Genrad Inc	Westford	MA	A	978 589-7000	16768
Ghg Electronic Services	Medford	MA	G	781 391-1147	12934
Gold Line Connector Inc	New Bedford	MA	F	508 999-5656	13391
Granite Reliable Power LLC	Marlborough	MA	G	508 251-7650	12763
Group Four Transducers Inc **(PA)**	East Longmeadow	MA	F	413 525-2705	10477
H & W Test Products Inc	Seekonk	MA	F	508 336-3200	15023
Hampden Engineering Corp	East Longmeadow	MA	D	413 525-3981	10478
Hid Global Corporation	Newton	MA	C	617 581-6200	13601
High Voltage Engineering Corp	Wakefield	MA	F	781 224-1001	15954
Honeywell Data Instruments Inc	Acton	MA	B	978 264-9550	7361
Ineoquest Technologies Inc **(PA)**	Westwood	MA	C	508 339-2497	16870
Inspectrology LLC	Sudbury	MA	E	978 212-3100	15659
Inventronics Inc	Tyngsboro	MA	G	978 649-9040	15891
Ion Track Instruments LLC	Wilmington	MA	D	978 658-3767	17007
James G Hachey Inc	Peabody	MA	G	781 229-6400	14344
Keysight Technologies Inc	Andover	MA	G	800 829-4444	7561
Kidde-Fenwal Inc **(HQ)**	Ashland	MA	A	508 881-2000	7663
Krohn-Hite Corporation	Brockton	MA	F	508 580-1660	9160
L T X International Inc	Norwood	MA	D	781 461-1000	14173
Laser Labs Inc	Pembroke	MA	G	781 826-4138	14415
Lynn Products Co	Lynn	MA	E	781 593-2500	12524
Magcap Engineering LLC	Canton	MA	F	781 821-2300	9754
Magellan Diagnostics Inc **(HQ)**	Chelmsford	MA	D	978 250-7000	9915
Magnos Incorporated	Hudson	MA	G	978 562-1173	11790
Matec Instrument Companies Inc **(PA)**	Northborough	MA	E	508 393-0155	14038
Microsemi Frequency Time Corp	Beverly	MA	D	978 232-0040	8155
Middlesex General Industries	Newburyport	MA	E	781 935-8870	13514
Mini-Systems Inc	Plainville	MA	E	508 695-2000	14528
Mks Instruments Inc	Lawrence	MA	C	978 975-2350	12058
Mti-Milliren Technologies Inc	Newburyport	MA	E	978 465-6064	13516
Mu Net Inc	Lexington	MA	F	781 861-8644	12245
Murata Power Solutions Inc **(DH)**	Westborough	MA	C	508 339-3000	16637
Nanomoleculardx	Pittsfield	MA	F	518 588-7815	14493
Novotechnik US Inc	Southborough	MA	G	508 485-2244	15363
Origo Automation Inc	Lowell	MA	G	877 943-5677	12417
Pharmatron Inc	Westborough	MA	F	603 645-6766	16643
Pitman An AGFA Company	Andover	MA	G	800 526-5441	7584
Power Systems Integrity Inc	Northborough	MA	G	508 393-1655	14045
Precise Time and Frequency LLC	Wakefield	MA	G	781 245-9090	15971
Programmed Test Sources Inc	Littleton	MA	F	978 486-3008	12320
Qorvo Inc	Chelmsford	MA	G	978 770-2158	9923
Quadtech Inc	Marlborough	MA	E	978 461-2100	12811
Relevant Energy Concepts Inc	Springfield	MA	G	413 733-7692	15501
Rika Denshi America Inc	Attleboro	MA	E	508 226-2080	7788
Rotek Instrument Corp	Waltham	MA	E	781 899-4611	16190
Scully Signal Company **(PA)**	Wilmington	MA	C	617 692-8600	17044
Seahorse Bioscience Inc **(HQ)**	Lexington	MA	E	978 671-1600	12263
Sifos Technologies Inc	Andover	MA	G	978 975-2100	7605
Spirent Communications Inc	Southborough	MA	G	774 463-0281	15367
Standex International Corp	Chicopee	MA	G	413 536-1311	10062
Tech180 Corp	Easthampton	MA	F	413 203-6123	10581
Teledyne Lecroy Inc	Marion	MA	E	508 748-0103	12707
Teradyne Inc **(PA)**	North Reading	MA	B	978 370-2700	13990
Teradyne Inc	Woburn	MA	C	978 370-2700	17306
Teradyne Inc	Bedford	MA	C	617 482-2700	8014
Teradyne Inc	North Reading	MA	B	978 370-2700	13991
Thermo Orion Inc **(HQ)**	Chelmsford	MA	E	800 225-1480	9937
Thermo Scientific Portable Ana	Billerica	MA	C	978 670-7460	8305
Victor Microwave Inc	Wakefield	MA	F	781 245-4472	15982
Wagner Lifescience LLC	Middleton	MA	G	978 539-8102	13105
Wayne Kerr Electronics Inc	Woburn	MA	G	781 938-8390	17317
Xcerra Corporation **(HQ)**	Norwood	MA	C	781 461-1000	14206
Xcerra Corporation	Norwood	MA	C	781 461-1000	14207
Xcerra Corporation	Norwood	MA	E	781 461-1000	14208
Ftircom LLC	Benton	ME	G	603 886-5555	5705
Mainely Metrology Inc	Smithfield	ME	G	207 362-5520	6989
Micronetixx Technologies LLC	Lewiston	ME	G	207 786-2000	6306
Aclara Technologies LLC	Somersworth	NH	F	603 749-8376	19826
Airmar Technology Corp **(PA)**	Milford	NH	B	603 673-9570	19044
Airmar Technology Corp	Milford	NH	F	603 673-9570	19045
Amphenol Corporation	Nashua	NH	B	603 879-3000	19114
ARC Technology Solutions LLC	Nashua	NH	E	603 883-3027	19117
Auriga Piv Tech Inc	Merrimack	NH	G	603 402-2955	18987
Bantry Components Inc	Manchester	NH	E	603 668-3210	18785
Digital Devices Inc	Wilton	NH	G	603 654-6240	19978
Eagle Test Systems Inc	Bedford	NH	F	603 624-5757	17639
Eastern Time Design Inc	Candia	NH	F	603 483-5876	17781
Electri-Temp Corporation	Pelham	NH	G	603 422-2509	19432
Electrocraft New Hampshire Inc **(DH)**	Dover	NH	E	603 742-3330	18021
Everett Charles Tech LLC	Nashua	NH	E	603 882-2621	19151
Everett Charles Tech LLC	Hudson	NH	G	603 882-2621	18389
Extech Instruments Corporation	Nashua	NH	D	887 439-8324	19152
Fluke Electronics Corporation	Salem	NH	G	603 537-2680	19735
H6 Systems Incorporated	Nashua	NH	G	603 880-4190	19175
Hoyt Elec Instr Works Inc	Concord	NH	D	603 753-6321	17909
Innovative Test Solutions LLC	Nashua	NH	G	603 288-0280	19188
Ion Physics Corp	Fremont	NH	G	603 895-5100	18177

	CITY	ST	EMP	PHONE	ENTRY #
Iworx Systems Inc	Dover	NH	F	603 742-2492	18030
Leusin Microwave LLC	Hampstead	NH	F	603 329-7270	18241
Martel Electronics Corp	Derry	NH	E	603 434-6033	17988
Monarch International Inc	Amherst	NH	E	603 883-3390	17577
Ocean Industries LLC	Hudson	NH	G	603 622-2481	18421
Omega Laboratories Inc	Hampstead	NH	F	978 768-7771	18247
Optical Fiber Systems Inc	New Ipswich	NH	G	603 291-0345	19309
Physical Measurement Tech	Marlborough	NH	G	603 876-9990	18964
Q A Technology Company Inc	Hampton	NH	D	603 926-1193	18269
Spectrum Services	Pelham	NH	G	603 635-2439	19447
Wilcom Inc	Belmont	NH	E	603 524-2622	17686
Xcalibur Communications	Manchester	NH	G	603 625-9555	18957
Calibrators Inc	Cumberland	RI	G	401 769-0333	20315
Everett Charles Tech LLC	Lincoln	RI	F	401 739-7310	20572
Hanna Instruments Inc **(PA)**	Woonsocket	RI	E	401 765-7500	21567
Interplex Industries Inc **(DH)**	Rumford	RI	F	718 961-6212	21188
Centrodyne Corp of America	South Burlington	VT	G	802 658-4715	22442
Omni Measurement Systems Inc	Colchester	VT	E	802 497-2253	21875
Red Nun Instrument Corporation	Bridport	VT	G	802 758-6000	21759
Synapse Ic Llc	Winooski	VT	G	802 881-4028	22725
Transmille Calibration Inc	Colchester	VT	G	802 846-7582	21882
Vermont Mold & Tool Corp	Barnet	VT	G	802 633-2300	21605

3826 Analytical Instruments

	CITY	ST	EMP	PHONE	ENTRY #
Albrayco Technologies Inc	Cromwell	CT	G	860 635-3369	845
Alpha 1c LLC	Sherman	CT	G	860 354-7979	3892
Applied Biosystems LLC	Norwalk	CT	G	781 271-0045	3102
Buck Scientific Inc	Norwalk	CT	D	203 853-9444	3116
Cam2 Technologies LLC	Danbury	CT	G	203 456-3025	884
Carestream Health Molecular	New Haven	CT	E	888 777-2072	2674
Connecticut Analytical Corp	Bethany	CT	F	203 393-9666	119
Czitek LLC	Danbury	CT	G	888 326-8186	896
Designs & Prototypes Ltd	Simsbury	CT	G	860 658-0458	3899
Energy Beam Sciences Inc	East Granby	CT	F	860 653-0411	1126
Hamilton Sndstrnd Space	Windsor Locks	CT	A	860 654-6000	5395
Idex Health & Science LLC	Bristol	CT	C	860 314-2880	570
Ihs Herold Inc **(DH)**	Norwalk	CT	D	203 857-0215	3171
Industrial Analytics Corp	Madison	CT	G	203 245-0380	1966
K A F Manufacturing Co Inc	Stamford	CT	E	203 324-3012	4234
Madison Technology Intl	Mystic	CT	G	860 245-0245	2442
Omega Engineering Inc **(HQ)**	Norwalk	CT	C	203 359-1660	3211
Owlstone Inc **(PA)**	Westport	CT	G	203 908-4848	5221
Perkinelmer Inc	Shelton	CT	G	203 925-4600	3851
Perkinelmer Hlth Sciences Inc	Shelton	CT	C	203 925-4600	3852
Prospect Products Incorporated	Newington	CT	E	860 666-0323	2896
Real-Time Analyzers Inc	Middletown	CT	G	860 635-9800	2218
Scots Landing	Fabyan	CT	G	860 923-0437	1410
Spectral LLC **(PA)**	Putnam	CT	G	860 928-7726	3635
Spectrogram Corporation	Madison	CT	G	203 245-2433	1977
Tomtec Inc	Hamden	CT	D	203 281-6790	1790
Trajan Scientific Americas Inc	Bethel	CT	G	203 830-4910	184
Wentworth Laboratories Inc	Brookfield	CT	G	203 775-9311	666
AB Sciex LLC	Framingham	MA	G	508 383-7300	10914
AB Sciex Sales LP	Framingham	MA	D	508 383-7700	10915
Acton Research Corporation	Acton	MA	E	941 556-2601	7334
Advanced Instruments LLC **(PA)**	Norwood	MA	D	781 320-9000	14122
Advanced Thermal Solutions Inc **(PA)**	Norwood	MA	E	781 769-2800	14123
Amnis Corporation	Billerica	MA	G	206 374-7000	8208
Andor Technology Inc	Concord	MA	E	978 405-1116	10109
Anova Data Inc	Westford	MA	G	978 577-6600	16753
Antec (usa) LLC	Boston	MA	G	888 572-0012	8367
Applied Biosystems LLC	Bedford	MA	F	781 271-0045	7958
Applied Biosystems LLC	Framingham	MA	G	508 877-1307	10922
Atc Group Services LLC	West Springfield	MA	E	337 234-8777	16509
Autogen Inc	Holliston	MA	E	508 429-5965	11557
Balaji International Inc	North Easton	MA	G	508 472-1953	13942
Behavioral Research Tools	Boston	MA	G	802 578-4874	8399
Bel Legacy Corporation	Boston	MA	C	508 923-5000	8400
Biochrom Us Inc	Holliston	MA	G	508 893-8999	11560
Biomass Commodities Corp	Williamstown	MA	G	413 458-5326	16955
Biomerieux Inc	Boston	MA	G	617 879-8000	8411
Bitome Inc	Jamaica Plain	MA	G	207 812-8099	11940
Block Engineering LLC	Southborough	MA	E	508 480-9643	15348
Bone Biologics Corporation **(PA)**	Boston	MA	G	732 661-2224	8420
Boston Piezo-Optics Inc	Bellingham	MA	F	508 966-4988	8032
Bruker Axs Inc	Billerica	MA	F	978 663-3660	8221
Bruker Biospin Mri Inc	Billerica	MA	F	978 667-9580	8222
Bruker Corporation **(PA)**	Billerica	MA	C	978 663-3660	8223
Bruker Daltonics Inc	Billerica	MA	G	978 663-2548	8224
Bruker Enrgy Supercon Tech Inc **(HQ)**	Billerica	MA	G	978 901-7550	8226
Bruker Optics Inc **(HQ)**	Billerica	MA	E	978 901-1528	8227
Bruker Scientific LLC **(HQ)**	Billerica	MA	C	978 667-9580	8228
Caliper Life Sciences Inc **(DH)**	Hopkinton	MA	C	203 954-9442	11694
Cape Bioresearch Inc	East Falmouth	MA	G	413 658-5426	10437
Cassini Usa Inc	Burlington	MA	G	781 487-7000	9244
Cohesive Technologies Inc **(HQ)**	Franklin	MA	E	508 528-7989	11028
Copious Imaging LLC	Lexington	MA	F	617 921-0485	12214

	CITY	ST	EMP	PHONE	ENTRY #
Corindus Inc	Waltham	MA	E	508 653-3335	16076
Covaris Inc **(PA)**	Woburn	MA	E	781 932-3959	17154
Day Zero Diagnostics Inc	Allston	MA	G	857 770-1125	7463
Doble Engineering Company **(HQ)**	Watertown	MA	F	617 926-4900	16279
Duke River Engineering Co	Newton	MA	G	617 965-7255	13586
E F Jeld Co Inc	North Billerica	MA	G	978 667-1416	13810
EMD Millipore Corporation	Burlington	MA	B	800 854-3417	9263
EMD Millipore Corporation	Burlington	MA	D	978 715-4321	9264
EMD Millipore Corporation	Billerica	MA	B	978 715-4321	8243
EMD Millipore Corporation	Waltham	MA	B	781 533-5858	16097
EMD Millipore Corporation	Taunton	MA	B	781 533-5754	15748
EMD Millipore Corporation	Bedford	MA	C	781 533-6000	7973
EMD Millipore Corporation	Bedford	MA	C	781 533-6000	7974
EMD Millipore Corporation	Danvers	MA	E	978 762-5100	10215
Evoqua Water Technologies LLC	Tewksbury	MA	E	978 863-4600	15817
Exergen Corporation	Watertown	MA	D	617 923-9900	16284
Eye Point Pharmac	Watertown	MA	G	617 926-5000	16286
Eyepoint Pharmaceuticals Inc **(PA)**	Watertown	MA	E	617 926-5000	16287
Fiberlock Technologies Inc	Andover	MA	F	978 623-9987	7548
Fluid Management Systems Inc	Watertown	MA	E	617 393-2396	16288
Galvanic Applied Sciences	North Billerica	MA	F	978 848-2701	13818
General Fluidics Corporation	Waltham	MA	G	617 543-3114	16118
Genomic Solutions Inc	Holliston	MA	E	734 975-4800	11572
Gnr USA Instruments LLC	Foxboro	MA	G	508 698-3816	10884
Harvard Bioscience Inc **(PA)**	Holliston	MA	C	508 893-8999	11575
Headwall Photonics Inc **(PA)**	Fitchburg	MA	F	978 353-4040	10829
High Voltage Engineering Corp	Wakefield	MA	F	781 224-1001	15954
Honle Uv America Inc	Marlborough	MA	G	508 229-7774	12773
Illinois Tool Works Inc	Norwood	MA	B	781 828-2500	14160
Imaging W Varex Holdings Inc	Waltham	MA	G	781 663-6900	16129
Intelicoat Technologies	West Springfield	MA	G	413 536-7800	16526
International Light Tech Inc	Peabody	MA	E	978 818-6180	14343
Ionsense Inc	Saugus	MA	F	781 231-1739	14987
Izon Science US Ltd	Medford	MA	G	617 945-5936	12937
Janis Research Company Inc **(PA)**	Woburn	MA	D	781 491-0888	17208
Janis Research Company LLC	Woburn	MA	D	781 491-0888	17209
Jeol Usa Inc **(HQ)**	Peabody	MA	C	978 535-5900	14345
Jsi Medical Systems Corp	Boston	MA	G	917 472-5022	8643
Kirstein Per	Upton	MA	G	508 473-9673	15908
Krohn-Hite Corporation	Brockton	MA	F	508 580-1660	9160
Kt Assocs Inc	Cambridge	MA	G	617 547-3737	9529
Leica Biosystems	Danvers	MA	F	978 471-0625	10232
Life Technologies Corporation	Framingham	MA	F	508 383-7700	10976
Listen Inc	Boston	MA	F	617 556-4104	8668
Lockheed Martin Sippican Inc **(HQ)**	Marion	MA	B	508 748-3399	12699
M R Resources Inc	Fitchburg	MA	E	978 696-3060	10831
Magellan Diagnostics Inc **(HQ)**	Chelmsford	MA	D	978 250-7000	9915
Magellan Diagnostics Inc	North Billerica	MA	E	978 856-2345	13838
Matec Instrument Companies Inc **(PA)**	Northborough	MA	E	508 393-0155	14038
Mettler-Toledo Intl Inc	Newton	MA	G	800 472-4646	13614
Millennium Research Labs Inc	Woburn	MA	G	781 935-0790	17233
Minuteman Laboratories Inc	Chelmsford	MA	F	978 263-2632	9917
Mtoz Biolabs Inc	Cambridge	MA	E	617 401-8103	9571
Nanosurf Inc	Woburn	MA	G	781 549-7361	17235
New England Photoconductor	Norton	MA	F	508 285-5561	14084
New Objective Inc	Woburn	MA	F	781 933-9560	17244
Nova Biomedical Corporation **(PA)**	Waltham	MA	A	781 894-0800	16162
Nova Instruments LLC **(PA)**	Wakefield	MA	G	781 897-1200	15966
Omniprobe Inc	Concord	MA	E	214 572-6800	10148
On-Site Analysis Inc **(DH)**	Chelmsford	MA	G	561 775-5756	9918
Organomation Associates Inc	Berlin	MA	F	978 838-7300	8092
Park Bio Services LLC	Groveland	MA	G	978 794-8500	11303
Particles Plus Inc **(PA)**	Stoughton	MA	F	781 341-6898	15613
Pelagic Electronics	East Falmouth	MA	G	508 540-1200	10446
Perkinelmer Inc	Cambridge	MA	G	617 577-7744	9609
Perkinelmer Inc	Hopkinton	MA	F	508 435-9500	11731
Perkinelmer Inc	Arlington	MA	G	617 350-9440	7633
Perkinelmer Inc	Boston	MA	E	617 596-9909	8776
Perkinelmer Inc **(PA)**	Waltham	MA	C	781 663-6900	16171
Perkinelmer Hlth Sciences Inc	North Billerica	MA	E	617 350-9024	13855
Perkinelmer Holdings Inc **(HQ)**	Wellesley	MA	G	781 663-6900	16380
Philips North America LLC	Natick	MA	C	508 647-1130	13271
Photonics N Picoquant Amer Inc	West Springfield	MA	G	413 562-6161	16542
Photonis Scientific Inc **(DH)**	Sturbridge	MA	D	508 347-4000	15646
Precision Systems Inc	Natick	MA	E	508 655-7010	13274
President Fllows Hrvard Cllege	Cambridge	MA	C	617 495-4043	9617
Proveris Scientific Corp	Hudson	MA	E	508 460-8822	11809
Pvd Products Inc	Wilmington	MA	F	978 694-9455	17040
Resonance Research Inc	Billerica	MA	E	978 671-0811	8291
Rigaku Analytical Devices Inc	Wilmington	MA	E	781 328-1024	17041
Schoeffel International Corp	Chelmsford	MA	E	978 256-4512	9931
Sciaps Inc **(PA)**	Woburn	MA	E	339 222-2585	17291
Semilab USA LLC	North Billerica	MA	F	508 647-8400	13863
Sensitech Inc **(DH)**	Beverly	MA	D	978 927-7033	8177
Siemens Hlthcare Dgnostics Inc	Norwood	MA	C	781 269-3000	14199
Sirius Analytical Inc	Billerica	MA	G	978 338-5790	8295
Skyray Instrument Inc	Braintree	MA	F	617 202-3879	9037
Specs Tii Inc	Mansfield	MA	G	508 618-1292	12661
Spectra Analysis Inc **(PA)**	Marlborough	MA	F	508 281-6232	12827
Spectra Analysis Instrs Inc	Marlborough	MA	F	508 281-6233	12828
Spectral Evolution Inc	Haverhill	MA	G	978 687-1833	11474
Spectris Inc **(HQ)**	Westborough	MA	F	508 768-6400	16650
Spectros Instruments Inc	Hopedale	MA	G	508 478-1648	11683
Studio of Engaging Learning	Brighton	MA	G	617 975-0268	9107
Ta Instruments-Waters LLC **(PA)**	Wakefield	MA	F	781 233-1717	15980
Thermo Envmtl Instrs LLC **(HQ)**	Franklin	MA	C	508 520-0430	11086
Thermo Fisher Scientific Inc **(PA)**	Waltham	MA	C	781 622-1000	16213
Thermo Fisher Scientific Inc	Amherst	MA	B	413 577-2600	7527
Thermo Fisher Scientific Inc	Framingham	MA	G	978 735-3091	11007
Thermo Fisher Scientific Inc	Chelmsford	MA	F	978 250-7000	9936
Thermo Fisher Scientific Inc	Tewksbury	MA	G	781 622-1000	15843
Thermo Fisher Scientific Inc	Bedford	MA	C	781 280-5600	8017
Thermo Fisher Scientific Inc	Billerica	MA	E	978 667-4016	8304
Thermo Fisher Scientific Inc	Franklin	MA	F	508 520-0430	11087
Thermo Fisher Scientific Inc	Danvers	MA	G	978 223-1540	10262
Thermo Fisher Scientific Inc	Wilmington	MA	D	978 275-0800	17055
Thermo Keytek LLC	Tewksbury	MA	D	978 275-0800	15844
Thermo Orion Inc **(HQ)**	Chelmsford	MA	E	800 225-1480	9937
Thermo Scntfic Prtble Anlytcal **(HQ)**	Tewksbury	MA	C	978 657-5555	15845
Thoratec Corporation	Burlington	MA	D	781 272-0139	9346
Thrive Bioscience Inc	Wakefield	MA	G	978 720-8048	15981
Umass Mem Mri Imaging Ctr LLC	Worcester	MA	E	508 756-7300	17492
Union Biometrica Inc **(PA)**	Holliston	MA	E	508 893-3115	11610
Vacuum Process Technology LLC	Plymouth	MA	E	508 732-7200	14589
Vacuum Technology Inc	Gloucester	MA	G	510 333-6562	11216
Verosound Inc	Sudbury	MA	G	978 440-7898	15672
Viken Detection Corporation	Burlington	MA	E	617 467-5526	9353
Virogen Corp	Watertown	MA	G	617 926-9167	16329
Wafer Inspection Services Inc	Orleans	MA	G	508 944-2851	14245
Waters Corporation	Milford	MA	G	508 478-0208	13152
Waters Corporation **(PA)**	Milford	MA	C	508 478-2000	13153
Waters Technologies Corp	Taunton	MA	F	508 482-5223	15798
Waters Technologies Corp	Beverly	MA	F	978 927-7468	8196
Waters Technologies Corp	Franklin	MA	E	508 482-4807	11097
Waters Technologies Corp **(HQ)**	Milford	MA	A	508 478-2000	13154
Waveguide Corporation	Cambridge	MA	G	617 892-9700	9699
Wellumina Health Inc	Danvers	MA	G	978 777-1854	10273
Williamson Corporation	Concord	MA	E	978 369-9607	10163
Allan Fuller	Benton	ME	G	603 886-5555	5703
American Healthcare	Scarborough	ME	F	888 567-7733	6904
Artel Inc	Westbrook	ME	E	207 854-0860	7180
Bio RAD Lab	Portland	ME	G	207 615-0571	6622
Dirigo Analytics LLC	Kennebunk	ME	G	978 376-5522	6232
Envirologix Inc	Portland	ME	D	207 797-0300	6661
Fhc Inc **(PA)**	Bowdoin	ME	D	207 666-8190	5787
Fluid Imaging Technologies Inc	Scarborough	ME	E	207 289-3200	6917
Hindsight Imaging Inc	Freeport	ME	G	607 793-3762	6080
Idexx Distribution Inc	Westbrook	ME	D	207 556-0637	7190
Idexx Laboratories Inc **(PA)**	Westbrook	ME	A	207 556-0300	7191
John Fancy Inc	Appleton	ME	G	207 785-3610	5526
Long Life Saunas	Bowdoinham	ME	G	802 349-0501	5789
Allen Datagraph Systems Inc	Salem	NH	E	603 216-6344	19705
Brailsford & Company Inc	Antrim	NH	E	603 588-2880	17593
Coherent Inc	Salem	NH	F	603 685-0900	19716
Diversified Enterprises-ADT	Claremont	NH	G	603 543-0038	17847
EMD Millipore Corporation	Jaffrey	NH	B	603 532-8711	18462
Environmental Test Pdts LLC **(PA)**	Hollis	NH	G	603 924-5010	18331
Environmental Test Pdts LLC	Jaffrey	NH	G	603 593-5268	18463
Flir Systems Inc	Nashua	NH	G	866 636-4487	19162
GL&v USA Inc	Nashua	NH	D	603 882-2711	19169
Hiden Analytical Inc **(DH)**	Peterborough	NH	G	603 924-5008	19472
Hindsight Imaging Inc	Manchester	NH	G	607 793-3762	18833
Integra Biosciences Corp	Hudson	NH	F	603 578-5800	18401
Kentek Corporation	Pittsfield	NH	E	603 223-4900	19502
Labsphere Inc	North Sutton	NH	C	603 927-4266	19392
M Braun Inc	Stratham	NH	D	603 773-9333	19872
Metavac LLC	Portsmouth	NH	E	631 207-2344	19595
Microelectrodes Inc	Bedford	NH	G	603 668-0692	17654
Opti-Sciences Inc	Hudson	NH	G	603 883-4400	18424
Poly-Vac Inc	Manchester	NH	C	603 647-7822	18903
Teledyne Instrs Leeman Labs	Hudson	NH	D	603 521-3299	18446
Teledyne Instruments Inc	Hudson	NH	D	603 886-8400	18447
Thermo Fisher Scientific Inc	Portsmouth	NH	B	603 433-7676	19625
Thermo Fisher Scientific Inc	Hudson	NH	G	603 595-0505	18448
Thermo Fisher Scientific Inc	Portsmouth	NH	G	603 431-8410	19626
Wilbur Technical Services LLC	Mont Vernon	NH	G	603 880-7100	19094
Dewetron Inc	East Greenwich	RI	F	401 284-3750	20360
Envirnmntal Compliance Systems	Cumberland	RI	G	401 334-0306	20320
Hanna Instruments Inc **(PA)**	Woonsocket	RI	E	401 765-7500	21567
Oldcastle Buildingenvelope Inc	Warwick	RI	G	866 653-2278	21398
Thermo Fisher Scientific Inc	North Kingstown	RI	G	401 294-1234	20745
Biotek Instruments Inc **(HQ)**	Winooski	VT	D	802 655-4040	22717
Elution Technologies LLC	Colchester	VT	G	802 540-0296	21862
Living Systems Instrumentation	Burlington	VT	G	802 863-5547	21794

	CITY	ST	EMP	PHONE	ENTRY #
Med Associates Inc **(PA)**	Fairfax	VT	D	802 527-2343	21977
Raj Communications Ltd	Williston	VT	F	802 658-4961	22687
Vermont Optechs Inc	Charlotte	VT	G	802 425-2040	21836

3827 Optical Instruments

	CITY	ST	EMP	PHONE	ENTRY #
4 D Technology Corporation	East Hampton	CT	G	860 365-0420	1154
Abet Technologies Inc	Milford	CT	G	203 540-9990	2234
Adaptive Optics Associates Inc	East Hartford	CT	F	860 282-4401	1170
Advanced Photonics Intl Inc	Fairfield	CT	G	203 259-0437	1413
Aecc/Pearlman Buying Group LLC	Middlebury	CT	F	203 598-3200	2153
Aperture Optical Sciences Inc	Higganum	CT	G	860 301-2589	1899
Aperture Optical Sciences Inc	Meriden	CT	G	860 301-2372	2076
Argyle Optics LLC	Milford	CT	G	203 451-3320	2245
Brightsight Llc	Woodstock	CT	G	860 208-0222	5494
Coating Design Group Inc	Stratford	CT	E	203 878-3663	4405
Coburn Technologies Inc **(PA)**	South Windsor	CT	C	860 648-6600	3951
Conoptics Inc	Danbury	CT	F	203 743-3349	892
CT Fiberoptics Inc	Somers	CT	F	860 763-4341	3915
Data Technology Inc	Tolland	CT	E	860 871-8082	4545
Flabeg Technical Glass US Corp	Naugatuck	CT	E	203 729-5227	2473
Gerber Coburn Optical Inc **(HQ)**	South Windsor	CT	C	800 843-1479	3972
Karl Stetson Associates LLC	Coventry	CT	G	860 742-8414	834
Macro Systems Inc	Shelton	CT	G	203 225-6266	3830
Nntechnology Moore Systems LLC	Bridgeport	CT	G	203 366-3224	458
Odis Inc	Storrs Mansfield	CT	G	860 450-8407	4385
Optical Design Associates	Stamford	CT	G	203 249-6408	4271
Optical Research Technologies	Wilton	CT	G	203 762-9063	5296
Orafol Americas Inc	Avon	CT	C	860 676-7100	41
Retina Systems Inc	Seymour	CT	E	203 881-1311	3763
Scope Technology Inc	Plainfield	CT	F	860 963-1141	3457
Tower Optical Company Inc	Norwalk	CT	G	203 866-4535	3260
UTC Fire SEC Americas Corp Inc	Newtown	CT	C	203 426-1180	2947
Zygo Corporation **(HQ)**	Middlefield	CT	G	860 347-8506	2169
Acton Research Corporation	Acton	MA	E	941 556-2601	7334
Adaptive Optics Associates Inc	Devens	MA	F	978 757-9600	10316
Adaptive Optics Associates Inc **(DH)**	Devens	MA	D	978 757-9600	10317
Adaptive Optics Associates Inc	Devens	MA	E	978 391-0000	10318
AMF Optical Solutions LLC	Woburn	MA	G	781 933-6125	17118
Amplitude Laser Inc	Boston	MA	G	617 401-2195	8365
AMS Qi Inc	Cambridge	MA	G	617 797-4709	9389
Angstrom Advanced Inc	Stoughton	MA	D	781 519-4765	15580
Applied Science Group Inc	Billerica	MA	E	781 275-4000	8212
Atlantic RES Mktg Systems Inc	West Bridgewater	MA	F	508 584-7816	16429
Atlantic Vision Inc	Shrewsbury	MA	G	508 845-8401	15103
Axsun Technologies Inc	Billerica	MA	D	978 262-0049	8217
Bae Systems Info & Elec Sys	Lexington	MA	B	603 885-4321	12208
Bauer Associates Inc	Natick	MA	G	508 310-0201	13236
Bern Optics Inc	Westfield	MA	E	413 568-6800	16674
Boston Piezo-Optics Inc	Bellingham	MA	F	508 966-4988	8032
Cambrdge RES Instrmntation Inc	Hopkinton	MA	E	781 935-9099	11695
Chromatra LLC	Beverly	MA	G	978 473-7005	8116
Eidolon Corporation	Natick	MA	G	781 400-0586	13253
Electro Optical Industries **(PA)**	Boston	MA	E	617 401-2196	8523
Enos Engineering LLC	Acton	MA	G	978 654-6522	7353
Eo Vista LLC	Acton	MA	F	978 635-8080	7354
Excel Technology Inc **(HQ)**	Bedford	MA	D	781 266-5700	7976
Excelitas Technologies Corp **(DH)**	Waltham	MA	E	781 522-5910	16104
Focused Resolutions Inc	Methuen	MA	G	978 794-7981	13022
Genscope Inc	East Longmeadow	MA	F	413 526-0802	10476
Gentex Optics Inc	Dudley	MA	B	508 713-5267	10375
Gtat Corporation	Salem	MA	E	978 745-0088	14917
Hardric Laboratories Inc	North Chelmsford	MA	E	978 251-1702	13895
Headwall Photonics Inc	Bolton	MA	D	978 353-4100	8319
Hilsinger Company Parent LLC **(PA)**	Plainville	MA	C	508 699-4406	14520
Hilsinger Holdings Inc	Plainville	MA	C	508 699-4406	14521
Holographix LLC	Marlborough	MA	F	978 562-4474	12772
I-Optics Corp	Burlington	MA	G	508 366-1600	9284
Idealab Inc	Franklin	MA	F	508 528-9260	11054
Incom Inc	Charlton	MA	C	508 909-2200	9851
Innovations In Optics Inc	Woburn	MA	G	781 933-4477	17202
Instrument Technology Inc	Westfield	MA	E	413 562-3512	16690
J P Mfg Inc	Southbridge	MA	E	508 764-2538	15389
Kinetic Systems Inc	Boston	MA	E	617 522-8700	8649
KLA Corporation	Westwood	MA	D	978 843-7670	16871
L3 Technologies Inc	Wilmington	MA	C	978 694-9991	17014
L3 Technologies Inc	Northampton	MA	A	413 586-2330	14009
Lexitek Inc	Watertown	MA	G	781 431-9604	16294
Lithoptek LLC	Natick	MA	G	408 533-5847	13264
Magnolia Optical Tech Inc	Woburn	MA	G	781 376-1505	17222
Materion Prcsion Optics Thin F **(DH)**	Westford	MA	F	978 692-7513	16778
N-Vision Optics LLC	Needham	MA	G	781 505-8360	13305
Nano Beam Technologies	Lexington	MA	G	617 548-9495	12246
Nanoptek Corporation	Shirley	MA	G	978 460-7107	15091
Newport Corporation	Franklin	MA	D	508 553-5035	11070
Newport Corporation	Wilmington	MA	D	978 296-1306	17030
Novotech Inc	Acton	MA	E	978 929-9458	7375
Opco Laboratory Inc	Fitchburg	MA	E	978 345-2522	10846
Ophir Optics LLC	Wilmington	MA	C	978 657-6410	17033
Optical Metrology Inc	North Andover	MA	G	978 657-6303	13721
Opticraft Inc	Woburn	MA	E	781 938-0456	17250
Optimum Technologies Inc	Southbridge	MA	F	508 765-8100	15398
Opto-Line International Inc	Wilmington	MA	F	978 658-7255	17035
Optometrics Corporation	Littleton	MA	E	978 772-1700	12316
Optos Inc	Marlborough	MA	D	508 787-1400	12803
Orpro Vision LLC	Billerica	MA	G	617 676-1101	8271
Plymouth Grating Lab Inc	Carver	MA	F	508 465-2274	9806
Precision Optics Corp Inc **(PA)**	Gardner	MA	E	978 630-1800	11123
Prior Scientific Inc **(HQ)**	Rockland	MA	F	781 878-8442	14820
Resident Artist Studio LLC	Boxborough	MA	G	978 635-9162	8969
Roper Scientific Inc	Acton	MA	E	978 268-0337	7381
Rubil Associates Inc	Billerica	MA	F	978 670-7192	8292
S I Howard Glass Company Inc	Worcester	MA	E	508 753-8146	17461
Scientific Solutions Inc	North Chelmsford	MA	F	978 251-4554	13910
Skylight Navigation Technology	Sherborn	MA	G	508 655-7516	15079
Tel Epion Inc	Billerica	MA	E	978 436-2300	8302
Thermo Vision Corp **(HQ)**	Franklin	MA	F	508 520-0083	11090
Thin Film Imaging Technologies	Greenfield	MA	F	413 774-6692	11280
Transom Scopes Inc	Westfield	MA	E	413 562-3606	16737
Twin Coast Metrology Inc	Acton	MA	G	508 517-4508	7392
United Lens Company Inc	Southbridge	MA	C	508 765-5421	15407
Vacuum Process Technology LLC	Plymouth	MA	E	508 732-7200	14589
Zibra Corporation	Westport	MA	F	508 636-6606	16853
Zygo Corporation	Franklin	MA	E	508 541-1268	11101
American Rheinmetall Def Inc **(PA)**	Biddeford	ME	G	207 571-5850	5717
American Rhnmetall Systems LLC	Biddeford	ME	E	207 571-5850	5718
Bulzeyepro	Augusta	ME	G	207 626-0000	5604
Lighthouse Imaging LLC	Windham	ME	G	207 893-8233	7240
QED Optical Inc	Houlton	ME	G	207 532-6772	6209
603 Optx Inc	Keene	NH	G	603 357-4900	18489
Ametek Precitech Inc **(HQ)**	Keene	NH	D	603 357-2510	18491
Andover Corporation	Salem	NH	E	603 893-6888	19707
Bond Optics LLC	Lebanon	NH	E	603 448-2300	18616
Cheshire Optical Inc	Laconia	NH	G	603 352-0602	18562
Clear Align LLC	Nashua	NH	F	603 889-2116	19134
Elbit Systems of America LLC	Merrimack	NH	F	603 889-2500	18999
General Dynamics Mission	Nashua	NH	C	603 864-6300	19165
Guidewire Technologies Inc	Salem	NH	E	603 894-4399	19740
Guild Optical Associates Inc	Amherst	NH	F	603 889-6247	17567
Janos Technology Inc	Keene	NH	G	603 757-0070	18507
Janos Technology LLC	Keene	NH	C	603 757-0070	18508
Km Holding Inc	Hudson	NH	F	603 566-2704	18407
Moore Nntechnology Systems LLC **(DH)**	Swanzey	NH	D	603 352-3030	19886
National Aperture Inc	Salem	NH	F	603 893-7393	19754
Optical Solutions Inc	Charlestown	NH	G	603 826-4411	17818
Optics 1 Inc	Bedford	NH	G	603 296-0469	17657
Optics 1 Inc **(DH)**	Bedford	NH	F	603 296-0469	17658
Prophotonix Limited **(PA)**	Salem	NH	E	603 893-8778	19761
Robert Cairns Company LLC	Plaistow	NH	G	603 382-0044	19522
Semigen Inc	Londonderry	NH	E	603 624-8311	18735
Silicon Sense Inc	Nashua	NH	G	603 891-4248	19261
Space Optics Research Labs LLC	Merrimack	NH	F	978 250-8640	19032
Stingray Optics LLC	Keene	NH	F	603 358-5577	18529
Wilcox Industries Corp **(PA)**	Newington	NH	C	603 431-1331	19329
Adolf Meller Company **(PA)**	Providence	RI	E	800 821-0180	20946
Adolf Meller Company	Providence	RI	E	401 331-3838	20947
Knight Optical (usa) LLC	North Kingstown	RI	G	401 521-7000	20721
Nippon American Limited	East Greenwich	RI	F	401 885-7353	20374
Pyramid Case Co Inc	Providence	RI	A	401 273-0643	21101
89 North Inc	Williston	VT	G	802 881-0302	22653
Chroma Technology Corp	Bellows Falls	VT	C	802 428-2500	21650
J & L Metrology Inc	Springfield	VT	E	802 885-8291	22503
Jack Russell	West Rutland	VT	G	802 438-5213	22617
KLA Corporation	Williston	VT	F	802 318-9100	22677
Lenco Inc	Rutland	VT	E	802 775-2505	22344
Omega Optical Incorporated	Brattleboro	VT	D	802 251-7300	21742
Vermont Precision Machine Svcs	Springfield	VT	G	802 885-8291	22511

3829 Measuring & Controlling Devices, NEC

	CITY	ST	EMP	PHONE	ENTRY #
Ai-Tek Instruments LLC	Cheshire	CT	E	203 271-6927	708
Airflo Instrument Company	Glastonbury	CT	G	860 633-9455	1536
American Design & Mfg Inc	South Windsor	CT	E	860 282-2719	3935
Atlantic Sensors & Contrls LLC	Milford	CT	G	203 878-8118	2246
Bauer Inc	Bristol	CT	D	860 583-9100	531
Bojak Company	Milford	CT	G	203 378-5086	2255
Clinton Instrument Company	Clinton	CT	E	860 669-7548	780
Comet Technologies USA Inc **(DH)**	Shelton	CT	E	203 447-3200	3790
Cooper-Atkins Corporation **(HQ)**	Middlefield	CT	C	860 349-3473	2162
Data Technology Inc	Tolland	CT	E	860 871-8082	4545
Eaton Aerospace LLC	Bethel	CT	E	203 796-6000	150
Edmunds Manufacturing Company **(PA)**	Farmington	CT	D	860 677-2813	1480
Electro-Methods Inc **(PA)**	South Windsor	CT	C	860 289-8661	3962
Gems Sensors Inc	Plainville	CT	F	800 378-1600	3492
Gold Line Connector Inc **(PA)**	Redding	CT	E	203 938-2588	3648
Habco Industries LLC	Glastonbury	CT	E	860 682-6800	1556

SIC

	CITY	ST	EMP	PHONE	ENTRY #
Harcosemco LLC	Branford	CT	C	203 483-3700	322
Hayward Turnstiles Inc	Milford	CT	G	203 877-7096	2296
Hitachi Aloka Medical Ltd	Wallingford	CT	D	203 269-5088	4752
Hitachi Aloka Medical Amer Inc	Wallingford	CT	D	203 269-5088	4753
Image Insight Inc	East Hartford	CT	G	860 528-9806	1202
Judge Tool & Gage Inc	Stratford	CT	G	800 214-5990	4426
Jurman Metrics Inc	Monroe	CT	F	203 261-9388	2405
Kahn Industries Inc	Wethersfield	CT	E	860 529-8643	5252
Lex Products LLC **(PA)**	Shelton	CT	C	203 363-3738	3828
Luxpoint Inc	Rocky Hill	CT	G	860 982-9588	3722
Megasonics Inc	New Canaan	CT	G	203 966-3404	2607
Miracle Instruments Co	Lebanon	CT	F	860 642-7745	1936
Mirion Tech Canberra Inc **(HQ)**	Meriden	CT	B	203 238-2351	2109
Mistras Group Inc	Waterford	CT	E	860 447-2474	4989
Omega Engineering Inc	Norwalk	CT	D	714 540-4914	3212
Owlstone Inc **(PA)**	Westport	CT	G	203 908-4848	5221
Perey Turnstiles Inc	Bridgeport	CT	E	203 333-9400	467
Pmd Scientific Inc	Bloomfield	CT	G	860 242-8177	252
Power-Dyne LLC	Middletown	CT	E	860 346-9283	2211
Pratt Whtney Msurement Systems	Bloomfield	CT	E	860 286-8181	254
Preferred Utilities Mfg Corp **(HQ)**	Danbury	CT	D	203 743-6741	974
Projects Inc	Glastonbury	CT	C	860 633-4615	1574
Q-Lane Turnstiles LLC	Sandy Hook	CT	F	860 410-1801	3745
Semco Instruments Inc **(DH)**	Branford	CT	C	661 257-2000	347
Semco Instruments Inc	Branford	CT	G	661 362-6117	348
Sens All Inc	Southington	CT	G	860 628-8379	4076
Simmonds Precision Pdts Inc	Danbury	CT	E	203 797-5000	994
Soldream Inc	Vernon Rockville	CT	E	860 871-6883	4683
Specialty Components Inc	Wallingford	CT	G	203 284-9112	4811
Sperian Protectn Instrumentatn	Middletown	CT	C	860 344-1079	2225
Strain Measurement Devices Inc	Wallingford	CT	E	203 294-5800	4814
Technisonic Research Inc	Fairfield	CT	G	203 368-3600	1457
Tek-Air Systems Inc	Monroe	CT	E	203 791-1400	2418
TLC Ultrasound Inc	New Milford	CT	G	860 354-6333	2830
Trans-Tek Inc	Ellington	CT	E	860 872-8351	1343
Unholtz-Dickie Corporation **(PA)**	Wallingford	CT	E	203 265-9875	4825
Weigh & Test Systems Inc	Riverside	CT	F	203 698-9681	3693
Abbess Instrs & Systems Inc	Holliston	MA	F	508 429-0002	11555
Accusonic Technologies **(DH)**	New Bedford	MA	F	508 495-6600	13348
Aclara Technologies LLC	Wellesley	MA	E	781 694-3300	16357
Adaptive Wreless Solutions LLC	Hudson	MA	F	978 875-6000	11751
Ade Technologies Inc **(HQ)**	Westwood	MA	D	781 467-3500	16857
Admet Inc	Norwood	MA	G	781 769-0850	14120
Advanced Measurement Tech Inc	Woburn	MA	D	781 938-7800	17111
Advanced Mechanical Tech Inc **(PA)**	Watertown	MA	E	617 923-4174	16263
Advanced Thermal Solutions Inc **(PA)**	Norwood	MA	E	781 769-2800	14123
Aja International Inc	Scituate	MA	E	781 545-7365	15005
Ametek Inc	Wilmington	MA	D	978 988-4101	16973
Anderson Power Products Inc **(HQ)**	Sterling	MA	D	978 422-3600	15535
Anova Data Inc	Westford	MA	G	978 577-6600	16753
Associated Envmtl Systems Inc **(PA)**	Acton	MA	C	978 772-0022	7342
Auburn Filtersense LLC	Beverly	MA	E	978 777-2460	8103
Axcelis Technologies Inc **(PA)**	Beverly	MA	C	978 787-4000	8106
Barrett Technology LLC	Newton	MA	E	617 252-9000	13566
Biotech Diagnostics	Newton	MA	G	617 332-8787	13570
Blueline NDT LLC	Bedford	MA	G	781 791-9511	7963
Bmi Surplus Inc	Hanover	MA	G	781 871-8868	11328
Capacitec Inc **(PA)**	Ayer	MA	F	978 772-6033	7913
Cape Cod Wind Wther Indicators	Harwich Port	MA	G	508 432-9475	11398
Chauvin Arnoux Inc	Foxboro	MA	F	508 698-2115	10878
Control Resources Inc	Littleton	MA	E	978 486-4160	12297
Convectronics Inc	Haverhill	MA	F	978 374-7714	11419
CTS Valpey Corporation **(HQ)**	Hopkinton	MA	E	508 435-6831	11699
David L Ellis Company Inc **(PA)**	Acton	MA	G	978 897-1795	7349
Doble Engineering Company **(HQ)**	Watertown	MA	F	617 926-4900	16279
Druck LLC **(HQ)**	Billerica	MA	C	978 437-1000	8238
Dynisco Instruments LLC	Billerica	MA	D	978 215-3401	8240
Dynisco Instruments LLC **(HQ)**	Franklin	MA	C	508 541-9400	11037
Dynisco LLC **(HQ)**	Franklin	MA	D	508 541-3195	11038
Dynisco Parent Inc	Billerica	MA	E	978 667-5301	8241
Electro-Fix Inc	Plainville	MA	E	508 695-0228	14518
Environmental Svcs Group Inc	Medway	MA	E	508 533-7683	12959
Fitbit Inc	Boston	MA	G	857 277-0594	8549
Forte Technology Inc	South Easton	MA	F	508 297-2363	15277
Foster-Miller Inc	Devens	MA	D	781 684-4000	10320
G T C Falcon Inc	Plymouth	MA	F	508 746-0200	14560
Gefran Isi Inc	North Andover	MA	E	781 729-0842	13708
Grozier Technical Systems Inc	Westwood	MA	G	781 762-4446	16867
Hamilton Thorne Inc **(PA)**	Beverly	MA	E	978 921-2050	8138
Hawk Measurement America LLC **(PA)**	Lawrence	MA	G	978 304-3000	12031
Hefring LLC	Boston	MA	G	617 206-5750	8593
Hitec Products Inc	Pepperell	MA	F	978 772-6963	14438
Ideal Industries Inc	Sterling	MA	C	978 422-3600	15540
IDS Imaging Dev Systems Inc	Stoneham	MA	F	781 787-0048	15565
Illinois Tool Works Inc	Norwood	MA	B	781 828-2500	14160
Insense Medical LLC	Hopkinton	MA	G	518 316-4759	11722
Instron Japan Company Ltd	Norwood	MA	B	781 828-2500	14165
Integrated Dynamics Engrg Inc **(HQ)**	Randolph	MA	E	781 326-5700	14687
Intelligent Medical Dvcs Inc	Foxboro	MA	G	617 871-6401	10888
International Light Tech Inc	Peabody	MA	E	978 818-6180	14343
Ion Track Instruments LLC	Wilmington	MA	D	978 658-3767	17007
ITW Instron	Norwood	MA	G	781 762-3216	14167
Johnson Controls Inc	Wrentham	MA	E	508 384-0018	17524
Kerfoot Technologies Inc	Mashpee	MA	F	508 539-3002	12881
Kinemetrics Inc	Harvard	MA	G	978 772-4774	11381
Kinetic Systems Inc	Boston	MA	E	617 522-8700	8649
Krohn-Hite Corporation	Brockton	MA	F	508 580-1660	9160
Lawrence Instron Corporation	Norwood	MA	C	781 828-2500	14174
Live Cell Technologies LLC	Boston	MA	G	646 662-4157	8669
Lockheed Martin Sippican Inc **(HQ)**	Marion	MA	B	508 748-3399	12699
M R Resources Inc	Fitchburg	MA	E	978 696-3060	10831
Magnetic Sciences Inc	Acton	MA	G	978 266-9355	7372
Massachusetts Mtls Tech LLC **(PA)**	Weston	MA	G	617 500-8325	16827
Massachusetts Mtls Tech LLC	Cambridge	MA	G	617 502-5636	9549
Matec Instrument Companies Inc **(PA)**	Northborough	MA	E	508 393-0155	14038
Maximum Inc	New Bedford	MA	F	508 995-2200	13417
Microsense LLC **(HQ)**	Lowell	MA	E	978 843-7670	12411
Millimeter Wave Systems LLC	Amherst	MA	G	413 345-6467	7519
Mistras Group Inc	Auburn	MA	E	508 832-5500	7844
Mks Instruments Inc	Lawrence	MA	C	978 975-2350	12058
Nanmac Corp	Holliston	MA	E	508 872-4811	11588
Neotron Inc	Wellesley	MA	G	781 239-3461	16376
Newton-Wellesley Health Care	Newton	MA	F	617 726-2142	13618
Nix Inc	Allston	MA	G	617 458-9407	7472
Nortekusa Inc	Boston	MA	G	617 205-5750	8739
On Grade USA	Northborough	MA	G	508 351-9480	14042
On Line Controls Inc	Hudson	MA	G	978 562-5353	11798
Onto Innovation Inc **(PA)**	Wilmington	MA	B	978 253-6200	17032
Oxford Instrs Msrement Systems	Concord	MA	D	978 369-9933	10149
Photonis Scientific Inc **(DH)**	Sturbridge	MA	D	508 347-4000	15646
Pinpoint Laser Systems Inc	Peabody	MA	E	978 532-8001	14362
Princeton Security Tech Inc **(HQ)**	Franklin	MA	G	609 924-7310	11074
Princton Gamma-Tech Instrs Inc	Franklin	MA	F	609 924-7310	11075
Prior Scientific Inc **(HQ)**	Rockland	MA	F	781 878-8442	14820
Quadtech Inc	Marlborough	MA	E	978 461-2100	12811
Quality Engineering Assoc Inc	Billerica	MA	F	978 528-2034	8280
Quantek Instruments	Grafton	MA	G	508 839-0108	11224
Radiation Monitoring Dvcs Inc **(HQ)**	Watertown	MA	E	617 668-6800	16310
Raywatch Inc	West Roxbury	MA	G	401 338-2211	16502
Redshift Bioanalytics Inc	Burlington	MA	G	781 345-7300	9329
Rmd Instruments Corp	Watertown	MA	E	617 668-6900	16312
Rotek Instrument Corp	Waltham	MA	E	781 899-4611	16190
Rudolph Technologies Inc **(HQ)**	Wilmington	MA	B	978 253-6200	17042
Schneeberger Inc **(DH)**	Woburn	MA	G	781 271-0140	17290
Schoeffel International Corp	Chelmsford	MA	E	978 256-4512	9931
Scintitech Inc	Shirley	MA	G	978 425-0800	15093
Sea Machines Robotics Inc **(PA)**	Boston	MA	G	617 455-6266	8841
Second Wind Systems Inc	Newton	MA	F	617 581-6090	13634
Semiconsoft Inc	Southborough	MA	F	617 388-6832	15364
Setra Systems Inc	Boxboro	MA	F	978 263-1400	8954
Spectris Inc **(HQ)**	Westborough	MA	F	508 768-6400	16650
Spire Metering Technology LLC	Marlborough	MA	F	978 263-7100	12829
Spiroll International Corp	Cambridge	MA	G	617 876-8141	9659
Technical Manufacturing Corp **(HQ)**	Peabody	MA	D	978 532-6330	14376
Teledyne Instruments Inc	North Falmouth	MA	E	508 563-1000	13956
Testing Machines Inc	Swansea	MA	G	302 613-5600	15717
Thermalogic Corporation	Hudson	MA	E	800 343-4492	11823
Thermo Electron Karlsruhe GMBH	Tewksbury	MA	G	978 513-3724	15842
Thermo Envmtl Instrs LLC **(HQ)**	Franklin	MA	C	508 520-0430	11086
Thermo Instrument Systems Inc	Waltham	MA	G	781 622-1000	16214
Thermo Process Instruments LP	Franklin	MA	C	508 553-6913	11089
TM Electronics Inc	Devens	MA	F	978 772-0970	10334
Toolmex Indus Solutions Inc **(PA)**	Northborough	MA	D	508 653-5110	14052
Trans Metrics Inc **(HQ)**	Watertown	MA	F	617 926-1000	16325
Triangle Engineering Inc	Hanover	MA	F	781 878-1500	11356
Trimble Inc	Marlborough	MA	G	508 381-5800	12838
United Innovations Inc	Holyoke	MA	F	413 533-7500	11663
Vaisala Inc	Newton	MA	D	617 467-1500	13647
Vaisala Inc	Woburn	MA	E	781 933-4500	17312
Verify LLC	Cambridge	MA	F	513 285-7258	9694
Viricor Inc	Sudbury	MA	G	508 733-5537	15673
Waters Corporation **(PA)**	Milford	MA	C	508 478-2000	13153
Waters Technologies Corp **(HQ)**	Milford	MA	A	508 478-2000	13154
Whoop Inc	Boston	MA	F	617 670-1074	8927
Wildlife Acoustics Inc	Maynard	MA	G	978 369-5225	12906
X Sonix	Boxborough	MA	G	978 266-2106	8972
Abbott Dgnstics Scrborough Inc **(DH)**	Scarborough	ME	D	207 730-5750	6901
Ibcontrols	Windham	ME	E	207 893-0080	7237
Idexx Distribution Inc	Westbrook	ME	D	207 556-0637	7190
Illinois Tool Works Inc	Mechanic Falls	ME	E	207 998-5140	6420
Intelligent Controls Inc **(HQ)**	Saco	ME	E	207 571-1123	6849
McGuire & Co Inc	Falmouth	ME	G	207 797-3323	6032
Rainwise Inc	Trenton	ME	E	800 762-5723	7101
Airmar Technology Corp **(PA)**	Milford	NH	B	603 673-9570	19044

	CITY	ST	EMP	PHONE	ENTRY #
Allard Nazarian Group Inc **(PA)**	Manchester	NH	C	603 668-1900	18774
ARC Technology Solutions LLC	Nashua	NH	E	603 883-3027	19117
Avid Corp	Portsmouth	NH	F	603 559-9700	19541
Beta Acquisition Inc	Thornton	NH	G	603 726-7500	19900
Cc1 Inc	Portsmouth	NH	E	603 319-2000	19548
Chauvin Arnoux Inc **(PA)**	Dover	NH	E	603 749-6434	18012
Enertrac Inc	Portsmouth	NH	F	603 821-0003	19559
Geokon LLC	Lebanon	NH	D	603 448-1562	18624
Geophysical Survey Systems Inc **(DH)**	Nashua	NH	D	603 893-1109	19167
Guidewire Technologies Inc	Salem	NH	E	603 894-4399	19740
Hampshire Controls Corporation	Dover	NH	F	603 749-9424	18026
Kimball Physics Inc	Wilton	NH	E	603 878-1616	19981
Microvision Inc	Seabrook	NH	E	603 474-5566	19810
Motorway Engineering Inc	Manchester	NH	F	603 668-6315	18878
National Aperture Inc	Salem	NH	F	603 893-7393	19754
Nexus Technology Inc	Nashua	NH	F	877 595-8116	19216
Northeast NDT Inc	Nashua	NH	G	603 595-4227	19219
Oztek Corp	Merrimack	NH	F	603 546-0090	19018
Proteq Solutions LLC	Nashua	NH	F	603 888-6630	19241
Rcd Components LLC **(HQ)**	Manchester	NH	D	603 666-4627	18909
RDF Corporation	Hudson	NH	D	603 882-5195	18432
Thomas Instruments Inc	Spofford	NH	G	603 363-4500	19858
United Sensor Corp	Amherst	NH	F	603 672-0909	17590
Vibrac LLC **(PA)**	Manchester	NH	F	603 882-6777	18950
Aspects Inc	Warren	RI	E	401 247-1854	21286
Astronova Inc **(PA)**	West Warwick	RI	B	401 828-4000	21479
Atec	Wakefield	RI	G	401 782-6950	21267
Calibrators Inc	Cumberland	RI	G	401 769-0333	20315
Crest Manufacturing Company	Lincoln	RI	E	401 333-1350	20566
Eppley Laboratory Inc	Newport	RI	F	401 847-1020	20664
Honeywell International Inc	Woonsocket	RI	C	401 769-7274	21568
Kearflex Engineering Company	Warwick	RI	F	401 781-4900	21382
Lindon Group Inc	East Providence	RI	G	401 272-2081	20430
Ocean Data Equipment Corp	Warwick	RI	F	401 454-1810	21397
Raytheon Company	Portsmouth	RI	D	401 847-8000	20938
Textron Inc **(PA)**	Providence	RI	B	401 421-2800	21134
Wuersch Time Inc	Coventry	RI	G	401 828-2525	20170
Alken Inc	Colchester	VT	E	802 655-3159	21856
Bachar Samawi Innovations LLC **(PA)**	West Dover	VT	G	802 464-0440	22605
Bowles Corporation	North Ferrisburgh	VT	F	802 425-3447	22225
Doble Engineering Company	Hinesburg	VT	C	802 482-2255	22022
Ion Science LLC	Waterbury	VT	G	802 244-5153	22583
Microstrain Inc	Williston	VT	F	802 862-6629	22681
Simmonds Precision Pdts Inc **(DH)**	Vergennes	VT	A	802 877-4000	22556

3841 Surgical & Medical Instrs & Apparatus

	CITY	ST	EMP	PHONE	ENTRY #
109 Design LLC **(PA)**	New Haven	CT	G	203 941-1812	2650
Abbott Associates Inc	Milford	CT	F	203 878-2370	2233
Acme Monaco Corporation **(PA)**	New Britain	CT	C	860 224-1349	2503
Aplicare Products LLC **(HQ)**	Meriden	CT	C	203 630-0500	2077
Auto Suture Company Australia	Norwalk	CT	G	203 845-1000	3106
Auto Suture Company UK	Norwalk	CT	B	203 845-1000	3107
Auto Suture Russia Inc	Norwalk	CT	G	203 845-1000	3108
Becton Dickinson and Company	Canaan	CT	B	860 824-5487	683
Bio-Med Devices Inc	Guilford	CT	D	203 458-0202	1693
Biorasis Inc	Storrs	CT	G	860 429-3592	4380
Blairden Precision Instrs Inc	Trumbull	CT	G	203 799-2000	4616
Boston Endo-Surgical Tech LLC	Bridgeport	CT	D	203 336-6479	385
Boston Scientific Corporation	Avon	CT	B	860 673-2500	33
C & W Manufacturing Co Inc	Glastonbury	CT	E	860 633-4631	1542
Calmare Therapeutics Inc **(PA)**	Fairfield	CT	G	203 368-6044	1417
Carwild Corporation **(PA)**	New London	CT	E	860 442-4914	2768
Cas Medical Systems Inc	Branford	CT	G	203 315-6953	301
Cas Medical Systems Inc **(HQ)**	Branford	CT	D	203 488-6056	302
Catachem Inc	Oxford	CT	G	203 262-0330	3394
Cirtec Medical Corp	Enfield	CT	C	860 814-3973	1349
Clinical Dynamics Conn LLC	Plantsville	CT	G	203 269-0090	3528
Connecticut Hypodermics Inc	Wallingford	CT	D	203 265-4881	4725
Convexity Scientific LLC	Fairfield	CT	G	949 637-1216	1425
Covidien Holding Inc	North Haven	CT	G	203 492-5000	3019
Covidien LP	North Haven	CT	B	203 492-6332	3020
Covidien LP	New Haven	CT	B	781 839-1722	2680
Covidien LP	North Haven	CT	A	203 492-5000	3021
Cygnus Medical LLC	Branford	CT	G	800 990-7489	308
Dcg-Pmi Inc	Bethel	CT	E	203 743-5525	142
Delfin Marketing Inc	Greenwich	CT	G	203 554-2707	1607
E M M Inc	Madison	CT	E	203 245-0306	1960
Eppendorf Manufacturing Corp	Enfield	CT	C	860 253-3400	1360
Frank Roth Co Inc	Stratford	CT	D	203 377-2155	4413
Furnace Source LLC	Terryville	CT	F	860 582-4201	4479
Gr Enterprises and Tech	Woodbridge	CT	G	203 387-1430	5467
Hamilton Sndstrnd Space	Windsor Locks	CT	A	860 654-6000	5395
Hitachi Aloka Medical Ltd	Wallingford	CT	D	203 269-5088	4752
Hitachi Aloka Medical Amer Inc	Wallingford	CT	D	203 269-5088	4753
Hobbs Medical Inc	Stafford Springs	CT	E	860 684-5875	4111
Hologic Inc	Danbury	CT	C	203 790-1188	933
Home Diagnostics Corp	Trumbull	CT	C	203 445-1170	4625
Ipsogen	Stamford	CT	G	203 504-8583	4229
Kbc Electronics Inc	Milford	CT	F	203 298-9654	2306
Lacey Manufacturing Co LLC	Bridgeport	CT	B	203 336-7427	443
Lambdavision Incorporated	Farmington	CT	G	860 486-6593	1489
Lee Company **(PA)**	Westbrook	CT	A	860 399-6281	5157
Lenses Only LLC	Bloomfield	CT	F	860 769-2020	239
Lorad Corporation	Danbury	CT	C	203 790-5544	950
Lumendi LLC	Westport	CT	G	203 528-0316	5210
M G M Instruments Inc **(PA)**	Hamden	CT	E	203 248-4008	1768
Marel Corporation	West Haven	CT	F	203 934-8187	5135
Medtronic Inc	North Haven	CT	E	203 492-5764	3039
Memry Corporation **(HQ)**	Bethel	CT	C	203 739-1100	170
Memry Corporation	Bethel	CT	G	203 739-1146	171
Microspecialities Inc	Middletown	CT	F	203 874-1832	2205
Monopol Corporation	Bristol	CT	F	860 583-3852	583
Natural Polymer Devices Inc	Farmington	CT	G	860 679-7894	1496
New Wave Surgical Corp	New Haven	CT	E	954 796-4126	2718
Newmark Medical Components Inc	Waterbury	CT	F	203 753-1158	4928
Novatek Medical Inc	Stamford	CT	G	203 356-0156	4263
Oerlikon AM Medical Inc	Shelton	CT	D	203 712-1030	3846
Oral Fluid Dynamics LLC	Farmington	CT	G	860 561-5036	1502
Orthozon Technologies LLC	Stamford	CT	G	203 989-4937	4274
Oxford Science Inc	Oxford	CT	F	203 881-3115	3417
Oxford Science Center LLC	Oxford	CT	G	203 751-1912	3418
Perosphere Technologies Inc	Danbury	CT	G	475 218-4600	967
Precision Engineered Pdts LLC	Bridgeport	CT	G	203 336-6479	473
Precision Metal Products Inc	Milford	CT	C	203 877-4258	2337
Respironics Novametrix LLC	Wallingford	CT	C	203 697-6475	4796
Saar Corporation	Farmington	CT	F	860 674-9440	1511
Sekisui Diagnostics LLC	Stamford	CT	G	203 602-7777	4313
Sequel Special Products LLC	Wolcott	CT	E	203 759-1020	5459
Sleep Management Solutions LLC **(HQ)**	Hartford	CT	F	888 497-5337	1871
Smiths Medical Asd Inc	Southington	CT	B	860 621-9111	4078
Southington Tool & Mfg Corp	Plantsville	CT	E	860 276-0021	3540
Spine Wave Inc	Shelton	CT	D	203 944-9494	3873
Stryker Corporation	East Hartford	CT	F	860 528-1111	1224
Summit Orthopedic Tech Inc	Milford	CT	E	203 693-2727	2370
Supernova Diagnostics Inc	New Canaan	CT	G	301 792-4345	2617
Surgiquest Inc	Milford	CT	D	203 799-2400	2373
Synectic Engineering Inc	Milford	CT	F	203 877-8488	2374
Tangen Biosciences Inc	Branford	CT	E	203 433-4045	354
Tarry Medical Products Inc	Danbury	CT	F	203 794-1438	998
Tomtec	Orange	CT	G	203 795-5030	3385
Ultimate Wireforms Inc	Bristol	CT	D	860 582-9111	621
United Ophthalmics LLC	Meriden	CT	G	203 745-8399	2144
United States Surgical Corp **(HQ)**	New Haven	CT	A	203 845-1000	2750
Utitec Inc **(HQ)**	Watertown	CT	D	860 945-0605	5032
Utitec Holdings Inc **(PA)**	Watertown	CT	G	860 945-0601	5033
Wallach Surgical Devices Inc **(PA)**	Trumbull	CT	E	203 799-2000	4644
Wallach Surgical Devices Inc	Trumbull	CT	F	800 243-2463	4645
Winslow Automatics Inc	New Britain	CT	D	860 225-6321	2591
149 Medical Inc	Bolton	MA	G	617 410-8123	8316
3M Company	Lexington	MA	B	651 733-1110	12199
3M Company	Haverhill	MA	G	978 420-0001	11403
Abiomed R&D Inc	Danvers	MA	G	978 646-1400	10191
Accellent Holdings Corp	Wilmington	MA	A	978 570-6900	16962
Accellent LLC **(DH)**	Wilmington	MA	C	978 570-6900	16963
Acuitybio Corporation	Newton	MA	G	617 515-9671	13554
Adoneh LLC	Concord	MA	G	978 618-0389	10107
Advansource Biomaterials Corp	Wilmington	MA	F	978 657-0075	16967
Agile Devices Inc	Boston	MA	G	617 416-5495	8344
Allen Medical Systems Inc **(DH)**	Acton	MA	F	978 263-7727	7338
American Optics Limited	Wellesley Hills	MA	F	905 631-5377	16395
Angiodynamics Inc	Marlborough	MA	F	508 658-7990	12712
Anika Therapeutics Inc **(PA)**	Bedford	MA	C	781 457-9000	7957
Annovation Biopharma Inc	Wayland	MA	G	617 724-0343	16332
Apogee Technology Inc **(PA)**	Norwood	MA	G	781 551-9450	14132
Applied Tissue Tech LLC	Hingham	MA	G	781 366-3848	11491
Archetype Hardware	Brighton	MA	G	707 303-6003	9094
Arctic Holdings LLC	West Harwich	MA	G	978 535-5351	16480
Aroma Spa & Laser Center Inc	Westford	MA	G	978 685-8883	16754
Arrow International Inc	Chelmsford	MA	D	978 250-5100	9871
Arrow Interventional Inc	Chelmsford	MA	E	919 433-4948	9872
Arteriocyte Med Systems Inc	Hopkinton	MA	F	508 497-9350	11690
Atc Technologies Inc **(PA)**	Wilmington	MA	F	781 939-0725	16975
Aurora Imaging Technology Inc **(PA)**	Danvers	MA	E	877 975-7530	10198
Autocam Medical Inc	Plymouth	MA	E	508 830-1442	14543
AV Medical Technologies Inc	Duxbury	MA	G	612 200-0118	10392
Avedro Inc **(HQ)**	Waltham	MA	D	781 768-3400	16040
Balancetek Corporation	Watertown	MA	G	781 910-9706	16272
Baril Corporation	Haverhill	MA	E	978 373-7910	11407
Beaver Medical LLC	Natick	MA	G	617 935-3500	13237
Beaver-Visitec Intl Holdings **(PA)**	Waltham	MA	F	847 739-3219	16043
Beaver-Visitec Intl Inc **(HQ)**	Waltham	MA	C	781 906-8080	16044
Beaver-Visitec Intl Inc	Waltham	MA	G	847 739-3219	16045
Becton Dickinson and Company	Andover	MA	D	978 901-7319	7539
Becton Dickinson and Company	Woburn	MA	B	781 935-5115	17128

SIC

	CITY	ST	EMP	PHONE	ENTRY #
Belmont Instrument LLC **(PA)**	Billerica	MA	E	978 663-0212	8218
Biodirection Inc	Southborough	MA	E	508 599-2400	15345
Biomerieux Inc	Boston	MA	G	617 879-8000	8411
Biostage Inc	Holliston	MA	E	774 233-7300	11561
Bitome Inc	Jamaica Plain	MA	G	207 812-8099	11940
Bl Healthcare Inc	Foxboro	MA	G	508 543-4150	10877
Boston Plstic Oral Srgery Fndt	Boston	MA	G	617 355-6058	8437
Boston Scientific Corporation **(PA)**	Marlborough	MA	B	508 683-4000	12727
Boston Scientific Corporation	Bedford	MA	G	781 259-2501	7964
Boston Scientific Corporation	Marlborough	MA	B	508 382-0200	12728
Boston Scientific Corporation	Quincy	MA	B	617 689-6000	14617
Boston Scientific Corporation	Watertown	MA	B	617 972-4000	16274
Boston Scientific Intl Corp	Marlborough	MA	G	508 683-4000	12729
Boston Transtec LLC	Newton	MA	G	617 930-6088	13572
Braintree Scientific Inc	Braintree	MA	G	781 348-0768	8993
Brimfield Precision LLC	Brimfield	MA	D	413 245-7144	9109
Btl Industries Inc	Marlborough	MA	C	866 285-1656	12730
C R Bard Inc	Chelmsford	MA	B	978 441-6202	9884
Cambridge Heart Inc **(PA)**	Foxborough	MA	E	978 654-7600	10912
Cambridge Interventional LLC	Burlington	MA	G	978 793-2674	9243
Cardiofocus Inc	Marlborough	MA	E	508 658-7200	12735
Castlewood Surgical	Groton	MA	G	978 448-3628	11285
Ceek Enterprises Inc	Melrose	MA	G	919 522-4837	12976
Cheetah Medical Inc **(PA)**	Newton	MA	E	617 964-0613	13577
Chmc Otlrynglgic Fundation Inc **(PA)**	Boston	MA	F	617 355-8290	8472
Clinical Instruments Intl	Burlington	MA	F	781 221-2266	9251
Cognex Germany Inc	Natick	MA	C	508 650-3000	13248
Cognoptix Inc	Concord	MA	G	978 263-0005	10121
Cold Chain Technologies Inc	Franklin	MA	D	508 429-1395	11029
Cold Chain Technologies Inc **(PA)**	Franklin	MA	D	508 429-1395	11030
Collaborative Med Concept LLC	Newton	MA	G	603 494-6056	13581
Concert Medical LLC	Norwell	MA	E	781 261-7400	14100
Conformis Inc **(PA)**	Billerica	MA	C	781 345-9001	8232
Corindus Vascular Robotics Inc **(PA)**	Waltham	MA	E	508 653-3335	16077
Covidien LP **(HQ)**	Mansfield	MA	A	763 514-4000	12622
Cristcot Inc	Concord	MA	G	978 212-6380	10125
Cytonome/St LLC	Bedford	MA	F	617 330-5030	7968
Cytovera Inc	Chestnut Hill	MA	G	617 682-8981	9985
Cytyc Corporation **(HQ)**	Marlborough	MA	B	508 263-2900	12744
Cytyc Corporation	Marlborough	MA	C	508 303-4746	12745
Dale Medical Products Inc **(PA)**	Franklin	MA	C	508 695-9316	11035
David Clark Company Inc **(PA)**	Worcester	MA	C	508 756-6216	17362
Davol Inc	Woburn	MA	E	781 932-5900	17165
Deerfield Corporation	Framingham	MA	G	508 877-0143	10941
Dentsply Ih Inc **(HQ)**	Waltham	MA	C	781 890-6800	16084
Depuy Mitek LLC	Raynham	MA	B	508 880-8100	14709
Depuy Synthes Products Inc **(DH)**	Raynham	MA	D	508 880-8100	14711
Depuy Synthes Sales Inc	Raynham	MA	G	508 880-8100	14712
Depuy Synthes Sales Inc	Bridgewater	MA	F	508 880-8100	9071
Diagnosys LLC **(PA)**	Lowell	MA	E	978 458-1600	12367
Diamond Diagnostics Inc **(PA)**	Holliston	MA	D	508 429-0450	11567
Differential Pipetting Inc	Gloucester	MA	G	978 515-3392	11177
Digilab Genomic Solutions Inc	Holliston	MA	D	508 893-3130	11568
Digital Cognition Tech Inc	Waltham	MA	E	617 433-1777	16087
Direx Systems Corp	Canton	MA	G	339 502-6013	9727
Draeger Medical Systems Inc	Andover	MA	C	800 437-2437	7545
Eagle Vision Inc	Dennis	MA	G	508 385-2283	10307
Earlysense Inc	Woburn	MA	F	781 373-3228	17172
Endodynamix Inc	Salem	MA	F	978 740-0400	14909
Endogen Inc	Woburn	MA	D	617 225-0055	17177
Eos Imaging Inc	Cambridge	MA	F	678 564-5400	9467
Escalon Digital Solutions Inc	Stoneham	MA	F	610 688-6830	15562
Etex Corporation	Braintree	MA	E	617 577-7270	9006
Everest Halthcare Holdings Inc **(DH)**	Waltham	MA	G	781 699-9000	16100
Everest Healthcare Texas Holdg	Waltham	MA	G	781 699-9000	16101
Exalpha Biologicals Inc	Shirley	MA	G	978 425-1370	15083
Eyenetra Inc	Cambridge	MA	G	973 229-3341	9477
Eyepoint Pharmaceuticals Inc **(PA)**	Watertown	MA	E	617 926-5000	16287
Fci Ophthalmics Inc	Pembroke	MA	G	781 826-9060	14404
Firefly Global	Belmont	MA	G	781 835-6548	8074
Five Star Manufacturing Inc	New Bedford	MA	D	508 998-1404	13387
Five Star Surgical Inc	New Bedford	MA	D	508 998-1404	13388
Fms New York Services LLC **(DH)**	Waltham	MA	G	781 699-9000	16108
Fresenius Med Care Hldings Inc **(DH)**	Waltham	MA	A	781 699-9000	16110
Fresenius Med Care Rnal Thrpie	Waltham	MA	G	781 699-9000	16111
Fresenius Med Care Vntures LLC **(DH)**	Waltham	MA	G	781 699-9000	16112
Fresenius Med Care W Wllow LLC	Waltham	MA	F	781 699-9000	16113
Fresenius Med Svcs Group LLC	Waltham	MA	G	781 699-9000	16114
Fresenius Medical Care North **(DH)**	Waltham	MA	D	781 699-9000	16115
Fresenius Usa Inc	Marlborough	MA	E	508 460-1150	12757
Fresenius USA Marketing Inc **(DH)**	Waltham	MA	F	781 699-9000	16116
Functional Assessment Tech Inc	North Billerica	MA	F	978 663-2800	13817
Green Heron Hlth Solutions Inc	Rockport	MA	G	978 309-8118	14835
Gregory Manufacturing Inc	Holyoke	MA	D	413 536-5432	11628
Guidant Corporation	Marlborough	MA	A	508 683-4000	12766
Gyrus Acmi LLC **(DH)**	Southborough	MA	C	508 804-2600	15359
Haemonetics Asia Incorporated **(HQ)**	Braintree	MA	G	781 848-7100	9015
Haemonetics Corporation **(PA)**	Braintree	MA	A	781 848-7100	9016
Hallowell Engrg & Mfg Corp	Pittsfield	MA	G	413 445-4263	14475
Hamilton Thorne Inc **(PA)**	Beverly	MA	E	978 921-2050	8138
Harvard Clinical Tech Inc	Natick	MA	E	508 655-2000	13259
Heartware International Inc **(DH)**	Framingham	MA	E	508 739-0950	10962
Hemedex Inc	Waltham	MA	F	617 577-1759	16126
Highland Labs Inc	Holliston	MA	E	508 429-2918	11577
Hightech American Indus Labs	Lexington	MA	E	781 862-9884	12229
Hologic Inc	Marlborough	MA	C	508 263-2900	12769
Hologic Inc **(PA)**	Marlborough	MA	C	508 263-2900	12771
Home Intensive Care Inc	Waltham	MA	G	781 699-9000	16127
Horsepower Technologies Inc	Lowell	MA	E	844 514-6773	12380
Hyalex Orthopaedics Inc	Lexington	MA	G	347 871-5850	12230
Hydrocision Inc	North Billerica	MA	E	978 474-9300	13824
Image Stream Medical Inc	Littleton	MA	D	978 486-8494	12309
Image Stream Medical LLC	Harvard	MA	G	978 456-9087	11380
Instrumentation Laboratory Co **(DH)**	Bedford	MA	A	781 861-0710	7982
Insulet Corporation **(PA)**	Acton	MA	B	978 600-7000	7365
Intact Medical Corporation	Framingham	MA	E	508 655-7820	10969
Intech Inc	Acton	MA	E	978 263-2210	7366
Integra Lifesciences Prod Corp	Mansfield	MA	G	781 971-5682	12637
Integra Luxtec Inc	North Billerica	MA	D	508 835-9700	13828
Integrated Ophthalmic Sys	Woburn	MA	G	617 571-8238	17205
Intelon Optics Inc	Lexington	MA	G	310 980-3087	12232
Invivo Thrputics Holdings Corp	Cambridge	MA	G	617 863-5500	9518
Iq Medical Devices LLC	Belmont	MA	F	617 484-3188	8076
Isolux LLC	Danvers	MA	G	978 774-9136	10226
Ivenix Inc	North Andover	MA	E	978 775-8050	13711
Ives Eeg Solutions LLC	Newburyport	MA	G	978 358-8006	13502
Jacobs Precision Corp	Avon	MA	G	508 588-2121	7888
Jarvis Surgical Inc	Westfield	MA	E	413 562-6659	16692
Jlp Machine and Welding LLC	Kingston	MA	G	781 585-1744	11958
Karl Storz Endovision Inc	Charlton	MA	B	508 248-9011	9852
Kirwan Enterprise LLC	Marshfield	MA	G	781 834-9500	12861
KS Manufacturing Inc	Allston	MA	D	508 427-5727	7468
Lab Medical Manufacturing Inc	Billerica	MA	D	978 663-2475	8262
Lake Region Manufacturing Inc **(HQ)**	Wilmington	MA	A	952 361-2515	17015
Lake Region Medical Inc **(HQ)**	Wilmington	MA	E	978 570-6900	17016
Lantheus Medical Imaging Inc **(HQ)**	North Billerica	MA	B	800 362-2668	13832
Lantheus Ml Intermediate Inc	North Billerica	MA	A	978 671-8001	13833
Laser Engineering	Milford	MA	G	508 520-2500	13124
Legacy Medical Solutions LLC	Tyngsboro	MA	G	978 655-6007	15893
Lemaitre Vascular Inc **(PA)**	Burlington	MA	C	781 221-2266	9297
Logan Instruments Inc	Braintree	MA	F	617 394-0601	9024
Lymol Medical Corp **(PA)**	Woburn	MA	F	781 935-0004	17219
M R P Group Inc (de)	Lawrence	MA	G	978 687-7979	12049
Maruho Htsujyo Innovations Inc **(PA)**	Norwell	MA	F	617 653-1617	14107
Mauna Kea Technologies Inc	Allston	MA	G	617 657-1550	7469
Mds Nxstage Corporation **(DH)**	Lawrence	MA	E	866 697-8243	12050
Medcon Biolab Technologies Inc	Grafton	MA	G	508 839-4203	11223
Medical Cmpression Systems Inc	Concord	MA	G	800 377-5804	10140
Medical Device Bus Svcs Inc	Raynham	MA	E	508 880-8100	14717
Medical Instrument Technology	Hyannis	MA	G	508 775-8682	11849
Medical Monofilament Mfg LLC	Plymouth	MA	G	508 746-7877	14565
Medical-Technical Gases Inc	North Billerica	MA	E	781 395-1946	13841
Medisight Corporation	Cambridge	MA	G	415 205-2764	9550
Medsix Inc	Jamaica Plain	MA	G	617 935-2716	11946
Medsource Tech Holdings LLC **(DH)**	Wilmington	MA	F	978 570-6900	17021
Medsource Technologies LLC **(DH)**	Wilmington	MA	F	978 570-6900	17022
Medtrnic Intrvntnal Vsclar Inc	Danvers	MA	A	978 777-0042	10238
Medtrnic Sofamor Danek USA Inc	Hopkinton	MA	G	508 497-0792	11727
Medtronic	Mansfield	MA	F	508 452-4203	12645
Medtronic Inc	Chicopee	MA	F	413 593-6400	10043
Medtronic Inc	Danvers	MA	F	978 739-3080	10239
Medtronic Inc	Danvers	MA	F	978 777-0042	10240
Merit Medical Systems Inc **(HQ)**	Rockland	MA	F	781 681-7900	14813
Microline Surgical Inc **(HQ)**	Beverly	MA	C	978 922-9810	8153
Mindgraph Medical Inc	Andover	MA	G	508 904-2563	7571
Mobius Imaging LLC	Shirley	MA	D	978 796-5068	15090
Moderna LLC **(HQ)**	Cambridge	MA	G	617 714-6500	9565
Morgan Scientific Inc **(PA)**	Haverhill	MA	F	978 521-4440	11454
Mossman Associates Inc	Milford	MA	G	508 488-6169	13130
Most Cardio Incorporated	Salem	MA	G	978 594-1614	14930
Nanoentek Inc	Waltham	MA	G	781 472-2558	16155
Needletech Products Inc	North Attleboro	MA	C	508 431-4000	13767
Nellcor Puritan Bennett LLC **(DH)**	Mansfield	MA	B	508 261-8000	12649
Nelmed Corporation	North Attleboro	MA	G	508 695-8817	13768
Neurologica Corp	Danvers	MA	C	978 564-8500	10242
Neurometrix Inc **(PA)**	Waltham	MA	E	781 890-9989	16159
Newton Laboratories Inc	Belmont	MA	G	617 484-7003	8078
Newton Scientific Inc	Charlestown	MA	E	617 354-9469	9840
Ninepoint Medical Inc	Bedford	MA	G	617 250-7190	7994
Nix Inc	Allston	MA	G	617 458-9407	7472
Nordson Med Design & Dev Inc **(HQ)**	Marlborough	MA	E	508 481-6233	12797
Northeast Ems Enterprises	Rehoboth	MA	G	508 252-6584	14755
Omarc LLC	Norwood	MA	G	781 702-6732	14187
Omnilife Science Inc	Raynham	MA	G	508 824-2444	14724

	CITY	ST	EMP	PHONE	ENTRY #
Opportunity/Discovery LLC	Wilmington	MA	G	781 301-1596	17034
Optim LLC	Sturbridge	MA	E	508 347-5100	15643
Oxford Immunotec USA Inc	Marlborough	MA	D	833 682-6933	12805
Palomar Medical Tech LLC **(DH)**	Burlington	MA	E	781 993-2330	9317
Paradigm Biodevices Inc	Rockland	MA	G	781 982-9950	14818
Park Bio Services LLC	Groveland	MA	G	978 794-8500	11303
Pep Industries LLC	Attleboro	MA	A	508 226-5600	7776
Phase-N Corporation	Boston	MA	G	617 737-0064	8777
Photo Diagnostic Systems Inc	Boxborough	MA	E	978 266-0420	8966
Plenoptika Inc **(PA)**	Cambridge	MA	G	617 862-2203	9612
Pointcare Technologies Inc	Marlborough	MA	E	508 281-6925	12808
Portela Soni Medical LLC	Attleboro	MA	G	508 818-2727	7780
Precision Biopsy Inc	Boston	MA	G	720 859-3553	8790
Precision Engineered Pdts LLC **(DH)**	Attleboro	MA	G	508 226-5600	7782
Precision Systems Inc	Natick	MA	E	508 655-7010	13274
Pressure Biosciences Inc	South Easton	MA	F	508 230-1828	15288
Primo Medical Group Inc **(PA)**	Stoughton	MA	C	781 297-5700	15617
Primrose Medical Inc	East Walpole	MA	F	508 660-8688	10529
Professnal Cntract Strlization	Taunton	MA	F	508 822-5524	15774
Rachiotek LLC	Wellesley	MA	G	407 923-0721	16383
Radius Medical Tech Inc	Stow	MA	F	978 263-4466	15635
Ranfac Corp	Avon	MA	D	508 588-4400	7894
Rebiscan Inc	Boston	MA	F	857 600-0982	8813
Reboot Medical Inc	Lowell	MA	G	818 621-6554	12426
Rest Ensured Medical Inc	Norwood	MA	G	603 225-2860	14195
Rhealth Corporation	Bedford	MA	E	617 913-7630	8006
Rph Enterprises Inc	Franklin	MA	D	508 238-3351	11076
Sangstat Medical LLC	Cambridge	MA	B	510 789-4300	9642
Schuerch Corporation	Abington	MA	F	781 982-7000	7330
Scion Medical Techologies LLC	Newton Upper Falls	MA	G	617 455-5186	13658
Sekisui Diagnostics LLC **(DH)**	Burlington	MA	C	781 652-7800	9336
Sevenoaks Biosystems	Cambridge	MA	G	617 299-0404	9648
Siemens Hlthcare Dgnostics Inc	Norwood	MA	C	781 551-7000	14198
Sil-Med Corporation	Taunton	MA	D	508 823-7701	15784
Smith & Nephew Inc	Andover	MA	E	978 749-1000	7608
Smith & Nephew Inc	Mansfield	MA	E	508 261-3600	12659
Smith & Nephew Inc	Mansfield	MA	E	508 261-3600	12660
Smith & Nephew Endoscopy Inc	Andover	MA	D	978 749-1000	7609
Smiths Medical Asd Inc	Westport	MA	G	508 636-6909	16847
Spirus Medical LLC	West Bridgewater	MA	G	781 297-7220	16456
Sqz Biotechnologies Company	Watertown	MA	G	617 758-8672	16319
SRS Medical Corp	North Billerica	MA	G	978 663-2800	13867
SRS Medical Systems Inc **(PA)**	North Billerica	MA	E	978 663-2800	13868
Steris Corporation	Northborough	MA	G	508 393-9323	14048
Stryker Corporation	Hopkinton	MA	B	508 416-5200	11739
Surgibox Inc	Brookline	MA	G	617 982-3908	9221
Surgical Specialties Corp **(HQ)**	Westwood	MA	C	781 751-1000	16876
Suture Concepts Inc	Beverly	MA	G	978 969-0070	8185
Swiss Precision Products Inc **(DH)**	North Oxford	MA	E	508 987-8003	13975
Symmetry Medical Inc	New Bedford	MA	C	508 998-1104	13453
Symptllgnce Med Infrmatics LLC	Franklin	MA	G	617 755-0576	11083
T & T Machine Products Inc	Rockland	MA	F	781 878-3861	14829
T2 Biosystems Inc **(PA)**	Lexington	MA	C	781 761-4646	12276
Target Therapeutics Inc **(HQ)**	Marlborough	MA	B	508 683-4000	12834
Team-At-Work	Groton	MA	G	978 448-8562	11295
Tecomet Inc	Wilmington	MA	D	978 642-2400	17051
Tecomet Inc **(PA)**	Wilmington	MA	C	978 642-2400	17052
Tegra Medical LLC **(HQ)**	Franklin	MA	C	508 541-4200	11084
Tei Biosciences Inc	Boston	MA	E	617 268-1616	8875
Teleflex Incorporated	Cambridge	MA	D	617 577-2200	9679
Telemed Systems Inc	Hudson	MA	E	978 567-9033	11821
Tetherx Inc	Southborough	MA	G	508 308-7845	15369
Therapeutic Innovations Inc	North Attleboro	MA	G	347 754-0252	13784
Tnco Inc	New Bedford	MA	D	781 447-6661	13454
USA Renewable LLC	Newton	MA	G	617 319-7237	13645
Uti Holding Company	Wilmington	MA	G	978 570-6900	17062
Valeritas Inc	Marlborough	MA	E	774 239-2498	12841
Vasca Inc	Tewksbury	MA	E	978 640-0431	15847
Verax Biomedical Incorporated	Marlborough	MA	F	508 755-7029	12842
Viamed Corp	South Easton	MA	F	508 238-0220	15294
Viant AS&o Holdings LLC	Wilmington	MA	G	866 899-1392	17063
Visionquest Holdings LLC	Littleton	MA	F	978 776-9518	12326
Windgap Medical Inc	Watertown	MA	G	617 440-3311	16330
Worldwide Innvtive Hlthcare In	Cambridge	MA	G	646 694-2273	9705
Xenotherapeutics LLC	Boston	MA	G	617 750-1907	8938
Zyno Medical LLC	Natick	MA	F	508 650-2008	13288
Abbott Dgnstics Scrborough Inc **(DH)**	Scarborough	ME	D	207 730-5750	6901
Atlantic Laser Clinic	York	ME	G	207 854-8200	7305
Idexx Distribution Inc	Westbrook	ME	D	207 556-0637	7190
Insphero Inc	Brunswick	ME	G	800 779-7558	5838
Mars Medical Products LLC	Skowhegan	ME	G	207 385-3278	6982
Medical Resources Inc	Brunswick	ME	E	207 721-1110	5842
Physician Engineered Products	Fryeburg	ME	G	207 935-1256	6101
Special Diversified Opp Inc	Windham	ME	E	207 856-6151	7254
Spin Analytical Inc	Berwick	ME	G	207 704-0160	5712
Sterizign Precision Tech LLC	Brunswick	ME	G	888 234-3074	5847
Accellent Endoscopy Inc	Laconia	NH	C	603 528-1211	18550

	CITY	ST	EMP	PHONE	ENTRY #
Aponos Medical Corporation	Kingston	NH	G	603 347-8229	18540
Apriomed Inc	Derry	NH	G	603 421-0875	17971
Atech Designs Inc	Dover	NH	G	603 926-8216	18006
Atrium Medical Corporation **(HQ)**	Merrimack	NH	B	603 880-1433	18986
Cytyc Corporation	Londonderry	NH	E	603 668-7688	18690
Design Standards Corp	Charlestown	NH	D	603 826-7744	17813
Dutch Ophthalmic Usa Inc	Exeter	NH	F	603 778-6929	18119
Getinge Group Logis Ameri LLC	Merrimack	NH	A	603 880-1433	19003
Grason & Associates LLC	Rindge	NH	G	603 899-3089	19649
Gtimd LLC	Amherst	NH	F	603 880-0277	17566
Hmd Inc	Jaffrey	NH	E	603 532-5757	18467
Icad Inc **(PA)**	Nashua	NH	C	603 882-5200	19181
Imagene Technology Inc	Lebanon	NH	F	603 448-9940	18625
Iometry Inc	Hanover	NH	G	603 643-5670	18294
KMC Systems Inc	Merrimack	NH	D	866 742-0442	19010
Lake Region Medical Inc	Laconia	NH	D	603 528-1211	18571
Lodestone Biomedical LLC	Lebanon	NH	G	617 686-5517	18628
Maxilon Laboratories Inc	Amherst	NH	G	603 594-9300	17575
Microcatheter Components LLC	Jaffrey	NH	G	603 532-0345	18473
Multi-Med Inc	Keene	NH	E	603 357-8733	18519
Neuraxis LLC	Derry	NH	G	603 912-5306	17991
New England Small Tube Corp	Litchfield	NH	D	603 429-1600	18652
Prepco Inc	Colebrook	NH	G	603 237-4080	17875
Prometheus Group of NH Ltd	Dover	NH	F	800 442-2325	18047
Qesidyne Inc	Hudson	NH	G	603 883-3116	18431
Robert Tyszko Od Pllc	Peterborough	NH	G	603 924-9591	19486
Seacoast Technologies Inc	Portsmouth	NH	G	603 766-9800	19619
Sims Portex Inc	Keene	NH	F	603 352-3812	18525
Smiths Medical Asd Inc	Keene	NH	E	603 352-3812	18526
Smiths Medical Asd Inc	Keene	NH	E	603 352-3812	18527
STA Fit For Women LLC	Keene	NH	G	603 357-8880	18528
Steralon Inc	Manchester	NH	G	603 296-0490	18930
Teleflex Incorporated	Jaffrey	NH	E	603 532-7706	18479
Tfx Medical Incorporated	Jaffrey	NH	B	603 532-7706	18480
Ticked Off Inc	Dover	NH	G	603 742-0925	18061
Vallum Corporation	Nashua	NH	G	603 577-1989	19277
Vapotherm Inc **(PA)**	Exeter	NH	B	603 658-0011	18135
Vascular Technology Inc	Nashua	NH	E	603 594-9700	19279
American Access Care RI LLC	Providence	RI	G	401 277-9729	20952
Astronova Inc	West Warwick	RI	C	401 828-4000	21480
Bi Medical LLC	Coventry	RI	G	866 246-3301	20139
Biomedical Structures LLC	Warwick	RI	E	401 223-0990	21336
Bnr Supplies	Cranston	RI	G	401 461-9132	20190
C R Bard Inc	Warwick	RI	B	401 825-8300	21338
Cadence Science Inc	Cranston	RI	C	401 942-1031	20193
Confluent Medical Tech Inc	Warwick	RI	G	401 223-0990	21344
Contech Medical Inc	Providence	RI	D	401 351-4890	20989
Davol Inc **(DH)**	Warwick	RI	E	401 825-8300	21350
Degania Silicone Inc **(PA)**	Smithfield	RI	G	401 349-5373	21219
Geotec Inc	Warwick	RI	E	401 228-7395	21366
Illuminoss Medical Inc	East Providence	RI	F	401 714-0008	20419
Luv2bu Inc	Cranston	RI	G	401 612-9585	20256
Nu-Lustre Finishing Corp	Providence	RI	D	401 521-7800	21079
Precision Electrolysis Needles	Barrington	RI	F	401 246-1155	20052
RJ Mansour Inc	Providence	RI	E	401 521-7800	21116
S2s Surgical LLC	East Greenwich	RI	G	401 398-1933	20378
Unetixs Vascular Inc	North Kingstown	RI	E	401 583-0089	20748
Ascension Technology Corp	Shelburne	VT	E	802 893-6657	22411
Biotek Instruments Inc **(HQ)**	Winooski	VT	D	802 655-4040	22717
Blair Campbell	Rutland	VT	G	802 773-7711	22325
Clarity Laboratories Inc	South Burlington	VT	G	802 658-6321	22443
Eric Lawhite Co	South Royalton	VT	G	802 763-7670	22491
Human Biomed Inc	South Burlington	VT	G	802 556-1394	22448
Lord Corporation **(DH)**	Williston	VT	D	802 862-6629	22680
PBL Incorporated	Colchester	VT	F	802 893-0111	21876
Raj Communications Ltd	Williston	VT	F	802 658-4961	22687
Simmedtec LLC	Williston	VT	G	802 872-5968	22691
Stromatec Inc	North Ferrisburgh	VT	G	802 425-2700	22228

3842 Orthopedic, Prosthetic & Surgical Appliances/Splys

	CITY	ST	EMP	PHONE	ENTRY #
Acme United Corporation **(PA)**	Fairfield	CT	C	203 254-6060	1412
Advanced Hearing Solutions LLC	Avon	CT	F	860 674-8558	31
Alternative Prosthetic Svcs	Bridgeport	CT	G	203 367-1212	370
Auto Suture Company Australia	Norwalk	CT	G	203 845-1000	3106
Auto Suture Company UK	Norwalk	CT	B	203 845-1000	3107
Avitus Orthopaedics Inc	Farmington	CT	F	860 637-9922	1466
Becton Dickinson and Company	Canaan	CT	B	860 824-5487	683
Beiersdorf Inc	Norwalk	CT	B	203 854-8000	3110
Beiersdorf North America Inc **(DH)**	Wilton	CT	F	203 563-5800	5277
Bio Med Packaging Systems Inc	Norwalk	CT	E	203 846-1923	3113
Biometrics Inc **(PA)**	Trumbull	CT	G	203 261-1162	4615
Brymill Corporation **(PA)**	Ellington	CT	F	860 875-2460	1330
Cardiopulmonary Corp	Milford	CT	E	203 877-1999	2261
Carwild Corporation **(PA)**	New London	CT	E	860 442-4914	2768
Comprhnsive Prsthetic Svcs LLC	Branford	CT	G	203 315-1400	305
Contemporary Products LLC	Middletown	CT	E	860 346-9283	2182
Cranial Technologies Inc	Madison	CT	F	203 318-8739	1958

	CITY	ST	EMP	PHONE	ENTRY #
Ctl Corporation	West Simsbury	CT	G	860 651-9173	5154
Danbury Ortho	Danbury	CT	G	203 797-1500	898
Elvex Corporation	Shelton	CT	F	203 743-2488	3800
Enduro Wheelchair Company	East Hartford	CT	G	860 289-0374	1194
Ethicon Inc	Southington	CT	B	860 621-9111	4048
Fire & Iron	West Haven	CT	G	203 934-3756	5123
First Aid Bandage Co Inc	New London	CT	F	860 443-8499	2773
Gordon Engineering Corp	Brookfield	CT	F	203 775-4501	645
Hamilton Standard Space	Windsor Locks	CT	E	860 654-6000	5396
Hanger Prsthetcs & Ortho Inc	Torrington	CT	G	860 482-5611	4581
Hanger Prsthetcs & Ortho Inc	North Haven	CT	G	203 230-0667	3029
Hanger Prsthetcs & Ortho Inc	Cromwell	CT	G	860 667-5300	854
Hanger Prsthetcs & Ortho Inc	Hartford	CT	F	860 545-9050	1829
Hanger Prsthetcs & Ortho Inc	Newington	CT	G	860 667-5370	2869
Hanger Prsthetcs & Ortho Inc	Vernon	CT	G	860 871-0905	4668
Hanger Prsthetcs & Ortho Inc	Stratford	CT	G	203 377-8820	4418
Hermell Products Inc	Bloomfield	CT	E	860 242-6550	225
Ict Business	Stamford	CT	G	203 595-9452	4219
K W Griffen Company	Norwalk	CT	E	203 846-1923	3183
Kbc Electronics Inc	Milford	CT	F	203 298-9654	2306
Kelyniam Global Inc	Collinsville	CT	F	800 280-8192	815
Leona Corp	Wethersfield	CT	G	860 257-3840	5256
Limbkeepers LLC	Lyme	CT	G	860 304-3250	1955
McIntire Company **(HQ)**	Bristol	CT	F	860 585-8559	580
McNeil Healthcare Inc	West Haven	CT	G	203 934-8187	5136
New England Ctr For Hring Rhab	Hampton	CT	G	860 455-1404	1798
New England Orthotic & Prost	Meriden	CT	G	203 634-7566	2112
New England Shoulder Elbow Soc	Farmington	CT	G	860 679-6600	1499
Orteoponix LLC	Storrs	CT	G	203 804-9775	4382
Playtex Products LLC **(HQ)**	Shelton	CT	D	203 944-5500	3856
Praxair Inc	Danbury	CT	D	800 772-9247	970
Prospect Designs Inc	New Hartford	CT	G	860 379-7858	2645
Respironics Inc	Wallingford	CT	C	203 697-6490	4795
Safety Dispatch Inc	Ridgefield	CT	G	203 885-5722	3682
Scapa Tapes North America LLC **(DH)**	Windsor	CT	C	860 688-8000	5361
Schaeffler Aerospace USA Corp **(DH)**	Danbury	CT	B	203 744-2211	984
Stride Inc	Middlebury	CT	F	203 758-8307	2159
Tangen Biosciences Inc	Branford	CT	E	203 433-4045	354
Teleflex Incorporated	Coventry	CT	E	860 742-8821	841
United Seating & Mobility LLC **(PA)**	Rocky Hill	CT	G	860 761-0700	3732
United States Surgical Corp **(HQ)**	New Haven	CT	A	203 845-1000	2750
Wellinks Inc	New Haven	CT	G	650 704-0714	2753
Westconn Orthopedic Laboratory	Danbury	CT	G	203 743-4420	1011
Zenith-Omni Hearing Center **(PA)**	New Haven	CT	G	203 624-9857	2763
3M Company	Haverhill	MA	G	978 420-0001	11403
A & S Transport Wheelchair Svc	Brockton	MA	G	617 701-4407	9113
A-T Surgical Mfg Co Inc	Holyoke	MA	E	413 532-4551	11615
Adaptive Mobility Equipment	Seekonk	MA	G	508 336-2556	15017
Adhesive Tapes Intl Inc	Easthampton	MA	G	203 792-8279	10554
Advanced Orthopedic Services **(PA)**	Hyannis	MA	G	508 771-5050	11833
Advanced Orthopedic Svcs Inc	Hyannis	MA	G	508 771-5050	11834
Advanced Research Development	North Andover	MA	G	781 285-8721	13687
Aearo Technologies LLC	Auburn	MA	B	317 692-6645	7822
Amatech Corporation **(DH)**	Acton	MA	E	978 263-5401	7340
Americal Sergical Company	Salem	MA	G	781 592-7200	14890
American Prosthetics Inc **(PA)**	Braintree	MA	G	617 328-0606	8987
American Surgical Company LLC	Salem	MA	E	781 592-7200	14891
Angel Guard Products Inc	Worcester	MA	G	508 791-1073	17339
Apothecary Products LLC	North Attleboro	MA	E	508 695-0727	13745
Arcam Cad To Metal Inc	Woburn	MA	F	781 281-1718	17121
Arrow Interventional Inc	Chelmsford	MA	E	919 433-4948	9872
Barnhardt Manufacturing Co	Colrain	MA	E	413 624-3471	10104
Bay State Elevator Company Inc **(PA)**	Agawam	MA	E	413 786-7000	7421
Bethcare Inc	Boston	MA	G	617 997-1069	8404
Bionx Medical Technologies Inc	Cambridge	MA	D	781 761-1545	9411
Bonesupport Inc	Wellesley	MA	G	781 772-1756	16364
Boston Artificial Limb Co	Burlington	MA	G	781 272-3132	9240
Boston Brace International	Burlington	MA	G	781 270-3650	9241
Boston Brace International Inc **(PA)**	Avon	MA	E	508 588-6060	7880
Boston Medical Products Inc	Shrewsbury	MA	E	508 898-9300	15105
Boston Orthotics Inc	Taunton	MA	E	508 821-7655	15733
Boston Scientific Corporation **(PA)**	Marlborough	MA	B	508 683-4000	12727
Brimfield Precision LLC	Brimfield	MA	D	413 245-7144	9109
Brownmed Inc **(PA)**	Boston	MA	E	857 317-3354	8447
Burke Medical Equipment Inc	Chicopee	MA	E	413 592-5464	10003
Chamberlain Group LLC	Great Barrington	MA	F	413 528-7744	11236
Continental Metal Pdts Co Inc	Woburn	MA	E	781 935-4400	17151
Cornell Orthotics Prosthetics **(PA)**	Beverly	MA	F	978 922-2866	8121
Covidien France Holdings Inc	Mansfield	MA	G	508 261-8000	12620
Covidien LLC	Mansfield	MA	G	508 261-8000	12621
Covidien LP **(HQ)**	Mansfield	MA	A	763 514-4000	12622
Covidien US Holdings Inc	Mansfield	MA	G	508 261-8000	12623
Crompton Park Oral Surgery & I	Worcester	MA	G	508 799-2550	17361
David Clark Company Inc **(PA)**	Worcester	MA	C	508 756-6216	17362
Depuy Spine LLC **(HQ)**	Raynham	MA	B	508 880-8100	14710
Depuy Synthes Sales Inc	Raynham	MA	F	508 880-8100	14713
Easter Seals Massachusetts	New Bedford	MA	F	508 992-3128	13382
Eddies Wheels Inc	Shelburne Falls	MA	F	413 625-0033	15069
Fleming Industries Inc	Chicopee	MA	D	413 593-3300	10026
Fosta-Tek Optics Inc **(PA)**	Leominster	MA	D	978 534-6511	12141
Fresenius Usa Inc	Marlborough	MA	E	508 460-1150	12757
Freudenberg Medical LLC	Gloucester	MA	E	978 281-2023	11184
Gentex Optics Inc **(DH)**	Dudley	MA	C	570 282-8531	10376
Genzyme Corporation **(DH)**	Cambridge	MA	A	617 252-7500	9489
Global RES Innovation Tech Inc	Charlestown	MA	G	617 383-4748	9835
Gta-Nht Inc **(HQ)**	Rockland	MA	C	781 331-5900	14804
Hanger Prosthethics & Orthotic	South Easton	MA	G	508 238-6760	15278
Hanger Prosthetics & Orthotics	Leominster	MA	G	978 466-7400	12149
Hanger Prsthetcs & Ortho Inc	Springfield	MA	G	413 734-0002	15474
Hanger Prsthetcs & Ortho Inc	Methuen	MA	G	978 683-5509	13026
Hanger Prsthetcs & Ortho Inc	Leominster	MA	G	978 466-7400	12150
Hayes Prosthetic Inc	West Springfield	MA	G	413 733-2287	16524
Hd Lifesciences LLC	Woburn	MA	G	866 949-5433	17198
Head Prone Inc	Cambridge	MA	G	617 864-0780	9506
Hearing Armor LLC	Needham	MA	F	781 789-5017	13300
Honeywell Data Instruments Inc	Acton	MA	B	978 264-9550	7361
Jahrling Ocular Prosthetics **(PA)**	Boston	MA	G	617 523-2280	8624
Liberating Technologies Inc	Holliston	MA	G	508 893-6363	11582
Louis M Gerson Co Inc **(PA)**	Middleboro	MA	E	508 947-4000	13065
Louis M Gerson Co Inc	Middleboro	MA	E	508 947-4000	13066
Lower Limb Technology	Auburndale	MA	G	617 916-1650	7864
Lower Limb Technology LLC	West Yarmouth	MA	F	508 775-0990	16580
Marine Polymer Tech Inc **(PA)**	Tewksbury	MA	E	781 270-3200	15820
Medical Device Bus Svcs Inc	Bridgewater	MA	G	508 828-6155	9083
Medical Device Bus Svcs Inc	Norton	MA	D	508 828-2726	14082
Medsix Inc	Jamaica Plain	MA	G	617 935-2716	11946
Medsource Technologies LLC **(DH)**	Wilmington	MA	F	978 570-6900	17022
Medtronic Inc	Danvers	MA	F	978 739-3080	10239
Medtronic Inc	Danvers	MA	F	978 777-0042	10240
Mike Murphy	Milford	MA	G	508 473-9943	13126
Ms Wheelchair Mass Foundation	Taunton	MA	G	774 501-1185	15766
Myomo Inc	Cambridge	MA	E	617 996-9058	9573
National Seating Mobility Inc	Chicopee	MA	G	413 420-0054	10048
Neogenix LLC **(PA)**	Norwood	MA	G	781 702-6732	14181
New England Blazers	Saugus	MA	G	617 448-3709	14992
New England Orthotic & Prost	Worcester	MA	G	508 890-8808	17431
New England Wheelchair Spt Inc	Dover	MA	G	508 785-0393	10351
New England Whlchair Athc Assn	Canton	MA	G	781 830-8751	9763
Nuclead Incorporated	Cambridge	MA	G	508 583-2699	9595
Numotion	Taunton	MA	G	401 681-2153	15769
O & P Iam Inc	Woburn	MA	G	781 239-3331	17248
Occlusion Prosthetics	Hyannis	MA	G	508 827-4377	11851
Omni Life Science Inc **(HQ)**	Raynham	MA	E	508 824-2444	14723
Oped Inc	Sudbury	MA	G	781 891-6733	15665
Ops-Core Inc	Boston	MA	F	617 670-3547	8755
Or-6 LLC	Sandwich	MA	G	617 515-1909	14971
Orthotic & Prosthetic Ctrs LLC	West Yarmouth	MA	G	508 775-7151	16581
Orthotic and Prosthetic Center	Braintree	MA	G	508 775-2570	9029
Orthotic Solutions Inc	Plymouth	MA	G	774 205-2278	14570
Orthotics Prosthetics Labs Inc	Northampton	MA	G	413 585-8622	14015
Orthotics West Inc	Holyoke	MA	G	413 736-3000	11647
Palomar Medical Products LLC	Burlington	MA	C	781 993-2300	9316
Panther Therapeutics Inc	Cambridge	MA	G	857 413-1698	9605
Pioneer Vly Orthtics Prsthtics	West Springfield	MA	G	413 788-9655	16545
Precision Orthot & Prosthetics	New Bedford	MA	G	508 991-5577	13443
Pro-Tech Orthopedics Inc	Raynham	MA	F	508 821-9600	14727
Prosthtic Orthtic Slutions LLC	West Springfield	MA	G	413 785-4047	16549
Ranfac Corp	Avon	MA	D	508 588-4400	7894
Rewalk Robotics Inc	Marlborough	MA	G	508 251-1154	12815
Rogerson Orthopedic Appls Inc	Boston	MA	F	617 268-1135	8826
Rph Enterprises Inc	Franklin	MA	D	508 238-3351	11076
Rrk Walker Inc	Mendon	MA	G	508 541-8100	12995
Safariland LLC	Dalton	MA	D	413 684-3104	10183
Safety & Gloves Inc	Foxboro	MA	G	800 221-0570	10900
Salk Company Inc	Allston	MA	E	617 782-4030	7474
Sals Clothing & Fabric Restor	Everett	MA	E	617 387-6726	10630
Smith & Nephew Inc	Lawrence	MA	G	978 208-0680	12075
Spinal Technology Inc **(PA)**	West Yarmouth	MA	D	508 775-0990	16582
Steelcraft Inc	Millbury	MA	E	508 865-4445	13176
Sunrise Prosthetics Orthotics	Milford	MA	G	508 473-9943	13145
Sunrise Prosthetics Orthotics **(PA)**	Worcester	MA	G	508 753-4738	17484
Surgical Specialties Corp **(HQ)**	Westwood	MA	C	781 751-1000	16876
Teleflex Medical Incorporated	Mansfield	MA	G	800 474-0178	12663
Tesco Associates Inc	Tyngsboro	MA	F	978 649-5527	15902
Tillotson Rubber Co Inc	Seekonk	MA	G	781 402-1731	15043
Touch Bionics	Mansfield	MA	G	774 719-2199	12666
United Prosthetics Inc	Quincy	MA	G	617 773-7140	14665
Visionaid Inc	Wareham	MA	E	508 295-3300	16258
W D C Holdings Inc	Attleboro	MA	D	508 699-4412	7806
Wadsworth Medical Tech Inc	Westborough	MA	G	508 789-6531	16657
Web Home Phoenix Fabrication	Kingston	MA	G	781 424-8076	11967
Wheelchair Recycler Custm & R	Marlborough	MA	G	978 760-4444	12851
Babac Inc	Winslow	ME	F	207 872-0889	7267
Boston Ocular Prosthetics Inc	Searsport	ME	G	800 824-2492	6948

	CITY	ST	EMP	PHONE	ENTRY #
Finetone Hearing Instruments	Windham	ME	G	207 893-2922	7233
Globe Footwear LLC **(HQ)**	Auburn	ME	G	207 784-9186	5569
Hanger Prosthetics & Orthotics	Waterville	ME	F	207 872-8779	7156
Hanger Prsthetcs & Ortho Inc	Augusta	ME	G	207 622-9792	5608
Hanger Prsthetcs & Ortho Inc	Auburn	ME	G	207 782-6907	5571
Hanger Prsthetcs & Ortho Inc	Portland	ME	G	207 773-4963	6668
Hardwood Products Company LP	Guilford	ME	B	207 876-3311	6158
Maine Artfl Limb Orthotics Co	Portland	ME	F	207 773-4963	6681
P C Northern Prosthetics	Presque Isle	ME	G	207 768-5348	6768
Pine Tree Orthopedic Lab Inc	Livermore Falls	ME	F	207 897-5558	6381
Puritan Medical Pdts Co LLC	Guilford	ME	B	207 876-3311	6160
Tena Group LLC	Windham	ME	G	207 893-2920	7256
Allied Orthotic Inc	Londonderry	NH	G	603 434-7722	18675
Allied Wheelchair	Hampton	NH	G	603 601-8174	18253
Arzol Corp	Keene	NH	G	603 352-5242	18493
Atrium Medical Corporation **(HQ)**	Merrimack	NH	B	603 880-1433	18986
Atrium Medical Corporation	Hudson	NH	G	603 880-1433	18375
Austin Medical Products Inc	Center Conway	NH	G	603 356-7004	17792
Bavec LLC	Dover	NH	G	603 290-5285	18007
Boston Brace International	Salem	NH	G	603 772-2388	19715
Capital Orthtics Prsthtics LLC	Manchester	NH	G	603 425-0106	18795
Capital Orthtics Prsthtics LLC **(PA)**	Concord	NH	G	603 226-0106	17888
Corflex Inc **(PA)**	Manchester	NH	E	603 623-3344	18806
Fdr Center For Prost	Nashua	NH	G	603 595-9255	19155
Fireye Inc **(DH)**	Derry	NH	C	603 432-4100	17979
Globe Manufacturing Co LLC **(DH)**	Pittsfield	NH	B	603 435-8323	19500
Grabber Construction Pdts Inc	Windham	NH	F	603 890-0455	20007
Hanger Prsthetcs & Ortho Inc	Somersworth	NH	G	603 742-0334	19839
Healthco International LLC	Colebrook	NH	F	603 255-3771	17871
Holase Incorporated	Portsmouth	NH	G	603 397-0038	19575
Imcor Inc	Nashua	NH	G	603 886-4300	19184
Kelly Manufacturing Company	Rumney	NH	G	603 786-9933	19697
Kisers Ortho Prosthetic Serv **(PA)**	Keene	NH	G	603 357-7666	18513
Labonville Inc	Gorham	NH	E	603 752-3221	18214
Monoplex Eye Prosthetics LLC	Bedford	NH	G	603 622-5200	17655
New England Brace Co Inc **(PA)**	Concord	NH	F	508 588-6060	17916
New Hampshire Prosthetics LLC	Portsmouth	NH	G	603 294-0010	19600
Next Step Bnics Prsthetics Inc **(PA)**	Manchester	NH	F	603 668-3831	18886
Poly-Vac Inc	Manchester	NH	C	603 647-7822	18903
Seabrook Medical LLC	Seabrook	NH	C	603 474-1919	19817
Silver Lake Fabrication	Belmont	NH	G	603 630-5658	17683
The Great N Woods Assoc/ Blind	Colebrook	NH	G	603 490-9877	17876
Tri-Med Inc	Peterborough	NH	G	603 924-7211	19491
AF Group Inc	Lincoln	RI	C	401 757-3910	20553
Ashaway Line & Twine Mfg Co	Ashaway	RI	D	401 377-2221	20031
Atlantic Footcare Inc	North Smithfield	RI	D	401 568-4918	20782
Bacou-Dalloz Safety Inc	Smithfield	RI	G	401 232-1200	21212
Carlow Orthpd & Prosthetic Inc **(PA)**	Cranston	RI	G	203 483-8488	20195
Cintas Corporation No 2	Pawtucket	RI	G	401 723-7300	20823
Custom Composite Mfg Inc	Cranston	RI	G	401 275-2230	20206
GF Health Products Inc	Warwick	RI	E	401 738-1500	21368
Honeywell Safety Pdts USA Inc	Smithfield	RI	G	800 500-4739	21232
Honeywell Safety Products Usa	Smithfield	RI	F	401 233-0333	21233
Impactwear International Lllp	Providence	RI	G	213 559-2454	21036
Jahrling Ocular Prosthetics	Cranston	RI	G	401 454-4168	20243
Johnson & Johnson	Cumberland	RI	C	401 762-6751	20330
New England Orthopedics Inc **(PA)**	Warwick	RI	G	401 739-9838	21396
Nunnery Orthtic Prosthetic LLC	North Kingstown	RI	G	401 294-4210	20731
Ocean Orthopedic Services Inc **(PA)**	North Providence	RI	F	401 725-5240	20768
Power Chair Recyclers Neng LLC	North Kingstown	RI	G	401 294-4111	20733
Rhode Island Limb Co **(PA)**	Cranston	RI	G	401 941-6230	20279
Rhode Island Limb Co	Pawtucket	RI	G	401 475-3501	20892
Sperian Protection Usa Inc **(DH)**	Smithfield	RI	E	401 232-1200	21250
Summer Infant Inc **(PA)**	Woonsocket	RI	D	401 671-6550	21581
Summer Infant Inc	Woonsocket	RI	G	401 671-6550	21582
Aadco Medical Inc	Randolph	VT	D	802 728-3400	22296
Brickyard Enterprises Inc	Ferrisburgh	VT	G	802 338-7267	21987
Gaffco Ballistics LLC	South Londonderry	VT	G	802 824-9899	22486
Revision Ballistics Ltd	Essex Junction	VT	E	802 879-7002	21956
Revision Military JV	Essex Junction	VT	B	802 879-7002	21957

3843 Dental Eqpt & Splys

	CITY	ST	EMP	PHONE	ENTRY #
Acme Monaco Corporation **(PA)**	New Britain	CT	C	860 224-1349	2503
Aero-Med Ltd	South Windsor	CT	G	860 659-2270	3933
Anna M Chisilenco-Raho	Milford	CT	G	203 877-0377	2244
Centrix Inc	Shelton	CT	C	203 929-5582	3788
J S Dental Manufacturing Inc	Ridgefield	CT	G	203 438-8832	3669
Jensen Industries Inc **(PA)**	North Haven	CT	D	203 285-1402	3033
Kinetic Instruments Inc	Bethel	CT	E	203 743-0080	167
Nova Dental LLC **(PA)**	North Haven	CT	G	203 234-3900	3044
Palmero Healthcare LLC	Stratford	CT	F	203 377-6424	4438
Pickadent Inc	Ridgefield	CT	G	203 431-8716	3675
Scott Woodford	Madison	CT	G	203 245-4266	1974
Ultimate Wireforms Inc	Bristol	CT	D	860 582-9111	621
Winslow Automatics Inc	New Britain	CT	D	860 225-6321	2591
3d Diagnostix Inc	Allston	MA	G	617 820-5279	7458
A2z Dental LLC	Marlborough	MA	G	844 442-5587	12708
Apogent Technologies Inc	Waltham	MA	A	781 622-1300	16035
Benco Dental	Hopkinton	MA	E	508 435-3000	11693
Bicon LLC **(PA)**	Boston	MA	E	617 524-4443	8406
Boston M4 Tech LLC	Woburn	MA	G	617 279-3172	17136
Cataki International Inc	Wareham	MA	E	508 295-9630	16243
Cendres+metaux USA Inc	Attleboro	MA	G	508 316-0962	7717
Convergent Dental Inc	Needham Heights	MA	E	508 500-5656	13323
Custom Atmated Prosthetics LLC **(DH)**	Stoneham	MA	G	781 279-2771	15559
Dental Dreams LLC	Brockton	MA	G	508 583-2256	9139
Dentovations Inc	Boston	MA	F	617 737-1199	8500
Dillon Laboratories Inc	Abington	MA	F	781 871-2333	7322
Encore Crown & Bridge Inc	Plymouth	MA	E	508 746-6025	14555
Ergonomic Products Inc	Fall River	MA	E	508 636-2263	10691
Independent Product Service **(PA)**	Amesbury	MA	G	978 352-8887	7491
Jacobs Precision Corp	Avon	MA	G	508 588-2121	7888
Keystone Dental Inc **(PA)**	Burlington	MA	D	781 328-3300	9294
Prosthetic Design Inc	Fitchburg	MA	G	978 345-2588	10850
Pulpdent Corporation	Watertown	MA	D	617 926-6666	16308
South Shore Dental Labs	Hanover	MA	G	781 924-5382	11351
Sterngold Dental LLC	Attleboro	MA	E	508 226-5660	7796
Straumann Usa LLC **(HQ)**	Andover	MA	C	978 747-2500	7612
Tekscan Inc	Boston	MA	D	617 464-4500	8876
New England Denture Cntr Bangr **(PA)**	Bangor	ME	F	207 941-6550	5655
Bausch Articulating Papers Inc	Nashua	NH	G	603 883-2155	19125
North East Ceramic Studio Inc	Bow	NH	G	603 225-9310	17724
William J Devaney	Portsmouth	NH	G	603 436-7603	19631
Dutchmen Dental LLC	Tiverton	RI	G	401 624-9177	21257

3844 X-ray Apparatus & Tubes

	CITY	ST	EMP	PHONE	ENTRY #
Bidwell Industrial Group Inc **(PA)**	Middletown	CT	E	860 346-9283	2178
Biowave Innovations LLC	Wilton	CT	C	203 982-8157	5278
Comet Technologies USA Inc **(DH)**	Shelton	CT	E	203 447-3200	3790
High Energy X-Rays Intl Corp	Wallingford	CT	G	203 909-9777	4751
Hologic Inc	Danbury	CT	C	203 790-1188	933
Kub Technologies Inc	Stratford	CT	E	203 364-8544	4429
Lorad Corporation	Danbury	CT	C	203 790-5544	950
Parker Medical Inc	New Milford	CT	G	860 350-3446	2822
Precision X-Ray Inc	North Branford	CT	F	203 484-2011	2972
Precision X-Ray Inc	North Branford	CT	F	203 484-2011	2973
Remote Technologies Inc **(PA)**	Greenwich	CT	G	203 661-2798	1641
Topex Inc	Danbury	CT	F	203 748-5918	999
Biolucent LLC	Marlborough	MA	G	508 263-2900	12726
Bruker Corporation **(PA)**	Billerica	MA	C	978 663-3660	8223
Cytyc Surgical Products LLC	Marlborough	MA	D	508 263-2900	12746
Eastern Diagnostic Imaging	Taunton	MA	F	508 828-2970	15746
Finch Therapeutics Inc	Somerville	MA	G	617 229-6499	15171
Grady Research Inc	Ayer	MA	G	978 772-3303	7921
Hologic Inc	Marlborough	MA	C	508 263-2900	12769
Hologic Inc	Marlborough	MA	C	508 263-2900	12770
Hologic Inc **(PA)**	Marlborough	MA	C	508 263-2900	12771
Hologic Foreign Sales Corp	Bedford	MA	A	781 999-7300	7980
Princeton Security Tech Inc **(HQ)**	Franklin	MA	G	609 924-7310	11074
Princton Gamma-Tech Instrs Inc	Franklin	MA	F	609 924-7310	11075
Protom International Inc	Wakefield	MA	E	781 245-3964	15973
Qsa Global Inc **(HQ)**	Burlington	MA	D	781 272-2000	9325
Saxslab US Inc	Amherst	MA	G	413 237-4309	7524
V J Electronix Inc	Chelmsford	MA	E	631 589-8800	9938
Vivid Technologies Inc	Woburn	MA	G	781 939-3986	17314
Hologic Inc	Londonderry	NH	C	603 668-7688	18702
Aadco Medical Inc	Randolph	VT	D	802 728-3400	22296

3845 Electromedical & Electrotherapeutic Apparatus

	CITY	ST	EMP	PHONE	ENTRY #
Abbey Aesthetics LLC	Avon	CT	G	860 242-0497	30
Amco Precision Tools Inc **(PA)**	Berlin	CT	E	860 828-5640	70
American Dream Unlimited LLC	Andover	CT	G	860 742-5055	2
Atlantic Inertial Systems Inc	Cheshire	CT	A	203 250-3500	714
Bio-Med Devices Inc	Guilford	CT	D	203 458-0202	1693
Charlies Ride	Windsor Locks	CT	G	860 916-3637	5388
Coherent Inc	Bloomfield	CT	E	860 243-9557	215
Defibtech LLC **(PA)**	Guilford	CT	D	866 333-4248	1700
Door Step Prep LLC	West Hartford	CT	G	860 550-0460	5066
Dynamic Lasers LLC	New Milford	CT	G	866 731-9610	2797
Eclipse Systems Inc	Branford	CT	G	203 483-0665	311
Epicurean Feast Medtron O	North Haven	CT	G	203 492-5000	3025
Focus Medical LLC	Bethel	CT	G	203 730-8885	154
Hobbs Medical Inc	Stafford Springs	CT	E	860 684-5875	4111
Home Diagnostics Corp	Trumbull	CT	C	203 445-1170	4625
Intracranial Bioanalytics LLC	Woodbridge	CT	G	914 490-1524	5468
Ivy Biomedical Systems Inc	Branford	CT	E	203 481-4183	326
Jeffrey Gold	Hamden	CT	G	203 281-5737	1762
Legnos Medical Inc	Groton	CT	F	860 446-8058	1680
Loon Medical Inc	Tolland	CT	G	860 373-0217	4550
Mobile Sense Technologies Inc	Darien	CT	G	203 914-5375	1029
Non-Invasive Med Systems LLC	Stamford	CT	G	914 462-0701	4260
Novatek Medical Inc	Stamford	CT	G	203 356-0156	4263
Philips Ultrasound Inc	Waterbury	CT	D	203 753-5215	4938
Pioneer Optics Company Inc	Bloomfield	CT	F	860 286-0071	251

	CITY	ST	EMP	PHONE	ENTRY #
Ram Technologies LLC	Guilford	CT	F	203 453-3916	1715
Respironics Novametrix LLC	Wallingford	CT	C	203 697-6475	4796
Respond Systems	Branford	CT	F	203 481-2810	341
Safe Laser Therapy LLC	Stamford	CT	G	203 261-4400	4308
Star Tech Instruments Inc	New Fairfield	CT	G	203 312-0767	2627
Teclens LLC	Stamford	CT	G	919 824-5224	4343
Tomtec Inc	Hamden	CT	D	203 281-6790	1790
United States Surgical Corp **(HQ)**	New Haven	CT	A	203 845-1000	2750
Walker Magnetics Group Inc **(HQ)**	Windsor	CT	E	508 853-3232	5378
149 Medical Inc	Bolton	MA	G	617 410-8123	8316
Abiomed Inc **(PA)**	Danvers	MA	B	978 646-1400	10189
Abiomed Cardiovascular Inc	Danvers	MA	D	978 777-5410	10190
Adherean Inc	Chestnut Hill	MA	G	617 652-0304	9981
Alip Corporation	Brighton	MA	G	857 234-6073	9092
American Optics Limited	Wellesley Hills	MA	F	905 631-5377	16395
Arteriocyte Med Systems Inc **(HQ)**	Hopkinton	MA	E	866 660-2674	11691
Ashametrics Inc	Cambridge	MA	G	617 694-1428	9394
Aurora Healthcare US Corp	Danvers	MA	F	978 204-5240	10197
Axio Inc	Leeds	MA	G	413 552-8355	12097
Axiomed Spine Corporation **(PA)**	Malden	MA	F	978 232-3990	12560
Balancetek	Boston	MA	G	617 320-4340	8389
Belmont Instrument LLC **(PA)**	Billerica	MA	E	978 663-0212	8218
Beltronics Inc	Needham	MA	F	617 244-8696	13293
Beta Bionics Inc	Boston	MA	F	949 293-2076	8403
Bewell Body Scan	Chestnut Hill	MA	G	617 754-0300	9982
Biolucent LLC	Marlborough	MA	G	508 263-2900	12726
Biomerieux Inc	Boston	MA	G	617 879-8000	8411
Biosensics LLC	Newton	MA	G	888 589-6213	13569
Bioview	Billerica	MA	G	978 670-4741	8219
Bitome Inc	Jamaica Plain	MA	G	207 812-8099	11940
Blink Neurotech Corp	Brighton	MA	G	917 767-6829	9096
Boston Microfluidics Inc	Cambridge	MA	E	857 239-9665	9419
Boston Scientific Corporation **(PA)**	Marlborough	MA	B	508 683-4000	12727
Brainwave Science LLC	Southborough	MA	G	774 760-1678	15351
Cambridge Heart Inc **(PA)**	Foxborough	MA	E	978 654-7600	10912
Candela Corporation **(DH)**	Marlborough	MA	C	508 969-1837	12734
Cape Colon Hydrotherapy	East Sandwich	MA	G	508 833-9855	10505
Cardiofocus Inc	Marlborough	MA	E	508 658-7200	12735
Cardiovascular Instrument	Wakefield	MA	F	781 245-7799	15945
Caritas Pet Imaging LLC	Norwood	MA	G	508 259-8919	14139
Centers of New England MRC	Haverhill	MA	G	978 241-8232	11414
Cerenova Inc	Cambridge	MA	G	715 212-2595	9435
Clozex Medical Inc	Wellesley	MA	G	781 237-1673	16365
Conmed Corporation	Westborough	MA	C	508 366-3668	16608
Cosman Medical LLC	Marlborough	MA	D	781 272-6561	12742
Covidien LP **(HQ)**	Mansfield	MA	A	763 514-4000	12622
Csa Medical Inc	Lexington	MA	D	443 921-8053	12215
Cynosure Inc **(HQ)**	Westford	MA	B	978 256-4200	16763
Delsys Inc	Natick	MA	F	508 545-8200	13251
Diagnosys LLC **(PA)**	Lowell	MA	E	978 458-1600	12367
Docbox Inc	Waltham	MA	F	978 987-2569	16089
Eldersafe Technologies Inc	Harvard	MA	F	617 852-3018	11375
Electrosonics Medical Inc	Boston	MA	G	216 357-3310	8524
Emri Systems LLP	Cambridge	MA	G	617 417-9798	9465
Epidemic Solutions Inc	Westwood	MA	G	504 722-3818	16865
Ergosuture Inc	Arlington	MA	G	339 234-6289	7625
Excelitas Tech Holdg Corp	Waltham	MA	F	781 522-5914	16102
General Electric Company **(PA)**	Boston	MA	A	617 443-3000	8558
Gys Tech LLC	Shirley	MA	F	530 613-9233	15084
Haemonetics Asia Incorporated **(HQ)**	Braintree	MA	G	781 848-7100	9015
Haemonetics Corporation **(PA)**	Braintree	MA	A	781 848-7100	9016
Heartlander Surgical Inc	Westwood	MA	G	781 320-9601	16868
Highland Instruments	Sharon	MA	G	617 504-6031	15051
Hologic Inc **(PA)**	Marlborough	MA	C	508 263-2900	12771
Hologic Inc	Marlborough	MA	C	508 263-2900	12769
Hydrodot Inc	Acton	MA	G	978 399-0206	7362
Inanovate Inc	Wellesley	MA	G	617 610-1712	16367
Infobionic Inc	Waltham	MA	E	978 674-8304	16133
Integer Holdings Corporation	Canton	MA	C	781 830-5800	9744
L3 Technologies Inc	Northampton	MA	A	413 586-2330	14009
Lake Region Manufacturing Inc **(HQ)**	Wilmington	MA	A	952 361-2515	17015
Lantos Technologies Inc	Wilmington	MA	G	781 443-7633	17017
Lockheed Martin Sippican Inc **(HQ)**	Marion	MA	B	508 748-3399	12699
Lumicell Inc	Newton	MA	G	617 404-1001	13611
Luxcath LLC	Boston	MA	G	617 419-1800	8674
M R Resources Inc	Fitchburg	MA	E	978 696-3060	10831
Medcool Inc	Wellesley	MA	G	617 512-4530	16372
Medicametrix Inc	Lowell	MA	G	617 694-1713	12407
Medtronic	Framingham	MA	G	508 739-0950	10984
Medtronic Inc	Danvers	MA	F	978 739-3080	10239
Medtronic Inc	Danvers	MA	F	978 777-0042	10240
Mettler-Toledo Process Analyti	Billerica	MA	D	781 301-8800	8265
Micro-Leads Inc	Somerville	MA	G	617 299-0295	15199
Micron Solutions Inc **(PA)**	Fitchburg	MA	G	978 345-5000	10838
Mindsciences Inc	Worcester	MA	G	516 658-2985	17418
Myolex Inc	Brookline	MA	G	888 382-8656	9210
Myriad Fiber Imaging Tech Inc	Dudley	MA	F	508 949-3000	10382
Nellcor Puritan Bennett LLC **(DH)**	Mansfield	MA	B	508 261-8000	12649
Neurasense Inc	Cambridge	MA	G	618 917-4686	9577
Neuroelectrics Corporation	Cambridge	MA	G	617 390-6447	9579
Neutron Therapeutics Inc	Danvers	MA	E	978 326-8999	10243
Nihon Khden Innovation Ctr Inc	Cambridge	MA	G	617 318-5904	9582
Northeast Monitoring Inc	Maynard	MA	G	978 461-3992	12902
Novanta Inc **(PA)**	Bedford	MA	C	781 266-5700	7996
NSM Marketing Inc	Medfield	MA	G	508 359-5297	12915
Nxstage Medical Inc **(DH)**	Lawrence	MA	B	978 687-4700	12067
Obsidian Therapeutics Inc	Cambridge	MA	G	339 364-6721	9596
Omnimedics	Melrose	MA	G	617 527-4590	12986
Opko Diagnostics LLC	Woburn	MA	G	781 933-8012	17249
Pace Medical Inc	Lexington	MA	F	781 862-4242	12252
Palomar Medical Products LLC	Burlington	MA	C	781 993-2300	9316
Palomar Medical Tech LLC **(DH)**	Burlington	MA	E	781 993-2330	9317
Pathmaker Neurosystems Inc	Boston	MA	G	617 968-3006	8768
Pendar Technologies LLC **(PA)**	Cambridge	MA	G	617 588-2128	9608
Perkinelmer Inc **(PA)**	Waltham	MA	C	781 663-6900	16171
Photonview Technologies	Newton	MA	G	781 366-4836	13626
Precision Optics Corp Inc **(PA)**	Gardner	MA	E	978 630-1800	11123
Proven Process Med Dvcs Inc	Mansfield	MA	D	508 261-0800	12652
Quanterix Corporation **(PA)**	Billerica	MA	C	617 301-9400	8281
Quanttus Inc	Newton	MA	G	617 401-2648	13628
Radiation Monitoring Dvcs Inc **(HQ)**	Watertown	MA	E	617 668-6800	16310
Respiratory Motion Inc	Watertown	MA	E	508 954-2706	16311
Reviveflow Inc	Chelmsford	MA	G	978 621-9466	9927
Sb Marketers Inc	Webster	MA	G	508 943-7162	16350
Sensomotoric Instruments Inc	Boston	MA	G	617 557-0010	8844
Smith & Nephew Inc	Mansfield	MA	E	508 261-3600	12660
Smith & Nephew Endoscopy Inc	Andover	MA	D	978 749-1000	7609
Solace Therapeutics Inc	Framingham	MA	G	508 283-1200	11006
Solos Endoscopy Inc	Boston	MA	G	617 360-9700	8852
Solx Inc	Sudbury	MA	G	978 808-6926	15668
Soundcure Inc	Boston	MA	G	408 938-5745	8855
Sparrows Little Tech LLC	Winchester	MA	G	781 799-6442	17096
Ssquare Detect Medical Devices	Andover	MA	G	978 202-5707	7611
Telemed Systems Inc	Hudson	MA	E	978 567-9033	11821
Teratech Corporation	Burlington	MA	E	781 270-4143	9344
Thermo Envmtl Instrs LLC **(HQ)**	Franklin	MA	C	508 520-0430	11086
Thermo Fisher Scientific Inc	Wilmington	MA	D	978 275-0800	17055
Thermo Fisher Scientific Inc **(PA)**	Waltham	MA	C	781 622-1000	16213
Thoratec Corporation	Burlington	MA	C	781 272-0139	9345
Thoratec Corporation	Burlington	MA	D	781 272-0139	9346
Tomophase Corporation	Burlington	MA	G	781 229-5700	9347
Translational Sciences Corp	Cambridge	MA	G	617 331-4014	9683
Transmedics Inc **(PA)**	Andover	MA	C	978 552-0443	7614
Transmedics Group Inc	Andover	MA	D	978 552-0900	7615
Vasca Inc	Tewksbury	MA	E	978 640-0431	15847
Vasotech Inc	Shrewsbury	MA	G	617 686-2770	15135
Vittamed Corporation **(PA)**	Westford	MA	G	617 977-4536	16799
Volcano Corporation	Billerica	MA	G	978 439-3560	8308
Zhang Fengling	Acton	MA	G	978 289-8606	7395
Zoll Medical Corporation **(HQ)**	Chelmsford	MA	A	978 421-9655	9942
Artel Inc	Westbrook	ME	E	207 854-0860	7180
David Saunders Inc	South Portland	ME	E	207 228-1888	7021
Electrnic Mobility Contrls LLC	Augusta	ME	F	207 512-8009	5607
Fhc Inc **(PA)**	Bowdoin	ME	D	207 666-8190	5787
Medrhythms Inc	Gorham	ME	G	207 447-2177	6121
Physician Engineered Products	Fryeburg	ME	G	207 935-1256	6101
Vuetek Scientific LLC	Gray	ME	F	207 657-6565	6143
Bmed Holding LLC	Durham	NH	G	603 868-1888	18075
Colonic Connection	Peterborough	NH	G	603 924-4449	19470
Mbraun	Stratham	NH	D	603 773-9333	19874
Memtec Corporation	Salem	NH	E	603 893-8080	19751
Monarch International Inc	Amherst	NH	E	603 883-3390	17577
Qesidyne Inc	Hudson	NH	G	603 883-3116	18431
Resonetics LLC **(PA)**	Nashua	NH	C	603 886-6772	19251
Sleepnet Corp	Hampton	NH	E	603 758-6600	18272
Azulite Inc	Providence	RI	G	916 801-8528	20967
Bio-Detek Incorporated	Pawtucket	RI	C	401 729-1400	20816
Criticare Technologies Inc	North Kingstown	RI	E	401 667-3837	20699
Hanna Instruments Inc **(PA)**	Woonsocket	RI	E	401 765-7500	21567
Natus Medical Incorporated	Warwick	RI	G	401 732-5251	21395
Lionheart Technologies Inc **(PA)**	Winooski	VT	C	802 655-4040	22721
Raj Communications Ltd	Williston	VT	F	802 658-4961	22687

3851 Ophthalmic Goods

	CITY	ST	EMP	PHONE	ENTRY #
Cashon	Groton	CT	G	786 325-4144	1666
Coburn Technologies Inc **(PA)**	South Windsor	CT	C	860 648-6600	3951
Encore Optics	South Windsor	CT	F	860 282-0082	3964
Gerber Coburn Optical Inc **(HQ)**	South Windsor	CT	C	800 843-1479	3972
Gerber Scientific LLC **(PA)**	Tolland	CT	C	860 871-8082	4548
Hoya Corporation	South Windsor	CT	B	860 289-5379	3982
Lenses Only LLC	Bloomfield	CT	F	860 769-2020	239
McLeod Optical Company Inc	Waterbury	CT	G	203 754-2187	4913
Pilla Inc	Ridgefield	CT	G	203 894-3265	3676
Precision Optical Co	East Hartford	CT	E	860 289-6023	1216

	CITY	ST	EMP	PHONE	ENTRY #
Shari M Roth MD	Avon	CT	G	860 676-2525	46
University Optics LLC	Dayville	CT	G	860 779-6123	1054
Worldscreen Inc	Watertown	CT	G	860 274-9218	5037
Aearo Technologies LLC	Auburn	MA	B	317 692-6645	7822
Andor Technology Ltd	Concord	MA	E	860 290-9211	10110
Bausch & Lomb Incorporated	Wilmington	MA	F	978 658-6111	16981
Beaver-Visitec Intl Inc **(HQ)**	Waltham	MA	C	781 906-8080	16044
Bomas Machine Specialties Inc	Somerville	MA	F	617 628-3831	15160
Chicopee Vision Center Inc	Springfield	MA	F	413 796-7570	15460
Claris Vision LLC	North Dartmouth	MA	G	508 994-1400	13917
Essilor Industries Corp	Dudley	MA	C	787 848-4130	10374
Eyes On Europe LLC	Milton	MA	G	617 696-9311	13191
Focal Point Opticians Inc **(PA)**	Newton	MA	G	617 965-2770	13593
Fosta-Tek Optics Inc **(PA)**	Leominster	MA	D	978 534-6511	12141
Gentex Optics Inc **(DH)**	Dudley	MA	C	570 282-8531	10376
Gentex Optics Inc	Dudley	MA	B	508 713-5267	10375
Hilsinger Company Parent LLC **(PA)**	Plainville	MA	C	508 699-4406	14520
Hilsinger Holdings Inc	Plainville	MA	C	508 699-4406	14521
Lensmaster Optical Company	Southbridge	MA	G	508 764-4958	15392
Lets Go Technology Inc **(PA)**	Worcester	MA	F	508 853-8200	17407
Menicon America Inc	North Billerica	MA	G	781 609-2042	13842
Nauset Optical	Orleans	MA	G	508 255-6394	14237
Northeast Lens Corp	Hopkinton	MA	E	617 964-6797	11730
Paramount Corp	New Bedford	MA	E	508 999-4442	13436
Randolph Engineering Inc	Randolph	MA	E	781 961-6070	14695
Skelmet Inc	Boston	MA	G	617 396-0612	8849
Spectacle Eye Ware Inc	Boston	MA	G	617 542-9600	8857
Vision Dynamics LLC	Worcester	MA	G	203 271-1944	17502
Visionaid Inc	Wareham	MA	E	508 295-3300	16258
Wilmington Partners LP	Wilmington	MA	C	978 658-6111	17067
McLeod Optical Company Inc	Augusta	ME	F	207 623-3841	5614
Milor Corporation Inc	Auburn	ME	G	207 783-4226	5581
Blanchard Contact Lens Inc	Manchester	NH	F	800 367-4009	18788
Galvion Ltd **(HQ)**	Portsmouth	NH	G	514 739-4444	19566
General Dynamics Mission	Nashua	NH	C	603 864-6300	19165
Jcptrading Inc	Manchester	NH	G	603 880-7042	18767
Sibs LLC	Meredith	NH	G	781 864-7498	18979
Accu Rx Inc	Johnston	RI	E	401 454-2920	20497
Dioptics Medical Products Inc	Smithfield	RI	D	805 781-3300	21221
Honeywell Safety Products Usa	Smithfield	RI	F	401 233-0333	21233
Jones Safety Equipment Company	East Providence	RI	G	401 434-4010	20424
McLeod Optical Company Inc **(PA)**	Warwick	RI	E	401 467-3000	21388
Precise Products Company	Lincoln	RI	F	401 724-7190	20592
Sperian Protection Usa Inc **(DH)**	Smithfield	RI	E	401 232-1200	21250
Uvex Distribution Inc	Smithfield	RI	F	401 232-1200	21251
Uvex Safety Manufacturing Ltd	Smithfield	RI	C	401 232-1200	21252
Galvion Ballistics Ltd	Newport	VT	F	802 334-2774	22199
Galvion Ballistics Ltd **(PA)**	Essex Junction	VT	C	802 879-7002	21940
Prolens Inc	North Troy	VT	G	802 988-1018	22242

3861 Photographic Eqpt & Splys

	CITY	ST	EMP	PHONE	ENTRY #
Bidwell Industrial Group Inc **(PA)**	Middletown	CT	E	860 346-9283	2178
Ebeam Film LLC	Shelton	CT	F	203 926-0100	3798
Kenyon Laboratories LLC	Higganum	CT	G	860 345-2097	1903
Reliance Business Systems Inc	North Haven	CT	G	203 281-4407	3058
Rosco Holdings Inc **(PA)**	Stamford	CT	D	203 708-8900	4306
Rosco Laboratories Inc **(HQ)**	Stamford	CT	E	203 708-8900	4307
Verico Technology LLC **(HQ)**	Enfield	CT	E	800 492-7286	1389
Vitec Production Solutions Inc **(HQ)**	Shelton	CT	D	203 929-1100	3887
Xerox Corporation **(HQ)**	Norwalk	CT	B	203 968-3000	3274
1 Beyond Inc	Boston	MA	F	617 591-2200	8326
3derm Systems Inc	Boston	MA	G	617 237-6041	8328
Adaptive Optics Associates Inc **(DH)**	Devens	MA	D	978 757-9600	10317
Advance Reproductions Corp	North Andover	MA	D	978 685-2911	13686
AGFA Corporation	Wilmington	MA	B	978 658-5600	16969
Avid Technology Inc **(PA)**	Burlington	MA	A	978 640-6789	9235
Avid Technology Inc	Burlington	MA	C	978 640-3063	9236
Broadcast Pix Inc	Chelmsford	MA	E	978 600-1100	9878
Deep Sea Systems Intl Inc	Cataumet	MA	G	508 540-6732	9812
Eastern Copy Fax Inc	Gloucester	MA	G	978 768-3808	11180
Editshare LLC	Allston	MA	G	617 782-0479	7464
Flir Systems Inc	North Billerica	MA	C	978 901-8000	13814
Fujifilm North America Corp	Bedford	MA	C	781 271-4400	7978
Georgia-Pacific LLC	Leominster	MA	C	978 537-4701	12144
Glidecam Industries Inc	Kingston	MA	F	781 585-7900	11957
Greensight Agronomics Inc	Boston	MA	G	617 633-4919	8580
Katz Eye Optics	Greenfield	MA	G	413 743-2523	11266
Kinoton America Distribution	Boston	MA	G	617 562-0003	8650
Laser Lightning LLC **(PA)**	East Douglas	MA	G	508 476-0138	10428
Precision Dynamics Corporation	Burlington	MA	D	888 202-3684	9321
Precision Dynamics Corporation	Billerica	MA	D	800 528-8005	8276
Process Solutions Inc	East Longmeadow	MA	G	413 525-5870	10489
Progress Enterprises LLC	Westfield	MA	F	413 562-2736	16717
R & B Splicer Systems Inc	Avon	MA	G	508 580-3500	7893
Scallop Imaging LLC	Marblehead	MA	E	617 849-6400	12692
Solutek Corporation	Boston	MA	E	617 445-5335	8853
Source Two Inc	Bondsville	MA	G	413 289-1251	8325
Valentine Tool & Stamping Inc	Norton	MA	F	508 285-6911	14091
Visual Departures Ltd	Ashley Falls	MA	G	413 229-2272	7675
Xenics Usa Inc	Beverly	MA	G	978 969-1706	8199
Evad Images	Lincoln	ME	G	207 794-2930	6352
27th Exposure LLC	Littleton	NH	G	603 444-5800	18653
Fastvision LLC	Nashua	NH	F	603 891-4317	19154
Flir Commercial Systems Inc	Nashua	NH	C	603 324-7824	19159
Flir Systems Inc	Nashua	NH	C	603 324-7783	19161
Fuser Technologies Corp	Nashua	NH	G	603 886-5186	19164
Hyndsight Vision Systems Inc	Peterborough	NH	G	603 924-1334	19473
Swaffield Enterprises Inc	Wolfeboro	NH	G	603 569-3017	20025
Verico Technology LLC	Nashua	NH	C	603 402-7573	19281
Clarke Industrial Engineering **(PA)**	North Kingstown	RI	G	401 667-7880	20696
Dewal Industries LLC	Narragansett	RI	C	401 789-9736	20637
Hutchison Company Inc	North Kingstown	RI	F	401 294-3503	20717
Sprint Systems of Photography	Woonsocket	RI	G	401 597-5790	21580
Grant John	Sheldon	VT	G	802 933-4808	22428

3873 Watch & Clock Devices & Parts

	CITY	ST	EMP	PHONE	ENTRY #
Accu-Time Systems Inc **(DH)**	Ellington	CT	E	860 870-5000	1324
Morristown Star Struck LLC	Bethel	CT	E	203 778-4925	173
Pyramid Time Systems LLC	Meriden	CT	E	203 238-0550	2120
Real Women International LLC	Southbury	CT	G	212 719-3130	4032
Timex Group Usa Inc **(DH)**	Middlebury	CT	C	203 346-5000	2160
Accu-Time Systems Inc	Boston	MA	G	860 870-5000	8336
Cape Cod Wind Wther Indicators	Harwich Port	MA	G	508 432-9475	11398
Centerline Machine Company Inc	Beverly	MA	F	978 524-8842	8115
Chelsea Clock LLC	Chelsea	MA	E	617 884-0250	9948
Electric Time Company Inc	Medfield	MA	E	508 359-4396	12913
Fraen Corporation **(PA)**	Reading	MA	C	781 205-5300	14734
Lampin Corporation **(PA)**	Uxbridge	MA	E	508 278-2422	15923
Faco Metal Products Inc	Cranston	RI	F	401 943-7127	20223
Paroline/Wright Design Inc	Pawtucket	RI	F	401 781-5300	20875
Wuersch Time Inc	Coventry	RI	G	401 828-2525	20170

39 MISCELLANEOUS MANUFACTURING INDUSTRIES

3911 Jewelry: Precious Metal

	CITY	ST	EMP	PHONE	ENTRY #
AG Jewelry Designs LLC **(PA)**	Stamford	CT	G	800 643-0978	4130
Brannkey Inc	Old Saybrook	CT	E	860 510-0501	3330
Carol Ackerman Designs	Collinsville	CT	G	860 693-1013	814
Elm City Mfg Jewelers Inc	Hamden	CT	G	203 248-2195	1747
Gemma Oro Inc	Westport	CT	G	203 227-0774	5197
George S Preisner Jewelers	Wallingford	CT	G	203 265-0057	4748
Goldworks	Danbury	CT	G	203 743-9668	925
Herff Jones LLC	Stratford	CT	F	203 368-9344	4419
Joseph A Cnte Mfg Jewelers Inc	Hamden	CT	G	203 248-9853	1764
Karavas Fashions Ltd	Norwalk	CT	F	203 866-4000	3184
Kenneth R Carson	Manchester	CT	G	860 247-2707	2016
Mrk Fine Arts LLC	New Canaan	CT	G	203 972-3115	2609
O C Tanner Company	Shelton	CT	G	203 944-5430	3844
Russell Amy Kahn **(PA)**	Ridgefield	CT	F	203 438-2133	3680
Silver Little Shop Inc	Avon	CT	G	860 678-1976	47
Silversmith Inc	Greenwich	CT	G	203 869-4244	1649
A & A Jewelers Inc	North Dartmouth	MA	G	508 992-5320	13915
AB Group Inc	Attleboro	MA	F	508 222-1404	7698
Adina Inc **(PA)**	Norwood	MA	E	781 762-4477	14119
Alan W Leavitt Company	Boston	MA	G	617 338-9335	8349
Alexis Bittar LLC	Boston	MA	G	617 236-0505	8354
Artinian Garabet Corporation	Concord	MA	F	978 371-7110	10113
Ashworth Assoc Mfg Whl Jwelers	North Attleboro	MA	F	508 695-1900	13747
Barmakian Brothers Ltd Partnr	Boston	MA	E	617 227-3724	8392
Block Jewelers Inc	Agawam	MA	G	413 789-2940	7424
Charles Thomae & Son Inc	Attleboro	MA	E	508 222-0785	7719
Design Jewelry	Belmont	MA	G	617 489-0764	8072
E A Dion Inc	Attleboro	MA	C	800 445-1007	7730
Edward Spencer	Boston	MA	G	617 426-0521	8519
EF Leach & Company	Attleboro	MA	B	508 643-3309	7731
Goldman-Kolber Inc	Norwood	MA	E	781 769-6362	14156
Hallmark Healy Group Inc **(DH)**	Attleboro	MA	C	508 222-9234	7744
Hummingbird Productions	Aquinnah	MA	G	508 645-3030	7620
J T Inman Co Inc	Attleboro Falls	MA	E	508 226-0080	7814
Jack Hodgdon	Attleboro	MA	G	508 223-9990	7754
Jewelry Creations	Norton	MA	G	508 285-4230	14079
Jewelry Solutions LLC	Canton	MA	G	781 821-6100	9748
John E Lepper Inc	Attleboro	MA	G	508 222-6723	7755
John Lewis Inc	Boston	MA	G	617 266-6665	8634
Khalsa Jot	Millis	MA	G	508 376-6206	13185
Lenn Arts Inc	Attleboro	MA	E	508 223-3400	7759
Lestage	Wrentham	MA	G	508 695-7038	17525
M S Company	Attleboro	MA	D	508 222-1700	7760
Marley Hall Inc	Attleboro	MA	G	508 226-2666	7763
McVan Inc	Attleboro	MA	E	508 431-2400	7766
Michael Vincent	Feeding Hills	MA	G	413 786-4911	10801
Michele Mercaldo	Boston	MA	G	617 350-7909	8704
Mr Idea Inc	Attleboro	MA	E	508 222-0155	7770
Newpro Designs Inc **(HQ)**	Norwood	MA	E	781 762-4477	14183

Employee Codes: A=Over 500 employees, B=251-500
C=101-250, D=51-100 E=20-50, F=10-19, G=3-9

	CITY	ST	EMP	PHONE	ENTRY #
North Attleboro Jewelry Co	Attleboro	MA	G	508 222-4660	7774
P&N Jewelry Inc	Chelsea	MA	G	617 889-3200	9963
Plainville Stock Company	Plainville	MA	D	508 699-4434	14533
Richline Group Inc	Attleboro	MA	C	774 203-1199	7787
Robbins Company	Attleboro	MA	C	508 222-2900	7789
RS Nazarian Inc	Boston	MA	F	617 723-3040	8829
Sweet Metal Finishing Inc	Attleboro	MA	E	508 226-4359	7799
Theme Merchandise Inc	Attleboro	MA	G	508 226-4717	7803
Touch Inc	Waltham	MA	F	781 894-8133	16216
Town & Country Fine Jwly Group	Chelsea	MA	A	617 345-4771	9973
W E Richards Co Inc	Attleboro	MA	F	508 226-1036	7807
We Dream In Colur LLC	Essex	MA	G	978 768-0168	10598
Whiting & Davis LLC	Attleboro Falls	MA	E	508 699-4412	7819
Zero Porosity Casting Inc	Waltham	MA	F	781 373-1951	16226
Daunis	Portland	ME	F	207 773-6011	6648
Gem Creations of Maine	Charlotte	ME	G	207 454-2139	5900
Michael Good Designs Inc	Rockport	ME	F	207 236-9619	6824
Pyramid Studios	Ellsworth	ME	G	207 667-3321	6020
Thomas Michaels Designers Inc	Camden	ME	G	207 236-2708	5870
Willis & Sons Inc	Bar Harbor	ME	G	207 288-4935	5671
Melvin Reisz	Portsmouth	NH	G	603 436-9188	19594
Song Even	Hinsdale	NH	G	603 256-6018	18321
Stoneman Custom Jewelers	Keene	NH	G	603 352-0811	18530
Thomas Jewelry Design Inc	Newport	NH	D	603 372-6102	19363
A & N Jewelry Company	North Providence	RI	G	401 431-9500	20751
A F F Inc **(PA)**	Greenville	RI	D	401 949-3000	20460
Accu-Tool Inc	Pawtucket	RI	G	401 725-5350	20806
Alviti Link All Inc	Johnston	RI	G	401 861-6656	20499
Anatolia Creations	Warwick	RI	G	401 737-4774	21323
Anatone Jewelry Co Inc	North Providence	RI	E	401 728-0490	20752
Arden Jewelry Mfg Co	Johnston	RI	E	401 274-9800	20500
Armbrust International Ltd	Providence	RI	C	401 781-3300	20957
Atamian Manufacturing Corp	Providence	RI	E	800 286-9614	20959
Avanti Jewelry Inc	Cranston	RI	F	401 944-9430	20186
Bazar Group Inc **(PA)**	East Providence	RI	E	401 434-2595	20391
Bliss Manufacturing Co Inc	Pawtucket	RI	E	401 729-1690	20818
Bu Inc	Providence	RI	F	401 831-2112	20976
Carla Corp	East Providence	RI	C	401 438-7070	20395
Cellini Inc **(PA)**	Kingston	RI	D	212 594-3812	20549
Chronomatic Inc	East Greenwich	RI	E	401 884-6361	20357
Creative Findings LLC	Pawtucket	RI	G	401 274-5579	20828
Creative Pins By Lynne	Greenville	RI	G	401 949-3665	20465
D & D Model Cleaning & Casting	Johnston	RI	G	401 274-4011	20505
Damico Mfg Co	Greenville	RI	G	401 949-0023	20466
Danecraft Inc **(PA)**	Providence	RI	D	401 941-7700	20993
Danecraft Inc	Providence	RI	C	401 941-7700	20994
David Grau	Providence	RI	G	401 831-0351	20995
Edgar Modeliers	Providence	RI	E	401 781-3506	21003
Esposito Jewelry Inc	Providence	RI	F	401 943-1900	21008
Fashion Accents LLC **(PA)**	Providence	RI	E	401 331-6626	21012
Fiesta Jewelry Corporation	Pawtucket	RI	G	212 564-6847	20839
First Card Co Inc	East Providence	RI	E	401 434-6140	20414
Gem-Craft Inc	Cranston	RI	E	401 854-1200	20231
Geo H Fuller and Son Company	Pawtucket	RI	E	401 722-6530	20843
Grant Foster Group L P	Smithfield	RI	F	401 231-4077	21229
Hadc	Providence	RI	G	401 274-1870	21024
Herff Jones LLC	Warwick	RI	F	401 331-1240	21370
Herff Jones LLC	Providence	RI	E	401 331-0888	21029
Imperial-Deltah Inc	East Providence	RI	D	401 434-2597	20420
J H Breakell & Company Inc	Newport	RI	F	401 849-3522	20667
Jcc Residual Ltd	Woonsocket	RI	E	508 699-4401	21572
JMS Casting Inc	Providence	RI	G	401 453-5990	21045
Jomay Inc	Cranston	RI	F	401 944-5240	20246
Kennedy Incorporated	North Kingstown	RI	F	401 295-7800	20720
Klitzner Industries Inc	Lincoln	RI	D	800 621-0161	20577
Lim Jewelry	Cranston	RI	G	401 946-9656	20254
Mag Jewelry Co Inc	Cranston	RI	E	401 942-1840	20257
Marketplace Inc Corporate	East Greenwich	RI	F	401 336-3000	20372
Martins Soldering	Johnston	RI	G	401 521-2280	20520
Muhammad Choudhry	Pawtucket	RI	G	401 726-1118	20862
Narragasett Jewelry Inc	Providence	RI	E	401 944-2200	21075
National Chain Company **(PA)**	Warwick	RI	D	401 732-3634	21393
Paroline/Wright Design Inc	Pawtucket	RI	F	401 781-5300	20875
Pearl Comet Inc	Lincoln	RI	G	401 475-1309	20589
Quinonez Mynor	Providence	RI	G	401 751-9292	21104
Racecar Jewelry Co Inc	Pawtucket	RI	G	401 475-5701	20888
Reed Allison Group Inc	Providence	RI	D	617 846-1237	21107
Rolyn Inc **(PA)**	Cranston	RI	E	401 944-0844	20281
Snow Findings Company Inc	West Warwick	RI	G	401 821-7712	21509
Stylecraft Inc	Cranston	RI	D	401 463-9944	20293
Tahoe Jewelry Inc	East Providence	RI	E	401 435-4114	20445
Tme Co Inc	Providence	RI	E	860 354-0686	21139
Twentieth Century Casting	Pawtucket	RI	G	401 728-6836	20907
Wehr Industries Inc	Warwick	RI	E	401 732-6565	21444
Wiesner Manufacturing Company	Warwick	RI	E	401 421-2406	21447
Designed Essence Enterprise	Burlington	VT	G	802 864-4238	21780
Emporium	Rutland	VT	G	802 773-4478	22334
PBL Incorporated	Colchester	VT	F	802 893-0111	21876

3914 Silverware, Plated & Stainless Steel Ware

	CITY	ST	EMP	PHONE	ENTRY #
Boardman Silversmiths Inc	Wallingford	CT	F	203 265-9978	4710
George S Preisner Jewelers	Wallingford	CT	G	203 265-0057	4748
Silversmith Inc	Greenwich	CT	G	203 869-4244	1649
Woodbury Pewterers Inc	Woodbury	CT	E	203 263-2668	5492
Alviti Creations Inc	Attleboro	MA	G	508 222-4030	7703
Conference Medal & Trophy Co	Buzzards Bay	MA	F	508 563-3600	9359
Dipwell Company Inc	Northampton	MA	G	413 587-4673	14004
George Guertin Trophy Inc	Auburn	MA	G	508 832-4001	7836
Good Taste LLC	Amesbury	MA	G	978 388-4026	7487
Greenfield Silver Inc **(PA)**	Greenfield	MA	D	413 774-2774	11262
Greg Asselin Studios Ltd	Norton	MA	G	508 222-7361	14078
J T Inman Co Inc	Attleboro Falls	MA	E	508 226-0080	7814
Jewelry Creations	Norton	MA	G	508 285-4230	14079
Roger Jette Silversmiths Inc	North Attleboro	MA	G	508 695-5555	13776
Syratech Acquisition Corp **(HQ)**	Medford	MA	C	781 539-0100	12949
Towle Manufacturing Company **(DH)**	Medford	MA	G	781 539-0100	12950
All Seasons Printing & Awards	Pelham	NH	G	603 881-7106	19427
J H Breakell & Company Inc	Newport	RI	F	401 849-3522	20667

3915 Jewelers Findings & Lapidary Work

	CITY	ST	EMP	PHONE	ENTRY #
A & J Tool Findings Co Inc	Plainville	MA	F	508 695-6631	14514
A Murphy James & Son Inc	Attleboro	MA	E	508 761-5060	7696
Alex and Ani LLC	Natick	MA	G	401 336-1397	13232
B & L Manufacturing Inc	Bellingham	MA	F	508 966-3066	8031
Cold River Mining Inc	Turners Falls	MA	G	413 863-5445	15876
Davriel Jewelers Inc	East Longmeadow	MA	G	413 525-4975	10471
Diamond Express Inc	Wilmington	MA	E	781 284-9402	16994
Edward Spencer	Boston	MA	G	617 426-0521	8519
EF Leach & Company	Attleboro	MA	B	508 643-3309	7731
FE Knight Inc **(PA)**	Franklin	MA	G	508 520-1666	11045
Fisk Industries Inc	Attleboro Falls	MA	G	508 695-3661	7813
Guyot Brothers Company Inc	Attleboro	MA	F	508 222-2000	7743
Hallmark Healy Group Inc **(DH)**	Attleboro	MA	C	508 222-9234	7744
Idex Health & Science LLC	Middleboro	MA	C	774 213-0200	13064
M S Company	Attleboro	MA	D	508 222-1700	7760
Richard H Bird & Co Inc	Waltham	MA	E	781 894-0160	16189
Ronald Pratt Company Inc	Attleboro	MA	E	508 222-9601	7790
J S Ritter Jewelers Supply LLC	Portland	ME	G	207 712-4744	6675
ALA Casting Co Inc	Warwick	RI	E	516 371-4350	21320
Alex and Ani LLC **(PA)**	Cranston	RI	B	401 633-1486	20175
Angelo Di Maria Inc	Providence	RI	E	401 274-0100	20954
APAC Tool Inc	North Providence	RI	F	401 724-6090	20753
Aro-Sac Inc	North Providence	RI	E	401 231-6655	20754
Automatic Findings	Cranston	RI	G	401 781-4810	20185
Claire Stewart LLC	East Providence	RI	C	401 467-7400	20396
Contract Fusion Inc	East Providence	RI	E	401 438-1298	20400
Creative Castings Inc	Pawtucket	RI	G	401 724-1070	20827
Crystal Hord Corporation	Pawtucket	RI	E	401 723-2989	20829
Dama Jewelry Technology Inc	East Providence	RI	E	401 272-6513	20402
Eagle Tool Inc	Providence	RI	F	401 421-5105	21001
Evans Findings Company Inc	East Providence	RI	E	401 434-5600	20412
Fashions By Gary Inc	Pawtucket	RI	F	401 726-1453	20838
Fulford Manufacturing Company **(PA)**	Riverside	RI	F	401 431-2000	21168
Geo H Fuller and Son Company	Pawtucket	RI	E	401 722-6530	20843
Jmt Epoxy	Providence	RI	G	401 331-9730	21046
L & M Torsion Spring Co Inc	Providence	RI	G	401 231-5635	21048
Lees Manufacturing Co Inc	Providence	RI	E	401 275-2383	21050
Lorac Company Inc	Providence	RI	E	401 781-3330	21057
Meloni Tool Co Inc	Johnston	RI	G	401 272-6513	20521
Natale & Sons Castings	Cranston	RI	G	401 467-4744	20266
Pruefer Metalworks Inc	Warwick	RI	F	401 785-4688	21407
Roland & Whytock Company	Providence	RI	E	401 781-1234	21117
Rolyn Inc **(PA)**	Cranston	RI	E	401 944-0844	20281
Salvadore Tool & Findings Inc **(PA)**	Providence	RI	E	401 331-6000	21119
Tercat Tool and Die Co Inc	Providence	RI	D	401 421-3371	21133
Tri-Bro Tool Company	Cranston	RI	F	401 781-6323	20305
Unit Tool Co	Warwick	RI	E	401 781-2647	21436
W R Cobb Company **(PA)**	East Providence	RI	C	401 438-7000	20448
Ablap Inc	Bradford	VT	G	802 748-5900	21698
Eastwind Lapidary Inc	Windsor	VT	G	802 674-5427	22707

3931 Musical Instruments

	CITY	ST	EMP	PHONE	ENTRY #
Austin Organs Incorporated	Hartford	CT	E	860 522-8293	1808
Broome & Co LLC	East Granby	CT	G	860 653-2106	1118
Broome & Company LLC	Windsor Locks	CT	G	860 623-0254	5387
Fender Musical Instrs Corp	New Hartford	CT	G	860 379-7575	2637
Sweetheart Flute Company LLC	Enfield	CT	G	860 749-8514	1387
Viz-Pro LLC	Winsted	CT	G	860 379-0055	5427
Zuckerman Hrpsichords Intl LLC	Stonington	CT	G	860 535-1715	4379
Action Organ Service	Foxboro	MA	G	508 543-2161	10875
Alternate Mode Inc	East Longmeadow	MA	G	413 594-5190	10464
Andover Organ Company Inc	Lawrence	MA	F	978 686-9600	11994
Anthem Music Group Inc	North Billerica	MA	G	978 667-3224	13793
Arista Flutes LLC	Bedford	MA	G	781 275-8821	7959

	CITY	ST	EMP	PHONE	ENTRY #
Avedis Zildjian Co **(PA)**	Norwell	MA	C	781 871-2200	14096
Brannen Brothers-Flutemakers	Woburn	MA	E	781 935-9522	17139
Burgett Brothers Incorporated	Haverhill	MA	E	978 374-8888	11411
C B Fisk Inc	Gloucester	MA	E	978 283-1909	11168
Eastman Wind Instruments Inc	Acton	MA	F	800 789-2216	7351
FA Finale Inc	Boston	MA	D	617 226-7888	8536
Fishman Transducers Inc	Andover	MA	D	978 988-9199	7549
G Finkenbeiner Inc	Waltham	MA	G	781 899-3138	16117
Keefe Piccolo Company Inc	Winchester	MA	G	781 369-1626	17090
Noack Organ Company Inc	Georgetown	MA	G	978 352-6266	11147
SE Shires Inc	Holliston	MA	E	508 634-6805	11601
Vater Percussion Inc	Holbrook	MA	E	781 767-1877	11540
Verne Q Powell Flutes Inc	Maynard	MA	D	978 461-6111	12905
Vindor Music Inc	Newton	MA	G	617 984-9831	13649
William S Haynes Co Inc	Acton	MA	G	978 268-0600	7393
Faucher Organ Company Inc	Biddeford	ME	G	207 283-1420	5732
NS Design	Nobleboro	ME	G	207 563-7705	6493
Pantheon Guitars LLC	Lewiston	ME	F	207 755-0003	6314
Richard Fisher	Prospect Harbor	ME	G	207 963-7184	6771
Woodsound Studio	Rockport	ME	G	207 596-7407	6827
Euphonon Co	Orford	NH	G	603 353-4882	19420
Guitabec USA Inc	Berlin	NH	E	603 752-1432	17697
Northwind Timber	Center Sandwich	NH	G	603 284-6123	17807
Alesis LP	Cumberland	RI	G	401 658-4032	20313
Clear Carbon & Components Inc	Bristol	RI	F	401 254-5085	20068
Your Heaven LLC	Providence	RI	G	401 273-7076	21158
A David Moore Inc	North Pomfret	VT	G	802 457-3914	22234
Cooperman Fife & Drum Co	Bellows Falls	VT	G	802 463-9750	21651
Stephen J Russell & Co	Chester	VT	G	802 869-2540	21850

3942 Dolls & Stuffed Toys

	CITY	ST	EMP	PHONE	ENTRY #
Anjar Co	Stamford	CT	G	203 321-1023	4140
Cabin Critters Inc	New Fairfield	CT	G	203 778-4552	2622
Oskr Inc	North Haven	CT	G	475 238-2634	3046
Oyo Sportstoys Inc	Hudson	MA	D	978 264-2000	11799
Hasbro Inc **(PA)**	Pawtucket	RI	A	401 431-8697	20845
Marcias Dollclothes	North Scituate	RI	G	401 742-3654	20780
Sproutel Inc	Providence	RI	G	914 806-6514	21126
Verve Inc	Providence	RI	G	401 351-6415	21149
Bonnies Bundles Dolls	Chester	VT	G	802 875-2114	21841
Hibernation Holding Co Inc	Shelburne	VT	B	802 985-3001	22419
R John Wright Dolls Inc	Bennington	VT	E	802 447-7072	21690
Vermont Teddy Bear Co Inc	Shelburne	VT	C	802 985-1319	22426

3944 Games, Toys & Children's Vehicles

	CITY	ST	EMP	PHONE	ENTRY #
Anjar Co	Stamford	CT	G	203 321-1023	4140
Col-Lar Enterprises Inc **(PA)**	New Milford	CT	F	203 798-1786	2793
Enterplay LLC	Guilford	CT	F	203 458-1128	1703
Essex Wood Products Inc	Colchester	CT	E	860 537-3451	802
Imagine 8 LLC	Madison	CT	G	203 421-0905	1964
Infinity Stone Inc	Waterbury	CT	F	203 575-9484	4888
Lego Systems Inc **(DH)**	Enfield	CT	A	860 749-2291	1368
Mark G Cappitella **(PA)**	East Haddam	CT	G	860 873-3093	1151
Mwb Toy Company LLC	Danbury	CT	G	212 598-4500	958
Poof-Alex Holdings LLC **(PA)**	Greenwich	CT	G	203 930-7711	1638
Ross Curtis Product Inc	Norwich	CT	G	860 886-6800	3289
Roto-Die Company Inc	East Windsor	CT	F	860 292-7030	1300
Skydog Kites LLC	Colchester	CT	G	860 365-0600	810
US Games Systems Inc	Stamford	CT	E	203 353-8400	4353
Burnham Associates Inc	Salem	MA	F	978 745-1788	14899
Canal Toys Usa Ltd	Westborough	MA	G	508 366-9060	16599
Cartamundi East Longmeadow LLC	East Longmeadow	MA	B	413 526-2000	10469
Ceaco Inc	Newton	MA	G	617 926-8080	13575
Charles Ro Mfg Co Inc	Malden	MA	G	781 322-6084	12565
Charles Thomae & Son Inc	Attleboro	MA	E	508 222-0785	7719
Edaron Inc **(PA)**	Holyoke	MA	C	413 533-7159	11624
Ferrari Classics Corporation	Southwick	MA	G	413 569-6179	15413
Gemini Games	Arlington	MA	G	781 643-6965	7628
Gold Water Technology Inc	Walpole	MA	G	781 551-3590	15992
Greenbrier Games LLP	Marlborough	MA	G	978 618-8442	12764
Hitpoint Inc **(PA)**	Springfield	MA	F	508 314-6070	15476
Innovative Development Inc	East Walpole	MA	G	508 668-9080	10525
Koplow Games Inc	Boston	MA	F	617 482-4011	8654
Leap Year Publishing LLC	North Andover	MA	F	978 688-9900	13717
Little Kids Inc	Seekonk	MA	E	401 454-7600	15026
Massachusetts Chess Assn **(PA)**	Lexington	MA	G	781 862-3799	12241
Monahan Products LLC	Hingham	MA	E	781 413-3000	11506
Neuromotion Inc	Boston	MA	F	415 676-9326	8726
Oyo Sportstoys Inc	Hudson	MA	D	978 264-2000	11799
Paul K Guillow Inc	Wakefield	MA	E	781 245-5255	15967
Voltree Power Inc	Canton	MA	G	781 858-4939	9794
West End Strollers	Boston	MA	G	617 720-6020	8922
Wicked Cornhole	Tewksbury	MA	G	978 851-7600	15849
Winning Moves Inc	Danvers	MA	F	978 777-7464	10274
Winning Solutions Inc	Manchester	MA	G	978 525-2813	12609
Wyrmwood Inc	Taunton	MA	G	508 837-0057	15801
Zen Art & Design Inc	Hadley	MA	F	800 215-6010	11312
Zepkas Antigues	Springfield	MA	G	413 782-2964	15530
Atlantic Standard Molding Inc	Portland	ME	F	207 797-0727	6613
Bluejacket Inc	Searsport	ME	F	207 548-9970	6947
Bruce Dennison	East Machias	ME	G	207 255-0954	5983
Different Drummer	Solon	ME	G	207 643-2572	6997
Elms Puzzles Inc	Harrison	ME	F	207 583-6262	6176
Jwd Premium Products	Liberty	ME	G	617 429-8867	6330
Delta Education LLC	Nashua	NH	B	800 258-1302	19144
Gail Wilson Designs	South Acworth	NH	G	603 835-6551	19852
Puzzle House	Jaffrey	NH	F	603 532-4442	18475
Sempco Inc	Nashua	NH	E	603 889-1830	19259
Two In One Manufacturing Inc	Nashua	NH	E	603 595-8212	19276
Willowtoys	Madison	NH	G	603 367-4657	18765
Ageless Innovation LLC **(PA)**	Pawtucket	RI	G	888 569-4255	20810
Hasbro Inc	Pawtucket	RI	F	401 726-2090	20846
Hasbro Inc	Providence	RI	F	401 280-2127	21026
Hasbro Inc	Pawtucket	RI	E	401 431-8412	20847
Hasbro Inc **(PA)**	Pawtucket	RI	A	401 431-8697	20845
Hasbro International Inc **(HQ)**	Pawtucket	RI	A	401 431-8697	20848
Homespun Samplar	Harrisville	RI	G	401 732-3181	20480
Sproutel Inc	Providence	RI	G	914 806-6514	21126
Cooperman Fife & Drum Co	Bellows Falls	VT	G	802 463-9750	21651
Green Mountain Blocks	Danville	VT	G	802 748-1341	21896
Learning Materials Workshop	Burlington	VT	G	802 862-0112	21793
Maple Landmark Inc	Middlebury	VT	E	802 388-0627	22114
Real Good Toys Inc	Montpelier	VT	G	802 479-2217	22159
Stave Puzzles Incorporated	Wilder	VT	E	802 295-5200	22648
Tom Stebbins DBA Kite Ene	Westford	VT	G	802 878-9650	22629
Vermont Christmas Company	Milton	VT	G	802 893-1670	22139
Vermont Hand Crafters Inc	Waterbury	VT	G	802 434-5044	22588

3949 Sporting & Athletic Goods, NEC

	CITY	ST	EMP	PHONE	ENTRY #
Ammunition Stor Components LLC	New Britain	CT	G	860 225-3548	2509
Aqua Massage International Inc	Mystic	CT	F	860 536-3735	2434
Bob Vess Building LLC	Cromwell	CT	G	860 729-2536	849
Brampton Technology Ltd	Newington	CT	G	860 667-7689	2849
Dewey J Manufacturing Company	Oxford	CT	G	203 264-3064	3399
Edgewater International LLC	Stafford Springs	CT	F	860 851-9014	4110
Europa Sports Products Inc	Windsor	CT	G	860 688-1110	5333
Fairfield Pool & Equipment Co **(PA)**	Fairfield	CT	G	203 334-3600	1431
Force3 Pro Gear LLC	Milford	CT	G	315 367-2331	2291
Gilman Corporation	Gilman	CT	E	860 887-7080	1534
Golf Galaxy LLC	Norwalk	CT	G	203 855-0500	3162
Group Works	Wilton	CT	G	203 834-7905	5290
Hamden Sports Center Inc	Hamden	CT	G	203 248-9898	1758
Homeland Fundraising	East Windsor	CT	G	860 386-6698	1286
International Soccer & Rugby	Southport	CT	G	203 254-1979	4096
Intersec LLC	Rocky Hill	CT	G	860 985-3158	3718
Jammar Mfg Co Inc	Niantic	CT	G	866 848-1113	2953
Jaypro Sports LLC	Waterford	CT	E	860 447-3001	4986
K & D Business Ventures LLC	Jewett City	CT	G	860 237-1458	1914
Marty Gilman Incorporated **(PA)**	Gilman	CT	D	860 889-7334	1535
Marty Gilman Incorporated	Bozrah	CT	G	860 889-7334	282
Mike Sadlak	Coventry	CT	G	860 742-0227	835
Pfd Studios	Marlborough	CT	G	860 295-8500	2068
Probatter Sports LLC	Milford	CT	G	203 874-2500	2342
Rampage LLC	Trumbull	CT	F	203 930-1022	4630
Road-Fit Enterprises LLC	Plainville	CT	G	860 371-5137	3514
Robert Louis Company Inc	Newtown	CT	G	203 270-1400	2935
Sadlak Industries LLC	Coventry	CT	E	860 742-0227	838
Samsara Fitness LLC	Chester	CT	F	860 895-8533	776
Swivel Machine Works Inc	Newtown	CT	G	203 270-6343	2940
Trassig Corp	Georgetown	CT	G	203 659-0456	1533
Tucci Lumber Co LLC	Norwalk	CT	G	203 956-6181	3262
Uniboard Corp	Putnam	CT	G	860 428-5979	3637
Wasp Archery Products Inc	Plymouth	CT	G	860 283-0246	3549
Wiffle Ball Incorporated	Shelton	CT	F	203 924-4643	3890
Wild Card Golf LLC	Hartford	CT	G	860 296-1661	1885
3 Play Inc **(PA)**	Walpole	MA	G	781 205-4820	15986
40 Up Tackle Company Inc	Westfield	MA	G	413 562-0385	16660
A & S Tackle Corp	Swansea	MA	G	508 679-8122	15702
Ace Archers Inc	Foxborough	MA	G	774 215-5292	10910
Ace Archers Inc	Foxboro	MA	G	508 697-5647	10874
Acushnet Company **(DH)**	Fairhaven	MA	A	508 979-2000	10635
Acushnet Company	Acushnet	MA	E	508 979-2000	7397
Acushnet Company	New Bedford	MA	A	508 979-2000	13349
Acushnet Company	New Bedford	MA	E	508 979-2000	13350
Acushnet Company	New Bedford	MA	E	508 979-2156	13351
Acushnet Company	Brockton	MA	A	508 979-2309	9115
Acushnet Company	Brockton	MA	E	508 979-2343	9116
Acushnet Holdings Corp **(HQ)**	Fairhaven	MA	E	800 225-8500	10636
Al Gags	Indian Orchard	MA	G	413 285-8023	11884
Aluma-Cast Corp	North Attleboro	MA	G	508 399-6650	13744
Amalgamated Titanium Intl Corp	Cambridge	MA	F	617 395-7700	9386
Ampac Enterprises Inc	Shirley	MA	D	978 425-6266	15080
B F M Mini Golf Driving Range	North Reading	MA	F	978 664-9276	13978
Barnstable Bat Inc	Centerville	MA	G	508 362-8046	9813

S I C

	CITY	ST	EMP	PHONE	ENTRY #
Big Daddy Boomerangs LLC	Springfield	MA	G	413 297-7079	15452
Billerica Backstage Rehearsal	Pinehurst	MA	G	978 670-1133	14447
Brewers Ledge Inc	Randolph	MA	G	781 961-5200	14671
Callaway Golf Company	Chicopee	MA	E	413 536-1200	10005
Cherry Hill Construction Corp	Pembroke	MA	G	781 826-6886	14394
Cohasset Sports Complex	Cohasset	MA	G	781 383-0278	10096
Cookes Skate Supplies Inc	Wilmington	MA	G	978 657-7586	16989
Cuesport Inc	Southfield	MA	G	413 229-6626	15410
Cybex International Inc	Medway	MA	C	508 533-4167	12958
Duane Smith	Attleboro	MA	G	508 222-9541	7729
Field Protection Agency LLC	Auburn	MA	G	508 832-0395	7834
Final Forge LLC	Plymouth	MA	G	857 244-0764	14557
Firejudge Worldwide Inc	Haverhill	MA	G	978 604-0009	11434
Fitness Em LLC	Uxbridge	MA	E	508 278-3209	15916
Fitnow Inc	Boston	MA	E	617 699-5585	8550
Foamaction Sports LLC	Rochester	MA	G	508 887-3721	14786
Foot Locker Retail Inc	Saugus	MA	G	781 231-0142	14981
Fuji Mats LLC	Methuen	MA	G	205 419-5080	13023
Great Neck Saw Mfrs Inc	Millbury	MA	E	508 865-4482	13166
Heartbreak Hill Running Co Inc	Newton	MA	G	617 467-4487	13599
Hogy Lure Company LLC	Falmouth	MA	G	617 699-5157	10791
Hollrock Engineering Inc	Hadley	MA	F	413 586-2256	11307
Home Grown Lacrosse LLC	North Andover	MA	G	978 208-2300	13709
Hudson Poly Bag Inc	Hudson	MA	F	978 562-7566	11776
Hydro-Test Products Inc	Stow	MA	F	978 897-4647	15632
Imperial Pools Inc	Taunton	MA	F	508 339-3830	15758
Insignia Athletics LLC	Worcester	MA	G	508 756-3633	17393
JB Sports LLC	Revere	MA	G	617 930-3044	14769
Larchmont Engineering Inc	Chelmsford	MA	G	978 250-1177	9912
Life+gear Inc	Wellesley Hills	MA	E	858 755-2099	16398
Macneill Engineering Co Inc	Westborough	MA	E	508 481-8830	16633
Mark Keup	Scituate	MA	G	781 544-4610	15009
Morse Diving Inc	Rockland	MA	G	781 733-1511	14815
Mylec Inc **(PA)**	Winchendon	MA	D	978 297-0089	17078
Neptune Inc	Attleboro	MA	G	508 222-8313	7771
New England Spt Ventures LLC	Boston	MA	G	617 267-9440	8732
Nonantum Boxing Club LLC	Newton	MA	G	617 340-3700	13619
North Point Brands LLC	North Adams	MA	G	339 707-3017	13683
Ocean Lures LLC	Rowley	MA	G	978 618-1982	14862
Outdoor Outfitters Inc	Orleans	MA	E	508 255-0455	14239
Outrageous Lures LLC	Plymouth	MA	G	347 509-8610	14571
Paradigm Sports Inc	Amesbury	MA	G	978 687-6687	7502
Perfect Curve Inc **(PA)**	Boston	MA	G	617 224-1600	8774
Promounds Inc **(PA)**	Braintree	MA	E	508 580-6171	9032
Pursuit Toboggan LLC	Fall River	MA	G	508 567-0550	10749
R J Shepherd Co Inc	Whitman	MA	G	781 447-5768	16927
R R Venture	Wellesley	MA	G	781 431-6170	16382
Reel Easy Inc	Newburyport	MA	G	978 476-7187	13528
Regal Sporting Technologies	Orange	MA	G	978 544-6571	14224
Savage Range Systems Inc	Westfield	MA	G	413 568-7001	16727
Sports Power Drive Inc	Holliston	MA	G	774 233-0175	11603
Sportsscarf LLC	Mattapoisett	MA	G	508 758-8176	12891
Stan Ray Products Co	Salem	MA	G	978 594-0667	14944
Stuart Sports Specialties Inc	Indian Orchard	MA	G	413 543-1524	11897
Surfari Inc	Gloucester	MA	F	978 704-9051	11214
Swimex Inc	Fall River	MA	E	508 646-1600	10768
Tennis Loft	Nantucket	MA	G	508 228-9228	13231
Thomas & Thomas Rodmakers	Greenfield	MA	E	413 475-3840	11281
Tom Waters Golf Shop	Manchester	MA	G	978 526-7311	12608
Velex Corporation	Cambridge	MA	G	617 440-4948	9691
Village Sports	Westport	MA	G	508 672-4284	16850
Will Kirkpatricks Decoy Shop	Hudson	MA	F	978 562-7841	11826
Winchester Fishing Inc	Gloucester	MA	G	978 282-0679	11219
Xthera Corporation	Franklin	MA	G	508 528-3100	11100
Austin Merrill	Scarborough	ME	G	207 219-0593	6906
Cedarworks of Maine Inc	Rockland	ME	E	207 596-0771	6788
Chambers Leasing	Houlton	ME	G	207 532-4381	6203
Corn Snow LLC	Farmington	ME	G	603 684-2427	6042
E Skip Grindle & Sons	Ellsworth	ME	G	207 460-0334	6017
Extreme Dim Wildlife Calls LLC	Hampden	ME	G	207 862-2825	6165
Grain Surfboards	York	ME	G	207 457-5313	7307
Gregg Stewart	Brewer	ME	G	207 989-0903	5796
Maine Lure Company LLC	Biddeford	ME	G	413 543-1524	5745
Maine Surfers Union	Portland	ME	G	207 771-7873	6690
Plantes Lobster Escape Vents	Somerville	ME	G	207 549-7204	6999
Power Gripps Usa Inc	Sorrento	ME	G	207 422-2051	7000
Pride Manufacturing Co LLC **(PA)**	Burnham	ME	C	207 487-3322	5855
Advanced Fitnes Components LLC	Hudson	NH	F	603 595-1967	18370
Athletic Innovation Inc	Rochester	NH	G	603 332-1212	19660
Atlantic Sports International	Langdon	NH	G	603 835-6948	18610
Bauer Hockey LLC	Exeter	NH	C	603 430-2111	18111
Bce Acquisition Us Inc **(HQ)**	Exeter	NH	G	603 430-2111	18112
Bobos Indoor Playground	Nashua	NH	G	603 718-8721	19128
Bps Diamond Sports Inc	Exeter	NH	G	253 891-8377	18114
Dennco Inc	Salem	NH	E	603 898-0004	19721
Fulling Mill Fly Fishing LLC	Claremont	NH	G	603 542-5480	17851
H R P Products Inc	Farmington	NH	F	603 330-3757	18142

	CITY	ST	EMP	PHONE	ENTRY #
Jenex Inc	Milford	NH	G	603 672-2600	19066
L L Bean Inc	West Lebanon	NH	G	603 298-6975	19955
Old Bh Inc **(PA)**	Exeter	NH	C	603 430-2111	18126
Pat Trap Inc	Henniker	NH	G	603 428-3396	18309
Pigeon Hold Targets	Merrimack	NH	G	603 420-8839	19021
Richardson Mfg Co Inc	Silver Lake	NH	G	603 367-9018	19825
Roces North America	West Lebanon	NH	G	603 298-2137	19961
Santa Cruz Gunlocks LLC	Webster	NH	G	603 746-7740	19945
Simbex LLC	Lebanon	NH	E	603 448-2367	18636
Ashaway Line & Twine Mfg Co	Ashaway	RI	D	401 377-2221	20031
Bacou Dalloz USA Inc	Smithfield	RI	F	401 757-2428	21211
Bennetts Sports Inc	Cranston	RI	G	401 943-7600	20189
Caron Alpine Technologies Inc	Tiverton	RI	G	401 624-8999	21254
East Greenwich Spine and Sport	East Greenwich	RI	F	401 886-5907	20364
Endless Wave Inc	Jamestown	RI	G	401 423-3400	20489
Gibbs Lures Inc	Cumberland	RI	G	401 726-2277	20321
Great American Recrtl Eqp	Cranston	RI	E	401 463-5587	20233
Grenade (usa) LLC	Cranston	RI	G	401 944-3960	20234
Hayward Industries Inc	North Kingstown	RI	G	401 583-1150	20714
Imagination Playground LLC	Providence	RI	G	678 604-7466	21035
Jonathan Knight	Wakefield	RI	G	401 263-3671	21273
Mearthane Products Corporation **(PA)**	Cranston	RI	C	401 946-4400	20260
North Sails Group LLC	Newport	RI	D	401 849-7997	20675
Parsonskellogg LLC	East Providence	RI	E	401 438-0650	20439
Planet Eclipse LLC	Warren	RI	G	401 247-9061	21302
Shegear Inc	Newport	RI	G	401 619-0072	20681
Waterrower Inc	Warren	RI	D	800 852-2210	21316
Bachar Samawi Innovations LLC **(PA)**	West Dover	VT	G	802 464-0440	22605
Balance Designs Inc	Manchester Center	VT	G	802 362-2893	22080
Burton Corporation **(PA)**	Burlington	VT	B	802 862-4500	21770
Burton Corporation	Burlington	VT	G	802 862-4500	21771
Burton Corporation	South Burlington	VT	D	802 652-3600	22441
Concept2 Inc **(PA)**	Morrisville	VT	E	802 888-7971	22166
Damascus Worldwide Inc	Rutland	VT	G	802 775-6062	22328
Forward Inc	Shelburne	VT	G	802 585-1098	22417
Gordini USA Inc **(PA)**	Essex Junction	VT	E	802 879-5211	21942
Killington Ltd	Killington	VT	D	802 422-3333	22053
Manufacturing Solutions Inc	Morrisville	VT	E	802 888-3289	22172
Michael Olden	Newport	VT	G	802 334-5525	22202
Northern Strike	Lyndonville	VT	G	802 427-3201	22071
Orvis Company	Manchester	VT	F	802 362-3750	22078
Perfect Storm Sports Tech LLC	Essex Junction	VT	G	802 662-2102	21954
Red Corp	Burlington	VT	D	802 862-4500	21806
Snowshoe Pond Mple Sgrwrks LLC	Enosburg Falls	VT	G	802 777-9676	21927
Sports Products Incorporated	Winooski	VT	G	802 655-2620	22724
Tsl Snowshoes LLC	Williston	VT	G	802 660-8232	22695
Vermont Ski Safety Equipment	Underhill	VT	G	802 899-4738	22549
Whistlekick LLC	Montpelier	VT	F	802 225-6676	22164
Wood Dynamics Corporation **(PA)**	South Pomfret	VT	G	802 457-3970	22489

3951 Pens & Mechanical Pencils

	CITY	ST	EMP	PHONE	ENTRY #
Bic Consumer Products Mfg Co	Milford	CT	C	203 783-2000	2254
Bic Corporation **(HQ)**	Shelton	CT	A	203 783-2000	3782
Bic USA Inc **(DH)**	Shelton	CT	C	203 783-2000	3783
Gillette Company	Bethel	CT	G	203 796-4000	155
EF Leach & Company	Attleboro	MA	B	508 643-3309	7731
Gillette Company	Andover	MA	A	781 662-9600	7552
Gillette Company **(HQ)**	Boston	MA	A	617 421-7000	8561
Hub Pen Company Inc **(PA)**	Braintree	MA	D	781 535-5500	9018
Precision Handling Devices **(PA)**	Westport	MA	F	508 679-5282	16845
Riveto Manufacturing Co	Orange	MA	E	978 544-2171	14226
Garland Industries Inc	Coventry	RI	E	401 821-1450	20147
Derand Precision	South Londonderry	VT	G	802 874-7161	22485

3952 Lead Pencils, Crayons & Artist's Mtrls

	CITY	ST	EMP	PHONE	ENTRY #
Bic Corporation **(HQ)**	Shelton	CT	A	203 783-2000	3782
Color Craft Ltd	East Granby	CT	F	800 509-6563	1121
Colors Ink	Wallingford	CT	G	203 269-4000	4722
Screening Ink LLC	Enfield	CT	G	860 212-0475	1381
Exit Five Gallery	West Barnstable	MA	G	508 375-1011	16407
Henry J Montville	Auburn	MA	G	508 832-6111	7837
Jen Mfg Inc	Millbury	MA	E	508 753-1076	13168
Pucker Gallery Inc	Somerville	MA	F	617 261-1817	15207
Scratch Art Company Inc **(PA)**	Avon	MA	F	508 583-8085	7895
Eco-Kids LLC	Portland	ME	G	207 899-2752	6659
Garland Industries Inc	Coventry	RI	E	401 821-1450	20147
Wood & Wood Inc	Waitsfield	VT	G	802 496-3000	22572

3953 Marking Devices

	CITY	ST	EMP	PHONE	ENTRY #
A D Perkins Company	New Haven	CT	G	203 777-3456	2651
A G Russell Company Inc	Hartford	CT	G	860 247-9093	1800
Acme Sign Co **(PA)**	Stamford	CT	F	203 324-2263	4128
American Rubber Stamp Company	Cheshire	CT	G	203 755-1135	710
D R S Desings	Bethel	CT	G	203 744-2858	140
Gutkin Enterprises LLC	Hamden	CT	G	203 777-5510	1752
Liftline Capital LLC	Old Saybrook	CT	F	860 395-0150	3342
Mbsw Inc	West Hartford	CT	D	860 243-0303	5086

	CITY	ST	EMP	PHONE	ENTRY #
Schwerdtle Stamp Company	Bridgeport	CT	E	203 330-2750	487
United Stts Sgn & Fbrction	Trumbull	CT	E	203 601-1000	4640
Van Deusen & Levitt Assoc Inc	Weston	CT	E	203 445-6244	5175
AA White Company	Uxbridge	MA	F	508 779-0821	15913
Duncan M Gillies Co Inc	West Boylston	MA	G	508 835-4445	16415
G3 Incorporated **(PA)**	Lowell	MA	E	978 805-5001	12372
Holmes Stamp Company	Salem	MA	G	978 744-1051	14922
Idemia America Corp **(DH)**	Billerica	MA	B	978 215-2400	8255
Lincoln Press Co Inc	Fall River	MA	E	508 673-3241	10723
Logan Stamp Works Inc	Boston	MA	G	617 569-2121	8670
Making Your Mark Inc	Quincy	MA	G	617 479-0999	14637
Opsec Security Inc	Boston	MA	F	617 226-3000	8756
Owl Stamp Company Inc	Lowell	MA	G	978 452-4541	12418
Rofin-Baasel Inc **(DH)**	Devens	MA	E	978 635-9100	10332
Royal Stamp Works Inc	Peabody	MA	G	978 531-5555	14367
Titus & Bean Graphics Inc	Kingston	MA	F	781 585-1355	11965
Valley Steel Stamp Inc	Greenfield	MA	E	413 773-8200	11282
Visimark Inc **(PA)**	Worcester	MA	E	866 344-7721	17501
Armstrong Family Inds Inc	Hermon	ME	E	207 848-7300	6183
Anco Signs & Stamps Inc	Manchester	NH	G	603 669-3779	18779
Granite State Stamps Inc	Manchester	NH	F	603 669-9322	18829
Global Rfid Systems N Amer LLC	Narragansett	RI	G	401 783-3818	20640
Henry A Evers Corp Inc	Providence	RI	F	401 781-4767	21028

3955 Carbon Paper & Inked Ribbons

	CITY	ST	EMP	PHONE	ENTRY #
Avcarb LLC	Lowell	MA	D	978 452-8961	12347
Encore Images Inc	Marblehead	MA	F	781 631-4568	12681
Electronics For Imaging Inc	Londonderry	NH	F	603 279-4635	18695
Vermont Toner Recharge Inc	Essex Junction	VT	G	802 864-7637	21964

3961 Costume Jewelry & Novelties

	CITY	ST	EMP	PHONE	ENTRY #
A Capela Do Santo Antonio Inc	New London	CT	G	860 447-3329	2764
Mystic Knotwork LLC	Mystic	CT	F	860 889-3793	2444
Smiling Dog	Middletown	CT	G	860 344-0707	2223
Swarovski North America Ltd	Stamford	CT	G	203 462-3357	4337
Swarovski North America Ltd	Trumbull	CT	G	203 372-0336	4634
AB Group Inc	Attleboro	MA	F	508 222-1404	7698
Adina Inc **(PA)**	Norwood	MA	E	781 762-4477	14119
American Biltrite Inc **(PA)**	Wellesley	MA	G	781 237-6655	16359
Ashworth Assoc Mfg Whl Jwelers	North Attleboro	MA	F	508 695-1900	13747
Barnstable Bracelet	West Barnstable	MA	G	508 362-1630	16404
Carole Sousa Jewelry	Boston	MA	G	617 232-4087	8460
Charles Thomae & Son Inc	Attleboro	MA	E	508 222-0785	7719
Conversation Concepts LLC	Fitchburg	MA	F	978 342-1414	10820
Gear2succeed LLC	Duxbury	MA	G	781 733-0559	10397
J & K Sales Company Inc	Rehoboth	MA	E	508 252-6235	14751
Joel Goldsmith Bagnal Inc	Wellesley	MA	G	781 235-8266	16368
K W Bristol Co Inc	North Attleboro	MA	G	508 699-4742	13760
Lenn Arts Inc	Attleboro	MA	E	508 223-3400	7759
Nano-Ice LLC	Brookline	MA	G	617 512-8811	9212
Newpro Designs Inc **(HQ)**	Norwood	MA	E	781 762-4477	14183
North Attleboro Jewelry Co	Attleboro	MA	G	508 222-4660	7774
Plastic Craft Novelty Co Inc	Attleboro	MA	E	508 222-1486	7777
Swarovski North America Ltd	Boston	MA	G	617 578-0705	8871
Swarovski US Holding Limited	Peabody	MA	G	978 531-4582	14374
Sweet Metal Finishing Inc	Attleboro	MA	E	508 226-4359	7799
Yankee Crafters Wampum Jewelry	South Yarmouth	MA	G	508 394-0575	15336
Victoria Ann Varga Inc	Cumberland Foreside	ME	G	207 781-4050	5933
Accu-Tool Inc	Pawtucket	RI	G	401 725-5350	20806
Aetna Manufacturing Company	Providence	RI	G	401 751-3260	20948
AG & G Inc **(PA)**	Johnston	RI	E	401 946-4330	20498
American Ring Co Inc **(PA)**	East Providence	RI	E	401 438-9060	20385
Amsco Ltd Inc	Cranston	RI	G	401 785-2860	20181
Barlow Designs Inc	East Providence	RI	G	401 438-7925	20390
Barrington Manufacturing Inc	Warren	RI	F	401 245-1737	21288
Bazar Group Inc **(PA)**	East Providence	RI	E	401 434-2595	20391
Bliss Manufacturing Co Inc	Pawtucket	RI	E	401 729-1690	20818
Chronomatic Inc	East Greenwich	RI	E	401 884-6361	20357
Clayton Company Inc	Providence	RI	G	401 421-2978	20984
Dama Jewelry Technology Inc	East Providence	RI	E	401 272-6513	20402
Danecraft Inc **(PA)**	Providence	RI	D	401 941-7700	20993
Decor Craft Inc	Providence	RI	E	401 621-2324	20996
Dina Inc	Cranston	RI	G	401 942-9633	20212
Esposito Jewelry Inc	Providence	RI	F	401 943-1900	21008
Fulford Manufacturing Company **(PA)**	Riverside	RI	F	401 431-2000	21168
Gennaro Inc	Cranston	RI	F	401 632-4100	20232
Gloria Duchin Inc	Rumford	RI	D	401 431-5016	21185
Ira Holtz & Associates	Cranston	RI	G	401 521-8960	20241
J P I Inc	Warwick	RI	G	401 737-7433	21377
Jcc Residual Ltd	Woonsocket	RI	E	508 699-4401	21572
Jewelry Holding Co Inc	West Warwick	RI	G	401 826-7934	21496
Jim Clift Design Inc	Coventry	RI	G	401 823-9680	20150
Jji International Inc	Cranston	RI	E	401 780-8668	20244
Jonette Jewelry Company	East Providence	RI	D	401 438-1941	20425
Josef Creations Inc **(PA)**	Chepachet	RI	E	401 421-4198	20135
Kennedy Incorporated	North Kingstown	RI	F	401 295-7800	20720
Kerissa Creations Inc	Greenville	RI	E	401 949-3700	20470
Klitzner Industries Inc	Lincoln	RI	D	800 621-0161	20577
Kmb International	Bristol	RI	F	401 253-6798	20088
Llmage Inc	Johnston	RI	E	401 369-7141	20518
Mag Jewelry Co Inc	Cranston	RI	E	401 942-1840	20257
Michael Healy Designs Inc	Manville	RI	G	401 597-5900	20610
Modern Manufacturing Inc	Johnston	RI	F	401 944-9230	20523
Pauley Co	Warwick	RI	F	401 467-2930	21400
Perry Blackburne Inc	North Providence	RI	E	401 231-7200	20771
R & D Manufacturing Company	Pawtucket	RI	F	401 305-7662	20887
Ramco Inc	Warwick	RI	G	401 739-4343	21409
Reed Allison Group Inc	Providence	RI	D	617 846-1237	21107
Rolyn Inc **(PA)**	Cranston	RI	E	401 944-0844	20281
Salvadore Tool & Findings Inc **(PA)**	Providence	RI	E	401 331-6000	21119
Stylecraft Inc	Cranston	RI	D	401 463-9944	20293
Swarovski Digital Business USA	Cranston	RI	G	888 207-9873	20294
Swarovski North America Ltd	Warwick	RI	G	401 732-0794	21433
Swarovski North America Ltd **(DH)**	Cranston	RI	A	401 463-6400	20295
Swarovski US Holding Limited **(HQ)**	Cranston	RI	G	401 463-6400	20296
Two Hands Inc	Providence	RI	E	401 785-2727	21142
Ubio Inc	Johnston	RI	E	401 541-9172	20544
Unit Tool Co	Warwick	RI	E	401 781-2647	21436
Wehr Industries Inc	Warwick	RI	E	401 732-6565	21444
Winkler Group Ltd **(PA)**	Rumford	RI	C	401 272-2885	21199
Winkler Group Ltd	Rumford	RI	E	401 751-6120	21200
Baked Beads Inc	Waitsfield	VT	F	802 496-2440	22560

3965 Fasteners, Buttons, Needles & Pins

	CITY	ST	EMP	PHONE	ENTRY #
Bees Knees Zipper Wax LLC	Berlin	CT	G	203 521-5727	75
Braxton Manufacturing Co Inc	Watertown	CT	C	860 274-6781	5000
Connectcut Prcsion Cmpnnts LLC	Torrington	CT	G	860 489-8621	4573
Eyelet Tech LLC	Wolcott	CT	E	203 879-5306	5442
Illinois Tool Works Inc	Naugatuck	CT	E	203 720-1676	2479
ITW Powertrain Fastening	Naugatuck	CT	G	203 720-1676	2480
J & J Precision Eyelet Inc	Thomaston	CT	D	860 283-8243	4505
Jo Vek Tool and Die Mfg Co	Waterbury	CT	G	203 755-1884	4892
Knight Inc	Waterbury	CT	G	203 754-6502	4895
Lord & Hodge Inc	Middletown	CT	F	860 632-7006	2201
Manchester Tl & Design ADP LLC	Hartford	CT	G	860 296-6541	1843
Metalform Acquisition LLC **(PA)**	New Britain	CT	E	860 224-2630	2553
Nucap US Inc **(DH)**	Wolcott	CT	E	203 879-1423	5450
Ogs Technologies Inc	Cheshire	CT	E	203 271-9055	749
Paneloc Corporation	Farmington	CT	E	860 677-6711	1505
Platt Brothers & Company **(PA)**	Waterbury	CT	D	203 753-4194	4940
Rings Wire Inc **(PA)**	Milford	CT	E	203 874-6719	2352
Rome Fastener Corporation	Milford	CT	E	203 874-6719	2354
Rome Fastener Sales Corp	Milford	CT	F	203 874-6719	2355
Stevens Company Incorporated	Thomaston	CT	D	860 283-8201	4515
Timber-Top Inc	Watertown	CT	G	860 274-6706	5029
US Button Corporation	Putnam	CT	C	860 928-2707	3638
Bees Knees Zipper Wax LLC	Fall River	MA	G	203 521-5727	10667
Briscon Electric Mfg Corp	Auburn	MA	F	508 832-3481	7830
Buckleguycom LLC	Newburyport	MA	G	978 213-9989	13475
Charles Thomae & Son Inc	Attleboro	MA	E	508 222-0785	7719
Great Northern Industries Inc **(PA)**	Boston	MA	C	617 262-4314	8578
M C Machine Co Inc	Hopedale	MA	G	508 473-3642	11677
Nixon Company Inc	Indian Orchard	MA	E	413 543-3701	11890
Reeves Coinc	Attleboro	MA	E	508 222-2877	7785
United Shoe Machinery Corp	Middleboro	MA	G	508 923-6001	13079
YKK (usa) Inc	Marlborough	MA	G	978 458-3200	12855
Allied Endeavers Inc	Waldoboro	ME	G	207 832-0511	7130
Velcro USA Inc **(DH)**	Manchester	NH	A	603 669-4880	18949
W H Bagshaw Co Inc	Nashua	NH	E	603 883-7758	19283
Precision Plsg Ornamentals Inc	Pawtucket	RI	E	401 728-9994	20883
Weller E E Co Inc/MCS Finshg	Providence	RI	E	401 461-4275	21152

3991 Brooms & Brushes

	CITY	ST	EMP	PHONE	ENTRY #
Liftline Capital LLC	Old Saybrook	CT	F	860 395-0150	3342
Loos & Co Inc	Pomfret	CT	F	860 928-6681	3553
Torrington Brush Works Inc	Torrington	CT	G	860 482-3517	4602
Angel Guard Products Inc	Worcester	MA	G	508 791-1073	17339
Butler Home Products LLC **(DH)**	Hudson	MA	F	508 597-8000	11761
Cardinal Comb & Brush Mfg Corp	Leominster	MA	E	978 537-6330	12125
Goode Brush Company	Nahant	MA	G	781 581-0280	13215
Jen Mfg Inc	Millbury	MA	E	508 753-1076	13168
R&R Sweeping Services Inc	East Bridgewater	MA	G	508 586-5705	10419
Sanderson-Macleod Incorporated	Palmer	MA	C	413 283-3481	14295
Howard P Fairfield LLC **(DH)**	Skowhegan	ME	E	207 474-9836	6976
American Brush Company Inc	Claremont	NH	F	603 542-9951	17834
Felton Inc	Londonderry	NH	D	603 425-0200	18697
Felton Brush	Londonderry	NH	F	603 425-0200	18698
ACS Industries Inc **(PA)**	Lincoln	RI	E	401 769-4700	20552
Tucel Industries Inc	Forest Dale	VT	F	802 247-6824	21993

3993 Signs & Advertising Displays

	CITY	ST	EMP	PHONE	ENTRY #
420 Sign Design Inc	Norwalk	CT	G	203 852-1255	3094
A D Perkins Company	New Haven	CT	G	203 777-3456	2651

	CITY	ST	EMP	PHONE	ENTRY #
ABC Sign Corporation	Shelton	CT	E	203 513-8110	3772
Accent Signs LLC	Stamford	CT	G	203 975-8688	4126
Acme Sign Co **(PA)**	Stamford	CT	F	203 324-2263	4128
Adamsahern Sign Solutions Inc	Hartford	CT	F	860 523-8835	1802
Applied Advertising Inc	Danbury	CT	F	860 640-0800	872
Arteffects Incorporated	Bloomfield	CT	E	860 242-0031	204
Asi Sign Systems Inc	East Berlin	CT	G	860 828-3331	1097
Automotive Coop Couponing Inc	Weston	CT	G	203 227-2722	5169
Barneys Sign Service Inc	Stratford	CT	G	203 878-3763	4396
Belmeade Group LLC	West Granby	CT	G	860 413-3569	5048
Big Prints LLC	East Haven	CT	G	203 469-1100	1243
Bristol Signart Inc	Bristol	CT	G	860 582-2577	538
Camaro Signs Inc **(PA)**	Yantic	CT	G	860 886-1553	5508
Century Sign LLC	Hamden	CT	G	203 230-9000	1737
City Sign	Hartford	CT	G	860 232-4803	1813
Compu-Signs LLC	Plainville	CT	G	860 747-1985	3474
Computer Sgns Old Saybrook LLC	Old Saybrook	CT	G	860 388-9773	3331
Concord Industries Inc	Norwalk	CT	E	203 750-6060	3131
Connecticut Container Corp **(PA)**	North Haven	CT	C	203 248-2161	3018
Connecticut Sign Craft Inc	Naugatuck	CT	G	203 729-0706	2468
Connecticut Sign Service LLC	Essex	CT	G	860 767-7446	1395
Corr/Dis Incorporated	Norwalk	CT	G	203 838-6075	3132
Creative Dimensions Inc	Cheshire	CT	E	203 250-6500	725
Derrick Mason **(PA)**	Norwich	CT	G	413 527-4282	3278
Displaycraft Inc	Plainville	CT	E	860 747-9110	3481
Dundorf Designs USA Inc	Salem	CT	G	860 859-2955	3738
East Coast Sign and Supply Inc	Bethel	CT	G	203 791-8326	149
Farmington Displays Inc	Farmington	CT	E	860 677-2497	1481
Fastsigns	Milford	CT	G	203 298-4075	2288
Fastsigns	Bristol	CT	G	860 583-8000	562
Gerber Scientific LLC **(PA)**	Tolland	CT	C	860 871-8082	4548
Granata Signs LLC	Stamford	CT	G	203 358-0780	4202
Horizons Unlimited Inc	Willimantic	CT	F	860 423-1931	5266
Image360	Wallingford	CT	F	203 949-0726	4755
Jaime M Camacho	Norwalk	CT	G	203 846-8221	3178
Jill Ghi	Canaan	CT	G	860 824-7123	688
John Oldham Studios Inc	Wethersfield	CT	E	860 529-3331	5251
John Rawlinson John Leary	Milford	CT	G	203 882-8484	2305
Jornik Man Corp	Stamford	CT	F	203 969-0500	4232
Lauretano Sign Group Inc	Terryville	CT	E	860 582-0233	4484
Lewtan Industries Corporation	West Hartford	CT	D	860 278-9800	5082
Lifetime Acrylic Signs Inc	Fairfield	CT	G	203 255-6751	1442
Lorence Sign Works LLC	Berlin	CT	G	860 829-9999	94
McIntire Company **(HQ)**	Bristol	CT	F	860 585-8559	580
Mr Skylight LLC	New Canaan	CT	G	203 966-6005	2608
New Haven Sign Company	Northford	CT	G	203 484-2777	3091
Nomis Enterprises	Wallingford	CT	G	631 821-3120	4778
Nu Line Design LLC	Wallingford	CT	G	203 949-0726	4779
Ogs Technologies Inc	Cheshire	CT	E	203 271-9055	749
Pattison Sign Group Inc	Bristol	CT	G	860 583-3000	592
Picture This Hartford Inc	East Hartford	CT	G	860 528-1409	1210
Point View Displays LLC	East Haven	CT	G	203 468-0887	1258
Precision Graphics Inc	East Berlin	CT	E	860 828-6561	1106
Prime Resources Corp	Bridgeport	CT	B	203 331-9100	474
Prokop Sign Co	Taftville	CT	G	860 889-6265	4471
Revolution Lighting **(HQ)**	Stamford	CT	G	203 504-1111	4299
Revolution Lighting Tech Inc	Stamford	CT	F	203 504-1111	4301
Revolution Lighting Tech Inc **(PA)**	Stamford	CT	C	203 504-1111	4300
Rising Sign Company Inc	Norwalk	CT	G	203 853-4155	3233
Rokap Inc	Wallingford	CT	G	203 265-6895	4799
S D & D Inc	East Berlin	CT	F	860 357-2603	1107
Semiotics LLC	Manchester	CT	G	860 644-5700	2047
Shiner Signs Inc	Meriden	CT	E	203 634-4331	2130
Siam Valee	Wallingford	CT	G	203 269-6888	4806
Sign A Rama	New London	CT	G	860 443-9744	2780
Sign A Rama	Orange	CT	G	203 795-5450	3384
Sign A Rama	Danbury	CT	G	203 792-4091	992
Sign Connection Inc	Vernon Rockville	CT	G	860 870-8855	4682
Sign Creations	Southport	CT	G	203 259-8330	4098
Sign Factory	Enfield	CT	F	860 763-1085	1384
Sign In Soft Inc	Shelton	CT	G	203 216-3046	3870
Sign Language LLC	Danbury	CT	G	203 778-2250	993
Sign Maintenance Service Co	Bridgeport	CT	G	203 336-1051	489
Sign Pro Inc	Plantsville	CT	F	860 229-1812	3539
Sign Professionals	Norwich	CT	G	860 823-1122	3291
Sign Stop Inc	East Hartford	CT	G	860 721-1411	1220
Sign Wizard	Hartford	CT	G	860 525-7729	1870
Signcenter LLC	Milford	CT	G	800 269-2130	2363
Signcrafters Inc	Stamford	CT	G	203 353-9535	4318
Signs By Anthony Inc	Norwalk	CT	G	203 866-1744	3245
Signs By Autografix	Branford	CT	G	203 481-6502	349
Signs Now LLC	Newington	CT	G	860 667-8339	2903
Signs of All Kinds	Manchester	CT	G	860 649-1989	2048
Signs of Success Inc	Stamford	CT	G	203 329-3374	4319
Signs Plus Inc **(PA)**	East Granby	CT	G	860 653-0547	1144
Signs Plus LLC	Willimantic	CT	G	860 423-3048	5269
Signs Unlimited Inc	Derby	CT	G	203 734-7446	1080

	CITY	ST	EMP	PHONE	ENTRY #
Speedi Sign LLC	Brookfield	CT	G	203 775-0700	658
Tims Sign & Lighting Service	Meriden	CT	G	203 634-8840	2143
United Stts Sgn & Fbrction	Trumbull	CT	E	203 601-1000	4640
US Highway Products Inc	Bridgeport	CT	F	203 336-0332	502
Wad Inc	East Berlin	CT	E	860 828-3331	1110
Wesport Signs	Norwalk	CT	G	203 286-7710	3270
Write Way Signs & Design Inc	Torrington	CT	G	860 482-8893	4609
A S P Enterprises Inc	Newton	MA	G	617 244-2762	13551
Accurate Graphics Inc	Lynn	MA	G	781 593-1630	12488
Ace Signs Inc	Springfield	MA	F	413 739-3814	15440
Acme Sign Corporation	Peabody	MA	G	978 535-6600	14306
Acryline Inc	North Attleboro	MA	E	508 695-0060	13742
Ad-A-Day Company Inc	Taunton	MA	E	508 824-8676	15719
Advanced Signing LLC	Medway	MA	E	508 533-9000	12955
Agnoli Sign Company Inc	Springfield	MA	E	413 732-5111	15443
All American Embroidery Inc	Wilmington	MA	G	978 657-0414	16970
Allmac Signs	Harwich	MA	G	508 430-4174	11387
Apifia Inc **(PA)**	Boston	MA	E	585 506-2787	8368
Apple Mill Holding Company Inc	Pembroke	MA	F	781 826-9706	14392
Architctral Graphics Signs Inc	Watertown	MA	G	617 924-0070	16269
B Luka Signs Inc	Taunton	MA	G	508 822-9022	15731
Back Bay Sign	Wilmington	MA	G	978 203-0570	16978
Back Bay Sign LLC	Wilmington	MA	E	781 475-1001	16979
Back Street Inc	Seekonk	MA	G	508 336-6333	15018
Baker Sign Works Inc	Fall River	MA	F	508 674-6600	10666
Batten Bros Inc	Wakefield	MA	F	781 245-4800	15943
Bay State Associates Inc	Lakeville	MA	E	508 947-6700	11973
Blazing Signworks Inc	Fitchburg	MA	G	800 672-4887	10812
C & D Signs Inc	Tewksbury	MA	E	978 851-2424	15809
Cadwell Products Company Inc	Holliston	MA	F	508 429-3100	11562
Callahan Sign LLC	Pittsfield	MA	G	413 443-5931	14462
Cape Ann Sign Co Inc	Ipswich	MA	G	978 356-0960	11909
Cheyne Awning & Sign Co	Pittsfield	MA	G	413 442-4742	14464
Chucks Sign Co	Chicopee	MA	G	413 592-3710	10012
Clayton LLC	Woburn	MA	E	617 250-8500	17144
Cole Sign Co	Tewksbury	MA	G	978 851-5502	15811
Colonial Brass Company	Taunton	MA	G	508 947-1098	15737
Color Media Group LLC	Boston	MA	F	617 620-0229	8480
Countryside Signs	Seekonk	MA	G	508 761-9530	15020
Creative Signworks	Millbury	MA	G	508 865-7330	13161
Cyr Sign & Banner Company	Medford	MA	G	781 395-7297	12928
Dahl Group	Boxford	MA	G	978 887-2598	8976
Dawns Sign Tech Incorporated	North Andover	MA	G	978 208-0012	13697
Dehaas Advertising & Design	Newburyport	MA	G	978 462-1997	13481
Design Communications Ltd **(PA)**	Avon	MA	D	617 542-9620	7886
Designflow Wraps Inc	Beverly	MA	G	978 729-5415	8126
Dg International Holdings Corp	Needham Heights	MA	G	781 577-2016	13328
Doranco Inc	Attleboro	MA	G	508 236-0290	7727
E A Dion Inc	Attleboro	MA	C	800 445-1007	7730
E V Yeuell Inc	Woburn	MA	E	781 933-2984	17171
East Coast Sign Company	Stoneham	MA	G	781 858-9382	15561
Eastern Etching and Mfg Co	Chicopee	MA	E	413 594-6601	10022
Eratech Inc	Ashfield	MA	F	413 628-3219	7650
Excel Sign & Decoration Corp	Natick	MA	G	617 479-8552	13255
Expansion Opportunities Inc	Northborough	MA	E	508 303-8200	14033
Expose Signs & Graphics Inc	Hopedale	MA	G	508 381-0941	11671
Far Reach Graphics Inc	Needham Heights	MA	G	781 444-4889	13332
Fastsigns of Attleboro	Rehoboth	MA	G	508 699-6699	14749
GAP Promotions LLC	Gloucester	MA	F	978 281-0335	11185
Gemini Sign Company Inc	Marlborough	MA	G	508 485-3343	12760
General Display Inc	Medway	MA	D	508 533-6676	12960
Gloucester Graphics Inc **(PA)**	Gloucester	MA	F	978 281-4500	11188
Grand Image Inc	Hudson	MA	E	888 973-2622	11775
Graphic Impact Signs Inc	Pittsfield	MA	E	413 499-0382	14474
Hamilton Sign & Design Inc	Worcester	MA	G	508 459-9731	17388
Harvey Signs Inc	Methuen	MA	G	978 794-2071	13027
Hassan Woodcarving & Sign Co	Cohasset	MA	G	781 383-6075	10100
Honorcraft LLC	Stoughton	MA	E	781 341-0410	15597
ID Graphics Group Inc	South Easton	MA	E	508 238-8500	15279
Idec	Canton	MA	G	617 527-7878	9742
Innovative Media Group Inc	Weymouth	MA	F	781 335-8773	16892
Insite Sign LLC	Duxbury	MA	G	781 934-5664	10399
Instant Sign Center	Norwood	MA	G	781 278-0150	14163
Intelligent Signage Inc	Longmeadow	MA	G	413 567-8399	12334
J K L Corp	Wilmington	MA	G	978 657-5575	17009
J Masse Sign	Plainville	MA	G	508 695-0534	14523
Jack Knight Co	Hanover	MA	G	781 340-1500	11344
JD Design LLC	Saugus	MA	G	781 941-2066	14989
Jim Haluck	South Easton	MA	G	508 230-8901	15283
Jnj Inc	Framingham	MA	G	508 620-0202	10973
JR Higgins Associates LLC	Acton	MA	E	978 266-1200	7367
Keating Communication Group	Canton	MA	G	781 828-9030	9749
Kiwi Signs & Mar Graphics LLC	Falmouth	MA	G	732 930-4121	10794
Lane Printing Co Inc	Holbrook	MA	F	781 767-4450	11529
Liddell Brothers Inc	Norwell	MA	E	781 293-2100	14106
Lyons Signs Inc	Worcester	MA	G	508.754-2501	17409
Magic Printing Inc	Framingham	MA	G	413 363-1711	10980

	CITY	ST	EMP	PHONE	ENTRY #
Mark Todisco	Stoneham	MA	G	781 438-5280	15567
Mass Sign & Decal Inc	Rockland	MA	G	781 878-7446	14812
Mediavue Systems Inc	Hingham	MA	E	781 926-0676	11502
Merrimack Engraving & Mkg Co	Methuen	MA	G	978 683-5335	13035
Metal Solutions LLC	Millbury	MA	G	774 276-0096	13171
Mike Gath	Tewksbury	MA	G	978 851-4373	15824
Moren Signs Inc	Agawam	MA	G	413 786-0349	7441
Multi Sign Inc	West Springfield	MA	G	413 732-9900	16533
Municipal Graphics Inc	Wrentham	MA	G	508 384-0925	17526
Mystic Scenic Studios Inc	Norwood	MA	D	781 440-0914	14180
New England Sign Group Inc	Worcester	MA	E	508 832-3471	17432
New England Wire Products Inc **(PA)**	Leominster	MA	C	800 254-9473	12171
New England Wooden Ware Corp **(PA)**	Gardner	MA	E	978 632-3600	11122
Newman Enterprises Inc	Framingham	MA	G	508 875-7446	10988
of Cape Cod Incorporated	South Yarmouth	MA	G	508 398-9100	15332
Owl Stamp Company Inc	Lowell	MA	G	978 452-4541	12418
P&G Graphic Solutions Inc	Springfield	MA	G	413 731-9213	15497
Paint Town Inc	Palmer	MA	G	413 283-2245	14290
Paulson Electric	Watertown	MA	G	617 926-5661	16305
Philadelphia Sign Co	Littleton	MA	F	978 486-0137	12318
Pilgrim Badge & Label Corp	Brockton	MA	D	508 436-6300	9171
Plymouth Sign Co Inc	South Yarmouth	MA	G	508 398-2721	15333
Poyant Signs Inc **(PA)**	New Bedford	MA	E	800 544-0961	13442
Pretorius Electric	West Bridgewater	MA	G	508 326-9492	16450
Quick Print Ltd Inc	Chelmsford	MA	G	978 256-1822	9924
Raven Creative Inc	Marblehead	MA	G	781 476-5529	12691
Ready 2 Run Graphics Signs Inc	Worcester	MA	G	508 459-9977	17453
Recognition Center Inc	Holliston	MA	G	508 429-5881	11598
Redi-Letters Express LLC	Worcester	MA	G	508 340-3284	17455
Reeves Coinc	Attleboro	MA	E	508 222-2877	7785
Reid Graphics Inc	Andover	MA	D	978 474-1930	7598
Rustic Marlin Designs LLC	Hanover	MA	E	508 376-1004	11350
Scg Signs	Plainville	MA	G	781 297-9400	14534
Sepinuck Sign Co Inc	Braintree	MA	G	781 849-1181	9036
Serrato Sign Co	Worcester	MA	G	508 756-7004	17472
Sew What Embroidery	Dalton	MA	G	413 684-0672	10184
Sign A Rama	Raynham	MA	G	508 822-7533	14730
Sign Art Inc	Malden	MA	F	781 322-3785	12596
Sign Company	Dennis Port	MA	E	508 760-5400	10314
Sign Design Inc	Brockton	MA	D	508 580-0094	9175
Sign Effects Inc	North Billerica	MA	G	978 663-0787	13864
Sign Post LLC	Roslindale	MA	G	617 469-4400	14843
Sign Shop Inc	Westfield	MA	G	413 562-1876	16730
Sign System Solutions LLC	Hopkinton	MA	F	508 497-6340	11735
Sign Techniques Inc	Chicopee	MA	F	413 594-8240	10060
Sign-A-Rama	Danvers	MA	G	978 774-0936	10257
Signature Signs	Dartmouth	MA	G	508 993-8511	10277
Signs & Sites Inc	Seekonk	MA	G	508 336-5858	15037
Signs By CAM Inc	Franklin	MA	G	508 528-0766	11080
Signs By Doug	Salisbury	MA	G	978 463-2222	14956
Signs By J Inc	Boston	MA	G	617 825-9855	8845
Signs By Russ Inc	Brockton	MA	G	508 580-2221	9176
Signs Plus	Milford	MA	G	508 478-5077	13144
Signs Solutions Unlimited	Reading	MA	G	781 942-0111	14743
Signs To Go Inc	Woburn	MA	G	781 938-7700	17296
Signworks Group Inc	Watertown	MA	F	617 924-0292	16316
Silver Screen Design Inc	Greenfield	MA	F	413 773-1692	11275
South Shore Signs	Marshfield	MA	G	781 834-1120	12868
Speedy Sign-A-Rama USA	Braintree	MA	G	781 849-1181	9038
SRP Signs	Somerville	MA	G	617 623-6222	15220
Strong Group Inc **(PA)**	Gloucester	MA	E	978 281-3300	11212
Sunrise Systems Elec Co Inc **(PA)**	Pembroke	MA	G	781 826-9706	14428
Sunshine Sign Company Inc	North Grafton	MA	C	508 839-5588	13965
Tim Gratuski	Leominster	MA	G	978 466-9000	12195
Titus & Bean Graphics Inc	Kingston	MA	F	781 585-1355	11965
United Sign Co Inc	Beverly	MA	G	978 927-9346	8193
Vacca Sign Service Inc	Newton	MA	G	617 332-3111	13646
Vinyl Approach	Paxton	MA	G	508 755-5279	14303
Visimark Inc	Auburn	MA	F	508 832-3471	7851
Vital Signs	Newton	MA	G	617 645-3946	13651
W S Sign Design Corp	Springfield	MA	G	413 241-6916	15522
Whitney Vgas Archctural Pdts	Needham	MA	G	781 449-1351	13317
William Crosby	Concord	MA	G	978 371-1111	10162
Affordable Exhibit Displays	Auburn	ME	G	207 782-6175	5548
Affordable Exhibit Displays	Auburn	ME	G	207 782-6175	5547
All Kinds of Signs LLC	Wells	ME	G	978 531-7100	7159
Amb Signs Inc **(PA)**	Dover Foxcroft	ME	G	207 564-3633	5959
American Nameplate	Brewer	ME	G	207 848-7187	5793
American Nameplate **(PA)**	Hermon	ME	G	207 848-7187	6182
Bailey Sign Inc	Westbrook	ME	E	207 774-2843	7181
Banana Banners	Bowdoinham	ME	G	207 666-3951	5788
Bangor Neon Inc	Bangor	ME	F	207 947-2766	5631
Banner Source	Yarmouth	ME	G	207 846-0915	7292
Bishop Crown Co	Winslow	ME	G	207 873-2350	7268
Blackbear Signworks Inc	Saco	ME	G	207 286-8004	6844
Caron Signs Co Inc	Hermon	ME	G	207 848-7889	6184
Carrot Signs	Brunswick	ME	G	207 725-0769	5834

	CITY	ST	EMP	PHONE	ENTRY #
Finyl Vinyl	Pittsfield	ME	G	207 487-2753	6590
Glidden Signs Inc	Scarborough	ME	F	207 396-6111	6919
Graphix Design	Old Town	ME	G	207 827-4412	6540
Leon Merchant Signs **(PA)**	Caribou	ME	G	207 498-2475	5885
Lynne Bailey	York	ME	G	207 363-7999	7310
Minuteman Sign Centers	Belfast	ME	G	207 338-2299	5694
Minuteman Sign Centers Inc **(PA)**	Augusta	ME	G	207 622-4171	5615
Neokraft Signs Inc	Lewiston	ME	E	207 782-9654	6310
Northern Signs	Fairfield	ME	G	207 465-2399	6028
Pattison Sign Group (ne) Inc	Limestone	ME	A	514 856-7756	6343
Plastics Supply of Maine Inc	Biddeford	ME	G	207 775-7778	5755
R S D Graphics Inc	East Waterboro	ME	G	207 247-6430	5986
Rising Revolution Studio LLC	Shapleigh	ME	G	207 636-7136	6959
Scott Stanton	Acton	ME	G	207 477-2956	5509
Sign Concepts	Portland	ME	F	207 699-2920	6727
Sign Design Inc	Portland	ME	F	207 856-2600	6728
Sign Guy Inc	Windham	ME	G	207 892-5851	7252
Sign Services Inc	Stetson	ME	F	207 296-2400	7066
Sign Systems of Maine Inc	Portland	ME	G	207 775-7110	6729
Signarama Saco	Saco	ME	G	207 494-8085	6858
Signs By MO	South Berwick	ME	G	207 384-2363	7004
Signworks Inc	Farmington	ME	G	207 778-3822	6053
Ssw Inc	Limington	ME	G	207 793-4440	6349
T R Sign Design Inc	Portland	ME	F	207 856-2600	6736
Yorks Signs	Skowhegan	ME	G	207 474-9331	6988
Advantage Signs Inc	Concord	NH	G	603 224-7446	17881
Albrite Signs LLC	Gorham	NH	G	603 466-5192	18210
All Signs Steve Main	Hillsboro	NH	G	603 464-5455	18312
Anco Signs & Stamps Inc	Manchester	NH	G	603 669-3779	18779
Assured Computing Technologies	Bedford	NH	G	603 627-8728	17631
Barlo Signs International Inc	Hudson	NH	D	603 880-8949	18377
Big Daddys Signs Florida Inc	Laconia	NH	G	800 535-2139	18558
Classic Signs Inc	Amherst	NH	F	603 883-0384	17555
Courrier Graphics Inc	Manchester	NH	G	603 626-7012	18808
Dales Paint n Place Inc	Newport	NH	G	603 863-5050	19344
Fast Signs	Salem	NH	G	603 894-7446	19731
Fastrax Signs	Stratham	NH	G	603 778-4799	19868
Fastrax Signs Inc	Brentwood	NH	G	603 775-7500	17749
First Sign & Corporate Image	Manchester	NH	G	603 627-0003	18822
Gemini Signs & Design Ltd	Conway	NH	G	603 447-3336	17952
Granite State Stamps Inc	Manchester	NH	F	603 669-9322	18829
Indaba Holdings Corp	Auburn	NH	F	603 437-1200	17611
Ink Outside Box Incorporated	Pelham	NH	G	603 635-2292	19435
J H Dunning Corporation	North Walpole	NH	E	603 445-5591	19394
Jutras Signs Inc	Bedford	NH	E	603 622-2344	17648
Loudon Screen Printing Inc	Epsom	NH	G	603 736-9420	18106
Maineline Graphics LLC	Antrim	NH	G	603 588-3177	17596
Marvel Signs & Designs LLC	Thornton	NH	G	603 726-4111	19901
Neopa Signs	Swanzey	NH	G	603 352-3305	19887
New England Signs & Awngs LLC	Hudson	NH	G	603 235-7205	18420
Northroad Wood Signs	Temple	NH	G	603 924-9330	19898
Oakridge Sign and Graphics LLC	New Ipswich	NH	G	603 878-1183	19308
Omni Signs LLC	Meredith	NH	G	603 279-1492	18976
Portsmouth Sign Company	Newington	NH	G	603 436-0047	19324
Powerplay Management LLC	Portsmouth	NH	E	603 436-3030	19609
Precision Letter Corporation	Manchester	NH	F	603 625-9625	18904
Sign Gallery	Hooksett	NH	G	603 622-7212	18360
Signs Happen Inc	Concord	NH	G	603 225-4081	17929
Sundance Sign & Design	Dover	NH	G	603 742-1517	18055
Valley Signs	Lebanon	NH	G	603 252-1977	18640
Yesco Sign and Ltg Concord	Tilton	NH	G	603 238-6988	19913
Zax Signage Corp	Greenland	NH	G	603 319-6178	18225
Accent Display Corp	Cranston	RI	E	401 461-8787	20171
Ahlers Designs Inc	Pawtucket	RI	G	401 365-1010	20811
Allmark International Inc	Smithfield	RI	G	401 232-7080	21208
B Sign Graphics Inc	Cranston	RI	G	401 943-6941	20187
Dasko Identification Products	East Providence	RI	F	401 435-6500	20403
Dexter Enterprises Corp	East Providence	RI	G	401 434-2300	20404
Dexter Sign Co	East Providence	RI	E	401 434-1100	20406
Elliott Sales Group Inc	Providence	RI	D	401 944-0002	21005
Fine Designs Inc	North Kingstown	RI	G	401 886-5000	20710
Finish Line Signs	Ashaway	RI	G	401 377-8454	20034
Gepp LLC	Warwick	RI	F	401 808-8004	21367
Hub-Federal Inc	Providence	RI	F	401 421-3400	21032
Hutchison Company Inc	North Kingstown	RI	F	401 294-3503	20717
Island Reflections Corporation	Narragansett	RI	G	401 782-2744	20641
Josef Creations Inc **(PA)**	Chepachet	RI	E	401 421-4198	20135
Mandeville Signs Inc	Lincoln	RI	E	401 334-9100	20581
Mastercast Ltd	Pawtucket	RI	F	401 726-3100	20858
Myriad Inc	Providence	RI	G	401 855-2000	21074
National Marker Company	North Smithfield	RI	D	401 762-9700	20792
Orion Ret Svcs & Fixturing Inc	Smithfield	RI	D	401 334-5000	21243
Progressive Displays Inc	Warren	RI	E	401 245-2909	21303
Resources Unlimited Inc	Cranston	RI	F	401 369-7329	20278
Riverview Signs & Graphics	Westerly	RI	G	401 596-7889	21537
Safe Guard Signs	Pawtucket	RI	E	401 725-9090	20894
Salute Spirits LLC	Newport	RI	G	609 306-2258	20678

S I C

	CITY	ST	EMP	PHONE	ENTRY #
Schofield Printing Inc	Pawtucket	RI	E	401 728-6980	20898
Scope Display & Box Co Inc **(PA)**	Cranston	RI	D	401 942-7150	20284
Traffic Signs & Safety Inc	Bristol	RI	G	401 396-9840	20106
Anything Printed LLC	Woodstock	VT	G	802 457-3414	22735
Artistic Woodworks Inc	Rochester	VT	G	802 767-3123	22316
Awesome Graphics Inc	Rutland	VT	G	802 773-6143	22324
Design Signs Inc	Essex Junction	VT	G	802 872-9906	21939
Dexter Products Inc	Swanton	VT	G	802 868-7085	22530
Diaco Communication Inc	South Burlington	VT	G	802 863-6233	22446
Great Big Graphics Inc **(PA)**	Morrisville	VT	G	802 888-5515	22167
Green Mountain Recognition	Rutland	VT	G	802 775-7063	22337
Gvh Studio Inc	Bennington	VT	G	802 379-1135	21671
Kerins Sign Service	Montpelier	VT	F	802 223-0357	22151
Letter Barn	Springfield	VT	G	802 885-5451	22505
R & W Gibson Corp	South Burlington	VT	G	802 864-4791	22463
Rule Signs	Randolph	VT	G	802 728-6030	22302
Sammel Sign Company	Essex Junction	VT	G	802 879-3360	21958
Sara Sassy Inc	South Burlington	VT	G	802 864-4791	22464
Sb Signs Inc	Williston	VT	G	802 879-7969	22690
Twin State Signs Inc	Essex Junction	VT	G	802 872-8949	21962
Wood & Wood Inc	Waitsfield	VT	G	802 496-3000	22572

3995 Burial Caskets

	CITY	ST	EMP	PHONE	ENTRY #
Dignified Endings LLC	East Hartford	CT	D	860 291-0575	1187
Cambium Corp	Athol	MA	F	978 249-7557	7685
Florence Casket Company	Florence	MA	D	413 584-4244	10866
Colony Casket Inc	Providence	RI	G	401 831-7100	20987

3996 Linoleum & Hard Surface Floor Coverings, NEC

	CITY	ST	EMP	PHONE	ENTRY #
Conformis Inc	Wallingford	CT	G	203 793-7178	4724
Industrial Floor Covering Inc	North Billerica	MA	G	978 362-8655	13826
Hampshire Hardwoods LLC	Laconia	NH	G	603 434-1144	18565
Natco Products Corporation **(PA)**	West Warwick	RI	B	401 828-0300	21504

3999 Manufacturing Industries, NEC

	CITY	ST	EMP	PHONE	ENTRY #
210 Innovations	Groton	CT	G	860 445-0210	1664
283 Industries Inc	Ridgefield	CT	G	203 276-8956	3653
A L C Inovators Inc	Milford	CT	G	203 877-8526	2232
Ace Beauty Supply Inc	Branford	CT	G	203 488-2416	284
Acme United Corporation **(PA)**	Fairfield	CT	C	203 254-6060	1412
Additive Experts LLC	New Britain	CT	G	860 351-3324	2505
Advanced Specialist LLC	Watertown	CT	G	860 945-9125	4997
Aero Precision Mfg LLC	Wallingford	CT	G	203 675-7625	4694
Alpine Management Group LLC	Westport	CT	G	954 531-1692	5180
American Hydrogen Northeast	Bridgeport	CT	E	203 449-4614	373
Ann S Davis	Lebanon	CT	F	860 642-7228	1932
Apiject Systems Corp **(PA)**	Stamford	CT	G	203 461-7121	4141
Atech Industries LLC	Orange	CT	G	203 887-4900	3359
Barrette Mechanical	Brooklyn	CT	G	860 774-0499	670
Bic Corporation **(HQ)**	Shelton	CT	A	203 783-2000	3782
Bic USA Inc **(DH)**	Shelton	CT	C	203 783-2000	3783
Biological Industries	Cromwell	CT	G	860 316-5197	848
Blackbird Manufacturing and De	Coventry	CT	G	860 331-3477	831
Bridgeport Proc & Mfg LLC	Bridgeport	CT	G	203 612-7733	389
Cad/CAM Dntl Stdio Mil Ctr Inc	Newtown	CT	G	203 733-3069	2917
Cardinal Shehan Center Inc	Bridgeport	CT	E	203 336-4468	395
Case Patterns Inc	Groton	CT	G	860 445-6722	1665
CCI Cyrus River Terminal LLC	Stamford	CT	G	203 761-8000	4159
Classic Tool & Mfg LLC	Waterbury	CT	G	203 755-6313	4858
Components For Mfg LLC **(PA)**	Mystic	CT	G	860 245-5326	2437
Components For Mfg LLC	Groton	CT	G	860 572-1671	1668
Conair Corporation **(PA)**	Stamford	CT	B	203 351-9000	4171
Connecticut Components Inc	Tolland	CT	G	860 633-0277	4541
Connecticut Metal Industries	Ansonia	CT	G	203 736-0790	11
Crystal Journey Candles LLC	Branford	CT	E	203 433-4735	307
Customized Foods Mfg LLC	Waterbury	CT	G	203 759-1645	4862
Cyro Industries	Orange	CT	G	203 269-4481	3363
Delcon Industries	Trumbull	CT	G	203 371-5711	4622
Delcon Industries LLC	Bridgeport	CT	G	203 331-9720	403
Delta-Source LLC	West Hartford	CT	F	860 461-1600	5065
Diversified Manufact	Ansonia	CT	G	203 734-0379	13
East Coast Precision Mfg	Chester	CT	G	860 322-4624	771
Ellis Manufacturing LLC	Plainville	CT	G	865 518-0531	3485
Ensign Bickford Industries	Simsbury	CT	F	203 843-2126	3901
Eyelash Extensions and More	West Hartford	CT	F	860 951-9355	5071
Fire Prevention Services	Norwalk	CT	F	203 866-6357	3152
Formatron Ltd	Farmington	CT	F	860 676-0227	1482
Four Twenty Industries LLC	Berlin	CT	G	860 818-3334	85
Fx Models LLC	Terryville	CT	G	860 589-5279	4480
G A Industries	Bristol	CT	G	860 261-5484	566
Garbeck Airflow Industries	Middletown	CT	G	860 301-5032	2186
Global Scenic Services Inc	Bridgeport	CT	E	203 334-2130	420
Go Green Industries LLC	New Milford	CT	G	914 772-0026	2801
Grohe Manufacturing	Ansonia	CT	G	203 516-5536	17
Gutkin Enterprises LLC	Hamden	CT	G	203 777-5510	1752
Hamden Grinding	Hamden	CT	G	203 288-2906	1753
Hannes Precision Industry Inc	Norwalk	CT	F	203 853-7276	3166
Hpi Manufacturing Inc	Hamden	CT	G	203 777-5395	1760
Hydro-Flex Inc	Stratford	CT	G	203 269-5599	4421
Isaac Industries	Danbury	CT	G	203 778-3239	935
J&P Mfg LLC	Plainville	CT	G	860 747-4790	3499
Jenray Products Inc	Brookfield	CT	E	914 375-5596	648
Jfs Industries	Thomaston	CT	G	203 592-0754	4506
JS Industries	Thompson	CT	G	860 928-0786	4534
K and R Precision Grinding	New Britain	CT	G	860 505-8030	2547
K F Machining	East Windsor	CT	G	860 292-6466	1289
Kent Billings LLC	Glastonbury	CT	G	860 659-1104	1561
Leisure Learning Products Inc	Stamford	CT	F	203 325-2800	4237
M P Robinson Production	Redding	CT	E	203 938-1336	3650
Manufacturing Productivi	Windsor	CT	G	860 916-8189	5346
Martin Mfg Services LLC	Killingworth	CT	G	860 663-1465	1927
MLS Acq Inc	East Windsor	CT	F	860 386-6878	1296
Modelvision Inc	New Milford	CT	G	860 355-3884	2814
Motive Industries LLC	North Windham	CT	G	860 423-2064	3083
Nano Pet Products LLC	Norwalk	CT	G	203 345-1330	3203
Norfolk Industries LLC	Greenwich	CT	G	860 618-8822	1635
Northeast Wood Products LLC	Uncasville	CT	E	860 862-6350	4647
O & G Industries Inc	Harwinton	CT	C	860 485-6600	1891
O & G Industries Inc	Beacon Falls	CT	C	203 881-5192	63
Oak Tree Moulding LLC	Woodstock	CT	G	860 455-3056	5499
Picture This Hartford Inc	East Hartford	CT	G	860 528-1409	1210
Pleasant Valley Fence Co Inc	Pleasant Valley	CT	F	860 379-0088	3546
Precision Express Mfg LLC	Bristol	CT	F	860 584-2627	597
Qds LLC	Shelton	CT	G	203 338-9668	3865
Raymond J Bykowski	Cheshire	CT	G	203 271-2385	758
Readydock Inc	Avon	CT	G	860 523-9980	44
Rlp Inc	Stamford	CT	G	203 359-2504	4303
Robert Audette **(PA)**	Cheshire	CT	G	203 872-3119	760
Rome Fastener Corporation	Milford	CT	E	203 874-6719	2354
RR Design	Bethel	CT	G	203 792-3419	176
Sadlak Manufacturing LLC	Coventry	CT	E	860 742-0227	839
Show Motion Inc	Milford	CT	E	203 866-1866	2362
Simkins Industries	East Haven	CT	G	203 787-7171	1262
Solidification Pdts Intl Inc	Northford	CT	G	203 484-9494	3092
Spv Industries LLC	West Hartford	CT	G	860 953-5928	5096
Tag Promotions Inc	Monroe	CT	G	800 909-4011	2417
Thermospas Hot Tub Products	Wallingford	CT	E	203 303-0005	4817
Thomas S Klise Co	Mystic	CT	G	860 536-4200	2453
Thomaston Industries Inc	Thomaston	CT	F	860 283-4358	4521
Three Kings Products LLC	Watertown	CT	G	860 945-5294	5028
Tjl Industries LLC	Cheshire	CT	G	203 250-2187	766
UST LLC **(HQ)**	Stamford	CT	G	203 817-3000	4355
Valore Inc	Norwalk	CT	G	203 854-4799	3264
Wmb Industries LLC	North Haven	CT	G	203 927-2822	3069
3d Educational Services Inc	Chelmsford	MA	G	978 364-2728	9864
99degrees Custom Inc	Lawrence	MA	G	978 655-3362	11988
Accurate Composites LLC	East Falmouth	MA	D	508 457-9097	10433
ACS Auxiliaries Group Inc	Attleboro	MA	G	508 399-3018	7700
Acushnet Mfg Hom	Acushnet	MA	G	508 763-2074	7398
Advanced CAM Manufacturing LLC	Hudson	MA	G	978 562-2825	11752
Advanced Electronic Technology	Ayer	MA	G	978 846-6487	7905
Ait Manufacturing LLC	Lawrence	MA	G	978 655-7257	11991
Alpha Fierce LLC	Merrimac	MA	G	781 518-3311	12999
Alpha Tech Pet Inc	Littleton	MA	F	978 486-3690	12291
Anthony Industries Inc	Woburn	MA	G	781 305-3750	17119
Apothecary Products LLC	North Attleboro	MA	E	508 695-0727	13745
Architectural Illusions	Boston	MA	G	617 338-8118	8374
Asian Art Society New England	Sherborn	MA	G	781 250-6311	15077
Atlantic Industrial Models LLC	Essex	MA	E	978 768-7686	10591
Ats Finishing Inc	North Andover	MA	G	978 975-0957	13692
B & B Mfg Co	Provincetown	MA	G	508 487-0858	14607
Barber Walters Industries LLC	Wellesley	MA	G	781 241-5433	16363
Battalion Co Inc **(PA)**	Lowell	MA	G	978 453-2824	12352
Blanche P Field LLC	Boston	MA	E	617 423-0714	8413
Callenstitch LLC	Concord	MA	E	978 369-9080	10120
Cape Cod Dog	Eastham	MA	G	508 255-4206	10548
Cara Armour	Waltham	MA	G	781 899-7297	16060
Cartamundi East Longmeadow LLC	East Longmeadow	MA	B	413 526-2000	10469
Champagne Tables & Pet Pdts	Southampton	MA	G	413 527-4370	15337
Christmas Studio	Monson	MA	G	413 267-3342	13203
CIM Industries Inc	Bridgewater	MA	G	800 543-3458	9067
Colton Hollow Candle Company	Monson	MA	G	413 267-3986	13205
Compound Manufacturing LLC	Greenfield	MA	G	413 773-8909	11258
Constant Velocity Mfg LLC	Spencer	MA	G	508 735-3399	15427
Cory Manufacturing Inc	West Bridgewater	MA	G	508 680-2111	16435
Cotuit Works	Cotuit	MA	G	508 428-3971	10169
Country Candle Co Inc **(PA)**	Millbury	MA	E	508 865-6061	13160
Createk-Stone Inc	Southbridge	MA	G	888 786-6389	15378
Creative Strands	Sutton	MA	G	508 865-1141	15681
Crow Haven Corner Inc	Salem	MA	G	978 745-8763	14904
Currys Leather Shop Inc	Randolph	MA	F	781 963-0679	14675
Custom Learning Designs Inc	Belmont	MA	D	617 489-1702	8071
David W Wallace	Shelburne Falls	MA	G	413 625-6523	15067
Davis Precision Mfg LLC	Lawrence	MA	G	978 794-0042	12015

	CITY	ST	EMP	PHONE	ENTRY #
Diamondhead USA Inc	West Springfield	MA	G	413 537-4806	16516
E R S Resources	Worcester	MA	G	508 421-3434	17368
East Coast Silks Inc	Chelmsford	MA	G	978 970-5510	9895
Elite Sem Inc	Medfield	MA	G	508 955-0414	12914
EMD Millipore Corporation **(DH)**	Burlington	MA	A	781 533-6000	9262
Envirocare Corporation **(PA)**	North Andover	MA	G	978 658-0123	13702
Farm Table At Kringle Candle	Bernardston	MA	G	413 648-5200	8093
Fire Defenses New England LLC	Danvers	MA	F	978 304-1506	10217
Fire-1 Manufacturing Inc	Mendon	MA	G	508 478-8473	12993
Four Lggers Doggie Daycare LLC	Beverly	MA	G	978 922-4182	8132
Freestyle Systems LLC	Shrewsbury	MA	G	508 845-4911	15113
G F L Industries	Leominster	MA	G	978 728-4800	12142
G H Allen Associates Inc	Ayer	MA	G	978 772-4010	7920
George Guertin Trophy Inc	Auburn	MA	G	508 832-4001	7836
Go Green Industries Inc	Westford	MA	G	978 496-1881	16769
Go Green Mfg Inc	Gardner	MA	G	978 928-4333	11118
Hartnett Co Inc	Woburn	MA	F	781 935-2600	17196
Harvard Double Reeds	Harvard	MA	G	978 772-1898	11376
Hci Cleaning Products LLC	Burlington	MA	G	508 864-5510	9281
Hedge Hog Industries	Springfield	MA	G	413 363-2528	15475
Hemenway & Associates	West Boylston	MA	G	508 835-2859	16417
Hex	Salem	MA	G	978 666-0765	14920
Highland Labs Inc	Holliston	MA	E	508 429-2918	11577
Hmh Religious Mfg Inc	Plainville	MA	F	508 699-9464	14522
Houghton Mifflin Harcourt Co **(PA)**	Boston	MA	B	617 351-5000	8606
Hydro-Test Products Inc	Stow	MA	F	978 897-4647	15632
Inspeedcom LLC	Sudbury	MA	G	978 397-6813	15660
International Light Tech Inc	Peabody	MA	E	978 818-6180	14343
Inverness Corporation **(DH)**	Attleboro	MA	E	774 203-1130	7752
J & J Music Boxes Inc	Pepperell	MA	F	978 433-5686	14439
Jab Industries Inc	Attleboro	MA	G	401 447-9668	7753
Keith Industrial Group Inc	Clinton	MA	G	978 365-5555	10082
King Gt Inc	Canton	MA	G	781 562-1554	9751
Kodiak Industries LLC	Billerica	MA	G	617 839-1298	8261
Lavoie Industries Llc	Fall River	MA	G	508 542-1062	10722
LS Starrett Company **(PA)**	Athol	MA	A	978 249-3551	7689
Luv Manufacturing	Malden	MA	G	857 277-3573	12578
Lzj Holdings Inc	Andover	MA	G	978 409-1091	7566
Magpie Industries LLC	Somerville	MA	G	617 623-3330	15193
Manomet Manufacturing Inc	New Bedford	MA	G	508 997-1795	13415
Mass Logic Inc	Boxboro	MA	G	978 635-1917	8953
Mbm Building Systems Ltd	Boston	MA	F	617 478-3466	8690
McF Electronic Services Inc	Lowell	MA	G	603 718-2256	12406
McNeilly Ems Educators Inc	Danvers	MA	G	978 375-7373	10236
Megatech Corporation	Tewksbury	MA	F	978 937-9600	15822
Milani Industries Inc	Stoughton	MA	G	781 344-3377	15608
Mole Hollow Candles Limited	Worcester	MA	E	508 756-7415	17423
Mooneytunco Inc	Weymouth	MA	G	781 331-4445	16894
MS Industries Inc	Lunenburg	MA	G	978 582-1492	12482
Mystic Industries Corp	Wakefield	MA	F	781 245-1950	15962
Mystic Scenic Studios Inc	Norwood	MA	D	781 440-0914	14180
National Fiber Technology LLC	Lawrence	MA	G	978 686-2964	12062
Neo Green Technology Corp	Woburn	MA	G	617 500-7103	17239
Nixon Company Inc	Indian Orchard	MA	E	413 543-3701	11890
Northeast Stamp & Engraving	Milford	MA	G	508 473-5818	13132
NV Candles LLC	Auburn	MA	G	774 234-6895	7846
Olimpia Industries Incorporate	Bellingham	MA	G	508 966-3392	8054
Partylite Inc **(HQ)**	Plymouth	MA	D	203 661-1926	14572
Partylite Worldwide LLC **(DH)**	Norwell	MA	C	888 999-5706	14110
Pawsitively Yummy	Tyngsboro	MA	G	603 889-3181	15898
PEI Realty Trust	Milford	MA	E	508 478-2025	13136
Pha Industries Inc	Orange	MA	F	978 544-8770	14222
Pilgrim Candle Company Inc **(PA)**	Westfield	MA	E	413 562-2635	16715
Prysm Inc	Concord	MA	E	408 586-1100	10152
R T Clark Manufacturing Inc	Clinton	MA	G	800 921-4330	10092
Red Hawk Fire & Security LLC	Holyoke	MA	G	413 568-4709	11650
Salon Monet	Boston	MA	G	617 425-0010	8836
Sandler & Sons Co	Medway	MA	G	508 533-8282	12970
Scharn Industries	Woburn	MA	F	781 376-9777	17289
Sheffield Pottery Inc	Sheffield	MA	E	413 229-7700	15065
Sjogren Industries Inc	Worcester	MA	F	508 987-3206	17474
Small Corp	Greenfield	MA	G	413 772-0889	11276
Std Manufacturing Inc	Stoughton	MA	G	781 828-4400	15623
Stilisti	Boston	MA	G	617 262-2234	8867
Stoney Industries Inc	Shrewsbury	MA	G	508 845-6731	15133
Stran & Company Inc **(PA)**	Quincy	MA	E	617 822-6950	14660
Swiss Ace Manufacturing Inc	Leominster	MA	G	978 860-3199	12191
Syratech Acquisition Corp **(HQ)**	Medford	MA	C	781 539-0100	12949
T J Holmes Co Inc	Chartley	MA	E	508 222-1723	9858
Thought Industries Inc	Boston	MA	G	617 669-7725	8884
Three Fays Power LLC	Ware	MA	G	413 427-2665	16238
Townie Frozen Desserts LLC	Hull	MA	G	781 925-6095	11831
Tyco International MGT Co LLC	Mansfield	MA	G	508 261-6200	12667
Unruly Studios Inc	Boston	MA	G	857 327-5080	8901
Uppermark LLC	Brookline	MA	G	413 303-9653	9224
US Standard Brands Inc	Walpole	MA	G	617 719-8796	16016
Validity Inc	Boxboro	MA	F	978 635-3400	8955
Vector 5 Collaborative LLC	Lunenburg	MA	G	978 348-2997	12485
Wendi C Smith	Yarmouth Port	MA	F	508 362-4595	17533
Whiffletree Cntry Str Gift Sp	Billerica	MA	G	978 663-6346	8309
Yankee Candle Company Inc **(DH)**	South Deerfield	MA	C	413 665-8306	15260
Yankee Candle Investments LLC **(DH)**	South Deerfield	MA	G	413 665-8306	15261
Yankee Holding Corp **(DH)**	South Deerfield	MA	G	413 665-8306	15262
Ycc Holdings LLC	South Deerfield	MA	A	413 665-8306	15263
Ymittos Candle Mfg Co	Lowell	MA	G	978 453-2824	12450
Zycal Bioceuticals Mfg LLC	Shrewsbury	MA	E	888 779-9225	15139
Affordable Exhibit Displays	Auburn	ME	G	207 782-6175	5547
Barringer Industries LLC	Scarborough	ME	G	207 730-7125	6908
Cellblock Fcs LLC	Standish	ME	F	603 276-5785	7061
Christmas Cove Designs Inc	Dresden	ME	G	207 350-1035	5965
Dakins Miniatures Inc **(PA)**	Searsport	ME	G	207 548-6084	6949
Danica Design Inc **(PA)**	Rockport	ME	G	207 236-3060	6819
Fetch Inc	Portland	ME	G	207 773-5450	6662
Gardner Chipmills Millinocket	Chester	ME	F	207 794-2223	5905
Gerrish Global Industries LLC	Naples	ME	G	207 595-2150	6460
Hope Association **(PA)**	Rumford	ME	D	207 364-4561	6835
Initial This Inc	Veazie	ME	G	207 992-7176	7127
Lie-Nielsen Toolworks Inc	Warren	ME	D	800 327-2520	7144
Lockwood Mfg Inc	Presque Isle	ME	F	207 764-4196	6760
Maine Cedar Hot Tubs Inc	Madison	ME	G	207 474-0953	6406
Maine Made Stuffcom	Lexington Twp	ME	G	207 628-3160	6329
Marca Manufacturing LLC	Gorham	ME	F	207 854-8471	6120
Moore-Clark USA Inc	Westbrook	ME	F	207 591-7077	7198
New Gen Industries	Cumberland Center	ME	G	207 400-1928	5930
Pams Wreaths	Harpswell	ME	G	207 751-7234	6174
Pike Industries Inc	Dover Foxcroft	ME	G	207 564-8444	5963
Planet Ventures Inc **(PA)**	Westbrook	ME	E	207 761-1515	7203
RFI Industries	Dexter	ME	G	443 255-8767	5956
Richard Fisher	Prospect Harbor	ME	G	207 963-7184	6771
Sea Point Chandlers LLC	Kittery Point	ME	G	207 703-2395	6261
Two Rivers Pet Products Inc	Turner	ME	E	207 225-3965	7112
Ultimate Industries	Kennebunkport	ME	G	617 923-1568	6248
Village Candle Inc	Wells	ME	C	207 251-4800	7168
Whitney Originals Inc	Whitneyville	ME	D	207 255-3392	7222
Alene Candles LLC **(PA)**	Milford	NH	C	603 673-5050	19046
Armstrong Industries Inc	Amherst	NH	G	715 629-1632	17551
Auto-Lock Broadhead Co LLC	Raymond	NH	G	603 895-0502	19634
Bryant Group Inc	Contoocook	NH	F	603 746-1166	17941
D D Bean & Sons Co **(PA)**	Jaffrey	NH	D	603 532-8311	18459
Endur Id Inc	Hampton	NH	G	603 758-1488	18262
Enviromart Industries Inc	Plaistow	NH	G	603 378-0154	19513
Ewe Kids Inc	Candia	NH	G	603 483-0984	17783
G&R Industries Inc	Goffstown	NH	G	603 626-3071	18202
Garaventa U S A Inc	Manchester	NH	G	603 669-6553	18824
GKN Aerospace New England Inc	Charlestown	NH	D	603 542-5135	17814
Hannan Technologies LLC	Danbury	NH	G	603 768-5656	17964
Happy House Amusement Inc	Goffstown	NH	E	603 497-4151	18203
Hlf Industries	Sandown	NH	G	603 303-2425	19785
Houghton Mifflin Harcourt Co	Portsmouth	NH	G	630 467-7000	19576
Huntley Benard Industries Inc	Nashua	NH	G	603 943-7813	19180
Image Factory LLC	Raymond	NH	G	603 895-3024	19639
Imed Mfg	Hampstead	NH	G	603 489-5184	18240
Ingu LLC	Portsmouth	NH	F	603 770-5969	19579
Integrity Laser Inc	Nashua	NH	G	603 930-1413	19189
Jab Manufacturing LLC	Salem	NH	G	603 328-8113	19743
Jim Carr Inc	Pelham	NH	G	603 635-2821	19437
Kevin S Boghigian	Nashua	NH	G	603 883-0236	19194
Key Industries	New Ipswich	NH	G	603 369-9634	19306
Keyspin Manufacturing	Merrimack	NH	G	603 420-8508	19009
Lupine Inc	Center Conway	NH	D	603 356-7371	17801
Marklin Candle Design LLC	Contoocook	NH	F	603 746-2211	17946
Mobilerobots Inc	Amherst	NH	E	603 881-7960	17576
Omni Components Corp **(PA)**	Hudson	NH	D	603 882-4467	18422
Porter Manufacturing	New Ipswich	NH	G	603 303-6846	19310
Ricor Usa Inc	Salem	NH	G	603 718-8903	19763
Sweeney Manufacturing	Seabrook	NH	G	603 814-4127	19820
Tack-Tiles Braille Systems LLC	Plaistow	NH	G	603 382-1904	19526
Valid Mfg Inc	Hudson	NH	F	603 880-0948	18449
Blackledge Industries LLC	Pawtucket	RI	G	401 270-6779	20817
Buick LLC	Hope Valley	RI	E	401 539-2432	20481
C&M Mfg Co Inc	Chepachet	RI	G	401 232-9633	20133
Cas Acquisition Co LLC	North Smithfield	RI	F	401 884-8556	20783
Dawn Industries Inc	West Warwick	RI	G	401 884-8175	21490
GA Rel Manufacturing Company	Providence	RI	E	401 331-5455	21019
Gloria Duchin Inc	Rumford	RI	D	401 431-5016	21185
Graco Awards Manufacturing Inc	Providence	RI	E	281 255-2161	21021
Hodges Badge Company Inc **(PA)**	Portsmouth	RI	C	401 682-2000	20923
Imperial Ceramics	Warwick	RI	G	401 732-0500	21375
International Insignia Corp	Providence	RI	D	401 784-0000	21039
Ira Green Inc	Providence	RI	C	800 663-7487	21040
Lance Industries	North Providence	RI	G	401 654-5394	20766
Mel-Co-Ed Inc	Pawtucket	RI	E	401 724-2160	20859
Michael Healy Designs Inc	Manville	RI	G	401 597-5900	20610
Mjh Crawford Industries I	Lincoln	RI	G	401 728-3443	20585

	CITY	ST	EMP	PHONE	ENTRY #
Numaco Packaging LLC	East Providence	RI	F	401 438-4952	20436
Officers Equipment Co	Providence	RI	E	703 221-1912	21082
Recognition Awards	Johnston	RI	G	401 365-1265	20535
RJ Mansour Inc	Providence	RI	E	401 521-7800	21116
Scope Display & Box Co Inc **(PA)**	Cranston	RI	D	401 942-7150	20284
Screencraft Tileworks LLC	Lincoln	RI	G	401 427-2816	20596
Song Wind Industries Inc	Barrington	RI	E	401 245-7582	20056
Splendid Loon Studio	Wakefield	RI	G	401 789-7879	21278
Up Country Inc	East Providence	RI	E	401 431-2940	20447
Urschel Tool Co	Cranston	RI	F	401 944-0600	20308
Advanced Animations	Stockbridge	VT	E	802 746-8974	22518
Aunt Sadies Inc	Lunenburg	VT	F	802 892-5267	22066
Dock Doctors LLC	Ferrisburgh	VT	E	802 877-6756	21988
Gibson Peggy Day	West Glover	VT	F	802 525-3034	22607
Green Mountain Cbd Inc	Hardwick	VT	G	802 595-3258	22012
Hazelett Strip-Casting Corp	Colchester	VT	G	802 951-6846	21865
Hyzer Industries	Montpelier	VT	G	802 223-8277	22150
Kids On Block - Vermont Inc	Burlington	VT	G	802 860-3349	21790
Leo D Bernstein & Sons Inc	Shaftsbury	VT	D	802 442-8029	22404
Leo D Bernstein and Sons Inc	Shaftsbury	VT	C	212 337-9578	22405
Porter Music Box Company Inc	Randolph	VT	G	802 728-9694	22301
Sullivan Industries LLC	Montpelier	VT	G	802 229-1909	22161
Travis M Bonnett	Saint Albans	VT	F	802 524-1890	22382
Vermont Center Wreaths Inc	Newport Center	VT	D	802 334-6432	22208
Vermont Juvenile Furn Mfg Inc	West Rutland	VT	F	802 438-2231	22620
Way Out Wax Inc	North Hyde Park	VT	F	802 730-8069	22233
Wheel House Designs Inc	Morrisville	VT	G	802 888-8552	22180

73 BUSINESS SERVICES

7372 Prepackaged Software

	CITY	ST	EMP	PHONE	ENTRY #
3 Story Software LLC	New Milford	CT	G	203 530-3224	2785
360alumni Inc	Weston	CT	G	203 253-5860	5167
Actualmeds Corporation	East Hartford	CT	G	888 838-9053	1169
Advanced Decisions Inc	Orange	CT	F	203 402-0603	3357
Advanced Reasoning	Waterford	CT	G	860 437-0508	4980
Afficiency Inc	Westport	CT	G	718 496-9071	5178
Agencyport Software Corp	Farmington	CT	G	860 674-6135	1464
API Wizard LLC	Ridgefield	CT	G	914 764-5726	3655
Appstract Ideas	Bristol	CT	G	860 857-1123	519
Array Technologies Inc	Glastonbury	CT	G	860 657-8086	1538
Art of Wellbeing LLC	Stamford	CT	G	917 453-3009	4144
Ataccama Corp US	Stamford	CT	F	203 564-1488	4145
Automatech Inc	Unionville	CT	F	860 673-5940	4653
Becaid LLC	New Haven	CT	G	203 915-6914	2665
Blue Sky Studios Inc	Greenwich	CT	C	203 992-6000	1600
Breach Intelligence Inc	Farmington	CT	E	844 312-7001	1469
Ca Inc	East Windsor	CT	E	800 225-5224	1281
CD Solutions Inc	Branford	CT	E	203 481-5895	303
Channel Sources LLC	Brookfield	CT	F	203 775-6464	638
Codebridge Software Inc	West Haven	CT	G	203 535-0517	5111
Community Brands Holdings LLC	Westport	CT	F	203 227-1255	5185
Computer Prgrm & Systems Inc **(PA)**	Stamford	CT	G	203 324-9203	4170
Computer Tech Express LLC	Norwalk	CT	G	203 810-4932	3130
Continuity Engine Inc	New Haven	CT	G	866 631-5556	2678
Coss Systems Inc (not Inc)	Old Greenwich	CT	G	732 447-7724	3307
Couponz Direct LLC	Greenwich	CT	G	212 655-9615	1604
Criterion Inc	Norwalk	CT	E	203 703-9000	3133
Cya Technologies Inc	Shelton	CT	E	203 513-3111	3792
Dataprep Inc	Orange	CT	E	203 795-2095	3364
Desrosier of Greenwich Inc	Greenwich	CT	F	203 661-2334	1608
Device42 Inc	West Haven	CT	F	203 409-7242	5116
Dmt Solutions Global Corp	Danbury	CT	A	203 233-6231	903
Dreamer Software LLC	Manchester	CT	G	860 645-1240	2003
Earnix Inc	Westport	CT	F	203 557-8077	5189
Enginuity Plm LLC **(HQ)**	Milford	CT	F	203 218-7225	2286
Epath Learning Inc	New London	CT	E	860 444-7900	2771
Fergtech Inc	Darien	CT	G	203 656-1139	1024
Fergtech Inc **(PA)**	Darien	CT	G	203 656-1139	1025
Flagpole Software LLC	Newtown	CT	G	203 426-5166	2921
Flexiinternational Sftwr Inc **(PA)**	Shelton	CT	E	203 925-3040	3803
Freethink Technologies Inc	Branford	CT	F	860 237-5800	317
Frevvo Inc	Branford	CT	F	203 208-3117	318
Gerber Scientific LLC **(PA)**	Tolland	CT	C	860 871-8082	4548
Golf Research Associates	Stamford	CT	G	203 968-1608	4201
Graybark Enterprises LLC	Fairfield	CT	G	203 255-4503	1436
Grayfin Security LLC	Madison	CT	G	203 800-6760	1961
Grey Wall Software LLC	New Haven	CT	F	203 782-5944	2693
Harpoon Acquisition Corp	Glastonbury	CT	A	860 815-5736	1557
Horizon Software Inc	Glastonbury	CT	G	860 633-2090	1559
Hotseat Chassis Inc	Waterbury	CT	G	860 582-5031	4884
Hypack Inc **(PA)**	Middletown	CT	F	860 635-1500	2191
Information Builders Inc	Hartford	CT	F	860 249-7229	1837
Information Resources Inc	Norwalk	CT	D	203 845-6400	3173
Information Tech Intl Corp	Manchester	CT	G	860 648-2570	2012
Inner Office Inc	Moosup	CT	G	860 564-6777	2427
Innovation Group	Farmington	CT	E	860 674-2900	1486
Innovative Software LLC	Hebron	CT	G	860 228-4144	1897
Insight Enterprises Inc	Easton	CT	G	203 374-2013	1320
Intellgent Clearing Netwrk Inc	North Haven	CT	G	203 972-0861	3031
It Helps LLC	New Milford	CT	G	860 799-8321	2806
Jpg Consulting Inc	Wilton	CT	G	203 247-2730	5292
Kol LLC	Woodbridge	CT	E	203 393-2924	5470
Lablite LLC	New Milford	CT	F	860 355-8817	2812
Locallive Networks Inc	Stamford	CT	G	877 355-6225	4238
Management Software Inc	Ledyard	CT	G	860 536-5177	1942
Mbsiinet Inc	Southbury	CT	F	888 466-2744	4030
Mental Canvas LLC	Madison	CT	G	475 329-0515	1968
Microsoft Corporation	Farmington	CT	E	860 678-3100	1492
Microtrain Inc	Newington	CT	G	860 666-7890	2882
Mind2mind Exchange LLC	Stamford	CT	G	203 856-0981	4250
Mindtrainr LLC	Stamford	CT	G	914 799-1515	4251
Mpi Systems Inc	Wilton	CT	G	203 762-2260	5295
Mvp Systems Software Inc	Unionville	CT	F	860 269-3112	4659
Navtech Systems Inc	Old Greenwich	CT	G	203 661-7800	3312
Neasi-Weber International	Norwalk	CT	G	203 857-4404	3206
New England Computer Svcs Inc	Branford	CT	E	475 221-8200	333
Nexvue Information Systems Inc	Stamford	CT	F	203 327-0800	4259
Nortonlifelock Inc	Glastonbury	CT	D	860 652-6600	1568
Nuance Communications Inc	Stratford	CT	G	781 565-5000	4436
Nxtid Inc	Oxford	CT	F	203 266-2103	3416
Open Solutions LLC **(HQ)**	Glastonbury	CT	C	860 815-5000	1569
Open Water Development LLC	Old Greenwich	CT	G	646 883-2062	3313
Oracle America Inc	Stamford	CT	D	203 703-3000	4273
Oracle Corporation	Middletown	CT	B	860 632-8329	2208
Orisha Oracle Inc	Bridgeport	CT	G	203 612-8989	461
Pathfinder Solutions Group LLC	Wilton	CT	G	203 247-2479	5298
Peerless Systems Corporation **(DH)**	Stamford	CT	F	203 350-0040	4281
Pitney Bowes Inc **(PA)**	Stamford	CT	A	203 356-5000	4285
Polymath Software	Willimantic	CT	G	860 423-5823	5268
Private Communications Corp	Sherman	CT	F	860 355-2718	3896
Prolink Inc	Glastonbury	CT	G	860 659-5928	1575
Protegrity Usa Inc **(PA)**	Stamford	CT	E	203 326-7200	4292
Qdiscovery LLC **(HQ)**	New London	CT	E	860 271-7080	2777
Qscend Technologies Inc	Waterbury	CT	E	203 757-6000	4948
Qualedi Inc	Shelton	CT	G	203 538-5320	3866
Qualedi Inc **(PA)**	Milford	CT	G	203 874-4334	2345
Radical Computing Corporation	Newington	CT	G	860 953-0240	2897
Richard Breault	Milford	CT	G	203 876-2707	2349
Rindle LLC	Norwalk	CT	G	551 482-2037	3232
Saleschain LLC	Waterbury	CT	F	203 262-1611	4951
Sas Institute Inc	Glastonbury	CT	E	860 633-4119	1577
Satori Audio LLC	Westport	CT	G	203 571-6050	5229
Scry Health Inc	Woodbridge	CT	F	203 936-8244	5478
Securities Software & Consulti	Windsor	CT	G	860 298-4500	5362
Servicetune Inc	Avon	CT	G	860 284-4445	45
Shibumicom Inc	Norwalk	CT	F	855 744-2864	3242
Shiloh Software Inc	Cheshire	CT	G	203 272-8456	761
Siggpay Inc	Norwalk	CT	G	203 957-8261	3243
Sigmund Software LLC	Danbury	CT	F	800 448-6975	991
Smartpay Solutions	Southington	CT	G	860 986-7659	4077
Software Cnslting Rsources Inc	Goshen	CT	G	860 491-2689	1587
SS&c Technologies Inc	Windsor	CT	G	860 930-5882	5364
SS&c Technologies Inc **(HQ)**	Windsor	CT	C	860 298-4500	5365
SS&c Technologies Holdings Inc **(PA)**	Windsor	CT	D	860 298-4500	5366
Stamford Risk Analytics LLC	Stamford	CT	F	203 559-0883	4332
Swing By Swing Golf Inc	Hartford	CT	G	310 922-8023	1874
Synergy Solutions LLC	Wilton	CT	G	203 762-1153	5306
Tagetik North America LLC	Stamford	CT	G	203 391-7520	4341
Tangoe Us Inc	Shelton	CT	B	203 859-9300	3877
Tangoe Us Inc **(HQ)**	Shelton	CT	C	973 257-0300	3878
Tavisca LLC	Stamford	CT	G	203 956-1000	4342
Technolutions Inc	New Haven	CT	E	203 404-4835	2743
Telenity Inc	Monroe	CT	C	203 445-2000	2419
Thebeamer LLC	East Hartford	CT	F	860 212-5071	1228
Think Ahead Software LLC **(PA)**	West Hartford	CT	G	860 463-9786	5098
Trinity Mobile Networks Inc	New Haven	CT	G	301 332-6401	2749
Trycycle Data Systems US Inc	Farmington	CT	G	860 558-1148	1520
Uniworld Bus Publications Inc	Darien	CT	G	201 384-4900	1036
Voice Glance LLC	Mystic	CT	F	800 260-3025	2456
Yourmembershipcom Inc	Groton	CT	G	860 271-7241	1690
Zillion Group Inc	Norwalk	CT	F	203 810-5400	3275
128 Technology Inc **(PA)**	Burlington	MA	E	781 203-8400	9227
3derm Systems Inc	Boston	MA	G	617 237-6041	8328
3wyc Inc	Newton	MA	G	617 584-7767	13550
AAF Microsystems Ltd	Westborough	MA	G	508 366-9100	16585
Able Software Corp	Billerica	MA	G	978 667-2400	8203
Able Software Corp **(PA)**	Lexington	MA	F	781 862-2804	12200
Accord Software Inc	Methuen	MA	G	978 687-2320	13010
Accounttech	Bedford	MA	G	781 276-1555	7956
Accufund Inc	Needham	MA	G	781 433-0233	13289
Acenna Data Inc	Cambridge	MA	G	443 878-9292	9371
Acktify Inc	Melrose	MA	G	781 462-3942	12974
Aclara Software Inc	Wellesley	MA	D	781 283-9160	16356

	CITY	ST	EMP	PHONE	ENTRY #
Acquia Inc **(PA)**	Boston	MA	C	888 922-7842	8337
Acronis North America Inc	Burlington	MA	F	781 782-9100	9228
Actifio Federal Inc	Needham	MA	F	781 795-9182	13290
Actuality Systems Inc	Arlington	MA	G	617 325-9230	7622
Actuate Corporation	Westborough	MA	G	508 870-9822	16587
Acumen Data Systems Inc	West Springfield	MA	F	413 737-4800	16504
Adanac Software Inc	Stow	MA	G	978 562-3466	15629
Adaptive Insights Inc	Framingham	MA	G	508 532-4947	10917
Adeptis Inc	Woburn	MA	G	781 569-5996	17110
Adobe Systems Incorporated	Newton	MA	D	617 467-6760	13555
Advance Systems Inc	Newton	MA	F	888 238-8704	13556
Advanced Career Tech Inc **(PA)**	Boston	MA	E	508 620-5904	8341
Advantage Data Inc **(PA)**	Boston	MA	E	212 227-8870	8342
Affinity Project Inc	Cambridge	MA	G	202 841-4011	9376
Agencyport Software Corp **(HQ)**	Boston	MA	D	866 539-6623	8343
Airworks Solutions Inc	Boston	MA	F	857 990-1060	8345
Aislebuyer Lllc	Boston	MA	F	617 606-7062	8346
Akamai Technologies Inc **(PA)**	Cambridge	MA	B	617 444-3000	9378
Akumo Software Inc	Boston	MA	F	617 466-9818	8348
Alfresco Software Inc **(PA)**	Wellesley	MA	D	888 317-3395	16358
Alignable Inc	Boston	MA	F	978 376-5852	8355
Alivia Capital LLC	Boston	MA	G	781 569-5212	8356
Alivia Capital LLC **(PA)**	Woburn	MA	G	781 569-5212	17116
All Around Active Co	Boxford	MA	G	978 561-1033	8973
Allocation Solutions LLC	Burlington	MA	G	339 234-5695	9231
Allscrpts Hlthcare Sltions Inc	Burlington	MA	A	800 720-7351	9232
Allure Security Technology Inc	Waltham	MA	G	877 669-8883	16031
Alm Works Inc **(PA)**	Newton	MA	G	617 600-4369	13560
Almusnet Inc	Woburn	MA	E	781 933-1846	17117
Amcs Group Inc	Boston	MA	E	610 932-4006	8358
American Well Corporation	Boston	MA	B	617 204-3500	8363
Anchor Labs Group Inc	Worcester	MA	G	508 500-9157	17338
Ansys Inc	Concord	MA	G	781 229-8900	10111
Apifia Inc **(PA)**	Boston	MA	E	585 506-2787	8368
Applause LLC	Framingham	MA	D	508 665-6910	10921
Applied Computer Engineering **(PA)**	Taunton	MA	G	508 824-4630	15725
Appneta Inc **(PA)**	Boston	MA	E	781 235-2470	8369
Apps Associates LLC	Acton	MA	C	978 399-0230	7341
Apriori Technologies Inc **(PA)**	Concord	MA	D	978 371-2006	10112
Architexa Inc	Cambridge	MA	G	617 500-7391	9391
Aries Systems Corporation	North Andover	MA	E	978 975-7570	13691
Armada Logistics Inc	Somerville	MA	G	855 727-6232	15156
Artech House Inc **(HQ)**	Norwood	MA	F	781 769-9750	14134
Askcody Inc	Boston	MA	G	617 455-2075	8377
Aspect Software Inc	Chelmsford	MA	E	978 250-7900	9873
Aspmd	Cambridge	MA	G	617 864-6844	9396
Asure Software Inc	Taunton	MA	G	512 437-2700	15727
Aternity Inc	Westborough	MA	C	508 475-0414	16590
Athenahealth Inc **(HQ)**	Watertown	MA	C	617 402-1000	16270
Athigo	Newton	MA	G	617 410-8834	13564
Atiim Inc	Boston	MA	F	800 735-4071	8381
Atlantis Technology Corp	Concord	MA	G	978 341-0999	10114
Atlas Devices LLC	Boston	MA	G	617 415-1657	8383
Atrex Energy Inc **(PA)**	Walpole	MA	E	781 461-8251	15988
Attivio Inc	Boston	MA	D	857 226-5040	8385
Autodesk Inc	Salem	MA	E	855 646-4868	14896
Automatech Inc **(PA)**	Plymouth	MA	G	508 830-0088	14544
Aviation Edge LLC	Belmont	MA	G	781 405-3246	8065
Avid Technology Inc **(PA)**	Burlington	MA	A	978 640-6789	9235
Aware Inc **(PA)**	Bedford	MA	D	781 276-4000	7962
Azara Healthcare LLC	Burlington	MA	G	781 365-2208	9237
Bamboo Rose LLC	Boston	MA	G	857 284-4360	8390
Bamboo Rose LLC **(PA)**	Gloucester	MA	G	978 281-3723	11164
Bancware Inc **(DH)**	Boston	MA	D	617 542-2800	8391
Baramundi Software Usa Inc	Framingham	MA	G	508 861-7561	10925
Bare Bones Software Inc	North Chelmsford	MA	F	978 251-0500	13885
Basho Technologies Inc **(PA)**	Cambridge	MA	E	617 714-1700	9403
Basis Technology Corporation	Cambridge	MA	G	617 386-2000	9404
Battery Ventures Vi LP	Waltham	MA	A	781 577-1000	16041
Beacon Application Svcs Corp **(PA)**	Framingham	MA	E	508 663-4433	10926
Beagle Learning Inc	Boston	MA	G	617 784-3817	8396
Beanstox Inc	Boston	MA	G	617 878-2102	8397
Belarc Inc	Maynard	MA	F	978 461-1100	12896
Beyondtrust Software Inc	Andover	MA	F	978 206-3700	7540
Bigtincan Mobile Pty Ltd	Waltham	MA	G	617 981-7557	16047
Biobright LLC **(PA)**	Boston	MA	G	617 444-9007	8410
Biomed Software Inc	Newton	MA	G	617 513-1298	13568
Bionetiks Co	New Bedford	MA	G	415 343-4990	13362
Biovia Corp	Milford	MA	G	508 497-9911	13109
Biq LLC	Southborough	MA	G	508 485-9896	15346
Biscom Inc	Westford	MA	D	978 250-1800	16757
Blackboard Inc	Brookline	MA	G	617 713-5471	9195
Blub0x Security Inc	Andover	MA	G	508 414-3517	7541
Blue Cow Software Inc	Lynnfield	MA	G	781 224-2583	12546
Blueconic Inc	Boston	MA	E	888 440-2583	8416
Blueday Inc	Boston	MA	G	978 461-4500	8417
Bluesnap Inc **(PA)**	Waltham	MA	E	781 790-5013	16049
BMC Software Inc	Needham	MA	G	781 810-4494	13294
Bombich Software Inc	Longmeadow	MA	G	413 935-2300	12331
Bonami Software Corporation	Acton	MA	G	978 264-6641	7346
Bonapp	Cambridge	MA	G	917 488-5202	9414
Boston Commerce Inc	Boston	MA	G	617 782-8998	8429
Boston Health Economics LLC	Boston	MA	F	781 290-0808	8432
Boston Software Corp	Needham Heights	MA	F	781 449-8585	13320
Botify Corporation	Cambridge	MA	G	617 576-2005	9421
Boxcar Media LLC	North Adams	MA	E	413 663-3384	13670
Boxever US Inc	Boston	MA	E	617 599-2420	8443
BRC Development LLC	Upton	MA	G	774 245-7750	15905
Bridgeme LLC	Newton	MA	G	617 310-4801	13573
Bring Up Inc	Cambridge	MA	G	617 803-4248	9422
Buildium LLC	Boston	MA	G	888 414-1988	8449
Bullhorn Inc **(PA)**	Boston	MA	C	617 478-9100	8450
Cadence Design Systems Inc	Chelmsford	MA	D	978 262-6404	9885
Cadnexus Inc	Woburn	MA	G	781 281-2672	17140
Cambridge Semantics Inc	Boston	MA	F	617 245-0517	8457
Carbon Black Inc **(DH)**	Waltham	MA	B	617 393-7400	16062
Carbon Black Federal Inc	Waltham	MA	G	617 393-7400	16063
Carbonite Inc **(PA)**	Boston	MA	C	617 587-1100	8458
Casenet LLC	Bedford	MA	D	781 357-2700	7966
Cassiopae US Inc	Burlington	MA	G	435 647-9940	9245
Cazena Inc	Waltham	MA	E	781 897-6380	16064
Celerity Solutions Inc **(PA)**	Dedham	MA	G	781 329-1900	10282
Centage Corporation	Natick	MA	D	800 366-5111	13243
Centra Software Inc **(DH)**	Lexington	MA	D	781 861-7000	12211
Cerence Inc **(PA)**	Burlington	MA	D	781 565-5507	9246
Cerner Corporation	Waltham	MA	D	781 434-2200	16065
Certeon Inc	Burlington	MA	E	781 425-5099	9247
Char Software Inc **(PA)**	Boston	MA	D	617 418-4422	8468
Check Point Software Tech Inc	Acton	MA	G	978 635-0300	7347
Cheshire Software Inc	Newton	MA	F	617 527-4000	13579
Chronologics LLC	Boston	MA	G	617 686-6770	8474
Cimcon Softwares Inc **(PA)**	Burlington	MA	D	978 692-9868	9249
City Pblcations Greater Boston	Wayland	MA	G	617 549-7622	16335
CLC Bio LLC **(PA)**	Beverly	MA	F	617 945-0178	8117
Clearway Software Corp	Medfield	MA	G	508 906-6333	12912
Client Server Engineering Svcs	Boston	MA	E	617 338-7898	8476
Clypd Inc	Somerville	MA	E	617 800-9481	15166
Computer Management Cons	Tewksbury	MA	G	603 595-0850	15812
Connance Inc	Auburndale	MA	G	781 577-5000	7859
Connectedview LLC	Westborough	MA	G	508 205-0243	16609
Connectrn Inc	Waltham	MA	G	781 223-2852	16075
Constellation Diagnostics Inc	Cambridge	MA	G	617 233-4554	9440
Cosmic Software Inc	Billerica	MA	F	978 667-2556	8234
Covered Security Inc	Boston	MA	G	781 218-9894	8485
Cow Town Productions Inc	Amherst	MA	G	413 259-1350	7514
Crew By True Rowing Inc	Cambridge	MA	G	617 398-7480	9444
Csp Inc **(PA)**	Lowell	MA	D	978 954-5038	12364
Cura Software Solutions Co	Bedford	MA	F	781 325-7158	7967
Cusa Technologies Inc	Mansfield	MA	E	508 339-7675	12626
Cyberark Software Inc **(HQ)**	Newton	MA	E	617 965-1544	13585
Cybtek Inc	Peabody	MA	G	978 532-7110	14327
Daedalus Software Inc	Cambridge	MA	E	617 851-5157	9448
Data Plus Incorporated	North Chelmsford	MA	F	978 888-6300	13892
Data Translation Inc **(PA)**	Norton	MA	D	508 481-3700	14076
Datadog Inc	Boston	MA	G	866 329-4466	8495
Datanational Corporation	Pembroke	MA	F	781 826-3400	14397
Datawatch Corporation **(HQ)**	Bedford	MA	D	978 441-2200	7970
David Corporation **(PA)**	Wakefield	MA	E	781 587-3008	15948
Davinci Group	Wakefield	MA	G	781 391-6009	15949
Dbmaestro Inc	Concord	MA	G	508 641-6108	10127
Deerwalk Inc **(PA)**	Lexington	MA	B	781 325-1775	12218
Defense Logics LLC	Waltham	MA	G	781 330-9195	16083
Delve Labs Inc	Boston	MA	F	617 820-9798	8498
Demiurge Game Development LLC	Cambridge	MA	E	617 354-7772	9452
Dg3 Group America Inc	Woburn	MA	G	617 241-5600	17167
Digital Guardian Inc **(PA)**	Waltham	MA	E	781 788-8180	16088
Digital Immunity LLC	Burlington	MA	G	508 630-0321	9257
Digital Paradigms Inc	Boston	MA	G	617 723-9400	8506
Dimensional Insight Inc **(PA)**	Burlington	MA	E	781 229-9111	9258
Divlan Inc	Cambridge	MA	G	347 338-8843	9454
Dmh Software	Acton	MA	G	978 263-0526	7350
Doorbell Inc	Cambridge	MA	G	516 375-5507	9456
Drizly Inc	Boston	MA	G	972 234-1033	8510
Duck Creek Technologies LLC **(PA)**	Boston	MA	E	857 239-5709	8511
Duck Creek Technologies LLC	Boston	MA	G	980 613-8044	8512
Dynamicops Inc	Burlington	MA	G	781 221-2136	9259
Dynatrace Inc **(PA)**	Waltham	MA	G	781 530-1000	16093
Dynatrace Holdings LLC **(HQ)**	Waltham	MA	C	781 530-1000	16094
Dynatrace International LLC **(DH)**	Waltham	MA	G	781 530-1000	16095
Eastgate Systems Inc	Watertown	MA	G	617 924-9044	16280
Ebsnet Inc	Groton	MA	G	978 448-9000	11288
Eclinicalworks LLC	Westborough	MA	E	508 836-2700	16616
Elastic Cloud Gate LLC	Natick	MA	G	617 500-8284	13254
Electra Vehicles Inc	Boston	MA	F	617 313-7848	8522

SIC

	CITY	ST	EMP	PHONE	ENTRY #
Elerts Corporation	Weymouth	MA	F	781 803-6362	16888
Ellucian	Waltham	MA	G	781 672-1800	16096
Emagine	East Taunton	MA	G	508 692-9522	10512
EMC Corporation	Southborough	MA	G	508 382-7556	15356
EMC Corporation **(HQ)**	Hopkinton	MA	B	508 435-1000	11706
EMC Corporation	Newton	MA	C	617 618-3400	13587
Endowmentsolutions LLC	Auburn	MA	G	617 308-7231	7833
Endurnce Intl Group Hldngs Inc **(PA)**	Burlington	MA	D	781 852-3200	9268
Envvisual Inc	Boston	MA	G	800 982-3221	8526
Epicenter	Westfield	MA	F	413 568-1360	16682
Equitrac Corporation	Burlington	MA	G	781 565-5000	9269
Era7 Bioinformatics Inc	Cambridge	MA	G	617 576-2005	9471
Erecruit Holdings LLC	Boston	MA	D	617 535-3720	8527
Erevnos Corporation	West Roxbury	MA	G	619 675-9536	16494
Eskill Corporation	North Chelmsford	MA	F	978 649-8010	13893
Etawiz LLC	Oxford	MA	G	774 823-5156	14260
Everbridge Inc **(PA)**	Burlington	MA	C	818 230-9700	9271
Evergage Inc	Somerville	MA	D	888 310-0589	15170
Everteam Inc	Boston	MA	F	650 596-1800	8530
Evertrue Inc	Boston	MA	E	617 460-3371	8531
Evervest Co	Boston	MA	G	585 697-4170	8532
Exa Corporation **(DH)**	Burlington	MA	D	781 564-0200	9272
Exari Group Inc **(PA)**	Boston	MA	G	617 938-3777	8533
Exari Systems Inc	Boston	MA	E	617 938-3777	8534
Expertek Systems Inc	Marlborough	MA	F	508 624-0006	12754
Extreme Protocol Solutions Inc	Uxbridge	MA	G	508 278-3600	15915
EZ Rater Systems Inc	Boxford	MA	G	978 887-8322	8977
Eze Castle Software Inc **(HQ)**	Boston	MA	C	617 316-1100	8535
Fablevision Learning LLC	Dedham	MA	F	781 320-3225	10289
Fein Academy LLC	Swampscott	MA	G	978 495-0777	15697
Finomial Corporation **(PA)**	Cambridge	MA	G	917 488-6050	9478
Finomial Corporation	Boston	MA	G	646 820-7637	8546
Fis Financial Systems LLC	Burlington	MA	G	952 935-3300	9274
Fis Systems International LLC	Boston	MA	G	617 728-7722	8548
Fitivity Inc	Shrewsbury	MA	G	508 308-5822	15112
Flimp Media	Hopkinton	MA	E	508 435-5220	11714
Floc LLC	Pembroke	MA	G	617 823-5798	14405
Fonzy Inc	Dedham	MA	G	857 342-3143	10290
Footsizer LLC	Sudbury	MA	G	617 337-3537	15657
Frameshift Labs Inc	Boston	MA	G	617 319-1357	8552
Fundtech Corporation	Burlington	MA	E	781 993-9100	9276
G360link	Boxborough	MA	G	978 266-1500	8963
Galaxy Software Inc	Quincy	MA	G	617 773-7790	14627
Gb and Smith Inc	Cambridge	MA	G	617 319-3563	9485
Gdm Software LLC	Boston	MA	G	617 416-6333	8556
Geisel Software Inc	Worcester	MA	F	508 853-5310	17380
Generative Labs Inc	Cambridge	MA	F	434 326-8061	9487
Geometric Informatics Inc	Somerville	MA	G	617 440-1078	15177
Ginger Software Inc	Newton	MA	E	617 755-0160	13596
Glogood Inc	Cambridge	MA	G	617 491-3500	9496
Good2gether	Concord	MA	G	978 371-3172	10132
Goodrich Corporation	Westford	MA	A	978 303-6700	16771
Gotuit Media Corp	Woburn	MA	E	801 592-5575	17193
Graphisoft North America Inc	Waltham	MA	E	617 485-4219	16122
Grid Solutions Corp	Marblehead	MA	G	781 718-4266	12684
Haystack ID	Boston	MA	G	617 422-0075	8591
Healersource	Allston	MA	G	212 464-7748	7467
Healigo Inc	Boston	MA	G	508 208-0461	8592
Health Helm Inc	Lowell	MA	G	508 951-2156	12379
Healthedge Software Inc **(PA)**	Burlington	MA	D	781 285-1300	9282
Heuristic Labs Inc	Westford	MA	G	347 994-0299	16772
Homeportfolio Inc	Newton	MA	D	617 559-1197	13602
Horizon International Inc	Belmont	MA	G	617 489-6666	8075
Hoylu Inc	Pembroke	MA	G	877 554-6958	14409
Hubengage Inc	Cambridge	MA	G	877 704-6662	9507
Hubspot Inc **(PA)**	Cambridge	MA	A	888 482-7768	9508
Hughes Riskapps LLC	Boston	MA	G	617 936-0301	8609
Human Care Systems Inc **(PA)**	Boston	MA	E	617 720-7838	8610
Hycu Inc	Boston	MA	A	617 681-9100	8612
I-Pass Patient Safety Inst Inc	Framingham	MA	G	617 932-7926	10964
Iet Solutions LLC **(DH)**	Canton	MA	E	818 838-0606	9743
IMD Soft Inc **(DH)**	Dedham	MA	E	781 449-5567	10292
Industrial Defender Inc	Foxboro	MA	D	508 718-6777	10887
Infinite Forest Inc	Cambridge	MA	F	617 299-1382	9514
Infinite Knot LLC	Whitinsville	MA	G	617 372-0707	16914
Inflight Corporation	Easthampton	MA	G	413 203-2056	10565
Infogix Inc	Burlington	MA	G	617 826-6020	9285
Informatics In Context Inc	Boston	MA	G	650 200-5110	8615
Information Builders Inc	Wakefield	MA	E	781 224-7660	15956
Infotree Inc	Acton	MA	G	978 263-8558	7363
Intac International Inc	Woburn	MA	E	781 272-4494	17204
Intelligent Bus Entrmt Inc	Watertown	MA	F	617 519-4172	16292
Intelligent Compression Tech	Quincy	MA	E	617 773-3369	14635
Intelycare Inc	Quincy	MA	F	617 971-8344	14636
Intempo Software Inc **(PA)**	Springfield	MA	F	800 950-2221	15479
Intuit Inc	Hyannis	MA	C	508 862-1050	11844
Inukshukbio Interactive Inc	Falmouth	MA	G	612 916-6606	10793
Irody	Boston	MA	G	781 262-0440	8621
Isubscribed Inc	Burlington	MA	E	844 378-4646	9288
Itext Software Corp	Somerville	MA	G	617 982-2646	15186
Itrica Corp	Boston	MA	G	617 340-7777	8623
Izotope Inc **(PA)**	Cambridge	MA	D	617 577-7799	9520
JD Software Inc	Salem	MA	G	888 419-9998	14924
Jda Software Group Inc	Boston	MA	G	857 305-8330	8626
Jedox Inc	Boston	MA	G	617 514-7300	8627
Jenzabar Inc **(PA)**	Boston	MA	D	617 492-9099	8628
Jiminny Inc	Boston	MA	G	917 940-5886	8631
JM Software Inc	Dracut	MA	G	978 957-9105	10361
Jobsmart Inc	Ashfield	MA	F	724 272-3448	7652
Jrni Inc	Boston	MA	G	857 305-6477	8642
Juriba Limited	Boston	MA	E	617 356-8681	8645
Kenexa Brassring Inc	Littleton	MA	C	781 530-5000	12312
Kenexa Compensation Inc **(DH)**	Needham	MA	E	877 971-9171	13303
Kewill Inc **(DH)**	Chelmsford	MA	D	978 482-2500	9908
Keylium Inc	Hingham	MA	G	781 385-9178	11500
Keynectup Inc	Wellesley	MA	G	781 325-3414	16369
Kitewheel LLC	Boston	MA	E	617 447-2138	8651
Kleermail LLC	Boston	MA	G	888 273-3420	8652
Klypper Inc	Chelmsford	MA	G	978 987-8548	9909
Knowledge Management Assoc LLC	Waltham	MA	G	781 250-2001	16139
KPM Technologies Inc	Andover	MA	G	617 721-8770	7563
Kronos Acquisition Corporation **(HQ)**	Lowell	MA	G	978 250-9800	12391
Kronos Incorporated	Waltham	MA	D	978 947-2990	16141
Kronos Incorporated **(DH)**	Lowell	MA	C	978 250-9800	12392
Kronos International MGT LLC	Lowell	MA	G	978 250-9800	12393
Kronos Parent Corporation **(PA)**	Lowell	MA	G	978 250-9800	12394
Kronos Solutions Inc **(DH)**	Lowell	MA	G	978 805-9971	12395
Ksplice Inc	Cambridge	MA	G	765 577-5423	9528
Kubotek Usa Inc	Marlborough	MA	E	508 229-2020	12785
Labthink International Inc	Medford	MA	F	617 830-2190	12938
Lantiq Broadband Holdco Inc	Bedford	MA	G	781 687-0400	7988
Lattix Inc	Andover	MA	G	978 474-4332	7565
Laveem Inc	Cambridge	MA	G	617 286-6517	9532
Leaderclips Inc	Wellesley	MA	G	248 808-1093	16370
Leading Market Technologies	Boston	MA	E	617 494-4747	8661
Leftfield Software	Boston	MA	G	617 524-3842	8662
Leveltrigger Inc	Somerville	MA	G	650 468-1098	15190
Levr Inc	Boston	MA	G	605 261-0083	8663
Lexia Learning Systems LLC	Concord	MA	E	800 435-3942	10138
Libring Technologies Inc	Cambridge	MA	G	617 553-1015	9535
Life Image Inc	Newton	MA	D	617 244-8411	13610
Lifeady Inc	Watertown	MA	G	781 632-1296	16295
Lincoln Learning Solutions LLC	Lincoln	MA	G	781 259-9696	12287
Linesider Communications Inc	Danvers	MA	E	617 671-0000	10233
Loadspring Solutions Inc **(PA)**	Wilmington	MA	F	978 685-9715	17018
Login VSI Inc	Woburn	MA	G	844 828-3693	17217
Logmein Inc **(PA)**	Boston	MA	C	781 638-9050	8671
Longwood Software Inc	Maynard	MA	F	978 897-2900	12900
Longworth Venture Partners LP **(PA)**	Norfolk	MA	E	781 663-3600	13663
Luzy Technologies LLC	Boston	MA	E	514 577-2295	8675
M B S Services Inc	Wellesley	MA	G	781 431-0945	16371
Machinemetrics Inc	Northampton	MA	G	413 341-5747	14011
Macromicro LLC	Boston	MA	G	617 818-1291	8678
Magnitude Software Inc	Burlington	MA	G	781 202-3200	9299
Makemesustainable Inc	Cambridge	MA	G	617 821-1375	9544
Materialise Dental Inc	Waltham	MA	E	443 557-0121	16149
Mathworks Inc	Natick	MA	G	508 647-7000	13266
Measurement Computing Corp **(HQ)**	Norton	MA	D	508 946-5100	14081
Meddata Group LLC	Danvers	MA	F	978 887-0039	10237
Medical Information Tech Inc **(PA)**	Westwood	MA	C	781 821-3000	16872
Meditech	Framingham	MA	G	781 821-3000	10983
Mega Na Inc	Raynham	MA	E	781 784-7684	14718
Memento Inc	Burlington	MA	D	781 221-3030	9301
Mendix Inc	Boston	MA	C	857 263-8200	8695
Mercury Systems Inc **(PA)**	Andover	MA	C	978 256-1300	7570
Merlinone Inc **(PA)**	Quincy	MA	E	617 328-6645	14639
Meta Software Corporation **(PA)**	Burlington	MA	F	781 238-0293	9302
Metacog Inc	Worcester	MA	G	508 798-6100	17413
Micro Financial Cmpt Systems	Medway	MA	G	508 533-1233	12967
Micro Focus Software Inc	Cambridge	MA	B	617 613-2000	9553
Micros Systems Inc	Westborough	MA	F	508 655-7500	16635
Microsoft Corporation	Cambridge	MA	E	781 398-4600	9554
Microsoft Corporation	Natick	MA	G	508 545-2957	13268
Microsoft Corporation	Cambridge	MA	C	857 453-6000	9555
Microsoft Corporation	Burlington	MA	G	781 487-6400	9303
Millennial Media Inc	Boston	MA	F	617 301-4550	8707
Mindedge Inc	Waltham	MA	F	781 250-1805	16150
Mindstorm Technologies Inc	Brookline	MA	G	781 642-1700	9209
Minuteman Software Associates	Arlington	MA	G	781 643-4918	7630
Mixfit Inc	Salem	MA	G	617 902-8082	14929
Mobilepro Corporation	Cambridge	MA	G	480 398-0909	9562
Mobilesuites Inc	Cambridge	MA	G	302 593-3055	9563
Modkit LLC	Cambridge	MA	G	617 838-1784	9567
Momedx Inc	Boston	MA	G	617 401-7780	8710

	CITY	ST	EMP	PHONE	ENTRY #
Monadnock Associates Inc **(PA)**	Watertown	MA	F	617 924-7032	16302
Monotype Imaging Inc **(DH)**	Woburn	MA	D	781 970-6000	17234
Morgan Scientific Inc **(PA)**	Haverhill	MA	F	978 521-4440	11454
Morphisec Inc	Boston	MA	E	617 209-2552	8712
Moviri Inc	Boston	MA	G	857 233-5705	8714
MTI Systems Inc	West Springfield	MA	E	413 733-1972	16532
Murphy Software Inc	Burlington	MA	G	781 710-8419	9304
Myinvenio US Corp	Boston	MA	G	408 464-0565	8718
Mysunbuddy Inc	Boston	MA	G	404 219-2640	8719
N & M Pro Solutions Inc	Lenox	MA	G	413 822-1009	12102
Netbrain Technologies Inc **(PA)**	Burlington	MA	C	781 221-7199	9306
Netcracker Technology Corp **(HQ)**	Waltham	MA	C	781 419-3300	16158
Netsuite	Boston	MA	G	877 638-7848	8723
New England Time Solutions Inc	Hampden	MA	G	888 222-3396	11322
New Frontier Advisors LLC **(PA)**	Boston	MA	G	617 482-1433	8733
Nexthink Inc	Boston	MA	E	617 576-2005	8736
North Atlantic Pubg Systems	Concord	MA	G	978 371-8989	10147
Nortonlifelock Inc	Cambridge	MA	D	781 530-2200	9584
Ntt Data Inc	Boston	MA	C	617 241-9200	8744
Nuance Communications Inc	Berkley	MA	G	508 821-5954	8088
Nuance Communications Inc **(PA)**	Burlington	MA	A	781 565-5000	9312
Oak Group Inc	Wellesley	MA	E	781 943-2200	16377
Oasisworks Inc	Wellesley	MA	G	617 329-5588	16378
Oatsystems Inc	Waltham	MA	D	781 907-6100	16165
Object Management Group Inc	Needham	MA	E	781 444-0404	13307
Onapsis Inc **(PA)**	Boston	MA	F	617 603-9932	8747
Onecloud Labs LLC	Boston	MA	F	781 437-7966	8749
Onepin Inc	Westborough	MA	E	508 475-1000	16640
Oneview Commerce Inc	Boston	MA	F	617 292-0400	8750
Online Marketing Solutions	Lowell	MA	F	978 937-2363	12416
Onshape Inc	Cambridge	MA	F	844 667-4273	9599
Open Text Inc	Boston	MA	G	617 378-3364	8752
Openair Inc	Boston	MA	D	617 351-0232	8753
Openbridge Inc	Boston	MA	G	857 234-1008	8754
Openeye Scientific Sftwr Inc	Cambridge	MA	G	617 374-8844	9600
Optirtc Inc	Boston	MA	F	844 678-4782	8757
Oracle America Inc	Waltham	MA	C	781 672-4280	16168
Oracle America Inc	Burlington	MA	F	781 744-0000	9313
Oracle Corporation	Cambridge	MA	B	617 497-7713	9602
Oracle Corporation	Burlington	MA	C	781 744-0000	9314
Oracle Otc Subsidiary LLC	Cambridge	MA	A	617 386-1000	9603
Oracle Systems Corporation	Lynn	MA	B	781 744-0900	12532
Orbotech Inc	Billerica	MA	F	978 667-6037	8270
Osprey Compliance Software LLC	Waltham	MA	G	888 677-7394	16169
Outsystems Inc	Boston	MA	F	617 837-6840	8763
Overtone Studio Inc	Framingham	MA	G	774 290-2900	10991
Owncloud Inc	Foxboro	MA	E	617 515-3664	10896
Panda Security	Burlington	MA	E	407 215-3020	9318
Paperpile LLC	Cambridge	MA	G	617 682-9250	9606
Para Research Inc	Gloucester	MA	F	978 282-1100	11201
Parametric Holdings Inc	Needham Heights	MA	G	781 370-5000	13342
Parametric Technology Corp	Boston	MA	G	781 370-5000	8764
Pathai Inc	Boston	MA	G	617 543-5250	8767
Patheer Inc **(PA)**	Quincy	MA	G	888 968-5936	14644
Paytronix Systems Inc **(PA)**	Newton	MA	D	617 649-3300	13623
Peelfly Inc	Everett	MA	G	860 608-3819	10625
Peergrade Inc **(PA)**	Boston	MA	F	857 302-4023	8772
Perceptive Automata Inc **(PA)**	Somerville	MA	F	617 299-1296	15203
Percussion Software Inc	Woburn	MA	C	781 438-9900	17260
Perillon Software Inc	Acton	MA	G	978 263-0412	7377
Picis Clinical Solutions Inc **(DH)**	Wakefield	MA	C	336 397-5336	15969
Planet Small Communications	Lawrence	MA	G	978 794-2201	12071
Planon Corporation	Braintree	MA	F	781 356-0999	9030
Plataine Inc	Waltham	MA	G	336 905-0900	16174
Plumriver LLC	Wellesley	MA	E	781 431-7477	16381
Plynk Connect Inc	Boston	MA	G	760 815-2955	8781
Pmweb Inc	Wakefield	MA	D	617 207-7080	15970
Pointillist Inc	Boston	MA	E	617 752-2214	8783
Pongo Software LLC	Northborough	MA	G	508 393-4528	14044
Pos Center Inc	Quincy	MA	G	617 797-5026	14646
Position Health Inc	Reading	MA	G	617 549-2403	14739
Power Advocate Inc	Boston	MA	G	415 615-0146	8787
Power Object Inc	Newton	MA	E	617 630-5701	13627
Power Pros Consulting Group	South Easton	MA	G	508 238-6629	15287
Power Steering Software	Cambridge	MA	G	617 520-2100	9614
Preservica Inc	Boston	MA	E	617 294-6676	8791
Preventy Inc	Cambridge	MA	G	617 981-0920	9618
Process Dynamics Inc	Bedford	MA	G	781 271-0944	8002
Profitect Inc **(HQ)**	Burlington	MA	F	781 290-0009	9323
Progress Software Corporation **(PA)**	Bedford	MA	B	781 280-4000	8003
Promisec Holdings LLC	Boston	MA	G	781 453-1105	8797
Protect & Heal Children Mass	Haverhill	MA	G	978 374-8304	11462
Proximie Inc	Bedford	MA	G	617 391-6824	8004
Psyton Software	Chestnut Hill	MA	G	617 308-5058	9992
Ptc Inc	Waltham	MA	C	617 792-7622	16179
Ptc Parametric Technology	Needham	MA	G	781 370-5699	13309
Pulse Network Inc	Norwood	MA	F	781 688-8000	14189
Pxt Payments Inc	Andover	MA	G	978 247-7164	7588
Q-Biz Solutions LLC	Watertown	MA	G	617 212-7684	16309
Qstream Inc **(PA)**	Burlington	MA	G	781 222-2020	9327
Quadrant LLC	Mansfield	MA	E	508 594-2700	12654
Qualcomm Incorporated	Boxborough	MA	B	858 587-1121	8968
Quality Solutions Inc **(PA)**	Newburyport	MA	E	978 465-7755	13525
Quantum Simulation Tech Inc	Cambridge	MA	G	847 626-5535	9622
Quest Software Inc	Swampscott	MA	E	781 592-0752	15699
Quickbase Inc **(PA)**	Cambridge	MA	C	855 725-2293	9623
Quickdoc Inc	Brookline	MA	G	617 738-1800	9217
Quinn Curtis Inc	Medfield	MA	G	508 359-6639	12918
Rapid7 Inc **(PA)**	Boston	MA	C	617 247-1717	8810
Raw Diamond Inc	Cambridge	MA	G	857 222-5601	9625
Red Frames Inc **(HQ)**	Boston	MA	F	617 477-8740	8814
Red Hat Inc	Westford	MA	F	978 392-1000	16788
Red Hat Inc	Westford	MA	F	978 692-3113	16789
Redi2 Technologies Inc	Boston	MA	E	617 910-3282	8815
Reify Health Inc	Boston	MA	G	617 861-8261	8817
Rejjee Inc	Cambridge	MA	G	617 283-5057	9628
Reklist LLC	Plymouth	MA	G	215 518-1637	14579
Renaissance International	Newburyport	MA	G	978 465-5111	13529
Research Applications and	Cambridge	MA	G	800 939-7238	9630
Research Cmpt Consulting Svcs **(PA)**	Canton	MA	G	781 821-1221	9774
Revulytics Inc **(PA)**	Waltham	MA	E	781 398-3400	16188
Riffr LLC	Boston	MA	G	617 851-5989	8821
Right Submission LLC	Newton	MA	G	617 407-9076	13631
Rivermeadow Software Inc	Westford	MA	G	617 448-4990	16790
Rm Education Inc **(HQ)**	Hyannis	MA	E	508 862-0700	11856
Roam Data Inc	Boston	MA	E	888 589-5885	8823
Rockstar New England Inc	Andover	MA	E	978 409-6272	7601
Rsa Security LLC **(DH)**	Bedford	MA	A	781 515-5000	8007
Rwwi Holdings LLC	Wellesley	MA	B	781 239-0700	16384
Saba Software Inc	Burlington	MA	G	781 238-6730	9331
Salesbrief Inc	Boston	MA	G	203 216-0270	8834
Salesforcecom Inc	Boston	MA	G	857 415-3510	8835
Saperion Inc	Auburndale	MA	C	781 899-1228	7868
Scheduling Systems Inc	Framingham	MA	G	508 620-0390	11002
School Yourself Inc	Brookline	MA	G	516 729-7478	9219
Schoolsuite LLC	Great Barrington	MA	G	800 671-1905	11245
Scout Out LLC	Hingham	MA	G	970 476-0209	11510
Sdl Xyenterprise LLC **(PA)**	Wakefield	MA	C	781 756-4400	15974
Sea Street Technologies Inc	Canton	MA	E	617 600-5150	9777
Seceon Inc	Westford	MA	E	978 923-0040	16791
Securelytix Inc	Newton	MA	G	617 283-5227	13635
Semantic Objects LLC	Newton	MA	F	617 272-0955	13636
Siemens Industry Software Inc	Waltham	MA	G	781 250-6800	16193
Silver Bay Software LLC	Dunstable	MA	G	800 364-2889	10391
Similarweb Inc	Burlington	MA	F	800 540-1086	9338
Simsoft Corp	Westborough	MA	G	508 366-5451	16649
Sinauer Associates Inc	Sunderland	MA	E	413 549-4300	15676
Skelmir LLC	Somerville	MA	F	617 625-1551	15215
Skillsoft Corporation	Norwood	MA	G	800 899-1038	14200
Skybuildersdotcom Inc	Cambridge	MA	G	617 876-5678	9653
Smart Software Inc	Belmont	MA	E	617 489-2743	8081
Smartco Services LLC	Taunton	MA	E	508 880-0816	15786
Smartstripe Software Corp	Lexington	MA	G	781 861-1812	12275
Smashfly Technologies Inc **(HQ)**	Concord	MA	F	978 369-3932	10157
Snowbound Software Corporation	Waltham	MA	D	617 607-2000	16195
Softmedia Inc	Walpole	MA	G	978 528-3266	16012
Software Concepts Inc	North Billerica	MA	F	978 584-0400	13865
Software Experts Inc	Westford	MA	F	978 692-5343	16793
Software Leverage Inc	Waltham	MA	G	781 894-3399	16197
Solemma LLC	Cambridge	MA	G	415 238-2231	9654
Solusoft Inc	North Andover	MA	E	978 375-6021	13728
Solutions Atlantic Inc	Boston	MA	G	617 423-2699	8854
Sophic Alliance Inc	East Falmouth	MA	G	508 495-3801	10449
Sorriso Technologies Inc	Acton	MA	E	978 635-3900	7387
Spatter Inc	Newton	MA	G	617 510-0498	13639
Springboard Retail Inc	Boston	MA	E	888 347-2191	8860
Sqdm	Woburn	MA	G	888 993-9674	17301
SS&c Technologies Inc	Burlington	MA	G	781 654-6498	9340
Ssh Government Solutions Inc	Waltham	MA	G	781 247-2124	16200
Standard Machines Inc	Newburyport	MA	G	978 462-4999	13536
Standard Molecular Inc	Cambridge	MA	G	617 401-3318	9661
Starfish Storage Corporation	Waltham	MA	G	781 250-3000	16201
Starwind Software Inc	Middleton	MA	G	617 449-7717	13102
Statistical Solutions Ltd	Boston	MA	F	617 535-7677	8864
Streetscan Inc	Burlington	MA	E	617 399-8236	9341
Stuart Karon	Newton	MA	G	802 649-1911	13641
Suse LLC	Cambridge	MA	E	617 613-2000	9667
Suse LLC	Cambridge	MA	F	617 613-2111	9668
Suspect Technologies Inc	Cambridge	MA	G	843 318-8278	9669
Symphony Talent LLC	Bedford	MA	F	781 275-2716	8013
Synopsys Inc	Westborough	MA	G	508 870-6500	16652
Sysaid Technologies Inc	Newton	MA	F	800 686-7047	13642
T I S Software Corp	Norfolk	MA	G	508 528-9027	13665
T Lex Inc	Brookline	MA	G	617 731-8606	9222

S
I
C

	CITY	ST	EMP	PHONE	ENTRY #
Tamale Software Inc **(DH)**	Boston	MA	G	617 443-1033	8872
Technologies 2010 Inc	Milford	MA	G	508 482-0164	13146
Tegos Technology Inc	Cambridge	MA	G	617 571-5077	9678
Teletypesetting Company Inc	Boston	MA	F	617 542-6220	8877
Televeh Inc	Auburndale	MA	F	857 400-1938	7871
Tex Apps 1 LLC	Boston	MA	D	781 375-6975	8878
Texthelp Inc	Woburn	MA	G	781 503-0421	17309
Tibco Software Inc	Boston	MA	D	617 859-6800	8885
Timelinx Software LLC	North Andover	MA	G	978 662-1171	13731
Toast Inc **(PA)**	Boston	MA	D	617 682-0225	8886
Tokay Software Incorporated	Framingham	MA	F	508 788-0896	11008
Tom Snyder Productions Inc **(HQ)**	Watertown	MA	D	617 600-2145	16324
Toolsgroup Inc	Boston	MA	E	617 263-0080	8887
Toucanect Inc	Boston	MA	G	617 437-1400	8889
Touch Ahead Software LLC	Boston	MA	F	866 960-9301	8890
Touchpoint Software Corp	Sudbury	MA	F	978 443-0094	15669
Triple Seat Software LLC	Acton	MA	G	978 635-0615	7391
Trumpit Inc **(PA)**	Winchester	MA	G	617 650-9292	17099
Tufin Software North Amer Inc	Boston	MA	F	781 685-4940	8893
Tulip Interfaces Inc **(PA)**	Somerville	MA	G	833 468-8547	15226
Typesafe Inc	Cambridge	MA	E	617 622-2200	9684
Unicom Engineering Inc **(HQ)**	Canton	MA	B	781 332-1000	9791
Unipoint Technologies	Auburndale	MA	G	617 952-4244	7872
Unit4 Business Software Inc **(DH)**	Burlington	MA	F	877 704-5974	9350
Uptodate Inc **(DH)**	Waltham	MA	D	781 392-2000	16218
Valora Technologies Inc	Bedford	MA	E	781 229-2265	8018
Vantage Reporting Inc	Dedham	MA	E	212 750-2256	10299
Vanu Inc	Lexington	MA	D	617 864-1711	12281
Varstreet Inc	Boston	MA	E	781 273-3979	8903
Vaultive Inc	Boston	MA	E	212 875-1210	8904
Vblearning LLC	Newton	MA	E	617 527-9999	13648
Veeam Software Corporation	Swampscott	MA	G	781 592-0752	15701
Veho Tech Inc	North Reading	MA	G	617 909-6026	13993
Vermilion Software	Boston	MA	G	617 279-0799	8907
Vertica Systems LLC	Cambridge	MA	C	617 386-4400	9696
Veteran Software Solutions LLC	Marlborough	MA	G	508 330-4553	12843
Via Science Inc **(PA)**	Somerville	MA	G	857 600-2171	15227
Vindor Music Inc	Newton	MA	G	617 984-9831	13649
Virtual Cove Inc	Natick	MA	G	781 354-0492	13287
Virtual Software Systems Inc	Burlington	MA	G	774 270-1207	9354
Visible Measures Corp **(PA)**	Boston	MA	E	617 482-0222	8912
Vision Consulting Group Inc	Holliston	MA	F	508 314-5378	11612
Visitrend LLC	Waltham	MA	F	857 919-2372	16220
Vivantio Inc	Boston	MA	E	617 982-0390	8913
Vizient Inc	Bedford	MA	F	781 271-0980	8019
VMS Software Inc	Bolton	MA	G	978 451-0110	8324
Walden Services Inc	Waltham	MA	G	781 642-7653	16222
Waters Corporation **(PA)**	Milford	MA	C	508 478-2000	13153
Wealth2kcom Inc	Boston	MA	F	781 989-5200	8918
Weather Build Inc	Cambridge	MA	G	617 460-5556	9700
Webport Global LLC	Boston	MA	G	617 385-5058	8919
Webteamwork	Stoughton	MA	G	781 344-8373	15628
Wellcoin Inc	Newton	MA	G	617 512-8617	13654
Westport Group Ltd	Belmont	MA	G	617 489-6581	8083
William Sever Inc	Worcester	MA	F	617 651-2483	17504
Wired Informatics LLC	Boston	MA	G	646 623-7459	8930
Wireover Co	Boston	MA	G	617 308-7993	8931
Wordstream Inc	Boston	MA	F	617 963-0555	8933
Work Play Sleep Inc	Cambridge	MA	G	617 902-0827	9703
Work Technology Corporation **(PA)**	Cambridge	MA	E	617 625-5888	9704
Workday Inc	Boston	MA	G	617 936-1100	8934
Workscape	Framingham	MA	G	508 861-5500	11016
Workscape Inc **(HQ)**	Marlborough	MA	C	508 573-9000	12852
Worldwide Information Inc	Beverly	MA	G	888 273-3260	8198
Wyebot Inc	Marlborough	MA	G	508 481-2603	12853
Zappix Inc	Burlington	MA	F	781 214-8124	9357
Zato Inc	Springfield	MA	G	617 834-8105	15529
Zlink Inc	Maynard	MA	G	978 309-3628	12907
Zoll Medical Corporation **(HQ)**	Chelmsford	MA	A	978 421-9655	9942
Zone & Co Sftwr Consulting LLC	Boston	MA	G	617 307-7068	8943
Zoran Corporation	Burlington	MA	C	408 523-6500	9358
Brian D Murphy	Sebec	ME	G	207 564-2737	6956
Bridge Education	Westbrook	ME	G	207 321-1111	7183
BSD Soft Ware	Durham	ME	G	207 522-5881	5968
Carbonite Inc	Lewiston	ME	G	617 927-3521	6279
Certify Inc **(PA)**	Portland	ME	E	207 773-6100	6635
Chimani Inc	Portland	ME	G	207 221-0266	6637
Coursestorm Inc	Orono	ME	G	207 866-0328	6553
Lilypad LLC	Cape Elizabeth	ME	G	207 200-0221	5877
Limmer Education LLC	Kennebunk	ME	G	207 482-0622	6238
Mathemtics Problem Solving LLC	Portland	ME	G	207 772-2846	6692
Nearpeer Inc	Portland	ME	G	207 615-0414	6699
Powerful ME	Portland	ME	G	207 370-8830	6714
Rockstep Solutions Inc	Portland	ME	G	844 800-7625	6723
Spindoc Inc	Augusta	ME	G	207 689-7010	5621
Subx Inc	Portland	ME	G	207 775-0808	6734
Tidestone Solutions	Portland	ME	G	207 761-2133	6739
Trio Software Corp	Bangor	ME	F	207 942-6222	5660
Tyler Technologies Inc	Yarmouth	ME	C	207 781-2260	7301
Tyler Technologies Inc	Yarmouth	ME	B	207 781-4606	7302
Advanced Entp Systems Corp	Salem	NH	E	508 431-7607	19703
Akken Inc	Nashua	NH	D	866 590-6695	19105
Akumina Inc	Nashua	NH	E	603 318-8269	19106
Alexander Lan Inc	Hollis	NH	F	603 880-8800	18325
Alignrevenue Inc	Bedford	NH	G	603 566-4117	17629
Allen Systems Group Inc	Nashua	NH	D	239 435-2200	19110
Amber Holding Inc **(DH)**	Nashua	NH	E	603 324-3000	19112
Ansys Inc	Lebanon	NH	G	603 653-8005	18612
Assuretec Holdings Inc **(PA)**	Manchester	NH	G	603 641-8443	18781
Autovirt Inc	Nashua	NH	G	603 546-2900	19119
Bid2win Software Inc	Portsmouth	NH	D	800 336-3808	19543
Bottomline Technologies De Inc **(PA)**	Portsmouth	NH	C	603 436-0700	19547
Brown Dog Software Inc	Danville	NH	G	603 382-2713	17967
C Sommer Software LLC	Derry	NH	G	603 432-6225	17974
CCA Global Partners Inc	Manchester	NH	F	603 626-0333	18797
Centric Software Inc	Lebanon	NH	G	603 448-3009	18618
CNi Corp	Milford	NH	G	603 249-5075	19050
Conest Software Systems Inc	Manchester	NH	E	603 437-9353	18802
Connectleader LLC	Salem	NH	C	800 955-5040	19718
Connexient LLC	Manchester	NH	F	603 669-1300	18803
Crawford Sftwr Consulting Inc	Londonderry	NH	G	603 537-9630	18689
Denali Software Inc	Nashua	NH	G	603 566-0991	19145
Eddefy Inc	Dover	NH	G	802 989-1934	18020
Emerlyn Software LLC	Center Conway	NH	G	603 447-6130	17795
Episerver Inc **(DH)**	Nashua	NH	C	603 594-0249	19150
Equinox Software Systems Inc	Westmoreland	NH	G	603 399-9970	19971
Eversolve LLC	Windham	NH	G	603 870-9739	20005
Expedience Software LLC	Manchester	NH	E	978 378-5330	18821
Fis Systems International LLC	Salem	NH	C	603 898-6185	19733
Hopto Inc **(PA)**	Concord	NH	F	800 472-7466	17908
Hydrocad Sftwr Solutions LLC	Chocorua	NH	G	603 323-8666	17831
Ibis LLC	Bedford	NH	E	603 471-0951	17645
Infinizone Corp	Hollis	NH	F	603 465-2917	18333
Inspectcheck LLC	Chichester	NH	G	603 223-0003	17829
Interactive Systems Inc	Nashua	NH	F	603 318-7700	19190
Intouch Software	West Lebanon	NH	G	603 643-1952	19954
Itag LLC	Merrimack	NH	F	603 429-8436	19008
Kana Software Inc	Bedford	NH	G	650 614-8300	17649
Kentico Software LLC	Bedford	NH	E	866 328-8998	17650
Lanmark Controls Inc	Hudson	NH	G	978 264-0200	18409
Lcm Group Inc	Nashua	NH	G	603 888-1248	19198
Learning Station LLC	Wilmot	NH	G	603 496-7896	19973
Loyalty Builders Inc **(PA)**	Portsmouth	NH	F	603 610-8800	19590
Mapleleaf Software Inc	Londonderry	NH	G	603 413-0419	18717
Meetingmatrix Intl Inc	Portsmouth	NH	E	603 610-1600	19593
Myturncom Pbc	Lebanon	NH	G	206 552-8488	18632
Narrative 1 Software LLC	Plymouth	NH	G	603 968-2233	19529
Newmarket Software Systems	Portsmouth	NH	G	603 436-7500	19601
Noblespirit Entp Sftwr LLC	Pittsfield	NH	G	603 435-8218	19504
Ntp Software of Ca Inc **(PA)**	Nashua	NH	G	603 641-6937	19221
NWare Technologies Inc	Dover	NH	G	603 617-3760	18043
Omada Technologies LLC	Portsmouth	NH	G	603 944-7124	19602
Oracle Corporation	Manchester	NH	E	603 668-4998	18896
Oracle Systems Corporation	Nashua	NH	B	603 897-3000	19225
Paton Data Company	Merrimack	NH	G	603 598-8070	19020
Perimeter Acquisition Corp **(HQ)**	Manchester	NH	F	603 645-1616	18900
Peruse Software Inc	Nashua	NH	G	603 626-0061	19230
Phario Solution	Nashua	NH	G	603 821-3804	19232
Pickup Patrol LLC	Mont Vernon	NH	G	603 310-9120	19093
Premier Packaging LLC	Hooksett	NH	G	603 485-7465	18354
Professnal Sftwr For Nrses Inc	Amherst	NH	F	800 889-7627	17582
Profitkey International Inc	Salem	NH	E	603 898-9800	19760
Protracker Software Inc	Hampton	NH	G	603 926-8085	18268
Regdox Solutions Inc	Nashua	NH	D	978 264-4460	19248
Retrieve LLC	Manchester	NH	E	603 413-0022	18910
River City Software LLC	Exeter	NH	G	603 686-5525	18130
SDC Solutions Inc	Bedford	NH	E	603 629-4242	17661
Simpliprotected LLC	Auburn	NH	G	603 669-7465	17613
Skillsoft Corporation **(DH)**	Nashua	NH	C	603 324-3000	19262
Ssi Investments I Limited **(DH)**	Nashua	NH	G	603 324-3000	19265
Ssi Investments II Limited	Nashua	NH	A	603 324-3000	19266
Strolid Inc	Windham	NH	F	978 655-8550	20010
Sungard Insurance Systems Inc	Manchester	NH	G	603 641-3636	18933
Syam Software Inc	Londonderry	NH	F	603 598-9575	18740
Synap Inc	Dover	NH	G	888 572-1150	18056
Teameda Inc	Manchester	NH	G	603 656-5200	18936
Techlok Inc	Manchester	NH	G	617 902-0322	18937
Thunderbolt Innovation LLC	Dover	NH	G	888 335-6234	18060
Tyler Technologies Inc	Merrimack	NH	E	603 578-6745	19038
Tyler Technologies Inc	Manchester	NH	G	800 288-8167	18943
Wind River Systems Inc	Nashua	NH	E	603 897-2000	19287
Andera Inc	Providence	RI	D	401 621-7900	20953
Ansys Inc	Providence	RI	G	401 455-1955	20955
Avtech Software Inc **(PA)**	Warren	RI	E	401 628-1600	21287

	CITY	ST	EMP	PHONE	ENTRY #
E Sphere Inc	Providence	RI	F	401 270-7512	21000
Forensicsoft Inc	East Greenwich	RI	G	401 489-7559	20367
Igt Global Solutions Corp	West Greenwich	RI	E	401 392-7025	21456
Kerb Inc	Providence	RI	D	401 491-9595	21047
Ocean State Software LLC	East Greenwich	RI	G	202 695-8049	20375
Opal Data Technology Inc	Providence	RI	G	401 435-0033	21085
Open SRC Prjct Fr Ntwk Dt ACS	Narragansett	RI	G	401 284-1304	20644
Oracle Corporation	Barrington	RI	B	401 245-1110	20050
Oracle Corporation	Warwick	RI	G	401 658-3900	21399
Quantifacts Inc	Riverside	RI	G	401 421-8300	21175
Schneider Electric It Corp **(DH)**	West Kingston	RI	A	401 789-5735	21471
Shelfdig LLC	Providence	RI	G	617 299-6335	21121
Simpatico Software Systems	Barrington	RI	F	401 246-1358	20055
Smiths Detection Inc	Middletown	RI	F	401 848-7678	20632
Tap Technologies Inc	Narragansett	RI	G	860 333-7834	20652
Voicescript Technologies	Warwick	RI	E	401 524-2246	21439
Zingon LLC	Providence	RI	G	716 491-0000	21159
Aurora North Software Inc	Burlington	VT	E	802 540-2504	21768
Bennington Microtchnlgy Center	North Bennington	VT	G	802 442-8975	22209
Cloud Forest Solutions Inc	Bondville	VT	G	802 353-2848	21697
Concepts Eti Inc	White River Junction	VT	D	802 296-2321	22637
Concepts Nrec LLC **(PA)**	White River Junction	VT	D	802 296-2321	22638
Conix Systems **(PA)**	Pawlet	VT	G	800 332-1899	22256
Core Value Software	Norwich	VT	F	802 473-3147	22247
Dealerpolicy LLC	Williston	VT	G	802 655-9000	22661
Faraday Inc	Middlebury	VT	G	800 442-1521	22110
Gametheory Inc	Burlington	VT	G	802 779-2322	21785
Gary F Girome	Milton	VT	G	802 893-7870	22128
Jamison Computer Services	Saint Albans	VT	G	802 527-9758	22370
Mach 7 Technologies Inc	South Burlington	VT	F	802 861-7745	22452
Mediware/Synergy Human & Socia	Essex Junction	VT	D	802 878-8514	21949
Natworks Inc	Northfield	VT	F	802 485-6818	22244
Notabli Inc	Burlington	VT	F	802 448-0810	21799
Piematrix Inc	Burlington	VT	F	802 318-4891	21803
Resource Engineering Inc	Waitsfield	VT	G	802 496-5888	22568
Richard Akerboom	White River Junction	VT	G	802 291-6116	22642
Social Sentinel Inc	Burlington	VT	F	800 628-0158	21810
Thinkmd Inc	Burlington	VT	G	802 734-7993	21812
Touchfight Games LLC	Shaftsbury	VT	G	802 753-7360	22407
Upper Access Inc	Hinesburg	VT	G	802 482-2988	22032
Vermont Systems Inc	Essex Junction	VT	D	802 879-6993	21963
Visible Electrophysiology LLC	Colchester	VT	F	802 847-4539	21889
Workwise LLC	Waterbury	VT	E	802 881-8178	22589

76 MISCELLANEOUS REPAIR SERVICES

7692 Welding Repair

	CITY	ST	EMP	PHONE	ENTRY #
Accurate Welding Services LLC	Windsor Locks	CT	F	860 623-9500	5380
Aerotek Welding Co Inc	North Granby	CT	G	860 653-0120	2993
Amk Welding Inc **(HQ)**	South Windsor	CT	E	860 289-5634	3937
Anderson Tool Company Inc	New Haven	CT	G	203 777-4153	2657
Ansonia Stl Fabrication Co Inc	Beacon Falls	CT	E	203 888-4509	53
B & F Machine Co Inc	New Britain	CT	D	860 225-6349	2512
C and B Welding LLC	Lebanon	CT	G	860 423-9047	1933
C V Tool Company Inc **(PA)**	Southington	CT	E	978 353-7901	4042
Cheshire Manufacturing Co Inc	Cheshire	CT	G	203 272-3586	721
City Welding	Hartford	CT	G	860 951-4714	1814
Ctr Welding	Danbury	CT	G	704 473-1587	894
D B F Industries Inc	New Britain	CT	E	860 827-8283	2525
Durant Machine Inc **(PA)**	Mystic	CT	G	860 536-7698	2438
Dyco Industries Inc	South Windsor	CT	E	860 289-4957	3958
East Windsor Metal Fabg Inc	South Windsor	CT	F	860 528-7107	3961
EZ Welding LLC	New Britain	CT	G	860 707-3100	2533
F & W Rentals Inc	Orange	CT	F	203 795-0591	3366
Farrell Prcsion Mtalcraft Corp	New Milford	CT	E	860 355-2651	2799
Fonda Fabricating & Welding Co	Plainville	CT	G	860 793-0601	3489
General Wldg & Fabrication Inc	Watertown	CT	F	860 274-9668	5010
Goodyfab Llc	North Branford	CT	G	203 927-3059	2964
H G Steinmetz Machine Works	Bethel	CT	F	203 794-1880	158
Harry Thommen Company	Bridgeport	CT	G	203 333-3637	424
J T Fantozzi Co Inc	Meriden	CT	G	203 238-7018	2096
Jeff Manufacturing Co Inc	Torrington	CT	F	860 482-8845	4582
Jims Welding Service LLC	Danbury	CT	G	203 744-2982	939
Joining Technologies Inc	East Granby	CT	D	860 653-0111	1130
K T I Turbo-Tech Inc	East Windsor	CT	F	860 623-2511	1290
Kell-Strom Tool Intl Inc	Wethersfield	CT	E	860 529-6851	5254
Kensington Welding & Trlr Co	Kensington	CT	G	860 828-3564	1918
Kin-Therm Inc	East Windsor	CT	F	860 623-2511	1291
KTI Bi-Metallix Inc	East Windsor	CT	F	860 623-2511	1293
KTI Inc **(HQ)**	East Windsor	CT	F	860 623-2511	1294
L M Gill Welding and Mfr LLC	Manchester	CT	E	860 647-9931	2018
Labco Welding Inc	Middletown	CT	G	860 632-2625	2200
Lemac Iron Works Inc	West Hartford	CT	G	860 232-7380	5081
LM Gill Welding & Mfg LLC	Manchester	CT	E	860 647-9931	2020
Lynn Welding Co Inc	Newington	CT	F	860 667-4400	2877
Mackenzie Mch & Mar Works Inc	East Haven	CT	G	203 777-3479	1254
Mainville Welding Co Inc	Meriden	CT	G	203 237-3103	2101
Marc Bouley	Willimantic	CT	G	860 450-1713	5267
Matias Importing & Distrg Corp	Newington	CT	G	860 666-5544	2880
Metal Industries Inc	Hartford	CT	G	860 296-6228	1847
Nct Inc	Newington	CT	F	860 666-8424	2886
New Canaan Forge LLC **(PA)**	New Canaan	CT	G	203 966-3858	2610
P & M Welding Co LLC	South Windsor	CT	G	860 528-2077	3999
Parama Corp	Bethel	CT	F	203 790-8155	174
Paul Welding Company Inc	Newington	CT	F	860 229-9945	2891
Phoenix Machine Inc	Seymour	CT	G	203 888-1135	3759
Quality Welding LLC	Bristol	CT	G	860 585-1121	599
Quality Welding Service LLC	Portland	CT	G	860 342-7202	3572
Recor Welding Center Inc	Southington	CT	G	860 573-1942	4073
Reliable Welding & Speed LLC	Enfield	CT	G	860 749-3977	1379
Reno Machine Company Inc	Newington	CT	D	860 666-5641	2898
S S Fabrications Inc	Eastford	CT	G	860 974-1910	1314
Sauciers Misc Metal Works LLC	Southington	CT	G	860 747-4577	4075
Somers Manufacturing Inc	Bristol	CT	G	860 314-1075	613
Sorge Industries Inc	Shelton	CT	G	203 924-8900	3872
Standard Welding Company Inc	East Hartford	CT	G	860 528-9628	1222
State Welding & Fabg Inc	Wallingford	CT	G	203 294-4071	4813
Thomas La Ganga	Torrington	CT	G	860 489-0920	4601
Tim Welding	North Branford	CT	G	203 488-3486	2981
Tinsley GROup-Ps&w Inc **(HQ)**	Milford	CT	D	919 742-5832	2376
Torrington Diesel Corporation	Torrington	CT	G	860 496-9948	4603
Total Fab LLC	East Haven	CT	F	475 238-8176	1266
Trico Welding Company LLC	Beacon Falls	CT	G	203 720-3782	66
United Steel Inc	East Hartford	CT	C	860 289-2323	1232
Weld-All Inc	Southington	CT	F	860 621-3156	4091
Welder Repair & Rental Svc Inc	Durham	CT	G	203 238-9284	1096
White Welding Company Inc	Waterbury	CT	G	203 753-1197	4978
Willies Welding Inc	Meriden	CT	G	203 237-6235	2151
A & M Welding Fabrication Inc	East Weymouth	MA	G	781 335-9548	10532
ABC Disposal Service Inc	New Bedford	MA	E	508 990-1911	13347
Advanced Welding & Design Inc	Woburn	MA	F	781 938-7644	17112
Aero Brazing Corp	Woburn	MA	F	781 933-7511	17114
Aero Manufacturing Corp	Beverly	MA	D	978 720-1000	8096
Alvin Johnson	East Longmeadow	MA	G	413 525-6334	10465
Amic Inc	Attleboro	MA	G	508 222-5300	7704
Ashmont Welding Company Inc	Bridgewater	MA	F	508 279-1977	9060
Aviation Welding	Uxbridge	MA	G	508 278-3041	15914
Baxter Inc	West Yarmouth	MA	G	508 228-8136	16578
Biasin Enterprises Inc	Lee	MA	G	413 243-0885	12089
Blue Fleet Welding Service	New Bedford	MA	F	508 997-5513	13363
Boston Forging & Welding Corp	Boston	MA	G	617 567-2300	8430
Boston Welding & Design Inc	Woburn	MA	F	781 932-0035	17137
Burton Frame and Trailer Inc	Pepperell	MA	G	978 433-2051	14437
Capeway Welding Inc	Plymouth	MA	F	508 747-6666	14549
Chicopee Welding & Tool Inc	Charlemont	MA	F	413 598-8215	9819
City Welding & Fabrication Inc	Worcester	MA	E	508 853-6000	17356
CM Murphy Welding Inc	Webster	MA	G	508 868-8511	16340
Complete Welding Services	Marshfield	MA	G	781 837-9024	12858
Composite Company Inc	Sherborn	MA	G	508 651-1681	15078
D Cronins Welding Service	Lawrence	MA	G	978 664-4488	12014
Danvers Engineering Co Inc	Danvers	MA	G	978 774-7501	10211
David Gilbert	Framingham	MA	G	508 879-1507	10940
DCB Welding and Fabrication	Lowell	MA	G	978 587-3883	12366
Diaute Bros	Braintree	MA	G	781 848-0524	9001
Dockside Repairs Inc	New Bedford	MA	F	508 993-6730	13380
East Cast Wldg Fabrication LLC	Newburyport	MA	E	978 465-2338	13484
Excalibur Welding and Piping	Rehoboth	MA	G	401 241-0548	14748
Falcon Precision Machine Co	Ludlow	MA	G	413 583-2117	12465
Feeney Fence Inc	Hyde Park	MA	G	617 364-1407	11866
First Place Welding Inc	Rutland	MA	G	508 886-4762	14881
Fitchburg Welding Co Inc	Westminster	MA	E	978 874-2911	16804
G and JW Elding Inc	East Taunton	MA	G	774 565-0223	10513
G and M Welding	Malden	MA	G	781 480-4247	12573
Gabcon Welding & Cnstr Co	Taunton	MA	D	508 822-2220	15751
Gem Welding	North Billerica	MA	G	978 362-3873	13821
Gill Metal Fab Inc	Brockton	MA	E	508 580-4445	9151
Harbor Welding	Gloucester	MA	G	978 281-5771	11192
Harris Tool & Die Company Inc	Fitchburg	MA	G	978 479-1842	10828
Herb Con Machine Company Inc	Saugus	MA	G	781 233-2755	14985
Herrick Everett Welding & Mch	Holland	MA	G	413 245-7533	11553
Horacios Welding & Shtmtl Inc	New Bedford	MA	F	508 985-9940	13395
Housatonic Welding Company	Housatonic	MA	G	413 274-6631	11742
Hubb Equipment Inc	Hubbardston	MA	G	978 928-4258	11744
International Beam Wldg Corp	West Springfield	MA	F	413 781-4368	16527
J & L Welding & Machine Co	Gloucester	MA	E	978 283-3388	11193
J E Schell Welding	East Freetown	MA	G	508 763-4658	10453
J F OMalley Welding Co	Worcester	MA	G	508 791-8671	17395
K & W Machine Works	Springfield	MA	G	413 543-3329	15483
K K Welding Inc	Hyde Park	MA	G	617 361-1780	11871
Kent Pearce	East Wareham	MA	G	508 295-3791	10531
Kielb Welding Enterprises	Springfield	MA	F	413 734-4544	15484
L W Tank Repair Incorporated	North Uxbridge	MA	F	508 234-6000	13995
Larkin Motors LLC	Bridgewater	MA	G	508 807-1333	9082
Ledgerock Welding and Fabg	Hudson	MA	G	978 562-6500	11785

	CITY	ST	EMP	PHONE	ENTRY #
Leo S Cavelier Inc	Acton	MA	G	978 369-2770	7368
Lima Fredy	Everett	MA	F	781 599-3055	10618
Linton Welding & Fabrication	Lawrence	MA	G	978 681-7736	12048
Lizotte Welding	East Freetown	MA	G	508 763-8784	10454
Malcom Co-Leister	Andover	MA	G	781 875-3121	7567
Marblehead Engineering	Essex	MA	F	978 432-1386	10595
McNamara Fabricating Co Inc	West Boylston	MA	F	774 243-7425	16422
Metrick Manufacturing Co Inc	Woburn	MA	G	781 935-1331	17228
Micro ARC Welding Service	Worcester	MA	G	508 852-6125	17414
Noremac Manufacturing Corp	Westborough	MA	E	508 879-7514	16639
O W Landergren Inc	Pittsfield	MA	E	413 442-5632	14497
Oleary Welding Corp	East Douglas	MA	G	508 476-9793	10431
Oliver Welding & Fabricating	Ipswich	MA	G	978 356-4488	11933
ORourke Welding Inc	Worcester	MA	G	508 755-6360	17437
Podgurski Wldg & Hvy Eqp Repr	Canton	MA	G	781 830-9901	9770
Quincy Steel & Welding Co Inc	Quincy	MA	G	617 472-1180	14651
R & M Precision Machine	Fall River	MA	G	508 678-2488	10750
R Moody Machine & Fabrication	Deerfield	MA	G	413 773-3329	10303
Rae Js	Shelburne Falls	MA	G	413 625-9228	15075
Ralph Seaver	Cherry Valley	MA	G	508 892-9486	9976
Raymond Spinazzola	Ashland	MA	G	508 881-3089	7667
Rens Welding & Fabricating	Taunton	MA	F	508 828-1702	15779
Roar Industries Inc	Holliston	MA	F	508 429-5952	11599
Roland Teiner Company Inc	Everett	MA	F	617 387-7800	10628
Shaw Welding Company Inc	Billerica	MA	F	978 667-0197	8293
Standex International Corp	North Billerica	MA	D	978 667-2771	13869
Tewksbury Welding Inc	Tewksbury	MA	G	978 851-7401	15841
Thermo Craft Engineering Corp	Lynn	MA	E	781 599-4023	12543
Triad Inc	Plainville	MA	G	508 695-2247	14537
Trivak Inc	Lowell	MA	E	978 453-7123	12440
Union Machine Company Lynn Inc **(PA)**	Groveland	MA	E	978 521-5100	11304
Villa Machine Associates Inc	Dedham	MA	F	781 326-5969	10300
Welch Welding and Trck Eqp Inc	North Chelmsford	MA	E	978 251-8726	13913
Welch Welding Inc	North Chelmsford	MA	G	978 251-8726	13914
Weld Rite	Jamaica Plain	MA	G	617 524-9747	11951
Welding Craftsmen Co Inc	South Easton	MA	F	508 230-7878	15295
Welfab Inc	North Billerica	MA	E	978 667-0180	13876
Brooks Welding & Machining Inc	Waterboro	ME	G	207 247-4141	7151
Churchs Welding & Fab Inc	Durham	ME	G	207 353-4249	5969
Days Auto Body Inc	Medway	ME	G	207 746-5310	6423
Dennis Welding & Marine Inc	Beals	ME	G	207 497-5998	5683
Derek White	Winterport	ME	G	207 223-5746	7277
Down East Shtmtl & Certif Wldg	Brewer	ME	G	207 989-3443	5795
Espositos Wldg & Fabrication	Surry	ME	G	207 667-2442	7076
Howies Wldg & Fabrication Inc	Jay	ME	G	207 645-2581	6220
M & M Sheet Metal & Welding	Presque Isle	ME	G	207 764-6443	6761
Maine Conveyor Inc	Windham	ME	G	207 854-5661	7241
Nichols Custom Welding Inc	Wilton	ME	E	207 645-3101	7227
North E Wldg & Fabrication Inc	Auburn	ME	E	207 786-2446	5583
Praxair Surface Tech Inc	Biddeford	ME	D	207 282-3787	5757
Ramsays Welding & Machine Inc	Lincoln	ME	F	207 794-8839	6359
Titan Chain & Welding	Oakland	ME	G	207 465-4144	6535
Troy Winger	Trenton	ME	G	207 667-1815	7103
Walts Machine Shop	Oquossoc	ME	G	207 864-5083	6548
Western Maine Welding & Piping	Strong	ME	G	207 652-2327	7074
3 D Welding	Claremont	NH	G	603 543-0866	17833
Ace Welding Co Inc	Merrimack	NH	E	603 424-9936	18984
Anderson Welding LLC	Dover	NH	G	603 996-6225	18005
Andy Croteau	Portsmouth	NH	G	603 436-8919	19536
ARC Maintenance Machining	Londonderry	NH	G	603 626-8046	18677
Baron Machine Company Inc	Laconia	NH	D	603 524-6800	18557
Bocra Industries Inc	Seabrook	NH	E	603 474-3598	19794
Brazen Innovations Inc	Marlow	NH	G	603 446-7919	18966
Bri-Weld Industries LLC	Auburn	NH	F	603 622-9480	17608
Burt General Repair & Welding	Lancaster	NH	G	603 788-4821	18597
Caron Fabrication LLC	Groveton	NH	G	603 631-0025	18231
Custom Welding & Fabrications	West Nottingham	NH	F	603 942-5170	19964
D M F Machine Co Inc	Londonderry	NH	G	603 434-4945	18691
East Coast Metal Works Co Inc	Kingston	NH	G	603 642-9600	18543
East Coast Welding	Gilford	NH	G	603 293-8384	18187
Erwin Precision Inc	Manchester	NH	G	603 623-2333	18819
Hollis Line Machine Co Inc **(PA)**	Hollis	NH	E	603 465-2251	18332
J & D Welding	Grafton	NH	G	603 523-7695	18216

	CITY	ST	EMP	PHONE	ENTRY #
Mahers Welding Service Inc	Northfield	NH	G	603 286-4851	19404
Mass Chassis	Kingston	NH	F	603 642-8967	18545
Mds Welding & Fabrication	Weare	NH	G	603 660-0772	19938
Northeast Wldg Bridge Repr LLC	New Boston	NH	G	603 396-8549	19295
Ralph L Osgood Inc	Claremont	NH	F	603 543-1703	17859
Recycling Mechanical Neng LLC	Allenstown	NH	F	603 268-8028	17541
Sean Byrnes Welding LLC	Thornton	NH	G	603 726-4315	19902
Smiths Tblar Systms-Lconia Inc	Laconia	NH	B	603 524-2064	18587
Starkey Welding Crane Service	Brentwood	NH	G	603 679-2553	17758
Stone Machine Co Inc	Chester	NH	F	603 887-4287	17826
Strafford Machine Inc	Strafford	NH	G	603 664-9758	19866
Valley Welding & Fabg Inc	Hollis	NH	E	603 465-3266	18340
Weidner Services LLC	Jaffrey	NH	F	603 532-4833	18481
Whites Welding Co Inc	Hampton	NH	G	603 926-2261	18280
Will-Mor Manufacturing Inc	Seabrook	NH	D	603 474-8971	19823
Artic Tool & Engrg Co LLC	Greenville	RI	F	401 785-2210	20461
Blouin General Welding & Fabg	Woonsocket	RI	G	401 762-4542	21551
Champlin Welding Inc	Narragansett	RI	G	401 782-4099	20636
Dexter Service Center	East Providence	RI	G	401 438-3900	20405
Formex Inc	East Greenwich	RI	E	401 885-9800	20368
Frontier Welding & Fabrication	Woonsocket	RI	G	401 769-0271	21565
Goldenrod Welding Inc	Cumberland	RI	G	401 725-9248	20322
Guill Tool & Engrg Co Inc	West Warwick	RI	D	401 822-8186	21493
Laser Fare Inc **(PA)**	Smithfield	RI	D	401 231-4400	21235
Luthers Repair Shop Inc	Bristol	RI	F	401 253-5550	20091
Microweld Co Inc	Riverside	RI	G	401 438-5985	21172
Providence Welding	Providence	RI	G	401 941-2700	21100
Robert B Evans Inc	Westerly	RI	G	401 596-2719	21538
Seven Star Inc	Newport	RI	G	401 683-6222	20680
West Warwick Welding Inc	West Warwick	RI	F	401 822-8200	21513
Browns Certified Welding Inc	Bristol	VT	F	802 453-3351	21762
Cave Manufacturing Inc	Brattleboro	VT	E	802 257-9253	21723
Giroux Body Shop Inc	Hinesburg	VT	F	802 482-2162	22025
Gloucester Associates Inc	Barre	VT	E	802 479-1088	21617
Metalworks Inc	Burlington	VT	G	802 863-0414	21796
Milton Vermont Sheet Metal Inc	Milton	VT	D	802 893-1581	22134
North Country Engineering Inc	Derby	VT	E	802 766-5396	21902
PG Adams Inc	South Burlington	VT	F	802 862-8664	22457
Raymond Reynolds Welding	Essex Junction	VT	G	802 879-4650	21955
Thomas Drake	Colchester	VT	G	802 655-0990	21881

7694 Armature Rewinding Shops

	CITY	ST	EMP	PHONE	ENTRY #
Aparos Electric Motor Service	Southington	CT	G	860 276-2044	4039
Bemat TEC LLC	Cromwell	CT	G	860 632-0049	847
Central Electric Inc	Dayville	CT	G	860 774-3054	1041
Cudzilo Enterprises Inc	Bethel	CT	G	203 748-4694	139
Electric Enterprise Inc	Stratford	CT	F	203 378-7311	4410
Jan Manufacturing Inc	Wolcott	CT	G	203 879-0580	5445
Palmers Elc Mtrs & Pumps Inc	Norwalk	CT	G	203 348-7378	3214
Precision Devices Inc **(PA)**	Wallingford	CT	F	203 265-9308	4788
Tibbys Electric Motor Service	Bethel	CT	G	203 748-4694	183
Total Control Inc	Wallingford	CT	G	203 269-4749	4822
Traver Electric Motor Co Inc	Waterbury	CT	E	203 753-5103	4966
Bay State Electric Motor Co	Methuen	MA	G	978 686-7089	13012
Delta Elc Mtr Repr Sls & Svc	Medford	MA	G	781 395-0551	12930
First Electric Motor Svc Inc	Woburn	MA	E	781 491-1100	17181
Hancock Electric Mtr Svcs Inc	Quincy	MA	G	617 472-5789	14631
Kalman Electric Motors Inc	Stoughton	MA	G	781 341-4900	15600
Maxon Precision Motors Inc **(HQ)**	Taunton	MA	E	508 677-0520	15763
Morse Electric Motors Co Inc	Gardner	MA	G	978 632-3733	11120
Reliance Electric Service	Holyoke	MA	G	413 533-3557	11651
Shepard & Parker Inc	Fitchburg	MA	G	978 343-3907	10852
Stearns Perry & Smith Co Inc	Quincy	MA	G	617 423-4775	14659
AC Electric Corp **(PA)**	Auburn	ME	E	207 784-7341	5545
AC Electric Corp	Bangor	ME	F	207 945-9487	5628
Moir Company Inc	Denmark	ME	F	207 452-2000	5951
Prime Electric Motors	Gorham	ME	F	207 591-7800	6128
Timken Motor & Crane Svcs LLC	Portland	ME	F	207 699-2501	6740
Algers Leo NH Elc Mtrs	Laconia	NH	G	603 524-3729	18555
Chase Electric Motors LLC	Hooksett	NH	G	603 669-2565	18346
Lawrence Fay	Manchester	NH	G	603 668-3811	18862
Wirewinders Inc	Milford	NH	G	603 673-1763	19083
Pioneer Motors and Drives Inc	South Burlington	VT	E	802 651-0114	22458

ALPHABETIC SECTION

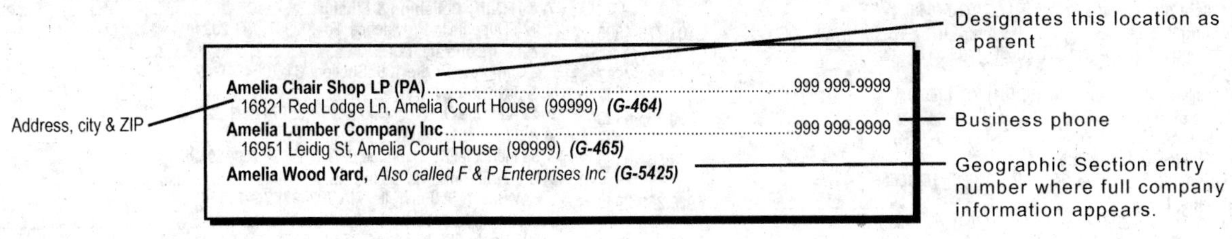

See footnotes for symbols and codes identification.

* Companies listed alphabetically.

* Complete physical or mailing address.

1 Beyond Inc 617 591-2200
529 Main St Ste 109 Boston MA (02129) ***(G-8326)***
1 Call Does It All and Then 413 584-5381
85 State Rd South Deerfield MA (01373) ***(G-15244)***
101.7 FM, Providence *Also called Boston Phoenix Inc* ***(G-20971)***
109 Design LLC (PA) 203 941-1812
55 Whitney Ave Fl 2 New Haven CT (06510) ***(G-2650)***
128 Technology Inc (PA) 781 203-8400
200 Summit Dr Burlington MA (01803) ***(G-9227)***
136 Express Printing Inc 401 253-0136
380 Metacom Ave Bristol RI (02809) ***(G-20059)***
136 Express Prtg & Copy Ctr, Bristol *Also called 136 Express Printing Inc* ***(G-20059)***
1366 Technologies Inc 781 861-1611
68 Preston Ct Bedford MA (01730) ***(G-7955)***
138 Barrows Street Realty Inc 508 285-2904
138 Barrows St Norton MA (02766) ***(G-14069)***
149 Medical Inc 617 410-8123
1173 Main St Bolton MA (01740) ***(G-8316)***
14th Star Brewing LLC 802 528-5988
133 N Main St Ste 7 Saint Albans VT (05478) ***(G-22362)***
16 Acres Optical, Springfield *Also called Chicopee Vision Center Inc* ***(G-15460)***
1634 Meadery 508 517-4058
3 Short St Ipswich MA (01938) ***(G-11899)***
16sur20 Management LLC 413 637-5061
30 Kemble St Lenox MA (01240) ***(G-12099)***
17 Chestnut Inc 800 897-3117
97 Tenney St Unit 1 Georgetown MA (01833) ***(G-11134)***
176 Willow Avenue LLC 401 635-2329
176 Willow Ave Little Compton RI (02837) ***(G-20603)***
1817 Shoppe Inc (PA) 508 347-2241
420 Main St Ste 1 Sturbridge MA (01566) ***(G-15636)***
1911 Office LLC 603 352-2448
20 Central Sq Keene NH (03431) ***(G-18488)***
1947 LLC 401 293-5500
208 Clock Tower Sq Portsmouth RI (02871) ***(G-20916)***
1st Casting Company 401 272-0750
64 Dyerville Ave Johnston RI (02919) ***(G-20495)***
2 Cool Promos 508 351-9700
1900 W Park Dr Ste 280 Westborough MA (01581) ***(G-16583)***
2 Dogs Treats LLC 617 286-4844
171 Neponset Ave Dorchester MA (02122) ***(G-10339)***
2 Girl A Trunk 203 762-0360
35 Dudley Rd Wilton CT (06897) ***(G-5272)***
2 Hawksley Drive, Oxford *Also called Nordic Shield Plastic Corp* ***(G-14270)***
20/20 Software Inc 203 316-5500
2001 W Main St Ste 270 Stamford CT (06902) ***(G-4122)***
200 Mill Plain Road LLC 203 254-0113
1411 Cross Hwy Fairfield CT (06824) ***(G-1411)***
210 Innovations 860 445-0210
210 Leonard Dr Groton CT (06340) ***(G-1664)***
2111 Hearst Ave, Lebanon *Also called Myturncom Pbc* ***(G-18632)***
21st, Marlborough *Also called Twentyfrst Cntury Bchmcals Inc* ***(G-12839)***
21st Century Foods Inc 617 522-7595
30 Germania St Ste 2 Boston MA (02130) ***(G-8327)***
21st Century Fox America Inc 203 563-6600
20 Westport Rd Wilton CT (06897) ***(G-5273)***
24m Technologies Inc 617 553-1012
130 Brookline St Ste 200 Cambridge MA (02139) ***(G-9366)***
269 Walpole Street LLC 781 762-1128
269 Walpole St Norwood MA (02062) ***(G-14115)***
270 University Ave LLC 781 407-0836
270 University Ave Westwood MA (02090) ***(G-16855)***
27th Exposure LLC 603 444-5800
53 Main St Littleton NH (03561) ***(G-18653)***
28 Kitchen Cabinet LLC 774 321-6099
28 Coolidge St Auburn MA (01501) ***(G-7820)***
283 Industries Inc 203 276-8956
3 Mallory Hill Rd Ridgefield CT (06877) ***(G-3653)***
290 Industrial Stitching Inc 978 355-0271
49 Main St South Barre MA (01074) ***(G-15234)***
2d Material Technologies LLC 603 763-4791
84 Todd Farm Ln New London NH (03257) ***(G-19312)***
2l Inc 978 567-8867
4 Kane Industrial Dr Hudson MA (01749) ***(G-11748)***
3 D Welding 603 543-0866
18 Old Newport Rd Claremont NH (03743) ***(G-17833)***
3 Little Figs LLC 617 623-3447
278 Highland Ave B Somerville MA (02143) ***(G-15150)***
3 M N Corp 508 586-4471
12 Perry Ave Brockton MA (02302) ***(G-9112)***
3 Play Inc (PA) 781 205-4820
1600 Providence Hwy Ste 1 Walpole MA (02081) ***(G-15986)***
3 Potato 4 LLC 978 744-0948
2 E India Square Mall Salem MA (01970) ***(G-14888)***
3 Story Software LLC 203 530-3224
63 Bridge St New Milford CT (06776) ***(G-2785)***
3-D Welding Inc 508 222-2500
5 Howard Ireland Dr Attleboro MA (02703) ***(G-7695)***
32 North Corporation 207 284-5010
16 Pomerleau St Biddeford ME (04005) ***(G-5716)***
325 Silver Street Inc 413 789-1800
325 Silver St Agawam MA (01001) ***(G-7415)***
360 Recycling LLC 413 562-0193
100 Sgt Tm Dion Way Westfield MA (01085) ***(G-16659)***
360alumni Inc 203 253-5860
1 Norfield Rd Weston CT (06883) ***(G-5167)***
3cross Brewing Company 508 615-8195
26 Cambridge St Worcester MA (01603) ***(G-17328)***
3d Diagnostix Inc 617 820-5279
24 Denby Rd 211 Allston MA (02134) ***(G-7458)***
3d Educational Services Inc 978 364-2728
321 Billerica Rd Ste 1 Chelmsford MA (01824) ***(G-9864)***
3d Logging Co Inc 603 915-3020
302 Howard St Berlin NH (03570) ***(G-17690)***
3d-Matrix, Cambridge *Also called 3dm Inc* ***(G-9367)***
3ddx, Allston *Also called 3d Diagnostix Inc* ***(G-7458)***
3derm Systems Inc 617 237-6041
101 Huntington Ave # 1300 Boston MA (02199) ***(G-8328)***
3des, Chelmsford *Also called 3d Educational Services Inc* ***(G-9864)***
3dfortify Inc 978 399-4075
28 Damrell St Ste B4 Boston MA (02127) ***(G-8329)***
3dm Inc 617 875-6204
245 1st St Cambridge MA (02142) ***(G-9367)***
3M, Tilton *Also called Innovative Paper Tech LLC* ***(G-19906)***
3M Company 781 871-1400
30 Commerce Rd Rockland MA (02370) ***(G-14788)***
3M Company 651 733-1110
10 Maguire Rd Ste 310 Lexington MA (02421) ***(G-12199)***
3M Company 978 256-3911
279 Billerica Rd Chelmsford MA (01824) ***(G-9865)***
3M Company 978 659-9000
55 Foundation Ave Ste 100 Haverhill MA (01835) ***(G-11402)***
3M Company 978 659-9000
501 Griffin Brook Park Dr Methuen MA (01844) ***(G-13007)***
3M Company 203 237-5541
400 Research Pkwy Meriden CT (06450) ***(G-2069)***
3M Company 978 420-0001
55 Ward Hill Ave Haverhill MA (01835) ***(G-11403)***
3M Purification Inc 860 684-8628
32 River Rd Stafford Springs CT (06076) ***(G-4103)***
3M Purification Inc (HQ) 203 237-5541
400 Research Pkwy Meriden CT (06450) ***(G-2070)***
3M Touch Systems Inc (HQ) 978 659-9000
501 Griffin Brook Dr Methuen MA (01844) ***(G-13008)***
3M Touch Systems Inc 978 659-9000
501 Griffin Brook Park Dr Methuen MA (01844) ***(G-13009)***

ALPHABETIC

(PA)=Parent Co (HQ)=Headquarters (DH)=Div Headquarters

3M Touch Systems Inc..........508 871-1840
115 Flanders Rd Westborough MA (01581) ***(G-16584)***
3p4, Salem *Also called 3 Potato 4 LLC* ***(G-14888)***
3t Lighting Inc..........203 775-1805
20 Pocono Rd Brookfield CT (06804) ***(G-631)***
3wyc Inc..........617 584-7767
117 Wallace St Newton MA (02461) ***(G-13550)***
4 D Technology Corporation..........860 365-0420
91 Daniel St East Hampton CT (06424) ***(G-1154)***
40 Up Tackle Company Inc..........413 562-0385
16 Union Ave Ste 5 Westfield MA (01085) ***(G-16660)***
40parklane LLC..........978 369-2940
4 Apple Rdg Unit 3 Maynard MA (01754) ***(G-12893)***
42 Design Fab Studio Inc..........413 203-4948
34 Front St Indian Orchard MA (01151) ***(G-11882)***
420 Sign Design Inc..........203 852-1255
25 Commerce St Norwalk CT (06850) ***(G-3094)***
4382412 Canada Inc..........802 225-5911
310 Hurricane Ln Unit 3 Williston VT (05495) ***(G-22652)***
494 Amherst St LLC..........470 430-4608
494 Amherst St Nashua NH (03063) ***(G-19102)***
4frng, Shelburne *Also called Forward Inc* ***(G-22417)***
4power LLC..........617 299-0068
56 Stiles Rd Ste 101 Salem NH (03079) ***(G-19701)***
508tees Screenprinting..........508 717-3835
211 Middle Rd Acushnet MA (02743) ***(G-7396)***
59 Beecher Street LLC..........631 734-6200
59 Beecher St Southbridge MA (01550) ***(G-15373)***
5n Plus Wisconsin Inc..........203 384-0331
120 Corporate Dr Trumbull CT (06611) ***(G-4610)***
603 Manufacturing LLC..........603 578-9876
21 Park Ave Hudson NH (03051) ***(G-18368)***
603 Optx Inc..........603 357-4900
80 Krif Rd Unit 14 Keene NH (03431) ***(G-18489)***
603 Screenprinting LLC..........603 505-7693
85 Lowell Rd Salem NH (03079) ***(G-19702)***
7 South Sandwich Company LLC..........802 388-3354
1396 Route 7 S Ste 4 Middlebury VT (05753) ***(G-22095)***
7 Waves Inc..........781 519-9389
97 Thayer Rd Braintree MA (02184) ***(G-8984)***
71 Pickett District Road LLC..........860 350-5964
71 Pickett District Rd New Milford CT (06776) ***(G-2786)***
73 75 Magazine Street LLC..........617 787-1913
1125 Commonwealth Ave Allston MA (02134) ***(G-7459)***
77 Mattatuck Heights LLC..........203 597-9338
77 Mattatuck Heights Rd Waterbury CT (06705) ***(G-4834)***
7ac Technologies Inc..........781 574-1348
100 Cummings Ctr Ste 265g Beverly MA (01915) ***(G-8094)***
7th Settlement Brewery LLC..........603 534-5292
47 Washington St Dover NH (03820) ***(G-18002)***
8 Raceway Drive LLC..........508 325-0040
8 Raceway Dr Nantucket MA (02554) ***(G-13216)***
8 Times LLC..........203 227-7575
12 Juniper Rd Westport CT (06880) ***(G-5177)***
861 Corp..........617 268-8855
226 W Broadway Boston MA (02127) ***(G-8330)***
89 North Inc..........802 881-0302
20 Winter Sport Ln # 135 Williston VT (05495) ***(G-22653)***
900 Industries Inc..........508 865-9600
16 Deborah Dr Sutton MA (01590) ***(G-15678)***
99degrees Custom Inc..........978 655-3362
15 Union St Ste 205 Lawrence MA (01840) ***(G-11988)***
A & A Architectural Wdwkg Inc..........413 568-9914
104 Mainline Dr Ste C Westfield MA (01085) ***(G-16661)***
A & A Industries Inc..........978 977-9660
320 Jubilee Dr Peabody MA (01960) ***(G-14304)***
A & A Jewelers Inc..........508 992-5320
279 State Rd North Dartmouth MA (02747) ***(G-13915)***
A & A Manufacturing Co Inc..........262 786-1500
457 State St North Haven CT (06473) ***(G-3000)***
A & A Products, Bangor *Also called Salibas Rug & Upholstery Clrs* ***(G-5658)***
A & A Products and Services..........860 683-0879
610 Hayden Station Rd Windsor CT (06095) ***(G-5312)***
A & B Ice Co, Bridgeport *Also called Leonard F Brooks* ***(G-445)***
A & D Components Inc..........860 582-9541
33 Stafford Ave Ste 2 Bristol CT (06010) ***(G-509)***
A & D Metal Inc..........413 485-7505
555 Southampton Rd Westfield MA (01085) ***(G-16662)***
A & D Print Shop..........207 764-2662
540 Main St Presque Isle ME (04769) ***(G-6751)***
A & D Tool Co..........413 543-3166
34 Front St Ste 5 Indian Orchard MA (01151) ***(G-11883)***
A & F Plating Co Inc..........401 861-3597
45 River Ave Providence RI (02908) ***(G-20943)***
A & G Centerless Grinding Inc..........781 281-0007
15 Linscott Rd Woburn MA (01801) ***(G-17102)***
A & G Dirtworks Inc..........207 290-5054
22 Caron Dr Howland ME (04448) ***(G-6213)***
A & G Manufacturing Co Inc..........781 581-1892
500 Lynnway Lynn MA (01905) ***(G-12487)***
A & H Composition and Prtg Inc..........401 438-1200
5 Almeida Ave East Providence RI (02914) ***(G-20383)***
A & H Duffy Polishing & Finshg..........401 785-9203
175 Dupont Dr Providence RI (02907) ***(G-20944)***
A & I Concentrate LLC..........203 447-1938
2 Corporate Dr Ste 136 Shelton CT (06484) ***(G-3771)***
A & J Grinding Service..........802 467-3038
42 A Frame Dr West Burke VT (05871) ***(G-22604)***
A & J Industries LLC..........508 278-4531
56 Industrial Dr Uxbridge MA (01569) ***(G-15912)***
A & J Tool Findings Co Inc..........508 695-6631
6 W Bacon St Plainville MA (02762) ***(G-14514)***
A & K Railroad Materials Inc..........203 495-8790
200 Benton St Hamden CT (06517) ***(G-1728)***
A & M Auto Machine Inc..........203 237-3502
711 E Main St Meriden CT (06450) ***(G-2071)***
A & M Tool & Die Company Inc..........508 764-3241
64 Mill St Ste 1 Southbridge MA (01550) ***(G-15374)***
A & M Welding Fabrication Inc..........781 335-9548
276 Libbey Indus Pkwy 2 East Weymouth MA (02189) ***(G-10532)***
A & N Jewelry Company..........401 431-9500
1029 Charles St Ste 2 North Providence RI (02904) ***(G-20751)***
A & P Coat Apron & Lin Sup Inc..........914 840-3200
420 Ledyard St Hartford CT (06114) ***(G-1799)***
A & P Woodworking Inc..........617 569-4664
136 Bennington St Boston MA (02128) ***(G-8331)***
A & R Machining Tool & Die..........508 985-0916
259 Samuel Barnet Blvd B New Bedford MA (02745) ***(G-13346)***
A & S Pharmaceutical Corp..........203 368-2538
480 Barnum Ave Ste 3 Bridgeport CT (06608) ***(G-364)***
A & S Tackle Corp..........508 679-8122
724 Locust St Swansea MA (02777) ***(G-15702)***
A & S Transport Wheelchair Svc..........617 701-4407
40 Highland St Brockton MA (02301) ***(G-9113)***
A & W Paving & Sealcoating..........207 743-6615
501 Elm Rd South Paris ME (04281) ***(G-7009)***
A A A Sheet Metal Inc..........781 523-1227
23 Winslow Dr Hanson MA (02341) ***(G-11359)***
A A E,, Wilmington *Also called All American Embroidery Inc* ***(G-16970)***
A A I, Canton *Also called Alexis Aerospace Inds LLC* ***(G-695)***
A A Mono Rite Acct Brd Sys, Watertown *Also called Peter Young Company* ***(G-16306)***
A A Plastic & Met Fabricators..........978 777-0367
250 North St Ste A2 Danvers MA (01923) ***(G-10188)***
A A S, Newington *Also called Advanced Adhesive Systems Inc* ***(G-2838)***
A American Stone & Countertop, Wallingford *Also called American Stonecrafters Inc* ***(G-4698)***
A Arena & Sons Inc..........508 435-3673
159 Ash St Hopkinton MA (01748) ***(G-11685)***
A B & D Machining Inc..........781 891-4120
56 Clematis Ave Waltham MA (02453) ***(G-16019)***
A B & F Sheet Metal..........203 272-9340
327 Sandbank Rd Cheshire CT (06410) ***(G-707)***
A B A Tool & Die Div, Manchester *Also called Aba-PGT Inc* ***(G-1980)***
A B B Power Transmission, Norwalk *Also called Asea Brown Boveri Inc* ***(G-3105)***
A B C Printing & Mailing, East Haven *Also called A B C Printing Inc* ***(G-1241)***
A B C Printing Inc..........203 468-1245
875 Foxon Rd East Haven CT (06513) ***(G-1241)***
A B Engineering & Co..........508 987-0318
3 Old Cudworth Rd Oxford MA (01540) ***(G-14251)***
A B Excavating Inc..........603 788-5110
653 Main St Lancaster NH (03584) ***(G-18596)***
A B Group, Attleboro *Also called W E Richards Co Inc* ***(G-7807)***
A B Metal Fabricators..........508 947-5577
155 Millenium Cir Lakeville MA (02347) ***(G-11969)***
A B Munroe Dairy Inc..........401 438-4450
151 N Brow St East Providence RI (02914) ***(G-20384)***
A B T Machine Co..........508 429-4355
1649 Washington St Ste 1 Holliston MA (01746) ***(G-11554)***
A Baileys LLC..........401 252-6002
57 Water Way Barrington RI (02806) ***(G-20042)***
A Barney's Sign, Stratford *Also called Barneys Sign Service Inc* ***(G-4396)***
A Bismark Company..........508 675-2002
5 Probber Ln Ste 1 Fall River MA (02720) ***(G-10648)***
A C Performance Center Ltd..........802 862-6074
306 Mallard Dr Colchester VT (05446) ***(G-21855)***
A C S, Stoughton *Also called Alpha Chemical Services Inc* ***(G-15579)***
A C T, Greenland *Also called Advanced Concrete Tech Inc-NH* ***(G-18219)***
A C T Manufacturing LLC..........860 289-8837
55 Glendale Rd South Windsor CT (06074) ***(G-3930)***
A Capela Do Santo Antonio Inc..........860 447-3329
35 Henry St New London CT (06320) ***(G-2764)***
A D & G Enterprises Inc..........508 528-0232
23 Forge Pkwy 1 Franklin MA (02038) ***(G-11019)***
A D Grinding..........860 747-6630
54 Lewis St Plainville CT (06062) ***(G-3460)***
A D M, Portsmouth *Also called Advanced Design & Mfg Inc* ***(G-19532)***
A D Perkins Company..........203 777-3456
43 Elm St New Haven CT (06510) ***(G-2651)***

A David Moore Inc 802 457-3914
6810 Pomfret Rd North Pomfret VT (05053) ***(G-22234)***
A Day Trip Com, Cohasset *Also called Tinytown Gazette* ***(G-10102)***
A F F Inc (PA) 401 949-3000
26 Lark Industrial Pkwy Greenville RI (02828) ***(G-20460)***
A F Fuels 603 672-7010
102 Route 13 Brookline NH (03033) ***(G-17769)***
A F I Med Electronic Eqp Repai, Walpole *Also called MV Mason Electronics Inc* ***(G-16004)***
A F M Engineering Corp 860 774-7518
24 Woodward Rd Brooklyn CT (06234) ***(G-668)***
A F Murphy Die & Mch Co Inc 617 328-3820
430 Hancock St Quincy MA (02171) ***(G-14612)***
A G C Incorporated (PA) 203 235-3361
106 Evansville Ave Meriden CT (06451) ***(G-2072)***
A G I Automation, Trumbull *Also called American Grippers Inc* ***(G-4611)***
A G Industries Inc 508 695-4219
75 Chestnut St North Attleboro MA (02760) ***(G-13741)***
A G Miller Company Inc 413 732-9297
53 Batavia St Springfield MA (01109) ***(G-15438)***
A G Russell Company Inc 860 247-9093
60 George St Hartford CT (06114) ***(G-1800)***
A Gerber Corp 203 918-1913
110 Idlewood Dr Stamford CT (06905) ***(G-4123)***
A H Mfg. Co., Johnston *Also called Packaging Company LLC* ***(G-20527)***
A Hardiman Machine Co Inc 860 623-8133
94 Newberry Rd East Windsor CT (06088) ***(G-1274)***
A Helium Plus Balloons LLC 860 833-1761
94 Albert Ave Wethersfield CT (06109) ***(G-5239)***
A I C Inc (PA) 978 352-4510
7 Martel Way Georgetown MA (01833) ***(G-11135)***
A I S, Leominster *Also called Affordable Intr Systems Inc* ***(G-12108)***
A I S, Hudson *Also called Ais Group Holdings LLC* ***(G-11753)***
A J R Inc 203 384-0400
67 Poland St Bridgeport CT (06605) ***(G-365)***
A Johnson Co 802 453-4884
995 S 116 Rd Bristol VT (05443) ***(G-21760)***
A L C Inovators Inc 203 877-8526
230 Pepes Farm Rd Ste C Milford CT (06460) ***(G-2232)***
A L Ellis Inc 508 672-4799
113 Griffin St Ste 1 Fall River MA (02724) ***(G-10649)***
A Line Design Inc 203 294-0080
18 Martin Trl Wallingford CT (06492) ***(G-4691)***
A Lot Bakery Products Inc 617 561-1122
255 Maverick St Boston MA (02128) ***(G-8332)***
A Luongo & Sons Incorporated 508 226-0788
160 Fireworks Cir Bridgewater MA (02324) ***(G-9059)***
A Lyons & Company Inc 978 526-4244
40 Beach St Unit 105 Manchester MA (01944) ***(G-12601)***
A M C Design and Manufacturing, Cranston *Also called Austrian Machine Corp* ***(G-20184)***
A M I, Winthrop *Also called Alternative Manufacturing Inc* ***(G-7279)***
A M I, Mystic *Also called Aqua Massage International Inc* ***(G-2434)***
A M T, Milton *Also called Advanced Machine and Tl Co Inc* ***(G-22124)***
A Murphy James & Son Inc 508 761-5060
1879 County St Attleboro MA (02703) ***(G-7696)***
A N C Tool and Manufacturing 508 757-0224
49 Gardner St Worcester MA (01610) ***(G-17329)***
A P C M G E, West Kingston *Also called Schneider Electric It Corp* ***(G-21471)***
A P M, Leominster *Also called Advanced Prototypes & Molding* ***(G-12107)***
A P M Sterngold, Attleboro *Also called Sterngold Dental LLC* ***(G-7796)***
A P S, Bridgeport *Also called Alternative Prosthetic Svcs* ***(G-370)***
A Papish Incorporated (PA) 203 744-0323
21 Taylor St Danbury CT (06810) ***(G-863)***
A Personal Touch Inc (PA) 781 447-0467
23 Commercial Waye Ste E Hanson MA (02341) ***(G-11360)***
A Printery, West Harwich *Also called R E K Management Inc* ***(G-16481)***
A R C O, Bridgeport *Also called Arcade Technology LLC* ***(G-376)***
A R Tool, Berlin *Also called Andy Rakowicz* ***(G-72)***
A S & C B Gould & Sons Inc 207 474-3930
9 Walton Mills Rd Cornville ME (04976) ***(G-5926)***
A S A P Engravers 508 234-6974
211 Mason Rd Whitinsville MA (01588) ***(G-16909)***
A S Fine Foods 203 322-3899
856 High Ridge Rd Stamford CT (06905) ***(G-4124)***
A S I, Manchester *Also called Assembly Specialists Inc* ***(G-18780)***
A S J Specialties LLC 203 284-8650
2 Toms Dr Wallingford CT (06492) ***(G-4692)***
A S P Enterprises Inc 617 244-2762
227 California St Newton MA (02458) ***(G-13551)***
A Schulman Custom Compounding 508 756-0002
53 Millbrook St Ste 2 Worcester MA (01606) ***(G-17330)***
A Sweet As Sugar Life-Cupcakes 603 591-8957
173 Pillsbury Rd Londonderry NH (03053) ***(G-18669)***
A T S, Ellington *Also called Accu-Time Systems Inc* ***(G-1324)***
A T S Cases Inc 508 393-9110
172 Otis St Ste 4 Northborough MA (01532) ***(G-14028)***
A Taste Afrcas - World Cuisine, White River Junction *Also called World Cuisine Concepts LLC* ***(G-22644)***
A To Z Boatworks Inc 781 545-6632
12 Chief Jstce Cshng Hwy Scituate MA (02066) ***(G-15004)***
A To Z Foods Inc 781 413-0221
797 Massachusetts Ave Arlington MA (02476) ***(G-7621)***
A V X, Biddeford *Also called AVX Tantalum Corporation* ***(G-5720)***
A W Chaffee (PA) 207 465-3234
164 Belgrade Rd Oakland ME (04963) ***(G-6528)***
A W Chaffee 207 426-8588
163 Hinckley Rd Clinton ME (04927) ***(G-5912)***
A W Chesterton Company (PA) 781 438-7000
860 Salem St Groveland MA (01834) ***(G-11298)***
A W Chesterton Company 781 438-7000
860 Salem St Groveland MA (01834) ***(G-11299)***
A X M S Inc 203 263-5046
27 Woodside Cir Woodbury CT (06798) ***(G-5480)***
A Young Casting 508 222-8188
35 County St Attleboro MA (02703) ***(G-7697)***
A Z Copy Center, Southington *Also called AZ Copy Center Inc* ***(G-4040)***
A&M Sand & Gravel LLC 207 223-4189
180 Coles Corner Rd Winterport ME (04496) ***(G-7275)***
A&R Plating Services LLC 860 274-9562
147 Riverside St Oakville CT (06779) ***(G-3295)***
A&S Brewing Collaborative LLC 617 368-5000
1 Design Center Pl # 850 Boston MA (02210) ***(G-8333)***
A&S Innersprings Usa LLC 860 298-0401
4 Market Cir Windsor CT (06095) ***(G-5313)***
A-1 Asphalt Paving 860 436-6085
925 New Britain Ave Rocky Hill CT (06067) ***(G-3700)***
A-1 Auto Frame, Worcester *Also called ORourke Welding Inc* ***(G-17437)***
A-1 Chrome and Polishing Corp 860 666-4593
125 Stamm Rd Newington CT (06111) ***(G-2836)***
A-1 Machining Co 860 223-6420
235 John Downey Dr New Britain CT (06051) ***(G-2501)***
A-1 Polishing Co 401 751-8944
8 Alcazar Ave Johnston RI (02919) ***(G-20496)***
A-1 Stairs By Wesconn Stairs, Danbury *Also called Wesconn Stairs Inc* ***(G-1008)***
A-D Scientific, Bellingham *Also called Accudyne Machine Tool Inc* ***(G-8027)***
A-Po-G Inc 207 774-7606
23 Evergreen Dr Portland ME (04103) ***(G-6608)***
A-S Catering, Stamford *Also called A S Fine Foods* ***(G-4124)***
A-T Surgical Mfg Co Inc 413 532-4551
115 Clemente St Holyoke MA (01040) ***(G-11615)***
A.H. Harris West Lebanon, West Lebanon *Also called Hd Supply Construction Supply* ***(G-19952)***
A1 Beyond Video Services, Boston *Also called 1 Beyond Inc* ***(G-8326)***
A1 Pallets Inc 978 838-2720
163 River Rd W Berlin MA (01503) ***(G-8090)***
A1 Screw Machine Products Inc 413 594-8939
717 Fuller Rd Chicopee MA (01020) ***(G-9995)***
A123 Systems LLC 617 778-5700
200 West St Waltham MA (02451) ***(G-16020)***
A1a Steel LLC 774 763-2503
120 Bernard E Saint Jean East Falmouth MA (02536) ***(G-10432)***
A2z Dental LLC 844 442-5587
5 Mount Royal Ave Ste 300 Marlborough MA (01752) ***(G-12708)***
AA & B Co 203 933-9110
284 2nd Ave West Haven CT (06516) ***(G-5107)***
AA Global Printing Inc 617 527-7629
22 Parker Ave Newton MA (02459) ***(G-13552)***
AA Pharmaceuticals Inc 617 935-1241
470 Wildwood Ave Ste 3 Woburn MA (01801) ***(G-17103)***
AA White Company 508 779-0821
867 Quaker Hwy Unit A Uxbridge MA (01569) ***(G-15913)***
AAA Atm Services 603 841-5615
25 1st St Amesbury MA (01913) ***(G-7476)***
AAA Radiator 781 662-7203
163 Beech Ave Melrose MA (02176) ***(G-12973)***
Aacc, Lawrence *Also called American Adhesive Coatings LLC* ***(G-11992)***
Aadco Medical Inc 802 728-3400
2279 Vt Route 66 Randolph VT (05060) ***(G-22296)***
AAF Microsystems Ltd 508 366-9100
21 E Main St Ste 3 Westborough MA (01581) ***(G-16585)***
Aag-All American Gasket, Brockton *Also called David A Payne* ***(G-9136)***
Aak Power Supply Corporation 603 382-2222
73 Newton Rd Pmb 2 # 103 Plaistow NH (03865) ***(G-19506)***
Aapi 203 268-2450
593 M St Monroe CT (06468) ***(G-2389)***
Aardvark Polymers 609 483-1013
73 Underwood Rd Ste 13 Woodstock CT (06281) ***(G-5493)***
Aaron Industries Corp 978 534-6135
20 Mohawk Dr Ste 1 Leominster MA (01453) ***(G-12105)***
Aastrom Biosciences Inc 617 761-8642
64 Sidney St Cambridge MA (02139) ***(G-9368)***
Aavid Corporation 603 528-3400
1 Aavid Cir Laconia NH (03246) ***(G-18549)***
AB Electronics Inc 203 740-2793
61 Commerce Dr Brookfield CT (06804) ***(G-632)***
AB Engineering & Company, Oxford *Also called A B Engineering & Co* ***(G-14251)***

ALPHABETIC

AB Group Inc 508 222-1404
40 John Williams St Attleboro MA (02703) ***(G-7698)***
AB Sciex LLC 508 383-7300
500 Old Connecticut Path B Framingham MA (01701) ***(G-10914)***
AB Sciex Sales LP 508 383-7700
500 Old Connecticut Path B Framingham MA (01701) ***(G-10915)***
AB&f Sheet Metal Products, Cheshire *Also called A B & F Sheet Metal* ***(G-707)***
Ab-Wey Machine & Die Co Inc 781 294-8031
51 School St Pembroke MA (02359) ***(G-14389)***
Aba-PGT Inc (PA) 860 649-4591
10 Gear Dr Manchester CT (06042) ***(G-1980)***
Aba-PGT Inc 860 872-2058
140 Bolton Rd Vernon Rockville CT (06066) ***(G-4677)***
Abaco Systems Technology Corp 256 382-8115
900 Technology Park Dr # 200 Billerica MA (01821) ***(G-8202)***
Abacus Automation Inc 802 442-3662
264 Shields Dr Bennington VT (05201) ***(G-21661)***
Abair Assemblies, Waterbury *Also called Abair Manufacturing Company* ***(G-4835)***
Abair Manufacturing Company 203 757-0112
250 Mill St Ste 2 Waterbury CT (06706) ***(G-4835)***
Abariscan Inc 978 462-0284
78 Lime St Newburyport MA (01950) ***(G-13467)***
Abas Accessories, Worcester *Also called Valkyrie Company Inc* ***(G-17496)***
ABB Enterprise Software Inc 860 747-7111
41 Woodford Ave Plainville CT (06062) ***(G-3461)***
ABB Enterprise Software Inc 617 574-1130
2 Oliver St Boston MA (02109) ***(G-8334)***
ABB Enterprise Software Inc 203 798-6210
152 Deer Hill Ave Ste 304 Danbury CT (06810) ***(G-864)***
ABB Enterprise Software Inc 860 285-0183
5 Waterside Xing Fl 3-2 Windsor CT (06095) ***(G-5314)***
ABB Enterprise Software Inc 203 329-8771
900 Long Ridge Rd Stamford CT (06902) ***(G-4125)***
ABB Finance (usa) Inc 919 856-2360
501 Merritt 7 Ste 2 Norwalk CT (06851) ***(G-3095)***
ABB Inc 203 790-8588
24 Commerce Dr Danbury CT (06810) ***(G-865)***
ABB Installation Products Inc 508 435-0101
86 South St Hopkinton MA (01748) ***(G-11686)***
Abba Fuels Inc 802 878-8095
1018 Vt Route 15 Underhill VT (05489) ***(G-22545)***
Abbas Shahrestanaki 617 548-0986
61 Endicott St Norwood MA (02062) ***(G-14116)***
Abbess Instrs & Systems Inc 508 429-0002
75 October Hill Rd Holliston MA (01746) ***(G-11555)***
Abbey Aesthetics LLC 860 242-0497
135 Cold Spring Rd Avon CT (06001) ***(G-30)***
Abbey Printing, Easthampton *Also called Abby Printing Co Inc* ***(G-10551)***
Abbey Water Treatment Inc 978 443-5001
419 Concord Rd Sudbury MA (01776) ***(G-15650)***
Abbott 978 577-3467
4 Robbins Rd Westford MA (01886) ***(G-16750)***
Abbott Associates Inc 203 878-2370
261a Pepes Farm Rd Milford CT (06460) ***(G-2233)***
Abbott Ball Company 860 236-5901
19 Railroad Pl West Hartford CT (06110) ***(G-5050)***
Abbott Dgnstics Scrborough Inc (HQ) 207 730-5750
10 Southgate Rd Scarborough ME (04074) ***(G-6901)***
Abbott Laboratories 508 849-2500
100 Research Dr Worcester MA (01605) ***(G-17331)***
Abbott Laboratories 603 891-3380
20 Trafalgar Sq Ste 459 Nashua NH (03063) ***(G-19103)***
Abbott Manufacturing, West Hartford *Also called Lewtan Industries Corporation* ***(G-5082)***
Abbott Printers, Boston *Also called E D Abbott Company Inc* ***(G-8514)***
Abbott Printing Company Inc 203 562-5562
912 Dixwell Ave Hamden CT (06514) ***(G-1729)***
Abbott-Action Inc (PA) 401 722-2100
3 Venus Way Attleboro MA (02703) ***(G-7699)***
Abbott-Action Inc 781 702-5710
10 Campanelli Cir Canton MA (02021) ***(G-9710)***
Abbvie Bioresearch Center, Worcester *Also called Abbvie Inc* ***(G-17332)***
Abbvie Inc 508 849-2500
100 Research Dr Worcester MA (01605) ***(G-17332)***
Abbvie Inc 617 335-7640
200 Sidney St Cambridge MA (02139) ***(G-9369)***
Abby Printing Co Inc 413 536-5269
58 Oneil St Easthampton MA (01027) ***(G-10551)***
Abbydabby 860 586-8832
2523 Albany Ave West Hartford CT (06117) ***(G-5051)***
ABC Disposal Service Inc 508 990-1911
994 Nash Rd New Bedford MA (02746) ***(G-13347)***
ABC Disposal Welding Shop, New Bedford *Also called ABC Disposal Service Inc* ***(G-13347)***
ABC Sign Corporation 203 513-8110
30 Controls Dr Ste 1 Shelton CT (06484) ***(G-3772)***
Abclonal-Neo Inc 617 412-1176
395 W Cummings Park Woburn MA (01801) ***(G-17104)***
Abco Tool & Die Inc 508 771-3225
11 Thornton Dr Hyannis MA (02601) ***(G-11832)***
Abcorp, Stamford *Also called American Banknote Corporation* ***(G-4135)***
Abcorp NA Inc 617 325-9600
225 Rivermoor St Ste 225 # 225 Boston MA (02132) ***(G-8335)***
Abcrosby & Company Inc 978 827-6064
20 S Maple Ave Ashburnham MA (01430) ***(G-7643)***
Abek LLC 860 314-3905
492 Birch St Bristol CT (06010) ***(G-510)***
Abet Technologies Inc 203 540-9990
168 Old Gate Ln Milford CT (06460) ***(G-2234)***
Abiomed Inc (PA) 978 646-1400
22 Cherry Hill Dr Danvers MA (01923) ***(G-10189)***
Abiomed Cardiovascular Inc 978 777-5410
22 Cherry Hill Dr Danvers MA (01923) ***(G-10190)***
Abiomed R&D Inc 978 646-1400
22 Cherry Hill Dr Danvers MA (01923) ***(G-10191)***
Abisee Inc 978 637-2900
30 Sudbury Rd Ste 1b Acton MA (01720) ***(G-7333)***
Ablap Inc 802 748-5900
226 Industrial Dr Bradford VT (05033) ***(G-21698)***
Able Coil and Electronics Co 860 646-5686
25 Howard Rd Bolton CT (06043) ***(G-273)***
Able Pest Control Service 508 559-7987
610 N Main St Ste 2 Brockton MA (02301) ***(G-9114)***
Able Software Corp 978 667-2400
655 Boston Rd Ste 1b Billerica MA (01821) ***(G-8203)***
Able Software Corp (PA) 781 862-2804
5 Appletree Ln Lexington MA (02420) ***(G-12200)***
About-Face Kitchens Inc 978 532-0212
27 Walnut St Ste 1h Peabody MA (01960) ***(G-14305)***
Abpro Corporation 617 225-0808
68 Cummings Park Woburn MA (01801) ***(G-17105)***
Abra-Cadabra EMB & Screen Prtg, Lakeville *Also called Abra-Cadabra Promotional AP* ***(G-11970)***
Abra-Cadabra Promotional AP 508 821-2002
155 Millenium Cir Ste 101 Lakeville MA (02347) ***(G-11970)***
ABS Pallet 508 246-1041
72 Laurelwood Dr Hopedale MA (01747) ***(G-11668)***
ABS Printing Inc 401 826-0870
173 Washington St West Warwick RI (02893) ***(G-21475)***
Absolute Haitian Corporation (PA) 508 459-5372
33 Southgate St Worcester MA (01610) ***(G-17333)***
Absolute Manufacturing Inc 978 433-0760
24 Lomar Park Ste F Pepperell MA (01463) ***(G-14435)***
Absolute Marble & Granite, Canton *Also called Vanity World Inc* ***(G-9792)***
Absolute Metal Finishing Inc 781 551-8235
90 Morse St Norwood MA (02062) ***(G-14117)***
Absolute Precision Co 203 767-9066
234 Bates Rock Rd Southbury CT (06488) ***(G-4021)***
Absolute Rstrtion Slant Sltons 603 518-5864
3 Tallwood Dr Ste 3 # 3 Bow NH (03304) ***(G-17706)***
Absolute Sheet Metal 978 667-0236
559 Boston Rd Billerica MA (01821) ***(G-8204)***
Absorbent Specialty Pdts LLC 401 722-1177
1 John C Dean Mem Blvd Cumberland RI (02864) ***(G-20312)***
Abstract Tool Inc 860 526-4635
500 Main St Ste 15 Deep River CT (06417) ***(G-1056)***
Abtech Inc 603 585-7106
126 Rte 12 N Fitzwilliam NH (03447) ***(G-18147)***
Abtelum Biomedical Inc 781 367-1696
175 Briar Ln Westwood MA (02090) ***(G-16856)***
AC, Auburn *Also called AC Electric Corp* ***(G-5545)***
AC Electric, Bangor *Also called AC Electric Corp* ***(G-5628)***
AC Electric Corp (PA) 207 784-7341
120 Merrow Rd Auburn ME (04210) ***(G-5545)***
AC Electric Corp 207 945-9487
40 Target Industrial Cir Bangor ME (04401) ***(G-5628)***
AC General Inc 978 568-8229
10 Technology Dr 316 Hudson MA (01749) ***(G-11749)***
AC Navigation LLC 508 359-5903
16 Ledgetree Rd Medfield MA (02052) ***(G-12908)***
AC Performance Ctr, Colchester *Also called A C Performance Center Ltd* ***(G-21855)***
Ac/DC Industrial Electric LLC 860 886-2232
44 Yantic Flats Rd Ste 2 Yantic CT (06389) ***(G-5506)***
Acacia Communications Inc (PA) 978 938-4896
3 Mill And Main Pl # 400 Maynard MA (01754) ***(G-12894)***
Academic Studies Press, Brookline *Also called Borderlines Foundation* ***(G-9197)***
Academy Marble & Granite LLC (PA) 203 791-2956
101 Wooster St Ste C Bethel CT (06801) ***(G-126)***
Academy Printing Service 860 828-5549
900 Farmington Ave Ste 2 Kensington CT (06037) ***(G-1916)***
Acana Northeast Inc 800 922-2629
360 Commerce Way Unit 3 Pembroke NH (03275) ***(G-19455)***
Acara Holdings LLC 603 434-3175
162 Pembroke Rd Concord NH (03301) ***(G-17879)***
Acbel (usa) Polytech Inc 508 625-1768
227 South St Hopkinton MA (01748) ***(G-11687)***
ACC, East Falmouth *Also called Associates of Cape Cod Inc* ***(G-10435)***
Accel Intl Holdings Inc 203 237-2700
508 N Colony St Meriden CT (06450) ***(G-2073)***

Accela Graphics Neng Inc 508 366-5999
74 Otis St Westborough MA (01581) ***(G-16586)***
Accelerated Media Tech Inc 508 459-0300
19 Technology Dr Auburn MA (01501) ***(G-7821)***
Accelerating Biologics, Cambridge *Also called Bioanalytix Inc* ***(G-9408)***
Accelerator Systems Inc 603 898-6010
3 Commerce Dr Ste 303 Atkinson NH (03811) ***(G-17602)***
Acceleron Inc 860 651-9333
21 Lordship Rd Ste 1 East Granby CT (06026) ***(G-1115)***
Acceleron Pharma Inc (PA) 617 649-9200
128 Sidney St Cambridge MA (02139) ***(G-9370)***
Accellent Endoscopy Inc 603 528-1211
45 Lexington Dr Laconia NH (03246) ***(G-18550)***
Accellent Holdings Corp 978 570-6900
100 Fordham Rd Wilmington MA (01887) ***(G-16962)***
Accellent Laconia, Laconia *Also called Lake Region Medical Inc* ***(G-18571)***
Accellent LLC (HQ) 978 570-6900
100 Fordham Rd Bldg C Wilmington MA (01887) ***(G-16963)***
Accent Banner LLC 781 391-7300
17 Locust St Medford MA (02155) ***(G-12920)***
Accent Display Corp 401 461-8787
1655 Elmwood Ave Ste 9 Cranston RI (02910) ***(G-20171)***
Accent On Industrial Metal Inc 413 785-1654
179 Page Blvd Springfield MA (01104) ***(G-15439)***
Accent Plating Company Inc 401 722-6306
25 Esten Ave Unit 5 Pawtucket RI (02860) ***(G-20805)***
Accent Printing Inc 781 487-9300
99 Chelmsford Rd Rear 13 North Billerica MA (01862) ***(G-13788)***
Accent Screenprinting 203 284-8601
186 Center St Wallingford CT (06492) ***(G-4693)***
Accent Signs LLC 203 975-8688
130 Lenox Ave Ste 21 Stamford CT (06906) ***(G-4126)***
Accenture Duck Creek, Boston *Also called Duck Creek Technologies LLC* ***(G-8511)***
Accenus, Dover *Also called Uraseal Inc* ***(G-18064)***
Access Intelligence 203 854-6730
761 Main Ave Ste 2 Norwalk CT (06851) ***(G-3096)***
Accord Software Inc 978 687-2320
42 Olympic Village Dr Methuen MA (01844) ***(G-13010)***
Accordant Energy LLC 802 772-7368
225 S Main St Ste 2 Rutland VT (05701) ***(G-22322)***
Accounting Web 978 331-1243
400 Tradecenter G755 Woburn MA (01801) ***(G-17106)***
Accounttech 781 276-1555
54 Middlesex Tpke Ste B2 Bedford MA (01730) ***(G-7956)***
Accu Packaging Inc 978 447-5590
210 Andover St Ste 3 Wilmington MA (01887) ***(G-16964)***
Accu Rx Inc 401 454-2920
100 Federal Way Johnston RI (02919) ***(G-20497)***
Accu-Care Supply Inc 401 438-7110
109 King Philip Rd Rumford RI (02916) ***(G-21179)***
Accu-Mill Technologies LLC 860 747-3921
161 Woodford Ave Ste 39 Plainville CT (06062) ***(G-3462)***
Accu-Rite Tool & Mfg Co 860 688-4844
23 Industrial Park Rd W B Tolland CT (06084) ***(G-4538)***
Accu-Time Systems Inc 860 870-5000
175 Federal St Ste 1225 Boston MA (02110) ***(G-8336)***
Accu-Time Systems Inc (HQ) 860 870-5000
420 Somers Rd Ellington CT (06029) ***(G-1324)***
Accu-Tool Inc 401 725-5350
250 Esten Ave Unit 101 Pawtucket RI (02860) ***(G-20806)***
Accubend LLC 860 378-0303
1657 Mrden Wtrbury Tpke Plantsville CT (06479) ***(G-3525)***
Accucon Inc 978 840-0337
12 Mount Pleasant Ave # 100 Leominster MA (01453) ***(G-12106)***
Accudie Inc 508 756-8482
532 Franklin St Worcester MA (01604) ***(G-17334)***
Accudynamics LLC 508 946-4545
240 Kenneth Welch Dr Lakeville MA (02347) ***(G-11971)***
Accudyne Machine Tool Inc 508 966-3110
128 Mendon St Bellingham MA (02019) ***(G-8027)***
Accufab Inc 781 894-5737
81 Rumford Ave Waltham MA (02453) ***(G-16021)***
Accufab Iron Works Inc 413 268-7133
82 S Main St Goshen MA (01032) ***(G-11222)***
Accufund Inc 781 433-0233
400 Hillside Ave Ste 5 Needham MA (02494) ***(G-13289)***
Accumet Engineering Inc 978 692-6180
123 Oak Hill Rd Westford MA (01886) ***(G-16751)***
Accumet Engineering Corp 978 568-8311
518 Main St Hudson MA (01749) ***(G-11750)***
Accumold Technologies Inc 203 384-9256
52 Carroll Ave Bridgeport CT (06607) ***(G-366)***
Accupaulo Holding Corporation (PA) 860 666-5621
33 Stafford Ave Ste 5 Bristol CT (06010) ***(G-511)***
Accuprobe Corporation 978 745-7878
35 Congress St Ste 201 Salem MA (01970) ***(G-14889)***
Accura Printing 802 476-4429
80 East Rd Barre VT (05641) ***(G-21607)***
Accurate Brazing Corporation 860 432-1840
4 Progress Dr Manchester CT (06042) ***(G-1981)***
Accurate Brazing Corporation (HQ) 603 945-3750
36 Cote Ave Ste 5 Goffstown NH (03045) ***(G-18197)***
Accurate Burring Company 860 747-8640
161 Woodford Ave Ste 19 Plainville CT (06062) ***(G-3463)***
Accurate Composites LLC 508 457-9097
33 Technology Park Dr East Falmouth MA (02536) ***(G-10433)***
Accurate Graphics Inc 781 593-1630
26 Alley St Lynn MA (01902) ***(G-12488)***
Accurate Metal Finishing Corp 781 963-7300
414 South St Randolph MA (02368) ***(G-14668)***
Accurate Mold Company Inc 860 301-1988
64 Nooks Hill Rd Cromwell CT (06416) ***(G-842)***
Accurate Molded Products Inc 401 739-2400
459 Warwick Industrial Dr Warwick RI (02886) ***(G-21317)***
Accurate Plastics, East Falmouth *Also called Accurate Composites LLC* ***(G-10433)***
Accurate Plastics Inc 508 457-9097
33 Technology Park Dr East Falmouth MA (02536) ***(G-10434)***
Accurate Rubber Products Inc 802 868-3063
22 Lake St Swanton VT (05488) ***(G-22529)***
Accurate Services Inc 508 674-5773
951 Broadway Ste 4 Fall River MA (02724) ***(G-10650)***
Accurate Threaded Products, Bristol *Also called Accupaulo Holding Corporation* ***(G-511)***
Accurate Threaded Products Co 860 666-5621
33 Stafford Ave Ste 5 Bristol CT (06010) ***(G-512)***
Accurate Tool & Die Inc 203 967-1200
16 Leon Pl Stamford CT (06902) ***(G-4127)***
Accurate Tool & Machine Inc 508 946-3414
155 Millenium Cir Ste 105 Lakeville MA (02347) ***(G-11972)***
Accurate Welding Services LLC 860 623-9500
7 Industrial Rd Windsor Locks CT (06096) ***(G-5380)***
Accurounds, Avon *Also called Boston Centerless Inc* ***(G-7881)***
Accurounds Inc 508 587-3500
15 Doherty Ave Avon MA (02322) ***(G-7874)***
Accusemble Electronics Inc 978 584-0072
5 Esquire Rd North Billerica MA (01862) ***(G-13789)***
Accusonic Technologies (HQ) 508 495-6600
259 Samuel Barnet Blvd New Bedford MA (02745) ***(G-13348)***
Accutech Machine Inc 978 922-7271
370 Andover St Danvers MA (01923) ***(G-10192)***
Accutech Packaging Inc 508 543-3800
157 Green St Foxboro MA (02035) ***(G-10873)***
Accutech Packaging Inc 508 543-3800
71 Hampden Rd Mansfield MA (02048) ***(G-12610)***
Accutrol LLC 203 445-9991
21 Commerce Dr Danbury CT (06810) ***(G-866)***
Accutron Inc 860 683-8300
149 Addison Rd Windsor CT (06095) ***(G-5315)***
Accutronics Inc 978 250-9144
10 Elizabeth Dr Ste 3 Chelmsford MA (01824) ***(G-9866)***
Accuturn Mfg Co LLC 860 289-6355
100 Commerce Way South Windsor CT (06074) ***(G-3931)***
Ace Archers Inc 774 215-5292
131 Morse St Foxborough MA (02035) ***(G-10910)***
Ace Archers Inc 508 697-5647
131 Morse St Foxboro MA (02035) ***(G-10874)***
Ace Beauty Supply Inc 203 488-2416
937 W Main St Branford CT (06405) ***(G-284)***
Ace Cabinet Company 860 225-6111
321 Ellis St Ste 18 New Britain CT (06051) ***(G-2502)***
Ace Castings, Colchester *Also called PBL Incorporated* ***(G-21876)***
Ace Finishing Co LLC 860 582-4600
225 Terryville Rd Bristol CT (06010) ***(G-513)***
Ace Machine Inc 603 329-6716
563 Rte 111 East Hampstead NH (03826) ***(G-18080)***
Ace Metal Finishing, Lawrence *Also called CIL Electroplating Inc* ***(G-12007)***
Ace Metal Finishing Inc 978 683-2082
125 Glenn St Lawrence MA (01843) ***(G-11989)***
Ace Moulding Co Inc 413 267-4875
91 Bethany Rd Monson MA (01057) ***(G-13201)***
Ace Precision Inc 413 789-7536
1123 Suffield St Agawam MA (01001) ***(G-7416)***
Ace Result LLC 612 559-3838
343 Vanderbilt Ave Norwood MA (02062) ***(G-14118)***
Ace Sailmakers 860 739-5999
3 Colton Rd East Lyme CT (06333) ***(G-1268)***
Ace Servicing Co Inc 203 795-1400
340 Edward Ct Orange CT (06477) ***(G-3356)***
Ace Signs Inc 413 739-3814
477 Cottage St Springfield MA (01104) ***(G-15440)***
Ace Technical Plastics Inc 860 278-2444
122 Park Ave J Hartford CT (06108) ***(G-1801)***
Ace Tire & Auto Center Inc 203 438-4042
861 Ethan Allen Hwy Ridgefield CT (06877) ***(G-3654)***
Ace Torwel Inc (HQ) 888 878-0898
38 Simpson Dr Framingham MA (01701) ***(G-10916)***
Ace Welding Co Inc 603 424-9936
715a Daniel Webster Hwy Merrimack NH (03054) ***(G-18984)***
Ace-Lon Corporation 781 322-7121
960 Eastern Ave Malden MA (02148) ***(G-12556)***

ALPHABETIC

Aceinna Inc 978 965-3200
1 Tech Dr Ste 325 Andover MA (01810) ***(G-7532)***
Acenna Data Inc 443 878-9292
10 Harvey St Cambridge MA (02140) ***(G-9371)***
Acer Therapeutics Inc (PA) 844 902-6100
300 Washington St Ste 351 Newton MA (02458) ***(G-13553)***
Acera Inc 978 998-4281
100 Cummings Ctr Ste 439c Beverly MA (01915) ***(G-8095)***
Acheson Company LLC 413 268-0246
6 Main St Williamsburg MA (01096) ***(G-16946)***
Acheson Properties, Williamsburg *Also called Acheson Company LLC* ***(G-16946)***
Achillion Pharmaceuticals Inc 203 624-7000
300 George St Ste 801 New Haven CT (06511) ***(G-2652)***
Aci - Pcb Inc 603 528-7711
254 Court St Ste A Laconia NH (03246) ***(G-18551)***
Aci Technology Inc 781 937-9888
215 Salem St Ste J Woburn MA (01801) ***(G-17107)***
Acitronics, Branford *Also called Schmitt Realty Holdings Inc* ***(G-346)***
Ack 60 Main LLC 508 228-1398
58 Main St Nantucket MA (02554) ***(G-13217)***
Ack Surf School LLC 508 325-2589
5 Amelia Dr Nantucket MA (02554) ***(G-13218)***
Ackles Steel & Iron Company 781 893-6818
12 Sun St Waltham MA (02453) ***(G-16022)***
Acktify Inc 781 462-3942
142 Franklin St Melrose MA (02176) ***(G-12974)***
Aclara Software Inc 781 283-9160
16 Laurel Ave Ste 100 Wellesley MA (02481) ***(G-16356)***
Aclara Technologies LLC 781 694-3300
16 Laurel Ave Ste 100 Wellesley MA (02481) ***(G-16357)***
Aclara Technologies LLC 603 749-8376
130 Main St Somersworth NH (03878) ***(G-19826)***
Acm Warehouse & Distribution 203 239-9557
77 Sackett Point Rd North Haven CT (06473) ***(G-3001)***
Acme Apparel, Gloucester *Also called Acme Merchandise and AP Inc* ***(G-11158)***
Acme Bookbinding Company, Charlestown *Also called Hf Group LLC* ***(G-9836)***
Acme Bookbinding Company Inc 617 242-1100
92 Cambridge St Charlestown MA (02129) ***(G-9823)***
Acme Merchandise and AP Inc 978 282-4800
46 Blackburn Ctr Ste 47 Gloucester MA (01930) ***(G-11158)***
Acme Monaco Corporation (PA) 860 224-1349
75 Winchell Rd New Britain CT (06052) ***(G-2503)***
Acme Precast Co Inc 508 548-9607
509 Thomas B Landers Rd West Falmouth MA (02574) ***(G-16477)***
Acme Press Inc 203 334-8221
95 Erna Ave Milford CT (06461) ***(G-2235)***
Acme Printing, Westwood *Also called Universal Wilde Inc* ***(G-16881)***
Acme Sales 603 434-8826
4 King George Dr Londonderry NH (03053) ***(G-18670)***
Acme Sign Co (PA) 203 324-2263
12 Research Dr Stamford CT (06906) ***(G-4128)***
Acme Sign Corporation 978 535-6600
3 Lakeland Park Dr Peabody MA (01960) ***(G-14306)***
Acme Staple Company Inc 603 934-2320
87 Hill Rd Franklin NH (03235) ***(G-18155)***
Acme Typesetting Service Co 860 953-1470
47 Cody St West Hartford CT (06110) ***(G-5052)***
Acme United Corporation (PA) 203 254-6060
55 Walls Dr Ste 201 Fairfield CT (06824) ***(G-1412)***
Acme United Corporation 508 481-5944
89 Hayes Memorial Dr Marlborough MA (01752) ***(G-12709)***
Acme Wire Products Co Inc 860 572-0511
1 Broadway Ave Mystic CT (06355) ***(G-2433)***
Acme-Shorey Precast Co Inc (PA) 508 432-0530
36 Great Western Rd Harwich MA (02645) ***(G-11386)***
Acme-Shorey Precast Co Inc 508 430-0956
351 Whites Path South Yarmouth MA (02664) ***(G-15324)***
Acmt Inc 860 645-0592
369 Progress Dr Manchester CT (06042) ***(G-1982)***
Acom Publishing Inc 413 267-4999
97 Main St Monson MA (01057) ***(G-13202)***
Acon Inc 508 230-8022
22 Bristol Dr South Easton MA (02375) ***(G-15268)***
Acorda Therapeutics, Chelsea *Also called Civitas Therapeutics Inc* ***(G-9949)***
Acorean Manufacturing, Fall River *Also called Alden Acoreana Realty Trust* ***(G-10652)***
Acorn Manufacturing Co Inc 508 339-4500
457 School St Mansfield MA (02048) ***(G-12611)***
Acorn Overhead Door 508 378-0441
249 Governors Rd Quincy MA (02169) ***(G-14613)***
Acoustic Magic Inc 978 440-9384
35 Peakham Rd Sudbury MA (01776) ***(G-15651)***
Acp Waterjet Inc 800 951-5127
325a New Boston St Woburn MA (01801) ***(G-17108)***
Acquia Inc (PA) 888 922-7842
53 State St Ste 1101 Boston MA (02109) ***(G-8337)***
Acquisitions Controlled Svcs 203 327-6364
55 Woodland Pl Apt 4 Stamford CT (06902) ***(G-4129)***
Acra-Cut, Acton *Also called Intech Inc* ***(G-7366)***
Acralube Inc 413 562-5019
54b Mainline Dr Westfield MA (01085) ***(G-16663)***
Acro-Matic Plastics, Leominster *Also called Crisci Tool and Die Inc* ***(G-12128)***
Acronis North America Inc 781 782-9100
1 Van De Graaff Dr # 301 Burlington MA (01803) ***(G-9228)***
Across Usa Inc 617 678-0350
91 Summer St 1 Everett MA (02149) ***(G-10599)***
Acryline Inc 508 695-0060
324 S Washington St North Attleboro MA (02760) ***(G-13742)***
ACS, Bedford *Also called Deborah Frost* ***(G-17638)***
ACS Auxiliaries Group Inc 508 399-3018
300 Turner St Attleboro MA (02703) ***(G-7700)***
ACS Division Biochemical Tech 617 216-6144
42 Chauncy St Ste 10a Boston MA (02111) ***(G-8338)***
ACS Group Inc 617 381-0822
27 Carter St Everett MA (02149) ***(G-10600)***
ACS Industries Inc (PA) 401 769-4700
1 New England Way Unit 1 # 1 Lincoln RI (02865) ***(G-20552)***
Acson Tool Company 203 334-8050
62 Carroll Ave Bridgeport CT (06607) ***(G-367)***
Act Manufacturing, South Windsor *Also called A C T Manufacturing LLC* ***(G-3930)***
Actega North America Inc 508 845-6600
577 Hartford Tpke Ste C Shrewsbury MA (01545) ***(G-15097)***
Actega Wit, Shrewsbury *Also called Actega North America Inc* ***(G-15097)***
Acti, Waltham *Also called Alkermes Cntrlled Therapeutics* ***(G-16030)***
Actifio Federal Inc 781 795-9182
105 Cabot St Ste 301e Needham MA (02494) ***(G-13290)***
Actimus Inc 617 438-9968
189 Coles Rd Cromwell CT (06416) ***(G-843)***
Action Apparel Inc (PA) 781 224-0777
100a Maple St Stoneham MA (02180) ***(G-15552)***
Action Container, Attleboro *Also called Abbott-Action Inc* ***(G-7699)***
Action Conveyor Tech Inc 401 722-2300
90 Douglas Pike Unit 1 Smithfield RI (02917) ***(G-21207)***
Action Organ Service 508 543-2161
77 Lakeview Rd Foxboro MA (02035) ***(G-10875)***
Action Packaging Systems Inc (PA) 860 222-9510
372 Somers Rd Ellington CT (06029) ***(G-1325)***
Action Precision Machining, Leominster *Also called Gdjr Machining Incorporated* ***(G-12143)***
Action Press, West Boylston *Also called Jen Ren Corporation* ***(G-16419)***
Action Screen Printing 207 795-7786
41 Chestnut St Ste 5 Lewiston ME (04240) ***(G-6272)***
Action Unlimited Newspaper, Concord *Also called Doncar Inc* ***(G-10129)***
Active Cutting Fluids, Burlington *Also called Sally Seaver* ***(G-9332)***
Actnano Inc (PA) 857 333-8631
100 Morrissey Blvd Boston MA (02125) ***(G-8339)***
Acton Custom Enterprises 603 279-0241
33 Wildwood Dr Holderness NH (03245) ***(G-18322)***
Acton Metal Processing Corp 781 893-5890
41 Athletic Field Rd Waltham MA (02451) ***(G-16023)***
Acton Research Corporation 941 556-2601
15 Discovery Way Acton MA (01720) ***(G-7334)***
Acton Woodworks Inc 978 263-0222
2 School St Acton MA (01720) ***(G-7335)***
Actronics Incorporated 781 890-7030
166 Bear Hill Rd Waltham MA (02451) ***(G-16024)***
Actuality Systems Inc 617 325-9230
1337 Massachusetts Ave Arlington MA (02476) ***(G-7622)***
Actualmeds Corporation 888 838-9053
222 Pitkin St Ste 107 East Hartford CT (06108) ***(G-1169)***
Actuaries Division, Stamford *Also called Computer Prgrm & Systems Inc* ***(G-4170)***
Actuate Corporation 508 870-9822
25 Smith St Westborough MA (01581) ***(G-16587)***
Acu Gage Systems, Hudson *Also called Ocean Industries LLC* ***(G-18421)***
Acucut Inc 860 793-7012
200 Town Line Rd Southington CT (06489) ***(G-4036)***
Acuitybio Corporation 617 515-9671
200 Upland Rd Newton MA (02460) ***(G-13554)***
Acumen Data Systems Inc 413 737-4800
2223 Westfield St West Springfield MA (01089) ***(G-16504)***
Acumentrics Rups LLC 617 932-7877
10 Walpole Park S Walpole MA (02081) ***(G-15987)***
Acuren Inspection Inc (HQ) 203 702-8740
30 Main St Ste 402 Danbury CT (06810) ***(G-867)***
Acuren Inspection Inc 207 786-7884
264 Merrow Rd Ste 3 Auburn ME (04210) ***(G-5546)***
Acuren Inspection Inc 203 869-6734
43 Arch St Greenwich CT (06830) ***(G-1592)***
Acushnet Company (HQ) 508 979-2000
333 Bridge St Fairhaven MA (02719) ***(G-10635)***
Acushnet Company 508 979-2000
4 Slocum St Acushnet MA (02743) ***(G-7397)***
Acushnet Company 508 979-2000
700 Belleville Ave New Bedford MA (02745) ***(G-13349)***
Acushnet Company 508 979-2000
215 Duchaine Blvd New Bedford MA (02745) ***(G-13350)***
Acushnet Company 508 979-2156
256 Samuel Barnet Blvd New Bedford MA (02745) ***(G-13351)***

Acushnet Company ... 508 979-2309
144 Field St Brockton MA (02302) ***(G-9115)***
Acushnet Company ... 508 979-2343
144 Field St Brockton MA (02302) ***(G-9116)***
Acushnet Holdings Corp (HQ) ... 800 225-8500
333 Bridge St Fairhaven MA (02719) ***(G-10636)***
Acushnet International Inc (HQ) ... 508 979-2000
333 Bridge St Fairhaven MA (02719) ***(G-10637)***
Acushnet Mfg Hom ... 508 763-2074
168 Lake St Acushnet MA (02743) ***(G-7398)***
Acushnet Rubber Company Inc ... 508 998-4000
744 Belleville Ave New Bedford MA (02745) ***(G-13352)***
Acusphere Inc ... 617 577-8800
38 Sidney St Cambridge MA (02139) ***(G-9372)***
Acusphere Inc (PA) ... 617 648-8800
99 Hayden Ave Ste 1 Lexington MA (02421) ***(G-12201)***
Ad Art America, Woodstock *Also called Vermont Flannel Co* ***(G-22740)***
Ad Hoc Energy LLC ... 508 507-8005
1492r Main St Millis MA (02054) ***(G-13182)***
Ad Label Inc ... 860 779-0513
59 N Society Rd Brooklyn CT (06234) ***(G-669)***
Ad M Holdings LLC ... 207 667-9696
23 Industrial Way Trenton ME (04605) ***(G-7096)***
Ad Plus Inc ... 617 859-3128
631 Tremont St Apt 2 Boston MA (02118) ***(G-8340)***
Ad Print ... 508 533-7411
96 Main St Medway MA (02053) ***(G-12952)***
Ad-A-Day Company Inc ... 508 824-8676
245 W Water St Taunton MA (02780) ***(G-15719)***
Ad-Tech, Hampton *Also called Adhesive Technologies Inc* ***(G-18252)***
Ada Fabricators Inc ... 978 262-9900
323 Andover St Ste 3 Wilmington MA (01887) ***(G-16965)***
Adam Burtt Tree and Log LLC ... 603 269-2019
39 Chapelle Rd Center Barnstead NH (03225) ***(G-17787)***
Adam E Mock and Son Logging An ... 603 648-2444
1354 Pleasant St Webster NH (03303) ***(G-19943)***
Adam Shade and Screen, Framingham *Also called Shade Adams & Screen Co* ***(G-11004)***
Adam Z Golas (PA) ... 860 224-7178
99 John Downey Dr New Britain CT (06051) ***(G-2504)***
Adamczyk Enterprises Inc ... 860 745-9830
3 Palomba Dr Enfield CT (06082) ***(G-1345)***
Adams Granite Company Inc ... 802 476-5281
58 Pitman Rd Websterville VT (05678) ***(G-22596)***
Adams Printing Inc ... 401 722-9222
545 Pawtucket Ave # 103 Pawtucket RI (02860) ***(G-20807)***
Adams Redemption Center ... 413 743-7691
56 Commercial St Ste 2 Adams MA (01220) ***(G-7408)***
Adams Specialty & Printing Co ... 413 743-9101
14 Pine St Ste 1 Adams MA (01220) ***(G-7409)***
Adamsahern Sign Solutions Inc ... 860 523-8835
30 Arbor St Unit 208 Hartford CT (06106) ***(G-1802)***
Adamsdale Concrete & Pdts Co ... 401 722-6725
551 Weeden St Pawtucket RI (02860) ***(G-20808)***
Adanac Software Inc ... 978 562-3466
174 Barton Rd Stow MA (01775) ***(G-15629)***
Adaptas Solutions (PA) ... 413 284-9975
7 3rd St Palmer MA (01069) ***(G-14277)***
Adaptive Fabrication LLC ... 802 380-3376
22 Browne Ct Unit 117 Brattleboro VT (05301) ***(G-21715)***
Adaptive Insights Inc ... 508 532-4947
50 Speen St Ste 300 Framingham MA (01701) ***(G-10917)***
Adaptive Mobility Equipment ... 508 336-2556
1551 Fall River Ave Seekonk MA (02771) ***(G-15017)***
Adaptive Networks Inc ... 781 444-4170
123 Highland Ave Needham MA (02494) ***(G-13291)***
Adaptive Optics Associates Inc ... 978 757-9600
115 Jackson Rd Devens MA (01434) ***(G-10316)***
Adaptive Optics Associates Inc (HQ) ... 978 757-9600
115 Jackson Rd Devens MA (01434) ***(G-10317)***
Adaptive Optics Associates Inc ... 860 282-4401
121 Prestige Park Cir East Hartford CT (06108) ***(G-1170)***
Adaptive Optics Associates Inc ... 978 391-0000
53 Jackson Rd Devens MA (01434) ***(G-10318)***
Adaptive Surface Tech Inc ... 617 360-7080
85 Bolton St Ste 122 Cambridge MA (02140) ***(G-9373)***
Adaptive Wireless Solutions LLC ... 978 875-6000
577 Main St Hudson MA (01749) ***(G-11751)***
Adax Machine Co Inc ... 603 598-6777
5 Flagstone Dr Hudson NH (03051) ***(G-18369)***
Adcole Corporation (HQ) ... 508 485-9100
669 Forest St Marlborough MA (01752) ***(G-12710)***
Add-A-Sign, Leominster *Also called Tim Gratuski* ***(G-12195)***
Addamo Manufacturing Inc ... 860 667-2601
360 Stamm Rd Newington CT (06111) ***(G-2837)***
Addilat Inc (PA) ... 781 258-9963
70 Conn St Woburn MA (01801) ***(G-17109)***
Addison County Asphalt Pdts ... 802 388-2338
34 Main St Middlebury VT (05753) ***(G-22096)***
Addison Independent, Middlebury *Also called Addison Press Inc* ***(G-22097)***
Addison Press Inc ... 802 388-4944
58 Maple St Middlebury VT (05753) ***(G-22097)***
Additive Circuits Inc ... 603 366-1578
254 Court St Ste A Laconia NH (03246) ***(G-18552)***
Additive Experts LLC ... 860 351-3324
1 Liberty Sq New Britain CT (06051) ***(G-2505)***
Addivant USA Holdings Corp., Danbury *Also called Si Group USA Hldings Usha Corp* ***(G-990)***
Addivant Usa, LLC, Danbury *Also called Si Group USA (usaa) LLC* ***(G-989)***
Ade Technologies Inc (HQ) ... 781 467-3500
80 Wilson Way Westwood MA (02090) ***(G-16857)***
Adept Mobilerobots, Amherst *Also called Mobilerobots Inc* ***(G-17576)***
Adept Screen Prtg & Graphics ... 207 353-6094
644 Lisbon St Lisbon Falls ME (04252) ***(G-6366)***
Adeptis Inc ... 781 569-5996
400 Tradecenter Ste 5900 Woburn MA (01801) ***(G-17110)***
Adg Printing Incorporated ... 978 667-9285
306 Boston Rd Ste 3 North Billerica MA (01862) ***(G-13790)***
Adherean Inc ... 617 652-0304
219 Crafts Rd Chestnut Hill MA (02467) ***(G-9981)***
Adhesive Applications Inc ... 413 527-7120
45 Ferry St Easthampton MA (01027) ***(G-10552)***
Adhesive Applications Inc ... 413 527-7120
41 Oneil St Easthampton MA (01027) ***(G-10553)***
Adhesive Engineering & Supply ... 603 895-4028
15 Batchelder Rd Seabrook NH (03874) ***(G-19790)***
Adhesive Innovations LLC ... 877 589-0544
Washington Ctr Ste 204 Dover NH (03820) ***(G-18003)***
Adhesive Packaging Spc Inc (HQ) ... 800 222-1117
103 Foster St Peabody MA (01960) ***(G-14307)***
Adhesive Tapes Intl Inc ... 203 792-8279
41 Oneil St Easthampton MA (01027) ***(G-10554)***
Adhesive Technologies Inc (PA) ... 603 926-1616
3 Merrill Industrial Dr Hampton NH (03842) ***(G-18252)***
Adhesives Prepregs, Plainfield *Also called Apcm Manufacturing LLC* ***(G-3448)***
ADI Polishing Inc ... 401 942-3955
81 Calder St Cranston RI (02920) ***(G-20172)***
ADI Print Solutions Inc ... 508 230-7024
22 Willow St 4 Chelsea MA (02150) ***(G-9943)***
Adidas Printing Inc ... 978 851-6337
20 Mulholland Dr Ipswich MA (01938) ***(G-11900)***
Adina Inc (PA) ... 781 762-4477
90 Kerry Pl Ste 5 Norwood MA (02062) ***(G-14119)***
Adirondack Guide Boat, North Ferrisburgh *Also called Martin Custom Boat Works LLC* ***(G-22226)***
Adirondack Guide Boat ... 802 425-3926
6821 Route 7 North Ferrisburgh VT (05473) ***(G-22224)***
Adjacent Bakery LLC ... 207 252-6722
5 Lincoln Ave Scarborough ME (04074) ***(G-6902)***
Adk Pressure Equipment Corp (HQ) ... 860 585-0050
745 Clark Ave Bristol CT (06010) ***(G-514)***
Adkins Printing Company ... 800 228-9745
40 South St Ste 2 New Britain CT (06051) ***(G-2506)***
Admet Inc ... 781 769-0850
51 Morgan Dr Ste 15 Norwood MA (02062) ***(G-14120)***
Admiral Packaging Inc ... 401 274-5588
10 Admiral St Providence RI (02908) ***(G-20945)***
Admix Inc ... 603 627-2340
144 Harvey Rd Londonderry NH (03053) ***(G-18671)***
Adobe Systems Incorporated ... 617 467-6760
275 Washington St Ste 300 Newton MA (02458) ***(G-13555)***
Adolf Jandris & Sons Inc ... 978 632-0089
202 High St Gardner MA (01440) ***(G-11102)***
Adolf Meller Company (PA) ... 800 821-0180
120 Corliss St Providence RI (02904) ***(G-20946)***
Adolf Meller Company ... 401 331-3838
120 Corliss St Providence RI (02904) ***(G-20947)***
Adolor Corporation ... 781 860-8660
65 Hayden Ave Lexington MA (02421) ***(G-12202)***
Adonai Spring Water Inc ... 844 273-7672
31 West St Unit 4 Randolph MA (02368) ***(G-14669)***
Adoneh LLC ... 978 618-0389
428 Lowell Rd Concord MA (01742) ***(G-10107)***
Ador Inc ... 860 583-2367
210 Redstone Hill Rd # 5 Bristol CT (06010) ***(G-515)***
ADP Rivet, Hartford *Also called Manchester Tl & Design ADP LLC* ***(G-1843)***
Adra Rand ... 978 274-2652
23 Hartland Way Acton MA (01720) ***(G-7336)***
Adt/Diversity Inc ... 508 222-9601
50 Perry Ave Attleboro MA (02703) ***(G-7701)***
Adva Optical Networking North ... 978 674-6800
300 Apollo Dr Chelmsford MA (01824) ***(G-9867)***
Advance Affrdale Hring Sltions, Avon *Also called Advanced Hearing Solutions LLC* ***(G-31)***
Advance Concrete Form Inc ... 603 669-4496
241 Pepsi Rd Manchester NH (03109) ***(G-18771)***
Advance Data Technology Inc ... 978 801-4376
132 Washington St Topsfield MA (01983) ***(G-15852)***
Advance Development & Mfg ... 203 453-4325
325 Soundview Rd Guilford CT (06437) ***(G-1691)***

ALPHABETIC

Advance Electronic Concepts 207 797-9825
26 Evergreen Dr Ste A Portland ME (04103) ***(G-6609)***
Advance Form & Supply, Manchester *Also called Advance Concrete Form Inc* ***(G-18771)***
Advance Heat Treating Co 203 380-8898
147 West Ave Bridgeport CT (06604) ***(G-368)***
Advance Machine & Tool Inc 413 499-4900
50 Greenway St Pittsfield MA (01201) ***(G-14448)***
Advance Machine Co Inc 978 897-5808
49 White Pond Rd Stow MA (01775) ***(G-15630)***
Advance Mold & Mfg Inc 860 432-5887
71 Utopia Rd Manchester CT (06042) ***(G-1983)***
Advance Mold Mfg Inc 860 783-5024
15 Teaberry Ridge Rd Ellington CT (06029) ***(G-1326)***
Advance Plastics Inc 508 987-7235
27 Industrial Park Rd E Oxford MA (01540) ***(G-14252)***
Advance Reproductions Corp 978 685-2911
100 Flagship Dr North Andover MA (01845) ***(G-13686)***
Advance Systems Inc 888 238-8704
79a Chapel St Newton MA (02458) ***(G-13556)***
Advance Welding, Springfield *Also called Kielb Welding Enterprises* ***(G-15484)***
Advanced Adhesive Systems Inc 860 953-4100
681 N Mountain Rd Newington CT (06111) ***(G-2838)***
Advanced Aerostructures Inc (PA) 413 315-9284
340 Mckinstry Ave Ste 300 Chicopee MA (01013) ***(G-9996)***
Advanced Air Systems Inc 781 878-5733
43 Highland Rd Ste J Abington MA (02351) ***(G-7319)***
Advanced Animations 802 746-8974
534 Vt Route 107 Stockbridge VT (05772) ***(G-22518)***
Advanced Battery Systems Inc 508 378-2284
274 Plymouth St Halifax MA (02338) ***(G-11313)***
Advanced Building Products Inc 207 490-2306
95 Cyro Dr Sanford ME (04073) ***(G-6870)***
Advanced Burner Solutions Corp 508 400-3289
4 Overlook Dr Medway MA (02053) ***(G-12953)***
Advanced CAM Manufacturing LLC 978 562-2825
526 Main St Hudson MA (01749) ***(G-11752)***
Advanced Career Tech Inc (PA) 508 620-5904
1 International Pl 19 Boston MA (02110) ***(G-8341)***
Advanced Chemical Company 401 785-3434
105-131 Bellows St Warwick RI (02888) ***(G-21318)***
Advanced Circuit Technolo 603 880-6000
91 Northeastern Blvd Nashua NH (03062) ***(G-19104)***
Advanced Cnc Machine Inc 603 625-6631
722 E Indus Pk Dr Unit 15 Manchester NH (03109) ***(G-18772)***
Advanced Concepts & Engrg LLC 207 270-3025
9 Zions Hill Rd Dexter ME (04930) ***(G-5955)***
Advanced Concrete Tech Inc-NH 603 431-5661
300 Portsmouth Ave Greenland NH (03840) ***(G-18219)***
Advanced Consulting 603 882-5529
8 Corona Ave Nashua NH (03063) ***(G-19099)***
Advanced Control Systems Corp 781 829-9228
222 Bolivar St Canton MA (02021) ***(G-9711)***
Advanced Custom Cabinets Inc 603 772-6211
13 Prescott Rd Brentwood NH (03833) ***(G-17743)***
Advanced Decisions Inc 203 402-0603
350 Woodland Ln Orange CT (06477) ***(G-3357)***
Advanced Def Slutions Tech LLC 860 243-1122
23 Britton Dr Bloomfield CT (06002) ***(G-199)***
Advanced Design & Mfg Inc 603 430-7573
350 Heritage Ave Unit 3 Portsmouth NH (03801) ***(G-19532)***
Advanced Diamond Solutions Inc 617 291-3497
12 Inman St Apt 15 Cambridge MA (02139) ***(G-9374)***
Advanced Digital Replication, Roslindale *Also called Harvey Bravman* ***(G-14838)***
Advanced Drainage Systems Inc 413 589-0515
58 Wyoming St Ludlow MA (01056) ***(G-12452)***
Advanced Drainage Systems Inc 860 529-8188
520 Cromwell Ave Rocky Hill CT (06067) ***(G-3701)***
Advanced Electronic Controls 413 736-3625
94 Doty Cir West Springfield MA (01089) ***(G-16505)***
Advanced Electronic Design Inc 508 699-0249
344 John L Dietsch Blvd Attleboro Falls MA (02763) ***(G-7810)***
Advanced Electronic Technology 978 846-6487
12 Shirley St Ayer MA (01432) ***(G-7905)***
Advanced Embroidery, Hyannis *Also called Threadhead Inc* ***(G-11859)***
Advanced Engineering Corp 978 777-7147
45 Prince St Danvers MA (01923) ***(G-10193)***
Advanced Entp Systems Corp 508 431-7607
1 Stiles Rd Ste 302 Salem NH (03079) ***(G-19703)***
Advanced Exhibits, Stockbridge *Also called Advanced Animations* ***(G-22518)***
Advanced Fitnes Components LLC 603 595-1967
17 Hampshire Dr Ste 18 Hudson NH (03051) ***(G-18370)***
Advanced Flexible Composites 802 681-7121
452 Morse Rd Bennington VT (05201) ***(G-21662)***
Advanced Frp Systems Inc 508 927-6915
106 Finnell Dr Ste 13 Weymouth MA (02188) ***(G-16883)***
Advanced Fuel Co LLC 860 642-4817
126 Pleasure Hill Rd North Franklin CT (06254) ***(G-2986)***
Advanced Graphics Inc 781 551-0550
470 Washington St Ste 20 Norwood MA (02062) ***(G-14121)***
Advanced Graphics Inc 203 378-0471
55 Old South Ave Stratford CT (06615) ***(G-4388)***
Advanced Hearing Solutions LLC 860 674-8558
47 W Main St Avon CT (06001) ***(G-31)***
Advanced ID Detection LLC 617 544-8030
23 Jayar Rd Medway MA (02053) ***(G-12954)***
Advanced Illumination Inc 802 767-3830
440 State Garage Rd Rochester VT (05767) ***(G-22315)***
Advanced Imaging Inc 978 658-7776
234 Ballardvale St Wilmington MA (01887) ***(G-16966)***
Advanced Indus Solutions Inc 207 832-0569
151 One Pie Rd Waldoboro ME (04572) ***(G-7129)***
Advanced Instruments LLC (PA) 781 320-9000
2 Technology Way Ste 1 Norwood MA (02062) ***(G-14122)***
Advanced Interconnections Corp 401 823-5200
5 Energy Way West Warwick RI (02893) ***(G-21476)***
Advanced Linen Group 203 877-3896
215 Pepes Farm Rd Milford CT (06460) ***(G-2236)***
Advanced Machine and Tl Co Inc 802 893-6322
63b Gonyeau Rd Milton VT (05468) ***(G-22124)***
Advanced Machine Services LLC (PA) 203 888-6600
2056 Thomaston Ave Waterbury CT (06704) ***(G-4836)***
Advanced Machine Technology 860 872-2664
5 Industrial Dr Ellington CT (06029) ***(G-1327)***
Advanced Materials Processing 978 251-3060
225 Stedman St Ste 14 Lowell MA (01851) ***(G-12339)***
Advanced Measurement Tech Inc 781 938-7800
10e Commerce Way Woburn MA (01801) ***(G-17111)***
Advanced Mechanical Tech Inc (PA) 617 923-4174
176 Waltham St Watertown MA (02472) ***(G-16263)***
Advanced Metal Systems Corp 508 429-0480
34 Pope Rd Bldg 5 Holliston MA (01746) ***(G-11556)***
Advanced Mfg Tech Inc 508 885-0249
2 Bixby Rd Spencer MA (01562) ***(G-15424)***
Advanced Micro Controls Inc 860 585-1254
20 Gear Dr Terryville CT (06786) ***(G-4473)***
Advanced Micro Devices Inc 978 795-2500
90 Central St Boxborough MA (01719) ***(G-8956)***
Advanced Mixing Technologies, Londonderry *Also called Admix Inc* ***(G-18671)***
Advanced Orthopedic Services (PA) 508 771-5050
680 Falmouth Rd Hyannis MA (02601) ***(G-11833)***
Advanced Orthopedic Svcs Inc 508 771-5050
680 Falmouth Rd Hyannis MA (02601) ***(G-11834)***
Advanced Photonics Intl Inc 203 259-0437
96 Lamplighter Ln Fairfield CT (06825) ***(G-1413)***
Advanced Polymerics Inc 603 328-8177
32 Hampshire Rd Salem NH (03079) ***(G-19704)***
Advanced Prcsion Castings Corp 203 736-9452
120 Pullman Dr Milford CT (06461) ***(G-2237)***
Advanced Precast Concrete, Old Lyme *Also called David Shuck* ***(G-3320)***
Advanced Print Solutions Inc (PA) 508 655-8434
45 Bishop Rd Sharon MA (02067) ***(G-15045)***
Advanced Print Technology Inc 978 342-0093
76 Laurel St Fitchburg MA (01420) ***(G-10809)***
Advanced Product Solutions LLC 203 745-4225
555 Sherman Ave Unit C16 Hamden CT (06514) ***(G-1730)***
Advanced Products Operation, North Haven *Also called Parker-Hannifin Corporation* ***(G-3049)***
Advanced Prototype Development 203 267-1262
7 Stiles Rd Southbury CT (06488) ***(G-4022)***
Advanced Prototypes & Molding 978 534-0584
21 Howe St Leominster MA (01453) ***(G-12107)***
Advanced Radon Mitigation Inc 603 644-1207
180 Londonderry Tpke # 1 Hooksett NH (03106) ***(G-18341)***
Advanced Reasoning 860 437-0508
82 Boston Post Rd Ste 3 Waterford CT (06385) ***(G-4980)***
Advanced Receiver Research 860 485-0310
535 Burlington Rd Harwinton CT (06791) ***(G-1886)***
Advanced Research Development 781 285-8721
805 Turnpike St Ste 1 North Andover MA (01845) ***(G-13687)***
Advanced Resources & Construct 207 265-2646
27 Commercial Rd Kingfield ME (04947) ***(G-6251)***
Advanced Self Defense 401 486-8135
1020 Putnam Pike Chepachet RI (02814) ***(G-20132)***
Advanced Sheetmetal Assoc LLC 860 349-1644
52 Indstrial Pk Access Rd Middlefield CT (06455) ***(G-2161)***
Advanced Signing LLC 508 533-9000
4 Industrial Park Rd Medway MA (02053) ***(G-12955)***
Advanced Sonic Proc Systems, Oxford *Also called Advanced Sonics LLC* ***(G-3387)***
Advanced Sonics LLC 203 266-4440
324 Christian St Oxford CT (06478) ***(G-3387)***
Advanced Specialist LLC 860 945-9125
162 Commercial St Watertown CT (06795) ***(G-4997)***
Advanced Specialty Metals, Nashua *Also called Powdered Metal Technology Corp* ***(G-19236)***
Advanced Thermal Solutions Inc (PA) 781 769-2800
89 Access Rd Ste 27 Norwood MA (02062) ***(G-14123)***
Advanced Torque Products LLC 860 828-1523
56 Budney Rd Newington CT (06111) ***(G-2839)***
Advanced Trimwright Inc 508 822-7745
103 Old Colony Ave Unit 8 East Taunton MA (02718) ***(G-10509)***

Advanced Vacuum Systems, Ayer *Also called Avs Incorporated* ***(G-7912)***
Advanced Welding & Design Inc....781 938-7644
6 Draper St Woburn MA (01801) ***(G-17112)***
Advanced Window Systems LLC....800 841-6544
14 Alcap Rdg Cromwell CT (06416) ***(G-844)***
Advanced Woodworking Technolog....978 937-1400
258 W Manchester St Lowell MA (01852) ***(G-12340)***
Advancepierre Foods Inc....207 541-2800
54 Saint John St Portland ME (04102) ***(G-6610)***
Advansource Biomaterials Corp....978 657-0075
229 Andover St Wilmington MA (01887) ***(G-16967)***
Advanstar Communications Inc....339 298-4200
70 Blanchard Rd Ste 301 Burlington MA (01803) ***(G-9229)***
Advantage Communications LLC....203 966-8390
43 Pine St New Canaan CT (06840) ***(G-2592)***
Advantage Data Inc (PA)....212 227-8870
1 Federal St Fl 25 Boston MA (02110) ***(G-8342)***
Advantage Media & Marketing....508 875-0011
225 Arlington St Ste D Framingham MA (01702) ***(G-10918)***
Advantage Mold Inc....603 647-6678
576 Mammoth Rd Ste 23 Londonderry NH (03053) ***(G-18672)***
Advantage Plastic Products Inc....603 227-9540
38 Henniker St Concord NH (03301) ***(G-17880)***
Advantage Sheet Metal Mfg LLC....203 720-0929
51 Elm St Naugatuck CT (06770) ***(G-2457)***
Advantage Signs Inc....603 224-7446
128 Hall St Ste C Concord NH (03301) ***(G-17881)***
Advantcraft Inc....508 498-4644
11 Juniper Rd Upton MA (01568) ***(G-15903)***
Advent Medical Products Inc....781 272-2813
55 Beaver Pond Rd Lincoln MA (01773) ***(G-12285)***
Advertiser-Democrat....207 743-7011
220 Main St Ste 1 Norway ME (04268) ***(G-6521)***
Advisor....203 239-4121
83 State St North Haven CT (06473) ***(G-3002)***
Advisor Perspectives Inc....781 376-0050
10 State St Fl 2nd Woburn MA (01801) ***(G-17113)***
Advocate Newspapers (PA)....617 387-2200
573 Broadway Everett MA (02149) ***(G-10601)***
Aearo Technologies LLC....317 692-6645
48 Sword St Ste 101 Auburn MA (01501) ***(G-7822)***
AEC Engineering....207 865-4190
172 Lower Main St Freeport ME (04032) ***(G-6071)***
Aecc/Pearlman Buying Group LLC....203 598-3200
1255 Middlebury Rd Middlebury CT (06762) ***(G-2153)***
Aegerion Pharmaceuticals Inc (HQ)....877 764-3131
245 1st St Ste 18 Cambridge MA (02142) ***(G-9375)***
Aegis Container, Milford *Also called Aegis Holdings LLC* ***(G-19042)***
Aegis Holdings LLC....603 673-8900
Riverway W Milford NH (03055) ***(G-19042)***
Aegis Semiconductor Security, Woburn *Also called Ii-VI Photonics (us) Inc* ***(G-17200)***
Aemc Instruments, Dover *Also called Chauvin Arnoux Inc* ***(G-18012)***
Aemc Instruments, Foxboro *Also called Chauvin Arnoux Inc* ***(G-10878)***
AEN Asphalt Inc....860 885-0500
34 Bozrah St Bozrah CT (06334) ***(G-279)***
Aeqrx Technologies Ltd....401 463-8822
50 Minnesota Ave Warwick RI (02888) ***(G-21319)***
Aer Control Systems LLC....203 772-4700
36 Nettleton Ave North Haven CT (06473) ***(G-3003)***
Aeration Technologies Inc....603 434-3539
3 Commercial Ln Ste F Londonderry NH (03053) ***(G-18673)***
Aerc Removals LLC....774 218-4212
11 Robert Toner Blvd North Attleboro MA (02763) ***(G-13743)***
Aereo Inc....617 861-8287
2 Rosenfeld Dr Ste F Hopedale MA (01747) ***(G-11669)***
Aerex Manufacturing, South Windsor *Also called ATI Ladish Machining Inc* ***(G-3939)***
Aerial Acoustics Corporation....978 988-1600
100 Research Dr Ste 4 Wilmington MA (01887) ***(G-16968)***
Aero - Bond Corp....413 734-2224
1 Allen St Ste 212 Springfield MA (01108) ***(G-15441)***
Aero Brazing Corp....781 933-7511
223 New Boston St Woburn MA (01801) ***(G-17114)***
Aero Component Services LLC....860 291-0417
781 Goodwin St East Hartford CT (06108) ***(G-1171)***
Aero Defense International LLC....603 644-0305
400 Bedford St Ste 136 Manchester NH (03101) ***(G-18773)***
Aero Gear Incorporated....860 688-0888
1050 Day Hill Rd Windsor CT (06095) ***(G-5316)***
Aero Manufacturing Corp....978 720-1000
100 Sam Fonzo Dr Ste 1 Beverly MA (01915) ***(G-8096)***
Aero Precision Mfg LLC....203 675-7625
71 S Turnpike Rd Wallingford CT (06492) ***(G-4694)***
Aero Surveillance Inc....978 691-5832
800 Turnpike St Ste 300 North Andover MA (01845) ***(G-13688)***
Aero Tube Technologies LLC....860 289-2520
425 Sullivan Ave Ste 8 South Windsor CT (06074) ***(G-3932)***
Aero Turbine Components Inc....508 755-2121
993 Millbury St Worcester MA (01607) ***(G-17335)***
Aero-Dynamics Inc....603 474-2547
142 Batchelder Rd Seabrook NH (03874) ***(G-19791)***
Aero-Med Ltd....860 659-2270
571 Nutmeg Rd N South Windsor CT (06074) ***(G-3933)***
Aero-Med Molding Technologies (PA)....203 735-2331
50 Westfield Ave Ansonia CT (06401) ***(G-4)***
Aerobond Composites LLC....413 734-2224
1 Allen St Ste 201 Springfield MA (01108) ***(G-15442)***
Aerocess Inc....860 357-2451
500 Four Rod Rd Ste 110 Berlin CT (06037) ***(G-67)***
Aerocision LLC....860 526-9700
12a Inspiration Ln Chester CT (06412) ***(G-767)***
Aerocor Inc....860 281-9274
59 Newberry Rd East Windsor CT (06088) ***(G-1275)***
Aerodynamics Metal Finishing, Seabrook *Also called Aero-Dynamics Inc* ***(G-19791)***
Aeroflex / Metelics Inc....603 641-3800
100 Chelmsford St Lowell MA (01851) ***(G-12341)***
Aeromics Inc....216 772-1004
11000 Cedar Ave Ste 270 Branford CT (06405) ***(G-285)***
Aeronautica Windpower LLC....508 732-8945
11 Resnik Rd Plymouth MA (02360) ***(G-14539)***
Aeroparts Plus Inc....802 489-5023
12 Gregory Dr Ste 1 South Burlington VT (05403) ***(G-22435)***
Aeroplas Corp International....603 465-7300
265b Proctor Hill Rd Hollis NH (03049) ***(G-18324)***
Aerosat Avionics LLC....603 943-8680
60 State Route 101a Amherst NH (03031) ***(G-17549)***
Aerospace, Berlin *Also called Amco Precision Tools Inc* ***(G-70)***
Aerospace Adhsive Bonding Tech....413 315-9349
340 Mckinstry Ave Ste 300 Chicopee MA (01013) ***(G-9997)***
Aerospace Fabricators Inc....781 899-4535
116 Harvard St Waltham MA (02453) ***(G-16025)***
Aerospace Metals Inc....860 522-3123
239 W Service Rd Hartford CT (06120) ***(G-1803)***
Aerospace Semiconductor Inc....978 688-1299
439 S Union St Unit 2105 Lawrence MA (01843) ***(G-11990)***
Aerospace Support Inc....413 789-3103
44 Russo Cir Agawam MA (01001) ***(G-7417)***
Aeroswiss LLC....203 634-4545
20 Powers Dr Meriden CT (06451) ***(G-2074)***
Aerotech Fasteners Inc....860 928-6300
1 Ridge Rd Putnam CT (06260) ***(G-3600)***
Aerotek Welding Co Inc....860 653-0120
51 Loomis St North Granby CT (06060) ***(G-2993)***
Aeroturn LLC....203 262-8309
115 Hurley Rd Ste 2c Oxford CT (06478) ***(G-3388)***
Aerovironment Inc....805 520-8350
141 S Bedford St Ste 250 Burlington MA (01803) ***(G-9230)***
Aeroweld Inc....603 524-8121
49 Blaisdell Ave Laconia NH (03246) ***(G-18553)***
Aertec....978 475-6385
11 Bartlet St Andover MA (01810) ***(G-7533)***
AES Corporation....978 535-7310
285 Newbury St Ste 1 Peabody MA (01960) ***(G-14308)***
Aesthetic Blacksmithing, Bridgeport *Also called Jozef Custom Ironworks Inc* ***(G-437)***
Aetna Insulated Wire LLC....757 460-3381
53 Old Wilton Rd Milford NH (03055) ***(G-19043)***
Aetna Jewelery Mfg, Providence *Also called Aetna Manufacturing Company* ***(G-20948)***
Aetna Manufacturing Company....401 751-3260
720 Harris Ave Providence RI (02909) ***(G-20948)***
Aetruim Incorporated....651 773-4200
4 Federal St Billerica MA (01821) ***(G-8205)***
AF Group Inc....401 757-3910
24 Albion Rd Ste 210 Lincoln RI (02865) ***(G-20553)***
Afc Cable Systems Inc....508 998-8277
260 Duchaine Blvd New Bedford MA (02745) ***(G-13353)***
Afcon Products Inc....203 393-9301
35 Sargent Dr Bethany CT (06524) ***(G-118)***
Afficiency Inc....718 496-9071
606 Post Rd E Westport CT (06880) ***(G-5178)***
Affinity Led Light LLC....978 378-5338
1 Washington St Ste 5121 Dover NH (03820) ***(G-18004)***
Affinity Led Lighting, Dover *Also called Affinity Led Light LLC* ***(G-18004)***
Affinity Project Inc....202 841-4011
3 Concord Ave Cambridge MA (02138) ***(G-9376)***
Affordable Conveyors Svcs LLC....860 582-1800
144 W Washington St Bristol CT (06010) ***(G-516)***
Affordable Exhibit Displays....207 782-6175
142 Turner St Auburn ME (04210) ***(G-5547)***
Affordable Exhibit Displays....207 782-6175
142 Turner St Auburn ME (04210) ***(G-5548)***
Affordable Intr Systems Inc (HQ)....978 562-7500
25 Tucker Dr Leominster MA (01453) ***(G-12108)***
Affordable Kitchen and Baths, Biddeford *Also called Lauzon Gilles* ***(G-5743)***
Affordable Water Trtmnt....860 423-3147
498 Stafford Rd Mansfield Center CT (06250) ***(G-2061)***
AFL Telecommunications LLC....603 528-7780
16 Eastgate Park Dr Belmont NH (03220) ***(G-17669)***
Africa China Mining Corp....617 921-5500
420 Washington St Ste 302 Braintree MA (02184) ***(G-8985)***
AG & G Inc (PA)....401 946-4330
21 Mill St Johnston RI (02919) ***(G-20498)***

A
L
P
H
A
B
E
T
I
C

AG Jewelry Designs LLC (PA)....800 643-0978
1 Stamford Plz Stamford CT (06901) ***(G-4130)***
AG Semiconductor Services LLC....203 322-5300
1111 Summer St Fl 4 Stamford CT (06905) ***(G-4131)***
AG Structures LLC....603 648-2987
96 Old Turnpike Rd Salisbury NH (03268) ***(G-19780)***
Against Grn Gourmet Foods LLC....802 258-3838
22 Browne Ct Unit 119 Brattleboro VT (05301) ***(G-21716)***
Agape Dermatology....401 396-2227
49 Seekonk St Unit 3 Providence RI (02906) ***(G-20949)***
Agar Machining & Welding Inc....401 724-2260
270 York Ave Pawtucket RI (02860) ***(G-20809)***
Agawam Novelty Company Inc....413 536-0471
354 Rowley St Agawam MA (01001) ***(G-7418)***
AGC Acquisition LLC....203 639-7125
106 Evansville Ave Meriden CT (06451) ***(G-2075)***
AGCO Corporation....603 826-4664
72 Hammond Acres Charlestown NH (03603) ***(G-17809)***
Ageless Innovation LLC (PA)....888 569-4255
161 Exchange St Unit 2a Pawtucket RI (02860) ***(G-20810)***
Agency Systems Group....978 422-8479
20 Kilburn Rd Sterling MA (01564) ***(G-15531)***
Agencyport Software Corp (HQ)....866 539-6623
22 Boston Wharf Rd 10 Boston MA (02210) ***(G-8343)***
Agencyport Software Corp....860 674-6135
190 Farmington Ave Farmington CT (06032) ***(G-1464)***
Agentus Therapeutics Inc (HQ)....701 674-4400
3 Forbes Rd Lexington MA (02421) ***(G-12203)***
Agenus Inc (PA)....781 674-4400
3 Forbes Rd Lexington MA (02421) ***(G-12204)***
AGFA Corporation....978 658-5600
200 Ballardvale St Wilmington MA (01887) ***(G-16969)***
AGFA Finance Group, Wilmington *Also called AGFA Corporation* ***(G-16969)***
Aggregate Inds - Northeast Reg....781 893-7562
537 South St Rear Waltham MA (02453) ***(G-16026)***
Aggregate Inds - Northeast Reg....781 344-1100
1101 Turnpike St Stoughton MA (02072) ***(G-15574)***
Aggregate Inds - Northeast Reg....508 384-3161
400 Green St Wrentham MA (02093) ***(G-17513)***
Aggregate Inds - Northeast Reg....508 398-8865
230 Great Western Rd South Dennis MA (02660) ***(G-15264)***
Aggregate Inds - Northeast Reg....508 881-1430
71 Spring St Ashland MA (01721) ***(G-7655)***
Aggregate Inds - Northeast Reg....508 822-7120
1500 King Philip St Raynham MA (02767) ***(G-14704)***
Aggregate Inds - Northeast Reg....508 821-9508
203 Fremont St Taunton MA (02780) ***(G-15720)***
Aggregate Inds - Northeast Reg....617 924-8550
48 Coolidge Ave Watertown MA (02472) ***(G-16264)***
Aggregate Inds - Northeast Reg....508 398-8865
230 Great Western Rd Dennis MA (02638) ***(G-10305)***
Aggregate Inds - Northeast Reg....781 941-7200
1715 Broadway Ste 1 Saugus MA (01906) ***(G-14975)***
Aggregate Industries....978 582-0261
1000 Reservoir Rd Lunenburg MA (01462) ***(G-12480)***
Aggregate Industries - Mwr Inc....603 427-1137
650 Peverly Hill Rd Portsmouth NH (03801) ***(G-19533)***
Aggregate Industries - Mwr Inc....781 941-7200
1715 Broadway Ste 1 Saugus MA (01906) ***(G-14976)***
Aggregate Industries - Mwr Inc....781 231-3400
1831 Broadway Saugus MA (01906) ***(G-14977)***
Aggregate Industries - Mwr Inc....781 337-2304
611 Pleasant St East Weymouth MA (02189) ***(G-10533)***
Aggregate Industries - Mwr Inc....781 344-1100
1101 Turnpike St Stoughton MA (02072) ***(G-15575)***
Aggregate Industries - Mwr Inc....508 754-4709
651 Lake St Shrewsbury MA (01545) ***(G-15098)***
Aggregate Industries - Mwr Inc....781 941-3108
1715 Broadway Ste 1 Saugus MA (01906) ***(G-14978)***
Aggregate Industries - Mwr Inc....603 243-3554
91 Chester Rd Raymond NH (03077) ***(G-19633)***
Agi Polymatrix LLC (HQ)....413 499-3550
45 Downing Industrial Par Pittsfield MA (01201) ***(G-14449)***
Agi-Shorewood Group Us LLC....203 324-4839
300 Atlantic St Ste 206 Stamford CT (06901) ***(G-4132)***
Agi-Shorewood U.S., Greenwich *Also called Atlas Agi Holdings LLC* ***(G-1594)***
Agile Devices Inc....617 416-5495
28 Damrell St Ste 101 Boston MA (02127) ***(G-8344)***
Agile Magnetics, Concord *Also called Regional Mfg Specialists Inc* ***(G-17926)***
Agilent Technologies Inc....978 794-3664
40 Shattuck Rd Ste 201 Andover MA (01810) ***(G-7534)***
Agilent Technologies Inc....413 593-2900
300 Griffith Rd Chicopee MA (01022) ***(G-9998)***
Agilent Technologies Inc....781 861-7200
121 Hartwell Ave Lexington MA (02421) ***(G-12205)***
Agilynx Inc....617 314-6463
4 Rodeo Cir Billerica MA (01821) ***(G-8206)***
Agios Pharmaceuticals Inc (PA)....617 649-8600
88 Sidney St Cambridge MA (02139) ***(G-9377)***
Agis Inc....508 591-8400
214 S Meadow Rd Plymouth MA (02360) ***(G-14540)***
Agissar Corporation....203 375-8662
526 Benton St Stratford CT (06615) ***(G-4389)***
AGM Industries Inc....508 587-3900
16 Jonathan Dr Brockton MA (02301) ***(G-9117)***
Agnoli Sign Company Inc....413 732-5111
722 Worthington St Springfield MA (01105) ***(G-15443)***
Agri-Mark Inc....802 388-6731
869 Exchange St Middlebury VT (05753) ***(G-22098)***
Agri-Mark Inc (PA)....978 552-5500
40 Shattuck Rd Ste 301 Andover MA (01810) ***(G-7535)***
Agri-Mark Inc....413 732-4168
958 Riverdale St West Springfield MA (01089) ***(G-16506)***
Agri-Mark Inc....781 740-0090
50 Derby St Ste 100 Hingham MA (02043) ***(G-11489)***
Agri-Mark Inc....802 496-1200
193 Home Farm Way Waitsfield VT (05673) ***(G-22559)***
Agri-Mark Cabot, Middlebury *Also called Agri-Mark Inc* ***(G-22098)***
Agricltral Resources Mass Dept....774 331-2818
38 Forest St Attleboro MA (02703) ***(G-7702)***
Agriphar Crop Solutions, Waterbury *Also called Macdermid AG Solutions Inc* ***(G-4903)***
Agrium Advanced Tech US Inc....978 422-3331
18 Legate Hill Rd Sterling MA (01564) ***(G-15532)***
Agway, Madison *Also called Burger-Roy Inc* ***(G-6404)***
Agwey Metal Designs Inc....508 747-1037
206 S Meadow Rd Plymouth MA (02360) ***(G-14541)***
Ah Nelsen Associates LLC....603 716-6687
23 Sunshine Dr Ste 23 # 23 Kingston NH (03848) ***(G-18538)***
Ahead LLC....508 985-9898
270 Samuel Barnet Blvd New Bedford MA (02745) ***(G-13354)***
Ahead Communications Systems....203 720-0227
6 Rubber Ave Naugatuck CT (06770) ***(G-2458)***
Ahlers Designs Inc....401 365-1010
999 Main St Unit 707 Pawtucket RI (02860) ***(G-20811)***
Ahlers Gifts.com, Pawtucket *Also called Ahlers Designs Inc* ***(G-20811)***
Ahlstrom Windsor Locks LLC....860 654-8629
3 Chirnside Rd Windsor Locks CT (06096) ***(G-5381)***
Ahlstrom-Munksjo Nonwovens LLC (HQ)....860 654-8300
2 Elm St Windsor Locks CT (06096) ***(G-5382)***
Ahlstrom-Munksjo Paper Inc....978 342-1080
100 Erdman Way Ste S-101 Leominster MA (01453) ***(G-12109)***
Ahlstrom-Munksjo USA Inc (HQ)....860 654-8300
2 Elm St Windsor Locks CT (06096) ***(G-5383)***
Ai Divestitures Inc....203 575-5727
245 Freight St Waterbury CT (06702) ***(G-4837)***
Ai-Tek Instruments LLC....203 271-6927
152 Knotter Dr Cheshire CT (06410) ***(G-708)***
Aidance Skincare & Topical Sol....401 432-7750
184 Burnside Ave Woonsocket RI (02895) ***(G-21547)***
Aileron Therapeutics Inc....774 444-0704
490 Arsenal Way Ste 210 Watertown MA (02472) ***(G-16265)***
Aim Joraco, Smithfield *Also called Automated Industrial Mch Inc* ***(G-21210)***
Aimco, Auburn *Also called Aimtek Inc* ***(G-7823)***
Aimtek Inc (PA)....508 832-5035
201 Washington St Auburn MA (01501) ***(G-7823)***
Aipco Inc....508 823-7003
75 John Hancock Rd Taunton MA (02780) ***(G-15721)***
Air Age Inc....203 431-9000
88 Danbury Rd Ste 2b Wilton CT (06897) ***(G-5274)***
Air Control Industries Inc....207 445-2518
76 Augusta Rockland Rd Windsor ME (04363) ***(G-7262)***
Air Energy Group LLC....508 230-9445
6 Norfolk Ave South Easton MA (02375) ***(G-15269)***
Air Handling Systems, Woodbridge *Also called Manufacturers Service Co Inc* ***(G-5471)***
Air Head Composting Toilet, Westbrook *Also called Eos Design LLC* ***(G-7188)***
Air Products and Chemicals Inc....508 435-3428
52 Wilson St Hopkinton MA (01748) ***(G-11688)***
Air Tool Sales & Service Co (PA)....860 673-2714
1 Burnham Ave Unionville CT (06085) ***(G-4652)***
Air Travel Journal, Boston *Also called Robert Weiss Associates Inc* ***(G-8825)***
Air Treatment Division, Amesbury *Also called Munters Corporation* ***(G-7498)***
Air-Lock Incorporated....203 878-4691
108 Gulf St Milford CT (06460) ***(G-2238)***
Air-Mart Heating & Cooling LLC....603 821-1416
225 Stedman St Ste 13 Lowell MA (01851) ***(G-12342)***
Air-Tite Holders Inc....413 664-2730
1560 Curran Hwy North Adams MA (01247) ***(G-13667)***
Air-Vac Engineering Co Inc (PA)....203 888-9900
30 Progress Ave Ste 2 Seymour CT (06483) ***(G-3748)***
Airborne Industries Inc....203 315-0200
6 Sycamore Way Ste 2 Branford CT (06405) ***(G-286)***
Aircraft, Plainville *Also called Top Flight Machine Tool LLC* ***(G-3520)***
Aircraft Forged Tool Company....860 347-3778
98 Cedar St Rockfall CT (06481) ***(G-3696)***
Airex LLC....603 841-2040
15 Lilac Ln Somersworth NH (03878) ***(G-19827)***
Airex Corporation....603 821-3065
17 Executive Dr Hudson NH (03051) ***(G-18371)***

Airflo Instrument Company 860 633-9455
53 Addison Rd Glastonbury CT (06033) *(G-1536)*
Airflow Direction Inc 978 462-9995
2 Livingston Ln Newbury MA (01951) *(G-13462)*
Airgas Usa LLC 978 439-1344
1 Plank St Billerica MA (01821) *(G-8207)*
Airgas Usa LLC 401 884-0201
120 Telmore Rd East Greenwich RI (02818) *(G-20351)*
Airgas Usa LLC 203 729-2159
120 Rado Dr Naugatuck CT (06770) *(G-2459)*
Airlinx Communications Inc 603 878-1926
111 Old Country Rd New Ipswich NH (03071) *(G-19302)*
Airloc Corporation 508 528-0022
5 Fisher St Franklin MA (02038) *(G-11020)*
Airmar Technology Corp (PA) 603 673-9570
35 Meadowbrook Dr Milford NH (03055) *(G-19044)*
Airmar Technology Corp 603 673-9570
40 Meadowbrook Dr Milford NH (03055) *(G-19045)*
Airpot Corporation 800 848-7681
35 Lois St Norwalk CT (06851) *(G-3097)*
Airs, Hudson *Also called American Ir Solutions LLC (G-18373)*
Airtight Ink, Richmond *Also called Z M Weapons High Performance (G-22313)*
Airtime Publishing Inc 203 454-4773
191 Post Rd W Westport CT (06880) *(G-5179)*
Airworks Solutions Inc 857 990-1060
180 Canal St Ste 303 Boston MA (02114) *(G-8345)*
Airxchange Inc 781 871-4816
85 Longwater Dr Rockland MA (02370) *(G-14789)*
Airy Technology Inc 781 341-1850
31 Tosca Dr Ste 8 Stoughton MA (02072) *(G-15576)*
Ais Global Holdings LLC 203 250-3500
250 Knotter Dr Cheshire CT (06410) *(G-709)*
Ais Group Holdings LLC (PA) 978 562-7500
4 Robert Rd Hudson MA (01749) *(G-11753)*
Ais Holdings Corp (HQ) 978 562-7500
25 Tucker Dr Ste 1 Leominster MA (01453) *(G-12110)*
Aislebuyer Lllc 617 606-7062
321 Summer St Fl 8 Boston MA (02210) *(G-8346)*
Ait Manufacturing LLC 978 655-7257
678 Andover St Lawrence MA (01843) *(G-11991)*
Aiudi Concrete Inc 860 399-9289
129 Norris Ave Westbrook CT (06498) *(G-5155)*
Aj Casey LLC 203 226-5961
597 Westport Ave C363 Norwalk CT (06851) *(G-3098)*
Aj Mfg 860 963-7622
999 Quaddick Town Farm Rd Thompson CT (06277) *(G-4530)*
AJ Precision Inc 413 568-9099
25 Century St Agawam MA (01001) *(G-7419)*
AJ Tuck Company 203 775-1234
32 Tucks Rd Brookfield CT (06804) *(G-633)*
Aja International Inc 781 545-7365
809 Country Way Scituate MA (02066) *(G-15005)*
Ajinomoto Cambrooke Inc (HQ) 508 782-2300
4 Copeland Dr Ayer MA (01432) *(G-7906)*
AK Stucco LLC 860 832-9589
47 Hatch St New Britain CT (06053) *(G-2507)*
AKa McHlngelo Strbuilder LLC 508 238-9054
31 Randall St North Easton MA (02356) *(G-13940)*
Aka Tool Inc 603 524-1868
477 Province Rd Ste 1 Laconia NH (03246) *(G-18554)*
Akamai Technologies Inc (PA) 617 444-3000
145 Broadway Cambridge MA (02142) *(G-9378)*
Akcea Therapeutics Inc (HQ) 617 207-0202
22 Boston Wharf Rd Fl 9 Boston MA (02210) *(G-8347)*
Akebia Therapeutics Inc (PA) 617 871-2098
245 1st St Ste 1400 Cambridge MA (02142) *(G-9379)*
Akken Inc 866 590-6695
98 Spit Brook Rd Ste 402 Nashua NH (03062) *(G-19105)*
AKO Inc 860 298-9765
50 Baker Hollow Rd Windsor CT (06095) *(G-5317)*
Akrivis Technologies LLC 617 233-4097
1 Broadway Fl 14 Cambridge MA (02142) *(G-9380)*
Akston Biosciences Corporation 978 969-3381
100 Cummings Ctr Ste 454c Beverly MA (01915) *(G-8097)*
Akumina Inc 603 318-8269
30 Temple St Ste 301 Nashua NH (03060) *(G-19106)*
Akumo Software Inc 617 466-9818
35 Channel Ctr St # 405 Boston MA (02210) *(G-8348)*
Al CU Met Inc 603 432-6220
3 Planeview Dr Londonderry NH (03053) *(G-18674)*
Al Gags 413 285-8023
34 Front St Indian Orchard MA (01151) *(G-11884)*
Al Woodworking 508 886-2883
173 Pleasantdale Rd Rutland MA (01543) *(G-14879)*
Al's Beverage Company, East Windsor *Also called Jmf Group LLC (G-1288)*
Al's Doughnuts, Boston *Also called 861 Corp (G-8330)*
Al's Goldfish Lure Co, Indian Orchard *Also called Stuart Sports Specialties Inc (G-11897)*
Al's Goldfish Lure Co., Biddeford *Also called Maine Lure Company LLC (G-5745)*
ALA Casting Co Inc 516 371-4350
185 Jefferson Blvd Warwick RI (02888) *(G-21320)*
Alacrity Semiconductors Inc 475 325-8435
4 Pin Oak Dr Ste B Branford CT (06405) *(G-287)*
Alacron Inc 603 891-2750
71 Spit Brook Rd Ste 200 Nashua NH (03060) *(G-19107)*
Alakai Technologies Corp 774 248-4964
22 Piazza Ln Hopkinton MA (01748) *(G-11689)*
Alan Stevens 207 547-3840
240 Philbrick Rd Sidney ME (04330) *(G-6961)*
Alan T Seeler Inc 603 744-3736
87 Nh Route 132 N New Hampton NH (03256) *(G-19301)*
Alan W Leavitt Company 617 338-9335
333 Washington St Ste 328 Boston MA (02108) *(G-8349)*
Alaris Usa LLC 207 517-5304
33r Main St Ste 1 Windham ME (04062) *(G-7228)*
Alarm Engineering, Georgetown *Also called L W Bills Co (G-11144)*
Alarm One 203 239-1714
142 Maple Ave North Haven CT (06473) *(G-3004)*
Alarmsafe Inc 978 658-6717
6 Omni Way Chelmsford MA (01824) *(G-9868)*
Albany Engnered Composites Inc 603 330-5851
216 Airport Dr Rochester NH (03867) *(G-19651)*
Albany Engnered Composites Inc 603 330-5993
216 Airport Dr Rochester NH (03867) *(G-19652)*
Albany Engnered Composites Inc 603 330-5800
216 Airport Dr Rochester NH (03867) *(G-19653)*
Albany Engnered Composites Inc (HQ) 603 330-5800
216 Airport Dr Rochester NH (03867) *(G-19654)*
Albany International Corp (PA) 603 330-5850
216 Airport Dr Rochester NH (03867) *(G-19655)*
Albany International Corp 603 330-5993
85 Innovation Dr Rochester NH (03867) *(G-19656)*
Albany Molecular Research Inc 781 672-4530
201 Jones Rd Ste 300 Waltham MA (02451) *(G-16027)*
Albany Safran Composites LLC (HQ) 603 330-5800
85 Innovation Dr Rochester NH (03867) *(G-19657)*
Albarrie Environmental Svcs, Auburn *Also called Albarrie Technical Fabrics Inc (G-5549)*
Albarrie Technical Fabrics Inc 207 786-0424
195 Center St Auburn ME (04210) *(G-5549)*
Albea Metal Americas, Watertown *Also called Covit America Inc (G-5004)*
Albea Thomaston Inc 860 283-2000
60 Electric Ave Thomaston CT (06787) *(G-4497)*
Albert Basse Associates Inc 781 344-3555
175 Campanelli Pkwy Stoughton MA (02072) *(G-15577)*
Albert Capone (PA) 617 629-2296
14 Bow St Somerville MA (02143) *(G-15151)*
Albert E Erickson Co 203 386-8931
1111 Honeyspot Rd Ste 1 Stratford CT (06615) *(G-4390)*
Albert K Stokes, Hudson *Also called Stokes Woodworking Co Inc (G-11820)*
Albert Kemperle Inc 401 826-5111
288 Lincoln Ave Warwick RI (02888) *(G-21321)*
Albert Kemperle Inc 860 727-0933
141 Locust St Hartford CT (06114) *(G-1804)*
Albert Landry 603 883-1919
100 Factory St Ste E1 Nashua NH (03060) *(G-19108)*
Albert Langin 603 635-3560
19 Hayden Rd Pelham NH (03076) *(G-19426)*
Albert M M Johnston IV 207 848-2561
527 Fuller Rd Hermon ME (04401) *(G-6181)*
Alberto Vasallo Jr 617 522-5060
175 Wm F Mcclellan Hwy Boston MA (02128) *(G-8350)*
Albion Beams Inc 978 526-4406
9 Spy Rock Hill Rd Manchester MA (01944) *(G-12602)*
Albion Manufacturing 207 873-5633
133 Halifax St Winslow ME (04901) *(G-7265)*
Albion Systems, Manchester *Also called Albion Beams Inc (G-12602)*
Albireo Pharma Inc 857 415-4774
10 Post Office Sq 500s Boston MA (02109) *(G-8351)*
Albireo Pharma Inc (PA) 857 254-5555
10 Post Office Sq Ste 502 Boston MA (02109) *(G-8352)*
Albisons Printing Inc 207 622-1941
124 Riverside Dr Augusta ME (04330) *(G-5603)*
Albrayco Technologies Inc 860 635-3369
38 River Rd Cromwell CT (06416) *(G-845)*
Albright Technologies Inc 978 466-5870
30 Patriots Cir Leominster MA (01453) *(G-12111)*
Albrite Signs LLC 603 466-5192
20 Libby St Gorham NH (03581) *(G-18210)*
ALC Sales Company LLC (PA) 203 877-8526
230 Pepes Farm Rd Ste C Milford CT (06460) *(G-2239)*
Alcan Packaging, Norwalk *Also called Cebal Americas (G-3121)*
Alcat Incorporated 203 878-0648
116 W Main St Milford CT (06460) *(G-2240)*
Alchemist - Waterbury, The, Stowe *Also called Alchemy Canning Ltd (G-22519)*
Alchemy Canning Ltd 802 244-7744
100 Cottage Club Rd Stowe VT (05672) *(G-22519)*
Alcides D Fortes D/B/A Custom 508 378-7815
225 Elm St East Bridgewater MA (02333) *(G-10405)*
Alco Construction Inc 603 305-8493
5 Christine Dr Unit 5-G Hudson NH (03051) *(G-18372)*

Alco Technology...508 678-7449
560 Ray St Fall River MA (02720) *(G-10651)*
Alcoa Global Fasteners Inc...412 553-4545
44 Campanelli Pkwy Stoughton MA (02072) *(G-15578)*
Alcom LLC (PA)...207 861-9800
6 Millennium Dr Winslow ME (04901) *(G-7266)*
Alcor-Usa Llc...603 398-1564
220 Stockbridge Corner Rd Alton NH (03809) *(G-17544)*
Alcresta Therapeutics Inc...617 431-3600
1 Newton Executive Park # 100 Newton MA (02462) *(G-13557)*
Aldam Press Inc...413 443-2800
163 South St Ste 4 Pittsfield MA (01201) *(G-14450)*
Aldatu Biosciences Inc...978 705-1036
201 Dexter Ave Watertown MA (02472) *(G-16266)*
Alden Acoreana Realty Trust (PA)...508 678-2098
210 Alden St Fall River MA (02723) *(G-10652)*
Alden and Broden Corporation...603 882-0330
13 Blue Ridge Rd Westford MA (01886) *(G-16752)*
Alden Corporation...203 879-8830
1 Hillside Dr Wolcott CT (06716) *(G-5432)*
Alden Hauk Inc...781 281-0154
215 Salem St Ste 10 Woburn MA (01801) *(G-17115)*
Alden Medical LLC (PA)...413 747-9717
360 Cold Spring Ave Ste 1 West Springfield MA (01089) *(G-16507)*
Alden New England, Middleboro *Also called Alden Shoe Company Inc (G-13050)*
Alden Shoe Company Inc...508 947-3926
1 Taunton St Middleboro MA (02346) *(G-13050)*
Alden Tool Company Inc...860 828-3556
199 New Park Dr Berlin CT (06037) *(G-68)*
Alden Yachts Brokerage, Bristol *Also called Alden Yachts Corporation (G-20060)*
Alden Yachts Corporation...401 683-4200
99 Poppasquash Rd Unit I Bristol RI (02809) *(G-20060)*
Aldeyra Therapeutics Inc (PA)...781 761-4904
131 Hartwell Ave Ste 320 Lexington MA (02421) *(G-12206)*
Aldlab Chemicals LLC...203 589-4934
410 Sackett Point Rd North Haven CT (06473) *(G-3005)*
Aldrich Marble & Granite Co...781 762-6111
83 Morse St Ste 3 Norwood MA (02062) *(G-14124)*
Aldrich Stone, Norwood *Also called Aldrich Marble & Granite Co (G-14124)*
Aleksandr S Yaskovich...508 822-7267
40 Weir St Taunton MA (02780) *(G-15722)*
Alene Candles LLC (PA)...603 673-5050
51 Scarborough Ln Milford NH (03055) *(G-19046)*
Alent Inc...203 575-5727
245 Freight St Waterbury CT (06702) *(G-4838)*
Alent USA Holding Inc...203 575-5727
245 Freight St Waterbury CT (06702) *(G-4839)*
Alepack LLC...508 274-5792
10 Alden Cir Mashpee MA (02649) *(G-12874)*
Alere Inc...207 730-5714
10 Southgate Rd Scarborough ME (04074) *(G-6903)*
Alere Scarborough, Inc., Scarborough *Also called Abbott Dgnstics Scrborough Inc (G-6901)*
Alere US Holdings LLC...781 647-3900
51 Sawyer Rd Waltham MA (02453) *(G-16028)*
Alert Fire Protection Inc...401 261-8836
40 Starline Way Unit 1 Cranston RI (02921) *(G-20173)*
Alert Products...603 357-3331
95 Krif Rd Keene NH (03431) *(G-18490)*
Alert Solutions Inc...401 427-2100
201 Hillside Rd Ste 2 Cranston RI (02920) *(G-20174)*
Alesis LP...401 658-4032
200 Scenic View Dr Cumberland RI (02864) *(G-20313)*
Alex and Ani LLC...401 336-1397
1245 Worcester St Natick MA (01760) *(G-13232)*
Alex and Ani LLC (PA)...401 633-1486
2000 Chapel View Blvd # 360 Cranston RI (02920) *(G-20175)*
Alexander Lan Inc...603 880-8800
175 Broad St Hollis NH (03049) *(G-18325)*
Alexander Moles...508 823-8864
306 Winthrop St Taunton MA (02780) *(G-15723)*
Alexanders Mech Solutions, Greenfield Twp *Also called Alexanders Welding & Mch Inc (G-6152)*
Alexanders Welding & Mch Inc...207 827-3300
79 Alexander Way Greenfield Twp ME (04418) *(G-6152)*
Alexandria Communications, South Burlington *Also called Alexandria Press (G-22436)*
Alexandria Press...802 497-0074
11 Harbor Ridge Rd South Burlington VT (05403) *(G-22436)*
Alexion Pharma LLC (HQ)...203 272-2596
100 College St New Haven CT (06510) *(G-2653)*
Alexion Pharmaceuticals Inc (PA)...475 230-2596
121 Seaport Blvd Boston MA (02210) *(G-8353)*
Alexis Aerospace Inds LLC...860 516-4602
200 Smith Way Canton CT (06019) *(G-695)*
Alexis Bittar LLC...617 236-0505
130 Newbury St Boston MA (02116) *(G-8354)*
Alexis Foods Inc (PA)...508 829-9111
160 Reservoir St Ste 4 Holden MA (01520) *(G-11541)*
Alexis Foods Inc...978 952-6777
173 Goldsmith St Littleton MA (01460) *(G-12290)*
Alexs Ugly Sauce LLC...617 300-0180
57 Prospect Ave Roslindale MA (02131) *(G-14837)*
Alfa International Corp...401 765-0503
32 Mechanic Ave Ste 99 Woonsocket RI (02895) *(G-21548)*
Alfa Laval Inc...978 465-5777
111 Parker St Newburyport MA (01950) *(G-13468)*
Alfa Laval Thermal-Food Ctr, Newburyport *Also called Alfa Laval Inc (G-13468)*
Alfa Nobel LLC...203 876-2823
94 Utica St Milford CT (06461) *(G-2241)*
Alfred J Cavallaro Inc...978 475-2466
470 S Main St Andover MA (01810) *(G-7536)*
Alfred N Gravel...401 765-4432
300 S Main St Woonsocket RI (02895) *(G-21549)*
Alfred St Germain...207 925-1135
38 Shotgun Gulch Rd Hiram ME (04041) *(G-6193)*
Alfred's Upholstrey and Co., Alfred *Also called Alfreds Upholstering & Custom (G-5514)*
Alfreds Upholstering & Custom...207 536-5565
181 Waterboro Rd Alfred ME (04002) *(G-5514)*
Alfresco Software Inc (PA)...888 317-3395
100 Worcester St Ste 203 Wellesley MA (02481) *(G-16358)*
Alfro Custom Manufacturing Co...203 264-6246
99 Old Woodbury Rd Southbury CT (06488) *(G-4023)*
Algers Leo NH Elc Mtrs...603 524-3729
459 Province Rd Laconia NH (03246) *(G-18555)*
Algonquin Industries Inc (PA)...508 966-4600
139 Farm St Bellingham MA (02019) *(G-8028)*
Algonquin Industries Inc (HQ)...203 453-4348
129 Soundview Rd Guilford CT (06437) *(G-1692)*
ALICE JAMES BOOKS, Farmington *Also called Alice James Poetry Coop Inc (G-6040)*
Alice James Poetry Coop Inc...207 778-7071
114 Prescott St Farmington ME (04938) *(G-6040)*
Alignable Inc...978 376-5852
205 Portland St Ste 500 Boston MA (02114) *(G-8355)*
Aligned Vision, Chelmsford *Also called Assembly Guidance Systems Inc (G-9874)*
Alignmeeting, Bedford *Also called Alignrevenue Inc (G-17629)*
Alignrevenue Inc...603 566-4117
3 Old Mill Rd Bedford NH (03110) *(G-17629)*
Alinabal Inc (HQ)...203 877-3241
28 Woodmont Rd Milford CT (06460) *(G-2242)*
Alinabal Inc...860 828-9933
384 Christian Ln Kensington CT (06037) *(G-1917)*
Alinabal Holdings Corporation (PA)...203 877-3241
28 Woodmont Rd Milford CT (06460) *(G-2243)*
Aline Systems Inc...781 990-1462
30 Doaks Ln Marblehead MA (01945) *(G-12673)*
Alinea Pharmaceuticals Inc...617 500-7867
101 Main St Ste 182 Cambridge MA (02142) *(G-9381)*
Alip Corporation...857 234-6073
60a Waverly St Brighton MA (02135) *(G-9092)*
Alivia Capital LLC...781 569-5212
100 Cambridge St Ste 1400 Boston MA (02114) *(G-8356)*
Alivia Capital LLC (PA)...781 569-5212
400 Tradecenter Ste 5900 Woburn MA (01801) *(G-17116)*
Alivia Technology, Boston *Also called Alivia Capital LLC (G-8356)*
Alivia Technology, Woburn *Also called Alivia Capital LLC (G-17116)*
Alkalol Company...617 304-3668
580 Harrison Ave Ste 400 Boston MA (02118) *(G-8357)*
Alken Inc...802 655-3159
40 Hercules Dr Colchester VT (05446) *(G-21856)*
Alkermes Inc (HQ)...781 609-6000
852 Winter St Waltham MA (02451) *(G-16029)*
Alkermes Cntrlled Therapeutics...877 706-0510
852 Winter St Waltham MA (02451) *(G-16030)*
All American Deleading Inc...781 953-1673
136 Nokomis Rd Hingham MA (02043) *(G-11490)*
All American Embroidery Inc...978 657-0414
789 Woburn St Ste 2 Wilmington MA (01887) *(G-16970)*
All American Septic & Sewer, Taunton *Also called Gabcon Welding & Cnstr Co (G-15751)*
All American Walls and Pavers...603 219-0822
1 N Curtisville Rd Concord NH (03301) *(G-17882)*
All Around Active Co...978 561-1033
15 Chapman Rd Boxford MA (01921) *(G-8973)*
All City Screen Printing Inc...781 665-0000
983 Main St Wakefield MA (01880) *(G-15940)*
All Five Tool Co Inc...860 583-1693
169 White Oak Dr Berlin CT (06037) *(G-69)*
All Granite & Marble Inc II...508 434-0611
379 Worcester Rd Charlton MA (01507) *(G-9846)*
All In One Dumpster Service...508 735-8979
4 John St Millbury MA (01527) *(G-13155)*
All Kinds of Signs LLC...978 531-7100
676 Post Rd Ste 1 Wells ME (04090) *(G-7159)*
All Metal Fabricators Inc...978 263-3904
82 Hayward Rd Acton MA (01720) *(G-7337)*
All Natures Elements...603 427-3535
190 Scribner Rd Fremont NH (03044) *(G-18173)*
All Panel Systems LLC...203 208-3142
9 Baldwin Dr Unit 1 Branford CT (06405) *(G-288)*

All Phase Dumpsters LLC 203 778-9104
30 Wolfpits Rd Bethel CT (06801) *(G-127)*
All Phase Htg Coolg Contr LLC 860 873-9680
500 Tater Hill Rd East Haddam CT (06423) *(G-1147)*
All Phase Steel Works LLC 203 375-8881
57 Trumbull St New Haven CT (06510) *(G-2654)*
All Power Manufacturing Co (HQ) 562 802-2640
1 Tribiology Ctr Oxford CT (06478) *(G-3389)*
All Pro Tint 508 992-8468
429 Allen St New Bedford MA (02740) *(G-13355)*
All Seasonal Fuel Inc 781 329-7800
1079 East St Dedham MA (02026) *(G-10279)*
All Seasons 603 560-7777
165 Ledge St Nashua NH (03060) *(G-19109)*
All Seasons Printing & Awards 603 881-7106
1 Industrial Park Dr # 20 Pelham NH (03076) *(G-19427)*
All Security Co Inc 508 993-4271
771 Kempton St New Bedford MA (02740) *(G-13356)*
All Set Press LLC 781 397-1993
988 Eastern Ave Malden MA (02148) *(G-12557)*
All Signs Steve Main 603 464-5455
17 Holman St Hillsboro NH (03244) *(G-18312)*
All Star Adhesive Products 401 247-1866
30 Cutler St Unit 201 Warren RI (02885) *(G-21283)*
All Star Fabrication Inc 978 887-7617
8 Hood Farm Rd Ipswich MA (01938) *(G-11901)*
All Star Sporting Goods, Shirley *Also called Ampac Enterprises Inc (G-15080)*
All States Asphalt Inc 860 774-7550
127 Attwaugan Crossing Rd Dayville CT (06241) *(G-1038)*
All Steel LLC 860 871-6023
240 Crystal Lake Rd Ellington CT (06029) *(G-1328)*
All Steel Fabricating Inc 508 839-4471
84 Creeper Hill Rd North Grafton MA (01536) *(G-13958)*
All Tech Auto/Truck Electric 203 790-8990
36 Kenosia Ave Ste B Danbury CT (06810) *(G-868)*
All-Test Pro LLC (PA) 860 399-4222
20 Research Pkwy Unit G&H Old Saybrook CT (06475) *(G-3327)*
All-Time Manufacturing Co Inc 860 848-9258
Bridge St Montville CT (06353) *(G-2421)*
Allagash Brewing Company 207 878-5385
50 Industrial Way Portland ME (04103) *(G-6611)*
Allagash Guide Inc 207 634-3748
292 River Rd Norridgewock ME (04957) *(G-6494)*
Allagash Maple Products Inc 207 431-1481
279 Back Rd Skowhegan ME (04976) *(G-6967)*
Allan Fuller 603 886-5555
304 Unity Rd Benton ME (04901) *(G-5703)*
Allan Ponn 781 438-4338
38 Montvale Ave Stoneham MA (02180) *(G-15553)*
Allard Lumber Company (PA) 802 254-4939
74 Glen Orne Dr Brattleboro VT (05301) *(G-21717)*
Allard Nazarian Group Inc (PA) 603 668-1900
124 Joliette St Manchester NH (03102) *(G-18774)*
Allard Nazarian Group Inc 603 314-0017
111 Joliette St Ste 9 Manchester NH (03102) *(G-18775)*
Allavita 802 225-6526
27 State St Montpelier VT (05602) *(G-22144)*
Allcoat Technology Inc 978 988-0880
100 Eames St Wilmington MA (01887) *(G-16971)*
Allearth Renewables Inc 802 872-9600
94 Harvest Ln Williston VT (05495) *(G-22654)*
Allegheny River Group Inc 508 634-0181
258 Main St Ste 305 Milford MA (01757) *(G-13107)*
Allegra Network LLC 508 528-5339
317 Union St Franklin MA (02038) *(G-11021)*
Allegra Print & Imaging, Brockton *Also called Fasprint Inc (G-9146)*
Allegra Print & Imaging, Providence *Also called Omo Inc (G-21084)*
Allegra Print & Imaging, Boston *Also called Milk Street Press Inc (G-8706)*
Allegra Print & Imaging, Shelton *Also called System Intgrtion Cnsulting LLC (G-3876)*
Allegra Print & Imaging 603 622-3821
128 S River Rd Ste 2 Bedford NH (03110) *(G-17630)*
Allegra Print & Imaging 508 339-3555
1 Fowler St Ste 3 Mansfield MA (02048) *(G-12612)*
Allegra Print & Imaging 401 884-9280
41 Rocky Hollow Rd East Greenwich RI (02818) *(G-20352)*
Allegra Print & Imaging No 196, Kingston *Also called Key Graphics Inc (G-20551)*
Allegra Print and Imaging, Waltham *Also called R & H Communications Inc (G-16181)*
Allegro Microsystems Inc 508 853-5000
955 Perimeter Rd Manchester NH (03103) *(G-18776)*
Allegro Microsystems LLC 508 853-5000
100 Crowley Dr Marlborough MA (01752) *(G-12711)*
Allegro Microsystems LLC (HQ) 603 626-2300
955 Perimeter Rd Manchester NH (03103) *(G-18777)*
Allen Datagraph Systems Inc 603 216-6344
45a Northwestern Dr Salem NH (03079) *(G-19705)*
Allen Manufacturing Inc 207 333-3385
41 Canal St Lewiston ME (04240) *(G-6273)*
Allen Medical Systems Inc (HQ) 978 263-7727
100 Discovery Way Ste 100 # 100 Acton MA (01720) *(G-7338)*
Allen Precision LLC 860 370-9881
1 Northgate Dr Windsor Locks CT (06096) *(G-5384)*
Allen Screen Printing, Brunswick *Also called Identity Group Holdings Corp (G-5837)*
Allen Systems Group Inc 239 435-2200
30 Temple St Fl 6 Nashua NH (03060) *(G-19110)*
Allen Woodworking LLC 617 306-6479
200 Center St Bellingham MA (02019) *(G-8029)*
Allen's Drain Cleaning Service, Presque Isle *Also called Allens Environmental Svcs Inc (G-6752)*
Allen-Bailey Tag & Label Inc 585 538-2324
100 Main St Ste 103 Whitinsville MA (01588) *(G-16910)*
Allena Labs 617 467-4577
142 North Rd Ste B Sudbury MA (01776) *(G-15652)*
Allena Pharmaceuticals Inc (PA) 617 467-4577
1 Newton Executive Park # 202 Newton MA (02462) *(G-13558)*
Allens Blueberry Freezer Inc (PA) 207 667-5561
244 Main St Ellsworth ME (04605) *(G-6013)*
Allens Environmental Svcs Inc 207 764-9336
27 Washburn Rd Presque Isle ME (04769) *(G-6752)*
Allergan Sales LLC 508 324-1481
927 Currant Rd Fall River MA (02720) *(G-10653)*
Allesco Industries Inc (PA) 401 943-0680
15 Amflex Dr Cranston RI (02921) *(G-20176)*
Alley Road LLC 207 633-3171
120 Commercial St Boothbay Harbor ME (04538) *(G-5781)*
Allgreenit LLC 860 516-4948
123 Farmington Ave # 162 Bristol CT (06010) *(G-517)*
Alliance Book Mfg Co Inc 781 294-0802
221 Mattakeesett St Pembroke MA (02359) *(G-14390)*
Alliance Cable Corp 508 824-5896
201 Alfred Lord Blvd Taunton MA (02780) *(G-15724)*
Alliance Energy LLC 203 933-2511
Merritt Pkwy New Haven CT (06535) *(G-2655)*
Alliance Graphics Inc 860 666-7992
16 Progress Cir Bldg 3 Newington CT (06111) *(G-2840)*
Alliance Leather Finishing 978 531-6771
58 Pulaski St Ste 2 Peabody MA (01960) *(G-14309)*
Alliance Paper Company Inc 508 324-9100
33 India St Pawtucket RI (02860) *(G-20812)*
Alliance Press, The, Brunswick *Also called Alliance Printers LLC (G-5828)*
Alliance Printers LLC 207 504-8200
3 Business Pkwy Ste 1 Brunswick ME (04011) *(G-5828)*
Alliance Sheet Metal 508 587-0314
21 Ledin Dr Avon MA (02322) *(G-7875)*
Alliance Upholstery Inc 413 731-7857
143 Main St Springfield MA (01105) *(G-15444)*
Alliance Water Treatment Co 203 323-9968
28 Coachlamp Ln Stamford CT (06902) *(G-4133)*
Allied Controls Inc 860 628-8443
25 Forest St Apt 14a Stamford CT (06901) *(G-4134)*
Allied Endeavers Inc 207 832-0511
760 Atlantic Hwy Waldoboro ME (04572) *(G-7130)*
Allied Engineering, Newington *Also called Allied Machining Co Inc (G-2841)*
Allied Fabrication Inc 978 667-5901
18 Republic Rd North Billerica MA (01862) *(G-13791)*
Allied Group Inc (PA) 401 461-1700
25 Amflex Dr Cranston RI (02921) *(G-20177)*
Allied Group Inc 401 946-6100
333 Bucklin St Providence RI (02907) *(G-20950)*
Allied Machined Products Corp 508 756-4290
4 Westec Dr Auburn MA (01501) *(G-7824)*
Allied Machining Co Inc 860 665-1228
50 Progress Cir Ste 3 Newington CT (06111) *(G-2841)*
Allied Metal Finishing L L C 860 290-8865
379 Chapel Rd South Windsor CT (06074) *(G-3934)*
Allied Orthotic Inc 603 434-7722
3 Commercial Ln Ste E Londonderry NH (03053) *(G-18675)*
Allied Printing Services Inc (PA) 860 643-1101
1 Allied Way Manchester CT (06042) *(G-1984)*
Allied Resin Technologies LLC 978 401-2267
25 Litchfield St Leominster MA (01453) *(G-12112)*
Allied Sealant Inc 978 254-7117
10 Jean Ave Ste 16 Chelmsford MA (01824) *(G-9869)*
Allied Sinterings Incorporated 203 743-7502
29 Briar Ridge Rd Danbury CT (06810) *(G-869)*
Allied Telesis Inc 603 334-6058
15 Rye St Portsmouth NH (03801) *(G-19534)*
Allied Tool & Fastener, Waldoboro *Also called Allied Endeavers Inc (G-7130)*
Allied Wheelchair 603 601-8174
725 Lafayette Rd Ste 3 Hampton NH (03842) *(G-18253)*
Allison Taylor, Branford *Also called Fyc Apparel Group LLC (G-319)*
Allmac Signs 508 430-4174
10 Captain Scott Rd Harwich MA (02645) *(G-11387)*
Allmark International Inc 401 232-7080
18 Industrial Dr Smithfield RI (02917) *(G-21208)*
Allnex USA Inc 203 269-4481
528 S Cherry St Wallingford CT (06492) *(G-4695)*
Allocation Solutions LLC 339 234-5695
1 Wall St Fl 6 Burlington MA (01803) *(G-9231)*

ALPHABETIC

Alloy Castings Co Inc...508 378-2541
151 W Union St East Bridgewater MA (02333) ***(G-10406)***
Alloy Engineering Co Inc (PA)...203 366-5253
304 Seaview Ave Bridgeport CT (06607) ***(G-369)***
Alloy Fabricators of Neng...781 986-6400
39 York Ave Randolph MA (02368) ***(G-14670)***
Alloy Holdings LLC...401 353-7500
160 Niantic Ave Providence RI (02907) ***(G-20951)***
Alloy Metals Inc (PA)...203 774-3270
34b Barnes Indus Rd S Wallingford CT (06492) ***(G-4696)***
Alloy Specialties Incorporated...860 646-4587
110 Batson Dr Manchester CT (06042) ***(G-1985)***
Alloy Welding & Mfg Co Inc...860 582-3638
233 Riverside Ave Bristol CT (06010) ***(G-518)***
Allpage Inc...508 995-6614
54 Conduit St New Bedford MA (02745) ***(G-13357)***
Allread Products Co LLC...860 589-3566
22 S Main St Terryville CT (06786) ***(G-4474)***
Allscrpts Hlthcare Sltions Inc...800 720-7351
1 Burlington Woods Dr # 3 Burlington MA (01803) ***(G-9232)***
Allstar Foundation For Urea Cy...978 658-5319
125 Federal St Wilmington MA (01887) ***(G-16972)***
Allstate Drilling Co...401 434-7458
227 Wampanoag Trl Riverside RI (02915) ***(G-21163)***
Allstate Fire Equipment, Danvers *Also called Fire Defenses New England LLC* ***(G-10217)***
Allstate Hood & Duct Inc...413 568-4663
88 Notre Dame St Westfield MA (01085) ***(G-16664)***
Allston Power LLC...617 562-4054
84 Lincoln St Brighton MA (02135) ***(G-9093)***
Allston-Brighton Tab...617 629-3387
20 Holland St Somerville MA (02144) ***(G-15152)***
Alltec Laser Technology...508 765-6666
50 Optical Dr Southbridge MA (01550) ***(G-15375)***
Alltech Inc...802 524-7460
90 Parah Dr Saint Albans VT (05478) ***(G-22363)***
Alltraxx LLC...603 610-7179
1950 Lafayette Rd Ste 202 Portsmouth NH (03801) ***(G-19535)***
Alltype Signs & Graphics, Framingham *Also called Jnj Inc* ***(G-10973)***
Allure Security Technology Inc...877 669-8883
200 5th Ave Ste 4010 Waltham MA (02451) ***(G-16031)***
Ally Automotive Inc...734 604-2257
16 Dalby St Ste 2 Newton MA (02458) ***(G-13559)***
Allyndale Corporation...860 824-7959
40 Allyndale Rd East Canaan CT (06024) ***(G-1111)***
Alm Media LLC...860 527-7900
201 Ann Uccello St Fl 4 Hartford CT (06103) ***(G-1805)***
Alm Works Inc (PA)...617 600-4369
181 Wells Ave Ste 204 Newton MA (02459) ***(G-13560)***
Almanac Publishing Co...207 755-2000
70 Mount Hope Ave Lewiston ME (04240) ***(G-6274)***
Almont Company Inc...617 269-8244
293 Libbey Indstrl Pkwy East Weymouth MA (02189) ***(G-10534)***
Almusnet Inc...781 933-1846
400 Tradecenter Ste 4900 Woburn MA (01801) ***(G-17117)***
Alnara Pharmaceuticals Inc...617 349-3690
840 Memorial Dr Cambridge MA (02139) ***(G-9382)***
Alnylam Alewife Mfg Fcilty, Cambridge *Also called Alnylam Pharmaceuticals Inc* ***(G-9383)***
Alnylam Pharmaceuticals Inc...617 551-8200
665 Concord Ave Cambridge MA (02138) ***(G-9383)***
Alnylam Pharmaceuticals Inc (PA)...617 551-8200
300 3rd St Ste 3 Cambridge MA (02142) ***(G-9384)***
Alnylam US Inc...617 551-8200
300 3rd St Ste 3 Cambridge MA (02142) ***(G-9385)***
Alo Systems, Lawrence *Also called Joe Batson* ***(G-12041)***
Alopexx Pharmaceuticals LLC...617 945-2510
100 Main St Ste 110 Concord MA (01742) ***(G-10108)***
Alpa Incorporated...802 662-8401
34 River Rd Essex Junction VT (05452) ***(G-21928)***
Alpha 1c LLC...860 354-7979
3 Leach Hollow Rd Sherman CT (06784) ***(G-3892)***
Alpha Chemical Services Inc...781 344-8688
46 Morton St Stoughton MA (02072) ***(G-15579)***
Alpha Design & Composition...603 435-8592
47 Manchester St Pittsfield NH (03263) ***(G-19497)***
Alpha Fierce LLC...781 518-3311
2 Prospect Hill St Merrimac MA (01860) ***(G-12999)***
Alpha Grainger Mfg Inc...508 520-4005
20 Discovery Way Franklin MA (02038) ***(G-11022)***
Alpha Graph Printshop...603 595-1444
97 Main St Ste 1 Nashua NH (03060) ***(G-19111)***
Alpha Innovation Inc...978 744-1100
86 Pleasant St Marblehead MA (01945) ***(G-12674)***
Alpha Instruments Inc...978 264-2966
468 Great Rd Ste 3 Acton MA (01720) ***(G-7339)***
Alpha Magnetics & Coils Inc...860 496-0122
527 Westledge Dr Torrington CT (06790) ***(G-4556)***
Alpha Plating and Finishing Co...860 747-5002
169 W Main St Plainville CT (06062) ***(G-3464)***
Alpha Press, Waltham *Also called Bruno Diduca* ***(G-16053)***
Alpha Tech Pet Inc...978 486-3690
25 Porter Rd Ste 210 Littleton MA (01460) ***(G-12291)***
Alpha Technologies Group Inc...603 635-2800
33 Bridge St Pelham NH (03076) ***(G-19428)***
Alpha-Core Inc...203 954-0050
6 Waterview Dr Shelton CT (06484) ***(G-3773)***
Alphabet Publishing, Branford *Also called Burns Walton* ***(G-300)***
AlphaGraphics, Salem *Also called Creative Ink* ***(G-14903)***
AlphaGraphics, Attleboro *Also called Rhode Island Mktg & Prtg Inc* ***(G-7786)***
AlphaGraphics, Wallingford *Also called Rf Printing LLC* ***(G-4797)***
AlphaGraphics, Nashua *Also called Alpha Graph Printshop* ***(G-19111)***
AlphaGraphics, Manchester *Also called Hurley Ink LLC* ***(G-18840)***
AlphaGraphics, Greenwich *Also called Turnstone Inc* ***(G-1658)***
AlphaGraphics, Framingham *Also called Elbonais Incorporated* ***(G-10945)***
AlphaGraphics, Worcester *Also called Documents On Demand Inc* ***(G-17366)***
AlphaGraphics, Stamford *Also called Melega Inc* ***(G-4249)***
AlphaGraphics, Providence *Also called Fairmont Sons LLC* ***(G-21010)***
AlphaGraphics LLC...203 230-0018
24 Rossotto Dr Hamden CT (06514) ***(G-1731)***
AlphaGraphics Pntshp of Future...603 645-0002
88 Harvey Rd Manchester NH (03103) ***(G-18778)***
Alphamed Incorporated...774 571-9415
150 Ellery St Wrentham MA (02093) ***(G-17514)***
Alpine Art & Mirror, Westport *Also called Alpine Management Group LLC* ***(G-5180)***
Alpine Kitchens, Woonsocket *Also called Gary Eldridge* ***(G-21566)***
Alpine Machine Co Inc...603 752-1441
355 Goebel St Berlin NH (03570) ***(G-17691)***
Alpine Management Group LLC...954 531-1692
25 Sylvan Rd S Ste B Westport CT (06880) ***(G-5180)***
Alpine Precision LLC...978 667-6333
23 Sullivan Rd North Billerica MA (01862) ***(G-13792)***
Alps Sportswear Mfg Co Inc...978 685-5159
5 Commonwealth Rd Ste 1a Natick MA (01760) ***(G-13233)***
Alrite Manufacturing Company, Bloomfield *Also called Kenneth Leroux* ***(G-237)***
Als Beverage Company Inc...860 627-7003
13 Revay Rd East Windsor CT (06088) ***(G-1276)***
Als Oil Service...508 853-2539
307 Hartford Tpke Shrewsbury MA (01545) ***(G-15099)***
Als Precision Machining LLC...603 647-1075
1356 Hooksett Rd Hooksett NH (03106) ***(G-18342)***
Alsco Industries Inc...508 347-1199
174 Charlton Rd Sturbridge MA (01566) ***(G-15637)***
Alseres Pharmaceuticals Inc...508 497-2360
275 Grove St Ste 2-400 Auburndale MA (02466) ***(G-7855)***
Alstom Power Co, Windsor *Also called GE Steam Power Inc* ***(G-5336)***
Alstom Power Co...860 688-1911
175 Addison Rd Windsor CT (06095) ***(G-5318)***
Alstom Renewable US LLC...860 688-1911
200 Great Pond Dr Windsor CT (06095) ***(G-5319)***
Altaeros Energies Inc...617 908-8464
28 Dane St Somerville MA (02143) ***(G-15153)***
Altair Avionics Corporation...781 762-8600
249 Vanderbilt Ave Ste 1 Norwood MA (02062) ***(G-14125)***
Altamira Lighting, Warren *Also called Brownlie Lamar Design Group* ***(G-21292)***
Altec Northeast LLC...508 320-9041
44 Chocksett Rd Sterling MA (01564) ***(G-15533)***
Altek Company...860 482-7626
89 Commercial Blvd Ste 1 Torrington CT (06790) ***(G-4557)***
Altek Electronics Inc...860 482-7626
89 Commercial Blvd Torrington CT (06790) ***(G-4558)***
Altenloh Brinck & Co US Inc...401 253-8600
280 Franklin St Bristol RI (02809) ***(G-20061)***
Alterio Tractor Pulling LLC...203 305-9812
37 Cold Spring Dr Oxford CT (06478) ***(G-3390)***
Alternate Energy Futures...917 745-7097
3121 Avalon Valley Dr Danbury CT (06810) ***(G-870)***
Alternate Finishing Inc...978 567-9205
15 Kane Industrial Dr Hudson MA (01749) ***(G-11754)***
Alternate Mode Inc...413 594-5190
30 Westwood Ave East Longmeadow MA (01028) ***(G-10464)***
Alternative Energy Retailer, Oxford *Also called Zackin Publications Inc* ***(G-3431)***
Alternative Fuel & Energy LLC...860 537-5345
31 Halls Hill Rd Colchester CT (06415) ***(G-798)***
Alternative Fuel Systems E LLC...603 231-1942
19 Twist Hill Rd Dunbarton NH (03046) ***(G-18072)***
Alternative Manufacturing Inc...207 377-9377
30 Summer St Ste B Winthrop ME (04364) ***(G-7279)***
Alternative Prosthetic Svcs...203 367-1212
191 Bennett St Bridgeport CT (06605) ***(G-370)***
Alternative Screen Printing...978 887-9927
426 Boston St Ste 150 Topsfield MA (01983) ***(G-15853)***
Althor Products LLC...860 386-6700
200 Old County Cir # 116 Windsor Locks CT (06096) ***(G-5385)***
Altman Orthotics & Prosthetics, Wethersfield *Also called Leona Corp* ***(G-5256)***
Alto Aviation, Sterling *Also called Alto Technologies Corporation* ***(G-15534)***
Alto Products Corp Al...860 747-2736
63 N Washington St Plainville CT (06062) ***(G-3465)***

Alto Technologies Corporation (PA)....978 422-9071
86 Leominster Rd Sterling MA (01564) ***(G-15534)***
Altra Industrial Motion Corp (PA)....781 917-0600
300 Granite St Ste 201 Braintree MA (02184) ***(G-8986)***
Alue Optics, Groton *Also called Cashon* ***(G-1666)***
Aluma-Cast Corp....508 399-6650
136 May St North Attleboro MA (02760) ***(G-13744)***
Alumasign, Brockton *Also called Sign Design Inc* ***(G-9175)***
Alumi-Nex Mold Inc....508 949-2200
155 Chase Ave Webster MA (01570) ***(G-16338)***
Aluminum Castings Inc....603 654-9695
4 Hampshire Hills Ln Wilton NH (03086) ***(G-19974)***
Aluminum Finishing Company Inc....203 333-1690
1575 Railroad Ave Bridgeport CT (06605) ***(G-371)***
Alvarado Custom Cabinetry LLC....203 831-0181
51 Midrocks Dr Norwalk CT (06851) ***(G-3099)***
Alvarium Beer Company LLC....860 306-3857
30 Biltmore St New Britain CT (06053) ***(G-2508)***
Alves Baking Co....508 673-8003
19 Norfolk St Fall River MA (02720) ***(G-10654)***
Alvest (usa) Inc (HQ)....860 602-3400
812 Bloomfield Ave Windsor CT (06095) ***(G-5320)***
Alvin J Coleman & Son Inc....603 447-3056
9 Nh Route 113 Albany NH (03818) ***(G-17534)***
Alvin Johnson....413 525-6334
26 Maple Ct East Longmeadow MA (01028) ***(G-10465)***
Alvin Products Inc....978 975-4580
85 Paris St Everett MA (02149) ***(G-10602)***
Alviti Creations Inc....508 222-4030
67 Mechanic St Unit 4 Attleboro MA (02703) ***(G-7703)***
Alviti Link All Inc....401 861-6656
165 Dyerville Ave Unit 1 Johnston RI (02919) ***(G-20499)***
Alzheon Inc....508 861-7709
111 Speen St Ste 306 Framingham MA (01701) ***(G-10919)***
AM Manufacturing LLC....860 573-1987
278 Oakwood Dr Ste 6 Glastonbury CT (06033) ***(G-1537)***
AM Technologies Inc....617 926-7920
108 Water St Watertown MA (02472) ***(G-16267)***
AMA Engineering Smartmove....508 636-7740
683 American Legion Hwy Westport MA (02790) ***(G-16835)***
Amag Pharmaceuticals Inc (PA)....617 498-3300
1100 Winter St Waltham MA (02451) ***(G-16032)***
Amal Fuel Inc....978 934-9704
5 Drum Hill Rd Chelmsford MA (01824) ***(G-9870)***
Amalgamated Culture Work Inc (PA)....800 272-2066
420 Pine St Burlington VT (05401) ***(G-21766)***
Amalgamated Titanium Intl Corp....617 395-7700
94 Hampshire St Apt C Cambridge MA (02139) ***(G-9386)***
Amaral Custom Fabrications Inc....401 396-5663
310 Bourne Ave Ste 5 Rumford RI (02916) ***(G-21180)***
Amaral's Linguica, New Bedford *Also called Lisbon Sausage Co Inc* ***(G-13408)***
Amaray, Pittsfield *Also called Agi Polymatrix LLC* ***(G-14449)***
Amaray Plastics....413 499-3550
45 Downing Industrial Par Pittsfield MA (01201) ***(G-14451)***
Amasa Technologies Inc....617 899-8223
1 Harmony Ln Andover MA (01810) ***(G-7537)***
Amastan Technologies Inc....978 258-1645
25 Commerce Way Ste 1 North Andover MA (01845) ***(G-13689)***
Amatech Corporation (HQ)....978 263-5401
100 Discovery Way Acton MA (01720) ***(G-7340)***
Amatech International, Acton *Also called Amatech Corporation* ***(G-7340)***
Amatex Corporation....603 524-2552
45 Primrose Dr S Laconia NH (03246) ***(G-18556)***
Amatom Electronic Hardware, Cromwell *Also called Carey Manufacturing Co Inc* ***(G-851)***
Amatom Electronic Hardwares, Cromwell *Also called Carey Manufacturing Co Inc* ***(G-850)***
Amazing Glaze....508 285-7234
41 New Taunton Ave Norton MA (02766) ***(G-14070)***
Amazon Food Service, Ludlow *Also called Amazon Fruit Corp* ***(G-12453)***
Amazon Fruit Corp....774 244-2820
1158 East St Ludlow MA (01056) ***(G-12453)***
Amb Audio-Video, Dover Foxcroft *Also called Amb Signs Inc* ***(G-5959)***
Amb Signs Inc (PA)....207 564-3633
25 North St Ste D Dover Foxcroft ME (04426) ***(G-5959)***
Amber Holding Inc (HQ)....603 324-3000
107 Northeastern Blvd Nashua NH (03062) ***(G-19112)***
Ambergen Inc (PA)....617 923-9990
313 Pleasant St Ste 4 Watertown MA (02472) ***(G-16268)***
Ambiance Painting LLC....203 354-8689
67 Murray St Norwalk CT (06851) ***(G-3100)***
Ambit Creative Group, Concord *Also called Dmr Print Inc* ***(G-10128)***
Ambix Manufacturing Inc....603 452-5247
1369 Nh Route 16 Albany NH (03818) ***(G-17535)***
Ambrose D Cedrone Lodge 1069....617 460-4664
196 Adams St Newton MA (02458) ***(G-13561)***
Ambrose G McCarthy Jr....207 474-8837
228 North Ave Skowhegan ME (04976) ***(G-6968)***
Ambur Machine Co Inc....508 234-6341
2376 Providence Rd Northbridge MA (01534) ***(G-14053)***
AMC, Newburyport *Also called Arwood Machine Corporation* ***(G-13469)***
Amci, Terryville *Also called Advanced Micro Controls Inc* ***(G-4473)***
Amco Precision Tools Inc (PA)....860 828-5640
921 Farmington Ave Berlin CT (06037) ***(G-70)***
Amcs Group Inc....610 932-4006
179 Lincoln St Lbby Boston MA (02111) ***(G-8358)***
AME, Seekonk *Also called Adaptive Mobility Equipment* ***(G-15017)***
Amenico, Pittsfield *Also called American Enrgy Indpendence LLC* ***(G-19498)***
Ameramesh Technologies Inc....508 324-9977
218 Shove St Fall River MA (02724) ***(G-10655)***
Amercian Digital Imaging, Chelsea *Also called ADI Print Solutions Inc* ***(G-9943)***
Americ An Novelty Inc....401 785-9850
692 Lafayette Rd Seabrook NH (03874) ***(G-19792)***
America Cable Assemblies Inc (PA)....413 283-2515
21 Wilbraham St Unit A12 Palmer MA (01069) ***(G-14278)***
America Extract Corporation....860 267-4444
31 E High St East Hampton CT (06424) ***(G-1155)***
Americad Technology Corporat....781 551-8220
700 Pleasant St Norwood MA (02062) ***(G-14126)***
Americal Sergical Company....781 592-7200
45 Congress St Salem MA (01970) ***(G-14890)***
American & Schoen Machinery Co....978 524-0168
100 Cummings Ctr Ste 140a Beverly MA (01915) ***(G-8098)***
American Academy Arts Sciences....617 491-2600
136 Irving St Cambridge MA (02138) ***(G-9387)***
American Access Care RI LLC....401 277-9729
100 Highland Ave Providence RI (02906) ***(G-20952)***
American Acoustical Products, Holliston *Also called Ward Process Inc* ***(G-11613)***
American Actuator Corporation....203 324-6334
292 Newtown Tpke Redding CT (06896) ***(G-3645)***
American Adhesive Coatings LLC (PA)....978 688-7400
12 Osgood St Lawrence MA (01843) ***(G-11992)***
American Alloy Wire Corp....203 426-3133
1 Wire Rd Newtown CT (06470) ***(G-2914)***
American Backplane Inc....860 567-2360
355 Bantam Lake Rd Morris CT (06763) ***(G-2430)***
American Bacon Boston Felt Inc....603 332-7000
31 Front St Rochester NH (03868) ***(G-19658)***
American Banknote Corporation (PA)....203 941-4090
1055 Washington Blvd Fl 6 Stamford CT (06901) ***(G-4135)***
American Battery Company LLC....781 440-0325
930 Washington St Norwood MA (02062) ***(G-14127)***
American Biltrite Inc (PA)....781 237-6655
57 River St Ste 302 Wellesley MA (02481) ***(G-16359)***
American Boat Builders....401 236-2466
1 Washington St Newport RI (02840) ***(G-20654)***
American Bolt & Nut Co Inc....617 884-3331
124 Carter St 38 Chelsea MA (02150) ***(G-9944)***
American Bookend Company LLC....401 932-2700
207 S Pier Rd Narragansett RI (02882) ***(G-20633)***
American Brush Company Inc....603 542-9951
112 Industrial Blvd Claremont NH (03743) ***(G-17834)***
American Business Service....603 659-2912
45 Harvey Mill Rd Lee NH (03861) ***(G-18642)***
American Calan Inc....603 942-7711
454 Jenness Pond Rd Northwood NH (03261) ***(G-19410)***
American Canvas & Aluminum, South Hadley *Also called Lyman Conrad* ***(G-15306)***
American Canvas Co, Boston *Also called Harry Miller Co LLC* ***(G-8590)***
American Canvas Company LLC....603 642-6665
63 Route 125 Ste 1 Kingston NH (03848) ***(G-18539)***
American Carbonation, Palmer *Also called American Dry Ice Corporation* ***(G-14279)***
American Chest Company, North Kingstown *Also called D Mac Consulting LLC* ***(G-20701)***
American Cladding Technologies....860 413-3098
15 International Dr East Granby CT (06026) ***(G-1116)***
American Collars Couplings Inc....860 379-7043
88 Hubbard St Winsted CT (06098) ***(G-5403)***
American Concrete Inds Inc (PA)....207 947-8334
982 Minot Ave Auburn ME (04210) ***(G-5550)***
American Concrete Inds Inc....207 947-8334
1717 Stillwater Ave Bangor ME (04401) ***(G-5629)***
American Copy Print....781 769-9077
1502 Boston Providence Tp Norwood MA (02062) ***(G-14128)***
American Copyprint, Norwood *Also called American Copy Print* ***(G-14128)***
American Craft Brewery LLC (HQ)....617 368-5000
1 Design Center Pl # 850 Boston MA (02210) ***(G-8359)***
American Crane and Hoist Corp....617 482-8383
1234 Washington St Boston MA (02118) ***(G-8360)***
American Crystal Works....603 356-7879
27 Seavey St North Conway NH (03860) ***(G-19371)***
American CT Rng Bnder Index &....860 868-7900
42 Sabbaday Ln Washington CT (06793) ***(G-4830)***
American Custom Design Wdwkg....603 286-3239
168 Sanborn Rd Tilton NH (03276) ***(G-19903)***
American Custom Displays....781 829-0585
348 Circuit St Ste 3 Hanover MA (02339) ***(G-11326)***
American Design & Mfg Inc....860 282-2719
145 Commerce Way South Windsor CT (06074) ***(G-3935)***
American Disposables Inc....413 967-6201
2705 Greenwich Rd Hardwick MA (01082) ***(G-11371)***

ALPHABETIC

American Distilling Inc..........860 267-4444
380 N Main St Marlborough CT (06447) *(G-2063)*
American Distilling Inc (PA)..........860 267-4444
31 E High St East Hampton CT (06424) *(G-1156)*
American Dream Unlimited LLC..........860 742-5055
212 Gilead Rd Andover CT (06232) *(G-2)*
American Drone Solutions LLC..........413 306-9427
50 Brooks Pl West Bridgewater MA (02379) *(G-16428)*
American Dry Ice Corporation (PA)..........413 283-9906
19 2nd St Palmer MA (01069) *(G-14279)*
American Dry Stripping, Milford *Also called Gybenorth Industries LLC (G-2295)*
American Dryer Corporation..........508 678-9000
88 Currant Rd Fall River MA (02720) *(G-10656)*
American Earth Anchors Inc..........508 520-8511
20 Grove St Ste 6 Franklin MA (02038) *(G-11023)*
American Electro Products, Farmington *Also called National Integrated Inds Inc (G-1495)*
American Electro Products Div, Waterbury *Also called National Integrated Inds Inc (G-4922)*
American Electro Products Inc..........203 756-7051
1358 Thomaston Ave Waterbury CT (06704) *(G-4840)*
American Enrgy Indpendence LLC..........603 228-3611
5 Main St Pittsfield NH (03263) *(G-19498)*
American Fiber Technologies, Bridgeport *Also called US Highway Products Inc (G-502)*
American Fnshg Specialists Inc..........203 367-0663
40 Cowles St Bridgeport CT (06607) *(G-372)*
American Foam Technologies Inc..........304 497-3000
221 3rd St Ste 101 Newport RI (02840) *(G-20655)*
American Folding Table Mfg, Northbridge *Also called Tent Connection Inc (G-14062)*
American Grippers Inc..........203 459-8345
171 Spring Hill Rd Trumbull CT (06611) *(G-4611)*
American Health Resources Inc..........508 588-7700
28 Hillington Dr North Easton MA (02356) *(G-13941)*
American Healthcare..........888 567-7733
6 Lincoln Ave Scarborough ME (04074) *(G-6904)*
American Heat Treating Inc..........203 268-1750
16 Commerce Dr Monroe CT (06468) *(G-2390)*
American Hydrogen Northeast..........203 449-4614
520 Savoy St Bridgeport CT (06606) *(G-373)*
American Imex Corporation..........203 261-5200
57 Maryanne Dr Monroe CT (06468) *(G-2391)*
American Industrial Rbr Pdts, Wallingford *Also called Jem Manufacturing Inc (G-4759)*
American Ink & Oil Corporation..........781 762-0026
61 Endicott St Ste 33 Norwood MA (02062) *(G-14129)*
American Insulated Panel Co, Taunton *Also called Aipco Inc (G-15721)*
American Ir Solutions LLC..........662 626-2477
1 Wall St Hudson NH (03051) *(G-18373)*
American Iron & Metal USA Inc (HQ)..........401 463-5605
25 Kenney Dr Cranston RI (02920) *(G-20178)*
American Journal, Falmouth *Also called Current Publishing LLC (G-6030)*
American Journal Trnsp..........508 927-4183
116 Court St Ste 4 Plymouth MA (02360) *(G-14542)*
American Keder Inc (PA)..........603 899-3233
22 Perkins Rd Rindge NH (03461) *(G-19646)*
American Library Association..........860 347-6933
575 Main St Ste 300 Middletown CT (06457) *(G-2170)*
American Lighthouse Foundation..........207 594-4174
186 Lighthouse Rd Owls Head ME (04854) *(G-6561)*
American Lighting Fixture Corp..........508 824-1970
58 Flanagan Dr Framingham MA (01701) *(G-10920)*
American Litho, Fairfield *Also called L R K Communications Inc (G-1441)*
American Machine Co..........508 366-9634
58 Hopkinton Rd Westborough MA (01581) *(G-16588)*
American Machining Tech Inc..........860 342-0005
141 Pickering St Portland CT (06480) *(G-3561)*
American Mailing Depot, Cheshire *Also called American Rubber Stamp Company (G-710)*
American Marine Products Inc..........954 782-1400
73 Southwest St Charlestown NH (03603) *(G-17810)*
American Marketing & Sales..........978 514-8929
20 Mohawk Dr Leominster MA (01453) *(G-12113)*
American Meadows Inc..........802 862-6560
2438 Shelburne Rd Shelburne VT (05482) *(G-22410)*
American Metal Master Mch Tl, Plantsville *Also called American Metal Masters LLC (G-3526)*
American Metal Masters LLC..........860 621-6911
141 Summer St Plantsville CT (06479) *(G-3526)*
American Metal Polishing..........978 726-7752
14 Commerce Rd Shrewsbury MA (01545) *(G-15100)*
American Metalcraft Co..........781 331-8588
55 Woodrock Rd Ste 12 East Weymouth MA (02189) *(G-10535)*
American Metalcrafters, Middletown *Also called Aztec Industries LLC (G-2175)*
American Metallizing..........860 289-1677
401 Governors Hwy South Windsor CT (06074) *(G-3936)*
American Molded Products Inc..........203 333-0183
130 Front St Bridgeport CT (06606) *(G-374)*
American Molding, Windsor Locks *Also called Awm LLC (G-5386)*
American Molding Corporation..........978 534-0009
35 Tisdale Ave Leominster MA (01453) *(G-12114)*
American Molding Product, Vernon Rockville *Also called Atlas Hobbing and Tool Co Inc (G-4678)*
American Mteorological Soc Inc (PA)..........617 227-2425
45 Beacon St Boston MA (02108) *(G-8361)*
American Nameplate..........207 848-7187
103 Center St Brewer ME (04412) *(G-5793)*
American Nameplate (PA)..........207 848-7187
21 White Pine Rd Ste 1 Hermon ME (04401) *(G-6182)*
American Natural Soda Ash Corp (PA)..........203 226-9056
15 Riverside Ave Ste 2 Westport CT (06880) *(G-5181)*
American Nut & Chocolate Inc..........617 427-1510
121 Newmarket Sq Boston MA (02118) *(G-8362)*
American Optics Limited..........905 631-5377
34 Washington St Ste 200 Wellesley Hills MA (02481) *(G-16395)*
American Outdoor Brands Corp (PA)..........800 331-0852
2100 Roosevelt Ave Springfield MA (01104) *(G-15445)*
American Outdoor Brands Sls Co..........207 532-7966
19 Aviation Dr Houlton ME (04730) *(G-6202)*
American Overhead Ret Div Inc..........860 876-4552
1885 S Main St Middletown CT (06457) *(G-2171)*
American Paper Recycling Corp (PA)..........800 422-3220
87 Central St Bldg 1 Mansfield MA (02048) *(G-12613)*
American Performance Pdts LLC..........203 269-4468
7 Atwater Pl Wallingford CT (06492) *(G-4697)*
American Plastic Products Inc..........203 596-2410
2114 Thomaston Ave Waterbury CT (06704) *(G-4841)*
American Plating, Cranston *Also called American Ring Co Inc (G-20179)*
American Players, Fall River *Also called American Power Source Inc (G-10657)*
American Police Beat, Cambridge *Also called On The Beat Inc (G-9598)*
American Polyfilm Inc (PA)..........203 483-9797
15 Baldwin Dr Branford CT (06405) *(G-289)*
American Power Design Inc..........603 894-4446
3 Industrial Dr Unit 6 Windham NH (03087) *(G-19998)*
American Power Devices Inc..........781 592-6090
69 Bennett St Ste 1 Lynn MA (01905) *(G-12489)*
American Power Service, Georgetown *Also called 17 Chestnut Inc (G-11134)*
American Power Source Inc (PA)..........508 672-8847
15 Shaw St Fall River MA (02724) *(G-10657)*
American Precision Mfg LLC..........203 734-1800
26 Beaver St Ste 1 Ansonia CT (06401) *(G-5)*
American Precision Mold Inc..........860 267-1356
58 E High St East Hampton CT (06424) *(G-1157)*
American Prefab Wood Pdts Co..........860 242-5468
1217 Blue Hills Ave Bloomfield CT (06002) *(G-200)*
American Prfmce Polymers LLC, Manchester *Also called Renco Corporation (G-12606)*
American Prfmce Polymers LLC..........603 237-8001
1 Beaver Dam Rd Ste 6 Manchester MA (01944) *(G-12603)*
American Printing Inc..........603 880-0277
6 Columbia Dr Unit B Amherst NH (03031) *(G-17550)*
American Prosthetics Inc (PA)..........617 328-0606
197 Quincy Ave Ste 102 Braintree MA (02184) *(G-8987)*
American Prtg & Envelope Inc..........508 832-6100
211 Southbridge St Auburn MA (01501) *(G-7825)*
American Pulley Cover, South Windsor *Also called Siftex Equipment Company (G-4009)*
American Railway Technologies..........860 291-1170
61 Alna Ln Ste 1 East Hartford CT (06108) *(G-1172)*
American Refacing Cstm Cab LLC..........860 647-0868
1 Mitchell Dr Manchester CT (06042) *(G-1986)*
American Rheinmetall Def Inc (PA)..........207 571-5850
15 Morin St Ste B Biddeford ME (04005) *(G-5717)*
American Rhnmetall Systems LLC..........207 571-5850
15 Morin St Ste B Biddeford ME (04005) *(G-5718)*
American Ring Co Inc (PA)..........401 438-9060
19 Grosvenor Ave East Providence RI (02914) *(G-20385)*
American Ring Co Inc..........401 467-4480
41 Wheatland Ave Cranston RI (02910) *(G-20179)*
American Roller Company LLC..........203 598-3100
84 Turnpike Dr Middlebury CT (06762) *(G-2154)*
American Rubber Stamp Company..........203 755-1135
35 Judson Ct Cheshire CT (06410) *(G-710)*
American Rural Fire Apparatus..........802 433-1554
154 Industry St Williamstown VT (05679) *(G-22649)*
American Saw & Mfg Company Inc..........413 525-3961
301 Chestnut St East Longmeadow MA (01028) *(G-10466)*
American SCrew & Barrels Inc..........978 630-1300
60 Linus Allain Ave Gardner MA (01440) *(G-11103)*
American Seal and Engrg Co Inc (HQ)..........203 789-8819
295 Indian River Rd Orange CT (06477) *(G-3358)*
American Sheet Metal LLC..........978 578-8360
4 Fanaras Dr Salisbury MA (01952) *(G-14948)*
American Silk Screening LLC..........860 828-5486
386 Deming Rd Berlin CT (06037) *(G-71)*
American Sleeve Bearing LLC..........860 684-8060
1 Spring St Stafford Springs CT (06076) *(G-4104)*
American Solartechnics LLC..........207 548-1122
24 Us Rt 1 Stockton Springs ME (04981) *(G-7068)*
American Specialty Co Inc..........203 929-5324
762 River Rd Shelton CT (06484) *(G-3774)*
American Specialty Pdts LLC..........860 871-2279
101 Industrial Park Rd Vernon CT (06066) *(G-4662)*
American Speedy Printing, Lebanon *Also called Just Rewards Inc (G-18626)*

American Speedy Printing, Methuen *Also called Color Images Inc* ***(G-13015)***
American Standard Company 860 628-9643
157 Water St Southington CT (06489) ***(G-4037)***
American Steel Fabricators Inc 603 547-6311
328 Sawmill Rd Greenfield NH (03047) ***(G-18218)***
American Stitch & Print Inc 203 239-5383
222 Elm St Ste 9 North Haven CT (06473) ***(G-3006)***
American Stonecrafters Inc 203 514-9725
224 S Whittlesey Ave Wallingford CT (06492) ***(G-4698)***
American Superconductor Corp (PA) 978 842-3000
114 E Main St Ayer MA (01432) ***(G-7907)***
American Surgical Company LLC 781 592-7200
45 Congress St Ste 153 Salem MA (01970) ***(G-14891)***
American Tinter 603 458-6379
5 Dublin Rd Windham NH (03087) ***(G-19999)***
American Tool & Mfg Corp 860 666-2255
125 Rockwell Rd Newington CT (06111) ***(G-2842)***
American Tool Company 401 333-0111
623 George Washington Hwy Lincoln RI (02865) ***(G-20554)***
American Trade Fairs Org 203 221-0114
250 Main St Ste 101 Westport CT (06880) ***(G-5182)***
American Trophy & Supply Co 401 438-3060
110 Russell Ave East Providence RI (02914) ***(G-20386)***
American Unmanned Systems LLC 203 406-7611
460 Summer St Stamford CT (06901) ***(G-4136)***
American Vehicles Sales LLC 860 886-0327
58 Yantic Flats Rd Yantic CT (06389) ***(G-5507)***
American Veteran Textile LLC 203 583-0576
674 Main St Fl 2 Ansonia CT (06401) ***(G-6)***
American Water Systems LLC 781 830-9722
9 Pequot Way Canton MA (02021) ***(G-9712)***
American Well Corporation 617 204-3500
75 State St Fl 26 Boston MA (02109) ***(G-8363)***
American Wire Corporation 203 426-3133
1 Wire Rd Newtown CT (06470) ***(G-2915)***
American Wood Products 203 248-4433
301 State St North Haven CT (06473) ***(G-3007)***
American Woolen Company Inc 860 684-2766
8 Furnace Ave Stafford Springs CT (06076) ***(G-4105)***
American-International Tl Inds 401 942-7855
99 Calder St Cranston RI (02920) ***(G-20180)***
American-Republican Inc (PA) 203 574-3636
389 Meadow St Waterbury CT (06702) ***(G-4842)***
American-Republican Inc 860 496-9301
122 Franklin St Torrington CT (06790) ***(G-4559)***
Americanbio Inc 508 655-4336
20 Dan Rd Canton MA (02021) ***(G-9713)***
Americansub 508 949-2320
137 Schofield Ave Dudley MA (01571) ***(G-10372)***
Americas Best Defense 774 745-5809
274 South St Shrewsbury MA (01545) ***(G-15101)***
Americraft Carton Inc 978 459-9328
164 Meadowcroft St Lowell MA (01852) ***(G-12343)***
Amerifix LLC 203 931-7290
278 Washington Ave West Haven CT (06516) ***(G-5108)***
Ameriforge Group Inc 603 863-1270
452 Sunapee St Newport NH (03773) ***(G-19342)***
Ames Color File Div, Somerville *Also called Ames Safety Envelope Company* ***(G-15154)***
Ames Companies Inc 802 446-2601
82 Creek Rd Wallingford VT (05773) ***(G-22573)***
Ames Safety Envelope Company (HQ) 617 684-1000
12 Tyler St Somerville MA (02143) ***(G-15154)***
Amesbury Foundry Co 978 388-0830
56 Mill St Amesbury MA (01913) ***(G-7477)***
Ametek Inc 203 265-6731
21 Toelles Rd Wallingford CT (06492) ***(G-4699)***
Ametek Inc 978 988-4101
50 Fordham Rd Wilmington MA (01887) ***(G-16973)***
Ametek Inc 508 998-4335
50 Welby Rd New Bedford MA (02745) ***(G-13358)***
Ametek Aegis, New Bedford *Also called HCC Aegis Inc* ***(G-13393)***
Ametek Arizona Instrument LLC 508 946-6200
11 Commerce Blvd Middleboro MA (02346) ***(G-13051)***
Ametek Arospc Pwr Holdings Inc (HQ) 978 988-4771
50 Fordham Rd Wilmington MA (01887) ***(G-16974)***
Ametek Brookfield, Middleboro *Also called Ametek Arizona Instrument LLC* ***(G-13051)***
Ametek Precitech Inc (HQ) 603 357-2510
44 Black Brook Rd Keene NH (03431) ***(G-18491)***
Ametek Scp Inc (HQ) 401 596-6658
52 Airport Rd Westerly RI (02891) ***(G-21515)***
Ametek Specialty Metal Pdts, Wallingford *Also called Ametek Inc* ***(G-4699)***
Amex Inc 617 569-5630
256 Marginal St Ste 3 Boston MA (02128) ***(G-8364)***
AMF Optical Solutions LLC 781 933-6125
30 Nashua St Ste 3 Woburn MA (01801) ***(G-17118)***
AMF Technologies, Rockland *Also called Arborway Metal Finishing Inc* ***(G-14792)***
AMG-Awetis Mfg Group Corp 603 286-1645
18 Colonial Dr Gilford NH (03249) ***(G-18182)***
Amgen Inc 401 392-1200
40 Technology Way Unit 1 West Greenwich RI (02817) ***(G-21452)***
Amgen Inc 617 444-5000
360 Binney St Cambridge MA (02142) ***(G-9388)***
Amgraph Packaging Inc 860 822-2000
90 Paper Mill Rd Baltic CT (06330) ***(G-48)***
Amherst Brewing Co Inc 413 253-4400
36 N Pleasant St Amherst MA (01002) ***(G-7511)***
Amherst College Public Affairs 413 542-2321
306 Converse Hl Amherst MA (01002) ***(G-7512)***
Amherst Label Inc 603 673-7849
15 Westchester Dr Milford NH (03055) ***(G-19047)***
Amherst Machine Co 413 549-4551
16 Cowls Rd Amherst MA (01002) ***(G-7513)***
AMI, Middleboro *Also called Andys Machine Inc* ***(G-13052)***
AMI Graphics Inc (PA) 603 664-7174
223 Drake Hill Rd Strafford NH (03884) ***(G-19865)***
Amic Inc 508 222-5300
60 Walton St Attleboro MA (02703) ***(G-7704)***
Amicus Hlthcare Lving Ctrs LLC 978 934-0000
2 Technology Dr North Chelmsford MA (01863) ***(G-13884)***
Amius Partners LLC 203 526-5926
180 E Rock Rd New Haven CT (06511) ***(G-2656)***
Amk Technical Services, South Windsor *Also called Amk Welding Inc* ***(G-3937)***
Amk Welding Inc (HQ) 860 289-5634
283 Sullivan Ave South Windsor CT (06074) ***(G-3937)***
Amkor Industrial Products Inc 508 799-4970
42 Lagrange St Worcester MA (01610) ***(G-17336)***
Amkor Technology Inc 781 438-7800
105 Central St Ste 2300 Stoneham MA (02180) ***(G-15554)***
Ammeraal Beltech Inc 401 732-8131
46 Warwick Industrial Dr Warwick RI (02886) ***(G-21322)***
Ammo and Bullet Manufacturing 978 807-7681
2210 Portland Rd Arundel ME (04046) ***(G-5527)***
Ammunition Stor Components LLC 860 225-3548
206 Newington Ave New Britain CT (06051) ***(G-2509)***
Amnis Corporation 206 374-7000
290 Concord Rd Billerica MA (01821) ***(G-8208)***
Amodex Products Inc 203 335-1255
1354 State St Bridgeport CT (06605) ***(G-375)***
Amodios Inc (PA) 203 573-1229
40 Falls Ave Ste 4 Waterbury CT (06708) ***(G-4843)***
Amorsa Therapeutics Inc 508 571-8240
7 Banfill Ln Southborough MA (01772) ***(G-15342)***
AMP, Warwick *Also called Accurate Molded Products Inc* ***(G-21317)***
AMP Corp, Lowell *Also called Advanced Materials Processing* ***(G-12339)***
AMP Timber Harvesting Inc 802 874-7260
449 Cross Rd West Townshend VT (05359) ***(G-22625)***
Ampac Enterprises Inc 978 425-6266
1 Main St Shirley MA (01464) ***(G-15080)***
Ampac Packaging LLC 413 572-2658
175 Ampad Rd Westfield MA (01085) ***(G-16665)***
Ampco Publishing & Prtg Corp 203 325-1509
130 Lenox Ave Ste 32 Stamford CT (06906) ***(G-4137)***
Amphenol, Wallingford *Also called Times Wire and Cable Company* ***(G-4820)***
Amphenol Advanced Sensors 978 294-8300
900 Middlesex Tpke Billerica MA (01821) ***(G-8209)***
Amphenol Alden, Brockton *Also called Amphenol Alden Products Co* ***(G-9118)***
Amphenol Alden Products Co (HQ) 508 427-7000
117 N Main St Brockton MA (02301) ***(G-9118)***
Amphenol Corporation 203 327-7300
50 Sunnyside Ave Stamford CT (06902) ***(G-4138)***
Amphenol Corporation 603 879-3000
91 Northeastern Blvd Nashua NH (03062) ***(G-19113)***
Amphenol Corporation 203 743-9272
4 Old Newtown Rd Ste 2 Danbury CT (06810) ***(G-871)***
Amphenol Corporation (PA) 203 265-8900
358 Hall Ave Wallingford CT (06492) ***(G-4700)***
Amphenol Corporation 203 287-2272
720 Sherman Ave Hamden CT (06514) ***(G-1732)***
Amphenol Corporation 603 879-3000
200 Innovative Way # 201 Nashua NH (03062) ***(G-19114)***
Amphenol International Ltd (HQ) 203 265-8900
358 Hall Ave Wallingford CT (06492) ***(G-4701)***
Amphenol Nexus Technologies 203 327-7300
50 Sunnyside Ave Stamford CT (06902) ***(G-4139)***
Amphenol Pcd Inc 978 921-1531
2 Technology Dr Peabody MA (01960) ***(G-14310)***
Amphenol Pcd Inc (HQ) 978 921-1531
72 Cherry Hill Dr Ste 2 Beverly MA (01915) ***(G-8099)***
Amphenol Printed Circuits, Nashua *Also called Amphenol Corporation* ***(G-19113)***
Amphenol Printed Circuits Inc 603 324-4500
91 Northeastern Blvd Nashua NH (03062) ***(G-19115)***
Amphenol Rf, Danbury *Also called Amphenol Corporation* ***(G-871)***
Ampleon USA Inc 401 830-5420
310 Grge Wash Hwy Ste 500 Smithfield RI (02917) ***(G-21209)***
Amplicea Therapeutics Inc 617 515-6755
53 Hancock Hill Dr Worcester MA (01609) ***(G-17337)***
Amplitude Laser Inc 617 401-2195
50 Milk St Fl 16 Boston MA (02109) ***(G-8365)***

ALPHABETIC

Ampol Tool Inc...203 932-3161
44 Hamilton St West Haven CT (06516) ***(G-5109)***
Amramp, Boston *Also called Gordon Industries Inc* ***(G-8575)***
Amri Burlington Inc (HQ)...781 270-7900
99 S Bedford St Burlington MA (01803) ***(G-9233)***
Amri Global, Burlington *Also called Amri Burlington Inc* ***(G-9233)***
Amro Tool Co...860 274-9766
127 Echo Lake Rd Ste 26 Watertown CT (06795) ***(G-4998)***
AMS, Boston *Also called American Mteorological Soc Inc* ***(G-8361)***
AMS Glass Bead Cabinets...413 566-0037
267 Allen St Hampden MA (01036) ***(G-11319)***
AMS Grinding Co Inc...508 588-2283
959 W Chestnut St Ste 1 Brockton MA (02301) ***(G-9119)***
AMS Qi Inc...617 797-4709
1 Broadway Fl 14 Cambridge MA (02142) ***(G-9389)***
Amsc, Ayer *Also called American Superconductor Corp* ***(G-7907)***
Amsco Ltd Inc...401 785-2860
35 5th Ave Cranston RI (02910) ***(G-20181)***
Amstep Products, Bristol *Also called Patwil LLC* ***(G-593)***
Amt, Spencer *Also called Advanced Mfg Tech Inc* ***(G-15424)***
Amt Acquisition Inc...401 247-1680
5 Greenlawn Ave Warren RI (02885) ***(G-21284)***
Amt Micropure Inc...203 226-7938
14 Mountain View Dr Weston CT (06883) ***(G-5168)***
Amtak Fasteners, East Providence *Also called Gripnail Corporation* ***(G-20416)***
Amtec Corporation...860 230-0006
30 Center Pkwy Plainfield CT (06374) ***(G-3447)***
Amti, Watertown *Also called Advanced Mechanical Tech Inc* ***(G-16263)***
Amtrol Inc (HQ)...401 884-6300
1400 Division Rd West Warwick RI (02893) ***(G-21477)***
Amtrol Intl Investments Inc (HQ)...401 884-6300
1400 Division Rd West Warwick RI (02893) ***(G-21478)***
Amusements Unlimited, Stamford *Also called Rlp Inc* ***(G-4303)***
Amwell, Boston *Also called American Well Corporation* ***(G-8363)***
An Designs Inc...860 618-0183
111 Putter Ln Torrington CT (06790) ***(G-4560)***
An Electronic Instrumentation...978 208-4555
300 Griffin Brook Dr Methuen MA (01844) ***(G-13011)***
An Rob, Natick *Also called Andrew Roberts Inc* ***(G-13235)***
Anacko Cordage Co...401 792-3936
102 Dean Knauss Dr Narragansett RI (02882) ***(G-20634)***
Anaconda Usa Inc...800 285-5721
154 E Central St Natick MA (01760) ***(G-13234)***
Analog Devices Inc (PA)...781 329-4700
1 Technology Way Norwood MA (02062) ***(G-14130)***
Analog Devices Intl Inc (HQ)...781 329-4700
1 Technology Way Norwood MA (02062) ***(G-14131)***
Analogic Corporation (HQ)...978 326-4000
8 Centennial Dr Peabody MA (01960) ***(G-14311)***
Analogic Corporation...978 977-3000
8 Centennial Dr Peabody MA (01960) ***(G-14312)***
Analysis Tech Inc...781 224-1223
6 Whittemore Ter Wakefield MA (01880) ***(G-15941)***
Anapo Plastics Corp...860 874-8174
222 Main St 214 Farmington CT (06032) ***(G-1465)***
Anaren Ceramics Inc...603 898-2883
27 Northwestern Dr Salem NH (03079) ***(G-19706)***
Anatech, Wakefield *Also called Analysis Tech Inc* ***(G-15941)***
Anatolia Creations...401 737-4774
1692 Warwick Ave Warwick RI (02889) ***(G-21323)***
Anatone Jewelry Co Inc...401 728-0490
10 Mark Dr North Providence RI (02904) ***(G-20752)***
Anchor...508 675-7151
887 Highland Ave Fall River MA (02720) ***(G-10658)***
Anchor Bend Glassworks LLC (PA)...401 667-7338
215 Shady Lea Rd Ste 100 North Kingstown RI (02852) ***(G-20690)***
Anchor Concrete...401 942-4800
30 Budlong Rd Cranston RI (02920) ***(G-20182)***
Anchor Labs Group Inc...508 500-9157
95 Prescott St Worcester MA (01605) ***(G-17338)***
Anchor Rubber Products LLC...860 667-2628
152 Rockwell Rd Ste C9 Newington CT (06111) ***(G-2843)***
Anchor-Seal Inc...978 515-6004
54 Great Republic Dr Gloucester MA (01930) ***(G-11159)***
Anchorage Inc...401 245-3300
57 Miller St Warren RI (02885) ***(G-21285)***
Anchorage Inc-Dyer Boats, Warren *Also called Anchorage Inc* ***(G-21285)***
Anco Engineering Inc...203 925-9235
217 Long Hill Cross Rd Shelton CT (06484) ***(G-3775)***
Anco Signs & Stamps Inc...603 669-3779
749 E Industrial Park Dr Manchester NH (03109) ***(G-18779)***
Anco Tool & Die Co Inc...401 438-5860
30 Almeida Ave East Providence RI (02914) ***(G-20387)***
Anco Tool & Manufacturing, Watertown *Also called Cgl Inc* ***(G-5002)***
Ancom Custom Cabinets...978 456-7780
22 Bryan Way Ayer MA (01432) ***(G-7908)***
Andaluna Enterprises Inc...617 335-3204
159 Indian Hill St West Newbury MA (01985) ***(G-16489)***
Andera Inc...401 621-7900
15 Park Row W Ste 200 Providence RI (02903) ***(G-20953)***
Andersen Corporation...508 235-0300
16 Currant Rd Fall River MA (02720) ***(G-10659)***
Andersn Greenwd Crosby Valve, Mansfield *Also called Crosby Valve & Gage Intl Inc* ***(G-12624)***
Anderson Airmotive Products Co, Fall River *Also called Steger Power Connection Inc* ***(G-10763)***
Anderson Components Corp...781 324-0350
61 Clinton St Malden MA (02148) ***(G-12558)***
Anderson David C & Assoc LLC (PA)...860 749-7547
9 Moody Rd Ste 1 Enfield CT (06082) ***(G-1346)***
Anderson Family Tree Farm Inc...207 463-2843
244 Winding Hill Rd Crystal ME (04747) ***(G-5928)***
Anderson Group, Enfield *Also called Anderson David C & Assoc LLC* ***(G-1346)***
Anderson Logging and Lumber...978 874-2751
36 Nichols St Westminster MA (01473) ***(G-16802)***
Anderson Manufacturing Company...203 263-2318
337 Quassapaug Rd Woodbury CT (06798) ***(G-5481)***
Anderson Power Products Inc (HQ)...978 422-3600
13 Pratts Junction Rd Sterling MA (01564) ***(G-15535)***
Anderson Publishing Inc...508 228-3866
27 Mill St Nantucket MA (02554) ***(G-13219)***
Anderson Publishing LLC...860 621-2192
24 Mooreland Dr Southington CT (06489) ***(G-4038)***
Anderson Specialty Company...860 953-6630
81 Custer St West Hartford CT (06110) ***(G-5053)***
Anderson Stair & Railing...203 288-0117
348 Sackett Point Rd North Haven CT (06473) ***(G-3008)***
Anderson Technologies Inc...860 663-2100
243 Roast Meat Hill Rd Killingworth CT (06419) ***(G-1924)***
Anderson Tool Company Inc...203 777-4153
85 Willow St Ste 3 New Haven CT (06511) ***(G-2657)***
Anderson Welding LLC...603 996-6225
3 Dean Dr Dover NH (03820) ***(G-18005)***
Andert Inc...860 974-3893
39 Boston Tpke Eastford CT (06242) ***(G-1312)***
Andon Electronics Corporation...401 333-0388
4 Court Dr Lincoln RI (02865) ***(G-20555)***
Andor Technology Inc...978 405-1116
300 Baker Ave Ste 150 Concord MA (01742) ***(G-10109)***
Andor Technology Ltd...860 290-9211
300 Baker Ave Ste 150 Concord MA (01742) ***(G-10110)***
Andover Corporation...603 893-6888
4 Commercial Dr Salem NH (03079) ***(G-19707)***
Andover Medical Dev Group...978 685-0838
51 S Canal St Unit 2 Lawrence MA (01843) ***(G-11993)***
Andover Organ Company Inc...978 686-9600
560 Broadway Lawrence MA (01841) ***(G-11994)***
Andover Publishing Company...978 475-7000
100 Turnpike St North Andover MA (01845) ***(G-13690)***
Andover Townsman, North Andover *Also called Eagle-Tribune Publishing Co* ***(G-13698)***
Andover Townsmen, North Andover *Also called Andover Publishing Company* ***(G-13690)***
Andre Furniture Industries...860 528-8826
55 Sandra Dr Ste 1 South Windsor CT (06074) ***(G-3938)***
Andrew Alliance Usa Inc...617 797-9071
135 Beaver St Ste 402 Waltham MA (02452) ***(G-16033)***
Andrew Irish Logging...207 562-8839
1264 Auburn Rd Peru ME (04290) ***(G-6583)***
Andrew J Foss Company Inc...603 755-2515
100 Cocheco Rd Farmington NH (03835) ***(G-18139)***
Andrew Roberts Inc...508 653-6412
215 Oak St Ste 1 Natick MA (01760) ***(G-13235)***
Andrew Rolden PC...978 391-4655
39 Main St Ayer MA (01432) ***(G-7909)***
Andrew T Johnson Company Inc (PA)...617 742-1610
15 Tremont Pl Boston MA (02108) ***(G-8366)***
Andrews Arboriculture LLC...203 565-8570
860 Andrew Mountain Rd Naugatuck CT (06770) ***(G-2460)***
Andrews Holdings Inc...978 772-4444
2 New England Way Ayer MA (01432) ***(G-7910)***
Andritz Shw Inc...860 496-8888
90 Commercial Blvd Torrington CT (06790) ***(G-4561)***
Andrus Power Solutions Inc...413 243-0043
690 Pleasant St Lee MA (01238) ***(G-12087)***
Andy Collazzo...978 539-8962
15 Mill St Danvers MA (01923) ***(G-10194)***
Andy Croteau...603 436-8919
285 Banfield Rd Portsmouth NH (03801) ***(G-19536)***
Andy Rakowicz...860 828-1620
600 Four Rod Rd Ste 4 Berlin CT (06037) ***(G-72)***
Andys Machine Inc...508 947-1192
23 Abbey Ln Middleboro MA (02346) ***(G-13052)***
Andys Silkscreen...207 672-3302
322 Main St Bingham ME (04920) ***(G-5769)***
Anexis LLC...978 921-6293
115 Valley St Beverly MA (01915) ***(G-8100)***
Angel Fuel LLC...203 597-8759
56 Knoll St Waterbury CT (06705) ***(G-4844)***

Angel Guard Products Inc 508 791-1073
120 Goddard Memorial Dr Worcester MA (01603) *(G-17339)*
Angelo Di Maria Inc 401 274-0100
395 Admiral St Providence RI (02908) *(G-20954)*
Angies Work Room Inc 508 761-5636
466 Washington St Ste 1 Attleboro MA (02703) *(G-7705)*
Angiodynamics Inc 508 658-7990
26 Forest St Marlborough MA (01752) *(G-12712)*
Angiotech, Westwood *Also called Surgical Specialties Corp (G-16876)*
Anglo Silver Liner Co 508 943-1440
21 Pearl St Webster MA (01570) *(G-16339)*
Anglo-Saxon Federation of Amer 978 346-9311
43 Grove St Merrimac MA (01860) *(G-13000)*
Angostura International Ltd 207 786-3200
176 First Flight Dr Auburn ME (04210) *(G-5551)*
Angstrom Advanced Inc 781 519-4765
95 Mill St Stoughton MA (02072) *(G-15580)*
Anika Therapeutics Inc (PA) 781 457-9000
32 Wiggins Ave Bedford MA (01730) *(G-7957)*
Anjar Co 203 321-1023
42 Russet Rd Stamford CT (06903) *(G-4140)*
Anjen Finishing 508 251-1532
432 Northboro Road Centl Marlborough MA (01752) *(G-12713)*
Ann S Davis 860 642-7228
754 Exeter Rd Lebanon CT (06249) *(G-1932)*
Anna M Chisilenco-Raho 203 877-0377
67 Cherry St Ste 2 Milford CT (06460) *(G-2244)*
Annovation Biopharma Inc 617 724-0343
2 Dairy Farm Ln Wayland MA (01778) *(G-16332)*
Anodic Incorporated 203 268-9966
1480 Monroe Tpke Stevenson CT (06491) *(G-4374)*
Anodizing, Waterbury *Also called Seidel Inc (G-4954)*
Anomatic Corporation 203 720-2367
50 Rado Dr Unit B Naugatuck CT (06770) *(G-2461)*
Anomet Products Inc 508 842-0174
830 Boston Tpke Shrewsbury MA (01545) *(G-15102)*
Anova Data Inc 978 577-6600
4 Technology Park Dr Westford MA (01886) *(G-16753)*
Ansa Company Inc 203 687-1664
130 Water St Norwalk CT (06854) *(G-3101)*
Ansac, Westport *Also called American Natural Soda Ash Corp (G-5181)*
Ansel Label and Packaging Corp 203 452-0311
204 Spring Hill Rd Ste 3 Trumbull CT (06611) *(G-4612)*
Anson Sailmakers Inc 603 431-6676
588 Portsmouth Ave Greenland NH (03840) *(G-18220)*
Ansonia Plastics LLC 203 736-5200
401 Birmingham Blvd Ansonia CT (06401) *(G-7)*
Ansonia Stl Fabrication Co Inc 203 888-4509
164 Pines Bridge Rd Beacon Falls CT (06403) *(G-53)*
Ansys Inc 781 229-8900
150 Baker Avenue Ext # 100 Concord MA (01742) *(G-10111)*
Ansys Inc 603 653-8005
10 Cavendish Ct Lebanon NH (03766) *(G-18612)*
Ansys Inc 401 455-1955
235 Promenade St Rm 485 Providence RI (02908) *(G-20955)*
Antaya Inc 401 941-7050
333 Strawbery F Rd 3 Warwick RI (02886) *(G-21324)*
Antaya Technologies Corp 401 921-3197
333 Strawberry Field Rd # 3 Warwick RI (02886) *(G-21325)*
Antec (usa) LLC 888 572-0012
1 Boston Pl Fl 26 Boston MA (02108) *(G-8367)*
Antec Scientific USA, Boston *Also called Antec (usa) LLC (G-8367)*
Antenna Associates Inc 508 583-3241
21 Burke Dr Brockton MA (02301) *(G-9120)*
Antenna Research Assoc Inc 781 829-4740
28 Riverside Dr Ste 2 Pembroke MA (02359) *(G-14391)*
Anterion Therapeutics Inc 617 240-0324
1 Loring Ave Ste B117 Salem MA (01970) *(G-14892)*
Anthem Music Group Inc 978 667-3224
2 Sterling Rd Unit 2 # 2 North Billerica MA (01862) *(G-13793)*
Anthony Automotive 207 582-7105
810 Brunswick Ave Gardiner ME (04345) *(G-6104)*
Anthony Corrado Inc 401 723 7600
125 Higginson Ave Lincoln RI (02865) *(G-20556)*
Anthony Galluzzo Corp 603 432-2681
14 Liberty Dr Londonderry NH (03053) *(G-18676)*
Anthony Industries Inc 781 305-3750
5r Green St Woburn MA (01801) *(G-17119)*
Anthony Manufacturing Co Inc 781 396-1400
410 Riverside Ave Medford MA (02155) *(G-12921)*
Anthony s Fuel 203 513-7400
56 Great Oak Rd Shelton CT (06484) *(G-3776)*
Anthroposophic Press Inc 212 414-2275
610 Main St Great Barrington MA (01230) *(G-11232)*
Anti-Pest-O, Yarmouth *Also called Holy Terra Products Inc (G-7295)*
Anti-Phishing Wkg Group Inc 404 434-7282
38 Rice St Ste 200 Cambridge MA (02140) *(G-9390)*
Antique Homes Magazine 508 476-7271
73 Wallis St East Douglas MA (01516) *(G-10424)*
Antiqueweb.com, Middlefield *Also called Times Publishing LLC (G-2167)*
Antiquity Tile, Hampden *Also called Wiseman & Spaulding Designs (G-6169)*
Antoine Mechanical Inc 207 897-4100
102 Main St Jay ME (04239) *(G-6219)*
Antoinette Leonard Associates, Woodstock *Also called Longhill Partners Inc (G-22738)*
Anton Enterprises Inc 401 781-3120
430 Wellington Ave Cranston RI (02910) *(G-20183)*
Antrim Controls & Systems 603 588-6297
76 N Bennington Rd Bennington NH (03442) *(G-17687)*
Antrim Wind Energy LLC 603 570-4842
155 Fleet St Portsmouth NH (03801) *(G-19537)*
Antron Engineering & Mch Co 508 966-2803
170 Mechanic St Bellingham MA (02019) *(G-8030)*
Anver Corporation 978 568-0221
36 Parmenter Rd Hudson MA (01749) *(G-11755)*
Anvil International LLC (HQ) 603 418-2800
2 Holland Way Exeter NH (03833) *(G-18110)*
Anvil International LLC 401 886-3000
160 Frenchtown Rd North Kingstown RI (02852) *(G-20691)*
Anvil Machine Co 603 635-9009
72 Russell Dr Pelham NH (03076) *(G-19425)*
Anvil Precision Machine, Pelham *Also called Anvil Machine Co (G-19425)*
Anything Printed LLC 802 457-3414
414 Woodstock Rd Woodstock VT (05091) *(G-22735)*
Aoa Xinetics, Devens *Also called Adaptive Optics Associates Inc (G-10316)*
Aoa Xinetics, Devens *Also called Adaptive Optics Associates Inc (G-10317)*
Aoa Xinetics, East Hartford *Also called Adaptive Optics Associates Inc (G-1170)*
Aoa Xinetics, Devens *Also called Adaptive Optics Associates Inc (G-10318)*
Aotco Metal Finishing Inc 781 275-0880
11 Suburban Park Dr Billerica MA (01821) *(G-8210)*
AP Disposition LLC 860 889-1344
387 N Main St Norwich CT (06360) *(G-3276)*
AP Dley Cstm Laminating Corp 603 437-6666
6 Ledge Rd Windham NH (03087) *(G-20000)*
AP Extrusion Inc 603 890-1086
10 Manor Pkwy Ste E Salem NH (03079) *(G-19708)*
AP Plastics LLC 800 222-1117
103 Foster St Peabody MA (01960) *(G-14313)*
APA LLC 781 986-5900
4 Campanelli Cir Canton MA (02021) *(G-9714)*
APAC Tool Inc 401 724-6090
49 Hurdis St North Providence RI (02904) *(G-20753)*
Apahouser Inc 508 786-0309
40 Hayes Memorial Dr Marlborough MA (01752) *(G-12714)*
Aparo's Electric Motor Repair, Southington *Also called Aparos Electric Motor Service (G-4039)*
Aparos Electric Motor Service 860 276-2044
134 Industrial Dr Southington CT (06489) *(G-4039)*
Apb Enterprises Inc 508 481-0966
160 Main St Marlborough MA (01752) *(G-12715)*
APC Paper Company Inc (PA) 603 542-0411
130 Sullivan St Claremont NH (03743) *(G-17835)*
APC Paper Group, Claremont *Also called APC Paper Company Inc (G-17835)*
APC Phno, Nashua *Also called Amphenol Printed Circuits Inc (G-19115)*
Apcm Manufacturing LLC 860 564-7817
1366 Norwich Rd Plainfield CT (06374) *(G-3448)*
Apco Products 860 767-2108
6 Essex Industrial Park Centerbrook CT (06409) *(G-701)*
Apct Global, Wallingford *Also called Apct-Ct Inc (G-4702)*
Apct-Ct Inc 203 284-1215
340 Quinnipiac St Unit 25 Wallingford CT (06492) *(G-4702)*
Apct-Wallingford Inc 203 269-3311
340 Quinnipiac St Unit 25 Wallingford CT (06492) *(G-4703)*
Apeak Inc 617 964-1709
63 Albert Rd Auburndale MA (02466) *(G-7856)*
Apellis Pharmaceuticals Inc (PA) 617 977-5700
100 5th Ave Waltham MA (02451) *(G-16034)*
Apem Inc (HQ) 978 372-1602
63 Neck Rd Haverhill MA (01835) *(G-11404)*
Aperture Optical Sciences Inc 860 301-2589
23 Soobitsky Rd Higganum CT (06441) *(G-1899)*
Aperture Optical Sciences Inc 860 301-2372
170 Pond View Dr Meriden CT (06450) *(G-2076)*
Apex Machine Tool Company Inc 860 677-2884
500 Knotter Dr Cheshire CT (06410) *(G-711)*
Apex Plastics, Nashua *Also called Spire Technology Solutions LLC (G-19264)*
Apex Press Inc 508 366-1110
122 Turnpike Rd Westborough MA (01581) *(G-16589)*
Apex Resource Technologies Inc 413 442-1414
17 Downing Three Park 2b Pittsfield MA (01201) *(G-14452)*
Apex Tool & Cutter Co Inc 203 888-8970
59 Old Turnpike Rd Beacon Falls CT (06403) *(G-54)*
API, Branford *Also called American Polyfilm Inc (G-289)*
API Electronics Inc 508 485-6350
400 Nickerson Rd Marlborough MA (01752) *(G-12716)*
API Technologies, Marlborough *Also called Cmt Filters Inc (G-12738)*
API Technologies Corp, Marlborough *Also called API Electronics Inc (G-12716)*
API Technologies Corp (PA) 855 294-3800
400 Nickerson Rd Ste 1 Marlborough MA (01752) *(G-12717)*

ALPHABETIC

API Technologies Corporation 508 485-0336
165 Cedar Hill St Marlborough MA (01752) ***(G-12718)***
API Technologies Corporation 508 251-6400
400 Nickerson Rd Ste 1 Marlborough MA (01752) ***(G-12719)***
API Wizard LLC 914 764-5726
10 Hamilton Rd Ridgefield CT (06877) ***(G-3655)***
Apifia Inc (PA) 585 506-2787
200 State St Mrktplace Ct Boston MA (02109) ***(G-8368)***
Apiject Systems Corp (PA) 203 461-7121
2 High Ridge Park Stamford CT (06905) ***(G-4141)***
APJ Test Consulting, Nashua *Also called Everett Charles Tech LLC* ***(G-19151)***
Aplicare Products LLC (HQ) 203 630-0500
550 Research Pkwy Meriden CT (06450) ***(G-2077)***
Apmar Usa Inc 413 781-5261
175 Progress Ave Springfield MA (01104) ***(G-15446)***
Apogee Corporation (PA) 860 963-1976
5 Highland Dr Putnam CT (06260) ***(G-3601)***
Apogee Corporation 860 632-3550
154 West St Ste C Cromwell CT (06416) ***(G-846)***
Apogee Machining Services Inc 978 740-4689
97 Canal St Salem MA (01970) ***(G-14893)***
Apogee Technology Inc (PA) 781 551-9450
129 Morgan Dr Norwood MA (02062) ***(G-14132)***
Apogent Technologies Inc 781 622-1300
81 Wyman St Waltham MA (02451) ***(G-16035)***
Apollo Steel LLC 603 532-1156
52 Fitzgerald Dr Jaffrey NH (03452) ***(G-18456)***
Aponos Medical Corporation 603 347-8229
17 Route 125 Bldg A7 Kingston NH (03848) ***(G-18540)***
Apothecary Products LLC 508 695-0727
90 George Leven Dr North Attleboro MA (02760) ***(G-13745)***
Appalachian Gap Distillery Inc 802 989-7359
88 Mainelli Rd Ste 2 Middlebury VT (05753) ***(G-22099)***
Appalachian Press 413 568-2621
11 Railroad Ave Westfield MA (01085) ***(G-16666)***
Appalachian Stitching Co LLC (PA) 603 444-4422
90 Badger St Littleton NH (03561) ***(G-18654)***
Appalchian Engineered Flrg Inc 802 988-1073
105 Industrial Park Dr North Troy VT (05859) ***(G-22240)***
Apparel 2000 LLC 781 740-6204
40 Reservoir Park Dr D Rockland MA (02370) ***(G-14790)***
Appels Printing & Mailing Bur 860 522-8189
307 Homestead Ave Hartford CT (06112) ***(G-1806)***
Apperian, Boston *Also called Red Frames Inc* ***(G-8814)***
Appetites 508 362-3623
2905 Main St Barnstable MA (02630) ***(G-7946)***
Applause LLC 508 665-6910
100 Pennsylvania Ave # 500 Framingham MA (01701) ***(G-10921)***
Apple Mill Holding Company Inc 781 826-9706
720 Washington St Pembroke MA (02359) ***(G-14392)***
Apple Steel Rule Die Co Inc 414 353-2444
88 Industry Ave Ste C Springfield MA (01104) ***(G-15447)***
Appleton Grp LLC 860 653-1603
2 Connecticut South Dr East Granby CT (06026) ***(G-1117)***
Applewood Controls Inc 978 486-9220
37 Ayer Rd Littleton MA (01460) ***(G-12292)***
Applicator Sales & Service, Salem *Also called Beacon Sales Acquisition Inc* ***(G-19712)***
Applied Advertising Inc 860 640-0800
71 Newtown Rd Ste 5 Danbury CT (06810) ***(G-872)***
Applied Biosystems LLC 781 271-0045
301 Merritt 7 Ste 23 Norwalk CT (06851) ***(G-3102)***
Applied Biosystems LLC 781 271-0045
2 Preston Ct Bedford MA (01730) ***(G-7958)***
Applied Biosystems LLC 508 877-1307
1455 Concord St Ste 8 Framingham MA (01701) ***(G-10922)***
Applied Bosystems Part Lf Tech, Bedford *Also called Applied Biosystems LLC* ***(G-7958)***
Applied Computer Engineering (PA) 508 824-4630
500 Myles Standish Blvd # 1 Taunton MA (02780) ***(G-15725)***
Applied Diamond Coatings LLC 860 349-3133
30 Ozick Dr Durham CT (06422) ***(G-1086)***
Applied Graphics Inc 978 241-5300
61 S Hunt Rd Amesbury MA (01913) ***(G-7478)***
Applied Laser Solutions Inc 203 739-0179
28 Commerce Dr Danbury CT (06810) ***(G-873)***
Applied Light Manufacturing 413 552-3600
48 Commercial St Holyoke MA (01040) ***(G-11616)***
Applied Machine Technology, Warren *Also called Amt Acquisition Inc* ***(G-21284)***
Applied Materials 978 282-2917
80 Blackburn Ctr Gloucester MA (01930) ***(G-11160)***
Applied Materials Inc 978 795-8000
80 Central St Ste 325 Boxborough MA (01719) ***(G-8957)***
Applied Nanofemto Tech LLC 978 761-4293
240 Varnum Ave Apt 12 Lowell MA (01854) ***(G-12344)***
Applied Nnstrctred Sltions LLC 978 670-6959
157 Concord Rd Billerica MA (01821) ***(G-8211)***
Applied Plastic Technology Inc 508 752-5924
169 Fremont St Worcester MA (01603) ***(G-17340)***
Applied Plastics Co Inc 781 762-1881
25 Endicott St Norwood MA (02062) ***(G-14133)***
Applied Plastics Tech Inc 401 253-0200
45 Broadcommon Rd Bristol RI (02809) ***(G-20062)***
Applied Porous Tech Inc 860 408-9793
2 Tunxis Rd Ste 103 Tariffville CT (06081) ***(G-4472)***
Applied Precision Technology 508 226-8700
81 West St Attleboro MA (02703) ***(G-7706)***
Applied Rubber & Plastics Inc 860 987-9018
100 Skitchewaug St Windsor CT (06095) ***(G-5321)***
Applied Science Group Inc 781 275-4000
900 Middlesex Tpke 5-5 Billerica MA (01821) ***(G-8212)***
Applied Science Laboratories, Billerica *Also called Applied Science Group Inc* ***(G-8212)***
Applied Tissue Tech LLC 781 366-3848
99 Derby St Ste 200 Hingham MA (02043) ***(G-11491)***
Applied Tool & Design LLC 603 740-2954
1 Mill Hill Rd Madbury NH (03823) ***(G-18760)***
Applied Water Management Inc 508 675-5755
21 Father Devalles Blvd # 1 Fall River MA (02723) ***(G-10660)***
Applitek Technologies Corp 401 467-0007
160 Georgia Ave Providence RI (02905) ***(G-20956)***
Appneta Inc (PA) 781 235-2470
285 Summer St Fl 4 Boston MA (02210) ***(G-8369)***
Apps Associates LLC 978 399-0230
40 Nagog Park Ste 105 Acton MA (01720) ***(G-7341)***
Appstract Ideas 860 857-1123
81 Martin Rd Bristol CT (06010) ***(G-519)***
Apraxis Software, Center Barnstead *Also called Our Town Publishing Inc* ***(G-17790)***
Aprea (us) Inc 857 239-9072
535 Boylston St Boston MA (02116) ***(G-8370)***
Aprea Therapeutics, Boston *Also called Aprea (us) Inc* ***(G-8370)***
Aprea Therapeutics Inc 617 463-9385
535 Boylston St Boston MA (02116) ***(G-8371)***
Apricot Home LLC 203 552-1791
15 Sheffield Way Greenwich CT (06831) ***(G-1593)***
April Cornell, Burlington *Also called Cornell Online LLC* ***(G-21776)***
April Metalworks 603 883-1510
31 Sagamore Park Rd Hudson NH (03051) ***(G-18374)***
April Twenty One Corporation 978 667-8472
749 Boston Rd Billerica MA (01821) ***(G-8213)***
Apriomed Inc 603 421-0875
45 S Main St Unit 2 Derry NH (03038) ***(G-17971)***
Apriori Technologies Inc (PA) 978 371-2006
300 Baker Ave Ste 170 Concord MA (01742) ***(G-10112)***
APS, Lee *Also called Andrus Power Solutions Inc* ***(G-12087)***
APS, Peabody *Also called Adhesive Packaging Spc Inc* ***(G-14307)***
APS Robotics & Integration LLC 860 526-1040
500 Main St Ste 9 Deep River CT (06417) ***(G-1057)***
APT, Fitchburg *Also called Advanced Print Technology Inc* ***(G-10809)***
Aptar Inc 860 489-6249
301 Ella Grasso Ave Torrington CT (06790) ***(G-4562)***
Aptargroup Inc 203 377-8100
125 Access Rd Stratford CT (06615) ***(G-4391)***
Aptech Graphics, North Providence *Also called Graphic Application Tech Inc* ***(G-20763)***
Aqua Bio Compliance Corp 508 798-2966
44 Richmond Ave Worcester MA (01602) ***(G-17341)***
Aqua Blasting Corp 860 242-8855
2 Northwood Dr Bloomfield CT (06002) ***(G-201)***
Aqua Massage International Inc 860 536-3735
1101 Noank Ledyard Rd Mystic CT (06355) ***(G-2434)***
Aqua Phoenix Limited 401 821-2732
72 Wood Cove Dr Coventry RI (02816) ***(G-20136)***
Aqua Solutions Inc 508 947-5777
154 W Grove St Ste D Middleboro MA (02346) ***(G-13053)***
Aqua Specialties 603 942-5671
561 1st Nh Tpke Northwood NH (03261) ***(G-19411)***
Aqua Systems Inc (PA) 603 778-8796
289 Exeter Rd Hampton Falls NH (03844) ***(G-18281)***
Aqua Tite Innovative Solutions 603 431-5555
1 Liberty Ln E Ste 117 Hampton NH (03842) ***(G-18254)***
Aqua Vitea Kombucha, Middlebury *Also called Aqua Vitea LLC* ***(G-22100)***
Aqua Vitea LLC 802 453-8590
153 Pond Ln Middlebury VT (05753) ***(G-22100)***
Aqua Vitea LLC 802 352-1049
8 Shard Villa Rd Salisbury VT (05769) ***(G-22398)***
Aquaback Technologies Inc 978 863-1000
4 Raymond Ave Ste 8 Salem NH (03079) ***(G-19709)***
Aquabotix Technology Corp 508 676-1000
21 Father Devalles Blvd # 8 Fall River MA (02723) ***(G-10661)***
Aquacomfort Solutions LLC 407 831-1941
15 Burton Dr Cheshire CT (06410) ***(G-712)***
Aqualogic Inc 203 248-8959
30 Devine St North Haven CT (06473) ***(G-3009)***
Aquamesh, Northbridge *Also called Riverdale Mills Corporation* ***(G-14060)***
Aquamotion Inc 401 785-3000
88 Jefferson Blvd Ste C Warwick RI (02888) ***(G-21326)***
Aquarion Water Company 401 596-2847
87 Margin St Westerly RI (02891) ***(G-21516)***
Aquas Group, East Providence *Also called Environmental Ctrl Systems Inc* ***(G-20410)***
Aquasent, Storrs Mansfield *Also called Aquatic Sensor Netwrk Tech LLC* ***(G-4383)***

Aquatic Sensor Netwrk Tech LLC 860 429-4303
30 Beacon Hill Dr Storrs Mansfield CT (06268) ***(G-4383)***
Aquawave of New England LLC 603 431-8975
195 Nh Ave Portsmouth NH (03801) ***(G-19538)***
Aquidneck Cstm Composites Inc 401 254-6911
69 Ballou Blvd Bristol RI (02809) ***(G-20063)***
Aquiline Drones LLC 860 361-7958
750 Main St Ste 319 Hartford CT (06103) ***(G-1807)***
Aqyr Technologies Inc 603 402-6099
12 Murphy Dr Ste 200 Nashua NH (03062) ***(G-19116)***
AR Metallizing Ltd 508 541-7700
24 Forge Pkwy Franklin MA (02038) ***(G-11024)***
Ar-Ro Engineering Company Inc (PA) 401 766-6669
16 Vincent Ave Ste 1 North Smithfield RI (02896) ***(G-20781)***
Araces Incorporated 413 499-9997
570 East St Pittsfield MA (01201) ***(G-14453)***
Aram Machine Co, North Billerica *Also called John A Kachagian* ***(G-13829)***
Aramid Rigging Inc 401 683-6966
14 Regatta Way Ste 3 Portsmouth RI (02871) ***(G-20917)***
Aratana Therapeutics Inc 617 425-9226
200 Clarendon St Fl 54 Boston MA (02116) ***(G-8372)***
Arbo Machine Co Inc 781 871-3449
45 Union St Rockland MA (02370) ***(G-14791)***
Arbon Equipment Corporation 410 796-5902
29 Griffin Rd S Bloomfield CT (06002) ***(G-202)***
Arborjet Inc 781 935-9070
99 Blueberry Hill Rd Woburn MA (01801) ***(G-17120)***
Arbortech Tools USA Corp 866 517-7869
45r Washington St Norwell MA (02061) ***(G-14094)***
Arborway Metal Finishing Inc 781 982-0137
401 Vfw Dr Rockland MA (02370) ***(G-14792)***
ARC Dynamics Inc 860 563-1006
28 Belamose Ave Ste C Rocky Hill CT (06067) ***(G-3702)***
ARC Enterprises, Kingfield *Also called Advanced Resources & Construct* ***(G-6251)***
ARC Maintenance Machining 603 626-8046
14 Tinker Ave Unit 2 Londonderry NH (03053) ***(G-18677)***
ARC Technology Solutions LLC 603 883-3027
165 Ledge St Ste 4 Nashua NH (03060) ***(G-19117)***
Arcade Industries Inc 508 832-6300
205 Southbridge St Auburn MA (01501) ***(G-7826)***
Arcade Snacks & Dried Fruits, Auburn *Also called Arcade Industries Inc* ***(G-7826)***
Arcade Technology LLC 203 366-3871
38 Union Ave Bridgeport CT (06607) ***(G-376)***
Arcadia, Stamford *Also called Wilson Partitions Inc* ***(G-4360)***
Arcadia Architectural Pdts Inc 203 316-8000
110 Viaduct Rd Stamford CT (06907) ***(G-4142)***
Arcam Cad To Metal Inc 781 281-1718
6 Gill St Woburn MA (01801) ***(G-17121)***
Arcast Inc 207 539-9638
5 Park Rd Oxford ME (04270) ***(G-6562)***
Arcast Inc 207 539-9638
264 Main St Oxford ME (04270) ***(G-6563)***
Arcat Inc 203 929-9444
173 Sherman St Fairfield CT (06824) ***(G-1414)***
Arccos Golf LLC 844 692-7226
700 Canal St Ste 19 Stamford CT (06902) ***(G-4143)***
Arch Parent Inc 860 336-4856
82 Storrs Rd Willimantic CT (06226) ***(G-5261)***
Arch Parent Inc 401 388-9802
13 Airport Rd Westerly RI (02891) ***(G-21517)***
Arch Parent Inc 413 504-1433
1129 Riverdale St West Springfield MA (01089) ***(G-16508)***
Archer Machine 207 637-3396
482 Sokokis Ave Limington ME (04049) ***(G-6346)***
Archer Roose Inc 646 283-4152
21 Drydock Ave Boston MA (02210) ***(G-8373)***
Archer Roose Wine, Boston *Also called Archer Roose Inc* ***(G-8373)***
Archerdx Inc 978 232-3570
123 Brimbal Ave Beverly MA (01915) ***(G-8101)***
Archetype Hardware 707 303-6003
124 Sutherland Rd Apt 9 Brighton MA (02135) ***(G-9094)***
Archimedia Solutions Group LLC (PA) 970 774-5400
11 Sylvan St Ste 5 Danvers MA (01923) ***(G-10195)***
Archtctral Graphics Signs Inc 617 924-0070
73 Oakland St Watertown MA (02472) ***(G-16269)***
Architects of Packaging Inc 413 568-3187
11 Mainline Dr Westfield MA (01085) ***(G-16667)***
Architectural Elements Inc 978 263-2482
972 Massachusetts Ave Boxboro MA (01719) ***(G-8951)***
Architectural Glazing Systems 508 588-4845
40 Murphy Dr Avon MA (02322) ***(G-7876)***
Architectural Illusions 617 338-8118
300 Summer St Apt 11 Boston MA (02210) ***(G-8374)***
Architectural Kitchens Inc 781 239-9750
310b Washington St Wellesley MA (02481) ***(G-16360)***
Architectural Openings Inc 617 776-9223
16 Garfield Ave Somerville MA (02145) ***(G-15155)***
Architectural Skylight Co Inc 207 247-6747
661 Main St Waterboro ME (04087) ***(G-7150)***
Architectural Star Ltg LLC 508 678-1900
21 Father Devalles Blvd # 12 Fall River MA (02723) ***(G-10662)***
Architectural Stone Group LLC 203 494-5451
9 Island Brook Ave Bridgeport CT (06606) ***(G-377)***
Architectural Supplements LLC 203 591-5505
567 S Leonard St Bldg 1b Waterbury CT (06708) ***(G-4845)***
Architectural Timber Mllwk Inc 413 586-3045
49 Mount Warner Rd Hadley MA (01035) ***(G-11305)***
Architexa Inc 617 500-7391
1035 Cambridge St Ste 1 Cambridge MA (02141) ***(G-9391)***
Arck Enterprises Inc 978 777-9166
100 High St Danvers MA (01923) ***(G-10196)***
Arclin Surfaces - E Longmeadow 678 781-5341
82 Deer Park Dr East Longmeadow MA (01028) ***(G-10467)***
Arconic Inc 860 379-3314
145 Price Rd Winsted CT (06098) ***(G-5404)***
Arconic Ttnium Engineered Pdts, Burlington *Also called Rmi Titanium Company LLC* ***(G-9330)***
Arcor Epoxy Inc 508 385-5598
117 Queen Anne Rd Harwich MA (02645) ***(G-11388)***
Arctic Holdings LLC 978 535-5351
198 Route 28 West Harwich MA (02671) ***(G-16480)***
Arctic Pack, New Bedford *Also called Packaging Products Corporation* ***(G-13434)***
Ard, North Andover *Also called Advanced Research Development* ***(G-13687)***
Arden Jewelry Mfg Co 401 274-9800
10 Industrial Ln Johnston RI (02919) ***(G-20500)***
Ardent Inc (PA) 860 528-6000
95 Leggett St East Hartford CT (06108) ***(G-1173)***
Ardent Concepts Inc 603 474-1760
4 Merrill Industrial Dr # 8 Hampton NH (03842) ***(G-18255)***
Ardent Displays & Packaging, East Hartford *Also called Ardent Inc* ***(G-1173)***
Ardent Mills LLC 978 772-6337
35 Nemco Way Ayer MA (01432) ***(G-7911)***
Ardeo Systems Inc 978 373-4680
17 Parkridge Rd Ste 2 Haverhill MA (01835) ***(G-11405)***
Arens Stoneworks Inc 603 436-8000
434 Portsmouth Ave Greenland NH (03840) ***(G-18221)***
Argix Direct, South Windsor *Also called L T A Group Inc* ***(G-3989)***
Argo Ems, Clinton *Also called Eastern Company* ***(G-785)***
Argos Corporation 508 828-5900
84 Independence Dr Taunton MA (02780) ***(G-15726)***
Argosy Publishing Inc (PA) 617 527-9999
109 Oak St Ste 102 Newton MA (02464) ***(G-13562)***
Argotec LLC (HQ) 413 772-2564
53 Silvio O Conte Dr Greenfield MA (01301) ***(G-11250)***
Argyle Associates Inc 603 226-4300
30 Terrill Park Dr Concord NH (03301) ***(G-17883)***
Argyle Optics LLC 203 451-3320
28 Tower St Milford CT (06460) ***(G-2245)***
Ariad Pharmaceuticals Inc 617 494-0400
40 Landsdowne St Cambridge MA (02139) ***(G-9392)***
Arico Engineering Inc 860 642-7040
841 Route 32 Ste 19 North Franklin CT (06254) ***(G-2987)***
Ariel Instant Printing 603 352-3663
26 Roxbury St Keene NH (03431) ***(G-18492)***
Aries Systems Corporation 978 975-7570
50 High St Ste 21 North Andover MA (01845) ***(G-13691)***
ARINC Incorporated 781 863-0711
175 Bedford St Ste 12 Lexington MA (02420) ***(G-12207)***
ARINC Research, Lexington *Also called ARINC Incorporated* ***(G-12207)***
Arion Jrnl of Hmnties Classics 617 353-6480
621 Commonwealth Ave Fl 4 Boston MA (02215) ***(G-8375)***
Arise Air Inc 888 359-2747
120 Palmer Rd Plympton MA (02367) ***(G-14590)***
Arise Computer, Woburn *Also called Aci Technology Inc* ***(G-17107)***
Arista Flutes LLC 781 275-8821
10 Railroad Ave Bedford MA (01730) ***(G-7959)***
Aristocrat Products Inc 508 529-3471
17 Taft St Ste 1 Upton MA (01568) ***(G-15904)***
Ariston Engraving & Machine Co 781 935-2328
56 Dragon Ct Woburn MA (01801) ***(G-17122)***
Ark of Safety 802 429-2537
265 French Rd West Newbury VT (05085) ***(G-22610)***
Ark Plasma 207 332-6999
9 Mountain Rd Alfred ME (04002) ***(G-5515)***
Ark-Les Connectors Corporation 781 297-6324
350 Revolutionary Dr East Taunton MA (02718) ***(G-10510)***
Arkwright Advanced Coating Inc 401 821-1000
538 Main St Fiskeville RI (02823) ***(G-20454)***
Arland Tool & Mfg Inc (PA) 508 347-3368
421 Main St Sturbridge MA (01566) ***(G-15638)***
Arland Tool & Mfg Inc 508 867-3085
45 Freight House Rd West Brookfield MA (01585) ***(G-16464)***
Arlin Mfg Co Inc 978 454-9165
239 Industrial Ave E Lowell MA (01852) ***(G-12345)***
Arlington Advocate, Concord *Also called Gatehouse Media LLC* ***(G-10130)***
Arlington Industries Inc 802 375-6139
2617 Vt Route 7a Arlington VT (05250) ***(G-21594)***

ALPHABETIC

Arlington Sample Book Co Inc (PA) 603 763-9082
100 Fernwood Point Rd Sunapee NH (03782) ***(G-19879)***
Arlington Swifty Printing Inc 781 646-8700
1386 Massachusetts Ave Arlington MA (02476) ***(G-7623)***
Arm Inc 978 264-7300
100 5th Ave Fl 5 Waltham MA (02451) ***(G-16036)***
Arm Centerless Grinding 978 352-2410
36 Jackman St Unit 14 Georgetown MA (01833) ***(G-11136)***
Armada Logistics Inc 855 727-6232
48 Grove St Ste 201 Somerville MA (02144) ***(G-15156)***
Armadillo Noise Vibration LLC 774 992-7156
1 Titleist Dr Acushnet MA (02743) ***(G-7399)***
Armanni Usa Inc 207 893-0557
39 Enterprise Dr Windham ME (04062) ***(G-7229)***
Armatron International Inc (PA) 781 321-2300
15 Highland Ave Malden MA (02148) ***(G-12559)***
Armbrust International Ltd 401 781-3300
735 Allens Ave Providence RI (02905) ***(G-20957)***
Armco Woodworking & Display 508 831-0990
115 Sw Cutoff Worcester MA (01604) ***(G-17342)***
Armed & Ready Alarm System 203 596-0327
112 Fieldwood Rd Waterbury CT (06704) ***(G-4846)***
Armenian Mirror-Spectator, Watertown *Also called Baikar Association Inc* ***(G-16271)***
Armetta LLC 860 788-2369
90 Industrial Park Rd Middletown CT (06457) ***(G-2172)***
Armin Innovative Products Inc 508 822-4629
1424 Somerset Ave Dighton MA (02715) ***(G-10335)***
Armor Box Company LLC 860 242-9981
29 Woods Rd Bloomfield CT (06002) ***(G-203)***
Armor Holdings Protech Div 413 445-4000
1595 East St Pittsfield MA (01201) ***(G-14454)***
Armor Roll, Jamaica Plain *Also called Weld Rite* ***(G-11951)***
Armored Auto Group, Danbury *Also called Armored Autogroup Inc* ***(G-874)***
Armored Autogroup Inc (HQ) 203 205-2900
44 Old Ridgebury Rd # 300 Danbury CT (06810) ***(G-874)***
Armored Autogroup Parent Inc (HQ) 203 205-2900
44 Old Ridgebury Rd # 300 Danbury CT (06810) ***(G-875)***
Armored Autogroup Sales Inc 203 205-2900
44 Old Ridgebury Rd # 300 Danbury CT (06810) ***(G-876)***
Armored Shield Technologies 714 848-5796
3655 W Mcfadden Ave Redding CT (06896) ***(G-3646)***
Arms, West Bridgewater *Also called Atlantic RES Mktg Systems Inc* ***(G-16429)***
Armset LLC 978 774-0035
2 De Bush Ave Middleton MA (01949) ***(G-13083)***
Armstrong Family Inds Inc 207 848-7300
1 Printers Dr Hermon ME (04401) ***(G-6183)***
Armstrong Industries Inc 715 629-1632
27 Old Milford Rd Amherst NH (03031) ***(G-17551)***
Armstrong Machine Co Inc 978 232-9466
117 Elliott St Ste 3 Beverly MA (01915) ***(G-8102)***
Armstrong Mold Corporation 781 749-3207
28 South St Ste 1 Hingham MA (02043) ***(G-11492)***
Armstrong Pharmaceuticals Inc (HQ) 617 323-7404
423 Lagrange St West Roxbury MA (02132) ***(G-16493)***
Armstrong Pharmaceuticals Inc 617 323-7404
25 John Rd Canton MA (02021) ***(G-9715)***
Arnitex LLC 203 869-1406
110 Orchard St Cos Cob CT (06807) ***(G-822)***
Arnold Bakeries 508 398-6588
17 Oyster Cove Rd Bass River MA (02664) ***(G-7953)***
Aro-Sac Inc 401 231-6655
1 Warren Ave North Providence RI (02911) ***(G-20754)***
Aroma Spa & Laser Center Inc 978 685-8883
225 Essex St Westford MA (01886) ***(G-16754)***
Aroostacast Inc 207 764-0077
217 Parsons Rd Presque Isle ME (04769) ***(G-6753)***
Aroostook Fiber Works, Ashland *Also called Roxanne L Tardie* ***(G-5540)***
Aroostook Republican, Presque Isle *Also called Northeast Publishing Company* ***(G-6764)***
Aroostook Trusses Inc 207 768-5817
655 Missile St Presque Isle ME (04769) ***(G-6754)***
Aroyan Alum Strefronts Windows, Abington *Also called Aroyan Inc* ***(G-7320)***
Aroyan Inc 781 421-3107
1423 Bedford St Ste 1 Abington MA (02351) ***(G-7320)***
Arqule Inc (PA) 781 994-0300
1 Wall St Ste 7 Burlington MA (01803) ***(G-9234)***
Arr, Harwinton *Also called Advanced Receiver Research* ***(G-1886)***
Arradiance LLC 508 202-0593
11a Beaver Brook Rd Littleton MA (01460) ***(G-12293)***
Arrakis Therapeutics Inc 617 913-0348
830 Winter St Ste 1 Waltham MA (02451) ***(G-16037)***
Array Technologies Inc 860 657-8086
21 Sequin Dr Glastonbury CT (06033) ***(G-1538)***
Arrigoni Winery 860 342-1999
209 Sand Hill Rd Portland CT (06480) ***(G-3562)***
Arris International, Westborough *Also called Ruckus Wireless Inc* ***(G-16645)***
Arris Technology Inc 678 473-8493
15 Sterling Dr Wallingford CT (06492) ***(G-4704)***
Arris Technology Inc 978 614-2900
900 Chelmsford St Lowell MA (01851) ***(G-12346)***
Arrow Concrete Products Inc (PA) 860 653-5063
560 Salmon Brook St Granby CT (06035) ***(G-1588)***
Arrow Diversified Tooling Inc 860 872-9072
17 Pinney St Ellington CT (06029) ***(G-1329)***
Arrow International Inc 978 250-5100
16 Elizabeth Dr Chelmsford MA (01824) ***(G-9871)***
Arrow Interventional Inc 919 433-4948
16 Elizabeth Dr Chelmsford MA (01824) ***(G-9872)***
Arrow Machine LLC 413 323-7280
151 N Washington St Belchertown MA (01007) ***(G-8021)***
Arrow Manufacturing Company 860 589-3900
16 Jeannette St Bristol CT (06010) ***(G-520)***
Arrow Moccasin Company 978 562-7870
120 Central St Ste 2 Hudson MA (01749) ***(G-11756)***
Arrow Tool Division, Wethersfield *Also called Merritt Machine Company* ***(G-5257)***
Arrow Window Shade Mfg Co 860 956-3570
1252 Berlin Tpke Wethersfield CT (06109) ***(G-5240)***
Arrow Window Shade Mfg Co Mrdn 860 563-4035
47 Oxford St Wethersfield CT (06109) ***(G-5241)***
Arrowhead Athletics, Andover *Also called Shawsheen Rubber Co Inc* ***(G-7604)***
ARS Products LLC 860 564-0208
43 Lathrop Road Ext Plainfield CT (06374) ***(G-3449)***
Art, Brentwood *Also called Asphalt Recovery Tech LLC* ***(G-17744)***
Art For A Cause LLC 248 645-3966
224 Libbey Indus Pkwy East Weymouth MA (02189) ***(G-10536)***
Art For Literacy, East Weymouth *Also called Art For A Cause LLC* ***(G-10536)***
Art Licensing Intl Inc 802 362-3662
6366 Vt Route 7a Arlington VT (05250) ***(G-21595)***
Art New England Magazine 617 259-1040
560 Harrison Ave Boston MA (02118) ***(G-8376)***
Art of Wellbeing LLC 917 453-3009
230 Saddle Hill Rd Stamford CT (06903) ***(G-4144)***
Art Shirt Co 617 625-2636
228 Lowell St Somerville MA (02144) ***(G-15157)***
Art Swiss Corporation 508 999-3281
1357 E Rodney French Blvd New Bedford MA (02744) ***(G-13359)***
Artco Offset Inc 781 830-7900
340 Turnpike St Ste 1-3b Canton MA (02021) ***(G-9716)***
Artcraft, Hudson *Also called United Stretch Design Corp* ***(G-11824)***
Artcraft Braid Co LLC 401 831-9077
11 Bonazzoli Ave Hudson MA (01749) ***(G-11757)***
Artcraft Co Inc 508 695-4042
200 John L Dietsch Blvd North Attleboro MA (02763) ***(G-13746)***
Artcrete Enterprises Inc 401 270-0700
53 Capitol View Ave Providence RI (02908) ***(G-20958)***
Artech House Inc (HQ) 781 769-9750
685 Canton St Norwood MA (02062) ***(G-14134)***
Artech Lubricants, Bethel *Also called Artech Packaging LLC* ***(G-128)***
Artech Packaging LLC 845 858-8558
18 Taylor Ave Ste 2 Bethel CT (06801) ***(G-128)***
Arteffects Incorporated 860 242-0031
27 Britton Dr Bloomfield CT (06002) ***(G-204)***
Artek, Antrim *Also called Riley Mountain Products Inc* ***(G-17597)***
Artel Inc 207 854-0860
25 Bradley Dr Westbrook ME (04092) ***(G-7180)***
Artel Video Systems Corp 978 263-5775
5b Lyberty Way Westford MA (01886) ***(G-16755)***
Artemas Industries Inc 603 755-9777
20 Sarah Greenfield Way Farmington NH (03835) ***(G-18140)***
Arteriocyte Med Systems Inc 508 497-9350
45 South St Hopkinton MA (01748) ***(G-11690)***
Arteriocyte Med Systems Inc (HQ) 866 660-2674
45 South St Ste 3c Hopkinton MA (01748) ***(G-11691)***
Artforms (PA) 800 828-8518
128 Maine St Brunswick ME (04011) ***(G-5829)***
Artfx Signs, Bloomfield *Also called Arteffects Incorporated* ***(G-204)***
Arthur G Russell Company Inc 860 583-4109
750 Clark Ave Bristol CT (06010) ***(G-521)***
Arthur H Gaebel Inc 978 263-4401
36 Sargent Rd Boxborough MA (01719) ***(G-8958)***
Arthurs Memorials Inc 603 356-5398
875 Eastman Rd Center Conway NH (03813) ***(G-17791)***
Artic Tool & Engrg Co LLC 401 785-2210
29 Lark Industrial Pkwy Greenville RI (02828) ***(G-20461)***
Artificial Limb Co, Cranston *Also called Rhode Island Limb Co* ***(G-20279)***
Artigiano Stained Glass 617 244-0141
1238 Chestnut St Newton MA (02464) ***(G-13563)***
Artinian Garabet Corporation 978 371-7110
39 Main St Concord MA (01742) ***(G-10113)***
Artisan Bread & Products LLC 914 843-4401
13 Dry Hill Rd Norwalk CT (06851) ***(G-3103)***
Artisan Industries Inc 781 893-6800
44 Campanelli Pkwy Stoughton MA (02072) ***(G-15581)***
Artisan Millwork Inc Cabi 401 721-5500
750 School St Pawtucket RI (02860) ***(G-20813)***
Artisan Surfaces Inc 802 885-8677
200 Clinton St Springfield VT (05156) ***(G-22499)***
Artistic Iron Works LLC 203 838-9200
11 Reynolds St Norwalk CT (06855) ***(G-3104)***

Artistic Label Company Inc 401 737-0666
60 Gilbane St Warwick RI (02886) ***(G-21327)***
Artistic Woodworks Inc 802 767-3123
606 Fiske Rd Unit 28 Rochester VT (05767) ***(G-22316)***
Artquick Corp 508 358-4864
72 Oxbow Rd Wayland MA (01778) ***(G-16333)***
Arts International Wholesale 508 822-7181
104 Forge River Pkwy Raynham MA (02767) ***(G-14705)***
Arts Ipswich 978 356-5335
134 Town Farm Rd Ipswich MA (01938) ***(G-11902)***
Arturo Milite and Spinella Bky, Waterbury *Also called Milite Bakery* ***(G-4916)***
Artvac Corporation 401 333-6120
17 New England Way Lincoln RI (02865) ***(G-20557)***
Arundel Machine Tool Co 207 985-8555
20 Technology Dr Arundel ME (04046) ***(G-5528)***
Arvest Press Inc 781 894-4844
252r Calvary St Waltham MA (02453) ***(G-16038)***
Arvinas Inc (PA) 203 535-1456
395 Winchester Ave New Haven CT (06511) ***(G-2658)***
Arwood Machine Corporation 978 463-3777
95 Parker St Ste 4 Newburyport MA (01950) ***(G-13469)***
Arzol Chemical Company, Keene *Also called Arzol Corp* ***(G-18493)***
Arzol Corp 603 352-5242
12 Norway Ave Ste 2 Keene NH (03431) ***(G-18493)***
As Liquidation I Company Inc (PA) 603 879-0205
62 State Route 101a 2b Amherst NH (03031) ***(G-17552)***
Asahi/America Inc (HQ) 781 321-5409
655 Andover St Lawrence MA (01843) ***(G-11995)***
Asahi/America Inc 800 343-3618
655 Andover St Lawrence MA (01843) ***(G-11996)***
ASAP, Dudley *Also called Americansub* ***(G-10372)***
ASAP Machine Sp & Fabrication 860 564-4114
89 Mill Brook Rd Plainfield CT (06374) ***(G-3450)***
ASC Duplicating Inc 802 229-0660
407 Barre St 1 Montpelier VT (05602) ***(G-22145)***
Asca Inc (PA) 603 433-6700
112 Corporate Dr Ste 1 Portsmouth NH (03801) ***(G-19539)***
Ascend Elevator Inc 215 703-0358
212 W Newberry Rd Bloomfield CT (06002) ***(G-205)***
Ascend Robotics LLC 978 451-0170
245 First St Ste 18 Cambridge MA (02142) ***(G-9393)***
Ascension Technology Corp 802 893-6657
120 Graham Way Ste 130 Shelburne VT (05482) ***(G-22411)***
Ascent Aerosystems LLC 330 554-6334
1061 East St Tewksbury MA (01876) ***(G-15806)***
Asco Power Technologies LP 508 624-0466
2 Maple St Marlborough MA (01752) ***(G-12720)***
Asct LLC 860 349-1121
30 Ozick Dr Durham CT (06422) ***(G-1087)***
Asd Lighting Corp 781 739-3977
120 Shawmut Rd Canton MA (02021) ***(G-9717)***
Asd-Lighting Corp 781 739-3977
625 University Ave Norwood MA (02062) ***(G-14135)***
Ase, Orange *Also called American Seal and Engrg Co Inc* ***(G-3358)***
Ase (us) Inc 781 305-5900
18 Commerce Way Ste 2900 Woburn MA (01801) ***(G-17123)***
Asea Brown Boveri Inc (HQ) 203 750-2200
501 Merritt 7 Norwalk CT (06851) ***(G-3105)***
Ashametrics Inc 617 694-1428
1035 Cambridge St Ste 8 Cambridge MA (02141) ***(G-9394)***
Ashaway Cement Products Inc 401 539-1010
65 Stilson Rd Wyoming RI (02898) ***(G-21588)***
Ashaway Line & Twine Mfg Co 401 377-2221
24 Laurel St Ashaway RI (02804) ***(G-20031)***
Ashcroft Inc (HQ) 203 378-8281
250 E Main St Stratford CT (06614) ***(G-4392)***
Ashcroft Inc 203 378-8281
250 E Main St Stratford CT (06614) ***(G-4393)***
Ashe America Inc 802 254-0200
23 Marlboro Rd Brattleboro VT (05301) ***(G-21718)***
Ashe Converting Equipment, Brattleboro *Also called Ashe America Inc* ***(G-21718)***
Ashland Cabinet Corp 508 303-8100
7 Turnpike Rd Southborough MA (01772) ***(G-15343)***
Ashland Electric Products Inc 603 335-1100
10 Indl Way Rochester NH (03867) ***(G-19659)***
Ashland LLC 508 235-7164
238 S Main St Assonet MA (02702) ***(G-7676)***
Ashleigh Inc (PA) 207 967-4311
8 Western Ave Ste 6 Kennebunk ME (04043) ***(G-6228)***
Ashley & Harmon Logging Inc 207 259-2043
230 Chases Mill Rd East Machias ME (04630) ***(G-5982)***
Ashmont Welding Company Inc 508 279-1977
10 Cranmore Dr Bridgewater MA (02324) ***(G-9060)***
Ashworth Assoc Mfg Whl Jwelers 508 695-1900
41 Richards Ave North Attleboro MA (02760) ***(G-13747)***
Ashworth Awards, North Attleboro *Also called Ashworth Assoc Mfg Whl Jwelers* ***(G-13747)***
Ashworth Bros Inc (PA) 508 674-4693
222 Milliken Blvd Ste 7 Fall River MA (02721) ***(G-10663)***
Ashworth International Inc 508 674-4693
222 Milliken Blvd Ste 7 Fall River MA (02721) ***(G-10664)***

Asi Modulex, East Berlin *Also called Wad Inc* ***(G-1110)***
Asi Sign Systems Inc 860 828-3331
100 Clark Dr East Berlin CT (06023) ***(G-1097)***
Asia Direct LLC 603 382-9485
91 Main St Ste 14 Plaistow NH (03865) ***(G-19507)***
Asian Art Society New England 781 250-6311
50 Old Orchard Rd Sherborn MA (01770) ***(G-15077)***
Asiana Noodle Shop 802 862-8828
88 Church St Burlington VT (05401) ***(G-21767)***
Asimov Inc 425 750-4182
700 Main St Cambridge MA (02139) ***(G-9395)***
Ask Services, North Kingstown *Also called Lightship Group LLC* ***(G-20723)***
Ask-Inttag LLC 802 288-7210
1000 River St Bldg 966d Essex Junction VT (05452) ***(G-21929)***
Askcody Inc 617 455-2075
745 Atlantic Ave Ste 100 Boston MA (02111) ***(G-8377)***
Asm Nexx Inc 978 436-4600
900 Middlesex Tpke Billerica MA (01821) ***(G-8214)***
Asml Us LLC 203 761-4000
77 Danbury Rd Wilton CT (06897) ***(G-5275)***
Aspect Inc 617 713-2813
50 Kenwood St Brookline MA (02446) ***(G-9194)***
Aspect Software Inc 978 250-7900
300 Apollo Dr Ste 1 Chelmsford MA (01824) ***(G-9873)***
Aspects Inc 401 247-1854
245 Child St Warren RI (02885) ***(G-21286)***
Aspell Saggers LLC 508 216-3264
60 James St North Attleboro MA (02760) ***(G-13748)***
Aspen Aerogels Inc (PA) 508 691-1111
30 Forbes Rd Bldg B Northborough MA (01532) ***(G-14029)***
Aspen Aerogels Inc 401 432-2612
3 Dexter Rd East Providence RI (02914) ***(G-20388)***
Aspen Aerogels RI LLC 401 432-2612
3 Dexter Rd East Providence RI (02914) ***(G-20389)***
Aspen Compressor LLC 508 281-5322
24 Saint Martin Dr Ste 2 Marlborough MA (01752) ***(G-12721)***
Aspen Products Group Inc 508 481-5058
184 Cedar Hill St Marlborough MA (01752) ***(G-12722)***
Aspen Systems, Marlborough *Also called Aspen Compressor LLC* ***(G-12721)***
Asphalt Recovery Tech LLC 603 778-1449
50 Pine Rd Brentwood NH (03833) ***(G-17744)***
Aspmd 617 864-6844
38 8th St Apt 5 Cambridge MA (02141) ***(G-9396)***
Assa Inc (HQ) 203 624-5225
110 Sargent Dr New Haven CT (06511) ***(G-2659)***
Assa Inc 800 235-7482
110 Sargent Dr New Haven CT (06511) ***(G-2660)***
Assa Abloy Accss & Edrss Hrdwr 860 225-7411
225 Episcopal Rd Berlin CT (06037) ***(G-73)***
Assa Abloy Entrance Sys US Inc 508 368-2600
1 A St 2b Auburn MA (01501) ***(G-7827)***
Assa Abloy Inc., New Haven *Also called Assa Inc* ***(G-2659)***
Assa Abloy USA, New Haven *Also called Sargent Manufacturing Company* ***(G-2735)***
Assa High Security Locks, New Haven *Also called Assa Inc* ***(G-2660)***
Assabet Machine Corp 978 562-7992
1145 Massachusetts Ave Boxborough MA (01719) ***(G-8959)***
Assayquant Technologies Inc 774 278-3302
260 Cedar Hill St Marlborough MA (01752) ***(G-12723)***
Assembly Guidance Systems Inc 978 244-1166
27 Industrial Ave Unit 4 Chelmsford MA (01824) ***(G-9874)***
Assembly Specialists Inc 603 624-9563
8030 S Willow St Unit 3-4 Manchester NH (03103) ***(G-18780)***
Associated Envmtl Systems, Acton *Also called Associated Envmtl Systems Inc* ***(G-7342)***
Associated Envmtl Systems Inc (PA) 978 772-0022
8 Post Office Sq Acton MA (01720) ***(G-7342)***
Associated Power Products, Newton *Also called Mega-Power Inc* ***(G-13613)***
Associated Training Svcs LLC 603 772-9002
5 Industrial Dr Brentwood NH (03833) ***(G-17745)***
Associated Training Svcs of NW, Brentwood *Also called Associated Training Svcs LLC* ***(G-17745)***
Associates of Cape Cod Inc (PA) 508 540-3444
124 Bernard E Saint Jean East Falmouth MA (02536) ***(G-10435)***
Assoction For Grvstone Studies 413 772-0836
278 Main St Ste 209 Greenfield MA (01301) ***(G-11251)***
Assonet Industries Inc 508 644-5001
17 Mill St Assonet MA (02702) ***(G-7677)***
Assurance Technology Corp 978 250-8060
303 Littleton Rd Chelmsford MA (01824) ***(G-9875)***
Assured Computing Technologies 603 627-8728
19 Harvey Rd Unit 13-15 Bedford NH (03110) ***(G-17631)***
Assuretec Holdings Inc (PA) 603 641-8443
62 Lowell St Ste 4 Manchester NH (03101) ***(G-18781)***
AST, Cambridge *Also called Adaptive Surface Tech Inc* ***(G-9373)***
Astenjohnson Inc 413 733-6603
40 Progress Ave Springfield MA (01104) ***(G-15448)***
Astenjohnson Inc 802 658-2040
192 Industrial Ave Williston VT (05495) ***(G-22655)***
Aster Enterprises Inc 978 264-0499
6 Eastern Rd Acton MA (01720) ***(G-7343)***

ALPHABETIC

Asterisk Typographics Inc ...802 476-8399
70 Smith St Barre VT (05641) ***(G-21608)***
Asti Company Inc ...860 482-2675
953 S Main St Torrington CT (06790) ***(G-4563)***
Astonish Results LP ...401 921-6220
300 Metro Center Blvd Warwick RI (02886) ***(G-21328)***
Astralite Inc ...203 775-0172
20 Pocono Rd Brookfield CT (06804) ***(G-634)***
Astro Aircom LLC ...860 688-3320
25 Northwood Dr Bloomfield CT (06002) ***(G-206)***
Astro Industries Inc ...860 828-6304
819 Farmington Ave Unit A Berlin CT (06037) ***(G-74)***
Astron Inc (PA) ...978 433-9500
21 Lomar Park Pepperell MA (01463) ***(G-14436)***
Astronics Aerosat Corporation ...603 879-0205
220 Hackett Hill Rd Manchester NH (03102) ***(G-18782)***
Astronova Inc (PA) ...401 828-4000
600 E Greenwich Ave West Warwick RI (02893) ***(G-21479)***
Astronova Inc ...401 828-4000
600 E Greenwich Ave West Warwick RI (02893) ***(G-21480)***
Asure Software Inc ...512 437-2700
30 Robert W Boyden Rd 500b Taunton MA (02780) ***(G-15727)***
Asylum Distillery ...203 209-0146
105 Waterville Rd Southport CT (06890) ***(G-4093)***
Asymmetrical Defense LLC ...978 597-6078
155 N End Rd Townsend MA (01469) ***(G-15868)***
At Comm Corp ...603 624-4424
150 Dow St Ste 404 Manchester NH (03101) ***(G-18783)***
AT Wall Company (HQ) ...401 739-0740
55 Service Ave Warwick RI (02886) ***(G-21329)***
AT&T Inc ...781 878-8169
10 Washington St Norwell MA (02061) ***(G-14095)***
Ata Piping, Windham *Also called Wardwell Piping Inc* ***(G-7259)***
Ataccama Corp US ...203 564-1488
263 Tresser Blvd Fl 9 Stamford CT (06901) ***(G-4145)***
Atamian Manufacturing Corp ...800 286-9614
910 Plainfield St Providence RI (02909) ***(G-20959)***
Atc Group Services LLC ...802 862-1980
171 Commerce St Williston VT (05495) ***(G-22656)***
Atc Group Services LLC ...337 234-8777
73 William Frank Dr West Springfield MA (01089) ***(G-16509)***
Atc Information Inc ...617 723-7030
85 E India Row Apt 16c Boston MA (02110) ***(G-8378)***
Atc Ponderosa B-I LLC ...617 375-7500
116 Huntington Ave Boston MA (02116) ***(G-8379)***
Atc Ponderosa K LLC ...617 375-7500
116 Huntington Ave Boston MA (02116) ***(G-8380)***
Atc Power Systems Inc ...603 429-0391
45 Depot St Merrimack NH (03054) ***(G-18985)***
Atc Screw Machine Inc ...781 939-0725
419 River St Haverhill MA (01832) ***(G-11406)***
Atc Technologies Inc (PA) ...781 939-0725
30b Upton Dr Wilmington MA (01887) ***(G-16975)***
Atco Lanair, Portsmouth *Also called Lanair Research & Development* ***(G-19584)***
Atco Plastics Inc ...508 695-3573
31 W Bacon St Plainville MA (02762) ***(G-14515)***
Atco-Aircraft Technical Co ...603 433-0081
521 Shattuck Way Ste 1 Newington NH (03801) ***(G-19321)***
Atec ...401 782-6950
214 High St Wakefield RI (02879) ***(G-21267)***
Atech Designs Inc ...603 926-8216
77 Spur Rd Dover NH (03820) ***(G-18006)***
Atech Industries LLC ...203 887-4900
879 Robert Treat Ext Orange CT (06477) ***(G-3359)***
Aternity Inc ...508 475-0414
200 Friberg Pkwy Ste 1004 Westborough MA (01581) ***(G-16590)***
Atfo, Westport *Also called American Trade Fairs Org* ***(G-5182)***
Atfsi, Hampstead *Also called Atkinson Thin Film Systems* ***(G-18236)***
Atg, Cambridge *Also called Oracle Otc Subsidiary LLC* ***(G-9603)***
Athan's Bakery, Brighton *Also called Athans Inc* ***(G-9095)***
Athans Inc ...617 783-0313
407 Washington St Brighton MA (02135) ***(G-9095)***
Athenahealth Inc (HQ) ...617 402-1000
311 Arsenal St Ste 14 Watertown MA (02472) ***(G-16270)***
Athens Industries Inc ...860 621-8957
220 West St Plantsville CT (06479) ***(G-3527)***
Athigo ...617 410-8834
61 Chapel St Newton MA (02458) ***(G-13564)***
Athletic Emblem & Lettering Co ...413 734-0415
189 Taylor St Springfield MA (01105) ***(G-15449)***
Athletic Innovation Inc ...603 332-1212
54 Allen St Ste 2 Rochester NH (03867) ***(G-19660)***
Athol Daily News, Athol *Also called Athol Press Inc* ***(G-7684)***
Athol Press Inc ...978 249-3535
225 Exchange St Athol MA (01331) ***(G-7684)***
Athol Screw Machine Products ...978 249-8072
123 New Athol Rd Orange MA (01364) ***(G-14213)***
ATI, Pawtucket *Also called Accu-Tool Inc* ***(G-20806)***
ATI Flat Rlled Pdts Hldngs LLC ...203 756-7414
271 Railroad Hill St Waterbury CT (06708) ***(G-4847)***
ATI Flowform Products LLC ...978 667-0202
12 Suburban Park Dr Billerica MA (01821) ***(G-8215)***
ATI Forged Products, East Hartford *Also called ATI Ladish Machining Inc* ***(G-1174)***
ATI Ladish Machining Inc (HQ) ...860 688-3688
311 Prestige Park Rd East Hartford CT (06108) ***(G-1174)***
ATI Ladish Machining Inc ...860 688-3688
34 S Satellite Rd South Windsor CT (06074) ***(G-3939)***
ATI Ladish Machining Inc ...860 688-3688
311 Prestige Park Rd East Hartford CT (06108) ***(G-1175)***
ATI Specialty Materials, New Britain *Also called Tdy Industries LLC* ***(G-2586)***
Atiim Inc ...800 735-4071
399 Boylston St Fl 6 Boston MA (02116) ***(G-8381)***
Atk Space Systems Inc ...508 497-9457
65 South St Ste 105 Hopkinton MA (01748) ***(G-11692)***
Atkinson Thin Film Systems ...603 329-7322
25 Garland Dr Hampstead NH (03841) ***(G-18236)***
Atlantic Air Products Mfg LLC ...603 410-3900
814 Route 3a Bow NH (03304) ***(G-17707)***
Atlantic Animal Health Inc ...781 289-9600
100 Mill St Revere MA (02151) ***(G-14763)***
Atlantic Atm LLC ...978 356-4051
383 Linebrook Rd Ipswich MA (01938) ***(G-11903)***
Atlantic Auto & Trck Parts LLC ...978 535-6777
245 Newbury St Rm 1 Peabody MA (01960) ***(G-14314)***
Atlantic Blanket Company Inc ...207 338-9691
231 Atlantic Hwy Northport ME (04849) ***(G-6520)***
Atlantic Boat Company ...207 664-2900
Flye Point Rd Brooklin ME (04616) ***(G-5813)***
Atlantic Bookbinders Inc ...978 365-4524
87 Flagg St South Lancaster MA (01561) ***(G-15315)***
Atlantic Braiding Machinery, Warwick *Also called Windmill Associates Inc* ***(G-21448)***
Atlantic Brewing Company, Bar Harbor *Also called Salisbury Cove Associates Inc* ***(G-5669)***
Atlantic Coastal Printing Inc ...207 284-4328
321 Elm St Ste 1 Biddeford ME (04005) ***(G-5719)***
Atlantic Cotton Company, Portland *Also called Atlantic Sportswear Inc* ***(G-6612)***
Atlantic Eqp Installers Inc ...203 284-0402
55 N Plains Industrial Rd Wallingford CT (06492) ***(G-4705)***
Atlantic Fabricating Co Inc ...860 291-9882
71 Edwin Rd South Windsor CT (06074) ***(G-3940)***
Atlantic Footcare Inc ...401 568-4918
229 Quaker Hwy Apt 3 North Smithfield RI (02896) ***(G-20782)***
Atlantic Fuels, Rye *Also called Nas Fuels LLC* ***(G-19699)***
Atlantic Hardchrome Ltd ...207 645-4300
128 Weld Rd Ste 4 Wilton ME (04294) ***(G-7224)***
Atlantic Industrial Models LLC ...978 768-7686
7 Essex Park Rd Essex MA (01929) ***(G-10591)***
Atlantic Inertial Systems, Cheshire *Also called Ais Global Holdings LLC* ***(G-709)***
Atlantic Inertial Systems Inc (HQ) ...203 250-3500
250 Knotter Dr Cheshire CT (06410) ***(G-713)***
Atlantic Inertial Systems Inc ...203 250-3500
250 Knotter Dr Cheshire CT (06410) ***(G-714)***
Atlantic Laboratories Inc ...207 832-5376
41 Cross St Waldoboro ME (04572) ***(G-7131)***
Atlantic Laser Clinic ...207 854-8200
433 Us Route 1 Ste 209 York ME (03909) ***(G-7305)***
Atlantic Lighting Inc ...508 678-5411
231 Commerce Dr Fall River MA (02720) ***(G-10665)***
Atlantic MBL & Gran Group Inc ...508 540-9770
59 Technology Park Dr East Falmouth MA (02536) ***(G-10436)***
Atlantic Metalcraft Co ...781 447-9900
14 Cooney Ln Middleboro MA (02346) ***(G-13054)***
Atlantic Microtool, Atkinson *Also called Cogent Mfg Solutions LLC* ***(G-17603)***
Atlantic Microtool ...603 898-3212
91 Stiles Rd Ste 207 Salem NH (03079) ***(G-19710)***
Atlantic Millwork, North Haven *Also called Elm City Manufacturing LLC* ***(G-3024)***
Atlantic Pipe Corporation ...860 747-5557
60 N Washington St Plainville CT (06062) ***(G-3466)***
Atlantic Poly Inc ...781 769-4260
86 Morse St Norwood MA (02062) ***(G-14136)***
Atlantic Power GP Inc ...617 977-2400
200 Clarendon St Ste 2502 Boston MA (02116) ***(G-8382)***
Atlantic Precision Spring Inc ...860 583-1864
125 Ronzo Rd Bristol CT (06010) ***(G-522)***
Atlantic Prefab Inc (PA) ...603 668-2648
19 Stoney Brook Dr Wilton NH (03086) ***(G-19975)***
Atlantic Printing Co Inc ...781 449-2700
5 Causeway Ln Medfield MA (02052) ***(G-12909)***
Atlantic Pwr Enrgy Svcs US LLC ...617 977-2400
3 Allied Dr Ste 155 Dedham MA (02026) ***(G-10280)***
Atlantic RES Mktg Systems Inc ...508 584-7816
230 W Center St West Bridgewater MA (02379) ***(G-16429)***
Atlantic Rubber Company Inc ...800 882-3666
37 Ayer Rd Ste 6 Littleton MA (01460) ***(G-12294)***
Atlantic Sensors & Contrls LLC ...203 878-8118
301 Brewster Rd Milford CT (06460) ***(G-2246)***
Atlantic Sports International ...603 835-6948
157 Village Rd Langdon NH (03602) ***(G-18610)***

Atlantic Sportswear Inc.....207 797-5028
36 Waldron Way Portland ME (04103) ***(G-6612)***
Atlantic Standard Molding Inc.....207 797-0727
380 Warren Ave Apt 2 Portland ME (04103) ***(G-6613)***
Atlantic Steel Fabricators Inc.....978 657-8292
238 Andover St Wilmington MA (01887) ***(G-16976)***
Atlantic Tool Company.....781 331-5550
18 Station St Weymouth MA (02189) ***(G-16884)***
Atlantic Turtle Top Inc.....508 839-1711
127 Ferry St South Grafton MA (01560) ***(G-15296)***
Atlantic Vision Inc.....508 845-8401
810 Boston Tpke Ste 2 Shrewsbury MA (01545) ***(G-15103)***
Atlantic Water Management.....401 397-8200
51 Fieldstone Dr Coventry RI (02816) ***(G-20137)***
Atlantic Wood & Cabinet Works.....207 885-0767
94 Broadturn Rd Scarborough ME (04074) ***(G-6905)***
Atlantic Woodcraft Inc.....860 749-4887
199 Moody Rd Enfield CT (06082) ***(G-1347)***
Atlantis Technology Corp.....978 341-0999
1620 Sudbury Rd Ste 1 Concord MA (01742) ***(G-10114)***
Atlantis Woodworking Inc.....978 745-5312
283 Derby St Salem MA (01970) ***(G-14894)***
Atlas Agi Holdings LLC.....203 622-9138
100 Northfield St Greenwich CT (06830) ***(G-1594)***
Atlas Atm Corp.....401 421-4183
1106 N Main St Providence RI (02904) ***(G-20960)***
Atlas Barrell & Pallet Inc.....401 568-2900
50 Old Mill St Harrisville RI (02830) ***(G-20477)***
Atlas Box and Crating Co Inc (PA).....508 865-1155
223 Wrcster Prvdence Tpke Sutton MA (01590) ***(G-15679)***
Atlas Brass & Aluminum Co.....413 732-4604
139 Meadow St Westfield MA (01085) ***(G-16668)***
Atlas Copco Compressors LLC.....518 765-3344
94 N Elm St Fl 4 Westfield MA (01085) ***(G-16669)***
Atlas Copco Compressors LLC.....413 493-7290
92 Interstate Dr West Springfield MA (01089) ***(G-16510)***
Atlas Devices LLC.....617 415-1657
56 Roland St Ste 114 Boston MA (02129) ***(G-8383)***
Atlas Distributing Inc.....508 791-6221
44 Southbridge St Auburn MA (01501) ***(G-7828)***
Atlas Fabrication Inc.....401 861-4911
491 Silver Spring St Providence RI (02904) ***(G-20961)***
Atlas Filtri North America LLC.....203 284-0080
1068 N Farms Rd Ste 3 Wallingford CT (06492) ***(G-4706)***
Atlas Founders Inc.....413 786-4210
90 Industrial Ln Agawam MA (01001) ***(G-7420)***
Atlas Global Ltg Solutions Inc (PA).....617 304-3264
338 Commercial St Boston MA (02109) ***(G-8384)***
Atlas Global Solutions, Sutton *Also called Atlas Box and Crating Co Inc* ***(G-15679)***
Atlas Hobbing and Tool Co Inc.....860 870-9226
20 Mountain St Vernon Rockville CT (06066) ***(G-4678)***
Atlas Industrial Services LLC.....203 315-4538
30 Ne Industrial Rd Branford CT (06405) ***(G-290)***
Atlas Machine Tool Inc.....508 284-3542
18 Sargent St Ste 1 Gloucester MA (01930) ***(G-11161)***
Atlas Metal Works LLC.....860 282-1030
48 Commerce Way South Windsor CT (06074) ***(G-3941)***
Atlas Metallizing Inc.....860 827-9777
5 East St New Britain CT (06051) ***(G-2510)***
Atlas Precision Mfg LLC.....860 290-9114
508 Burnham St South Windsor CT (06074) ***(G-3942)***
Atlas Press Worcester Inc.....508 835-9440
211 Shrewsbury St Ste 1 West Boylston MA (01583) ***(G-16409)***
Atlas Pyrovision Entertainment (PA).....603 532-8324
136 Old Sharon Rd Jaffrey NH (03452) ***(G-18457)***
Atlas Screen Process, Webster *Also called Jaf Corporation* ***(G-16344)***
Atlas Stamping & Mfg Corp.....860 757-3233
729 N Mountain Rd Newington CT (06111) ***(G-2844)***
Atlee Corp.....978 681-1003
30 Commerce Way Ste 2 Tewksbury MA (01876) ***(G-15807)***
Atlee Delaware Incorporated.....978 681-1003
9 Clinton Rd Melrose MA (02176) ***(G-12975)***
Atmi, Inc., Danbury *Also called Entegris Prof Solutions Inc* ***(G 913)***
Atmosair, Fairfield *Also called Clean Air Group Inc* ***(G-1420)***
Atoll-Bio USA Inc.....978 281-4595
468 Washington St Gloucester MA (01930) ***(G-11162)***
Atom Adhesives.....401 413-9902
226 S Main St Providence RI (02903) ***(G-20962)***
Atom Marketing Inc (PA).....781 982-9930
127 American Elm Ave Hanover MA (02339) ***(G-11327)***
Atomic Cafe (PA).....978 910-0489
45 Mason St Ste 1 Salem MA (01970) ***(G-14895)***
Atomic Led Inc.....401 265-0222
81 W Greenville Rd Greenville RI (02828) ***(G-20462)***
Atp Industries LLC (PA).....860 479-5007
75 Northwest Dr Plainville CT (06062) ***(G-3467)***
Atrenne Cmpt Solutions LLC (HQ).....508 588-6110
10 Mupac Dr Brockton MA (02301) ***(G-9121)***
Atrenne Cmpt Solutions LLC.....508 588-6110
11 Burke Dr Brockton MA (02301) ***(G-9122)***
Atrex Energy Inc (PA).....781 461-8251
19 Walpole Park S Walpole MA (02081) ***(G-15988)***
Atrium Medical Corporation (HQ).....603 880-1433
40 Continental Blvd Merrimack NH (03054) ***(G-18986)***
Atrium Medical Corporation.....603 880-1433
29 Flagstone Dr Hudson NH (03051) ***(G-18375)***
Ats Finishing Inc.....978 975-0957
2350 Turnpike St North Andover MA (01845) ***(G-13692)***
Ats Precision, New Hampton *Also called Alan T Seeler Inc* ***(G-19301)***
Attar Software USA, Newburyport *Also called Renaissance International* ***(G-13529)***
Atticus Bakery LLC.....203 562-9007
360 James St New Haven CT (06513) ***(G-2661)***
Attivio Inc.....857 226-5040
100 Summer St Ste 3150 Boston MA (02110) ***(G-8385)***
Attleboro Pancakes Inc.....508 399-8189
383 Washington St Attleboro MA (02703) ***(G-7707)***
Attleboro Sand & Gravel Corp.....508 222-2870
125 Tiffany St Attleboro MA (02703) ***(G-7708)***
Attleboro Scholarship Co.....508 226-4414
89 N Main St Attleboro MA (02703) ***(G-7709)***
ATW Companies Inc (PA).....401 244-1002
125 Metro Center Blvd # 3001 Warwick RI (02886) ***(G-21330)***
ATW Electronics Inc.....617 304-3579
24 Spice St Ste 2 Charlestown MA (02129) ***(G-9824)***
Au New Haven LLC.....203 468-0342
30 Lenox St New Haven CT (06513) ***(G-2662)***
Au Soleil.....617 535-6040
711 Boylston St Ste 5 Boston MA (02116) ***(G-8386)***
Aube Precision Tool Co Inc.....413 589-9048
54 Moody St Ludlow MA (01056) ***(G-12454)***
Auburn Filtersense LLC.....978 777-2460
800 Cummings Ctr Ste 355w Beverly MA (01915) ***(G-8103)***
Auburn International Inc.....978 777-2460
800 Cummings Ctr Ste 355w Beverly MA (01915) ***(G-8104)***
Auburn Manufacturing Company.....860 346-6677
29 Stack St Middletown CT (06457) ***(G-2173)***
Auburn Manufacturing Inc.....207 345-8271
5125 Walker Rd Mechanic Falls ME (04256) ***(G-6417)***
Auburn Manufacturing Inc (PA).....207 345-8271
34 Walker Rd Mechanic Falls ME (04256) ***(G-6418)***
Auburn Systems LLC.....978 777-2460
800 Cummings Ctr Ste 355w Beverly MA (01915) ***(G-8105)***
Auciello Iron Works Inc (PA).....978 568-8382
560 Main St Ste 6 Hudson MA (01749) ***(G-11758)***
Aucoins Press Inc.....508 885-0800
104 Main St Spencer MA (01562) ***(G-15425)***
Aucoins Printing.....508 885-3595
37 Mcdonald St Spencer MA (01562) ***(G-15426)***
Audette Group LLC.....401 667-5884
144 Westminster St # 302 Providence RI (02903) ***(G-20963)***
Audio Accessories Inc.....603 446-3335
25 Mill St Marlow NH (03456) ***(G-18965)***
Audio File Publications Inc.....207 774-7563
37 Silver St Portland ME (04101) ***(G-6614)***
Audio Line, Marlow *Also called Audio Accessories Inc* ***(G-18965)***
Audio Video Designs.....508 325-9989
9 Windy Way Nantucket MA (02554) ***(G-13220)***
Audiofile Magazine, Portland *Also called Audio File Publications Inc* ***(G-6614)***
Audioworks Inc.....203 876-1133
260 Old Gate Ln Milford CT (06460) ***(G-2247)***
Audubon Copy Shppe of Firfield.....203 259-4311
540 Barnum Ave Ste 4 Bridgeport CT (06608) ***(G-378)***
Auger Electric LLC.....603 335-5633
25 Hampshire Ave Rochester NH (03867) ***(G-19661)***
Aunt Sadies Inc.....802 892-5267
108 S Lunenburg Rd Lunenburg VT (05906) ***(G-22066)***
Auriga Measurement Systems.....978 452-7700
2 Executive Dr Chelmsford MA (01824) ***(G-9876)***
Auriga Measurement Systems (PA).....978 452-7700
302 Willow Brook Dr Wayland MA (01778) ***(G-16334)***
Auriga Microwave, Wayland *Also called Auriga Measurement Systems* ***(G-16334)***
Auriga Piv Tech Inc.....603 402-2955
30 Daniel Webster Hwy Merrimack NH (03054) ***(G-18987)***
Aurora Biosystems LLC.....603 766-1947
1 New Hampshire Ave Portsmouth NH (03801) ***(G-19540)***
Aurora Flight Sciences Corp.....617 500-4800
150 Cambridgepark Dr Fl 4 Cambridge MA (02140) ***(G-9397)***
Aurora Fuel Company Inc.....401 345-5996
191 Pulaski St West Warwick RI (02893) ***(G-21481)***
Aurora Fuel Company Inc.....401 821-5996
92 Pond St West Warwick RI (02893) ***(G-21482)***
Aurora Healthcare US Corp.....978 204-5240
8 Electronics Ave Ste 1 Danvers MA (01923) ***(G-10197)***
Aurora Imaging Technology Inc (PA).....877 975-7530
8 Electronics Ave Ste 1 Danvers MA (01923) ***(G-10198)***
Aurora Imaging Technology Inc.....617 522-6900
165 Worcester St Wellesley MA (02481) ***(G-16361)***
Aurora North Software Inc.....802 540-2504
29 Church St Ste 303 Burlington VT (05401) ***(G-21768)***
Aurora Plastics, Lunenburg *Also called S&E Specialty Polymers LLC* ***(G-12483)***

Aurora Wind Project LLC..........978 409-9712
100 Brdgestone Sq Ste 300 Andover MA (01810) ***(G-7538)***
Austin Electronics, Chester *Also called Whelen Engineering Company Inc* ***(G-778)***
Austin Hard Chrome..........401 421-0840
57 Sprague St Providence RI (02907) ***(G-20964)***
Austin Machine & Fabrication, Sanford *Also called Jr Robert Austin* ***(G-6878)***
Austin Medical Products Inc..........603 356-7004
66 Eastern Ave Center Conway NH (03813) ***(G-17792)***
Austin Merrill..........207 219-0593
162 Pleasant Hill Rd Scarborough ME (04074) ***(G-6906)***
Austin Organs Incorporated..........860 522-8293
156 Woodland St Hartford CT (06105) ***(G-1808)***
Austin Powder Company..........860 564-5466
332 Ekonk Hill Rd Sterling CT (06377) ***(G-4365)***
Austin Print..........978 369-8591
23 Allen Farm Ln Concord MA (01742) ***(G-10115)***
Austin Rubber Stamps, Kensington *Also called Academy Printing Service* ***(G-1916)***
Austrian Machine Corp..........401 946-4090
25 Stamp Farm Rd Cranston RI (02921) ***(G-20184)***
Autac Incorporated (PA)..........203 481-3444
25 Thompson Rd Branford CT (06405) ***(G-291)***
Autac Incorporated..........203 481-3444
25 Thompson Rd Branford CT (06405) ***(G-292)***
Autajon Packg - Boston Corp..........603 595-0700
100 Northwest Blvd Nashua NH (03063) ***(G-19118)***
Authentic Designs Inc..........802 394-7715
154 Mill Rd West Rupert VT (05776) ***(G-22614)***
Authentic Log Homes Inc..........802 472-5096
1670 Craftsbury Rd Hardwick VT (05843) ***(G-22009)***
Autism Support Daily..........802 985-8773
42 Oakhill Rd Shelburne VT (05482) ***(G-22412)***
Auto Body Supplies and Paint..........508 791-4111
90 Washington St Worcester MA (01610) ***(G-17343)***
Auto Chlor Systems Co, Foxboro *Also called Conopco Inc* ***(G-10880)***
Auto Electric Service LLC..........603 642-5990
191 Crawley Falls Rd A8 Brentwood NH (03833) ***(G-17746)***
Auto Hunter Magazine, Saugus *Also called Hunter Associates Inc* ***(G-14986)***
Auto Industrial Machine Inc..........978 777-3772
3 Electronics Ave Ste 2 Danvers MA (01923) ***(G-10199)***
Auto Merchandising Depot, Weston *Also called Automotive Coop Couponing Inc* ***(G-5169)***
Auto Suture Company Australia..........203 845-1000
150 Glover Ave Norwalk CT (06850) ***(G-3106)***
Auto Suture Company UK..........203 845-1000
150 Glover Ave Norwalk CT (06850) ***(G-3107)***
Auto Suture Russia Inc..........203 845-1000
150 Glover Ave Norwalk CT (06850) ***(G-3108)***
Auto-Chlor System NY Cy Inc..........508 543-6767
140 Washington St Ste 1 Foxboro MA (02035) ***(G-10876)***
Auto-Lock Broadhead Co LLC..........603 895-0502
59 Batchelder Rd Raymond NH (03077) ***(G-19634)***
Auto/Truck Repair, Groveton *Also called Caron Fabrication LLC* ***(G-18231)***
Autocam Medical Inc..........508 830-1442
24 Aldrin Rd Plymouth MA (02360) ***(G-14543)***
Autocrat Coffee, Lincoln *Also called Finlay EXT Ingredients USA Inc* ***(G-20574)***
Autodesk Inc..........855 646-4868
120 Washington St Ste 202 Salem MA (01970) ***(G-14896)***
Autogen Inc..........508 429-5965
84 October Hill Rd Ste 5 Holliston MA (01746) ***(G-11557)***
Automatech Inc..........860 673-5940
21 Westview Ter Unionville CT (06085) ***(G-4653)***
Automatech Inc (PA)..........508 830-0088
138 Industrial Park Rd Plymouth MA (02360) ***(G-14544)***
Automated Finishing Co Inc..........508 222-6262
90 County St Attleboro MA (02703) ***(G-7710)***
Automated Industrial Mch Inc..........401 232-1710
347 Farnum Pike Smithfield RI (02917) ***(G-21210)***
Automatic Findings..........401 781-4810
19 5th Ave Cranston RI (02910) ***(G-20185)***
Automatic Machine Pdts Sls Co..........508 822-4226
400 Constitution Dr Taunton MA (02780) ***(G-15728)***
Automatic Machine Products..........860 346-7064
40 Liberty St Middletown CT (06457) ***(G-2174)***
Automatic Machine Products Co..........508 822-4226
400 Constitution Dr Taunton MA (02780) ***(G-15729)***
Automatic Rolls of New England, Dayville *Also called Northeast Foods Inc* ***(G-1049)***
Automatic Specialties Inc..........508 481-2370
422 Northboro Rd Central Marlborough MA (01752) ***(G-12724)***
Automation Inc..........860 236-5991
707 Oakwood Ave West Hartford CT (06110) ***(G-5054)***
Automec Inc..........781 893-3403
82 Calvary St Waltham MA (02453) ***(G-16039)***
Automotive & Miniature Ltg, Hillsborough *Also called Osram Sylvania Inc* ***(G-18317)***
Automotive Coop Couponing Inc..........203 227-2722
27 Cardinal Rd Weston CT (06883) ***(G-5169)***
Automotive Mach Shop Sup..........508 586-6706
630 N Main St West Bridgewater MA (02379) ***(G-16430)***
Autospool, Bristol *Also called HMC Holding Corporation* ***(G-20084)***
Autotech Inc..........802 497-2482
246 Main St Winooski VT (05404) ***(G-22716)***
Autotronics LLC (PA)..........207 543-6262
129 Us Route 1 Frenchville ME (04745) ***(G-6090)***
Autovirt Inc..........603 546-2900
12 Murphy Dr Nashua NH (03062) ***(G-19119)***
Autumn Harp Inc..........802 453-4807
61 Pine St Bristol VT (05443) ***(G-21761)***
Autumn Rose Quarry, Graniteville *Also called Rock of Ages Corporation* ***(G-22002)***
Autumn-Harp Inc..........802 857-4600
26 Thompson Dr Essex Junction VT (05452) ***(G-21930)***
AV Medical Technologies Inc..........612 200-0118
20 Ryans Ln Duxbury MA (02332) ***(G-10392)***
Ava Anderson, Johnston *Also called Phe Investments LLC* ***(G-20529)***
Avacea..........617 294-0261
102 Edith St Everett MA (02149) ***(G-10603)***
Avalanche Downhill Racing Inc..........860 537-4306
12 Davidson Rd Colchester CT (06415) ***(G-799)***
Avalon Advanced Tech Repr Inc..........860 254-5442
59 Newberry Rd East Windsor CT (06088) ***(G-1277)***
Avantgarde Molecular LLC..........617 549-2238
63 Great Rd Ste 107 Maynard MA (01754) ***(G-12895)***
Avanti Jewelry Inc..........401 944-9430
140 Comstock Pkwy Unit 5 Cranston RI (02921) ***(G-20186)***
Avara Pharmaceutical Svcs Inc (HQ)..........203 918-1659
401 Merritt 7 Norwalk CT (06851) ***(G-3109)***
Avatar, East Windsor *Also called Avalon Advanced Tech Repr Inc* ***(G-1277)***
Avaya Inc..........908 953-6000
600 Technology Park Dr # 1 Billerica MA (01821) ***(G-8216)***
Avcarb LLC..........978 452-8961
2 Indl Ave Lowell MA (01851) ***(G-12347)***
Avcarb Material Solutions, Lowell *Also called Avcarb LLC* ***(G-12347)***
Avco Corporation (HQ)..........401 421-2800
40 Westminster St Providence RI (02903) ***(G-20965)***
Aved Electronics LLC..........978 453-6393
95 Billerica Ave North Billerica MA (01862) ***(G-13794)***
Avedis Zildjian Co (PA)..........781 871-2200
22 Longwater Dr Norwell MA (02061) ***(G-14096)***
Avedro Inc (HQ)..........781 768-3400
201 Jones Rd Waltham MA (02451) ***(G-16040)***
Avenger Filter Force, Ipswich *Also called Avenger Inc* ***(G-11904)***
Avenger Inc..........978 356-7311
53 Mitchell Rd Ipswich MA (01938) ***(G-11904)***
Aveo Pharmaceuticals Inc..........617 299-5000
12 Emily St Cambridge MA (02139) ***(G-9398)***
Aveo Pharmaceuticals Inc (PA)..........617 588-1960
1 Broadway Fl 14 Cambridge MA (02142) ***(G-9399)***
Aveo Securities Corporation..........617 588-1960
1 Broadway Fl 14 Cambridge MA (02142) ***(G-9400)***
Avery Abrasives Inc..........203 372-3513
2225 Reservoir Ave Ste 1 Trumbull CT (06611) ***(G-4613)***
Avery Dennison Corporation..........978 353-2100
224 Industrial Rd Fitchburg MA (01420) ***(G-10810)***
Avery Dennison Corporation..........508 948-3500
1700 W Park Dr Ste 400 Westborough MA (01581) ***(G-16591)***
Avery Dennison Corporation..........603 217-4144
7 Fruite St Unit 7 # 7 Belmont NH (03220) ***(G-17670)***
Avery Dennison Corporation..........508 988-8200
175 Crossing Blvd Ste 510 Framingham MA (01702) ***(G-10923)***
Avery Dennison Fastener Div, Fitchburg *Also called Avery Dennison Corporation* ***(G-10810)***
Avery Dnnson Dgtal Ink Sltions, Belmont *Also called Avery Dennison Corporation* ***(G-17670)***
Averys Beverage LLC..........860 224-0830
520 Corbin Ave New Britain CT (06052) ***(G-2511)***
Aveta Biomics Inc..........339 927-5994
110 Great Rd Ste 302 Bedford MA (01730) ***(G-7960)***
Avian Technologies LLC..........603 526-2420
116 Newport Rd Ste 4-6b New London NH (03257) ***(G-19313)***
Aviation Edge LLC..........781 405-3246
43 Lantern Rd Belmont MA (02478) ***(G-8065)***
Aviation Welding..........508 278-3041
73 Commerce Dr Uxbridge MA (01569) ***(G-15914)***
Aviatron Inc (us)..........802 865-9318
25 Customs Dr South Burlington VT (05403) ***(G-22437)***
Avid Corp..........603 559-9700
222 International Dr # 195 Portsmouth NH (03801) ***(G-19541)***
Avid Technology Inc (PA)..........978 640-6789
75 Network Dr Burlington MA (01803) ***(G-9235)***
Avid Technology Inc..........978 640-3063
65 Network Dr Burlington MA (01803) ***(G-9236)***
Avila Textiles Inc..........508 828-5882
620 Spring St North Dighton MA (02764) ***(G-13929)***
Avilite Corp..........603 626-4388
59 Daniel Webster Hwy # 100 Merrimack NH (03054) ***(G-18988)***
Avitide Inc..........603 965-2100
16 Cavendish Ct Ste 151 Lebanon NH (03766) ***(G-18613)***
Avitus Orthopaedics Inc..........860 637-9922
400 Farmington Ave R2826 Farmington CT (06032) ***(G-1466)***
Avlite Systems, Tilton *Also called Sealite Usa LLC* ***(G-19911)***
Avocus Publishing Inc..........603 357-0236
4 White Brook Rd Gilsum NH (03448) ***(G-18195)***

Avolon Aerospace New York Inc 203 663-5490
700 Canal St 2nd Stamford CT (06902) *(G-4146)*
Avon Cabinet Company 508 587-9122
501 W Main St Avon MA (02322) *(G-7877)*
Avon Cstm EMB & Screenprinting 781 341-4663
4 Brentwood Ave Avon MA (02322) *(G-7878)*
Avon Custom EMB & Screen Prtg, Avon *Also called Avon Cstm EMB & Screenprinting (G-7878)*
Avon Custom Mixing Svcs Inc 781 767-0511
55 High St Holbrook MA (02343) *(G-11521)*
Avon Food Company LLC 781 341-4981
30 James Massey Ln Stoughton MA (02072) *(G-15582)*
Avrobio Inc (PA) 617 914-8420
1 Kendall Sq Ste B2001 Cambridge MA (02139) *(G-9401)*
Avs Incorporated 978 772-0710
60 Fitchburg Rd Ayer MA (01432) *(G-7912)*
Avtec Industries Inc 978 562-2300
5 Bacon St Wellesley MA (02482) *(G-16362)*
Avtech Software Inc (PA) 401 628-1600
16 Cutler St Warren RI (02885) *(G-21287)*
Avvio Networks Inc 781 271-0002
11 Donovan Dr Bedford MA (01730) *(G-7961)*
AVX Tantalum Corporation 207 282-5111
401 Hill St Biddeford ME (04005) *(G-5720)*
AW Airflo Industries Inc 978 465-6260
52 Parker St Newburyport MA (01950) *(G-13470)*
AW Perkins Company 802 773-3600
36 Curtis Ave Rutland VT (05701) *(G-22323)*
Aware Inc (PA) 781 276-4000
40 Middlesex Tpke Bedford MA (01730) *(G-7962)*
Awesome Graphics Inc 802 773-6143
77 Woodstock Ave Rutland VT (05701) *(G-22324)*
Awl Assoc 413 436-9600
2345b Main St Warren MA (01083) *(G-16259)*
Awm LLC 860 386-1000
100 D Neil Hagen Dr Windsor Locks CT (06096) *(G-5386)*
Awnair, Stafford Springs *Also called Tetrault & Sons Inc (G-4117)*
Awning Guy LLC 401 787-0097
182 Waterman St Providence RI (02906) *(G-20966)*
Axcelis Technologies Inc (PA) 978 787-4000
108 Cherry Hill Dr Beverly MA (01915) *(G-8106)*
Axel Plastics RES Labs Inc 718 672-8300
50 Cambridge Dr Monroe CT (06468) *(G-2392)*
Axels Custom Woodworking LLC 203 869-1317
45 Rodwell Ave Greenwich CT (06830) *(G-1595)*
Axenics Inc (PA) 978 774-9393
161 S Main St Middleton MA (01949) *(G-13084)*
Axerra Networks Inc 203 906-3570
30 Bear Run Woodbury CT (06798) *(G-5482)*
Axerra Networks Limited, Woodbury *Also called Axerra Networks Inc (G-5482)*
Axiam Inc (PA) 978 281-3550
58 Blackburn Ctr Gloucester MA (01930) *(G-11163)*
Axio Inc 413 552-8355
77 Grove Ave Leeds MA (01053) *(G-12097)*
Axiom Microdevices Inc 781 376-3000
20 Sylvan Rd Woburn MA (01801) *(G-17124)*
Axiom Wire and Cable 508 498-8899
20 Townsend Rd Ste C Attleboro MA (02703) *(G-7711)*
Axiomatics, Wilmington *Also called Trexel Inc (G-17059)*
Axiomed Spine Corporation (PA) 978 232-3990
350 Main St Ste 31 Malden MA (02148) *(G-12560)*
Axiomx Inc 203 208-1034
688 E Main St Branford CT (06405) *(G-293)*
Axis Cnc Incorporated 413 967-6803
39 Gould Rd Ware MA (01082) *(G-16228)*
Axis Laser 203 284-9455
7 Atwater Pl Wallingford CT (06492) *(G-4707)*
Axis Machining Inc 401 766-9911
549 River St Woonsocket RI (02895) *(G-21550)*
Axis Technologies Inc 978 275-9908
39 Wilbur St Ste 2 Lowell MA (01851) *(G-12348)*
Axis-Shield Poc As 508 285-4870
15 Commerce Way Ste E Norton MA (02766) *(G-14071)*
Axon Communications Inc 781 849-6700
6 Brooks Dr Braintree MA (02184) *(G-8988)*
Axsun Technologies Inc 978 262-0049
1 Fortune Dr Billerica MA (01821) *(G-8217)*
Axygen Bioscience Inc 978 442-2200
836 North St Tewksbury MA (01876) *(G-15808)*
Ayan Electric Inc 978 256-6306
225 Stedman St Ste 7 Lowell MA (01851) *(G-12349)*
AZ Copy Center Inc 860 621-7325
298 Captain Lewis Dr Southington CT (06489) *(G-4040)*
Azara Healthcare LLC 781 365-2208
70 Blanchard Rd Ste 401 Burlington MA (01803) *(G-9237)*
Azelis Americas LLC 212 915-8178
154 Pioneer Dr Leominster MA (01453) *(G-12115)*
Azores Corp (HQ) 978 253-6200
16 Jonspin Rd Wilmington MA (01887) *(G-16977)*
Aztec Industries LLC 860 343-1960
695 High St Middletown CT (06457) *(G-2175)*
Azulite Inc 916 801-8528
10 Davol Sq Providence RI (02903) *(G-20967)*
Azurity Pharmaceuticals (PA) 855 379-0382
8 Cabot Rd Woburn MA (01801) *(G-17125)*
Azz Inc 774 854-0700
51 Alder St Medway MA (02053) *(G-12956)*
B & A Company Inc 203 876-7527
160 Wampus Ln Milford CT (06460) *(G-2248)*
B & A Design Inc 860 871-0134
255 Bamforth Rd Vernon Rockville CT (06066) *(G-4679)*
B & B Embroidery Inc 207 465-2846
82 Libby Hill Rd Oakland ME (04963) *(G-6529)*
B & B Equipment LLC 860 342-5773
80 Main St Ste D Portland CT (06480) *(G-3563)*
B & B Mfg Co 508 487-0858
186 Bradford St Provincetown MA (02657) *(G-14607)*
B & B Ventures Ltd Lblty Co 203 481-1700
550 E Main St Ste 27 Branford CT (06405) *(G-294)*
B & C Sand & Gravel Company 203 335-6640
412 Housatonic Ave Bridgeport CT (06604) *(G-379)*
B & C Tooling Company Inc 781 447-5292
844 Bedford St Whitman MA (02382) *(G-16920)*
B & D Machine Inc 860 871-9226
30 Industrial Park Rd E Tolland CT (06084) *(G-4539)*
B & D Pallet Co, Westfield *Also called B&D Pallet Bldg & Indus Sup (G-16670)*
B & D Precision Inc 781 438-8644
41 Elm St Ste 7 Stoneham MA (02180) *(G-15555)*
B & E Juices Inc 203 333-1802
550 Knowlton St Bridgeport CT (06608) *(G-380)*
B & E Tool Company Inc 413 569-5585
10 Hudson Dr Southwick MA (01077) *(G-15411)*
B & F Machine Co Inc 860 225-6349
145 Edgewood Ave New Britain CT (06051) *(G-2512)*
B & G Cabinet 978 465-6455
253 Low St Ste 8 Newburyport MA (01950) *(G-13471)*
B & G Forming Technology Inc 203 235-2169
956 Old Colony Rd Meriden CT (06451) *(G-2078)*
B & J Manufacturing Corp 508 822-1990
55 Constitution Dr Taunton MA (02780) *(G-15730)*
B & K Enterprises Inc 508 881-1168
223 Main St Ashland MA (01721) *(G-7656)*
B & L Manufacturing Inc 508 966-3066
8 Williams Way Bellingham MA (02019) *(G-8031)*
B & L Plastics Inc 401 723-3000
535 Prospect St Pawtucket RI (02860) *(G-20814)*
B & L Tool and Machine Company 860 747-2721
76 Northwest Dr Plainville CT (06062) *(G-3468)*
B & M Plastics Inc 401 728-0404
511 York Ave Pawtucket RI (02861) *(G-20815)*
B & M Printing Inc 401 334-3190
1300 Mendon Rd Cumberland RI (02864) *(G-20314)*
B & P Plating Equipment LLC 860 589-5799
74 Broderick Rd Bristol CT (06010) *(G-523)*
B & R Bartlett Enterprises 207 448-7060
592 Us Route One Amity ME (04471) *(G-5522)*
B & R Machine Inc 413 589-0246
305a Moody St Ste A Ludlow MA (01056) *(G-12455)*
B & R Machine Works Inc 203 798-0595
23 Henry St Bethel CT (06801) *(G-129)*
B & R Metal Products Inc 781 593-0888
120 Broadway Lynn MA (01904) *(G-12490)*
B & T Millworks 207 591-5740
62 Sanford Dr Gorham ME (04038) *(G-6109)*
B & T Pallet Recycling Inc 207 784-9048
13 Fireslate Pl Lewiston ME (04240) *(G-6275)*
B and G Enterprise LLC (PA) 203 562-7232
178 Chapel St New Haven CT (06513) *(G-2663)*
B and M, Milton *Also called Proforma Printing & Promotion (G-13199)*
B and R Modern Hand Tool Inc 207 773-6706
54 E Kidder St Portland ME (04103) *(G-6615)*
B C Ames Incorporated 781 893-0095
1644 Concord St Framingham MA (01701) *(G-10924)*
B C T, East Providence *Also called Camirob Corp (G-20394)*
B C T, Naugatuck *Also called Business Cards Tomorrow Inc (G-2464)*
B Copy, Portland *Also called Cybercopy Inc (G-6646)*
B E Publishing 401 294-2490
346 Smith St North Kingstown RI (02852) *(G-20692)*
B F M Mini Golf Driving Range 978 664-9276
327 Main St North Reading MA (01864) *(G-13978)*
B Fresh 401 349-0001
37 Lark Industrial Pkwy A Greenville RI (02828) *(G-20463)*
B G Peck Company Inc 978 686-4181
50 Shepard St Lawrence MA (01843) *(G-11997)*
B H Davis Co 860 923-2771
227 Riverside Dr Thompson CT (06277) *(G-4531)*
B H S Industries Ltd 203 284-9764
23 N Plains Industrial Rd # 3 Wallingford CT (06492) *(G-4708)*

ALPHABETIC

B H Shoe Holdings Inc (HQ) 203 661-2424
124 W Putnam Ave Ste 1 Greenwich CT (06830) ***(G-1596)***
B Hall & Sons Logging Inc 603 482-7741
63 Hall Rd Errol NH (03579) ***(G-18108)***
B L C Investments Inc 203 877-1888
228a Rowe Ave Milford CT (06461) ***(G-2249)***
B L R, Old Saybrook *Also called Bff Holdings Inc* ***(G-3328)***
B Luka Signs Inc 508 822-9022
39 Tremont St Taunton MA (02780) ***(G-15731)***
B M I South, Thomaston *Also called Biedermann Mfg Inds Inc* ***(G-4499)***
B Marine Corp 207 633-3171
120 Commercial St Boothbay Harbor ME (04538) ***(G-5782)***
B N M Printing & Promotion 617 464-1120
71 Commercial St Ste 304 Boston MA (02109) ***(G-8387)***
B O E, Saint Johnsbury *Also called Blue Ox Enterprise Inc* ***(G-22387)***
B P Logging 603 237-4131
158 Creampoke Rd Stewartstown NH (03576) ***(G-19860)***
B R S Inc 508 697-5448
1453 Plymouth St Bridgewater MA (02324) ***(G-9061)***
B S T Systems Inc 860 564-4078
78 Plainfield Pike Plainfield CT (06374) ***(G-3451)***
B Sign Graphics Inc 401 943-6941
141 Rome Dr Cranston RI (02921) ***(G-20187)***
B T Building Systems, Southport *Also called Thomas Bernhard Building Sys* ***(G-4102)***
B T S Graphics LLC 860 274-6422
36 Zoar Ave Ste 2 Oakville CT (06779) ***(G-3296)***
B V T V Inc 508 737-7754
109 Carlson Ln Marstons Mills MA (02648) ***(G-12871)***
B Vitalini, Milford *Also called Vita-Crete Inc* ***(G-13151)***
B&B Logging LLC 860 982-2425
298 Brainard Hill Rd Higganum CT (06441) ***(G-1900)***
B&B Micro Manufacturing Inc 413 281-9431
121 Union St Ste N1 Adams Adams MA (01220) ***(G-7410)***
B&C Kitchen and Bath, Enfield *Also called Atlantic Woodcraft Inc* ***(G-1347)***
B&D Pallet Bldg & Indus Sup 413 568-9624
997 Western Ave Westfield MA (01085) ***(G-16670)***
B&E Precision Arcft Components, Southwick *Also called B & E Tool Company Inc* ***(G-15411)***
B&G Foods Inc 207 772-8341
1 Beanpot Cir Portland ME (04103) ***(G-6616)***
B&J Sheet Metal 617 590-2295
232 Turtle Pond Pkwy Hyde Park MA (02136) ***(G-11862)***
B&K Enterprises, Ashland *Also called B & K Enterprises Inc* ***(G-7656)***
B&N Aerospace Inc 860 665-0134
44 Rockwell Rd Newington CT (06111) ***(G-2845)***
B&R Sand and Gravel 860 464-5099
1358 Baldwin Hill Rd Gales Ferry CT (06335) ***(G-1525)***
B&T Screw Machine Co Inc 860 314-4410
571 Broad St Bristol CT (06010) ***(G-524)***
B-C-D Metal Products Inc 781 397-9922
205 Maplewood St Malden MA (02148) ***(G-12561)***
B-P Products Inc 203 288-0200
100 Sanford St Hamden CT (06514) ***(G-1733)***
B-Sweet LLC 203 452-0499
444 Main St Ste C Monroe CT (06468) ***(G-2393)***
B/E Aerospace Inc 978 546-1331
31 Pooles Ln Rockport MA (01966) ***(G-14834)***
B/E Aerospace Inc 603 926-5700
94 Tide Mill Rd Hampton NH (03842) ***(G-18256)***
B/E Aerospace Inc 203 380-5000
650 Long Beach Blvd Stratford CT (06615) ***(G-4394)***
B2w, Portsmouth *Also called Bid2win Software Inc* ***(G-19543)***
Baa Creations 860 464-1339
13 Lambtown Rd Ledyard CT (06339) ***(G-1939)***
Babac Inc 207 872-0889
166 China Rd Winslow ME (04901) ***(G-7267)***
Babbco, Raynham *Also called C H Babb Co Inc* ***(G-14706)***
Babcock & King Incorporated (PA) 203 336-7989
750 Commerce Dr Fairfield CT (06825) ***(G-1415)***
Babcock Power Capital Corp (HQ) 978 646-3300
222 Rosewood Dr Fl 3 Danvers MA (01923) ***(G-10200)***
Babcock Power Inc (PA) 978 646-3300
6 Kimball Ln Ste 210 Lynnfield MA (01940) ***(G-12545)***
Babcock Power Inc Research Ctr 508 792-4800
45 Mckeon Rd Worcester MA (01610) ***(G-17344)***
Babin Machine Inc 508 588-9189
14 Upland Rd Brockton MA (02301) ***(G-9123)***
Babin Machine Tool, Brockton *Also called Babin Machine Inc* ***(G-9123)***
Babtech Inc 207 594-7106
410 Main St Rockland ME (04841) ***(G-6784)***
Baby Briefcase LLC 617 696-7668
51 Randolph Ave Milton MA (02186) ***(G-13189)***
Bachar Samawi Innovations LLC (PA) 802 464-0440
266a Handle Rd West Dover VT (05356) ***(G-22605)***
Back Bay Sign 978 203-0570
65 Industrial Way Wilmington MA (01887) ***(G-16978)***
Back Bay Sign LLC 781 475-1001
65i Industrial Way Wilmington MA (01887) ***(G-16979)***
Back Cove Yachts, Rockland *Also called North End Composites LLC* ***(G-6806)***
Back Street Inc 508 336-6333
128 Highland Ave Seekonk MA (02771) ***(G-15018)***
Backcountry Magazine 802 644-6794
168 Main St Jeffersonville VT (05464) ***(G-22045)***
Backer Hotwatt Inc 978 777-0000
16a Electronics Ave Danvers MA (01923) ***(G-10201)***
Backporch Publishing 603 357-8761
16 Russell St Keene NH (03431) ***(G-18494)***
Backseat Gorilla Applications 978 658-6161
41 Garden Ave Wilmington MA (01887) ***(G-16980)***
Backus Distillery LLC 802 999-2255
379 Kennison Rd Westfield VT (05874) ***(G-22626)***
Backwash Brew Holdings LLC 207 659-2300
15 Hardy St Brewer ME (04412) ***(G-5794)***
Bacon Industries Inc 508 384-0780
65 Warren Dr Wrentham MA (02093) ***(G-17515)***
Bacou Dalloz USA Inc 401 757-2428
900 Douglas Pike Ste 100 Smithfield RI (02917) ***(G-21211)***
Bacou-Dalloz Eye & Face Protec, Smithfield *Also called Honeywell Safety Products Usa* ***(G-21233)***
Bacou-Dalloz Safety Inc 401 232-1200
900 Douglas Pike Ste 100 Smithfield RI (02917) ***(G-21212)***
Bae Systems Elctronic Solution 603 885-3653
65 Spit Brook Rd Nashua NH (03060) ***(G-19120)***
Bae Systems Info & Elec Sys (HQ) 603 885-4321
65 Spit Brook Rd Nashua NH (03060) ***(G-19121)***
Bae Systems Info & Elec Sys 603 885-4321
65 River Rd Hudson NH (03051) ***(G-18376)***
Bae Systems Info & Elec Sys 603 885-4321
95 Canal St Nashua NH (03064) ***(G-19122)***
Bae Systems Info & Elec Sys 603 885-4321
130 Daniel Webster Hwy Merrimack NH (03054) ***(G-18989)***
Bae Systems Info & Elec Sys 603 885-4321
144 Daniel Webster Hwy # 24 Merrimack NH (03054) ***(G-18990)***
Bae Systems Info & Elec Sys 603 885-4321
2 Forbes Rd Lexington MA (02421) ***(G-12208)***
Bae Systems Info & Elec Sys 603 885-3653
65 Spit Brook Rd Nashua NH (03060) ***(G-19123)***
Bae Systems Info & Elec Sys 603 885-3770
9 Canal St Nashua NH (03064) ***(G-19124)***
Bae Systems Info & Elec Sys 781 273-3388
600 District Ave Burlington MA (01803) ***(G-9238)***
Bae Systems Info & Elec Sys 603 647-5367
2 Industrial Dr Londonderry NH (03053) ***(G-18678)***
Bae Systems Tech Sol Srvc Inc 508 833-9562
1 Flat Rock Hill Rd Sagamore MA (02561) ***(G-14883)***
Bae Systems Tech Sol Srvc Inc 207 449-3577
149 Front St Bath ME (04530) ***(G-5673)***
Bae Systems Tech Sol Srvc Inc 401 846-5500
76 Hammarlund Way Ste 3 Middletown RI (02842) ***(G-20616)***
Baena Ben & Matthew, Bridgeport *Also called Ben Baena & Son* ***(G-382)***
Bafs Inc (PA) 207 942-5226
61 Florida Ave Ste 101 Bangor ME (04401) ***(G-5630)***
Bag Balm, Lyndonville *Also called Vermonts Original LLC* ***(G-22076)***
Bagdon Advertising Inc 508 366-5500
32 South St Westborough MA (01581) ***(G-16592)***
Bagel Boy Inc 978 682-8646
485 S Union St Lawrence MA (01843) ***(G-11998)***
Bagel Boys Inc (PA) 860 657-4400
85 Nutmeg Ln Glastonbury CT (06033) ***(G-1539)***
Bagela Usa LLC 203 944-0525
70 Platt Rd Shelton CT (06484) ***(G-3777)***
Bagge Inc 508 429-8080
150 Kuniholm Dr Ste 4 Holliston MA (01746) ***(G-11558)***
Bagrout Inc 413 949-0743
44 Monroe St Ware MA (01082) ***(G-16229)***
Baikar Association Inc (PA) 617 924-4420
755 Mount Auburn St Watertown MA (02472) ***(G-16271)***
Bailey Avenue Kitchens 203 438-4868
904 Ethan Allen Hwy Ridgefield CT (06877) ***(G-3656)***
Bailey Sign Inc 207 774-2843
9 Thomas Dr Westbrook ME (04092) ***(G-7181)***
Bailey Works, Newmarket *Also called Baileyworks Inc* ***(G-19330)***
Baileyworks Inc 603 292-6485
55 Main St 213 Newmarket NH (03857) ***(G-19330)***
Baingan LLC 203 924-2626
94 River Rd Shelton CT (06484) ***(G-3778)***
Baird & Bartlett Coi NC 508 588-9400
319 Manley St West Bridgewater MA (02379) ***(G-16431)***
Bak Precision Industries, Cranston *Also called Estate Agency Inc* ***(G-20221)***
Bak Precision Industries, Cranston *Also called Estate Agency Inc* ***(G-20222)***
Bake-N-Joy Foods, North Andover *Also called Frozen Batters Inc* ***(G-13706)***
Baked Beads Inc 802 496-2440
6973 Main St Waitsfield VT (05673) ***(G-22560)***
Bakelite N Sumitomo Amer Inc (HQ) 860 645-3851
24 Mill St Manchester CT (06042) ***(G-1987)***
Baker Bags, Tamworth *Also called Creative Filtration Systems* ***(G-19891)***

Baker Commodities Inc.....802 658-0721
354 Avenue B Williston VT (05495) *(G-22657)*
Baker Commodities Inc.....978 454-8811
134 Billerica Ave North Billerica MA (01862) *(G-13795)*
Baker Commodities Inc.....207 622-3505
1607 Riverside Dr Vassalboro ME (04989) *(G-7124)*
Baker Commodities Inc.....401 821-3003
4 Riverdale Ct Warwick RI (02886) *(G-21331)*
Baker Company Inc (PA).....207 324-8773
175 Gate House Rd Sanford ME (04073) *(G-6871)*
Baker Company, The, Sanford *Also called Baker Company Inc (G-6871)*
Baker Graphics Inc.....603 625-5427
143 Middle St Ste 1 Manchester NH (03101) *(G-18784)*
Baker Hghes Olfld Oprtions LLC.....508 668-0400
1600 Providence Hwy Ste 4 Walpole MA (02081) *(G-15989)*
Baker Parts Inc.....508 636-3121
135 Potter St New Bedford MA (02740) *(G-13360)*
Baker Petrolite LLC.....781 849-9699
82 Winthrop Ave Braintree MA (02184) *(G-8989)*
Baker Petrolite S Suelnis, Braintree *Also called Baker Petrolite LLC (G-8989)*
Baker Salmon Christopher.....603 588-4000
375 Keene Rd Antrim NH (03440) *(G-17592)*
Baker Sign Works Inc.....508 674-6600
75 Ferry St Ste 5 Fall River MA (02721) *(G-10666)*
Baker's Dozen Bakery, Colchester *Also called Bakers Dozen Inc (G-21857)*
Bakers Dozen Inc.....802 879-4001
70 Roosevelt Hwy Ste 2 Colchester VT (05446) *(G-21857)*
Bakery Engineering/Winkler Inc.....203 929-8630
2 Trap Falls Rd Ste 105 Shelton CT (06484) *(G-3779)*
Bakery To Go Inc.....617 482-1015
314 Shawmut Ave Boston MA (02118) *(G-8388)*
Bal International Inc.....203 359-6775
281 Tresser Blvd Fl 12 Stamford CT (06901) *(G-4147)*
Balaji International Inc.....508 472-1953
2 Oak Leaf Ln North Easton MA (02356) *(G-13942)*
Balance Designs Inc.....802 362-2893
245 Airport Rd Manchester Center VT (05255) *(G-22080)*
Balancetek.....617 320-4340
19 Joy St Boston MA (02114) *(G-8389)*
Balancetek Corporation.....781 910-9706
18 Winsor Ave Watertown MA (02472) *(G-16272)*
Balchen Tool & Machine, Jonesport *Also called Larry Balchen (G-6227)*
Balderdash Cellars.....413 464-4629
502 East St Ste B Pittsfield MA (01201) *(G-14455)*
Balding Precision Inc.....203 878-9135
61 Woodmont Rd Milford CT (06460) *(G-2250)*
Baldwin Cooke, New Hartford *Also called Executive Greetings Inc (G-2636)*
Baldwin Lawn Furniture LLC.....860 347-1306
440 Middlefield St Ste 1 Middletown CT (06457) *(G-2176)*
Balfor Industries Inc.....203 828-6473
327 Riggs St Oxford CT (06478) *(G-3391)*
Ball & Roller Bearing Co LLC.....860 355-4161
46 Old State Rd Ste 4 New Milford CT (06776) *(G-2787)*
Ball and Chain Forge.....207 878-2217
56 Warren Ave Ste 106 Portland ME (04103) *(G-6617)*
Ball Slides Inc.....508 359-4348
102 Adams St Medfield MA (02052) *(G-12910)*
Ball Supply Corporation.....860 673-3364
52 Old Mill Rd Avon CT (06001) *(G-32)*
Ballard Unmanned Systems Inc.....508 687-4970
153 Northboro Rd Ste 1 Southborough MA (01772) *(G-15344)*
Ballistic Fluid Technologies (PA).....603 654-3065
352 Center Rd Unit 3 Lyndeborough NH (03082) *(G-18757)*
Balsam Woods Farm.....860 265-1800
4 Clinton St Stafford Springs CT (06076) *(G-4106)*
Baltasar & Sons Inc.....203 723-0425
186 Sheridan Dr Naugatuck CT (06770) *(G-2462)*
Balyo Inc.....781 281-7957
78b Olympia Ave Woburn MA (01801) *(G-17126)*
Bam Lab LLC.....603 973-9388
186 Blackwater Rd Somersworth NH (03878) *(G-19828)*
Bamboo Rose LLC.....857 284-4360
98 N Washington St Boston MA (02114) *(G-8390)*
Bamboo Rose LLC (PA).....978 281-3723
17 Rogers St Gloucester MA (01930) *(G-11164)*
Bamboo Rose Software, Gloucester *Also called Bamboo Rose LLC (G-11164)*
Banacek Invstgtons Srch Recove.....781 784-1400
1075 Providence Hwy Sharon MA (02067) *(G-15046)*
Banana Banners.....207 666-3951
160 Main St Bowdoinham ME (04008) *(G-5788)*
Banas Sand & Gravel Co Inc.....413 583-8321
246 Fuller St Ludlow MA (01056) *(G-12456)*
Bancroft Custom Woodworks.....413 738-7001
3223 Hancock Rd Williamstown MA (01267) *(G-16954)*
Bancware Inc (HQ).....617 542-2800
100 High St Fl 19 Boston MA (02110) *(G-8391)*
Bandera Acquisition LLC (HQ).....480 553-6400
2 Hampshire St Foxborough MA (02035) *(G-10911)*
Bangor Daily News, Bangor *Also called Bangor Publishing Company (G-5632)*
Bangor Daily News, Belfast *Also called Bangor Publishing Company (G-5685)*
Bangor Daily News Hancock Bur, Ellsworth *Also called Bangor Publishing Company (G-6014)*
Bangor Millwork & Supply Inc.....207 878-8548
460 Riverside St Portland ME (04103) *(G-6618)*
Bangor Neon Inc.....207 947-2766
1567 Hammond St Bangor ME (04401) *(G-5631)*
Bangor Publishing Company (PA).....207 990-8000
1 Merchants Plz Bangor ME (04401) *(G-5632)*
Bangor Publishing Company.....207 338-3034
26 Spring St Belfast ME (04915) *(G-5685)*
Bangor Publishing Company.....207 667-9393
98 Main St Ste B Ellsworth ME (04605) *(G-6014)*
Bangs Island Mussels, Portland *Also called Wild Ocean Aquaculture LLC (G-6745)*
Bank & Business Forms Inc.....603 357-0567
6 Kingsbury St Keene NH (03431) *(G-18495)*
Bank Sails, Norwalk *Also called Mbm Sales (G-3193)*
Banks White Poliaris Co Inc.....781 293-3033
500 Industrial Dr Halifax MA (02338) *(G-11314)*
Banner & Awning Works, Oakville *Also called Banner Works (G-3297)*
Banner Mold & Die Co Inc.....978 534-6558
251 Florence St Leominster MA (01453) *(G-12116)*
Banner Source.....207 846-0915
387b E Elm St Yarmouth ME (04096) *(G-7292)*
Banner Works.....203 597-9999
15 Rockland Ave Oakville CT (06779) *(G-3297)*
Bannerama Instant Signs Inc.....781 899-4744
10 Sibley Rd Weston MA (02493) *(G-16822)*
Bannish Lumber Inc.....413 354-2279
632 Route 20 Chester MA (01011) *(G-9980)*
Bantam Sheet Metal.....860 567-9690
1160 Bantam Rd Bantam CT (06750) *(G-52)*
Bantry Components Inc.....603 668-3210
160 Bouchard St Manchester NH (03103) *(G-18785)*
Baobab Asset Management LLC.....203 340-5700
2 Greenwich Office Park # 300 Greenwich CT (06831) *(G-1597)*
Bar Co American, North Haven *Also called American Wood Products (G-3007)*
Bar Harbor Foods, Whiting *Also called Looks Gourmet Food Co Inc (G-7221)*
Bar Work Manufacturing Co Inc.....203 753-4103
1198 Highland Ave Waterbury CT (06708) *(G-4848)*
Bar-Plate Manufacturing Co.....203 397-0033
1180 Sherman Ave Hamden CT (06514) *(G-1734)*
Baramundi Software Usa Inc.....508 861-7561
550 Cochituate Rd Ste 25 Framingham MA (01701) *(G-10925)*
Baranowski Woodworking Co Inc.....508 690-1515
14 Washington St East Bridgewater MA (02333) *(G-10407)*
Barbara Brownie LLC.....603 601-2886
22 Watsons Ln Hampton NH (03842) *(G-18257)*
Barbaras Bakery Inc (HQ).....800 343-0590
500 Nickerson Rd Marlborough MA (01752) *(G-12725)*
Barber Elc Enclosures Mfg Inc.....508 699-4872
30 Chestnut St North Attleboro MA (02760) *(G-13749)*
Barber Foods (HQ).....207 482-5500
56 Milliken St Portland ME (04103) *(G-6619)*
Barber Foods.....207 772-1934
70 Saint John St Portland ME (04102) *(G-6620)*
Barber Walters Industries LLC.....781 241-5433
142 Oakland St Wellesley MA (02481) *(G-16363)*
Barbour Corporation (PA).....508 583-8200
1001 N Montello St Brockton MA (02301) *(G-9124)*
Barbour Plastics, Brockton *Also called Barbour Corporation (G-9124)*
Barbour Plastics Inc (HQ).....508 583-8200
1001 N Montello St Brockton MA (02301) *(G-9125)*
Barbour Stockwell Inc.....781 933-5200
45 6th Rd Woburn MA (01801) *(G-17127)*
Barclay Furniture Associates.....413 536-8084
532 Main St Ste 6 Holyoke MA (01040) *(G-11617)*
Barclay Water Management Inc.....617 926-3400
55 Chapel St Ste 400 Newton MA (02458) *(G-13565)*
Barco Engineering Co, Tilton *Also called Barco Manufacturing Inc (G-19904)*
Barco Manufacturing Inc.....603 286-3324
505 W Main St Tilton NH (03276) *(G-19904)*
Bardell Office Sty & Sups, East Haven *Also called Bardell Printing Corp (G-1242)*
Bardell Printing Corp.....203 469-2441
42 Michael St East Haven CT (06513) *(G-1242)*
Barden Corporation, The, Danbury *Also called Schaeffler Aerospace USA Corp (G-984)*
Bardon Industries Inc.....401 884-1814
3377 S County Trl East Greenwich RI (02818) *(G-20353)*
Bardon Trimount Inc.....508 384-3161
400 Green St Wrentham MA (02093) *(G-17516)*
Bardons Technology, East Greenwich *Also called Bardon Industries Inc (G-20353)*
Bare Bones Software Inc.....978 251-0500
73 Princeton St Ste 206 North Chelmsford MA (01863) *(G-13885)*
Barett and Gould Inc.....603 464-6400
31 Norton Dr Hillsborough NH (03244) *(G-18314)*
Bargain News Free Classified A.....203 377-3000
720 Barnum Avenue Cutoff Stratford CT (06614) *(G-4395)*

ALPHABETIC

Bariatrix Nutrition Corp.......802 527-2500
308 Industrial Park Rd Fairfax VT (05454) ***(G-21972)***
Baril Corporation.......978 373-7910
50 Ward Hill Ave Haverhill MA (01835) ***(G-11407)***
Barile Printers LLC.......860 224-0127
43 Viets St New Britain CT (06053) ***(G-2513)***
Barker Screen Printers, Meriden *Also called Multiprints Inc* ***(G-2111)***
Barker Steel LLC.......207 883-3444
51 Us Route 1 Ste H Scarborough ME (04074) ***(G-6907)***
Barker Steel LLC.......413 665-2381
73 Old State Rd South Deerfield MA (01373) ***(G-15245)***
Barker Steel LLC.......413 568-7803
287 Lockhouse Rd Westfield MA (01085) ***(G-16671)***
Barker Steel LLC.......860 282-1860
30 Talbot Ln South Windsor CT (06074) ***(G-3943)***
Barlo Manufacturing.......203 481-3426
4 Beaver Rd Ste 1 Branford CT (06405) ***(G-295)***
Barlo Signs International Inc.......603 880-8949
158 Greeley St Hudson NH (03051) ***(G-18377)***
Barlow Architectural Mllwk LLC.......603 329-6026
30 Gigante Dr Hampstead NH (03841) ***(G-18237)***
Barlow Designs Inc.......401 438-7925
20 Commercial Way East Providence RI (02914) ***(G-20390)***
Barlow Metal Stamping Inc.......860 583-1387
2 Barlow St Bristol CT (06010) ***(G-525)***
Barlow Wood Products.......603 673-2642
119 Melendy Rd Milford NH (03055) ***(G-19048)***
Barmakian Brothers Ltd Partnr.......617 227-3724
333 Washington St Ste 701 Boston MA (02108) ***(G-8392)***
Barn Door Screen Printers.......603 447-5369
56 Pleasant St Conway NH (03818) ***(G-17950)***
Barnard Die Inc.......781 246-3117
431 Water St Frnt Wakefield MA (01880) ***(G-15942)***
Barnard Water Jet Cutting, Wakefield *Also called Barnard Die Inc* ***(G-15942)***
Barnes Aerospace, Windsor *Also called Barnes Group Inc* ***(G-5322)***
Barnes Aerospace W Chester Div, Bristol *Also called Barnes Group Inc* ***(G-528)***
Barnes Concrete Co Inc.......860 928-7242
873 Providence Pike Putnam CT (06260) ***(G-3602)***
Barnes Group Inc (PA).......860 583-7070
123 Main St Bristol CT (06010) ***(G-526)***
Barnes Group Inc.......860 298-7740
169 Kennedy Rd Windsor CT (06095) ***(G-5322)***
Barnes Group Inc.......860 582-9581
18 Main St Bristol CT (06010) ***(G-527)***
Barnes Group Inc.......860 298-7740
80 Scott Swamp Rd Farmington CT (06032) ***(G-1467)***
Barnes Group Inc.......513 759-3503
123 Main St Bristol CT (06010) ***(G-528)***
Barnes Technical Products LLC.......203 931-8852
15 High St New Haven CT (06510) ***(G-2664)***
Barney & Co California LLC.......559 442-1752
4 Belfield Rd Cape Elizabeth ME (04107) ***(G-5874)***
Barney Rabin Company Inc.......781 639-0593
2 Foss Ter Marblehead MA (01945) ***(G-12675)***
Barneys Sign Service Inc.......203 878-3763
45 Seymour St Ste 3 Stratford CT (06615) ***(G-4396)***
Barnhardt Manufacturing Co.......413 624-3471
247 Main Rd Colrain MA (01340) ***(G-10104)***
Barnstable Bat Inc.......508 362-8046
40 Pleasant Pines Ave Centerville MA (02632) ***(G-9813)***
Barnstable Bracelet.......508 362-1630
160 Percival Dr West Barnstable MA (02668) ***(G-16404)***
Barnstable Patriot Newsppr Inc.......508 771-1427
4 Ocean Ave Hyannis MA (02601) ***(G-11835)***
Barnstable Riding, New Bedford *Also called Niche Inc* ***(G-13427)***
Baron & Young Co Inc.......860 589-3235
400 Middle St Ste 13 Bristol CT (06010) ***(G-529)***
Baron Machine Company Inc.......603 524-6800
40 Primrose Dr S Laconia NH (03246) ***(G-18557)***
Baron Technology Inc.......203 452-0515
62 Spring Hill Rd Trumbull CT (06611) ***(G-4614)***
Barrday Advanced Mtl Solutions, Millbury *Also called Barrday Corporation* ***(G-13156)***
Barrday Corporation (HQ).......508 581-2100
86 Providence St Bldg 3 Millbury MA (01527) ***(G-13156)***
Barre Gazette, Barre *Also called Turley Publications Inc* ***(G-7952)***
Barre Precision Products Inc.......860 647-1913
199 Hopriver Rd Bolton CT (06043) ***(G-274)***
Barre Tile Inc.......802 476-0912
187 Mechanic St Lebanon NH (03766) ***(G-18614)***
Barrel House Z LLC.......339 207-7888
95 Woodrock Rd Weymouth MA (02189) ***(G-16885)***
Barrett Technology Inc.......617 252-9000
139 Main St Cambridge MA (02142) ***(G-9402)***
Barrett Technology LLC.......617 252-9000
73 Chapel St Ste D Newton MA (02458) ***(G-13566)***
Barrette Mechanical.......860 774-0499
36 Bush Hill Rd Brooklyn CT (06234) ***(G-670)***
Barrette Outdoor Living Inc.......800 866-8101
8 Morin St Biddeford ME (04005) ***(G-5721)***
Barringer Industries LLC.......207 730-7125
2 Washington Ave Scarborough ME (04074) ***(G-6908)***
Barrington Manufacturing Inc.......401 245-1737
8 Rockland Rd Warren RI (02885) ***(G-21288)***
Barrington Print & Copy LLC.......401 943-8300
133 Central St Ste 1 Warwick RI (02886) ***(G-21332)***
Barrington Printing, Warwick *Also called Barrington Print & Copy LLC* ***(G-21332)***
Barrup Farms Inc.......802 334-2331
516 Lower Quarry Rd Derby VT (05829) ***(G-21899)***
Barry Callebaut USA LLC.......802 524-9711
400 Industrial Park Rd Saint Albans VT (05478) ***(G-22364)***
Barry Controls, Hopkinton *Also called Hutchinson Arospc & Indust Inc* ***(G-11719)***
Barry Industries Inc.......508 226-3350
60 Walton St Attleboro MA (02703) ***(G-7712)***
Barry Manufacturing Co Inc.......781 598-1055
15 Bubier St Lynn MA (01901) ***(G-12491)***
Bart Truck Equipment LLC.......413 737-2766
358 River St West Springfield MA (01089) ***(G-16511)***
Bart's Homemade, Greenfield *Also called Snows Nice Cream Co Inc* ***(G-11277)***
Bartlett Maine Estate Winery.......207 546-2408
175 Chicken Mill Pond Rd Gouldsboro ME (04607) ***(G-6135)***
Bartlett Winery, Gouldsboro *Also called Bartlett Maine Estate Winery* ***(G-6135)***
Bartletts Bench and Wire Inc (PA).......207 354-0138
574 Cushing Rd Friendship ME (04547) ***(G-6092)***
Bartley Machine & Mfg Co Inc.......978 388-0085
35 Water St Amesbury MA (01913) ***(G-7479)***
Barton Corporation Salisbury.......603 760-2669
34 Folly Mill Rd Ste 4 Seabrook NH (03874) ***(G-19793)***
Barton Rice Corporation.......508 966-2194
12 Hawksley Rd Oxford MA (01540) ***(G-14253)***
Basco Leather Goods, Worcester *Also called Valkyrie Company Inc* ***(G-17497)***
Basement Designs Inc.......508 693-4442
110 California Ave Oak Bluffs MA (02557) ***(G-14209)***
Basement LLC.......508 762-9080
316 Main St Unit 1 Worcester MA (01608) ***(G-17345)***
Basho Technologies Inc (PA).......617 714-1700
485 Msschsetts Ave Ste 1a Cambridge MA (02139) ***(G-9403)***
Basin Timber LLC.......802 343-4694
3721 Vt Route 109 Belvidere Center VT (05442) ***(G-21658)***
Basis Audio Inc.......603 889-4776
26 Clinton Dr Ste 116 Hollis NH (03049) ***(G-18326)***
Basis Technology Corporation.......617 386-2000
101 Main St Ste 1400 Cambridge MA (02142) ***(G-9404)***
Bass Cabinetry and Mllwk LLC.......207 754-0087
228 Sawyer Rd Greene ME (04236) ***(G-6147)***
Bass Plating Company.......860 243-2557
82 Old Windsor Rd Bloomfield CT (06002) ***(G-207)***
Bass Precision Products.......978 922-3608
62 Bridge St Beverly MA (01915) ***(G-8107)***
Bass Products LLC.......860 585-7923
435 Lake Ave Bristol CT (06010) ***(G-530)***
Bass Ready Rooter, New Bedford *Also called D J Bass Inc* ***(G-13376)***
Bass River Marine Canvas LLC.......781 856-5145
239 Great Western Rd South Dennis MA (02660) ***(G-15265)***
Bassett & Cassidy Inc.......978 452-9595
1527 Middlesex St Lowell MA (01851) ***(G-12350)***
Bassette Printers LLC.......413 781-7140
326 Barton Ave Belchertown MA (01007) ***(G-8022)***
Bast Road Collection, West Rupert *Also called Authentic Designs Inc* ***(G-22614)***
Bateman & Slade Inc.......617 423-5556
263 Main St Ste 3 Stoneham MA (02180) ***(G-15556)***
Bates & Klinke, Taunton *Also called B & J Manufacturing Corp* ***(G-15730)***
Bates Abrasive Products Inc.......773 586-8700
6 Carol Dr Lincoln RI (02865) ***(G-20558)***
Bates Bros Seam Face Gran Co.......781 337-1150
611 Pleasant St East Weymouth MA (02189) ***(G-10537)***
Bates Plastics Inc.......401 781-7711
60 Glen Rd Cranston RI (02920) ***(G-20188)***
Bath Iron Works Corporation (HQ).......207 443-3311
700 Washington St Stop 1 Bath ME (04530) ***(G-5674)***
Bath Iron Works Corporation.......207 442-1266
Mallet Park Brunswick ME (04011) ***(G-5830)***
Bath Systems Massachusetts Inc.......508 521-2700
25 Turnpike St West Bridgewater MA (02379) ***(G-16432)***
Batian Peak Coffee.......978 663-2305
10 Hurd St Lowell MA (01852) ***(G-12351)***
Battalion Co Inc (PA).......978 453-2824
325 Chelmsford St Lowell MA (01851) ***(G-12352)***
Batten Bros Inc.......781 245-4800
893 Main St Wakefield MA (01880) ***(G-15943)***
Batten Sign, Wakefield *Also called Batten Bros Inc* ***(G-15943)***
Battenfeld of America Inc.......401 823-0700
31 James P Murphy Ind Hwy West Warwick RI (02893) ***(G-21483)***
Battenkill Communications LLP.......802 362-3981
5515 Main St Manchester Center VT (05255) ***(G-22081)***
Battery Resourcers LLC.......206 948-6325
54 Rockdale St Worcester MA (01606) ***(G-17346)***
Battery Ventures Vi LP.......781 577-1000
930 Winter St Ste 2500 Waltham MA (02451) ***(G-16041)***

Battilana & Associates 802 457-3375
6 Swain St Woodstock VT (05091) ***(G-22736)***
Battle Road Press 603 924-7600
216a Old Jaffrey Rd Peterborough NH (03458) ***(G-19467)***
Bauer Inc 860 583-9100
175 Century Dr Bristol CT (06010) ***(G-531)***
Bauer Associates Inc 508 310-0201
8 Tech Cir Natick MA (01760) ***(G-13236)***
Bauer Compressor North East, Monroe *Also called Bauer Compressors Inc* ***(G-2394)***
Bauer Compressors Inc 203 445-9514
60 Twin Brook Ter Monroe CT (06468) ***(G-2394)***
Bauer Hockey LLC 603 430-2111
100 Domain Dr Ste 1 Exeter NH (03833) ***(G-18111)***
Bauhan Publishing 603 567-4430
44 Main St Peterborough NH (03458) ***(G-19468)***
Bausch & Lomb Incorporated 978 658-6111
100 Research Dr Ste 2 Wilmington MA (01887) ***(G-16981)***
Bausch Advanced Tech Inc (PA) 860 669-7380
115 Nod Rd Clinton CT (06413) ***(G-779)***
Bausch Articulating Papers Inc 603 883-2155
12 Murphy Dr Unit 4 Nashua NH (03062) ***(G-19125)***
Bavarian Chocolate Haus Inc 603 356-2663
2483 White Mountain Hwy North Conway NH (03860) ***(G-19372)***
Bavec LLC 603 290-5285
6 Jefferson Dr Dover NH (03820) ***(G-18007)***
Baxalta US Inc 312 656-8021
650 Kendall Dr Cambridge MA (02142) ***(G-9405)***
Baxter Bros Inc 203 637-4559
1030 E Putnam Ave Greenwich CT (06830) ***(G-1598)***
Baxter Crane & Rigging, West Yarmouth *Also called Baxter Inc* ***(G-16578)***
Baxter Inc 508 228-8136
10 Bayview St West Yarmouth MA (02673) ***(G-16578)***
Baxter Investment Management, Greenwich *Also called Baxter Bros Inc* ***(G-1598)***
Baxter Sand & Gravel Inc 413 536-3370
652 Prospect St Chicopee MA (01020) ***(G-9999)***
Bay Crane Service Conn Inc 203 785-8000
37 Nettleton Ave North Haven CT (06473) ***(G-3010)***
Bay State Associates Inc 508 947-6700
101 Charles Eldridge Rd Lakeville MA (02347) ***(G-11973)***
Bay State Blackboard, Braintree *Also called Designer Board Specialties* ***(G-9000)***
Bay State Cast Products Inc 413 736-1028
41 Brookdale Dr Springfield MA (01104) ***(G-15450)***
Bay State Crucible Co 508 824-5121
740 W Water St Taunton MA (02780) ***(G-15732)***
Bay State Electric Motor Co 978 686-7089
20 Aegean Dr Ste 6 Methuen MA (01844) ***(G-13012)***
Bay State Elevator Company Inc (PA) 413 786-7000
275 Silver St Agawam MA (01001) ***(G-7421)***
Bay State Envelope Inc (PA) 508 337-8900
440 Chauncy St Mansfield MA (02048) ***(G-12614)***
Bay State Espresso 978 686-5049
35 Walnut St Haverhill MA (01830) ***(G-11408)***
Bay State Galvanizing Inc 617 389-0671
128 Spring St 132 Everett MA (02149) ***(G-10604)***
Bay State Machine Inc 860 230-0054
21 Center Pkwy Plainfield CT (06374) ***(G-3452)***
Bay State Milling Company (PA) 617 328-4423
100 Congress St Ste 2 Quincy MA (02169) ***(G-14614)***
Bay State Partition & Fix Co 617 782-1113
37 Antwerp St Boston MA (02135) ***(G-8393)***
Bay State Plating Inc 413 533-6927
18 N Bridge St Holyoke MA (01040) ***(G-11618)***
Bay State Scale & Systems Inc 781 993-9035
7 Ray Ave Burlington MA (01803) ***(G-9239)***
Bay State Scale Co, Burlington *Also called Bay State Scale & Systems Inc* ***(G-9239)***
Bay State Specialty Co, Lakeville *Also called Bay State Associates Inc* ***(G-11973)***
Bay State Spring Corp 508 829-5702
1864 Main St Jefferson MA (01522) ***(G-11952)***
Bay State Surface Technologies 508 832-5035
201 Washington St Auburn MA (01501) ***(G-7829)***
Bay State Swiss CAM Design 603 859-7552
286 Henry Wilson Hwy Alton NH (03809) ***(G-17545)***
Bay Steel Co Inc (PA) 781 294-8308
87 Lake St Halifax MA (02338) ***(G-11315)***
Bay Steel Co Inc 508 697-7083
81 Bridge St Bridgewater MA (02324) ***(G-9062)***
Bay Tact Corporation 860 315-7372
440 Route 198 Woodstock Valley CT (06282) ***(G-5503)***
Bayard Inc (HQ) 860 437-3012
1 Montauk Ave Ste 3 New London CT (06320) ***(G-2765)***
Baycorp Holdings Ltd (PA) 603 294-4850
953 Islington St Ste 22 Portsmouth NH (03801) ***(G-19542)***
Bayer Clothing Group Inc (PA) 203 661-4140
503 Riversville Rd Greenwich CT (06831) ***(G-1599)***
Bayhead Products Corporation 603 742-3000
173 Crosby Rd Dover NH (03820) ***(G-18008)***
Bayley Quality Seafood Inc 207 883-4581
21 Snow Canning Rd Scarborough ME (04074) ***(G-6909)***
Baynets Safety Systems, Colchester *Also called International Cordage East Ltd* ***(G-804)***

Bayside Print Services, Portland *Also called Davic Inc* ***(G-6649)***
Baystate Lightning Protection 508 697-7727
55 Three Rivers Dr Bridgewater MA (02324) ***(G-9063)***
Baystate Machine Co., Easthampton *Also called Northampton Machine Co Inc* ***(G-10571)***
Bayview Graphics 781 878-3340
21 Bayview St North Weymouth MA (02191) ***(G-13996)***
Bayview Marine Inc 401 737-3111
781 Oakland Beach Ave Warwick RI (02889) ***(G-21333)***
Bazar Group Inc (PA) 401 434-2595
795 Waterman Ave East Providence RI (02914) ***(G-20391)***
Bazzano, J Cedar Products, Pleasant Valley *Also called Pleasant Valley Fence Co Inc* ***(G-3546)***
Bb Metal Fabrication Inc 802 265-8375
653 River St Fair Haven VT (05743) ***(G-21965)***
Bb Walpole Liquidation NH Inc 617 303-0113
220 Clarendon St Boston MA (02116) ***(G-8394)***
Bb Walpole Liquidation NH Inc 603 756-2882
35 Main St Walpole NH (03608) ***(G-19915)***
Bb Walpole Liquidation NH Inc 617 491-4340
52d Brattle St Cambridge MA (02138) ***(G-9406)***
Bb Walpole Liquidation NH Inc (PA) 603 756-3701
47 Main St Unit 1 Walpole NH (03608) ***(G-19916)***
Bbb & Machine Inc 508 273-0050
1 Thatcher Ln Wareham MA (02571) ***(G-16240)***
BBC Printing and Products Inc 781 647-4646
21 Hill Rd Waltham MA (02451) ***(G-16042)***
BBCg LLC 617 796-8800
273 Lenox St Ste 8 Norwood MA (02062) ***(G-14137)***
BBH Apparrel 207 633-0601
45 Commercial St Boothbay Harbor ME (04538) ***(G-5783)***
Bbhs Thermal Solutions Corp 781 718-2352
18 Ellis St Malden MA (02148) ***(G-12562)***
Bbi Enzymes USA Ltd 608 709-5270
1037 Forest Ave Portland ME (04103) ***(G-6621)***
Bbmc Inc 413 443-3333
1 N Main St Hancock MA (01237) ***(G-11324)***
Bbt North America Corporation 603 552-1100
50 Wentworth Ave Londonderry NH (03053) ***(G-18679)***
Bbu Inc 413 593-2700
21 Taxiway Dr Chicopee MA (01022) ***(G-10000)***
Bc Nichols Machine LLC 603 926-2333
7 Kershaw Ave Ste 2 Hampton NH (03842) ***(G-18258)***
Bce Acquisition Us Inc (HQ) 603 430-2111
100 Domain Dr Exeter NH (03833) ***(G-18112)***
Bcr Technology Center 207 885-9700
83 Mussey Rd Scarborough ME (04074) ***(G-6910)***
BCT Reporting LLC 860 302-1876
55 Whiting St Ste 1a Plainville CT (06062) ***(G-3469)***
Bd Bioscience, Woburn *Also called Becton Dickinson and Company* ***(G-17128)***
BE Peterson Inc 508 436-7900
40 Murphy Dr Ste 2 Avon MA (02322) ***(G-7879)***
Be Semiconductor Inds USA Inc (HQ) 603 626-4700
14 Keewaydin Dr Salem NH (03079) ***(G-19711)***
Be Youneeq LLC 603 244-3933
62 Langford Rd Raymond NH (03077) ***(G-19635)***
Beacon Application Svcs Corp (PA) 508 663-4433
40 Speen St Ste 305 Framingham MA (01701) ***(G-10926)***
Beacon Communications Inc (PA) 401 732-3100
1944 Warwick Ave Ste W4 Warwick RI (02889) ***(G-21334)***
Beacon Group Inc (PA) 860 594-5200
549 Cedar St Newington CT (06111) ***(G-2846)***
Beacon Hill Chocolates 617 725-1900
91 Charles St Ste 1 Boston MA (02114) ***(G-8395)***
Beacon Hill Times, The, Revere *Also called Independent Newspaper Group* ***(G-14768)***
Beacon Industries Inc 860 594-5200
549 Cedar St Newington CT (06111) ***(G-2847)***
Beacon Power, Tyngsboro *Also called BP Fly Corporation* ***(G-15886)***
Beacon Press, Boston *Also called Unitarian Universalist Assn* ***(G-8897)***
Beacon Press Inc 207 282-1535
457 Alfred St Biddeford ME (04005) ***(G-5722)***
Beacon Sales Acquisition Inc 207 797 7950
15 Keewaydin Dr Salem NH (03079) ***(G-19712)***
Bead Electronics, Milford *Also called Bead Industries Inc* ***(G-2251)***
Bead Industries Inc (PA) 203 301-0270
11 Cascade Blvd Milford CT (06460) ***(G-2251)***
Beadery Craft Products, The, Hope Valley *Also called Buick LLC* ***(G-20481)***
Beagle Learning Inc 617 784-3817
281 Summer St Fl 2 Boston MA (02210) ***(G-8396)***
Beans Inc 860 945-9234
2213 Litchfield Rd Watertown CT (06795) ***(G-4999)***
Beanstox Inc 617 878-2102
60 State St Ste 700 Boston MA (02109) ***(G-8397)***
Beantown Bedding LLC 781 608-9915
137 Main St Hingham MA (02043) ***(G-11493)***
Bear Country Powersports LLC 603 482-3370
54 Main St Errol NH (03579) ***(G-18109)***
Bear Hands Brewing Company 860 576-5374
13 Palmer Ct Central Village CT (06332) ***(G-705)***

Bear Hill Lumber Co 207 929-5225
668 Hollis Rd Hollis Center ME (04042) *(G-6198)*
Bear Hydraulics Inc 401 732-5832
45 Fullerton Rd Warwick RI (02886) *(G-21335)*
Bear Paw Lumber Corp (PA) 207 935-3052
103 Main St Fryeburg ME (04037) *(G-6095)*
Bear Pond Dumpster LLC 207 224-0337
250 Bear Pond Rd Turner ME (04282) *(G-7105)*
Bear Swamp Power Company LLC 207 723-4341
1024 Central St Millinocket ME (04462) *(G-6438)*
Beard Concrete Co Derby Inc (PA) 203 874-2533
127 Boston Post Rd Milford CT (06460) *(G-2252)*
Beard Concrete Co Derby Inc 203 735-4641
37 Main St Derby CT (06418) *(G-1068)*
Beard Concrete Company, Milford *Also called Beard Concrete Co Derby Inc (G-2252)*
Beardsley Publishing Corp 203 263-0888
45 Main St N Woodbury CT (06798) *(G-5483)*
Beardsworth Group Inc 860 283-4014
1085 Waterbury Rd Thomaston CT (06787) *(G-4498)*
Bearicuda Bins, Litchfield *Also called Bearicuda Inc (G-1945)*
Bearicuda Inc 860 361-6860
3 West St Ste 3e Litchfield CT (06759) *(G-1945)*
Beasley Woodworks LLC 401 529-5099
22 Laurel Rd Charlestown RI (02813) *(G-20130)*
Beau Ties Limited of Vermont, Middlebury *Also called Btl Holdings LLC (G-22105)*
Beaumac Company Inc 603 736-9321
382 Suncook Valley Hwy Epsom NH (03234) *(G-18104)*
Beautyflame, Westborough *Also called TFC Enterprises LLC (G-16656)*
Beaver Medical LLC 617 935-3500
10 Coleman Ct Natick MA (01760) *(G-13237)*
Beaver-Visitec Intl Holdings (PA) 847 739-3219
411 Waverley Oaks Rd # 229 Waltham MA (02452) *(G-16043)*
Beaver-Visitec Intl Inc (HQ) 781 906-8080
500 Totten Pond Rd # 500 Waltham MA (02451) *(G-16044)*
Beaver-Visitec Intl Inc 847 739-3219
411 Waverley Oaks Rd # 229 Waltham MA (02452) *(G-16045)*
Becaid LLC 203 915-6914
5 Science Park Ste 29 New Haven CT (06511) *(G-2665)*
Becks Printing Co 413 664-7411
16 Protection Ave North Adams MA (01247) *(G-13668)*
Beckson Manufacturing Inc (PA) 203 366-3644
165 Holland Ave Bridgeport CT (06605) *(G-381)*
Beckwood Services Inc 603 382-3840
27 Hale Spring Rd Plaistow NH (03865) *(G-19508)*
Becon Incorporated (PA) 860 243-1428
522 Cottage Grove Rd Bloomfield CT (06002) *(G-208)*
Becton Dickinson and Company 860 824-5487
Grace Way Rr 7 Canaan CT (06018) *(G-683)*
Becton Dickinson and Company 978 901-7319
200 Bulfinch Dr Ste 1 Andover MA (01810) *(G-7539)*
Becton Dickinson and Company 781 935-5115
6 Henshaw St Woburn MA (01801) *(G-17128)*
Bed Works, The, Bangor *Also called Waterworks (G-5663)*
Bedard Sheet Metal Company 413 572-3774
123 Summit Lock Rd Ste 2 Westfield MA (01085) *(G-16672)*
Bedford Freeman & Worth 617 426-7440
75 Arlington St Fl 8 Boston MA (02116) *(G-8398)*
Bedjet LLC 401 404-5250
217 Goddard Row Newport RI (02840) *(G-20656)*
Bedoukian Research Inc (PA) 203 830-4000
6 Commerce Dr Danbury CT (06810) *(G-877)*
Bedrock Automtn Platforms Inc 781 821-0280
171 Forbes Blvd Ste 1000 Mansfield MA (02048) *(G-12615)*
Bee Fiberglass, Taunton *Also called JMS Manufacturing Inc (G-15760)*
BEE International Inc 508 238-5558
46 Eastman St Ste 5 South Easton MA (02375) *(G-15270)*
Bee-Commerce.com, Weston *Also called Woods End Inc (G-5176)*
Beech River Mill 603 539-2636
30 Route 16b Center Ossipee NH (03814) *(G-17802)*
Beechcraft Defense Co LLC 401 457-2485
40 Westminster St Fl 5 Providence RI (02903) *(G-20968)*
Beede Electrical Instr Co Inc 603 753-6362
75 Frontage Rd 106 North Stonington CT (06359) *(G-3071)*
Beehive Heat Treating Svcs Inc 203 866-1635
373 Katona Dr Fairfield CT (06824) *(G-1416)*
Beeken/Parsons Inc 802 985-2913
1611 Harbor Rd Shelburne VT (05482) *(G-22413)*
Beep On Beacon, Brookline *Also called Blackboard Inc (G-9195)*
Beer King, Rutland *Also called Bullock & Block Ltd (G-22326)*
Beer Saver USA 207 299-2826
16 Sylvan Cir Kennebunk ME (04043) *(G-6229)*
Beerd Brewing Co LLC 585 771-7428
22 Bayview Ave Stonington CT (06378) *(G-4375)*
Bees Knees Zipper Wax LLC 203 521-5727
11 Courtney St Apt 11 # 11 Fall River MA (02720) *(G-10667)*
Bees Knees Zipper Wax LLC 203 521-5727
3 Canoe Birch Ct Berlin CT (06037) *(G-75)*
Bees Manufacturing LLC 781 400-1280
40 Wildwood Dr Needham MA (02492) *(G-13292)*
Bees Wrap LLC 802 643-2132
383 Exchange St Middlebury VT (05753) *(G-22101)*
Beetle Inc 508 295-8585
3 Thatcher Ln Wareham MA (02571) *(G-16241)*
Begell House Inc 203 456-6161
50 North St Danbury CT (06810) *(G-878)*
Behavioral Research Tools 802 578-4874
191 W Canton St Boston MA (02116) *(G-8399)*
BEI Holdings Inc 203 741-9300
6 Capital Dr Wallingford CT (06492) *(G-4709)*
Beiersdorf Inc (HQ) 203 563-5800
45 Danbury Rd Wilton CT (06897) *(G-5276)*
Beiersdorf Inc 203 854-8000
360 Dr Martin Luther King Norwalk CT (06854) *(G-3110)*
Beiersdorf North America Inc (HQ) 203 563-5800
45 Danbury Rd Wilton CT (06897) *(G-5277)*
Beigene Usa Inc (HQ) 781 801-1887
55 Cambrdge Pkwy Ste 700w Cambridge MA (02142) *(G-9407)*
Bel Air Finishing Supply Corp 401 667-7902
101 Circuit Dr North Kingstown RI (02852) *(G-20693)*
Bel Legacy Corporation 508 923-5000
84 State St Fl 11 Boston MA (02109) *(G-8400)*
Bel Power Inc 508 870-9775
2400 Computer Dr Westborough MA (01581) *(G-16593)*
Belanger Sheet Metal Inc 207 474-8990
689 Malbons Mills Rd Skowhegan ME (04976) *(G-6969)*
Belanger Welding & Fabrication 207 657-5558
118 Sabbathday Rd New Gloucester ME (04260) *(G-6464)*
Belarc Inc 978 461-1100
2 Mill And Main Pl # 520 Maynard MA (01754) *(G-12896)*
Belco Fuel Company Inc 781 331-6521
38 Mountain Ash Ln Pembroke MA (02359) *(G-14393)*
Belden Inc 508 754-4858
324 Clark St Worcester MA (01606) *(G-17347)*
Belden Inc 978 573-0908
210 Andover St Unit 48 Peabody MA (01960) *(G-14315)*
Belden Inc 978 537-8911
128 Tolman Ave Leominster MA (01453) *(G-12117)*
Beldotti Bakeries 203 348-9029
605 Newfield Ave Stamford CT (06905) *(G-4148)*
Belfast Bay Brewing Company 866 338-5722
14 Cliff Ln Belfast ME (04915) *(G-5686)*
Belgiums Chocolate Source Inc 781 283-5787
480 Adams St Ste 202 Milton MA (02186) *(G-13190)*
Belimo Air Controls USA, Danbury *Also called Belimo Aircontrols (usa) Inc (G-879)*
Belimo Aircontrols (usa) Inc (HQ) 800 543-9038
33 Turner Rd Danbury CT (06810) *(G-879)*
Belimo Automation AG 203 749-3319
33 Turner Rd Danbury CT (06810) *(G-880)*
Belimo Customization USA Inc 203 791-9915
33 Turner Rd Danbury CT (06810) *(G-881)*
Belisle Machine Works Inc 603 669-8902
180 Revere Ave Manchester NH (03109) *(G-18786)*
Bell and Howell LLC 860 526-9561
6 Winter Ave Deep River CT (06417) *(G-1058)*
Bell Helicopter Korea Inc 401 421-2800
40 Westminster St Providence RI (02903) *(G-20969)*
Bell Label Co., Lewiston *Also called Bell Manufacturing Co (G-6276)*
Bell Manufacturing Co 207 784-2961
777 Main St Lewiston ME (04240) *(G-6276)*
Bell Power Systems LLC 860 767-7502
34 Plains Rd Essex CT (06426) *(G-1393)*
Bell Rubber 781 400-7262
477 Washington St Abington MA (02351) *(G-7321)*
Bella Casa Roofing LLC 475 619-0393
585 Cove Rd Apt 2 Stamford CT (06902) *(G-4149)*
Bellamy-Robie, Boston *Also called American Crane and Hoist Corp (G-8360)*
Bellecraft Woodworking Inc 978 297-2672
540 River St Winchendon MA (01475) *(G-17071)*
Bellingham Metal Works LLC 617 519-5958
101 Jefferson Rd Franklin MA (02038) *(G-11025)*
Bellofatto Electrical 781 284-4164
26 Geneva St Revere MA (02151) *(G-14764)*
Bellows Inc 401 766-5331
194 School St Forestdale RI (02824) *(G-20455)*
Belmar Company 781 935-2233
10 Draper St Ste 30 Woburn MA (01801) *(G-17129)*
Belmeade Group LLC 860 413-3569
46 Simsbury Rd West Granby CT (06090) *(G-5048)*
Belmeade Signs, West Granby *Also called Belmeade Group LLC (G-5048)*
Belmont Boatworks LLC 207 342-2885
163 Augusta Rd Belmont ME (04952) *(G-5701)*
Belmont Corporation 860 589-5700
60 Crystal Pond Pl Bristol CT (06010) *(G-532)*
Belmont Instrument LLC (PA) 978 663-0212
780 Boston Rd Ste 3 Billerica MA (01821) *(G-8218)*
Belmont Medical Technologies, Billerica *Also called Belmont Instrument LLC (G-8218)*
Belmont Printing Company 617 484-0833
46 Brighton St Belmont MA (02478) *(G-8066)*

Beloit Ptry Jrnl Fundation Inc 207 522-1303
271 N Gorham Rd Gorham ME (04038) *(G-6110)*
Belt Technologies Inc (PA) 413 786-9922
11 Bowles Rd Agawam MA (01001) *(G-7422)*
Beltronics Inc 617 244-8696
124 Crescent Rd Ste 7 Needham MA (02494) *(G-13293)*
Belvoir Media Group, Norwalk *Also called Belvoir Publications Inc (G-3112)*
Belvoir Media Group LLC 203 857-3128
535 Cnncticut Ave Ste 100 Norwalk CT (06854) *(G-3111)*
Belvoir Publications Inc (PA) 203 857-3100
800 Connecticut Ave 4w02 Norwalk CT (06854) *(G-3112)*
Bemat TEC LLC 860 632-0049
114 West St Cromwell CT (06416) *(G-847)*
Bematek Systems Inc 978 744-5816
96 Swampscott Rd Ste 7 Salem MA (01970) *(G-14897)*
Bemis Associates Inc (PA) 978 425-6761
1 Bemis Way Shirley MA (01464) *(G-15081)*
Bemis Associates Inc 978 425-6761
100 Ayer Rd Shirley MA (01464) *(G-15082)*
Ben & Bills Chocolate Emporium 508 548-7878
209 Main St Falmouth MA (02540) *(G-10787)*
Ben & Blls Chclat Emporium Inc (PA) 413 584-5695
143 Main St Northampton MA (01060) *(G-13997)*
Ben & Jerrys Homemade Inc 203 488-9666
120 Northwood Rd Newington CT (06111) *(G-2848)*
Ben Art Manufacturing Co Inc 203 758-4435
109 Waterbury Rd Prospect CT (06712) *(G-3583)*
Ben Baena & Son 203 334-8568
218 Charles St Bridgeport CT (06606) *(G-382)*
Ben Barretts LLC 860 928-9373
129 Robbins Rd Thompson CT (06277) *(G-4532)*
Ben Franklin Design Mfg Co Inc 413 786-4220
938 Suffield St Agawam MA (01001) *(G-7423)*
Ben Franklin Manufacturing, Agawam *Also called Ben Franklin Design Mfg Co Inc (G-7423)*
Ben Jordan Logging LLC 207 694-2011
21 Granite St Millinocket ME (04462) *(G-6439)*
Ben Savage Logging Inc 207 735-6699
30 North Rd Sebec ME (04481) *(G-6955)*
Bench Dogs 207 845-2084
747 Waldoboro Rd Washington ME (04574) *(G-7148)*
Bench Systems, Lewiston *Also called Maine Barrel & Display Company (G-6303)*
Benchmark Carbide 800 523-8570
616 Dwight St Springfield MA (01104) *(G-15451)*
Benchmark Electronics Inc 603 879-7000
100 Innovative Way # 100 Nashua NH (03062) *(G-19126)*
Benco Dental 508 435-3000
63 South St Ste 194 Hopkinton MA (01748) *(G-11693)*
Benco Precision Machining Inc 978 281-2055
10 Pond Rd Gloucester MA (01930) *(G-11165)*
Bendon Gear & Machine Inc 781 878-8100
100 Weymouth St Ste A1 Rockland MA (02370) *(G-14793)*
Benevento Asphalt, Wilmington *Also called Benevento Sand & Stone Corp (G-16983)*
Benevento Asphalt Corp 978 658-5300
900 Salem St Wilmington MA (01887) *(G-16982)*
Benevento Sand & Stone Corp 978 658-4762
200 Salem St Wilmington MA (01887) *(G-16983)*
Benevolent Tech For Hlth, Boston *Also called Bethcare Inc (G-8404)*
Benjamin Chase Co, Londonderry *Also called Anthony Galluzzo Corp (G-18676)*
Benjamin Martin Corp 781 326-8311
115 Commerce Way Dedham MA (02026) *(G-10281)*
Benjamin Mndlowitz Photography, Brooklin *Also called Noah Publications (G-5821)*
Benjamin Moore & Co 508 473-8900
49 Sumner St Milford MA (01757) *(G-13108)*
Benjamin River Marine Inc 207 359-2244
64 Benjamin River Dr Brooklin ME (04616) *(G-5814)*
Bennett Goding & Cooper Inc 978 682-8868
738 Main St Waltham MA (02451) *(G-16046)*
Bennettisville Printing, Hebron *Also called Bennettsville Holdings LLC (G-1895)*
Bennetts Sports Inc 401 943-7600
900 Phenix Ave Cranston RI (02921) *(G-20189)*
Bennettsville Holdings LLC 860 444-9400
33 Pendleton Dr A Hebron CT (06248) *(G-1895)*
Bennice Molding Co 203 440-2543
184 Gravel St Apt 42 Meriden CT (06450) *(G-2079)*
Bennington Army and Navy Inc 802 447-0020
451 Main St 453 Bennington VT (05201) *(G-21663)*
Bennington Banner, Bennington *Also called North Eastern Publishing Co (G-21686)*
Bennington Microtchnlgy Center 802 442-8975
441 Water St North Bennington VT (05257) *(G-22209)*
Bennington Potters Inc (PA) 800 205-8033
324 County St Bennington VT (05201) *(G-21664)*
Bennington Shriff GLC Slar LLC 802 233-3370
811 Us Route 7 S Bennington VT (05201) *(G-21665)*
Bennington Sports & Graphic, Bennington *Also called Bennington Army and Navy Inc (G-21663)*
Benoit & Company 413 283-8348
1240 Park St Palmer MA (01069) *(G-14280)*
Bens Sugar Shack 603 924-3177
83 Webster Hwy Temple NH (03084) *(G-19896)*
Benson Enterprises Inc 508 583-5401
87 Union St North Easton MA (02356) *(G-13943)*
Benson Neptune Inc (HQ) 401 821-7140
6 Jefferson Dr Coventry RI (02816) *(G-20138)*
Benson Woodhomes, Walpole *Also called Benson Woodworking Company Inc (G-19917)*
Benson Woodworking Company Inc 603 756-3600
6 Blackjack Xing Walpole NH (03608) *(G-19917)*
Bent Water Brewing Co 781 780-9948
180 Commercial St Lynn MA (01905) *(G-12492)*
Bent's Cookie Factory, Milton *Also called G H Bent Company (G-13192)*
Bentley Mills Inc 617 439-0405
27 Drydock Ave Ste 7 Boston MA (02210) *(G-8401)*
Bentley Pharmaceuticals Inc (HQ) 603 658-6100
2 Holland Way Exeter NH (03833) *(G-18113)*
Bentley Publishers, Cambridge *Also called Robert Bentley Inc (G-9636)*
Benu Biopharma Inc 508 208-5634
50 Lands End Ln Sudbury MA (01776) *(G-15653)*
Benz, Edwin H Co, Providence *Also called E H Benz Co Inc (G-20999)*
Beon Home Inc 617 600-8329
8 Barberry Ln North Easton MA (02356) *(G-13944)*
Bera Company, Rochester *Also called Inner Traditions International (G-22317)*
Bercen Division, Cranston *Also called Cranston Print Works Company (G-20203)*
Berg LLC (PA) 617 588-0083
500 Old Connecticut Path # 3 Framingham MA (01701) *(G-10927)*
Bergan Architectural Wdwkg Inc 860 346-0869
55 N Main St Middletown CT (06457) *(G-2177)*
Bergen Pipe Supports Inc (HQ) 781 935-9550
225 Merrimac St Woburn MA (01801) *(G-17130)*
Berger Corporation 508 255-3267
2 Lots Hollow Rd Orleans MA (02653) *(G-14230)*
Bergeron Machine Inc 978 577-6235
65 Powers Rd Westford MA (01886) *(G-16756)*
Bergquist Family Entps Inc 781 449-9196
89 Central Ave Needham Heights MA (02494) *(G-13318)*
Bering Technology Inc 408 364-6500
5086 Main St Waitsfield VT (05673) *(G-22561)*
Berkmatics Inc 413 664-6152
59 Demond Ave North Adams MA (01247) *(G-13669)*
Berkshire Brewing Company Inc (PA) 413 665-6600
12 Railroad St South Deerfield MA (01373) *(G-15246)*
Berkshire Bridge & Iron Co Inc 413 684-3182
140 E Housatonic St Dalton MA (01226) *(G-10174)*
Berkshire Concrete Corp (HQ) 413 443-4734
550 Cheshire Rd Pittsfield MA (01201) *(G-14456)*
Berkshire Corporation (HQ) 413 528-2602
21 River St Great Barrington MA (01230) *(G-11233)*
Berkshire Custom Coating Inc 413 442-3757
50 Downing Industrial Par Pittsfield MA (01201) *(G-14457)*
Berkshire Group Ltd 413 562-7200
184 Falcon Dr Westfield MA (01085) *(G-16673)*
Berkshire Mnufactured Pdts Inc 978 462-8161
116 Parker St Newburyport MA (01950) *(G-13472)*
Berkshire Mountain Distlrs Inc 413 229-0219
1640 Home Rd Great Barrington MA (01230) *(G-11234)*
Berkshire Mtn Bky Pizza Cafe, Pittsfield *Also called Berkshire Mtn Bky Pizza Cafe (G-14458)*
Berkshire Mtn Bky Pizza Cafe 413 464-9394
180 Elm St Ste A Pittsfield MA (01201) *(G-14458)*
Berkshire Photonics LLC 860 868-0412
88 Bee Brook Rd Washington Depot CT (06794) *(G-4832)*
Berkshire Precision Tool LLC 413 499-3875
9 Betnr Industrial Dr Pittsfield MA (01201) *(G-14459)*
Berkshire Publishing Group LLC 413 528-0206
122 Castle St Great Barrington MA (01230) *(G-11235)*
Berkshire Record, Great Barrington *Also called Limestone Communications (G-11241)*
Berkshire Reference Works, Great Barrington *Also called Berkshire Publishing Group LLC (G-11235)*
Berkshire Screen 413 212-8360
95 Davis St Pittsfield MA (01201) *(G-14460)*
Berkshire Spt & Sew What EMB, Dalton *Also called Sew What Embroidery (G-10184)*
Berkshire Sterile Mfg Inc 413 243-0330
480 Pleasant St Lee MA (01238) *(G-12088)*
Berkshire Totes For Tots Inc 413 442-7048
89 Egremont Ave Pittsfield MA (01201) *(G-14461)*
Berlin Daily Sun 603 752-5858
164 Main St Ste 1 Berlin NH (03570) *(G-17692)*
Berlin Foundary & Achine Co, Berlin *Also called Bfmc LLC (G-17693)*
Berlin Operations, East Berlin *Also called Paradigm Prcision Holdings LLC (G-1105)*
Berlyn Reporter, Meredith *Also called Salmon Press LLC (G-18978)*
Bermer Precision Products LLC 508 764-2521
94 Ashland Ave Southbridge MA (01550) *(G-15376)*
Bermer Tool & Die Inc 508 764-2521
81 Ashland Ave Southbridge MA (01550) *(G-15377)*
Bern Optics Inc 413 568-6800
579 Southampton Rd Ste 1 Westfield MA (01085) *(G-16674)*
Bernard Ginn and Sons Inc 207 234-2187
54 Perkins Rd Winterport ME (04496) *(G-7276)*
Bernardinos Bakery Inc (PA) 413 592-1944
105 Exchange St Chicopee MA (01013) *(G-10001)*

ALPHABETIC

Bernardo Manufacuring, Rumford *Also called Winkler Group Ltd* ***(G-21199)***
Bernell Tool & Mfg Co........203 756-4405
181 Mulloy Rd Waterbury CT (06705) ***(G-4849)***
Berry Global Inc........508 918-1715
25 Forge Pkwy Franklin MA (02038) ***(G-11026)***
Berry Global Inc........812 424-2904
44 Oneil St Easthampton MA (01027) ***(G-10555)***
Berry Global Inc........508 325-0004
8 Amelia Dr Ste 1 Nantucket MA (02554) ***(G-13221)***
Berry Global Inc........401 254-0600
51 Ballou Blvd Bristol RI (02809) ***(G-20064)***
Berry Global Films LLC........978 532-2000
199 Rosewood Dr Ste 240 Danvers MA (01923) ***(G-10202)***
Berry Logging/R A Berry & Sons........207 634-4808
24 Maple St Norridgewock ME (04957) ***(G-6495)***
Berry Manufacturing, Pawtucket *Also called Professional Images Inc* ***(G-20884)***
Berry Plastics Corp........413 529-2183
122 Pleasant St Easthampton MA (01027) ***(G-10556)***
Berry Plastics Corporation........413 527-1250
44 Oneil St Easthampton MA (01027) ***(G-10557)***
Berry Twist........857 362-7455
200 Faneuil Hall Mkt Pl Boston MA (02109) ***(G-8402)***
Berstein Display, Shaftsbury *Also called Leo D Bernstein and Sons Inc* ***(G-22405)***
Berthon Usa Inc........401 846-8404
40 May St & The New Prt Newport RI (02840) ***(G-20657)***
Bertoldo Engraving, Wakefield *Also called Bertoldo Inc* ***(G-15944)***
Bertoldo Inc........781 324-9145
43 Wiley St Wakefield MA (01880) ***(G-15944)***
Bertram & Leithner Inc........978 459-7474
210 Stedman St Lowell MA (01851) ***(G-12353)***
Bertram Sirkin........860 656-7446
200 Mohegan Dr West Hartford CT (06117) ***(G-5055)***
Berube Tool & Die Inc........603 382-2224
34 Main St Plaistow NH (03865) ***(G-19509)***
Bes Cu Inc........860 582-8660
400 Middle St Bristol CT (06010) ***(G-533)***
Besam Entrance Solutions, Auburn *Also called Assa Abloy Entrance Sys US Inc* ***(G-7827)***
Besheer Artile Studios, Bedford *Also called Besheer Studios* ***(G-17632)***
Besheer Studios........603 472-5288
27 Mcintosh Ln Bedford NH (03110) ***(G-17632)***
Besi USA, Salem *Also called Be Semiconductor Inds USA Inc* ***(G-19711)***
Bess Home Fashions Inc........401 828-0300
155 Brookside Ave West Warwick RI (02893) ***(G-21484)***
Bessette Holdings Inc........860 289-6000
95 Leggett St East Hartford CT (06108) ***(G-1176)***
Best Felts Inc........207 596-0566
17 Dexter St Ext Thomaston ME (04861) ***(G-7081)***
Best Foods Baking Co. Now., Orange *Also called Bimbo Bakeries Usa Inc* ***(G-3360)***
Best Home Fashions, West Warwick *Also called Natco Home Fashions Inc* ***(G-21503)***
Best Machine Inc........603 895-4018
79 Beede Hill Rd Fremont NH (03044) ***(G-18174)***
Best Management Products Inc........860 434-0277
9 Matthews Dr Unit A1-A2 East Haddam CT (06423) ***(G-1148)***
Best Manager Products, East Haddam *Also called Best Management Products Inc* ***(G-1148)***
Best Manufacturing, Seekonk *Also called Tillotson Corporation* ***(G-15042)***
Best Products, Poultney *Also called Macryan Inc* ***(G-22273)***
Best Quality Printing, Hyde Park *Also called Ted Best* ***(G-11881)***
Bestway Food and Fuel........860 447-0729
6 Boston Post Rd Waterford CT (06385) ***(G-4981)***
Bestway of New England Inc........978 368-7667
840 Sterling Rd South Lancaster MA (01561) ***(G-15316)***
Beta Acquisition Inc........603 726-7500
202 Tamarack Rd Thornton NH (03285) ***(G-19900)***
Beta Bionics Inc........949 293-2076
8 Saint Marys St Ste 936 Boston MA (02215) ***(G-8403)***
Beta Dyne Inc........508 697-1993
110 Elm St Unit 12 Bridgewater MA (02324) ***(G-9064)***
Beta Pharma Inc........203 315-5062
1 Enterprise Dr Ste 408 Shelton CT (06484) ***(G-3780)***
Beta Shim Co........203 926-1150
11 Progress Dr Shelton CT (06484) ***(G-3781)***
Bete Fog Nozzle Inc (PA)........413 772-0846
50 Greenfield St Greenfield MA (01301) ***(G-11252)***
Beth Bowley, Rockland *Also called Babtech Inc* ***(G-6784)***
Beth Mueller Design, Barre *Also called Beth Mueller Inc* ***(G-21609)***
Beth Mueller Inc........802 476-3582
13 Pleasant St Barre VT (05641) ***(G-21609)***
Beth Veneto........617 472-4729
215 Samoset Ave Ste 15 Quincy MA (02169) ***(G-14615)***
Bethcare Inc........617 997-1069
110 Chauncy St Boston MA (02111) ***(G-8404)***
Bethel Citizen, Albany Twp *Also called Citizen Printers Incorporated* ***(G-5512)***
Bethel Division, Bethel *Also called Vanderbilt Chemicals LLC* ***(G-189)***
Bethel Mail Service........203 730-1399
211 Greenwood Ave Ste 2 Bethel CT (06801) ***(G-130)***
Bethel Mail Service Center, Bethel *Also called Bethel Mail Service* ***(G-130)***
Bethel Printing & Graphics........203 748-7034
81 Greenwood Ave Ste 10 Bethel CT (06801) ***(G-131)***
Bethel Sand & Gravel Co........203 743-4469
2 Maple Avenue Ext Bethel CT (06801) ***(G-132)***
Betkoski Brothers LLC........203 723-8262
332 Bethany Rd Beacon Falls CT (06403) ***(G-55)***
Betlan Corporation........203 270-7898
31 Pecks Ln Ste 7 Newtown CT (06470) ***(G-2916)***
Betoel Publishers, Stamford *Also called Kieffer Associates Inc* ***(G-4235)***
Better Baking By Beth........860 482-4706
270 W Hill Rd Torrington CT (06790) ***(G-4564)***
Better Bottling Solutions LLC........219 308-5616
25 Harrington St Newton MA (02460) ***(G-13567)***
Better Life LLC........603 647-0077
8030 S Willow St Unit 1-4 Manchester NH (03103) ***(G-18787)***
Better Maintenance Sheet Metal........978 948-7067
48 Railroad Ave Rowley MA (01969) ***(G-14846)***
Better Molded Products Inc (PA)........860 589-0066
95 Valley St Ste 2 Bristol CT (06010) ***(G-534)***
Better Pallets Inc........203 230-9549
10 Corbin Cir Branford CT (06405) ***(G-296)***
Betty Reez Whoopiez........207 865-1735
67 Carter Rd Freeport ME (04032) ***(G-6072)***
Betx LLC........860 459-1681
440 Cedar Ln New Hartford CT (06057) ***(G-2632)***
Betz Tool Company Inc........203 878-1187
70 Raton Rd Ste K Milford CT (06461) ***(G-2253)***
Beverage Publications Inc........203 288-3375
2508 Whitney Ave Apt N Hamden CT (06518) ***(G-1735)***
Beverly Citizen, Beverly *Also called Gatehouse Media Mass I Inc* ***(G-8134)***
Beverly Citizen........978 927-2777
48 Dunham Rd Beverly MA (01915) ***(G-8108)***
Beverly Feldman, Norwalk *Also called Aj Casey LLC* ***(G-3098)***
Beverly Hills Hlth & Buty Pdts, Bow *Also called Riverview Labs Inc* ***(G-17729)***
Beverly Pallet Company Inc........978 356-1121
51 Mitchell Rd Ipswich MA (01938) ***(G-11905)***
Beverly Qiagen Inc........978 927-7027
100 Cummings Ctr Ste 407j Beverly MA (01915) ***(G-8109)***
Beverly Shade Shoppe........978 922-0374
81 Bridge St Ste C Beverly MA (01915) ***(G-8110)***
Bevi, Charlestown *Also called Hydration Labs Incorporated* ***(G-9837)***
Bevin Bells, East Hampton *Also called Bevin Bros Manufacturing Co* ***(G-1158)***
Bevin Bros Manufacturing Co........860 267-4431
17 Watrous St East Hampton CT (06424) ***(G-1158)***
Bevovations LLC (PA)........978 227-5469
320 Industrial Rd Leominster MA (01453) ***(G-12118)***
Bewell Body Scan........617 754-0300
25 Boylston St Ste LI07 Chestnut Hill MA (02467) ***(G-9982)***
Bey-Low Molds........860 482-6561
80 Sunrise Dr Torrington CT (06790) ***(G-4565)***
Beyond Shaker LLC........617 461-6608
124a Cummings Park Woburn MA (01801) ***(G-17131)***
Beyondtrust Software Inc........978 206-3700
200 Brickstone Sq Ste G03 Andover MA (01810) ***(G-7540)***
BF Goodrich Aerspce Aircrft In........802 877-2911
100 Panton Rd Vergennes VT (05491) ***(G-22552)***
Bff Holdings Inc (HQ)........860 510-0100
141 Mill Rock Rd E Old Saybrook CT (06475) ***(G-3328)***
BFI Print Communications Inc (PA)........781 447-1199
255 State St Fl 7 Boston MA (02109) ***(G-8405)***
Bfmc LLC........603 752-4550
489 Goebel St Berlin NH (03570) ***(G-17693)***
Bh Media Inc (HQ)........617 426-3000
100 Grossman Dr Ste 400 Braintree MA (02184) ***(G-8990)***
Bhs-Torin, Manchester *Also called L M Gill Welding and Mfr LLC* ***(G-2017)***
Bi Medical LLC........866 246-3301
1372 Main St Coventry RI (02816) ***(G-20139)***
Bi-Metalix, East Windsor *Also called KTI Bi-Metallix Inc* ***(G-1293)***
Bi-Qem Inc........413 584-2472
238 Nonotuck St Florence MA (01062) ***(G-10864)***
Biasin Enterprises Inc........413 243-0885
515 Marble St Lee MA (01238) ***(G-12089)***
Bic Consumer Products Mfg Co........203 783-2000
565 Bic Dr Milford CT (06461) ***(G-2254)***
Bic Corporation (HQ)........203 783-2000
1 Bic Way Ste 1 # 1 Shelton CT (06484) ***(G-3782)***
Bic Graphic USA, Shelton *Also called Bic Corporation* ***(G-3782)***
Bic USA Inc (HQ)........203 783-2000
1 Bic Way Ste 1 # 1 Shelton CT (06484) ***(G-3783)***
Bicon LLC (PA)........617 524-4443
501 Arborway Boston MA (02130) ***(G-8406)***
Bicron Electronics Company (PA)........860 482-2524
427 Goshen Rd Torrington CT (06790) ***(G-4566)***
Bid2win Software Inc........800 336-3808
99 Bow St Ste 500 Portsmouth NH (03801) ***(G-19543)***
Biddeford Saco Courier, Biddeford *Also called Mainely Newspapers Inc* ***(G-5746)***
Bidirectional Display Inc........617 599-8282
8 Monument Pl Acton MA (01720) ***(G-7344)***

Bidwell Industrial Group Inc (PA) 860 346-9283
2055 S Main St Middletown CT (06457) ***(G-2178)***

Biedermann Mfg Inds Inc 860 283-8268
135 S Main St Thomaston CT (06787) ***(G-4499)***

Biena LLC 617 202-5210
119 Braintree St Ste 409 Boston MA (02134) ***(G-8407)***

Biena Foods, Boston *Also called Biena LLC* ***(G-8407)***

Big 3 Precision Products Inc 508 429-4774
140 Lowland St Holliston MA (01746) ***(G-11559)***

Big Belly Solar Inc 888 820-0300
150 A St Ste 103 Needham Heights MA (02494) ***(G-13319)***

Big Bill, Newport *Also called Codet-Newport Corporation* ***(G-22192)***

Big Daddy Boomerangs LLC 413 297-7079
88 Coral Rd Springfield MA (01118) ***(G-15452)***

Big Daddy Brews LLC 603 569-5647
1 Bioteau Dr East Kingston NH (03827) ***(G-18084)***

Big Daddys Signs Florida Inc 800 535-2139
24 Lexington Dr Laconia NH (03246) ***(G-18558)***

Big Dipper 603 742-7075
222 Route 108 Somersworth NH (03878) ***(G-19829)***

Big Dog Disposal Inc 508 695-9539
72 Pond St Seekonk MA (02771) ***(G-15019)***

Big Foote Crushing LLC 603 345-0695
1225 River Rd Weare NH (03281) ***(G-19932)***

Big G Seafood Inc 508 994-5113
48 Antonio Costa Ave New Bedford MA (02740) ***(G-13361)***

Big Pond Wireless LLC 781 593-2321
1230 Furnace Brook Pkwy North Reading MA (01864) ***(G-13979)***

Big Prints LLC 203 469-1100
15 Baer Cir Ste 2 East Haven CT (06512) ***(G-1243)***

Big Purple Cupcake LLC 203 483-8738
6 Conifer Dr Branford CT (06405) ***(G-297)***

Big Rock Oyster Company Inc 774 408-7951
501 Depot St Harwich MA (02645) ***(G-11389)***

Bigelow Tea, Fairfield *Also called RC Bigelow Inc* ***(G-1451)***

Bigfoot Seo Strategies 617 448-4848
27 Smith St Unit 1305 Marblehead MA (01945) ***(G-12676)***

Bigtincan Mobile Pty Ltd 617 981-7557
260 Charles St Ste 101 Waltham MA (02453) ***(G-16047)***

Bigwood Corporation 508 477-2220
57 Industrial Dr Mashpee MA (02649) ***(G-12875)***

Bike & Ski Touring Ctr of Neng 802 388-6666
74 Main St Middlebury VT (05753) ***(G-22102)***

Bike Center, The, Middlebury *Also called Bike & Ski Touring Ctr of Neng* ***(G-22102)***

Bike Track Inc 802 457-3275
19 Central St Ste D Woodstock VT (05091) ***(G-22737)***

Bikers Outfitters, The, Revere *Also called L & J Leathers Manufacturing* ***(G-14770)***

Bilbe Controls, Bristol *Also called Rostra Vernatherm LLC* ***(G-609)***

Bill Lztte Archtctural GL Alum 401 383-9535
400 Wampanoag Trl Riverside RI (02915) ***(G-21164)***

Bill Martel 617 776-1040
2 Bradley St Ste S8 Somerville MA (02145) ***(G-15158)***

Bill Willard Inc 413 584-1054
1350 Main St Ste 1505 Springfield MA (01103) ***(G-15453)***

Billard Corporation 508 888-4964
290 Route 130 Unit 1 Sandwich MA (02563) ***(G-14961)***

Billerica Backstage Rehearsal 978 670-1133
749 Boston Rd Pinehurst MA (01866) ***(G-14447)***

Billerica Minute-Man, Concord *Also called Gatehouse Media Mass I Inc* ***(G-10131)***

Billings Diesel & Marine Svc 207 367-2328
Moose Island Rd Stonington ME (04681) ***(G-7069)***

Billy Hill Tubs LLC 978 422-8800
47 Chocksett Rd Sterling MA (01564) ***(G-15536)***

Biltrite Corporation 617 884-3124
31 Highland St Chelsea MA (02150) ***(G-9945)***

Biltrite Manufacturing Plant, Chelsea *Also called Biltrite Corporation* ***(G-9945)***

Bimbo Bakeries Usa Inc 508 336-7735
63 Fall River Ave Rehoboth MA (02769) ***(G-14745)***

Bimbo Bakeries Usa Inc 203 932-1000
284 Bull Hill Ln Orange CT (06477) ***(G-3360)***

Bimbo Bakeries Usa Inc 207 883-5252
3 Lincoln Ave Scarborough ME (04074) ***(G-6911)***

Bimbo Bakeries Usa Inc 860 691-1180
9 Freedom Way Portland CT (06480) ***(G-3564)***

Bimbo Bakeries Usa Inc 508 923-1023
45 Leona Dr Middleboro MA (02346) ***(G-13055)***

Bimbo Bakeries Usa Inc 781 306-0221
4110 Mystic Valley Pkwy Medford MA (02155) ***(G-12922)***

Bimbo Bakeries Usa Inc 603 626-7405
3 E Point Dr Hooksett NH (03106) ***(G-18343)***

Bimbo Bakeries Usa Inc 802 748-1389
1188 Memorial Dr Saint Johnsbury VT (05819) ***(G-22386)***

Bimbo Bakeries Usa Inc 413 543-5328
1964 Boston Rd Ste 3 Wilbraham MA (01095) ***(G-16933)***

Bimbo Bakeries Usa Inc 603 448-4227
91 Mechanic St Lebanon NH (03766) ***(G-18615)***

Bindery Solutions Inc (PA) 802 372-3492
225 W Shore Rd Grand Isle VT (05458) ***(G-21997)***

Bingham & Taylor Corp (HQ) 540 825-8334
1022 Elm St Rocky Hill CT (06067) ***(G-3703)***

Bio Defense Corporation 617 778-1800
12 Channel St Ste 9 Boston MA (02210) ***(G-8408)***

Bio Energy Inc 617 822-1220
739 Washington St Boston MA (02124) ***(G-8409)***

Bio Green 603 570-6159
124 Heritage Ave Unit 15 Portsmouth NH (03801) ***(G-19544)***

Bio Holdings Inc 401 683-5400
45 Highpoint Ave Ste 3 Portsmouth RI (02871) ***(G-20918)***

Bio Med Packaging Systems Inc 203 846-1923
100 Pearl St Norwalk CT (06850) ***(G-3113)***

Bio Pharmaceutical, Boston *Also called Puretech Health LLC* ***(G-8799)***

Bio RAD Lab 207 615-0571
1045 Riverside St Portland ME (04103) ***(G-6622)***

Bio-Catalytic Enterprises Inc 413 739-9148
1 Allen St Ste 201 Springfield MA (01108) ***(G-15454)***

Bio-Concept Laboratories Inc 603 437-4990
13 Industrial Way Salem NH (03079) ***(G-19713)***

Bio-Detek Incorporated 401 729-1400
525 Narragansett Park Dr Pawtucket RI (02861) ***(G-20816)***

Bio-Med Devices Inc 203 458-0202
61 Soundview Rd Guilford CT (06437) ***(G-1693)***

Bio-Mold Division, Wilmington *Also called Neu-Tool Design Inc* ***(G-17029)***

Bio-Oregon, Westbrook *Also called Moore-Clark USA Inc* ***(G-7198)***

Bio-Tek Instruments, Winooski *Also called Lionheart Technologies Inc* ***(G-22721)***

Bioanalytix Inc 857 829-3200
790 Memorial Dr Cambridge MA (02139) ***(G-9408)***

Bioarray Genetics Inc 508 577-0205
400 Farmington Ave Farmington CT (06032) ***(G-1468)***

Biobright LLC (PA) 617 444-9007
2 Park Plz Ste 605 Boston MA (02116) ***(G-8410)***

Biochrom Us Inc 508 893-8999
84 October Hill Rd Ste 10 Holliston MA (01746) ***(G-11560)***

Bioclinica Inc 860 701-0082
234 Bank St New London CT (06320) ***(G-2766)***

Biodesign International Inc 207 283-6500
60 Industrial Park Rd Saco ME (04072) ***(G-6843)***

Biodirection Inc 508 599-2400
144 Trnpike Rd Sthborough Southborough Southborough MA (01772) ***(G-15345)***

Bioenergy International LLC 617 657-5200
3 Batterymarch Park # 301 Quincy MA (02169) ***(G-14616)***

Biofibers Capital Group LLC 203 561-6133
14 Amidon Dr Ashford CT (06278) ***(G-25)***

Biogen Inc (PA) 617 679-2000
225 Binney St Cambridge MA (02142) ***(G-9409)***

Biogen MA Inc (HQ) 617 679-2000
225 Binney St Cambridge MA (02142) ***(G-9410)***

Biohaven Pharmaceuticals, New Haven *Also called Biohaven Phrm Holdg Co Ltd* ***(G-2667)***

Biohaven Pharmaceuticals Inc 203 404-0410
215 Church St New Haven CT (06510) ***(G-2666)***

Biohaven Phrm Holdg Co Ltd 203 404-0410
215 Church St New Haven CT (06510) ***(G-2667)***

Biohelix Corporation 978 927-5056
500 Cummings Ctr Ste 5550 Beverly MA (01915) ***(G-8111)***

Biological Industries 860 316-5197
100 Sebethe Dr Ste A3 Cromwell CT (06416) ***(G-848)***

Biologics Production, Winslow *Also called Lohmann Animal Health Intl Inc* ***(G-7270)***

Biolucent LLC 508 263-2900
250 Campus Dr Marlborough MA (01752) ***(G-12726)***

Biom, Cambridge *Also called Bionx Medical Technologies Inc* ***(G-9411)***

Biomass Commodities Corp 413 458-5326
227 Adams Rd Williamstown MA (01267) ***(G-16955)***

Biomass Energy LLC 540 872-3300
125 Powder Forest Dr Weatogue CT (06089) ***(G-5041)***

Biomed Health Inc 860 657-2258
70 Oakwood Dr Ste 8 Glastonbury CT (06033) ***(G-1540)***

Biomed Packing Systems, Norwalk *Also called K W Griffen Company* ***(G-3183)***

Biomed Software Inc 617 513-1298
72 Kensington St Newton MA (02460) ***(G-13568)***

Biomedical Polymers Inc 978 632-2555
16 Chocksett Rd Sterling MA (01564) ***(G-15537)***

Biomedical Structures LLC 401 223-0990
60 Commerce Dr Warwick RI (02886) ***(G-21336)***

Biomerieux Inc 617 879-8000
201 Wshington St Ste 4030 Boston MA (02108) ***(G-8411)***

Biometrics Inc (PA) 203 261-1162
115 Technology Dr Cp102 Trumbull CT (06611) ***(G-4615)***

Bionetiks Co 415 343-4990
145 Union St Apt 8 New Bedford MA (02740) ***(G-13362)***

Bionostics Inc 978 772-7070
7 Jackson Rd Devens MA (01434) ***(G-10319)***

Bionx Medical Technologies Inc 781 761-1545
27 Moulton St Cambridge MA (02138) ***(G-9411)***

Biopharm Engineered Systems, Andover *Also called Jgp Enterprises Inc* ***(G-7559)***

Biopharma of Cape Cod Inc 508 428-5823
656 Putnam Ave Cotuit MA (02635) ***(G-10168)***

Biophysical Devices Inc 617 629-0304
27 Columbus Ave Somerville MA (02143) ***(G-15159)***

Bioprocessh2o LLC......401 683-5400
45 Highpoint Ave Portsmouth RI (02871) *(G-20919)*
Bioprocessing Inc......207 457-0025
1045 Riverside St Portland ME (04103) *(G-6623)*
Bioraft, Cambridge *Also called Research Applications and (G-9630)*
Biorasis Inc......860 429-3592
23 Fellen Rd Storrs CT (06268) *(G-4380)*
Biosan Laboratories Inc......603 437-0861
8 Bowers Rd Derry NH (03038) *(G-17972)*
Bioscience Beads Division, West Warwick *Also called Colloidal Science Solutions (G-21487)*
Biosensics LLC......888 589-6213
57 Chapel St Ste 200 Newton MA (02458) *(G-13569)*
Biosolutions, Meriden *Also called Brand-Nu Laboratories Inc (G-2080)*
Biosolve Company......781 482-7900
24 Victory Ln Dracut MA (01826) *(G-10354)*
Biostage Inc......774 233-7300
84 October Hill Rd Ste 11 Holliston MA (01746) *(G-11561)*
Biotech Diagnostics......617 332-8787
109 Lovett Rd Newton MA (02459) *(G-13570)*
Biotech Source Inc (PA)......207 894-5690
12 Studio Dr Windham ME (04062) *(G-7230)*
Biotek Instruments Inc (HQ)......802 655-4040
100 Tigan St Winooski VT (05404) *(G-22717)*
Bioverativ Inc (HQ)......781 663-4400
225 2nd Ave Waltham MA (02451) *(G-16048)*
Biovia Corp......508 497-9911
9 Industrial Rd Ste 4 Milford MA (01757) *(G-13109)*
Bioview......978 670-4741
44 Manning Rd Ste 4 Billerica MA (01821) *(G-8219)*
Biowave Innovations LLC......203 982-8157
274 Ridgefield Rd Wilton CT (06897) *(G-5278)*
Bioxcel Therapeutics Inc......475 238-6837
555 Long Wharf Dr New Haven CT (06511) *(G-2668)*
Biq LLC......508 485-9896
37 Valley Rd Southborough MA (01772) *(G-15346)*
Birch Point Paper Products Inc......978 422-1447
750 Crawford St Fitchburg MA (01420) *(G-10811)*
Bird Precision, Waltham *Also called Richard H Bird & Co Inc (G-16189)*
Birds & Beans LLC......857 233-2722
27 Summer St South Dartmouth MA (02748) *(G-15236)*
Birdtrack Press......203 389-7789
26 Mckinley Ave New Haven CT (06515) *(G-2669)*
Birk Manufacturing Inc......800 531-2070
14 Capitol Dr East Lyme CT (06333) *(G-1269)*
Birken Manufacturing Company......860 242-2211
3 Old Windsor Rd Bloomfield CT (06002) *(G-209)*
Birkett Woodworking LLC......860 361-9142
14 Benedict Rd Morris CT (06763) *(G-2431)*
Birkhauser, Boston *Also called Walter De Gruyter Inc (G-8915)*
Birnam Wood Games, Burlington *Also called Gametheory Inc (G-21785)*
Birnn Chocolates Vermont Inc......802 860-1047
102 Kimball Ave Ste 4 South Burlington VT (05403) *(G-22438)*
Birotech Inc......203 968-5080
29 Sunnyside Ave Ste 4 Stamford CT (06902) *(G-4150)*
Bisco Environmental Inc......508 738-5100
55 Ferncroft Rd Ste 110 Danvers MA (01923) *(G-10203)*
Biscom Inc......978 250-1800
10 Technology Park Dr # 102 Westford MA (01886) *(G-16757)*
Bishop Crown Co......207 873-2350
404 Nowell Rd Winslow ME (04901) *(G-7268)*
Biszko Contracting Corp......508 679-0518
20 Development St Fall River MA (02721) *(G-10668)*
Bite Tech Inc......203 987-6898
20 Glover Ave Ste 1 Norwalk CT (06850) *(G-3114)*
Bitflow Inc......781 932-2900
400 W Cummings Park # 5050 Woburn MA (01801) *(G-17132)*
Bitome Inc......207 812-8099
18 Park Ln Jamaica Plain MA (02130) *(G-11940)*
Bittersweet Herb Farm, Shelburne Falls *Also called David W Wallace (G-15067)*
Bittid LLC......781 570-2077
81 Walnut St Winchester MA (01890) *(G-17083)*
Bittware Inc (HQ)......603 226-0404
45 S Main St Ste L100 Concord NH (03301) *(G-17884)*
Bittware Fpga Cmpt Systems, Concord *Also called Bittware Inc (G-17884)*
Bixby & Co LLC......207 691-1778
1 Sea Street Pl Rockland ME (04841) *(G-6785)*
Bixby International Corp......978 462-4100
1 Preble Rd Newburyport MA (01950) *(G-13473)*
Biz Tek Printing and Mktg LLC......508 248-3377
5 North St Ste 7 Ware MA (01082) *(G-16230)*
Biz Wiz Print & Copy Ctr LLC (PA)......860 721-0040
781 Cromwell Ave Ste E Rocky Hill CT (06067) *(G-3704)*
Bizcard Xpress LLC......860 324-6840
26 Killingworth Rd Higganum CT (06441) *(G-1901)*
Bizunite, Manchester *Also called CCA Global Partners Inc (G-18797)*
Bji Enterprises, Westport *Also called Dartmouth Awning Co Inc (G-16838)*
Bjm Pumps LLC......860 399-5937
123 Spencer Plain Rd # 1 Old Saybrook CT (06475) *(G-3329)*

Bjorklund Corp......401 944-6400
17 Freese St Providence RI (02908) *(G-20970)*
Bki Worldwide, Salem *Also called Cooking Solutions Group Inc (G-19719)*
Bkmfg Corp......860 738-2200
200 International Way Winsted CT (06098) *(G-5405)*
Bl Healthcare Inc......508 543-4150
100 Foxboro Blvd Ste 230 Foxboro MA (02035) *(G-10877)*
Bl Printing Shop......203 334-7779
3442 Fairfield Ave Bridgeport CT (06605) *(G-383)*
Black & Decker (us) Inc......860 563-5800
662 Silas Deane Hwy Wethersfield CT (06109) *(G-5242)*
Black & Decker (us) Inc......860 225-5111
700 Stanley Dr New Britain CT (06053) *(G-2514)*
Black & Decker (us) Inc (HQ)......860 225-5111
1000 Stanley Dr New Britain CT (06053) *(G-2515)*
Black & Decker (us) Inc......413 526-5150
301 Chestnut St East Longmeadow MA (01028) *(G-10468)*
Black & Decker (us) Inc......781 329-3407
377 University Ave Westwood MA (02090) *(G-16858)*
Black & Decker Corporation......603 356-7595
41 Settelers Grn North Conway NH (03860) *(G-19373)*
Black and White Printing......401 265-7811
501 Gleasondale Rd Ste 9 Stow MA (01775) *(G-15631)*
Black Bear Graphics......207 265-4593
51 W Kingfield Rd Kingfield ME (04947) *(G-6252)*
Black Bear Graphics Inc......207 778-9715
805 Farmington Falls Rd # 8 Farmington ME (04938) *(G-6041)*
Black Bear Tree Svc......802 345-2815
3466 Franklin St Brandon VT (05733) *(G-21707)*
Black Beauty Driveway Sealing......802 860-7113
60 Mercier Dr Colchester VT (05446) *(G-21858)*
Black Cove Cabinetry......207 883-8901
137 Pleasant Hill Rd Scarborough ME (04074) *(G-6912)*
Black Diamond Drill Grinders......978 465-3799
17 Viking Ter Shrewsbury MA (01545) *(G-15104)*
Black Diamond Group Inc......781 932-4173
300 Tradecenter Ste 5550 Woburn MA (01801) *(G-17133)*
Black Diamond Mfg & Engrg Inc......978 352-6716
8 Searle St Georgetown MA (01833) *(G-11137)*
Black Dog Corporation......401 683-5858
1 Maritime Dr Ste 3 Portsmouth RI (02871) *(G-20920)*
Black Dog Screen Printing......207 426-9041
27 Main St Clinton ME (04927) *(G-5913)*
Black Earth Compost LLC......262 227-1067
2 Hillside Rd Gloucester MA (01930) *(G-11166)*
Black Earth Technologies Inc......508 397-1335
2575 County St Dighton MA (02715) *(G-10336)*
Black Flannel Brewing Co LLC......802 488-0089
21 Essex Way Ste 201 Essex Junction VT (05452) *(G-21931)*
Black Ice Publishers......508 481-0910
130 Main St Southborough MA (01772) *(G-15347)*
Black Oxide Co Inc......508 757-0340
100 Grand St Ste 3 Worcester MA (01610) *(G-17348)*
Black Rock Tech Group LLC......203 916-7200
211 State St Ste 203 Bridgeport CT (06604) *(G-384)*
Black Shield Driveway Sealer, Abington *Also called Kol-Tar Inc (G-7326)*
Black Tooth Games Brand, Lincoln *Also called Simply Media Inc (G-12289)*
Blackbear Signworks Inc......207 286-8004
19 Industrial Park Rd Saco ME (04072) *(G-6844)*
Blackbird Manufacturing and De......860 331-3477
112 Gardner Tavern Ln Coventry CT (06238) *(G-831)*
Blackboard Inc......617 713-5471
1187 Beacon St Brookline MA (02446) *(G-9195)*
Blackburn Energy Inc......800 342-9194
11 Chestnut St Amesbury MA (01913) *(G-7480)*
Blackhawk Machine Products Inc......401 232-7563
6 Industrial Dr Smithfield RI (02917) *(G-21213)*
Blackledge Industries LLC......401 270-6779
255 Main St Pawtucket RI (02860) *(G-20817)*
Blacklightning Publishing Inc......802 439-6462
252 Riddle Pond Rd West Topsham VT (05086) *(G-22621)*
Blacksmith Prtg & Copy Ctr LLC......603 569-6300
90a Center St Wolfeboro NH (03894) *(G-20015)*
Blackstone Industries LLC......203 792-8622
16 Stony Hill Rd Bethel CT (06801) *(G-133)*
Blackstone Valley Prestain......401 568-9745
730 Broncos Hwy Mapleville RI (02839) *(G-20611)*
Blackthorne Forge Ltd......802 426-3369
3821 Us Route 2 Marshfield VT (05658) *(G-22092)*
Blacktrace Inc......617 848-1211
156 Norwell Ave Norwell MA (02061) *(G-14097)*
Blackwold Inc......860 526-0800
212 Middlesex Ave Chester CT (06412) *(G-768)*
Blade Tech Systems Inc......508 830-9506
100 Armstrong Rd Ste 103 Plymouth MA (02360) *(G-14545)*
Blair Campbell......802 773-7711
298 Us Route 4 E Rutland VT (05701) *(G-22325)*
Blairden Precision Instrs Inc......203 799-2000
95 Corporate Dr Trumbull CT (06611) *(G-4616)*

Blake Press Inc....617 742-8700
11 Beacon St Bsmt Boston MA (02108) ***(G-8412)***
Blakeslee Prestress Inc (PA)....203 315-7090
At Mc Dermott Rd Rr 139 Branford CT (06405) ***(G-298)***
Blanchard Awnings, Wakefield *Also called William Blanchard Co Inc* ***(G-15985)***
Blanchard Contact Lens Inc....800 367-4009
8025 S Willow St Ste 211 Manchester NH (03103) ***(G-18788)***
Blanchard Press Inc....617 426-6690
249 Mystic Valley Pkwy Winchester MA (01890) ***(G-17084)***
Blanchard Printing....603 891-1505
16 Pinebrook Rd Nashua NH (03062) ***(G-19127)***
Blanche P Field LLC....617 423-0714
1 Design Center Pl # 336 Boston MA (02210) ***(G-8413)***
Blank Industries Inc....855 887-3123
17 Brent Dr Hudson MA (01749) ***(G-11759)***
Blase Manufacturing Company (PA)....203 375-5646
60 Watson Blvd Ste 3 Stratford CT (06615) ***(G-4397)***
Blase Tool & Manufacturing Co, Stratford *Also called Blase Manufacturing Company* ***(G-4397)***
Blastech Overhaul & Repair....860 243-8811
86 W Dudley Town Rd Bloomfield CT (06002) ***(G-210)***
Blazing Signworks Inc....800 672-4887
57 Sarah Ln Fitchburg MA (01420) ***(G-10812)***
Blendco Systems LLC....800 537-7797
630 Beaulieu St Holyoke MA (01040) ***(G-11619)***
Blessed Creek....860 416-3692
908 Overhill Dr Suffield CT (06078) ***(G-4460)***
Blethen Maine Newspapers, Augusta *Also called Seattle Times Company* ***(G-5619)***
Blethen Maine Newspapers Inc....207 791-6650
390 Congress St Portland ME (04101) ***(G-6624)***
Blevins Company....207 882-6396
178 Boothbay Rd Edgecomb ME (04556) ***(G-5999)***
Blink, North Reading *Also called Immedia Semiconductor Inc* ***(G-13985)***
Blink Neurotech Corp....917 767-6829
48 Englewood Ave 3 Brighton MA (02135) ***(G-9096)***
Blinky Products, Ayer *Also called Plastic Assembly Corporation* ***(G-7934)***
Bliss Logging....603 279-5674
47 Old Center Harbor Rd Meredith NH (03253) ***(G-18971)***
Bliss Manufacturing Co Inc....401 729-1690
50 Bacon St Pawtucket RI (02860) ***(G-20818)***
Blitz Foods LLC....617 243-7446
75 Park Plz Ste 3 Boston MA (02116) ***(G-8414)***
Block Engineering LLC....508 480-9643
132 Turnpike Rd Ste 110 Southborough MA (01772) ***(G-15348)***
Block Island Software, Acton *Also called Sorriso Technologies Inc* ***(G-7387)***
Block Island Times, The, Block Island *Also called Manisses Inc* ***(G-20058)***
Block Jewelers Inc....413 789-2940
299 Walnut St Ste 1 Agawam MA (01001) ***(G-7424)***
Block Mems LLC....508 251-3100
132 Turnpike Rd Ste 110 Southborough MA (01772) ***(G-15349)***
Blodget Oven Company, The, Essex Junction *Also called GS Blodgett Corporation* ***(G-21944)***
Bloom & Company Inc....617 923-1526
694 Mount Auburn St Watertown MA (02472) ***(G-16273)***
Bloom Boss LLC....774 777-5208
251 W Central St Natick MA (01760) ***(G-13238)***
Bloomfield Wood & Melamine Inc....860 243-3226
1 Griffin Rd S Bloomfield CT (06002) ***(G-211)***
Blouin Display, Dover *Also called Mfb Holdings LLC* ***(G-18036)***
Blouin General Welding & Fabg....401 762-4542
574 2nd Ave Woonsocket RI (02895) ***(G-21551)***
Blount Boats Inc....401 245-8300
461 Water St Warren RI (02885) ***(G-21289)***
Blount Fine Foods Corp (PA)....774 888-1300
630 Currant Rd Fall River MA (02720) ***(G-10669)***
Blount Fine Foods Corp....401 245-8800
383-93 Water St Warren RI (02885) ***(G-21290)***
Blow Molded Specialties, Pawtucket *Also called B & L Plastics Inc* ***(G-20814)***
BLT, Shelburne *Also called Brett Lewis Threads Ltd* ***(G-22414)***
Bltees....413 289-0050
21 Wilbraham St Unit A4 Palmer MA (01069) ***(G-14281)***
Blub0x Security Inc....508 414-3517
9 Bartlet St Ste 334 Andover MA (01810) ***(G-7541)***
Blue Anchor Woodworks Inc....781 631-2390
208 Beacon St Marblehead MA (01945) ***(G-12677)***
Blue Atlantic Fabricators LLC....617 874-8503
256 Marginal St Ste 2 Boston MA (02128) ***(G-8415)***
Blue Barn Inc....617 894-6987
708 Whitney St Gardner MA (01440) ***(G-11104)***
Blue Bell Mattress Company LLC....860 292-6372
24 Thompson Rd East Windsor CT (06088) ***(G-1278)***
Blue Buffalo Company Ltd (HQ)....203 762-9751
11 River Rd Ste 200 Wilton CT (06897) ***(G-5279)***
Blue Buffalo Pet Products Inc (HQ)....203 762-9751
11 River Rd Ste 103 Wilton CT (06897) ***(G-5280)***
Blue Chip Tool....860 875-7999
40 Tolland Stage Rd D4 Tolland CT (06084) ***(G-4540)***

Blue Cow Software Inc....781 224-2583
50 Salem St Ste 103a Lynnfield MA (01940) ***(G-12546)***
Blue Dawg Pwr Wash Southern NH....603 498-9473
567 Main St Hampstead NH (03841) ***(G-18238)***
Blue Fleet Welding Service....508 997-5513
102 Wamsutta St New Bedford MA (02740) ***(G-13363)***
Blue Hill Cabinet & Woodwork....207 374-2260
517 Pleasant St Blue Hill ME (04614) ***(G-5770)***
Blue Hill Transformer, Holliston *Also called Total Recoil Magnetics Inc* ***(G-11609)***
Blue Magic Inc....781 639-8428
60 Village St Marblehead MA (01945) ***(G-12678)***
Blue Moon Foods Inc....802 295-1165
568 N Main St Ste 1 White River Junction VT (05001) ***(G-22635)***
Blue Moon Sorbet, White River Junction *Also called Blue Moon Foods Inc* ***(G-22635)***
Blue Ox Enterprise Inc....802 274-4494
2085 New Boston Rd Saint Johnsbury VT (05819) ***(G-22387)***
Blue Ox Malthouse LLC....207 649-0018
41 Capital Ave Lisbon Falls ME (04252) ***(G-6367)***
Blue Rhino of Ne....413 781-3694
1709 Page Blvd Springfield MA (01104) ***(G-15455)***
Blue Sky Inc....207 772-0073
987 Riverside St Portland ME (04103) ***(G-6625)***
Blue Sky Studios Inc....203 992-6000
1 American Ln Ste 301 Greenwich CT (06831) ***(G-1600)***
Blue Sky/Vifx, Greenwich *Also called Blue Sky Studios Inc* ***(G-1600)***
Blue Tree LLC....603 436-0831
9 Sheafe St Portsmouth NH (03801) ***(G-19545)***
Bluebird Graphic Sols, Woburn *Also called Clayton LLC* ***(G-17144)***
Bluecatbio MA Inc....978 405-2533
58 Elsinore St Concord MA (01742) ***(G-10116)***
Blueconic Inc....888 440-2583
207 South St Ste 671 Boston MA (02111) ***(G-8416)***
Bluecrest, Danbury *Also called Dmt Solutions Global Corp* ***(G-903)***
Blueday Inc....978 461-4500
50 Federal St Fl 2 Boston MA (02110) ***(G-8417)***
Bluefin Biomedicine Inc....978 712-8105
32 Tozer Rd Beverly MA (01915) ***(G-8112)***
Bluejacket Inc....207 548-9970
160 E Main St Searsport ME (04974) ***(G-6947)***
Bluejay Diagnostics Inc....978 631-0152
360 Msschstts Ave Ste 203 Acton MA (01720) ***(G-7345)***
Blueline NDT LLC....781 791-9511
34 Dunelm Rd Bedford MA (01730) ***(G-7963)***
Bluemoon Oyster Co Lcc....781 585-6000
10 Wendell Pond Rd Duxbury MA (02332) ***(G-10393)***
Blueprint Medicines Corp (PA)....617 374-7580
45 Sidney St Cambridge MA (02139) ***(G-9412)***
Bluesnap Inc (PA)....781 790-5013
800 South St Ste 640 Waltham MA (02453) ***(G-16049)***
Bluewater Designs, Bristol *Also called Patriot Manufacturing LLC* ***(G-591)***
Bluewater Farms, North Easton *Also called Graystone Limited LLC* ***(G-13946)***
Bluezone Products Inc....781 937-0202
225 Wildwood Ave Woburn MA (01801) ***(G-17134)***
Blushift Aerospace Inc....207 619-1703
74 Orion St 116 Brunswick ME (04011) ***(G-5831)***
Blvd Graphix....207 325-2583
22 Main St Limestone ME (04750) ***(G-6339)***
Blw LLC....802 246-4500
22 Browne Ct Unit 105 Brattleboro VT (05301) ***(G-21719)***
Bm Undercar Warehouse....516 736-0476
115 Carter St Chelsea MA (02150) ***(G-9946)***
BMC Software Inc....781 810-4494
250 1st Ave Ste 205 Needham MA (02494) ***(G-13294)***
Bmco Industries Inc....401 781-6884
4646 Post Rd Apt 1 East Greenwich RI (02818) ***(G-20354)***
Bmd, Guilford *Also called Bio-Med Devices Inc* ***(G-1693)***
Bmed Holding LLC....603 868-1888
16 Strafford Ave Durham NH (03824) ***(G-18075)***
Bmi, Warren *Also called Barrington Manufacturing Inc* ***(G-21288)***
Bmi Cad Services Inc....860 658-0808
8a Herman Dr Simsbury CT (06070) ***(G-3897)***
Bmi Surplus Inc....781 871-8868
149 King St Hanover MA (02339) ***(G-11328)***
Bml Tool & Mfg Corp....203 880-9485
67 Enterprise Dr Monroe CT (06468) ***(G-2395)***
BNL Industries Inc....860 870-6222
30 Industrial Park Rd Vernon CT (06066) ***(G-4663)***
Bnr Supplies....401 461-9132
18 Gallup Ave Cranston RI (02910) ***(G-20190)***
Bnz Materials Inc....978 663-3401
400 Iron Horse Park North Billerica MA (01862) ***(G-13796)***
Boaopharma Inc....508 315-8080
19 Erie Dr Ste 1 Natick MA (01760) ***(G-13239)***
Boardman Silversmiths Inc....203 265-9978
22 N Plains Industrial Rd 6c Wallingford CT (06492) ***(G-4710)***
Bob Bean Company Inc....603 818-4390
44 Nashua Rd Unit 2 Londonderry NH (03053) ***(G-18680)***
Bob Bergeron....978 352-7615
132 Tenney St Georgetown MA (01833) ***(G-11138)***

ALPHABETIC

Bob The Baker LLC...203 775-1032
594 Federal Rd Brookfield CT (06804) *(G-635)*
Bob Vess Building LLC...860 729-2536
605 Main St Cromwell CT (06416) *(G-849)*
Bob Walker Inc...207 642-2083
365 Northeast Rd Standish ME (04084) *(G-7060)*
Bobbex Inc...800 792-4449
523 Pepper St Ste B Monroe CT (06468) *(G-2396)*
Bobby OS Foods LLC...603 458-2502
21 Connell Dr Salem NH (03079) *(G-19714)*
Bobby Pins...401 461-3400
2208 Broad St Cranston RI (02905) *(G-20191)*
Bobken Automatics, Waterbury *Also called Oakville Quality Products LLC (G-4931)*
Bobken Automatics Inc...203 757-5525
1495 Thomaston Ave Ste 2 Waterbury CT (06704) *(G-4850)*
Bobos Indoor Playground...603 718-8721
522 Amherst St Nashua NH (03063) *(G-19128)*
Boc Gases, Bellingham *Also called Messer LLC (G-8050)*
Boc Gases, Stoughton *Also called Messer LLC (G-15607)*
Boc Gases...617 878-2090
60 State St Boston MA (02109) *(G-8418)*
Boc Gasses At Mit...617 374-9992
77 Massachusetts Ave 22 Cambridge MA (02139) *(G-9413)*
Boc Group Inc...978 658-5410
301 Ballardvale St Wilmington MA (01887) *(G-16984)*
Boccelli...860 862-9300
1 Mohegan Sun Blvd 621c Uncasville CT (06382) *(G-4646)*
Bocra Industries Inc...603 474-3598
140 Batchelder Rd Seabrook NH (03874) *(G-19794)*
Body Covers, Laconia *Also called Vantastic Inc (G-18591)*
Body Rags, Pelham *Also called C K Productions Inc (G-19429)*
Bodycote Hot Isostatic Prsg, Andover *Also called Bodycote Imt Inc (G-7542)*
Bodycote Imt Inc (HQ)...978 470-0876
155 River St Andover MA (01810) *(G-7542)*
Bodycote Thermal Proc Inc...860 225-7691
675 Christian Ln Berlin CT (06037) *(G-76)*
Bodycote Thermal Proc Inc...978 356-3818
11 Old Right Rd Ste C Ipswich MA (01938) *(G-11906)*
Bodycote Thermal Proc Inc...508 754-1724
284 Grove St Worcester MA (01605) *(G-17349)*
Bodycote Thermal Proc Inc...603 524-7886
187 Water St Laconia NH (03246) *(G-18559)*
Bodycote Thermal Proc Inc...860 282-1371
45 Connecticut Ave South Windsor CT (06074) *(G-3944)*
Boehringer Ingelheim Corp (HQ)...203 798-9988
900 Ridgebury Rd Ridgefield CT (06877) *(G-3657)*
Boehringer Ingelheim Pharma (HQ)...203 798-9988
900 Ridgebury Rd Ridgefield CT (06877) *(G-3658)*
Boehringer Ingelheim USA Corp (HQ)...203 798-9988
900 Ridgebury Rd Ridgefield CT (06877) *(G-3659)*
Boehrnger Ingelheim Roxane Inc...203 798-5555
175 Briar Ridge Rd Ridgefield CT (06877) *(G-3660)*
Boeing Company...978 369-9522
49 Edgewood Rd Concord MA (01742) *(G-10117)*
Boeing Company...860 627-9393
1 Hartfield Blvd Ste 112 East Windsor CT (06088) *(G-1279)*
Bogaris Corporation...617 505-6696
29 Sargent Beechwood Brookline MA (02445) *(G-9196)*
Boggs Mobile Homes, Warren *Also called Leland Boggs II (G-7143)*
Bogner of America Inc (HQ)...802 861-6900
128 Lakeside Ave Ste 302 Burlington VT (05401) *(G-21769)*
Bogner's, Manchester *Also called Manchester Packing Company Inc (G-2024)*
Bohndell Sails, Rockport *Also called E S Bohndell & Co Inc (G-6821)*
Bojak Company...203 378-5086
152 Old Gate Ln D Milford CT (06460) *(G-2255)*
Bold Wood Interiors LLC...203 907-4077
138 Haven St New Haven CT (06513) *(G-2670)*
Bolduc Brothers Log & Shipg...207 353-5990
397 Ridge Rd Lisbon Falls ME (04252) *(G-6368)*
Bolducs Machine Works Inc...860 455-1232
207 Miller Rd North Windham CT (06235) *(G-3078)*
Boles Enterprises Inc...603 622-4282
143 Middle St Ste 1 Manchester NH (03101) *(G-18789)*
Bolger & OHearn Inc...508 676-1518
47 Slade St Fall River MA (02724) *(G-10670)*
Bolger Products...978 355-2226
28 Summer St Barre MA (01005) *(G-7949)*
Bolinda Publishing Inc...207 722-3185
186 S Long Swamp Rd Jackson ME (04921) *(G-6218)*
Bollore Inc...860 774-2930
60 Louisa Viens Dr Dayville CT (06241) *(G-1039)*
Bollywood Delights Inc...508 740-1908
6 Lynbrook Rd Southborough MA (01772) *(G-15350)*
Bolstridge Logging LLC...603 859-8241
159 Brackett Rd New Durham NH (03855) *(G-19300)*
Bolton Aerospace, Manchester *Also called Pas Technologies Inc (G-2037)*
Bolton Printing Co...978 365-4844
553 Wattaquadock Hill Rd Bolton MA (01740) *(G-8317)*
Boman Precision Tech Inc...203 415-8350
67 Erna Ave Milford CT (06461) *(G-2256)*
Bomar Inc...603 826-5781
73 Southwest St Charlestown NH (03603) *(G-17811)*
Bomar Machine LLC...860 505-7299
600 Four Rod Rd Ste 7 Berlin CT (06037) *(G-77)*
Bomas Machine Specialties Inc...617 628-3831
334 Washington St Somerville MA (02143) *(G-15160)*
Bomb Cosmetics, Salem *Also called Fizz Time (G-19734)*
Bombadils Spirit Shop Inc...860 423-9661
135 Storrs Rd 8 Mansfield Center CT (06250) *(G-2062)*
Bombardier Mass Transit, Boston *Also called Bombardier Services Corp (G-8419)*
Bombardier Services Corp...617 464-0323
2 Frontage Rd Boston MA (02118) *(G-8419)*
Bombich Software Inc...413 935-2300
63 Greenacre Ave Longmeadow MA (01106) *(G-12331)*
Bomco Inc...978 283-9000
125 Gloucester Ave Gloucester MA (01930) *(G-11167)*
Bonamar Corp...617 965-3400
1105 Washington St Newton MA (02465) *(G-13571)*
Bonami Software Corporation...978 264-6641
34 Hammond St Acton MA (01720) *(G-7346)*
Bonapp...917 488-5202
14 Story St Cambridge MA (02138) *(G-9414)*
Bond Adhesives & Coatings Corp...603 474-3811
896 Lafayette Rd Seabrook NH (03874) *(G-19795)*
Bond Optics LLC...603 448-2300
76 Etna Rd Lebanon NH (03766) *(G-18616)*
Bond Polymers International, Seabrook *Also called Bond Adhesives & Coatings Corp (G-19795)*
Bond Printing Company Inc...781 871-3990
104 Plain St Hanover MA (02339) *(G-11329)*
Bond-Bilt Garages Inc...203 269-3375
30 N Plains Industrial Rd # 16 Wallingford CT (06492) *(G-4711)*
Bonded Abrasives, Worcester *Also called Saint-Gobain Abrasives Inc (G-17464)*
Bonded Concrete Inc...413 229-2075
49 Clayton Rd Ashley Falls MA (01222) *(G-7672)*
Bone Biologics Corporation (PA)...732 661-2224
321 Columbus Ave Ste 3fl Boston MA (02116) *(G-8420)*
Bonesupport Inc...781 772-1756
60 William St Ste 330 Wellesley MA (02481) *(G-16364)*
Boniface Tool & Die Inc...508 764-3248
181 Southbridge Rd Dudley MA (01571) *(G-10373)*
Bonito Manufacturing Inc...203 234-8786
445 Washington Ave North Haven CT (06473) *(G-3011)*
Bonneaus Vermont Maple...802 744-2742
224 Buck Hill Rd Lowell VT (05847) *(G-22059)*
Bonnies Bundles Dolls...802 875-2114
250 North St Chester VT (05143) *(G-21841)*
Bonsal American Inc...508 987-8188
Old Webster Rd Oxford MA (01540) *(G-14254)*
Bonsal American Inc...860 824-7733
43 Clayton Rd Canaan CT (06018) *(G-684)*
Bonsal American Inc...413 243-0053
110 Marble St Lee MA (01238) *(G-12090)*
Bonsal American Inc...860 824-7733
43 Clayton Rd Canaan CT (06018) *(G-685)*
Bonsal American Inc...508 791-6366
18 Mccracken Rd Millbury MA (01527) *(G-13157)*
Book Automation Inc...860 354-7900
458 Danbury Rd Ste B10 New Milford CT (06776) *(G-2788)*
Book Mktg Works, Avon *Also called Publishing Directions LLC (G-42)*
Book-Mart Press Inc...978 251-6000
15 Wellman Ave North Chelmsford MA (01863) *(G-13886)*
Books On Disk, Boston *Also called Teletypesetting Company Inc (G-8877)*
Boostercom...855 631-6850
275 Grove St Ste 1-305 Auburndale MA (02466) *(G-7857)*
Boot Strap Press, Northampton *Also called Council On Intl Pub Affirs Inc (G-14002)*
Booth Felt Co Inc...603 330-3334
1 Progress Dr Ste 1 # 1 Dover NH (03820) *(G-18009)*
Borderlines Foundation...617 365-9438
1577 Beacon St Brookline MA (02446) *(G-9197)*
Borealis Press Inc...207 370-6020
35 Tenney Hl Blue Hill ME (04614) *(G-5771)*
Borg Design Inc...978 562-1559
19 Brent Dr Hudson MA (01749) *(G-11760)*
Boro Sand & Stone Corp (PA)...508 699-2911
192 Plain St North Attleboro MA (02760) *(G-13750)*
Boro Sand & Stone Corp...508 238-7222
87 Eastman St South Easton MA (02375) *(G-15271)*
Borroughs Corporation...603 895-3991
22 Jennifer Ln Raymond NH (03077) *(G-19636)*
Borroughs Manufacturing, Raymond *Also called Borroughs Corporation (G-19636)*
Bosal Foam and Fiber (PA)...207 793-2245
171 Washington St Limerick ME (04048) *(G-6332)*
Bosal Foam Products, Limerick *Also called Bosal Foam and Fiber (G-6332)*
Bose Corporation (PA)...508 879-7330
100 The Mountain Rd Framingham MA (01701) *(G-10928)*

Bose Corporation....508 766-1265
145 Pennsylvania Ave Framingham MA (01701) ***(G-10929)***
Bossonnet Inc....508 986-2308
121 Flanders Rd Westborough MA (01581) ***(G-16594)***
Bostik Inc....978 777-0100
211 Boston St Middleton MA (01949) ***(G-13085)***
Boston America Corp....781 933-3535
55 6th Rd Ste 8 Woburn MA (01801) ***(G-17135)***
Boston and Maine Corporation (HQ)....978 663-1130
1700 Iron Horse Park North Billerica MA (01862) ***(G-13797)***
Boston Artificial Limb Co....781 272-3132
44 Middlesex Tpke Burlington MA (01803) ***(G-9240)***
Boston Atlantic Corp....508 754-4076
7 Harris Ct Worcester MA (01610) ***(G-17350)***
Boston Atlantic Gasket and Rbr, Worcester *Also called Boston Atlantic Corp* ***(G-17350)***
Boston Atmtc Sprnklr Fbrcation....781 681-5122
10 Commerce Rd 2 Rockland MA (02370) ***(G-14794)***
Boston Bagel Inc....617 364-6900
101 Sprague St Ste 3 Hyde Park MA (02136) ***(G-11863)***
Boston Baking Inc....617 364-6900
101 Sprague St Ste 3 Boston MA (02136) ***(G-8421)***
Boston Beer Company Inc....617 368-5080
30 Germania St Ste 1 Boston MA (02130) ***(G-8422)***
Boston Beer Company Inc (PA)....617 368-5000
1 Design Center Pl # 850 Boston MA (02210) ***(G-8423)***
Boston Beer Corporation (HQ)....617 368-5000
1 Design Center Pl # 850 Boston MA (02210) ***(G-8424)***
Boston Billows Inc....603 598-1200
55 Lake St Ste 7 Nashua NH (03060) ***(G-19129)***
Boston Biochem Inc....617 241-7072
840 Memorial Dr Ste 3 Cambridge MA (02139) ***(G-9415)***
Boston Biomedical Pharma Inc....617 674-6800
640 Memorial Dr Cambridge MA (02139) ***(G-9416)***
Boston Biopharma LLC....617 780-9300
30 Page Rd Weston MA (02493) ***(G-16823)***
Boston Blacksmith Inc....617 364-1499
46 Business St Boston MA (02136) ***(G-8425)***
Boston Boatworks LLC....617 561-9111
333 Terminal St Charlestown MA (02129) ***(G-9825)***
Boston Brace International....603 772-2388
23 Stiles Rd Ste 218 Salem NH (03079) ***(G-19715)***
Boston Brace International....781 270-3650
50 Mall Rd Ste G10 Burlington MA (01803) ***(G-9241)***
Boston Brace International Inc (PA)....508 588-6060
20 Ledin Dr Ste 1 Avon MA (02322) ***(G-7880)***
Boston Brands of Maine, Lewiston *Also called Mr Boston Brands LLC* ***(G-6308)***
Boston Business Journal Inc....617 330-1000
70 Franklin St Ste 800 Boston MA (02110) ***(G-8426)***
Boston Business Printing Inc....617 482-7955
115 Broad St Bsmt Boston MA (02110) ***(G-8427)***
Boston Centerless Inc....508 587-3500
15 Doherty Ave Avon MA (02322) ***(G-7881)***
Boston Chinese News Inc....617 354-4154
1105 Mass Ave Apt 3e Cambridge MA (02138) ***(G-9417)***
Boston Chipyard The Inc....617 742-9537
257 Faneuil Hall Pl Boston MA (02109) ***(G-8428)***
Boston Commerce Inc....617 782-8998
119 Braintree St Ste 510 Boston MA (02134) ***(G-8429)***
Boston Critic Inc....617 324-1360
30 Wadsworth St Cambridge MA (02142) ***(G-9418)***
Boston Design Guide Inc....978 443-9886
277 Concord Rd Sudbury MA (01776) ***(G-15654)***
Boston Endo-Surgical Tech, Bridgeport *Also called Precision Engineered Pdts LLC* ***(G-473)***
Boston Endo-Surgical Tech LLC....203 336-6479
1146 Barnum Ave Bridgeport CT (06610) ***(G-385)***
Boston Environmental LLC....603 334-1000
600 State St Ste 7 Portsmouth NH (03801) ***(G-19546)***
Boston Executive Helicopters....781 603-6186
209 Access Rd Norwood MA (02062) ***(G-14138)***
Boston Fabrications....781 762-9185
39 Franklin R Mckay Rd Attleboro MA (02703) ***(G-7713)***
Boston Family Boat Building....617 522-5366
133 Paul Gore St Jamaica Plain MA (02130) ***(G-11941)***
Boston Fog LLC....888 846-4145
18 Walnut St Belmont NH (03220) ***(G-17671)***
Boston Forging & Welding Corp....617 567-2300
336 Border St Boston MA (02128) ***(G-8430)***
Boston Garage....339 788-9580
145 Webster St Ste D Hanover MA (02339) ***(G-11330)***
Boston Globe, Boston *Also called Ne Media Group Inc* ***(G-8721)***
Boston Globe LLC....617 929-2684
53 State St Fl 23 Boston MA (02109) ***(G-8431)***
Boston Hatian Reporter, Boston *Also called Boston Neighborhood News Inc* ***(G-8435)***
Boston Health Economics LLC....781 290-0808
265 Franklin St Ste 1100 Boston MA (02110) ***(G-8432)***
Boston Helicopters, North Andover *Also called North Andover Flight Academy* ***(G-13720)***
Boston Herald, Braintree *Also called Bh Media Inc* ***(G-8990)***
Boston Irish Reporter....617 436-1222
150 Munt Vrnon St Ste 120 Dorchester MA (02125) ***(G-10340)***
Boston Iron Works, Everett *Also called Lima Fredy* ***(G-10618)***
Boston Lamb & Veal Co Inc....617 442-3644
155 Hampden St Boston MA (02119) ***(G-8433)***
Boston Ltigation Solutions LLC....617 933-9780
100 Franklin St Boston MA (02110) ***(G-8434)***
Boston M4 Tech LLC....617 279-3172
500 W Cummings Park # 1500 Woburn MA (01801) ***(G-17136)***
Boston Machine Inc....978 458-7722
10 Tracy Rd Chelmsford MA (01824) ***(G-9877)***
Boston Magazine, Boston *Also called Metro Corp* ***(G-8702)***
Boston Medical Products Inc....508 898-9300
70 Chestnut St Shrewsbury MA (01545) ***(G-15105)***
Boston Microfluidics Inc....857 239-9665
125 Cambridgepark Dr # 101 Cambridge MA (02140) ***(G-9419)***
Boston Model Bakery....203 562-9491
169 Washington Ave New Haven CT (06519) ***(G-2671)***
Boston Neighborhood News Inc....617 436-1222
150 Munt Vrnon St Ste 120 Boston MA (02125) ***(G-8435)***
Boston Ocular Prosthetics Inc....800 824-2492
133 Mortland Rd Searsport ME (04974) ***(G-6948)***
Boston Oncology LLC....857 209-5052
245 First St Ste 1800 Cambridge MA (02142) ***(G-9420)***
Boston Orthotics Inc....508 821-7655
30 Rob W Boyden Rd 1100 Taunton MA (02780) ***(G-15733)***
Boston Orthotics & Prosthetics, Salem *Also called Boston Brace International* ***(G-19715)***
Boston Paper Board Corp....617 666-1154
40 Roland St Boston MA (02129) ***(G-8436)***
Boston Phoenix Inc (PA)....617 536-5390
1 Chestnut St Ste 1 # 1 Providence RI (02903) ***(G-20971)***
Boston Piezo-Optics Inc....508 966-4988
38b Maple St Bellingham MA (02019) ***(G-8032)***
Boston Plstic Oral Srgery Fndt....617 355-6058
300 Longwood Ave Boston MA (02115) ***(G-8437)***
Boston Pretzel Bakery Inc....617 522-9494
284 Amory St Ste 2 Boston MA (02130) ***(G-8438)***
Boston Process Tech Inc....978 854-5579
10 Technology Dr Ste 1a Peabody MA (01960) ***(G-14316)***
Boston Red Sox Yearbook, Jamaica Plain *Also called Dunfey Publishing Company Inc* ***(G-11943)***
Boston Retail Products Inc (PA)....781 395-7417
400 Riverside Ave Medford MA (02155) ***(G-12923)***
BOSTON REVIEW, Cambridge *Also called Boston Critic Inc* ***(G-9418)***
Boston Salads and Provs Inc....617 307-6340
57 Food Mart Rd Boston MA (02118) ***(G-8439)***
Boston Sand & Gravel Company (PA)....617 227-9000
100 N Washington St Fl 2 Boston MA (02114) ***(G-8440)***
Boston Sand & Gravel Company....617 242-5540
40 Bunker Hill Indus Park Charlestown MA (02129) ***(G-9826)***
Boston Sand & Gravel Company....508 888-8002
181 Kiahs Way Sandwich MA (02563) ***(G-14962)***
Boston Sand & Gravel Company....603 330-3999
69 N Coast Rd Rochester NH (03868) ***(G-19662)***
Boston Sash & Millwork Inc....508 880-8808
667 Spring St North Dighton MA (02764) ***(G-13930)***
Boston Scientific Corporation (PA)....508 683-4000
300 Boston Scientific Way Marlborough MA (01752) ***(G-12727)***
Boston Scientific Corporation....860 673-2500
85 Bridgewater Dr Avon CT (06001) ***(G-33)***
Boston Scientific Corporation....781 259-2501
140 Hanscom Dr Bedford MA (01730) ***(G-7964)***
Boston Scientific Corporation....508 382-0200
100 Boston Scientific Way Marlborough MA (01752) ***(G-12728)***
Boston Scientific Corporation....617 689-6000
500 Commander Shea Blvd Quincy MA (02171) ***(G-14617)***
Boston Scientific Corporation....617 972-4000
480 Pleasant St Watertown MA (02472) ***(G-16274)***
Boston Scientific Intl Corp....508 683-4000
300 Boston Scientific Way Marlborough MA (01752) ***(G-12729)***
Boston Ship Repair LLC....617 330-5045
32a Drydock Ave Boston MA (02210) ***(G-8441)***
Boston Smoked Fish Company LLC....617 819-5476
Bays 16 20 Boston Fish Pe Ys St Ba Boston MA (02210) ***(G-8442)***
Boston Software Corp....781 449-8585
189 Reservoir St Needham Heights MA (02494) ***(G-13320)***
Boston Sports Journal LLC....617 306-0166
4 Daniels Rd Medway MA (02053) ***(G-12957)***
Boston Steel & Mfg Co....781 324-3000
89 Newark St Haverhill MA (01832) ***(G-11409)***
Boston Steel Fabricators Inc....781 767-1540
610 South St Holbrook MA (02343) ***(G-11522)***
Boston Tag and Label Inc....781 893-9080
296 Newton St Ste 4 Waltham MA (02453) ***(G-16050)***
Boston Trailer Manufacturing....508 668-2242
1 Production Rd Walpole MA (02081) ***(G-15990)***
Boston Transtec LLC....617 930-6088
481 Dudley Rd Newton MA (02459) ***(G-13572)***
Boston Turning Works....617 924-4747
120 Elm St Watertown MA (02472) ***(G-16275)***
Boston Welding & Design Inc....781 932-0035
7 Micro Dr Woburn MA (01801) ***(G-17137)***

Boston Winery LLC...617 265-9463
26 Ericsson St Dorchester MA (02122) ***(G-10341)***
Boston Wood Art...508 353-4129
5 Maple Ave Natick MA (01760) ***(G-13240)***
BOSTON'S CHILDREN HOSPTIAL, Boston *Also called Chmc Otlrynglgic Fundation Inc* ***(G-8472)***
Boston-Power Inc (PA)...508 366-0885
2200 W Park Dr Ste 320 Westborough MA (01581) ***(G-16595)***
Bostoncounters LLC...781 281-1622
78h Olympia Ave Woburn MA (01801) ***(G-17138)***
Bostonia Magazine, Brookline *Also called Trustees of Boston University* ***(G-9223)***
Bostonian Shoe Co, Waltham *Also called C & J Clark America Inc* ***(G-16054)***
Bostonsportsjournal.com, Medway *Also called Boston Sports Journal LLC* ***(G-12957)***
Bosworth Company...401 438-1110
930 Waterman Ave East Providence RI (02914) ***(G-20392)***
Botelho Wood Working...774 240-7235
21 Reuben St Fall River MA (02723) ***(G-10671)***
Botify Corporation...617 576-2005
185 Alewife Brook Pkwy Cambridge MA (02138) ***(G-9421)***
Bottle & Cork, North Grafton *Also called JCB Inc* ***(G-13961)***
Botto's Bakery, Portland *Also called Mathews Bakery Inc* ***(G-6693)***
Bottom Line Inc (PA)...203 973-5900
3 Landmark Sq Ste 230 Stamford CT (06901) ***(G-4151)***
Bottom Line Publications, Stamford *Also called Bottom Line Inc* ***(G-4151)***
Bottomline Technologies De Inc (PA)...603 436-0700
325 Corporate Dr Ste 300 Portsmouth NH (03801) ***(G-19547)***
Bouchard Family Farm Products...207 834-3237
3 Strip Rd Fort Kent ME (04743) ***(G-6058)***
Boucher Company Inc...603 356-6455
19 Upper W Side Rd North Conway NH (03860) ***(G-19374)***
Boucher Con Foundation Sups...508 947-4279
80 Cambridge St Middleboro MA (02346) ***(G-13056)***
Bouckaert Industrial Textiles...401 769-5474
235 Singleton St Woonsocket RI (02895) ***(G-21552)***
Boudreaus Welding Co Inc...860 774-2771
1029 N Main St Dayville CT (06241) ***(G-1040)***
Boudrieau Tool & Die Inc...603 899-5795
1032 Nh Route 119 Unit 9 Rindge NH (03461) ***(G-19647)***
Bouffard Metal Goods, Waterbury *Also called H&T Waterbury Inc* ***(G-4880)***
Boulder Technologies LLC...603 740-8402
6 Faraday Dr Dover NH (03820) ***(G-18010)***
Boulevard Machine & Gear Inc...413 788-6466
785 Page Blvd Springfield MA (01104) ***(G-15456)***
Boulia-Gorrell Lumber Co Inc...603 524-1300
176 Fair St Laconia NH (03246) ***(G-18560)***
Bounce Imaging Inc...716 310-8281
114 Western Ave Ste 1 Allston MA (02134) ***(G-7460)***
Bouncepad North America Inc...617 804-0110
50 Termi St Unit 710bldg Charlestown MA (02129) ***(G-9827)***
Bourdon Forge Co Inc...860 632-2740
99 Tuttle Rd Middletown CT (06457) ***(G-2179)***
Bourdons Institutional Sls Inc...603 542-8709
85 Plains Rd Claremont NH (03743) ***(G-17836)***
Bourg Collaters System, New Bedford *Also called C P Bourg Inc* ***(G-13369)***
Bourgeois Guitars, Lewiston *Also called Pantheon Guitars LLC* ***(G-6314)***
Bourgeois Machine Co...978 774-6240
15 Bixby Ave Middleton MA (01949) ***(G-13086)***
Boutin McQuiston Inc (PA)...802 863-8038
365 Dorset St South Burlington VT (05403) ***(G-22439)***
Boutwell Owens & Co Inc (PA)...978 343-3067
251 Authority Dr Fitchburg MA (01420) ***(G-10813)***
Bouyea-Fassetts, Rutland *Also called Unilever Bestfoods North Amer* ***(G-22357)***
Bovano Industries Incorporated...203 272-3208
830 S Main St Ofc A Cheshire CT (06410) ***(G-715)***
Bovano of Cheshire, Cheshire *Also called Bovano Industries Incorporated* ***(G-715)***
Boves of Vermont Inc...802 862-7235
8 Catamount Dr Milton VT (05468) ***(G-22125)***
Bovie Screen Process Prtg Co Inc...603 224-0651
4 Northeast Ave Bow NH (03304) ***(G-17708)***
Bowles Corporation...802 425-3447
445 Longpoint Rd North Ferrisburgh VT (05473) ***(G-22225)***
Boxcar Media LLC...413 663-3384
102 Main St North Adams MA (01247) ***(G-13670)***
Boxerbrand, East Weymouth *Also called Almont Company Inc* ***(G-10534)***
Boxever US Inc...617 599-2420
34 Farnsworth St Fl 4 Boston MA (02210) ***(G-8443)***
Boxford Designs LLC...603 216-2399
55 Walnut Hill Rd Derry NH (03038) ***(G-17973)***
Boyajian Inc...781 828-9966
144 Will Dr Canton MA (02021) ***(G-9718)***
Boyce Highlands Furn Co Inc...603 753-1042
14 Whitney Rd Concord NH (03301) ***(G-17885)***
Boyd Coatings, Hudson *Also called Precision Coating Co Inc* ***(G-11806)***
Boydco Inc (PA)...401 438-6900
101 Commercial Way East Providence RI (02914) ***(G-20393)***
Boyden Valley Winery LLC...802 644-8151
64 Vt Route 104 Cambridge VT (05444) ***(G-21822)***
Boyle Engineering...802 388-6966
91 Court St Middlebury VT (05753) ***(G-22103)***
Boynton Machine Company Inc...781 899-9900
101 Clematis Ave Ste 6 Waltham MA (02453) ***(G-16051)***
BP Countertop Design Co LLC...203 732-1620
101 Elizabeth St Ste 1 Derby CT (06418) ***(G-1069)***
BP Fly Corporation (PA)...978 649-9114
65 Middlesex Rd Tyngsboro MA (01879) ***(G-15886)***
BP Logging...207 398-4457
562 Main St Saint Francis ME (04774) ***(G-6866)***
BP Lubricants USA Inc...508 791-3201
692 Millbury St 94 Worcester MA (01607) ***(G-17351)***
Bpi, New Bedford *Also called Baker Parts Inc* ***(G-13360)***
Bprex Halthcare Brookville Inc...203 754-4141
574 E Main St Waterbury CT (06702) ***(G-4851)***
Bps Diamond Sports Inc...253 891-8377
100 Domain Dr Exeter NH (03833) ***(G-18114)***
Bps Division, Bristol *Also called Freudenberg-Nok General Partnr* ***(G-17763)***
Brackett Machine Inc...207 854-9789
355 Saco St Westbrook ME (04092) ***(G-7182)***
Bracone Metal Spinning Inc...860 628-5927
39 Depaolo Dr Southington CT (06489) ***(G-4041)***
Brad Kettle...860 546-9929
4 Howe Rd Canterbury CT (06331) ***(G-692)***
Brad's Logging, Canterbury *Also called Brad Kettle* ***(G-692)***
Brada Manufacturing Inc...401 739-3774
46 Warwick Industrial Dr Warwick RI (02886) ***(G-21337)***
Bradbury Barrel Co, Bridgewater *Also called E G W Bradbury Enterprises* ***(G-5805)***
Bradbury Enterprises, Rumford *Also called Clinton G Bradbury Inc* ***(G-6833)***
Bradbury Mtn Metalworks LLC...207 688-5009
56 Minot Rd Pownal ME (04069) ***(G-6748)***
Bradford & Bigelow Inc...978 904-3112
3 Perkins Way Newburyport MA (01950) ***(G-13474)***
Bradford Coatings Inc...978 459-4100
75 Rogers St Lowell MA (01852) ***(G-12354)***
Bradford Coatings, LLC, Lowell *Also called Bradford Coatings Inc* ***(G-12354)***
Bradford Distillery LLC (PA)...781 378-2491
604 First Parish Rd Scituate MA (02066) ***(G-15006)***
Bradford Distillery LLC...781 385-7145
3 Pond Park Rd Ste 4 Hingham MA (02043) ***(G-11494)***
Bradford Finshg Powdr Coat Inc...978 469-9965
2 S Grove St Haverhill MA (01835) ***(G-11410)***
Bradford Machine, Brattleboro *Also called Cave Manufacturing Inc* ***(G-21723)***
Bradford Machine Inc...603 938-2355
8 Bacon Rd Bradford NH (03221) ***(G-17739)***
Bradford Press Inc...401 621-7195
91 Atwells Ave Providence RI (02903) ***(G-20972)***
Bradford Price Book, Littleton *Also called Harrison Publishing House Inc* ***(G-18661)***
Bradford Soap Mexico Inc (HQ)...401 821-2141
200 Providence St West Warwick RI (02893) ***(G-21485)***
Bradford White Corp...603 332-0116
20 Industrial Way Rochester NH (03867) ***(G-19663)***
Bradford Woodworking, Northampton *Also called Craig F Bradford* ***(G-14003)***
Bradley Goodwin Pattern Co...401 461-5220
216 Oxford St Providence RI (02905) ***(G-20973)***
Bradley Oil Company...508 336-4400
513 Winthrop St Rehoboth MA (02769) ***(G-14746)***
Brady Business Forms Inc...978 458-2585
171 Lincoln St Ste 1 Lowell MA (01852) ***(G-12355)***
Brady Enterprises Inc (PA)...781 682-6280
167 Moore Rd East Weymouth MA (02189) ***(G-10538)***
Brady Enterprises Inc...781 337-7057
45 Finnell Dr Weymouth MA (02188) ***(G-16886)***
Brady Screenprint Inc...207 284-8531
464 Elm St Biddeford ME (04005) ***(G-5723)***
Brady-Built Sunrooms, Auburn *Also called Marvic Inc* ***(G-7842)***
Braemar Machine Co...860 585-1903
550 Broad St Bristol CT (06010) ***(G-535)***
Brahmin Leather Works LLC...509 994-4000
77 Alden Rd Fairhaven MA (02719) ***(G-10638)***
Braided Products Company...401 434-0300
9 Industrial Way Riverside RI (02915) ***(G-21165)***
Brailsford & Company Inc...603 588-2880
15 Elm Ave Antrim NH (03440) ***(G-17593)***
Brain Fingerprinting Tech, Southborough *Also called Brainwave Science LLC* ***(G-15351)***
Braintree Forum & Observer...781 843-2937
91 Washington St Braintree MA (02184) ***(G-8991)***
Braintree Printing Inc...781 848-5300
230 Wood Rd Braintree MA (02184) ***(G-8992)***
Braintree Scientific Inc...781 348-0768
60 Columbian St W Braintree MA (02184) ***(G-8993)***
Brainwave Science LLC...774 760-1678
257 Turnpike Rd Ste 220 Southborough MA (01772) ***(G-15351)***
Brampton Technology Ltd...860 667-7689
61 Maselli Rd Newington CT (06111) ***(G-2849)***
Branch Olive Oil Company LLC...781 775-8788
210 Andover St Peabody MA (01960) ***(G-14317)***
Branch River Plastics Inc...401 232-0270
15 Thurber Blvd Smithfield RI (02917) ***(G-21214)***

Brand & Oppenheimer Co Inc 781 271-0000
4 Preston Ct Ste 200 Bedford MA (01730) *(G-7965)*
Brand & Oppenheimer Co Inc (PA) 401 293-5500
208 Clock Tower Sq Portsmouth RI (02871) *(G-20921)*
Brand Dielectrics Inc 508 828-1200
30 Robert W Boyden Rd 900a Taunton MA (02780) *(G-15734)*
Brand-Nu Laboratories Inc (PA) 203 235-7989
377 Research Pkwy Ste 2 Meriden CT (06450) *(G-2080)*
Branding Company Inc 203 793-1923
5 C St Westerly RI (02891) *(G-21518)*
Brandstrom Instruments Inc 203 544-9341
85 Ethan Allen Hwy Ridgefield CT (06877) *(G-3661)*
Brandywine Materials LLC 781 281-2746
308 E School St Woonsocket RI (02895) *(G-21553)*
Branford Open Mri & Diagnostic 203 481-7800
1208 Main St Branford CT (06405) *(G-299)*
Brannen Brothers-Flutemakers 781 935-9522
58 Dragon Ct Woburn MA (01801) *(G-17139)*
Brannen Flutes, Woburn *Also called Brannen Brothers-Flutemakers (G-17139)*
Brannkey Inc 860 510-0501
137 Mill Rock Rd E Old Saybrook CT (06475) *(G-3330)*
Branon Family Maple Orchards 802 827-3914
539 Branon Rd Fairfield VT (05455) *(G-21982)*
Branon Shady Maples Inc 802 827-6605
1097 North Rd Fairfield VT (05455) *(G-21983)*
Branson Ultrasonics Corp (HQ) 203 796-0400
41 Eagle Rd Ste 1 Danbury CT (06810) *(G-882)*
Branson Ultrasonics Corp 978 262-9040
267 Boston Rd Ste 4 North Billerica MA (01862) *(G-13798)*
Brant Industries Inc (PA) 203 661-3344
80 Field Point Rd Ste 3 Greenwich CT (06830) *(G-1601)*
Brantner and Associates Inc 401 326-9368
15 Gray Ln Ste 109 Ashaway RI (02804) *(G-20032)*
Brasco Technologies LLC 203 484-4291
76 Woodland Dr Northford CT (06472) *(G-3086)*
Brass Butterfly Inc 802 287-9818
169 Main St Poultney VT (05764) *(G-22270)*
Brass City Technologies LLC (PA) 203 723-7021
1344 New Haven Rd Naugatuck CT (06770) *(G-2463)*
Brass Foundry 207 236-3200
531 Park St West Rockport ME (04865) *(G-7178)*
Brass Traditions, Terryville *Also called Malco Inc (G-4485)*
Brattleboro Kiln Dry & Milling 802 254-4528
1103 Vernon St Brattleboro VT (05301) *(G-21720)*
Brattleboro Reformer, Brattleboro *Also called New England Newspapers Inc (G-21740)*
Brattleworks Company Inc 978 410-5078
134 Chelsea St Gardner MA (01440) *(G-11105)*
Brava Enterprises LLC 207 241-2420
86 Main St Lewiston ME (04240) *(G-6277)*
Bravo LLC (PA) 866 922-9222
349 Wetherell St Manchester CT (06040) *(G-1988)*
Bravo LLC 860 896-1899
1084 Hartford Tpke Vernon CT (06066) *(G-4664)*
Bravo Maslow LLC 912 580-0044
2 Cityview Ln Apt 605 Quincy MA (02169) *(G-14618)*
Bravo Pet Store, Manchester *Also called Bravo LLC (G-1988)*
Braxton Manufacturing Co Inc 860 274-6781
858 Echo Lake Rd Watertown CT (06795) *(G-5000)*
Brayton Wilson Cole Corp 781 803-6624
70 Sharp St Hingham MA (02043) *(G-11495)*
Brazecom Industries LLC 603 529-2080
45 B And B Ln Weare NH (03281) *(G-19933)*
Brazen Innovations Inc 603 446-7919
40 Davis Dr Marlow NH (03456) *(G-18966)*
Brazilian Times 617 625-5559
311 Broadway Somerville MA (02145) *(G-15161)*
Brazonics Inc (HQ) 603 758-6237
94 Tide Mill Rd Hampton NH (03842) *(G-18259)*
BRC Development LLC 774 245-7750
28 Rockwood Ln Upton MA (01568) *(G-15905)*
Breach Intelligence Inc 844 312-7001
6 S Ridge Rd Farmington CT (06032) *(G-1469)*
Bread & Chocolate Inc 802 429-2920
1538 Industrial Park Wells River VT (05081) *(G-22600)*
Bread and Wine Publishing LLC 860 649-3109
220 Charter Oak St Manchester CT (06040) *(G-1989)*
Breakaway Brew Haus LLC 860 647-9811
5 Steel Crossing Rd Bolton CT (06043) *(G-275)*
Breakfast Woodworks Inc 203 458-8888
135 Leetes Island Rd Guilford CT (06437) *(G-1694)*
Breakthrough Coatings, Buzzards Bay *Also called Creative Stone Systems Inc (G-9360)*
Breakwater Foods LLC 617 335-6475
82 Sanderson Ave Lynn MA (01902) *(G-12493)*
Breed Nutrition Inc 508 840-3888
5 Old Bliss St Rehoboth MA (02769) *(G-14747)*
Breeze Publications Inc 401 334-9555
6 Blckstone Vly Pl Ste 20 Lincoln RI (02865) *(G-20559)*
Breezy Hill, Oxford *Also called Jackson Caldwell (G-6567)*
Breezy Hill Lumber Co 603 496-8870
78 Province Rd Barnstead NH (03218) *(G-17615)*
Bremser Technologies Inc 203 378-8486
305 Sniffens Ln Stratford CT (06615) *(G-4398)*
Bren Corporation 401 943-8200
1763 Plainfield Pike Johnston RI (02919) *(G-20501)*
Brendan C Kinnane Inc 508 679-8479
394 Kilburn St Fall River MA (02724) *(G-10672)*
Brenmar Molding Inc 978 343-3198
1361 Rindge Rd Fitchburg MA (01420) *(G-10814)*
Brennan Machine Co Inc 781 293-3997
820 Monponsett St Hanson MA (02341) *(G-11361)*
Brentwood Box Company Inc 603 895-0829
33 Lane Rd Raymond NH (03077) *(G-19637)*
Brescias Printing Services Inc 860 528-4254
66 Connecticut Blvd East Hartford CT (06108) *(G-1177)*
Bresna Hand Ice, Gloucester *Also called Cape Pond Ice Company (G-11172)*
Brett Lewis Threads Ltd 802 985-1166
118 Peeper Pond Ln Shelburne VT (05482) *(G-22414)*
Brettuns Village.com, Lewiston *Also called Brettunsvillagecom (G-6278)*
Brettunsvillagecom 207 782-7863
557 Lincoln St Lewiston ME (04240) *(G-6278)*
Brew Your Own, Manchester Center *Also called Battenkill Communications LLP (G-22081)*
Brewer Banner Designs 508 996-6006
77 Forest St New Bedford MA (02740) *(G-13364)*
Brewer Electric & Utilities In 508 771-2040
110 Old Town House Rd South Yarmouth MA (02664) *(G-15325)*
Brewer Fitness, Randolph *Also called Brewers Ledge Inc (G-14671)*
Brewers Ledge Inc 781 961-5200
87 York Ave Randolph MA (02368) *(G-14671)*
Brewers Supply Group Inc 401 275-4920
250 Niantic Ave Providence RI (02907) *(G-20974)*
Brewmasters Brewing Svcs LLC 413 268-2199
4 Main St Williamsburg MA (01096) *(G-16947)*
Brewster Ice Co 508 896-3593
Main St Brewster MA (02631) *(G-9052)*
Bri Metal Works Inc 203 368-1649
105 Island Brook Ave Bridgeport CT (06606) *(G-386)*
Bri-Weld Industries LLC 603 622-9480
55 Gold Ledge Ave Auburn NH (03032) *(G-17608)*
Brian Berlepsch 203 484-9799
21 Commerce Dr Ste 2 North Branford CT (06471) *(G-2959)*
Brian D Murphy 207 564-2737
24 Frandy Ln Sebec ME (04481) *(G-6956)*
Brian Leopold 508 465-0345
53 Myles Standish Dr Carver MA (02330) *(G-9802)*
Brian Safa 203 271-3499
80 Royalwood Ct Cheshire CT (06410) *(G-716)*
Brian Summer 413 625-9990
46 Conway St Ste B Shelburne Falls MA (01370) *(G-15066)*
Brians Machine Shop LLC 603 224-4333
27 Industrial Park Dr # 1 Concord NH (03301) *(G-17886)*
Briar Hill, Poultney *Also called Quarry Slate Industries Inc (G-22274)*
Briarwood Printing Company Inc 860 747-6805
301 Farmington Ave Plainville CT (06062) *(G-3470)*
Bricins Inc 860 482-0250
347 Technology Park Dr Torrington CT (06790) *(G-4567)*
Brick Kiln Place LLC 781 826-6027
200 Boston Ave Ste 2530 Medford MA (02155) *(G-12924)*
Brickell Brands LLC 877 598-0060
101 Mcalister Farm Rd Portland ME (04103) *(G-6626)*
Brickell Men's Products, Portland *Also called Brickell Brands LLC (G-6626)*
Brickyard Enterprises Inc 802 338-7267
239 Brickyard Rd Ferrisburgh VT (05456) *(G-21987)*
Brico LLC 860 242-7068
6c Northwood Dr Bloomfield CT (06002) *(G-212)*
Bride & Groom, Sutton *Also called Chevalier Associates Inc (G-15680)*
Brideau Shtmtl & Fabrication 978 537-3372
29 Phillips St Leominster MA (01453) *(G-12119)*
Bridge & Byron Inc 603 225-5221
45 S State St Concord NH (03301) *(G-17887)*
Bridge 12 Technologies Inc 617 674-2766
37 Loring Dr Framingham MA (01702) *(G-10930)*
Bridge Building Images, Milton *Also called Vermont Christmas Company (G-22139)*
Bridge Byron Printers, Concord *Also called Bridge & Byron Inc (G-17887)*
Bridge Education 207 321-1111
90 E Bridge St Westbrook ME (04092) *(G-7183)*
Bridge Publishing LLC 508 681-8914
155 Smoke Valley Rd Osterville MA (02655) *(G-14246)*
Bridgeme LLC 617 310-4801
273 Otis St Newton MA (02465) *(G-13573)*
Bridgeport Boatwork Inc (PA) 860 536-9651
837 Seaview Ave Bridgeport CT (06607) *(G-387)*
Bridgeport Burial Vault Co 203 375-7375
544 Surf Ave Stratford CT (06615) *(G-4399)*
Bridgeport Fittings LLC 203 377-5944
705 Lordship Blvd Stratford CT (06615) *(G-4400)*
Bridgeport Insulated Wire Co (PA) 203 333-3191
51 Brookfield Ave Bridgeport CT (06610) *(G-388)*
Bridgeport Insulated Wire Co 203 375-9579
514 Surf Ave Stratford CT (06615) *(G-4401)*

A L P H A B E T I C

Bridgeport Magnetics Group Inc.....203 954-0050
6 Waterview Dr Shelton CT (06484) *(G-3784)*
Bridgeport Nat Bindery Inc.....413 789-1981
662 Silver St Agawam MA (01001) *(G-7425)*
Bridgeport Proc & Mfg LLC.....203 612-7733
155 Davenport St Bridgeport CT (06607) *(G-389)*
Bridgeport Tl & Stamping Corp.....203 336-2501
35 Burr Ct Bridgeport CT (06605) *(G-390)*
Bridges Point Boat Yard Inc.....207 359-2713
23 Bridges Point Ln Brooklin ME (04616) *(G-5815)*
Bridgesat Inc.....617 419-1800
100 High St Fl 28 Boston MA (02110) *(G-8444)*
Bridgewater Prtg Copy Ctr LLC.....508 697-5227
100 Broad St Bridgewater MA (02324) *(G-9065)*
Bridgewater Raynham Sand Stone, Bridgewater *Also called B R S Inc* *(G-9061)*
Bridgewater Trophy, Bridgewater *Also called Modern Marking Products Inc* *(G-9085)*
Bridgton News Corp.....207 647-2851
118 Main St Bridgton ME (04009) *(G-5806)*
Bridgton News The, Bridgton *Also called Bridgton News Corp* *(G-5806)*
Brigade Tactical Corp.....603 682-7063
400 Bedford St Ste Sw05 Manchester NH (03101) *(G-18790)*
Briggs Lumber Products.....508 886-2054
336 E County Rd Rutland MA (01543) *(G-14880)*
Briggs Lumber Products.....978 630-4207
104 E Broadway Gardner MA (01440) *(G-11106)*
Brightec Inc.....508 647-9710
8 Pleasant St Fl 1c Natick MA (01760) *(G-13241)*
Brightman Corp.....508 644-2620
181 S Main St Assonet MA (02702) *(G-7678)*
Brightman Lumber Co, Assonet *Also called Brightman Corp* *(G-7678)*
Brighton & Hove Mold Ltd.....203 264-3013
115 Hurley Rd Ste 2c Oxford CT (06478) *(G-3392)*
Brightsight Llc.....860 208-0222
9 Hebert Ln Woodstock CT (06281) *(G-5494)*
Brill Academic Publishers, Boston *Also called Brill Usa Inc* *(G-8445)*
Brill Usa Inc.....617 263-2323
2 Liberty Sq Fl 11 Boston MA (02109) *(G-8445)*
Brillacademic Publishers Inc.....617 742-5277
112 Water St Ste 400 Boston MA (02109) *(G-8446)*
Brimatco Corporation.....203 272-0044
1486 Highland Ave Ste 10 Cheshire CT (06410) *(G-717)*
Brimfield Flemarket.com, Sturbridge *Also called Journal of Antq & Collectibles* *(G-15639)*
Brimfield Hwy Dept, Brimfield *Also called Town of Brimfield* *(G-9111)*
Brimfield Precision LLC.....413 245-7144
68 Mill Ln Brimfield MA (01010) *(G-9109)*
Bring Up Inc.....617 803-4248
618 Cambridge St Cambridge MA (02141) *(G-9422)*
Brio Promotions, Rockland *Also called Trems Inc* *(G-6812)*
Brion Rieff Boatbuilder Inc.....207 359-4455
130 Reach Rd Brooklin ME (04616) *(G-5816)*
Briscon Electric Mfg Corp.....508 832-3481
93 Bancroft St Auburn MA (01501) *(G-7830)*
Bristal Cushion & ACC LLC.....401 247-4499
6 Commercial Way Warren RI (02885) *(G-21291)*
Bristol Inc (HQ).....860 945-2200
1100 Buckingham St Watertown CT (06795) *(G-5001)*
Bristol Adult Resource Ctr Inc.....860 583-8721
97 Peck Ln Bristol CT (06010) *(G-536)*
Bristol Bay LLC.....978 744-4272
70 Washington St Ste 310 Salem MA (01970) *(G-14898)*
Bristol Cushions Inc.....401 247-4499
31 Birchwood Dr Bristol RI (02809) *(G-20065)*
Bristol Instrument Gears Inc.....860 583-1395
164 Central St Ste 1 Bristol CT (06010) *(G-537)*
Bristol Marine, Bristol *Also called Lenmarine Inc* *(G-20089)*
Bristol Myers Squibb.....781 209-2309
100 Binney St Cambridge MA (02142) *(G-9423)*
Bristol Phoenix.....401 253-6000
1 Bradford St Bristol RI (02809) *(G-20066)*
Bristol Place Inc.....508 226-2300
555 Pleasant St Ste 201 Attleboro MA (02703) *(G-7714)*
Bristol Press.....860 584-0501
188 Main St Torrington CT (06790) *(G-4568)*
Bristol Seafood LLC.....207 761-4251
5 Portland Fish Pier Portland ME (04101) *(G-6627)*
Bristol Signart Inc.....860 582-2577
550 Broad St Bristol CT (06010) *(G-538)*
Bristol Tool & Die Company.....860 582-2577
550 Broad St Ste 13 Bristol CT (06010) *(G-539)*
Bristol-Myers Squibb Company.....978 667-9532
331 Trebble Cove Rd Billerica MA (01821) *(G-8220)*
Brite Strike Tctcal Illmntion, Duxbury *Also called Brite-Strike Technologies Inc* *(G-10394)*
Brite-Strike Technologies Inc.....781 585-3525
1145 Franklin St Duxbury Duxbury MA (02332) *(G-10394)*
British Beer Company Inc.....978 577-6034
149 Littleton Rd Westford MA (01886) *(G-16758)*
British Precision Inc.....860 633-3343
20 Sequin Dr Glastonbury CT (06033) *(G-1541)*
Brittany Company Inc.....203 269-7859
193 S Cherry St Wallingford CT (06492) *(G-4712)*
Brittany Global Tech Corp.....508 999-3281
1357 E Rodney French Blvd New Bedford MA (02744) *(G-13365)*
Brn Corporation.....603 726-3800
3279 Us Route 3 Campton NH (03223) *(G-17775)*
Broad Peak Manufacturing LLC.....203 678-4664
10 Beaumont Rd Ste 1 Wallingford CT (06492) *(G-4713)*
Broadband Communication Div, Wallingford *Also called Ruckus Wireless Inc* *(G-4802)*
Broadcast Pix Inc.....978 600-1100
27 Industrial Ave Unit 5 Chelmsford MA (01824) *(G-9878)*
Broadcastmed Inc.....860 953-2900
195 Farmington Ave Farmington CT (06032) *(G-1470)*
Broadcom Corporation.....978 719-1300
200 Brickstone Sq Ste 401 Andover MA (01810) *(G-7543)*
Broadstone Industries.....978 691-2790
195 Circuit Ave Lowell MA (01852) *(G-12356)*
Broadstripes LLC.....203 350-9824
129 Church St Ste 805 New Haven CT (06510) *(G-2672)*
Broadway Station, Oak Bluffs *Also called Basement Designs Inc* *(G-14209)*
Brochu Logging Inc.....207 453-2982
178 E Benton Rd Benton ME (04901) *(G-5704)*
Brockway Ferry Corporation (PA).....860 767-8231
59 Plains Rd Essex CT (06426) *(G-1394)*
Brockway-Smith Company.....413 247-9674
125 Chestnut St West Hatfield MA (01088) *(G-16482)*
Brodeur Machine Company Inc.....508 995-2662
62 Wood St New Bedford MA (02745) *(G-13366)*
Brodeur Machine Company Bus Tr.....508 995-2662
62 Wood St New Bedford MA (02745) *(G-13367)*
Brody Printing Company Inc.....203 384-9313
265 Central Ave Bridgeport CT (06607) *(G-391)*
Broen-Lab Inc.....205 956-9444
15 Constitution Dr # 122 Bedford NH (03110) *(G-17633)*
Brogans Custom Woodworking.....978 502-8013
30 Main St Westminster MA (01473) *(G-16803)*
Broil King, Winsted *Also called Bkmfg Corp* *(G-5405)*
Broleco Inc (PA).....978 689-3200
200 Sutton St Ste 226 North Andover MA (01845) *(G-13693)*
Bromar.....207 474-3784
17 Parlin St Skowhegan ME (04976) *(G-6970)*
Bronze Craft Corporation.....603 883-7747
37 Will St Nashua NH (03060) *(G-19130)*
Brook & Whittle Limited (HQ).....203 483-5602
20 Carter Dr Guilford CT (06437) *(G-1695)*
Brook Broad Brewing LLC.....860 623-1000
122 Prospect Hill Rd East Windsor CT (06088) *(G-1280)*
Brook Heath Studio.....413 337-5736
24 W Main St Heath MA (01346) *(G-11488)*
Brook Hollow Sand & Gravel.....603 231-0238
317 S River Rd Bedford NH (03110) *(G-17634)*
Brook Pond Machining Inc.....413 562-7411
170b Lockhouse Rd Westfield MA (01085) *(G-16675)*
Brook Wiles Logging Inc.....207 398-4105
209 Allagash Rd Allagash ME (04774) *(G-5518)*
Brooke Taylor Winery LLC (PA).....860 974-1263
848 Route 171 Woodstock CT (06281) *(G-5495)*
Brookfeld Mdcl/Srgical Sup Inc.....203 775-0862
60 Old New Milford Rd Brookfield CT (06804) *(G-636)*
Brookfield Industries Inc.....860 283-6211
99 W Hillside Ave Thomaston CT (06787) *(G-4500)*
Brookfield Phrm Compounding, Brookfield *Also called Brookfeld Mdcl/Srgical Sup Inc* *(G-636)*
Brookfield Power Neng LLC.....207 723-4341
1024 Central St Millinocket ME (04462) *(G-6440)*
Brookfield Tractor Prfmce Eqp, Brookfield *Also called Dave Ross* *(G-640)*
Brookfield Wire Company Inc (HQ).....508 867-6474
231 E Main St West Brookfield MA (01585) *(G-16465)*
Brooklin Boat Yard Inc (PA).....207 359-2236
44 Center Hbr Rd Ste 44 Brooklin ME (04616) *(G-5817)*
Brookline Print Center.....617 926-0300
85 River St Ste 7 Waltham MA (02453) *(G-16052)*
Brookline T A B.....617 566-3585
254 2nd Ave Needham Heights MA (02494) *(G-13321)*
Brookline Textiles Inc.....802 748-1933
Lower Waterford Rd Lower Waterford VT (05848) *(G-22060)*
Brooklyn Sand & Gravel LLC.....860 779-3980
42 Junior Ave Danielson CT (06239) *(G-1012)*
Brooks Associates Inc (PA).....781 871-3400
300 Longwater Dr Unit 3 Norwell MA (02061) *(G-14098)*
Brooks Automation Inc.....978 262-2795
12 Elizabeth Dr Chelmsford MA (01824) *(G-9879)*
Brooks Automation Inc (PA).....978 262-2400
15 Elizabeth Dr Chelmsford MA (01824) *(G-9880)*
Brooks Precision Machining.....978 256-7477
4 Kidder Rd Chelmsford MA (01824) *(G-9881)*
Brooks Welding & Machining Inc.....207 247-4141
897 West Rd Waterboro ME (04087) *(G-7151)*
Brookside Flvors Ingrdents LLC (HQ).....203 595-4520
201 Tresser Blvd Ste 320 Stamford CT (06901) *(G-4152)*

Brookwood Laminating Inc 860 774-5001
275 Putnam Rd Wauregan CT (06387) *(G-5038)*
Brookwood Roll Goods Group, Wauregan *Also called Brookwood Laminating Inc (G-5038)*
Broome & Co LLC 860 653-2106
62 Turkey Hills Rd East Granby CT (06026) *(G-1118)*
Broome & Company LLC 860 623-0254
12 Copper Dr Windsor Locks CT (06096) *(G-5387)*
Broomfield Laboratories Inc 978 779-6600
164 Still River Rd Bolton MA (01740) *(G-8318)*
Brosseau Fuels LLC 802 888-9209
2148 Cadys Falls Rd Morrisville VT (05661) *(G-22165)*
Brothers & Sons Sugar House 860 489-2719
998 Saw Mill Hill Rd Torrington CT (06790) *(G-4569)*
Brothers Machining Corp 508 286-9136
364 Reservoir St Norton MA (02766) *(G-14072)*
Broude International Editions 413 458-8131
141 White Oaks Rd Williamstown MA (01267) *(G-16956)*
Brouillette Hvac & Shtmtl Inc 508 822-4800
13 Stevens St East Taunton MA (02718) *(G-10511)*
Brouillette Realty LLC 401 499-4867
48 Barrington Ave Barrington RI (02806) *(G-20043)*
Brown & Sharpe Pumps, North Kingstown *Also called Bsm Pump Corp (G-20694)*
Brown Country Services LLC 802 464-5200
131 Route 100 West Dover VT (05356) *(G-22606)*
Brown Dog Software Inc 603 382-2713
24 Colby Rd Danville NH (03819) *(G-17967)*
Brown Fox Printing Inc (PA) 207 883-9525
253 Us Route 1 Scarborough ME (04074) *(G-6913)*
Brown Med, Boston *Also called Brownmed Inc (G-8447)*
Brown Novelty Co Inc 802 388-2502
406 E Main St Middlebury VT (05753) *(G-22104)*
Brown Publishing Network Inc (PA) 781 547-7600
10 City Sq Ste 3 Charlestown MA (02129) *(G-9828)*
Brown Shop, North Haven *Also called J O Brown & Son Inc (G-6511)*
Brown Wood Products, Middlebury *Also called Brown Novelty Co Inc (G-22104)*
Browne Hansen LLC 203 269-0557
44 School House Rd Wallingford CT (06492) *(G-4714)*
Brownell & Company Inc (PA) 860 873-8625
423 E Haddam Moodus Rd Moodus CT (06469) *(G-2423)*
Brownell Boat Stands Inc 508 758-3671
5 Boat Rock Rd Mattapoisett MA (02739) *(G-12885)*
Brownell Boat Trailers Inc 508 996-3110
129 Alden Rd Fairhaven MA (02719) *(G-10639)*
Brownell Boatstands, Mattapoisett *Also called Brownell Boat Stands Inc (G-12885)*
Brownell Trailers LLC 508 996-3110
129 Alden Rd Fairhaven MA (02719) *(G-10640)*
Brownlie Lamar Design Group 401 714-9371
79 Joyce St Warren RI (02885) *(G-21292)*
Brownmed Inc (PA) 857 317-3354
101 Federal St Fl 29 Boston MA (02110) *(G-8447)*
Browns Certified Welding Inc 802 453-3351
275 S 116 Rd Bristol VT (05443) *(G-21762)*
Browns Greens 207 326-4636
715 Coastal Rd Brooksville ME (04617) *(G-5824)*
Browns Quarried Slate Pdts Inc 802 468-2297
2504 S Street Ext Castleton VT (05735) *(G-21827)*
Browns River Bindery Inc 802 878-3335
1 Allen Martin Dr Essex Junction VT (05452) *(G-21932)*
Browns River Maple 802 878-2880
375 Browns River Rd Essex Junction VT (05452) *(G-21933)*
Browns Rver Rec Prsrvtion Svcs, Essex Junction *Also called Browns River Bindery Inc (G-21932)*
Browser Daily 860 469-5534
211 Spencer Hill Rd Winsted CT (06098) *(G-5406)*
Brox Industries Inc (PA) 978 454-9105
1471 Methuen St Dracut MA (01826) *(G-10355)*
Brozzian LLC 774 280-9338
5 Sunset Dr Whitinsville MA (01588) *(G-16911)*
Bruce A Pettengill 207 933-2578
129 Bog Rd Leeds ME (04263) *(G-6268)*
Bruce Barrowclough 978 524-0022
140 Elliott St Bldg A Beverly MA (01915) *(G-8113)*
Bruce C Smith Logging 207 255-3259
45 Smith Ln Machiasport ME (04655) *(G-6397)*
Bruce Dennison 207 255-0954
599 Jacksonville Rd East Machias ME (04630) *(G-5983)*
Bruce Diamond Corporation 508 222-3755
1231 County St Attleboro MA (02703) *(G-7715)*
Bruce Luong DBA Pure Froyo 978 996-7800
108 Merrimack St Lowell MA (01852) *(G-12357)*
Bruce Park Sports EMB LLC 203 853-4488
20 Chatham Dr Norwalk CT (06854) *(G-3115)*
Bruce Waite Logging Inc 802 867-2213
88 Snow Rd Dorset VT (05251) *(G-21907)*
Bruin Plastics Co Inc 401 568-3081
61 Joslin Rd Glendale RI (02826) *(G-20459)*
Bruker Axs Inc 978 663-3660
40 Manning Rd Billerica MA (01821) *(G-8221)*
Bruker Biospin Mri Inc 978 667-9580
15 Fortune Dr Billerica MA (01821) *(G-8222)*
Bruker Corporation (PA) 978 663-3660
40 Manning Rd Billerica MA (01821) *(G-8223)*
Bruker Daltonics Inc 978 663-2548
15 Fortune Dr Billerica MA (01821) *(G-8224)*
Bruker Detection Corporation 978 663-3660
40 Manning Rd Billerica MA (01821) *(G-8225)*
Bruker Enrgy Supercon Tech Inc (HQ) 978 901-7550
15 Fortune Dr Billerica MA (01821) *(G-8226)*
Bruker Optics Inc (HQ) 978 901-1528
40 Manning Rd Billerica MA (01821) *(G-8227)*
Bruker Scientific LLC (HQ) 978 667-9580
40 Manning Rd Billerica MA (01821) *(G-8228)*
Brumberg Publications Inc 617 734-1979
124 Harvard St Ste 9 Brookline MA (02446) *(G-9198)*
Bruno Diduca 781 894-5300
57 Harvard St Waltham MA (02453) *(G-16053)*
Brunswick Enclosure Company 978 670-1124
25 Sullivan Rd Ste 6 North Billerica MA (01862) *(G-13799)*
Brunswick Instant Printing Inc 207 729-6854
44 Cushing St Brunswick ME (04011) *(G-5832)*
Brunswick Publishing LLC 207 729-3311
3 Business Pkwy Brunswick ME (04011) *(G-5833)*
Brushfoil LLC 203 453-7403
1 Shoreline Dr Ste 6 Guilford CT (06437) *(G-1696)*
Bruso-Holmes Inc 802 878-8337
34 Park St Ste 10 Essex Junction VT (05452) *(G-21934)*
Bryan, Woburn *Also called Lymol Medical Corp (G-17219)*
Bryan Heavens Logging & Firewo 860 485-1712
50 Shingle Mill Rd Harwinton CT (06791) *(G-1887)*
Bryan Oncor Inc 617 957-9858
141 Powder House Blvd Somerville MA (02144) *(G-15162)*
Bryant Group Inc 603 746-1166
28 Riverside Dr Contoocook NH (03229) *(G-17941)*
Bryant Sheet Metal & Cnstr 781 826-4113
301 Winter St Ste 3 Hanover MA (02339) *(G-11331)*
Bryce, Northampton *Also called Heavenly Chocolate (G-14008)*
Bryka Skystocks LLC 845 507-8200
549 Cedar St Newington CT (06111) *(G-2850)*
Brymill Corporation (PA) 860 875-2460
105 Windermere Ave Ste 3b Ellington CT (06029) *(G-1330)*
Brymill Cryogenic Sys, Ellington *Also called Brymill Corporation (G-1330)*
Bryt Manufacturing 860 224-4772
23 John St New Britain CT (06051) *(G-2516)*
BSD Soft Ware 207 522-5881
10 Brookside Dr Durham ME (04222) *(G-5968)*
BSD Software, Durham *Also called BSD Soft Ware (G-5968)*
Bsg Handcraft 508 636-5154
250 Niantic Ave Providence RI (02907) *(G-20975)*
Bsm Pump Corp 401 471-6350
180 Frenchtown Rd North Kingstown RI (02852) *(G-20694)*
BT Copy & Printing Center, Ware *Also called Biz Tek Printing and Mktg LLC (G-16230)*
Btd Precision Inc 413 594-2783
75 Marion St Chicopee MA (01013) *(G-10002)*
Btl Holdings LLC 917 596-3660
69 Industrial Ave Middlebury VT (05753) *(G-22105)*
Btl Industries Inc 866 285-1656
362 Elm St Marlborough MA (01752) *(G-12730)*
Btu International Inc (HQ) 978 667-4111
23 Esquire Rd North Billerica MA (01862) *(G-13800)*
Btu Overseas Ltd (HQ) 978 667-4111
23 Esquire Rd North Billerica MA (01862) *(G-13801)*
Bu Inc 401 831-2112
812 Charles St Providence RI (02904) *(G-20976)*
Bubble Mneia Dssert Noodle Bar 207 773-9559
15 Temple St Portland ME (04101) *(G-6628)*
Bubier Meats, Greene *Also called Bubiers Meats (G-6148)*
Bubiers Meats 207 946-7761
194 Sprague Mills Rd Greene ME (04236) *(G-6148)*
Buchanan Minerals LLC (HQ) 304 392-1000
57 Danbury Rd Ste 201 Wilton CT (06897) *(G-5281)*
Buck Brothers, Millbury *Also called Great Neck Saw Mfrs Inc (G-13166)*
Buck Scientific Inc 203 853-9444
58 Fort Point St Norwalk CT (06855) *(G-3116)*
Buck's Ice Cream, Milford *Also called Bucks Spumoni Company Inc (G-2257)*
Buckeye Cleaning Center, East Weymouth *Also called Buckeye International Inc (G-10539)*
Buckeye International Inc 617 827-2137
65 Mathewson Dr Ste Q East Weymouth MA (02189) *(G-10539)*
Buckleguycom LLC 978 213-9989
15 Graf Rd Newburyport MA (01950) *(G-13475)*
Buckley Co Inc 781 545-7975
31 Hollycrest Rd Scituate MA (02066) *(G-15007)*
Bucks Spumoni Company Inc 203 874-2007
229 Pepes Farm Rd Milford CT (06460) *(G-2257)*
Budco Products Corp 401 767-2590
60 Kindergarten St Woonsocket RI (02895) *(G-21554)*
Budd Foods, Manchester *Also called Msn Corporation (G-18879)*
Budget Printing Center, Taunton *Also called Aleksandr S Yaskovich (G-15722)*

A L P H A B E T I C

Budget Printing Concord LLC.....978 369-4630
97 Thoreau St Concord MA (01742) ***(G-10118)***
Budgetcard Inc.....508 695-8762
171 Commonwealth Ave Attleboro Falls MA (02763) ***(G-7811)***
Budiproducts.....617 470-3086
404 Marlborough St Boston MA (02115) ***(G-8448)***
Budney Aerospace Inc.....860 828-0585
131 New Park Dr Berlin CT (06037) ***(G-78)***
Budney Overhaul & Repair Ltd.....860 828-0585
131 New Park Dr Berlin CT (06037) ***(G-79)***
Budrad Engineering Co LLC.....203 452-7310
26 Patmar Cir Monroe CT (06468) ***(G-2397)***
Buffalo Industrial Fabrics Inc.....203 553-9400
372 Danbury Rd Ste 199 Wilton CT (06897) ***(G-5282)***
Buick LLC.....401 539-2432
106 Canonchet Rd Hope Valley RI (02832) ***(G-20481)***
Builders Choice Kitchen & Bath.....413 569-9802
796 College Hwy Southwick MA (01077) ***(G-15412)***
Builders Concrete East LLC.....860 456-4111
79 Boston Post Rd North Windham CT (06256) ***(G-3079)***
Builders Supply of Cape Cod.....508 888-0444
18 Jan Sebastian Dr Sandwich MA (02563) ***(G-14963)***
Building Blocks, Newton *Also called Homeportfolio Inc* ***(G-13602)***
Building Envelope Systems LLC.....508 381-0429
20 High St Plainville MA (02762) ***(G-14516)***
Buildium LLC.....888 414-1988
3 Center Plz Ste 400 Boston MA (02108) ***(G-8449)***
Built Rite Manufacturing Inc.....802 228-7293
750 E Hill Rd Ludlow VT (05149) ***(G-22061)***
Built-Rite Tool and Die Inc.....978 751-8432
11 Jytek Rd Leominster MA (01453) ***(G-12120)***
Built-Rite Tool and Die Inc.....978 365-3867
851 Sterling Rd Lancaster MA (01523) ***(G-11981)***
Built-Rite Tool and Die Inc (PA).....978 368-7250
807 Sterling Rd Lancaster MA (01523) ***(G-11982)***
Bulcast LLC.....617 901-6836
55 Crosby Rd Chestnut Hill MA (02467) ***(G-9983)***
Bull Data Systems Inc (HQ).....978 294-6000
285 Billerica Rd Ste 200 Chelmsford MA (01824) ***(G-9882)***
Bull Display, Middletown *Also called Bull Metal Products Inc* ***(G-2180)***
Bull Hn Info Systems Inc.....978 256-1033
285 Billerica Rd Ste 200 Chelmsford MA (01824) ***(G-9883)***
Bull Metal Products Inc.....860 346-9691
191 Saybrook Rd Middletown CT (06457) ***(G-2180)***
Bulletin Newspapers Inc.....617 361-1406
695 Truman Hwy Ste 99 Hyde Park MA (02136) ***(G-11864)***
Bulletin Newspapers Inc (PA).....617 361-8400
695 Truman Hwy Ste 99 Hyde Park MA (02136) ***(G-11865)***
Bullhorn Inc (PA).....617 478-9100
100 Summer St Ste 1700 Boston MA (02110) ***(G-8450)***
Bullock & Block Ltd.....802 773-3350
57 Crescent St Rutland VT (05701) ***(G-22326)***
Bully Boy Distillers.....617 442-6000
35 Cedric St Roxbury MA (02119) ***(G-14870)***
Bulzeyepro.....207 626-0000
1069 S Belfast Ave Augusta ME (04330) ***(G-5604)***
Bumboosa LLC.....508 539-1373
25 Brewster Rd Mashpee MA (02649) ***(G-12876)***
Bumper Boats Inc.....401 841-8200
9 Connell Hwy Newport RI (02840) ***(G-20658)***
Bumwraps Inc (PA).....802 326-4080
578 Vt Route 242 Montgomery Center VT (05471) ***(G-22141)***
Bumwraps Inc.....802 326-4080
158 Main St Ste 3 Newport VT (05855) ***(G-22190)***
Bunnell Rocky Log & Forest Mgt.....603 638-4983
523 Littleton Rd Monroe NH (03771) ***(G-19089)***
Bunsen Rush Laboratories Inc.....203 397-0820
270 Amity Rd Ste 124 Woodbridge CT (06525) ***(G-5463)***
Bunting & Lyon Inc.....203 272-4623
615 Broad Swamp Rd Cheshire CT (06410) ***(G-718)***
Bunzl Maine.....207 772-9825
150 Read St Portland ME (04103) ***(G-6629)***
Buon Appetito From Italy LLC.....860 437-3668
15 Shaw St New London CT (06320) ***(G-2767)***
Burbak Companies.....603 654-2291
361 Forest Rd Wilton NH (03086) ***(G-19976)***
Burbak Plastic, Wilton *Also called Burbak Companies* ***(G-19976)***
Burdick Chocolates, Walpole *Also called Bb Walpole Liquidation NH Inc* ***(G-19916)***
Burdon Enterprises LLC.....860 345-4882
20 Reisman Trl Higganum CT (06441) ***(G-1902)***
Bureau of National Affairs Inc.....781 843-9422
150 Fairways Edge Dr Marshfield MA (02050) ***(G-12856)***
Burell Bros Inc.....860 455-9681
Rr 97 Hampton CT (06247) ***(G-1796)***
Burger-Roy Inc.....207 696-3978
66 Main St Madison ME (04950) ***(G-6404)***
Burgess Machine, Middleton *Also called Bourgeois Machine Co* ***(G-13086)***
Burgess Sugarhouse LLC.....802 899-5228
251 Irish Settlement Rd Underhill VT (05489) ***(G-22546)***
Burgett Brothers Incorporated.....978 374-8888
35 Duncan St Haverhill MA (01830) ***(G-11411)***
Burk Technology Inc.....978 486-0086
7 Beaver Brook Rd Littleton MA (01460) ***(G-12295)***
Burke Medical Equipment Inc.....413 592-5464
516 Montgomery St Chicopee MA (01020) ***(G-10003)***
Burke Mountain Bird Seed, Lyndonville *Also called Northeast Agricultural Sls Inc* ***(G-22070)***
Burke Precision Machine Co Inc.....860 408-1394
7 Hatchett Hill Rd East Granby CT (06026) ***(G-1119)***
Burlington Foundry Co Inc.....781 272-1182
13 Adams St Burlington MA (01803) ***(G-9242)***
Burlington Free Press, Burlington *Also called McClure Newspapers Inc* ***(G-21795)***
Burlington Free Press, Burlington *Also called Gannett Co Inc* ***(G-21786)***
Burlington Machine Inc.....978 284-6525
340b Fordham Rd Wilmington MA (01887) ***(G-16985)***
Burlington Petroleum Equipment.....802 864-5155
32 San Remo Dr South Burlington VT (05403) ***(G-22440)***
Burlington Union.....781 229-0918
9 Myrna Rd Lexington MA (02420) ***(G-12209)***
Burlodge USA Inc.....336 776-1010
24 Pearson St Litchfield NH (03052) ***(G-18651)***
Burndy Americas Inc (HQ).....603 647-5000
47 E Industrial Pk Dr Manchester NH (03109) ***(G-18791)***
Burndy Americas Intl Holdg LLC.....603 647-5000
47 E Industrial Pk Dr Manchester NH (03109) ***(G-18792)***
Burndy LLC.....603 647-5000
47 Industrial Dr Londonderry NH (03053) ***(G-18681)***
Burndy LLC.....203 792-1115
185 Grassy Plain St Bethel CT (06801) ***(G-134)***
Burndy LLC.....603 745-8114
Connector Road Route 3 Lincoln NH (03251) ***(G-18645)***
Burndy LLC.....603 647-5119
7 Aviation Park Dr Londonderry NH (03053) ***(G-18682)***
Burndy LLC.....603 745-8114
34 Bern Dibner Dr Lincoln NH (03251) ***(G-18646)***
Burndy LLC.....603 444-6781
150 Burndy Rd Littleton NH (03561) ***(G-18655)***
Burndy LLC (HQ).....603 647-5000
47 E Industrial Park Dr Manchester NH (03109) ***(G-18793)***
Burnell Controls Inc.....978 646-9992
153 Andover St Ste 202 Danvers MA (01923) ***(G-10204)***
Burner Booster, The, Medway *Also called Advanced Burner Solutions Corp* ***(G-12953)***
Burnham & Morrill, Portland *Also called B&G Foods Inc* ***(G-6616)***
Burnham Associates Inc.....978 745-1788
14 Franklin St Salem MA (01970) ***(G-14899)***
Burns Walton.....203 422-5222
29 Milo Dr Branford CT (06405) ***(G-300)***
Burns Industries Incorporated.....603 881-8336
34 Pepperell Rd Hollis NH (03049) ***(G-18327)***
Burns Machine LLC.....603 524-4080
516 Province Rd Laconia NH (03246) ***(G-18561)***
Burnside Supermarket LLC.....860 291-9965
1150 Burnside Ave East Hartford CT (06108) ***(G-1178)***
Burr Industries Inc.....978 774-2527
495 Newbury St Danvers MA (01923) ***(G-10205)***
Burr Signs, Scarborough *Also called Glidden Signs Inc* ***(G-6919)***
Burrillville Town of Inc.....401 568-6296
141 Clair River Dr Oakland RI (02858) ***(G-20798)***
Burrillville Waste Water, Oakland *Also called Burrillville Town of Inc* ***(G-20798)***
Burroughs Machine Tool Pdts.....207 745-5558
1 Isthmus Rd Charleston ME (04422) ***(G-5899)***
Burt General Repair & Welding.....603 788-4821
330 Portland St Lancaster NH (03584) ***(G-18597)***
Burt's Repair, Lancaster *Also called Burt General Repair & Welding* ***(G-18597)***
Burtco Inc.....802 722-3358
185 Rte 123 Westminster Station VT (05159) ***(G-22633)***
Burton Corporation (PA).....802 862-4500
180 Queen City Park Rd Burlington VT (05401) ***(G-21770)***
Burton Corporation.....802 862-4500
266 Queen City Park Rd Burlington VT (05401) ***(G-21771)***
Burton Corporation.....802 652-3600
30 Technology Park Way South Burlington VT (05403) ***(G-22441)***
Burton Frame and Trailer Inc.....978 433-2051
106 Brookline St Pepperell MA (01463) ***(G-14437)***
Burton Manufacturing Center, South Burlington *Also called Burton Corporation* ***(G-22441)***
Burton Wire & Cable Inc.....603 624-2427
4 Brookside West Hooksett NH (03106) ***(G-18344)***
Bushwick Metals LLC.....203 630-2459
130 Research Pkwy Ste 203 Meriden CT (06450) ***(G-2081)***
Business Card Express, Concord *Also called Acara Holdings LLC* ***(G-17879)***
Business Cards Overnight Inc.....978 974-9271
15 Union St Ste 19 Lawrence MA (01840) ***(G-11999)***
Business Cards Tomorrow Inc.....203 723-5858
69 Raytkwich Rd Naugatuck CT (06770) ***(G-2464)***
Business Financial Pubg LLC.....802 865-9886
380 Hurricane Ln Ste 202 Williston VT (05495) ***(G-22658)***
Business Journals Inc (PA).....203 853-6015
50 Day St Fl 3 Norwalk CT (06854) ***(G-3117)***
Business New Haven, New Haven *Also called Second Wind Media Limited* ***(G-2736)***

Business People Vermont, Williston *Also called Mill Publishing Inc* ***(G-22682)***
Business Printer, The, Charlton *Also called Dns Inc* ***(G-9849)***
Business Resources Inc.........508 433-4600
1500 W Park Dr Westborough MA (01581) ***(G-16596)***
Business West.........413 781-8600
1441 Main St Ste 604 Springfield MA (01103) ***(G-15457)***
Business West On Line, Springfield *Also called Business West* ***(G-15457)***
Buswell Manufacturing Co Inc.........203 334-6069
229 Merriam St Bridgeport CT (06604) ***(G-392)***
Butch Eaton Logging & Trucki.........603 522-3894
1496 Province Lake Rd East Wakefield NH (03830) ***(G-18094)***
Butcher Block Inc.........800 258-4304
19 Syd Clarke Dr Claremont NH (03743) ***(G-17837)***
Butler & Macmaster Engines, Hallowell *Also called Melton Sales and Service Inc* ***(G-6163)***
Butler Architectural Wdwkg Inc.........508 985-9980
200 Theodore Rice Blvd New Bedford MA (02745) ***(G-13368)***
Butler Automatic Inc (PA).........508 923-0544
41 Leona Dr Middleboro MA (02346) ***(G-13057)***
Butler Home Products LLC (HQ).........508 597-8000
2 Cabot Rd Ste 1 Hudson MA (01749) ***(G-11761)***
Butler Metal Fabricators Inc.........413 306-5762
91 Pinevale St Indian Orchard MA (01151) ***(G-11885)***
Butlers Rv Services Corp.........508 987-0234
254 Sutton Ave Oxford MA (01540) ***(G-14255)***
Buttergirl Baking Co.........857 891-6625
12 Moon Hill Rd Lexington MA (02421) ***(G-12210)***
Butternut Mountain Farm, Morrisville *Also called Vermont Maple Sugar Co Inc* ***(G-22178)***
Butternut Mountain Farm, Johnson *Also called Vermont Maple Sugar Co Inc* ***(G-22052)***
Butternuts Good Dishes Inc.........603 569-6869
12 Railroad Ave Wolfeboro NH (03894) ***(G-20016)***
Buttura & Sons Inc.........802 476-6646
109 Boynton St Barre VT (05641) ***(G-21610)***
Buttura Gherardi Gran Artisans, Barre *Also called Buttura & Sons Inc* ***(G-21610)***
Buy Boxescom LLC.........617 305-7865
1 Boston Pl Ste 3400 Boston MA (02108) ***(G-8451)***
Buy Monthly Publishing Inc.........802 244-6620
2687 Waterbury-Stowe Rd Waterbury Center VT (05677) ***(G-22590)***
Buyers Digest, Fairfax *Also called Gannett River States Pubg Corp* ***(G-21975)***
Buyers Digest Press Inc.........802 893-4214
57 Yankee Park Rd Fairfax VT (05454) ***(G-21973)***
Buzzafricocom.........617 903-0152
7 Chestnut St Lynn MA (01902) ***(G-12494)***
Buzzards Bay Brewing Inc.........508 636-2288
98 Horseneck Rd Westport MA (02790) ***(G-16836)***
Buzzworthy Baking LLC.........978 254-5910
454 Harrington Ave Concord MA (01742) ***(G-10119)***
Bway Corporation.........978 537-4911
196 Industrial Rd Leominster MA (01453) ***(G-12121)***
Bwi of MA LLC.........978 534-4065
248 Industrial Rd Leominster MA (01453) ***(G-12122)***
Bwt Pharma & Biotech Inc.........508 485-4291
417 South St Ste 5 Marlborough MA (01752) ***(G-12731)***
By Design Screen Printing, Everett *Also called Byd Corp* ***(G-10605)***
Byd Corp.........617 394-0799
167 Bow St Ste 2 Everett MA (02149) ***(G-10605)***
Byer Manufacturing Company.........207 866-2171
74 Mill St Orono ME (04473) ***(G-6552)***
Byer of Maine, Orono *Also called Byer Manufacturing Company* ***(G-6552)***
Byrne Group Inc.........203 573-0100
170 Grand St Waterbury CT (06702) ***(G-4852)***
Byrne Sand & Gravel Co Inc.........508 947-0724
210 Wood St Middleboro MA (02346) ***(G-13058)***
Byrne Woodworking Inc.........203 953-3205
170 Herbert St Bridgeport CT (06604) ***(G-393)***
Byron Lord Inc.........203 287-9881
18 Bailey Rd Old Lyme CT (06371) ***(G-3315)***
C & A Machine Co Inc.........860 667-0605
49 Progress Cir Newington CT (06111) ***(G-2851)***
C & C Fabricating Inc.........978 356-9980
24 Hayward St Ste A Ipswich MA (01938) ***(G-11907)***
C & C Fiberglass Components.........401 254-4342
75 Ballou Blvd Bristol RI (02009) ***(G-20067)***
C & C Lamination.........413 594-6910
34 Pajak St Chicopee MA (01013) ***(G-10004)***
C & C Logging.........860 683-0071
416 Pigeon Hill Rd Windsor CT (06095) ***(G-5323)***
C & C Machine Inc.........978 649-0285
78 Progress Ave Tyngsboro MA (01879) ***(G-15887)***
C & C Metals Engineering Inc.........508 835-9011
104 Hartwell St West Boylston MA (01583) ***(G-16410)***
C & C Scale Co Inc.........508 947-0001
17 Hybrid Dr Lakeville MA (02347) ***(G-11974)***
C & C Thermoforming Inc.........413 289-1900
111 Breckenridge St Ste A Palmer MA (01069) ***(G-14282)***
C & D, Deblois *Also called Jasper Wyman & Son* ***(G-5946)***
C & D Signs Inc.........978 851-2424
170 Lorum St Tewksbury MA (01876) ***(G-15809)***
C & G Machine Tool Co Inc.........413 467-9556
180 W State St Granby MA (01033) ***(G-11227)***
C & G Precisions Products Inc.........203 879-6989
14 Venus Dr Wolcott CT (06716) ***(G-5433)***
C & H Air Inc.........508 746-5511
246 S Meadow Rd Ste 29 Plymouth MA (02360) ***(G-14546)***
C & J Clark America Inc (HQ).........617 964-1222
60 Tower Rd Waltham MA (02451) ***(G-16054)***
C & J Clark Latin America.........617 243-4100
60 Tower Rd Waltham MA (02451) ***(G-16055)***
C & J Jewelry, Providence *Also called Narragasett Jewelry Inc* ***(G-21075)***
C & K Components LLC (PA).........617 969-3700
1601 Trapelo Rd Ste 178 Waltham MA (02451) ***(G-16056)***
C & L Aviation Group (PA).........207 217-6050
40 Wyoming Ave Bangor ME (04401) ***(G-5633)***
C & M Machine Products Inc.........603 594-8100
25 Flagstone Dr Hudson NH (03051) ***(G-18378)***
C & M Tool and Die LLC.........781 893-1880
36 Rumford Ave Waltham MA (02453) ***(G-16057)***
C & M Tool and Mfg Inc.........781 899-1709
39 Emerson Rd Waltham MA (02451) ***(G-16058)***
C & O Box & Printing Company.........508 881-1760
84 Pheasant Hill Rd Hooksett NH (03106) ***(G-18345)***
C & O Box Co, Hooksett *Also called C & O Box & Printing Company* ***(G-18345)***
C & P Precision Machine Co, Stoughton *Also called James E Cofran* ***(G-15599)***
C & R Printing, Bristol *Also called Ronald Bottino* ***(G-608)***
C & R Usn, Bath *Also called Supervisor of Shipbuilding* ***(G-5681)***
C & S Engineering Inc.........203 235-5727
956 Old Colony Rd Meriden CT (06451) ***(G-2082)***
C & S Machine Co Inc.........401 431-1830
55 Pawtucket Ave Ste F Rumford RI (02916) ***(G-21181)***
C & T Print Finishing Inc.........860 282-0616
67 Commerce Way South Windsor CT (06074) ***(G-3945)***
C & W Co Inc.........401 941-6311
231 Georgia Ave Providence RI (02905) ***(G-20977)***
C & W Manufacturing Co Inc.........860 633-4631
74 Eastern Blvd Glastonbury CT (06033) ***(G-1542)***
C and B Welding LLC.........860 423-9047
20 Hillside Dr Lebanon CT (06249) ***(G-1933)***
C and M Micro-Tool Inc.........508 230-3535
18 Plymouth Dr South Easton MA (02375) ***(G-15272)***
C B Boatworks Inc.........207 562-8849
146 Tower Rd Peru ME (04290) ***(G-6584)***
C B Enterprises Division, Manchester *Also called Whiteledge Inc* ***(G-2058)***
C B Fisk Inc.........978 283-1909
21 Kondelin Rd Gloucester MA (01930) ***(G-11168)***
C B P Corp (PA).........207 985-9767
39 Limerick Rd Unit 2 Arundel ME (04046) ***(G-5529)***
C C Distributors, West Greenwich *Also called Rhode Island Distrg Co LLC* ***(G-21465)***
C C F, Seabrook *Also called Communction Cmpnent Flters Inc* ***(G-19797)***
C C I, Leominster *Also called Carbon Composites Inc* ***(G-12124)***
C Cowles & Company (PA).........203 865-3117
126 Bailey Rd North Haven CT (06473) ***(G-3012)***
C E Bradely Lab Inc.........802 257-1122
55 Bennett Dr Brattleboro VT (05301) ***(G-21721)***
C E Bradley Laboratories (PA).........802 257-1122
56 Bennett Dr Brattleboro VT (05301) ***(G-21722)***
C E D, Oxford *Also called Consulting Engrg Dev Svcs Inc* ***(G-3398)***
C E D Corp.........781 834-9312
791 Keene St Duxbury MA (02332) ***(G-10395)***
C E I, Wallingford *Also called Component Engineers Inc* ***(G-4723)***
C F D Engineering Company (PA).........203 758-4148
194 Cook Rd Prospect CT (06712) ***(G-3584)***
C F D Engineering Company.........203 754-2807
105 Avenue Of Industry Waterbury CT (06705) ***(G-4853)***
C F Jameson & Co Inc.........978 462-4097
69 Purchase St Newburyport MA (01950) ***(G-13476)***
C H Babb Co Inc.........508 977-0600
445 Paramount Dr Raynham MA (02767) ***(G-14706)***
C H Yates Rubber Corp.........508 674-3378
222 Sykes Rd Fall River MA (02720) ***(G-10673)***
C I Medical, Norton *Also called Creative Imprints Inc* ***(G-14074)***
C J Brand & Son.........860 536-9266
9 Overlook Ave Mystic CT (06355) ***(G-2435)***
C J Cranam Inc.........207 739-1016
15 Madison Ave Oxford ME (04270) ***(G-6564)***
C J S Millwork Inc.........203 708-0080
425 Fairfield Ave Ste 12 Stamford CT (06902) ***(G-4153)***
C K Productions Inc.........603 893-5069
60a Pulpit Rock Rd Pelham NH (03076) ***(G-19429)***
C L Hauthaway & Sons Corp.........781 592-6444
638 Summer St Lynn MA (01905) ***(G-12495)***
C L O V, Winooski *Also called Creative Labels Vermont Inc* ***(G-22720)***
C M G Precision.........413 547-8124
45 State St Ludlow MA (01056) ***(G-12457)***
C Mather Company Inc.........860 528-5667
339 Chapel Rd South Windsor CT (06074) ***(G-3946)***
C N C Router Technologies.........203 744-6651
4 Barnard Dr Danbury CT (06810) ***(G-883)***

ALPHABETIC

C Newspaper Inc.....978 412-1800
55 Market St Ste 208 Ipswich MA (01938) ***(G-11908)***
C O Jelliff Corporation (PA).....203 259-1615
354 Pequot Ave Ste 300 Southport CT (06890) ***(G-4094)***
C P Bourg Inc (PA).....508 998-2171
50 Samuel Barnet Blvd New Bedford MA (02745) ***(G-13369)***
C P Media, Auburn *Also called Community Newspaper Company **(G-7832)***
C P W, Cranston *Also called Cranston Print Works Company **(G-20202)***
C Q P Bakery.....978 557-5626
19 Blanchard St Lawrence MA (01843) ***(G-12000)***
C R Bard Inc.....978 441-6202
1 Executive Dr Ste 303 Chelmsford MA (01824) ***(G-9884)***
C R Bard Inc.....401 825-8300
100 Crossings Blvd Warwick RI (02886) ***(G-21338)***
C R Bard Ep, Chelmsford *Also called C R Bard Inc **(G-9884)***
C R I, Hopkinton *Also called Cri Rubber LLC **(G-11698)***
C R I, Hopkinton *Also called Cambrdge RES Instrmntation Inc **(G-11695)***
C R Scott Marine Wdwkg Co.....401 849-0715
43 3rd St Fl 2 Newport RI (02840) ***(G-20659)***
C S H Industries Inc.....508 747-1990
15 Appollo 11 Rd Plymouth MA (02360) ***(G-14547)***
C S I, Milford *Also called Charge Solutions Inc **(G-2264)***
C S I Keyboards Inc.....978 532-8181
56 Pulaski St Unit 1 Peabody MA (01960) ***(G-14318)***
C S Sprong & Co, Williamsburg *Also called CJ Sprong & Co Inc **(G-16948)***
C Sherman Johnson Company.....860 873-8697
1 Matthews Dr East Haddam CT (06423) ***(G-1149)***
C Sjoberg & Son Inc.....401 461-8220
415 Station St Cranston RI (02910) ***(G-20192)***
C Sommer Software LLC.....603 432-6225
11 Symphony Ln Derry NH (03038) ***(G-17974)***
C T C, Hopkinton *Also called Control Technology Corporation **(G-11697)***
C T L Land Management Inc.....207 845-2841
142 Hopkins Rd Washington ME (04574) ***(G-7149)***
C V C, Methuen *Also called Central Vacuum Cleaners **(G-13013)***
C V C, Lawrence *Also called Central Vacuum Cleaners **(G-12004)***
C V Tool Company Inc.....978 353-7901
12 Baltic Ln Ste 1 Fitchburg MA (01420) ***(G-10815)***
C V Tool Company Inc (PA).....978 353-7901
44 Robert Porter Rd Southington CT (06489) ***(G-4042)***
C W Mock Logging.....603 938-6096
142 Fairgrounds Rd Bradford NH (03221) ***(G-17740)***
C W Paine Yacht Design Inc.....207 236-2166
59 Sea St Camden ME (04843) ***(G-5866)***
C W Timber, Colebrook *Also called W Craig Washburn **(G-17877)***
C Z Machine Shop, East Hampstead *Also called Cz Machine Inc **(G-18081)***
C&C Machine Shop Inc.....207 667-6910
328 Bucksport Rd Ste 1 Ellsworth ME (04605) ***(G-6015)***
C&G Precision Parts, Wolcott *Also called C & G Precisions Products Inc **(G-5433)***
C&L Engine Solutions LLC.....307 217-6050
40 Wyoming Ave Bangor ME (04401) ***(G-5634)***
C&M Mfg Co Inc.....401 232-9633
1879 Snake Hill Rd Chepachet RI (02814) ***(G-20133)***
C&S Chmcal Sprtons Sensors LLC.....603 491-9511
338 N Pembroke Rd Pembroke NH (03275) ***(G-19456)***
C-B Manufacturing & Tool Co.....860 583-5402
118 Napco Dr Terryville CT (06786) ***(G-4475)***
C-O Bella Rouge At Belissino.....207 318-5214
472 Ocean St South Portland ME (04106) ***(G-7017)***
C-R Control Systems Inc.....603 727-9149
85 Mechanic St Unit B2 Lebanon NH (03766) ***(G-18617)***
C-R Machine Co Inc (PA).....978 663-3989
13 Alexander Rd Ste 10 Billerica MA (01821) ***(G-8229)***
C-V Machine Company LLC.....603 356-5189
236 Kearsarge Rd North Conway NH (03860) ***(G-19375)***
C/A Design, Dover *Also called Costello/April Design Inc **(G-18015)***
C2c Systems Inc.....508 870-2205
112 Turnpike Rd Ste 111 Westborough MA (01581) ***(G-16597)***
C3i Inc.....603 929-9989
8 Commerce Way Exeter NH (03833) ***(G-18115)***
C5bio.....617 955-4626
69 Chestnut St Cambridge MA (02139) ***(G-9424)***
C7, Bridgewater *Also called Control 7 Inc **(G-9068)***
C8 Sciences, New Haven *Also called Becaid LLC **(G-2665)***
Ca Inc.....800 225-5224
160 Bridge St Ste 300 East Windsor CT (06088) ***(G-1281)***
CA J&L Enterprises Inc.....781 963-6666
15 Marshall St Canton MA (02021) ***(G-9719)***
Caap Co Inc.....203 877-0375
152 Pepes Farm Rd Milford CT (06460) ***(G-2258)***
Cab Screen Printing.....508 695-8421
32 Reardons Field Ln North Attleboro MA (02763) ***(G-13751)***
Cabin Critters Inc.....203 778-4552
3 Dunham Dr Ste A New Fairfield CT (06812) ***(G-2622)***
Cabinet Assembly Systems Corp.....401 884-8556
1485 S County Trl Unit 4 East Greenwich RI (02818) ***(G-20355)***
Cabinet Harward Specialti.....860 231-1192
50 Chelton Ave West Hartford CT (06110) ***(G-5056)***
Cabinet House LLC.....781 424-2259
33 Tara Dr Norwell MA (02061) ***(G-14099)***
Cabinet Maker, Brookline *Also called Mark Allen Cabinetry LLC **(G-17772)***
Cabinet Masters Inc.....603 425-6428
4 Beaver Lake Rd Derry NH (03038) ***(G-17975)***
Cabinet Resources Ct Inc.....860 352-2030
180 Cherry Brook Rd Canton CT (06019) ***(G-696)***
Cabinet Warehouse LLC (PA).....508 281-2077
636 Boston Post Rd E Marlborough MA (01752) ***(G-12732)***
Cabinet Works, Lyman *Also called Mike Guillemette & Sons **(G-6391)***
Cabinets For Less LLC.....603 935-7551
679 Mast Rd Manchester NH (03102) ***(G-18794)***
Cable Assemblies Inc.....603 889-4090
13 Columbia Dr Unit 17 Amherst NH (03031) ***(G-17553)***
Cable Electronics Inc.....860 953-0300
221 Newfield Ave Ste 2 Hartford CT (06106) ***(G-1809)***
Cable Management LLC.....860 670-1890
290 Pratt St Ste 1108 Meriden CT (06450) ***(G-2083)***
Cable Manufacturing Business, Redding *Also called Armored Shield Technologies **(G-3646)***
Cable Technology Inc.....860 429-7889
73 River Rd Willington CT (06279) ***(G-5270)***
Cabletron, Salem *Also called Enterasys Networks Inc **(G-19725)***
Cabot Coach Builders Inc (PA).....978 374-4530
99 Newark St Haverhill MA (01832) ***(G-11412)***
Cabot Corporation (PA).....617 345-0100
2 Seaport Ln Ste 1300 Boston MA (02210) ***(G-8452)***
Cabot Corporation.....978 671-4000
157 Concord Rd Billerica MA (01821) ***(G-8230)***
Cabot Corporation.....978 556-8400
50 Rogers Rd Ste 1 Haverhill MA (01835) ***(G-11413)***
Cabot Creamery, Andover *Also called Agri-Mark Inc **(G-7535)***
Cabot Creamery, Hingham *Also called Agri-Mark Inc **(G-11489)***
Cabot Creamery, Waitsfield *Also called Agri-Mark Inc **(G-22559)***
Cabot Creamery.....888 792-2268
869 Exchange St Middlebury VT (05753) ***(G-22106)***
Cabot Creamery Cooperative Inc.....978 552-5500
193 Home Farm Way Waitsfield VT (05673) ***(G-22562)***
Cabot Heritage Corp.....978 745-5532
176 North St Salem MA (01970) ***(G-14900)***
Cabot Hill Naturals Inc.....800 747-4372
62 Bridge St Lancaster NH (03584) ***(G-18598)***
Cabot Hills Maple LLC.....802 426-3463
979 Thistle Hill Rd Cabot VT (05647) ***(G-21819)***
Cabot Market Letter, Salem *Also called Cabot Heritage Corp **(G-14900)***
Cabot Specialty Chemicals Inc (HQ).....617 345-0100
2 Seaport Ln Ste 1300 Boston MA (02210) ***(G-8453)***
Cad CAM Machine LLC.....860 410-9788
150 Robert Jackson Way Plainville CT (06062) ***(G-3471)***
Cad Management Resources Inc.....207 221-2911
60 Pineland Dr Ste 107 New Gloucester ME (04260) ***(G-6465)***
Cad Tech Machine Incorporated.....978 692-0677
7 Littleton Rd Ste D1 Westford MA (01886) ***(G-16759)***
Cad/CAM Dntl Stdio Mil Ctr Inc.....203 733-3069
184 Mount Pleasant Rd Newtown CT (06470) ***(G-2917)***
Cadcom Inc.....203 877-0640
110 Raton Rd Milford CT (06461) ***(G-2259)***
Cadence Aerospace, Westfield *Also called Tell Tool Inc **(G-16732)***
Cadence Ct Inc.....860 370-9780
4 Kenny Roberts Mem Dr Suffield CT (06078) ***(G-4461)***
Cadence Design Systems Inc.....978 262-6404
270 Billerica Rd Chelmsford MA (01824) ***(G-9885)***
Cadence Science Inc.....401 942-1031
2080 Plainfield Pike Cranston RI (02921) ***(G-20193)***
Cadesk Company LLC (PA).....203 268-8083
88 Cottage St Trumbull CT (06611) ***(G-4617)***
Cadi Co Inc (PA).....203 729-1111
60 Rado Dr Naugatuck CT (06770) ***(G-2465)***
Cadi Company, Naugatuck *Also called Cadi Co Inc **(G-2465)***
Cadillac Gage Textron Inc (HQ).....978 657-5111
201 Lowell St Wilmington MA (01887) ***(G-16986)***
Cadmanage, New Gloucester *Also called Cad Management Resources Inc **(G-6465)***
Cadmus.....203 595-3000
200 1st Stamford Pl Fl 2 Stamford CT (06902) ***(G-4154)***
Cadnexus Inc.....781 281-2672
100 Tower Office Park K Woburn MA (01801) ***(G-17140)***
Cado Manufacturing Inc.....978 343-2989
1 Princeton Rd Ste 2 Fitchburg MA (01420) ***(G-10816)***
Cado Products Inc.....978 343-2989
1b Princeton Rd Fitchburg MA (01420) ***(G-10817)***
Cadrus Therapeutics Inc.....508 344-9719
67 Millbrook St Ste 422 Worcester MA (01606) ***(G-17352)***
Cadwell Company, Holliston *Also called Cadwell Products Company Inc **(G-11562)***
Cadwell Products Company Inc.....508 429-3100
3 Kuniholm Dr Holliston MA (01746) ***(G-11562)***
Cafe Refugee Inc.....603 499-7415
2 Stewart Ave Claremont NH (03743) ***(G-17838)***
Cai Inks, Georgetown *Also called A I C Inc **(G-11135)***

Caine Machining Inc 860 738-1619
43 Meadow St Winsted CT (06098) *(G-5407)*
Cairns Robert Company, Plaistow *Also called Robert Cairns Company LLC (G-19522)*
Cakes For All Seasons LLC 207 432-9192
10 W Point Ln Ste 206 Biddeford ME (04005) *(G-5724)*
Cakewalk Bakers LLC 617 903-4352
12 Farnsworth St Fl 1 Boston MA (02210) *(G-8454)*
Cal Brown Paving, Gales Ferry *Also called Calvin Brown (G-1526)*
Cal Chemical Corporation 401 821-0320
592 Arnold Rd Coventry RI (02816) *(G-20140)*
Cala Fruit Distributors Inc 401 725-8189
71 Dexter St Pawtucket RI (02860) *(G-20819)*
Calais Press Inc 207 454-8613
23 Washington St Ste 1 Calais ME (04619) *(G-5864)*
Calco, Saint Johnsbury *Also called Caledonia Inc (G-22388)*
Calculator Training 860 355-8255
94 Buckingham Rd New Milford CT (06776) *(G-2789)*
Caldwell Cmmnications Advisors 617 425-7318
500 Harrison Ave Ste 3r Boston MA (02118) *(G-8455)*
Caleb Churchill 207 215-7949
5 Hisler Mt Rd Somerville ME (04348) *(G-6998)*
Caledonia Inc (PA) 802 748-2319
2878 Vt Route 18 Saint Johnsbury VT (05819) *(G-22388)*
Caledonia Spirits Inc 802 472-8000
46 Buffalo Mtn Commons Dr Hardwick VT (05843) *(G-22010)*
Caledonian Record Pubg Co Inc (PA) 802 748-8121
190 Federal St Saint Johnsbury VT (05819) *(G-22389)*
Caledonian Record Pubg Co Inc 603 444-7141
263 Main St Littleton NH (03561) *(G-18656)*
Caledonian-Record, Saint Johnsbury *Also called Caledonian Record Pubg Co Inc (G-22389)*
Calendar Press Inc 978 531-1860
28 Winter St Peabody MA (01960) *(G-14319)*
Caliber Company (PA) 413 642-4260
100 Springdale Rd Westfield MA (01085) *(G-16676)*
Calibrators Inc 401 769-0333
38 Morning Glory Rd Cumberland RI (02864) *(G-20315)*
Caliper Life Sciences Inc (HQ) 203 954-9442
68 Elm St Hopkinton MA (01748) *(G-11694)*
Caliper Woodworking Corp 781 322-9760
49 Clinton St Malden MA (02148) *(G-12563)*
Calise & Sons Bakery Inc (PA) 401 334-3444
2 Quality Dr Lincoln RI (02865) *(G-20560)*
Calista Therapeutics Inc 401 345-5979
32 Riverside Dr Lincoln RI (02865) *(G-20561)*
Calkins Rock Products Inc 802 626-5755
34 Calkins Dr Lyndonville VT (05851) *(G-22067)*
Calkins Sand & Gravel, Lyndonville *Also called Calkins Rock Products Inc (G-22067)*
Calkins Sand & Gravel Inc 802 334-8418
3258 Vt Route 14 N Newport VT (05855) *(G-22191)*
Call Construction, Levant *Also called Kevin Call (G-6271)*
Call, The, Woonsocket *Also called Rhode Island Media Group (G-21578)*
Callahan Sign Company, Pittsfield *Also called Callahan Sign LLC (G-14462)*
Callahan Sign LLC 413 443-5931
8 Federico Dr Unit B Pittsfield MA (01201) *(G-14462)*
Callahan, Robert, Tilton *Also called Nes Embroidery Inc (G-19908)*
Callaway Cars Inc 860 434-9002
3 High St Old Lyme CT (06371) *(G-3316)*
Callaway Companies Inc (PA) 860 434-9002
3 High St Old Lyme CT (06371) *(G-3317)*
Callaway Golf Ball Oprtons Inc 207 737-4324
County Rd Richmond ME (04357) *(G-6781)*
Callaway Golf Company 413 536-1200
425 Meadow St Chicopee MA (01013) *(G-10005)*
Callenstitch LLC 978 369-9080
52 Domino Dr Concord MA (01742) *(G-10120)*
Callico Metals Inc 401 398-8238
512 Old Baptist Rd North Kingstown RI (02852) *(G-20695)*
Calling All Cargo LLC 603 740-1900
69 Venture Dr Unit 4 Dover NH (03820) *(G-18011)*
Calmare Therapeutics Inc (PA) 203 368-6044
1375 Kings Hwy Ste 400 Fairfield CT (06824) *(G-1417)*
Calorique LLC 508 291-2000
2380 Cranberry Hwy Unit 6 West Wareham MA (02576) *(G-16567)*
Calvin Brown 860 536-6178
259 Gallup Hill Rd Gales Ferry CT (06339) *(G-1526)*
Calvin Johnson 802 685-3205
620 Vermont Rm 110 Chelsea VT (05038) *(G-21837)*
Calyx Containers LLC 617 249-6870
500 Lincoln St Ste 2 Allston MA (02134) *(G-7461)*
Calzone Ltd (PA) 203 367-5766
225 Black Rock Ave Bridgeport CT (06605) *(G-394)*
Calzone Case Company, Bridgeport *Also called Calzone Ltd (G-394)*
CAM Dvlpment McRo Cmpnents Inc 802 265-3240
84 Blissville Rd Hydeville VT (05750) *(G-22039)*
CAM Engineering Inc 978 300-5073
8 Jefts St Townsend MA (01469) *(G-15869)*
CAM Group LLC 860 646-2378
130 Chapel Rd Manchester CT (06042) *(G-1990)*
CAM Logging, Skowhegan *Also called Ambrose G McCarthy Jr (G-6968)*
CAM Mfg Inc 207 764-4199
1215 Airport Dr Presque Isle ME (04769) *(G-6755)*
Cam2 Technologies LLC 203 456-3025
6 Finance Dr Danbury CT (06810) *(G-884)*
Camar Corp 508 845-9263
55 Church St Northborough MA (01532) *(G-14030)*
Camara Metalworks 508 636-7822
1126 American Legion Hwy Westport MA (02790) *(G-16837)*
Camara Slate Products Inc 802 265-3200
963 S Main St Fair Haven VT (05743) *(G-21966)*
Camaro Signs Inc (PA) 860 886-1553
58 Yantic Flats Rd Unit 1 Yantic CT (06389) *(G-5508)*
Cambex Corporation 508 217-4508
337 Turnpike Rd Ste 200 Southborough MA (01772) *(G-15352)*
Cambex Corporation (PA) 508 983-1200
115 Flanders Rd Westborough MA (01581) *(G-16598)*
Cambium Corp 978 249-7557
339 Main St Athol MA (01331) *(G-7685)*
Cambrdge RES Instrmntation Inc 781 935-9099
68 Elm St Hopkinton MA (01748) *(G-11695)*
Cambrdge Sund MGT Holdings LLC (HQ) 781 547-7100
404 Wyman St Ste 200 Waltham MA (02451) *(G-16059)*
Cambridge Brands Mfg Inc 617 491-2500
810 Main St Cambridge MA (02139) *(G-9425)*
Cambridge Brewing Co Inc 617 494-1994
1 Kendall Sq Ste B1102 Cambridge MA (02139) *(G-9426)*
Cambridge Brickhouse Inc 978 725-8001
60 Island St Ste 2 Lawrence MA (01840) *(G-12001)*
Cambridge Chronicle, Somerville *Also called Gatehouse Media Mass I Inc (G-15176)*
Cambridge Electronics Inc 617 710-7013
15 Amherst Rd Belmont MA (02478) *(G-8067)*
Cambridge Electronics Laborato 617 629-2805
20 Chester St Somerville MA (02144) *(G-15163)*
Cambridge Fund Raising Assoc 508 359-0019
15 Brook St Ste 6 Medfield MA (02052) *(G-12911)*
Cambridge Heart Inc (PA) 978 654-7600
124 Washington St Foxborough MA (02035) *(G-10912)*
Cambridge Interventional LLC 978 793-2674
78 Cambridge St Burlington MA (01803) *(G-9243)*
Cambridge Isotope Labs, Tewksbury *Also called Cambridge Isotope Labs Inc (G-15810)*
Cambridge Isotope Labs Inc (HQ) 978 749-8000
3 Highwood Dr Tewksbury MA (01876) *(G-15810)*
Cambridge Offsett Printing, Fall River *Also called Potters Printing Inc (G-10747)*
Cambridge Polymer Group Inc 617 629-4400
56 Roland St Ste 310 Boston MA (02129) *(G-8456)*
Cambridge Precision Machine Co 802 253-9269
347 Baird Rd Stowe VT (05672) *(G-22520)*
Cambridge Printing Co Inc 617 547-0270
47 7th St Cambridge MA (02141) *(G-9427)*
Cambridge Proteome, Woburn *Also called Abclonal-Neo Inc (G-17104)*
Cambridge Semantics Inc 617 245-0517
1 Beacon St Ste 3400 Boston MA (02108) *(G-8457)*
Cambridge Soundworks Inc 781 329-2777
26 Dartmouth St Westwood MA (02090) *(G-16859)*
Cambridge Soundworks Inc 781 829-8818
1422 Washington St Hanover MA (02339) *(G-11332)*
Cambridge Specialty Co Inc 860 828-3579
588 Four Rod Rd Berlin CT (06037) *(G-80)*
Cambridge Technology, Bedford *Also called Novanta Corporation (G-7995)*
Cambridgeport 781 302-3347
21 Pacella Park Dr Randolph MA (02368) *(G-14672)*
Cambridgeport Air Systems Inc 978 465-8481
4 Carleton Dr Georgetown MA (01833) *(G-11139)*
Cambrooke Therapeutics, Inc., Ayer *Also called Ajinomoto Cambrooke Inc (G-7906)*
Camco Display & Screen Prtg, Providence *Also called Cathedral Art Metal Co Inc (G-20981)*
Camco Manufacturing Inc 978 537-6777
165 Pioneer Dr Leominster MA (01453) *(G-12123)*
Camden Designs, Wells *Also called Village Candle Inc (G-7168)*
Camden Herald 207 236-8511
91 Camden St Ste 403 Rockland ME (04841) *(G-6786)*
Camden Printing Inc 207 236-4112
12 Moran Dr Ste F Rockland ME (04841) *(G-6787)*
Camelot Enterprises Inc (PA) 781 341-9100
213 Turnpike St Ste 1 Stoughton MA (02072) *(G-15583)*
Camelot Tools LLC 508 981-7443
800 Main St Holden MA (01520) *(G-11542)*
Camera Works Inc 603 898-7175
34 Londonderry Rd Unit A2 Londonderry NH (03053) *(G-18683)*
Cameron International Corp 860 633-0277
256 Oakwood Dr Ste 1 Glastonbury CT (06033) *(G-1543)*
Cameron International Corp 207 793-2289
14 Business Park Rd Limerick ME (04048) *(G-6333)*
Camerota Truck Parts, Bow *Also called S Camerota & Sons Inc (G-17730)*
Camerota Truck Parts, North Haven *Also called S Camerota & Sons Inc (G-3060)*
Cametoid Technologies Inc 860 646-4667
150 Colonial Rd Manchester CT (06042) *(G-1991)*
Camger Coatings Systems Inc 508 528-5787
364 Main St Norfolk MA (02056) *(G-13659)*

A L P H A B E T I C

Camiant Inc 508 486-9996
200 Nickerson Rd Ste 200 # 200 Marlborough MA (01752) ***(G-12733)***
Camio Custom Cabinetry Inc 781 562-1573
130 Jackson St Ste 2 Canton MA (02021) ***(G-9720)***
Camirob Corp 401 435-4477
30 Risho Ave East Providence RI (02914) ***(G-20394)***
Campaignsthatwincom LLC 508 667-6365
210 Park Ave 210 # 210 Worcester MA (01609) ***(G-17353)***
Campus Yellow Pages LLC 860 523-9909
79 High Wood Rd West Hartford CT (06117) ***(G-5057)***
Canadian American Resources 802 223-2271
104 Main St Montpelier VT (05602) ***(G-22146)***
Canadian Chains, Norridgewock *Also called Jackman Equipment* ***(G-6497)***
Canal Toys Usa Ltd 508 366-9060
1700 W Park Dr Ste 120 Westborough MA (01581) ***(G-16599)***
Canalside Printing 508 759-4141
443 Shore Rd Monument Beach MA (02553) ***(G-13214)***
Canam Bridges US Inc 603 542-5202
386 River Rd Claremont NH (03743) ***(G-17839)***
Canberra Industries, Inc., Meriden *Also called Mirion Tech Canberra Inc* ***(G-2109)***
Candela Corporation (HQ) 508 969-1837
251 Locke Dr Marlborough MA (01752) ***(G-12734)***
Candle Cabin, The, North Hyde Park *Also called Way Out Wax Inc* ***(G-22233)***
Candlewick Press Inc 617 661-3330
99 Dover St Ste 3 Somerville MA (02144) ***(G-15164)***
Candlewood Machine Pdts LLC 860 350-2211
46 Old State Rd Ste 6 New Milford CT (06776) ***(G-2790)***
Candlewood Stars Inc 203 994-8826
60 Newtown Rd Ste 32 Danbury CT (06810) ***(G-885)***
Candlewood Tool & Machine Shop 860 355-1892
24 Martha Ln Gaylordsville CT (06755) ***(G-1529)***
Candy House Confections, Bennington *Also called McCains Vermont Products Inc* ***(G-21682)***
Canevari Plastics Inc 203 878-4319
10 Furniture Row Milford CT (06460) ***(G-2260)***
Cannan Fuels 508 339-3317
157 Pratt St Mansfield MA (02048) ***(G-12616)***
Cannelli Printing Co Inc 203 932-1719
39 Wood St West Haven CT (06516) ***(G-5110)***
Canner Incorporated 978 448-3063
1 Cannery Row West Groton MA (01472) ***(G-16479)***
Canniff Monument, Roslindale *Also called W C Canniff & Sons Inc* ***(G-14845)***
Cannondale Sports Group, Wilton *Also called Cycling Sports Group Inc* ***(G-5286)***
Cano Corporation (PA) 978 342-0953
225 Industrial Rd Fitchburg MA (01420) ***(G-10818)***
Canoga Perkins Corporation 203 888-7914
100 Bank St Seymour CT (06483) ***(G-3749)***
Canopy Timber Alternatives 802 388-1548
30 Grist Mill Rd Middlebury VT (05753) ***(G-22107)***
Canson Inc 413 538-9250
21 Industrial Dr South Hadley MA (01075) ***(G-15300)***
Cantata Media LLC 203 951-9885
132b Water St Norwalk CT (06854) ***(G-3118)***
Canton Citizen Inc 781 821-4418
866 Washington St Ste 1 Canton MA (02021) ***(G-9721)***
Canton Journal 781 828-0006
254 2nd Ave Needham MA (02494) ***(G-13295)***
Canvas and Sail Repair Company, Westbrook *Also called Liberty Services LLC* ***(G-5159)***
Canvas Link Inc 508 366-3323
10 Old Flanders Rd Westborough MA (01581) ***(G-16600)***
Canvasmith 207 379-2121
31 Fort St Fairhaven MA (02719) ***(G-10641)***
Canvasworks Inc 207 985-2419
8 Bragdon Ln Kennebunk ME (04043) ***(G-6230)***
Cap, Stoneham *Also called Custom Atmated Prosthetics LLC* ***(G-15559)***
Cap-Tech Products Inc 860 490-5078
61 Arrow Rd Ste 11 Wethersfield CT (06109) ***(G-5243)***
Capacitec Inc (PA) 978 772-6033
87 Fitchburg Rd Ayer MA (01432) ***(G-7913)***
Capco Crane & Hoist Inc 978 948-2998
58 Forest Ridge Dr Rowley MA (01969) ***(G-14847)***
Capco Plastics Inc (PA) 401 272-3833
297 Dexter St Providence RI (02907) ***(G-20978)***
Capco Steel Erection Company 401 383-9388
33 Acorn St Unit 2 Providence RI (02903) ***(G-20979)***
Cape Ann Brewing Company Inc 978 281-4782
11 Rogers St Gloucester MA (01930) ***(G-11169)***
Cape Ann Olive Oil Company 978 281-1061
57 Main St Gloucester MA (01930) ***(G-11170)***
Cape Ann Sign & Screen, Ipswich *Also called Cape Ann Sign Co Inc* ***(G-11909)***
Cape Ann Sign Co Inc 978 356-0960
43 S Main St Ipswich MA (01938) ***(G-11909)***
Cape Bioresearch Inc 413 658-5426
7 Smilin Jack Ln East Falmouth MA (02536) ***(G-10437)***
Cape Cod, Harwich *Also called Coastal Image Inc* ***(G-11391)***
Cape Cod Beer Inc 508 790-4200
1336 Phinneys Ln Barnstable MA (02630) ***(G-7947)***
Cape Cod Braided Rug Co Inc 508 432-3133
75 Olde Homestead Dr Marstons Mills MA (02648) ***(G-12872)***
Cape Cod Chronicle, Chatham *Also called Hyora Publications Inc* ***(G-9860)***
Cape Cod Cupola Co Inc 508 994-2119
78 State Rd North Dartmouth MA (02747) ***(G-13916)***
Cape Cod Dog 508 255-4206
3 Main St Unit 1 Eastham MA (02642) ***(G-10548)***
Cape Cod Door Mats, Hyannis *Also called Cape Cod Drmats of Distinction* ***(G-11836)***
Cape Cod Drmats of Distinction 508 790-0070
105 Ferndoc St Ste E1 Hyannis MA (02601) ***(G-11836)***
Cape Cod Fence Co 508 398-2293
20 N Main St South Yarmouth MA (02664) ***(G-15326)***
Cape Cod Flag Poles, Division, Harwich Port *Also called Cape Cod Wind Wther Indicators* ***(G-11398)***
Cape Cod Life LLC 508 419-7381
13 Steeple St Ste 204 Mashpee MA (02649) ***(G-12877)***
Cape Cod Life Publications, Mashpee *Also called Cape Cod Life LLC* ***(G-12877)***
Cape Cod Manufacturing 508 477-1188
94 Industrial Dr Ste 1 Mashpee MA (02649) ***(G-12878)***
Cape Cod Metal Polsg Cloths, Dennis *Also called Cape Cod Polish Company Inc* ***(G-10306)***
Cape Cod Polish Company Inc 800 682-4246
27 Kondelin Rd Gloucester MA (01930) ***(G-11171)***
Cape Cod Polish Company Inc 508 385-5099
348 Hokum Rock Rd Dennis MA (02638) ***(G-10306)***
Cape Cod Potato Chips, Hyannis *Also called Snyders-Lance Inc* ***(G-11858)***
Cape Cod Provisions, Pocasset *Also called Cape Cod Sweets LLC* ***(G-14594)***
Cape Cod Ready Mix Inc 508 255-4600
300 Rt 6a Orleans MA (02653) ***(G-14231)***
Cape Cod Sailmakers Inc 508 563-3080
4b Long Hill Rd Cataumet MA (02534) ***(G-9810)***
Cape Cod Shipbuilding Co 508 295-3550
7 Narrows Rd Wareham MA (02571) ***(G-16242)***
Cape Cod Sweets LLC 508 564-5840
31 Jonathan Bourne Dr # 1 Pocasset MA (02559) ***(G-14594)***
Cape Cod Textile, Sandwich *Also called Gonco Inc* ***(G-14968)***
Cape Cod Wind Wther Indicators 508 432-9475
Allan Harbor Marine Harwich Port MA (02646) ***(G-11398)***
Cape Cod Winery 508 457-5592
681 Sandwich Rd East Falmouth MA (02536) ***(G-10438)***
Cape Colon Hydrotherapy 508 833-9855
74 Mill Rd East Sandwich MA (02537) ***(G-10505)***
Cape Courier, Falmouth *Also called Upstairs* ***(G-6036)***
Cape Pond Ice Company (PA) 978 283-0174
104 Commercial St Gloucester MA (01930) ***(G-11172)***
Cape Pond Ice Company 978 688-2300
48 Winthrop Ave Lawrence MA (01843) ***(G-12002)***
Cape Pond Ice Company 978 531-4853
26 Walnut St Peabody MA (01960) ***(G-14320)***
Cape Setups LLC 508 375-6444
1611 Main St West Barnstable MA (02668) ***(G-16405)***
Cape Simulations, Natick *Also called Capesym Inc* ***(G-13242)***
Cape Strobe Emergency Lighting 508 776-0911
10 Captains Ln Harwich MA (02645) ***(G-11390)***
Cape Technologies LLC 207 741-2995
120 Thadeus St Ste 2 South Portland ME (04106) ***(G-7018)***
Capesym Inc 508 653-7100
6 Huron Dr Ste 1 Natick MA (01760) ***(G-13242)***
Capeway Bearing & Machine Inc 508 747-2800
100 Camelot Dr Plymouth MA (02360) ***(G-14548)***
Capeway Printing & Copy Center 781 878-1600
71 Reservoir Park Dr Rockland MA (02370) ***(G-14795)***
Capeway Welding Inc 508 747-6666
9 Appollo 11 Rd Plymouth MA (02360) ***(G-14549)***
Capeway Yarns Inc 401 624-1311
209 Horizon Dr Tiverton RI (02878) ***(G-21253)***
Capewell Aerial Systems LLC (PA) 860 610-0700
105 Nutmeg Rd S South Windsor CT (06074) ***(G-3947)***
Capital Cities Communications 203 784-8800
8 Elm St New Haven CT (06510) ***(G-2673)***
Capital Design & Engrg Inc 203 798-6027
35 Eagle Rd Ste 2 Danbury CT (06810) ***(G-886)***
Capital Orthtics Prsthtics LLC 603 425-0106
15 Nelson St Manchester NH (03103) ***(G-18795)***
Capital Orthtics Prsthtics LLC (PA) 603 226-0106
246 Pleasant St Ste 200 Concord NH (03301) ***(G-17888)***
Capital Venture, Stamford *Also called Scinetx LLC* ***(G-4310)***
Capitol Copy Inc 603 226-2679
1 Eagle Sq Ste 15 Concord NH (03301) ***(G-17889)***
Capitol Cupcake Company LLC 802 522-3576
64 Meadowbrook Dr Montpelier VT (05602) ***(G-22147)***
Capitol Distributors Inc 603 224-3348
114 Hall St Concord NH (03301) ***(G-17890)***
Capitol Electronics Inc 203 744-3300
11 Francis J Clarke Cir Bethel CT (06801) ***(G-135)***
Capitol Machine Inc Preci 860 410-0758
30 Hayden Ave Ste B Plainville CT (06062) ***(G-3472)***
Capitol Printing Co Inc 860 522-1547
52 Pratt St Hartford CT (06103) ***(G-1810)***
Capitol Sausage & Provs Inc 860 527-5510
101 Reserve Rd Bldg 14 Hartford CT (06114) ***(G-1811)***

Capitol Stationery Company 401 943-5333
1286 Cranston St Cranston RI (02920) ***(G-20194)***
Capone Foods, Somerville *Also called Albert Capone* ***(G-15151)***
Capone Iron Corporation 978 948-8000
20 Turcotte Memorial Dr Rowley MA (01969) ***(G-14848)***
Capralogics Inc 413 477-6866
235 Czesky Rd Gilbertville MA (01031) ***(G-11153)***
Capricorn Investors II LP 203 861-6600
30 E Elm St Greenwich CT (06830) ***(G-1602)***
Capricorn Products LLC 207 321-0014
12 Rice St Ste 2 Portland ME (04103) ***(G-6630)***
Caproni Sugar Bush, North Adams *Also called Mary Ann Caproni* ***(G-13679)***
Capstan Atlantic 508 384-3100
10 Cushing Dr Wrentham MA (02093) ***(G-17517)***
Captain Bonneys Creamery 774 218-3586
267 New Bedford Rd Rochester MA (02770) ***(G-14784)***
Captain Dustys Ice Cream 978 744-0777
143 Derby St Salem MA (01970) ***(G-14901)***
Car Buyers Market 516 482-0292
30 Nutmeg Dr Ste B Trumbull CT (06611) ***(G-4618)***
Cara Armour 781 899-7297
80 Trapelo Rd Waltham MA (02452) ***(G-16060)***
Cara Incorporated 401 732-6535
333 Strawberry Field Rd # 2 Warwick RI (02886) ***(G-21339)***
Cara Therapeutics Inc 203 406-3700
107 Elm St Fl 9 Stamford CT (06902) ***(G-4155)***
Carala Ventures Ltd 800 483-6449
120 Research Dr Stratford CT (06615) ***(G-4402)***
Carando Foods, Springfield *Also called Smithfield Foods Inc* ***(G-15506)***
Carando Gourmet Foods Corp (PA) 413 737-0183
175 Main St Agawam MA (01001) ***(G-7426)***
Carando Gourmet Frozen Foods, Agawam *Also called Carando Gourmet Foods Corp* ***(G-7426)***
Caraustar Industries Inc 978 665-2632
100 Newark Ave Fitchburg MA (01420) ***(G-10819)***
Caraustar Industries Inc 413 593-9700
70 Better Way Chicopee MA (01022) ***(G-10006)***
Carbide Solutions LLC 860 515-8665
800 Marshall Phelps Rd Windsor CT (06095) ***(G-5324)***
Carbide Specialities 781 899-1300
38 Guinan St Waltham MA (02451) ***(G-16061)***
Carbide Technology Inc 860 621-8981
55 Captain Lewis Dr Southington CT (06489) ***(G-4043)***
Carbon Black Inc (HQ) 617 393-7400
1100 Winter St Ste 4900 Waltham MA (02451) ***(G-16062)***
Carbon Black Federal Inc 617 393-7400
1100 Winter St Ste 4900 Waltham MA (02451) ***(G-16063)***
Carbon Composites Inc 978 840-0707
12 Jytek Rd Leominster MA (01453) ***(G-12124)***
Carbon Felt Inc 603 542-0202
98 Plains Rd Claremont NH (03743) ***(G-17840)***
Carbon Products Inc 860 749-0614
40 Scitico Rd Somersville CT (06072) ***(G-3923)***
Carbonite Inc 617 927-3521
18 Mollison Way Lewiston ME (04240) ***(G-6279)***
Carbonite Inc (PA) 617 587-1100
2 Avenue De Lafayette # 6 Boston MA (02111) ***(G-8458)***
Carbtrol Corporation 203 337-4340
200 Benton St Stratford CT (06615) ***(G-4403)***
Cardan Robotics, Shirley *Also called Gys Tech LLC* ***(G-15084)***
Cardi Materials LLC (PA) 401 739-8300
400 Lincoln Ave Warwick RI (02888) ***(G-21340)***
Cardinal Comb & Brush Mfg Corp 978 537-6330
106 Carter St Ste 3 Leominster MA (01453) ***(G-12125)***
Cardinal Comb Mfg, Leominster *Also called Cardinal Comb & Brush Mfg Corp* ***(G-12125)***
Cardinal Communications Inc 603 382-4800
23 Atkinson Depot Rd Plaistow NH (03865) ***(G-19510)***
Cardinal Health 414 LLC 860 291-9135
131 Hartland St Ste 8 East Hartford CT (06108) ***(G-1179)***
Cardinal Printing Co Inc 207 452-2931
33 E Main St Denmark ME (04022) ***(G-5948)***
Cardinal Shehan Center Inc 203 336-4468
1494 Main St Bridgeport CT (06604) ***(G-395)***
Cardinal Shoe Corporation 978 686-9706
468 N Canal St Ste 3 Lawrence MA (01840) ***(G-12003)***
Cardiofocus Inc 508 658-7200
500 Nicksn Rd Ste 500200 Marlborough MA (01752) ***(G-12735)***
Cardiopulmonary Corp 203 877-1999
200 Cascade Blvd Ste B Milford CT (06460) ***(G-2261)***
Cardiovascular Instrument 781 245-7799
102 Foundry St Wakefield MA (01880) ***(G-15945)***
Cardioxyl Pharmaceuticals Inc 919 869-8586
5 Research Pkwy Wallingford CT (06492) ***(G-4715)***
Cardurion Pharmaceuticals Inc 617 863-8088
350 Mssachusetts Ave Fl 3 Flr 3 Cambridge MA (02139) ***(G-9428)***
Care New England Health System 401 739-9255
11 Knight St Bldg C10 Warwick RI (02886) ***(G-21341)***
Career Press Inc (PA) 201 848-0310
65 Parker St Ste 7 Newburyport MA (01950) ***(G-13477)***
Carefree Building Co Inc (PA) 860 267-7600
48 Westchester Rd Colchester CT (06415) ***(G-800)***
Carefree Small Buildings, Colchester *Also called Carefree Building Co Inc* ***(G-800)***
Carestream Health Molecular 888 777-2072
4 Science Park New Haven CT (06511) ***(G-2674)***
Carestream Molecular Imaging, New Haven *Also called Carestream Health Molecular* ***(G-2674)***
Carey Automatic Door LLC 203 267-4278
35 Forest Rd Southbury CT (06488) ***(G-4024)***
Carey Brothers Inc 508 222-7234
12 Hiawatha Rd Harwich Port MA (02646) ***(G-11399)***
Carey Manufacturing Co Inc (PA) 860 829-1803
5 Pasco Hill Rd Unit A Cromwell CT (06416) ***(G-850)***
Carey Manufacturing Co Inc 860 829-1803
5 Pasco Hill Rd Unit B Cromwell CT (06416) ***(G-851)***
Cargill, Ayer *Also called Ardent Mills LLC* ***(G-7911)***
Caribe Cmmnctions Publications 617 522-5060
175 Wm F Mcclellan Hwy Boston MA (02128) ***(G-8459)***
Caribe Communications, Boston *Also called Alberto Vasallo Jr* ***(G-8350)***
Carigent Therapeutics Inc 203 887-2873
5 Science Park Ste 10 New Haven CT (06511) ***(G-2675)***
Caring Pharmacy 2, Dorchester *Also called Vietaz Inc* ***(G-10349)***
Caritas Pet Imaging LLC 508 259-8919
800 Washington St Ste 1 Norwood MA (02062) ***(G-14139)***
Carl Associates Inc 860 749-7620
1257 John Fitch Blvd 3 South Windsor CT (06074) ***(G-3948)***
Carl Fisher Co Inc 413 736-3661
42 Wilcox St Springfield MA (01105) ***(G-15458)***
Carl Perry 860 834-4459
91 Highview Ter Middletown CT (06457) ***(G-2181)***
Carla Corp 401 438-7070
33 Sutton Ave East Providence RI (02914) ***(G-20395)***
Carlas Pasta Inc 860 436-4042
50 Talbot Ln South Windsor CT (06074) ***(G-3949)***
Carli Farm & Equipment LLC 860 908-3227
40 Mill Ln Salem CT (06420) ***(G-3737)***
Carlin Combustion Tech Inc 413 525-7700
126 Bailey Rd North Haven CT (06473) ***(G-3013)***
Carlin Combustion Tech Inc (HQ) 203 680-9401
126 Bailey Rd North Haven CT (06473) ***(G-3014)***
Carling Technologies Inc (PA) 860 793-9281
60 Johnson Ave Plainville CT (06062) ***(G-3473)***
Carlingswitch, Plainville *Also called Carling Technologies Inc* ***(G-3473)***
Carlisle Communications Inc 978 369-7921
662a Bedford Rd Carlisle MA (01741) ***(G-9797)***
Carlisle Construction Mtls LLC 888 746-1114
15 Franklin St Portland ME (04101) ***(G-6631)***
CARLISLE MOSQUITO, Carlisle *Also called Carlisle Communications Inc* ***(G-9797)***
Carlisle Publications 603 622-4056
40 Cascade Cir Manchester NH (03103) ***(G-18796)***
Carlo Gavazzi Incorporated 508 588-6110
10 Mupac Dr Brockton MA (02301) ***(G-9126)***
Carlow Orthpd & Prsthetic Inc (PA) 203 483-8488
1580 Pontiac Ave Ste 2 Cranston RI (02920) ***(G-20195)***
Carlson Sheet Metal 860 354-4660
24 Bostwick Pl New Milford CT (06776) ***(G-2791)***
Carlstrom Pressed Metal Co Inc 508 366-4472
65 Fisher St Westborough MA (01581) ***(G-16601)***
Carlton Forge Works 860 873-9730
37 Eli Chapman Rd Moodus CT (06469) ***(G-2424)***
Carlton Industries Corp 203 288-5605
33 Rossotto Dr Hamden CT (06514) ***(G-1736)***
Carlyle Johnson Machine Co LLC (PA) 860 643-1531
291 Boston Tpke Bolton CT (06043) ***(G-276)***
Carnegie Communications LLC 978 692-5092
210 Littleton Rd Ste 100 Westford MA (01886) ***(G-16760)***
Carnegie Dartlet LLC (PA) 978 692-5092
210 Littleton Rd Ste 100 Westford MA (01886) ***(G-16761)***
Carnegie Tool Inc 203 866-0744
25 Perry Ave Ste 12 Norwalk CT (06850) ***(G-3119)***
Carol Ackerman Designs 860 693-1013
107 Main St Collinsville CT (06019) ***(G-814)***
Carole Sousa Jewelry 617 232-4087
64 Cypress St Ste 1 Boston MA (02132) ***(G-8460)***
Carolyn's Handmade, Maynard *Also called 40parklane LLC* ***(G-12893)***
Caron Alpine Technologies Inc 401 624-8999
164 Nanaquaket Rd Tiverton RI (02878) ***(G-21254)***
Caron Fabrication LLC 603 631-0025
115 Lancaster Rd Groveton NH (03582) ***(G-18231)***
Caron Signs Co Inc 207 848-7889
41 Daves Way Hermon ME (04401) ***(G-6184)***
Carpe Diem Coffee Roasting Co 207 676-2233
150 Wells St North Berwick ME (03906) ***(G-6505)***
Carpenter Powder Products Inc 401 769-5600
500 Park East Dr Woonsocket RI (02895) ***(G-21555)***
Carpenters Boat Shop Inc 207 677-2614
440 Old County Rd Pemaquid ME (04558) ***(G-6579)***
Carpin Manufacturing Inc 203 574-2556
411 Austin Rd Waterbury CT (06705) ***(G-4854)***

Carr Management Inc (PA)......603 888-1315
1 Tara Blvd Ste 303 Nashua NH (03062) ***(G-19131)***
Carr Tool Co Inc......603 669-0177
19 Tinker Ave Unit 2 Londonderry NH (03053) ***(G-18684)***
Carr-Dee Corp......781 391-4500
37 Linden St Medford MA (02155) ***(G-12925)***
Carriage House Companies Inc......860 647-1909
42 Steeplechase Dr Manchester CT (06040) ***(G-1992)***
Carriage Hse Developments LLC......339 221-4253
253 Swanton St Winchester MA (01890) ***(G-17085)***
Carriage Towne News......603 642-4499
14 Church St Kingston NH (03848) ***(G-18541)***
Carrick Pharmaceuticals Inc......617 623-0525
16 Highland Rd Somerville MA (02144) ***(G-15165)***
Carrier Access - Trin Networks......203 778-8222
61 Commerce Dr Brookfield CT (06804) ***(G-637)***
Carrier Chipping Inc......207 858-4277
100 Carrier Ln Skowhegan ME (04976) ***(G-6971)***
Carrier Corporation......860 728-7000
426 Colt Hwy Farmington CT (06032) ***(G-1471)***
Carrier Manufacturing Inc......860 223-2264
70a Saint Claire Ave New Britain CT (06051) ***(G-2517)***
Carrier Wldg & Fabrication LLC......207 645-3100
469 Depot St Wilton ME (04294) ***(G-7225)***
Carrington International LLC......603 867-8957
293 High St Candia NH (03034) ***(G-17780)***
Carris Financial Corp (PA)......802 773-9111
49 Main St Proctor VT (05765) ***(G-22283)***
Carris Plastics, Proctor *Also called Carris Reels Inc* ***(G-22284)***
Carris Plastics, Center Rutland *Also called Carris Reels Inc* ***(G-21831)***
Carris Reels Connecticut Inc......860 749-8308
11 Randolph St Enfield CT (06082) ***(G-1348)***
Carris Reels Inc (HQ)......802 773-9111
49 Main St Proctor VT (05765) ***(G-22284)***
Carris Reels Inc......802 773-9111
628 Us Business Rte Center Rutland VT (05736) ***(G-21831)***
Carroll Coatings Company Inc (PA)......401 781-4942
150 Ernest St Providence RI (02905) ***(G-20980)***
Carroll Concrete, Newport *Also called Newport Sand & Gravel Co Inc* ***(G-19352)***
Carroll Concrete Co, Peterborough *Also called Newport Sand & Gravel Co Inc* ***(G-19480)***
Carroll Concrete Co, Randolph *Also called Newport Sand & Gravel Co Inc* ***(G-22300)***
Carroll Concrete Co, Guildhall *Also called Newport Sand & Gravel Co Inc* ***(G-22006)***
Carroll Concrete Co, Charlestown *Also called Newport Sand & Gravel Co Inc* ***(G-17817)***
Carroll Concrete Co, Newport *Also called Newport Sand & Gravel Co Inc* ***(G-22204)***
Carroll Concrete Co......802 229-0191
379 Granger Rd Barre VT (05641) ***(G-21611)***
Carroll Concrete Co Inc......603 863-1765
8 Reeds Mill Rd Newport NH (03773) ***(G-19343)***
Carrot Signs......207 725-0769
6 Bay Bridge Rd Brunswick ME (04011) ***(G-5834)***
Carrubba Incorporated......203 878-0605
70 Research Dr Milford CT (06460) ***(G-2262)***
Cars Realty LLC......401 231-1389
17 Ferncrest Dr Johnston RI (02919) ***(G-20502)***
Cartamundi East Longmeadow LLC......413 526-2000
443 Shaker Rd East Longmeadow MA (01028) ***(G-10469)***
Carten Controls Inc......203 699-2100
604 W Johnson Ave Cheshire CT (06410) ***(G-719)***
Carten-Fujikin Incorporated......203 699-2134
604 W Johnson Ave Cheshire CT (06410) ***(G-720)***
Carter Machine Inc......802 426-3501
360 Pattys Xing Marshfield VT (05658) ***(G-22093)***
Carus Publishing......603 924-7209
20 Depot St Unit 310 Peterborough NH (03458) ***(G-19466)***
Carvers' Guild, West Groton *Also called Canner Incorporated* ***(G-16479)***
Carwild Corporation (PA)......860 442-4914
3 State Pier Rd New London CT (06320) ***(G-2768)***
Cas Acquisition Co LLC......401 884-8556
20 Providence Pike North Smithfield RI (02896) ***(G-20783)***
Cas America, North Smithfield *Also called Cas Acquisition Co LLC* ***(G-20783)***
Cas America, East Greenwich *Also called Cabinet Assembly Systems Corp* ***(G-20355)***
Cas Medical Systems Inc......203 315-6953
32 E Industrial Rd Branford CT (06405) ***(G-301)***
Cas Medical Systems Inc (HQ)......203 488-6056
44 E Industrial Rd Branford CT (06405) ***(G-302)***
Cas of New England, South Easton *Also called Connected Automotive* ***(G-15274)***
Casa Antigua......781 584-8240
129 Oxford St Lynn MA (01901) ***(G-12496)***
Casa Systems Inc (PA)......978 688-6706
100 Old River Rd Ste 100 # 100 Andover MA (01810) ***(G-7544)***
Casanna Designs......401 835-4029
41 Charles Dr Unit 1 Tiverton RI (02878) ***(G-21255)***
Casaro Labs Ltd......203 353-8500
1100 Summer St Ste 203 Stamford CT (06905) ***(G-4156)***
Cascaded Purchase Holdings Inc (PA)......603 448-1090
35 Connctcut Rver Bend Rd Claremont NH (03743) ***(G-17841)***
Cascades Auburn Fiber Inc......207 753-5300
586 Lewiston Junction Rd Auburn ME (04210) ***(G-5552)***
Cascades Holding US Inc......203 426-5871
1 Edmund Rd Newtown CT (06470) ***(G-2918)***
Casco Bay Butter Company LLC......207 712-9148
146 Maine Ave Portland ME (04103) ***(G-6632)***
Casco Bay Diesel LLC......207 878-9377
429 Warren Ave Unit 5 Portland ME (04103) ***(G-6633)***
Casco Bay Fibers......207 869-5429
15 Main St Freeport ME (04032) ***(G-6073)***
Casco Bay Sbstnce Abuse Rsrces......207 773-7993
205 Ocean Ave Portland ME (04103) ***(G-6634)***
Casco Bay Steel Structures Inc......207 780-6722
1 Wallace Ave South Portland ME (04106) ***(G-7019)***
Casco Products Corporation (HQ)......203 922-3200
1000 Lafayette Blvd # 100 Bridgeport CT (06604) ***(G-396)***
Case Assembly Solutions Inc......508 238-5665
19 Norfolk Ave Ste B South Easton MA (02375) ***(G-15273)***
Case Concepts Intl LLC (PA)......203 883-8602
112 Prospect St Unit A Stamford CT (06901) ***(G-4157)***
Case Future Corporation Inc......401 944-0402
27 Mill St Johnston RI (02919) ***(G-20503)***
Case Hard......401 635-8201
56 Indian Rd Little Compton RI (02837) ***(G-20604)***
Case Patterns & Wood Products, Groton *Also called Case Patterns Inc* ***(G-1665)***
Case Patterns Inc......860 445-6722
257 South Rd Groton CT (06340) ***(G-1665)***
Case Technology Inc......978 356-6011
26 Hayward St Ipswich MA (01938) ***(G-11910)***
Casenet LLC......781 357-2700
36 Crosby Dr Bedford MA (01730) ***(G-7966)***
Casepick Systems, LLC, Wilmington *Also called Symbotic LLC* ***(G-17050)***
Cashon......786 325-4144
350 W Shore Ave Groton CT (06340) ***(G-1666)***
Cask & Kiln Kitchen LLC......802 464-2275
228 Stowe Hill Rd Wilmington VT (05363) ***(G-22700)***
Casma Therapeutics Inc......857 777-4248
400 Technology Sq Ste 201 Cambridge MA (02139) ***(G-9429)***
Casmed, Branford *Also called Cas Medical Systems Inc* ***(G-301)***
Caspari Inc (PA)......203 888-1100
99 Cogwheel Ln Seymour CT (06483) ***(G-3750)***
Casper's Janitorial Service, Lincoln *Also called Jordan Millworks Inc* ***(G-6356)***
Caspi Cards and Art......617 964-8888
137 Lowell Ave Newton MA (02460) ***(G-13574)***
Caspian Arms Ltd......802 472-6454
75 Cal Foster Dr Wolcott VT (05680) ***(G-22729)***
Cassa Floor Design Inc......508 845-0600
420 Boston Tpke Shrewsbury MA (01545) ***(G-15106)***
Cassidy Bros Forge Inc......978 948-7303
282 Newburyport Tpke Rowley MA (01969) ***(G-14849)***
Cassini Usa Inc......781 487-7000
1 Wall St Fl 6 Burlington MA (01803) ***(G-9244)***
Cassiopae US Inc......435 647-9940
1 Van De Graaff Dr # 102 Burlington MA (01803) ***(G-9245)***
Cast Coat Inc......508 587-4502
354 West St Ste 1 West Bridgewater MA (02379) ***(G-16433)***
Cast Global Manufacturing Corp......203 828-6147
66 Prokop Rd Oxford CT (06478) ***(G-3393)***
Castaldo Products Mfg Co Inc......508 520-1666
120 Constitution Blvd Franklin MA (02038) ***(G-11027)***
Castaldo Proudcts, Franklin *Also called FE Knight Inc* ***(G-11045)***
Caste Glass......401 934-2959
102 Pole Bridge Rd North Scituate RI (02857) ***(G-20776)***
Castechnologies Inc......508 222-2915
40 Townsend Rd Attleboro MA (02703) ***(G-7716)***
Caster Crative Photography LLC......401 364-3545
280 Old Mill Rd Charlestown RI (02813) ***(G-20131)***
Castle Beverages Inc......203 732-0883
105 Myrtle Ave Ansonia CT (06401) ***(G-8)***
Castle Complements Printing Co......978 250-9122
74 Bridge St Chelmsford MA (01824) ***(G-9886)***
Castle Interiors, Ludlow *Also called Huot Enterprises Inc* ***(G-12468)***
Castle Island Brewing Co LLC......781 951-2029
31 Astor Ave Norwood MA (02062) ***(G-14140)***
Castle Machine Co......978 356-2151
59 Old Right Rd Ipswich MA (01938) ***(G-11911)***
Castle Machine Company, Ipswich *Also called Castle Machine Co* ***(G-11911)***
Castle Plastics Inc......978 534-6220
11 Francis St Leominster MA (01453) ***(G-12126)***
Castlewood Surgical......978 448-3628
20 Whiley Rd Groton MA (01450) ***(G-11285)***
Castonguay Meats Inc......207 897-4989
252 Gibbs Mill Rd Livermore ME (04253) ***(G-6373)***
Castrol Industrial N Amer Inc......860 928-5100
251 Kennedy Dr Putnam CT (06260) ***(G-3603)***
Cat LLC......860 953-1807
819 N Mountain Rd Hartford CT (06111) ***(G-1812)***
Catabasis Pharmaceuticals Inc......617 349-1971
1 Kendall Sq Ste B14202 Cambridge MA (02139) ***(G-9430)***
Catachem Inc......203 262-0330
353 Christian St Ste 2 Oxford CT (06478) ***(G-3394)***

Cataki International Inc 508 295-9630
14 Kendrick Rd Ste 5 Wareham MA (02571) *(G-16243)*
Catalyst Medical LLC 857 928-8817
23 Oak St Belmont MA (02478) *(G-8068)*
Catalyst/Spring I Ltd Partner 617 884-9410
191 Williams St Chelsea MA (02150) *(G-9947)*
Catamount Glassware Co Inc 802 442-5438
309 County St Bennington VT (05201) *(G-21666)*
Catamount North Cabinetry LLC 802 264-9009
15 Corporate Dr Essex Junction VT (05452) *(G-21935)*
Catania Oils, Ayer *Also called Catania-Spagna Corporation (G-7914)*
Catania-Spagna Corporation 978 772-7900
3 Nemco Way Ayer MA (01432) *(G-7914)*
Catanzaro Food Products Inc 401 255-1700
203 Concord St Unit 457 Pawtucket RI (02860) *(G-20820)*
Cataumet Sawmills, East Falmouth *Also called Theodore Wolf Inc (G-10450)*
Catch Kings, The, Scarborough *Also called Austin Merrill (G-6906)*
Catek, Tiverton *Also called Caron Alpine Technologies Inc (G-21254)*
Catelectric Corp (PA) 860 912-0800
33 Island Cir S Groton CT (06340) *(G-1667)*
Cathedral Art Metal Co Inc 401 273-7200
25 Manton Ave Providence RI (02909) *(G-20981)*
Catholic Transcript Inc 860 286-2828
467 Bloomfield Ave Bloomfield CT (06002) *(G-213)*
Catholic Transcript Online, Bloomfield *Also called Catholic Transcript Inc (G-213)*
Caton Connector Corp 781 585-4315
26 Wapping Rd Ste 1 Kingston MA (02364) *(G-11955)*
Catskill Gran Countertops Inc 860 667-1555
156 Pane Rd Ste A Newington CT (06111) *(G-2852)*
Causeway Graphics 508 309-6592
27 Cochituate Rd Framingham MA (01701) *(G-10931)*
Cavanagh Company 401 949-4000
610 Putnam Pike Greenville RI (02828) *(G-20464)*
Cave Manufacturing Inc 802 257-9253
22 Browne Ct Unit 104 Brattleboro VT (05301) *(G-21723)*
Cavium Inc 508 357-4111
600 Nickerson Rd Marlborough MA (01752) *(G-12736)*
Cavtech Industries 203 437-8764
217 Interstate Ln Waterbury CT (06705) *(G-4855)*
Caya Construction Co 508 234-5082
76 Sutton St Northbridge MA (01534) *(G-14054)*
Cazena Inc 781 897-6380
1601 Trapelo Rd Ste 205 Waltham MA (02451) *(G-16064)*
CB Logging 207 231-4952
194 Fox Rd New Canada ME (04743) *(G-6462)*
CB Seating Etc LLC (PA) 203 359-3880
324 Strawberry Hill Ave Norwalk CT (06851) *(G-3120)*
CB Sports Inc 781 322-0307
359 Washington St Ste C Malden MA (02148) *(G-12564)*
CB Ventures LLC 603 434-3175
162 Pembroke Rd Concord NH (03301) *(G-17891)*
Cbc Co, Coventry *Also called Charles Boggini Company LLC (G-832)*
Cbis, West Brookfield *Also called Concrete Block Insulating Syst (G-16466)*
CBS Manufacturing Company 860 653-8100
35 Kripes Rd East Granby CT (06026) *(G-1120)*
CC Electronx, Limington *Also called Chip Component Electronx (G-6347)*
Cc-Teknologies Inc 508 444-8810
21 Marsden St Brockton Brockton MA (02302) *(G-9127)*
Cc1 Inc 603 319-2000
170 West Rd Ste 7 Portsmouth NH (03801) *(G-19548)*
CCA Global Partners Inc 603 626-0333
670 North Commercial St # 300 Manchester NH (03101) *(G-18797)*
CCC Media LLC 860 225-4601
1 Court St New Britain CT (06051) *(G-2518)*
Cch Tagetik, Stamford *Also called Tagetik North America LLC (G-4341)*
CCI, Putnam *Also called Central Construction Inds LLC (G-3604)*
CCI Corpus Christi LLC 203 564-8100
2200 Atlantic St Ste 800 Stamford CT (06902) *(G-4158)*
CCI Cyrus River Terminal LLC 203 761-8000
2200 Atlantic St Ste 800 Stamford CT (06902) *(G-4159)*
CCI Robinsons Bend LLC 203 564-8571
2200 Atlantic St Ste 800 Stamford CT (06902) *(G-4160)*
Cciyes, Tolland *Also called Connecticut Components Inc (G-4541)*
CCL Industries Corporation (HQ) 203 926-1253
15 Controls Dr Shelton CT (06484) *(G-3785)*
CCL Label, Shelton *Also called CCL Industries Corporation (G-3785)*
CCL Label Inc 203 926-1253
15 Controls Dr Shelton CT (06484) *(G-3786)*
CCL Label Inc (HQ) 508 872-4511
161 Worcester Rd Ste 603 Framingham MA (01701) *(G-10932)*
CCL Label (delaware) Inc (HQ) 203 926-1253
15 Controls Dr Shelton CT (06484) *(G-3787)*
CCM Logging Land Clearing LLC 603 387-1853
369 Burnt Hill Rd New London NH (03257) *(G-19314)*
Ccr Products LLC 860 953-0499
167 South St West Hartford CT (06110) *(G-5058)*
CCS Marine Inc 508 587-8877
124 Turnpike St Ste 12 West Bridgewater MA (02379) *(G-16434)*

CD Racing Products 203 264-7822
91 Willenbrock Rd Ste B3 Oxford CT (06478) *(G-3395)*
CD Solutions Inc 203 481-5895
420 E Main St Ste 16 Branford CT (06405) *(G-303)*
CD Works, Beverly *Also called Zerious Electronic Pubg Corp (G-8201)*
Cde, Danbury *Also called Capital Design & Engrg Inc (G-886)*
CDF Corporation (PA) 508 747-5858
77 Industrial Park Rd Plymouth MA (02360) *(G-14550)*
Cdi LLC A Valley Forge Co 508 587-7000
637 N Montello St Brockton MA (02301) *(G-9128)*
CDI Meters Inc 508 867-3178
3r Green St Ste 2 Woburn MA (01801) *(G-17141)*
Cdiled LLC 413 530-2921
21 Wilbraham St Palmer MA (01069) *(G-14283)*
Cdl Print Mail LLC 978 410-5148
205 School St Ste 102 Gardner MA (01440) *(G-11107)*
Cdp Manufacturing LLC 508 588-6400
15 Jonathan Dr Ste 6 Brockton MA (02301) *(G-9129)*
Ceac, Sandy Hook *Also called Conn Engineering Assoc Corp (G-3741)*
Ceaco Inc 617 926-8080
70 Bridge St Ste 200 Newton MA (02458) *(G-13575)*
Cebal Americas (PA) 203 845-6356
101 Merritt 7 Ste 2 Norwalk CT (06851) *(G-3121)*
Cecelia New York LLC 917 392-4536
23 Chestnut St Darien CT (06820) *(G-1021)*
Ceda Company Inc 860 666-1593
36 Holmes Rd Newington CT (06111) *(G-2853)*
Cedar Chest Inc 413 584-3860
150 Main St Ste 1 Northampton MA (01060) *(G-13998)*
Cedar Craft Fence Co 401 397-7765
8 Doe Run Coventry RI (02816) *(G-20141)*
Cedar Swamp Log & Lumber 860 974-2344
45 Hager Rd Woodstock CT (06281) *(G-5496)*
Cedarapids, Westport *Also called Terex Usa LLC (G-5234)*
Cedarworks of Maine Inc (PA) 207 596-1010
799 Commercial St Rockport ME (04856) *(G-6817)*
Cedarworks of Maine Inc 207 596-0771
12 Merrill Dr Rockland ME (04841) *(G-6788)*
Cedarworks Playsets, Rockport *Also called Cedarworks of Maine Inc (G-6817)*
Cedarworks Playsets, Rockland *Also called Cedarworks of Maine Inc (G-6788)*
Cedilla Therapeutics Inc 617 581-9333
38 Sidney St Ste 200 Cambridge MA (02139) *(G-9431)*
Ceek Enterprises Inc 919 522-4837
1 City Hall Plz Melrose MA (02176) *(G-12976)*
Cei Flowmaster Products LLC 603 880-0094
18 Park Ave Hudson NH (03051) *(G-18379)*
Celeno Communications 617 500-3683
464 Common St Ste 279 Belmont MA (02478) *(G-8069)*
Celerity Solutions Inc (PA) 781 329-1900
990 Washington St Ste 304 Dedham MA (02026) *(G-10282)*
Celeros Inc 248 478-2800
1188 Centre St Ste 1 Newton MA (02459) *(G-13576)*
Celeros Separations, Newton *Also called Celeros Inc (G-13576)*
Celestial Monitoring Corp (HQ) 401 782-1045
24 Celestial Dr Ste B Narragansett RI (02882) *(G-20635)*
Celestica Arden Hills, Merrimack *Also called Celestica LLC (G-18991)*
Celestica LLC 603 657-3000
11 Continental Blvd # 103 Merrimack NH (03054) *(G-18991)*
Celgene Avilomics Research Inc 857 706-1311
200 Cambridgepark Dr Cambridge MA (02140) *(G-9432)*
Celgene Corporation 857 225-2309
100 Macy St Unit F174 Amesbury MA (01913) *(G-7481)*
Celios Corporation 978 877-2044
39 Sagamore Ave Portsmouth NH (03801) *(G-19549)*
Cell Nique 888 417-9343
12 Old Stage Coach Rd Weston CT (06883) *(G-5170)*
Cell Press Inc 617 397-2800
50 Hampshire St Cambridge MA (02139) *(G-9433)*
Cellanyx Diagnostics LLC 571 212-9991
100 Cummings Ctr Ste 451d Beverly MA (01915) *(G-8114)*
Cellar Crafts 603 673-3615
73 Old Milford Rd Mont Vernon NH (03057) *(G-19092)*
Cellar Door Winery (PA) 207 763-4478
367 Youngtown Rd Lincolnville ME (04849) *(G-6361)*
Cellaria Biosciences LLC 617 981-4208
26 Bennett Rd Boxford MA (01921) *(G-8974)*
Cellassist LLC (PA) 413 559-1256
54 Hobson St Springfield MA (01109) *(G-15459)*
Cellay LLC 617 995-1307
100 Inman St Ste 207 Cambridge MA (02139) *(G-9434)*
Cellblock Fcs LLC 603 276-5785
234 Northeast Rd Ste 5 Standish ME (04084) *(G-7061)*
Cellgenix USA 603 373-0408
1 Nh Ave Portsmouth NH (03801) *(G-19550)*
Cellini Inc (PA) 212 594-3812
35 Roxanna Ln Kingston RI (02881) *(G-20549)*
Cellmark Inc 401 723-4200
402 Walcott St Pawtucket RI (02860) *(G-20821)*

ALPHABETIC

Cellmark Pulp & Paper Inc....203 299-5050
80 Washington St Ste 1 Norwalk CT (06854) ***(G-3122)***
Celtic Co, West Hartford *Also called Component Concepts Inc* ***(G-5062)***
Celyad Inc....857 990-6900
2 Seaport Ln Boston MA (02210) ***(G-8461)***
Cem Group LLC (HQ)....860 675-5000
258 Spielman Hwy Ste 7 Burlington CT (06013) ***(G-675)***
Cemcolift Elevator Systems, Bloomfield *Also called Ascend Elevator Inc* ***(G-205)***
Cement Well Concrete Products....413 283-8450
104 Mason St Palmer MA (01069) ***(G-14284)***
Cemex Materials LLC....413 562-3647
69 Neck Rd Westfield MA (01085) ***(G-16677)***
Cendres+metaux USA Inc....508 316-0962
93 Tyler St Attleboro MA (02703) ***(G-7717)***
Cengage Learning Inc (PA)....617 289-7918
200 Pier 4 Blvd Ste 400 Boston MA (02210) ***(G-8462)***
Cengage Lrng Holdings II Inc (PA)....617 289-7700
20 Channel Ctr St Boston MA (02210) ***(G-8463)***
Censa Pharmaceuticals Inc (PA)....617 225-7700
65 William St Ste 200 Wellesley Hills MA (02481) ***(G-16396)***
Centage Corporation....800 366-5111
24 Superior Dr Ste 201 Natick MA (01760) ***(G-13243)***
Centco Architectural Metals....508 456-1888
523 Spring St East Bridgewater MA (02333) ***(G-10408)***
Center Broach & Machine Co....203 235-6329
525 N Colony St Meriden CT (06450) ***(G-2084)***
Center For Discovery....203 955-1381
1320 Mill Hill Rd Southport CT (06890) ***(G-4095)***
Center For Northern Woodlands....802 439-6292
16 On The Cmn Lyme NH (03768) ***(G-18753)***
Center For Work and Family, Chestnut Hill *Also called Trustees of Boston College* ***(G-9993)***
Center Harbor Sails LLC....207 359-2003
Reach Rd Brooklin ME (04616) ***(G-5818)***
Center Manufacturing Corp....978 356-8420
17 Hayward St Ste 2 Ipswich MA (01938) ***(G-11912)***
Center Point Inc....207 568-3717
600 Brooks Rd Knox ME (04986) ***(G-6262)***
Center Point Publishing, Knox *Also called Center Point Inc* ***(G-6262)***
Centerline Machine Company Inc....978 524-8842
60 Park St Beverly MA (01915) ***(G-8115)***
Centerline Technologies LLC....978 568-1330
577 Main St Ste 270 Hudson MA (01749) ***(G-11762)***
Centers of New England MRC....978 241-8232
1 Park Way Haverhill MA (01830) ***(G-11414)***
Centorr Vaccum Industries, Nashua *Also called CVI Group Inc* ***(G-19100)***
Centorr/Vacuum Industries LLC (PA)....603 595-7233
55 Northstern Blvd Unit 2 Nashua NH (03062) ***(G-19132)***
Centra Software Inc (HQ)....781 861-7000
430 Bedford St Ste 220 Lexington MA (02420) ***(G-12211)***
Central Admxture Phrm Svcs Inc....781 376-0032
55 6th Rd Woburn MA (01801) ***(G-17142)***
Central Coating Tech Inc....508 835-6225
165 Shrewsbury St West Boylston MA (01583) ***(G-16411)***
Central Conn Cmmunications LLC....860 225-4601
1 Court St Fl 4 New Britain CT (06051) ***(G-2519)***
Central Connecticut Coating....860 528-8281
52 Village St East Hartford CT (06108) ***(G-1180)***
Central Connecticut Sls & Mfg....860 667-1411
37 Stanwell Rd Newington CT (06111) ***(G-2854)***
Central Construction Inds LLC....860 963-8902
30 Harris St Putnam CT (06260) ***(G-3604)***
Central Electric Inc....860 774-3054
364 Putnam Pike Dayville CT (06241) ***(G-1041)***
Central Falls Provision Co....401 725-7020
847 High St Central Falls RI (02863) ***(G-20112)***
Central Garden & Pet Company....508 884-5426
125 John Hancock Rd Ste 5 Taunton MA (02780) ***(G-15735)***
Central MA Waterjet Inc....508 769-4308
32 Grafton St Millbury MA (01527) ***(G-13158)***
Central Maine Cold Storage....419 215-7955
84 Heritage Park Rd Bucksport ME (04416) ***(G-5854)***
Central Maine Crane Inc....207 465-2229
523 Belgrade Rd Oakland ME (04963) ***(G-6530)***
Central Maine Crate Inc....207 873-5880
34 Clairmont Ave Oakland ME (04963) ***(G-6531)***
Central Maine Fabrication, Oakland *Also called Floyd Baker Metal Fabrication* ***(G-6533)***
Central Maine Morning Sentinel....207 873-3341
31 Front St Waterville ME (04901) ***(G-7153)***
Central Maine Online....207 872-2985
800 W River Rd Waterville ME (04901) ***(G-7154)***
Central Marble & Granite LLC....203 734-4644
22 Maple St Ansonia CT (06401) ***(G-9)***
Central Mass Installations....508 612-3092
250 Worcester St Unit 6 West Boylston MA (01583) ***(G-16412)***
Central Mass Powdr Coating Inc....978 365-1700
32 Greeley St Clinton MA (01510) ***(G-10077)***
Central Math, Auburn *Also called Cmsr Services LLC* ***(G-7831)***
Central Metal Finishing Inc....978 291-0500
80 Flagship Dr North Andover MA (01845) ***(G-13694)***

Central Pallet & Box....860 224-4416
271 John Downey Dr New Britain CT (06051) ***(G-2520)***
Central Printing & Supply....781 322-1220
21 Bradley Ave Haverhill MA (01832) ***(G-11415)***
Central Steel Rule Die Inc....508 853-2663
46 W Mountain St Worcester MA (01606) ***(G-17354)***
Central Street Corporation....207 947-8049
80 Central St Bangor ME (04401) ***(G-5635)***
Central Vacuum Cleaners (PA)....978 682-5294
476 Lowell St Ste 1 Methuen MA (01844) ***(G-13013)***
Central Vacuum Cleaners....978 682-5295
250 Canal St Lawrence MA (01840) ***(G-12004)***
Centre Machine, Weare *Also called Jr Frank Bolton* ***(G-19936)***
Centrexion Therapeutics Corp....617 837-6911
200 State St Ste 6 Boston MA (02109) ***(G-8464)***
Centric Software Inc....603 448-3009
115 Etna Rd Fl 2 Lebanon NH (03766) ***(G-18618)***
Centricut Manufacturing LLC....603 298-6191
16 Airpark Rd West Lebanon NH (03784) ***(G-19948)***
Centritec Seals LLC....860 594-7183
222 Pitkin St Ste 104 East Hartford CT (06108) ***(G-1181)***
Centrix Inc....203 929-5582
770 River Rd Shelton CT (06484) ***(G-3788)***
Centrodyne Corp of America....802 658-4715
75 Ethan Allen Dr South Burlington VT (05403) ***(G-22442)***
Centroid Wire and Cable LLC....603 227-0900
155 River Rd Unit 28 Bow NH (03304) ***(G-17709)***
Century Acquisition....518 758-7229
49 Clayton Rd Canaan CT (06018) ***(G-686)***
Century Box, Methuen *Also called Gooby Industries Corp* ***(G-13024)***
Century Concrete, Ashley Falls *Also called Bonded Concrete Inc* ***(G-7672)***
Century Food Service Inc....508 995-3221
107 S Main St Acushnet MA (02743) ***(G-7400)***
Century Magnetics Intl....603 934-4931
20 Canal St Ste 401 Franklin NH (03235) ***(G-18156)***
Century Products, New Canaan *Also called Contek International Corp* ***(G-2595)***
Century Robotics LLC....603 540-2576
548 Donald St Ste 12 Bedford NH (03110) ***(G-17635)***
Century Sheet Metal Inc....401 433-1380
19 Maple Ave Riverside RI (02915) ***(G-21166)***
Century Sign LLC....203 230-9000
2666 State St Hamden CT (06517) ***(G-1737)***
Century Spring Mfg Co Inc....860 582-3344
100 Wooster Ct Bristol CT (06010) ***(G-540)***
Century Tool and Design Inc....860 621-6748
260 Canal St Milldale CT (06467) ***(G-2383)***
Century Tool Co Inc....860 923-9523
753 Thompson Rd Thompson CT (06277) ***(G-4533)***
Century-Ty Wood Mfg Inc....508 429-4011
79 Lowland St Holliston MA (01746) ***(G-11563)***
Cenveo Inc....203 595-3000
200 1st Stamford Pl Stamford CT (06902) ***(G-4161)***
Cenveo Enterprises Inc (PA)....203 595-3000
200 First Stamford Pl # 2 Stamford CT (06902) ***(G-4162)***
Cenveo Worldwide Limited (HQ)....203 595-3000
200 First Stamford Pl # 2 Stamford CT (06902) ***(G-4163)***
Cequr Corporation....508 486-0010
734 Forest St Ste 100 Marlborough MA (01752) ***(G-12737)***
Ceramco Inc....603 447-2090
1467 E Main St Center Conway NH (03813) ***(G-17793)***
Ceramic Process Systems....508 222-0614
111 Worcester St Taunton MA (02780) ***(G-15736)***
Ceramic To Metal Seals Inc....781 665-5002
78 Stone Pl Ste 4 Melrose MA (02176) ***(G-12977)***
Ceramics Grinding Co Inc....978 461-5935
12 Walnut St Maynard MA (01754) ***(G-12897)***
Cerbone Bakery, Stamford *Also called Beldotti Bakeries* ***(G-4148)***
Cerence Inc (PA)....781 565-5507
15 Wayside Rd Burlington MA (01803) ***(G-9246)***
Cerenova Inc....715 212-2595
11 Douglas St Cambridge MA (02139) ***(G-9435)***
Ceres LLC (PA)....833 237-3767
190 College St Burlington VT (05401) ***(G-21772)***
Ceres Natural Remedies, Burlington *Also called Ceres LLC* ***(G-21772)***
Cerevance Inc (PA)....408 220-5722
1 Marina Park Dr Fl 14 Boston MA (02210) ***(G-8465)***
Ceric Fab Systems, Ayer *Also called Ceric Fabrication Co Inc* ***(G-7915)***
Ceric Fabrication Co Inc....978 772-9034
70 Nemco Way Ayer MA (01432) ***(G-7915)***
Cerner Corporation....781 434-2200
51 Sawyer Rd Ste 600 Waltham MA (02453) ***(G-16065)***
Cerner DHT, Waltham *Also called Cerner Corporation* ***(G-16065)***
Cerrito Furniture Inds Inc....203 481-2580
7 Venice St Branford CT (06405) ***(G-304)***
Cerritos Upholstery Concepts, Branford *Also called Cerrito Furniture Inds Inc* ***(G-304)***
Cersosimo Lumber Company Inc (PA)....802 254-4508
1103 Vernon St Brattleboro VT (05301) ***(G-21724)***
Cersosimo Lumber Company Inc....413 477-6258
18 Shunpike Rd Hardwick MA (01037) ***(G-11373)***

Cersosimo Lumber Company Inc 603 786-9482
3997 Rumney Route 25 Rumney NH (03266) ***(G-19695)***
Certainteed Corporation 508 655-9731
22 Winter St Natick MA (01760) ***(G-13244)***
Certeon Inc 781 425-5099
5 Wall St Fl 5 # 5 Burlington MA (01803) ***(G-9247)***
Certify Inc (PA) 207 773-6100
20 York St Ste 201 Portland ME (04101) ***(G-6635)***
Cessna Aircraft, Oxford *Also called Textron Aviation Inc* ***(G-3427)***
Cesyl Mills Inc 508 865-6129
95 W Main St Millbury MA (01527) ***(G-13159)***
CET Inc 203 882-8057
270 Rowe Ave Ste D Milford CT (06461) ***(G-2263)***
CET Technology LLC 603 894-6100
27a Roulston Rd Windham NH (03087) ***(G-20001)***
Ceylon R Morehouse Logging 802 695-4660
617 Sawmill Rd Concord VT (05824) ***(G-21890)***
CFM Test & Balance Corp 203 778-1900
14 Depot Pl Ste 2 Bethel CT (06801) ***(G-136)***
Cg Roxane LLC 603 476-8844
455 Ossipee Rd Moultonborough NH (03254) ***(G-19095)***
Cgear Uniforms, Newport *Also called Shegear Inc* ***(G-20681)***
Cgit Westboro Inc 508 836-4000
30 Oak St Westborough MA (01581) ***(G-16602)***
Cgl Inc 860 945-6166
1094 Echo Lake Rd Watertown CT (06795) ***(G-5002)***
Chabaso Bakery, New Haven *Also called Atticus Bakery LLC* ***(G-2661)***
Chaco Inc 781 769-5557
99 Central St Norwood MA (02062) ***(G-14141)***
Chadwick & Trefethen Inc 603 436-2568
50 Borthwick Ave Portsmouth NH (03801) ***(G-19551)***
Chair City Meats Inc 978 630-1050
766 W Broadway Gardner MA (01440) ***(G-11108)***
Chair City Wayside, Gardner *Also called Ralph Curcio Co Inc* ***(G-11124)***
Challenging Tms, Pzzl Plyrs Wk, Westerly *Also called CM Publications Inc* ***(G-21519)***
Chamberlain Group LLC 413 528-7744
934 Main St Great Barrington MA (01230) ***(G-11236)***
Chamberlain Machine LLC 603 756-2560
17 Huntington Ln Walpole NH (03608) ***(G-19918)***
Chamberlain Manufacturing Corp 508 996-5621
117 King St New Bedford MA (02745) ***(G-13370)***
Chamberlain Release, Owner, Lyndonville *Also called Northern Strike* ***(G-22071)***
Chambers Leasing 207 532-4381
381 North St Houlton ME (04730) ***(G-6203)***
Champagne Tables & Pet Pdts 413 527-4370
15 Old County Rd Southampton MA (01073) ***(G-15337)***
Champlain Chocolate Company 802 864-1808
290 Boyer Cir Williston VT (05495) ***(G-22659)***
Champlain Construction Co Inc 802 388-2652
189 Birchard Park Middlebury VT (05753) ***(G-22108)***
Champlain Distilleries 802 378-5059
139 E Shore Rd South Hero VT (05486) ***(G-22480)***
Champlain Precision Inc (PA) 802 453-7225
235 Campground Rd New Haven VT (05472) ***(G-22184)***
Champlain Software, Gloucester *Also called Para Research Inc* ***(G-11201)***
Champlin Boat Works, Narragansett *Also called Champlin Welding Inc* ***(G-20636)***
Champlin Welding Inc 401 782-4099
556 Point Judith Rd Narragansett RI (02882) ***(G-20636)***
Champlin-Packrite Inc 860 951-9217
151 Batson Dr Manchester CT (06042) ***(G-1993)***
Chand Eisenmann Metallurgical, Burlington *Also called Cem Group LLC* ***(G-675)***
Chang Shing Tofu Inc 617 868-8878
37 Rogers St Cambridge MA (02142) ***(G-9436)***
Change Logic 617 274-8661
233 Needham St Ste 300 Newton Upper Falls MA (02464) ***(G-13657)***
Change Water Labs Inc 917 292-5160
413 Broadway Cambridge MA (02138) ***(G-9437)***
Changs Publishing Company 617 542-1230
216 Lincoln St Boston MA (02111) ***(G-8466)***
Channel Alloys 203 975-1404
301 Merritt 7 Ste 1 Norwalk CT (06851) ***(G-3123)***
Channel Fish Co Inc 617 569-3200
370 E Eagle St Boston MA (02128) ***(G-8467)***
Channel Sources LLC 203 775-6464
246 Federal Rd Ste A12-1 Brookfield CT (06804) ***(G-638)***
Channel Sources Company, Brookfield *Also called Channel Sources LLC* ***(G-638)***
Channelbind International Corp (PA) 864 579-7072
45 Centre St Concord NH (03301) ***(G-17892)***
Channing Bete Company Inc (PA) 413 665-7611
1 Community Pl South Deerfield MA (01373) ***(G-15247)***
Channing-Bete, South Deerfield *Also called Channing Bete Company Inc* ***(G-15247)***
Chante, Cranston *Also called Rolyn Inc* ***(G-20281)***
Chapco Inc (PA) 860 526-9535
10 Denlar Dr Chester CT (06412) ***(G-769)***
Chapins Wood Products Inc (PA) 781 294-0758
6 Delia Way Halifax MA (02338) ***(G-11316)***
Chapman & Wheeler Inc 207 824-2224
Mason St Bethel ME (04217) ***(G-5714)***
Chapman Fuel 978 452-9656
210 Cross St Lowell MA (01854) ***(G-12358)***
Char Software Inc (PA) 617 418-4422
2 Center Plz Fl 3 Boston MA (02108) ***(G-8468)***
Charbert Fabrics, Chestnut Hill *Also called Charbert Inc* ***(G-9984)***
Charbert Inc 401 364-7751
830 Boylston St Ste 209 Chestnut Hill MA (02467) ***(G-9984)***
Chardan Ltd 508 992-0854
453 S Main St Ste 1 Attleboro MA (02703) ***(G-7718)***
Charge Analytics LLC 978 201-7952
34 Silvermine Rd Boxford MA (01921) ***(G-8975)***
Charge Solutions Inc 203 871-7282
205 Research Dr Unit 1011 Milford CT (06460) ***(G-2264)***
Charles A Richardson Inc 508 339-8600
330 Otis St Mansfield MA (02048) ***(G-12617)***
Charles Boggini Company LLC 860 742-2652
733 Bread And Milk St Coventry CT (06238) ***(G-832)***
Charles Clay Ltd 203 662-0125
149 Cherry St New Canaan CT (06840) ***(G-2593)***
Charles Curtis LLC 802 274-0060
462 Hill St Danville VT (05828) ***(G-21895)***
Charles E Tuttle Co Inc (HQ) 802 773-8930
364 Innovation Dr North Clarendon VT (05759) ***(G-22214)***
Charles J Angelo Mfg Group LLC 860 646-2378
130 Chapel Rd Manchester CT (06042) ***(G-1994)***
Charles Lane Inc 207 365-4606
55 Ester Rd Sherman Mills ME (04776) ***(G-6960)***
Charles Lane Trucking, Sherman Mills *Also called Charles Lane Inc* ***(G-6960)***
Charles Leonard Steel Svcs LLC 603 225-0211
183 Pembroke Rd Concord NH (03301) ***(G-17893)***
Charles McCann 413 442-3922
27 Hungerford St Pittsfield MA (01201) ***(G-14463)***
Charles Pike & Sons 860 455-9968
311 Providence Tpke Hampton CT (06247) ***(G-1797)***
Charles River Apparel Inc 781 793-5300
1205 Providence Hwy Sharon MA (02067) ***(G-15047)***
Charles River Laboratories Inc 860 376-1240
425 Pendleton Hill Rd Voluntown CT (06384) ***(G-4689)***
Charles River Laboratories Inc 860 889-1389
1 Wisconsin Ave Ste 100 Norwich CT (06360) ***(G-3277)***
Charles River Laboratories Inc 860 429-7261
67 Baxter Rd Storrs CT (06268) ***(G-4381)***
Charles Ro Mfg Co Inc 781 322-6084
662 Cross St Ste 1 Malden MA (02148) ***(G-12565)***
Charles Rosenberg, Burlington *Also called Cherrybrook Kitchen LLC* ***(G-9248)***
Charles Shackleton & Miranda T 802 672-5175
The Mill Rte 4 Bridgewater VT (05034) ***(G-21757)***
Charles Smith Steel LLC 603 753-9844
115 N Main St Boscawen NH (03303) ***(G-17702)***
Charles Supper Company Inc 508 655-4610
15 Tech Cir Ste 1 Natick MA (01760) ***(G-13245)***
Charles Thomae & Son Inc 508 222-0785
15 Maynard St Attleboro MA (02703) ***(G-7719)***
Charles Webb Inc (PA) 781 569-0444
470 Wildwood Ave Ste 7 Woburn MA (01801) ***(G-17143)***
Charles Webb Desgr Woodworker, Woburn *Also called Charles Webb Inc* ***(G-17143)***
Charlesbridge Publishing Inc (PA) 617 926-0329
85 Main St Ste 5 Watertown MA (02472) ***(G-16276)***
Charlestown Bridge 617 241-8500
87 Warren St Charlestown MA (02129) ***(G-9829)***
Charlie Horse Screen Printing/ 207 985-3293
1468 Portland Rd Arundel ME (04046) ***(G-5530)***
Charlies Ride 860 916-3637
389 North St Windsor Locks CT (06096) ***(G-5388)***
Charlotte News 802 425-4949
823 Ferry Rd Charlotte VT (05445) ***(G-21832)***
Charm Sciences Inc (PA) 978 687-9200
659 Andover St Lawrence MA (01843) ***(G-12005)***
Charr Custom Boat Company 508 375-0028
20 Corporation Rd Yarmouth Port MA (02675) ***(G-17529)***
Charron Wood Products Inc 802 369-0166
28 River St Ste 8 Windsor VT (05089) ***(G-22706)***
Charter Dev & Consulting Corp 802 878-5005
57 River Rd Unit 1023 Essex Junction VT (05452) ***(G-21936)***
Charter Industries Inc 401 245-0850
329 Market St Warren RI (02885) ***(G-21293)***
Charter Nex Films Inc 413 863-3171
18 Industrial Blvd Turners Falls MA (01376) ***(G-15875)***
Charter Oak Automation LLC 203 562-0699
340 Quinnipiac St Ste 19 Wallingford CT (06492) ***(G-4716)***
Chas G Allen Realty LLC 978 355-2911
25 Williamsville Rd Barre MA (01005) ***(G-7950)***
Chas W House & Sons Inc 860 673-2518
19 Perry St Unionville CT (06085) ***(G-4654)***
Chasco Inc 603 436-2141
15 Banfield Rd Unit 6 Portsmouth NH (03801) ***(G-19552)***
Chase Associates Inc 207 882-7526
304 Boothbay Rd Edgecomb ME (04556) ***(G-6000)***
Chase Construction, Westwood *Also called Chase Corporation* ***(G-16862)***

ALPHABETIC

Chase Corp 508 819-4200
26 Summer St Bridgewater MA (02325) ***(G-9066)***
Chase Corp Inc 781 332-0700
295 University Ave Westwood MA (02090) ***(G-16860)***
Chase Corporation (PA) 781 332-0700
295 University Ave Westwood MA (02090) ***(G-16861)***
Chase Corporation 203 285-1244
149 Amity Rd Woodbridge CT (06525) ***(G-5464)***
Chase Corporation 508 731-2710
24 Dana Rd Oxford MA (01540) ***(G-14256)***
Chase Corporation 781 963-2600
19 Highland Ave Randolph MA (02368) ***(G-14673)***
Chase Corporation 781 329-3259
295 University Ave Westwood MA (02090) ***(G-16862)***
Chase Electric Motors LLC 603 669-2565
78 Londonderry Tpke G1 Hooksett NH (03106) ***(G-18346)***
Chase Graphics Inc 860 315-9006
124 School St Putnam CT (06260) ***(G-3605)***
Chase Machine Co Inc 401 821-8879
324 Washington St West Warwick RI (02893) ***(G-21486)***
Chase Media Group 914 962-3871
31 Pecks Ln Ste 3 Newtown CT (06470) ***(G-2919)***
Chase Press, Newtown *Also called Shop Smart Central Inc* ***(G-2936)***
Chase S Daily LLC 207 338-0555
96 Main St Belfast ME (04915) ***(G-5687)***
Chase Speciality Coating 781 332-0700
295 University Ave Westwood MA (02090) ***(G-16863)***
Chase's Daily, Belfast *Also called Chase S Daily LLC* ***(G-5687)***
Chases Daily LLC 207 930-0464
623 N Palermo Rd Freedom ME (04941) ***(G-6070)***
Chassis Dynamics Inc 203 262-6272
91 Willenbrock Rd Ste A1 Oxford CT (06478) ***(G-3396)***
Chassis Engineering LLC 978 948-0826
445 Newburyport Tpke Rowley MA (01969) ***(G-14850)***
Chatco, Brockton *Also called Chatham Plastic Ventures Inc* ***(G-9130)***
Chatham Furn Reproductions 603 394-0089
39 Highland Rd South Hampton NH (03827) ***(G-19855)***
Chatham Jam & Jelly Shop, West Chatham *Also called Jam & Jelly Chatham* ***(G-16474)***
Chatham Plastic Ventures Inc 518 392-5761
1200 W Chestnut St Brockton MA (02301) ***(G-9130)***
Chaucer Accessories Inc 978 373-1566
143 Essex St Ste 3 Haverhill MA (01832) ***(G-11416)***
Chaucer Leather, Haverhill *Also called Chaucer Accessories Inc* ***(G-11416)***
Chaudhary LLC 401 954-9695
371 Benefit St Pawtucket RI (02861) ***(G-20822)***
Chauncey Wings Sons Inc 413 772-6611
78 Pierce St Greenfield MA (01301) ***(G-11253)***
Chauvin Arnoux Inc (PA) 603 749-6434
15 Faraday Dr Dover NH (03820) ***(G-18012)***
Chauvin Arnoux Inc 508 698-2115
200 Foxboro Blvd Ste 300 Foxboro MA (02035) ***(G-10878)***
Chebli Architectural Woodwork 781 642-0733
50 Sun St Waltham MA (02453) ***(G-16066)***
Check Mate Service Line LLC 401 231-7296
375 Putnam Pike Smithfield RI (02917) ***(G-21215)***
Check Point Software Tech Inc 978 635-0300
179 Great Rd Ste 111a Acton MA (01720) ***(G-7347)***
Checksforlesscom 800 245-5775
200 Riverside Indus Pkwy Portland ME (04103) ***(G-6636)***
Checon Corporation (PA) 508 643-0940
30 Larsen Way North Attleboro MA (02763) ***(G-13752)***
Cheeky Fishing, North Adams *Also called North Point Brands LLC* ***(G-13683)***
Cheetah Medical Inc (PA) 617 964-0613
1320 Centre St Ste 400 Newton MA (02459) ***(G-13577)***
Chef Creations LLC 407 228-0069
330 Lynnway Ste 301 Lynn MA (01901) ***(G-12497)***
Chefs Equipment Emporium, Wallingford *Also called Demartino Fixture Co Inc* ***(G-4733)***
Chelsea Clock LLC 617 884-0250
101 2nd St Chelsea MA (02150) ***(G-9948)***
Chelsea Green Publishing Co 802 295-6300
85 N Main St Ste 120 White River Junction VT (05001) ***(G-22636)***
Chelsea Industries Inc (HQ) 617 232-6060
46a Glen Ave Newton MA (02459) ***(G-13578)***
Chelsea Record, Revere *Also called Independant Newspaper Group* ***(G-14767)***
Chem Quest Inc 207 856-2993
1 Liberty Ln E Ste 212 Hampton NH (03842) ***(G-18260)***
Chem-Tainer Industries Inc 401 467-2750
530 Wellington Ave Ste 5 Cranston RI (02910) ***(G-20196)***
Chem-Tron, Danbury *Also called Chemical-Electric Corporation* ***(G-888)***
Chem-Tron Pntg Pwdr Cating Inc 203 743-5131
92 Taylor St Danbury CT (06810) ***(G-887)***
Chemart Company 401 333-9200
11 New England Way Lincoln RI (02865) ***(G-20562)***
Chemart Company (PA) 401 333-9200
15 New England Way Lincoln RI (02865) ***(G-20563)***
Chemcage US LLC 617 504-9548
97 Giles Rd East Kingston NH (03827) ***(G-18085)***
Chemco Corporation 978 687-9000
46 Stafford St Lawrence MA (01841) ***(G-12006)***
Chemessence Inc 860 355-4108
180 Sunny Valley Rd # 15 New Milford CT (06776) ***(G-2792)***
Chemetal Division, Easthampton *Also called October Company Inc* ***(G-10572)***
Chemetal Division, Easthampton *Also called October Company Inc* ***(G-10573)***
Chemi-Graphic Inc 413 589-0151
340 State St Ludlow MA (01056) ***(G-12458)***
Chemical & Metallurgical Div, Exeter *Also called Osram Sylvania Inc* ***(G-18127)***
Chemical Coatings Corp 401 331-9000
35 Livingston St Providence RI (02904) ***(G-20982)***
Chemical-Electric Corporation 203 743-5131
92 Taylor St Danbury CT (06810) ***(G-888)***
Chemin Pharma LLC 203 208-2811
4 Research Dr Woodbridge CT (06525) ***(G-5465)***
Chemiplastica Inc 413 584-2472
238 Nonotuck St Florence MA (01062) ***(G-10865)***
Chemotex Protective Coatings (PA) 860 349-0144
15 Commerce Cir Durham CT (06422) ***(G-1088)***
Chemrock Corporation 207 594-8225
94 Buttermilk Ln Thomaston ME (04861) ***(G-7082)***
Chemtrac Systems 978 448-0061
5 Lakeside Dr Groton MA (01450) ***(G-11286)***
Chemtrade Chemicals US LLC 603 926-0191
239 Drakeside Rd Hampton NH (03842) ***(G-18261)***
Chemtura Receivables LLC 203 573-3327
199 Benson Rd Waterbury CT (06749) ***(G-4856)***
Chemtura USA, Shelton *Also called Lanxess Solutions US Inc* ***(G-3824)***
Chen Hsi Pin 781 986-7900
25 Warren St Randolph MA (02368) ***(G-14674)***
Cherise Cpl LLC 203 238-3482
57 S Broad St Meriden CT (06450) ***(G-2085)***
Cherner Chair Company LLC 203 894-4702
218 North St Ridgefield CT (06877) ***(G-3662)***
Cherry Hill Construction Corp 781 826-6886
722 Washington St Pembroke MA (02359) ***(G-14394)***
Cherry Point Products Inc 207 546-0930
54 Wyman Rd Milbridge ME (04658) ***(G-6431)***
Cherry Pond Designs Inc 603 586-7795
716 Meadows Rd Jefferson NH (03583) ***(G-18482)***
Cherry Pond Furniture, Jefferson *Also called Cherry Pond Designs Inc* ***(G-18482)***
Cherry Semiconductor Corp 401 885-3600
2000 S County Trl East Greenwich RI (02818) ***(G-20356)***
Cherry Valley Welding, Cherry Valley *Also called Ralph Seaver* ***(G-9976)***
Cherrybrook Kitchen LLC 781 272-0400
20 Mall Rd Ste 410 Burlington MA (01803) ***(G-9248)***
Cherryfield Foods Inc (HQ) 207 546-7573
320 Ridge Rd Cherryfield ME (04622) ***(G-5902)***
Cheshire Division, Cheshire *Also called Atlantic Inertial Systems Inc* ***(G-714)***
Cheshire Herald, Wallingford *Also called True Publishing Company* ***(G-4823)***
Cheshire Manufacturing Co Inc 203 272-3586
312 E Johnson Ave Ste 1 Cheshire CT (06410) ***(G-721)***
Cheshire Optical Inc 603 352-0602
53c Davis Pl Laconia NH (03246) ***(G-18562)***
Cheshire Software Inc 617 527-4000
1170 Walnut St Newton MA (02461) ***(G-13579)***
Chessco Industries Inc (PA) 203 255-2804
1330 Post Rd E Ste 2 Westport CT (06880) ***(G-5183)***
Chester Boatworks 860 526-2227
444 Main St Deep River CT (06417) ***(G-1059)***
Chester Braley 239 841-0019
25 Howards Ln Epsom NH (03234) ***(G-18105)***
Chester Brothers 802 655-4159
146 W Canal St Winooski VT (05404) ***(G-22718)***
Chester Forest Products Inc 603 887-4123
143 Halls Village Rd Chester NH (03036) ***(G-17823)***
Chester H Chapman 207 625-3349
374 Spec Pond Rd Porter ME (04068) ***(G-6600)***
Chesters Custom Woodworking 802 259-3232
1292 Frost Hill Rd Belmont VT (05730) ***(G-21657)***
Chevalier Associates Inc 508 770-0092
176 Worcester Prov Tpke 101a Sutton MA (01590) ***(G-15680)***
Chew Publishing Inc 401 808-0648
190 E Main Rd Ste 3 Middletown RI (02842) ***(G-20617)***
Chewbarka's Tags, Johnston *Also called Fred Ricci Tool Co Inc* ***(G-20512)***
Cheyne Awning & Sign Co 413 442-4742
275 Hungerford St Pittsfield MA (01201) ***(G-14464)***
CHI Foods LLC 310 309-1186
79 10th St Providence RI (02906) ***(G-20983)***
Chiasma Inc 617 928-5300
140 Kendrick St Bldg Ce Needham MA (02494) ***(G-13296)***
Chic LLC 781 312-7800
2 Corporate Park Dr Pembroke MA (02359) ***(G-14395)***
Chick Trucking Inc 603 659-3566
Rr 152 Newmarket NH (03857) ***(G-19331)***
Chicken Soup For Soul LLC 203 861-4000
132 E Putnam Ave Ste 20 Cos Cob CT (06807) ***(G-823)***
Chicken Soup For Soul Entrmt I (HQ) 855 398-0443
132 E Putnam Ave Fl 2w Cos Cob CT (06807) ***(G-824)***
Chicopee Foundations Inc (PA) 413 536-3370
652 Prospect St Chicopee MA (01020) ***(G-10007)***

Chicopee Foundations Inc 413 594-4700
158 New Lombard Rd Chicopee MA (01020) ***(G-10008)***
Chicopee Provision Company Inc 413 594-4765
19 Sitarz Ave Chicopee MA (01013) ***(G-10009)***
Chicopee Register Newspaper 413 592-3599
333 Front St Ste 5 Chicopee MA (01013) ***(G-10010)***
Chicopee Tribune 413 552-3775
582 Britton St Chicopee MA (01020) ***(G-10011)***
Chicopee Vision Center Inc 413 796-7570
1907 Wilbraham Rd Springfield MA (01129) ***(G-15460)***
Chicopee Welding & Tool Inc 413 598-8215
94 W Hawley Rd Charlemont MA (01339) ***(G-9819)***
Chicos Wine and Spirits, Pittsfield *Also called Kwik Mart* ***(G-14479)***
Chief Executive Group LLC (PA) 785 832-0303
9 W Broad St Ste 430 Stamford CT (06902) ***(G-4164)***
Chief Executive Group LP (PA) 203 930-2700
9 W Broad St Ste 430 Stamford CT (06902) ***(G-4165)***
Chief Executive Magazine, Stamford *Also called Chief Executive Group LP* ***(G-4165)***
Chief Logging & Cnstr Inc 802 584-3868
2494 Stone Rd South Ryegate VT (05069) ***(G-22495)***
Chiero Sabor Restaurant, Marlborough *Also called Morais Marizete* ***(G-12795)***
Child Evngelism Fellowship Inc 203 879-2154
730 Bound Line Rd Wolcott CT (06716) ***(G-5434)***
Child Safety Solutions Inc 207 226-3870
75 Mechanic St Rockland ME (04841) ***(G-6789)***
Childrens Health Market Inc 203 762-2938
27 Cannon Rd Ste 1b Wilton CT (06897) ***(G-5283)***
Chilmark Archtctural Wdwkg LLC 508 856-9200
705 Plantation St Worcester MA (01605) ***(G-17355)***
Chilmark Chocolates Inc 508 645-3013
583 State Rd Chilmark MA (02535) ***(G-10072)***
Chilton Furniture and Paint, Freeport *Also called Chilton Paint Co Inc ME* ***(G-6074)***
Chilton Paint Co Inc ME 207 865-4443
184 Lower Main St Freeport ME (04032) ***(G-6074)***
Chimani Inc 207 221-0266
148 Middle St Ste 1d Portland ME (04101) ***(G-6637)***
Chinamerica Food Manufacture 617 426-1818
81 Tyler St A Boston MA (02111) ***(G-8469)***
Chinese Spaghetti Factory 617 542-0224
73 Essex St Boston MA (02111) ***(G-8470)***
Chinese Spaghetti Factory Inc 617 445-7714
83 Newmarket Sq Boston MA (02118) ***(G-8471)***
Chip Component Electronx 207 510-7608
13 Airport Dr Limington ME (04049) ***(G-6347)***
Chip In A Bottle LLC 203 460-0665
837 Whalley Ave Ste 1 New Haven CT (06515) ***(G-2676)***
Chipping & Logging 207 625-4056
37 Cross Rd Porter ME (04068) ***(G-6601)***
Chips, Peabody *Also called Component Hndng Inspctn Pckn* ***(G-14325)***
Chisholm and Hunt Printers Inc 978 283-0318
14 Whittemore St Gloucester MA (01930) ***(G-11173)***
Chisletts Boating & Design LLC 603 755-6815
35 Industrial Park Dover NH (03820) ***(G-18013)***
Chittenden Environmental 802 578-0194
8195 Williston Rd Williston VT (05495) ***(G-22660)***
Chmc Otlrynglgic Fundation Inc (PA) 617 355-8290
300 Longwood Ave Boston MA (02115) ***(G-8472)***
Chocolate Therapy 508 875-1571
60 Worcester Rd Ste 10 Framingham MA (01702) ***(G-10933)***
Chocorua Valley Lumber Company 508 883-6878
1210 Pulaski Blvd Bellingham MA (02019) ***(G-8033)***
Choice Foods 508 332-2442
770 S Main St Rm Main Bellingham MA (02019) ***(G-8034)***
Choice Graphics Inc 978 948-2789
140 Central St Ste 4 Rowley MA (01969) ***(G-14851)***
Choice Magazine, Middletown *Also called American Library Association* ***(G-2170)***
Choice Printing & Product LLC 401 438-3838
150 Newport Ave Rumford RI (02916) ***(G-21182)***
Choice Woodworking Inc 978 207-0289
25 Nutter Rd North Reading MA (01864) ***(G-13980)***
Choklit Mold Ltd 401 725-7377
23 Carrington St Lincoln RI (02865) ***(G-20564)***
Chomerics Division, Hudson *Also called Parker-Hannifin Corporation* ***(G-18425)***
Chooseco LLC 802 496-2595
49 Fiddlers Grn Waitsfield VT (05673) ***(G-22563)***
Chopper One Inc 207 444-5476
215 Old Main St Eagle Lake ME (04739) ***(G-5973)***
Chris & Zack LLC 203 298-0742
385 Boston Post Rd Orange CT (06477) ***(G-3361)***
Chris Clark 802 356-0044
1848 Parker Rd Vershire VT (05079) ***(G-22558)***
Chris Cross LLC 203 386-8426
294 Benton St Stratford CT (06615) ***(G-4404)***
Chris Davis Stoneware Pottery 207 363-7561
81 Seabury Rd York ME (03909) ***(G-7306)***
Chris J Seamans 802 287-9399
4370 Vermont Route 140 Middletown Springs VT (05757) ***(G-22123)***
Chris Martin (PA) 508 580-0069
36 E Main St Avon MA (02322) ***(G-7882)***
Chrisandras Interiors Inc 802 228-2075
72 Pond St A Ludlow VT (05149) ***(G-22062)***
Christeyns Laundry Tech LLC 617 203-2169
100 Laurel St Ste 120 East Bridgewater MA (02333) ***(G-10409)***
Christhopher Dinatale 781 834-4248
15 Bailey Ter Marshfield MA (02050) ***(G-12857)***
Christian Science Monitor, Boston *Also called Christian Science Pubg Soc* ***(G-8473)***
Christian Science Pubg Soc (PA) 617 450-2000
210 Massachusetts Ave Boston MA (02115) ***(G-8473)***
Christmas Cove Designs Inc 207 350-1035
438 Middle Rd Dresden ME (04342) ***(G-5965)***
Christmas Studio 413 267-3342
252 Main St Monson MA (01057) ***(G-13203)***
Christopher Condors 203 852-8181
23 1st St Ste 1 Norwalk CT (06855) ***(G-3124)***
Christopher's Towing, Chelmsford *Also called Christphrs Emrgncy Eqptmnt &* ***(G-9887)***
Christopher-Gordon Publishing 781 762-5577
3 Bailey St Foxboro MA (02035) ***(G-10879)***
Christopoulos Designs Inc 203 576-1110
195 Dewey St Bridgeport CT (06605) ***(G-397)***
Christphrs Emrgncy Eqptmnt & 978 265-8363
76 Riverneck Rd Chelmsford MA (01824) ***(G-9887)***
Christy Machine Company 207 748-1092
270 Oldfields Rd South Berwick ME (03908) ***(G-7001)***
Chroma Color, Leominster *Also called Hudson Color Concentrates LLC* ***(G-12153)***
Chroma Technology Corp 802 428-2500
10 Imtec Ln Bellows Falls VT (05101) ***(G-21650)***
Chromalloy Component Svcs Inc 203 924-1666
415 Howe Ave Shelton CT (06484) ***(G-3789)***
Chromalloy Component Svcs Inc 860 688-7798
601 Marshall Phelps Rd Windsor CT (06095) ***(G-5325)***
Chromalloy Connecticut, Windsor *Also called Chromalloy Gas Turbine LLC* ***(G-5326)***
Chromalloy Gas Turbine LLC 860 688-7798
601 Marshall Phelps Rd Windsor CT (06095) ***(G-5326)***
Chromatic Press US Inc 860 796-7667
84 Woodrow St West Hartford CT (06107) ***(G-5059)***
Chromatics Inc 203 743-6868
19 Francis J Clarke Cir Bethel CT (06801) ***(G-137)***
Chromatra LLC 978 473-7005
100 Cummings Ctr Ste 231g Beverly MA (01915) ***(G-8116)***
Chronicle Inc 802 525-3531
133 Water St Barton VT (05822) ***(G-21647)***
Chronicle Printing Company 860 423-8466
1 Chronicle Rd Willimantic CT (06226) ***(G-5262)***
Chronicle, The, Willimantic *Also called Chronicle Printing Company* ***(G-5262)***
Chronoflex, Wilmington *Also called Advansource Biomaterials Corp* ***(G-16967)***
Chronologics LLC 617 686-6770
3 Arlington St Boston MA (02116) ***(G-8474)***
Chronomatic Inc 401 884-6361
1503 S County Trl East Greenwich RI (02818) ***(G-20357)***
Chuck Roast Equipment Inc (PA) 603 447-5492
90 Odell Hill Rd Conway NH (03818) ***(G-17951)***
Chuck Rose Inc 603 746-2311
100 Chase Farm Rd Contoocook NH (03229) ***(G-17942)***
Chuckles Inc 603 669-4228
11925 S Willow St Manchester NH (03103) ***(G-18798)***
Chucks Sign Co 413 592-3710
658 Fuller Rd Chicopee MA (01020) ***(G-10012)***
Church & Maple Glass Studio 802 863-3880
37 N Prospect St Apt 5 Burlington VT (05401) ***(G-21773)***
Churchill Coatings Corporation 508 394-6573
243 Pleasant St South Yarmouth MA (02664) ***(G-15327)***
Churchill Corporation 781 665-4700
344 Franklin St Melrose MA (02176) ***(G-12978)***
Churchill Wallstone & Gravel, Somerville *Also called Caleb Churchill* ***(G-6998)***
Churchs Welding & Fab Inc 207 353-4249
103 Old Brunswick Rd Durham ME (04222) ***(G-5969)***
Churyk, Stefan M, New Milford *Also called S M Churyk Iron Works Inc* ***(G-2826)***
Chute Chemical Agency 207 532-4370
11 Putnam Ave Houlton ME (04730) ***(G-6204)***
CIA Ink, Fall River *Also called Corporate Image Apparel Inc* ***(G-10680)***
Cianbro Fbrcation Coating Corp 207 487-3311
335 Hunnewell Ave Pittsfield ME (04967) ***(G-6588)***
Cico, Norwalk *Also called Twenty Five Commerce Inc* ***(G-3263)***
Cid Performance Tool, Saco *Also called Coastal Industrial Distrs* ***(G-6845)***
Ciden Technologies, West Springfield *Also called Alden Medical LLC* ***(G-16507)***
Cidra Chemical Management Inc (HQ) 203 265-0035
50 Barnes Park Rd N # 103 Wallingford CT (06492) ***(G-4717)***
Cidra Corporate Services Inc 203 265-0035
50 Barnes Park Rd N Wallingford CT (06492) ***(G-4718)***
Cidra Corporation 203 265-0035
50 Barnes Park Rd N # 103 Wallingford CT (06492) ***(G-4719)***
Cidra Mineral Processing Inc 203 265-0035
50 Barnes Park Rd N Wallingford CT (06492) ***(G-4720)***
Cidra Oilsands Inc (HQ) 203 265-0035
50 Barnes Park Rd N Wallingford CT (06492) ***(G-4721)***
Cielo Therapeutics Inc 617 649-2005
1 Meadowland Dr Hopkinton MA (01748) ***(G-11696)***

ALPHABETIC

CIL Electroplating Inc (PA)....978 683-2082
125 Glenn St Lawrence MA (01843) ***(G-12007)***
CIL Electroplating Inc....978 683-2082
9 Mill St Lawrence MA (01840) ***(G-12008)***
Cil Inc....978 685-8300
400 Canal St Lawrence MA (01840) ***(G-12009)***
CIM Industries Inc....800 543-3458
26 Summer St Bridgewater MA (02325) ***(G-9067)***
CIM Industries Inc....603 924-9481
23 Elm St Ste 2 Peterborough NH (03458) ***(G-19469)***
Cimbali Usa Inc....203 254-6046
418 Meadow St Ste 203 Fairfield CT (06824) ***(G-1418)***
Cimcon Softwares Inc (PA)....978 692-9868
200 Summit Dr Ste 500s Burlington MA (01803) ***(G-9249)***
Cimetrics Inc....617 350-7550
180 Lincoln St Ste 3 Boston MA (02111) ***(G-8475)***
Cimpress USA Incorporated (HQ)....866 614-8002
275 Wyman St Ste 100 Waltham MA (02451) ***(G-16067)***
Cinco Medical, Wakefield *Also called Cardiovascular Instrument* ***(G-15945)***
Cintas Corporation....203 272-2036
10 Diana Ct Cheshire CT (06410) ***(G-722)***
Cintas Corporation....207 307-2448
293 Target Cir Bangor ME (04401) ***(G-5636)***
Cintas Corporation No 2....401 723-7300
700 Narragansett Park Dr Pawtucket RI (02861) ***(G-20823)***
Cipem USA Inc....347 642-1106
44b Grove St Unit 78 Melrose MA (02176) ***(G-12979)***
Circadian Information....781 439-6326
2 Main St Ste 310 Stoneham MA (02180) ***(G-15557)***
Circle Metal Finishing Inc....978 682-4297
55 Chase St Ste 3 Methuen MA (01844) ***(G-13014)***
Circle Twelve Inc....508 620-5360
945 Concord St Framingham MA (01701) ***(G-10934)***
Circle Wire, Pepperell *Also called Astron Inc* ***(G-14436)***
Circlet Press Inc....617 864-0663
1770 Mass Ave Ste 278 Cambridge MA (02140) ***(G-9438)***
Circor International Inc (PA)....781 270-1200
30 Corporate Dr Ste 200 Burlington MA (01803) ***(G-9250)***
Circor Naval Solutions LLC (HQ)....413 436-7711
82 Bridge St Warren MA (01083) ***(G-16260)***
Circuit Connect Inc....603 880-7447
4 State St Nashua NH (03063) ***(G-19133)***
Circuit Design, Taunton *Also called Darrell Wheaton* ***(G-15740)***
Circuit Express Inc....603 537-9392
16 Westgate Rd Derry NH (03038) ***(G-17976)***
Circuit Systems Inc (PA)....413 562-5019
54 Mainline Dr Ste B Westfield MA (01085) ***(G-16678)***
Circuit Technology Inc....603 424-2200
6a Continental Blvd Merrimack NH (03054) ***(G-18992)***
Circuit Technology Center Inc....978 374-5000
22 Parkridge Rd Haverhill MA (01835) ***(G-11417)***
Circuitest Services, Hudson *Also called Everett Charles Tech LLC* ***(G-18389)***
Circuitmedic, Haverhill *Also called Circuit Technology Center Inc* ***(G-11417)***
Circulation....508 676-2526
207 Pocasset St Fall River MA (02721) ***(G-10674)***
Cirillo Manufacturing Group....203 484-5010
34 Panagrosi St East Haven CT (06512) ***(G-1244)***
Cirtec Medical Corp....860 814-3973
99 Print Shop Rd Enfield CT (06082) ***(G-1349)***
Cirtech, Merrimack *Also called Circuit Technology Inc* ***(G-18992)***
Cirtronics Corporation....603 249-9190
528 Route 13 S Ste 130 Milford NH (03055) ***(G-19049)***
Cisco Brewers Inc....508 325-5929
5 Bartlett Farm Rd Nantucket MA (02554) ***(G-13222)***
Cisco Systems Inc....978 936-1246
10 Fox Vine Ln Scituate MA (02066) ***(G-15008)***
Cisco Systems Inc....408 526-4000
1414 Massachusetts Ave Boxborough MA (01719) ***(G-8960)***
Cisco Systems Inc....203 229-2300
383 Main Ave Ste 7 Norwalk CT (06851) ***(G-3125)***
Cisco Systems Inc....860 284-5500
50 Stanford Dr Farmington CT (06032) ***(G-1472)***
Citadel Computer Corporation....603 672-5500
16 Columbia Dr Amherst NH (03031) ***(G-17554)***
Citius Printing & Graphics LLC....781 547-5550
20 Clematis Ave Waltham MA (02453) ***(G-16068)***
Citiworks Corp....508 761-7400
20 Rutledge Dr Attleboro MA (02703) ***(G-7720)***
Citizen Cider LLC....802 448-3278
316 Pine St Ste 114 Burlington VT (05401) ***(G-21774)***
Citizen News....203 746-4669
Candle Wood Cor Rm 39 New Fairfield CT (06812) ***(G-2623)***
Citizen Printers Incorporated....207 824-2444
19 Crooked River Cswy Albany Twp ME (04217) ***(G-5512)***
Citra Labs LLC....781 848-9386
55 Messina Dr Ste 4 Braintree MA (02184) ***(G-8994)***
Citra Solv LLC....203 778-0881
188 Shadow Lake Rd Ridgefield CT (06877) ***(G-3663)***
City Data Cable Co....203 327-7917
34 Parker Ave Stamford CT (06906) ***(G-4166)***
City Fresh Foods Inc....617 606-7123
69 Shirley St Roxbury MA (02119) ***(G-14871)***
City Fresh Foods Inc....617 606-7123
77 Shirley St Roxbury MA (02119) ***(G-14872)***
City Machine Corporation....413 538-9766
155 N Canal St Holyoke MA (01040) ***(G-11620)***
City of Chicopee....413 594-1870
1356 Burnett Rd Chicopee MA (01020) ***(G-10013)***
City Pblcations Greater Boston....617 549-7622
18 Lake Shore Dr Wayland MA (01778) ***(G-16335)***
City Sign....860 232-4803
1811 Park St Hartford CT (06106) ***(G-1813)***
City Stitchers, Derby *Also called Rss Enterprises LLC* ***(G-1078)***
City Welding....860 951-4714
84 Wellington St Hartford CT (06106) ***(G-1814)***
City Welding & Fabrication Inc....508 853-6000
10 Ararat St Ste 1 Worcester MA (01606) ***(G-17356)***
Cityscapes Books, Brookline *Also called Pagoda Group LLC* ***(G-9214)***
Cives Corporation....207 622-6141
103 Lipman Rd Augusta ME (04330) ***(G-5605)***
Cives Steel, Augusta *Also called Cives Corporation* ***(G-5605)***
Civitas Therapeutics Inc....617 884-3004
190 Everett Ave Chelsea MA (02150) ***(G-9949)***
CJ Corrado & Sons Inc....508 655-8434
45 Bishop Rd Sharon MA (02067) ***(G-15048)***
CJ Shaughnessy Crane Svc Inc....781 924-1168
520 Bodwell Street Ext Avon MA (02322) ***(G-7883)***
CJ Sprong & Co Inc....413 628-4410
1679 West Rd Williamsburg MA (01096) ***(G-16948)***
Cjmco, Bolton *Also called Carlyle Johnson Machine Co LLC* ***(G-276)***
Ckh Industries Inc....860 563-2999
365 Silas Deane Hwy Ste 1 Wethersfield CT (06109) ***(G-5244)***
Ckm Coatings....603 642-5728
191 Crawley Falls Rd # 12 Brentwood NH (03833) ***(G-17747)***
CKS Packaging Inc....203 729-0716
10 Great Hill Rd Naugatuck CT (06770) ***(G-2466)***
Claire Lathrop Band Mill Inc....802 453-3606
44 South St Bristol VT (05443) ***(G-21763)***
Claire Stewart LLC....401 467-7400
800 Waterman Ave East Providence RI (02914) ***(G-20396)***
Clancy Woodworking LLC....860 355-3655
12 Anderson Rd E Sherman CT (06784) ***(G-3893)***
Clanol Systems Inc....203 637-9909
1374 E Putnam Ave Old Greenwich CT (06870) ***(G-3306)***
Clarcor Eng MBL Solutions LLC (HQ)....860 920-4200
60 Prestige Park Rd East Hartford CT (06108) ***(G-1182)***
Claremont Sales Corporation....860 349-4499
35 Winsome Rd Durham CT (06422) ***(G-1089)***
Clarendon Harwood Bowls, West Rutland *Also called McCormacks Machine Co Inc* ***(G-22618)***
Clarex, Bedford *Also called Dmi Nutraceuticals Inc* ***(G-7971)***
Clariant Plas Coatings USA LLC....207 784-0733
17 Foss Rd Lewiston ME (04240) ***(G-6280)***
Clariant Plas Coatings USA LLC....508 829-6321
85 Industrial Dr Holden MA (01520) ***(G-11543)***
Clarios....860 886-9021
39 Route 2 Ledyard CT (06339) ***(G-1940)***
Clarios....603 222-2400
477 Congress St Fl 6 Portland ME (04101) ***(G-6638)***
Clarios....603 222-2400
915 Holt Ave Unit 7 Manchester NH (03109) ***(G-18799)***
Clarios....781 213-3463
39 Salem St Lynnfield MA (01940) ***(G-12547)***
Clarios....678 297-4040
71 Deerfield Ln Meriden CT (06450) ***(G-2086)***
Claris Vision LLC....508 994-1400
51 State Rd North Dartmouth MA (02747) ***(G-13917)***
Clarity Laboratories Inc....802 658-6321
20 Kimball Ave South Burlington VT (05403) ***(G-22443)***
Clark & Sons Seamless Gutter....413 732-3934
48 Woodcrest Ct Chicopee MA (01020) ***(G-10014)***
Clark Boat-Yard....401 423-3625
110 Racquet Rd Jamestown RI (02835) ***(G-20488)***
Clark Hammerbeam Corporation....781 461-1946
886 Washington St Dedham MA (02026) ***(G-10283)***
Clark Island Boat Works....207 594-4112
4 Rein Rd South Thomaston ME (04858) ***(G-7045)***
Clark Manner Marguarite....860 444-7679
601 Broad St New London CT (06320) ***(G-2769)***
Clark Metal Fabrication Inc....207 330-6322
1463 Auburn Rd Turner ME (04282) ***(G-7106)***
Clark Paint & Varnish Company....413 733-3554
966 Union St West Springfield MA (01089) ***(G-16512)***
Clark Paint Factory, West Springfield *Also called Clark Paint & Varnish Company* ***(G-16512)***
Clark Pallet, Mount Vernon *Also called Edgar Clark & Sons Pallet Inc* ***(G-6458)***
Clark Publishing....603 431-1238
44 Pearson St Portsmouth NH (03801) ***(G-19553)***
Clark Solutions....978 568-3400
10 Brent Dr Hudson MA (01749) ***(G-11763)***

Clark's, Newport *Also called TW Clark Pulp & Logging LLC* ***(G-6487)***
Clarke Distribution Corp 203 838-9385
64 S Main St Norwalk CT (06854) ***(G-3126)***
Clarke Industrial Engineering (PA) 401 667-7880
42 Whitecap Dr North Kingstown RI (02852) ***(G-20696)***
Clarkie Industries 508 404-0202
182 Grant St North Attleboro MA (02760) ***(G-13753)***
Clarks Machine Shop, Clinton *Also called Clarks Machine Shop* ***(G-5914)***
Clarks Machine Shop 207 426-8977
58 Pleasant St Clinton ME (04927) ***(G-5914)***
Clarks Steel Drum Company 781 396-1109
76 Wolcott St Medford MA (02155) ***(G-12926)***
Clarktron Products Inc 203 333-6517
1525 Kings Hwy Ste 7 Fairfield CT (06824) ***(G-1419)***
Clarkworks Machine 978 692-2556
496 Groton Rd Ste 5 Westford MA (01886) ***(G-16762)***
Classic Boat Shop Inc 207 244-3374
Rr 102 Bernard ME (04612) ***(G-5706)***
Classic Coil Company Inc 860 583-7600
205 Century Dr Bristol CT (06010) ***(G-541)***
Classic Copy & Printing, Cambridge *Also called John Karl Dietrich & Assoc* ***(G-9521)***
Classic Embroidery Co 401 434-9632
855 Waterman Ave East Providence RI (02914) ***(G-20397)***
Classic Engineering LLC 978 526-9003
19 Kettle Cove Ln Unit 2 Gloucester MA (01930) ***(G-11174)***
Classic Envelope Inc 508 731-6747
120 Gilboa St Unit 1 East Douglas MA (01516) ***(G-10425)***
Classic Images Inc 860 243-8365
16 Walts Hl Bloomfield CT (06002) ***(G-214)***
Classic Kitchen Design Inc 508 775-3075
127 Airport Rd Hyannis MA (02601) ***(G-11837)***
Classic Kitchens & Interiors, Hyannis *Also called Classic Kitchen Design Inc* ***(G-11837)***
Classic Label Inc 203 389-3535
10 Research Dr Woodbridge CT (06525) ***(G-5466)***
Classic Letter Press Inc 508 221-7496
77 Diane Ave South Yarmouth MA (02664) ***(G-15328)***
Classic Millwork Design Co, Webster *Also called Louis Richards* ***(G-16348)***
Classic Signs Inc 603 883-0384
13 Columbia Dr Unit 16 Amherst NH (03031) ***(G-17555)***
Classic Sporting Enterprises 802 525-3623
214 Higgins Ln Barton VT (05822) ***(G-21648)***
Classic Tool & Mfg Inc 203 755-6313
112 Porter St Waterbury CT (06708) ***(G-4857)***
Classic Tool & Mfg LLC 203 755-6313
112 Porter St Waterbury CT (06708) ***(G-4858)***
Classic Woodworks Inc 508 563-9922
1231 Rte 28a Cataumet MA (02534) ***(G-9811)***
Classics of Golf, Stratford *Also called Carala Ventures Ltd* ***(G-4402)***
Clay Furniture Industries Inc 860 643-7580
41 Chapel St Manchester CT (06042) ***(G-1995)***
Clayground 401 884-4888
5600 Post Rd Unit 109 East Greenwich RI (02818) ***(G-20358)***
Clayton LLC 617 250-8500
17 Everberg Rd Ste E Woburn MA (01801) ***(G-17144)***
Clayton Company Inc 401 421-2978
999 Chalkstone Ave Providence RI (02908) ***(G-20984)***
Clayton Offroad Manufacturer 475 238-8251
99 Commerce St East Haven CT (06512) ***(G-1245)***
CLC Bio LLC (PA) 617 945-0178
100 Cummings Ctr Ste 407j Beverly MA (01915) ***(G-8117)***
Clean Air Group Inc 203 335-3700
418 Meadow St Ste 204 Fairfield CT (06824) ***(G-1420)***
Clean Products LLC 508 676-9355
537 Quequechan St Fall River MA (02721) ***(G-10675)***
Clean Up Group 203 668-8323
82 Jodi Dr Meriden CT (06450) ***(G-2087)***
Cleanbasins Inc 978 670-5838
272 Rangeway Rd North Billerica MA (01862) ***(G-13802)***
Cleanbrands LLC 877 215-7378
240 Bald Hill Rd Warwick RI (02886) ***(G-21342)***
Cleaner Home Living, Hudson *Also called Butler Home Products LLC* ***(G-11761)***
Cleanpart-East, Southbridge *Also called Lsa Cleanpart LLC* ***(G 15393)***
Cleanrest, Warwick *Also called Cleanbrands LLC* ***(G-21342)***
Clear & Colored Coatings LLC (PA) 203 879-1379
222 Spindle Hill Rd Wolcott CT (06716) ***(G-5435)***
Clear Align LLC 603 889-2116
24 Simon St Nashua NH (03060) ***(G-19134)***
Clear Automation LLC 860 621-2955
85 Robert Porter Rd Southington CT (06489) ***(G-4044)***
Clear Carbon & Components Inc 401 254-5085
108 Tupelo St Bristol RI (02809) ***(G-20068)***
Clear Choice Inc 401 421-5275
40 Agnes St Providence RI (02909) ***(G-20985)***
Clear Water Manufacturing Corp (PA) 860 372-4907
900 Wells Rd Wethersfield CT (06109) ***(G-5245)***
Clearesult Consulting Inc 508 836-9500
50 Washington St Ste 3000 Westborough MA (01581) ***(G-16603)***
Clearh2o 207 221-0039
34 Danforth St Portland ME (04101) ***(G-6639)***
Clearly Clean Products LLC (PA) 860 646-1040
225 Oakland Rd Ste 401 South Windsor CT (06074) ***(G-3950)***
Clearmotion Inc 617 313-0822
400 Research Dr Wilmington MA (01887) ***(G-16987)***
Clearmotion Inc (PA) 617 313-0822
805 Middlesex Tpke Billerica MA (01821) ***(G-8231)***
Clearspan, South Windsor *Also called Engineering Services & Pdts Co* ***(G-3965)***
Clearway Software Corp 508 906-6333
266 Main St Ste 39 Medfield MA (02052) ***(G-12912)***
Cleco Manufacturing, Hudson *Also called Concrete Systems Inc* ***(G-18380)***
Clematis Machine & Fixture Co 781 894-0777
42 Clematis Ave Waltham MA (02453) ***(G-16069)***
Clement Machine Tool Co Inc 401 438-7248
30 Central Ave East Providence RI (02914) ***(G-20398)***
Clementia Pharmaceuticals USA 857 226-5588
275 Grove St Ste 2-400 Auburndale MA (02466) ***(G-7858)***
Clemson Sheet Metal LLC 860 871-9369
344 Somers Rd Unit 1 Vernon Rockville CT (06066) ***(G-4680)***
Clever Green Cabinets LLC 508 963-6776
738 Main St Waltham MA (02451) ***(G-16070)***
Cleverfoodies Inc 888 938-7984
70 S Winooski Ave Ste 141 Burlington VT (05401) ***(G-21775)***
Click Bond Inc 860 274-5435
18 Park Rd Watertown CT (06795) ***(G-5003)***
Client Server Engineering Svcs 617 338-7898
177 Tremont St Boston MA (02111) ***(G-8476)***
Clifford Lumber LLP 802 482-2325
24 Gardner Cir Hinesburg VT (05461) ***(G-22021)***
Cliflex Bellows Corporation 617 268-5774
45 W 3rd St Boston MA (02127) ***(G-8477)***
Cliggott Publishing, Darien *Also called Ubm LLC* ***(G-1035)***
Clinical Dynamics Conn LLC 203 269-0090
1210 Mrden Waterbury Tpke Plantsville CT (06479) ***(G-3528)***
Clinical Instruments Intl 781 221-2266
63 2nd Ave Burlington MA (01803) ***(G-9251)***
Clint S Custom Woodworkin 860 887-1476
628 River Rd Jewett City CT (06351) ***(G-1910)***
Clint Sales & Manufacturing 978 927-3010
117 Elliott St Ste 2 Beverly MA (01915) ***(G-8118)***
Clinton G Bradbury Inc 207 562-8014
1180 Route 2 Ste 5 Rumford ME (04276) ***(G-6833)***
Clinton Instrument Company 860 669-7548
295 E Main St Clinton CT (06413) ***(G-780)***
Clinton Nypro, Clinton *Also called Nypro Inc* ***(G-10086)***
Clio Designs Incorporated 781 449-9500
1000 Highland Ave Ste 2 Needham MA (02494) ***(G-13297)***
Clives Jams LLC 617 294-9766
32 Freeman Ave Everett MA (02149) ***(G-10606)***
Clivus Multrum Inc 978 725-5591
15 Union St Ste 412 Lawrence MA (01840) ***(G-12010)***
Clivus New England Inc 978 794-9400
60 Island St Ste 8 Lawrence MA (01840) ***(G-12011)***
Cloak & Dagger Creations 978 486-4414
61 Gilson Rd Littleton MA (01460) ***(G-12296)***
Clondalkin Pharma & Healthcare 860 342-1987
264 Freestone Ave Portland CT (06480) ***(G-3565)***
Cloodloc, Stamford *Also called Novatek Medical Inc* ***(G-4263)***
Cloos Woodworking Inc 401 528-8629
8 Alcazar Ave Johnston RI (02919) ***(G-20504)***
Clopay Corporation 203 230-9116
285 State St Ste 4 North Haven CT (06473) ***(G-3015)***
Clos De La Tech 508 648-2505
3 Judy Ann Dr East Falmouth MA (02536) ***(G-10439)***
Cloth N Canvas Recovery Inc 802 658-6826
354 Prim Rd Colchester VT (05446) ***(G-21859)***
Cloud Forest Solutions Inc 802 353-2848
4 Stoney Hill Rd Bondville VT (05340) ***(G-21697)***
Cloutier Sand & Gravel 603 636-1100
890 Northside Rd Stark NH (03582) ***(G-19859)***
Clover Hill Forest LLC 860 672-0394
20 Hurlburt Pl Cornwall CT (06753) ***(G-819)***
Cloverdale Cleaner, West Cornwall *Also called Cloverdale Inc* ***(G-5046)***
Cloverdale Inc 860 672-0216
5 Smith Pl West Cornwall CT (06796) ***(G-5046)***
Clozex Medical Inc 781 237-1673
36 Washington St Ste 220 Wellesley MA (02481) ***(G-16365)***
Clp Pb LLC 617 252-5213
53 State St Ste 9 Boston MA (02109) ***(G-8478)***
Clss, Concord *Also called Charles Leonard Steel Svcs LLC* ***(G-17893)***
Cly-Del Manufacturing Company 203 574-2100
151 Sharon Rd Waterbury CT (06705) ***(G-4859)***
Clypd Inc 617 800-9481
212 Elm St Ste 4 Somerville MA (02144) ***(G-15166)***
CM Almy & Son Inc 207 487-3232
133 Ruth St Pittsfield ME (04967) ***(G-6589)***
CM Bedding Group Inc 508 673-1001
451 Quarry St Fall River MA (02723) ***(G-10676)***
CM Labs, Scarborough *Also called GM Specialties Inc* ***(G-6922)***

ALPHABETIC

CM Murphy Welding Inc 508 868-8511
75 Lakeside Ave Webster MA (01570) ***(G-16340)***
CM Publications Inc 401 596-9358
6 Bayview Dr Westerly RI (02891) ***(G-21519)***
CM Technology, North Reading *Also called Creative Motion Technology* ***(G-13981)***
CMC, Newton *Also called Collaborative Med Concept LLC* ***(G-13581)***
Cmd Logging 603 986-5055
520 N Barnstead Rd Center Barnstead NH (03225) ***(G-17788)***
Cme, North Adams *Also called Cordmaster Engineering Co Inc* ***(G-13671)***
CMI, Attleboro *Also called Composite Modules* ***(G-7723)***
CMI, Ayer *Also called Creative Materials Inc* ***(G-7916)***
CMI, East Weymouth *Also called Cutlass Marine Inc* ***(G-10540)***
CMI Specialty Products Inc 860 585-0409
105 Redstone Hill Rd Bristol CT (06010) ***(G-542)***
Cmio Magazine Publications 617 851-6671
152 Washington St Newton MA (02458) ***(G-13580)***
Cml Services Inc 207 772-5032
35 Bradley Dr Stop 1 Westbrook ME (04092) ***(G-7184)***
Cmn Enterprises, Tilton *Also called Yesco Sign and Ltg Concord* ***(G-19913)***
Cmp, Woburn *Also called Continental Metal Pdts Co Inc* ***(G-17151)***
CMS, Nashua *Also called Custom Manufacturing Svcs Inc* ***(G-19141)***
CMS Enterprise Inc 508 995-2372
255 Popes Is New Bedford MA (02740) ***(G-13371)***
Cmsr Services LLC 774 210-2513
482 Southbridge St Ste 3 Auburn MA (01501) ***(G-7831)***
Cmt Filters Inc 508 258-6400
400 Nickerson Rd Marlborough MA (01752) ***(G-12738)***
Cmt Materials Inc 508 226-3901
107 Frank Mossberg Dr Attleboro MA (02703) ***(G-7721)***
Cmyk Print Services 207 228-3838
49 Woodspell Rd Scarborough ME (04074) ***(G-6914)***
CN Brown Company 207 892-5955
357 Roosevelt Trl Windham ME (04062) ***(G-7231)***
CN Custom Cabinets Inc 978 300-5531
365 Main St Townsend MA (01469) ***(G-15870)***
Cnc Design & Counsulting LLC 603 686-5437
63 Route 125 Ste 4 Kingston NH (03848) ***(G-18542)***
CNc International Ltd Partnr 401 769-6100
20 Privilege St Woonsocket RI (02895) ***(G-21556)***
Cnc Mill Specs, Haverhill *Also called Dustin W Ciampa* ***(G-11427)***
Cnc North Inc 603 542-3361
16 Industrial Blvd Claremont NH (03743) ***(G-17842)***
Cnc Specialties Inc 413 267-5051
85 Bethany Rd Monson MA (01057) ***(G-13204)***
CNE Machine Company 508 668-4110
2000 Main St Ste 7 Walpole MA (02081) ***(G-15991)***
Cnh Technologies Inc 781 933-0362
10a Henshaw St Woburn MA (01801) ***(G-17145)***
CNi Corp 603 249-5075
468 Route 13 S Ste A Milford NH (03055) ***(G-19050)***
Cns Outdoor Technologies LLC 413 475-3840
627 Barton Rd Greenfield MA (01301) ***(G-11254)***
Co Op Creamery 802 524-6581
140 Federal St Saint Albans VT (05478) ***(G-22365)***
Co Press 413 525-6686
388 Chapin St Ludlow MA (01056) ***(G-12459)***
Co-Op Printing, Ludlow *Also called Co Press* ***(G-12459)***
Coach Inc 203 372-0208
5065 Main St Ste P2114 Trumbull CT (06611) ***(G-4619)***
Coach Leatherware, Lee *Also called Tapestry Inc* ***(G-12096)***
Coast Maine Organic Pdts Inc (PA) 207 879-0002
145 Newbury St Fl 3 Portland ME (04101) ***(G-6640)***
Coast of Maine, Inc., Portland *Also called Coast Maine Organic Pdts Inc* ***(G-6640)***
Coast To Coast Ff & E Installa 603 433-0164
2 Spring Hill Rd Greenland NH (03840) ***(G-18222)***
Coastal Aquacultural Supply 401 467-9370
100 Glen Rd Cranston RI (02920) ***(G-20197)***
Coastal Extreme Brewing Co LLC 401 849-5232
293 Jt Connell Rd Newport RI (02840) ***(G-20660)***
Coastal Group Inc 860 452-4148
145 Chestnut Hill Rd Killingworth CT (06419) ***(G-1925)***
Coastal Image Inc 508 430-7870
129 Queen Anne Rd Harwich MA (02645) ***(G-11391)***
Coastal Industrial Distrs 207 286-3319
6 Willey Rd Saco ME (04072) ***(G-6845)***
Coastal Industries Inc 978 373-1543
77 Newark St Haverhill MA (01832) ***(G-11418)***
Coastal Inflatables LLC 603 490-7606
16 Swampscott St Newmarket NH (03857) ***(G-19332)***
Coastal N Counters Inc 508 539-3500
92 Industrial Dr Mashpee MA (02649) ***(G-12879)***
Coastal Pallet Corporation 203 333-1892
135 E Washington Ave Bridgeport CT (06604) ***(G-398)***
Coastal Plastics Inc 401 539-2446
35 Mechanic St Hope Valley RI (02832) ***(G-20482)***
Coastal Printing, Newburyport *Also called Harborside Printing Co Inc* ***(G-13495)***
Coastal Seafoods Inc (PA) 203 431-0453
35 Brentwood Ave Ste 4 Fairfield CT (06825) ***(G-1421)***
Coastal Steel Corporation 860 443-4073
10 Mallard Ln Waterford CT (06385) ***(G-4982)***
Coastal T Shirts Inc 207 784-4184
205 Washington St S Auburn ME (04210) ***(G-5553)***
Coastal Tooling, Killingworth *Also called Coastal Group Inc* ***(G-1925)***
Coastal Woodworking Inc 207 563-1072
16 Sand Hill Dr Nobleboro ME (04555) ***(G-6492)***
Coastal Woodworks & Display, Nobleboro *Also called Coastal Woodworking Inc* ***(G-6492)***
Coaters Inc 508 996-5700
305 Nash Rd Unit 1 New Bedford MA (02746) ***(G-13372)***
Coating Application Tech 781 491-0699
219 New Boston St Woburn MA (01801) ***(G-17146)***
Coating Design Group Inc 203 878-3663
430 Sniffens Ln Stratford CT (06615) ***(G-4405)***
Coating Systems Inc 978 937-3712
90 Phoenix Ave Lowell MA (01852) ***(G-12359)***
Coatings Adhesives Inks 978 352-7273
7 Martel Way Georgetown MA (01833) ***(G-11140)***
Coatings and Coverings 774 237-0882
4 Jilfrey Way Harwich MA (02645) ***(G-11392)***
Cobal-USA Altrnative Fuels LLC 203 751-1974
40 James St Ansonia CT (06401) ***(G-10)***
Cobb Lumber Inc 802 824-5228
1683 Springhill Rd South Londonderry VT (05155) ***(G-22484)***
Cobb/Ballou Findings, East Providence *Also called W R Cobb Company* ***(G-20448)***
Cobble Mountain Inc 802 439-5232
1051 Village Rd East Corinth VT (05040) ***(G-21913)***
Cobham 603 418-9786
32 Industrial Dr Exeter NH (03833) ***(G-18116)***
Cobham Antenna Systems, Exeter *Also called Cobham* ***(G-18116)***
Cobham Exeter Inc 603 775-5200
11 Continental Dr Exeter NH (03833) ***(G-18117)***
Cobham Metelics, Londonderry *Also called Macom Tech Sltons Holdings Inc* ***(G-18716)***
Cobra Powder Coating 207 391-3060
29 Stagecoach Rd Lyman ME (04002) ***(G-6388)***
Cobra Precision Machining Corp 603 434-8424
3 Craneway Hooksett NH (03106) ***(G-18347)***
Cobra Precision Products Inc 401 766-3333
2131 Providence Pike North Smithfield RI (02896) ***(G-20784)***
Coburn Technologies Inc (PA) 860 648-6600
83 Gerber Rd W South Windsor CT (06074) ***(G-3951)***
Coca Cola Btlg Co of Cape Cod 508 888-0001
370 Route 130 Sandwich MA (02563) ***(G-14964)***
Coca-Cola, Sandwich *Also called Coca Cola Btlg Co of Cape Cod* ***(G-14964)***
Coca-Cola, Farmington *Also called Farmington Coca Cola Btlg Dstr* ***(G-6047)***
Coca-Cola, South Portland *Also called Maine Soft Drink Association* ***(G-7032)***
Coca-Cola Bottling Company 603 623-6033
99 Eddy Rd Manchester NH (03102) ***(G-18800)***
Coca-Cola Bottling Company 207 942-5546
91 Dowd Rd Bangor ME (04401) ***(G-5637)***
Coca-Cola Bottling Company 508 888-0001
370 Route 130 Sandwich MA (02563) ***(G-14965)***
Coca-Cola Bottling Company 603 926-0404
118 Stard Rd Seabrook NH (03874) ***(G-19796)***
Coca-Cola Bottling Company 802 654-3800
733 Hercules Dr Colchester VT (05446) ***(G-21860)***
Coca-Cola Bottling Company 603 437-3530
7 Symmes Dr Londonderry NH (03053) ***(G-18685)***
Coca-Cola Bottling Company 603 267-8834
495 Depot St Belmont NH (03220) ***(G-17672)***
Coca-Cola Bottling Company 207 773-5505
316 Western Ave South Portland ME (04106) ***(G-7020)***
Coca-Cola Bottling Company 978 459-9378
160 Industrial Ave E Lowell MA (01852) ***(G-12360)***
Coca-Cola Bottling Company 207 764-4481
1005 Airport Dr Presque Isle ME (04769) ***(G-6756)***
Coca-Cola Company 860 443-2816
150 Parkway S Waterford CT (06385) ***(G-4983)***
Coca-Cola Refreshments USA Inc 401 331-1981
95 Pleasant Valley Pkwy Providence RI (02908) ***(G-20986)***
Coca-Cola Refreshments USA Inc 413 586-8450
45 Industrial Dr Northampton MA (01060) ***(G-13999)***
Coca-Cola Refreshments USA Inc 413 772-2617
180 Silvio O Conte Dr Greenfield MA (01301) ***(G-11255)***
Cocchia Norwalk Grape Co 203 855-7911
25 Ely Ave Norwalk CT (06854) ***(G-3127)***
Coccomo Brothers Drilling LLC 860 828-1632
1897 Berlin Tpke Berlin CT (06037) ***(G-81)***
Cochin Rubbers Intl LLC (PA) 877 289-0364
241 Francis Ave Mansfield MA (02048) ***(G-12618)***
Cocofuel 401 209-8099
39 Ashburton Dr Cranston RI (02921) ***(G-20198)***
Cocomama Foods Inc 978 621-2126
406 W 1st St Boston MA (02127) ***(G-8479)***
Coddington Brewing Co, Middletown *Also called D & H Inc* ***(G-20618)***
Code Briefcase 603 487-2381
77 Beard Rd New Boston NH (03070) ***(G-19292)***
Codebridge Software Inc 203 535-0517
91 Honor Rd West Haven CT (06516) ***(G-5111)***

Codet-Newport Corporation (HQ)........802 334-5811
294 Crawford Rd Newport VT (05855) ***(G-22192)***
Codling Brothers Logging........802 454-7177
1165 Maple Hill Rd Plainfield VT (05667) ***(G-22266)***
Cody Brewing Company........978 387-4329
36 Main St Ste 4 Amesbury MA (01913) ***(G-7482)***
Coelho Fuel Inc........978 458-8252
493 Princeton Blvd Lowell MA (01851) ***(G-12361)***
Coffee News USA Inc (PA)........207 941-0860
1 Cumberland Pl Ste 102 Bangor ME (04401) ***(G-5638)***
Cogent Engineering Inc........978 977-3310
119 Foster St Bldg 8 Peabody MA (01960) ***(G-14321)***
Cogent Mfg Solutions LLC........603 898-3212
115 Fieldstone Ln Atkinson NH (03811) ***(G-17603)***
Coghlin Companies Inc (PA)........508 753-2354
27 Otis St Westborough MA (01581) ***(G-16604)***
Cognex Corporation (PA)........508 650-3000
1 Vision Dr Natick MA (01760) ***(G-13246)***
Cognex Corporation........508 650-3044
801 Worcester St Natick MA (01760) ***(G-13247)***
Cognex Germany Inc........508 650-3000
1 Vision Dr Natick MA (01760) ***(G-13248)***
Cognex International Inc (HQ)........508 650-3000
1 Vision Dr Natick MA (01760) ***(G-13249)***
Cogniscent Inc........508 863-0069
410 Concord Rd Weston MA (02493) ***(G-16824)***
Cognoptix Inc........978 263-0005
100 Main St Ste 110 Concord MA (01742) ***(G-10121)***
Cogworks Ltd........603 588-3333
10 Water St Antrim NH (03440) ***(G-17594)***
Cogz Systems LLC........203 263-7882
58 Steeple View Ln Woodbury CT (06798) ***(G-5484)***
Cohasa Publishing Inc........802 222-5281
Rr 5 Bradford VT (05033) ***(G-21699)***
Cohasset Sports Complex........781 383-0278
34 Crocker Ln Cohasset MA (02025) ***(G-10096)***
Cohens United Baking Inc........508 754-0232
26 Washburn St Worcester MA (01610) ***(G-17357)***
Coherent Inc........860 243-9557
1280 Blue Hills Ave Ste A Bloomfield CT (06002) ***(G-215)***
Coherent Inc........603 685-0900
32 Hampshire Rd Salem NH (03079) ***(G-19716)***
Coherent Bloomfield, Bloomfield *Also called Coherent Inc* ***(G-215)***
Coherent Salem, Salem *Also called Coherent Inc* ***(G-19716)***
Coherent-Deos LLC........860 243-9557
1280 Blue Hills Ave Ste A Bloomfield CT (06002) ***(G-216)***
Cohesion, Andover *Also called Nsight Inc* ***(G-7579)***
Cohesive Biotechnologies, Franklin *Also called Cohesive Technologies Inc* ***(G-11028)***
Cohesive Technologies Inc (HQ)........508 528-7989
101 Constitution Blvd F Franklin MA (02038) ***(G-11028)***
Cohos Counters LLC........603 788-4928
272 Main St Lancaster NH (03584) ***(G-18599)***
Coils Plus Inc........203 879-0755
30 Town Line Rd Wolcott CT (06716) ***(G-5436)***
Col-Lar Enterprises Inc (PA)........203 798-1786
37 S End Plz New Milford CT (06776) ***(G-2793)***
Colburntreat LLC........802 654-8603
276 E Allen St Ste 5 Winooski VT (05404) ***(G-22719)***
Colby Footwear Inc........603 332-2283
364 Route 108 Somersworth NH (03878) ***(G-19830)***
Colchester Bulletin Bulletin, Norwich *Also called Gatehouse Media Conn Holdings* ***(G-3281)***
Colcord Machine Co Inc........508 634-8840
2 Rosenfeld Dr Ste G Hopedale MA (01747) ***(G-11670)***
Cold Atlantic Seafood Inc........508 996-3352
38 Bethel St New Bedford MA (02740) ***(G-13373)***
Cold Brew Coffee Company LLC........860 250-4410
27 E Ridge Ct Cheshire CT (06410) ***(G-723)***
Cold Brook Energy, Hermon *Also called Dysarts* ***(G-6185)***
Cold Chain Technologies Inc........508 429-1395
135 Constitution Blvd Franklin MA (02038) ***(G-11029)***
Cold Chain Technologies Inc (PA)........508 429-1395
135 Constitution Blvd Franklin MA (02038) ***(G-11030)***
Cold Corners Mapleworks LLC........802 551-2270
2893 North Rd Fairfield VT (05455) ***(G-21984)***
Cold Hollow Precision Inc........802 933-5542
154 Butternut Hollow Rd Enosburg Falls VT (05450) ***(G-21923)***
Cold River Furniture, South Acworth *Also called Maynard & Maynard Furn Makers* ***(G-19853)***
Cold River Logging LLC........860 334-9506
195 Tuckie Rd North Windham CT (06256) ***(G-3080)***
Cold River Materials, East Swanzey *Also called Lane Construction Corporation* ***(G-18093)***
Cold River Mining Inc........413 219-3315
246 Silver St Greenfield MA (01301) ***(G-11256)***
Cold River Mining Inc........413 863-5445
17 Masonic Ave Turners Falls MA (01376) ***(G-15876)***
Cold River Stitching LLC........207 515-0039
89 Lovell Rd Fryeburg ME (04037) ***(G-6096)***
Coldstash Inc........617 780-5603
879 Hopkins Hill Rd West Greenwich RI (02817) ***(G-21453)***
Coldtub, West Harwich *Also called Arctic Holdings LLC* ***(G-16480)***
Cole Cabinet Co Inc........401 467-4343
530 Wellington Ave Cranston RI (02910) ***(G-20199)***
Cole S Crew Machine Products........203 723-1418
69 Dodge Ave North Haven CT (06473) ***(G-3016)***
Cole Sign Co........978 851-5502
1615 Shawsheen St Ste 5 Tewksbury MA (01876) ***(G-15811)***
Coleman Concrete Inc........603 447-5936
9 Nh Route 113 Albany NH (03818) ***(G-17536)***
Coleman Concrete Division, Albany *Also called Alvin J Coleman & Son Inc* ***(G-17534)***
Coleman Drilling & Blasting........860 376-3813
1458 Hopeville Rd Voluntown CT (06384) ***(G-4690)***
Coleman Manufacturing Co Inc........617 389-0380
48 Waters Ave Everett MA (02149) ***(G-10607)***
Coley Pharmaceutical Group Inc........781 431-9000
93 Worcester St Ste 101 Wellesley MA (02481) ***(G-16366)***
Colin Bartlett & Sons Inc........207 532-2214
592 Us Route One Amity ME (04471) ***(G-5523)***
Collaborative Med Concept LLC........603 494-6056
43 Ruane Rd Newton MA (02465) ***(G-13581)***
Collabric........207 945-5095
1017 School St Veazie ME (04401) ***(G-7126)***
Collagen Medical LLC........857 928-8817
23 Oak St Belmont MA (02478) ***(G-8070)***
Collegiate House, Medford *Also called Collegiate Uniforms Inc* ***(G-12927)***
Collegiate Uniforms Inc........781 219-4952
970 Fellsway Ste 1 Medford MA (02155) ***(G-12927)***
Collegium Pharmaceutical Inc........781 713-3699
100 Technology Center Dr # 300 Stoughton MA (02072) ***(G-15584)***
Collins Compost........860 749-3416
11 Powder Hill Rd Enfield CT (06082) ***(G-1350)***
Collins Lighting & Assoc LLC........603 893-1106
17 Dawn St Salem NH (03079) ***(G-19717)***
Collins Manufacturing Inc........978 768-2553
239 Western Ave Essex MA (01929) ***(G-10592)***
Collins Pattern & Mold, Fremont *Also called Robert A Collins* ***(G-18180)***
Collins Precision Machining........603 882-2474
55 Lake St Ste 7 Nashua NH (03060) ***(G-19135)***
Collins Sheet Metal Inc........207 384-4428
510 Portland St Berwick ME (03901) ***(G-5708)***
Colloidal Science Solutions........401 826-3641
1454 Main St Ste 24 West Warwick RI (02893) ***(G-21487)***
Collt Mfg Inc........508 376-2525
1375 Main St Millis MA (02054) ***(G-13183)***
Colonial Blacksmith........508 420-5326
5 Christina Ln Sandwich MA (02563) ***(G-14966)***
Colonial Brass Company........508 947-1098
42 Connie St Taunton MA (02780) ***(G-15737)***
Colonial Bronze Company........860 489-9233
511 Winsted Rd Torrington CT (06790) ***(G-4570)***
Colonial Coatings Inc........203 783-9933
66 Erna Ave Milford CT (06461) ***(G-2265)***
Colonial Corrugated Pdts Inc........203 597-1707
118 Railroad Hill St Waterbury CT (06708) ***(G-4860)***
Colonial Cutlery Intl Inc........401 737-0024
606 Ten Rod Rd North Kingstown RI (02852) ***(G-20697)***
Colonial Electronic Mfrs Inc........603 881-8244
1 Chestnut St Ste 203 Nashua NH (03060) ***(G-19136)***
Colonial Engravers, Salem *Also called Colonial Key & Engraving* ***(G-14902)***
Colonial Green Products LLC........207 614-6660
Airport Plaza Mall 1725 5 Airport Plaza Mall Sanford ME (04073) ***(G-6872)***
Colonial Green Products LLC (PA)........603 532-7005
1032 Nh Route 119 Unit 6 Rindge NH (03461) ***(G-19648)***
Colonial Iron Shop Inc........860 763-0659
15 Dust House Rd Enfield CT (06082) ***(G-1351)***
Colonial Key & Engraving........978 745-8237
1 Florence St Ste 2 Salem MA (01970) ***(G-14902)***
Colonial Knife Company, North Kingstown *Also called Colonial Cutlery Intl Inc* ***(G-20697)***
Colonial Landscape Corp........978 448-3329
66 North St Groton MA (01450) ***(G-11287)***
Colonial Lithograph Inc........508 222-1832
129 Bank St Ste 5 Attleboro MA (02703) ***(G-7722)***
Colonial Machine & Tool Co Inc........401 826-1883
5 Salvas Ave Coventry RI (02816) ***(G-20142)***
Colonial Machine Company........781 233-0026
16 Albert Rd Peabody MA (01960) ***(G-14322)***
Colonial Marble Co Inc........617 389-1130
25 Garvey St Everett MA (02149) ***(G-10608)***
Colonial Medical Supply Co Inc........603 328-5130
31 Lowell Rd Unit 6 Windham NH (03087) ***(G-20002)***
Colonial Mills Inc........401 724-6279
77 Pawtucket Ave Rumford RI (02916) ***(G-21183)***
Colonial Ornamental Iron Works........978 531-1474
77 Walnut St Ste 3 Peabody MA (01960) ***(G-14323)***
Colonial Print & Imaging, Old Greenwich *Also called Clanol Systems Inc* ***(G-3306)***
Colonial Printers of Windsor........860 627-5433
1 Concorde Way Windsor Locks CT (06096) ***(G-5389)***
Colonial Printing Inc (PA)........401 691-3400
333 Strawberry Field Rd # 11 Warwick RI (02886) ***(G-21343)***
Colonial Printing Inc........401 367-6690
176 Broadway Newport RI (02840) ***(G-20661)***

ALPHABETIC

Colonial Spring Company, Bristol *Also called Triple A Spring Ltd Partnr* ***(G-620)***
Colonial Stone Yard, Groton *Also called Colonial Landscape Corp* ***(G-11287)***
Colonial Times Publishing......781 274-9997
805 Massachusetts Ave Lexington MA (02420) ***(G-12212)***
Colonial Village Refinishing......781 740-8844
165 Beal St Hingham MA (02043) ***(G-11496)***
Colonial Welding Service, Torrington *Also called Thomas La Ganga* ***(G-4601)***
Colonial Wood Products Inc......203 932-9003
250 Callegari Dr West Haven CT (06516) ***(G-5112)***
Colonial Woodworking Inc......603 938-5131
65 Main St Bradford NH (03221) ***(G-17741)***
Colonial Woodworking Inc......203 866-5844
145 Water St Norwalk CT (06854) ***(G-3128)***
Colonic Connection......603 924-4449
77 Hancock Rd Ste C Peterborough NH (03458) ***(G-19470)***
Coloniel Printing, Manchester *Also called Boles Enterprises Inc* ***(G-18789)***
Colony Casket Inc......401 831-7100
50 Curtis St Providence RI (02909) ***(G-20987)***
Color Change Technology Inc......978 377-0050
30 Massachusetts Ave North Andover MA (01845) ***(G-13695)***
Color Craft Ltd......800 509-6563
14 Airport Park Rd East Granby CT (06026) ***(G-1121)***
Color Film Media Group LLC (PA)......203 202-2929
45 Keeler Ave Norwalk CT (06854) ***(G-3129)***
Color Images Inc......978 688-4994
99 West St Methuen MA (01844) ***(G-13015)***
Color Media Group LLC......617 620-0229
4 Copley Pl Ste 120 Boston MA (02116) ***(G-8480)***
Colorgraphix LLC......203 264-5212
91 Willenbrock Rd Ste B5 Oxford CT (06478) ***(G-3397)***
Colormark Inc......603 595-2244
25 Progress Ave Ste A Nashua NH (03062) ***(G-19137)***
Colors Ink......203 269-4000
40 Capital Dr Wallingford CT (06492) ***(G-4722)***
Colt Defense Holding, West Hartford *Also called Colt Defense LLC* ***(G-5060)***
Colt Defense LLC (HQ)......860 232-4489
547 New Park Ave West Hartford CT (06110) ***(G-5060)***
Colt Heel Div Montello Heel, Brockton *Also called Montello Heel Mfg Inc* ***(G-9167)***
Colt Refining Inc (PA)......603 429-9966
12a Star Dr Merrimack NH (03054) ***(G-18993)***
Colton Enterprises Inc......802 746-8033
1697 Rte 100 Pittsfield VT (05762) ***(G-22262)***
Colton Hollow Candle Company......413 267-3986
101 Wilbraham Rd Monson MA (01057) ***(G-13205)***
Colts Manufacturing Co LLC (HQ)......860 236-6311
547 New Park Ave West Hartford CT (06110) ***(G-5061)***
Colts Plastics Company Inc......860 774-2277
969 N Main St Dayville CT (06241) ***(G-1042)***
Colucid Pharmaceuticals Inc......857 285-6495
222 3rd St Ste 1320 Cambridge MA (02142) ***(G-9439)***
Columbia ASC Inc......978 683-2205
165 S Broadway Ste 167 Lawrence MA (01843) ***(G-12012)***
Columbia Electrical Contrs Inc......508 366-8297
27 Otis St Ste 300 Westborough MA (01581) ***(G-16605)***
Columbia Forest Products Inc......207 760-3800
395 Missile St Presque Isle ME (04769) ***(G-6757)***
Columbia Forest Products Inc......802 334-6711
115 Columbia Way Newport VT (05855) ***(G-22193)***
Columbia Forest Products Inc......802 334-3600
324 Bluff Rd Newport VT (05855) ***(G-22194)***
Columbia Manufacturing Inc......860 228-2259
165 Route 66 E Columbia CT (06237) ***(G-817)***
Columbia Manufacturing Inc......413 562-3664
1 Cycle St Westfield MA (01085) ***(G-16679)***
Columbia Tech, Westborough *Also called Coghlin Companies Inc* ***(G-16604)***
Columbia Tech, Westborough *Also called Columbia Electrical Contrs Inc* ***(G-16605)***
Comanche Clean Energy Corp......203 326-4570
1 Dock St Ste 101 Stamford CT (06902) ***(G-4167)***
Comark LLC (PA)......508 359-8161
440 Fortune Blvd Milford MA (01757) ***(G-13110)***
Combat Weapons Development LLC......603 978-0244
322 Circle Rd Manchester NH (03103) ***(G-18801)***
Comdec Incorporated......978 462-3399
25 Hale St Newburyport MA (01950) ***(G-13478)***
Comengs Inc......203 792-7306
5 Shelter Rock Rd Ste 7 Danbury CT (06810) ***(G-889)***
Comet Technologies USA Inc (HQ)......203 447-3200
100 Trap Falls Road Ext Shelton CT (06484) ***(G-3790)***
Comex Machinery......203 334-2196
145 Front St Bridgeport CT (06606) ***(G-399)***
Comfortable Environments......203 876-2140
11 Terrell Dr Milford CT (06461) ***(G-2266)***
Comicana Inc......203 968-0748
61 Studio Rd Stamford CT (06903) ***(G-4168)***
Command Chemical Corporation......203 319-1857
2490 Black Rock Tpke # 359 Fairfield CT (06825) ***(G-1422)***
Command Corporation......800 851-6012
59 Rainbow Rd East Granby CT (06026) ***(G-1122)***
Commerce Connect Media Inc......800 547-7377
830 Post Rd E Fl 2 Westport CT (06880) ***(G-5184)***
Commercial Fisheries News, Deer Isle *Also called Compass Publications Inc* ***(G-5947)***
Commercial Gear Sprocket Inc......508 668-1073
618 Washington St East Walpole MA (02032) ***(G-10522)***
Commercial Machine Inc......413 583-3670
305 Moody St Ste B Ludlow MA (01056) ***(G-12460)***
Commercial Screenprint EMB Inc......207 942-2862
130 Thatcher St Bangor ME (04401) ***(G-5639)***
Commercial Sewing Inc......860 482-5509
65 Grant St Torrington CT (06790) ***(G-4571)***
Common Crossing Inc......508 822-8225
11 N Main St Berkley MA (02779) ***(G-8084)***
Common Sense Engineered Pdts......203 888-8695
164 Pines Bridge Rd Beacon Falls CT (06403) ***(G-56)***
Common Sense Marketing......603 763-2441
9 Central St Sunapee NH (03782) ***(G-19880)***
Common Sense Real Estate Guide, Sunapee *Also called Common Sense Marketing* ***(G-19880)***
COMMONS, THE, Brattleboro *Also called Vermont Independent Media Inc* ***(G-21751)***
Commonwealth Biofuel......978 881-0478
77 Parker St Newburyport MA (01950) ***(G-13479)***
Commonwealth Editions, Beverly *Also called Memoirs Unlimited Inc* ***(G-8151)***
Commonwealth Fuel Corp......617 884-5444
281 Eastern Ave Waltham MA (02451) ***(G-16071)***
Commonwealth Liquids LLC......508 676-9355
537 Quequechan St Fall River MA (02721) ***(G-10677)***
Commonwealth Packaging Corp......413 593-1482
1146 Sheridan St Chicopee MA (01022) ***(G-10015)***
Commonwlth Soap Toiletries Inc (PA)......508 676-9355
537 Quequechan St Fall River MA (02721) ***(G-10678)***
Commonwlth Ventr Funding Group (PA)......781 684-0095
391 Totten Pond Rd # 402 Waltham MA (02451) ***(G-16072)***
Commscope Technologies LLC......203 699-4100
33 Union City Rd Ste 2 Prospect CT (06712) ***(G-3585)***
Commtank Cares Inc......781 224-1021
84 New Salem St Wakefield MA (01880) ***(G-15946)***
Communction Cmpnent Flters Inc (PA)......603 294-4685
145 Batchelder Rd Seabrook NH (03874) ***(G-19797)***
Communication Ink Inc......978 977-4595
140 Summit St Peabody MA (01960) ***(G-14324)***
Communication Networks LLC......203 796-5300
3 Corporate Dr Danbury CT (06810) ***(G-890)***
Communications & Pwr Inds LLC......978 922-6000
150 Sohier Rd Beverly MA (01915) ***(G-8119)***
Community Advertiser......207 582-8486
20 Peter Path Farmingdale ME (04344) ***(G-6038)***
Community Advocate, Westborough *Also called Bagdon Advertising Inc* ***(G-16592)***
Community Brands Holdings LLC......203 227-1255
180 Post Rd E Ste 200 Westport CT (06880) ***(G-5185)***
Community Newspaper, Beverly *Also called Gatehouse Media Mass I Inc* ***(G-8135)***
Community Newspaper, Chelmsford *Also called Gatehouse Media Mass I Inc* ***(G-9902)***
Community Newspaper......508 339-8977
5 Cohannat St Framingham MA (01701) ***(G-10935)***
Community Newspaper Company, Concord *Also called Lancaster Times Inc* ***(G-10137)***
Community Newspaper Company......508 721-5600
475 Washington St Auburn MA (01501) ***(G-7832)***
Community Newspaper Inc......781 639-4800
122 Washington St Marblehead MA (01945) ***(G-12679)***
Community of Jesus Inc (PA)......508 255-1094
5 Bay View Dr Orleans MA (02653) ***(G-14232)***
Community Shopper, Worcester *Also called Worcester Tlegram Gazette Corp* ***(G-17507)***
Comnav Engineering Inc......207 221-8524
430 Riverside St Portland ME (04103) ***(G-6641)***
Companion Industries Inc......860 628-0504
891 W Queen St Southington CT (06489) ***(G-4045)***
Company of Coca-Cola Bottling......781 672-8624
80 2nd Ave Waltham MA (02451) ***(G-16073)***
Company of Coca-Cola Bottling......617 622-5400
275 Wyman St Waltham MA (02451) ***(G-16074)***
Company of Coca-Cola Bottling......508 836-5200
2 Sassacus Dr Westborough MA (01581) ***(G-16606)***
Company of Coca-Cola Bottling......860 569-0037
471 Main St 471 # 471 East Hartford CT (06118) ***(G-1183)***
Company of Coca-Cola Bottling......413 448-8296
180 Silvio O Conte Dr Greenfield MA (01301) ***(G-11257)***
Company of Coca-Cola Bottling......203 905-3900
333 Ludlow St Ste 8 Stamford CT (06902) ***(G-4169)***
Company of Coca-Cola Bottling......781 449-4300
9 B St Needham Heights MA (02494) ***(G-13322)***
Company of Coca-Cola Bottling......413 586-8450
45 Industrial Dr Northampton MA (01060) ***(G-14000)***
Company of Craftsmen......860 536-4189
43 W Main St Mystic CT (06355) ***(G-2436)***
Companystuffcom Inc......978 282-1525
45 S Main St Ipswich MA (01938) ***(G-11913)***
Compass Company......978 635-0303
13 Gioconda Ave Acton MA (01720) ***(G-7348)***

Compass Publications Inc 207 348-1057
161 Perez Xrd Deer Isle ME (04627) ***(G-5947)***
Competition Engineering Inc 203 453-5200
80 Carter Dr Guilford CT (06437) ***(G-1697)***
Competitive Edge Coatings LLC 860 882-0762
185 Nutmeg Rd S South Windsor CT (06074) ***(G-3952)***
Complete Cvrage Wodpriming LLC 603 485-1122
288 Pinewood Rd Allenstown NH (03275) ***(G-17538)***
Complete Welding Services 781 837-9024
1235 Main St Marshfield MA (02050) ***(G-12858)***
Complex Mold & Machine 603 536-1221
1137 Route 175 Plymouth NH (03264) ***(G-19528)***
Component Concepts Inc 860 523-4066
26 Hammick Rd West Hartford CT (06107) ***(G-5062)***
Component Engineers Inc 203 269-0557
108 N Plains Indus Rd Wallingford CT (06492) ***(G-4723)***
Component Hndng Inspctn Pckn 978 535-3997
83 Pine St Ste 13 Peabody MA (01960) ***(G-14325)***
Component Sources Intl 508 986-2300
121 Flanders Rd Westborough MA (01581) ***(G-16607)***
Component Technologies Corpora 401 965-2699
14 Grizwald Ave Barrington RI (02806) ***(G-20044)***
Component Technologies Inc (PA) 860 667-1065
68 Holmes Rd Newington CT (06111) ***(G-2855)***
Components Division, Bristol *Also called Freudenberg-Nok General Partnr* ***(G-17764)***
Components For Mfg LLC (PA) 860 245-5326
800 Flanders Rd Unit 3-5 Mystic CT (06355) ***(G-2437)***
Components For Mfg LLC 860 572-1671
26 High St Groton CT (06340) ***(G-1668)***
Composimold 888 281-2674
903 Western Ave Manchester ME (04351) ***(G-6408)***
Composite Company Inc 508 651-1681
19 Kendall Ave Sherborn MA (01770) ***(G-15078)***
Composite Energy Tech Inc 401 253-2670
52 Ballou Blvd Bristol RI (02809) ***(G-20069)***
Composite Engineering Inc 978 371-3132
277 Baker Ave Concord MA (01742) ***(G-10122)***
Composite McHining Experts LLC 203 624-0664
222 Universal Dr Bldg 1 North Haven CT (06473) ***(G-3017)***
Composite Modules 508 226-6969
61 Union St Attleboro MA (02703) ***(G-7723)***
Compost Plant L3c 401 644-6179
21 Mount Hope Ave Providence RI (02906) ***(G-20988)***
Compost Plant, The, Providence *Also called Compost Plant L3c* ***(G-20988)***
Compound Manufacturing LLC 413 773-8909
43 Warner St Greenfield MA (01301) ***(G-11258)***
COMPOUNDING SOLUTIONS, Lewiston *Also called Neal Specialty Compounding LLC* ***(G-6309)***
Compressor Energy Services LLC 603 491-2200
49 Church Rd Bedford NH (03110) ***(G-17636)***
Comprhnsive Prsthetic Svcs LLC 203 315-1400
21 Business Park Dr Branford CT (06405) ***(G-305)***
Compton Paper & Novelty, Harrisville *Also called Desnoyers Enterprises Inc* ***(G-20478)***
Comptronics, Waltham *Also called A B & D Machining Inc* ***(G-16019)***
Comptus, Thornton *Also called Beta Acquisition Inc* ***(G-19900)***
Compu Signs, Lebanon *Also called Valley Signs* ***(G-18640)***
Compu-Gard Inc 508 679-8845
1432 Gar Hwy Swansea MA (02777) ***(G-15703)***
Compu-Signs LLC 860 747-1985
105 E Main St Plainville CT (06062) ***(G-3474)***
Compucision LLC 860 355-9790
29 S End Plz New Milford CT (06776) ***(G-2794)***
Computech Inc 207 777-7468
31 Mill St Auburn ME (04210) ***(G-5554)***
Computer Components Inc 860 653-9909
18 Kripes Rd East Granby CT (06026) ***(G-1123)***
Computer Express LLC 860 829-1310
365 New Britain Rd Ste D Berlin CT (06037) ***(G-82)***
Computer Management Cons 603 595-0850
500 Clark Rd Ste 3a Tewksbury MA (01876) ***(G-15812)***
Computer Network Integrators, Milford *Also called CNi Corp* ***(G-19050)***
Computer Prgrm & Systems Inc (PA) 203 324-9203
1011 High Ridge Rd # 208 Stamford CT (06905) ***(G-4170)***
Computer Sgns Old Saybrook LLC 860 388-9773
460 Boston Post Rd Old Saybrook CT (06475) ***(G-3331)***
Computer Tech Express LLC 203 810-4932
95 New Canaan Ave Norwalk CT (06850) ***(G-3130)***
Computr Imprntble Lbl Systms 877 512-8763
1500 District Ave Burlington MA (01803) ***(G-9252)***
Computron Metal Products Inc 781 447-2265
66 Pond St Whitman MA (02382) ***(G-16921)***
Computype Inc 603 225-5500
38 Locke Rd Ste 4 Concord NH (03301) ***(G-17894)***
Comsat Inc 203 264-4091
2120 River Rd Southbury CT (06488) ***(G-4025)***
Comstock Industries Inc 603 279-7045
Foundry Ave Meredith NH (03253) ***(G-18972)***
Comstock Press 401 596-8719
58 Benson Ave Westerly RI (02891) ***(G-21520)***
Comtech PST Corp 978 887-5754
417 Boston St Topsfield MA (01983) ***(G-15854)***
Comtorgage Corporation 401 765-0900
58 Industrial Dr Slatersville RI (02876) ***(G-21203)***
Comtran Cable LLC 508 399-7004
330 Turner St Attleboro MA (02703) ***(G-7724)***
Comunidade News 203 730-0175
4 Laurel St Danbury CT (06810) ***(G-891)***
Comvac Systems Inc 860 265-3658
3 Peerless Way Ste U Enfield CT (06082) ***(G-1352)***
Con-Tec Inc 203 723-8942
41 Raytkwich Rd Naugatuck CT (06770) ***(G-2467)***
Conair Corporation 800 492-7464
314 Ella Grasso Ave Torrington CT (06790) ***(G-4572)***
Conair Corporation (PA) 203 351-9000
1 Cummings Point Rd Stamford CT (06902) ***(G-4171)***
Conant Controls Inc 781 395-2240
215 Salem St Ste K Woburn MA (01801) ***(G-17147)***
Conard Corporation 860 659-0591
101 Commerce St Glastonbury CT (06033) ***(G-1544)***
Concentric Fabrication LLC 774 955-5692
179 Riverside Ave Somerset MA (02725) ***(G-15142)***
Concentric Fabrication LLC 508 672-4098
7 Coombs St Middleboro MA (02346) ***(G-13059)***
Concept Chemicals Inc 781 740-0711
9 Eldridge Ct Hingham MA (02043) ***(G-11497)***
Concept Machining Inc 978 663-4999
25 Sullivan Rd Ste 7 North Billerica MA (01862) ***(G-13803)***
Concept Manufacturing Company, Waltham *Also called Swiss Concept Inc* ***(G-16203)***
Concept Tool and Design Inc 603 622-0216
28 Daniel Plummer Rd # 9 Goffstown NH (03045) ***(G-18198)***
Concept Tooling Inc 508 754-6466
242 Stafford St Worcester MA (01603) ***(G-17358)***
Concept2 Inc (PA) 802 888-7971
105 Industrial Park Dr Morrisville VT (05661) ***(G-22166)***
Concepts Eti Inc 802 296-2321
217 Billings Farm Rd White River Junction VT (05001) ***(G-22637)***
Concepts Nrec LLC (PA) 802 296-2321
217 Billings Farm Rd White River Junction VT (05001) ***(G-22638)***
Concert Medical LLC 781 261-7400
77 Accord Park Dr Ste A3 Norwell MA (02061) ***(G-14100)***
Concert Pharmaceuticals Inc (PA) 781 860-0045
65 Hayden Ave Ste 3000n Lexington MA (02421) ***(G-12213)***
Concession Master, Chestnut Hill *Also called Di An Enterprises Inc* ***(G-9986)***
Conco Wood Working Inc 203 934-9665
755 1st Ave West Haven CT (06516) ***(G-5113)***
Concord Awning & Canvas, Bow *Also called Yarra Design & Fabrication LLC* ***(G-17736)***
Concord Distributing, Norwalk *Also called Concord Industries Inc* ***(G-3131)***
Concord Foods LLC 508 580-1700
10 Minuteman Way Brockton MA (02301) ***(G-9131)***
Concord Industries Inc 203 750-6060
19 Willard Rd Norwalk CT (06851) ***(G-3131)***
Concord Litho Group Inc (PA) 603 224-1202
92 Old Turnpike Rd Concord NH (03301) ***(G-17895)***
Concord Medical Products, Lincoln *Also called Advent Medical Products Inc* ***(G-12285)***
Concord Monitor 603 224-5301
44 S Shore Dr Contoocook NH (03229) ***(G-17943)***
Concord Photo Engraving Co 603 225-3681
12 Commercial St Concord NH (03301) ***(G-17896)***
Concord Print Sltions Copy Svc, Concord *Also called Walnut Bottom Inc* ***(G-17939)***
Concord Sand and Gravel Inc 603 435-6787
14 Presby Ln Loudon NH (03307) ***(G-18747)***
Concord Teacakes Etcetera Inc 978 369-7644
59 Commonwealth Ave Concord MA (01742) ***(G-10123)***
Concord Teacakes Etcetera Inc (PA) 978 369-2409
30 Domino Dr Ste 1 Concord MA (01742) ***(G-10124)***
Concordia Ltd 203 483-0221
5 Enterprise Dr North Branford CT (06471) ***(G-2960)***
Concrete & Mortar Packg LLC 508 473-1799
12 S Free St Milford MA (01757) ***(G-13111)***
Concrete Block Insulating Syst 508 867-4241
25 Freight House Rd West Brookfield MA (01585) ***(G-16466)***
Concrete Pdts of Londonderry 978 658-2645
773 Salem St Wilmington MA (01887) ***(G-16988)***
Concrete Products 860 423-4144
356 Tuckie Rd North Windham CT (06256) ***(G-3081)***
Concrete Sol. Prod. Contact or, Nashua *Also called Flir Systems Inc* ***(G-19162)***
Concrete Supplement Co 860 567-5556
272 Norfolk Rd Litchfield CT (06759) ***(G-1946)***
Concrete Systems Inc 603 432-1840
15 Independence Dr Londonderry NH (03053) ***(G-18686)***
Concrete Systems Inc 603 886-5472
14 Park Ave Hudson NH (03051) ***(G-18380)***
Concretebenchmolds LLC 800 242-1809
75 Angelica Dr Framingham MA (01701) ***(G-10936)***
Condomdepot Co 860 747-1338
186 Camp St Plainville CT (06062) ***(G-3475)***
Condon Mfg Co Inc 413 543-1250
310 Verge St Springfield MA (01129) ***(G-15461)***

ALPHABETIC

Condor Press, Norwalk *Also called Christopher Condors* ***(G-3124)***
Conductrf, Methuen *Also called Electronic Assemblies Mfg Inc* ***(G-13019)***
Conest Software Systems Inc 603 437-9353
592 Harvey Rd Manchester NH (03103) ***(G-18802)***
Confer Health Inc 617 433-8810
56 Roland St Ste 208 Charlestown MA (02129) ***(G-9830)***
Conference Medal & Trophy Co 508 563-3600
530 Macarthur Blvd Buzzards Bay MA (02532) ***(G-9359)***
Confidential Copy, Cranston *Also called Crosstown Press Inc* ***(G-20205)***
Confluent Maine, Windham *Also called Tube Hollows International* ***(G-7258)***
Confluent Medical Tech Inc 401 223-0990
60 Commerce Dr Warwick RI (02886) ***(G-21344)***
Conform Automotive, Auburn *Also called Detroit Technologies Inc* ***(G-5560)***
Conform Gissing Intl LLC 207 784-1118
125 Allied Rd Auburn ME (04210) ***(G-5555)***
Conformis Inc 203 793-7178
10 Beaumont Rd Ste 4 Wallingford CT (06492) ***(G-4724)***
Conformis Inc (PA) 781 345-9001
600 Technology Park Dr # 3 Billerica MA (01821) ***(G-8232)***
Congruity 360 LLC 508 689-9516
456 Bedford St Fall River MA (02720) ***(G-10679)***
Conix Systems (PA) 800 332-1899
441 W Tinmouth Rd Pawlet VT (05761) ***(G-22256)***
Conklin Limestone Company 401 334-2330
25 Wilbur Rd Lincoln RI (02865) ***(G-20565)***
Conklin-Sherman Company Incthe 203 881-0190
59 Old Turnpike Rd Beacon Falls CT (06403) ***(G-57)***
Conley Casting Supply Corp (PA) 401 461-4710
124 Maple St Warwick RI (02888) ***(G-21345)***
Conmed Corporation 508 366-3668
134 Flanders Rd Westborough MA (01581) ***(G-16608)***
Conn Daily Campus 860 486-3407
11 Dog Ln Storrs Mansfield CT (06268) ***(G-4384)***
Conn Engineering Assoc Corp 203 426-4733
27 Philo Curtis Rd Sandy Hook CT (06482) ***(G-3741)***
Connance Inc 781 577-5000
275 Grove St Ste 1-100 Auburndale MA (02466) ***(G-7859)***
Conneaut Industries Inc 401 392-1110
89 Hopkins Hill Rd West Greenwich RI (02817) ***(G-21454)***
Connectcut Crnial Fcial Imgery 860 643-2940
483 Middle Tpke W Ste 102 Manchester CT (06040) ***(G-1996)***
Connectcut Hspnic Yellow Pages 860 560-8713
2074 Park St Ste 2 Hartford CT (06106) ***(G-1815)***
Connectcut Prcsion Cmpnnts LLC 860 489-8621
588 S Main St Rear Torrington CT (06790) ***(G-4573)***
Connectcut Prcsion Cstings Inc 603 542-3373
20 Wentworth Pl Claremont NH (03743) ***(G-17843)***
Connectcut Rver Vly Yllow Pges 603 727-4700
103 Hanover St Ste 9 Lebanon NH (03766) ***(G-18619)***
Connectcut Shreline Developers 860 669-4424
10 Long Hill Rd Clinton CT (06413) ***(G-781)***
Connectcut Spring Stmping Corp 860 677-1341
48 Spring Ln Farmington CT (06032) ***(G-1473)***
Connected Automotive 508 238-5855
87 Eastman St South Easton MA (02375) ***(G-15274)***
Connectedview LLC 508 205-0243
1 Research Dr Ste 310b Westborough MA (01581) ***(G-16609)***
Connecticut Advanced Products 860 659-2260
41c New London Tpke Glastonbury CT (06033) ***(G-1545)***
Connecticut Analytical Corp 203 393-9666
696 Amity Rd Ste 13 Bethany CT (06524) ***(G-119)***
Connecticut Anodizing Finshg 203 367-1765
128 Logan St Bridgeport CT (06607) ***(G-400)***
Connecticut Beverage Journal, Hamden *Also called Beverage Publications Inc* ***(G-1735)***
Connecticut Carpentry LLC 203 639-8585
290 Pratt St Ofc Meriden CT (06450) ***(G-2088)***
Connecticut Coining Inc 203 743-3861
10 Trowbridge Dr Bethel CT (06801) ***(G-138)***
Connecticut Components Inc 860 633-0277
60 Industrial Park Rd W # 2 Tolland CT (06084) ***(G-4541)***
Connecticut Concrete Form Inc 860 674-1314
168 Brickyard Rd Farmington CT (06032) ***(G-1474)***
Connecticut Container Corp (PA) 203 248-2161
455 Sackett Point Rd North Haven CT (06473) ***(G-3018)***
Connecticut Cue Parts, Wolcott *Also called Jan Manufacturing Inc* ***(G-5445)***
Connecticut Die Cutting Svc, East Hartford *Also called Bessette Holdings Inc* ***(G-1176)***
Connecticut Diesel and Marine 203 481-1010
287 Woodmont Rd Milford CT (06460) ***(G-2267)***
Connecticut Dist Svcs Ltd, East Hartford *Also called Burnside Supermarket LLC* ***(G-1178)***
Connecticut Engravers, Milford *Also called Ideas Inc* ***(G-2299)***
Connecticut Fabricating Co Inc 203 878-3465
15 Warfield St Milford CT (06461) ***(G-2268)***
Connecticut Galvanizing, Glastonbury *Also called Highway Safety Corp* ***(G-1558)***
Connecticut Greenstar Inc 203 368-1522
1157 Melville Ave Fairfield CT (06825) ***(G-1423)***
Connecticut Hone Incorporated 860 747-3884
9 Grace Ave Plainville CT (06062) ***(G-3476)***
Connecticut Hypodermics Inc 203 265-4881
519 Main St Wallingford CT (06492) ***(G-4725)***
Connecticut Iron Works Inc 203 869-0657
59 Davenport Ave Greenwich CT (06830) ***(G-1603)***
Connecticut Laminating Co Inc 203 787-2184
162 James St New Haven CT (06513) ***(G-2677)***
Connecticut Law Book Co Inc 203 458-8000
39 Chaffinch Island Rd Guilford CT (06437) ***(G-1698)***
Connecticut Machine & Welding 203 502-2605
425 Harding Ave Stratford CT (06615) ***(G-4406)***
Connecticut Mch Tooling & Cast 203 874-8300
93 Research Dr Milford CT (06460) ***(G-2269)***
Connecticut Metal Industries 203 736-0790
1 Riverside Dr Ste G Ansonia CT (06401) ***(G-11)***
Connecticut Metalworks, Newington *Also called J OConnor LLC* ***(G-2873)***
Connecticut Millwork Inc 860 875-2860
80 Spring St Vernon CT (06066) ***(G-4665)***
Connecticut Newspapers Inc 203 964-2200
75 Tresser Blvd Stamford CT (06901) ***(G-4172)***
Connecticut Parent Magazine 203 483-1700
420 E Main St Ste 18 Branford CT (06405) ***(G-306)***
Connecticut Plasma Tech LLC 860 289-5500
273 Chapel Rd South Windsor CT (06074) ***(G-3953)***
Connecticut Post, Norwalk *Also called Medianews Group Inc* ***(G-3195)***
Connecticut Precast Corp 203 268-8688
555 Fan Hill Rd Monroe CT (06468) ***(G-2398)***
Connecticut Refining Co, New Haven *Also called Alliance Energy LLC* ***(G-2655)***
Connecticut Screen Works Inc 203 269-4499
121 N Plains Indus Rd Wallingford CT (06492) ***(G-4726)***
Connecticut Sign Craft Inc 203 729-0706
47 Cherry St Naugatuck CT (06770) ***(G-2468)***
Connecticut Sign Service LLC 860 767-7446
25 Saybrook Rd Ste 6 Essex CT (06426) ***(G-1395)***
Connecticut Solid Surface LLC 860 410-9800
361 East St Plainville CT (06062) ***(G-3477)***
Connecticut Spring & Stamping, Farmington *Also called Connectcut Spring Stmping Corp* ***(G-1473)***
Connecticut Stone Supplies Inc (PA) 203 882-1000
138 Woodmont Rd Milford CT (06460) ***(G-2270)***
Connecticut Tool & Cutter Co 860 314-1740
280 Redstone Hill Rd # 1 Bristol CT (06010) ***(G-543)***
Connecticut Tool & Mfg Co LLC 860 846-0800
35 Corp Ave Plainville CT (06062) ***(G-3478)***
Connecticut Tool Co Inc 860 928-0565
6 Highland Dr Putnam CT (06260) ***(G-3606)***
Connecticut Trade Company Inc 203 368-0398
1157 Melville Ave Fairfield CT (06825) ***(G-1424)***
Connecticut Valley Bindery 860 229-7637
1 Hartford Sq Ste 28w New Britain CT (06052) ***(G-2521)***
Connecticut Valley Inds LLC 860 388-0822
8 Center Rd Old Saybrook CT (06475) ***(G-3332)***
Connecticut Valley Winery LLC 860 489-9463
1480 Litchfield Tpke New Hartford CT (06057) ***(G-2633)***
Connectivity Works Inc 207 843-0854
182 Bagaduce Rd Holden ME (04429) ***(G-6196)***
Connectleader LLC 800 955-5040
7 Stiles Rd Ste 102 Salem NH (03079) ***(G-19718)***
Connectrn Inc 781 223-2852
203 Crescent St Ste 403 Waltham MA (02453) ***(G-16075)***
Connell Communications Inc 603 924-7271
149 Emerald St Unit O Keene NH (03431) ***(G-18496)***
Connell Limited Partnership (PA) 617 737-2700
1 International Pl Fl 31 Boston MA (02110) ***(G-8481)***
Connelly 3 Pubg Group Inc 860 664-4988
10 W Main St Fl 2 Clinton CT (06413) ***(G-782)***
Conner Bottling Works, Newfields *Also called Thomas H Conner* ***(G-19320)***
Connexient LLC 603 669-1300
33 S Coml St Ste 302 Manchester NH (03101) ***(G-18803)***
Connexus Manufacturing LLC 978 568-1831
312 Main St Hudson MA (01749) ***(G-11764)***
Connoisseurs Products Corp (PA) 800 851-5333
17 Presidential Way Woburn MA (01801) ***(G-17148)***
Connolly Printing LLC 781 932-8885
17b Gill St Woburn MA (01801) ***(G-17149)***
Connors Design Ltd 508 481-1930
257 Simarano Dr Ste 105 Marlborough MA (01752) ***(G-12739)***
Conntext Labels 413 528-3303
5 Butternut Ln Ste 2 Great Barrington MA (01230) ***(G-11237)***
Conntrol International Inc 860 928-0567
135 Park Rd Putnam CT (06260) ***(G-3607)***
Conopco Inc 708 606-0540
75 Merritt Blvd Trumbull CT (06611) ***(G-4620)***
Conopco Inc 508 543-6767
140 Washington St Ste 1 Foxboro MA (02035) ***(G-10880)***
Conopco Inc 860 669-8601
1 John St Clinton CT (06413) ***(G-783)***
Conopco Inc 203 381-3557
75 Merritt Blvd Trumbull CT (06611) ***(G-4621)***
Conoptics Inc 203 743-3349
19 Eagle Rd Danbury CT (06810) ***(G-892)***
Conproco Corp (PA) 603 743-5800
388 High St Somersworth NH (03878) ***(G-19831)***

Conproco Corp ...603 743-5800
655 River Rd Bow NH (03304) *(G-17710)*
Conquip Systems LLC ...860 526-7883
78 Turkey Hill Rd Chester CT (06412) *(G-770)*
Conrad-Jarvis Corp ...401 722-8700
217 Conant St Pawtucket RI (02860) *(G-20824)*
Conseal International Inc ...781 278-0010
90 Kerry Pl Ste 2 Norwood MA (02062) *(G-14142)*
Consoldted Inds Acqsition Corp ...203 272-5371
677 Mixville Rd Cheshire CT (06410) *(G-724)*
Consoldted Precision Pdts Corp ...781 848-3333
205 Wood Rd Braintree MA (02184) *(G-8995)*
Consoldted Utlities Corporaion ...978 562-3500
503 River Rd Hudson MA (01749) *(G-11765)*
Consolidated Coating Company, Bellingham *Also called Manning Way Cpitl Partners LLC* *(G-8044)*
Consolidated Concrete Corp (PA) ...401 438-4700
835 Taunton Ave Unit 1 East Providence RI (02914) *(G-20399)*
Consolidated Concrete Corp ...401 828-4700
10 Reservoir Rd Coventry RI (02816) *(G-20143)*
Consolidated Cont Holdings LLC ...508 485-2109
1 Dangelo Dr Marlborough MA (01752) *(G-12740)*
Consolidated Container Co LLC ...802 658-6588
8 Harbor View Rd South Burlington VT (05403) *(G-22444)*
Consolidated Container Co LLC ...508 520-8800
1253 W Central St Franklin MA (02038) *(G-11031)*
Consolidated Container Co LLC ...603 329-6747
27 Industrial Dr Londonderry NH (03053) *(G-18687)*
Consolidated Container Co LLC ...603 624-6055
27 Industrial Dr Londonderry NH (03053) *(G-18688)*
Consolidated Container Co LLC ...207 772-7468
364 Forest Ave Portland ME (04101) *(G-6642)*
Consolidated Thread Mills, Fall River *Also called Dhm Thread Corporation* *(G-10682)*
Constant Velocity Mfg LLC ...508 735-3399
221 N Spencer Rd Spencer MA (01562) *(G-15427)*
Constellation Brands Inc ...617 249-5082
1 Batterymarch Park Quincy MA (02169) *(G-14619)*
Constellation Diagnostics Inc ...617 233-4554
700 Main St Cambridge MA (02139) *(G-9440)*
Constlltion Phrmaceuticals Inc ...617 714-0555
215 1st St Ste 200 Cambridge MA (02142) *(G-9441)*
Constrction Summary of NH Main ...603 627-8856
734 Chestnut St Manchester NH (03104) *(G-18804)*
Construction Service, Wilbraham *Also called Cs-Ma LLC* *(G-16934)*
Construction Service Division, Wilbraham *Also called Dauphinais & Son Inc* *(G-16935)*
Construction Source MGT LLC ...508 484-5100
33 Commercial St Raynham MA (02767) *(G-14707)*
Consulting Engrg Dev Svcs Inc ...203 828-6528
3 Fox Hollow Rd Oxford CT (06478) *(G-3398)*
Contact Edition, Northampton *Also called Contact Quarterly* *(G-14001)*
Contact Inc ...207 882-6116
788 Boothbay Rd Edgecomb ME (04556) *(G-6001)*
Contact Quarterly ...413 586-1181
221 Pine St Ste 112 Northampton MA (01062) *(G-14001)*
Contacts411, Whitinsville *Also called Infinite Knot LLC* *(G-16914)*
Containment Solutions Inc ...860 651-4371
35 Ichabod Rd Simsbury CT (06070) *(G-3898)*
Contech Engnered Solutions LLC ...781 932-4201
10 Tower Office Park Woburn MA (01801) *(G-17150)*
Contech Engnered Solutions LLC ...413 283-7611
41 Fenton St Palmer MA (01069) *(G-14285)*
Contech Engnered Solutions LLC ...207 885-9830
71 Us Route 1 Ste F Scarborough ME (04074) *(G-6915)*
Contech Medical Inc ...401 351-4890
99 Hartford Ave Providence RI (02909) *(G-20989)*
Contek International Corp ...203 972-3406
93 Cherry St New Canaan CT (06840) *(G-2594)*
Contek International Corp ...203 972-7330
60 Field Crest Rd New Canaan CT (06840) *(G-2595)*
Contempo Card Co Inc (PA) ...401 272-4210
69 Tingley St Ste 1a Providence RI (02903) *(G-20990)*
Contemporary Apparel Inc ...508 339-3523
127 N Main St Mansfield MA (02048) *(G-12619)*
Contemporary Cabinet Designs ...781 769-7979
416 Lenox St Ste B Norwood MA (02062) *(G-14143)*
Contemporary Products LLC ...860 346-9283
2055 S Main St Middletown CT (06457) *(G-2182)*
Context Labs Inc ...617 902-0932
222 3rd St Ste 2242 Cambridge MA (02142) *(G-9442)*
Conti Precision Tool Co Inc ...978 632-6224
104 E Broadway Gardner MA (01440) *(G-11109)*
Continental Braze Supply LLC ...603 948-1016
5 Sampson Rd Rochester NH (03867) *(G-19664)*
Continental Cable LLC ...800 229-5131
253 Monument Rd Hinsdale NH (03451) *(G-18319)*
Continental Consolidated Inds, Worcester *Also called Continental Woodcraft Inc* *(G-17359)*
Continental Consumer Products, Stamford *Also called Continental Fragrances Ltd* *(G-4173)*
Continental Fragrances Ltd ...800 542-5903
333 Ludlow St 2nd Stamford CT (06902) *(G-4173)*
Continental Machine Pdts Inc ...617 567-7396
400 Border St Boston MA (02128) *(G-8482)*
Continental Machine Tl Co Inc ...860 223-2896
533 John Downey Dr New Britain CT (06051) *(G-2522)*
Continental Marble & Granite, Plainville *Also called Mark Dzidzk* *(G-3504)*
Continental Metal Pdts Co Inc ...781 935-4400
35 Olympia Ave Woburn MA (01801) *(G-17151)*
Continental Stone MBL Gran Inc ...978 422-8700
287 Leominster Rd Sterling MA (01564) *(G-15538)*
Continental Stone, Inc., Sterling *Also called Continental Stone MBL Gran Inc* *(G-15538)*
Continental Woodcraft Inc (PA) ...508 581-9560
7 Coppage Dr Worcester MA (01603) *(G-17359)*
Contintential Microwave ...603 775-5200
32 Industrial Dr Exeter NH (03833) *(G-18118)*
Continuity Engine Inc ...866 631-5556
59 Elm St New Haven CT (06510) *(G-2678)*
Continuus Pharmaceutical ...781 281-0099
25 Olympia Ave Woburn MA (01801) *(G-17152)*
Continuus Pharmaceuticals Inc ...781 281-0226
25r Olympia Ave Woburn MA (01801) *(G-17153)*
Contitech Thermopol LLC ...603 692-6300
10 Interstate Dr Somersworth NH (03878) *(G-19832)*
Contitech Thermopol LLC ...603 692-6300
35 Industrial Way Ste 204 Rochester NH (03867) *(G-19665)*
Contitech Thermopol LLC (HQ) ...603 692-6300
9 Interstate Dr Somersworth NH (03878) *(G-19833)*
Contoocook River Lumber Inc ...603 428-3636
54 Main St Henniker NH (03242) *(G-18303)*
Contorq Components LLC ...860 225-3366
433 John Downey Dr New Britain CT (06051) *(G-2523)*
Contour Semiconductor Inc ...978 670-4100
85 Rangeway Rd Ste 1 North Billerica MA (01862) *(G-13804)*
Contract Decor Intl Inc ...508 587-7000
637 N Montello St Brockton MA (02301) *(G-9132)*
Contract Engineering Inc ...978 921-0501
128 Park St Ste B5 Beverly MA (01915) *(G-8120)*
Contract Fusion Inc ...401 438-1298
99 Massasoit Ave East Providence RI (02914) *(G-20400)*
Contract Glass Service Inc ...978 262-1323
44 Dunham Rd Billerica MA (01821) *(G-8233)*
Contract Mfg Tech LLC ...603 692-4488
2 Crescent Ave Dover NH (03820) *(G-18014)*
Contributions, Medfield *Also called Cambridge Fund Raising Assoc* *(G-12911)*
Control 7 Inc ...508 697-3197
55 Scotland Blvd Bridgewater MA (02324) *(G-9068)*
Control Concepts Inc (PA) ...860 928-6551
100 Park St Putnam CT (06260) *(G-3608)*
Control Resources Inc ...978 486-4160
11 Beaver Brook Rd Littleton MA (01460) *(G-12297)*
Control Technology Corporation (PA) ...508 435-9596
25 South St Hopkinton MA (01748) *(G-11697)*
Controlled Chaos ...802 274-5321
116 Free St Portland ME (04101) *(G-6643)*
Controlled Fluidics LLC ...603 673-4323
18 Hollow Oak Ln Milford NH (03055) *(G-19051)*
Controls For Automation Inc ...508 802-6005
25 Constitution Dr Taunton MA (02780) *(G-15738)*
Contronautics Incorporated ...978 568-8883
31 Wilkins St Hudson MA (01749) *(G-11766)*
Conval Inc ...860 749-0761
96 Phoenix Ave Enfield CT (06082) *(G-1353)*
Convanta Holliston ...508 429-9750
115 Washington St Holliston MA (01746) *(G-11564)*
Convectronics Inc ...978 374-7714
111 Neck Rd Haverhill MA (01835) *(G-11419)*
Convergent - Photonics LLC ...413 598-5200
711 E Main St Chicopee MA (01020) *(G-10016)*
Convergent Dental Inc ...508 500-5656
140 Kendrick St Ste C110 Needham Heights MA (02494) *(G-13323)*
Convergent Networks Inc ...978 262-0231
500 Boylston St Fl 4 Boston MA (02116) *(G-8483)*
Convergent Solutions LLC ...203 293-3534
3 Baywood Ln Westport CT (06880) *(G-5186)*
Conversation Concepts LLC ...978 342-1414
339 Broad St Ste 2 Fitchburg MA (01420) *(G-10820)*
Converter Consultants LLC ...203 729-1031
1058 Rubber Ave Naugatuck CT (06770) *(G-2469)*
Converting McHy Adhesives LLC ...860 561-0226
50 Sleepy Hollow Rd Newington CT (06111) *(G-2856)*
Convexity Scientific LLC ...949 637-1216
418 Meadow St Fairfield CT (06824) *(G-1425)*
Conveyor Installation, Smithfield *Also called Action Conveyor Tech Inc* *(G-21207)*
Conveytrex LLC ...508 812-4333
1658 Gar Hwy Swansea MA (02777) *(G-15704)*
Conviber Inc ...724 274-6300
2 Hawksley Rd Unit F Oxford MA (01540) *(G-14257)*
Conway Daily Sun, Berlin *Also called Berlin Daily Sun* *(G-17692)*
Conway Daily Sun, North Conway *Also called Country News Club Inc* *(G-19376)*
Conway Hardwood Products LLC ...860 355-4030
37 Gaylord Rd Gaylordsville CT (06755) *(G-1530)*

A L P H A B E T I C

Conway Pallet Inc 413 268-3343
270 Williamsburg Rd Williamsburg MA (01096) *(G-16949)*
Conway, Jeremiah, Gaylordsville *Also called Conway Hardwood Products LLC (G-1530)*
Cook & Cook Cabinetry, Scarborough *Also called Atlantic Wood & Cabinet Works (G-6905)*
Cook Company, Upton *Also called Cook Forest Products Inc (G-15906)*
Cook Forest Products Inc 508 634-3300
252 Milford St Upton MA (01568) *(G-15906)*
Cookes Skate Supplies Inc 978 657-7586
446 Main St Wilmington MA (01887) *(G-16989)*
Cooking Solutions Group Inc (HQ) 603 893-9701
11 Keewaydin Dr Ste 300 Salem NH (03079) *(G-19719)*
Cooks Butlr Great Soups Sauces, Bristol *Also called Great Soups Inc (G-20082)*
Cool Air Creations Inc 401 830-5780
10 Business Park Dr Smithfield RI (02917) *(G-21216)*
Cool Gear International LLC 508 830-3440
10 Cordage Park Cir # 212 Plymouth MA (02360) *(G-14551)*
Cool-It LLC 203 284-4848
340 Quinnipiac St Wallingford CT (06492) *(G-4727)*
Coolcomposites Inc 510 717-9125
25 Chilcott Pl Ste 1 Jamaica Plain MA (02130) *(G-11942)*
Cooley Incorporated (HQ) 401 724-9000
50 Esten Ave Pawtucket RI (02860) *(G-20825)*
Cooley Incorporated 401 721-6374
5 Slater Rd Cranston RI (02920) *(G-20200)*
Cooley Building Products, Pawtucket *Also called Cooley Incorporated (G-20825)*
Cooliance Inc 401 921-6500
60 Alhambra Rd Ste 1 Warwick RI (02886) *(G-21346)*
Coop's Microcreamery, Boston *Also called Samarc Inc (G-8837)*
Cooper Controls, Essex Junction *Also called Cooper Lighting Inc (G-21937)*
Cooper Crouse-Hinds LLC 860 683-4300
1200 Kennedy Rd Windsor CT (06095) *(G-5327)*
Cooper Eldred Boat Builders 508 540-7130
267 Sippewissett Rd Falmouth MA (02540) *(G-10788)*
Cooper Interconnect Inc 617 389-7080
222 Williams St Chelsea MA (02150) *(G-9950)*
Cooper Lighting Inc 800 767-3674
16 Perkins Dr Essex Junction VT (05452) *(G-21937)*
Cooper Marketing Group Inc 203 797-9386
41 Eagle Rd Ste 2 Danbury CT (06810) *(G-893)*
Cooper Products Inc 603 524-3367
210 Fair St Laconia NH (03246) *(G-18563)*
Cooper Surgical, Trumbull *Also called Blairden Precision Instrs Inc (G-4616)*
Cooper-Atkins Corporation (HQ) 860 349-3473
33 Reeds Gap Rd Middlefield CT (06455) *(G-2162)*
Cooperman Fife & Drum Co 802 463-9750
1007 Route 121 Bellows Falls VT (05101) *(G-21651)*
Coopersurgical Inc 203 453-1700
393 Soundview Rd Guilford CT (06437) *(G-1699)*
Coorstek Inc 860 653-8071
10 Airport Park Rd East Granby CT (06026) *(G-1124)*
Coorstek Inc 603 673-7560
47 Powers St Milford NH (03055) *(G-19052)*
Coorstek Inc 774 317-2600
5 Norton Dr Worcester MA (01606) *(G-17360)*
Coorstek East Granby, East Granby *Also called Coorstek Inc (G-1124)*
Coorstek Milford, Milford *Also called Coorstek Inc (G-19052)*
Coorstek Worcester, Worcester *Also called Coorstek Inc (G-17360)*
Copar Industries, Middletown *Also called Armetta LLC (G-2172)*
Cope & Scribe Incorporated 508 410-7100
29 Rodman St West Brookfield MA (01585) *(G-16467)*
Copies and More, Peterborough *Also called Savron Graphics Inc (G-19487)*
Copious Imaging LLC 617 921-0485
83 Hartwell Ave Lexington MA (02421) *(G-12214)*
Copley Controls Corporation (HQ) 781 828-8090
20 Dan Rd Canton MA (02021) *(G-9722)*
Copp Excavating Inc 207 926-4988
190 Pinkham Brook Rd Durham ME (04222) *(G-5970)*
Copp Logging LLC 603 479-4828
27 Danville Rd Fremont NH (03044) *(G-18175)*
Copper Lease, Stewartstown *Also called Kheops International Inc (G-19862)*
Copper Maid, Bow *Also called Pen & Inc (G-17726)*
Coprico Inc 617 889-0520
40 Washington Ave Chelsea MA (02150) *(G-9951)*
Copy Caps 508 349-1300
50 Somerset Ave Wellfleet MA (02667) *(G-16401)*
Copy Print Company 401 228-3900
176 N View Ave Cranston RI (02920) *(G-20201)*
Copy Print/Etc, Cranston *Also called Copy Print Company (G-20201)*
Copy Stop Inc 203 288-6401
2371 Whitney Ave Hamden CT (06518) *(G-1738)*
Copy World, East Providence *Also called A & H Composition and Prtg Inc (G-20383)*
Copycat Print Shop, East Longmeadow *Also called Shafiis Inc (G-10492)*
Copycat Print Shop, West Springfield *Also called Western Mass Copying Prtg Inc (G-16565)*
Corbeil Enterprises Inc 603 744-2867
12 Bristol Rd Bristol NH (03222) *(G-17762)*
Corbin & Son Logging Inc 802 484-3329
2334 Route 106 Reading VT (05062) *(G-22305)*
Corbin Russwin 860 225-7411
110 Sargent Dr New Haven CT (06511) *(G-2679)*
Corbin Russwin Arch Hdwr, Berlin *Also called Assa Abloy Accss & Edrss Hrdwr (G-73)*
Corbus Pharmaceuticals Inc 617 963-1000
500 River Ridge Dr # 200 Norwood MA (02062) *(G-14144)*
Corbus Phrmctcals Holdings Inc (PA) 617 963-0100
500 River Ridge Dr Norwood MA (02062) *(G-14145)*
Corcoran Machine Co 603 445-5258
76 Weeks Rd Charlestown NH (03603) *(G-17812)*
Corden Pharma Intl Inc 781 305-3332
639 Granite St Ste 408 Braintree MA (02184) *(G-8996)*
Cordenpharma 617 401-2828
500 Kendall St Cambridge MA (02142) *(G-9443)*
Cordmaster Engineering Co Inc 413 664-9371
1544 Curran Hwy North Adams MA (01247) *(G-13671)*
Core Assemblies Inc 603 293-0270
21 Meadowbrook Ln Unit 4 Gilford NH (03249) *(G-18183)*
Core Concepts Inc 508 528-0070
305 Union St Ste 7 Franklin MA (02038) *(G-11032)*
Core Elastomers 603 319-6912
170 West Rd Ste 2 Portsmouth NH (03801) *(G-19554)*
Core Value Software 802 473-3147
316 Main St Norwich VT (05055) *(G-22247)*
Coredge Networks Inc 617 267-5205
50 Commonwealth Ave # 504 Boston MA (02116) *(G-8484)*
Corenco, Warwick *Also called Baker Commodities Inc (G-21331)*
Corenco Div, North Billerica *Also called Baker Commodities Inc (G-13795)*
Corero Network Security Inc 978 212-1500
293 Boston Post Rd W # 310 Marlborough MA (01752) *(G-12741)*
Corey Madden Logging Inc 207 827-1632
6 Madden Ln Greenbush ME (04418) *(G-6146)*
Corfin Industries LLC 603 893-9900
1050 Perimeter Rd Manchester NH (03103) *(G-18805)*
Corflex Inc (PA) 603 623-3344
669 E Industrial Pk Dr Manchester NH (03109) *(G-18806)*
Coriant America Inc (HQ) 978 250-2900
220 Mill Rd Chelmsford MA (01824) *(G-9888)*
Corindus Inc 508 653-3335
309 Waverley Oaks Rd # 105 Waltham MA (02452) *(G-16076)*
Corindus Vascular Robotics Inc (PA) 508 653-3335
309 Waverly Oaks Rd # 10 Waltham MA (02452) *(G-16077)*
Corinth Acquisition Corp (PA) 203 504-6260
2777 Summer St Ste 206 Stamford CT (06905) *(G-4174)*
Cork Technologies, Lawrence *Also called North American Chemical Co (G-12066)*
Cork Technologies LLC 978 687-9500
29 S Canal St Ste 204 Lawrence MA (01843) *(G-12013)*
Cormiers Self Defense Aca 508 596-7326
72 Morton St Holliston MA (01746) *(G-11565)*
Corn Snow LLC 603 684-2427
161 Maple Ave Farmington ME (04938) *(G-6042)*
Cornell Online LLC 802 448-3281
131 Battery St Burlington VT (05401) *(G-21776)*
Cornell Orthotics Prosthetics (PA) 978 922-2866
100 Cummings Ctr Ste 207h Beverly MA (01915) *(G-8121)*
Cornell-Carr Co Inc 203 261-2529
626 Main St Monroe CT (06468) *(G-2399)*
Corner Washers Inc 617 370-0350
223 Harvard Ave Allston MA (02134) *(G-7462)*
Cornerstone Propane, Keene *Also called Keene Gas Corporation (G-18510)*
Corning Incorporated 207 985-3111
2 Alfred Rd Kennebunk ME (04043) *(G-6231)*
Corning Incorporated 603 357-7662
69 Island St Ste T Keene NH (03431) *(G-18497)*
Corningware Corelle & More 207 865-3942
1 Freeport Village Sta Freeport ME (04032) *(G-6075)*
Cornwall & Patterson Div, Branford *Also called Pratt-Read Corporation (G-339)*
Corona Films Inc 978 597-6444
241 Dudley Rd West Townsend MA (01474) *(G-16566)*
Coronado Group LLC (PA) 203 761-1291
57 Danbury Rd Ste 201 Wilton CT (06897) *(G-5284)*
Coronet Awning Company, Taunton *Also called Taunton Venetian Blind Inc (G-15789)*
Corotec Corp 860 678-0038
145 Hyde Rd Farmington CT (06032) *(G-1475)*
Corporate, Windsor *Also called ABB Enterprise Software Inc (G-5314)*
Corporate Connecticut Mag LLC 860 257-0500
912 Silas Deane Hwy Wethersfield CT (06109) *(G-5246)*
Corporate Connection, Salem *Also called Holmes Stamp Company (G-14922)*
Corporate Image Apparel Inc 508 676-3099
596 Airport Rd Fall River MA (02720) *(G-10680)*
Corporate Press 781 769-6656
89 Access Rd Ste 17 Norwood MA (02062) *(G-14146)*
Corporation, Hudson *Also called AC General Inc (G-11749)*
Corporation Niton, Billerica *Also called Thermo Scientific Portable Ana (G-8305)*
Corr/Dis Incorporated 203 838-6075
38 Burchard Ln Norwalk CT (06853) *(G-3132)*
Corrado Block, Lincoln *Also called Anthony Corrado Inc (G-20556)*
Corrados Canvas & Cushions Inc 401 253-5511
47 Gooding Ave Bristol RI (02809) *(G-20070)*

Corru Seals Inc 203 284-0319
24 Capital Dr Wallingford CT (06492) ***(G-4728)***
Corrugated Packaging Inc 978 342-6076
215 Cleghorn Fitchburg MA (01420) ***(G-10821)***
Corrugated Stitcher Service 508 823-2844
88 Jerome St Berkley MA (02779) ***(G-8085)***
Cortina Famous Schools, Wilton *Also called Cortina Learning Intl Inc* ***(G-5285)***
Cortina Learning Intl Inc (PA) 800 245-2145
33 Catalpa Rd Wilton CT (06897) ***(G-5285)***
Cortron Inc 978 975-5445
59 Technology Dr Lowell MA (01851) ***(G-12362)***
Corvus Publishing LLC 401 595-8937
221 Washington Rd Barrington RI (02806) ***(G-20045)***
Cory Manufacturing Inc 508 680-2111
343 Manley St West Bridgewater MA (02379) ***(G-16435)***
Cos Cob T V & Video, Cos Cob *Also called Sean Mecesery* ***(G-829)***
Cosman Medical LLC 781 272-6561
300 Boston Scientific Way Marlborough MA (01752) ***(G-12742)***
Cosmic Bakers of Vermont LLC 802 524-0800
30 S Main St Saint Albans VT (05478) ***(G-22366)***
Cosmic Software Inc 978 667-2556
17 Bridge St Ste 101 Billerica MA (01821) ***(G-8234)***
Cosmo, Byfield *Also called Starensier Inc* ***(G-9365)***
Cosmos Food Products Inc 800 942-6766
200 Callegari Dr West Haven CT (06516) ***(G-5114)***
Coss Systems Inc (not Inc) 732 447-7724
26 Arcadia Rd Old Greenwich CT (06870) ***(G-3307)***
Costa Precision Mfg Corp (PA) 603 542-5229
59 Plains Rd Claremont NH (03743) ***(G-17844)***
Costal, Georgetown *Also called Bob Bergeron* ***(G-11138)***
Costantino's Venda Ravioli, Providence *Also called Venda Ravioli Inc* ***(G-21147)***
Costantino's Venda Ravioli, Providence *Also called Venda Ravioli Inc* ***(G-21148)***
Costello/April Design Inc 603 749-6755
180 Crosby Rd Dover NH (03820) ***(G-18015)***
Costume Works Inc 617 623-7510
36 Alston St Somerville MA (02143) ***(G-15167)***
Cote Machine 603 673-0211
281 Mason Rd Milford NH (03055) ***(G-19053)***
Coto Technology, North Kingstown *Also called Kearney-National Inc* ***(G-20719)***
Coto Technology Inc 401 943-2686
66 Whitecap Dr North Kingstown RI (02852) ***(G-20698)***
Cotswold Furniture Makers, Hinesburg *Also called Greenrange Furniture Company* ***(G-22027)***
Cotta Truck Equipment 508 269-1960
30 Bedford Park Ste 4 Bridgewater MA (02324) ***(G-9069)***
Cottages & Grdns Publications, Norwalk *Also called Dulce Domum LLC* ***(G-3145)***
Cotter Brothers Corporation 978 777-5001
8 Southside Rd Danvers MA (01923) ***(G-10206)***
Cotter Corporation 978 774-6777
8 Southside Rd Danvers MA (01923) ***(G-10207)***
Cotter Machine Co Inc (PA) 508 291-7400
7 Little Brook Rd West Wareham MA (02576) ***(G-16568)***
Cotton's Woolens, Dresden *Also called Christmas Cove Designs Inc* ***(G-5965)***
Cotuit Works 508 428-3971
50 Shell Ln Cotuit MA (02635) ***(G-10169)***
Coulter Press, Worcester *Also called Worcester Tlegram Gazette Corp* ***(G-17508)***
Council On Intl Pub Affirs Inc (PA) 212 972-9878
3 Mont View Ave Northampton MA (01060) ***(G-14002)***
Counter Culture 781 439-9810
60 Main St Saugus MA (01906) ***(G-14979)***
Counter Pro Inc 603 647-2444
210 Lincoln St Manchester NH (03103) ***(G-18807)***
Counter Productions Inc 508 587-0416
103 Liberty St Brockton MA (02301) ***(G-9133)***
Counter Tech Inc 603 352-1882
180 Emerald St Ste 50 Keene NH (03431) ***(G-18498)***
Counteredge LLC 781 891-0050
108 Clematis Ave Unit 2 Waltham MA (02453) ***(G-16078)***
Counterra LLC 781 821-2100
399 Neponset St Ste 202 Canton MA (02021) ***(G-9723)***
Counters, Newington *Also called Catskill Gran Countertops Inc* ***(G-2852)***
Counterwerks Inc 508 553-9600
200 Center St Bellingham MA (02019) ***(G-8035)***
Country Bed Shop Inc 978 386-7550
328 Richardson Rd Ashby MA (01431) ***(G-7646)***
Country Candle Co Inc (PA) 508 865-6061
22 West St Millbury MA (01527) ***(G-13160)***
Country Carpenters Inc 860 228-2276
326 Gilead St Hebron CT (06248) ***(G-1896)***
Country Courier, Barre *Also called Ta Update Inc* ***(G-21642)***
Country Kitchen, Lewiston *Also called Lepage Bakeries Park St LLC* ***(G-6298)***
Country Kitchen, Belmont *Also called Lepage Bakeries Park St LLC* ***(G-17677)***
Country Kitchen, Hudson *Also called Lepage Bakeries Park St LLC* ***(G-18410)***
Country Life LLC 781 659-1321
335 Washington St Ste 3 Norwell MA (02061) ***(G-14101)***
Country Log Homes Inc 413 229-8084
27 Rockwall Ct Goshen CT (06756) ***(G-1582)***
Country News Club Inc 603 356-2999
64 Seavey St North Conway NH (03860) ***(G-19376)***
Country Press, New London *Also called Echo Communications Inc* ***(G-19316)***
Country Press Inc 508 947-4485
1 Commercial Dr Lakeville MA (02347) ***(G-11975)***
Country Pure Foods Inc 330 753-2293
58 West Rd Ellington CT (06029) ***(G-1331)***
Country Riders Snow Mobile CLB 802 988-2255
974 N Jay Rd Jay VT (05859) ***(G-22044)***
Country Shop Robb Fmly Ltd 802 258-9087
827 Ames Hill Rd Brattleboro VT (05301) ***(G-21725)***
Country Standard Time 617 969-0331
54 Ballard St Newton MA (02459) ***(G-13582)***
Countryside Butchers 207 282-2882
50 Washington St Biddeford ME (04005) ***(G-5725)***
Countryside Signs 508 761-9530
102 Pond St Unit F1 Seekonk MA (02771) ***(G-15020)***
Countryside Woodcraft 413 862-3276
665 Huntington Rd Russell MA (01071) ***(G-14877)***
County Communications 603 394-7070
207 Amesbury Rd Kensington NH (03833) ***(G-18535)***
County Concrete & Cnstr Co 207 483-4409
125 Pit Rd Columbia Falls ME (04623) ***(G-5919)***
County Concrete Corp (PA) 413 499-3359
290 Hubbard Ave Dalton MA (01226) ***(G-10175)***
County Courier Inc 802 933-4375
342 Main St N Enosburg Falls VT (05450) ***(G-21924)***
County Heat Treat, Millbury *Also called United-County Industries Corp* ***(G-13179)***
County of Lincoln 207 882-5276
54 Huntoon Hill Rd Wiscasset ME (04578) ***(G-7284)***
County Street Ice Cream Corp 508 674-3357
2977 County St Somerset MA (02726) ***(G-15143)***
Couponz Direct LLC 212 655-9615
25 Lewis St Ste 303 Greenwich CT (06830) ***(G-1604)***
Courage Therapeutics Inc 617 216-9921
64 Homer St Newton MA (02459) ***(G-13583)***
Courant Specialty Products Inc 860 241-3795
285 Broad St Hartford CT (06115) ***(G-1816)***
Courier Communications LLC (HQ) 978 251-6000
15 Wellman Ave North Chelmsford MA (01863) ***(G-13887)***
Courier Companies Inc (PA) 978 251-6000
15 Wellman Ave North Chelmsford MA (01863) ***(G-13888)***
Courier Epic, North Chelmsford *Also called Courier New Media Inc* ***(G-13890)***
Courier Intl Holdings LLC 978 251-6000
15 Wellman Ave North Chelmsford MA (01863) ***(G-13889)***
Courier New Media Inc (HQ) 978 251-3945
15 Wellman Ave North Chelmsford MA (01863) ***(G-13890)***
Courier Printing Inc 413 442-3242
26 1st St Pittsfield MA (01201) ***(G-14465)***
Courier Publications, Rockland *Also called Village Netmedia Inc* ***(G-6813)***
Courrier Graphics Inc 603 626-7012
1875 S Willow St Ste B2 Manchester NH (03103) ***(G-18808)***
Course Technology, Boston *Also called Cengage Learning Inc* ***(G-8462)***
Coursestorm Inc 207 866-0328
148 Main St Orono ME (04473) ***(G-6553)***
Courtsmart Digital Systems Inc 978 251-3300
51 Middlesex St Unit 128 North Chelmsford MA (01863) ***(G-13891)***
Cousineau Forest Products, Henniker *Also called Cousineau Lumber Inc* ***(G-18304)***
Cousineau Lumber Inc 603 428-7155
1310 Old Concord Rd Henniker NH (03242) ***(G-18304)***
Cousineau Wood Products ME LLC 207 635-4445
3 Valley Rd North Anson ME (04958) ***(G-6500)***
Cousins Sawmill 207 445-2467
Rr 105 Windsor ME (04363) ***(G-7263)***
Couturier Ino 203 238-4555
5 Cross St Meriden CT (06451) ***(G-2089)***
Covalent Coating Tech LLC 860 214-6452
222 Pitkin St East Hartford CT (06108) ***(G-1184)***
Covalnce Spcalty Adhesives LLC 812 424-2904
25 Forge Pkwy Franklin MA (02038) ***(G-11033)***
Covalnce Spcalty Adhesives LLC 401 253-2595
51 Ballou Blvd Bristol RI (02809) ***(G-20071)***
Covarls Inc (PA) 781 932-3959
14 Gill St Unit H Woburn MA (01801) ***(G-17154)***
Cove Metal Company Inc (PA) 401 724-3500
160 Grenville St Pawtucket RI (02860) ***(G-20826)***
Cove Press, Stamford *Also called US Games Systems Inc* ***(G-4353)***
Cove Shoe Company Division, Greenwich *Also called HH Brown Shoe Company Inc* ***(G-1620)***
Cove Textile Machinery Co, Pawtucket *Also called Cove Metal Company Inc* ***(G-20826)***
Cove Woodworking Inc 978 704-9773
5 Hesperus Ave Gloucester MA (01930) ***(G-11175)***
Coventry Log Homes 603 747-8177
108 S Court St Woodsville NH (03785) ***(G-20030)***
Covered Security Inc 781 218-9894
170 Milk St Ste 2 Boston MA (02109) ***(G-8485)***
Coveris Advanced Coatings 413 539-5547
69 William Frank Dr West Springfield MA (01089) ***(G-16513)***
Coveside Conservation Products, Portland *Also called A-Po-G Inc* ***(G-6608)***

ALPHABETIC

Covestro LLC 412 777-2000
8 Fairview Way South Deerfield MA (01373) *(G-15248)*
Covey Engineering, Peabody *Also called John Covey* *(G-14346)*
Covidien, Mansfield *Also called Nellcor Puritan Bennett LLC* *(G-12649)*
Covidien France Holdings Inc 508 261-8000
15 Hampshire St Mansfield MA (02048) *(G-12620)*
Covidien Holding Inc 203 492-5000
195 Mcdermott Rd North Haven CT (06473) *(G-3019)*
Covidien LLC 508 261-8000
15 Hampshire St Mansfield MA (02048) *(G-12621)*
Covidien LP 203 492-6332
195 Mcdermott Rd North Haven CT (06473) *(G-3020)*
Covidien LP 781 839-1722
555 Long Wharf Dr Fl 4 New Haven CT (06511) *(G-2680)*
Covidien LP (HQ) 763 514-4000
15 Hampshire St Mansfield MA (02048) *(G-12622)*
Covidien LP 203 492-5000
60 Middletown Ave North Haven CT (06473) *(G-3021)*
Covidien US Holdings Inc 508 261-8000
15 Hampshire St Mansfield MA (02048) *(G-12623)*
Covit America Inc 860 274-6791
1 Seemar Rd Watertown CT (06795) *(G-5004)*
Cow Town Productions Inc 413 259-1350
233 N Pleasant St Amherst MA (01002) *(G-7514)*
Cowles Products Company Inc 203 865-3110
126 Bailey Rd North Haven CT (06473) *(G-3022)*
Cowles Stamping Inc 203 865-3117
126 Bailey Rd North Haven CT (06473) *(G-3023)*
Cox Machine 207 342-2267
39 Belfast Augusta Rd W Searsmont ME (04973) *(G-6944)*
Cox Woodworking Inc 603 399-7704
5 Route 63 Westmoreland NH (03467) *(G-19970)*
CP, Torrington *Also called Connectcut Prcsion Cmpnnts LLC* *(G-4573)*
CP Solar Thermal LLC 860 877-2238
210 Century Dr Bristol CT (06010) *(G-544)*
CPC Plastics Inc 401 828-0820
770 Main St West Warwick RI (02893) *(G-21488)*
Cph Program & Machine Tool Des 603 716-3849
134 Haines St 17 Nashua NH (03060) *(G-19138)*
CPI Radant Tech Div Inc 978 562-3866
100 Adams St Clinton MA (01510) *(G-10078)*
Cpk Manufacturing LLC 207 622-6229
681 Riverside Dr Augusta ME (04330) *(G-5606)*
CPM Acquisition Corp 319 232-8444
18 Continental Blvd Merrimack NH (03054) *(G-18994)*
CPM Acquisition Corp 603 423-6300
18 Continental Blvd Merrimack NH (03054) *(G-18995)*
CPM U.S.A. Merr, Merrimack *Also called CPM Acquisition Corp* *(G-18995)*
Cpo Science, Nashua *Also called Delta Education LLC* *(G-19144)*
CPS Technologies Corp 508 222-0614
111 S Worcester St Norton MA (02766) *(G-14073)*
Cr Technology Inc 978 681-5305
55 Chase St Ste 3 Methuen MA (01844) *(G-13016)*
Cr-TEC Engineering Inc 203 318-9500
15 Orchard Park Rd A20 Madison CT (06443) *(G-1957)*
Craft Inc 508 761-7917
1929 County St Attleboro MA (02703) *(G-7725)*
Craft Beer Guild Distrg VT LLC (PA) 781 585-5165
35 Elder Ave Kingston MA (02364) *(G-11956)*
Craft Beer Guild of Vermont, Kingston *Also called Craft Beer Guild Distrg VT LLC* *(G-11956)*
Craft Brew Alliance Inc 603 430-8600
35 Corporate Dr Portsmouth NH (03801) *(G-19555)*
Craft Corrugated Box Inc 508 998-2115
4674 Acushnet Ave New Bedford MA (02745) *(G-13374)*
Craft Interiors 781 321-8695
13 Irving St Malden MA (02148) *(G-12566)*
Craftline, North Haven *Also called Platt-Labonia of N Haven Inc* *(G-3052)*
Craftmens Corner 413 782-3783
940 Boston Rd Springfield MA (01119) *(G-15462)*
Craftsmen Printing Group Inc 203 327-2817
104 Lincoln Ave Stamford CT (06902) *(G-4175)*
Craig AAR 978 691-0024
800 Turnpike St Ste 300 North Andover MA (01845) *(G-13696)*
Craig F Bradford 413 586-4500
190 Industrial Dr Ste 1 Northampton MA (01060) *(G-14003)*
Crain Communications Inc 617 357-9090
77 Franklin St Lbby Boston MA (02110) *(G-8486)*
Cramaro Tarpaulin Systems Inc 508 393-3062
51 Sw Cutoff Northborough MA (01532) *(G-14031)*
Cramer Company 860 291-8402
105 Nutmeg Rd S South Windsor CT (06074) *(G-3954)*
Cramer Fabrics Inc 603 742-3838
20 Venture Dr Dover NH (03820) *(G-18016)*
Cramik Enterprises Inc 401 596-8171
34 Canal St Ste 1 Westerly RI (02891) *(G-21521)*
Cranberry Country Machine & Tl 508 923-1107
15 Summer St Middleboro MA (02346) *(G-13060)*
Crane & Co Inc 413 684-6856
66 Downing Industrial Par Pittsfield MA (01201) *(G-14466)*
Crane & Co Inc (HQ) 617 648-3799
1 Beacon St Ste 1702 Boston MA (02108) *(G-8487)*
Crane & Co Inc 413 684-2600
17 Downing Industrial Par Pittsfield MA (01201) *(G-14467)*
Crane & Co Inc 413 664-4321
1466 Curran Hwy North Adams MA (01247) *(G-13672)*
Crane & Co Inc 413 684-2600
30 South St Dalton MA (01226) *(G-10176)*
Crane & Co Inc 413 684-2600
800 Main St Dalton MA (01226) *(G-10177)*
Crane Aerospace Inc (HQ) 203 363-7300
100 Stamford Pl Stamford CT (06902) *(G-4176)*
Crane Co (PA) 203 363-7300
100 1st Stamford Pl # 300 Stamford CT (06902) *(G-4177)*
Crane Composition Inc 774 338-5183
23 Ploughed Neck Rd East Sandwich MA (02537) *(G-10506)*
Crane Controls Inc (HQ) 203 363-7300
100 Stamford Pl Stamford CT (06902) *(G-4178)*
Crane Currency, Boston *Also called Crane & Co Inc* *(G-8487)*
Crane Currency, Nashua *Also called Crane Security Tech Inc* *(G-19139)*
Crane Currency Us LLC 617 648-3710
1 Beacon St Ste 1702 Boston MA (02108) *(G-8488)*
Crane Data LLC 508 439-4419
110 Turnpike Rd Ste 213 Westborough MA (01581) *(G-16610)*
Crane Intl Holdings Inc (HQ) 203 363-7300
100 Stamford Pl Stamford CT (06902) *(G-4179)*
Crane Mdsg Systems Inc 781 501-5800
990 Washington St Ste 205 Dedham MA (02026) *(G-10284)*
Crane Payment Solutions Inc (HQ) 603 685-6999
1 Executive Park Dr # 202 Bedford NH (03110) *(G-17637)*
Crane Pro Services, Chelmsford *Also called Konecranes Inc* *(G-9910)*
Crane Security Tech Inc 603 881-1860
1 Cellu Dr Nashua NH (03063) *(G-19139)*
Crane Stationery LLC 413 664-2256
1466 Curran Hwy North Adams MA (01247) *(G-13673)*
Cranes Contract Cutting Inc 207 667-9008
350 Douglas Hwy Lamoine ME (04605) *(G-6263)*
Cranial Technologies Inc 203 318-8739
1343 Boston Post Rd Madison CT (06443) *(G-1958)*
Crank Shop Inc 802 878-3615
23 Kellogg Rd Essex Junction VT (05452) *(G-21938)*
Cranston Print Works Company (PA) 401 943-4800
1381 Cranston St Cranston RI (02920) *(G-20202)*
Cranston Print Works Company 800 525-0595
1381 Cranston St Cranston RI (02920) *(G-20203)*
Cranston Print Works Company 401 397-2442
25 Hopkins Hill Rd West Greenwich RI (02817) *(G-21455)*
Cranston Trucking, West Greenwich *Also called Cranston Print Works Company* *(G-21455)*
Crawford Chandler Agency Inc 413 528-3035
642 Harmon Rd Monterey MA (01245) *(G-13213)*
Crawford Sftwr Consulting Inc 603 537-9630
1e Commons Dr Unit 26 Londonderry NH (03053) *(G-18689)*
Crazy Foam International LLC 781 985-5048
181 Wells Ave Ste 105 Newton MA (02459) *(G-13584)*
Crazy Russian Girls Whole 802 681-3983
101 Main St Bennington VT (05201) *(G-21667)*
CRC Chrome Corporation 203 630-1008
169 Pratt St R Meriden CT (06450) *(G-2090)*
Crdn of Greater New Hampshire, Nashua *Also called Roll Tide of Nh LLC* *(G-19255)*
Createk-Stone Inc 888 786-6389
833 Main St Ste 2 Southbridge MA (01550) *(G-15378)*
Createx Colors, East Granby *Also called Color Craft Ltd* *(G-1121)*
Creatics LLC 781 843-2202
60 Columbian St Braintree MA (02184) *(G-8997)*
Creative Apparel Assoc LLC (HQ) 207 342-2814
318 Augusta Rd Belmont ME (04952) *(G-5702)*
Creative Apparel Assoc LLC 207 564-0235
62 Engdahl Dr Dover Foxcroft ME (04426) *(G-5960)*
Creative Bronze Inc 401 823-7340
21 Brayton St Unit 2 West Warwick RI (02893) *(G-21489)*
Creative Business, Marshfield *Also called Stysil Enterprises Ltd* *(G-12870)*
Creative Canvas 207 633-2056
514 Wiscasset Rd Boothbay ME (04537) *(G-5776)*
Creative Castings Inc 401 724-1070
1090 Main St Pawtucket RI (02860) *(G-20827)*
Creative Celebrations 978 774-7737
46 Longbow Rd Danvers MA (01923) *(G-10208)*
Creative Communications, New London *Also called Bayard Inc* *(G-2765)*
Creative Digital Imaging 207 973-0500
24 Dowd Rd Bangor ME (04401) *(G-5640)*
Creative Digital Inc 401 942-0771
85 Wildflower Dr Cranston RI (02921) *(G-20204)*
Creative Dimensions Inc 203 250-6500
345 Mccausland Ct Cheshire CT (06410) *(G-725)*
Creative Embroidery LLC 207 777-6300
213 Washington St S Auburn ME (04210) *(G-5556)*
Creative Envelope Inc 860 963-1231
26 Highland Dr Putnam CT (06260) *(G-3609)*

Creative Exchange Inc 978 863-9955
3 Brook St Chelmsford MA (01824) *(G-9889)*
Creative Extrusion & Tech Inc 508 587-2290
230 Elliot St Brockton MA (02302) *(G-9134)*
Creative Filtration Systems 603 323-2000
Rr 25 Tamworth NH (03886) *(G-19891)*
Creative Findings LLC 401 274-5579
270 Broadway Pawtucket RI (02860) *(G-20828)*
Creative Hydronics Intl Inc 508 524-3535
42 Diandy Rd Sagamore Beach MA (02562) *(G-14885)*
Creative Imprints Inc 508 285-7650
15 Commerce Way Ste A Norton MA (02766) *(G-14074)*
Creative Ink, Salem *Also called Design Copy Printers Inc* *(G-14906)*
Creative Ink 978 741-2244
167 Boston St Salem MA (01970) *(G-14903)*
Creative Kitchen & Bath Inc 508 477-3347
451 Nathan Ellis Hwy Mashpee MA (02649) *(G-12880)*
Creative Labels Vermont Inc 802 655-7654
11 Tigan St Winooski VT (05404) *(G-22720)*
Creative Ltg Designs Decor LLC 603 448-2066
227 Mechanic St Ste 2 Lebanon NH (03766) *(G-18620)*
Creative Marketing Services 802 775-9500
27 Wales St Rutland VT (05701) *(G-22327)*
Creative Materials Inc 978 391-4700
12 Willow Rd Ayer MA (01432) *(G-7916)*
Creative Media Applications 203 226-0544
22 Old Orchard Dr Weston CT (06883) *(G-5171)*
Creative Mobile Systems Inc 860 649-6272
189 Adams St Manchester CT (06042) *(G-1997)*
Creative Motion Technology 978 664-6218
45 Main St North Reading MA (01864) *(G-13981)*
Creative Pins By Lynne 401 949-3665
6 Country Dr Greenville RI (02828) *(G-20465)*
Creative Publishing Corp Amer (PA) 978 532-5880
2 1st Ave Ste 103 Peabody MA (01960) *(G-14326)*
Creative Rack Solutions Inc 203 755-2102
365 Thomaston Ave Waterbury CT (06702) *(G-4861)*
Creative Services 413 525-4993
788 Somers Rd East Longmeadow MA (01028) *(G-10470)*
Creative Signworks 508 865-7330
20 West St Millbury MA (01527) *(G-13161)*
Creative Stone LLC 203 624-1882
42 Vista Dr East Haven CT (06512) *(G-1246)*
Creative Stone & Tile, East Haven *Also called Creative Stone LLC* *(G-1246)*
Creative Stone Systems Inc 866 608-7625
169 Clay Pond Rd Ste 1 Buzzards Bay MA (02532) *(G-9360)*
Creative Strands 508 865-1141
3 Boston Rd Ste 7 Sutton MA (01590) *(G-15681)*
Creative Success Alliance Corp 781 878-7114
100 Weymouth St Ste D2 Rockland MA (02370) *(G-14796)*
Creative Threads LLC 603 466-2752
43a Dublin St Gorham NH (03581) *(G-18211)*
Credit Card Supplies Corp 508 485-4230
105 Bartlett St Marlborough MA (01752) *(G-12743)*
Credo Reference Limited 617 292-6100
50 Milk St Fl 16 Boston MA (02109) *(G-8489)*
Creed-Monarch Inc 860 225-7884
1 Pucci Park New Britain CT (06051) *(G-2524)*
Creighton Kayla 508 612-0685
315 Linwood Ave Whitinsville MA (01588) *(G-16912)*
Cremark Inc 207 874-7720
10 Exchange St Ste 208 Portland ME (04101) *(G-6644)*
Crescent Industries Company 207 777-3500
191 Washington St S Auburn ME (04210) *(G-5557)*
Crescent Mnfacturing Operating 860 673-1921
700 George Wash Tpke Burlington CT (06013) *(G-676)*
Crest Manufacturing Company 401 333-1350
5 Hood Dr Lincoln RI (02865) *(G-20566)*
Crest Printing Co Inc 617 889-1171
152 Vinton St Melrose MA (02176) *(G-12980)*
Crest Studios 802 365-4200
1096 Vt Route 30 Townshend VT (05353) *(G-22541)*
Crew By True Rowing Inc 617 398-7480
243 Bent St Apt 5 Cambridge MA (02141) *(G-9444)*
Crh Americas Inc 978 840-1176
14 Monument Sq Ste 302 Leominster MA (01453) *(G-12127)*
Cri Rubber LLC (HQ) 508 657-8488
5 Ridge Rd Hopkinton MA (01748) *(G-11698)*
Cri-Sil LLC 207 283-6422
359 Hill St Biddeford ME (04005) *(G-5726)*
Cri-Sil Silicone Technologies, Biddeford *Also called Cri-Sil LLC* *(G-5726)*
Cri-Tech Inc 781 826-5600
85 Winter St Hanover MA (02339) *(G-11333)*
Cricket Press Inc 860 521-9279
236 Park Rd West Hartford CT (06119) *(G-5063)*
Cricket Press Inc 978 526-7131
50 Summer St Manchester MA (01944) *(G-12604)*
Cricket Radio LLC 802 825-8368
260 Battery St Burlington VT (05401) *(G-21777)*
Crimson Press 781 914-3111
16 Spencer St Stoneham MA (02180) *(G-15558)*
Crimsonbikes LLC 617 958-1727
1001 Mass Ave Ste 1 Cambridge MA (02138) *(G-9445)*
Crisci Tool and Die Inc 978 537-4102
32 Jungle Rd Ste 1 Leominster MA (01453) *(G-12128)*
Cristcot Inc 978 212-6380
9 Damonmill Sq Ste 4a Concord MA (01742) *(G-10125)*
Cristcot LLC 978 212-6380
9 Damonmill Sq Ste 4a Concord MA (01742) *(G-10126)*
Cristek Interconnects Inc 978 735-2161
663 Lawrence St Lowell MA (01852) *(G-12363)*
Cristy Corporation 978 343-4330
260 Authority Dr Fitchburg MA (01420) *(G-10822)*
Criterion Inc 203 703-9000
501 Merritt 7 Ste 1 Norwalk CT (06851) *(G-3133)*
Critical Prcess Filtration Inc (PA) 603 595-0140
1 Chestnut St Ste 221 Nashua NH (03060) *(G-19140)*
Criticare Technologies Inc 401 667-3837
125 Commerce Park Rd North Kingstown RI (02852) *(G-20699)*
Crocetti-Oakdale Packing Inc (PA) 508 587-0035
378 Pleasant St East Bridgewater MA (02333) *(G-10410)*
Crocetti-Oakdale Packing Inc 508 941-0458
12 Taylor Ave Brockton MA (02302) *(G-9135)*
Crocker Architectural Shtmtl 508 987-9900
129 Southbridge Rd North Oxford MA (01537) *(G-13970)*
Crockergraphics Inc 781 444-7020
80 Spring Rd Needham Heights MA (02494) *(G-13324)*
Crompton Park Oral Surgery & I 508 799-2550
59 Quinsigamond Ave Worcester MA (01610) *(G-17361)*
Cromwell Chronicle 860 257-8715
222 Dividend Rd Rocky Hill CT (06067) *(G-3705)*
Cronin Cabinet Marine LLP 508 248-7026
164 Sturbridge Rd Ste 20 Charlton MA (01507) *(G-9847)*
Crooked Face Creamery LLC 207 858-5096
552 River Rd Norridgewock ME (04957) *(G-6496)*
Crosby Designs, Concord *Also called William Crosby* *(G-10162)*
Crosby Machine Company Inc 508 867-3121
17 Freight House Rd West Brookfield MA (01585) *(G-16468)*
Crosby Valve & Gage Intl Inc 508 384-3121
55 Cabot Blvd Mansfield MA (02048) *(G-12624)*
Cross Machine Inc 603 752-6111
167 Glen Ave Berlin NH (03570) *(G-17694)*
Crossed Genres 617 335-2101
204 Arthur St Framingham MA (01702) *(G-10937)*
Crossknots Woodworking 603 237-8392
545 Hollow Rd Stewartstown NH (03576) *(G-19861)*
Crossroads Deli & Fuel LLC 860 824-8474
123 Johnson Rd Falls Village CT (06031) *(G-1462)*
Crosstown Press Inc 401 941-4061
829 Park Ave Cranston RI (02910) *(G-20205)*
Croteau Development Group Inc 860 684-3605
25 West St Stafford Springs CT (06076) *(G-4107)*
Crow Haven Corner Inc 978 745-8763
125 Essex St Salem MA (01970) *(G-14904)*
Crowley Cheese Incorporated 802 259-2340
14 Crowley Ln Mount Holly VT (05758) *(G-22181)*
Crown Equipment Corporation 781 933-3366
2 Presidential Way Woburn MA (01801) *(G-17155)*
Crown Equipment Corporation 207 773-5890
82 Scott Dr Westbrook ME (04092) *(G-7185)*
Crown Lift Trucks, Woburn *Also called Crown Equipment Corporation* *(G-17155)*
Crown Lift Trucks, Westbrook *Also called Crown Equipment Corporation* *(G-7185)*
Crown Molding Etc LLC 203 287-9424
148 Gillies Rd Hamden CT (06517) *(G-1739)*
Crown Point Cabinetry Corp 603 542-1273
462 River Rd Claremont NH (03743) *(G-17845)*
Crown Point Realty Corp Inc 603 543-1208
153 Charlestown Rd Claremont NH (03743) *(G-17846)*
Crown Poly Inc 781 883-4979
19 Country Club Way Norton MA (02766) *(G-14075)*
Crown Properties & HM Sls LLC 603 964-2005
203 Lafayette Rd North Hampton NH (03862) *(G-19382)*
Crrc LLC 860 635-2200
46 Nooks Hill Rd Cromwell CT (06416) *(G-852)*
Crrc MA Corporation 617 415-7190
655 Page Blvd Springfield MA (01104) *(G-15463)*
CRS Steam Inc 978 630-2308
35 Chatham St Gardner MA (01440) *(G-11110)*
Crucial Cmponent Machining LLC 603 223-0012
27 Industrial Park Dr # 5 Concord NH (03301) *(G-17897)*
Crue Brew Brewery LLC 508 272-6090
293 Whippoorwill Dr Raynham MA (02767) *(G-14708)*
Cruising Direct Sails, Portsmouth *Also called North Sails Group LLC* *(G-20933)*
Crush Club LLC 203 626-9545
65 S Colony St Wallingford CT (06492) *(G-4729)*
Cruz Construction Company Inc 401 727-3770
23 Maple St Ste 6 Cumberland RI (02864) *(G-20316)*
Crww Specialty Composites Inc 401 539-8555
49 Mechanic St Hope Valley RI (02832) *(G-20483)*

ALPHABETIC

Crymed Technologies, Lexington *Also called Csa Medical Inc* ***(G-12215)***
Cryogas International, Lexington *Also called Gasworld Publishing LLC* ***(G-12225)***
Crystal Engineering Co Inc....978 465-7007
2 Stanley Tucker Dr Newburyport MA (01950) ***(G-13480)***
Crystal Fairfield Tech LLC....860 354-2111
8 S End Plz New Milford CT (06776) ***(G-2795)***
Crystal Hord Corporation....401 723-2989
33 York Ave Ste 45 Pawtucket RI (02860) ***(G-20829)***
Crystal Ice Co Inc....508 997-7522
178 Front St New Bedford MA (02740) ***(G-13375)***
Crystal Journey Candles LLC....203 433-4735
69 N Branford Rd Branford CT (06405) ***(G-307)***
Crystal Rock Holdings Inc (HQ)....860 945-0661
1050 Buckingham St Watertown CT (06795) ***(G-5005)***
Crystal Spring Water Co Inc (PA)....207 782-1521
24 Brickyard Cir Auburn ME (04210) ***(G-5558)***
Crystal Stamping....401 724-5880
51 Charlton Ave Pawtucket RI (02860) ***(G-20830)***
Crystal Stamping Corp....401 724-5880
2984 Post Rd Wakefield RI (02879) ***(G-21268)***
Crystal Tool and Machine Co....860 870-7431
114 Brooklyn St Vernon CT (06066) ***(G-4666)***
Crystal Tool LLC....860 510-0113
50 Connally Dr Old Saybrook CT (06475) ***(G-3333)***
Cs-Ma LLC....413 733-6631
2420 Boston Rd Wilbraham MA (01095) ***(G-16934)***
Csa Medical Inc....443 921-8053
91 Hartwell Ave Ste 1 Lexington MA (02421) ***(G-12215)***
CSC Cocoa LLC....203 846-5611
36 Grove St New Canaan CT (06840) ***(G-2596)***
Csg Inc....207 846-9567
247 Portland St Ste 5 Yarmouth ME (04096) ***(G-7293)***
Csi, Harwinton *Also called Spring Computerized Inds LLC* ***(G-1893)***
Csi Mfg Inc....508 986-2300
121 Flanders Rd Westborough MA (01581) ***(G-16611)***
Csl Building Group LLC (PA)....616 669-6692
10 Park Pl Lee MA (01238) ***(G-12091)***
Csp Inc (PA)....978 954-5038
175 Cabot St Ste 210 Lowell MA (01854) ***(G-12364)***
Cspi, Lowell *Also called Csp Inc* ***(G-12364)***
CST, Fall River *Also called Commonwlth Soap Toiletries Inc* ***(G-10678)***
Csw, Wallingford *Also called Connecticut Screen Works Inc* ***(G-4726)***
Csw Inc (PA)....413 589-1311
45 Tyburski Rd Ludlow MA (01056) ***(G-12461)***
CT Acquisitions LLC....888 441-0537
1 Grand St Wallingford CT (06492) ***(G-4730)***
CT Composites & Marine Svc LLC....860 282-0100
620 Sullivan Ave South Windsor CT (06074) ***(G-3955)***
CT Conveyor LLC....860 637-2926
320 Terryville Rd Bristol CT (06010) ***(G-545)***
CT Dumpster LLC....203 521-0779
32 Birch Ave Milford CT (06460) ***(G-2271)***
CT Fiberoptics Inc....860 763-4341
64 Field Rd Ste 11 Somers CT (06071) ***(G-3915)***
CT Pellet, Torrington *Also called Scott Olson Enterprises LLC* ***(G-4598)***
CT Precast, Monroe *Also called Connecticut Precast Corp* ***(G-2398)***
CT Tool, Plainville *Also called Connecticut Tool & Mfg Co LLC* ***(G-3478)***
CT Woodworking LLC....860 884-9586
438 Route 32 North Franklin CT (06254) ***(G-2988)***
Ctech Adhesives....860 482-5947
39 Maple Hollow Rd New Hartford CT (06057) ***(G-2634)***
CTI, Newington *Also called Component Technologies Inc* ***(G-2855)***
CTI Industries Inc (HQ)....203 795-0070
283 Indian River Rd Orange CT (06477) ***(G-3362)***
Ctl Corporation....860 651-9173
10 Rocklyn Ct West Simsbury CT (06092) ***(G-5154)***
Ctr, Bridgeport *Also called Palmieri Industries Inc* ***(G-462)***
Ctr Enterprises....978 794-2093
60 Railroad St Ste 1 Haverhill MA (01835) ***(G-11420)***
Ctr Welding....704 473-1587
39 Padanaram Rd Danbury CT (06811) ***(G-894)***
CTS Services LLC....203 268-5865
15 Rayo Dr Shelton CT (06484) ***(G-3791)***
CTS Valpey Corporation (HQ)....508 435-6831
75 South St Hopkinton MA (01748) ***(G-11699)***
Cubic Wafer Inc....603 546-0600
10 Al Paul Ln Ste 204 Merrimack NH (03054) ***(G-18996)***
Cubist Pharmaceuticals LLC....781 860-8660
65 Hayden Ave Lexington MA (02421) ***(G-12216)***
Cudzilo Enterprises Inc....203 748-4694
40 Taylor Ave Bethel CT (06801) ***(G-139)***
Cue Inc....617 591-9500
19 Norfolk Ave Ste D South Easton MA (02375) ***(G-15275)***
Cue Biopharma Inc (PA)....617 949-2680
21 Erie St Ste 1 Cambridge MA (02139) ***(G-9446)***
Cuenca Vision, Boston *Also called La Semana Newspaper* ***(G-8658)***
Cuero Operating....203 253-8651
34 Meeker Rd Westport CT (06880) ***(G-5187)***
Cuescript Inc....203 763-4030
555 Lordship Blvd Unit F Stratford CT (06615) ***(G-4407)***
Cuesport Inc....413 229-6626
1415 Canaan Southfield Rd Southfield MA (01259) ***(G-15410)***
Cuivre & Co LLC....401 965-4569
5 Division St Bldg G East Greenwich RI (02818) ***(G-20359)***
Cuizina Foods Company....425 486-7000
330 Lynnway Ste 102 Lynn MA (01901) ***(G-12498)***
Culligan Water Technologies, Colchester *Also called Everett M Windover Inc* ***(G-21863)***
Cullinan Manufacturing Inc....978 465-1110
25 Howlett St Topsfield MA (01983) ***(G-15855)***
Cultec Inc....203 775-4416
878 Federal Rd Brookfield CT (06804) ***(G-639)***
Culver Company LLC....978 463-1700
104 Bridge Rd Salisbury MA (01952) ***(G-14949)***
Cumberland Foundry Co Inc....401 658-3300
310 W Wrentham Rd Cumberland RI (02864) ***(G-20317)***
Cuming Microwave Corporation (HQ)....508 521-6700
264 Bodwell St Avon MA (02322) ***(G-7884)***
Cummings Printing Company, Hooksett *Also called Lew A Cummings Co Inc* ***(G-18352)***
Cummins Inc....413 737-2659
177 Rocus St Ste 1 Springfield MA (01104) ***(G-15464)***
Cummins Northeast LLC....781 329-1750
100 Allied Dr Dedham MA (02026) ***(G-10285)***
Cunniff Corp (PA)....508 540-6232
36 Round Pond Dr East Falmouth MA (02536) ***(G-10440)***
Cunningham Engineering Inc....978 774-4169
9 Electronics Ave Danvers MA (01923) ***(G-10209)***
Cunningham Industries Inc....203 324-2942
102 Lincoln Ave Ste 3 Stamford CT (06902) ***(G-4180)***
Cunningham Machine Co Inc....978 256-7541
35 Hunt Rd Chelmsford MA (01824) ***(G-9890)***
Cunningham Tech LLC (PA)....860 738-8759
39 Maple Hollow Rd New Hartford CT (06057) ***(G-2635)***
Cupcake Rowe LLC....603 673-0489
25 Wyman Ln Milford NH (03055) ***(G-19054)***
Cupcake Town....774 284-4667
237 West St Mansfield MA (02048) ***(G-12625)***
Cura Software Solutions Co....781 325-7158
34 Crosby Dr Bedford MA (01730) ***(G-7967)***
Curagen Corporation (HQ)....908 200-7500
119 4th Ave Needham Heights MA (02494) ***(G-13325)***
Curator....603 756-3888
108 Wentworth Rd Walpole NH (03608) ***(G-19919)***
Curbside Compost LLC....914 646-6890
65 Spring Valley Rd Ridgefield CT (06877) ***(G-3664)***
Curevac Inc....617 694-1537
34 Farnsworth St Ste 101 Boston MA (02210) ***(G-8490)***
Curirx Inc....978 658-2962
205 Lowell St 1c Wilmington MA (01887) ***(G-16990)***
Curis Inc (PA)....617 503-6500
4 Maguire Rd Lexington MA (02421) ***(G-12217)***
Current Ltg Employeeco LLC....216 266-2906
745 Atlantic Ave Boston MA (02111) ***(G-8491)***
Current Publishing LLC....207 854-2577
5 Fundy Rd Ste 1 Falmouth ME (04105) ***(G-6030)***
Curriculum Associates LLC....978 313-1331
12 Beacon St Ste 510 Boston MA (02108) ***(G-8492)***
Curriculum Associates LLC....978 313-1276
1 Distribution Center Cir # 200 Littleton MA (01460) ***(G-12298)***
Curriculum Associates LLC (PA)....978 667-8000
153 Rangeway Rd North Billerica MA (01862) ***(G-13805)***
Currier Engineering....781 449-7706
316 Hunnewell St Needham MA (02494) ***(G-13298)***
Curry Copy and Printing Center, Manchester *Also called Baker Graphics Inc* ***(G-18784)***
Curry Copy Center of Keene....603 352-9542
7 Emerald St Apt 204 Keene NH (03431) ***(G-18499)***
Curry Copy Ctr W Springfield, West Springfield *Also called Paper Plus Inc* ***(G-16540)***
Curry Printing, Westborough *Also called J T Gardner Inc* ***(G-16627)***
Curry Printing, Worcester *Also called J T Gardner Inc* ***(G-17396)***
Curry Printing & Copy Center, Auburn *Also called J T Gardner Inc* ***(G-7839)***
Curry Printing & Copy Center, Westborough *Also called J T Gardner Inc* ***(G-16628)***
Curry Printing & Copy Center....207 772-5897
10 City Ctr Portland ME (04101) ***(G-6645)***
Curry Printing & Marketing, Auburn *Also called Computech Inc* ***(G-5554)***
Curry Printing & Office Sups, Keene *Also called Curry Copy Center of Keene* ***(G-18499)***
Curry's Leather Products, Randolph *Also called Currys Leather Shop Inc* ***(G-14675)***
Currys Leather Shop Inc....781 963-0679
314 High St Randolph MA (02368) ***(G-14675)***
Curtain Manufacturers Plus....508 675-8680
113 Griffin St Fall River MA (02724) ***(G-10681)***
Curtil North America LLC....661 294-0030
12 Betnr Industrial Dr Pittsfield MA (01201) ***(G-14468)***
Curtis Corporation A Del Corp....203 426-5861
44 Berkshire Rd Sandy Hook CT (06482) ***(G-3742)***
Curtis Industries LLC (PA)....508 853-2200
70 Hartwell St West Boylston MA (01583) ***(G-16413)***
Curtis Packaging Corporation....203 426-5861
44 Berkshire Rd Sandy Hook CT (06482) ***(G-3743)***

Curtis Products LLC 203 754-4155
70 Halcyon Dr Bristol CT (06010) *(G-546)*
Curtis Tractor Cab, West Boylston *Also called Curtis Industries LLC (G-16413)*
Curtis Universal Joint Co Inc 413 737-0281
4 Birnie Ave Springfield MA (01107) *(G-15465)*
Curtiss Woodworking Inc 203 527-9305
123 Union City Rd Prospect CT (06712) *(G-3586)*
Curtiss Wright Surface Tech, Wakefield *Also called Metal Improvement Company LLC (G-15961)*
Curtiss-Wright Surface Tech, Wilmington *Also called Metal Improvement Company LLC (G-17023)*
Curved Glass Distributors, Derby *Also called Whalley Glass Company (G-1083)*
Cusa Technologies Inc 508 339-7675
800 S Main St Ste 301 Mansfield MA (02048) *(G-12626)*
Cushs Homegrown LLC 860 739-7373
4 Green Valley Lake Rd Old Lyme CT (06371) *(G-3318)*
Cusson Sash Company 860 659-0354
128 Addison Rd Glastonbury CT (06033) *(G-1546)*
Custom & Miller Box Company 401 431-9007
25 Almeida Ave East Providence RI (02914) *(G-20401)*
Custom & Precision Pdts Inc 203 281-0818
2893 State St Rear Hamden CT (06517) *(G-1740)*
Custom Arospc Components LLC 781 935-4940
30 Nashua St Ste 3 Woburn MA (01801) *(G-17156)*
Custom Atmated Prosthetics LLC (HQ) 781 279-2771
85 Maple St Ste 1 Stoneham MA (02180) *(G-15559)*
Custom Banner & Graphics LLC 603 332-2067
184 Milton Rd Rochester NH (03868) *(G-19666)*
Custom Canvas & Upholstery LLC 207 241-8518
134 Main St Ste 8 Lewiston ME (04240) *(G-6281)*
Custom Carbide Corp 413 732-7470
616 Dwight St Springfield MA (01104) *(G-15466)*
Custom Chrome Plating 203 265-5667
400 S Orchard St Wallingford CT (06492) *(G-4731)*
Custom Coatings 508 771-8830
104 Enterprise Rd Hyannis MA (02601) *(G-11838)*
Custom Composite Mfg Inc 401 275-2230
21 Palmer Ave Cranston RI (02920) *(G-20206)*
Custom Composite Technologies 207 442-7007
15 Wing Farm Pkwy Bath ME (04530) *(G-5675)*
Custom Computer Systems Inc 508 393-8899
36 Woodland Rd Northborough MA (01532) *(G-14032)*
Custom Convyrs Fabrication Inc 508 922-0283
140 Southbridge Rd North Oxford MA (01537) *(G-13971)*
Custom Cordage LLC, Waldoboro *Also called Advanced Indus Solutions Inc (G-7129)*
Custom Covers 860 669-4169
20 Riverside Dr Clinton CT (06413) *(G-784)*
Custom Crafted Enterprises 508 695-2878
123 John L Dietsch Sq North Attleboro MA (02763) *(G-13754)*
Custom Crft Ktchns By Rizio BR 203 268-0271
8 Maple Dr Monroe CT (06468) *(G-2400)*
Custom Design Incorporated 401 294-0200
370 Commerce Park Rd North Kingstown RI (02852) *(G-20700)*
Custom Design Service Corp 203 748-1105
6 Ohehyahtah Pl Danbury CT (06810) *(G-895)*
Custom Design Woodworks LLC 860 434-0515
10 Maywood Dr Old Lyme CT (06371) *(G-3319)*
Custom Die Cut Inc 603 437-3090
3 Lexington Rd Unit 1a Windham NH (03087) *(G-20003)*
Custom Flow Solutions LLC 401 487-2957
61 Dora St Providence RI (02909) *(G-20991)*
Custom Food Pdts Holdings LLC 310 637-0900
411 W Putnam Ave Greenwich CT (06830) *(G-1605)*
Custom Furniture & Design LLC 860 567-3519
601 Bantam Rd Litchfield CT (06759) *(G-1947)*
Custom Glass and Alum Co Inc 978 640-5800
120 Lumber Ln Unit 4 Tewksbury MA (01876) *(G-15813)*
Custom House LLC 860 873-1259
8 Matthews Dr Ste 3 East Haddam CT (06423) *(G-1150)*
Custom Interiors 860 738-8754
152 Colebrook River Rd Winchester Center CT (06098) *(G-5310)*
Custom Iron Works Inc 401 826-3310
1600 Flat River Rd Coventry RI (02816) *(G-20144)*
Custom Ktchens By Chmpagne Inc 508 528-7919
170 Grove St Franklin MA (02038) *(G-11034)*
Custom Learning Designs Inc 617 489-1702
375 Concord Ave Ste 101 Belmont MA (02478) *(G-8071)*
Custom Machine & Tool Co Inc 781 924-1003
301 Winter St Ste 2 Hanover MA (02339) *(G-11334)*
Custom Machine LLC 781 935-4940
30 Nashua St Ste 2 Woburn MA (01801) *(G-17157)*
Custom Manufacturing Svcs Inc 603 883-1355
235 Main Dunstable Rd Nashua NH (03062) *(G-19141)*
Custom Marine Canvas LLC 860 572-9547
71 Marsh Rd Groton CT (06340) *(G-1669)*
Custom Metal Crafters Inc 860 953-4210
815 N Mountain Rd Newington CT (06111) *(G-2857)*
Custom Metal Crafters CMC, Newington *Also called Custom Metal Crafters Inc (G-2857)*
Custom Metal Fabrication 413 584-8200
40 Audubon Rd Leeds MA (01053) *(G-12098)*
Custom Mmic Design Svcs Inc 978 467-4290
300 Apollo Dr Chelmsford MA (01824) *(G-9891)*
Custom Mtal Fabricators VT LLC 802 888-0033
327 Ferry St Hyde Park VT (05655) *(G-22035)*
Custom Office Furn Boston Inc 781 933-9970
10 Atlantic Ave Ste 3 Woburn MA (01801) *(G-17158)*
Custom Pallets Inc 508 867-2411
2 Mill St Brookfield MA (01506) *(G-9189)*
Custom Plastics Machining Inc 781 937-9700
9 Presidential Way Ste D Woburn MA (01801) *(G-17159)*
Custom Printing & Copy Inc (PA) 860 290-6890
16 Debra St Enfield CT (06082) *(G-1354)*
Custom Publishing Design Group 860 513-1213
35 Cold Spring Rd Ste 321 Rocky Hill CT (06067) *(G-3706)*
Custom Quality Silk Screen 781 878-0760
333 Weymouth St Ste 5 Rockland MA (02370) *(G-14797)*
Custom Seamless Gutters Inc 401 726-3137
260 Pawtucket Ave Frnt Pawtucket RI (02860) *(G-20831)*
Custom Seasonings Inc 978 762-6300
12 Heritage Way Gloucester MA (01930) *(G-11176)*
Custom Sports Sleeves LLC 508 344-9749
49 Royal Oaks Way Leominster MA (01453) *(G-12129)*
Custom Sportswear Mfg 203 879-4420
14 Town Line Rd Wolcott CT (06716) *(G-5437)*
Custom Steel Fabrication Corp 978 774-4555
26 Lonergan Rd Middleton MA (01949) *(G-13087)*
Custom Stitch 978 988-1344
379 Middlesex Ave Wilmington MA (01887) *(G-16991)*
Custom Tees Plus 203 752-1071
365 Whalley Ave New Haven CT (06511) *(G-2681)*
Custom TS n More LLC 203 438-1592
135 Ethan Allen Hwy Ridgefield CT (06877) *(G-3665)*
Custom Welding & Fabrications 603 942-5170
127 Old Turnpike Rd West Nottingham NH (03291) *(G-19964)*
Custom Window Decorators 207 784-4113
1486 Lisbon St Lewiston ME (04240) *(G-6282)*
Custom Woods Designs M Marion 413 566-8230
76 Bennett Rd Hampden MA (01036) *(G-11320)*
Custom Woodturning 401 625-5909
381 State Ave Tiverton RI (02878) *(G-21256)*
Custom Woodworking Brentwood 603 887-6766
10 Edwards Mill Rd Chester NH (03036) *(G-17824)*
Custom Woodworking LLC 978 928-3366
12 Old Westminster Rd Hubbardston MA (01452) *(G-11743)*
Customer Fulfillment Center, Quincy *Also called Boston Scientific Corporation (G-14617)*
Customized Foods Mfg LLC 203 759-1645
8 S Commons Rd Waterbury CT (06704) *(G-4862)*
Customscoop, Manchester *Also called Eoutreach Solutions LLC (G-18817)*
Cut Rite Instruments, Taunton *Also called Diamond Plated Technology Inc (G-15743)*
Cutanea Life Sciences Inc 484 568-0100
120 Presidential Way # 330 Woburn MA (01801) *(G-17160)*
Cutispharma Inc 800 461-7449
841 Woburn St Wilmington MA (01887) *(G-16992)*
Cutlass Marine Inc 781 740-1260
55 Woodrock Rd Ste 8 East Weymouth MA (02189) *(G-10540)*
Cutter & Locke Inc (PA) 802 889-3500
234 Monarch Hill Rd Tunbridge VT (05077) *(G-22542)*
Cutting Edge Carbide Tech Inc 888 210-9670
36 School St Leominster MA (01453) *(G-12130)*
Cutting Edge Technologies, Plymouth *Also called Richards Micro-Tool LLC (G-14580)*
Cutting Edge Texstyles, Bedford *Also called Brand & Oppenheimer Co Inc (G-7965)*
Cutting Tool Technologies Inc 603 654-2550
327 Forest Rd Wilton NH (03086) *(G-19977)*
Cv Machine Co & Hobby Shop, North Conway *Also called C-V Machine Company LLC (G-19375)*
CVI Group Inc (PA) 603 595-7233
55 Northstern Blvd Unit 2 Nashua NH (03062) *(G-19100)*
CW Hood Yachts Inc 781 631-0192
3 Beacon St Ste 4 Marblehead MA (01945) *(G-12680)*
Cwl Enterprises Inc (HQ) 303 790-8023
200 First Stamford Pl # 2 Stamford CT (06902) *(G-4181)*
Cx Thin Films LLC 401 461-5500
1515 Elmwood Ave Cranston RI (02910) *(G-20207)*
Cxe Equipment Services LLC 603 437-2477
33 Beckman Lndg Seabrook NH (03874) *(G-19798)*
Cxo Media Inc (HQ) 508 766-5696
492 Old Connecticut Path # 200 Framingham MA (01701) *(G-10938)*
Cya Technologies Inc 203 513-3111
3 Enterprise Dr Ste 408 Shelton CT (06484) *(G-3792)*
Cyalume Technologies Inc (HQ) 888 451-4885
96 Windsor St West Springfield MA (01089) *(G-16514)*
Cyberark Software Inc (HQ) 617 965-1544
60 Wells Ave Ste 103 Newton MA (02459) *(G-13585)*
Cybercopy Inc 207 775-2679
1006 Forest Ave Ste 1 Portland ME (04103) *(G-6646)*
Cybertools For Libraries, Boston *Also called Cybertools Inc (G-8493)*

ALPHABETIC

Cybertools Inc...978 772-9200
75 Arlington St 500 Boston MA (02116) *(G-8493)*
Cybex International Inc...508 533-4167
51 Alder St Medway MA (02053) *(G-12958)*
Cybtek Inc...978 532-7110
147 Summit St Ste 3b3 Peabody MA (01960) *(G-14327)*
Cycle Engineering Inc...413 967-3818
132 Gilbertville Rd Ware MA (01082) *(G-16231)*
Cycle-TEC...508 966-0066
74 Mendon St Bellingham MA (02019) *(G-8036)*
Cyclerion Therapeutics Inc (PA)...857 327-8778
301 Binney St Cambridge MA (02142) *(G-9447)*
Cycling Sports Group Inc (HQ)...608 268-8916
1 Cannondale Way Wilton CT (06897) *(G-5286)*
Cyclone Microsystems Inc...203 786-5536
25 Marne St Hamden CT (06514) *(G-1741)*
Cyclone Pcie Systems LLC...203 786-5536
25 Marne St Hamden CT (06514) *(G-1742)*
Cyclones Arena...603 880-4424
20 Constitution Dr Hudson NH (03051) *(G-18381)*
Cygnus Business Media, Westport *Also called Commerce Connect Media Inc* *(G-5184)*
Cygnus Medical LLC...800 990-7489
965 W Main St Ste 2 Branford CT (06405) *(G-308)*
Cylinder Vodka Inc...203 979-0792
101 Washington Blvd # 1223 Stamford CT (06902) *(G-4182)*
Cyn Environmental Services, Stoughton *Also called Cyn Oil Corporation* *(G-15585)*
Cyn Oil Corporation...781 341-8074
1771 Washington St Stoughton MA (02072) *(G-15585)*
Cynosure Inc (HQ)...978 256-4200
5 Carlisle Rd Westford MA (01886) *(G-16763)*
Cynthia Carroll Pallian...207 646-1600
2049 Post Rd Wells ME (04090) *(G-7160)*
Cyr Sign & Banner Company...781 395-7297
40 Canal St Ste 2 Medford MA (02155) *(G-12928)*
Cyr Woodworking Inc...860 232-1991
139 Summit St Newington CT (06111) *(G-2858)*
Cyro Industries...203 269-4481
25 Executive Blvd 1 Orange CT (06477) *(G-3363)*
Cyro Industry...207 324-6000
1796 Main St Sanford ME (04073) *(G-6873)*
Cyta Therapeutics Inc...617 947-1416
165 New Boston St Woburn MA (01801) *(G-17161)*
Cytec Industries Inc...203 321-2200
1937 W Main St Ste 1 Stamford CT (06902) *(G-4183)*
Cytocure LLC...978 232-1243
100 Cummings Ctr Ste 430c Beverly MA (01915) *(G-8122)*
Cytonome/St LLC...617 330-5030
9 Oak Park Dr Bedford MA (01730) *(G-7968)*
Cytosol Laboratories Inc...781 848-9386
55 Messina Dr Ste 4 Braintree MA (02184) *(G-8998)*
Cytovera Inc...617 682-8981
10 Hammond Pond Pkwy # 102 Chestnut Hill MA (02467) *(G-9985)*
Cytyc Corporation...603 668-7688
2 E Perimeter Rd Londonderry NH (03053) *(G-18690)*
Cytyc Corporation (HQ)...508 263-2900
250 Campus Dr Marlborough MA (01752) *(G-12744)*
Cytyc Corporation...508 303-4746
445 Simarano Dr Marlborough MA (01752) *(G-12745)*
Cytyc Surgical Products LLC...508 263-2900
250 Campus Dr Marlborough MA (01752) *(G-12746)*
Cz Machine Inc...603 382-4259
110 Hunt Rd East Hampstead NH (03826) *(G-18081)*
Czitek LLC...888 326-8186
4 Ford Ln Danbury CT (06811) *(G-896)*
D & B Machining Inc...401 726-2347
53 John St Cumberland RI (02864) *(G-20318)*
D & B Tool Co LLC...203 878-6026
83 Erna Ave Milford CT (06461) *(G-2272)*
D & D Model Cleaning & Casting...401 274-4011
2 Leah St Johnston RI (02919) *(G-20505)*
D & D Precision Machine Co Inc...508 946-8010
395 Plymouth St Middleboro MA (02346) *(G-13061)*
D & E Screw Machine Pdts Inc...508 658-7344
34 Bill Bromage Dr Colebrook NH (03576) *(G-17866)*
D & G Machine Products Inc...207 854-1500
50 Eisenhower Dr Westbrook ME (04092) *(G-7186)*
D & H Inc...401 847-6690
210 Coddington Hwy Middletown RI (02842) *(G-20618)*
D & H Print Management Ltd...781 829-0209
300 Oak St Ste 1925 Pembroke MA (02359) *(G-14396)*
D & J Fuels LLC...207 646-5561
287 Perry Oliver Rd Wells ME (04090) *(G-7161)*
D & L Associates Inc...781 400-5068
679 Highland Ave Rear Needham Heights MA (02494) *(G-13326)*
D & L Engineering Company...203 375-5856
564 Surf Ave Stratford CT (06615) *(G-4408)*
D & M Screw Machine Pdts LLC...860 410-9781
97 Forestville Ave Plainville CT (06062) *(G-3479)*
D & M Tool Company Inc...860 236-6037
17 Grassmere Ave West Hartford CT (06110) *(G-5064)*
D & P Instruments, Simsbury *Also called Designs & Prototypes Ltd* *(G-3899)*
D & R Products Co Inc...978 562-4137
455 River Rd Hudson MA (01749) *(G-11767)*
D & S Manufacturing, Southwick *Also called Tova Industries Inc* *(G-15419)*
D & S Plating Co Inc...413 533-7771
102 Cabot St Ste 6 Holyoke MA (01040) *(G-11621)*
D & T Spinning Inc...802 228-2925
608 Fletcher Hill Rd South Woodstock VT (05071) *(G-22497)*
D & W Tool Findings Inc...401 727-3030
304 Cottage St Pawtucket RI (02860) *(G-20832)*
D 2 Incorporated...508 329-2046
6 Otis Park Dr Ste 1 Bourne MA (02532) *(G-8945)*
D A Mfg Co LLC...978 297-1059
261 Lincoln Ave Winchendon MA (01475) *(G-17072)*
D B F Industries Inc...860 827-8283
145 Edgewood Ave New Britain CT (06051) *(G-2525)*
D B S Industries Inc...978 373-4748
144 Hilldale Ave Haverhill MA (01832) *(G-11421)*
D C Hall Rental Service, North Branford *Also called Halls Rental Service LLC* *(G-2966)*
D C Industrial Sales, Warren *Also called David P Cioe* *(G-21294)*
D C M Services, Framingham *Also called David Gilbert* *(G-10940)*
D C Speeney Sons Pyrotechnics...603 532-9323
531 North St Jaffrey NH (03452) *(G-18458)*
D Cedrone Inc...508 405-4260
7 Hiram Rd Framingham MA (01701) *(G-10939)*
D Clement Inc...978 649-3263
130 Pond St Dunstable MA (01827) *(G-10389)*
D Cronins Welding Service...978 664-4488
70 State St Lawrence MA (01843) *(G-12014)*
D D Bean & Sons Co (PA)...603 532-8311
207 Peterborough St Jaffrey NH (03452) *(G-18459)*
D D G Fabrication...603 883-9292
29 Crown St Nashua NH (03060) *(G-19142)*
D D M Metal Finishing Co Inc...860 872-4683
25 Industrial Park Rd W Tolland CT (06084) *(G-4542)*
D E Enterprise Inc...207 594-9544
680 Commercial St Rockport ME (04856) *(G-6818)*
D F & B Precision Mfg Inc...860 354-5663
180 Sunny Valley Rd Ste 3 New Milford CT (06776) *(G-2796)*
D F Carter Co Inc...978 977-0444
147 Summit St Ste 7 Peabody MA (01960) *(G-14328)*
D F I, Hudson *Also called Detroit Forming Inc* *(G-18385)*
D F Moody LLC...207 474-6029
1284 E Ridge Rd Cornville ME (04976) *(G-5927)*
D F Richard Inc...603 742-2020
124 Broadway Dover NH (03820) *(G-18017)*
D G C, Gardner *Also called Data Guide Cable Corporation* *(G-11111)*
D G Robertson Inc...802 864-6027
3016 Williston Rd South Burlington VT (05403) *(G-22445)*
D J Bass Inc...508 678-4499
84 Bates St New Bedford MA (02745) *(G-13376)*
D J Fabricators Inc...978 356-0228
94 Turnpike Rd Ipswich MA (01938) *(G-11914)*
D K Schulman...860 868-4300
239 New Milford Tpke New Preston CT (06777) *(G-2834)*
D L A Disposition Services, Groton *Also called United States Dept of Navy* *(G-1689)*
D L S Detailing...603 878-2554
755 Turnpike Rd New Ipswich NH (03071) *(G-19303)*
D Lasser Ceramics...802 824-5383
6405 Vt Route 100 Londonderry VT (05148) *(G-22057)*
D M F Machine Co Inc...603 434-4945
48 Harvey Rd Londonderry NH (03053) *(G-18691)*
D M G Enterprises...207 726-4603
160 Belyea Rd Edmunds Twp ME (04628) *(G-6005)*
D M Printing Service Inc...603 883-1897
3 Central St Hudson NH (03051) *(G-18382)*
D Mac Consulting LLC (PA)...401 500-3879
50 Reynolds St North Kingstown RI (02852) *(G-20701)*
D Moore Associates, Atkinson *Also called Accelerator Systems Inc* *(G-17602)*
D N Hylan Associates Inc...207 359-9807
53 Benjamin River Dr Brooklin ME (04616) *(G-5819)*
D P Engineering Inc...203 421-7965
211 Summer Hill Rd Madison CT (06443) *(G-1959)*
D R Designs Inc...207 622-3303
980 Western Ave Manchester ME (04351) *(G-6409)*
D R S Desings...203 744-2858
217 Greenwood Ave Bethel CT (06801) *(G-140)*
D S C, Salem *Also called Data Electronic Devices Inc* *(G-19720)*
D S Graphics Inc (PA)...978 970-1359
120 Stedman St Lowell MA (01851) *(G-12365)*
D S Greene Co Inc...781 245-2644
431 Water St Wakefield MA (01880) *(G-15947)*
D Simpson Inc...401 232-3638
13 Industrial Dr Smithfield RI (02917) *(G-21217)*
D V C, Woburn *Also called Digital Vdeo Cmmunications Inc* *(G-17168)*
D V Die Cutting Inc...978 777-0300
45 Prince St Danvers MA (01923) *(G-10210)*
D W Clark Inc (PA)...508 378-4014
692 N Bedford St East Bridgewater MA (02333) *(G-10411)*

D&B Tool Co., Milford *Also called Morning Star Tool LLC* ***(G-2316)***
D&P Media For Print Inc..........978 685-2210
46 Bridle Path Ln Methuen MA (01844) ***(G-13017)***
D&S Engineered Products, Attleboro *Also called Bruce Diamond Corporation* ***(G-7715)***
D-Lew Inc..........508 481-7709
216 Boston Rd Southborough MA (01772) ***(G-15353)***
D. F. Richard Energy, Dover *Also called D F Richard Inc* ***(G-18017)***
D40 Gravel LLP..........802 673-5494
71 Cliff St Newport VT (05855) ***(G-22195)***
Da Capo Press, Boston *Also called Hachette Book Group Inc* ***(G-8587)***
Da Capo Press..........617 252-5200
53 State St Ste 9 Boston MA (02109) ***(G-8494)***
Da Capo Publishing Inc..........802 864-5684
255 S Champlain St Ste 5 Burlington VT (05401) ***(G-21778)***
Da Costa Awning Co, Taunton *Also called Da Costa Awnings & Canvas Spc* ***(G-15739)***
Da Costa Awnings & Canvas Spc..........508 822-4944
16 Winter St Taunton MA (02780) ***(G-15739)***
Da Rosas..........508 693-0110
46 Circuit Ave Oak Bluffs MA (02557) ***(G-14210)***
Da Silva Klanko Ltd..........203 756-4932
70 Deerwood Ln Unit 8 Waterbury CT (06704) ***(G-4863)***
Daaquam Lumber Maine Inc (HQ)..........207 435-6401
1203 Aroostook Scenic Hwy Masardis ME (04732) ***(G-6415)***
Dac Systems Inc..........203 924-7000
4 Armstrong Rd Ste 12 Shelton CT (06484) ***(G-3793)***
Dacruz Manufacturing Inc..........860 584-5315
100 Broderick Rd Bristol CT (06010) ***(G-547)***
Dadanco - Mestek, Westfield *Also called Mestek Inc* ***(G-16700)***
Daddys Private Stock LLC..........207 399-7154
185 Whitten Rd Canaan ME (04924) ***(G-5872)***
Dads..........508 248-9774
417 Worcester Rd Charlton MA (01507) ***(G-9848)***
Daedalus Software Inc..........617 851-5157
215 First St Ste 7 Cambridge MA (02142) ***(G-9448)***
Dag Machine and Tool Inc..........401 724-0450
92 Pleasant St 1 Pawtucket RI (02860) ***(G-20833)***
Dahl Group..........978 887-2598
196 Middleton Rd Boxford MA (01921) ***(G-8976)***
Dahlicious Holdings LLC..........978 401-2103
320 Hamilton St Ste 3 Leominster MA (01453) ***(G-12131)***
Dahlicious LLC..........505 200-0396
320 Hamilton St Ste 3 Leominster MA (01453) ***(G-12132)***
Dahlstrom & Company Inc..........508 429-3367
50 October Hill Rd Holliston MA (01746) ***(G-11566)***
Daikin U S Corporation..........401 738-0261
10 Globe St Warwick RI (02886) ***(G-21347)***
Dailey Precast LLC..........802 442-4418
381 Airport Rd Shaftsbury VT (05262) ***(G-22402)***
Dailey-Mc Neil, Kensington *Also called Dan Dailey Inc* ***(G-18536)***
Daily Campus, The, Storrs Mansfield *Also called Conn Daily Campus* ***(G-4384)***
Daily Catch..........617 734-2700
441 Harvard St Brookline MA (02446) ***(G-9199)***
Daily Fantasy Spt Rankings LLC..........609 273-8408
175 Mount Vernon St Dover NH (03820) ***(G-18018)***
Daily Fare LLC..........203 743-7300
13 Durant Ave Bethel CT (06801) ***(G-141)***
Daily Gardener..........802 223-7851
2930 Dugar Brook Rd Calais VT (05648) ***(G-21821)***
Daily General Counsel Pllc..........617 721-4342
12 Stedman St Brookline MA (02446) ***(G-9200)***
Daily Grind..........508 279-9952
23 Central Sq Bridgewater MA (02324) ***(G-9070)***
Daily Hampshire Gazette..........413 527-4000
72 Main St Easthampton MA (01027) ***(G-10558)***
Daily Herald Brown Inc..........401 351-3372
195 Angell St Providence RI (02906) ***(G-20992)***
Daily Impressions LLC..........203 508-5305
60 Village Cir Hamden CT (06514) ***(G-1743)***
Daily Juice Press LLC..........781 261-6099
132 Chief Justice Cushing Cohasset MA (02025) ***(G-10097)***
Daily Mart..........860 529-5210
2204 Silas Deane Hwy Rocky Hill CT (06067) ***(G-3707)***
Daily News Tribune..........781 329-5008
254 2nd Ave Ste 1 Needham Heights MA (02494) ***(G-13327)***
Daily News-Mercury, Malden *Also called Eastern Mddlsex Press Pblctons* ***(G-12569)***
Daily Paper..........508 790-8800
644 W Main St Hyannis MA (02601) ***(G-11839)***
Daily Portsmouth..........603 767-1395
114 Crescent Way Portsmouth NH (03801) ***(G-19556)***
Daily Printing Inc..........978 927-4630
25 West St Beverly MA (01915) ***(G-8123)***
Daily Rider LLC..........802 497-1269
1541 North Ave Burlington VT (05408) ***(G-21779)***
Daily Stroll LLC..........678 770-4531
2001 Commonwealth Ave Brighton MA (02135) ***(G-9097)***
Daily Times Chronicle, Woburn *Also called Daily Woburn Times Inc* ***(G-17162)***
Daily Voice, Norwalk *Also called Cantata Media LLC* ***(G-3118)***
Daily Woburn Times Inc (PA)..........781 933-3700
1 Arrow Dr Ste 1 # 1 Woburn MA (01801) ***(G-17162)***
Daily Woburn Times Inc..........978 658-2346
1 Arrow Dr Wilmington MA (01887) ***(G-16993)***
Daily Woburn Times Inc..........781 944-2200
531 Main St Reading MA (01867) ***(G-14733)***
Dakin Road Investments Inc..........978 443-4020
162 Ayer Rd Littleton MA (01460) ***(G-12299)***
Dakins Miniatures Inc (PA)..........207 548-6084
21 Prospect St Searsport ME (04974) ***(G-6949)***
Dakota Systems Inc..........978 275-0600
1057 Broadway Rd Dracut MA (01826) ***(G-10356)***
Daktari Diagnostics Inc..........617 336-3299
85 Bolton St Ste 229 Cambridge MA (02140) ***(G-9449)***
Dal-Trac Oil Company..........508 222-3935
143 Fisher St Attleboro MA (02703) ***(G-7726)***
Dalau Incorporated..........603 670-1031
19 Star Dr Unit 6 Merrimack NH (03054) ***(G-18997)***
Dalbergia LLC (PA)..........860 870-2500
58 Gerber Dr Tolland CT (06084) ***(G-4543)***
Dale A Thomas and Sons Inc..........207 722-3505
148 Moosehead Trail Hwy Brooks ME (04921) ***(G-5823)***
Dale E Crawford..........603 473-2738
2453 Lovell Lake Rd Sanbornville NH (03872) ***(G-19782)***
Dale E Percy Inc..........802 253-8503
269 Weeks Hill Rd Stowe VT (05672) ***(G-22521)***
Dale Engineering & Son Inc..........781 541-6055
3 Alfred Cir Bedford MA (01730) ***(G-7969)***
Dale Medical Products Inc (PA)..........508 695-9316
40 Kenwood Cir Ste 7 Franklin MA (02038) ***(G-11035)***
Dale Rand Printing Inc..........207 773-8198
508 Riverside St Ste A Portland ME (04103) ***(G-6647)***
Dale Vishay Electronics LLC..........603 881-7799
22 Clinton Dr Hollis NH (03049) ***(G-18328)***
Dalegip America Inc..........207 323-1880
34 Kidder Point Rd Searsport ME (04974) ***(G-6950)***
Dales Paint n Place Inc..........603 863-5050
449 Sunapee St Ste 6 Newport NH (03773) ***(G-19344)***
Dalla Corte Lumber..........860 875-9480
12 Minor Rd Stafford Springs CT (06076) ***(G-4108)***
Dalton Electric Heating Co Inc..........978 356-9844
28 Hayward St Ipswich MA (01938) ***(G-11915)***
Dalton Enterprises Inc (PA)..........203 272-3221
131 Willow St Cheshire CT (06410) ***(G-726)***
Dalton Manufacturing Company..........978 388-2227
6 Clark St Amesbury MA (01913) ***(G-7483)***
Daly Bros Bedding Co Inc..........207 282-9583
25 Edwards Ave Biddeford ME (04005) ***(G-5727)***
Dama, Johnston *Also called Meloni Tool Co Inc* ***(G-20521)***
Dama Jewelry Technology Inc..........401 272-6513
800 Waterman Ave East Providence RI (02914) ***(G-20402)***
Damark Woodcraft Inc..........978 373-6670
115 Hale St Haverhill MA (01830) ***(G-11422)***
Damascus Worldwide Inc..........802 775-6062
194 Seward Rd Rutland VT (05701) ***(G-22328)***
Damico Mfg Co..........401 949-0023
22 Lark Industrial Pkwy C Greenville RI (02828) ***(G-20466)***
Dampits LLC..........203 210-7946
98 Ridgefield Rd Wilton CT (06897) ***(G-5287)***
Dampney Company Inc..........617 389-2805
85 Paris St Everett MA (02149) ***(G-10609)***
Dan Beard Inc..........203 924-4346
64 Hawthorne Ave Shelton CT (06484) ***(G-3794)***
Dan Dailey Inc..........603 778-2303
2 North Rd Kensington NH (03833) ***(G-18536)***
Dan-Kar Plastics Products..........781 935-9221
192 New Boston St C Woburn MA (01801) ***(G-17163)***
Dan-Ray Machine Co Inc..........978 374-7611
93 Essex St Haverhill MA (01832) ***(G-11423)***
Dana Hardy..........207 757-8445
1285 Dyer Brook Rd Dyer Brook ME (04747) ***(G-5972)***
Dana Robes Boat Builders..........207 529-2433
75 Southern Point Rd Round Pond ME (04564) ***(G-6829)***
Danafilms Corp..........508 366-8884
5 Otis St Westborough MA (01581) ***(G-16612)***
Danaher Tool Group..........203 284-7000
61 Barnes Industrial Park Wallingford CT (06492) ***(G-4732)***
Danalevi Corp..........413 626-8120
732 Daniel Shays Hwy Belchertown MA (01007) ***(G-8023)***
Danalevi Powerboats, Belchertown *Also called Danalevi Corp* ***(G-8023)***
Danas Boat Shop..........207 882-7205
214 N End Rd Westport Island ME (04578) ***(G-7216)***
Danbury Aviation, Danbury *Also called Santoto LLC* ***(G-983)***
Danbury Metal Finishing Inc..........203 748-5044
124 West St Danbury CT (06810) ***(G-897)***
Danbury Ortho..........203 797-1500
2 Riverview Dr Danbury CT (06810) ***(G-898)***
Danbury Sheet Metal, Bethel *Also called Varnum Enterprises LLC* ***(G-190)***
Danbury Square Box Company..........203 744-4611
1a Broad St Danbury CT (06810) ***(G-899)***
Dance Paws LLC..........617 945-3044
82 Normandy Ave Cambridge MA (02138) ***(G-9450)***

ALPHABETIC

Danecraft Inc (PA)............401 941-7700
1 Baker St Providence RI (02905) ***(G-20993)***
Danecraft Inc............401 941-7700
1 Baker St Providence RI (02905) ***(G-20994)***
DAngelo Burial Vaults............508 528-0385
30 Raymond St Franklin MA (02038) ***(G-11036)***
Danglers Inc............401 274-7742
35 Oakdale Ave Johnston RI (02919) ***(G-20506)***
Dani Instruments, Inc., Marlborough *Also called Spectra Analysis Instrs Inc* ***(G-12828)***
Danica Candle Works, Rockport *Also called Danica Design Inc* ***(G-6819)***
Danica Design Inc (PA)............207 236-3060
569 West St Rockport ME (04856) ***(G-6819)***
Daniel Johnston & Co Inc............603 525-9330
19 Boutwell Rd Hancock NH (03449) ***(G-18284)***
Daniel L Dunnells Logging Inc............207 793-2901
58 Maplecrest Rd Parsonsfield ME (04047) ***(G-6574)***
Daniel Preston............603 579-0525
7 Industrial Dr Hudson NH (03051) ***(G-18383)***
Daniel Wheeler............603 528-6363
180 Stark St Gilford NH (03249) ***(G-18184)***
Daniele Inc............401 568-6228
105 Davis Dr Pascoag RI (02859) ***(G-20799)***
Daniele International Inc............401 568-6228
105 Davis Dr Pascoag RI (02859) ***(G-20800)***
Daniele International Inc............401 568-6228
180 Davis Dr Pascoag RI (02859) ***(G-20801)***
Daniele International Inc (PA)............401 568-6228
1000 Danielle Dr Mapleville RI (02839) ***(G-20612)***
Danjon Manufacturing Corp............203 272-7258
1075 S Main St Cheshire CT (06410) ***(G-727)***
Danly IEM, Boston *Also called Connell Limited Partnership* ***(G-8481)***
Danny Boy Fisheries Inc............207 829-6622
628 New Gloucester Rd North Yarmouth ME (04097) ***(G-6516)***
Danone Holdings Inc............203 229-7000
208 Harbor Dr Fl 3 Stamford CT (06902) ***(G-4184)***
Dans Logging & Construction............603 237-4040
219 Reed Rd Colebrook NH (03576) ***(G-17867)***
Dans Machine............413 529-9635
14a Nashawannuck St Easthampton MA (01027) ***(G-10559)***
Dante Confection............978 262-2242
19 Sterling Rd Ste 6 North Billerica MA (01862) ***(G-13806)***
Dante Ltd............860 376-0204
633 Plainfield Rd Jewett City CT (06351) ***(G-1911)***
Danver, Wallingford *Also called CT Acquisitions LLC* ***(G-4730)***
Danvers Engineering Co Inc............978 774-7501
88 Holten St Ste 3 Danvers MA (01923) ***(G-10211)***
Danvers Herald............978 774-0505
152 Sylvan St Danvers MA (01923) ***(G-10212)***
Danvers Industrial Packg Corp............978 777-0020
39 Tozer Rd Beverly MA (01915) ***(G-8124)***
Danversbank............978 468-2243
25 Railroad Ave South Hamilton MA (01982) ***(G-15314)***
Darby Pop LLC............207 799-4202
66 Cross Hill Rd Cape Elizabeth ME (04107) ***(G-5875)***
DArcy Saw LLC............800 569-1264
10 Canal Bank Rd Windsor Locks CT (06096) ***(G-5390)***
Dari-Farms Ice Cream Co Inc............860 872-8313
55 Gerber Dr Tolland CT (06084) ***(G-4544)***
Darien Times, New Canaan *Also called Hersam Publishing Company* ***(G-2601)***
Dark Harbor Boatyard Corp............207 734-2246
700 Acre Is Islesboro ME (04848) ***(G-6215)***
Dark Matter Chocolate LLC............303 718-3835
407 Washington St Cambridge MA (02139) ***(G-9451)***
Darlene Springo, Ellsworth *Also called H W Dunn & Son Inc* ***(G-6019)***
Darling Boatworks Inc............802 425-2004
821 Ferry Rd Charlotte VT (05445) ***(G-21833)***
Darlington Fabrics Corporation............401 596-2816
36 Beach St Westerly RI (02891) ***(G-21522)***
Darly Custom Technology Inc............860 298-7966
276 Addison Rd Windsor CT (06095) ***(G-5328)***
Darmariscotta Pottery Inc............207 563-8843
Northey Sq Damariscotta ME (04543) ***(G-5935)***
Darrel L Tibbetts............207 897-4932
115 Hathaway Hill Rd Livermore ME (04253) ***(G-6374)***
Darrell C McGuire & Sons Inc............207 532-0511
1157 Hodgdon Corner Rd Houlton ME (04730) ***(G-6205)***
Darrell Wheaton............508 824-1669
200 Myles Standish Blvd # 3 Taunton MA (02780) ***(G-15740)***
Dart Products Screen Printing, Bridgeport *Also called Bl Printing Shop* ***(G-383)***
Dartex Coatings Inc............401 766-1500
22 Steel St Slatersville RI (02876) ***(G-21204)***
Dartmouth Awning Co Inc............508 636-6838
45 Beeden Rd Westport MA (02790) ***(G-16838)***
Dartmouth Feeders & Traps Inc............774 202-6594
53 Russells Mills Rd South Dartmouth MA (02748) ***(G-15237)***
Dartmouth Inc............603 646-2600
6175 Robinson Hall Hanover NH (03755) ***(G-18286)***
Dartmouth Journal Services Inc............802 244-1457
5 Pilgrim Park Rd Ste 5 # 5 Waterbury VT (05676) ***(G-22582)***
Dartmouth Undying Inc............603 643-2143
14 Dunster Dr Hanover NH (03755) ***(G-18287)***
DARTMOUTH, THE, Hanover *Also called Dartmouth Inc* ***(G-18286)***
Darwin A Lewis Inc............802 457-4521
243 Densmore Hill Rd Hartland VT (05048) ***(G-22015)***
Dasan Zhone Solutions Inc............510 777-7000
112 Corporate Dr Ste 1 Portsmouth NH (03801) ***(G-19557)***
Dasco Signs, Acton *Also called Scott Stanton* ***(G-5509)***
Dasco Supply LLC............203 388-0095
43 Homestead Ave Stamford CT (06902) ***(G-4185)***
Dasco Welded Products Inc............203 754-9353
2038 Thomaston Ave Waterbury CT (06704) ***(G-4864)***
Dasein Inc............781 756-0380
109 Cambridge St Winchester MA (01890) ***(G-17086)***
Dasko Identification Products............401 435-6500
66 Commercial Way Unit 1 East Providence RI (02914) ***(G-20403)***
Dasko Label, East Providence *Also called Dasko Identification Products* ***(G-20403)***
Data Associates Business Trust............781 890-0110
280 Bear Hill Rd Waltham MA (02451) ***(G-16079)***
Data Binding Inc............401 738-7901
10 New England Way Warwick RI (02886) ***(G-21348)***
Data Electronic Devices Inc............603 893-2047
32 Northwestern Dr Salem NH (03079) ***(G-19720)***
Data Guide Cable Corporation............978 632-0900
232 Sherman St Gardner MA (01440) ***(G-11111)***
Data Industrial Corporation............508 758-6390
6 County Rd Ste 6 # 6 Mattapoisett MA (02739) ***(G-12886)***
Data Management Incorporated............860 677-8586
557 New Britain Ave Unionville CT (06085) ***(G-4655)***
Data Plus Incorporated............978 888-6300
55 Middlesex St Unit 219 North Chelmsford MA (01863) ***(G-13892)***
Data Print Inc............781 935-3350
18 Cranes Ct Woburn MA (01801) ***(G-17164)***
Data Signal Corporation............203 882-5393
16 Higgins Dr Milford CT (06460) ***(G-2273)***
Data Technology Inc............860 871-8082
24 Industrial Park Rd W Tolland CT (06084) ***(G-4545)***
Data Translation Inc (PA)............508 481-3700
10 Commerce Way Ste E Norton MA (02766) ***(G-14076)***
Data-Graphics Inc............860 667-0435
240 Hartford Ave Newington CT (06111) ***(G-2859)***
Data3sixty, Burlington *Also called Infogix Inc* ***(G-9285)***
Datacon Inc............781 273-5800
60 Blanchard Rd Burlington MA (01803) ***(G-9253)***
Datadog Inc............866 329-4466
33 Arch St Boston MA (02110) ***(G-8495)***
Datanational Corporation............781 826-3400
100 Schoosett St Ste 2a Pembroke MA (02359) ***(G-14397)***
Datanyze Inc (HQ)............415 237-3434
170 Data Dr Waltham MA (02451) ***(G-16080)***
Datapaq Inc............603 537-2680
3 Corporate Park Dr # 1 Derry NH (03038) ***(G-17977)***
Dataprep Inc............203 795-2095
109 Boston Post Rd Ste 2 Orange CT (06477) ***(G-3364)***
Dataquest Korea Inc............239 561-4862
56 Top Gallant Rd Stamford CT (06902) ***(G-4186)***
Datawatch Corporation (HQ)............978 441-2200
4 Crosby Dr Bedford MA (01730) ***(G-7970)***
Datel Inc............508 964-5131
120 Forbes Blvd Ste 125 Mansfield MA (02048) ***(G-12627)***
Datex Microcomputer Service, Milford *Also called Richard Breault* ***(G-2349)***
Daughters of St Paul Inc............617 522-2566
77 Dudley Rd Billerica MA (01821) ***(G-8235)***
Daunis............207 773-6011
616 Congress St Ste 2 Portland ME (04101) ***(G-6648)***
Daunis Fine Jewelry, Portland *Also called Daunis* ***(G-6648)***
Dauphinais & Son Inc............508 839-9258
8 Shrewsbury St North Grafton MA (01536) ***(G-13959)***
Dauphinais & Son Inc............413 596-3964
2420 Boston Rd Wilbraham MA (01095) ***(G-16935)***
Dav-Tech Plating Inc............508 485-8472
40 Cedar Hill St Marlborough MA (01752) ***(G-12747)***
Davco............603 768-3517
1397 Us Route 4 Danbury NH (03230) ***(G-17963)***
Dave and Jeff Logging & Firewd............802 355-0465
84 May Farm Rd Barton VT (05822) ***(G-21649)***
Dave Ross............203 775-4327
92 S Lake Shore Dr Brookfield CT (06804) ***(G-640)***
Daves Mrktplace Smthfield Inc............401 830-5650
371 Putnam Pike Ste 590 Smithfield RI (02917) ***(G-21218)***
Daves Paving and Construction............203 753-4992
105 Waterbury Rd Ste 5 Prospect CT (06712) ***(G-3587)***
Daves Sheet Metal Inc............978 454-3144
13 Chuck Dr Bldg 5 Dracut MA (01826) ***(G-10357)***
Daves Sitework and Sawmill............603 313-0787
850 Templeton Tpke Fitzwilliam NH (03447) ***(G-18148)***
Davic Inc............207 774-0093
417 Congress St Portland ME (04101) ***(G-6649)***
Davico Inc............508 998-1150
95 Brook St New Bedford MA (02746) ***(G-13377)***

Davico Manufacturing, New Bedford *Also called Davico Inc* ***(G-13377)***
David A Payne...508 588-7500
291 Howard St Brockton MA (02302) ***(G-9136)***
David Bird LLC...207 832-0569
151 One Pie Rd Waldoboro ME (04572) ***(G-7132)***
David Clark Company Inc (PA)...508 756-6216
360 Franklin St Worcester MA (01604) ***(G-17362)***
David Corporation (PA)...781 587-3008
301 Edgewater Pl Ste 116 Wakefield MA (01880) ***(G-15948)***
David Derewianka...860 649-1983
459 Dennison Rdg Manchester CT (06040) ***(G-1998)***
David Gilbert...508 879-1507
10 Olympic St Framingham MA (01701) ***(G-10940)***
David Grau...401 831-0351
11 Dorrance St Providence RI (02903) ***(G-20995)***
David King & Co Inc...617 482-6950
134 Beach St Boston MA (02111) ***(G-8496)***
David L Ellis Company Inc (PA)...978 897-1795
310 Old High St Acton MA (01720) ***(G-7349)***
David Lefort...781 826-9033
13 Arrowhead Path Halifax MA (02338) ***(G-11317)***
David Michaud...207 377-8037
61 Birch St Winthrop ME (04364) ***(G-7280)***
David P Cioe...401 247-0079
59 Baker St Warren RI (02885) ***(G-21294)***
David P Deveney Memorial Co...781 396-7772
165 Mystic Ave Medford MA (02155) ***(G-12929)***
David Packard Company Inc...508 987-2998
15 Industrial Park Rd E Oxford MA (01540) ***(G-14258)***
David R Burl...603 235-2661
56 N Mast St Goffstown NH (03045) ***(G-18199)***
David R Godine Publisher Inc (PA)...617 451-9600
15 Court Sq Ste 320 Boston MA (02108) ***(G-8497)***
David R Godine Publisher Inc...603 532-4100
426 Nutting Rd Jaffrey NH (03452) ***(G-18460)***
David Rich Co, Wellesley *Also called Watson Printing Co Inc* ***(G-16393)***
David Saunders Inc...207 228-1888
192 Gannett Dr South Portland ME (04106) ***(G-7021)***
David Sevigny Inc...978 297-2775
62 Hale St Winchendon MA (01475) ***(G-17073)***
David Shuck...860 434-8562
Hatchetts Hill Rd Old Lyme CT (06371) ***(G-3320)***
David W Wallace...413 625-6523
635 Mohawk Trl Shelburne Falls MA (01370) ***(G-15067)***
David Weisman LLC...203 322-9978
30 Mill Valley Ln Stamford CT (06903) ***(G-4187)***
Davidon Alloys, Warwick *Also called Davidon Industries Inc* ***(G-21349)***
Davidon Industries Inc...401 737-8380
87 Dewey Ave Warwick RI (02886) ***(G-21349)***
Davids Drapery...781 849-9499
264 Middle St Braintree MA (02184) ***(G-8999)***
Davin Machining and Welding Co...617 884-8933
1 Winnisimmet St Ste 1 # 1 Chelsea MA (02150) ***(G-9952)***
Davinci Arms LLC...413 583-4327
100 State St Bldg 123-A Ludlow MA (01056) ***(G-12462)***
Davinci Biomedical RES Pdts...978 368-3477
40 Maple Ave South Lancaster MA (01561) ***(G-15317)***
Davinci Group...781 391-6009
6 Cowdry Ln Wakefield MA (01880) ***(G-15949)***
Davis Art Images, Worcester *Also called Davis Publications Inc* ***(G-17364)***
Davis Corp of Worcester Inc (PA)...508 754-7201
50 Portland St Worcester MA (01608) ***(G-17363)***
Davis Enterprises Inc...781 461-8444
51 Legacy Blvd Dedham MA (02026) ***(G-10286)***
Davis Precision Mfg LLC...978 794-0042
250 Canal St Ste 27 Lawrence MA (01840) ***(G-12015)***
Davis Press...401 624-9331
79 Sherry Ave Bristol RI (02809) ***(G-20072)***
Davis Publications, Worcester *Also called Davis Corp of Worcester Inc* ***(G-17363)***
Davis Publications Inc...508 754-7201
50 Portland St Fl 3 Worcester MA (01608) ***(G-17364)***
Davis Village Solutions LLC...603 878-3662
167 Davis Village Rd New Ipswich NH (03071) ***(G-19304)***
Davis-Standard LLC (HQ)...860 599-1010
1 Extrusion Dr Pawcatuck CT (06379) ***(G-3432)***
Davis-Standard Holdings Inc (PA)...860 599-1010
1 Extrusion Dr Pawcatuck CT (06379) ***(G-3433)***
Davol Inc (HQ)...401 825-8300
100 Crossings Blvd Warwick RI (02886) ***(G-21350)***
Davol Inc...781 932-5900
160 New Boston St Woburn MA (01801) ***(G-17165)***
Davol/Taunton Printing Inc...508 824-4305
330 Winthrop St Ste 3 Taunton MA (02780) ***(G-15741)***
Davriel Jewelers Inc...413 525-4975
37 Harkness Ave East Longmeadow MA (01028) ***(G-10471)***
Davriel Promotions, East Longmeadow *Also called Davriel Jewelers Inc* ***(G-10471)***
Dawid Manufacturing Inc...203 734-1800
26 Beaver St Ansonia CT (06401) ***(G-12)***
Dawn Auger...508 587-0363
156 Grove St Brockton MA (02302) ***(G-9137)***
Dawn Brainard...802 334-2780
415 Union St Newport VT (05855) ***(G-22196)***
Dawn Enterprises LLC...860 646-8200
275 Progress Dr Ste B Manchester CT (06042) ***(G-1999)***
Dawn Industries Inc...401 884-8175
1300 Division Rd West Warwick RI (02893) ***(G-21490)***
Dawns Sign Tech Incorporated...978 208-0012
33 Flagship Dr North Andover MA (01845) ***(G-13697)***
Dawson Forte LLP...781 467-0170
47 Harvard St Westwood MA (02090) ***(G-16864)***
Day Fred A Co LLC...860 589-0531
11 Commerce Dr Bristol CT (06010) ***(G-548)***
Day Bros...207 743-0508
25 Dat Rd Oxford ME (04270) ***(G-6565)***
Day Machine Systems Inc...860 229-3440
221 South St Bldg F2 New Britain CT (06051) ***(G-2526)***
Day Publishing Company (HQ)...860 701-4200
47 Eugene Oneill Dr New London CT (06320) ***(G-2770)***
Day Zero Diagnostics Inc...857 770-1125
127 Western Ave Allston MA (02134) ***(G-7463)***
Day's Welding, Medway *Also called Days Auto Body Inc* ***(G-6423)***
Day, The, New London *Also called Day Publishing Company* ***(G-2770)***
Day-O-Lite Fluorescent Fixs, Warwick *Also called SCW Corporation* ***(G-21423)***
Daybrake Donuts Inc...203 368-4962
941 Madison Ave Bridgeport CT (06606) ***(G-401)***
Dayken Pallet, Leeds *Also called Gerrity Company Incorporated* ***(G-6269)***
Dayon Manufacturing Inc...860 677-8561
1820 New Britain Ave Farmington CT (06032) ***(G-1476)***
Days Auto Body Inc...207 746-5310
16 Main Rd Medway ME (04460) ***(G-6423)***
Dayton Bag & Burlap Co...860 653-8191
10 Hazelwood Rd Ste A5 East Granby CT (06026) ***(G-1125)***
Dayton Sand & Gravel Inc...207 499-2306
928 Goodwins Mills Rd Dayton ME (04005) ***(G-5944)***
Dayton Superior Corporation...401 885-1934
3970 Post Rd Warwick RI (02886) ***(G-21351)***
DB&f Industries, New Britain *Also called D B F Industries Inc* ***(G-2525)***
Dbi Woodworks Inc...781 739-2060
491 W Main St Ste 1 Avon MA (02322) ***(G-7885)***
Dbmaestro Inc...508 641-6108
300 Baker Ave Ste 300 # 300 Concord MA (01742) ***(G-10127)***
DC & D Inc...860 623-2941
42 Skinner Rd Broad Brook CT (06016) ***(G-628)***
DC Scaffold Inc...508 580-5100
400 West St Ste 2 West Bridgewater MA (02379) ***(G-16436)***
DCB Welding and Fabrication...978 587-3883
143 Meadowcroft St Lowell MA (01852) ***(G-12366)***
Dcci, New Haven *Also called Dow Cover Company Incorporated* ***(G-2683)***
Dcg Precision Manufacturing, Bethel *Also called Dcg-Pmi Inc* ***(G-142)***
Dcg-Pmi Inc...203 743-5525
9 Trowbridge Dr Bethel CT (06801) ***(G-142)***
DCI, Providence *Also called Decor Craft Inc* ***(G-20996)***
Dci Inc (PA)...603 838-6544
265 S Main St Lisbon NH (03585) ***(G-18648)***
Dci Inc...802 763-7847
324 Waterman Rd South Royalton VT (05068) ***(G-22490)***
Ddfhklt Inc...413 733-7441
233 Western Ave West Springfield MA (01089) ***(G-16515)***
Dds Services Ltd...781 837-3997
30 Oak St Pembroke MA (02359) ***(G-14398)***
De Mari Pasta Dies USA Inc...978 454-4099
48 Chuck Dr Dracut MA (01826) ***(G-10358)***
De Muerte Usa LLC...860 331-7085
73 Morningside St W Hartford CT (06112) ***(G-1817)***
De Ross Pallet Co, Oxford *Also called Lelanite Corporation* ***(G-14266)***
DEA LLC...401 349-3446
1861 Smith St North Providence RI (02911) ***(G-20755)***
Deacon Giles Inc...781 883-8256
75 Canal St Salem MA (01970) ***(G-14905)***
Deadwood Pallets...774 214-8628
93 Salisbury St Bellingham MA (02019) ***(G-8037)***
Dealerpolicy LLC...802 655-9000
2300 St George Rd Williston VT (05495) ***(G-22661)***
Dean Machine Incorporated...401 919-5100
25 Sharpe Dr Cranston RI (02920) ***(G-20208)***
Dean Paige Welding Inc...978 939-8187
377 State Rd Baldwinville MA (01436) ***(G-7943)***
Deangelis Iron Work Inc...508 238-4310
305 Depot St South Easton MA (02375) ***(G-15276)***
Dearborn Bortec Inc...207 935-2502
12 Budrich Dr Fryeburg ME (04037) ***(G-6097)***
Dearborn Crane and Engrg Co...781 897-4100
110 Winn St Ste 205 Woburn MA (01801) ***(G-17166)***
Debco Machine Inc...508 655-4469
85 North Ave Natick MA (01760) ***(G-13250)***
Deborah Frost...603 882-3100
20 Commerce Park North # 106 Bedford NH (03110) ***(G-17638)***
Deborah Ludington...603 766-1651
16 Autumn Pond Park Greenland NH (03840) ***(G-18223)***

ALPHABETIC

Debrasong Publishing LLC 413 204-4682
82-3 Mount Archer Rd Lyme CT (06371) *(G-1954)*
Deburr Co 860 621-6634
201 Atwater St Plantsville CT (06479) *(G-3529)*
Deburring House Inc 860 828-0889
230 Berlin St East Berlin CT (06023) *(G-1098)*
Decas Cranberry Co Inc (PA) 508 866-8506
4 Old Forge Way Ste 1 Carver MA (02330) *(G-9803)*
Decas Cranberry Products Inc 508 866-8506
4 Old Forge Way Ste 1 Carver MA (02330) *(G-9804)*
Decco 508 329-1391
108 Milk St Westborough MA (01581) *(G-16613)*
Deciphera Pharmaceuticals LLC 781 209-6400
200 Smith St Waltham MA (02451) *(G-16081)*
Deciphera Pharmaceuticals Inc (PA) 781 209-6400
200 Smith St Rm 1 Waltham MA (02451) *(G-16082)*
Decitek Corp 508 366-1011
145 Flanders Rd Westborough MA (01581) *(G-16614)*
Decker Machine Works Inc 413 628-3300
201 Munson St Greenfield MA (01301) *(G-11259)*
Decks R US 860 505-0726
35 Carlton St Fl 2 New Britain CT (06053) *(G-2527)*
Deco Interior Finishes Inc 508 994-9436
189 Popes Is New Bedford MA (02740) *(G-13378)*
Deco Products Inc 860 528-4304
34 Nelson St Ste C East Hartford CT (06108) *(G-1185)*
Decor Craft Inc 401 621-2324
133 Mathewson St Providence RI (02903) *(G-20996)*
Decorative Window Ware, Poultney *Also called Brass Butterfly Inc* *(G-22270)*
Decorator Services Inc 203 384-8144
25 Wells St Ste 1 Bridgeport CT (06604) *(G-402)*
Decorators Sewing Shoppe Inc 401 453-3500
1 Salzillo St Johnston RI (02919) *(G-20507)*
Dedham Recycled Gravel Inc 781 329-1044
1039 East St Dedham MA (02026) *(G-10287)*
Dee Kay Designs Inc (PA) 401 539-2400
177 Skunk Hill Rd Hope Valley RI (02832) *(G-20484)*
Dee Zee Ice LLC 860 276-3500
93 Industrial Dr Southington CT (06489) *(G-4046)*
Deep River Fuel Terminals LLC 860 342-4619
29 Myrtle Rd Portland CT (06480) *(G-3566)*
Deep Sea Systems Intl Inc 508 540-6732
1130 Rte 28a Cataumet MA (02534) *(G-9812)*
Deepwater Buoyancy Inc 207 468-2565
394 Hill St Biddeford ME (04005) *(G-5728)*
Deer Creek Fabrics Inc 203 964-0922
509 Glenbrook Rd Stamford CT (06906) *(G-4188)*
Deerfield Corporation 508 877-0143
6 Doyle Cir Framingham MA (01701) *(G-10941)*
Deerfield Machine & Tool Co, North Adams *Also called Denault Inc* *(G-13674)*
Deerfield Optics, Framingham *Also called Deerfield Corporation* *(G-10941)*
Deerfield Valley News, Wilmington *Also called Vermont Media Corp* *(G-22705)*
Deermont Corpopration 802 775-5759
113 S Main St Rutland VT (05701) *(G-22329)*
Deerwalk Inc (PA) 781 325-1775
430 Bedford St Ste 175 Lexington MA (02420) *(G-12218)*
Defense Integration 617 515-2470
15 W Elm Ter Brockton MA (02301) *(G-9138)*
Defense Logics LLC 781 330-9195
66 Stow St Waltham MA (02453) *(G-16083)*
Defense Manufacturers Inc 603 332-4186
26 Willand Dr Somersworth NH (03878) *(G-19834)*
Defense Support Solutions LLC 978 989-9460
60 Island St Ste 2 Lawrence MA (01840) *(G-12016)*
Defeo Manufacturing Inc 203 775-0254
115 Commerce Dr Brookfield CT (06804) *(G-641)*
Defiance Graphics Corp 978 948-2789
140 Central St Rowley MA (01969) *(G-14852)*
Defibtech LLC (PA) 866 333-4248
741 Boston Post Rd # 201 Guilford CT (06437) *(G-1700)*
Deflex Innovations Inc 603 215-6738
22 Jericho Rd Berlin NH (03570) *(G-17695)*
Degania Medical, Smithfield *Also called Degania Silicone Inc* *(G-21219)*
Degania Silicone Inc (PA) 401 349-5373
14 Thurber Blvd Smithfield RI (02917) *(G-21219)*
Degreasing Devices Co 508 765-0045
105 Dresser St Southbridge MA (01550) *(G-15379)*
Degree Controls Inc (PA) 603 672-8900
18 Meadowbrook Dr Milford NH (03055) *(G-19055)*
Dehaas Advertising & Design 978 462-1997
10 Dorothy E Lucey Dr Newburyport MA (01950) *(G-13481)*
Deitsch Plastic Company Inc 203 934-6601
14 Farwell St West Haven CT (06516) *(G-5115)*
Deja Brew Inc 508 842-8991
510 Boston Tpke Shrewsbury MA (01545) *(G-15107)*
Dejana Trck Utility Eqp Co LLC 401 231-9797
9 Business Park Dr Smithfield RI (02917) *(G-21220)*
Dejana Truck & Utility Eqp, Smithfield *Also called Dejana Trck Utility Eqp Co LLC* *(G-21220)*
Dek Tillett Ltd 413 229-8764
1373 Boardman St Sheffield MA (01257) *(G-15059)*

Del Arbour LLC 203 882-8501
152 Old Gate Ln Milford CT (06460) *(G-2274)*
Del-Tron Precision Inc 203 778-2727
5 Trowbridge Dr Ste 1 Bethel CT (06801) *(G-143)*
Dela Incorporated (PA) 978 372-7783
175 Ward Hill Ave Ste 1 Haverhill MA (01835) *(G-11424)*
Dela Lamimnation Solutions, Haverhill *Also called Dela Incorporated* *(G-11424)*
Delany & Long Ltd 203 532-0010
41 Chestnut St Greenwich CT (06830) *(G-1606)*
Delaware Valley Corp 978 459-6932
600 Woburn St Tewksbury MA (01876) *(G-15814)*
Delcon Industries 203 371-5711
31 Frenchtown Rd Trumbull CT (06611) *(G-4622)*
Delcon Industries LLC 203 331-9720
560 N Washington Ave # 4 Bridgeport CT (06604) *(G-403)*
Delfin Marketing Inc 203 554-2707
500 W Putnam Ave Ste 400 Greenwich CT (06830) *(G-1607)*
Delicate Decadence LLC 802 479-7948
15 Cottage St Ste 4 Barre VT (05641) *(G-21612)*
Delice, Roxbury *Also called Jean Charles Blondine* *(G-14873)*
Dell Acquisition LLC 860 677-8545
35 Corporate Ave Plainville CT (06062) *(G-3480)*
Dell EMC, Hopkinton *Also called EMC Corporation* *(G-11706)*
Dell EMC, Bellingham *Also called EMC Corporation* *(G-8038)*
Dell Inc 603 579-9630
300 Innovative Way # 301 Nashua NH (03062) *(G-19143)*
Dell Manufacturing, Plainville *Also called Dell Acquisition LLC* *(G-3480)*
Dell'amore Pasta Sauce, Colchester *Also called Dellamore Enterprises Inc* *(G-21861)*
Dellamore Enterprises Inc 802 655-6264
948 Hercules Dr Ste 1 Colchester VT (05446) *(G-21861)*
Delltech Inc 203 878-8266
175 Buckingham Ave Milford CT (06460) *(G-2275)*
Delsys Inc 508 545-8200
23 Strathmore Rd Ste 1 Natick MA (01760) *(G-13251)*
Delta Education LLC 800 258-1302
80 Northwest Blvd Nashua NH (03063) *(G-19144)*
Delta Elc Mtr Repr Sls & Serv, Medford *Also called Delta Elc Mtr Repr Sls & Svc* *(G-12930)*
Delta Elc Mtr Repr Sls & Svc 781 395-0551
101 Hicks Ave Medford MA (02155) *(G-12930)*
Delta Electronics Mfg Corp 978 927-1060
416 Cabot St Beverly MA (01915) *(G-8125)*
Delta Elevator Service Corp (HQ) 860 676-6152
1 Farm Springs Rd Canton CT (06019) *(G-697)*
Delta Magnetics and Controls 781 963-2544
275 Centre St Ste 16 Holbrook MA (02343) *(G-11523)*
Delta Mechanical Seals, Fall River *Also called Northeast Equipment Inc* *(G-10740)*
Delta Molding, Leominster *Also called Lolli Company Inc* *(G-12163)*
Delta-Ray Industries Inc 203 367-9903
805 Housatonic Ave Bridgeport CT (06604) *(G-404)*
Delta-Source LLC 860 461-1600
138 Beacon Hill Dr West Hartford CT (06117) *(G-5065)*
Deltran Inc 508 699-7506
65 John L Dietsch Blvd A Attleboro Falls MA (02763) *(G-7812)*
Deluxe Corporation 978 597-8715
12 South St Townsend MA (01469) *(G-15871)*
Delve Labs Inc 617 820-9798
31 Saint James Ave Boston MA (02116) *(G-8498)*
Delvec, Saugus *Also called Sonnys Pizza Inc* *(G-14998)*
Demaich Industries Inc 401 944-3576
70 Mill St Johnston RI (02919) *(G-20508)*
Demakes Enterprises Inc (PA) 781 417-1100
37 Waterhill St Lynn MA (01905) *(G-12499)*
Demakes Enterprises Inc 781 586-0212
34 Riley Way Lynn MA (01905) *(G-12500)*
Demandq Inc 617 401-2165
480 Pleasant St Ste B110 Watertown MA (02472) *(G-16277)*
Demars 978 388-2349
3 Essex St Amesbury MA (01913) *(G-7484)*
Demartino Fixture Co Inc 203 269-3971
920 S Colony Rd Wallingford CT (06492) *(G-4733)*
Deme, Mechanic Falls *Also called Downeast Machine & Engrg Inc* *(G-6419)*
Demiurge Game Development LLC 617 354-7772
130 Prospect St Cambridge MA (02139) *(G-9452)*
Demosthenes Greek-AM Demo 617 628-7766
218 Somerville Ave Somerville MA (02143) *(G-15168)*
Dems Fuel Inc 978 660-0018
87 Littleton Rd Chelmsford MA (01824) *(G-9892)*
Demsey Manufacturing Co Inc 860 274-6209
78 New Wood Rd Watertown CT (06795) *(G-5006)*
Demusz Mfg Co Inc 860 528-9845
303 Burnham St East Hartford CT (06108) *(G-1186)*
Den Mar Corporation 508 999-3295
1005 Reed Rd North Dartmouth MA (02747) *(G-13918)*
Den Technologies Corp 401 263-7579
5 Compass Cir Boylston MA (01505) *(G-8979)*
Denali Software Inc 603 566-0991
154 Broad St Ste 1535 Nashua NH (03063) *(G-19145)*
Denault Inc 413 664-6771
79 Walden St North Adams MA (01247) *(G-13674)*

Denco Counter-Bore LLC 860 276-0782
30 Peters Cir Southington CT (06489) ***(G-4047)***
Denison Pharmaceuticals LLC 401 723-5500
1 Powder Hill Rd Lincoln RI (02865) ***(G-20567)***
Dennco Inc 603 898-0004
21 Northwestern Dr Salem NH (03079) ***(G-19721)***
Dennecrepe Corporation 978 630-8669
70 Fredette St Gardner MA (01440) ***(G-11112)***
Dennis Ducharme 802 426-3796
87 Bailey Pond Rd Marshfield VT (05658) ***(G-22094)***
Dennis Frigon 207 672-4076
Rr 201 Caratunk ME (04925) ***(G-5881)***
Dennis Thompson 603 595-6813
315 Derry Rd Ste 14 Hudson NH (03051) ***(G-18384)***
Dennis Trudel 603 635-7208
72 Russell Dr Unit 3 Pelham NH (03076) ***(G-19430)***
Dennis Welding & Marine Inc 207 497-5998
179 Alley Bays Rd Beals ME (04611) ***(G-5683)***
Denny Mikes cue Stuff Inc (PA) 207 591-5084
55 Bradley Dr Ste A Westbrook ME (04092) ***(G-7187)***
Denny S Sweet Onion Rings 781 598-5317
21 Neptune Blvd Lynn MA (01902) ***(G-12501)***
Denominator Company Inc 203 263-3210
744 Main St S Woodbury CT (06798) ***(G-5485)***
Dens Sand & Gravel 860 642-6478
970 Goshen Hill Rd Ext Lebanon CT (06249) ***(G-1934)***
Dent Herb Company, Lancaster *Also called Cabot Hill Naturals Inc* ***(G-18598)***
Dental Dreams LLC 508 583-2256
698 Crescent St Brockton MA (02302) ***(G-9139)***
Dental Kaleidoscope Magazine 781 821-8898
2184 Washington St Canton MA (02021) ***(G-9724)***
Dental Studios of Western Mass 413 787-9920
120 Lyman St South Hadley MA (01075) ***(G-15301)***
Denton Auto Inc 802 586-2828
2200 Wild Branch Rd Craftsbury VT (05826) ***(G-21892)***
Dentovations Inc 617 737-1199
100 Cambridge St Ste 104 Boston MA (02114) ***(G-8499)***
Dentovations Inc 617 737-1199
100 Franklin St Boston MA (02110) ***(G-8500)***
Dentovations Company, Boston *Also called Dentovations Inc* ***(G-8499)***
Dentsply Ih Inc (HQ) 781 890-6800
590 Lincoln St Waltham MA (02451) ***(G-16084)***
Dentsply Implants, Waltham *Also called Dentsply Ih Inc* ***(G-16084)***
Depot Millworks 603 444-1656
54 Cottage St Littleton NH (03561) ***(G-18657)***
Depuy Mitek LLC 508 880-8100
325 Paramount Dr Raynham MA (02767) ***(G-14709)***
Depuy Orthopaedics, Bridgewater *Also called Medical Device Bus Svcs Inc* ***(G-9083)***
Depuy Spine LLC (HQ) 508 880-8100
325 Paramount Dr Raynham MA (02767) ***(G-14710)***
Depuy Synthes Products Inc (HQ) 508 880-8100
325 Paramount Dr Raynham MA (02767) ***(G-14711)***
Depuy Synthes Sales Inc 508 880-8100
325 Paramount Dr Raynham MA (02767) ***(G-14712)***
Depuy Synthes Sales Inc 508 880-8100
325 Paramount Dr Raynham MA (02767) ***(G-14713)***
Depuy Synthes Sales Inc 508 880-8100
50 Scotland Blvd Bridgewater MA (02324) ***(G-9071)***
Der-Tex Corporation 207 284-5931
1 Lehner Rd Saco ME (04072) ***(G-6846)***
Derand Precision 802 874-7161
354 Mountain Rd South Londonderry VT (05155) ***(G-22485)***
Derby Cellular Products Inc 203 735-4661
680 Bridgeport Ave Ste 3 Shelton CT (06484) ***(G-3795)***
Derek Ciccone 508 476-2105
334 Se Main St East Douglas MA (01516) ***(G-10426)***
Derek White 207 223-5746
15 Memorial Dr Winterport ME (04496) ***(G-7277)***
Deringer-Ney Inc (PA) 860 242-2281
353 Woodland Ave Bloomfield CT (06002) ***(G-217)***
Dermalogix Partners Inc 207 883-4103
672 Us Route 1 Scarborough ME (04074) ***(G-6916)***
Derosa Printing Company Inc 860 646-1698
485 Middle Tpke E Manchester CT (06040) ***(G-2000)***
Derrick Clifford Logging LLC 802 948-2798
133 Raymond Hill Rd Orwell VT (05760) ***(G-22254)***
Derrick Mason (PA) 413 527-4282
2 Nelson St Norwich CT (06360) ***(G-3278)***
Derry News, Derry *Also called Eagle-Tribune Publishing Co* ***(G-17978)***
Des Printing, Barrington *Also called Rlcp Inc* ***(G-20054)***
Descal Inc 781 736-9400
1275 Main St Ste 1 Waltham MA (02451) ***(G-16085)***
Deschenes & Cooper Architectur 860 599-2481
25 White Rock Bridge Rd Pawcatuck CT (06379) ***(G-3434)***
Desco Electronics Inc 508 643-1950
36 Bacon Sq Plainville MA (02762) ***(G-14517)***
Desco Industries Inc 603 332-0717
73 Allen St Rochester NH (03867) ***(G-19667)***
Desco Industries Inc 781 821-8370
1 Colgate Way Canton MA (02021) ***(G-9725)***
Desco Industries Inc 781 821-8370
1 Colgate Way Canton MA (02021) ***(G-9726)***
Desert Harvest Solar Farm LLC 978 531-2222
2 Centennial Dr Ste 4f Peabody MA (01960) ***(G-14329)***
Design Architectural Heating 207 784-0309
141 Howe St Lewiston ME (04240) ***(G-6283)***
Design Communications Ltd (PA) 617 542-9620
85 Bodwell St Avon MA (02322) ***(G-7886)***
Design Consultants Associates 603 329-4541
1 Owens Ct Hampstead NH (03841) ***(G-18239)***
Design Copy Printers Inc 978 741-2244
167 Boston St Salem MA (01970) ***(G-14906)***
Design Engineering Inc 860 482-4120
245 E Elm St Torrington CT (06790) ***(G-4574)***
Design Fab, Windham *Also called Rbw Inc* ***(G-7246)***
Design Fab Inc 207 786-2446
928 Minot Ave Auburn ME (04210) ***(G-5559)***
Design Fabricators Inc 401 944-5294
72 Stamp Farm Rd Cranston RI (02921) ***(G-20209)***
Design Flow Wraps, Beverly *Also called Designflow Wraps Inc* ***(G-8126)***
Design Idea Printing 860 896-0103
344 Somers Rd Ellington CT (06029) ***(G-1332)***
Design Jewelry 617 489-0764
6 Apollo Rd Belmont MA (02478) ***(G-8072)***
Design Label Manufacturing Inc (PA) 860 739-6266
12 Nottingham Dr Old Lyme CT (06371) ***(G-3321)***
Design Mark Industries Inc 800 451-3275
3 Kendrick Rd Wareham MA (02571) ***(G-16244)***
Design Research Optics, East Greenwich *Also called Nippon American Limited* ***(G-20374)***
Design Signs Inc 802 872-9906
4 Andrew Dr Essex Junction VT (05452) ***(G-21939)***
Design Standards Corp 603 826-7744
957 Claremont Rd Charlestown NH (03603) ***(G-17813)***
Designed Essence Enterprise 802 864-4238
52 Church St Ste 2b Burlington VT (05401) ***(G-21780)***
Designer Board Specialties 781 794-9413
144 Lundquist Dr Braintree MA (02184) ***(G-9000)***
Designer Sinks & Faucets 781 924-1768
74 Maplewood Dr Hanover MA (02339) ***(G-11335)***
Designer Stained Glass 508 763-3255
4 Perkins Ln Acushnet MA (02743) ***(G-7401)***
Designers Metalcraft 508 378-0404
530 Spring St East Bridgewater MA (02333) ***(G-10412)***
Designers' Circle, Burlington *Also called Designed Essence Enterprise* ***(G-21780)***
Designflow Wraps Inc 978 729-5415
51 Park St Beverly MA (01915) ***(G-8126)***
Designing Element 203 849-3076
6 Barnum Ave Norwalk CT (06851) ***(G-3134)***
Designing Health Inc 661 257-1705
302 Benton Dr East Longmeadow MA (01028) ***(G-10472)***
Designpak, Marlborough *Also called Egoh Packaging Inc* ***(G-12752)***
Designs & Prototypes Ltd 860 658-0458
1280 Hopmeadow St Ste E Simsbury CT (06070) ***(G-3899)***
Designs By Lainie 781 592-2126
300 Lynn Shore Dr Apt 802 Lynn MA (01902) ***(G-12502)***
Designtex Group Inc 207 774-2689
14 Industrial Way Portland ME (04103) ***(G-6650)***
Desjardins Woodworking Inc 860 491-9972
211 East St N Goshen CT (06756) ***(G-1583)***
Desk Top Graphics Inc (HQ) 617 832-1927
1 1st Ave Peabody MA (01960) ***(G-14330)***
Desk Top Graphics Inc 207 828-0041
477 Congress St Ste 2b Portland ME (04101) ***(G-6651)***
Desk Top Solutions Inc 781 890-7500
335 Bear Hill Rd Waltham MA (02451) ***(G-16086)***
Desktop Engineering Magazine, Dublin *Also called Helmers Publishing Inc* ***(G-18068)***
Desktop Metal Inc (PA) 978 224-1244
63 3rd Ave Burlington MA (01803) ***(G-9254)***
Desnoyers Enterprises Inc 800 922-4445
1160 Mount Pleasant Rd Harrisville RI (02830) ***(G-20478)***
Desrosier of Greenwich Inc 203 661-2334
103 Mason St Greenwich CT (06830) ***(G-1608)***
Dessureau Machines Inc 802 476-4561
53 Granite St Barre VT (05641) ***(G-21613)***
Destination Map Only In WA, Waitsfield *Also called Discovery Map Intl Inc* ***(G-22564)***
Destiny Publishers, Merrimac *Also called Anglo-Saxon Federation of Amer* ***(G-13000)***
Destrail 818 687-7037
45 Museum St Apt D Cambridge MA (02138) ***(G-9453)***
Detail Woodworking Ltd 617 323-8100
19 Linnell Cir Billerica MA (01821) ***(G-8236)***
Detectogen Inc 508 330-1709
5 Jacob Amsden Rd Westborough MA (01581) ***(G-16615)***
Detotec North America Inc 860 230-0078
363 Ekonk Hill Rd Moosup CT (06354) ***(G-2425)***
Detotec North America Inc 860 564-1012
401 Snake Meadow Hill Rd Sterling CT (06377) ***(G-4366)***
Detroit Forming Inc 603 598-2767
15 Sagamore Park Rd Hudson NH (03051) ***(G-18385)***

ALPHABETIC

Detroit Technologies Inc 207 784-1118
125 Allied Rd Auburn ME (04210) ***(G-5560)***
Devar Inc 203 368-6751
706 Bostwick Ave Bridgeport CT (06605) ***(G-405)***
Development Associates Inc 401 884-1350
300 Old Baptist Rd North Kingstown RI (02852) ***(G-20702)***
Development Resources, Westborough *Also called Business Resources Inc* ***(G-16596)***
Deveney & White Inc 617 288-3080
664 Gallivan Blvd Boston MA (02124) ***(G-8501)***
Deveney & White Monuments, Boston *Also called Deveney & White Inc* ***(G-8501)***
Deveney, David P Memorial Co, Medford *Also called David P Deveney Memorial Co* ***(G-12929)***
Device Technologies Inc 508 229-2000
155 Northboro Rd Ste 8 Southborough MA (01772) ***(G-15354)***
Device42 Inc 203 409-7242
600 Saw Mill Rd West Haven CT (06516) ***(G-5116)***
Devincentis Press Inc 781 605-3796
988 Eastern Ave Malden MA (02148) ***(G-12567)***
Devon Precision Industries Inc 203 879-1437
251 Munson Rd Wolcott CT (06716) ***(G-5438)***
Devon Precision Industries., Wolcott *Also called Devon Precision Industries Inc* ***(G-5438)***
Devon's Place, Mansfield *Also called Driscolls Restaurant* ***(G-12629)***
Devprotek Inc 603 577-5557
4 Clinton Dr Hollis NH (03049) ***(G-18329)***
Devtech Pet Inc (PA) 603 889-8311
12 Howe Dr Amherst NH (03031) ***(G-17556)***
Dewal Industries LLC 401 789-9736
15 Ray Trainor Dr Narragansett RI (02882) ***(G-20637)***
Dewalt Service Center 050, Wethersfield *Also called Black & Decker (us) Inc* ***(G-5242)***
Dewetron Inc 401 284-3750
2850 S County Trl Unit 1 East Greenwich RI (02818) ***(G-20360)***
Dewey J Manufacturing Company 203 264-3064
112 Willenbrock Rd Oxford CT (06478) ***(G-3399)***
Dewitt Machine & Fabrication 207 732-3530
1152 Medford Center Rd Medford ME (04463) ***(G-6422)***
Dexmet Corporation 203 294-4440
22 Barnes Industrial Rd S Wallingford CT (06492) ***(G-4734)***
Dexter Co The, East Providence *Also called Dexter Enterprises Corp* ***(G-20404)***
Dexter Crane Service, East Providence *Also called Dexter Sign Co* ***(G-20406)***
Dexter Enterprises Corp 401 434-2300
70 Waterman Ave East Providence RI (02914) ***(G-20404)***
Dexter Innvative Solutions LLC 978 544-2751
61 E River St Orange MA (01364) ***(G-14214)***
Dexter Precision Products, Orange *Also called Leavitt Machine Co* ***(G-14220)***
Dexter Products Inc 802 868-7085
716 Vt Route 78 Swanton VT (05488) ***(G-22530)***
Dexter Service Center 401 438-3900
80 Waterman Ave East Providence RI (02914) ***(G-20405)***
Dexter Sign Co 401 434-1100
70 Waterman Ave East Providence RI (02914) ***(G-20406)***
Dexter-Russell Inc 800 343-6042
44 River St Southbridge MA (01550) ***(G-15380)***
Deyulio Sausage Company LLC 203 348-1863
1501 State St Bridgeport CT (06605) ***(G-406)***
Dff Corp 413 786-8880
59 Gen Creighto Agawam MA (01001) ***(G-7427)***
Dfi-Electroplating, North Providence *Also called DFI-Ep LLC* ***(G-20756)***
DFI-Ep LLC 401 943-9900
50 Waterman Ave North Providence RI (02911) ***(G-20756)***
Dfs In-Home Services 845 405-6464
15 Great Pasture Rd Danbury CT (06810) ***(G-900)***
Dg International Holdings Corp 781 577-2016
75 2nd Ave Ste 720 Needham Heights MA (02494) ***(G-13328)***
Dg Marshall Associates Inc 508 943-2394
11 Old Worcester Rd Webster MA (01570) ***(G-16341)***
Dg Precision Manufacturing, Woodbury *Also called Duda and Goodwin Inc* ***(G-5486)***
Dg3 Digital Pubg Solutions, Woburn *Also called Dg3 Group America Inc* ***(G-17167)***
Dg3 Group America Inc 617 241-5600
500 W Cummings Park # 4500 Woburn MA (01801) ***(G-17167)***
Dgf Indstrial Innvations Group 603 528-6591
25 Waterford Pl Gilford NH (03249) ***(G-18185)***
DH Custom Woodworks 781 784-5951
68 Ames St Sharon MA (02067) ***(G-15049)***
DH Hardwick & Sons Inc 603 588-6618
301 Francestown Rd Bennington NH (03442) ***(G-17688)***
DH Industries USA Inc 781 229-5814
67 S Bedford St Ste 400w Burlington MA (01803) ***(G-9255)***
Dhf LLC 603 778-2440
424 Route 125 Unit 6 Brentwood NH (03833) ***(G-17748)***
Dhm Thread Corporation 508 672-0032
192 Anawan St Ste 301 Fall River MA (02721) ***(G-10682)***
Di An Enterprises Inc 617 469-0819
85 Wallis Rd Chestnut Hill MA (02467) ***(G-9986)***
Di MO Tool, Middleboro *Also called Di-MO Manufacturing Inc* ***(G-13062)***
Di-Cor Industries Inc 860 585-5583
139 Center St Bristol CT (06010) ***(G-549)***
Di-El Tool & Manufacturing 203 235-2169
69 Research Pkwy Ste 1 Meriden CT (06450) ***(G-2091)***
Di-MO Manufacturing Inc 508 947-2200
35 Harding St Middleboro MA (02346) ***(G-13062)***
Diaco Communication Inc 802 863-6233
3073 Williston Rd South Burlington VT (05403) ***(G-22446)***
Diacom Corporation 603 880-1900
5 Howe Dr Amherst NH (03031) ***(G-17557)***
Diacritech Inc 617 236-7500
4 S Market St Fl 4 # 4 Boston MA (02109) ***(G-8502)***
Diageo Americas Inc 203 229-2100
801 Main Ave Norwalk CT (06851) ***(G-3135)***
Diageo Americas Supply Inc 203 229-2100
801 Main Ave Norwalk CT (06851) ***(G-3136)***
Diageo Investment Corporation 203 229-2100
801 Main Ave Norwalk CT (06851) ***(G-3137)***
Diageo North America Inc 508 324-9800
800 S Main St Mansfield MA (02048) ***(G-12628)***
Diageo North America Inc (HQ) 203 229-2100
801 Main Ave Norwalk CT (06851) ***(G-3138)***
Diageo PLC 203 229-2100
801 Main Ave Norwalk CT (06851) ***(G-3139)***
Diagnosys LLC (PA) 978 458-1600
55 Technology Dr Ste 1 Lowell MA (01851) ***(G-12367)***
Diakosmisis Corporation 617 776-7714
561 Windsor St Ste B301 Somerville MA (02143) ***(G-15169)***
Dial Fabrics Co Inc 508 822-5333
20 Cushman St Taunton MA (02780) ***(G-15742)***
Diamond Antenna Microwave Corp 978 486-0039
59 Porter Rd Littleton MA (01460) ***(G-12300)***
Diamond Casting and Mch Co Inc 603 465-2263
95 Proctor Hill Rd Hollis NH (03049) ***(G-18330)***
Diamond Deans Dollhouse Co, Montpelier *Also called Real Good Toys Inc* ***(G-22159)***
Diamond Diagnostics -USA, Holliston *Also called Diamond Diagnostics Inc* ***(G-11567)***
Diamond Diagnostics Inc (PA) 508 429-0450
333 Fiske St Holliston MA (01746) ***(G-11567)***
Diamond Express Inc 781 284-9402
155 West St Ste 3 Wilmington MA (01887) ***(G-16994)***
Diamond Ironworks Inc 978 794-4640
109 Blanchard St Lawrence MA (01843) ***(G-12017)***
Diamond Machining Technology, Marlborough *Also called Acme United Corporation* ***(G-12709)***
Diamond Machining Technology, Marlborough *Also called Vogel Capital Inc* ***(G-12846)***
Diamond Music Co 603 635-2083
5 Leonard Dr Pelham NH (03076) ***(G-19431)***
Diamond Plated Technology Inc 508 823-2711
28 Godfrey St Taunton MA (02780) ***(G-15743)***
Diamond Rf LLC 978 486-0039
59 Porter Rd Littleton MA (01460) ***(G-12301)***
Diamond Solar Group LLC 978 808-9288
460 Boston St Ste 1 Topsfield MA (01983) ***(G-15856)***
Diamond Stl & Fabrication LLC 781 245-3255
80 New Salem St Ste 9 Wakefield MA (01880) ***(G-15950)***
Diamond Systems, Pelham *Also called Diamond Music Co* ***(G-19431)***
Diamond Trucking, Fort Kent *Also called Guimond Logging* ***(G-6060)***
Diamond USA Inc (HQ) 978 256-6544
85 Rangeway Rd Ste 3 North Billerica MA (01862) ***(G-13807)***
Diamond Water Systems Inc 413 536-8186
863 Montgomery St Chicopee MA (01013) ***(G-10017)***
Diamond Windows Doors Mfg Inc 617 282-1688
99 E Cottage St Boston MA (02125) ***(G-8503)***
Diamond-Roltran LLC 978 486-0039
59 Porter Rd Ste 2 Littleton MA (01460) ***(G-12302)***
Diamondhead USA Inc 413 537-4806
622 Union St West Springfield MA (01089) ***(G-16516)***
Diamondsharp Corporation 603 445-2224
20 Blanchard Brook Cir Walpole NH (03608) ***(G-19920)***
Diannes Fine Desserts Inc (PA) 978 463-3832
4 Graf Rd Newburyport MA (01950) ***(G-13482)***
Diannes Fine Desserts Inc 978 463-3881
1 Perry Way Newburyport MA (01950) ***(G-13483)***
Diaper To Go, Agawam *Also called Agawam Novelty Company Inc* ***(G-7418)***
Dias Infrared Corp 845 987-8152
75 Sterling St West Boylston MA (01583) ***(G-16414)***
Diaute Bros 781 848-0524
475 Quincy Ave Braintree MA (02184) ***(G-9001)***
Diba Industries Inc (HQ) 203 744-0773
4 Precision Rd Danbury CT (06810) ***(G-901)***
Dibs, Providence *Also called Kerb Inc* ***(G-21047)***
Dicerna Pharmaceuticals Inc 617 621-8097
33 Hayden Ave Lexington MA (02421) ***(G-12219)***
Dichtomatik Americas LP 603 628-7030
100 Commercial St Manchester NH (03101) ***(G-18809)***
Dick Muller Designer/Craftsman 413 625-0016
21 High St Shelburne Falls MA (01370) ***(G-15068)***
Dickinson's Cosmetics, East Hampton *Also called T N Dickinson Company* ***(G-1166)***
Dicks Baking 207 284-3779
351 Pleasant River Rd Milo ME (04463) ***(G-6445)***
Dickson Eagle, Warwick *Also called E G & G Sealol Eagle Inc* ***(G-21357)***
Dickson Product Development 203 846-2128
14 Perry Ave Norwalk CT (06850) ***(G-3140)***

Dicon Connections Inc........203 481-8080
33 Fowler Rd North Branford CT (06471) *(G-2961)*
Dicronite Dry Lube, Westfield *Also called Circuit Systems Inc (G-16678)*
Dictaphone Corporation (HQ)........203 381-7000
3191 Broadbridge Ave Stratford CT (06614) *(G-4409)*
Diebolt & Company........860 434-2222
341 Shaker Rd East Longmeadow MA (01028) *(G-10473)*
Diecast Connections Co Inc........413 592-8444
10 Cordage Park Cir # 222 Plymouth MA (02360) *(G-14552)*
Diecast Manufacturer (PA)........978 667-6784
67 Faulkner St North Billerica MA (01862) *(G-13808)*
Diecraft Compacting Tool Inc........203 879-3019
36 James Pl Wolcott CT (06716) *(G-5439)*
Diecutting Tooling Svcs Inc (PA)........413 331-3500
680 Meadow St Chicopee MA (01013) *(G-10018)*
Diehl Graphics Co........978 297-1598
128 Maple St Winchendon MA (01475) *(G-17074)*
Dielectric Products........617 924-5688
178 Orchard St Watertown MA (02472) *(G-16278)*
Dielectrics Inc (HQ)........413 594-8111
300 Burnett Rd Chicopee MA (01020) *(G-10019)*
Diemat Inc........978 499-0900
19 Central St Ste 9 Byfield MA (01922) *(G-9362)*
Dienes Corporation........508 885-6301
27 W Main St Spencer MA (01562) *(G-15428)*
Dietze & Associates LLC........203 762-3500
88 Danbury Rd Ste 1a Wilton CT (06897) *(G-5288)*
Dietze Associates, Wilton *Also called Dietze & Associates LLC (G-5288)*
Different Drummer........207 643-2572
211 Eaton Hill Rd Solon ME (04979) *(G-6997)*
Differential Pipetting Inc........978 515-3392
11 Dory Rd Gloucester MA (01930) *(G-11177)*
Differential Pressure Plus........203 481-2545
67 N Branford Rd Ste 4 Branford CT (06405) *(G-309)*
Difruscia Industries Inc........401 943-9900
1425 Cranston St Cranston RI (02920) *(G-20210)*
Dig Media Group Inc........617 418-9075
24 Spice St Ste 203 Boston MA (02129) *(G-8504)*
Dig Rite Company Inc........401 862-5895
311 Pippin Orchard Rd Cranston RI (02921) *(G-20211)*
Digatron Power Electronics Inc........203 446-8000
50 Waterview Dr Shelton CT (06484) *(G-3796)*
Digilab Inc........508 305-2410
105 South St Hopkinton MA (01748) *(G-11700)*
Digilab Genomic Solutions Inc........508 893-3130
84 October Hill Rd Ste 7 Holliston MA (01746) *(G-11568)*
Digipress Inc (PA)........617 832-1927
1 1st Ave Peabody MA (01960) *(G-14331)*
Digital Alloys Incorporated........617 557-3432
37 North Ave Burlington MA (01803) *(G-9256)*
Digital Cognition Tech Inc........617 433-1777
210 Bear Hill Rd Ste 301 Waltham MA (02451) *(G-16087)*
Digital Devices Inc........603 654-6240
28 Howard St Wilton NH (03086) *(G-19978)*
Digital Graphics Inc........781 270-3670
101 Billerica Ave Bldg 6n North Billerica MA (01862) *(G-13809)*
Digital Guardian Inc (PA)........781 788-8180
275 Wyman St Ste 250 Waltham MA (02451) *(G-16088)*
Digital Image Fidelity LLC........508 577-8496
25 South Ave Whitman MA (02382) *(G-16922)*
Digital Immunity LLC........508 630-0321
60 Mall Rd Ste 309 Burlington MA (01803) *(G-9257)*
Digital Ink Printing LLC........603 692-6002
72 High St Somersworth NH (03878) *(G-19835)*
Digital Lumens Incorporated........617 723-1200
374 Congress St Ste 601 Boston MA (02210) *(G-8505)*
Digital Paradigms Inc........617 723-9400
151 Tremont St Ste 110 Boston MA (02111) *(G-8506)*
Digital Press Printers LLC........802 863-5579
128 Commerce St Williston VT (05495) *(G-22662)*
Digital Printer Service........860 395-7942
159 Mountain Dr Gilford NH (03249) *(G-18186)*
Digital Printing Concepts Inc........401 431-2110
985 Waterman Ave East Providence RI (02914) *(G-20407)*
Digital Vdeo Cmmunications Inc........781 932-6882
500 W Cummings Park # 2000 Woburn MA (01801) *(G-17168)*
Digitry Company Inc (PA)........207 774-0300
449 Forest Ave Ste 210 Portland ME (04101) *(G-6652)*
Dignified Endings LLC........860 291-0575
15 Stanley St East Hartford CT (06108) *(G-1187)*
Dijitized Communications Inc........603 473-2144
58 Route 153 Middleton NH (03887) *(G-19039)*
Dike Corporation (PA)........978 208-7046
1 Broadway Ste 1b Lawrence MA (01840) *(G-12018)*
Dilla St Corp........508 478-3419
130 Cedar St Milford MA (01757) *(G-13112)*
Dillon Dental Laboratories, Abington *Also called Dillon Laboratories Inc (G-7322)*
Dillon Laboratories Inc........781 871-2333
4 Thicket St Abington MA (02351) *(G-7322)*
Diluigis Inc........978 750-9900
41 Popes Ln Danvers MA (01923) *(G-10213)*
Dimark Incorporated........781 447-7990
205 Commercial St Whitman MA (02382) *(G-16923)*
Dimark Precision Machining........781 447-7990
745 Washington St Pembroke MA (02359) *(G-14399)*
Dimension Lumber........207 897-9973
85 Jug Hill Rd Peru ME (04290) *(G-6585)*
Dimension-Polyant Inc........860 928-8300
78 Highland Dr Putnam CT (06260) *(G-3610)*
Dimensional Insight Inc (PA)........781 229-9111
60 Mall Rd Ste 210 Burlington MA (01803) *(G-9258)*
Dina Inc........401 942-9633
357 Dyer Ave Cranston RI (02920) *(G-20212)*
Dingee Machine Co, Cornish *Also called Larry Dingee (G-17962)*
Dinner Daily LLC........978 392-5887
26 Colonial Dr Westford MA (01886) *(G-16764)*
Dinning Out -Main Coast, Wolfeboro Falls *Also called Panoramic Publishing Group LLC (G-20028)*
Diocesan Press Inc........508 675-3857
887 Highland Ave Fall River MA (02720) *(G-10683)*
Dion Label Printing Inc........413 568-3713
539 North Rd Westfield MA (01085) *(G-16680)*
Dion Signs and Service Inc........401 724-4459
125 Samuel Barnet Blvd New Bedford MA (02745) *(G-13379)*
Dionex, Chelmsford *Also called Magellan Diagnostics Inc (G-9915)*
Dionne & Sons Fuel Oil, Coventry *Also called Dionne & Sons Piping Dynamics (G-20145)*
Dionne & Sons Piping Dynamics........401 821-9266
599 Arnold Rd Coventry RI (02816) *(G-20145)*
Dioptics Medical Products Inc........805 781-3300
500 Washington Hwy Smithfield RI (02917) *(G-21221)*
Dipwell Company Inc........413 587-4673
82 Industrial Dr Unit 3 Northampton MA (01060) *(G-14004)*
Direct Display Publishing Inc........207 443-4800
765 High St Ste 5 Bath ME (04530) *(G-5676)*
Direct Sales LLC (PA)........203 371-2373
440 Sky Top Dr Fairfield CT (06825) *(G-1426)*
Direx Systems Corp........339 502-6013
956 Turnpike St Canton MA (02021) *(G-9727)*
Dirigo Analytics LLC........978 376-5522
14 Oak Bluff Rd Kennebunk ME (04043) *(G-6232)*
Dirigo Stitching Inc........207 474-8421
40 Dane Ave Skowhegan ME (04976) *(G-6972)*
Discerning Palate LLC (PA)........603 279-8600
21 Corliss Hill Rd Meredith NH (03253) *(G-18973)*
Disco Chick........860 788-6203
170 Main St Middletown CT (06457) *(G-2183)*
Discount Beverages Plus Cig........603 356-8844
1130 Eastman Rd Center Conway NH (03813) *(G-17794)*
Discount Liquors, Lynn *Also called Market Square Beverage Co Inc (G-12525)*
Discover Maine Magazine, Portland *Also called Cremark Inc (G-6644)*
Discovery Map Intl Inc........802 316-4060
5197 Main St Unit 8 Waitsfield VT (05673) *(G-22564)*
Dispatch........781 837-8700
1248 Ferry St Marshfield MA (02050) *(G-12859)*
Dispatch News........978 458-7100
491 Dutton St Lowell MA (01854) *(G-12368)*
Dispatch Plant, Chicopee *Also called Chicopee Foundations Inc (G-10008)*
Dispersion Services LLC........603 577-9520
25 Front St Ste 201 Nashua NH (03064) *(G-19146)*
Displaycraft Inc........860 747-9110
335 S Washington St Plainville CT (06062) *(G-3481)*
Displays For Less, Warren *Also called Progressive Displays Inc (G-21303)*
Distance Racing Products........207 453-2644
441 Center Rd Fairfield ME (04937) *(G-6026)*
Distillation Tech Pdts LLC........603 935-7070
285 Lindstrom Ln Manchester NH (03104) *(G-18766)*
Distillery Network Inc........603 997-6786
21 W Auburn St Ste 30 Manchester NH (03101) *(G-18810)*
Distinct Element........617 322-3979
52 Ormond St Mattapan MA (02126) *(G-12883)*
Distinctive Designs USA, Salem *Also called Dundorf Designs USA Inc (G-3738)*
Distinctive Steering Wheels........860 274-9087
189 Chimney Rd Watertown CT (06795) *(G-5007)*
Distribution & Control Product........781 324-0070
730 Eastern Ave Malden MA (02148) *(G-12568)*
Ditech........978 463-0665
144 Elm St Byfield MA (01922) *(G-9363)*
Dittmar & McNeil CPA S Inc........401 921-2600
501 Centerville Rd # 103 Warwick RI (02886) *(G-21352)*
Ditusa Corporation........978 335-5259
19 Shepherd St Gloucester MA (01930) *(G-11178)*
Div Cabot Road LLC........781 396-3122
1 Cabot Rd Medford MA (02155) *(G-12931)*
Div of Bttnfeld Glcester Engrg, Newport *Also called Shrinkfast Marketing (G-19358)*
Diversified Biotech Inc........781 326-6709
65 Commerce Way Dedham MA (02026) *(G-10288)*
Diversified Business Systems, Haverhill *Also called D B S Industries Inc (G-11421)*

A L P H A B E T I C

Diversified Decorating Sales 603 532-4557
32 Fitzgerald Dr Jaffrey NH (03452) *(G-18461)*
Diversified Enterprises-ADT 603 543-0038
101 Mulberry St Ste 2n Claremont NH (03743) *(G-17847)*
Diversified Industrial Sup LLC 800 244-3647
100 Terminal St Charlestown MA (02129) *(G-9831)*
Diversified Machining Inc 978 562-2213
9 Bonazzoli Ave Ste 24 Hudson MA (01749) *(G-11768)*
Diversified Manufact 203 734-0379
1 Riverside Dr Ste H Ansonia CT (06401) *(G-13)*
Diversified Metal Crafters Inc 401 305-7700
4 Carol Dr Lincoln RI (02865) *(G-20568)*
Diversified Printing Solutions 203 826-7198
128 E Liberty St Danbury CT (06810) *(G-902)*
Diversitech Corporation 800 699-0453
391 W Water St Taunton MA (02780) *(G-15744)*
Diversity Studio Inc 978 250-5553
160 Ayer Rd 14 Littleton MA (01460) *(G-12303)*
Divine Stoneworks LLC 774 221-6006
60 Pleasant St Ashland MA (01721) *(G-7657)*
Divine Treasure 860 643-2552
404 Middle Tpke W Manchester CT (06040) *(G-2001)*
Division 5 LLC 860 752-4127
99 Cooper Ln Stafford Springs CT (06076) *(G-4109)*
Divlan Inc 347 338-8843
69 Harvey St Apt 1 Cambridge MA (02140) *(G-9454)*
Divya Marigowda 781 863-5189
39 Woodpark Cir Lexington MA (02421) *(G-12220)*
Dixie Consumer Products LLC 978 537-4701
149 Hamilton St Leominster MA (01453) *(G-12133)*
Dixon Bros Millwork Inc 781 261-9962
200 Wales St Abington MA (02351) *(G-7323)*
Diy Awards LLC (PA) 800 810-1216
1 Atlantic St Ste 705 Stamford CT (06901) *(G-4189)*
Dj Instruments, Franklin *Also called Dynisco Instruments LLC* *(G-11037)*
Dj Instruments, Franklin *Also called Dynisco LLC* *(G-11038)*
Dj Microlaminates Inc 978 261-3188
490 Boston Post Rd Sudbury MA (01776) *(G-15655)*
Dj Wholesale Club Inc 978 649-2525
3 Westech Dr Tyngsboro MA (01879) *(G-15888)*
Djd Enterprises LLC 617 803-6875
330 Columbia St Cambridge MA (02141) *(G-9455)*
DJM Precision Machining 978 922-0407
200 Rantoul St Rear Beverly MA (01915) *(G-8127)*
Dkd Solutions Inc 508 762-9114
77 E Worcester St Worcester MA (01604) *(G-17365)*
Dl Distributors LLC 203 931-1724
343 Beach St West Haven CT (06516) *(G-5117)*
Dl Technology LLC 978 374-6451
216 River St Haverhill MA (01832) *(G-11425)*
Dla Document Services 401 841-6011
47 Chandler St Newport RI (02841) *(G-20662)*
Dlt, Pelham *Also called Dennis Trudel* *(G-19430)*
Dlz Architectural Mill Work 860 883-7562
510 Ledyard St Hartford CT (06114) *(G-1818)*
Dm Inc 802 425-2119
28 Industrial Dr Milton VT (05468) *(G-22126)*
Dm Semiconductor Company Inc 603 898-7750
24 Keewaydin Dr Ste 5 Salem NH (03079) *(G-19722)*
DManielly Express 401 490-2900
918 Atwells Ave Providence RI (02909) *(G-20997)*
Dmar Environmental LLC 508 331-1884
184 Stone St Ste 1 Clinton MA (01510) *(G-10079)*
Dmf Engineering, Londonderry *Also called D M F Machine Co Inc* *(G-18691)*
Dmh Software 978 263-0526
143 Butternut Holw Acton MA (01718) *(G-7350)*
Dmi Nutraceuticals Inc 617 999-7219
1 Oak Park Dr Ste 2 Bedford MA (01730) *(G-7971)*
Dmi Technology Corp (PA) 603 742-3330
1 Progress Dr Dover NH (03820) *(G-18019)*
Dmjl Consulting LLC 978 989-0790
145 Milk St Methuen MA (01844) *(G-13018)*
Dmr Industries Inc 603 335-0325
181 Milton Rd Rochester NH (03868) *(G-19668)*
Dmr Print Inc (PA) 617 876-3688
13 Dover St Concord MA (01742) *(G-10128)*
DMS Machining & Fabrication, Barre *Also called Gloucester Associates Inc* *(G-21617)*
Dmt Export Inc 508 481-5944
85 Hayes Memorial Dr # 1 Marlborough MA (01752) *(G-12748)*
Dmt Solutions Global Corp 203 233-6231
37 Executive Dr Danbury CT (06810) *(G-903)*
Dns Inc 508 248-5901
123 Hammond Hill Rd Charlton MA (01507) *(G-9849)*
Doble Engineering Company (HQ) 617 926-4900
85 Walnut St Watertown MA (02472) *(G-16279)*
Doble Engineering Company 802 482-2255
110 Riggs Rd Hinesburg VT (05461) *(G-22022)*
Docbox Inc 978 987-2569
760 Main St 2-4 Waltham MA (02451) *(G-16089)*
Dock Doctors LLC 802 877-6756
19 Little Otter Ln Ferrisburgh VT (05456) *(G-21988)*
Dockside Repairs Inc 508 993-6730
14 Hervey Tichon Ave New Bedford MA (02740) *(G-13380)*
Doctor Stuff LLC 203 785-8475
20 N Plains Industrial Rd # 1 Wallingford CT (06492) *(G-4735)*
Document Archives Imaging LLC 603 656-5209
451 Pepsi Rd Ste C Manchester NH (03109) *(G-18811)*
Documents On Demand Inc 508 793-0956
184 Main St Worcester MA (01608) *(G-17366)*
Docuprint & Imaging Inc 203 776-6000
27 Whitney Ave New Haven CT (06510) *(G-2682)*
Docuprint Express Ltd 508 895-9090
1 Bert Dr Ste 14 West Bridgewater MA (02379) *(G-16437)*
Docuprintnow, New Haven *Also called Docuprint & Imaging Inc* *(G-2682)*
Docuserve Inc 508 786-5820
72 Cedar Hill St Ste B Marlborough MA (01752) *(G-12749)*
Dodge Company Inc (PA) 800 443-6343
9 Progress Rd Billerica MA (01821) *(G-8237)*
Dodge Woodworking LLC 603 642-6188
7 Cove Rd East Kingston NH (03827) *(G-18086)*
Dodgeskiboots, Essex Junction *Also called Perfect Storm Sports Tech LLC* *(G-21954)*
Dodlin Hill Stone Company LLC 207 465-6463
49 Allagash Dr Oakland ME (04963) *(G-6532)*
Dog Gone Smart, Norwalk *Also called Nano Pet Products LLC* *(G-3203)*
Doggie Passport 603 315-8243
214 Heathrow Ave Manchester NH (03104) *(G-18812)*
Dogwatch Inc (PA) 508 650-0600
10 Michigan Dr Natick MA (01760) *(G-13252)*
Dolan LLC 617 451-7300
10 Milk St Ste 1000 Boston MA (02108) *(G-8507)*
Dolan-Jenner Industries Inc 978 263-1400
159 Swanson Rd Boxborough MA (01719) *(G-8961)*
Dolly Plow Inc 781 293-9828
53 Mattakeesett St Pembroke MA (02359) *(G-14400)*
Dome Enterprises Trust (PA) 401 738-7900
10 New England Way Warwick RI (02886) *(G-21353)*
Dome Industries, Warwick *Also called Dome Publishing Company Inc* *(G-21354)*
Dome Publishing Company Inc (HQ) 401 738-7900
10 New England Way Warwick RI (02886) *(G-21354)*
Domestic Kitchens Inc 203 368-1651
515 Commerce Dr Fairfield CT (06825) *(G-1427)*
Dometic Uk Blind Systems Ltd 802 362-5258
91 Manchester Valley Rd Manchester Center VT (05255) *(G-22082)*
Dometic US Blind Systems, Manchester Center *Also called Dometic Uk Blind Systems Ltd* *(G-22082)*
Dominics Decorating Inc 203 838-1827
6 Allen Ct Norwalk CT (06851) *(G-3141)*
Dominion & Grimm USA 802 524-9625
164 Yankee Park Rd Fairfax VT (05454) *(G-21974)*
Dominion Rebar Company 401 724-9200
30 Lockbridge St Pawtucket RI (02860) *(G-20834)*
Domino Media Group Inc 877 223-7844
16 Taylor Pl Westport CT (06880) *(G-5188)*
Domino.com, Westport *Also called Domino Media Group Inc* *(G-5188)*
Domtar Paper Company LLC 207 427-6400
144 Main St Baileyville ME (04694) *(G-5624)*
Don S Screw Machine Pdts LLC 860 283-6448
247 Old Northfield Rd Thomaston CT (06787) *(G-4501)*
Don-May of Wakefield Inc 401 789-9339
128 Main St Wakefield RI (02879) *(G-21269)*
Donahue Industries Inc 508 845-6501
5 Industrial Dr Shrewsbury MA (01545) *(G-15108)*
Donald A Jhnson Fine Wdwkg LLC 603 356-9080
199 Dundee Rd Intervale NH (03845) *(G-18454)*
Donald G Lockard 401 965-3182
11 Setting Sun Dr Westerly RI (02891) *(G-21523)*
Donald McIntire 207 778-3581
300 Porter Hill Rd Farmington ME (04938) *(G-6043)*
Donali Systems Integration Inc 860 715-5432
128 Tanner Marsh Rd Guilford CT (06437) *(G-1701)*
Doncar Inc 978 371-2442
100 Domino Dr 1 Concord MA (01742) *(G-10129)*
Doncasters Inc 860 446-4803
835 Poquonnock Rd Groton CT (06340) *(G-1670)*
Doncasters Inc (HQ) 860 449-1603
835 Poquonnock Rd Groton CT (06340) *(G-1671)*
Doncasters Inc 413 785-1801
160 Cottage St Springfield MA (01104) *(G-15467)*
Doncasters Precision Castings-, Groton *Also called Doncasters Inc* *(G-1670)*
Doncasters US Hldings 2018 Inc 860 677-1376
835 Poquonnock Rd Groton CT (06340) *(G-1672)*
Donham Crafts, Naugatuck *Also called Unimetal Surface Finishing LLC* *(G-2498)*
Donnelley Financial LLC 978 251-4000
5 Cornell Pl Wilmington MA (01887) *(G-16995)*
Donnin Publishing Inc 203 453-8866
800 Village Walk Guilford CT (06437) *(G-1702)*
Donovan Marine-Atlantic, Biddeford *Also called ME Industries* *(G-5749)*

Donut Stop 203 924-7133
368 Howe Ave Shelton CT (06484) *(G-3797)*
Donwell Company 860 649-5374
130 Sheldon Rd Manchester CT (06042) *(G-2002)*
Doolittles Print Serve Inc 603 543-0700
84 Elm St Claremont NH (03743) *(G-17848)*
Doom Forest Distillery LLC 207 462-1990
29 Chadwick Ln Pittston ME (04345) *(G-6592)*
Dooney & Bourke Inc (PA) 203 853-7515
1 Regent St Norwalk CT (06855) *(G-3142)*
Door Craft, Epping *Also called Flexi-Door Corporation* *(G-18099)*
Door Step Prep LLC 860 550-0460
51 Thomson Rd West Hartford CT (06107) *(G-5066)*
Doorbell Inc 516 375-5507
10 Holyoke Pl 277 Cambridge MA (02138) *(G-9456)*
Doorbell.me, Cambridge *Also called Doorbell Inc* *(G-9456)*
Doosan Fuel Cell America Inc (HQ) 860 727-2200
195 Governors Hwy South Windsor CT (06074) *(G-3956)*
Dorado Tankers Pool Inc 203 662-2600
20 Glover Ave Norwalk CT (06850) *(G-3143)*
Doranco Inc 508 236-0290
81 West St Attleboro MA (02703) *(G-7727)*
Dorchester Beer Holdings LLC 617 869-7092
1250 Massachusetts Ave Boston MA (02125) *(G-8508)*
Dorchester Reporter, Dorchester *Also called Boston Irish Reporter* *(G-10340)*
Dorel Juvenile Group Inc 800 544-1108
25 Forbes Blvd Unit 4 Foxboro MA (02035) *(G-10881)*
Dorie Enterprises Inc 508 761-7588
470 Colvin St Attleboro MA (02703) *(G-7728)*
Dormakaba USA Inc 781 963-0182
480 S Main St Randolph MA (02368) *(G-14676)*
Dorn Equipment Corp 781 662-9300
27 Upham St Melrose MA (02176) *(G-12981)*
Dorothy Cox Chocolates, Wareham *Also called Dorothy Coxs Candies Inc* *(G-16245)*
Dorothy Coxs Candies Inc 774 678-0654
8 Kendrick Rd Unit 4-5 Wareham MA (02571) *(G-16245)*
Dosco Sheet Metal and Mfg 508 865-9998
6 Grafton St Millbury MA (01527) *(G-13162)*
Doss Corporation 860 721-7384
102 Orchard Hill Dr Wethersfield CT (06109) *(G-5247)*
Double A Plastics Co Inc 413 267-4403
85 Bethany Rd Monson MA (01057) *(G-13206)*
Double Diamond Sportswear, Shelburne *Also called Gsg Inc* *(G-22418)*
Double Diamond Sugar House 508 479-4950
21 Edgewater Dr Dover MA (02030) *(G-10350)*
Double E Company LLC (PA) 508 588-8099
319 Manley St Ste 301 West Bridgewater MA (02379) *(G-16438)*
Doubletree 860 589-7766
42 Century Dr Bristol CT (06010) *(G-550)*
Dough Connection Corporation 877 693-6844
32a Holton St Woburn MA (01801) *(G-17169)*
Dough Masters, Auburn *Also called Management Controls LLC* *(G-5579)*
Dougherty Tool Company Inc 508 485-5566
148 Marlboro Rd Southborough MA (01772) *(G-15355)*
Douglas Bros Div, Portland *Also called Robert Mitchell Co Inc* *(G-6722)*
Douglas DK Company Incorporate 413 567-8572
299 Bliss Rd Longmeadow MA (01106) *(G-12332)*
Douglas Dynamics LLC 207 701-4200
50 Gordon Dr Rockland ME (04841) *(G-6790)*
Douglas Moss 203 854-5559
28 Knight St Ste 5 Norwalk CT (06851) *(G-3144)*
Douglas Wine & Spirits Inc 401 353-6400
1661 Mineral Spring Ave North Providence RI (02904) *(G-20757)*
Dover Microsystems Inc 781 577-0300
203 Crescent St Ste 108 Waltham MA (02453) *(G-16090)*
Dover Motion, Boxborough *Also called Invetech Inc* *(G-8964)*
Dow Chemical Company 508 229-7676
455 Forest St Marlborough MA (01752) *(G-12750)*
Dow Cover Company Incorporated 203 469-5394
373 Lexington Ave New Haven CT (06513) *(G-2683)*
Dow Div of UTC 860 683-7340
360 Bloomfield Ave Windsor CT (06095) *(G-5329)*
Dow Jones & Company Inc 413 598-4000
200 Burnett Rd Chicopee MA (01020) *(G-10020)*
Dow Jones & Company Inc 212 416-3858
84 2nd Ave Chicopee MA (01020) *(G-10021)*
Down E Emulsions Ltd Lblty Co 207 947-8624
58 Bennett St Bangor ME (04401) *(G-5641)*
Down East Enterprise Inc 207 594-9544
680 Commercial St Rockport ME (04856) *(G-6820)*
Down East Inc 207 647-5443
11 Depot St Bridgton ME (04009) *(G-5807)*
Down East Shtmtl & Certif Wldg 207 989-3443
19 Sparks Ave Brewer ME (04412) *(G-5795)*
Down Wind Dockside Svcs LLC 401 619-1990
5 Merton Rd Newport RI (02840) *(G-20663)*
Downeast Boats & Composites 207 326-9400
The New Rd Rr 175 Penobscot ME (04476) *(G-6581)*
Downeast Cider House LLC 857 301-8881
256 Marginal St Ste 2 Boston MA (02128) *(G-8509)*
Downeast Fishing Gear Inc 207 667-3131
12 Bar Harbor Rd Trenton ME (04605) *(G-7097)*
Downeast Graphics & Prtg Inc 207 667-5582
477 Washington Jct Rd Ellsworth ME (04605) *(G-6016)*
Downeast Machine & Engrg Inc 207 345-8111
26 Maple St Mechanic Falls ME (04256) *(G-6419)*
Downeast Networking Services 772 485-4304
98 Chestnut St Portland ME (04101) *(G-6653)*
Downeast Wire Trap Company 207 434-5791
141 Evergreen Point Rd Jonesboro ME (04648) *(G-6224)*
Downeast Woodworks 207 781-4800
9 Lavers Pond Rd Freeport ME (04032) *(G-6076)*
Downs Sails 978 750-8140
57 N Putnam St Danvers MA (01923) *(G-10214)*
Doyle Manchester Sailmakers, South Dartmouth *Also called Doyle Sailmakers Inc* *(G-15238)*
Doyle Sail Makers, East Greenwich *Also called Doyle Sails* *(G-20362)*
Doyle Sailmakers Inc (PA) 978 740-5950
96 Swampscott Rd Ste 8 Salem MA (01970) *(G-14907)*
Doyle Sailmakers Inc 401 884-4227
1 Division St Ste 1 # 1 East Greenwich RI (02818) *(G-20361)*
Doyle Sailmakers Inc 508 992-6322
278 Elm St South Dartmouth MA (02748) *(G-15238)*
Doyle Sails 401 884-4227
1 Division St Ste 1 # 1 East Greenwich RI (02818) *(G-20362)*
Dp Marine LLC 917 705-7435
34 Lockwood Ln Riverside CT (06878) *(G-3690)*
Dp2 LLC Head 203 655-0747
25 Old Kings Hwy N Darien CT (06820) *(G-1022)*
Dpal Technologies, Durham *Also called Bmed Holding LLC* *(G-18075)*
Dpc Quality Pump Service 203 874-6877
544 Bridgeport Ave Milford CT (06460) *(G-2276)*
Dr Bessette Naturals 413 277-6188
71 Greenwich Rd Ware MA (01082) *(G-16232)*
Dr Biron Incorporated (PA) 603 622-5222
9 Old Falls Rd Manchester NH (03103) *(G-18813)*
Dr Guilbeault Air Comprsr LLC 603 598-0891
17 Park Ave Hudson NH (03051) *(G-18386)*
Dr Lucys LLC 757 233-9495
1 Scale Ave Ste 14 Rutland VT (05701) *(G-22330)*
Dr Pepper Bottling Co Portland 207 773-4258
250 Canco Rd Portland ME (04103) *(G-6654)*
DR Templeman Company 860 747-2709
1 Northwest Dr Plainville CT (06062) *(G-3482)*
Dra-Cor Industries Inc 508 580-3770
65 N Main St Brockton MA (02301) *(G-9140)*
Dracut Kitchen & Bath 978 453-3869
18 Chuck Dr Dracut MA (01826) *(G-10359)*
Draeger Medical Systems Inc 800 437-2437
6 Tech Dr Andover MA (01810) *(G-7545)*
Dragon Products Company Inc 207 879-2328
960 Ocean Ave Portland ME (04103) *(G-6655)*
Dragon Products Company LLC (HQ) 207 774-6355
57 Atlantic Pl South Portland ME (04106) *(G-7022)*
Dragon Products Company LLC 207 594-5555
107 New County Rd Thomaston ME (04861) *(G-7083)*
Dragonlab LLC 860 436-9221
1275 Cromwell Ave Ste C6 Rocky Hill CT (06067) *(G-3708)*
Draher Machine Company 203 753-0179
30 Tosun Rd Wolcott CT (06716) *(G-5440)*
Drainage Products, Windsor Locks *Also called TWC Trans World Consulting* *(G-5402)*
Draka Cableteq, North Dighton *Also called Prysmian Cbles Systems USA LLC* *(G-13935)*
Draka Cableteq USA, North Dighton *Also called Prysmian Cbles Systems USA LLC* *(G-13936)*
Draka Fibre Technology 508 822-0246
761 Warner Blvd Taunton MA (02780) *(G-15745)*
Dramatic Dffrence Publications 207 778-9696
139 Adams Cir Farmington ME (04938) *(G-6044)*
Drape It Inc 781 209-1912
131 Lexington St Waltham MA (02452) *(G-16091)*
Draper Knitting Company Inc 781 828-0029
28 Draper Ln Ste 1 Canton MA (02021) *(G-9728)*
Draper Metal Fabrication Inc 781 961-3146
260 Centre St Unit A Holbrook MA (02343) *(G-11524)*
Draper Metals 508 584-4617
652 W Rear Center St West Bridgewater MA (02379) *(G-16439)*
Drc Precision Machining Co 781 438-4500
74 Maple St Ste B Stoneham MA (02180) *(G-15560)*
Dream Spirit Publishers 207 283-0667
17 Alpine Ln Arundel ME (04046) *(G-5531)*
Dreamer Software LLC 860 645-1240
17 Mckinley St Manchester CT (06040) *(G-2003)*
Dreamtech Water Solutions LLC 603 513-7829
159 Main St Ste 100 Nashua NH (03060) *(G-19147)*
Dresco Belting Co Inc 781 335-1350
122 East St East Weymouth MA (02189) *(G-10541)*
Drew's All Natural, Chester *Also called Drews LLC* *(G-21842)*

Drews LLC (HQ) 802 875-1184
926 Vermont Route 103 S Chester VT (05143) *(G-21842)*
Drews LLC 781 935-6045
10 Kennedy Rd Woburn MA (01801) *(G-17170)*
Dri-Air Industries Inc 860 627-5110
16 Thompson Rd East Windsor CT (06088) *(G-1282)*
Dried Materials Unlimited, Cheshire *Also called Raymond J Bykowski (G-758)*
Driggin Sandra DBA Extra Extra 617 773-6996
21 Mayor Thomas J Mcgrath Quincy MA (02169) *(G-14620)*
Drill Rite Carbide Tool Co 860 583-3200
6 Orchard St Terryville CT (06786) *(G-4476)*
Drill-Out, Wolcott *Also called Alden Corporation (G-5432)*
Drink Maple Inc 978 610-6408
144 North Rd Ste 1050 Sudbury MA (01776) *(G-15656)*
Drinkmaple 802 528-5279
75 N Elm St Saint Albans VT (05478) *(G-22367)*
Driscolls Restaurant 508 261-1574
535 S Main St Mansfield MA (02048) *(G-12629)*
Drive-O-Rama Inc 508 394-0028
Drive O Rama Inc Dennis Port MA (02639) *(G-10312)*
Driveway Medics LLC 508 761-6921
10 Vista Ct Seekonk MA (02771) *(G-15021)*
Driveways By R Stanley Inc 401 789-8600
794 Slocum Rd Saunderstown RI (02874) *(G-21201)*
Driving Impressions, East Providence *Also called Parsonskellogg LLC (G-20439)*
Drizly Inc 972 234-1033
334 Boylston St Ste 301 Boston MA (02116) *(G-8510)*
Droitcour Company 401 737-4646
28 Graystone St Warwick RI (02886) *(G-21355)*
Drop, Essex Junction *Also called Gordini USA Inc (G-21942)*
Dropwise Technologies Corp 617 945-5180
1035 Cambridge St Ste 15b Cambridge MA (02141) *(G-9457)*
Drs Development LLC 774 271-0533
10 Marion Rd Rochester MA (02770) *(G-14785)*
Drs Naval Power Systems Inc 203 366-5211
141 North Ave Bridgeport CT (06606) *(G-407)*
Drs Naval Power Systems Inc 203 798-3000
21 South St Danbury CT (06810) *(G-904)*
Drs Naval Power Systems Inc 203 798-3000
21 South St Danbury CT (06810) *(G-905)*
Drs Naval Power Systems Inc 203 366-5211
206 Island Brook Ave Bridgeport CT (06606) *(G-408)*
Drs Power Technology Inc 978 343-9719
166 Boulder Dr Ste 201 Fitchburg MA (01420) *(G-10823)*
Drt Aerospace LLC 413 789-1800
325 Silver St Agawam MA (01001) *(G-7428)*
Drt Aerospace LLC 203 781-8020
620 Research Pkwy Meriden CT (06450) *(G-2092)*
Drt Aerospace LLC 860 379-0783
200 Price Rd Winsted CT (06098) *(G-5408)*
Drt Power Systems, Winsted *Also called Drt Aerospace LLC (G-5408)*
Druck LLC (HQ) 978 437-1000
1100 Tech Park Dr Ste 300 Billerica MA (01821) *(G-8238)*
Druck, Inc., Billerica *Also called Druck LLC (G-8238)*
Dryvit Holdings Inc (HQ) 401 822-4100
1 Energy Way Providence RI (02903) *(G-20998)*
Dryvit Systems Inc (HQ) 401 822-4100
1 Energy Way West Warwick RI (02893) *(G-21491)*
Ds Smith Packaging, Lowell *Also called Interstate Cont Lowell LLC (G-12383)*
DSA Printing & Publishing Inc 978 256-3900
14 Alpha Rd Chelmsford MA (01824) *(G-9893)*
Dsaencore LLC (PA) 203 740-4200
50 Pocono Rd Brookfield CT (06804) *(G-642)*
Dsk Engineering and Technology 413 289-6485
180 Elm St Ste 201 Waltham MA (02453) *(G-16092)*
DSM Coating Resins Inc 800 458-0014
730 Main St Wilmington MA (01887) *(G-16996)*
DSM Metal Fabrication Inc 207 282-6740
129 Precourt St Biddeford ME (04005) *(G-5729)*
Dso Manufacturing Company Inc 860 224-2641
390 John Downey Dr New Britain CT (06051) *(G-2528)*
Dss Circuits Inc 508 852-8061
29 Oriental St Worcester MA (01605) *(G-17367)*
Dssi, Cataumet *Also called Deep Sea Systems Intl Inc (G-9812)*
Dst Output East LLC (HQ) 816 221-1234
125 Ellington Rd South Windsor CT (06074) *(G-3957)*
Dti, Southborough *Also called Device Technologies Inc (G-15354)*
Du-Lite Corporation 860 347-2505
171 River Rd Middletown CT (06457) *(G-2184)*
Dual Control Inc 603 627-4114
8 Delta Dr Unit D Londonderry NH (03053) *(G-18692)*
Duane Smith 508 222-9541
139 Glendale Rd Attleboro MA (02703) *(G-7729)*
Dublin Steel Corporation 413 289-1218
95 2nd St Palmer MA (01069) *(G-14286)*
Duc-Pac Corporation 413 525-3302
21 Baldwin St East Longmeadow MA (01028) *(G-10474)*
Ducas Logging Inc 207 834-5506
6 Dumond Rd Wallagrass ME (04781) *(G-7138)*
Ducharme Logging, Marshfield *Also called Dennis Ducharme (G-22094)*
Ducharme Machine Shop Inc 802 476-6575
1668 Mcglynn Rd Graniteville VT (05654) *(G-21999)*
Duck Creek Technologies LLC (PA) 857 239-5709
22 Boston Wharf Rd Fl 10 Boston MA (02210) *(G-8511)*
Duck Creek Technologies LLC 980 613-8044
22 Boston Wharf Rd Fl 10 Boston MA (02210) *(G-8512)*
Duckhill River Corp 978 657-6186
520 Main St Wilmington MA (01887) *(G-16997)*
Ducktrap River of Maine LLC 207 338-6280
57 Little River Dr Belfast ME (04915) *(G-5688)*
Ductco LLC 860 243-0350
13 Britton Dr Bloomfield CT (06002) *(G-218)*
Duda and Goodwin Inc 203 263-4353
90 Washington Rd Woodbury CT (06798) *(G-5486)*
Duelmark Aerospace Corporation 802 644-2603
96 John Putnam Memorial Cambridge VT (05444) *(G-21823)*
Dufresnes Sugar House 413 268-7509
113 Goshen Rd Williamsburg MA (01096) *(G-16950)*
Duggan Associates Inc 508 879-3277
375 Worcester Rd Framingham MA (01701) *(G-10942)*
Duhamel Family Farm LLC 802 868-4954
107 Franklin Rd Highgate Center VT (05459) *(G-22019)*
Duke River Engineering Co 617 965-7255
30 Ossipee Rd Newton MA (02464) *(G-13586)*
Dulce Domum LLC 203 227-1400
40 Richards Ave Ste 4 Norwalk CT (06854) *(G-3145)*
Dumond Chemicals Inc 609 655-7700
695 West Ave Milford CT (06461) *(G-2277)*
Duncan Galvanizing Corporation 617 389-8440
69 Norman St Ste 2 Everett MA (02149) *(G-10610)*
Duncan M Gillies Co Inc 508 835-4445
66 Central St West Boylston MA (01583) *(G-16415)*
Dundee Holding Inc (HQ) 860 677-1376
36 Spring Ln Farmington CT (06032) *(G-1477)*
Dundorf Designs USA Inc 860 859-2955
426 Forsyth Rd Salem CT (06420) *(G-3738)*
Dunfey Publishing Company Inc 617 522-3267
39 Eliot St Jamaica Plain MA (02130) *(G-11943)*
Dunkin' Donuts, Auburndale *Also called Speedway LLC (G-7870)*
Dunlap Weavers, Orland *Also called Two Islands Corporation (G-6551)*
Dunn & Co Inc 978 368-8505
75 Green St Ste 1 Clinton MA (01510) *(G-10080)*
Dunn Industries Inc 603 666-4800
123 Abby Rd Manchester NH (03103) *(G-18814)*
Dunn Paper Holdings Inc 860 289-7496
2 Forbes St East Hartford CT (06108) *(G-1188)*
Dunn Paper LLC 860 466-4141
2 Forbes St East Hartford CT (06108) *(G-1189)*
Dunn Woodworks 603 363-4180
168 Friedsam Dr Chesterfield NH (03443) *(G-17828)*
Dunning Sand & Gravel Company 860 677-1616
105 Brickyard Rd Farmington CT (06032) *(G-1478)*
Dunphey Associates Supply Co, Stamford *Also called Dasco Supply LLC (G-4185)*
Duparquet Copper Cookware, East Greenwich *Also called Cuivre & Co LLC (G-20359)*
Dupliform Casting Co 508 485-9333
158 Winter St Marlborough MA (01752) *(G-12751)*
Dupont, North Billerica *Also called E I Du Pont De Nemours & Co (G-13811)*
Dupont Packaging Inc 413 552-0048
68 Winter St 4b Holyoke MA (01040) *(G-11622)*
Dupont Water Technologies, North Kingstown *Also called International Dioxcide Inc (G-20718)*
Dur A Flex Motor Sports 401 739-0202
875 W Shore Rd Warwick RI (02889) *(G-21356)*
Dur-Mate, Mystic *Also called Durant Machine Inc (G-2438)*
Dura Kote Technology Ltd 401 331-6460
2 Industrial Ln Johnston RI (02919) *(G-20509)*
Durable Technologies, Worcester *Also called Visimark Inc (G-17501)*
Duracell Company (HQ) 203 796-4000
14 Research Dr Bethel CT (06801) *(G-144)*
Duracell Company 203 796-4000
Berkshire Corporate Bldg Bethel CT (06801) *(G-145)*
Duracell Manufacturing Inc 203 796-4000
15 Research Dr Bethel CT (06801) *(G-146)*
Duracell Manufacturing LLC 203 796-4000
14 Research Dr Bethel CT (06801) *(G-147)*
Duracell US Holding LLC (HQ) 203 796-4000
14 Research Dr Bethel CT (06801) *(G-148)*
Duraflow LLC 978 851-7439
120 Lumber Ln Unit 15 Tewksbury MA (01876) *(G-15815)*
Duralectra-Chn LLC 401 597-5000
1 Shorr Ct Woonsocket RI (02895) *(G-21557)*
Duralite Incorporated 860 379-3113
15 School St Riverton CT (06065) *(G-3694)*
Durant Machine Inc (PA) 860 536-7698
664 Noank Rd Mystic CT (06355) *(G-2438)*
Durant Prfmce Coatings Inc 781 289-1400
112 Railroad Ave Revere MA (02151) *(G-14765)*

Durant Tool Company Inc 401 781-7800
200 Circuit Dr North Kingstown RI (02852) *(G-20703)*
Durantes Pasta Inc 203 387-5560
78 Fenwick St West Haven CT (06516) *(G-5118)*
Durasol Systems Inc 802 864-3009
19 Echo Pl Williston VT (05495) *(G-22663)*
Durasol Systems Inc 802 388-7309
38b Pond Ln Middlebury VT (05753) *(G-22109)*
Durastone Corporation 401 723-7100
150 Higginson Ave Lincoln RI (02865) *(G-20569)*
Durbin Machine Inc 860 342-1602
101 Airline Ave Portland CT (06480) *(G-3567)*
Durco Manufacturing Co Inc 203 575-0446
493 S Leonard St Waterbury CT (06708) *(G-4865)*
Durfee Enterprises, Coventry *Also called Masiello Enterprises Inc (G-20155)*
Durgin and Crowell Lbr Co Inc 603 763-2860
231 Fisher Corner Rd New London NH (03257) *(G-19315)*
Durham Manufacturing Company (PA) 860 349-3427
201 Main St Durham CT (06422) *(G-1090)*
Durkee-Mower Inc 781 593-8007
2 Empire St Lynn MA (01902) *(G-12503)*
Duro-Fiber Co Inc 603 881-4200
11 Park Ave Hudson NH (03051) *(G-18387)*
Duro-Last Inc 413 631-0050
84 Westover Rd Ludlow MA (01056) *(G-12463)*
Duro-Last Roofing Company, Ludlow *Also called Duro-Last Inc (G-12463)*
Durol Company 203 288-3383
2580 State St Hamden CT (06517) *(G-1744)*
Durol Cosmetic Laboratories, West Haven *Also called Durol Laboratories LLC (G-5119)*
Durol Laboratories LLC 866 611-9694
5 Knight Ln West Haven CT (06516) *(G-5119)*
Duromar Inc 781 826-2525
706 Washington St Pembroke MA (02359) *(G-14401)*
Durridge Company Inc 978 667-9556
900 Technology Park Dr # 200 Billerica MA (01821) *(G-8239)*
Durstin Machine & Mfg 860 485-1257
57 Westleigh Dr Harwinton CT (06791) *(G-1888)*
Dusa Pharmaceuticals Inc (HQ) 978 657-7500
25 Upton Dr Wilmington MA (01887) *(G-16998)*
Dusobox Co Inc 978 372-7192
233 Neck Rd Haverhill MA (01835) *(G-11426)*
Dustin W Ciampa 603 571-4325
65 Avco Rd Unit M Haverhill MA (01835) *(G-11427)*
Dutch Ophthalmic Usa Inc 603 778-6929
10 Continental Dr Bldg 1 Exeter NH (03833) *(G-18119)*
Dutch Wharf Boat Yard & Marina 203 488-9000
70 Maple St Branford CT (06405) *(G-310)*
Dutchmen Dental LLC 401 624-9177
1359 Main Rd Tiverton RI (02878) *(G-21257)*
Dutile Glines & Higgins Inc 603 622-0452
146 Londonderry Tpke # 12 Hooksett NH (03106) *(G-18348)*
Duva Distributors Inc 508 841-8182
479 Hartford Tpke Shrewsbury MA (01545) *(G-15109)*
Duvaltex (us) Inc (HQ) 207 873-3331
9 Oak St Guilford ME (04443) *(G-6157)*
Duxbury Clipper Inc 781 934-2811
11 S Station St Duxbury MA (02332) *(G-10396)*
Duxbury Composite Products 603 585-9100
57 Creamery Rd Fitzwilliam NH (03447) *(G-18149)*
Duz Manufacturing Inc 203 874-1032
87 Opal St Milford CT (06461) *(G-2278)*
DVE Manufacturing Inc 207 783-9895
550 Lisbon St Lewiston ME (04240) *(G-6284)*
Dwight R Mills Inc 207 625-3965
271 Federal Rd Porter ME (04068) *(G-6602)*
Dwyer Aluminum Mast Company 203 484-0419
2 Commerce Dr Ste 1 North Branford CT (06471) *(G-2962)*
Dyax Corp 617 349-0200
300 Shire Way Lexington MA (02421) *(G-12221)*
Dycem Corporation (HQ) 401 738-4420
33 Appian Way Smithfield RI (02917) *(G-21222)*
Dyco Industries Inc 860 289-4957
229 S Satellite Rd South Windsor CT (06074) *(G-3958)*
Dyeables Inc 207 778-9871
374 High St Farmington ME (04938) *(G-6045)*
Dyer S Docking Systems Corp 603 942-5122
404 Stage Rd West Nottingham NH (03291) *(G-19965)*
Dykeman Welding & Fabrication, Tewksbury *Also called Mark Dykeman (G-15821)*
Dykrex Wire Die Machinery Div, Worcester *Also called Sancliff Inc (G-17469)*
Dymax Corporation 860 626-7006
51 Greenwoods Rd Torrington CT (06790) *(G-4575)*
Dymax Materials Inc (HQ) 860 482-1010
51 Greenwoods Rd Torrington CT (06790) *(G-4576)*
Dymax Oligomers & Coatings, Torrington *Also called Dymax Corporation (G-4575)*
Dymax Oligomers & Coatings 860 626-7006
318 Industrial Ln Torrington CT (06790) *(G-4577)*
Dymco, Bristol *Also called Dynamic Manufacturing Company (G-551)*
Dymotek Corporation 800 788-1984
24 Scitico Rd Somers CT (06071) *(G-3916)*
Dymotek Corporation 860 875-2868
7 Main St Ellington CT (06029) *(G-1333)*
Dyna Roll Inc 603 474-2547
146 Batchelder Rd Seabrook NH (03874) *(G-19799)*
Dynamic Bldg Enrgy Sltions LLC (PA) 860 599-1872
183 Provdnc New London North Stonington CT (06359) *(G-3072)*
Dynamic Controls Hs Inc 860 654-6000
1 Hamilton Rd Windsor Locks CT (06096) *(G-5391)*
Dynamic Converting Systems 401 333-4363
623 George Washington Hwy Lincoln RI (02865) *(G-20570)*
Dynamic Flight Systems 203 449-7211
303 Stanley Rd Monroe CT (06468) *(G-2401)*
Dynamic Gunver Technologies, Manchester *Also called Paradigm Manchester Inc (G-2032)*
Dynamic Lasers LLC 866 731-9610
324 Candlewood Mtn Rd New Milford CT (06776) *(G-2797)*
Dynamic Manufacturing Company 860 589-2751
95 Valley St Ste 5 Bristol CT (06010) *(G-551)*
Dynamic Racing Transm LLC 203 315-0138
104-5 Enterprise Dr North Branford CT (06471) *(G-2963)*
Dynamic Urethanes Inc 207 657-3770
42 Yarmouth Rd Gray ME (04039) *(G-6138)*
Dynamicops Inc 781 221-2136
1 Wall St Fl 2 Burlington MA (01803) *(G-9259)*
Dynapower Company LLC (PA) 802 860-7200
85 Meadowland Dr South Burlington VT (05403) *(G-22447)*
Dynasol Industries Inc 781 821-8888
330 Pine St Canton MA (02021) *(G-9729)*
Dynasty Production 617 361-5297
36 Tileston St Boston MA (02113) *(G-8513)*
Dynatrace Inc (PA) 781 530-1000
1601 Trapelo Rd Ste 116 Waltham MA (02451) *(G-16093)*
Dynatrace Holdings LLC (HQ) 781 530-1000
1601 Trapelo Rd Ste 116 Waltham MA (02451) *(G-16094)*
Dynatrace International LLC (HQ) 781 530-1000
1601 Trapelo Rd Ste 116 Waltham MA (02451) *(G-16095)*
Dynavac, Hingham *Also called Vacuum Technology Associates (G-11513)*
Dynawash, East Berlin *Also called Edro Corporation (G-1099)*
Dynawave Cable Incorporated 978 469-9448
135 Ward Hill Ave Haverhill MA (01835) *(G-11428)*
Dynawave Incorporated 978 469-0555
135 Ward Hill Ave Ste 3 Haverhill MA (01835) *(G-11429)*
Dynex/Rivett Inc 508 881-5110
54 Nickerson Rd Ashland MA (01721) *(G-7658)*
Dynisco Instruments LLC 978 215-3401
37 Manning Rd Ste 2 Billerica MA (01821) *(G-8240)*
Dynisco Instruments LLC (HQ) 508 541-9400
38 Forge Pkwy Franklin MA (02038) *(G-11037)*
Dynisco LLC (HQ) 508 541-3195
38 Forge Pkwy Franklin MA (02038) *(G-11038)*
Dynisco Parent Inc 978 667-5301
37 Manning Rd Ste 2 Billerica MA (01821) *(G-8241)*
Dyno Nobel Inc 860 843-2000
660 Hopmeadow St Simsbury CT (06070) *(G-3900)*
Dysarts 207 947-8649
530 Coldbrook Rd Hermon ME (04401) *(G-6185)*
Dzi 413 527-4500
150 Pleasant St Ste 320 Easthampton MA (01027) *(G-10560)*
E & A Enterprises Inc 203 250-8050
10 Capital Dr A Wallingford CT (06492) *(G-4736)*
E & D Manufacturing 978 345-0183
1006 Ashburnham St Fitchburg MA (01420) *(G-10824)*
E & E Tool & Manufacturing Co 860 738-8577
100 International Way Winsted CT (06098) *(G-5409)*
E & G Graphics 802 773-3111
2 Clover St Rutland VT (05701) *(G-22331)*
E & J Andrychowski Farms 860 423-4124
257 Brick Top Rd Windham CT (06280) *(G-5311)*
E & J Gallo Winery 781 213-5050
401 Edgewater Pl Ste 195 Wakefield MA (01880) *(G-15951)*
E & J Parts Cleaning Inc 203 757-1716
1669 Thomaston Ave Waterbury CT (06704) *(G-4866)*
E & M Enterprises Inc 401 274-7405
16 Sunnyside Ave Johnston RI (02919) *(G-20510)*
E & S Gauge Company, Tolland *Also called E and S Gage Inc (G-4546)*
E A Dion Inc 800 445-1007
33 Franklin R Mckay Rd Attleboro MA (02703) *(G-7730)*
E A M, Biddeford *Also called Eami Inc (G-5730)*
E A M T Inc 401 762-1500
841 Park East Dr Woonsocket RI (02895) *(G-21558)*
E and S Gage Inc 860 872-5917
38 Gerber Dr Tolland CT (06084) *(G-4546)*
E B Asphalt & Landscaping LLC 860 639-1921
60 Terminal Way Norwich CT (06360) *(G-3279)*
E B Buffing, Bristol *Also called Etherington Brothers Inc (G-557)*
E B Frye & Son Inc 603 654-6581
12 Frye Mill Rd Wilton NH (03086) *(G-19979)*
E C I, Westfield *Also called Transcon Technologies Inc (G-16736)*
E C S, Fall River *Also called Teknikor Automtn & Contrls Inc (G-10771)*
E C S, Cumberland *Also called Envirnmntal Compliance Systems (G-20320)*

ALPHABETIC

E Crane Computing Inc.....603 226-4041
16 Centre St Ste 3 Concord NH (03301) ***(G-17898)***
E D A X International Division, Natick *Also called Philips North America LLC* ***(G-13271)***
E D Abbott Company Inc.....617 267-5550
179 Mass Ave Boston MA (02115) ***(G-8514)***
E D I, Lincoln *Also called Electrochemical Devices Inc* ***(G-20571)***
E D I, Taunton *Also called Eastern Diagnostic Imaging* ***(G-15746)***
E F D, East Providence *Also called Nordson Efd LLC* ***(G-20435)***
E F Inc.....978 630-3800
88 Suffolk Ln Gardner MA (01440) ***(G-11113)***
E F Jeld Co Inc.....978 667-1416
152 Rangeway Rd North Billerica MA (01862) ***(G-13810)***
E F Shea Neng Con Pdts I, Amesbury *Also called Shea Concrete Products Inc* ***(G-7508)***
E G & G Sealol Eagle Inc.....401 732-0333
33 Plan Way Bldg 5 Warwick RI (02886) ***(G-21357)***
E G W Bradbury Enterprises.....207 429-8141
100 Main Rd Bridgewater ME (04735) ***(G-5805)***
E Gs Gauging Incorporated.....978 663-2300
200 Research Dr Wilmington MA (01887) ***(G-16999)***
E H Benz Co Inc.....401 331-5650
73 Maplehurst Ave Providence RI (02908) ***(G-20999)***
E H Metalcraft Company Inc.....508 580-0870
396 West St West Bridgewater MA (02379) ***(G-16440)***
E H Publishing Inc (PA).....508 663-1500
111 Speen St Ste 200 Framingham MA (01701) ***(G-10943)***
E I Du Pont De Nemours & Co.....978 663-7113
331 Treble Cove Rd North Billerica MA (01862) ***(G-13811)***
E I J Inc.....802 889-3432
467 Vt Route 110 Tunbridge VT (05077) ***(G-22543)***
E I Printing Co.....207 797-4838
200 Riverside Indus Pkwy Portland ME (04103) ***(G-6656)***
E Ink Corporation.....617 499-6000
1000 Technology Park Dr Billerica MA (01821) ***(G-8242)***
E J Carrier Inc.....207 668-4457
Rr 201 Jackman ME (04945) ***(G-6216)***
E J White Fuel.....781 878-0802
89 Spring St Rockland MA (02370) ***(G-14798)***
E M Crosby Boat Works.....508 362-7100
48 Lombard Ave West Barnstable MA (02668) ***(G-16406)***
E M K Inc.....207 474-2666
89 Lambert Rd Skowhegan ME (04976) ***(G-6973)***
E M M Inc.....203 245-0306
8 Bishop Ln Madison CT (06443) ***(G-1960)***
E Magazine, Norwalk *Also called Douglas Moss* ***(G-3144)***
E O Manufacturing Company Inc.....203 932-5981
474 Frontage Rd West Haven CT (06516) ***(G-5120)***
E P M Co Inc.....860 589-3233
147 Terryville Rd Bristol CT (06010) ***(G-552)***
E P S I, Haverhill *Also called Enginered Pressure Systems Inc* ***(G-11432)***
E Paint Company.....508 540-4412
25 Research Rd East Falmouth MA (02536) ***(G-10441)***
E Print Inc.....603 594-0009
10 Rebel Rd Hudson NH (03051) ***(G-18388)***
E R Hinman & Sons Inc.....860 673-9170
77 Milford St Burlington CT (06013) ***(G-677)***
E R Hitchcock Company.....860 229-2024
191 John Downey Dr New Britain CT (06051) ***(G-2529)***
E R S Resources.....508 421-3434
95 Prescott Pl Worcester MA (01605) ***(G-17368)***
E S Bohndell & Co Inc.....207 236-3549
198 Commercial St Rockport ME (04856) ***(G-6821)***
E S D Systems, Canton *Also called Desco Industries Inc* ***(G-9726)***
E S I, Hanover *Also called Eyesaver International Inc* ***(G-11337)***
E S Ritchie & Sons Inc.....781 826-5131
243 Oak St Pembroke MA (02359) ***(G-14402)***
E S Sports Corporation.....413 534-5634
47 Jackson St Holyoke MA (01040) ***(G-11623)***
E Skip Grindle & Sons.....207 460-0334
485 North St Ellsworth ME (04605) ***(G-6017)***
E Sphere Inc.....401 270-7512
255 Promenade St Apt 162 Providence RI (02908) ***(G-21000)***
E T Duval & Son Inc.....978 537-7596
386 Main St Leominster MA (01453) ***(G-12134)***
E T I, Cheshire *Also called Electro-Tech Inc* ***(G-729)***
E V Yeuell Inc.....781 933-2984
17 Gill St Woburn MA (01801) ***(G-17171)***
E W Sykes General Contractors.....978 249-7655
5567 S Athol Rd Athol MA (01331) ***(G-7686)***
E W Winship Ltd Inc.....508 228-1908
51 Main St Nantucket MA (02554) ***(G-13223)***
E Z Telecom.....617 466-0826
227 Broadway Chelsea MA (02150) ***(G-9953)***
E&B Printing LLC.....401 353-5777
1375 Mineral Spring Ave # 5 North Providence RI (02904) ***(G-20758)***
E&D Machining Inc.....978 667-4848
19 Sterling Rd Ste 5a North Billerica MA (01862) ***(G-13812)***
E&M Logging & Land Clearing LL.....802 896-6091
338 Mill Rd Wardsboro VT (05355) ***(G-22576)***

E&S Automotive Operations LLC.....203 332-4555
425 Boston Ave Bridgeport CT (06610) ***(G-409)***
E-B Manufacturing Company Inc.....860 632-8563
825 Middle St Middletown CT (06457) ***(G-2185)***
E-I-E-I-o Incorporated.....508 324-9311
502 Bedford St Fall River MA (02720) ***(G-10684)***
E-J Electric T & D LLC.....203 626-9625
53 N Plains Industrial Rd Wallingford CT (06492) ***(G-4737)***
E-Lite Technologies Inc.....203 371-2070
2285 Reservoir Ave Trumbull CT (06611) ***(G-4623)***
E-Skylight.com, Waterboro *Also called Architectural Skylight Co Inc* ***(G-7150)***
E-Z Crete LLC.....603 313-6462
502 Winchester St Keene NH (03431) ***(G-18500)***
E-Z Crete LLC.....603 313-6462
250 Hancock Rd Harrisville NH (03450) ***(G-18301)***
E-Z Switch Manufacturing Inc.....203 874-7766
463 Naugatuck Ave Milford CT (06460) ***(G-2279)***
E-Z Tools Inc.....203 838-2102
5 Poplar St Norwalk CT (06855) ***(G-3146)***
E. C. Mitchell Co., Middleton *Also called Ewm Corp* ***(G-13088)***
E. P. Tool & Machine, Northfield *Also called Eptam Plastics Ltd* ***(G-19400)***
E.F. Cook Company, Lincoln *Also called Johnston Dandy Company* ***(G-6355)***
EA Patten Co LLC.....860 649-2851
303 Wetherell St Manchester CT (06040) ***(G-2004)***
Eab Testing Inc.....978 548-7626
27 Congress St Ste 305-18 Salem MA (01970) ***(G-14908)***
Eagle America Inc.....401 732-0333
33 Plan Way Bldg 5 Warwick RI (02886) ***(G-21358)***
Eagle Copy Center.....603 225-3713
29 Beacon Hill Rd Windham NH (03087) ***(G-20004)***
Eagle Div, Warwick *Also called John Crane Sealol Inc* ***(G-21381)***
Eagle Electric Service LLC.....860 868-9898
145 Flanders Rd Bethlehem CT (06751) ***(G-194)***
Eagle Fire Safety Inc.....978 256-3777
56 Bridge St Chelmsford MA (01824) ***(G-9894)***
Eagle Industries Inc.....207 929-3700
118 Hollis Rd Hollis Center ME (04042) ***(G-6199)***
Eagle Industries Inc.....401 596-8111
15 Gray Ln Ste 403 Ashaway RI (02804) ***(G-20033)***
Eagle Manufacturing Co Inc.....860 537-3759
13 Homonick Rd Colchester CT (06415) ***(G-801)***
Eagle Pattern & Casting Co.....401 943-7154
14 Oneida St Cranston RI (02920) ***(G-20213)***
Eagle Publications Inc.....603 543-3100
45 Crescent St Claremont NH (03743) ***(G-17849)***
Eagle Screen Co LLC.....401 722-9315
100 Dexter St Ste 1 Pawtucket RI (02860) ***(G-20835)***
Eagle Test Systems Inc.....603 624-5757
2 Commerce Dr Ste 102 Bedford NH (03110) ***(G-17639)***
Eagle Times, Claremont *Also called Eagle Publications Inc* ***(G-17849)***
Eagle Tissue LLC.....860 282-2535
70 Bidwell Rd South Windsor CT (06074) ***(G-3959)***
Eagle Tool Inc.....401 421-5105
430 Kinsley Ave Providence RI (02909) ***(G-21001)***
Eagle Tribune, The, North Andover *Also called Eagle-Tribune Publishing Co* ***(G-13699)***
Eagle Vision Inc.....508 385-2283
1017 Main St Dennis MA (02638) ***(G-10307)***
Eagle Woodworking Inc.....978 681-6194
678 Andover St Ste 1 Lawrence MA (01843) ***(G-12019)***
Eagle-Tribune Publishing Co (HQ).....978 946-2000
100 Turnpike St North Andover MA (01845) ***(G-13698)***
Eagle-Tribune Publishing Co.....978 374-0321
181 Merrimack St Haverhill MA (01830) ***(G-11430)***
Eagle-Tribune Publishing Co.....978 946-2000
100 Turnpike St North Andover MA (01845) ***(G-13699)***
Eagle-Tribune Publishing Co.....978 282-0077
36 Whittemore St Gloucester MA (01930) ***(G-11179)***
Eagle-Tribune Publishing Co.....603 437-7000
46 W Broadway Derry NH (03038) ***(G-17978)***
Eaglepicher Technologies LLC.....401 471-6580
2000 S County Trl East Greenwich RI (02818) ***(G-20363)***
Eaglepicher Yardney Division, East Greenwich *Also called Eaglepicher Technologies LLC* ***(G-20363)***
Eami Inc.....207 283-3001
19 Pomerleau St Biddeford ME (04005) ***(G-5730)***
Earl W Gerrish & Sons Inc.....207 965-2171
2 Charlottes Rd Brownville ME (04414) ***(G-5826)***
Early Advantage LLC.....203 259-6480
426 Mine Hill Rd Fairfield CT (06824) ***(G-1428)***
Early American Industries Assn.....508 439-2215
167 Bakerville Rd South Dartmouth MA (02748) ***(G-15239)***
Earlysense Inc.....781 373-3228
800 W Cummings Park # 6400 Woburn MA (01801) ***(G-17172)***
Earmark, Hamden *Also called Farmington River Holdings LLC* ***(G-1749)***
Earnix Inc.....203 557-8077
191 Post Rd W Westport CT (06880) ***(G-5189)***
Eartec Company Inc.....401 789-8700
145 Dean Knauss Dr Narragansett RI (02882) ***(G-20638)***

Earth Animal Ventures Inc 717 271-6393
49 John St Stamford CT (06902) ***(G-4190)***
Earth Engineered Systems 203 231-4614
630 Hawthorne Ave Derby CT (06418) ***(G-1070)***
Earth Sky + Water LLC 603 654-7649
28 Howard St Wilton NH (03086) ***(G-19980)***
Earths Elements Inc 508 697-2277
1070 Vernon St Bridgewater MA (02324) ***(G-9072)***
Earthworks Granite & Marble 781 356-3544
89 Pearl St Ste 4 Braintree MA (02184) ***(G-9002)***
Eas Holdings LLC (HQ) 781 449-3056
15 Crawford St Needham Heights MA (02494) ***(G-13329)***
Eased Edges, Laconia *Also called Outdoor Enhancements LLC* ***(G-18580)***
East Bay Ice Co Inc 401 434-7485
1109 S Broadway East Providence RI (02914) ***(G-20408)***
East Bay Manufacturers Inc 401 254-2960
400 Franklin St Bristol RI (02809) ***(G-20073)***
East Bay Newspapers, Bristol *Also called Phoenix-Times Publishing Co* ***(G-20098)***
East Bay Printing & Copying, Warren *Also called Saffron Group Inc* ***(G-21305)***
East Boston Times Inc 617 567-9600
40 Central Sq Boston MA (02128) ***(G-8515)***
East Branch Engrg & Mfg Inc 860 355-9661
57 S End Plz New Milford CT (06776) ***(G-2798)***
East Cast Wldg Fabrication LLC 978 465-2338
104 Parker St Newburyport MA (01950) ***(G-13484)***
East Coast Concrete Pdts LLC 603 883-3042
5 Northern Blvd Ste 15 Amherst NH (03031) ***(G-17558)***
East Coast Fabrication Inc 508 990-7918
137 Popes Is New Bedford MA (02740) ***(G-13381)***
East Coast Fabrications 508 295-1982
9 Acoaxet Ln West Wareham MA (02576) ***(G-16569)***
East Coast Filter Inc 716 649-2326
560 Washington St Ste 3 Wrentham MA (02093) ***(G-17518)***
East Coast Filter Corp 508 883-7744
61 Main St Ste 3 Blackstone MA (01504) ***(G-8311)***
East Coast Florist & Silks, Chelmsford *Also called East Coast Silks Inc* ***(G-9895)***
East Coast Induction Inc 508 587-2800
506 N Warren Ave Brockton MA (02301) ***(G-9141)***
East Coast Interiors Inc 508 995-4200
4 Ledgewood Blvd North Dartmouth MA (02747) ***(G-13919)***
East Coast Laminiating Company 401 729-0097
362 Abbott Run Valley Rd Cumberland RI (02864) ***(G-20319)***
East Coast Lightning Eqp Inc 860 379-9072
24 Lanson Dr Winsted CT (06098) ***(G-5410)***
East Coast Marble & Gran Corp 781 760-0207
142 Lynnfield St Lynn MA (01904) ***(G-12504)***
East Coast Metal Hose Inc 203 723-7459
41 Raytkwich Rd Naugatuck CT (06770) ***(G-2470)***
East Coast Metal Works Co Inc 603 642-9600
21 Route 125 Unit 2 Kingston NH (03848) ***(G-18543)***
East Coast Packaging LLC (PA) 860 675-8500
210 Main St Unit 1182 Farmington CT (06034) ***(G-1479)***
East Coast Perfection Coating, Holliston *Also called Bagge Inc* ***(G-11558)***
East Coast Plastics Inc 508 429-8080
763 Waverley St Ste 3 Framingham MA (01702) ***(G-10944)***
East Coast Precision Mfg 860 322-4624
221 Middlesex Ave Chester CT (06412) ***(G-771)***
East Coast Precision Mfg LLC 978 887-5920
63 Pond Meadow Rd Killingworth CT (06419) ***(G-1926)***
East Coast Printing Inc 781 331-5635
2 Keith Way Ste 5 Hingham MA (02043) ***(G-11498)***
East Coast Publications Inc (PA) 781 878-4540
17 Accord Park Dr Ste 207 Norwell MA (02061) ***(G-14102)***
East Coast Roof Specialties, Winsted *Also called East Coast Lightning Eqp Inc* ***(G-5410)***
East Coast Sign and Supply Inc 203 791-8326
11 Francis J Clarke Cir Bethel CT (06801) ***(G-149)***
East Coast Sign Company 781 858-9382
125 North St Stoneham MA (02180) ***(G-15561)***
East Coast Silks Inc 978 970-5510
55 Drum Hill Rd Chelmsford MA (01824) ***(G-9895)***
East Coast Stairs Co Inc 860 528-7096
125 Bidwell Rd South Windsor CT (06074) ***(G-3960)***
East Coast Welding 603 293-8384
1979 Lake Shore Rd Gilford NH (03249) ***(G-18187)***
East Coast Woodworking Inc 207 442-0025
6 Crooker Rd Brunswick ME (04011) ***(G-5835)***
East Greenwich Spine and Sport 401 886-5907
1351 S County Trl Ste 100 East Greenwich RI (02818) ***(G-20364)***
East Hartford Lamination Co 860 633-4637
110 Commerce St Glastonbury CT (06033) ***(G-1547)***
East Hartford Operations, East Hartford *Also called ATI Ladish Machining Inc* ***(G-1175)***
East Longmeadow Business Svcs 413 525-6111
25 Lake Dr Enfield CT (06082) ***(G-1355)***
East Meets West, Boston *Also called Bakery To Go Inc* ***(G-8388)***
East Passage Boatwrights Inc 401 253-5535
257 Franklin St Unit 8 Bristol RI (02809) ***(G-20074)***
East Providence Mohawks 401 829-1411
78 Vine St East Providence RI (02914) ***(G-20409)***
East Rock Brewing Company LLC 203 530-3484
285 Nicoll St New Haven CT (06511) ***(G-2684)***
East Shore Production 207 775-5353
48 Free St Ste 302 Portland ME (04101) ***(G-6657)***
East Shore Wire Rope 203 469-5204
5 Old Bradley St East Haven CT (06512) ***(G-1247)***
East West Boston LLC 617 598-3000
12 Channel St Ste 301 Boston MA (02210) ***(G-8516)***
East Windsor Metal Fabg Inc 860 528-7107
91 Glendale Rd South Windsor CT (06074) ***(G-3961)***
Eastcoast Bio, North Berwick *Also called McWilliams Inc* ***(G-6509)***
Easter Seals Massachusetts 508 992-3128
256 Union St New Bedford MA (02740) ***(G-13382)***
Eastern Boats Inc 603 652-9213
11 Industrial Way Milton NH (03851) ***(G-19084)***
Eastern Broach Inc 860 828-4800
10 Sparks St Plainville CT (06062) ***(G-3483)***
Eastern Cabinet Shop Inc 617 361-7575
1450 Hyde Park Ave Boston MA (02136) ***(G-8517)***
Eastern Cast Hardware Co Inc 413 733-7690
77 Heywood Ave West Springfield MA (01089) ***(G-16517)***
Eastern Company (PA) 203 729-2255
112 Bridge St Naugatuck CT (06770) ***(G-2471)***
Eastern Company 860 526-0800
212 Middlesex Ave Chester CT (06412) ***(G-772)***
Eastern Company 860 669-2233
1 Heritage Park Rd Clinton CT (06413) ***(G-785)***
Eastern Connecticut 860 423-1972
42 Boston Post Rd Willimantic CT (06226) ***(G-5263)***
Eastern Copy Fax Inc 978 768-3808
42 Blackburn Ctr Gloucester MA (01930) ***(G-11180)***
Eastern Copy-Fax, Gloucester *Also called Eastern Copy Fax Inc* ***(G-11180)***
Eastern Design Inc 401 765-0558
70 New River Rd Manville RI (02838) ***(G-20607)***
Eastern Diagnostic Imaging 508 828-2970
597 Winthrop St Taunton MA (02780) ***(G-15746)***
Eastern Electric Cnstr Co 860 485-1100
75 North Rd Harwinton CT (06791) ***(G-1889)***
Eastern Etching and Mfg Co 413 594-6601
35 Lower Grape St Bldg 1 Chicopee MA (01013) ***(G-10022)***
Eastern Ice Company Inc 508 672-1800
281 Commerce Dr Fall River MA (02720) ***(G-10685)***
Eastern Inc 203 563-9535
95 Locust Ave New Canaan CT (06840) ***(G-2597)***
Eastern Index Inc 781 581-1100
154 Lynnway Unit 402 Lynn MA (01902) ***(G-12505)***
Eastern Industrial Products 781 826-9511
737 Washington St Pembroke MA (02359) ***(G-14403)***
Eastern Machine & Design Corp 781 293-6391
1062 Main St Hanson MA (02341) ***(G-11362)***
Eastern Manufacturing Company 401 231-8330
9 Humbert St North Providence RI (02911) ***(G-20759)***
Eastern Marble & Granite LLC 203 882-8221
201 Buckingham Ave Milford CT (06460) ***(G-2280)***
Eastern Mass Machined Products 978 462-9301
164 Elm St Salisbury MA (01952) ***(G-14950)***
Eastern Mddlsex Press Pblctons (PA) 781 321-8000
277 Commercial St Malden MA (02148) ***(G-12569)***
Eastern Metal Industries Inc 781 231-5220
910 Broadway Rear Saugus MA (01906) ***(G-14980)***
Eastern Metal Treating Inc 860 763-4311
28 Bacon Rd Enfield CT (06082) ***(G-1356)***
Eastern Metal Works Inc 203 878-6995
333 Woodmont Rd Milford CT (06460) ***(G-2281)***
Eastern Metals Inc 603 818-8639
4 Old Nashua Rd Londonderry NH (03053) ***(G-18693)***
Eastern Packaging Inc 978 685-7723
283 Lowell St Lawrence MA (01840) ***(G-12020)***
Eastern Plastics, Bristol *Also called Idex Health & Science LLC* ***(G-570)***
Eastern Precast Company Inc 203 775-0230
1 Commerce Dr Brookfield CT (06804) ***(G-643)***
Eastern Precision Machining Co (PA) 978 356-2372
25 Plains Rd Ipswich MA (01938) ***(G-11916)***
Eastern Resins Corp 401 769-6700
1174 River St Woonsocket RI (02895) ***(G-21559)***
Eastern Screw Company 401 943-0680
15 Amflex Dr Cranston RI (02921) ***(G-20214)***
Eastern Systems Group, Waitsfield *Also called Eastern Systems Inc* ***(G-22565)***
Eastern Systems Inc (PA) 802 496-1000
5197 Main St Unit 4 Waitsfield VT (05673) ***(G-22565)***
Eastern Time Design Inc 603 483-5876
143 Raymond Rd Candia NH (03034) ***(G-17781)***
Eastern Tool Corporation 781 395-1472
58 Swan St Medford MA (02155) ***(G-12932)***
Eastern Woods Music Publishing 508 238-3270
159 Cotuit Rd Sandwich MA (02563) ***(G-14967)***
Eastgate Systems Inc 617 924-9044
134 Main St Ste 2a Watertown MA (02472) ***(G-16280)***
Easthampton Machine & Tool Inc 413 527-8770
72 Parsons St Easthampton MA (01027) ***(G-10561)***

Easthampton Precision Mfg Inc....413 527-1650
16 Arthur St Easthampton MA (01027) *(G-10562)*
Eastman Industries (PA)....207 878-5353
70 Ingersol Dr Portland ME (04103) *(G-6658)*
Eastman Wind Instruments Inc....800 789-2216
68 Nonset Path Acton MA (01720) *(G-7351)*
Easton Brewing Company LLC....203 921-7263
53 Ridgeway Rd Easton CT (06612) *(G-1317)*
Easton Journal....508 230-7964
159 Main St Milford MA (01757) *(G-13113)*
Eastside Electric Inc....860 485-0700
178 Birge Park Rd Harwinton CT (06791) *(G-1890)*
Eastwind Communications Inc....508 862-8600
75 Perseverance Way Hyannis MA (02601) *(G-11840)*
Eastwind Diamond Abrasives, Windsor *Also called Eastwind Lapidary Inc (G-22707)*
Eastwind Lapidary Inc....802 674-5427
61 Main St Windsor VT (05089) *(G-22707)*
Eastwood Printing Inc....860 529-6673
501 Middletown Ave Wethersfield CT (06109) *(G-5248)*
Easy Access Distribution Inc....781 893-3999
141 Middlesex Tpke Ste 4 Burlington MA (01803) *(G-9260)*
Easy Graphics Inc....203 622-0001
31 Saint Roch Ave Ste 1 Greenwich CT (06830) *(G-1609)*
Easy Locate LLC....617 216-3654
32 Addison St Arlington MA (02476) *(G-7624)*
Easy Way Cleaners, Woburn *Also called Easy Way Dry Cleaners Inc (G-17173)*
Easy Way Dry Cleaners Inc....781 933-1473
227 Main St Woburn MA (01801) *(G-17173)*
Eat Drink Lucky....207 450-9060
10 Fieldstone Rd Cape Elizabeth ME (04107) *(G-5876)*
Eating Well Inc (HQ)....802 425-5700
120 Graham Way Ste 100 Shelburne VT (05482) *(G-22415)*
Eatingwell Media Group, Shelburne *Also called Eating Well Inc (G-22415)*
Eaton Aerospace LLC....203 796-6000
15 Durant Ave Bethel CT (06801) *(G-150)*
Eaton Corporation....508 520-2444
165 Grove St Ste 10 Franklin MA (02038) *(G-11039)*
Eaton Corporation....203 796-6000
15 Durant Ave Bethel CT (06801) *(G-151)*
Eaton Electric Holdings LLC....860 683-4300
1200 Kennedy Rd Windsor CT (06095) *(G-5330)*
Eaton Farm Confectioners Inc....508 865-5235
370 Main St Ste 1200 Worcester MA (01608) *(G-17369)*
Eaton Mountain Ski Area, Skowhegan *Also called E M K Inc (G-6973)*
Eaton Trap Co Inc....207 443-3617
12 Birchwood Rd Woolwich ME (04579) *(G-7289)*
Eaton Woodworking, Natick *Also called Boston Wood Art (G-13240)*
Eaton Wright Line, Worcester *Also called Wright Line LLC (G-17510)*
Eba, East Longmeadow *Also called Alvin Johnson (G-10465)*
EBA&d, Simsbury *Also called Ensign-Bickford Arospc Def Co (G-3903)*
Ebano Woodworks Inc....978 879-7206
616 Essex St Ste 1 Lawrence MA (01841) *(G-12021)*
Ebara Technologies Inc....978 465-1983
69 Parker St B Newburyport MA (01950) *(G-13485)*
Ebeam Film LLC....203 926-0100
240 Long Hill Cross Rd Shelton CT (06484) *(G-3798)*
Ebl Products Inc....860 290-3737
22 Prestige Park Cir East Hartford CT (06108) *(G-1190)*
Ebner Furnaces....603 552-3806
51 Harvey Rd Unit C Londonderry NH (03053) *(G-18694)*
Ebsco Publishing Inc (HQ)....978 356-6500
10 Estes St Ipswich MA (01938) *(G-11917)*
Ebscohost, Ipswich *Also called Ebsco Publishing Inc (G-11917)*
Ebsnet Inc....978 448-9000
274e Main St Groton MA (01450) *(G-11288)*
Ebws LLC....802 765-4180
61 Rockbottom Rd Strafford VT (05072) *(G-22526)*
EC Holdings Inc....203 846-1651
2 Muller Ave Norwalk CT (06851) *(G-3147)*
ECB Motor Company Inc....508 717-5441
1520 Alfred Rd Lyman ME (04002) *(G-6389)*
Ecc Holdings Inc (HQ)....401 331-9000
35 Livingston St Providence RI (02904) *(G-21002)*
Eccles Carleton, Easton *Also called Eccles-Lehman Inc (G-1318)*
Eccles-Lehman Inc....203 268-0605
44 Sanford Dr Easton CT (06612) *(G-1318)*
Echelon Industries Corporation....413 562-6659
53 Airport Rd Westfield MA (01085) *(G-16681)*
Echo Communications Inc....603 526-6006
59 Pleasant St New London NH (03257) *(G-19316)*
Echo Hill Orchards, Monson *Also called Colton Hollow Candle Company (G-13205)*
Echo Industries Inc....978 544-7000
61 R W Moore Ave Orange MA (01364) *(G-14215)*
ECI Screen Print Inc....860 283-9849
15 Mountain View Rd Watertown CT (06795) *(G-5008)*
Ecin Industries Inc....508 675-6920
1 Ace St Unit 2 Fall River MA (02720) *(G-10686)*
Eckel Industries Inc (PA)....978 772-0840
100 Groton Shirley Rd Ayer MA (01432) *(G-7917)*
Eckert Ziegler Radiopharma Inc (PA)....508 497-0060
63 South St Ste 110 Hopkinton MA (01748) *(G-11701)*
Eckoustic Division, Ayer *Also called Eckel Industries Inc (G-7917)*
Eclinicalworks LLC....508 836-2700
114 Turnpike Rd Westborough MA (01581) *(G-16616)*
Eclipse Mfg Inc....920 457-2311
44 Pleasant St Ware MA (01082) *(G-16233)*
Eclipse Systems Inc....203 483-0665
14 Commercial St Ub Branford CT (06405) *(G-311)*
Eco Division, Somerville *Also called Tracer Technologies Inc (G-15224)*
Eco Services LLC....603 682-0963
23 Durham Point Rd Durham NH (03824) *(G-18076)*
Eco Touch Inc....603 319-1762
22 Canal St Unit 125 Somersworth NH (03878) *(G-19836)*
Eco-Kids LLC....207 899-2752
273 Presumpscot St Ste 4 Portland ME (04103) *(G-6659)*
Eco2 Office Inc....508 478-8511
231 E Main St Milford MA (01757) *(G-13114)*
Ecochlor Inc....978 263-5478
22 Silver Hill Rd Acton MA (01720) *(G-7352)*
Ecochlor Inc....978 298-1463
14 Nason St Ste 309 Maynard MA (01754) *(G-12898)*
Ecoflik LLC....860 460-4419
1 Old Bridge Rd Old Lyme CT (06371) *(G-3322)*
Ecogenics, Trumbull *Also called Lady Anne Cosmetics Inc (G-4626)*
Ecohouse LLC....207 529-2700
45 Cora Cressy Rd Bremen ME (04551) *(G-5791)*
Ecolab Inc....781 688-2100
1 Edgewater Dr Ste 210 Norwood MA (02062) *(G-14147)*
Ecolab Inc....978 658-2423
240 Ballardvale St Ste D Wilmington MA (01887) *(G-17000)*
Ecologic Energy Solutions LLC....203 889-0505
48 Union St Ste 14 Stamford CT (06906) *(G-4191)*
Ecological Fibers Inc (PA)....978 537-0003
40 Pioneer Dr Lunenburg MA (01462) *(G-12481)*
Ecological Fibers Inc....401 725-9700
730 York Ave Pawtucket RI (02861) *(G-20836)*
Ecometics Inc....203 853-7856
19 Concord St Norwalk CT (06854) *(G-3148)*
Econocorp Inc....781 986-7500
72 Pacella Park Dr Randolph MA (02368) *(G-14677)*
Economizer USA, Attleboro *Also called ACS Auxiliaries Group Inc (G-7700)*
Economou Plumbing & Heating....978 957-6953
49 Settlers Way Dracut MA (01826) *(G-10360)*
Economy Coupon & Printing Inc....781 279-8555
11 Mason St Peabody MA (01960) *(G-14332)*
Economy Printing, Danbury *Also called Paul Dewitt (G-965)*
Economy Printing, Peabody *Also called Economy Coupon & Printing Inc (G-14332)*
Economy Printing & Copy Center (PA)....203 792-5610
128 E Liberty St Ste 4 Danbury CT (06810) *(G-906)*
Economy Printing & Copy Center....203 438-7401
971 Ethan Allen Hwy Ridgefield CT (06877) *(G-3666)*
Economy Spring, Southington *Also called Matthew Warren Inc (G-4065)*
Ecoshel Inc (PA)....207 274-3508
126 Clark Siding Rd Ashland ME (04732) *(G-5536)*
Ecosystem Consulting Svc Inc....860 742-0744
30 Mason St Coventry CT (06238) *(G-833)*
Ecovent Corp....620 983-6863
24 Cambridge St Ste 6 Charlestown MA (02129) *(G-9832)*
Ecrm Imaging Systems, North Andover *Also called Ecrm Incorporated (G-13700)*
Ecrm Incorporated (PA)....800 537-3276
25 Commerce Way Ste 1 North Andover MA (01845) *(G-13700)*
Ect2, Burlington *Also called Emerging Cpd Trtmnt Techngy (G-9266)*
Ed Branson....413 625-2933
634 Bellus Rd Ashfield MA (01330) *(G-7649)*
Ed Branson Glass, Ashfield *Also called Ed Branson (G-7649)*
Ed Sanders....603 788-3626
36 Bunker Hill St Lancaster NH (03584) *(G-18600)*
Edac Nd Inc....860 633-9474
81 National Dr Glastonbury CT (06033) *(G-1548)*
Edac Technologies LLC....860 789-2511
68 Prospect Hill Rd East Windsor CT (06088) *(G-1283)*
Edac Technologies LLC (HQ)....203 806-2090
5 Mckee Pl Cheshire CT (06410) *(G-728)*
Edac Technologies LLC....860 667-2134
275 Richard St Newington CT (06111) *(G-2860)*
Edal Industries Inc....203 467-2591
51 Commerce St East Haven CT (06512) *(G-1248)*
Edaron Inc (PA)....413 533-7159
100 Appleton St Holyoke MA (01040) *(G-11624)*
Edco Industries Inc....203 333-8982
203 Dekalb Ave Bridgeport CT (06607) *(G-410)*
Eddefy Inc....802 989-1934
7 Riverside Dr Dover NH (03820) *(G-18020)*
Eddies Wheels Inc....413 625-0033
140 State St Shelburne Falls MA (01370) *(G-15069)*
Edelman Metalworks Inc....203 744-7331
36 Butterfield Rd Newtown CT (06470) *(G-2920)*

Edesia Inc 401 272-5521
550 Romano Vineyard Way North Kingstown RI (02852) ***(G-20704)***
Edesia Enterprises LLC 401 272-5521
550 Romano Vineyard Way North Kingstown RI (02852) ***(G-20705)***
Edesia Industries LLC 401 272-5521
550 Romano Vineyard Way North Kingstown RI (02852) ***(G-20706)***
Edgar Clark & Son Inc 207 685-4568
Rr 41 Readfield ME (04355) ***(G-6776)***
Edgar Clark & Sons Pallet Inc 207 685-3888
1495 Pond Rd Mount Vernon ME (04352) ***(G-6458)***
Edgar Modeliers 401 781-3506
95 Hathaway St Ste 37 Providence RI (02907) ***(G-21003)***
Edge Velocity Corporation 603 912-5618
68 Stiles Rd Ste G Salem NH (03079) ***(G-19723)***
Edgecomb Boat Works 207 882-5038
957 Boothbay Rd Edgecomb ME (04556) ***(G-6002)***
Edgeone LLC 508 291-0960
4 Little Brook Rd West Wareham MA (02576) ***(G-16570)***
Edgeone LLC 508 291-0057
4 Little Brook Rd West Wareham MA (02576) ***(G-16571)***
Edgetech Instruments Inc 508 263-5900
399 River Rd Hudson MA (01749) ***(G-11769)***
Edgewater International LLC 860 851-9014
17 Middle River Dr Stafford Springs CT (06076) ***(G-4110)***
Edgewater Marine Inds LLC 508 992-6555
90 Hatch St Unit 1 New Bedford MA (02745) ***(G-13383)***
Edgewell Per Care Brands LLC 802 442-5551
401 Gage St Bennington VT (05201) ***(G-21668)***
Edgewell Per Care Brands LLC 802 524-2151
75 Swanton Rd Saint Albans VT (05478) ***(G-22368)***
Edgewell Per Care Brands LLC 203 882-2300
10 Leighton Rd Milford CT (06460) ***(G-2282)***
Edgewell Per Care Brands LLC (HQ) 203 944-5500
6 Research Dr Shelton CT (06484) ***(G-3799)***
Edgewell Personal Care Company 203 882-2308
10 Leighton Rd Milford CT (06460) ***(G-2283)***
Edible Green Mountains LLC 802 768-8356
2584 Richville Rd Manchester Center VT (05255) ***(G-22083)***
Edic Bi Weekly 617 918-5406
43 Hawkins St Ste 2 Boston MA (02114) ***(G-8518)***
Edison Coatings Inc 860 747-2220
3 Northwest Dr Plainville CT (06062) ***(G-3484)***
Edison Press, Sanford *Also called RH Rosenfield Co* ***(G-6889)***
Editas Medicine Inc 617 401-9000
11 Hurley St Cambridge MA (02141) ***(G-9458)***
Editorial Ofc Indtrl Lser Solt, Sturbridge *Also called Penwell* ***(G-15645)***
Editshare LLC 617 782-0479
119 Braintree St Ste 173 Allston MA (02134) ***(G-7464)***
Edmund Carr 781 817-5616
230 Evergreen Ave Braintree MA (02184) ***(G-9003)***
Edmunds Gages, Farmington *Also called Edmunds Manufacturing Company* ***(G-1480)***
Edmunds Manufacturing Company (PA) 860 677-2813
45 Spring Ln Farmington CT (06032) ***(G-1480)***
Edrive Actuators Inc 860 953-0588
385 Stamm Rd Newington CT (06111) ***(G-2861)***
Edro Corporation 860 828-0311
37 Commerce St East Berlin CT (06023) ***(G-1099)***
Edsan Chemical Company Inc 203 624-3123
150 Whittier Rd New Haven CT (06515) ***(G-2685)***
Edsanders.com, Lancaster *Also called Ed Sanders* ***(G-18600)***
Edson Corporation 508 822-0100
9 2nd St Taunton MA (02780) ***(G-15747)***
Edson Manufacturing Inc 203 879-1411
10 Venus Dr Wolcott CT (06716) ***(G-5441)***
Educational Assessment Svcs, South Burlington *Also called Clarity Laboratories Inc* ***(G-22443)***
Educational Directions Inc 401 683-3523
156 Anthony Rd Portsmouth RI (02871) ***(G-20922)***
Educational Instrument, Nashua *Also called Sempco Inc* ***(G-19259)***
Educators Publishing Service, Cambridge *Also called School Specialty Inc* ***(G-9647)***
Edward Bernard Inc 207 732-3987
Main St West Enfield ME (04493) ***(G-7170)***
Edward Elgar Publishing Inc 413 584-5551
9 Dewey Ct Northampton MA (01060) ***(G-14005)***
Edward F Briggs Disposal Inc 401 294-6391
Carrs Pond Rd East Greenwich RI (02818) ***(G-20365)***
Edward Group Inc 802 775-1029
194 Seward Rd Rutland VT (05701) ***(G-22332)***
Edward Segal Inc 860 283-5821
360 Reynolds Bridge Rd Thomaston CT (06787) ***(G-4502)***
Edward Spencer 617 426-0521
44 School St Lbby A Boston MA (02108) ***(G-8519)***
Edwards Ltd 207 439-2400
9 Ranger Dr Kittery ME (03904) ***(G-6255)***
Edwards Vacuum LLC 978 262-7565
12 Elizabeth Dr Chelmsford MA (01824) ***(G-9896)***
Edwards Vacuums Inc 978 753-3647
1 Highwood Dr Ste 101 Tewksbury MA (01876) ***(G-15816)***
Edwards Wines LLC 860 535-0202
74 Chester Maine Rd North Stonington CT (06359) ***(G-3073)***
Edwards, Jonathan Winery, North Stonington *Also called Edwards Wines LLC* ***(G-3073)***
Edwoods Firewood & Logging 401 568-6585
529 Cooper Hill Rd Mapleville RI (02839) ***(G-20613)***
Eemax Inc (HQ) 203 267-7890
400 Captain Neville Dr Waterbury CT (06705) ***(G-4867)***
EF Leach & Company 508 643-3309
8 N Main St Ste 500 Attleboro MA (02703) ***(G-7731)***
EFC, Waterbury *Also called Electronic Film Capacitors* ***(G-4869)***
Efficiency Plus 603 539-8125
49 Leavitt Rd Center Ossipee NH (03814) ***(G-17803)***
Effihealth LLC 888 435-3108
259 Main St Apt 3 Stamford CT (06901) ***(G-4192)***
Efitzgerald Publishing LLC 860 904-7250
319 Ridgewood Rd West Hartford CT (06107) ***(G-5067)***
Egan Church Supply, Millbury *Also called Country Candle Co Inc* ***(G-13160)***
Egan, Sterling, Nrm, Brookes, Pawcatuck *Also called Davis-Standard Holdings Inc* ***(G-3433)***
Eglean Inc 617 229-5863
35 Kingston St Apt 2 Boston MA (02111) ***(G-8520)***
Eglean.com, Boston *Also called Eglean Inc* ***(G-8520)***
Egoh Packaging Inc 508 460-6683
175 Maple St Marlborough MA (01752) ***(G-12752)***
Egs Electrcl Grp Nelson Heat T, East Granby *Also called Appleton Grp LLC* ***(G-1117)***
Egyptian Cotton Tshirts LLC 781 272-7922
11 Makechnie Rd Burlington MA (01803) ***(G-9261)***
Ehl Kitchens, Glastonbury *Also called East Hartford Lamination Co* ***(G-1547)***
Ei-Envrnmental Integration LLC 413 219-9547
278 Old Greenfield Rd Shelburne Falls MA (01370) ***(G-15070)***
Eichenauer Inc 603 863-1454
292 Sunapee St Newport NH (03773) ***(G-19345)***
Eidolon Corporation 781 400-0586
3 Erie Dr Natick MA (01760) ***(G-13253)***
Eigenlight Corporation 603 692-9200
13 Water St Apt B Newmarket NH (03857) ***(G-19333)***
Eikon Corporation 978 662-5200
300 Brickstone Sq Ste 201 Andover MA (01810) ***(G-7546)***
Eimskip USA Inc 207 221-5268
468 Commercial St Portland ME (04101) ***(G-6660)***
Eip Pharma Inc 617 945-9146
210 Broadway Ste 201 Cambridge MA (02139) ***(G-9459)***
Eis, Milford *Also called Engineered Inserts & Systems* ***(G-2285)***
Eis Wire & Cable Inc 413 536-0152
775 New Ludlow Rd South Hadley MA (01075) ***(G-15302)***
Eisai Inc 978 837-4616
35 Cambridgepark Dr # 200 Cambridge MA (02140) ***(G-9460)***
Ej Usa Inc 508 586-3130
1125 Pearl St Brockton MA (02301) ***(G-9142)***
Ek-Ris Cable Company Inc 860 223-4327
503 Burritt St Apt 7 New Britain CT (06053) ***(G-2530)***
Ekeys4 Cars 978 655-3135
8 Marblehead St North Andover MA (01845) ***(G-13701)***
Ekto Manufacturing Corp 207 324-4427
83 Eagle Dr Sanford ME (04073) ***(G-6874)***
El Mar Inc 860 729-7232
38 Cody St 2 West Hartford CT (06110) ***(G-5068)***
El Mundo Newspapers, Boston *Also called Caribe Cmmnctions Publications* ***(G-8459)***
El Paissa Butchershop 617 567-0493
1010 Bennington St Boston MA (02128) ***(G-8521)***
El Paso Prod Oil Gas Texas LP 860 293-1990
490 Capitol Ave Hartford CT (06106) ***(G-1819)***
El-Op US Inc 603 889-2500
220 Daniel Webster Hwy Merrimack NH (03054) ***(G-18998)***
Elan Pharma 415 885-6780
300 Technology Sq Ste 3 Cambridge MA (02139) ***(G-9461)***
Elan Publishing Company Inc 603 253-6002
72 Whittier Hwy Unit 3 Moultonborough NH (03254) ***(G-19096)***
Elanco Animal Health, Hopkinton *Also called Eli Lilly and Company* ***(G-11702)***
Elastic Cloud Gate LLC 617 500-8284
93 E Central St Unit 5 Natick MA (01760) ***(G-13254)***
Elbe-Cesco Inc 508 676-8531
649 Alden St Fall River MA (02723) ***(G-10687)***
Elbit Systems of America LLC 603 889-2500
220 Daniel Webster Hwy Merrimack NH (03054) ***(G-18999)***
Elbonais Incorporated 508 626-2318
1451 Concord St Ste 1 Framingham MA (01701) ***(G-10945)***
Elc Acquisition Corporation 203 743-4059
6 Trowbridge Dr Bethel CT (06801) ***(G-152)***
Elco Inc (PA) 207 784-3996
9 Enterprise St Lewiston ME (04240) ***(G-6285)***
Elco Precision Machining, Lewiston *Also called Elco Inc* ***(G-6285)***
Elder Printing & Supply Co Div, Williamstown *Also called McClelland Press Inc* ***(G-16958)***
Eldersafe Technologies Inc 617 852-3018
127 Poor Farm Rd Harvard MA (01451) ***(G-11375)***
Eldorado Stone 617 947-6722
36 Walnut St Rochester NH (03867) ***(G-19669)***
Eldorado Usa Inc 203 208-2282
322 E Main St Ste 2 Branford CT (06405) ***(G-312)***

Eldred Wheeler Company 781 924-5067
199 Winter St Ste 3 Hanover MA (02339) ***(G-11336)***
Eldur AG, Bangor *Also called Eldur Corporation* ***(G-5642)***
Eldur Corporation 207 942-6592
448 Griffin Rd Bangor ME (04401) ***(G-5642)***
Electra Dyne Company Inc 508 746-3270
56 Jordan Rd Plymouth MA (02360) ***(G-14553)***
Electra Vehicles Inc 617 313-7848
22 Boston Wharf Rd Fl 7 Boston MA (02210) ***(G-8522)***
Electrcal Instllations Inc Eii 603 253-4525
397 Whittier Hwy Moultonborough NH (03254) ***(G-19097)***
Electri-Cable Assemblies, Shelton *Also called Premier Mfg Group Inc* ***(G-3863)***
Electri-Temp Corporation 603 422-2509
10 Bridge St Unit 7 Pelham NH (03076) ***(G-19432)***
Electric Boat Corporation 860 433-0503
210 Mitchell St Groton CT (06340) ***(G-1673)***
Electric Boat Corporation 860 433-3000
75 Eastern Point Rd Groton CT (06340) ***(G-1674)***
Electric Boat Corporation (HQ) 860 433-3000
75 Eastern Point Rd Groton CT (06340) ***(G-1675)***
Electric Boat Corporation 401 268-2410
165 Dillabur Ave North Kingstown RI (02852) ***(G-20707)***
Electric Boat Fairwater Div, Groton *Also called Electric Boat Corporation* ***(G-1674)***
Electric Cable Compounds Inc 203 723-2590
108 Rado Dr Naugatuck CT (06770) ***(G-2472)***
Electric Enterprise Inc 203 378-7311
1410 Stratford Ave Stratford CT (06615) ***(G-4410)***
Electric Time Company Inc 508 359-4396
97 West St Medfield MA (02052) ***(G-12913)***
Electrical Safety Products LLC 781 249-5007
375 Main St Bldg 100 Woburn MA (01801) ***(G-17174)***
Electrix LLC 203 776-5577
45 Spring St New Haven CT (06519) ***(G-2686)***
Electrnic Mobility Contrls LLC 207 512-8009
26 Gabriel Dr Augusta ME (04330) ***(G-5607)***
Electrnic Shtmtal Crftsmen Inc 781 341-3260
120 Central St Stoughton MA (02072) ***(G-15586)***
Electro Mech Specialists LLC 860 887-2613
6 Commerce Park Rd Bozrah CT (06334) ***(G-280)***
Electro Optical Industries (PA) 617 401-2196
50 Milk St Fl 16 Boston MA (02109) ***(G-8523)***
Electro Standards Lab Inc 401 946-1390
36 Western Industrial Dr Cranston RI (02921) ***(G-20215)***
Electro Standards Laboratories, Cranston *Also called Electro Standards Lab Inc* ***(G-20215)***
Electro Switch Corp 781 607-3306
180 King Ave Weymouth MA (02188) ***(G-16887)***
Electro-Fix Inc 508 695-0228
300 South St Plainville MA (02762) ***(G-14518)***
Electro-Flex Heat, West Hartford *Also called Manufacturers Coml Fin LLC* ***(G-5084)***
Electro-Mechanical Tech Co 978 562-7898
34 Tower St Hudson MA (01749) ***(G-11770)***
Electro-Methods Inc (PA) 860 289-8661
330 Governors Hwy South Windsor CT (06074) ***(G-3962)***
Electro-Methods Inc 860 289-8661
525 Nutmeg Rd N South Windsor CT (06074) ***(G-3963)***
Electro-Prep Inc 508 291-2880
14 Kendrick Rd Ste 3 Wareham MA (02571) ***(G-16246)***
Electro-Tech Inc 203 271-1976
408 Sandbank Rd Cheshire CT (06410) ***(G-729)***
Electro-Term Inc 413 734-6469
50 Warehouse St Springfield MA (01118) ***(G-15468)***
Electro-Term/Hollingsworth, Springfield *Also called Electro-Term Inc* ***(G-15468)***
Electrochem Inc 781 938-5300
400 W Cummings Park # 5600 Woburn MA (01801) ***(G-17175)***
Electrochem Solutions Inc 781 575-0800
670 Paramount Dr Raynham MA (02767) ***(G-14714)***
Electrochemical Devices Inc (PA) 401 333-6112
29 Kennedy Blvd Lincoln RI (02865) ***(G-20571)***
Electrocraft Inc (HQ) 855 697-7966
2 Marin Way Ste 3 Stratham NH (03885) ***(G-19867)***
Electrocraft New Hampshire Inc (HQ) 603 742-3330
1 Progress Dr Dover NH (03820) ***(G-18021)***
Electrodes Incorporated 203 878-7400
160 Cascade Blvd Milford CT (06460) ***(G-2284)***
Electrodes Incorporated 508 757-2295
218 Franklin St Worcester MA (01604) ***(G-17370)***
Electrodyne Systems, Scarborough *Also called Gauss Corporation* ***(G-6918)***
Electrolizing Inc 401 861-5900
20 Houghton St Providence RI (02904) ***(G-21004)***
Electrolyzer Corp 978 363-5349
22 Bachelor St West Newbury MA (01985) ***(G-16490)***
Electron Solutions Inc 781 674-2440
1 Briggs Rd Lexington MA (02421) ***(G-12222)***
Electronic Assemblies Mfg Inc 978 374-6840
126 Merrimack St Methuen MA (01844) ***(G-13019)***
Electronic Assembly Service, Sanford *Also called Marja Corporation* ***(G-6882)***
Electronic Connection Corp 860 243-3356
112 Porter St Waterbury CT (06708) ***(G-4868)***
Electronic Distribution Corp 413 536-3400
698 Chicopee St Chicopee MA (01013) ***(G-10023)***
Electronic Film Capacitors 203 755-5629
41 Interstate Ln Waterbury CT (06705) ***(G-4869)***
Electronic Finishing Company, Bridgeport *Also called Park Distributories Inc* ***(G-464)***
Electronic House, Framingham *Also called E H Publishing Inc* ***(G-10943)***
Electronic Imaging Mtls Inc 603 357-1459
20 Forge St Keene NH (03431) ***(G-18501)***
Electronic Magazine, Stamford *Also called Informa Business Media Inc* ***(G-4223)***
Electronic Products Inds Inc 978 462-8101
85 Parker St Newburyport MA (01950) ***(G-13486)***
Electronic Publishing Services 508 544-1254
529 Main St Charlestown MA (02129) ***(G-9833)***
Electronic Spc Conn Inc 203 288-1707
19 Hamden Park Dr Hamden CT (06517) ***(G-1745)***
Electronic Test Energy Co, West Roxbury *Also called Etec Inc* ***(G-16495)***
Electronics Aid Inc 603 876-4161
32 Roxbury Rd Marlborough NH (03455) ***(G-18959)***
Electronics For Imaging Inc 603 279-6800
79 E Wilder Rd Ste 1 West Lebanon NH (03784) ***(G-19949)***
Electronics For Imaging Inc 603 279-4635
12 Innovatiion Way Londonderry NH (03053) ***(G-18695)***
Electropac Co Inc 603 622-3711
70 Pembroke Rd Ste 1 Concord NH (03301) ***(G-17899)***
Electroplating Co, Worcester *Also called Reliable Plating Co Inc* ***(G-17458)***
Electropolishing Systems Inc 508 830-1717
24 Aldrin Rd Plymouth MA (02360) ***(G-14554)***
Electrosonics Medical Inc 216 357-3310
2 Oliver St Ste 616 Boston MA (02109) ***(G-8524)***
Electrostat 781 885-2135
24 Petipas Ln Randolph MA (02368) ***(G-14678)***
Electrotech Inc 207 596-0556
344 Park St Rockland ME (04841) ***(G-6791)***
Electroweave Inc 508 752-8932
425 Shrewsbury St Worcester MA (01604) ***(G-17371)***
Elecyr Corporation 617 905-6800
871 Islington St Ste A100 Portsmouth NH (03801) ***(G-19558)***
Elegant Publishing Inc 401 245-9726
120 Amaral St Ste 3 Riverside RI (02915) ***(G-21167)***
Elegant Stitches Inc 413 447-9452
237 1st St Pittsfield MA (01201) ***(G-14469)***
Elektrisola Incorporated (PA) 603 796-2114
126 High St Boscawen NH (03303) ***(G-17703)***
Element 119 LLC 860 358-0119
296 Reynolds Bridge Rd Thomaston CT (06787) ***(G-4503)***
Element All Stars 207 576-6931
746 Main St Lewiston ME (04240) ***(G-6286)***
Element Brainerd LLC 617 487-8114
65 Brainerd Rd Allston MA (02134) ***(G-7465)***
Element Hanover - Lebanon 603 646-8108
25 Foothill St Lebanon NH (03766) ***(G-18621)***
Element Industries Inc 401 253-8802
48 Ballou Blvd Bristol RI (02809) ***(G-20075)***
Element LLC 508 394-3032
581 Main St West Dennis MA (02670) ***(G-16475)***
Element Marketing 802 448-4252
80 Pinebrook Rd Waitsfield VT (05673) ***(G-22566)***
Element Metal Arts 631 896-9683
215 Shady Lea Rd North Kingstown RI (02852) ***(G-20708)***
Element One LLC 203 344-1553
1 N Water St Ste 100 Norwalk CT (06854) ***(G-3149)***
Element Precision LLC 774 318-1777
10 Cabot St Southbridge MA (01550) ***(G-15381)***
Element Solutions Inc 203 575-5850
245 Freight St Waterbury CT (06702) ***(G-4870)***
Elemental Development LLC 802 318-1041
519 Sherman Hollow Rd Hinesburg VT (05461) ***(G-22023)***
Elemental Energies 207 641-5070
27 N Berwick Rd Wells ME (04090) ***(G-7162)***
Elemental Innovation Inc 603 259-4400
5 Puzzle Ln Newton NH (03858) ***(G-19365)***
Elemental Scents LLC 617 504-2559
24 Hancock St Auburndale MA (02466) ***(G-7860)***
Elements East LLC 508 528-1902
44 Main St Franklin MA (02038) ***(G-11040)***
Elements LLC 860 231-8011
945 Farmington Ave West Hartford CT (06107) ***(G-5069)***
Elenel Industries Inc (PA) 508 478-2025
500 Fortune Blvd Milford MA (01757) ***(G-13115)***
Elerts Corporation 781 803-6362
1132 Main St Ste 300 Weymouth MA (02190) ***(G-16888)***
Eli Engineering Co Inc 401 822-1494
354 Hopkins Hill Rd Coventry RI (02816) ***(G-20146)***
Eli Lilly and Company 508 435-8326
3 Maria Ln Hopkinton MA (01748) ***(G-11702)***
Eli Lilly and Company 317 209-6287
450 Kendall St Fl 3 Cambridge MA (02142) ***(G-9462)***
Elicio Therapeutics Inc 617 945-2077
1 Kendall Sq Bldg 1400w Cambridge MA (02139) ***(G-9463)***

Elie Baking Corporation..........508 584-4890
204 N Montello St Brockton MA (02301) ***(G-9143)***
Elite..........617 407-9300
129a Galen St Watertown MA (02472) ***(G-16281)***
Elite Adhesives LLC..........978 852-8269
61 Standish Rd Haverhill MA (01832) ***(G-11431)***
Elite Custom Compounding Inc..........401 921-2136
303 Kilvert St Warwick RI (02886) ***(G-21359)***
Elite Division, Ludlow *Also called James Austin Company* ***(G-12469)***
Elite Manufacturing Svcs Corp..........978 688-6150
8 Industrial Way Ste B3 Salem NH (03079) ***(G-19724)***
Elite Metal Fabricators Inc..........413 547-2588
100 State St Bldg 203 Ludlow MA (01056) ***(G-12464)***
Elite Sem Inc..........508 955-0414
266 Main St Ste 27 Medfield MA (02052) ***(G-12914)***
Elizabeth Arden Inc..........508 384-9018
1 Premium Outlet Blvd Wrentham MA (02093) ***(G-17519)***
Elizabeth Eakins, Norwalk *Also called Holland & Sherry Inc* ***(G-3169)***
Eljen Corporation..........860 610-0426
125 Mckee St East Hartford CT (06108) ***(G-1191)***
Elkay Plastics..........781 932-9800
101 Commerce Way Woburn MA (01801) ***(G-17176)***
Elkins & Co Inc..........207 633-0109
103 Industrial Park Rd Boothbay ME (04537) ***(G-5777)***
Ellab Inc..........603 417-3363
74 Northeastern Blvd Nashua NH (03062) ***(G-19148)***
Ellen McLaughlin..........207 746-3398
Rr 157 Medway ME (04460) ***(G-6424)***
Ellington Printery Inc..........860 875-3310
25 West Rd Ste B Ellington CT (06029) ***(G-1334)***
Elliott Auto Supply Co Inc..........978 772-9882
95 Fitchburg Rd Ayer MA (01432) ***(G-7918)***
Elliott Group, Providence *Also called Elliott Sales Group Inc* ***(G-21005)***
Elliott Sales Group Inc..........401 944-0002
111 Dupont Dr Providence RI (02907) ***(G-21005)***
Ellipson Data LLC..........203 227-5520
21 Bridge Sq Westport CT (06880) ***(G-5190)***
Ellis Boat Co Inc..........207 244-9221
265 Seawall Rd Southwest Harbor ME (04679) ***(G-7046)***
Ellis Manufacturing LLC..........865 518-0531
161 Woodford Ave Ste 62 Plainville CT (06062) ***(G-3485)***
Ellison Surface Tech - W LLC..........802 773-4278
112 Quality Ln Rutland VT (05701) ***(G-22333)***
Ellison Surface Tech Inc..........802 775-9300
106 Innovation Dr North Clarendon VT (05759) ***(G-22215)***
Ellsworth American Inc..........207 667-2576
30 Water St Ellsworth ME (04605) ***(G-6018)***
Ellucian..........781 672-1800
230 3rd Ave Waltham MA (02451) ***(G-16096)***
Elm City Cheese Company Inc..........203 865-5768
2240 State St Hamden CT (06517) ***(G-1746)***
Elm City Manufacturing LLC..........203 248-1969
370 Sackett Point Rd North Haven CT (06473) ***(G-3024)***
Elm City Mfg Jewelers Inc..........203 248-2195
29 Marne St Hamden CT (06514) ***(G-1747)***
Elm Industries Inc..........413 734-7762
380 Union St Ste 67 West Springfield MA (01089) ***(G-16518)***
Elm Press Incorporated..........860 583-3600
16 Tremco Dr Terryville CT (06786) ***(G-4477)***
Elm Street Vault Inc..........207 284-4855
38 Landry St Biddeford ME (04005) ***(G-5731)***
Elm-Cap Industries Inc..........860 953-1060
111 South St West Hartford CT (06110) ***(G-5070)***
Elma & Sana LLC..........617 529-4532
550 Newtown Rd Ste 800 Littleton MA (01460) ***(G-12304)***
Elmco/Mpc Tool Company LLC (PA)..........401 253-3611
3 Peter Rd Bristol RI (02809) ***(G-20076)***
Elmet Technologies LLC..........207 333-6100
1560 Lisbon St Lewiston ME (04240) ***(G-6287)***
Elmo Motion Control Inc..........603 821-9979
42 Technology Way Nashua NH (03060) ***(G-19149)***
Elms Puzzles Inc..........207 583-6262
Hobbs Hill Ln Harrison ME (04040) ***(G-6176)***
Elmwood Countertop Inc..........401 785-1677
50 Webb St Cranston RI (02920) ***(G-20216)***
Elot Inc (PA)..........203 388-1808
51 Forest Ave Apt 117 Old Greenwich CT (06870) ***(G-3308)***
Elottery, Old Greenwich *Also called Elot Inc* ***(G-3308)***
Elpakco Inc (PA)..........978 392-0400
2 Carl Thompson Rd Westford MA (01886) ***(G-16765)***
Elpakco Inc..........603 968-9950
Main St Ashland NH (03217) ***(G-17598)***
Elscott Manufacturing LLC (PA)..........207 422-6747
38 Route 1 Gouldsboro ME (04607) ***(G-6136)***
Elsevier Inc..........781 663-5200
50 Hampshire St Fl 5 Cambridge MA (02139) ***(G-9464)***
Eltec Industries Inc (PA)..........207 541-9085
171 Wardtown Rd Freeport ME (04032) ***(G-6077)***
Eltek USA Inc..........603 421-0020
250 Commercial St # 2022 Manchester NH (03101) ***(G-18815)***
Elution Technologies LLC..........802 540-0296
480 Hercules Dr Ste 1 Colchester VT (05446) ***(G-21862)***
Elvex Corporation..........203 743-2488
2 Mountain View Dr Shelton CT (06484) ***(G-3800)***
Ely Tool Inc..........413 732-2347
455 Cottage St Springfield MA (01104) ***(G-15469)***
Em &M Builders LLC..........508 497-3446
59 Oakhurst Rd Hopkinton MA (01748) ***(G-11703)***
Em Screen Systems Inc..........508 865-9995
45 River St Ste A Millbury MA (01527) ***(G-13163)***
Em-Bolt, Colchester *Also called Jen Col Innovations LLC* ***(G-21869)***
Em4 Inc (HQ)..........781 275-7501
7 Oak Park Dr Bedford MA (01730) ***(G-7972)***
Ema Services Inc..........978 251-4044
105 State Route 101a # 6 Amherst NH (03031) ***(G-17559)***
Emack & Bolio's, Brookline *Also called Gone Troppo Inc* ***(G-9201)***
Emagine..........508 692-9522
73 Stevens St 1e East Taunton MA (02718) ***(G-10512)***
Embassy Creations, Providence *Also called Pyramid Case Co Inc* ***(G-21101)***
Embedded Now Inc..........508 246-8196
13 Water St Ste 2 Holliston MA (01746) ***(G-11569)***
EMBlem&badge, Johnston *Also called Recognition Awards* ***(G-20535)***
Embr Labs Inc..........413 218-0629
24 Roland St 102 Charlestown MA (02129) ***(G-9834)***
Embraer Executive Jet Svcs LLC..........860 804-4600
41 Perimeter Rd Windsor Locks CT (06096) ***(G-5392)***
Embraer Executive Jets, Windsor Locks *Also called Embraer Executive Jet Svcs LLC* ***(G-5392)***
Embrodery By Evrything Per LLC..........603 444-0130
42 Cottage St Littleton NH (03561) ***(G-18658)***
Embroider-Ism LLC..........508 375-6461
10 Hillside Dr Centerville MA (02632) ***(G-9814)***
Embroidery Clinic LLC..........781 843-5293
53 Plain St Ste 2 Braintree MA (02184) ***(G-9004)***
Embroidery Creat Londonderry, Londonderry *Also called Martin D Marguerite* ***(G-18718)***
Embroidery Loft..........978 681-1155
60 Pine St Ste F Methuen MA (01844) ***(G-13020)***
Embroidery Place..........508 842-5311
10 Broushane Cir Shrewsbury MA (01545) ***(G-15110)***
Embroidme of Londonderry NH, Londonderry *Also called Stitches By Kayo Inc* ***(G-18739)***
EMC, Augusta *Also called Electrnic Mobility Contrls LLC* ***(G-5607)***
EMC Corporation..........508 249-5883
228 South St Hopkinton MA (01748) ***(G-11704)***
EMC Corporation..........508 382-7556
21 Coslin Dr Bldg 4 Southborough MA (01772) ***(G-15356)***
EMC Corporation..........508 346-2900
171 South St Hopkinton MA (01748) ***(G-11705)***
EMC Corporation (HQ)..........508 435-1000
176 South St Hopkinton MA (01748) ***(G-11706)***
EMC Corporation..........508 613-2022
7 Maddie Way Bellingham MA (02019) ***(G-8038)***
EMC Corporation..........617 618-3400
95 Wells Ave Ste 215 Newton MA (02459) ***(G-13587)***
EMC Corporation..........508 435-0369
117 South St Hopkinton MA (01748) ***(G-11707)***
EMC Corporation..........800 445-2588
80 South St Hopkinton MA (01748) ***(G-11708)***
EMC Corporation..........508 435-1000
50 Constitution Blvd Franklin MA (02038) ***(G-11041)***
EMC Corporation..........508 528-2546
109 Constitution Blvd # 2 Franklin MA (02038) ***(G-11042)***
EMC Corporation..........508 634-2774
5 Technology Dr Milford MA (01757) ***(G-13116)***
EMC Corporation..........866 438-3622
111 Constitution Blvd Franklin MA (02038) ***(G-11043)***
EMC Corporation..........203 418-4500
2150 Post Rd Fl 5 Fairfield CT (06824) ***(G-1429)***
EMC Corporation..........800 275-8777
55 Constitution Blvd Franklin MA (02038) ***(G-11044)***
EMC Global Holdings Company..........508 544-2852
176 South St Hopkinton MA (01748) ***(G-11709)***
EMC International Holdings Inc (HQ)..........508 435-1000
176 South St Hopkinton MA (01748) ***(G-11710)***
EMC Investment Corporation..........508 435-1000
176 South St Hopkinton MA (01748) ***(G-11711)***
EMC SERVICES, Cranston *Also called Energy MGT & Ctrl Svcs Inc* ***(G-20217)***
EMC Test Design LLC..........508 292-1833
521 California St Newton MA (02460) ***(G-13588)***
Emc2, Hopkinton *Also called EMC International Holdings Inc* ***(G-11710)***
Emc7 LLC..........203 429-4355
149 Brookview Ave Fairfield CT (06825) ***(G-1430)***
Emco Engineering Inc..........508 314-8305
118 Will Dr Canton MA (02021) ***(G-9730)***
Emco Services Inc..........508 674-5504
37 Slade St Fall River MA (02724) ***(G-10688)***
Emco/Fgs LLC..........617 389-0076
1 Rex Dr Braintree MA (02184) ***(G-9005)***
EMD Millipore Corporation (HQ)..........781 533-6000
400 Summit Dr Burlington MA (01803) ***(G-9262)***

ALPHABETIC

EMD Millipore Corporation....800 854-3417
400 Summit Dr Burlington MA (01803) ***(G-9263)***
EMD Millipore Corporation....603 532-8711
11 Prescott Rd Jaffrey NH (03452) ***(G-18462)***
EMD Millipore Corporation....978 715-4321
400 Summit Dr Burlington MA (01803) ***(G-9264)***
EMD Millipore Corporation....978 715-4321
290 Concord Rd 2 Billerica MA (01821) ***(G-8243)***
EMD Millipore Corporation....781 533-5858
300 2nd Ave Waltham MA (02451) ***(G-16097)***
EMD Millipore Corporation....781 533-5754
530 John Hancock Rd Taunton MA (02780) ***(G-15748)***
EMD Millipore Corporation....781 533-6000
75 Wiggins Ave Bedford MA (01730) ***(G-7973)***
EMD Millipore Corporation....781 533-6000
80 Ashby Rd Bedford MA (01730) ***(G-7974)***
EMD Millipore Corporation....978 762-5100
17 Cherry Hill Dr Danvers MA (01923) ***(G-10215)***
EMD Pharmaceuticals, Burlington *Also called EMD Serono Inc* ***(G-9265)***
EMD Pharmaceuticals, Rockland *Also called EMD Serono Inc* ***(G-14799)***
EMD Serono Inc....781 982-9000
290 Concord Rd Billerica MA (01821) ***(G-8244)***
EMD Serono Inc....978 715-1804
400 Summit Dr Fl 4 Burlington MA (01803) ***(G-9265)***
EMD Serono Inc (HQ)....781 982-9000
1 Technology Pl Rockland MA (02370) ***(G-14799)***
EMD Serono Inc....781 261-7500
4 Batterymarch Park # 200 Quincy MA (02169) ***(G-14621)***
EMD Serono Biotech Center Inc....978 294-1100
45a Middlesex Tpke Billerica MA (01821) ***(G-8245)***
EMD Serono Biotech Center Inc (HQ)....800 283-8088
1 Technology Pl Rockland MA (02370) ***(G-14800)***
EMD Serono Biotech Center Inc....978 294-1100
4 Batterymarch Park Ste 2 Quincy MA (02169) ***(G-14622)***
EMD Serono Holding Inc....781 982-9000
1 Technology Pl Rockland MA (02370) ***(G-14801)***
EMD Serono Research Inst Inc (HQ)....781 982-9000
1 Technology Pl Rockland MA (02370) ***(G-14802)***
Emergent Biodefense Ops....718 302-3000
50 Shawmut Rd Canton MA (02021) ***(G-9731)***
Emerging Cpd Trtmnt Techngy....617 886-7400
70 Blanchard Rd Ste 204 Burlington MA (01803) ***(G-9266)***
Emerlyn Software LLC....603 447-6130
1620 E Main St 209 Center Conway NH (03813) ***(G-17795)***
Emerson Apparatus Company....207 856-0055
59 Sanford Dr Unit 12 Gorham ME (04038) ***(G-6111)***
Emerson Automation Solutions....508 594-4356
55 Cabot Blvd Mansfield MA (02048) ***(G-12630)***
Emerson Automation Solutions....508 594-4410
55 Cabot Blvd Mansfield MA (02048) ***(G-12631)***
Emerson Electric Co....774 266-4136
9 Oxford Rd Mansfield MA (02048) ***(G-12632)***
Emerson Process Management....978 689-2800
12 Ballard Way Lawrence MA (01843) ***(G-12022)***
Emerson Rmote Automtn Solution, Watertown *Also called Bristol Inc* ***(G-5001)***
Emery Floor Inc....802 635-7652
2938 Plot Rd Johnson VT (05656) ***(G-22049)***
Emga Foods LLC....978 532-0000
26 Walnut St Peabody MA (01960) ***(G-14333)***
Emhart Glass Inc (HQ)....860 298-7340
123 Great Pond Dr Windsor CT (06095) ***(G-5331)***
Emhart Glass Manufacturing Inc (HQ)....860 298-7340
123 Great Pond Dr Windsor CT (06095) ***(G-5332)***
Emhart Teknologies LLC....877 364-2781
4 Shelter Rock Rd Danbury CT (06810) ***(G-907)***
Emhart Teknologies LLC....203 790-5000
Shelter Rock Danbury CT (06810) ***(G-908)***
EMI Inc....860 669-1199
4 Heritage Park Rd Clinton CT (06413) ***(G-786)***
Emilee's Italian Ice, Hartford *Also called Poppys LLC* ***(G-1860)***
Emily Post Institute Inc....802 860-1814
444 S Union St Ste 340 Burlington VT (05401) ***(G-21781)***
Emissive Energy Corp....401 294-2030
135 Circuit Dr North Kingstown RI (02852) ***(G-20709)***
Emm Precision Inc....603 356-8892
619 E Conway Rd Center Conway NH (03813) ***(G-17796)***
Emme Controls LLC....503 793-3792
32 Valley St Fl C Bristol CT (06010) ***(G-553)***
Emme E2ms LLC....860 845-8810
32 Valley St Fl C Bristol CT (06010) ***(G-554)***
Emosyn America Inc....203 794-1100
7 Commerce Dr Danbury CT (06810) ***(G-909)***
Empco Inc (PA)....860 589-3233
147 Terryville Rd Bristol CT (06010) ***(G-555)***
Empco Prcision Swiss Screw Mch, Bristol *Also called Empco Inc* ***(G-555)***
Empire Denture Center, Bangor *Also called New England Denture Cntr Bangr* ***(G-5655)***
Empire Industries Inc....860 647-1431
180 Olcott St Manchester CT (06040) ***(G-2005)***
Empire Printing Systems LLC....860 633-3333
63 Hebron Ave Ste C Glastonbury CT (06033) ***(G-1549)***
Empire Tool LLC....203 735-7467
259 Roosevelt Dr Derby CT (06418) ***(G-1071)***
Emporium....802 773-4478
133 Strongs Ave Rutland VT (05701) ***(G-22334)***
EMR Global Inc....203 452-8166
265 Prestige Park Rd East Hartford CT (06108) ***(G-1192)***
Emri Systems LLP....617 417-9798
41 Kinnaird St Cambridge MA (02139) ***(G-9465)***
Ems Engnred Mtls Solutions LLC (HQ)....508 342-2100
39 Perry Ave Attleboro MA (02703) ***(G-7732)***
Emsc LLC....203 268-5101
2009 Summer St Ste 201 Stamford CT (06905) ***(G-4193)***
Emseal Joint Systems Ltd....508 836-0280
25 Bridle Ln Westborough MA (01581) ***(G-16617)***
Emtec Metal Products, Bridgeport *Also called Hispanic Enterprises Inc* ***(G-425)***
Enanta Pharmaceuticals Inc....617 607-0800
500 Arsenal St Watertown MA (02472) ***(G-16282)***
Enchanted World Boxes Inc....617 492-6941
445 Concord Ave Cambridge MA (02138) ***(G-9466)***
Encite LLC....781 750-8241
1 North Ave Ste E Burlington MA (01803) ***(G-9267)***
Enco, Plaistow *Also called Environmental Container Svcs* ***(G-19514)***
Enco Container Services Inc....603 382-8481
4 Wilder Dr Ste 7 Plaistow NH (03865) ***(G-19511)***
Enco Industries Inc....603 382-8481
4 Wilder Dr Ste 7 Plaistow NH (03865) ***(G-19512)***
Encon Evaporators, Hooksett *Also called PSI Water Systems Inc* ***(G-18356)***
Encore Crown & Bridge Inc....508 746-6025
37 Industrial Park Rd Plymouth MA (02360) ***(G-14555)***
Encore Dental Laboratory, Plymouth *Also called Encore Crown & Bridge Inc* ***(G-14555)***
Encore Images Inc....781 631-4568
21 Lime St Ste 12 Marblehead MA (01945) ***(G-12681)***
Encore Optics....860 282-0082
140 Commerce Way South Windsor CT (06074) ***(G-3964)***
ENDEAVOR ROBOTICS, Bedford *Also called Irobot Corporation* ***(G-7985)***
Endicott Custom Machine LLC....603 865-1323
462 Sunapee St Newport NH (03773) ***(G-19346)***
Endiprev Usa LLC....401 519-3600
10 Dorrance St Ste 700 Providence RI (02903) ***(G-21006)***
Endless Wave Inc....401 423-3400
11 Howland Ave Jamestown RI (02835) ***(G-20489)***
Endo Graphics Inc....203 778-1557
41 Kenosia Ave Ste 102 Danbury CT (06810) ***(G-910)***
Endodynamix Inc....978 740-0400
121 Loring Ave Ste 910 Salem MA (01970) ***(G-14909)***
Endogen Inc....617 225-0055
30 Commerce Way Woburn MA (01801) ***(G-17177)***
Endoto Corp....860 289-8033
43 Franklin St East Hartford CT (06108) ***(G-1193)***
Endowmentsolutions LLC....617 308-7231
8 Booth Rd Auburn MA (01501) ***(G-7833)***
Endur Id Inc....603 758-1488
8 Merrill Industrial Dr # 4 Hampton NH (03842) ***(G-18262)***
Endurance Brewing Company LLC....617 725-0256
72 Joy St Apt 18 Boston MA (02114) ***(G-8525)***
Endurnce Intl Group Hldngs Inc (PA)....781 852-3200
10 Corporate Dr Ste 300 Burlington MA (01803) ***(G-9268)***
Enduro Wheelchair Company....860 289-0374
750 Tolland St East Hartford CT (06108) ***(G-1194)***
Ene Systems of Nh Inc....603 856-0330
155 River Rd Unit 10 Bow NH (03304) ***(G-17711)***
Enefco International Inc (PA)....207 514-7218
1130 Minot Ave Auburn ME (04210) ***(G-5561)***
Ener-Tek International Inc....401 471-6580
2000 S County Trl East Greenwich RI (02818) ***(G-20366)***
Enercon (PA)....207 657-7000
25 Northbrook Dr Gray ME (04039) ***(G-6139)***
Enercon....207 657-7001
234 First Flight Dr Auburn ME (04210) ***(G-5562)***
Enercon Technologies, Gray *Also called Enercon* ***(G-6139)***
Energex Pellet Fuel Inc....603 298-7007
20 Airpark Rd West Lebanon NH (03784) ***(G-19950)***
Energizer, Shelton *Also called Edgewell Per Care Brands LLC* ***(G-3799)***
Energizer Manufacturing Inc....802 442-6301
401 Gage St Bennington VT (05201) ***(G-21669)***
Energy Beam Sciences Inc....860 653-0411
29 Kripes Rd Ste B East Granby CT (06026) ***(G-1126)***
Energy MGT & Ctrl Svcs Inc....401 946-1440
116 Budlong Rd Cranston RI (02920) ***(G-20217)***
Energy Release, Leominster *Also called Uspack Inc* ***(G-12197)***
Energy Release LLC....978 466-9700
14 Brent Dr Hudson MA (01749) ***(G-11771)***
Energy Resources Group Inc (PA)....603 335-2535
23 Commerce Pkwy Farmington NH (03835) ***(G-18141)***
Energy Saving Products and Sls....860 675-6443
713 George Washington Tpk Burlington CT (06013) ***(G-678)***
Energy Sciences Inc....978 694-9000
42 Industrial Way Ste 1 Wilmington MA (01887) ***(G-17001)***

Energy Smart Building Inc 802 453-4438
22 Varney Hill Rd Starksboro VT (05487) *(G-22515)*
Energy Tech LLC 860 345-3993
63 Church Hill Rd Haddam CT (06438) *(G-1726)*
Energy Today Inc 603 425-8933
373 S Willow St 254 Manchester NH (03103) *(G-18816)*
Energyblox Inc 203 230-3000
21 Overlook Dr Hamden CT (06514) *(G-1748)*
Energetic Baltic Ml 603 252-0804
80 Baltic St Enfield NH (03748) *(G-18097)*
Enertrac Inc 603 821-0003
100 Market St Unit 302 Portsmouth NH (03801) *(G-19559)*
Enfield Collision, Enfield *Also called Adamczyk Enterprises Inc (G-1345)*
Enfield Publishing & Dist Co 603 632-7377
234 May St Enfield NH (03748) *(G-18098)*
Enfield Technologies LLC 203 375-3100
50 Waterview Dr Ste 120 Shelton CT (06484) *(G-3801)*
Enfield Transit Mix Inc 860 763-0864
84 Broadbrook Rd Enfield CT (06082) *(G-1357)*
Enflo Corporation (PA) 860 589-0014
315 Lake Ave Bristol CT (06010) *(G-556)*
Engage2excel, Attleboro *Also called Robbins Company (G-7789)*
Engelhard Corp Scales 207 853-2501
30 Staniels Rd Eastport ME (04631) *(G-5994)*
Engement Company Inc 978 561-3008
58 Main St Ste 2 Topsfield MA (01983) *(G-15857)*
Engine Alliance LLC 860 565-2239
124 Hebron Ave Ste 200 Glastonbury CT (06033) *(G-1550)*
Engineered Assembly & Services 781 834-9085
210 King Phillips Pathe Marshfield MA (02050) *(G-12860)*
Engineered Coatings Inc 860 567-5556
272 Norfolk Rd Litchfield CT (06759) *(G-1948)*
Engineered Inserts & Systems (PA) 203 301-3334
26 Quirk Rd Milford CT (06460) *(G-2285)*
Engineered Monofilaments Corp 802 863-6823
21 Commerce St Williston VT (05495) *(G-22664)*
Engineered Polymer Industries, Cheshire *Also called Osterman & Company Inc (G-752)*
Engineered Polymers Inds Inc 203 272-2233
726 S Main St Cheshire CT (06410) *(G-730)*
Engineered Precision Products, Pembroke *Also called Richard Gilbert (G-14424)*
Engineered Printing Solutions, East Dorset *Also called Pad Print Machinery of Vermont (G-21915)*
Engineered Syntactic Systems, Attleboro *Also called Cmt Materials Inc (G-7721)*
Engineering, Andover *Also called Schneider Automation Inc (G-7602)*
Engineering Powders Division, Woonsocket *Also called Technic Inc (G-21585)*
Engineering Services & Pdts Co (PA) 860 528-1119
1395 John Fitch Blvd South Windsor CT (06074) *(G-3965)*
Engineered Pressure Systems Inc 978 469-8280
165 Ferry Rd Haverhill MA (01835) *(G-11432)*
Enginering Components Pdts LLC 860 747-6222
35 Forshaw Ave Plainville CT (06062) *(G-3486)*
Enginred Plas Sltons Group Inc 781 762-3913
76 Astor Ave Ste 101 Norwood MA (02062) *(G-14148)*
Enginred Syntactic Systems LLC 508 226-3907
107 Frank Mossberg Dr Attleboro MA (02703) *(G-7733)*
Enginuity Plm LLC (HQ) 203 218-7225
440 Wheelers Farms Rd Milford CT (06461) *(G-2286)*
Englander, North Billerica *Also called World Sleep Products Inc (G-13879)*
Enhanced Mfg Solutions LLC 203 488-5796
33 Business Park Dr Ste 4 Branford CT (06405) *(G-313)*
Enjet Aero Danvers LLC (HQ) 978 777-1980
13 Mill St Danvers MA (01923) *(G-10216)*
Enjet Aero Malden LLC 781 321-0366
60 Winter St Malden MA (02148) *(G-12570)*
Enjet Aero New Britain LLC 860 356-0330
150 John Downey Dr New Britain CT (06051) *(G-2531)*
Enlivity Corporation 617 964-5237
345 Upland Ave Newton MA (02461) *(G-13589)*
Eno Massachusetts 781 297-7331
200 Tosca Dr Stoughton MA (02072) *(G-15587)*
Enon Copy Inc (PA) 970 927-0757
409 Cabot St Ste 4 Beverly MA (01915) *(G-8128)*
Enos Engineering LLC 978 654-6522
914 Main St Acton MA (01720) *(G-7353)*
Enow Inc 401 732-7080
133 Hallene Rd B2 Warwick RI (02886) *(G-21360)*
Enpure Process Systems Inc 401 447-3976
54 Ingleside Ave Cranston RI (02905) *(G-20218)*
Ens Microwave LLC 203 794-7940
14 Commerce Dr Danbury CT (06810) *(G-911)*
Ensign Bickford Industries 203 843-2126
100 Grist Mill Ln Simsbury CT (06070) *(G-3901)*
Ensign-Bckford Rnwble Enrgies 860 843-2000
125 Powder Forest Dr Simsbury CT (06070) *(G-3902)*
Ensign-Bickford Arospc Def Co (HQ) 860 843-2289
640 Hopmeadow St Simsbury CT (06070) *(G-3903)*
Ensign-Bickford Company (HQ) 860 843-2001
125 Powder Forest Dr Simsbury CT (06070) *(G-3904)*
Ensign-Bickford Industries Inc 860 658-4411
630 Hopmeadow St Rm 20 Simsbury CT (06070) *(G-3905)*
Ensign-Bickford Industries Inc 860 843-2000
175 Powder Forest Dr Weatogue CT (06089) *(G-5042)*
Ensign-Bickford Industries Inc 781 693-1870
1601 Trapelo Rd Ste 284 Waltham MA (02451) *(G-16098)*
Ensinger Prcsion Cmponents Inc 860 928-7911
11 Danco Rd Putnam CT (06260) *(G-3611)*
Ensio Resources Inc 603 224-0221
431 River Rd Bow NH (03304) *(G-17712)*
Entasis Thrputics Holdings Inc (PA) 781 810-0120
35 Gatehouse Dr Waltham MA (02451) *(G-16099)*
Entec Polymers 508 865-2001
166 Stone School Rd Sutton MA (01590) *(G-15682)*
Entech Manufacturing LLC 603 934-1288
234 Hill Rd Franklin NH (03235) *(G-18157)*
Entegris Inc 978 436-6575
9 Crosby Dr Bedford MA (01730) *(G-7975)*
Entegris Inc 800 766-2681
7 Commerce Dr Danbury CT (06810) *(G-912)*
Entegris Inc (PA) 978 436-6500
129 Concord Rd Billerica MA (01821) *(G-8246)*
Entegris Inc 978 436-6500
129 Concord Rd Bldg 2 Billerica MA (01821) *(G-8247)*
Entegris Prof Solutions Inc (HQ) 203 794-1100
7 Commerce Dr Danbury CT (06810) *(G-913)*
Enterade USA 781 352-5450
100 Rver Ridge Dr Ste 112 Norwood MA (02062) *(G-14149)*
Enterasys Networks Inc (HQ) 603 952-5000
9 Northstern Blvd Ste 300 Salem NH (03079) *(G-19725)*
Enterplay LLC 203 458-1128
800 Village Walk Ste 307 Guilford CT (06437) *(G-1703)*
Enterprise Castings LLC 207 782-5511
40 South Ave Lewiston ME (04240) *(G-6288)*
Enterprise Foundry, Lewiston *Also called Enterprise Castings LLC (G-6288)*
Enterprise Newsmedia LLC (HQ) 585 598-0030
400 Crown Colony Dr Quincy MA (02169) *(G-14623)*
Enterprise Newsmedia LLC 781 769-5535
1091 Washington St Norwood MA (02062) *(G-14150)*
Enterprise Prtg & Pdts Corp 401 438-3838
150 Newport Ave Rumford RI (02916) *(G-21184)*
Enterprise Publications (PA) 508 548-4700
50 Depot Ave Falmouth MA (02540) *(G-10789)*
Enterprise Publications 508 457-9180
35 Technology Park Dr West Falmouth MA (02574) *(G-16478)*
Enterprise Publishing Co LLC 585 598-0030
10 Purchase St Fall River MA (02720) *(G-10689)*
Enterprise, The, Fall River *Also called Enterprise Publishing Co LLC (G-10689)*
Entrees Made Easy 203 261-5777
100 Cross Hill Rd Monroe CT (06468) *(G-2402)*
Entwistle Company (HQ) 508 481-4000
6 Bigelow St Hudson MA (01749) *(G-11772)*
Envax Products Inc 203 264-8181
349 Christian St Oxford CT (06478) *(G-3400)*
Envelopes & More Inc 860 286-7570
124 Francis Ave Newington CT (06111) *(G-2862)*
Envie Company Inc 866 700-6410
5 Cabot Pl Stoughton MA (02072) *(G-15588)*
Envirem Organics Ltd 207 948-4500
39 Cornshop Rd Unity ME (04988) *(G-7115)*
Envirnmntal Compliance Systems 401 334-0306
3294 Mendon Rd Cumberland RI (02864) *(G-20320)*
Enviro-Tote Inc 603 647-7171
15 Industrial Dr Londonderry NH (03053) *(G-18696)*
Envirocare Corporation (PA) 978 658-0123
167 Coventry Ln North Andover MA (01845) *(G-13702)*
Envirologix Inc 207 797-0300
500 Riverside Indus Pkwy Portland ME (04103) *(G-6661)*
Enviromart Industries Inc 603 378-0154
4 Wilder Dr Plaistow NH (03865) *(G-19513)*
Environics Inc 860 872-1111
69 Industrial Park Rd E Tolland CT (06084) *(G-4547)*
Environmantal Systems Cor 800 953-5167
18 Jansen Ct Hartford CT (06110) *(G-1820)*
Environmedics Div, Westford *Also called Genrad Inc (G-16768)*
Environmental Container Svcs 603 382-8481
4 Wilder Dr Ste 7 Plaistow NH (03865) *(G-19514)*
Environmental Ctrl Systems Inc 401 437-8612
830 Waterman Ave East Providence RI (02914) *(G-20410)*
Environmental Division, Beverly *Also called TK&k Services LLC (G-8192)*
Environmental Energy & Finance 978 807-0027
20 Walters Way Newry ME (04261) *(G-6490)*
Environmental Improvements (PA) 781 857-2375
545 N Quincy St Abington MA (02351) *(G-7324)*
Environmental Packg Tech Inc 603 378-0340
4 Wilder Dr Ste 7 Plaistow NH (03865) *(G-19515)*
Environmental Science Tech Inc 603 378-0809
4 Wilder Dr Ste 7 Plaistow NH (03865) *(G-19516)*
Environmental Svcs Group Inc 508 533-7683
11 Awl St Medway MA (02053) *(G-12959)*

A L P H A B E T I C

Environmental Test Pdts LLC (PA)......603 924-5010
29 Shipley Dr Hollis NH (03049) ***(G-18331)***
Environmental Test Pdts LLC......603 593-5268
45 Knight St 1 Jaffrey NH (03452) ***(G-18463)***
Envision, Cumberland *Also called Plastics Plus Inc* ***(G-20339)***
Envvisual Inc......800 982-3221
56 Roland St Boston MA (02129) ***(G-8526)***
Eo Vista LLC......978 635-8080
42 Nagog Park Ste 200 Acton MA (01720) ***(G-7354)***
Eon Designs, Norwich *Also called One and Co Inc* ***(G-3288)***
Eos Design LLC (PA)......740 392-3642
775 Main St S481 Westbrook ME (04092) ***(G-7188)***
Eos Imaging Inc......678 564-5400
185 Alewife Brook Pkwy # 205 Cambridge MA (02138) ***(G-9467)***
Eos Photonics Inc......617 945-9137
30 Spinelli Pl Ste A Cambridge MA (02138) ***(G-9468)***
Eoutreach Solutions LLC......603 410-5000
835 Hanover St Ste 204 Manchester NH (03104) ***(G-18817)***
Eows Midland Inc......203 358-5705
1 Landmark Sq Fl 11 Stamford CT (06901) ***(G-4194)***
Epaint Company, East Falmouth *Also called E Paint Company* ***(G-10441)***
Epath Learning Inc......860 444-7900
300 State St Ste 400 New London CT (06320) ***(G-2771)***
Epec LLC (PA)......508 995-5171
176 Samuel Barnet Blvd New Bedford MA (02745) ***(G-13384)***
Epec Engineered Technologies, New Bedford *Also called Epec LLC* ***(G-13384)***
Ephesian Arms Inc......508 674-7030
112 Tripp St Fall River MA (02724) ***(G-10690)***
Epi, Manchester *Also called Erwin Precision Inc* ***(G-18819)***
Epi II Inc......978 462-1514
30 Green St Newburyport MA (01950) ***(G-13487)***
Epic By Nextec, Greenwich *Also called Nextec Applications Inc* ***(G-1634)***
Epic Enterprises Inc......978 772-2340
11 Copeland Dr Ayer MA (01432) ***(G-7919)***
Epic Technologies Inc......781 932-7870
500 W Cummings Park # 6950 Woburn MA (01801) ***(G-17178)***
Epicenter......413 568-1360
1 Arch Rd Westfield MA (01085) ***(G-16682)***
Epicurean Feast Medtron O......203 492-5000
195 Mcdermott Rd North Haven CT (06473) ***(G-3025)***
Epidemic Solutions Inc......504 722-3818
7 Youngs Rd Westwood MA (02090) ***(G-16865)***
Epifanes North America Inc......207 354-0804
70 Water St Thomaston ME (04861) ***(G-7084)***
Epirus Biopharmaceuticals Inc (PA)......617 600-3497
124 Washington St Ste 101 Foxboro MA (02035) ***(G-10882)***
Episerver Inc (HQ)......603 594-0249
542 Amherst St Nashua NH (03063) ***(G-19150)***
Epivax Inc......401 272-2123
188 Valley St Ste 424 Providence RI (02909) ***(G-21007)***
Epizyme Inc......617 229-5872
400 Technology Sq Ste 4 Cambridge MA (02139) ***(G-9469)***
Epo-Tek, Billerica *Also called Epoxy Technology Inc* ***(G-8248)***
Epoch Times Boston-Chinese......617 968-8019
32 Oxford St Cambridge MA (02138) ***(G-9470)***
Epoxalot Jewelry......508 699-0767
38 Peck St North Attleboro MA (02760) ***(G-13755)***
Epoxies Inc......401 946-5564
21 Starline Way Cranston RI (02921) ***(G-20219)***
Epoxies, Etc, Cranston *Also called Fri Resins Holding Company* ***(G-20228)***
Epoxies, Etc, Cranston *Also called Epoxies Inc* ***(G-20219)***
Epoxy Technology Inc (PA)......978 667-3805
14 Fortune Dr Billerica MA (01821) ***(G-8248)***
Epoxyset, Woonsocket *Also called Epoxytech Inc* ***(G-21560)***
Epoxytech Inc......401 726-4500
718 Park East Dr Woonsocket RI (02895) ***(G-21560)***
Eppendorf Inc (HQ)......732 287-1200
175 Freshwater Blvd Enfield CT (06082) ***(G-1358)***
Eppendorf Holding Inc (HQ)......860 253-3417
175 Freshwater Blvd Enfield CT (06082) ***(G-1359)***
Eppendorf Manufacturing Corp......860 253-3400
175 Freshwater Blvd Enfield CT (06082) ***(G-1360)***
EPPING VFD, Columbia Falls *Also called Epping Volunteer Fire District* ***(G-5920)***
Epping Volunteer Fire District......207 483-2036
392 Us Rte 1 Columbia Falls ME (04623) ***(G-5920)***
Eppley Laboratory Inc......401 847-1020
12 Sheffield Ave Newport RI (02840) ***(G-20664)***
Epropelled Inc (PA)......978 703-1350
116 John St Ste 205 Lowell MA (01852) ***(G-12369)***
Eps Polymer Distribution Inc......508 925-5932
165 Memorial Dr Ste D Shrewsbury MA (01545) ***(G-15111)***
Epsg, Norwood *Also called Enginred Plas Sltons Group Inc* ***(G-14148)***
Eptam Plastics Ltd (PA)......603 286-8009
2 Riverside Business Park Northfield NH (03276) ***(G-19400)***
Epv Plastics Corporation......508 987-2595
2 Hawksley Rd Unit A Oxford MA (01540) ***(G-14259)***
Equinature LLC......774 217-8057
1961 Quaker St Northbridge MA (01534) ***(G-14055)***
Equinature Products, Northbridge *Also called Equinature LLC* ***(G-14055)***
Equinox Publishing......802 497-0276
987 Bay Rd Shelburne VT (05482) ***(G-22416)***
Equinox Software Systems Inc......603 399-9970
90 Overman Rd Westmoreland NH (03467) ***(G-19971)***
Equipois LLC......603 668-1900
124 Joliette St Manchester NH (03102) ***(G-18818)***
Equitrac Corporation......781 565-5000
1 Wayside Rd Burlington MA (01803) ***(G-9269)***
ER Enterprises LLC......617 296-9140
51 Winchester St Ste 203 Newton MA (02461) ***(G-13590)***
ER Lewin Inc......508 384-0363
25 Cushing Dr Wrentham MA (02093) ***(G-17520)***
ERA Replica Automobiles, New Britain *Also called International Automobile Entps* ***(G-2543)***
ERA Wire Inc......203 933-0480
19 Locust St West Haven CT (06516) ***(G-5121)***
Era7 Bioinformatics Inc......617 576-2005
Cic 14th Flr 1 Broadway Cambridge MA (02142) ***(G-9471)***
Eratech Inc......413 628-3219
225 Smith Rd Ashfield MA (01330) ***(G-7650)***
Erecruit Holdings LLC......617 535-3720
100 Summer St Ste 1700 Boston MA (02110) ***(G-8527)***
Erevnos Corporation......619 675-9536
142 Keystone St West Roxbury MA (02132) ***(G-16494)***
Ergonomic Products Inc......508 636-2263
198 Airport Rd Fall River MA (02720) ***(G-10691)***
Ergosuture Inc......339 234-6289
196 Jason St Arlington MA (02476) ***(G-7625)***
Eric Carle LLC......413 586-2046
84 North St Northampton MA (01060) ***(G-14006)***
Eric Carle Studio, Northampton *Also called Eric Carle LLC* ***(G-14006)***
Eric Dow Boatbuilder......207 359-2277
71 Reach Rd Brooklin ME (04616) ***(G-5820)***
Eric Goetz Custom Sailboats......401 253-2670
15 Broadcommon Rd Bristol RI (02809) ***(G-20077)***
Eric Lawhite Co......802 763-7670
2907 Dairy Hill Rd South Royalton VT (05068) ***(G-22491)***
Erich Husemoller Import & Expo......413 585-9855
116 Pleasant St Ste 229 Easthampton MA (01027) ***(G-10563)***
Erie Scientific Company, Portsmouth *Also called Erie Scientific LLC* ***(G-19560)***
Erie Scientific LLC (HQ)......603 430-6859
20 Post Rd Portsmouth NH (03801) ***(G-19560)***
Erimar System Integration......603 483-4000
39 Hemlock Dr Candia NH (03034) ***(G-17782)***
Erin Murphy......928 525-2056
824 Roosevelt Trl Windham ME (04062) ***(G-7232)***
Ermel Precision Machining Inc......603 673-7336
24 Route 13 Brookline NH (03033) ***(G-17770)***
Ernest Johnson......508 259-6727
146 Phelps St Marlborough MA (01752) ***(G-12753)***
Ernest Johnson Co, Marlborough *Also called Ernest Johnson* ***(G-12753)***
Ernest R Palmer Lumber Co Inc......207 876-2725
30 N Dexter Rd Sangerville ME (04479) ***(G-6899)***
Erolls Inc......978 544-0100
158 Gov Dukakis Dr Orange MA (01364) ***(G-14216)***
Ersa Inc......401 348-4000
83 Tom Harvey Rd Westerly RI (02891) ***(G-21524)***
Erving Industries Inc (PA)......413 422-2700
97 E Main St Erving MA (01344) ***(G-10589)***
Erving Paper Mills, Erving *Also called Erving Industries Inc* ***(G-10589)***
Erving Paper Mills Inc......413 422-2700
97 E Main St Erving MA (01344) ***(G-10590)***
Erwin Precision Inc......603 623-2333
150 Dow St Ste 7 Manchester NH (03101) ***(G-18819)***
Erytech Pharma Inc......360 320-3325
1 Main St Ste 300 Cambridge MA (02142) ***(G-9472)***
ES Metal Fabrications Inc......860 585-6067
11 Allread Dr Terryville CT (06786) ***(G-4478)***
Es Products, Bristol *Also called Altenloh Brinck & Co US Inc* ***(G-20061)***
Escalon Digital Solutions Inc......610 688-6830
91 Montvale Ave Ste 320 Stoneham MA (02180) ***(G-15562)***
Eschdale Lawn & Grdn Pdts LLC......207 757-7268
881 Smyrna Center Rd Smyrna Mills ME (04780) ***(G-6991)***
Esco Technologies Inc......508 429-4441
75 October Hill Rd Holliston MA (01746) ***(G-11570)***
Esco Tool, Holliston *Also called Esco Technologies Inc* ***(G-11570)***
Escountertops LLC......413 732-8128
3 Century Way West Springfield MA (01089) ***(G-16519)***
Esi, Wilmington *Also called Energy Sciences Inc* ***(G-17001)***
Eskill Corporation......978 649-8010
7 Technology Dr Ste 101 North Chelmsford MA (01863) ***(G-13893)***
Esmail Riyaz......978 689-3837
3 Cloverfield Dr Andover MA (01810) ***(G-7547)***
Esmond Manufacturing Company......401 942-9103
169 N View Ave Cranston RI (02920) ***(G-20220)***
ESP Solutions Services LLC......508 285-0017
580 Myles Standish Blvd # 2 Taunton MA (02780) ***(G-15749)***
Esposito Jewelry Inc......401 943-1900
225 Dupont Dr Ste 1 Providence RI (02907) ***(G-21008)***

Espositos Wldg & Fabrication...207 667-2442
159 Blue Hill Rd Surry ME (04684) ***(G-7076)***
Essential Life Solutions Ltd...781 341-7240
308 Tosca Dr Stoughton MA (02072) ***(G-15589)***
Essential Trading Systems Corp...860 295-8100
9 Austin Dr Ste 3 Marlborough CT (06447) ***(G-2064)***
Essentra Porous Technologies, Chicopee *Also called Porex Cleanroom Products Inc* ***(G-10052)***
Essex Bay Engineering Inc...978 412-9600
19 Mitchell Rd Ipswich MA (01938) ***(G-11918)***
Essex Column Corp...978 352-7670
95 Tenney St Ste 1 Georgetown MA (01833) ***(G-11141)***
Essex Concrete Products Inc...860 767-1768
141 Westbrook Rd Essex CT (06426) ***(G-1396)***
Essex County Brewing Co LLC...978 587-2254
58 Pulaski St Bldg A Peabody MA (01960) ***(G-14334)***
Essex Engineering Inc...781 595-2114
20 Day St Lynn MA (01905) ***(G-12506)***
Essex Engineering & Mfg Co, Lynn *Also called Essex Engineering Inc* ***(G-12506)***
Essex Manufacturing Co...802 864-4584
301 Avenue D Ste 15 Williston VT (05495) ***(G-22665)***
Essex Printing, Methuen *Also called Essex Ruling & Printing Co* ***(G-13021)***
Essex Ruling & Printing Co...978 682-2457
154 Haverhill St Ste 2 Methuen MA (01844) ***(G-13021)***
Essex Wood Products Inc...860 537-3451
75 Mill St Colchester CT (06415) ***(G-802)***
Essilor Industries Corp...787 848-4130
183 W Main St Dudley MA (01571) ***(G-10374)***
Essity...413 289-1221
1st St Palmer MA (01069) ***(G-14287)***
Est, Inc Government Services, Plaistow *Also called Environmental Science Tech Inc* ***(G-19516)***
Estate Agency Inc (PA)...401 942-0700
1001 Reservoir Ave Cranston RI (02910) ***(G-20221)***
Estate Agency Inc...401 946-5380
25 Western Industrial Dr Cranston RI (02921) ***(G-20222)***
Esteem Manufacturing Corp...860 282-9964
175 S Satellite Rd South Windsor CT (06074) ***(G-3966)***
Eta Devices Inc...617 577-8300
245 First St Cambridge MA (02142) ***(G-9473)***
Etawiz LLC...774 823-5156
1 Maid Marion St Oxford MA (01540) ***(G-14260)***
Etc, Marlborough *Also called Essential Trading Systems Corp* ***(G-2064)***
Etc Components Usa Inc...508 353-7075
346 Franklin St Worcester MA (01604) ***(G-17372)***
Etched Image LLC...401 225-6095
1800 Mineral Spring Ave # 101 North Providence RI (02904) ***(G-20760)***
Etco Incorporated (PA)...401 467-2400
25 Bellows St Warwick RI (02888) ***(G-21361)***
Etec Inc...617 477-4308
25 Worley St West Roxbury MA (02132) ***(G-16495)***
Etex Corporation...617 577-7270
55 Messina Dr Braintree MA (02184) ***(G-9006)***
Ethan Allen Interiors Inc (PA)...203 743-8000
25 Lake Avenue Ext Danbury CT (06811) ***(G-914)***
Etherington Brothers Inc...860 585-5624
33 Stafford Ave Ste 2 Bristol CT (06010) ***(G-557)***
Ethicon Endo - Surgery, Southington *Also called Ethicon Inc* ***(G-4048)***
Ethicon Inc...860 621-9111
201 W Queen St Southington CT (06489) ***(G-4048)***
Ethnic Publishers Inc...617 227-8929
5 Prince St Boston MA (02113) ***(G-8528)***
Ethosenergy Component Repr LLC...203 949-8144
34 Capital Dr Wallingford CT (06492) ***(G-4738)***
Ethosenergy Tc Inc...413 593-0500
1310 Sheridan St Chicopee MA (01022) ***(G-10024)***
Ethosenergy Tc Inc (HQ)...802 257-2721
2140 Westover Rd Chicopee MA (01022) ***(G-10025)***
Ethosenergy Tc Inc...978 353-3089
9 Leominster Connector # 301 Leominster MA (01453) ***(G-12135)***
ETM Manufacturing, Littleton *Also called Sajawi Corporation* ***(G-12323)***
Eugene F Delfino Company Inc...978 221-6496
72 Amble Rd Chelmsford MA (01824) ***(G-9897)***
Euphonon Co...603 353-4882
69 Archertown Rd Orford NH (03777) ***(G-19420)***
Eureka Blank Book Co, Holyoke *Also called Eureka Lab Book Inc* ***(G-11625)***
Eureka Lab Book Inc...413 534-5671
110 Winter St Holyoke MA (01040) ***(G-11625)***
Euro Precision Inc...413 229-0004
125 Sheffield Business Pa Ashley Falls MA (01222) ***(G-7673)***
Euro-Pro Holdco LLC...617 243-0235
89 A St 100 Needham Heights MA (02494) ***(G-13330)***
Euroduna Americas Inc...508 888-2710
81 Sanderson Dr Plymouth MA (02360) ***(G-14556)***
Europa Sports Products Inc...860 688-1110
755 Rainbow Rd Windsor CT (06095) ***(G-5333)***
European Cabinet Design Inc...781 769-7100
2 Sumner St Norwood MA (02062) ***(G-14151)***
European Cubicles LLC...617 681-6700
38 3rd Ave Ste 100w Boston MA (02129) ***(G-8529)***
European Custom Casework Inc...401 356-0400
473 Saint Paul St North Smithfield RI (02896) ***(G-20785)***
Eurosled, Walpole *Also called 3 Play Inc* ***(G-15986)***
Eurosocks North America Inc...401 739-6500
300 Centerville Rd # 450 Warwick RI (02886) ***(G-21362)***
Eusa Pharma (us) LLC...617 584-8012
15 Wayside Rd Ste 2 Burlington MA (01803) ***(G-9270)***
Eustis Chair, Cambridge *Also called Eustis Enterprises Inc* ***(G-9474)***
Eustis Enterprises Inc...978 827-3103
431 Huron Ave Cambridge MA (02138) ***(G-9474)***
Ev Launchpad LLC...603 828-2919
1465 Woodbury Ave 384 Portsmouth NH (03801) ***(G-19561)***
Ev Rite Tool Inc...413 568-1433
132 Elm St Westfield MA (01085) ***(G-16683)***
Evad Images...207 794-2930
48 Main St Lincoln ME (04457) ***(G-6352)***
Evans & Faulkner, Watertown *Also called McDermott Pallotta Inc* ***(G-16300)***
Evans Capacitor Company...401 435-3555
72 Boyd Ave East Providence RI (02914) ***(G-20411)***
Evans Company, East Providence *Also called Evans Findings Company Inc* ***(G-20412)***
Evans Cooling Systems Inc (PA)...860 668-1114
1 Mountain Rd Ste 1 # 1 Suffield CT (06078) ***(G-4462)***
Evans Findings Company Inc...401 434-5600
33 Eastern Ave East Providence RI (02914) ***(G-20412)***
Evans Industries Inc...978 887-8561
249 Boston St Topsfield MA (01983) ***(G-15858)***
Evans Machine Co Inc...508 584-8085
32 N Manchester St Brockton MA (02302) ***(G-9144)***
Evans Printing Co...603 856-8238
155 River Rd Unit 15 Bow NH (03304) ***(G-17713)***
Evans Welding & Construction, Westerly *Also called Robert B Evans Inc* ***(G-21538)***
Ever Better Eating Inc...603 435-5119
5 Main St Pittsfield NH (03263) ***(G-19499)***
Ever Ready Press...203 734-5157
78 Clifton Ave Ansonia CT (06401) ***(G-14)***
Everbridge Inc (PA)...818 230-9700
25 Corporate Dr Ste 400 Burlington MA (01803) ***(G-9271)***
Evercel Inc (PA)...781 741-8800
1055 Washington Blvd Fl 8 Stamford CT (06901) ***(G-4195)***
Everest Halthcare Holdings Inc (HQ)...781 699-9000
920 Winter St Waltham MA (02451) ***(G-16100)***
Everest Healthcare Texas Holdg...781 699-9000
920 Winter St Waltham MA (02451) ***(G-16101)***
Everest Herald Ltd Partnership...617 744-0620
25 Norseman Ave Watertown MA (02472) ***(G-16283)***
Everest Isles LLC...203 561-5128
616 N Elm St Wallingford CT (06492) ***(G-4739)***
Everett Charles Tech LLC...401 739-7310
6 Court Dr Lincoln RI (02865) ***(G-20572)***
Everett Charles Tech LLC...603 882-2621
41 Simon St Ste 1b Nashua NH (03060) ***(G-19151)***
Everett Charles Tech LLC...603 882-2621
7 Park Ave Hudson NH (03051) ***(G-18389)***
Everett Custom Woodworking...508 435-7675
32 W Main St Hopkinton MA (01748) ***(G-11712)***
Everett J Prescott Inc...401 333-8588
38 Albion Rd Lincoln RI (02865) ***(G-20573)***
Everett M Windover Inc...802 865-0000
154 Brentwood Dr Unit 1 Colchester VT (05446) ***(G-21863)***
Everett Print, Bridgeport *Also called Integrated Print Solutions Inc* ***(G-431)***
Evergage Inc...888 310-0589
212 Elm St Ste 4 Somerville MA (02144) ***(G-15170)***
Evergreen Cabinetry LLC...603 833-6881
44 Evergreen Valley Rd Milton NH (03851) ***(G-19085)***
Evergreen Custom Printing Inc...207 782-2327
63 Broad St Auburn ME (04210) ***(G-5563)***
Evergreen Embroidery...603 726-4271
239 Riverside Dr Campton NH (03223) ***(G-17776)***
Evergreen Enterprises Inc...508 823-2377
23 Howland Rd Berkley MA (02779) ***(G-8086)***
Evergreen Landscaping Inc...207 451-5007
Ledge Ln Berwick ME (03901) ***(G-5709)***
Everhot, Watertown *Also called Therma-Flow Inc* ***(G-16322)***
Everlast Products LLC...203 250-7111
150 Knotter Dr Cheshire CT (06410) ***(G-731)***
Everlasting Images Inc...207 351-3277
1272 Us Route 1 Cape Neddick ME (03902) ***(G-5878)***
Eversolve LLC...603 870-9739
8 Woodvue Rd Windham NH (03087) ***(G-20005)***
Everteam Inc...650 596-1800
745 Atlantic Ave Boston MA (02111) ***(G-8530)***
Evertrue Inc...617 460-3371
290 Congress St Fl 7 Boston MA (02210) ***(G-8531)***
Evervest Co...585 697-4170
21 School St Boston MA (02108) ***(G-8532)***
Everybody Water LLC...855 374-6539
35 Elm Ct Cohasset MA (02025) ***(G-10098)***

ALPHABETIC

Everyday Speech, Upton *Also called BRC Development LLC* ***(G-15905)***
Everything 2 Wheels LLC 860 225-2453
230 South St New Britain CT (06051) ***(G-2532)***
Evoaero Inc 860 289-2520
425 Sullivan Ave Ste 5 South Windsor CT (06074) ***(G-3967)***
Evogence, Rocky Hill *Also called Frontier Vision Tech Inc* ***(G-3709)***
Evonic Cyro, Wallingford *Also called Allnex USA Inc* ***(G-4695)***
Evoqua Water Technologies LLC 860 528-6512
88 Nutmeg Rd S South Windsor CT (06074) ***(G-3968)***
Evoqua Water Technologies LLC 978 863-4600
558 Clark Rd Tewksbury MA (01876) ***(G-15817)***
Evoqua Water Technologies LLC 978 934-9349
10 Technology Dr Lowell MA (01851) ***(G-12370)***
Evotec (us) Inc 650 228-1400
33 Business Park Dr # 6 Branford CT (06405) ***(G-314)***
Evs New Hampshire Inc 603 352-3000
50 Optical Ave Keene NH (03431) ***(G-18502)***
Evse Llc 860 745-2433
89 Phoenix Ave Enfield CT (06082) ***(G-1361)***
Ewald Instruments Corp 860 491-9042
95 Wooster Ct Ste 3 Bristol CT (06010) ***(G-558)***
Ewe Kids Inc 603 483-0984
1 Tower Hill Rd Candia NH (03034) ***(G-17783)***
Ewing Controls Inc 413 774-7500
321 Deerfield St Greenfield MA (01301) ***(G-11260)***
Ewm Corp (PA) 978 774-1191
88 Boston St Middleton MA (01949) ***(G-13088)***
Ewp, Colchester *Also called Essex Wood Products Inc* ***(G-802)***
Exa Corporation (HQ) 781 564-0200
55 Network Dr Burlington MA (01803) ***(G-9272)***
Exacom Inc 603 228-0706
99 Airport Rd Ste 3 Concord NH (03301) ***(G-17900)***
Exact Change 617 492-5405
5 Brewster St Cambridge MA (02138) ***(G-9475)***
Exact Components, Topsfield *Also called Graham Whitehead & Manger Co* ***(G-15861)***
Exact Dispensing Systems 207 563-2299
1130 Route 1 Newcastle ME (04553) ***(G-6482)***
Exalpha Biologicals Inc 978 425-1370
2 Shaker Rd Ste B101 Shirley MA (01464) ***(G-15083)***
Exarca Pharmaceuticals LLC 617 620-2776
20 Meriam St Lexington MA (02420) ***(G-12223)***
Exari Group Inc (PA) 617 938-3777
745 Boylston St Boston MA (02116) ***(G-8533)***
Exari Systems Inc 617 938-3777
745 Boylston St Ste 201 Boston MA (02116) ***(G-8534)***
Exatel Visual Systems Inc 781 221-7400
111 S Bedford St Ste 201 Burlington MA (01803) ***(G-9273)***
Excalibur Shelving Systems Inc 603 746-6200
292 Burnham Intervale Rd Contoocook NH (03229) ***(G-17944)***
Excalibur Welding and Piping 401 241-0548
45 Providence St Rehoboth MA (02769) ***(G-14748)***
Excel Dryer Inc 413 525-4531
357 Chestnut St East Longmeadow MA (01028) ***(G-10475)***
Excel Graphix 781 642-6736
35 Arnold Rd Norwood MA (02062) ***(G-14152)***
Excel Sign & Decoration Corp 617 479-8552
4 Eastleigh Ln Natick MA (01760) ***(G-13255)***
Excel Spring & Stamping LLC 860 585-1495
61 E Main St Ste 2 Bristol CT (06010) ***(G-559)***
Excel Technology Inc (HQ) 781 266-5700
125 Middlesex Tpke Bedford MA (01730) ***(G-7976)***
Excel Tool & Die Co Inc 617 472-0473
69 Sumner St Quincy MA (02169) ***(G-14624)***
Excelimmune Inc 617 262-8055
376 Hale St Rm 329 Beverly MA (01915) ***(G-8129)***
Excelimmune Inc (PA) 781 262-8055
1776 Massachusetts Ave Lexington MA (02420) ***(G-12224)***
Excelitas Tech Holdg Corp 781 522-5914
200 West St Ste E403 Waltham MA (02451) ***(G-16102)***
Excelitas Tech Holdings LLC (PA) 781 522-5900
200 West St Ste E403 Waltham MA (02451) ***(G-16103)***
Excelitas Technologies Corp 800 775-6786
35 Congress St Ste 2021 Salem MA (01970) ***(G-14910)***
Excelitas Technologies Corp (HQ) 781 522-5910
200 West St Waltham MA (02451) ***(G-16104)***
Excell Solutions Inc 978 663-6100
18 Esquire Rd North Billerica MA (01862) ***(G-13813)***
Excella Graphics 781 763-7768
300 Main St Malden MA (02148) ***(G-12571)***
Excello Tool Engrg & Mfg Co 203 878-4073
37 Warfield St Milford CT (06461) ***(G-2287)***
Excelsior Printing, North Adams *Also called Ghp Media Inc* ***(G-13675)***
Executive Force Protection LLC 617 470-9230
245 1st St Ste 1800 Cambridge MA (02142) ***(G-9476)***
Executive Greetings Inc (HQ) 860 379-9911
120 Industrial Park Rd New Hartford CT (06057) ***(G-2636)***
Executive Office Services Inc 203 373-1333
2085 Madison Ave Bridgeport CT (06606) ***(G-411)***
Executive Press Inc 860 793-0060
27 East St Plainville CT (06062) ***(G-3487)***
Executive Printing Darien LLC 203 655-4691
1082 Post Rd Darien CT (06820) ***(G-1023)***
Executive Wine & Spirits Inc 603 647-8048
34 1st Ave Manchester NH (03104) ***(G-18820)***
Executrain, Boston *Also called International Data Group Inc* ***(G-8618)***
Exemplar Laboratories LLC 508 676-6726
200 Riggenbach Rd Fall River MA (02720) ***(G-10692)***
Exemplar Pharma LLC 508 676-6726
927 Currant Rd Fall River MA (02720) ***(G-10693)***
Exemplar Pharmaceuticals, Fall River *Also called Exemplar Pharma LLC* ***(G-10693)***
Exergen Corporation 617 923-9900
400 Pleasant St Watertown MA (02472) ***(G-16284)***
Exeter Analytical Inc (PA) 978 251-1411
7 Doris Dr Ste 6a North Chelmsford MA (01863) ***(G-13894)***
Exeter Cabinet Company Inc 603 778-8113
16 Kingston Rd Unit 5 Exeter NH (03833) ***(G-18120)***
Exit 5 Gallery, West Barnstable *Also called Exit Five Gallery* ***(G-16407)***
Exit Five Gallery 508 375-1011
1085 Main St West Barnstable MA (02668) ***(G-16407)***
Exocetus Autonomous Systems 860 512-7260
7 Laser Ln Wallingford CT (06492) ***(G-4740)***
Exothermics Inc 603 821-5660
14 Columbia Dr Amherst NH (03031) ***(G-17560)***
Exotic Foods 508 422-9540
53 Sumner St Milford MA (01757) ***(G-13117)***
Expanded Rubber Products Inc 207 985-4141
62 Portland Rd Ste 9 Kennebunk ME (04043) ***(G-6233)***
Expanded Rubber Products Inc (PA) 207 324-8226
41 Industrial Ave Sanford ME (04073) ***(G-6875)***
Expansion Opportunities Inc 508 303-8200
35 Lyman St Ste 1 Northborough MA (01532) ***(G-14033)***
Expedience Software LLC 978 378-5330
1087 Elm St Ste 249 Manchester NH (03101) ***(G-18821)***
Experimental Prototype Pdts Co 860 289-4948
248 Chapel Rd South Windsor CT (06074) ***(G-3969)***
Expert Embroidery 203 269-9675
121 N Plains Indus Ste G Wallingford CT (06492) ***(G-4741)***
Expertees, Danvers *Also called T-Shirts N Jeans Inc* ***(G-10260)***
Expertek Systems Inc 508 624-0006
100 Locke Dr Ste 4 Marlborough MA (01752) ***(G-12754)***
Expose Signs & Graphics Inc 508 381-0941
13 Airport Rd Hopedale MA (01747) ***(G-11671)***
Express Assemblyproducts LLC 603 424-5590
10 Northern Blvd Ste 14b Amherst NH (03031) ***(G-17561)***
Express Cntertops Kit Flrg LLC 203 283-4909
303 Boston Post Rd Orange CT (06477) ***(G-3365)***
Express Company, Sandwich *Also called Billard Corporation* ***(G-14961)***
Express Copy Inc 802 362-0501
275c Manchester Valley Rd Manchester Center VT (05255) ***(G-22084)***
Expressive Design Group Inc 413 315-6296
49 Garfield St Holyoke MA (01040) ***(G-11626)***
Expressway Lube Centers 203 744-2511
225 White St Danbury CT (06810) ***(G-915)***
Exstar 339 293-9334
4 Manison St Ste A Stoneham MA (02180) ***(G-15563)***
Extech Instruments Corporation 887 439-8324
9 Townsend W Nashua NH (03063) ***(G-19152)***
Extend Biosciences Inc 732 599-8580
90 Bridge St Ste 100 Newton MA (02458) ***(G-13591)***
Extile.com, Stamford *Also called Pauls Marble Depot LLC* ***(G-4279)***
Extra Extra Daily, Quincy *Also called Driggin Sandra DBA Extra Extra* ***(G-14620)***
Extra Fuel 203 330-0613
540 Boston Ave Bridgeport CT (06610) ***(G-412)***
Extra Origin Foods, Belmont *Also called Longrun LLC* ***(G-8077)***
Extra Virgin Foods Company, Watertown *Also called Extra Virgin Foods Inc* ***(G-16285)***
Extra Virgin Foods Inc 617 407-9161
71 Arlington St Watertown MA (02472) ***(G-16285)***
Extrafresh LLC 413 567-8995
25 Andover Rd Longmeadow MA (01106) ***(G-12333)***
Extreme Dim Wildlife Calls LLC 207 862-2825
208 Kennebec Rd Hampden ME (04444) ***(G-6165)***
Extreme Networks Inc 603 952-5000
9 Northeastern Blvd Salem NH (03079) ***(G-19726)***
Extreme Protocol Solutions Inc 508 278-3600
10 River Rd Ste 102e Uxbridge MA (01569) ***(G-15915)***
Extrusion Alternatives Inc 603 430-9600
19 Post Rd Portsmouth NH (03801) ***(G-19562)***
Exxonmobil Oil Corporation 781 963-7252
93 Mazzeo Dr Randolph MA (02368) ***(G-14679)***
Exxonmobil Pipeline Company 413 736-1881
145 Albany St Springfield MA (01105) ***(G-15470)***
Eye Ear It LLC 203 487-8949
19 Pomperaug Rd Woodbury CT (06798) ***(G-5487)***
Eye Point Pharmac 617 926-5000
400 Pleasant St Watertown MA (02472) ***(G-16286)***
Eyedeal Scanning LLC 617 519-8696
124 Crescent Rd Ste 3b Needham MA (02494) ***(G-13299)***
Eyegate Pharmaceuticals Inc (PA) 781 788-9043
271 Waverly Oaks Rd # 10 Waltham MA (02452) ***(G-16105)***

Eyelash Extensions and More 860 951-9355
998 Farmington Ave West Hartford CT (06107) *(G-5071)*
Eyelet Crafters Inc 203 757-9221
2712 S Main St Waterbury CT (06706) *(G-4871)*
Eyelet Design Inc 203 754-4141
574 E Main St Waterbury CT (06702) *(G-4872)*
Eyelet Tech LLC 203 879-5306
10 Venus Dr Wolcott CT (06716) *(G-5442)*
Eyelet Toolmakers Inc 860 274-5423
40 Callender Rd Watertown CT (06795) *(G-5009)*
Eyemax LLC 781 424-9281
74 Chestnut St Weston MA (02493) *(G-16825)*
Eyenetra Inc 973 229-3341
2 James Way Cambridge MA (02141) *(G-9477)*
Eyepoint Pharmaceuticals Inc (PA) 617 926-5000
480 Pleasant St Ste B300 Watertown MA (02472) *(G-16287)*
Eyepvideo Systems LLC 603 382-2547
25 Olde Rd Danville NH (03819) *(G-17968)*
Eyes On Europe LLC 617 696-9311
44 Fox Hill Ln Milton MA (02186) *(G-13191)*
Eyesaver International Inc 781 829-0808
348 Circuit St Ste 2 Hanover MA (02339) *(G-11337)*
Eylward Timber Co 203 265-4276
13 Quince St Wallingford CT (06492) *(G-4742)*
EZ Rater Systems Inc 978 887-8322
93 Killam Hill Rd Boxford MA (01921) *(G-8977)*
EZ Welding LLC 860 707-3100
244 Garry Dr New Britain CT (06052) *(G-2533)*
Eze Castle Software Inc (HQ) 617 316-1100
12 Farnsworth St Fl 6 Boston MA (02210) *(G-8535)*
Ezenia Inc (PA) 603 589-7600
401 Main St Ste 205 Salem NH (03079) *(G-19727)*
Ezequelle Logging Inc 413 258-0265
165 Sandisfield Rd Sandisfield MA (01255) *(G-14960)*
Ezflow Limited Partnership (HQ) 860 577-7064
4 Business Park Rd Old Saybrook CT (06475) *(G-3334)*
Ezra J Leboff Co Inc 617 783-4200
74 Lincoln St Brighton MA (02135) *(G-9098)*
Eztousecom Directories 207 974-3171
592 Hammond St Bangor ME (04401) *(G-5643)*
F & D Plastics Inc (PA) 978 668-5140
23 Jytek Dr Leominster MA (01453) *(G-12136)*
F & L Iron Work Inc 203 777-0751
105 Barclay St New Haven CT (06519) *(G-2687)*
F & M Tool & Die Co Inc 978 537-0290
25 Jytek Rd Leominster MA (01453) *(G-12137)*
F & M Tool & Plastics Inc 978 840-1897
175 Pioneer Dr Leominster MA (01453) *(G-12138)*
F & S Wood Products 401 423-1048
39 Frigate St Jamestown RI (02835) *(G-20490)*
F & W Rentals Inc 203 795-0591
164 Boston Post Rd Orange CT (06477) *(G-3366)*
F A D C O, Bristol *Also called Day Fred A Co LLC* *(G-548)*
F A Wildnauer Woodwork, South Berwick *Also called F A Wilnauer Woodwork Inc* *(G-7002)*
F A Wilnauer Woodwork Inc 207 384-4824
28 Witchtrot Rd South Berwick ME (03908) *(G-7002)*
F B Washburn Candy Corporation 508 588-0820
137 Perkins Ave Brockton MA (02302) *(G-9145)*
F C Hammond & Son Lbr Co Inc 603 523-4353
11 Hammonds Way Canaan NH (03741) *(G-17778)*
F D Grave & Son Inc 203 239-9394
85 State St Ste C North Haven CT (06473) *(G-3026)*
F D I, Farmington *Also called Farmington Displays Inc* *(G-1481)*
F E Knight, Franklin *Also called Castaldo Products Mfg Co Inc* *(G-11027)*
F F I, Smithfield *Also called Fiberglass Fabricators Inc* *(G-21224)*
F F J, Pawtucket *Also called Geo H Fuller and Son Company* *(G-20843)*
F F Screw Products Inc 860 621-4567
888 W Queen St Southington CT (06489) *(G-4049)*
F H Peterson Machine Corp 781 341-4930
143 South St Stoughton MA (02072) *(G-15590)*
F J Weidner Inc 203 469-4202
34 Tyler Street Ext East Haven CT (06512) *(G-1249)*
F L C Machined Products Co 978 948-7525
47 Main St Rowley MA (01969) *(G-14853)*
F L Tripp & Sons Inc 508 636-4058
Cherry & Webb Ln Westport Point MA (02791) *(G-16854)*
F M, Cheshire *Also called Fiber Mountain Inc* *(G-732)*
F M C, Somersworth *Also called Fall Machine Company LLC* *(G-19837)*
F M C Marine Colloid Division, Rockland *Also called FMC Corporation* *(G-6795)*
F M Callahan and Son Inc 781 324-5101
22 Sharon St Malden MA (02148) *(G-12572)*
F M I, Hudson *Also called Fabco Mfg Inc* *(G-11773)*
F M S, Watertown *Also called Fluid Management Systems Inc* *(G-16288)*
F P, Leominster *Also called First Plastics Corp* *(G-12139)*
F R Carroll Inc 207 793-8615
25 Doles Ridge Rd Limerick ME (04048) *(G-6334)*
F R Mahony Associates 978 597-0703
41 Bayberry Hill Rd Townsend MA (01474) *(G-15872)*
F T International, Auburn *Also called Free-Flow Packaging Intl Inc* *(G-7835)*
F T Smith Sand & Gravel, North Brookfield *Also called FT Smith Trckg & Excvtg Inc* *(G-13880)*
F V Sea Breeze LLC 401 792-0188
28 Serenity Way Wakefield RI (02879) *(G-21270)*
F W Derbyshire Inc 508 883-2385
38 Main St Blackstone MA (01504) *(G-8312)*
F W Lombard Company (PA) 978 827-5333
246 Lakeview Dr Winchendon MA (01475) *(G-17075)*
F W Webb Company 203 865-6124
650 Boulevard New Haven CT (06519) *(G-2688)*
F2nyc, Pawtucket *Also called Fiesta Jewelry Corporation* *(G-20839)*
F3 Mfg Inc 207 692-7178
977 W River Rd Unit 3 Waterville ME (04901) *(G-7155)*
FA Finale Inc 617 226-7888
24 Prime Park Way Ste 305 Boston MA (02116) *(G-8536)*
Fab Braze Corp (PA) 781 893-6777
5 Progress Ave Nashua NH (03062) *(G-19153)*
Fabco Engineering, Fall River *Also called Fall River Boiler & Welding Co* *(G-10695)*
Fabco Mfg Inc 978 568-8519
14 Bonazzoli Ave Hudson MA (01749) *(G-11773)*
Fabco Wrap, New London *Also called First Aid Bandage Co Inc* *(G-2773)*
Faber Family Associates Lpa (PA) 603 681-0484
6 Northwestern Dr Salem NH (03079) *(G-19728)*
Faber Industries LLC (HQ) 603 681-0484
6 Northwestern Dr Salem NH (03079) *(G-19729)*
Faber Polivol LLC (HQ) 603 681-0484
6 Northwestern Dr Salem NH (03079) *(G-19730)*
Fablevision Learning LLC 781 320-3225
368 Washington St Ste 207 Dedham MA (02026) *(G-10289)*
Fabor Fourslide Inc 203 753-4380
44 Railroad Hill St Waterbury CT (06708) *(G-4873)*
Fabri TEC Engineering Inc 401 783-0051
25 Walts Way Narragansett RI (02882) *(G-20639)*
Fabricate LLC 207 288-5113
64 Mount Desert St Bar Harbor ME (04609) *(G-5665)*
Fabricated Metals, Amherst *Also called Greenfield Industries Inc* *(G-17565)*
Fabricgraphics, Pawcatuck *Also called Guidera Marketing Services* *(G-3436)*
Fabrique Ltd 203 481-5400
28 School St Branford CT (06405) *(G-315)*
Fabrizio Corporation 781 396-1400
410 Riverside Ave Medford MA (02155) *(G-12933)*
Fabtron Corporation 781 891-4430
80 Calvary St Waltham MA (02453) *(G-16106)*
Fabula Nebulae LLC 917 545-9049
31 Gilmore Ln Holden ME (04429) *(G-6197)*
Fabworx Solutions Inc 603 224-9679
10 Ferry St Ste 136 Concord NH (03301) *(G-17901)*
Faces Typography Inc 401 273-4455
40 Rice St 1 Providence RI (02907) *(G-21009)*
Faco Metal Products Inc 401 943-7127
22 Thunder Trl Cranston RI (02921) *(G-20223)*
Fad Tool Company LLC 860 582-7890
95 Valley St Ste 7 Bristol CT (06010) *(G-560)*
Fadden Chipping & Logging Inc 603 939-2462
1708 E Conway Rd Center Conway NH (03813) *(G-17797)*
Fadden Construction, North Woodstock *Also called J H Faddens & Sons* *(G-19398)*
Fadden Trucking, Center Conway *Also called Fadden Chipping & Logging Inc* *(G-17797)*
Fag Bearings LLC (HQ) 203 790-5474
200 Park Ave Danbury CT (06810) *(G-916)*
FAg Holding Corporation (HQ) 203 790-5474
200 Park Ave Danbury CT (06810) *(G-917)*
Fagan Design & Fabrication 203 937-1874
44 Railroad Ave West Haven CT (06516) *(G-5122)*
Faille Precision Machining 860 822-1964
118 W Main St Baltic CT (06330) *(G-49)*
Fair Haven Slate, Poultney *Also called Taran Bros Inc* *(G-22279)*
Fair Winds Press and Quiver 978 282-9590
100 Cummings Ctr Ste 406l Beverly MA (01915) *(G-8130)*
Fairchild Auto-Mated Parts Inc 860 379-2725
10 White St Winsted CT (06098) *(G-5411)*
Fairchild Energy LLC 207 775-8100
82 Running Hill Rd South Portland ME (04106) *(G-7023)*
Fairchild Semiconductor Corp (HQ) 207 775-8100
82 Running Hill Rd South Portland ME (04106) *(G-7024)*
Fairchild Semiconductor Corp 207 775-8100
333 Western Ave South Portland ME (04106) *(G-7025)*
Fairchild Semiconductor W Corp 207 775-8100
82 Running Hill Rd South Portland ME (04106) *(G-7026)*
Fairdeal Mfg Co, Chepachet *Also called Josef Creations Inc* *(G-20135)*
Fairfield County Look 203 869-0077
6 Wyckham Hill Ln Greenwich CT (06831) *(G-1610)*
Fairfield County Millwork 203 393-9751
20 Sargent Dr Bethany CT (06524) *(G-120)*
Fairfield Pool & Equipment Co (PA) 203 334-3600
278 Meadow St Fairfield CT (06824) *(G-1431)*
Fairfield Processing Corp (PA) 203 744-2090
88 Rose Hill Ave Danbury CT (06810) *(G-918)*

ALPHABETIC

Fairfield Wood Works, Stratford *Also called Fairfield Woodworks LLC* ***(G-4411)***
Fairfield Woodworks LLC 203 380-9842
365 Sniffens Ln Stratford CT (06615) ***(G-4411)***
Fairmont Sons LLC (PA) 401 351-4000
20 Westminster St Providence RI (02903) ***(G-21010)***
Fairmount Foundry Inc 401 769-1585
25 2nd Ave Woonsocket RI (02895) ***(G-21561)***
Fairview Machine Company Inc 978 887-2141
427 Boston St Topsfield MA (01983) ***(G-15859)***
Fairview Millwork Inc 603 929-4449
344 State Route 107 Seabrook NH (03874) ***(G-19800)***
Falcon Performance Footwear, Auburn *Also called Globe Footwear LLC* ***(G-5568)***
Falcon Performance Ftwr LLC 207 784-9186
27 Wrights Lndg Auburn ME (04210) ***(G-5564)***
Falcon Precision Machine Co 413 583-2117
97 Center St Ludlow MA (01056) ***(G-12465)***
Falcon Press 860 763-2293
13 Rockland Dr Enfield CT (06082) ***(G-1362)***
Fall Machine Company LLC 603 750-7100
10 Willand Dr Somersworth NH (03878) ***(G-19837)***
Fall Prevention Alarms Inc 508 765-5050
186 Hamilton St Southbridge MA (01550) ***(G-15382)***
Fall River Apparel Inc 508 677-1975
1 Ace St Unit 3 Fall River MA (02720) ***(G-10694)***
Fall River Boiler & Welding Co 508 677-4479
994 Jefferson St Ste 2 Fall River MA (02721) ***(G-10695)***
Fall River Mfg Co Inc 508 675-1125
540 Currant Rd Fall River MA (02720) ***(G-10696)***
Fall River Modern Printing Co 508 673-9421
798 Plymouth Ave Fall River MA (02721) ***(G-10697)***
Fall River Ready-Mix Con LLC 508 675-7540
245 Tripp St Fall River MA (02724) ***(G-10698)***
Fall River Tool & Die Co Inc 508 674-4621
994 Jefferson St Ste 2 Fall River MA (02721) ***(G-10699)***
Fallon Fine Cabinetry 781 453-6988
171 Reservoir St Needham Heights MA (02494) ***(G-13331)***
Falls Fuel LLC 203 744-3835
5 Laughlin Rd Bethel CT (06801) ***(G-153)***
Falmer 781 593-0088
168 Broad St Fl 2 Lynn MA (01901) ***(G-12507)***
Falmer Associates Inc 978 745-4000
96 Swampscott Rd Ste 10 Salem MA (01970) ***(G-14911)***
Falmer Thermal Spray, Salem *Also called Falmer Associates Inc* ***(G-14911)***
Falmouth Enterprise, Falmouth *Also called Enterprise Publications* ***(G-10789)***
Falmouth Products Inc 508 548-6686
530 Thomas B Landers Rd East Falmouth MA (02536) ***(G-10442)***
Falmouth Ready Mix Inc 508 548-6100
475 Thomas B Landers Rd East Falmouth MA (02536) ***(G-10443)***
Falmouth Sheet Metal, East Falmouth *Also called Cunniff Corp* ***(G-10440)***
Famars USA LLC 401 397-5500
87 Kingstown Rd Unit C330 Richmond RI (02898) ***(G-21161)***
Families and Wealth LLC 617 558-5800
1075 Washington St Newton MA (02465) ***(G-13592)***
Family Memorials Inc 802 476-7831
36 Burnham St Barre VT (05641) ***(G-21614)***
Family Raceway LLC 860 896-0171
11 Earl St Vernon CT (06066) ***(G-4667)***
Family Yarns Inc 207 269-3852
15 Family Cir Etna ME (04434) ***(G-6025)***
Famous Amos of Boston, Canton *Also called Murray Biscuit Company LLC* ***(G-9758)***
Faneuil Kitchen Cabinet, Hingham *Also called Colonial Village Refinishing* ***(G-11496)***
Far Industries Inc 508 644-3122
11 Ridge Hill Rd Assonet MA (02702) ***(G-7679)***
Far Reach Graphics Inc 781 444-4889
15 Kearney Rd Needham Heights MA (02494) ***(G-13332)***
Faraday Inc 800 442-1521
5 Court St Middlebury VT (05753) ***(G-22110)***
Farber Industrial Fabricating 401 725-2492
55 Moss St Pawtucket RI (02860) ***(G-20837)***
Fargo Ta LLC 617 345-0066
745 Atlantic Ave Fl 8 Boston MA (02111) ***(G-8537)***
Faria Beede Instruments Inc 860 848-9271
75 Frontage Rd Ste 106 North Stonington CT (06359) ***(G-3074)***
Faria Marine Instruments, North Stonington *Also called Faria Beede Instruments Inc* ***(G-3074)***
Farm Coast Brewery LLC 401 816-5021
241 Cornell Rd Tiverton RI (02878) ***(G-21258)***
Farm Table At Kringle Candle 413 648-5200
219 South St Bernardston MA (01337) ***(G-8093)***
Farm Truck Institute 207 400-2242
1265 Middle Rd Dresden ME (04342) ***(G-5966)***
Farmer Brown Service Inc 978 897-7550
54 Knox Trl Bldg 2m Acton MA (01720) ***(G-7355)***
Farmer Willies Inc 401 441-2997
50 Terminal St Bldg Providence RI (02906) ***(G-21011)***
Farmers Almanac, Lewiston *Also called Almanac Publishing Co* ***(G-6274)***
Farmington Chipping Enterprise 207 778-4888
Town Farm Rd Farmington ME (04938) ***(G-6046)***
Farmington Coca Cola Btlg Dstr 207 778-4733
282 Farmington Falls Rd Farmington ME (04938) ***(G-6047)***
Farmington Displays Inc 860 677-2497
21 Hyde Rd Ste 2 Farmington CT (06032) ***(G-1481)***
Farmington Engineering Inc 800 428-7584
73 Defco Park Rd North Haven CT (06473) ***(G-3027)***
Farmington Mtal Fbrication LLC 860 404-7415
139 Center St Ste 2001 Bristol CT (06010) ***(G-561)***
Farmington River Holdings LLC 203 777-2130
1125 Dixwell Ave Hamden CT (06514) ***(G-1749)***
Faro Technologies Inc 603 893-6200
1 Wall St Ste 105 Hudson NH (03051) ***(G-18390)***
Farrar Press Inc 508 799-9874
707 Pleasant St Paxton MA (01612) ***(G-14301)***
Farrar Sails Inc 860 447-0382
6 Union St Ste 6 # 6 New London CT (06320) ***(G-2772)***
Farrel Corporation (HQ) 203 736-5500
1 Farrel Blvd Ansonia CT (06401) ***(G-15)***
Farrel Pomini, Ansonia *Also called Farrel Corporation* ***(G-15)***
Farrell Prcsion Mtalcraft Corp 860 355-2651
192 Danbury Rd New Milford CT (06776) ***(G-2799)***
Farrins Boat Shop 207 563-5510
19 Sproul Rd Walpole ME (04573) ***(G-7140)***
Farsounder Inc 401 784-6700
151 Lavan St Warwick RI (02888) ***(G-21363)***
Fasano Corp 401 785-9646
333 Wellington Ave Cranston RI (02910) ***(G-20224)***
Fashion Accents LLC (PA) 401 331-6626
100 Nashua St Providence RI (02904) ***(G-21012)***
Fashion Accessories First, Greenville *Also called A F F Inc* ***(G-20460)***
Fashions By Gary Inc 401 726-1453
108 Tweed St Pawtucket RI (02861) ***(G-20838)***
Fashions Inc (PA) 617 338-0163
535 Albany St Ste 2 Boston MA (02118) ***(G-8538)***
Fasprint Inc (PA) 508 588-9961
195 Liberty St Ste 1 Brockton MA (02301) ***(G-9146)***
Fasstech, North Billerica *Also called Functional Assessment Tech Inc* ***(G-13817)***
Fast, Stratford *Also called Food Atmtn - Svc Tchniques Inc* ***(G-4412)***
Fast Forms Printing & Paper 207 941-8383
229 Swan Rd Hermon ME (04401) ***(G-6186)***
Fast Mailing 617 605-8693
55 Teed Dr Randolph MA (02368) ***(G-14680)***
Fast Signs 603 894-7446
345 S Broadway Salem NH (03079) ***(G-19731)***
Fastcap Systems Corporation 857 239-7500
21 Drydock Ave Fl 8e Boston MA (02210) ***(G-8539)***
Fastcast Consortium Inc 508 853-4500
40 Rockdale St Worcester MA (01606) ***(G-17373)***
Fastech Inc 781 964-3010
18 Washington St Ste 33 Canton MA (02021) ***(G-9732)***
Fastforms, Boston *Also called BFI Print Communications Inc* ***(G-8405)***
Fastrax Signs 603 778-4799
68 Portsmouth Ave Stratham NH (03885) ***(G-19868)***
Fastrax Signs Inc 603 775-7500
67 Route 27 Brentwood NH (03833) ***(G-17749)***
Fastserv/Northeast, Norwalk *Also called Corr/Dis Incorporated* ***(G-3132)***
Fastsigns, West Springfield *Also called Multi Sign Inc* ***(G-16533)***
Fastsigns, Salem *Also called Fast Signs* ***(G-19731)***
FASTSIGNS, Manchester *Also called Semiotics LLC* ***(G-2047)***
Fastsigns, Manchester *Also called Courrier Graphics Inc* ***(G-18808)***
Fastsigns, Needham Heights *Also called Far Reach Graphics Inc* ***(G-13332)***
Fastsigns, Seekonk *Also called Back Street Inc* ***(G-15018)***
Fastsigns, Woburn *Also called Signs To Go Inc* ***(G-17296)***
Fastsigns 203 298-4075
1015 Bridgeport Ave Milford CT (06460) ***(G-2288)***
Fastsigns 860 583-8000
1290 Farmington Ave Bristol CT (06010) ***(G-562)***
Fastsigns of Attleboro 508 699-6699
5 Greenwood Dr Rehoboth MA (02769) ***(G-14749)***
Fastvision LLC 603 891-4317
71 Spit Brook Rd Ste 201 Nashua NH (03060) ***(G-19154)***
Fat City Sports, New Milford *Also called Jb Muze Enterprises* ***(G-2807)***
Fat Hat Clothing Co 802 296-6646
1 Quechee Main St Quechee VT (05059) ***(G-22294)***
Faucher Organ Company Inc 207 283-1420
31 Sokokis Rd Biddeford ME (04005) ***(G-5732)***
Faux Designs 617 965-0142
72 Rowe St Auburndale MA (02466) ***(G-7861)***
Faverco Inc 617 247-1440
16 Aberdeen St Boston MA (02215) ***(G-8540)***
Favorite Fuels LLC 603 967-4889
1 Crank Rd Hampton Falls NH (03844) ***(G-18282)***
Fay Electric Motors, Manchester *Also called Lawrence Fay* ***(G-18862)***
Fbn Plastics Inc 603 894-4326
338 N Main St Salem NH (03079) ***(G-19732)***
Fc Meyer Packaging LLC (HQ) 203 847-8500
108 Main St Ste 3 Norwalk CT (06851) ***(G-3150)***

FC Phillips Inc 781 344-9400
471 Washington St Stoughton MA (02072) ***(G-15591)***
FCA LLC 203 857-0825
26 2nd St Norwalk CT (06855) ***(G-3151)***
Fci Electrical-Brundy Products 603 444-6781
150 Burndy Rd Littleton NH (03561) ***(G-18659)***
Fci Ophthalmics Inc 781 826-9060
30 Corporate Park Dr # 310 Pembroke MA (02359) ***(G-14404)***
Fd Plastics, Leominster *Also called F & D Plastics Inc* ***(G-12136)***
FDA Group LLC 413 330-7476
3 Bridle Ridge Dr North Grafton MA (01536) ***(G-13960)***
FDM Adhesives LLC 978 423-3553
5 Lavantie St Haverhill MA (01830) ***(G-11433)***
Fdr Center For Prost 603 595-9255
39 Simon St Ste 7 Nashua NH (03060) ***(G-19155)***
FE Knight Inc (PA) 508 520-1666
120 Constitution Blvd Franklin MA (02038) ***(G-11045)***
Fea, Littleton *Also called Forest Economic Advisors LLC* ***(G-12306)***
Feature Products Ltd 603 669-0800
18 Cote Ave Ste 13 Goffstown NH (03045) ***(G-18200)***
Feature Ring Co, Chelsea *Also called Town & Country Fine Jwly Group* ***(G-9973)***
Fed, Dedham *Also called Dedham Recycled Gravel Inc* ***(G-10287)***
Fedco, Wallingford *Also called Fiberglass Engr & Design Co* ***(G-4743)***
Federal Electronics Inc 401 944-6200
75 Stamp Farm Rd Cranston RI (02921) ***(G-20225)***
Federal Metal Finishing Inc 617 242-3371
18 Dorrance St Boston MA (02129) ***(G-8541)***
Federal Prison Industries 203 743-6471
Rr 37 Danbury CT (06811) ***(G-919)***
Federal Specialties Inc 413 782-6900
140 Norman St West Springfield MA (01089) ***(G-16520)***
Federici Brands LLC 203 762-7667
195 Danbury Rd Wilton CT (06897) ***(G-5289)***
Fedex Office & Print Svcs Inc 603 298-5891
267 Plainfield Rd West Lebanon NH (03784) ***(G-19951)***
Fedex Office & Print Svcs Inc 978 275-0574
61 Drum Hill Rd Chelmsford MA (01824) ***(G-9898)***
Fedhal Foods Inc 508 595-9178
560 Lincoln St Worcester MA (01605) ***(G-17374)***
Feed Commodities Intl Inc 802 334-2942
758 S Yard Rd Newport VT (05855) ***(G-22197)***
Feeleys Company Inc 617 773-1711
232 Water St 238 Quincy MA (02169) ***(G-14625)***
Feeney Fence Inc 617 364-1407
120 Business St Ste 5 Hyde Park MA (02136) ***(G-11866)***
Feeney's Welding and Fence Co., Hyde Park *Also called Feeney Fence Inc* ***(G-11866)***
Fein Academy LLC 978 495-0777
21 Bay View Dr Swampscott MA (01907) ***(G-15697)***
Fein Things 508 778-5200
1656 Falmouth Rd Centerville MA (02632) ***(G-9815)***
Fel Tech Hammer Division, Worcester *Also called Frank E Lashua Inc* ***(G-17379)***
Feldhaus Consulting LLC 603 276-0508
110 Crestview Rd Belmont MA (02478) ***(G-8073)***
Felicia Oil Co Inc 978 283-3808
78 Commercial St Gloucester MA (01930) ***(G-11181)***
Felicia Winkfield 401 849-3029
2 Lowndes St Newport RI (02840) ***(G-20665)***
Fellows Corporation 802 674-6500
7 Everett Ln Windsor VT (05089) ***(G-22708)***
Felton Inc 603 425-0200
7 Burton Dr Londonderry NH (03053) ***(G-18697)***
Felton Brush 603 425-0200
7 Burton Dr Londonderry NH (03053) ***(G-18698)***
Fender Musical Instrs Corp 860 379-7575
37 Greenwoods Rd New Hartford CT (06057) ***(G-2637)***
Fenn LLC 860 259-6600
80 Clark Dr Unit 5d East Berlin CT (06023) ***(G-1100)***
Fenton Corp 203 221-2788
191 Post Rd W Westport CT (06880) ***(G-5191)***
Fenway Cmmunications Group Inc 617 226-1900
870 Commonwealth Ave F Boston MA (02215) ***(G-8542)***
Fergtech Inc 203 656-1139
28 Thorndal Cir Ste 1 Darien CT (06820) ***(G-1024)***
Fergtech Inc (PA) 203 656-1139
19 Wilson Ridge Rd Darien CT (06820) ***(G-1025)***
Ferguson Perforating Company (HQ) 401 941-8876
130 Ernest St Providence RI (02905) ***(G-21013)***
Fernandes Precast Company 401 349-4907
356 Washington Hwy Smithfield RI (02917) ***(G-21223)***
Fernwood Inc (PA) 207 363-7891
24 Logging Rd Cape Neddick ME (03902) ***(G-5879)***
Feroleto Steel Company Inc (HQ) 203 366-3263
300 Scofield Ave Bridgeport CT (06605) ***(G-413)***
Ferraiolo Construction Inc 207 582-6162
279 Main St Ste 1 Rockland ME (04841) ***(G-6792)***
Ferrara For Contemporary AP, Mansfield *Also called Contemporary Apparel Inc* ***(G-12619)***
Ferrari Classics Corporation 413 569-6179
120 Berkshire Ave Southwick MA (01077) ***(G-15413)***
Ferraro Custom Woodwork LLC 203 876-1280
29 Eastern Steel Rd Milford CT (06460) ***(G-2289)***
Ferre Form Metal Products 860 274-3280
25 Falls Ave Oakville CT (06779) ***(G-3298)***
Ferreira Concrete Forms Inc 401 639-0931
7 Tallman Ave East Providence RI (02914) ***(G-20413)***
Ferris Power Products, Bourne *Also called Hamilton Ferris Co Inc* ***(G-8946)***
Ferrite Microwave Tech LLC 603 881-5234
165 Ledge St Ste 2 Nashua NH (03060) ***(G-19156)***
Ferron Mold and Tool LLC 860 774-5555
154 Louisa Viens Dr Dayville CT (06241) ***(G-1043)***
Ferrotec (usa) Corporation (HQ) 603 472-6800
33 Constitution Dr Bedford NH (03110) ***(G-17640)***
Fetch Inc 207 773-5450
195 Commercial St Portland ME (04101) ***(G-6662)***
Feteria Tool & Findings 508 222-7788
1285 County St Attleboro MA (02703) ***(G-7734)***
Ff Screw Products, Southington *Also called F F Screw Products Inc* ***(G-4049)***
Fgs, Braintree *Also called Financial Graphic Services Inc* ***(G-9007)***
Fgx International, Smithfield *Also called Dioptics Medical Products Inc* ***(G-21221)***
Fhc Inc (PA) 207 666-8190
1201 Main St Bowdoin ME (04287) ***(G-5787)***
Fiandaca, Boston *Also called Fashions Inc* ***(G-8538)***
Fiba Technologies Inc (PA) 508 887-7100
53 Ayer Rd Littleton MA (01460) ***(G-12305)***
Fiber Materials Inc (HQ) 207 282-5911
5 Morin St Biddeford ME (04005) ***(G-5733)***
Fiber Mountain Inc 203 806-4040
700 W Johnson Ave Ste 100 Cheshire CT (06410) ***(G-732)***
Fibercape Internet Services, Falmouth *Also called Homeland Security Wireless Inc* ***(G-10792)***
Fiberglas Fabrications 508 255-9409
36 Giddiah Hill Rd Orleans MA (02653) ***(G-14233)***
Fiberglass Building Pdts Inc 847 650-3045
546a Plymouth St Halifax MA (02338) ***(G-11318)***
Fiberglass Engr & Design Co 203 265-1644
25 N Plains Industrial Hw Wallingford CT (06492) ***(G-4743)***
Fiberglass Fabricators Inc 401 231-3552
964 Douglas Pike Smithfield RI (02917) ***(G-21224)***
Fiberglass Plus Inc 802 878-2066
2355 Us Route 2 North Hero VT (05474) ***(G-22230)***
Fiberlock Technologies Inc 978 623-9987
150 Dascomb Rd Andover MA (01810) ***(G-7548)***
Fiberon Technologies Inc (PA) 508 616-9500
287 Turnpike Rd Westborough MA (01581) ***(G-16618)***
Fiberoptic Resale Corp 603 496-1258
21 Technology Way Ste 4e5 Nashua NH (03060) ***(G-19157)***
Fiberoptics Technology Inc (PA) 860 928-0443
1 Quasset Rd Pomfret CT (06258) ***(G-3550)***
Fiberoptics Technology Inc 860 928-0443
1 Fiber Rd Pomfret CT (06258) ***(G-3551)***
Fiberspar Linepipe LLC 281 854-2636
800 Purchase St Ste 502 New Bedford MA (02740) ***(G-13385)***
Fiberspar Spoolable Products (PA) 508 291-9000
28 Pattersons Brook Rd West Wareham MA (02576) ***(G-16572)***
Fibertec Inc 508 697-5100
35 Scotland Blvd Bridgewater MA (02324) ***(G-9073)***
Fibertech Networks LLC 978 264-6000
80 Central St Boxborough MA (01719) ***(G-8962)***
Fibre Optic Plus Inc 860 646-3581
585 Nutmeg Rd N South Windsor CT (06074) ***(G-3970)***
Fibredyne, Dover *Also called Pentair Rsdntial Fltration LLC* ***(G-18045)***
Fiddlehead Focus 207 316-2243
90 E Main St 1 Fort Kent ME (04743) ***(G-6059)***
Fidelis EMC 978 655-3390
149 Lancaster Rd North Andover MA (01845) ***(G-13703)***
Fidelux Lighting LLC (HQ) 860 436-5000
100 Great Meadow Rd # 600 Hartford CT (06109) ***(G-1821)***
Field Pendleton 508 829-2470
1951 Main St Jefferson MA (01522) ***(G-11953)***
Field Protection Agency LLC 508 832-0395
38 Silver St Auburn MA (01501) ***(G-7834)***
Field Sytems Division, Shrewsbury *Also called Neles USA Inc* ***(G-15125)***
Fielding Manufacturing, Cranston *Also called Fielding Mfg Zinc Diecasting* ***(G-20227)***
Fielding Manufacturing Inc 401 461-0400
780 Wellington Ave Cranston RI (02910) ***(G-20226)***
Fielding Mfg Zinc Diecasting 401 461-0400
780 Wellington Ave Cranston RI (02910) ***(G-20227)***
Fieldston Clothes Inc (HQ) 508 646-2900
40 County St Fall River MA (02723) ***(G-10700)***
Fiesta Jewelry Corporation 212 564-6847
250 East Ave Pawtucket RI (02860) ***(G-20839)***
Fife, Westport *Also called Flottec International Sls Corp* ***(G-5195)***
Fife Packaging LLC 603 753-2669
77 Merrimack St Penacook NH (03303) ***(G-19465)***
Figulo Corporation 617 269-0807
22 Elkins St Boston MA (02127) ***(G-8543)***
Fil-Tech Inc 617 227-1133
190 Old Colony Ave Ste 1 Boston MA (02127) ***(G-8544)***

Filcorp Industries Inc 802 893-1882
63 Gonyeau Rd B Milton VT (05468) ***(G-22127)***

Filerx.com, Portland *Also called Precision Direct Inc* ***(G-6715)***

Filmx Technologies 860 779-3403
20 Louisa Viens Dr Dayville CT (06241) ***(G-1044)***

Filtech Inc 617 227-1133
6 Pinckney St Boston MA (02114) ***(G-8545)***

Filter Fab Inc 860 749-6381
23b Eleanor Rd Somers CT (06071) ***(G-3917)***

Filter Fabrication, Somers *Also called Filter Fab Inc* ***(G-3917)***

Filter-Kleen Manufacturing Co 978 692-5137
3 Broadway St Westford MA (01886) ***(G-16766)***

Filtered Air Systems Inc 781 491-0508
100 Ashburton Ave Ste 3 Woburn MA (01801) ***(G-17179)***

Filtered By Forest LLC 978 590-3203
115 Nahant St Unit 1 Lynn MA (01902) ***(G-12508)***

Filters Inc 401 722-8999
593 Mineral Spring Ave Pawtucket RI (02860) ***(G-20840)***

Filtersense, Beverly *Also called Impolit Envmtl Ctrl Corp* ***(G-8140)***

Filtration & Separation Div, Haverhill *Also called Parker-Hannifin Corporation* ***(G-11457)***

Filtrex Corp 508 226-7711
150 Bank St Attleboro MA (02703) ***(G-7735)***

Filtrine Manufacturing Co Inc (PA) 603 352-5500
15 Kit St Keene NH (03431) ***(G-18503)***

Fimor North America Inc (HQ) 203 272-3219
50 Grandview Ct Cheshire CT (06410) ***(G-733)***

Final Forge LLC 857 244-0764
246 S Meadow Rd Ste 13 Plymouth MA (02360) ***(G-14557)***

Financial Graphic Services Inc 617 389-0076
1 Rex Dr Braintree MA (02184) ***(G-9007)***

Financial Prtg Solutions LLC 860 886-9931
21a River Rd Preston CT (06365) ***(G-3580)***

Finch Therapeutics Inc 617 229-6499
200 Innerbelt Rd Ste 400 Somerville MA (02143) ***(G-15171)***

Fine Designs Inc 401 886-5000
6855 Post Rd North Kingstown RI (02852) ***(G-20710)***

Fine Edge Tool Company Inc 508 222-7511
13 Maynard St Attleboro MA (02703) ***(G-7736)***

Fine Food Services Inc 860 445-5276
223 Thames St Groton CT (06340) ***(G-1676)***

Fine Line Graphics Inc 401 349-3300
90 Douglas Pike Unit 4 Smithfield RI (02917) ***(G-21225)***

Fine Line Graphics Inc (PA) 401 349-3300
90 Douglas Pike Unit 3 Smithfield RI (02917) ***(G-21226)***

Fine Line Woodworking Inc 978 263-4322
972 Massachusetts Ave Boxboro MA (01719) ***(G-8952)***

Fine Magazine 617 721-7372
9 Fowle St Woburn MA (01801) ***(G-17180)***

Fine Pets LLC 203 833-1517
229 Stanwich Rd Greenwich CT (06830) ***(G-1611)***

Fine Print Booksellers 207 967-9989
28 Dock Sq Kennebunkport ME (04046) ***(G-6244)***

Fine Print New England Inc 860 953-0660
711 N Mountain Rd Newington CT (06111) ***(G-2863)***

Fine Woodcrafters, Littleton *Also called Oak Gallery Inc* ***(G-12314)***

Finelines, Peabody *Also called Ksg Enterprises Inc* ***(G-14349)***

Finesse Solutions Inc 978 255-1296
5 Perry Way Newburyport MA (01950) ***(G-13488)***

Finest Kind 207 499-7176
975 South St Dayton ME (04005) ***(G-5945)***

Finetech 603 627-8989
60 State Route 101a Amherst NH (03031) ***(G-17562)***

Finetone Hearing Instruments 207 893-2922
2 Plaza Dr Windham ME (04062) ***(G-7233)***

Finicky Pet Food Inc 508 991-8448
68 Blackmer St New Bedford MA (02744) ***(G-13386)***

Finish Line Signs 401 377-8454
28 Main St Ashaway RI (02804) ***(G-20034)***

Finishers Technology Corp 860 829-1000
319 Main St East Berlin CT (06023) ***(G-1101)***

Finishield Corp 603 641-2164
5 George Ave Londonderry NH (03053) ***(G-18699)***

Finishing Solutions LLC 860 705-8231
28 Jurach Rd Colchester CT (06415) ***(G-803)***

Finite Industries, Windsor *Also called Scapa Tapes North America LLC* ***(G-5361)***

Finite Smt, Merrimack *Also called Finite Surface Mount Tech LLC* ***(G-19000)***

Finite Surface Mount Tech LLC 603 423-0300
33 Elm St Ste B Merrimack NH (03054) ***(G-19000)***

Finlay EXT Ingredients USA Inc (HQ) 800 288-6272
10 Blackstone Valley Pl Lincoln RI (02865) ***(G-20574)***

Finlay EXT Ingredients USA Inc 401 769-5490
1268 Park East Dr Woonsocket RI (02895) ***(G-21562)***

Finomial Corporation (PA) 917 488-6050
30 Kelley St Cambridge MA (02138) ***(G-9478)***

Finomial Corporation 646 820-7637
101 Arch St Ste 400 Boston MA (02110) ***(G-8546)***

Finyl Vinyl 207 487-2753
71 Crawford Rd Pittsfield ME (04967) ***(G-6590)***

Fiore Artisan Olive Oils 207 801-8549
86 Hammond St Bangor ME (04401) ***(G-5644)***

Fiore Machine Inc 413 543-5767
140 Michon St Indian Orchard MA (01151) ***(G-11886)***

Fire & Iron 203 934-3756
298 Platt Ave West Haven CT (06516) ***(G-5123)***

Fire Defenses New England LLC 978 304-1506
44 Garden St Ste 1 Danvers MA (01923) ***(G-10217)***

Fire Dept, White River Junction *Also called Town of Hartford* ***(G-22643)***

Fire Emergency Maint Co LLC 781 334-3100
29 Stillman Rd Lynnfield MA (01940) ***(G-12548)***

Fire Prevention Services 203 866-6357
13 Winfield St Norwalk CT (06855) ***(G-3152)***

Fire Protection Team LLC 603 641-2550
78 Londonderry Tpke 10 Hooksett NH (03106) ***(G-18349)***

Fire Technology Inc 860 276-2181
122 Spring St Southington CT (06489) ***(G-4050)***

Fire-1 Manufacturing Inc 508 478-8473
70 Millville Rd Mendon MA (01756) ***(G-12993)***

Fireball Heat Treating Co Inc 508 222-2617
34 John Williams St Attleboro MA (02703) ***(G-7737)***

Firebrand Technologies, Newburyport *Also called Quality Solutions Inc* ***(G-13525)***

Firefly Global 781 835-6548
556 Trapelo Rd Belmont MA (02478) ***(G-8074)***

Firehouse Discount Oil LLC (PA) 860 404-1827
17 Depot Pl Ste C Unionville CT (06085) ***(G-4656)***

Firejudge Worldwide Inc 978 604-0009
21 Westland Ter Haverhill MA (01830) ***(G-11434)***

Fireslate 2 Inc 508 273-0047
3065 Cranberry Hwy A24 East Wareham MA (02538) ***(G-10530)***

Fireye Inc (HQ) 603 432-4100
3 Manchester Rd Derry NH (03038) ***(G-17979)***

First Aid Bandage Co Inc 860 443-8499
3 State Pier Rd New London CT (06320) ***(G-2773)***

First Aviation Services Inc (PA) 203 291-3300
15 Riverside Ave Westport CT (06880) ***(G-5192)***

First Card Co Inc 401 434-6140
79 Commercial Way East Providence RI (02914) ***(G-20414)***

First Choice Printing Inc 207 353-8006
60 Capital Ave Lisbon Falls ME (04252) ***(G-6369)***

First Electric Motor Svc Inc 781 491-1100
73 Olympia Ave Woburn MA (01801) ***(G-17181)***

First Electronics Corporation 617 288-2430
71 Von Hillern St Ste 1 Dorchester MA (02125) ***(G-10342)***

First Equity Group Inc (PA) 203 291-7700
15 Riverside Ave Ste 1 Westport CT (06880) ***(G-5193)***

First Fabricators Co Inc 978 356-2901
27 Turnpike Rd Ipswich MA (01938) ***(G-11919)***

First Impression Printing Inc 781 344-8855
178 Tosca Dr Stoughton MA (02072) ***(G-15592)***

First Impressions Embroidery 603 606-1400
1261 Hooksett Rd Ste 1 Hooksett NH (03106) ***(G-18350)***

First Light Technologies Inc 802 287-4195
212 Ideal Way Poultney VT (05764) ***(G-22271)***

First Magazine LLC 617 965-0504
49 Helene Rd Waban MA (02468) ***(G-15936)***

First Place USA, Hamden *Also called Gutkin Enterprises LLC* ***(G-1752)***

First Place Welding Inc 508 886-4762
183 E County Rd Rutland MA (01543) ***(G-14881)***

First Plastics Corp 978 537-0367
22 Jytek Rd Leominster MA (01453) ***(G-12139)***

First Print Inc 781 729-7714
109 Cambridge St Winchester MA (01890) ***(G-17087)***

First Quality Metal Products 781 585-5820
171 Palmer Rd Ste D Plympton MA (02367) ***(G-14591)***

First Sign & Corporate Image 603 627-0003
107 Hollis St Manchester NH (03101) ***(G-18822)***

First Step Print Shop LLC 802 899-2708
22 Park St Underhill VT (05489) ***(G-22547)***

First Wind Holdings Inc 617 960-2888
179 Lincoln St Ste 500 Boston MA (02111) ***(G-8547)***

Fis, Needham Heights *Also called Flexible Information Systems* ***(G-13333)***

Fis Financial Systems LLC 952 935-3300
3 Van De Graaff Dr Ste 2 Burlington MA (01803) ***(G-9274)***

Fis Systems International LLC 617 728-7722
75 Federal St 101 Boston MA (02110) ***(G-8548)***

Fis Systems International LLC 603 898-6185
9 Northstern Blvd Ste 400 Salem NH (03079) ***(G-19733)***

Fisher LLC (PA) 207 701-4200
50 Gordon Dr Rockland ME (04841) ***(G-6793)***

Fisher Controls Intl LLC 860 599-1140
95 Pendleton Hill Rd North Stonington CT (06359) ***(G-3075)***

Fisher Engineering 207 701-4200
50 Gordon Dr Rockland ME (04841) ***(G-6794)***

Fisher Engineering Division, Rockland *Also called Douglas Dynamics LLC* ***(G-6790)***

Fisher Footwear LLC 203 302-2800
777 W Putnam Ave Greenwich CT (06830) ***(G-1612)***

Fisher Logging 413 498-2615
275 S Mountain Rd Northfield MA (01360) ***(G-14063)***

Fisher Mfg Systems Inc (PA) 203 269-3846
20 N Plains Industrial Rd # 12 Wallingford CT (06492) ***(G-4744)***
Fisher Products, Wallingford *Also called Fisher Mfg Systems Inc* ***(G-4744)***
Fisher Sails, Dennis *Also called Olsen Marine* ***(G-10308)***
Fisher Scientific Intl LLC (HQ) 781 622-1000
81 Wyman St Waltham MA (02451) ***(G-16107)***
Fisher Sigerson Morrison LLC 203 302-2800
777 W Putnam Ave Greenwich CT (06830) ***(G-1613)***
Fishermens Daily Catch LLC 401 252-1190
70 Sherman Ave Bristol RI (02809) ***(G-20078)***
Fishing Hot Spots Inc 715 365-5555
9 Townsend W Nashua NH (03063) ***(G-19158)***
Fishman Corporation 508 435-2115
192 South St Hopkinton MA (01748) ***(G-11713)***
Fishman Transducers Inc 978 988-9199
3 Riverside Dr Ste 1 Andover MA (01810) ***(G-7549)***
Fisk Industries Inc 508 695-3661
100 John L Dietsch Blvd A Attleboro Falls MA (02763) ***(G-7813)***
Fit America Inc 309 839-1695
150 Cordaville Rd Ste 100 Southborough MA (01772) ***(G-15357)***
Fit N Stitch Inc 401 294-3492
486 Dry Bridge Rd North Kingstown RI (02852) ***(G-20711)***
Fitbit Inc 857 277-0594
1 Marina Park Dr Ste 1 # 1 Boston MA (02210) ***(G-8549)***
Fitchburg Pattern and Model Co 978 342-0770
21 Myrtle Ave Fitchburg MA (01420) ***(G-10825)***
Fitchburg Welding Co Inc 978 874-2911
4 Depot Rd Westminster MA (01473) ***(G-16804)***
Fitivity Inc 508 308-5822
15 Meadowsweet Rd Shrewsbury MA (01545) ***(G-15112)***
Fitness Elemnet 860 670-2855
267 Chapman St New Britain CT (06051) ***(G-2534)***
Fitness Em LLC 508 278-3209
660 Douglas St Uxbridge MA (01569) ***(G-15916)***
Fitnow Inc 617 699-5585
101 Tremont St Ste 900 Boston MA (02108) ***(G-8550)***
Fitz Machine Inc 781 245-5966
4 Railroad Ave Ste 5 Wakefield MA (01880) ***(G-15952)***
Fitzgerald & Wood Inc 203 488-2553
85 Rogers St Ste 3 Branford CT (06405) ***(G-316)***
Fitzgerald-Norwalk Awning Co 203 847-5858
131 Main St Norwalk CT (06851) ***(G-3153)***
Fitzhugh Electrical Corp 203 453-3171
361 Long Hill Rd Guilford CT (06437) ***(G-1704)***
Fitzpatrick Company, The, Westwood *Also called Idex Mpt Inc* ***(G-16869)***
Fitzwater Engineering Corp 401 647-7600
271 Plainfield Pike North Scituate RI (02857) ***(G-20777)***
Five Star Companies, New Bedford *Also called Five Star Surgical Inc* ***(G-13388)***
Five Star Manufacturing Inc 508 998-1404
163 Samuel Barnet Blvd New Bedford MA (02745) ***(G-13387)***
Five Star Plating LLC 978 655-4081
7a Broadway Lawrence MA (01840) ***(G-12023)***
Five Star Products Inc 203 336-7900
60 Parrott Dr Shelton CT (06484) ***(G-3802)***
Five Star Surgical Inc 508 998-1404
163 Samuel Barnet Blvd New Bedford MA (02745) ***(G-13388)***
Fives N Amercn Combustn Inc 860 739-3466
287 Boston Post Rd East Lyme CT (06333) ***(G-1270)***
Fives N Amercn Combustn Inc 216 271-6000
999 Andrews St Southington CT (06489) ***(G-4051)***
Fizz Time 603 870-0000
11 Industrial Way Bldg C Salem NH (03079) ***(G-19734)***
Fjb America LLC 203 682-2424
8 Wright St Ste 107 Westport CT (06880) ***(G-5194)***
Flabeg Technical Glass US Corp 203 729-5227
451 Church St Naugatuck CT (06770) ***(G-2473)***
Flag & Gift Store Ltd 508 675-6400
79 Pheasant Ridge Rd Seekonk MA (02771) ***(G-15022)***
Flag Hill Distillery LLC 603 659-2949
297 N River Rd Lee NH (03861) ***(G-18643)***
Flag Hill Winery & Vinyrd LLC 603 659-2949
297 N River Rd Lee NH (03861) ***(G-18644)***
Flag-Works Over America LLC 603 225-2530
6 N Main St Concord NH (03301) ***(G-17902)***
Flagg Palmer Precast Inc 508 987-3400
1 Industrial Park Rd W Oxford MA (01540) ***(G-14261)***
Flagpole Software LLC 203 426-5166
19 Scudder Rd Newtown CT (06470) ***(G-2921)***
Flagraphics Inc 617 776-7549
30 Alston St Somerville MA (02143) ***(G-15172)***
Flagship Converters Inc 203 792-0034
205 Shelter Rock Rd Danbury CT (06810) ***(G-920)***
Flagship Press Inc 978 975-3100
150 Flagship Dr North Andover MA (01845) ***(G-13704)***
Flagstone Inc 207 227-5883
235 Griffin Ridge Rd Mapleton ME (04757) ***(G-6411)***
Flame Laminating Corporation (PA) 978 725-9527
2350 Turnpike St Bldg B North Andover MA (01845) ***(G-13705)***
Flametech Steels Inc 978 686-9518
600 Essex St Lawrence MA (01841) ***(G-12024)***

Flanagan Brothers Inc 860 633-3558
25 Mill St Glastonbury CT (06033) ***(G-1551)***
Flanagan Brothers, Inc, Glastonbury *Also called Edac Nd Inc* ***(G-1548)***
Flange Inc 978 343-9200
21 Myrtle Ave Fitchburg MA (01420) ***(G-10826)***
Flange Lock LLC 203 861-9400
57 Old Post Rd No 2 Ste 3 Greenwich CT (06830) ***(G-1614)***
Flash Card Inc 603 625-0803
44 Huse Rd Manchester NH (03103) ***(G-18823)***
Flashbags LLC 802 999-8981
70 S Winooski Ave Burlington VT (05401) ***(G-21782)***
Flat Rock Tile and Stone 603 542-0678
181 Washington St Claremont NH (03743) ***(G-17850)***
Flavor & The Menu, Freeport *Also called Flavor Unlimited Inc* ***(G-6078)***
Flavor Unlimited Inc 207 865-4432
5 Brook Hill Rd Freeport ME (04032) ***(G-6078)***
Flavrz Beverage Corporation 978 879-4567
33 Commercial St Ste 3 Gloucester MA (01930) ***(G-11182)***
Flavrz Organic Beverages LLC 203 716-8082
25 Hamilton Ln Darien CT (06820) ***(G-1026)***
Fleet Management LLC 800 722-6654
89 Phoenix Ave Enfield CT (06082) ***(G-1363)***
Fleetwood Industries Inc 860 747-6750
4 Northwest Dr Plainville CT (06062) ***(G-3488)***
Fleetwood Multi-Media Inc 781 599-2400
20 Wheeler St Ste 202 Lynn MA (01902) ***(G-12509)***
Fleetwood On Site Cnfrnce, Lynn *Also called Fleetwood Multi-Media Inc* ***(G-12509)***
Fleming & Son Corp 617 623-3047
40 White St Somerville MA (02144) ***(G-15173)***
Fleming Industries Inc 413 593-3300
102 1st Ave Chicopee MA (01020) ***(G-10026)***
Fleming Printing, Somerville *Also called Fleming & Son Corp* ***(G-15173)***
Flemish Master Weavers Inc 207 324-6600
96 Gate House Rd Sanford ME (04073) ***(G-6876)***
Fletcher Granite LLC (HQ) 978 692-1312
535 Groton Rd Westford MA (01886) ***(G-16767)***
Fletcher-Terry Company LLC (PA) 860 828-3400
91 Clark Dr East Berlin CT (06023) ***(G-1102)***
Flex O Fold North America Inc 781 631-3190
91 Front St Marblehead MA (01945) ***(G-12682)***
Flex Technology Incorporated 603 883-1500
6 George Ave Londonderry NH (03053) ***(G-18700)***
Flex-O-Graphic Prtg Plate Inc 508 752-8100
33 Arctic St Ste 4 Worcester MA (01604) ***(G-17375)***
Flex-Print-Labels 603 929-3088
10 Merrill Industrial Dr Hampton NH (03842) ***(G-18263)***
Flex-Rest Inc 508 797-4046
7 Brookfield St Worcester MA (01605) ***(G-17376)***
Flexaust Company Inc 978 465-0445
40r Merrimac St Ste 401w Newburyport MA (01950) ***(G-13489)***
Flexaust Inc 978 388-1005
10 Industrial Way Ste 2 Amesbury MA (01913) ***(G-7485)***
Flexcar 617 995-4231
25 1st St Ste 11 Cambridge MA (02141) ***(G-9479)***
Flexcon Company Inc (PA) 508 885-8200
1 Flexcon Industrial Park Spencer MA (01562) ***(G-15429)***
Flexcon Industrial LLC (HQ) 210 798-1900
1 S Spencer Rd Spencer MA (01562) ***(G-15430)***
Flexcon Industries Inc 781 986-2424
300 Pond St Ste 1 Randolph MA (02368) ***(G-14681)***
Flexenergy Inc 603 430-7000
30 Nh Ave Portsmouth NH (03801) ***(G-19563)***
Flexenergy Holdings LLC (PA) 603 430-7000
30 Nh Ave Portsmouth NH (03801) ***(G-19564)***
Flexenergy.com, Portsmouth *Also called Flexenergy Inc* ***(G-19563)***
Flexhead Industries Inc 508 893-9596
56 Lowland St Holliston MA (01746) ***(G-11571)***
Flexi Brace, Revere *Also called JB Sports LLC* ***(G-14769)***
Flexi-Door Corporation 603 679-2286
277 Pleasant St Epping NH (03042) ***(G-18099)***
Flexible Information Systems 781 326-9977
62 Lynn Rd Needham Heights MA (02494) ***(G-13333)***
Flexiinternational Sftwr Inc (PA) 203 925-3040
2 Trap Falls Rd Ste 501 Shelton CT (06484) ***(G-3803)***
Flexion Therapeutics Inc (PA) 781 305-7777
10 Mall Rd Ste 301 Burlington MA (01803) ***(G-9275)***
Flexo Concepts, Plymouth *Also called Blade Tech Systems Inc* ***(G-14545)***
Flexo Label Solutions LLC 860 243-9300
500 Main St Ste 6 Deep River CT (06417) ***(G-1060)***
Flexogrphic Print Slutions LLC 603 570-6339
1 Hardy Rd 306 Bedford NH (03110) ***(G-17641)***
Flexor Energy Company 207 866-3527
99 Bennoch Rd Orono ME (04473) ***(G-6554)***
Flight Enhancements Corp 912 257-0440
47 Oakcrest Rd Oxford CT (06478) ***(G-3401)***
Flight Support Inc 203 562-1415
101 Sackett Point Rd North Haven CT (06473) ***(G-3028)***
Flimp Media 508 435-5220
2 Hayden Rowe St Ste 2 # 2 Hopkinton MA (01748) ***(G-11714)***

ALPHABETIC

Flint Group US LLC...781 763-0600
45 Reservoir Park Dr Rockland MA (02370) ***(G-14803)***
Flintec Inc...978 562-4548
18 Kane Industrial Dr Hudson MA (01749) ***(G-11774)***
Flir Commercial Systems Inc...603 324-7824
9 Townsend W Ste 1 Nashua NH (03063) ***(G-19159)***
Flir Maritime Us Inc...603 324-7900
9 Townsend W Nashua NH (03063) ***(G-19160)***
Flir Surveillance, Inc., North Billerica *Also called Flir Systems Inc* ***(G-13814)***
Flir Systems Inc...603 324-7783
9 Townsend W Ste 1 Nashua NH (03063) ***(G-19161)***
Flir Systems Inc...866 636-4487
9 Townsend W Ste 1 Nashua NH (03063) ***(G-19162)***
Flir Systems Inc...978 901-8000
25 Esquire Rd North Billerica MA (01862) ***(G-13814)***
Flir Systems-Boston Inc (HQ)...978 901-8000
25 Esquire Rd North Billerica MA (01862) ***(G-13815)***
Flir Unmnned Grund Systems Inc (HQ)...978 769-9333
19 Alpha Rd Ste 101 Chelmsford MA (01824) ***(G-9899)***
Flo Chemical Corp...978 827-5101
20 Puffer St Ashburnham MA (01430) ***(G-7644)***
Flo-Matic, Brattleboro *Also called C E Bradley Laboratories* ***(G-21722)***
Floc LLC...617 823-5798
125 Church St Ste 90-136 Pembroke MA (02359) ***(G-14405)***
Flodesign Sonics Inc...413 596-5900
380 Main St Wilbraham MA (01095) ***(G-16936)***
Flojet, Beverly *Also called Flow Control LLC* ***(G-8131)***
Florence Casket Company...413 584-4244
16 Bardwell St Florence MA (01062) ***(G-10866)***
Florence Crushed Stone, Florence *Also called Troy Minerals Inc* ***(G-21992)***
Florian Tools, Southington *Also called American Standard Company* ***(G-4037)***
Flottec International Sls Corp...973 588-4717
3 Meeker Rd Westport CT (06880) ***(G-5195)***
Flour Bakery Cafe, Boston *Also called Cakewalk Bakers LLC* ***(G-8454)***
Flow Chemicals, Ashburnham *Also called Flo Chemical Corp* ***(G-7644)***
Flow Control LLC...978 281-0440
100 Cummings Ctr Beverly MA (01915) ***(G-8131)***
Flow Grinding Corp (PA)...781 933-5300
70 Conn St Woburn MA (01801) ***(G-17182)***
Flow Resources Inc (HQ)...860 666-1200
135 Day St Ste 1 Newington CT (06111) ***(G-2864)***
Flowers Boat Works Inc...207 563-7404
21 Ridge Rd Walpole ME (04573) ***(G-7141)***
Flowserve Corporation...203 877-4252
408 Woodmont Rd Milford CT (06460) ***(G-2290)***
Flowserve US Inc...978 682-5248
280 Merrimack St Lawrence MA (01843) ***(G-12025)***
Flowtron Outdoor Products Div, Malden *Also called Armatron International Inc* ***(G-12559)***
Floyd Baker Metal Fabrication...207 465-9346
263 Belgrade Rd Oakland ME (04963) ***(G-6533)***
Flue Gas Solutions Inc...207 893-1510
19 Commons Ave Windham ME (04062) ***(G-7234)***
Fluent Technologies Inc...781 939-0900
331 Montvale Ave Ste 300 Woburn MA (01801) ***(G-17183)***
Fluid Coating Technology Inc...860 963-2505
48 Industrial Park Rd Putnam CT (06260) ***(G-3612)***
Fluid Controls Division, New Britain *Also called Parker-Hannifin Corporation* ***(G-2561)***
Fluid Dynamics LLC (PA)...860 791-6325
192 Sheldon Rd Manchester CT (06042) ***(G-2006)***
Fluid Eqp Solutions Neng LLC...855 337-6633
7 Walters Way Exeter NH (03833) ***(G-18121)***
Fluid Imaging Technologies Inc...207 289-3200
200 Enterprise Dr Scarborough ME (04074) ***(G-6917)***
Fluid Management Systems Inc...617 393-2396
580 Pleasant St Watertown MA (02472) ***(G-16288)***
Fluidform Inc...978 287-4698
42 Nagog Park Ste 110 Acton MA (01720) ***(G-7356)***
Fluidx, Woburn *Also called Opko Diagnostics LLC* ***(G-17249)***
Fluigent Inc...978 934-5283
600 Suffolk St Ste M2d2 Lowell MA (01854) ***(G-12371)***
Fluke Electronics Corporation...603 537-2680
87 Stiles Rd Ste 206 Salem NH (03079) ***(G-19735)***
Fluke Networks, Salem *Also called Fluke Electronics Corporation* ***(G-19735)***
Fluoropolymer Resources LLC (PA)...860 423-7622
99 Erver Dr Rvrview Sq Ii Riverview East Hartford CT (06108) ***(G-1195)***
Fluted Partition Inc (PA)...203 368-2548
850 Union Ave Bridgeport CT (06607) ***(G-414)***
Fluted Partition Inc...203 334-3500
850 Union Ave Bridgeport CT (06607) ***(G-415)***
Fly Rod & Reel, Rockport *Also called D E Enterprise Inc* ***(G-6818)***
Flying Colors, Boston *Also called Faverco Inc* ***(G-8540)***
FMC, Topsfield *Also called Fairview Machine Company Inc* ***(G-15859)***
FMC Corporation...207 594-3200
341 Park St Rockland ME (04841) ***(G-6795)***
FMI Chemical Inc...860 243-3222
4 Northwood Dr Bloomfield CT (06002) ***(G-219)***
FMI Paint & Chemical Inc...860 218-2210
14 Eastern Park Rd East Hartford CT (06108) ***(G-1196)***
Fmp Products...203 422-0686
100 Melrose Ave Ste 206 Greenwich CT (06830) ***(G-1615)***
Fms New York Services LLC (HQ)...781 699-9000
920 Winter St Waltham MA (02451) ***(G-16108)***
Foam Brewers...802 399-2511
112 Lake St Burlington VT (05401) ***(G-21783)***
Foam Concepts Inc...508 278-7255
44 Rivulet St Uxbridge MA (01569) ***(G-15917)***
Foam Laminates of Vermont, Starksboro *Also called Energy Smart Building Inc* ***(G-22515)***
Foam Plastics New England Inc...203 758-6651
32 Gramar Ave Waterbury CT (06712) ***(G-4874)***
Foam Pro Inc...207 212-9657
6 State St Bangor ME (04401) ***(G-5645)***
Foamaction Sports LLC...508 887-3721
298 Neck Rd Rochester MA (02770) ***(G-14786)***
Foamtech LLC...978 343-4022
1 Nursery Ln Fitchburg MA (01420) ***(G-10827)***
Focal Point Opticians Inc (PA)...617 965-2770
882 Walnut St Newton MA (02459) ***(G-13593)***
Focal Point Technologies...508 830-9716
15 Richards Rd Plymouth MA (02360) ***(G-14558)***
Focus Medical LLC...203 730-8885
23 Francis J Clarke Cir Bethel CT (06801) ***(G-154)***
Focus Now Solutions LLC...203 247-9038
1140 Post Rd Fairfield CT (06824) ***(G-1432)***
Focus Technologies Inc...860 829-8998
600 Four Rod Rd Ste 5 Berlin CT (06037) ***(G-83)***
Focused Resolutions Inc...978 794-7981
40 Arrowwood St Methuen MA (01844) ***(G-13022)***
Fog Pharmaceuticals Inc...617 945-9510
100 Acorn Park Dr Fl 6 Cambridge MA (02140) ***(G-9480)***
Fog Pharmaceuticals Inc...781 929-9187
245 1st St Cambridge MA (02142) ***(G-9481)***
Fogg Flavor Labs LLC...978 808-1732
59 Prospect St West Newbury MA (01985) ***(G-16491)***
Fogg Lumbering Inc...207 732-4087
153 Tannery Rd Lowell ME (04493) ***(G-6385)***
Foilmark Inc (HQ)...978 225-8200
5 Malcolm Hoyt Dr Newburyport MA (01950) ***(G-13490)***
Foilmark Inc...860 243-0343
40 E Newberry Rd Bloomfield CT (06002) ***(G-220)***
Folder-Glr Techl Svs Grp LLC...603 635-7400
30 Pulpit Rock Rd Pelham NH (03076) ***(G-19433)***
Foley Fish, New Bedford *Also called M F Fley Incrprtd-New Bdford* ***(G-13413)***
Foleys Pump Service Inc...203 792-2236
30 Miry Brook Rd Danbury CT (06810) ***(G-921)***
Folio Associates, Hyannis *Also called Gatco Inc* ***(G-11842)***
Follenderwerks Inc...802 362-0911
30 Ayers St Apt 1 Barre VT (05641) ***(G-21615)***
Fonda Fabricating & Welding Co...860 793-0601
50 Milford Street Ext Plainville CT (06062) ***(G-3489)***
Fontaine Logging...802 472-6140
62 Center Rd Hardwick VT (05843) ***(G-22011)***
Fonzy Inc...857 342-3143
190 Milton St Dedham MA (02026) ***(G-10290)***
Food Atmtn - Svc Tchniques Inc (PA)...203 377-4414
905 Honeyspot Rd Stratford CT (06615) ***(G-4412)***
Foot Locker Retail Inc...781 231-0142
1201 Broadway Saugus MA (01906) ***(G-14981)***
Footprint Pwr Acquisitions LLC...978 740-8411
24 Fort Ave Salem MA (01970) ***(G-14912)***
Footsizer LLC...617 337-3537
365 Boston Post Rd # 300 Sudbury MA (01776) ***(G-15657)***
Footsox Inc...800 338-0833
16 Whittemore St Gloucester MA (01930) ***(G-11183)***
Footwear Specialties Inc...207 284-5003
16 Pomerleau St Biddeford ME (04005) ***(G-5734)***
For Astellas Institute (HQ)...508 756-1212
33 Locke Dr Marlborough MA (01752) ***(G-12755)***
Force3 Pro Gear LLC...315 367-2331
45 Banner Dr 1 Milford CT (06460) ***(G-2291)***
Forced Exposure Inc...781 321-0320
60 Lowell St Arlington MA (02476) ***(G-7626)***
Forecast International Inc...203 426-0800
22 Commerce Rd Ste 1 Newtown CT (06470) ***(G-2922)***
Forecaster Publishing Inc...207 781-3661
295 Gannett Dr South Portland ME (04106) ***(G-7027)***
Foredom Electric Co, Bethel *Also called Blackstone Industries LLC* ***(G-133)***
Forensicon, New London *Also called Qdiscovery LLC* ***(G-2777)***
Forensicsoft Inc...401 489-7559
5700 Post Rd Unit 10 East Greenwich RI (02818) ***(G-20367)***
Forest Chester Products Inc...207 794-2303
Rr 116 Lincoln ME (04457) ***(G-6353)***
Forest Economic Advisors LLC...978 496-6336
298 Great Rd Littleton MA (01460) ***(G-12306)***
Forest Manufacturing Corp...603 647-6991
8 Grey Point Ave Auburn NH (03032) ***(G-17609)***
Forest Products Associates, Greenfield *Also called Leon M Fiske Company Inc* ***(G-11268)***
Forest Remodeling...413 222-7953
122 Hampden Rd Somers CT (06071) ***(G-3918)***

Forester Moulding & Lumber 978 840-3100
152 Hamilton St Ste A Leominster MA (01453) *(G-12140)*
Forestville Machine Co Inc 860 747-6000
355 S Washington St Plainville CT (06062) *(G-3490)*
Forge Baking Company Inc 617 764-5365
12 Elder Ter Arlington MA (02474) *(G-7627)*
Forgotten Traditions LLC 603 344-2231
49 Silver Lake Rd Tilton NH (03276) *(G-19905)*
Form Centerless Grinding Inc 508 520-0900
1 Kenwood Cir Franklin MA (02038) *(G-11046)*
Form Factor, Southbury *Also called Micro-Probe Incorporated (G-4031)*
Form Roll Die Corp (PA) 508 755-2010
217 Stafford St Worcester MA (01603) *(G-17377)*
Form Roll Die Corp 508 755-5302
88 Webster Pl Worcester MA (01603) *(G-17378)*
Form-All Plastics Corporation 203 634-1137
104 Gracey Ave Meriden CT (06451) *(G-2093)*
Formatron Ltd 860 676-0227
21 Hyde Rd Farmington CT (06032) *(G-1482)*
Formatt Printing Inc 401 475-6666
1063 Mineral Spring Ave North Providence RI (02904) *(G-20761)*
Formed Fiber Technologies, LLC, Auburn *Also called Conform Gissing Intl LLC (G-5555)*
Formex Inc 401 885-9800
3305 S County Trl East Greenwich RI (02818) *(G-20368)*
Formlabs Inc (PA) 617 932-5227
35 Medford St Ste 201 Somerville MA (02143) *(G-15174)*
Forrati Manufacturing & Tl LLC 860 426-1105
411 Summer St Plantsville CT (06479) *(G-3530)*
Forrest Machine Inc 860 563-1796
236 Christian Ln Berlin CT (06037) *(G-84)*
Forrest P Hicks II 603 586-9819
28 Meadows Rd Jefferson NH (03583) *(G-18483)*
Fort Hill Sign Products Inc 781 321-4320
13 Airport Rd Hopedale MA (01747) *(G-11672)*
Forte Carbon Fiber Products, Ledyard *Also called Forte Rts Inc (G-1941)*
Forte Rts Inc 860 464-5221
14 Lorenz Industrial Pkwy Ledyard CT (06339) *(G-1941)*
Forte Technology Inc 508 297-2363
58 Norfolk Ave Ste 4 South Easton MA (02375) *(G-15277)*
Forterra Pipe & Precast LLC 508 881-2000
400 Main St Ashland MA (01721) *(G-7659)*
Forterra Pipe & Precast LLC 401 782-2600
170 Fiore Industrial Dr Peace Dale RI (02879) *(G-20913)*
Forterra Pipe & Precast LLC 860 564-9000
174 All Hallows Rd Wauregan CT (06387) *(G-5039)*
Fortier Boats Inc 508 673-5253
34 Riverside Ave Somerset MA (02725) *(G-15144)*
Fortifiber Corporation 508 222-3500
55 Starkey Ave Attleboro MA (02703) *(G-7738)*
Fortiming Corporation 508 281-5980
209 Main St Marlborough MA (01752) *(G-12756)*
Fortis LLC 617 600-4178
76 Sutton St Unit 151 Northbridge MA (01534) *(G-14056)*
Fortress Biotech Inc 781 652-4500
95 Sawyer Rd Ste 110 Waltham MA (02453) *(G-16109)*
Fortuna's Italian Market, Sandgate *Also called Fortunas Sausage Co LLC (G-22400)*
Fortunas Sausage Co LLC 802 375-0200
723 Stannard Rd Sandgate VT (05250) *(G-22400)*
Fortune Inc (PA) 207 878-5760
256 Read St Portland ME (04103) *(G-6663)*
Forum Plastics LLC 203 754-0777
105 Progress Ln Waterbury CT (06705) *(G-4875)*
Forward Enterprises Inc 508 882-0265
182 Crawford Rd Oakham MA (01068) *(G-14212)*
Forward Inc 802 585-1098
237 Morse Dr Shelburne VT (05482) *(G-22417)*
Forward Merch LLC 603 742-4377
111 Venture Dr Dover NH (03820) *(G-18022)*
Forward Photonics LLC 617 767-3519
500 W Cummings Park # 1900 Woburn MA (01801) *(G-17184)*
Fosta-Tek Optics Inc (PA) 978 534-6511
320 Hamilton St Ste 1 Leominster MA (01453) *(G-12141)*
Foster Carroll Inc 508 497-0060
2 Chestnut St Hopkinton MA (01748) *(G-11715)*
Foster Corporation (HQ) 860 928-4102
45 Ridge Rd Putnam CT (06260) *(G-3613)*
Foster Delivery Science, Putnam *Also called Foster Corporation (G-3613)*
Foster Delivery Science Inc (HQ) 860 928-4102
36 Ridge Rd Putnam CT (06260) *(G-3614)*
Foster Delivery Science Inc 860 630-4515
45 Ridge Rd Putnam CT (06260) *(G-3615)*
Foster Industries Inc 802 472-6147
75 Cal Foster Dr Wolcott VT (05680) *(G-22730)*
Foster-Miller Inc 781 684-4000
116 Queenstown St Devens MA (01434) *(G-10320)*
Fosters Daily Dmcrat Fstrs Sun 603 431-4888
111 Nh Ave Portsmouth NH (03801) *(G-19565)*
Fosters Promotional Goods 781 631-3824
16 Anderson St Ste 101 Marblehead MA (01945) *(G-12683)*
Foto Factory, Littleton *Also called 27th Exposure LLC (G-18653)*
Fougera Pharmaceuticals Inc 203 265-2086
524 S Cherry St Wallingford CT (06492) *(G-4745)*
Foundation Armor LLC 866 306-0246
472 Amherst St Unit 14 Nashua NH (03063) *(G-19163)*
Foundation Cigar Company LLC 203 738-9377
110 Day Hill Rd Windsor CT (06095) *(G-5334)*
Foundry Div of Edson, Taunton *Also called Edson Corporation (G-15747)*
Foundry Foods Inc 314 982-3204
383 Main Ave Fl 5 Norwalk CT (06851) *(G-3154)*
Fountain Dispensers Co Inc 401 461-8400
35 Greenwich St Providence RI (02907) *(G-21014)*
Fountain Plating Company Inc 413 781-4651
492 Prospect Ave West Springfield MA (01089) *(G-16521)*
Four Color Ink LLC 860 395-5471
2 Business Park Rd Old Saybrook CT (06475) *(G-3335)*
Four Elements Salon & Spa 508 672-3111
875 State Rd Unit 2 Westport MA (02790) *(G-16839)*
Four In One LLC 978 250-0751
12 Alpha Rd Chelmsford MA (01824) *(G-9900)*
Four Lggers Doggie Daycare LLC 978 922-4182
950 Cummings Ctr Ste 101x Beverly MA (01915) *(G-8132)*
Four M Studios, Springfield *Also called Meredith Corporation (G-15488)*
Four Saps Sugar Shack Corp 603 858-5159
10 Fredette Dr Lyndeborough NH (03082) *(G-18758)*
Four Seasons Cooler Eqp LLC 203 263-0705
150 Brushy Hill Rd Woodbury CT (06798) *(G-5488)*
Four Seasons Fence, Portsmouth *Also called Chasco Inc (G-19552)*
Four Seasons Trattoria Inc 508 760-6600
1077 Route 28 South Yarmouth MA (02664) *(G-15329)*
Four Star Manufacturing Co 860 583-1614
400 Riverside Ave Bristol CT (06010) *(G-563)*
Four Twenty Industries LLC 860 818-3334
314 Deming Rd Berlin CT (06037) *(G-85)*
Fournier Steel Fabrication 207 443-6404
341 State Rd West Bath ME (04530) *(G-7169)*
Fourslide Spring Stamping Inc 860 583-1688
87 Cross St Bristol CT (06010) *(G-564)*
Fourth Street Press Inc 978 232-9251
3 Ellis Sq Beverly MA (01915) *(G-8133)*
Fowler Printing and Graphics 781 986-8900
132 York Ave Randolph MA (02368) *(G-14682)*
Fox Brothers Furniture Studio 978 462-7726
39 Liberty St Newburyport MA (01950) *(G-13491)*
Fox Modular Homes Inc 413 243-1950
225 Housatonic St Lee MA (01238) *(G-12092)*
Foxon Company 401 421-2386
235 W Park St Providence RI (02908) *(G-21015)*
Foxon Park Beverages Inc 203 467-7874
103 Foxon Blvd East Haven CT (06513) *(G-1250)*
Foxrock Granite LLC 617 249-8015
100 Newport Ave Quincy MA (02171) *(G-14626)*
Foxx Life Sciences LLC 603 890-3699
6 Delaware Dr Salem NH (03079) *(G-19736)*
Fpr Pinedale LLC 203 542-6000
58 Commerce Rd Stamford CT (06902) *(G-4196)*
Fr Flow Ctrl Vlves US Bdco Inc (PA) 978 744-5690
29 Old Right Rd Ipswich MA (01938) *(G-11920)*
Fractal Antenna Systems Inc 781 290-5308
213 Burlington Rd Ste 105 Bedford MA (01730) *(G-7977)*
Fraen Corporation (PA) 781 205-5300
80 New Crossing Rd Reading MA (01867) *(G-14734)*
Fraen Corporation 781 937-8825
324 New Boston St Woburn MA (01801) *(G-17185)*
Fraen Machining Corporation (PA) 781 205-5400
324 New Boston St Woburn MA (01801) *(G-17186)*
Fraen Mechatronics LLC 781 439-5934
80 New Crossing Rd Reading MA (01867) *(G-14735)*
Frain & Associates Inc 508 644-3424
8 Chester St Assonet MA (02702) *(G-7680)*
Fraivillig Technologies Co 512 784-5698
145 Pinckney St Apt 401 Boston MA (02114) *(G-8551)*
Fram Group Operations LLC 203 830-7800
39 Old Ridgebury Rd Danbury CT (06810) *(G-922)*
Framatone Connectors USA, Bethel *Also called Burndy LLC (G-134)*
Frame Center of Norwood Inc (PA) 781 762-2535
460 Bearses Way Hyannis MA (02601) *(G-11841)*
Frame My Tvcom LLC 978 912-7200
419 River St Haverhill MA (01832) *(G-11435)*
Framer's Gallery, The, Auburn *Also called Henry J Montville (G-7837)*
Framery, The, Nashua *Also called Herbert Mosher (G-19177)*
Frameshift Labs Inc 617 319-1357
129 Newbury St Ste 400 Boston MA (02116) *(G-8552)*
Framingham Engraving Co 508 877-7867
20 Nadine Rd Framingham MA (01701) *(G-10946)*
Framingham Source 508 315-7176
124 Fay Rd Framingham MA (01702) *(G-10947)*
Framingham Tab, Framingham *Also called Gatehouse Media Mass I Inc (G-10948)*
Francer Industries Inc 781 337-2882
44 Wharf St East Weymouth MA (02189) *(G-10542)*

Frank B Struzik Inc....401 766-6880
129 Ballou St Woonsocket RI (02895) **(G-21563)**
Frank E Lashua Inc (PA)....508 552-0023
1 Pullman St Worcester MA (01606) **(G-17379)**
Frank J Newman & Son Inc....401 231-0550
44 Newman Ave Johnston RI (02919) **(G-20511)**
Frank L Reed Inc....413 596-3861
2443 Boston Rd Wilbraham MA (01095) **(G-16937)**
Frank Morrow Company....401 941-3900
129 Baker St Providence RI (02905) **(G-21016)**
Frank Passarella Inc....401 295-4943
375 Earle Dr North Kingstown RI (02852) **(G-20712)**
Frank Printing Co R....203 265-6152
184 Center St Wallingford CT (06492) **(G-4746)**
Frank Roth Co Inc....203 377-2155
1795 Stratford Ave Stratford CT (06615) **(G-4413)**
Frank Shatz & Co....401 739-1822
61 Dewey Ave Ste D Warwick RI (02886) **(G-21364)**
Frank Wiggins (PA)....603 863-3151
501 Sunapee St Guild NH (03754) **(G-18235)**
Frank Wiggins....603 863-1537
79 Bascom Rd Newport NH (03773) **(G-19347)**
Franke Associates Inc....207 743-6654
2 Industry Dr South Paris ME (04281) **(G-7010)**
Franklin Area Survival Center....413 863-9549
96 4th St Turners Falls MA (01376) **(G-15877)**
Franklin Country Fabricators, Greenfield *Also called Franklin County Fabricators* **(G-11261)**
Franklin County Fabricators....413 774-3518
144 Adams Rd Greenfield MA (01301) **(G-11261)**
Franklin Fixtures Inc (PA)....508 291-1475
20 Pattersons Brook Rd # 1 West Wareham MA (02576) **(G-16573)**
Franklin Group....207 778-2075
187 Wilton Rd Farmington ME (04938) **(G-6048)**
Franklin Journal, The, Farmington *Also called Franklin Group* **(G-6048)**
Franklin Paint Company Inc....800 486-0304
259 Cottage St Franklin MA (02038) **(G-11047)**
Franklin Print Shoppe Inc....860 496-9516
48 Main St Torrington CT (06790) **(G-4578)**
Franklin Robotics Inc....617 513-7666
85 Rangeway Rd Ste 3 North Billerica MA (01862) **(G-13816)**
Franklin Sheet Metal Works Inc....508 528-3600
231 Cottage St Franklin MA (02038) **(G-11048)**
Franklin's Printing, Farmington *Also called Nemi Publishing Inc* **(G-6052)**
Fraqtir, West Haven *Also called Light Fantastic Realty Inc* **(G-5131)**
Frasal Tool Co Inc....860 666-3524
14 Foster St Newington CT (06111) **(G-2865)**
Fred C Weld Inc....603 675-6147
102 Root Hill Rd Cornish NH (03745) **(G-17960)**
Fred C Weld Logging, Cornish *Also called Fred C Weld Inc* **(G-17960)**
Fred F Waltz Co Inc....401 769-4900
97 Industrial Dr North Smithfield RI (02896) **(G-20786)**
Fred Ricci Tool Co Inc....401 464-9911
165 Dyerville Ave Unit 2 Johnston RI (02919) **(G-20512)**
Fred Wieninger & Son, Milbridge *Also called Frederick Wieninger Monuments* **(G-6432)**
Fredenberg-Nok Seals Division, Ashland *Also called Freudenberg-Nok General Partnr* **(G-17599)**
Frederick Purdue Company Inc (PA)....203 588-8000
201 Tresser Blvd Stamford CT (06901) **(G-4197)**
Frederick Wieninger Monuments....207 546-2356
178 Main St Milbridge ME (04658) **(G-6432)**
Fredericks Jf Aero LLC....860 677-2646
25 Spring Ln Farmington CT (06032) **(G-1483)**
Fredericks Pastries (PA)....603 882-7725
109 State Route 101a # 4 Amherst NH (03031) **(G-17563)**
Free Aire, Warren *Also called R H Travers Company* **(G-22578)**
Free Flow Power Corporation....978 283-2822
239 Causeway St Ste 300 Boston MA (02114) **(G-8553)**
Free Press....413 585-1533
40 Main St Ste 301 Florence MA (01062) **(G-10867)**
Free Press Inc....207 594-4408
8 N Main St Ste 101 Rockland ME (04841) **(G-6796)**
Free Times, West Warwick *Also called Kent County Daily Times* **(G-21498)**
Free-Flow Packaging Intl Inc....508 832-5369
4 Saint Mark St Auburn MA (01501) **(G-7835)**
Freeaire Refrigeration, Buzzards Bay *Also called Mv3 LLC* **(G-9361)**
Freebird Semiconductor Corp....617 955-7152
17 Parkridge Rd Ste 5e Haverhill MA (01835) **(G-11436)**
Freeda S Foods LLC....781 662-6474
3 Citation Ave Stoneham MA (02180) **(G-15564)**
Freedom Digital Printing LLC....508 881-6940
200 Butterfield Dr Ste A2 Ashland MA (01721) **(G-7660)**
Freedom Press....860 599-5390
30 Sunrise Ave Pawcatuck CT (06379) **(G-3435)**
Freedom Technologies LLC....860 633-0452
80 Timrod Trl Glastonbury CT (06033) **(G-1552)**
Freeman Bedford....617 399-4000
75 Arlington St Ste 8000 Boston MA (02116) **(G-8554)**
Freeport Manufacturing Company....207 865-9340
89 Wardtown Rd Freeport ME (04032) **(G-6079)**
Freestyle Systems LLC....508 845-4911
238 Cherry St Ste 1 Shrewsbury MA (01545) **(G-15113)**
Freethink Technologies Inc....860 237-5800
35 Ne Industrial Rd # 201 Branford CT (06405) **(G-317)**
Freezer Hill Mulch Company LLC....203 758-3725
845 Carrington Rd Bethany CT (06524) **(G-121)**
Freihofer Baking Co....207 947-2387
1172 Hammond St Bangor ME (04401) **(G-5646)**
Freihofer Charles Baking Co....203 729-4545
1041 New Haven Rd Naugatuck CT (06770) **(G-2474)**
Freihofer's Bakery Outlet, Hooksett *Also called Bimbo Bakeries Usa Inc* **(G-18343)**
Freihofer's Bakery Outlet, Wilbraham *Also called Bimbo Bakeries Usa Inc* **(G-16933)**
Frelonic, Saco *Also called Der-Tex Corporation* **(G-6846)**
FREMONT ENGINEERING, Fremont *Also called Fremont Machine & Tool Co Inc* **(G-18176)**
Fremont Machine & Tool Co Inc....603 895-9445
810 Main St Fremont NH (03044) **(G-18176)**
French River Mtls Thompson LLC....860 450-9574
307 Reardon Rd North Grosvenordale CT (06255) **(G-2994)**
French Webb & Co Inc....207 338-6706
21 Front St Belfast ME (04915) **(G-5689)**
Frequency Therapeutics Inc (PA)....866 389-1970
19 Presidential Way Fl 2 Woburn MA (01801) **(G-17187)**
Frequency Therapeutics Inc....978 436-0704
400 Farmington Ave Farmington CT (06032) **(G-1484)**
Frescobene Foods LLC....203 610-4688
185 Red Oak Rd Fairfield CT (06824) **(G-1433)**
Fresenius Kabi Compounding LLC....224 358-1150
20 Dan Rd Canton MA (02021) **(G-9733)**
Fresenius Med Care Hldings Inc (HQ)....781 699-9000
920 Winter St Waltham MA (02451) **(G-16110)**
Fresenius Med Care Rnal Thrpie....781 699-9000
920 Winter St Waltham MA (02451) **(G-16111)**
Fresenius Med Care Vntures LLC (HQ)....781 699-9000
920 Winter St Waltham MA (02451) **(G-16112)**
Fresenius Med Care W Wllow LLC....781 699-9000
920 Winter St Waltham MA (02451) **(G-16113)**
Fresenius Med Svcs Group LLC....781 699-9000
920 Winter St Ste 3142 Waltham MA (02451) **(G-16114)**
Fresenius Medical Care N Amer, Waltham *Also called Fresenius Med Care Hldings Inc* **(G-16110)**
Fresenius Medical Care North (HQ)....781 699-9000
920 Winter St Ste A Waltham MA (02451) **(G-16115)**
Fresenius Usa Inc....508 460-1150
360 Cedar Hill St Marlborough MA (01752) **(G-12757)**
Fresenius USA Marketing Inc (HQ)....781 699-9000
920 Winter St Waltham MA (02451) **(G-16116)**
Fresh Interiors, West Dennis *Also called Element LLC* **(G-16475)**
Freshiana LLC....800 301-8071
375 Greenwich Ave Apt 6 Greenwich CT (06830) **(G-1616)**
Freudenberg Medical LLC....978 281-2023
92 Blackburn Ctr Gloucester MA (01930) **(G-11184)**
Freudenberg Nok, Gloucester *Also called Freudenberg Medical LLC* **(G-11184)**
Freudenberg-Nok General Partnr....603 286-1600
19 Axle Dr Northfield NH (03276) **(G-19401)**
Freudenberg-Nok General Partnr....603 286-1600
6 Axle Dr Northfield NH (03276) **(G-19402)**
Freudenberg-Nok General Partnr....603 934-7800
450 Pleasant St Bristol NH (03222) **(G-17763)**
Freudenberg-Nok General Partnr....603 744-0371
450 Pleasant St Bristol NH (03222) **(G-17764)**
Freudenberg-Nok General Partnr....603 968-7187
125 Main St Ashland NH (03217) **(G-17599)**
Frevvo Inc....203 208-3117
500 E Main St Ste 330 Branford CT (06405) **(G-318)**
Frg Publications....413 734-3411
380 Union St Ste 100 West Springfield MA (01089) **(G-16522)**
Fri Resins Holding Company....401 946-5564
21 Starline Way Cranston RI (02921) **(G-20228)**
Friction Force, Prospect *Also called Red Barn Innovations* **(G-3595)**
Friday Engineering Inc....781 932-8686
17 Everberg Rd Woburn MA (01801) **(G-17188)**
Friend Box Company Inc....978 774-0240
90 High St Danvers MA (01923) **(G-10218)**
Friends Foundry Inc....401 769-0160
416 Pond St Woonsocket RI (02895) **(G-21564)**
Friends Historic Bristol Inc....401 451-2735
495 Hope St Unit 8 Bristol RI (02809) **(G-20079)**
Frigon, Dennis Logging, Caratunk *Also called Dennis Frigon* **(G-5881)**
Fringe Factory....508 992-7563
119 Coggeshall St New Bedford MA (02746) **(G-13389)**
Frito-Lay North America Inc....978 657-8344
337 Ballardvale St Wilmington MA (01887) **(G-17002)**
Frito-Lay North America Inc....860 412-1000
1886 Upper Maple St Dayville CT (06241) **(G-1045)**
Frito-Lay North America Inc....781 348-1500
100 Commerce Dr Braintree MA (02184) **(G-9008)**
Fritz Glass....508 394-0441
36 Upper County Rd Dennis Port MA (02639) **(G-10313)**

Fronek Anchor Darling Entp....603 528-1931
86 Doris Ray Ct Laconia NH (03246) *(G-18564)*
Front Door Records, Aquinnah *Also called Hummingbird Productions* *(G-7620)*
Front Porch Brewing....203 679-1096
226 N Plins Ind Rd Unit 4 Wallingford CT (06492) *(G-4747)*
Front Run Organx Inc....978 356-7133
17 Hayward St Ste 3 Ipswich MA (01938) *(G-11921)*
Frontier Design Group LLC....603 448-6283
31 Old Etna Rd Ste N5 Lebanon NH (03766) *(G-18622)*
Frontier Forge Inc....207 265-2151
37 Depot St Kingfield ME (04947) *(G-6253)*
Frontier Manufacturing Inc....401 722-0852
245 Esten Ave Pawtucket RI (02860) *(G-20841)*
Frontier Vision Tech Inc....860 953-0240
2080 Silas Deane Hwy # 203 Rocky Hill CT (06067) *(G-3709)*
Frontier Welding & Fabrication....401 769-0271
63 Transit St Woonsocket RI (02895) *(G-21565)*
Frost Beer Works LLC....949 945-4064
171 Commerce St Hinesburg VT (05461) *(G-22024)*
Frost Cedar Products Inc....207 566-5912
Fahi Pond Rd North Anson ME (04958) *(G-6501)*
Frostbite Cupcakes....508 801-6706
230 Chestnut Oak Rd Chepachet RI (02814) *(G-20134)*
Frozen Batters Inc....508 683-1414
351 Willow St North Andover MA (01845) *(G-13706)*
Frozen Cups LLC....978 918-1872
265 Merrimack St Ste 6 Lawrence MA (01843) *(G-12026)*
Frozen Desserts, Winchester *Also called Philip RS Sorbets* *(G-17095)*
Frueii....401 499-5887
68 Dorrance St 177 Providence RI (02903) *(G-21017)*
Frugal Printer Inc....603 894-6333
47a Northwestern Dr Salem NH (03079) *(G-19737)*
Fruit & Nut House, Warwick *Also called Lady Ann Candies* *(G-21384)*
Fruit Basket World Division....617 389-8989
210 Beacham St Everett MA (02149) *(G-10611)*
Fruitaceuticals, Sagamore *Also called Naturex-Dbs LLC* *(G-14884)*
Fruitbud Juice LLC....203 790-8200
131 West St Danbury CT (06810) *(G-923)*
Fruta Juice Bar LLC....203 690-9168
295 Fairfield Ave Bridgeport CT (06604) *(G-416)*
Fry Company J M....781 575-1520
480 Neponset St Ste 11b Canton MA (02021) *(G-9734)*
Frye's Measure Mill, Wilton *Also called E B Frye & Son Inc* *(G-19979)*
Fryer Corporation....203 888-9944
43 Old State Road 67 Oxford CT (06478) *(G-3402)*
Fsb Inc....203 404-4700
24 New Park Dr Berlin CT (06037) *(G-86)*
Fsb North America, Berlin *Also called Fsb Inc* *(G-86)*
Fsm Plasticoid Mfg Inc....860 623-1361
32 North Rd East Windsor CT (06088) *(G-1284)*
FSNB Enterprises Inc....203 254-1947
12 Woodacre Ln Monroe CT (06468) *(G-2403)*
FT Smith Trckg & Excvtg Inc....508 867-0400
53 Brooks Pond Rd North Brookfield MA (01535) *(G-13880)*
Ftc Inc (PA)....207 354-2545
570 Cushing Rd Friendship ME (04547) *(G-6093)*
FTC Enterprise Inc....508 378-2799
170 W Union St East Bridgewater MA (02333) *(G-10413)*
Ftircom LLC....603 886-5555
304 Unity Rd Benton ME (04901) *(G-5705)*
Fuccillo Ready Mix Inc....508 540-2821
548 Thomas B Landers Rd East Falmouth MA (02536) *(G-10444)*
Fuchs Lubricants Co....203 469-2336
281 Silver Sands Rd East Haven CT (06512) *(G-1251)*
Fuchs Northeast Division, East Haven *Also called Fuchs Lubricants Co* *(G-1251)*
Fudge Factory Inc....888 669-7425
4367 Main St Manchester Center VT (05255) *(G-22085)*
Fuel America....617 782-0999
152 Chestnut Hill Ave Brighton MA (02135) *(G-9099)*
Fuel Cell Manufacturing, Torrington *Also called Fuelcell Energy Inc* *(G-4579)*
Fuel Co....401 467-8773
9 Hylestead St Providence RI (02905) *(G-21018)*
Fuel First....203 735-5097
575 Main St Ansonia CT (06401) *(G-16)*
Fuel First Elm Inc....413 732-5732
173 Elm St West Springfield MA (01089) *(G-16523)*
Fuel For Fire Inc....508 975-4573
13 Tech Cir Natick MA (01760) *(G-13256)*
Fuel For Humanity Inc....203 255-5913
11 Hedley Farms Rd Westport CT (06880) *(G-5196)*
Fuel Gym LLC....781 315-8001
385 Main St Wakefield MA (01880) *(G-15953)*
Fuel Lab....860 677-4987
20 Burnt Hill Rd Farmington CT (06032) *(G-1485)*
Fuel Magazine....413 247-5579
38 Elm St Apt 7 Hatfield MA (01038) *(G-11400)*
Fuel On Line Corp....888 475-2552
1127 North Ave Ste 27169 Burlington VT (05408) *(G-21784)*
Fuel Source Inc....781 469-8449
960 Providence Hwy Norwood MA (02062) *(G-14153)*
Fuel Training Studio LLC....617 694-5489
75 Merrimac St Newburyport MA (01950) *(G-13492)*
Fuelcell Energy Inc....860 496-1111
539 Technology Park Dr Torrington CT (06790) *(G-4579)*
Fueling Services LLC....401 764-0711
141 Shun Pike Johnston RI (02919) *(G-20513)*
Fuji Clean Usa LLC....207 406-2927
41 Greenwood Rd Ste 2 Brunswick ME (04011) *(G-5836)*
Fuji Film Microdisk USA, Bedford *Also called Fujifilm North America Corp* *(G-7978)*
Fuji Mats LLC....205 419-5080
12 Cameron Way Methuen MA (01844) *(G-13023)*
Fujifilm Dimatix Inc....603 443-5300
109 Etna Rd Lebanon NH (03766) *(G-18623)*
Fujifilm Microdisks U.S.a, Bedford *Also called Fujifilm Rcrding Media USA Inc* *(G-7979)*
Fujifilm North America Corp....781 271-4400
45 Crosby Dr Bedford MA (01730) *(G-7978)*
Fujifilm Rcrding Media USA Inc (HQ)....781 271-4400
45 Crosby Dr Bedford MA (01730) *(G-7979)*
Fulcrum Design....802 442-6441
107 Rutter Rd Bennington VT (05201) *(G-21670)*
Fulcrum Promotions & Printing....203 909-6362
75 Wheeler Ave Apt 102 Bridgeport CT (06606) *(G-417)*
Fulcrum Therapeutics Inc....617 651-8851
26 Landsdowne St Ste 525 Cambridge MA (02139) *(G-9482)*
Fulcrum Thrptics Scrities Corp....617 651-8851
26 Landsdowne St Ste 525 Cambridge MA (02139) *(G-9483)*
Fulcrum9 Systems Inc....978 549-3868
5 Jay Ln Acton MA (01720) *(G-7357)*
Fulflex, Brattleboro *Also called Garflex Inc* *(G-21728)*
Fulford Findings, Providence *Also called Salvadore Tool & Findings Inc* *(G-21119)*
Fulford Manufacturing Company (PA)....401 431-2000
65 Tripps Ln Riverside RI (02915) *(G-21168)*
Fulghum Fibres Inc....207 427-6560
224 Main St Baileyville ME (04694) *(G-5625)*
Full Circle Padding Inc....508 285-2500
253 Mansfield Ave Unit 5 Norton MA (02766) *(G-14077)*
Full Court Press....207 464-0002
855 Main St Ste 2 Westbrook ME (04092) *(G-7189)*
Full Line Graphics Inc....508 238-1914
68 Cheryl Cir Taunton MA (02780) *(G-15750)*
Full Sun Company....802 989-7011
616 Exchange St Unit 2 Middlebury VT (05753) *(G-22111)*
Fuller Allan Analytical Instrs, Benton *Also called Allan Fuller* *(G-5703)*
Fuller Box Co Inc (PA)....508 695-2525
150 Chestnut St North Attleboro MA (02760) *(G-13756)*
Fuller Box Co Inc....401 725-4300
1152 High St Central Falls RI (02863) *(G-20113)*
Fuller Machine Co Inc....603 835-6559
5 Gilsum Mine Rd Alstead NH (03602) *(G-17542)*
Fuller Packaging, Central Falls *Also called Fuller Box Co Inc* *(G-20113)*
Fuller Sand & Gravel Inc....802 293-5700
9 N Main St Danby VT (05739) *(G-21893)*
Fulling Mill Fly Fishing LLC....603 542-5480
329 River Rd Claremont NH (03743) *(G-17851)*
Functional Assessment Tech Inc....978 663-2800
76 Treble Cove Rd Ste 3 North Billerica MA (01862) *(G-13817)*
Functional Coatings LLC....978 462-0746
13 Malcolm Hoyt Dr Newburyport MA (01950) *(G-13493)*
Fundtech Corporation....781 993-9100
2400 District Ave Ste 150 Burlington MA (01803) *(G-9276)*
Funkhouser Industrial Products....860 653-1972
10 Hazelwood Rd Ste 3b East Granby CT (06026) *(G-1127)*
Furbush Roberts Prtg Co Inc....207 945-9409
435 Odlin Rd Bangor ME (04401) *(G-5647)*
Furlongs Cottage Candies....781 762-4124
1355 Bston Prvidence Tpke Norwood MA (02062) *(G-14154)*
Furnace Source LLC....860 582-4201
99 Agney Ave Terryville CT (06786) *(G-4479)*
Furnished Quarters LLC....212 367-9400
303 3rd St Cambridge MA (02142) *(G-9404)*
Furniture Design Services Inc....978 531-3250
119 Foster St Bldg 13 Peabody MA (01960) *(G-14335)*
Furs By Prezioso Ltd....203 230-2930
2969 Whitney Ave Ste 201 Hamden CT (06518) *(G-1750)*
Fused Fiberoptics LLC....508 765-1652
79 Golf St Southbridge MA (01550) *(G-15383)*
Fuser Technologies Corp....603 886-5186
472 Amherst St Unit 22 Nashua NH (03063) *(G-19164)*
Fusion Optix Inc....781 995-0805
17 Wheeling Ave Woburn MA (01801) *(G-17189)*
Future Foam Inc....508 339-0354
47 Maple St Mansfield MA (02048) *(G-12633)*
Future Graphics, Taunton *Also called Michael M Almeida* *(G-15765)*
Future Manufacturing Inc....860 584-0685
75 Center St Bristol CT (06010) *(G-565)*
Futureguard Building Pdts Inc (PA)....800 858-5818
101 Merrow Rd Auburn ME (04210) *(G-5565)*

ALPHABETIC

Fv Misty Blue LLC 609 884-3000
16 Broadcommon Rd Bristol RI (02809) **(G-20080)**
Fwm Inc 603 578-3366
11 Friars Dr Hudson NH (03051) **(G-18391)**
Fx Group 508 987-1366
2 Hawksley Rd Unit B Oxford MA (01540) **(G-14262)**
Fx Models LLC 860 589-5279
111 Seymour Rd Terryville CT (06786) **(G-4480)**
Fyc Apparel Group LLC 203 466-6525
158 Commerce St East Haven CT (06512) **(G-1252)**
Fyc Apparel Group LLC (PA) 203 481-2420
30 Thompson Rd Branford CT (06405) **(G-319)**
G & A Machine Inc 603 894-6965
168 Lawrence Rd Salem NH (03079) **(G-19738)**
G & A Plating & Polishing Co, Cranston *Also called Jrb Associates Inc* **(G-20247)**
G & A Plating & Polishing Co 401 351-8693
94 Silver Spring St North Providence RI (02904) **(G-20762)**
G & G Products LLC 207 985-9100
70 Twine Mill Rd Ste 1 Kennebunk ME (04043) **(G-6234)**
G & G Silk Screening 508 830-1075
187 Court St Plymouth MA (02360) **(G-14559)**
G & G Tool & Die Corp 603 625-9744
36 Cote Ave Ste 3 Goffstown NH (03045) **(G-18201)**
G & H Manufacturing Inc 413 562-2035
455 North Rd Westfield MA (01085) **(G-16684)**
G & L Tool Corp 413 786-2535
952 Suffield St Agawam MA (01001) **(G-7429)**
G & M Tool Company 203 888-9354
45 Highland Rd Seymour CT (06478) **(G-3751)**
G & R Enterprises Incorporated 860 549-6120
101 Kinsley St Hartford CT (06103) **(G-1822)**
G & W Foundry Corp 508 581-8719
50 Howe Ave Ste G Millbury MA (01527) **(G-13164)**
G A Industries 860 261-5484
630 Emmett St Unit 1 Bristol CT (06010) **(G-566)**
G and JW Elding Inc 774 565-0223
468 Wren St East Taunton MA (02718) **(G-10513)**
G and M Welding 781 480-4247
59 Waite St Malden MA (02148) **(G-12573)**
G and W Precision 413 397-3361
226 Greenfield Rd South Deerfield MA (01373) **(G-15249)**
G and W Precision Inc 413 665-0983
199 Long Plain Rd C Whately MA (01093) **(G-16905)**
G B Enterprises 413 210-4658
82 Spring St Amherst MA (01002) **(G-7515)**
G C Management Corp (PA) 207 244-5363
78 Seal Cove Rd Southwest Harbor ME (04679) **(G-7047)**
G E C, Gloucester *Also called Gloucester Engineering Co Inc* **(G-11186)**
G F Grinding Tool Mfg Co Inc 203 757-6244
649 Captain Neville Dr Waterbury CT (06705) **(G-4876)**
G F L Industries 978 728-4800
29 June St Leominster MA (01453) **(G-12142)**
G Finkenbeiner Inc 781 899-3138
33 Rumford Ave Waltham MA (02453) **(G-16117)**
G H Allen Associates Inc 978 772-4010
179 W Main St Ayer MA (01432) **(G-7920)**
G H Bent Company 617 322-9287
7 Pleasant St Milton MA (02186) **(G-13192)**
G J Logging 207 764-3826
1561 State Rd Mapleton ME (04757) **(G-6412)**
G K Services, Hartford *Also called G&K Services LLC* **(G-1823)**
G M Allen & Son Inc 207 469-7060
267 Front Ridge Rd Orland ME (04472) **(G-6549)**
G M F Woodworking LLC 203 788-8979
22 Sunset Hill Ave Norwalk CT (06851) **(G-3155)**
G M I, Holyoke *Also called Gregory Manufacturing Inc* **(G-11628)**
G M L of NH Inc 603 237-5231
104 Titus Hill Rd Colebrook NH (03576) **(G-17868)**
G M T Manufacturing Co Inc 860 628-6757
220 West St Plantsville CT (06479) **(G-3531)**
G P 2 Technologies Inc 603 226-0336
157 River Rd Unit 18 Bow NH (03304) **(G-17714)**
G P Tool Co Inc 203 744-0310
59 James St Danbury CT (06810) **(G-924)**
G Pro Industrial Services 207 766-1671
5 Drapeau St Biddeford ME (04005) **(G-5735)**
G R Logging Inc 207 868-2692
107 Jefferson St Van Buren ME (04785) **(G-7120)**
G S Davidson Co Inc 617 389-4000
55 Concord St North Reading MA (01864) **(G-13982)**
G S P Coatings Inc 802 257-5858
101 John Seitz Dr Brattleboro VT (05301) **(G-21726)**
G S Precision Inc (PA) 802 257-5200
101 John Seitz Dr Brattleboro VT (05301) **(G-21727)**
G S S, Watertown *Also called Global Steering Systems LLC* **(G-5011)**
G Scatchard Lamps, Westford *Also called G Scatchard Ltd* **(G-22628)**
G Scatchard Ltd 802 899-2181
958 Vt Route 128 15 Westford VT (05494) **(G-22628)**
G Schoepferinc 203 250-7794
460 Cook Hill Rd Cheshire CT (06410) **(G-734)**
G T C Falcon Inc 508 746-0200
130 Industrial Park Rd Plymouth MA (02360) **(G-14560)**
G T R Finishing Corporation 508 588-3240
1 Jonathan Dr Brockton MA (02301) **(G-9147)**
G T R Manufacturing Corp 508 588-3240
1 Jonathan Dr Brockton MA (02301) **(G-9148)**
G Tanury Plating Co Inc 401 232-2330
100 Railroad Ave Johnston RI (02919) **(G-20514)**
G Thomas and Sons Inc 860 935-5174
573 Fabyan Rd North Grosvenordale CT (06255) **(G-2995)**
G V S Jewelers, Belmont *Also called Design Jewelry* **(G-8072)**
G W Lumber & Millwork Inc (PA) 802 860-7370
1860 Williston Rd Ste 3 Williston VT (05495) **(G-22666)**
G W Plastics Inc 802 234-9941
239 Pleasant St Bethel VT (05032) **(G-21694)**
G W Plastics Inc (PA) 802 234-9941
239 Pleasant St Bethel VT (05032) **(G-21695)**
G W Plastics Inc 802 763-2194
272 Waterman Rd South Royalton VT (05068) **(G-22492)**
G W Plastics Inc 802 233-0319
101 Commerce Park Sharon VT (05065) **(G-22408)**
G Woodcraft 203 846-4168
11 Ruby St Norwalk CT (06850) **(G-3156)**
G&E Steel Fabricators Inc 978 741-0391
4 Florence St Unit 5 Salem MA (01970) **(G-14913)**
G&F Medical Inc 978 560-2622
709 Main St Fiskdale MA (01518) **(G-10806)**
G&F Precision Molding Inc (PA) 508 347-9132
709 Main St Fiskdale MA (01518) **(G-10807)**
G&K Services LLC 860 856-4400
96 Murphy Rd Hartford CT (06114) **(G-1823)**
G&R Industries Inc 603 626-3071
4 Cote Ave Ste 9 Goffstown NH (03045) **(G-18202)**
G&S Logging 603 237-4929
12 Lombard St Colebrook NH (03576) **(G-17869)**
G.H. Grimm Company, Swanton *Also called Leader Evaporator Co Inc* **(G-22531)**
G3 Incorporated (PA) 978 805-5001
71 Willie St Lowell MA (01854) **(G-12372)**
G360link 978 266-1500
85 Swanson Rd Ste 110 Boxborough MA (01719) **(G-8963)**
G4s Technology Software 781 457-0700
1 Executive Dr Chelmsford MA (01824) **(G-9901)**
G5 Scientific LLC 781 272-7877
10 Fred St Burlington MA (01803) **(G-9277)**
GA Gear, Portland *Also called Blue Sky Inc* **(G-6625)**
GA Rel Manufacturing Company 401 331-5455
564 Manton Ave Providence RI (02909) **(G-21019)**
Gabcon Welding & Cnstr Co 508 822-2220
15 Hamilton St Taunton MA (02780) **(G-15751)**
Gac Chemical, Searsport *Also called General Alum New England Corp* **(G-6952)**
Gac Chemical Corporation (PA) 207 548-2525
34 Kidder Point Rd Searsport ME (04974) **(G-6951)**
Gac Inc 860 633-1768
160 Oak St Ste 412 Glastonbury CT (06033) **(G-1553)**
Gaffco Ballistics LLC 802 824-9899
114 Horton Rd South Londonderry VT (05155) **(G-22486)**
Gagne & Son Con Blocks Inc 207 495-3313
270 Riverside Dr Auburn ME (04210) **(G-5566)**
Gagne & Sons Logging Co LLC 603 449-2255
146 Ferry Rd Dummer NH (03588) **(G-18070)**
Gaia Chemical Corporation 860 355-2730
23 George Washington Plz Gaylordsville CT (06755) **(G-1531)**
Gail Wilson Designs 603 835-6551
420 Grout Hill Rd South Acworth NH (03607) **(G-19852)**
Gaines Trucking Inc 401 862-2993
35 Roosters Way Middletown RI (02842) **(G-20619)**
Galasso Materials LLC 860 527-1825
60 S Main St East Granby CT (06026) **(G-1128)**
Galaxie Labs Inc 781 272-3750
18 A St Burlington MA (01803) **(G-9278)**
Galaxie Salsa Co 207 939-3392
62 Webster Rd Buxton ME (04093) **(G-5856)**
Galaxy Fuel LLC 203 878-8173
180 New Haven Ave Milford CT (06460) **(G-2292)**
Galaxy Software Inc 617 773-7790
200 Falls Blvd Unit B301 Quincy MA (02169) **(G-14627)**
Galilean Seafood Inc 401 253-3030
16 Broadcommon Rd Bristol RI (02809) **(G-20081)**
Galileo Press, Inc., Quincy *Also called Rheinwerk Publishing Inc* **(G-14654)**
Gallant Machine Works Inc 508 799-2919
6 Ek Ct Shrewsbury MA (01545) **(G-15114)**
Galleria Stone 603 424-2884
714 Daniel Webster Hwy Merrimack NH (03054) **(G-19001)**
Gallery Leather Co Inc 207 667-9474
27 Industrial Way Trenton ME (04605) **(G-7098)**
Gallivan Company Inc 508 543-5233
71 Elm St Ste 9 Foxboro MA (02035) **(G-10883)**
Galvanic Applied Sciences 978 848-2701
101 Billerica Ave 5-104 North Billerica MA (01862) **(G-13818)**

Galvion Ballistics Ltd.......802 334-2774
30 Industrial Dr Ste 10 Newport VT (05855) *(G-22198)*
Galvion Ballistics Ltd.......802 334-2774
30 Industrial Dr Ste 100 Newport VT (05855) *(G-22199)*
Galvion Ballistics Ltd (PA).......802 879-7002
7 Corporate Dr Essex Junction VT (05452) *(G-21940)*
Galvion Ltd (HQ).......514 739-4444
200 International Dr # 250 Portsmouth NH (03801) *(G-19566)*
Gametheory Inc.......802 779-2322
266 Main St Burlington VT (05401) *(G-21785)*
Gamewright, Newton *Also called Ceaco Inc* *(G-13575)*
Gamit Signs, Stoneham *Also called Mark Todisco* *(G-15567)*
Gammelgarden Creamery.......802 823-5757
431 Quarry Hill Rd Pownal VT (05261) *(G-22281)*
Gammon Milam.......207 364-2889
286 Andover Rd Rumford ME (04276) *(G-6834)*
Gamut Publishing.......860 296-6128
563 Franklin Ave Hartford CT (06114) *(G-1824)*
Gandin Brothers Inc.......802 584-3521
87 Stoneshed Rd South Ryegate VT (05069) *(G-22496)*
Gangi Printing Inc.......617 776-6071
17 Kensington Ave Somerville MA (02145) *(G-15175)*
Gannett Co Inc.......802 863-3441
100 Bank St Ste 700 Burlington VT (05401) *(G-21786)*
Gannett River States Pubg Corp.......802 893-4214
57 Yankee Park Rd Fairfax VT (05454) *(G-21975)*
Gannon & Scott Inc.......401 463-5550
33 Kenney Dr Cranston RI (02920) *(G-20229)*
GAP Promotions LLC.......978 281-0335
1 Washington St Gloucester MA (01930) *(G-11185)*
Gapolymer, Woodstock *Also called Aardvark Polymers* *(G-5493)*
Gar Kenyon Aerospace & Defense, Meriden *Also called Saf Industries LLC* *(G-2128)*
Garan Enterprises Inc.......413 594-4991
129 Broadway St Chicopee MA (01020) *(G-10027)*
Garaventa U S A Inc.......603 669-6553
999 Candia Rd Bldg 2 Manchester NH (03109) *(G-18824)*
Garbeck Airflow Industries.......860 301-5032
442 Arbutus St Middletown CT (06457) *(G-2186)*
Garden By Artech, Leominster *Also called Allied Resin Technologies LLC* *(G-12112)*
Garden Light Natural Foods Mkt, East Hartford *Also called Garden of Light Inc* *(G-1197)*
Garden of Light Inc.......860 895-6622
127 Park Ave Ste 100 East Hartford CT (06108) *(G-1197)*
Garden World Inc.......781 233-9510
24r Bennett Hwy Ste 3 Saugus MA (01906) *(G-14982)*
Gardner Chipmills Millinocket.......207 794-2223
820 S Chester Rd Chester ME (04457) *(G-5905)*
Gardner Mattress Corporation (PA).......978 744-1810
254 Canal St Salem MA (01970) *(G-14914)*
Gardner News Incorporated.......978 632-8000
309 Central St Gardner MA (01440) *(G-11114)*
Gardner Tool & Stamping Co.......978 632-0823
13 Travers St Gardner MA (01440) *(G-11115)*
Gardoc Inc (HQ).......603 673-6400
86 Powers St Milford NH (03055) *(G-19056)*
Gare Incorporated.......978 373-9131
165 Rosemont St Haverhill MA (01832) *(G-11437)*
Garelick Farms LLC (HQ).......508 528-9000
1199 W Central St Ste 1 Franklin MA (02038) *(G-11049)*
Garelick Farms LLC.......781 599-1300
10 Creek Brook Dr Haverhill MA (01832) *(G-11438)*
Garelick Farms LLC.......508 528-9000
1199 W Central St Franklin MA (02038) *(G-11050)*
Garfields Smokehouse Inc.......603 469-3225
163 Main St Meriden NH (03770) *(G-18983)*
Garflex Inc.......802 257-5256
32 Justin Holden Dr Brattleboro VT (05301) *(G-21728)*
Garland Industries Inc.......401 821-1450
1 S Main St Coventry RI (02816) *(G-20147)*
Garland Lumber Company Inc.......603 356-5636
636 E Conway Rd Center Conway NH (03813) *(G-17798)*
Garland Transportation Corp.......603 356-5636
636 E Conway Rd Center Conway NH (03813) *(G-17799)*
Garland Writing Instruments, Coventry *Also called Garland Industries Inc* *(G-20147)*
Garlic Press Inc.......802 864-0670
237 Commerce St Ste 102 Williston VT (05495) *(G-22667)*
Garlic Press Inc.......802 864-0670
237 Commerce St Williston VT (05495) *(G-22668)*
Garlock Prtg & Converting Corp.......978 630-1028
77 Industrial Rowe Gardner MA (01440) *(G-11116)*
Garlock Prtg & Converting Corp (PA).......978 630-1028
164 Fredette St Gardner MA (01440) *(G-11117)*
Garmac Screw Machine Inc.......203 723-6911
70 Great Hill Rd Naugatuck CT (06770) *(G-2475)*
Garmin International Inc.......800 561-5105
2 Delorme Dr Ste 2 # 2 Yarmouth ME (04096) *(G-7294)*
Garner Leach Inc.......508 695-9395
262 Broad St North Attleboro MA (02760) *(G-13757)*
Garner Leach Inc.......508 226-5660
23 Frank Mossberg Dr Attleboro MA (02703) *(G-7739)*
Garrett G Gilpatric.......603 744-3286
231 Peaked Hill Rd Bristol NH (03222) *(G-17765)*
Garrett Printing & Graphics.......860 589-6710
331 Riverside Ave Bristol CT (06010) *(G-567)*
Gartland Distributors LLC.......207 282-9456
4 Dusty Acres Biddeford ME (04005) *(G-5736)*
Garuka Bars, Montgomery Center *Also called Gorilla Bars Inc* *(G-22143)*
Garvin Industries Inc.......603 647-5410
81 Priscilla Ln Auburn NH (03032) *(G-17610)*
Gary Blake Car Buffs.......603 778-0563
58 Portsmouth Ave Exeter NH (03833) *(G-18122)*
Gary Eldridge.......401 769-0026
32 Mechanic Ave Ste 225 Woonsocket RI (02895) *(G-21566)*
Gary F Girome.......802 893-7870
25 Quarry Ln Milton VT (05468) *(G-22128)*
Gary Green Trucking Logging.......207 225-3433
517 General Turner Hl Rd Turner ME (04282) *(G-7107)*
Gary Hullihen.......413 283-2383
5 Beebe Rd Monson MA (01057) *(G-13207)*
Gary Kellner.......781 329-0404
524 High St Westwood MA (02090) *(G-16866)*
Gary M Pomeroy Logging Inc.......207 848-3171
1909 Hammond St Hermon ME (04401) *(G-6187)*
Gary Tool Company.......203 377-3077
26 Grant St Stratford CT (06615) *(G-4414)*
Gas Turbine Fuel Systems Div, Devens *Also called Parker-Hannifin Corporation* *(G-10329)*
Gasbarre Products Inc.......401 467-5200
81 Western Industrial Dr A Cranston RI (02921) *(G-20230)*
Gaskin Manufacturing Corp.......508 695-8949
17 Cross St Unit 8 Plainville MA (02762) *(G-14519)*
Gaspars Sausage Co Inc.......508 998-2012
384 Faunce Corner Rd North Dartmouth MA (02747) *(G-13920)*
Gaspee Publishing.......401 272-3668
22 Parsonage St Providence RI (02903) *(G-21020)*
Gasworld Publishing LLC.......781 862-0624
5 Militia Dr Ste 16 Lexington MA (02421) *(G-12225)*
Gatco Inc.......508 815-4910
297 North St Ste 212 Hyannis MA (02601) *(G-11842)*
Gatehouse Media LLC.......781 829-9305
600 Cordwainer Dr Norwell MA (02061) *(G-14103)*
Gatehouse Media LLC.......781 275-7204
9 Meriam St Lexington MA (02420) *(G-12226)*
Gatehouse Media LLC.......978 263-4736
150 Baker Avenue Ext # 101 Concord MA (01742) *(G-10130)*
Gatehouse Media LLC.......508 676-8211
207 Pocasset St Fall River MA (02721) *(G-10701)*
Gatehouse Media LLC.......508 880-9000
5 Cohannet St Taunton MA (02780) *(G-15752)*
Gatehouse Media LLC.......860 886-0106
10 Railroad Ave Norwich CT (06360) *(G-3280)*
Gatehouse Media Conn Holdings.......860 887-9211
10 Railroad Ave Norwich CT (06360) *(G-3281)*
Gatehouse Media Mass I Inc.......781 233-2040
72 Cherry Hill Dr Beverly MA (01915) *(G-8134)*
Gatehouse Media Mass I Inc (HQ).......585 598-0030
48 Dunham Rd Beverly MA (01915) *(G-8135)*
Gatehouse Media Mass I Inc.......508 626-4412
33 New York Ave Framingham MA (01701) *(G-10948)*
Gatehouse Media Mass I Inc.......781 235-4000
15 Pacella Park Dr Randolph MA (02368) *(G-14683)*
Gatehouse Media Mass I Inc.......508 295-1190
24 Sandwich Rd Wareham MA (02571) *(G-16247)*
Gatehouse Media Mass I Inc.......508 626-3859
40 Mechanic St Marlborough MA (01752) *(G-12758)*
Gatehouse Media Mass I Inc.......978 667-2156
150 Baker Avenue Ext # 101 Concord MA (01742) *(G-10131)*
Gatehouse Media Mass I Inc.......508 634-7522
197 Main St Milford MA (01757) *(G-13118)*
Gatehouse Media Mass I Inc.......617 629-3381
20 40 Holland St Somerville MA (02144) *(G-15176)*
Gatehouse Media Mass I Inc.......781 487-7200
2 Commercial St Sharon MA (02067) *(G-15050)*
Gatehouse Media Mass I Inc.......781 861-9110
9 Meriam St Ste 11 Lexington MA (02420) *(G-12227)*
Gatehouse Media Mass I Inc.......781 639-4800
48 Dunham Rd Beverly MA (01915) *(G-8136)*
Gatehouse Media Mass I Inc.......781 682-4850
91 Washington St Weymouth MA (02188) *(G-16889)*
Gatehouse Media Mass I Inc.......978 256-7196
15 Fletcher St Chelmsford MA (01824) *(G-9902)*
Gates Moore Lighting.......203 847-3231
224 Bible Hill Rd Hillsborough NH (03244) *(G-18315)*
Gateway Digital Inc.......203 853-4929
16 Testa Pl Norwalk CT (06854) *(G-3157)*
Gateway Mastering Studios Inc.......207 828-9400
428 Cumberland Ave Portland ME (04101) *(G-6664)*
Gateway Press, Lincoln *Also called Lincoln News* *(G-6357)*
Gateway Printing.......508 295-0505
174 Main St Wareham MA (02571) *(G-16248)*
Gath Signs, Tewksbury *Also called Mike Gath* *(G-15824)*

ALPHABETIC

Gauss Corporation.......207 883-4121
1 Gibson Rd Scarborough ME (04074) ***(G-6918)***
Gava Group Inc.......781 878-9889
691 Main St Hanover MA (02339) ***(G-11338)***
Gavitt Wire and Cable Co Inc.......508 867-6476
62 Central St West Brookfield MA (01585) ***(G-16469)***
Gaylord West.......802 285-6438
1762 Rice Hill Rd Franklin VT (05457) ***(G-21994)***
Gaylord, Richard N, Westfield *Also called Westfield Grinding Wheel Co* ***(G-16744)***
Gaynor Industries Corporation.......978 658-5500
98 Eames St Wilmington MA (01887) ***(G-17003)***
Gaynor Minden Inc.......212 929-0087
468 Canal St Lawrence MA (01840) ***(G-12027)***
Gazette Printing Co Inc.......413 527-7700
58 Oneil St Easthampton MA (01027) ***(G-10564)***
Gazette Publications Inc.......617 524-2626
7 Harris Ave Boston MA (02130) ***(G-8555)***
Gb and Smith Inc.......617 319-3563
90 Sherman St Cambridge MA (02140) ***(G-9485)***
Gbg Industries, Hinsdale *Also called Continental Cable LLC* ***(G-18319)***
Gbo Inc.......207 772-0302
340 Presumpscot St Portland ME (04103) ***(G-6665)***
Gca Logging Inc.......207 639-3941
118 River Rd Avon ME (04966) ***(G-5623)***
Gckm Machines.......617 584-6266
14 Hawthorn St Newton MA (02458) ***(G-13594)***
Gcn Media Services, Norwalk *Also called Gcn Publishing Inc* ***(G-3158)***
Gcn Publishing Inc.......203 665-6211
194 Main St Ste 2nw Norwalk CT (06851) ***(G-3158)***
Gcp Applied Technologies Inc (PA).......617 876-1400
62 Whittemore Ave Cambridge MA (02140) ***(G-9486)***
Gd-Ots Williston, Williston *Also called General Dynamics-Ots Inc* ***(G-22670)***
Gdjr Machining Incorporated.......978 365-3568
823 Lancaster St Leominster MA (01453) ***(G-12143)***
Gdm Software LLC.......617 416-6333
225 Franklin St Boston MA (02110) ***(G-8556)***
Gds Manufacturing Company.......802 862-7610
32 Boyer Cir Williston VT (05495) ***(G-22669)***
GE, Plainville *Also called ABB Enterprise Software Inc* ***(G-3461)***
GE Aviation.......513 552-3272
1000 Western Ave Lynn MA (01901) ***(G-12510)***
GE Energy Management Svcs Inc.......603 692-2100
130 Main St Somersworth NH (03878) ***(G-19838)***
GE Energy Parts Intl LLC (HQ).......617 443-3000
41 Farnsworth St Boston MA (02210) ***(G-8557)***
GE Engine Svcs UNC Holdg I Inc.......518 380-0767
71 Shelton Ave New Haven CT (06511) ***(G-2689)***
GE Enrgy Pwr Cnversion USA Inc.......203 373-2211
3135 Eon Tpke Fairfield CT (06828) ***(G-1434)***
GE Grid Solutions LLC.......425 250-2695
175 Addison Rd Windsor CT (06095) ***(G-5335)***
GE Healthcare Inc (HQ).......800 526-3593
100 Results Way Marlborough MA (01752) ***(G-12759)***
GE Healthcare Life Sciences, Marlborough *Also called GE Healthcare Inc* ***(G-12759)***
GE Healthcare Life Sciences, Marlborough *Also called Global Lf Scnces Sltons USA LL* ***(G-12761)***
GE Infrastructure Sensing LLC (HQ).......978 437-1000
1100 Technology Park Dr # 100 Billerica MA (01821) ***(G-8249)***
GE Oil & Gas Esp Inc.......405 670-1431
78 Black Rock Tpke Redding CT (06896) ***(G-3647)***
GE Panametrics Inc.......978 670-6454
1100 Tech Park Dr Ste 100 Billerica MA (01821) ***(G-8250)***
GE Renewable Energy USA, Windsor *Also called Alstom Renewable US LLC* ***(G-5319)***
GE Sensing & Inspection Tech, Billerica *Also called GE Infrastructure Sensing LLC* ***(G-8249)***
GE Steam Power Inc.......860 688-1911
853 S West St Feeding Hills MA (01030) ***(G-10798)***
GE Steam Power Inc (HQ).......866 257-8664
175 Addison Rd Windsor CT (06095) ***(G-5336)***
GE Transportation Parts LLC.......816 650-6171
3135 Easton Tpke Fairfield CT (06828) ***(G-1435)***
Gear Works Inc.......802 885-5039
76 Pearl St Ste 1 Springfield VT (05156) ***(G-22500)***
Gear/Tronics Inc.......781 933-1400
100 Chelmsford Rd North Billerica MA (01862) ***(G-13819)***
Gear/Tronics Industries Inc.......781 933-1400
100 Chelmsford Rd North Billerica MA (01862) ***(G-13820)***
Gear2succeed LLC.......781 733-0559
81 Marshall St Duxbury MA (02332) ***(G-10397)***
Gebelein Group Inc.......617 361-6611
1715 Hyde Park Ave Hyde Park MA (02136) ***(G-11867)***
GEC Durham Industries Inc (PA).......508 995-2636
255 Samuel Barnet Blvd New Bedford MA (02745) ***(G-13390)***
Geer Construction Co Inc.......860 376-5321
852 Voluntown Rd Jewett City CT (06351) ***(G-1912)***
Geer Sand & Gravel, Jewett City *Also called Geer Construction Co Inc* ***(G-1912)***
Gefran Inc (HQ).......781 729-5249
400 Willow St North Andover MA (01845) ***(G-13707)***
Gefran Isi Inc.......781 729-0842
400 Willow St North Andover MA (01845) ***(G-13708)***
Geib Refining Corporation.......401 738-8560
399 Kilvert St Warwick RI (02886) ***(G-21365)***
Geiger of Austria Inc.......802 388-3156
38 Pond Ln Middlebury VT (05753) ***(G-22112)***
Geisel Software Inc.......508 853-5310
67 Millbrook St Ste 520 Worcester MA (01606) ***(G-17380)***
Geisser Industry, Riverside *Also called Allstate Drilling Co* ***(G-21163)***
Gelato Giuliana LLC.......203 772-0607
240 Sargent Dr Ste 9 New Haven CT (06511) ***(G-2690)***
Gelder Aerospace LLC.......203 283-9524
12 Commerce Dr Shelton CT (06484) ***(G-3804)***
Gem Creations of Maine.......207 454-2139
14 Sherrard Ln Charlotte ME (04666) ***(G-5900)***
Gem Gravure Co Inc (PA).......781 878-0456
112 School St Hanover MA (02339) ***(G-11339)***
Gem Label & Tape Company.......401 724-1300
65 Blackstone Ave # 6532 Pawtucket RI (02860) ***(G-20842)***
Gem Manufacturing Co Inc (PA).......203 574-1466
78 Brookside Rd Waterbury CT (06708) ***(G-4877)***
Gem Welding.......978 362-3873
12 Republic Rd North Billerica MA (01862) ***(G-13821)***
Gem-Craft Inc.......401 854-1200
1420 Elmwood Ave Cranston RI (02910) ***(G-20231)***
Gemco Manufacturing Co Inc.......860 628-5529
555 W Queen St Southington CT (06489) ***(G-4052)***
Gemforms, Portland *Also called Printgraphics of Maine Inc* ***(G-6716)***
Gemgraphics Inc.......603 352-7112
415 Marlboro St Keene NH (03431) ***(G-18504)***
Gemini Firfield Screenprinting.......603 357-3847
149 Emerald St Unit N Keene NH (03431) ***(G-18505)***
Gemini Games.......781 643-6965
197 Forest St Arlington MA (02474) ***(G-7628)***
Gemini Screen Printing & EMB, Brockton *Also called Gemini Screenprinting & EMB Co* ***(G-9149)***
Gemini Screenprinting & EMB Co.......508 586-8223
959 W Chestnut St Brockton MA (02301) ***(G-9149)***
Gemini Sign Company Inc.......508 485-3343
128 S Bolton St Marlborough MA (01752) ***(G-12760)***
Gemini Signs & Design Ltd.......603 447-3336
226 W Main St Conway NH (03818) ***(G-17952)***
Gemini Valve, Raymond *Also called Parker & Harper Companies Inc* ***(G-19643)***
Gemma Oro Inc.......203 227-0774
2 Coach Ln Westport CT (06880) ***(G-5197)***
Gems Publishing Usa Inc.......508 872-0066
12 Walnut St Framingham MA (01702) ***(G-10949)***
Gems Sensors & Controls, Plainville *Also called Gems Sensors Inc* ***(G-3491)***
Gems Sensors Inc (HQ).......860 747-3000
1 Cowles Rd Plainville CT (06062) ***(G-3491)***
Gems Sensors Inc.......800 378-1600
1 Cowles Rd Plainville CT (06062) ***(G-3492)***
Gen-El-Mec Associates Inc.......203 828-6566
2 Fox Hollow Rd Oxford CT (06478) ***(G-3403)***
Genband US LLC.......972 521-5800
3 Federal St Billerica MA (01821) ***(G-8251)***
Genconnex, Hingham *Also called New England Gen-Connect LLC* ***(G-11507)***
Geneisis Sprinkler Systems.......508 428-1842
21 Fir Ln Osterville MA (02655) ***(G-14247)***
Genelec Inc.......508 652-0900
7 Tech Cir Natick MA (01760) ***(G-13257)***
General Abrasives Inc.......802 763-7264
Back River Rd Sharon VT (05065) ***(G-22409)***
General Airmotive Pwr Pdts LLC.......508 674-6400
994 Jefferson St Ste 10 Fall River MA (02721) ***(G-10702)***
General Alum New England Corp.......207 548-2525
34 Kidder Point Rd Searsport ME (04974) ***(G-6952)***
General Cable Industries Inc.......603 668-1620
345 Mcgregor St Manchester NH (03102) ***(G-18825)***
General Cable Industries Inc.......860 456-8000
1600 Main St Willimantic CT (06226) ***(G-5264)***
General Cable Industries Inc.......401 333-4848
3 Carol Dr Lincoln RI (02865) ***(G-20575)***
General Datacomm Inc (HQ).......203 729-0271
353 Christian St Ste 4 Oxford CT (06478) ***(G-3404)***
General Datacomm Inds Inc (PA).......203 729-0271
353 Christian St Ste 4 Oxford CT (06478) ***(G-3405)***
General Display Inc.......508 533-6676
6 Industrial Park Rd Medway MA (02053) ***(G-12960)***
General Dynamics.......508 880-4521
425 John Quincy Adams Rd Taunton MA (02780) ***(G-15753)***
General Dynamics Corporation.......413 494-2313
100 Plastics Ave Pittsfield MA (01201) ***(G-14470)***
General Dynamics Corporation.......207 442-3245
700 Washington St Bath ME (04530) ***(G-5677)***
General Dynamics Corporation.......413 494-3137
34 E Windsor Rd Rm 2563 Hinsdale MA (01235) ***(G-11520)***
General Dynamics Def.......413 494-1110
100 Plastics Ave Pittsfield MA (01201) ***(G-14471)***

General Dynamics Electric Boat, Groton *Also called Electric Boat Corporation* ***(G-1675)***
General Dynamics Mission 781 410-9635
150 Rustcraft Rd Dedham MA (02026) ***(G-10291)***
General Dynamics Mission 603 864-6300
24 Simon St Nashua NH (03060) ***(G-19165)***
General Dynamics Mission 508 880-4000
400 John Quincy Adams Rd Taunton MA (02780) ***(G-15754)***
General Dynamics Mission 954 846-3000
89 A St Needham Heights MA (02494) ***(G-13334)***
General Dynamics Mission Syste 617 715-7000
553 South St Quincy MA (02169) ***(G-14628)***
General Dynamics Ordnance 860 404-0162
65 Sandscreen Rd Avon CT (06001) ***(G-34)***
General Dynamics-Ots Inc 802 662-7000
326 Ibm Rd Bldg 862 Williston VT (05495) ***(G-22670)***
General Dynamics-Ots Inc 207 283-3611
291 North St Saco ME (04072) ***(G-6847)***
General Dynmics Mssion Systems 413 494-1110
100 Plastics Ave Pittsfield MA (01201) ***(G-14472)***
General Dynmics Mssion Systems 508 880-4000
20 Constitution Dr Taunton MA (02780) ***(G-15755)***
General Electric Company (PA) 617 443-3000
5 Necco St Boston MA (02210) ***(G-8558)***
General Electric Company 781 598-7303
1000 Western Ave Lynn MA (01905) ***(G-12511)***
General Electric Company 603 666-8300
31 Industrial Park Dr Hooksett NH (03106) ***(G-18351)***
General Electric Company 203 396-1572
1285 Boston Ave Bridgeport CT (06610) ***(G-418)***
General Electric Company 802 775-9842
210 Columbian Ave Rutland VT (05701) ***(G-22335)***
General Electric Company 781 594-0100
1000 Western Ave Lynn MA (01910) ***(G-12512)***
General Electric Company 508 870-5200
1400 Computer Dr Ste 3 Westborough MA (01581) ***(G-16619)***
General Electric Company 207 786-5100
135 Rodman Rd Auburn ME (04210) ***(G-5567)***
General Electric Company 617 608-6008
1 Gateway Ctr Ste 251 Newton MA (02458) ***(G-13595)***
General Electric Company 617 444-8777
6 Mcelway Rd Harwich MA (02645) ***(G-11393)***
General Electric Company 207 941-2500
534 Griffin Rd Bangor ME (04401) ***(G-5648)***
General Electric Company 518 385-7164
901 Main Ave Ste 103 Norwalk CT (06851) ***(G-3159)***
General Electro Components 860 659-3573
122 Naubuc Ave Ste A7 Glastonbury CT (06033) ***(G-1554)***
General Findings, Attleboro *Also called EF Leach & Company* ***(G-7731)***
General Fluidics Corporation 617 543-3114
1601 Trapelo Rd Waltham MA (02451) ***(G-16118)***
General Ftting Heat Trnsf Pdts, Porter *Also called Chester H Chapman* ***(G-6600)***
General Heat Treating Co 203 755-5441
80 Fulkerson Dr Waterbury CT (06708) ***(G-4878)***
General Instrs Wrline Networks, Lowell *Also called Ruckus Wireless Inc* ***(G-12430)***
General Kinetics LLC 603 627-8547
10 Commerce Park North # 6 Bedford NH (03110) ***(G-17642)***
General Lighting Division, Exeter *Also called Osram Sylvania Inc* ***(G-18128)***
General Machine & Foundry, Wilton *Also called Aluminum Castings Inc* ***(G-19974)***
General Machine Company Inc 860 426-9295
1223 Mount Vernon Rd Southington CT (06489) ***(G-4053)***
General Machine Inc 413 533-5744
56 Jackson St Ste 1 Holyoke MA (01040) ***(G-11627)***
General Manufacturing Corp 978 667-5514
154 Rangeway Rd North Billerica MA (01862) ***(G-13822)***
General Marine Inc 207 284-7517
56 Landry St Biddeford ME (04005) ***(G-5737)***
General Metal Finishing LLC 508 222-9683
42 Frank Mossberg Dr Attleboro MA (02703) ***(G-7740)***
General Packaging Products Inc 203 846-1340
3 Valley View Rd Apt 9 Norwalk CT (06851) ***(G-3160)***
General Plating Inc 401 421-0219
16 Sunnyside Ave Johnston RI (02919) ***(G-20515)***
General Pneumatics, Meriden *Also called Saf Industries LLC* ***(G-2127)***
General Polymer Inc 401 723-6660
59 Foundry St Central Falls RI (02863) ***(G-20114)***
General Products & Gear Corp 978 948-8146
120 Haverhill St Rowley MA (01969) ***(G-14854)***
General Seating Solutions LLC 860 242-3307
45 S Satellite Rd Ste 5 South Windsor CT (06074) ***(G-3971)***
General Sheet Metal Works Inc 203 333-6111
120 Silliman Ave Bridgeport CT (06605) ***(G-419)***
General Steel Products Co Inc 617 387-5400
16 Russell Rd Lexington MA (02420) ***(G-12228)***
General Wire Products Inc 508 752-8260
425 Shrewsbury St Worcester MA (01604) ***(G-17381)***
General Wldg & Fabrication Inc 860 274-9668
977 Echo Lake Rd Watertown CT (06795) ***(G-5010)***
General Woodworking Inc (PA) 978 458-6625
105 Pevey St Lowell MA (01851) ***(G-12373)***
General Woodworking Inc 978 251-4070
299 Western Ave Lowell MA (01851) ***(G-12374)***
Generation Four Inc 781 899-3180
713 Main St Waltham MA (02451) ***(G-16119)***
Generative Labs Inc 434 326-8061
70 Pacific St Cambridge MA (02139) ***(G-9487)***
Generator Power Solutions Neng 603 577-1766
29 Dickerman St Nashua NH (03060) ***(G-19166)***
Generators On Demand LLC 860 662-4090
61-1 Buttonball Rd Old Lyme CT (06371) ***(G-3323)***
Genere Food, Providence *Also called Plastic Services Entps Inc* ***(G-21090)***
Genesis Alkali LLC 215 299-6773
1 Stamford Plz 263 Stamford CT (06901) ***(G-4198)***
Genest Landscape Masonry 207 892-3778
45 Enterprise Dr Windham ME (04062) ***(G-7235)***
Genest Precast, Sanford *Also called Richard Genest Inc* ***(G-6890)***
Geneve Holdings Inc (PA) 203 358-8000
96 Cummings Point Rd Stamford CT (06902) ***(G-4199)***
Genfoot America Inc 802 893-4280
33 Catamount Dr Milton VT (05468) ***(G-22129)***
Genfoot America Inc 603 575-5114
673 Industrial Park Rd Littleton NH (03561) ***(G-18660)***
Genlyte Group Incorporated 781 418-7900
3000 Minuteman Rd Andover MA (01810) ***(G-7550)***
GENLYTE THOMAS GROUP LLC, Andover *Also called Genlyte Thomas Group LLC* ***(G-7551)***
Genlyte Thomas Group LLC 978 659-3732
200 Minuteman Rd Ste 205 Andover MA (01810) ***(G-7551)***
Genlyte Thomas Group LLC 781 418-7900
3 Burlington Woods Dr # 100 Burlington MA (01803) ***(G-9279)***
Gennaro Inc 401 632-4100
1725 Pontiac Ave Cranston RI (02920) ***(G-20232)***
Genoa Sausage Co Inc 781 933-3115
14 Industrial Pkwy Woburn MA (01801) ***(G-17190)***
Genocea Biosciences Inc 617 876-8191
100 Acorn Park Dr Fl 5 Cambridge MA (02140) ***(G-9488)***
Genomic Solutions Inc 734 975-4800
84 October Hill Rd Ste 7 Holliston MA (01746) ***(G-11572)***
Genovese Manufacturing Co 860 582-9944
8 Bombard Ct Terryville CT (06786) ***(G-4481)***
Genplex Inc 207 474-3500
7 Industrial Park Rd # 1 Skowhegan ME (04976) ***(G-6974)***
Genrad Inc 978 589-7000
7 Technology Park Dr Westford MA (01886) ***(G-16768)***
Genscope Inc 413 526-0802
18 Deer Park Dr East Longmeadow MA (01028) ***(G-10476)***
Gentest Corporation 781 935-5115
6 Henshaw St Woburn MA (01801) ***(G-17191)***
Gentex Corporation 603 657-1200
645 Harvey Rd Ste 1 Manchester NH (03103) ***(G-18826)***
Gentex Optics Inc 508 713-5267
183 W Main St Dudley MA (01571) ***(G-10375)***
Gentex Optics Inc (HQ) 570 282-8531
183 W Main St Dudley MA (01571) ***(G-10376)***
Gentle Machine Co LLC 603 532-9363
39 Hadley Rd Jaffrey NH (03452) ***(G-18464)***
Genuine Jamaican 802 633-2676
609 Barnet Center Rd Barnet VT (05821) ***(G-21604)***
Genuine Local, Meredith *Also called Discerning Palate LLC* ***(G-18973)***
Genvario Awning Co 203 847-5858
131 Main St Norwalk CT (06851) ***(G-3161)***
Genx International Inc (PA) 203 453-1700
393 Soundview Rd Guilford CT (06437) ***(G-1705)***
Genzyme Allston, Boston *Also called Genzyme Corporation* ***(G-8559)***
Genzyme Biosurgery, Cambridge *Also called Genzyme Corporation* ***(G-9490)***
Genzyme Corporation 508 271-3631
31 New York Ave Framingham MA (01701) ***(G-10950)***
Genzyme Corporation 508 271-2642
200 Crossing Blvd Framingham MA (01702) ***(G-10951)***
Genzyme Corporation (HQ) 617 252-7500
50 Binney St Cambridge MA (02142) ***(G-9489)***
Genzyme Corporation 617 252-7500
78 New York Ave Framingham MA (01701) ***(G-10952)***
Genzyme Corporation 508 370-9690
80 New York Ave Framingham MA (01701) ***(G-10953)***
Genzyme Corporation 508 271-2919
55 Cambridge Pkwy Ste 19 Cambridge MA (02142) ***(G-9490)***
Genzyme Corporation 617 768-9292
41 Everett St Natick MA (01760) ***(G-13258)***
Genzyme Corporation 617 252-7500
114 Western Ave Allston MA (02134) ***(G-7466)***
Genzyme Corporation 508 351-2699
11 Forbes Rd Northborough MA (01532) ***(G-14034)***
Genzyme Corporation 781 487-5728
153 2nd Ave Waltham MA (02451) ***(G-16120)***
Genzyme Corporation 508 351-2600
1 Research Dr Ste 200 Westborough MA (01581) ***(G-16620)***
Genzyme Corporation 508 872-8400
1 The Mountain Rd Framingham MA (01701) ***(G-10954)***
Genzyme Corporation 508 872-8400
1 Kendall Sq Cambridge MA (02139) ***(G-9491)***

ALPHABETIC

Genzyme Corporation....617 252-7500
1 Kendall Sq Ste 113 Cambridge MA (02139) ***(G-9492)***
Genzyme Corporation....617 494-8484
500 St Kendall Cambridge MA (02142) ***(G-9493)***
Genzyme Corporation....508 898-9001
3400 Computer Dr Westborough MA (01581) ***(G-16621)***
Genzyme Corporation....617 779-3100
500 Soldiers Field Rd Boston MA (02134) ***(G-8559)***
Genzyme Corporation....508 872-8400
51 New York Ave Framingham MA (01701) ***(G-10955)***
Genzyme Corporation....508 872-8400
45 New York Ave Framingham MA (01701) ***(G-10956)***
Genzyme Corporation....508 872-8400
74 New York Ave Framingham MA (01701) ***(G-10957)***
Genzyme Corporation....508 872-8400
68 New York Ave Framingham MA (01701) ***(G-10958)***
Genzyme Genetics, Westborough *Also called Genzyme Corporation* ***(G-16621)***
Genzyme Securities Corporation....617 252-7500
50 Binney St Cambridge MA (02142) ***(G-9494)***
Genzyme Therapeutics Division, Cambridge *Also called Genzyme Corporation* ***(G-9489)***
Geo H Fuller and Son Company....401 722-6530
151 Exchange St Pawtucket RI (02860) ***(G-20843)***
Geo Knight & Co Inc....508 588-0186
52 Perkins St Brockton MA (02302) ***(G-9150)***
Geoffroy Labs, Londonderry *Also called Rob Geoffroy* ***(G-18734)***
Geographics Australia, Norwalk *Also called Royal Consumer Products LLC* ***(G-3234)***
Geokon LLC....603 448-1562
48 Spencer St Lebanon NH (03766) ***(G-18624)***
Geometric Engineering Co....978 352-4651
97 Tenney St Unit 7 Georgetown MA (01833) ***(G-11142)***
Geometric Informatics Inc....617 440-1078
387 Somerville Ave Apt 2 Somerville MA (02143) ***(G-15177)***
Geonautics Manufacturing Inc....978 462-7161
506 Merrimac St Newburyport MA (01950) ***(G-13494)***
Geoorbital Inc....617 651-1102
17 Rev Nzreno Prperzi Way Somerville MA (02143) ***(G-15178)***
Geophysical Survey Systems Inc (HQ)....603 893-1109
40 Simon St Ste 1 Nashua NH (03060) ***(G-19167)***
George A Vollans....508 257-6241
27 New St Nantucket MA (02554) ***(G-13224)***
George Baggett....207 785-5442
158 Feyler Rd Union ME (04862) ***(G-7113)***
George Dawe....978 388-5565
23 Noel St Amesbury MA (01913) ***(G-7486)***
George Gordon Associates Inc....603 424-5204
12 Continental Blvd Merrimack NH (03054) ***(G-19002)***
George Guertin Trophy Inc....508 832-4001
32 Auburn St Auburn MA (01501) ***(G-7836)***
George Howell Coffee Co LLC....978 635-9033
312 School St Acton MA (01720) ***(G-7358)***
George J Foster Co Inc....603 332-2200
90 N Main St Rochester NH (03867) ***(G-19670)***
George L Martin....802 254-5838
218 Main St Brattleboro VT (05301) ***(G-21729)***
George Publishing Company....781 826-4996
167 Elm St Pembroke MA (02359) ***(G-14406)***
George R King....508 821-3826
27 Gretchen Way Raynham MA (02767) ***(G-14715)***
George R Roberts Company, Alfred *Also called Nicmar Industries* ***(G-5516)***
George S Preisner Jewelers....203 265-0057
150 Center St Wallingford CT (06492) ***(G-4748)***
George Schmithet and Company, Guilford *Also called Schmitt Realty Holdings Inc* ***(G-1719)***
George Weston Bakeries....413 443-6095
703 W Housatonic St Pittsfield MA (01201) ***(G-14473)***
George's Textile, Lowell *Also called Gilbride Enterprises LLC* ***(G-12375)***
Georges Bank LLC....617 423-3474
310 Northern Ave Areac Boston MA (02210) ***(G-8560)***
Georgetown Pottery....207 371-2801
755 Five Islands Rd Georgetown ME (04548) ***(G-6106)***
Georgia Stone Industries Inc (HQ)....401 232-2040
15 Branch Pike Smithfield RI (02917) ***(G-21227)***
Georgia-Pacific LLC....207 827-7711
1 Portland St Old Town ME (04468) ***(G-6538)***
Georgia-Pacific LLC....207 427-4077
144 Main St Baileyville ME (04694) ***(G-5626)***
Georgia-Pacific LLC....781 440-3600
315 Norwood Park S Ste 1 Norwood MA (02062) ***(G-14155)***
Georgia-Pacific LLC....978 537-4701
149 Hamilton St Leominster MA (01453) ***(G-12144)***
Georgia-Pacific LLC....603 433-8000
170 Shattuck Way Newington NH (03801) ***(G-19322)***
Geosonics Inc....203 271-2504
416 Highland Ave Ste D Cheshire CT (06410) ***(G-735)***
Geotec Inc....401 228-7395
89 Bellows St Warwick RI (02888) ***(G-21366)***
Gepp LLC....401 808-8004
83 Vermont Ave Bldg 3-4 Warwick RI (02888) ***(G-21367)***
Gerald F Dalton & Sons Inc....508 238-5374
51 Rockland St North Easton MA (02356) ***(G-13945)***
Gerard F Scalley....781 933-3009
18 Dartmouth St Woburn MA (01801) ***(G-17192)***
Gerard Farms Inc....781 858-1013
447 Water St Framingham MA (01701) ***(G-10959)***
Gerard Poulin & Sons Logging....207 246-3537
115 Poulin Dr Readfield ME (04355) ***(G-6777)***
Gerard R Davis Ltd....401 766-8760
521 Providence Pike North Smithfield RI (02896) ***(G-20787)***
Gerber Coburn Optical Inc (HQ)....800 843-1479
55 Gerber Rd E South Windsor CT (06074) ***(G-3972)***
Gerber Scientific LLC (PA)....860 871-8082
24 Indl Pk Rd W Tolland CT (06084) ***(G-4548)***
Gerber Technology LLC (HQ)....860 871-8082
24 Industrial Park Rd W Tolland CT (06084) ***(G-4549)***
Gerdau Ameristeel US Inc....860 351-9029
75 Neal Ct Plainville CT (06062) ***(G-3493)***
Gerlach Sheet Metal....603 782-6136
303 W Haven Rd Manchester NH (03104) ***(G-18827)***
Gerrish Global Industries LLC....207 595-2150
90 Pleasant View Dr Naples ME (04055) ***(G-6460)***
Gerrity Company Incorporated....207 933-2804
152 Bog Rd Leeds ME (04263) ***(G-6269)***
Ges Control Systems Inc....905 336-5517
22 Grandview Dr Dover NH (03820) ***(G-18023)***
Gessner Company, Charlton *Also called Ghm Industries Inc* ***(G-9850)***
Getchell & Son Inc....401 231-3850
950 Douglas Pike Smithfield RI (02917) ***(G-21228)***
Getchell Bros Inc....207 490-0809
1913 Main St Sanford ME (04073) ***(G-6877)***
Getinge AB, Merrimack *Also called Getinge Group Logis Ameri LLC* ***(G-19003)***
Getinge Group Logis Ameri LLC....603 880-1433
40 Continental Blvd Merrimack NH (03054) ***(G-19003)***
GF Health Products Inc....401 738-1500
33 Plan Way Bldg 2 Warwick RI (02886) ***(G-21368)***
GF Machining Solutions LLC....508 474-1100
150 Hopping Brook Rd Holliston MA (01746) ***(G-11573)***
Gforce Grafix Corporation....978 840-4401
12 Mount Pleasant Ave Leominster MA (01453) ***(G-12145)***
Gfxco LLC....401 722-8888
66 Stearns St Pawtucket RI (02861) ***(G-20844)***
Gg Inks, South Hadley *Also called Ggs Custom Metals Inc* ***(G-15303)***
Gg Sportswear Inc....860 296-4441
241 Ledyard St Ste B10 Hartford CT (06114) ***(G-1825)***
Ggs Custom Metals Inc....413 315-4344
785 New Ludlow Rd South Hadley MA (01075) ***(G-15303)***
Ghg Electronic Services....781 391-1147
49 Baxter St Medford MA (02155) ***(G-12934)***
Ghi Sign Service, Canaan *Also called Jill Ghi* ***(G-688)***
Ghm Industries Inc (PA)....508 248-3941
100 Sturbridge Rd Unit A Charlton MA (01507) ***(G-9850)***
Ghp Media Inc....413 663-3771
123 Mass Moca Way North Adams MA (01247) ***(G-13675)***
Ghp Media Inc (PA)....203 479-7500
475 Heffernan Dr West Haven CT (06516) ***(G-5124)***
Gl Plastek LLC....603 569-5100
5 Wickers Dr Wolfeboro NH (03894) ***(G-20017)***
Gl Plastek Ltd Partnership....603 569-5100
5 Wickers Dr Wolfeboro NH (03894) ***(G-20018)***
Gl Plastek Wolfeboro, Wolfeboro *Also called PSI Molded Plastics NH Inc* ***(G-20024)***
Giannetti Mfg Services Inc....413 532-9736
28 Michael Dr South Hadley MA (01075) ***(G-15304)***
Gibbs Lures Inc....401 726-2277
1 Hatch St Cumberland RI (02864) ***(G-20321)***
Gibson Peggy Day....802 525-3034
2492 Parker Rd West Glover VT (05875) ***(G-22607)***
Giddings Equipment, Pittsford *Also called Giddings Manufacturing Co Inc* ***(G-22263)***
Giddings Manufacturing Co Inc....802 483-2292
1448 Us Route 7 Pittsford VT (05763) ***(G-22263)***
Gifford's Famous Ice Cream, Skowhegan *Also called Giffords Dairy Inc* ***(G-6975)***
Giffords Dairy Inc....207 474-9821
25 Hathaway St Skowhegan ME (04976) ***(G-6975)***
Gilbert Manufacturing Co, Ipswich *Also called Larsdale Inc* ***(G-11928)***
Gilbride Enterprises LLC....978 452-0878
360 Merrimack St Lowell MA (01852) ***(G-12375)***
Gilchrist Metal Fabg Co Inc (PA)....603 889-2600
18 Park Ave Hudson NH (03051) ***(G-18392)***
Gilcris Enterprises Inc....802 226-7764
283 Peaceful Valley Rd Proctorsville VT (05153) ***(G-22288)***
Gill Design Inc....603 890-1237
3 Industrial Dr Unit 5 Windham NH (03087) ***(G-20006)***
Gill Metal Fab Inc....508 580-4445
170 Oak Hill Way Brockton MA (02301) ***(G-9151)***
Gilles Champagne....603 237-5272
Edwards St Colebrook NH (03576) ***(G-17870)***
Gillette Company (HQ)....617 421-7000
1 Gillette Park Boston MA (02127) ***(G-8561)***
Gillette Company....617 268-1363
1 Gillette Park Boston MA (02127) ***(G-8562)***

Gillette Company........781 662-9600
30 Burtt Rd Andover MA (01810) ***(G-7552)***
Gillette Company........203 796-4000
14 Research Dr Bethel CT (06801) ***(G-155)***
Gillette De Mexico Inc........617 421-7000
800 Boylston St Boston MA (02199) ***(G-8563)***
Gillians Foods Inc........781 586-0086
45 Congress St Ste 106 Salem MA (01970) ***(G-14915)***
Gillies W Technologies LLC........508 852-2502
250 Barber Ave Worcester MA (01606) ***(G-17382)***
Gillis Lumber Inc........207 448-2218
231 Maple St Danforth ME (04424) ***(G-5941)***
Gilman Corporation........860 887-7080
1 Polly Ln Gilman CT (06336) ***(G-1534)***
Gilman Gear, Gilman *Also called Marty Gilman Incorporated* ***(G-1535)***
Gilman Gear, Bozrah *Also called Marty Gilman Incorporated* ***(G-282)***
Giltron Inc........508 359-4310
620 Spring St 90-1 North Dighton MA (02764) ***(G-13931)***
Gilway Technical Lamp, Peabody *Also called International Light Tech Inc* ***(G-14343)***
Gima LLC........860 296-4441
241 Ledyard St Ste B10 Hartford CT (06114) ***(G-1826)***
Gimasport, Hartford *Also called Gima LLC* ***(G-1826)***
Giner Elx Inc........781 392-0300
89 Rumford Ave Auburndale MA (02466) ***(G-7862)***
Giner Life Sciences Inc........781 529-0576
89 Rumford Ave Auburndale MA (02466) ***(G-7863)***
Ginerlabs, Auburndale *Also called Giner Life Sciences Inc* ***(G-7863)***
Ginger Bettys, Quincy *Also called Beth Veneto* ***(G-14615)***
Ginger Software Inc........617 755-0160
128 Chestnut St Newton MA (02465) ***(G-13596)***
Gingham Ventures LLC (PA)........617 206-1197
6 Liberty Sq Ste 2151 Boston MA (02109) ***(G-8564)***
Gingras Lumber Inc........413 229-2182
77 Clayton Rd Ashley Falls MA (01222) ***(G-7674)***
Ginkgo Bioworks Inc........814 422-5362
27 Drydock Ave Ste 8 Boston MA (02210) ***(G-8565)***
Ginsco Inc........508 677-4767
1572 President Ave Fall River MA (02720) ***(G-10703)***
Ginsco Inc (PA)........508 677-4767
1706 President Ave Fall River MA (02720) ***(G-10704)***
Ginsco Inc........508 990-3350
272 State Rd North Dartmouth MA (02747) ***(G-13921)***
Ginseng Up Corporation (PA)........508 799-6178
16 Plum St Worcester MA (01604) ***(G-17383)***
Giovanni, Middleboro *Also called Malden Intl Designs Inc* ***(G-13067)***
Giral LLC........802 238-7852
1 Lawson Ln Ste 120 Burlington VT (05401) ***(G-21787)***
Girardin Moulding Inc........860 623-4486
564 Halfway House Rd Windsor Locks CT (06096) ***(G-5393)***
Girome, Gary F and Associates, Milton *Also called Gary F Girome* ***(G-22128)***
Girouard Tool & Die Inc........978 534-4147
218 Viscoloid Ave Leominster MA (01453) ***(G-12146)***
Girouard Tool Corp........978 534-4147
218 Viscoloid Ave Leominster MA (01453) ***(G-12147)***
Giroux Body Shop Inc........802 482-2162
10370 Route 116 Hinesburg VT (05461) ***(G-22025)***
Giv, Barre *Also called Granite Industries Vermont Inc* ***(G-21618)***
Givens Marine Survival Svc Co........617 441-5400
550 Main Rd Tiverton RI (02878) ***(G-21259)***
GJM Manufacturing Inc........508 222-9322
453 S Main St Attleboro MA (02703) ***(G-7741)***
GK Mechanical Systems LLC........203 775-4970
934 Federal Rd Ste 1b Brookfield CT (06804) ***(G-644)***
GKN Aerospace New England Inc........603 542-5135
1105 River Rd Charlestown NH (03603) ***(G-17814)***
GKN Aerospace Newington LLC........800 667-8502
183 Louis St Newington CT (06111) ***(G-2866)***
GKN Aerospace Newington LLC (HQ)........860 667-8502
183 Louis St Newington CT (06111) ***(G-2867)***
GKN Arspace Svcs Strctures LLC........860 613-0236
1000 Corporate Row Cromwell CT (06416) ***(G-853)***
GKS Service Company Inc........603 483-2122
196 Brown Rd Candia NH (03034) ***(G-17784)***
GL&v USA Inc (HQ)........603 882-2711
1 Cellu Dr Ste 200 Nashua NH (03063) ***(G-19168)***
GL&v USA Inc........603 882-2711
1 Cellu Dr Ste 200 Nashua NH (03063) ***(G-19169)***
GL&v USA Inc........413 637-2424
175 Crystal St Lenox MA (01240) ***(G-12100)***
Glacier Computer LLC (PA)........860 355-7552
46 Bridge St Ste 1 New Milford CT (06776) ***(G-2800)***
Glacier Computer LLC........603 882-1560
10 Northern Blvd Ste 2 Amherst NH (03031) ***(G-17564)***
Glad Products Company........781 848-6272
220 Forbes Rd Braintree MA (02184) ***(G-9009)***
Glass By Petze........508 428-0971
130 Westwind Cir Osterville MA (02655) ***(G-14248)***
Glass Dimension Inc........978 768-7984
197 Western Ave Essex MA (01929) ***(G-10593)***
Glass Industries America LLC........203 269-6700
340 Quinnipiac St Unit 9 Wallingford CT (06492) ***(G-4749)***
Glass Molders Pottery Pla........508 634-2932
42 Taft St Milford MA (01757) ***(G-13119)***
Glass Pro Inc........603 436-2882
364 Middle Rd Brentwood NH (03833) ***(G-17750)***
Glass Technologies Division, Central Falls *Also called Osram Sylvania Inc* ***(G-20122)***
Glasshouse, Pomfret Center *Also called LLC Glass House* ***(G-3556)***
Glastonbury Citizen Inc........860 633-4691
87 Nutmeg Ln Glastonbury CT (06033) ***(G-1555)***
Glastonbury Southern Gage Div, Colchester *Also called Q Alpha Inc* ***(G-806)***
Glaxosmithkline LLC........617 828-9028
100 Catherine Dr Braintree MA (02184) ***(G-9010)***
Glaxosmithkline LLC........978 853-6490
37 Grove St Topsfield MA (01983) ***(G-15860)***
Glaxosmithkline LLC........203 232-5145
186 Beecher Dr Southbury CT (06488) ***(G-4026)***
Glaxosmithkline LLC........401 934-2834
176 Snake Hill Rd North Scituate RI (02857) ***(G-20778)***
Glenn LLC........800 521-0065
300 Jefferson Blvd # 206 Warwick RI (02888) ***(G-21369)***
Glenn S Viles & Sons Inc........207 635-2493
Elm St North Anson ME (04958) ***(G-6502)***
Glenn, Inc., Warwick *Also called Glenn LLC* ***(G-21369)***
Glenns Gardening & Woodworking........617 548-7977
491 Arborway Apt 20 Boston MA (02130) ***(G-8566)***
Glenwood Kitchens USA........508 875-1180
1291 Worcester Rd Ste 3 Framingham MA (01701) ***(G-10960)***
Glenwood Press, Everett *Also called Green Summer* ***(G-10612)***
Glidden Signs Inc........207 396-6111
40a Manson Libby Rd Scarborough ME (04074) ***(G-6919)***
Glidecam Industries Inc........781 585-7900
23 Joseph St Kingston MA (02364) ***(G-11957)***
Glines Rhodes Inc........508 385-8828
381 Satucket Rd Brewster MA (02631) ***(G-9053)***
Glixx Laboratories Inc........781 333-5348
63 South St Ste 130 Hopkinton MA (01748) ***(G-11716)***
Global Advanced Metals USA Inc (PA)........781 996-7300
100 Worcester St Ste 200 Wellesley Hills MA (02481) ***(G-16397)***
Global Biotechnologies Inc........800 755-8420
19 Rigby Rd Scarborough ME (04074) ***(G-6920)***
Global Brass & Copper LLC (PA)........203 597-5000
215 Piedmont St Waterbury CT (06706) ***(G-4879)***
Global Coding Solutions, Carver *Also called Brian Leopold* ***(G-9802)***
Global Connector Tech Ltd........978 208-1618
354 Merrimack St Ste 260 Lawrence MA (01843) ***(G-12028)***
Global E.D.M. Supplies, New Britain *Also called Makino Inc* ***(G-2549)***
Global Engineered Mtls Corp........401 725-2100
200 Sayles Hill Rd Manville RI (02838) ***(G-20608)***
Global Enterprises Inc........508 399-8270
699 Washington St Attleboro MA (02703) ***(G-7742)***
Global Filtration Systems........603 651-8777
615 Center St Wolfeboro NH (03894) ***(G-20019)***
Global Fire Products Inc........617 750-1125
745 Atlantic Ave Fl 8 Boston MA (02111) ***(G-8567)***
Global Foundries, Essex Junction *Also called Globalfoundries US 2 LLC* ***(G-21941)***
Global ID Technologies, Narragansett *Also called Global Rfid Systems N Amer LLC* ***(G-20640)***
Global Interconnect Inc........508 563-6306
11 Jonathan Bourne Dr Pocasset MA (02559) ***(G-14595)***
Global Laminates........603 373-8081
300 Constitution Ave Portsmouth NH (03801) ***(G-19567)***
Global Lf Scnces Sltons USA LL........508 475-2000
14 Walkup Dr Westborough MA (01581) ***(G-16622)***
Global Lf Scnces Sltons USA LL........508 480-9235
170 Locke Dr Marlborough MA (01752) ***(G-12761)***
Global Light Co LLC........617 620-2084
328 Harvard St Apt 3 Cambridge MA (02139) ***(G-9495)***
Global Materials Inc........978 322-1900
1449 Middlesex St Lowell MA (01851) ***(G-12376)***
Global Palate Foods LLC........203 543-3028
161 Cross Hwy Westport CT (06880) ***(G-5198)***
Global Pallet & Packaging LLC........603 969-6660
148 Batchelder Rd Seabrook NH (03874) ***(G-19801)***
Global Pallet Solutions LLC........860 826-5000
271 John Downey Dr New Britain CT (06051) ***(G-2535)***
Global Plastics LLC (HQ)........603 782-2835
99 Middle St Ste 1 Manchester NH (03101) ***(G-18828)***
Global Prints Inc........800 578-4278
65 Sprague St Ste 25 Hyde Park MA (02136) ***(G-11868)***
Global RES Innovation Tech Inc........617 383-4748
56 Roland St Ste 102b Charlestown MA (02129) ***(G-9835)***
Global Rfid Systems N Amer LLC........401 783-3818
1004 Boston Neck Rd # 7 Narragansett RI (02882) ***(G-20640)***
Global Scenic Services Inc........203 334-2130
46 Brookfield Ave Bridgeport CT (06610) ***(G-420)***
Global Steering Systems LLC (PA)........860 945-5400
156 Park Rd Watertown CT (06795) ***(G-5011)***

ALPHABETIC

Global Tower Holdings LLC ...617 375-7500
116 Huntington Ave Boston MA (02116) ***(G-8568)***
Global Transfer, Attleboro *Also called Global Enterprises Inc* ***(G-7742)***
Global Trbine Cmpnent Tech LLC ...860 528-4722
125 S Satellite Rd South Windsor CT (06074) ***(G-3973)***
Global Value Lighting LLC (PA) ...401 535-4002
1350 Division Rd Ste 204 West Warwick RI (02893) ***(G-21492)***
Global Values VT LLC ...802 476-8000
25 S Front St Barre VT (05641) ***(G-21616)***
Globaldie, Auburn *Also called Enefco International Inc* ***(G-5561)***
Globalfoundries US 2 LLC ...408 462-4452
1000 River St Essex Junction VT (05452) ***(G-21941)***
Globe Composite Solutions LLC ...781 871-3700
200 Shuman Ave Ste 100 Stoughton MA (02072) ***(G-15593)***
Globe Composite Solutions Ltd ...781 871-3700
200 Shuman Ave Stoughton MA (02072) ***(G-15594)***
Globe Environmental Corp ...203 481-5586
131 Commercial Pkwy 1b Branford CT (06405) ***(G-320)***
Globe Footwear LLC ...207 784-9186
27 Wrights Lndg Auburn ME (04210) ***(G-5568)***
Globe Footwear LLC (HQ) ...207 784-9186
27 Wrights Lndg Auburn ME (04210) ***(G-5569)***
Globe Manufacturing Co LLC (HQ) ...603 435-8323
37 Loudon Rd Pittsfield NH (03263) ***(G-19500)***
Globe Pequot Press, Guilford *Also called Morris Communications Co LLC* ***(G-1712)***
Globe Tool & Met Stampg Co Inc ...860 621-6807
95 Robert Porter Rd Southington CT (06489) ***(G-4054)***
Globeco Maine LLC ...207 809-2671
19 Fowler Farm Rd Scarborough ME (04074) ***(G-6921)***
Glogood Inc ...617 491-3500
27 Gray Gdns E Cambridge MA (02138) ***(G-9496)***
Gloria Duchin Inc ...401 431-5016
201 Narragansett Park Dr Rumford RI (02916) ***(G-21185)***
Gloria J Gordon Logging ...207 684-4462
74 Norton Hill Rd Strong ME (04983) ***(G-7071)***
Gloria Jean Photography ...603 485-7176
347 Pembroke St Pembroke NH (03275) ***(G-19457)***
Gloucester Associates Inc ...802 479-1088
10 Transport Dr 1 Barre VT (05641) ***(G-21617)***
Gloucester Daily Times, Gloucester *Also called Eagle-Tribune Publishing Co* ***(G-11179)***
Gloucester Engineering Co Inc (HQ) ...978 281-1800
11 Dory Rd Gloucester MA (01930) ***(G-11186)***
Gloucester Engineering Co Inc ...978 515-7008
18 Sargent St Gloucester MA (01930) ***(G-11187)***
Gloucester Graphics Inc (PA) ...978 281-4500
19 Pond Rd Gloucester MA (01930) ***(G-11188)***
Glover Company Inc ...207 236-8644
17 Rockville St Rockport ME (04856) ***(G-6822)***
Glsynthesis Inc ...508 754-6700
298 Highland St Worcester MA (01602) ***(G-17384)***
Gluer-TEC, Pelham *Also called Folder-Glr Techl Svs Grp LLC* ***(G-19433)***
Gluertec, Pelham *Also called Ss & G LLC* ***(G-19448)***
Glv US Holding Inc, Nashua *Also called Valmet Inc* ***(G-19278)***
Glycozym Usa Inc ...425 985-2556
100 Cummings Ctr Ste 430j Beverly MA (01915) ***(G-8137)***
Glyne Manufacturing Co Inc ...203 375-4495
380 E Main St Stratford CT (06614) ***(G-4415)***
Glyt, Andover *Also called Genlyte Group Incorporated* ***(G-7550)***
GM Merc Inc ...508 878-1305
158 W Main St Hopkinton MA (01748) ***(G-11717)***
GM Specialties Inc ...207 883-8300
1 Commercial Rd Scarborough ME (04074) ***(G-6922)***
Gmf Engineering Inc ...781 233-0315
15 Main St Saugus MA (01906) ***(G-14983)***
Gmn Usa LLC ...800 686-1679
181 Business Park Dr Bristol CT (06010) ***(G-568)***
Gmo Threshold Logging II LLC ...617 330-7500
40 Rowes Wharf Ste 600 Boston MA (02110) ***(G-8569)***
Gmo Threshold Logging LLC ...617 330-7500
40 Rowes Wharf Ste 600 Boston MA (02110) ***(G-8570)***
Gmo Thrshold Tmber Hldings LLC ...617 330-7500
40 Rowes Wharf Ste 600 Boston MA (02110) ***(G-8571)***
Gmt Composites, Bristol *Also called Element Industries Inc* ***(G-20075)***
Gmt Mfg, Plantsville *Also called G M T Manufacturing Co Inc* ***(G-3531)***
Gn Audio USA Inc (HQ) ...800 826-4656
900 Chelmsford St Lowell MA (01851) ***(G-12377)***
Gn Netcom, Inc., Lowell *Also called Gn Audio USA Inc* ***(G-12377)***
Gnr USA Instruments LLC ...508 698-3816
6 Nason Ln Foxboro MA (02035) ***(G-10884)***
Go East Promotions, Warwick *Also called Gepp LLC* ***(G-21367)***
Go Green Industries LLC ...914 772-0026
23 Meredith Ln New Milford CT (06776) ***(G-2801)***
Go Green Industries Inc ...978 496-1881
2 Doris Rd Westford MA (01886) ***(G-16769)***
Go Green Mfg Inc ...978 928-4333
232 Chapel St Gardner MA (01440) ***(G-11118)***
Go2 Media Inc ...617 457-7870
10 High St Ste 1002 Boston MA (02110) ***(G-8572)***
Goamericago Beverages LLC ...802 897-7700
2139 Quiet Valley Rd Shoreham VT (05770) ***(G-22432)***
Godfreys Sawmill LLC ...802 326-4868
926 Deep Gibou Rd Montgomery Center VT (05471) ***(G-22142)***
Godin Land Clearing ...508 885-9666
28 Marble Rd Spencer MA (01562) ***(G-15431)***
Godiva Chocolatier Inc ...781 843-0466
250 Granite St Ste 168 Braintree MA (02184) ***(G-9011)***
Goetz Composites, Bristol *Also called Composite Energy Tech Inc* ***(G-20069)***
Goffstown News, Manchester *Also called Neighborhood News* ***(G-18882)***
Gold Line Connector Inc (PA) ...203 938-2588
40 Great Pasture Rd Redding CT (06896) ***(G-3648)***
Gold Line Connector Inc ...508 999-5656
263 Brook St Unit 2 New Bedford MA (02745) ***(G-13391)***
Gold Line Manufacturing, New Bedford *Also called Gold Line Connector Inc* ***(G-13391)***
Gold Medal Bakery Inc (PA) ...508 674-5766
21 Penn St Fall River MA (02724) ***(G-10705)***
Gold Water Technology Inc ...781 551-3590
25 Walpole Park S Walpole MA (02081) ***(G-15992)***
Golden Fleece Mfg Group LLC (HQ) ...978 686-3833
25 Computer Dr Haverhill MA (01832) ***(G-11439)***
Golden Manet Press Inc ...617 773-2423
86 Robertson St Quincy MA (02169) ***(G-14629)***
Golden Sun Inc ...800 575-7960
5 High Ridge Park Ste 200 Stamford CT (06905) ***(G-4200)***
Goldenrod Welding Inc ...401 725-9248
37 Elizabeth St Cumberland RI (02864) ***(G-20322)***
Goldline Controls Inc (HQ) ...401 583-1100
61 Whitecap Dr North Kingstown RI (02852) ***(G-20713)***
Goldman-Kolber Inc ...781 769-6362
185 Dean St Ste 204 Norwood MA (02062) ***(G-14156)***
Goldslager Conveyor Company ...203 795-9886
73 Fernwood Rd Hamden CT (06517) ***(G-1751)***
Goldworks ...203 743-9668
5 Locust Ave Danbury CT (06810) ***(G-925)***
Golf Course News, Yarmouth *Also called United Publications Inc* ***(G-7303)***
Golf Galaxy LLC ...203 855-0500
595 Connecticut Ave Ste 4 Norwalk CT (06854) ***(G-3162)***
Golf Research Associates ...203 968-1608
2810 High Ridge Rd Stamford CT (06903) ***(G-4201)***
Golf Shop The, Manchester *Also called Tom Waters Golf Shop* ***(G-12608)***
Golf Tips, Braintree *Also called Werner Publishing Corporation* ***(G-9049)***
Golfsmith, Norwalk *Also called Golf Galaxy LLC* ***(G-3162)***
Golik Machine Co ...860 610-0095
154 Commerce Way South Windsor CT (06074) ***(G-3974)***
Gonco Inc (PA) ...508 833-3900
338 Route 130 Sandwich MA (02563) ***(G-14968)***
Gone Baking LLC ...603 305-6026
64 Settlers Ct Bedford NH (03110) ***(G-17643)***
Gone Troppo Inc (PA) ...617 739-7995
108 Codman Rd Brookline MA (02445) ***(G-9201)***
Gooby Industries Corp ...978 689-0100
45 Chase St Ste 45 # 45 Methuen MA (01844) ***(G-13024)***
Gooch & Housego Boston, Bedford *Also called Em4 Inc* ***(G-7972)***
Good Cause Greetings Inc ...413 543-1515
30 W Colonial Rd Wilbraham MA (01095) ***(G-16938)***
Good Hues Custom Powdr Coating ...603 434-8034
227 Rockingham Rd Derry NH (03038) ***(G-17980)***
Good Taste LLC ...978 388-4026
36 Main St Ste 2 Amesbury MA (01913) ***(G-7487)***
Good Tern Press Inc ...508 277-5500
15 Channel Ctr St Apt 616 Boston MA (02210) ***(G-8573)***
Good To-Go LLC ...207 451-9060
484 Us Route 1 Kittery ME (03904) ***(G-6256)***
Good Wives Inc ...781 596-0070
86 Sanderson Ave Ste 3 Lynn MA (01902) ***(G-12513)***
Good2gether ...978 371-3172
23 Anson Rd Concord MA (01742) ***(G-10132)***
Goodbev Inc ...617 545-5240
7 Chestnut St Lynn MA (01902) ***(G-12514)***
Goodcopy Printing & Graphics, New Haven *Also called Goodcopy Printing Center Inc* ***(G-2691)***
Goodcopy Printing Center Inc ...203 624-0194
110 Hamilton St New Haven CT (06511) ***(G-2691)***
Goode Brush Company ...781 581-0280
89 Bass Point Rd Nahant MA (01908) ***(G-13215)***
Goodrich, West Hartford *Also called Triumph Eng Ctrl Systems LLC* ***(G-5100)***
Goodrich Corporation, Vergennes *Also called Simmonds Precision Pdts Inc* ***(G-22556)***
Goodrich Corporation ...505 345-9031
100 Wooster Hts Danbury CT (06810) ***(G-926)***
Goodrich Corporation ...978 532-2350
5th St Peabody MA (01960) ***(G-14336)***
Goodrich Corporation ...978 303-6700
9 Technology Park Dr Westford MA (01886) ***(G-16770)***
Goodrich Corporation ...203 797-5000
100 Wooster Hts Danbury CT (06810) ***(G-927)***
Goodrich Corporation ...978 303-6700
7 Technology Park Dr Westford MA (01886) ***(G-16771)***

Goodrich Corporation ... 802 877-4000
100 Panton Rd Vergennes VT (05491) *(G-22553)*
Goodrich Sensors and Integrate, Cheshire *Also called Atlantic Inertial Systems Inc (G-713)*
Goodridge Lumber ... 802 755-6298
183 Bailey Hazen Rd E Albany VT (05820) *(G-21592)*
Goodspeed Machine Company ... 978 297-0296
15 Summer Dr Winchendon MA (01475) *(G-17076)*
Goodyfab Llc ... 203 927-3059
88 Totoket Rd North Branford CT (06471) *(G-2964)*
Goong ... 860 216-3041
798 Silver Ln East Hartford CT (06118) *(G-1198)*
Goose Hummock Shop, Orleans *Also called Outdoor Outfitters Inc (G-14239)*
Goose Valley Natural Foods LLC ... 617 914-0126
100 City Hall Plz Ste 305 Boston MA (02108) *(G-8574)*
Gordini USA Inc (PA) ... 802 879-5211
67 Allen Martin Dr Essex Junction VT (05452) *(G-21942)*
Gordon Corporation ... 860 628-4775
170 Spring St Unit 3 Southington CT (06489) *(G-4055)*
Gordon Engineering Corp ... 203 775-4501
67 Del Mar Dr Brookfield CT (06804) *(G-645)*
Gordon Industries Inc (PA) ... 857 401-1114
202 W 1st St Boston MA (02127) *(G-8575)*
Gordon Products Incorporated ... 203 775-4501
67 Del Mar Dr Brookfield CT (06804) *(G-646)*
Gordon Rubber and Pkg Co Inc ... 203 735-7441
10 Cemetery Ave Derby CT (06418) *(G-1072)*
Gordons of Beverly, Beverly *Also called Theological Threads Inc (G-8190)*
Gordons Window Decor Inc (PA) ... 802 655-7777
8 Leroy Rd Williston VT (05495) *(G-22671)*
Gordons Window Decor Centl V T, Williston *Also called Gordons Window Decor Inc (G-22671)*
Goremote ... 508 384-0139
1 Premium Outlet Blvd Wrentham MA (02093) *(G-17521)*
Gorgeous Gelato LLC ... 207 699-4309
434 Fore St Portland ME (04101) *(G-6666)*
Gorham Brick & Block Inc ... 603 752-3631
331 Western Ave Berlin NH (03570) *(G-17696)*
Gorham Growl ... 207 839-4795
2 Main St Gorham ME (04038) *(G-6112)*
Gorham Sand & Gravel ... 603 466-2291
42 Lancaster Rd Gorham NH (03581) *(G-18212)*
Gorilla Bars Inc ... 802 309-4997
650 Fisher Rd Montgomery Center VT (05471) *(G-22143)*
Gorilla Circuits ... 603 864-0283
207 Main St Nashua NH (03060) *(G-19170)*
Gorilla Graphics Inc ... 860 704-8208
52 N Main St Middletown CT (06457) *(G-2187)*
Gorilla Gym, Cambridge *Also called Velex Corporation (G-9691)*
Gorman Machine Corp ... 508 923-9462
122 E Grove St Middleboro MA (02346) *(G-13063)*
Gortons, Gloucester *Also called Gortons Inc (G-11189)*
Gortons Inc (HQ) ... 978 283-3000
128 Rogers St Gloucester MA (01930) *(G-11189)*
Gosolar NH LLC ... 603 948-1189
232 Cales Hwy Barrington NH (03825) *(G-17618)*
Goss Lumber Co Inc ... 603 428-3363
841 Flanders Rd Henniker NH (03242) *(G-18305)*
Gossamer Press ... 207 827-9881
259 Main St Ste 1 Old Town ME (04468) *(G-6539)*
Got Ice LLC ... 508 228-1156
8 Miacomet Ave Nantucket MA (02554) *(G-13225)*
Got Interface ... 781 547-5700
135 Beaver St Ste 206 Waltham MA (02452) *(G-16121)*
Gotham Chemical Company Inc ... 203 854-6644
21 South St Norwalk CT (06854) *(G-3163)*
Gotham Ink In Color, Marlborough *Also called Gotham Ink of New England Inc (G-12762)*
Gotham Ink of New England Inc ... 508 485-7911
255 E Main St Marlborough MA (01752) *(G-12762)*
Gotuit Media Corp ... 801 592-5575
400 Tradecenter Ste 3890 Woburn MA (01801) *(G-17193)*
Gotuit Video, Woburn *Also called Gotuit Media Corp (G-17193)*
Goulet Enterprises Inc ... 860 379-0793
115 New Hartford Rd Pleasant Valley CT (06063) *(G-3545)*
Goulet Printery, Pleasant Valley *Also called Goulet Enterprises Inc (G-3545)*
Gourmet Oils and Vinegars Neng ... 603 269-2271
21 Maple St Center Barnstead NH (03225) *(G-17789)*
Government Sales, Hartford *Also called Government Surplus Sales Inc (G-1827)*
Government Surplus Sales Inc ... 860 247-7787
69 Francis Ave Hartford CT (06106) *(G-1827)*
Governor Supply Co ... 978 870-6888
22 Hunter Ln Lancaster MA (01523) *(G-11983)*
Govt Comm Sys., Bedford *Also called L3harris Technologies Inc (G-7987)*
Gowdey Reed, Central Falls *Also called Reed Gowdey Company (G-20123)*
Gowell Candy Shop Inc ... 508 583-2521
727 N Main St Brockton MA (02301) *(G-9152)*
Gowell's Home Made Candy, Brockton *Also called Gowell Candy Shop Inc (G-9152)*
GP Aggregate Corp ... 978 283-5318
19 Pond Rd Gloucester MA (01930) *(G-11190)*
GP Industries ... 860 859-9938
500 Norwich Ave Ste 7 Taftville CT (06380) *(G-4470)*
GP&g, Rowley *Also called General Products & Gear Corp (G-14854)*
Gp2 Technologies, Bow *Also called G P 2 Technologies Inc (G-17714)*
GPA ... 860 410-0624
10 Farmington Valley Dr # 5 Plainville CT (06062) *(G-3494)*
Gpd Optoelectronics Corp ... 603 894-6865
7 Manor Pkwy Salem NH (03079) *(G-19739)*
Gpx International Tire Corp (PA) ... 781 321-3910
124 Washington St Ste 101 Foxboro MA (02035) *(G-10885)*
Gr Enterprises and Tech ... 203 387-1430
3 Penny Ln Woodbridge CT (06525) *(G-5467)*
Grabber Construction Pdts Inc ... 603 890-0455
10 Industrial Dr Unit 12 Windham NH (03087) *(G-20007)*
Grace Machine Company LLC ... 860 828-8789
46 Woodlawn Rd Ste A Berlin CT (06037) *(G-87)*
Grace Ormonde Marriage Inc ... 401 245-9726
120 Amaral St Ste 3 Riverside RI (02915) *(G-21169)*
Grace Ormonde Wedding Style, Riverside *Also called Grace Ormonde Marriage Inc (G-21169)*
Gracie Maes Kitchen LLC ... 860 885-8250
383 Bethel Rd Griswold CT (06351) *(G-1663)*
Graco Awards Manufacturing Inc ... 281 255-2161
177 Georgia Ave Providence RI (02905) *(G-21021)*
Gradar Metals, Milford *Also called B L C Investments Inc (G-2249)*
Graduation Solutions LLC ... 914 934-5991
200 Pemberwick Rd Greenwich CT (06831) *(G-1617)*
Graduation Source, Greenwich *Also called Graduation Solutions LLC (G-1617)*
Grady Research Inc ... 978 772-3303
323 W Main St Ste 1 Ayer MA (01432) *(G-7921)*
Grafted Coatings Inc ... 203 377-9979
400 Surf Ave Stratford CT (06615) *(G-4416)*
Grafton News Holdings LLC ... 508 839-2259
100 Front St Ste 500 Worcester MA (01608) *(G-17385)*
Grafton News, The, Worcester *Also called Grafton News Holdings LLC (G-17385)*
Grafton Village Cheese Co LLC ... 802 843-2221
400 Linden St Brattleboro VT (05301) *(G-21730)*
Graham Field Bandage, Warwick *Also called GF Health Products Inc (G-21368)*
Graham Tool and Machine LLC ... 860 585-1261
9 Container Dr Terryville CT (06786) *(G-4482)*
Graham Whitehead & Manger Co (PA) ... 203 922-9225
462 Boston St Ste 2-1 Topsfield MA (01983) *(G-15861)*
Grain Surfboards ... 207 457-5313
73 Webber Rd York ME (03909) *(G-7307)*
Grainpro Inc (PA) ... 978 371-7118
200 Baker Ave Ste 309 Concord MA (01742) *(G-10133)*
Granata Sign Co, Stamford *Also called Granata Signs LLC (G-4202)*
Granata Signs LLC ... 203 358-0780
80 Lincoln Ave 90 Stamford CT (06902) *(G-4202)*
Grand Embroidery Inc ... 203 888-7484
225 Christian St Oxford CT (06478) *(G-3406)*
Grand Image Inc ... 888 973-2622
560 Main St Ste 3 Hudson MA (01749) *(G-11775)*
Grand Imprints, Oxford *Also called Grand Embroidery Inc (G-3406)*
Grand View Winery Co LLC ... 802 456-8810
2039 Max Gray Rd Plainfield VT (05667) *(G-22267)*
Grande Brothers Inc ... 617 323-6169
72 Martin St West Roxbury MA (02132) *(G-16496)*
Grandstream Networks Inc (PA) ... 617 566-9300
126 Brookline Ave Ste 3 Boston MA (02215) *(G-8576)*
Grandten Distilling LLC ... 617 269-0497
383 Dorchester Ave # 130 Boston MA (02127) *(G-8577)*
Graney John F Metal Design LLC ... 413 528-6744
1920 N Main St Sheffield MA (01257) *(G-15060)*
Graney Metal Designs, Sheffield *Also called Graney John F Metal Design LLC (G-15060)*
Granger Lynch Corp ... 508 756-6244
18 Mccracken Rd Ste 1 Millbury MA (01527) *(G-13165)*
Granite & Kitchen Studio LLC ... 860 290-4444
313 Pleasant Valley Rd South Windsor CT (06074) *(G-3975)*
Granite 3 LLC ... 603 566-0339
24 Twillingate Rd Temple NH (03084) *(G-19897)*
Granite Brook LLC ... 781 788-9700
199 Church St Weston MA (02493) *(G-16826)*
Granite Industries Vermont Inc ... 800 451-3236
Vanneti Pl Barre VT (05641) *(G-21618)*
Granite LLC ... 860 586-8132
116 Willard Ave Newington CT (06111) *(G-2868)*
Granite Mountain Inds LLC ... 978 369-0014
174 Cash St 7 South Portland ME (04106) *(G-7028)*
Granite Power Technologies, Manchester *Also called Vicor Corporation (G-18951)*
Granite Print LLC ... 617 479-5777
90 Palmer St Quincy MA (02169) *(G-14630)*
Granite Quill Publishers ... 603 464-3388
246 W Main St Hillsborough NH (03244) *(G-18316)*
Granite Reliable Power LLC ... 508 251-7650
200 Donald Lynch Blvd # 300 Marlborough MA (01752) *(G-12763)*
Granite State Candy Shoppe LLC (PA) ... 603 225-2591
13 Warren St Concord NH (03301) *(G-17903)*

ALPHABETIC

Granite State Casting...603 878-2759
127 Fitchburg Rd Mason NH (03048) ***(G-18967)***
Granite State Concrete Co Inc...603 673-3327
408 Elm St Milford NH (03055) ***(G-19057)***
Granite State Cover and Canvas...603 382-5462
144 Main St Plaistow NH (03865) ***(G-19517)***
Granite State Finishing Inc...603 880-4130
141 Canal St Unit 2 Nashua NH (03064) ***(G-19171)***
Granite State Forest Products...603 428-7890
1104 Old Concord Rd Henniker NH (03242) ***(G-18306)***
Granite State Log Homes Inc (PA)...603 536-4949
17 King Rd Campton NH (03223) ***(G-17777)***
Granite State Manufacturing, Manchester *Also called Allard Nazarian Group Inc* ***(G-18774)***
Granite State Plasma Cutting...603 536-4415
10 Pleasant St Ste 400 Portsmouth NH (03801) ***(G-19568)***
Granite State Plastics Inc...603 669-6715
37 Executive Dr Hudson NH (03051) ***(G-18393)***
Granite State Stamps Inc...603 669-9322
8025 S Willow St Ste 102 Manchester NH (03103) ***(G-18829)***
Granitech LLC...860 620-1733
409 Canal St Ste 4 Plantsville CT (06479) ***(G-3532)***
Grannick's Bitter Apple Co, Norwalk *Also called Valore Inc* ***(G-3264)***
Granny Blossom Specialty...802 645-0507
425 Vt Route 30 Wells VT (05774) ***(G-22599)***
Granny Blossom's, Wells *Also called Granny Blossom Specialty* ***(G-22599)***
Grannys Got It...203 879-0042
724 Wolcott Rd Ste 3 Wolcott CT (06716) ***(G-5443)***
Grant John...802 933-4808
16 Sheldon Hts Sheldon VT (05483) ***(G-22428)***
Grant Foster Group L P...401 231-4077
500 Washington Hwy Smithfield RI (02917) ***(G-21229)***
Grant Larkin...413 698-2599
937 Summit Rd Richmond MA (01254) ***(G-14779)***
Grant Manufacturing & Mch Co...203 366-4557
90 Silliman Ave Bridgeport CT (06605) ***(G-421)***
Grant Riveters USA, Bridgeport *Also called Riveting Systems USA LLC* ***(G-483)***
Granta USA Ltd...440 207-6051
62 E Starrs Plain Rd Danbury CT (06810) ***(G-928)***
Granville Manufacturing Co...802 767-4747
45 Mill Rd Ofc Rte 100 Granville VT (05747) ***(G-22003)***
Graphene Composites Usa Inc...401 261-5811
177 N Main St Providence RI (02903) ***(G-21022)***
Graphenea Inc...415 568-6243
1 Broadway Fl 14 Cambridge MA (02142) ***(G-9497)***
Graphic Application Tech Inc...401 233-2100
60 Waterman Ave North Providence RI (02911) ***(G-20763)***
Graphic Arts Finishers Inc...617 241-9292
185 Countryside Rd Newton MA (02459) ***(G-13597)***
Graphic Arts Repair...781 843-7954
76 Bradley Road Ext Braintree MA (02184) ***(G-9012)***
Graphic Awards & Trophy, Norton *Also called Greg Asselin Studios Ltd* ***(G-14078)***
Graphic Consumer Services Inc...603 483-5355
208 Brown Rd Candia NH (03034) ***(G-17785)***
Graphic Developments Inc...781 878-2222
70 Mayflower Dr Hanover MA (02339) ***(G-11340)***
Graphic Edge Inc...802 855-8840
155 Seward Rd Rutland VT (05701) ***(G-22336)***
Graphic Excellence LLC...413 733-6691
1441 Main St Springfield MA (01103) ***(G-15471)***
Graphic Explosion Inc...207 576-3210
41 Delcliffe Ln Lewiston ME (04240) ***(G-6289)***
Graphic Fllfillment Finshg Inc...781 727-8845
145 Union St Ste 3 Holbrook MA (02343) ***(G-11525)***
Graphic Image Inc...203 877-8787
561 Boston Post Rd Milford CT (06460) ***(G-2293)***
Graphic Impact Signs Inc...413 499-0382
575 Dalton Ave Pittsfield MA (01201) ***(G-14474)***
Graphic Ink Incorporated...401 431-5081
629 Warren Ave East Providence RI (02914) ***(G-20415)***
Graphic Litho, Lawrence *Also called High-Speed Process Prtg Corp* ***(G-12035)***
Graphic Packaging Intl LLC...860 567-4196
133 Goodhouse Rd Litchfield CT (06759) ***(G-1949)***
Graphic Packaging Intl LLC...603 230-5100
80 Commercial St Concord NH (03301) ***(G-17904)***
Graphic Packaging Intl LLC...603 230-5486
80 Commercial St Concord NH (03301) ***(G-17905)***
Graphic Packaging Intl LLC...603 230-5100
80 Commercial St Concord NH (03301) ***(G-17906)***
Graphic Packaging Intl LLC...603 224-2333
80 Commercial St Concord NH (03301) ***(G-17907)***
Graphic Printing Co, West Springfield *Also called Ddfhklt Inc* ***(G-16515)***
Graphic Utilities Incorporated...207 370-9178
191 Development Dr Limestone ME (04750) ***(G-6340)***
Graphicast Inc...603 532-4481
36 Knight St Jaffrey NH (03452) ***(G-18465)***
Graphics Press LLC...203 272-9187
1161 Sperry Rd Cheshire CT (06410) ***(G-736)***
Graphics Source Co...413 543-0700
18 Pequot Rd Southampton MA (01073) ***(G-15338)***
Graphis Electrical Controls, Dover *Also called Ges Control Systems Inc* ***(G-18023)***
Graphisoft North America Inc...617 485-4219
60 Hickory Dr Ste 101 Waltham MA (02451) ***(G-16122)***
Graphite Die Mold Inc...860 349-4444
18 Airline Rd Durham CT (06422) ***(G-1091)***
Graphiti Screenprinting Signs, York *Also called Lynne Bailey* ***(G-7310)***
Graphix Design...207 827-4412
489 Kirkland Rd Old Town ME (04468) ***(G-6540)***
Graphix Plus Inc...508 677-2122
52 Queen St Fall River MA (02724) ***(G-10706)***
Grason & Associates LLC...603 899-3089
1134 Nh Route 119 Rindge NH (03461) ***(G-19649)***
Grass Roots Creamery...860 653-6303
4 Park Pl Granby CT (06035) ***(G-1589)***
Grassetti Sales Associates...413 737-2283
160 Progress Ave Springfield MA (01104) ***(G-15472)***
Grassroots of New England...401 333-1963
202 Nate Whipple Hwy Cumberland RI (02864) ***(G-20323)***
Grate Products LLC...800 649-6140
31 Sanford Rd Westport MA (02790) ***(G-16840)***
Grate Technologies, Coventry *Also called R B L Holdings Inc* ***(G-20163)***
Gravel Doctor Midcoast Maine...207 633-1099
15 Halls Ln Bristol ME (04539) ***(G-5812)***
Gravel Electric Inc...401 265-6041
27 Indigo Farm Rd Harrisville RI (02830) ***(G-20479)***
Gravel Hill Partners LLC...603 277-9074
34 Macdonald Dr Hanover NH (03755) ***(G-18288)***
Gravel Public House...508 384-0888
36 South St Wrentham MA (02093) ***(G-17522)***
Graves Concrete, East Templeton *Also called Ragged Hill Incorporated* ***(G-10520)***
Gray Enterprises, Charlestown *Also called Pompanette LLC* ***(G-17819)***
Gray Rock Concrete...802 379-5393
54 W Milton Rd Milton VT (05468) ***(G-22130)***
Graybark Enterprises LLC...203 255-4503
20 Governors Ln Fairfield CT (06824) ***(G-1436)***
Graycer Screw Products Co Inc...508 966-1810
113 Depot St Bellingham MA (02019) ***(G-8039)***
Grayfin Micro, Madison *Also called Grayfin Security LLC* ***(G-1961)***
Grayfin Security LLC...203 800-6760
82 Bradley Rd Madison CT (06443) ***(G-1961)***
Graystone Limited LLC (PA)...855 356-1027
50 Oliver St Ste 102 North Easton MA (02356) ***(G-13946)***
Graytron Inc...413 625-2456
888 Baptist Corner Rd Ashfield MA (01330) ***(G-7651)***
Graywolf Sensing Solutions LLC (PA)...203 402-0477
6 Research Dr Ste 110 Shelton CT (06484) ***(G-3805)***
Graziano Redi-Mix Inc...508 697-8350
60 1st St Bridgewater MA (02324) ***(G-9074)***
Great, Woodbridge *Also called Gr Enterprises and Tech* ***(G-5467)***
Great American Recrtl Eqp...401 463-5587
24 Stafford Ct Cranston RI (02920) ***(G-20233)***
Great Atlantic Seafood, Biddeford *Also called Lukas Foods Inc* ***(G-5744)***
Great Barrington Auto Sup Inc...413 528-0838
227 Stockbridge Rd Great Barrington MA (01230) ***(G-11238)***
Great Bay Gazette...603 793-2620
6 2nd St Exeter NH (03833) ***(G-18123)***
Great Big Graphics Inc (PA)...802 888-5515
355 Industrial Park Dr Morrisville VT (05661) ***(G-22167)***
Great Brook Lumber Inc...207 457-1063
766 Upper Guinea Rd Lebanon ME (04027) ***(G-6265)***
Great Lakes Chemical Corp (HQ)...203 573-2000
2 Armstrong Rd Ste 101 Shelton CT (06484) ***(G-3806)***
Great Neck Saw Mfrs Inc...508 865-4482
100 Riverlin St Millbury MA (01527) ***(G-13166)***
Great Northern Docks Inc (PA)...207 693-3770
1114 Roosevelt Trl Naples ME (04055) ***(G-6461)***
Great Northern Industries Inc (PA)...617 262-4314
266 Beacon St Ste 2 Boston MA (02116) ***(G-8578)***
Great Oak Publications Inc...978 664-4761
7 Bow St Ste 2 North Reading MA (01864) ***(G-13983)***
Great Rhythm Brewing Co LLC...603 300-8588
229 Miller Ave Portsmouth NH (03801) ***(G-19569)***
Great Soups Inc...401 253-3200
67 Gooding Ave Bristol RI (02809) ***(G-20082)***
Great Threads...413 323-9402
6 Berkshire Ave Belchertown MA (01007) ***(G-8024)***
Great Wine, The, Acton *Also called Hirsch Retail Store Inc* ***(G-7360)***
Greater Manchester Sports...603 627-3892
35 Benjamin St Manchester NH (03109) ***(G-18830)***
Greater New Milford Spectrum, New Milford *Also called Local Media Group Inc* ***(G-2813)***
Greatheart Inc...978 475-8732
89 N Main St Ste 3 Andover MA (01810) ***(G-7553)***
Greco Bros Inc...401 421-9306
1 Greco Ln Providence RI (02909) ***(G-21023)***
Greco Industries Inc...203 798-7804
14 Trowbridge Dr Bethel CT (06801) ***(G-156)***
Greek Elements LLC...203 594-2022
49 Journeys End Rd New Canaan CT (06840) ***(G-2598)***

Green Brothers Fabricating 508 880-3608
15 4th St Taunton MA (02780) ***(G-15756)***
Green Burial Massachusetts 413 863-4634
270 Mountain Rd Gill MA (01354) ***(G-11156)***
Green Dragon Bindery Inc 508 842-8250
265 Boylston St Shrewsbury MA (01545) ***(G-15115)***
Green Egg Design LLC 860 541-5411
750 Main St Ste 506 Hartford CT (06103) ***(G-1828)***
Green Heron Hlth Solutions Inc 978 309-8118
47a High St Rockport MA (01966) ***(G-14835)***
Green Manor Corporation (PA) 860 643-8111
306 Progress Dr Manchester CT (06042) ***(G-2007)***
Green Maountain Yogurt, West Newbury *Also called Ark of Safety* ***(G-22610)***
Green Mountain Awning Inc 802 438-2951
36 Marble St West Rutland VT (05777) ***(G-22615)***
Green Mountain Baking Co, Auburn *Also called Lepage Bakeries Park St LLC* ***(G-5576)***
Green Mountain Beverages, Middlebury *Also called Vermont Hard Cider Company LLC* ***(G-22120)***
Green Mountain Blocks 802 748-1341
316 Vance Rd Danville VT (05828) ***(G-21896)***
Green Mountain Book Bargains, North Pomfret *Also called Trafalgar Square Farm Inc* ***(G-22235)***
Green Mountain Cbd Inc 802 595-3258
273 Kate Brook Rd Hardwick VT (05843) ***(G-22012)***
Green Mountain Chipping Inc (PA) 802 899-1239
Rr 15 Underhill VT (05489) ***(G-22548)***
Green Mountain Chocolate Co (PA) 508 473-9060
1 Rosenfeld Dr Hopedale MA (01747) ***(G-11673)***
Green Mountain Coffee Roasters, Burlington *Also called Keurig Green Mountain Inc* ***(G-9293)***
Green Mountain Compost 802 660-4949
1042 Redmond Rd Williston VT (05495) ***(G-22672)***
Green Mountain Custom Barrels, Conway *Also called Green Mtn Rifle Barrel Co Inc* ***(G-17953)***
Green Mountain Distillers LLC 802 498-4848
2919 Laporte Rd Morrisville VT (05661) ***(G-22168)***
Green Mountain Fly Wheeler 802 223-1595
550 Stewart Rd Montpelier VT (05602) ***(G-22148)***
Green Mountain Forest Products 802 868-2306
962 Morey Rd Highgate Center VT (05459) ***(G-22020)***
Green Mountain Fragrances Inc 802 490-2268
185 Meeting House Ln Brattleboro VT (05301) ***(G-21731)***
Green Mountain Gazebo 802 869-1212
237 Kimball Hill Rd Westminster VT (05158) ***(G-22630)***
Green Mountain Glass LLC 603 826-4660
3 Depot St Charlestown NH (03603) ***(G-17815)***
Green Mountain Greengo, Chester *Also called Hume Specialties Inc* ***(G-21843)***
Green Mountain Honey Farms 802 877-3396
Rr 7 Ferrisburg VT (05456) ***(G-21986)***
Green Mountain Knitting, Medway *Also called Plastic Monofil Co Ltd* ***(G-12969)***
Green Mountain Knitting Inc 800 361-1190
28 Industrial Dr Milton VT (05468) ***(G-22131)***
Green Mountain Marinades 802 434-3731
191 Dick Brown Rd Bristol NH (03222) ***(G-17766)***
Green Mountain Metals of VT 603 542-0005
2 Wentworth Pl Claremont NH (03743) ***(G-17852)***
Green Mountain Monogram Inc 802 757-2553
14 Creamery St Wells River VT (05081) ***(G-22601)***
Green Mountain Mulch, Derby *Also called Barrup Farms Inc* ***(G-21899)***
Green Mountain Recognition 802 775-7063
9 Grandview Ter Rutland VT (05701) ***(G-22337)***
Green Mountain Risk MGT Inc 802 763-7773
191 Kibling Hill Rd Strafford VT (05072) ***(G-22527)***
Green Mountain Risk MGT LLC 802 683-8586
660 Central Ave Ste 201 Dover NH (03820) ***(G-18024)***
Green Mountain Smokehouse 802 674-6653
341 Us Route 5 S Windsor VT (05089) ***(G-22709)***
Green Mountain Spinnery Inc 802 387-4528
7 Brickyard Ln East Dummerston VT (05346) ***(G-21919)***
Green Mountain Vista Inc 802 862-0159
223 Avenue D 10 Williston VT (05495) ***(G 22673)***
Green Mtn Grn & Barrel LLC 802 324-5838
17 Christmas Hill Rd Richmond VT (05477) ***(G-22311)***
Green Mtn Maple Sug Ref Co Inc 802 644-2625
204 Boarding House Hl Rd Belvidere Center VT (05442) ***(G-21659)***
Green Mtn Organic Crmry LLC 802 482-6455
10516 Route 116 Ste 100 Hinesburg VT (05461) ***(G-22026)***
Green Mtn Rifle Barrel Co Inc 603 447-1095
153 W Main St Conway NH (03818) ***(G-17953)***
Green Publishing, West Springfield *Also called Frg Publications* ***(G-16522)***
Green Ray Led Intl LLC (PA) 203 485-1435
115 E Putnam Ave Ste 3 Greenwich CT (06830) ***(G-1618)***
Green Solar LLC 413 552-4114
933 E Columbus Ave Springfield MA (01105) ***(G-15473)***
Green Summer 617 387-0120
308 Main St Everett MA (02149) ***(G-10612)***
Greenbrier Games LLP 978 618-8442
12 Bicknell St Marlborough MA (01752) ***(G-12764)***
Greencore Oars LLC 508 586-8418
121 Liberty St Brockton MA (02301) ***(G-9153)***
Greene Industries Inc 401 884-7530
65 Rocky Hollow Rd East Greenwich RI (02818) ***(G-20369)***
Greene Lyon Group Inc 617 290-2276
18 S Hunt Rd Unit 6 Amesbury MA (01913) ***(G-7488)***
Greener 3000 LLC 781 589-5777
800 Boylston St Fl 16 Boston MA (02199) ***(G-8579)***
Greener Group LLC 978 441-3900
123 Bolt St Lowell MA (01852) ***(G-12378)***
Greenerd Press & Mch Co LLC (PA) 603 889-4101
41 Crown St Nashua NH (03060) ***(G-19172)***
Greenfield Industries Inc 603 883-6423
5 Manhattan Dr Amherst NH (03031) ***(G-17565)***
Greenfield Silver Inc (PA) 413 774-2774
298 Federal St Greenfield MA (01301) ***(G-11262)***
Greenhaven Cabinetry & Millwor 860 535-1106
338 Elm St Stonington CT (06378) ***(G-4376)***
Greenleaf Bfuels New Haven LLC 203 672-9028
100 Waterfront St New Haven CT (06512) ***(G-2692)***
Greenmaker Industries Conn LLC 860 761-2830
697 Oakwood Ave West Hartford CT (06110) ***(G-5072)***
Greenport Foods LLC 203 221-2673
191 Post Rd W Westport CT (06880) ***(G-5199)***
Greenrange Furniture Company 802 747-8564
2778 Shelburne Falls Rd Hinesburg VT (05461) ***(G-22027)***
Greenscape of Clinton LLC 860 669-1880
13 Janes Ln Clinton CT (06413) ***(G-787)***
Greensight Agronomics Inc 617 633-4919
12 Channel St Ste 605 Boston MA (02210) ***(G-8580)***
Greenstone Precast 207 926-5704
1 Oz Dr New Gloucester ME (04260) ***(G-6466)***
Greentree Marketing Inc 508 877-2581
10 Central St Framingham MA (01701) ***(G-10961)***
Greenville Ready Mix Inc 401 539-2333
Skunk Hill Rd Ashaway RI (02804) ***(G-20035)***
Greenwald Industries, Chester *Also called Blackwold Inc* ***(G-768)***
Greenwich Gofer 203 637-8425
56 Halsey Dr Old Greenwich CT (06870) ***(G-3309)***
Greenwich Magazine, Westport *Also called Moffly Publications Inc* ***(G-5216)***
Greenwich Sentinel 203 883-1430
28 Bruce Park Ave Greenwich CT (06830) ***(G-1619)***
Greenwich Time, Norwalk *Also called Hearst Corporation* ***(G-3167)***
Greenwich Time 203 253-2922
44 Columbus Pl Apt 9 Stamford CT (06907) ***(G-4203)***
Greenwood Associates, Wareham *Also called Electro-Prep Inc* ***(G-16246)***
Greenwood Emrgncy Vehicles LLC (HQ) 508 695-7138
530 John Dietsch Blvd North Attleboro MA (02763) ***(G-13758)***
Greenwood Mill Inc 802 626-0800
599 Goose Green Rd Bradford VT (05033) ***(G-21700)***
Greenwood Publishing Group LLC 603 431-7894
361 Hanover St Portsmouth NH (03801) ***(G-19570)***
Greenwood Publishing Group LLC (HQ) 617 351-5000
125 High St Boston MA (02110) ***(G-8581)***
Greg Asselin Studios Ltd 508 222-7361
27 Walker St Norton MA (02766) ***(G-14078)***
Greg Manning Logging LLC 802 439-6255
1388 Center Rd Corinth VT (05039) ***(G-21891)***
Greg Robbins and Associates 888 699-8876
15 Park Pl Branford CT (06405) ***(G-321)***
Gregg Stewart 207 989-0903
17 Doughty Dr Ste 106 Brewer ME (04412) ***(G-5796)***
Gregor Technologies LLC 860 482-2569
529 Technology Park Dr Torrington CT (06790) ***(G-4580)***
Gregory Engineering Corp 508 481-0480
105 Bartlett St Marlborough MA (01752) ***(G-12765)***
Gregory Manufacturing Inc 413 536-5432
102 Cabot St Ste 2 Holyoke MA (01040) ***(G-11628)***
Gregory Woodworks LLC 203 794-0726
6 Sympaug Park Rd Bethel CT (06801) ***(G-157)***
Gregstrom Corporation 781 935-6600
64 Holton St Woburn MA (01801) ***(G-17194)***
Greif Inc 740 549-6000
491 North St Windsor Locks CT (06096) ***(G-5394)***
Gremarco Industries Inc 508 867-5244
131 E Main St West Brookfield MA (01585) ***(G-16470)***
Grenade (usa) LLC 401 944-3960
815 Reservoir Ave Ste 1a Cranston RI (02910) ***(G-20234)***
Grenier Fuels LLC 207 602-1400
184 Lewis Ave Saco ME (04072) ***(G-6848)***
Grenier Print Shop Inc 617 522-2225
3702 Washington St Boston MA (02130) ***(G-8582)***
Greniers Garden & Bakery 802 244-8057
1413 Guptil Rd Waterbury Center VT (05677) ***(G-22591)***
Grey Force Cooling 508 441-1753
214 Neck Rd Rochester MA (02770) ***(G-14787)***
Grey Wall Software LLC 203 782-5944
195 Church St Fl 14 New Haven CT (06510) ***(G-2693)***
Greylock Press LLC 978 530-1740
6 Granite Road Ext Peabody MA (01960) ***(G-14337)***

ALPHABETIC

Greylock Sand & Gravel LLC..........413 441-4967
5 Mill St Adams MA (01220) ***(G-7411)***
Greystone, North Providence *Also called Induplate Inc* ***(G-20765)***
Greystone of Lincoln Inc (PA)..........401 333-0444
7 Wellington Rd Lincoln RI (02865) ***(G-20576)***
Grid Solutions Corp..........781 718-4266
132 One Half Wash St Marblehead MA (01945) ***(G-12684)***
Gridiron Capital LLC (PA)..........203 972-1100
220 Elm St Fl 2 New Canaan CT (06840) ***(G-2599)***
Griffin Green..........203 266-5727
190 Hard Hill Rd N Bethlehem CT (06751) ***(G-195)***
Griffin Manufacturing Co Inc..........508 677-0048
502 Bedford St Fall River MA (02720) ***(G-10707)***
Griffin Publishing Co Inc..........781 829-4700
21 Chestnut St Duxbury MA (02332) ***(G-10398)***
Griffin Report Food Marketing, Duxbury *Also called Griffin Publishing Co Inc* ***(G-10398)***
Griffith Company..........203 333-5557
239 Asylum St Bridgeport CT (06610) ***(G-422)***
Grill Daddy Brush Company..........888 840-7552
29 Arcadia Rd Old Greenwich CT (06870) ***(G-3310)***
Grillo Services LLC..........203 877-5070
1183 Oronoque Rd Milford CT (06461) ***(G-2294)***
Grimco Inc..........800 542-9941
221 South St Unit G1 New Britain CT (06051) ***(G-2536)***
Grimm, G H Co, Rutland *Also called Leader Evaporatorinc* ***(G-22343)***
Grind..........401 223-1212
1401 Park Ave Unit 1 Cranston RI (02920) ***(G-20235)***
Grindrite, Waitsfield *Also called Wintersteiger Inc* ***(G-22571)***
Gringo Jack's, Manchester Center *Also called Gringo Kitchens LLC* ***(G-22086)***
Gringo Kitchens LLC..........802 362-0836
5103 Main St Manchester Center VT (05255) ***(G-22086)***
Grinnell Cabinet Makers Inc..........401 781-1080
169 Mill St Cranston RI (02905) ***(G-20236)***
Grip Pod Systems Intl LLC..........239 233-3694
77 Childs Dr Dover NH (03820) ***(G-18025)***
Gripnail Corporation..........401 431-1791
97 Dexter Rd East Providence RI (02914) ***(G-20416)***
Gripwet Inc..........207 239-0486
55 Devereaux Cir South Portland ME (04106) ***(G-7029)***
Grist For Mill LLC..........603 744-0405
2 Central St Bristol NH (03222) ***(G-17767)***
Griswold LLC..........860 564-3321
1 River St Moosup CT (06354) ***(G-2426)***
Griswold Machine & Fabrication..........860 376-9891
8 Sheldon Rd Jewett City CT (06351) ***(G-1913)***
Griswold Rubber Company, Moosup *Also called Griswold LLC* ***(G-2426)***
Griswold Textile Print Inc..........401 596-2784
84 White Rock Rd Westerly RI (02891) ***(G-21525)***
Grit, Charlestown *Also called Global RES Innovation Tech Inc* ***(G-9835)***
Grizzly Graphix, Sheldon *Also called Grant John* ***(G-22428)***
Grohe Manufacturing..........203 516-5536
26 Beaver St Ste 2 Ansonia CT (06401) ***(G-17)***
Grolen Communications Inc..........603 645-0101
814 Elm St Ste 101 Manchester NH (03101) ***(G-18831)***
Groov-Pin Corporation (PA)..........770 251-5054
331 Farnum Pike Smithfield RI (02917) ***(G-21230)***
Grossman Marketing Group, Somerville *Also called Massachusetts Envelope Co Inc* ***(G-15195)***
Grote & Weigel Inc (PA)..........860 242-8528
76 Granby St Bloomfield CT (06002) ***(G-221)***
Groton Herald Inc..........978 448-6061
161 Main St Groton MA (01450) ***(G-11289)***
Groton Pallet Incorporated..........978 448-5651
183 Kemp St Groton MA (01450) ***(G-11290)***
Groton Timberworks of Vermont..........802 584-4446
2126 Scott Hwy Groton VT (05046) ***(G-22005)***
Groton Wind LLC..........603 786-2862
590 Groton Hollow Rd Rumney NH (03266) ***(G-19696)***
Ground Support Products Corp..........860 491-3348
42 Winter St Ste 5 Pembroke MA (02359) ***(G-14407)***
Group Artic Inc..........781 848-2174
55 Messina Dr Braintree MA (02184) ***(G-9013)***
Group Four Transducers Inc (PA)..........413 525-2705
22 Deer Park Dr East Longmeadow MA (01028) ***(G-10477)***
Group Works..........203 834-7905
50 Powder Horn Hill Rd Wilton CT (06897) ***(G-5290)***
Groupglobalnet Corp..........857 212-4012
768 Morton St Boston MA (02126) ***(G-8583)***
Grove Labs Inc..........703 608-8178
28 Dane St Somerville MA (02143) ***(G-15179)***
Grove Products Inc..........978 534-5188
17 Marguerite Ave Ste 1 Leominster MA (01453) ***(G-12148)***
Grove Street Enterprises Inc..........413 698-3301
508 Canaan Rd Richmond MA (01254) ***(G-14780)***
Grove Systems Inc..........860 663-2555
572 Route 148 Deep River CT (06419) ***(G-1061)***
Grover Gundrilling LLC..........207 743-7051
59 Industrial Dr Oxford ME (04270) ***(G-6566)***

Growth I M33 L P..........617 877-0046
888 Boylston St Ste 500 Boston MA (02199) ***(G-8584)***
Grozier Technical Systems Inc..........781 762-4446
11 Stanford Dr Westwood MA (02090) ***(G-16867)***
Gruenewald Mfg Co Inc..........978 777-0200
250 North St Ste A10 Danvers MA (01923) ***(G-10219)***
GS Blodgett Corporation..........603 225-5688
509 Route 3a Bow NH (03304) ***(G-17715)***
GS Blodgett Corporation..........802 871-3287
19 Thompson Dr Essex Junction VT (05452) ***(G-21943)***
GS Blodgett Corporation (HQ)..........802 860-3700
42 Allen Martin Dr Essex Junction VT (05452) ***(G-21944)***
GS Blodgett Corporation..........802 860-3700
42 Allen Martin Dr Essex Junction VT (05452) ***(G-21945)***
GS Inc..........207 593-7730
12 Moran Dr Ste A1 Rockland ME (04841) ***(G-6797)***
GS Precision Inc-Keene Div..........603 355-1166
18 Bradco St Keene NH (03431) ***(G-18506)***
Gs Rubber Industries LLC..........508 672-0742
104 Anawan St Ste 2 Fall River MA (02721) ***(G-10708)***
Gs Thermal Solutions Inc..........475 289-4625
144 Old Brookfield Rd C Danbury CT (06811) ***(G-929)***
GSC, Lancaster *Also called Governor Supply Co* ***(G-11983)***
Gsg Inc..........802 828-6221
3986 Harbor Rd Shelburne VT (05482) ***(G-22418)***
Gsk Innovations..........508 566-5212
17 Woodland Rd East Walpole MA (02032) ***(G-10523)***
Gsoft, Lexington *Also called Divya Marigowda* ***(G-12220)***
Gsoutfitting..........413 773-0247
58 Summer St Greenfield MA (01301) ***(G-11263)***
Gsp Worldwide, Pembroke *Also called Ground Support Products Corp* ***(G-14407)***
Gsr Global Corporation..........781 687-9191
700 Technology Park Dr # 210 Billerica MA (01821) ***(G-8252)***
Gssi, Nashua *Also called Geophysical Survey Systems Inc* ***(G-19167)***
Gt Advanced Cz LLC..........603 883-5200
243 Daniel Webster Hwy Merrimack NH (03054) ***(G-19004)***
Gt Advanced Technologies..........508 954-8249
1 Industrial Dr Unit 1 # 1 Danvers MA (01923) ***(G-10220)***
Gt Advanced Technologies Inc..........978 498-4294
35 Congress St Ste 251 Salem MA (01970) ***(G-14916)***
Gt Advanced Technologies Inc (PA)..........603 883-5200
5 Wentworth Dr Ste 1 Hudson NH (03051) ***(G-18394)***
Gt Advanced Technologies Ltd..........603 883-5200
5 Wentworth Dr Hudson NH (03051) ***(G-18395)***
Gta-Nht Inc (HQ)..........781 331-5900
30 Commerce Rd Rockland MA (02370) ***(G-14804)***
Gtat, Hudson *Also called Gt Advanced Technologies Inc* ***(G-18394)***
Gtat Corporation..........603 883-5200
20 Trafalgar Sq Nashua NH (03063) ***(G-19173)***
Gtat Corporation..........978 745-0088
27 Congress St Salem MA (01970) ***(G-14917)***
Gtat Corporation (HQ)..........603 883-5200
5 Wentworth Dr 1 Hudson NH (03051) ***(G-18396)***
Gtb Innovative Solutions Inc..........413 733-0146
507 Southampton Rd Ste 1 Westfield MA (01085) ***(G-16685)***
Gtech, Braintree *Also called Igt Global Solutions Corp* ***(G-9019)***
Gtimd Catheter Solutions, Amherst *Also called Gtimd LLC* ***(G-17566)***
Gtimd LLC..........603 880-0277
6 Columbia Dr Amherst NH (03031) ***(G-17566)***
Gtrpet Smf LLC..........203 661-1229
10 Mead Ave Unit B Cos Cob CT (06807) ***(G-825)***
Gtxcel Inc..........508 804-3092
144 Turnpike Rd Ste 140 Southborough MA (01772) ***(G-15358)***
Guardair Corporation..........413 594-4400
47 Veterans Dr Chicopee MA (01022) ***(G-10028)***
Guardian Envmtl Tech Inc..........860 350-2200
208 Sawyer Hill Rd New Milford CT (06776) ***(G-2802)***
Guardian Indus Pdts Inc Mass..........508 384-0060
150 Dedham St Norfolk MA (02056) ***(G-13660)***
Guardian Technologies Inc..........603 594-0430
4 Townsend W Nashua NH (03063) ***(G-19174)***
Guardion Inc..........603 769-7265
151 S Bedford St 7 Burlington MA (01803) ***(G-9280)***
Guarducci Stained GL Studios..........413 528-6287
64 Stoney Brook Rd Great Barrington MA (01230) ***(G-11239)***
Guasa Salsa Vzla..........203 981-7011
9 Rainbow Rd Norwalk CT (06851) ***(G-3164)***
Guertin Graphics & Awards Inc..........508 754-0200
136 Southbridge St Worcester MA (01608) ***(G-17386)***
Guertin's Awards Plus, Auburn *Also called George Guertin Trophy Inc* ***(G-7836)***
Guess Inc..........781 843-3147
250 Granite St Ste B Braintree MA (02184) ***(G-9014)***
Guhring Inc..........860 216-5948
121 W Ddley Town Rd Ste C Bloomfield CT (06002) ***(G-222)***
Guia Commercial Portugues Inc..........401 438-1740
100 Warren Ave East Providence RI (02914) ***(G-20417)***
Guida's Milk & Ice Cream, New Britain *Also called Guida-Seibert Dairy Company* ***(G-2537)***
Guida-Seibert Dairy Company (PA)..........860 224-2404
433 Park St New Britain CT (06051) ***(G-2537)***

Guidant Corporation 508 683-4000
300 Boston Scientific Way Marlborough MA (01752) ***(G-12766)***

Guide & Directory, Needham Heights *Also called Bergquist Family Entps Inc* ***(G-13318)***

Guidera Marketing Services 860 599-8880
21 Pawcatuck Ave Pawcatuck CT (06379) ***(G-3436)***

Guidewire Technologies Inc 603 894-4399
26 Keewaydin Dr Ste A Salem NH (03079) ***(G-19740)***

Guiding Channels Co 508 853-0781
93 Longmeadow Ave Worcester MA (01606) ***(G-17387)***

Guild Optical Associates Inc 603 889-6247
11 Columbia Dr Unit 13 Amherst NH (03031) ***(G-17567)***

Guill Tool & Engrg Co Inc 401 822-8186
10 Pike St West Warwick RI (02893) ***(G-21493)***

Guill Tool and Engrg Co Inc 401 828-7600
20 Pike St West Warwick RI (02893) ***(G-21494)***

Guimond Logging 207 834-6329
760 Aroostook Rd Fort Kent ME (04743) ***(G-6060)***

Guinness America Inc 203 229-2100
801 Main Ave Norwalk CT (06851) ***(G-3165)***

Guitabec USA Inc 603 752-1432
42 Industrial Park Dr Berlin NH (03570) ***(G-17697)***

Gulemo Inc 860 456-1151
2 Birch St Willimantic CT (06226) ***(G-5265)***

Gulf Manufacturing Inc 860 529-8601
645 Cromwell Ave Rocky Hill CT (06067) ***(G-3710)***

Gulf of Maine Inc 207 726-4620
736 Leighton Point Rd Pembroke ME (04666) ***(G-6580)***

Gulfstream Aerospace Corp 860 210-1469
142 Second Hill Rd New Milford CT (06776) ***(G-2803)***

Gulfstream Aerospace Corp 912 965-3000
95 Old County Rd East Granby CT (06026) ***(G-1129)***

Gulfstream Aerospace Corp 413 562-5866
33 Elise St Westfield MA (01085) ***(G-16686)***

Gun F X Tactical Development (PA) 207 797-8200
28 Stroudwater Rd Unit 10 Portland ME (04102) ***(G-6667)***

Guncanco Ltd 978 352-3320
117 W Main St Georgetown MA (01833) ***(G-11143)***

Gunworks International L L C 860 388-4591
4 Center Rd Old Saybrook CT (06475) ***(G-3336)***

Gurit (usa) Inc 401 396-5008
115 Broadcommon Rd Bristol RI (02809) ***(G-20083)***

Gurit Uk, Bristol *Also called Gurit (usa) Inc* ***(G-20083)***

Gus & Ruby Letterpress LLC 603 319-1717
29 Congress St Portsmouth NH (03801) ***(G-19571)***

Gustafson Machine 978 281-2012
44 Whittemore St Ste 5 Gloucester MA (01930) ***(G-11191)***

Gustare Oils & Vinegars (PA) 508 945-4505
461 Main St Chatham MA (02633) ***(G-9859)***

Gutermann Inc 603 200-0340
55 Main St Apt 409 Newmarket NH (03857) ***(G-19334)***

Gutkin Enterprises LLC 203 777-5510
1349 Dixwell Ave Ste 1 Hamden CT (06514) ***(G-1752)***

Gutter People, The, Raymond *Also called Gutter Wholesalers Inc* ***(G-6773)***

Gutter Wholesalers Inc 207 655-7407
145 Webbs Mills Rd 93-1 Raymond ME (04071) ***(G-6773)***

Guy Little Press Inc (PA) 207 795-0650
235 N River Rd Auburn ME (04210) ***(G-5570)***

Guy Ravenelle 860 564-3200
71 Black Hill Rd Central Village CT (06332) ***(G-706)***

Guy T Piro & Sons 617 776-2840
483 Medford St Somerville MA (02145) ***(G-15180)***

Guyot Brothers Company Inc 508 222-2000
20 John Williams St Attleboro MA (02703) ***(G-7743)***

Gvd Corporation (PA) 617 661-0060
45 Spinelli Pl Cambridge MA (02138) ***(G-9498)***

Gvh Studio Inc 802 379-1135
40 Pageant St Bennington VT (05201) ***(G-21671)***

Gvs North America, Sanford *Also called Maine Manufacturing LLC* ***(G-6881)***

Gwb Corporation 508 896-9486
9 Bartlet St Ste 55 Andover MA (01810) ***(G-7554)***

Gwilliam Company Inc 860 354-2884
46 Old State Rd New Milford CT (06776) ***(G-2804)***

Gxt Green Inc 978 735-4367
505 Middlesex Tpke # 11 Billerica MA (01821) ***(G-8253)***

Gybenorth Industries LLC 203 876-9876
80 Wampus Ln Ste 13 Milford CT (06460) ***(G-2295)***

Gyrus Acmi LLC (HQ) 508 804-2600
136 Turnpike Rd Ste 300 Southborough MA (01772) ***(G-15359)***

Gys Tech LLC 530 613-9233
Phoenix Pk 2 Shker Rd Ste Phoenix Park Shirley MA (01464) ***(G-15084)***

H & B Tool & Engineering Co 860 528-9341
481 Sullivan Ave South Windsor CT (06074) ***(G-3976)***

H & B Woodworking Co 860 793-6991
105 E Main St Plainville CT (06062) ***(G-3495)***

H & C Sales Inc 781 344-6445
107 Tosca Dr Stoughton MA (02072) ***(G-15595)***

H & H Engineering Co Inc 978 682-0567
6 Pine St Methuen MA (01844) ***(G-13025)***

H & H Marine Inc 207 546-7477
932 Us Route 1 Ste 1 Steuben ME (04680) ***(G-7067)***

H & R Machine Co Inc 413 743-5610
101 Alger St Adams MA (01220) ***(G-7412)***

H & S Machine Company Inc 978 686-2321
35 Marston St Lawrence MA (01841) ***(G-12029)***

H & S Tool and Engineering Inc 508 672-6509
777 Airport Rd Fall River MA (02720) ***(G-10709)***

H & S Woodworks L T D 914 391-3926
161 Merryall Rd New Milford CT (06776) ***(G-2805)***

H & T Specialty Co Inc 781 893-3866
56 Clematis Ave Waltham MA (02453) ***(G-16123)***

H & W Machine LLC 860 828-7679
37 Willow Brook Dr Berlin CT (06037) ***(G-88)***

H & W Test Products Inc 508 336-3200
58 Industrial Ct Seekonk MA (02771) ***(G-15023)***

H 6, Nashua *Also called H6 Systems Incorporated* ***(G-19175)***

H Arthur York Logging Inc (PA) 207 746-5883
157 Main Rd Medway ME (04460) ***(G-6425)***

H Arthur York Logging Inc 207 746-5912
163 Turnpike Rd Medway ME (04460) ***(G-6426)***

H B M, Marlborough *Also called Hottinger Bldwin Msrements Inc* ***(G-12775)***

H B Smith Company Inc 413 568-3148
61 Union St Ste 7 Westfield MA (01085) ***(G-16687)***

H Barber & Sons Inc 203 729-9000
15 Raytkwich Rd Naugatuck CT (06770) ***(G-2476)***

H C Haynes, Winn *Also called Herbert C Haynes Inc* ***(G-7264)***

H C Starck Inc (HQ) 617 630-5800
45 Industrial Pl Newton MA (02461) ***(G-13598)***

H E Moore Corp (PA) 617 268-1262
45 Lakeshore Dr Norfolk MA (02056) ***(G-13661)***

H E Moore Corp 617 268-1262
485 E 1st St Boston MA (02127) ***(G-8585)***

H F Staples & Co Inc 603 889-8600
9 Webb Dr Ste 5 Merrimack NH (03054) ***(G-19005)***

H G Cockrill Corp 508 429-2005
349 Fiske St Holliston MA (01746) ***(G-11574)***

H G Steinmetz Machine Works 203 794-1880
2 Turnage Ln Bethel CT (06801) ***(G-158)***

H H Arnold Co Inc 781 878-0346
529 Liberty St Rockland MA (02370) ***(G-14805)***

H Hirschmann Ltd 802 438-4447
467 Sheldon Ave West Rutland VT (05777) ***(G-22616)***

H I Five Renewables 978 384-8032
8 Church St Merrimac MA (01860) ***(G-13001)***

H Krevit and Company Inc 203 772-3350
73 Welton St New Haven CT (06511) ***(G-2694)***

H L Handy Company Inc 802 387-4040
22 W Hill Rd Putney VT (05346) ***(G-22289)***

H Larosee and Sons Inc 978 562-9417
140 E Main St Westborough MA (01581) ***(G-16623)***

H Loeb Corporation 508 996-3745
419 Sawyer St Unit 2 New Bedford MA (02746) ***(G-13392)***

H O Wire Co Inc 508 243-7177
215 Shrewsbury St West Boylston MA (01583) ***(G-16416)***

H O Zimman Inc 781 598-9230
152 Lynnway Lynn MA (01902) ***(G-12515)***

H P Fairfield LLC 207 885-4895
65 Pleasant Hill Rd Scarborough ME (04074) ***(G-6923)***

H R P Products Inc 603 330-3757
101 Nh Route 11 Farmington NH (03835) ***(G-18142)***

H W Dunn & Son Inc 207 667-8121
146 Water St Ellsworth ME (04605) ***(G-6019)***

H&H Custom Metal Fabg Inc 603 382-2818
6 Duston Ave Plaistow NH (03865) ***(G-19518)***

H&H Propeller Shop Inc (PA) 978 744-3806
0 Essex St Salem MA (01970) ***(G-14918)***

H&L Instruments LLC 603 964-1818
34 Post Rd North Hampton NH (03862) ***(G-19383)***

H&M Metals LLC 603 889-8320
9a Columbia Dr Amherst NH (03031) ***(G-17568)***

H&T Waterbury Inc 203 574-2240
984 Waterville St Waterbury CT (06710) ***(G-4880)***

H-O Products Corporation 860 379-9875
12 Munro St Winsted CT (06098) ***(G-5412)***

H.K. Klitzner Company Division, Lincoln *Also called Klitzner Industries Inc* ***(G-20577)***

H.krevit, New Haven *Also called New Haven Chlor-Alkali LLC* ***(G-2714)***

H2o Wear, Wilton *Also called Waterwear Inc* ***(G-19991)***

H2ohh, Portland *Also called Shed Happens Inc* ***(G-6725)***

H6 Systems Incorporated 603 880-4190
55 Lake St Ste 11 Nashua NH (03060) ***(G-19175)***

Haartz Auto Fabric, Acton *Also called Haartz Corporation* ***(G-7359)***

Haartz Corporation (PA) 978 264-2600
87 Hayward Rd Acton MA (01720) ***(G-7359)***

Habasit Abt Inc 860 632-2211
150 Industrial Park Rd Middletown CT (06457) ***(G-2188)***

Habasit America Inc 860 632-2211
150 Industrial Park Rd Middletown CT (06457) ***(G-2189)***

Habco Industries LLC 860 682-6800
172 Oak St Glastonbury CT (06033) ***(G-1556)***

ALPHABETIC

(PA)=Parent Co (HQ)=Headquarters (DH)=Div Headquarters

Habitat Post & Beam Inc 413 665-4006
21 Elm St South Deerfield MA (01373) ***(G-15250)***
Habitat Virtual Village, South Deerfield *Also called Habitat Post & Beam Inc* ***(G-15250)***
Hachette Book Group Inc 617 227-0730
3 Center Plz Boston MA (02108) ***(G-8586)***
Hachette Book Group Inc 617 227-0730
53 State St Ste 9 Boston MA (02109) ***(G-8587)***
Hackett Publishing Company 617 497-6303
847 Massachusetts Ave Cambridge MA (02139) ***(G-9499)***
Hadc 401 274-1870
85 Whipple St Providence RI (02908) ***(G-21024)***
Hadco Corporation (HQ) 603 421-3400
12a Manor Pkwy Salem NH (03079) ***(G-19741)***
Hadley Printing Company Inc 413 536-8517
58 N Canal St Holyoke MA (01040) ***(G-11629)***
Hadley Propeller Inc 413 585-0500
28 Stockwell Rd Hadley MA (01035) ***(G-11306)***
Haemonetics Asia Incorporated (HQ) 781 848-7100
400 Wood Rd Braintree MA (02184) ***(G-9015)***
Haemonetics Corporation (PA) 781 848-7100
400 Wood Rd Braintree MA (02184) ***(G-9016)***
Haffordlogging 603 478-0142
553 W Main St Hillsboro NH (03244) ***(G-18313)***
Hagan Design and Machine Inc 603 292-1101
8 Forbes Rd Newmarket NH (03857) ***(G-19335)***
Hague Textiles Inc (PA) 508 678-7556
168 Stevens St Fall River MA (02721) ***(G-10710)***
Hague Textiles Inc 508 678-7556
168 Stevens St Fall River MA (02721) ***(G-10711)***
Hai Labs, Lexington *Also called Hightech American Indus Labs* ***(G-12229)***
Haigh-Farr Inc 603 644-6170
43 Harvey Rd Bedford NH (03110) ***(G-17644)***
Haines Manufacturing Co, Presque Isle *Also called Harold Haines Inc* ***(G-6758)***
Hair Designs By Debbie Tin 603 887-0643
144 North Rd Sandown NH (03873) ***(G-19784)***
Hair Studio At Lafayette 207 604-5005
2 Storer St Ste 105 Kennebunk ME (04043) ***(G-6235)***
Hairenik Association Inc 617 926-3974
80 Bigelow Ave Watertown MA (02472) ***(G-16289)***
Haiti Projects Inc 978 969-1064
335 Water St Hanover MA (02339) ***(G-11341)***
Hajan LLC 860 223-2005
788 W Main St New Britain CT (06053) ***(G-2538)***
Halbro America Inc 401 438-2727
885 Warren Ave East Providence RI (02914) ***(G-20418)***
Halco Inc 203 575-9450
114 Porter St Waterbury CT (06708) ***(G-4881)***
Hale Brothers Inc 603 474-2511
16 Stard Rd Seabrook NH (03874) ***(G-19802)***
Haley Construction Inc 207 778-9990
116 Pierpole Rd Farmington ME (04938) ***(G-6049)***
Half-Time Ventures Inc 978 369-2907
103 Meadowbrook Rd Carlisle MA (01741) ***(G-9798)***
Hall Industries, North Branford *Also called Hall Machine Systems Inc* ***(G-2965)***
Hall Machine Systems Inc (HQ) 203 481-4275
8c Commerce Dr North Branford CT (06471) ***(G-2965)***
Hallmark Healy Group Inc (HQ) 508 222-9234
49 Pearl St Attleboro MA (02703) ***(G-7744)***
Hallmark Sweet/Ekru Inc 508 226-9600
49 Pearl St Attleboro MA (02703) ***(G-7745)***
Hallowell EMC, Pittsfield *Also called Hallowell Engrg & Mfg Corp* ***(G-14475)***
Hallowell Engrg & Mfg Corp 413 445-4263
239 West St Pittsfield MA (01201) ***(G-14475)***
Halls Edge Inc 203 653-2281
420 Fairfield Ave Ste 3 Stamford CT (06902) ***(G-4204)***
Halls Rental Service LLC 203 488-0383
45 Cedar Lake Rd North Branford CT (06471) ***(G-2966)***
Halo Maritime Defense Systems, Newton *Also called Elemental Innovation Inc* ***(G-19365)***
Hamco Tank Systems LLC 603 878-0585
815 Hurricane Hill Rd Mason NH (03048) ***(G-18968)***
Hamden Brewing Company LLC 203 247-4677
819 Bridgeport Ave Shelton CT (06484) ***(G-3807)***
Hamden Grinding 203 288-2906
555 Sherman Ave Ste 11 Hamden CT (06514) ***(G-1753)***
Hamden Journal LLC 203 668-6307
99 Burke St Hamden CT (06514) ***(G-1754)***
Hamden Metal Service Company 203 281-1522
2 Broadway Hamden CT (06518) ***(G-1755)***
Hamden Press Inc 203 624-0554
1054 Dixwell Ave Hamden CT (06514) ***(G-1756)***
Hamden Sheet Metal Inc 203 776-1472
1079 Dixwell Ave Hamden CT (06514) ***(G-1757)***
Hamden Sports Center Inc 203 248-9898
2858 Whitney Ave Hamden CT (06518) ***(G-1758)***
Hamilton Branch, South Hamilton *Also called Danversbank* ***(G-15314)***
Hamilton Elevator Interiors 781 233-9540
6 Belair St Saugus MA (01906) ***(G-14984)***
Hamilton Ferris Co Inc 508 743-9901
3 Angelo Dr Bourne MA (02532) ***(G-8946)***
Hamilton Precision LLC 603 524-7622
274 Jamestown Rd Belmont NH (03220) ***(G-17673)***
Hamilton Sign & Design Inc 508 459-9731
545 Sw Cutoff Worcester MA (01607) ***(G-17388)***
Hamilton Sndstrnd Space 860 654-6000
1 Hamilton Rd Windsor Locks CT (06096) ***(G-5395)***
Hamilton Standard Space 860 654-6000
1 Hamilton Rd Windsor Locks CT (06096) ***(G-5396)***
Hamilton Storage Tech Inc (HQ) 508 544-7000
3 Forge Pkwy Franklin MA (02038) ***(G-11051)***
Hamilton Storage Tech Inc 508 544-7000
3 Forge Pkwy Franklin MA (02038) ***(G-11052)***
Hamilton Sundstrand Corp (HQ) 860 654-6000
1 Hamilton Rd Windsor Locks CT (06096) ***(G-5397)***
Hamilton Thorne Inc (PA) 978 921-2050
100 Cummings Ctr Ste 465e Beverly MA (01915) ***(G-8138)***
Hamilton Tool Inc 401 421-8870
26 Turner St Providence RI (02908) ***(G-21025)***
Hamiltonbookcom LLC 860 824-0275
147 Route 7 S Falls Village CT (06031) ***(G-1463)***
Hamlethub LLC 203 431-6400
37 Danbury Rd Ste 202 Ridgefield CT (06877) ***(G-3667)***
Hamlin Cabinets Corp 508 384-8371
112 Pond St Norfolk MA (02056) ***(G-13662)***
Hammamatsu Corporation 603 883-3888
20 Sunland Dr Hudson NH (03051) ***(G-18397)***
Hammar & Sons Inc 603 635-2292
71 Bridge St Pelham NH (03076) ***(G-19434)***
Hammond Lumber, Canaan *Also called F C Hammond & Son Lbr Co Inc* ***(G-17778)***
Hampden Engineering Corp 413 525-3981
99 Shaker Rd East Longmeadow MA (01028) ***(G-10478)***
Hampden Fence Supply Inc 413 786-4390
80 Industrial Ln Agawam MA (01001) ***(G-7430)***
Hampden Hat & Cap Co Division, Springfield *Also called Athletic Emblem & Lettering Co* ***(G-15449)***
Hampden Papers Inc (PA) 413 536-1000
100 Water St Holyoke MA (01040) ***(G-11630)***
Hampford Research Inc (PA) 203 375-1137
54 Veterans Blvd Stratford CT (06615) ***(G-4417)***
Hampshire Chemical Corp (HQ) 603 888-2320
2 E Spit Brook Rd Nashua NH (03060) ***(G-19176)***
Hampshire Controls Corporation 603 749-9424
1 Grove St Dover NH (03820) ***(G-18026)***
Hampshire Hardwoods LLC 603 434-1144
53 Captains Walk Laconia NH (03246) ***(G-18565)***
Hampstead Copy Center, East Hampstead *Also called Ram Printing Incorporated* ***(G-18082)***
Hampstead Copy Center, East Hampstead *Also called Ram Printing Incorporated* ***(G-18083)***
Hampton Door Company Inc 413 568-5730
14 Coleman Ave Westfield MA (01085) ***(G-16688)***
Hampton North Fisheries Inc 603 463-5874
163 Stevens Hill Rd Nottingham NH (03290) ***(G-19414)***
Hampton Sand and Gravel 603 601-2275
564 Lafayette Rd Hampton NH (03842) ***(G-18264)***
Hamworthy Peabody Combustn Inc (HQ) 203 922-1199
6 Armstrong Rd Ste 2 Shelton CT (06484) ***(G-3808)***
Hancock Electric Mtr Svcs Inc 617 472-5789
231 Willard St Quincy MA (02169) ***(G-14631)***
Hancock Marine Inc 508 678-0301
300 River St Fall River MA (02720) ***(G-10712)***
Hancor Inc 802 886-8403
30 Precision Dr Springfield VT (05156) ***(G-22501)***
Handyaid Co 413 786-9865
106 S Westfield St Feeding Hills MA (01030) ***(G-10799)***
Handyscape LLC 860 318-1067
43 Sandy Pine Dr Southington CT (06489) ***(G-4056)***
Hanesbrands Inc 603 424-6737
80 Premium Outlets Blvd # 365 Merrimack NH (03054) ***(G-19006)***
Hanford Cabinet & Wdwkg Co 860 388-5055
102 Ingham Hill Rd Old Saybrook CT (06475) ***(G-3337)***
Hanger Clinic, Leominster *Also called Hanger Prosthetics & Orthotics* ***(G-12149)***
Hanger Prosthethics & Orthotic 508 238-6760
67 Belmont St South Easton MA (02375) ***(G-15278)***
Hanger Prosthetics & Orthotics 978 466-7400
100 Erdman Way Ste S-100 Leominster MA (01453) ***(G-12149)***
Hanger Prosthetics & Orthotics 207 872-8779
325 Kennedy Memorial Dr Waterville ME (04901) ***(G-7156)***
Hanger Prsthetcs & Ortho Inc 860 482-5611
811 E Main St Ste B Torrington CT (06790) ***(G-4581)***
Hanger Prsthetcs & Ortho Inc 207 622-9792
24 Stone St Augusta ME (04330) ***(G-5608)***
Hanger Prsthetcs & Ortho Inc 603 742-0334
7 Marsh Brook Dr Ste 201 Somersworth NH (03878) ***(G-19839)***
Hanger Prsthetcs & Ortho Inc 203 230-0667
260 State St North Haven CT (06473) ***(G-3029)***
Hanger Prsthetcs & Ortho Inc 207 782-6907
600 Turner St Ste 2b Auburn ME (04210) ***(G-5571)***
Hanger Prsthetcs & Ortho Inc 860 667-5300
10 Countyline Dr Cromwell CT (06416) ***(G-854)***
Hanger Prsthetcs & Ortho Inc 860 545-9050
282 Washington St 1b Hartford CT (06106) ***(G-1829)***

Hanger Prsthetcs & Ortho Inc 860 667-5370
181 Patricia M Genova Dr Newington CT (06111) ***(G-2869)***
Hanger Prsthetcs & Ortho Inc 860 871-0905
428 Hartford Tpke Ste 103 Vernon CT (06066) ***(G-4668)***
Hanger Prsthetcs & Ortho Inc 413 734-0002
1985 Main St Springfield MA (01103) ***(G-15474)***
Hanger Prsthetcs & Ortho Inc 978 683-5509
100 Milk St Ste 120 Methuen MA (01844) ***(G-13026)***
Hanger Prsthetcs & Ortho Inc 978 466-7400
100 Erdman Way Ste S-100 Leominster MA (01453) ***(G-12150)***
Hanger Prsthetcs & Ortho Inc 203 377-8820
1985 Barnum Ave Stratford CT (06615) ***(G-4418)***
Hanger Prsthetcs & Ortho Inc 207 773-4963
959 Brighton Ave Portland ME (04102) ***(G-6668)***
Hanington Bros Inc 207 765-2681
488 Us Hwy 2 Macwahoc Plt ME (04451) ***(G-6399)***
Hanington Timberlands 207 456-7003
95 Main St Reed Plt ME (04497) ***(G-6779)***
Hanks Protein Plus, Pawtucket *Also called Pbuttri LLC* ***(G-20877)***
Hanna Instruments Inc (PA) 401 765-7500
584 Park East Dr Woonsocket RI (02895) ***(G-21567)***
Hannaford & Dumas Corporation 781 503-0100
26 Conn St Woburn MA (01801) ***(G-17195)***
Hannah Engineering Inc 978 777-5892
150 Maple St Danvers MA (01923) ***(G-10221)***
Hannah International Foods Inc 603 474-5805
1 Depot Ln Seabrook NH (03874) ***(G-19803)***
Hannan Technologies LLC 603 768-5656
208 Dean Rd Danbury NH (03230) ***(G-17964)***
Hannes Precision Industry Inc 203 853-7276
74 Fort Point St Norwalk CT (06855) ***(G-3166)***
Hans Kissle Company LLC 978 556-4500
9 Haverhill St Haverhill MA (01830) ***(G-11440)***
Hansa Consult North Amer LLC 603 422-8833
200 International Dr Portsmouth NH (03801) ***(G-19572)***
Hanson Whitman Express 781 293-0420
1000 Main St Hanson MA (02341) ***(G-11363)***
Hants White LLC 207 429-9786
24 E Ridge Rd Mars Hill ME (04758) ***(G-6414)***
Happy Bird Baking Company LLC 603 759-0714
24 Long Hill Rd Peterborough NH (03458) ***(G-19471)***
Happy House Amusement Inc 603 497-4151
70 Depot St Goffstown NH (03045) ***(G-18203)***
Har-Conn Chrome Company (PA) 860 236-6801
603 New Park Ave West Hartford CT (06110) ***(G-5073)***
Harbar LLC 781 828-0848
320 Turnpike St Canton MA (02021) ***(G-9735)***
Harbisonwalker Intl Inc 203 934-7960
163 Boston Post Rd West Haven CT (06516) ***(G-5125)***
Harbor Candy Shop Inc 207 646-8078
248 Main St Ogunquit ME (03907) ***(G-6537)***
Harbor House Cottages, Biddeford *Also called Salo Bay Trading Co* ***(G-5762)***
Harbor Print Shop 207 633-4176
59 Corey Ln Boothbay ME (04537) ***(G-5778)***
Harbor Publications Inc 203 245-8009
1 Orchard Park Rd Ste 8 Madison CT (06443) ***(G-1962)***
Harbor Technologies, Augusta *Also called Kw Boats* ***(G-5612)***
Harbor Welding 978 281-5771
5 Marsh St Gloucester MA (01930) ***(G-11192)***
Harborside Printing Co Inc 978 462-2026
3 Graf Rd Ste 5 Newburyport MA (01950) ***(G-13495)***
Harbour Biomed 617 682-3679
1 Broadway Fl 14 Cambridge MA (02142) ***(G-9500)***
Harbus News Corporation 617 495-6528
Harvard Busines Schl Bldg Boston MA (02163) ***(G-8588)***
Harcosemco, Branford *Also called Semco Instruments Inc* ***(G-347)***
Harcosemco, Branford *Also called Semco Instruments Inc* ***(G-348)***
Harcosemco LLC 203 483-3700
186 Cedar St Branford CT (06405) ***(G-322)***
Harcourt Achieve, Boston *Also called Hmh Supplemental Publishers* ***(G-8600)***
Hard Core Spral Tube Wnders In 603 775-0230
50 Pine Rd Brentwood NH (03833) ***(G-17751)***
Hard-Core Self Defense 203 231-2344
500 River Rd Shelton CT (06484) ***(G-3809)***
Hardcore Sweet Cupcakes LLC 203 808-5547
784 Cooke St Waterbury CT (06710) ***(G-4882)***
Hardigg Case Center, Northampton *Also called Hardigg Industries Inc* ***(G-14007)***
Hardigg Industries Inc 413 665-2163
99 Industrial Dr Ste 1 Northampton MA (01060) ***(G-14007)***
Harding Metals Inc 603 942-5573
42 Harding Dr Northwood NH (03261) ***(G-19412)***
Harding Print, Whitman *Also called Harry B Harding & Son Inc* ***(G-16924)***
Harding Sails Inc 508 748-0334
732 Mill St Marion MA (02738) ***(G-12697)***
Harding Sails Nb, Marion *Also called Harding Sails Inc* ***(G-12697)***
Hardline Heat Treating Inc 508 764-6669
134 Ashland Ave Southbridge MA (01550) ***(G-15384)***
Hardric Laboratories Inc 978 251-1702
55 Middlesex St North Chelmsford MA (01863) ***(G-13895)***
Hardrock Granite Co Inc 802 479-3606
95 Boynton St Barre VT (05641) ***(G-21619)***
Hardware Products Company, Chelsea *Also called Catalyst/Spring I Ltd Partner* ***(G-9947)***
Hardwick Dry Kilns, Brattleboro *Also called Cersosimo Lumber Company Inc* ***(G-21724)***
Hardwick Gazette Newspaper, Hardwick *Also called Hardwick Gazette Print Shop* ***(G-22013)***
Hardwick Gazette Print Shop 802 472-6521
42 S Main St Hardwick VT (05843) ***(G-22013)***
Hardwick Laminators Inc 413 477-6600
268 Main St Gilbertville MA (01031) ***(G-11154)***
Hardwickvmeyard & Winery 413 967-7763
3305 Greenwich Rd Hardwick MA (01082) ***(G-11372)***
Hardwood Design Inc 401 294-2235
24 Dorset Mill Rd Exeter RI (02822) ***(G-20450)***
Hardwood Products Company LP 207 876-3311
31 School St Guilford ME (04443) ***(G-6158)***
Hardy Doric Inc 978 250-1113
22 Progress Ave Chelmsford MA (01824) ***(G-9903)***
Harjani Hitesh 860 913-6032
850 Hartford Tpke H109 Waterford CT (06385) ***(G-4984)***
Harkness Industries, Inc., Cheshire *Also called Fimor North America Inc* ***(G-733)***
Harmac Rebar & Steel Corp 207 935-3531
103 Corn Shop Rd Fryeburg ME (04037) ***(G-6098)***
Harman Becker Automotive Syste 203 328-3501
400 Atlantic St Ste 15 Stamford CT (06901) ***(G-4205)***
Harman Consumer Inc 203 328-3500
400 Atlantic St Ste 1500 Stamford CT (06901) ***(G-4206)***
Harman Consumer Group Division, Stamford *Also called Harman International Inds Inc* ***(G-4208)***
Harman International Inds Inc (HQ) 203 328-3500
400 Atlantic St Ste 15 Stamford CT (06901) ***(G-4207)***
Harman International Inds Inc 203 328-3500
400 Atlantic St Ste 15 Stamford CT (06901) ***(G-4208)***
Harman International Inds Inc 203 328-3500
400 Atlantic St Fl 5 Stamford CT (06901) ***(G-4209)***
Harman KG Holding LLC (HQ) 203 328-3500
400 Atlantic St Ste 1500 Stamford CT (06901) ***(G-4210)***
Harmonic Drive LLC (HQ) 978 532-1800
247 Lynnfield St Peabody MA (01960) ***(G-14338)***
Harmonized Cookery 802 598-9206
450 Sparrow Farm Rd Montpelier VT (05602) ***(G-22149)***
Harmons Clam Cakes 207 967-4100
165 Read St Portland ME (04103) ***(G-6669)***
Harmony Metal Products North 603 536-6012
10 Pleasant St Ste 400 Portsmouth NH (03801) ***(G-19573)***
Harodite Industries Inc (PA) 508 824-6961
66 South St Taunton MA (02780) ***(G-15757)***
Harold C Moore II 207 595-5683
604 Ryerson Hill Rd South Paris ME (04281) ***(G-7011)***
Harold Estey Lumber Inc 603 432-5184
9 Old Nashua Rd Londonderry NH (03053) ***(G-18701)***
Harold Haines Inc 207 762-1411
243 Main St Presque Isle ME (04769) ***(G-6758)***
Harper Bros Printing Inc 978 667-9459
25 Sullivan Rd Ste 3 North Billerica MA (01862) ***(G-13823)***
Harpoon Acquisition Corp 860 815-5736
455 Winding Brook Dr Glastonbury CT (06033) ***(G-1557)***
Harpoon Brewery, Windsor *Also called Mbbc Vermont LLC* ***(G-22712)***
Harpoon Brewery, Boston *Also called Mass Bay Brewing Company Inc* ***(G-8682)***
Harpoon Productions 781 383-0500
445 Beechwood St Ste 1 Cohasset MA (02025) ***(G-10099)***
Harrel, Pawcatuck *Also called Davis-Standard LLC* ***(G-3432)***
Harriman Pit, Milford *Also called Penobscot Sand Grav Stone LLC* ***(G-6437)***
Harrington Air Systems LLC 781 341-1999
80 Rosedale Rd Watertown MA (02472) ***(G-16290)***
Harrington's of Vermont, Richmond *Also called Harringtons In Vermont Inc* ***(G-22312)***
Harringtons In Vermont Inc (PA) 802 434-7500
210 Main Rd Richmond VT (05477) ***(G-22312)***
Harris Envmtl Systems Inc 978 470-8600
11 Connector Rd Andover MA (01810) ***(G-7555)***
Harris Steel, South Deerfield *Also called Barker Steel LLC* ***(G-15245)***
Harris Tool & Die Company Inc 978 479-1842
655 Westminster St Fitchburg MA (01420) ***(G-10828)***
Harrison Enterprise LLC 914 665-8348
237 Asylum St Bridgeport CT (06610) ***(G-423)***
Harrison Publishing House Inc 603 444-0820
995 Industrial Park Rd Littleton NH (03561) ***(G-18661)***
Harrison Redi-Mix Corp 802 849-6688
1803 Skunk Hill Rd Fairfax VT (05454) ***(G-21976)***
Harrison Specialty Co Inc (PA) 781 828-8180
15 University Rd Ste A Canton MA (02021) ***(G-9736)***
Harrison Specialty Co Inc 781 828-8180
15 University Rd Ste A Canton MA (02021) ***(G-9737)***
Harrisville Designs Inc (PA) 603 827-3333
69 Main St Fl 2 Harrisville NH (03450) ***(G-18302)***
Harry B Harding & Son Inc 781 447-3941
15 Colebrook Blvd Whitman MA (02382) ***(G-16924)***
Harry Miller Co Inc 617 427-2300
850 Albany St Boston MA (02119) ***(G-8589)***

Harry Miller Co LLC (PA).....617 427-2300
19 Hampden St Boston MA (02119) **(G-8590)**
Harry Thommen Company.....203 333-3637
3404 Fairfield Ave Bridgeport CT (06605) **(G-424)**
Harrys Machined Parts.....508 366-1455
15 Belmont St Northborough MA (01532) **(G-14035)**
Harrys Mold & Machine Inc.....508 697-6432
275 Elm St Bridgewater MA (02324) **(G-9075)**
Harsha Inc.....860 439-1466
850 Hartford Tpke Waterford CT (06385) **(G-4985)**
Hart Tool & Engineering.....203 264-9776
339 Christian St Oxford CT (06478) **(G-3407)**
Hartford, Newport *Also called Eichenauer Inc* **(G-19345)**
Hartford Advocate, Hartford *Also called New Mass Media Inc* **(G-1852)**
Hartford Aircraft Products.....860 242-8228
94 Old Poquonock Rd Bloomfield CT (06002) **(G-223)**
Hartford Business Supply Inc.....860 233-2138
1718 Park St Hartford CT (06106) **(G-1830)**
Hartford Courant Company.....860 678-1330
80 Darling Dr Avon CT (06001) **(G-35)**
Hartford Courant Company.....860 560-3747
141 South St Ste E West Hartford CT (06110) **(G-5074)**
Hartford Courant Company LLC (HQ).....860 241-6200
285 Broad St Hartford CT (06115) **(G-1831)**
Hartford Courant Company LLC.....860 525-5555
121 Wawarme Ave Hartford CT (06114) **(G-1832)**
Hartford Courant South BR Off, Hartford *Also called Hartford Courant Company LLC* **(G-1832)**
Hartford Cpl Co-Op Inc.....860 296-5636
75 Airport Rd Hartford CT (06114) **(G-1833)**
Hartford Division, Hartford *Also called Terex Utilities Inc* **(G-1877)**
Hartford Electric Sup Co Inc.....860 760-4887
70 Inwood Rd Rocky Hill CT (06067) **(G-3711)**
Hartford Fine Art & Framing Co, East Hartford *Also called Picture This Hartford Inc* **(G-1210)**
Hartford Flavor Company LLC.....860 604-9767
30 Arbor St Unit 107 Hartford CT (06106) **(G-1834)**
Hartford Gauge Co.....860 233-9619
23 Brook St West Hartford CT (06110) **(G-5075)**
Hartford Industrial Finshg Co.....860 243-2040
25 Northwood Dr Bloomfield CT (06002) **(G-224)**
Hartford Jet Center LLC.....860 548-9334
20 Lindbergh Dr Hartford CT (06114) **(G-1835)**
Hartford Monthly Meeting.....860 232-3631
144 Quaker Ln S West Hartford CT (06119) **(G-5076)**
Hartford Technologies Inc.....860 571-3602
1022 Elm St Rocky Hill CT (06067) **(G-3712)**
Hartford Toner & Cartridge Inc (PA).....860 292-1280
6 Wapping Rd Broad Brook CT (06016) **(G-629)**
Hartland Inc.....207 785-4350
61 Hope St Rockport ME (04856) **(G-6823)**
Hartmann, Mansfield *Also called Hl Operating LLC* **(G-12635)**
Hartmann Incorporated.....508 851-1400
575 West St Ste 110 Mansfield MA (02048) **(G-12634)**
Hartnett Co Inc.....781 935-2600
946 Main St Woburn MA (01801) **(G-17196)**
Hartwell Asscoiates.....617 686-7571
24 Thorndike St Cambridge MA (02141) **(G-9501)**
Harty Integrated Solutions, New Haven *Also called Harty Press Inc* **(G-2695)**
Harty Press Inc.....203 562-5112
25 James St New Haven CT (06513) **(G-2695)**
Harvard Bioscience Inc (PA).....508 893-8999
84 October Hill Rd Ste 10 Holliston MA (01746) **(G-11575)**
Harvard Bus Schl Pubg Corp (HQ).....617 783-7400
20 Guest St Ste 700 Brighton MA (02135) **(G-9100)**
Harvard Business Review, Boston *Also called President Fllows Hrvard Cllege* **(G-8792)**
Harvard Business Review, Brighton *Also called Harvard Bus Schl Pubg Corp* **(G-9100)**
Harvard Clinical Tech Inc.....508 655-2000
22 Pleasant St Natick MA (01760) **(G-13259)**
Harvard Crimson Inc.....617 576-6600
14 Plympton St Cambridge MA (02138) **(G-9502)**
Harvard Double Reeds.....978 772-1898
69 S Shaker Rd Harvard MA (01451) **(G-11376)**
Harvard Environmental Services, Westwood *Also called Gary Kellner* **(G-16866)**
Harvard Folding Box Co Inc.....978 683-2802
15 Union St Ste 555 Lawrence MA (01840) **(G-12030)**
Harvard Instant Printing.....781 893-2622
36 Elm St Waltham MA (02453) **(G-16124)**
Harvard Lampoon Inc.....617 495-7801
44 Bow St Cambridge MA (02138) **(G-9503)**
Harvard Machinery, Harvard *Also called Harvard Products Inc* **(G-11378)**
Harvard Magazine Inc.....617 495-5746
7 Ware St Cambridge MA (02138) **(G-9504)**
Harvard Manufacturing Inc.....978 425-5375
2 Shaker Rd Ste C104 Shirley MA (01464) **(G-15085)**
Harvard Observatory Model Shop, Cambridge *Also called President Fllows Hrvard Cllege* **(G-9615)**
Harvard Press.....978 456-3700
5 Littleton Rd Harvard MA (01451) **(G-11377)**
Harvard Products Inc.....978 772-0309
325 Ayer Rd Ste A105 Harvard MA (01451) **(G-11378)**
Harvard Scientific Corporation.....617 876-5033
799 Concord Ave Cambridge MA (02138) **(G-9505)**
Harvard University Press, Cambridge *Also called President Fllows Hrvard Cllege* **(G-9616)**
Harvest Hill Holdings LLC (PA).....203 914-1620
1 High Ridge Park Fl 2 Stamford CT (06905) **(G-4211)**
Harvest of Barnstable, Yarmouth Port *Also called Wendi C Smith* **(G-17533)**
Harvest Yeast, Gloucester *Also called Tekkware Inc* **(G-11215)**
Harvey Bigelow Designs, Fall River *Also called Ecin Industries Inc* **(G-10686)**
Harvey Bravman.....617 323-9969
4394 Washington St Roslindale MA (02131) **(G-14838)**
Harvey Industries Inc.....781 935-7990
33 Commonwealth Ave Woburn MA (01801) **(G-17197)**
Harvey Industries Inc.....603 622-4232
725 Huse Rd Manchester NH (03103) **(G-18832)**
Harvey Signs Inc.....978 794-2071
30 Osgood St Methuen MA (01844) **(G-13027)**
Harveys Bakeries.....603 749-5149
6 Progress Dr Dover NH (03820) **(G-18027)**
Harwest Holdings One Inc.....860 423-8334
1102 Windham Rd South Windham CT (06266) **(G-3925)**
Harwich Oracle.....508 247-3200
5 Namskaket Rd Orleans MA (02653) **(G-14234)**
Hasbro Inc (PA).....401 431-8697
1027 Newport Ave Pawtucket RI (02861) **(G-20845)**
Hasbro Inc.....401 726-2090
1011 Newport Ave Pawtucket RI (02861) **(G-20846)**
Hasbro Inc.....401 280-2127
1 Hasbro Pl Providence RI (02903) **(G-21026)**
Hasbro Inc.....401 431-8412
200 Narragansett Park Dr Pawtucket RI (02861) **(G-20847)**
Hasbro International Inc (HQ).....401 431-8697
1027 Newport Ave Pawtucket RI (02861) **(G-20848)**
Hasler Inc.....203 301-3400
19 Forest Pkwy Shelton CT (06484) **(G-3810)**
Hass Bros Inc.....508 336-9323
190 Providence St Rehoboth MA (02769) **(G-14750)**
Hassan Woodcarving & Sign Co.....781 383-6075
799 Chief Jstice Cshing Cohasset MA (02025) **(G-10100)**
Hat Trick Graphics LLC.....203 748-1128
87 Sand Pit Rd Ste 1 Danbury CT (06810) **(G-930)**
Hata Hi-Tech Machining LLC.....203 333-9139
1 Riverside Dr Ste E Ansonia CT (06401) **(G-18)**
Haulaway Dumpster Disposal.....781 871-1234
800 Hingham St Rockland MA (02370) **(G-14806)**
Hauser Chocolatier, Westerly *Also called Hauser Foods Inc* **(G-21526)**
Hauser Foods Inc.....401 596-8866
59 Tom Harvey Rd Westerly RI (02891) **(G-21526)**
Hauthane, Lynn *Also called C L Hauthaway & Sons Corp* **(G-12495)**
Haverhill Gazette, Haverhill *Also called Eagle-Tribune Publishing Co* **(G-11430)**
Hawk Integrated Plastics LLC.....860 337-0310
1 Commerce Dr Columbia CT (06237) **(G-818)**
Hawk Measurement America LLC (PA).....978 304-3000
90 Glenn St Ste 100b Lawrence MA (01843) **(G-12031)**
Hawk Motors Inc.....207 363-4716
1100 Us Route 1 York ME (03909) **(G-7308)**
Hawk Quality Products Inc.....603 432-3319
125 Rockingham Rd Derry NH (03038) **(G-17981)**
Hawkes & Huberdeau Woodworking.....978 388-7747
23 Noel St Ste 5 Amesbury MA (01913) **(G-7489)**
Hawkes Motorsports LLC.....603 660-9864
129a S Mast St Goffstown NH (03045) **(G-18204)**
Hawkins Machine Company Inc.....401 828-1424
374 Hopkins Hill Rd Coventry RI (02816) **(G-20148)**
Hawleys Fine Woodwork.....802 483-2575
1 River Rd Chittenden VT (05737) **(G-21854)**
Hawtan Leathers LLC.....978 465-3791
75 Parker St Newburyport MA (01950) **(G-13496)**
Hawthorn Creative Group LLC.....603 610-0533
33 Jewell Ct Portsmouth NH (03801) **(G-19574)**
Hayden Manufacturing Co Inc.....508 295-0497
50 Carver Rd West Wareham MA (02576) **(G-16574)**
Haydon Kerk Mtion Slutions Inc.....203 756-7441
1500 Meriden Rd Waterbury CT (06705) **(G-4883)**
Haydon Kerk Mtion Slutions Inc.....603 465-7227
56 Meadowbrook Dr Milford NH (03055) **(G-19058)**
Haydon Motion Europe, Waterbury *Also called Tritex Corporation* **(G-4967)**
Hayes Prosthetic Inc.....413 733-2287
1309 Riverdale St West Springfield MA (01089) **(G-16524)**
Hayes Recycled Pallets.....802 247-4620
16 Maple St Brandon VT (05733) **(G-21708)**
Hayley Custom Stair Co Inc.....802 861-6400
19 Gauthier Dr Essex Junction VT (05452) **(G-21946)**
Haylons Market LLC.....860 739-9509
157 W Main St Ste 1 Niantic CT (06357) **(G-2951)**
Haystack ID.....617 422-0075
100 Franklin St Boston MA (02110) **(G-8591)**

Hayward Industries Inc 401 583-1150
61 Whitecap Dr North Kingstown RI (02852) ***(G-20714)***
Hayward Turnstiles Inc 203 877-7096
160 Wampus Ln Milford CT (06460) ***(G-2296)***
Hayward Tyler Inc (HQ) 802 655-4444
480 Roosevelt Hwy Colchester VT (05446) ***(G-21864)***
Hazard Marine A Div Ltd Inds 508 943-7531
4 Town Forest Rd Webster MA (01570) ***(G-16342)***
Hazelett Strip-Casting Corp 802 951-6846
63 Brentwood Dr Colchester VT (05446) ***(G-21865)***
Hazen Paper Company (PA) 413 538-8204
240 S Water St Holyoke MA (01040) ***(G-11631)***
HB Logging LLC 603 638-4983
523 Littleton Rd Monroe NH (03771) ***(G-19090)***
HB Precision Products 401 767-4340
21 Lark Industrial Pkwy A Greenville RI (02828) ***(G-20467)***
HB Printing, Northborough *Also called Tomandtim Enterprises LLC* ***(G-14051)***
Hbh Prestain Inc (PA) 802 375-9723
1223 E Arlington Rd Arlington VT (05250) ***(G-21596)***
Hbi Boat LLC 860 536-7776
145 Pearl St Groton CT (06340) ***(G-1677)***
Hbl America Inc (HQ) 860 257-9800
712 Brook St Ste 107 Rocky Hill CT (06067) ***(G-3713)***
Hbl Batteries, Rocky Hill *Also called Hbl America Inc* ***(G-3713)***
HCC Aegis Inc (HQ) 508 998-3141
50 Welby Rd New Bedford MA (02745) ***(G-13393)***
Hci Cleaning Products LLC 508 864-5510
2 Burlington Woods Dr Burlington MA (01803) ***(G-9281)***
Hcp Packaging Usa Inc 603 256-3141
370 Monument Rd Hinsdale NH (03451) ***(G-18320)***
Hd Bennett Machine Co Inc 508 867-0154
3 Crooks Cross Rd North Brookfield MA (01535) ***(G-13881)***
Hd Lifesciences LLC 866 949-5433
12 Gill St Ste 4500 Woburn MA (01801) ***(G-17198)***
Hd Merrimack 978 681-9969
60 Island St Ste 4 Lawrence MA (01840) ***(G-12032)***
Hd Supply Construction Supply 603 298-6072
17 Plaza Heights Rd # 3 West Lebanon NH (03784) ***(G-19952)***
Hdm Systems Corporation 617 562-4054
84 Lincoln St Brighton MA (02135) ***(G-9101)***
Head 2 Toe 781 944-0286
167 Pleasant St Reading MA (01867) ***(G-14736)***
Head Prone Inc 617 864-0780
777 Concord Ave Ste 103 Cambridge MA (02138) ***(G-9506)***
Headwall Photonics Inc 978 353-4100
580 Main St Bolton MA (01740) ***(G-8319)***
Headwall Photonics Inc (PA) 978 353-4040
601 River St Fitchburg MA (01420) ***(G-10829)***
Headwaters Inc 781 715-6404
134 Pleasant St Marblehead MA (01945) ***(G-12685)***
Healersource 212 464-7748
50 Gordon St Ste 2 Allston MA (02134) ***(G-7467)***
Healigo Inc 508 208-0461
472 Jamaicaway Boston MA (02130) ***(G-8592)***
Health Enterprises, North Attleboro *Also called Apothecary Products LLC* ***(G-13745)***
Health Helm Inc 508 951-2156
110 Canal St Fl 4 Lowell MA (01852) ***(G-12379)***
Health Monitor, Newtown *Also called The Bee Publishing Company* ***(G-2943)***
Health Pro, Portland *Also called Casco Bay Sbstnce Abuse Rsrces* ***(G-6634)***
Healthcare Publishing Inc 508 655-4489
25 Washington Ave Ste 4 Natick MA (01760) ***(G-13260)***
Healthco International LLC 603 255-3771
1 Wilderness Rd Colebrook NH (03576) ***(G-17871)***
Healthedge Software Inc (PA) 781 285-1300
30 Corporate Dr Ste 150 Burlington MA (01803) ***(G-9282)***
Healthquarters Inc 978 922-4490
900 Cummings Ctr Beverly MA (01915) ***(G-8139)***
Healthstar Inc 781 428-3696
62 Johnson Ln Braintree MA (02184) ***(G-9017)***
Healthy Harvest Inc 203 245-3786
42 Godman Rd Madison CT (06443) ***(G-1963)***
Healthy Homeworks 207 415-4245
17 Kellogg St Portland ME (04101) ***(G-6670)***
Healthy Life Snack Inc 781 575-6744
905 Turnpike St Ste D2 Canton MA (02021) ***(G-9738)***
Healy Plaques, Manville *Also called Michael Healy Designs Inc* ***(G-20610)***
Hearing Armor LLC 781 789-5017
378 Hillside Ave Needham MA (02494) ***(G-13300)***
Hearst Communications Inc 508 793-9100
100 Front St Ste 500 Worcester MA (01608) ***(G-17389)***
Hearst Corporation 203 438-6544
42 Vitti St New Canaan CT (06840) ***(G-2600)***
Hearst Corporation 203 926-2080
1000 Bridgeport Ave Shelton CT (06484) ***(G-3811)***
Hearst Corporation 203 625-4445
301 Merritt 7 Ste 1 Norwalk CT (06851) ***(G-3167)***
Heart of Vermont Inc 802 476-3098
131 S Main St Ste 5 Barre VT (05641) ***(G-21620)***
Heart Quali Home Heati Produ 802 888-5232
317 Stafford Ave Morrisville VT (05661) ***(G-22169)***
Heartbreak Hill Running Co Inc 617 467-4487
638 Commonwealth Ave Newton MA (02459) ***(G-13599)***
Hearth Warming, Laconia *Also called Village West Publishing Inc* ***(G-18592)***
Hearthstone Stoves, Morrisville *Also called Heart Quali Home Heati Produ* ***(G-22169)***
Heartlander Surgical Inc 781 320-9601
90 Wildwood Dr Westwood MA (02090) ***(G-16868)***
Heartware International Inc (HQ) 508 739-0950
500 Old Connecticut Path Framingham MA (01701) ***(G-10962)***
Heartwood Cabinetmakers LLC 508 634-2004
51 N Main St Uxbridge MA (01569) ***(G-15918)***
Heartwood Cabinetry 860 295-0304
345 N Main St Marlborough CT (06447) ***(G-2065)***
Heat Exchanger Products Corp 781 749-0220
55 Industrial Park Rd Hingham MA (02043) ***(G-11499)***
Heat Fab Inc 413 863-2242
130 Industrial Blvd Turners Falls MA (01376) ***(G-15878)***
Heat Trace Products LLC 978 534-2810
233 Florence St Leominster MA (01453) ***(G-12151)***
Heat Treating, East Granby *Also called Specialty Steel Treating Inc* ***(G-1145)***
Heat-Flo Inc 508 278-2400
15 Megan Ct Uxbridge MA (01569) ***(G-15919)***
Heatbath Corporation (HQ) 413 452-2000
107 Front St Indian Orchard MA (01151) ***(G-11887)***
Heaters Inc 860 739-5477
11 Freedom Way Unit D5 Niantic CT (06357) ***(G-2952)***
Heath Lumber, North Hyde Park *Also called M B Heath & Sons Lumber Inc* ***(G-22232)***
Heatmaker Parts & Service 617 930-0036
95 Main St Reading MA (01867) ***(G-14737)***
Heavenly Chocolate 413 586-0038
150 Main St Northampton MA (01060) ***(G-14008)***
Heavy Metal Corp 401 944-2002
1 Park Row Ste 300 Providence RI (02903) ***(G-21027)***
Heb Manufacturing Company Inc 802 685-4821
67 Vt Rte 110 Chelsea VT (05038) ***(G-21838)***
Hebert Candies, Shrewsbury *Also called Hebert Retail LLC* ***(G-15116)***
Hebert Foundry & Machine Inc 603 524-2065
113 Fair St Laconia NH (03246) ***(G-18566)***
Hebert Foundry & Machine Co, Laconia *Also called Hebert Foundry & Machine Inc* ***(G-18566)***
Hebert Manufacturing Company (PA) 603 524-2065
113 Fair St Laconia NH (03246) ***(G-18567)***
Hebert Retail LLC 508 845-8051
574 Hartford Tpke Shrewsbury MA (01545) ***(G-15116)***
Hedge Hog Industries 413 363-2528
86 Princeton St Springfield MA (01109) ***(G-15475)***
Heffron Asphalt Corp (PA) 781 935-1455
68 Winter St North Reading MA (01864) ***(G-13984)***
Heffron Materials, North Reading *Also called Heffron Asphalt Corp* ***(G-13984)***
Hefring LLC 617 206-5750
280 Summer St Boston MA (02210) ***(G-8593)***
Heidi Jos LLC 603 774-5375
55 Crystal Ave Derry NH (03038) ***(G-17982)***
Heila Technologies Inc 954 829-4839
444 Somerville Ave Ste 2 Somerville MA (02143) ***(G-15181)***
Heinrich LLC 781 891-9591
156 Bishops Forest Dr Waltham MA (02452) ***(G-16125)***
Heise Industries Inc 860 828-6538
196 Commerce St East Berlin CT (06023) ***(G-1103)***
Heka Instruments Incorporated 516 882-1155
84 October Hill Rd Ste 10 Holliston MA (01746) ***(G-11576)***
Helander Products Inc 860 669-7953
26 Knollwood Dr Clinton CT (06413) ***(G-788)***
Helfrich Bros Boiler Works Inc 978 975-2464
39 Merrimack St Lawrence MA (01843) ***(G-12033)***
Helfrich Construction Svcs LLC 978 683-7244
39 Merrimack St Lawrence MA (01843) ***(G-12034)***
Heli Modified Inc 207 625-4642
20 Industrial Way Cornish ME (04020) ***(G-5925)***
Helical Solutions LLC 866 543-5422
29 Sanford Dr Gorham ME (04038) ***(G-6113)***
Helium Plus Inc 203 304-1880
17 Pebble Rd Newtown CT (06470) ***(G-2923)***
Helix Power Corporation 781 718-7282
28 Dane St Somerville MA (02143) ***(G-15182)***
Helixbind Inc 508 460-1028
181 Cedar Hill St Ste 3 Marlborough MA (01752) ***(G-12767)***
Hellgren Logging LLC 207 778-0401
156 Ernies Way Temple ME (04984) ***(G-7079)***
Hellier, Danbury *Also called Acuren Inspection Inc* ***(G-867)***
Helmers Publishing Inc 603 563-1631
1283 Main St Dublin NH (03444) ***(G-18068)***
Helmick & Schechter Inc 617 332-2433
447 Lowell Ave Apt 3 Newton MA (02460) ***(G-13600)***
Hemedex Inc 617 577-1759
564 Main St Ste 300 Waltham MA (02452) ***(G-16126)***
Hemenway & Associates 508 835-2859
127 Worcester St West Boylston MA (01583) ***(G-16417)***
Hendersons Redware 207 942-9013
53 Downing Rd Bangor ME (04401) ***(G-5649)***

ALPHABETIC

Hendrick Manufacturing Corp (PA)....781 631-4400
32 Commercial St Salem MA (01970) ***(G-14919)***
Hendrickson Advertising Inc....978 422-8087
118 Leominster Rd Sterling MA (01564) ***(G-15539)***
Hendrickson Publishers LLC....978 532-6546
140 Summit St Peabody MA (01960) ***(G-14339)***
Hendrickson Publishers Inc....800 358-3111
140 Summit St Peabody MA (01960) ***(G-14340)***
Henkel Consumer Goods Inc (HQ)....475 210-0230
200 Elm St Stamford CT (06902) ***(G-4212)***
Henkel Corporation....508 230-1100
167 Batchelder Rd Seabrook NH (03874) ***(G-19804)***
Henkel Locktite....603 474-5541
1 Deer Xing Seabrook NH (03874) ***(G-19805)***
Henkel Loctite Corporation (HQ)....860 571-5100
1 Henkel Way Rocky Hill CT (06067) ***(G-3714)***
Henkel of America Inc (HQ)....860 571-5100
1 Henkel Way Rocky Hill CT (06067) ***(G-3715)***
Henkel US Operations Corp (HQ)....860 571-5100
1 Henkel Way Rocky Hill CT (06067) ***(G-3716)***
Henniker Redi-Mix, Henniker *Also called Michie Corporation* ***(G-18307)***
Henry A Evers Corp Inc....401 781-4767
72 Oxford St Providence RI (02905) ***(G-21028)***
Henry J Montville....508 832-6111
567 Southbridge St Ste 15 Auburn MA (01501) ***(G-7837)***
Henry N Sawyer Co Inc....617 242-4610
586 Rutherford Ave Boston MA (02129) ***(G-8594)***
Henry Perkins Company....508 697-6978
180 Broad St Bridgewater MA (02324) ***(G-9076)***
Henry Thayer Company....203 226-0940
65 Adams Rd Easton CT (06612) ***(G-1319)***
Henrys Railings....617 333-0535
1690 Hyde Park Ave Boston MA (02136) ***(G-8595)***
Hepco, Hingham *Also called Heat Exchanger Products Corp* ***(G-11499)***
Herald Association Inc....802 747-6121
27 Wales St Rutland VT (05701) ***(G-22338)***
Herald News, The, Fall River *Also called Gatehouse Media LLC* ***(G-10701)***
Herald of Randolph....802 728-3232
30 Pleasant St Randolph VT (05060) ***(G-22297)***
Herb Allure Inc....207 584-3550
201 Tannery Loop Amherst ME (04605) ***(G-5521)***
Herb Chambers Brookline Inc....617 278-3920
308 Boylston St Brookline MA (02445) ***(G-9202)***
Herb Con Machine Company Inc....781 233-2755
6 Bow Street Ext Saugus MA (01906) ***(G-14985)***
Herbasway Laboratories LLC....203 269-6991
101 N Plains Indstrl Rd Wallingford CT (06492) ***(G-4750)***
Herbert C Haynes Inc (PA)....207 736-3412
40 Route 168 Winn ME (04495) ***(G-7264)***
Herbert C Haynes Inc....207 848-5930
40 Freedom Pkwy Hermon ME (04401) ***(G-6188)***
Herbert L Hardy and Son Inc....207 757-8550
1454 Dyerbrook Smyrna Mills ME (04780) ***(G-6992)***
Herbert Mosher....603 882-4357
60 Main St Ste 2 Nashua NH (03060) ***(G-19177)***
Hercules Press....617 323-1950
91 Spring St Boston MA (02132) ***(G-8596)***
Hercules Pulp and Paper Div, Chicopee *Also called Solenis LLC* ***(G-10061)***
Hercules Slr (us) Inc (PA)....508 993-0010
44 South St New Bedford MA (02740) ***(G-13394)***
Herend Store , The, Manchester *Also called J Yeager Inc* ***(G-22077)***
Herfco Inc....978 772-4758
9 Great Rd Shirley MA (01464) ***(G-15086)***
Herff Jones LLC....203 266-7170
39 Terrell Farm Rd Bethlehem CT (06751) ***(G-196)***
Herff Jones LLC....401 331-1240
150 Herff Jones Way Warwick RI (02888) ***(G-21370)***
Herff Jones LLC....203 368-9344
71 Vought Pl Stratford CT (06614) ***(G-4419)***
Herff Jones LLC....401 331-0888
10 Temple St Providence RI (02905) ***(G-21029)***
Herff Jones - Dieges & Clust, Warwick *Also called Herff Jones LLC* ***(G-21370)***
Hergon Design Inc....781 286-0663
188 Lincoln St Revere MA (02151) ***(G-14766)***
Heritage Concrete Corp....401 294-1524
535 South County Trl Exeter RI (02822) ***(G-20451)***
Heritage Joinery Ltd....802 485-6107
1688 Route 12 Northfield VT (05663) ***(G-22243)***
Heritage Lanterns....207 893-1134
85 Sandbar Rd Windham ME (04062) ***(G-7236)***
Heritage Post & Beam....802 223-6319
449 East Rd Barre VT (05641) ***(G-21621)***
Heritage Press Inc....508 888-2111
335 Cotuit Rd Unit 3 Sandwich MA (02563) ***(G-14969)***
Heritage Print Solutions, Sandwich *Also called Heritage Press Inc* ***(G-14969)***
Heritage Printers, Hartford *Also called G & R Enterprises Incorporated* ***(G-1822)***
Heritage Printing Co, Farmington *Also called Donald McIntire* ***(G-6043)***
Heritage Wharf Company LLC....508 990-1011
218 Elm St Dartmouth MA (02748) ***(G-10275)***
Herley Industries Inc....781 729-9450
10 Sonar Dr Woburn MA (01801) ***(G-17199)***
Herley New England, Woburn *Also called Herley Industries Inc* ***(G-17199)***
Herman Schmidt Precision Workh....860 289-3347
26 Sea Pave Rd South Windsor CT (06074) ***(G-3977)***
Hermann Schmidt Company Inc....860 289-3347
26 Sea Pave Rd South Windsor CT (06074) ***(G-3978)***
Hermell Products Inc....860 242-6550
9 Britton Dr Bloomfield CT (06002) ***(G-225)***
Hermit Woods Inc....603 253-7968
72 Main St Meredith NH (03253) ***(G-18974)***
Hermon Sand & Gravel LLC....207 848-5977
23 Timberview Dr Hermon ME (04401) ***(G-6189)***
Hermtech Inc....860 758-7528
8 Thompson Rd Ste 9 East Windsor CT (06088) ***(G-1285)***
Hero Coatings, Newburyport *Also called Functional Coatings LLC* ***(G-13493)***
Hero Coatings Inc....978 462-0746
13 Malcolm Hoyt Dr Newburyport MA (01950) ***(G-13497)***
Heron Machine & Engrg Inc....413 547-6308
100 State St Bldg 217 Ludlow MA (01056) ***(G-12466)***
Herrick & Cowell Company Inc....203 288-2578
839 Sherman Ave Hamden CT (06514) ***(G-1759)***
Herrick & White Ltd....401 658-0440
3 Flat St Cumberland RI (02864) ***(G-20324)***
Herrick Everett Welding & Mch....413 245-7533
51 E Brimfield Rd Holland MA (01521) ***(G-11553)***
Herrick Mill Work Inc....603 746-5092
290 Burnham Intervale Rd Contoocook NH (03229) ***(G-17945)***
Herrick's Welding and Machine, Holland *Also called Herrick Everett Welding & Mch* ***(G-11553)***
Herrmann Pepi Crystal Inc....603 528-1020
3 Waterford Pl Gilford NH (03249) ***(G-18188)***
Hersam Acorn Cmnty Pubg LLC....203 261-2548
205 Spring Hill Rd Trumbull CT (06611) ***(G-4624)***
Hersam Acorn Cmnty Pubg LLC (HQ)....203 438-6544
16 Bailey Ave Ridgefield CT (06877) ***(G-3668)***
Hersam Acorn Newspapers LLC....802 362-3535
Rr 7 Manchester Center VT (05255) ***(G-22087)***
Hersam Publishing Company....203 966-9541
42 Vitti St New Canaan CT (06840) ***(G-2601)***
Hersey Clutch Co....508 255-2533
8 Commerce Dr Orleans MA (02653) ***(G-14235)***
Hess Corporation....508 580-6530
244 W Center St West Bridgewater MA (02379) ***(G-16441)***
Hessel Industries Inc....203 736-2317
95 Roosevelt Dr Derby CT (06418) ***(G-1073)***
Heuristic Labs Inc....347 994-0299
16 Byrne Ave Westford MA (01886) ***(G-16772)***
Hevc Advance LLC....617 367-4802
28 State St Ste 3202 Boston MA (02109) ***(G-8597)***
Heveatex Corporation....508 675-0181
106 Ferry St Ste 1 Fall River MA (02721) ***(G-10713)***
Hewlett Packard HP Autonomy So....508 476-0000
120 Turnpike Rd Southborough MA (01772) ***(G-15360)***
Hex....978 666-0765
246 Essex St Frnt Salem MA (01970) ***(G-14920)***
Hex Design Inc (PA)....802 442-3309
215 Benmont Ave Bennington VT (05201) ***(G-21672)***
Hexagon Holdings Inc (HQ)....401 886-2000
250 Circuit Dr North Kingstown RI (02852) ***(G-20715)***
Hexagon Metrology Inc (HQ)....401 886-2000
250 Circuit Dr North Kingstown RI (02852) ***(G-20716)***
Hexagon Mfg Intelligence, North Kingstown *Also called Hexagon Metrology Inc* ***(G-20716)***
Hexcel Corporation (PA)....203 969-0666
281 Tresser Blvd Ste 1503 Stamford CT (06901) ***(G-4213)***
Hexcel Corporation....925 520-3232
250 Nutmeg Rd S South Windsor CT (06074) ***(G-3979)***
Hexcel Pottsville Corporation....203 969-0666
2 Stamford Plz 16thf Stamford CT (06901) ***(G-4214)***
Hexi, Wallingford *Also called High Energy X-Rays Intl Corp* ***(G-4751)***
Heyes Forest Products Inc....978 544-8801
34 Daniel Shays Hwy Orange MA (01364) ***(G-14217)***
Heyoka Solutions LLC....866 389-8578
19 Howes Ln Falmouth MA (02540) ***(G-10790)***
Hf Group LLC....617 242-1100
92 Cambridge St Charlestown MA (02129) ***(G-9836)***
Hfo Chicago LLC....860 285-0709
910 Day Hill Rd Windsor CT (06095) ***(G-5337)***
Hg Tech LLC....203 632-5946
162 Spencer St Naugatuck CT (06770) ***(G-2477)***
Hgh Industries LLC....860 644-1150
43 Sally Dr South Windsor CT (06074) ***(G-3980)***
Hgi Incorporated....978 388-2808
10 Industrial Way Amesbury MA (01913) ***(G-7490)***
HH Brown Shoe Company Inc (HQ)....203 661-2424
124 W Putnam Ave Ste 1a Greenwich CT (06830) ***(G-1620)***
Hhc LLC....860 456-0677
340 Progress Dr Manchester CT (06042) ***(G-2008)***
Hht, Ansonia *Also called Hata Hi-Tech Machining LLC* ***(G-18)***

HI Heat Company Inc...860 528-9315
32 Glendale Rd South Windsor CT (06074) *(G-3981)*
HI Tech Mch & Fabrication LLC...866 972-2077
15 Gray Ln Ashaway RI (02804) *(G-20036)*
HI Tech Profiles Inc...401 377-2040
401 Main St Ashaway RI (02804) *(G-20037)*
HI Tune Wax, Whately *Also called HI Tunes (G-16906)*
HI Tunes...435 962-0405
207 River Rd Whately MA (01093) *(G-16906)*
Hi-De Liners Inc...978 544-7801
131 W Main St Orange MA (01364) *(G-14218)*
Hi-Rel Group LLC...860 767-9031
16 Plains Rd Essex CT (06426) *(G-1397)*
Hi-Rel Products LLC...860 767-9031
16 Plains Rd Essex CT (06426) *(G-1398)*
Hi-Tech Inc...401 454-4086
50 Perry Ave Attleboro MA (02703) *(G-7746)*
Hi-Tech Fabricating Inc...203 284-0894
30 Knotter Dr Cheshire CT (06410) *(G-737)*
Hi-Tech Fabricators Inc...603 672-3766
10 Scarborough Ln Milford NH (03055) *(G-19059)*
Hi-Tech Metals Inc...508 966-0332
139 Farm St Bellingham MA (02019) *(G-8040)*
Hi-Tech Mold & Tool Inc...413 443-9184
1 Technology Dr W Pittsfield MA (01201) *(G-14476)*
HI-Tech Packaging Inc...203 378-2700
1 Bruce Ave Stratford CT (06615) *(G-4420)*
Hi-Tech Plating Inc...617 389-3400
69 Norman St Ste 2 Everett MA (02149) *(G-10613)*
HI-Tech Polishing Inc...860 665-1399
50 Progress Cir Ste 3 Newington CT (06111) *(G-2870)*
Hi-Temp Products Corp...203 744-3025
88 Taylor St Danbury CT (06810) *(G-931)*
Hi-Vue Maples LLC...802 752-8888
224 Stvens Mills Slide Rd Richford VT (05476) *(G-22306)*
Hi-Way Concrete Pdts Co Inc...508 295-0834
2746 Cranberry Hwy Wareham MA (02571) *(G-16249)*
Hibernation Holding Co Inc...802 985-3001
6655 Shelburne Rd Shelburne VT (05482) *(G-22419)*
Hibernian Machine Tool Service...603 878-1917
948 Turnpike Rd New Ipswich NH (03071) *(G-19305)*
Hickey Logging...207 724-3648
16 West Rd West Gardiner ME (04345) *(G-7172)*
Hicks and Otis Prints Inc...203 846-2087
9 Wilton Ave Norwalk CT (06851) *(G-3168)*
Hicks Loggings, Jefferson *Also called Forrest P Hicks II (G-18483)*
Hicks Machine Inc...603 756-3671
65 Maplewood Cir Walpole NH (03608) *(G-19921)*
Hid Global Corporation...617 581-6200
1320 Centre St Ste 201a Newton MA (02459) *(G-13601)*
Hidden Moon Brewing, Londonderry *Also called Moonlight Meadery LLC (G-18724)*
Hiden Analytical Inc (HQ)...603 924-5008
75 Hancock Rd Ste H Peterborough NH (03458) *(G-19472)*
Higgins Fabrication LLC...719 930-6437
40 Johnson St Ste 5 Bangor ME (04401) *(G-5650)*
Higginson Book Company...978 745-7170
10 Colonial Rd Salem MA (01970) *(G-14921)*
Higgs Energy LLC...860 213-5561
66 Franklin St Norwich CT (06360) *(G-3282)*
High Country Gardens, Shelburne *Also called American Meadows Inc (G-22410)*
High Energy X-Rays Intl Corp...203 909-9777
57 N Plains Industrial Rd B Wallingford CT (06492) *(G-4751)*
High Grade Finishing Co LLC...860 749-8883
6 Print Shop Rd Enfield CT (06082) *(G-1364)*
High Grade Furnishing, Enfield *Also called High Grade Finishing Co LLC (G-1364)*
High Grade Sales, Lynn *Also called High Grade Shade & Screen Co (G-12516)*
High Grade Shade & Screen Co...781 592-5027
41 Sutton St Lynn MA (01901) *(G-12516)*
High Liner Foods USA Inc...978 977-5305
801 Jubilee Dr Peabody MA (01960) *(G-14341)*
High Performance Med Solutions, Ashaway *Also called Hitachi Cable America Inc (G-20038)*
High Pine Well Drilling Inc...207 929-4122
116 Webster Rd Buxton ME (04093) *(G-5857)*
High Prfmce Composites Ltd...401 274-8560
99 Power St Providence RI (02906) *(G-21030)*
High Ridge Brands Co (HQ)...203 674-8080
333 Ludlow St Ste 2 Stamford CT (06902) *(G-4215)*
High Ridge Copy Inc...203 329-1889
1009 High Ridge Rd Stamford CT (06905) *(G-4216)*
High Ridge Printing & Copy Ctr, Stamford *Also called High Ridge Copy Inc (G-4216)*
High School Counselor Connect, West Hartford *Also called Campus Yellow Pages LLC (G-5057)*
High Speed Routing LLC...603 527-8027
42 Newark St Haverhill MA (01832) *(G-11441)*
High Speed Technologies Inc...603 483-0333
1357 Route 3a 9 Bow NH (03304) *(G-17716)*
High Standard Inc...603 532-8000
81 Turnpike Rd Jaffrey NH (03452) *(G-18466)*
High Tech Harvesting LLC...603 229-0750
7333 Oak Hill Rd Loudon NH (03307) *(G-18748)*
High Tech Machinists Inc...978 256-1600
177 Riverneck Rd Chelmsford MA (01824) *(G-9904)*
High Tech Precision Mfg L L C...860 621-7242
43 Aircraft Rd Southington CT (06489) *(G-4057)*
High Technology Coating Div, New Bedford *Also called Brodeur Machine Company Bus Tr (G-13367)*
High Voltage Engineering Corp...781 224-1001
401 Edgewater Pl Ste 680 Wakefield MA (01880) *(G-15954)*
High Voltage Maintenance Corp...508 668-9205
24 Walpole Park S Ste 3 Walpole MA (02081) *(G-15993)*
High Voltage Outsourcing LLC...203 456-3101
1 Corporate Dr Danbury CT (06810) *(G-932)*
High-Speed Process Prtg Corp...978 683-2766
130 Shepard St Lawrence MA (01843) *(G-12035)*
Highland Instruments...617 504-6031
2 Manns Hill Cres Sharon MA (02067) *(G-15051)*
Highland Labs Inc...508 429-2918
163 Woodland St Holliston MA (01746) *(G-11577)*
Highland Logging Inc...207 436-1113
39 Station Rd Wallagrass ME (04781) *(G-7139)*
Highland Manufacturing Inc...860 646-5142
5 Glen Rd Ste 4 Manchester CT (06040) *(G-2009)*
Highland Press of Athol Inc...978 249-6588
59 Marble St Athol MA (01331) *(G-7687)*
Highland Sugarworks Inc...802 479-1747
49 Parker Rd Websterville VT (05678) *(G-22597)*
Highland Tool Co Inc...603 882-6907
20 Simon St Nashua NH (03060) *(G-19178)*
Highliner Rope Co LLC...207 372-6300
71 Seal Harbor Rd Saint George ME (04860) *(G-6869)*
Hightech American Indus Labs...781 862-9884
320 Massachusetts Ave Lexington MA (02420) *(G-12229)*
Hightech Extracts LLC...207 590-3251
5 Drapeau St Biddeford ME (04005) *(G-5738)*
Hightechspeed LLC...978 600-8222
8 Federal Way Ste 4 Groveland MA (01834) *(G-11300)*
Highway Safety Corp (PA)...860 659-4330
239 Commerce St Ste C Glastonbury CT (06033) *(G-1558)*
Highway Vehicle/Safety Report, Branford *Also called Stamler Publishing Company (G-351)*
Higson Inc...508 678-4970
917 S Main St Fall River MA (02724) *(G-10714)*
Higson Seafood, Fall River *Also called Higson Inc (G-10714)*
Hilco Athletic & Graphics Inc...401 822-1775
55 Greenhill St West Warwick RI (02893) *(G-21495)*
Hilco Vision, Plainville *Also called Hilsinger Company Parent LLC (G-14520)*
Hildex Farm, Sugar Hill *Also called Pollys Pancake Parlor (G-19878)*
Hill Farmstead LLC...802 533-7450
403 Hill Rd Greensboro Bend VT (05842) *(G-22004)*
Hill Farmstead Brewery, Greensboro Bend *Also called Hill Farmstead LLC (G-22004)*
Hill Tim Fine Woodworking...207 854-1387
11 Little Wing Ln Gorham ME (04038) *(G-6114)*
Hiller Printing, New Bedford *Also called Victoria H Bradshaw (G-13457)*
Hilliard's Chocolate System, West Bridgewater *Also called Jimsan Enterprises Inc (G-16442)*
Hilliards House Candy Inc (PA)...508 238-6231
316 Main St North Easton MA (02356) *(G-13947)*
Hillman Enterprises (PA)...508 761-6967
24 Angeline St Attleboro MA (02703) *(G-7747)*
Hills Pallet Company...603 988-8624
362 Route 108 Somersworth NH (03878) *(G-19840)*
Hills Point Industries LLC (PA)...917 515-8650
191 Post Rd W Westport CT (06880) *(G-5200)*
Hillsgrove Machine Inc...603 776-5090
45 Dudley Rd Alton NH (03809) *(G-17546)*
Hillside Capital Inc De Corp (HQ)...203 618-0202
201 Tresser Blvd Ste 200 Stamford CT (06901) *(G-4217)*
Hillside Engineering Inc...978 762-6640
10r Rainbow Ter Ste A Danvers MA (01923) *(G-10222)*
Hillside Plastics Inc...413 863 2222
262 Millers Falls Rd Turners Falls MA (01376) *(G-15879)*
Hillside Press...617 742-1922
192 Green St Melrose MA (02176) *(G-12982)*
Hillside Solid Surfaces...802 479-2508
Gable Pl Ste 37 Barre VT (05641) *(G-21622)*
Hillside Stone Product, Barre *Also called Hillside Solid Surfaces (G-21622)*
Hillside Stone Products Inc...802 479-2508
37 Gable Pl Barre VT (05641) *(G-21623)*
Hilltop Candies...508 583-0895
15 Jonathan Dr Ste 3 Brockton MA (02301) *(G-9154)*
Hilltop Cooperative...603 895-6476
2 Parker Ave Raymond NH (03077) *(G-19638)*
Hilltop Orchard, Richmond *Also called Grove Street Enterprises Inc (G-14780)*
Hilltop Wood Crafts...508 754-3915
126 Pakachoag St Auburn MA (01501) *(G-7838)*
Hilltown Pork Inc...413 357-6661
243 Sodom St Granville MA (01034) *(G-11230)*

ALPHABETIC

Hilsinger Company Parent LLC (PA) 508 699-4406
33 W Bacon St Plainville MA (02762) ***(G-14520)***
Hilsinger Holdings Inc 508 699-4406
33 W Bacon St Plainville MA (02762) ***(G-14521)***
Hinckley Co, Portsmouth *Also called Talaria Company LLC* ***(G-20941)***
Hinckley Company, The, Portsmouth *Also called Talaria Company LLC* ***(G-20940)***
Hinckley Company, The, Trenton *Also called Talaria Company LLC* ***(G-7102)***
Hinckley Yacht Services, Southwest Harbor *Also called Talaria Company LLC* ***(G-7052)***
Hindley Manufacturing Co Inc 401 722-2550
9 Havens St Cumberland RI (02864) ***(G-20325)***
Hindsight Imaging Inc 607 793-3762
3 Waterford Way Unit 112 Manchester NH (03102) ***(G-18833)***
Hindsight Imaging Inc 607 793-3762
23 Staples Point Rd Freeport ME (04032) ***(G-6080)***
Hinesburg Record 802 482-2350
327 Charlotte Rd Hinesburg VT (05461) ***(G-22028)***
Hinman Lumber, Burlington *Also called E R Hinman & Sons Inc* ***(G-677)***
Hint Peripherals Corp 203 634-4468
46 Gracey Ave Meriden CT (06451) ***(G-2094)***
Hiperfax Inc 207 764-4319
470 State St Presque Isle ME (04769) ***(G-6759)***
Hippopress LLC (PA) 603 625-1855
49 Hollis St Manchester NH (03101) ***(G-18834)***
Hirsch Retail Store Inc 978 621-4634
52 Eaton Dr Acton MA (01719) ***(G-7360)***
HIRSCHMANN WINDOWS AND DOORS, West Rutland *Also called H Hirschmann Ltd* ***(G-22616)***
Hirst Fuel LLC 401 789-6376
83 Birchwood Dr Wakefield RI (02879) ***(G-21271)***
His Vineyard Inc 203 790-1600
2 Vail Rd Bethel CT (06801) ***(G-159)***
Hispanic Communications LLC 203 674-6793
400 Main St Stamford CT (06901) ***(G-4218)***
Hispanic Communications LLC 203 624-8007
51 Elm St New Haven CT (06510) ***(G-2696)***
Hispanic Enterprises Inc 203 588-9334
200 Cogswell St Bridgeport CT (06610) ***(G-425)***
Historic Map Works 207 756-5215
3 Cottage Rd Portland ME (04106) ***(G-6671)***
Historical Art Prints 203 262-6680
464 Burr Rd Southbury CT (06488) ***(G-4027)***
Historical Publications, Tunbridge *Also called Cutter & Locke Inc* ***(G-22542)***
Hitachi Aloka Medical Ltd 203 269-5088
10 Fairfield Blvd Wallingford CT (06492) ***(G-4752)***
Hitachi Aloka Medical Amer Inc 203 269-5088
10 Fairfield Blvd Wallingford CT (06492) ***(G-4753)***
Hitachi Cable America Inc 603 669-4347
900 Holt Ave Manchester NH (03109) ***(G-18835)***
Hitachi Cable America Inc 401 315-5100
15 Gray Ln Ste 201 Ashaway RI (02804) ***(G-20038)***
Hitachi Protection Platform, Marlborough *Also called Sepaton Inc* ***(G-12824)***
Hitbro Realty LLC 860 824-1370
78 High St Canaan CT (06018) ***(G-687)***
Hitchcock Press Inc 413 538-8811
8 Hanover St Holyoke MA (01040) ***(G-11632)***
Hitchcock Printers, New Britain *Also called E R Hitchcock Company* ***(G-2529)***
Hitchiner Ferrous USA Division, Milford *Also called Hitchiner Manufacturing Co Inc* ***(G-19061)***
Hitchiner Manufacturing Co Inc (PA) 603 673-1100
594 Elm St Milford NH (03055) ***(G-19060)***
Hitchiner Manufacturing Co Inc 603 673-1100
1 Scarborough Ln Milford NH (03055) ***(G-19061)***
Hitchiner Manufacturing Co Inc 603 732-1935
117 Old Wilton Rd Milford NH (03055) ***(G-19062)***
Hitchiner Manufacturing Co Inc 603 673-1100
Hitchiner Way Milford NH (03055) ***(G-19063)***
Hitchiner Plant 1, Milford *Also called Hitchiner Manufacturing Co Inc* ***(G-19063)***
Hitec Products Inc 978 772-6963
4 Lomar Park Pepperell MA (01463) ***(G-14438)***
Hitech Chrome Pltg & Polsg Lc 860 456-8070
30 Baker Rd North Windham CT (06256) ***(G-3082)***
Hitech Div, Peterborough *Also called New Hmpshire Ball Bearings Inc* ***(G-19479)***
Hitech Metals, Bellingham *Also called Hi-Tech Metals Inc* ***(G-8040)***
Hitpoint Inc (PA) 508 314-6070
1350 Main St Ste 1300 Springfield MA (01103) ***(G-15476)***
Hittite Microwave LLC (HQ) 978 250-3343
2 Elizabeth Dr Chelmsford MA (01824) ***(G-9905)***
HJ Baker & Bro LLC (PA) 203 682-9200
2 Corporate Dr Ste 545 Shelton CT (06484) ***(G-3812)***
HK Chain Usa Inc 401 782-0402
1058 Kingstown Rd Unit 8 Wakefield RI (02879) ***(G-21272)***
Hkd Snowmakers, Natick *Also called Snow Economics Inc* ***(G-13279)***
Hl Operating LLC (HQ) 508 851-1400
575 West St Ste 110 Mansfield MA (02048) ***(G-12635)***
Hlf Industries 603 303-2425
210 Fremont Rd Sandown NH (03873) ***(G-19785)***
HM Machine LLC 603 948-1178
44 Venture Dr Dover NH (03820) ***(G-18028)***
HM Machine LLC 603 617-3450
5 Faraday Dr Dover NH (03820) ***(G-18029)***
HM Publishing Corp 617 251-5000
222 Berkeley St Boston MA (02116) ***(G-8598)***
HMC Corporation (PA) 603 746-3399
284 Maple St Hopkinton NH (03229) ***(G-18362)***
HMC Holding Corporation (PA) 401 253-5501
68 Buttonwood St Bristol RI (02809) ***(G-20084)***
Hmd Inc 603 532-5757
81 Turnpike Rd Jaffrey NH (03452) ***(G-18467)***
Hmh, Boston *Also called Houghton Mifflin Harcourt Co* ***(G-8606)***
Hmh, Portsmouth *Also called Houghton Mifflin Harcourt Co* ***(G-19576)***
Hmh Publishers LLC (HQ) 617 351-5000
125 High St Boston MA (02110) ***(G-8599)***
Hmh Religious Mfg Inc 508 699-9464
11 Mirimichi St Plainville MA (02762) ***(G-14522)***
Hmh Supplemental Publishers 407 345-2000
222 Berkeley St Boston MA (02116) ***(G-8600)***
Hnu, Sandwich *Also called Pid Analyzers LLC* ***(G-14972)***
Ho Toy Noodles Inc (PA) 617 426-0247
1490 Central St Stoughton MA (02072) ***(G-15596)***
Hob Industries Inc 203 879-3028
750 Bound Line Rd Wolcott CT (06716) ***(G-5444)***
Hobbs Medical Inc 860 684-5875
8 Spring St Stafford Springs CT (06076) ***(G-4111)***
Hobbs Tavern & Brewing Co LLC 603 539-2000
2415 Route 16 West Ossipee NH (03890) ***(G-19966)***
Hobo, Bourne *Also called Onset Computer Corporation* ***(G-8948)***
Hobson and Motzer Incorporated (PA) 860 349-1756
30 Airline Rd Durham CT (06422) ***(G-1092)***
Hockey Magazine, The, Rockland *Also called Regional Spt Media Group LLC* ***(G-14821)***
Hockey12com 781 910-2877
12 Beaumont Ave Billerica MA (01821) ***(G-8254)***
Hodgdon Shipbuilding LLC 207 563-7033
6 Angell Ln Damariscotta ME (04543) ***(G-5936)***
Hodgdon Shipbuilding LLC (HQ) 207 633-4194
14 School St East Boothbay ME (04544) ***(G-5976)***
Hodgdon Yachts Inc 207 737-2802
150 Main St Ste 12 Richmond ME (04357) ***(G-6782)***
Hodgdon Yachts Inc (PA) 207 737-2802
14 School St East Boothbay ME (04544) ***(G-5977)***
Hodges Badge Company Inc (PA) 401 682-2000
1170 E Main Rd Portsmouth RI (02871) ***(G-20923)***
Hoffmann-La Roche Inc 203 871-2303
15 Commercial St Branford CT (06405) ***(G-323)***
Hogy Lure Company LLC 617 699-5157
15 Simpson Ln Falmouth MA (02540) ***(G-10791)***
Holase Incorporated 603 397-0038
75 Rochester Ave Portsmouth NH (03801) ***(G-19575)***
Holbrook Sun Inc 781 767-4000
15 Pacella Park Dr # 200 Randolph MA (02368) ***(G-14684)***
Holden, Keene *Also called Evs New Hampshire Inc* ***(G-18502)***
Holden Trap Rock Co, Holden *Also called Massachusetts Broken Stone Co* ***(G-11547)***
Holden Trap Rock Company, Berlin *Also called Massachusetts Broken Stone Co* ***(G-8091)***
Holden Wine & Spirits Inc 508 829-6632
140 Reservoir St Holden MA (01520) ***(G-11544)***
Hole In One 508 255-5359
4295 Us 6 Eastham MA (02642) ***(G-10549)***
Hole In One Donut Shop, Eastham *Also called Hole In One* ***(G-10549)***
Holiday Farm Inc 413 684-0444
Holiday Cottage Rd Dalton MA (01226) ***(G-10178)***
Hollan Publishing Inc 978 704-9342
4 Butler Ave Manchester MA (01944) ***(G-12605)***
Holland & Sherry Inc (PA) 212 628-1950
5 Taft St Norwalk CT (06854) ***(G-3169)***
Holland Company Inc 413 743-1292
153 Howland Ave Adams MA (01220) ***(G-7413)***
Holland Drug Inc 207 778-5419
624 Wilton Rd Farmington ME (04938) ***(G-6050)***
Holland Woodworking 413 527-6588
224 Pomeroy Meadow Rd Southampton MA (01073) ***(G-15339)***
Holland Woodworking Inc 508 481-2990
666 Brigham St Marlborough MA (01752) ***(G-12768)***
Hollands Boat Shop Inc 207 338-3155
7 Mill Ln Belfast ME (04915) ***(G-5690)***
Hollingsworth & Vose Company (PA) 508 850-2000
112 Washington St East Walpole MA (02032) ***(G-10524)***
Hollis Controls Inc (PA) 603 595-2482
131 Daniel Webster Hwy Nashua NH (03060) ***(G-19179)***
Hollis Industries Inc 508 429-4328
1485 Washington St Holliston MA (01746) ***(G-11578)***
Hollis Line Machine Co Inc 603 465-2251
128 Old Wilton Rd Milford NH (03055) ***(G-19064)***
Hollis Line Machine Co Inc (PA) 603 465-2251
295 S Merrimack Rd Hollis NH (03049) ***(G-18332)***
Hollow Frost Publishers 860 974-2081
411 Barlow Cemetery Rd Woodstock CT (06281) ***(G-5497)***
Hollrock Engineering Inc 413 586-2256
294 Russell St Hadley MA (01035) ***(G-11307)***

Holly Press Inc 203 846-1720
8 College St Norwalk CT (06851) ***(G-3170)***
Holm Corrugated Container Inc 860 628-5559
Metals Dr Southington CT (06489) ***(G-4058)***
Holmes Stamp Company 978 744-1051
128 Margin St Salem MA (01970) ***(G-14922)***
Holmris US Inc 603 232-3490
250 Commercial St # 2008 Manchester NH (03101) ***(G-18836)***
Holmspray, Chartley *Also called T J Holmes Co Inc* ***(G-9858)***
Holo-Krome USA 800 879-6205
61 Barnes Industrial Park Wallingford CT (06492) ***(G-4754)***
Hologic Inc 508 263-2900
250 Campus Dr Marlborough MA (01752) ***(G-12769)***
Hologic Inc 508 263-2900
445 Simarano Dr Marlborough MA (01752) ***(G-12770)***
Hologic Inc 203 790-1188
36 Apple Ridge Rd Danbury CT (06810) ***(G-933)***
Hologic Inc (PA) 508 263-2900
250 Campus Dr Marlborough MA (01752) ***(G-12771)***
Hologic Inc 603 668-7688
2 E Perimeter Rd Londonderry NH (03053) ***(G-18702)***
Hologic Foreign Sales Corp 781 999-7300
35 Crosby Dr Bedford MA (01730) ***(G-7980)***
Holographix LLC 978 562-4474
140 Locke Dr Ste A Marlborough MA (01752) ***(G-12772)***
Holometrology, Coventry *Also called Karl Stetson Associates LLC* ***(G-834)***
Holy Cross Book Store, Brookline *Also called Holy Cross Orthodox Press* ***(G-9203)***
Holy Cross Orthodox Press 800 245-0599
50 Goddard Ave Brookline MA (02445) ***(G-9203)***
Holy Donut 207 303-0137
398 Us Route 1 Scarborough ME (04074) ***(G-6924)***
Holy Terra Products Inc 207 846-4170
253 Royall Point Rd Yarmouth ME (04096) ***(G-7295)***
Holyoke Machine Company (PA) 413 534-5612
514 Main St Holyoke MA (01040) ***(G-11633)***
Home Diagnostics Corp 203 445-1170
1 Trefoil Dr Trumbull CT (06611) ***(G-4625)***
Home Grown Lacrosse LLC 978 208-2300
400 Osgood St North Andover MA (01845) ***(G-13709)***
Home Heating Services Corp 617 625-8255
2 Alpine St Somerville MA (02144) ***(G-15183)***
Home Intensive Care Inc 781 699-9000
920 Winter St Waltham MA (02451) ***(G-16127)***
Home Kore Mfg Co Mass Inc 508 947-0000
210 Kenneth Welch Dr Lakeville MA (02347) ***(G-11976)***
Home Market Foods Inc (PA) 781 948-1500
140 Morgan Dr Ste 100 Norwood MA (02062) ***(G-14157)***
Home of St Julien Macaroons, Sandown *Also called White Oak Farms* ***(G-19789)***
Home Pdts Intl - N Amer Inc 978 534-6536
106 Carter St Leominster MA (01453) ***(G-12152)***
Homefree LLC 603 898-0172
10 Industrial Dr Unit 11 Windham NH (03087) ***(G-20008)***
Homegrown Lumber 603 447-3800
230 Heath Rd Center Conway NH (03813) ***(G-17800)***
Homeland Company 401 884-2427
69 Highpoint Dr East Greenwich RI (02818) ***(G-20370)***
Homeland Fuels Company LLC 781 737-1892
40 Shawmut Rd Ste 200 Canton MA (02021) ***(G-9739)***
Homeland Fundraising 860 386-6698
38 Borrup Rd East Windsor CT (06088) ***(G-1286)***
Homeland Security Wireless Inc 508 299-1404
5 Robinson Rd Falmouth MA (02540) ***(G-10792)***
Homemade Lbtons By Ccchia Sons, Norwalk *Also called Cocchia Norwalk Grape Co* ***(G-3127)***
Homeportfolio Inc 617 559-1197
288 Walnut St Ste 500 Newton MA (02460) ***(G-13602)***
Homes and Land Magazine, Portsmouth *Also called Reid Publication Inc* ***(G-19614)***
Homespun Samplar 401 732-3181
1716 Round Top Rd Harrisville RI (02830) ***(G-20480)***
Homestead Baking Co 401 434-0551
145 N Broadway Rumford RI (02916) ***(G-21186)***
Homestead Kitchen Centre LLC 603 642-8022
53 Church St Unit 18 Kingston NH (03848) ***(G-18544)***
Hometown Design Mix, Vineyard Haven *Also called Mix* ***(G-15934)***
Hometown Fuel DBA Hometo 207 325-4411
3 Van Buren Rd Limestone ME (04750) ***(G-6341)***
Homewood Cabinet Co Inc 860 599-2441
262 S Broad St Pawcatuck CT (06379) ***(G-3437)***
Honematic Machine Corporation 508 869-2131
222 Shrewsbury St Boylston MA (01505) ***(G-8980)***
Hones LLC 603 643-4223
12 South St Ste 3 Hanover NH (03755) ***(G-18289)***
Honey Cell Inc (PA) 203 925-1818
850 Union Ave Bridgeport CT (06607) ***(G-426)***
Honey Hill Farm 413 659-3141
98 W Mineral Rd Millers Falls MA (01349) ***(G-13180)***
Honeywell Authorized Dealer, Danvers *Also called Burnell Controls Inc* ***(G-10204)***
Honeywell Data Instruments Inc 978 264-9550
100 Discovery Way Acton MA (01720) ***(G-7361)***
Honeywell International Inc 781 298-2700
65 Shawmut Rd Unit 5 Canton MA (02021) ***(G-9740)***
Honeywell International Inc 401 757-2560
10 Thurber Blvd Smithfield RI (02917) ***(G-21231)***
Honeywell International Inc 203 484-7161
12 Clintonville Rd Northford CT (06472) ***(G-3087)***
Honeywell International Inc 207 846-3350
10 Princess Rd Yarmouth ME (04096) ***(G-7296)***
Honeywell International Inc 877 841-2840
203 Cornerstone Dr Williston VT (05495) ***(G-22674)***
Honeywell International Inc 401 769-7274
245 Railroad St Woonsocket RI (02895) ***(G-21568)***
Honeywell International Inc 973 455-2000
65 Acceri Rd Ste 1 Warwick RI (02886) ***(G-21371)***
Honeywell International Inc 203 484-7161
12 Clintonville Rd Northford CT (06472) ***(G-3088)***
Honeywell International Inc 203 484-6202
12 Clintonville Rd Northford CT (06472) ***(G-3089)***
Honeywell International Inc 401 762-6200
245 Rlroad St Wnsocket Ri Woonsocket Ri Woonsocket RI (02895) ***(G-21569)***
Honeywell International Inc 401 769-7274
245 Railroad St Woonsocket RI (02895) ***(G-21570)***
Honeywell International Inc 203 484-7161
12 Clintonville Rd North Branford CT (06471) ***(G-2967)***
Honeywell International Inc 508 490-7100
250 Turnpike Rd Southborough MA (01772) ***(G-15361)***
Honeywell International Inc 203 484-7161
1 Fire Lite Pl 4 Northford CT (06472) ***(G-3090)***
Honeywell International Inc 978 774-3007
199 Rosewood Dr Ste 300 Danvers MA (01923) ***(G-10223)***
Honeywell Robert Warner 978 358-8080
14 Hawthorne Rd Newburyport MA (01950) ***(G-13498)***
Honeywell Safety Pdts USA Inc 800 500-4739
10 Thurber Bouevard Smithfield RI (02828) ***(G-21232)***
Honeywell Safety Products, Smithfield *Also called Sperian Protection Usa Inc* ***(G-21250)***
Honeywell Safety Products Usa 401 233-0333
10 Thurber Blvd Smithfield RI (02917) ***(G-21233)***
Honle Uv America Inc 508 229-7774
261 Cedar Hill St Ste 5 Marlborough MA (01752) ***(G-12773)***
Honora Winery & Vineyard Inc 802 368-2930
1950 Collins Rd Brattleboro VT (05301) ***(G-21732)***
Honorcraft LLC 781 341-0410
292 Page St Ste A Stoughton MA (02072) ***(G-15597)***
Hood Sailmakers, Groton *Also called Custom Marine Canvas LLC* ***(G-1669)***
Hood Sailmakers Inc (PA) 401 849-9400
23 Johnny Cake Hill Rd Middletown RI (02842) ***(G-20620)***
Hoodco Systems Inc 978 851-7473
30 Barry Dr Tewksbury MA (01876) ***(G-15818)***
Hooke Laboratories Inc 617 475-5114
439 S Union St Lawrence MA (01843) ***(G-12036)***
Hookfast Specialties Inc 401 781-4466
63 Seymour St Providence RI (02905) ***(G-21031)***
Hope & Main 401 245-7400
691 Main St Warren RI (02885) ***(G-21295)***
Hope Association (PA) 207 364-4561
85 Lincoln Ave Rumford ME (04276) ***(G-6835)***
Hope Buffinton Packaging Inc 401 725-3646
575 Lonsdale Ave Central Falls RI (02863) ***(G-20115)***
Hope Global, Cumberland *Also called Nfa Corp* ***(G-20334)***
Hope Kit Cbinets Stone Sup LLC (PA) 203 610-6147
1901 Commerce Dr Bridgeport CT (06605) ***(G-427)***
Hope-Bffnton Pckging Group LLC 401 725-3646
575 Lonsdale Ave Central Falls RI (02863) ***(G-20116)***
Hopkington Independent 508 435-5188
32 South St Westborough MA (01581) ***(G-16624)***
Hopkins Hill Sand & Stone LLC 401 739-8300
400 Lincoln Ave Warwick RI (02888) ***(G-21372)***
Hopkins Press 401 231-9654
345 Woonasquatucket Ave North Providence RI (02911) ***(G-20764)***
Hopkinton Crier 508 626-3939
33 New York Ave Framingham MA (01701) ***(G-10963)***
Hopp Companies Inc 800 889-8425
3 Simm Ln Ste 2 Newtown CT (06470) ***(G-2924)***
Hoppe Technologies Inc 413 592-9213
107 First Ave Chicopee MA (01020) ***(G-10029)***
Hopps Company 617 481-1379
20 Braintree Ave Quincy MA (02169) ***(G-14632)***
Hopto Inc (PA) 800 472-7466
6 Loudon Rd Ste 200 Concord NH (03301) ***(G-17908)***
Horacios Welding & Shtmtl Inc 508 985-9940
64 John Vertente Blvd New Bedford MA (02745) ***(G-13395)***
Horberg Industries Inc 203 334-9444
19 Staples St Bridgeport CT (06604) ***(G-428)***
Horizon House Publications Inc (PA) 781 769-9750
685 Canton St Norwood MA (02062) ***(G-14158)***
Horizon International Inc 617 489-6666
385 Concord Ave Ste 104 Belmont MA (02478) ***(G-8075)***
Horizon Manufacturing & Design 802 384-3715
56 Burnett Rd Westminster W VT (05346) ***(G-22634)***

ALPHABETIC

Horizon Sales......978 779-0487
56 Powder Hill Rd Bolton MA (01740) **(G-8320)**
Horizon Sheet Metal Inc......413 734-6966
109 Cadwell Dr Springfield MA (01104) **(G-15477)**
Horizon Software Inc......860 633-2090
148 Eastern Blvd Ste 208 Glastonbury CT (06033) **(G-1559)**
Horizons Unlimited Inc......860 423-1931
90 S Park St Ste 1 Willimantic CT (06226) **(G-5266)**
Horlick Company Inc......781 963-0090
91 Pacella Park Dr Randolph MA (02368) **(G-14685)**
Horn Book Inc......617 278-0225
300 Fenway Ste P311 Boston MA (02115) **(G-8601)**
Horn Book Magazine, Boston *Also called Horn Book Inc* **(G-8601)**
Horn Corporation (PA)......800 832-7020
580 Fort Pond Rd Lancaster MA (01523) **(G-11984)**
Horner Millwork Corp......781 826-7770
55 Corporate Park Dr # 1 Pembroke MA (02359) **(G-14408)**
Horsepower Technologies Inc......844 514-6773
175 Cabot St Ste 500 Lowell MA (01854) **(G-12380)**
Horst Engrg De Mexico LLC......860 289-8209
36 Cedar St East Hartford CT (06108) **(G-1199)**
Horton Brasses Inc......860 635-4400
49 Nooks Hill Rd Cromwell CT (06416) **(G-855)**
Hosetech Plus More Inc......413 385-0035
83 Carmelinas Cir Ludlow MA (01056) **(G-12467)**
Hoshizaki America Inc......508 251-7060
360 Cedar Hill St Marlborough MA (01752) **(G-12774)**
Hosokawa Alpine American Div, Northborough *Also called Hosokawa Micron International* **(G-14037)**
Hosokawa Alpine American Inc......508 655-1123
455 Whitney St Northborough MA (01532) **(G-14036)**
Hosokawa Micron International......508 655-1123
455 Whitney St Northborough MA (01532) **(G-14037)**
Hosokawa Micron Intl Inc......860 828-0541
63 Fuller Way Berlin CT (06037) **(G-89)**
Hosokawa Polymer Systems Div, Berlin *Also called Hosokawa Micron Intl Inc* **(G-89)**
Hostar Mar Trnspt Systems Inc......508 295-2900
1 Kendrick Rd Wareham MA (02571) **(G-16250)**
Hot Plates Company......508 429-1445
83 Nickerson Rd Ste 1e Ashland MA (01721) **(G-7661)**
Hot Stepz Magazine......617 959-6403
42 Edson St Dorchester MA (02124) **(G-10343)**
Hot Stuff Rl Inc......401 781-7500
70 Jefferson Blvd Warwick RI (02888) **(G-21373)**
Hot Tools Inc......781 639-1000
24 Tioga Way Marblehead MA (01945) **(G-12686)**
Hotham & Sons Lumber Inc......207 926-4231
Town Farm Rd New Gloucester ME (04260) **(G-6467)**
Hotrod Hotline......208 562-0470
106 Main St North Adams MA (01247) **(G-13676)**
Hotseat Chassis Inc......860 582-5031
20 S Commons Rd Waterbury CT (06704) **(G-4884)**
Hottinger Bldwin Msrements Inc (HQ)......508 624-4500
19 Bartlett St Marlborough MA (01752) **(G-12775)**
Houghton Mifflin LLC......617 351-5000
222 Berkeley St Lbby 1 Boston MA (02116) **(G-8602)**
Houghton Mifflin Co Intl Inc......617 351-5000
222 Berkeley St Boston MA (02116) **(G-8603)**
Houghton Mifflin Harcourt, Boston *Also called Hmh Publishers LLC* **(G-8599)**
Houghton Mifflin Harcourt......617 351-5000
125 High St Ste 900 Boston MA (02110) **(G-8604)**
Houghton Mifflin Harcourt (HQ)......617 351-5000
125 High St Ste 900 Boston MA (02110) **(G-8605)**
Houghton Mifflin Harcourt Co (PA)......617 351-5000
125 High St Ste 900 Boston MA (02110) **(G-8606)**
Houghton Mifflin Harcourt Co......630 467-7000
361 Hanover St Portsmouth NH (03801) **(G-19576)**
Houghton Mifflin Harcourt Pubg (HQ)......617 351-5000
125 High St Ste 900 Boston MA (02110) **(G-8607)**
Houghton Mifflin Holdings Inc (PA)......617 351-5000
125 High St Ste 900 Boston MA (02110) **(G-8608)**
Houghton Mifflin Publishing, Boston *Also called Houghton Mifflin Harcourt Pubg* **(G-8607)**
Houle Bros Granite Co Inc......802 476-6825
25 S Front St Barre VT (05641) **(G-21624)**
Houlton Farms Dairy Inc (PA)......207 532-3170
Commonwealth Ave Houlton ME (04730) **(G-6206)**
Houlton Pioneer Times, Houlton *Also called Northeast Publishing Company* **(G-6208)**
Houlton Powers Boards, Houlton *Also called Chambers Leasing* **(G-6203)**
Housatonic Welding Company......413 274-6631
57 Van Dusenfled Rd Housatonic MA (01236) **(G-11742)**
Housatonic Wire Co......203 888-9670
109 River St Seymour CT (06483) **(G-3752)**
House of Kobrin, Everett *Also called Reliable Fabrics Inc* **(G-10626)**
House of Laurila......603 224-8123
1138 Hopkinton Rd Hopkinton NH (03229) **(G-18363)**
House of Primavera, Providence *Also called Danecraft Inc* **(G-20994)**
House of Stainless Inc......800 556-3470
1637 Elmwood Ave Cranston RI (02910) **(G-20237)**
House of Troy, Hyde Park *Also called Light Logic Inc* **(G-22037)**
House of Villeroy & Boch, Kittery *Also called Villeroy & Boch Usa Inc* **(G-6259)**
Housing Devices Inc......781 395-5200
407r Mystic Ave Ste 32b Medford MA (02155) **(G-12935)**
Houston Macdermid Inc......203 575-5700
245 Freight St Waterbury CT (06702) **(G-4885)**
Houston Weber Systems Inc......203 481-0115
31 Business Park Dr Ste 3 Branford CT (06405) **(G-324)**
Howard Boats LLC......508 362-6859
Beale Way Barnstable MA (02630) **(G-7948)**
Howard Engineering LLC......203 729-5213
687 Wooster St Naugatuck CT (06770) **(G-2478)**
Howard Foods Inc (PA)......978 774-6207
5 Ray St Danvers MA (01923) **(G-10224)**
Howard P Fairfield LLC (HQ)......207 474-9836
9 Green St Skowhegan ME (04976) **(G-6976)**
Howard P Fairfield LLC......802 888-2092
87 Old Creamery Rd B Morrisville VT (05661) **(G-22170)**
Howard P Fairfield LLC......207 885-4895
65 Pleasant Hill Rd Scarborough ME (04074) **(G-6925)**
Howard Precision Inc......603 293-8012
359 Hounsell Ave Gilford NH (03249) **(G-18189)**
Howard Printing Inc......802 254-3550
14 Noahs Ln Brattleboro VT (05301) **(G-21733)**
Howard Products Incorporated......508 757-2440
7 Brookfield St Worcester MA (01605) **(G-17390)**
Howard S I Glass Co, Worcester *Also called S I Howard Glass Company Inc* **(G-17461)**
Howard Tool Company......207 942-1203
547 Odlin Rd Bangor ME (04401) **(G-5651)**
Howards Fuel Co Inc......603 635-9955
24 Jane St Manchester NH (03104) **(G-18837)**
Howarth Bkkping Income Tax Svc, Westport *Also called Howarth Specialty Company* **(G-16841)**
Howarth Specialty Company......508 674-8950
37 E Briggs Rd Westport MA (02790) **(G-16841)**
Howestemco Inc......508 528-6500
50 Earls Way Franklin MA (02038) **(G-11053)**
Howies Wldg & Fabrication Inc......207 645-2581
1148 Main St Jay ME (04239) **(G-6220)**
Howland Tool & Machine Ltd......508 763-8472
159 Chace Rd East Freetown MA (02717) **(G-10452)**
Howmet Castings & Services Inc......860 379-3314
145 Price Rd Winsted CT (06098) **(G-5413)**
Howmet Corporation......203 481-3451
4 Commercial St Branford CT (06405) **(G-325)**
Hoy Printing Corp......207 284-5531
120 Main St Biddeford ME (04005) **(G-5739)**
Hoya Corporation......860 289-5379
580 Nutmeg Rd N South Windsor CT (06074) **(G-3982)**
Hoya Optcal Labs Amrc-Hartford, South Windsor *Also called Hoya Corporation* **(G-3982)**
Hoylu Inc......877 554-6958
50 Corporate Park Dr # 270 Pembroke MA (02359) **(G-14409)**
Hoylu Boston, Pembroke *Also called Hoylu Inc* **(G-14409)**
Hoyt Elec Instr Works Inc......603 753-6321
23 Meter St Concord NH (03303) **(G-17909)**
Hoyt Manufacturing Co Inc......860 628-2050
37 W Center St Ste Ll1 Southington CT (06489) **(G-4059)**
HP Hood LLC (PA)......617 887-8441
6 Kimball Ln Ste 400 Lynnfield MA (01940) **(G-12549)**
HP Hood LLC......860 623-4435
1250 East St S Suffield CT (06078) **(G-4463)**
HP Hood LLC......203 304-9151
153 S Main St Newtown CT (06470) **(G-2925)**
HP Hood LLC......207 774-9861
349 Park Ave Portland ME (04102) **(G-6672)**
HP Hood LLC......413 786-2178
233 Main St Agawam MA (01001) **(G-7431)**
HP Hood LLC......413 789-8194
86 Oak Ln Feeding Hills MA (01030) **(G-10800)**
HP Hood LLC......978 535-3385
18 Blackstone St Peabody MA (01960) **(G-14342)**
HP Inc......650 857-1501
550 King St Littleton MA (01460) **(G-12307)**
HP Inc......800 222-5547
153 Taylor St Littleton MA (01460) **(G-12308)**
Hpi, Gilford *Also called Howard Precision Inc* **(G-18189)**
Hpi Manufacturing Inc......203 777-5395
375 Morse St Hamden CT (06517) **(G-1760)**
Hpm LLC......508 958-5565
52 Fox Run Rd Bellingham MA (02019) **(G-8041)**
Hrd Press, Pelham *Also called Human Resource Dev Press* **(G-14388)**
HRF Fastener Systems Inc......860 589-0750
70 Horizon Dr Bristol CT (06010) **(G-569)**
Hsb Aircraft Components LLC......860 505-7349
80 Production Ct New Britain CT (06051) **(G-2539)**
HT Machine Co Inc......508 949-1105
15 Town Forest Rd Webster MA (01570) **(G-16343)**
Hub & Federal Sign, Providence *Also called Hub-Federal Inc* **(G-21032)**
Hub Automotive Rebuilders, Ipswich *Also called Jnc Rebuilders Inc* **(G-11925)**

Hub Consolidated Inc....802 948-2209
690 Route 73 Orwell VT (05760) *(G-22255)*
Hub Folding Box Company Inc....508 339-0005
774 Norfolk St Mansfield MA (02048) *(G-12636)*
Hub Pen Company Inc (PA)....781 535-5500
1525 Washington St Ste 1 Braintree MA (02184) *(G-9018)*
Hub-Federal Inc....401 421-3400
135 Dean St Providence RI (02903) *(G-21032)*
Hubb Equipment Inc....978 928-4258
31 Old Boston Tpke Hubbardston MA (01452) *(G-11744)*
Hubbard Rake Co....207 497-5949
1561 Mason Bay Rd Jonesport ME (04649) *(G-6226)*
Hubbardton Forge LLC....802 468-3090
154 Route 30 S Castleton VT (05735) *(G-21828)*
Hubbell Incorporated (PA)....475 882-4000
40 Waterview Dr Shelton CT (06484) *(G-3813)*
Hubbell Incorporated....800 346-4175
7 Aviation Park Dr Londonderry NH (03053) *(G-18703)*
Hubbell Incorporated....203 426-2555
14 Prospect Dr Newtown CT (06470) *(G-2926)*
Hubbell Incorporated....603 647-5000
47 E Industrial Park Dr Manchester NH (03109) *(G-18838)*
Hubbell Incorporated Delaware....475 882-4800
40 Waterview Dr Shelton CT (06484) *(G-3814)*
Hubbell Incorporated Delaware (HQ)....475 882-4000
40 Waterview Dr Shelton CT (06484) *(G-3815)*
Hubbell Premise Wiring Inc....860 535-8326
23 Clara Dr Ste 103 Mystic CT (06355) *(G-2439)*
Hubbell Wiring Device....203 882-4800
185 Plains Rd Milford CT (06461) *(G-2297)*
Hubengage Inc....877 704-6662
1035 Cambridge St Ste 1 Cambridge MA (02141) *(G-9507)*
Huber + Shner Platis Photonics....781 275-5080
213 Burlington Rd Ste 123 Bedford MA (01730) *(G-7981)*
Huber Engineered Woods LLC....207 488-6700
333 Station Rd Easton ME (04740) *(G-5989)*
Hubergroup Usa Inc....860 687-1617
147 Addison Rd Windsor CT (06095) *(G-5338)*
Hubscrub Co Inc....603 624-4243
1015 Candia Rd Unit 1 Manchester NH (03109) *(G-18839)*
Hubspot Inc (PA)....888 482-7768
25 1st St Ste 200 Cambridge MA (02141) *(G-9508)*
Hudson Color Concentrates LLC....978 537-3538
50 Francis St Leominster MA (01453) *(G-12153)*
Hudson Company, Cranston *Also called Hudson Terminal Corp (G-20239)*
Hudson Liquid Asphalts, Providence *Also called Hudson Terminal Corp (G-21033)*
Hudson Liquid Asphalts Inc (PA)....401 274-2200
2000 Chapel View Blvd # 380 Cranston RI (02920) *(G-20238)*
Hudson Poly Bag Inc....978 562-7566
578 Main St Hudson MA (01749) *(G-11776)*
Hudson Terminal Corp (PA)....401 274-2200
29 Terminal Rd Providence RI (02905) *(G-21033)*
Hudson Terminal Corp....401 941-0500
2000 Chapel View Blvd # 380 Cranston RI (02920) *(G-20239)*
Hueson Corp....508 234-6372
134 Ferry St South Grafton MA (01560) *(G-15297)*
Hugard Inc....508 986-2300
121 Flanders Rd Westborough MA (01581) *(G-16625)*
Hugger Design, Greenwich *Also called Puppy Hugger (G-1639)*
Hughes Riskapps LLC....617 936-0301
139a Charles St Pmb 382 Boston MA (02114) *(G-8609)*
Huhtamaki Inc....207 795-6000
11 Fireslate Pl Lewiston ME (04240) *(G-6290)*
Huhtamaki Inc....207 873-3351
242 College Ave Waterville ME (04901) *(G-7157)*
Hull Times, The, Hull *Also called S & S Publications Inc (G-11830)*
Hullihen Machine, Monson *Also called Gary Hullihen (G-13207)*
Human Biomed Inc....802 556-1394
159 Crispin Dr South Burlington VT (05403) *(G-22448)*
Human Body Recon Company....603 895-2920
11 Meindl Way Nottingham NH (03290) *(G-19415)*
Human Care Systems Inc (PA)....617 720-7838
1 Faneuil Hall Sq Boston MA (02109) *(G-8610)*
Human Resource Dev Press (PA)....413 253-3488
22 Amherst Rd Pelham MA (01002) *(G-14388)*
Human Resources, Weatogue *Also called Ensign-Bickford Industries Inc (G-5042)*
Humanscale Corporation....617 338-0077
179 South St Fl 1 Boston MA (02111) *(G-8611)*
Hume Specialties Inc....802 875-3117
291 Pleasant St Chester VT (05143) *(G-21843)*
Hummel Bros Inc....203 787-4113
180 Sargent Dr New Haven CT (06511) *(G-2697)*
Hummingbird Productions....508 645-3030
4 Pilot S Ldg Aquinnah MA (02535) *(G-7620)*
Humphrey Mh & Sons Inc....207 625-4965
92 Mudgett Rd Parsonsfield ME (04047) *(G-6575)*
Humphreys Industrial Pdts Inc....603 692-5005
22 Nadeau Dr Rochester NH (03867) *(G-19671)*
Humphreys Pharmacal Inc....860 267-8710
31 E High St East Hampton CT (06424) *(G-1159)*
Hunt Boatbuilders Inc....401 324-4205
1909 Alden Lndg Portsmouth RI (02871) *(G-20924)*
Hunt Yachts LLC....401 324-4201
1909 Alden Lndg Portsmouth RI (02871) *(G-20925)*
Hunter Associates Inc....781 233-9100
92 Walnut St Ste 3 Saugus MA (01906) *(G-14986)*
Hunter Panels, Portland *Also called Carlisle Construction Mtls LLC (G-6631)*
Hunting Dearborn Inc....207 935-2171
6 Dearborn Dr Fryeburg ME (04037) *(G-6099)*
Huntington Graphics....802 660-3605
168 Battery St Ste 2 Burlington VT (05401) *(G-21788)*
Huntington Logging....603 272-9322
28 Arron Rd Piermont NH (03779) *(G-19492)*
Huntley Benard Industries Inc....603 943-7813
5 Pine Street Ext Nashua NH (03060) *(G-19180)*
Hunts Seafood Inc....978 255-2636
17 North End Blvd Ste A Salisbury MA (01952) *(G-14951)*
Huot Enterprises Inc....413 589-7422
54 Moody St Ludlow MA (01056) *(G-12468)*
Hurley Ink LLC....603 645-0002
8 Perimeter Rd Manchester NH (03103) *(G-18840)*
Hurley Manufacturing, New Hartford *Also called New Hartford Industrial Park (G-2643)*
Hurley Manufacturing Company....860 379-8506
37 Greenwoods Rd New Hartford CT (06057) *(G-2638)*
Hurley Precision Machining LLC....603 474-1879
19 Batchelder Rd Seabrook NH (03874) *(G-19806)*
Hurley's Boston Soda Breads, Hyde Park *Also called SMH Fine Foods Inc (G-11879)*
Husky Fuel....203 783-0783
62 Larkey Rd Oxford CT (06478) *(G-3408)*
Husky Meadows Farm, Greenwich *Also called Norfolk Industries LLC (G-1635)*
Hussey Corporation (PA)....207 676-2271
38 Dyer St Ext North Berwick ME (03906) *(G-6506)*
Hussey Seating Co, North Berwick *Also called Hussey Corporation (G-6506)*
Hussey Seating Company....207 676-2271
38 Dyer St Ext North Berwick ME (03906) *(G-6507)*
Huston & Company Wood Design....207 967-2345
226 Log Cabin Rd Arundel ME (04046) *(G-5532)*
Hutchinson Arospc & Indust Inc (HQ)....508 417-7000
82 South St Hopkinton MA (01748) *(G-11718)*
Hutchinson Arospc & Indust Inc....508 417-7000
82 South St Hopkinton MA (01748) *(G-11719)*
Hutchinson Arospc & Indust Inc....508 417-7000
82 South St Hopkinton MA (01748) *(G-11720)*
Hutchinson Machine....603 329-9545
12 Industrial Way Unit 7 Atkinson NH (03811) *(G-17604)*
Hutchinson Precision Ss Inc....860 779-0300
39 Wauregan Rd Danielson CT (06239) *(G-1013)*
Hutchinson Sealing Systems Inc....603 772-3771
171 Exeter Rd 169 Newfields NH (03856) *(G-19317)*
Hutchison Co Advg Display....508 234-4681
369 Douglas Rd Whitinsville MA (01588) *(G-16913)*
Hutchison Company Advg Display, North Kingstown *Also called Hutchison Company Inc (G-20717)*
Hutchison Company Inc....401 294-3503
376 Dry Bridge Rd Ste J1 North Kingstown RI (02852) *(G-20717)*
Hvo, Danbury *Also called High Voltage Outsourcing LLC (G-932)*
Hw Graphics....860 278-2338
92 Wyndemere Ln Windsor CT (06095) *(G-5339)*
Hwang Bishop Designs Ltd....401 245-9557
30 Cutler St Unit 209 Warren RI (02885) *(G-21296)*
Hxi LLC....978 772-7774
12 Lancaster County Rd # 1 Harvard MA (01451) *(G-11379)*
Hxi Millimeter Wave Products, Harvard *Also called Hxi LLC (G-11379)*
Hy-Liner Rope Co, Saint George *Also called Highliner Rope Co LLC (G-6869)*
Hy-Temp Inc....508 222-6626
34 John Williams St Attleboro MA (02703) *(G-7748)*
Hy-Ten Die & Development Corp....603 673-1611
38 Powers St Milford NH (03055) *(G-19065)*
Hy-Ten Plastics, Milford *Also called Hy-Ten Die & Development Corp (G-19065)*
Hy9 Corporation....508 698-1040
124 Washington St Ste 101 Foxboro MA (02035) *(G-10886)*
Hyalex Orthopaedics Inc....347 871-5850
99 Hayden Ave Ste 360 Lexington MA (02421) *(G-12230)*
Hycon Inc....603 644-1414
349 E Industrial Park Dr Manchester NH (03109) *(G-18841)*
Hycu Inc....617 681-9100
109 State St Boston MA (02109) *(G-8612)*
Hyde Athletic Industries, Waltham *Also called Saucony Inc (G-16191)*
Hyde Clothes Div, Greenwich *Also called Bayer Clothing Group Inc (G-1599)*
Hyde Group Inc (PA)....800 872-4933
54 Eastford Rd Southbridge MA (01550) *(G-15385)*
Hyde Park Bulletin, Hyde Park *Also called Bulletin Newspapers Inc (G-11865)*
Hyde Park Bulletin Newspaper, Hyde Park *Also called Bulletin Newspapers Inc (G-11864)*
Hyde Park Concrete Inc....617 364-5485
8 B St Hyde Park MA (02136) *(G-11869)*
Hyde Tools, Southbridge *Also called Hyde Group Inc (G-15385)*
Hyde Tools....508 764-4344
54 Eastford Rd Southbridge MA (01550) *(G-15386)*

ALPHABETIC

Hydration Labs Incorporated 617 333-8191
529 Main St Ste 311 Charlestown MA (02129) ***(G-9837)***
Hydraulic Solutions of Ne 207 859-9955
709 China Rd Winslow ME (04901) ***(G-7269)***
Hydro Honing Laboratories Inc (PA) 860 289-4328
8 Eastern Park Rd East Hartford CT (06108) ***(G-1200)***
Hydro Quip Inc (PA) 508 399-5771
108 Pond St Seekonk MA (02771) ***(G-15024)***
Hydro Service & Supplies Inc 203 265-3995
975 Middle St Ste K Middletown CT (06457) ***(G-2190)***
Hydro-Flex Inc 203 269-5599
534 Surf Ave Stratford CT (06615) ***(G-4421)***
Hydro-Slave, Rockland *Also called Marine Hydraulic Engrg Co* ***(G-6803)***
Hydro-Test Products Inc 978 897-4647
85 Hudson Rd Stow MA (01775) ***(G-15632)***
Hydrocad Sftwr Solutions LLC 603 323-8666
216 Chocorua Mountain Hwy Chocorua NH (03817) ***(G-17831)***
Hydrochemical Techniques Inc 860 527-6350
253 Locust St Hartford CT (06114) ***(G-1836)***
Hydrocision Inc 978 474-9300
267 Boston Rd Ste 28 North Billerica MA (01862) ***(G-13824)***
Hydroclean Rstrtn Clng Systms, Hartford *Also called Hydrochemical Techniques Inc* ***(G-1836)***
Hydrodot Inc 978 399-0206
3 Post Office Sq Ste K Acton MA (01720) ***(G-7362)***
Hydrofera, Manchester *Also called Hhc LLC* ***(G-2008)***
Hydrofera LLC 860 456-0677
340 Progress Dr Manchester CT (06042) ***(G-2010)***
Hydrogen Energy California LLC 978 287-9529
30 Monument Sq Ste 235 Concord MA (01742) ***(G-10134)***
Hydrogen Highway LLC 203 871-1000
242 Branford Rd North Branford CT (06471) ***(G-2968)***
Hydroid Inc (PA) 508 563-6565
1 Henry Dr Pocasset MA (02559) ***(G-14596)***
Hydroid LLC 508 563-6565
1 Henry Dr Pocasset MA (02559) ***(G-14597)***
Hydrolevel Company 203 776-0473
126 Bailey Rd North Haven CT (06473) ***(G-3030)***
Hydrolevel Div, North Haven *Also called C Cowles & Company* ***(G-3012)***
Hydronics Manufacturing Inc 978 528-4335
150 Rangeway Rd North Billerica MA (01862) ***(G-13825)***
Hydrotec Inc 203 264-6700
115 Hurley Rd Ste 7a Oxford CT (06478) ***(G-3409)***
Hydrotech Services Inc 508 699-5977
38b George Leven Dr North Attleboro MA (02760) ***(G-13759)***
Hyertherm Inc 603 643-3441
20 Airpark Rd West Lebanon NH (03784) ***(G-19953)***
Hygrade Precision Tech Inc 860 747-5773
329 Cooke St Plainville CT (06062) ***(G-3496)***
Hylie Products Incorporated 203 439-8786
30 Grandview Ct Cheshire CT (06410) ***(G-738)***
Hyndsight Vision Systems Inc 603 924-1334
49 Vose Farm Rd Ste 120 Peterborough NH (03458) ***(G-19473)***
Hyora Publications Inc 508 430-2700
60 Munson Meeting Way C Chatham MA (02633) ***(G-9860)***
Hypack Inc (PA) 860 635-1500
56 Bradley St Middletown CT (06457) ***(G-2191)***
Hyperion Catalysis Intl Inc (PA) 617 354-9678
38 Smith Pl Cambridge MA (02138) ***(G-9509)***
Hypertherm Inc (PA) 603 643-3441
21 Great Hollow Rd Hanover NH (03755) ***(G-18290)***
Hypertherm Inc 603 643-3441
1 Etna Rd Hanover NH (03755) ***(G-18291)***
Hypertherm Inc 603 643-3441
9 Great Hollow Rd Hanover NH (03755) ***(G-18292)***
Hypoxyprobe Inc 781 272-6888
121 Middlesex Tpke Ste 2 Burlington MA (01803) ***(G-9283)***
Hysen Technologies Inc (PA) 401 312-6500
1725 Mendon Rd Unit 205 Cumberland RI (02864) ***(G-20326)***
Hytek Plumbing and Heating LLC 860 389-1122
241 Krug Rd Preston CT (06365) ***(G-3581)***
Hytex Decorative Textiles, Randolph *Also called Hytex Industries Inc* ***(G-14686)***
Hytex Industries Inc 781 963-4400
58 York Ave Randolph MA (02368) ***(G-14686)***
Hyzer Industries 802 223-8277
108 Main St Montpelier VT (05602) ***(G-22150)***
I & I Sling Inc 781 575-0600
1400 Boston Providence Tp Norwood MA (02062) ***(G-14159)***
I & J Machine Tool Company 203 877-5376
230 Woodmont Rd Ste V Milford CT (06460) ***(G-2298)***
I and U LLC 860 803-1491
66 Mattatuck Heights Rd Waterbury CT (06705) ***(G-4886)***
I B A Inc 508 865-2507
19 River St Millbury MA (01527) ***(G-13167)***
I B A Print Shop, Millbury *Also called I B A Inc* ***(G-13167)***
I B S, Waltham *Also called Industrial Biomedical Sensors* ***(G-16132)***
I C Haus Corp 802 372-8340
9 Dodge Ter Grand Isle VT (05458) ***(G-21998)***
I C I, South Easton *Also called International Coil Inc* ***(G-15280)***
I C T, Southbury *Also called International Contact Tech* ***(G-4028)***
I C T, Waltham *Also called Instrumentation & Control Tech* ***(G-16135)***
I Copy 401 788-8277
99 Fortin Rd Ste 115 Kingston RI (02881) ***(G-20550)***
I E A, Brookfield *Also called Imperial Elctrnic Assembly Inc* ***(G-647)***
I F Engineering Corp 860 935-0280
3 Foshay Rd Dudley MA (01571) ***(G-10377)***
I G Marston Company 781 767-2894
8 Mear Rd Holbrook MA (02343) ***(G-11526)***
I H T, North Quincy *Also called Industrial Heat Treating Inc* ***(G-13977)***
I L S, Holyoke *Also called International Laser Systems* ***(G-11634)***
I M P, Chicopee *Also called International Metal Pdts Inc* ***(G-10033)***
I M S, Leominster *Also called Innovative Mold Solutions Inc* ***(G-12155)***
I Make News 617 864-4400
1254 Chestnut St Newton MA (02464) ***(G-13603)***
I N I Screen Printing 774 206-1341
2812 Acushnet Ave New Bedford MA (02745) ***(G-13396)***
I Q Technology LLC 860 749-7255
9 Moody Rd Ste 18 Enfield CT (06082) ***(G-1365)***
I R Sources Inc 603 672-0582
28 Old Milford Rd Brookline NH (03033) ***(G-17771)***
I R T, Laconia *Also called Infra Red Technology Inc* ***(G-18568)***
I Shalom, Bristol *Also called New York Accessory Group Inc* ***(G-20095)***
I T C, Bridgeport *Also called Innovative ARC Tubes Corp* ***(G-430)***
I T C, Lenox *Also called Innovative Tooling Company Inc* ***(G-12101)***
I T S, Bedford *Also called Interntonal Totalizing Systems* ***(G-7983)***
I T W Foils, Newburyport *Also called Foilmark Inc* ***(G-13490)***
I V I Corp 781 826-3195
265 Oak St Pembroke MA (02359) ***(G-14410)***
I'M Safe Productions, Rockland *Also called Child Safety Solutions Inc* ***(G-6789)***
I-Optics Corp 508 366-1600
1 Wall St Fl 6 Burlington MA (01803) ***(G-9284)***
I-Pass Institute, Framingham *Also called I-Pass Patient Safety Inst Inc* ***(G-10964)***
I-Pass Patient Safety Inst Inc 617 932-7926
161 Worcester Rd Ste 402 Framingham MA (01701) ***(G-10964)***
I-Web, Avon *Also called Integrated Web Finishing Syst* ***(G-7887)***
I2biomed Inc 857 259-4410
365 Garfield Rd Concord MA (01742) ***(G-10135)***
Iae, East Hartford *Also called International Aero Engines LLC* ***(G-1203)***
Iae International Aero Engs AG 860 565-1773
400 Main St Ms121-10 East Hartford CT (06108) ***(G-1201)***
Ian Marie Inc 978 463-6742
11 Malcolm Hoyt Dr Newburyport MA (01950) ***(G-13499)***
IBC Advanced Alloys Inc-Belac 978 284-8900
55 Jonspin Rd Wilmington MA (01887) ***(G-17004)***
IBC Communications Inc 978 455-9692
6 Stonehill Rd North Chelmsford MA (01863) ***(G-13896)***
Ibcontrols 207 893-0080
3 Pope Rd Windham ME (04062) ***(G-7237)***
Ibex Outdoor Clothing LLC 802 359-4239
132 Ballardvale Dr White River Junction VT (05001) ***(G-22639)***
Ibis LLC 603 471-0951
10 Corporate Dr Ste 100 Bedford NH (03110) ***(G-17645)***
Ibrattleboro 802 257-7475
41 Cedar St Brattleboro VT (05301) ***(G-21734)***
Ibs - Interplast Group, North Dighton *Also called Inteplast Group Corporation* ***(G-13932)***
Ic-Haus, Grand Isle *Also called I C Haus Corp* ***(G-21998)***
Icad Inc (PA) 603 882-5200
98 Spit Brook Rd Ste 100 Nashua NH (03062) ***(G-19181)***
Ice Cream Equipment Supply, North Haverhill *Also called L E Jackson Coropration* ***(G-19389)***
Ice Cream Machine Co 401 333-5053
4288 Diamond Hill Rd Cumberland RI (02864) ***(G-20327)***
Ice Effects 781 871-7070
83 E Water St Ste 15 Rockland MA (02370) ***(G-14807)***
Ice Treat Inc 617 889-0300
170 Everett Ave Unit 3 Chelsea MA (02150) ***(G-9954)***
Icf, Johnston *Also called Industrial & Commercial Finshg* ***(G-20516)***
ICP Construction Inc (HQ) 978 623-9980
150 Dascomb Rd Andover MA (01810) ***(G-7556)***
ICP Construction Inc 508 829-0035
150 Dascomb Rd Andover MA (01810) ***(G-7557)***
ICP Group, Andover *Also called Innovative Chem Pdts Group LLC* ***(G-7558)***
Ics, Guilford *Also called International Comm Svcs Inc* ***(G-1706)***
Ics Corp 978 362-0057
100 Business Park Dr # 13 Tyngsboro MA (01879) ***(G-15889)***
Ict Business 203 595-9452
17 Bridge St Stamford CT (06905) ***(G-4219)***
ID Graphics Group Inc 508 238-8500
9 Bristol Dr South Easton MA (02375) ***(G-15279)***
ID Sign Group, South Easton *Also called ID Graphics Group Inc* ***(G-15279)***
ID Technology LLC 603 598-1553
237 Main Dunstable Rd Nashua NH (03062) ***(G-19182)***
Ida International Inc 203 736-9249
200 Roosevelt Dr Derby CT (06418) ***(G-1074)***

Ida Publishing Co Inc 203 661-9090
282 Railroad Ave Ste 4 Greenwich CT (06830) ***(G-1621)***
Ideal Bias Binding Corp 508 748-2712
35 Bullivant Farm Rd Marion MA (02738) ***(G-12698)***
Ideal Box Company, Lawrence *Also called Harvard Folding Box Co Inc* ***(G-12030)***
Ideal Box Company 978 683-2802
15 Union St Ste 455 Lawrence MA (01840) ***(G-12037)***
Ideal Compost Company 603 924-5050
439 Old Greenfield Rd Peterborough NH (03458) ***(G-19474)***
Ideal Concrete Block Co (PA) 978 692-3076
45 Powers Rd Westford MA (01886) ***(G-16773)***
Ideal Engineering Co Inc 508 966-2324
105 Depot St Bellingham MA (02019) ***(G-8042)***
Ideal Industries Inc 978 422-3600
13 Pratts Junction Rd Sterling MA (01564) ***(G-15540)***
Ideal Instrument Co Inc 781 828-0881
863 Washington St Canton MA (02021) ***(G-9741)***
Ideal Kitchens of Palmer (PA) 413 532-2253
838 Grattan St Chicopee MA (01020) ***(G-10030)***
Ideal Little Things, Marion *Also called Ideal Bias Binding Corp* ***(G-12698)***
Ideal Packaging Solutions, Biddeford *Also called Paul Israelson* ***(G-5754)***
Ideal Plating & Polsg Co Inc 401 455-1700
175 Public St Providence RI (02903) ***(G-21034)***
Ideal Press, Bristol *Also called Davis Press* ***(G-20072)***
Ideal Printing Co Inc 203 777-7626
228 Food Terminal Plz New Haven CT (06511) ***(G-2698)***
Ideal Tape Co Inc 978 458-6833
1400 Middlesex St Lowell MA (01851) ***(G-12381)***
Ideal Tape Co-A Div Amercn Bil, Lowell *Also called Ideal Tape Co Inc* ***(G-12381)***
Idealab Inc 508 528-9260
305 Union St Ste 10 Franklin MA (02038) ***(G-11054)***
Ideapaint, Boston *Also called Innovative Chem Pdts Group LLC* ***(G-8616)***
Ideas Inc 978 453-6864
160 Tanner St Lowell MA (01852) ***(G-12382)***
Ideas Inc 203 878-9686
80a Rowe Ave Milford CT (06461) ***(G-2299)***
Idec 617 527-7878
60 Shawmut Rd Ste 5 Canton MA (02021) ***(G-9742)***
Idemia America Corp (HQ) 978 215-2400
296 Concord Rd Ste 300 Billerica MA (01821) ***(G-8255)***
Idemia Identity & SEC USA LLC 860 529-2559
101 Hammer Mill Rd Rocky Hill CT (06067) ***(G-3717)***
Idenix Pharmaceuticals Inc (HQ) 617 995-9800
320 Bent St Cambridge MA (02141) ***(G-9510)***
Idenix Pharmaceuticals Inc 617 876-5883
60 Hampshire St Cambridge MA (02139) ***(G-9511)***
Identification Concepts, Concord *Also called Computype Inc* ***(G-17894)***
Identification Products Corp 203 334-5969
1073 State St Bridgeport CT (06605) ***(G-429)***
Identity Group Holdings Corp 207 510-6800
43 Bibber Pkwy Brunswick ME (04011) ***(G-5837)***
Idevices LLC 860 352-5252
50 Tower Ln Avon CT (06001) ***(G-36)***
Idex Health & Science LLC 774 213-0200
16 Leona Dr Middleboro MA (02346) ***(G-13064)***
Idex Health & Science LLC 860 314-2880
110 Halcyon Dr Bristol CT (06010) ***(G-570)***
Idex Mpt Inc (HQ) 630 530-3333
90 Glacier Dr Ste 1000 Westwood MA (02090) ***(G-16869)***
Idexx Distribution Inc 207 556-0637
1 Idexx Dr Westbrook ME (04092) ***(G-7190)***
Idexx Laboratories Inc (PA) 207 556-0300
1 Idexx Dr Westbrook ME (04092) ***(G-7191)***
Idg (HQ) 508 875-5000
1 Exeter Plz Fl 15 Boston MA (02116) ***(G-8613)***
Idg Brokerage Services, Framingham *Also called Idg Communications Inc* ***(G-10966)***
Idg Communications Inc (HQ) 508 872-8200
5 Speen St Framingham MA (01701) ***(G-10965)***
Idg Communications Inc 508 766-5300
492 Old Connecticut Path Framingham MA (01701) ***(G-10966)***
Idg Corporate Services Group 508 875-5000
5 Speen St Ste 5 # 5 Framingham MA (01701) ***(G-10967)***
Idg List Services, Framingham *Also called International Data Group Inc* ***(G-10970)***
Idg Paper Services 508 875-5000
492 Old Connecticut Path # 410 Framingham MA (01701) ***(G-10968)***
Idg Woit Modem 781 861-6541
30 Edgewood Rd Lexington MA (02420) ***(G-12231)***
IDI, Milford *Also called Interface Devices Incorporated* ***(G-2303)***
IDS, Manchester *Also called Integrated Deicing Svcs LLC* ***(G-18843)***
IDS Highway Safety Inc 401 333-0740
136 Scott Rd Cumberland RI (02864) ***(G-20328)***
IDS Imaging Dev Systems Inc 781 787-0048
92 Montvale Ave Ste 2950 Stoneham MA (02180) ***(G-15565)***
Ie Chemical Systems Inc 603 888-4777
402 S Main St Nashua NH (03060) ***(G-19183)***
Iemct 203 683-4382
205 Research Dr Ste 8 Milford CT (06460) ***(G-2300)***
Iep, Stoughton *Also called International Event Products* ***(G-15598)***
Iet Solutions LLC (HQ) 818 838-0606
25 Dan Rd Canton MA (02021) ***(G-9743)***
If I Only Had A Nickel 603 225-3972
7 Jordan Ave Concord NH (03301) ***(G-17910)***
Ifco Systems Us LLC 207 883-0244
7 Washington Ave Scarborough ME (04074) ***(G-6926)***
Ifg Industries LLC (HQ) 603 681-0484
6 Northwestern Dr Salem NH (03079) ***(G-19742)***
Iggy's Bread of The World, Cambridge *Also called Iggys Bread Ltd* ***(G-9512)***
Iggys Bread Ltd 617 491-7600
205 Arlington St Ste 4 Watertown MA (02472) ***(G-16291)***
Iggys Bread Ltd (PA) 617 491-7600
130 Fawcett St Cambridge MA (02138) ***(G-9512)***
Iggys Bread of The World, Watertown *Also called Iggys Bread Ltd* ***(G-16291)***
Igitt Inc 401 841-5544
210 Airport Access Rd Middletown RI (02842) ***(G-20621)***
Igm, Holbrook *Also called I G Marston Company* ***(G-11526)***
Igt Global Solutions Corp 781 849-5642
60 Columbian St Braintree MA (02184) ***(G-9019)***
Igt Global Solutions Corp 401 392-7025
55 Technology Way West Greenwich RI (02817) ***(G-21456)***
Iheartcommunications Inc 603 436-7300
815 Lafayette Rd Portsmouth NH (03801) ***(G-19577)***
Iheartcommunications Inc 802 655-0093
265 Hegeman Ave Colchester VT (05446) ***(G-21866)***
IHOP, Attleboro *Also called Attleboro Pancakes Inc* ***(G-7707)***
Ihs Herold Inc (HQ) 203 857-0215
200 Connecticut Ave Ste 8 Norwalk CT (06854) ***(G-3171)***
Ii-VI Photonics (us) Inc (HQ) 781 938-1222
78a Olympia Ave Woburn MA (01801) ***(G-17200)***
Ikigai Foods LLC 203 954-8083
19 Beverly Hill Dr Shelton CT (06484) ***(G-3816)***
IL Pharma Inc 617 355-6910
1 Broadway Fl 14 Cambridge MA (02142) ***(G-9513)***
Ilios Dynamics, Waltham *Also called Ilios Inc* ***(G-16128)***
Ilios Inc 781 466-6481
45 1st Ave Waltham MA (02451) ***(G-16128)***
Illinois Tool Works Inc 207 998-5140
31 Winterbrook Rd Mechanic Falls ME (04256) ***(G-6420)***
Illinois Tool Works Inc 508 821-9828
166 Stoneybrook Rd Raynham MA (02767) ***(G-14716)***
Illinois Tool Works Inc 860 646-8153
375 New State Rd Manchester CT (06042) ***(G-2011)***
Illinois Tool Works Inc 978 874-0151
180 State Rd E Westminster MA (01473) ***(G-16805)***
Illinois Tool Works Inc 508 520-0083
35 Parkwood Dr Ste 10 Hopkinton MA (01748) ***(G-11721)***
Illinois Tool Works Inc 203 720-1676
29 Rado Dr Naugatuck CT (06770) ***(G-2479)***
Illinois Tool Works Inc 978 777-1100
30 Endicott St Danvers MA (01923) ***(G-10225)***
Illinois Tool Works Inc 203 574-2119
1240 Wolcott St Waterbury CT (06705) ***(G-4887)***
Illinois Tool Works Inc 860 435-2574
14 Brook St Lakeville CT (06039) ***(G-1930)***
Illinois Tool Works Inc 781 828-2500
825 University Ave Norwood MA (02062) ***(G-14160)***
Illinois Tool Works Inc 781 878-7015
56 Air Station Indus Park Rockland MA (02370) ***(G-14808)***
Illumination Devices, Williston *Also called 4382412 Canada Inc* ***(G-22652)***
Illuminoss Medical Inc 401 714-0008
993 Waterman Ave East Providence RI (02914) ***(G-20419)***
Imabiotech Corp 978 362-1825
44 Manning Rd Billerica MA (01821) ***(G-8256)***
Image Award Ribbons, Portsmouth *Also called Hodges Badge Company Inc* ***(G-20923)***
Image Awnings Inc 603 569-6680
509 S Main St Wolfeboro NH (03894) ***(G-20020)***
Image Factory 508 295-3876
50 Portside Dr Pocasset MA (02559) ***(G-14598)***
Image Factory LLC 603 895-3024
20 Chester Rd Raymond NH (03077) ***(G-19639)***
Image Ink Inc 860 665-9792
102 Pane Rd Ste A Newington CT (06111) ***(G-2871)***
Image Insight Inc 860 528-9806
87 Church St East Hartford CT (06108) ***(G-1202)***
Image One Prtg & Graphics Inc 203 459-1880
838 Main St Ste L Monroe CT (06468) ***(G-2404)***
Image Polymers Company (HQ) 978 296-0194
384 Lowell St Ste 207 Wakefield MA (01880) ***(G-15955)***
Image Printing & Copying Inc 401 737-9311
33 Plan Way Bldg 7 Warwick RI (02886) ***(G-21374)***
Image Processing, Darien *Also called Schmitt Realty Holdings Inc* ***(G-1031)***
Image Resolutions Inc 781 659-0900
382 Washington St Unit 2 Norwell MA (02061) ***(G-14104)***
Image Software Services Inc 978 425-3600
2 Shaker Rd Ste D103 Shirley MA (01464) ***(G-15087)***
Image Source International Inc 508 801-9252
53a Portside Dr Pocasset MA (02559) ***(G-14599)***

ALPHABETIC

Image Stream Medical Inc....978 486-8494
1 Monarch Dr Ste 102 Littleton MA (01460) ***(G-12309)***
Image Stream Medical LLC....978 456-9087
20 White Ln Harvard MA (01451) ***(G-11380)***
Image Tek Mfg Inc....802 885-6208
280 Clinton St Springfield VT (05156) ***(G-22502)***
Image360....203 949-0726
163 N Plains Indus Rd Wallingford CT (06492) ***(G-4755)***
Imagene Technology Inc....603 448-9940
85 Mechanic St Lebanon NH (03766) ***(G-18625)***
Imagetek Manufacturing, Springfield *Also called Image Tek Mfg Inc* ***(G-22502)***
Imagewise, Hampton Falls *Also called Kensington Group Incorporated* ***(G-18283)***
Imagination Playground LLC....678 604-7466
292 Charles St Providence RI (02904) ***(G-21035)***
Imagine 8 LLC....203 421-0905
26 Eagle Meadow Rd Madison CT (06443) ***(G-1964)***
Imagine Publishing, Watertown *Also called Charlesbridge Publishing Inc* ***(G-16276)***
Imagineering Inc....207 596-6483
6 Gordon Dr Rockland ME (04841) ***(G-6798)***
Imaging Data Corporation....978 365-9353
67 Plain St Clinton MA (01510) ***(G-10081)***
Imaging Division, Burlington *Also called Zoran Corporation* ***(G-9358)***
Imaging Solutions & More....413 331-4100
324 Shawinigan Dr Chicopee MA (01020) ***(G-10031)***
Imaging W Varex Holdings Inc....781 663-6900
940 Winter St Waltham MA (02451) ***(G-16129)***
Imani Magazine/Fmi....203 809-2565
15 Boylston St West Haven CT (06516) ***(G-5126)***
Imanova, Leominster *Also called Nova Packaging Systems Inc* ***(G-12174)***
Imanova Packaging....978 537-8534
7 New Lancaster Rd Leominster MA (01453) ***(G-12154)***
IMC Internet, North Haven *Also called Interactive Marketing Corp* ***(G-3032)***
Imcor Inc....603 886-4300
74 Northeastrn Blvd 19a Nashua NH (03062) ***(G-19184)***
IMD Soft Inc (HQ)....781 449-5567
980-990 Wash St Ste 115 Dedham MA (02026) ***(G-10292)***
Imdx, Foxboro *Also called Intelligent Medical Dvcs Inc* ***(G-10888)***
Imed Mfg....603 489-5184
9 Gigante Dr Hampstead NH (03841) ***(G-18240)***
Imeldas Fabrics & Designs....207 778-0665
5 Starks Rd New Sharon ME (04955) ***(G-6476)***
Imerys Kaolin Inc....207 741-2118
27 Main St South Portland ME (04106) ***(G-7030)***
Imerys Talc America Inc....802 228-6400
73 E Hill Rd Ludlow VT (05149) ***(G-22063)***
Imerys Usa Inc....207 238-9267
1329 Waterville Rd Skowhegan ME (04976) ***(G-6977)***
Imi Inc....978 373-9190
140 Hilldale Ave Haverhill MA (01832) ***(G-11442)***
IMI Precision Engineering, Farmington *Also called Norgren Inc* ***(G-1500)***
Immedia Semiconductor Inc....978 296-4950
100 Riverpark Dr Fl 1 North Reading MA (01864) ***(G-13985)***
Immucell Corporation (PA)....207 878-2770
56 Evergreen Dr Portland ME (04103) ***(G-6673)***
Immunex Rhode Island Corp....401 392-1200
40 Technology Way West Greenwich RI (02817) ***(G-21457)***
Immunogen Inc (PA)....781 895-0600
830 Winter St Waltham MA (02451) ***(G-16130)***
Immunogen Securities Corp....617 995-2500
830 Winter St Ste 6 Waltham MA (02451) ***(G-16131)***
Impact Plastics, Putnam *Also called Apogee Corporation* ***(G-3601)***
Impact Plastics, Cromwell *Also called Apogee Corporation* ***(G-846)***
Impact Protection Systems Inc....508 737-8850
41 Wilton Dr Centerville MA (02632) ***(G-9816)***
Impact Sales & Marketing LLC....860 523-5366
48 Carlyle Rd West Hartford CT (06117) ***(G-5077)***
Impactwear International Lllp....213 559-2454
16 Elbow St Providence RI (02903) ***(G-21036)***
Impellimax Inc....603 886-9569
165 Ledge St Ste 3 Nashua NH (03060) ***(G-19185)***
Imperia Corporation....508 894-3000
306 Rumstick Rd Barrington RI (02806) ***(G-20046)***
Imperial Bag and Paper....508 541-7220
111 Constitution Blvd Franklin MA (02038) ***(G-11055)***
Imperial Ceramics....401 732-0500
1621 Warwick Ave Warwick RI (02889) ***(G-21375)***
Imperial Elctrnic Assembly Inc....203 740-8425
1000 Federal Rd Brookfield CT (06804) ***(G-647)***
Imperial Embroidery, West Roxbury *Also called Imperial Monogram Company Inc* ***(G-16497)***
Imperial Graphics, Milford *Also called Imperial Grphic Cmmnctions Inc* ***(G-2301)***
Imperial Grphic Cmmnctions Inc....203 650-3478
22 Way St Milford CT (06460) ***(G-2301)***
Imperial Image Inc....978 251-0420
55 Middlesex St North Chelmsford MA (01863) ***(G-13897)***
Imperial Metal Finishing Inc....203 377-1229
920 Honeyspot Rd Stratford CT (06615) ***(G-4422)***
Imperial Metalworks LLC....203 791-8567
92 Coolidge Ave Stamford CT (06906) ***(G-4220)***
Imperial Monogram Company Inc....617 323-0100
1733 Centre St West Roxbury MA (02132) ***(G-16497)***
Imperial Pearl, East Providence *Also called Bazar Group Inc* ***(G-20391)***
Imperial Pearl Syndicate, East Providence *Also called Imperial-Deltah Inc* ***(G-20420)***
Imperial Pools Inc....508 339-3830
90 John Hancock Rd Taunton MA (02780) ***(G-15758)***
Imperial-Deltah Inc....401 434-2597
795 Waterman Ave East Providence RI (02914) ***(G-20420)***
Impolit Envmtl Ctrl Corp....978 927-4619
800 Cummings Ctr Ste 355w Beverly MA (01915) ***(G-8140)***
Imposition Graphics, North Branford *Also called Brian Berlepsch* ***(G-2959)***
Impreglon Inc....401 766-3353
222 Goldstein Dr Woonsocket RI (02895) ***(G-21571)***
Impress Systems Inc....978 441-2022
7 Stuart Rd Chelmsford MA (01824) ***(G-9906)***
Impression Point Inc....203 353-8800
500 West Ave Ste 4 Stamford CT (06902) ***(G-4221)***
Impressions Plus Inc....617 479-5777
89 Penn St Quincy MA (02169) ***(G-14633)***
Imprint Boston Inc....857 251-9383
620 Blue Hill Ave Dorchester MA (02121) ***(G-10344)***
Imprint Inc....401 949-1177
22 Lark Industrial Pkwy E Greenville RI (02828) ***(G-20468)***
Imprint Industrial Service Co, Greenville *Also called Imprint Inc* ***(G-20468)***
Imprint Marketing....508 315-3433
9 Wedgewood Rd Natick MA (01760) ***(G-13261)***
Imprinted Sportswear Inc....413 732-5271
1458 Riverdale St Ste B West Springfield MA (01089) ***(G-16525)***
Impulse Packaging Inc....401 434-5588
34 Eden Rd Rockport MA (01966) ***(G-14836)***
IMS, Milford *Also called Enginuity Plm LLC* ***(G-2286)***
In Building Cellular, Peabody *Also called James G Hachey Inc* ***(G-14344)***
In Compliance Magazine, Littleton *Also called Page Same Publishing Inc* ***(G-12317)***
In Store Experience Inc....203 221-4777
49 Richmondville Ave # 102 Westport CT (06880) ***(G-5201)***
In Style Fragrances, Waterford *Also called Harjani Hitesh* ***(G-4984)***
In The Mix....603 557-2078
2 Vernon St Nashua NH (03064) ***(G-19186)***
In Your Own Words LLC....207 946-5049
582 Quaker Ridge Rd Greene ME (04236) ***(G-6149)***
Inanovate Inc....617 610-1712
56 Beechwood Rd Wellesley MA (02482) ***(G-16367)***
Inanycase.com, Pittsfield *Also called Apex Resource Technologies Inc* ***(G-14452)***
Inc, Akumina, Nashua *Also called Akumina Inc* ***(G-19106)***
Inc, Waterbury, Waterbury *Also called Wces Inc* ***(G-4977)***
Incase Inc....508 478-6500
118 Salisbury St Holden MA (01520) ***(G-11545)***
Incident Control Systems LLC....508 984-8820
92 Gifford St 33 New Bedford MA (02744) ***(G-13397)***
Incjet Inc....860 823-3090
31 Clinton Ave Ste 2 Norwich CT (06360) ***(G-3283)***
Incom Inc....508 909-2200
294 Southbridge Rd Charlton MA (01507) ***(G-9851)***
Incon, Saco *Also called Intelligent Controls Inc* ***(G-6849)***
Incon Inc....603 595-0550
21 Flagstone Dr Hudson NH (03051) ***(G-18398)***
Incoporated Villge of Orlean, Orleans *Also called Village of Orleans* ***(G-22253)***
Incredible Foods Inc....617 491-6600
75 Sprague St Boston MA (02136) ***(G-8614)***
Incredibrew Inc....603 891-2477
112 Daniel Webster Hwy # 1 Nashua NH (03060) ***(G-19187)***
Incure Inc....860 748-2979
1 Hartford Sq Ste 16w New Britain CT (06052) ***(G-2540)***
Indaba Holdings Corp....603 437-1200
66 Gold Ledge Ave Auburn NH (03032) ***(G-17611)***
Indars Stairs LLC....860 208-3826
39 W Town St Lebanon CT (06249) ***(G-1935)***
Indeco North America Inc....203 713-1030
135 Research Dr Milford CT (06460) ***(G-2302)***
Independant Newspaper Group....781 485-0588
385 Broadway Ste 105 Revere MA (02151) ***(G-14767)***
Independence Park....203 421-9396
38 Sheffield Ln Madison CT (06443) ***(G-1965)***
Independent Brewers Untd Corp (HQ)....802 862-6114
431 Pine St Ste G12 Burlington VT (05401) ***(G-21789)***
Independent Color Press LLC....603 539-5959
189 Wakefield St Rochester NH (03867) ***(G-19672)***
Independent Fermentations....508 789-9940
127 Camelot Dr Ste 3 Plymouth MA (02360) ***(G-14561)***
Independent Metalworx Inc....203 520-4089
4 Hershey Dr Ste 1a Ansonia CT (06401) ***(G-19)***
Independent News....413 522-5046
12 Main St Ste 1 Shelburne Falls MA (01370) ***(G-15071)***
Independent Newspaper, Boston *Also called East Boston Times Inc* ***(G-8515)***
Independent Newspaper Group....781 485-0588
385 Broadway Revere MA (02151) ***(G-14768)***
Independent Product Service (PA)....978 352-8887
55 Congress St Apt 174 Amesbury MA (01913) ***(G-7491)***

Independent Rowing News Inc....603 448-5090
53 S Main St Ste 201 Hanover NH (03755) *(G-18293)*
Indepenent Plating Co....508 756-0301
35 New St Worcester MA (01605) *(G-17391)*
Index Millwork, Milton *Also called Index Packaging Inc (G-19086)*
Index Packaging Inc....603 350-0018
1055 White Mountain Hwy Milton NH (03851) *(G-19086)*
India Weekly Co....203 699-8419
328 Industrial Ave Cheshire CT (06410) *(G-739)*
Indian Meadow Herbals LLC....207 565-3010
1284 Macomber Mill Rd Eastbrook ME (04634) *(G-5988)*
Indian News, Monson *Also called Acom Publishing Inc (G-13202)*
Indian River Sand LLC....413 977-0646
200 Falls Blvd Unit E308 Quincy MA (02169) *(G-14634)*
Indieferm, Plymouth *Also called Independent Fermentations (G-14561)*
Indigo Coast Inc....860 592-0088
17 Meadow St Kent CT (06757) *(G-1922)*
Induplate, Lincoln *Also called Greystone of Lincoln Inc (G-20576)*
Induplate Inc (PA)....401 231-5770
1 Greystone Ave Ste 1 # 1 North Providence RI (02911) *(G-20765)*
Indusol Inc....508 865-9516
11 Depot St Sutton MA (01590) *(G-15683)*
Industrial & Commercial Finshg....401 942-4680
1339 Plainfield St Johnston RI (02919) *(G-20516)*
Industrial Analytics Corp....203 245-0380
1 Orchard Park Rd Ste 10 Madison CT (06443) *(G-1966)*
Industrial Automation, Plainville *Also called Enginering Components Pdts LLC (G-3486)*
Industrial Biomedical Sensors....781 891-4201
1377 Main St Waltham MA (02451) *(G-16132)*
Industrial Chemical, Wakefield *Also called Maranatha Industries Inc (G-15960)*
Industrial Cnnctons Sltons LLC....860 747-7677
41 Woodford Ave Plainville CT (06062) *(G-3497)*
Industrial Cutting Tools Inc....413 562-2996
351 N Elm St Westfield MA (01085) *(G-16689)*
Industrial Defender Inc....508 718-6777
225 Foxboro Blvd Foxboro MA (02035) *(G-10887)*
Industrial Etching Inc....413 525-4110
21 Fisher Ave East Longmeadow MA (01028) *(G-10479)*
Industrial Flame Cutting Inc....203 723-4897
45 Lancaster Dr Beacon Falls CT (06403) *(G-58)*
Industrial Floor Covering Inc....978 362-8655
148 Rangeway Rd Unit Cd North Billerica MA (01862) *(G-13826)*
Industrial Floor Finishes, Div, Bedford *Also called Perma Incorporated (G-8000)*
Industrial Forrest Products LL....203 863-9486
21 Stanwich Rd Greenwich CT (06830) *(G-1622)*
Industrial Foundry Corporation....508 278-5523
Elmdale Rd Uxbridge MA (01569) *(G-15920)*
Industrial Heat Treating Inc....617 328-1010
22 Densmore St 26 North Quincy MA (02171) *(G-13977)*
Industrial Heater Corp....203 250-0500
30 Knotter Dr Cheshire CT (06410) *(G-740)*
INDUSTRIAL INTERNET CONSORTIUM, Needham *Also called Object Management Group Inc (G-13307)*
Industrial Lbling Systems Corp....978 649-7004
100 Business Park Dr Tyngsboro MA (01879) *(G-15890)*
Industrial Marine Elec Inc....603 434-2309
8025 S Willow St Ste 207 Manchester NH (03103) *(G-18842)*
Industrial Metal Pdts Co Inc....781 762-3330
15 Merchant St Sharon MA (02067) *(G-15052)*
Industrial Pallet LLC....860 234-0962
29 Gregory Rd Princeton MA (01541) *(G-14605)*
Industrial Pallet LLC....860 974-0093
27 Chaplin Rd Eastford CT (06242) *(G-1313)*
Industrial Polymers & Chem Inc (PA)....508 845-6112
508 Boston Tpke Shrewsbury MA (01545) *(G-15117)*
Industrial Prcision Components, Bridgeport *Also called Comex Machinery (G-399)*
Industrial Press Inc....212 889-6330
32 Haviland St 3 Norwalk CT (06854) *(G-3172)*
Industrial Production Supplies....508 226-1776
19 Franklin St Attleboro MA (02703) *(G-7749)*
Industrial Prssure Washers LLC....860 608-6153
500 Ridge Rd Wethersfield CT (06109) *(G-5249)*
Industrial Realty Trust, Newburyport *Also called Epi II Inc (G-13487)*
Industrial Safety Products LLC....802 338-9035
195 Acorn Ln Colchester VT (05446) *(G-21867)*
Industrial Sales Corp (PA)....203 227-5988
727 Post Rd E Westport CT (06880) *(G-5202)*
Industrial Sales Supply, Westport *Also called Industrial Sales Corp (G-5202)*
Industrial Service Company, Greenville *Also called Richard Chiovitti (G-20474)*
Industrial Shipg Entps MGT LLC....203 504-5800
2187 Atlantic St Stamford CT (06902) *(G-4222)*
Industrial Stl Boiler Svcs Inc....413 532-7788
939 Chicopee St Ste 2 Chicopee MA (01013) *(G-10032)*
Industrial Trucks & Equipment, Brockton *Also called Ite LLC (G-9156)*
Industrial Video & Ctrl Co LLC....617 467-3059
330 Nevada St Newton MA (02460) *(G-13604)*
Industrial Wood Product Co....203 735-2374
84 Platt Rd Shelton CT (06484) *(G-3817)*

Industronics Service, South Windsor *Also called Jad LLC (G-3983)*
Ineoquest Technologies Inc (PA)....508 339-2497
247 Station Dr Ste Ne2 Westwood MA (02090) *(G-16870)*
Ineos Melamines LLC....413 730-3811
730b Worcester St Springfield MA (01151) *(G-15478)*
Ineos Nova Lcc....978 297-2265
26 Belmont Ave Winchendon MA (01475) *(G-17077)*
Inert Corporation....978 462-4415
1 Industrial Way Amesbury MA (01913) *(G-7492)*
Inertia Dynamics LLC....860 379-1252
31 Industrial Park Rd New Hartford CT (06057) *(G-2639)*
Inertia Dynamics Inc....860 379-1252
31 Industrial Park Rd New Hartford CT (06057) *(G-2640)*
Infab Refractories Inc....207 783-2075
150 Summer St Lewiston ME (04240) *(G-6291)*
Infineon Tech Americas Corp....978 640-3893
1 Highwood Dr Ste 302 Tewksbury MA (01876) *(G-15819)*
Infineon Tech Americas Corp....802 769-6824
1000 River St Essex Junction VT (05452) *(G-21947)*
Infinite Compost....617 922-6419
44 Myopia Rd Hyde Park MA (02136) *(G-11870)*
Infinite Creative Entps Inc....603 910-5000
72 Stard Rd Unit 4 Seabrook NH (03874) *(G-19807)*
Infinite Electronics Intl Inc....978 459-8800
495r Billerica Ave North Billerica MA (01862) *(G-13827)*
Infinite Forest Inc....617 299-1382
172 Charles St Ste B Cambridge MA (02141) *(G-9514)*
Infinite Graphic Solutions....781 938-6333
15 Cranes Ct Woburn MA (01801) *(G-17201)*
Infinite Imaging, Portsmouth *Also called Powerplay Management LLC (G-19609)*
Infinite Imaging Inc (PA)....603 436-3030
933 Islington St Portsmouth NH (03801) *(G-19578)*
Infinite Imaging Inc....207 363-4402
470 Us Route 1 Ste 1 York ME (03909) *(G-7309)*
Infinite Knot LLC....617 372-0707
466 Carpenter Rd Whitinsville MA (01588) *(G-16914)*
Infinity....508 753-1981
346 Franklin St Ste 2 Worcester MA (01604) *(G-17392)*
Infinity Pharmaceuticals Inc (PA)....617 453-1000
1100 Massachusetts Ave # 4 Cambridge MA (02138) *(G-9515)*
Infinity Printing, Danbury *Also called Hat Trick Graphics LLC (G-930)*
Infinity Stone Inc....203 575-9484
1261 Meriden Rd Waterbury CT (06705) *(G-4888)*
Infinity Tapes LLC....978 686-0632
300 Canal St Ste 7 Lawrence MA (01840) *(G-12038)*
Infinizone Corp....603 465-2917
99 Pine Hill Rd Hollis NH (03049) *(G-18333)*
Infirst Healthcare Inc....203 222-1300
8 Church Ln Westport CT (06880) *(G-5203)*
Inflight Corporation....413 203-2056
1 Cottage St Ste 5-19 Easthampton MA (01027) *(G-10565)*
Infobionic Inc....978 674-8304
200 5th Ave Ste 4030 Waltham MA (02451) *(G-16133)*
Infogix Inc....617 826-6020
15 New England Exec Park Burlington MA (01803) *(G-9285)*
Infolibria Inc....781 392-2200
271 Waverley Oaks Rd Waltham MA (02452) *(G-16134)*
Inforce, North Kingstown *Also called Emissive Energy Corp (G-20709)*
Inform Inc....203 924-9929
25 Brook St Ste 200 Shelton CT (06484) *(G-3818)*
Informa Business Media Inc....203 358-9900
11 Riverbend Dr S Stamford CT (06907) *(G-4223)*
Informa Business Media Inc....203 358-9900
11 River Band Dry S Stamford CT (06906) *(G-4224)*
Informatics In Context Inc....650 200-5110
1 Boston Pl Ste 2600 Boston MA (02108) *(G-8615)*
Information Builders Inc....781 224-7660
500 Edgewater Dr Ste 568 Wakefield MA (01880) *(G-15956)*
Information Builders Inc....860 249-7229
100 Pearl St Fl 14 Hartford CT (06103) *(G-1837)*
Information Gatekeepers Inc....617 782-5033
72 Thornberry Rd Winchester MA (01890) *(G-17088)*
Information Resources Inc....203 845-6400
383 Main Ave Ste 20 Norwalk CT (06851) *(G-3173)*
Information Server Co....978 443-1871
3 Camperdown Ln Sudbury MA (01776) *(G-15658)*
Information Tech Intl Corp....860 648-2570
440 Oakland St Manchester CT (06042) *(G-2012)*
Information Today Inc....203 761-1466
88 Danbury Rd Ste 2c Wilton CT (06897) *(G-5291)*
Informtion Consulting Svcs Inc....207 596-7783
2a Gordon Dr Rockland ME (04841) *(G-6799)*
Infors USA Inc....781 335-3108
25 Mathewson Dr Weymouth MA (02189) *(G-16890)*
Infotrak National Data Service....781 276-1711
67 Holmes St Needham MA (02492) *(G-13301)*
Infotree Inc....978 263-8558
30 Nagog Park Ste 210 Acton MA (01720) *(G-7363)*
Infotrends Cap Ventures, Weymouth *Also called Infotrends Research Group (G-16891)*

ALPHABETIC

Infotrends Research Group.....781 616-2100
97 Libbey Industrial Pkwy # 300 Weymouth MA (02189) ***(G-16891)***
Infra Red Technology Inc.....603 524-1177
60 Bay St Ste 7 Laconia NH (03246) ***(G-18568)***
Inframetrics, North Billerica *Also called Flir Systems-Boston Inc* ***(G-13815)***
Infutronix LLC.....508 650-2007
177 Pine St Natick MA (01760) ***(G-13262)***
Ingenico Mobile Solutions, Boston *Also called Roam Data Inc* ***(G-8823)***
Ingenven Flrplymer Slutions LL.....603 601-0877
70 High St Hampton NH (03842) ***(G-18265)***
Ingersoll-Rand Company.....508 573-1524
362 Elm St Marlborough MA (01752) ***(G-12776)***
Ingerson Transportation.....603 586-4335
36 Alderbrook Dr Jefferson NH (03583) ***(G-18484)***
Ingleside Corporation.....774 847-9386
38 South St Wrentham MA (02093) ***(G-17523)***
Ingleside Corporation.....781 769-6656
89 Access Rd Ste 17 Norwood MA (02062) ***(G-14161)***
Ingu LLC.....603 770-5969
210 West Rd Portsmouth NH (03801) ***(G-19579)***
Iniram Precision Machinery, Middleton *Also called Iniram Precision Mch Tl LLC* ***(G-13089)***
Iniram Precision Mch Tl LLC.....978 854-3037
333 N Main St Middleton MA (01949) ***(G-13089)***
Initial Ideas Inc (PA).....802 773-6310
142 West St Rutland VT (05701) ***(G-22339)***
Initial Ideas Inc.....802 775-1685
378 Quality Ln Rutland VT (05701) ***(G-22340)***
Initial Step Monogramming.....860 665-0542
635 New Park Ave Ste 2a West Hartford CT (06110) ***(G-5078)***
Initial This Inc.....207 992-7176
25 Silver Rdg Veazie ME (04401) ***(G-7127)***
Injectech Engineering LLC (PA).....860 379-9781
19 Pioneer Rd New Hartford CT (06057) ***(G-2641)***
Injected Solutions Inc.....413 499-5800
840 Cheshire Rd Lanesborough MA (01237) ***(G-11987)***
Ink Etcetera Corporation.....978 263-1555
165 Great Rd Acton MA (01720) ***(G-7364)***
Ink Inc Publishing Service.....617 576-6740
280 Green St Fl 2 Cambridge MA (02139) ***(G-9516)***
Ink Mill Corp.....603 217-4144
7 Fruite St G Belmont NH (03220) ***(G-17674)***
Ink N Thredz, Medway *Also called Itg Group Inc* ***(G-12962)***
Ink Outside Box Incorporated.....603 635-2292
71 Bridge St Pelham NH (03076) ***(G-19435)***
Inkberry.....603 876-4880
107 Main St Marlborough NH (03455) ***(G-18960)***
Inkbit LLC.....617 433-8842
200 Boston Ave Ste 1850 Medford MA (02155) ***(G-12936)***
Inkify LLC.....617 304-6642
25 Walpole Park S Ste 8 Walpole MA (02081) ***(G-15994)***
Inkspot Press.....802 447-1768
736 Main St Bennington VT (05201) ***(G-21673)***
Inkspot Press of Manchester, Manchester Center *Also called Thompson Printing Inc* ***(G-22091)***
Inkstone Inc.....508 587-5200
129 Liberty St Brockton MA (02301) ***(G-9155)***
Inkstone Printing, Brockton *Also called Inkstone Inc* ***(G-9155)***
Inland Technologies.....207 761-6951
140 Jetport Blvd Portland ME (04102) ***(G-6674)***
Inline Plastics Corp (PA).....203 924-5933
42 Canal St Shelton CT (06484) ***(G-3819)***
Inmetal, Sharon *Also called Industrial Metal Pdts Co Inc* ***(G-15052)***
Innarah Inc.....203 873-0015
838 Woodend Rd Stratford CT (06615) ***(G-4423)***
Inner Office Inc.....860 564-6777
49 Daggett St Moosup CT (06354) ***(G-2427)***
Inner Traditions International (PA).....802 767-3174
1 Park St Rochester VT (05767) ***(G-22317)***
Inner-Tite Corp.....508 829-6361
110 Industrial Dr Holden MA (01520) ***(G-11546)***
Innocor Foam Technical.....978 462-5400
122 Parker St Newburyport MA (01950) ***(G-13500)***
Innopad Inc.....978 253-4204
50 Winchester Rd Newton MA (02458) ***(G-13605)***
Innophase Corp.....860 399-2269
18 Sea Scape Dr Westbrook CT (06498) ***(G-5156)***
Innoteq Inc (PA).....203 659-4444
555 Lordship Blvd Stratford CT (06615) ***(G-4424)***
Innovasea Systems Inc.....207 322-3219
52 S Main St Morrill ME (04952) ***(G-6454)***
Innovation Group.....860 674-2900
76 Batterson Park Rd Farmington CT (06032) ***(G-1486)***
Innovation Pharmaceuticals Inc (PA).....978 921-4125
100 Cummings Ctr Ste 151b Beverly MA (01915) ***(G-8141)***
Innovations In Optics Inc.....781 933-4477
82 Cummings Park Woburn MA (01801) ***(G-17202)***
Innovative ARC Tubes Corp.....203 333-1031
1240 Central Ave Bridgeport CT (06607) ***(G-430)***
Innovative Chem Pdts Group LLC (PA).....978 623-9980
150 Dascomb Rd Andover MA (01810) ***(G-7558)***
Innovative Chem Pdts Group LLC.....800 393-5250
1 Beacon St Boston MA (02108) ***(G-8616)***
Innovative Coatings Inc.....508 533-6101
24 Jayar Rd Medway MA (02053) ***(G-12961)***
Innovative Components LLC.....860 621-7220
635 Old Turnpike Rd Plantsville CT (06479) ***(G-3533)***
Innovative Designs, Leominster *Also called American Marketing & Sales* ***(G-12113)***
Innovative Development Inc.....508 668-9080
153 Washington St Ste 9 East Walpole MA (02032) ***(G-10525)***
Innovative Machine & Sup Inc.....603 239-8082
40 Snow Rd Winchester NH (03470) ***(G-19992)***
Innovative Media Group Inc.....781 335-8773
36 Finnell Dr Ste 3 Weymouth MA (02188) ***(G-16892)***
Innovative Mold Solutions Inc.....978 840-1503
42 Jungle Rd Leominster MA (01453) ***(G-12155)***
Innovative Paper Tech LLC.....603 286-4891
1 Paper Trail Tilton NH (03276) ***(G-19906)***
Innovative Products & Eqp Inc.....603 246-5858
20 Executive Dr Hudson NH (03051) ***(G-18399)***
Innovative Publishing Co LLC.....267 266-8876
91 Litchfield Rd Edgartown MA (02539) ***(G-10585)***
Innovative Software LLC.....860 228-4144
94 Country Ln Hebron CT (06248) ***(G-1897)***
Innovative Systems, Meriden *Also called Southwick & Meister Inc* ***(G-2133)***
Innovative Test Solutions LLC.....603 288-0280
41 Simon St Ste 2f Nashua NH (03060) ***(G-19188)***
Innovative Tooling Company Inc.....413 637-1031
180 Pittsfield Rd Lenox MA (01240) ***(G-12101)***
Innovion Corporation.....978 267-4064
265 Ballardvale St Wilmington MA (01887) ***(G-17005)***
Innovive LLC.....617 500-1691
129 Concord Rd Billerica MA (01821) ***(G-8257)***
Innovtive McHning Slutions Inc.....207 515-2033
15 Ayer Dr Norway ME (04268) ***(G-6522)***
Inofab LLC.....603 435-5082
26 Broadway St Pittsfield NH (03263) ***(G-19501)***
Inofab-Nnovation Infabrication.....603 491-2946
46 Aiden Cir Belmont NH (03220) ***(G-17675)***
Inotec, Middletown *Also called Carl Perry* ***(G-2181)***
Inov8v Energy LLC.....603 632-7333
738 Goose Pond Rd Canaan NH (03741) ***(G-17779)***
Inovar Packaging Group LLC.....978 463-4004
8 Opportunity Way Newburyport MA (01950) ***(G-13501)***
Inozyme Pharma Inc (PA).....857 330-4340
280 Summer St Fl 5 Boston MA (02210) ***(G-8617)***
Inphotonics Inc.....781 440-0202
111 Downey St Norwood MA (02062) ***(G-14162)***
Inquirer and Mirror Inc.....508 228-0001
1 Old South Rd Nantucket MA (02554) ***(G-13226)***
Inquiring News.....860 983-7587
51 Gilbert Ave Bloomfield CT (06002) ***(G-226)***
Inreach Inc.....207 846-7104
2 Delorme Dr Yarmouth ME (04096) ***(G-7297)***
Inriver Tank & Boat Inc.....978 287-9534
152 Commonwealth Ave # 21 Concord MA (01742) ***(G-10136)***
Insense Medical LLC.....518 316-4759
4 Wyman Ln Hopkinton MA (01748) ***(G-11722)***
Inside Premier Health, Brunswick *Also called Medical Resources Inc* ***(G-5842)***
Inside Track Cabling Inc.....603 886-8013
18 West Rd Hudson NH (03051) ***(G-18400)***
Insight Enterprises Inc.....203 374-2013
78 Gate Ridge Rd Easton CT (06612) ***(G-1320)***
Insight Media LLC.....203 831-8464
3 Morgan Ave Ste 2 Norwalk CT (06851) ***(G-3174)***
Insight Plus Technology LLC.....860 930-4763
191 Redstone Hill Rd Bristol CT (06010) ***(G-571)***
Insignia Athletics LLC.....508 756-3633
60 Fremont St Worcester MA (01603) ***(G-17393)***
Insite Sign LLC.....781 934-5664
40 Tremont St Ste 50 Duxbury MA (02332) ***(G-10399)***
Insource Design & Mfg Tech LLC.....603 718-8228
39 Depot St Merrimack NH (03054) ***(G-19007)***
Inspectcheck LLC.....603 223-0003
160 Dover Rd Unit 6 Chichester NH (03258) ***(G-17829)***
Inspectrology LLC.....978 212-3100
142 North Rd Ste N Sudbury MA (01776) ***(G-15659)***
Inspeedcom LLC.....978 397-6813
10 Hudson Rd Sudbury MA (01776) ***(G-15660)***
Insphero Inc.....800 779-7558
74 Orion St Brunswick ME (04011) ***(G-5838)***
Inspire Hope Foundtn For Urea.....781 817-6664
95 Linda Rd Braintree MA (02184) ***(G-9020)***
Installed Building Pdts Inc.....203 889-0505
43 Crescent St Apt 19 Stamford CT (06906) ***(G-4225)***
Instant Imprints, Meriden *Also called Team Destination Inc* ***(G-2138)***
Instant Offset Press Inc.....508 790-1100
115 Enterprise Rd Hyannis MA (02601) ***(G-11843)***

Instant Sign Center 781 278-0150
1400 Boston Providence Tp Norwood MA (02062) ***(G-14163)***
Instantron Co Inc 401 433-6800
3712 Pawtucket Ave Riverside RI (02915) ***(G-21170)***
Instinctive Works LLC 203 434-8094
5 Spicer Ct Westport CT (06880) ***(G-5204)***
Institute For Scial Cltral Cmm 508 548-9063
47 Barrows St Dedham MA (02026) ***(G-10293)***
Instron Applications Lab 800 564-8378
825 University Ave Norwood MA (02062) ***(G-14164)***
Instron Japan Company Ltd 781 828-2500
825 University Ave Norwood MA (02062) ***(G-14165)***
Instrument & Valve Services Co 508 842-7000
238 Cherry St Ste D Shrewsbury MA (01545) ***(G-15118)***
Instrument Technology, Westfield *Also called Transom Scopes Inc* ***(G-16737)***
Instrument Technology Inc 413 562-3512
33 Airport Rd Westfield MA (01085) ***(G-16690)***
Instrumentation & Control Tech 781 273-5052
738 Main St Ste 219 Waltham MA (02451) ***(G-16135)***
Instrumentation Laboratory Co (HQ) 781 861-0710
180 Hartwell Rd Bedford MA (01730) ***(G-7982)***
Insty-Prints of Bedford Inc 603 622-3821
25 S River Rd Bedford NH (03110) ***(G-17646)***
Insulated Wire Inc 203 791-1999
2c Park Lawn Dr Bethel CT (06801) ***(G-160)***
Insulation Technology Inc 508 697-6926
35 1st St Bridgewater MA (02324) ***(G-9077)***
Insulectro 603 629-4403
8 Akira Way Londonderry NH (03053) ***(G-18704)***
Insulet Corporation (PA) 978 600-7000
100 Nagog Park Acton MA (01720) ***(G-7365)***
Insulfab Plastics Inc 603 934-2770
155 N Main St Franklin NH (03235) ***(G-18158)***
Insulpane Connecticut Inc 800 922-3248
30 Edmund St Hamden CT (06517) ***(G-1761)***
Insulsafe Textiles Inc 207 782-7011
55 Holland St Lewiston ME (04240) ***(G-6292)***
Insultab Inc 781 935-0800
45 Industrial Pkwy Ste 1 Woburn MA (01801) ***(G-17203)***
Insys Micro Inc 917 566-5045
40 Richards Ave Ste 3 Norwalk CT (06854) ***(G-3175)***
Intac International Inc 781 272-4494
15 Commonwealth Ave # 202 Woburn MA (01801) ***(G-17204)***
Intact Medical Corporation 508 655-7820
550 Cochituate Rd Ste 25 Framingham MA (01701) ***(G-10969)***
Intec Automation Inc 603 332-7733
5 Sampson Rd Rochester NH (03867) ***(G-19673)***
Intech Inc 978 263-2210
979 Main St Acton MA (01720) ***(G-7366)***
Integer Holdings Corporation 781 830-5800
670 Paramount Dr Canton MA (02021) ***(G-9744)***
Integra Biosciences Corp 603 578-5800
2 Wentworth Dr Hudson NH (03051) ***(G-18401)***
Integra Lifesciences Prod Corp 781 971-5682
11 Cabot Blvd Mansfield MA (02048) ***(G-12637)***
Integra Luxtec Inc 508 835-9700
85 Rangeway Rd Ste 1 North Billerica MA (01862) ***(G-13828)***
Integra Test Division, Bedford *Also called Teradyne Inc* ***(G-8014)***
Integra-Cast Inc 860 225-7600
265 Newington Ave New Britain CT (06051) ***(G-2541)***
Integral Industries Inc 860 953-0686
111 Holmes Rd Newington CT (06111) ***(G-2872)***
Integral Technologies Inc (HQ) 860 741-2281
120 Post Rd Enfield CT (06082) ***(G-1366)***
Integrated Clean Tech Inc 413 281-2555
25 Ontario St Pittsfield MA (01201) ***(G-14477)***
Integrated Deicing Svcs LLC (HQ) 603 647-1717
175 Ammon Dr Manchester NH (03103) ***(G-18843)***
Integrated Deicing Svcs LLC 603 647-1717
175 Ammon Dr Unit 106 Manchester NH (03103) ***(G-18844)***
Integrated Design & Mfg LLC 603 692-5563
15 Interstate Dr Somersworth NH (03878) ***(G-19841)***
Integrated Dynamic Metals Corp 508 624-7271
66 Brigham St Unit A Marlborough MA (01752) ***(G-12777)***
Integrated Dynamics Engrg Inc (HQ) 781 326-5700
68 Mazzeo Dr Randolph MA (02368) ***(G-14687)***
Integrated Electronics, Ayer *Also called Superconductivity Inc* ***(G-7940)***
Integrated Ophthalmic Sys 617 571-8238
596 Main St Woburn MA (01801) ***(G-17205)***
Integrated Packg Systems Inc 860 623-2623
256 Main St Ste D East Windsor CT (06088) ***(G-1287)***
Integrated Print Solutions Inc 203 330-0200
35 Benham Ave Ste 2 Bridgeport CT (06605) ***(G-431)***
Integrated Web Finishing Syst 508 580-5809
175 Bodwell St Avon MA (02322) ***(G-7887)***
Integrity Composites LLC 207 571-0743
8 Morin St Biddeford ME (04005) ***(G-5740)***
Integrity Cylinder Sales LLC 860 267-6667
17 Watrous St East Hampton CT (06424) ***(G-1160)***
Integrity Graphics Inc 800 343-1248
42 Carver Cir Simsbury CT (06070) ***(G-3906)***
Integrity Graphics LLC 339 987-5533
21 Mazzeo Dr Ste 101 Randolph MA (02368) ***(G-14688)***
Integrity Industries Inc 203 312-9788
1 Saw Mill Rd Ste 7 New Fairfield CT (06812) ***(G-2624)***
Integrity Laser Inc 603 930-1413
6 Spruce St Unit 2 Nashua NH (03060) ***(G-19189)***
Integrity Manufacturing LLC 860 678-1599
1451 New Britain Ave # 1 Farmington CT (06032) ***(G-1487)***
Integro LLC 860 832-8960
30 Peter Ct New Britain CT (06051) ***(G-2542)***
Intel Massachusetts Inc 978 553-4000
75 Reed Rd Hudson MA (01749) ***(G-11777)***
INTEL Network Systems Inc (HQ) 978 553-4000
77 Reed Rd Hudson MA (01749) ***(G-11778)***
Intelicoat Technologies 413 536-7800
69 William Frank Dr West Springfield MA (01089) ***(G-16526)***
Intelitek Inc 800 221-2763
18 Tsienneto Rd Derry NH (03038) ***(G-17983)***
Intellgent Clearing Netwrk Inc 203 972-0861
110 Washington Ave North Haven CT (06473) ***(G-3031)***
Intellgent Office Intriors LLC 978 808-7884
5 Waltham St Wilmington MA (01887) ***(G-17006)***
Intellia Therapeutics Inc (PA) 857 285-6200
40 Erie St Cambridge MA (02139) ***(G-9517)***
Intellicut Inc 617 417-5236
2 De Bush Ave Unit A8 Middleton MA (01949) ***(G-13090)***
Intelligent Building Controls, Windham *Also called Ibcontrols* ***(G-7237)***
Intelligent Bus Entrmt Inc 617 519-4172
480 Pleasant St Ste C210 Watertown MA (02472) ***(G-16292)***
Intelligent Compression Tech 617 773-3369
1250 Hancock St Ste 701n Quincy MA (02169) ***(G-14635)***
Intelligent Controls Inc (HQ) 207 571-1123
34 Spring Hill Rd Saco ME (04072) ***(G-6849)***
Intelligent Medical Dvcs Inc 617 871-6401
124 Washington St Ste 101 Foxboro MA (02035) ***(G-10888)***
Intelligent Platforms LLC 413 586-7884
4 Bay Rd Ste 105 Hadley MA (01035) ***(G-11308)***
Intelligent Signage Inc 413 567-8399
28 Greenmeadow Dr Longmeadow MA (01106) ***(G-12334)***
Intellihome of Vermont L L C 802 464-2499
18 Coldbrook Rd Wilmington VT (05363) ***(G-22701)***
Intellisense Software Corp 781 933-8098
220 Broadway Ste 102 Lynnfield MA (01940) ***(G-12550)***
Intellitech International Inc 978 212-7200
43 Broad St Ste B404 Hudson MA (01749) ***(G-11779)***
Intelon Optics Inc 310 980-3087
91 Hartwell Ave Ste 301 Lexington MA (02421) ***(G-12232)***
Intelvideo, Stamford *Also called Xintekidel Inc* ***(G-4362)***
Intelycare Inc 617 971-8344
1515 Hancock St Ste 203 Quincy MA (02169) ***(G-14636)***
Intempo Software Inc (PA) 800 950-2221
191 Chestnut St Fl 5 Springfield MA (01103) ***(G-15479)***
Inteplast Engineered Films Inc 508 366-8884
5 Otis St Westborough MA (01581) ***(G-16626)***
Inteplast Group Corporation 508 880-7640
455 Somerset Ave North Dighton MA (02764) ***(G-13932)***
Inter-All Corporation 413 467-7181
25 W State St Granby MA (01033) ***(G-11228)***
Inter-Connection Tech Inc 978 975-7510
250 Canal St Lawrence MA (01840) ***(G-12039)***
Inter-Ego Systems Inc (PA) 516 576-9052
131 Main St Ste 1 Hatfield MA (01038) ***(G-11401)***
Interactive Marketing Corp 203 248-5324
399 Sackett Point Rd North Haven CT (06473) ***(G-3032)***
Interactive Media Corp 508 376-4245
1360 Main St Millis MA (02054) ***(G-13184)***
Interactive Systems Inc 603 318-7700
61 Spit Brook Rd Ste 406 Nashua NH (03060) ***(G-19190)***
Intercept Boat Corp 781 294-8100
171 Mattakeesett St Ste 9 Pembroke MA (02359) ***(G-14411)***
Interconnect Technology Inc 603 883-3116
3 Christine Dr Hudson NH (03051) ***(G-18402)***
Interdynamics, Salem *Also called Mostmed Inc* ***(G-14931)***
Interface Devices Incorporated 203 878-4648
230 Depot Rd Milford CT (06460) ***(G-2303)***
Interface Prcsion Bnchwrks Inc 978 544-8866
150 Quabbin Blvd Orange MA (01364) ***(G-14219)***
Interface Technology, Bridgeport *Also called A J R Inc* ***(G-365)***
Intergrated Control Systems 802 658-6385
38 Eastwood Dr South Burlington VT (05403) ***(G-22449)***
Interior Design Center, Quincy *Also called New England Worldwide Export* ***(G-14642)***
Interior Wdwkg Solutions Inc 401 261-6329
47 Pettaconsett Ave Cranston RI (02920) ***(G-20240)***
Interlott Technologies Inc 401 463-6392
55 Technology Way West Greenwich RI (02817) ***(G-21458)***
International Aero Engines LLC 860 565-5515
400 Main St East Hartford CT (06108) ***(G-1203)***

A L P H A B E T I C

International Automobile Entps (PA) 860 224-0253
608 E Main St Ste 612 New Britain CT (06051) ***(G-2543)***
International Automobile Entps 860 224-0253
608 E Main St New Britain CT (06051) ***(G-2544)***
International Beam Wldg Corp 413 781-4368
63 Doty Cir West Springfield MA (01089) ***(G-16527)***
International Chromium Pltg Co 401 421-0205
2 Addison Pl Providence RI (02909) ***(G-21037)***
International Coil Inc 508 580-8515
8 Norfolk Ave Unit 2 South Easton MA (02375) ***(G-15280)***
International Comm Svcs Inc 401 580-8888
2 Burgis Ln Guilford CT (06437) ***(G-1706)***
International Contact Tech 203 264-5757
1432 Old Waterbury Rd # 6 Southbury CT (06488) ***(G-4028)***
International Cordage East Ltd 860 873-5000
226 Upton Rd Colchester CT (06415) ***(G-804)***
International Crmic Engrg Corp (PA) 508 853-4700
235 Brooks St Worcester MA (01606) ***(G-17394)***
International Data Group, Boston *Also called Idg* ***(G-8613)***
International Data Group Inc (PA) 508 875-5000
1 Exeter Plz Fl 15 Boston MA (02116) ***(G-8618)***
International Data Group Inc 508 766-5632
3 Speen St Ste 300 Framingham MA (01701) ***(G-10970)***
International Data Group Inc 508 935-4719
5 Speen St Ste 1 Framingham MA (01701) ***(G-10971)***
International Dioxcide Inc 401 295-8800
40 Whitecap Dr North Kingstown RI (02852) ***(G-20718)***
International Elevator Corp 203 302-1023
97 Valley Rd Cos Cob CT (06807) ***(G-826)***
International Energy MGT, Milford *Also called Iemct* ***(G-2300)***
International Etching Inc 401 781-6800
7 Ninigret Ave Providence RI (02907) ***(G-21038)***
International Event Products 781 341-0929
1490 Central St Ste D Stoughton MA (02072) ***(G-15598)***
International Food Products 781 769-6666
422 Walpole St Ste B Norwood MA (02062) ***(G-14166)***
International Header, Smithfield *Also called RI Carbide Tool Co* ***(G-21248)***
International Innovations Inc 802 454-7764
1127 Max Gray Rd Plainfield VT (05667) ***(G-22268)***
International Insignia Corp 401 784-0000
1280 Eddy St Providence RI (02905) ***(G-21039)***
International Journal of Arts 401 333-1804
55 Farm Dr Cumberland RI (02864) ***(G-20329)***
International Laser Systems 413 533-4372
362 Race St Holyoke MA (01040) ***(G-11634)***
International Light Tech Inc 978 818-6180
10 Technology Dr Ste 2 Peabody MA (01960) ***(G-14343)***
International Metal Pdts Inc 413 532-2411
1165 Montgomery St Chicopee MA (01013) ***(G-10033)***
International Mktg Strategies 203 406-0106
1 Stamford Lndg Stamford CT (06902) ***(G-4226)***
International Paper - 16 Inc (HQ) 203 329-8544
281 Tresser Blvd Stamford CT (06901) ***(G-4227)***
International Paper Company 207 784-4051
175 Allied Rd Auburn ME (04210) ***(G-5572)***
International Paper Company 860 928-7901
175 Park Rd Putnam CT (06260) ***(G-3616)***
International Pipe & Stl Corp 203 481-7102
4 Enterprise Dr North Branford CT (06471) ***(G-2969)***
International Press of Boston 617 623-3016
387 Somerville Ave Apt 3 Somerville MA (02143) ***(G-15184)***
International Robotics Inc 914 630-1060
761 Stillwater Rd Stamford CT (06902) ***(G-4228)***
International Soccer & Rugby 203 254-1979
3683 Post Rd Southport CT (06890) ***(G-4096)***
International Sole & Lea Corp 508 588-0905
520 Depot St South Easton MA (02375) ***(G-15281)***
International Stone Inc 781 937-3300
10 Ryan Rd Woburn MA (01801) ***(G-17206)***
International Stone Products (PA) 802 476-6636
21 Metro Way Barre VT (05641) ***(G-21625)***
International Technologies Inc 401 467-6907
115 Maple St Warwick RI (02888) ***(G-21376)***
International Yacht Restoratio 401 846-2587
449 Thames St Unit 100 Newport RI (02840) ***(G-20666)***
Interntnal Br-Tech Sltions Inc (PA) 413 739-2271
225 Armory St Springfield MA (01104) ***(G-15480)***
Interntonal MBL Gran Entps Inc 860 296-0741
110 Airport Rd Hartford CT (06114) ***(G-1838)***
Interntonal Micro Photonix Inc 978 685-3800
120 Willow St North Andover MA (01845) ***(G-13710)***
Interntonal Science Foundation 703 869-1853
385 Somerville Ave Somerville MA (02143) ***(G-15185)***
Interntonal Totalizing Systems (PA) 978 521-8867
10 Paul Revere Rd Bedford MA (01730) ***(G-7983)***
Interplex Engineered Pdts Inc (HQ) 508 399-6810
54 Venus Way Attleboro MA (02703) ***(G-7750)***
Interplex Engineered Pdts Inc 401 434-6543
231 Ferris Ave Rumford RI (02916) ***(G-21187)***
Interplex Engineered Products, Rumford *Also called Interplex Industries Inc* ***(G-21189)***
Interplex Etch Logic LLC 508 399-6810
54 Venus Way Attleboro MA (02703) ***(G-7751)***
Interplex Industries Inc (HQ) 718 961-6212
231 Ferris Ave Rumford RI (02916) ***(G-21188)***
Interplex Industries Inc 401 434-6543
231 Ferris Ave Rumford RI (02916) ***(G-21189)***
Interplex Metal Logic 401 434-6543
231 Ferris Ave Rumford RI (02916) ***(G-21190)***
Interplex Metals Ri Inc 401 732-9999
231 Ferris Ave Rumford RI (02916) ***(G-21191)***
Interpolymer Corporation (HQ) 781 828-7120
200 Dan Rd Canton MA (02021) ***(G-9745)***
Interpro LLC 860 526-5869
630 Industrial Park Rd Deep River CT (06417) ***(G-1062)***
Interpro Rapid Technology, Deep River *Also called Interpro LLC* ***(G-1062)***
Interrotech 207 778-4907
57 Main St New Sharon ME (04955) ***(G-6477)***
Intersec LLC 860 985-3158
1275 Cromwell Ave Ste B3 Rocky Hill CT (06067) ***(G-3718)***
Intersense Incorporated 781 541-6330
700 Technology Park Dr # 102 Billerica MA (01821) ***(G-8258)***
Intersil Design Center, Concord *Also called Renesas Electronics Amer Inc* ***(G-10156)***
Interstate + Lakeland Lbr Corp 203 531-8050
184 S Water St Greenwich CT (06830) ***(G-1623)***
Interstate Battery Southern ME, Lewiston *Also called Tim Kat Inc* ***(G-6325)***
Interstate Cont Lowell LLC (HQ) 978 458-4555
240 Industrial Ave E Lowell MA (01852) ***(G-12383)***
Interstate Design Company Inc 413 786-7730
84 Gold St Agawam MA (01001) ***(G-7432)***
Interstate Gasket Company Inc 508 234-5500
55 Gilmore Dr Sutton MA (01590) ***(G-15684)***
Interstate Manufacturing Assoc 603 863-4855
45 Lower Main St Sunapee NH (03782) ***(G-19881)***
Interstate Manufacturing Co 413 789-8674
84 Gold St Agawam MA (01001) ***(G-7433)***
Interstate Mat Corporation 508 238-0116
32 Norfolk Ave Ste 4 South Easton MA (02375) ***(G-15282)***
Interstate Specialty Pdts Inc 800 984-1811
55 Gilmore Dr Sutton MA (01590) ***(G-15685)***
Interstate Tax Corporation 203 854-0704
83 East Ave Ste 110 Norwalk CT (06851) ***(G-3176)***
Intersurface Dynamics Inc 203 778-9995
21 Francis J Clarke Cir Bethel CT (06801) ***(G-161)***
Interticketcom Inc (PA) 781 275-5724
2 Glenridge Dr Bedford MA (01730) ***(G-7984)***
Intervale Farm & Gardens, Burlington *Also called William R Raap* ***(G-21817)***
Inteset Systems, Hanover *Also called Inteset Technologies LLC* ***(G-11342)***
Inteset Technologies LLC 781 826-1560
51 Mill St Ste 21 Hanover MA (02339) ***(G-11342)***
Intest Thermal Solutions, Mansfield *Also called Temptronic Corporation* ***(G-12664)***
Intlaero Beta Corp 317 821-2000
400 Main St East Hartford CT (06108) ***(G-1204)***
Intouch Labels and Packg Inc 800 370-2693
181 Industrial Ave E Lowell MA (01852) ***(G-12384)***
Intouch Software 603 643-1952
37 Wildwood Dr West Lebanon NH (03784) ***(G-19954)***
Intracranial Bioanalytics LLC 914 490-1524
22 Richard Sweet Dr Woodbridge CT (06525) ***(G-5468)***
Intrasonics Inc 860 283-8040
1401 Waterbury Rd Thomaston CT (06787) ***(G-4504)***
Intrnatl Chromium Plating Co, Providence *Also called International Chromium Pltg Co* ***(G-21037)***
Intuit Inc 508 862-1050
75 Perseverance Way Ste 3 Hyannis MA (02601) ***(G-11844)***
Intuit- Eclispe, Hyannis *Also called Intuit Inc* ***(G-11844)***
Inukshukbio Interactive Inc 612 916-6606
104 Woods Hole Rd Falmouth MA (02540) ***(G-10793)***
Invensense Inc (PA) 857 268-4400
100 Summer St Boston MA (02110) ***(G-8619)***
Invensys Systems Argentina 508 543-8750
38 Neponset Ave Foxboro MA (02035) ***(G-10889)***
Inventec Prfmce Chem USA LLC 860 526-8300
500 Main St Ste 18 Deep River CT (06417) ***(G-1063)***
Inventronics Inc 978 649-9040
130 Middlesex Rd Ste 14 Tyngsboro MA (01879) ***(G-15891)***
Inverness Corporation (HQ) 774 203-1130
49 Pearl St Attleboro MA (02703) ***(G-7752)***
Inversant Inc 617 423-0331
561 Boylston St Boston MA (02116) ***(G-8620)***
Invetech Inc 508 475-3400
159 Swanson Rd Boxborough MA (01719) ***(G-8964)***
Invision Inc 207 725-7123
48 Melden Dr Brunswick ME (04011) ***(G-5839)***
Invivo Thrputics Holdings Corp 617 863-5500
1 Kendall Sq Ste B14402 Cambridge MA (02139) ***(G-9518)***
Iometry Inc 603 643-5670
9 Morrison Rd Hanover NH (03755) ***(G-18294)***
Ion Design Group, Portland *Also called Sign Systems of Maine Inc* ***(G-6729)***

Ion Physics Corp 603 895-5100
373 Main St Fremont NH (03044) ***(G-18177)***
Ion Science LLC....802 244-5153
162 S Main St Waterbury VT (05676) ***(G-22583)***
Ion Track Instruments LLC....978 658-3767
205 Lowell St Wilmington MA (01887) ***(G-17007)***
Ionbond LLC....603 610-4460
195 Nh Ave Portsmouth NH (03801) ***(G-19580)***
Ionic Pharmaceuticals LLC....978 509-4980
189 Tappan St Brookline MA (02445) ***(G-9204)***
Ionsense Inc....781 231-1739
999 Broadway Ste 404 Saugus MA (01906) ***(G-14987)***
Iovino Bros Sporting Goods....203 790-5966
2 Lee Mac Ave Ste 2 # 2 Danbury CT (06810) ***(G-934)***
Ipac Fabrics Inc....508 845-6112
508 Boston Tpke Shrewsbury MA (01545) ***(G-15119)***
IPC Information Systems, Old Saybrook *Also called IPC Systems Inc* ***(G-3338)***
IPC Information Systems, Fairfield *Also called IPC Systems Inc* ***(G-1437)***
IPC Systems Inc....203 339-7000
8 Custom Dr Old Saybrook CT (06475) ***(G-3338)***
IPC Systems Inc....860 271-4100
777 Commerce Dr Ste 100 Fairfield CT (06825) ***(G-1437)***
Ipg Photonics Corporation (PA)....508 373-1100
50 Old Webster Rd Oxford MA (01540) ***(G-14263)***
Ipg Photonics Corporation....508 229-2130
377 Simarano Dr Ste 302 Marlborough MA (01752) ***(G-12778)***
Ipg Photonics Corporation....603 518-3200
200 Innovative Way # 1390 Nashua NH (03062) ***(G-19191)***
Ipg Photonics Corporation....508 506-2812
259 Cedar Hill St Marlborough MA (01752) ***(G-12779)***
Ipn Industries Inc....603 623-8626
8 Ricker Ave Londonderry NH (03053) ***(G-18705)***
Ipotec LLC....603 778-2882
41 Industrial Park Dr Exeter NH (03833) ***(G-18124)***
Ippolito Stonecraft, Seekonk *Also called Phillip Ippolito* ***(G-15033)***
Ips, Amesbury *Also called Independent Product Service* ***(G-7491)***
Ipsen Bioscience Inc....617 679-8500
1 Kendall Sq Ste B7401 Cambridge MA (02139) ***(G-9519)***
Ipsogen....203 504-8583
700 Canal St Ste 5 Stamford CT (06902) ***(G-4229)***
Ipswich Brewery, Ipswich *Also called Mercury Brewing & Dist Co* ***(G-11930)***
Ipswich Cabinetry Inc....978 356-1123
4 Poplar St Ipswich MA (01938) ***(G-11922)***
Ipswich Chronicle....978 356-5141
2 Washington St Ipswich MA (01938) ***(G-11923)***
Iq Medical Devices LLC....617 484-3188
50 Summit Rd Belmont MA (02478) ***(G-8076)***
Iqe Kc LLC....508 824-6696
200 John Hancock Rd Taunton MA (02780) ***(G-15759)***
IQF Custom Packing LLC....508 646-0400
140 Waldron Rd Fall River MA (02720) ***(G-10715)***
IR Industries Inc....203 790-8273
21 Francis J Clarke Cir Bethel CT (06801) ***(G-162)***
Ira Green Inc....800 663-7487
177 Georgia Ave Providence RI (02905) ***(G-21040)***
Ira Holtz & Associates....401 521-8960
2220 Plainfield Pike 4w Cranston RI (02921) ***(G-20241)***
Iradion Laser Inc....401 762-5100
1 Technology Dr Uxbridge MA (01569) ***(G-15921)***
Irish Inc (PA)....207 224-7605
625 Plains Rd Turner ME (04282) ***(G-7108)***
Irobot Corporation (PA)....781 430-3000
8 Crosby Dr Bedford MA (01730) ***(G-7985)***
Irody....781 262-0440
30 Newbury St Ste 3 Boston MA (02116) ***(G-8621)***
Iron Craft Fabricating LLC....860 923-9869
34 Corttiss Rd North Grosvenordale CT (06255) ***(G-2996)***
Iron Duck Division, Chicopee *Also called Fleming Industries Inc* ***(G-10026)***
Iron Horse Standing Seam Roofg, Tunbridge *Also called E I J Inc* ***(G-22543)***
Iron Man Machine, Pittsfield *Also called Charles McCann* ***(G-14463)***
Ironman Inc....989 386-8975
150 Rumford Ave Apt 230 Mansfield MA (02048) ***(G-12638)***
Ironwood Pharmaceuticals Inc (PA)....617 621-7722
100 Summer St Ste 2300 Boston MA (02110) ***(G-8622)***
Irrigation Automtn Systms Inc....800 549-4551
1 Main St Ste 10 Whitinsville MA (01588) ***(G-16915)***
Irving Consumer Products Inc....781 273-3222
25 Burlington Mall Rd # 608 Burlington MA (01803) ***(G-9286)***
Irving Tissue Corporation....781 273-3222
25 Burlington Mall Rd Burlington MA (01803) ***(G-9287)***
Irving Woodlands LLC....207 562-4400
24 Hall Hill Rd Dixfield ME (04224) ***(G-5957)***
Irving Woodlands LLC (HQ)....207 834-5767
1798 St John Rd St John Plt ME (04743) ***(G-7058)***
Irwin Industrial Tool Company....413 525-3961
301 Chestnut St East Longmeadow MA (01028) ***(G-10480)***
Irwin Industrial Tool Company....207 856-6111
37 Bartlett Rd Gorham ME (04038) ***(G-6115)***

Isaac Industries....203 778-3239
108 Stadley Rough Rd Danbury CT (06811) ***(G-935)***
Isaacson Lumber Co Inc....207 897-2115
133 Park St Livermore Falls ME (04254) ***(G-6378)***
Isabellenhuette USA, Swansea *Also called Isotek Corporation* ***(G-15705)***
Iselann Moss Industries Inc....401 463-5950
41 Slater Rd Cranston RI (02920) ***(G-20242)***
Ishigaki USA Ltd....603 433-3334
280 Heritage Ave Unit J Portsmouth NH (03801) ***(G-19581)***
ISI-Exeter, Nashua *Also called Interactive Systems Inc* ***(G-19190)***
Isilon Systems LLC....206 315-7500
176 South St Hopkinton MA (01748) ***(G-11723)***
Island Ad-Vantages, Stonington *Also called Penobscot Bay Press Inc* ***(G-7070)***
Island Approaches Inc....207 348-2459
300 Sunset Rd Sunset ME (04683) ***(G-7075)***
Island Desserts LLC....508 660-2200
24 Walpole Park S Ste 1 Walpole MA (02081) ***(G-15995)***
Island Lobster Supply....207 863-4807
E Main St Vinalhaven ME (04863) ***(G-7128)***
Island Mooring Supplies LLC....401 447-5387
68 John Oldham Rd Prudence Island RI (02872) ***(G-21160)***
Island News Enterprise....401 423-3200
45 Narragansett Ave Jamestown RI (02835) ***(G-20491)***
Island Reflections Corporation....401 782-2744
83 Conanicus Rd Narragansett RI (02882) ***(G-20641)***
Island Sand & Gravel Pit, Shelton *Also called Dan Beard Inc* ***(G-3794)***
Islander....802 372-5600
2355 Us Route 2 North Hero VT (05474) ***(G-22231)***
Ism Capital Corporation Ltd....401 454-8519
940 Waterman Ave East Providence RI (02914) ***(G-20421)***
Isolux LLC....978 774-9136
100 Ferncroft Rd Ste 110 Danvers MA (01923) ***(G-10226)***
Isopur Fluid Technologies Inc....860 599-1872
183 Provi New Londo Tpke North Stonington CT (06359) ***(G-3076)***
Isotech North America Inc....802 863-8050
158 Brentwood Dr Ste 4 Colchester VT (05446) ***(G-21868)***
Isotek Corporation....508 673-2900
1199 Gar Hwy Swansea MA (02777) ***(G-15705)***
Isovolta Inc....802 775-5528
477 Windcrest Rd Rutland VT (05701) ***(G-22341)***
Isp, Sutton *Also called Interstate Specialty Pdts Inc* ***(G-15685)***
Isp Freetown Fine Chem Inc....508 672-0634
238 S Main St Assonet MA (02702) ***(G-7681)***
Isr (ntllgnce Srvllance Reconn....203 797-5000
100 Wooster Hts Danbury CT (06810) ***(G-936)***
ISS, Shirley *Also called Image Software Services Inc* ***(G-15087)***
Isto Biologics, Hopkinton *Also called Arteriocyte Med Systems Inc* ***(G-11691)***
Isubscribed Inc....844 378-4646
15 Network Dr Fl 3 Burlington MA (01803) ***(G-9288)***
Isun International Group LLC....508 835-9000
235 W Boylston St Ste A West Boylston MA (01583) ***(G-16418)***
It Helps LLC....860 799-8321
54 Boxwood Ln New Milford CT (06776) ***(G-2806)***
It'll Be Pizza, Scarborough *Also called Itllbe LLC* ***(G-6927)***
Itaconix Corporation....603 775-4400
2 Marin Way Ste 1 Stratham NH (03885) ***(G-19869)***
Itaconix LLC....603 775-4400
2 Marin Way Stratham NH (03885) ***(G-19870)***
Itag LLC....603 429-8436
11 Marty Dr Merrimack NH (03054) ***(G-19008)***
Ital Marble Co Inc....781 595-4859
500 Lynnway Lynn MA (01905) ***(G-12517)***
Ital-Tech Machined Pdts LLC....978 373-6773
3 Federal Way Groveland MA (01834) ***(G-11301)***
Italian Bakery Products Co....207 782-8312
225 Bartlett St Lewiston ME (04240) ***(G-6293)***
Italian Choppers LLC....508 648-6816
64 High St Southbridge MA (01550) ***(G-15387)***
Ite LLC....508 313-5600
140 Manley St Brockton MA (02301) ***(G-9156)***
Itech Data Services Inc....802 383-1500
20 Kimball Ave Ste 303n South Burlington VT (05403) ***(G-22450)***
Iterum Therapeutics Inc....860 391-8349
20 Research Pkwy Old Saybrook CT (06475) ***(G-3339)***
Itext Software Corp....617 982-2646
265 Medford St Ste 500 Somerville MA (02143) ***(G-15186)***
Itg Group Inc....508 645-4994
4 Main St Ste H Medway MA (02053) ***(G-12962)***
Ithaca Peripherals Div, Wallingford *Also called Magnetec Corporation* ***(G-4768)***
Ithaco Space Systems Inc....607 272-7640
100 Wooster Hts Danbury CT (06810) ***(G-937)***
ITI, Westfield *Also called Instrument Technology Inc* ***(G-16690)***
ITI, Hudson *Also called Interconnect Technology Inc* ***(G-18402)***
Itllbe LLC....207 730-7301
5 Lincoln Ave Scarborough ME (04074) ***(G-6927)***
Itnh Inc....603 669-6900
150 Dow St Manchester NH (03101) ***(G-18845)***
Itrica Corp....617 340-7777
125 High St Fl 2 Boston MA (02110) ***(G-8623)***

ALPHABETIC

Its A Corker 781 729-9630
29 Arthur St Winchester MA (01890) ***(G-17089)***
Its Classified Inc 802 222-5152
900 S Main St Bradford VT (05033) ***(G-21701)***
Its New England Inc 203 265-8100
8 Capital Dr Wallingford CT (06492) ***(G-4756)***
ITT Corporation 781 932-5665
10 Mill St Woburn MA (01801) ***(G-17207)***
ITT Standard 860 683-2144
1036 Poquonock Ave Windsor CT (06095) ***(G-5340)***
ITT Water & Wastewater USA Inc (HQ) 262 548-8181
1 Greenwich Pl Ste 2 Shelton CT (06484) ***(G-3820)***
ITW Devcon Inc 978 777-1100
30 Endicott St Danvers MA (01923) ***(G-10227)***
ITW Drawform Inc 203 574-3200
1240 Wolcott St Waterbury CT (06705) ***(G-4889)***
ITW EF&c US, Westminster *Also called Illinois Tool Works Inc* ***(G-16805)***
ITW Foilmark, Bloomfield *Also called Foilmark Inc* ***(G-220)***
ITW Instron 781 762-3216
825 University Ave Norwood MA (02062) ***(G-14167)***
ITW Nutmeg, Naugatuck *Also called Illinois Tool Works Inc* ***(G-2479)***
ITW Plymers Salants N Amer Inc 781 681-0418
56 Air Station Indus Park Rockland MA (02370) ***(G-14809)***
ITW Powertrain Fastening 203 720-1676
29 Rado Dr Naugatuck CT (06770) ***(G-2480)***
Iva Corporation 978 443-5800
142 North Rd Ste R Sudbury MA (01776) ***(G-15661)***
Ivek Corp 802 886-2238
10 Fairbanks Rd North Springfield VT (05150) ***(G-22236)***
Ivenix Inc 978 775-8050
50 High St Ste 50 # 50 North Andover MA (01845) ***(G-13711)***
Ives Eeg Solutions LLC 978 358-8006
25 Storey Ave Newburyport MA (01950) ***(G-13502)***
Ivy Biomedical Systems Inc 203 481-4183
11 Business Park Dr # 10 Branford CT (06405) ***(G-326)***
Iwaki America Incorporated (HQ) 508 429-1440
5 Boynton Rd Holliston MA (01746) ***(G-11579)***
Iwaki Pumps Inc (HQ) 508 429-1440
5 Boynton Rd Holliston MA (01746) ***(G-11580)***
Iworx Systems Inc 603 742-2492
62 Littleworth Rd Dover NH (03820) ***(G-18030)***
Ixys Intgrted Circuits Div LLC 978 524-6700
78 Cherry Hill Dr Beverly MA (01915) ***(G-8142)***
Iyrs, Newport *Also called International Yacht Restoratio* ***(G-20666)***
Izon Science US Ltd 617 945-5936
196 Boston Ave Ste 3500 Medford MA (02155) ***(G-12937)***
Izotope Inc (PA) 617 577-7799
60 Hampshire St Cambridge MA (02139) ***(G-9520)***
Izzi B'S Allergen Free Cupcake, Norwalk *Also called Izzi BS Allergy Free LLC* ***(G-3177)***
Izzi BS Allergy Free LLC 203 810-4378
22 Knight St Norwalk CT (06851) ***(G-3177)***
Izzi Clothes, Fall River *Also called Fieldston Clothes Inc* ***(G-10700)***
Izzy Industries Inc 603 219-0596
701 Riverwood Dr Pembroke NH (03275) ***(G-19458)***
J & B Metal Finishing 978 874-5944
1 Leominster St Westminster MA (01473) ***(G-16806)***
J & B Metal Products Company 781 233-7506
341 Central St Saugus MA (01906) ***(G-14988)***
J & B Service Company LLC 203 743-9357
12 Trowbridge Dr Bethel CT (06801) ***(G-163)***
J & D Associates Corp 508 478-9770
355 Purchase St Milford MA (01757) ***(G-13120)***
J & D Embroidering Co 860 822-9777
26 Bushnell Hollow Rd A Baltic CT (06330) ***(G-50)***
J & D Machine 603 624-9717
728 E Indus Pk Dr Unit 5 Manchester NH (03109) ***(G-18846)***
J & D Welding 603 523-7695
377 Kinsman Rd Grafton NH (03240) ***(G-18216)***
J & E Specialty Inc 603 742-6357
519 Central Ave Dover NH (03820) ***(G-18031)***
J & G Machining Company Inc 860 379-7038
100 Whiting St Ste 1 Winsted CT (06098) ***(G-5414)***
J & J Machining 401 397-2782
2059 Victory Hwy Coventry RI (02816) ***(G-20149)***
J & J Moulding, Pomfret Center *Also called Jakes Jr Lawrence* ***(G-3555)***
J & J Music Boxes Inc 978 433-5686
10 Lomar Park Pepperell MA (01463) ***(G-14439)***
J & J Precision Eyelet Inc 860 283-8243
116 Waterbury Rd Thomaston CT (06787) ***(G-4505)***
J & J Technologies Inc 508 291-3803
18 Kendrick Rd Wareham MA (02571) ***(G-16251)***
J & K Sales Company Inc 508 252-6235
225 Pleasant St Rehoboth MA (02769) ***(G-14751)***
J & L Machine Co Inc 860 649-3539
62 Batson Dr Manchester CT (06042) ***(G-2013)***
J & L Metrology Inc 802 885-8291
280 Clinton St Springfield VT (05156) ***(G-22503)***
J & L Tool Company Inc 203 265-6237
368 N Cherry Street Ext Wallingford CT (06492) ***(G-4757)***
J & L Welding & Machine Co 978 283-3388
19 Arthur St 25 Gloucester MA (01930) ***(G-11193)***
J & M Cabinet Shop Inc 508 660-6660
2050 Main St Walpole MA (02081) ***(G-15996)***
J & M Enterprises Inc 207 968-2729
33 Howe Rd Fairfield ME (04937) ***(G-6027)***
J & M Logging Inc 207 622-6353
35 Harold Dr Sidney ME (04330) ***(G-6962)***
J & M Machining Inc 207 474-7300
313 North Ave Skowhegan ME (04976) ***(G-6978)***
J & M Plumbing & Cnstr LLC 860 319-3082
16 West St Norwich CT (06360) ***(G-3284)***
J & O Construction Inc 508 586-4900
4 Brian Dr Brockton MA (02301) ***(G-9157)***
J & R Graphics Inc 781 871-7577
155 Webster St Ste L Hanover MA (02339) ***(G-11343)***
J & R Langley Co Inc 603 622-9653
169 S Main St Manchester NH (03102) ***(G-18847)***
J & R Plastics 508 995-0893
226 Nyes Ln Acushnet MA (02743) ***(G-7402)***
J & R Projects 203 879-2347
1509 Wolcott Rd Waterbury CT (06716) ***(G-4890)***
J & S Business Products Inc 877 425-4049
17 Main St Ste 5 Ayer MA (01432) ***(G-7922)***
J & S Logging 207 864-5617
3039 Main St Rangeley ME (04970) ***(G-6772)***
J & T Printing LLC 860 529-4628
46 2 Silas Deane Hwy Wethersfield CT (06109) ***(G-5250)***
J + J Branford Inc (PA) 203 488-5637
145 N Mn St Branford CT (06405) ***(G-327)***
J A Black Company 207 338-4040
3 Blacks Lndg Belfast ME (04915) ***(G-5691)***
J and L Sand 207 499-2545
221 S Waterboro Rd Lyman ME (04002) ***(G-6390)***
J and R Pre Cast Inc 508 822-3311
16 County St Berkley MA (02779) ***(G-8087)***
J Arnold Mittleman 860 346-6562
29 Stack St Middletown CT (06457) ***(G-2192)***
J B A Products 603 539-5034
234 Granite Rd Effingham NH (03882) ***(G-18095)***
J B Concrete Products Inc 860 928-9365
1 Arch St Putnam CT (06260) ***(G-3617)***
J B Foley Printing Company 401 467-3616
1469 Broad St Providence RI (02905) ***(G-21041)***
J B J Machine Company Inc 207 676-3380
12 Elm St North Berwick ME (03906) ***(G-6508)***
J B Sash & Door Company Inc 617 884-8940
280 2nd St Chelsea MA (02150) ***(G-9955)***
J B Silk Screen Printing, North Branford *Also called Concordia Ltd* ***(G-2960)***
J Burdon Division, Milford *Also called Ridge View Associates Inc* ***(G-2351)***
J C B Leasing Inc 603 529-7974
14 B And B Ln Weare NH (03281) ***(G-19934)***
J C Custom Woodworking, Medway *Also called Joel Cassidy* ***(G-12963)***
J C Enterprises Inc 508 881-7228
300 Eliot St Ste 12 Ashland MA (01721) ***(G-7662)***
J C Image Inc 802 527-1557
88 Walnut St Saint Albans VT (05478) ***(G-22369)***
J C Logging Inc 207 794-4349
350 Transalpine Rd Lincoln ME (04457) ***(G-6354)***
J Carvalho LLC 774 206-1435
166 Essex St New Bedford MA (02745) ***(G-13398)***
J Crosier Mold Polishing 413 663-6262
133 Mohawk Trl Florida MA (01247) ***(G-10871)***
J D & Associates 860 546-2112
115 John Brook Rd Canterbury CT (06331) ***(G-693)***
J D Paulsen 207 647-5679
249 Portland Rd Bridgton ME (04009) ***(G-5808)***
J Dana Design Inc 413 477-6844
232 Lucas Rd Hardwick MA (01037) ***(G-11374)***
J E Schell Welding 508 763-4658
253 Bullock Rd East Freetown MA (02717) ***(G-10453)***
J F Kessler Inc 781 828-0134
283 Neponset St Canton MA (02021) ***(G-9746)***
J F M, Merrimac *Also called James F Mullen Co Inc* ***(G-13002)***
J F OMalley Welding Co 508 791-8671
1177 Millbury St Worcester MA (01607) ***(G-17395)***
J F Tool Inc 860 349-3063
205 Main St Ste C Rockfall CT (06481) ***(G-3697)***
J Foster Ice Cream 860 651-1499
894 Hopmeadow St Simsbury CT (06070) ***(G-3907)***
J G Machine Co Inc 978 447-5279
21 Concord St Wilmington MA (01887) ***(G-17008)***
J G Maclellan Con Co Inc (PA) 978 458-1223
180 Phoenix Ave Lowell MA (01852) ***(G-12385)***
J G Performance Inc 781 871-1404
43 Highland Rd Abington MA (02351) ***(G-7325)***
J H Breakell & Company Inc 401 849-3522
132 Spring St Newport RI (02840) ***(G-20667)***
J H Dunning Corporation 603 445-5591
1 Dunning Dr North Walpole NH (03609) ***(G-19394)***

J H Faddens & Sons 603 745-2406
99 Main St North Woodstock NH (03262) (G-19398)
J H Metal Finishing Inc (PA) 860 223-6412
1146 East St New Britain CT (06051) (G-2545)
J I L Software, Sebec Also called Brian D Murphy (G-6956)
J I Morris Company 508 764-4394
394 Elm St Southbridge MA (01550) (G-15388)
J J Box Co Inc 203 367-1211
25 Admiral St Bridgeport CT (06605) (G-432)
J J Concrete Foundations 203 798-8310
15 Stony Hill Rd Bethel CT (06801) (G-164)
J J Industries Conn Inc 860 628-4655
125 W Queen St Southington CT (06489) (G-4060)
J J Plank Corporation 920 733-4479
16 Plank Industrial Dr Farmington NH (03835) (G-18143)
J J Ryan Corporation 860 628-0393
355 Atwater St Plantsville CT (06479) (G-3534)
J J Traskos Mfg Inc 401 348-2080
113 Canal St Westerly RI (02891) (G-21527)
J Joy Associates Inc 781 871-1569
273 Weymouth St Ste 2 Rockland MA (02370) (G-14810)
J K Adams Company Inc 802 362-2303
1430 Route 30 Dorset VT (05251) (G-21908)
J K L Corp 978 657-5575
12 Bay St Ste 105 Wilmington MA (01887) (G-17009)
J M Compounds Inc 203 376-9854
290 Pratt St Ofc Meriden CT (06450) (G-2095)
J M Sheet Metal LLC 860 747-5537
161 Woodford Ave Ste 11 Plainville CT (06062) (G-3498)
J Mack Studios LLC 401 932-8600
101 Cross St Westerly RI (02891) (G-21528)
J Magazine Inc 617 515-1822
338 Saint Paul St Apt 6 Brookline MA (02446) (G-9205)
J Masse Sign 508 695-0534
5 Madison St Unit B Plainville MA (02762) (G-14523)
J N G Hadeka Slate Flooring 802 265-3351
773 Briar Hill Rd West Pawlet VT (05775) (G-22611)
J O Brown & Son Inc 207 867-4621
1 Main St North Haven ME (04853) (G-6511)
J OConnor LLC 860 665-7702
309 Pane Rd Ste 1 Newington CT (06111) (G-2873)
J P I Inc 401 737-7433
405 Kilvert St Ste E Warwick RI (02886) (G-21377)
J P Licks Homemade Ice Cream 781 329-9100
704 Legacy Pl Dedham MA (02026) (G-10294)
J P Mfg Inc 508 764-2538
13 Lovely St Southbridge MA (01550) (G-15389)
J P Moriarty & Co Inc 617 628-3000
22 Clifton St Ste 1 Somerville MA (02144) (G-15187)
J P Precision Machine Co 413 592-8191
90 Exchange St Chicopee MA (01013) (G-10034)
J R Liggett Ltd Inc 603 675-2055
973 Nh Route 12a Cornish NH (03745) (G-17961)
J R Logging Inc 603 237-8010
41 Spring St Colebrook NH (03576) (G-17872)
J R S, Canton Also called Jewelry Solutions LLC (G-9748)
J R V Smita Company LLC 781 828-6490
566 Washington St Canton MA (02021) (G-9747)
J S Dental, Ridgefield Also called J S Dental Manufacturing Inc (G-3669)
J S Dental Manufacturing Inc 203 438-8832
196 N Salem Rd Ridgefield CT (06877) (G-3669)
J S McCarthy Printing, Augusta Also called Letter Systems Inc (G-5613)
J S Ritter Jewelers Supply LLC 207 712-4744
50 Cove St Portland ME (04101) (G-6675)
J S Wholesale Fuels 207 622-4332
867 Western Ave Manchester ME (04351) (G-6410)
J T C Printing, Needham Heights Also called D & L Associates Inc (G-13326)
J T Fantozzi Co Inc 203 238-7018
95 Fair St Meriden CT (06451) (G-2096)
J T Gardner Inc (PA) 800 540-4993
190 Turnpike Rd Westborough MA (01581) (G-16627)
J T Gardner Inc 508 832-2036
567 Southbridge St Ste 14 Auburn MA (01501) (G-7839)
J T Gardner Inc 508 366-2679
144 E Main St Westborough MA (01581) (G-16628)
J T Gardner Inc 508 751-6600
165 Southbridge St Worcester MA (01608) (G-17396)
J T Inman Co Inc 508 226-0080
31 Larsen Way Attleboro Falls MA (02763) (G-7814)
J T Machine Co Inc 508 476-1508
175 Davis St East Douglas MA (01516) (G-10427)
J T Manufacturing Corporation 603 821-5720
60b Pulpit Rock Rd Pelham NH (03076) (G-19436)
J Tefft Logging & Firewoo 401 539-9838
33 Fenner Hill Rd Hope Valley RI (02832) (G-20485)
J Voisine & Son Logging Inc 207 436-0932
771 Aroostook Rd Fort Kent ME (04743) (G-6061)
J W Fishers Mfg Inc 508 822-7330
1953 County St East Taunton MA (02718) (G-10514)
J W Machining Inc 978 562-5611
17 Bonazzoli Ave Hudson MA (01749) (G-11780)
J W Precision Company Inc 603 868-6574
373 Route 4 Barrington NH (03825) (G-17619)
J Weston Walch Publisher 207 772-2846
40 Walch Dr Portland ME (04103) (G-6676)
J Yeager Inc (PA) 802 362-0810
4542 Main St Manchester VT (05254) (G-22077)
J&J Machine Company Inc 508 481-8166
66b Brigham St Marlborough MA (01752) (G-12780)
J&L, Gloucester Also called J & L Welding & Machine Co (G-11193)
J&L Plastic Molding LLC 203 265-6237
368 N Cherry Street Ext Wallingford CT (06492) (G-4758)
J&P Mfg LLC 860 747-4790
125 Robert Jackson Way F Plainville CT (06062) (G-3499)
J-A Industries Incorporated 508 297-1648
6 Eleanore Strasse North Easton MA (02356) (G-13948)
J-K Tool Co Inc 413 789-0613
41 Russo Cir Agawam MA (01001) (G-7434)
J-Pac LLC (HQ) 603 692-9955
25 Centre Rd Somersworth NH (03878) (G-19842)
J-Pac Medical, Somersworth Also called J-Pac LLC (G-19842)
J-Tech Automation LLC 401 934-2435
205 Sandy Brook Rd North Scituate RI (02857) (G-20779)
J-Teck Usa Inc 203 791-2121
50 Miry Brook Rd Danbury CT (06810) (G-938)
J. Weston Walch, Publisher, Portland Also called Mathemtics Problem Solving LLC (G-6692)
J.S. McCarthy Printers, Augusta Also called JS McCarthy Co Inc (G-5609)
Ja Apparel Corp 580 990-4580
689 Belleville Ave New Bedford MA (02745) (G-13399)
Jab Industries Inc 401 447-9668
185 Washington St Attleboro MA (02703) (G-7753)
Jab Manufacturing LLC 603 328-8113
51 Northwestern Dr Ste E Salem NH (03079) (G-19743)
Jack Dilling 978 928-4002
122 Worcester Rd Hubbardston MA (01452) (G-11745)
Jack Hodgdon 508 223-9990
67 Mechanic St Unit 3 Attleboro MA (02703) (G-7754)
Jack Knight Co 781 340-1500
972 Washington St Ste 2 Hanover MA (02339) (G-11344)
Jack Russell 802 438-5213
186 Marble St West Rutland VT (05777) (G-22617)
Jack's Custom Woodworking, Woburn Also called Jarica Inc (G-17210)
Jack's Machine Company, Scituate Also called South Shore Manufacturing Inc (G-15014)
Jackiestees 617 799-8404
238 Rantoul St Beverly MA (01915) (G-8143)
Jackman Cash Fuel, Jackman Also called Jackman Lumber Inc (G-6217)
Jackman Equipment 207 858-0690
617 Skowhegan Rd Norridgewock ME (04957) (G-6497)
Jackman Lumber Inc 207 858-0321
318 Varney Rd Skowhegan ME (04976) (G-6979)
Jackman Lumber Inc (PA) 207 668-4407
548 Main St Jackman ME (04945) (G-6217)
Jackson Bond Enterprises LLC 603 742-2350
39 Industrial Park Dover NH (03820) (G-18032)
Jackson Bookbinding Co Inc 401 231-0800
21 Lark Industrial Pkwy B Greenville RI (02828) (G-20469)
Jackson Caldwell 207 539-2325
266 Hebron Rd Oxford ME (04270) (G-6567)
Jackson Corrugated Cont Corp 860 767-3373
45 River Rd Essex CT (06426) (G-1399)
Jackson Sgrhuse Vgtable Stands 207 539-4613
50 Hebron Rd Oxford ME (04270) (G-6568)
Jackson Square Laundromat, Jamaica Plain Also called Jason Santelli Enterprises LLC (G-11944)
Jaco Inc 508 553-1000
140 Constitution Blvd Franklin MA (02038) (G-11056)
Jacob Burdin Logging 207 564-3384
115 Downs Rd Sebec ME (04481) (G-6957)
Jacobs Precision Corp 508 588-2121
21 Ledin Dr Ste B Avon MA (02322) (G-7888)
Jacobs Vehicle Systems Inc 860 243-5222
22 E Dudley Town Rd Bloomfield CT (06002) (G-227)
Jacobsen Woodworking Co Inc 203 531-9050
3 Oak St W Greenwich CT (06830) (G-1624)
Jacquelines Gourmet Cookies, Salem Also called Jacquelines Wholesale Bky Inc (G-14923)
Jacquelines Wholesale Bky Inc 978 744-8600
96 Swampscott Rd Ste 1 Salem MA (01970) (G-14923)
Jad LLC 860 289-1551
489 Sullivan Ave South Windsor CT (06074) (G-3983)
Jade Engineered Plastics Inc 401 253-4440
121 Broadcommon Rd Bristol RI (02809) (G-20085)
Jade Manufacturing Company Inc 401 737-2400
132 Meadow St Warwick RI (02886) (G-21378)
Jaeger Usa Inc 603 332-5816
104 Pickering Rd Rochester NH (03867) (G-19674)
Jaf Corporation 508 943-8519
37 Market St Webster MA (01570) (G-16344)

A L P H A B E T I C

Jagger Brothers.......207 324-5622
5 Water St Springvale ME (04083) ***(G-7053)***
Jagger Spun Division, Springvale *Also called Jagger Brothers* ***(G-7053)***
Jagtar, Cos Cob *Also called Arnitex LLC* ***(G-822)***
Jahrling Ocular Prosthetics (PA).......617 523-2280
50 Staniford St Fl 8 Boston MA (02114) ***(G-8624)***
Jahrling Ocular Prosthetics.......401 454-4168
120 Dudley St Ste 202 Cranston RI (02905) ***(G-20243)***
Jaime M Camacho.......203 846-8221
345 Main Ave Norwalk CT (06851) ***(G-3178)***
Jain America Foods Inc.......413 593-8883
1000 Sheridan St Chicopee MA (01022) ***(G-10035)***
Jak Designs LLC.......330 689-6849
2 Sayward St Kennebunk ME (04043) ***(G-6236)***
Jak Designs LLC (PA).......207 204-0396
24 Ocean Ave Kennebunkport ME (04046) ***(G-6245)***
Jake Brake, Bloomfield *Also called Jacobs Vehicle Systems Inc* ***(G-227)***
Jakes Jr Lawrence.......860 974-3744
405 Brooklyn Rd Pomfret Center CT (06259) ***(G-3555)***
Jakes Mint Chew LLC.......978 304-0528
10r Rainbow Ter Ste H Danvers MA (01923) ***(G-10228)***
Jam & Jelly Chatham.......508 945-3052
10 Vineyard Ave West Chatham MA (02669) ***(G-16474)***
Jam Company.......203 655-3260
1770 Post Rd Darien CT (06820) ***(G-1027)***
Jam Fuel LLC.......802 345-6118
5087 Us Route 5 N 1 Windsor VT (05089) ***(G-22710)***
Jam Plastics, Burlington *Also called Precision Dynamics Corporation* ***(G-9321)***
Jam Plastics Inc.......978 537-2570
22 Tucker Dr Leominster MA (01453) ***(G-12156)***
Jamaica Cottage Shop Inc.......802 297-3760
170 Winhall Station Rd South Londonderry VT (05155) ***(G-22487)***
Jamaica Plain Porchfest Inc.......617 320-6230
50 Dunster Rd Boston MA (02130) ***(G-8625)***
James A Kiley Company.......617 776-0344
15 Linwood St Somerville MA (02143) ***(G-15188)***
James A McBrady Inc.......207 883-4176
29 Parkway Dr Scarborough ME (04074) ***(G-6928)***
James Austin Company.......413 589-1600
203 West Ave Ludlow MA (01056) ***(G-12469)***
James Cable LLC (PA).......781 356-8701
15 Braintree Hill Park # 102 Braintree MA (02184) ***(G-9021)***
James Callahan.......914 641-2852
55 Buck Hill Rd Ridgefield CT (06877) ***(G-3670)***
James Communications, Braintree *Also called James Cable LLC* ***(G-9021)***
James Devaney Fuel Co.......781 326-7608
111 River St Dedham MA (02026) ***(G-10295)***
James E Cofran.......781 341-0897
106 Cabral Cir Stoughton MA (02072) ***(G-15599)***
James F Mullen Co Inc.......978 346-0045
51 E Main St Merrimac MA (01860) ***(G-13002)***
James G Hachey Inc.......781 229-6400
1r Newbury St Ste 309 Peabody MA (01960) ***(G-14344)***
James H Carville.......207 353-2625
134 Bowdoinham Rd Lisbon Falls ME (04252) ***(G-6370)***
James H Rich Boatyard.......207 244-3208
Main St Rr 102 Bernard ME (04612) ***(G-5707)***
James Ippolito & Co Conn Inc.......203 366-3840
1069 Conn Ave Ste 16 Bridgeport CT (06607) ***(G-433)***
James J Licari (PA).......203 333-5000
300 N Washington Ave Bridgeport CT (06604) ***(G-434)***
James J Scott LLC.......860 571-9200
38 New Britain Ave Ste 3 Rocky Hill CT (06067) ***(G-3719)***
James L Gallagher Inc.......508 758-3102
408 W Main Rd Little Compton RI (02837) ***(G-20605)***
James L Howard and Company Inc.......860 242-3581
10 Britton Dr Bloomfield CT (06002) ***(G-228)***
James M Dunn.......207 212-2963
45 Ledge Hill Rd Hebron ME (04238) ***(G-6180)***
James M Munch.......802 353-3114
48 Route 37 S Sherman CT (06784) ***(G-3894)***
James Manufacturing, North Haven *Also called Jeskey LLC* ***(G-3034)***
James Monroe Wire & Cable Corp (PA).......978 368-0131
767 Sterling Rd South Lancaster MA (01561) ***(G-15318)***
James Newspapers Inc (PA).......207 743-7011
1 Pikes Hl Norway ME (04268) ***(G-6523)***
James Newspapers Inc.......207 364-7893
69 Congress St Rumford ME (04276) ***(G-6836)***
James Thompson Native Lumber.......401 377-2837
385 Woodville Rd Hopkinton RI (02833) ***(G-20487)***
James Wright Precision Pdts.......860 928-7756
20 Mechanics St Putnam CT (06260) ***(G-3618)***
Jamestown Boat Yard Inc.......401 423-0600
60 Racquet Rd Jamestown RI (02835) ***(G-20492)***
Jamestown Industries Inc.......603 286-3301
270 Tilton Rd Ste 4 Northfield NH (03276) ***(G-19403)***
Jamestown Press, Jamestown *Also called Island News Enterprise* ***(G-20491)***
Jamieson Laser LLC.......860 482-3375
50 Thomaston Rd Litchfield CT (06759) ***(G-1950)***
Jamison Computer Services.......802 527-9758
1624 Cline Rd Saint Albans VT (05478) ***(G-22370)***
Jamlab Enterprises.......978 688-8750
190 Haverhill St Methuen MA (01844) ***(G-13028)***
Jammar Mfg Co Inc.......866 848-1113
26 Industrial Park Rd Niantic CT (06357) ***(G-2953)***
Jan Manufacturing Inc.......203 879-0580
14 Town Line Rd Ste 8 Wolcott CT (06716) ***(G-5445)***
Jan Woodworks Renovation.......413 563-2534
61 Bowdoin St Westfield MA (01085) ***(G-16691)***
Janco Inc (PA).......603 742-0043
50 Goodwin Rd Rollinsford NH (03869) ***(G-19691)***
Janco Electronics Inc.......603 742-1581
50 Goodwin Rd Rollinsford NH (03869) ***(G-19692)***
Jane Diagnostics Inc.......617 651-2295
201 Freeman St Apt A7 Brookline MA (02446) ***(G-9206)***
Janice Miller.......603 629-9995
150 Dow St Ste 4 Manchester NH (03101) ***(G-18848)***
Janik Sausage Co Inc.......860 749-4661
136 Hazard Ave Enfield CT (06082) ***(G-1367)***
Janis Research Company Inc (PA).......781 491-0888
225 Wildwood Ave Woburn MA (01801) ***(G-17208)***
Janis Research Company LLC.......781 491-0888
225 Wildwood Ave Woburn MA (01801) ***(G-17209)***
Janitorial Commercial Gen Svc, Hamden *Also called Daily Impressions LLC* ***(G-1743)***
Janna Ugone & Associates Inc.......413 527-5530
1 Cottage St Unit 6 Easthampton MA (01027) ***(G-10566)***
Jannel Manufacturing Inc.......781 767-0666
5 Mear Rd Holbrook MA (02343) ***(G-11527)***
Janos Technology Inc.......603 757-0070
55 Black Brook Rd Keene NH (03431) ***(G-18507)***
Janos Technology LLC.......603 757-0070
55 Black Brook Rd Keene NH (03431) ***(G-18508)***
Jaquith Caibide Corp.......978 356-7770
31 Turnpike Rd Ipswich MA (01938) ***(G-11924)***
Jarden Corporation.......203 264-9717
288 Christian St Ste 11 Oxford CT (06478) ***(G-3410)***
Jarden LLC.......203 845-5300
301 Merritt 7 Ste 5 Norwalk CT (06851) ***(G-3179)***
Jarden LLC.......207 645-2574
5 Mill St East Wilton ME (04234) ***(G-5987)***
Jared Manufacturing Co Inc.......203 846-1732
25 Perry Ave Norwalk CT (06850) ***(G-3180)***
Jarica Inc.......781 935-1907
3 Aberjona Dr Woburn MA (01801) ***(G-17210)***
Jarvenpaa & Sons.......978 874-2231
233 S Ashburnham Rd Westminster MA (01473) ***(G-16807)***
Jarvis Airfoil Inc.......860 342-5000
528 Glastonbury Tpke Portland CT (06480) ***(G-3568)***
Jarvis Company Inc (PA).......603 332-9000
100 Jarvis Ave Rochester NH (03868) ***(G-19675)***
Jarvis Cutting Tools Inc.......603 332-9000
100 Jarvis Ave Rochester NH (03868) ***(G-19676)***
Jarvis Precision Polishing.......860 589-5822
190 Century Dr Bristol CT (06010) ***(G-572)***
Jarvis Products, Middletown *Also called Penco Corporation* ***(G-2209)***
Jarvis Products Corporation (HQ).......860 347-7271
33 Anderson Rd Middletown CT (06457) ***(G-2193)***
Jarvis Surgical Inc.......413 562-6659
53 Airport Rd Westfield MA (01085) ***(G-16692)***
JAS F Mullen Co Inc.......978 346-0045
51 E Main St Merrimac MA (01860) ***(G-13003)***
Jason Patenaude Excavating Inc.......802 766-4567
311 Fortin Rd Derby VT (05829) ***(G-21900)***
Jason S Landry.......603 783-1154
263 Route 129 Loudon NH (03307) ***(G-18749)***
Jason Santelli Enterprises LLC.......617 942-2205
274 Centre St Jamaica Plain MA (02130) ***(G-11944)***
Jasper & Bailey Sail Makers, Newport *Also called Jasper Aaron* ***(G-20668)***
Jasper Aaron.......401 847-8796
64 Halsey St Unit 11 Newport RI (02840) ***(G-20668)***
Jasper Wyman & Son.......207 546-3381
Rr 193 Cherryfield ME (04622) ***(G-5903)***
Jasper Wyman & Son.......207 638-2201
601 Rte 193 Deblois ME (04622) ***(G-5946)***
Jasper Wyman & Son (PA).......207 546-3800
280 Main St Milbridge ME (04658) ***(G-6433)***
Jasper Wyman & Son.......207 546-2311
7 Wyman Rd Milbridge ME (04658) ***(G-6434)***
Jasper Wyman & Son.......207 546-3381
178 Main St Cherryfield ME (04622) ***(G-5904)***
Java Skin Care, Saunderstown *Also called Java Worx International LLC* ***(G-21202)***
Java Worx International LLC.......866 609-3258
28 Bow Run Saunderstown RI (02874) ***(G-21202)***
Jaw Precision Machining LLC.......860 535-0615
44 Taugwonk Spur Rd # 1 Stonington CT (06378) ***(G-4377)***
Jay Engineering Corp.......978 250-0115
35 Hunt Rd Ste B Chelmsford MA (01824) ***(G-9907)***
Jay Packaging Group Inc (PA).......401 244-1300
100 Warwick Industrial Dr Warwick RI (02886) ***(G-21379)***

Jay Sons Screw Mch Pdts Inc 860 621-0141
197 Burritt St Milldale CT (06467) *(G-2384)*
Jaybird & Mais Inc 978 686-8659
360 Merrimack St Ste 20 Lawrence MA (01843) *(G-12040)*
Jaye's Studio, Stamford *Also called Malabar Bay LLC (G-4243)*
Jaymill, Manchester *Also called Janice Miller (G-18848)*
Jaypro Sports LLC 860 447-3001
976 Hartford Tpke Ste B Waterford CT (06385) *(G-4986)*
JB Dawn Products, Dover *Also called Booth Felt Co Inc (G-18009)*
JB Filtration LLC 860 333-7962
18 River Road Dr Essex CT (06426) *(G-1400)*
Jb Muze Enterprises 860 355-5949
180 Sunny Valley Rd Ste 9 New Milford CT (06776) *(G-2807)*
JB Sports LLC 617 930-3044
121 Morris St Revere MA (02151) *(G-14769)*
Jbjs, Needham *Also called Journal of Bone Jint Srgery In (G-13302)*
Jbl, Stamford *Also called Harman Consumer Inc (G-4206)*
JBM Carmel LLC 802 442-9110
14 Morse Rd Bennington VT (05201) *(G-21674)*
Jbm Service Inc 978 939-8004
686 Patriots Rd Templeton MA (01468) *(G-15803)*
JBM Sherman Carmel Inc 802 442-5115
14 Morse Rd Bennington VT (05201) *(G-21675)*
Jbnj Foods Incorporated 781 293-0912
48 Phillips St Hanson MA (02341) *(G-11364)*
JC Clocks Company Inc 508 998-8442
9 Ventura Dr North Dartmouth MA (02747) *(G-13922)*
JC Millwork Inc 207 293-4204
191 Cottle Hill Rd Mount Vernon ME (04352) *(G-6459)*
JCB Inc 508 839-5550
197 Worcester St North Grafton MA (01536) *(G-13961)*
Jcc Residual Ltd 508 699-4401
811 Park East Dr Woonsocket RI (02895) *(G-21572)*
JCM Design & Display Inc 401 781-0470
610 Manton Ave Ste 1 Providence RI (02909) *(G-21042)*
JCP Trading Inc 603 232-0967
35 Elm St Manchester NH (03101) *(G-18849)*
Jcptrading Inc 603 880-7042
35 Elm St Manchester NH (03101) *(G-18767)*
JD Design LLC 781 941-2066
184 Broadway Ste 11 Saugus MA (01906) *(G-14989)*
JD Software Inc 888 419-9998
27 Congress St Ste 505 Salem MA (01970) *(G-14924)*
Jda Software Group Inc 857 305-8330
320 Congress St Ste 401 Boston MA (02210) *(G-8626)*
Jean Charles Blondine 857 247-9369
28 Mount Pleasant Ave Roxbury MA (02119) *(G-14873)*
Jeba Graphics LLC 603 532-7726
32 Fitzgerald Dr Jaffrey NH (03452) *(G-18468)*
Jedox Inc 617 514-7300
50 Milk St Fl 16 Boston MA (02109) *(G-8627)*
Jeff Cummings Services LLC 603 456-3706
268 Bean Rd Warner NH (03278) *(G-19927)*
Jeff Manufacturing Co Inc 860 482-8845
679 Riverside Ave Torrington CT (06790) *(G-4582)*
Jeff Schiff 617 887-0202
120 Eastern Ave Ste 205 Chelsea MA (02150) *(G-9956)*
Jeffco Fibres Inc (PA) 508 943-0440
12 Park St Webster MA (01570) *(G-16345)*
Jefferson Rubber Products, Worcester *Also called Jefferson Rubber Works Inc (G-17397)*
Jefferson Rubber Works Inc 508 791-3600
17 Coppage Dr Worcester MA (01603) *(G-17397)*
Jeffrey Gold 203 281-5737
2440 Whitney Ave Ste 6 Hamden CT (06518) *(G-1762)*
Jeio Tech Inc 781 376-0700
19 Alexander Rd Ste 7 Billerica MA (01821) *(G-8259)*
Jeld-Wen Inc 802 228-2020
146 Pleasant St Ext Ludlow VT (05149) *(G-22064)*
Jeld-Wen Inc 802 886-1728
36 Precision Dr Ste 130 North Springfield VT (05150) *(G-22237)*
Jeld-Wen Doors, North Springfield *Also called Jeld-Wen Inc (G-22237)*
Jem Electronics Inc 508 520-3105
23 National Dr Franklin MA (02038) *(G-11057)*
Jem Manufacturing Inc 203 250-9404
20 N Plains Industrial Rd # 12 Wallingford CT (06492) *(G-4759)*
JEM Precision Grinding Inc 860 633-0152
35 Nutmeg Ln Glastonbury CT (06033) *(G-1560)*
Jem Precision Technologies 508 672-0666
1567 N Main St Ste 1 Fall River MA (02720) *(G-10716)*
Jem Precision Technology, Fall River *Also called Jem Precision Technologies (G-10716)*
Jembow Inc 603 774-6055
92 Woodhill Rd Bow NH (03304) *(G-17717)*
Jen Col Innovations LLC 802 448-3053
875 Roosevelt Hwy Ste 130 Colchester VT (05446) *(G-21869)*
Jen Mfg Inc 508 753-1076
3 Latti Farm Rd Millbury MA (01527) *(G-13168)*
Jen Ren Corporation 508 835-3331
45 Sterling St Ste 11 West Boylston MA (01583) *(G-16419)*
Jen-Coat Inc (HQ) 413 875-9855
132 N Elm St Westfield MA (01085) *(G-16693)*
Jena Piezosystem Inc 508 634-6688
2 Rosenfeld Dr Ste B Hopedale MA (01747) *(G-11674)*
Jenex Inc 603 672-2600
172b South St Milford NH (03055) *(G-19066)*
Jenkins Sugar Group Inc 203 853-3000
16 S Main St Ste 202 Norwalk CT (06854) *(G-3181)*
Jenne Machine LLC 802 626-1106
180 Commercial Ln Lyndonville VT (05851) *(G-22068)*
Jennings Yacht Services 860 625-1368
800 Flanders Rd Mystic CT (06355) *(G-2440)*
Jenray Products Inc 914 375-5596
4 Production Dr Brookfield CT (06804) *(G-648)*
Jens & Marie Inc 401 475-9991
2 Thomas St Ste 1 Providence RI (02903) *(G-21043)*
Jensen Cabinet Co 603 554-8363
27 Dearborn St Milford NH (03055) *(G-19067)*
Jensen Dental, North Haven *Also called Jensen Industries Inc (G-3033)*
Jensen Industries Inc (PA) 203 285-1402
50 Stillman Rd North Haven CT (06473) *(G-3033)*
Jensen Machine Co 860 666-5438
721 Russell Rd Newington CT (06111) *(G-2874)*
Jenson Enterprises LLC 802 497-3530
1891 Williston Rd South Burlington VT (05403) *(G-22451)*
Jenzabar Inc (PA) 617 492-9099
101 Huntington Ave # 2200 Boston MA (02199) *(G-8628)*
Jeol Usa Inc (HQ) 978 535-5900
11 Dearborn Rd Peabody MA (01960) *(G-14345)*
Jericho Woodworking 802 295-9399
3221 Jericho St White River Junction VT (05001) *(G-22640)*
Jerome Martin Paul 207 422-3965
12 Martin Rd North Sullivan ME (04664) *(G-6513)*
Jerome Ridel 860 379-1774
15 Hampsted Rd West Granby CT (06090) *(G-5049)*
Jerrys Custom Upholstery 508 697-2183
259 Plain St Bridgewater MA (02324) *(G-9078)*
Jerrys Printing & Graphics LLC 203 384-0015
1183 Broad St Bridgeport CT (06604) *(G-435)*
Jeskey LLC 203 772-6675
69 Dodge Ave North Haven CT (06473) *(G-3034)*
Jesko Tool & Knife 413 543-1520
34 Front St Indian Orchard MA (01151) *(G-11888)*
Jessicas Discount Fuel 207 310-1966
247 Allen Rd Pownal ME (04069) *(G-6749)*
Jet Coating Co 508 869-2158
240 Shrewsbury St Boylston MA (01505) *(G-8981)*
Jet Electro Finishing, Barrington *Also called Jet Electro-Finishing Co Inc (G-20047)*
Jet Electro-Finishing Co Inc 401 728-5809
408 Middle Hwy Barrington RI (02806) *(G-20047)*
Jet Graphics LLC 508 580-5809
175 Bodwell St Ste 1 Avon MA (02322) *(G-7889)*
Jet Industries Inc 413 786-2010
307 Silver St Agawam MA (01001) *(G-7435)*
Jet Machined Products LLC 508 378-3200
221 Highland St East Bridgewater MA (02333) *(G-10414)*
Jet Press 508 478-1814
323 Main St Milford MA (01757) *(G-13121)*
Jet Process Corporation 203 985-6000
57 Dodge Ave North Haven CT (06473) *(G-3035)*
Jet Service Envelope Co Inc (PA) 802 229-9335
80 East Rd Barre VT (05641) *(G-21626)*
Jet Tech Inc 781 599-8685
52 Alley St Lynn MA (01902) *(G-12518)*
Jet Tool & Cutter Mfg Inc 860 621-5381
125 W Queen St Southington CT (06489) *(G-4061)*
Jet-Co Precision Machining 603 882-7958
286 Lowell Rd Hudson NH (03051) *(G-18403)*
Jetco, Hudson *Also called Jet-Co Precision Machining (G-18403)*
Jeto Engineering Inc 978 768-6472
191 Western Ave Essex MA (01929) *(G-10594)*
Jewel Case Corporation 401 943-1400
110 Dupont Dr Providence RI (02907) *(G-21044)*
Jeweled Cross, Woonsocket *Also called Jcc Residual Ltd (G-21572)*
Jewell Instruments LLC (PA) 603 669-5121
850 Perimeter Rd Manchester NH (03103) *(G-18850)*
Jewell Woodworks LLC 603 679-8025
79 Stage Rd Nottingham NH (03290) *(G-19416)*
Jewelry Creations 508 285-4230
123 Reservoir St Norton MA (02766) *(G-14079)*
Jewelry Holding Co Inc 401 826-7934
30 Fairview Ave West Warwick RI (02893) *(G-21496)*
Jewelry Solutions LLC 781 821-6100
448 Turnpike St Ste 2 Canton MA (02021) *(G-9748)*
Jewish Advocate Pubg Corp 617 523-6232
15 School St Fl 2 Boston MA (02108) *(G-8629)*
Jewish Journal 978 745-4111
27 Congress St Ste 501 Salem MA (01970) *(G-14925)*
Jewish Journal, The, Salem *Also called North Shore Jewish Press Ltd (G-14932)*

A L P H A B E T I C

Jewish Leader Newspaper....860 442-7395
28 Channing St New London CT (06320) ***(G-2774)***
Jewish Ledger, Hartford *Also called NRG Connecticut LLC* ***(G-1855)***
Jewish Times, Boston *Also called Jewish Advocate Pubg Corp* ***(G-8629)***
Jf Griffin Publishing LLC....413 458-4800
148 Main St Williamstown MA (01267) ***(G-16957)***
Jf Hutchinson Co....207 926-3676
616b Lewiston Rd New Gloucester ME (04260) ***(G-6468)***
Jf2 LLC....508 429-1022
215 Hopping Brook Rd Holliston MA (01746) ***(G-11581)***
JFd Tube & Coil Products Inc....203 288-6941
7 Hamden Park Dr Hamden CT (06517) ***(G-1763)***
Jfj Services LLC....860 395-1922
17 Forest Glen Rd Old Saybrook CT (06475) ***(G-3340)***
Jfm No 3 Corp....207 782-2726
800 Center St Auburn ME (04210) ***(G-5573)***
Jfs Industries....203 592-0754
90 Walnut St Apt B Thomaston CT (06787) ***(G-4506)***
JG Manufacturing Corp....978 681-8400
1980 Turnpike St Ste 3 North Andover MA (01845) ***(G-13712)***
Jgp Enterprises Inc....978 691-2737
200 Bulfinch Dr Ste 160 Andover MA (01810) ***(G-7559)***
Jgs Properties LLC....203 378-7508
1805 Stratford Ave Stratford CT (06615) ***(G-4425)***
JH Lynch & Sons Inc....401 434-7100
835 Taunton Ave East Providence RI (02914) ***(G-20422)***
JH Smith Co Inc (PA)....413 772-0191
330 Chapman St Greenfield MA (01301) ***(G-11264)***
Jhb Enterprises, Marstons Mills *Also called Cape Cod Braided Rug Co Inc* ***(G-12872)***
Jhs Restoration Inc....860 757-3870
170 Strong Rd South Windsor CT (06074) ***(G-3984)***
Jiffy Print Inc....207 947-4490
494 Broadway Bangor ME (04401) ***(G-5652)***
Jiffy Print Copy Center, Fall River *Also called Lincoln Press Co Inc* ***(G-10723)***
Jill Ghi....860 824-7123
532 Ashley Falls Rd Canaan CT (06018) ***(G-688)***
Jill Rosenwald Ceramic Design....617 422-0787
369 Congress St Fl 2 Boston MA (02210) ***(G-8630)***
Jim Brown....207 789-5188
2596 Atlantic Hwy Lincolnville ME (04849) ***(G-6362)***
Jim Carr Inc....603 635-2821
100 Bridge St Pelham NH (03076) ***(G-19437)***
Jim Clift Design Inc....401 823-9680
5 Grandview St Coventry RI (02816) ***(G-20150)***
Jim Haluck....508 230-8901
65 Belmont St South Easton MA (02375) ***(G-15283)***
Jim Lovejoy Cabinetmaker....413 229-9008
75 Main St Sheffield MA (01257) ***(G-15061)***
Jim's Metal Fabrication, New Gloucester *Also called Jf Hutchinson Co* ***(G-6468)***
Jiminny Inc....917 940-5886
745 Atlantic Ave Boston MA (02111) ***(G-8631)***
Jims Salad Co....207 948-2613
557 Albion Rd Unity ME (04988) ***(G-7116)***
Jims Welding Service LLC....203 744-2982
18 Finance Dr Danbury CT (06810) ***(G-939)***
Jimsan Enterprises Inc....508 587-3666
275 E Center St West Bridgewater MA (02379) ***(G-16442)***
Jimtown Sand and Gravel Inc....603 752-4622
1803 Riverside Dr Berlin NH (03570) ***(G-17698)***
Jj Portland News LLC....860 342-1432
264 Main St Middletown CT (06457) ***(G-2194)***
Jji International Inc....401 780-8668
1 Weingeroff Blvd Cranston RI (02910) ***(G-20244)***
JJT Engineering Inc....978 657-4137
3b Lopez Rd Wilmington MA (01887) ***(G-17010)***
Jk Antennas Inc....845 228-8700
72 Grays Bridge Rd Ste D Brookfield CT (06804) ***(G-649)***
Jk Motorsports....203 255-9120
500 Grasmere Ave Fairfield CT (06824) ***(G-1438)***
Jkb Daira Inc (PA)....203 642-4824
22 S Smith St Norwalk CT (06855) ***(G-3182)***
JKL Specialty Foods Inc....203 541-3990
417 Shippan Ave Ste 2 Stamford CT (06902) ***(G-4230)***
Jl Aerotech Inc....860 248-8628
475 Buckland Rd Ste 103 South Windsor CT (06074) ***(G-3985)***
JL Lucas Machinery Co Inc....203 597-1300
429 Brookside Rd Waterbury CT (06708) ***(G-4891)***
Jlc Tech LLC....781 826-8162
370 Corporate Park Dr Pembroke MA (02359) ***(G-14412)***
Jlg Technologies LLC....508 424-2338
371 Turnpike Rd Ste 200 Southborough MA (01772) ***(G-15362)***
Jlp Machine and Welding LLC....781 585-1744
10 Winter St Kingston MA (02364) ***(G-11958)***
Jlp Services Inc....508 667-5498
6 Kenwood Dr Rutland MA (01543) ***(G-14882)***
Jls Tool & Die Inc....978 304-3111
13 Eddington St Middleton MA (01949) ***(G-13091)***
JM Huber Corporation....207 488-2051
333 Station Rd Easton ME (04740) ***(G-5990)***
JM Logging Forestry, Sherman *Also called James M Munch* ***(G-3894)***
JM Software Inc....978 957-9105
32 Elene St Dracut MA (01826) ***(G-10361)***
Jmc Asset Holdings Inc....781 447-9264
162 Industrial Blvd Ste 7 Hanson MA (02341) ***(G-11365)***
Jmd Duct Fabrication LLC....603 235-9314
25 Brown Ridge Rd Weare NH (03281) ***(G-19935)***
Jmd Industries Inc....603 882-3198
1 Park Ave Hudson NH (03051) ***(G-18404)***
Jmd Manufacturing Inc....508 620-6563
59 Fountain St Ste 5 Framingham MA (01702) ***(G-10972)***
Jmf Group LLC....860 627-7003
13 Revay Rd East Windsor CT (06088) ***(G-1288)***
Jmh Industries Inc....401 438-2500
889 Waterman Ave East Providence RI (02914) ***(G-20423)***
Jmk Inc....603 886-4100
15 Caldwell Dr Amherst NH (03031) ***(G-17569)***
Jmk Logging LLC....207 227-2964
555 Pulcifur Rd Mapleton ME (04757) ***(G-6413)***
JMS Casting Inc....401 453-5990
183 Public St Providence RI (02903) ***(G-21045)***
JMS Graphics Inc....203 598-7555
850 Straits Tpke Ste 204 Middlebury CT (06762) ***(G-2155)***
JMS Manufacturing Inc....508 675-1141
22 5th St Unit 8 Taunton MA (02780) ***(G-15760)***
Jmsc Enterprises Inc....603 468-1010
95 Ledge Rd Unit 4 Seabrook NH (03874) ***(G-19808)***
Jmt Epoxy....401 331-9730
25 Western Industrial Dr # 3 Cranston RI (02921) ***(G-20245)***
Jmt Epoxy....401 331-9730
95 Hartford Ave Rear Bldg Providence RI (02909) ***(G-21046)***
Jnc Rebuilders Inc....978 356-2996
91 Turnpike Rd Ste 5 Ipswich MA (01938) ***(G-11925)***
Jnj Inc....508 620-0202
505 Worcester Rd Framingham MA (01701) ***(G-10973)***
Jnj Industries Inc....508 553-0529
290 Beaver St Franklin MA (02038) ***(G-11058)***
Jnp Coffee LLC....858 518-7437
8 Kalamat Farms Cir Shrewsbury MA (01545) ***(G-15120)***
Jo Vek Tool and Die Mfg Co....203 755-1884
2121 Thomaston Ave Waterbury CT (06704) ***(G-4892)***
Joan Fabrics LLC....978 454-3777
134 Middle St Ste 300 Lowell MA (01852) ***(G-12386)***
Joan Imports, Johnston *Also called Arden Jewelry Mfg Co* ***(G-20500)***
Jobart Inc (PA)....978 689-4414
37 1/2 Oakland Ave Methuen MA (01844) ***(G-13029)***
Jobin Machine Inc....860 953-1631
37 Custer St West Hartford CT (06110) ***(G-5079)***
Jobsmart Inc....724 272-3448
1157 Bug Hill Rd Ashfield MA (01330) ***(G-7652)***
Jodys Quick Print....978 777-6114
14 East St Middleton MA (01949) ***(G-13092)***
Joe Batson....978 689-0072
530 Essex St Lawrence MA (01840) ***(G-12041)***
Joe Martin....401 823-1860
3 Bridal Ave Unit 1 West Warwick RI (02893) ***(G-21497)***
Joe Passarelli & Co....203 877-1434
67 Andrews Ave Milford CT (06460) ***(G-2304)***
Joe Valentine Machine Company....203 356-9776
77 Southfield Ave Ste 2 Stamford CT (06902) ***(G-4231)***
Joe's Paint Center, Branford *Also called J + J Branford Inc* ***(G-327)***
Joel Cassidy....508 533-5887
54 Holliston St Medway MA (02053) ***(G-12963)***
Joel Goldsmith Bagnal Inc....781 235-8266
101 Central St Wellesley MA (02482) ***(G-16368)***
Joes Custom Polishing....802 479-9266
874 E Barre Rd East Barre VT (05649) ***(G-21911)***
Jogalite-Bikealite, Silver Lake *Also called Nitefighter International* ***(G-19824)***
Johansons Boatworks....207 596-7060
11 Farwell Dr Rockland ME (04841) ***(G-6800)***
John A Kachagian....978 663-8511
34 Sullivan Rd Ste 15 North Billerica MA (01862) ***(G-13829)***
John Brown US LLC....617 449-4354
1 South Sta Fl 3 Boston MA (02110) ***(G-8632)***
John C Whyte....603 530-1168
43 Mutton Rd Salisbury NH (03268) ***(G-19781)***
John Carlevale....401 392-1926
640 Weaver Hill Rd West Greenwich RI (02817) ***(G-21459)***
John Carter Fire Escape Svcs....617 990-7387
70 G St Boston MA (02127) ***(G-8633)***
John Costin Studio....207 985-7221
1 Colonel Gelardi Dr # 104 Kennebunk ME (04043) ***(G-6237)***
John Covey....978 535-4681
6 Cobb Ave Peabody MA (01960) ***(G-14346)***
John Crane Inc....401 463-8700
75 Commerce Dr Warwick RI (02886) ***(G-21380)***
John Crane Sealol Inc (HQ)....401 732-0715
75 Commerce Dr 101 Warwick RI (02886) ***(G-21381)***
John Deere Authorized Dealer, Sanford *Also called North Country Tractor Inc* ***(G-6884)***
John Deere Authorized Dealer, Londonderry *Also called Siteone Landscape Supply LLC* ***(G-18737)***

John Deere Authorized Dealer, Essex *Also called Bell Power Systems LLC* ***(G-1393)***
John Deere Authorized Dealer, Marlborough *Also called Knm Holdings LLC* ***(G-12783)***
John Deere Authorized Dealer, Dover *Also called North Country Tractor Inc* ***(G-18041)***
John E Lepper Inc....508 222-6723
10 Tappan Ave Attleboro MA (02703) ***(G-7755)***
John E Ruggles & Co....508 992-9766
123 Sawyer St Unit 1 New Bedford MA (02746) ***(G-13400)***
John F Wielock....508 943-5366
27 Mill Rd Dudley MA (01571) ***(G-10378)***
John Fancy Inc....207 785-3610
118 Jones Hill Rd Appleton ME (04862) ***(G-5526)***
John H Collins & Son Co....401 722-0775
Dunnell Ln Pawtucket RI (02862) ***(G-20849)***
John Harvard's Brew House, Framingham *Also called John Harvards Brewhouse Llc* ***(G-10974)***
John Harvards Brewhouse Llc....508 875-2337
1 Worcester Rd Framingham MA (01701) ***(G-10974)***
John Hychko....203 757-3458
299 Sheffield St Waterbury CT (06704) ***(G-4893)***
John J Marr....603 939-2698
Main St Rr 113 Conway NH (03818) ***(G-17954)***
John J Pawloski Lumber Inc....203 794-0737
4 Pleasantview Ter Bethel CT (06801) ***(G-165)***
John June Custom Cabinetry LLC....203 334-1720
541 Fairfield Ave Bridgeport CT (06604) ***(G-436)***
John Karl Dietrich & Assoc....617 868-4140
26 Central Sq Cambridge MA (02139) ***(G-9521)***
John Khiel III Log Chpping Inc....207 452-2157
65 Bull Ring Rd Denmark ME (04022) ***(G-5949)***
John Latka & Co Inc....413 562-4374
204 Southampton Rd Westfield MA (01085) ***(G-16694)***
John Lewis Inc....617 266-6665
352 Msschstts Ave Apt 515 Boston MA (02115) ***(G-8634)***
John M Kriskey Carpentry....203 531-0194
129 N Water St Greenwich CT (06830) ***(G-1625)***
John Mc Leod Ltd (PA)....802 464-8175
111 W Main St Wilmington VT (05363) ***(G-22702)***
John Oldham Studios Inc....860 529-3331
888 Wells Rd Wethersfield CT (06109) ***(G-5251)***
John P Pow Company Inc....617 269-6040
49 D St Boston MA (02127) ***(G-8635)***
John Rawlinson John Leary....203 882-8484
316 Boston Post Rd Milford CT (06460) ***(G-2305)***
John Seavey Acadia Fuel....207 664-6050
711 Bar Harbor Rd Trenton ME (04605) ***(G-7099)***
John Wiley & Sons Inc....802 287-4326
1966 Hillside Rd Poultney VT (05764) ***(G-22272)***
John Zink -Todd Combustn Group, Shelton *Also called John Zink Company LLC* ***(G-3821)***
John Zink Company, Shelton *Also called Hamworthy Peabody Combustn Inc* ***(G-3808)***
John Zink Company LLC....203 925-0380
2 Armstrong Rd Fl 3 Shelton CT (06484) ***(G-3821)***
Johncarlo Woodworking Inc....413 562-4002
30 Clifton St Westfield MA (01085) ***(G-16695)***
Johnny H Castonguay....207 897-5945
140 Shackley Hill Rd Livermore ME (04253) ***(G-6375)***
Johns Bay Boat Co....207 644-8261
90 Poorhouse Cove Rd South Bristol ME (04568) ***(G-7005)***
Johns Building Supply Co Inc....413 442-7846
891 Crane Ave Ste 1 Pittsfield MA (01201) ***(G-14478)***
Johns Manville, West Boylston *Also called Johns Manville Corporation* ***(G-16420)***
Johns Manville Corporation....774 261-8500
10 Bunkerhill Pkwy West Boylston MA (01583) ***(G-16420)***
Johns Manville Corporation....207 784-0123
51 Lexington St Lewiston ME (04240) ***(G-6294)***
Johns Manville Corporation....207 283-8000
15 Lund Rd Saco ME (04072) ***(G-6850)***
Johnson & Johnson, Raynham *Also called Medical Device Bus Svcs Inc* ***(G-14717)***
Johnson & Johnson....401 647-1493
78 E Killingly Rd Foster RI (02825) ***(G-20456)***
Johnson & Johnson....401 762-6751
1300 Highland Corporate D Cumberland RI (02864) ***(G-20330)***
Johnson Abrasives Co Inc....603 532-4434
49 Fitzgerald Dr Jaffrey NH (03452) ***(G-18469)***
Johnson Contrls Authorized Dlr, New Haven *Also called F W Webb Company* ***(G-2688)***
Johnson Controls, Ledyard *Also called Clarios* ***(G-1940)***
Johnson Controls, Portland *Also called Clarios* ***(G-6638)***
Johnson Controls, Manchester *Also called Clarios* ***(G-18799)***
Johnson Controls, Lynnfield *Also called Clarios* ***(G-12547)***
Johnson Controls, Meriden *Also called Clarios* ***(G-2086)***
Johnson Controls Inc....860 571-3300
27 Inwood Rd Rocky Hill CT (06067) ***(G-3720)***
Johnson Controls Inc....860 688-7151
21 Griffin Rd N Ste 4 Windsor CT (06095) ***(G-5341)***
Johnson Controls Inc....508 384-0018
78 South St Wrentham MA (02093) ***(G-17524)***
Johnson Controls Inc....617 992-2073
33 Avenue Louis Pasteur Boston MA (02115) ***(G-8636)***
Johnson Filaments, Williston *Also called Astenjohnson Inc* ***(G-22655)***
Johnson Gage Company....860 242-5541
534 Cottage Grove Rd Bloomfield CT (06002) ***(G-229)***
Johnson Marble and Granite....802 459-3303
61 Main St Proctor VT (05765) ***(G-22285)***
Johnson Marine, East Haddam *Also called C Sherman Johnson Company* ***(G-1149)***
Johnson Matthey Phrm Mtls Inc (HQ)....978 784-5000
25 Patton Rd Devens MA (01434) ***(G-10321)***
Johnson Matthey Phrm Mtls Inc....978 784-5000
70 Flagship Dr North Andover MA (01845) ***(G-13713)***
Johnson Matthey Phrm Svcs, North Andover *Also called Johnson Matthey Phrm Mtls Inc* ***(G-13713)***
Johnson Millwork Inc....860 267-4693
222 Quarry Hill Rd East Hampton CT (06424) ***(G-1161)***
Johnson Otdoors Watercraft Inc (HQ)....207 827-5513
125 Gilman Falls Ave B Old Town ME (04468) ***(G-6541)***
Johnson Precision, Hudson *Also called Mrpc Northeast LLC* ***(G-18417)***
Johnson Printing & Graphics....207 439-2567
384 Harold L Dow Hwy # 15 Eliot ME (03903) ***(G-6007)***
Johnson Ultramar Fuel Service, Lancaster *Also called Ultramar Inc* ***(G-18608)***
Johnson Woolen Mills LLC....802 635-2271
51 Lower Main St E Johnson VT (05656) ***(G-22050)***
Johnsons Boatyard Inc....207 766-3319
88 Island Ave Long Island ME (04050) ***(G-6383)***
Johnsons Food Products Corp....617 265-3400
1 Mount Vernon St Boston MA (02108) ***(G-8637)***
Johnston Dandy Company (PA)....207 794-6571
148 Main St Lincoln ME (04457) ***(G-6355)***
Johnston Dandy Company....413 315-4596
78 N Canal St Holyoke MA (01040) ***(G-11635)***
Johnston Logging, Hermon *Also called Albert M M Johnston IV* ***(G-6181)***
Johnstone Company Inc....203 239-5834
222 Sackett Point Rd North Haven CT (06473) ***(G-3036)***
Joinery Shop Inc....617 242-4718
92 Arlington Ave Charlestown MA (02129) ***(G-9838)***
Joining Technologies Inc....860 653-0111
17 Connecticut South Dr B East Granby CT (06026) ***(G-1130)***
Jojoscupcakes LLC....401 297-4900
77 Isle Of Capri Rd Coventry RI (02816) ***(G-20151)***
Jolen Cream Bleach Corp....203 259-8779
25 Walls Dr Fairfield CT (06824) ***(G-1439)***
Jolie Jewels, Cranston *Also called Jji International Inc* ***(G-20244)***
Jolie Montre, Southbury *Also called Real Women International LLC* ***(G-4032)***
Jolley Precast Inc....860 774-9066
463 Putnam Rd Danielson CT (06239) ***(G-1014)***
Joma Incorporated....203 759-0848
185 Interstate Ln Waterbury CT (06705) ***(G-4894)***
Joma Diamond Tool Company....413 525-0760
46 Baldwin St Ste A East Longmeadow MA (01028) ***(G-10481)***
Jomay Inc....401 944-5240
66 Libera St Cranston RI (02920) ***(G-20246)***
Jon Barrett Associates Inc....401 846-8226
555 Thames St Newport RI (02840) ***(G-20669)***
Jon Goodman....413 586-9650
102 Petticoat Hill Rd Williamsburg MA (01096) ***(G-16951)***
Jon Goodman Photogravure, Williamsburg *Also called Jon Goodman* ***(G-16951)***
Jon Shafts & Stuff....603 518-5033
347 Massabesic St Manchester NH (03103) ***(G-18851)***
Jon Strong Low Impact Log LLC....603 487-5298
141 Riverdale Rd New Boston NH (03070) ***(G-19293)***
Jonal Labs Logistics LLC....203 634-4444
468 Center St Meriden CT (06450) ***(G-2097)***
Jonathan Clowes Sculpture....603 835-6441
98 March Hill Rd Walpole NH (03608) ***(G-19922)***
Jonathan Knight....401 263-3671
74 Table Rock Rd Wakefield RI (02879) ***(G-21273)***
Jones & Bartlett Learning LLC (PA)....978 443-5000
5 Wall St Fl 3 Burlington MA (01803) ***(G-9289)***
Jones & Company, East Providence *Also called Jones Safety Equipment Company* ***(G-20424)***
Jones & Vining Incorporated (PA)....508 232-7470
1115 W Chestnut St Ste 2 Brockton MA (02301) ***(G-9158)***
Jones & Vining Incorporated....207 784-3547
765 Webster St Lewiston ME (04240) ***(G-6295)***
Jones Metal Products Co Inc....860 289-8023
22 Schwier Rd Ste 1 South Windsor CT (06074) ***(G-3986)***
Jones Safety Equipment Company....401 434-4010
325 Massasoit Ave East Providence RI (02914) ***(G-20424)***
Jonette Jewelry Company....401 438-1941
373 Taunton Ave East Providence RI (02914) ***(G-20425)***
Jonmandy Corporation....860 482-2354
151 Ella Grasso Ave Ste 3 Torrington CT (06790) ***(G-4583)***
Jor Services LLC....203 594-7774
4 Parting Brook Rd New Canaan CT (06840) ***(G-2602)***
Joraco Inc....401 232-1710
347 Farnum Pike Smithfield RI (02917) ***(G-21234)***
Jordan Associates....603 246-8998
Rr 145 Pittsburg NH (03592) ***(G-19494)***
Jordan Bros Seafood Co Inc....508 583-9797
314 Northern Ave Boston MA (02210) ***(G-8638)***

Jordan Brothers Seafood, Boston *Also called Jordan Bros Seafood Co Inc* ***(G-8638)***
Jordan Enterprises Inc.......508 481-2948
40 Hudson St Ste B Marlborough MA (01752) ***(G-12781)***
Jordan Family Chipping Inc.......207 625-8890
Rr 160 Kezar Falls ME (04047) ***(G-6249)***
Jordan Millworks Inc.......207 794-6178
Rr 3 Box 1882 Lincoln ME (04457) ***(G-6356)***
Jordan Saw Mill L L C.......860 774-0247
201 Saw Mill Hill Rd Sterling CT (06377) ***(G-4367)***
Jordan Sawmill, Sterling *Also called Jordan Saw Mill L L C* ***(G-4367)***
Jordan Tree Harvesters Inc (PA).......207 625-4378
River St Kezar Falls ME (04047) ***(G-6250)***
Jordi Labs LLC.......508 719-8543
200 Gilbert St Mansfield MA (02048) ***(G-12639)***
Jorgensen Tool & Stamping Inc.......603 524-5813
23 Fruite St Belmont NH (03220) ***(G-17676)***
Jornal Dos Sports LLC.......857 888-9186
30 Oakland St 1 Melrose MA (02176) ***(G-12983)***
Jornik Man Corp.......203 969-0500
652 Glenbrook Rd Ste 2 Stamford CT (06906) ***(G-4232)***
Josef Creations Inc (PA).......401 421-4198
141 Jackson School Hse Rd Chepachet RI (02814) ***(G-20135)***
Joseph A Cnte Mfg Jewelers Inc.......203 248-9853
2582 Whitney Ave Hamden CT (06518) ***(G-1764)***
Joseph A Owen Jr.......978 486-3318
56 Wychwood Hts Littleton MA (01460) ***(G-12310)***
Joseph A Thomas Ltd.......401 253-1330
24 Broadcommon Rd Bristol RI (02809) ***(G-20086)***
Joseph Abboud Mfg Corp (HQ).......508 999-1301
689 Belleville Ave New Bedford MA (02745) ***(G-13401)***
Joseph Abboud Mfg Corp.......508 961-1726
11 Belleville Rd New Bedford MA (02745) ***(G-13402)***
Joseph C La Fond Co Inc.......401 769-3744
340 Old River Rd Manville RI (02838) ***(G-20609)***
Joseph Freedman Co Inc (PA).......888 677-7818
115 Stevens St Springfield MA (01104) ***(G-15481)***
Joseph Freedman Co Inc.......413 781-4444
40 Albany St Springfield MA (01105) ***(G-15482)***
Joseph J McFadden Jr.......860 354-6794
87 Danbury Rd New Milford CT (06776) ***(G-2808)***
Joseph K Delano Sawmill Inc.......508 994-8752
158 Cross Rd North Dartmouth MA (02747) ***(G-13923)***
Joseph Lotuff Sr.......413 967-5964
44 E Main St Ware MA (01082) ***(G-16234)***
Joseph Merritt & Company Inc.......203 743-6734
4c Chrstpher Columbus Ave Danbury CT (06810) ***(G-940)***
Joseph Nachado.......508 644-3404
5 Berkley Ave Assonet MA (02702) ***(G-7682)***
Joseph P Carrara & Sons Inc (PA).......802 775-2301
167 N Shrewsbury Rd North Clarendon VT (05759) ***(G-22216)***
Joseph P Carrara & Sons Inc.......802 388-6363
2464 Case St Middlebury VT (05753) ***(G-22113)***
Joseph's Online Bakery, Lawrence *Also called Middle East Bakery Inc* ***(G-12057)***
Josephs Gourmet Pasta Company.......978 521-1718
262 Primrose St Haverhill MA (01830) ***(G-11443)***
Josh Smpson Cntemporary GL Inc.......413 625-6145
30 Frank Williams Rd Shelburne Falls MA (01370) ***(G-15072)***
Joshua LLC (PA).......203 624-0080
90 Hamilton St New Haven CT (06511) ***(G-2699)***
Josselyns Sawmill Inc.......603 586-4507
243 Bailey Rd Jefferson NH (03583) ***(G-18485)***
Jotas Corporation.......781 273-1155
158 Cambridge St Ste 158 # 158 Burlington MA (01803) ***(G-9290)***
Jotul North America Inc.......207 797-5912
55 Hutcherson Dr Gorham ME (04038) ***(G-6116)***
Jounce Therapeutics Inc (PA).......857 259-3840
780 Memorial Dr Cambridge MA (02139) ***(G-9522)***
Journal LLC (PA).......802 228-3600
8 High St Ludlow VT (05149) ***(G-22065)***
Journal Computing In Higher.......413 549-5150
127 Sunset Ave Amherst MA (01002) ***(G-7516)***
Journal Emergency Management, Weston *Also called Prime National Publishing Corp* ***(G-16830)***
Journal Infectious Diseases.......617 367-1848
225 Friend St Boston MA (02114) ***(G-8639)***
Journal Inquirer, Manchester *Also called Green Manor Corporation* ***(G-2007)***
Journal Inquirer, Manchester *Also called Journal Publishing Company Inc* ***(G-2014)***
Journal Jewish, Salem *Also called Jewish Journal* ***(G-14925)***
Journal of Antq & Collectibles.......508 347-1960
46 Hall Rd Sturbridge MA (01566) ***(G-15639)***
Journal of Bone Jint Srgery In.......781 449-9780
20 Pickering St Ste 3 Needham MA (02492) ***(G-13302)***
Journal of Commerce Inc.......617 439-7099
88 Black Falcon Ave # 240 Boston MA (02210) ***(G-8640)***
Journal of Interdiscplinary.......781 862-4089
14 Barberry Rd Lexington MA (02421) ***(G-12233)***
Journal Opinion, Bradford *Also called Cohasa Publishing Inc* ***(G-21699)***
Journal Opinion Inc.......802 222-5281
48 Main St Bradford VT (05033) ***(G-21702)***
Journal Publishing Company Inc.......860 646-0500
306 Progress Dr Manchester CT (06042) ***(G-2014)***
Journal Register Company.......508 678-3844
207 Pocasset St Fall River MA (02721) ***(G-10717)***
Journal Roman Archaeology LLC.......401 683-1955
95 Peleg Rd Portsmouth RI (02871) ***(G-20926)***
Journal Transcript Newspapers, Winthrop *Also called Village Netmedia Inc* ***(G-17101)***
Journeyman Press, The, Newburyport *Also called Ian Marie Inc* ***(G-13499)***
Jouve of North America Inc (HQ).......802 254-6073
70 Landmark Hill Dr Brattleboro VT (05301) ***(G-21735)***
Joval Machine Co Inc.......203 284-0082
515 Main St Yalesville CT (06492) ***(G-5505)***
Jovan Machine Co Inc.......203 879-2855
1133 Wolcott Rd Ste A Wolcott CT (06716) ***(G-5446)***
Jovek Tool and Die.......860 261-5020
474 Birch St Bristol CT (06010) ***(G-573)***
Jovil Universal LLC.......203 792-6700
10 Precision Rd Danbury CT (06810) ***(G-941)***
Jowa Usa Inc.......978 486-9800
59 Porter Rd Littleton MA (01460) ***(G-12311)***
Joy Carole Creations Inc.......203 794-1401
42 Mill Plain Rd Danbury CT (06811) ***(G-942)***
Joyce Printers Inc.......203 389-4452
16 Research Dr Woodbridge CT (06525) ***(G-5469)***
Joyn Bio LLC.......978 549-3723
27 Drydock Ave Ste 8 Boston MA (02210) ***(G-8641)***
Jozef Custom Ironworks Inc.......203 384-6363
250 Smith St Bridgeport CT (06607) ***(G-437)***
JP Carrara & Sons, Middlebury *Also called Joseph P Carrara & Sons Inc* ***(G-22113)***
JP Lillis Enterprises Inc (PA).......508 888-8394
7 Jan Sebastian Dr Sandwich MA (02563) ***(G-14970)***
JP Moriarty Millwork, Somerville *Also called J P Moriarty & Co Inc* ***(G-15187)***
JP Obelisk Inc.......508 942-6248
10 Duck Farm Ln Bridgewater MA (02324) ***(G-9079)***
JP Plastics Inc.......508 697-4202
45 1st St Bridgewater MA (02324) ***(G-9080)***
JP Precision Machine Co, Chicopee *Also called J P Precision Machine Co* ***(G-10034)***
JP Sealcoating Inc.......508 954-3510
6 Gentian Rd Norton MA (02766) ***(G-14080)***
JP Sercel Associates Inc.......603 595-7048
220 Hackett Hill Rd Manchester NH (03102) ***(G-18852)***
Jpg Consulting Inc.......203 247-2730
65 Heather Ln Wilton CT (06897) ***(G-5292)***
Jph Graphics LLC.......978 744-7873
87 Canal St Salem MA (01970) ***(G-14926)***
JPS and Sons, Rehoboth *Also called Hass Bros Inc* ***(G-14750)***
Jpsa, Manchester *Also called JP Sercel Associates Inc* ***(G-18852)***
JPsexton LLC.......860 748-2048
460 Hayden Station Rd Windsor CT (06095) ***(G-5342)***
Jr & Sons Construction.......508 326-7884
17 Sodom Rd Westport MA (02790) ***(G-16842)***
Jr Chemical Coatings LLC.......508 896-3383
139 Queen Anne Rd Harwich MA (02645) ***(G-11394)***
Jr Fabrication, New Portland *Also called Justin Jordan* ***(G-6474)***
Jr Frank Bolton.......603 529-3633
58 Carding Mill Rd Weare NH (03281) ***(G-19936)***
JR Grady Company LLC.......978 458-3662
63 Middlesex St Ste 7 North Chelmsford MA (01863) ***(G-13898)***
JR Higgins Associates LLC.......978 266-1200
898 Main St Acton MA (01720) ***(G-7367)***
Jr Hinds Const Serv.......603 496-2344
60 Ridge Rd Tilton NH (03276) ***(G-19907)***
JR Poirier Tool & Machine Co.......603 882-9279
4 Manhattan Dr Amherst NH (03031) ***(G-17570)***
Jr Robert Austin.......207 490-1500
56 Jagger Mill Rd Sanford ME (04073) ***(G-6878)***
Jra, Portsmouth *Also called Journal Roman Archaeology LLC* ***(G-20926)***
Jrb Associates Inc.......401 351-8693
2 2nd Ave Cranston RI (02910) ***(G-20247)***
Jrk Precision Machine.......413 789-7200
25 Century St Agawam MA (01001) ***(G-7436)***
Jrni Inc.......857 305-6477
179 Lincoln St Boston MA (02111) ***(G-8642)***
JS Industries.......860 928-0786
526 Quaddick Rd Thompson CT (06277) ***(G-4534)***
JS International Inc.......508 675-4722
485 Commerce Dr Fall River MA (02720) ***(G-10718)***
JS McCarthy Co Inc (PA).......207 622-6241
15 Darin Dr Augusta ME (04330) ***(G-5609)***
JS McCarthy Co Inc.......203 355-7600
652 Glenbrook Rd 4-101 Stamford CT (06906) ***(G-4233)***
Js Pallet Co Inc.......401 723-0223
60 Lockbridge St Pawtucket RI (02860) ***(G-20850)***
Jsi Medical Systems Corp.......917 472-5022
1 Boston Pl Ste 2600 Boston MA (02108) ***(G-8643)***
Jsi Quality Cabinetry, Fall River *Also called JS International Inc* ***(G-10718)***
Jsi Store Fixtures Inc (PA).......207 943-5203
140 Park St Milo ME (04463) ***(G-6446)***

Jsp Fabrication Inc 603 826-3868
49 Hammond Rd Charlestown NH (03603) ***(G-17816)***
Jsr Merchandising, Dover *Also called Forward Merch LLC* ***(G-18022)***
Jt Machine Shop, East Douglas *Also called J T Machine Co Inc* ***(G-10427)***
Jtc Precision Swiss Inc 603 935-9830
850 E Indus Pk Dr Ste 1 Manchester NH (03109) ***(G-18853)***
JTL Falcon Title Examiner 978 377-0223
105 Hyatt Ave Haverhill MA (01835) ***(G-11444)***
Jubali, Boston *Also called Life Force Beverages LLC* ***(G-8665)***
Judd Wire Inc (HQ) 413 863-9402
124 Turnpike Rd Turners Falls MA (01376) ***(G-15880)***
Judge Tool & Gage Inc 800 214-5990
555 Lordship Blvd Unit A Stratford CT (06615) ***(G-4426)***
Judge Tool Sales Company, Stratford *Also called Judge Tool & Gage Inc* ***(G-4426)***
Judith Jackson Inc 203 698-3011
1535 E Putnam Ave Apt 406 Old Greenwich CT (06870) ***(G-3311)***
Jules A Gourdeau Inc 978 922-0102
94 Corning St Beverly MA (01915) ***(G-8144)***
Julian Materials LLC 802 875-6564
3643 Vt Route 103 N Chester VT (05143) ***(G-21844)***
Julie Cecchini 413 562-2042
74 Tannery Rd Southwick MA (01077) ***(G-15414)***
Julie Industries Inc (PA) 978 276-0820
2 Dundee Park Dr Ste 302a Andover MA (01810) ***(G-7560)***
Juliet Marine Systems Inc 603 319-8412
101 Shattuck Way Ste 2 Portsmouth NH (03801) ***(G-19582)***
Julima Cheese Inc 978 939-8800
212 Freight Shed Rd Baldwinville MA (01436) ***(G-7944)***
Julius Koch USA Inc 508 995-9565
15 Crooks Way Mattapoisett MA (02739) ***(G-12887)***
Jumbo Donuts 508 278-9977
5 Douglas St Uxbridge MA (01569) ***(G-15922)***
Jumbo Plastics Inc 978 537-7835
218 Willard St Leominster MA (01453) ***(G-12157)***
Jumptap, Boston *Also called Millennial Media Inc* ***(G-8707)***
Junction Frame Shop Inc 802 296-2121
55 S Main St White River Junction VT (05001) ***(G-22641)***
Junes Place 508 533-5037
122 Main St Medway MA (02053) ***(G-12964)***
Juniper Pharmaceuticals Inc (HQ) 617 639-1500
33 Arch St Ste 1000 Boston MA (02110) ***(G-8644)***
Junora Ltd 207 284-4900
16 Pomerleau St Biddeford ME (04005) ***(G-5741)***
Jupiter Communications LLC 475 238-7082
755 1st Ave West Haven CT (06516) ***(G-5127)***
Juriba Limited 617 356-8681
30 Newbury St Boston MA (02116) ***(G-8645)***
Jurman Metrics Inc 203 261-9388
555 Hammertown Rd Monroe CT (06468) ***(G-2405)***
Just Breakfast & Things 860 376-4040
15 River Rd Lisbon CT (06351) ***(G-1943)***
Just Counters 603 627-2027
28 Daniel Plummer Rd # 3 Goffstown NH (03045) ***(G-18205)***
Just Naturals & Company LLC 603 471-0944
5 Cotton Cir Bedford NH (03110) ***(G-17647)***
Just Publications Inc 617 739-5878
8 Alton Pl Ste 2 Brookline MA (02446) ***(G-9207)***
Just Rentals, Brookline *Also called Just Publications Inc* ***(G-9207)***
Just Rewards Inc 603 448-6800
443 Miracle Mile Ste 3 Lebanon NH (03766) ***(G-18626)***
Just Right Awnings & Signs 603 740-8416
7 Industrial Park Dover NH (03820) ***(G-18033)***
Just Soap 413 625-6990
1079 Hawley Rd Ashfield MA (01330) ***(G-7653)***
Justin Jordan 207 628-4123
92 River Rd New Portland ME (04961) ***(G-6474)***
Justleathercom 207 641-8313
1284 N Berwick Rd Wells ME (04090) ***(G-7163)***
Jutras Signs Inc 603 622-2344
30 Harvey Rd Unit 8 Bedford NH (03110) ***(G-17648)***
Jutras Signs & Flags, Bedford *Also called Jutras Signs Inc* ***(G-17648)***
JV Precision Machine Co 203 888-0748
71 Cogwheel Ln Seymour CT (06483) ***(G-3753)***
Jwd Premium Products 617 429-8867
27 W Main St Liberty ME (04949) ***(G-6330)***
K & B Rock Crushing LLC 603 622-1188
20 Commercial Ct Auburn NH (03032) ***(G-17612)***
K & C Industries Inc 508 520-4600
3 Kenwood Cir Franklin MA (02038) ***(G-11059)***
K & D Business Ventures LLC 860 237-1458
39 1/2 Wedgewood Dr Jewett City CT (06351) ***(G-1914)***
K & D Distributing, Windham *Also called K & D Millworks Inc* ***(G-7238)***
K & D Millworks Inc 207 892-5188
7 Danielle Dr Windham ME (04062) ***(G-7238)***
K & E Auto Machine L L C 203 723-7189
628 Prospect St Naugatuck CT (06770) ***(G-2481)***
K & E Plastics Inc 802 375-0011
141 Morse Rd Bennington VT (05201) ***(G-21676)***
K & G Corp 860 643-1133
219 Adams St Manchester CT (06042) ***(G-2015)***
K & K Black Oxide LLC 860 223-1805
50 Peter Ct New Britain CT (06051) ***(G-2546)***
K & K Precision Manufacturing 860 828-7681
54 Clark Dr Ste F East Berlin CT (06023) ***(G-1104)***
K & K Thermoforming Inc 508 764-7700
380 Elm St Southbridge MA (01550) ***(G-15390)***
K & R Machine Co Corp 413 568-9335
99 Springdale Rd Westfield MA (01085) ***(G-16696)***
K & W Machine Works 413 543-3329
146 Verge St Springfield MA (01129) ***(G-15483)***
K & W Webbing Company Inc 401 725-4441
403 Roosevelt Ave Central Falls RI (02863) ***(G-20117)***
K A D Machine & Tool, Chicopee *Also called Kad Machine Inc* ***(G-10036)***
K A F Manufacturing Co Inc 203 324-3012
14 Fahey St Stamford CT (06907) ***(G-4234)***
K A Switch, Milford *Also called Kilo Ampere Switch Corporation* ***(G-2307)***
K A T, East Longmeadow *Also called Alternate Mode Inc* ***(G-10464)***
K and C Plastics Inc 978 537-0605
18 Crawford St Leominster MA (01453) ***(G-12158)***
K and R Precision Grinding 860 505-8030
39 John St New Britain CT (06051) ***(G-2547)***
K B Logging Inc 207 757-8818
3276 Us Route 2 Smyrna Mills ME (04780) ***(G-6993)***
K B Welding, Pembroke *Also called Kevin Bonney* ***(G-14414)***
K F Brick Plant, South Windsor *Also called Redland Brick Inc* ***(G-4007)***
K F Machining 860 292-6466
36 Newberry Rd East Windsor CT (06088) ***(G-1289)***
K H Cornell International Inc 203 392-3660
59 Amity Rd New Haven CT (06515) ***(G-2700)***
K Int L Woodworking 781 440-0512
59 Earle St Norwood MA (02062) ***(G-14168)***
K K Welding Inc 617 361-1780
107 Providence St Hyde Park MA (02136) ***(G-11871)***
K L Mason & Sons Inc 207 224-7628
Rr 4 North Turner ME (04266) ***(G-6515)***
K M C Bearings, West Greenwich *Also called Kmc Inc* ***(G-21460)***
K M Morin Logging Inc 207 399-8835
749 Hinckley Rd Clinton ME (04927) ***(G-5915)***
K M T Machining 508 529-6953
41 Grove St Upton MA (01568) ***(G-15907)***
K P I, Wilton *Also called Kimball Physics Inc* ***(G-19981)***
K S E Inc 413 549-5506
665 Amherst Rd Ste 1 Sunderland MA (01375) ***(G-15675)***
K T I, East Windsor *Also called Kin-Therm Inc* ***(G-1291)***
K T I Kin Therm, East Windsor *Also called KTI Inc* ***(G-1294)***
K T I Turbo-Tech Inc 860 623-2511
3 Thompson Rd East Windsor CT (06088) ***(G-1290)***
K V A Electronics 978 262-2264
77 Alexander Rd Ste 1 Billerica MA (01821) ***(G-8260)***
K W Aggregates 207 452-8888
65 Bull Ring Rd Denmark ME (04022) ***(G-5950)***
K W Bristol Co Inc 508 699-4742
4 Bruce Ave North Attleboro MA (02760) ***(G-13760)***
K W Griffen Company 203 846-1923
100 Pearl St Norwalk CT (06850) ***(G-3183)***
K&H Group Inc 802 442-5455
473 Bowen Rd Bennington VT (05201) ***(G-21677)***
K&M/Nordic Co Inc 401 431-5150
5 Tripps Ln Riverside RI (02915) ***(G-21171)***
K-Tec LLC 860 283-8875
33 River St Ste 2 Thomaston CT (06787) ***(G-4507)***
K-Tech International 860 489-9399
56 Ella Grasso Ave Torrington CT (06790) ***(G-4584)***
K2w LLC 617 818-2613
30 Grant St Waltham MA (02453) ***(G-16136)***
K6 Manufacturing Inc 603 888-4669
15 Macdonald Dr Nashua NH (03062) ***(G-19192)***
Kabinet Korner Inc 781 324-9600
212 Maplewood St Malden MA (02148) ***(G-12574)***
Kables and Konnector Services 978 897-4852
13 Vernon St Maynard MA (01754) ***(G-12899)***
Kacerguis Farms Inc 203 405-1202
78 Crane Hollow Rd Bethlehem CT (06751) ***(G-197)***
Kad Machine Inc 413 538-8684
28 Holgate Ave Chicopee MA (01020) ***(G-10036)***
Kadant Fibergen Inc (HQ) 781 275-3600
8 Alfred Cir Bedford MA (01730) ***(G-7986)***
Kadant Inc 508 791-8171
35 Sword St Auburn MA (01501) ***(G-7840)***
Kadant Inc (PA) 978 776-2000
1 Technology Park Dr # 210 Westford MA (01886) ***(G-16774)***
Kadant Inc 508 791-8171
35 Sword St Auburn MA (01501) ***(G-7841)***
Kadmon Corporation LLC 724 778-6125
55 Cambrdge Pkwy Ste 300e Cambridge MA (02142) ***(G-9523)***
Kady International, Scarborough *Also called Kritzer Industries Inc* ***(G-6930)***

ALPHABETIC

Kafa Group LLC...475 275-0090
800 Union Ave Bridgeport CT (06607) ***(G-438)***
Kahla Porcelain USA, Boston *Also called Reach Distribution Inc* ***(G-8811)***
Kahn Industries Inc...860 529-8643
885 Wells Rd Wethersfield CT (06109) ***(G-5252)***
Kahr Arms Inc...508 635-1414
130 Goddard Memorial Dr Worcester MA (01603) ***(G-17398)***
Kal-Lite Division, Bow *Also called Kalwall Corporation* ***(G-17718)***
Kala Pharmaceuticals Inc...781 996-5252
490 Arsenal Way Ste 120 Watertown MA (02472) ***(G-16293)***
Kaleido Biosciences Inc (PA)...617 674-9000
65 Hayden Ave Lexington MA (02421) ***(G-12234)***
Kalion Inc...617 698-2113
92 Elm St Milton MA (02186) ***(G-13193)***
Kalman Electric Motors Inc...781 341-4900
471 Page St Stoughton MA (02072) ***(G-15600)***
Kalow Technologies LLC...802 775-4633
238 Innovation Dr North Clarendon VT (05759) ***(G-22217)***
Kalvista Pharmaceuticals Inc (PA)...857 999-0075
55 Cambrdge Pkwy Ste 901e Cambridge MA (02142) ***(G-9524)***
Kalwall Corporation (PA)...603 627-3861
1111 Candia Rd Manchester NH (03109) ***(G-18854)***
Kalwall Corporation...603 224-6881
40 River Rd Bow NH (03304) ***(G-17718)***
Kam Weld Technologies, Norwood *Also called Kamweld Technologies Inc* ***(G-14169)***
Kaman Aerospace Corporation (HQ)...860 242-4461
1332 Blue Hills Ave Bloomfield CT (06002) ***(G-230)***
Kaman Aerospace Corporation...860 242-4461
30 Old Windsor Rd Bloomfield CT (06002) ***(G-231)***
Kaman Aerospace Corporation...860 242-4461
30 Old Windsor Rd Bloomfield CT (06002) ***(G-232)***
Kaman Aerospace Corporation...860 632-1000
217 Smith St Middletown CT (06457) ***(G-2195)***
Kaman Aerospace Group Inc (HQ)...860 243-7100
1332 Blue Hills Ave Bloomfield CT (06002) ***(G-233)***
Kaman Automation, Inc., Bloomfield *Also called Ruby Automation LLC* ***(G-258)***
Kaman Composites - Vermont Inc...802 442-9964
25 Performance Dr Bennington VT (05201) ***(G-21678)***
Kaman Corporation (PA)...860 243-7100
1332 Blue Hills Ave Bloomfield CT (06002) ***(G-234)***
Kaman Corporation...860 632-1000
217 Smith St Middletown CT (06457) ***(G-2196)***
Kaman Fluid Power, LLC, Bloomfield *Also called Ruby Fluid Power LLC* ***(G-259)***
Kaman Precision Products Inc...860 632-1000
217 Smith St Middletown CT (06457) ***(G-2197)***
Kamatics Corporation (HQ)...860 243-9704
1330 Blue Hills Ave Bloomfield CT (06002) ***(G-235)***
Kamatics Corporation...860 243-7230
1331 Blue Hills Ave Bloomfield CT (06002) ***(G-236)***
Kamel Peripherals Inc (PA)...508 435-7771
88a Elm St Ste 7 Hopkinton MA (01748) ***(G-11724)***
Kaminario Inc (PA)...877 982-2555
75 2nd Ave Ste 620 Needham Heights MA (02494) ***(G-13335)***
Kammetal Inc (PA)...718 722-9991
300 Great Hill Rd Naugatuck CT (06770) ***(G-2482)***
Kamrowski Metal Refinishing, Framingham *Also called Kamrowski Refinishing Co Inc* ***(G-10975)***
Kamrowski Metal Refinishing...508 877-0367
80 K St Boston MA (02127) ***(G-8646)***
Kamrowski Refinishing Co Inc...508 877-0367
12 Bradford Rd Framingham MA (01701) ***(G-10975)***
Kamweld Technologies Inc...781 762-6922
90 Access Rd Norwood MA (02062) ***(G-14169)***
Kan Pak LLC...203 933-6631
425 Main St N Southbury CT (06488) ***(G-4029)***
Kana Software Inc...650 614-8300
10 Corporate Dr Ste 2206 Bedford NH (03110) ***(G-17649)***
Kangas Inc...207 635-3745
51 New Portland Rd North Anson ME (04958) ***(G-6503)***
Kanguru Solutions, Millis *Also called Interactive Media Corp* ***(G-13184)***
Kantahdin Welding...207 528-2924
79 Potato Row Patten ME (04765) ***(G-6578)***
Kanu Inc...603 437-6311
33 Londonderry Rd Unit 12 Londonderry NH (03053) ***(G-18706)***
Kanzaki Specialty Papers Inc (HQ)...413 967-6204
20 Cummings St Ware MA (01082) ***(G-16235)***
Kapcom LLC...203 891-5112
86 John St East Haven CT (06513) ***(G-1253)***
Kappa Sails LLC...860 399-8899
25 Whippoorwill Dr Gales Ferry CT (06335) ***(G-1527)***
Kapson Printing Service Inc...617 265-2543
10 Winter St Dorchester MA (02122) ***(G-10345)***
Kapstone Paper and Packg Corp...860 928-2211
25 Intervale St Putnam CT (06260) ***(G-3619)***
Karas Engineering Co Inc...860 355-3153
20 Old Route 7 Plz New Milford CT (06776) ***(G-2809)***
Karavas Fashions Ltd...203 866-4000
17 Wall St Norwalk CT (06850) ***(G-3184)***
Karger S Publishers Inc...860 675-7834
26 W Avon Rd Unionville CT (06085) ***(G-4657)***
Karl Gschwind Machineworks LLC...603 434-4211
6 Tinkham Ave Derry NH (03038) ***(G-17984)***
Karl Stetson Associates LLC...860 742-8414
2060 South St Coventry CT (06238) ***(G-834)***
Karl Storz Endovision Inc...508 248-9011
91 Carpenter Hill Rd Charlton MA (01507) ***(G-9852)***
Karls Boat Shop Inc...508 432-4488
50 Great Western Rd Harwich MA (02645) ***(G-11395)***
Karuna Therapeutics Inc...857 449-2244
33 Arch St Ste 3110 Boston MA (02110) ***(G-8647)***
Karyopharm Therapeutics Inc (PA)...617 658-0600
85 Wells Ave Fl 2 Newton MA (02459) ***(G-13606)***
Kasalis Inc...781 273-6200
11 North Ave Burlington MA (01803) ***(G-9291)***
Kase Printing Inc...603 883-9223
13 Hampshire Dr Ste 12 Hudson NH (03051) ***(G-18405)***
Kasheta Power Equipment...860 528-8421
1275 John Fitch Blvd South Windsor CT (06074) ***(G-3987)***
Kasi Infrared, Newport *Also called R Filion Manufacturing Inc* ***(G-19355)***
Kasper, Clinton *Also called Nine West Holdings Inc* ***(G-791)***
Katahdin Cedar Log Homes, Oakfield *Also called Katahdin Forest Products Co* ***(G-6527)***
Katahdin Forest Products Co (PA)...800 845-4533
205 Smyrna Rd Oakfield ME (04763) ***(G-6527)***
Katahdin Hill Co...781 862-7566
29 Marrett St Lexington MA (02421) ***(G-12235)***
Katahdin Industries Inc (PA)...781 329-1420
51 Parmenter Rd Hudson MA (01749) ***(G-11781)***
Katahdin Regional Dev Corp...207 447-6913
217 Penobscot Ave Millinocket ME (04462) ***(G-6441)***
Katahdin Welding, Patten *Also called Kantahdin Welding* ***(G-6578)***
Katalyst Kombucha LLC...413 773-9700
324 Wells St Greenfield MA (01301) ***(G-11265)***
Kate's Canvas Works, Gloucester *Also called Katherine McAloon* ***(G-11194)***
Kate's Creamery, Kennebunkport *Also called Kates Homemade Butter Inc* ***(G-6246)***
Kates Homemade Butter Inc...207 934-5134
24 Dairy Ln Kennebunkport ME (04046) ***(G-6246)***
Katherine McAloon...978 525-2223
32 Lexington Ave Gloucester MA (01930) ***(G-11194)***
Kathy Clark...508 655-3666
37 Oak Knoll Rd Natick MA (01760) ***(G-13263)***
Katona Bakery LLC...203 337-5349
1189 Post Rd Ste 3b Fairfield CT (06824) ***(G-1440)***
Katz Eye Optics...413 743-2523
14 Greenway Ln Greenfield MA (01301) ***(G-11266)***
Kav Machine Company Inc...603 642-5251
7 Orchard Ln East Kingston NH (03827) ***(G-18087)***
Kay Gee Sign and Graphics, Auburn *Also called Visimark Inc* ***(G-7851)***
Kay Gee Sign and Graphics Co, Worcester *Also called New England Sign Group Inc* ***(G-17432)***
Kayaku Advanced Materials Inc (PA)...617 965-5511
200 Flanders Rd Westborough MA (01581) ***(G-16629)***
Kayaku Advanced Materials Inc...617 965-5511
20 Ossipee Rd Newton MA (02464) ***(G-13607)***
Kaycee Group...603 505-5754
21 Bear Meadow Rd Londonderry NH (03053) ***(G-18707)***
Kayem Foods Inc (PA)...781 933-3115
75 Arlington St Chelsea MA (02150) ***(G-9957)***
Kayjay Foods Inc...978 833-0728
119 Patriots Rd East Templeton MA (01438) ***(G-10519)***
Kaytec Inc...802 848-7010
1 Memorial Dr Richford VT (05476) ***(G-22307)***
KB Custom Stair Builders Inc...203 234-0836
101 Powdered Metal Rd # 1 North Haven CT (06473) ***(G-3037)***
KB Logging, Smyrna Mills *Also called K B Logging Inc* ***(G-6993)***
Kbc Electronics Inc...203 298-9654
273 Pepes Farm Rd Milford CT (06460) ***(G-2306)***
Kbioscience LLC...978 232-9430
100 Cummings Ctr Ste 420h Beverly MA (01915) ***(G-8145)***
Kbj Manufacturing Inc...860 585-7257
137 Stafford Ave Bristol CT (06010) ***(G-574)***
Kbs Building Systems Inc...207 739-2222
41 Main St South Paris ME (04281) ***(G-7012)***
Kbs Homes, South Paris *Also called Modular Fun I Inc* ***(G-7014)***
Kc Crafts LLC...860 426-9797
384 Old Turnpike Rd Plantsville CT (06479) ***(G-3535)***
Kc Precision Machining LLC...978 356-8900
23 Old Right Rd Unit 1 Ipswich MA (01938) ***(G-11926)***
Kcb Solutions LLC...978 425-0400
900 Mount Laurel Cir Shirley MA (01464) ***(G-15088)***
Kcm Oil...802 447-7371
2155 East Rd Shaftsbury VT (05262) ***(G-22403)***
Kco Numet Inc...203 375-4995
235 Edison Rd Orange CT (06477) ***(G-3367)***
Kdg, Seymour *Also called Kinetic Development Group LLC* ***(G-3754)***
Kdo LLC...508 802-1347
8 Broadway Ave Taunton MA (02780) ***(G-15761)***

Ke Printing & Graphics, Canton *Also called Keating Communication Group* ***(G-9749)***
Kearflex Engineering Company 401 781-4900
66 Cypress St Warwick RI (02888) ***(G-21382)***
Kearney-National Inc 401 943-2686
66 Whitecap Dr North Kingstown RI (02852) ***(G-20719)***
Keating Communication Group 781 828-9030
956 Turnpike St Canton MA (02021) ***(G-9749)***
Keating Concrete, Lunenburg *Also called Wakefield Investments Inc* ***(G-12486)***
Keating Wilbert Vault Company 413 543-1226
1840 Boston Rd Wilbraham MA (01095) ***(G-16939)***
Kedron Sugar Makers, South Woodstock *Also called Kendle Enterprises* ***(G-22498)***
Keebler Company 508 520-7223
17 Forge Pkwy Franklin MA (02038) ***(G-11060)***
Keebowil Inc (PA) 603 352-4232
353 West St Keene NH (03431) ***(G-18509)***
Keebowil Inc 802 775-3572
126 Spruce St Rutland VT (05701) ***(G-22342)***
Keefe Piccolo Company Inc 781 369-1626
54 Church St Winchester MA (01890) ***(G-17090)***
Keeling Company Inc 860 349-0916
107 Shore Dr Old Lyme CT (06371) ***(G-3324)***
Keeling's, Old Lyme *Also called Keeling Company Inc* ***(G-3324)***
Keen Woodworking 802 259-2963
2817 Shunpike Rd Mount Holly VT (05758) ***(G-22182)***
Keena Corporation 617 928-3493
21 Barnstable Rd Newton MA (02465) ***(G-13608)***
Keene Bradford Esq PC 781 246-4545
7 Kimball Ln Lynnfield MA (01940) ***(G-12551)***
Keene Gas Corporation 603 352-4134
64 Main St Ste A Keene NH (03431) ***(G-18510)***
Keene Publishing Corporation 603 352-1234
60 West St Keene NH (03431) ***(G-18511)***
Keene Sentinel, Keene *Also called Keene Publishing Corporation* ***(G-18511)***
Keezer Sportswear, Weymouth *Also called Premier Services Inc* ***(G-16898)***
Keith Industrial Group Inc 978 365-5555
104 Sterling St Ste 5 Clinton MA (01510) ***(G-10082)***
Keith's Sports Ltd II, Rutland *Also called Graphic Edge Inc* ***(G-22336)***
Keiver Willard-Lumber Corp 978 462-7193
11 Graf Rd 13 Newburyport MA (01950) ***(G-13503)***
Kel Log Inc (PA) 603 752-2000
743 E Side River Rd Milan NH (03588) ***(G-19040)***
Kel Log Inc 603 752-2000
580 Main St Gorham NH (03581) ***(G-18213)***
Kell-Strom Tool Co Inc (PA) 860 529-6851
214 Church St Wethersfield CT (06109) ***(G-5253)***
Kell-Strom Tool Intl Inc 860 529-6851
214 Church St Wethersfield CT (06109) ***(G-5254)***
Kelleher Marketing, East Windsor *Also called Homeland Fundraising* ***(G-1286)***
Keller Products Incorporated 603 224-5502
164 River Rd Bow NH (03304) ***(G-17719)***
Keller Products Inc 978 264-1911
180 Middlesex St North Chelmsford MA (01863) ***(G-13899)***
Kellerhaus Inc 603 366-4466
259 Endicott St N Laconia NH (03246) ***(G-18569)***
Kelley Bros New England LLC 207 517-4100
4 Delta Dr Ste 3 Westbrook ME (04092) ***(G-7192)***
Kelley Bros New England LLC 603 748-0274
16 Celina Ave Nashua NH (03063) ***(G-19193)***
Kelley Bros New England LLC (HQ) 603 881-5559
17 Hampshire Dr Ste 20 Hudson NH (03051) ***(G-18406)***
Kelley Bros New England LLC 802 865-5133
87 Holly Ct Williston VT (05495) ***(G-22675)***
Kelley Direct Solutions, Portsmouth *Also called Kelley Solutions Inc* ***(G-19583)***
Kelley Metal Corp 401 434-8795
115 Valley St East Providence RI (02914) ***(G-20426)***
Kelley Solutions Inc 603 431-3881
210 West Rd Unit 7 Portsmouth NH (03801) ***(G-19583)***
Kelley Wood Products Inc 978 345-7531
85 River St Fitchburg MA (01420) ***(G-10830)***
Kellogg Bros Inc 413 569-6029
377 N Loomis St Southwick MA (01077) ***(G-15415)***
Kellogg Company 860 665-9920
52 Hollow Tree Ln Newington CT (06111) ***(G-2875)***
Kellogg Hardwoods Inc 203 797-1992
11 Diamond Ave Bethel CT (06801) ***(G-166)***
Kellsport Industries Inc 508 646-0855
22 Boomer St Fall River MA (02720) ***(G-10719)***
Kelly Lumber Sales Inc 207 435-4950
101 Brunswick St Old Town ME (04468) ***(G-6542)***
Kelly Manufacturing Company 603 786-9933
106 Water St Rumney NH (03266) ***(G-19697)***
Kelly Trucking, Gorham *Also called Kel Log Inc* ***(G-18213)***
Kelsey Mfg Division, East Berlin *Also called Finishers Technology Corp* ***(G-1101)***
Keltron Corporation (HQ) 781 894-8710
101 1st Ave Ste 4a Waltham MA (02451) ***(G-16137)***
Kelyniam Global Inc 800 280-8192
97 River Rd Ste A Collinsville CT (06019) ***(G-815)***
Kemby Manufacturing 860 582-2850
56 E Orchard St Terryville CT (06786) ***(G-4483)***
Kemp Technologies Inc 631 418-8407
7 Virginia Dr Rochdale MA (01542) ***(G-14781)***
Kemper Manufacturing Corp 203 934-1600
5 Clinton Pl West Haven CT (06516) ***(G-5128)***
Kemtuff, Williston *Also called Gds Manufacturing Company* ***(G-22669)***
Ken-Labs, Higganum *Also called Kenyon Laboratories LLC* ***(G-1903)***
Kenco Printing 781 391-9500
24b Rockingham St Lowell MA (01852) ***(G-12387)***
Kendall Press, Cambridge *Also called M & C Press Inc* ***(G-9541)***
Kendall Productions 617 661-0402
26 Cpl Mcternan St 2 Cambridge MA (02139) ***(G-9525)***
Kendle Enterprises 802 457-3015
109 Kendle Rd South Woodstock VT (05071) ***(G-22498)***
Kenexa Brassring Inc 781 530-5000
550 King St Littleton MA (01460) ***(G-12312)***
Kenexa Compensation Inc (HQ) 877 971-9171
160 Gould St Needham MA (02494) ***(G-13303)***
Kennametal Inc 802 626-3331
34 Sanderson St Greenfield MA (01301) ***(G-11267)***
Kennebec Cabinet Company, Bath *Also called Kennebec Company* ***(G-5679)***
Kennebec Cabinetry Inc 207 442-0813
37 Wing Farm Pkwy Bath ME (04530) ***(G-5678)***
Kennebec Company 207 443-2131
1 Front St Ste 3 Bath ME (04530) ***(G-5679)***
Kennebec Company, The, Bath *Also called Kennebec Cabinetry Inc* ***(G-5678)***
Kennebec Marine Company 207 773-0392
162 Spurwink Rd Scarborough ME (04074) ***(G-6929)***
Kennebec Technologies 207 626-0188
150 Church Hill Rd Augusta ME (04330) ***(G-5610)***
Kennebunkport Brewing Company, Kennebunk *Also called Ashleigh Inc* ***(G-6228)***
Kennebunkport Pie Company LLC 207 205-4466
40 Maine St Ste 124 Kennebunkport ME (04046) ***(G-6247)***
Kennedy Incorporated 401 295-7800
21 Circuit Dr North Kingstown RI (02852) ***(G-20720)***
Kennedy Gustafson and Cole Inc 860 828-2594
100 White Oak Dr Berlin CT (06037) ***(G-90)***
Kennedy Information LLC 603 357-8100
24 Railroad St Keene NH (03431) ***(G-18512)***
Kennedy Sheet Metal Inc 781 331-7764
1319 Pleasant St East Weymouth MA (02189) ***(G-10543)***
Kenneth Crosby Co Inc 508 497-0048
103 South St Hopkinton MA (01748) ***(G-11725)***
Kenneth Leroux 860 769-9800
105 Filley St Unit C Bloomfield CT (06002) ***(G-237)***
Kenneth Lynch & Sons Inc 203 762-8363
114 Willenbrock Rd Oxford CT (06478) ***(G-3411)***
Kenneth R Carson 860 247-2707
34 Cole St Manchester CT (06042) ***(G-2016)***
Kennetron Inc 508 828-9363
103 Old Colony Ave Unit 3 East Taunton MA (02718) ***(G-10515)***
Kenney Manufacturing Company (PA) 401 739-2200
1000 Jefferson Blvd Warwick RI (02886) ***(G-21383)***
Kennison Machine Company, Rockland *Also called Kenniston Machines* ***(G-6801)***
Kenniston Machines 207 594-7810
30 Moran Dr Rockland ME (04841) ***(G-6801)***
Keno Graphic Services Inc 203 925-7722
1 Parrott Dr Ste 100 Shelton CT (06484) ***(G-3822)***
Kenoco Inc 207 620-7260
347 Maine Ave Farmingdale ME (04344) ***(G-6039)***
Kens Foods Inc (PA) 508 229-1100
1 Dangelo Dr Marlborough MA (01752) ***(G-12782)***
Kensco Inc (PA) 203 734-8827
41 Clifton Ave Ansonia CT (06401) ***(G-20)***
Kensington Glass and Frmng Co 860 828-9428
124 Woodlawn Rd Berlin CT (06037) ***(G-91)***
Kensington Group Incorporated 603 926-6742
113 Lafayette Rd Hampton Falls NH (03844) ***(G-18283)***
Kensington Welding & Trlr Co 860 828-3564
1114 Farmington Ave Kensington CT (06037) ***(G-1918)***
Kensol-Franklin Inc 508 528-2000
842 Union St Ste 1 Franklin MA (02038) ***(G-11061)***
Kent Billings LLC 860 659-1104
320 Spring Street Ext Glastonbury CT (06033) ***(G-1561)***
Kent County Daily Times 401 789-9744
1353 Main St West Warwick RI (02893) ***(G-21498)***
Kent Fabrications Inc 339 244-4533
171 Mattakeesett St Pembroke MA (02359) ***(G-14413)***
Kent Falls Brewing Company 860 398-9645
33 Camps Rd Kent CT (06757) ***(G-1923)***
Kent Nutrition Group Inc 207 622-1530
10 Dalton Rd Augusta ME (04330) ***(G-5611)***
Kent Nutrition Group Inc 802 848-7718
1 Webster St Richford VT (05476) ***(G-22308)***
Kent Nutrition Group Inc 802 247-9599
57 Alta Woods Brandon VT (05733) ***(G-21709)***
Kent Nutrition Group Inc 207 892-9411
43 Main St Windham ME (04062) ***(G-7239)***
Kent Nutrition Group Inc 603 437-3400
15 Buttrick Rd Londonderry NH (03053) ***(G-18708)***

ALPHABETIC

Kent Pearce...508 295-3791
3039 Cranberry Hwy East Wareham MA (02538) ***(G-10531)***
Kent's Welding & Radiator Svc, East Wareham *Also called Kent Pearce* ***(G-10531)***
Kentek Corporation...603 223-4900
32 Broadway St Pittsfield NH (03263) ***(G-19502)***
Kentico Software LLC...866 328-8998
15 Constitution Dr Ste 2g Bedford NH (03110) ***(G-17650)***
Kentron Technologies Inc...978 988-9100
155 West St Ste 10 Wilmington MA (01887) ***(G-17011)***
Kenway Composites, Augusta *Also called Cpk Manufacturing LLC* ***(G-5606)***
Kenya Coffee and Tea Import, Lowell *Also called Batian Peak Coffee* ***(G-12351)***
Kenyon Composites...617 803-3198
321 Western Ave Gloucester MA (01930) ***(G-11195)***
Kenyon Industries Inc...401 364-7761
36 Sherman Ave Kenyon RI (02836) ***(G-20548)***
Kenyon International Inc...860 664-4906
8 Heritage Park Rd Clinton CT (06413) ***(G-789)***
Kenyon Laboratories LLC...860 345-2097
12 Scovil Rd Higganum CT (06441) ***(G-1903)***
Kenyon Woodworking Inc...617 524-6883
179 Boylston St Jamaica Plain MA (02130) ***(G-11945)***
Keo Milling Cutters LLC...800 523-5233
273 Main St Athol MA (01331) ***(G-7688)***
Kerb Inc...401 491-9595
301 Promenade St Providence RI (02908) ***(G-21047)***
Kerber Saw Mill...802 257-0614
3550 Coolidge Hwy Guilford VT (05301) ***(G-22007)***
Kerfoot Technologies Inc...508 539-3002
766 Falmouth Rd Ste B12 Mashpee MA (02649) ***(G-12881)***
Kerigans Fuel Inc...203 334-3646
258 Dekalb Ave Bridgeport CT (06607) ***(G-439)***
Kerins Sign Service...802 223-0357
E Montpelier Rd Rr 2 Montpelier VT (05602) ***(G-22151)***
Kerissa Creations Inc...401 949-3700
15 Lark Industrial Pkwy E Greenville RI (02828) ***(G-20470)***
Kerite, Seymour *Also called Marmon Utility LLC* ***(G-3755)***
Kerk Motion Products, Milford *Also called Haydon Kerk Mtion Slutions Inc* ***(G-19058)***
Kernco Inc...978 777-1956
28 Harbor St Danvers MA (01923) ***(G-10229)***
Kerr Leathers Inc...978 852-0660
63 Jefferson Ave Salem MA (01970) ***(G-14927)***
Kerrigan Paper Products Inc...978 374-4797
293 Neck Rd Haverhill MA (01835) ***(G-11445)***
Kerrin Graphics & Printing...508 765-1339
42 W Dudley Rd Dudley MA (01571) ***(G-10379)***
Kerry Inc...207 775-7060
40 Quarry Rd Ste 200 Portland ME (04103) ***(G-6677)***
Kerry R Wood...203 221-7780
2 Hideaway Ln Westport CT (06880) ***(G-5205)***
Kershner Sign, South Burlington *Also called R & W Gibson Corp* ***(G-22463)***
Kervick Entreprises, Worcester *Also called Fastcast Consortium Inc* ***(G-17373)***
Kervick Family Foundation Inc...508 853-4500
40 Rockdale St Worcester MA (01606) ***(G-17399)***
Keryx Biopharmaceuticals Inc (HQ)...617 871-2098
245 1st St Cambridge MA (02142) ***(G-9526)***
Kessler Machine Works, Canton *Also called J F Kessler Inc* ***(G-9746)***
Kestrel Health Information Inc...802 482-4000
206 Commerce St Williston VT (05495) ***(G-22676)***
Kestrel Tooling Company...207 721-0609
40 Rymat Rd Topsham ME (04086) ***(G-7090)***
Ketcham Supply Co Inc...508 997-4787
111 Myrtle St New Bedford MA (02740) ***(G-13403)***
Ketcham Traps...508 997-4787
111 Myrtle St New Bedford MA (02740) ***(G-13404)***
Kettle Cuisine LLC (PA)...617 409-1100
330 Lynnway Lynn MA (01901) ***(G-12519)***
Kettlepizza LLC...888 205-1931
1755 Osgood St North Andover MA (01845) ***(G-13714)***
Keurig Dr Pepper Inc...781 575-4033
250 Royall St Canton MA (02021) ***(G-9750)***
Keurig Dr Pepper Inc (PA)...781 418-7000
53 South Ave Burlington MA (01803) ***(G-9292)***
Keurig Green Mountain Inc...781 246-3466
53 South Ave Burlington MA (01803) ***(G-9293)***
Kevin Bonney...781 826-6439
79 Water St Pembroke MA (02359) ***(G-14414)***
Kevin Call...207 884-7786
4206 Union St Levant ME (04456) ***(G-6271)***
Kevin Cradock Woodworking Inc...617 524-2405
119 Business St Hyde Park MA (02136) ***(G-11872)***
Kevin Lyman Roofing Co...508 697-8244
123 Green St Bridgewater MA (02324) ***(G-9081)***
Kevin S Boghigian...603 883-0236
141 Canal St Unit 4 Nashua NH (03064) ***(G-19194)***
Kevins Woodworks LLC...508 989-8692
221 London St Fall River MA (02723) ***(G-10720)***
Kewill Inc (HQ)...978 482-2500
1 Executive Dr Ste 201 Chelmsford MA (01824) ***(G-9908)***
Key Container Corporation (PA)...401 723-2000
21 Campbell St Pawtucket RI (02861) ***(G-20851)***
Key Graphics Inc...401 826-2425
7 Caitlin Ct Kingston RI (02881) ***(G-20551)***
Key Industries...603 369-9634
65 Turnpike Rd Unit B New Ipswich NH (03071) ***(G-19306)***
Key Polymer Corporation...978 683-9411
17 Shepard St Lawrence MA (01843) ***(G-12042)***
Key Polymer Holdings LLC...978 683-9411
17 Shepard St Lawrence MA (01843) ***(G-12043)***
Keylium Inc...781 385-9178
47 Lafayette Ave Hingham MA (02043) ***(G-11500)***
Keynectup Inc...781 325-3414
30 Grove St Wellesley MA (02482) ***(G-16369)***
Keysight Technologies Inc...800 829-4444
40 Shattuck Rd Andover MA (01810) ***(G-7561)***
Keyspin Manufacturing...603 420-8508
21 Continental Blvd Merrimack NH (03054) ***(G-19009)***
Keystone Dental Inc (PA)...781 328-3300
154 Middlesex Tpke Ste 2 Burlington MA (01803) ***(G-9294)***
Keystone Paper & Box Co Inc...860 291-0027
31 Edwin Rd South Windsor CT (06074) ***(G-3988)***
Keystone Precision & Engrg...978 433-8484
16 Lomar Park Ste 3 Pepperell MA (01463) ***(G-14440)***
Keystone Precision Inc...978 433-8484
16 Lomar Park Ste 3 Pepperell MA (01463) ***(G-14441)***
Keystone Press, Manchester *Also called Dr Biron Incorporated* ***(G-18813)***
Keystone Press LLC...603 622-5222
9 Old Falls Rd Manchester NH (03103) ***(G-18768)***
Keystone Printing Ink Co...781 762-6974
180 Kerry Pl Ste C Norwood MA (02062) ***(G-14170)***
Keystone Rv Company...203 367-9847
2660 North Ave Bridgeport CT (06604) ***(G-440)***
Keyway Inc...860 571-9181
3 Wells Rd Wethersfield CT (06109) ***(G-5255)***
Kezaer Trailbrakers, Hiram *Also called Alfred St Germain* ***(G-6193)***
Kgc, Berlin *Also called Kennedy Gustafson and Cole Inc* ***(G-90)***
Khalsa Jot...508 376-6206
368 Village St Millis MA (02054) ***(G-13185)***
Kheops International Inc (PA)...603 237-8188
232 Us Route 3 Stewartstown NH (03576) ***(G-19862)***
Khmerpost USA LLC...978 677-7163
45 Merrimack St Lowell MA (01852) ***(G-12388)***
Khoury Fuel Inc...781 251-0993
386 Main St Melrose MA (02176) ***(G-12984)***
Ki Inc...203 641-5492
342 Cedarwood Dr Orange CT (06477) ***(G-3368)***
Kickemuit Industries LLC...508 675-0594
177 Riverside Ave Somerset MA (02725) ***(G-15145)***
Kicteam Inc...207 514-7030
1130 Minot Ave Auburn ME (04210) ***(G-5574)***
Kidde Fire System, Ashland *Also called Kidde-Fenwal Inc* ***(G-7663)***
Kidde-Fenwal Inc (HQ)...508 881-2000
400 Main St Ashland MA (01721) ***(G-7663)***
Kiddie Bumbper Boats, Newport *Also called Bumper Boats Inc* ***(G-20658)***
Kidpub Press LLC...617 407-2337
433 Smith St North Attleboro MA (02760) ***(G-13761)***
Kids On Block - Vermont Inc...802 860-3349
294 N Winooski Ave # 125 Burlington VT (05401) ***(G-21790)***
Kidsbooks LLC...617 425-0300
569 Boylston St Ste 200 Boston MA (02116) ***(G-8648)***
Kieffer Associates Inc...203 323-3437
86 Wallacks Dr Stamford CT (06902) ***(G-4235)***
Kielb Welding Enterprises...413 734-4544
150 Brookdale Dr Springfield MA (01104) ***(G-15484)***
Kielo America Inc...203 431-3999
163 Branchville Rd Ridgefield CT (06877) ***(G-3671)***
Kilcourse Specialty Products...860 210-2075
46 Old State Rd Ste 3 New Milford CT (06776) ***(G-2810)***
Kilder Corporation...978 663-8800
7 Executive Park Dr North Billerica MA (01862) ***(G-13830)***
Killeen Machine and Tl Co Inc...508 754-1714
33 Hermon St Worcester MA (01610) ***(G-17400)***
Killingly Asphalt Products, Dayville *Also called All States Asphalt Inc* ***(G-1038)***
Killington Ltd...802 422-3333
4763 Killington Rd Killington VT (05751) ***(G-22053)***
Killington Cabinets...802 773-3960
281 Rebecca Ln Killington VT (05751) ***(G-22054)***
Killington Resort & Pico Mtn, Killington *Also called Killington Ltd* ***(G-22053)***
Killoran Contracting Inc...617 298-5248
5 Eager Rd Milton MA (02186) ***(G-13194)***
Kilo Ampere Switch Corporation...203 877-5994
230 Woodmont Rd Ste 27 Milford CT (06460) ***(G-2307)***
Kim's Nail Salon, Stratford *Also called Kims Nail Corporation* ***(G-4428)***
Kimark Specialty Box Company...603 668-1336
34 Beech St Manchester NH (03103) ***(G-18855)***
Kimball Physics Inc...603 878-1616
311 Kimball Hill Rd Wilton NH (03086) ***(G-19981)***
Kimball Wood Products, Wolfeboro *Also called Kimballs Lumber Center LLC* ***(G-20021)***

Kimballs Lumber Center LLC (PA)......603 569-2477
25 Varney Rd Wolfeboro NH (03894) ***(G-20021)***
Kimberly-Clark Corporation......860 210-1602
58 Pickett District Rd New Milford CT (06776) ***(G-2811)***
Kimberly-Clark Corporation......508 520-1355
38 Pawn St Ste 108 Franklin MA (02038) ***(G-11062)***
Kimberly-Clark Corporation......973 986-8454
137 Ryegate Ter Stratford CT (06615) ***(G-4427)***
Kimberly-Clark Corporation......972 281-1200
352 Papermill Rd East Ryegate VT (05042) ***(G-21920)***
Kimchuk Incorporated (PA)......203 790-7800
1 Corporate Dr Ste 1 # 1 Danbury CT (06810) ***(G-943)***
Kimchuk Incorporated......203 798-0799
4 Finance Dr Danbury CT (06810) ***(G-944)***
Kims Nail Corporation......203 380-8608
7365 Main St Ste 11 Stratford CT (06614) ***(G-4428)***
Kimtek Corporation......802 754-9000
326 Industrial Park Ln Orleans VT (05860) ***(G-22248)***
Kin-Therm Inc......860 623-2511
3 Thompson Rd East Windsor CT (06088) ***(G-1291)***
Kinamor Incorporated......203 269-0380
63 N Plains Industrial Rd Wallingford CT (06492) ***(G-4760)***
Kinamor Plastics, Wallingford *Also called Kinamor Incorporated* ***(G-4760)***
Kindelan Woodworking......603 434-3253
179 Rockingham Rd Derry NH (03038) ***(G-17985)***
Kinder Industries Inc......401 253-7076
75 Tupelo St Bristol RI (02809) ***(G-20087)***
Kinderma LLC......860 796-5503
55 Village Pl Glastonbury CT (06033) ***(G-1562)***
Kinderwagon Company......617 256-7599
5 Gooseberry Rd Newport RI (02840) ***(G-20670)***
Kinefac Corporation......508 754-6901
156 Goddard Memorial Dr Worcester MA (01603) ***(G-17401)***
Kinemetrics Inc......978 772-4774
325 Ayer Rd Ste A118 Harvard MA (01451) ***(G-11381)***
Kinepower Company Division, Worcester *Also called Kinefac Corporation* ***(G-17401)***
Kinetic Development Group LLC......203 888-4321
71 Cogwheel Ln Seymour CT (06483) ***(G-3754)***
Kinetic Fuel LLC......508 668-8278
31 Lavender Ln Walpole MA (02081) ***(G-15997)***
Kinetic Instruments Inc......203 743-0080
17 Berkshire Blvd Bethel CT (06801) ***(G-167)***
Kinetic Systems Inc......617 522-8700
20 Arboretum Rd Boston MA (02131) ***(G-8649)***
Kinetic Tool Co Inc......860 627-5882
5 Craftsman Rd Ste 7 East Windsor CT (06088) ***(G-1292)***
Kinex Cappers LLC (PA)......603 883-2400
13 Columbia Dr Unit 4 Amherst NH (03031) ***(G-17571)***
Kinfolk Memorials Inc......802 479-1423
Lowery Rd East Barre VT (05649) ***(G-21912)***
King & Co Architectural Wdwkg, Marlborough *Also called King & Co Architectural Wdwkg* ***(G-18961)***
King & Co Architectural Wdwkg......603 876-4900
8 Roxbury Rd Marlborough NH (03455) ***(G-18961)***
King Fisher Co Inc......978 596-0214
81 Old Ferry Rd Lowell MA (01854) ***(G-12389)***
King Forest Industries Inc (PA)......603 764-5711
53 E Side Rd Wentworth NH (03282) ***(G-19946)***
King Gt Inc......781 562-1554
480 Neponset St Ste 4a Canton MA (02021) ***(G-9751)***
King Kalipers Inc......978 977-4994
58 Pulaski St Ste 21 Peabody MA (01960) ***(G-14347)***
King Koil Northeast, East Windsor *Also called Blue Bell Mattress Company LLC* ***(G-1278)***
King Manufacturing Co Inc......603 532-6455
295 Squantum Rd Jaffrey NH (03452) ***(G-18470)***
King of Covers Inc (PA)......860 379-2427
154 Torrington Rd Winsted CT (06098) ***(G-5415)***
King Printing Company Inc......978 458-2345
181 Industrial Ave E Lowell MA (01852) ***(G-12390)***
Kingdom Pellets LLC......802 747-1093
1105 Route 7b Central North Clarendon VT (05759) ***(G-22218)***
Kingfield Wood Products, Kingfield *Also called Frontier Forge Inc* ***(G-6253)***
Kings Cornr Woodturning Wdwkg......603 529-0063
502 Barnard Hill Rd Weare NH (03281) ***(G-19937)***
Kings Draperies Inc......508 230-0055
17 Davis Ave Brockton MA (02301) ***(G-9159)***
Kingsland Co......860 542-6981
7 Colebrook Rd Norfolk CT (06058) ***(G-2957)***
Kingslide USA Inc......978 475-0120
16 Haverhill St Andover MA (01810) ***(G-7562)***
Kingston Aluminum Foundry Inc......781 585-6631
7 Pembroke St Kingston MA (02364) ***(G-11959)***
Kingston Block Co Inc......781 585-6400
72 Main St Kingston MA (02364) ***(G-11960)***
Kingston Krafts......401 272-0292
15 Industrial Rd Unit 2 Cranston RI (02920) ***(G-20248)***
Kingston Manufacturing Co Inc......781 585-4476
3 Pleasant St Kingston MA (02364) ***(G-11961)***
Kingston Materials, Kingston *Also called Torromeo Industries Inc* ***(G-18546)***
Kingston Wind Independence LLC......781 871-8200
649 Broad St East Weymouth MA (02189) ***(G-10544)***
Kingswood Kitchens Co Inc......203 792-8700
70 Beaver St Danbury CT (06810) ***(G-945)***
Kingswood Press, The, Wolfeboro *Also called Swaffield Enterprises Inc* ***(G-20025)***
Kingswood Sales Inc......603 522-6636
2499 White Mountain Hwy Sanbornville NH (03872) ***(G-19783)***
Kiniksa Pharmaceuticals Corp......781 431-9100
100 Hayden Ave Ste 1 Lexington MA (02421) ***(G-12236)***
Kinne Electric Service Company......603 622-0441
155 Webster St Manchester NH (03104) ***(G-18856)***
Kinoton America Distribution......617 562-0003
8 Goodenough St Boston MA (02135) ***(G-8650)***
Kinross Cashmere, Westwood *Also called Dawson Forte LLP* ***(G-16864)***
Kintai Therapeutics Inc......617 409-7395
26 Landsdowne St Ste 4 Cambridge MA (02139) ***(G-9527)***
Kip Inc......860 677-0272
72 Spring Ln Farmington CT (06032) ***(G-1488)***
Kirby George Jr Paint Co Inc......508 997-9008
163 Mount Vernon St New Bedford MA (02740) ***(G-13405)***
Kirchoff Wohlberg Inc......212 644-2020
897 Boston Post Rd Madison CT (06443) ***(G-1967)***
Kirk Electronics & Plastic......401 467-8585
85 Glen Rd Cranston RI (02920) ***(G-20249)***
Kirkland Newspaper Inc......207 778-2075
187 Wilton Rd Farmington ME (04938) ***(G-6051)***
Kirkwood Direct, Wilmington *Also called Kirkwood Holdings Inc* ***(G-17012)***
Kirkwood Holdings Inc (PA)......978 658-4200
904 Main St Wilmington MA (01887) ***(G-17012)***
Kirstein Per......508 473-9673
158 East St Upton MA (01568) ***(G-15908)***
Kirwan Enterprise LLC......781 834-9500
180 Enterprise Dr Marshfield MA (02050) ***(G-12861)***
Kisers Ortho Prosthetic Serv (PA)......603 357-7666
25 Avon St Keene NH (03431) ***(G-18513)***
Kita Usa Inc......774 331-2265
64 Water St Attleboro MA (02703) ***(G-7756)***
Kitchen Cab Resurfacing LLC......203 334-2857
136 Merriam St Bridgeport CT (06604) ***(G-441)***
Kitchen Center RI Inc......401 640-6514
121 Terrace Ave Pawtucket RI (02860) ***(G-20852)***
Kitchen Kraftsmen......860 616-1240
77 Pierson Ln Ste A Windsor CT (06095) ***(G-5343)***
Kitchen Store, The, Dorset *Also called J K Adams Company Inc* ***(G-21908)***
Kitchens & Bath of Norwood......781 255-1448
520 Boston Providence Norwood MA (02062) ***(G-14171)***
Kitchens By US, East Bridgewater *Also called Kitchens R US Inc* ***(G-10415)***
Kitchens R US Inc......508 378-7474
494 N Bedford St East Bridgewater MA (02333) ***(G-10415)***
Kitewheel LLC......617 447-2138
186 South St Ste 301 Boston MA (02111) ***(G-8651)***
Kiwanis Fndtion Middletown Inc......860 638-8135
340 Chamberlain Hill Rd Middletown CT (06457) ***(G-2198)***
Kiwi Signs & Mar Graphics LLC......732 930-4121
56 Scranton Ave Falmouth MA (02540) ***(G-10794)***
KLA Corporation......802 318-9100
57 Day Ln 20 Williston VT (05495) ***(G-22677)***
KLA Corporation......978 843-7670
60 Glacier Dr Ste 4000 Westwood MA (02090) ***(G-16871)***
KLA Systems Inc......508 359-7361
31 Mill St Assonet MA (02702) ***(G-7683)***
Klauber Brothers, West Warwick *Also called Leavers Lace Corporation* ***(G-21499)***
Klear-Vu Corporation (PA)......508 674-5723
600 Airport Rd Fall River MA (02720) ***(G-10721)***
Kleeberg Sheet Metal Inc......413 589-1854
65 Westover Rd Ludlow MA (01056) ***(G-12470)***
Kleenline LLC......978 463-0827
6 Opportunity Way Rear Newburyport MA (01950) ***(G-13504)***
Kleermail LLC......888 273-3420
30 Newbury St Ste 3 Boston MA (02116) ***(G-8652)***
Klein Design Inc......978 281-5276
99 Sadler St Gloucester MA (01930) ***(G-11196)***
Klein Marine Systems Inc......603 893-6131
11 Klein Dr Salem NH (03079) ***(G-19744)***
Kline Chemistry Laboratory, New Haven *Also called Yale University* ***(G-2759)***
Klitzner Industries Inc......800 621-0161
26 Kirkbrae Dr Lincoln RI (02865) ***(G-20577)***
Klone Lab LLC......978 378-3434
115 Water St Ste A Newburyport MA (01950) ***(G-13505)***
Kluber Lubric North America LP......603 647-4104
32 Industrial Dr Londonderry NH (03053) ***(G-18709)***
Kluber Lubrication N Amer LP......800 447-2238
32 Industrial Dr Londonderry NH (03053) ***(G-18710)***
Kluber Lubrication NA LP (HQ)......603 647-4104
32 Industrial Dr Londonderry NH (03053) ***(G-18711)***
Klx Aerospace Solutions, Stratford *Also called B/E Aerospace Inc* ***(G-4394)***
Klypper Inc......978 987-8548
12 Brush Hill Rd Chelmsford MA (01824) ***(G-9909)***

ALPHABETIC

Km Foods Inc...781 894-7616
47 Graymore Rd Waltham MA (02451) ***(G-16138)***
Km Holding Inc...603 566-2704
120 Derry St Hudson NH (03051) ***(G-18407)***
Kmb International...401 253-6798
8 Robin Dr Bristol RI (02809) ***(G-20088)***
Kmc Inc...401 392-1900
20 Technology Way West Greenwich RI (02817) ***(G-21460)***
KMC Systems Inc...866 742-0442
220 Daniel Webster Hwy Merrimack NH (03054) ***(G-19010)***
Kms Machine Works Inc...508 822-3151
447 Winthrop St Taunton MA (02780) ***(G-15762)***
Knapp Container Inc...203 888-0511
17 Old Turnpike Rd Beacon Falls CT (06403) ***(G-59)***
Knb Design LLC...203 777-6661
91 Shelton Ave New Haven CT (06511) ***(G-2701)***
Knd Machine Co...508 336-5509
61 Blanding Rd Rehoboth MA (02769) ***(G-14752)***
Kneebinding Inc...802 760-3026
782 Mountain Rd Stowe VT (05672) ***(G-22522)***
Kneeland Bros Inc...978 948-3919
51 Wethersfield St Rowley MA (01969) ***(G-14855)***
Knight Inc...203 754-6502
47 Stevens St Waterbury CT (06704) ***(G-4895)***
Knight Industries Inc...802 773-8777
20 Innovation Dr North Clarendon VT (05759) ***(G-22219)***
Knight Kitchens, North Clarendon *Also called Knight Industries Inc* ***(G-22219)***
Knight Machine & Tool Co Inc...413 532-2507
11 Industrial Dr South Hadley MA (01075) ***(G-15305)***
Knight Manufacturing, Waterbury *Also called Knight Inc* ***(G-4895)***
Knight Optical (usa) LLC...401 521-7000
1130 Ten Rod Rd Ste D102 North Kingstown RI (02852) ***(G-20721)***
Knight Underwater Bearing Llc...207 251-0001
2 Knight Ln Cape Neddick ME (03902) ***(G-5880)***
Knight, Jack Sign Co, Hanover *Also called Jack Knight Co* ***(G-11344)***
Knm Holdings LLC...508 229-1400
410 Forest St Ste 3 Marlborough MA (01752) ***(G-12783)***
Knobby Krafters Inc...508 222-7272
129 Bank St Ste 5 Attleboro MA (02703) ***(G-7757)***
Knoll Inc...617 695-0220
281 Summer St Fl 1 Boston MA (02210) ***(G-8653)***
Knoll Inc...860 395-2093
5 Connolly Dr Old Saybrook CT (06475) ***(G-3341)***
Knowledge Management Assoc LLC...781 250-2001
77 Rumford Ave Ste 2 Waltham MA (02453) ***(G-16139)***
Knowlton Machine Company...207 854-8471
5 Sanford Dr Gorham ME (04038) ***(G-6117)***
Knowlton Machine Engineering, Gorham *Also called Knowlton Machine Company* ***(G-6117)***
Knox Enterprises Inc (PA)...203 226-6408
830 Post Rd E Ste 205 Westport CT (06880) ***(G-5206)***
Knox Industries Inc...203 226-6408
830 Post Rd E Ste 205 Westport CT (06880) ***(G-5207)***
Knox Machine Co Inc...207 273-2296
936 Eastern Rd Warren ME (04864) ***(G-7142)***
Koan Biotherapeutics Inc...617 968-7882
15 Laura Rd Waban MA (02468) ***(G-15937)***
Kobyluck Ready-Mix Inc...860 444-9604
24 Industrial Dr Waterford CT (06385) ***(G-4987)***
Kobyluck Sand and Gravel Inc...860 444-9600
24 Industrial Dr Waterford CT (06385) ***(G-4988)***
Koch Industries Inc...207 767-2161
5 Central Ave South Portland ME (04106) ***(G-7031)***
Koch Membrane Systems, Inc., Wilmington *Also called Koch Separation Solutions Inc* ***(G-17013)***
Koch Separation Solutions Inc (HQ)...978 694-7000
850 Main St Wilmington MA (01887) ***(G-17013)***
Kochman Reidt & Haigh Inc...781 573-1500
471 Page St Ste 8 Stoughton MA (02072) ***(G-15601)***
Koda Industries Indiana LLC...781 891-3066
51 Sawyer Rd Ste 420 Waltham MA (02453) ***(G-16140)***
Kodiak Industries LLC...617 839-1298
17 Ciccone Way Billerica MA (01821) ***(G-8261)***
Kodiak Machining Co Inc...978 356-9876
20 Hayward St Ipswich MA (01938) ***(G-11927)***
Koffee Kup Bakery Inc (PA)...802 863-2696
59 Rathe Rd Ste A Colchester VT (05446) ***(G-21870)***
Koffee Kup Bakery Inc...603 225-6149
28 Dunklee Rd Ste 3 Bow NH (03304) ***(G-17720)***
Kohler Mix Specialties LLC...860 666-1511
100 Milk Ln Newington CT (06111) ***(G-2876)***
Kohv Eyewear, Meredith *Also called Sibs LLC* ***(G-18979)***
Kokos Machine Co, Dudley *Also called Ryszard A Kokosinski* ***(G-10383)***
Kol LLC...203 393-2924
12 Cassway Rd Woodbridge CT (06525) ***(G-5470)***
Kol-Tar Inc...781 871-0883
699 Adams St Abington MA (02351) ***(G-7326)***
Kollsman Inc (HQ)...603 889-2500
220 Daniel Webster Hwy Merrimack NH (03054) ***(G-19011)***
Kolltan Pharmaceuticals Inc (HQ)...203 773-3000
300 George St Ste 530 New Haven CT (06511) ***(G-2702)***
Komor Mfg Co, Rehoboth *Also called J & K Sales Company Inc* ***(G-14751)***
Komtek Technologies, Worcester *Also called Kt Acquisition LLC* ***(G-17402)***
Kondelin Associates Inc (HQ)...978 281-3663
10 Centennial Dr Ste 105 Peabody MA (01960) ***(G-14348)***
Konecranes Inc...978 256-5525
25 Industrial Ave Ste 1 Chelmsford MA (01824) ***(G-9910)***
Kongsberg Actuation (HQ)...860 668-1285
1 Firestone Dr Suffield CT (06078) ***(G-4464)***
Kongsberg Automotive, Suffield *Also called Kongsberg Actuation* ***(G-4464)***
Kongsberg Dgtal Simulation Inc...860 405-2300
170 Leonard Dr Groton CT (06340) ***(G-1678)***
Konneco International LLC...401 767-3690
34 Georgianna Ave North Smithfield RI (02896) ***(G-20788)***
Konnext Inc...978 567-0800
7 Kane Industrial Dr # 2 Hudson MA (01749) ***(G-11782)***
Konrad Prefab LLC...802 885-6780
260 Clinton St Springfield VT (05156) ***(G-22504)***
Kool Ink LLC...860 242-0303
21 Old Windsor Rd Ste B Bloomfield CT (06002) ***(G-238)***
Koolart USA, Haddam *Also called Moonlight Media LLC* ***(G-1727)***
Kopin Corporation (PA)...508 870-5959
125 North Dr Westborough MA (01581) ***(G-16630)***
Kopin Display Corporation (PA)...508 870-5959
125 North Dr Westborough MA (01581) ***(G-16631)***
Koplow Games Inc...617 482-4011
369 Congress St Fl 5 Boston MA (02210) ***(G-8654)***
Korber Hats, Fall River *Also called Whole Earth Hat Co Inc* ***(G-10783)***
Korner Bagel Partnership...508 336-5204
23 Circle Dr Seekonk MA (02771) ***(G-15025)***
Korner Kare...860 491-3731
175 North St Goshen CT (06756) ***(G-1584)***
Korolath of New England Inc (HQ)...781 933-6004
310 Salem St Woburn MA (01801) ***(G-17211)***
Korolath of New England Inc...978 562-7366
498 River Rd Hudson MA (01749) ***(G-11783)***
Kosco Oil, Oxford *Also called Butlers Rv Services Corp* ***(G-14255)***
Koss Industries Inc...802 863-5004
191 Loomis St Burlington VT (05401) ***(G-21791)***
Koster Keunen Inc...860 945-3333
1021 Echo Lake Rd Watertown CT (06795) ***(G-5012)***
Koster Keunen LLC (PA)...860 945-3333
1021 Echo Lake Rd Watertown CT (06795) ***(G-5013)***
Koster Keunen Mfg Inc...860 945-3333
1021 Echo Lake Rd Watertown CT (06795) ***(G-5014)***
Kovacs Machine and Tool Co...203 269-4949
50 N Plains Industrial Rd Wallingford CT (06492) ***(G-4761)***
Kovil Manufacturing LLC...203 699-9425
1486 Highland Ave Ste 2 Cheshire CT (06410) ***(G-741)***
Kowalski Furinture Design, Spencer *Also called Robert Kowalski* ***(G-15435)***
Kp Building Products Inc...866 850-4447
402 Boyer Cir Williston VT (05495) ***(G-22678)***
KPM Analytics Inc (PA)...774 462-6700
113 Cedar St Ste 1 Milford MA (01757) ***(G-13122)***
KPM Analytics North Amer Corp (PA)...508 473-9901
113 Cedar St Ste 3 Milford MA (01757) ***(G-13123)***
KPM Technologies Inc...617 721-8770
77 Main St Andover MA (01810) ***(G-7563)***
Kpt Company Inc...978 558-4009
14 Clarendon St Malden MA (02148) ***(G-12575)***
Kraft Foods, Woburn *Also called Kraft Heinz Foods Company* ***(G-17212)***
Kraft Foods, Mansfield *Also called Kraft Heinz Foods Company* ***(G-12640)***
Kraft Group LLC (PA)...508 384-4230
1 Patriot Pl Foxboro MA (02035) ***(G-10890)***
Kraft Heinz Foods Company...781 933-2800
1 Hill St Woburn MA (01801) ***(G-17212)***
Kraft Heinz Foods Company...508 763-3311
111 Forbes Blvd Mansfield MA (02048) ***(G-12640)***
Krafty Kakes Inc...203 284-0299
39 N Plains Industrial Rd E Wallingford CT (06492) ***(G-4762)***
Kramer Printing Company Inc...203 933-5416
270 Front Ave West Haven CT (06516) ***(G-5129)***
Krav Maga Southington, Plantsville *Also called Ladrdefense LLC* ***(G-3536)***
Kravet Inc...617 428-0370
1 Design Center Pl # 300 Boston MA (02210) ***(G-8655)***
Krazy Korner Bagel & Deli, Seekonk *Also called Korner Bagel Partnership* ***(G-15025)***
Kreate & Print Inc...781 255-0505
14 Central St Norwood MA (02062) ***(G-14172)***
Krell Industries LLC...203 298-4000
45 Connair Rd Ste 1 Orange CT (06477) ***(G-3369)***
Krest Products Corp...978 537-1244
707 Lancaster St Leominster MA (01453) ***(G-12159)***
Kretetek Industries LLC...603 402-3073
66 River Rd Hudson NH (03051) ***(G-18408)***
Kritzer Industries Inc...207 883-4141
30 Parkway Dr Scarborough ME (04074) ***(G-6930)***
Krl Electronics, Manchester *Also called Bantry Components Inc* ***(G-18785)***

Krofta Technologies LLC (HQ) 413 236-5634
401 South St Dalton MA (01226) ***(G-10179)***
Krohn-Hite Corporation 508 580-1660
15 Jonathan Dr Ste 4 Brockton MA (02301) ***(G-9160)***
Kronos Acquisition Corporation (HQ) 978 250-9800
900 Chelmsford St # 312 Lowell MA (01851) ***(G-12391)***
Kronos Incorporated 978 947-2990
200 West St Ste 4a Waltham MA (02451) ***(G-16141)***
Kronos Incorporated (HQ) 978 250-9800
900 Chelmsford St # 312 Lowell MA (01851) ***(G-12392)***
Kronos International MGT LLC 978 250-9800
900 Chelmsford St # 312 Lowell MA (01851) ***(G-12393)***
Kronos Parent Corporation (PA) 978 250-9800
900 Chelmsford St # 312 Lowell MA (01851) ***(G-12394)***
Kronos Solutions Inc (HQ) 978 805-9971
900 Chelmsford St # 312 Lowell MA (01851) ***(G-12395)***
Krueger International Inc 617 542-4043
109 Broad St Boston MA (02110) ***(G-8656)***
KS Manufacturing Inc 508 427-5727
9 Sawyer Ter Allston MA (02134) ***(G-7468)***
Ksaria Corporation (PA) 866 457-2742
300 Griffin Brook Dr Methuen MA (01844) ***(G-13030)***
Ksaria Service Corporation 978 933-0000
300 Griffin Brook Dr Methuen MA (01844) ***(G-13031)***
KSD Custom Wood Products Inc 603 796-2951
102 High St Boscawen NH (03303) ***(G-17704)***
Ksg Enterprises Inc 978 977-7357
77 Walnut St Ste 8 Peabody MA (01960) ***(G-14349)***
Ksplice Inc 765 577-5423
1 Main St Ste 7f Cambridge MA (02142) ***(G-9528)***
Kt Acquisition LLC 508 853-4500
40 Rockdale St Worcester MA (01606) ***(G-17402)***
Kt Assocs Inc 617 547-3737
19 Cottage St Cambridge MA (02139) ***(G-9529)***
Ktcr Holding 203 227-4115
4 Pheasant Ln Westport CT (06880) ***(G-5208)***
KTI Bi-Metallix Inc 860 623-2511
3 Thompson Rd East Windsor CT (06088) ***(G-1293)***
KTI Inc (HQ) 860 623-2511
3 Thompson Rd East Windsor CT (06088) ***(G-1294)***
Ktron Inc 508 229-0919
90 Bartlett St Marlborough MA (01752) ***(G-12784)***
Ktt Enterprises LLC 203 288-7883
15 Marne St Hamden CT (06514) ***(G-1765)***
Kub, Cape Neddick *Also called Knight Underwater Bearing Llc* ***(G-5880)***
Kub Technologies Inc 203 364-8544
111 Research Dr Stratford CT (06615) ***(G-4429)***
Kubotek Usa Inc 508 229-2020
2 Mount Royal Ave Ste 500 Marlborough MA (01752) ***(G-12785)***
Kubtec, Stratford *Also called Kub Technologies Inc* ***(G-4429)***
Kuehne New Haven LLC 203 508-6703
71 Welton St New Haven CT (06511) ***(G-2703)***
Kullson Holding Company Inc 207 783-3442
21 Old Farm Rd Lewiston ME (04240) ***(G-6296)***
Kusa LLC 603 912-5325
8 Industrial Way Ste D1 Salem NH (03079) ***(G-19745)***
Kva Electronics, Billerica *Also called K V A Electronics* ***(G-8260)***
Kvh Industries Inc 401 847-3327
75 Enterprise Ctr Middletown RI (02842) ***(G-20622)***
Kvh Industries Inc (PA) 401 847-3327
50 Enterprise Ctr Middletown RI (02842) ***(G-20623)***
Kw Boats (HQ) 207 622-6229
681 Riverside Dr Augusta ME (04330) ***(G-5612)***
Kw Steel Structures LLC 857 342-7838
50 School St Walpole MA (02081) ***(G-15998)***
Kwant Elements Intl LLC 203 625-5553
464 Valley Rd Cos Cob CT (06807) ***(G-827)***
Kwik Kopy Printing 978 232-3552
100 Cummings Ctr Ste 210d Beverly MA (01915) ***(G-8146)***
Kwik Mart 413 464-7902
1245 W Housatonic St Pittsfield MA (01201) ***(G-14479)***
Kwik Print Inc 413 528-2885
35 Bridge St Great Barrington MA (01230) ***(G-11240)***
Kws Inc 207 832-5095
110 One Pie Rd Waldoboro ME (04572) ***(G-7133)***
Kx Technologies LLC (HQ) 203 799-9000
55 Railroad Ave West Haven CT (06516) ***(G-5130)***
Kyle Equipment Co Inc 978 422-8448
14 Legate Hill Rd Sterling MA (01564) ***(G-15541)***
Kyler Seafood Inc 508 984-5150
2 Washburn St New Bedford MA (02740) ***(G-13406)***
Kyler's, New Bedford *Also called Kyler Seafood Inc* ***(G-13406)***
Kyon Pharma Inc 617 567-2436
156 Porter St Apt 249 Boston MA (02128) ***(G-8657)***
L & A Tent Awning, Lewiston *Also called Lewiston-Auburn Tent & Awng Co* ***(G-6301)***
L & B Associates Inc 802 868-5210
1088 Cook Rd Saint Albans VT (05478) ***(G-22371)***
L & B Beverage Inc 401 434-9991
227 N Brow St Ste A East Providence RI (02914) ***(G-20427)***
L & G Fabricators Inc 802 447-0965
137 Harwood Hill Rd Bennington VT (05201) ***(G-21679)***
L & J Enterprises Inc 781 233-1966
67 Maplewood St Malden MA (02148) ***(G-12576)***
L & J Leathers Manufacturing 781 289-6466
1039 Broadway Revere MA (02151) ***(G-14770)***
L & J of New England Inc 508 756-8080
15 Sagamore Rd Ste 2 Worcester MA (01605) ***(G-17403)***
L & J Screen Printers Inc 508 791-7320
15 Sagamore Rd Worcester MA (01605) ***(G-17404)***
L & L Concrete Products Inc 508 987-8175
28 Linwood St Oxford MA (01540) ***(G-14264)***
L & L Fabricators, Nashua *Also called Albert Landry* ***(G-19108)***
L & L Mechanical LLC 860 491-4007
28 Pie Hill Rd Goshen CT (06756) ***(G-1585)***
L & L Noodle Inc 617 889-6888
22 Willow St Chelsea MA (02150) ***(G-9958)***
L & L Race Cars 978 420-7852
47 Frost Rd Tyngsboro MA (01879) ***(G-15892)***
L & M Machine Inc 617 294-0378
115 Tremont St Everett MA (02149) ***(G-10614)***
L & M Manufacturing Co Inc 860 379-2751
37 Greenwoods Rd New Hartford CT (06057) ***(G-2642)***
L & M Sheds LLC 603 679-5243
66 N River Rd Epping NH (03042) ***(G-18100)***
L & M Torsion Spring Co Inc 401 231-5635
22 Fisher St Providence RI (02906) ***(G-21048)***
L & P Gate Company Inc 860 296-8009
83 Meadow St Hartford CT (06114) ***(G-1839)***
L & P Paper Inc 508 248-3265
267 Southbridge Rd Charlton MA (01507) ***(G-9853)***
L & R Manufacturing Co Inc 508 853-0562
340 Tacoma St Worcester MA (01605) ***(G-17405)***
L & S Industries Inc (PA) 508 995-4654
32 Lambeth St New Bedford MA (02745) ***(G-13407)***
L & S Industries Inc 508 998-7900
72 S Main St Acushnet MA (02743) ***(G-7403)***
L A B, Bristol *Also called Lab Security Systems Corp* ***(G-575)***
L B Products, Fall River *Also called Elbe-Cesco Inc* ***(G-10687)***
L Brown and Sons Printing Inc 802 476-3164
14 Jefferson St 20 Barre VT (05641) ***(G-21627)***
L C M Tool Co 203 757-1575
68 Diane Ter Waterbury CT (06705) ***(G-4896)***
L D G Corporation 781 337-7155
143 Moore Rd East Weymouth MA (02189) ***(G-10545)***
L E A, Jefferson *Also called Leading Edge Attachments Inc* ***(G-11954)***
L E Jackson Coropration 603 787-6036
2858 Drtmouth College Hwy North Haverhill NH (03774) ***(G-19389)***
L E Taylor and Sons Inc 207 625-4056
37 Cross Rd Porter ME (04068) ***(G-6603)***
L E Weed and Son, Newport *Also called Newport Concrete Block Co* ***(G-19351)***
L F Pease Co 401 438-2850
21 Massasoit Ave East Providence RI (02914) ***(G-20428)***
L H C Inc (PA) 781 592-6444
638 Summer St Lynn MA (01905) ***(G-12520)***
L H Thompson Inc 207 989-3280
54 Wilson St Brewer ME (04412) ***(G-5797)***
L Hardy Company Inc (PA) 508 757-3480
17 Mill St Worcester MA (01603) ***(G-17406)***
L Hewitt Rand 413 664-8171
55 Chenaille Ter North Adams MA (01247) ***(G-13677)***
L L Bean Inc 603 298-6975
8 Glen Rd Ste 29 West Lebanon NH (03784) ***(G-19955)***
L L Bean Inc 207 552-2000
5 Campus Dr Desert Freeport ME (04033) ***(G-6081)***
L L Bean Inc 207 725-0300
8 Industrial Pkwy Brunswick ME (04011) ***(G-5840)***
L M C, Southington *Also called Light Metals Coloring Co Inc* ***(G-4062)***
L M C Light Iron Inc 207 793-9957
151 Range E Rd Limerick ME (04048) ***(G-6335)***
L M Gill Welding and Mfr LLC (PA) 860 647-9931
1422 Tolland Tpke Manchester CT (06042) ***(G-2017)***
L M Gill Welding and Mfr LLC 860 647-9931
1422 Tolland Tpke Manchester CT (06042) ***(G-2018)***
L M I, Acton *Also called Liquid Metronics Incorporated* ***(G-7369)***
L M T Communications Inc 203 426-4568
84 S Main St Newtown CT (06470) ***(G-2927)***
L M T Magazine, Newtown *Also called L M T Communications Inc* ***(G-2927)***
L P Macadams Company Inc 203 366-3647
50 Austin St Bridgeport CT (06604) ***(G-442)***
L R Brown Manufacturing Co 203 265-5639
53 Prince St Wallingford CT (06492) ***(G-4763)***
L R Fuel Systems 603 848-3835
151 South Rd Gilmanton NH (03237) ***(G-18193)***
L R K Communications Inc 203 372-1456
96 Toll House Ln Fairfield CT (06825) ***(G-1441)***
L Ray Packing Company 207 546-2355
27 Wyman Rd Milbridge ME (04658) ***(G-6435)***

ALPHABETIC

L S Hardwood Floor 617 288-0339
14 Arcadia St Dorchester MA (02122) ***(G-10346)***
L S I, Orange *Also called Light Sources Inc* ***(G-3371)***
L S N E, Manchester *Also called Lyophilization Svcs Neng Inc* ***(G-18866)***
L Suzio Asphalt Co Inc 203 237-8421
975 Westfield Rd Meriden CT (06450) ***(G-2098)***
L T A Group Inc 860 291-9911
694 Nutmeg Rd N South Windsor CT (06074) ***(G-3989)***
L T I, Holliston *Also called Liberating Technologies Inc* ***(G-11582)***
L T Technologies 508 456-0315
612 Plymouth St Ste 12 East Bridgewater MA (02333) ***(G-10416)***
L T X International Inc 781 461-1000
825 University Ave Norwood MA (02062) ***(G-14173)***
L W Bills Co 978 352-6660
79 Park St Georgetown MA (01833) ***(G-11144)***
L W Tank Repair Incorporated 508 234-6000
410 N Main St North Uxbridge MA (01538) ***(G-13995)***
L&E Floorcovering 508 473-0723
10 Mellen St Hopedale MA (01747) ***(G-11675)***
L&P Aerospace Acquisition LLC 860 635-8811
422 Timber Ridge Rd Middletown CT (06457) ***(G-2199)***
L-3 Advanced Systems Divisions, Burlington *Also called L3 Technologies Inc* ***(G-9295)***
L-Com Inc (HQ) 978 682-6936
50 High St North Andover MA (01845) ***(G-13715)***
L-Com Global Connectivity, North Andover *Also called L-Com Inc* ***(G-13715)***
L-Tronics Inc 781 893-6672
195 Fox Rd Unit 111 Waltham MA (02451) ***(G-16142)***
L-Tronics Inc 781 893-6672
30 Clematis Ave Ste 2 Waltham MA (02453) ***(G-16143)***
L3 Essco Inc 978 568-5100
90 Nemco Way Ayer MA (01432) ***(G-7923)***
L3 Henschel, Ayer *Also called L3 Technologies Inc* ***(G-7925)***
L3 Open Water Power, Foxboro *Also called L3 Technologies Inc* ***(G-10891)***
L3 Secrity Dtction Systems Inc 781 939-3800
179-181 Ferry Rd Haverhill MA (01835) ***(G-11446)***
L3 Technologies Inc 978 462-2400
90 Nemco Way Ayer MA (01432) ***(G-7924)***
L3 Technologies Inc 413 586-2330
50 Prince St Northampton MA (01060) ***(G-14009)***
L3 Technologies Inc 617 895-6841
124 Washington St Ste 101 Foxboro MA (02035) ***(G-10891)***
L3 Technologies Inc 978 784-1999
90 Nemco Way Ayer MA (01432) ***(G-7925)***
L3 Technologies Inc 781 270-2100
1 Wall St Ste 7 Burlington MA (01803) ***(G-9295)***
L3 Technologies Inc 978 694-9991
65 Jonspin Rd Wilmington MA (01887) ***(G-17014)***
L3harris Technologies Inc 508 966-9500
5 Sand Castle Ln Bellingham MA (02019) ***(G-8043)***
L3harris Technologies Inc 603 689-1450
85 Northwest Blvd Nashua NH (03063) ***(G-19195)***
L3harris Technologies Inc 603 689-1450
85 Northwest Blvd Ste B Nashua NH (03063) ***(G-19196)***
L3harris Technologies Inc 781 538-4148
175 Middlesex Tpke Ste 2 Bedford MA (01730) ***(G-7987)***
L3harris Technologies Inc 978 905-3500
150 Apollo Dr Chelmsford MA (01824) ***(G-9911)***
La Bella Bride Magazine 401 397-5795
13 Northup Plat Rd Coventry RI (02816) ***(G-20152)***
La Casona Bakery, Central Falls *Also called La Casona Restaurant Inc* ***(G-20118)***
La Casona Restaurant Inc 401 727-0002
768 Broad St Central Falls RI (02863) ***(G-20118)***
La Chance Brick, Auburn *Also called Rjf - Morin Brick LLC* ***(G-5595)***
La Chance Controls 860 342-2212
175 Penfield Hill Rd Portland CT (06480) ***(G-3569)***
La Creme Chocolat Inc 443 841-2458
110 Standish Neck Rd Standish ME (04084) ***(G-7062)***
La Foe Brian 802 754-8837
151 Tarbox Hill Rd Orleans VT (05860) ***(G-22249)***
La Perle & Sons Granite Co 802 476-6463
140 Railroad St Barre VT (05641) ***(G-21628)***
La Pietra Custom Marble & Gran, Brookfield *Also called La Pietra Thinstone Veneer* ***(G-650)***
La Pietra Thinstone Veneer 203 775-6162
1106 Federal Rd Brookfield CT (06804) ***(G-650)***
La Semana Newspaper 617 427-6212
903 Albany St Boston MA (02119) ***(G-8658)***
La Valley Wood Inc 207 316-6263
101 Industrial Dr Van Buren ME (04785) ***(G-7121)***
La Voz Hispana De Connecticut, New Haven *Also called Hispanic Communications LLC* ***(G-2696)***
Laars Heating Systems Company 603 335-6300
20 Industrial Way Rochester NH (03867) ***(G-19677)***
Lab Frnture Instlltons Sls Inc 978 646-0600
11 River St Ste 2 Middleton MA (01949) ***(G-13093)***
Lab Medical Manufacturing Inc 978 663-2475
28 Cook St Billerica MA (01821) ***(G-8262)***
Lab Publications LLC 781 598-9779
47 Paradise Rd Swampscott MA (01907) ***(G-15698)***
Lab Security Systems Corp 860 589-6037
700 Emmett St Bristol CT (06010) ***(G-575)***
Labco Welding Inc 860 632-2625
129 Industrial Park Rd Middletown CT (06457) ***(G-2200)***
Label Art, Wilton *Also called W S Packaging* ***(G-19990)***
Label Haus Inc 978 777-1773
3 Southside Rd Ste B Danvers MA (01923) ***(G-10230)***
Label One, Old Saybrook *Also called Privateer Ltd* ***(G-3349)***
Label Tech Inc 603 692-2005
16 Interstate Dr Somersworth NH (03878) ***(G-19843)***
Labelprint America, Newburyport *Also called Inovar Packaging Group LLC* ***(G-13501)***
Labelprint America Inc 978 463-4004
8 Opportunity Way Newburyport MA (01950) ***(G-13506)***
Labfitout, Wakefield *Also called Stem Solutions LLC* ***(G-15978)***
Lablite LLC 860 355-8817
8 S Main St New Milford CT (06776) ***(G-2812)***
Labminds Inc 844 956-8327
285 Washington St Ste 3 Somerville MA (02143) ***(G-15189)***
Labombard Machine 978 688-7773
55 Chase St Methuen MA (01844) ***(G-13032)***
Labonville Inc 603 752-3221
500 Main St Trlr 21 Gorham NH (03581) ***(G-18214)***
Labonville Safety, Gorham *Also called Labonville Inc* ***(G-18214)***
Labpulse Medical, East Granby *Also called Energy Beam Sciences Inc* ***(G-1126)***
Labree's Bakery, Old Town *Also called Labrees Inc* ***(G-6543)***
Labrees Inc 207 827-6121
169 Gilman Falls Ave Old Town ME (04468) ***(G-6543)***
Labsphere Inc 603 927-4266
231 Shaker St North Sutton NH (03260) ***(G-19392)***
Labtech Inc (PA) 508 435-5500
114 South St Hopkinton MA (01748) ***(G-11726)***
Labthink International Inc 617 830-2190
200 Rivers Edge Dr Ste 1 Medford MA (02155) ***(G-12938)***
Labwear.com, Bridgeport *Also called Sassone Labwear LLC* ***(G-485)***
Lac Landscaping LLC 203 807-1067
60 Country Ln Milford CT (06461) ***(G-2308)***
Lace Unlimited, Pawtucket *Also called Frontier Manufacturing Inc* ***(G-20841)***
Lacerta Group Inc 508 339-3312
50 Suffolk Rd Mansfield MA (02048) ***(G-12641)***
Lacerta Group Inc (PA) 508 339-3312
360 Forbes Blvd Mansfield MA (02048) ***(G-12642)***
Lacey Manufacturing Co LLC 203 336-7427
1146 Barnum Ave Bridgeport CT (06610) ***(G-443)***
Laconia Daily Sun, Laconia *Also called Lakes Region News Club Inc* ***(G-18572)***
Laconia Magnetics Inc 603 528-2766
Prescott Hill Rd Laconia NH (03246) ***(G-18570)***
Lacucina Express 413 566-8015
9 Allen St Hampden MA (01036) ***(G-11321)***
LAD Welding & Fabrication 603 228-6617
33 Fisherville Rd Concord NH (03303) ***(G-17911)***
Ladd Research Industries, Williston *Also called Raj Communications Ltd* ***(G-22687)***
Laddawn Inc (HQ) 800 446-3639
155 Jackson Rd Devens MA (01434) ***(G-10322)***
Ladesco Inc 603 623-3772
150 Dow St Ste 401 Manchester NH (03101) ***(G-18857)***
Ladrdefense LLC 860 637-8488
243 Canal St Plantsville CT (06479) ***(G-3536)***
Lady Ann Candies 401 738-4321
86 Warwick Industrial Dr # 1 Warwick RI (02886) ***(G-21384)***
Lady Anne Cosmetics Inc 203 372-6972
78 Russ Rd Trumbull CT (06611) ***(G-4626)***
Lafarge North America Inc 203 468-6068
410 Waterfront St New Haven CT (06512) ***(G-2704)***
Lafayette Distributors Cpl Inc 603 430-9405
369 Lafayette Rd Hampton NH (03842) ***(G-18266)***
Lafoe Logging LLC 802 754-8837
151 Tarbox Hill Rd Orleans VT (05860) ***(G-22250)***
Lagasse & Lewis LLC 603 382-5898
38 Main St Plaistow NH (03865) ***(G-19519)***
Laird Technologies Inc 603 627-7877
1 Perimeter Rd Ste 1 # 1 Manchester NH (03103) ***(G-18858)***
Laird Woodworking Inc 508 892-8877
863 Pleasant St Rochdale MA (01542) ***(G-14782)***
Lake Champlain Chocolates, Williston *Also called Champlain Chocolate Company* ***(G-22659)***
Lake Champlain Trnsp Co 802 660-3495
King Street Dock Burlington VT (05401) ***(G-21792)***
Lake Grinding Company 203 336-3767
231 Asylum St Bridgeport CT (06610) ***(G-444)***
Lake Machine Co Inc 603 542-8884
12 Balcom Pl Claremont NH (03743) ***(G-17853)***
Lake Manufacturing Co Inc 978 465-1617
6 Opportunity Way Newburyport MA (01950) ***(G-13507)***
Lake Region Manufacturing Inc (HQ) 952 361-2515
100 Fordham Rd Ste 3 Wilmington MA (01887) ***(G-17015)***
Lake Region Medical, Wilmington *Also called Lake Region Manufacturing Inc* ***(G-17015)***
Lake Region Medical, Wilmington *Also called Accellent LLC* ***(G-16963)***
Lake Region Medical Inc (HQ) 978 570-6900
100 Fordham Rd Ste 3 Wilmington MA (01887) ***(G-17016)***

Lake Region Medical Inc 603 528-1211
45 Lexington Dr Laconia NH (03246) *(G-18571)*
Lakes Region News Club Inc 603 527-9299
1127 Union Ave Laconia NH (03246) *(G-18572)*
Lakes Region Tubular Pdts Inc 603 528-2838
51 Growth Rd Laconia NH (03246) *(G-18573)*
Lakeside Management Corp 508 695-3252
3 Belcher St Plainville MA (02762) *(G-14524)*
Lakeville Journal Company LLC (PA) 860 435-9873
33 Bissell St Lakeville CT (06039) *(G-1931)*
Lakeville Journal, The, Lakeville *Also called Lakeville Journal Company LLC (G-1931)*
Lakewood Industries Inc 413 499-3550
40 Downing Industrial Par Pittsfield MA (01201) *(G-14480)*
Lakewood Logging Inc 207 431-4052
132 Lakewood Rd Madison ME (04950) *(G-6405)*
Lakewood Mold, Pittsfield *Also called Lakewood Industries Inc (G-14480)*
Lakonia Greek Products LLC 207 282-4002
10 W Point Ln Unit 202 Biddeford ME (04005) *(G-5742)*
Lally Column Corp 508 828-5997
138 Plain Dr Stoughton MA (02072) *(G-15602)*
Lam Therapeutics Inc 203 458-7100
530 Old Whitfield St Guilford CT (06437) *(G-1707)*
Lama Yeshe Wisdom Archive Inc 781 259-4466
6 Goose Pond Rd Lincoln MA (01773) *(G-12286)*
Lamb & Ritchie Company Inc 781 941-2700
90 Broadway Saugus MA (01906) *(G-14990)*
Lamb Knitting Machine Corp 413 592-2501
66 New Lombard Rd Chicopee MA (01020) *(G-10037)*
Lamb Printing Company Inc 413 662-2495
48 Cherry St North Adams MA (01247) *(G-13678)*
Lambdavision Incorporated 860 486-6593
400 Farmington Ave Mc6409 Farmington CT (06032) *(G-1489)*
Lamberti Packing Company 203 562-0436
207 Food Terminal Plz # 207 New Haven CT (06511) *(G-2705)*
Lambient Technologies LLC 857 242-3963
649 Msschusetts Ave Ste 4 Cambridge MA (02139) *(G-9530)*
Lamco Chemical Company Inc 617 884-8470
212 Arlington St Chelsea MA (02150) *(G-9959)*
Lamcotec, Monson *Also called Laminating Coating Tech Inc (G-13208)*
Lamell Lumber Corporation 802 878-2475
82a Jericho Rd Essex Junction VT (05452) *(G-21948)*
Laminated Products Inc 401 762-0711
32 Mechanic Ave Ste 204 Woonsocket RI (02895) *(G-21573)*
Laminating Coating Tech Inc 413 267-4808
152 Bethany Rd Monson MA (01057) *(G-13208)*
Laminted Plas Dstrs Fbricators, North Billerica *Also called Kilder Corporation (G-13830)*
Lamitech 781 878-7708
800 Hingham St Ste 200 Rockland MA (02370) *(G-14811)*
Lamor USA Corporation 203 888-7700
2 Enterprise Dr Ste 404 Shelton CT (06484) *(G-3823)*
Lampin Corporation (PA) 508 278-2422
38 River Rd Uxbridge MA (01569) *(G-15923)*
Lamplighter Brewing Co LLC 207 650-3325
284 Broadway Cambridge MA (02139) *(G-9531)*
Lamprey River Screen Print 603 659-9959
25 N Main St Newmarket NH (03857) *(G-19336)*
Lamson and Goodnow LLC 413 625-0201
45 Conway St Shelburne Falls MA (01370) *(G-15073)*
Lamson and Goodnow Mfg, Shelburne Falls *Also called Lamson and Goodnow LLC (G-15073)*
Lamson and Goodnow Mfg Co 413 625-6311
45 Conway St Shelburne Falls MA (01370) *(G-15074)*
Lamsonsharp, Shelburne Falls *Also called Lamson and Goodnow Mfg Co (G-15074)*
Lamtec Inc 207 774-6560
2301 Congress St Portland ME (04102) *(G-6678)*
Lanair Research & Development 603 433-6134
521 Shattuck Way Portsmouth NH (03801) *(G-19584)*
Lancaster Herrald, Pittsburg *Also called Jordan Associates (G-19494)*
Lancaster Times Inc 978 368-3393
150 Baker Avenue Ext # 101 Concord MA (01742) *(G-10137)*
Lance Industries 401 654-5394
1119 Douglas Ave North Providence RI (02904) *(G-20766)*
Lance Industries Inc (PA) 401 365-6272
55 Industrial Cir Ste 3 Lincoln RI (02865) *(G-20578)*
Lance International, Westport *Also called Robert Warren LLC (G-5227)*
Lance Williams & Son Logging & 603 569-3349
157 Ledge Hill Rd Center Tuftonboro NH (03816) *(G-17808)*
Lanco Assembly Systems Inc (PA) 207 773-2060
12 Thomas Dr Westbrook ME (04092) *(G-7193)*
Lanco Integrated, Westbrook *Also called Lanco Assembly Systems Inc (G-7193)*
Land & Sea Fuel 207 733-0005
417 S Lubec Rd Lubec ME (04652) *(G-6386)*
Land and Sea Inc 603 226-3966
25 Henniker St Concord NH (03301) *(G-17912)*
Land of Nod Winery LLC 860 824-5225
99 Lower Rd East Canaan CT (06024) *(G-1112)*
Landa Pressure Washers of RI 401 463-8303
11 Comstock Pkwy Cranston RI (02921) *(G-20250)*

Lander Inc 413 448-8734
20 Keeler St Bldg D Pittsfield MA (01201) *(G-14481)*
Landfil Gas Prodcrs of Plnvlle 508 695-3252
3 Belcher St Plainville MA (02762) *(G-14525)*
Landmark Finish Inc 978 470-2040
12 Dundee Park Dr Andover MA (01810) *(G-7564)*
Landmark Window Fashions Inc 781 767-3535
5 Mear Rd Ste 4 Holbrook MA (02343) *(G-11528)*
Landry Enterprises Inc 508 528-9122
41 Summer St Franklin MA (02038) *(G-11063)*
Lane Construction Corporation 603 352-2006
Oliver Hl Rd Off Rte 32 S East Swanzey NH (03446) *(G-18093)*
Lane Printing Co Inc 781 767-4450
210 S Franklin St Holbrook MA (02343) *(G-11529)*
Lane PRInting& Advertising, Holbrook *Also called Lane Printing Co Inc (G-11529)*
Lanford Manufacturing Corp 978 557-0240
43 Merrimack St Lawrence MA (01843) *(G-12044)*
Langer Associates Inc 603 626-4388
55 South Commercial St B2 Manchester NH (03101) *(G-18859)*
Langstrom Metals Inc 508 839-5224
84 Creeper Hill Rd North Grafton MA (01536) *(G-13962)*
Lank Machining Co LLC 207 286-9549
113 Mountain Rd Arundel ME (04046) *(G-5533)*
Lanmark Controls Inc 978 264-0200
1 Wall St Ste C-103 Hudson NH (03051) *(G-18409)*
Lanoco Specialty Wire Pdts Inc 508 865-1500
7 John Rd Sutton MA (01590) *(G-15686)*
Lansen Mold Co Inc 413 443-5328
1 Main St Hancock MA (01237) *(G-11325)*
Lantheus Holdings Inc (PA) 978 671-8001
331 Treble Cove Rd North Billerica MA (01862) *(G-13831)*
Lantheus Medical Imaging Inc (HQ) 800 362-2668
331 Treble Cove Rd North Billerica MA (01862) *(G-13832)*
Lantheus MI Intermediate Inc 978 671-8001
331 Treble Cove Rd North Billerica MA (01862) *(G-13833)*
Lantiq Broadband Holdco Inc 781 687-0400
40 Middlesex Tpke Bedford MA (01730) *(G-7988)*
Lantos Technologies Inc 781 443-7633
50 Concord St Ste E-300 Wilmington MA (01887) *(G-17017)*
Lanxess Solutions US Inc 203 723-2237
400 Elm St Naugatuck CT (06770) *(G-2483)*
Lanxess Solutions US Inc (HQ) 203 573-2000
2 Armstrong Rd Ste 101 Shelton CT (06484) *(G-3824)*
Laplume & Sons Printing Inc 978 683-1009
1 Farley St Lawrence MA (01843) *(G-12045)*
Lapoint Industries Inc (PA) 207 777-3100
65 First Flight Dr Auburn ME (04210) *(G-5575)*
Lapointe Hudson Broach Co Inc 978 562-7943
11 Brent Dr Hudson MA (01749) *(G-11784)*
Laporte Division, Concord *Also called Graphic Packaging Intl LLC (G-17906)*
Larad Equipment Corp 508 473-2700
18 Menfi Way Hopedale MA (01747) *(G-11676)*
Laraway Mountain Maple 802 644-5433
1959 Codding Hollow Rd Waterville VT (05492) *(G-22595)*
Larchmont Engineering Inc 978 250-1177
11 Billerica Rd Chelmsford MA (01824) *(G-9912)*
Larchmont Engineering Inc 603 622-8825
180 Zachary Rd Ste 3 Manchester NH (03109) *(G-18860)*
Larco Machines Co Inc 860 647-9769
239 Hopriver Rd Bolton CT (06043) *(G-277)*
Larcoline Inc (PA) 802 864-5440
113 Acorn Ln Ste 2 Colchester VT (05446) *(G-21871)*
Larcoline Inc 802 229-0660
7 Main St Montpelier VT (05602) *(G-22152)*
Lariat Biosciences Inc 603 244-9657
39 John St Chelsea MA (02150) *(G-9960)*
Larkin Iron Works Inc 617 333-9710
9 B St Hyde Park MA (02136) *(G-11873)*
Larkin Motors LLC 508 807-1333
25 Firwrks Cir Brdgewater Bridgewater Bridgewater MA (02324) *(G-9082)*
Larose Rf Systems, Millis *Also called Radio Frequency Company Inc (G-13186)*
Larry Balchen 207 497-5621
1834 Mason Bay Rd Jonesport ME (04649) *(G-6227)*
Larry Dingee 603 542-9682
195 Nh Route 120 Cornish NH (03745) *(G-17962)*
Larry's Auto Machine & Supply, Groton *Also called Larrys Auto Machine LLC (G-1679)*
Larrys Auto Machine LLC 860 449-9112
175 Leonard Dr Groton CT (06340) *(G-1679)*
Larsdale Inc (PA) 978 356-9995
4 S Main St Ste 7 Ipswich MA (01938) *(G-11928)*
Larson Tool & Stamping Company 508 222-0897
90 Olive St Attleboro MA (02703) *(G-7758)*
Larson Worldwide Inc 781 659-2115
95 Mount Blue St Norwell MA (02061) *(G-14105)*
Lasalle Donuts Inc 401 272-9773
251 Smith St Providence RI (02908) *(G-21049)*
Laser Advantage LLC 603 886-9464
4 Townsend W Ste 2 Nashua NH (03063) *(G-19197)*
Laser Body Solutions, Hamden *Also called Jeffrey Gold (G-1762)*

A L P H A B E T I C

Laser Engineering 508 520-2500
113 Cedar St Ste S5 Milford MA (01757) ***(G-13124)***

Laser Fare Inc (PA) 401 231-4400
1 Industrial Dr S Smithfield RI (02917) ***(G-21235)***

Laser Focus World, Nashua *Also called Pennwell Corporation* ***(G-19229)***

Laser Group Publishing Inc 603 880-8909
177 E Industrial Park Dr Manchester NH (03109) ***(G-18861)***

Laser Labs Inc 781 826-4138
70 Corporate Park Dr # 1245 Pembroke MA (02359) ***(G-14415)***

Laser Laser Inc 617 615-2292
1895 Centre St Ste 205 West Roxbury MA (02132) ***(G-16498)***

Laser Light Engines Inc 603 952-4550
8 Industrial Way Ste C6 Salem NH (03079) ***(G-19746)***

Laser Lightning LLC (PA) 508 476-0138
174 Davis St East Douglas MA (01516) ***(G-10428)***

Laser Process Mfg Inc 978 531-6003
2 Centennial Dr Ste 6 Peabody MA (01960) ***(G-14350)***

Laser Projection Technologies 603 421-0209
8 Delta Dr Unit 9 Londonderry NH (03053) ***(G-18712)***

Laser Tool Company Inc 860 283-8284
98 N Main St Thomaston CT (06787) ***(G-4508)***

Lasercomp Ta, Wakefield *Also called Ta Instruments-Waters LLC* ***(G-15980)***

Lasercraze 978 689-7700
1580 Osgood St Ste 2210 North Andover MA (01845) ***(G-13716)***

Laserperformance North America, Portsmouth *Also called Quarter Moon Incorporated* ***(G-20937)***

Laservall North America LLC 401 724-0076
136 Newell Ave Pawtucket RI (02860) ***(G-20853)***

Laserwords Maine 207 782-9595
1775 Lisbon St Lewiston ME (04240) ***(G-6297)***

Lash Boat Yard, Friendship *Also called Wesley Lash* ***(G-6094)***

Lash Lamour 617 247-1871
129 Newbury St Fl 2 Boston MA (02116) ***(G-8659)***

Lashway Firewood Co, Williamsburg *Also called Lashway Logging Inc* ***(G-16952)***

Lashway Logging Inc 413 268-3600
67 Main St Williamsburg MA (01096) ***(G-16952)***

Lassy Tools Inc 860 747-2748
96 Bohemia St Plainville CT (06062) ***(G-3500)***

Lasting Impressions, Bethel *Also called D R S Desings* ***(G-140)***

Latex Foam International LLC (HQ) 203 924-0700
510 River Rd Shelton CT (06484) ***(G-3825)***

Latex Foam Intl Holdings Inc (PA) 203 924-0700
510 River Rd Shelton CT (06484) ***(G-3826)***

Latex Foam Products, Shelton *Also called Latex Foam International LLC* ***(G-3825)***

Lathrop Mill, Bristol *Also called Claire Lathrop Band Mill Inc* ***(G-21763)***

Laticrete Supercap LLC 203 393-4558
91 Amity Rd Bethany CT (06524) ***(G-122)***

Lattice Semi-Conductor, Burlington *Also called Lattice Semiconductor Corp* ***(G-9296)***

Lattice Semiconductor Corp 781 229-5819
67 S Bedford St Ste 400w Burlington MA (01803) ***(G-9296)***

Lattix Inc 978 474-4332
8 Harper Cir Andover MA (01810) ***(G-7565)***

Latva Machine Inc 603 863-5155
744 John Stark Hwy Newport NH (03773) ***(G-19348)***

Laughing Whale, Searsport *Also called Bluejacket Inc* ***(G-6947)***

Launchworks LLC 978 338-3045
123 Brimbal Ave Beverly MA (01915) ***(G-8147)***

Launchworks Manufacturing Lab, Beverly *Also called Launchworks LLC* ***(G-8147)***

Laura Marr Productions LLC 207 856-9700
155 Warren Ave Ste C Westbrook ME (04092) ***(G-7194)***

Laurel Tool & Manufacturing 860 889-5354
177 Franklin St Norwich CT (06360) ***(G-3285)***

Laurelbrook Ntral Rsources LLC 860 824-5843
12 Casey Hill Rd East Canaan CT (06024) ***(G-1113)***

Laurence Sharpe 603 744-8175
208 Plumer Hill Rd Alexandria NH (03222) ***(G-17537)***

Lauretano Sign Group Inc 860 582-0233
1 Tremco Dr Terryville CT (06786) ***(G-4484)***

Laurin Publishing Co Inc (PA) 413 499-0514
100 West St Pittsfield MA (01201) ***(G-14482)***

Lauzon Gilles 207 286-0600
428 Elm St Biddeford ME (04005) ***(G-5743)***

Lauzon Machine and Engrg Inc 802 442-3116
757 Main St Bennington VT (05201) ***(G-21680)***

Lauzon's Machine & Engineering, Bennington *Also called Lauzon Machine and Engrg Inc* ***(G-21680)***

Lavallee Machinery Inc 508 764-2896
831 Main St Southbridge MA (01550) ***(G-15391)***

LAvant Garde Inc 805 522-0045
Perkins Way Unit 1 Newburyport MA (01950) ***(G-13508)***

Laveem Inc 617 286-6517
255 Main St Ste 6 Cambridge MA (02142) ***(G-9532)***

Lavelle Machine & Tool Co Inc 978 692-8825
485 Groton Rd Westford MA (01886) ***(G-16775)***

Lavigne Manufacturing Inc 401 490-4627
15 Western Industrial Dr Cranston RI (02921) ***(G-20251)***

Lavoie Industries Llc 508 542-1062
969 Charles St Fall River MA (02724) ***(G-10722)***

Lawrence Crankshaft Inc 978 372-0504
500 Groveland St Haverhill MA (01830) ***(G-11447)***

Lawrence Fay 603 668-3811
93 Depot Rd Manchester NH (03103) ***(G-18862)***

Lawrence Fuel Inc 978 984-5255
233 Winthrop Ave Lawrence MA (01843) ***(G-12046)***

Lawrence Holdings Inc (PA) 203 949-1600
34b Barnes Indus Rd S Wallingford CT (06492) ***(G-4764)***

Lawrence Instron Corporation 781 828-2500
825 University Ave Norwood MA (02062) ***(G-14174)***

Lawrence Lyon 802 685-7790
100 N Main St Chelsea VT (05038) ***(G-21839)***

Lawrence Metal Forming Corp 978 535-1200
7 Lakeland Park Dr Peabody MA (01960) ***(G-14351)***

Lawrence Parson 207 935-3737
510 Hampshire Rd Brownfield ME (04010) ***(G-5825)***

Lawrence Pumps, Lawrence *Also called Flowserve US Inc* ***(G-12025)***

Lawrence Ready-Mix, Sandwich *Also called Boston Sand & Gravel Company* ***(G-14962)***

Lawrence Sigler 978 464-2027
314 Ball Hill Rd Princeton MA (01541) ***(G-14606)***

Lawrence Textile Inc 978 689-4355
1 Logan St Lawrence MA (01841) ***(G-12047)***

Lawson Hemphill Inc 508 679-5364
1658 Grnd Army Rpblc Hwy Swansea MA (02777) ***(G-15706)***

Lawyers Weekly LLC (PA) 617 451-7300
40 Court St Fl 5 Boston MA (02108) ***(G-8660)***

Laylas Falafel 203 685-2830
936 High Ridge Rd Stamford CT (06905) ***(G-4236)***

Lbry Inc 267 210-4292
521 Pine St Manchester NH (03104) ***(G-18863)***

Lc Technology Solutions Inc 978 255-1620
2c Fanaras Dr Salisbury MA (01952) ***(G-14952)***

Lcd Lighting Inc 203 799-7877
37 Robinson Blvd Orange CT (06477) ***(G-3370)***

Lcm Group Inc 603 888-1248
3 Taggart Dr Ste C Nashua NH (03060) ***(G-19198)***

Lcs Controls Inc 802 767-3128
1678 Vt Route 100 S Rochester VT (05767) ***(G-22318)***

Ld Assoc LLC 203 452-9393
16 Georges Ln Monroe CT (06468) ***(G-2406)***

LD Plastics Inc 508 584-7651
1130 Pearl St Brockton MA (02301) ***(G-9161)***

LDB Manufacturing, Cranston *Also called LDB Tool and Findings Inc* ***(G-20252)***

LDB Tool and Findings Inc 401 944-6000
2380 Plainfield Pike Cranston RI (02921) ***(G-20252)***

Ldc Inc 401 861-4667
22 First St East Providence RI (02914) ***(G-20429)***

Le Masurier Granite Quarry 978 251-3841
Ledge Rd North Chelmsford MA (01863) ***(G-13900)***

LE Weed & Son LLC (PA) 603 863-1540
187 S Main St Newport NH (03773) ***(G-19349)***

Leach Garner-A Brkshire Hathaw, Attleboro *Also called Hallmark Healy Group Inc* ***(G-7744)***

Lead Conversion Plus 802 497-1557
710 Everest Rd Milton VT (05468) ***(G-22132)***

Leader Dist Systems Inc 802 254-6093
1566 Putney Rd Brattleboro VT (05301) ***(G-21736)***

Leader Evaporator Co Inc (PA) 802 868-5444
49 Jonergin Dr Swanton VT (05488) ***(G-22531)***

Leader Evaporatorinc 802 775-5411
2 Pine St Rutland VT (05701) ***(G-22343)***

Leader Publishing Co Inc 617 387-4570
28 Church St Everett MA (02149) ***(G-10615)***

Leaderclips Inc 248 808-1093
17 Pembroke Rd Wellesley MA (02482) ***(G-16370)***

Leading Edge Attachments Inc (PA) 508 829-4855
72 Heather Cir Jefferson MA (01522) ***(G-11954)***

Leading Edge Concepts Inc 203 797-1200
15 Berkshire Blvd Ste A Bethel CT (06801) ***(G-168)***

Leading Edge Safety Systems, Madison *Also called Pucuda Inc* ***(G-1972)***

Leading Edge Tool Co,, Lyndonville *Also called Mark Hunter* ***(G-22069)***

Leading Market Technologies 617 494-4747
58 Winter St Ste 5 Boston MA (02108) ***(G-8661)***

Leahy Press Inc 802 223-2100
79 River St Montpelier VT (05602) ***(G-22153)***

Leaktite Corporation (PA) 978 537-8000
40 Francis St Leominster MA (01453) ***(G-12160)***

Leap Therapeutics Inc (PA) 617 714-0360
47 Thorndike St Ste B1-1 Cambridge MA (02141) ***(G-9533)***

Leap Year Publishing LLC 978 688-9900
16 High St Ste 300 North Andover MA (01845) ***(G-13717)***

Learning Materials Workshop 802 862-0112
58 Henry St Burlington VT (05401) ***(G-21793)***

Learning Station LLC 603 496-7896
88 Stone Bridge Rd Wilmot NH (03287) ***(G-19973)***

Leather Man Limited, Essex *Also called Brockway Ferry Corporation* ***(G-1394)***

Leatherby 860 658-6166
19 Deer Park Rd Weatogue CT (06089) ***(G-5043)***

Leavers Lace Corporation (PA) 401 397-5555
144 Mishnock Rd West Greenwich RI (02817) ***(G-21461)***

Leavers Lace Corporation 401 828-8117
100 Pulaski St West Warwick RI (02893) ***(G-21499)***
Leavitt & Parris Inc 207 797-0100
256 Read St Portland ME (04103) ***(G-6679)***
Leavitt Corporation (HQ) 617 389-2600
100 Santilli Hwy Everett MA (02149) ***(G-10616)***
Leavitt Jewelers, Boston *Also called Alan W Leavitt Company* ***(G-8349)***
Leavitt Logging LLC 802 644-1440
4269 Vt Route 109 Belvidere Center VT (05442) ***(G-21660)***
Leavitt Machine Co 978 544-3872
24 E River St Orange MA (01364) ***(G-14220)***
Lebanon Prcision Bearing Plant, Lebanon *Also called Timken Company* ***(G-18638)***
Lebanon Screw Products Inc 802 674-6347
39 Park Rd Windsor VT (05089) ***(G-22711)***
Lecam Machine Inc 508 588-2300
7 Renker Dr Easton MA (02356) ***(G-10584)***
Leclaire Fuel Oil LLC 203 922-1512
97 Unit 3 Bridgeport Ave Shelton CT (06484) ***(G-3827)***
Lectro Engineering Inc 781 891-9640
39 Calvary St Fl 2 Waltham MA (02453) ***(G-16144)***
Leddynamics Inc 802 728-4533
296 Beanville Rd Randolph VT (05060) ***(G-22298)***
Ledgerock Welding and Fabg 978 562-6500
6 Loring St Hudson MA (01749) ***(G-11785)***
Ledgeview Printing, Westford *Also called May Graphics & Printing Inc* ***(G-16779)***
Ledor Jewelry, Plainville *Also called Titus Engraving & Stonesetting* ***(G-14536)***
Lee Brown Co LLC 860 379-4706
91 Old Forge Rd Riverton CT (06065) ***(G-3695)***
Lee Burial Vaults, North Dighton *Also called Precast Vault Co Inc* ***(G-13933)***
Lee Burial Vaults, Braintree *Also called Precast Vault Co Inc* ***(G-9031)***
Lee Company (PA) 860 399-6281
2 Pettipaug Rd Westbrook CT (06498) ***(G-5157)***
Lee Company 860 399-6281
55 Bokum Rd Essex CT (06426) ***(G-1401)***
Lee Company 860 399-6281
22 Pequot Park Rd Westbrook CT (06498) ***(G-5158)***
Lee Electric Inc 978 777-0070
128 Maple St Danvers MA (01923) ***(G-10231)***
Lee Manufacturing Inc 203 284-0466
46 Barnes Industrial Rd S Wallingford CT (06492) ***(G-4765)***
Lee Merchant Signs, Caribou *Also called Leon Merchant Signs* ***(G-5885)***
Lee Spring Company LLC 860 584-0991
245 Lake Ave Bristol CT (06010) ***(G-576)***
Lee Tool Co Inc 413 583-8750
40 Ravenwood Dr Ludlow MA (01056) ***(G-12471)***
Leed - Himmel Industries Inc 203 288-8484
75 Leeder Hill Dr Hamden CT (06517) ***(G-1766)***
Leedon Webbing Co Inc 401 722-1043
86 Tremont St Central Falls RI (02863) ***(G-20119)***
Leek Building Products Inc 203 853-3883
205 Wilson Ave Ste 3 Norwalk CT (06854) ***(G-3185)***
Leelynd Corp 203 753-9137
546 S Main St Waterbury CT (06706) ***(G-4897)***
Leemar Casting Company Inc 401 276-2844
27 Mill St Unit 2 Johnston RI (02919) ***(G-20517)***
Lees Concrete Inc 207 974-4936
974 Odlin Rd Bangor ME (04401) ***(G-5653)***
Lees Manufacturing Co Inc 401 275-2383
160 Niantic Ave Providence RI (02907) ***(G-21050)***
Lefort Fine Furniture, Halifax *Also called David Lefort* ***(G-11317)***
Left-Tees Designs Bayou LLC 603 437-6630
15 W Broadway Ste 2 Derry NH (03038) ***(G-17986)***
Leftfield Software 617 524-3842
153 South St Boston MA (02130) ***(G-8662)***
Legacy Global Sports LP 603 373-7262
290 Heritage Ave Unit 2 Portsmouth NH (03801) ***(G-19585)***
Legacy Machine & Mfg LLC 978 388-0956
43 Clinton St Amesbury MA (01913) ***(G-7493)***
Legacy Medical Solutions LLC 978 655-6007
90 Progress Ave 3 Tyngsboro MA (01879) ***(G-15893)***
Legacy Publishing Group Inc 800 322-3866
75 Green St Ste 1 Clinton MA (01510) ***(G-10083)***
Legacy Woodworking LLC 203 440-9710
912 Old Colony Rd Meriden CT (06451) ***(G-2099)***
Legal Affairs Inc 203 865-2520
115 Blake Rd Hamden CT (06517) ***(G-1767)***
LEGAL AFFAIRS MAGAZINE, Hamden *Also called Legal Affairs Inc* ***(G-1767)***
Legends & Heroes 617 571-6990
365 Astin Post Rd Ste 210 Sudbury MA (01776) ***(G-15662)***
Legere Group Ltd 860 674-0392
80 Darling Dr Avon CT (06001) ***(G-37)***
Legere Woodworking, Avon *Also called Legere Group Ltd* ***(G-37)***
Leggett & Platt 1010, Woburn *Also called Leggett & Platt Incorporated* ***(G-17213)***
Leggett & Platt Incorporated 508 987-8706
23 Dana Rd Oxford MA (01540) ***(G-14265)***
Leggett & Platt Incorporated 336 956-5000
3040 Junior Home Rd Woburn MA (01801) ***(G-17213)***
Legion Flying Club Inc 413 467-7844
70 Kendall St Granby MA (01033) ***(G-11229)***
Legnos Medical Inc 860 446-8058
973 North Rd Groton CT (06340) ***(G-1680)***
Lego Brand Retail, Enfield *Also called Lego Systems Inc* ***(G-1368)***
Lego Systems Inc (HQ) 860 749-2291
555 Taylor Rd Enfield CT (06082) ***(G-1368)***
Legrand, West Hartford *Also called Ortronics Inc* ***(G-5088)***
Legrand Holding Inc (HQ) 860 233-6251
60 Woodlawn St West Hartford CT (06110) ***(G-5080)***
Legu Tool and Mold LLC 207 850-1450
32 Smada Dr Sanford ME (04073) ***(G-6879)***
Lehi Sheet Metal Corporation 508 366-8550
245 Flanders Rd Westborough MA (01581) ***(G-16632)***
Lehigh Cement Company 800 833-4157
55 Fields Point Dr Providence RI (02905) ***(G-21051)***
Lehigh Cement Company LLC 401 467-6750
Municipal Whrf 25 Tremial Municipal Wharf Providence RI (02905) ***(G-21052)***
Lehouillier Maple Orchard 802 888-6465
798 Sterling View Rd Hyde Park VT (05655) ***(G-22036)***
Lehvoss North America LLC 860 495-2046
185 S Broad St Ste 2b Pawcatuck CT (06379) ***(G-3438)***
Leica Biosystems 978 471-0625
38 Cherry Hill Dr Danvers MA (01923) ***(G-10232)***
Leighton Logging, Barnstead *Also called Steve Leighton* ***(G-17617)***
Leightons Custom Machining 207 296-2601
Exeter Rd Stetson ME (04488) ***(G-7065)***
Leipold Inc 860 298-9791
545 Marshall Phelps Rd Windsor CT (06095) ***(G-5344)***
Leisure Group, Stamford *Also called Leisure Learning Products Inc* ***(G-4237)***
Leisure Learning Products Inc 203 325-2800
652 Glenbrook Rd Bldg 8 Stamford CT (06906) ***(G-4237)***
Leisure Manufacturing 978 373-3831
42 Phoenix Row Haverhill MA (01832) ***(G-11448)***
Leisure Time Canvas 413 785-5500
140 Norman St West Springfield MA (01089) ***(G-16528)***
Leland Boggs II 207 273-2610
715 Camden Rd Warren ME (04864) ***(G-7143)***
Lelanite Corporation (PA) 508 987-2637
1 Cudworth Rd Webster MA (01570) ***(G-16346)***
Lelanite Corporation 508 987-1771
Town Forest Rd Oxford MA (01540) ***(G-14266)***
Lemac Iron Works Inc 860 232-7380
18 Brainard Rd West Hartford CT (06117) ***(G-5081)***
Lemaitre Vascular Inc (PA) 781 221-2266
63 2nd Ave Burlington MA (01803) ***(G-9297)***
Lemire R & Sons LLC 603 588-3718
237 Elm Ave Antrim NH (03440) ***(G-17595)***
Lemire R & Sons Logging, Antrim *Also called Lemire R & Sons LLC* ***(G-17595)***
Len Libby Candy Shops, Scarborough *Also called Len Libbys Inc* ***(G-6931)***
Len Libbys Inc 207 883-4897
419 Us Route 1 Scarborough ME (04074) ***(G-6931)***
Len-Tex Corp 603 445-2342
18 Len Tex Ln North Walpole NH (03609) ***(G-19395)***
Len-Tex Wallcoverings, North Walpole *Also called Len-Tex Corp* ***(G-19395)***
Lenco Armored Vehicles, Pittsfield *Also called Lenco Industries Inc* ***(G-14483)***
Lenco Inc 802 775-2505
175 Quality Ln Rutland VT (05701) ***(G-22344)***
Lenco Industries Inc 413 443-7359
10 Betnr Industrial Dr Pittsfield MA (01201) ***(G-14483)***
Leni's Textiles, Canton *Also called Lenis Inc* ***(G-9752)***
Lenis Inc 781 401-3273
480 Neponset St Ste 4a Canton MA (02021) ***(G-9752)***
Lenmarine Inc (PA) 401 253-2200
99 Poppasquash Rd Unit 1 Bristol RI (02809) ***(G-20089)***
Lenmarine Inc 508 678-1234
1 Main St Somerset MA (02726) ***(G-15146)***
Lenn Arts Inc 508 223-3400
65 Newcomb St Attleboro MA (02703) ***(G-7759)***
Lennartz Enterprises LLC 978 663-6100
18 Esquire Rd North Billerica MA (01862) ***(G-13834)***
Lennox Roofing Inc 508 328-5780
23 Belcher St Abington MA (02351) ***(G-7327)***
Lennys Screen Printing 781 267-5977
78 Quincy Ave Braintree MA (02184) ***(G-9022)***
Lenox, East Longmeadow *Also called Newell Brands Inc* ***(G-10484)***
Lenox, East Longmeadow *Also called American Saw & Mfg Company Inc* ***(G-10466)***
Lenox Division, East Longmeadow *Also called Irwin Industrial Tool Company* ***(G-10480)***
Lenox Lumber Co 413 637-2744
325 Partridge Rd Pittsfield MA (01201) ***(G-14484)***
Lenses Only LLC 860 769-2020
812 Park Ave Bloomfield CT (06002) ***(G-239)***
Lensmaster Optical Company 508 764-4958
28 Sandersdale Rd Ste 1 Southbridge MA (01550) ***(G-15392)***
Lentros Engineering Inc 508 881-1160
280 Eliot St Ashland MA (01721) ***(G-7664)***
Lenze Americas Corporation (HQ) 508 278-9100
630 Douglas St Uxbridge MA (01569) ***(G-15924)***
Leo Coons Jr 508 995-3300
1091 Main St Acushnet MA (02743) ***(G-7404)***

ALPHABETIC

Leo D Bernstein & Sons Inc 802 442-8029
372 Vt Route 67 E Shaftsbury VT (05262) *(G-22404)*
Leo D Bernstein and Sons Inc 212 337-9578
372 Vt Route 67 E Shaftsbury VT (05262) *(G-22405)*
Leo S Cavelier Inc 978 369-2770
14 Wetherbee St Acton MA (01720) *(G-7368)*
Leo's Machine & Welding, Acushnet *Also called Leo Coons Jr (G-7404)*
Leominster Champion 978 534-6006
285 Central St Ste 202b Leominster MA (01453) *(G-12161)*
Leominster Ice & Oil Co, Leominster *Also called Leominster Ice Company Inc (G-12162)*
Leominster Ice Company Inc 978 537-5322
5 Chestnut St Leominster MA (01453) *(G-12162)*
Leon Levin, Pembroke *Also called Chic LLC (G-14395)*
Leon M Fiske Company Inc 413 772-6833
75 Oak Hill Rd Greenfield MA (01301) *(G-11268)*
Leon Merchant Signs (PA) 207 498-2475
72 Madawaska Rd Caribou ME (04736) *(G-5885)*
Leon's Upholstery, New London *Also called Clark Manner Marguarite (G-2769)*
Leona Corp 860 257-3840
638 Silas Deane Hwy Wethersfield CT (06109) *(G-5256)*
Leonard F Brooks (PA) 203 335-4934
199 Asylum St Bridgeport CT (06610) *(G-445)*
Leonard Philbrick Inc 603 635-3500
18 Atwood Rd Pelham NH (03076) *(G-19438)*
Leoni Wire Inc 413 593-6618
301 Griffith Rd Chicopee MA (01022) *(G-10038)*
Leopard Snow Publishing LLC 603 742-7714
171 Durham Rd Dover NH (03820) *(G-18034)*
Leos Kitchen & Stair Corp 860 225-7363
48 John St New Britain CT (06051) *(G-2548)*
Lepage Bakeries Park St LLC 207 783-9161
354 Lisbon St Lewiston ME (04240) *(G-6298)*
Lepage Bakeries Park St LLC 207 783-9161
11 Adamian Dr Auburn ME (04210) *(G-5576)*
Lepage Bakeries Park St LLC (HQ) 207 783-9161
11 Adamian Dr Auburn ME (04210) *(G-5577)*
Lepage Bakeries Park St LLC 603 524-9104
438 Union Rd Belmont NH (03220) *(G-17677)*
Lepage Bakeries Park St LLC 603 880-4446
2 Security Dr Hudson NH (03051) *(G-18410)*
Leprechaun Sheepskin Company 413 339-4355
464 Tea St Charlemont MA (01339) *(G-9820)*
Leslie W Robertson 207 824-2764
494 Bear River Rd Newry ME (04261) *(G-6491)*
Lesro Industries Inc 800 275-7545
1 Griffin Rd S Bloomfield CT (06002) *(G-240)*
Lessard & Sons Logging Inc 603 752-5767
1775 Hutchins St Berlin NH (03570) *(G-17699)*
Lessard & Sons Trucking, Berlin *Also called Lessard & Sons Logging Inc (G-17699)*
Lesser Evil 203 529-3555
18 Finance Dr Danbury CT (06810) *(G-946)*
Lestage 508 695-7038
360 Spring St Wrentham MA (02093) *(G-17525)*
Lets Go Inc 617 495-9659
67 Mount Auburn St Cambridge MA (02138) *(G-9534)*
Lets Go Technology Inc (PA) 508 853-8200
799 W Boylston St Worcester MA (01606) *(G-17407)*
Lets Yo Yogurt 413 525-4002
436 N Main St East Longmeadow MA (01028) *(G-10482)*
Letter Barn 802 885-5451
128 Union St Springfield VT (05156) *(G-22505)*
Letter Man Press, West Lebanon *Also called Letterman Press LLC (G-19956)*
Letter Systems Inc (PA) 207 622-7126
15 Darin Dr Augusta ME (04330) *(G-5613)*
Letterman Press LLC 603 543-0500
1 Glen Rd Ste 222 West Lebanon NH (03784) *(G-19956)*
Letterpress Services Inc 413 732-0399
85 Phelon Ave West Springfield MA (01089) *(G-16529)*
Leusin Microwave LLC 603 329-7270
6 Gigante Dr Hampstead NH (03841) *(G-18241)*
Levaggis Candies 781 335-1231
1186 Main St South Weymouth MA (02190) *(G-15321)*
Levasseur Precision Inc 603 524-6766
13 Artisan Ct Unit A Gilford NH (03249) *(G-18190)*
Leveillee Archtctral Mllwk Inc 508 885-9731
23 S Spencer Rd Spencer MA (01562) *(G-15432)*
Leveltrigger Inc 650 468-1098
212 Elm St Somerville MA (02144) *(G-15190)*
Levesque Farm Pallets 207 868-3905
182 Marquis Rd Van Buren ME (04785) *(G-7122)*
Leviton Manufacturing Co Inc 401 273-4875
1 State St Ste 400 Providence RI (02908) *(G-21053)*
Levr Inc 605 261-0083
260 Everett St Ste 2 Boston MA (02128) *(G-8663)*
Lew A Cummings Co Inc 603 625-6901
4 Peters Brook Dr Hooksett NH (03106) *(G-18352)*
Lewicki & Sons Excavating Inc 508 695-0122
15 Wilmarth Ln Plainville MA (02762) *(G-14526)*
Lewis and Saunders 603 528-1871
144 Lexington Dr Laconia NH (03246) *(G-18574)*
Lewis Bible Bindery, Hartland *Also called Darwin A Lewis Inc (G-22015)*
Lewis Graphics Inc 401 943-8300
269 Macklin St Cranston RI (02920) *(G-20253)*
Lewis R Martino 203 463-4430
328 Oxford Rd Oxford CT (06478) *(G-3412)*
Lewiston Daily Sun (PA) 207 784-3555
104 Park St Lewiston ME (04240) *(G-6299)*
Lewiston Daily Sun 207 784-5411
104 Park St Lewiston ME (04240) *(G-6300)*
Lewiston Daily Sun 207 364-8728
69 Congress St Rumford ME (04276) *(G-6837)*
Lewiston-Auburn Tent & Awng Co 207 784-7353
240 River Rd Lewiston ME (04240) *(G-6301)*
Lewmar Inc (HQ) 203 458-6200
351 New Whitfield St Guilford CT (06437) *(G-1708)*
Lewmar Marine, Guilford *Also called Lewmar Inc (G-1708)*
Lewtan Industries Corporation 860 278-9800
57 Loomis Dr Apt A1 West Hartford CT (06107) *(G-5082)*
Lex Products LLC (PA) 203 363-3738
15 Progress Dr Shelton CT (06484) *(G-3828)*
Lex-Aire Products Inc 978 663-7202
34 Sullivan Rd Ste 2 North Billerica MA (01862) *(G-13835)*
Lexia Learning Systems LLC 800 435-3942
300 Baker Ave Ste 320 Concord MA (01742) *(G-10138)*
Lexington Cat Clinic, Littleton *Also called Alpha Tech Pet Inc (G-12291)*
Lexington Data Incorporated 603 899-5673
316 Main St Rindge NH (03461) *(G-19650)*
Lexington Graphics 781 863-9510
76 Bedford St Ste 6 Lexington MA (02420) *(G-12237)*
Lexington Lighting Group LLC 860 564-4512
181 Narragansett Park Dr Rumford RI (02916) *(G-21192)*
Lexington Minuteman, Lexington *Also called Gatehouse Media Mass I Inc (G-12227)*
Lexington Press Inc 781 862-8900
15 Meriam St Lexington MA (02420) *(G-12238)*
Lexisnexis, Newton *Also called Relx Inc (G-13629)*
Lexitek Inc 781 431-9604
50 Hunt St Ste 120 Watertown MA (02472) *(G-16294)*
Lfi Inc (PA) 401 231-4400
1 Industrial Dr S Smithfield RI (02917) *(G-21236)*
Lfr Chassis Inc 508 425-3117
20 Sewall St Shrewsbury MA (01545) *(G-15121)*
Lgl Group Inc 407 298-2000
140 Greenwich Ave Ste 4 Greenwich CT (06830) *(G-1626)*
LH Gault & Son Incorporated 203 227-5181
11 Ferry Ln W Westport CT (06880) *(G-5209)*
Lhq Bicycle Components, Amherst *Also called Lifestyle Hq LLC (G-7517)*
Libbys Boat Shop 207 497-5487
12 Hixey Head Rd Beals ME (04611) *(G-5684)*
Liberated Images Inc 978 532-1880
119 Foster St Peabody MA (01960) *(G-14352)*
Liberating Technologies Inc 508 893-6363
325 Hopping Brook Rd A Holliston MA (01746) *(G-11582)*
Liberty Construction Svcs LLC 617 602-4001
65 Allerton St Roxbury MA (02119) *(G-14874)*
Liberty Engineering Inc 617 965-6644
26 Farwell St Newton MA (02460) *(G-13609)*
Liberty Enrgy Utlities NH Corp (HQ) 905 287-2061
15 Buttrick Rd Londonderry NH (03053) *(G-18713)*
Liberty Garage Inc 203 778-0222
51 Sugar Hollow Rd Ste 1 Danbury CT (06810) *(G-947)*
Liberty Glass and Met Inds Inc 860 923-3623
339 Riverside Dr North Grosvenordale CT (06255) *(G-2997)*
Liberty Graphics Inc 207 589-4596
Main St Liberty ME (04949) *(G-6331)*
Liberty Intercept, Braintree *Also called Liberty Packaging Co Inc (G-9023)*
Liberty Machine LLC 603 435-6613
409 Parade Rd Barnstead NH (03218) *(G-17616)*
Liberty Mtals Min Holdings LLC (PA) 617 654-4374
175 Berkeley St Boston MA (02116) *(G-8664)*
Liberty Packaging Co Inc 781 849-3355
22 Raleigh Rd Braintree MA (02184) *(G-9023)*
Liberty Plastics Company, Attleboro *Also called Applied Precision Technology (G-7706)*
Liberty Press Inc 603 641-1991
660 Mast Rd Manchester NH (03102) *(G-18864)*
Liberty Printing Co Inc 508 586-6810
99 Lawrence St Brockton MA (02302) *(G-9162)*
Liberty Publishing Inc 978 777-8200
100 Cummings Ctr Beverly MA (01915) *(G-8148)*
Liberty Research Co Inc (PA) 603 332-2730
7 Nadeau Dr Rochester NH (03867) *(G-19678)*
Liberty Screen Print Co LLC 203 632-5449
141 S Main St Beacon Falls CT (06403) *(G-60)*
Liberty Services LLC 860 399-0077
790 Boston Post Rd Ste 2 Westbrook CT (06498) *(G-5159)*
Liberty Utilities, Londonderry *Also called Liberty Enrgy Utlities NH Corp (G-18713)*
Libring Technologies Inc 617 553-1015
1 Broadway Fl 14 Cambridge MA (02142) *(G-9535)*
Licari Woodworking, Bridgeport *Also called James J Licari (G-434)*

Liddell Brothers Inc.......781 293-2100
61 Accord Park Dr Norwell MA (02061) *(G-14106)*
Lie-Nielsen Toolworks Inc.......800 327-2520
264 Stirling Rd Warren ME (04864) *(G-7144)*
Liebl Printing Co.......603 237-8650
15 Forbes Hill Rd Colebrook NH (03576) *(G-17873)*
Life Force Beverages LLC.......551 265-9482
196 Quincy St Boston MA (02121) *(G-8665)*
Life Global, Guilford *Also called Genx International Inc (G-1705)*
Life Image Inc.......617 244-8411
1 Gteway Ctr St Ste 200 Newton MA (02458) *(G-13610)*
Life Is Good (PA).......603 594-6100
15 Hudson Park Dr Hudson NH (03051) *(G-18411)*
Life Is Good Design Center, Hudson *Also called Life Is Good Wholesale Inc (G-18412)*
Life Is Good Wholesale Inc.......603 594-6100
15 Hudson Park Dr Hudson NH (03051) *(G-18412)*
Life Knives, Millis *Also called Khalsa Jot (G-13185)*
Life Publications.......860 953-0444
106 South St Ste 5 West Hartford CT (06110) *(G-5083)*
Life Study Fllwship Foundation.......203 655-1436
90 Heights Rd Darien CT (06820) *(G-1028)*
Life Technologies Corporation.......508 383-7700
500 Old Connecticut Path # 10 Framingham MA (01701) *(G-10976)*
Life+gear Inc.......858 755-2099
21 Cushing Rd Wellesley Hills MA (02481) *(G-16398)*
Lifeady Inc.......781 632-1296
72 Winsor Ave Watertown MA (02472) *(G-16295)*
Lifecanvas Technologies Inc.......404 274-1953
1035 Cambridge St Ste 9 Cambridge MA (02141) *(G-9536)*
Lifegas, Marlborough *Also called Linde Gas North America LLC (G-12786)*
Lifeglobal Group, The, Guilford *Also called Coopersurgical Inc (G-1699)*
Lifeimage, Newton *Also called Life Image Inc (G-13610)*
Lifeline Systems Company.......207 777-8827
100 Campus Ave Ste G1 Lewiston ME (04240) *(G-6302)*
Lifeline Systems Company.......603 653-1610
1 Medical Center Dr Lebanon NH (03756) *(G-18627)*
Lifeline Systems Company (HQ).......508 988-1000
111 Lawrence St Framingham MA (01702) *(G-10977)*
Lifeline Systems Company.......508 988-3000
111 Lawrence St Framingham MA (01702) *(G-10978)*
Lifeline Systems Securities, Framingham *Also called Lifeline Systems Company (G-10978)*
Lifestyle Hq LLC.......310 741-8489
158 High Point Dr Amherst MA (01002) *(G-7517)*
Lifetime Acrylic Signs Inc.......203 255-6751
593 Cascade Dr Fairfield CT (06825) *(G-1442)*
Lifetime Brands Inc.......401 333-2040
999 Main St Unit 115 Pawtucket RI (02860) *(G-20854)*
Liftbag Usa Inc.......401 884-8801
6946 Post Rd N Kingstown North Kingstown RI (02852) *(G-20722)*
Liftline Capital LLC.......860 395-0150
7 Center Rd W Old Saybrook CT (06475) *(G-3342)*
Light Engines LLC.......508 347-3647
29 Library Ln S Sturbridge MA (01566) *(G-15640)*
Light Fantastic Realty Inc.......203 934-3441
114 Boston Post Rd West Haven CT (06516) *(G-5131)*
Light Logic Inc.......802 888-7984
902 Silver Ridge Rd Hyde Park VT (05655) *(G-22037)*
Light Metal Platers LLC.......781 899-8855
70 Clematis Ave Waltham MA (02453) *(G-16145)*
Light Metals Coloring Co Inc.......860 621-0145
270 Spring St Southington CT (06489) *(G-4062)*
Light Rock Beverage, Danbury *Also called Light Rock Spring Water Co (G-948)*
Light Rock Spring Water Co.......203 743-2251
9 Balmforth Ave Danbury CT (06810) *(G-948)*
Light Sources Inc (PA).......203 799-7877
37 Robinson Blvd Orange CT (06477) *(G-3371)*
Light Sources Inc.......203 799-7877
70 Cascade Blvd Milford CT (06460) *(G-2309)*
Lightblocks Inc.......603 889-1115
32 Hampshire Rd Salem NH (03079) *(G-19747)*
Lighthouse Imaging LLC.......207 893-8233
765 Roosevelt Trl Windham ME (04062) *(G-7240)*
Lighthouse International LLC.......860 528-4722
125 S Satellite Rd South Windsor CT (06074) *(G-3990)*
Lighthouse Manufacturing LLC.......978 532-5999
35 Mirona Road Ext Portsmouth NH (03801) *(G-19586)*
Lighthouse Printing LLC.......860 388-2677
315 Boston Post Rd Ste 3 Old Saybrook CT (06475) *(G-3343)*
Lighthouse Publications.......401 396-9888
30 Bradford St Bristol RI (02809) *(G-20090)*
Lighthouse Publications (PA).......508 534-9291
350 Kidds Hill Rd Hyannis MA (02601) *(G-11845)*
Lighthouse Technology Partners, Greenwich *Also called Desrosier of Greenwich Inc (G-1608)*
Lighthouse Woodworks LLC.......781 223-4302
175 Wlliam F Mcclllan Hwy Boston MA (02128) *(G-8666)*
Lighting Edge Inc.......860 767-8968
50 West Ave Ste 4 Essex CT (06426) *(G-1402)*
Lighting Quotient, The, West Haven *Also called Sylvan R Shemitz Designs LLC (G-5147)*
Lighting Solutions Inc.......207 772-2738
52 Middle Rd Falmouth ME (04105) *(G-6031)*
Lightmatter Inc.......857 244-0460
61 Chatham St Fl 5 Boston MA (02109) *(G-8667)*
Lightninglabel.com, Stamford *Also called Cenveo Worldwide Limited (G-4163)*
Lightolier, Fall River *Also called Signify North America Corp (G-10761)*
Lightship Group LLC (PA).......401 294-3341
606 Ten Rod Rd Unit 6 North Kingstown RI (02852) *(G-20723)*
Lightspeed Mfg Co LLC.......978 521-7676
63 Neck Rd Haverhill MA (01835) *(G-11449)*
Lignetics New England Inc.......603 532-4666
141 Old Sharon Rd Jaffrey NH (03452) *(G-18471)*
Lignetics New England Inc.......603 532-4666
415 Squantum Rd Jaffrey NH (03452) *(G-18472)*
Lignetics New England Inc.......413 284-1050
21 Wilbraham St Unit B13 Palmer MA (01069) *(G-14288)*
Lignetics of Maine.......207 684-3457
30 Norton Hill Rd Strong ME (04983) *(G-7072)*
Lil' Dogs, Agawam *Also called Pros Choice Inc (G-7448)*
Lilly's Fresh Pasta, Everett *Also called Lillys Gastronomia Italian (G-10617)*
Lillys Gastronomia Italian.......617 387-9666
208 Main St Everett MA (02149) *(G-10617)*
Lilypad LLC.......207 200-0221
17 Cole Field Rd Cape Elizabeth ME (04107) *(G-5877)*
Lim Jewelry.......401 946-9656
90 Libera St Ste 12 Cranston RI (02920) *(G-20254)*
Lima Fredy.......781 599-3055
69 Norman St Ste 17 Everett MA (02149) *(G-10618)*
Llmage Inc.......401 369-7141
4 Industrial Ln Johnston RI (02919) *(G-20518)*
Limb-It-Less Logging LLC.......860 227-0987
182 Saybrook Rd Essex CT (06426) *(G-1403)*
Limbkeepers LLC.......860 304-3250
25 Joshuatown Rd Lyme CT (06371) *(G-1955)*
Limerick Dough Boy.......207 793-4145
8 Maple St Limerick ME (04048) *(G-6336)*
Limerick Machine Company Inc.......207 793-2288
81 Central Ave Limerick ME (04048) *(G-6337)*
Limestone Communications (PA).......413 528-5380
21 Elm St Great Barrington MA (01230) *(G-11241)*
Limington Lumber Company.......207 625-3286
411 Pequawket Trl East Baldwin ME (04024) *(G-5974)*
Limlaws Pulpwood Inc.......802 439-3503
261 Vt Route 25 West Topsham VT (05086) *(G-22622)*
Limmer Education LLC.......207 482-0622
1 Sayward St Kennebunk ME (04043) *(G-6238)*
Limo Chipping and Land Query, West Topsham *Also called Limlaws Pulpwood Inc (G-22622)*
Lincoln County News, Newcastle *Also called Lincoln County Publishing Co (G-6483)*
Lincoln County Publishing Co.......207 563-3171
116 Mills Rd Newcastle ME (04553) *(G-6483)*
Lincoln Creamery Inc.......401 724-1050
276 Front St Frnt 1 Lincoln RI (02865) *(G-20579)*
Lincoln Electric Holdings Inc.......508 366-7070
6 N Main St Ste 205 Uxbridge MA (01569) *(G-15925)*
Lincoln Hoist, North Grafton *Also called Lincoln Precision Machining Co (G-13963)*
Lincoln Learning Solutions LLC.......781 259-9696
23 Birchwood Ln Lincoln MA (01773) *(G-12287)*
Lincoln News.......207 794-6532
78 W Broadway Lincoln ME (04457) *(G-6357)*
Lincoln Packing Co.......401 943-0878
7 Industrial Rd Cranston RI (02920) *(G-20255)*
Lincoln Precision Machine Inc.......860 923-9358
923 Thompson Rd Thompson CT (06277) *(G-4535)*
Lincoln Precision Machining Co.......508 839-2175
121 Creeper Hill Rd North Grafton MA (01536) *(G-13963)*
Lincoln Press Co Inc.......508 673-3241
407 Pleasant St Fall River MA (02721) *(G-10723)*
Lincoln Tool & Machine Corp.......508 485-2940
43 Parmenter Rd Hudson MA (01749) *(G-11786)*
Lincoln, RI Plant, Lincoln *Also called General Cable Industries Inc (G-20575)*
Linde Gas North America LLC.......508 229-8118
50 Dangelo Dr Ste 1 Marlborough MA (01752) *(G-12786)*
Linden Photonics Inc.......978 392-7985
1 Park Dr Ste 10 Westford MA (01886) *(G-16776)*
Lindon Group Inc.......401 272-2081
28 Sutton Ave East Providence RI (02914) *(G-20430)*
Lindt & Sprungli (usa) Inc (HQ).......603 778-8100
1 Fine Chocolate Pl Stratham NH (03885) *(G-19871)*
Line Bore Industries Inc.......508 987-6509
3 Harlan Dr Oxford MA (01540) *(G-14267)*
Line Electric, Glastonbury *Also called General Electro Components (G-1554)*
Line-X Merrimack Valley LLC.......603 224-7792
617 Route 3a Bow NH (03304) *(G-17721)*
Linear & Metric Co.......603 432-1700
37 Harvey Rd Londonderry NH (03053) *(G-18714)*
Linear Technology LLC.......978 656-4750
15 Research Pl North Chelmsford MA (01863) *(G-13901)*

Linemaster Switch Corporation 860 630-4920
29 Plaine Hill Rd Woodstock CT (06281) ***(G-5498)***
Linemaster Switch Corporation 860 564-7713
16 Center Pkwy Plainfield CT (06374) ***(G-3453)***
Linesider Brewing Company LLC 401 398-7700
1485 S County Trl Ste 201 East Greenwich RI (02818) ***(G-20371)***
Linesider Communications Inc 617 671-0000
55 Ferncroft Rd Ste 120 Danvers MA (01923) ***(G-10233)***
Linesider Technologies, Danvers *Also called Linesider Communications Inc* ***(G-10233)***
Lingard Cabinet Co LLC 860 647-9886
540 N Main St Ste 2 Manchester CT (06042) ***(G-2019)***
Lingol Corporation 203 265-3608
415 S Cherry St Wallingford CT (06492) ***(G-4766)***
Link AKC, Stamford *Also called Wagz Inc* ***(G-4356)***
Link Enterprises Corp 413 585-9869
82 Industrial Dr Northampton MA (01060) ***(G-14010)***
Link Metal Corporation 603 569-5085
45 Bay St Wolfeboro NH (03894) ***(G-20022)***
Linkletter and Sons Inc 207 654-2301
115 Harmony Rd Athens ME (04912) ***(G-5541)***
Linmel Associates Inc 508 481-6699
160 Main St Marlborough MA (01752) ***(G-12787)***
Lins Propane Trucks Corp 508 669-6665
2281 Cedar St Dighton MA (02715) ***(G-10337)***
Linton Welding & Fabrication 978 681-7736
4 Home St Lawrence MA (01841) ***(G-12048)***
Linvar LLC 860 951-3818
2189 Silas Deane Hwy # 15 Rocky Hill CT (06067) ***(G-3721)***
Linx Consulting LLC 508 461-6333
661 S Main St Ste 7 Webster MA (01570) ***(G-16347)***
Lion Gold Mining Llc 617 785-2345
110 Central Ave Malden MA (02148) ***(G-12577)***
Lion Labels Inc 508 230-8211
15 Hampden Dr South Easton MA (02375) ***(G-15284)***
Lionano Inc 607 216-8156
19 Presidential Way # 103 Woburn MA (01801) ***(G-17214)***
Lionheart Technologies Inc (PA) 802 655-4040
100 Tigan St Winooski VT (05404) ***(G-22721)***
Lipid Genomics Inc 443 465-3495
400 Farmington Ave R1718 Farmington CT (06032) ***(G-1490)***
Lipomed Inc 617 577-7222
150 Cambridgepark Dr # 705 Cambridge MA (02140) ***(G-9537)***
Liquid Blue Inc 401 333-6200
6 Linlew Dr Derry NH (03038) ***(G-17987)***
Liquid Measurement Systems Inc 802 528-8100
141 Morse Dr Milton VT (05468) ***(G-22133)***
Liquid Metronics Incorporated 978 263-9800
8 Post Office Sq Ste 1 Acton MA (01720) ***(G-7369)***
Liquidpiston Inc 860 838-2677
1292a Blue Hills Ave Bloomfield CT (06002) ***(G-241)***
Liquidsky Technologies Inc (PA) 857 389-9893
89 Access Rd Norwood MA (02062) ***(G-14175)***
Liquiglide Inc 617 901-0700
75 Sidney St Fl 5 Cambridge MA (02139) ***(G-9538)***
Lirakis Safety Harness Inc 401 846-5356
18 Sheffield Ave Newport RI (02840) ***(G-20671)***
Lisa Jo Rudy 508 540-7293
21 Ridgeview Dr Falmouth MA (02540) ***(G-10795)***
Lisa Lee Creations Inc 203 479-4462
10 Selden St New Haven CT (06525) ***(G-2706)***
Lisa Signs Inc 781 935-1821
2 Norwood Cir Woburn MA (01801) ***(G-17215)***
Lisbon Sausage Co Inc 508 993-7645
433 S 2nd St New Bedford MA (02740) ***(G-13408)***
Lisha & Nirali Fuel LLC 908 433-6504
223 Maple St Middleton MA (01949) ***(G-13094)***
Lista International, Holliston *Also called Stanley Industrial & Auto LLC* ***(G-11604)***
Listen Inc 617 556-4104
580 Harrison Ave Ste 3w Boston MA (02118) ***(G-8668)***
Litchfield International Inc 860 567-8824
457 Bantam Rd Ste 12 Litchfield CT (06759) ***(G-1951)***
Litchfield Sand & Gravel 603 424-6515
1 Continental Dr Londonderry NH (03053) ***(G-18715)***
Lite Control, Plympton *Also called Litecontrol Corporation* ***(G-14592)***
Litecontrol Corporation 781 294-0100
65 Spring St Plympton MA (02367) ***(G-14592)***
Litho-Craft Inc 781 729-1789
1 Lowell Ave Winchester MA (01890) ***(G-17091)***
Lithographics Inc 860 678-1660
55 Spring Ln Farmington CT (06032) ***(G-1491)***
Lithoptek LLC 408 533-5847
8 Tech Cir Natick MA (01760) ***(G-13264)***
Litron LLC 413 789-0700
207 Bowles Rd Agawam MA (01001) ***(G-7437)***
Little Acre Gourmet Foods 603 749-7227
7 W Knox Marsh Rd Dover NH (03820) ***(G-18035)***
Little Bits Manufacturing Inc 860 923-2772
694 Riverside Dr North Grosvenordale CT (06255) ***(G-2998)***
Little Delights Bakery 978 455-0040
132 Merrimack St Lowell MA (01852) ***(G-12396)***
Little Enterprises Inc 978 356-7422
31 Locust Rd Ipswich MA (01938) ***(G-11929)***
Little Gottage Baking 207 432-2930
32 Guillemette St Sanford ME (04073) ***(G-6880)***
Little Harbor Window Co Inc 207 698-1332
11 Little Harbor Rd Berwick ME (03901) ***(G-5710)***
Little Harbor Window Company, Berwick *Also called Little Harbor Window Co Inc* ***(G-5710)***
Little House By Andre Inc 802 878-8733
69 Creek Farm Plz Ste 3 Colchester VT (05446) ***(G-21872)***
Little John's Sign Factory, Enfield *Also called Sign Factory* ***(G-1384)***
Little Kids Inc 401 454-7600
1015 Newman Ave Seekonk MA (02771) ***(G-15026)***
Little Notch Bakery 207 244-4043
11 Apple Ln Southwest Harbor ME (04679) ***(G-7048)***
Little Rhody Brand, Johnston *Also called Rhode Island Provision Co Inc* ***(G-20537)***
Little Rhody Machine Repair 401 828-1919
7 Alice St Coventry RI (02816) ***(G-20153)***
Little River Hot Glass Studio, Stowe *Also called Little River Hotglass Studio* ***(G-22523)***
Little River Hotglass Studio 802 253-0889
593 Moscow Rd Stowe VT (05672) ***(G-22523)***
Little Shop of Olive Oils Inc 508 533-5522
23 Broken Tree Rd Medway MA (02053) ***(G-12965)***
Littleton Millwork Inc 603 444-2677
44 Lafayette Ave Littleton NH (03561) ***(G-18662)***
Liturgical Publications Inc 203 966-6470
87 Lambert Rd New Canaan CT (06840) ***(G-2603)***
Liuzzi Cheese, Hamden *Also called Ndr Liuzzi Inc* ***(G-1774)***
Live Cell Technologies LLC 646 662-4157
4 Longfellow Pl Apt 1805 Boston MA (02114) ***(G-8669)***
Live Wire Marketing Corp 603 969-8771
26 Massabesic St Manchester NH (03103) ***(G-18865)***
Livermall Falls Advertiser, Farmington *Also called Kirkland Newspaper Inc* ***(G-6051)***
Living Acres LLC 207 778-2390
251 Weeks Mills Rd New Sharon ME (04955) ***(G-6478)***
Living Magazine 203 283-5290
162 Bridgeport Ave Milford CT (06460) ***(G-2310)***
Living Power Systems Inc 617 496-8328
16 Divinity Ave 3085 Cambridge MA (02138) ***(G-9539)***
Living Systems Instrumentation 802 863-5547
156 Battery St Ste 5 Burlington VT (05401) ***(G-21794)***
Livingstone Studios 401 475-1145
85 Industrial Cir Ste 113 Lincoln RI (02865) ***(G-20580)***
Lizotte Welding 508 763-8784
12 Carpenter Ln East Freetown MA (02717) ***(G-10454)***
Lizotte's Machine & Welding, East Freetown *Also called Lizotte Welding* ***(G-10454)***
LJL Enterprises Inc 781 639-2714
20 Webster St Fl 4 Peabody MA (01960) ***(G-14353)***
Ljm Packaging Co Inc 401 295-2660
330 Romano Vineyard Way North Kingstown RI (02852) ***(G-20724)***
LKM Industries Inc 781 935-9210
44 6th Rd Ste 2 Woburn MA (01801) ***(G-17216)***
Lkq Precious Metals Inc 401 762-0094
800 Central St North Smithfield RI (02896) ***(G-20789)***
LL Bean Mfg Bus, Brunswick *Also called L L Bean Inc* ***(G-5840)***
LLC Cochran Cousins 802 222-0440
170 Boyer Cir Ste 20 Williston VT (05495) ***(G-22679)***
LLC Dow Gage 860 828-5327
169 White Oak Dr 6037 Berlin CT (06037) ***(G-92)***
LLC Dow Gage 860 828-5327
169 White Oak Dr Berlin CT (06037) ***(G-93)***
LLC Glass House 860 974-1665
50 Swedetown Rd Pomfret Center CT (06259) ***(G-3556)***
Lloyd Labs 781 224-0083
24 Fitch Ct Wakefield MA (01880) ***(G-15957)***
Lloyds Woodworking Inc 978 562-9007
86 River St Hudson MA (01749) ***(G-11787)***
Lm, Newport *Also called Latva Machine Inc* ***(G-19348)***
Lm Gill Welding & Mfg, Manchester *Also called L M Gill Welding and Mfr LLC* ***(G-2018)***
LM Gill Welding & Mfg LLC 860 647-9931
1422 Tolland Tpke Manchester CT (06042) ***(G-2020)***
Lmg Rhode Island Holdings Inc 401 849-3300
272 Valley Rd Middletown RI (02842) ***(G-20624)***
Lmg Rhode Island Holdings Inc (HQ) 585 598-0030
119 Harris Ave Providence RI (02902) ***(G-21054)***
LMI Liquidation Corporation 781 593-2561
15 Marion St Lynn MA (01905) ***(G-12521)***
Lmj Enterprises LLC (PA) 207 794-3489
445 Main St Lincoln ME (04457) ***(G-6358)***
LMS, Milton *Also called Liquid Measurement Systems Inc* ***(G-22133)***
Lna Laser Technology, Pawtucket *Also called Laservall North America LLC* ***(G-20853)***
Lo Stocco Motors 203 797-9618
19 Chestnut St Danbury CT (06810) ***(G-949)***
Loadspring Solutions Inc (PA) 978 685-9715
187 Ballardvale St B210 Wilmington MA (01887) ***(G-17018)***
Loanworks Servicing LLC 203 402-7304
3 Corporate Dr Ste 208 Shelton CT (06484) ***(G-3829)***
Loaves & Fishes Ministries 860 524-1730
646 Prospect Ave Hartford CT (06105) ***(G-1840)***

Lobster Rx...207 949-2028
99 Forest Ave Orono ME (04473) *(G-6555)*
Lobster Unlimited, Orono *Also called Lobster Rx (G-6555)*
Local Juice Inc...508 813-9282
539 South St Hyannis MA (02601) *(G-11846)*
Local Media Group Inc...508 775-1200
319 Main St Hyannis MA (02601) *(G-11847)*
Local Media Group Inc...508 997-7411
25 Elm St New Bedford MA (02740) *(G-13409)*
Local Media Group Inc...603 436-1800
111 New Hampshire Ave Portsmouth NH (03801) *(G-19587)*
Local Media Group Inc...860 354-2273
45 Main St New Milford CT (06776) *(G-2813)*
Local Media Group Inc...508 947-1760
25 Elm St New Bedford MA (02740) *(G-13410)*
Local Tortilla LLC...413 387-7140
113 Bay Rd Hadley MA (01035) *(G-11309)*
Locallive Networks Inc...877 355-6225
175 Atlantic St Ste 2 Stamford CT (06901) *(G-4238)*
Localytics, Boston *Also called Char Software Inc (G-8468)*
Location Lube Inc...508 888-5000
164 Mid Tech Dr Unit H West Yarmouth MA (02673) *(G-16579)*
Locked In Steel...603 233-8299
16 Abbott St Hudson NH (03051) *(G-18365)*
Lockett Medical Corporation (PA)...401 421-6599
3 Richmond Sq Providence RI (02906) *(G-21055)*
Lockheed Martin - RMS, Burlington *Also called Lockheed Martin Corp - Boston (G-9298)*
Lockheed Martin Corp - Boston...781 565-1100
35 Corporate Dr Ste 250 Burlington MA (01803) *(G-9298)*
Lockheed Martin Corporation...978 256-4113
16 Maple Rd Chelmsford MA (01824) *(G-9913)*
Lockheed Martin Corporation...978 256-4113
16 Maple Rd Chelmsford MA (01824) *(G-9914)*
Lockheed Martin Corporation...508 460-0086
5 Mount Royal Ave Marlborough MA (01752) *(G-12788)*
Lockheed Martin Corporation...781 862-6222
2 Forbes Rd Lexington MA (02421) *(G-12239)*
Lockheed Martin Corporation...413 236-3400
75 S Church St Ste 401 Pittsfield MA (01201) *(G-14485)*
Lockheed Martin Corporation...603 885-5295
144 Daniel Webster Hwy Merrimack NH (03054) *(G-19012)*
Lockheed Martin Corporation...603 885-4321
410 Amherst St Ste 200 Nashua NH (03063) *(G-19199)*
Lockheed Martin Corporation...603 885-4321
95 Canal St Nashua NH (03064) *(G-19200)*
Lockheed Martin Corporation...207 442-1112
590 Washington St Bath ME (04530) *(G-5680)*
Lockheed Martin Global Inc...401 849-3703
76 Hammarlund Way Ste 1 Middletown RI (02842) *(G-20625)*
Lockheed Martin Info. Tech, Middletown *Also called Lockheed Martin Global Inc (G-20625)*
Lockheed Martin Mis Fire Ctrl, Chelmsford *Also called Lockheed Martin Corporation (G-9914)*
Lockheed Martin Rso, Bath *Also called Lockheed Martin Corporation (G-5680)*
Lockheed Martin Services LLC...978 275-9730
175 Cabot St Ste 415 Lowell MA (01854) *(G-12397)*
Lockheed Martin Sippican Inc (HQ)...508 748-3399
7 Barnabas Rd Marion MA (02738) *(G-12699)*
Lockheed Martin Sippican Inc...774 553-6282
7 Barnabas Rd Marion MA (02738) *(G-12700)*
Lockheed Window Corp...401 568-3061
925 S Main St Pascoag RI (02859) *(G-20802)*
Lockwood Mfg Inc...207 764-4196
135 Parsons St Presque Isle ME (04769) *(G-6760)*
Lodestone Biomedical LLC...617 686-5517
16 Cavendish Ct Lebanon NH (03766) *(G-18628)*
Log Cabin Bldg Co & Sawmill...603 788-3036
3 Walker Dr Lancaster NH (03584) *(G-18601)*
Log House Designs Inc (PA)...603 694-3373
184 Butter Hill Rd Chatham NH (03813) *(G-17822)*
Logan Grate Inc...617 569-5280
42 Lynde St Everett MA (02149) *(G-10619)*
Logan Instruments Inc...617 394-0601
101a French Ave Braintree MA (02184) *(G-9024)*
Logan Stamp Works Inc...617 569-2121
104 Meridian St 106 Boston MA (02128) *(G-8670)*
Logantech, Waterbury *Also called Proxtalkercom LLC (G-4947)*
Logic Seal LLC...203 598-3400
10 Sparks St Plainville CT (06062) *(G-3501)*
Logicbio Therapeutics Inc...617 230-0399
99 Erie St Ste 1 Cambridge MA (02139) *(G-9540)*
Login VSI Inc...844 828-3693
300 Tradecenter Ste 3460 Woburn MA (01801) *(G-17217)*
Logmein Inc (PA)...781 638-9050
320 Summer St Ste 100 Boston MA (02210) *(G-8671)*
Logo Sportswear Inc...203 678-4700
12 Beaumont Rd Wallingford CT (06492) *(G-4767)*
Lohmann Animal Health Intl Inc...207 873-3989
375 China Rd Winslow ME (04901) *(G-7270)*
Lohnes Pallet...781 878-6801
72 B St Hanover MA (02339) *(G-11345)*
Lohnes' Pallet Co, Hanover *Also called Lohnes Pallet (G-11345)*
Lolas Italian Harvest LLC...508 651-0524
9 Main St Natick MA (01760) *(G-13265)*
Lolli Company Inc...978 537-8343
637 Lancaster St Leominster MA (01453) *(G-12163)*
Lollipop Kids LLC...203 664-1799
13 Woodland Drive Ext Redding CT (06896) *(G-3649)*
Lolo Bags, New Canaan *Also called Putu LLC (G-2613)*
Long Falls Paperboard LLC...802 257-0365
161 Wellington Rd Brattleboro VT (05301) *(G-21737)*
Long Island Pipe New Hampshire, Salem *Also called Long Island Pipe Supply NH Inc (G-19748)*
Long Island Pipe Supply Inc...860 688-1780
1220 Kennedy Rd Windsor CT (06095) *(G-5345)*
Long Island Pipe Supply NH Inc...603 685-3200
50 Northwestern Dr Ste 6b Salem NH (03079) *(G-19748)*
LONG ISLAND PIPE SUPPLY OF ALBANY, INC., Windsor *Also called Long Island Pipe Supply Inc (G-5345)*
Long Life Saunas...802 349-0501
112 Pond Rd Ste G Bowdoinham ME (04008) *(G-5789)*
Long Live Beerworks Inc...203 980-0121
58 Hudson St Providence RI (02909) *(G-21056)*
Long Meadow Farms Quilts...802 334-5532
305 Union St Ste A Newport VT (05855) *(G-22200)*
Long Range LLC...603 934-3009
26 Cannery St Franklin NH (03235) *(G-18159)*
Long Trail Brewing Company...802 672-5011
5520 Us Route 4 Bridgewater Corners VT (05035) *(G-21758)*
Long Trail Glass Distributor, Rutland *Also called Emporium (G-22334)*
Longcap Lamson Products LLC...413 642-8135
79 Mainline Dr Westfield MA (01085) *(G-16697)*
Longford's Own, Stamford *Also called Longfords Ice Cream Ltd (G-4239)*
Longfords Ice Cream Ltd...914 935-9469
425 Fairfield Ave Ste 25 Stamford CT (06902) *(G-4239)*
Longhill Partners Inc (PA)...802 457-4000
4 Sunset Farms Woodstock VT (05091) *(G-22738)*
Longhini LLC...212 219-1230
41 Longhini Ln New Haven CT (06519) *(G-2707)*
Longmeadow Package Store Inc...413 567-3201
400 Longmeadow St Longmeadow MA (01106) *(G-12335)*
Longray Inc...781 862-5137
14 Taft Ave Lexington MA (02421) *(G-12240)*
Longrun LLC...617 758-8674
464 Common St U207 Belmont MA (02478) *(G-8077)*
Longto Tree Service...802 274-9308
887 Mink Hl Bradford VT (05033) *(G-21703)*
Longwood Software Inc...978 897-2900
107 Main St Maynard MA (01754) *(G-12900)*
Longworth Venture Partners LP (PA)...781 663-3600
17 Chickadee Dr Norfolk MA (02056) *(G-13663)*
Lonza Biologics Inc...603 610-4696
40 Goosebay Dr Portsmouth NH (03801) *(G-19588)*
Lonza Biologics Inc (HQ)...603 610-4500
101 International Dr Portsmouth NH (03801) *(G-19589)*
Lonza Rockland Inc...207 594-3400
191 Thomaston St Rockland ME (04841) *(G-6802)*
Lonza Wood Protection...203 229-2900
501 Merritt 7 Norwalk CT (06851) *(G-3186)*
Lookout Solutions LLC...203 750-0307
7 Lookout Rd Norwalk CT (06850) *(G-3187)*
Looks Gourmet Food Co Inc (HQ)...207 259-3341
1112 Cutler Rd Whiting ME (04691) *(G-7221)*
Loon Medical Inc...860 373-0217
1 Technology Dr Tolland CT (06084) *(G-4550)*
Loop Weekly...978 683-8800
238 Pleasant St Methuen MA (01844) *(G-13033)*
Loos & Co Inc (PA)...860 928-7981
16b Mashamoquet Rd Pomfret CT (06258) *(G-3552)*
Loos & Co Inc...860 928-6681
Rr 101 Pomfret CT (06258) *(G-3553)*
Lopesdzine...508 857-0121
1 Bert Dr Ste 3 West Bridgewater MA (02379) *(G-16443)*
Lorac Company Inc...401 781-3330
97 Johnson St Providence RI (02905) *(G-21057)*
Lorac Union Tool, Providence *Also called Lorac Company Inc (G-21057)*
Lorad Corporation...203 790-5544
36 Apple Ridge Rd Danbury CT (06810) *(G-950)*
Lorad Medical Systems, Danbury *Also called Lorad Corporation (G-950)*
Loral Press Inc...603 362-5549
7 Main St Atkinson NH (03811) *(G-17605)*
Lord & Hodge Inc...860 632-7006
362 Industrial Park Rd # 4 Middletown CT (06457) *(G-2201)*
Lord Corporation (HQ)...802 862-6629
459 Hurricane Ln Ste 102 Williston VT (05495) *(G-22680)*
Lord Hobo Brewing Company LLC...781 281-0809
5 Draper St Woburn MA (01801) *(G-17218)*
Lord Microstrain, Williston *Also called Lord Corporation (G-22680)*

ALPHABETIC

Lorence Sign Works LLC 860 829-9999
55 Willow Brook Dr Berlin CT (06037) ***(G-94)***
Lorence Signworks, Berlin *Also called Lorence Sign Works LLC* ***(G-94)***
Lorenco Industries Inc 203 743-6962
25 Henry St Bethel CT (06801) ***(G-169)***
Lorenzos Bakery LLC 508 287-9974
1533 Acushnet Ave New Bedford MA (02746) ***(G-13411)***
Loreto Publications Inc 603 239-6671
139a Tully Brook Rd Fitzwilliam NH (03447) ***(G-18150)***
Lorex Plastics Co Inc 203 286-0020
221 Wilson Ave Norwalk CT (06854) ***(G-3188)***
Loric Tool Inc 860 928-0171
95 Gaumond Rd North Grosvenordale CT (06255) ***(G-2999)***
Lorimer Studios LLC 401 714-0014
35 Brown St North Kingstown RI (02852) ***(G-20725)***
Loring Industries LLC 207 328-7005
14 Colorado Rd Limestone ME (04750) ***(G-6342)***
Lorusso Corp (PA) 508 668-6520
3 Belcher St Plainville MA (02762) ***(G-14527)***
Lorusso, SM & Son, Wrentham *Also called S M Lorusso & Sons Inc* ***(G-17528)***
Lorusso-Bristol Stone, East Weymouth *Also called S M Lorusso & Sons Inc* ***(G-10546)***
Los Angles Tmes Cmmnctions LLC 203 965-6434
250 Harbor Dr Stamford CT (06902) ***(G-4240)***
Lost Nation Brewing LLC 802 851-8041
87 Old Creamery Rd Morrisville VT (05661) ***(G-22171)***
Lost Sock Corporation 978 664-0730
26 Hillview Rd North Reading MA (01864) ***(G-13986)***
Loto Lighting LLc 617 776-3115
1 Fitchburg St Apt C305 Somerville MA (02143) ***(G-15191)***
Lou-Jan Tool & Die Inc 203 272-3536
161 E Johnson Ave Cheshire CT (06410) ***(G-742)***
Loud Technologies Inc 508 234-6158
1 Main St Ste 1 # 1 Whitinsville MA (01588) ***(G-16916)***
Loudon Screen Printing Inc 603 736-9420
1929 Dover Rd Epsom NH (03234) ***(G-18106)***
Louie and Teds Blacktop Inc 508 678-4948
105 Buffington St Swansea MA (02777) ***(G-15707)***
Louis C Morin Company Inc 978 670-1222
19 Sterling Rd Ste 4 North Billerica MA (01862) ***(G-13836)***
Louis E Allyn Sons Inc 860 542-5741
270 Ashpohtag Rd Norfolk CT (06058) ***(G-2958)***
Louis Electric Co Inc 203 879-5483
1584 Wolcott Rd Wolcott CT (06716) ***(G-5447)***
Louis Garneau USA Inc 802 334-5885
3916 Us Route 5 Derby VT (05829) ***(G-21901)***
Louis M Gerson Co Inc (PA) 508 947-4000
16 Commerce Blvd Ste D Middleboro MA (02346) ***(G-13065)***
Louis M Gerson Co Inc 508 947-4000
15 Sumner Ave Middleboro MA (02346) ***(G-13066)***
Louis Press Inc 401 351-9229
39 Greenville Ave Apt 1 Johnston RI (02919) ***(G-20519)***
Louis Richards 508 671-9017
661 S Main St Ste 1 Webster MA (01570) ***(G-16348)***
Louis Rodriguz 203 777-6937
145 Adeline St New Haven CT (06519) ***(G-2708)***
Louis W Mian Inc (PA) 617 241-7900
547 Rutherford Ave Boston MA (02129) ***(G-8672)***
Lovallo Metalspinning 413 743-3947
915 N State Rd Cheshire MA (01225) ***(G-9979)***
Love 'n Herbs, Waterbury *Also called Da Silva Klanko Ltd* ***(G-4863)***
Lovejoy Curtis LLC 413 737-0281
4 Birnie Ave Springfield MA (01107) ***(G-15485)***
Lovejoy Tool Company Inc 802 885-2194
133 Main St Springfield VT (05156) ***(G-22506)***
Lovell Lumber Co Inc 207 925-6455
3 Mill Rd Lovell ME (04051) ***(G-6384)***
Lovett & Hall Woodworks 207 650-5139
77 Egypt Rd Gray ME (04039) ***(G-6140)***
Lowe Manufacturing, Plainville *Also called D & M Screw Machine Pdts LLC* ***(G-3479)***
Lowell Corporation 508 835-2900
65 Hartwell St West Boylston MA (01583) ***(G-16421)***
Lowell Digisonde Intl LLC 978 735-4752
175 Cabot St Ste 200 Lowell MA (01854) ***(G-12398)***
Lowell Sun, Lowell *Also called Dispatch News* ***(G-12368)***
Lowell Sun Publishing Company (HQ) 978 459-1300
491 Dutton St Ste 2 Lowell MA (01854) ***(G-12399)***
Lowell's Boat Shop, Amesbury *Also called Newbury Port Meritown Society* ***(G-7501)***
Lower Cape Sand and Gravel Inc 508 255-2839
2740 Nauset Rd Eastham MA (02642) ***(G-10550)***
Lower Limb Technology 617 916-1650
130 Rumford Ave Auburndale MA (02466) ***(G-7864)***
Lower Limb Technology LLC 508 775-0990
191 Mid Tech Dr West Yarmouth MA (02673) ***(G-16580)***
Loxo Oncology Inc (HQ) 203 653-3880
281 Tresser Blvd Fl 9 Stamford CT (06901) ***(G-4241)***
Loyal Fence Company LLC 203 530-7046
1 Lorraine Ter Rockfall CT (06481) ***(G-3698)***
Loyalty Builders Inc (PA) 603 610-8800
210 Commerce Way Ste 250 Portsmouth NH (03801) ***(G-19590)***
LP Hometown Pizza LLC 860 589-1208
90 Burlington Ave Bristol CT (06010) ***(G-577)***
Lpg Metal Crafts LLC 860 982-3573
54 Carol Dr Plainville CT (06062) ***(G-3502)***
LPI Printing and Graphic Inc 781 438-5400
18 Spencer St Stoneham MA (02180) ***(G-15566)***
Lps Enterprises Inc 508 763-3830
128 Braley Rd Bldg A3 East Freetown MA (02717) ***(G-10455)***
Lq Mechatronics Inc 203 433-4430
2 Sycamore Way Branford CT (06405) ***(G-328)***
Lrp Conferences LLC 203 663-0100
35 Nutmeg Dr Trumbull CT (06611) ***(G-4627)***
Lrv Properties LLC 401 714-7001
94 Ridge St Providence RI (02909) ***(G-21058)***
LS Starrett Company (PA) 978 249-3551
121 Crescent St Athol MA (01331) ***(G-7689)***
LS Starrett Company 978 249-3551
121 Crescent St Athol MA (01331) ***(G-7690)***
Lsa Cleanpart LLC 508 765-4848
10 Cabot St Ste 100 Southbridge MA (01550) ***(G-15393)***
Lsc Communications Inc 978 251-6000
15 Wellman Ave North Chelmsford MA (01863) ***(G-13902)***
Lsne, Bedford *Also called Lyophilization Svcs Neng Inc* ***(G-17651)***
LTI Group, Pittsfield *Also called LTI Smart Glass Inc* ***(G-14486)***
LTI Smart Glass Inc 413 637-5001
14 Federico Dr Pittsfield MA (01201) ***(G-14486)***
Lts Inc 207 774-1104
37 Danforth St Portland ME (04101) ***(G-6680)***
LTS Group Holdings LLC (HQ) 978 264-6001
80 Central St Ste 240 Boxborough MA (01719) ***(G-8965)***
LTX Credence, Norwood *Also called L T X International Inc* ***(G-14173)***
Lubrication Management, Danbury *Also called Expressway Lube Centers* ***(G-915)***
Lubrite LLC 781 871-1420
145 Webster St Ste J Hanover MA (02339) ***(G-11346)***
Lubrite Technologies, Hanover *Also called Lubrite LLC* ***(G-11346)***
Lubrite Technology, Hanover *Also called US Bronze Foundry & Mch Inc* ***(G-11358)***
Lubrizol Global Management 978 642-5051
207 Lowell St Wilmington MA (01887) ***(G-17019)***
Luca 401 289-2251
139 Water St Warren RI (02885) ***(G-21297)***
Lucci Corp 603 567-4301
375 Jaffrey Rd Ste 7 Peterborough NH (03458) ***(G-19475)***
Luce Dirt Excavation 207 785-3478
2879 N Union Rd Union ME (04862) ***(G-7114)***
Lucerne Farms 207 488-2520
40 Easton Line Rd Fort Fairfield ME (04742) ***(G-6056)***
Luces Pure Maple Syrup 207 696-3732
54 Sugar Maple Dr Anson ME (04911) ***(G-5525)***
Luchon Cabinet Woodwork 860 684-5037
140 Buckley Hwy Stafford Springs CT (06076) ***(G-4112)***
Luck Industrial Sales Inc 617 924-0728
46 Quincy St Watertown MA (02472) ***(G-16296)***
Luckey LLC 203 285-3819
184 Chapel St New Haven CT (06513) ***(G-2709)***
Ludlow Corporation (HQ) 508 261-8000
15 Hampshire St Mansfield MA (02048) ***(G-12643)***
Ludlow Jute Company Limited, Mansfield *Also called Ludlow Corporation* ***(G-12643)***
Ludlow Printing and Copy Ctr 413 583-5220
44 Sewall St Ste 1 Ludlow MA (01056) ***(G-12472)***
Ludlow Tool 413 786-6360
68 Moylan Ln Agawam MA (01001) ***(G-7438)***
Ludlow Tool Co 413 786-6415
46 Moylan Ln Agawam MA (01001) ***(G-7439)***
Luis Pressure Washer 203 706-7399
47 Esther Ave Waterbury CT (06708) ***(G-4898)***
Lujean Printing Co Inc 508 428-8700
4507 Falmouth Rd Cotuit MA (02635) ***(G-10170)***
Lukas Foods Inc 207 284-7052
64 Landry St Biddeford ME (04005) ***(G-5744)***
Luke's Toy Factory, Danbury *Also called Mwb Toy Company LLC* ***(G-958)***
Lulla Smith 207 230-0832
44 Timbercliffe Dr Camden Me Camden ME (04843) ***(G-5867)***
Lululemon USA Inc 603 431-0871
60 State St Portsmouth NH (03801) ***(G-19591)***
Lumacera Innovative Mtls Inc 978 302-6475
83 East St Pepperell MA (01463) ***(G-14442)***
Lumber Outlet, Campton *Also called Granite State Log Homes Inc* ***(G-17777)***
Lumendi LLC 203 528-0316
253 Post Rd W Westport CT (06880) ***(G-5210)***
Lumenpulse Lighting Corp 617 307-5700
10 Post Office Sq Ste 900 Boston MA (02109) ***(G-8673)***
Lumentum Operations LLC 408 546-5483
45 Griffin Rd S Bloomfield CT (06002) ***(G-242)***
Lumetta Inc 401 691-3994
33 Minnesota Ave Warwick RI (02888) ***(G-21385)***
Lumicell Inc 617 404-1001
275 Washington St Ste 200 Newton MA (02458) ***(G-13611)***
Lumigent Technologies, Andover *Also called Beyondtrust Software Inc* ***(G-7540)***

Lumina Power Inc 978 241-8260
26 Ward Hill Ave Haverhill MA (01835) ***(G-11450)***
Luminescent Systems Inc 603 643-7766
4 Lucent Dr Lebanon NH (03766) ***(G-18629)***
Lunaform LLC 207 422-3306
66 Cedar Ln North Sullivan ME (04664) ***(G-6514)***
Lunch Bundles Inc 802 272-3051
202 Barnum Rd Bristol VT (05443) ***(G-21764)***
Lund Precision Products Inc 617 413-0236
175 Bay Shore Rd Hyannis MA (02601) ***(G-11848)***
Lunder Manufacturing Inc 207 284-5961
44 Spring Hill Rd Saco ME (04072) ***(G-6851)***
Lundys Company Inc 781 595-8639
34 Boston St Lynn MA (01904) ***(G-12522)***
Lunt Silversmiths, Greenfield *Also called Greenfield Silver Inc* ***(G-11262)***
Lupi-Marchigiano Bakery, New Haven *Also called Boston Model Bakery* ***(G-2671)***
Lupine Inc 603 356-7371
16 Lupine Ln Center Conway NH (03813) ***(G-17801)***
Lupis Inc 203 562-9491
169 Washington Ave New Haven CT (06519) ***(G-2710)***
Luscombe Ave Waiting Room 508 299-8051
21 Luscombe Ave Woods Hole MA (02543) ***(G-17327)***
Luster-On Products Inc 413 739-2541
54 Waltham Ave Springfield MA (01109) ***(G-15486)***
Lutco Bearings Inc 508 756-6296
677 Cambridge St Ste 1 Worcester MA (01610) ***(G-17408)***
Luther's Welding, Bristol *Also called Luthers Repair Shop Inc* ***(G-20091)***
Luthers Repair Shop Inc 401 253-5550
500 Wood St Bristol RI (02809) ***(G-20091)***
Lutronic USA 888 588-7644
19 Fortune Dr Billerica MA (01821) ***(G-8263)***
Luv Manufacturing 857 277-3573
513 Broadway Malden MA (02148) ***(G-12578)***
Luv2bu Inc 401 612-9585
17 Yard St Cranston RI (02920) ***(G-20256)***
Luvata Waterbury Inc 203 753-5215
2121 Thomaston Ave Ste 1 Waterbury CT (06704) ***(G-4899)***
Luvetrak, Marlborough *Also called On-Site Analysis Inc* ***(G-12802)***
Luxcath LLC 617 419-1800
33 Arch St Fl 32 Boston MA (02110) ***(G-8674)***
Luxpoint Inc 860 982-9588
101 Hammer Mill Rd Ste K Rocky Hill CT (06067) ***(G-3722)***
Luxuriance Biopharma Inc 617 817-6679
8 N Branch Rd Concord MA (01742) ***(G-10139)***
Luzy Technologies LLC 514 577-2295
778 Boylston St Apt 6b Boston MA (02199) ***(G-8675)***
Lwi Metalworks, Morrisville *Also called S & A Trombley Corporation* ***(G-22176)***
Lyco Enterprises Inc 603 888-2640
171 Taylor St Nashua NH (03060) ***(G-19201)***
Lydall Inc (PA) 860 646-1233
1 Colonial Rd Manchester CT (06042) ***(G-2021)***
Lydall Thermal Acoustical Inc 860 646-1233
1 Colonial Rd Manchester CT (06042) ***(G-2022)***
Lyfeshot LLC 978 451-4662
360 Massachusetts Ave # 103 Acton MA (01720) ***(G-7370)***
Lyman Conrad (PA) 413 538-8200
228 Lathrop St South Hadley MA (01075) ***(G-15306)***
Lyman Morse Boatbuilding Inc (PA) 207 354-6904
84 Knox St Thomaston ME (04861) ***(G-7085)***
Lyman Morse Boatbuilding Inc 207 354-6904
19 Elltee Cir Thomaston ME (04861) ***(G-7086)***
Lyman Products Corporation (PA) 860 632-2020
475 Smith St Middletown CT (06457) ***(G-2202)***
Lyman Products Corporation 860 632-2020
475 Smith St Middletown CT (06457) ***(G-2203)***
Lyman Sheet Metal Co Inc 413 527-0848
281 College Hwy Southampton MA (01073) ***(G-15340)***
Lyme Green Heat 603 359-8837
135 Mud Turtle Pond Rd Lyme NH (03768) ***(G-18754)***
Lymol Medical Corp (PA) 781 935-0004
4 Plympton St Woburn MA (01801) ***(G-17219)***
Lyn-Lad Group Ltd (PA) 781 598-6010
20 Boston St Lynn MA (01904) ***(G-12523)***
Lynch Corp 203 452-3007
140 Greenwich Ave Ste 3 Greenwich CT (06830) ***(G-1627)***
Lyndon Furniture, Saint Johnsbury *Also called Lyndon Woodworking Inc* ***(G-22390)***
Lyndon Woodworking Inc (PA) 802 748-0100
1135 Industrial Pkwy Saint Johnsbury VT (05819) ***(G-22390)***
Lyne Laboratories Inc 508 583-8700
10 Burke Dr Brockton MA (02301) ***(G-9163)***
Lynn Products Co 781 593-2500
400 Boston St Ste 1 Lynn MA (01905) ***(G-12524)***
Lynn Publishing Group, Saint Albans *Also called Milton Independent Inc* ***(G-22372)***
Lynn Welding Co Inc 860 667-4400
75 Rockwell Rd Ste 1 Newington CT (06111) ***(G-2877)***
Lynn Yarrington 802 453-4221
602 Laffin Rd New Haven VT (05472) ***(G-22185)***
Lynne Bailey 207 363-7999
180 Woodbridge Rd Unit 9 York ME (03909) ***(G-7310)***
Lynwood Laboratories Inc 781 449-6776
945 Great Plain Ave Ste 1 Needham MA (02492) ***(G-13304)***
Lynx System Developers Inc 978 556-9780
179 Ward Hill Ave Haverhill MA (01835) ***(G-11451)***
Lyon Manufacturing LLC 203 876-7386
215 Research Dr Ste 4 Milford CT (06460) ***(G-2311)***
Lyons Signs Inc 508 754-2501
1454 Grafton St Worcester MA (01604) ***(G-17409)***
Lyons Surface Plate Co, Chelsea *Also called Lawrence Lyon* ***(G-21839)***
Lyons Tool and Die Company 203 238-2689
185 Research Pkwy Meriden CT (06450) ***(G-2100)***
Lyophilization Svcs Neng Inc (PA) 603 626-5763
1 Sundial Ave Ste 112 Manchester NH (03103) ***(G-18866)***
Lyophilization Svcs Neng Inc 603 668-5763
25 Commerce Dr Bedford NH (03110) ***(G-17651)***
Lyophilization Svcs Neng Inc 603 626-9559
19 Harvey Rd Ste 5&7 Bedford NH (03110) ***(G-17652)***
Lytron Incorporated 781 933-7300
9 Forbes Rd Woburn MA (01801) ***(G-17220)***
Lzj Holdings Inc 978 409-1091
3 Dundee Park Dr Ste B06 Andover MA (01810) ***(G-7566)***
M & A Advnced Design Cnstr Inc (PA) 603 329-9515
1 Gigante Dr Hampstead NH (03841) ***(G-18242)***
M & A Plastics Inc 978 319-9930
95 Jones Ave Dracut MA (01826) ***(G-10362)***
M & B Automotive Machine Shop 203 348-6134
443 Elm St Stamford CT (06902) ***(G-4242)***
M & B Enterprise LLC 203 298-9781
155 New Haven Ave Derby CT (06418) ***(G-1075)***
M & C Powersports 207 713-3128
443 Church Hill Rd Leeds ME (04263) ***(G-6270)***
M & C Press Inc 617 354-2584
1 Main St Ste 105 Cambridge MA (02142) ***(G-9541)***
M & D Coatings LLC 203 380-9466
167 Avon St Stratford CT (06615) ***(G-4430)***
M & G Metal Inc 413 664-4057
161 River Rd Clarksburg MA (01247) ***(G-10073)***
M & H Engineering Co Inc 978 777-1222
183 Newbury St Ste 1 Danvers MA (01923) ***(G-10234)***
M & K Engineering Inc 781 933-1760
166 New Boston St Woburn MA (01801) ***(G-17221)***
M & K Industries Inc 978 514-9850
177 Florence St Leominster MA (01453) ***(G-12164)***
M & L Asphalt Services LLC 603 355-1230
19 West St Swanzey NH (03446) ***(G-19884)***
M & M Carbide Inc 860 628-2002
290 Center St Southington CT (06489) ***(G-4063)***
M & M Garment Manufacturing 617 389-7787
167 Bow St Ste 2 Everett MA (02149) ***(G-10620)***
M & M Glass Blowing Co Inc 603 598-8195
2 Townsend W Ste 11a Nashua NH (03063) ***(G-19202)***
M & M Glassblowing, Nashua *Also called M & M Glass Blowing Co Inc* ***(G-19202)***
M & M Label Co Inc 781 321-2737
380 Pearl St Malden MA (02148) ***(G-12579)***
M & M Precast Corp 203 743-5559
39 Padanaram Rd Danbury CT (06811) ***(G-951)***
M & M Printing Rush Service 508 476-4495
20 Yew St East Douglas MA (01516) ***(G-10429)***
M & M Scale Company Inc 781 321-2737
380 Pearl St Malden MA (02148) ***(G-12580)***
M & M Sheet Metal & Welding 207 764-6443
32 Industrial St Presque Isle ME (04769) ***(G-6761)***
M & R Builders, Searsport *Also called Dakins Miniatures Inc* ***(G-6949)***
M & R Manufacturing Inc 860 666-5066
111 Carr Ave Newington CT (06111) ***(G-2878)***
M & R Screen Printing Inc 508 996-0419
95 Rodney French Blvd New Bedford MA (02744) ***(G-13412)***
M & T Manufacturing Co 401 789-0472
30 Hopkins Ln Peace Dale RI (02879) ***(G-20914)***
M & Z Engineering Inc 860 496-0282
643 Riverside Ave Torrington CT (06790) ***(G-4585)***
M A D Signs 508 273-7887
2510 Cranberry Hwy Ste 6 Wareham MA (02571) ***(G-16252)***
M A Haskell & Sons LLC 207 993-2265
174 Mann Rd China ME (04358) ***(G-5910)***
M and J Supply, Providence *Also called Sturbridge Associates III LLC* ***(G-21129)***
M B Eastman Logging Inc 207 625-8020
146 North Rd Parsonsfield ME (04047) ***(G-6576)***
M B Heath & Sons Lumber Inc 802 635-2538
6 Heath Rd North Hyde Park VT (05665) ***(G-22232)***
M B Machine, Willimantic *Also called Marc Bouley* ***(G-5267)***
M B S Services Inc 781 431-0945
37 Bay State Rd Wellesley MA (02481) ***(G-16371)***
M Braun Inc 603 773-9333
14 Marin Way Stratham NH (03885) ***(G-19872)***
M C Machine Co Inc 508 473-3642
98 Mill St Hopedale MA (01747) ***(G-11677)***
M C Test Service Inc 781 218-7550
101 Billerica Ave Bldg 7 North Billerica MA (01862) ***(G-13837)***

ALPHABETIC

M Cubed Technologies Inc (HQ) 203 304-2940
31 Pecks Ln Ste 8 Newtown CT (06470) ***(G-2928)***
M Cubed Technologies Inc 203 452-2333
921 Main St Monroe CT (06468) ***(G-2407)***
M D F Powder Coat Systems LLC 401 683-7525
207 Highpoint Ave Ste 300 Portsmouth RI (02871) ***(G-20927)***
M D L, Needham Heights *Also called Microwave Development Labs Inc* ***(G-13337)***
M Drug LLC 207 973-9444
33 Whiting Hill Rd Ste 4 Brewer ME (04412) ***(G-5798)***
M E Baker Company (PA) 508 620-5304
945 Concord St Framingham MA (01701) ***(G-10979)***
M E C, Gilford *Also called Metz Electronics Corp* ***(G-18191)***
M F Engineering Company Inc 401 253-6163
7 Peter Rd Bristol RI (02809) ***(G-20092)***
M F Fley Incrprtd-New Bdford 508 997-0773
77 Wright St New Bedford MA (02740) ***(G-13413)***
M G A Cast Stone Inc 207 926-5993
7 Oxford Homes Ln Oxford ME (04270) ***(G-6569)***
M G M Instruments Inc (PA) 203 248-4008
925 Sherman Ave Hamden CT (06514) ***(G-1768)***
M H S Architectural Millwork, Marlborough *Also called Mike Sequore* ***(G-18962)***
M I R Inc 203 888-2541
103 Breault Rd Beacon Falls CT (06403) ***(G-61)***
M J C Machine Inc 603 889-0300
2 W Otterson St Nashua NH (03060) ***(G-19203)***
M J Gordon Company Inc 413 448-6066
141 North St 302 Pittsfield MA (01201) ***(G-14487)***
M J Industries Inc 978 352-6190
4 Carleton Dr Georgetown MA (01833) ***(G-11145)***
M K S, Andover *Also called Mks Instruments Inc* ***(G-7574)***
M K S Astex Products, Wilmington *Also called Mks Instruments Inc* ***(G-17024)***
M M Newman Corporation 781 631-7100
24 Tioga Way Marblehead MA (01945) ***(G-12687)***
M P, Salem *Also called Micro-Precision Tech Inc* ***(G-19752)***
M P E, Branford *Also called Madison Polymeric Engrg Inc* ***(G-330)***
M P I, Seymour *Also called Microboard Processing Inc* ***(G-3757)***
M P I, Winchester *Also called MJW Mass Inc* ***(G-17092)***
M P Robinson Production 203 938-1336
77 Topstone Rd Redding CT (06896) ***(G-3650)***
M Piette & Sons Lumber Inc 802 754-8876
6 Seminole Ln Irasburg VT (05845) ***(G-22040)***
M R D Design & Manufacturing 413 543-2012
1294 Worcester St Rear Indian Orchard MA (01151) ***(G-11889)***
M R F, Allenstown *Also called Materials Research Frncs Inc* ***(G-17539)***
M R P Group Inc (de) 978 687-7979
49 Blanchard St Ste 405 Lawrence MA (01843) ***(G-12049)***
M R Resources Inc 978 696-3060
160 Authority Dr Fitchburg MA (01420) ***(G-10831)***
M S Company 508 222-1700
61 School St Attleboro MA (02703) ***(G-7760)***
M S G, Amherst *Also called Manufacturing Services Group* ***(G-17572)***
M Squared Lasers Inc 408 667-0553
1 Broadway Fl 14 Cambridge MA (02142) ***(G-9542)***
M T D Corporation 203 261-3721
171 Spring Hill Rd Trumbull CT (06611) ***(G-4628)***
M T G, Westfield *Also called Manufacturing Tech Group Inc* ***(G-16698)***
M T I, Mystic *Also called Madison Technology Intl* ***(G-2442)***
M T S Tool LLC 860 945-0875
27 Main St Ste 2 Oakville CT (06779) ***(G-3299)***
M V Mason Elec Inc 508 668-6200
442 High Plain St Walpole MA (02081) ***(G-15999)***
M&G Berman Inc 203 834-8754
67 Pond Rd Wilton CT (06897) ***(G-5293)***
M&M Label Company, Malden *Also called M & M Scale Company Inc* ***(G-12580)***
M-Fab LLC 860 496-0055
52 Norwood St Torrington CT (06790) ***(G-4586)***
M-Tech 978 649-4563
67 Westech Dr Tyngsboro MA (01879) ***(G-15894)***
M.A.C. Systems, Canton *Also called Siemens Industry Inc* ***(G-9779)***
M/A Com, Chelmsford *Also called L3harris Technologies Inc* ***(G-9911)***
M/A-Com, Lowell *Also called Macom Metelics LLC* ***(G-12400)***
M/A-Com, Lowell *Also called Macom Technology Solutions Inc* ***(G-12403)***
M/K Systems Inc 978 857-9228
300 Andover St Unit 213 Peabody MA (01960) ***(G-14354)***
M1 Project LLC 617 906-6032
930 Commonwealth Ave Boston MA (02215) ***(G-8676)***
M2 Inc 802 655-2364
170 Franklin St Winooski VT (05404) ***(G-22722)***
M8trix Tech LLC 617 925-7030
45 Dan Rd Canton MA (02021) ***(G-9753)***
M8trix Technology, Canton *Also called M8trix Tech LLC* ***(G-9753)***
MA Haskell Fuel Co LLC 207 993-2265
1166 Route 3 China ME (04358) ***(G-5911)***
MA Mfg LLC 978 400-9991
325 Authority Dr Fitchburg MA (01420) ***(G-10832)***
Mac Dermid Elec Solution, Waterbury *Also called Macdermid Incorporated* ***(G-4901)***
Mac Observer Inc 603 868-2030
18 Denbow Rd Ste 101 Durham NH (03824) ***(G-18077)***
Maca, Lexington *Also called Massachusetts Chess Assn* ***(G-12241)***
Macala Tool Inc 860 763-2580
7 Moody Rd Bldg 5 Enfield CT (06082) ***(G-1369)***
Macdermid Incorporated (HQ) 203 575-5700
245 Freight St Waterbury CT (06702) ***(G-4900)***
Macdermid Incorporated 802 885-8089
260 Clinton St Springfield VT (05156) ***(G-22507)***
Macdermid Incorporated 203 575-5700
245 Freight St Waterbury CT (06702) ***(G-4901)***
Macdermid Acumen Inc 203 575-5700
245 Freight St Waterbury CT (06702) ***(G-4902)***
Macdermid AG Solutions Inc 203 575-5727
245 Freight St Waterbury CT (06702) ***(G-4903)***
Macdermid Anion Inc 203 575-5700
245 Freight St Waterbury CT (06702) ***(G-4904)***
Macdermid Brazil Inc 203 575-5700
245 Freight St Waterbury CT (06702) ***(G-4905)***
Macdermid Enthone Inc (HQ) 203 934-8611
350 Frontage Rd West Haven CT (06516) ***(G-5132)***
Macdermid Overseas Asia Ltd (HQ) 203 575-5799
245 Freight St Waterbury CT (06702) ***(G-4906)***
Macdermid Prfmce Solutions, Waterbury *Also called Macdermid Incorporated* ***(G-4900)***
Macdermid Printing Solutions 203 575-5727
245 Freight St Waterbury CT (06702) ***(G-4907)***
Macdermid South America Inc 203 575-5700
245 Freight St Waterbury CT (06702) ***(G-4908)***
Macdermid South Atlantic Inc 203 575-5700
245 Freight St Waterbury CT (06702) ***(G-4909)***
Macdiarmid Machine Corp 978 465-3546
7 Perry Way Ste 13 Newburyport MA (01950) ***(G-13509)***
Macdonald Associates, Manchester *Also called Queen City Sounds Inc* ***(G-18908)***
Macdonald Cabinet & 508 346-3221
580 Washington St South Easton MA (02375) ***(G-15285)***
Mace Adhesives Coatings Co Inc 508 943-9052
38 Roberts Rd Dudley MA (01571) ***(G-10380)***
Macgregor Bay Corporation 413 283-8747
50 Depot St Belchertown MA (01007) ***(G-8025)***
Mach 7 Technologies Inc 802 861-7745
120 Kimball Ave Ste 210 South Burlington VT (05403) ***(G-22452)***
Mach Machine Inc 978 274-5700
569 Main St Hudson MA (01749) ***(G-11788)***
Machine Craft Company Inc 603 225-0958
114 Hall St Concord NH (03301) ***(G-17913)***
Machine Incorporated 781 297-3700
879 Turnpike St Stoughton MA (02072) ***(G-15603)***
Machine Shop, Pascoag *Also called Sandberg Enterprises Inc* ***(G-20804)***
Machine Shop, Niantic *Also called Niantic Tool Inc* ***(G-2955)***
Machine Shop, The, Bristol *Also called Corbeil Enterprises Inc* ***(G-17762)***
Machine Technology Inc 978 927-1900
148 Sohier Rd Beverly MA (01915) ***(G-8149)***
Machine Trailers, Winslow *Also called Alcom LLC* ***(G-7266)***
Machined Integrations LLC 603 420-8871
1507 Columbia Cir Merrimack NH (03054) ***(G-19013)***
Machinemetrics Inc 413 341-5747
47 Pleasant St Northampton MA (01060) ***(G-14011)***
Machinery Service Co Inc 207 882-6788
166 W Alna Rd Wiscasset ME (04578) ***(G-7285)***
Machinex Company Inc 401 231-3230
350 Washington Hwy Smithfield RI (02917) ***(G-21237)***
Machining For Electronics Inc 978 562-7554
4 Bigelow St Hudson MA (01749) ***(G-11789)***
Machining Innovations Inc 207 465-2500
279 Summer St Oakland ME (04963) ***(G-6534)***
Maciel John 978 897-5865
4 Rickey Dr Maynard MA (01754) ***(G-12901)***
Mack Associates, Pelham *Also called Albert Langin* ***(G-19426)***
Mack Group Inc (PA) 802 375-2511
608 Warm Brook Rd Arlington VT (05250) ***(G-21597)***
Mack Molding Company Inc (HQ) 802 375-2511
608 Warm Brook Rd Arlington VT (05250) ***(G-21598)***
Mack Molding Company Inc 802 375-0500
79 E Arlington Rd Arlington VT (05250) ***(G-21599)***
Mack Prototype Inc 978 632-3700
424 Main St Gardner MA (01440) ***(G-11119)***
Mack Technologies Inc (HQ) 978 392-5500
27 Carlisle Rd Westford MA (01886) ***(G-16777)***
Mackenzie Couture ACC Inc 781 334-2805
1 Friendship Ln Lynnfield MA (01940) ***(G-12552)***
Mackenzie Machine & Design Inc 339 933-8157
171 Mattakeesett St Ste 2 Pembroke MA (02359) ***(G-14416)***
Mackenzie Mch & Mar Works Inc 203 777-3479
36 Morgan Ter East Haven CT (06512) ***(G-1254)***
Mackenzie Vault Inc 413 525-8827
165 Benton Dr East Longmeadow MA (01028) ***(G-10483)***
Mackinnon Printing Co Inc 978 263-8435
6 Ledgerock Way Unit 7 Acton MA (01720) ***(G-7371)***

Mackson Mfg Co Inc.....860 589-4035
139 Center St Ste 2002 Bristol CT (06010) *(G-578)*
Maclean Precision Mch Co Inc.....603 367-9011
1928 Village Rd Madison NH (03849) *(G-18763)*
Macleay Interactive Design Inc.....207 495-2208
17 Richardson Rd Rome ME (04963) *(G-6828)*
Maclellan Co.....781 891-5462
121 Felton St Waltham MA (02453) *(G-16146)*
Macmillan Publishing Group LLC.....646 307-5617
75 Arlington St Fl 8 Boston MA (02116) *(G-8677)*
Macneill Engineering Co Inc.....508 481-8830
1700 W Park Dr Ste 310 Westborough MA (01581) *(G-16633)*
Macom Metelics LLC.....978 656-2500
100 Chelmsford St Lowell MA (01851) *(G-12400)*
Macom Tech Sltons Holdings Inc.....603 641-3800
54 Grenier Field Rd Londonderry NH (03053) *(G-18716)*
Macom Tech Sltons Holdings Inc (PA).....978 656-2500
100 Chelmsford St Lowell MA (01851) *(G-12401)*
Macom Technology Solutions Inc.....978 656-2500
121 Hale St Lowell MA (01851) *(G-12402)*
Macom Technology Solutions Inc (HQ).....978 656-2500
100 Chelmsford St Lowell MA (01851) *(G-12403)*
Macomber Looms.....207 363-2808
130 Beech Ridge Rd York ME (03909) *(G-7311)*
Macraigor Systems LLC (PA).....617 264-4459
227 Cypress St Ste 1 Brookline MA (02445) *(G-9208)*
Macraigor Systems,, Brookline *Also called Macraigor Systems LLC (G-9208)*
Macris Industries Inc.....860 514-7003
8 Summit St Mystic CT (06355) *(G-2441)*
Macristy Industries Inc (PA).....860 225-4637
610 N Mountain Rd Newington CT (06111) *(G-2879)*
Macro Systems Inc.....203 225-6266
20 Hubbell Ln Shelton CT (06484) *(G-3830)*
Macromicro LLC.....617 818-1291
20 Rowes Wharf Apt 409 Boston MA (02110) *(G-8678)*
Macryan Inc.....802 287-4788
244 Lewis Rd Poultney VT (05764) *(G-22273)*
Macton Corporation.....203 267-1500
116 Willenbrock Rd Oxford CT (06478) *(G-3413)*
Macy Industries Inc.....603 623-5568
5 Lehoux Dr Hooksett NH (03106) *(G-18353)*
Mad Gabs Inc.....207 854-1679
25 Yarmouth Crossing Dr Yarmouth ME (04096) *(G-7298)*
Mad River Distillers.....802 496-6973
156 Cold Springs Farm Rd Warren VT (05674) *(G-22577)*
Mad River Distillers.....617 262-1990
321 Beacon St Boston MA (02116) *(G-8679)*
Mad River Media.....802 496-9173
House Fuller Waitsfield VT (05673) *(G-22567)*
Mad Sportswear LLC.....203 932-4868
100 Putney Dr West Haven CT (06516) *(G-5133)*
Madden Timberlands Inc.....207 827-0112
92 Beechwood Ave Old Town ME (04468) *(G-6544)*
Maddog LLC.....203 878-0147
33 Tall Pine Rd Milford CT (06461) *(G-2312)*
Madewell Manufacturing Co Inc.....508 997-0768
651 Orchard St New Bedford MA (02744) *(G-13414)*
Madgetech Inc (PA).....603 456-2011
6 Warner Rd Warner NH (03278) *(G-19928)*
Madigan Millwork Inc.....860 673-7601
150 New Britain Ave Unionville CT (06085) *(G-4658)*
Madison Cable Corporation.....508 752-2884
125 Goddard Memorial Dr Worcester MA (01603) *(G-17410)*
Madison Company (PA).....203 488-4477
27 Business Park Dr Branford CT (06405) *(G-329)*
Madison Group Inc.....781 853-0029
1330 Broadway Revere MA (02151) *(G-14771)*
Madison Lumber Mill Inc.....603 539-4145
71 Marcella Dr Rr 41 Madison NH (03849) *(G-18764)*
Madison Nobile Media, Revere *Also called Madison Group Inc (G-14771)*
Madison Polymeric Engrg Inc.....203 488-4554
965 W Main St Ste 2 Branford CT (06405) *(G-330)*
Madison Technology Intl.....860 245-0245
375 Allyn St Unit 1 Mystic CT (06355) *(G-2442)*
Madtown Logging LLC.....207 728-6260
185 Lavoie Ave Madawaska ME (04756) *(G-6400)*
Mafcote International Inc (HQ).....203 644-1200
108 Main St Ste 3 Norwalk CT (06851) *(G-3189)*
Mag Jewelry Co Inc.....401 942-1840
838 Dyer Ave Cranston RI (02920) *(G-20257)*
Magazine Columbiano.....617 365-3182
545 Malden St Revere MA (02151) *(G-14772)*
Magcap Engineering LLC.....781 821-2300
100 Energy Dr Canton MA (02021) *(G-9754)*
Magcor Inc.....203 445-0302
14 Wrabel Cir Monroe CT (06468) *(G-2408)*
Magellan Arospc Haverhill Inc.....978 774-6000
20 Computer Dr Haverhill MA (01832) *(G-11452)*
Magellan Diagnostics Inc (HQ).....978 250-7000
22 Alpha Rd Chelmsford MA (01824) *(G-9915)*
Magellan Diagnostics Inc.....978 856-2345
101 Billerica Ave Ste 4-2 North Billerica MA (01862) *(G-13838)*
Magenta Therapeutics Inc.....857 242-0170
100 Technology Sq Cambridge MA (02139) *(G-9543)*
Magic Hat Brewing Company, Burlington *Also called Independent Brewers Untd Corp (G-21789)*
Magic Hat Brewing Company & Pe.....802 658-2739
5 Bartlett Bay Rd South Burlington VT (05403) *(G-22453)*
Magic Industries Inc.....860 949-8380
140 Bozrah St Bozrah CT (06334) *(G-281)*
Magic Kitch'n, Bow *Also called Pitco Frialator Inc (G-17727)*
Magic Lantern Movie Theatre, Bridgton *Also called Down East Inc (G-5807)*
Magic Printing Inc.....413 363-1711
945 Concord St Framingham MA (01701) *(G-10980)*
Magiq Technologies Inc (PA).....617 661-8300
11 Ward St Ste 300 Somerville MA (02143) *(G-15192)*
Magmotor Technologies Inc.....508 835-4305
10 Coppage Dr Worcester MA (01603) *(G-17411)*
Magna Standard Mfg Co Inc.....203 874-0444
122 Cascade Blvd Milford CT (06460) *(G-2313)*
Magna Steel Sales Inc.....203 888-0300
2 Alliance Cir Beacon Falls CT (06403) *(G-62)*
Magnani Press Incorporated.....860 236-2802
120 New Park Ave Hartford CT (06106) *(G-1841)*
Magnat-Fairview LLC.....413 593-5742
1102 Sheridan St Chicopee MA (01022) *(G-10039)*
Magnatech LLC.....860 653-2573
6 Kripes Rd East Granby CT (06026) *(G-1131)*
Magnatech Dsd Co, The, East Granby *Also called Magnatech LLC (G-1131)*
Magneli Materials LLC.....203 644-8560
33 Weeburn Dr New Canaan CT (06840) *(G-2604)*
Magnemotion Inc.....978 757-9100
139 Barnum Rd Devens MA (01434) *(G-10323)*
Magnesium Interactive LLC.....917 609-1306
171 Roseville Rd Westport CT (06880) *(G-5211)*
Magnetec Corporation.....203 949-9933
7 Laser Ln Wallingford CT (06492) *(G-4768)*
Magnetic Sciences Inc.....978 266-9355
367 Arlington St Acton MA (01720) *(G-7372)*
Magnetic Seal Corp.....401 247-2800
365 Market St Warren RI (02885) *(G-21298)*
Magnetic Technologies Ltd.....508 987-3303
43 Town Forest Rd Oxford MA (01540) *(G-14268)*
Magnetika East Ltd.....508 485-7555
34 Saint Martin Dr Ste 11 Marlborough MA (01752) *(G-12789)*
Magnetometric Devices, Salem *Also called Stellar Manufacturing Inc (G-19771)*
Magnitude Software Inc.....781 202-3200
2400 District Ave Ste 320 Burlington MA (01803) *(G-9299)*
Magnolia Optical Tech Inc.....781 376-1505
52b Cummings Park Ste 314 Woburn MA (01801) *(G-17222)*
Magnos Incorporated.....978 562-1173
9 Robert Rd Hudson MA (01749) *(G-11790)*
Magnus Molding, Pittsfield *Also called Modern Mold & Tool Inc (G-14491)*
Magnus Molding Inc.....413 443-1192
1995 East St Pittsfield MA (01201) *(G-14488)*
Magoon Logging LLC.....603 435-9918
863 Route 129 Loudon NH (03307) *(G-18750)*
Magpie Industries LLC.....617 623-3330
416 Highland Ave Somerville MA (02144) *(G-15193)*
Maguire Lace & Warping Inc.....401 821-1290
65 Stone St Coventry RI (02816) *(G-20154)*
Maguire Lace Works, Coventry *Also called Maguire Lace & Warping Inc (G-20154)*
Magwen Diamond Pdts Inc.....508 375-9152
10 Knollwood Dr Yarmouth Port MA (02675) *(G-17530)*
Mahar Excavating & Logging.....802 442-2954
592 Coleville Rd Bennington VT (05201) *(G-21681)*
Mahers Welding Service Inc.....603 286-4851
103 Park St Northfield NH (03276) *(G-19404)*
Mail-A-Map, Madison *Also called Harbor Publications Inc (G-1962)*
Maillet Construction.....603 582-2810
129 Campbell Mill Rd Mason NH (03048) *(G-18969)*
Maillouxs Vermont Cntry Farms, Ferrisburg *Also called Green Mountain Honey Farms (G-21986)*
Mailly Manufacturing Company.....203 879-1445
54 Wakelee Rd Wolcott CT (06716) *(G-5448)*
Main Campus Newspaper, The, Orono *Also called University of Maine System (G-6560)*
Main Industrial Tires Ltd (PA).....713 676-0251
107 Audubon Rd Ste 2 Wakefield MA (01880) *(G-15958)*
Main Street Cheese LLC.....603 525-3300
37 Main St Hancock NH (03449) *(G-18285)*
Maine Antique Digest Inc.....207 832-7534
911 Main St Waldoboro ME (04572) *(G-7134)*
Maine Artfl Limb & Orthotics, Portland *Also called Maine Artfl Limb Orthotics Co (G-6681)*
Maine Artfl Limb Orthotics Co.....207 773-4963
959 Brighton Ave Rear Portland ME (04102) *(G-6681)*
Maine Authors Publishing.....207 594-0090
12 High St Thomaston ME (04861) *(G-7087)*
Maine Bag Co, Caribou *Also called Maine Potato Growers Inc (G-5886)*

ALPHABETIC

Maine Balsam Fir Prodcts.....207 674-5090
16 Morse Hill Rd West Paris ME (04289) ***(G-7176)***
Maine Balsam Fir Products, West Paris *Also called Maine Balsam Fir Prodcts* ***(G-7176)***
Maine Barrel & Display Company.....207 784-6700
21 Fireslate Pl Lewiston ME (04240) ***(G-6303)***
Maine Bats Hrbors Publications.....207 594-8622
218 Main St Camden ME (04847) ***(G-5868)***
Maine Beer Company LLC.....207 221-5711
525 Us Route 1 Freeport ME (04032) ***(G-6082)***
Maine Bio-Fuel Inc.....207 878-3001
51 Ingersol Dr Portland ME (04103) ***(G-6682)***
Maine Biotechnology Svcs Inc.....207 797-5454
1037r Forest Ave Portland ME (04103) ***(G-6683)***
Maine Blueberry Equipment Co.....207 483-4156
250 Epping Rd Columbia ME (04623) ***(G-5918)***
Maine Boats Homes & Harbors, Camden *Also called Maine Bats Hrbors Publications* ***(G-5868)***
Maine Cage Factory, Auburn *Also called Scott-Lynn Mfg* ***(G-5598)***
Maine Camp Outfitters, Sunset *Also called Island Approaches Inc* ***(G-7075)***
Maine Cat Co Inc.....207 529-6500
300 Waldoboro Rd Bremen ME (04551) ***(G-5792)***
Maine Cedar Hot Tubs Inc.....207 474-0953
Wesserunsett Rd Madison ME (04950) ***(G-6406)***
Maine Cedar Specialty Products.....207 532-4034
1938 Ludlow Rd Ludlow ME (04730) ***(G-6387)***
Maine Cleaners Supply Inc.....207 657-3166
143 Cumberland Rd North Yarmouth ME (04097) ***(G-6517)***
Maine Coast Marketing.....207 781-9801
160 Presumpscot St Ste 1 Portland ME (04103) ***(G-6684)***
Maine Coast Nordic.....207 255-6714
133 Smalls Point Rd Machiasport ME (04655) ***(G-6398)***
Maine Container LLC.....603 888-1315
115 Poland Spring Dr Poland ME (04274) ***(G-6594)***
Maine Conveyor Inc (PA).....207 854-5661
259 New Portland Rd Gorham ME (04038) ***(G-6118)***
Maine Conveyor Inc.....207 854-5661
5 Maynard Rogers Rd Windham ME (04062) ***(G-7241)***
Maine Cookie Co., The, Kennebunkport *Also called Kennebunkport Pie Company LLC* ***(G-6247)***
Maine Craft Distilling LLC.....207 798-2528
123 Washington Ave Portland ME (04101) ***(G-6685)***
Maine Crisp Company LLC (PA).....207 213-9296
10 Railroad Sq Waterville ME (04901) ***(G-7158)***
Maine Custom Woodlands LLC.....207 353-9020
1326 Hallowell Rd Durham ME (04222) ***(G-5971)***
Maine Distilleries LLC.....207 865-4828
437 Us Route 1 Freeport ME (04032) ***(G-6083)***
Maine Dock & Dredge LLC.....207 660-5577
107 George Wright Rd Woolwich ME (04579) ***(G-7290)***
Maine Fabricators Inc.....207 839-8555
18 Mitchell Hill Rd Gorham ME (04038) ***(G-6119)***
Maine Fiber Company LLC.....207 699-4550
465 Congress St Ste 701 Portland ME (04101) ***(G-6686)***
Maine Heritage Timber LLC.....207 723-9200
450 Golden Rd Millinocket ME (04462) ***(G-6442)***
Maine Heritage Weavers.....207 933-2605
904 Main St Monmouth ME (04259) ***(G-6449)***
Maine Industrial P & R Corp.....207 563-5532
21 Teague St Newcastle ME (04553) ***(G-6484)***
Maine Innkeepers Association, Skowhegan *Also called Maine Stitching Spc LLC* ***(G-6981)***
Maine Lure Company LLC.....413 543-1524
40 Main St Ste 13-114 Biddeford ME (04005) ***(G-5745)***
Maine Machine Products Company.....207 743-6344
79 Prospect Ave South Paris ME (04281) ***(G-7013)***
Maine Made Furniture, Rumford *Also called Premium Log Yards Inc* ***(G-6842)***
Maine Made Stuffcom.....207 628-3160
1687 Long Falls Dam Rd Lexington Twp ME (04961) ***(G-6329)***
Maine Manufacturing LLC.....207 324-1754
63 Community Dr Sanford ME (04073) ***(G-6881)***
Maine Market Refrigeration LLC (PA).....207 685-3504
98 Morris Springer Rd Fayette ME (04349) ***(G-6055)***
Maine Meal LLC.....207 779-4185
4 Madison Ave Fl 2 Skowhegan ME (04976) ***(G-6980)***
Maine Medicinals Inc.....207 737-8717
555 Gardiner Rd Dresden ME (04342) ***(G-5967)***
Maine Micro Furnace Inc.....207 329-9207
1368 Riverside St Portland ME (04103) ***(G-6687)***
Maine Mlclar Qulty Contrls Inc.....207 885-1072
23 Mill Brook Rd Saco ME (04072) ***(G-6852)***
Maine Mold & Machine Inc.....207 388-2732
208 Town Farm Rd Hartford ME (04220) ***(G-6177)***
Maine Nwsppers In Educatn Fund.....207 791-6650
390 Congress St Portland ME (04101) ***(G-6688)***
Maine Parts & Machine Inc.....207 797-0024
68 Waldron Way Portland ME (04103) ***(G-6689)***
Maine Plastics, Portland *Also called Consolidated Container Co LLC* ***(G-6642)***
Maine Point, Southwest Harbor *Also called T Henri Inc* ***(G-7051)***
Maine Poly Aquisition Corp.....207 946-7000
933 Route 202 Greene ME (04236) ***(G-6150)***
Maine Post & Beam LLC.....207 751-6793
1274 North Rd North Yarmouth ME (04097) ***(G-6518)***
Maine Potato Growers Inc.....207 764-3131
56 Sincock St Caribou ME (04736) ***(G-5886)***
Maine Power Express LLC.....203 661-0055
485 W Putnam Ave Greenwich CT (06830) ***(G-1628)***
Maine Pure.....207 256-8111
37 W View Dr Fryeburg ME (04037) ***(G-6100)***
Maine Pursuit LLC.....207 549-7972
279 E River Rd Whitefield ME (04353) ***(G-7217)***
Maine Pursuits, Whitefield *Also called Maine Pursuit LLC* ***(G-7217)***
Maine Radio.....207 883-2929
68 Mussey Rd Scarborough ME (04074) ***(G-6932)***
Maine Rubber International.....877 648-1949
107 Audubon Rd Ste 2 Wakefield MA (01880) ***(G-15959)***
Maine Sailing Partners LLC.....207 865-0850
111 Reach Rd Harpswell ME (04079) ***(G-6173)***
Maine Scale LLC.....207 777-9500
4 Washington St N Ste 1 Auburn ME (04210) ***(G-5578)***
Maine Seafood Ventures LLC.....207 303-0165
1016 Portland Rd Saco ME (04072) ***(G-6853)***
Maine Soft Drink Association.....207 773-5505
316 Western Ave South Portland ME (04106) ***(G-7032)***
Maine Standard Biofuels, Portland *Also called Maine Bio-Fuel Inc* ***(G-6682)***
Maine Stitching Spc LLC.....207 812-5207
40 Dane Ave Skowhegan ME (04976) ***(G-6981)***
Maine Sunday Telegram, Portland *Also called Mtm Oldco Inc* ***(G-6696)***
Maine Surfers Union.....207 771-7873
15 Free St Portland ME (04101) ***(G-6690)***
Maine Tire, Wakefield *Also called Maine Rubber International* ***(G-15959)***
Maine Tool & Machine LLC.....207 725-0038
27 Canal St Lisbon Falls ME (04252) ***(G-6371)***
Maine Toolroom Inc.....207 883-2455
8 Washington Ave Scarborough ME (04074) ***(G-6933)***
Maine Turnpike Authority.....207 829-4531
108 Blackstrap Rd Cumberland Center ME (04021) ***(G-5929)***
Maine Wild Blueberry Company (HQ).....207 255-8364
78 Elm St Machias ME (04654) ***(G-6392)***
Maine Wild Blueberry Company.....207 255-8364
50 Elm St Machias ME (04654) ***(G-6393)***
Maine Wood & Design LLC.....207 363-5270
55 Witchtrot Rd York ME (03909) ***(G-7312)***
Maine Wood Flooring, Portage *Also called Maine Woods Company LLC* ***(G-6598)***
Maine Wood Treaters Inc.....207 345-8411
58 Walker Rd Mechanic Falls ME (04256) ***(G-6421)***
Maine Woods Company LLC.....207 435-4393
92 Fish Lake Rd Portage ME (04768) ***(G-6598)***
Maine Woods Pellet Company LLC.....207 654-2237
164 Harmony Rd Athens ME (04912) ***(G-5542)***
Maine Woolens LLC.....207 725-7900
15 Paul St Brunswick ME (04011) ***(G-5841)***
Maine-Line Leather, Lewiston *Also called Maineline Industries Inc* ***(G-6304)***
Maine-OK Enterprises Inc.....207 633-4620
97 Townsend Ave Boothbay Harbor ME (04538) ***(G-5784)***
Mainebiz, Portland *Also called New England Business Media LLC* ***(G-6700)***
Maineline Graphics LLC.....603 588-3177
1 High St Antrim NH (03440) ***(G-17596)***
Maineline Industries Inc.....207 782-6622
850 Main St Ste 3 Lewiston ME (04240) ***(G-6304)***
Mainely Maple LLC.....207 634-3073
165 Burrill Hill Rd Norridgewock ME (04957) ***(G-6498)***
Mainely Metrology Inc.....207 362-5520
921 Smithfield Rd Smithfield ME (04978) ***(G-6989)***
Mainely Newspapers Inc.....207 282-4337
180 Main St Biddeford ME (04005) ***(G-5746)***
Mainely Trees Inc.....207 684-3301
26 S Main St Strong ME (04983) ***(G-7073)***
Mainline Energy Systems Inc.....860 429-9663
95 June St Northbridge MA (01534) ***(G-14057)***
Mainline Heating & Supply, Northbridge *Also called Mainline Energy Systems Inc* ***(G-14057)***
Mainline Paint Mfg Co.....401 726-3650
768 Main St Pawtucket RI (02860) ***(G-20855)***
Maintenance Tech Inc.....207 797-7233
235 Riverside Indus Pkwy Portland ME (04103) ***(G-6691)***
Mainville Welding Co Inc.....203 237-3103
55 Goffe St Meriden CT (06451) ***(G-2101)***
Mair-Mac Machine Company Inc.....508 895-9001
86 N Montello St Brockton MA (02301) ***(G-9164)***
Maitri Learning LLC.....413 529-2868
131 Tob Hill Rd Westhampton MA (01027) ***(G-16801)***
Majestic Marble & Granite Inc.....781 830-1020
253 Revere St Canton MA (02021) ***(G-9755)***
Majilite Corporation.....978 441-6800
1530 Broadway Rd Dracut MA (01826) ***(G-10363)***
Majilite Manufacturing Inc.....978 441-6800
1530 Broadway Rd Dracut MA (01826) ***(G-10364)***
Majilly, Pomfret Center *Also called Tonmar LLC* ***(G-3559)***
Make Archtectural Metalworking.....508 273-7603
2358 Cranberry Hwy West Wareham MA (02576) ***(G-16575)***

Makemesustainable Inc 617 821-1375
91 Kinnaird St Ste 2 Cambridge MA (02139) *(G-9544)*

Makers Natural Green Wreaths, Newport Center *Also called Vermont Center Wreaths Inc (G-22208)*

Making Your Mark Inc 617 479-0999
121 Liberty St Quincy MA (02169) *(G-14637)*

Makino Inc 860 223-0236
255 Myrtle St New Britain CT (06053) *(G-2549)*

Makscientific LLC 781 365-0958
151 S Bedford St 104 Burlington MA (01803) *(G-9300)*

Malabar Bay LLC 203 359-9714
1127 High Ridge Rd # 159 Stamford CT (06905) *(G-4243)*

Malagar Group LLC 603 778-1372
188 Bunker Hill Ave Stratham NH (03885) *(G-19873)*

Malco Inc 860 584-0446
38 Napco Dr Terryville CT (06786) *(G-4485)*

Malco Saw Co Inc 401 942-7380
22 Field St Cranston RI (02920) *(G-20258)*

Malcolm Bradsher Co Inc 603 679-3888
181 Exeter Rd Epping NH (03042) *(G-18101)*

Malcolm L Pettegrow Inc 207 244-3514
135 Seal Cove Rd Southwest Harbor ME (04679) *(G-7049)*

Malcom Co-Leister 781 875-3121
25 Abbot St Andover MA (01810) *(G-7567)*

Malden Centerless Grinding Co 781 324-7991
910 Eastern Ave Malden MA (02148) *(G-12581)*

Malden Intl Designs Inc 508 946-2270
19 Cowan Dr Middleboro MA (02346) *(G-13067)*

Maley Laser Processing Inc 401 732-8400
1280 Jefferson Blvd Warwick RI (02886) *(G-21386)*

Malik Embossing Corp 978 745-6060
28 Varney St Salem MA (01970) *(G-14928)*

Mallard Printing Inc 508 675-5733
657 Quarry St Ste 9 Fall River MA (02723) *(G-10724)*

Malone Brothers Inc 508 379-3662
1699 Gar Hwy Swansea MA (02777) *(G-15708)*

Maloney Marine Rigging Inc 207 633-6788
Ebeneck Rd Bth Bay Rgnbt West Southport ME (04576) *(G-7179)*

Malta Food Pantry Inc 860 725-0944
19 Woodland St Ste 37 Hartford CT (06105) *(G-1842)*

Mama Rosies Co Inc 617 242-4300
10 Dorrance St Boston MA (02129) *(G-8680)*

Mamco, Westerly *Also called Maxson Automatic Machinery Co (G-21530)*

Management Controls LLC 207 753-6844
265 Rodman Rd Auburn ME (04210) *(G-5579)*

Management Roundtable Inc 781 891-8080
321 Walnut St Ste 222 Newton MA (02460) *(G-13612)*

Management Software Inc 860 536-5177
547 Colonel Ledyard Hwy Ledyard CT (06339) *(G-1942)*

Manchester Lumber Inc 802 635-2315
66 River Rd E Johnson VT (05656) *(G-22051)*

Manchester Molding and Mfg Co 860 643-2141
96 Sheldon Rd Manchester CT (06042) *(G-2023)*

Manchester Packing, Vernon *Also called Bravo LLC (G-4664)*

Manchester Packing Company Inc 860 646-5000
349 Wetherell St Manchester CT (06040) *(G-2024)*

Manchester Tl & Design ADP LLC 860 296-6541
465 Ledyard St Hartford CT (06114) *(G-1843)*

Manchester, NH Plant, Manchester *Also called General Cable Industries Inc (G-18825)*

Mandes Inc 781 344-6915
593 Washington St Stoughton MA (02072) *(G-15604)*

Mandeville Signs Inc 401 334-9100
676 George Washington Hwy Lincoln RI (02865) *(G-20581)*

Manfucturer, Charlton *Also called Incom Inc (G-9851)*

Mange LLC 917 880-2104
30 Summer St Apt 1 Somerville MA (02143) *(G-15194)*

Mango Dsp Inc 203 857-4008
83 East Ave Ste 115 Norwalk CT (06851) *(G-3190)*

Mango Intllgent Vdeo Solutions, Norwalk *Also called Mango Dsp Inc (G-3190)*

Manisses Inc 401 466-2222
1 Ocean Ave Block Island RI (02807) *(G-20058)*

Mann Publishing Group, Rollinsford *Also called Mann Publishing Incorporated (G-19693)*

Mann Publishing Incorporated 603 601-0325
710 Main St Fl 6 Rollinsford NH (03869) *(G-19693)*

Manna Mix 213 519-0719
5 Schoolhouse Rd Newport NH (03773) *(G-19350)*

Manning Brothers Wood Products 603 286-4896
27 Sargent St Northfield NH (03276) *(G-19405)*

Manning Way Cpitl Partners LLC 508 966-4800
5 Williams Way Bellingham MA (02019) *(G-8044)*

Manomet Manufacturing Inc 508 997-1795
194 Riverside Ave New Bedford MA (02746) *(G-13415)*

Manroland Goss Web Systems AMR (HQ) 603 750-6600
121 Technology Dr Ste 1 Durham NH (03824) *(G-18078)*

Mansfield Machinery Co Inc 508 339-7973
27 Rock St Mansfield MA (02048) *(G-12644)*

Mansfield News, Framingham *Also called Community Newspaper (G-10935)*

Mansir Printing LLC 413 536-4250
24 Shawmut Ave Holyoke MA (01040) *(G-11636)*

Mantrose-Haeuser Co Inc (HQ) 203 454-1800
100 Nyala Farms Rd Westport CT (06880) *(G-5212)*

Mantrose-Haeuser Co Inc 203 454-1800
113 Olive St Attleboro MA (02703) *(G-7761)*

Manufacturers Associates Inc 203 931-4344
45 Railroad Ave West Haven CT (06516) *(G-5134)*

Manufacturers Coml Fin LLC 860 242-6287
1022 Boulevard West Hartford CT (06119) *(G-5084)*

Manufacturers Service Co Inc 203 389-9595
5 Lunar Dr Woodbridge CT (06525) *(G-5471)*

Manufactures Technologies, West Springfield *Also called MTI Systems Inc (G-16532)*

Manufacturing, Burlington *Also called Computr Imprntble Lbl Systms (G-9252)*

Manufacturing, Merrimac *Also called JAS F Mullen Co Inc (G-13003)*

Manufacturing Productivi 860 916-8189
910 Day Hill Rd Windsor CT (06095) *(G-5346)*

Manufacturing Service Corp 508 865-2550
11 Waters St Millbury MA (01527) *(G-13169)*

Manufacturing Services, Millbury *Also called Manufacturing Service Corp (G-13169)*

Manufacturing Services Group 603 883-1022
105 State Route 101a # 6 Amherst NH (03031) *(G-17572)*

Manufacturing Solutions Inc 802 888-3289
153 Stafford Ave Morrisville VT (05661) *(G-22172)*

Manufacturing Tech Group Inc 413 562-4337
85 Servistar Indus Way Westfield MA (01085) *(G-16698)*

Manufctrers Pattern Fndry Corp 413 732-8117
25 Mill River Ln Springfield MA (01105) *(G-15487)*

Manufctring Resource Group Inc 781 440-9700
930 Washington St Norwood MA (02062) *(G-14176)*

Manufcturers Mart Publications, Georgetown *Also called Guncanco Ltd (G-11143)*

Manutech Industries 413 447-7794
17 Taconic Park Dr Pittsfield MA (01201) *(G-14489)*

Map of Month 401 274-4288
1 Richmond Sq Ste 150e Providence RI (02906) *(G-21059)*

Map Printing Inc 508 676-5177
54 Mcdonald St Fall River MA (02720) *(G-10725)*

Mapeco Products, Oxford *Also called Walz & Krenzer Inc (G-3429)*

Maple Brook Farm, North Bennington *Also called Mountain Mozzarella LLC (G-22210)*

Maple Craft Foods LLC 203 913-7066
6 Cider Mill Rd Sandy Hook CT (06482) *(G-3744)*

Maple Grove Farms Vermont Inc (HQ) 802 748-5141
1052 Portland St Saint Johnsbury VT (05819) *(G-22391)*

Maple Guild, Island Pond *Also called Sweet Tree Holdings 1 LLC (G-22042)*

Maple Guys LLC 603 654-2415
327 Forest Rd Wilton NH (03086) *(G-19982)*

Maple Heights Farm 603 286-7942
133 Reservoir Rd Northfield NH (03276) *(G-19406)*

Maple Landmark Inc 802 388-0627
1297 Exchange St Middlebury VT (05753) *(G-22114)*

Maple Landmark Woodcraft, Middlebury *Also called Maple Landmark Inc (G-22114)*

Maple Leaf Cpitl Ventures Corp (PA) 781 569-6311
322 Mystic Ave Medford MA (02155) *(G-12939)*

Maple Leaf Malt & Brewing 802 464-9900
3 N Main St Wilmington VT (05363) *(G-22703)*

Maple Nut Kitchen LLC 603 354-3219
43 Darling Rd Keene NH (03431) *(G-18514)*

Maple On Tap 802 498-4477
378 Mccullough Hill Rd Montpelier VT (05602) *(G-22154)*

Maple Print Services Inc 860 381-5470
39 Wedgewood Dr Jewett City CT (06351) *(G-1915)*

Maple Road Service Station 413 567-6233
773 Maple Rd Longmeadow MA (01106) *(G-12336)*

Maple Valley Creamery 413 588-4881
102 Mill Valley Rd Hadley MA (01035) *(G-11310)*

Maplegate Media Group Inc 203 826-7557
1503 Sienna Dr Danbury CT (06810) *(G-952)*

Mapleleaf Software Inc 603 413-0419
254 Nashua Rd Londonderry NH (03053) *(G-18717)*

Maplewood Machine Co Inc 508 673-6710
271 Anthony St Fall River MA (02721) *(G-10726)*

Mar Lee Companies Tech Ctrs, Fitchburg *Also called Mar-Lee Companies Inc (G-10833)*

Mar-Lee Companies Inc 978 343-9600
190 Authority Dr Fitchburg MA (01420) *(G-10833)*

Mar-Lee Companies Inc 978 348-1291
180 Authority Dr Fitchburg MA (01420) *(G-10834)*

Maranatha Industries Inc (PA) 781 245-0038
24 Fitch Ct Wakefield MA (01880) *(G-15960)*

Marblehead Engineering 978 432-1386
7 Essex Park Rd Essex MA (01929) *(G-10595)*

Marblehead Weather Gmts LLC 781 639-1060
100 Hoods Ln Ste U8 Marblehead MA (01945) *(G-12688)*

Marborough Enterprise 508 485-5200
40 Mechanic St Marlborough MA (01752) *(G-12790)*

Marbuo Inc 508 994-7700
634 State Rd Unit E2 North Dartmouth MA (02747) *(G-13924)*

Marc Bouley 860 450-1713
28 Young St Willimantic CT (06226) *(G-5267)*

Marc J Riendeau 802 748-6252
676 Morrill Rd Danville VT (05828) *(G-21897)*

Marc Johnson 860 774-3315
16 Depot Rd Danielson CT (06239) ***(G-1015)***
Marc Tool & Die Inc 203 758-5933
23 Oak Ln Prospect CT (06712) ***(G-3588)***
Marca Machine Engineering, Gorham *Also called Marca Manufacturing LLC* ***(G-6120)***
Marca Manufacturing LLC 207 854-8471
5 Sanford Dr Gorham ME (04038) ***(G-6120)***
Marcello Sausage Co 401 275-1952
7 Industrial Rd Cranston RI (02920) ***(G-20259)***
Marchand Machine Works Inc 508 883-4040
435 Wrentham Rd Bellingham MA (02019) ***(G-8045)***
Marcias Dollclothes 401 742-3654
965 Chopmist Hill Rd North Scituate RI (02857) ***(G-20780)***
Marcott Designs 508 226-2680
48 Eddy St Ste 2 Attleboro MA (02703) ***(G-7762)***
Marcou Construction Company 603 774-6511
250 Mansion Rd Dunbarton NH (03046) ***(G-18073)***
Marcus Company Inc 413 534-3303
750 Main St Holyoke MA (01040) ***(G-11637)***
Marcus Printing Co, Holyoke *Also called Marcus Company Inc* ***(G-11637)***
Mardon Manufacturing Company 978 948-7040
237r Main St Rowley MA (01969) ***(G-14856)***
Marel Corporation 203 934-8187
5 Saw Mill Rd West Haven CT (06516) ***(G-5135)***
Marena Industries Inc 860 528-9701
433 School St East Hartford CT (06108) ***(G-1205)***
Marena Machinery Sales Div, East Hartford *Also called Marena Industries Inc* ***(G-1205)***
Marenna Amusements LLC 203 623-4386
88 Marsh Hill Rd Orange CT (06477) ***(G-3372)***
Maretron LLP 602 861-1707
60 Johnson Ave Plainville CT (06062) ***(G-3503)***
Margaret Quint Logging 603 447-3957
161 Jack Frost Ln Conway NH (03818) ***(G-17955)***
Margies Sweet Surrender 781 925-2271
179 Nantasket Rd Hull MA (02045) ***(G-11828)***
Maria's Ravioli, Medford *Also called Marias Food Products Inc* ***(G-12940)***
Mariah Group LLC 802 747-4000
92 Park St Rutland VT (05701) ***(G-22345)***
Marias Food Products Inc 781 396-4110
48 Suffolk St Medford MA (02155) ***(G-12940)***
Marie Deprofio 781 894-9793
11 Harrington Rd Waltham MA (02452) ***(G-16147)***
Marilu Foods Inc 401 348-2858
3 Gilleo Dr Westerly RI (02891) ***(G-21529)***
Marine Bioproducts 617 847-1426
39 Broad St Quincy MA (02169) ***(G-14638)***
Marine Canvas Shop, Newbury *Also called Salt Marsh Canvas* ***(G-13465)***
Marine Hydraulic Engrg Co (PA) 207 594-9525
17 Gordon Dr Rockland ME (04841) ***(G-6803)***
Marine Money, Stamford *Also called International Mktg Strategies* ***(G-4226)***
Marine Polymer Tech Inc (PA) 781 270-3200
159 Lorum St Tewksbury MA (01876) ***(G-15820)***
Marine Product Team, Mansfield *Also called Emerson Automation Solutions* ***(G-12631)***
Mariner Ablngton Edition 781 878-4489
165 Enterprise Dr Marshfield MA (02050) ***(G-12862)***
Marinero Express 809 East 203 487-0636
809 E Main St Stamford CT (06902) ***(G-4244)***
Mario Precision Products 203 758-3101
19 Wihbey Dr Prospect CT (06712) ***(G-3589)***
Marion Manufacturing Company 203 272-5376
1675 Reinhard Rd Cheshire CT (06410) ***(G-743)***
Marion Mfg Co 401 331-4343
87 Corliss St Providence RI (02904) ***(G-21060)***
Marios Oil Corp 617 202-8259
22 Forest Ave Everett MA (02149) ***(G-10621)***
Marios Welding 508 646-1038
185 Welcome St Fall River MA (02721) ***(G-10727)***
Maritime Marine Group, Augusta *Also called Spb LLC* ***(G-5620)***
Maritox, Pawtucket *Also called Blackledge Industries LLC* ***(G-20817)***
Marja Corporation 207 324-2994
14 Dale St Sanford ME (04073) ***(G-6882)***
Marjan Inc 203 573-1742
44 Railroad Hill St Waterbury CT (06708) ***(G-4910)***
Marjorie Royer Interiors Inc 978 774-0533
50 N Liberty St Middleton MA (01949) ***(G-13095)***
Mark Allen Cabinetry LLC 603 491-7570
13 Columbia Dr Unit 3 Amherst NH (03031) ***(G-17573)***
Mark Allen Cabinetry LLC (PA) 603 321-3163
232 Route 13 Brookline NH (03033) ***(G-17772)***
Mark D Skiest 508 754-0639
4 Parker Rd Shrewsbury MA (01545) ***(G-15122)***
Mark Dykeman 978 691-1100
805 Chandler St Tewksbury MA (01876) ***(G-15821)***
Mark Dzidzk 860 793-2767
20k Hultenius St Plainville CT (06062) ***(G-3504)***
Mark G Cappitella (PA) 860 873-3093
31 Bogue Ln East Haddam CT (06423) ***(G-1151)***
Mark Gauvin 508 758-2324
7 Noyes Ave Mattapoisett MA (02739) ***(G-12888)***
Mark Goodwin Wooden Bowls 866 478-4065
63 Balcom Rd Foster RI (02825) ***(G-20457)***
Mark Hunter 802 626-8407
315 Hill St Lyndonville VT (05851) ***(G-22069)***
Mark Karotkin 860 202-7821
17 Grassmere Ave Hartford CT (06110) ***(G-1844)***
Mark Keup 781 544-4610
105 Front St Scituate MA (02066) ***(G-15009)***
Mark Richey Wdwkg & Design Inc 978 499-3800
40 Parker St Newburyport MA (01950) ***(G-13510)***
Mark Todisco 781 438-5280
24 Spencer St Stoneham MA (02180) ***(G-15567)***
Mark V Laboratory Inc 860 653-7201
18 Kripes Rd East Granby CT (06026) ***(G-1132)***
Mark Welch 603 835-6347
713 River Rd Walpole NH (03608) ***(G-19923)***
Mark Welch Logging, Walpole *Also called Mark Welch* ***(G-19923)***
Markal Finishing Co Inc 203 384-8219
400 Bostwick Ave Bridgeport CT (06605) ***(G-446)***
Markarian Electric LLC 617 393-9700
586 Pleasant St Ste 5 Watertown MA (02472) ***(G-16297)***
Market Square Beverage Co Inc 781 593-2150
3 Market Sq Lynn MA (01905) ***(G-12525)***
Marketing Sltons Unlimited LLC 860 523-0670
109 Talcott Rd West Hartford CT (06110) ***(G-5085)***
Marketing Worldwide Corp (PA) 631 444-8090
423 Main St 3 Rockland ME (04841) ***(G-6804)***
Marketplace Inc Corporate 401 336-3000
816 Middle Rd East Greenwich RI (02818) ***(G-20372)***
Markforged Inc (PA) 866 496-1805
480 Pleasant St Watertown MA (02472) ***(G-16298)***
Markforged Inc 617 666-1935
4 Suburban Park Dr Billerica MA (01821) ***(G-8264)***
Markforged Inc 617 666-1935
85 School St Watertown MA (02472) ***(G-16299)***
Marklin Candle Design LLC 603 746-2211
28 Riverside Dr Contoocook NH (03229) ***(G-17946)***
Markow Race Cars 860 610-0776
701 Nutmeg Rd N Ste 1 South Windsor CT (06074) ***(G-3991)***
Marks Printing House Inc 207 338-5460
17 Main St Belfast ME (04915) ***(G-5692)***
Marks Wells & Pumps Inc 508 528-1741
55 Maple St Bellingham MA (02019) ***(G-8046)***
Marlboro Plastics, Marlborough *Also called Consolidated Cont Holdings LLC* ***(G-12740)***
Marlborough Foundry Inc 508 485-2848
555 Maple St Marlborough MA (01752) ***(G-12791)***
Marlborough Plastics Inc 860 295-9124
350 N Main St Marlborough CT (06447) ***(G-2066)***
Marley Hall Inc 508 226-2666
453 S Main St Ste 4 Attleboro MA (02703) ***(G-7763)***
Marlow Watson Inc (HQ) 800 282-8823
37 Upton Technology Park Wilmington MA (01887) ***(G-17020)***
Marmon Aerospace & Defense LLC 603 622-3500
680 Hayward St Manchester NH (03103) ***(G-18867)***
Marmon Utility 603 249-1302
53 Old Wilton Rd Milford NH (03055) ***(G-19068)***
Marmon Utility LLC (HQ) 603 673-2040
53 Old Wilton Rd Milford NH (03055) ***(G-19069)***
Marmon Utility LLC 203 881-5358
49 Day St Seymour CT (06483) ***(G-3755)***
Marmon Utility LLC 603 673-2040
116 State Route 101a Amherst NH (03031) ***(G-17574)***
Maro Display Inc 401 294-5551
112 Dillabur Ave North Kingstown RI (02852) ***(G-20726)***
Maroney Associates Inc 781 767-3970
63 Plymouth St Holbrook MA (02343) ***(G-11530)***
Maros Products Incorporated 401 885-1788
36 Bellair Ave Unit 4 Warwick RI (02886) ***(G-21387)***
Marox Corporation 413 536-1300
373 Whitney Ave Holyoke MA (01040) ***(G-11638)***
Marr Office Equipment Inc 401 725-5186
751 Main St Pawtucket RI (02860) ***(G-20856)***
Mars Incorporated 508 966-0022
444 Hartford Ave Bellingham MA (02019) ***(G-8047)***
Mars 2000 Inc 401 421-5275
45 Troy St Providence RI (02909) ***(G-21061)***
Mars Architectural Millwork 203 579-2632
55 Randall Ave Ste A Bridgeport CT (06606) ***(G-447)***
Mars Associates, Ashland *Also called Ecoshel Inc* ***(G-5536)***
Mars Manufacturing Co Inc 401 769-9663
32 Mechanic Ave Ste 100 Woonsocket RI (02895) ***(G-21574)***
Mars Medical Products LLC 207 385-3278
184 Norridgewock Ave Skowhegan ME (04976) ***(G-6982)***
Mars Plastics, Providence *Also called Mars 2000 Inc* ***(G-21061)***
Marsam Metal Finishing Co 860 826-5489
206 Newington Ave New Britain CT (06051) ***(G-2550)***
Marsars Water Rescue Systems 203 924-7315
8 Algonkin Rd Shelton CT (06484) ***(G-3831)***
Marsh Botanical Garden, New Haven *Also called Yale University* ***(G-2761)***

Marshall Marine Corp 508 994-0414
55 Shipyard Ln South Dartmouth MA (02748) ***(G-15240)***
Marshall Specialty Grinding 207 623-3700
40 Beech St Chelsea ME (04330) ***(G-5901)***
Marspec-Abernaqui-America 603 964-4063
103 Exeter Rd North Hampton NH (03862) ***(G-19384)***
Martel Binding, Somerville *Also called Bill Martel* ***(G-15158)***
Martel Electronics Corp 603 434-6033
3 Corporate Park Dr # 1 Derry NH (03038) ***(G-17988)***
Martells Metal Works 508 226-0136
76 Dewey Ave Attleboro MA (02703) ***(G-7764)***
Martha's Vineyard Printing Co, Oak Bluffs *Also called Da Rosas* ***(G-14210)***
Marthas Seastreak Vineyard LLC 617 896-0293
49 State Pier New Bedford MA (02740) ***(G-13416)***
Marthas Vineyard Times 508 693-6100
30 Beach Rd Vineyard Haven MA (02568) ***(G-15933)***
Martin Cabinet Inc (PA) 860 747-5769
336 S Washington St Ste 2 Plainville CT (06062) ***(G-3505)***
Martin Cabinet Inc 860 747-5769
500 Broad St Bristol CT (06010) ***(G-579)***
Martin Carmichael 207 827-2858
1095 Main Rd Cardville ME (04418) ***(G-5882)***
Martin Carmichael Hvy Eqp Repr, Cardville *Also called Martin Carmichael* ***(G-5882)***
Martin Custom Boat Works LLC 802 318-7882
6821 Route 7 North Ferrisburgh VT (05473) ***(G-22226)***
Martin D Marguerite 603 421-9654
80 Nashua Rd Ste 15 Londonderry NH (03053) ***(G-18718)***
Martin Forest Products 207 498-6723
369 Albair Rd Caribou ME (04736) ***(G-5887)***
Martin Intl Enclosures LLC 603 474-2626
14 Woodworkers Way Seabrook NH (03874) ***(G-19809)***
Martin Mfg Services LLC 860 663-1465
96 Cow Hill Rd Killingworth CT (06419) ***(G-1927)***
Martin Quarry, East Corinth *Also called Martin R L & W B Inc* ***(G-21914)***
Martin R L & W B Inc 802 439-5797
8678 Vt Route 25 East Corinth VT (05040) ***(G-21914)***
Martin Rosols Inc 860 223-2707
45 Grove St New Britain CT (06053) ***(G-2551)***
Martin Sprocket & Gear Inc 508 634-3990
357 Fortune Blvd Milford MA (01757) ***(G-13125)***
Martin Woodworks, West Warwick *Also called Joe Martin* ***(G-21497)***
Martins Cheese Co Inc 508 636-2357
221 Sodom Rd Westport MA (02790) ***(G-16843)***
Martins Farm Recycling 413 774-5631
341 Plain Rd Greenfield MA (01301) ***(G-11269)***
Martins News Shop 617 267-1334
143 Hemenway St Apt 4 Boston MA (02115) ***(G-8681)***
Martins Soldering 401 521-2280
10 Alcazar Ave Johnston RI (02919) ***(G-20520)***
Marty Gilman Incorporated (PA) 860 889-7334
30 Gilman Rd Gilman CT (06336) ***(G-1535)***
Marty Gilman Incorporated 860 889-7334
1 Commerce Park Rd Bozrah CT (06334) ***(G-282)***
Maru Ltd DBA Greenleaf Metals 802 985-5200
1022 Mason Hl N Starksboro VT (05487) ***(G-22516)***
Maruho Htsujyo Innovations Inc (PA) 617 653-1617
55 Accord Park Dr Norwell MA (02061) ***(G-14107)***
Marus Printing 802 436-2044
115 Merritt Rd Hartland VT (05048) ***(G-22016)***
Marvel Abrasive Products, Lincoln *Also called Bates Abrasive Products Inc* ***(G-20558)***
Marvel Abrasives Products LLC 800 621-0673
6 Carol Dr Lincoln RI (02865) ***(G-20582)***
Marvel Signs & Designs LLC 603 726-4111
2524 Nh Route 175 Thornton NH (03285) ***(G-19901)***
Marver Med Inc 781 341-9372
1063 Turnpike St Stoughton MA (02072) ***(G-15605)***
Marvic Inc 508 798-2600
160 Southbridge St Auburn MA (01501) ***(G-7842)***
Mary Ann Caproni 413 663-7330
452 Walker St North Adams MA (01247) ***(G-13679)***
Mary Lee Harris 802 468-5370
825 Sand Hill Rd Castleton VT (05735) ***(G-21829)***
Masbro Polishing Company Inc 401 722-2227
5 Lori Ellen Dr Smithfield RI (02917) ***(G-21238)***
Mascaros Woodcraft Co Inc (PA) 413 594-4255
101 Front St Chicopee MA (01013) ***(G-10040)***
Mascon Inc 781 938-5800
5 Commonwealth Ave Unit 3 Woburn MA (01801) ***(G-17223)***
Masiello Enterprises Inc 401 826-1883
5 Salvas Ave Coventry RI (02816) ***(G-20155)***
Masimo Semiconductor Inc 603 595-8900
25 Sagamore Park Rd Hudson NH (03051) ***(G-18413)***
Mason & Hamlin, Haverhill *Also called Burgett Brothers Incorporated* ***(G-11411)***
Mason Box Company 800 842-9526
517 Mineral Spring Ave Pawtucket RI (02860) ***(G-20857)***
Mason Grapevine LLC 603 878-4272
780 Starch Mill Rd Mason NH (03048) ***(G-18970)***
Mason Grapevine, The, Mason *Also called Mason Grapevine LLC* ***(G-18970)***
Mason Industries Inc 508 485-8494
40 Cedar Hill St Marlborough MA (01752) ***(G-12792)***
Mason Medical Communications 203 227-9252
10 Covlee Dr Westport CT (06880) ***(G-5213)***
Mason Pallet Inc 207 897-6270
233 Strickland Loop Rd Livermore Falls ME (04254) ***(G-6379)***
Mason's Brewing, Brewer *Also called Backwash Brew Holdings LLC* ***(G-5794)***
Masonry & More Inc 508 740-8537
34 Benson Ave Framingham MA (01702) ***(G-10981)***
Masquerade 603 275-0717
4 Joanna Rd Salem NH (03079) ***(G-19749)***
Mass Automation Corporation 508 759-0770
6 Colonel Dr Unit 1 Bourne MA (02532) ***(G-8947)***
Mass Bay Brewing Company Inc (PA) 617 574-9551
306 Northern Ave Boston MA (02210) ***(G-8682)***
Mass Cabinets Inc 978 738-0600
99 Cross St Methuen MA (01844) ***(G-13034)***
Mass Chassis 603 642-8967
68 Route 125 Kingston NH (03848) ***(G-18545)***
Mass Coating Corp 347 325-0001
7 Endean Dr East Walpole MA (02032) ***(G-10526)***
Mass Design Inc (PA) 603 886-6460
41 Simon St Ste 2c Nashua NH (03060) ***(G-19204)***
Mass Engineering & Tank Inc 508 947-8669
29 Abbey Ln Middleboro MA (02346) ***(G-13068)***
Mass Logic Inc 978 635-1917
648 Stow Rd Boxboro MA (01719) ***(G-8953)***
Mass Machine Inc 781 467-3550
24 Walpole Park S Ste 14 Walpole MA (02081) ***(G-16000)***
Mass Metalworks LLC 508 533-7500
89 Main St Ste 104 Medway MA (02053) ***(G-12966)***
Mass Printing & Forms Inc 781 396-1970
352 Park St Ste 202w North Reading MA (01864) ***(G-13987)***
Mass Sign & Decal Inc 781 878-7446
443 Webster St Ste 2 Rockland MA (02370) ***(G-14812)***
Mass Tank Sales Corp 508 947-8826
29 Abbey Ln Middleboro MA (02346) ***(G-13069)***
Mass Transfer Systems, Walpole *Also called North Amrcn Fltration Mass Inc* ***(G-16005)***
Mass Vac Inc 978 667-2393
247 Rangeway Rd North Billerica MA (01862) ***(G-13839)***
Mass Web Printing Company Inc 508 832-5317
150 Chestnut St Ste 1 Providence RI (02903) ***(G-21062)***
Mass-Flex Research Inc 781 391-3640
18 Canal St Ste 3 Medford MA (02155) ***(G-12941)***
Massa Products Corporation 781 749-3120
280 Lincoln St Hingham MA (02043) ***(G-11501)***
Massachsetts Prosecutors Guide 617 696-6729
30 Hinckley Rd Milton MA (02186) ***(G-13195)***
Massachstts Med Dvcs Jurnl LLC 617 358-5631
8 Saint Marys St Ste 611 Boston MA (02215) ***(G-8683)***
Massachstts Rebuild Svc Export, West Brookfield *Also called Mrse* ***(G-16472)***
Massachusetts Bay Tech Inc 781 344-8809
378 Page St Ste 7 Stoughton MA (02072) ***(G-15606)***
Massachusetts Bev Aliance LLC 617 701-6238
190 Mechanic St Bellingham MA (02019) ***(G-8048)***
Massachusetts Beverage Bus, Boston *Also called New Beverage Publications Inc* ***(G-8728)***
Massachusetts Broken Stone Co (PA) 978 838-9999
332 Sawyerhill Rd Berlin MA (01503) ***(G-8091)***
Massachusetts Broken Stone Co 508 829-5353
2077 N Main St Holden MA (01520) ***(G-11547)***
Massachusetts Chess Assn (PA) 781 862-3799
234 Manor Ter Lexington MA (02420) ***(G-12241)***
Massachusetts Clean Energy Ctr 617 315-9355
63 Franklin St Fl 3 Boston MA (02110) ***(G-8684)***
Massachusetts Container Corp 508 481-1100
300 Cedar Hill St Marlborough MA (01752) ***(G-12793)***
Massachusetts Control Ctr Inc 978 649-1128
40 Westech Dr Tyngsboro MA (01879) ***(G-15895)***
Massachusetts Daily Collegian, Amherst *Also called University of Massachusetts* ***(G-7530)***
Massachusetts Envelope Co Inc (PA) 617 623-8000
30 Cobble Hill Rd Somerville MA (02143) ***(G-15195)***
Massachusetts Envelope Co Inc 860 727-9100
10 Midland St Hartford CT (06120) ***(G-1845)***
Massachusetts Importing Co 781 395-1210
255 Main St Medford MA (02155) ***(G-12942)***
Massachusetts Institute Tech 617 253-1541
84 Masschstts Ave Ste 483 Cambridge MA (02139) ***(G-9545)***
Massachusetts Institute Tech 617 253-5646
1 Rogers St Cambridge MA (02142) ***(G-9546)***
Massachusetts Institute Tech 617 253-1000
400 Main St Cambridge MA (02142) ***(G-9547)***
Massachusetts Institute Tech 617 253-7183
77 Mass Ave Ste E60 Cambridge MA (02139) ***(G-9548)***
Massachusetts Machine Works 781 467-3550
24 Walpole Park S Ste 14 Walpole MA (02081) ***(G-16001)***
Massachusetts Medical Society (PA) 781 893-4610
860 Winter St Waltham MA (02451) ***(G-16148)***
Massachusetts Medical Society 617 734-9800
10 Shattuck St Boston MA (02115) ***(G-8685)***

ALPHABETIC

Massachusetts Mtls Tech LLC (PA) 617 500-8325
12 Gowell Ln Weston MA (02493) ***(G-16827)***
Massachusetts Mtls Tech LLC 617 502-5636
810 Memorial Dr Ste 105 Cambridge MA (02139) ***(G-9549)***
Massachusetts Natural Fert Inc 978 874-0744
65 Bean Porridge Hill Rd Westminster MA (01473) ***(G-16808)***
Massachusetts Repro Ltd 617 227-2237
1 Milk St Lbby Lbby Boston MA (02109) ***(G-8686)***
Massachusetts Review Inc 413 545-2689
211 Hicks Way Amherst MA (01003) ***(G-7518)***
MASSACHUSETTS REVIEW, THE, Amherst *Also called Massachusetts Review Inc* ***(G-7518)***
Massachusetts Thermal Tstg Lab, Franklin *Also called Cold Chain Technologies Inc* ***(G-11029)***
Massage Chairs For Less 603 882-7580
3 Cardinal Cir Nashua NH (03063) ***(G-19205)***
Massasoit/Tackband Inc 413 593-6731
118 Dulong Cir Chicopee MA (01022) ***(G-10041)***
Massbiologics 617 474-3000
460 Walk Hill St Boston MA (02126) ***(G-8687)***
Masscec, Boston *Also called Massachusetts Clean Energy Ctr* ***(G-8684)***
Massconn Distribute Cpl 860 882-0717
12 Commerce Way South Windsor CT (06074) ***(G-3992)***
Massdevice, Boston *Also called Massachstts Med Dvcs Jurnl LLC* ***(G-8683)***
MASSHEFA, Boston *Also called Poweroptions Inc* ***(G-8788)***
Massinvestor Incorporated 617 620-4606
10 Farmer Rd Arlington MA (02476) ***(G-7629)***
Massmicro LLC 781 828-6110
50 Energy Dr Canton MA (02021) ***(G-9756)***
Massmicroelectronics LLC 781 828-6110
50 Energy Dr Ste 202 Canton MA (02021) ***(G-9757)***
Master Engrv & Printery Inc (PA) 203 723-2779
45 Westridge Dr Waterbury CT (06708) ***(G-4911)***
Master Printing & Signs 617 623-8270
60 Union Sq Somerville MA (02143) ***(G-15196)***
Master Tool & Machine Inc 860 747-2581
13 Grace Ave Plainville CT (06062) ***(G-3506)***
Master Welders, Braintree *Also called Diaute Bros* ***(G-9001)***
Master-Halco Inc 508 583-7474
63 Manley St West Bridgewater MA (02379) ***(G-16444)***
Mastercast Ltd 401 726-3100
56 Barnes St Pawtucket RI (02860) ***(G-20858)***
Mastercraft Tool and Mch Co 860 628-5551
100 Newell St Southington CT (06489) ***(G-4064)***
Masterman & Kovil, Cheshire *Also called Kovil Manufacturing LLC* ***(G-741)***
Masters Machine Company Inc 207 529-5191
500 Lower Round Pond Rd Round Pond ME (04564) ***(G-6830)***
Masterwork 781 995-3354
10 Draper St Ste 35 Woburn MA (01801) ***(G-17224)***
Mastriani Gourmet Food LLC 203 368-9556
570 Barnum Ave Bridgeport CT (06608) ***(G-448)***
Mastro Lighting Mfg Co Inc (PA) 401 467-7700
555 Elmwood Ave Providence RI (02907) ***(G-21063)***
Mat Game Set 603 277-9763
51 Pinnacle Rd Lyme NH (03768) ***(G-18755)***
Matallurgical Perspectives 413 596-4283
4 Meeting House Ln Wilbraham MA (01095) ***(G-16940)***
Matec Instrument Companies Inc (PA) 508 393-0155
56 Hudson St Ste 3 Northborough MA (01532) ***(G-14038)***
Material Concrete Corp 401 765-0204
618 Greenville Rd North Smithfield RI (02896) ***(G-20790)***
Material Promotions Inc 203 757-8900
145 Railroad Hill St Waterbury CT (06708) ***(G-4912)***
Materialise Dental Inc 443 557-0121
590 Lincoln St Waltham MA (02451) ***(G-16149)***
Materials Development Corp 781 391-0400
10 Lowell Junction Rd Andover MA (01810) ***(G-7568)***
Materials Proc Dev Group LLC 203 269-6617
7 Swan Ave Wallingford CT (06492) ***(G-4769)***
Materials Research Frncs Inc 603 485-2394
65 Pinewood Rd Unit 2 Allenstown NH (03275) ***(G-17539)***
Materion Lrge Area Catings LLC (HQ) 216 486-4200
300 Lamberton Rd Windsor CT (06095) ***(G-5347)***
Materion Prcsion Optics Thin F (HQ) 978 692-7513
2 Lyberty Way Westford MA (01886) ***(G-16778)***
Materion Technical Mtls Inc 401 333-1700
5 Wellington Rd Lincoln RI (02865) ***(G-20583)***
Mathemtics Problem Solving LLC 207 772-2846
40 Walch Dr Portland ME (04103) ***(G-6692)***
Mathertops, South Windsor *Also called C Mather Company Inc* ***(G-3946)***
Matheson Tri-Gas Inc 207 775-0515
75 Scott Dr Westbrook ME (04092) ***(G-7195)***
Mathews Bakery Inc 207 773-9647
550 Washington Ave Portland ME (04103) ***(G-6693)***
Mathews Brothers Company (PA) 207 338-3360
22 Perkins Rd Belfast ME (04915) ***(G-5693)***
Mathworks Inc 508 647-7000
1 Lakeside Campus Dr Natick MA (01760) ***(G-13266)***
Mathworks Lakeside Campus, Natick *Also called Mathworks Inc* ***(G-13266)***
Matias Importing & Distrg Co, Newington *Also called Matias Importing & Distrg Corp* ***(G-2880)***
Matias Importing & Distrg Corp 860 666-5544
135 Fenn Rd Newington CT (06111) ***(G-2880)***
Matkim Industries Inc 508 987-3599
2 Hawksley Rd Unit D Oxford MA (01540) ***(G-14269)***
Matouk Textile Works Inc 508 997-3444
925 Airport Rd Fall River MA (02720) ***(G-10728)***
Matrivax Research & Dev Corp 617 385-7640
650 Albany St Ste 117 Boston MA (02118) ***(G-8688)***
Matrix Aerospace Corp 603 542-0191
421 River Rd Claremont NH (03743) ***(G-17854)***
Matrix Air, Newport *Also called Pollution Research & Dev Corp* ***(G-19353)***
Matrix Apparel Group LLC 203 740-7837
29 Candlewood Dr New Fairfield CT (06812) ***(G-2625)***
Matrix I LLC 401 434-3040
1 Catamore Blvd Ste 3 East Providence RI (02914) ***(G-20431)***
Matrix Metal Products Inc 508 226-2374
53 County St Attleboro MA (02703) ***(G-7765)***
Matrixchem Inc 347 727-6886
3992 Route 121 Cambridgeport VT (05141) ***(G-21824)***
Mattapoisett Millworks, Mattapoisett *Also called Mark Gauvin* ***(G-12888)***
Matthew Associates Inc 617 965-6126
92 Crofton Rd Waban MA (02468) ***(G-15938)***
Matthew Fisel ND 203 453-0122
20 Dunk Rock Rd Guilford CT (06437) ***(G-1709)***
Matthew Warren Inc 860 621-7358
29 Depaolo Dr Southington CT (06489) ***(G-4065)***
Matthew Warren Inc 203 888-2133
95 Silvermine Rd Ste 1 Seymour CT (06483) ***(G-3756)***
Matthews Printing Co 203 265-0363
10 Marshall St Wallingford CT (06492) ***(G-4770)***
Mattingly Products Company 207 635-2719
25 Folon Rd North Anson ME (04958) ***(G-6504)***
Matts Maple Syrup 802 464-9788
370 Higley Hill Rd Brattleboro VT (05301) ***(G-21738)***
Mauna Kea Technologies Inc 617 657-1550
24 Denby Rd Ste 140 Allston MA (02134) ***(G-7469)***
Maurer & Shepherd Joyners 860 633-2383
122 Naubuc Ave Ste B4 Glastonbury CT (06033) ***(G-1563)***
Maurices Country Meat Mkt LLC 860 546-9588
155 Gooseneck Hill Rd Canterbury CT (06331) ***(G-694)***
Mauser Packg Solutions Holdg 978 728-5000
25 Tucker Dr Leominster MA (01453) ***(G-12165)***
Mavel Americas Inc 617 242-2204
121 Mount Vernon St Boston MA (02108) ***(G-8689)***
Maverick Arms Inc 203 230-5300
7 Grasso Ave North Haven CT (06473) ***(G-3038)***
Maverick Photonics LLC 603 540-4434
2107 Elm St Manchester NH (03104) ***(G-18868)***
Mavrck, Boston *Also called Apifia Inc* ***(G-8368)***
Max Pharmaceutical LLC 603 472-2813
238 Joppa Hill Rd Bedford NH (03110) ***(G-17653)***
Max Productions LLC 203 838-2795
167 Main St Ste 1 Norwalk CT (06851) ***(G-3191)***
Max Roads LLC 603 895-5200
10 Twins Rd Raymond NH (03077) ***(G-19640)***
Max-Tek LLC 860 372-4900
48 N Plains Industrial Rd # 1 Wallingford CT (06492) ***(G-4771)***
Max-Tek Ue Superabrasive Mch, Wallingford *Also called Max-Tek LLC* ***(G-4771)***
Maxam Initiation Systems LLC 860 774-3507
74 Dixon Rd Sterling CT (06377) ***(G-4368)***
Maxam North America Inc 860 774-2333
74 Dixon Rd Sterling CT (06377) ***(G-4369)***
Maxam Tire North America Inc 844 629-2662
300 Rosewood Dr Ste 102 Danvers MA (01923) ***(G-10235)***
Maxant Industries Inc 978 772-0576
58 Barnum Rd Devens MA (01434) ***(G-10324)***
Maxi Green Inc 802 657-3586
1184 Prim Rd Ste 2 Colchester VT (05446) ***(G-21873)***
Maxilon Laboratories Inc 603 594-9300
105 State Route 101a # 8 Amherst NH (03031) ***(G-17575)***
Maxim Integrated Products Inc 978 934-7600
8 Technology Dr North Chelmsford MA (01863) ***(G-13903)***
Maximum Inc 508 995-2200
30 Samuel Barnet Blvd New Bedford MA (02745) ***(G-13417)***
Maximus 978 728-8000
11 Mill St Ste 2 Lowell MA (01852) ***(G-12404)***
Maxon Corporation 978 795-1285
75 Discovery Way Acton MA (01720) ***(G-7373)***
Maxon Precision Motors Inc (HQ) 508 677-0520
125 Dever Rd Taunton MA (02780) ***(G-15763)***
Maxson Automatic Machinery Co (PA) 401 596-0162
70 Airport Rd Westerly RI (02891) ***(G-21530)***
Maxym Technologies Inc 207 283-8601
17 Landry St Biddeford ME (04005) ***(G-5747)***
May Graphics & Printing Inc 978 392-1302
359 Littleton Rd Westford MA (01886) ***(G-16779)***
Mayan Corporation 203 854-4711
79 Day St Norwalk CT (06854) ***(G-3192)***

Mayarc Industries Inc 860 871-1872
54 Minor Hill Rd Ellington CT (06029) *(G-1335)*
Mayborn Group, Stamford *Also called Mayborn Usa Inc (G-4245)*
Mayborn Usa Inc 781 269-7490
1010 Washington Blvd # 11 Stamford CT (06901) *(G-4245)*
Maybrook Inc 603 898-0811
8 Willow St Ste 2 Salem NH (03079) *(G-19750)*
Mayfield Plastics Inc 508 865-8150
68 Providence Rd Sutton MA (01590) *(G-15687)*
Mayflower Brewing Company LLC 508 746-2674
12 Resnik Rd Plymouth MA (02360) *(G-14562)*
Mayhew Basque Plastics LLC 978 537-5219
100 Simplex Dr Ste 3 Westminster MA (01473) *(G-16809)*
Mayhew Steel Products Inc (PA) 413 625-6351
199 Industrial Blvd Turners Falls MA (01376) *(G-15881)*
Mayhew Tools, Turners Falls *Also called Mayhew Steel Products Inc (G-15881)*
Maynard & Maynard Furn Makers 603 835-2969
21 Beryl Rd South Acworth NH (03607) *(G-19853)*
Mayville House 207 824-6545
158 Mayville Rd Bethel ME (04217) *(G-5715)*
MB Aerospace 860 653-0569
99 Rainbow Rd East Granby CT (06026) *(G-1133)*
MB Sport LLC (PA) 203 966-1985
31 Grove St New Canaan CT (06840) *(G-2605)*
Mbbc Vermont LLC 802 674-5491
336 Ruth Carney Dr Windsor VT (05089) *(G-22712)*
Mbf Holdings LLC 203 302-2812
777 W Putnam Ave Greenwich CT (06830) *(G-1629)*
Mbf Printing 774 233-0337
118 Washington St Holliston MA (01746) *(G-11583)*
MBI Graphics & Printing Corp 508 765-0658
97 Worcester St Southbridge MA (01550) *(G-15394)*
MBL International Corporation (HQ) 781 939-6964
15a Constitution Way Woburn MA (01801) *(G-17225)*
Mbm Building Systems Ltd 617 478-3466
160 Federal St Boston MA (02110) *(G-8690)*
Mbm Sales 203 866-3674
40 Quintard Ave Norwalk CT (06854) *(G-3193)*
Mbo Advertising Services 781 837-5897
184 Standish St Marshfield MA (02050) *(G-12863)*
Mbraun 603 773-9333
14 Marin Way Stratham NH (03885) *(G-19874)*
Mbs Fabrication Inc (PA) 508 765-0900
270 Ashland Ave Southbridge MA (01550) *(G-15395)*
Mbsiinet Inc 888 466-2744
194 Main St N Southbury CT (06488) *(G-4030)*
Mbsw Inc 860 243-0303
41 Plainfield Rd West Hartford CT (06117) *(G-5086)*
Mbt, Stoughton *Also called Massachusetts Bay Tech Inc (G-15606)*
Mbw Incorporated 978 544-6462
184 Gov Dukakis Dr Orange MA (01364) *(G-14221)*
Mbw Tractor Sales LLC 207 384-2001
540 Route 4 Berwick ME (03901) *(G-5711)*
Mc Assembly, North Billerica *Also called M C Test Service Inc (G-13837)*
Mc Assembly International LLC 781 729-1073
101 Billerica Ave Bldg 7 North Billerica MA (01862) *(G-13840)*
Mc Crossins Logging Inc 207 826-2225
549 E Ridge Rd Cardville ME (04418) *(G-5883)*
MC Faulkner & Sons Inc 207 929-4545
28 Hague Rd Buxton ME (04093) *(G-5858)*
Mc Garvin Engineering Co 978 454-2741
35 Maple St Ste 1 Lowell MA (01852) *(G-12405)*
Mc Guire Manufacturing Co Inc 203 699-1801
60 Grandview Ct Cheshire CT (06410) *(G-744)*
Mc Kenney Machine & Tool Co, Corinna *Also called McKenney Machine & Tool Co (G-5921)*
Mc Kinney Products Company 800 346-7707
225 Episcopal Rd 1 Berlin CT (06037) *(G-95)*
Mc Kinnon Printing Co Inc 781 592-3677
101 Naples Rd Revere MA (02151) *(G-14773)*
Mc10 Inc 617 234-4448
10 Maguire Rd Bldg 31fl Lexington MA (02421) *(G-12242)*
McAllister Fuels Inc 802 782-5293
5023 Corliss Rd Richford VT (05476) *(G-22309)*
McAllister Machine Inc 207 282-8655
7 Pomerleau St 102 Biddeford ME (04005) *(G-5748)*
McBey John 603 934-2858
55 Industrial Park Dr Franklin NH (03235) *(G-18160)*
McBey Machines, Franklin *Also called McBey John (G-18160)*
McBooks Press Inc 607 272-2114
246 Goose Ln Ste 200 Guilford CT (06437) *(G-1710)*
McBreairty Ransford 207 498-3182
163 Brown Rd Woodland ME (04736) *(G-7288)*
McC, East Walpole *Also called Mass Coating Corp (G-10526)*
McC Materials Inc 860 309-9491
243 Union St North Adams MA (01247) *(G-13680)*
McCabe Sand & Gravel Co Inc 508 823-0771
120 Berkley St Taunton MA (02780) *(G-15764)*
McCafferty Logging LLC 207 212-8600
243 N Buckfield Rd Buckfield ME (04220) *(G-5852)*
McCain Foods Usa Inc 207 488-2561
319 Richardson Rd Easton ME (04740) *(G-5991)*
McCain Foods Usa Inc 207 488-2561
Station Rd Easton ME (04740) *(G-5992)*
McCains Vermont Products Inc 802 447-2610
1541 West Rd Bennington VT (05201) *(G-21682)*
McCann Fabrication 207 926-4118
1027 Lewiston Rd New Gloucester ME (04260) *(G-6469)*
McCarthy Bros Fuel Co Inc 508 867-5515
33 Lakeshore Dr West Brookfield MA (01585) *(G-16471)*
McClave Philbrick & Giblin 860 572-7710
929 Flanders Rd Mystic CT (06355) *(G-2443)*
McClelland Press Inc (PA) 413 663-5750
103 North St Williamstown MA (01267) *(G-16958)*
McClure Newspapers Inc 802 863-3441
100 Bank St Ste 700 Burlington VT (05401) *(G-21795)*
McCormacks Machine Co Inc 802 438-2345
5383 Walker Mt Rd West Rutland VT (05777) *(G-22618)*
McCrea Capital Advisors Inc 617 276-3388
202 Neponset Valley Pkwy Hyde Park MA (02136) *(G-11874)*
McCrea's Candies, Hyde Park *Also called McCrea Capital Advisors Inc (G-11874)*
McCullough Crushing Inc (PA) 802 223-5693
548 Mccullough Hill Rd Middlesex VT (05602) *(G-22122)*
McDermott Pallotta Inc 617 924-2318
376 Arsenal St Watertown MA (02472) *(G-16300)*
McDonald Duvall Design Inc 207 596-7940
10 Farwell Dr Rockland ME (04841) *(G-6805)*
McDonald Stain Glass Ltd 207 633-4815
7 Wall Point Rd Boothbay Harbor ME (04538) *(G-5785)*
McE - Monroe, Hudson *Also called Mercury Systems Inc (G-18366)*
McElroy Electronics Corp 978 425-4055
27 Fredonian St 33 Shirley MA (01464) *(G-15089)*
McF Electronic Services Inc 603 718-2256
39 1st St Lowell MA (01850) *(G-12406)*
McGill Airflow LLC 802 442-1900
452 Harwood Hill Rd Bennington VT (05201) *(G-21683)*
McGirr Graphics Incorporated 508 747-6400
19 Richards Rd Plymouth MA (02360) *(G-14563)*
McGirr Graphics Incorporated 508 747-6400
19 Richards Rd Plymouth MA (02360) *(G-14564)*
McGuire & Co Inc 207 797-3323
27 Gray Rd Falmouth ME (04105) *(G-6032)*
McGuire Controls, Falmouth *Also called McGuire & Co Inc (G-6032)*
McInnis USA Inc 203 890-9950
850 Canal St Stamford CT (06902) *(G-4246)*
McIntire Brass Works Inc 617 547-1819
14 Horace St Somerville MA (02143) *(G-15197)*
McIntire Company (HQ) 860 585-8559
745 Clark Ave Bristol CT (06010) *(G-580)*
McKearney Associates Inc (PA) 617 269-7600
850 Summer St Ste 102 Boston MA (02127) *(G-8691)*
McKeena Printing, Manchester *Also called Murroneys Printing Inc (G-18880)*
McKenney Machine & Tool Co 207 278-7091
400 Exeter Rd Corinna ME (04928) *(G-5921)*
McKnight Management Co Inc (PA) 508 540-5051
505 Palmer Ave Falmouth MA (02540) *(G-10796)*
McLane Research Labs Inc (PA) 508 495-4000
121 Bernard E Saint Jean East Falmouth MA (02536) *(G-10445)*
McLean Communications LLC 603 624-1442
50 Dow St Manchester NH (03101) *(G-18869)*
McLeod Optical Company Inc (PA) 401 467-3000
50 Jefferson Park Rd Warwick RI (02888) *(G-21388)*
McLeod Optical Company Inc 207 623-3841
179 Mount Vernon Ave Augusta ME (04330) *(G-5614)*
McLeod Optical Company Inc 203 754-2187
451 Meriden Rd Ste 3 Waterbury CT (06705) *(G-4913)*
McM Stamping Corporation 203 792-3080
66 Beaver Brook Rd Danbury CT (06810) *(G-953)*
MCM Technologies Inc 401 785-9204
175 Dupont Dr Providence RI (02907) *(G-21064)*
McManus E Vq Gp LLC 781 935-2483
14 Winter Rd Woburn MA (01801) *(G-17226)*
McMellon Bros Incorporated 203 375-5685
915 Honeyspot Rd Stratford CT (06615) *(G-4431)*
McMullin Manufacturing Corp 203 740-3360
70 Pocono Rd Brookfield CT (06804) *(G-651)*
McNairn Packaging Inc (PA) 413 568-1989
6 Elise St Westfield MA (01085) *(G-16699)*
McNally Industries Inc 603 654-5361
Tremont St Wilton NH (03086) *(G-19983)*
McNamara Fabricating Co Inc 774 243-7425
215 Shrewsbury St West Boylston MA (01583) *(G-16422)*
McNeil Healthcare Inc 203 934-8187
5 Saw Mill Rd West Haven CT (06516) *(G-5136)*
McNeilly Ems Educators Inc 978 375-7373
125 Liberty St Ste 102 Danvers MA (01923) *(G-10236)*
McPherson, Chelmsford *Also called Schoeffel International Corp (G-9931)*
McQuade Tidd Industries 207 532-2675
154 Steelstone St Houlton ME (04730) *(G-6207)*
MCS, North Billerica *Also called Microwave Cmpnents Specialists (G-13845)*

MCS, Westborough *Also called Microwave Cmpnents Systems Inc* ***(G-16636)***
McStowe Engineering & Met Pdts....508 378-7400
548 Spring St East Bridgewater MA (02333) ***(G-10417)***
McStowe Engrg & Met Pdts Co, East Bridgewater *Also called McStowe Engineering & Met Pdts* ***(G-10417)***
McVan Inc....508 431-2400
35 Frank Mossberg Dr Attleboro MA (02703) ***(G-7766)***
McWeeney Marketing Group Inc....203 891-8100
53 Robinson Blvd Orange CT (06477) ***(G-3373)***
McWilliams Inc....207 676-7639
211 Wells St Ste 1 North Berwick ME (03906) ***(G-6509)***
MD Chemicals LLC....508 314-9664
120 Jeffrey Ave Ste 2 Holliston MA (01746) ***(G-11584)***
MD Cosmetic Laser & Botox Ctr, Ferrisburgh *Also called Meadham Inc* ***(G-21989)***
MD Solarsciences Corporation....203 857-0095
9 W Broad St Ste 320 Stamford CT (06902) ***(G-4247)***
MD Stetson Company Inc....781 986-6161
92 York Ave Randolph MA (02368) ***(G-14689)***
Mdm, Quincy *Also called A F Murphy Die & Mch Co Inc* ***(G-14612)***
Mdm Products LLC....203 877-7070
105 Woodmont Rd Milford CT (06460) ***(G-2314)***
Mds Nxstage Corporation (HQ)....866 697-8243
350 Merrimack St Lawrence MA (01843) ***(G-12050)***
Mds Welding & Fabrication....603 660-0772
30 B And B Ln Weare NH (03281) ***(G-19938)***
ME and Ollies....603 319-1561
2454 Lafayette Rd Ste 21 Portsmouth NH (03801) ***(G-19592)***
ME Industries....207 286-2030
19 Pomerleau St Biddeford ME (04005) ***(G-5749)***
ME Tomacelli Inc....207 633-7553
55 Industrial Park Rd Boothbay ME (04537) ***(G-5779)***
Me-92 Operations Inc....401 831-9200
10 Houghton St Providence RI (02904) ***(G-21065)***
Meade Daily Group LLC....860 399-7342
103 Cold Spring Dr Westbrook CT (06498) ***(G-5160)***
Meadham Inc....802 878-1236
34 Middlebrook Rd Ferrisburgh VT (05456) ***(G-21989)***
Meadow Manufacturing Inc....860 357-3785
120 Old Brickyard Ln Kensington CT (06037) ***(G-1919)***
Means Pre-Cast Co Inc....781 843-1909
151 Adams St Braintree MA (02184) ***(G-9025)***
Mearthane Products Corporation (PA)....401 946-4400
16 Western Industrial Dr Cranston RI (02921) ***(G-20260)***
Measured Air Performance LLC....603 606-8350
250 Commercial St # 2015 Manchester NH (03101) ***(G-18870)***
Measurement Computing Corp (HQ)....508 946-5100
10 Commerce Way Ste C1 Norton MA (02766) ***(G-14081)***
Measurement Systems, Glastonbury *Also called Cameron International Corp* ***(G-1543)***
Measurement Systems Inc....203 949-3500
50 Barnes Park Rd N # 102 Wallingford CT (06492) ***(G-4772)***
Meb Enterprises Inc....203 599-0273
496 S Broad St Meriden CT (06450) ***(G-2102)***
Mec, North Adams *Also called Meehan Electronics Corporation* ***(G-13681)***
Mecha Noodle Bar....203 691-9671
201 Crown St New Haven CT (06510) ***(G-2711)***
Mechancal Engnered Systems LLC....203 400-4658
180 Jonathan Rd New Canaan CT (06840) ***(G-2606)***
Mechancal Engrg Met Fbrication, Methuen *Also called H & H Engineering Co Inc* ***(G-13025)***
Mechanical Drv Components Inc....413 535-2000
317 Meadow St Ste 6a Chicopee MA (01013) ***(G-10042)***
Mechanical Specialties Inc....401 267-4410
1143 Main St Pmb 782 Wyoming RI (02898) ***(G-21589)***
Med Associates Inc (PA)....802 527-2343
166 Industrial Park Rd Fairfax VT (05454) ***(G-21977)***
Med Print, Ellington *Also called Ellington Printery Inc* ***(G-1334)***
Med-Tech, North Billerica *Also called Medical-Technical Gases Inc* ***(G-13841)***
Medalco Metals Inc (PA)....413 586-6010
23 College St Ste 3 South Hadley MA (01075) ***(G-15307)***
Medallion Gallery Inc....617 236-8283
350 Boylston St Boston MA (02116) ***(G-8692)***
Medcon Biolab Technologies Inc....508 839-4203
50 Brigham Hill Rd Grafton MA (01519) ***(G-11223)***
Medcool Inc....617 512-4530
30 Washington St Wellesley MA (02481) ***(G-16372)***
Meddata Group LLC....978 887-0039
300 Rosewood Dr Ste 250 Danvers MA (01923) ***(G-10237)***
Meddevice Concepts LLC....617 834-7420
34 Fuller St Edgartown MA (02539) ***(G-10586)***
Medelco Inc....203 275-8070
54 Washburn St Bridgeport CT (06605) ***(G-449)***
Medex Southington, Southington *Also called Smiths Medical Asd Inc* ***(G-4078)***
Medford Transcript....781 396-1982
57 High St Medford MA (02155) ***(G-12943)***
Medi - Print Inc (PA)....781 324-4455
200 Maplewood St Malden MA (02148) ***(G-12582)***
Medi - Print Inc....617 566-7594
660 Huntin Ave Boston MA (02115) ***(G-8693)***
Media Links Inc....860 206-9163
431-C Hayden Station Rd Windsor CT (06095) ***(G-5348)***
Media One LLC....203 745-5825
44 Hawley Rd Hamden CT (06517) ***(G-1769)***
Media Scope International Inc....508 643-2988
51 Stoddard Dr North Attleboro MA (02760) ***(G-13762)***
Media Ventures Inc....203 852-6570
200 Connecticut Ave # 23 Norwalk CT (06854) ***(G-3194)***
Medianews Group Inc....978 772-0777
78 Barnum Rd Devens MA (01434) ***(G-10325)***
Medianews Group Inc....203 333-0161
301 Merritt 7 Ste 1 Norwalk CT (06851) ***(G-3195)***
Medianews Group Inc....978 343-6911
808 Main St Fitchburg MA (01420) ***(G-10835)***
Mediascope International, North Attleboro *Also called Media Scope International Inc* ***(G-13762)***
Mediatek USA Inc....781 503-8000
120 Presidential Way Woburn MA (01801) ***(G-17227)***
Mediatek Woburn, Woburn *Also called Mediatek USA Inc* ***(G-17227)***
Mediavue Systems Inc....781 926-0676
35 Pond Park Rd Ste 14 Hingham MA (02043) ***(G-11502)***
Medical Arts Press Inc....508 253-5000
500 Staples Dr 30352v Framingham MA (01702) ***(G-10982)***
Medical Asthtics Assoc Neng PC....978 263-5376
274 Great Rd Ste 2a Acton MA (01720) ***(G-7374)***
Medical Cmpnent Spcialists Inc....508 966-0992
42 Williams Way Bellingham MA (02019) ***(G-8049)***
Medical Cmpression Systems Inc....800 377-5804
2352 Main St Ste 102 Concord MA (01742) ***(G-10140)***
Medical Device & Biologics, Malden *Also called Nanofuse Biologics LLC* ***(G-12584)***
Medical Device Bus Svcs Inc....508 880-8100
325 Paramount Dr Raynham MA (02767) ***(G-14717)***
Medical Device Bus Svcs Inc....508 828-6155
50 Scotland Blvd Bridgewater MA (02324) ***(G-9083)***
Medical Device Bus Svcs Inc....508 828-2726
15 Commerce Way Norton MA (02766) ***(G-14082)***
Medical Device Fabrication, Jaffrey *Also called Hmd Inc* ***(G-18467)***
Medical Information Tech Inc (PA)....781 821-3000
Meditech Cir Westwood MA (02090) ***(G-16872)***
Medical Instrument Technology....508 775-8682
110 Breeds Hill Rd Ste 9 Hyannis MA (02601) ***(G-11849)***
Medical Isotopes Inc....603 635-2255
100 Bridge St Pelham NH (03076) ***(G-19439)***
Medical Monofilament Mfg LLC....508 746-7877
121 Camelot Dr Ste 2 Plymouth MA (02360) ***(G-14565)***
Medical Publishing Assoc....617 530-6222
55 Temple Pl Boston MA (02111) ***(G-8694)***
Medical Resources Inc....207 721-1110
11 Medical Center Dr # 1 Brunswick ME (04011) ***(G-5842)***
Medical-Technical Gases Inc....781 395-1946
8 Executive Park Dr North Billerica MA (01862) ***(G-13841)***
Medicametrix Inc....617 694-1713
600 Suffolk St Lowell MA (01854) ***(G-12407)***
Medici Gelalto, Barrington *Also called A Baileys LLC* ***(G-20042)***
Medicredits, Lenox *Also called N & M Pro Solutions Inc* ***(G-12102)***
Medina Plating Corp....330 725-4155
17 Kestree Dr Londonderry NH (03053) ***(G-18719)***
Medisight Corporation....415 205-2764
38 Spring St Cambridge MA (02141) ***(G-9550)***
Meditech....781 821-3000
550 Cochituate Rd Framingham MA (01701) ***(G-10983)***
Mediterranean Custom Cabinets....508 588-5498
318 Manley St Ste 1 West Bridgewater MA (02379) ***(G-16445)***
Mediterranean Snack Fd Co LLC....973 402-2644
1111 Summer St Ste 5a Stamford CT (06905) ***(G-4248)***
Mediware/Synergy Human & Socia....802 878-8514
25 New England Dr Essex Junction VT (05452) ***(G-21949)***
Medrhythms Inc....207 447-2177
4 Old Dynamite Way Gorham ME (04038) ***(G-6121)***
Medsix Inc....617 935-2716
101 S Huntington Ave Jamaica Plain MA (02130) ***(G-11946)***
Medsource Tech Holdings LLC (HQ)....978 570-6900
100 Fordham Rd Bldg C Wilmington MA (01887) ***(G-17021)***
Medsource Technologies LLC (HQ)....978 570-6900
100 Fordham Rd Ste 1 Wilmington MA (01887) ***(G-17022)***
Medtrnic Intrvntnal Vsclar Inc....978 777-0042
37a Cherry Hill Dr Danvers MA (01923) ***(G-10238)***
Medtrnic Sofamor Danek USA Inc....508 497-0792
239 South St Ste 2 Hopkinton MA (01748) ***(G-11727)***
Medtronic....508 452-4203
15 Hampshire St Mansfield MA (02048) ***(G-12645)***
Medtronic....508 739-0950
500 Old Connecticut Path # 3 Framingham MA (01701) ***(G-10984)***
Medtronic Inc....203 492-5764
60 Middletown Ave North Haven CT (06473) ***(G-3039)***
Medtronic Inc....978 739-3080
35 Cherry Hill Dr Danvers MA (01923) ***(G-10239)***
Medtronic Inc....978 777-0042
37 Cherry Hill Dr Danvers MA (01923) ***(G-10240)***
Medtronic Inc....413 593-6400
2 Ludlow Park Dr Chicopee MA (01022) ***(G-10043)***

Medusa Brewing Company Inc 978 310-1933
111 Main St Hudson MA (01749) *(G-11791)*
Meehan Electronics Corporation 413 664-9371
1544 Curran Hwy North Adams MA (01247) *(G-13681)*
Meetingmatrix Intl Inc 603 610-1600
195 Nh Ave Portsmouth NH (03801) *(G-19593)*
Mega Manufacturing LLC 860 666-5555
115 Pane Rd Newington CT (06111) *(G-2881)*
Mega Na Inc 781 784-7684
175 Paramount Dr Unit 302 Raynham MA (02767) *(G-14718)*
Mega Resveratrol, Danbury *Also called Candlewood Stars Inc (G-885)*
Mega-Power Inc 800 982-4339
44 Oak St Ste 1 Newton MA (02464) *(G-13613)*
Megafood, Derry *Also called Biosan Laboratories Inc (G-17972)*
Meganutra Inc (PA) 781 762-9600
128 Carnegie Row Ste 107 Norwood MA (02062) *(G-14177)*
Megaprint Inc 603 536-2900
1177 Nh Route 175 Holderness NH (03245) *(G-18323)*
Megapulse Incorporated 781 538-5299
23 Crosby Dr Bedford MA (01730) *(G-7989)*
Megasonics Inc 203 966-3404
205 Benedict Hill Rd New Canaan CT (06840) *(G-2607)*
Megatech Corporation 978 937-9600
525 Woburn St Ste 3 Tewksbury MA (01876) *(G-15822)*
Megawave Corporation 978 615-7200
234 Brooks St 3 Worcester MA (01606) *(G-17412)*
Meister Abrasives Usa Inc 401 294-4503
201 Circuit Dr North Kingstown RI (02852) *(G-20727)*
Mel-Co-Ed Inc 401 724-2160
381 Roosevelt Ave Pawtucket RI (02860) *(G-20859)*
Melco, Meriden *Also called Meriden Electronics Corp (G-2103)*
Melega Inc 203 961-8703
47 W Main St Stamford CT (06902) *(G-4249)*
Melexis Inc 603 223-2362
15 Trafalgar Sq Ste 100 Nashua NH (03063) *(G-19206)*
Mellanox Technologies Inc 978 439-5400
100 Apollo Dr Ste 302 Chelmsford MA (01824) *(G-9916)*
Mellen Company Inc (PA) 603 228-2929
40 Chenell Dr Concord NH (03301) *(G-17914)*
Mellen Company Inc 603 648-2121
1260 Battle St Webster NH (03303) *(G-19944)*
Meller Optics, Inc., Providence *Also called Adolf Meller Company (G-20946)*
Meller Optics, Inc., Providence *Also called Adolf Meller Company (G-20947)*
Mellos North End Mfg Co Inc 508 673-2320
63 N Court St Fall River MA (02720) *(G-10729)*
Melon, Leeds *Also called Axio Inc (G-12097)*
Meloni Tool Co Inc 401 272-6513
25 Oakdale Ave Johnston RI (02919) *(G-20521)*
Melrose Free Press Inc 781 665-4000
48 Dunham Rd Beverly MA (01915) *(G-8150)*
Melt Cognition 781 275-6400
7 Alfred Cir Bedford MA (01730) *(G-7990)*
Melton Sales and Service Inc 207 623-8895
323 Water St Hallowell ME (04347) *(G-6163)*
Melville Candy Corporation 800 638-8063
28 York Ave Randolph MA (02368) *(G-14690)*
Melville Old Time Candy & Pdts, Randolph *Also called Melville Candy Corporation (G-14690)*
Melvin L Yoder 207 278-3539
16 Bolstridge Rd Corinna ME (04928) *(G-5922)*
Melvin Reisz 603 436-9188
49 Market St Portsmouth NH (03801) *(G-19594)*
Mem-Co Fittings Inc 603 329-9633
45 Gigante Dr Hampstead NH (03841) *(G-18243)*
Membrane Structure Solutions 908 520-0112
71 Summer St Hingham MA (02043) *(G-11503)*
Membrane-Switchescom 508 277-2892
10 Ocean St Lynn MA (01902) *(G-12526)*
Memco, Jay *Also called Antoine Mechanical Inc (G-6219)*
Memento Inc 781 221-3030
55 Network Dr Burlington MA (01803) *(G-9301)*
Memoir Network 207 353-5454
95 Gould Rd Lisbon ME (04252) *(G-6364)*
Memoirs Unlimited Inc 978 985-3206
266 Cabot St Ste 2 Beverly MA (01915) *(G-8151)*
Memorial Sandblast Inc 802 476-7086
15 Blackwell St Barre VT (05641) *(G-21629)*
Memory Lane Collections, Danbury *Also called Visual Impact LLC (G-1005)*
Memphremagog Press Printers, Newport *Also called Dawn Brainard (G-22196)*
Memry Corporation (HQ) 203 739-1100
3 Berkshire Blvd Bethel CT (06801) *(G-170)*
Memry Corporation 203 739-1146
8 Berkshire Blvd Bethel CT (06801) *(G-171)*
Memsic Inc (HQ) 978 738-0900
1 Tech Dr Ste 325 Andover MA (01810) *(G-7569)*
Memtec Corporation 603 893-8080
68 Stiles Rd Ste D Salem NH (03079) *(G-19751)*
Menard Manufacturing 802 438-5173
162 Misty Mdws West Rutland VT (05777) *(G-22619)*
Menchies Frozen Yogurt 781 740-1245
15 Shipyard Dr Ste 1e Hingham MA (02043) *(G-11504)*
Mendix Inc 857 263-8200
22 Boston Wharf Rd Fl 8 Boston MA (02210) *(G-8695)*
Menicon America Inc 781 609-2042
76 Treble Cove Rd Ste 3 North Billerica MA (01862) *(G-13842)*
Meninno Brothers Gourmet Foods, Danvers *Also called R Walters Foods (G-10249)*
Meno Publishing Inc 781 209-2665
460 Hillside Ave Ste 6 Needham Heights MA (02494) *(G-13336)*
Meno Reunion Books, Needham Heights *Also called Meno Publishing Inc (G-13336)*
Menon Laboratories Inc 339 224-2787
28 Dane St Somerville MA (02143) *(G-15198)*
Mental Canvas LLC 475 329-0515
61 Hartford Ave Madison CT (06443) *(G-1968)*
Menton Machine Co Inc 781 293-8394
1299 Main St Hanson MA (02341) *(G-11366)*
Mepp Tool Co Inc 860 289-8230
81 Commerce St Glastonbury CT (06033) *(G-1564)*
Mer+ge 512 665-2266
217 Reservoir Rd Chestnut Hill MA (02467) *(G-9987)*
Mercaldo Studio, Boston *Also called Michele Mercaldo (G-8704)*
Mercantile Development Inc 203 922-8880
10 Waterview Dr Shelton CT (06484) *(G-3832)*
Merchant Machine Inc 508 672-1991
50 Merchant St Fall River MA (02723) *(G-10730)*
Merchants Fabrication Inc (PA) 508 784-6700
23 Golf St Southbridge MA (01550) *(G-15396)*
Merchants Metals LLC 413 562-9981
390 Burnett Rd Chicopee MA (01020) *(G-10044)*
Merck Group 781 858-3284
80 Ashby Rd Bedford MA (01730) *(G-7991)*
Merck Research Laboratories 617 992-2000
33 Avenue Louis Pasteur Boston MA (02115) *(G-8696)*
Merck Sharp & Dohme Corp 781 860-8660
65 Hayden Ave Lexington MA (02421) *(G-12243)*
Merck Sharp & Dohme Corp 617 992-2074
33 Avenue Louis Pasteur Boston MA (02115) *(G-8697)*
Mercolino Bakery 413 733-9595
287 Frank Smith Rd Longmeadow MA (01106) *(G-12337)*
Mercuria Energy Trading Inc 203 413-3355
33 Benedict Pl Ste 1 Greenwich CT (06830) *(G-1630)*
Mercury Brewing & Dist Co 978 356-3329
2 Brewery Pl Ipswich MA (01938) *(G-11930)*
Mercury Learning and Info LLC 781 934-0500
455 Washington St Duxbury MA (02331) *(G-10400)*
Mercury Systems Inc 203 792-7474
267 Lowell Rd Ste A Hudson NH (03051) *(G-18366)*
Mercury Systems Inc 603 883-2900
267 Lowell Rd Ste 101 Hudson NH (03051) *(G-18414)*
Mercury Systems Inc (PA) 978 256-1300
50 Minuteman Rd Andover MA (01810) *(G-7570)*
Mercury Wire Products Inc 508 885-6363
1 Mercury Dr Spencer MA (01562) *(G-15433)*
Mereco Technologies Group Inc (HQ) 401 822-9300
8 Ricker Ave Londonderry NH (03053) *(G-18720)*
Meredith Corporation 413 733-4040
1300 Liberty St Springfield MA (01104) *(G-15488)*
Merida LLC 508 675-6572
1 Currant Rd Ste 1 # 1 Fall River MA (02720) *(G-10731)*
Meriden Electronics Corp 203 237-8811
1777 N Colony Rd Meriden CT (06450) *(G-2103)*
Meriden Manufacturing Inc 203 237-7481
230 State Street Ext Meriden CT (06450) *(G-2104)*
Meriden Precision Plastics LLC 203 235-3261
290 Pratt St Ste 18 Meriden CT (06450) *(G-2105)*
Meridian Custom Woodworking In 508 587-4400
443 Summer St 1 Brockton MA (02302) *(G-9165)*
Meridian Industrial Group LLC 413 538-9880
529 S East St Holyoke MA (01040) *(G-11639)*
Meridian Operations LLC 860 564-8811
1414 Norwich Rd Plainfield CT (06374) *(G-3454)*
Meridian Printing Inc 401 885-4882
1538 S County Trl East Greenwich RI (02818) *(G-20373)*
Merit Machine Manufacturing 978 342-7677
25 Willow St Fitchburg MA (01420) *(G-10836)*
Merit Medical Systems Inc (HQ) 781 681-7900
1050 Hingham St Fl 1 Rockland MA (02370) *(G-14813)*
Meritronics, Oxford *Also called Power Trans Co Inc (G-3419)*
Merl Inc 203 237-8811
1777 N Colony Rd Meriden CT (06450) *(G-2106)*
Merle Schloff 802 352-4246
Prospect St Salisbury VT (05769) *(G-22399)*
Merlinone Inc (PA) 617 328-6645
17 Whitney Rd Quincy MA (02169) *(G-14639)*
Merlyn, Putnam *Also called Control Concepts Inc (G-3608)*
Merriam-Webster Incorporated (HQ) 413 734-3134
47 Federal St Springfield MA (01105) *(G-15489)*
Merrick Services 508 802-3751
368 Greenwood St Millbury MA (01527) *(G-13170)*

A L P H A B E T I C

Merrifield Paint Company Inc 860 529-1583
47 Inwood Rd Rocky Hill CT (06067) ***(G-3723)***
Merrill Blueberry Farms Inc 207 667-2541
63 Thorsen Rd Hancock ME (04640) ***(G-6170)***
Merrill Corporation 860 249-7220
100 Pearl St Fl 14 Hartford CT (06103) ***(G-1846)***
Merrill Corporation 617 535-1500
101 Federal St Ste 2102 Boston MA (02110) ***(G-8698)***
Merrill Graphics Incorporated 781 843-0666
35 Crescent Ave Braintree MA (02184) ***(G-9026)***
Merrill Industries Inc 860 871-1888
26 Village St Ellington CT (06029) ***(G-1336)***
Merrill Industries LLC 860 871-1888
26 Village St Ellington CT (06029) ***(G-1337)***
Merrill Oil LLC 203 387-1130
517 Amity Rd Woodbridge CT (06525) ***(G-5472)***
Merrill's Metal Shop, Wilton *Also called McNally Industries Inc* ***(G-19983)***
Merrimac Spool and Reel Co Inc 978 372-7777
203 Essex St Haverhill MA (01832) ***(G-11453)***
Merrimac Tool Company Inc (PA) 978 388-7159
91 High St Amesbury MA (01913) ***(G-7494)***
Merrimac Vly Alum Brass Fndry 978 388-0830
56 Mill St Amesbury MA (01913) ***(G-7495)***
Merrimack Engraving & Mkg Co 978 683-5335
55 Chase St Methuen MA (01844) ***(G-13035)***
Merrimack Manufacturing Co 207 647-3566
217 Harrison Rd Bridgton ME (04009) ***(G-5809)***
Merrimack Micro LLC 603 809-4183
76 Jessica Dr Merrimack NH (03054) ***(G-19014)***
Merrimack Pharmaceuticals Inc 617 441-1000
1 Broadway Fl 14 Cambridge MA (02142) ***(G-9551)***
Merrimack Valley Water Assn 978 975-1800
15 Union St Ste 800 Lawrence MA (01840) ***(G-12051)***
Merritt Extruder Corp 203 230-8100
15 Marne St Hamden CT (06514) ***(G-1770)***
Merritt Machine Company 860 257-4484
61 Arrow Rd Ste 5 Wethersfield CT (06109) ***(G-5257)***
Merritt, Joseph & Company, Danbury *Also called Joseph Merritt & Company Inc* ***(G-940)***
Merry Christmas From Heaven, Weymouth *Also called Mooneytunco Inc* ***(G-16894)***
Mersana Therapeutics Inc (PA) 617 498-0020
840 Memorial Dr Ste 4 Cambridge MA (02139) ***(G-9552)***
Mersen USA Ep Corp (HQ) 805 351-8400
374 Merrimac St Newburyport MA (01950) ***(G-13511)***
Mery Manufacturing, Rockfall *Also called Rogers Manufacturing Company* ***(G-3699)***
Mesco Corporation 401 683-2677
1676 E Main Rd Bay A Portsmouth RI (02871) ***(G-20928)***
Messer LLC 508 236-0222
525 Pleasant St Attleboro MA (02703) ***(G-7767)***
Messer LLC 508 966-3148
92a Depot St Bellingham MA (02019) ***(G-8050)***
Messer LLC 802 878-6339
Ibm Plant Essex Junction VT (05452) ***(G-21950)***
Messer LLC 207 475-3102
9 Ranger Dr Kittery ME (03904) ***(G-6257)***
Messer LLC 781 341-4575
97 Maple St Stoughton MA (02072) ***(G-15607)***
Messer Petroleum Equipment, Westbrook *Also called Messer Truck Equipment* ***(G-7196)***
Messer Truck Equipment (PA) 207 854-9751
170 Warren Ave Westbrook ME (04092) ***(G-7196)***
Messiah Development LLC 203 368-2405
210 Congress St Bridgeport CT (06604) ***(G-450)***
Mestek Inc (PA) 470 898-4533
260 N Elm St Westfield MA (01085) ***(G-16700)***
Mestek Inc 207 426-2351
76 Hinckley Rd Clinton ME (04927) ***(G-5916)***
Mestek Inc 413 564-5530
260 N Elm St Westfield MA (01085) ***(G-16701)***
Mestek Inc 413 568-9571
260 N Elm St Westfield MA (01085) ***(G-16702)***
Mestek Inc 413 568-9571
260 N Elm St Westfield MA (01085) ***(G-16703)***
Met Tech Inc 203 254-9319
1901 Post Rd Fairfield CT (06824) ***(G-1443)***
Met-Craft, Oxford *Also called Cast Global Manufacturing Corp* ***(G-3393)***
Meta Software Corporation (PA) 781 238-0293
15 New England Exec Park Burlington MA (01803) ***(G-9302)***
Metabolix, Woburn *Also called Yield10 Bioscience Inc* ***(G-17326)***
Metacog Inc 508 798-6100
55 Linden St Worcester MA (01609) ***(G-17413)***
Metal Bellows, Sharon *Also called Senior Operations LLC* ***(G-15056)***
Metal Components 401 886-7979
250 Old Baptist Rd North Kingstown RI (02852) ***(G-20728)***
Metal Fabrications, Biddeford *Also called DSM Metal Fabrication Inc* ***(G-5729)***
Metal Fish LLC 978 930-0637
100 Wotton St North Chelmsford MA (01863) ***(G-13904)***
Metal Graphic, Waltham *Also called Knowledge Management Assoc LLC* ***(G-16139)***
Metal Guy LLC 401 474-0234
1 Washington St Newport RI (02840) ***(G-20672)***
Metal Housings Enclosures 978 567-3324
34 Tower St Hudson MA (01749) ***(G-11792)***
Metal Improvement Company LLC 860 635-9994
20 Tuttle Pl Ste 6 Middletown CT (06457) ***(G-2204)***
Metal Improvement Company LLC 781 246-3848
1 Nablus Rd Wakefield MA (01880) ***(G-15961)***
Metal Improvement Company LLC 860 224-9148
1 John Downey Dr New Britain CT (06051) ***(G-2552)***
Metal Improvement Company LLC 860 688-6201
145 Addison Rd Windsor CT (06095) ***(G-5349)***
Metal Improvement Company LLC 860 523-9901
12 Thompson Rd East Windsor CT (06088) ***(G-1295)***
Metal Improvement Company LLC 978 658-0032
201 Ballardvale St Wilmington MA (01887) ***(G-17023)***
Metal Industries Inc 860 296-6228
806r Wethersfield Ave Hartford CT (06114) ***(G-1847)***
Metal Magic Inc 207 667-8519
979 Bar Harbor Rd Trenton ME (04605) ***(G-7100)***
Metal Men 413 533-0513
280 Ludlow Rd Chicopee MA (01020) ***(G-10045)***
Metal Plus LLC 860 379-1327
214 Wallens Hill Rd Winsted CT (06098) ***(G-5416)***
Metal Processing Co Inc 978 649-1289
75 Westech Dr Tyngsboro MA (01879) ***(G-15896)***
Metal Solutions LLC 774 276-0096
1 Herricks Ln Millbury MA (01527) ***(G-13171)***
Metal Specialties Inc 207 786-4268
300 Rodman Rd Auburn ME (04210) ***(G-5580)***
Metal Spraying Co Inc 401 725-2722
900 Lonsdale Ave Central Falls RI (02863) ***(G-20120)***
Metal Suppliers Online LLC 603 329-0101
35 Gigante Dr Hampstead NH (03841) ***(G-18244)***
Metal Tronics Inc 978 659-6960
400 E Main St Georgetown MA (01833) ***(G-11146)***
Metal Works, Limington *Also called Archer Machine* ***(G-6346)***
Metal Works Inc 603 332-9323
24 Industrial Dr Londonderry NH (03053) ***(G-18721)***
Metal-Flex Welded Bellows Inc 802 334-5550
149 Lakemont Rd Newport VT (05855) ***(G-22201)***
Metalcrafters Inc 978 683-7097
104 Pleasant Valley St Methuen MA (01844) ***(G-13036)***
Metalform Acquisition LLC (PA) 860 224-2630
555 John Downey Dr New Britain CT (06051) ***(G-2553)***
Metalform Company, New Britain *Also called Metalform Acquisition LLC* ***(G-2553)***
Metalgrommets.com, Dighton *Also called Armin Innovative Products Inc* ***(G-10335)***
Metallium Inc 508 728-9074
11 Duff St Watertown MA (02472) ***(G-16301)***
Metallizing Service Co Inc (PA) 860 953-1144
11 Cody St Hartford CT (06110) ***(G-1848)***
Metallon Inc 860 283-8265
1415 Waterbury Rd Thomaston CT (06787) ***(G-4509)***
Metallurgical Solutions Inc 401 941-2100
85 Aldrich St Providence RI (02905) ***(G-21066)***
Metalogic Industries LLC 508 461-6787
115 Schofield Ave Dudley MA (01571) ***(G-10381)***
Metalor Technologies USA Corp (HQ) 508 699-8800
255 John L Dietsch Blvd North Attleboro MA (02763) ***(G-13763)***
Metalor USA Refining Corp (HQ) 508 699-8800
255 John L Dietsch Blvd North Attleboro MA (02763) ***(G-13764)***
Metalpro Inc 860 388-1811
50 School House Rd Old Saybrook CT (06475) ***(G-3344)***
Metalsmiths Inc 617 265-4040
15 Banton St Boston MA (02124) ***(G-8699)***
Metalworks Inc 802 863-0414
205 Flynn Ave Burlington VT (05401) ***(G-21796)***
Metamorphic Materials Inc 860 738-8638
122 Colebrook River Rd Winsted CT (06098) ***(G-5417)***
Metaphor Bronze Tileworks LLC 207 342-2597
245 S Main St Morrill ME (04952) ***(G-6455)***
Metastat Inc (PA) 617 531-6500
27 Drydock Ave Ste 2 Boston MA (02210) ***(G-8700)***
Metavac LLC 631 207-2344
20 Post Rd Portsmouth NH (03801) ***(G-19595)***
Metelics Corp 408 737-8197
100 Chelmsford St Lowell MA (01851) ***(G-12408)***
Meteor Globl Mfg Solutions Inc 617 733-6506
87 Munn Rd Monson MA (01057) ***(G-13209)***
Meteor Gms, Monson *Also called Meteor Globl Mfg Solutions Inc* ***(G-13209)***
Metfab Engineering Inc 508 695-1007
332 John L Dietsch Blvd Attleboro Falls MA (02763) ***(G-7815)***
Methods & Machining Svcs Inc 401 942-5700
140 Uxbridge St Cranston RI (02920) ***(G-20261)***
Methods 3d Inc 978 443-5388
65 Union Ave Sudbury MA (01776) ***(G-15663)***
Metric Mfg, Woburn *Also called Metrick Manufacturing Co Inc* ***(G-17228)***
Metrick Manufacturing Co Inc 781 935-1331
142 Bedford Rd Ste 3 Woburn MA (01801) ***(G-17228)***
Metro Inc (PA) 401 461-2200
1 Metro Park Dr Cranston RI (02910) ***(G-20262)***

Metro Boston LLC 617 210-7905
234 Congress St Fl 4 Boston MA (02110) ***(G-8701)***
Metro Corp 617 262-9700
300 Massachusetts Ave Boston MA (02115) ***(G-8702)***
Metro Group Inc 781 932-9911
64 Cummings Park Woburn MA (01801) ***(G-17229)***
Metro Home Video, Cranston *Also called Metro Inc* ***(G-20262)***
Metro Sign & Awning, Tewksbury *Also called C & D Signs Inc* ***(G-15809)***
Metroblity Optical Systems Inc 781 255-5300
101 Billerica Ave Bldg 7 North Billerica MA (01862) ***(G-13843)***
Metropltan Cbinets Countertops, Norwood *Also called Metropolitan Cab Distrs Corp* ***(G-14178)***
Metropolitan Cab & Countertops, Natick *Also called Metropolitan Cab Distrs Corp* ***(G-13267)***
Metropolitan Cab Distrs Corp 508 651-8950
10 Mercer Rd Natick MA (01760) ***(G-13267)***
Metropolitan Cab Distrs Corp (PA) 781 949-8900
505 University Ave Norwood MA (02062) ***(G-14178)***
Metsa Board Americas Corp 203 229-0037
301 Merritt 7 Ste 2 Norwalk CT (06851) ***(G-3196)***
Metso Automation, Shrewsbury *Also called Neles USA Inc* ***(G-15126)***
Metso Fabric, Winthrop *Also called Valmet Inc* ***(G-7283)***
Metso Usa Inc (HQ) 617 369-7850
133 Federal St Ste 302 Boston MA (02110) ***(G-8703)***
Mettler Packaging LLC 508 738-2201
90 New State Hwy Ste 1 Raynham MA (02767) ***(G-14719)***
Mettler-Toledo Ingold, Inc., Billerica *Also called Mettler-Toledo Process Analyti* ***(G-8265)***
Mettler-Toledo Intl Inc 800 472-4646
150 Wells Ave Newton MA (02459) ***(G-13614)***
Mettler-Toledo Process Analyti 781 301-8800
900 Middlesex Tpke 8-1 Billerica MA (01821) ***(G-8265)***
Mettler-Toledo Thornton Inc 978 262-0210
900 Middlesex Tpke 8-1 Billerica MA (01821) ***(G-8266)***
Metz Communication Corporation 603 528-2590
151c Elm St Laconia NH (03246) ***(G-18575)***
Metz Electronics Corp 603 524-8806
7 Countryside Dr Gilford NH (03249) ***(G-18191)***
Metzger/Mcguire Inc 603 224-6122
807 Route 3a Bow NH (03304) ***(G-17722)***
Metzys Taqueria LLC 978 992-1451
17 55th St Newburyport MA (01950) ***(G-13512)***
Mevatec Corp 603 885-4321
65 Spit Brook Rd Nashua NH (03060) ***(G-19207)***
Mexi-Grill LLC 203 574-2127
495 Union St Waterbury CT (06706) ***(G-4914)***
Mexichem Spcalty Compounds Inc (HQ) 978 537-8071
170 Pioneer Dr Leominster MA (01453) ***(G-12166)***
Meyer Gage Co Inc 860 528-6526
230 Burnham St South Windsor CT (06074) ***(G-3993)***
Meyer Wire & Cable Company LLC 203 281-0817
1072 Sherman Ave Hamden CT (06514) ***(G-1771)***
Meyers Gluten Free Baking LLC 978 381-9629
1025 Hale St Beverly MA (01915) ***(G-8152)***
Mezzanine Safeti Gates Inc 978 768-3000
174 Western Ave Essex MA (01929) ***(G-10596)***
Mfb Holdings LLC 603 742-0104
27 Production Dr Dover NH (03820) ***(G-18036)***
Mfg Electronics Inc 978 671-5490
70 Treble Cove Rd Ste 1 North Billerica MA (01862) ***(G-13844)***
Mfi Corp 802 658-6600
44 Lakeside Ave Burlington VT (05401) ***(G-21797)***
Mg Print and Promotions 603 343-2534
1 Washington St Ste 501 Dover NH (03820) ***(G-18037)***
Mg2 Technologies LLC 978 739-1068
41 Sherwood Ave Danvers MA (01923) ***(G-10241)***
MGA Emblem Co, Cheshire *Also called Robert Audette* ***(G-760)***
Mgb Machine Inc 401 253-0055
60 Magnolia St Bristol RI (02809) ***(G-20093)***
Mgb Us Inc 774 415-0060
157 Grove St Ste 30 Franklin MA (02038) ***(G-11064)***
Mgc's Cstm Made Wooden, East Haddam *Also called Mark G Cappitella* ***(G-1151)***
Mgi Energy, Northborough *Also called Sundrum Solar Inc* ***(G-14049)***
Mgi Inc 207 817-3280
21 White Pine Rd Ste 7 Hermon ME (04401) ***(G-6190)***
MGI usa Inc 203 312-1200
23 Forest Ave Danbury CT (06810) ***(G-954)***
Mgs Group-Hall Industries The, North Branford *Also called MGS Manufacturing Inc* ***(G-2970)***
MGS Manufacturing Inc 203 481-4275
8c Commerce Dr North Branford CT (06471) ***(G-2970)***
MH Rhodes Cramer LLC 860 291-8402
105 Nutmeg Rd S South Windsor CT (06074) ***(G-3994)***
MH Stallman Company Inc (PA) 401 331-5129
292 Charles St Providence RI (02904) ***(G-21067)***
Mhgc, Wareham *Also called Viabella Holdings LLC* ***(G-16257)***
Miami Heat Discount Fuel 508 991-2875
391 Main St Fairhaven MA (02719) ***(G-10642)***
Miami Wabash Paper LLC (HQ) 203 847-8500
108 Main St Ste 3 Norwalk CT (06851) ***(G-3197)***
Miano Printing Services Inc 617 935-2830
330 Woodland St Holliston MA (01746) ***(G-11585)***
Mica-Tron Products Corp 781 767-2163
275 Centre St Ste 13 Holbrook MA (02343) ***(G-11531)***
Michael Brisebois 413 527-9590
6 Industrial Pkwy Easthampton MA (01027) ***(G-10567)***
Michael Good Designs Inc 207 236-9619
325 Commercial St Rockport ME (04856) ***(G-6824)***
Michael Healy Designs Inc 401 597-5900
60 New River Rd Manville RI (02838) ***(G-20610)***
Michael Humphries Wdwkg Inc 413 498-0018
158 Birnam Rd Northfield MA (01360) ***(G-14064)***
Michael Humphries Woodworking 413 498-2187
105 Main St Northfield MA (01360) ***(G-14065)***
Michael M Almeida 508 823-4957
330 Winthrop St Unit 1 Taunton MA (02780) ***(G-15765)***
Michael Monteiro 508 481-1881
667 Farm Rd Ste 1 Marlborough MA (01752) ***(G-12794)***
Michael Olden 802 334-5525
1670 E Main St Newport VT (05855) ***(G-22202)***
Michael Perra Inc 603 644-2110
640 Harvard St Ste 2 Manchester NH (03103) ***(G-18871)***
Michael V Morin 207 459-1200
1298 Main St B Sanford ME (04073) ***(G-6883)***
Michael Vincent 413 786-4911
20 Liquori Dr Feeding Hills MA (01030) ***(G-10801)***
Michaelson Fluid Power Inc 401 232-7070
9 Rocky Hill Rd Smithfield RI (02917) ***(G-21239)***
Michaud Machine Company, Winthrop *Also called David Michaud* ***(G-7280)***
Michaud Tool Co Inc 860 582-6785
122 Napco Dr Terryville CT (06786) ***(G-4486)***
Micheals Provision, Fall River *Also called Miranda Brothers Inc* ***(G-10735)***
Michele Mercaldo 617 350-7909
276 Shawmut Ave Boston MA (02118) ***(G-8704)***
Michele Schiano Di Cola Inc 203 265-5301
11 S Colony St Wallingford CT (06492) ***(G-4773)***
Michele's Totally Awesome Gour, Londonderry *Also called Micheles Sweet Shoppe LLC* ***(G-18722)***
Micheles Sweet Shoppe LLC 603 425-2946
123 Nashua Rd Unit 14 Londonderry NH (03053) ***(G-18722)***
Michell Instruments Inc 978 484-0005
319 Newburyport Tpke # 207 Rowley MA (01969) ***(G-14857)***
Michie Corporation 603 428-7426
173 Buxton Industrial Dr Henniker NH (03242) ***(G-18307)***
Mickey Herbst 203 993-5879
32 Laurel St Fairfield CT (06825) ***(G-1444)***
Micon Die Corporation 413 478-5029
85 Phelon Ave West Springfield MA (01089) ***(G-16530)***
Micon Steel Rule Die, West Springfield *Also called Micon Die Corporation* ***(G-16530)***
Micrex Corporation 508 660-1900
17 Industrial Rd Walpole MA (02081) ***(G-16002)***
Micro Abrasives Corporation 413 562-3641
720 Southampton Rd Westfield MA (01085) ***(G-16704)***
Micro ARC Welding Service 508 852-6125
33 Pullman St Worcester MA (01606) ***(G-17414)***
Micro Bends Corp 603 924-0022
365 Jaffrey Rd Peterborough NH (03458) ***(G-19476)***
Micro Care Corporation (PA) 860 827-0626
595 John Downey Dr New Britain CT (06051) ***(G-2554)***
Micro Care Marketing Svcs Div, New Britain *Also called Micro Care Corporation* ***(G-2554)***
Micro Electronics Inc 508 761-9161
1005 Newman Ave Seekonk MA (02771) ***(G-15027)***
Micro Financial Cmpt Systems 508 533-1233
89 Main St Ste 204 Medway MA (02053) ***(G-12967)***
Micro Financial Systems, Medway *Also called Micro Financial Cmpt Systems* ***(G-12967)***
Micro Focus Software Inc 617 613-2000
150 Cambridgepark Dr # 800 Cambridge MA (02140) ***(G-9553)***
Micro Insert Inc 860 621-5789
183 Clark St Milldale CT (06467) ***(G-2385)***
Micro Machine & Electronics 978 466-9350
283 Whitney St Leominster MA (01453) ***(G-12167)***
Micro Magnetics Inc 508 672-4489
617 Airport Rd Fall River MA (02720) ***(G-10732)***
Micro Matic, Naugatuck *Also called Advantage Sheet Metal Mfg LLC* ***(G-2457)***
Micro Metal Components Inc 603 463-5986
19 Brown Rd Deerfield NH (03037) ***(G-17970)***
Micro Precision LLC 860 423-4575
1102 Windham Rd South Windham CT (06266) ***(G-3926)***
Micro Source Discovery Systems 860 350-8078
11 George Washington Plz Gaylordsville CT (06755) ***(G-1532)***
Micro Tech Mfg Inc 508 752-5212
100 Grand St Ste 1 Worcester MA (01610) ***(G-17415)***
Micro Tech Production Mch Co 603 434-1743
1 Commercial Ln Londonderry NH (03053) ***(G-18723)***
Micro Weld Fabtec Corp 603 234-6531
19 Spring St Windham NH (03087) ***(G-20009)***
Micro Wire Products Inc 508 584-0200
120 N Main St Brockton MA (02301) ***(G-9166)***

Micro Wire Transm Systems Inc 802 876-7901
8 Ewing Pl Essex Junction VT (05452) ***(G-21951)***
Micro-Leads Inc 617 299-0295
255 Elm St Ste 300 Somerville MA (02144) ***(G-15199)***
Micro-Mech Inc 978 356-2966
33 Turnpike Rd Ipswich MA (01938) ***(G-11931)***
Micro-Precision Inc (PA) 603 763-2394
6 Main St Sunapee NH (03782) ***(G-19882)***
Micro-Precision Tech Inc 603 893-7600
10 Manor Pkwy Ste C Salem NH (03079) ***(G-19752)***
Micro-Probe Incorporated 203 267-6446
2 Pomperaug Office Park # 103 Southbury CT (06488) ***(G-4031)***
Microbest Inc 203 597-0355
670 Captain Neville Dr # 1 Waterbury CT (06705) ***(G-4915)***
Microbiotix Inc 508 757-2800
1 Innovation Dr Ste 14 Worcester MA (01605) ***(G-17416)***
Microboard Processing Inc 203 881-4300
36 Cogwheel Ln Seymour CT (06483) ***(G-3757)***
Microbot Medical Inc (PA) 781 875-3605
25 Recreation Park Dr # 108 Hingham MA (02043) ***(G-11505)***
Microcal LLC 413 586-7720
22 Industrial Dr E Northampton MA (01060) ***(G-14012)***
Microcatheter Components LLC 603 532-0345
82 Fitzgerald Dr Unit 1a Jaffrey NH (03452) ***(G-18473)***
Microchem, Westborough *Also called Kayaku Advanced Materials Inc* ***(G-16629)***
Microchip Technologies, Westborough *Also called Microchip Technology Inc* ***(G-16634)***
Microchip Technology Inc 774 760-0087
112 Turnpike Rd Ste 100 Westborough MA (01581) ***(G-16634)***
Microcut Inc 781 582-8090
8 Aldrin Rd Plymouth MA (02360) ***(G-14566)***
Microcut Laser Designs, Chester *Also called Paul Thomas* ***(G-21848)***
Microdisplay Report, Norwalk *Also called Insight Media LLC* ***(G-3174)***
Microdyne Technologies 860 747-9473
64 Neal Ct Plainville CT (06062) ***(G-3507)***
Microelectrodes Inc 603 668-0692
40 Harvey Rd Bedford NH (03110) ***(G-17654)***
Microfab Inc 603 621-9522
180 Zachary Rd Ste 1 Manchester NH (03109) ***(G-18872)***
Microfluidics Intl Corp 617 969-5452
90 Glacier Dr Ste 1000 Westwood MA (02090) ***(G-16873)***
Microline Surgical Inc (HQ) 978 922-9810
50 Dunham Rd Ste 1500 Beverly MA (01915) ***(G-8153)***
Micromatics Machine Co Inc 603 889-2115
9 Clinton Dr Hollis NH (03049) ***(G-18334)***
Micrometal Technologies Inc (PA) 978 462-3600
5 New Pasture Rd Newburyport MA (01950) ***(G-13513)***
Micrometals Tech Corp 508 792-1615
12 Jacques St Worcester MA (01603) ***(G-17417)***
Micromod Automation & Controls 585 321-9209
10 Capital Dr Wallingford CT (06492) ***(G-4774)***
Micromod Automtn & Contrls LLC 585 321-9200
10 Capital Dr Wallingford CT (06492) ***(G-4775)***
Micron Corporation 781 769-5771
89 Access Rd Ste 5 Norwood MA (02062) ***(G-14179)***
Micron Plastics Inc 978 772-6900
30 Faulkner St Ayer MA (01432) ***(G-7926)***
Micron Products Inc 978 345-5000
25 Sawyer Passway Fitchburg MA (01420) ***(G-10837)***
Micron Solutions Inc (PA) 978 345-5000
25 Sawyer Passway Fitchburg MA (01420) ***(G-10838)***
Micronetixx Microwave LLC 207 786-2000
1 Gendron Dr Lewiston ME (04240) ***(G-6305)***
Micronetixx Technologies LLC 207 786-2000
70 Commercial St Ste 1 Lewiston ME (04240) ***(G-6306)***
Micronics, Beverly *Also called Bruce Barrowclough* ***(G-8113)***
Micronics Engneered Filtration, Portsmouth *Also called Micronics Filtration LLC* ***(G-19596)***
Micronics Filtration LLC (HQ) 603 433-1299
300 Constitution Ave # 201 Portsmouth NH (03801) ***(G-19596)***
Microphase Corporation 203 866-8000
100 Trap Falls Road Ext # 400 Shelton CT (06484) ***(G-3833)***
Microplasmic Corporation 978 548-9762
17 Esquire Dr Peabody MA (01960) ***(G-14355)***
Microprint, Waltham *Also called Desk Top Solutions Inc* ***(G-16086)***
Micros Systems Inc 508 655-7500
1800 W Park Dr Ste 250 Westborough MA (01581) ***(G-16635)***
Microscale Inc 781 995-2245
800 W Cummings Park # 3350 Woburn MA (01801) ***(G-17230)***
Microsemi Corp- Massachusetts 978 442-5600
75 Technology Dr Lowell MA (01851) ***(G-12409)***
Microsemi Corp- Massachusetts 978 794-1666
6 Lake St Ste 1 Lawrence MA (01841) ***(G-12052)***
Microsemi Corp- Massachusetts 978 620-2600
6 Lake St Ste 1 Lawrence MA (01841) ***(G-12053)***
Microsemi Corp-Colorado 480 941-6300
6 Lake St Ste 1 Lawrence MA (01841) ***(G-12054)***
Microsemi Corporation 781 665-1071
6 Lake St Ste 1 Lawrence MA (01841) ***(G-12055)***
Microsemi Corporation 978 442-5637
75 Technology Dr Lowell MA (01851) ***(G-12410)***
Microsemi Corporation 978 232-3793
48 Abby Rd Manchester NH (03103) ***(G-18873)***
Microsemi Corporation 978 232-3793
890 East St Ste 3 Tewksbury MA (01876) ***(G-15823)***
Microsemi Corporation 978 232-0040
163 Cabot St Beverly MA (01915) ***(G-8154)***
Microsemi Frequency Time Corp 978 232-0040
34 Tozer Rd Beverly MA (01915) ***(G-8155)***
Microsemi Nes Inc 978 794-1666
6 Lake St Lawrence MA (01841) ***(G-12056)***
Microsemi-Cdi, Lawrence *Also called Microsemi Corporation* ***(G-12055)***
Microsemi-Lawrence, Lawrence *Also called Microsemi Corp- Massachusetts* ***(G-12053)***
Microsemi-Lowell, Lowell *Also called Microsemi Corp- Massachusetts* ***(G-12409)***
Microsense LLC (HQ) 978 843-7670
205 Industrial Ave E Lowell MA (01852) ***(G-12411)***
Microsoft Corporation 781 398-4600
255 Main St Ste 401 Cambridge MA (02142) ***(G-9554)***
Microsoft Corporation 508 545-2957
1245 Worcester St # 3072 Natick MA (01760) ***(G-13268)***
Microsoft Corporation 857 453-6000
1 Memorial Dr Ste 1 # 1 Cambridge MA (02142) ***(G-9555)***
Microsoft Corporation 781 487-6400
5 Wayside Rd Burlington MA (01803) ***(G-9303)***
Microsoft Corporation 860 678-3100
74 Batterson Park Rd # 100 Farmington CT (06032) ***(G-1492)***
Microsorb Technologies Inc 401 767-2269
8 Independence Way # 124 Franklin MA (02038) ***(G-11065)***
Microspec Corporation 603 924-4300
327 Jaffrey Rd Peterborough NH (03458) ***(G-19477)***
Microspecialities Inc 203 874-1832
430 Smith St Middletown CT (06457) ***(G-2205)***
Micross Express 781 938-0866
400 W Cummings Park # 6900 Woburn MA (01801) ***(G-17231)***
Microstrain Inc 802 862-6629
459 Hurricane Ln Ste 102 Williston VT (05495) ***(G-22681)***
Microtech Inc 203 272-3234
1425 Highland Ave Cheshire CT (06410) ***(G-745)***
Microtek Inc 413 593-1025
2070 Westover Rd Chicopee MA (01022) ***(G-10046)***
Microtrain Inc 860 666-7890
23 Judge Ln Newington CT (06111) ***(G-2882)***
Microtraining Assoc Inc 781 982-8984
141 Walnut St Hanover MA (02339) ***(G-11347)***
Microtronic Inc 508 627-8951
5 Peases Point Rd Edgartown MA (02539) ***(G-10587)***
Microvision Inc 603 474-5566
20 London Ln Seabrook NH (03874) ***(G-19810)***
Microwave Cmpnents Specialists 978 667-1215
34 Sullivan Rd Ste 10 North Billerica MA (01862) ***(G-13845)***
Microwave Cmpnents Systems Inc 508 466-8400
131 Flanders Rd Westborough MA (01581) ***(G-16636)***
Microwave Components Inc 978 453-6016
1794 Bridge St Ste 21r Dracut MA (01826) ***(G-10365)***
Microwave Development Labs Inc 781 292-6600
135 Crescent Rd Needham Heights MA (02494) ***(G-13337)***
Microwave Engineering Corp 978 685-2776
1551 Osgood St North Andover MA (01845) ***(G-13718)***
Microwave Video Systems LLC 781 665-6600
165c Tremont St Melrose MA (02176) ***(G-12985)***
Microweld Co Inc 401 438-5985
285 Wampanoag Trl Riverside RI (02915) ***(G-21172)***
Mid Cape Restoration 207 929-4759
335 Cape Rd Hollis Center ME (04042) ***(G-6200)***
Mid State Assembly & Packg Inc 203 634-8740
604 Pomeroy Ave Meriden CT (06450) ***(G-2107)***
Mid State Machine Products (PA) 207 873-6136
83 Verti Dr Winslow ME (04901) ***(G-7271)***
Mid State Sheet Metal & Wldg 207 933-5603
119 Packard Rd Monmouth ME (04259) ***(G-6450)***
Mid-Coast Machine, Boothbay *Also called ME Tomacelli Inc* ***(G-5779)***
Mid-State Manufacturing Inc 860 621-6855
1610 Mriden Waterburytpke Milldale CT (06467) ***(G-2386)***
Mid-VT Molding LLC 802 234-9777
768 S Main St Bethel VT (05032) ***(G-21696)***
Midas Technology Inc 781 938-0069
400 W Cummings Park # 6400 Woburn MA (01801) ***(G-17232)***
Midconn Precision Mfg LLC 860 584-1340
190 Century Dr Ste 9 Bristol CT (06010) ***(G-581)***
Middlbury Bee-Intelligencer-Ct 203 577-6800
2030 Straits Tpke Middlebury CT (06762) ***(G-2156)***
Middle East Bakery Inc (PA) 978 688-2221
30 International Way Lawrence MA (01843) ***(G-12057)***
Middle Quarter Animal Hospital 203 263-4772
726 Main St S Woodbury CT (06798) ***(G-5489)***
Middleboro Gazette, New Bedford *Also called Local Media Group Inc* ***(G-13410)***
Middlebury Print & Copy, Shoreham *Also called S M T Graphics LLC* ***(G-22433)***
Middlesex General Industries 781 935-8870
2 New Pasture Rd Ste 7 Newburyport MA (01950) ***(G-13514)***
Middlesex News 508 626-3800
33 New York Ave Framingham MA (01701) ***(G-10985)***

Middlesex Research Mfg Co Inc..........978 562-3697
27 Apsley St Hudson MA (01749) ***(G-11793)***
Middlesex Truck & Auto Bdy Inc..........617 442-3000
65 Gerard St Boston MA (02119) ***(G-8705)***
Middlesex Truck & Coach, Boston *Also called Middlesex Truck & Auto Bdy Inc* ***(G-8705)***
Middleton Aerospace, Haverhill *Also called Magellan Arospc Haverhill Inc* ***(G-11452)***
Middletown Engine Center, East Hartford *Also called Pratt & Whitney Company Inc* ***(G-1212)***
Middletown Printing Co Inc..........860 347-5700
512 Main St Middletown CT (06457) ***(G-2206)***
Midget Louver Company Inc..........203 783-1444
671 Naugatuck Ave Milford CT (06461) ***(G-2315)***
Midland Co Inc..........401 397-4425
91 Maple Valley Rd Coventry RI (02816) ***(G-20156)***
Midstate Mold & Engineering..........508 520-0011
20 Liberty Way Ste D Franklin MA (02038) ***(G-11066)***
Midsun Specialty Products Inc..........860 378-0111
378 Four Rod Rd Berlin CT (06037) ***(G-96)***
Midtown Machine & Tool, Colchester *Also called Thomas Drake* ***(G-21881)***
Midway United Limited..........781 400-1742
21a Highland Cir Needham Heights MA (02494) ***(G-13338)***
Midwest Price Companies, West Paris *Also called Price Companies Inc* ***(G-7177)***
Miedge, Bedford *Also called Ibis LLC* ***(G-17645)***
Mija Industries Inc..........781 871-5629
11 Commerce Rd Ste C Rockland MA (02370) ***(G-14814)***
Mikco Manufacturing Inc..........203 269-2250
14 Village Ln Wallingford CT (06492) ***(G-4776)***
Mike Gath..........978 851-4373
509 Main St Tewksbury MA (01876) ***(G-15824)***
Mike Guillemette & Sons..........207 324-6221
136 Howitt Rd Lyman ME (04002) ***(G-6391)***
Mike Lowell Logging & Wood..........802 279-6993
678 Brook Rd Wolcott VT (05680) ***(G-22731)***
Mike Maine Pickle..........207 488-6881
46 White Rd Easton ME (04740) ***(G-5993)***
Mike Murphy..........508 473-9943
2 S Main St Milford MA (01757) ***(G-13126)***
Mike Orzel Logging..........413 320-3367
150 Federal St Northampton MA (01062) ***(G-14013)***
Mike Sadlak..........860 742-0227
712 Bread Milk St Unit A6 Coventry CT (06238) ***(G-835)***
Mike Sequore..........603 876-4634
7 Roxbury Rd Marlborough NH (03455) ***(G-18962)***
Mike's Engine Stand, Naugatuck *Also called K & E Auto Machine L L C* ***(G-2481)***
Mikes and Sons..........207 762-6310
87 State St Presque Isle ME (04769) ***(G-6762)***
Mikes Machine Co Inc..........508 619-3168
24 Commonwealth Ave South Yarmouth MA (02664) ***(G-15330)***
Mikes Precision Machine Inc..........978 667-9793
14 Hadley St North Billerica MA (01862) ***(G-13846)***
Mikini Embroidery, Sanford *Also called Michael V Morin* ***(G-6883)***
Mikrolar Inc..........603 617-2508
7 Scott Rd Ste 5 Hampton NH (03842) ***(G-18267)***
Mikros Manufacturing Inc..........603 690-2020
24 Colonel Ashley Ln Claremont NH (03743) ***(G-17855)***
Milacron Marketing Company LLC..........978 238-7100
428 Newburyport Tpke Rowley MA (01969) ***(G-14858)***
Milani Industries Inc..........781 344-3377
61 Marys Way Stoughton MA (02072) ***(G-15608)***
Milara Inc..........508 533-5322
49 Maple St Milford MA (01757) ***(G-13127)***
Milbar Labs Inc..........203 467-1577
20 Commerce St East Haven CT (06512) ***(G-1255)***
Miles Kedex Co Inc..........978 874-1403
1 Rowtier Rd Westminster MA (01473) ***(G-16810)***
Miles Press Inc..........508 752-6430
14 Sword St Ste 5 Auburn MA (01501) ***(G-7843)***
Milford Daily News, Milford *Also called Gatehouse Media Mass I Inc* ***(G-13118)***
Milford Fabricating Co., Orange *Also called Valley Tool and Mfg LLC* ***(G-3386)***
Milford Fuel..........207 827-2701
240 Main Rd Milford ME (04461) ***(G-6436)***
Milford Manufacturing Svcs LLC..........508 478-8544
4 Business Way Hopedale MA (01747) ***(G-11678)***
Milford Mirror, The, Shelton *Also called Hearst Corporation* ***(G-3811)***
Milford Woodworking Company..........508 473-2335
294 West St Milford MA (01757) ***(G-13128)***
Military Art China, Contoocook *Also called Bryant Group Inc* ***(G-17941)***
Militarylife Publishing LLC..........203 402-7234
4 Research Dr Shelton CT (06484) ***(G-3834)***
Milite Bakery..........203 753-9451
53 Interstate Ln Waterbury CT (06705) ***(G-4916)***
Milk Street Press Inc..........617 742-7900
8 Faneuil Hall Market Pl Boston MA (02109) ***(G-8706)***
Mill City Iron Fabricators..........978 957-6833
479 Textile Ave Dracut MA (01826) ***(G-10366)***
Mill City Leather Works..........603 935-9974
31 Lavista St Manchester NH (03103) ***(G-18874)***
Mill Fudge Factory, The, Bristol *Also called Grist For Mill LLC* ***(G-17767)***
Mill Machine Tool & Die Co..........860 628-6700
280 Mill St Southington CT (06489) ***(G-4066)***
Mill Manufacturing Inc..........203 367-9572
105 Willow St Bridgeport CT (06610) ***(G-451)***
Mill Publishing Inc..........802 862-4109
237 Commerce St Ste 202 Williston VT (05495) ***(G-22682)***
Mill River Lumber Ltd..........802 775-0032
2639 Middle Rd North Clarendon VT (05759) ***(G-22220)***
Mill Valley Molding Inc..........413 247-9313
15 West St West Hatfield MA (01088) ***(G-16483)***
Mill Valley Molding LLC..........413 247-9313
15 West St West Hatfield MA (01088) ***(G-16484)***
Millard Jewelry Division, Warwick *Also called Millard Wire Company* ***(G-21389)***
Millard Wire Company (PA)..........401 737-9330
449 Warwick Industrial Dr Warwick RI (02886) ***(G-21389)***
Millard Wire Company..........401 737-9330
259 Industrial Dr Warwick RI (02886) ***(G-21390)***
Millbrae Energy LLC (PA)..........203 742-2800
500 W Putnam Ave Ste 400 Greenwich CT (06830) ***(G-1631)***
Millbrook Distillery LLC..........203 637-2231
687 River Rd Cos Cob CT (06807) ***(G-828)***
Millbrook Press Inc..........203 740-2220
2 Old New Milford Rd 2e Brookfield CT (06804) ***(G-652)***
Millen Industries Inc (PA)..........203 847-8500
108 Main St Ste 4 Norwalk CT (06851) ***(G-3198)***
Millennial Media Inc..........617 301-4550
155 Seaport Blvd Ste 800 Boston MA (02210) ***(G-8707)***
Millennial Net Inc..........978 569-1921
24 Hartwell Ave Ste 2 Lexington MA (02421) ***(G-12244)***
Millennium Die Group Inc..........413 283-3500
2022 Bridge St Three Rivers MA (01080) ***(G-15851)***
Millennium Pharmaceuticals Inc..........617 679-7000
1 Kendall Sq Bldg 200 Cambridge MA (02139) ***(G-9556)***
Millennium Pharmaceuticals Inc..........617 679-7000
40 Landsdowne St Cambridge MA (02139) ***(G-9557)***
Millennium Pharmaceuticals Inc..........617 679-7000
45 Sidney St Cambridge MA (02139) ***(G-9558)***
Millennium Pharmaceuticals Inc..........617 679-7000
35 Landsdowne St Cambridge MA (02139) ***(G-9559)***
Millennium Pharmaceuticals Inc..........617 679-7000
640 Memorial Dr Ste 3w Cambridge MA (02139) ***(G-9560)***
Millennium Plastics Inc..........978 372-4822
154 Center St Groveland MA (01834) ***(G-11302)***
Millennium Plating Company Inc..........978 454-0526
75 Phoenix Ave Lowell MA (01852) ***(G-12412)***
Millennium Precision LLC..........603 644-1555
234 Abby Rd Manchester NH (03103) ***(G-18875)***
Millennium Press Inc..........413 821-0028
570 Silver St Agawam MA (01001) ***(G-7440)***
Millennium Printing Corp..........781 337-0002
317 Libbey Pkwy Weymouth MA (02189) ***(G-16893)***
Millennium Research Labs Inc..........781 935-0790
160 New Boston St Woburn MA (01801) ***(G-17233)***
Miller Castings Inc..........860 822-9991
30 Pautipaug Hill Rd North Franklin CT (06254) ***(G-2989)***
Miller Company..........203 235-4474
275 Pratt St Meriden CT (06450) ***(G-2108)***
Miller Corrugated Box Co..........401 739-7020
289 Kilvert St Warwick RI (02886) ***(G-21391)***
Miller Drug Whiting Hill Phrm, Brewer *Also called M Drug LLC* ***(G-5798)***
Miller Electric Mfg LLC..........401 828-0087
11 Grandview St Coventry RI (02816) ***(G-20157)***
Miller Firewood & Logging Inc..........401 539-7707
1741 Ten Rod Rd Exeter RI (02822) ***(G-20452)***
Miller Fuel LLC..........860 675-6121
28 Monce Rd Burlington CT (06013) ***(G-679)***
Miller H C Wood Working Inc..........508 429-4220
93 Bartzak Dr Holliston MA (01746) ***(G-11586)***
Miller Professional Trans Svc..........860 871-6818
8 Bancroft Rd Vernon CT (06066) ***(G-4669)***
Millers Petroleum Systems Inc..........413 499-2134
875 Crane Ave Pittsfield MA (01201) ***(G-14490)***
Millers Wood Working..........802 730 9374
1967 Cote Hill Rd Morrisville VT (05661) ***(G-22173)***
Millibar Inc..........508 488-9870
122 South St Rear Hopkinton MA (01748) ***(G-11728)***
Millies Pierogi, Chicopee *Also called Garan Enterprises Inc* ***(G-10027)***
Millimeter Wave Systems LLC..........413 345-6467
9 Research Dr Ste 8 Amherst MA (01002) ***(G-7519)***
Millincket Fabrication Mch Inc (PA)..........207 723-9733
432 Katahdin Ave Millinocket ME (04462) ***(G-6443)***
Milliporesigma, Burlington *Also called EMD Millipore Corporation* ***(G-9262)***
Millrite Machine Inc..........413 562-9212
587 Southampton Rd Westfield MA (01085) ***(G-16705)***
Mills Coffee Roasting Co..........401 781-7860
1058 Broad St Providence RI (02905) ***(G-21068)***
Mills Industries Inc..........603 528-4217
167 Water St Laconia NH (03246) ***(G-18576)***
Millstone Med Outsourcing LLC (PA)..........508 679-8384
580 Commerce Dr Fall River MA (02720) ***(G-10733)***

Millturn Manufacturing Co ... 203 248-1602
1203 Ridge Rd North Haven CT (06473) ***(G-3040)***
Millwood Inc ... 203 248-7902
33 Stiles Ln North Haven CT (06473) ***(G-3041)***
Millwork City Internet Svcs ... 207 370-5020
3 Parsons Ln York ME (03909) ***(G-7313)***
Millwork Masters Ltd (PA) ... 603 358-3038
69 Island St Ste B Keene NH (03431) ***(G-18515)***
Millwork One Inc ... 401 738-6990
60 Kenney Dr Cranston RI (02920) ***(G-20263)***
Millwork Shop LLC ... 860 489-8848
39 Putter Ln Torrington CT (06790) ***(G-4587)***
Milo Chip LLC ... 207 943-2682
29 High St Milo ME (04463) ***(G-6447)***
Milor Corporation Inc ... 207 783-4226
120 Center St Ste 204 Auburn ME (04210) ***(G-5581)***
Milpower Source Inc ... 603 267-8865
7 Field Ln Belmont NH (03220) ***(G-17678)***
Milton Independent Inc ... 802 893-2028
281 N Main St Saint Albans VT (05478) ***(G-22372)***
Milton Times Inc ... 617 696-7758
3 Boulevard St Ste 5 Milton MA (02186) ***(G-13196)***
Milton Vermont Sheet Metal Inc ... 802 893-1581
103 Gonyeau Rd Milton VT (05468) ***(G-22134)***
Miltronics Mfg Svcs Inc ... 603 352-3333
95 Krif Rd Keene NH (03431) ***(G-18516)***
Mimforms LLC ... 800 445-1245
50 Washington St Fl 7 Norwalk CT (06854) ***(G-3199)***
Mimir Insights, Cambridge *Also called Acenna Data Inc* ***(G-9371)***
Mimoco Inc ... 617 783-1100
475 Hillside Ave Ste 1 Needham Heights MA (02494) ***(G-13339)***
Mina Custom Print ... 617 520-4797
766a Cambridge St Cambridge MA (02141) ***(G-9561)***
Minarik Automation & Control, Bloomfield *Also called Minarik Corporation* ***(G-243)***
Minarik Corporation ... 860 687-5000
1 Vision Way Bloomfield CT (06002) ***(G-243)***
Minarik Corporation ... 781 329-2700
38 Forge Pkwy Ste 150 Franklin MA (02038) ***(G-11067)***
Mind2mind Exchange LLC ... 203 856-0981
32 Mill Brook Rd Stamford CT (06902) ***(G-4250)***
Mindedge Inc ... 781 250-1805
271 Waverley Oaks Rd Waltham MA (02452) ***(G-16150)***
Mindful Elements LLC ... 508 845-2833
112 South St Shrewsbury MA (01545) ***(G-15123)***
Mindgraph Medical Inc ... 508 904-2563
11 Pipers Gln Andover MA (01810) ***(G-7571)***
Mindsciences Inc ... 516 658-2985
45 Hickory Dr Worcester MA (01609) ***(G-17418)***
Mindstorm Technologies Inc ... 781 642-1700
2 Saint Paul St Apt 405 Brookline MA (02446) ***(G-9209)***
Mindstream, South Burlington *Also called Step Ahead Innovations Inc* ***(G-22468)***
Mindtrainr LLC ... 914 799-1515
107 Revonah Cir Stamford CT (06905) ***(G-4251)***
Mine Hill Distillery ... 860 210-1872
5 Mine Hill Rd Roxbury CT (06783) ***(G-3736)***
Mineral Technology, Canaan *Also called Minteq International Inc* ***(G-689)***
Minerva Neurosciences Inc (PA) ... 617 600-7373
1601 Trapelo Rd Ste 284 Waltham MA (02451) ***(G-16151)***
Mini LLC ... 203 464-5495
66 Church St Naugatuck CT (06770) ***(G-2484)***
Mini Pops Inc ... 781 436-5864
19 Robin Rd Sharon MA (02067) ***(G-15053)***
Mini-Broach Machine Co Inc ... 978 386-7959
1266 Main St Ashby MA (01431) ***(G-7647)***
Mini-Systems Inc (PA) ... 508 695-1420
20 David Rd North Attleboro MA (02760) ***(G-13765)***
Mini-Systems Inc ... 508 695-0203
45 Frank Mossberg Dr Attleboro MA (02703) ***(G-7768)***
Mini-Systems Inc ... 508 695-2000
168 E Bacon St Plainville MA (02762) ***(G-14528)***
MINI-SYSTEMS THIN FILM DIV, North Attleboro *Also called Mini-Systems Inc* ***(G-13765)***
Miniature Casting Corporation ... 401 463-5090
21 Slater Rd Cranston RI (02920) ***(G-20264)***
Miniature Nut & Screw Corp ... 860 953-4490
820 N Mountain Rd Newington CT (06111) ***(G-2883)***
Minike Card Care ... 508 853-4490
532 W Boylston St Worcester MA (01606) ***(G-17419)***
Minteq International Inc ... 860 824-5435
30 Daisy Hill Rd Canaan CT (06018) ***(G-689)***
Minute Man Airfield ... 978 897-3933
302 Boxboro Rd Stow MA (01775) ***(G-15633)***
Minute Man Press ... 203 891-6251
5 Hamden Park Dr Hamden CT (06517) ***(G-1772)***
Minute Man Press ... 401 619-1650
687 W Main Rd Middletown RI (02842) ***(G-20626)***
Minuteman Governance Inc ... 508 837-3004
43 Forest Ln Hopkinton MA (01748) ***(G-11729)***
Minuteman Implant Club Inc ... 413 549-4108
2 Westview Ter Natick MA (01760) ***(G-13269)***
Minuteman Laboratories Inc ... 978 263-2632
7a Stuart Rd Chelmsford MA (01824) ***(G-9917)***
Minuteman Leaseguard, Hudson *Also called Minuteman Seamless Gutters* ***(G-11794)***
Minuteman Metal LLC ... 207 217-8908
469 Depot St Wilton ME (04294) ***(G-7226)***
Minuteman Newspaper (PA) ... 203 226-8877
1175 Post Rd E Ste 3e Westport CT (06880) ***(G-5214)***
Minuteman Pre-Hung Door Co, Acton *Also called Sb Development Corp* ***(G-7384)***
Minuteman Press, Concord *Also called Minuteman Printing Corp* ***(G-10141)***
Minuteman Press, Lowell *Also called Bassett & Cassidy Inc* ***(G-12350)***
Minuteman Press, Hamden *Also called Minute Man Press* ***(G-1772)***
Minuteman Press, Waltham *Also called Generation Four Inc* ***(G-16119)***
Minuteman Press, Middletown *Also called Minute Man Press* ***(G-20626)***
Minuteman Press, Colchester *Also called Larcoline Inc* ***(G-21871)***
Minuteman Press, North Conway *Also called P2k Printing LLC* ***(G-19378)***
Minuteman Press, Beverly *Also called Enon Copy Inc* ***(G-8128)***
Minuteman Press, Milford *Also called Eco2 Office Inc* ***(G-13114)***
Minuteman Press, Londonderry *Also called Bob Bean Company Inc* ***(G-18680)***
Minuteman Press, Enfield *Also called P & M Investments LLC* ***(G-1373)***
Minuteman Press, Marlborough *Also called Apb Enterprises Inc* ***(G-12715)***
Minuteman Press, Montpelier *Also called ASC Duplicating Inc* ***(G-22145)***
Minuteman Press, Milford *Also called S and Z Graphics LLC* ***(G-2358)***
Minuteman Press, Burlington *Also called Jotas Corporation* ***(G-9290)***
Minuteman Press, East Haven *Also called Sabar Graphics LLC* ***(G-1260)***
Minuteman Press, Greenwich *Also called Easy Graphics Inc* ***(G-1609)***
Minuteman Press, Monroe *Also called FSNB Enterprises Inc* ***(G-2403)***
Minuteman Press, Middletown *Also called Middletown Printing Co Inc* ***(G-2206)***
Minuteman Press, Stamford *Also called P & S Printing LLC* ***(G-4275)***
Minuteman Press, Milford *Also called Rgp Corp* ***(G-13141)***
Minuteman Press, Hartford *Also called Capitol Printing Co Inc* ***(G-1810)***
Minuteman Press, Canton *Also called J R V Smita Company LLC* ***(G-9747)***
Minuteman Press, Vernon Rockville *Also called Vernon Printing Co Inc* ***(G-4688)***
Minuteman Press, Seekonk *Also called Mrf Enterprises Inc* ***(G-15030)***
Minuteman Press, Norwalk *Also called Max Productions LLC* ***(G-3191)***
Minuteman Press, Providence *Also called Peak Printing Inc* ***(G-21088)***
Minuteman Press, Dedham *Also called Davis Enterprises Inc* ***(G-10286)***
Minuteman Press, Warwick *Also called Summit Printing LLC* ***(G-21431)***
Minuteman Press, Billerica *Also called Ralph Traynham* ***(G-8282)***
Minuteman Press, Andover *Also called Seventy Nine N Main St Prtg* ***(G-7603)***
Minuteman Press, New London *Also called New London Printing Co LLC* ***(G-2775)***
Minuteman Press, North Dartmouth *Also called Marbuo Inc* ***(G-13924)***
Minuteman Press, Boston *Also called Fenway Cmmunications Group Inc* ***(G-8542)***
Minuteman Press ... 617 361-7400
1279 Hyde Park Ave Hyde Park MA (02136) ***(G-11875)***
Minuteman Press ... 508 775-9890
1694 Falmouth Rd Centerville MA (02632) ***(G-9817)***
Minuteman Press ... 978 465-2242
188 Route 1 Unit E Newburyport MA (01950) ***(G-13515)***
Minuteman Press ... 508 673-1407
435 Columbia St Fall River MA (02721) ***(G-10734)***
Minuteman Press ... 978 345-0818
386 Summer St Fitchburg MA (01420) ***(G-10839)***
Minuteman Press ... 508 336-3050
294 Taunton Ave Seekonk MA (02771) ***(G-15028)***
Minuteman Press ... 860 529-4628
462 Silas Deane Hwy Wethersfield CT (06109) ***(G-5258)***
Minuteman Press ... 508 778-0220
223 Barnstable Rd Hyannis MA (02601) ***(G-11850)***
Minuteman Press Intl Inc ... 617 244-7001
1383 Washington St Newton MA (02465) ***(G-13615)***
Minuteman Press Intl Inc ... 603 718-1439
217 W Hollis St Nashua NH (03060) ***(G-19208)***
Minuteman Press of Bristol ... 860 589-1100
98 Farmington Ave Bristol CT (06010) ***(G-582)***
Minuteman Press of Danbury ... 203 743-6755
12 Mill Plain Rd Ste 10 Danbury CT (06811) ***(G-955)***
Minuteman Press of Johnston ... 401 944-0667
1999 Plainfield Pike # 3 Johnston RI (02919) ***(G-20522)***
Minuteman Press of Pawtucket ... 401 305-6644
805 Central Ave Pawtucket RI (02861) ***(G-20860)***
Minuteman Press Worcester Inc ... 508 757-5450
122 Green St Ste 1 Worcester MA (01604) ***(G-17420)***
Minuteman Printing Corp ... 978 369-2808
20 Beharrell St Ste 1 Concord MA (01742) ***(G-10141)***
Minuteman Seamless Gutters ... 978 562-1744
2 Kane Industrial Dr Hudson MA (01749) ***(G-11794)***
Minuteman Sign Centers ... 207 338-2299
171 High St Ste 1 Belfast ME (04915) ***(G-5694)***
Minuteman Sign Centers Inc (PA) ... 207 622-4171
297 State St Augusta ME (04330) ***(G-5615)***
Minuteman Software Associates ... 781 643-4918
63 Foster St Arlington MA (02474) ***(G-7630)***
Minuteman Spring Company Inc ... 508 299-6100
34 Howe Ave Millbury MA (01527) ***(G-13172)***

Minuteman Thrift Shop, Bedford *Also called Officers Wives Club* ***(G-7998)***
Minuteman Tress, Waterbury *Also called Byrne Group Inc* ***(G-4852)***
Minuteman Vermont Print & Mail, Montpelier *Also called Larcoline Inc* ***(G-22152)***
Mioe Inc 978 494-9460
300 Brickstone Sq Andover MA (01810) ***(G-7572)***
Miracle Instruments Co 860 642-7745
1667 Exeter Rd Lebanon CT (06249) ***(G-1936)***
Mirak Building Trust 781 643-8000
1125 Massachusetts Ave Arlington MA (02476) ***(G-7631)***
Miranda Brothers Inc 508 672-0982
317 Lindsey St Fall River MA (02720) ***(G-10735)***
Miranda Vineyard LLC 860 491-9906
42 Ives Rd Goshen CT (06756) ***(G-1586)***
Miravia LLC (PA) 802 425-6483
236 Lucys Ln Charlotte VT (05445) ***(G-21834)***
Miricle Wood, Merrimack *Also called H F Staples & Co Inc* ***(G-19005)***
Mirion Tech Canberra Inc (HQ) 203 238-2351
800 Research Pkwy Meriden CT (06450) ***(G-2109)***
Mirror Polishing & Pltg Co Inc 203 574-5400
346 Huntingdon Ave Waterbury CT (06708) ***(G-4917)***
Miss Print 603 279-5939
1 Meredith Center Rd Meredith NH (03253) ***(G-18975)***
Mission Allergy Inc 203 364-1570
28 Hawleyville Rd Hawleyville CT (06440) ***(G-1894)***
Mister BS Jerky Co 203 631-2758
25 Harness Dr Meriden CT (06450) ***(G-2110)***
Mister Sister 401 421-6969
268 Wickenden St Providence RI (02903) ***(G-21069)***
Mistras Group Inc 860 447-2474
6 Mill Ln Waterford CT (06385) ***(G-4989)***
Mistras Group Inc 508 832-5500
2 Millbury St Auburn MA (01501) ***(G-7844)***
Mistras Services, Auburn *Also called Mistras Group Inc* ***(G-7844)***
Mit, Cambridge *Also called Massachusetts Institute Tech* ***(G-9547)***
MIT, Cambridge *Also called Technology Review Inc* ***(G-9677)***
Mit Press, The, Cambridge *Also called Massachusetts Institute Tech* ***(G-9546)***
Mitch Rosen Extraordinary Gunl 603 647-2971
540 North Commercial St Manchester NH (03101) ***(G-18876)***
Mitchell Differential Inc 508 755-3790
384 Hartford Tpke Shrewsbury MA (01545) ***(G-15124)***
Mitchell Machine Incorporated (PA) 413 739-9693
224 Hancock St Springfield MA (01109) ***(G-15490)***
Mitchell Sand & Gravel LLC 603 357-0881
20 Payne Rd Winchester NH (03470) ***(G-19993)***
Mitchell Tees & Signs Inc 802 483-6866
41 Gloriosa Dr Pittsford VT (05763) ***(G-22264)***
Mitchell-Bate Company 203 233-0862
365 Thomaston Ave Waterbury CT (06702) ***(G-4918)***
Mitchs Maples Sugar House 802 875-5240
2440 Green Mountain Tpke Chester VT (05143) ***(G-21845)***
Mitee-Bite Products LLC 603 539-4538
340 Route 16b Center Ossipee NH (03814) ***(G-17804)***
Mitton Millworks 978 475-7761
53 Gould Rd Andover MA (01810) ***(G-7573)***
MIW Corp 508 672-4029
1205 Bay St Fall River MA (02724) ***(G-10736)***
Mix 508 693-8240
4 Union St Vineyard Haven MA (02568) ***(G-15934)***
Mix & Company, Wellesley *Also called Mix and Company Ltd* ***(G-16373)***
Mix and Company Ltd 781 235-0028
68 Central St Wellesley MA (02482) ***(G-16373)***
Mix Marketing Corp 401 954-6121
68 Old Pine Rd Narragansett RI (02882) ***(G-20642)***
Mix Up Printer 401 334-4291
1060 Great Rd Lincoln RI (02865) ***(G-20584)***
Mixfit Inc 617 902-8082
26 Aborn St Salem MA (01970) ***(G-14929)***
Mixx Frozen Yogurt Inc (PA) 617 782-6499
66 Brighton Ave Allston MA (02134) ***(G-7470)***
Miyoshi America Inc (HQ) 860 779-3990
110 Louisa Viens Dr Dayville CT (06241) ***(G-1046)***
Miyoshi America Inc 860 779-3990
313 Lake Rd Dayville CT (06241) ***(G-1047)***
Miyoshi America Inc 860 779-3990
90 Louisa Viens Dr Dayville CT (06241) ***(G-1048)***
Mj Machine Inc 508 697-5329
1 1st St 9 Bridgewater MA (02324) ***(G-9084)***
Mj Research Inc (HQ) 510 724-7000
245 Winter St Ste 100 Waltham MA (02451) ***(G-16152)***
Mj Tool & Manufacturing Inc 860 352-2688
11 Herman Dr Ste B Simsbury CT (06070) ***(G-3908)***
MJB Logging Inc 207 231-1376
1139 St John Rd Fort Kent ME (04743) ***(G-6062)***
Mjh Crawford Industries I 401 728-3443
11 Browne Hill Ct Lincoln RI (02865) ***(G-20585)***
MJM Holdings Inc (PA) 603 838-6624
130 N Main St Lisbon NH (03585) ***(G-18649)***
MJM Marga LLC 203 729-0600
28 Raytkwich Rd Naugatuck CT (06770) ***(G-2485)***
MJW Mass Inc 781 721-0332
37 East St Winchester MA (01890) ***(G-17092)***
MK Fuel Inc 413 245-7507
341 Sturbridge Rd Brimfield MA (01010) ***(G-9110)***
Mk Logging 207 436-1809
38 Cleveland Ave Frenchville ME (04745) ***(G-6091)***
Mk Services Corp 978 777-2196
194 S Main St Middleton MA (01949) ***(G-13096)***
Mkb Machine & Tool Mfg 860 828-5728
600 Four Rod Rd Ste 3 Berlin CT (06037) ***(G-97)***
Mkind Inc 603 493-6882
150 Dow St Ste 4 Manchester NH (03101) ***(G-18877)***
Mkl Stone LLC 781 844-9811
100 Ashland St Everett MA (02149) ***(G-10622)***
Mkrs Corporation 203 762-2662
32 Blueberry Hill Pl Wilton CT (06897) ***(G-5294)***
Mks Astex Products, Methuen *Also called Mks Instruments Inc* ***(G-13037)***
Mks Instruments Inc (PA) 978 645-5500
2 Tech Dr Ste 201 Andover MA (01810) ***(G-7574)***
Mks Instruments Inc 978 284-4000
90 Industrial Way Wilmington MA (01887) ***(G-17024)***
Mks Instruments Inc 978 975-2350
17 Ballard Way Lawrence MA (01843) ***(G-12058)***
Mks Instruments Inc 978 645-5500
6 Shattuck Rd Andover MA (01810) ***(G-7575)***
Mks Instruments Inc 978 738-3721
6 Shattuck Rd Andover MA (01810) ***(G-7576)***
Mks Instruments Inc 978 682-3512
651 Lowell St Methuen MA (01844) ***(G-13037)***
Mks Msc Inc 978 284-4000
90 Industrial Way Wilmington MA (01887) ***(G-17025)***
Mlc Services LLC 781 366-1132
35 Jeffrey Ave Holliston MA (01746) ***(G-11587)***
Mlk Business Forms Inc 203 624-6304
25 James St New Haven CT (06513) ***(G-2712)***
MLS Acq Inc 860 386-6878
32 North Rd East Windsor CT (06088) ***(G-1296)***
MLS Screw Machine Corp 401 435-3850
10 Dexter Rd East Providence RI (02914) ***(G-20432)***
MLS Sheet Metal LLC 781 275-2265
39 Crosby Dr Bedford MA (01730) ***(G-7992)***
MM Reif Ltd 617 442-9500
850 Albany St Boston MA (02119) ***(G-8708)***
Mmd Art Service, Seekonk *Also called Countryside Signs* ***(G-15020)***
Mmqci, Saco *Also called Maine Mlclar Qulty Contrls Inc* ***(G-6852)***
Mobile Marine Canvas Co, South Harpswell *Also called Seth Hetherington* ***(G-7008)***
Mobile Mini Inc 866 344-4092
77 Bridge Rd Salisbury MA (01952) ***(G-14953)***
Mobile Mini Inc 860 668-1888
911 S St Mach 1 Indus Par 1 Mach Suffield CT (06078) ***(G-4465)***
Mobile Mini Inc 508 427-5395
125 Manley St West Bridgewater MA (02379) ***(G-16446)***
Mobile Monitor Tech LLC 617 965-5057
831 Beacon St Ste 202 Newton Centre MA (02459) ***(G-13656)***
Mobile Semiconductor Corp 802 399-2449
237 Commerce St Williston VT (05495) ***(G-22683)***
Mobile Sense Technologies Inc 203 914-5375
24 Cliff Ave Darien CT (06820) ***(G-1029)***
Mobile Specialties 978 416-0107
610 S Union St Lawrence MA (01843) ***(G-12059)***
Mobilepro Corporation 480 398-0909
25 Mount Auburn St Cambridge MA (02138) ***(G-9562)***
Mobilerobots Inc 603 881-7960
10 Columbia Dr Amherst NH (03031) ***(G-17576)***
Mobilesuites Inc 302 593-3055
35 Brookline St Apt 5 Cambridge MA (02139) ***(G-9563)***
Mobius Imaging LLC 978 796-5068
2 Shaker Rd Ste F100 Shirley MA (01464) ***(G-15090)***
Moble Internet Access Inc 978 273-2390
300 Oak St Ste 1010 Pembroke MA (02359) ***(G-14417)***
Mockingbird Studios Inc 508 339-6755
905 S Main St Mansfield MA (02048) ***(G-12646)***
Mocktail Beverages Inc 855 662-5824
88 Walnut Rd Wenham MA (01984) ***(G-16403)***
Modean Industries Inc 203 371-6625
15 Lucielle Dr Easton CT (06612) ***(G-1321)***
Model Engineering, Holbrook *Also called Nadco International Inc* ***(G-11532)***
Model Works, Newington *Also called Pal Corporation* ***(G-2889)***
Modeltronix 508 529-3567
13 Grove St Upton MA (01568) ***(G-15909)***
Modelvision Inc 860 355-3884
566 Danbury Rd Ste 4 New Milford CT (06776) ***(G-2814)***
Modem Srismitha 617 323-0080
1811 Centre St West Roxbury MA (02132) ***(G-16499)***
Modern Architechtural Glazing, Worcester *Also called Modern Mfg Inc Worcester* ***(G-17421)***
Modern Dispersions Inc (PA) 978 534-3370
78 Maguerite Ave Leominster MA (01453) ***(G-12168)***
Modern Distillery Age 203 971-8710
228 Silvermine Ave Norwalk CT (06850) ***(G-3200)***

ALPHABETIC

Modern Elec Fax & Computers, Fairfield *Also called Modern Electronic Fax & Cmpt* ***(G-1445)***
Modern Electronic Fax & Cmpt 203 292-6520
65 Milton St Fairfield CT (06824) ***(G-1445)***
Modern Graphics Inc 781 331-5000
28 Glendale Rd Quincy MA (02169) ***(G-14640)***
Modern Heritage LLC 781 913-8261
237 Wethersfield St Rowley MA (01969) ***(G-14859)***
Modern Jewelry, Johnston *Also called Modern Manufacturing Inc* ***(G-20523)***
Modern Manufacturing Inc 401 944-9230
47 Homeland St Johnston RI (02919) ***(G-20523)***
Modern Marking Products Inc 508 697-6066
43 Central Sq Bridgewater MA (02324) ***(G-9085)***
Modern Metal Finishing Inc 203 267-1510
110 Willenbrock Rd Oxford CT (06478) ***(G-3414)***
Modern Metal Solutions LLC 603 402-3022
12 Park Ave Hudson NH (03051) ***(G-18415)***
Modern Mfg Inc Worcester 508 791-7151
12 Brussels St Worcester MA (01610) ***(G-17421)***
Modern Mold & Tool Inc (PA) 413 443-1192
1995 East St Pittsfield MA (01201) ***(G-14491)***
Modern Nutrition & Biotech 203 244-5830
61 Overlook Dr Ridgefield CT (06877) ***(G-3672)***
Modern Objects Inc 203 378-5785
5 River Dr Norwalk CT (06855) ***(G-3201)***
Modern Plastics 401 732-0415
380 Jefferson Blvd Ste A Warwick RI (02886) ***(G-21392)***
Modern Rug & Awning Co, Fitchburg *Also called Moderne Rug Inc* ***(G-10840)***
Modern Sheetmetal Inc 508 798-6665
243 Stafford St Ste 2 Worcester MA (01603) ***(G-17422)***
Modern Shoe Company LLC 617 333-7470
101 Sprague St Ste 1 Hyde Park MA (02136) ***(G-11876)***
Modern Tractor & Truck Service 508 761-4425
400 Pine St Seekonk MA (02771) ***(G-15029)***
Modern Woodcrafts LLC 860 677-7371
72 Northwest Dr Plainville CT (06062) ***(G-3508)***
Modern Woodworks Co 508 543-9830
131 Morse St Ste 4 Foxboro MA (02035) ***(G-10892)***
Moderna Inc (PA) 617 714-6500
200 Technology Sq Cambridge MA (02139) ***(G-9564)***
Moderna LLC (HQ) 617 714-6500
200 Tech Sq Cambridge MA (02139) ***(G-9565)***
Moderna Therapeutics, Cambridge *Also called Moderna LLC* ***(G-9565)***
Moderna Therapeutics Inc 617 714-6500
200 Technology Sq Cambridge MA (02139) ***(G-9566)***
Moderne Rug Inc 978 343-3210
123 Airport Rd Fitchburg MA (01420) ***(G-10840)***
Modernist Pantry LLC 207 200-3817
25 Harold L Dow Hwy Eliot ME (03903) ***(G-6008)***
Modine Manufacturing Company 401 792-1231
604 Liberty Ln West Kingston RI (02892) ***(G-21467)***
Modkit LLC 617 838-1784
254 Garden St Cambridge MA (02138) ***(G-9567)***
Modu Form Inc (PA) 978 345-7942
172 Industrial Rd Fitchburg MA (01420) ***(G-10841)***
Modu Form Inc 978 345-7942
172 Industrial Rd Fitchburg MA (01420) ***(G-10842)***
Modular Air Filtration Systems 508 823-4900
450 Richmond St Raynham MA (02767) ***(G-14720)***
Modular Fun I Inc 207 739-2400
300 Park St South Paris ME (04281) ***(G-7014)***
Modulease Corporation 508 695-4145
212 Mount Hope St North Attleboro MA (02760) ***(G-13766)***
Moduline, Brockton *Also called Gill Metal Fab Inc* ***(G-9151)***
Modus Media Inc 781 663-5000
1601 Trapelo Rd Ste 170 Waltham MA (02451) ***(G-16153)***
Modutec, Manchester *Also called Jewell Instruments LLC* ***(G-18850)***
Moeller Instrument Company Inc 800 243-9310
126 Main St Ivoryton CT (06442) ***(G-1907)***
Moffly Publications Inc 203 222-0600
205 Main St Ste 1 Westport CT (06880) ***(G-5215)***
Moffly Publications Inc (PA) 203 222-0600
205 Main St Ste 1 Westport CT (06880) ***(G-5216)***
Mohawk Industries Inc 203 739-0260
4 Nabby Rd Danbury CT (06811) ***(G-956)***
Mohawk Industries Inc 508 660-8935
15 Walpole Park S Ste 8 Walpole MA (02081) ***(G-16003)***
Mohawk Industries Inc 706 629-7721
180 Church St Torrington CT (06790) ***(G-4588)***
Mohawk Manufacturing Company 860 632-2345
1270 Newfield St Middletown CT (06457) ***(G-2207)***
Mohawk Shade & Blind Co Inc 617 868-6000
2098 Massachusetts Ave Cambridge MA (02140) ***(G-9568)***
Mohawk Tool and Die Mfg Co Inc 203 367-2181
25 Wells St Ste 4 Bridgeport CT (06604) ***(G-452)***
Mohican Valley Concrete Corp 203 254-7133
195 Ardmore St Fairfield CT (06824) ***(G-1446)***
Mohican Vly Sand & Grav Corp 203 254-7133
195 Ardmore St Fairfield CT (06824) ***(G-1447)***
Moir Company Inc 207 452-2000
67 E Main St Denmark ME (04022) ***(G-5951)***
Mojo Cold Brewed Coffee Inc 617 877-2997
30 Henderson Rd St Lot Beverly MA (01915) ***(G-8156)***
Mold Makers Inc 508 588-4212
1 Old West St West Bridgewater MA (02379) ***(G-16447)***
Mold Threads Inc 203 483-1420
21 W End Ave Branford CT (06405) ***(G-331)***
Molding Technologies LLC 860 395-3230
304 Boston Post Rd Ste 1 Old Saybrook CT (06475) ***(G-3345)***
Molding Tooling and Design 207 247-4077
64 Landry St Biddeford ME (04005) ***(G-5750)***
Moldmakers, West Bridgewater *Also called Mold Makers Inc* ***(G-16447)***
Moldmaster Engineering Inc 413 442-5793
187 Newell St Pittsfield MA (01201) ***(G-14492)***
Moldpro Inc 603 357-2523
36 Denman Thompson Hwy Swanzey NH (03446) ***(G-19885)***
Molds Plus Inc 207 795-0000
41 Chestnut St Ste 1a Lewiston ME (04240) ***(G-6307)***
Moldvision LLC 860 315-1025
316 County Home Rd Thompson CT (06277) ***(G-4536)***
Mole Hollow Candles Limited 508 756-7415
5 Wheeler Ave Worcester MA (01609) ***(G-17423)***
Molecular Health Inc 832 482-3898
70 Fargo St Ste 902 Boston MA (02210) ***(G-8709)***
Molly Merchandising Unlimited 508 829-2544
907 Main St Holden MA (01520) ***(G-11548)***
Molnycke, Palmer *Also called Essity* ***(G-14287)***
Mom Central 617 332-6819
440 Beacon St Chestnut Hill MA (02467) ***(G-9988)***
Momedx Inc 617 401-7780
285 Columbus Ave Unit 301 Boston MA (02116) ***(G-8710)***
Momenta Pharmaceuticals Inc (PA) 617 491-9700
301 Binney St Cambridge MA (02142) ***(G-9569)***
Moms Organic Munchies 207 869-4078
174 Lower Main St Ste 21 Freeport ME (04032) ***(G-6084)***
Monadnock Associates Inc (PA) 617 924-7032
3 Brook St Watertown MA (02472) ***(G-16302)***
Monadnock Grinding LLC 603 585-7275
98 Royalston Rd Fitzwilliam NH (03447) ***(G-18151)***
Monadnock Land Clearing 603 878-2803
932 Fitchburg Rd Greenville NH (03048) ***(G-18227)***
Monadnock Land Clearing & Chip, Greenville *Also called Monadnock Land Clearing* ***(G-18227)***
Monadnock Ledger, Concord *Also called Newspapers of New Hampshire* ***(G-17918)***
Monadnock Ledger, Peterborough *Also called Newspapers of New Hampshire* ***(G-19481)***
Monadnock Log Home Svcs LLC 603 876-4800
24 Red Gate Rd Jaffrey NH (03452) ***(G-18474)***
Monadnock Paper Mills Inc (PA) 603 588-3311
117 Antrim Rd Bennington NH (03442) ***(G-17689)***
Monadnock Shopper News, Keene *Also called Shakour Publishers Inc* ***(G-18524)***
Monaghan Printing Company 508 991-8087
59 Alden Rd Fairhaven MA (02719) ***(G-10643)***
Monahan Associates 207 771-0900
2 Cotton St 200 Portland ME (04101) ***(G-6694)***
Monahan Products LLC 781 413-3000
60 Sharp St Ste 3 Hingham MA (02043) ***(G-11506)***
Monarch International Inc 603 883-3390
15 Columbia Dr Amherst NH (03031) ***(G-17577)***
Monarch Metal Finishing Co Inc 401 785-3200
189 Georgia Ave Providence RI (02905) ***(G-21070)***
Monarch Monitoring, Amherst *Also called Monarch International Inc* ***(G-17577)***
Monarch Plastic LLC 860 653-2000
514r Salmon Brook St Granby CT (06035) ***(G-1590)***
Mondelez Global LLC 781 878-0103
188 Ledgewood Dr Hanover MA (02339) ***(G-11348)***
Moneyletters, Holliston *Also called PRI Financial Publishing* ***(G-11597)***
Moneysworth & Best USA Inc 603 968-3301
1 Cedar Ln Ashland NH (03217) ***(G-17600)***
Monkey-Trunks 603 367-4427
1853 White Mountain Hwy Tamworth NH (03886) ***(G-19892)***
Monks Manufacturing Co Inc 978 657-8282
1 Upton Dr Wilmington MA (01887) ***(G-17026)***
Mono Crete Step Co of CT LLC 203 748-8419
12 Trowbridge Dr Bethel CT (06801) ***(G-172)***
Mono Die Cutting Co Inc 401 434-1274
7 Hemingway Dr Riverside RI (02915) ***(G-21173)***
Monogramit LLC 860 779-0694
9 S Main St Brooklyn CT (06234) ***(G-671)***
Monoplex Eye Prosthetics LLC 603 622-5200
169 S River Rd Unit 14a Bedford NH (03110) ***(G-17655)***
Monopol Corporation 860 583-3852
394 Riverside Ave Bristol CT (06010) ***(G-583)***
Monotype Imaging Inc (HQ) 781 970-6000
600 Unicorn Park Dr Woburn MA (01801) ***(G-17234)***
Monsanto Company 617 551-7200
245 1st St Ste 2 Cambridge MA (02142) ***(G-9570)***
Montachsett Tcci Burial Vaults, Leominster *Also called Montachsett Tcci Burial Vaults* ***(G-12169)***
Montachsett Tcci Burial Vaults 978 537-6190
38 Castle St Leominster MA (01453) ***(G-12169)***

Montague Industries Inc ...413 863-4301
15 Rastallis St Turners Falls MA (01376) ***(G-15882)***
Montague Machine Company, Turners Falls *Also called Montague Industries Inc* ***(G-15882)***
Montague Reporter Incorporated ...413 863-8666
177 Avenue A Turners Falls MA (01376) ***(G-15883)***
Montalvo Corporation ...207 856-2501
50 Hutcherson Dr Gorham ME (04038) ***(G-6122)***
Montecito Roadhouse Inc ...207 856-6811
1102 Bridgton Rd Westbrook ME (04092) ***(G-7197)***
Monteiro Machine Company, Marlborough *Also called Michael Monteiro* ***(G-12794)***
Montello Heel Mfg Inc ...508 586-0603
13 Emerson Ave Ste 4 Brockton MA (02301) ***(G-9167)***
Montiones Biscotti (PA) ...508 285-7004
253 Mansfield Ave Norton MA (02766) ***(G-14083)***
Montpelier Granite Works Inc ...802 223-2581
43 Granite Shed Ln Montpelier VT (05602) ***(G-22155)***
Montville Sewer Plant, Uncasville *Also called Town of Montville* ***(G-4650)***
Monument Industries Inc ...802 442-8187
159 Phyllis Ln Bennington VT (05201) ***(G-21684)***
Monument Street Entps LLC ...781 820-1888
51 Ministerial Dr Concord MA (01742) ***(G-10142)***
Monument View Apts LP ...802 863-8424
100 Bank St Ste 400 Burlington VT (05401) ***(G-21798)***
Monumental Estates LLC ...802 442-7339
253 Fox Hill Rd Bennington VT (05201) ***(G-21685)***
Monzite Corporation (HQ) ...617 429-7050
165 Ledge St Nashua NH (03060) ***(G-19209)***
Moo Inc ...401 434-3561
14 Blackstone Valley Pl Lincoln RI (02865) ***(G-20586)***
Moo.com, Lincoln *Also called Moo Inc* ***(G-20586)***
Moody Investments LLC ...401 423-0121
716 South County Trl Exeter RI (02822) ***(G-20453)***
Moody Machine Products Inc ...401 941-5130
141 Carolina Ave Providence RI (02905) ***(G-21071)***
Moon Cutter Co Inc ...203 288-9249
2969 State St Hamden CT (06517) ***(G-1773)***
Moonbat City Baking Co LLC ...207 323-4955
129 Main St Apt 3 Belfast ME (04915) ***(G-5695)***
Mooneytunco Inc ...781 331-4445
65 Mathewson Dr Ste C Weymouth MA (02189) ***(G-16894)***
Moonlight Ltd ...508 584-0094
244 Liberty St Ste 11 Brockton MA (02301) ***(G-9168)***
Moonlight Meadery LLC ...603 216-2162
23 Londonderry Rd Unit 17 Londonderry NH (03053) ***(G-18724)***
Moonlight Media LLC ...860 345-3595
95 Bridge Rd Bldg 4b Haddam CT (06438) ***(G-1727)***
Moonlighting LLC ...203 740-8964
4 Jackson Dr Brookfield CT (06804) ***(G-653)***
Moonlite Graphics Co Inc ...401 635-2962
175 W Main Rd Little Compton RI (02837) ***(G-20606)***
Mooradian Cover Company, Hyde Park *Also called Sorenson Sewing Inc* ***(G-11880)***
Moore Co, Attleboro *Also called Jack Hodgdon* ***(G-7754)***
Moore Company (PA) ...401 596-2816
36 Beach St Westerly RI (02891) ***(G-21531)***
Moore Company ...401 596-2816
36 Beach St Westerly RI (02891) ***(G-21532)***
Moore Company ...401 596-0219
48 Canal St Westerly RI (02891) ***(G-21533)***
Moore Company ...401 596-2816
36 Beach St Westerly RI (02891) ***(G-21534)***
Moore Nntechnology Systems LLC (HQ) ...603 352-3030
230 Old Homestead Hwy Swanzey NH (03446) ***(G-19886)***
Moore Tool Company Inc (HQ) ...203 366-3224
800 Union Ave Bridgeport CT (06607) ***(G-453)***
Moore Woodworking Inc ...508 364-7338
300 Polpis Rd Nantucket MA (02554) ***(G-13227)***
Moore-Clark USA Inc ...207 591-7077
15 Saunders Way Ste 500e Westbrook ME (04092) ***(G-7198)***
Moores Sawmill Inc ...860 242-3003
171 Mountain Ave Bloomfield CT (06002) ***(G-244)***
Moose Creek Home Center Inc ...207 224-7497
2319 Auburn Rd Turner ME (04282) ***(G-7109)***
Moose Mountain Food Co., Wells River *Also called Bread & Chocolate Inc* ***(G-22600)***
Moose Mountain Logging Inc ...603 491-3667
55 Brewster Hill Rd Tamworth NH (03886) ***(G-19893)***
Moose River Lumber Company Inc ...207 668-4426
25 Talpey Rd Moose River ME (04945) ***(G-6453)***
Moose's Tale Food & Ale, Boston *Also called Sunday River Brewing Co Inc* ***(G-8869)***
Moosehead Cedar Log Homes, Greenville Junction *Also called Moosehead Wood Components Inc* ***(G-6154)***
Moosehead Cedar Log Homes ...802 464-7609
225 Vermont 9 Wilmington VT (05363) ***(G-22704)***
Moosehead Country Log Homes ...207 695-3730
Greenville Industral Park Greenville ME (04441) ***(G-6153)***
Moosehead Wood Components Inc ...207 695-3730
441 Pritham Ave Greenville Junction ME (04442) ***(G-6154)***
Moosewood Millworks LLC ...207 435-4950
42 American Realty Rd Ashland ME (04732) ***(G-5537)***
Moquin and Daley PA ...617 536-0606
24 School St Ste 704 Boston MA (02108) ***(G-8711)***
Mor-Wire & Cable Inc ...978 453-1782
50 Newhall St Ste 1 Lowell MA (01852) ***(G-12413)***
Morais Marizete ...508 460-8200
416 Boston Post Rd E # 3 Marlborough MA (01752) ***(G-12795)***
Moran Tool & Die, Bolton *Also called Barre Precision Products Inc* ***(G-274)***
Morano Gelato Inc ...603 643-4233
55 S Main St Hanover NH (03755) ***(G-18295)***
Moren Signs Inc ...413 786-0349
101 Ramah Cir S Agawam MA (01001) ***(G-7441)***
Morgan Advanced Ceramics Inc ...508 995-1725
225 Theodore Rice Blvd New Bedford MA (02745) ***(G-13418)***
Morgan Advanced Ceramics Inc ...603 598-9122
4 Park Ave Hudson NH (03051) ***(G-18416)***
Morgan Enterprises Inc ...985 377-3216
110 Blackstone River Rd Worcester MA (01607) ***(G-17424)***
Morgan Mill Metals LLC ...401 270-9944
25 Morgan Mill Rd Johnston RI (02919) ***(G-20524)***
Morgan Scientific Inc (PA) ...978 521-4440
151 Essex St Ste 8 Haverhill MA (01832) ***(G-11454)***
Morin Brothers ...207 834-5361
41 Charette Hill Rd Fort Kent ME (04743) ***(G-6063)***
Morin Corporation (HQ) ...860 584-0900
685 Middle St Bristol CT (06010) ***(G-584)***
Morin East, Bristol *Also called Morin Corporation* ***(G-584)***
Morin Engine Services LLC ...603 880-3009
151 W Hollis St Nashua NH (03060) ***(G-19210)***
Morning Star Farm, Lyndeborough *Also called Nadeau Logging* ***(G-18759)***
Morning Star Marble & Gran Inc ...207 725-7309
47 Park Dr Topsham ME (04086) ***(G-7091)***
Morning Star Tool LLC ...203 878-6026
83 Erna Ave Milford CT (06461) ***(G-2316)***
Morningstar Stone & Tile, Topsham *Also called Morning Star Marble & Gran Inc* ***(G-7091)***
Mornsun America LLC ...978 293-3923
13 Country Club Ln Milford MA (01757) ***(G-13129)***
Moroso Performance Pdts Inc (PA) ...203 453-6571
80 Carter Dr Guilford CT (06437) ***(G-1711)***
Morphisec Inc ...617 209-2552
745 Atlantic Ave Ste 211 Boston MA (02111) ***(G-8712)***
Morris & Broms LLC ...401 781-3134
900 Wellington Ave Cranston RI (02910) ***(G-20265)***
Morris and Butler ...603 918-0355
3 Grandview Ter North Hampton NH (03862) ***(G-19385)***
Morris Communications Co LLC ...203 458-4500
246 Goose Ln Ste 200 Guilford CT (06437) ***(G-1712)***
Morris Logging ...207 834-6210
158 Volette Settlement Rd Fort Kent ME (04743) ***(G-6064)***
Morris Transparent Box Co ...401 438-6116
945 Warren Ave East Providence RI (02914) ***(G-20433)***
Morris Yacht Inc (PA) ...207 667-6235
53 Granville Rd Bass Harbor ME (04653) ***(G-5672)***
Morris Yachts LLC ...207 667-2499
1 Little Harbor Lndg # 1 Portsmouth RI (02871) ***(G-20929)***
Morrison Berkshire Inc ...413 663-6501
865 Church St North Adams MA (01247) ***(G-13682)***
Morrison Millwork and Str Fixs ...207 892-9418
270 Roosevelt Trl Windham ME (04062) ***(G-7242)***
Morrison's Forest Products, Harmony *Also called Tracy J Morrison* ***(G-6172)***
Morristown Star Struck LLC ...203 778-4925
8 Francis J Clarke Cir Bethel CT (06801) ***(G-173)***
Morse Diving Inc ...781 733-1511
199 Weymouth St Ste 4 Rockland MA (02370) ***(G-14815)***
Morse Electric Motors Co Inc ...978 632-3733
380 E Broadway Gardner MA (01440) ***(G-11120)***
Morse Farm Inc ...802 223-2740
1168 County Rd Montpelier VT (05602) ***(G-22156)***
Morse Ready Mix LLC ...508 809-4644
24 Cross St Plainville MA (02762) ***(G-14529)***
Morse Sand & Gravel Corp ...508 809-4644
125 Tiffany St Attleboro MA (02703) ***(G-7769)***
Morse Watchmans Inc ...203 264-1108
2 Morse Rd Oxford CT (06478) ***(G-3415)***
Morses Sauerkraut ...207 832-5569
3856 Washington Rd Waldoboro ME (04572) ***(G-7135)***
Morton & Company Inc ...978 657-7726
11 Eames St Wilmington MA (01887) ***(G-17027)***
Morton Buildings Inc ...413 562-7028
563 Southampton Rd Westfield MA (01085) ***(G-16706)***
Morton International LLC ...401 274-7258
144 Allens Ave Providence RI (02903) ***(G-21072)***
Mosaic Records Inc ...203 327-7111
425 Fairfield Ave Ste 1 Stamford CT (06902) ***(G-4252)***
Moscow Mills Incorporated ...802 253-2036
435 Moscow Rd Stowe VT (05672) ***(G-22524)***
Moscow Mills Inc ...802 253-2036
11 Averill St Apt 1 Barre VT (05641) ***(G-21630)***
Moseley Corporation ...508 520-4004
31 Hayward St Ste A2 Franklin MA (02038) ***(G-11068)***
Moser Thos Cabinetmakers, Freeport *Also called Thos Moser Cabinetmakers Inc* ***(G-6087)***

A L P H A B E T I C

Mosher Company Inc 413 598-8341
15 Exchange St Chicopee MA (01013) ***(G-10047)***
Mossberg Corporation (PA) 203 230-5300
7 Grasso Ave North Haven CT (06473) ***(G-3042)***
Mossman Associates Inc 508 488-6169
9 Village Cir Milford MA (01757) ***(G-13130)***
Most Cardio Incorporated 978 594-1614
121 Loring Ave Ste 600 Salem MA (01970) ***(G-14930)***
Mostmed Inc 978 740-0400
121 Loring Ave Ste 920 Salem MA (01970) ***(G-14931)***
Mother Myricks, Manchester Center *Also called Fudge Factory Inc* ***(G-22085)***
Mother's Kitchen, New Britain *Also called Rich Products Corporation* ***(G-2573)***
Motion Technology Inc 508 460-9800
10 Forbes Rd Northborough MA (01532) ***(G-14039)***
Motive Industries LLC 860 423-2064
356 Tuckie Rd North Windham CT (06256) ***(G-3083)***
Motive Power 857 350-3765
34 Farnsworth St Boston MA (02210) ***(G-8713)***
Moto Tassinari Inc 603 298-6646
2 Technology Dr West Lebanon NH (03784) ***(G-19957)***
Motorcyclists Post 203 929-9409
11 Haven Ln Shelton CT (06484) ***(G-3835)***
Motorola Mobility LLC 847 523-5000
111 Locke Dr Ste 3 Marlborough MA (01752) ***(G-12796)***
Motorola Solutions Inc 508 261-4502
20 Cabot Blvd M2280 Mansfield MA (02048) ***(G-12647)***
Motorway Engineering Inc 603 668-6315
85 Hancock St Manchester NH (03101) ***(G-18878)***
Mott Corporation (PA) 860 793-6333
84 Spring Ln Farmington CT (06032) ***(G-1493)***
Mott Corporation 800 289-6688
75 Spring Ln Farmington CT (06032) ***(G-1494)***
Mouldcam Inc 401 396-5522
115 Broadcommon Rd Bristol RI (02809) ***(G-20094)***
Mount Desert Island Ice Cream 207 460-5515
325 Main St Bar Harbor ME (04609) ***(G-5666)***
Mount Desert Islander 207 288-0556
310 Main St Bar Harbor ME (04609) ***(G-5667)***
Mount Desert Spring Water, Southwest Harbor *Also called G C Management Corp* ***(G-7047)***
Mount Tom Box Co Inc 413 781-5300
21 Campbell St Pawtucket RI (02861) ***(G-20861)***
Mount Tom Box Company Inc 413 781-5300
190 Interstate Dr West Springfield MA (01089) ***(G-16531)***
Mount Warner Vineyards LLC 413 531-4046
85 Mount Warner Rd Hadley MA (01035) ***(G-11311)***
Mount Washington Vly Mtn Ear 603 447-6336
79 Main St Lancaster NH (03584) ***(G-18602)***
Mountain Cider LLC 802 483-2270
99 West Rd N Chittenden VT (05763) ***(G-22183)***
Mountain Corporation 603 876-3630
10 Wilcox Ct Marlborough NH (03455) ***(G-18963)***
Mountain Corporation (PA) 603 355-2272
59 Optical Ave Keene NH (03431) ***(G-18517)***
Mountain Dairy, Storrs Mansfield *Also called Willard J Stearns & Sons Inc* ***(G-4387)***
Mountain Firewood Kiln 603 444-6954
1536 Broomstick Hill Rd Littleton NH (03561) ***(G-18663)***
Mountain Fluid Power, Auburn *Also called Mountain Machine Works* ***(G-5582)***
Mountain Machine Works 207 783-6680
2589 Hotel Rd Auburn ME (04210) ***(G-5582)***
Mountain Mozzarella LLC 802 440-9950
441 Water St North Bennington VT (05257) ***(G-22210)***
Mountain Ridge Pet Supply, Nashua *Also called Kevin S Boghigian* ***(G-19194)***
Mountain Road Farm 802 644-5138
656 Vermont Route 108 S Jeffersonville VT (05464) ***(G-22046)***
Mountain Times, The, Killington *Also called Outer Limits Publishing LLC* ***(G-22055)***
Mountain Tops Custom T-Shirts (PA) 207 985-1919
39 Limerick Rd Unit 6 Arundel ME (04046) ***(G-5534)***
Mountain View Machine 413 527-6837
26 Pleasant St Southampton MA (01073) ***(G-15341)***
Mountain View Skids 802 933-2623
5290 Boston Post Rd Enosburg Falls VT (05450) ***(G-21925)***
Mountain Weavers, Manchester Center *Also called Rihm Management Inc* ***(G-22089)***
Mountainbase Mold & Mfg, Easthampton *Also called Michael Brisebois* ***(G-10567)***
Moveras LLC 603 685-0404
22 Northwestern Dr Salem NH (03079) ***(G-19753)***
Moviri Inc 857 233-5705
211 Congress St Ste 400 Boston MA (02110) ***(G-8714)***
Mozzarella House, Peabody *Also called Emga Foods LLC* ***(G-14333)***
Mozzicato Fmly Investments LLC 860 296-0426
631 Ridge Rd Wethersfield CT (06109) ***(G-5259)***
Mp Optical Communications Inc (PA) 978 456-7728
283 Littleton Rd Harvard MA (01451) ***(G-11382)***
Mp Systems Inc 860 687-3460
34 Bradley Park Rd East Granby CT (06026) ***(G-1134)***
Mpac, Greene *Also called Maine Poly Aquisition Corp* ***(G-6150)***
Mpb Corporation (HQ) 603 352-0310
7 Optical Ave Keene NH (03431) ***(G-18518)***
Mpb Corporation 603 448-3000
336 Mechanic St Lebanon NH (03766) ***(G-18630)***
Mpb Corporation 603 448-3000
334 Mechanic St Lebanon NH (03766) ***(G-18631)***
Mpi Systems Inc 203 762-2260
28 Powder Horn Hill Rd Wilton CT (06897) ***(G-5295)***
MPingo Multi Casting 413 241-2500
146 Chestnut St Springfield MA (01103) ***(G-15491)***
MPS, Holliston *Also called Miano Printing Services Inc* ***(G-11585)***
MPS Plastics Incorporated 860 295-1161
351 N Main St Marlborough CT (06447) ***(G-2067)***
Mpx 207 774-6116
2301 Congress St Portland ME (04102) ***(G-6695)***
Mr Boltons Music Inc 646 578-8081
31 Kings Hwy N Westport CT (06880) ***(G-5217)***
Mr Boston Brands LLC (HQ) 207 783-1433
21 Saratoga St Lewiston ME (04240) ***(G-6308)***
Mr Dumpster 781 233-3006
145 Dorchester St Ste 292 Boston MA (02127) ***(G-8715)***
Mr Gutter Inc 413 536-7451
740 High St Ste 2 Holyoke MA (01040) ***(G-11640)***
Mr Idea Inc 508 222-0155
100 Frank Mossberg Dr Attleboro MA (02703) ***(G-7770)***
Mr O'S Sporting Goods Store, Newport *Also called Michael Olden* ***(G-22202)***
Mr Plow 508 207-8999
222 E Central St Natick MA (01760) ***(G-13270)***
Mr Sandless Central Mass 508 864-6517
191 Fairhaven Rd Worcester MA (01606) ***(G-17425)***
Mr Skylight LLC 203 966-6005
411 South Ave New Canaan CT (06840) ***(G-2608)***
MRC Global (us) Inc 207 767-3861
169 Front St Bldg 9 South Portland ME (04106) ***(G-7033)***
MRC Global (us) Inc 508 966-3205
47 S Maple St Bellingham MA (02019) ***(G-8051)***
Mrd Woodworking LLC 401 789-3933
32 Frank Ave West Kingston RI (02892) ***(G-21468)***
Mrf Enterprises Inc 508 336-3050
294 Taunton Ave Seekonk MA (02771) ***(G-15030)***
Mrg, Norwood *Also called Manufctring Resource Group Inc* ***(G-14176)***
Mrh Tool LLC 203 878-3359
124 Research Dr Ste A Milford CT (06460) ***(G-2317)***
Mrk Fine Arts LLC 203 972-3115
65 Locust Ave Ste 301 New Canaan CT (06840) ***(G-2609)***
Mrl, Woburn *Also called Millennium Research Labs Inc* ***(G-17233)***
Mrnd LLC 860 749-0256
75 Hazard Ave Ste 1 Enfield CT (06082) ***(G-1370)***
Mrp Manufacturing LLC 603 435-5337
23 Catamount Rd Pittsfield NH (03263) ***(G-19503)***
Mrp Trading Innovations LLC 978 762-3900
85 Sam Fonzo Dr Beverly MA (01915) ***(G-8157)***
Mrpc Northeast LLC 603 880-3616
12 Executive Dr Hudson NH (03051) ***(G-18417)***
Mrs Macks Bakery Inc 508 753-0610
1393 Grafton St Ste 5 Worcester MA (01604) ***(G-17426)***
Mrs Mitchells Kitchen Inc 413 322-8816
514 Westfield Rd Holyoke MA (01040) ***(G-11641)***
Mrse 508 867-5083
192 W Main St West Brookfield MA (01585) ***(G-16472)***
Mrsi Systems LLC 978 667-9449
101 Billerica Ave Bldg 3 North Billerica MA (01862) ***(G-13847)***
Mrv Communications, Chelmsford *Also called Adva Optical Networking North* ***(G-9867)***
Ms Design CT, Oxford *Also called Susan Martovich* ***(G-3426)***
Ms Global, Wyoming *Also called Mechanical Specialties Inc* ***(G-21589)***
MS Industries Inc 978 582-1492
450 Leominster Rd Lunenburg MA (01462) ***(G-12482)***
Ms Wheelchair Mass Foundation 774 501-1185
19 Scadding St Taunton MA (02780) ***(G-15766)***
MSC Manufacturing Inc 781 888-8587
12 Industrial Way Rockland MA (02370) ***(G-14816)***
MSI, Beverly *Also called Microline Surgical Inc* ***(G-8153)***
MSI, Ledyard *Also called Management Software Inc* ***(G-1942)***
MSI Transducers Corp 978 486-0404
543 Great Rd Littleton MA (01460) ***(G-12313)***
Msj Investments Inc 860 684-9956
72 W Stafford Rd Ste 3 Stafford Springs CT (06076) ***(G-4113)***
Msm Protein Technologies Inc 617 504-9548
97 Giles Rd East Kingston NH (03827) ***(G-18088)***
Msn Corporation 603 623-3528
431 Somerville St Manchester NH (03103) ***(G-18879)***
MSP Digital Marketing 617 868-5778
117 Western Ave Allston MA (02134) ***(G-7471)***
Msr Utility 978 649-0002
209 Pleasant St Dunstable MA (01827) ***(G-10390)***
MST, North Smithfield *Also called Lkq Precious Metals Inc* ***(G-20789)***
Mt Tom Generating Company LLC 413 536-9586
200 Easthampton Rd Holyoke MA (01040) ***(G-11642)***
Mtd Inc 401 397-5460
2471 Flat River Rd Coventry RI (02816) ***(G-20158)***
Mtd Micro Molding Inc 508 248-0111
15 Trolley Crossing Rd Charlton MA (01507) ***(G-9854)***
MTI, Georgetown *Also called Metal Tronics Inc* ***(G-11146)***

MTI Polyexe Corporation 603 778-1449
50 Pine Rd Brentwood NH (03833) ***(G-17752)***
MTI Systems Inc 413 733-1972
1111 Elm St Ste 6 West Springfield MA (01089) ***(G-16532)***
MTI Unified Communications LLC 774 352-1110
5 Dupont Ave Unit 5-5 South Yarmouth MA (02664) ***(G-15331)***
Mti-Milliren Technologies Inc 978 465-6064
2 New Pasture Rd Ste 10 Newburyport MA (01950) ***(G-13516)***
Mtj Manufacturing Inc 203 334-4939
127 Wilmot Ave Bridgeport CT (06607) ***(G-454)***
Mtm Corporation 860 742-9600
643 Route 6 Andover CT (06232) ***(G-3)***
Mtm Oldco Inc (PA) 207 791-6650
1 City Ctr Fl 5 Portland ME (04101) ***(G-6696)***
Mtoz Biolabs Inc 617 401-8103
210 Broadway 201 Cambridge MA (02139) ***(G-9571)***
Mtr Precision Machining Inc 860 928-9440
60a Bradley Rd Pomfret Center CT (06259) ***(G-3557)***
MTS Associates Londonderry LLC 603 425-2562
55 Hall Rd Londonderry NH (03053) ***(G-18725)***
Mtu Aero Engines N Amer Inc 860 258-9700
795 Brook St 5 Rocky Hill CT (06067) ***(G-3724)***
Mu Net Inc 781 861-8644
442 Marrett Rd Ste 9 Lexington MA (02421) ***(G-12245)***
Mudpie Potters 413 548-3939
13 Montague Rd Leverett MA (01054) ***(G-12198)***
Mueller Corporation 508 456-4500
530 Spring St East Bridgewater MA (02333) ***(G-10418)***
Mueller Water Products Inc 508 923-2870
48 Leona Dr Ste C Middleboro MA (02346) ***(G-13070)***
Mug Factory, The, Milford *Also called Northeast Stamp & Engraving* ***(G-13132)***
Muhammad Choudhry 401 726-1118
530 Broadway Pawtucket RI (02860) ***(G-20862)***
Muir Envelope Div, Newington *Also called Muir Envelope Plus Inc* ***(G-2884)***
Muir Envelope Plus Inc 860 953-6847
124 Francis Ave Newington CT (06111) ***(G-2884)***
Mulch Ferris Products LLC 203 790-1155
6 Plumtrees Rd Danbury CT (06810) ***(G-957)***
Mullen Testers, Chicopee *Also called Standex International Corp* ***(G-10062)***
Multec Communications 781 294-4992
319 Centre Ave Ste 166 Rockland MA (02370) ***(G-14817)***
Multex Automation Corporation 617 347-7278
263 Huntington Ave Boston MA (02115) ***(G-8716)***
Multi Sign Inc 413 732-9900
777 Riverdale St West Springfield MA (01089) ***(G-16533)***
Multi Touch Surface Inc 408 634-9224
25 Lewis St Apt 3 Somerville MA (02143) ***(G-15200)***
Multi-Cable Corp 860 589-9035
37 Horizon Dr Bristol CT (06010) ***(G-585)***
Multi-Color Corporation 401 884-7100
311 Wilbert Way North Kingstown RI (02852) ***(G-20729)***
Multi-Fab Plastics, Dorchester *Also called Multifab Plastics Inc* ***(G-10347)***
Multi-Med Inc 603 357-8733
26 Victoria Ct Keene NH (03431) ***(G-18519)***
Multicultural Media, Barre *Also called Stephen McArthur* ***(G-21640)***
Multifab Plastics Inc 617 287-1411
889 Dorchester Ave Dorchester MA (02125) ***(G-10347)***
Multigrains Inc 978 691-6100
117 Water St Lawrence MA (01841) ***(G-12060)***
Multigrains Bakery, Lawrence *Also called Multigrains Inc* ***(G-12060)***
Multiplicity, Natick *Also called Kathy Clark* ***(G-13263)***
Multiprints Inc 203 235-4409
812 Old Colony Rd Meriden CT (06451) ***(G-2111)***
Mumm Engineering Inc 203 445-9777
57 Wells Rd Monroe CT (06468) ***(G-2409)***
Mumster Engineering, Manchester *Also called Whale Water Systems Inc* ***(G-22079)***
Mundos Crazy Music Pubg Corp 781 438-1704
21 Whipple Ave Stoneham MA (02180) ***(G-15568)***
Municipal Graphics Inc 508 384-0925
30 Commercial Dr Wrentham MA (02093) ***(G-17526)***
Municipal Market Analytics Inc (PA) 978 287-0014
75 Main St Fl 2 Concord MA (01742) ***(G-10143)***
Munis, Yarmouth *Also called Tyler Technologies Inc* ***(G-7301)***
Munk Pack Inc 203 769-5005
222 Railroad Ave Ste 2 Greenwich CT (06830) ***(G-1632)***
Munro Woodworking 508 966-2654
315 Farm St Bellingham MA (02019) ***(G-8052)***
Munroe Tool Co Inc 401 826-1040
134 Howard Ave Coventry RI (02816) ***(G-20159)***
Munsey Screw Machine Products 978 667-4053
3 Executive Park Dr Ste 3 # 3 North Billerica MA (01862) ***(G-13848)***
Munters Cargocaire, Amesbury *Also called Munters USA Inc* ***(G-7500)***
Munters Corporation 978 241-1100
79 Monroe St Amesbury MA (01913) ***(G-7496)***
Munters Corporation 978 388-2666
79 Monroe St Amesbury MA (01913) ***(G-7497)***
Munters Corporation (HQ) 978 241-1100
79 Monroe St Amesbury MA (01913) ***(G-7498)***
Munters Moisture Control Svcs 978 388-4900
79 Monroe St Amesbury MA (01913) ***(G-7499)***
Munters USA Inc 978 241-1100
79 Monroe St Amesbury MA (01913) ***(G-7500)***
Munters Zeol, Amesbury *Also called Munters Corporation* ***(G-7497)***
Murata Power Solutions Inc (HQ) 508 339-3000
129 Flanders Rd Westborough MA (01581) ***(G-16637)***
Murata Pwr Sltons Portland LLC 508 339-3000
129 Flanders Rd Westborough MA (01581) ***(G-16638)***
Murdock Webbing Company Inc (PA) 401 724-3000
27 Foundry St Central Falls RI (02863) ***(G-20121)***
Murphy Software Inc 781 710-8419
3 Fairfax St Burlington MA (01803) ***(G-9304)***
Murphy, JAS A & Son, Attleboro *Also called A Murphy James & Son Inc* ***(G-7696)***
Murray Biscuit Company LLC 781 760-0220
55 North St Canton MA (02021) ***(G-9758)***
Murray's Auto Recycling Center, Londonderry *Also called MTS Associates Londonderry LLC* ***(G-18725)***
Murroneys Printing Inc 603 623-4677
2626 Brown Ave Ste 4 Manchester NH (03103) ***(G-18880)***
Museum Collection, Providence *Also called Fashion Accents LLC* ***(G-21012)***
Mushield Company Inc 603 666-4433
9 Ricker Ave Londonderry NH (03053) ***(G-18726)***
Musical Playground 508 778-6679
142 Willow Run Dr Centerville MA (02632) ***(G-9818)***
Mussel Bound LLC 774 212-5488
80 Joe Long Rd Brewster MA (02631) ***(G-9054)***
Mutual Beef Co Inc 617 442-3238
126 Newmarket Sq Boston MA (02118) ***(G-8717)***
MV Mason Electronics Inc 508 668-6200
486 High Plain St Walpole MA (02081) ***(G-16004)***
Mv Products Division, North Billerica *Also called Mass Vac Inc* ***(G-13839)***
Mv3 LLC 617 658-4420
11 Mizzen Ln Buzzards Bay MA (02532) ***(G-9361)***
Mvk Silt Sock 978 204-9483
250 Main St Rowley MA (01969) ***(G-14860)***
Mvp Systems Software Inc 860 269-3112
29 Mill St Ste 8 Unionville CT (06085) ***(G-4659)***
Mwave Industries LLC 207 892-0011
33r Main St Ste 1 Windham ME (04062) ***(G-7243)***
Mwb Toy Company LLC 212 598-4500
128 E Liberty St Danbury CT (06810) ***(G-958)***
My Citizens News 203 729-2228
389 Meadow St Waterbury CT (06702) ***(G-4919)***
My Print and Copy LLC 978 232-3552
100 Cummings Ctr Ste 210d Beverly MA (01915) ***(G-8158)***
My Slide Lines LLC 203 324-1642
173 Main St Norwalk CT (06851) ***(G-3202)***
My Tool Company Inc 203 755-2333
1212 S Main St Waterbury CT (06706) ***(G-4920)***
My-T-Man Screen Printing Inc 603 622-7740
540 North Commercial St Manchester NH (03101) ***(G-18881)***
Mycabinetsonline 401 722-3863
24 Ballou Ave Lincoln RI (02865) ***(G-20587)***
Myco Tool & Manufacturing Inc 860 875-7340
176 Bolton Rd Ste 6 Vernon CT (06066) ***(G-4670)***
Myinvenio US Corp 408 464-0565
50 Milk St Fl 16 Boston MA (02109) ***(G-8718)***
Myjove Corporation 617 945-9051
1 Alewife Ctr Ste 200 Cambridge MA (02140) ***(G-9572)***
Mykrolis, Billerica *Also called Entegris Inc* ***(G-8247)***
Mylan Technologies Inc (HQ) 802 527-7792
110 Lake St Saint Albans VT (05478) ***(G-22373)***
Mylan Technologies Inc 802 527-7792
700 Industrial Park Rd Saint Albans VT (05478) ***(G-22374)***
Mylec Inc (PA) 978 297-0089
37 Commercial Dr Winchendon MA (01475) ***(G-17078)***
Mymetics Corporation 410 216-5345
150 Chestnut St Providence RI (02903) ***(G-21073)***
Myolex Inc 888 382-8656
1309 Beacon St Ste 300 Brookline MA (02446) ***(G-9210)***
Myomo Inc 617 996 9058
1 Broadway Fl 14 Cambridge MA (02142) ***(G-9573)***
Myri, Quincy *Also called Bioenergy International LLC* ***(G-14616)***
Myriad Engineering Co Inc 508 731-6416
96 Southbridge Rd North Oxford MA (01537) ***(G-13972)***
Myriad Fiber Imaging Tech Inc 508 949-3000
56 Southbridge Rd Dudley MA (01571) ***(G-10382)***
Myriad Inc 401 855-2000
10 Eagle St Fl 5 Providence RI (02908) ***(G-21074)***
Myriant Lake Providence Inc 617 657-5200
3 Batterymarch Park Fl 3 # 3 Quincy MA (02169) ***(G-14641)***
Myrin Institute Inc 413 528-4422
187 Main St Great Barrington MA (01230) ***(G-11242)***
Mysdispensers Inc 617 327-1124
511 Beech St Roslindale MA (02131) ***(G-14839)***
Myson, Williston *Also called Rettig USA Inc* ***(G-22688)***
Mystic Industries Corp 781 245-1950
474 Main St Wakefield MA (01880) ***(G-15962)***

ALPHABETIC

Mystic Knotwork LLC..........860 889-3793
25 Cottrell St Ste 1 Mystic CT (06355) ***(G-2444)***
Mystic Millwork, Norwood *Also called Mystic Scenic Studios Inc* ***(G-14180)***
Mystic Mountain Maples LLC..........802 524-6163
77 Rock Island Rd Saint Albans VT (05478) ***(G-22375)***
Mystic Parker Printing Inc..........781 321-4948
66 Willow St Malden MA (02148) ***(G-12583)***
Mystic River Foundry LLC..........860 536-7634
2 Broadway Ave Mystic CT (06355) ***(G-2445)***
Mystic River Press, Mystic *Also called Record-Journal Newspaper* ***(G-2450)***
Mystic Scenic Studios Inc..........781 440-0914
293 Lenox St Norwood MA (02062) ***(G-14180)***
Mystic Stainless & Alum Inc..........860 536-2236
23 Jackson Ave Mystic CT (06355) ***(G-2446)***
Mystic Valley Foundry Inc..........617 547-1819
14 Horace St Somerville MA (02143) ***(G-15201)***
Mystic Woodworks..........207 273-3937
199 Camden Rd Warren ME (04864) ***(G-7145)***
Mystockoptions.com, Brookline *Also called Mystockplancom Inc* ***(G-9211)***
Mystockplancom Inc..........617 734-1979
124 Harvard St Ste 9 Brookline MA (02446) ***(G-9211)***
Mysunbuddy Inc..........404 219-2640
1 Center Plz Ste 320 Boston MA (02108) ***(G-8719)***
Myturncom Pbc..........206 552-8488
16 Cavendish Ct Lebanon NH (03766) ***(G-18632)***
N & B Manufacturing Co Inc..........860 667-3204
215 Pascone Pl Newington CT (06111) ***(G-2885)***
N & M Pro Solutions Inc..........413 822-1009
212 East St Lenox MA (01240) ***(G-12102)***
N A Railrunner Inc..........781 860-7245
55 Old Bedford Rd Ste 106 Lincoln MA (01773) ***(G-12288)***
N B Baking Co..........508 992-5413
98 County St New Bedford MA (02744) ***(G-13419)***
N C Hunt Inc..........207 563-8503
237 Route One Damariscotta ME (04543) ***(G-5937)***
N E C H E A R, Hampton *Also called New England Ctr For Hring Rhab* ***(G-1798)***
N E E, Fall River *Also called New England Electropolishing* ***(G-10737)***
N E I A, Lexington *Also called New England Immunology Assoc* ***(G-12249)***
N E Industrial Coatings, Worcester *Also called New England Indus Coatings* ***(G-17430)***
N E K, Fitchburg *Also called New England Keyboard Inc* ***(G-10843)***
N E M T R LLC..........413 259-1444
29 Highland Dr Shutesbury MA (01072) ***(G-15140)***
N E O, Pawtucket *Also called New England Overseas Corp* ***(G-20867)***
N E P, Norton *Also called New England Photoconductor* ***(G-14084)***
N Excellence Wood Inc..........860 345-2050
323 Hidden Lake Rd Higganum CT (06441) ***(G-1904)***
N Ferrara Inc..........508 679-2440
10 Riverside Ave Somerset MA (02725) ***(G-15147)***
N H Central Concrete Corp..........603 428-7900
4 Bradford Rd Henniker NH (03242) ***(G-18308)***
N Kamenske & Co Inc..........603 888-1007
19 Fairhaven Rd Nashua NH (03060) ***(G-19211)***
N News LLC..........802 439-6054
4 Swamp Rd Topsham VT (05076) ***(G-22540)***
N P Medical Inc..........978 365-9721
101 Union St Clinton MA (01510) ***(G-10084)***
N R G Barriers, Saco *Also called Johns Manville Corporation* ***(G-6850)***
N R M, Canton *Also called National Resource MGT Inc* ***(G-9759)***
N S R Metal Works..........508 732-0190
5 Raffaele Rd Ste 2 Plymouth MA (02360) ***(G-14567)***
N T L, Derry *Also called Nel-Tech Labs Incorporated* ***(G-17990)***
N T P Republic, Holyoke *Also called Ntp/Republic Clear Thru Corp* ***(G-11645)***
N W P Inc..........802 442-4749
171 Church St Pownal VT (05261) ***(G-22282)***
N Y C O A, Manchester *Also called Nylon Corporation America Inc* ***(G-18890)***
N&N Manufacturing Inc (PA)..........978 465-1110
25 Howlett St Topsfield MA (01983) ***(G-15862)***
N&N Manufacturing Co, Topsfield *Also called Cullinan Manufacturing Inc* ***(G-15855)***
N-M Letters Inc..........401 245-5565
389 Nayatt Rd Barrington RI (02806) ***(G-20048)***
N-Tek Inc..........978 687-4010
22 Ballard Rd Lawrence MA (01843) ***(G-12061)***
N-Vision Optics LLC..........781 505-8360
220 Reservoir St Ste 26 Needham MA (02494) ***(G-13305)***
N/A, Westford *Also called Suburban Machine* ***(G-16794)***
N12 Technologies Inc..........857 259-6622
124 Washington St Ste 101 Foxboro MA (02035) ***(G-10893)***
N2 Biomedical LLC..........781 275-6001
1 Patriots Park Bedford MA (01730) ***(G-7993)***
N2bm Nutrition Inc..........978 241-2851
10b Elm St Salisbury MA (01952) ***(G-14954)***
NA Manosh Inc..........802 888-5722
120 Northgate Plz Ste B Morrisville VT (05661) ***(G-22174)***
Nabs Bindery, Waltham *Also called Nabs Inc* ***(G-16154)***
Nabs Inc..........781 899-7719
180 Elm St Ste 5 Waltham MA (02453) ***(G-16154)***
Nabson Inc..........617 323-1101
45 Independence Dr Taunton MA (02780) ***(G-15767)***
Nadco International Inc..........781 767-1797
604 South St Holbrook MA (02343) ***(G-11532)***
Nadeau Logging..........603 654-2594
649 Forest Rd Lyndeborough NH (03082) ***(G-18759)***
Nadeau Logging Inc..........207 834-6338
48 Summer Ave Fort Kent ME (04743) ***(G-6065)***
Naepac..........802 497-3654
338 Commerce St Unit 10 Williston VT (05495) ***(G-22684)***
Nafp Inc..........978 682-1855
983 Riverside Dr Methuen MA (01844) ***(G-13038)***
Nagel Machine Company Inc..........401 827-8962
27 Wightman St West Warwick RI (02893) ***(G-21500)***
Nahas Selim..........617 595-8808
56 Ripley St Newton MA (02459) ***(G-13616)***
Naheks Inc..........207 848-7770
15 Elaine Dr Hermon ME (04401) ***(G-6191)***
Naiad Dynamics Us Inc (HQ)..........203 929-6355
50 Parrott Dr Shelton CT (06484) ***(G-3836)***
Naiad Inflatables Newport Inc..........401 683-6700
4 Thurston Ave Newport RI (02840) ***(G-20673)***
Naiad Marine Systems, Shelton *Also called Naiad Dynamics Us Inc* ***(G-3836)***
Naked Nutrient By Deseo LLC..........646 809-4943
55 Crystal Ave Unit 7 Derry NH (03038) ***(G-17989)***
Nalas Engineering Services..........860 861-3691
1 Winnenden Rd Norwich CT (06360) ***(G-3286)***
Nameplates For Industry, New Bedford *Also called Nfi LLC* ***(G-13426)***
Nancy Larson Publishers Inc..........860 434-0800
27 Talcott Farm Rd Old Lyme CT (06371) ***(G-3325)***
Nancy Lawrence..........207 774-7276
3 Wharf St Portland ME (04101) ***(G-6697)***
Nandu Press..........207 767-3144
53 Goudy St South Portland ME (04106) ***(G-7034)***
Nanmac, Holliston *Also called Patriot Worldwide Inc* ***(G-11595)***
Nanmac Corp..........508 872-4811
1657 Washington St Unit B Holliston MA (01746) ***(G-11588)***
Nano Beam Technologies..........617 548-9495
5 Tricorne Rd Lexington MA (02421) ***(G-12246)***
Nano Ops Inc..........617 543-2921
8 Elder Rd Needham MA (02494) ***(G-13306)***
Nano Pet Products LLC..........203 345-1330
10 Hoyt St Norwalk CT (06851) ***(G-3203)***
Nano-Audio..........781 416-5096
21 Pine Plain Rd Wellesley MA (02481) ***(G-16374)***
Nano-Ice LLC..........617 512-8811
20 Chapel St Apt C611 Brookline MA (02446) ***(G-9212)***
Nanobiosym Inc..........781 391-7979
245 1st St Ste 18 Cambridge MA (02142) ***(G-9574)***
Nanobiosym Inc..........781 391-7979
200 Boston Ave Ste 4700 Medford MA (02155) ***(G-12944)***
Nanocap Technologies LLC (PA)..........860 521-9743
17 Morningcrest Dr Hartford CT (06117) ***(G-1849)***
Nanoentek Inc..........781 472-2558
240 Bear Hill Rd Ste 101 Waltham MA (02451) ***(G-16155)***
Nanofuse Biologics LLC..........978 232-3990
350 Main St Fl 2 Malden MA (02148) ***(G-12584)***
Nanolab Inc..........781 609-2722
22 Bedford St Waltham MA (02453) ***(G-16156)***
Nanomoleculardx..........518 588-7815
105 Elm St Pittsfield MA (01201) ***(G-14493)***
Nanoptek Corporation..........978 460-7107
2 Shaker Rd Shirley MA (01464) ***(G-15091)***
Nanoramic, Boston *Also called Fastcap Systems Corporation* ***(G-8539)***
Nanosemi Inc..........781 472-2832
200 5th Ave Ste 2020 Waltham MA (02451) ***(G-16157)***
Nanospire Inc..........207 929-6226
25 Jesse Daniel Dr Buxton ME (04093) ***(G-5859)***
Nanosurf Inc..........781 549-7361
300 Tradecenter Ste 5450 Woburn MA (01801) ***(G-17235)***
Nanotech Consulting, Upton *Also called Kirstein Per* ***(G-15908)***
Nanotechsys, Swanzey *Also called Moore Nntechnology Systems LLC* ***(G-19886)***
Nantero Inc..........781 932-5338
25b Olympia Ave Woburn MA (01801) ***(G-17236)***
Nantucket Bake Shop Inc..........508 228-2797
17 1/2 Old South Rd Ste C Nantucket MA (02554) ***(G-13228)***
Nantucket Beadboard Co Inc..........603 330-3338
109 Chestnut Hill Rd Rochester NH (03867) ***(G-19679)***
Nantucket Chronicle LLC..........508 257-6683
39 Low Beach Rd Siasconset MA (02564) ***(G-15141)***
Nantucket Glass & Mirror Inc..........508 228-3713
15 Sun Island Rd Nantucket MA (02554) ***(G-13229)***
Nantucket Ice House, Nantucket *Also called Got Ice LLC* ***(G-13225)***
Nantucket Looms, Nantucket *Also called E W Winship Ltd Inc* ***(G-13223)***
Nantucket Pavers Inc..........508 336-5800
71 Fall River Ave Rehoboth MA (02769) ***(G-14753)***
Nap Brothers Parlor Frame Inc..........860 633-9998
122 Naubuc Ave Ste B3 Glastonbury CT (06033) ***(G-1565)***
NAPA Auto Parts, Great Barrington *Also called Great Barrington Auto Sup Inc* ***(G-11238)***

Napp Printing Plate Dist Inc 203 575-5727
245 Freight St Waterbury CT (06702) ***(G-4921)***
Narragansett Bus Forms Inc 401 331-2000
21 Massasoit Ave East Providence RI (02914) ***(G-20434)***
Narragansett Coated Paper, Pawtucket *Also called Ecological Fibers Inc* ***(G-20836)***
Narragansett Imaging Usa LLC 401 762-3800
51 Industrial Dr North Smithfield RI (02896) ***(G-20791)***
Narragansett Screw Co 860 379-4059
119 Rowley St Winsted CT (06098) ***(G-5418)***
Narragansett Shipwrights Inc 401 846-3312
1 Spring Wharf Newport RI (02840) ***(G-20674)***
Narragasett Jewelry Inc 401 944-2200
100 Dupont Dr Ste 1 Providence RI (02907) ***(G-21075)***
Narrative 1 Software LLC 603 968-2233
1 Bridge St Ste 301 Plymouth NH (03264) ***(G-19529)***
Nas Fuels LLC 603 964-6967
296 Lafayette Rd Rye NH (03870) ***(G-19699)***
Nash Mfg & Grinding Svcs 413 301-5416
572 Saint James Ave Springfield MA (01109) ***(G-15492)***
Nashoba Valley Extract LLC 978 201-5245
15 Sudbury Rd Stow MA (01775) ***(G-15634)***
Nashoba Valley Spirits Limited 978 779-5521
100 Wattaquadock Hill Rd Bolton MA (01740) ***(G-8321)***
Nashoba Valley Winery, Bolton *Also called Nashoba Valley Spirits Limited* ***(G-8321)***
Nashua Circuits Inc 603 882-1773
29 Crown St Nashua NH (03060) ***(G-19212)***
Nashua Corporation 603 880-1110
59 Daniel Webster Hwy A Merrimack NH (03054) ***(G-19015)***
Nashua Fabrication Co Inc 603 889-2181
7 Security Dr Hudson NH (03051) ***(G-18418)***
Nashua Foundries Inc 603 882-4811
5 Foundry St Nashua NH (03060) ***(G-19213)***
Nashua Sand & Gravel LLC 603 459-8662
22 West Rd Hudson NH (03051) ***(G-18419)***
Nason Machine Company 508 865-3545
26 Cobblestone Ln East Douglas MA (01516) ***(G-10430)***
Nason's Stone House Farm, West Boxford *Also called Stone House Farm Inc* ***(G-16408)***
Nasoya Foods Inc 978 772-6880
1 New England Way Ayer MA (01432) ***(G-7927)***
Nasoya Foods Usa LLC 978 772-6880
1 New England Way Ayer MA (01432) ***(G-7928)***
Nat Chiavettione Inc 508 336-4142
702 Warren Ave Swansea MA (02777) ***(G-15709)***
Nat's Garage, Swansea *Also called Nat Chiavettione Inc* ***(G-15709)***
Natale & Sons Castings 401 467-4744
441 Niantic Ave Cranston RI (02910) ***(G-20266)***
Natale Co Safetycare LL 781 933-7205
5 W Dexter Ave Woburn MA (01801) ***(G-17237)***
Natco Home Fashions Inc 401 828-0300
155 Brookside Ave West Warwick RI (02893) ***(G-21501)***
Natco Home Fashions Inc 401 828-0300
155 Brookside Ave West Warwick RI (02893) ***(G-21502)***
Natco Home Fashions Inc (PA) 401 828-0300
155 Brookside Ave Ste 3 West Warwick RI (02893) ***(G-21503)***
Natco Products Corporation (PA) 401 828-0300
155 Brookside Ave West Warwick RI (02893) ***(G-21504)***
Natgun Corporation (HQ) 781 224-5180
11 Teal Rd Wakefield MA (01880) ***(G-15963)***
Nathan Airchime Inc 860 423-4575
1102 Windham Rd South Windham CT (06266) ***(G-3927)***
Nathaniel S Wilson Sailmaker 207 633-5071
15 Lincoln St East Boothbay ME (04544) ***(G-5978)***
Natick Center Graphics, Sharon *Also called CJ Corrado & Sons Inc* ***(G-15048)***
National Aperture Inc 603 893-7393
5 Northwestern Dr Salem NH (03079) ***(G-19754)***
National Braille Press Inc 617 425-2400
88 Saint Stephen St Boston MA (02115) ***(G-8720)***
National Chain Company (PA) 401 732-3634
55 Access Rd Ste 500 Warwick RI (02886) ***(G-21393)***
National Chimney Supply 802 861-2217
3 Green Tree Dr South Burlington VT (05403) ***(G-22454)***
National Chromium Company Inc 860 928-7965
10 Senexet Rd Putnam CT (06260) ***(G-3620)***
National Clothes Pin Co Inc 802 223-7332
1 Granite St Montpelier VT (05602) ***(G-22157)***
National Con Tnks / Frguard JV 978 505-5533
82 Tarbell Spring Rd Concord MA (01742) ***(G-10144)***
National Conveyors Company Inc 860 653-0374
33 Nicholson Rd Ste 2 East Granby CT (06026) ***(G-1135)***
National Cthlic Bthics Ctr Inc 401 289-0680
119 Bay Spring Ave Barrington RI (02806) ***(G-20049)***
National Die Company 203 879-1408
64 Wolcott Rd Wolcott CT (06716) ***(G-5449)***
National Embroidery, Portsmouth *Also called Next Event Corporation* ***(G-20931)***
National Fiber, Belchertown *Also called Macgregor Bay Corporation* ***(G-8025)***
National Fiber Technology LLC 978 686-2964
15 Union St Ste 320 Lawrence MA (01840) ***(G-12062)***
National Filter Media Corp 207 377-2626
40 Winada Dr Winthrop ME (04364) ***(G-7281)***
National Filter Media Corp 203 741-2225
9 Fairfield Blvd Wallingford CT (06492) ***(G-4777)***
National Filter Media Corp 207 377-2626
12 Winada Dr Winthrop ME (04364) ***(G-7282)***
National Grape Coop Assn Inc 978 371-1000
555 Virginia Rd Concord MA (01742) ***(G-10145)***
National Hanger Company Inc 800 426-4377
276 Water St North Bennington VT (05257) ***(G-22211)***
National Integrated Inds Inc (PA) 860 677-7995
322 Main St Farmington CT (06032) ***(G-1495)***
National Integrated Inds Inc 203 756-7051
1358 Thomaston Ave Waterbury CT (06704) ***(G-4922)***
National Klip, Montpelier *Also called National Clothes Pin Co Inc* ***(G-22157)***
National Magnetic Sensors Inc 860 621-6816
141 Summer St Ste 3 Plantsville CT (06479) ***(G-3537)***
National Marker Company 401 762-9700
100 Providence Pike North Smithfield RI (02896) ***(G-20792)***
National Medical Care-Npd, Marlborough *Also called Fresenius Usa Inc* ***(G-12757)***
National Meter Industries Inc 603 669-5790
10 Commerce Park North 11a Bedford NH (03110) ***(G-17656)***
National Nonwovens Inc (PA) 413 527-3445
110 Pleasant St Easthampton MA (01027) ***(G-10568)***
National Nonwovens Inc 413 527-3445
27 Mechanic St Easthampton MA (01027) ***(G-10569)***
National Nonwovens Inc 413 527-3445
180 Pleasant St Easthampton MA (01027) ***(G-10570)***
National Poetry Foundation 207 581-3814
5752 Neville Hall Orono ME (04469) ***(G-6556)***
National Relocation & RE Mag, Norwalk *Also called Relocation Information Svc Inc* ***(G-3229)***
National Resource MGT Inc (PA) 781 828-8877
480 Neponset St Ste 2a Canton MA (02021) ***(G-9759)***
National Ribbon LLC 860 742-6966
1159 Main St Coventry CT (06238) ***(G-836)***
National Screw Manufacturing 203 469-7109
259 Commerce St East Haven CT (06512) ***(G-1256)***
National Seating Mobility Inc 413 420-0054
150 Padgette St Ste F Chicopee MA (01022) ***(G-10048)***
National Service Systems Inc 781 344-6504
1600 Washington St Stoughton MA (02072) ***(G-15609)***
National Shooting Sports Found 203 426-1320
11 Mile Hill Rd Ste A Newtown CT (06470) ***(G-2929)***
National Spring & Stamping Inc 860 283-0203
135 S Main St Ste 8 Thomaston CT (06787) ***(G-4510)***
National Store Fronts Co Inc 508 584-8880
10 Tracy Dr Avon MA (02322) ***(G-7890)***
National Store Supply, North Bennington *Also called National Hanger Company Inc* ***(G-22211)***
National System, Stoughton *Also called National Service Systems Inc* ***(G-15609)***
National Tool & CAM, Newington *Also called M & R Manufacturing Inc* ***(G-2878)***
National Velour Corporation 401 737-8300
36 Bellair Ave Warwick RI (02886) ***(G-21394)***
National Vinyl LLC 413 420-0548
7 Coburn St Chicopee MA (01013) ***(G-10049)***
National Water Main Clg Co 617 361-5533
25 Marshall St Canton MA (02021) ***(G-9760)***
Native Sun Studio, Gilford *Also called Daniel Wheeler* ***(G-18184)***
Natural Nutmeg LLC 860 206-9500
53 Mountain View Ave Avon CT (06001) ***(G-38)***
Natural Polymer Devices Inc 860 679-7894
400 Farmington Ave Mc6409 Farmington CT (06032) ***(G-1496)***
Natural Rocks Spring Water Ice 207 451-2110
299 Harold L Dow Hwy Eliot ME (03903) ***(G-6009)***
Naturalase, Bethel *Also called Focus Medical LLC* ***(G-154)***
Naturally Maine 207 423-6443
1 Parkview Ct Ste 132 Biddeford ME (04005) ***(G-5751)***
Naturcom Enterprises LLC 802 222-4277
203 Depot St Bradford VT (05033) ***(G-21704)***
Nature Plus Inc 203 380-0316
55 Rachel Dr Stratford CT (06615) ***(G-4432)***
Natures First Inc (PA) 203 795-8400
58 Robinson Blvd Ste C Orange CT (06477) ***(G-3374)***
Natures View Inc 800 506-5307
15 Maplerow Ave Ste A Waterbury CT (06705) ***(G-4923)***
Naturex-Dbs LLC 774 247-0022
39 Pleasant St Sagamore MA (02561) ***(G-14884)***
Naturopatches Vermont Inc 800 340-9083
9 Spencer Dr Bellows Falls VT (05101) ***(G-21652)***
Natus Medical Incorporated 401 732-5251
200 Metro Center Blvd Warwick RI (02886) ***(G-21395)***
Natworks Inc 802 485-6818
454 S Main St Northfield VT (05663) ***(G-22244)***
Naugatuck Elec Indus Sup LLC 203 723-1082
68 Radnor Ave Naugatuck CT (06770) ***(G-2486)***
Naugatuck Recovery Inc (HQ) 203 723-1122
300 Great Hill Rd Naugatuck CT (06770) ***(G-2487)***
Naugatuck Stair Company Inc 203 729-7134
51 Elm St Naugatuck CT (06770) ***(G-2488)***
Naugatuck Vly Photo Engrv Inc 203 756-7345
2148 S Main St Waterbury CT (06706) ***(G-4924)***

ALPHABETIC

Naugler Co Inc.......978 463-9199
5 Perry Way Ste 1 Newburyport MA (01950) *(G-13517)*
Naugler Engineering, Newburyport *Also called Naugler Co Inc (G-13517)*
Naugler Mold & Engineering.......978 922-5634
60 Dunham Rd Beverly MA (01915) *(G-8159)*
Nauset Engineer Equipment.......508 339-2662
51 Fram Dr Mansfield MA (02048) *(G-12648)*
Nauset Lantern Shop.......508 255-1009
52 Rt 6a Orleans MA (02653) *(G-14236)*
Nauset Optical.......508 255-6394
9 West Rd Ste 12 Orleans MA (02653) *(G-14237)*
Nauta Roll Corporation.......860 267-2027
7 Whippoorwill Hollow Rd East Hampton CT (06424) *(G-1162)*
Nautel Maine Inc.......207 947-8200
201 Target Industrial Cir Bangor ME (04401) *(G-5654)*
Navarrete Foods Inc.......508 735-7319
50 Terminal St Charlestown MA (02129) *(G-9839)*
Navico Inc.......603 324-2042
10 Al Paul Ln Ste 101 Merrimack NH (03054) *(G-19016)*
Navigator Publishing LLC.......207 822-4350
30 Danforth St Ste 307 Portland ME (04101) *(G-6698)*
Navionics Inc.......508 291-6000
6 Thatcher Ln Wareham MA (02571) *(G-16253)*
Navitor Pharmaceuticals Inc.......857 285-4300
1030 Massachusetts Ave Cambridge MA (02138) *(G-9575)*
Navtec Rigging Solutions Inc.......203 458-3163
37 Stanton Rd Clinton CT (06413) *(G-790)*
Navtech Systems Inc.......203 661-7800
322 Sound Beach Ave Old Greenwich CT (06870) *(G-3312)*
Navy Product Team, Mansfield *Also called Emerson Automation Solutions (G-12630)*
Nbr Diamond Tool Corp.......603 394-2113
22 Exeter Rd Unit 2 South Hampton NH (03827) *(G-19856)*
NC Brands LP.......203 295-2300
40 Richards Ave Ste 2 Norwalk CT (06854) *(G-3204)*
NC Converting Inc.......508 336-6510
32 Hollister Rd Seekonk MA (02771) *(G-15031)*
Nca Inc.......860 974-2310
500 Hampton Rd Abington CT (06230) *(G-1)*
Ncab Group Usa Inc (PA).......603 329-4551
10 Starwood Dr Hampstead NH (03841) *(G-18245)*
Nci Holdings Inc (PA).......203 295-2300
40 Richards Ave Ste 2 Norwalk CT (06854) *(G-3205)*
NCR Corporation.......617 558-2000
180 Wells Ave Newton MA (02459) *(G-13617)*
Nct, Kennebunk *Also called Northeast Coating Tech Inc (G-6239)*
Nct Inc.......860 666-8424
20 Holmes Rd Newington CT (06111) *(G-2886)*
ND Otm LLC.......207 401-2879
24 Portland St Old Town ME (04468) *(G-6545)*
ND Paper Inc.......207 364-4521
35 Hartford St Rumford ME (04276) *(G-6838)*
ND Paper LLC.......207 364-4521
35 Hartford St Rumford ME (04276) *(G-6839)*
Ndr Liuzzi Inc.......203 287-8477
86 Rossotto Dr Hamden CT (06514) *(G-1774)*
Ndz Performance, Cheshire *Also called New Designz Inc (G-747)*
Ne Choice Cabinet.......781 245-3800
85 Farm St Wakefield MA (01880) *(G-15964)*
Ne Dumpster.......603 438-6402
20 C St Nashua NH (03060) *(G-19214)*
Ne Media Group Inc (PA).......617 929-2000
1 Exchange Pl Ste 201 Boston MA (02109) *(G-8721)*
Ne Stainless Steel Fab.......781 335-0121
86 Finnell Dr Ste 23 Weymouth MA (02188) *(G-16895)*
Nea, Auburn *Also called Northast Emrgncy Apparatus LLC (G-5584)*
Neal Specialty Compounding LLC.......207 777-1122
258 Goddard Rd Lewiston ME (04240) *(G-6309)*
Near East Bakery, Brockton *Also called Elie Baking Corporation (G-9143)*
Nearpeer Inc.......207 615-0414
63 Federal St Portland ME (04101) *(G-6699)*
Neasi-Weber International.......203 857-4404
17 Little Fox Ln Norwalk CT (06850) *(G-3206)*
Neat As A Pin.......603 627-3504
40 Palomino Ln Bedford NH (03110) *(G-17628)*
Neatheat, Sagamore Beach *Also called Creative Hydronics Intl Inc (G-14885)*
Neato Products LLC.......203 466-5170
37 Eastern Steel Rd Milford CT (06460) *(G-2318)*
Nebs, Groton *Also called New England Business Svc Inc (G-11291)*
Neci LLC.......781 828-4883
530 Turnpike St Canton MA (02021) *(G-9761)*
Necs, Branford *Also called New England Computer Svcs Inc (G-333)*
Necs, Stratford *Also called Hydro-Flex Inc (G-4421)*
Necsel Intllctual Property Inc.......802 877-6432
101 Panton Rd Ste 1 Vergennes VT (05491) *(G-22554)*
Necsel Ip, Vergennes *Also called Necsel Intllctual Property Inc (G-22554)*
Nectar Cappuccino Group, South Burlington *Also called Sunny Sky Products LLC (G-22469)*
Ned Acquisition Corp.......508 798-8546
18 Grafton St Worcester MA (01604) *(G-17427)*
Nedap Inc.......844 876-3327
25 Corporate Dr Ste 101 Burlington MA (01803) *(G-9305)*
Nedap Retail North America, Burlington *Also called Nedap Inc (G-9305)*
Nedc Sealing Solutions, Methuen *Also called New England Die Cutting Inc (G-13039)*
Need To Build Muscle, Salisbury *Also called N2bm Nutrition Inc (G-14954)*
Needham Certified Welding Corp.......781 444-7470
225 Highland Ave Rear Needham Heights MA (02494) *(G-13340)*
Needham Electric Supply LLC.......603 569-0643
26 Bay St Wolfeboro NH (03894) *(G-20023)*
Needletech Products Inc.......508 431-4000
452 John L Dietsch Blvd North Attleboro MA (02763) *(G-13767)*
Neeltran Inc.......860 350-5964
71 Pickett District Rd New Milford CT (06776) *(G-2815)*
Neenah Foundry Company.......781 344-1711
1595 Central St Stoughton MA (02072) *(G-15610)*
Neenah Northeast LLC (HQ).......413 533-0699
70 Front St West Springfield MA (01089) *(G-16534)*
Neenah Technical Materials.......413 684-7488
1080 Dalton Ave Pittsfield MA (01201) *(G-14494)*
Neenah Technical Materials Inc (HQ).......678 518-3343
Ashuelot Park Ii 448 Hbbr Dalton MA (01226) *(G-10180)*
Neenah Technical Materials Inc.......413 684-7874
448 Hubbard Ave Pittsfield MA (01201) *(G-14495)*
Neew England Badge, Framingham *Also called Framingham Engraving Co (G-10946)*
Nefab Packaging North East LLC.......800 258-4692
23 Williams Way Bellingham MA (02019) *(G-8053)*
Nefm, Leominster *Also called New England Fab Mtls Inc (G-12170)*
Negeg, Merrimac *Also called Northast Green Enrgy Group Inc (G-13004)*
Negm Electric LLC.......603 692-4806
302 Main St Somersworth NH (03878) *(G-19844)*
Nehp Inc.......802 652-1444
1193 S Brownell Rd Ste 35 Williston VT (05495) *(G-22685)*
Nei, Canton *Also called Unicom Engineering Inc (G-9791)*
Nei Stamping, Lebanon *Also called New England Industries Inc (G-18633)*
Neighborhood Beer Company Inc.......603 418-7124
27 Chisholm Farm Dr Stratham NH (03885) *(G-19875)*
Neighborhood News.......603 206-7800
100 William Loeb Dr Manchester NH (03109) *(G-18882)*
Neiss Corp.......860 872-8528
29 Naek Rd Vernon CT (06066) *(G-4671)*
Nel Group LLC.......860 683-0190
154 Broad St Windsor CT (06095) *(G-5350)*
Nel-Tech Labs Incorporated.......603 425-1096
4 Ash Street Ext Derry NH (03038) *(G-17990)*
Neles USA Inc.......508 852-0200
28 Bowditch Dr Worcester MA (01605) *(G-17428)*
Neles USA Inc (HQ).......508 852-0200
44 Bowditch Dr Shrewsbury MA (01545) *(G-15125)*
Neles USA Inc.......508 852-0200
44 Bowditch Dr Shrewsbury MA (01545) *(G-15126)*
Neles USA Inc.......508 852-0200
42 Bowditch Dr Shrewsbury MA (01545) *(G-15127)*
Nelipak Corporation (PA).......401 946-2699
21 Amflex Dr Cranston RI (02921) *(G-20267)*
Nelipak Healthcare Packaging, Cranston *Also called Nelipak Corporation (G-20267)*
Nellcor Puritan Bennett LLC (HQ).......508 261-8000
15 Hampshire St Mansfield MA (02048) *(G-12649)*
Nelmed Corporation.......508 695-8817
1 Thyme Ln North Attleboro MA (02760) *(G-13768)*
Nelson & Miller Associates.......203 356-9694
5 Hillandale Ave Ste F Stamford CT (06902) *(G-4253)*
Nelson & Power Inc.......781 933-0679
5 Washington Ter Woburn MA (01801) *(G-17238)*
Nelson Air Corporation.......603 673-3908
559 Route 13 S Milford NH (03055) *(G-19070)*
Nelson Apostle Inc.......860 953-4633
11 Sherman St Hartford CT (06110) *(G-1850)*
Nelson Heat Treating Co Inc.......203 754-0670
2046 N Main St Waterbury CT (06704) *(G-4925)*
Nelson Robotics Corp.......603 856-7421
26 Monroe St Concord NH (03301) *(G-17915)*
Nelson Stud Welding Inc.......800 635-9353
36 Spring Ln Farmington CT (06032) *(G-1497)*
Nelson Tool & Machine Co Inc.......860 589-8004
675 Emmett St Bristol CT (06010) *(G-586)*
Nemerever Vineyards LLC.......617 320-6994
535 Hammond St Chestnut Hill MA (02467) *(G-9989)*
Nemi Publishing Inc.......207 778-4801
553 Wilton Rd Farmington ME (04938) *(G-6052)*
Nemonix Engineering Inc.......508 393-7700
580 Main St Ste 5 Bolton MA (01740) *(G-8322)*
Nemtec Inc.......203 272-0788
B 8 Trackside Cheshire CT (06410) *(G-746)*
Nemucore Med Innovations Inc.......617 943-9983
33 Kirkland Cir Wellesley MA (02481) *(G-16375)*
Neo Green Technology Corp.......617 500-7103
395 W Cummings Park Woburn MA (01801) *(G-17239)*

Neo Markets Inc 603 766-8716
953 Islington St Ste 22 Portsmouth NH (03801) *(G-19597)*
Neo Scientific, Woburn *Also called Neo Green Technology Corp (G-17239)*
Neogenix LLC (PA) 781 702-6732
588 Pleasant St Ste 2 Norwood MA (02062) *(G-14181)*
Neokraft Signs Inc 207 782-9654
647 Pleasant St Lewiston ME (04240) *(G-6310)*
Neon Goose 781 925-5118
34 Brookline Ave Hull MA (02045) *(G-11829)*
Neon Pipe 207 285-7420
313 Main St Ste C Corinth ME (04427) *(G-5924)*
Neopa Signs 603 352-3305
114 S Winchester St Swanzey NH (03446) *(G-19887)*
Neoperl Inc 203 756-8891
171 Mattatuck Heights Rd Waterbury CT (06705) *(G-4926)*
Neopost USA Inc (HQ) 203 301-3400
478 Wheelers Farms Rd Milford CT (06461) *(G-2319)*
Neops, Worcester *Also called New England Orthotic & Prost (G-17431)*
Neotron Inc 781 239-3461
5 Hayden Pl Wellesley MA (02481) *(G-16376)*
Neovii Biotech Na Inc 781 966-3830
430 Bedford St Ste 195 Lexington MA (02420) *(G-12247)*
Nepco, Presque Isle *Also called Northeast Packaging Co (G-6763)*
Neptco Incorporated (HQ) 401 722-5500
30 Hamlet St Pawtucket RI (02861) *(G-20863)*
Neptune Garment Company 617 482-3980
242 E Berkeley St Ste 3 Boston MA (02118) *(G-8722)*
Neptune Inc 508 222-8313
39 Slater St Attleboro MA (02703) *(G-7771)*
Neptune-Benson, LLC, Coventry *Also called Benson Neptune Inc (G-20138)*
Nereg, Boston *Also called Northast Renewable Enrgy Group (G-8742)*
Nerjan Development Company 203 325-3228
101 West Ave Stamford CT (06902) *(G-4254)*
Nes Embroidery Inc 603 293-4664
100 Autumn Dr Unit 2 Tilton NH (03276) *(G-19908)*
Nes Worldwide Inc 413 485-5038
3 Progress Ave Westfield MA (01085) *(G-16707)*
Neses, Farmington *Also called New England Shoulder Elbow Soc (G-1499)*
Neshobe River Winery 802 247-8002
79 Stone Mill Dam Rd Brandon VT (05733) *(G-21710)*
Neshobe Wood Products Inc 802 247-3805
56 Pearl St Brandon VT (05733) *(G-21711)*
Nessen Lighting, Brookfield *Also called 3t Lighting Inc (G-631)*
Nest, Litchfield *Also called New England Small Tube Corp (G-18652)*
Nestech Machine Systems Inc 802 482-4575
223 Commerce St Hinesburg VT (05461) *(G-22029)*
Nestle 508 828-3954
455 John Hancock Rd Taunton MA (02780) *(G-15768)*
Nestle Usa Inc 860 928-0082
151 Mashamoquet Rd Pomfret Center CT (06259) *(G-3558)*
Nestle Usa Inc 978 988-2030
240 Ballardvale St Wilmington MA (01887) *(G-17028)*
Nestor Inc (PA) 401 274-5345
42 Oriental St Fl 3 Providence RI (02908) *(G-21076)*
Nestor Traffic Systems Inc (PA) 401 714-7781
1080 Main St Pawtucket RI (02860) *(G-20864)*
Net Results In Cad Inc 603 249-9995
1 Overlook Dr Ste 1 # 1 Amherst NH (03031) *(G-17578)*
Net Vantage Point Inc 781 860-9158
149 E Emerson Rd Lexington MA (02420) *(G-12248)*
Net.com, Westford *Also called Network Equipment Tech Inc (G-16780)*
Netbrain Technologies Inc (PA) 781 221-7199
15 Network Dr Ste 2 Burlington MA (01803) *(G-9306)*
Netco Extruded Plastics, Hudson *Also called Xponent Global Inc (G-11827)*
Netco Extruded Plastics Inc 978 562-3485
30 Tower St Hudson MA (01749) *(G-11795)*
Netcracker Technology Corp (HQ) 781 419-3300
95 Sawyer Rd Waltham MA (02453) *(G-16158)*
Netsource Inc (PA) 860 649-6000
260 Progress Dr Manchester CT (06042) *(G-2025)*
Netsuite 877 638-7848
268 Summer St Ste 400 Boston MA (02210) *(G-8723)*
Nettwerk Music Group LLC 617 497-8200
15 Richdale Ave Cambridge MA (02140) *(G-9576)*
Netw, New Britain *Also called New England Traveling Wire LLC (G-2557)*
Network Equipment Tech Inc (HQ) 510 713-7300
4 Technology Park Dr Westford MA (01886) *(G-16780)*
Network World Inc 800 622-1108
492 Old Connecticut Path # 311 Framingham MA (01701) *(G-10986)*
Netzsch Instruments N Amer LLC (HQ) 781 272-5353
129 Middlesex Tpke Burlington MA (01803) *(G-9307)*
Netzsch USA Holdings Inc (PA) 781 272-5353
37 North Ave Burlington MA (01803) *(G-9308)*
Neu Spclty Engineered Mtls LLC 203 239-9629
15 Corporate Dr North Haven CT (06473) *(G-3043)*
Neu-Tool Design Inc 978 658-5881
220 Ballardvale St Ste A Wilmington MA (01887) *(G-17029)*
Neudorfer Inc 802 244-5338
183 Crossett Hl Waterbury VT (05676) *(G-22584)*
Neudorfer Tables, Waterbury *Also called Neudorfer Inc (G-22584)*
Neuform Pharmaceuticals 617 559-9822
450 Lexington St Ste 101 Auburndale MA (02466) *(G-7865)*
Neurasense Inc 618 917-4686
2016 Mass Ave Apt 23 Cambridge MA (02140) *(G-9577)*
Neuraxis LLC 603 912-5306
16 Route 111 Ste 2 Derry NH (03038) *(G-17991)*
Neuro Phage Phrmaceuticals Inc 617 941-7004
222 3rd St Cambridge MA (02142) *(G-9578)*
Neurobo Pharmaceuticals Inc (PA) 617 313-7331
177 Huntington Ave # 1700 Boston MA (02115) *(G-8724)*
Neurobo Therapeutics Inc 617 313-7331
177 Huntington Ave # 1700 Boston MA (02115) *(G-8725)*
Neuroelectrics Corporation 617 390-6447
210 Broadway Ste 2 Cambridge MA (02139) *(G-9579)*
Neurogastrx Incorporated 781 730-4006
600 Unicorn Park Dr Woburn MA (01801) *(G-17240)*
Neurohydrate LLC 203 799-7900
4637 Main St Unit 5 Bridgeport CT (06606) *(G-455)*
Neurologica Corp 978 564-8500
14 Electronics Ave Danvers MA (01923) *(G-10242)*
Neurometrix Inc (PA) 781 890-9989
1000 Winter St Waltham MA (02451) *(G-16159)*
Neuromotion Inc 415 676-9326
200 Portland St Boston MA (02114) *(G-8726)*
Neuromotion Labs, Boston *Also called Neuromotion Inc (G-8726)*
Neutrasafe Corporation 781 616-3951
421 Page St Ste 1 Stoughton MA (02072) *(G-15611)*
Neutron Therapeutics Inc 978 326-8999
1 Industrial Dr Ste 1 # 1 Danvers MA (01923) *(G-10243)*
Nevamar Company LLC (HQ) 203 925-1556
1 Corporate Dr Ste 725 Shelton CT (06484) *(G-3837)*
Nevamar Distributors, Shelton *Also called Nevamar Company LLC (G-3837)*
Nevells Pallet Inc 207 547-4605
97 Pond Rd Sidney ME (04330) *(G-6963)*
Nevron Plastics Inc 781 233-1310
124 Ballard St Saugus MA (01906) *(G-14991)*
Nevron Plastics and Metals, Saugus *Also called Nevron Plastics Inc (G-14991)*
New Age Ems, Norwood *Also called Ppi/Time Zero Inc (G-14188)*
New Age Ems Inc 508 226-6090
527 Pleasant St Attleboro MA (02703) *(G-7772)*
New Age Motorsports LLC 203 268-1999
501 Pepper St Monroe CT (06468) *(G-2410)*
New American Food Products, Methuen *Also called Nafp Inc (G-13038)*
New American Paintings, Boston *Also called Open Studios Press Inc (G-8751)*
New Amtrol Holdings Inc (HQ) 614 438-3210
1400 Division Rd West Warwick RI (02893) *(G-21505)*
New Annex Plating Inc 401 349-0911
9 Warren Ave North Providence RI (02911) *(G-20767)*
New Balance Athletics Inc 207 634-3033
20 Depot St Norridgewock ME (04957) *(G-6499)*
New Balance Athletics Inc 207 474-2042
10 Walnut St Skowhegan ME (04976) *(G-6983)*
New Balance Athletics Inc (HQ) 617 783-4000
100 Guest St Fl 5 Boston MA (02135) *(G-8727)*
New Balance Athletics Inc 978 685-8400
5 S Union St Lawrence MA (01843) *(G-12063)*
New Balance Licensing LLC 800 343-4648
20 Guest St Fl 8 Brighton MA (02135) *(G-9102)*
New Bedford Salchicharia Inc (PA) 508 992-6257
6 Rockdale Ave New Bedford MA (02740) *(G-13420)*
New Bedford Scale Co Inc 508 997-6730
144 Francis St New Bedford MA (02740) *(G-13421)*
New Bedford Thread Co Inc 508 996-8584
10 Howland Rd Fairhaven MA (02719) *(G-10644)*
New Beverage Publications Inc 617 598-1900
55 Clarendon St Ste 1 Boston MA (02116) *(G-8728)*
New Boston Bulletin 603 487-5200
74 Thornton Rd New Boston NH (03070) *(G-19294)*
New Brand Sebsatians LLC 617 624-7999
100 Summer St Boston MA (02110) *(G-8729)*
New Britain Heat Treating Corp 860 223-0684
5 Grant Ave Enfield CT (06082) *(G-1371)*
New Britain Herald , The, New Britain *Also called Central Conn Cmmunications LLC (G-2519)*
New Can Company, Holbrook *Also called New Can Holdings Inc (G-11534)*
New Can Company Inc (HQ) 781 767-1650
1 Mear Rd Holbrook MA (02343) *(G-11533)*
New Can Holdings Inc (PA) 781 767-1650
1 Mear Rd Holbrook MA (02343) *(G-11534)*
New Canaan Advertiser, New Canaan *Also called Hearst Corporation (G-2600)*
New Canaan Forge LLC (PA) 203 966-3858
26 Burtis Ave New Canaan CT (06840) *(G-2610)*
New Canaan Olive Oil LLC 845 240-3294
47 Blachley Rd Stamford CT (06902) *(G-4255)*
New Canaan Stone Service LLC 401 829-8293
2 Deer Run Trl Johnston RI (02919) *(G-20525)*
New Chapter Inc (HQ) 800 543-7279
90 Technology Dr Brattleboro VT (05301) *(G-21739)*
New Charter Distribution, Brattleboro *Also called New Chapter Inc (G-21739)*

A L P H A B E T I C

New Designz Inc 860 384-1809
278 Sanbank Rd Cheshire CT (06410) ***(G-747)***
New England Abrasives 508 893-9540
35 Louis St Holliston MA (01746) ***(G-11589)***
New England Airfoil Pdts Inc 860 677-1376
36 Spring Ln Farmington CT (06032) ***(G-1498)***
New England Alpaca Fiber Pool 508 672-6032
645 Sanford Rd Westport MA (02790) ***(G-16844)***
New England Antiques Journal, Ware *Also called Turley Publications Inc* ***(G-16239)***
New England Apple Products Co, Leominster *Also called Bevovations LLC* ***(G-12118)***
New England Beverages LLC 203 208-4517
137 N Branford Rd Branford CT (06405) ***(G-332)***
New England Blazers 617 448-3709
4 Hickory Ln Saugus MA (01906) ***(G-14992)***
New England Bldg Solutions LLC 603 323-0012
9 Winding Way Scarborough ME (04074) ***(G-6934)***
New England Blinds 508 868-5399
7 Honeycrisp Way Sterling MA (01564) ***(G-15542)***
New England Boring Contractors 860 633-4649
129 Kreiger Ln Ste A Glastonbury CT (06033) ***(G-1566)***
New England Brace Co Inc (PA) 508 588-6060
2 Greenwood Ave Concord NH (03301) ***(G-17916)***
New England Braiding Co Inc 603 669-1987
610 Gold St Manchester NH (03103) ***(G-18883)***
New England Brewing Co LLC 203 387-2222
175 Amity Rd Woodbridge CT (06525) ***(G-5473)***
New England Bride Inc 781 334-6093
29 Durham Dr Lynnfield MA (01940) ***(G-12553)***
New England Bride Magazine, Lynnfield *Also called New England Bride Inc* ***(G-12553)***
New England Bridge Products 781 592-2444
93 Brookline St Lynn MA (01902) ***(G-12527)***
New England Broach Co Inc 413 665-7064
199-A Long Plain Rd Whately MA (01093) ***(G-16907)***
New England Business Media LLC 207 761-8379
48 Free St Ste 109 Portland ME (04101) ***(G-6700)***
New England Business Media LLC (PA) 508 755-8004
172 Shrewsbury St Ste 1 Worcester MA (01604) ***(G-17429)***
New England Business Svc Inc (HQ) 978 448-6111
500 Main St Groton MA (01471) ***(G-11291)***
New England Cabinet Co Inc 860 747-9995
580 E Main St New Britain CT (06051) ***(G-2555)***
New England Cap Company 203 736-6184
756 Derby Ave Seymour CT (06483) ***(G-3758)***
New England Carbide Inc 978 887-0313
428 Boston St Ste A Topsfield MA (01983) ***(G-15863)***
New England Castings LLC 207 642-3029
234 Northeast Rd Ste 2 Standish ME (04084) ***(G-7063)***
New England Chrome Plating 860 528-7176
63 Thomas St East Hartford CT (06108) ***(G-1206)***
New England Clock, North Haven *Also called Bonito Manufacturing Inc* ***(G-3011)***
New England Cm Inc 508 541-1307
31 Hayward St Ste H Franklin MA (02038) ***(G-11069)***
New England Cnc Inc 203 288-8241
46 Manila Ave Hamden CT (06514) ***(G-1775)***
New England Coffee Company, Norwood *Also called New England Partnership Inc* ***(G-14182)***
New England Compounding Center, Boston *Also called New England Compounding Phrm* ***(G-8730)***
New England Compounding Phrm 800 994-6322
100 High St Ste 2400 Boston MA (02110) ***(G-8730)***
New England Computer Svcs Inc 475 221-8200
322 E Main St Branford CT (06405) ***(G-333)***
New England Copperworks 401 232-9899
25 Maple Ave Smithfield RI (02917) ***(G-21240)***
New England Counter Top, Attleboro *Also called Dorie Enterprises Inc* ***(G-7728)***
New England Country Foods LLC 617 682-3650
1 Broadway Ste 12 Cambridge MA (02142) ***(G-9580)***
New England Country Pies LLC 781 596-0176
161b Pleasant St Lynn MA (01901) ***(G-12528)***
New England Crane Inc 207 782-7353
500 Potash Hill Rd Unit 1 Tyngsboro MA (01879) ***(G-15897)***
New England Ctr For Hring Rhab 860 455-1404
354 Hartford Tpke Hampton CT (06247) ***(G-1798)***
New England Custom Wood Wkg 508 991-8038
350 North St New Bedford MA (02740) ***(G-13422)***
New England Custom Woodworking, New Bedford *Also called New England Custom Wood Wkg* ***(G-13422)***
New England Denture Cntr Bangr (PA) 207 941-6550
58 Fruit St Bangor ME (04401) ***(G-5655)***
New England Die Co Inc 203 574-5140
48 Ford Ave Waterbury CT (06708) ***(G-4927)***
New England Die Cutting Inc 978 374-0789
96 Milk St Methuen MA (01844) ***(G-13039)***
New England Distilling Co 207 878-9759
26 Evergreen Dr Portland ME (04103) ***(G-6701)***
New England Drapery & Blind, Woburn *Also called New England Drapery Assoc Inc* ***(G-17241)***
New England Drapery Assoc Inc 781 944-7536
5 Conn St Ste 2 Woburn MA (01801) ***(G-17241)***
New England Drmtlgcal Soc Bret 203 432-0092
333 Cedar St New Haven CT (06510) ***(G-2713)***
New England Eagle Machine Inc 978 874-0017
25 Theodore Dr Ste 3 Westminster MA (01473) ***(G-16811)***
New England Electropolishing 508 672-6616
220 Shove St Fall River MA (02724) ***(G-10737)***
New England Embroidery Company 603 447-3878
Rr 16 Conway NH (03818) ***(G-17956)***
New England Emulsions Corp 508 429-5550
201 Lowland St Holliston MA (01746) ***(G-11590)***
New England Etching Co Inc 413 532-9482
23 Spring St Holyoke MA (01040) ***(G-11643)***
New England Extrusion Inc 413 863-3171
18 Industrial Blvd Turners Falls MA (01376) ***(G-15884)***
New England Fab Mtls Inc 978 466-7823
101 Crawford St Leominster MA (01453) ***(G-12170)***
New England Fast Ferry, New Bedford *Also called Marthas Seastreak Vineyard LLC* ***(G-13416)***
New England Fencewrights Inc 508 999-3337
249 Brownell Ave New Bedford MA (02740) ***(G-13423)***
New England Fiberglass Repair (PA) 203 866-1690
144 Water St Norwalk CT (06854) ***(G-3207)***
New England Filter Co Inc 401 722-8999
560 Mineral Spring Ave 2-123 Pawtucket RI (02860) ***(G-20865)***
New England Filter Company Inc (PA) 203 531-0500
21 S Water St Ste 2a Greenwich CT (06830) ***(G-1633)***
New England Fine Woodworking 860 526-5799
37 Castle View Dr Chester CT (06412) ***(G-773)***
New England Fleece Company 508 678-5550
147 Plymouth Ave Fall River MA (02721) ***(G-10738)***
New England Foam Products LLC (PA) 860 524-0121
760 Windsor St Hartford CT (06120) ***(G-1851)***
New England Fuels & Energy LLC 860 585-5917
86 Allen St Terryville CT (06786) ***(G-4487)***
New England Gen-Connect LLC 617 571-6884
35 Pond Park Rd Ste 11 Hingham MA (02043) ***(G-11507)***
New England Gran Cabinets LLC 860 310-2981
8 Cody St West Hartford CT (06110) ***(G-5087)***
New England Gravel Haulers 508 922-4518
38 Winthrop St Rehoboth MA (02769) ***(G-14754)***
New England Grinding and MA 203 333-1885
30 Radel St Bridgeport CT (06607) ***(G-456)***
New England Home 617 938-3991
530 Harrison Ave Ste 302 Boston MA (02118) ***(G-8731)***
New England Home Magazine, Boston *Also called New England Home* ***(G-8731)***
New England Homes Inc 603 436-8830
277 Locust St Dover NH (03820) ***(G-18038)***
New England Image & Print Inc 401 769-3708
585 Smithfield Rd North Smithfield RI (02896) ***(G-20793)***
New England Immunology Assoc 781 863-5774
217 Concord Ave Lexington MA (02421) ***(G-12249)***
New England Indus Coatings 508 754-1066
50 Lagrange St Worcester MA (01610) ***(G-17430)***
New England Industries Inc 603 448-5330
85 Etna Rd Lebanon NH (03766) ***(G-18633)***
New England Innovations Corp 603 742-6247
4 Progress Dr Dover NH (03820) ***(G-18039)***
New England Installations, Pembroke *Also called Dolly Plow Inc* ***(G-14400)***
New England Joinery Works Inc 860 767-3377
19 Bokum Rd Essex CT (06426) ***(G-1404)***
New England Journal Medicine, Waltham *Also called Massachusetts Medical Society* ***(G-16148)***
New England Journal Medicine, Boston *Also called Massachusetts Medical Society* ***(G-8685)***
New England Keyboard Inc 978 345-8332
1 Princeton Rd Ste 1 # 1 Fitchburg MA (01420) ***(G-10843)***
New England Kitchen Design Ctr 203 268-2626
401 Monroe Tpke Ste 4 Monroe CT (06468) ***(G-2411)***
New England Laser Inc 978 587-3914
1 Centennial Dr Ste 1 # 1 Peabody MA (01960) ***(G-14356)***
New England Low Vision, Worcester *Also called Lets Go Technology Inc* ***(G-17407)***
New England Materials LLC 203 261-5500
64 Cambridge Dr Monroe CT (06468) ***(G-2412)***
New England Metalform Inc 508 695-9340
380 South St Plainville MA (02762) ***(G-14530)***
New England Nautical LLC 603 601-3166
1950 Lafayette Rd Ste 200 Portsmouth NH (03801) ***(G-19598)***
New England Newspapers Inc 401 722-4000
2 Dexter St Ste 2 # 2 Pawtucket RI (02860) ***(G-20866)***
New England Newspapers Inc 802 254-2311
62 Black Mountain Rd Brattleboro VT (05301) ***(G-21740)***
New England Newspapers Inc (HQ) 413 447-7311
75 S Church St Ste L1 Pittsfield MA (01201) ***(G-14496)***
New England Nonwovens LLC 203 891-0851
283 Dogburn Rd West Haven CT (06516) ***(G-5137)***
New England Olive Oil Company 978 610-6776
191 Sudbury Rd Concord MA (01742) ***(G-10146)***

New England Ortho Neuro LLC 203 200-7228
2080 Whitney Ave Ste 290 Hamden CT (06518) ***(G-1776)***
New England Orthopedics Inc (PA) 401 739-9838
220 Toll Gate Rd Ste A Warwick RI (02886) ***(G-21396)***
New England Orthotic & Prost 508 890-8808
405 Grove St Ste 2 Worcester MA (01605) ***(G-17431)***
New England Orthotic & Prost 203 634-7566
61 Pomeroy Ave Unit 2a Meriden CT (06450) ***(G-2112)***
New England Outdoor Wood Pdts, Methuen *Also called Jobart Inc* ***(G-13029)***
New England Outerwear 207 240-3069
550 Lisbon St Lewiston ME (04240) ***(G-6311)***
New England Overseas Corp 401 722-3800
358 Lowden St Pawtucket RI (02860) ***(G-20867)***
New England Pallets Skids Inc 413 583-6628
250 West St Ludlow MA (01056) ***(G-12473)***
New England Paper Tube Co Inc 401 725-2610
200 Conant St Pawtucket RI (02860) ***(G-20868)***
New England Partnership Inc 800 225-3537
30 Walpole St Norwood MA (02062) ***(G-14182)***
New England Peptide Inc 978 630-0020
65 Zub Ln Gardner MA (01440) ***(G-11121)***
New England Pet Distr Ctr LLC 781 937-3600
268 W Cummings Park Woburn MA (01801) ***(G-17242)***
New England Photoconductor 508 285-5561
253 Mansfield Ave Norton MA (02766) ***(G-14084)***
New England Plasma Dev Corp 860 928-6561
14 Highland Dr Putnam CT (06260) ***(G-3621)***
New England Plastics Corp (PA) 781 933-6004
310 Salem St Ste 2 Woburn MA (01801) ***(G-17243)***
New England Plastics Corp 508 995-7334
126 Duchaine Blvd New Bedford MA (02745) ***(G-13424)***
New England Pottery, Taunton *Also called Central Garden & Pet Company* ***(G-15735)***
New England Precision Inc 800 293-4112
281 Beanville Rd Randolph VT (05060) ***(G-22299)***
New England Printing LLC 860 745-3600
1 Anngina Dr Enfield CT (06082) ***(G-1372)***
New England Printing Corp 603 431-0142
599 Lafayette Rd Ste 4 Portsmouth NH (03801) ***(G-19599)***
New England Prtzel Popcorn Inc 978 687-0342
15 Bay State Rd Lawrence MA (01841) ***(G-12064)***
New England Publishing Group, Swansea *Also called New England RE Bulltin* ***(G-15710)***
New England RE Bulltin 508 675-8884
1610 Gar Hwy Swansea MA (02777) ***(G-15710)***
New England Real Estate Jurnl, Norwell *Also called East Coast Publications Inc* ***(G-14102)***
New England Runner 781 987-1730
320 Washington St Norwell MA (02061) ***(G-14108)***
New England Salt Co LLC 207 262-9779
500 Odlin Rd Bangor ME (04401) ***(G-5656)***
New England Sand & Gravel Co 508 877-2460
Corner Danforth & Birch Framingham MA (01701) ***(G-10987)***
New England Scenic LLC 781 562-1792
8 Carver Cir Canton MA (02021) ***(G-9762)***
New England Sheets LLC (PA) 978 487-2500
36 Saratoga Blvd Devens MA (01434) ***(G-10326)***
New England Shirt Co LLC 508 672-2223
657 Quarry St 33 Fall River MA (02723) ***(G-10739)***
New England Shoulder Elbow Soc 860 679-6600
232 Farmington Ave Farmington CT (06030) ***(G-1499)***
New England Showcase, Brattleboro *Also called Howard Printing Inc* ***(G-21733)***
New England Shrlines Companies 781 826-0140
704 Washington St Pembroke MA (02359) ***(G-14418)***
New England Sign Group Inc 508 832-3471
33 Arctic St Worcester MA (01604) ***(G-17432)***
New England Signs & Awngs LLC 603 235-7205
315 Derry Rd Ste 3 Hudson NH (03051) ***(G-18420)***
New England Small Tube Corp 603 429-1600
480 Charles Bancroft Hwy # 3 Litchfield NH (03052) ***(G-18652)***
New England Smoked Seafood 802 773-4628
46 Hazel St Rutland VT (05701) ***(G-22346)***
New England Solar Hot Wtr Inc 781 536-8633
54 Corporate Park Dr # 510 Pembroke MA (02359) ***(G-14419)***
New England Solid Surfaces, Hudson *Also called Daniel Preston* ***(G-18383)***
New England Spt Ventures LLC 617 267-9440
4 Jersey St Boston MA (02215) ***(G-8732)***
New England Stained Glass 508 699-6965
478 Old Post Rd North Attleboro MA (02760) ***(G-13769)***
New England Stair Company Inc 203 924-0606
1 White St Shelton CT (06484) ***(G-3838)***
New England Standard Corp 203 876-7733
16 Honey St Milford CT (06461) ***(G-2320)***
New England Stone Industries, Smithfield *Also called Georgia Stone Industries Inc* ***(G-21227)***
New England Sugars LLC 508 792-3801
1120 Millbury St Worcester MA (01607) ***(G-17433)***
New England Tape Co, Hudson *Also called Netco Extruded Plastics Inc* ***(G-11795)***
New England Technology Group 617 864-5551
1 Davenport St Ste 1 # 1 Cambridge MA (02140) ***(G-9581)***
New England Tile & Stone Inc 914 481-4488
85 Old Long Ridge Rd # 2 Stamford CT (06903) ***(G-4256)***
New England Time Solutions Inc 888 222-3396
112 E Longmeadow Rd Fl 2 Hampden MA (01036) ***(G-11322)***
New England Tool & Automtn Inc 860 827-9389
321 Ellis St Ste 17 New Britain CT (06051) ***(G-2556)***
New England Tooling Inc 800 866-5105
145 Chestnut Hill Rd Killingworth CT (06419) ***(G-1928)***
New England Trads Cstm Mllwrks, Gorham *Also called B & T Millworks* ***(G-6109)***
New England Traffic Solutions, Glastonbury *Also called Gac Inc* ***(G-1553)***
New England Traveling Wire LLC 860 223-6297
162 Whiting St New Britain CT (06051) ***(G-2557)***
New England Ultimate Finishing 413 532-7777
709 Main St Holyoke MA (01040) ***(G-11644)***
New England Vlts Monuments LLC 603 449-2165
8 Laurel Ln Milan NH (03588) ***(G-19041)***
New England Water Jet Cutting 508 993-9235
84 Gifford St New Bedford MA (02744) ***(G-13425)***
New England Water Systems, Nashua *Also called Richard Arikian* ***(G-19253)***
New England Welding Inc 508 580-2024
145 Bodwell St Avon MA (02322) ***(G-7891)***
New England Wheelchair Spt Inc 508 785-0393
20 Haven St Dover MA (02030) ***(G-10351)***
New England Wheels Inc (PA) 978 663-9724
33 Manning Rd Billerica MA (01821) ***(G-8267)***
New England Whlchair Athc Assn 781 830-8751
3 Randolph St Canton MA (02021) ***(G-9763)***
New England Wire Products Inc (PA) 800 254-9473
9 Mohawk Dr Leominster MA (01453) ***(G-12171)***
New England Wire Tech Corp (HQ) 603 838-6624
130 N Main St Lisbon NH (03585) ***(G-18650)***
New England Wirecloth Co LLC 978 343-4998
123 Kelly Ave Fitchburg MA (01420) ***(G-10844)***
New England Wood Products LLC 401 789-7474
535 Liberty Ln West Kingston RI (02892) ***(G-21469)***
New England Wood Systems, Amesbury *Also called George Dawe* ***(G-7486)***
New England Woodcraft Inc 802 247-8211
481 North St Brandon VT (05733) ***(G-21712)***
New England Wooden Ware Corp (PA) 978 632-3600
205 School St Ste 201 Gardner MA (01440) ***(G-11122)***
New England Woodworking Co, Middletown *Also called Igitt Inc* ***(G-20621)***
New England Woodworks 207 324-6343
10 Coleco Ln Springvale ME (04083) ***(G-7054)***
New England Worldwide Export 617 472-0251
247 Water St Quincy MA (02169) ***(G-14642)***
New Fairfield Press Inc 203 746-2700
3 Dunham Dr New Fairfield CT (06812) ***(G-2626)***
New Frontier Advisors LLC (PA) 617 482-1433
155 Federal St Ste 1000 Boston MA (02110) ***(G-8733)***
New Gen Industries 207 400-1928
10 Native Way Cumberland Center ME (04021) ***(G-5930)***
New Generation Research Inc 617 573-9550
88 Broad St Fl 2 Boston MA (02110) ***(G-8734)***
New Hampshire Bindery Inc 603 224-0441
81 Dow Rd Bow NH (03304) ***(G-17723)***
New Hampshire Boring Inc 508 584-8201
1215 W Chestnut St Brockton MA (02301) ***(G-9169)***
New Hampshire Forge Inc 603 357-5692
15 Forge St Keene NH (03431) ***(G-18520)***
New Hampshire Industries, Claremont *Also called Cascaded Purchase Holdings Inc* ***(G-17841)***
New Hampshire Machine Products 603 772-4404
10 Kingston Rd Exeter NH (03833) ***(G-18125)***
New Hampshire Optical Sys Inc 603 391-2909
10 N Southwood Dr Nashua NH (03063) ***(G-19215)***
New Hampshire Plastics LLC 603 669-8523
1 Bouchard St Manchester NH (03103) ***(G-18884)***
New Hampshire Prcsn Metal, Londonderry *Also called Nhp Stratham Inc* ***(G-18728)***
New Hampshire Precision Met (PA) 603 668-6777
15 Industrial Dr Londonderry NH (03053) ***(G-18727)***
New Hampshire Print Mail Svcs, Concord *Also called Argyle Associates Inc* ***(G-17883)***
New Hampshire Prosthetics LLC 603 294-0010
30 International Dr # 201 Portsmouth NH (03801) ***(G-19600)***
New Hampshire Stamping Co Inc 603 641-1234
9 Lance Ln Ste 2 Goffstown NH (03045) ***(G-18206)***
New Hampshire Stl Erectors Inc 603 668-3464
17 Lamy Dr Goffstown NH (03045) ***(G-18207)***
New Hampshire Union Leader, Manchester *Also called Union Leader Corporation* ***(G-18944)***
New Hampshirecom 603 314-0447
1662 Elm St Ste 100 Manchester NH (03101) ***(G-18885)***
New Hartford Industrial Park 860 379-8506
37 Greenwoods Rd New Hartford CT (06057) ***(G-2643)***
New Haven Awning Co, New Haven *Also called B and G Enterprise LLC* ***(G-2663)***
New Haven Chlor-Alkali LLC 203 772-3350
73 Welton St New Haven CT (06511) ***(G-2714)***
New Haven Companies Inc 203 469-6421
41 Washington Ave East Haven CT (06512) ***(G-1257)***
New Haven Naturopathic Center 203 387-8661
14 Judwin Ave New Haven CT (06515) ***(G-2715)***
New Haven Register LLC 203 789-5200
100 Gando Dr New Haven CT (06513) ***(G-2716)***

ALPHABETIC

New Haven Sheet Metal Co....203 468-0341
42 Foxon St New Haven CT (06513) ***(G-2717)***
New Haven Sign Company....203 484-2777
1831 Middletown Ave Northford CT (06472) ***(G-3091)***
New Hmpshire Ball Bearings Inc (HQ)....603 924-3311
175 Jaffrey Rd Peterborough NH (03458) ***(G-19478)***
New Hmpshire Ball Bearings Inc....603 524-0004
155 Lexington Dr Laconia NH (03246) ***(G-18577)***
New Hmpshire Ball Bearings Inc....603 924-3311
175 Jaffrey Rd Peterborough NH (03458) ***(G-19479)***
New Hmpshire Stl Fbrcators Inc....603 668-3464
17 Lamy Dr Goffstown NH (03045) ***(G-18208)***
New Horizon Machine Co Inc....203 316-9355
36 Ludlow St Stamford CT (06902) ***(G-4257)***
New Hrizons EMB Screenprinting....802 651-9801
5 Laurette Dr Essex Junction VT (05452) ***(G-21952)***
New Leaf Pharmaceutical....203 270-4167
77 S Main St Newtown CT (06470) ***(G-2930)***
New Life Logging....802 767-9142
440 Clay Hill Rd Rochester VT (05767) ***(G-22319)***
New Line USA Inc....860 498-0347
247 Brigham Tavern Rd Coventry CT (06238) ***(G-837)***
New London Printing Co LLC....860 701-9171
147 State St Ste 1 New London CT (06320) ***(G-2775)***
New Machine Products LLC....203 790-5520
81 Beaver Brook Rd Ste B Danbury CT (06810) ***(G-959)***
New Market Press Inc....802 388-6397
16 Creek Rd Ste 5a Middlebury VT (05753) ***(G-22115)***
New Mass Media Inc....860 241-3617
285 Broad St Hartford CT (06115) ***(G-1852)***
New Method Plating Co Inc....508 754-2671
43 Hammond St Worcester MA (01610) ***(G-17434)***
New Milford Block & Supply....860 355-1101
574 Danbury Rd New Milford CT (06776) ***(G-2816)***
New Milford Commission....860 354-3758
123 West St New Milford CT (06776) ***(G-2817)***
New Milford Farms Inc....860 210-0250
60 Boardman Rd New Milford CT (06776) ***(G-2818)***
New Milfrd Water Pollutn Cntrl, New Milford *Also called New Milford Commission* ***(G-2817)***
New Objective Inc....781 933-9560
2 Constitution Way Woburn MA (01801) ***(G-17244)***
New Page Books, Newburyport *Also called Career Press Inc* ***(G-13477)***
New Precision Technology LLC....800 243-4565
98 Fort Path Rd Ste B Madison CT (06443) ***(G-1969)***
New Resources Group Inc....203 366-1000
955 Conn Ave Ste 1211 Bridgeport CT (06607) ***(G-457)***
New Tech Replacement Part Co, Bristol *Also called Rgd Technologies Corp* ***(G-605)***
New Tek Design Group Inc....508 835-4544
18 Worcester St West Boylston MA (01583) ***(G-16423)***
New Valence Robotics Corp....857 529-6397
12 Channel St Ste 601 Boston MA (02210) ***(G-8735)***
New Wave Surgical Corp....954 796-4126
555 Long Wharf Dr Fl 2 New Haven CT (06511) ***(G-2718)***
New York Accessory Group Inc....401 245-6096
500 Wood St Unit 21 Bristol RI (02809) ***(G-20095)***
New York Bagel Co, Fall River *Also called Ginsco Inc* ***(G-10704)***
New York Bagel Co, North Dartmouth *Also called Ginsco Inc* ***(G-13921)***
New York Graphic Society, Norwalk *Also called Portfolio Arts Group Ltd* ***(G-3222)***
New-Com Metal Products Corp....781 767-7520
29 Teed Dr Randolph MA (02368) ***(G-14691)***
New-Indy Cntinerboard Hold LLC (HQ)....508 384-4230
5100 Jurupa St Foxboro MA (02035) ***(G-10894)***
Newark America, Fitchburg *Also called Caraustar Industries Inc* ***(G-10819)***
Newbama Steel Inc....603 382-2261
213 Haverhill Rd East Kingston NH (03827) ***(G-18089)***
Newberry Enterprise....207 892-8596
18 Swett Rd Windham ME (04062) ***(G-7244)***
Newbo Interiors, Manchester *Also called Nouveau Interiors LLC* ***(G-18889)***
Newbury Port Meritown Society....978 834-0050
459 Main St Amesbury MA (01913) ***(G-7501)***
Newbury Port Olive Oil, West Newbury *Also called Andaluna Enterprises Inc* ***(G-16489)***
Newcarb, Topsfield *Also called New England Carbide Inc* ***(G-15863)***
Newcastle Systems Inc....781 935-3450
73 Ward Hill Ave Haverhill MA (01835) ***(G-11455)***
Newco Condenser Inc....475 882-4000
40 Waterview Dr Shelton CT (06484) ***(G-3839)***
Newco Lighting Inc (HQ)....475 882-4000
40 Waterview Dr Shelton CT (06484) ***(G-3840)***
Newcomb Spring Corp....860 621-0111
235 Spring St Southington CT (06489) ***(G-4067)***
Newcomb Springs Connecticut....860 621-0111
235 Spring St Southington CT (06489) ***(G-4068)***
Newcorr Packaging Inc....508 393-9256
66 Lyman St Northborough MA (01532) ***(G-14040)***
Newedge Signal Solutions LLC....978 425-5400
323 W Main St Ste 1 Ayer MA (01432) ***(G-7929)***
Newell Brands Inc....413 526-5150
301 Chestnut St East Longmeadow MA (01028) ***(G-10484)***
Newfab, Auburn *Also called North E Wldg & Fabrication Inc* ***(G-5583)***
Newfound Wood Works Inc (PA)....603 744-6872
67 Danforth Brook Rd Bristol NH (03222) ***(G-17768)***
Newhall Labs, Stamford *Also called Golden Sun Inc* ***(G-4200)***
Newhart Plastics Inc....203 877-5367
10 Furniture Row Milford CT (06460) ***(G-2321)***
Newjen Corp....413 543-4888
488 Tea St Charlemont MA (01339) ***(G-9821)***
Newly Weds Foods Inc....617 926-7600
70 Grove St 80 Watertown MA (02472) ***(G-16303)***
Newman Associates, Canton *Also called Westwood Systems Inc* ***(G-9795)***
Newman Enterprises Inc....508 875-7446
280 Worcester Rd Ste 118 Framingham MA (01702) ***(G-10988)***
Newman's Own Organics, Westport *Also called Newmans Own Inc* ***(G-5218)***
Newmans Own Inc (PA)....203 222-0136
1 Morningside Dr N Ste 1 # 1 Westport CT (06880) ***(G-5218)***
Newmark Medical Components Inc....203 753-1158
2670 S Main St Waterbury CT (06706) ***(G-4928)***
Newmarket Sand & Gravel, Newmarket *Also called Chick Trucking Inc* ***(G-19331)***
Newmarket Software Systems....603 436-7500
75 Nh Ave Ste 300 Portsmouth NH (03801) ***(G-19601)***
Newmind Robotics LLC....239 322-2997
44 Royal Crest Dr Apt 6 North Andover MA (01845) ***(G-13719)***
Newmont Slate Co Inc (PA)....802 645-0203
720 Vt Route 149 West Pawlet VT (05775) ***(G-22612)***
Newport Concrete Block Co....603 863-1540
187 S Main St Newport NH (03773) ***(G-19351)***
Newport Corporation....508 553-5035
8 Forge Pkwy Ste 2 Franklin MA (02038) ***(G-11070)***
Newport Corporation....978 296-1306
90 Industrial Way Wilmington MA (01887) ***(G-17030)***
Newport Creamery LLC....401 946-4000
35 Sockanosset Cross Rd Cranston RI (02920) ***(G-20268)***
Newport Daily News, The, Middletown *Also called Lmg Rhode Island Holdings Inc* ***(G-20624)***
Newport Electric Corporation....401 293-0527
200 Highpoint Ave Ste B5 Portsmouth RI (02871) ***(G-20930)***
Newport Electronics, Norwalk *Also called Omega Engineering Inc* ***(G-3212)***
Newport Furniture Parts Corp....802 334-5428
450 Main St Newport VT (05855) ***(G-22203)***
Newport Indus Fabrication Inc....207 368-4344
445 Elm St Newport ME (04953) ***(G-6485)***
Newport Jerky Company....347 913-6882
116 Meadow St Carver MA (02330) ***(G-9805)***
Newport Life Magazine Inc....401 841-0200
272 Valley Rd 2 Middletown RI (02842) ***(G-20627)***
Newport Rocking Chair Center, Newport *Also called Newport Furniture Parts Corp* ***(G-22203)***
Newport Sand & Gravel Co Inc....802 868-4119
1st St Swanton VT (05488) ***(G-22532)***
Newport Sand & Gravel Co Inc (PA)....603 298-0199
8 Reeds Mill Rd Newport NH (03773) ***(G-19352)***
Newport Sand & Gravel Co Inc....603 924-1999
399 Jaffrey Rd Peterborough NH (03458) ***(G-19480)***
Newport Sand & Gravel Co Inc....802 728-5055
37 Central St Randolph VT (05060) ***(G-22300)***
Newport Sand & Gravel Co Inc....802 328-3384
429 Breault Rd Guildhall VT (05905) ***(G-22006)***
Newport Sand & Gravel Co Inc....603 826-4444
368 Springfield Rd Charlestown NH (03603) ***(G-17817)***
Newport Sand & Gravel Co Inc....802 334-2000
2014 Alderbrook Rd Newport VT (05855) ***(G-22204)***
Newport Sand and Gravel, Newport *Also called Carroll Concrete Co Inc* ***(G-19343)***
Newport Storm Brewery, Newport *Also called Coastal Extreme Brewing Co LLC* ***(G-20660)***
Newport Tool & Die Inc....401 847-6711
1219 Aquidneck Ave Middletown RI (02842) ***(G-20628)***
Newport Wire & Cable, Warren *Also called Charter Industries Inc* ***(G-21293)***
Newprint Offset Inc....781 891-6002
405 Waltham St Lexington MA (02421) ***(G-12250)***
Newpro Designs Inc (HQ)....781 762-4477
90 Kerry Pl Ste 5 Norwood MA (02062) ***(G-14183)***
News & Sentinel Inc....603 237-5501
6 Bridge St Colebrook NH (03576) ***(G-17874)***
News 12 Connecticut....203 849-1321
28 Cross St Norwalk CT (06851) ***(G-3208)***
News and Citizen Inc....802 888-2212
417 Brooklyn St Morrisville VT (05661) ***(G-22175)***
News Gazette, Everett *Also called Leader Publishing Co Inc* ***(G-10615)***
News Star Inc....401 567-7077
170 Pascoag Main St Pascoag RI (02859) ***(G-20803)***
News Times....203 744-5100
333 Main St Danbury CT (06810) ***(G-960)***
Newsbank Inc....203 966-1100
58 Pine St Ste 1 New Canaan CT (06840) ***(G-2611)***
Newspaper Space Buyers....203 967-6452
149 Rowayton Ave Ste 2 Norwalk CT (06853) ***(G-3209)***
Newspapers New England Inc (PA)....603 224-5301
1 Monitor Dr Concord NH (03301) ***(G-17917)***
Newspapers of Massachusetts....978 544-2118
14 Hope St Greenfield MA (01301) ***(G-11270)***
Newspapers of New Hampshire (HQ)....603 224-5301
1 Monitor Dr Concord NH (03301) ***(G-17918)***

Newspapers of New Hampshire ... 603 924-7172
20 Grove St Peterborough NH (03458) ***(G-19481)***
Newstamp Lighting Corp ... 508 238-7073
227 Bay Rd North Easton MA (02356) ***(G-13949)***
Newstamp Lighting Co, North Easton *Also called Newstamp Lighting Corp* ***(G-13949)***
Newstress Inc ... 603 736-9000
1640 Dover Rd Epsom NH (03234) ***(G-18107)***
Newtec America Inc ... 203 323-0042
1055 Washington Blvd Fl 6 Stamford CT (06901) ***(G-4258)***
Newton Laboratories Inc ... 617 484-7003
10 Meadows Ln Belmont MA (02478) ***(G-8078)***
Newton Scientific Inc ... 617 354-9469
529 Main St Ste 600 Charlestown MA (02129) ***(G-9840)***
Newton-Wellesley Health Care ... 617 726-2142
2014 Washington St Newton MA (02462) ***(G-13618)***
Newtown Sports Group ... 508 341-1238
15 Anthony Ridge Rd Newtown CT (06470) ***(G-2931)***
Newtron Inc ... 617 969-1100
132 Charles St Ste 201 Auburndale MA (02466) ***(G-7866)***
Nexcelom Bioscience LLC ... 978 327-5340
360 Merrimack St Ste 47 Lawrence MA (01843) ***(G-12065)***
Nexprene, Shirley *Also called Tpe Solutions Inc* ***(G-15096)***
Next Event Corporation ... 401 683-0070
3390 E Main Rd Unit 1 Portsmouth RI (02871) ***(G-20931)***
Next Step Bnics Prsthetics Inc (PA) ... 603 668-3831
155 Dow St Ste 200 Manchester NH (03101) ***(G-18886)***
Nextcea Inc ... 800 225-1645
600 W Cummings Park # 6375 Woburn MA (01801) ***(G-17245)***
Nextchar LLC ... 877 582-1825
99 Pulpit Hill Rd Amherst MA (01002) ***(G-7520)***
Nextec Applications Inc (PA) ... 203 661-1484
11 Turner Dr Greenwich CT (06831) ***(G-1634)***
Nextek Inc ... 978 577-6214
2 Park Dr Ste 1 Westford MA (01886) ***(G-16781)***
Nextgen Adhesive, Burlington *Also called Ngac LLC* ***(G-9309)***
Nexthink Inc ... 617 576-2005
294 Washington St Ste 510 Boston MA (02108) ***(G-8736)***
Nextmove Technologies LLC ... 603 654-1280
1 Kerk St Hollis NH (03049) ***(G-18335)***
Nexus Energyguide, Wellesley *Also called Aclara Software Inc* ***(G-16356)***
Nexus Print Group Inc ... 617 429-9666
49 Westvale Rd Milton MA (02186) ***(G-13197)***
Nexus Technology Inc ... 877 595-8116
78 Northastern Blvd Ste 2 Nashua NH (03062) ***(G-19216)***
Nexvac Inc (PA) ... 603 887-0015
56 Giordani Ln Sandown NH (03873) ***(G-19786)***
Nexvue Information Systems Inc ... 203 327-0800
65 Broad St Stamford CT (06901) ***(G-4259)***
Neyra Industries Inc ... 860 289-4359
239 Sullivan Ave South Windsor CT (06074) ***(G-3995)***
Nfa Corp ... 401 333-8947
50 Martin St Cumberland RI (02864) ***(G-20331)***
Nfa Corp ... 401 333-8990
50 Martin St Cumberland RI (02864) ***(G-20332)***
Nfa Corp ... 401 333-8990
50 Martin St Cumberland RI (02864) ***(G-20333)***
Nfa Corp ... 401 333-8990
50 Martin St Cumberland RI (02864) ***(G-20334)***
Nfi LLC ... 508 998-9021
213 Theodore Rice Blvd New Bedford MA (02745) ***(G-13426)***
Ngac LLC ... 781 258-0008
25 B St Burlington MA (01803) ***(G-9309)***
Ngraver Company ... 860 823-1533
67 Wawecus Hill Rd Bozrah CT (06334) ***(G-283)***
NH Rapid Machining LLC ... 603 821-5200
22 Charron Ave Nashua NH (03063) ***(G-19217)***
NH Signs, Auburn *Also called Indaba Holdings Corp* ***(G-17611)***
NH Woodworks LLC ... 603 361-4727
70 Powers St Milford NH (03055) ***(G-19071)***
Nhbb, Peterborough *Also called New Hmpshire Ball Bearings Inc* ***(G-19478)***
Nhp Stratham Inc ... 603 668-6777
15 Industrial Dr Londonderry NH (03053) ***(G-18728)***
Nhrc LLC ... 603 485-2248
415 4th Range Rd Pembroke NH (03275) ***(G-19459)***
Nhrpa ... 603 340-5583
172 Pembroke Rd Concord NH (03301) ***(G-17919)***
Nhv America Inc ... 978 682-4900
100 Griffin Brook Dr Methuen MA (01844) ***(G-13040)***
Niagara Bottling LLC ... 909 226-7353
380 Woodland Ave Bloomfield CT (06002) ***(G-245)***
Niagara Cutter Athol Inc ... 978 249-2788
273 Main St Athol MA (01331) ***(G-7691)***
Niantic Awning & Sunroom Co, Niantic *Also called Niantic Awning Company* ***(G-2954)***
Niantic Awning Company ... 860 739-0161
193 Pennsylvania Ave Niantic CT (06357) ***(G-2954)***
Niantic Seal Inc ... 401 334-6870
17 Powder Hill Rd Lincoln RI (02865) ***(G-20588)***
Niantic Seal Nrtheast Rbr Pdts, Lincoln *Also called Niantic Seal Inc* ***(G-20588)***
Niantic Tool Inc ... 860 739-2182
32 Industrial Park Rd Niantic CT (06357) ***(G-2955)***
Nibmor Inc ... 207 502-7540
10 W Point Ln Biddeford ME (04005) ***(G-5752)***
Nibr, Cambridge *Also called Novartis Inst For Biomedical R* ***(G-9590)***
Niche Inc ... 508 990-4202
57 Cove St New Bedford MA (02744) ***(G-13427)***
Nicholas Brealey North America, Boston *Also called Nicholas Brealey Pubg Inc* ***(G-8737)***
Nicholas Brealey Pubg Inc ... 617 523-3801
20 Park Plz Ste 610 Boston MA (02116) ***(G-8737)***
Nichols Candies Inc ... 978 283-9850
1 Crafts Rd Gloucester MA (01930) ***(G-11197)***
Nichols Custom Welding Inc ... 207 645-3101
128 Weld Rd Ste 2 Wilton ME (04294) ***(G-7227)***
Nichols Development, Wilton *Also called Nichols Custom Welding Inc* ***(G-7227)***
Nichols Portland LLC (PA) ... 207 774-6121
2400 Congress St Portland ME (04102) ***(G-6702)***
Nichols Woodworking LLC (PA) ... 860 350-4223
136 Walker Brook Rd S Washington Depot CT (06794) ***(G-4833)***
Nicholsons, Wallingford *Also called Corru Seals Inc* ***(G-4728)***
Nickel Corporaxion ... 401 351-6555
836 Hope St Providence RI (02906) ***(G-21077)***
Nickerson Stonecrafters of Cao ... 508 255-8600
300 Rt 6a Orleans MA (02653) ***(G-14238)***
Nickle Creek Vineyard LLC ... 401 369-3694
12 King Rd Foster RI (02825) ***(G-20458)***
Nickson Industries Inc ... 860 747-1671
336 Woodford Ave Plainville CT (06062) ***(G-3509)***
Nicmar Industries ... 207 324-6571
192 Biddeford Rd Alfred ME (04002) ***(G-5516)***
Nicols Brothers Inc ... 207 364-7032
29 Industrial Park Rd Rumford ME (04276) ***(G-6840)***
Nicols Brothers Logging Inc ... 207 364-8685
197 Poplar Hill Rd Mexico ME (04257) ***(G-6428)***
Nidec America Corporation ... 860 653-2144
16 International Dr East Granby CT (06026) ***(G-1136)***
Nightsea, Bedford *Also called Blueline NDT LLC* ***(G-7963)***
Nihon Khden Innovation Ctr Inc ... 617 318-5904
237 Putnam Ave Cambridge MA (02139) ***(G-9582)***
Nike Inc ... 413 243-1861
530 Prime Outlets Blvd Lee MA (01238) ***(G-12093)***
Nike Inc ... 781 564-9929
25 Corporate Dr Ste 360 Burlington MA (01803) ***(G-9310)***
Nikel Precision Group LLC ... 207 282-6080
419 Hill St Biddeford ME (04005) ***(G-5753)***
Nikotrack LLC ... 401 683-7525
300 Highpoint Ave Ste 1b Portsmouth RI (02871) ***(G-20932)***
Nilsen Canvas Products ... 207 797-4863
212 Warren Ave Portland ME (04103) ***(G-6703)***
Nimbus Lakshmi Inc ... 857 999-2009
130 Prospect St Ste 301 Cambridge MA (02139) ***(G-9583)***
Nine Dragons Paper - Rumford, Rumford *Also called ND Paper Inc* ***(G-6838)***
Nine West Holdings Inc ... 860 669-3799
20 Killingworth Tpke # 125 Clinton CT (06413) ***(G-791)***
Ninepoint Medical Inc ... 617 250-7190
12 Oak Park Dr Ste 2 Bedford MA (01730) ***(G-7994)***
Ninos Ironworks ... 617 389-6603
57 Kelvin St Everett MA (02149) ***(G-10623)***
Ninth Sense Inc ... 617 835-4472
8 Saint Marys St Ste 611 Boston MA (02215) ***(G-8738)***
Nippon American Limited ... 401 885-7353
3 Cedar Rock Mdws East Greenwich RI (02818) ***(G-20374)***
Niro Companies LLC ... 860 982-5645
100 Harding St Berlin CT (06037) ***(G-98)***
Nirogyone Therapeutics LLC ... 508 439-2197
10 Laurel Ave Northborough MA (01532) ***(G-14041)***
Nirvana Chocolates, Milton *Also called Belgiums Chocolate Source Inc* ***(G-13190)***
Nishi Enterprises Inc ... 603 749-0113
442 Central Ave Dover NH (03820) ***(G-18040)***
Nissin Ion Equipment Usa Inc ... 978 362-2590
34 Sullivan Rd North Billerica MA (01862) ***(G-13849)***
Nitefighter International ... 603 367-4741
114 High St Silver Lake NH (03875) ***(G-19824)***
Nitor Corp ... 413 998-0510
5 Whalley Way Southwick MA (01077) ***(G-15416)***
Nitrotap Ltd ... 401 247-2141
100 Child St Warren RI (02885) ***(G-21299)***
Nitto Denko Avecia Inc (HQ) ... 508 532-2500
125 Fortune Blvd Milford MA (01757) ***(G-13131)***
Nix Inc ... 617 458-9407
114 Western Ave Allston MA (02134) ***(G-7472)***
Nixie Sparkling Water LLC ... 617 784-8671
149 Cross St Chatham MA (02633) ***(G-9861)***
Nixon Company Inc ... 413 543-3701
161 Main St Indian Orchard MA (01151) ***(G-11890)***
Nixon Machine, Wilton *Also called Robert Nixon* ***(G-19985)***
Njf Packaging Enterprise ... 508 428-1255
245 Westwind Cir Osterville MA (02655) ***(G-14249)***

A L P H A B E T I C

Njm Packaging LLC (HQ) 603 448-0300
77 Bank St Lebanon NH (03766) ***(G-18634)***
Nmg, Plaistow *Also called Plaistow Cabinet Co Inc* ***(G-19520)***
Nmi, Wellesley *Also called Nemucore Med Innovations Inc* ***(G-16375)***
Nntechnology Moore Systems LLC 203 366-3224
800 Union Ave Bridgeport CT (06607) ***(G-458)***
No 7 Sand & Gravel, North Sullivan *Also called Jerome Martin Paul* ***(G-6513)***
No Butts Bin Company Inc 203 245-5924
16 Birch Ln Madison CT (06443) ***(G-1970)***
Noack Organ Company Inc 978 352-6266
36 W Main St Georgetown MA (01833) ***(G-11147)***
Noah Publications 207 359-2131
751 Rich Rd Brooklin ME (04616) ***(G-5821)***
Noble Fire Brick Company Inc (PA) 860 623-9256
40 Woolam Rd East Windsor CT (06088) ***(G-1297)***
Noble Industrial Furnace Co, East Windsor *Also called Noble Fire Brick Company Inc* ***(G-1297)***
Noblespirit Entp Sftwr LLC 603 435-8218
51 Dowboro Rd Pittsfield NH (03263) ***(G-19504)***
Nocion Therapeutics Inc 781 812-6176
100 Beaver St Ste 301 Waltham MA (02453) ***(G-16160)***
Noco Energy Corp 802 864-6626
461 Avenue D Williston VT (05495) ***(G-22686)***
Noco Lubricants, Williston *Also called Noco Energy Corp* ***(G-22686)***
Noel Specialty Foods, Rutland *Also called New England Smoked Seafood* ***(G-22346)***
Noeveon Inc 978 642-5004
207 Lowell St Wilmington MA (01887) ***(G-17031)***
Nofet LLC 203 848-9064
227 Church St Apt 5j New Haven CT (06510) ***(G-2719)***
Noise Reduction Products Inc 603 835-6400
97 Lower Cemetery Rd Langdon NH (03602) ***(G-18611)***
Nolan Industries Inc 203 865-8160
67 Mill River St New Haven CT (06511) ***(G-2720)***
Nolas Fresh Foods LLC 617 283-2644
99 Walter St Roslindale MA (02131) ***(G-14840)***
Nomis Enterprises 631 821-3120
90 Northford Rd Wallingford CT (06492) ***(G-4778)***
Non-Invasive Med Systems LLC 914 462-0701
1 Harbor Point Rd # 2050 Stamford CT (06902) ***(G-4260)***
Nonantum Boxing Club LLC 617 340-3700
75 Adams St Newton MA (02458) ***(G-13619)***
Nonwovens Inc 978 251-8612
100 Wotton St North Chelmsford MA (01863) ***(G-13905)***
Noodle Lab LLC 617 717-4370
417 Crescent Ave Apt 3 Chelsea MA (02150) ***(G-9961)***
Noodle Revolution 401 596-9559
87 Oak St Westerly RI (02891) ***(G-21535)***
Noon Family Sheep Farm 207 324-3733
Sunset Rd Springvale ME (04083) ***(G-7055)***
Nooney Controls Corporation (PA) 401 294-6000
466 Dry Bridge Rd North Kingstown RI (02852) ***(G-20730)***
Nootelligence, Fairfield *Also called Focus Now Solutions LLC* ***(G-1432)***
Nopco, Avon *Also called Boston Brace International Inc* ***(G-7880)***
Nopco of Burlington, Burlington *Also called Boston Brace International* ***(G-9241)***
Nops Metal Works 802 382-9300
1479 Route 7 S Middlebury VT (05753) ***(G-22116)***
Nora Systems Inc (HQ) 603 894-1021
9 Northeastern Blvd Salem NH (03079) ***(G-19755)***
Norcell Inc (HQ) 203 254-5292
2 Corporate Dr Fl 5 Shelton CT (06484) ***(G-3841)***
Norco, Framingham *Also called Greentree Marketing Inc* ***(G-10961)***
Norcross Corporation 617 969-7020
255 Newtonville Ave Ste 1 Newton MA (02458) ***(G-13620)***
Nordic American Smokeless Inc 203 207-9977
100 Mill Plain Rd Ste 115 Danbury CT (06811) ***(G-961)***
Nordic Shield Plastic Corp 508 987-5361
2 Hawksley Rd Unit E Oxford MA (01540) ***(G-14270)***
Nordson Efd LLC (HQ) 401 431-7000
40 Catamore Blvd East Providence RI (02914) ***(G-20435)***
Nordson Med Design & Dev Inc (HQ) 508 481-6233
261 Cedar Hill St Ste 1 Marlborough MA (01752) ***(G-12797)***
Nordson Medical (nh) Inc (HQ) 603 327-0600
29 Northwestern Dr Salem NH (03079) ***(G-19756)***
Noreaster Yachts Inc 203 877-4339
29 Roselle St Milford CT (06461) ***(G-2322)***
Noremac Manufacturing Corp 508 879-7514
62 Hopkinton Rd Westborough MA (01581) ***(G-16639)***
Norfolk Asphalt Company Inc 508 668-3100
3 Belcher St Plainville MA (02762) ***(G-14531)***
Norfolk Corporation 781 319-0400
145 Enterprise Dr Marshfield MA (02050) ***(G-12864)***
Norfolk Factory Direct Kitchen 781 848-5333
265 Wood Rd Braintree MA (02184) ***(G-9027)***
Norfolk Industries LLC 860 618-8822
21 Deer Park Dr Greenwich CT (06830) ***(G-1635)***
Norfolk Iron Works Inc 508 482-9162
227 River Rd Uxbridge MA (01569) ***(G-15926)***
Norgaard Machine Inc 413 789-1291
370 Garden St Feeding Hills MA (01030) ***(G-10802)***
Norge Forge Press, Salem *Also called Salem House Press* ***(G-14940)***
Norgren, Farmington *Also called Kip Inc* ***(G-1488)***
Norgren Inc 860 677-0272
72 Spring Ln Farmington CT (06032) ***(G-1500)***
Norilsk Nickel USA Inc 203 730-0676
3 Turtle Ridge Ct Ridgefield CT (06877) ***(G-3673)***
Norking Company Inc 508 222-3100
53 County St Attleboro MA (02703) ***(G-7773)***
Norm Brown Logging 802 537-4474
240 Hulett Hill Rd Benson VT (05743) ***(G-21692)***
Norman Ellis 508 853-5833
14 Sword St Ste 5 Auburn MA (01501) ***(G-7845)***
Norman White Inc 207 636-1636
28 Grant Rd Shapleigh ME (04076) ***(G-6958)***
Norpin Mfg Co Inc 413 599-1628
2342 Boston Rd Wilbraham MA (01095) ***(G-16941)***
Norris Enterprises Inc 781 982-8158
605 Main St Hanover MA (02339) ***(G-11349)***
Norris Litho, Hanover *Also called Norris Enterprises Inc* ***(G-11349)***
Norse Inc 860 482-1532
100 South Rd Torrington CT (06790) ***(G-4589)***
Norteast Woodworking Inc 603 895-4271
24 Old Manchester Rd Raymond NH (03077) ***(G-19641)***
Nortek Inc 413 781-4777
70 Doty Cir West Springfield MA (01089) ***(G-16535)***
Nortekusa Inc 617 205-5750
21 Drydock Ave Ste 740e Boston MA (02210) ***(G-8739)***
North Amercn Spring Tl Co Div, Berlin *Also called All Five Tool Co Inc* ***(G-69)***
North American Auto Equipment 866 607-4022
86 Washington St Unit D2 Plainville MA (02762) ***(G-14532)***
North American Chemical Co 978 687-9500
19 S Canal St Ste 2 Lawrence MA (01843) ***(G-12066)***
North American Kelp, Waldoboro *Also called Atlantic Laboratories Inc* ***(G-7131)***
North American Metals, Londonderry *Also called Upcycle Solutions Inc* ***(G-18743)***
North American Plastics Ltd 603 644-1660
349 E Industrial Prk Dr Manchester NH (03109) ***(G-18887)***
North American Steel Corp 978 535-7587
1 Gwinnett Rd Peabody MA (01960) ***(G-14357)***
North American Supaflu Systems 207 883-1155
15 Holly St Ste 201b Scarborough ME (04074) ***(G-6935)***
North Amrcn Fltration Mass Inc 508 660-9016
23 Walpole Park S Ste 12 Walpole MA (02081) ***(G-16005)***
North Andover Flight Academy 978 689-7600
492 Sutton St North Andover MA (01845) ***(G-13720)***
North ATL Cstm Fabrication Inc 207 839-8410
3 Eisenhower Dr Westbrook ME (04092) ***(G-7199)***
North Atlantic Inc 207 774-6025
2 Portland Fish Portland ME (04101) ***(G-6704)***
North Atlantic Pubg Systems 978 371-8989
66 Commonwealth Ave Ste 5 Concord MA (01742) ***(G-10147)***
North Attleboro Jewelry Co 508 222-4660
112 Bank St Attleboro MA (02703) ***(G-7774)***
North Bridge Woodworking 978 433-0148
7 Lomar Park Unit 2 Pepperell MA (01463) ***(G-14443)***
North Chelmsford Digital, North Chelmsford *Also called Lsc Communications Inc* ***(G-13902)***
North Coast Sea-Foods Corp (PA) 617 345-4400
5 Drydock Ave Boston MA (02210) ***(G-8740)***
North Coast Sea-Foods Corp 508 997-0766
43 Blackmer St New Bedford MA (02744) ***(G-13428)***
North Conway Olive Oil Company 603 307-1066
2730 White Mountain Hwy North Conway NH (03860) ***(G-19377)***
North Country Comforters 207 584-2196
912 Great Pond Rd Great Pond ME (04408) ***(G-6145)***
North Country Engineering Inc 802 766-5396
106 John Taplin Rd Derby VT (05829) ***(G-21902)***
North Country Hard Cider LLC 603 834-9915
3 Front St Lowr Mill Rollinsford NH (03869) ***(G-19694)***
North Country Press 207 948-2208
126 Main St Unity ME (04988) ***(G-7117)***
North Country Smokehouse, Claremont *Also called Butcher Block Inc* ***(G-17837)***
North Country Tractor Inc 207 324-5646
8 Shaws Ridge Rd Sanford ME (04073) ***(G-6884)***
North Country Tractor Inc 603 742-5488
10 Littleworth Rd Dover NH (03820) ***(G-18041)***
North Country Wind Bells Inc 207 677-2224
544 State Route 32 Round Pond ME (04564) ***(G-6831)***
North E Wldg & Fabrication Inc 207 786-2446
928 Minot Ave Auburn ME (04210) ***(G-5583)***
North East Ceramic Studio Inc 603 225-9310
2 Noyes Ln Bow NH (03304) ***(G-17724)***
North East Cutting Die Corp 603 436-8952
29 Industrial Park Dover NH (03820) ***(G-18042)***
North East Fasteners Corp 860 589-3242
8 Tremco Dr Terryville CT (06786) ***(G-4488)***
North East Form Engineering 978 454-5290
44 Stedman St Ste 9 Lowell MA (01851) ***(G-12414)***
North East Indus Coatings Inc 978 356-1200
9 Old Right Rd Unit C Ipswich MA (01938) ***(G-11932)***

North East Knitting Inc....401 727-0500
179 Conant St Pawtucket RI (02860) ***(G-20869)***
North East Materials Group LLC....802 479-7004
751 Graniteville Rd Graniteville VT (05654) ***(G-22000)***
North East Precision Inc....802 748-1440
3606 Memorial Dr Saint Johnsbury VT (05819) ***(G-22392)***
North East Printing McHy Inc....603 474-7455
146 Batchelder Rd Seabrook NH (03874) ***(G-19811)***
North East Products, Dover *Also called New England Innovations Corp* ***(G-18039)***
North East Silicon Tech Inc....508 999-2001
11 David St New Bedford MA (02744) ***(G-13429)***
North Eastern Publishing Co....802 447-7567
425 Main St Bennington VT (05201) ***(G-21686)***
North Easton Companies Inc....774 259-0172
23 Wedgewood Dr North Easton MA (02356) ***(G-13950)***
North Easton Machine Co Inc....508 238-6219
218 Elm St North Easton MA (02356) ***(G-13951)***
North End Composites LLC....207 594-8427
23 Merrill Dr Rockland ME (04841) ***(G-6806)***
North End Oil Service Co Inc....413 734-7057
1003 Saint James Ave Springfield MA (01104) ***(G-15493)***
North End Press Inc....617 227-8929
5 Prince St Boston MA (02113) ***(G-8741)***
North Hartland Tool Corp....802 295-3196
14 Evarts Rd North Hartland VT (05052) ***(G-22229)***
North Haven Eqp & Lsg LLC....203 795-9494
212 Argyle Rd Orange CT (06477) ***(G-3375)***
North Oxford Mills, North Oxford *Also called Weymouth Braided Rug Co Inc* ***(G-13976)***
North Point Brands LLC....339 707-3017
60 Roberts Dr E North Adams MA (01247) ***(G-13683)***
North Reading Transcript, North Reading *Also called Great Oak Publications Inc* ***(G-13983)***
North River Graphics Inc....781 826-6866
100 Corporate Park Dr # 1730 Pembroke MA (02359) ***(G-14420)***
North River Press Pubg Corp....413 528-0034
27 Rosseter St Ste 1 Great Barrington MA (01230) ***(G-11243)***
North Sails Group LLC....401 683-7997
1 Maritime Dr Ste 1 # 1 Portsmouth RI (02871) ***(G-20933)***
North Sails Group LLC (HQ)....203 874-7548
125 Old Gate Ln Ste 7 Milford CT (06460) ***(G-2323)***
North Sails Group LLC....401 849-7997
449 Thames St Unit 400 Newport RI (02840) ***(G-20675)***
North Sales Rhode Island, Portsmouth *Also called Rhode Northsales Island Inc* ***(G-20939)***
North Shannon, Norwalk *Also called Swedish News Inc* ***(G-3253)***
North Shore Compost LLC....781 581-3489
56 Sanderson Ave Lynn MA (01902) ***(G-12529)***
North Shore Jewish Press Ltd....978 745-4111
27 Congress St Ste 501 Salem MA (01970) ***(G-14932)***
North Shore Laboratories Corp....978 531-5954
44 Endicott St Peabody MA (01960) ***(G-14358)***
North Shore Logging Inc....207 398-4173
1005 Main St Saint Francis ME (04774) ***(G-6867)***
North Shore Marble & Granite, Danvers *Also called Steven Tedesco* ***(G-10258)***
North Shore Printing Inc....978 664-2609
281 Main St North Reading MA (01864) ***(G-13988)***
North Shore Steel Co Inc (PA)....781 598-1645
16 Oakville St Lynn MA (01905) ***(G-12530)***
North Star Monthly, The, Danville *Also called Northstar Publishing LLC* ***(G-21898)***
North Taste, Plymouth *Also called Northice* ***(G-14569)***
North Technology Group, Milford *Also called North Sails Group LLC* ***(G-2323)***
North/Win Ltd....978 537-5518
272 Nashua St Leominster MA (01453) ***(G-12172)***
Northampton Machine Co Inc....413 529-2530
16 Industrial Pkwy Easthampton MA (01027) ***(G-10571)***
Northast Cab Cntrtop Dstrs Inc....617 296-2100
140 Campanelli Dr Ste 1 Braintree MA (02184) ***(G-9028)***
Northast Emrgncy Apparatus LLC....207 753-0080
440 Washington St N Auburn ME (04210) ***(G-5584)***
Northast Green Enrgy Group Inc....978 478-8425
49 W Main St Merrimac MA (01860) ***(G-13004)***
Northast Lghtning Prtction LLC....860 243-0010
10 Peters Rd Bloomfield CT (06002) ***(G-246)***
Northast Prformer Publications....617 627-9200
24 Dane St Somerville MA (02143) ***(G-15202)***
Northast Renewable Enrgy Group....617 878-2063
60 State St Ste 700 Boston MA (02109) ***(G-8742)***
Northbridge Companies....781 272-2424
15 3rd Ave Ste 1 Burlington MA (01803) ***(G-9311)***
Northeast Aggregate Corp....802 524-2627
1881 Sheldon Rd Saint Albans VT (05478) ***(G-22376)***
Northeast Agricultural Sls Inc (PA)....802 626-3351
205 East St Lyndonville VT (05851) ***(G-22070)***
Northeast Agricultural Sls Inc....207 487-6273
36 North Rd Detroit ME (04929) ***(G-5952)***
NORTHEAST BIG BUCK CLUB, Paxton *Also called Northeast Outdoors Inc* ***(G-14302)***
Northeast Biodiesel LLC....413 772-8891
179 Silvio O Conte Dr Greenfield MA (01301) ***(G-11271)***
Northeast Buffinton Group Inc....401 434-1107
75 Tripps Ln Riverside RI (02915) ***(G-21174)***
Northeast Building Products....508 786-5600
362 Elm St Marlborough MA (01752) ***(G-12798)***
Northeast Building Supply LLC....781 294-0400
91 Franklin St Hanson MA (02341) ***(G-11367)***
Northeast Cabinet Design....203 438-1709
18 Bailey Ave Ridgefield CT (06877) ***(G-3674)***
Northeast Cabinet Designs LLC....603 329-3465
2 Mary E Clark Dr Ste 2 # 2 Hampstead NH (03841) ***(G-18246)***
Northeast Carbide Inc....860 628-2515
525 W Queen St Southington CT (06489) ***(G-4069)***
Northeast Circuit Tech LLC....860 633-1967
112 Sherwood Dr Glastonbury CT (06033) ***(G-1567)***
Northeast Coating Tech Inc....207 985-3232
105 York St Kennebunk ME (04043) ***(G-6239)***
Northeast Coatings Inc....401 649-1552
19 Hezekiah Dr Warren RI (02885) ***(G-21300)***
Northeast Custom Chrome Nashua....603 566-6165
123 Tolles St Nashua NH (03064) ***(G-19218)***
Northeast Data Destruction LLC....800 783-6766
73 Plymouth St Mansfield MA (02048) ***(G-12650)***
Northeast Document Conservatio....978 470-1010
100 Brickstone Sq Ste 401 Andover MA (01810) ***(G-7577)***
Northeast Doran Inc....207 474-2000
N Ave Industrial Park Skowhegan ME (04976) ***(G-6984)***
Northeast Drill Supply....603 878-0998
36a Brown Dr Greenville NH (03048) ***(G-18228)***
Northeast E D M Inc....978 462-4663
4 Mulliken Way Ste 3 Newburyport MA (01950) ***(G-13518)***
Northeast Electronics Corp....203 878-3511
455 Bic Dr Milford CT (06461) ***(G-2324)***
Northeast Ems Enterprises....508 252-6584
1 Apple Valley Dr Rehoboth MA (02769) ***(G-14755)***
Northeast Equipment Inc....508 324-0083
44 Probber Ln Fall River MA (02720) ***(G-10740)***
Northeast Equipment Design Inc....781 740-0007
150 Recreation Park Dr # 6 Hingham MA (02043) ***(G-11508)***
Northeast Fluid Technologies, Maynard *Also called Northeast Monitoring Inc* ***(G-12902)***
Northeast Foods Inc....860 779-1117
328 Lake Rd Dayville CT (06241) ***(G-1049)***
Northeast Fuel Systems LLC....603 365-4103
53 Turbine Way Ste 47 Merrimack NH (03054) ***(G-19017)***
Northeast Hot-Fill Co-Op Inc....978 772-2338
25 Copeland Dr Ayer MA (01432) ***(G-7930)***
Northeast Innovations Inc....603 226-4000
145 Sheep Davis Rd Pembroke NH (03275) ***(G-19460)***
Northeast Kingdom Balsam, West Glover *Also called Gibson Peggy Day* ***(G-22607)***
Northeast Knitting Mills Inc (PA)....508 678-7553
69 Alden St Fall River MA (02723) ***(G-10741)***
Northeast Laboratory Svcs Inc (PA)....207 873-7711
227 China Rd Winslow ME (04901) ***(G-7272)***
Northeast Lens Corp....617 964-6797
118 South St Hopkinton MA (01748) ***(G-11730)***
Northeast Manufacturing Co Inc....781 438-3022
35 Spencer St Stoneham MA (02180) ***(G-15569)***
Northeast Manufacturing Inc....401 683-2075
300 Highpoint Ave Ste D Portsmouth RI (02871) ***(G-20934)***
Northeast Metal Co....413 568-1981
1022 Berkshire Ave Indian Orchard MA (01151) ***(G-11891)***
Northeast Metal Spinning Inc....603 898-2232
13 Industrial Way Atkinson NH (03811) ***(G-17606)***
Northeast Metals Tech LLC....978 948-2633
289 Newburyport Tpke Rowley MA (01969) ***(G-14861)***
Northeast Millwork Corp....401 624-7744
500 Eagleville Rd Tiverton RI (02878) ***(G-21260)***
Northeast Minority News Inc....860 249-6065
3580 Main St Ste 1 Hartford CT (06120) ***(G-1853)***
Northeast Monitoring Inc....978 461-3992
141 Parker St Ste 101 Maynard MA (01754) ***(G-12902)***
Northeast NDT Inc....603 595-4227
379 Amherst St Ste 208 Nashua NH (03063) ***(G-19219)***
Northeast Outdoors Inc....508 752-8762
390 Marshall St Paxton MA (01612) ***(G-14302)***
Northeast Packaging Co (PA)....207 764-6271
875 Skyway St Presque Isle ME (04769) ***(G-6763)***
Northeast Packaging Co....207 496-3141
56 Sincock St Caribou ME (04736) ***(G-5888)***
Northeast Panel Co LLC....860 678-9078
325 Main St Ste 3 Farmington CT (06032) ***(G-1501)***
Northeast Pellets LLC....207 435-6230
53 Realty Rd Ashland ME (04732) ***(G-5538)***
Northeast Performer Magazine, Somerville *Also called Northast Prformer Publications* ***(G-15202)***
Northeast Plastics Inc....781 245-5512
5 Del Carmine St Wakefield MA (01880) ***(G-15965)***
Northeast Printing & Graphics....508 746-8689
179 Court St Plymouth MA (02360) ***(G-14568)***
Northeast Products, Peterborough *Also called Lucci Corp* ***(G-19475)***
Northeast Publishing Company (HQ)....207 764-4471
260 Missile St Presque Isle ME (04769) ***(G-6764)***

A L P H A B E T I C

Northeast Publishing Company.....207 532-2281
23 Court St Houlton ME (04730) ***(G-6208)***
Northeast Publishing Company.....207 764-4471
260 Missile St Presque Isle ME (04769) ***(G-6765)***
Northeast Publishing Company.....207 768-5431
40 North St Ste 2 Presque Isle ME (04769) ***(G-6766)***
Northeast Publishing Company.....207 564-8355
12 E Main St Ste A Dover Foxcroft ME (04426) ***(G-5961)***
Northeast Quality Services LLC.....860 632-7242
14 Alcap Rdg Cromwell CT (06416) ***(G-856)***
Northeast Reprographics, Bangor *Also called Central Street Corporation* ***(G-5635)***
Northeast Sample Co, Haverhill *Also called Leisure Manufacturing* ***(G-11448)***
Northeast Sand & Gravel.....603 213-6133
17 Old Nashua Rd Ste 14 Amherst NH (03031) ***(G-17579)***
Northeast Sand and Gravel LLC.....603 305-9429
214 Appleton Rd New Ipswich NH (03071) ***(G-19307)***
Northeast Screen Graphics, East Longmeadow *Also called Industrial Etching Inc* ***(G-10479)***
Northeast Sealcoat, Millbury *Also called Granger Lynch Corp* ***(G-13165)***
Northeast Ship Repair Inc (PA).....617 330-5045
32a Drydock Ave Boston MA (02210) ***(G-8743)***
Northeast Silk Screen Inc.....603 883-6933
78 Northastern Blvd Ste 1 Nashua NH (03062) ***(G-19220)***
Northeast Stair Company LLC.....860 875-3358
185 Buff Cap Rd Tolland CT (06084) ***(G-4551)***
Northeast Stamp & Engraving.....508 473-5818
3 E Main St Milford MA (01757) ***(G-13132)***
Northeast Stihl, Oxford *Also called Stihl Incorporated* ***(G-3425)***
Northeast Thermography, Wallingford *Also called E & A Enterprises Inc* ***(G-4736)***
Northeast Timber Exchange LLC (PA).....802 875-1037
535 Cummings Rd Chester VT (05143) ***(G-21846)***
Northeast Time Trak Systems.....207 774-2336
79 Bradley Dr Ste A Westbrook ME (04092) ***(G-7200)***
Northeast Tool & Die Co Inc.....207 743-7273
16 Aldrich Ave Norway ME (04268) ***(G-6524)***
Northeast Treaters Inc (PA).....413 323-7811
201 Springfield Rd Belchertown MA (01007) ***(G-8026)***
Northeast Twr Svc.....508 533-1620
64 Acorn Dr Uxbridge MA (01569) ***(G-15927)***
Northeast Wldg Bridge Repr LLC.....603 396-8549
58 Riverdale Rd New Boston NH (03070) ***(G-19295)***
Northeast Wood Products, Pownal *Also called N W P Inc* ***(G-22282)***
Northeast Wood Products LLC.....860 862-6350
13 Crow Hill Rd Uncasville CT (06382) ***(G-4647)***
Northeast Woodworking Products.....603 895-4271
24 Old Manchester Rd Raymond NH (03077) ***(G-19642)***
Northeastern Importing Corp.....401 276-0654
483 Elmgrove Ave Providence RI (02906) ***(G-21078)***
Northeastern Metals Corp.....203 348-8088
130 Lenox Ave Ste 23 Stamford CT (06906) ***(G-4261)***
Northeastern Nonwovens Inc.....603 332-5900
7 Amarosa Dr Unit 3 Rochester NH (03868) ***(G-19680)***
Northeastern Publishing Co.....508 429-5588
112 Central St Holliston MA (01746) ***(G-11591)***
Northeastern Rustic Furni.....207 757-8300
2761 Us Route 2 Smyrna Mills ME (04780) ***(G-6994)***
Northend Agents LLC.....860 244-2445
150 Trumbull St Fl 4 Hartford CT (06103) ***(G-1854)***
Northern Air Inc.....508 823-4900
450 Richmond St Raynham MA (02767) ***(G-14721)***
Northern Berkshire Pregnancy.....413 346-4291
98 Church St Ste 1 North Adams MA (01247) ***(G-13684)***
Northern Champlain Islander, North Hero *Also called Islander* ***(G-22231)***
Northern Design Precast Inc.....603 783-8989
51 International Dr Loudon NH (03307) ***(G-18751)***
Northern Graphics Inc.....978 646-9925
161 S Main St Ste 210 Middleton MA (01949) ***(G-13097)***
Northern Industries Inc (PA).....401 769-4305
429 Tiogue Ave Coventry RI (02816) ***(G-20160)***
Northern Light, Biddeford *Also called Beacon Press Inc* ***(G-5722)***
Northern Mosoleum, Barre *Also called Global Values VT LLC* ***(G-21616)***
Northern Outdoor Lighting.....978 987-9845
14 Bixby Ln Westford MA (01886) ***(G-16782)***
Northern Pelagic Group LLC.....508 979-1171
4 Fish Is New Bedford MA (02740) ***(G-13430)***
Northern Power Systems Inc (HQ).....802 461-2955
29 Pitman Rd Ste 1 Barre VT (05641) ***(G-21631)***
Northern Power Systems Corp (PA).....802 461-2955
29 Pitman Rd Barre VT (05641) ***(G-21632)***
Northern Printers Inc.....207 769-1231
30 Dudley St Presque Isle ME (04769) ***(G-6767)***
Northern Products Inc.....978 840-3383
645 Lancaster St Leominster MA (01453) ***(G-12173)***
Northern RI Conservation Dst.....401 934-0840
2283 Hartford Ave Johnston RI (02919) ***(G-20526)***
Northern Signs.....207 465-2399
105 Martin Stream Rd Fairfield ME (04937) ***(G-6028)***
Northern Strike.....802 427-3201
842 Calendar Brook Rd Lyndonville VT (05851) ***(G-22071)***
Northern Tack.....207 217-7584
4 River Rd Calais ME (04619) ***(G-5865)***
Northern Tool Mfg Co Inc.....413 732-5549
170 Progress Ave Springfield MA (01104) ***(G-15494)***
Northern Turf Prfessionals Inc.....207 522-8598
251 Old Portland Rd Brunswick ME (04011) ***(G-5843)***
Northice.....781 985-5225
624 Long Pond Rd Plymouth MA (02360) ***(G-14569)***
Northlight Studio Press, Montpelier *Also called Leahy Press Inc* ***(G-22153)***
Northmen Defense LLC.....860 908-9308
24 Old Colchester Rd Ext Oakdale CT (06370) ***(G-3294)***
Northpoint Printing Svcs Inc.....781 895-1900
230 2nd Ave Ste 3 Waltham MA (02451) ***(G-16161)***
Northport LLC.....207 247-7600
61 Sokokis Trl East Waterboro ME (04030) ***(G-5985)***
Northport Wood Products, East Waterboro *Also called Northport LLC* ***(G-5985)***
Northroad Wood Signs.....603 924-9330
203 Old Revolutionary Rd Temple NH (03084) ***(G-19898)***
Northrop Grumman Corporation.....860 282-4461
121 Prestige Park Cir East Hartford CT (06108) ***(G-1207)***
Northrop Grumman Corporation.....978 772-0352
115 Jackson Rd Devens MA (01434) ***(G-10327)***
Northrop Grumman Info Systems, Andover *Also called Northrop Grumman Systems Corp* ***(G-7578)***
Northrop Grumman Systems Corp.....978 247-7812
100 Brickstone Sq Ste G03 Andover MA (01810) ***(G-7578)***
Northrup & Gibson Entps LLC.....401 423-2152
386 Beacon Ave Jamestown RI (02835) ***(G-20493)***
Northshire Brewery Inc.....802 681-0201
108 County St Bennington VT (05201) ***(G-21687)***
Northstar Biosciences LLC.....203 689-5399
2514 Boston Post Rd 4r Guilford CT (06437) ***(G-1713)***
Northstar Direct LLC.....603 627-3334
249 Gay St Manchester NH (03103) ***(G-18888)***
Northstar Publishing LLC.....802 684-1056
29 Hill St Danville VT (05828) ***(G-21898)***
Northwest Connecticut Mfg Co.....860 379-1553
95 Beech Hill Rd Colebrook CT (06021) ***(G-813)***
Northwest Precision Inc.....207 364-7597
37 Canal St Rumford ME (04276) ***(G-6841)***
Northwind Timber.....603 284-6123
379 N Sandwich Rd Center Sandwich NH (03227) ***(G-17807)***
Northwind Wood, Center Sandwich *Also called Northwind Timber* ***(G-17807)***
Northwood Canoe Co.....207 564-3667
336 Range Rd Atkinson ME (04426) ***(G-5544)***
Northwoods Publications LLC.....207 732-4880
57 Old County Rd N West Enfield ME (04493) ***(G-7171)***
Northwoods Sporting Journal, West Enfield *Also called Northwoods Publications LLC* ***(G-7171)***
Norton Land Clearing and Log.....978 391-4029
5 Robbins Rd Ayer MA (01432) ***(G-7931)***
Nortonlifelock Inc.....781 530-2200
2 Canal Park Ste 5 Cambridge MA (02141) ***(G-9584)***
Nortonlifelock Inc.....860 652-6600
200 Glastonbury Blvd # 30 Glastonbury CT (06033) ***(G-1568)***
Norwalk Awning Company, Norwalk *Also called Fitzgerald-Norwalk Awning Co* ***(G-3153)***
Norwalk Compreseer Company.....203 386-1234
1650 Stratford Ave Stratford CT (06615) ***(G-4433)***
Norwalk Compressor Inc.....203 386-1234
1650 Stratford Ave Stratford CT (06615) ***(G-4434)***
Norwalk Powdered Metals Inc.....203 338-8000
30 Moffitt St Stratford CT (06615) ***(G-4435)***
Norwell Mfg Co Inc.....508 822-2831
82 Stevens St East Taunton MA (02718) ***(G-10516)***
Norwood Bulletin, Norwood *Also called Enterprise Newsmedia LLC* ***(G-14150)***
Norwood Sheet Metal Corp.....781 762-0720
744 Bston Prvdnce Tpke St Norwood MA (02062) ***(G-14184)***
Norwood Woodworking Inc.....781 762-8367
640 Pleasant St Ste 1 Norwood MA (02062) ***(G-14185)***
Notabli Inc.....802 448-0810
209 College St Ste 3w Burlington VT (05401) ***(G-21799)***
Notch Inc.....203 258-9141
501 Massachusetts Ave Cambridge MA (02139) ***(G-9585)***
Notes, The, Yarmouth *Also called SMA Inc* ***(G-7300)***
Nottingham Wood Products.....802 766-2791
108 John Taplin Rd Derby VT (05829) ***(G-21903)***
Noujaim Tool Co Inc.....203 753-4441
412 Chase River Rd Waterbury CT (06704) ***(G-4929)***
Nouveau Interiors LLC.....603 398-1732
60 Rogers St Manchester NH (03103) ***(G-18889)***
Nouveau Packaging LLC.....508 880-0300
65 Ryan Dr Unit F1 Raynham MA (02767) ***(G-14722)***
Nova Analytics Corporation.....781 897-1208
100 Cummings Ctr Ste 535n Beverly MA (01915) ***(G-8160)***
Nova Biomedical Corporation (PA).....781 894-0800
200 Prospect St Waltham MA (02453) ***(G-16162)***
Nova Biomedical Corporation.....781 894-0800
39 Manning Rd Billerica MA (01821) ***(G-8268)***

Nova Dental LLC (PA) 203 234-3900
41 Middletown Ave Ste 2 North Haven CT (06473) ***(G-3044)***
Nova Idea Inc 781 281-2183
124 Cummings Park Woburn MA (01801) ***(G-17246)***
Nova Instruments Corporation (PA) 781 897-1200
600 Unicorn Park Dr Ste 4 Woburn MA (01801) ***(G-17247)***
Nova Instruments LLC (PA) 781 897-1200
500 Edgewater Dr Wakefield MA (01880) ***(G-15966)***
Nova Machining LLC 860 675-8131
16 E Shore Blvd Unionville CT (06085) ***(G-4660)***
Nova Packaging Systems Inc 978 537-8534
7 New Lancaster Rd Leominster MA (01453) ***(G-12174)***
Nova Sports Usa Inc 508 473-6540
6 Industrial Rd Ste 2 Milford MA (01757) ***(G-13133)***
Novacel Inc (HQ) 413 283-3468
21 3rd St Palmer MA (01069) ***(G-14289)***
Novaerus US Inc (PA) 813 304-2468
35 Melrose Pl Stamford CT (06902) ***(G-4262)***
Novagenesis 781 784-1149
77 Norwood St Sharon MA (02067) ***(G-15054)***
Novamont North America Inc 203 744-8801
1000 Bridgeport Ave # 304 Shelton CT (06484) ***(G-3842)***
Novanta Corporation (HQ) 781 266-5700
125 Middlesex Tpke Bedford MA (01730) ***(G-7995)***
Novanta Inc (PA) 781 266-5700
125 Middlesex Tpke Bedford MA (01730) ***(G-7996)***
Novartis Corporation 617 871-3594
22 Windsor St Cambridge MA (02139) ***(G-9586)***
Novartis Corporation 617 871-8000
400 Technology Sq Ste 7 Cambridge MA (02139) ***(G-9587)***
Novartis Corporation 617 871-8000
500 Technology Sq Cambridge MA (02139) ***(G-9588)***
Novartis Inst For Biomedical R 617 871-7523
100 Technology Sq Cambridge MA (02139) ***(G-9589)***
Novartis Inst For Biomedical R (HQ) 617 871-8000
250 Massachusetts Ave Cambridge MA (02139) ***(G-9590)***
Novartis Vccnes Dagnostics Inc 617 871-7000
350 Massachusetts Ave Cambridge MA (02139) ***(G-9591)***
Novartis Vccnes Dagnostics Inc 617 871-7000
350 Massachusetts Ave Cambridge MA (02139) ***(G-9592)***
Novatek Medical Inc 203 356-0156
1 Strawberry Hill Ave Stamford CT (06902) ***(G-4263)***
Novel Iron Works Inc 603 436-7950
250 Ocean Rd Greenland NH (03840) ***(G-18224)***
Novel Tees Screen Prtg EMB LLC 860 643-6008
81 Tolland Tpke Manchester CT (06042) ***(G-2026)***
Novel-Tees Unlimited LLC 860 643-6008
81 Tolland Tpke Manchester CT (06042) ***(G-2027)***
Novelion Therapeutics Inc 877 764-3131
1 Main St 800 Cambridge MA (02142) ***(G-9593)***
Novell, Cambridge *Also called Micro Focus Software Inc* ***(G-9553)***
Novelsat Inc 617 658-1419
25 Tanglewood Rd Newton MA (02459) ***(G-13621)***
Novelty Plastics, Cumberland *Also called Nfa Corp* ***(G-20332)***
Novelty Textile Mills LLC 860 774-5000
24 Spithead Rd Waterford CT (06385) ***(G-4990)***
November Defense LLC 401 662-7902
71 Teakwood Dr W Coventry RI (02816) ***(G-20161)***
Novo Nordisk US Bio Prod Inc 603 298-3169
9 Technology Dr West Lebanon NH (03784) ***(G-19958)***
Novo Precision LLC 860 583-0517
150 Dolphin Rd Bristol CT (06010) ***(G-587)***
Novogy Inc 617 674-5800
85 Bolton St Ste 124 Cambridge MA (02140) ***(G-9594)***
Novolac Epoxy Technologies Inc (PA) 508 385-5598
172 Queen Anne Rd Harwich MA (02645) ***(G-11396)***
Novotech Inc 978 929-9458
916 Main St Acton MA (01720) ***(G-7375)***
Novotechnik US Inc 508 485-2244
155 Northboro Rd Ste 31 Southborough MA (01772) ***(G-15363)***
Novy International Inc 203 743-7720
6 Abbott St Danbury CT (06810) ***(G-962)***
Now Publishers Inc 781 871-0245
167 Washington St Ste 20 Norwell MA (02061) ***(G-14109)***
Nowak Products Inc 860 666-9685
101 Rockwell Rd Newington CT (06111) ***(G-2887)***
Noxxon Pharma Inc 617 232-0638
51 Fairview Rd Weston MA (02493) ***(G-16828)***
Noyes Sheet Metal 508 482-9302
66 Sumner St Milford MA (01757) ***(G-13134)***
Npc Processing Inc 802 660-0496
97 Executive Dr Shelburne VT (05482) ***(G-22420)***
Npi Medical, Ansonia *Also called Ansonia Plastics LLC* ***(G-7)***
Npm, Stratford *Also called Norwalk Powdered Metals Inc* ***(G-4435)***
Nq Industries Inc 860 258-3466
1275 Cromwell Ave Ste A9 Rocky Hill CT (06067) ***(G-3725)***
NRG Connecticut LLC 860 231-2424
36 Woodland St Ste 1 Hartford CT (06105) ***(G-1855)***
Nrt Inc 508 533-4588
74 Main St Unit 16 Medway MA (02053) ***(G-12968)***
Nrz Companies Inc 508 856-7237
774 W Boylston St Worcester MA (01606) ***(G-17435)***
NS Converters LLC 508 628-1501
400 Boston Post Rd 2d Sudbury MA (01776) ***(G-15664)***
NS Design 207 563-7705
134 Back Meadow Rd Nobleboro ME (04555) ***(G-6493)***
Nsa Industries LLC (PA) 802 748-5007
210 Pierce Rd Saint Johnsbury VT (05819) ***(G-22393)***
Nsight Inc 781 273-6300
300 Brickstone Sq Ste 201 Andover MA (01810) ***(G-7579)***
NSK Steering Systems Amer Inc 802 442-5448
110 Shields Dr Bennington VT (05201) ***(G-21688)***
NSM Marketing Inc 508 359-5297
2 Newell Dr Medfield MA (02052) ***(G-12915)***
Nssa, Bennington Plant, Bennington *Also called NSK Steering Systems Amer Inc* ***(G-21688)***
Nteco Inc 203 656-1154
10 Center St Darien CT (06820) ***(G-1030)***
Ntp Software of Ca Inc (PA) 603 641-6937
427 Amherst St Ut381 Nashua NH (03063) ***(G-19221)***
Ntp/Republic Clear Thru Corp 413 493-6800
475 Canal St Holyoke MA (01040) ***(G-11645)***
Ntt Data Inc 617 241-9200
100 City Sq Ste 1 Boston MA (02129) ***(G-8744)***
Nu Chrome Corp 508 557-1418
32 Industrial Ct Seekonk MA (02771) ***(G-15032)***
Nu Line Design LLC 203 949-0726
21 N Plains Industrial Rd Wallingford CT (06492) ***(G-4779)***
Nu Line Signs, Wallingford *Also called Nu Line Design LLC* ***(G-4779)***
Nu-Cast Inc 603 432-1600
29 Grenier Field Rd Londonderry NH (03053) ***(G-18729)***
Nu-Lustre Finishing Corp 401 521-7800
1 Magnolia St Providence RI (02909) ***(G-21079)***
Nu-Stone Mfg & Distrg LLC 860 564-6555
160 Sterling Rd Sterling CT (06377) ***(G-4370)***
Nu-Truss Inc 413 562-3861
52 Steiger Dr Westfield MA (01085) ***(G-16708)***
Nuance Communications Inc 508 821-5954
151 Bryant St Berkley MA (02779) ***(G-8088)***
Nuance Communications Inc (PA) 781 565-5000
1 Wayside Rd Burlington MA (01803) ***(G-9312)***
Nuance Communications Inc 781 565-5000
3191 Broadbridge Ave Fl 2 Stratford CT (06614) ***(G-4436)***
Nucap US Inc (HQ) 203 879-1423
238 Wolcott Rd Wolcott CT (06716) ***(G-5450)***
Nucedar Mills, Chicopee *Also called Jain America Foods Inc* ***(G-10035)***
Nuclead Incorporated 508 583-2699
100 Pacific St Cambridge MA (02139) ***(G-9595)***
Nucor Bar Mill Group, Wallingford *Also called Nucor Steel Connecticut Inc* ***(G-4780)***
Nucor Steel Connecticut Inc 203 265-0615
35 Toelles Rd Wallingford CT (06492) ***(G-4780)***
Nufern 860 408-5000
7 Airport Park Rd East Granby CT (06026) ***(G-1137)***
Nuforj LLC 413 530-0349
1350 Main St Springfield MA (01103) ***(G-15495)***
Nuimage Awnings, Auburn *Also called Futureguard Building Pdts Inc* ***(G-5565)***
Numa Tool Company (PA) 860 923-9551
646 Thompson Rd Thompson CT (06277) ***(G-4537)***
Numaco Packaging LLC 401 438-4952
82 Boyd Ave East Providence RI (02914) ***(G-20436)***
Numark International Inc 954 761-7550
200 Scenic View Dr Cumberland RI (02864) ***(G-20335)***
Numberall Stamp & Tool Co 207 876-3541
1 High St Sangerville ME (04479) ***(G-6900)***
Numeric Inc 413 732-6544
195 Wayside Ave West Springfield MA (01089) ***(G-16536)***
Numeric Machining Company, West Springfield *Also called Numeric Inc* ***(G-16536)***
Numerical Control Technology, Newington *Also called Nct Inc* ***(G-2886)***
Numet Machining Techniques LLC 203 375-4995
235 Edison Rd Orange CT (06477) ***(G-3376)***
Numotion, Rocky Hill *Also called United Seating & Mobility LLC* ***(G-3732)***
Numotion 401 681-2153
300 Myles Standish Blvd Taunton MA (02780) ***(G-15769)***
Nunnery Orthtic Prosthetic LLC 401 294-4210
7408 Post Rd North Kingstown RI (02852) ***(G-20731)***
Nuovo Pasta Productions Ltd 203 380-4090
1330 Honeyspot Road Ext Stratford CT (06615) ***(G-4437)***
Nutek Aerospace Corp 860 355-3169
180 Sunny Valley Rd Ste 2 New Milford CT (06776) ***(G-2819)***
Nutex Industries Inc 508 993-2501
127 Rodney French Blvd # 4 New Bedford MA (02744) ***(G-13431)***
Nutfield Cabinetry LLC 603 498-6252
8 Shelly Dr Derry NH (03038) ***(G-17992)***
Nutfield Publishing LLC 603 537-2760
2 Litchfield Rd Londonderry NH (03053) ***(G-18730)***
Nutmeg Architectural Wdwrk Inc 203 325-4434
48 Union St Ste 14 Stamford CT (06906) ***(G-4264)***
Nutmeg Brewing Rest Group LLC 203 256-2337
819 Bridgeport Ave Shelton CT (06484) ***(G-3843)***

ALPHABETIC

Nutmeg Container Corporation (HQ)....860 963-6727
100 Canal St Putnam CT (06260) ***(G-3622)***
Nutmeg Utility Products Inc (PA)....203 250-8802
1755 Highland Ave Cheshire CT (06410) ***(G-748)***
Nutmeg Wire....860 822-8616
14 Main St Baltic CT (06330) ***(G-51)***
Nutra-Blend LLC....802 988-4474
53 E Main St North Troy VT (05859) ***(G-22241)***
Nutragenesis LLC....802 257-5345
76 Highland St Ste 208 Brattleboro VT (05301) ***(G-21741)***
Nutrasweet Company....706 303-5600
500 Totten Pond Rd 6 Waltham MA (02451) ***(G-16163)***
Nutrasweet Company....706 303-5600
500 Totten Pond Rd Ste 61 Waltham MA (02451) ***(G-16164)***
Nutricopia Inc....808 832-2080
15 E State St Ste 1 Montpelier VT (05602) ***(G-22158)***
Nutron Manufacturing Inc....860 887-4550
5 Wisconsin Ave Norwich CT (06360) ***(G-3287)***
Nutron Motor Company, Lyman *Also called ECB Motor Company Inc* ***(G-6389)***
Nuvelution Pharma Inc....781 924-1148
31 Schoosett St Pembroke MA (02359) ***(G-14421)***
Nuvera Fuel Cells LLC....617 245-7500
129 Concord Rd Bldg 1 Billerica MA (01821) ***(G-8269)***
Nuway Tobacco Company....860 289-6414
200 Sullivan Ave Ste 2 South Windsor CT (06074) ***(G-3996)***
NV Bots, Boston *Also called New Valence Robotics Corp* ***(G-8735)***
NV Candles LLC....774 234-6895
3 Jacobson Dr Ste 2 Auburn MA (01501) ***(G-7846)***
NWare Technologies Inc....603 617-3760
6 Old Rochester Rd # 202 Dover NH (03820) ***(G-18043)***
Nxp Usa Inc....401 830-5410
310 Washington Hwy Smithfield RI (02917) ***(G-21241)***
Nxstage Medical Inc (HQ)....978 687-4700
350 Merrimack St Lawrence MA (01843) ***(G-12067)***
Nxtid Inc....203 266-2103
288 Christian St Oxford CT (06478) ***(G-3416)***
Nyacol Nano Technologies Inc....508 881-2220
211 Megunko Rd Ashland MA (01721) ***(G-7665)***
Nylco, Clinton *Also called Worthen Industries Inc* ***(G-10095)***
Nylco Division, Nashua *Also called Worthen Industries Inc* ***(G-19289)***
Nyle Systems LLC....207 989-4335
12 Stevens Rd Unit B Brewer ME (04412) ***(G-5799)***
Nylo Metal Finishing LLC....203 574-5477
730 N Main St Ste 1 Waterbury CT (06704) ***(G-4930)***
Nylon Corporation America Inc....603 627-5150
333 Sundial Ave Manchester NH (03103) ***(G-18890)***
Nyltech North America....603 627-5150
333 Sundial Ave Manchester NH (03103) ***(G-18891)***
Nynex, Natick *Also called Verizon Communications Inc* ***(G-13285)***
Nypro Finpack Clinton....978 368-6021
25 School St Clinton MA (01510) ***(G-10085)***
Nypro Inc....978 784-2006
112 Barnum Rd Devens MA (01434) ***(G-10328)***
Nypro Inc (HQ)....978 365-8100
101 Union St Clinton MA (01510) ***(G-10086)***
Nypromold Inc (PA)....978 365-4547
144 Pleasant St Clinton MA (01510) ***(G-10087)***
Nzymsys Inc....877 729-4190
642 Hilliard St Ste 1208 Manchester CT (06042) ***(G-2028)***
O & E High-Tech Corporation....617 497-1108
139 Washington St Medford MA (02155) ***(G-12945)***
O & G Industries Inc....860 485-6600
255 Lower Bogue Rd Harwinton CT (06791) ***(G-1891)***
O & G Industries Inc....203 977-1618
686 Canal St Stamford CT (06902) ***(G-4265)***
O & G Industries Inc....203 881-5192
105 Breault Rd Beacon Falls CT (06403) ***(G-63)***
O & G Industries Inc....203 366-4586
240 Bostwick Ave Bridgeport CT (06605) ***(G-459)***
O & G Industries Inc....203 748-5694
9 Segar St Danbury CT (06810) ***(G-963)***
O & G Industries Inc....203 729-4529
Railroad Ave Ext Beacon Falls CT (06403) ***(G-64)***
O & G Industries Inc....860 354-4438
271 Danbury Rd New Milford CT (06776) ***(G-2820)***
O & P Iam Inc....781 239-3331
400 W Cummings Park # 4950 Woburn MA (01801) ***(G-17248)***
O A Both Corporation....508 881-4100
40 Nickerson Rd Ashland MA (01721) ***(G-7666)***
O Brien D G Inc....603 474-5571
1 Chase Park Rd Seabrook NH (03874) ***(G-19812)***
O C M Inc....508 675-7711
42 8th St Fall River MA (02720) ***(G-10742)***
O C Tanner Company....203 944-5430
2 Corporate Dr Ste 935 Shelton CT (06484) ***(G-3844)***
O C White Company....413 289-1751
4226 Church St Thorndike MA (01079) ***(G-15850)***
O E M Concepts (HQ)....207 283-6500
60 Industrial Park Rd Saco ME (04072) ***(G-6854)***
O E M Controls Inc (PA)....203 929-8431
10 Controls Dr Shelton CT (06484) ***(G-3845)***
O E M Health Information Inc....978 921-7300
8 West St Beverly MA (01915) ***(G-8161)***
O E M Press, Beverly *Also called O E M Health Information Inc* ***(G-8161)***
O F Mossberg & Sons Inc (HQ)....203 230-5300
7 Grasso Ave North Haven CT (06473) ***(G-3045)***
O M Y A Inc....802 499-8131
62 Main St Proctor VT (05765) ***(G-22286)***
O S C, Oxford *Also called Oxford Science Center LLC* ***(G-3418)***
O S Walker Company Inc (HQ)....508 853-3232
600 Day Hill Rd Windsor CT (06095) ***(G-5351)***
O W Heat Treat Inc....860 430-6709
77 Great Pond Rd South Glastonbury CT (06073) ***(G-3924)***
O W Landergren Inc....413 442-5632
1500 W Housatonic St Pittsfield MA (01201) ***(G-14497)***
O'Malley J F Welding, Worcester *Also called J F OMalley Welding Co* ***(G-17395)***
O'Neil Company, The, North Yarmouth *Also called Maine Cleaners Supply Inc* ***(G-6517)***
O-A, Agawam *Also called 325 Silver Street Inc* ***(G-7415)***
O/K Machinery Corporation....508 303-8286
73 Bartlett St Marlborough MA (01752) ***(G-12799)***
Oak Barrel Imports LLC....617 286-2524
421r Essex St Beverly MA (01915) ***(G-8162)***
Oak Gallery Inc (PA)....978 486-9846
160 Ayer Rd Unit 5 Littleton MA (01460) ***(G-12314)***
Oak Group Inc....781 943-2200
892 Worcester St Ste 250 Wellesley MA (02482) ***(G-16377)***
Oak Tree Moulding LLC....860 455-3056
7 Pole Bridge Rd Woodstock CT (06281) ***(G-5499)***
Oakridge Sign and Graphics LLC....603 878-1183
42 Poor Farm Rd New Ipswich NH (03071) ***(G-19308)***
Oakum Bay Sail Co....781 631-8983
9 State St Marblehead MA (01945) ***(G-12689)***
Oakville Quality Products LLC....203 757-5525
1495 Thomaston Ave Ste 2 Waterbury CT (06704) ***(G-4931)***
Oakwood Cabinetry....603 927-4713
26 Thayer Pond Rd Concord NH (03301) ***(G-17920)***
Oasis Coffee Corp....203 847-0554
327 Main Ave Norwalk CT (06851) ***(G-3210)***
Oasis Pharmaceuticals LLC....781 752-6094
64 Fifer Ln Lexington MA (02420) ***(G-12251)***
Oasisworks Inc....617 329-5588
14 Mica Ln Ste 204 Wellesley MA (02481) ***(G-16378)***
Oasys Water Inc....617 963-0450
124 Washington St Ste 101 Foxboro MA (02035) ***(G-10895)***
Oatmeal Studios Inc....802 967-8014
Town Rd 35 Rochester VT (05767) ***(G-22320)***
Oatsystems Inc....781 907-6100
309 Waverley Oaks Rd # 306 Waltham MA (02452) ***(G-16165)***
Oberlin LLC....401 588-8755
186 Union St Providence RI (02903) ***(G-21080)***
Oberon Company, New Bedford *Also called Paramount Corp* ***(G-13436)***
Oberthur Technologies, Billerica *Also called Idemia America Corp* ***(G-8255)***
Object Management Group Inc....781 444-0404
109 Highland Ave Ste 303 Needham MA (02494) ***(G-13307)***
Oborain....413 376-8854
7 Ripley Rd Montague MA (01351) ***(G-13212)***
OBrien Consolidated Inds....207 783-8543
680 Lisbon St Ste 1 Lewiston ME (04240) ***(G-6312)***
OBrien Publications Inc....781 378-2126
20 Schofield Rd Cohasset MA (02025) ***(G-10101)***
OBs Woodcrafts Inc....508 679-0480
314 Swansom Rd Swansea MA (02777) ***(G-15711)***
Observer, The, Southington *Also called Step Saver Inc* ***(G-4082)***
Obsidian Therapeutics Inc....339 364-6721
1030 Mass Ave Ste 400 Cambridge MA (02138) ***(G-9596)***
Occlusion Prosthetics....508 827-4377
17 School St Hyannis MA (02601) ***(G-11851)***
Ocean Cliff Corporation....508 990-7900
362 S Front St New Bedford MA (02740) ***(G-13432)***
Ocean Crest Seafood Inc....978 281-0232
88 Commercial St Gloucester MA (01930) ***(G-11198)***
Ocean Crest Seafoods Inc (PA)....978 281-0232
88 Commercial St Gloucester MA (01930) ***(G-11199)***
Ocean Data Equipment Corp....401 454-1810
222 Metro Center Blvd Warwick RI (02886) ***(G-21397)***
Ocean Farm Technologies Inc....207 322-4322
52 S Main St Morrill ME (04952) ***(G-6456)***
Ocean Industries LLC....603 622-2481
12 Park Ave Hudson NH (03051) ***(G-18421)***
Ocean Laminating Films, Cranston *Also called Wheeler Avenue LLC* ***(G-20311)***
Ocean Link Inc....401 683-4434
1 Maritime Dr Ste 10 Portsmouth RI (02871) ***(G-20935)***
Ocean Lures LLC....978 618-1982
4 Ice Pond Dr Rowley MA (01969) ***(G-14862)***
Ocean Marine Fabricating....508 999-5554
201 1/2 Popes Is New Bedford MA (02740) ***(G-13433)***
Ocean Navigator, Portland *Also called Navigator Publishing LLC* ***(G-6698)***

Ocean Organics Corp....207 832-4305
141 One Pie Rd Waldoboro ME (04572) ***(G-7136)***
Ocean Orthopedic Services Inc (PA)....401 725-5240
872 Charles St North Providence RI (02904) ***(G-20768)***
Ocean Premier Seafood Inc....603 206-4787
174 Calef Rd Ste 1 Manchester NH (03103) ***(G-18892)***
Ocean Publishing....603 812-5557
911 Ocean Blvd Apt 7 Rye NH (03870) ***(G-19700)***
Ocean Rigging LLC....800 624-2101
1 Bostwick Ave Bridgeport CT (06605) ***(G-460)***
Ocean Side Publications....401 331-8426
95 Putnam St East Providence RI (02914) ***(G-20437)***
Ocean Spray (europe) Ltd....508 946-1000
1 Ocean Spray Dr Middleboro MA (02349) ***(G-13071)***
Ocean Spray Cranberries Inc (PA)....508 946-1000
1 Ocean Spray Dr Middleboro MA (02349) ***(G-13072)***
Ocean Spray Cranberries Inc....508 947-4940
152 Bridge St Middleboro MA (02346) ***(G-13073)***
Ocean Spray Cranberries Inc....508 866-5306
60 Federal Rd South Carver MA (02366) ***(G-15235)***
Ocean Spray International Inc (HQ)....508 946-1000
1 Ocean Spray Dr Middleboro MA (02349) ***(G-13074)***
Ocean Spray Intl Svcs Inc (HQ)....508 946-1000
1 Ocean Spray Dr Lakeville MA (02347) ***(G-11977)***
Ocean State Book Binding Inc....401 528-1172
225 Dupont Dr Providence RI (02907) ***(G-21081)***
Ocean State Cpl Inc....401 431-0153
40 Jordan St East Providence RI (02914) ***(G-20438)***
Ocean State Creations, North Providence *Also called Anatone Jewelry Co Inc* ***(G-20752)***
Ocean State Innovations, Portsmouth *Also called Brand & Oppenheimer Co Inc* ***(G-20921)***
Ocean State Printers, Pawtucket *Also called Adams Printing Inc* ***(G-20807)***
Ocean State Scale Balance LLC....401 340-6622
31b Reservoir Rd Coventry RI (02816) ***(G-20162)***
Ocean State Shellfish Coop....401 789-2065
20 Walts Way Narragansett RI (02882) ***(G-20643)***
Ocean State Software LLC....202 695-8049
151 Tanglewood Dr East Greenwich RI (02818) ***(G-20375)***
Ocean Tug & Barge Engrg Corp....508 473-0545
258 Main St Ste 401 Milford MA (01757) ***(G-13135)***
OConnell Logging LLC....978 568-9740
27 Zina Rd Hudson MA (01749) ***(G-11796)***
Oct, Whitinsville *Also called Omni Control Technology Inc* ***(G-16917)***
October Company Inc (PA)....413 527-9380
51 Ferry St Easthampton MA (01027) ***(G-10572)***
October Company Inc....413 529-0718
39 Oneil St Easthampton MA (01027) ***(G-10573)***
Ocular Therapeutix Inc (PA)....781 357-4000
24 Crosby Dr Bedford MA (01730) ***(G-7997)***
Odat Machine Inc....207 854-2455
20 Sanford Dr Gorham ME (04038) ***(G-6123)***
Odd Jobs Handyman Service LLC....203 397-5275
19 Grouse Ln Woodbridge CT (06525) ***(G-5474)***
Oddball Brewing Co....603 210-5654
6 Glass St Pembroke NH (03275) ***(G-19461)***
Oddo Print Shop & Copy Center, Torrington *Also called Oddo Print Shop Inc* ***(G-4590)***
Oddo Print Shop Inc....860 489-6585
142 E Main St Torrington CT (06790) ***(G-4590)***
Odhner Holographics....603 673-8651
5 Lake Front St Amherst NH (03031) ***(G-17580)***
Odis Inc....860 450-8407
22 Quail Run Rd Storrs Mansfield CT (06268) ***(G-4385)***
Odorox Iaq Inc....203 541-5577
1266 E Main St Ste 700r Stamford CT (06902) ***(G-4266)***
Odwalla Inc....336 877-1634
102 Longwood Ave Brookline MA (02446) ***(G-9213)***
Odyn, Somerville *Also called Armada Logistics Inc* ***(G-15156)***
OEM Sources LLC....203 283-5415
214 Broadway Milford CT (06460) ***(G-2325)***
Oerlikon AM Medical Inc....203 712-1030
10 Constitution Blvd S Shelton CT (06484) ***(G-3846)***
Oerlikon Blzers Cating USA Inc....413 786-9380
30 General Agawam MA (01001) ***(G-7442)***
Oesco Inc....413 369-4335
8 Ashfield Rd Conway MA (01341) ***(G-10164)***
of Cape Cod Incorporated....508 398-9100
12 Whites Path Ste 6 South Yarmouth MA (02664) ***(G-15332)***
Offbeet Composting Llc....603 568-2756
90 Bolt St Lowell MA (01852) ***(G-12415)***
Office Management Systems....617 921-2966
84 Central Dr Stoughton MA (02072) ***(G-15612)***
Officers Equipment Co....703 221-1912
177 Georgia Ave Providence RI (02905) ***(G-21082)***
Officers Wives Club....781 274-8079
11 Barksdale St Bldg 1614 Bedford MA (01731) ***(G-7998)***
Offset Prep Inc....617 472-7887
91 Newbury Ave Quincy MA (02171) ***(G-14643)***
Offshore Fuel....207 963-7068
130 Route 1 Gouldsboro ME (04607) ***(G-6137)***
Offshore Marine Outfitters....207 363-8862
15 Hannaford Dr York ME (03909) ***(G-7314)***
Ofs Brightwave LLC....508 347-2261
50 Hall Rd Sturbridge MA (01566) ***(G-15641)***
Ofs Fitel LLC....860 678-0371
55 Darling Dr Avon CT (06001) ***(G-39)***
Ofs Fitel LLC....508 347-2261
50 Hall Rd Sturbridge MA (01566) ***(G-15642)***
Ofs Specialty Photonics Div, Avon *Also called Ofs Fitel LLC* ***(G-39)***
Ogden Newspapers NH LLC....603 882-2741
110 Main St Ste 1 Nashua NH (03060) ***(G-19222)***
Ogee Inc....802 540-8082
1 Lawson Ln Ste 130 Burlington VT (05401) ***(G-21800)***
Ogle Specialty, Meriden *Also called Couturier Ino* ***(G-2089)***
Ogs Technologies Inc....203 271-9055
1855 Peck Ln Cheshire CT (06410) ***(G-749)***
Ohlson Packaging LLC (HQ)....508 977-0004
490 Constitution Dr Taunton MA (02780) ***(G-15770)***
Oil Purification Systems Inc....203 346-1800
2176 Thomaston Ave Waterbury CT (06704) ***(G-4932)***
Oizero9 Inc....207 324-3582
31 Smada Dr Sanford ME (04073) ***(G-6885)***
OK Durable Packaging Inc....508 303-8067
73 Bartlett St Marlborough MA (01752) ***(G-12800)***
OK Engineering Inc....978 562-1010
14 Main St Ste 10 Hudson MA (01749) ***(G-11797)***
Okay Industries Inc....860 225-8707
245 New Park Dr Berlin CT (06037) ***(G-99)***
Okay Medical Products Mfg, Berlin *Also called Okay Industries Inc* ***(G-99)***
Okchem Inc....978 992-1811
47 3rd St Ste 3 Cambridge MA (02141) ***(G-9597)***
Okonite Company....401 333-3500
5 Industrial Rd Cumberland RI (02864) ***(G-20336)***
Olaf Pharmaceutical Inc....508 755-3570
1 Innovation Dr Worcester MA (01605) ***(G-17436)***
Old Bh Inc (PA)....603 430-2111
100 Domain Dr Exeter NH (03833) ***(G-18126)***
Old Cambridge Products Corp....860 243-1761
244 Woodland Ave Bloomfield CT (06002) ***(G-247)***
Old Castle Foods LLC....203 426-1344
13 Old Castle Dr Newtown CT (06470) ***(G-2932)***
Old Coach Home Sales....860 774-1379
242 Harris Rd Sterling CT (06377) ***(G-4371)***
Old Creamery Grocery Store....413 634-5560
445 Berkshire Trl Cummington MA (01026) ***(G-10173)***
Old Dublin Road Inc....603 924-3861
130 Grove St Peterborough NH (03458) ***(G-19482)***
Old Dutch Mustard Co Inc....516 466-0522
68 Old Wilton Rd Greenville NH (03048) ***(G-18229)***
Old Fashion Milk Paint Co Inc....978 448-6336
436 Main St Groton MA (01450) ***(G-11292)***
Old Hancock Glassworks, Antrim *Also called Baker Salmon Christopher* ***(G-17592)***
Old Ironsides Energy LLC....617 366-2030
10 Saint James Ave Ste 19 Boston MA (02116) ***(G-8745)***
Old Materials New England, Leominster *Also called Crh Americas Inc* ***(G-12127)***
Old Neighborhood Foods....781 595-1557
37 Waterhill St Lynn MA (01905) ***(G-12531)***
Old Neighborhood Foods Div, Lynn *Also called Demakes Enterprises Inc* ***(G-12499)***
Old Newbury Crafters, Amesbury *Also called Good Taste LLC* ***(G-7487)***
Old Ni Incorporated....203 327-7300
50 Sunnyside Ave Stamford CT (06902) ***(G-4267)***
Old Route Two Spirits Inc....802 424-4864
69 Pitman Rd Barre VT (05641) ***(G-21633)***
Old Salt Box Publishing & Dist....978 750-8090
20 Locust St Danvers MA (01923) ***(G-10244)***
Old San Juan Bakery Inc....413 534-5555
408 High St Holyoke MA (01040) ***(G-11646)***
Old School Apparel....781 231-0753
341 Central St Ste A Saugus MA (01906) ***(G-14993)***
Old Timers Timber Frames....802 376-9529
37 Westminster W Rd Saxtons River VT (05154) ***(G-22401)***
Old Town Canoe, Old Town *Also called Johnson Otdoors Watercraft Inc* ***(G-6541)***
Old York Quarry Inc....603 772-6061
285 Bell Marsh Rd York ME (03909) ***(G-7315)***
Oldcastle Apg Northeast Inc....781 506-9473
46 Spring St Holbrook MA (02343) ***(G-11535)***
Oldcastle Buildingenvelope Inc....866 653-2278
333 Straw Field Rd 3 Warwick RI (02886) ***(G-21398)***
Oldcastle Infrastructure Inc....508 336-7600
41 Almeida Rd Rehoboth MA (02769) ***(G-14756)***
Oldcastle Infrastructure Inc....978 486-9600
265 Foster St Littleton MA (01460) ***(G-12315)***
Oldcastle Infrastructure Inc....860 673-3291
151 Old Farms Rd Avon CT (06001) ***(G-40)***
Oldcastle Lawn & Garden Inc....207 998-5580
481 Spring Water Rd Poland ME (04274) ***(G-6595)***
Oldcastle Materials Inc....603 669-2373
1 Sundial Ave Ste 310 Manchester NH (03103) ***(G-18893)***
Oldcastle North Atlantic, Holbrook *Also called Oldcastle Apg Northeast Inc* ***(G-11535)***
Oldcastle Precast Inc....508 867-8312
41 Almeida Rd Rehoboth MA (02769) ***(G-14757)***

A L P H A B E T I C

Olde Bostonian...617 282-9300
66 Von Hillern St Boston MA (02125) **(G-8746)**
Olde Burnside Brewing Co LLC...860 528-2200
780 Tolland St East Hartford CT (06108) **(G-1208)**
Olde Village Monogramming Inc...413 528-3904
2 Stillwell St Ste 1 Great Barrington MA (01230) **(G-11244)**
Oldenburg Group Inc...603 542-9548
169 Pleasant St Ste 3 Claremont NH (03743) **(G-17856)**
Oldenburg Group Incorporated...603 542-9548
423 River Rd Claremont NH (03743) **(G-17857)**
Oldfashioned Milk Paint Co, Groton *Also called Old Fashion Milk Paint Co Inc* **(G-11292)**
Oleary Welding Corp...508 476-9793
124 Davis St East Douglas MA (01516) **(G-10431)**
Oligo Factory Inc...508 275-3561
70 Bartzak Dr 1 Holliston MA (01746) **(G-11592)**
Olimpia Industries Incorporate...508 966-3392
175 North St Bellingham MA (02019) **(G-8054)**
Olive Capizzano Oils & Vinegar...860 495-2187
5 Coggswell St Ste 1 Pawcatuck CT (06379) **(G-3439)**
Olive Chiappetta Oil LLC...203 223-3655
50 Mathews St Stamford CT (06902) **(G-4268)**
Olive Fiore Oils & Vinegars...207 596-0276
503 Main St Rockland ME (04841) **(G-6807)**
Olive Lakonian Oil LLC...603 264-5025
561 Spruce St Manchester NH (03103) **(G-18894)**
Olive Mannys Oil Inc...413 233-2532
1872 Boston Rd Wilbraham MA (01095) **(G-16942)**
Olive Newburyport Oil...978 462-7700
50 Water St Ste 403 Newburyport MA (01950) **(G-13519)**
Olive Northampton Oil Co...413 537-7357
150 Main St Ste 14 Northampton MA (01060) **(G-14014)**
Olive Nutmeg Oil...860 354-7300
25 Main St New Milford CT (06776) **(G-2821)**
Olive Oils and Balsamics LLC...860 563-0105
35 New Rd Rocky Hill CT (06067) **(G-3726)**
Olive Sabor Oil Co...860 922-7483
22 Brookford Rd Somers CT (06071) **(G-3919)**
Olive Wildrose Oil...603 767-0597
24 Great Hill Rd South Berwick ME (03908) **(G-7003)**
Oliver Barrette Millwrights...401 421-3750
6 Fox Pl Providence RI (02903) **(G-21083)**
Oliver Welding & Fabricating...978 356-4488
30 Avery St Ipswich MA (01938) **(G-11933)**
Olives Oil...802 864-4908
87 Waybury Rd Colchester VT (05446) **(G-21874)**
Olivia's Croutons., Brandon *Also called Olivias Croutons Company Inc* **(G-21713)**
Olivias Croutons Company Inc...802 465-8245
2014 Frstdale Rd Brandon Brandon VT (05733) **(G-21713)**
Olsen & Silk Abrasives...978 744-4720
35 Congress St Salem MA (01970) **(G-14933)**
Olsen Marine...508 385-2180
357 Hokum Rock Rd Dennis MA (02638) **(G-10308)**
Olson Brothers Company...860 747-6844
272 Camp St Plainville CT (06062) **(G-3510)**
Olson S Logging LLC...207 474-8835
15 Strickland Rd Canaan ME (04924) **(G-5873)**
Olympic Adhesives Inc (PA)...800 829-1871
670 Canton St Norwood MA (02062) **(G-14186)**
Olympic Engineering Service...978 373-2789
65 Avco Rd Unit C Haverhill MA (01835) **(G-11456)**
Olympic STEel-Ps&w, Milford *Also called Tinsley GROup-Ps&w Inc* **(G-2376)**
Olympic Systems Corporation...781 721-2740
15 Lowell Ave Winchester MA (01890) **(G-17093)**
Olympus Surgical Tech Amer, Southborough *Also called Gyrus Acmi LLC* **(G-15359)**
Om Cass Swiss, Seymour *Also called New England Cap Company* **(G-3758)**
Omada Technologies LLC...603 944-7124
36 Maplewood Ave Portsmouth NH (03801) **(G-19602)**
Omar Coffee Company...860 667-8889
41 Commerce Ct Newington CT (06111) **(G-2888)**
Omarc LLC...781 702-6732
588 Pleasant St Ste 2 Norwood MA (02062) **(G-14187)**
Omega Engineering Inc (HQ)...203 359-1660
800 Connecticut Ave 5n01 Norwalk CT (06854) **(G-3211)**
Omega Engineering Inc...714 540-4914
800 Cnncticut Ave Ste 5n1 Norwalk CT (06854) **(G-3212)**
Omega Engineering Inc...203 359-7922
1 Omega Dr Stamford CT (06907) **(G-4269)**
Omega Filters, Brattleboro *Also called Omega Optical Incorporated* **(G-21742)**
Omega Laboratories Inc...978 768-7771
8 Gigante Dr Hampstead NH (03841) **(G-18247)**
Omega Olive Oil Inc...781 585-3179
47 Newcombs Mill Rd Kingston MA (02364) **(G-11962)**
Omega Optical Incorporated...802 251-7300
21 Omega Dr Brattleboro VT (05301) **(G-21742)**
Omegadyne, Norwalk *Also called Omega Engineering Inc* **(G-3211)**
Omerin Usa Inc...475 343-3450
95 Research Pkwy Meriden CT (06450) **(G-2113)**
Omg Inc (HQ)...413 789-0252
153 Bowles Rd Agawam MA (01001) **(G-7443)**
Omg Inc...413 786-0516
95 Bowles Rd Agawam MA (01001) **(G-7444)**
OMI International Corporation...203 575-5727
350 Frontage Rd West Haven CT (06516) **(G-5138)**
Omichron Corp...802 824-3136
340 Melendy Hill Rd South Londonderry VT (05155) **(G-22488)**
Omni Components Corp (PA)...603 882-4467
46 River Rd Ste 1 Hudson NH (03051) **(G-18422)**
Omni Control Technology Inc...508 234-9121
1 Main St Ste 4 Whitinsville MA (01588) **(G-16917)**
Omni Digital Printers, Lawrence *Also called S A N Inc* **(G-12073)**
Omni Glass Inc...978 667-6664
55 High St Ste 4 North Billerica MA (01862) **(G-13850)**
Omni Life Science Inc (HQ)...508 824-2444
480 Paramount Dr Raynham MA (02767) **(G-14723)**
Omni Manufacturing Co Inc...413 568-6175
51 Church St Westfield MA (01085) **(G-16709)**
Omni Measurement Systems Inc...802 497-2253
808 Hercules Dr Colchester VT (05446) **(G-21875)**
Omni Medical Systems, Colchester *Also called Omni Measurement Systems Inc* **(G-21875)**
Omni Metals Company Inc...603 692-6664
14 Interstate Dr Somersworth NH (03878) **(G-19845)**
Omni Mold Systems LLC...888 666-4755
21 Kimball Heights Ln Lisbon CT (06351) **(G-1944)**
Omni Press Inc...207 780-6664
141 Preble St Portland ME (04101) **(G-6705)**
Omni Signs LLC...603 279-1492
6 Wall St Meredith NH (03253) **(G-18976)**
Omni Spectra, Manchester *Also called Xma Corporation* **(G-18958)**
Omni Technologies Corp...603 679-2211
195 Route 125 Brentwood NH (03833) **(G-17753)**
Omni-Trol Industries Inc...781 284-8000
15 Whitmore Rd Revere MA (02151) **(G-14774)**
Omnicolor Printing, Rumford *Also called Village Press Inc* **(G-21198)**
Omnicron Electronics...860 928-0377
554 Liberty Hwy Ste 2 Putnam CT (06260) **(G-3623)**
Omniglass, North Billerica *Also called Omni Glass Inc* **(G-13850)**
Omnilife Science Inc...508 824-2444
175 Paramount Dr Unit 5 Raynham MA (02767) **(G-14724)**
Omnimedics...617 527-4590
33 Chipman Ave Melrose MA (02176) **(G-12986)**
Omniprobe Inc...214 572-6800
300 Baker Ave Ste 150 Concord MA (01742) **(G-10148)**
Omnova Solutions Inc...978 342-5831
83 Authority Dr Fitchburg MA (01420) **(G-10845)**
Omo Inc...401 421-5160
102 Waterman St Unit 2 Providence RI (02906) **(G-21084)**
Omron Microscan Systems Inc...603 598-8400
486 Amherst St Nashua NH (03063) **(G-19223)**
Omtec Corp...508 481-3322
181 Liberty St Marlborough MA (01752) **(G-12801)**
Omtec Ball Transfers, Marlborough *Also called Omtec Corp* **(G-12801)**
Omya Inc...802 459-3311
206 Omya W Whipple Florence VT (05744) **(G-21991)**
Omya Inc...802 459-3311
39 Main St Proctor VT (05765) **(G-22287)**
On Board Solutions LLC...603 373-6500
200 International Dr # 195 Portsmouth NH (03801) **(G-19603)**
On Deck Sports, Braintree *Also called Promounds Inc* **(G-9032)**
On Grade USA...508 351-9480
276 W Main St Rear Northborough MA (01532) **(G-14042)**
On Line Controls Inc...978 562-5353
9a Kane Industrial Dr Hudson MA (01749) **(G-11798)**
On Pins & Needles...603 625-6573
20 Allen St Manchester NH (03102) **(G-18895)**
On Semiconductor, East Greenwich *Also called Semicndctor Cmpnnts Inds of RI* **(G-20379)**
On Site Printing & Copying...781 449-1871
679 Highland Ave Needham Heights MA (02494) **(G-13341)**
On The Ball Cutnhaul...603 851-3283
N Main St Laconia NH (03246) **(G-18578)**
On The Beat Inc...617 491-8878
43 Thorndike St Ste 2-4 Cambridge MA (02141) **(G-9598)**
On The Road Inc...207 273-3780
2243 Camden Rd Warren ME (04864) **(G-7146)**
On The Spot...508 583-6070
120 S Main St West Bridgewater MA (02379) **(G-16448)**
On Time Screen Printing & Embr...203 874-4581
155 New Haven Ave Derby CT (06418) **(G-1076)**
On Time Software, Groton *Also called Ebsnet Inc* **(G-11288)**
On Track Karting Inc (PA)...203 626-0464
984 N Colony Rd Wallingford CT (06492) **(G-4781)**
On-Site Analysis Inc (HQ)...561 775-5756
1 Executive Dr Ste 101 Chelmsford MA (01824) **(G-9918)**
On-Site Analysis Inc...508 460-7778
72 Cedar Hill St Marlborough MA (01752) **(G-12802)**
Onapsis Inc (PA)...617 603-9932
60 State St Ste 1020 Boston MA (02109) **(G-8747)**
Once Upon A Kiln...508 657-1739
15 N Main St Ste C8 Bellingham MA (02019) **(G-8055)**

Oncoarendi Therapeutics LLC 609 571-0306
125 Devonshire Ln Madison CT (06443) ***(G-1971)***
Oncomed Phrm Svcs MA Inc 781 209-5470
150 Bear Hill Rd Waltham MA (02451) ***(G-16166)***
Oncosynergy Inc 617 755-9156
380 Greenwich Ave Greenwich CT (06830) ***(G-1636)***
One and Co Inc 860 892-5180
154 N Main St Norwich CT (06360) ***(G-3288)***
One Call Does It All, South Deerfield *Also called 1 Call Does It All and Then* ***(G-15244)***
One Eye Open Brewing Co LLC 207 536-4176
55 Pitt St Apt 2 Portland ME (04103) ***(G-6706)***
One Kid LLC (PA) 203 254-9978
188 Compo Rd S Westport CT (06880) ***(G-5219)***
One Off Apparel Inc 508 835-8883
18 Worcester St West Boylston MA (01583) ***(G-16424)***
One Source Print and Promo LLC 860 635-3257
150 Salem Dr Cromwell CT (06416) ***(G-857)***
Onebin 617 851-6402
19 Stanhope St Apt 1b Boston MA (02116) ***(G-8748)***
Onecloud Labs LLC 781 437-7966
250 Summer St Boston MA (02210) ***(G-8749)***
Onepin Inc 508 475-1000
2200 W Park Dr Ste 440 Westborough MA (01581) ***(G-16640)***
Onesource Printing 207 784-1538
170 Summer St Lewiston ME (04240) ***(G-6313)***
Oneview Commerce Inc 617 292-0400
70 Fargo St Ste 905 Boston MA (02210) ***(G-8750)***
Onguard, Waltham *Also called K2w LLC* ***(G-16136)***
Onix Corporation 866 290-5362
71 Main St Caribou ME (04736) ***(G-5889)***
Online Defense Products LLC 603 845-3211
142 Lowell Rd Unit 17385 Hudson NH (03051) ***(G-18423)***
Online Marketing Solutions 978 937-2363
128 Warren St Lowell MA (01852) ***(G-12416)***
Online Moderation Inc 617 686-7737
11 Woodland Rd Dover MA (02030) ***(G-10352)***
Online Print Resources 617 539-3961
19 Moore St Winthrop MA (02152) ***(G-17100)***
Onofrios Ultimate Foods Inc 203 469-4014
35 Wheeler St New Haven CT (06512) ***(G-2721)***
Onset Computer Corporation 508 759-9500
470 Macarthur Blvd Bourne MA (02532) ***(G-8948)***
Onshape Inc 844 667-4273
1 Alewife Ctr Ste 130 Cambridge MA (02140) ***(G-9599)***
Onsite Drug Testing Neng 603 226-3858
2 Industrial Park Dr # 2 Concord NH (03301) ***(G-17921)***
Onsite Services Inc 860 669-3988
23 Meadow Rd Clinton CT (06413) ***(G-792)***
Onto Innovation Inc (PA) 978 253-6200
16 Jonspin Rd Wilmington MA (01887) ***(G-17032)***
Ontraget Promotional, Stoneham *Also called LPI Printing and Graphic Inc* ***(G-15566)***
Onvio LLC 603 685-0404
20 Northwestern Dr Salem NH (03079) ***(G-19757)***
Onvio Servo LLC 603 685-0404
20 Northwestern Dr Salem NH (03079) ***(G-19758)***
Onyx Specialty Papers Inc 413 243-1231
40 Willow St South Lee MA (01260) ***(G-15319)***
Onyx Spectrum Technology 978 686-7000
15 Union St Ste 525 Lawrence MA (01840) ***(G-12068)***
Oomph LLC 203 216-9848
5 Elm St New Canaan CT (06840) ***(G-2612)***
Op USA Inc 978 658-5135
6 Ledgerock Way Unit 4 Acton MA (01720) ***(G-7376)***
Opac Inc (PA) 401 231-3552
964 Douglas Pike Smithfield RI (02917) ***(G-21242)***
Opal Data Technology Inc 401 435-0033
1 Richmond Sq Ste 230e Providence RI (02906) ***(G-21085)***
Opalala Inc 508 646-0950
994 Jefferson St Ste 10 Fall River MA (02721) ***(G-10743)***
Opco Inc 207 882-6783
916 Cross Point Rd Edgecomb ME (04556) ***(G-6003)***
Opco Laboratory Inc 978 345-2522
704 River St Fitchburg MA (01420) ***(G-10846)***
Oped Inc 781 891-6733
383 Boston Post Rd Ste 2 Sudbury MA (01776) ***(G-15665)***
Opel Connecticut Solar LLC 203 612-2366
3 Corporate Dr Ste 204 Shelton CT (06484) ***(G-3847)***
Open Solutions LLC (HQ) 860 815-5000
455 Winding Brook Dr # 101 Glastonbury CT (06033) ***(G-1569)***
Open SRC Prjct Fr Ntwk Dt ACS 401 284-1304
165 Dean Knauss Dr Narragansett RI (02882) ***(G-20644)***
Open Studios Press Inc 617 778-5265
450 Harrison Ave Ste 304 Boston MA (02118) ***(G-8751)***
Open Text Inc 617 378-3364
200 State St Fl 12 Boston MA (02109) ***(G-8752)***
Open Water Development LLC 646 883-2062
14 Cove Ridge Ln Old Greenwich CT (06870) ***(G-3313)***
Openair Inc 617 351-0232
211 Congress St Fl 8 Boston MA (02110) ***(G-8753)***
Openbridge Inc 857 234-1008
119 Braintree St Ste 413 Boston MA (02134) ***(G-8754)***
Openclinica LLC 617 621-8585
460 Totten Pond Rd Waltham MA (02451) ***(G-16167)***
OPENDAP, Narragansett *Also called Open SRC Prjct Fr Ntwk Dt ACS* ***(G-20644)***
Openeye Scientific Sftwr Inc 617 374-8844
222 Third St Ste 3120 Cambridge MA (02142) ***(G-9600)***
Ophir Optics, Wilmington *Also called Newport Corporation* ***(G-17030)***
Ophir Optics LLC 978 657-6410
90 Industrial Way Wilmington MA (01887) ***(G-17033)***
Opko Diagnostics LLC 781 933-8012
4 Constitution Way Ste E Woburn MA (01801) ***(G-17249)***
Opportunity/Discovery LLC 781 301-1596
220 Ballardvale St Ste C Wilmington MA (01887) ***(G-17034)***
Ops-Core Inc 617 670-3547
12 Channel St Ste 901b Boston MA (02210) ***(G-8755)***
Opsec Security Inc 617 226-3000
330 Congress St Fl 3 Boston MA (02210) ***(G-8756)***
Optamark CT LLC 203 325-1180
15 Bank St Ste 1 Stamford CT (06901) ***(G-4270)***
Optamark LLC (PA) 508 643-1017
865 E Washington St North Attleboro MA (02760) ***(G-13770)***
Optamark Printing & Marketing, North Attleboro *Also called Tantar Corp* ***(G-13783)***
Optamark Prtg & Mktg Companies, North Attleboro *Also called Optamark LLC* ***(G-13770)***
Optek Systems Inc 978 448-9376
97 Long Hill Rd Groton MA (01450) ***(G-11293)***
Opteon Corporation 617 520-6658
119 Mount Auburn St Cambridge MA (02138) ***(G-9601)***
Opti-Sciences Inc 603 883-4400
8 Winn Ave Hudson NH (03051) ***(G-18424)***
Optical Design Associates 203 249-6408
600 Summer St Stamford CT (06901) ***(G-4271)***
Optical Energy Technologies 203 357-0626
472 Westover Rd Stamford CT (06902) ***(G-4272)***
Optical Fiber Systems Inc 603 291-0345
829b Turnpike Rd New Ipswich NH (03071) ***(G-19309)***
Optical Metrology Inc 978 657-6303
1600 Osgood St Ste 1-150 North Andover MA (01845) ***(G-13721)***
Optical Polymers Lab Corp 401 722-0710
200 Weeden St Pawtucket RI (02860) ***(G-20870)***
Optical Research Technologies 203 762-9063
310 Hurlbutt St Wilton CT (06897) ***(G-5296)***
Optical Solutions Inc 603 826-4411
26 Bull Run Charlestown NH (03603) ***(G-17818)***
Opticonx Inc 888 748-6855
45 Danco Rd Putnam CT (06260) ***(G-3624)***
Opticraft Inc 781 938-0456
17d Everberg Rd Woburn MA (01801) ***(G-17250)***
Optics 1 Inc 603 296-0469
2 Cooper Ln Bedford NH (03110) ***(G-17657)***
Optics 1 Inc (HQ) 603 296-0469
2 Cooper Ln Bedford NH (03110) ***(G-17658)***
Optim Inc 508 765-5879
64 Mill St Southbridge MA (01550) ***(G-15397)***
Optim LLC 508 347-5100
64 Technology Park Rd Sturbridge MA (01566) ***(G-15643)***
Optimet, North Andover *Also called Optical Metrology Inc* ***(G-13721)***
Optimum Bindery Services Neng, Nashua *Also called Optimum Bindery Svcs of Neng* ***(G-19224)***
Optimum Bindery Svcs of Neng 603 886-3889
120 Nrthstern Blvd Unit 1 Nashua NH (03062) ***(G-19224)***
Optimum Sportswear Inc 978 689-2290
34 Groton St Fl 1 Lawrence MA (01843) ***(G-12069)***
Optimum Technologies Inc 508 765-8100
114 Pleasant St Southbridge MA (01550) ***(G-15398)***
Optinova Americas Inc 203 743-0908
22 Shelter Rock Ln # 24 Danbury CT (06810) ***(G-964)***
Optirtc Inc 844 678-4782
356 Boylston St Fl 2 Boston MA (02116) ***(G-8757)***
Opto-Line International Inc 978 658-7255
265 Ballardvale St Ste 3 Wilmington MA (01887) ***(G-17035)***
Optometrics Corporation 978 772-1700
521 Great Rd Ste 1 Littleton MA (01460) ***(G-12316)***
Optomistic Products Inc 207 865-9181
61 N Main St Leominster MA (01453) ***(G-12175)***
Optos Inc 508 787-1400
500 Nickerson Rd Ste 201 Marlborough MA (01752) ***(G-12803)***
Optos North America, Marlborough *Also called Optos Inc* ***(G-12803)***
Optowares Incorporated 781 427-7106
15 Presidential Way Woburn MA (01801) ***(G-17251)***
Optris Ir Sensing LLC 603 766-6060
200 International Dr # 170 Portsmouth NH (03801) ***(G-19604)***
Opus Telecom Inc 508 875-4444
119 Herbert St Framingham MA (01702) ***(G-10989)***
Or-6 LLC 617 515-1909
49 Boardley Rd Sandwich MA (02563) ***(G-14971)***
Or-Live, Inc., Farmington *Also called Broadcastmed Inc* ***(G-1470)***
Oraceutical LLC 413 243-6634
815 Pleasant St Lee MA (01238) ***(G-12094)***

ALPHABETIC

Oracle America Inc 781 672-4280
580 Winter St Waltham MA (02451) ***(G-16168)***
Oracle America Inc 781 744-0000
10 Van De Graaff Dr Burlington MA (01803) ***(G-9313)***
Oracle America Inc 203 703-3000
900 Long Ridge Rd Bldg 1 Stamford CT (06902) ***(G-4273)***
Oracle Corporation 860 632-8329
54 Shady Hill Ln Middletown CT (06457) ***(G-2208)***
Oracle Corporation 401 245-1110
3 Veritas Way Barrington RI (02806) ***(G-20050)***
Oracle Corporation 401 658-3900
20 Altieri Way Warwick RI (02886) ***(G-21399)***
Oracle Corporation 617 497-7713
101 Main St Ste 1 Cambridge MA (02142) ***(G-9602)***
Oracle Corporation 603 668-4998
150 Dow St Ste 301 Manchester NH (03101) ***(G-18896)***
Oracle Corporation 781 744-0000
10 Van De Graaff Dr Ste 1 Burlington MA (01803) ***(G-9314)***
Oracle Otc Subsidiary LLC 617 386-1000
1 Main St Ste 7 Cambridge MA (02142) ***(G-9603)***
Oracle Systems Corporation 603 897-3000
1 Oracle Dr Ste 1 # 1 Nashua NH (03062) ***(G-19225)***
Oracle Systems Corporation 781 744-0900
124 Ocean St Lynn MA (01902) ***(G-12532)***
Orafol Americas Inc 860 676-7100
120 Darling Dr Avon CT (06001) ***(G-41)***
Oral Fluid Dynamics LLC 860 561-5036
400 Farmington Ave R1844 Farmington CT (06032) ***(G-1502)***
Oram Corporate Advisors 617 701-7430
189 Wells Ave Ste 100 Newton MA (02459) ***(G-13622)***
Orange Cheese Company 917 603-4378
5 Hampton Close Orange CT (06477) ***(G-3377)***
Orange Democrat 203 298-4575
297 Boston Post Rd Orange CT (06477) ***(G-3378)***
Orange Research Inc 203 877-5657
140 Cascade Blvd Milford CT (06460) ***(G-2326)***
Orange Restoration Labs, Orange *Also called Sally Conant* ***(G-3383)***
Orange Shutter Studios 413 544-8403
85 Poplar Ave West Springfield MA (01089) ***(G-16537)***
Orbetron LLC 651 983-2872
45 Industrial Rd Ste 208 Cumberland RI (02864) ***(G-20337)***
Orbit Design LLC 203 393-0171
290 Pratt St Meriden CT (06450) ***(G-2114)***
Orbit Plastics Corp 978 465-5300
45 Prince St Danvers MA (01923) ***(G-10245)***
Orbital Biosciences LLC (PA) 978 887-5077
4 Winsor Ln Topsfield MA (01983) ***(G-15864)***
Orbograph USA, Billerica *Also called Orbotech Inc* ***(G-8270)***
Orbotech Inc 978 667-6037
44 Manning Rd Ste 1 Billerica MA (01821) ***(G-8270)***
Orca Inc 860 223-4180
199 Whiting St New Britain CT (06051) ***(G-2558)***
Orchard Equipment & Supply Co, Conway *Also called Oesco Inc* ***(G-10164)***
Orchard Tool Die Inc 413 433-1233
34 Front St Ste 29 Indian Orchard MA (01151) ***(G-11892)***
Ordway Electric & Machine 802 476-8011
1599 Carrier Rd Graniteville VT (05654) ***(G-22001)***
Ore Offshore, West Wareham *Also called Edgeone LLC* ***(G-16570)***
OReilly Media Inc 617 354-5800
2 Avenue De Lafayette # 6 Boston MA (02111) ***(G-8758)***
Organic Project The, Duxbury *Also called W2w Partners LLC* ***(G-10404)***
Organic Studio 13 LLC 770 369-0756
110 Kenyon Ave Unit 13 Pawtucket RI (02861) ***(G-20871)***
Organogenesis Inc (HQ) 781 575-0775
85 Dan Rd Canton MA (02021) ***(G-9764)***
Organomation Associates Inc 978 838-7300
266 River Rd W Berlin MA (01503) ***(G-8092)***
Oriental Chow Mein Co, Fall River *Also called O C M Inc* ***(G-10742)***
Oriental Research Partners 781 642-1216
61 Tripp St Framingham MA (01702) ***(G-10990)***
Original Brdford Soap Wrks Inc (HQ) 401 821-2141
200 Providence St West Warwick RI (02893) ***(G-21506)***
Original Gourmet Food Co LLC 603 894-1200
52 Stiles Rd Ste 201 Salem NH (03079) ***(G-19759)***
Original Irregular 207 265-2773
239 Main St Ste 1 Kingfield ME (04947) ***(G-6254)***
Origio Midatlantic Devices Inc 856 762-2000
75 Corporate Dr Trumbull CT (06611) ***(G-4629)***
Origo Automation Inc 877 943-5677
175 Cabot St Ste 100 Lowell MA (01854) ***(G-12417)***
Origyn Inc 781 888-8834
780 Boylston St Apt 25k Boston MA (02199) ***(G-8759)***
Orion Enterprises Inc (HQ) 913 342-1653
1600 Osgood St Ste 2005 North Andover MA (01845) ***(G-13722)***
Orion Entrance Control Inc 603 527-4187
76a Lexington Dr Laconia NH (03246) ***(G-18579)***
Orion Fittings, North Andover *Also called Orion Enterprises Inc* ***(G-13722)***
Orion Fittings Inc 978 689-6150
815 Chestnut St North Andover MA (01845) ***(G-13723)***
Orion Industries Incorporated 978 772-0020
1 Orion Park Dr Ayer MA (01432) ***(G-7932)***
ORION MAGAZINE, Great Barrington *Also called The Orion Society Inc* ***(G-11248)***
Orion Manufacturing LLC 860 572-2921
800 Flanders Rd Unit 4-8 Mystic CT (06355) ***(G-2447)***
Orion Red, Smithfield *Also called Orion Ret Svcs & Fixturing Inc* ***(G-21243)***
Orion Ret Svcs & Fixturing Inc 401 334-5000
270 Jenckes Hill Rd Smithfield RI (02917) ***(G-21243)***
Orion Ropeworks Inc (PA) 207 877-2224
953 Benton Ave Winslow ME (04901) ***(G-7273)***
Orion Ropeworks LLC 207 877-2224
953 Benton Ave Winslow ME (04901) ***(G-7274)***
Orion Society, The, Great Barrington *Also called Myrin Institute Inc* ***(G-11242)***
Orisha Oracle Inc 203 612-8989
59 Regent St Bridgeport CT (06606) ***(G-461)***
Orleans Packing & Dist Co, Hyde Park *Also called Gebelein Group Inc* ***(G-11867)***
Oro, Brattleboro *Also called C E Bradely Lab Inc* ***(G-21721)***
Orono House of Pizza 207 866-5505
154 Park St Orono ME (04473) ***(G-6557)***
Orono Spectral Solutions Inc 866 269-8007
25 Freedom Pkwy Hermon ME (04401) ***(G-6192)***
ORourke Welding Inc 508 755-6360
851 Millbury St Worcester MA (01607) ***(G-17437)***
Orpro Vision LLC 617 676-1101
44 Manning Rd Ste 4 Billerica MA (01821) ***(G-8271)***
Orsted North America Inc 857 284-1430
1 International Pl # 2610 Boston MA (02110) ***(G-8760)***
Orteoponix LLC 203 804-9775
22 Scottron Dr Storrs CT (06268) ***(G-4382)***
Orthotic & Prosthetic Ctrs LLC 508 775-7151
126b Mid Tech Dr West Yarmouth MA (02673) ***(G-16581)***
Orthotic and Prosthetic Center 508 775-2570
197 Quincy Ave Ste 102 Braintree MA (02184) ***(G-9029)***
Orthotic Solutions Inc 774 205-2278
2277 State Rd Ste 5 Plymouth MA (02360) ***(G-14570)***
Orthotics Prosthetics Labs Inc 413 585-8622
241 King St Ste 123 Northampton MA (01060) ***(G-14015)***
Orthotics West Inc 413 736-3000
49 Liberty St Holyoke MA (01040) ***(G-11647)***
Orthozon Technologies LLC 203 989-4937
175 Atlantic St Ste 206 Stamford CT (06901) ***(G-4274)***
Ortronics Inc (HQ) 860 445-3900
125 Eugene Oneill Dr # 140 New London CT (06320) ***(G-2776)***
Ortronics Inc 877 295-3472
60 Woodlawn St West Hartford CT (06110) ***(G-5088)***
Ortronics Legrand 860 767-3515
14 Windermere Way Ivoryton CT (06442) ***(G-1908)***
Orvis Company 802 362-3750
4182 Main St Manchester VT (05254) ***(G-22078)***
Orwell Sand & Gravel 802 345-6028
1200 Park Hill Rd Benson VT (05743) ***(G-21693)***
Osaap America LLC 877 652-7227
10 Kidder Rd Chelmsford MA (01824) ***(G-9919)***
Oscar Jobs 860 583-7834
165 Riverside Ave Bristol CT (06010) ***(G-588)***
Oscomp Systems Inc (PA) 617 418-4640
337 Summer St 40 Boston MA (02210) ***(G-8761)***
Osda Contract Services Inc 203 878-2155
291 Pepes Farm Rd Milford CT (06460) ***(G-2327)***
Osda Inc 203 878-2155
98 Quirk Rd Milford CT (06460) ***(G-2328)***
Osf Flavors Inc (PA) 860 298-8350
40 Baker Hollow Rd Windsor CT (06095) ***(G-5352)***
Osgood Welding, Claremont *Also called Ralph L Osgood Inc* ***(G-17859)***
Oshea Mary Lynn Weaving Studio 802 545-2090
2672 Weybridge Rd Middlebury VT (05753) ***(G-22117)***
Oshkosh Corporation 800 392-9921
6 Wayside Rd Burlington MA (01803) ***(G-9315)***
Oshkosh Corporation 860 653-5548
35 Nicholson Rd East Granby CT (06026) ***(G-1138)***
OSI, Charlestown *Also called Optical Solutions Inc* ***(G-17818)***
Oskr Inc 475 238-2634
14a Buell St North Haven CT (06473) ***(G-3046)***
Oslo Switch Inc 203 272-2794
30 Diana Ct Cheshire CT (06410) ***(G-750)***
Oslo Switches, Cheshire *Also called Oslo Switch Inc* ***(G-750)***
Osprey Compliance Software LLC 888 677-7394
275 2nd Ave Ste 2 Waltham MA (02451) ***(G-16169)***
Osram Sylvania Inc 603 772-4331
131 Portsmouth Ave Exeter NH (03833) ***(G-18127)***
Osram Sylvania Inc 603 669-5350
131 Portsmouth Ave Exeter NH (03833) ***(G-18128)***
Osram Sylvania Inc (HQ) 978 570-3000
200 Ballardvale St # 305 Wilmington MA (01887) ***(G-17036)***
Osram Sylvania Inc 978 750-3900
200 Ballardvale St # 305 Wilmington MA (01887) ***(G-17037)***
Osram Sylvania Inc 401 723-1378
1193 Broad St Central Falls RI (02863) ***(G-20122)***

Osram Sylvania Inc 603 464-7235
275 W Main St Hillsborough NH (03244) *(G-18317)*
Osram Sylvania Inc 978 750-1529
71 Cherry Hill Dr Beverly MA (01915) *(G-8163)*
Ossipee Aggregates Corporation (HQ) 617 227-9000
100 N Washington St Boston MA (02114) *(G-8762)*
Ossipee Chipping Inc 603 539-5097
400 Route 25 E Center Ossipee NH (03814) *(G-17805)*
Ossipee Mountain Land Co LLC 603 323-7677
844 Whittier Rd Tamworth NH (03886) *(G-19894)*
Ostby Barton Division, Lincoln *Also called Everett Charles Tech LLC (G-20572)*
Oster Pewter, North Kingstown *Also called Callico Metals Inc (G-20695)*
Osterman & Company Inc (PA) 203 272-2233
726 S Main St Cheshire CT (06410) *(G-751)*
Osterman & Company Inc 203 272-2233
726 S Main St Cheshire CT (06410) *(G-752)*
Osterman Trading Div, Cheshire *Also called Osterman & Company Inc (G-751)*
Other Paper 802 864-6670
1340 Williston Rd Ste 201 South Burlington VT (05403) *(G-22455)*
Otis Elevator Company, Canton *Also called Delta Elevator Service Corp (G-697)*
Otis Elevator Company (HQ) 860 674-3000
1 Carrier Pl Farmington CT (06032) *(G-1503)*
Otis Elevator Company 860 290-3318
5 Farm Springs Rd Farmington CT (06032) *(G-1504)*
Otis Enterprises Marine Corp 207 548-6362
85 Prospect St Searsport ME (04974) *(G-6953)*
Otis Gazette 207 398-9001
14 Dickey Rd Allagash ME (04774) *(G-5519)*
Ottaway Newspapers 508 775-1200
319 Main St Hyannis MA (02601) *(G-11852)*
Otter Creek Awning, Williston *Also called Durasol Systems Inc (G-22663)*
Otter Creek Brewing Co LLC 802 388-0727
793 Exchange St Middlebury VT (05753) *(G-22118)*
Otter Creek Furniture, Salisbury *Also called Merle Schloff (G-22399)*
Otterman Logging & Excavating 802 439-5714
11 Branch Road Pvt West Topsham VT (05086) *(G-22623)*
Ouellette Industries Inc 508 695-0964
100 John L Dietsch Blvd B Attleboro Falls MA (02763) *(G-7816)*
Ouellette Sand & Gravel Inc 207 445-4131
80 Southern Oaks Dr South China ME (04358) *(G-7006)*
Ouimette Printing Inc 413 736-5926
40 Kelso Ave West Springfield MA (01089) *(G-16538)*
Our Family Farms Massachusetts, Greenfield *Also called Pioneer Vly Milk Mktg Coop Inc (G-11272)*
Our Place - Shop For Men Inc (PA) 401 231-2370
2044 Smith St North Providence RI (02911) *(G-20769)*
Our Place For Tuxedos, North Providence *Also called Our Place - Shop For Men Inc (G-20769)*
Our Town Crier 203 400-5000
36 Lyons Plains Rd Westport CT (06880) *(G-5220)*
Our Town Publishing, Medway *Also called Nrt Inc (G-12968)*
Our Town Publishing Inc 603 776-2500
1080 N Barnstead Rd Center Barnstead NH (03225) *(G-17790)*
Out & About Magazine 413 783-6704
21 Kay St Springfield MA (01109) *(G-15496)*
Out Sweet Tooth Cupcakes 207 272-4363
18 Romano Rd South Portland ME (04106) *(G-7035)*
Outdoor Enhancements LLC 603 524-8090
343 Court St Laconia NH (03246) *(G-18580)*
Outdoor Life Channel, Stamford *Also called Los Angles Tmes Cmmnctions LLC (G-4240)*
Outdoor Outfitters Inc 508 255-0455
15 Rt 6a Orleans MA (02653) *(G-14239)*
Outer Light Brewing Co LLC 475 201-9972
266 Bridge St Ste 1 Groton CT (06340) *(G-1681)*
Outer Limits Publishing LLC 802 422-2399
5465 Rte 4 Killington VT (05751) *(G-22055)*
Outerlmits Offshore Powerboats 401 253-7300
3 Minturn Farm Rd Bristol RI (02809) *(G-20096)*
Outland Engineering Inc 800 797-3709
167 Cherry St Pmb 280 Milford CT (06460) *(G-2329)*
Outlast Uniform Corporation 617 889-0510
6 Hancock St Chelsea MA (02150) *(G-9962)*
Outlaw Audio LLC 508 286-4110
10b Commerce Way Ste B Norton MA (02766) *(G-14085)*
Outpost Exploration LLC 203 762-7206
7 Broad Axe Ln Wilton CT (06897) *(G-5297)*
Outpost Journal 401 569-1211
532 Kinsley Ave Unit 501 Providence RI (02909) *(G-21086)*
Outrageous Lures LLC 347 509-8610
118 Long Pond Rd Ste C Plymouth MA (02360) *(G-14571)*
Outsource Electronic Mfg 401 615-0705
29 Linwood Dr North Kingstown RI (02852) *(G-20732)*
Outsystems Inc 617 837-6840
55 Thomson Pl Boston MA (02210) *(G-8763)*
Ov Loop Inc 781 640-2234
240 Newbury St Danvers MA (01923) *(G-10246)*
Oventrop Corp 860 413-9173
29 Kripes Rd East Granby CT (06026) *(G-1139)*
Overhaul Support Services LLC 860 653-1980
18 Connecticut South Dr East Granby CT (06026) *(G-1140)*
Overhaul Support Services LLC (PA) 860 264-2101
5 Connecticut South Dr East Granby CT (06026) *(G-1141)*
Overlook Industries Inc 413 527-4344
193 Northampton St Ste 2 Easthampton MA (01027) *(G-10574)*
Overseas Project Advancement 978 255-1816
61 Turkey Hill Rd West Newbury MA (01985) *(G-16492)*
Overtone Labs Inc 978 682-1257
60 Island St Ste 1 Lawrence MA (01840) *(G-12070)*
Overtone Studio Inc 774 290-2900
492 Old Connecticut Path # 102 Framingham MA (01701) *(G-10991)*
Ovl Manufacturing Inc LLC 860 829-0271
49 Cambridge Hts Berlin CT (06037) *(G-100)*
Ovtene Inc 617 852-4828
11 Sassamon Trl Ste 221 Marion MA (02738) *(G-12701)*
Owen Gray & Son 207 989-3575
300 Chamberlain St Brewer ME (04412) *(G-5800)*
Owen Gray and Son, Brewer *Also called Owen Gray & Son (G-5800)*
Owen Tool and Mfg Co Inc 860 628-6540
149 Aircraft Rd Southington CT (06489) *(G-4070)*
Owl Separation Systems LLC 603 559-9297
25 Nimble Hill Rd Newington NH (03801) *(G-19323)*
Owl Stamp Company Inc 978 452-4541
142 Middle St Lowell MA (01852) *(G-12418)*
Owlstamp Visual Solutions, Lowell *Also called Owl Stamp Company Inc (G-12418)*
Owlstone Inc (PA) 203 908-4848
19 Ludlow Rd Ste 202 Westport CT (06880) *(G-5221)*
Owncloud Inc 617 515-3664
124 Washington St Ste 101 Foxboro MA (02035) *(G-10896)*
Ox Paper Tube and Core Inc 508 879-1141
89 October Hill Rd Holliston MA (01746) *(G-11593)*
Oxbow Creative LLC 802 870-0354
47 Maple St Ste 332 Burlington VT (05401) *(G-21801)*
Oxford Asphalt Inc 508 987-0321
190 Old Webster Rd Oxford MA (01540) *(G-14271)*
Oxford Asphalt Mfg & Pav, Oxford *Also called Oxford Asphalt Inc (G-14271)*
Oxford Diagnostic Laboratories, Marlborough *Also called Oxford Immunotec Inc (G-12804)*
Oxford General Industries Inc 203 758-4467
3 Gramar Ave Prospect CT (06712) *(G-3590)*
Oxford Graphics, Peabody *Also called Kondelin Associates Inc (G-14348)*
Oxford Immunotec Inc (HQ) 508 481-4648
700 Nickerson Rd Ste 200 Marlborough MA (01752) *(G-12804)*
Oxford Immunotec USA Inc 833 682-6933
700 Nickerson Rd Ste 200 Marlborough MA (01752) *(G-12805)*
Oxford Industries Conn Inc 860 225-3700
221 South St Bldg H New Britain CT (06051) *(G-2559)*
Oxford Instrs Msrement Systems 978 369-9933
300 Baker Ave Ste 150 Concord MA (01742) *(G-10149)*
Oxford Instruments America, Concord *Also called Oxford Instrs Msrement Systems (G-10149)*
Oxford Performance Mtls Inc 860 698-9300
30 S Satellite Rd South Windsor CT (06074) *(G-3997)*
Oxford Polymers, New Britain *Also called Oxford Industries Conn Inc (G-2559)*
Oxford Science Inc 203 881-3115
178 Christian St Oxford CT (06478) *(G-3417)*
Oxford Science Center LLC 203 751-1912
Iii One American Way Oxford CT (06478) *(G-3418)*
Oxford Spring 5301, Oxford *Also called Leggett & Platt Incorporated (G-14265)*
Oxford Timber Inc 207 539-9656
60 E Oxford Rd Oxford ME (04270) *(G-6570)*
Oxpekk Performance Mtls Inc 860 698-9300
30 S Satellite Rd South Windsor CT (06074) *(G-3998)*
Oyo Sportstoys Inc 978 264-2000
108 Forest Ave Hudson MA (01749) *(G-11799)*
Oyster Creek Mushrooms Company 207 563-1076
61 Standpipe Rd Damariscotta ME (04543) *(G-5938)*
Oztek Corp 603 546-0090
11 Continental Blvd # 104 Merrimack NH (03054) *(G-19018)*
Ozzie Printing Inc 978 657-9400
24b Conn St Woburn MA (01801) *(G-17252)*
P & B Fabrics Inc 800 351-9087
45 Washington St Ste 47 Pawtucket RI (02860) *(G-20872)*
P & B Manufacturing, Providence *Also called Reed Allison Group Inc (G-21107)*
P & D Machine Inc 603 883-1814
29 Mason St Nashua NH (03060) *(G-19226)*
P & K Custom Acrylics Inc 781 388-2601
40 Faulkner St Malden MA (02148) *(G-12585)*
P & M Brick & Block Inc 617 924-6020
213 Arlington St Watertown MA (02472) *(G-16304)*
P & M Investments LLC 860 745-3600
1 Anngina Dr Enfield CT (06082) *(G-1373)*
P & M Tool & Die Inc 603 942-5636
372 1st Nh Tpke Northwood NH (03261) *(G-19413)*
P & M Welding Co LLC 860 528-2077
38 Edwin Rd South Windsor CT (06074) *(G-3999)*
P & R Machines 508 883-8727
22 David Dr Blackstone MA (01504) *(G-8313)*

ALPHABETIC

P & S Printing LLC...203 327-9818
513 Summer St Stamford CT (06901) ***(G-4275)***
P A G Industries Inc...978 265-5610
70 Princeton St Ste 2 North Chelmsford MA (01863) ***(G-13906)***
P A S, Lee *Also called Protective Armored Systems Inc **(G-12095)***
P A W Inc...413 589-0399
200 State St Bldg 102 Ludlow MA (01056) ***(G-12474)***
P and L Trucking...802 875-2819
31 Toma Rd Chester VT (05143) ***(G-21847)***
P C I Group...203 327-0410
652 Glenbrook Rd 3-201 Stamford CT (06906) ***(G-4276)***
P C Northern Prosthetics...207 768-5348
117 Academy St Presque Isle ME (04769) ***(G-6768)***
P C S, Taunton *Also called Professnal Cntract Strlization **(G-15774)***
P Craft Jewelry, Attleboro *Also called Plastic Craft Novelty Co Inc **(G-7777)***
P E P, Attleboro *Also called Precision Engineered Pdts LLC **(G-7782)***
P E P, Fryeburg *Also called Physician Engineered Products **(G-6101)***
P G L Industries Inc...508 679-8845
1432 Gar Hwy Swansea MA (02777) ***(G-15712)***
P G of New England, Concord *Also called Photographic Corp New England **(G-10150)***
P G T, Franklin *Also called Princton Gamma-Tech Instrs Inc **(G-11075)***
P I C, Windsor *Also called Purchasing & Inventory Cons **(G-22713)***
P J Albert Inc...978 345-7828
199 Upham St Fitchburg MA (01420) ***(G-10847)***
P L Woodworking...860 354-6855
4 Deer Hill Rd Sherman CT (06784) ***(G-3895)***
P M C, Malden *Also called Palmer Manufacturing Co Llc **(G-12586)***
P M I, East Windsor *Also called Plasticoid Manufacturing Inc **(G-1298)***
P M I, Woonsocket *Also called Polyurethane Molding Inds Inc **(G-21576)***
P M Kelly Inc...207 435-6654
27 Clark Rd Ashland ME (04732) ***(G-5539)***
P M S Manufactured Pdts Inc...978 281-2600
10 Sadler St Gloucester MA (01930) ***(G-11200)***
P M Tile and Grout Care, Bridgewater *Also called Paul McNamara **(G-9086)***
P P I, Williamstown *Also called Progressive Plastics Inc **(G-22650)***
P S M P, Biddeford *Also called Precision Screw Mch Pdts Inc **(G-5758)***
P Straker Ltd...508 996-4804
8 Middle St South Dartmouth MA (02748) ***(G-15241)***
P T I, Enfield *Also called Pti Industries Inc **(G-1376)***
P T P Machining Inc...800 872-3400
25 Sullivan Rd Ste 7 North Billerica MA (01862) ***(G-13851)***
P T Tool & Machine, Derby *Also called Peter Tasi **(G-1077)***
P V D, Wilmington *Also called Pvd Products Inc **(G-17040)***
P&G Graphic Solutions Inc...413 731-9213
784 Page Blvd Springfield MA (01104) ***(G-15497)***
P&G Metal Components Corp...860 243-2220
98 Filley St Bloomfield CT (06002) ***(G-248)***
P&L Machine, Littleton *Also called Dakin Road Investments Inc **(G-12299)***
P&M Cnc Machining, Northwood *Also called P & M Tool & Die Inc **(G-19413)***
P&M Welding, South Windsor *Also called P & M Welding Co LLC **(G-3999)***
P&N Jewelry Inc...617 889-3200
312 Broadway Chelsea MA (02150) ***(G-9963)***
P&P Tool & Die Corp...203 874-2571
72 Erna Ave Milford CT (06461) ***(G-2330)***
P-A-R Precision Inc...860 491-4181
15 Town Line Rd Wolcott CT (06716) ***(G-5451)***
P-Q Controls Inc (PA)...860 583-6994
95 Dolphin Rd Bristol CT (06010) ***(G-589)***
P-Q Controls Inc...207 564-7141
64 Park St Dover Foxcroft ME (04426) ***(G-5962)***
P.J. Noyes, Lancaster *Also called Trividia Mfg Solutions **(G-18606)***
P.M.c, Danbury *Also called PMC Engineering LLC **(G-968)***
P/A Industries Inc (PA)...860 243-8306
522 Cottage Grove Rd B Bloomfield CT (06002) ***(G-249)***
P2 Science Inc...203 821-7457
4 Research Dr Woodbridge CT (06525) ***(G-5475)***
P2k Printing LLC...603 356-2010
1305 White Mountain Hwy North Conway NH (03860) ***(G-19378)***
Pac Products, Yalesville *Also called Joval Machine Co Inc **(G-5505)***
Pace Associates Inc...781 433-0639
370 Weston Rd Wellesley MA (02482) ***(G-16379)***
Pace Industries LLC...978 667-8400
67 Faulkner St North Billerica MA (01862) ***(G-13852)***
Pace Medical Inc...781 862-4242
2643 Massachusetts Ave Lexington MA (02421) ***(G-12252)***
Pacheco Gear Inc...508 763-5709
24 Middleboro Rd East Freetown MA (02717) ***(G-10456)***
Pacific Pathway, Wellesley Hills *Also called Life+gear Inc **(G-16398)***
Pacific Printing Inc...413 585-5700
19 Damon Rd Northampton MA (01060) ***(G-14016)***
Package Industries Inc...508 865-5871
15 Harback Rd Sutton MA (01590) ***(G-15688)***
Package Machinery Company Inc...413 315-3801
80 Commercial St Holyoke MA (01040) ***(G-11648)***
Package Printing Company Inc...413 736-2748
33 Myron St West Springfield MA (01089) ***(G-16539)***
Package Steel Buildings, Sutton *Also called Package Industries Inc **(G-15688)***
Package Steel Systems Inc...508 865-5871
15 Harback Rd Sutton MA (01590) ***(G-15689)***
Packaging and Crating Tech LLC...203 759-1799
150 Mattatuck Heights Rd Waterbury CT (06705) ***(G-4933)***
Packaging Company LLC (PA)...401 943-5040
1 Carding Ln Johnston RI (02919) ***(G-20527)***
Packaging Concepts Assoc LLC...860 489-0480
230 Ella Grasso Ave Torrington CT (06790) ***(G-4591)***
Packaging Corporation America...978 256-4586
33 Glen Ave Chelmsford MA (01824) ***(G-9920)***
Packaging Corporation America...413 584-6132
525 Mount Tom Rd Northampton MA (01060) ***(G-14017)***
Packaging Corporation America...413 562-0610
61 Turnpike Industrial Rd Westfield MA (01085) ***(G-16710)***
Packaging Devices Inc (PA)...508 548-0224
61 Homestead Ln Teaticket MA (02536) ***(G-15802)***
Packaging Products Corporation (PA)...508 997-5150
198 Herman Melville Blvd New Bedford MA (02740) ***(G-13434)***
Packaging Specialties Inc...978 462-1300
3 Opportunity Way Newburyport MA (01950) ***(G-13520)***
Packard Inc...203 758-6219
6 Industrial Rd Prospect CT (06712) ***(G-3591)***
Packard Specialties, Prospect *Also called Packard Inc **(G-3591)***
Paclantic Inc...603 542-8600
91 Main St Ste C Claremont NH (03743) ***(G-17858)***
Paclantic Boot Company, Claremont *Also called Paclantic Inc **(G-17858)***
Paco Assensio Woodworking LLC...203 536-2608
15 Meadow St Norwalk CT (06854) ***(G-3213)***
Pacon Corporation...508 370-0780
79 Main St Ste 202 Framingham MA (01702) ***(G-10992)***
Pacos Tacos Mobile Mex LLC...401 793-0515
262 S Clarendon St Cranston RI (02910) ***(G-20269)***
Pacothane Technologies (PA)...781 729-0927
37 East St Winchester MA (01890) ***(G-17094)***
Pacothane Technologies...781 756-3163
76 Holton St Woburn MA (01801) ***(G-17253)***
Pact Inc...203 759-1799
150 Mattatuck Heights Rd Waterbury CT (06705) ***(G-4934)***
Pactiv Corporation...203 288-7722
458 Sackett Point Rd North Haven CT (06473) ***(G-3047)***
Pad Print Machinery of Vermont...802 362-0844
201 Tennis Way East Dorset VT (05253) ***(G-21915)***
Padco Inc...508 753-8486
19 Wells St Worcester MA (01604) ***(G-17438)***
Padebco Custom Boats Inc...207 529-5106
Anchor Inn Rd Round Pond ME (04564) ***(G-6832)***
Padlock Therapeutics Inc...978 381-9601
200 Cambridge Park Dr Cambridge MA (02140) ***(G-9604)***
Page Belting Company Inc...603 796-2463
104 High St Boscawen NH (03303) ***(G-17705)***
Page Mc Lellan Inc...401 397-2795
136 Mishnock Rd West Greenwich RI (02817) ***(G-21462)***
Page Same Publishing Inc...978 486-4684
531 King St Ste 5 Littleton MA (01460) ***(G-12317)***
Page Street Publishing Company...978 594-8758
27 Congress St Ste 105 Salem MA (01970) ***(G-14934)***
Pagell Corporation...508 429-2998
74 Lowland St Holliston MA (01746) ***(G-11594)***
Pagepro Wireless...603 749-5600
332 Central Ave Dover NH (03820) ***(G-18044)***
Pagio Inc...508 756-5006
84 Winter St Worcester MA (01604) ***(G-17439)***
Pagoda Group LLC...617 833-3137
1038 Beacon St Apt 304 Brookline MA (02446) ***(G-9214)***
Pain DAvignon II Inc...508 771-9771
15 Hinckley Rd Unit C Hyannis MA (02601) ***(G-11853)***
Paine Incense Co, Auburn *Also called Paine Products Inc **(G-5585)***
Paine Products Inc...207 782-0931
17 Sunset Ave Auburn ME (04210) ***(G-5585)***
Paine Publishing LLC...603 682-0735
51 Durham Point Rd Durham NH (03824) ***(G-18079)***
Paint & Powder Works LLC...860 225-2019
35 M And S Ct New Britain CT (06051) ***(G-2560)***
Paint Town Inc...413 283-2245
21 Wilbraham St Unit A2 Palmer MA (01069) ***(G-14290)***
Pairpoint Crystal, Reading *Also called Pgc Acquisition LLC **(G-14738)***
Pajama Gram Company, Shelburne *Also called Vermont Teddy Bear Co Inc **(G-22426)***
Pak 2000 Inc...603 569-3700
16 Page Hill Rd Lancaster NH (03584) ***(G-18603)***
Pakpro Inc...978 474-5018
11 W Knoll Rd Andover MA (01810) ***(G-7580)***
Pal Corporation...860 666-9211
45 Maselli Rd Newington CT (06111) ***(G-2889)***
Pal Technologies LLC...860 953-1984
9 Tolles St West Hartford CT (06110) ***(G-5089)***
Palace Manufacturing Co, North Billerica *Also called Lennartz Enterprises LLC **(G-13834)***
Paladin Commercial Prtrs LLC...860 953-4900
300 Hartford Ave Newington CT (06111) ***(G-2890)***

Palaka Corp 978 531-6252
18 Northfield Rd Peabody MA (01960) ***(G-14359)***
Paleo Products LLC 401 305-3473
560 Mineral Spring Ave Pawtucket RI (02860) ***(G-20873)***
Paleonola, Pawtucket *Also called Paleo Products LLC* ***(G-20873)***
Palisades Ltd 401 789-0295
1080 Kingstown Rd Peace Dale RI (02879) ***(G-20915)***
Pall Corporation 508 871-5394
20 Walkup Dr Westborough MA (01581) ***(G-16641)***
Pall Northborough (HQ) 978 263-9888
50 Bearfoot Rd Ste 1 Northborough MA (01532) ***(G-14043)***
Palladin Precision Pdts Inc 203 574-0246
57 Bristol St Waterbury CT (06708) ***(G-4935)***
Palleon Pharma Inc 857 285-5904
266 2nd Ave Ste 202 Waltham MA (02451) ***(G-16170)***
Pallet Guys LLC 203 691-6716
102 Bailey Rd North Haven CT (06473) ***(G-3048)***
Pallet Inc LLC 203 227-8148
41 Charcoal Hill Rd Westport CT (06880) ***(G-5222)***
Pallet Removal, Rockland *Also called Timothy Sills* ***(G-14830)***
Palletone of Maine Inc 207 897-5711
231 Park St Livermore Falls ME (04254) ***(G-6380)***
Pallets Recreated 978 345-5936
169 Clarendon St Fitchburg MA (01420) ***(G-10848)***
Pallflex Products Company 860 928-7761
125 Kennedy Dr Putnam CT (06260) ***(G-3625)***
Pallian & Company, Wells *Also called Cynthia Carroll Pallian* ***(G-7160)***
Palmer Foundry Inc 413 283-2976
22 Mount Dumplin Rd Palmer MA (01069) ***(G-14291)***
Palmer Industries Inc 800 398-9676
862r Charles St North Providence RI (02904) ***(G-20770)***
Palmer Manufacturing Co Llc (HQ) 781 321-0480
243 Medford St Malden MA (02148) ***(G-12586)***
Palmer Manufacturing Co LLC 781 321-0480
1 2nd St Ste 1 # 1 Peabody MA (01960) ***(G-14360)***
Palmero Healthcare LLC 203 377-6424
120 Goodwin Pl Stratford CT (06615) ***(G-4438)***
Palmers Elc Mtrs & Pumps Inc 203 348-7378
40 Osborne Ave Norwalk CT (06855) ***(G-3214)***
Palmieri Industries Inc 203 384-6020
118 Burr Ct Ste 1 Bridgeport CT (06605) ***(G-462)***
Palmisano Printing LLC 860 582-6883
319 Queen St Bristol CT (06010) ***(G-590)***
Paloma Pharmaceuticals Inc 617 407-6314
37 Neillian Cres Jamaica Plain MA (02130) ***(G-11947)***
Palomar Medical Products LLC 781 993-2300
15 Network Dr Burlington MA (01803) ***(G-9316)***
Palomar Medical Products, Inc., Burlington *Also called Palomar Medical Products LLC* ***(G-9316)***
Palomar Medical Tech LLC (HQ) 781 993-2330
15 Network Dr Burlington MA (01803) ***(G-9317)***
Palomar Printing 508 856-7237
232 W Boylston St West Boylston MA (01583) ***(G-16425)***
Pams Wreaths 207 751-7234
46 Clark Shore Rd Harpswell ME (04079) ***(G-6174)***
Pan De Oro Brand, Hartford *Also called Severance Foods Inc* ***(G-1868)***
Pan Del Cielo, Waterbury *Also called I and U LLC* ***(G-4886)***
Panacol-Usa Inc 860 738-7449
142 Industrial Ln Torrington CT (06790) ***(G-4592)***
Panagrafix Inc 203 691-5529
50 Fresh Meadow Rd West Haven CT (06516) ***(G-5139)***
Panam Railways, North Billerica *Also called Boston and Maine Corporation* ***(G-13797)***
Panasnic DVC Slutions Lab Mass, Sudbury *Also called Qualtre Inc* ***(G-15666)***
Pancon Corporation (PA) 781 297-6000
350 Revolutionary Dr East Taunton MA (02718) ***(G-10517)***
Panda Security 407 215-3020
77 S Bedford St Ste 350 Burlington MA (01803) ***(G-9318)***
Panda Software, Burlington *Also called Panda Security* ***(G-9318)***
Paneloc Corporation 860 677-6711
142 Brickyard Rd Farmington CT (06032) ***(G-1505)***
Panolam Industries Inc (HQ) 203 925-1556
1 Corporate Dr Ste 725 Shelton CT (06484) ***(G-3848)***
Panolam Industries Intl Inc 207 784-9111
1 Pionite Rd Auburn ME (04210) ***(G-5586)***
Panolam Industries Intl Inc (PA) 203 925-1556
1 Corporate Dr Ste 725 Shelton CT (06484) ***(G-3849)***
Panolam Surface System, Shelton *Also called Panolam Industries Inc* ***(G-3848)***
Panolam Surface Systems, Shelton *Also called Panolam Industries Intl Inc* ***(G-3849)***
Panolam Surface Systems 203 925-1556
1 Pionite Rd Auburn ME (04210) ***(G-5587)***
Panoramic Publishing Group LLC 603 569-5257
83 Center St Wolfeboro Falls NH (03896) ***(G-20028)***
Pantheon Guitars LLC 207 755-0003
41 Canal St Lewiston ME (04240) ***(G-6314)***
Panther Therapeutics Inc 857 413-1698
700 Main St Cambridge MA (02139) ***(G-9605)***
Panthera, Great Barrington *Also called Wainwright USA LLC* ***(G-11249)***

Panza Woodwork & Supply LLC 203 934-3430
4 Hugo St West Haven CT (06516) ***(G-5140)***
Paper Age, Cohasset *Also called OBrien Publications Inc* ***(G-10101)***
Paper Alliance LLC 203 315-3116
45 Ne Industrial Rd Branford CT (06405) ***(G-334)***
Paper Mill and Indus Rbr Pdts, Farmington *Also called Schaeferrolls Inc* ***(G-18144)***
Paper Packaging and Panache 401 253-2273
418 Hope St Bristol RI (02809) ***(G-20097)***
Paper Plus Inc 413 785-1363
91 Union St 1 West Springfield MA (01089) ***(G-16540)***
Paper Thermometer Co Inc 603 547-2034
62 Colin Dr Manchester NH (03103) ***(G-18897)***
Papergraphics Print & Copy 603 880-1835
4 John Tyler St Ste A Merrimack NH (03054) ***(G-19019)***
Paperpile LLC 617 682-9250
28 Glenwood Ave Apt 2 Cambridge MA (02139) ***(G-9606)***
Papers & Presents 781 235-1079
10 Lanark Rd Wellesley Hills MA (02481) ***(G-16399)***
Papish, Leo & Company, Danbury *Also called A Papish Incorporated* ***(G-863)***
Par Manufacturing Inc 860 677-1797
1824 New Britain Ave Farmington CT (06032) ***(G-1506)***
Par Thread Grinding, Farmington *Also called Par Manufacturing Inc* ***(G-1506)***
Para Research Inc 978 282-1100
85 Eastern Ave Ste G106 Gloucester MA (01930) ***(G-11201)***
Paraclete Press Inc (HQ) 508 255-4685
36 Southern Eagle Cartway Brewster MA (02631) ***(G-9055)***
Paraclete Press Inc 508 255-4685
39 Eldridge Rd Brewster MA (02631) ***(G-9056)***
Paradigm Biodevices Inc 781 982-9950
800 Hingham St Ste 207s Rockland MA (02370) ***(G-14818)***
Paradigm Manchester Inc 860 646-4048
203 Sheldon Rd Bldg 2 Manchester CT (06042) ***(G-2029)***
Paradigm Manchester Inc 860 646-4048
186 Adams St S Bldg 3 Manchester CT (06040) ***(G-2030)***
Paradigm Manchester Inc (HQ) 860 646-4048
967 Parker St Manchester CT (06042) ***(G-2031)***
Paradigm Manchester Inc 860 649-2888
255 Sheldon Rd Bldg 4 Manchester CT (06042) ***(G-2032)***
Paradigm Manchester Inc 860 646-4048
151 Sheldon Rd Manchester CT (06042) ***(G-2033)***
Paradigm Prcision Holdings LLC 860 829-3663
134 Commerce St East Berlin CT (06023) ***(G-1105)***
Paradigm Prcision Holdings LLC 978 278-7100
1 2nd St Peabody MA (01960) ***(G-14361)***
Paradigm Prcision Holdings LLC 860 649-2888
967 Parker St Manchester CT (06042) ***(G-2034)***
Paradigm Prcision Holdings LLC 781 321-0480
243 Medford St Malden MA (02148) ***(G-12587)***
Paradigm Precision, Manchester *Also called Paradigm Manchester Inc* ***(G-2029)***
Paradigm Precision, Manchester *Also called Paradigm Manchester Inc* ***(G-2030)***
Paradigm Precision, Manchester *Also called Paradigm Manchester Inc* ***(G-2031)***
Paradigm Sports Inc 978 687-6687
12 Oakland St 5 Amesbury MA (01913) ***(G-7502)***
Paradise Hlls Vnyrd Winery LLC 203 284-0123
15 Windswept Hill Rd Wallingford CT (06492) ***(G-4782)***
Paragon Electronic Systems 603 645-7630
255 Coolidge Ave Manchester NH (03102) ***(G-18898)***
Paragon Mfg Inc 413 562-7202
61 Union St Ste 108 Westfield MA (01085) ***(G-16711)***
Paragon Products Inc 860 388-1363
175 Elm St Ste 1 Old Saybrook CT (06475) ***(G-3346)***
Paragon Tool Company Inc 860 647-9935
121 Adams St S Manchester CT (06040) ***(G-2035)***
Paragraph 11 LLC 781 281-1143
5 Draper St Woburn MA (01801) ***(G-17254)***
Parallel Products of Neng (HQ) 508 884-5100
969 Shawmut Ave New Bedford MA (02746) ***(G-13435)***
Parallel Systems Corp 978 352-7100
118 Tenney St Georgetown MA (01833) ***(G-11148)***
Parama Corp 203 790-8155
7 Trowbridge Dr Bethel CT (06801) ***(G-174)***
Parametric Holdings Inc 781 370-5000
140 Kendrick St Needham Heights MA (02494) ***(G-13342)***
Parametric Technology Corp 781 370-5000
121 Seaport Blvd Boston MA (02210) ***(G-8764)***
Paramount Corp 508 999-4442
22 Logan St New Bedford MA (02740) ***(G-13436)***
Paramount Machine Company Inc 860 643-5549
138 Sanrico Dr Manchester CT (06042) ***(G-2036)***
Paramount Publishing Inc/ 603 472-3528
24 S Hills Dr Bedford NH (03110) ***(G-17659)***
Paramount South Boston 617 269-9999
667 E Broadway Boston MA (02127) ***(G-8765)***
Paramount Tool LLC 508 672-0844
473 Pleasant St Fall River MA (02721) ***(G-10744)***
Parason Machine Inc 860 526-3565
1000 Industrial Park Rd Deep River CT (06417) ***(G-1064)***
Paratek Pharmaceuticals Inc (PA) 617 807-6600
75 Park Plz Ste 4 Boston MA (02116) ***(G-8766)***

ALPHABETIC

Paratronix Inc 508 222-8979
200 Flanders Rd Westborough MA (01581) ***(G-16642)***
Pardi Mfg Inc 508 835-7887
185 Shrewsbury St West Boylston MA (01583) ***(G-16426)***
Parece JP Company 781 662-8640
165c Tremont St Melrose MA (02176) ***(G-12987)***
Parent Co Applications Inc (PA) 802 233-3612
20 Hillside Cir Essex Junction VT (05452) ***(G-21953)***
Parexel International LLC 978 313-3435
2 Federal St Billerica MA (01821) ***(G-8272)***
Parfums De Coeur Ltd (PA) 203 655-8807
750 E Main St Stamford CT (06902) ***(G-4277)***
Paricon Technologies Corp 508 823-0876
500 Myles Standish Blvd Taunton MA (02780) ***(G-15771)***
Paridise Foods LLC 203 283-3903
828 New Haven Ave Milford CT (06460) ***(G-2331)***
Parish Associates Inc 203 335-4100
1383 Kings Hwy Fairfield CT (06824) ***(G-1448)***
Parish Publishing, New Canaan *Also called Liturgical Publications Inc* ***(G-2603)***
Parisi Associates LLC 978 667-8700
6 Omni Way Chelmsford MA (01824) ***(G-9921)***
Park Advnced Cmposite Mtls Inc 203 755-1344
172 E Aurora St Ste A Waterbury CT (06708) ***(G-4936)***
Park Bio Services LLC 978 794-8500
154 Center St Groveland MA (01834) ***(G-11303)***
Park Distributories Inc (PA) 203 579-2140
347 Railroad Ave Bridgeport CT (06604) ***(G-463)***
Park Distributories Inc 203 366-7200
347 Railroad Ave Bridgeport CT (06604) ***(G-464)***
Park Press Printers, Saugus *Also called Gmf Engineering Inc* ***(G-14983)***
Park Printers 401 728-8650
496 Power Rd Pawtucket RI (02860) ***(G-20874)***
Park Street Press Inc 207 743-7702
8 High St South Paris ME (04281) ***(G-7015)***
Park-PMC Liquidation Corp 860 928-0401
161 Park Rd Putnam CT (06260) ***(G-3626)***
Parker, East Hartford *Also called Clarcor Eng MBL Solutions LLC* ***(G-1182)***
Parker & Harper Companies Inc (PA) 603 895-4761
2 Otter Ct Raymond NH (03077) ***(G-19643)***
Parker Hannifin Chomerics, Woburn *Also called Parker-Hannifin Corporation* ***(G-17255)***
Parker Hannifin Corpora 978 346-0578
13 Little Pond Rd Merrimac MA (01860) ***(G-13005)***
Parker Medical Inc 860 350-3446
5 Old Town Park Rd # 34 New Milford CT (06776) ***(G-2822)***
Parker Motor Design, Portsmouth *Also called Parker-Hannifin Corporation* ***(G-19605)***
Parker Press Inc 781 321-4948
66 Willow St Malden MA (02148) ***(G-12588)***
Parker-Hannifin Corporation 781 939-4278
70 Dragon Ct Woburn MA (01801) ***(G-17255)***
Parker-Hannifin Corporation 781 935-4850
8 Commonwealth Ave Woburn MA (01801) ***(G-17256)***
Parker-Hannifin Corporation 860 827-2300
95 Edgewood Ave New Britain CT (06051) ***(G-2561)***
Parker-Hannifin Corporation 603 880-4807
16 Flagstone Dr Hudson NH (03051) ***(G-18425)***
Parker-Hannifin Corporation 978 784-1200
14 Robbins Pond Rd Devens MA (01434) ***(G-10329)***
Parker-Hannifin Corporation 978 858-0505
242 Neck Rd Haverhill MA (01835) ***(G-11457)***
Parker-Hannifin Corporation 603 433-6400
15 Rye St Ste 307 Portsmouth NH (03801) ***(G-19605)***
Parker-Hannifin Corporation 203 239-3341
33 Defco Park Rd North Haven CT (06473) ***(G-3049)***
Parker-Hannifin Corporation 603 595-1500
26 Clinton Dr Ste 103 Hollis NH (03049) ***(G-18336)***
Parker-Hannifin Corporation 781 935-4850
77 Dragon Ct Woburn MA (01801) ***(G-17257)***
Parker-Hannifin Corporation 973 575-4844
26 Clinton Dr Ste 103 Hollis NH (03049) ***(G-18337)***
Parkmatic Car Prkg Systems LLC 802 495-0903
145 Pine Haven Shores Rd Shelburne VT (05482) ***(G-22421)***
Parkway Manufacturing Co Inc 508 559-6686
1 Bert Dr Ste 11 West Bridgewater MA (02379) ***(G-16449)***
Parlee Cycles Inc 978 998-4880
69 Federal St Beverly MA (01915) ***(G-8164)***
Parlex 978 946-2500
145 Milk St Methuen MA (01844) ***(G-13041)***
Parmaco LLC 860 573-7118
111 Warner Ct Glastonbury CT (06033) ***(G-1570)***
Paroline/Wright Design Inc 401 781-5300
89 Harris St Pawtucket RI (02861) ***(G-20875)***
Parrot The & Bird Emporium 413 569-5555
360 N Westfield St Ste 12 Feeding Hills MA (01030) ***(G-10803)***
Parson's Kitchen, Brownfield *Also called Lawrence Parson* ***(G-5825)***
Parsonskellogg LLC 401 438-0650
2290 Pawtucket Ave East Providence RI (02914) ***(G-20439)***
Particles Plus Inc (PA) 781 341-6898
31 Tosca Dr Ste 8 Stoughton MA (02072) ***(G-15613)***
Partner Therapeutics Inc (PA) 781 727-4259
19 Muzzey St Ste 105 Lexington MA (02421) ***(G-12253)***
Partners Printing Inc 207 773-0439
800 Main St Ste 1 South Portland ME (04106) ***(G-7036)***
Partnership Resources 978 256-0499
139 Billerica Rd Ste 1 Chelmsford MA (01824) ***(G-9922)***
Parts Tool and Die Inc 413 821-9718
344 Shoemaker Ln Agawam MA (01001) ***(G-7445)***
Parts Per Million Inc 508 479-5438
904 Main St Cotuit MA (02635) ***(G-10171)***
Party Design, Brockton *Also called Dawn Auger* ***(G-9137)***
Partylite Inc (HQ) 203 661-1926
59 Armstrong Rd Plymouth MA (02360) ***(G-14572)***
Partylite Worldwide LLC (HQ) 888 999-5706
600 Cordwainer Dr Ste 202 Norwell MA (02061) ***(G-14110)***
Pas, Bethany *Also called Plastic Assembly Systems LLC* ***(G-123)***
Pas Technologies Inc 860 649-2727
321 Progress Dr Manchester CT (06042) ***(G-2037)***
Pascale Industries Inc 508 673-3307
939 Currant Rd Fall River MA (02720) ***(G-10745)***
Pashi Inc 617 304-2742
167 Bow St Ste 3 Everett MA (02149) ***(G-10624)***
Passifora Personal Products 603 809-6762
5 Booth St Nashua NH (03060) ***(G-19227)***
Passur Aerospace Inc (PA) 203 622-4086
1 Landmark Sq Ste 1900 Stamford CT (06901) ***(G-4278)***
Pasta Bene Inc 508 583-1515
1050 Pearl St Ste 1 Brockton MA (02301) ***(G-9170)***
Pasta Patch Inc 401 884-1234
183 Old Forge Rd East Greenwich RI (02818) ***(G-20376)***
Pastry Shop 203 238-0483
31 Main St Meriden CT (06451) ***(G-2115)***
Pasture Hill Millwork LLC 603 335-4175
84 Estes Rd Rochester NH (03867) ***(G-19681)***
Pat Gagne Logging 603 449-2479
236 Ferry Rd Dummer NH (03588) ***(G-18071)***
Pat Trap Inc 603 428-3396
632 Western Ave Henniker NH (03242) ***(G-18309)***
Patchology, Norwood *Also called Rare Beauty Brands Inc* ***(G-14191)***
Patenaude Lumber Company Inc 603 428-3224
628 Rush Rd Henniker NH (03242) ***(G-18310)***
Paterson Group Inc 781 935-7036
225 Merrimac St Woburn MA (01801) ***(G-17258)***
Pathai Inc 617 543-5250
120 Brookline Ave Boston MA (02215) ***(G-8767)***
Patheer Inc (PA) 888 968-5936
180 Old Colony Ave # 200 Quincy MA (02170) ***(G-14644)***
Pathfinder Cell Therapy Inc 617 245-0289
12 Bow St Cambridge MA (02138) ***(G-9607)***
Pathfinder Solutions Group LLC 203 247-2479
116 Danbury Rd Unit 5232 Wilton CT (06897) ***(G-5298)***
Pathfire Inc 972 581-2000
75 2nd Ave Ste 720 Needham Heights MA (02494) ***(G-13343)***
Pathmaker Neurosystems Inc 617 968-3006
1 International Pl # 1400 Boston MA (02110) ***(G-8768)***
Pathway Lighting Products Inc 860 388-6881
175 Elm St 5 Old Saybrook CT (06475) ***(G-3347)***
Pathway The Lighting Source, Old Saybrook *Also called Pathway Lighting Products Inc* ***(G-3347)***
Paton Data Company 603 598-8070
19 Peaslee Rd Merrimack NH (03054) ***(G-19020)***
Patricia Poke 860 354-4193
20 Maple Ln New Milford CT (06776) ***(G-2823)***
Patricia Seybold Group Inc 617 742-5200
208 Allston St Apt 3 Brighton MA (02135) ***(G-9103)***
Patricia Spratt For Home LLC 860 434-9291
60 Lyme St Old Lyme CT (06371) ***(G-3326)***
Patricias Presents, New Milford *Also called Patricia Poke* ***(G-2823)***
Patrick T Conley Atty ....
200 Allens Ave Ste 4 Providence RI (02903) ***(G-21087)***
Patricks Inc 207 990-9303
629 Broadway Bangor ME (04401) ***(G-5657)***
Patriot Armored Systems LLC 413 637-1060
140 Crystal St Lenox Dale MA (01242) ***(G-12104)***
Patriot Coatings Inc 978 567-9006
17 Kane Industrial Dr # 2 Hudson MA (01749) ***(G-11800)***
Patriot Customs Incorporated 508 764-7342
134 Ashland Ave Southbridge MA (01550) ***(G-15399)***
Patriot Cyber Defense LLC 603 231-7000
35 Walnut St Rochester NH (03867) ***(G-19682)***
Patriot Envelope LLC 860 529-1553
501 Middletown Ave Wethersfield CT (06109) ***(G-5260)***
Patriot Foundry & Castings LLC 603 934-3919
324 Hill Rd Franklin NH (03235) ***(G-18161)***
Patriot Glass, Bow *Also called Ensio Resources Inc* ***(G-17712)***
Patriot Manufacturing, Acton *Also called David L Ellis Company Inc* ***(G-7349)***
Patriot Manufacturing LLC 860 506-2213
205 Cross St Bristol CT (06010) ***(G-591)***
Patriot Newspaper, Webster *Also called Yankee Shopper* ***(G-16354)***
Patriot Worldwide Inc 800 786-4669
1657 Washington St Ste 3 Holliston MA (01746) ***(G-11595)***

Patriot-News Co...617 345-0971
1 International Pl # 180 Boston MA (02110) *(G-8769)*
Patrol, Attleboro Falls *Also called Advanced Electronic Design Inc* *(G-7810)*
Patsys Bus Sales and Service...603 226-2222
31 Hall St Concord NH (03301) *(G-17922)*
Patten Machine Inc...978 562-9847
299 Central St Hudson MA (01749) *(G-11801)*
Pattison Sign Group (ne) Inc...514 856-7756
125 Kansas Rd Ste 100 Limestone ME (04750) *(G-6343)*
Pattison Sign Group Inc...860 583-3000
2074 Perkins St Bristol CT (06010) *(G-592)*
Patwil LLC...860 589-9085
190 Century Dr Ste 102 Bristol CT (06010) *(G-593)*
Paul A Morse...802 334-9160
553 Vt Route 100 Newport Center VT (05857) *(G-22207)*
Paul Dewitt...203 792-5610
128 E Liberty St Ste 4 Danbury CT (06810) *(G-965)*
Paul E Luke Inc...207 633-4971
15 Lukes Gulch East Boothbay ME (04544) *(G-5979)*
Paul E Wentworth...207 923-3547
1000 Cross Hill Rd Vassalboro ME (04989) *(G-7125)*
Paul H Gesswein & Company Inc...860 388-0652
40 River St Old Saybrook CT (06475) *(G-3348)*
Paul H Murphy & Co Inc...617 472-7707
634 Willard St Quincy MA (02169) *(G-14645)*
Paul H Warren Forest Products...207 362-3681
195 Warren Hill Rd Smithfield ME (04978) *(G-6990)*
Paul Israelson...512 574-4737
14 Sky Oaks Dr Biddeford ME (04005) *(G-5754)*
Paul K Guillow Inc...781 245-5255
40 New Salem St Wakefield MA (01880) *(G-15967)*
Paul King Foundry Inc...401 231-3120
92 Allendale Ave Johnston RI (02919) *(G-20528)*
Paul M Depalma Fuel LLC...781 812-0156
41 Cranberry Rd Weymouth MA (02188) *(G-16896)*
Paul McNamara...508 245-5654
110 Dundee Dr Bridgewater MA (02324) *(G-9086)*
Paul Morse Logging, Newport Center *Also called Paul A Morse* *(G-22207)*
Paul N Foulkes Inc...207 965-9481
801 Barnard Rd Williamsburg Twp ME (04414) *(G-7223)*
Paul Parrino...508 668-2936
25 Coney St East Walpole MA (02032) *(G-10527)*
Paul R Hicks...413 625-2623
1255 Route 2 E Charlemont MA (01339) *(G-9822)*
Paul Revere Press Inc...781 289-4031
5 Birch Rd Newton NH (03858) *(G-19366)*
Paul Thomas...802 875-4004
244 Main St Chester VT (05143) *(G-21848)*
Paul Welding Company Inc...860 229-9945
157 Kelsey St Newington CT (06111) *(G-2891)*
Paul White Woodcarving...508 888-1394
295 Route 6a East Sandwich MA (02537) *(G-10507)*
Paul Young Precast Company...508 966-4333
81 Depot St Bellingham MA (02019) *(G-8056)*
Paul's Pasta Shop, Groton *Also called Fine Food Services Inc* *(G-1676)*
Paul's Prosperous Printing, Wilton *Also called Prosperous Printing LLC* *(G-5300)*
Pauley Co...401 467-2930
1924 Elmwood Ave Warwick RI (02888) *(G-21400)*
Pauls Marble Depot LLC...203 978-0669
40 Warshaw Pl Ste 1 Stamford CT (06902) *(G-4279)*
Pauls Sugar House...413 268-3544
16 Depot Rd Haydenville MA (01039) *(G-11487)*
Pauls Wire Rope & Sling Inc...203 481-3469
4 Indian Neck Ave Branford CT (06405) *(G-335)*
Paulson Electric...617 926-5661
75 Partridge St Watertown MA (02472) *(G-16305)*
Pauway Corp...203 265-3939
63 N Cherry St Ste 2 Wallingford CT (06492) *(G-4783)*
Pavelok...603 225-7283
10 Dunklee Rd Ste 35 Bow NH (03304) *(G-17725)*
Pavement Warehouse...401 233-3200
11 Calista St Greenville RI (02828) *(G-20471)*
Pavers By Ideal, Westford *Also called Ideal Concrete Block Co* *(G-16773)*
Pavestone LLC...508 947-6001
18 Cowan Dr Middleboro MA (02346) *(G-13075)*
Paw Print Offset/Digital, South Burlington *Also called Paw Prints Press Inc* *(G-22456)*
Paw Print Pantry LLC (PA)...860 447-8442
33 Gurley Rd East Lyme CT (06333) *(G-1271)*
Paw Print Pantry LLC...860 447-8442
214 Flanders Rd Ste A Niantic CT (06357) *(G-2956)*
Paw Prints Press Inc...802 865-2872
12 Gregory Dr Ste 8 South Burlington VT (05403) *(G-22456)*
Pawsitively Yummy...603 889-3181
440 Middlesex Rd Tyngsboro MA (01879) *(G-15898)*
Pawtucket Hot Mix...401 722-4488
25 Concord St Pawtucket RI (02860) *(G-20876)*
Pawtucket Times, The, Pawtucket *Also called New England Newspapers Inc* *(G-20866)*
Pax Incorporated Printers...401 847-1157
687 W Main Rd Middletown RI (02842) *(G-20629)*
Paxxus Inc...860 242-0663
16 Southwood Dr Bloomfield CT (06002) *(G-250)*
Payne Engrg Fabrication Co Inc...781 828-9046
28 Draper Ln Ste 3 Canton MA (02021) *(G-9765)*
Paytronix Systems Inc (PA)...617 649-3300
80 Bridge St Ste 400 Newton MA (02458) *(G-13623)*
Pb & J Discoveries LLC...617 903-7253
113 Belmont St Newton MA (02460) *(G-13624)*
Pbd Productions LLC...508 482-9300
3b Landing Ln Hopedale MA (01747) *(G-11679)*
PBI, South Easton *Also called Pressure Biosciences Inc* *(G-15288)*
PBL Incorporated...802 893-0111
158 Brentwood Dr Ste 2 Colchester VT (05446) *(G-21876)*
PBM Nutritionals LLC (HQ)...802 527-0521
147 Industrial Park Rd Milton VT (05468) *(G-22135)*
Pbs Plastics Inc...603 868-1717
219 Old Concord Tpke Barrington NH (03825) *(G-17620)*
Pbuttri LLC...401 996-5583
160 Smithfield Ave Unit C Pawtucket RI (02860) *(G-20877)*
PC Whizdom, Merrimack *Also called Robert Veinot* *(G-19025)*
PCA, Northampton *Also called Packaging Corporation America* *(G-14017)*
PCA, Torrington *Also called Packaging Concepts Assoc LLC* *(G-4591)*
PCA Systems, Adams *Also called Holland Company Inc* *(G-7413)*
Pca/Chelmsford 310, Chelmsford *Also called Packaging Corporation America* *(G-9920)*
PCA/Supply Services 302b, Westfield *Also called Packaging Corporation America* *(G-16710)*
Pcb Connect Inc...781 806-5670
1 Merchant St Sharon MA (02067) *(G-15055)*
PCC Specialty Products Inc...508 753-6530
28 Sword St Auburn MA (01501) *(G-7847)*
PCC Strcturals Alum Operations, Northfield *Also called PCC Structurals Groton* *(G-19407)*
PCC Structurals Groton...603 286-4301
24 Granite St Northfield NH (03276) *(G-19407)*
PCC Structurals Groton (HQ)...860 405-3700
839 Poquonnock Rd Groton CT (06340) *(G-1682)*
PCC Structurals Groton...603 286-4301
35 Industrial Park Dr Franklin NH (03235) *(G-18162)*
Pcg Machine Shop, Hartland *Also called Precision Cutter Grinding Inc* *(G-22017)*
PCI Synthesis, Devens *Also called Polycarbon Industries Inc* *(G-10330)*
PCI Synthesis, Newburyport *Also called Polycarbon Industries Inc* *(G-13521)*
PCL Fixtures Inc...401 334-4646
275 Ferris Ave Unit A Rumford RI (02916) *(G-21193)*
Pcs Metro...401 574-6105
328 Warren Ave East Providence RI (02914) *(G-20440)*
Pcx Aerostructures LLC...860 666-2471
300 Fenn Rd Newington CT (06111) *(G-2892)*
Pcx Aerostructures LLC (PA)...860 666-2471
300 Fenn Rd Newington CT (06111) *(G-2893)*
Pd & E Electronics LLC...603 964-3165
180 Lafayette Rd Unit 13 North Hampton NH (03862) *(G-19386)*
PDC Brands, Stamford *Also called Parfums De Coeur Ltd* *(G-4277)*
PDC International Corp (PA)...203 853-1516
8 Sheehan Ave Norwalk CT (06854) *(G-3215)*
PDI, Middletown *Also called Plastic Design Intl Inc* *(G-2210)*
Pdi International Inc...978 446-0840
1100 Gorham St Lowell MA (01852) *(G-12419)*
Pdk Worldwide, Fall River *Also called PDk Worldwide Entps Inc* *(G-10746)*
PDk Worldwide Entps Inc (PA)...508 676-2155
10 N Main St Ste 3g Fall River MA (02720) *(G-10746)*
Pdq Inc (PA)...860 529-9051
24 Evans Rd Rocky Hill CT (06067) *(G-3727)*
PDQ Graphics, Newport *Also called Colonial Printing Inc* *(G-20661)*
Pe Wentworth, Vassalboro *Also called Paul E Wentworth* *(G-7125)*
Peaceful Daily Inc...203 909-2961
800 Village Walk Ste 103 Guilford CT (06437) *(G-1714)*
Peacemedia Foundation, Brattleboro *Also called Vtfolkus* *(G-21753)*
Peachwave of Watertown...203 942-4949
1156 Main St Watertown CT (06795) *(G-5015)*
Peacock Cabinetry...203 862-9333
9 Bettswood Rd Norwalk CT (06851) *(G-3216)*
Peak Manufacturing, Fitchburg *Also called MA Mfg LLC* *(G-10832)*
Peak Manufacturing, Fitchburg *Also called Portance Corp* *(G-10849)*
Peak Printing Inc...401 351-0500
88 Orange St Providence RI (02903) *(G-21088)*
Peak Scientific Inc (HQ)...866 647-1649
19 Sterling Rd Ste 1 North Billerica MA (01862) *(G-13853)*
Peak Scientific Instruments...978 262-1384
19 Sterling Rd Ste 5 North Billerica MA (01862) *(G-13854)*
Peaked Wind Power LLC...603 570-4842
155 Fleet St Portsmouth NH (03801) *(G-19606)*
Peaks Tarps...978 365-5555
89 Parker St Ste 5 Clinton MA (01510) *(G-10088)*
Peanut Butter and Jelly...203 504-2280
500 Bedford St Apt 227 Stamford CT (06901) *(G-4280)*
Pear Tree Pharmaceuticals Inc...617 500-3871
275 Grove St Ste 2-400 Auburndale MA (02466) *(G-7867)*
Pearce Processing Systems...978 283-3800
8 Kettle Cove Ln Gloucester MA (01930) *(G-11202)*

ALPHABETIC

Pearl Comet Inc 401 475-1309
16 Jason Dr Lincoln RI (02865) ***(G-20589)***
Pearl Die Cutting & Finishing 781 721-6900
110 Commerce Way Ste E Woburn MA (01801) ***(G-17259)***
Pearlco of Boston Inc 781 821-1010
5 Whitman Rd Canton MA (02021) ***(G-9766)***
Pearson Composites LLC 401 245-1200
373 Market St Warren RI (02885) ***(G-21301)***
Pearson Education Inc 617 848-6000
501 Boylston St Boston MA (02116) ***(G-8770)***
Pearson Education Inc 781 687-8800
22 Crosby Dr Bedford MA (01730) ***(G-7999)***
Pearson Education Holdings Inc 617 671-2000
501 Boylston St Ste 900 Boston MA (02116) ***(G-8771)***
Pearson Eductl Measurement, Boston *Also called Pearson Education Inc* ***(G-8770)***
Pearson Machine Company LLC 781 341-9416
81 Tosca Dr Stoughton MA (02072) ***(G-15614)***
Pease & Curren Incorporated 401 738-6449
75 Pennsylvania Ave Warwick RI (02888) ***(G-21401)***
Pease Awning & Sunroom Co, East Providence *Also called L F Pease Co* ***(G-20428)***
Pease Boat Works & Marine Rlwy 508 945-7800
43 Eliphamets Ln Chatham MA (02633) ***(G-9862)***
Peavey Manufacturing Company 207 843-7861
526 Main Rd Eddington ME (04428) ***(G-5997)***
PEC Detailing Co Inc 508 660-8954
33 Delcor Dr Walpole MA (02081) ***(G-16006)***
Peck Precision Fabrication, Lawrence *Also called B G Peck Company Inc* ***(G-11997)***
Peco Pallet 845 642-2780
34 Lake St Apt 2 Brighton MA (02135) ***(G-9104)***
Pedipress Inc 413 549-3918
301 Spencer Dr Amherst MA (01002) ***(G-7521)***
Pedro Oharas 207 783-6200
134 Main St Ste 2 Lewiston ME (04240) ***(G-6315)***
Pedro Reese 802 265-3658
1078 River St Fair Haven VT (05743) ***(G-21967)***
Pedro Slate, Fair Haven *Also called Pedro Reese* ***(G-21967)***
Pedros Inc 978 657-7101
147 Essex St Haverhill MA (01832) ***(G-11458)***
Peekaboopumpkin.com, Stamford *Also called Thomas Design Group LLC* ***(G-4345)***
Peel People LLC 773 255-9886
140 N Main St Unit 4a Attleboro MA (02703) ***(G-7775)***
Peel, LLC, Everett *Also called Peelfly Inc* ***(G-10625)***
Peeled Inc 212 706-2001
30 Martin St Ste 3b1 Cumberland RI (02864) ***(G-20338)***
Peeled Snacks, Cumberland *Also called Peeled Inc* ***(G-20338)***
Peelfly Inc 860 608-3819
25 Charlton St Apt 425 Everett MA (02149) ***(G-10625)***
Peening Technologies Conn, East Hartford *Also called Hydro Honing Laboratories Inc* ***(G-1200)***
Peening Technologies Eqp LLC 860 289-4328
8 Eastern Park Rd East Hartford CT (06108) ***(G-1209)***
Peergrade Inc (PA) 857 302-4023
361 Newbury St Ste 412 Boston MA (02115) ***(G-8772)***
Peerless Granite Co Inc 802 476-3061
35 S Front St Barre VT (05641) ***(G-21634)***
Peerless Handcuff Co Inc 413 732-2156
181 Doty Cir West Springfield MA (01089) ***(G-16541)***
Peerless Precision Inc 413 562-2359
22 Mainline Dr Westfield MA (01085) ***(G-16712)***
Peerless Systems Corporation (HQ) 203 350-0040
1055 Washington Blvd Fl 8 Stamford CT (06901) ***(G-4281)***
Peg Kearsarge Co Inc 603 374-2341
14 Mill St Bartlett NH (03812) ***(G-17627)***
Pegasus Capital Advisors LP (PA) 203 869-4400
750 E Main St Stamford CT (06902) ***(G-4282)***
Pegasus Glassworks Inc 508 347-5656
66 Technology Park Rd Sturbridge MA (01566) ***(G-15644)***
Pegasus Inc 508 429-2461
39 Locust St Holliston MA (01746) ***(G-11596)***
Pegasus Manufacturing, Middletown *Also called L&P Aerospace Acquisition LLC* ***(G-2199)***
Pegco Process Labs, Bartlett *Also called Peg Kearsarge Co Inc* ***(G-17627)***
Peggy Lawton Kitchens Inc 508 668-1215
255 Washington St East Walpole MA (02032) ***(G-10528)***
PEI Realty Trust 508 478-2025
500 Fortune Blvd Milford MA (01757) ***(G-13136)***
Peinert Boatworks Inc 508 758-3020
46 Marion Rd Mattapoisett MA (02739) ***(G-12889)***
Peko Creations Ltd 401 722-6661
390 Pine St Pawtucket RI (02860) ***(G-20878)***
Pel Associates LLC (PA) 860 446-9921
187 Ledgewood Rd Apt 407 Groton CT (06340) ***(G-1683)***
Pelagic Electronics 508 540-1200
174 Lake Shore Dr East Falmouth MA (02536) ***(G-10446)***
Pelham Machine & Tool Co, Pelham *Also called Leonard Philbrick Inc* ***(G-19438)***
Pelham Plastics Inc 603 886-7226
42 Dick Tracy Dr Pelham NH (03076) ***(G-19440)***
Pelican Products Inc 413 525-3990
60 Shaker Rd Ste 14 East Longmeadow MA (01028) ***(G-10485)***
Pelican Products Inc 413 665-2163
147 N Main St South Deerfield MA (01373) ***(G-15251)***
Pell Engineering and Mfg 603 598-6855
29 Industrial Park Dr Pelham NH (03076) ***(G-19441)***
Pella Corporation 401 662-2621
25 Narragansett Blvd Portsmouth RI (02871) ***(G-20936)***
Pella Corporation 401 247-0309
39 Baron Rd Barrington RI (02806) ***(G-20051)***
Pella Window Door, Portsmouth *Also called Pella Corporation* ***(G-20936)***
Pella Window Door, Barrington *Also called Pella Corporation* ***(G-20051)***
Pelletier & Pelletier 207 834-2296
14 E Main St Fort Kent ME (04743) ***(G-6066)***
PELLETIER AWNING DBA, Beverly *Also called R H M Group Inc* ***(G-8169)***
Pelletier Lube Service 802 622-0725
298 E Montpelier Rd Barre VT (05641) ***(G-21635)***
Pelletier Manufacturing Inc 207 723-6500
400 Golden Rd Millinocket ME (04462) ***(G-6444)***
Pelletier Millwrights LLC 860 564-8936
161 Moosup Pond Rd Danielson CT (06239) ***(G-1016)***
Pellion Technologies Inc 617 547-3191
1337 Massachusetts Ave Arlington MA (02476) ***(G-7632)***
Pellys Sports 413 301-0889
152 Main St Indian Orchard MA (01151) ***(G-11893)***
Pemberton's Gourmet, Gray *Also called Pembertons Food Inc* ***(G-6141)***
Pembertons Food Inc 207 657-6446
32 Lewiston Rd Bldg 1b Gray ME (04039) ***(G-6141)***
Pemko Manufacturing Co 901 365-2160
110 Sargent Dr New Haven CT (06511) ***(G-2722)***
Pen & Inc 603 225-7522
155 River Rd Unit 8 Bow NH (03304) ***(G-17726)***
Pen Ro Group, Pittsfield *Also called Pen Ro Mold and Tool Inc* ***(G-14498)***
Pen Ro Mold and Tool Inc 413 499-0464
343 Pecks Rd Ste 5 Pittsfield MA (01201) ***(G-14498)***
Penco Corporation 860 347-7271
33 Anderson Rd Middletown CT (06457) ***(G-2209)***
Pendar Technologies LLC (PA) 617 588-2128
30 Spinelli Pl Cambridge MA (02138) ***(G-9608)***
Penelope Wurr Glass 802 387-5607
719 W Hill Rd Putney VT (05346) ***(G-22290)***
Peninsula Publishing 203 292-5621
1630 Post Rd E Unit 312 Westport CT (06880) ***(G-5223)***
Peninsula Skincare Labs Inc 650 339-4299
7 Bulfinch Pl Ste 3 Boston MA (02114) ***(G-8773)***
Penmor Lithographers Inc 207 784-1341
8 Lexington St Lewiston ME (04240) ***(G-6316)***
Pennsylvania Globe Gaslight Co 203 484-7749
300 Shaw Rd North Branford CT (06471) ***(G-2971)***
Pennwell Corporation 603 891-9425
98 Spit Brook Rd Nashua NH (03062) ***(G-19228)***
Pennwell Corporation 603 891-0123
98 Spit Brook Rd Nashua NH (03062) ***(G-19229)***
Penny Marketing Ltd Partnr (PA) 203 866-6688
6 Prowitt St Norwalk CT (06855) ***(G-3217)***
Penny Press Inc (PA) 203 866-6688
6 Prowitt St Norwalk CT (06855) ***(G-3218)***
Penny Press Inc 203 866-6688
185 Plains Rd Ste 100e Milford CT (06461) ***(G-2332)***
Penny Publications LLC 203 866-6688
185 Plains Rd Ste 201e Milford CT (06461) ***(G-2333)***
Penny Publications LLC (PA) 203 866-6688
6 Prowitt St Norwalk CT (06855) ***(G-3219)***
Penny Straker Gardens, South Dartmouth *Also called P Straker Ltd* ***(G-15241)***
Pennysaver 603 536-3160
607 Tenney Mountain Hwy # 137 Plymouth NH (03264) ***(G-19530)***
Pennysaver The, Plymouth *Also called Pennysaver* ***(G-19530)***
Pennysaver, The, Warwick *Also called Beacon Communications Inc* ***(G-21334)***
Penobscot Bay Brewery, Winterport *Also called Winterport Winery Inc* ***(G-7278)***
Penobscot Bay Press Inc (PA) 207 367-2200
138 Main St Stonington ME (04681) ***(G-7070)***
Penobscot Bay Press Inc 207 374-2341
13 Main St Blue Hill ME (04614) ***(G-5772)***
Penobscot McCrum LLC 207 338-4360
28 Pierce St Belfast ME (04915) ***(G-5696)***
Penobscot Sand Grav Stone LLC 207 827-2829
392 Main Rd Milford ME (04461) ***(G-6437)***
Penobscot Times Inc 207 827-4451
282 Main St Old Town ME (04468) ***(G-6546)***
Penta-Tech Coated Products LLC (PA) 207 862-3105
58 Main Rd N Hampden ME (04444) ***(G-6166)***
Pentair Electronic Packaging, Warwick *Also called Schroff Inc* ***(G-21421)***
Pentair Electronic Packaging, Warwick *Also called Pep Central Inc* ***(G-21402)***
Pentair Rsdntial Fltration LLC 603 749-1610
47 Crosby Rd Dover NH (03820) ***(G-18045)***
Pentair Valves & Contrls US LP 508 594-4410
55 Cabot Blvd Mansfield MA (02048) ***(G-12651)***
Penwell 508 347-8245
15 Country Hill Rd Sturbridge MA (01566) ***(G-15645)***
Pep Be-St, Bridgeport *Also called Boston Endo-Surgical Tech LLC* ***(G-385)***

Pep Central Inc ... 401 732-3770
170 Commerce Dr Warwick RI (02886) *(G-21402)*
Pep Connecticut Plastics, Wallingford *Also called Precision Engineered Pdts LLC (G-4789)*
Pep General Metal Finishing, Attleboro *Also called General Metal Finishing LLC (G-7740)*
Pep Industries LLC ... 508 226-5600
110 Frank Mossberg Dr Attleboro MA (02703) *(G-7776)*
Pep Micropep, East Providence *Also called Matrix I LLC (G-20431)*
Pepin Granite Company Inc ... 802 476-6103
58 Granite St Barre VT (05641) *(G-21636)*
Peppercorn Food Service Inc ... 781 639-6035
91 Pitman Rd Marblehead MA (01945) *(G-12690)*
Pepperell Braiding Company Inc (PA) ... 978 433-2133
22 Lowell St Pepperell MA (01463) *(G-14444)*
Pepperell International ... 508 878-7987
34 Prospect St Pepperell MA (01463) *(G-14445)*
Pepsi ... 781 986-5249
663 North St Randolph MA (02368) *(G-14692)*
Pepsi Bottling Group Inc ... 978 772-2340
11 Copeland Dr Ayer MA (01432) *(G-7933)*
Pepsi Cola Bottling Aroostook ... 207 760-3000
52 Industrial St Ste 1 Presque Isle ME (04769) *(G-6769)*
Pepsi Cola Bottling Co ... 802 254-6093
1566 Putney Rd Brattleboro VT (05301) *(G-21743)*
Pepsi-Cola Btlg of Wrcster Inc (PA) ... 508 829-6551
90 Industrial Dr Holden MA (01520) *(G-11549)*
Pepsi-Cola Btlg of Wrcster Inc ... 860 774-4007
135 Louisa Viens Dr Dayville CT (06241) *(G-1050)*
Pepsi-Cola Metro Btlg Co Inc ... 203 375-2484
355 Benton St Stratford CT (06615) *(G-4439)*
Pepsi-Cola Metro Btlg Co Inc ... 207 623-1313
80 Anthony Ave Augusta ME (04330) *(G-5616)*
Pepsi-Cola Metro Btlg Co Inc ... 401 468-3221
24 Kenney Dr Cranston RI (02920) *(G-20270)*
Pepsi-Cola Metro Btlg Co Inc ... 401 468-3300
1400 Pontiac Ave Cranston RI (02920) *(G-20271)*
Pepsi-Cola Metro Btlg Co Inc ... 860 848-1231
260 Gallivan Ln Uncasville CT (06382) *(G-4648)*
Pepsi-Cola Metro Btlg Co Inc ... 203 234-9014
27 Leonardo Dr North Haven CT (06473) *(G-3050)*
Pepsi-Cola Metro Btlg Co Inc ... 603 625-5764
127 Pepsi Rd Manchester NH (03109) *(G-18899)*
Pepsi-Cola Metro Btlg Co Inc ... 207 973-2217
19 Penobscot Meadow Dr Hampden ME (04444) *(G-6167)*
Pepsi-Cola Metro Btlg Co Inc ... 860 688-6281
55 International Dr Windsor CT (06095) *(G-5353)*
Pepsi-Cola Metro Btlg Co Inc ... 207 784-5791
191 Merrow Rd Auburn ME (04210) *(G-5588)*
Pepsi-Cola Metro Btlg Co Inc ... 207 773-4258
250 Canco Rd Portland ME (04103) *(G-6707)*
Pepsico, Presque Isle *Also called Pepsi Cola Bottling Aroostook (G-6769)*
Pepsico, Holden *Also called Pepsi-Cola Btlg of Wrcster Inc (G-11549)*
Pepsico, Stratford *Also called Pepsi-Cola Metro Btlg Co Inc (G-4439)*
Pepsico, Ayer *Also called Pepsi Bottling Group Inc (G-7933)*
Pepsico, Dayville *Also called Pepsi-Cola Btlg of Wrcster Inc (G-1050)*
Pepsico, North Haven *Also called Pepsi-Cola Metro Btlg Co Inc (G-3050)*
Pepsico, Randolph *Also called Pepsi (G-14692)*
Pepsico, Windsor *Also called Pepsi-Cola Metro Btlg Co Inc (G-5353)*
Pepsico, Portland *Also called Pepsi-Cola Metro Btlg Co Inc (G-6707)*
Pepsico ... 508 216-1681
2 Hampshire St Ste 104 Foxboro MA (02035) *(G-10897)*
Pepsico ... 203 974-8912
150 Munson St New Haven CT (06511) *(G-2723)*
Pepsico Inc ... 508 869-1000
311 Main St Boylston MA (01505) *(G-8982)*
Pepsico Inc ... 781 767-6622
663 North St Randolph MA (02368) *(G-14693)*
Pequod Inc ... 508 858-5123
94 Front St New Bedford MA (02740) *(G-13437)*
Pequonnock Ironworks Inc ... 203 336-2178
621 Knowlton St Bridgeport CT (06608) *(G-465)*
Pequot ... 800 620-1492
1000 Lafayette Blvd # 1100 Bridgeport CT (06604) *(G-466)*
Perceptive Automata Inc (PA) ... 617 299-1296
230 Somerville Ave 2 Somerville MA (02143) *(G-15203)*
Percision Electronics, Marshfield *Also called Precision Electronics Corp (G-12865)*
Percussion Software Inc ... 781 438-9900
600 Unicorn Park Dr Ste 2 Woburn MA (01801) *(G-17260)*
Peregrine Manufacturing, Brooklyn *Also called Uninsred Alttude Cnnection Inc (G-673)*
Peregrine Turbine Tech LLC ... 207 687-8333
29 S Point Dr Wiscasset ME (04578) *(G-7286)*
Perennial Elements LLC ... 860 536-8593
15 Mystic Hill Rd Mystic CT (06355) *(G-2448)*
Perey Turnstiles Inc ... 203 333-9400
308 Bishop Ave Bridgeport CT (06610) *(G-467)*
Perfect Curve Inc (PA) ... 617 224-1600
137 South St Fl 3 Boston MA (02111) *(G-8774)*
Perfect Fit ... 207 278-3333
39 Stetson Rd Corinna ME (04928) *(G-5923)*
Perfect Fit Industries LLC ... 603 485-7161
25 Canal St Allenstown NH (03275) *(G-17540)*
Perfect Infinity Inc ... 203 906-0442
167 Cherry St Ste 145 Milford CT (06460) *(G-2334)*
Perfect Print LLC ... 401 347-2370
195 Dupont Dr Providence RI (02907) *(G-21089)*
Perfect Stitch Emroidery Inc ... 207 743-2830
19 James Rd South Paris ME (04281) *(G-7016)*
Perfect Storm Sports Tech LLC ... 802 662-2102
5b David Dr Essex Junction VT (05452) *(G-21954)*
Perfections Group, Hudson *Also called Locked In Steel (G-18365)*
Perfectsoftware, Norwalk *Also called Criterion Inc (G-3133)*
Performance Chemicals LLC ... 603 228-1200
40 Industrial Park Dr Franklin NH (03235) *(G-18163)*
Performance Compounding Inc ... 860 599-5616
185 S Broad St Ste 2a Pawcatuck CT (06379) *(G-3440)*
Performance Connection Systems ... 203 868-5517
599 W Main St Meriden CT (06451) *(G-2116)*
Performance Motion Devices Inc ... 978 266-1210
1 Technology Park Dr # 5 Westford MA (01886) *(G-16783)*
Performance Products Painting ... 207 783-4222
63 Omni Cir Auburn ME (04210) *(G-5589)*
Performance Tool Inc ... 413 568-6643
41 Jefferson St Ste 2 Westfield MA (01085) *(G-16713)*
Performer Publications Inc ... 617 627-9200
24 Dane St Somerville MA (02143) *(G-15204)*
Peri Formwork Systems Inc ... 857 524-5182
11 Elkins St Ste 110 Boston MA (02127) *(G-8775)*
Perillon Software Inc ... 978 263-0412
33 Nagog Park Ste 205 Acton MA (01720) *(G-7377)*
Perimeter Acquisition Corp (HQ) ... 603 645-1616
540 North Commercial St Manchester NH (03101) *(G-18900)*
Perimeter Technology, Manchester *Also called Perimeter Acquisition Corp (G-18900)*
Period Lighting Fixtures Inc ... 413 664-7141
167 River Rd Clarksburg MA (01247) *(G-10074)*
Periodic Tableware LLC ... 310 428-4250
415 Howe Ave Ste 110 Shelton CT (06484) *(G-3850)*
Peristere LLC ... 860 783-5301
95 Hilliard St Manchester CT (06042) *(G-2038)*
Perkinelmer Inc (PA) ... 781 663-6900
940 Winter St Waltham MA (02451) *(G-16171)*
Perkinelmer Inc ... 617 577-7744
245 1st St Cambridge MA (02142) *(G-9609)*
Perkinelmer Inc ... 508 435-9500
68 Elm St Bldg 2 Hopkinton MA (01748) *(G-11731)*
Perkinelmer Inc ... 617 350-9440
32 Glen Ave Arlington MA (02474) *(G-7633)*
Perkinelmer Inc ... 203 925-4600
710 Bridgeport Ave Shelton CT (06484) *(G-3851)*
Perkinelmer Inc ... 617 596-9909
549 Albany St Boston MA (02118) *(G-8776)*
Perkinelmer Hlth Sciences Inc (HQ) ... 781 663-6900
940 Winter St Waltham MA (02451) *(G-16172)*
Perkinelmer Hlth Sciences Inc ... 617 350-9024
331 Treble Cove Rd North Billerica MA (01862) *(G-13855)*
Perkinelmer Hlth Sciences Inc ... 203 925-4600
710 Bridgeport Ave Shelton CT (06484) *(G-3852)*
Perkinelmer Holdings Inc (HQ) ... 781 663-6900
940 Winter St Wellesley MA (02481) *(G-16380)*
Perkins Brothers Corp ... 781 858-3031
92 Evans Dr Stoughton MA (02072) *(G-15615)*
Perkins Pre-Coat, Stoughton *Also called Perkins Brothers Corp (G-15615)*
Perley Burrill Fuel ... 781 593-9292
906 Lynnfield St Lynnfield MA (01940) *(G-12554)*
Perma Incorporated ... 978 667-5161
605 Springs Rd Bedford MA (01730) *(G-8000)*
Permatex Inc (PA) ... 860 543-7500
10 Columbus Blvd Ste 1 Hartford CT (06106) *(G-1856)*
Permatex, Inc./ A Division ITW, Hartford *Also called Permatex Inc (G-1856)*
Perosphere Inc ... 203 885-1111
20 Kenosia Ave Danbury CT (06810) *(G-966)*
Perosphere Technologies Inc ... 475 218-4600
108 Mill Plain Rd Ste 301 Danbury CT (06811) *(G-967)*
Peroxygen Systems Inc ... 248 835-9026
116 John St Ste 315 Lowell MA (01852) *(G-12420)*
Perras Lumber Co Inc ... 603 636-1830
45 Perras Rd Groveton NH (03582) *(G-18232)*
Perras Pallet LLC ... 603 631-1169
44 Perras Rd Lancaster NH (03584) *(G-18604)*
Perrigo Nutritionals, Milton *Also called PBM Nutritionals LLC (G-22135)*
Perry Blackburne Inc ... 401 231-7200
330 Woonasquatucket Ave North Providence RI (02911) *(G-20771)*
Perry Packaging, Westwood *Also called Romanow Packaging LLC (G-16875)*
Perry Paving ... 401 732-1730
20 Keystone Dr Warwick RI (02889) *(G-21403)*
Perry Technology Corporation ... 860 738-2525
120 Industrial Park Rd New Hartford CT (06057) *(G-2644)*
Perseus Books Group, Boston *Also called Clp Pb LLC (G-8478)*

ALPHABETIC

Persimmon Technologies Corp......781 587-0677
200 Harvard Mill Sq Wakefield MA (01880) ***(G-15968)***
Persistor Instruments Inc......508 420-1600
153 Lovells Ln Ste A Marstons Mills MA (02648) ***(G-12873)***
Personal Care Appliances Div, Stamford *Also called Conair Corporation* ***(G-4171)***
Perspecta Svcs & Solutions Inc (HQ)......781 684-4000
350 2nd Ave Bldg 1 Waltham MA (02451) ***(G-16173)***
Peruse Software Inc......603 626-0061
436 Amherst St Ste 222 Nashua NH (03063) ***(G-19230)***
Pet Gear, West Rutland *Also called Vermont Juvenile Furn Mfg Inc* ***(G-22620)***
Pete and Gerrys Organics LLC......603 638-2827
140 Buffum Rd Monroe NH (03771) ***(G-19091)***
Peter E Randall Publisher LLC......603 431-5667
5 Greenleaf Woods Dr Portsmouth NH (03801) ***(G-19607)***
Peter Forg Manufacturing Co......617 625-0337
50 Park St Somerville MA (02143) ***(G-15205)***
Peter Galbert......978 660-5580
7 Gardenside St Roslindale MA (02131) ***(G-14841)***
Peter Limmer & Sons Inc......603 356-5378
Rr 16 Box A Intervale NH (03845) ***(G-18455)***
Peter Marques......603 447-2344
87 Main St Conway NH (03818) ***(G-17957)***
Peter Paquin Cranberries, Middleboro *Also called Wood St Wood Co* ***(G-13082)***
Peter Paul Electronics Co Inc......860 229-4884
480 John Downey Dr New Britain CT (06051) ***(G-2562)***
Peter Pierce......603 524-8312
390 Durrell Mountain Rd Belmont NH (03220) ***(G-17679)***
Peter Pierce Logging, Belmont *Also called Peter Pierce* ***(G-17679)***
Peter Tasi......203 732-6540
10 Francis St Derby CT (06418) ***(G-1077)***
Peter Thrasher......
93 S Washington St North Attleboro MA (02760) ***(G-13771)***
Peter Young Company......617 923-1101
11 Boyd St Watertown MA (02472) ***(G-16306)***
Peterboro Tool Company Inc......603 924-3034
Upper Union St Peterborough NH (03458) ***(G-19483)***
Peterborough Basket Company, Peterborough *Also called Old Dublin Road Inc* ***(G-19482)***
Petermans Boards and Bowls Inc......413 863-2116
61 French King Hwy Gill MA (01354) ***(G-11157)***
Peterson and Nash Inc......781 826-9085
846 Main St Norwell MA (02061) ***(G-14111)***
Petnet Solutions Inc......865 218-2000
350 Wshington St Unit 268 Woburn MA (01801) ***(G-17261)***
Petrofiber Corporation (PA)......603 627-0416
1994 Maple St Hopkinton NH (03229) ***(G-18364)***
Petron Automation Inc......860 274-9091
65 Mountain View Rd Watertown CT (06795) ***(G-5016)***
Petrunti Design & Wdwkg LLC......860 953-5332
23c Andover Dr West Hartford CT (06110) ***(G-5090)***
Pettengill Printing, Leeds *Also called Bruce A Pettengill* ***(G-6268)***
Pexagon Technology Inc......203 458-3364
14 Business Park Dr Ste E Branford CT (06405) ***(G-336)***
Pexco LLC......978 249-5343
764 S Athol Rd Athol MA (01331) ***(G-7692)***
Pez Candy Inc (HQ)......203 795-0531
35 Prindle Hill Rd Orange CT (06477) ***(G-3379)***
Pez Manufacturing Corp......203 795-0531
35 Prindle Hill Rd Orange CT (06477) ***(G-3380)***
PF Laboratories Inc (HQ)......973 256-3100
201 Tresser Blvd Ste 324 Stamford CT (06901) ***(G-4283)***
Pf Pro Fnshg Silkscreening Inc......603 329-8344
13 Gigante Dr Hampstead NH (03841) ***(G-18248)***
PFC Logging Inc......207 448-7998
46 Snow Farm Rd Danforth ME (04424) ***(G-5942)***
Pfd Studios......860 295-8500
213 Flood Rd Marlborough CT (06447) ***(G-2068)***
Pfeiffer Vacuum Inc (HQ)......603 578-6500
24 Trafalgar Sq Nashua NH (03063) ***(G-19231)***
Pfizer Inc......978 799-8657
3 Starr Cir Westford MA (01886) ***(G-16784)***
Pfizer Inc......203 401-0100
1 Howe St New Haven CT (06511) ***(G-2724)***
Pfizer Inc......860 441-4100
100 Eastern Point Rd Groton CT (06340) ***(G-1684)***
Pfizer Inc......978 247-1000
1 Burtt Rd Andover MA (01810) ***(G-7581)***
Pfr Machine Co......413 568-7603
15 Ponders Hollow Rd Westfield MA (01085) ***(G-16714)***
PG Adams Inc......802 862-8664
1215 Airport Pkwy South Burlington VT (05403) ***(G-22457)***
Pg Imtech of Californ......401 521-2490
27 Dexter Rd East Providence RI (02914) ***(G-20441)***
Pgc Acquisition LLC......508 888-2344
74 Pleasant St Reading MA (01867) ***(G-14738)***
Pgc Wire & Cable LLC......603 821-7300
17 Hampshire Dr Ste 1 Hudson NH (03051) ***(G-18426)***
Pgi, Lowell *Also called Plenus Group Inc* ***(G-12422)***
Pgxhealthholding Inc (PA)......203 786-3400
5 Science Park New Haven CT (06511) ***(G-2725)***
Pha Industries Inc......978 544-8770
153 Quabbin Blvd Orange MA (01364) ***(G-14222)***
Phadean Engineering Co Inc......888 204-0900
44 Summer St Shrewsbury MA (01545) ***(G-15128)***
Phario Solution......603 821-3804
11 Northeastern Blvd # 340 Nashua NH (03062) ***(G-19232)***
Pharm Eco Laboratories, Devens *Also called Johnson Matthey Phrm Mtls Inc* ***(G-10321)***
Pharma Compliance Group LLC......508 377-4561
24 Glendale View Dr Hampden MA (01036) ***(G-11323)***
Pharma Interface Analysis LLC......978 448-6137
101 Castle Dr Groton MA (01450) ***(G-11294)***
Pharma Launcher LLC......508 812-0850
290 Pleasant St Apt 219 Watertown MA (02472) ***(G-16307)***
Pharma Models LLC......617 630-1729
700 Centre St Newton MA (02458) ***(G-13625)***
Pharma Models LLC......617 306-2281
257 Simarano Dr Marlborough MA (01752) ***(G-12806)***
Pharmacal Research Labs Inc......203 755-4908
562 Captain Neville Dr # 1 Waterbury CT (06705) ***(G-4937)***
Pharmaceutical RES Assoc Inc (HQ)......203 588-8000
201 Tresser Blvd Stamford CT (06901) ***(G-4284)***
Pharmaceutical Resources, Brockton *Also called Lyne Laboratories Inc* ***(G-9163)***
Pharmaceutical Strtgs Stfng LL......781 835-2300
477 Main St Stoneham MA (02180) ***(G-15570)***
Pharmahealth Specialty/Lon......508 998-8000
132 Alden Rd Fairhaven MA (02719) ***(G-10645)***
Pharmalucence Inc (HQ)......781 275-7120
29 Dunham Rd Billerica MA (01821) ***(G-8273)***
Pharmask Inc......508 359-6700
28 Bridge St Medfield MA (02052) ***(G-12916)***
Pharmate Inc......617 800-5804
1555 Mass Ave Ste B Cambridge MA (02138) ***(G-9610)***
Pharmatron Inc......603 645-6766
2400 Computer Dr Westborough MA (01581) ***(G-16643)***
Pharmavite Corp......860 651-1885
10 Station St Simsbury CT (06070) ***(G-3909)***
Pharyx Inc......617 792-0524
325 New Boston St Unit 6 Woburn MA (01801) ***(G-17262)***
Phase N, Boston *Also called Phase-N Corporation* ***(G-8777)***
Phase-N Corporation......617 737-0064
256 Marginal St Ste 7 Boston MA (02128) ***(G-8777)***
Phat Thai......802 863-8827
100 North St Ste 1 Burlington VT (05401) ***(G-21802)***
Phe Investments LLC......401 289-2900
1 Carding Ln Johnston RI (02919) ***(G-20529)***
Philadelphia Sign Co......978 486-0137
50 Porter Rd Littleton MA (01460) ***(G-12318)***
Philbrick's Mobile Services, Stratham *Also called Malagar Group LLC* ***(G-19873)***
Philip Cups, Bridgeport *Also called Harrison Enterprise LLC* ***(G-423)***
Philip Machine Company Inc......401 353-7383
190 York Ave Pawtucket RI (02860) ***(G-20879)***
Philip RS Sorbets......781 721-6330
750 Main St Winchester MA (01890) ***(G-17095)***
Philipp Manufacturing Co Inc......413 527-4444
19 Ward Ave Easthampton MA (01027) ***(G-10575)***
Philippine Pot Partners LLC......401 789-7372
6 Princess Pine Rd Lincoln RI (02865) ***(G-20590)***
Philips Advanced Metrology Sys......508 647-8400
47 Manning Rd Billerica MA (01821) ***(G-8274)***
Philips Consumer Lifestyle, Andover *Also called Philips Holding USA Inc* ***(G-7582)***
Philips Hlthcare Infrmtics Inc......508 988-1000
111 Lawrence St Framingham MA (01702) ***(G-10993)***
Philips Holding USA Inc (HQ)......978 687-1501
3000 Minuteman Rd Ste 109 Andover MA (01810) ***(G-7582)***
Philips Lifeline, Framingham *Also called Lifeline Systems Company* ***(G-10977)***
Philips Lighting, Burlington *Also called Genlyte Thomas Group LLC* ***(G-9279)***
Philips Medical Systems Hsg (PA)......978 687-1501
3000 Minuteman Rd Andover MA (01810) ***(G-7583)***
Philips North America LLC......508 647-1130
12 Michigan Dr Natick MA (01760) ***(G-13271)***
Philips Ultrasound Inc......203 753-5215
1875 Thomaston Ave Ste 5 Waterbury CT (06704) ***(G-4938)***
Phillip Ippolito......508 336-9616
1970 Fall River Ave Seekonk MA (02771) ***(G-15033)***
Phillips Candy House Inc......617 282-2090
818 Wlliam T Mrrssey Blvd Boston MA (02122) ***(G-8778)***
Phillips Enterprises Inc......413 586-5860
149 Easthampton Rd Northampton MA (01060) ***(G-14018)***
Phillips Fuel Systems......203 908-3323
109 Holland Ave Bridgeport CT (06605) ***(G-468)***
Phillips Packaging......413 289-1070
1633 N Main St Palmer MA (01069) ***(G-14292)***
Phillips Precision Inc......508 869-3344
240 Shrewsbury St Boylston MA (01505) ***(G-8983)***
Phillips Pump LLC......203 576-6688
661 Lindley St Bridgeport CT (06606) ***(G-469)***
Phillips Pumps, Bridgeport *Also called Phillips Pump LLC* ***(G-469)***
Phillips, R J Associates, Bozrah *Also called Ngraver Company* ***(G-283)***

Phillips-Medisize LLC 978 365-1262
1 Union St Clinton MA (01510) ***(G-10089)***
Phillips-Moldex Company, Putnam *Also called Park-PMC Liquidation Corp* ***(G-3626)***
Phils Tree Service and Log 603 352-0202
34 Dale Dr Keene NH (03431) ***(G-18521)***
Phinney Lumber Co 207 839-3336
519 Fort Hill Rd Gorham ME (04038) ***(G-6124)***
Phio Pharmaceuticals Corp (PA) 508 767-3681
257 Simarano Dr Ste 101 Marlborough MA (01752) ***(G-12807)***
Phio Pharmaceuticals Corp 508 767-3861
60 Prescott St Ste 8 Worcester MA (01605) ***(G-17440)***
Phoenix Inc 508 399-7100
257 Pine St Seekonk MA (02771) ***(G-15034)***
Phoenix Company of Chicago Inc (PA) 630 595-2300
22 Great Hill Rd Naugatuck CT (06770) ***(G-2489)***
Phoenix Diagnostics Inc 508 655-8310
8 Tech Cir Natick MA (01760) ***(G-13272)***
Phoenix Electric Corp 781 821-0200
40 Hudson Rd Canton MA (02021) ***(G-9767)***
Phoenix Feeds Organix LLC 802 453-6684
5482 Ethan Allen Hwy New Haven VT (05472) ***(G-22186)***
Phoenix Machine Inc 203 888-1135
279 Pearl St Seymour CT (06483) ***(G-3759)***
Phoenix Poultry Corporation 413 732-1433
8 Wheeler Dr Enfield CT (06082) ***(G-1374)***
Phoenix Press Inc 203 865-5555
15 James St New Haven CT (06513) ***(G-2726)***
Phoenix Resources 603 863-9096
193 Lempster Coach Rd Goshen NH (03752) ***(G-18215)***
Phoenix Screen Printing 603 578-9599
61 Bridge St Nashua NH (03060) ***(G-19233)***
Phoenix Sheet Metal 508 994-4046
53 Cove Rd South Dartmouth MA (02748) ***(G-15242)***
Phoenix Trading Co Inc (PA) 617 794-8368
92 Blandin Ave Ste J Framingham MA (01702) ***(G-10994)***
Phoenix Vintners LLC 877 340-9869
127 High St Ipswich MA (01938) ***(G-11934)***
Phoenix Wire Inc 802 372-4561
31 Tracy Rd South Hero VT (05486) ***(G-22481)***
Phoenix Workstation Division, Lowell *Also called General Woodworking Inc* ***(G-12373)***
Phoenix Workstations, Lowell *Also called General Woodworking Inc* ***(G-12374)***
Phoenix-Times Publishing Co 401 253-6000
1 Bradford St Bristol RI (02809) ***(G-20098)***
Phoenixsongs Biologicals Inc 203 433-4329
33 Business Park Dr 1a Branford CT (06405) ***(G-337)***
Phosphorex Incorporated 508 435-9100
106 South St Hopkinton MA (01748) ***(G-11732)***
Photo Diagnostic Systems Inc 978 266-0420
85 Swanson Rd Ste 110 Boxborough MA (01719) ***(G-8966)***
Photo Etch Technology, Lowell *Also called G3 Incorporated* ***(G-12372)***
Photo Fab Engineering, Milford *Also called Elenel Industries Inc* ***(G-13115)***
Photo Tool Engineering Inc 978 805-5000
71 Willie St Lowell MA (01854) ***(G-12421)***
Photobert Cheatsheets, West Hartford *Also called Bertram Sirkin* ***(G-5055)***
Photofabrication Engrg Inc (HQ) 508 478-2025
500 Fortune Blvd Milford MA (01757) ***(G-13137)***
Photographic Corp New England 978 369-3002
177 Old Bedford Rd Fl 2 Concord MA (01742) ***(G-10150)***
Photomachining Inc 603 882-9944
4 Industrial Park Dr # 40 Pelham NH (03076) ***(G-19442)***
Photon Bounce 617 708-1231
19 Elmore St Roxbury MA (02119) ***(G-14875)***
Photonex Corporation 978 723-2200
200 Metrowest Tech Dr Maynard MA (01754) ***(G-12903)***
Photonic Marketing Corporation 401 333-3538
22 Ducarl Dr Lincoln RI (02865) ***(G-20591)***
Photonic Systems Inc 978 670-4990
900 Middlesex Tpke 5-2 Billerica MA (01821) ***(G-8275)***
Photonic Systems Inc 978 369-0729
100 Wildwood Dr Carlisle MA (01741) ***(G-9799)***
Photonics Media, Pittsfield *Also called Laurin Publishing Co Inc* ***(G-14482)***
Photonics N Picoquant Amer Inc 413 562-6161
9 Trinity Dr West Springfield MA (01089) ***(G-16542)***
Photonis Scientific Inc (HQ) 508 347-4000
660 Main St Sturbridge MA (01518) ***(G-15646)***
Photonis Usa, Inc., Sturbridge *Also called Photonis Scientific Inc* ***(G-15646)***
Photonview Technologies 781 366-4836
500 Lowell Ave Newton MA (02460) ***(G-13626)***
Photonwares Corporation (PA) 781 935-1200
15 Presidential Way Woburn MA (01801) ***(G-17263)***
Photronics Inc (PA) 203 775-9000
15 Secor Rd Brookfield CT (06804) ***(G-654)***
Photronics Texas Inc 203 546-3039
15 Secor Rd Brookfield CT (06804) ***(G-655)***
Photronics Texas I LLC 203 775-9000
15 Secor Rd Brookfield CT (06804) ***(G-656)***
Photronix Inc 781 221-0442
35 Sandy Brook Rd Burlington MA (01803) ***(G-9319)***
Physical Measurement Tech 603 876-9990
4 Ling St Marlborough NH (03455) ***(G-18964)***
Physician Engineered Products 207 935-1256
103 Smith St Fryeburg ME (04037) ***(G-6101)***
Piantedosi Baking Co 781 321-3400
240 Commercial St Malden MA (02148) ***(G-12589)***
Piantedosi Baking Co Inc (PA) 781 321-3400
240 Commercial St Malden MA (02148) ***(G-12590)***
Piatek Machine Company Inc 401 728-9930
25 Monticello Rd Pawtucket RI (02861) ***(G-20880)***
Pica Mfg Solutions Inc 603 845-3258
4 Ash Street Ext Unit 3 Derry NH (03038) ***(G-17993)***
Piches Screen Printing & EMB, Belmont *Also called Piches Ski Shop Inc* ***(G-17680)***
Piches Ski Shop Inc 603 524-4413
282 Daniel Webster Hwy Belmont NH (03220) ***(G-17680)***
Picis Clinical Solutions Inc (HQ) 336 397-5336
100 Quannapowitt Pkwy # 405 Wakefield MA (01880) ***(G-15969)***
Pick & Mix Corp 860 521-1521
1234 Farmington Ave Ste 3 West Hartford CT (06107) ***(G-5091)***
Pickadent Inc 203 431-8716
196 N Salem Rd Ste 2 Ridgefield CT (06877) ***(G-3675)***
Picken Printing Inc 978 251-0730
10 Middlesex St North Chelmsford MA (01863) ***(G-13907)***
Pickens Woodworking 207 725-8955
141 Tedford Rd Topsham ME (04086) ***(G-7092)***
Pickup Patrol LLC 603 310-9120
2 Wallace Ln Mont Vernon NH (03057) ***(G-19093)***
Pickwick 781 545-0884
59 Glades Rd Scituate MA (02066) ***(G-15010)***
Piconics Inc 978 649-7501
26 Cummings Rd Tyngsboro MA (01879) ***(G-15899)***
Pictex Corporation 617 375-5801
1260 Boylston St Boston MA (02215) ***(G-8779)***
Picture Frame Inc 207 729-7765
81 Main St Topsham ME (04086) ***(G-7093)***
Picture Frame Products Inc 781 648-7719
34 Hamilton Rd Apt 301 Arlington MA (02474) ***(G-7634)***
Picture Framer, Topsham *Also called Picture Frame Inc* ***(G-7093)***
Picture This Hartford Inc 860 528-1409
80 Pitkin St East Hartford CT (06108) ***(G-1210)***
Pid Analyzers LLC 774 413-5281
2 Washington Cir Ste 4 Sandwich MA (02563) ***(G-14972)***
Pie Guy The, Salem *Also called Withrow Inc* ***(G-19779)***
Pie Guy, The, Manchester *Also called Souhegan Management Corp* ***(G-18927)***
Pieco Holdings, Worcester *Also called Table Talk Pies Inc* ***(G-17485)***
Piematrix Inc 802 318-4891
106 Main St Burlington VT (05401) ***(G-21803)***
Pier Ice Plant Inc 401 789-6090
132 Kingstown Rd Narragansett RI (02882) ***(G-20645)***
Pierce Biotechnology Inc 781 622-1000
30 Commerce Way Ste 2 Woburn MA (01801) ***(G-17264)***
Pierce Machine Co Inc (PA) 413 684-0056
74 E Housatonic St Dalton MA (01226) ***(G-10181)***
Pierce Point Laser 207 854-0133
170 Forest St Westbrook ME (04092) ***(G-7201)***
Piezo Systems Inc 781 933-4850
65 Tower Office Park Woburn MA (01801) ***(G-17265)***
Pig + Poet Restaurant 207 236-3391
52 High St Camden ME (04843) ***(G-5869)***
Pig Rock Sausages LLC 617 851-9422
52 Dyer Ave Milton MA (02186) ***(G-13198)***
Pigeon Hold Targets 603 420-8839
75 Baboosic Lake Rd Merrimack NH (03054) ***(G-19021)***
Pika Energy Inc 207 887-9105
35 Bradley Dr Stop 1 Westbrook ME (04092) ***(G-7202)***
Pike Industries Inc 207 564-8444
53 Spaulding Rd Dover Foxcroft ME (04426) ***(G-5963)***
Pike Powder Coating LLC 617 779-7311
318 Lincoln St Allston MA (02134) ***(G-7473)***
Pilgrim Badge & Label Corp 508 436-6300
1200 W Chestnut St Brockton MA (02301) ***(G-9171)***
Pilgrim Candle Company Inc (PA) 413 562-2635
36 Union Ave Westfield MA (01085) ***(G-16715)***
Pilgrim Foods Co, Greenville *Also called Old Dutch Mustard Co Inc* ***(G-18229)***
Pilgrim Innovative Plas LLC 508 732-0297
127 Industrial Park Rd Plymouth MA (02360) ***(G-14573)***
Pilgrim Nuts, Oxford *Also called Walz & Krenzer Inc* ***(G-3430)***
Pilgrim Plastics, Taunton *Also called Star Printing Corp* ***(G-15787)***
Pilgrim Plastics Products Co, Brockton *Also called Pilgrim Badge & Label Corp* ***(G-9171)***
Pilgrim Tool & Die Inc 508 753-0190
565 Southbridge St Worcester MA (01610) ***(G-17441)***
Pilla Inc 203 894-3265
908 Ethan Allen Hwy Ridgefield CT (06877) ***(G-3676)***
Pillsbury Company LLC 617 884-9800
100 Justin Dr Ste 2 Chelsea MA (02150) ***(G-9964)***
Pilot Machine Designers Inc 203 866-2227
32 Hemlock Pl Norwalk CT (06854) ***(G-3220)***
Pilot Precision Properties LLC 413 350-5200
15 Merrigan Way South Deerfield MA (01373) ***(G-15252)***

ALPHABETIC

Pilot Seasonings, Waterbury *Also called Amodios Inc* ***(G-4843)***
Pin Hsiao & Associates LLC....206 818-0155
146a S Main St Milford MA (01757) ***(G-13138)***
Pin Stop....508 824-1886
87 Lakeview Dr Raynham MA (02767) ***(G-14725)***
Pin-Line, Warwick *Also called Wehr Industries Inc* ***(G-21444)***
Pine and Baker Mfg Inc....978 851-1215
166 Lorum St Tewksbury MA (01876) ***(G-15825)***
Pine and Baker, Inc., Tewksbury *Also called Pine and Baker Mfg Inc* ***(G-15825)***
Pine Baker Inc....978 851-1215
166 Lorum St Tewksbury MA (01876) ***(G-15826)***
Pine Land Farm Cheese Factory....207 688-6400
92 Creamery Ln New Gloucester ME (04260) ***(G-6470)***
Pine Meadow Machine Co Inc....860 623-4494
5 Webb St Windsor Locks CT (06096) ***(G-5398)***
Pine Ridge Gravel LLC....860 873-2500
24 Mount Parnassus Rd East Haddam CT (06423) ***(G-1152)***
Pine River Logging....603 833-1340
314 Hutchens Pond Rd Effingham NH (03882) ***(G-18096)***
Pine State Drilling & Hardware, Athens *Also called Pine State Drilling Inc* ***(G-5543)***
Pine State Drilling Inc....207 654-2771
Rr 150 Athens ME (04912) ***(G-5543)***
Pine State Pest Solutions Inc....207 795-1100
546 Poland Rd Auburn ME (04210) ***(G-5590)***
Pine State Premium Shavings, Lincoln *Also called Lmj Enterprises LLC* ***(G-6358)***
Pine Tree Concrete Products....508 883-7072
151 Lincoln St Millville MA (01529) ***(G-13187)***
Pine Tree Gravel Inc....207 862-4983
436 Meadow Rd Hampden ME (04444) ***(G-6168)***
Pine Tree Lumber, Chesterville *Also called Wood-Mizer Holdings Inc* ***(G-5909)***
Pine Tree Orthopedic Lab Inc....207 897-5558
175 Park St Livermore Falls ME (04254) ***(G-6381)***
Pinestream Communications Inc....781 893-6836
52 Pine St Weston MA (02493) ***(G-16829)***
Ping Electronics Inc....781 275-4731
240 Hartwell Rd Bedford MA (01730) ***(G-8001)***
Pinkberry....617 547-0573
1380 Massachusetts Ave Cambridge MA (02138) ***(G-9611)***
Pinkham's Guitar, Rockport *Also called Woodsound Studio* ***(G-6827)***
Pinnacle Aerospace Mfg LLC....203 258-3398
361 Field Point Rd Greenwich CT (06830) ***(G-1637)***
Pinnacle Loud Speakers, Hatfield *Also called Inter-Ego Systems Inc* ***(G-11401)***
Pinnacle Polymers LLC....203 313-4116
31 Bailey Ave Ste 4 Ridgefield CT (06877) ***(G-3677)***
Pinpoint Laser Systems Inc....978 532-8001
56 Pulaski St Unit 5 Peabody MA (01960) ***(G-14362)***
Pinpoint Promotions & Prtg LLC....203 301-4273
45 Railroad Ave West Haven CT (06516) ***(G-5141)***
Pinto Manufacturing Llc....860 659-9543
122 Naubuc Ave Ste A6 Glastonbury CT (06033) ***(G-1571)***
Pioneer Basements, Westport *Also called Grate Products LLC* ***(G-16840)***
Pioneer Brewing Company LLC....508 347-7500
195 Arnold Rd Fiskdale MA (01518) ***(G-10808)***
Pioneer Capital Corp....860 683-2005
651 Day Hill Rd Windsor CT (06095) ***(G-5354)***
Pioneer Consolidated Corp....508 987-8438
96 Southbridge Rd North Oxford MA (01537) ***(G-13973)***
Pioneer Cover All, North Oxford *Also called Pioneer Consolidated Corp* ***(G-13973)***
Pioneer Instnl Solutions....617 723-2277
85 Devonshire St Fl 8 Boston MA (02109) ***(G-8780)***
Pioneer Metal Products Inc....978 372-2100
19 Pillsbury Rd Sandown NH (03873) ***(G-19787)***
Pioneer Motors and Drives Inc....802 651-0114
30 Berard Dr Unit 6 South Burlington VT (05403) ***(G-22458)***
Pioneer Optics Company Inc....860 286-0071
35 Griffin Rd S Bloomfield CT (06002) ***(G-251)***
Pioneer Packaging Inc (PA)....413 378-6930
220 Padgette St Chicopee MA (01022) ***(G-10050)***
Pioneer Plastics Corporation....207 784-9111
1 Pionite Rd Auburn ME (04210) ***(G-5591)***
Pioneer Plastics Corporation....207 784-9111
1 Pionite Rd Auburn ME (04210) ***(G-5592)***
Pioneer Plastics Corporation (HQ)....203 925-1556
1 Corporate Dr Ste 725 Shelton CT (06484) ***(G-3853)***
Pioneer Precision Grinding....413 739-3371
175 New Bridge St West Springfield MA (01089) ***(G-16543)***
Pioneer Precision Products (PA)....860 828-5838
2311 Chamberlain Hwy Berlin CT (06037) ***(G-101)***
Pioneer Valley Books, Northampton *Also called Pioneer Vly Eductl Press Inc* ***(G-14019)***
Pioneer Valley Plating Co....413 535-1424
51 San Souci Dr South Hadley MA (01075) ***(G-15308)***
Pioneer Valley Printing Co....413 739-2855
62 Ely Ave West Springfield MA (01089) ***(G-16544)***
Pioneer Vly Eductl Press Inc....413 727-3573
155 Industrial Dr Northampton MA (01060) ***(G-14019)***
Pioneer Vly Milk Mktg Coop Inc....413 772-2332
324 Wells St Greenfield MA (01301) ***(G-11272)***
Pioneer Vly Orthtics Prsthtics....413 788-9655
138 Doty Cir West Springfield MA (01089) ***(G-16545)***
Pionite Decorative Surfaces, Auburn *Also called Panolam Industries Intl Inc* ***(G-5586)***
Pionite Decorative Surfaces, Shelton *Also called Pioneer Plastics Corporation* ***(G-3853)***
PIP Foundation Inc....508 757-0103
7 Bishop St Framingham MA (01702) ***(G-10995)***
PIP Itsa Inc....978 927-5717
13 Holly Ln Beverly MA (01915) ***(G-8165)***
PIP Printing, East Longmeadow *Also called Postal Instant Press* ***(G-10487)***
PIP Printing, Beverly *Also called PIP Itsa Inc* ***(G-8165)***
PIP Printing, Manchester *Also called Sazacks Inc* ***(G-2045)***
PIP Printing, Portsmouth *Also called New England Printing Corp* ***(G-19599)***
Pipe Dream Cupcakes LLC....978 397-6470
195 Amberville Rd North Andover MA (01845) ***(G-13724)***
Pipe Supports Group, Woburn *Also called Bergen Pipe Supports Inc* ***(G-17130)***
Piping Specialties Inc....207 878-3955
36 Rainmaker Dr Portland ME (04103) ***(G-6708)***
Pirate Dog Brand LLC....978 745-4786
4 Florence St Unit 3 Salem MA (01970) ***(G-14935)***
Pirit Heated Hose, East Dorset *Also called Sykes Hollow Innovations Ltd* ***(G-21917)***
Piro Printing, Somerville *Also called Guy T Piro & Sons* ***(G-15180)***
Pisani Steel Fabrication Inc....203 720-0679
360 Prospect St Ste 1 Naugatuck CT (06770) ***(G-2490)***
Piscataquis Observer, Dover Foxcroft *Also called Northeast Publishing Company* ***(G-5961)***
Pison Technology Inc....540 394-0998
258 Harvard St Ste 312 Brookline MA (02446) ***(G-9215)***
Pistritto Marble Imports Inc....860 296-5263
97 Airport Rd Hartford CT (06114) ***(G-1857)***
Pitcherville Sand & Grav Corp....603 878-0035
36 Brown Dr Greenville NH (03048) ***(G-18226)***
Pitcherville Sand and Gravel....781 365-1721
40 Mall Rd Burlington MA (01803) ***(G-9320)***
Pitco Frialator Inc (HQ)....603 225-6684
553 Route 3a Bow NH (03304) ***(G-17727)***
Pitco Frialator Inc....603 225-6684
39 Sheep Davis Rd Pembroke NH (03275) ***(G-19462)***
Pitco Frialator Inc....603 225-6684
10 Ferry St Concord NH (03301) ***(G-17923)***
Pith Products LLC....860 487-4859
39 Nott Hwy Unit 1 Ashford CT (06278) ***(G-26)***
Pitman An AGFA Company....800 526-5441
160 Dascomb Rd Andover MA (01810) ***(G-7584)***
Pitney Bowes Inc (PA)....203 356-5000
3001 Summer St Ste 3 Stamford CT (06905) ***(G-4285)***
Pitney Bowes Inc....401 435-8500
70 Catamore Blvd Ste 1 East Providence RI (02914) ***(G-20442)***
Pitney Bowes Inc....203 356-5000
300 Stamford Pl Ste 200 Stamford CT (06902) ***(G-4286)***
Pitney Bowes Inc....207 773-2345
970 Baxter Blvd Ste 203 Portland ME (04103) ***(G-6709)***
Pitney Bowes Inc....203 922-4000
27 Waterview Dr Shelton CT (06484) ***(G-3854)***
Pitney Bowes Inc....603 352-7766
640 Marlboro St Ste 5 Keene NH (03431) ***(G-18522)***
Pitney Bowes Inc....203 356-5000
27 Waterview Dr Shelton CT (06484) ***(G-3855)***
Pittsfield Gazette Inc....413 443-2010
10 Wendell Avenue Ext # 101 Pittsfield MA (01201) ***(G-14499)***
Pittsfield Plastics Engrg Inc....413 442-0067
1510 W Housatonic St Pittsfield MA (01201) ***(G-14500)***
Pittsfield Rye Bakery Inc....413 443-9141
1010 South St Pittsfield MA (01201) ***(G-14501)***
Pivotal Aero Wind Turbines Inc....781 803-2982
555 Bridge St Weymouth MA (02191) ***(G-16897)***
Pixels 2 Press LLC....203 642-3740
26 Pearl St Ste 8 Norwalk CT (06850) ***(G-3221)***
Pj Diversified Machining Inc....603 459-8655
12b Star Dr Ste 3 Merrimack NH (03054) ***(G-19022)***
PJ Keating Company....508 992-3542
72 S Main St Acushnet MA (02743) ***(G-7405)***
PJ Schwalbenberg & Assoc....207 354-0700
26 Spear Mill Rd Cushing ME (04563) ***(G-5934)***
Pjf Trucking and Logging LLC....802 463-3343
35 Schoolbus Depot Rd Bellows Falls VT (05101) ***(G-21653)***
Pjs To Your Door LLC....978 462-0699
71 Green St Newbury MA (01951) ***(G-13463)***
Places To Go LLC....774 202-7756
1 Wamsutta St New Bedford MA (02740) ***(G-13438)***
Placon Corporation....413 785-1553
1227 Union Street Ext West Springfield MA (01089) ***(G-16546)***
Plainville Electro Plating Co....860 525-5328
21 Forest Hills Dr Hartford CT (06117) ***(G-1858)***
Plainville Machine & Tl Co Inc....860 589-5595
65 Ronzo Rd Bristol CT (06010) ***(G-594)***
Plainville Plating Company Inc....860 747-1624
21 Forestville Ave Plainville CT (06062) ***(G-3511)***
Plainville Special Tool, Plainville *Also called Alto Products Corp Al* ***(G-3465)***
Plainville Stock Company....508 699-4434
104 South St Plainville MA (02762) ***(G-14533)***
Plaistow Cabinet Co Inc....603 382-1098
56 Newton Rd Plaistow NH (03865) ***(G-19520)***

Plan Tech Inc 603 783-4767
7031 Shaker Rd Unit J Loudon NH (03307) ***(G-18752)***
Plane Fantasy 617 734-4950
30 Rangeley Rd Chestnut Hill MA (02467) ***(G-9990)***
Planet Eclipse LLC 401 247-9061
130 Franklin St Bldg L4l5 Warren RI (02885) ***(G-21302)***
Planet Small Communications 978 794-2201
15 Union St Ste 5 Lawrence MA (01840) ***(G-12071)***
Planet Technologies Inc 800 255-3749
96 Danbury Rd Ridgefield CT (06877) ***(G-3678)***
Planet Ventures Inc (PA) 207 761-1515
85 Bradley Dr Westbrook ME (04092) ***(G-7203)***
Planon Corporation 781 356-0999
45 Braintree Hill Park # 400 Braintree MA (02184) ***(G-9030)***
Plansee USA LLC (HQ) 508 553-3800
115 Constitution Blvd Franklin MA (02038) ***(G-11071)***
Plant Snacks LLC 617 480-6265
60 Kendrick St Ste 200 Needham MA (02494) ***(G-13308)***
Plantes Lobster Escape Vents 207 549-7204
3628 Turner Ridge Rd Somerville ME (04348) ***(G-6999)***
Plas-TEC Coatings Inc 860 289-6029
68 Mascolo Rd South Windsor CT (06074) ***(G-4000)***
Plas-Tech Inc 207 854-8324
22 Bartlett Rd Gorham ME (04038) ***(G-6125)***
Plaskolite LLC 800 628-5084
113 Silver St Sheffield MA (01257) ***(G-15062)***
Plaskolite LLC 800 628-5084
119 Salisbury Rd Sheffield MA (01257) ***(G-15063)***
Plaskolite Massachusetts LLC 413 229-8711
119 Salisbury Rd Sheffield MA (01257) ***(G-15064)***
Plasma Coatings, Middlebury *Also called American Roller Company LLC* ***(G-2154)***
Plasma Coatings Inc 203 598-3100
758 E Main St Waterbury CT (06702) ***(G-4939)***
Plasma Giken Limited Company 508 640-7708
6 Viking Rd Webster MA (01570) ***(G-16349)***
Plasma Technology Incorporated 860 282-0659
70 Rye St South Windsor CT (06074) ***(G-4001)***
Plasmine Technology Inc 207 797-5009
33 Bishop St Portland ME (04103) ***(G-6710)***
Plastech Machining Fabrication 603 228-7601
25 Dunklee Rd Bow NH (03304) ***(G-17728)***
Plastech Manufacturing, East Windsor *Also called Trento Group LLC* ***(G-1308)***
Plasti-Clip Corporation 603 672-1166
38 Perry Rd Milford NH (03055) ***(G-19072)***
Plasti-Graphics Inc 781 599-7766
102 Central Ave Lynn MA (01901) ***(G-12533)***
Plastic Assembly Corporation 978 772-4725
1 Sculley Rd Unit A Ayer MA (01432) ***(G-7934)***
Plastic Assembly Systems LLC 203 393-0639
19 Sargent Dr Bethany CT (06524) ***(G-123)***
Plastic Concepts Inc 978 663-7996
2 Sterling Rd Unit 2 # 2 North Billerica MA (01862) ***(G-13856)***
Plastic Craft Novelty Co Inc 508 222-1486
12 Dunham St Apt A Attleboro MA (02703) ***(G-7777)***
Plastic Design Inc 978 251-4830
180 Middlesex St Ste 2 North Chelmsford MA (01863) ***(G-13908)***
Plastic Design Intl Inc (PA) 860 632-2001
111 Industrial Park Rd Middletown CT (06457) ***(G-2210)***
Plastic Distributing, Littleton *Also called Polyone Corporation* ***(G-12319)***
Plastic Distrs Fabricators Inc 978 374-0300
419 River St Haverhill MA (01832) ***(G-11459)***
Plastic Fabricators Corp 781 933-6007
310 Salem St Woburn MA (01801) ***(G-17266)***
Plastic Factory LLC 203 908-3468
678 Howard Ave Bridgeport CT (06605) ***(G-470)***
Plastic Forming Company Inc (PA) 203 397-1338
20 S Bradley Rd Woodbridge CT (06525) ***(G-5476)***
Plastic Industries, Nashua *Also called Carr Management Inc* ***(G-19131)***
Plastic Industries Inc (HQ) 603 888-1315
1 Tara Blvd Nashua NH (03062) ***(G-19234)***
Plastic Molding Mfg Inc (PA) 978 567-1000
34 Tower St Hudson MA (01749) ***(G-11802)***
Plastic Molding Technology 203 881-1811
92 Cogwheel Ln Seymour CT (06483) ***(G-3760)***
Plastic Monofil Co Ltd 732 629-7701
8 Tulip Way Medway MA (02053) ***(G-12969)***
Plastic Monofil Co Ltd 802 893-1543
28 Industrial Dr Milton VT (05468) ***(G-22136)***
Plastic Moulding Manufacturing, Hudson *Also called Restech Plastic Molding LLC* ***(G-11812)***
Plastic Services Entps Inc 401 490-3811
100 Niantic Ave Ste 104 Providence RI (02907) ***(G-21090)***
Plastic Solutions LLC 203 266-5675
263 Hickory Ln Bethlehem CT (06751) ***(G-198)***
Plastic Techniques Inc 603 622-5570
27 Springfield Rd Goffstown NH (03045) ***(G-18209)***
Plastic Technologies MD Inc 802 658-6588
8 Harbor Rd South Burlington VT (05403) ***(G-22459)***
Plastic Technologies NY LLC 802 658-6588
8 Harbor View Rd South Burlington VT (05403) ***(G-22460)***
Plastic Technology Division, Mansfield *Also called Hub Folding Box Company Inc* ***(G-12636)***
Plastican Inc 978 728-5000
196 Industrial Rd Leominster MA (01453) ***(G-12176)***
Plasticoid Manufacturing Inc 860 623-1361
32 North Rd Rear East Windsor CT (06088) ***(G-1298)***
Plastics and Concepts Conn Inc 860 657-9655
101 Laurel Trl Glastonbury CT (06033) ***(G-1572)***
Plastics Group, Woonsocket *Also called Ralco Industries Inc* ***(G-21577)***
Plastics Group of Whelen, The, Charlestown *Also called Whelen Engineering Co* ***(G-17821)***
Plastics Plus Inc 401 727-1447
51 Abbott St Ste 1 Cumberland RI (02864) ***(G-20339)***
Plastics Supply of Maine Inc 207 775-7778
6 Pomerleau St Biddeford ME (04005) ***(G-5755)***
Plastock, Putnam *Also called Ensinger Prcsion Cmponents Inc* ***(G-3611)***
Plastonics Inc 860 249-5455
230 Locust St Hartford CT (06114) ***(G-1859)***
Plastron Company, Westfield *Also called Sonicron Systems Corporation* ***(G-16731)***
Plataine Inc 336 905-0900
465 Waverley Oaks Rd # 420 Waltham MA (02452) ***(G-16174)***
Plating For Electronics Inc 781 893-2368
94 Calvary St Waltham MA (02453) ***(G-16175)***
Plating Supplies Intl Inc 413 786-2020
71 Ramah Cir N Agawam MA (01001) ***(G-7446)***
Plating Technology Inc 508 996-4006
41 Coffin Ave New Bedford MA (02746) ***(G-13439)***
Platinum Recognition LLC (PA) 401 305-6700
862 Charles St North Providence RI (02904) ***(G-20772)***
Platt & Labonia Company LLC 800 505-9099
70-80 Stoddard Ave North Haven CT (06473) ***(G-3051)***
Platt Brothers & Company (PA) 203 753-4194
2670 S Main St Waterbury CT (06706) ***(G-4940)***
Platt Brothers Realty II LLC 203 562-5112
25 James St New Haven CT (06513) ***(G-2727)***
Platt-Labonia of N Haven Inc 203 239-5681
70 Stoddard Ave North Haven CT (06473) ***(G-3052)***
Play To Win Inc 603 669-6770
183 Hayward St Manchester NH (03103) ***(G-18901)***
Play-It Productions Inc 212 695-6530
167b Lebanon Ave Colchester CT (06415) ***(G-805)***
Playtex Products LLC (HQ) 203 944-5500
6 Research Dr Ste 400 Shelton CT (06484) ***(G-3856)***
Pleasant Bay Boat Spar Co LLC 508 240-0058
80 Rayber Rd Orleans MA (02653) ***(G-14240)***
Pleasant Printing Co 508 222-3366
163 Pleasant St Ste 5 Attleboro MA (02703) ***(G-7778)***
Pleasant River Lumber Company (PA) 207 564-8520
432 Milo Rd Dover Foxcroft ME (04426) ***(G-5964)***
Pleasant River Pine, Hancock *Also called Prl Hancock LLC* ***(G-6171)***
Pleasant Street Designs Inc 978 682-3910
1 Aegean Dr Methuen MA (01844) ***(G-13042)***
Pleasant Valley Fence Co Inc 860 379-0088
Rr 181 Pleasant Valley CT (06063) ***(G-3546)***
Plenoptika Inc (PA) 617 862-2203
955 Msschstts Ave Box 339 Cambridge MA (02139) ***(G-9612)***
Plenus Group Inc 978 970-3832
101 Phoenix Ave Lowell MA (01852) ***(G-12422)***
Plouffs Monument Co Inc 802 933-4346
1087 Colton Rd Enosburg Falls VT (05450) ***(G-21926)***
Plp Composite Technologies 603 585-9100
57 Creamery Rd Fitzwilliam NH (03447) ***(G-18152)***
Plumb Pak, Winchester *Also called The Keeney Manufacturing Co* ***(G-19996)***
Plumb Pak Medical, Newington *Also called The Keeney Manufacturing Co* ***(G-2906)***
Plumbers of RI 401 919-0980
10 Rosario Dr Providence RI (02909) ***(G-21091)***
Plumriver LLC 781 431-7477
94 Edmunds Rd Wellesley MA (02481) ***(G-16381)***
Plumrose Usa Inc 802 868-7314
14 Jonergin Dr Swanton VT (05488) ***(G-22533)***
Plymouth Awning Co 508 746-3740
4 Brookside Ave Plymouth MA (02360) ***(G-14574)***
Plymouth Bay Winery 508 746-2100
114 Water St Plymouth MA (02360) ***(G-14575)***
Plymouth Grating Lab Inc 508 465-2274
5 Commerce Way Carver MA (02330) ***(G-9806)***
Plymouth Rubber Company LLC 781 828-0220
104 Revere St Canton MA (02021) ***(G-9768)***
Plymouth Rubber Europa SA 781 828-0220
960 Turnpike St Ste 2a Canton MA (02021) ***(G-9769)***
Plymouth Sign Co Inc 508 398-2721
63 Old Main St South Yarmouth MA (02664) ***(G-15333)***
Plymouth Spring Company Inc 860 584-0594
281 Lake Ave Bristol CT (06010) ***(G-595)***
Plynk Connect Inc 760 815-2955
19 Stanhope St Apt 2c Boston MA (02116) ***(G-8781)***
PM Colors Inc 401 521-7280
10 Industrial Ln Johnston RI (02919) ***(G-20530)***
PMC Engineering LLC 203 792-8686
11 Old Sugar Hollow Rd Danbury CT (06810) ***(G-968)***

ALPHABETIC

PMC Lighting Inc 401 738-7266
100 Gilbane St Warwick RI (02886) ***(G-21404)***
PMC Technologies LLC 203 222-0000
31 Glenwood Rd Weston CT (06883) ***(G-5172)***
Pmd Scientific Inc 860 242-8177
105 W Ddley Town Rd Ste F Bloomfield CT (06002) ***(G-252)***
PMG, West Boylston *Also called Precision Machine & Gear Inc* ***(G-16427)***
PMI, Wolcott *Also called Precision Methods Incorporated* ***(G-5452)***
PMS Mfg, Gloucester *Also called P M S Manufactured Pdts Inc* ***(G-11200)***
PMS Printing Inc (PA) 860 563-1676
175 Benton Dr Ste 100 East Longmeadow MA (01028) ***(G-10486)***
Pmt Group Inc (PA) 203 367-8675
800 Union Ave Bridgeport CT (06607) ***(G-471)***
Pmweb Inc 617 207-7080
1 Pope St Wakefield MA (01880) ***(G-15970)***
Pnderosa K Atc Acquisition Inc 617 375-7500
116 Huntington Ave Boston MA (02116) ***(G-8782)***
Pne Energy Supply LLC 603 413-6602
1087 Elm St Ste 414 Manchester NH (03101) ***(G-18902)***
Pneucleus Technologies LLC 603 921-5300
19a Clinton Dr Hollis NH (03049) ***(G-18338)***
Pneutek Inc 603 595-0302
17 Friars Dr Ste D Hudson NH (03051) ***(G-18427)***
Pneutronics Division, Hollis *Also called Parker-Hannifin Corporation* ***(G-18337)***
Pobco Inc 508 791-6376
99 Hope Ave Worcester MA (01603) ***(G-17442)***
Poc, Gardner *Also called Precision Optics Corp Inc* ***(G-11123)***
Pocahontas Spring Water Co (PA) 978 774-2690
42 School St Middleton MA (01949) ***(G-13098)***
Pocasset Machine Corporation 508 563-5572
7 Commerce Park Rd Pocasset MA (02559) ***(G-14600)***
Podgurski Wldg & Hvy Eqp Repr 781 830-9901
8 Springdale Ave Ste 2 Canton MA (02021) ***(G-9770)***
Podunk Popcorn 860 648-9565
245 Barber Hill Rd South Windsor CT (06074) ***(G-4002)***
Poets Corner Press Inc 508 228-1051
16a Amelia Dr Nantucket MA (02554) ***(G-13230)***
Pohto Etch Tech, Lowell *Also called Photo Tool Engineering Inc* ***(G-12421)***
Point Lighting Corporation 860 243-0600
61-65 W Dudley Town Rd Bloomfield CT (06002) ***(G-253)***
Point Machine Company 860 828-6901
588 Four Rod Rd Berlin CT (06037) ***(G-102)***
Point View Displays LLC 203 468-0887
200 Morgan Ave East Haven CT (06512) ***(G-1258)***
Pointcare Technologies Inc 508 281-6925
19 Brigham St Unit 9 Marlborough MA (01752) ***(G-12808)***
Pointillist Inc 617 752-2214
321 Summer St Fl 8 Boston MA (02210) ***(G-8783)***
Polamer Precision Inc 860 259-6200
105 Alton Brooks Way New Britain CT (06053) ***(G-2563)***
Polar Beverages, Worcester *Also called Polar Corp* ***(G-17443)***
Polar Cap Ice Co, Sandwich *Also called JP Lillis Enterprises Inc* ***(G-14970)***
Polar Controls Inc 978 425-2233
2 Shaker Rd Ste F220 Shirley MA (01464) ***(G-15092)***
Polar Corp (PA) 508 753-6383
1001 Southbridge St Worcester MA (01610) ***(G-17443)***
Polar Corporation 860 223-7891
59 High St Ste 11 New Britain CT (06051) ***(G-2564)***
Polar Focus Inc 413 665-2044
20 Industrial Dr E South Deerfield MA (01373) ***(G-15253)***
Polar Fuel Inc 508 543-5200
95 Washington St Foxboro MA (02035) ***(G-10898)***
Polar Industries Inc (PA) 203 758-6651
32 Gramar Ave Prospect CT (06712) ***(G-3592)***
Polaris Contract Mfg Inc 508 748-3399
15 Barnabas Rd Marion MA (02738) ***(G-12702)***
Polaris Management Inc 203 261-6399
30 Silver Hill Rd Easton CT (06612) ***(G-1322)***
Polaris Sheet Metal Inc 978 281-5644
18 Sargent St Ste 1 Gloucester MA (01930) ***(G-11203)***
Polarity, Farmington *Also called Breach Intelligence Inc* ***(G-1469)***
Polartec LLC (PA) 978 659-5109
300 Brickstone Sq Ste 401 Andover MA (01810) ***(G-7585)***
Polhemus, Colchester *Also called Alken Inc* ***(G-21856)***
Polifil Inc 401 767-2700
1112 River St Woonsocket RI (02895) ***(G-21575)***
Polka Dog Bakery, Boston *Also called Polka Dog Designs LLC* ***(G-8784)***
Polka Dog Designs LLC (PA) 617 338-5155
256 Shawmut Ave Boston MA (02118) ***(G-8784)***
Pollution Research & Dev Corp (PA) 603 863-7553
475 Sunapee St Ste 4 Newport NH (03773) ***(G-19353)***
Pollys Pancake Parlor 603 823-5575
672 Route 117 Sugar Hill NH (03586) ***(G-19878)***
Polnox Corporation 978 735-4438
225 Stedman St Ste 23 Lowell MA (01851) ***(G-12423)***
Polstal Corporation 203 849-7788
10 Admiral Ln Wilton CT (06897) ***(G-5299)***
Poly Mold Inc Building 1, Cheshire *Also called Polymold Corp* ***(G-753)***
Poly Plating Inc 413 593-5477
2096 Westover Rd Chicopee MA (01022) ***(G-10051)***
Poly-Cel Inc 508 229-8310
53 Brigham St Unit 2 Marlborough MA (01752) ***(G-12809)***
Poly-Ject Inc 603 882-6570
8 Manhattan Dr Amherst NH (03031) ***(G-17581)***
Poly-Mark Corp 978 368-1300
99 Parker St Clinton MA (01510) ***(G-10090)***
Poly-Metal Finishing Inc 413 781-4535
1 Allen St Ste 218 Springfield MA (01108) ***(G-15498)***
Poly-Tech Diamond Co Inc 508 695-3561
4 East St North Attleboro MA (02760) ***(G-13772)***
Poly-Vac Inc 603 647-7822
253 Abby Rd Manchester NH (03103) ***(G-18903)***
Polycarbon Industries Inc 978 772-2111
88 Jackson Rd Devens MA (01434) ***(G-10330)***
Polycarbon Industries Inc (HQ) 978 462-5555
9 Opportunity Way Newburyport MA (01950) ***(G-13521)***
Polycast, Stamford *Also called Spartech LLC* ***(G-4327)***
Polycom Inc 978 292-5000
600 Federal St Ste 1 Andover MA (01810) ***(G-7586)***
Polyexe Corporation 603 778-1143
50 Pine Rd Brentwood NH (03833) ***(G-17754)***
Polyfiber LLC 508 222-3500
55 Starkey Ave Attleboro MA (02703) ***(G-7779)***
Polyfoam Corp 508 234-6323
2355 Providence Rd Northbridge MA (01534) ***(G-14058)***
Polyfoam Corporation 401 781-3220
60 Glen Rd Cranston RI (02920) ***(G-20272)***
Polymath Software 860 423-5823
42 Carey St Willimantic CT (06226) ***(G-5268)***
Polymedex Discovery Group Inc (PA) 860 928-4102
45 Ridge Rd Putnam CT (06260) ***(G-3627)***
Polymer Corporation 413 267-5524
1 3rd St Palmer MA (01069) ***(G-14293)***
Polymer Corporation (HQ) 781 871-4606
180 Pleasant St Rockland MA (02370) ***(G-14819)***
Polymer Engineered Pdts Inc (PA) 203 324-3737
595 Summer St Ste 2 Stamford CT (06901) ***(G-4287)***
Polymer Films Inc 203 932-3000
301 Heffernan Dr West Haven CT (06516) ***(G-5142)***
Polymer Injection Molding, Palmer *Also called Polymer Corporation* ***(G-14293)***
Polymer Liquid Resin Casting, Rockland *Also called Polymer Corporation* ***(G-14819)***
Polymer Resources Ltd (PA) 203 324-3737
656 New Britain Ave Farmington CT (06032) ***(G-1507)***
Polymer Solutions Inc 401 423-1638
200 Weeden St Pawtucket RI (02860) ***(G-20881)***
Polymer Technologies LLC 603 883-4002
4 Bud Way Ste 14 Nashua NH (03063) ***(G-19235)***
Polymer Technology, Wilmington *Also called Wilmington Partners LP* ***(G-17067)***
Polymeric Converting LLC 860 623-1335
5 Old Depot Hill Rd Enfield CT (06082) ***(G-1375)***
Polymetallurgical LLC 508 695-9312
262 Broad St North Attleboro MA (02760) ***(G-13773)***
Polymold Corp 203 272-2622
951 S Meriden Rd Cheshire CT (06410) ***(G-753)***
Polyneer Inc 508 998-5225
259 Samuel Barnet Blvd D New Bedford MA (02745) ***(G-13440)***
Polyone Corporation 203 327-6010
70 Carlisle Pl Stamford CT (06902) ***(G-4288)***
Polyone Corporation 978 772-0764
305 Foster St Ste 103 Littleton MA (01460) ***(G-12319)***
Polyonics Corporation 978 462-3600
24 Graf Rd Newburyport MA (01950) ***(G-13522)***
Polypolish Products Div, Bethel *Also called Intersurface Dynamics Inc* ***(G-161)***
Polyrack North America Corp 401 770-1500
1600 Highland Corp Dr Cumberland RI (02864) ***(G-20340)***
Polytec Inc 508 417-1040
1 Cabot Rd Ste 102 Hudson MA (01749) ***(G-11803)***
Polytech Filtration Systems 978 562-7700
100 Forest Ave Hudson MA (01749) ***(G-11804)***
Polytechnic Inc 401 724-3608
110 Tweed St Pawtucket RI (02861) ***(G-20882)***
Polytronics Corporation 860 683-2442
800 Marshall Phelps Rd 1hi Windsor CT (06095) ***(G-5355)***
Polyurethane Molding Inds Inc 401 765-6700
100 Founders Dr Woonsocket RI (02895) ***(G-21576)***
Polyvinyl Films Inc 508 865-3558
19 Depot St Sutton MA (01590) ***(G-15690)***
Polyworks LLC 401 769-0994
1 Tupperware Dr Ste 7 North Smithfield RI (02896) ***(G-20794)***
Pomeroy & Co Inc 617 241-0234
18 Spice St Ste 1 Charlestown MA (02129) ***(G-9841)***
Pompanette, Charlestown *Also called Bomar Inc* ***(G-17811)***
Pompanette LLC (PA) 717 569-2300
73 Southwest St Charlestown NH (03603) ***(G-17819)***
Pond Cove Millwork Inc 207 773-6819
22 Mill Brook Rd Saco ME (04072) ***(G-6855)***
Pondera Nutraceuticals, Pownal *Also called Pondera Pharmaceuticals Inc* ***(G-6750)***

Pondera Pharmaceuticals Inc 207 688-4494
209 Chadsey Rd Pownal ME (04069) *(G-6750)*

Pongo Resume, Northborough *Also called Pongo Software LLC (G-14044)*

Pongo Software LLC 508 393-4528
168 E Main St Northborough MA (01532) *(G-14044)*

Ponn Machine Cutting Co 781 937-3373
20 Cross St Woburn MA (01801) *(G-17267)*

Ponn Rubber Co, Stoneham *Also called Allan Ponn (G-15553)*

Pony Shack Cider Company 781 367-4060
188 Picnic St Boxborough MA (01719) *(G-8967)*

Poof-Alex Holdings LLC (PA) 203 930-7711
10 Glenville St Ste 1 Greenwich CT (06831) *(G-1638)*

Pool Environments Inc 207 839-8225
10 Elm St Gorham ME (04038) *(G-6126)*

Poole Sheet Metal & Wldg Inc 603 679-3860
35 Commercial Dr 1 Brentwood NH (03833) *(G-17755)*

Pop Color, Williston *Also called Garlic Press Inc (G-22667)*

Pop Tops Company Inc 508 580-2580
10 Plymouth Dr South Easton MA (02375) *(G-15286)*

Pop Tops Sportswear, South Easton *Also called Pop Tops Company Inc (G-15286)*

Popcorn Movie Poster Co LLC 860 610-0000
1 Cherry St East Hartford CT (06108) *(G-1211)*

Pope Sails and Rigging Inc 207 596-7293
237 Park St Rockland ME (04841) *(G-6808)*

Poplar Hill Machine Inc 413 369-4252
2077 Roaring Brook Rd Conway MA (01341) *(G-10165)*

Poplar Tool & Mfg Co Inc 203 333-4369
420 Poplar St Bridgeport CT (06605) *(G-472)*

Poppys LLC 860 778-9044
260 Steele Rd Hartford CT (06117) *(G-1860)*

Pops Donuts 203 876-1210
587 New Haven Ave Milford CT (06460) *(G-2335)*

Popular Precast Products 508 966-4622
26 N Main St Bellingham MA (02019) *(G-8057)*

Poputees Co 401 497-6512
278 Lincoln St Blackstone MA (01504) *(G-8314)*

Popzup LLC 978 502-1737
1 Washington St Ste 5110 Dover NH (03820) *(G-18046)*

Porex Cleanroom Products Inc 800 628-8606
2255 Westover Rd Chicopee MA (01022) *(G-10052)*

Porobond Products LLC 203 234-7747
80 Sanford St Hamden CT (06514) *(G-1777)*

Porogen Corporation (HQ) 781 491-0807
35a Cabot Rd Woburn MA (01801) *(G-17268)*

Port Canvas Company, Arundel *Also called C B P Corp (G-5529)*

Port City Coffee Roasters, Portsmouth *Also called Red 23 Holdings Inc (G-19613)*

Port City Graphics Inc 207 450-6299
664a Main St Gorham ME (04038) *(G-6127)*

Port Cy Lf Communications Inc 207 781-4644
9 Ocean Ter Cumberland Foreside ME (04110) *(G-5932)*

Port Electronics Corporation 800 253-8510
60 Island St Ste 306 Lawrence MA (01840) *(G-12072)*

Port Printing Solutions Inc 207 741-5200
525 Main St Ste A South Portland ME (04106) *(G-7037)*

Port-O-Lite Company Inc 603 352-3205
1 Railroad St West Swanzey NH (03469) *(G-19967)*

Porta Door Co 203 888-6191
65 Cogwheel Ln Seymour CT (06483) *(G-3761)*

Porta Phone Co Inc 401 789-8700
145 Dean Knauss Dr Narragansett RI (02882) *(G-20646)*

Porta Phones, Narragansett *Also called Porta Phone Co Inc (G-20646)*

Porta-Brace Inc 802 442-8171
160 Benmont Ave Ste 100 Bennington VT (05201) *(G-21689)*

Portable Sawmill 207 843-7216
218 Blackcap Rd Eddington ME (04428) *(G-5998)*

Portage Lkers Snwmbile CLB Inc 207 415-0506
22b School St Portage ME (04768) *(G-6599)*

Portal Inc 800 966-3030
10 Tracy Dr Avon MA (02322) *(G-7892)*

Portance Corp 978 400-9991
325 Authority Dr Fitchburg MA (01420) *(G-10849)*

Portela Soni Medical LLC 508 818-2727
57 Totten Rd Attleboro MA (02703) *(G-7780)*

Porter Machine Inc 401 397-8889
765 Victory Hwy Unit 1 West Greenwich RI (02817) *(G-21463)*

Porter Manufacturing 603 303-6846
371 Turnpike Rd New Ipswich NH (03071) *(G-19310)*

Porter Music Box Company Inc 802 728-9694
33 Sunset Hill Rd Randolph VT (05060) *(G-22301)*

Porter Preston Inc 203 753-1113
61 Mattatuck Heights Rd # 2 Waterbury CT (06705) *(G-4941)*

Porter Sargent Publishers Inc 617 922-0076
2 Lan Dr Ste 100 Westford MA (01886) *(G-16785)*

Porter Square Press, Cambridge *Also called Somerville Quick Print Inc (G-9656)*

Porter-Ferguson, West Boylston *Also called Lowell Corporation (G-16421)*

Portfolio Arts Group Ltd 203 661-2400
129 Glover Ave Norwalk CT (06850) *(G-3222)*

Portion Meat Associates Inc 401 421-2438
356 Valley St Providence RI (02908) *(G-21092)*

Portland Connecticut Mch Sp, Portland *Also called Transportation Conn Dept (G-3579)*

Portland Magazine, Portland *Also called Portland Monthly Inc (G-6711)*

Portland Mattress Makers Inc (PA) 207 772-2276
25 Edwards Ave Biddeford ME (04005) *(G-5756)*

Portland Monthly Inc 207 775-4339
722 Congress St Portland ME (04102) *(G-6711)*

Portland Pudgy Inc 207 761-2428
48 Tyng St Portland ME (04102) *(G-6712)*

Portland Sand & Gravel Inc 207 829-2196
61 Rose Dr Cumberland Center ME (04021) *(G-5931)*

Portland Slitting Co Inc 860 342-1500
193 Pickering St Portland CT (06480) *(G-3570)*

Portland Stone Ware Co Inc (PA) 978 459-7272
50 Mcgrath Rd Dracut MA (01826) *(G-10367)*

Portland Stone Works Inc 207 878-6832
50 Allen Ave Portland ME (04103) *(G-6713)*

Portland Stoneworks, Portland *Also called Portland Stone Works Inc (G-6713)*

Portland Valve LLC (HQ) 704 289-6511
82 Bridge St Warren MA (01083) *(G-16261)*

Portland Valve LLC 978 284-4000
90 Industrial Way Warren MA (01083) *(G-16262)*

Portmanteau, Portland *Also called Nancy Lawrence (G-6697)*

Portsmouth Naval Shipyard, Portsmouth *Also called United States Dept of Navy (G-19627)*

Portsmouth Naval Shipyard 207 438-1000
Code 612 5 Bldg 153 6th Portsmouth NH (03804) *(G-19608)*

Portsmouth Sign Company 603 436-0047
19 Nimble Hill Rd Newington NH (03801) *(G-19324)*

Portuamerica Inc 413 589-0095
60 Lehigh St Ludlow MA (01056) *(G-12475)*

Porvair Filtration Group Inc 207 493-3027
15 Armco Ave Caribou ME (04736) *(G-5890)*

Pos Center Inc 617 797-5026
5 Beale St Quincy MA (02170) *(G-14646)*

Position Health Inc 617 549-2403
123 Haven St Ste 2689 Reading MA (01867) *(G-14739)*

Post & Beam Homes Inc 860 267-2060
4 Sexton Hill Rd East Hampton CT (06424) *(G-1163)*

Post Mortem Services LLC 860 675-1103
82 Knollwood Rd Farmington CT (06032) *(G-1508)*

Post Woodworking Inc 603 382-4951
163 Kingston Rd Danville NH (03819) *(G-17969)*

Post-Gazette Publishers, Boston *Also called Ethnic Publishers Inc (G-8528)*

Postal Instant Press (PA) 413 525-4044
175 Benton Dr Ste 100 East Longmeadow MA (01028) *(G-10487)*

Postdoc Ventures LLC 617 492-3555
1668 Massachusetts Ave Cambridge MA (02138) *(G-9613)*

Potomac Electric Corp 617 364-0400
1 Westinghouse Plz A17 Boston MA (02136) *(G-8785)*

Potter Family Maple 802 578-0937
544 King Rd Bakersfield VT (05441) *(G-21603)*

Potters Printing Inc 617 547-3161
822 Eastern Ave Fall River MA (02723) *(G-10747)*

Pottery Shop, The, York *Also called Chris Davis Stoneware Pottery (G-7306)*

Potting Shed Inc 617 899-6290
43 Bradford St Ste 3 Concord MA (01742) *(G-10151)*

Poulin Grain Inc 802 681-1605
1873 Vt Route 67 E North Bennington VT (05257) *(G-22212)*

Poulin Grain Inc 802 868-3323
24 Depot St Swanton VT (05488) *(G-22534)*

Poultney Pallet Inc 802 265-4444
10 Winham Ln Fair Haven VT (05743) *(G-21968)*

Pourer Fedora LLC 617 267-0333
35 Marlborough St Boston MA (02116) *(G-8786)*

Powder Horn Press Inc (PA) 508 746-8777
301 Court St Apt 1 Plymouth MA (02360) *(G-14576)*

Powder Pro Powder Coating Inc 508 991-5999
195 Riverside Ave New Bedford MA (02746) *(G-13441)*

Powdered Metal Technology Corp 617 642-4135
76 Northwest Blvd 29-A Nashua NH (03063) *(G-19236)*

Powell and Mahoney LLC 978 745-4332
39 Norman St Salem MA (01970) *(G-14936)*

Power Advocate Inc 415 615-0146
179 Lincoln St Ste 100 Boston MA (02111) *(G-8787)*

Power Chair Recyclers Neng LLC 401 294-4111
6802 Post Rd North Kingstown RI (02852) *(G-20733)*

Power Controls Inc 203 284-0235
801 N Main Street Ext Wallingford CT (06492) *(G-4784)*

Power Cover Usa LLC 203 755-2687
37 Commons Ct Ste 3 Waterbury CT (06704) *(G-4942)*

Power Equipment Co Inc (PA) 508 226-3410
7 Franklin R Mckay Rd Attleboro MA (02703) *(G-7781)*

Power Fuels LLC 203 699-0099
143 Main St Cheshire CT (06410) *(G-754)*

Power Graphics Printing 978 851-8988
1921 Main St Ste 4 Tewksbury MA (01876) *(G-15827)*

Power Gripps Usa Inc 207 422-2051
41 Pomola Ave Sorrento ME (04677) *(G-7000)*

Power Guide Marketing Inc (PA) 508 853-7357
540 W Boylston St Rear Worcester MA (01606) *(G-17444)*

ALPHABETIC

Power Object Inc 617 630-5701
123 Ridge Ave Newton MA (02459) *(G-13627)*
Power Pros Consulting Group 508 238-6629
20 Hampden Dr Ste 4 South Easton MA (02375) *(G-15287)*
Power Solutions LLC (PA) 800 876-9373
8 Filko Ave Unit 5 Swansea MA (02777) *(G-15713)*
Power Steering Software 617 520-2100
15 Mount Auburn St Cambridge MA (02138) *(G-9614)*
Power Strategies LLC 203 254-9926
2384 Redding Rd Fairfield CT (06824) *(G-1449)*
Power Systems Division, South Windsor *Also called United Technologies Corp (G-4018)*
Power Systems Integrity Inc 508 393-1655
100 Otis St Ste 6 Northborough MA (01532) *(G-14045)*
Power Trans Co Inc 203 881-0314
315 Riggs St Ste 2 Oxford CT (06478) *(G-3419)*
Power-Dyne LLC 860 346-9283
2055 S Main St Middletown CT (06457) *(G-2211)*
Power-Dyne LLC/Bidwll Indstrl, Middletown *Also called Power-Dyne LLC (G-2211)*
Powerbox (usa) Inc 303 439-7211
15 Constitution Dr Ste 1a Bedford NH (03110) *(G-17660)*
Powerdocks LLC 401 253-3103
1090 Hope St Bristol RI (02809) *(G-20099)*
Powerdyne International Inc 401 739-3300
145 Phenix Aveste 1 Cranston RI (02920) *(G-20273)*
Powerfab Inc 603 424-3900
715a Daniel Webster Hwy Merrimack NH (03054) *(G-19023)*
Powerful ME 207 370-8830
10 Beacon St Portland ME (04103) *(G-6714)*
Powergraphics Printing, Tewksbury *Also called Power Graphics Printing (G-15827)*
Powerhearth, Plainfield *Also called International Innovations Inc (G-22268)*
Powerhold Inc 860 349-1044
63 Old Indian Trl Middlefield CT (06455) *(G-2163)*
Powerhouse Botanic Distillery 978 930-8281
184 High Rd Newbury MA (01951) *(G-13464)*
Poweroptions Inc 617 737-8480
129 South St Fl 5 Boston MA (02111) *(G-8788)*
Powerplay Management LLC 603 436-3030
933 Islington St Portsmouth NH (03801) *(G-19609)*
Powerscreen Connecticut Inc 860 627-6596
140 Nutmeg Rd S South Windsor CT (06074) *(G-4003)*
Powerscreen England, South Windsor *Also called Powerscreen Connecticut Inc (G-4003)*
Powersure Fuel Rcndtioning LLC 978 886-2476
17 Alden Rd Andover MA (01810) *(G-7587)*
Powertronics, Candia *Also called Eastern Time Design Inc (G-17781)*
Powerwash Co 508 823-9274
40 Gatsby Dr Raynham MA (02767) *(G-14726)*
Poyant Signs Inc (PA) 800 544-0961
125 Samuel Barnet Blvd New Bedford MA (02745) *(G-13442)*
Pozzi Fmly Wine & Spirits LLC 646 422-9134
37 Old Well Rd Stamford CT (06907) *(G-4289)*
Pp Manufacturing Corporation 508 766-2700
175 Crossing Blvd Ste 200 Framingham MA (01702) *(G-10996)*
Ppc Books Ltd 203 226-6644
335 Post Rd W Westport CT (06880) *(G-5224)*
PPG 9431, Hartford *Also called PPG Industries Inc (G-1861)*
PPG Industries Inc 802 863-6387
60 San Remo Dr South Burlington VT (05403) *(G-22461)*
PPG Industries Inc 203 750-9553
106 Main St Norwalk CT (06851) *(G-3223)*
PPG Industries Inc 203 562-5173
390 East St New Haven CT (06511) *(G-2728)*
PPG Industries Inc 203 744-4977
211 White St Danbury CT (06810) *(G-969)*
PPG Industries Inc 203 294-4440
22 Barnes Industrial Rd S Wallingford CT (06492) *(G-4785)*
PPG Industries Inc 860 522-9544
292 Murphy Rd Hartford CT (06114) *(G-1861)*
PPG Industries Inc 617 268-4111
272 Dorchester Ave Boston MA (02127) *(G-8789)*
PPG Painters Supply, Norwalk *Also called PPG Industries Inc (G-3223)*
PPG Painters Supply, New Haven *Also called PPG Industries Inc (G-2728)*
PPG Painters Supply, Danbury *Also called PPG Industries Inc (G-969)*
Ppi/Time Zero Inc 508 226-6090
1400 Boston Providence Tp Norwood MA (02062) *(G-14188)*
Ppi/Time Zero Inc 781 881-2400
140 Carando Dr Springfield MA (01104) *(G-15499)*
Ppk Inc 203 376-9180
41 Montoya Dr Branford CT (06405) *(G-338)*
Ppm, Framingham *Also called Pp Manufacturing Corporation (G-10996)*
Pr-Mx Holdings Company LLC (HQ) 203 925-0012
25 Forest Pkwy Shelton CT (06484) *(G-3857)*
PRA Holdings Inc 203 853-0123
1 Stamford Forum Stamford CT (06901) *(G-4290)*
Practical Automation Inc (HQ) 203 882-5640
45 Woodmont Rd Milford CT (06460) *(G-2336)*
Praecis Inc 603 277-9288
6 Chambers Cir West Lebanon NH (03784) *(G-19959)*
Praecis Pharmaceuticals Inc 781 795-4100
830 Winter St Ste 1 Waltham MA (02451) *(G-16176)*
Praktikatalyst Pharma LLC 413 442-1857
25 Juliana Dr Pittsfield MA (01201) *(G-14502)*
Pralines Central, Wallingford *Also called Pralines Inc (G-4786)*
Pralines Inc 203 284-8847
30 N Plains Industrial Rd # 12 Wallingford CT (06492) *(G-4786)*
Pralines of Plainville 860 410-1151
107 New Britain Ave Plainville CT (06062) *(G-3512)*
Pratt & Whitney, East Hartford *Also called United Technologies Corp (G-1233)*
Pratt & Whitney, East Hartford *Also called United Technologies Corp (G-1235)*
Pratt & Whitney 800 742-5877
52 Pettengill Rd Londonderry NH (03053) *(G-18731)*
Pratt & Whitney Aircraft Nelc, Londonderry *Also called Pratt & Whitney (G-18731)*
Pratt & Whitney Company Inc (HQ) 860 565-4321
400 Main St East Hartford CT (06108) *(G-1212)*
Pratt & Whitney Eng Svcs Inc 860 610-2631
126 Silver Ln Apt 19 East Hartford CT (06118) *(G-1213)*
Pratt & Whitney Engine Svcs 203 934-2806
415 Washington Ave North Haven CT (06473) *(G-3053)*
Pratt & Whitney Engine Svcs 860 344-4000
1 Aircraft Rd Middletown CT (06457) *(G-2212)*
Pratt & Whitney Engine Svcs 207 676-4100
113 Wells St North Berwick ME (03906) *(G-6510)*
Pratt & Whitney Engine Svcs 860 565-4321
400 Main St Ste 1 East Hartford CT (06118) *(G-1214)*
Pratt & Whitney Services Inc 860 565-5489
400 Main St East Hartford CT (06108) *(G-1215)*
Pratt & Whitneys Repair &, East Hartford *Also called United Technologies Corp (G-1238)*
Pratt Whitney-Spare Parts Div, East Hartford *Also called United Technologies Corp (G-1236)*
Pratt Whtney Cstmer Trning Ctr, East Hartford *Also called Pratt & Whitney Engine Svcs (G-1214)*
Pratt Whtney Msurement Systems 860 286-8181
66 Douglas St Bloomfield CT (06002) *(G-254)*
Pratt-Read Corporation (PA) 860 625-3620
193 Turtle Bay Dr Branford CT (06405) *(G-339)*
Prattville Machine & Tl Co Inc 978 538-5229
240 Jubilee Dr Fl 2 Peabody MA (01960) *(G-14363)*
Praxair Inc 800 772-9247
10 Riverview Dr Danbury CT (06810) *(G-970)*
Praxair Inc 203 793-1200
10 Research Pkwy Wallingford CT (06492) *(G-4787)*
Praxair Inc 203 720-2477
120 Rado Dr Naugatuck CT (06770) *(G-2491)*
Praxair Inc 860 292-5400
1 U Car St Suffield CT (06078) *(G-4466)*
Praxair Inc (HQ) 203 837-2000
10 Riverview Dr Danbury CT (06810) *(G-971)*
Praxair Distribution Inc 860 349-0305
89 Commerce Cir Durham CT (06422) *(G-1093)*
Praxair Distribution Inc (HQ) 203 837-2000
10 Riverview Dr Danbury CT (06810) *(G-972)*
Praxair Distribution Inc 401 767-3450
21 Steel St Slatersville RI (02876) *(G-21205)*
Praxair Distribution Inc 203 837-2000
273 Washington St Auburn MA (01501) *(G-7848)*
Praxair Distribution Inc 203 837-2162
55 Old Ridgebury Rd Danbury CT (06810) *(G-973)*
Praxair Surface, Concord *Also called Tafa Incorporated (G-17934)*
Praxair Surface Tech Inc 603 224-9585
146 Pembroke Rd Ste 1 Concord NH (03301) *(G-17924)*
Praxair Surface Tech Inc 207 282-3787
24 Landry St Biddeford ME (04005) *(G-5757)*
Praxair Surface Tech Inc 860 646-0700
1366 Tolland Tpke Manchester CT (06042) *(G-2039)*
Praxis Bindery, Easthampton *Also called Praxis Bookbinding (G-10576)*
Praxis Bookbinding 413 527-7275
1 Cottage St Unit 18 Easthampton MA (01027) *(G-10576)*
Prazi USA Inc 508 747-1490
214 S Meadow Rd Rear S Plymouth MA (02360) *(G-14577)*
Pre -Clinical Safety Inc 860 739-9797
69 Quarry Dock Rd East Lyme CT (06333) *(G-1272)*
Precast Specialties Corp 781 878-7220
999 Adams St Abington MA (02351) *(G-7328)*
Precast Vault Co Inc 508 252-4886
131 Autumn St North Dighton MA (02764) *(G-13933)*
Precast Vault Co Inc (PA) 508 252-4886
131 Adams St Braintree MA (02184) *(G-9031)*
Preceding Inc 617 953-6173
27 Strathmore Rd Natick MA (01760) *(G-13273)*
Precidiag, Natick *Also called Preceding Inc (G-13273)*
Precious Alloy Refining LLC 774 296-5000
1595 Central St Stoughton MA (02072) *(G-15616)*
Precious Metals Reclaiming Svc (PA) 781 326-3442
253 Revere St B Canton MA (02021) *(G-9771)*
Precise Circuit Company Inc 203 924-2512
155 Myrtle St Shelton CT (06484) *(G-3858)*
Precise Industries Inc 978 453-8490
639 Lakeview Ave Lowell MA (01850) *(G-12424)*
Precise Products Company 401 724-7190
21 Lower Rd Lincoln RI (02865) *(G-20592)*

Precise Time and Frequency LLC.......781 245-9090
501 Audubon Rd Wakefield MA (01880) *(G-15971)*
Precise Turning and Mfg.......413 562-0052
28 Ramah Cir N Agawam MA (01001) *(G-7447)*
Precision Aerospace Inc.......203 888-3022
88 Cogwheel Ln Seymour CT (06483) *(G-3762)*
Precision Assemblies.......781 324-9054
19 Shurtleff St Malden MA (02148) *(G-12591)*
Precision Assisted Plastics, West Warwick *Also called CPC Plastics Inc (G-21488)*
Precision Biopsy Inc.......720 859-3553
100 High St Ste 2800 Boston MA (02110) *(G-8790)*
Precision Circuit Corporation.......508 479-8843
580 Myles Standish Blvd # 2 Taunton MA (02780) *(G-15772)*
Precision Coating, Woonsocket *Also called Duralectra-Chn LLC (G-21557)*
Precision Coating Co Inc (HQ).......781 329-1420
51 Parmenter Rd Hudson MA (01749) *(G-11805)*
Precision Coating Co Inc.......978 562-7561
51 Parmenter Rd Hudson MA (01749) *(G-11806)*
Precision Components Group.......413 333-4184
190 Doty Cir West Springfield MA (01089) *(G-16547)*
Precision Components Inc.......603 924-3597
77 Hancock Rd Ste 1 Peterborough NH (03458) *(G-19484)*
Precision Composites VT LLC.......802 626-5900
630 Gilman Rd Lyndonville VT (05851) *(G-22072)*
Precision Cutter Grinding Inc.......802 436-2039
7 Ferry Rd Hartland VT (05048) *(G-22017)*
Precision Deburring Inc.......860 583-4662
139 Center St Ste 5002 Bristol CT (06010) *(G-596)*
Precision Depaneling Mchs LLC.......540 248-1381
326 Main St Unit 11 Fremont NH (03044) *(G-18178)*
Precision Design, Milford *Also called Plasti-Clip Corporation (G-19072)*
Precision Devices Inc (PA).......203 265-9308
55 N Plains Industrial Rd Wallingford CT (06492) *(G-4788)*
Precision Digital Corporation.......508 655-7300
233 South St Hopkinton MA (01748) *(G-11733)*
Precision Dip Coating LLC.......203 805-4564
176 Chase River Rd Waterbury CT (06704) *(G-4943)*
Precision Direct Inc.......207 321-3677
200 Riverside Indus Pkwy Portland ME (04103) *(G-6715)*
Precision Dynamics Corporation.......888 202-3684
85 Terrace Hall Ave Burlington MA (01803) *(G-9321)*
Precision Dynamics Corporation.......800 528-8005
3 Federal St Ste 300 Billerica MA (01821) *(G-8276)*
Precision Electrolysis Needles.......401 246-1155
166 Bay Spring Ave Barrington RI (02806) *(G-20052)*
Precision Electronic Assembly.......203 452-1839
133 Bart Rd Monroe CT (06468) *(G-2413)*
Precision Electronics Corp.......781 834-6677
427 Plain St Marshfield MA (02050) *(G-12865)*
Precision Engineered Pdts LLC.......203 336-6479
1146 Barnum Ave Bridgeport CT (06610) *(G-473)*
Precision Engineered Pdts LLC.......203 265-3299
6 Northrop Indus Pk Rd W Wallingford CT (06492) *(G-4789)*
Precision Engineered Pdts LLC.......508 528-6500
50 Earls Way Franklin MA (02038) *(G-11072)*
Precision Engineered Pdts LLC (HQ).......508 226-5600
110 Frank Mossberg Dr Attleboro MA (02703) *(G-7782)*
Precision Engineering Inc.......508 278-5700
29 Industrial Dr Uxbridge MA (01569) *(G-15928)*
Precision Express Mfg LLC.......860 584-2627
630 Emmett St Unit 3 Bristol CT (06010) *(G-597)*
Precision Feeding Systems Inc.......413 525-9200
45 Deer Park Dr East Longmeadow MA (01028) *(G-10488)*
Precision Finishing Svcs Inc.......860 882-1073
60 Ezra Silva Ln Windsor CT (06095) *(G-5356)*
Precision Graphics Inc.......860 828-6561
10 Clark Dr East Berlin CT (06023) *(G-1106)*
Precision Grinding Company.......860 229-9652
33 Charles St New Britain CT (06051) *(G-2565)*
Precision Handling Devices (PA).......508 679-5282
758b State Rd Westport MA (02790) *(G-16845)*
Precision Images Inc.......508 824-6200
620 Spring St North Dighton MA (02764) *(G-13934)*
Precision Industrial Metals.......978 562-1800
1 Brent Dr Hudson MA (01749) *(G-11807)*
Precision Letter Corporation.......603 625-9625
396 Pepsi Rd Manchester NH (03109) *(G-18904)*
Precision Litho, South Hadley *Also called Verico Technology LLC (G-15312)*
Precision Lumber Inc.......603 764-9450
576 Buffalo Rd Wentworth NH (03282) *(G-19947)*
Precision Machine & Gear Inc.......508 835-7888
104 Hartwell St West Boylston MA (01583) *(G-16427)*
Precision Machine and Gears.......860 822-6993
21 Country Club Dr North Franklin CT (06254) *(G-2990)*
Precision Machine Shop, Atkinson *Also called Hutchinson Machine (G-17604)*
Precision Machining, Whitman *Also called Dimark Incorporated (G-16923)*
Precision Machinists Co Inc.......508 528-2325
9 Forge Pkwy Franklin MA (02038) *(G-11073)*
Precision Manufacturing LLC.......203 790-4663
153 Gracty Plain St A12 Bethel CT (06801) *(G-175)*
Precision Metal Fabrication, Newburyport *Also called AW Airflo Industries Inc (G-13470)*
Precision Metal Products Inc.......203 877-4258
307 Pepes Farm Rd Milford CT (06460) *(G-2337)*
Precision Metals and Plas Mfg, Winsted *Also called Precision Metals and Plastics (G-5419)*
Precision Metals and Plastics.......860 238-4320
118 Colebrook River Rd # 7 Winsted CT (06098) *(G-5419)*
Precision Methods Incorporated.......203 879-1429
40 North St Wolcott CT (06716) *(G-5452)*
Precision Mfg Solutions, Biddeford *Also called Nikel Precision Group LLC (G-5753)*
Precision Mfg Tool & Tl Design, Bethel *Also called Precision Manufacturing LLC (G-175)*
Precision Model-Fab Inc.......603 883-6680
134 Haines St Unit A Nashua NH (03060) *(G-19237)*
Precision Optical Co.......860 289-6023
351 Burnham St East Hartford CT (06108) *(G-1216)*
Precision Optics Corp Inc (PA).......978 630-1800
22 E Broadway Gardner MA (01440) *(G-11123)*
Precision Orthot & Prosthetics.......508 991-5577
203 Popes Is New Bedford MA (02740) *(G-13443)*
Precision Pasta Dies Inc.......978 866-7720
198 Compass Cir Hyannis MA (02601) *(G-11854)*
Precision Pcb Inc (PA).......781 447-6285
7 Oakdale Farm Rd Whitman MA (02382) *(G-16925)*
Precision Pcb Products Inc.......508 966-9484
7 Oakdale Farm Rd Whitman MA (02382) *(G-16926)*
Precision Placement Mchs Inc (PA).......603 895-5112
326 Main St Unit 11 Fremont NH (03044) *(G-18179)*
Precision Plastic Fab.......203 775-7047
5d Del Mar Dr Brookfield CT (06804) *(G-657)*
Precision Plastic Products Inc.......860 342-2233
151 Freestone Ave Portland CT (06480) *(G-3571)*
Precision Plastics Inc.......978 658-5345
18 Dadant Dr Wilmington MA (01887) *(G-17038)*
Precision Plsg Ornamentals Inc.......401 728-9994
601 Mineral Spring Ave # 2 Pawtucket RI (02860) *(G-20883)*
Precision Print and Copy Inc.......802 877-3711
12 Main St Ste 1 Vergennes VT (05491) *(G-22555)*
Precision Punch + Tooling Corp (PA).......860 229-9902
304 Christian Ln Berlin CT (06037) *(G-103)*
Precision Punch + Tooling Corp.......860 225-4159
304 Christian Ln Berlin CT (06037) *(G-104)*
Precision Resource Inc (PA).......203 925-0012
25 Forest Pkwy Shelton CT (06484) *(G-3859)*
Precision Resource Mexico, Shelton *Also called Pr-Mx Holdings Company LLC (G-3857)*
Precision Roll, Sanbornville *Also called Kingswood Sales Inc (G-19783)*
Precision Screw Mch Pdts Inc.......207 283-0121
30 Gooch St Biddeford ME (04005) *(G-5758)*
Precision Sensing Devices Inc.......508 359-2833
93 West St Ste D Medfield MA (02052) *(G-12917)*
Precision Sensors, Milford *Also called United Electric Controls Co (G-2377)*
Precision Sensors Inc.......203 877-2795
340 Woodmont Rd Milford CT (06460) *(G-2338)*
Precision Speed Mfg LLC.......860 635-8811
422 Timber Ridge Rd Middletown CT (06457) *(G-2213)*
Precision Spools, Pittsfield *Also called Pittsfield Plastics Engrg Inc (G-14500)*
Precision Sportswear Inc.......508 674-3034
54 Front St Unit 3 Fall River MA (02721) *(G-10748)*
Precision Stone Works Inc.......774 261-4420
224 Cherry St Ste C Shrewsbury MA (01545) *(G-15129)*
Precision Swiss Screw Machine, Bristol *Also called E P M Co Inc (G-552)*
Precision Systems Inc.......508 655-7010
16 Tech Cir Ste 100 Natick MA (01760) *(G-13274)*
Precision Tape & Label Co Inc.......508 278-7700
322 West St Uxbridge MA (01569) *(G-15929)*
Precision Technologies Inc.......978 649-8715
42 Westech Dr Tyngsboro MA (01879) *(G-15900)*
Precision Threaded Products, Bristol *Also called Thompson Aerospace LLC (G-617)*
Precision Tool & Components.......203 874-9215
195 Rock Ln Milford CT (06460) *(G-2339)*
Precision Tool & Molding LLC.......603 437-6685
22 Manchester Rd Unit 10 Derry NH (03038) *(G-17994)*
Precision Tool and Die, Derry *Also called Precision Tool & Molding LLC (G-17994)*
Precision Trned Cmponents Corp.......401 232-3377
331 Farnum Pike Smithfield RI (02917) *(G-21244)*
Precision Valley Finishing.......802 885-3150
135 Main St Springfield VT (05156) *(G-22508)*
Precision Wire Cutting.......860 485-1494
9 Windmill Rd Harwinton CT (06791) *(G-1892)*
Precision Woodcraft Inc.......860 693-3641
16 Cheryl Dr Canton CT (06019) *(G-698)*
Precision Woodcraft ME, Canton *Also called Precision Woodcraft Inc (G-698)*
Precision Woodworking.......617 479-7604
50 Samoset Ave Quincy MA (02169) *(G-14647)*
Precision X-Ray Inc.......203 484-2011
15 Commerce Dr North Branford CT (06471) *(G-2972)*
Precision X-Ray Inc.......203 484-2011
15 Comm Dr Unit 1 North Branford CT (06471) *(G-2973)*
Precisive LLC.......781 850-4469
651 Lowell St Methuen MA (01844) *(G-13043)*

Precix, New Bedford *Also called Acushnet Rubber Company Inc* ***(G-13352)***
Preferred Concrete Corp.....508 763-5500
66 Braley Rd East Freetown MA (02717) ***(G-10457)***
Preferred Foam Products Inc.....860 669-3626
140 Killingworth Tpke Clinton CT (06413) ***(G-793)***
Preferred Instruments, Danbury *Also called Preferred Utilities Mfg Corp* ***(G-974)***
Preferred Manufacturing Co.....203 239-0727
68 Old Broadway E North Haven CT (06473) ***(G-3054)***
Preferred PDT & Mktg Group LLC.....203 567-0221
415 Howe Ave Ste 103 Shelton CT (06484) ***(G-3860)***
Preferred Precision, Shelton *Also called Preferred Tool & Die Inc* ***(G-3861)***
Preferred Publications Inc.....978 697-4180
10 Fiorenza Dr Wilmington MA (01887) ***(G-17039)***
Preferred Tool & Die Inc (PA).....203 925-8525
30 Forest Pkwy Shelton CT (06484) ***(G-3861)***
Preferred Tool & Die Inc.....203 925-8525
19 Forest Pkwy Shelton CT (06484) ***(G-3862)***
Preferred Utilities Mfg Corp (HQ).....203 743-6741
31-35 South St Danbury CT (06810) ***(G-974)***
Preforms Plus.....603 889-8311
3 Capitol St Nashua NH (03063) ***(G-19101)***
Preisner, George S Pewter Co, Wallingford *Also called George S Preisner Jewelers* ***(G-4748)***
Prematech Advanced Ceramics, Worcester *Also called Prematech LLC* ***(G-17445)***
Prematech LLC.....508 791-9549
160 Goddard Memorial Dr Worcester MA (01603) ***(G-17445)***
Prematechnoligies LLC.....508 791-9549
160 Goddard Memorial Dr Worcester MA (01603) ***(G-17446)***
Premier Graphics LLC.....800 414-1624
860 Honeyspot Rd Ste 1 Stratford CT (06615) ***(G-4440)***
Premier Mfg Group Inc.....203 924-6617
10 Mountain View Dr Shelton CT (06484) ***(G-3863)***
Premier Packaging LLC.....603 485-7465
47 Post Rd Hooksett NH (03106) ***(G-18354)***
Premier Prtg Mailing Solutions, Stratford *Also called Premier Graphics LLC* ***(G-4440)***
Premier Roll & Tool Inc.....508 695-2551
10 Alice Agnew Dr North Attleboro MA (02763) ***(G-13774)***
Premier Services Inc.....781 335-9305
106 Finnell Dr Ste 5 Weymouth MA (02188) ***(G-16898)***
Premiere Packg Partners LLC.....203 694-0003
197 Huntingdon Ave Waterbury CT (06708) ***(G-4944)***
Premium Log Yards Inc (PA).....207 364-7500
1180 Route 2 Ste 5 Rumford ME (04276) ***(G-6842)***
Premium Poultry Co.....401 467-3200
850 Eddy St Providence RI (02905) ***(G-21093)***
Premium Sund Slutions Amer LLC (PA).....781 968-5511
301 Edgewater Pl Ste 100 Wakefield MA (01880) ***(G-15972)***
Prentis Printing Solutions Inc.....203 634-1266
35 Pratt St Meriden CT (06450) ***(G-2117)***
Prepco Inc.....603 237-4080
6 Sanel Dr Colebrook NH (03576) ***(G-17875)***
Presby Plastics Inc.....603 837-3826
143 Airport Rd Whitefield NH (03598) ***(G-19972)***
Prescient Pharma, Canton *Also called Prescientpharma LLC* ***(G-9772)***
Prescientpharma LLC.....617 955-0490
580 Washington St Canton MA (02021) ***(G-9772)***
Presco Incorporated.....203 397-8722
8 Lunar Dr Ste 4 Woodbridge CT (06525) ***(G-5477)***
Presco Engineering, Woodbridge *Also called Presco Incorporated* ***(G-5477)***
Prescott Cabinet Co.....860 495-0176
31 Buckingham St Pawcatuck CT (06379) ***(G-3441)***
Prescott Metal (PA).....207 283-0115
565 Elm St Biddeford ME (04005) ***(G-5759)***
Present Arms Inc.....413 575-4656
34 Front St Ste 326 Indian Orchard MA (01151) ***(G-11894)***
Preservica Inc.....617 294-6676
50 Milk St Fl 16 Boston MA (02109) ***(G-8791)***
President Fllows Hrvard Cllege, Cambridge *Also called President Fllows Hrvard Cllege* ***(G-9617)***
President Fllows Hrvard Cllege.....617 495-2020
60 Garden St Cambridge MA (02138) ***(G-9615)***
President Fllows Hrvard Cllege.....617 783-7888
60 Harvard Way Boston MA (02163) ***(G-8792)***
President Fllows Hrvard Cllege.....617 495-9897
79 Garden St Cambridge MA (02138) ***(G-9616)***
President Fllows Hrvard Cllege.....617 495-4043
16 Divinity Ave Rm B061 Cambridge MA (02138) ***(G-9617)***
President Press Inc.....617 773-1235
100 Columbia St Quincy MA (02169) ***(G-14648)***
Presidium USA Inc.....203 674-9374
100 Stamford Pl Stamford CT (06902) ***(G-4291)***
Press Ganey.....800 232-8032
70 Westview St Ste 6 Lexington MA (02421) ***(G-12254)***
Press Room, The, West Falmouth *Also called Enterprise Publications* ***(G-16478)***
Press Tech Company Inc.....401 377-4800
125 Main St Ashaway RI (02804) ***(G-20039)***
Press-It LLC.....781 935-0035
84 Washington St Woburn MA (01801) ***(G-17269)***
Pressed For Time Printing Inc.....617 267-4113
133 South St Boston MA (02111) ***(G-8793)***
Pressroom Incorporated.....978 283-5562
32 River Rd Gloucester MA (01930) ***(G-11204)***
Presstek Overseas Corp (HQ).....603 595-7000
200 Innovative Way Nashua NH (03062) ***(G-19238)***
Pressue Techniques.....978 686-2211
39 Flagship Dr North Andover MA (01845) ***(G-13725)***
Pressure Biosciences Inc.....508 230-1828
14 Norfolk Ave South Easton MA (02375) ***(G-15288)***
Pressure Blast Mfg Co Inc.....800 722-5278
205 Nutmeg Rd S Ste E South Windsor CT (06074) ***(G-4004)***
Pressure Techniques Intl Corp.....978 686-2211
114 Hale St Haverhill MA (01830) ***(G-11460)***
Prestige Custom Mirror & Glass.....781 647-0878
182 High St Waltham MA (02453) ***(G-16177)***
Prestige Metal Finishing LLC.....860 974-1999
44 Bradford Corner Rd Woodstock Valley CT (06282) ***(G-5504)***
Prestige Remodeling, Stratford *Also called Chris Cross LLC* ***(G-4404)***
Prestige Tool Mfg LLC.....203 874-0360
154 Old Gate Ln Milford CT (06460) ***(G-2340)***
Presto Lifts, Norton *Also called WB Engineering Inc* ***(G-14093)***
Presto Lifts, Falmouth *Also called WB Engineering Inc* ***(G-6037)***
Preston Engravers, East Windsor *Also called Roto-Die Company Inc* ***(G-1300)***
Preston Ridge Vineyard LLC.....860 383-4278
26 Miller Rd Preston CT (06365) ***(G-3582)***
Prestone Products Corporation.....203 731-7880
55 Federal Rd Danbury CT (06810) ***(G-975)***
Presumpscot Water Power Co.....207 856-4000
89 Cumberland St Westbrook ME (04092) ***(G-7204)***
Pretorius Electric.....508 326-9492
267a S Main St West Bridgewater MA (02379) ***(G-16450)***
Pretorius Electric and Sign, West Bridgewater *Also called Pretorius Electric* ***(G-16450)***
Pretty Instant LLC.....888 551-6765
300 Summer St Apt 14b Boston MA (02210) ***(G-8794)***
Preventative Maintenance Corp.....860 683-1180
55 Tunxis St Poquonock CT (06064) ***(G-3560)***
Prevently Inc.....617 981-0920
30 Cambridgepark Dr 412 Cambridge MA (02140) ***(G-9618)***
Preyco Mfg Co Inc.....203 574-4545
1184 N Main St Waterbury CT (06704) ***(G-4945)***
Prezioso Furs, Hamden *Also called Furs By Prezioso Ltd* ***(G-1750)***
Prfrred Lancaster Partners LLC.....717 299-0782
200 Berkeley St Boston MA (02116) ***(G-8795)***
PRI Financial Publishing.....508 429-5949
479 Washington St Holliston MA (01746) ***(G-11597)***
Price Companies Inc.....207 674-3663
23 Bethel Rd West Paris ME (04289) ***(G-7177)***
Price-Driscoll Corporation.....860 442-3575
17 Industrial Dr Waterford CT (06385) ***(G-4991)***
Priced Right Fuel LLC.....203 856-7031
29 Golden Hill St Norwalk CT (06854) ***(G-3224)***
Pride India Inc (PA).....617 202-9659
329 Summit Ave Apt 7 Brighton MA (02135) ***(G-9105)***
Pride Manufacturing Co LLC (PA).....207 487-3322
10 N Main St Burnham ME (04922) ***(G-5855)***
Pride Manufacturing Co LLC.....207 876-2719
169 Water St Guilford ME (04443) ***(G-6159)***
Pride Manufacturing Machine Sp, Guilford *Also called Pride Manufacturing Co LLC* ***(G-6159)***
Pride of India, Brighton *Also called Pride India Inc* ***(G-9105)***
Pride Sports, Burnham *Also called Pride Manufacturing Co LLC* ***(G-5855)***
Pridecraft Inc.....978 685-2831
109 Sutton St North Andover MA (01845) ***(G-13726)***
Pridemaxx Fine Wood Cabinetry.....508 527-8700
1034 East St Walpole MA (02081) ***(G-16007)***
Prima America Corporation.....603 631-5407
248 State St Groveton NH (03582) ***(G-18233)***
Prima Electro North Amer LLC, Chicopee *Also called Convergent - Photonics LLC* ***(G-10016)***
Prima North America Inc.....413 598-5200
711 E Main St Chicopee MA (01020) ***(G-10053)***
Prima Products.....508 553-8875
2 Spruce Tree Ln Forestdale MA (02644) ***(G-10872)***
Primary Colors Inc.....508 839-3202
9 Millennium Dr North Grafton MA (01536) ***(G-13964)***
Primary Graphics Corporation.....781 575-0411
175 W Water St Taunton MA (02780) ***(G-15773)***
Prime Electric Motors.....207 591-7800
72 Sanford Dr Gorham ME (04038) ***(G-6128)***
Prime Engineered Components, Watertown *Also called Prime Screw Machine Pdts Inc* ***(G-5019)***
Prime Engneered Components Inc.....860 274-6773
1012 Buckingham St Watertown CT (06795) ***(G-5017)***
Prime Line, Bridgeport *Also called Prime Resources Corp* ***(G-474)***
Prime National Publishing Corp.....781 899-2702
470 Boston Post Rd Ste 1 Weston MA (02493) ***(G-16830)***
Prime Publishers Inc.....860 274-6721
449 Main St Watertown CT (06795) ***(G-5018)***
Prime Resources Corp.....203 331-9100
1100 Boston Ave Bldg 1 Bridgeport CT (06610) ***(G-474)***

Prime Screw Machine Pdts Inc (PA) 860 274-6773
1012 Buckingham St Watertown CT (06795) **(G-5019)**
Prime Tanning Compan, Hartland *Also called Tasman Industries Inc* **(G-6179)**
Prime Technology LLC 203 481-5721
344 Twin Lakes Rd North Branford CT (06471) **(G-2974)**
Primearray Systems Inc 978 455-9488
1500 District Ave Burlington MA (01803) **(G-9322)**
Primetals Technologies USA LLC 508 755-6111
40 Crescent St Worcester MA (01605) **(G-17447)**
Primevigilance Inc 781 703-5540
1601 Trapelo Rd Waltham MA (02451) **(G-16178)**
Primmbiotech Inc 617 308-8135
8 Rutledge St West Roxbury MA (02132) **(G-16500)**
Primo Medical Group Inc (PA) 781 297-5700
75 Mill St Stoughton MA (02072) **(G-15617)**
Primrose Medical Inc 508 660-8688
286 Union St East Walpole MA (02032) **(G-10529)**
Princeton Instruments, Acton *Also called Roper Scientific Inc* **(G-7381)**
Princeton Security Tech Inc (HQ) 609 924-7310
27 Forge Pkwy Franklin MA (02038) **(G-11074)**
Princeton Technology Corp 603 595-1987
33 Constitution Dr Hudson NH (03051) **(G-18428)**
Princton Gamma-Tech Instrs Inc 609 924-7310
27 Forge Pkwy Franklin MA (02038) **(G-11075)**
Print & Post Services 203 336-0055
1 Seaview Ave Bridgeport CT (06607) **(G-475)**
Print All of Boston Inc 617 361-7400
1279 Hyde Park Ave Boston MA (02136) **(G-8796)**
Print Buyers International LLC 617 730-5951
118 Arlington Rd Chestnut Hill MA (02467) **(G-9991)**
Print Central, Norwood *Also called Chaco Inc* **(G-14141)**
Print Factory Inc 603 880-4519
15 Factory St Nashua NH (03060) **(G-19239)**
Print House, Malden *Also called Medi - Print Inc* **(G-12582)**
Print House LLC 860 652-0803
22 Kreiger Ln Ste 6 Glastonbury CT (06033) **(G-1573)**
Print Management Systems Inc 781 944-1041
26 Conn St Woburn MA (01801) **(G-17270)**
Print Master LLC 860 482-8152
1219 E Main St Torrington CT (06790) **(G-4593)**
Print Resource 508 433-4660
1500 W Park Dr Ste 215 Westborough MA (01581) **(G-16644)**
Print Shop 413 458-6039
30 Spring St Williamstown MA (01267) **(G-16959)**
Print Shop of Wolcott LLC 203 879-3353
450 Wolcott Rd Wolcott CT (06716) **(G-5453)**
Print Shops Inc 401 885-1226
70 Cliff St East Greenwich RI (02818) **(G-20377)**
Print Source Ltd 203 876-1822
116a Research Dr Ste D Milford CT (06460) **(G-2341)**
Print Synergy Solutions LLC 508 587-5200
129 Liberty St Brockton MA (02301) **(G-9172)**
Print Tech, Williston *Also called Digital Press Printers LLC* **(G-22662)**
Print Works, Presque Isle *Also called Northeast Publishing Company* **(G-6765)**
Print Works Inc 508 589-4626
25 South St Ste 2b Hopkinton MA (01748) **(G-11734)**
Printcraft Inc 401 739-0700
3076 Post Rd Warwick RI (02886) **(G-21405)**
Printech, Stamford *Also called JS McCarthy Co Inc* **(G-4233)**
Printed Communications 860 436-9619
400 Chapel Rd Ste L1 South Windsor CT (06074) **(G-4005)**
Printed Matter Inc 603 778-2990
27 Pleasant St Newfields NH (03856) **(G-19318)**
Printers, Hartford *Also called Hartford Business Supply Inc* **(G-1830)**
Printers Square Inc 603 623-0802
105 Faltin Dr Manchester NH (03103) **(G-18905)**
Printfusion LLC 603 283-0007
331 Flat Roof Mill Rd Swanzey NH (03446) **(G-19888)**
Printgraphics of Maine Inc 207 347-5700
116 Riverside Indtl Pkwy Portland ME (04103) **(G-6716)**
Printguard Inc 508 890-8822
1521 Grafton Rd Millbury MA (01527) **(G-13173)**
Printhouse, The, Boston *Also called Medi - Print Inc* **(G-8693)**
Printing & Graphic Services, New Haven *Also called Yale University* **(G-2758)**
Printing & Graphic Services 978 667-6950
505 Middlesex Tpke Unit 8 Billerica MA (01821) **(G-8277)**
Printing Brokersof Maine, Belfast *Also called J A Black Company* **(G-5691)**
Printing Depot, Worcester *Also called Sanchez Octavio Storage* **(G-17468)**
Printing Place Inc 781 272-7209
26 Philip Cir Melrose MA (02176) **(G-12988)**
Printing Plus, Waterbury *Also called Sheila P Patrick* **(G-4956)**
Printing Plus 401 596-6970
179 Main St Westerly RI (02891) **(G-21536)**
Printing Services, Amherst *Also called University of Massachusetts* **(G-7531)**
Printing Services Inc 508 655-2535
21 Tyler Ct Natick MA (01760) **(G-13275)**
Printing Solutions Inc 978 392-9903
6 Carlisle Rd Ste 6 # 6 Westford MA (01886) **(G-16786)**
Printing Store, The, Hamden *Also called Copy Stop Inc* **(G-1738)**
Printing Unlimited, Holbrook *Also called Maroney Associates Inc* **(G-11530)**
Printmaster, Norwood *Also called Ingleside Corporation* **(G-14161)**
Printpro Silkscreen & EMB 978 556-1695
233 Neck Rd Haverhill MA (01835) **(G-11461)**
Prints Charming Printers Inc 207 633-6663
1036b Wiscasset Rd Boothbay ME (04537) **(G-5780)**
Printsake Inc 508 419-7393
681 Falmouth Rd Ste C12 Mashpee MA (02649) **(G-12882)**
Printsmith Needham, Wellesley *Also called Pace Associates Inc* **(G-16379)**
Printsource, Bristol *Also called Warwick Group Inc* **(G-20109)**
Printsource, Wakefield *Also called Don-May of Wakefield Inc* **(G-21269)**
Printsynergy Solutions, Brockton *Also called Print Synergy Solutions LLC* **(G-9172)**
Printworks, Leominster *Also called Thomas B Fullen* **(G-12194)**
Printworld, North Kingstown *Also called R J H Printing Inc* **(G-20735)**
Prior Scientific Inc (HQ) 781 878-8442
80 Reservoir Park Dr Rockland MA (02370) **(G-14820)**
Priority Press, Enfield *Also called East Longmeadow Business Svcs* **(G-1355)**
Prism Products LLC 781 581-1740
319 Lynnway Ste 303a Lynn MA (01901) **(G-12534)**
Prism Streetlights Inc 401 792-9900
344 Main St Wakefield RI (02879) **(G-21274)**
Prismatrix Lighting, Rumford *Also called Lexington Lighting Group LLC* **(G-21192)**
Prismic Pharmaceuticals Inc 971 506-6415
650 South Rd Holden MA (01520) **(G-11550)**
Prison Legal News 802 257-1342
35 Yorkshire Cir Brattleboro VT (05301) **(G-21744)**
Private Communications Corp 860 355-2718
39 Holiday Point Rd Sherman CT (06784) **(G-3896)**
Private Wifi, Sherman *Also called Private Communications Corp* **(G-3896)**
Privateer Ltd 860 526-1837
5 Center Rd W Old Saybrook CT (06475) **(G-3349)**
Privateer International LLC 978 356-0477
28 Mitchell Rd Ipswich MA (01938) **(G-11935)**
Prl Hancock LLC 207 564-8520
71 Salems Rd Washington J Washington Jctn Hancock ME (04640) **(G-6171)**
Pro Am Enterprises Inc 781 662-8888
180 Tremont St Melrose MA (02176) **(G-12989)**
Pro Axis Machining 603 595-1616
25 Front St Ste 101c Nashua NH (03064) **(G-19240)**
Pro Counters New England LLC 203 347-8663
1 Chestnut St Ansonia CT (06401) **(G-21)**
Pro Design & Manufacturing 603 819-4131
13 Elm St Newton NH (03858) **(G-19367)**
Pro Dough Inc 603 623-6844
8030 S Willow St Unit 2-7 Manchester NH (03103) **(G-18906)**
Pro Lingua Associates Inc 802 257-7779
74 Cotton Mill Hl A315 Brattleboro VT (05301) **(G-21745)**
Pro Pel Plastech Inc 413 665-2282
4 Industrial Dr E South Deerfield MA (01373) **(G-15254)**
Pro Pel Plastech Inc (PA) 413 665-3379
378 Long Plain Rd South Deerfield MA (01373) **(G-15255)**
Pro Scientific Inc 203 267-4600
99 Willenbrock Rd Oxford CT (06478) **(G-3420)**
Pro Star Prcsion Machining LLC 603 518-8570
438 Kelly Ave Londonderry NH (03053) **(G-18732)**
Pro Tech Machine Inc 508 867-7994
200 Fiskdale Rd Brookfield MA (01506) **(G-9190)**
Pro Tool & Machine 413 732-8940
349 Cold Spring Ave West Springfield MA (01089) **(G-16548)**
Pro Tool and Design Inc 860 828-4667
230 Deming Rd Berlin CT (06037) **(G-105)**
Pro-Cut Cnc Machine Inc 603 623-5533
7 Lehoux Dr Hooksett NH (03106) **(G-18355)**
Pro-Fab Metal Products, Lynn *Also called Profab Metal Products Inc* **(G-12535)**
Pro-Line, Haverhill *Also called R W Hatfield Company Inc* **(G-11466)**
Pro-Lock USA LLC 203 382-3428
62 Church St Monroe CT (06468) **(G-2414)**
Pro-Manufactured Products Inc 860 564-2197
29 Center Pkwy Plainfield CT (06374) **(G-3455)**
Pro-Tech Orthopedics Inc 508 821-9600
95 Ryan Dr Ste 8 Raynham MA (02767) **(G-14727)**
Pro-Vac Inc 207 324-1846
342 Jordan Springs Rd Alfred ME (04002) **(G-5517)**
Probatter Sports LLC 203 874-2500
49 Research Dr Ste 1 Milford CT (06460) **(G-2342)**
Process Cooling Systems Inc 978 537-1996
213 Nashua St Leominster MA (01453) **(G-12177)**
Process Dynamics Inc 781 271-0944
209 Burlington Rd Bedford MA (01730) **(G-8002)**
Process Solutions Inc 413 525-5870
198 Benton Dr East Longmeadow MA (01028) **(G-10489)**
Procoat Products Inc 781 767-2270
260 Centre St Ste 1 Holbrook MA (02343) **(G-11536)**
Procraft Corporation 603 487-2080
416 River Rd New Boston NH (03070) **(G-19296)**
Procter & Gamble Company 207 753-4000
2879 Hotel Rd Auburn ME (04210) **(G-5593)**

ALPHABETIC

Proctor Piper Log Homes, Proctorsville *Also called Gilcris Enterprises Inc* ***(G-22288)***
Prodrive Technologies Inc....617 475-1617
15 University Rd Ste A Canton MA (02021) ***(G-9773)***
Product Resources LLC....978 524-8500
4 Mulliken Way Newburyport MA (01950) ***(G-13523)***
Production Basics Inc....617 926-8100
31 Dunham Rd Ste 3 Billerica MA (01821) ***(G-8278)***
Production Decorating Co Inc....203 574-2975
184 Railroad Hill St Waterbury CT (06708) ***(G-4946)***
Production Equipment Company....800 758-5697
401 Liberty St Meriden CT (06450) ***(G-2118)***
Production Honing Inc....413 568-9238
327 N Elm St Westfield MA (01085) ***(G-16716)***
Production Machine Sales & Svc....401 461-6830
74 Alton St Cranston RI (02910) ***(G-20274)***
Production Process, Manchester *Also called Industrial Marine Elec Inc* ***(G-18842)***
Production Tool & Grinding....978 544-8206
273 Main St Athol MA (01331) ***(G-7693)***
Producto Corporation (HQ)....203 366-3224
800 Union Ave Bridgeport CT (06607) ***(G-476)***
Producto Machine Company, The, Bridgeport *Also called Producto Corporation* ***(G-476)***
Prodways....763 568-7966
316 Daniel Webster Hwy Merrimack NH (03054) ***(G-19024)***
Prof Tool Grind Inc....508 230-3535
18 Plymouth Dr South Easton MA (02375) ***(G-15289)***
Profab Metal Products Inc....781 599-8500
541 Chestnut St Lynn MA (01904) ***(G-12535)***
Professional Boat Builder, Brooklin *Also called Woodenboat Publications Inc* ***(G-5822)***
Professional Graphics Inc....203 846-4291
25 Perry Ave Norwalk CT (06850) ***(G-3225)***
Professional Images Inc....401 725-7000
274 Broadway Pawtucket RI (02860) ***(G-20884)***
Professional Lithography Inc....413 532-9473
630 New Ludlow Rd South Hadley MA (01075) ***(G-15309)***
Professional Media Group, Trumbull *Also called Lrp Conferences LLC* ***(G-4627)***
Professional Tl Grinding Inc (PA)....508 230-3535
18 Plymouth Dr South Easton MA (02375) ***(G-15290)***
Professional Tool Grinding, South Easton *Also called Prof Tool Grind Inc* ***(G-15289)***
Professnal Cntract Strlization....508 822-5524
40 Myles Standish Blvd Taunton MA (02780) ***(G-15774)***
Professnal Sftwr For Nrses Inc....800 889-7627
4 Limbo Ln Amherst NH (03031) ***(G-17582)***
Proffe Publishing....603 654-1070
6 Mountain Meadow Trl Wilton NH (03086) ***(G-19984)***
Profile Metal Forming Inc (HQ)....603 659-8323
10 Forbes Rd Newmarket NH (03857) ***(G-19337)***
Profile News....617 325-1515
1895 Centre St Ste 10 West Roxbury MA (02132) ***(G-16501)***
Profiles Incorporated....413 283-7790
7 First St Palmer MA (01069) ***(G-14294)***
Profit Ect, Burlington *Also called Profitect Inc* ***(G-9323)***
Profitect Inc (HQ)....781 290-0009
200 Summit Dr Ste 405 Burlington MA (01803) ***(G-9323)***
Profitkey International Inc....603 898-9800
50 Stiles Rd Salem NH (03079) ***(G-19760)***
Proflow Inc....203 230-4700
303 State St North Haven CT (06473) ***(G-3055)***
Proflow Process Equipment, North Haven *Also called Proflow Inc* ***(G-3055)***
Proforma Piper Printing....603 934-5055
600 Laconia Rd Tilton NH (03276) ***(G-19909)***
Proforma Platinum Group, Raynham *Also called George R King* ***(G-14715)***
Proforma Printing & Promotion, Boston *Also called B N M Printing & Promotion* ***(G-8387)***
Proforma Printing & Promotion....617 464-1120
33 Gaskins Rd Milton MA (02186) ***(G-13199)***
Progeo Group Inc....603 286-1942
10 Timberline Dr Tilton NH (03276) ***(G-19910)***
Program LLC....781 281-0751
289 Elm St Ste 2 Marlborough MA (01752) ***(G-12810)***
Programmed Test Sources Inc....978 486-3008
9 Beaver Brook Rd Littleton MA (01460) ***(G-12320)***
Progress Enterprises LLC....413 562-2736
3 Progress Ave Westfield MA (01085) ***(G-16717)***
Progress Pallet Inc....508 923-1930
98 W Grove St Middleboro MA (02346) ***(G-13076)***
Progress Software Corporation (PA)....781 280-4000
14 Oak Park Dr Bedford MA (01730) ***(G-8003)***
Progressive Displays Inc....401 245-2909
605 Main St Warren RI (02885) ***(G-21303)***
Progressive Manufacturing Inc....603 298-5778
20 Airpark Rd West Lebanon NH (03784) ***(G-19960)***
Progressive Marble Fabrication....781 963-6029
43 York Ave Randolph MA (02368) ***(G-14694)***
Progressive Plastics Inc....802 433-1563
85 Industry St Williamstown VT (05679) ***(G-22650)***
Progressive Sheetmetal LLC....860 436-9884
36 Mascolo Rd South Windsor CT (06074) ***(G-4006)***
Progressive Stamping Co De Inc....248 299-7100
36 Spring Ln Farmington CT (06032) ***(G-1509)***
Proiron LLC....203 934-7967
1 Calgery Dr West Haven CT (06516) ***(G-5143)***
Project Plasma Holdings Corp (HQ)....508 244-6400
37 Birch St Milford MA (01757) ***(G-13139)***
Project Resources Inc....508 295-7444
16 Kendrick Rd Ste 6 Wareham MA (02571) ***(G-16254)***
Projects Inc....860 633-4615
65 Sequin Dr Glastonbury CT (06033) ***(G-1574)***
Prokop Sign Co....860 889-6265
338 Norwich Ave Ste 1 Taftville CT (06380) ***(G-4471)***
Prokop Signs & Graphics, Taftville *Also called Prokop Sign Co* ***(G-4471)***
Prolamina, Westfield *Also called Jen-Coat Inc* ***(G-16693)***
Prolamina Corporation....413 562-2315
175 Ampad Rd Westfield MA (01085) ***(G-16718)***
Prolamina Westfield Plant 2, Westfield *Also called Prolamina Corporation* ***(G-16718)***
Prolens Inc....802 988-1018
47 Main St North Troy VT (05859) ***(G-22242)***
Proline Products LLC....603 652-7337
34 Industrial Way Milton NH (03851) ***(G-19087)***
Prolink Inc....860 659-5928
148 Eastern Blvd Ste 104 Glastonbury CT (06033) ***(G-1575)***
Prolume Inc....203 268-7778
525 Fan Hill Rd Ste E Monroe CT (06468) ***(G-2415)***
Prom Software Inc....802 862-7500
150 Dorset St Ste 294 South Burlington VT (05403) ***(G-22462)***
Proman Inc....860 827-8778
60 Saint Claire Ave Ste 2 New Britain CT (06051) ***(G-2566)***
Promax Supply LLC....781 620-1602
142 Franklin St Melrose MA (02176) ***(G-12990)***
Promedior Inc....781 538-4200
81 Hartwell Ave Ste 105 Lexington MA (02421) ***(G-12255)***
Promet Marine Service Corp....401 467-3730
242 Allens Ave Providence RI (02905) ***(G-21094)***
Prometheus Group of NH Ltd....800 442-2325
1 Washington St Ste 3171 Dover NH (03820) ***(G-18047)***
Promise Propane....860 685-0676
110 Holmes Rd Newington CT (06111) ***(G-2894)***
Promisec Holdings LLC....781 453-1105
1 Boston Pl Ste 2600 Boston MA (02108) ***(G-8797)***
Promounds Inc (PA)....508 580-6171
150 Wood Rd Ste 200 Braintree MA (02184) ***(G-9032)***
Pronto Printer of Newington....860 666-2245
2406 Berlin Tpke Newington CT (06111) ***(G-2895)***
Proofing House Press, Salem *Also called Frugal Printer Inc* ***(G-19737)***
Prophotonix Limited (PA)....603 893-8778
13 Red Roof Ln Ste 200 Salem NH (03079) ***(G-19761)***
Proprint, Boston *Also called Pressed For Time Printing Inc* ***(G-8793)***
Proprint Inc....401 944-3855
1145 Atwood Ave Johnston RI (02919) ***(G-20531)***
Proquip USA, Marblehead *Also called Marblehead Weather Gmts LLC* ***(G-12688)***
Pros Choice Inc....413 583-3435
700 Silver St Agawam MA (01001) ***(G-7448)***
Prosensing Inc....413 549-4402
107 Sunderland Rd Amherst MA (01002) ***(G-7522)***
Prospect Designs Inc....860 379-7858
11 Prospect St New Hartford CT (06057) ***(G-2645)***
Prospect Machine Products Inc....203 758-4448
139 Union City Rd Prospect CT (06712) ***(G-3593)***
Prospect Printing LLC....203 758-6007
16 Waterbury Rd Prospect CT (06712) ***(G-3594)***
Prospect Products Incorporated....860 666-0323
43 Kelsey St Newington CT (06111) ***(G-2896)***
Prosperous Printing LLC....203 834-1962
35 Danbury Rd Ste 4 Wilton CT (06897) ***(G-5300)***
Prosthetic and Orthotic Labs, Milford *Also called Mike Murphy* ***(G-13126)***
Prosthetic Design Inc....978 345-2588
1141 South St Ste 2 Fitchburg MA (01420) ***(G-10850)***
Prosthtic Orthtic Slutions LLC....413 785-4047
66 Myron St West Springfield MA (01089) ***(G-16549)***
Prostrong Inc....781 829-0000
300 Oak St Ste 1120 Pembroke MA (02359) ***(G-14422)***
Prosys Finishing Tech Inc....401 781-1011
1420 Elmwood Ave Cranston RI (02910) ***(G-20275)***
Protac, New Haven *Also called Arvinas Inc* ***(G-2658)***
Protavic America Inc....603 623-8624
8 Ricker Ave Londonderry NH (03053) ***(G-18733)***
Protech Associates Inc....978 462-1241
4 Court St Newburyport MA (01950) ***(G-13524)***
Protech Digital Services LLC....207 899-9237
189 Tripp Lake Rd Poland ME (04274) ***(G-6596)***
Protect & Heal Children Mass....978 374-8304
57 5th Ave Haverhill MA (01830) ***(G-11462)***
Protective Armored Systems Inc....413 637-1060
100 Valley St Lee MA (01238) ***(G-12095)***
Protective Technologies Svcs....603 964-9421
216 Lafayette Rd Unit 201 North Hampton NH (03862) ***(G-19387)***
Protectowire Co Inc....781 826-3878
60 Washington St Pembroke MA (02359) ***(G-14423)***

Protegrity Usa Inc (PA)........203 326-7200
333 Ludlow St Ste 8 Stamford CT (06902) ***(G-4292)***
Protein Holdings Inc (PA)........207 771-0965
10 Moulton St Ste 5 Portland ME (04101) ***(G-6717)***
Protein Plus Peanut Butter Co........401 996-5583
4 View St Lincoln RI (02865) ***(G-20593)***
Protein Products Inc........508 954-6020
76 Carlton Ln North Andover MA (01845) ***(G-13727)***
Protein Sciences Corporation (HQ)........203 686-0800
1000 Research Pkwy Meriden CT (06450) ***(G-2119)***
Protek Power North America Inc........978 567-9615
43 Broad St Ste B206 Hudson MA (01749) ***(G-11808)***
Protek-Sure, Orleans *Also called Hersey Clutch Co* ***(G-14235)***
Proteostasis Therapeutics Inc........617 225-0096
80 Guest St Ste 500 Boston MA (02135) ***(G-8798)***
Proteowise Inc........203 430-4187
34 Bryan Rd Branford CT (06405) ***(G-340)***
Proteq Solutions LLC........603 888-6630
76 Northeastern Blvd 38a Nashua NH (03062) ***(G-19241)***
Proteus Industries Inc........978 281-9545
33 Commercial St Ste 4 Gloucester MA (01930) ***(G-11205)***
Proto Industrial Tools, New Britain *Also called Stanley Industrial & Auto LLC* ***(G-2585)***
Proto Part Inc........603 883-6531
71 Pine Rd Unit F Hudson NH (03051) ***(G-18429)***
Protom International Inc........781 245-3964
500 Edgewater Dr Ste 522 Wakefield MA (01880) ***(G-15973)***
Proton Energy Systems Inc........203 678-2000
10 Technology Dr Wallingford CT (06492) ***(G-4790)***
Proton Onsite, Wallingford *Also called Proton Energy Systems Inc* ***(G-4790)***
Protonex Technology Corp, Southborough *Also called Ballard Unmanned Systems Inc* ***(G-15344)***
Protopac Inc........860 274-6796
120 Echo Lake Rd Watertown CT (06795) ***(G-5020)***
Protopac Printing Services, Watertown *Also called Protopac Inc* ***(G-5020)***
Prototek Manufacturing, Contoocook *Also called Prototek Shtmtal Fbrcation LLC* ***(G-17947)***
Prototek Shtmtal Fbrcation LLC (PA)........603 746-2001
244 Burnham Intervale Rd Contoocook NH (03229) ***(G-17947)***
Prototype Plastic Mold Co Inc........860 632-2800
35 Industrial Park Pl Middletown CT (06457) ***(G-2214)***
Prototype Services Inc........508 478-8887
17 Airport Rd Hopedale MA (01747) ***(G-11680)***
Protracker Software Inc........603 926-8085
6 Merrill Industrial Dr # 7 Hampton NH (03842) ***(G-18268)***
Protronix Inc........203 269-5858
28 Parker St Wallingford CT (06492) ***(G-4791)***
Proudfoot Company Inc........203 459-0031
588 Pepper St Monroe CT (06468) ***(G-2416)***
Proven Process Med Dvcs Inc........508 261-0800
110 Forbes Blvd Mansfield MA (02048) ***(G-12652)***
Provencal Manufacturing Inc (PA)........603 772-6716
12 New Rd Newfields NH (03856) ***(G-19319)***
Proveris Scientific Corp........508 460-8822
2 Cabot Rd Ste 5 Hudson MA (01749) ***(G-11809)***
Providence Braid Company........401 722-2120
358 Lowden St Pawtucket RI (02860) ***(G-20885)***
Providence Business News........401 273-2201
400 Westminster St # 600 Providence RI (02903) ***(G-21095)***
Providence Cable Corporation........401 632-7650
12 Peppermint Ln Johnston RI (02919) ***(G-20532)***
Providence Casting Inc........401 231-0860
3 Warren Ave North Providence RI (02911) ***(G-20773)***
Providence Journal Company........401 277-7000
75 Fountain St Providence RI (02902) ***(G-21096)***
Providence Label & Tag Co........401 751-6677
315 Harris Ave Providence RI (02909) ***(G-21097)***
Providence Machine and Tl Work........401 751-1526
126 Bellows St Warwick RI (02888) ***(G-21406)***
Providence Metallizing Co Inc (PA)........401 722-5300
51 Fairlawn Ave Pawtucket RI (02860) ***(G-20886)***
Providence Mint Inc........401 272-7760
1205 Westminster St Providence RI (02909) ***(G-21098)***
Providence Spillproof Cntrs........401 723-4900
60 Valley St Apt 4 Providence RI (02909) ***(G-21099)***
Providence Visitor, Providence *Also called Visitor Printing Co* ***(G-21151)***
Providence Welding........401 941-2700
101 Poe St Providence RI (02905) ***(G-21100)***
Province Automation, Sanford *Also called Oizero9 Inc* ***(G-6885)***
Province Kiln Dried Firewood........603 524-4447
428 South Rd Belmont NH (03220) ***(G-17681)***
Provincetown Arts Press Inc (PA)........508 487-3167
650 Commercial St Provincetown MA (02657) ***(G-14608)***
Proximie Inc........617 391-6824
143 Great Rd Bedford MA (01730) ***(G-8004)***
Proxtalkercom LLC (PA)........203 721-6074
327 Huntingdon Ave Waterbury CT (06708) ***(G-4947)***
Proxy Manufacturing Inc........978 687-3138
55 Chase St Ste 7 Methuen MA (01844) ***(G-13044)***
Prozone, Lee *Also called Csl Building Group LLC* ***(G-12091)***

Prue Foundry Inc........508 385-3011
52 Paddocks Path Dennis MA (02638) ***(G-10309)***
Pruefer Metalworks Inc........401 785-4688
320 Elm St Warwick RI (02888) ***(G-21407)***
Prysm Inc........408 586-1100
45 Winthrop St Ste D Concord MA (01742) ***(G-10152)***
Prysmian Cbles Systems USA LLC........508 822-5444
22 Joseph Warner Blvd North Dighton MA (02764) ***(G-13935)***
Prysmian Cbles Systems USA LLC........508 822-0246
761 Joseph Warner Blvd Taunton MA (02780) ***(G-15775)***
Prysmian Cbles Systems USA LLC........508 822-5444
20 Joseph E Warner Blvd North Dighton MA (02764) ***(G-13936)***
Psd Inc........860 305-6346
80 Caroline Rd East Haven CT (06512) ***(G-1259)***
Psg Framing, Somerville *Also called Pucker Gallery Inc* ***(G-15207)***
Psg Framing Inc........617 261-1817
130 Broadway Somerville MA (02145) ***(G-15206)***
PSI, Northborough *Also called Power Systems Integrity Inc* ***(G-14045)***
PSI Controls, Portland *Also called Piping Specialties Inc* ***(G-6708)***
PSI Molded Plastics NH Inc........603 569-5100
5 Wickers Dr Wolfeboro NH (03894) ***(G-20024)***
PSI Plus Inc........860 267-6667
17 Watrous St East Hampton CT (06424) ***(G-1164)***
PSI Water Systems Inc (PA)........603 624-5110
1368 Hooksett Rd Hooksett NH (03106) ***(G-18356)***
Psjl Corporation (PA)........978 313-2500
780 Boston Rd Ste 4 Billerica MA (01821) ***(G-8279)***
Psjl Corporation........978 313-2550
41 Industrial Dr Exeter NH (03833) ***(G-18129)***
Pss, Wakefield *Also called Premium Sund Slutions Amer LLC* ***(G-15972)***
Psyton Software........617 308-5058
50 Vine St Chestnut Hill MA (02467) ***(G-9992)***
Pt Plus At Whitney Field........978 534-5922
31 Cinema Blvd Leominster MA (01453) ***(G-12178)***
Ptc As LLC........339 440-5818
6 Kimball Ln Lynnfield MA (01940) ***(G-12555)***
Ptc Inc........617 792-7622
230 3rd Ave Waltham MA (02451) ***(G-16179)***
Ptc Parametric Technology........781 370-5699
159 Laurel Dr Needham MA (02492) ***(G-13309)***
Ptc Therapeutics Gt Inc........781 799-9179
245 First St Ste 1800 Cambridge MA (02142) ***(G-9619)***
Pti Industries Inc (HQ)........800 318-8438
2 Peerless Way Enfield CT (06082) ***(G-1376)***
Ptp Machining........603 204-5446
21 West Rd Hudson NH (03051) ***(G-18430)***
Pts, Littleton *Also called Programmed Test Sources Inc* ***(G-12320)***
Pttgc Innovation America Corp (HQ)........617 657-5234
45 Cummings Park Woburn MA (01801) ***(G-17271)***
Public Scales........207 784-9466
32 Lexington St Lewiston ME (04240) ***(G-6317)***
Public Works Dept, Wilton *Also called Town of Wilton* ***(G-5308)***
Publishers Design & Prod Svcs........508 833-8300
349 Old Plymouth Rd Sagamore Beach MA (02562) ***(G-14886)***
Publishing Dimensions LLC........203 856-7716
15 Treadwell Ln Weston CT (06883) ***(G-5173)***
Publishing Directions LLC........860 673-7650
50 Lovely St Avon CT (06001) ***(G-42)***
Publishing Packagers, Westport *Also called Ppc Books Ltd* ***(G-5224)***
Publishing Solutions Group Inc........617 274-9001
400 W Cummings Park # 2600 Woburn MA (01801) ***(G-17272)***
Pucker Gallery Inc........617 261-1817
130 Broadway Rear Somerville MA (02145) ***(G-15207)***
Pucks Putters & Fuel LLC........203 877-5457
10 Robert Dennis Dr Milford CT (06461) ***(G-2343)***
Pucks Putters & Fuel LLC (PA)........203 494-3952
784 River Rd Shelton CT (06484) ***(G-3864)***
Pucuda Inc........860 526-8004
14 New Rd Madison CT (06443) ***(G-1972)***
Puffer International Inc........413 562-9100
24 Elm St Ste 2 Westfield MA (01085) ***(G-16719)***
Puffer International Inc........413 527-1069
139 Meadow St Westfield MA (01085) ***(G-16720)***
Puleos Dairy........978 590-7611
376 Highland Ave Salem MA (01970) ***(G-14937)***
Pulmatrix Inc (PA)........781 357-2333
99 Hayden Ave Ste 390 Lexington MA (02421) ***(G-12256)***
Pulmatrix Operating Co Inc........781 357-2333
99 Hayden Ave Ste 390 Lexington MA (02421) ***(G-12257)***
Pulp Paper Products Inc........860 806-0143
30 Norwood St Torrington CT (06790) ***(G-4594)***
Pulpdent Corporation........617 926-6666
80 Oakland St Watertown MA (02472) ***(G-16308)***
Pulse Network Inc........781 688-8000
10 Oceana Way Norwood MA (02062) ***(G-14189)***
Pulver Precision LLC........860 763-0763
38 Bacon Rd Enfield CT (06082) ***(G-1377)***
Pumc Holding Corporation (PA)........203 743-6741
31-35 South St Danbury CT (06810) ***(G-976)***

Pumping Systems Inc 508 588-6868
67 Water St Braintree MA (02184) ***(G-9033)***
Pumpkin Harbor Designs Inc 802 644-6588
950 N Cambridge Rd Jeffersonville VT (05464) ***(G-22047)***
Puppy Hugger 203 661-4858
121 North St Greenwich CT (06830) ***(G-1639)***
Puratos Corporation 781 688-8560
83 Morse St Norwood MA (02062) ***(G-14190)***
Purbeck Isle Inc (PA) 207 623-5119
36 Anthony Ave Ste 104 Augusta ME (04330) ***(G-5617)***
Purchasing & Inventory Cons 802 674-2620
1706 Brook Rd Windsor VT (05089) ***(G-22713)***
Purchasing Dept, Pittsfield *Also called Crane & Co Inc* ***(G-14466)***
Purdue Pharma, Stamford *Also called Frederick Purdue Company Inc* ***(G-4197)***
Purdue Pharma LP 203 588-8000
201 Tresser Blvd Fl 1 Stamford CT (06901) ***(G-4293)***
Purdue Pharma LP (PA) 203 588-8000
201 Tresser Blvd Fl 1 Stamford CT (06901) ***(G-4294)***
Purdue Pharma Manufacturing LP 252 265-1924
201 Tresser Blvd Fl 1 Stamford CT (06901) ***(G-4295)***
Pure Cold Press 617 487-8948
326 Harvard St Brookline MA (02446) ***(G-9216)***
Pure Element 603 235-4373
8 Birch St Derry NH (03038) ***(G-17995)***
Pure Energy Corporation (PA) 201 843-8100
101 Middlesex Tpke Ste 6 Burlington MA (01803) ***(G-9324)***
Pure Energy of America, Burlington *Also called Pure Energy Corporation* ***(G-9324)***
Pure Gold Sugaring LLC 802 467-3921
20 Craig Pond Rd Sutton VT (05867) ***(G-22528)***
Pure Imaging 781 537-6992
9 Fowle St Woburn MA (01801) ***(G-17273)***
Pure One Systems, Lawrence *Also called Merrimack Valley Water Assn* ***(G-12051)***
Pure Pup Love Inc 207 588-8111
20 Cloverleaf Ln Scarborough ME (04074) ***(G-6936)***
Purecoat International LLC 561 844-0100
30 Brighton St Belmont MA (02478) ***(G-8079)***
Purecoat North LLC 617 489-2750
39 Hittinger St Belmont MA (02478) ***(G-8080)***
Purely Organic Products LLC 212 826-9150
1 New Hampshire Ave # 125 Portsmouth NH (03801) ***(G-19610)***
Purestat Engineered Tech, Lewiston *Also called Kullson Holding Company Inc* ***(G-6296)***
Puretech Health LLC (PA) 617 482-2333
6 Tide St Ste 400 Boston MA (02210) ***(G-8799)***
Purewood Cabinetry 603 378-2001
6 W Main St Newton NH (03858) ***(G-19368)***
Purfx Inc 860 399-4045
51 Brookwood Dr Westbrook CT (06498) ***(G-5161)***
Purification Technologies LLC (HQ) 860 526-7801
67 Winthrop Rd Chester CT (06412) ***(G-774)***
Puritan Capital, Hollis *Also called Puritan Press Inc* ***(G-18339)***
Puritan Food Co Inc 617 269-5650
17 Food Mart Rd Boston MA (02118) ***(G-8800)***
Puritan Ice Cream Co of Boston 617 524-3580
3895 Washington St Boston MA (02131) ***(G-8801)***
Puritan Icecream Inc 617 524-7500
3895 Washington St Roslindale MA (02131) ***(G-14842)***
Puritan Industries Inc 860 693-0791
122 Powder Mill Rd Collinsville CT (06019) ***(G-816)***
Puritan Medical Pdts Co LLC 207 876-3311
31 School St Guilford ME (04443) ***(G-6160)***
Puritan Medical Products, Guilford *Also called Hardwood Products Company LP* ***(G-6158)***
Puritan Press Inc (PA) 603 889-4500
95 Runnells Bridge Rd Hollis NH (03049) ***(G-18339)***
Purposeenergy Inc (PA) 617 202-9156
800 W Cummings Park # 3400 Woburn MA (01801) ***(G-17274)***
Pursuit Toboggan LLC 508 567-0550
75 Ferry St Ste 5 Fall River MA (02721) ***(G-10749)***
Push603radio.com, Manchester *Also called Live Wire Marketing Corp* ***(G-18865)***
Pussums Cat Company, Turner *Also called Two Rivers Pet Products Inc* ***(G-7112)***
Putnam Plastics Corporation 860 774-1559
40 Louisa Viens Dr Dayville CT (06241) ***(G-1051)***
Putnam Rf Machining LLC 603 623-0700
720 Union St Manchester NH (03104) ***(G-18769)***
Putney Mountain Winery 802 387-5925
8 Bellows Falls Rd Putney VT (05346) ***(G-22291)***
Putney Pasta Company Inc 802 257-4800
28 Vernon St Ste 434 Brattleboro VT (05301) ***(G-21746)***
Putu LLC 203 594-9700
48 Elm St New Canaan CT (06840) ***(G-2613)***
Puzzle House 603 532-4442
426 Nutting Rd Jaffrey NH (03452) ***(G-18475)***
Pv Engineering & Mfg Inc 978 465-1221
88 Rabbit Rd Salisbury MA (01952) ***(G-14955)***
Pvd Products Inc 978 694-9455
35 Upton Dr Ste 200 Wilmington MA (01887) ***(G-17040)***
Pvh Corp 508 384-0070
475 Washington St Ste 6 Wrentham MA (02093) ***(G-17527)***
Pvh Corp 508 945-4063
1238 Main St Chatham MA (02633) ***(G-9863)***
Pw Power Systems LLC (HQ) 860 368-5900
628 Hebron Ave Ste 400 Glastonbury CT (06033) ***(G-1576)***
Pw Precision Machine LLC 203 889-8615
12 Scovil Rd Unit B Higganum CT (06441) ***(G-1905)***
Pwh Corporation 978 373-9111
55 Ward Hill Ave Haverhill MA (01835) ***(G-11463)***
Pxt Payments Inc 978 247-7164
300 Brickstone Sq Ste 201 Andover MA (01810) ***(G-7588)***
PYC Deborring LLC F/K/A C & 860 828-6806
500 Four Rod Rd Ste 114 Berlin CT (06037) ***(G-106)***
Pynchon Press Co Inc 413 315-8798
873 Grattan St Chicopee MA (01020) ***(G-10054)***
Pyne-Davidson Company 860 522-9106
237 Weston St Hartford CT (06120) ***(G-1862)***
Pyramid Case Co Inc 401 273-0643
122 Manton Ave Providence RI (02909) ***(G-21101)***
Pyramid Checks & Printing 207 878-9832
208 Riverside Indus Pkwy Portland ME (04103) ***(G-6718)***
Pyramid Mold Inc 413 442-6198
495 Churchill St Pittsfield MA (01201) ***(G-14503)***
Pyramid Printing and Advg Inc 781 337-7609
54 Mathewson Dr 60 Weymouth MA (02189) ***(G-16899)***
Pyramid Printing and Digital, Weymouth *Also called Pyramid Printing and Advg Inc* ***(G-16899)***
Pyramid Productions, Danbury *Also called Joy Carole Creations Inc* ***(G-942)***
Pyramid Studios 207 667-3321
10 State St Ellsworth ME (04605) ***(G-6020)***
Pyramid Time Systems LLC 203 238-0550
45 Gracey Ave Meriden CT (06451) ***(G-2120)***
Pyromate Inc 603 924-4251
270 Old Dublin Rd Peterborough NH (03458) ***(G-19485)***
Q LLC 603 294-0047
4 Cutts St Unit 3 Portsmouth NH (03801) ***(G-19611)***
Q A S 617 345-3000
125 Summer St Ste 1910 Boston MA (02110) ***(G-8802)***
Q A Technology Company Inc 603 926-1193
110 Towle Farm Rd Hampton NH (03842) ***(G-18269)***
Q Alpha Inc 860 357-7340
87 Upton Rd Colchester CT (06415) ***(G-806)***
Q E A, Billerica *Also called Quality Engineering Assoc Inc* ***(G-8280)***
Q Pin2s Billiards 413 285-7971
885 Riverdale St West Springfield MA (01089) ***(G-16550)***
Q S T, Saint Albans *Also called QST Inc* ***(G-22377)***
Q-Biz Solutions LLC 617 212-7684
480 Pleasant St Ste B200 Watertown MA (02472) ***(G-16309)***
Q-Jet DSI Inc 203 230-4700
303 State St North Haven CT (06473) ***(G-3056)***
Q-Lane Turnstiles LLC 860 410-1801
52 Riverside Rd Sandy Hook CT (06482) ***(G-3745)***
Q6 Integration Inc 508 266-0638
126 Clubhouse Ln Northbridge MA (01534) ***(G-14059)***
Qba Inc 860 963-9438
24 Woodland Dr Woodstock CT (06281) ***(G-5500)***
Qbit Semiconductor Ltd 351 205-0005
1 Monarch Dr Ste 203 Littleton MA (01460) ***(G-12321)***
Qbm New York Inc 716 821-1475
30 Caroline St Providence RI (02904) ***(G-21102)***
Qc Industries Inc (PA) 781 344-1000
60 Maple St Mansfield MA (02048) ***(G-12653)***
Qci Inc 508 399-8983
257 Pine St Seekonk MA (02771) ***(G-15035)***
Qdiscovery LLC (HQ) 860 271-7080
125 Eugene Oneill Dr # 140 New London CT (06320) ***(G-2777)***
Qds LLC 203 338-9668
120 Long Hill Cross Rd Shelton CT (06484) ***(G-3865)***
QED, Stoneham *Also called Queues Enforth Development Inc* ***(G-15571)***
QED Optical Inc 207 532-6772
2 Washburn St Houlton ME (04730) ***(G-6209)***
QEP Co Inc 978 368-8991
179 Brook St Clinton MA (01510) ***(G-10091)***
Qesidyne Inc 603 883-3116
4 Candy Ln Unit 1 Hudson NH (03051) ***(G-18431)***
Qg LLC 508 828-4400
1133 County St Taunton MA (02780) ***(G-15776)***
Qg Printing Corp 978 534-8351
27 Nashua St Leominster MA (01453) ***(G-12179)***
Qg Printing II Corp 860 741-0150
96 Phoenix Ave Enfield CT (06082) ***(G-1378)***
Qinetiq North America, Devens *Also called Foster-Miller Inc* ***(G-10320)***
Qinetiq North America, Inc., Waltham *Also called Perspecta Svcs & Solutions Inc* ***(G-16173)***
Qmagiq LLC 603 821-3092
22 Cotton Rd Ste 180 Nashua NH (03063) ***(G-19242)***
Qmd Medical, Milton *Also called Green Mountain Knitting Inc* ***(G-22131)***
Qmdi Press 860 642-8074
841 Route 32 Ste 19 North Franklin CT (06254) ***(G-2991)***
Qnp Technologies, East Glastonbury *Also called Quality Name Plate Inc* ***(G-1114)***
Qol Publications, Manchester *Also called Hippopress LLC* ***(G-18834)***
Qorvo Inc 978 770-2158
2 Executive Dr Chelmsford MA (01824) ***(G-9923)***

Qpharmetra LLC (PA) 978 655-1943
9 Nollet Dr Andover MA (01810) *(G-7589)*
Qpl, Chelmsford *Also called Quick Print Ltd Inc (G-9924)*
Qrsts LLC 617 625-3335
561 Windsor St Ste B101 Somerville MA (02143) *(G-15208)*
Qs Tehcnoligies Divison, Meriden *Also called Omerin Usa Inc (G-2113)*
Qsa Global Inc (HQ) 781 272-2000
30 North Ave Ste 3 Burlington MA (01803) *(G-9325)*
Qscend Technologies Inc 203 757-6000
231 Bank St Waterbury CT (06702) *(G-4948)*
Qsimulate, Cambridge *Also called Quantum Simulation Tech Inc (G-9622)*
Qsonica LLC 203 426-0101
53 Church Hill Rd Newtown CT (06470) *(G-2933)*
Qsr International Americas Inc 617 607-5112
35 Corporate Dr Ste 140 Burlington MA (01803) *(G-9326)*
Qsr Steel Corporation LLC 860 548-0248
121 Elliott St E Hartford CT (06114) *(G-1863)*
QST Inc 802 524-7704
300 Industrial Park Rd Saint Albans VT (05478) *(G-22377)*
Qstream Inc (PA) 781 222-2020
3 Burlington Woods Dr # 303 Burlington MA (01803) *(G-9327)*
Qteros LLC 413 531-6884
99 Pulpit Hill Rd Amherst MA (01002) *(G-7523)*
Qtran Inc 203 367-8777
155 Hill St Ste 3 Milford CT (06460) *(G-2344)*
Quabbin Inc 978 544-3872
158 Gov Dukakis Dr Orange MA (01364) *(G-14223)*
Quabbin Inc 978 249-8891
11 Falls Rd Royalston MA (01368) *(G-14876)*
Quabbin Vly Frmng Cmpnents Div, Palmer *Also called Shedworks Inc (G-14296)*
Quabbin Wire & Cable Co Inc (PA) 413 967-6281
10 Maple St Ware MA (01082) *(G-16236)*
Quad/Graphics Inc 413 525-8552
245 Benton Dr East Longmeadow MA (01028) *(G-10490)*
Quad/Graphics Inc 860 741-0150
27 Nashua St Leominster MA (01453) *(G-12180)*
Quad/Graphics Inc 508 692-3100
50 John Hancock Rd Taunton MA (02780) *(G-15777)*
Quad/Graphics Inc 781 231-7200
110 Commerce Way Ste F Woburn MA (01801) *(G-17275)*
Quad/Graphics Inc 203 288-2468
291 State St North Haven CT (06473) *(G-3057)*
Quad/Graphics Inc 781 917-1601
370 Libbey Industri Weymouth MA (02189) *(G-16900)*
Quadgraphics, Leominster *Also called Quad/Graphics Inc (G-12180)*
Quadra-Tek, Arlington *Also called Arlington Industries Inc (G-21594)*
Quadrant LLC 508 594-2700
120 Forbes Blvd Ste A Mansfield MA (02048) *(G-12654)*
Quadtech Inc 978 461-2100
734 Forest St Ste 500 Marlborough MA (01752) *(G-12811)*
Qual-Craft, Mansfield *Also called Qc Industries Inc (G-12653)*
Qualcomm Incorporated 978 318-0650
30 Monument Sq Ste 235 Concord MA (01742) *(G-10153)*
Qualcomm Incorporated 858 587-1121
100 Burtt Rd Ste 123 Andover MA (01810) *(G-7590)*
Qualcomm Incorporated 858 587-1121
90 Central St Ste 1 Boxborough MA (01719) *(G-8968)*
Qualedi Inc 203 538-5320
1 Trap Falls Rd Ste 206 Shelton CT (06484) *(G-3866)*
Qualedi Inc (PA) 203 874-4334
121 W Main St Ste 4 Milford CT (06460) *(G-2345)*
Quality Air Metals Inc 781 986-9967
283 Centre St Ste B Holbrook MA (02343) *(G-11537)*
Quality Automatics Inc (PA) 860 945-4795
15 Mclennan Dr Oakville CT (06779) *(G-3300)*
Quality Babbitting Services 603 642-7147
25 Pheasant Run East Kingston NH (03827) *(G-18090)*
Quality Care Drg/Cntrbrook LLC 860 767-0206
33 Main St Centerbrook CT (06409) *(G-702)*
Quality Carton Converting LLC 978 556-5008
175 Ward Hill Ave Ste 4 Haverhill MA (01835) *(G-11464)*
Quality Coils Incorporated (PA) 860 584-0927
748 Middle St Bristol CT (06010) *(G-598)*
Quality Components Rp 603 864-8196
5 Orchard Ln Pelham NH (03076) *(G-19443)*
Quality Containers of Neng 207 846-5420
247 Portland St Ste 2 Yarmouth ME (04096) *(G-7299)*
Quality Controls Inc 603 286-3321
200 Tilton Rd Northfield NH (03276) *(G-19408)*
Quality Die Cutting Inc (PA) 978 374-8027
506 River St Haverhill MA (01832) *(G-11465)*
Quality Engineering Assoc Inc 978 528-2034
755 Middlesex Tpke Ste 3 Billerica MA (01821) *(G-8280)*
Quality Envelope & Printing Co 508 947-8878
22 Cambridge St Ste H Middleboro MA (02346) *(G-13077)*
Quality Fabricators LLC 603 905-9012
246 Calef Hwy Barrington NH (03825) *(G-17621)*
Quality Fuel 401 822-9482
1086 Main St West Warwick RI (02893) *(G-21507)*
Quality Incense 339 224-0655
316 Rindge Ave Unit 6 Cambridge MA (02140) *(G-9620)*
Quality Kitchen Corp Delaware 203 744-2000
131 West St Ste 1 Danbury CT (06810) *(G-977)*
Quality Laser Inc 617 479-7374
36 6th Rd Woburn MA (01801) *(G-17276)*
Quality Loose Leaf Co 413 534-5891
62 Lyman St South Hadley MA (01075) *(G-15310)*
Quality Machine, New Milford *Also called Joseph J McFadden Jr (G-2808)*
Quality Machine Inc 860 354-6794
87 Danbury Rd New Milford CT (06776) *(G-2824)*
Quality Machine Inc 603 382-2334
31 Kingston Rd Plaistow NH (03865) *(G-19521)*
Quality Machining Co Inc 413 562-0389
96b1 Mainline Dr Westfield MA (01085) *(G-16721)*
Quality Metal Craft Inc 617 479-7374
135 Old Colony Ave Quincy MA (02170) *(G-14649)*
Quality Name Plate Inc 860 633-9495
22 Fisher Hill Rd East Glastonbury CT (06025) *(G-1114)*
Quality Packaging & Graphics 413 568-1923
280 Lockhouse Rd Westfield MA (01085) *(G-16722)*
Quality Paving, Woodland *Also called McBreairty Ransford (G-7288)*
Quality Press Inc 603 889-7211
126 Hall St Ste I Concord NH (03301) *(G-17925)*
Quality Printers Inc 860 443-2800
141 Shaw St New London CT (06320) *(G-2778)*
Quality Printing & Graphics, Fairfield *Also called Mickey Herbst (G-1444)*
Quality Printing Company Inc 413 442-4166
3 Federico Dr Pittsfield MA (01201) *(G-14504)*
Quality Printing Services Inc 401 434-4321
103 Wilson Ave Rumford RI (02916) *(G-21194)*
Quality Rolling Deburring Inc 860 283-0271
135 S Main St Ste 3 Thomaston CT (06787) *(G-4511)*
Quality Screw Machine Pdts Inc 401 231-8900
9 Industrial Dr S Smithfield RI (02917) *(G-21245)*
Quality Sheet Metal Inc 203 729-2244
17 Clark Rd Naugatuck CT (06770) *(G-2492)*
Quality Sign Crafters, Willimantic *Also called Horizons Unlimited Inc (G-5266)*
Quality Solutions Inc (PA) 978 465-7755
44 Merrimac St Ste 22 Newburyport MA (01950) *(G-13525)*
Quality Spraying Stenciling Co 401 861-2413
175 Dupont Dr Providence RI (02907) *(G-21103)*
Quality Stairs Inc 203 367-8390
70 Logan St Bridgeport CT (06607) *(G-477)*
Quality Welding LLC 860 585-1121
61 E Main St Bldg C Bristol CT (06010) *(G-599)*
Quality Welding Service LLC 860 342-7202
265 Brownstone Ave Portland CT (06480) *(G-3572)*
Quality Wire Edm Inc 860 583-9867
329 Redstone Hill Rd Bristol CT (06010) *(G-600)*
Quality Woodworks LLC 203 736-9200
1 Riverside Dr Ansonia CT (06401) *(G-22)*
Qualitytrainingportal.com, Waitsfield *Also called Resource Engineering Inc (G-22568)*
Qualtre Inc (HQ) 508 658-8360
144 North Rd Ste 2250 Sudbury MA (01776) *(G-15666)*
Quantance Inc (PA) 650 293-3300
20 Sylvan Rd Woburn MA (01801) *(G-17277)*
Quantek Instruments 508 839-0108
183 Magill Dr Grafton MA (01519) *(G-11224)*
Quanterix Corporation (PA) 617 301-9400
900 Middlesex Tpke 1-1 Billerica MA (01821) *(G-8281)*
Quantifacts Inc 401 421-8300
100 Amaral St Ste 2 Riverside RI (02915) *(G-21175)*
Quantrix, Portland *Also called Subx Inc (G-6734)*
Quanttus Inc 617 401-2648
2 Newton Executive Park # 104 Newton MA (02462) *(G-13628)*
Quantum Bpower Southington LLC 860 201-0621
49 Depaolo Dr Southington CT (06489) *(G-4071)*
Quantum Circuits Inc 203 891-6216
25 Science Park Ste 203 New Haven CT (06511) *(G-2729)*
Quantum Corporation LLC 802 505-5088
46 Worcester Village Rd Worcester VT (05682) *(G-22743)*
Quantum Designs LLC (PA) 617 491-6600
161 First St Ste 3 Cambridge MA (02142) *(G-9621)*
Quantum Discoveries Inc 857 272-9998
53 State St Ste 500 Boston MA (02109) *(G-8803)*
Quantum Simulation Tech Inc 847 626-5535
625 Massachusetts Ave Cambridge MA (02139) *(G-9622)*
Quarry Brothers Incorporated 508 252-9922
466 Winthrop St Rehoboth MA (02769) *(G-14758)*
Quarry Slate Industries Inc 802 287-9701
325 Upper Rd Poultney VT (05764) *(G-22274)*
Quarry Tap Room LLC 207 213-6173
122 Water St Hallowell ME (04347) *(G-6164)*
Quarter LLC 617 848-1249
867 Boylston St Boston MA (02116) *(G-8804)*
Quarter Line Drssge Unlmted 978 476-6554
79 Jewett St Rear Georgetown MA (01833) *(G-11149)*
Quarter Moon Incorporated (PA) 401 683-0400
200 Highpoint Ave Portsmouth RI (02871) *(G-20937)*

ALPHABETIC

Quarter Point Woodworking LLC (PA)..........207 926-1032
483 Intervale Rd New Gloucester ME (04260) *(G-6471)*
Quarter Point Woodworking LLC..........207 892-7022
7b Commons Ave Windham ME (04062) *(G-7245)*
Quarter Productions..........774 217-8073
3 Hillside Ave Amesbury MA (01913) *(G-7503)*
Quarterly Review of Wines..........781 721-0525
22 Safford St Quincy MA (02171) *(G-14650)*
Quarterly Review Wines Mag, Quincy *Also called Quarterly Review of Wines (G-14650)*
Quarterly Update..........508 540-0848
32 Quail Hollow Rd North Falmouth MA (02556) *(G-13953)*
Quarto Pubg Group USA Inc..........978 282-9590
100 Cummings Ctr Ste 265g Beverly MA (01915) *(G-8166)*
Quartzite Processing Inc..........781 322-3611
6 Holyoke St Malden MA (02148) *(G-12592)*
Quatum Inc..........860 666-3464
43 Maselli Rd Hartford CT (06111) *(G-1864)*
Quayside Publishing Group..........978 282-9590
100 Cummings Ctr Ste 406l Beverly MA (01915) *(G-8167)*
Queen Bee Vineyard Inc..........413 267-9329
173 Moulton Hill Rd Monson MA (01057) *(G-13210)*
Queen City Examiner..........603 289-6835
112 Auburn St Manchester NH (03103) *(G-18907)*
Queen City Printers Inc..........802 864-4566
701 Pine St Burlington VT (05401) *(G-21804)*
Queen City Soil & Stone DBA..........802 318-2411
20 Ferguson Ave Burlington VT (05401) *(G-21805)*
Queen City Sounds Inc..........603 668-4306
419 Somerville St Manchester NH (03103) *(G-18908)*
Queen Screw & Mfg Inc..........781 894-8110
60 Farwell St Waltham MA (02453) *(G-16180)*
Quemere International LLC..........914 934-8366
234 Middle St Middletown CT (06457) *(G-2215)*
Quero Shoes, Westport *Also called Cuero Operating (G-5187)*
Quest Drape..........781 859-0300
46 Cummings Park Woburn MA (01801) *(G-17278)*
Quest Plastics Inc..........860 489-1404
89 Commercial Blvd Ste 3 Torrington CT (06790) *(G-4595)*
Quest Software Inc..........781 592-0752
45 New Ocean St Swampscott MA (01907) *(G-15699)*
Questech Corporation (PA)..........802 773-1228
92 Park St Rutland VT (05701) *(G-22347)*
Questech Metals, Rutland *Also called Questech Corporation (G-22347)*
Questech Tile LLC..........802 773-1228
92 Park St Rutland VT (05701) *(G-22348)*
Questex Brazil LLC..........617 219-8300
3 Speen St Ste 300 Framingham MA (01701) *(G-10997)*
Queues Enforth Development Inc..........781 870-1100
92 Montvale Ave Ste 4300 Stoneham MA (02180) *(G-15571)*
Quick Copy, Fall River *Also called Fall River Modern Printing Co (G-10697)*
Quick Copy Center, Biddeford *Also called R & W Engraving Inc (G-5760)*
Quick Fab Inc..........401 848-0055
307 Oliphant Ln Unit 8 Middletown RI (02842) *(G-20630)*
Quick Fitting Inc..........401 734-9500
30 Plan Way Warwick RI (02886) *(G-21408)*
Quick Machine Services LLC..........203 634-8822
290 Pratt St Ste 4 Meriden CT (06450) *(G-2121)*
Quick Manufacturing Co..........978 750-4202
4 Electronics Ave Danvers MA (01923) *(G-10247)*
Quick Print Color Center..........207 282-6480
74 Industrial Park Rd # 102 Saco ME (04072) *(G-6856)*
Quick Print Ltd Inc..........978 256-1822
27 Industrial Ave Unit 4a Chelmsford MA (01824) *(G-9924)*
Quick Removal Service, Maynard *Also called Maciel John (G-12901)*
Quick Stop Printing..........508 797-4788
340 Shrewsbury St Worcester MA (01604) *(G-17448)*
Quick Turn Machine Company Inc..........860 623-2569
1000 Old County Cir # 105 Windsor Locks CT (06096) *(G-5399)*
Quick-Loc, Lincoln *Also called Quik Loc Inc (G-18647)*
Quick-Sling, Taunton *Also called Diversitech Corporation (G-15744)*
Quickbase Inc (PA)..........855 725-2293
150 Cambridgepark Dr # 500 Cambridge MA (02140) *(G-9623)*
Quickdoc Inc..........617 738-1800
1415 Beacon St Ste 119 Brookline MA (02446) *(G-9217)*
Quickpoint Corporation..........978 371-3267
23b Bradford St Concord MA (01742) *(G-10154)*
Quickprint of Rutland , The, Rutland *Also called Edward Group Inc (G-22332)*
Quicksplint Company, Rutland *Also called Blair Campbell (G-22325)*
Quidel Corporation..........866 800-5458
500 Cummings Ctr # 55500 Beverly MA (01915) *(G-8168)*
Quiet Logistics..........978 391-4439
66 Saratoga Blvd Devens MA (01434) *(G-10331)*
Quik Loc Inc..........603 745-7008
21 Arthur Salem Way Lincoln NH (03251) *(G-18647)*
Quikprint, Southborough *Also called D-Lew Inc (G-15353)*
Quikrete Companies LLC..........603 778-2123
44 Jubal Martin Rd Brentwood NH (03833) *(G-17756)*
Quilted Threads LLC..........603 428-6622
116 Main St Henniker NH (03242) *(G-18311)*
Quincy Steel & Welding Co Inc..........617 472-1180
444 Sea St Quincy MA (02169) *(G-14651)*
Quincy Sun Publishing Co Inc..........617 471-3100
1372 Hancock St Ste 102 Quincy MA (02169) *(G-14652)*
Quinlan Publishing Co Inc (PA)..........617 439-0076
23 Drydock Ave Fl 2 Boston MA (02210) *(G-8805)*
Quinlan Publishing Group, Boston *Also called Quinlan Publishing Co Inc (G-8805)*
Quinn Curtis Inc..........508 359-6639
18 Hearthstone Dr Medfield MA (02052) *(G-12918)*
Quinn Manufacturing Inc..........978 524-0310
149 Village Post Rd Danvers MA (01923) *(G-10248)*
Quinnipiac Valley Times..........203 675-9483
2301 State St Hamden CT (06517) *(G-1778)*
Quinonez Enterprises, Providence *Also called Quinonez Mynor (G-21104)*
Quinonez Mynor..........401 751-9292
249 Admiral St Providence RI (02908) *(G-21104)*
Quintal Burial Vaults..........508 669-5717
3425 Sharps Lot Rd Dighton MA (02715) *(G-10338)*
Quirion Luc (PA)..........802 673-8386
96 Western Ave Newport VT (05855) *(G-22205)*
Quirk Wire Co Inc..........508 867-3155
146 E Main St West Brookfield MA (01585) *(G-16473)*
Quoddy Tides Inc..........207 853-4806
123 Water St Eastport ME (04631) *(G-5995)*
Quoddy Tides Newspaper, Eastport *Also called Quoddy Tides Inc (G-5995)*
Quonset Point Facility, North Kingstown *Also called Electric Boat Corporation (G-20707)*
R & B Apparel Plus LLC..........860 333-1757
78 Plaza Ct Groton CT (06340) *(G-1685)*
R & B Splicer Systems Inc..........508 580-3500
145 Bodwell St Avon MA (02322) *(G-7893)*
R & D Manufacturing Company..........401 305-7662
60 Dunnell Ln Pawtucket RI (02860) *(G-20887)*
R & D Precision Inc..........203 284-3396
63 N Cherry St Ste 1 Wallingford CT (06492) *(G-4792)*
R & D Services LLC..........860 628-5205
45 Old Turnpike Rd Southington CT (06489) *(G-4072)*
R & D Technologies Inc..........401 885-6400
60 Romano Vineyard Way North Kingstown RI (02852) *(G-20734)*
R & D Tl Engrg Four-Slide Prod, Cranston *Also called R & D Tl Engrg Four-Slide Prod (G-20276)*
R & D Tl Engrg Four-Slide Prod..........401 942-9710
101 Libera St Cranston RI (02920) *(G-20276)*
R & H Communications Inc (PA)..........781 893-6221
187 Lexington St Ste 4 Waltham MA (02452) *(G-16181)*
R & I Manufacturing Co..........860 589-6364
118 Napco Dr Terryville CT (06786) *(G-4489)*
R & J Tool Inc (PA)..........603 366-4925
945 Scenic Rd Laconia NH (03246) *(G-18581)*
R & K Cookies LLC..........860 613-2893
9 Smith Farm Rd Cromwell CT (06416) *(G-858)*
R & K Machine..........603 528-0221
53 Blaisdell Ave Laconia NH (03246) *(G-18582)*
R & M Precision Machine..........508 678-2488
130 Moorland St Fall River MA (02724) *(G-10750)*
R & N Inc..........207 948-2613
557 Albion Rd Unity ME (04988) *(G-7118)*
R & P Plastics LLC..........978 297-1115
202 Spruce St Winchendon MA (01475) *(G-17079)*
R & R Corrugated Container Inc..........860 584-1194
360 Minor St Bristol CT (06010) *(G-601)*
R & R Lumber Company Inc..........207 848-3726
1435 Fuller Rd Carmel ME (04419) *(G-5893)*
R & R Machine, Blackstone *Also called Roland Le Gare (G-8315)*
R & R Machine Industries Inc..........401 766-2505
147 Industrial Dr North Smithfield RI (02896) *(G-20795)*
R & R McHy & Rebuilding Co, Bristol *Also called Richard Dahlen (G-606)*
R & R Pallet Corp..........203 272-2784
120 Schoolhouse Rd Cheshire CT (06410) *(G-755)*
R & R Polishing Co Inc..........401 831-6335
37 Fletcher Ave Cranston RI (02920) *(G-20277)*
R & S Welding, Ashland *Also called Raymond Spinazzola (G-7667)*
R & W Engraving Inc..........207 286-3020
30 Morin St Biddeford ME (04005) *(G-5760)*
R & W Gibson Corp..........802 864-4791
208 White St South Burlington VT (05403) *(G-22463)*
R A Cummings Inc..........207 777-7100
82 Goldthwaite Rd Auburn ME (04210) *(G-5594)*
R A Lalli, Stratford *Also called Jgs Properties LLC (G-4425)*
R A Thomas Logging Inc..........207 876-2722
58 Butter St Guilford ME (04443) *(G-6161)*
R A Tool Co..........203 877-2998
230 Woodmont Rd Ste Y Milford CT (06460) *(G-2346)*
R and L Amey, Pittsburg *Also called Roy E Amey (G-19495)*
R B C, Oxford *Also called Roller Bearing Co Amer Inc (G-3423)*
R B L Holdings Inc..........401 821-2200
6 Jefferson Dr Coventry RI (02816) *(G-20163)*
R B Logging Inc..........207 398-3176
1327 Main St Saint Francis ME (04774) *(G-6868)*

R B Machine Co Inc 508 830-0567
5 Raffaele Rd Plymouth MA (02360) ***(G-14578)***
R C Brayshaw & Co Inc (PA) 603 456-3101
45 Waterloo St Warner NH (03278) ***(G-19929)***
R D Fence Co, North Billerica *Also called RD Contractors Inc* ***(G-13859)***
R D S Machine Inc (PA) 603 863-4131
3 Putnam Rd Newport NH (03773) ***(G-19354)***
R D Webb Co Inc 508 650-0110
6 Huron Dr Ste 3a Natick MA (01760) ***(G-13276)***
R Ducharme Inc 413 534-4516
451 Mckinstry Ave Chicopee MA (01020) ***(G-10055)***
R E F Machine Company Inc 860 349-9344
24 West St Middlefield CT (06455) ***(G-2164)***
R E K Management Inc 508 775-3005
33 Route 28 West Harwich MA (02671) ***(G-16481)***
R E M, Southington *Also called REM Chemicals Inc* ***(G-4074)***
R F Consulting LLC (PA) 207 233-8846
192 Lower Flying Point Rd Freeport ME (04032) ***(G-6085)***
R F H Company Inc 203 853-2863
79 Rockland Rd Ste 3 Norwalk CT (06854) ***(G-3226)***
R F Hunter Co Inc 603 742-9565
113 Crosby Rd Ste 9 Dover NH (03820) ***(G-18048)***
R F Integration Inc (PA) 978 654-6770
85 Rangeway Rd Ste 1 North Billerica MA (01862) ***(G-13857)***
R F Mc Manus Company Inc 617 241-8081
7 Sherman St Charlestown MA (02129) ***(G-9842)***
R Filion Manufacturing Inc 603 865-1893
931 John Stark Hwy Newport NH (03773) ***(G-19355)***
R G J Associates Inc 978 443-7642
11 Hop Brook Ln Sudbury MA (01776) ***(G-15667)***
R G L Inc 860 653-7254
121 Rainbow Rd East Granby CT (06026) ***(G-1142)***
R G M Metals Inc 978 562-9773
5 Parmenter Rd Hudson MA (01749) ***(G-11810)***
R H Cheney Inc 508 222-7300
25 Townsend Rd Attleboro MA (02703) ***(G-7783)***
R H Foster Inc 207 868-2983
83 Main St Van Buren ME (04785) ***(G-7123)***
R H Le Mieur Corp 978 939-8741
638 Patriots Rd Templeton MA (01468) ***(G-15804)***
R H M Group Inc 978 745-4710
51 Park St Beverly MA (01915) ***(G-8169)***
R H Murphy Co Inc 603 889-2255
3 Howe Dr Ste 3 # 3 Amherst NH (03031) ***(G-17583)***
R H Spencer Company 978 463-0433
141 Main St Byfield MA (01922) ***(G-9364)***
R H Travers Company 802 496-5205
200 Burnt Mountain Rd Warren VT (05674) ***(G-22578)***
R H Wales & Son Inc 207 925-1363
376 Mcneil Rd Fryeburg ME (04037) ***(G-6102)***
R Hueter Co 978 927-3482
416 Cabot St Beverly MA (01915) ***(G-8170)***
R I Baker Co Inc (PA) 413 663-3791
163 River Rd Clarksburg MA (01247) ***(G-10075)***
R I Heat Treating Co Inc 401 467-9200
81 Aldrich St Providence RI (02905) ***(G-21105)***
R J Brass Inc 860 793-2336
26 Ashford Rd Plainville CT (06062) ***(G-3513)***
R J H Printing Inc 401 885-6262
6770 Post Rd North Kingstown RI (02852) ***(G-20735)***
R J Shepherd Co Inc 781 447-5768
7 Marble St Whitman MA (02382) ***(G-16927)***
R John Wright Dolls Inc 802 447-7072
2402 West Rd Bennington VT (05201) ***(G-21690)***
R K Machine Company LLC 860 224-7545
200 Myrtle St New Britain CT (06053) ***(G-2567)***
R K Solutions Inc 413 351-1401
81 Ramah Cir S Ste 1 Agawam MA (01001) ***(G-7449)***
R L Balla Inc 603 835-6529
338 Beryl Mountain Rd South Acworth NH (03607) ***(G-19854)***
R L Barry Inc 508 226-3350
60 Walton St Attleboro MA (02703) ***(G-7784)***
R L Cook Timber Harvesting 603 239-6424
811 Manning Hill Rd Winchester NH (03470) ***(G-19994)***
R L Fisher Inc 860 951-8110
30 Bartholomew Ave Hartford CT (06106) ***(G-1865)***
R L Hachey Company 781 891-4237
16 Pine Hill Cir Waltham MA (02451) ***(G-16182)***
R L Turick Co Inc 860 693-2230
186 Main St New Hartford CT (06057) ***(G-2646)***
R M Electronics, Methuen *Also called An Electronic Instrumentation* ***(G-13011)***
R M Machine LLC 413 331-0576
32 Dulong Cir Chicopee MA (01022) ***(G-10056)***
R Moody Machine & Fabrication 413 773-3329
667 River Rd Deerfield MA (01342) ***(G-10303)***
R Murphy Company Inc 978 772-3481
13 Groton Harvard Rd Ayer MA (01432) ***(G-7935)***
R N Haskins Printing Inc 207 465-2155
1795 Pond Rd Sidney ME (04330) ***(G-6964)***

R P Woodworking Inc 508 987-3722
4 Pioneer Dr North Oxford MA (01537) ***(G-13974)***
R Pepin & Sons Inc 207 324-6125
59 Shaw Rd Sanford ME (04073) ***(G-6886)***
R R Donnelley & Sons Company 860 649-5570
151 Redstone Rd Manchester CT (06042) ***(G-2040)***
R R Donnelley & Sons Company 617 345-4300
20 Custom House St # 650 Boston MA (02110) ***(G-8806)***
R R Donnelley & Sons Company 860 773-6140
60 Security Dr Avon CT (06001) ***(G-43)***
R R Donnelley & Sons Company 617 360-2000
65 Sprague St Hyde Park MA (02136) ***(G-11877)***
R R I, Billerica *Also called Resonance Research Inc* ***(G-8291)***
R R Leduc Corp 413 536-4329
100 Bobala Rd Holyoke MA (01040) ***(G-11649)***
R R Sprinkler Inc 802 868-2423
28 Canada St Swanton VT (05488) ***(G-22535)***
R R Venture 781 431-6170
25 Paine St Wellesley MA (02481) ***(G-16382)***
R S D Graphics Inc 207 247-6430
158 Main St East Waterboro ME (04030) ***(G-5986)***
R S Enterprise, West Granby *Also called Jerome Ridel* ***(G-5049)***
R S Nasarian, Boston *Also called RS Nazarian Inc* ***(G-8829)***
R S Pidacks Inc 207 897-4622
1801 Federal Rd Livermore ME (04253) ***(G-6376)***
R T Clark Manufacturing Inc 800 921-4330
104 Sterling St Bldg C Clinton MA (01510) ***(G-10092)***
R T G, Manchester *Also called K & G Corp* ***(G-2015)***
R T R, Stockbridge *Also called Rtr Technologies Inc* ***(G-15551)***
R W E Inc 860 974-1101
91 Highland Dr Putnam CT (06260) ***(G-3628)***
R W Hatfield Company Inc (PA) 978 521-2600
10 Avco Rd Ste 1 Haverhill MA (01835) ***(G-11466)***
R Walters Foods 978 646-8950
144 Pine St Danvers MA (01923) ***(G-10249)***
R Woodworking Larson Inc 860 646-7904
192 Sheldon Rd Manchester CT (06042) ***(G-2041)***
R&B Powder Coating LLC 802 287-2300
60 Firehouse Ln Poultney VT (05764) ***(G-22275)***
R&R Logging Forest Management 207 483-4612
Ridge Rd Addison ME (04606) ***(G-5510)***
R&R Sweeping Services Inc 508 586-5705
6 Winterfield Dr East Bridgewater MA (02333) ***(G-10419)***
R&R Tool & Die LLC 860 627-9197
94 Newberry Rd East Windsor CT (06088) ***(G-1299)***
R&V Industries Inc 207 324-5200
90 Community Dr Sanford ME (04073) ***(G-6887)***
R-D Mfg Inc 860 739-3986
6 Colton Rd East Lyme CT (06333) ***(G-1273)***
R.A.w, Somerville *Also called Qrsts LLC* ***(G-15208)***
R2b Inc 207 797-0019
94 Abby Ln Portland ME (04103) ***(G-6719)***
Ra Pharmaceuticals Inc 617 401-4060
87 Cambridgepark Dr Cambridge MA (02140) ***(G-9624)***
RA Smythe LLC 860 398-5764
439 Higby Rd Middletown CT (06457) ***(G-2216)***
Racecar Jewelry Co Inc 401 475-5701
19 Mendon Ave Pawtucket RI (02861) ***(G-20888)***
Racemaker Press 617 391-0911
39 Church St Boston MA (02116) ***(G-8807)***
Rachad Fuel Inc 781 273-0292
161 Bedford St Burlington MA (01803) ***(G-9328)***
Rachels Table LLC 401 949-5333
37 Lark Industrial Pkwy H Greenville RI (02828) ***(G-20472)***
Rachiotek LLC 407 923-0721
70 Walnut St Wellesley MA (02481) ***(G-16383)***
Racing Mart Fuels LLC 508 878-7664
27 Canal St Nashua NH (03064) ***(G-19243)***
Racing Times 203 298-2899
428 Main St Wallingford CT (06492) ***(G-4793)***
Rack Attack USA LLP 508 665-4361
745 Worcester Rd Framingham MA (01701) ***(G-10998)***
Rackliffe Pottery Inc 207 374-2297
Ellsworth Rd Rr 172 Blue Hill ME (04614) ***(G-5773)***
Radar Technology Inc 978 463-6064
2 New Pasture Rd Newburyport MA (01950) ***(G-13526)***
Radcliff Wire Inc 312 876-1754
97 Ronzo Rd Bristol CT (06010) ***(G-602)***
Radeco of Ct Inc 860 564-1220
17 West Pkwy Plainfield CT (06374) ***(G-3456)***
Radenna LLC 781 248-8826
60 1/2 Cold Spring Rd Westford MA (01886) ***(G-16787)***
Rader Industries Inc 203 334-6739
115 Island Brook Ave Bridgeport CT (06606) ***(G-478)***
Radiall Usa Inc 203 776-2813
777 Northrop Rd Wallingford CT (06492) ***(G-4794)***
Radiation Monitoring Dvcs Inc (HQ) 617 668-6800
44 Hunt St Ste 2 Watertown MA (02472) ***(G-16310)***
Radical Computing Corporation 860 953-0240
705 N Mountain Rd A210 Newington CT (06111) ***(G-2897)***

ALPHABETIC

Radio Act Corporation 617 731-6542
101 Winthrop Rd Brookline MA (02445) ***(G-9218)***
Radio Engineering Assoc Inc 978 597-0010
79 Tyler Rd Townsend MA (01469) ***(G-15873)***
Radio Frequency Company Inc 508 376-9555
150 Dover Rd Millis MA (02054) ***(G-13186)***
Radio Frequency Systems, Meriden *Also called RFS Americas* ***(G-2125)***
Radio Frequency Systems Inc (HQ) 203 630-3311
200 Pond View Dr Meriden CT (06450) ***(G-2122)***
Radio Systems, North Reading *Also called Big Pond Wireless LLC* ***(G-13979)***
Radio Waves, North Billerica *Also called Infinite Electronics Intl Inc* ***(G-13827)***
Radiodetection, Raymond *Also called SPX Corporation* ***(G-6774)***
Radius Health Inc (PA) 617 551-4000
950 Winter St Waltham MA (02451) ***(G-16183)***
Radius Medical Tech Inc 978 263-4466
46 Edson St Stow MA (01775) ***(G-15635)***
Radius Mfg & Fabrication Inc 603 529-0801
164 Concord Stage Rd Weare NH (03281) ***(G-19939)***
Radius Pipesystems Corp 857 263-7161
465 Commonwealth Ave # 2 Boston MA (02215) ***(G-8808)***
Radon Environmental Monitoring, Medway *Also called Environmental Svcs Group Inc* ***(G-12959)***
Radonaway, Haverhill *Also called Spruce Environmental Tech Inc* ***(G-11475)***
Rae Js 413 625-9228
2231 Mohawk Trl Shelburne Falls MA (01370) ***(G-15075)***
Raf Electronic Hardware, Seymour *Also called Matthew Warren Inc* ***(G-3756)***
Rag and Bone Bindery Ltd 401 728-0762
1088 Main St Frnt 1 Pawtucket RI (02860) ***(G-20889)***
Ragged Hill Incorporated 978 939-5712
147 Gardner Rd East Templeton MA (01438) ***(G-10520)***
Ragozzino Foods Inc (PA) 203 238-2553
10 Ames Ave Meriden CT (06451) ***(G-2123)***
Raid Inc 978 683-6444
200 Brickstone Sq Ste 302 Andover MA (01810) ***(G-7591)***
Railing Pro Inc 401 539-7998
5 Summit Rd Hope Valley RI (02832) ***(G-20486)***
Railings Unlimited 508 679-5678
20 Weybosset St Fall River MA (02723) ***(G-10751)***
Rain Carbon Inc (HQ) 203 406-0535
10 Signal Rd Stamford CT (06902) ***(G-4296)***
Rain Cii Carbon LLC 203 406-0535
10 Signal Rd Stamford CT (06902) ***(G-4297)***
Rainbow Graphics Inc 860 646-8997
118 Adams St S Manchester CT (06040) ***(G-2042)***
Rainbow Shack 413 743-4031
85 Summer St Ste 3 Adams MA (01220) ***(G-7414)***
Rainville Printing Entps Inc 603 485-3422
272 Cross Rd Pembroke NH (03275) ***(G-19463)***
Rainwise Inc 800 762-5723
18 River Field Rd Trenton ME (04605) ***(G-7101)***
Raitto Engineering & Mfg Inc 413 477-6637
36 Mill St Wheelwright MA (01094) ***(G-16908)***
Raj Communications Ltd 802 658-4961
83 Holly Ct Williston VT (05495) ***(G-22687)***
Rajessa LLC 508 540-4420
117 Bernard E Saint Jean East Falmouth MA (02536) ***(G-10447)***
Ralco Industries Inc (PA) 401 765-1000
1112 River St Woonsocket RI (02895) ***(G-21577)***
Ralph Curcio Co Inc 978 632-1120
372 E Brdway Bldg 372to # 372 Gardner MA (01440) ***(G-11124)***
Ralph L Osgood Inc 603 543-1703
144 Grissom Ln Claremont NH (03743) ***(G-17859)***
Ralph Seaver 508 892-9486
51 Redfield Rd Cherry Valley MA (01611) ***(G-9976)***
Ralph Traynham 978 667-0977
258 Salem Rd Ste 10 Billerica MA (01821) ***(G-8282)***
Ralph's Blacksmith Shop, Northampton *Also called Smj Metal Co Inc* ***(G-14021)***
Ram Belting Company Inc 860 438-7029
100 Production Ct Ste 3 New Britain CT (06051) ***(G-2568)***
Ram Printing Incorporated (PA) 603 382-7045
Rr 111 East Hampstead NH (03826) ***(G-18082)***
Ram Printing Incorporated 603 382-3400
3 Commerce Park Dr East Hampstead NH (03826) ***(G-18083)***
Ram Technologies LLC 203 453-3916
29 Soundview Rd Ste 12 Guilford CT (06437) ***(G-1715)***
Ramar-Hall Inc 860 349-1081
26 Old Indian Trl Middlefield CT (06455) ***(G-2165)***
Ramblers Way Farm Inc 888 793-9665
6 Commerce Dr Kennebunk ME (04043) ***(G-6240)***
Ramblers Way Farm Inc 207 699-4600
75 Market St Ste 101 Portland ME (04101) ***(G-6720)***
Ramblers Way Farm Inc 603 319-5141
100 Market St Unit 100 # 100 Portsmouth NH (03801) ***(G-19612)***
Ramco Inc 401 739-4343
205 Hallene Rd Unit 207 Warwick RI (02886) ***(G-21409)***
Ramco Machine LLC 978 948-3778
27 Turcotte Memorial Dr Rowley MA (01969) ***(G-14863)***
Ramdial Parts and Services LLC 860 296-5175
18 Adelaide St Hartford CT (06114) ***(G-1866)***

Ramdy Corporation 860 274-3713
40 Mclennan Dr Oakville CT (06779) ***(G-3301)***
Rampage LLC 203 930-1022
38 Palisade Ave Trumbull CT (06611) ***(G-4630)***
Ramsays Welding & Machine Inc 207 794-8839
289 Enfield Rd Lincoln ME (04457) ***(G-6359)***
Ramsbottom Printing Inc 508 730-2220
135 Waldron Rd Fall River MA (02720) ***(G-10752)***
Ramtel Corporation 401 231-3340
115 Railroad Ave Johnston RI (02919) ***(G-20533)***
Ran Woodworking 508 248-4818
160 Center Depot Rd Charlton MA (01507) ***(G-9855)***
Ran/All Metal Technology Inc 603 668-1907
7a E Point Dr Hooksett NH (03106) ***(G-18357)***
Rancloes Logging LLC 603 237-4474
822 Hollow Rd Stewartstown NH (03576) ***(G-19863)***
Rancourt & Co Shoecrafters Inc 207 782-1577
9 Bridge St Lewiston ME (04240) ***(G-6318)***
Rancourt & Co., Lewiston *Also called Rancourt & Co Shoecrafters Inc* ***(G-6318)***
Rand Barthel Treasurer 508 473-3305
50 Asylum St Mendon MA (01756) ***(G-12994)***
Rand Corporation 617 338-2059
20 Park Plz Ste 920 Boston MA (02116) ***(G-8809)***
Rand Grantwriting 617 524-5367
49 Orchardhill Rd Jamaica Plain MA (02130) ***(G-11948)***
Rand Kevin 802 454-1440
656 Vermont Route 14 Plainfield VT (05667) ***(G-22269)***
Rand Machine & Fabrication Co 203 272-1352
1486 Highland Ave Ste 2 Cheshire CT (06410) ***(G-756)***
Rand Media Co LLC 203 226-8727
265 Post Rd W Westport CT (06880) ***(G-5225)***
Rand Sheaves & Pulleys LLC 203 272-1352
1486 Highland Ave Cheshire CT (06410) ***(G-757)***
Rand Whitney 860 354-6063
7 Nutmeg Dr New Milford CT (06776) ***(G-2825)***
Rand Whitney-Greenwood St, Worcester *Also called Rand-Whitney Container LLC* ***(G-17451)***
Rand-Whitney Container Board L 860 848-1900
1 Rand Whitney Way Worcester MA (01607) ***(G-17449)***
Rand-Whitney Container LLC 603 822-7300
15 Stonewall Dr Dover NH (03820) ***(G-18049)***
Rand-Whitney Container LLC (HQ) 508 890-7000
1 Rand Whitney Way Worcester MA (01607) ***(G-17450)***
Rand-Whitney Container LLC 774 420-2425
2 Rand Whitney Way Worcester MA (01607) ***(G-17451)***
Rand-Whitney Container LLC 401 729-7900
455 Narragansett Park Dr Pawtucket RI (02861) ***(G-20890)***
Rand-Whitney Container Newtown, Newtown *Also called Rand-Whitney Group LLC* ***(G-2934)***
Rand-Whitney Group LLC 203 426-5871
1 Edmund Rd Newtown CT (06470) ***(G-2934)***
Rand-Whitney Group LLC (HQ) 508 791-2301
1 Rand Whitney Way Worcester MA (01607) ***(G-17452)***
Rand-Whitney Recycling LLC 860 848-1900
370 Route 163 Montville CT (06353) ***(G-2422)***
Randolph Engineering Inc 781 961-6070
26 Thomas Patten Dr Randolph MA (02368) ***(G-14695)***
Randolph Sunglasses, Randolph *Also called Randolph Engineering Inc* ***(G-14695)***
Ranfac Corp 508 588-4400
30 Doherty Ave Ste A Avon MA (02322) ***(G-7894)***
Ranger Automation Systems Inc 508 842-6500
9 Railroad Ave Millbury MA (01527) ***(G-13174)***
Ranor Inc 978 874-0591
1 Bella Dr Westminster MA (01473) ***(G-16812)***
Rapid Assault Tools, South Portland *Also called Granite Mountain Inds LLC* ***(G-7028)***
Rapid Finishing Corp 603 889-4234
43 Simon St Nashua NH (03060) ***(G-19244)***
Rapid Group 603 821-7300
15 Charron Ave Nashua NH (03063) ***(G-19245)***
Rapid Manufacturing Group LLC 603 402-4020
15 Charron Ave Nashua NH (03063) ***(G-19246)***
Rapid Micro Biosystems Inc (PA) 978 349-3200
1001 Pawtucket Blvd 280 Lowell MA (01854) ***(G-12425)***
Rapid Mold Evolution 603 673-1027
27 Ox Brook Woods Rd Milford NH (03055) ***(G-19073)***
Rapid Reproduction, Wilmington *Also called Duckhill River Corp* ***(G-16997)***
Rapid Sheet Metal LLC 603 821-5300
15 Charron Ave Nashua NH (03063) ***(G-19247)***
Rapid7 Inc (PA) 617 247-1717
120 Causeway St Ste 400 Boston MA (02114) ***(G-8810)***
Rapidex 860 285-8818
875 Marshall Phelps Rd Windsor CT (06095) ***(G-5357)***
Rapidprint, Middletown *Also called Bidwell Industrial Group Inc* ***(G-2178)***
Rapiscan Systems Inc 866 430-1913
23 Frontage Rd Andover MA (01810) ***(G-7592)***
Rare Beauty Brands Inc 888 243-0646
83 Morse St Ste 8a Norwood MA (02062) ***(G-14191)***
Rare Reminder Incorporated 860 563-9386
222 Dividend Rd Rocky Hill CT (06067) ***(G-3728)***

Raredon Resources Inc 413 586-0941
30 N Maple St Ste 2 Florence MA (01062) *(G-10868)*
Ras-Tech, Brentwood *Also called Recycled Asp Shingle Tech LLC (G-17757)*
Rathbuns Sawmill Inc 401 397-3996
239 Plain Rd West Greenwich RI (02817) *(G-21464)*
Rau Brothers Inc 978 297-1381
480 Central St Winchendon MA (01475) *(G-17080)*
Ravago Americas LLC 203 855-6000
10 Westport Rd Wilton CT (06897) *(G-5301)*
Ravco Wood Products, Central Village *Also called Guy Ravenelle (G-706)*
Rave Brothers LLC 207 773-7727
443b Western Ave South Portland ME (04106) *(G-7038)*
Rave X, South Portland *Also called Rave Brothers LLC (G-7038)*
Raven Creative Inc 781 476-5529
15a Sewall St Marblehead MA (01945) *(G-12691)*
Raven Technology LLC 207 729-7904
14 Industrial Pkwy Brunswick ME (04011) *(G-5844)*
Raven Ventures LLC, North Chelmsford *Also called Courier Communications LLC (G-13887)*
Raw Diamond Inc 857 222-5601
10 Kirkland Pl Cambridge MA (02138) *(G-9625)*
Raw Sea Foods Inc 508 673-0111
481 Currant Rd Fall River MA (02720) *(G-10753)*
Rawson Development Inc 860 928-4536
205 Munyan Rd Putnam CT (06260) *(G-3629)*
Rawson Manufacturing Inc (PA) 860 928-4458
99 Canal St Putnam CT (06260) *(G-3630)*
Ray Green Corp 707 544-2662
115 E Putnam Ave Ste 1 Greenwich CT (06830) *(G-1640)*
Ray Machine Corporation 860 582-8202
84 Town Hill Rd Terryville CT (06786) *(G-4490)*
Ray Scituate Precast Con Corp 781 837-1747
120 Clay Pit Rd Marshfield MA (02050) *(G-12866)*
Ray's Extrusion Dies Tubing Co, Swanton *Also called Raymond Gadues Inc (G-22536)*
Rayco Inc 860 357-4693
206 Newington Ave Fl 2 New Britain CT (06051) *(G-2569)*
Rayco Inc 978 388-1039
125 Cedar St Amesbury MA (01913) *(G-7504)*
Rayco Metal Finishing Inc 860 347-7434
134 Mill St Middletown CT (06457) *(G-2217)*
Rayes Mustard Mill 207 853-4451
83 Washington St Eastport ME (04631) *(G-5996)*
Rayflex Company Inc 203 336-2173
1061 Howard Ave Bridgeport CT (06605) *(G-479)*
Raym-Co Inc 860 678-8292
62 Spring Ln Farmington CT (06032) *(G-1510)*
Raymon Tool LLC 203 248-2199
79 Rossotto Dr Hamden CT (06514) *(G-1779)*
Raymond Agler 978 281-5048
16 Pleasant St Gloucester MA (01930) *(G-11206)*
Raymond Gadues Inc 802 868-2033
Rr 78 Box East Swanton VT (05488) *(G-22536)*
Raymond J Bykowski 203 271-2385
1685 Reinhard Rd Cheshire CT (06410) *(G-758)*
Raymond L Martin, Webster *Also called Linx Consulting LLC (G-16347)*
Raymond Reynolds Welding 802 879-4650
15 West St Essex Junction VT (05452) *(G-21955)*
Raymond Spinazzola 508 881-3089
13 Forest Ave Ashland MA (01721) *(G-7667)*
Raymond Thibault 508 281-5500
155 N Pough Rd Walpole MA (02081) *(G-16008)*
Raynham Tool & Die Inc 508 822-4489
150 Broadway Raynham MA (02767) *(G-14728)*
Raypax Manufacturing Co Inc 203 758-7416
21 Tremont St Waterbury CT (06708) *(G-4949)*
Rays Newspapers 401 728-1364
9 Maplecrest Dr Pawtucket RI (02861) *(G-20891)*
Raysecur Inc (PA) 844 729-7328
125 Cambridgepark Dr # 301 Cambridge MA (02140) *(G-9626)*
Raysolution LLC 765 714-0645
43 Linwood St Andover MA (01810) *(G-7593)*
Raytech Industries Div, Middletown *Also called Lyman Products Corporation (G-2202)*
Raytheon Arabian Systems Co 978 858 4547
880 Technology Park Dr Billerica MA (01821) *(G-8283)*
Raytheon Company 978 470-5000
350 Lowell St Andover MA (01810) *(G-7594)*
Raytheon Company (PA) 781 522-3000
870 Winter St Waltham MA (02451) *(G-16184)*
Raytheon Company 978 440-1000
1001 Boston Post Rd E Marlborough MA (01752) *(G-12812)*
Raytheon Company 781 522-3000
465 Centre St Quincy MA (02169) *(G-14653)*
Raytheon Company 401 847-8000
1847 W Main Rd Portsmouth RI (02871) *(G-20938)*
Raytheon Company 781 522-3000
362 Lowell St Andover MA (01810) *(G-7595)*
Raytheon Company 413 494-8042
540 Merrill Rd Pittsfield MA (01201) *(G-14505)*
Raytheon Company 860 446-4900
11 Main St Ste 3 Mystic CT (06355) *(G-2449)*
Raytheon Company 978 858-5000
50 Apple Hill Dr Tewksbury MA (01876) *(G-15828)*
Raytheon Company 978 256-6054
49 Amble Rd Chelmsford MA (01824) *(G-9925)*
Raytheon Company 508 877-5231
6 Huron Dr Framingham MA (01701) *(G-10999)*
Raytheon Company 310 647-9438
1001 Boston Post Rd E Marlborough MA (01752) *(G-12813)*
Raytheon Company 781 862-6800
420 Bedford St Ste 120 Lexington MA (02420) *(G-12258)*
Raytheon Company 781 933-1863
235 Presidential Way Woburn MA (01801) *(G-17279)*
Raytheon Company 339 645-6000
225 Presidential Way Woburn MA (01801) *(G-17280)*
Raytheon Company 603 635-6800
50 Bush Hill Rd Pelham NH (03076) *(G-19444)*
Raytheon Company 978 858-5000
50 Apple Hill Dr Tewksbury MA (01876) *(G-15829)*
Raytheon Company 508 490-1000
1001 Boston Post Rd E Marlborough MA (01752) *(G-12814)*
Raytheon Company 978 470-6922
350 Lowell St Andover MA (01810) *(G-7596)*
Raytheon Company 978 858-4700
50 Apple Hill Dr Tewksbury MA (01876) *(G-15830)*
Raytheon Company 978 313-0201
90 Salem Rd North Billerica MA (01862) *(G-13858)*
Raytheon European MGT Systems 978 858-4547
880 Technology Park Dr Billerica MA (01821) *(G-8284)*
Raytheon International Inc (PA) 781 522-3000
870 Winter St Waltham MA (02451) *(G-16185)*
Raytheon Intl Support Co 978 858-4547
880 Technology Park Dr Billerica MA (01821) *(G-8285)*
Raytheon Italy Liaison Company 978 684-5300
358 Lowell St Andover MA (01810) *(G-7597)*
Raytheon Korean Support Co 978 858-4547
880 Technology Park Dr Billerica MA (01821) *(G-8286)*
Raytheon Lgstics Spport Trning (HQ) 310 647-9438
180 Hartwell Rd Bedford MA (01730) *(G-8005)*
Raytheon Middle E Systems Co 978 858-4547
880 Technology Park Dr Billerica MA (01821) *(G-8287)*
Raytheon Radar Ltd 978 858-4547
880 Technology Park Dr Billerica MA (01821) *(G-8288)*
Raytheon Sutheast Asia Systems (HQ) 978 470-5000
880 Technology Park Dr Billerica MA (01821) *(G-8289)*
Raytheon Systems Support Co (HQ) 978 851-2134
50 Apple Hill Dr Tewksbury MA (01876) *(G-15831)*
Raytheon Tchnical ADM Svcs Ltd 978 858-4547
880 Technology Park Dr Billerica MA (01821) *(G-8290)*
Raywatch Inc 401 338-2211
107 Montclair Ave 2 West Roxbury MA (02132) *(G-16502)*
Razor Tool Inc 781 654-1582
6 Adele Rd Woburn MA (01801) *(G-17281)*
RB Graphics Inc 603 624-4025
45 Londonderry Tpke Hooksett NH (03106) *(G-18358)*
Rba, Narragansett *Also called Rocky Brook Associates Inc (G-20647)*
Rbc Bearings Incorporated (PA) 203 267-7001
102 Willenbrock Rd Oxford CT (06478) *(G-3421)*
Rbc Industries Inc 401 941-3000
80 Cypress St Warwick RI (02888) *(G-21410)*
Rbc Linear Precision Pdts Inc 203 255-1511
60 Round Hill Rd Fairfield CT (06824) *(G-1450)*
Rbc Prcision Pdts - Bremen Inc (HQ) 203 267-7001
102 Willenbrock Rd Oxford CT (06478) *(G-3422)*
Rbd Electronics Inc (PA) 413 442-1111
63 Flansburg Ave Dalton MA (01226) *(G-10182)*
Rbf Frozen Desserts LLC 516 474-6488
240 Park Rd Ste 3 West Hartford CT (06119) *(G-5092)*
Rbw Inc 207 786-2446
113 Nash Rd Windham ME (04062) *(G-7246)*
RC Bigelow Inc (PA) 888 244-3569
201 Black Rock Tpke Fairfield CT (06825) *(G-1451)*
RC Connectors LLC 860 413-2196
146 Hopmeadow St Weatogue CT (06089) *(G-5044)*
Rcd Components LLC (HQ) 603 666-4627
520 E Industrial Park Manchester NH (03109) *(G-18909)*
RCO Renovations Inc 508 668-5524
2 Willow St South Walpole MA (02071) *(G-15320)*
RD Contractors Inc 978 667-6545
220 Boston Rd North Billerica MA (01862) *(G-13859)*
RDF Corporation 603 882-5195
23 Elm Ave Hudson NH (03051) *(G-18432)*
RDS Machine LLC 603 863-4131
248 N Main St Newport NH (03773) *(G-19356)*
RE Kimball & Co Inc 978 388-1826
73 Merrimac St Amesbury MA (01913) *(G-7505)*
Re-Style Your Closets LLC 860 658-9450
86 E Weatogue St Simsbury CT (06070) *(G-3910)*
REA Associates Inc 209 521-2727
325 Boston Rd North Billerica MA (01862) *(G-13860)*
REA Magnet Wire Company Inc 203 738-6100
129 Soundview Rd Guilford CT (06437) *(G-1716)*

A L P H A B E T I C

REA-Craft Press Incorporated....508 543-8710
10 Wall St Foxboro MA (02035) ***(G-10899)***
Reach Distribution Inc....617 542-6466
6 Tide St Boston MA (02210) ***(G-8811)***
Reactel Inc....203 773-0135
315 Peck St Fl 3 New Haven CT (06513) ***(G-2730)***
Ready 2 Run Graphics Signs Inc....508 459-9977
240 Barber Ave Ste R Worcester MA (01606) ***(G-17453)***
Ready 4....857 233-5455
285 3rd St Unit 221 Cambridge MA (02142) ***(G-9627)***
Ready Slump, Cambridge *Also called Verify LLC* ***(G-9694)***
Ready Tool Company (HQ)....860 524-7811
1 Carney Rd West Hartford CT (06110) ***(G-5093)***
Ready4 Print LLC....203 345-0376
2051 Main St Bridgeport CT (06604) ***(G-480)***
Readydock Inc....860 523-9980
46 W Avon Rd Ste 302 Avon CT (06001) ***(G-44)***
Readys Window Products Inc....978 851-3963
98 N Billerica Rd Tewksbury MA (01876) ***(G-15832)***
Real Data Corp....603 669-3822
280 Summer St Fl 8 Boston MA (02210) ***(G-8812)***
Real Estate Guide, Andover *Also called Greatheart Inc* ***(G-7553)***
Real Estate Journal of RI Inc....401 831-7778
1343 Hartford Ave Ste 2 Johnston RI (02919) ***(G-20534)***
Real Good Toys Inc....802 479-2217
22 Gallison Hill Rd # 1 Montpelier VT (05602) ***(G-22159)***
Real Goods Solar Inc....508 992-1416
50 Conduit St New Bedford MA (02745) ***(G-13444)***
Real Pickles Coperative Inc....413 774-2600
311 Wells St Greenfield MA (01301) ***(G-11273)***
Real Women International LLC....212 719-3130
385 Main St S Ste 404 Southbury CT (06488) ***(G-4032)***
Real-Time Analyzers Inc....860 635-9800
362 Industrial Park Rd # 8 Middletown CT (06457) ***(G-2218)***
Realist, The, Somerville *Also called Rosenoff Reports Inc* ***(G-15213)***
Realmaplesyrup.com, Stafford Springs *Also called Balsam Woods Farm* ***(G-4106)***
Realtime Dx Inc....508 479-9818
106 N Hancock St Lexington MA (02420) ***(G-12259)***
Realty Publishing Center Inc....401 331-2505
572 Smith St Providence RI (02908) ***(G-21106)***
Rebars & Mesh Inc....978 374-2244
111 Avco Rd Haverhill MA (01835) ***(G-11467)***
Rebion, Boston *Also called Rebiscan Inc* ***(G-8813)***
Rebiscan Inc....857 600-0982
100 Cambridge St 14 Boston MA (02114) ***(G-8813)***
Reboot Medical Inc....818 621-6554
110 Canal St Fl 4 Lowell MA (01852) ***(G-12426)***
Rebtek Diamnd Blades Bits LLC....802 476-6520
423 E Montpelier Rd Barre VT (05641) ***(G-21637)***
Rec Components, Stafford Springs *Also called Edgewater International LLC* ***(G-4110)***
REc Manufacturing Corp....508 634-7999
50 Mellen St Hopedale MA (01747) ***(G-11681)***
Recall Services Healthwatch....978 369-7253
389 Lindsay Pond Rd Concord MA (01742) ***(G-10155)***
Recognition Awards....401 365-1265
16 Sunnyside Ave Johnston RI (02919) ***(G-20535)***
Recognition Center Inc....508 429-5881
326 Woodland St Holliston MA (01746) ***(G-11598)***
Recognition Products, Lebanon *Also called Ann S Davis* ***(G-1932)***
Recor Welding Center Inc....860 573-1942
86 Gannet Dr Southington CT (06489) ***(G-4073)***
Record Journal, The, Meriden *Also called Southington Citizen* ***(G-2132)***
Record-Journal Newspaper (PA)....203 235-1661
500 S Broad St Ste 2 Meriden CT (06450) ***(G-2124)***
Record-Journal Newspaper....860 536-9577
15 Holmes St Ste 3 Mystic CT (06355) ***(G-2450)***
Recovery Zone, Manchester *Also called Peristere LLC* ***(G-2038)***
Rectorseal....508 673-7561
1244 Davol St Fall River MA (02720) ***(G-10754)***
Rectorseal Corporation....508 673-7561
1244 Davol St Fall River MA (02720) ***(G-10755)***
Recycled Asp Shingle Tech LLC....603 778-1449
50 Pine Rd Brentwood NH (03833) ***(G-17757)***
Recycling Mechanical Neng LLC....603 268-8028
44 Ferry St Allenstown NH (03275) ***(G-17541)***
Red 23 Holdings Inc....603 433-3011
801 Islington St Ste 24 Portsmouth NH (03801) ***(G-19613)***
Red 7 Media LLC (HQ)....203 853-2474
10 Norden Pl Ste 202 Norwalk CT (06855) ***(G-3227)***
Red Apple Cheese LLC (PA)....203 755-5579
27 Siemon Co Dr Ste 231w Watertown CT (06795) ***(G-5021)***
Red Barn Innovations....203 393-0778
8 Tress Rd Prospect CT (06712) ***(G-3595)***
Red Barn Woodworkers....860 379-3158
118 Laurel Way Winsted CT (06098) ***(G-5420)***
Red Brick Clothing Co....603 882-4100
17 Dracut Rd Unit A Hudson NH (03051) ***(G-18433)***
Red Bull LLC....860 519-1018
460 Woodland Ave Bloomfield CT (06002) ***(G-255)***
Red Corp....802 862-4500
180 Queen City Park Rd Burlington VT (05401) ***(G-21806)***
Red Fish-Blue Fish Dye Works....603 692-3900
145 Green St Somersworth NH (03878) ***(G-19846)***
Red Frames Inc (HQ)....617 477-8740
285 Summer St Fl 2 Boston MA (02210) ***(G-8814)***
Red Hat Inc....978 392-1000
314 Little 10 Rd 10th Westford MA (01886) ***(G-16788)***
Red Hat Inc....978 692-3113
3 Lan Dr Ste 100 Westford MA (01886) ***(G-16789)***
Red Hawk Fire & Security LLC....413 568-4709
9 Sullivan Rd Holyoke MA (01040) ***(G-11650)***
Red Lessons Restaurant, Barrington *Also called Song Wind Industries Inc* ***(G-20056)***
Red Mill....207 655-7520
46 Red Mill Rd Casco ME (04015) ***(G-5895)***
Red Mill Graphics Incorporated....978 251-4081
14 Alpha Rd Chelmsford MA (01824) ***(G-9926)***
Red Nun Instrument Corporation....802 758-6000
1627 Middle Rd Bridport VT (05734) ***(G-21759)***
Red Oak Sourcing LLC....401 742-0701
2 Hampshire St Ste 200 Foxborough MA (02035) ***(G-10913)***
Red Oak Winnery LLC....781 558-1702
6 Fox Hollow Dr Saugus MA (01906) ***(G-14994)***
Red Rocket Site 2....860 581-8019
47 Industrial Park Rd Centerbrook CT (06409) ***(G-703)***
Red Rose Desserts....860 603-2670
125 Lebanon Ave Colchester CT (06415) ***(G-807)***
Red Shield Heating Oil, Windham *Also called CN Brown Company* ***(G-7231)***
Red Slate Quarry, Poultney *Also called Taran Bros Inc* ***(G-22278)***
Red Spot Printing....781 894-2211
182 Newton St Waltham MA (02453) ***(G-16186)***
Red Sun Press Inc....617 524-6822
94 Green St Jamaica Plain MA (02130) ***(G-11949)***
Red-E-Made, Brockton *Also called Concord Foods LLC* ***(G-9131)***
Red-E-Mix, Boston *Also called A Lot Bakery Products Inc* ***(G-8332)***
Redco Audio Inc....203 502-7600
1701 Stratford Ave Stratford CT (06615) ***(G-4441)***
Redden Publishing Co LLC....207 236-0767
160 Mistic Ave Rockport ME (04856) ***(G-6825)***
Redding Creamery LLC....203 938-2766
2 Marli Ln Redding CT (06896) ***(G-3651)***
Redemption Rock Brewery Co....978 660-5526
333 Shrewsbury St Worcester MA (01604) ***(G-17454)***
Redemption Rock Brewing Co, Worcester *Also called Redemption Rock Brewery Co* ***(G-17454)***
Redi-Letters Express LLC....508 340-3284
1051 Millbury St Ste B Worcester MA (01607) ***(G-17455)***
Redi-Mix Services Incorporated....508 823-0771
120 Berkley St Taunton MA (02780) ***(G-15778)***
Redi2 Technologies Inc....617 910-3282
211 Congress St 200 Boston MA (02110) ***(G-8815)***
Redifoils LLC....860 342-1500
193 Pickering St Portland CT (06480) ***(G-3573)***
Redimix Companies Inc (HQ)....603 524-4434
3 Eastgate Park Dr Belmont NH (03220) ***(G-17682)***
Redland Brick Inc....860 528-1311
1440 John Fitch Blvd South Windsor CT (06074) ***(G-4007)***
Redshift Bioanalytics Inc....781 345-7300
131 Middlesex Tpke Ste 1 Burlington MA (01803) ***(G-9329)***
Redwheel/Weiser LLC (PA)....978 465-0504
65 Parker St Ste 7 Newburyport MA (01950) ***(G-13527)***
Ree Machine Works Inc....978 663-9105
34 Sullivan Rd Ste 7 North Billerica MA (01862) ***(G-13861)***
Reebok International Ltd (HQ)....781 401-5000
25 Drydock Ave Ste 110 Boston MA (02210) ***(G-8816)***
Reed & Prince Mfg Corp....978 466-6903
272 Nashua St Leominster MA (01453) ***(G-12181)***
Reed & Stefanow Machine Tl Co....860 583-7834
165 Riverside Ave Bristol CT (06010) ***(G-603)***
Reed Allison Group Inc....617 846-1237
144 Wayland Ave Ste 1 Providence RI (02906) ***(G-21107)***
Reed Gowdey Company....401 723-6114
325 Illinois St Central Falls RI (02863) ***(G-20123)***
Reed Machinery Inc (PA)....508 595-9090
10a New Bond St Worcester MA (01606) ***(G-17456)***
Reed Wax, Reading *Also called Roger A Reed Inc* ***(G-14741)***
Reeds Inc....203 890-0557
201 Merritt 7 Norwalk CT (06851) ***(G-3228)***
Reeds Ferry Small Buildings....603 883-1362
3 Tracy Ln Hudson NH (03051) ***(G-18434)***
Reef To Rainforest Media LLC....802 985-9977
140 Webster Rd Shelburne VT (05482) ***(G-22422)***
Reel Easy Inc....978 476-7187
68 Curzon Mill Rd Newburyport MA (01950) ***(G-13528)***
Reeves Coinc....508 222-2877
51 Newcomb St Attleboro MA (02703) ***(G-7785)***
Refco Manufacturing Us Inc....413 746-3094
66 Industry Ave Ste 8 Springfield MA (01104) ***(G-15500)***

Reflek Corp 508 603-6807
240 Crawford St Fall River MA (02724) *(G-10756)*
Reform Biologics LLC 617 871-2101
12 Gill St Ste 4650 Woburn MA (01801) *(G-17282)*
Refresco Beverages US Inc 508 763-3515
65 Chace Rd East Freetown MA (02717) *(G-10458)*
Reg Riendeau Logging, Orleans *Also called Reginald J Riendeau (G-22251)*
Regal Press Inc 207 667-5227
265 Water St Ellsworth ME (04605) *(G-6021)*
Regal Press Incorporated (PA) 781 769-3900
79 Astor Ave Norwood MA (02062) *(G-14192)*
Regal Sleeving & Tubing LLC 603 659-5555
89 Crest Dr Somersworth NH (03878) *(G-19847)*
Regal Sporting Technologies 978 544-6571
100 Prentiss St Orange MA (01364) *(G-14224)*
Regan S Pingree 207 639-5706
989 Park St Phillips ME (04966) *(G-6586)*
Regco Corporation 978 521-4370
46 Rogers Rd Haverhill MA (01835) *(G-11468)*
Regdox Solutions Inc 978 264-4460
1 Tara Blvd Ste 300 Nashua NH (03062) *(G-19248)*
Regen Power Systems LLC 203 328-3045
113 Michael Ln Orange MA (01364) *(G-14225)*
Regenie's All Natural Snacks, Haverhill *Also called Regco Corporation (G-11468)*
Regenocell Therapeutics Inc 508 651-1598
16 David Dr Natick MA (01760) *(G-13277)*
Regent Controls Inc 203 732-6200
29 Lark Industrial Pkwy Greenville RI (02828) *(G-20473)*
Reginald J Riendeau 802 754-6003
109 River Rd Orleans VT (05860) *(G-22251)*
Reginaspices 207 632-5544
47 Edgeworth Ave Portland ME (04103) *(G-6721)*
Regine Printing Co Inc 401 943-3404
208 Laurel Hill Ave Providence RI (02909) *(G-21108)*
Reginold D Ricker 207 234-4811
3222 Western Ave Newburgh ME (04444) *(G-6480)*
Regional Industries Inc 978 750-8787
301 Newbury St 332 Danvers MA (01923) *(G-10250)*
Regional Mfg Specialists Inc 800 805-8991
24 Chenell Dr Concord NH (03301) *(G-17926)*
Regional Spt Media Group LLC 781 871-9271
800 Hingham St Rockland MA (02370) *(G-14821)*
Regional Stairs LLC 860 290-1242
183 Prestige Park Rd East Hartford CT (06108) *(G-1217)*
Register, The, Orleans *Also called Harwich Oracle (G-14234)*
Reheat Co Inc 978 777-4441
10 School St Danvers MA (01923) *(G-10251)*
Rehoboth Reporter, Rehoboth *Also called Target Marketing Group Inc (G-14761)*
Reid Graphics Inc 978 474-1930
7 Connector Rd Andover MA (01810) *(G-7598)*
Reid Publication Inc 603 433-2200
2456 Lafayette Rd Ste 6 Portsmouth NH (03801) *(G-19614)*
Reidville Hydraulics & Mfg Inc 860 496-1133
175 Industrial Ln Torrington CT (06790) *(G-4596)*
Reifenhauser Incorporated 847 669-9972
27 Garden St Ste B Danvers MA (01923) *(G-10252)*
Reify Health Inc 617 861-8261
745 Atlantic Ave Boston MA (02111) *(G-8817)*
Reiley Power, Worcester *Also called Riley Power Inc (G-17459)*
Reilly Foam Corp 860 243-8200
16 Britton Dr Bloomfield CT (06002) *(G-256)*
Reily Foods Company 504 524-6131
100 Charles St Malden MA (02148) *(G-12593)*
Reinforced Structures For Elec 508 754-5316
50 Suffolk St Worcester MA (01604) *(G-17457)*
Rejjee Inc 617 283-5057
7 Newport Rd Apt 8 Cambridge MA (02140) *(G-9628)*
Reklaw Machine Inc 508 699-9255
142 Old Post Rd North Attleboro MA (02760) *(G-13775)*
Reklist LLC 215 518-1637
94 Carver Rd Plymouth MA (02360) *(G-14579)*
Rel-Tech Electronics Inc 203 877-8770
215 Pepes Farm Rd Milford CT (06460) *(G-2347)*
Relays Unlimited, East Granby *Also called Computer Components Inc (G-1123)*
Relcor Inc 561 844-8335
10 Jacobs Meadow Rd East Sandwich MA (02537) *(G-10508)*
Relentless Inc 401 295-2585
100 Davisville Pier Rd North Kingstown RI (02852) *(G-20736)*
Relevant Energy Concepts Inc 413 733-7692
1833 Roosevelt Ave Springfield MA (01109) *(G-15501)*
Reliable 978 230-2689
77 Mill St Winchendon MA (01475) *(G-17081)*
Reliable Electro Plating Inc 508 222-0620
304 W Main St Chartley MA (02712) *(G-9857)*
Reliable Fabrics Inc 617 387-5321
29 Henderson St Everett MA (02149) *(G-10626)*
Reliable Fuel Incorporated 401 624-2903
550 Fish Rd Tiverton RI (02878) *(G-21261)*
Reliable Plating, Chartley *Also called Reliable Electro Plating Inc (G-9857)*
Reliable Plating & Polsg Co 203 366-5261
80 Bishop Ave Bridgeport CT (06607) *(G-481)*
Reliable Plating Co Inc 508 755-9434
523 Southbridge St Worcester MA (01610) *(G-17458)*
Reliable Scales & Systems LLC 860 380-0600
150 Village St Bristol CT (06010) *(G-604)*
Reliable Screw Mch Pdts Inc 978 531-0520
119r Foster St Bldg 6-2 Peabody MA (01960) *(G-14364)*
Reliable Shade & Screen Co 617 776-9538
14 Sterling St 2 Somerville MA (02144) *(G-15209)*
Reliable Silver Corporation 203 574-7732
302 Platts Mill Rd Naugatuck CT (06770) *(G-2493)*
Reliable Spring Company, Bristol *Also called Oscar Jobs (G-588)*
Reliable Tool & Die Inc 203 877-3264
435 Woodmont Rd Milford CT (06460) *(G-2348)*
Reliable Truss & Components In 508 339-8020
71 Maple St Mansfield MA (02048) *(G-12655)*
Reliable Welding & Speed LLC 860 749-3977
85 North St Enfield CT (06082) *(G-1379)*
Reliance Business Systems Inc 203 281-4407
420 Sackett Point Rd # 8 North Haven CT (06473) *(G-3058)*
Reliance Electric Service 413 533-3557
573 S Canal St Holyoke MA (01040) *(G-11651)*
Reliance Engineering, Leominster *Also called Built-Rite Tool and Die Inc (G-12120)*
Reliance Engineering Division, Lancaster *Also called Built-Rite Tool and Die Inc (G-11982)*
Reliance Steel Inc (PA) 802 655-4810
94 S Oak Cir Colchester VT (05446) *(G-21877)*
Reliance Steel Vermont Inc 802 655-4810
94 S Oak Cir Colchester VT (05446) *(G-21878)*
Relocation Information Svc Inc 203 855-1234
69 East Ave Ste 4 Norwalk CT (06851) *(G-3229)*
Relx Inc 860 219-0733
15 Cobbler Way Windsor CT (06095) *(G-5358)*
Relx Inc 203 840-4800
383 Main Ave Fl 3 Norwalk CT (06851) *(G-3230)*
Relx Inc 603 898-9664
8 Industrial Way Bldg C Salem NH (03079) *(G-19762)*
Relx Inc 603 431-7894
361 Hanover St Portsmouth NH (03801) *(G-19615)*
Relx Inc 781 663-5200
50 Hampshire St 5 Cambridge MA (02139) *(G-9629)*
Relx Inc 617 558-4925
313 Washington St Ste 401 Newton MA (02458) *(G-13629)*
Relyco Sales Inc 603 742-0999
121 Broadway Dover NH (03820) *(G-18050)*
REM Chemicals Inc (PA) 860 621-6755
325 W Queen St Southington CT (06489) *(G-4074)*
Rema Dri-Vac Corp 203 847-2464
45 Ruby St Norwalk CT (06850) *(G-3231)*
Remcon-North Corporation 603 279-7091
7-9 Enterprise Ct Meredith NH (03253) *(G-18977)*
Reminc, Middletown *Also called Research Engineering & Mfg Inc (G-20631)*
Reminder Broadcaster 860 875-3366
130 Old Town Rd Vernon CT (06066) *(G-4672)*
Reminder Media, Vernon *Also called Reminder Broadcaster (G-4672)*
Reminder Publications 413 525-3947
280 N Main St Ste 1 East Longmeadow MA (01028) *(G-10491)*
Reminder, The, Coventry *Also called Stevens Publishing Inc (G-20165)*
Remote Technologies Inc (PA) 203 661-2798
57 Old Mill Rd Greenwich CT (06831) *(G-1641)*
Remtec Incorporated 781 762-5732
5 Endicott St Norwood MA (02062) *(G-14193)*
Remtec Incorporated (PA) 781 762-9191
100 Morse St Ste 7 Norwood MA (02062) *(G-14194)*
Renaissance Glassworks Inc 603 882-1779
3 Pine St Ste 1 Nashua NH (03060) *(G-19249)*
Renaissance Greeting Cards Inc 207 324-4153
10 Renaissance Way Sanford ME (04073) *(G-6888)*
Renaissance International 978 465-5111
204 High St Newburyport MA (01950) *(G-13529)*
Renaissance Sheet Metal L 401 294-3703
8 Fishing Cove Rd North Kingstown RI (02852) *(G-20737)*
Renaissnce Elec Cmmnctions LLC (PA) 978 772-7774
12 Lancaster County Rd Harvard MA (01451) *(G-11383)*
Renbrandt Inc 617 445-8910
32 Blackburn Ctr Gloucester MA (01930) *(G-11207)*
Renchel Tool Inc 860 315-9017
51 Ridge Rd Putnam CT (06260) *(G-3631)*
Renco Corporation (PA) 978 526-8494
1 Beaver Dam Rd Ste 6 Manchester MA (01944) *(G-12606)*
Renesas Electronics Amer Inc 978 805-6900
300 Baker Ave Ste 300 # 300 Concord MA (01742) *(G-10156)*
Renetx Bio Inc 203 444-6642
157 Church St Fl 19 New Haven CT (06510) *(G-2731)*
Renew Energy 802 891-6774
7 Clapper Rd Milton VT (05468) *(G-22137)*
Renewable Fuels Vermont LLC 802 362-1516
114 Cemetery St Manchester Center VT (05255) *(G-22088)*
Renewable NRG Systems, Hinesburg *Also called Doble Engineering Company (G-22022)*

ALPHABETIC

Rennaissance Electronic Corp.....978 772-7774
12 Lancaster County Rd Harvard MA (01451) ***(G-11384)***
Rennline Design, Milton *Also called Rennline Inc* ***(G-22138)***
Rennline Inc.....802 893-7366
32 Catamount Dr Milton VT (05468) ***(G-22138)***
Reno Machine Company Inc.....860 666-5641
170 Pane Rd Ste 1 Newington CT (06111) ***(G-2898)***
Renova Lighting Systems Inc.....800 635-6682
36 Bellair Ave Unit 4 Warwick RI (02886) ***(G-21411)***
Renovators Supply Inc.....413 423-3300
Renovators Old Ml Millers Falls MA (01349) ***(G-13181)***
Rens Welding & Fabricating.....508 828-1702
988 Crane Ave S Ste 1 Taunton MA (02780) ***(G-15779)***
Rensup.com, Old Mill Marketing, Millers Falls *Also called Renovators Supply Inc* ***(G-13181)***
Rentschler Biopharma Inc.....508 282-5800
27 Maple St Milford MA (01757) ***(G-13140)***
Repair Dept, Athol *Also called LS Starrett Company* ***(G-7690)***
Repligen Corporation (PA).....781 250-0111
41 Seyon St Ste 100 Waltham MA (02453) ***(G-16187)***
Replimune Group Inc.....781 995-2443
18 Commerce Way Woburn MA (01801) ***(G-17283)***
Repose Fire Logs LLC.....207 595-8035
1301 Bridgton Rd Sebago ME (04029) ***(G-6954)***
Repro Craft Inc.....413 533-4937
354 Montcalm St Chicopee MA (01020) ***(G-10057)***
Republic Iron Works Inc.....413 594-8819
40 Champion Dr Chicopee MA (01020) ***(G-10058)***
Republican Company (HQ).....413 788-1000
1860 Main St Springfield MA (01103) ***(G-15502)***
Republican Journal, Belfast *Also called Village Netmedia Inc* ***(G-5698)***
Republican-American, Waterbury *Also called American-Republican Inc* ***(G-4842)***
Rer Machine Co.....508 248-3029
15 H Putnam Rd Charlton MA (01507) ***(G-9856)***
RES-Tech Corporation (HQ).....978 567-1000
34 Tower St Hudson MA (01749) ***(G-11811)***
RES-Tech Corporation.....860 828-1504
114 New Park Dr Berlin CT (06037) ***(G-107)***
Resavue Inc.....203 878-0944
48 Grannis Rd Orange CT (06477) ***(G-3381)***
Resavue Exhibits, Orange *Also called Resavue Inc* ***(G-3381)***
Research Applications and.....800 939-7238
222 3rd St Ste 234 Cambridge MA (02142) ***(G-9630)***
Research Cmpt Cnsulting Servic, Canton *Also called Research Cmpt Consulting Svcs* ***(G-9774)***
Research Cmpt Consulting Svcs (PA).....781 821-1221
960 Turnpike St Canton MA (02021) ***(G-9774)***
Research Engineering & Mfg Inc.....401 841-8880
55 Hammarlund Way Middletown RI (02842) ***(G-20631)***
Research In Motion Rf Inc (HQ).....603 598-8880
22 Technology Way Fl 5 Nashua NH (03060) ***(G-19250)***
Research Lab Supply Co, Canton *Also called Precious Metals Reclaiming Svc* ***(G-9771)***
Reservoir Genomics Inc.....412 304-5063
38 Tremont St Apt 1 Cambridge MA (02139) ***(G-9631)***
Resident Artist Studio LLC.....978 635-9162
438 Hill Rd Boxborough MA (01719) ***(G-8969)***
Resilience Therapeutics Inc.....617 780-2375
536 Bay Rd Duxbury MA (02332) ***(G-10401)***
Resin Designs LLC (HQ).....781 935-3133
11 State St Woburn MA (01801) ***(G-17284)***
Resin Systems Corporation.....603 673-1234
62 State Route 101a Ste 1 Amherst NH (03031) ***(G-17584)***
Resinall Corp (HQ).....203 329-7100
3065 High Ridge Rd Stamford CT (06903) ***(G-4298)***
Resolute FP US Inc.....203 292-6560
97 Village Ln Southport CT (06890) ***(G-4097)***
Resonance Research Inc.....978 671-0811
31 Dunham Rd Ste 1 Billerica MA (01821) ***(G-8291)***
Resonetics LLC (PA).....603 886-6772
26 Whipple St Nashua NH (03060) ***(G-19251)***
Resource Colors LLC.....978 537-3700
517 Lancaster St Leominster MA (01453) ***(G-12182)***
Resource Engineering Inc.....802 496-5888
80 Mobus Rd Waitsfield VT (05673) ***(G-22568)***
Resources Unlimited Inc.....401 369-7329
140 Comstock Pkwy Cranston RI (02921) ***(G-20278)***
Respiratory Motion Inc.....508 954-2706
80 Coolidge Hill Rd Watertown MA (02472) ***(G-16311)***
Respironics Inc.....203 697-6490
5 Technology Dr Wallingford CT (06492) ***(G-4795)***
Respironics Novametrix LLC.....203 697-6475
5 Technology Dr Wallingford CT (06492) ***(G-4796)***
Respond Systems.....203 481-2810
20 Baldwin Dr Branford CT (06405) ***(G-341)***
Response Technologies LLC.....401 585-5918
1505 Main St Ste B West Warwick RI (02893) ***(G-21508)***
Rest Ensured Medical Inc.....603 225-2860
661 Pleasant St Ste 99 Norwood MA (02062) ***(G-14195)***
Restech Plastic Molding, Hudson *Also called RES-Tech Corporation* ***(G-11811)***
Restech Plastic Molding, Berlin *Also called RES-Tech Corporation* ***(G-107)***
Restech Plastic Molding LLC (HQ).....978 567-1000
34 Tower St Hudson MA (01749) ***(G-11812)***
Restopedic Inc.....203 393-1520
695 Amity Rd Bethany CT (06524) ***(G-124)***
Restorbio Inc.....857 315-5521
500 Boylston St Ste 1300 Boston MA (02116) ***(G-8818)***
Resurrection Defense LLC.....603 313-1040
71 Richmond Rd Winchester NH (03470) ***(G-19995)***
Retail Sales Inc.....781 963-8169
75 York Ave Ste A Randolph MA (02368) ***(G-14696)***
Retcomp Inc.....603 487-5010
2nd New Hampshire Tpke S New Boston NH (03070) ***(G-19297)***
Retina Systems Inc.....203 881-1311
146 Day St Seymour CT (06483) ***(G-3763)***
Retrieve LLC.....603 413-0022
50 Commercial St Ste 35s Manchester NH (03101) ***(G-18910)***
Retrieve Technologies, Manchester *Also called Retrieve LLC* ***(G-18910)***
Retromedia Inc.....401 349-4640
20 Cedar Swamp Rd Ste 8 Smithfield RI (02917) ***(G-21246)***
Rettig USA Inc.....802 654-7500
948 Hercules Dr Ste 5 Colchester VT (05446) ***(G-21879)***
Rettig USA Inc.....802 654-7500
45 Krupp Dr Williston VT (05495) ***(G-22688)***
Revere Independent.....781 485-0588
385 Broadway Ste 105 Revere MA (02151) ***(G-14775)***
Revere Pharmaceuticals Inc.....781 718-9033
36 Orvis Rd Arlington MA (02474) ***(G-7635)***
Revision Automotive Inc.....401 944-4444
275 Niantic Ave Providence RI (02907) ***(G-21109)***
Revision Ballistics Ltd.....802 879-7002
7 Corporate Dr Essex Junction VT (05452) ***(G-21956)***
Revision Heat LLC.....207 221-5677
266 Gray Rd Windham ME (04062) ***(G-7247)***
Revision Military, Essex Junction *Also called Revision Ballistics Ltd* ***(G-21956)***
Revision Military JV.....802 879-7002
7 Corporate Dr Essex Junction VT (05452) ***(G-21957)***
Revival Brewing Company.....401 372-7009
505 Atwood Ave Providence RI (02903) ***(G-21110)***
Reviveflow Inc.....978 621-9466
119 Drum Hill Rd Ste 272 Chelmsford MA (01824) ***(G-9927)***
Revo Biologics Inc.....508 370-5451
300 Charlton Rd Spencer MA (01562) ***(G-15434)***
Revo Biologics Inc (HQ).....508 620-9700
175 Crossing Blvd Framingham MA (01702) ***(G-11000)***
Revolution Armor, New Bedford *Also called Incident Control Systems LLC* ***(G-13397)***
Revolution Composites LLC.....781 255-1111
340 Vanderbilt Ave Norwood MA (02062) ***(G-14196)***
Revolution Lighting, Stamford *Also called Seesmart Inc* ***(G-4312)***
Revolution Lighting (HQ).....203 504-1111
177 Broad St Fl 12 Stamford CT (06901) ***(G-4299)***
Revolution Lighting Tech Inc (PA).....203 504-1111
177 Broad St Fl 12 Stamford CT (06901) ***(G-4300)***
Revolution Lighting Tech Inc.....203 504-1111
177 Broad St Fl 12 Stamford CT (06901) ***(G-4301)***
Revulytics Inc (PA).....781 398-3400
130 Turner St Waltham MA (02453) ***(G-16188)***
Rewalk Robotics Inc.....508 251-1154
200 Donald Lynch Blvd # 100 Marlborough MA (01752) ***(G-12815)***
Rex Cut Products Incorporated.....508 678-1985
960 Airport Rd Fall River MA (02720) ***(G-10757)***
Rex Forge Div, Plantsville *Also called J J Ryan Corporation* ***(G-3534)***
Rex Lumber Company (PA).....800 343-0567
840 Main St Acton MA (01720) ***(G-7378)***
Rexa Inc.....508 584-1199
4 Manley St West Bridgewater MA (02379) ***(G-16451)***
Rexa Electraulic Actuation, West Bridgewater *Also called Rexa Inc* ***(G-16451)***
Reynolds Carbide Die Co Inc.....860 283-8246
27 Reynolds Bridge Rd Thomaston CT (06787) ***(G-4512)***
Rf Biocidics Inc.....617 419-1800
33 Arch St Fl 29 Boston MA (02110) ***(G-8819)***
Rf Logic LLC (PA).....603 578-9876
21 Park Ave Hudson NH (03051) ***(G-18435)***
Rf Printing LLC.....203 265-9939
200 Church St Ste 5 Wallingford CT (06492) ***(G-4797)***
Rf Venue Inc.....800 795-0817
72 Nickerson Rd Ashland MA (01721) ***(G-7668)***
Rf1 Holding Company (PA).....855 294-3800
400 Nickerson Rd Marlborough MA (01752) ***(G-12816)***
Rfbf Dye Works, Somersworth *Also called Red Fish-Blue Fish Dye Works* ***(G-19846)***
RFI Industries.....443 255-8767
32 Main St Dexter ME (04930) ***(G-5956)***
RFS Americas.....203 630-3311
175 Corporate Ct Meriden CT (06450) ***(G-2125)***
Rgc Millwork Incorporated.....978 275-9529
175a Old Canal Dr Lowell MA (01851) ***(G-12427)***
Rgd Technologies Corp.....860 589-0756
50 Emmett St Bristol CT (06010) ***(G-605)***
Rgm Enterprises Inc.....603 644-3336
880 2nd St Manchester NH (03102) ***(G-18911)***

Rgp Corp 508 478-8511
231 E Main St Ste C Milford MA (01757) ***(G-13141)***
RH Laboratories Inc 603 459-5900
1 Tanguay Ave Nashua NH (03063) ***(G-19252)***
RH Rosenfield Co 207 324-1798
2066 Main St Sanford ME (04073) ***(G-6889)***
Rhapsody Natural Foods Inc 802 563-2172
752 Danville Hill Rd Cabot VT (05647) ***(G-21820)***
Rhealth Corporation 617 913-7630
1 Oak Park Dr Ste 2 Bedford MA (01730) ***(G-8006)***
Rhee Gold Company 508 285-6650
155 Pine St Norton MA (02766) ***(G-14086)***
Rheinwerk Publishing Inc 781 228-5070
2 Heritage Dr Ste 305 Quincy MA (02171) ***(G-14654)***
Rhenovia Incorporated 310 382-4079
185 Alewife Brook Pkwy Cambridge MA (02138) ***(G-9632)***
Rhine Inc 781 710-7121
51 Church St Weston MA (02493) ***(G-16831)***
Rhino Energy Holdings LLC 203 862-7000
411 W Putnam Ave Ste 125 Greenwich CT (06830) ***(G-1642)***
Rhino Foods Inc (PA) 802 862-0252
179 Queen City Park Rd Burlington VT (05401) ***(G-21807)***
Rhino Shelters, Milford *Also called Mdm Products LLC* ***(G-2314)***
Rhode Island Beverage Journal 203 288-3375
2508 Whitney Ave Hamden CT (06518) ***(G-1780)***
Rhode Island Centerless Inc 401 942-0403
24 Morgan Mill Rd Johnston RI (02919) ***(G-20536)***
Rhode Island Chemical Corp 401 274-3905
754 Branch Ave Providence RI (02904) ***(G-21111)***
Rhode Island Distrg Co LLC 401 822-6400
119 Hopkins Hill Rd West Greenwich RI (02817) ***(G-21465)***
Rhode Island Driveshaft & Sup, Warwick *Also called Rhode Island Driveshaft Sup Co* ***(G-21412)***
Rhode Island Driveshaft Sup Co 401 941-0210
3 Jefferson Blvd Warwick RI (02888) ***(G-21412)***
Rhode Island Family Guide 401 247-0850
29 Chapin Rd Barrington RI (02806) ***(G-20053)***
Rhode Island Frt Syrup Co Inc 401 231-0040
250 Putnam Pike Smithfield RI (02917) ***(G-21247)***
Rhode Island Limb Co (PA) 401 941-6230
1559 Elmwood Ave Cranston RI (02910) ***(G-20279)***
Rhode Island Limb Co 401 475-3501
59 Prospect St Pawtucket RI (02860) ***(G-20892)***
Rhode Island Media Group 401 762-3000
75 Main St Woonsocket RI (02895) ***(G-21578)***
Rhode Island Mktg & Prtg Inc 401 351-4000
41 Deerfield Rd Unit 11 Attleboro MA (02703) ***(G-7786)***
Rhode Island Monthly 401 649-4800
717 Allens Ave Ste 105 Providence RI (02905) ***(G-21112)***
Rhode Island Precision Co 401 421-6661
25 Dorr St Providence RI (02908) ***(G-21113)***
Rhode Island Provision Co Inc 401 831-0815
5 Day St Johnston RI (02919) ***(G-20537)***
Rhode Island Publications Soc 401 273-1787
200 Allens Ave Ste 1 Providence RI (02903) ***(G-21114)***
Rhode Island Raceway LLC 860 701-0192
846 Vauxhall Street Ext Quaker Hill CT (06375) ***(G-3643)***
Rhode Island Ready Mix LLC 401 539-8222
35 Stilson Rd Wyoming RI (02898) ***(G-21590)***
Rhode Island Sheet Metal 508 557-1140
30 Palmer Meadow Ln Rehoboth MA (02769) ***(G-14759)***
Rhode Island Ventilating Co 401 723-8920
29 Aurora Dr Cumberland RI (02864) ***(G-20341)***
Rhode Island Wiring Service 401 789-1955
567 Liberty Ln West Kingston RI (02892) ***(G-21470)***
Rhode Northsales Island Inc 401 683-7997
1 Maritime Dr Ste 1 # 1 Portsmouth RI (02871) ***(G-20939)***
Rhodes Pharmaceuticals LP 401 262-9200
498 Washington St Coventry RI (02816) ***(G-20164)***
Rhody Rug Inc 401 728-5903
9 Powder Hill Rd Lincoln RI (02865) ***(G-20594)***
Rhythm Rhyme Results LLC 617 674-7524
155 Brookline St Apt 8 Cambridge MA (02139) ***(G-9633)***
Rhythm Pharmaceuticals Inc 857 264-4280
222 Berkeley St Ste 1200 Boston MA (02116) ***(G-8820)***
RI Carbide Tool Co 401 231-1020
339 Farnum Pike Smithfield RI (02917) ***(G-21248)***
RI Knitting Co Inc 508 822-5333
20 Cushman St Taunton MA (02780) ***(G-15780)***
RI Waterjet LLC 781 801-2500
3 Long Lane Ct Newport RI (02840) ***(G-20676)***
Ribco Supply Co, Clarksburg *Also called R I Baker Co Inc* ***(G-10075)***
Ricciardi Marble and Granite 508 790-2734
174 Airport Rd Hyannis MA (02601) ***(G-11855)***
Ricco Vishnu 203 449-0124
79 Sage Ave Bridgeport CT (06610) ***(G-482)***
Ricco Vishnu Brew House, Bridgeport *Also called Swagnificent Ent LLC* ***(G-498)***
Rice Packaging Inc 860 870-7057
356 Somers Rd Ellington CT (06029) ***(G-1338)***
Rich Logging 207 357-7863
62 Richards Ave Mexico ME (04257) ***(G-6429)***
Rich Plastic Products Inc 203 235-4241
57 High St Meriden CT (06450) ***(G-2126)***
Rich Products Corporation 866 737-8884
263 Myrtle St New Britain CT (06053) ***(G-2570)***
Rich Products Corporation 800 356-7094
263 Myrtle St New Britain CT (06053) ***(G-2571)***
Rich Products Corporation 860 827-8000
1 Celebration Way New Britain CT (06053) ***(G-2572)***
Rich Products Corporation 609 589-3049
263 Myrtle St New Britain CT (06053) ***(G-2573)***
Rich Snob Fashions, Bridgeport *Also called Ricco Vishnu* ***(G-482)***
Rich Technology International 207 883-7424
28 Pond View Dr Scarborough ME (04074) ***(G-6937)***
Richard A Tibbetts 207 539-5073
73 Longview Dr Oxford ME (04270) ***(G-6571)***
Richard Akerboom 802 291-6116
85 N Main St Ste 245 White River Junction VT (05001) ***(G-22642)***
Richard Arikian 603 881-5427
339 Broad St Nashua NH (03063) ***(G-19253)***
Richard Breault 203 876-2707
117 North St Milford CT (06460) ***(G-2349)***
Richard Cantwell Woodworking 508 984-7921
611 Belleville Ave New Bedford MA (02745) ***(G-13445)***
Richard Chiovitti 401 949-1177
22 Lark Industrial Pkwy Greenville RI (02828) ***(G-20474)***
Richard D Johnson & Son Inc 401 377-4312
440 Main St Ashaway RI (02804) ***(G-20040)***
Richard Dahlen 860 584-8226
350 Riverside Ave Bristol CT (06010) ***(G-606)***
Richard Dudgeon Inc 203 336-4459
24 Swift Pl Waterbury CT (06710) ***(G-4950)***
Richard Dupuis Logging Inc 603 636-2986
107 Thompson Rd Groveton NH (03582) ***(G-18234)***
Richard Fisher 207 963-7184
56 W Bay Rd Prospect Harbor ME (04669) ***(G-6771)***
Richard Genest Inc 207 324-7215
238 Country Club Rd Sanford ME (04073) ***(G-6890)***
Richard Gilbert 508 337-8774
52 Adams Ave Pembroke MA (02359) ***(G-14424)***
Richard H Bird & Co Inc 781 894-0160
1 Spruce St Waltham MA (02453) ***(G-16189)***
Richard Manufacturing Co Inc 203 874-3617
250 Rock Ln Milford CT (06460) ***(G-2350)***
Richard Pg Millwork Co Inc 508 776-2433
4022 Main St Cummaquid MA (02637) ***(G-10172)***
Richard Townsend 603 664-5987
43 Hall Rd Barrington NH (03825) ***(G-17622)***
Richards Arklay S Co Inc 617 527-4385
72 Winchester St Newton MA (02461) ***(G-13630)***
Richards Dean Custom Wdwkg 978 768-7104
17 Winthrop St Essex MA (01929) ***(G-10597)***
Richards Design, East Falmouth *Also called Rajessa LLC* ***(G-10447)***
Richards Design Inc 508 540-4420
117 Bernard E Saint Jean East Falmouth MA (02536) ***(G-10448)***
Richards Machine Tool Co Inc 860 436-2938
187 Stamm Rd Newington CT (06111) ***(G-2899)***
Richards Metal Products Inc 203 879-2555
14 Swiss Ln Wolcott CT (06716) ***(G-5454)***
Richards Micro-Tool LLC 508 746-6900
250 Cherry St Plymouth MA (02360) ***(G-14580)***
Richardson Landscaping Corp 401 423-1505
25 Clarke St Jamestown RI (02835) ***(G-20494)***
Richardson Mfg Co Inc 603 367-9018
4 High St Silver Lake NH (03875) ***(G-19825)***
Richardson's Maptech, New Bedford *Also called Edgewater Marine Inds LLC* ***(G-13383)***
Richardson-Allen Inc 207 284-8402
38 Pearl St Biddeford ME (04005) ***(G-5761)***
Richardsons Ice Cream 781 944-9121
50 Walkers Brook Dr Reading MA (01867) ***(G-14740)***
Richelieu Foods Inc (HQ) 781 786-6800
222 Forbes Rd Ste 401 Braintree MA (02184) ***(G-9034)***
Richie Navigation, Pembroke *Also called E S Ritchie & Sons Inc* ***(G-14402)***
Richie's Classic Italian Ice, Everett *Also called Richies King Slush Mfg Co Inc* ***(G-10627)***
Richies King Slush Mfg Co Inc 800 287-5874
3 Garvey St Everett MA (02149) ***(G-10627)***
Richline Group Inc 774 203-1199
49 Pearl St Attleboro MA (02703) ***(G-7787)***
Richmand Textiles Inc 508 839-6600
20 Milford Rd South Grafton MA (01560) ***(G-15298)***
Richmond Contract Mfg 207 737-4385
85 White Rd Bowdoinham ME (04008) ***(G-5790)***
Richmond Graphic Products Inc 401 233-2700
188 Progress Ave Providence RI (02909) ***(G-21115)***
Richmond Sand & Stone LLC 401 539-7770
35 Stilson Rd Richmond RI (02898) ***(G-21162)***
Rickenbacker Resources Inc 978 475-4520
77 Main St Andover MA (01810) ***(G-7599)***

A L P H A B E T I C

Rickie D Osgood Sr......207 674-3529
8 Osgood Ln Greenwood ME (04255) **(G-6155)**
Ricks Sheet Metal Inc......774 488-9576
82 Lea Ln Fall River MA (02721) **(G-10758)**
Ricks Truck & Trailer Repair......603 464-3636
39 Merrill Rd Hillsborough NH (03244) **(G-18318)**
Rickss Motorsport Electrics......603 329-9901
48 Gigante Dr Hampstead NH (03841) **(G-18249)**
Ricor Usa Inc......603 718-8903
200 Main St Ste 1 Salem NH (03079) **(G-19763)**
Ridco Casting Co......401 724-0400
6 Beverage Hill Ave Pawtucket RI (02860) **(G-20893)**
Ridge View Associates Inc......203 878-8560
122 Cascade Blvd Milford CT (06460) **(G-2351)**
Ridgefield Overhead Door LLC......203 431-3667
703 Danbury Rd Ste 4 Ridgefield CT (06877) **(G-3679)**
Ridgetop Cabinetry......207 563-8249
26 Carter Ridge Rd Boothbay Harbor ME (04538) **(G-5786)**
Ridgeway Racing, Vernon *Also called Crystal Tool and Machine Co* **(G-4666)**
Riding Enhancement Designs, Burlington *Also called Burton Corporation* **(G-21770)**
Ridlons Metal Shop......207 655-7997
627 Roosevelt Trl Casco ME (04015) **(G-5896)**
Rife Mltplwave Oscillators LLC......508 737-8468
2114 Main St Brewster MA (02631) **(G-9057)**
Riff Company Inc......203 272-4899
1484 Highland Ave Ste 7 Cheshire CT (06410) **(G-759)**
Riffr LLC......617 851-5989
7 Faneuil Hall Market Pl # 4 Boston MA (02109) **(G-8821)**
Rigaku Analytical Devices Inc......781 328-1024
30 Upton Dr Ste 2 Wilmington MA (01887) **(G-17041)**
Rigby Precision Products, Bridgton *Also called J D Paulsen* **(G-5808)**
Right Height Manufacturing, Manchester *Also called Mkind Inc* **(G-18877)**
Right Submission LLC......617 407-9076
59 High St Newton MA (02464) **(G-13631)**
Righthand Robotics Inc......617 501-0085
237 Washington St Somerville MA (02143) **(G-15210)**
Rigstar Rigging, Northampton *Also called Link Enterprises Corp* **(G-14010)**
Rihani Plastics Inc......401 942-7393
14 Suez St Cranston RI (02920) **(G-20280)**
Rihm Management Inc......802 867-5325
140 Powderhorn Rd Manchester Center VT (05255) **(G-22089)**
Rika Denshi America Inc......508 226-2080
112 Frank Mossberg Dr Attleboro MA (02703) **(G-7788)**
Riley Kitchen & Bath Co Inc......401 253-2205
369 Metacom Ave Bristol RI (02809) **(G-20100)**
Riley Mountain Products Inc......603 588-7234
10 Water St Antrim NH (03440) **(G-17597)**
Riley Power Inc......508 852-7100
26 Forest St Ste 300 Marlborough MA (01752) **(G-12817)**
Riley Power Inc......508 852-7100
5 Neponset St Worcester MA (01606) **(G-17459)**
Rimol Greenhouse Systems Inc......603 629-9004
40 Londonderry Tpke 2d Hooksett NH (03106) **(G-18359)**
Rinco Ultrasonics USA Inc......203 744-4500
87 Sand Pit Rd Ste 1b Danbury CT (06810) **(G-978)**
Rindle LLC......551 482-2037
3 Richards Ave Norwalk CT (06854) **(G-3232)**
Rings Wire Inc (PA)......203 874-6719
257 Depot Rd Milford CT (06460) **(G-2352)**
Rintec Corporation......860 274-3697
30 Mclennan Dr Oakville CT (06779) **(G-3302)**
Ripano Stoneworks Ltd......603 886-6655
90 E Hollis St Nashua NH (03060) **(G-19254)**
Ripley, Cromwell *Also called Crrc LLC* **(G-852)**
Ripley Odm LLC......603 524-8350
143 Lake St Ste 1e Laconia NH (03246) **(G-18583)**
Ripley Tools LLC (PA)......860 635-2200
46 Nooks Hill Rd Cromwell CT (06416) **(G-859)**
Riptide Synthetics Inc......617 945-8832
108 Amory St Apt 1 Cambridge MA (02139) **(G-9634)**
Ris, Montpelier *Also called Russian Information Services* **(G-22160)**
Rise Brewing Co, Stamford *Also called Riseandshine Corporation* **(G-4302)**
Riseandshine Corporation (PA)......917 599-7541
425 Fairfield Ave 1a11 Stamford CT (06902) **(G-4302)**
Risha Rishi LLC......860 346-7645
596 Washington St Middletown CT (06457) **(G-2219)**
Rising Revolution Studio LLC......207 636-7136
118 Granny Kent Pond Rd Shapleigh ME (04076) **(G-6959)**
Rising Sign Company Inc......203 853-4155
50 Commerce St Ste 1 Norwalk CT (06850) **(G-3233)**
Ritas of Milford......203 301-4490
175 Boston Post Rd Milford CT (06460) **(G-2353)**
Ritch Herald & Linda......203 661-8634
10 Fort Hill Ln Greenwich CT (06831) **(G-1643)**
Rite Aid Pharmacy, Colchester *Also called Maxi Green Inc* **(G-21873)**
Ritec Inc......401 738-3660
60 Alhambra Rd Ste 5 Warwick RI (02886) **(G-21413)**
Ritronics Inc......401 732-8175
60 Alhambra Rd Ste 1 Warwick RI (02886) **(G-21414)**
River City Software LLC......603 686-5525
108 Kingston Rd Exeter NH (03833) **(G-18130)**
River Falls Manufacturing Co......508 646-2900
40 County St Fall River MA (02723) **(G-10759)**
River Mill Co......860 669-5915
43 River Rd Clinton CT (06413) **(G-794)**
River Point Station, Warwick *Also called International Technologies Inc* **(G-21376)**
River Street Metal Finishing......781 843-9351
35 Johnson Ln Braintree MA (02184) **(G-9035)**
River Valley Oil Service LLC......860 342-5670
695 Portland Cobalt Rd Portland CT (06480) **(G-3574)**
Riverbed Technology Inc......617 250-5300
125 Cambridgepark Dr # 302 Cambridge MA (02140) **(G-9635)**
Riverdale Mills Corporation......508 234-8715
130 Riverdale St Northbridge MA (01534) **(G-14060)**
Riverdale Window and Door Corp......401 231-6000
2 Esmond St Smithfield RI (02917) **(G-21249)**
Rivermeadow Software Inc......617 448-4990
319 Littleton Rd Ste 305 Westford MA (01886) **(G-16790)**
Rivers Edge Sugar House......860 429-1510
326 Mansfield Rd Ashford CT (06278) **(G-27)**
Riverside Baking Company LLC......203 451-0331
1891 Post Rd Fairfield CT (06824) **(G-1452)**
Riverside Engineering Co Inc......978 531-1556
12 County St Peabody MA (01960) **(G-14365)**
Riverside Sheet Metal & Contg......781 396-0070
15 Reardon Rd 15 # 15 Medford MA (02155) **(G-12946)**
Riverside Specialty Foods Inc......603 474-5805
1 Depot Ln Seabrook NH (03874) **(G-19813)**
Riverton Memorial Inc......802 485-3371
2074 Route 12 Riverton VT (05663) **(G-22314)**
Riverview Labs Inc......603 715-2759
24 Dunklee Rd Ste 14 Bow NH (03304) **(G-17729)**
Riverview Machine Company Inc......413 533-5366
102 Cabot St Ste 1 Holyoke MA (01040) **(G-11652)**
Riverview Signs & Graphics......401 596-7889
17 Riverview Ave Westerly RI (02891) **(G-21537)**
Riverwalk Brewing......978 499-2337
40 Parker St Ste 4 Newburyport MA (01950) **(G-13530)**
Rivet Direct Inc......866 474-8387
54 Knox Trl Unit 2h1 Acton MA (01720) **(G-7379)**
Riveting Systems USA LLC......203 366-4557
90 Silliman Ave Bridgeport CT (06605) **(G-483)**
Riveto Manufacturing Co......978 544-2171
36 S Main St Orange MA (01364) **(G-14226)**
Rivinius & Sons Inc......781 933-5620
225 Salem St Woburn MA (01801) **(G-17285)**
Rivkind Associates Inc (PA)......781 269-2415
30 Twin Brooks Dr South Easton MA (02375) **(G-15291)**
Rj 15 Inc......860 585-0111
115 Cross St Bristol CT (06010) **(G-607)**
Rj Cabinetry LLC......203 515-8401
943 Post Rd E Westport CT (06880) **(G-5226)**
RJ Mansour Inc......401 521-7800
1 Magnolia St Providence RI (02909) **(G-21116)**
Rj Marine Industries......508 248-9933
1 Hawksley Rd Oxford MA (01540) **(G-14272)**
Rj Newbury, Windham *Also called Newberry Enterprise* **(G-7244)**
Rj Printing LLC......617 523-7656
98 N Washington St Ste B2 Boston MA (02114) **(G-8822)**
Rjb Meat Processing......401 781-5315
466 Atlantic Ave Warwick RI (02888) **(G-21415)**
Rjd Woodworking LLC......508 984-4315
92 Long Rd Fairhaven MA (02719) **(G-10646)**
Rjf - Morin Brick LLC......207 784-9375
130 Morin Brick Rd Auburn ME (04210) **(G-5595)**
Rjtb Group LLC......203 531-7216
253 Mill St Greenwich CT (06830) **(G-1644)**
Rk Machine, New Britain *Also called R K Machine Company LLC* **(G-2567)**
RK Manufacturing Corp Conn......203 797-8700
34 Executive Dr Ste 2 Danbury CT (06810) **(G-979)**
Rl Controls LLC......781 932-3349
2 Gill St Woburn MA (01801) **(G-17286)**
Rlcp Inc......401 461-6560
262 New Meadow Rd Barrington RI (02806) **(G-20054)**
Rlf Homes, Hartford *Also called R L Fisher Inc* **(G-1865)**
Rlp Inc......203 359-2504
12 Magee Ave Stamford CT (06902) **(G-4303)**
Rm Education Inc (HQ)......508 862-0700
310 Barnstable Rd Ste 101 Hyannis MA (02601) **(G-11856)**
Rm Educational Software,, Hyannis *Also called Rm Education Inc* **(G-11856)**
Rm Printing......860 621-0498
384 Old Turnpike Rd Plantsville CT (06479) **(G-3538)**
RMA Manufacturing LLC......603 352-0053
735 W Swanzey Rd West Swanzey NH (03469) **(G-19968)**
Rmd Instruments Corp......617 668-6900
44 Hunt St Ste 2 Watertown MA (02472) **(G-16312)**
Rme Filters Inc......603 595-4573
98 State Route 101a Amherst NH (03031) **(G-17585)**
Rmi, Stafford Springs *Also called Msj Investments Inc* **(G-4113)**

Rmi Inc...860 875-3366
130 Old Town Rd Vernon Rockville CT (06066) ***(G-4681)***
Rmi Titanium Company LLC...781 272-5967
8 A St Burlington MA (01803) ***(G-9330)***
RMS Media Group Inc...978 623-8020
300 Brickstone Sq Ste 904 Andover MA (01810) ***(G-7600)***
Rna Medical Division, Devens *Also called Bionostics Inc* ***(G-10319)***
Ro 59 Inc...781 341-1222
1 Cabot Pl Ste 3 Stoughton MA (02072) ***(G-15618)***
Road Bike, Norwalk *Also called Tam Communications Inc* ***(G-3254)***
Road-Fit Enterprises LLC...860 371-5137
98 Whiting St Plainville CT (06062) ***(G-3514)***
Roam Data Inc...888 589-5885
101 Federal St Ste 700 Boston MA (02110) ***(G-8823)***
Roaming Raceway and RR LLC...413 531-3390
755 Sheldon St Suffield CT (06078) ***(G-4467)***
Roar Industries Inc...508 429-5952
120 Jeffrey Ave Ste 1 Holliston MA (01746) ***(G-11599)***
Roaring Brook Veterenary Hosp, Canton *Also called Veterinary Medical Associates* ***(G-700)***
Rob Geoffroy...603 425-2517
176 Litchfield Rd Londonderry NH (03053) ***(G-18734)***
Robb Curtco Media LLC...978 264-7500
1 Acton Pl Ste 203 Acton MA (01720) ***(G-7380)***
Robbins Beef Co Inc...617 269-1826
35 Food Mart Rd 37 Boston MA (02118) ***(G-8824)***
Robbins Company...508 222-2900
400 Oneil Blvd Attleboro MA (02703) ***(G-7789)***
Robbins Lumber Inc...207 342-5221
53 Ghent Rd Searsmont ME (04973) ***(G-6945)***
Robbins Manufacturing Co Inc...508 675-2555
1200 Airport Rd Fall River MA (02720) ***(G-10760)***
Robco Steel Fabricators, Wells River *Also called Rowden Bros Corporation* ***(G-22602)***
Roberge Sharon, Somersworth *Also called Big Dipper* ***(G-19829)***
Robert A Collins...603 895-2345
130 Scribner Rd Fremont NH (03044) ***(G-18180)***
Robert A Randall...401 847-3118
12 Barney St Newport RI (02840) ***(G-20677)***
Robert Audette (PA)...203 872-3119
1732 S Main St Cheshire CT (06410) ***(G-760)***
Robert B Evans Inc...401 596-2719
128 Oak St Westerly RI (02891) ***(G-21538)***
Robert Babb & Sons...207 892-9692
28 Lotts Dr Windham ME (04062) ***(G-7248)***
Robert Bagdasarian, Riverside *Also called Microweld Co Inc* ***(G-21172)***
Robert Bentley Inc...617 547-4170
1734 Massachusetts Ave Cambridge MA (02138) ***(G-9636)***
Robert Cairns Company LLC...603 382-0044
2 Red Oak Dr Unit H Plaistow NH (03865) ***(G-19522)***
Robert Daigle & Sons Inc...207 834-3676
603 New Canada Rd New Canada ME (04743) ***(G-6463)***
Robert Dugrenier Associates, Townshend *Also called Crest Studios* ***(G-22541)***
Robert Emmet Company Inc...508 997-2651
51 Chancery St New Bedford MA (02740) ***(G-13446)***
Robert Gaynor...207 288-4398
758 Norway Dr Bar Harbor ME (04609) ***(G-5668)***
Robert H Thoms...617 876-0662
15 Meacham Rd Cambridge MA (02140) ***(G-9637)***
Robert J Moran Inc...978 486-4718
410 Great Rd Littleton MA (01460) ***(G-12322)***
Robert Kowalski...508 885-5392
22 Cherry St Spencer MA (01562) ***(G-15435)***
Robert L Lovallo...203 324-6655
127 Myrtle Ave Stamford CT (06902) ***(G-4304)***
Robert Louis Company Inc...203 270-1400
31 Shepard Hill Rd Newtown CT (06470) ***(G-2935)***
Robert Mitchell Co Inc (HQ)...207 797-6771
423 Riverside Indus Pkwy Portland ME (04103) ***(G-6722)***
Robert Murphy...978 745-7170
10 Colonial Rd Ste 5 Salem MA (01970) ***(G-14938)***
Robert Nixon...603 654-2285
328 Abbott Hill Rd Wilton NH (03086) ***(G-19985)***
Robert Russell Co Inc...508 226-4140
38 Park St Rehoboth MA (02769) ***(G-14760)***
Robert Timmons Jr...207 892-3366
22 Commons Ave 8 Windham ME (04062) ***(G-7249)***
Robert Tyszko Od Pllc...603 924-9591
129 Wilton Rd Peterborough NH (03458) ***(G-19486)***
Robert Veinot...603 424-1799
11 Plasic Rd Merrimack NH (03054) ***(G-19025)***
Robert W Carr & Sons Inc...207 637-2885
83 Millturn Rd Limington ME (04049) ***(G-6348)***
Robert W Libby...207 625-8285
483 Old Meetinghouse Rd Porter ME (04068) ***(G-6604)***
Robert W Libby and Sons, Porter *Also called Robert W Libby* ***(G-6604)***
Robert Warren LLC (PA)...203 247-3347
1 Sprucewood Ln Westport CT (06880) ***(G-5227)***
Robert Weiss Associates Inc...617 561-4000
256 Marginal St Ste 2 Boston MA (02128) ***(G-8825)***
Roberts & Sons Printing Inc...413 283-9356
1791 Boston Rd Springfield MA (01129) ***(G-15503)***
Roberts Brothers Lumber Co...413 628-3333
1450 Spruce Corner Rd Ashfield MA (01330) ***(G-7654)***
Roberts Enterprises Inc...508 867-7640
32 W Main St Brookfield MA (01506) ***(G-9191)***
Roberts Machine and Engrg...978 779-5039
42 Flanagan Rd Bolton MA (01740) ***(G-8323)***
Roberts Machine Shop Inc...978 927-6111
117 Elliott St Ste 7 Beverly MA (01915) ***(G-8171)***
Roberts Manufacturing Company, Springfield *Also called Grassetti Sales Associates* ***(G-15472)***
Roberts Polishing Co...401 946-8922
928 Plainfield St Johnston RI (02919) ***(G-20538)***
Roberts Prototype Machining...978 251-4200
108 Middlesex St Ste 12 North Chelmsford MA (01863) ***(G-13909)***
Robertson Frm Log Land Claring, Newry *Also called Leslie W Robertson* ***(G-6491)***
Robertson-Chase Fibers LLC...978 453-2837
16 Esquire Rd Ste 2 North Billerica MA (01862) ***(G-13862)***
Robes Dana Wood Craftsmen (PA)...603 643-9355
3 Great Hollow Rd Hanover NH (03755) ***(G-18296)***
Robillards Apple Crisp...802 748-4451
184 Barker Ave Saint Johnsbury VT (05819) ***(G-22394)***
Robin Industries Inc...401 253-8350
125 Thames St Bristol RI (02809) ***(G-20101)***
Robin Rug, Bristol *Also called Robin Industries Inc* ***(G-20101)***
Robinson Manufacturing Co (PA)...207 539-4481
283 King St Oxford ME (04270) ***(G-6572)***
Robinson Precision Tools Corp...603 889-1625
315 Derry Rd Ste 15 Hudson NH (03051) ***(G-18436)***
Robinson Tape & Label Inc...203 481-5581
32 Park Dr E Ste 1 Branford CT (06405) ***(G-342)***
Robinson-Greaves Marine Pntg...207 313-6132
26 Whippoorwill Trl Wells ME (04090) ***(G-7164)***
Roblo Woodworks, Stamford *Also called Robert L Lovallo* ***(G-4304)***
Roces North America...603 298-2137
10 Technology Dr Ste 1b West Lebanon NH (03784) ***(G-19961)***
Roche Bros Barrel & Drum Co...978 454-9135
161 Phoenix Ave Lowell MA (01852) ***(G-12428)***
Roche Engineering LLC...508 287-1964
4 Marks Ln East Freetown MA (02717) ***(G-10459)***
Roche Manufacturing Inc...978 454-9135
161 Phoenix Ave Lowell MA (01852) ***(G-12429)***
Roche Tool & Die...508 485-6460
170 Maple St Marlborough MA (01752) ***(G-12818)***
Rocheleau Blow Molding Systems, Fitchburg *Also called Rocheleau Tool and Die Co Inc* ***(G-10851)***
Rocheleau Tool and Die Co Inc...978 345-1723
117 Indl Rd Fitchburg MA (01420) ***(G-10851)***
Rochester Bituminous Products...508 295-8001
83 Kings Hwy West Wareham MA (02576) ***(G-16576)***
Rochester Electronics LLC (PA)...978 462-9332
16 Malcolm Hoyt Dr Newburyport MA (01950) ***(G-13531)***
Rochester Electronics LLC...978 462-1248
18 Malcolm Hoyt Dr Newburyport MA (01950) ***(G-13532)***
Rochester Shoe Tree Co Inc (PA)...603 968-3301
1 Cedar Ln Ashland NH (03217) ***(G-17601)***
Rochester Times Newspaper, Rochester *Also called Salmon Press LLC* ***(G-19686)***
Rochester USA...603 332-0717
73 Allen St Rochester NH (03867) ***(G-19683)***
Rock Bottom Stone Factory Outl...508 634-9300
235 E Main St Milford MA (01757) ***(G-13142)***
Rock of Ages Corporation...802 476-3119
558 Graniteville Rd Graniteville VT (05654) ***(G-22002)***
Rock Shop, Bar Harbor *Also called Willis & Sons Inc* ***(G-5671)***
Rock Valley Tool LLC...413 527-2350
54 Oneil St Easthampton MA (01027) ***(G-10577)***
Rock-Tenn Missisquoi Mill, Sheldon Springs *Also called Westrock Cp LLC* ***(G-22431)***
Rocket Books Inc...203 372-1818
34 Ridgeway Rd Easton CT (06612) ***(G-1323)***
Rockland Equipment Company LLC...781 871-4400
171 Vfw Dr Rockland MA (02370) ***(G-14822)***
Rockland Marine Corporation...207 594-7860
79 Mechanic St Rockland ME (04841) ***(G-6809)***
Rockport Custom Publishing LLC...978 522-4316
100 Cummings Ctr Ste 207p Beverly MA (01915) ***(G-8172)***
Rockport Marine Inc...207 236-9651
1 Main St Rockport ME (04856) ***(G-6826)***
Rockport Publishing, Beverly *Also called Quayside Publishing Group* ***(G-8167)***
Rockport Steel, Rockport *Also called Glover Company Inc* ***(G-6822)***
Rockstar New England Inc...978 409-6272
3 Dundee Park Dr Ste 102 Andover MA (01810) ***(G-7601)***
Rockstep Solutions Inc...844 800-7625
48 Free St Ste 200 Portland ME (04101) ***(G-6723)***
Rockwell Art & Framing LLC (PA)...203 762-8311
151 Old Ridgefield Rd # 101 Wilton CT (06897) ***(G-5302)***
Rockwell Automation Inc...978 441-9500
2 Executive Dr Chelmsford MA (01824) ***(G-9928)***

ALPHABETIC

Rockwell Automation Inc.....508 357-8400
100 Nickerson Rd Fl 1 Marlborough MA (01752) ***(G-12819)***
Rockwood Service Corporation (PA).....203 869-6734
43 Arch St Greenwich CT (06830) ***(G-1645)***
Rocky Brook Associates Inc.....401 789-0259
155 Dean Knauss Dr Narragansett RI (02882) ***(G-20647)***
Rod Jakes Shop LLC.....207 595-0677
400 N Bridgton Rd Ste A Bridgton ME (04009) ***(G-5810)***
Rodco Engineering, Wilmington *Also called JJT Engineering Inc* ***(G-17010)***
Rodney Hunt-Fontaine Inc (HQ).....978 544-2511
46 Mill St Orange MA (01364) ***(G-14227)***
Roebic Laboratories Inc (PA).....203 795-1283
25 Connair Rd Orange CT (06477) ***(G-3382)***
Roehm America LLC.....207 324-6000
1796 Main St Sanford ME (04073) ***(G-6891)***
Roehm America LLC.....203 269-4481
528 S Cherry St Wallingford CT (06492) ***(G-4798)***
Roehr Tool Corp.....978 562-4488
52 Old Willard Rd Unit 1 Leominster MA (01453) ***(G-12183)***
Roetech, Orange *Also called Roebic Laboratories Inc* ***(G-3382)***
Rofin-Baasel Inc (HQ).....978 635-9100
68 Barnum Rd Devens MA (01434) ***(G-10332)***
Roger A Reed Inc.....781 944-4640
167 Pleasant St Reading MA (01867) ***(G-14741)***
Roger Jette Silversmiths Inc.....508 695-5555
52 Orne St North Attleboro MA (02760) ***(G-13776)***
Roger Reed.....802 933-2535
351 Central St Sheldon VT (05483) ***(G-22429)***
Roger Tool and Die Company Inc.....508 853-3757
33 Pullman St Worcester MA (01606) ***(G-17460)***
Rogerjettesilversmiths, North Attleboro *Also called Rsj LLC* ***(G-13777)***
Rogers Cabinets.....781 762-5700
604 Pleasant St Norwood MA (02062) ***(G-14197)***
Rogers Corporation.....508 746-3311
63 Smiths Ln Kingston MA (02364) ***(G-11963)***
Rogers Corporation.....860 928-3622
245 Woodstock Rd Woodstock CT (06281) ***(G-5501)***
Rogers Foam Automotive Corp.....617 623-3010
20 Vernon St Ste 1 Somerville MA (02145) ***(G-15211)***
Rogers Foam Corporation (PA).....617 623-3010
20 Vernon St Ste 1 Somerville MA (02145) ***(G-15212)***
Rogers General Machining Inc.....413 532-4673
181 Ludlow Rd Chicopee MA (01020) ***(G-10059)***
Rogers Manufacturing Company.....860 346-8648
72 Main St Rockfall CT (06481) ***(G-3699)***
Rogers Printing Co Inc.....978 537-9791
136 Pond St Ste 1 Leominster MA (01453) ***(G-12184)***
Rogerson Orthopedic Appls Inc.....617 268-1135
483 Southampton St Boston MA (02127) ***(G-8826)***
Rohm Haas Electronic Mtls LLC (HQ).....508 481-7950
455 Forest St Marlborough MA (01752) ***(G-12820)***
Rohm Haas Electronic Mtls LLC.....978 689-1503
455 Forest St Marlborough MA (01752) ***(G-12821)***
Rokap Inc.....203 265-6895
1002 Yale Ave Wallingford CT (06492) ***(G-4799)***
Rokon International Inc.....603 335-3200
50 Railroad Ave Rochester NH (03839) ***(G-19684)***
Rol-Flo Engineering Inc.....401 596-0060
85a Tom Harvey Rd Westerly RI (02891) ***(G-21539)***
Rol-Vac Limited Partnership.....860 928-9929
207 Tracy Rd Dayville CT (06241) ***(G-1052)***
Roland & Whytock Company.....401 781-1234
75 Oxford St Ste 202 Providence RI (02905) ***(G-21117)***
Roland Gatchell.....978 352-6132
119 Thurlow St Georgetown MA (01833) ***(G-11150)***
Roland H Ripley & Son Inc.....603 436-1926
59 Cass St Portsmouth NH (03801) ***(G-19616)***
Roland H Tyler Logging Inc.....207 562-7282
Canton Point Rd Dixfield ME (04224) ***(G-5958)***
Roland J Soucy Company LLC.....603 635-3265
52 Marsh Rd Pelham NH (03076) ***(G-19445)***
Roland Le Gare.....508 883-2869
25 Rhode Island Ave Blackstone MA (01504) ***(G-8315)***
Roland Levesque.....207 834-6244
185 Volette Settlement Rd Fort Kent ME (04743) ***(G-6067)***
Roland Teiner Company Inc.....617 387-7800
134 Tremont St Everett MA (02149) ***(G-10628)***
Roll Tide of Nh LLC.....603 417-2498
4 Townsend W Ste 13 Nashua NH (03063) ***(G-19255)***
Rollease Acmeda Inc (PA).....203 964-1573
750 E Main St 7 Stamford CT (06902) ***(G-4305)***
Roller Bearing Co Amer Inc (HQ).....203 267-7001
102 Willenbrock Rd Oxford CT (06478) ***(G-3423)***
Roller Bearing Co Amer Inc.....203 758-8272
86 Benson Rd Middlebury CT (06762) ***(G-2157)***
Roller Bearing Co Amer Inc.....203 267-7001
1 Tribiology Ctr Oxford CT (06478) ***(G-3424)***
Rolling Thunder Express, Newport *Also called Rolling Thunder Press Inc* ***(G-6486)***
Rolling Thunder Press Inc.....207 368-2028
134a Main St Newport ME (04953) ***(G-6486)***
Rollins Printing Incorporated.....203 248-3200
3281 Whitney Ave Hamden CT (06518) ***(G-1781)***
Rollins Transmission Service, Stratford *Also called Connecticut Machine & Welding* ***(G-4406)***
Rollprint Packaging, Bloomfield *Also called Paxxus Inc* ***(G-250)***
Rolls Battery of New England.....978 745-3333
7 Oak St Salem MA (01970) ***(G-14939)***
Rolls-Royce Marine North Amer (HQ).....508 668-9610
110 Norfolk St Walpole MA (02081) ***(G-16009)***
Roly Safeti-Gate, Essex *Also called Mezzanine Safeti Gates Inc* ***(G-10596)***
Rolyn Inc (PA).....401 944-0844
189 Macklin St Cranston RI (02920) ***(G-20281)***
Roma Marble Inc.....413 583-5017
15 Westover Rd Ludlow MA (01056) ***(G-12476)***
Roma Stone.....508 430-1200
181 Queen Anne Rd Harwich MA (02645) ***(G-11397)***
Roman Woodworking.....860 490-5989
1181 East St New Britain CT (06051) ***(G-2574)***
Romano Investments Inc.....401 691-3400
333 Strawberry Field Rd # 11 Warwick RI (02886) ***(G-21416)***
Romanow Inc (PA).....781 320-9200
346 University Ave Westwood MA (02090) ***(G-16874)***
Romanow Container, Westwood *Also called Romanow Inc* ***(G-16874)***
Romanow Packaging LLC.....781 320-8309
346 University Ave Westwood MA (02090) ***(G-16875)***
Romax Inc.....502 327-8555
14 Barretts Rd Hudson MA (01749) ***(G-11813)***
Romco Contractors Inc.....860 243-8872
12 E Newberry Rd Bloomfield CT (06002) ***(G-257)***
Rome Fastener Corporation.....203 874-6719
257 Depot Rd Milford CT (06460) ***(G-2354)***
Rome Fastener Sales Corp.....203 874-6719
257 Depot Rd Milford CT (06460) ***(G-2355)***
Romulus Craft.....802 685-3869
8495 Vt Route 110 Washington VT (05675) ***(G-22580)***
Ron Lavallee.....248 705-3231
27 Campground Rd Belgrade ME (04917) ***(G-5699)***
Ron Ledger Son Logging.....207 532-2423
81 Lycette Rd Amity ME (04471) ***(G-5524)***
Ron-Bet Company Inc.....207 439-5868
99 State Rd Ste 1 Kittery ME (03904) ***(G-6258)***
Rona Incorporated.....401 737-4388
70 Dewey Ave Warwick RI (02886) ***(G-21417)***
Ronald Bottino.....860 585-9505
381 Riverside Ave Bristol CT (06010) ***(G-608)***
Ronald F Birrell.....413 219-6729
78 Parsons Way Becket MA (01223) ***(G-7954)***
Ronald Pratt Company Inc.....508 222-9601
50 Perry Ave Attleboro MA (02703) ***(G-7790)***
Rondo America Incorporated.....203 723-5831
209 Great Hill Rd Naugatuck CT (06770) ***(G-2494)***
Rondo Packaging Systems, Naugatuck *Also called Rondo America Incorporated* ***(G-2494)***
Ronnie Marvin Enterprises.....603 444-5017
33 Hillview Ter Littleton NH (03561) ***(G-18664)***
Ronnie Sellers Productions, South Portland *Also called Sellers Publishing Inc* ***(G-7040)***
Ronnie's Olde Fashioned Slush, North Easton *Also called Slush Connection Inc* ***(G-13952)***
Rontex America Inc.....603 883-5076
1 Caldwell Dr Amherst NH (03031) ***(G-17586)***
Roodle Rice & Noodle Bar.....203 269-9899
1263 S Broad St Wallingford CT (06492) ***(G-4800)***
Roopers Main St, Lewiston *Also called Roopers Redemption & Bev Ctr* ***(G-6319)***
Roopers Redemption & Bev Ctr.....207 782-1482
694 Main St Lewiston ME (04240) ***(G-6319)***
Rooterman, Providence *Also called Plumbers of RI* ***(G-21091)***
Rootpath Genomics.....857 209-1060
325 Vassar St Ste 2a Cambridge MA (02139) ***(G-9638)***
Rootpath Genomics Inc.....501 258-0969
43 Charles St Ste 2 Boston MA (02114) ***(G-8827)***
Rope Co LLC.....207 838-4358
39 Deer Run Rd Spruce Head ME (04859) ***(G-7057)***
Roper Scientific Inc.....978 268-0337
15 Discovery Way Acton MA (01720) ***(G-7381)***
Rosario Cabinets Inc.....781 329-0639
49 Lower East St Ste 2 Dedham MA (02026) ***(G-10296)***
Rosco Glame, Central Falls *Also called Rosco Laboratories Inc* ***(G-20124)***
Rosco Holdings Inc (PA).....203 708-8900
52 Harbor View Ave Stamford CT (06902) ***(G-4306)***
Rosco Laboratories Inc (HQ).....203 708-8900
52 Harbor View Ave Stamford CT (06902) ***(G-4307)***
Rosco Laboratories Inc.....401 725-6765
31 Walnut St Central Falls RI (02863) ***(G-20124)***
Rosco Manufacturing Llc.....401 228-0120
500 High St Central Falls RI (02863) ***(G-20125)***
Rose Alley Ale House, New Bedford *Also called Pequod Inc* ***(G-13437)***
Rose Therese Caps & Gown Co, Brockton *Also called Therese Rose Manufacturing* ***(G-9183)***
Rosellis Machine & Mfg Co.....413 562-4317
248 Root Rd Westfield MA (01085) ***(G-16723)***

Rosemount Inc.....508 261-2928
9 Oxford Rd Mansfield MA (02048) ***(G-12656)***
Rosencrntz Gldnstern Banknotes.....603 654-6160
6 Burns Hill Rd Wilton NH (03086) ***(G-19986)***
Rosenfeld Concrete Corp (HQ).....508 473-7200
75 Plain St Hopedale MA (01747) ***(G-11682)***
Rosenoff Reports Inc.....617 628-7783
26a Aberdeen Rd Somerville MA (02144) ***(G-15213)***
Ross Curtis Product Inc.....860 886-6800
45 Church St Norwich CT (06360) ***(G-3289)***
Ross Custom Switches, Norwich *Also called Ross Curtis Product Inc* ***(G-3289)***
Ross Mfg & Design LLC.....203 878-0187
124 Research Dr Ste A Milford CT (06460) ***(G-2356)***
Rosscommon Quilts Inc.....617 436-5848
15 Fairfax St Dorchester MA (02124) ***(G-10348)***
Rostra Tool Company.....203 488-8665
30 E Industrial Rd Branford CT (06405) ***(G-343)***
Rostra Vernatherm LLC.....860 582-6776
106 Enterprise Dr Bristol CT (06010) ***(G-609)***
Rotadyne, Marlborough *Also called Rotation Dynamics Corporation* ***(G-12822)***
Rotair Aerospace Corporation.....203 576-6545
964 Crescent Ave Bridgeport CT (06607) ***(G-484)***
Rotating Composite Tech LLC.....860 829-6809
49 Cambridge Hts Kensington CT (06037) ***(G-1920)***
Rotation Dynamics Corporation.....508 481-0900
33 Hayes Memorial Dr Marlborough MA (01752) ***(G-12822)***
Rotek Instrument Corp.....781 899-4611
390 Main St Waltham MA (02452) ***(G-16190)***
Roto Hardware Systems, Chester *Also called Roto-Frank of America Inc* ***(G-775)***
Roto-Die Company Inc.....860 292-7030
7d Pasco Dr East Windsor CT (06088) ***(G-1300)***
Roto-Frank of America Inc.....860 526-4996
14 Inspiration Ln Chester CT (06412) ***(G-775)***
Rotondo Precast, Rehoboth *Also called Oldcastle Infrastructure Inc* ***(G-14756)***
Rotondo Precast, Avon *Also called Oldcastle Infrastructure Inc* ***(G-40)***
Rougeluxe Apothecary Inc.....508 696-0900
21 Kennebec Ave Oak Bluffs MA (02557) ***(G-14211)***
Round Top Ice Cream Inc.....207 563-5307
526 Main St Damariscotta ME (04543) ***(G-5939)***
Roundtown Inc.....415 425-6891
45 Prospect St Cambridge MA (02139) ***(G-9639)***
Roussel Logging Inc.....207 728-3250
386 11th Ave Madawaska ME (04756) ***(G-6401)***
Rousselot Peabody Inc.....978 573-3700
227 Washington St Peabody MA (01960) ***(G-14366)***
Rovers Speacial Vehicles, Exeter *Also called Moody Investments LLC* ***(G-20453)***
Rowden Bros Corporation.....802 757-2807
416 Ryegate Rd Wells River VT (05081) ***(G-22602)***
Rowe Contracting Co.....781 620-0052
90 Woodcrest Dr Melrose MA (02176) ***(G-12991)***
Rowe Machine Co.....603 926-0029
143 N Shore Rd Hampton NH (03842) ***(G-18270)***
Rowland Technologies Inc.....203 269-9500
320 Barnes Rd Wallingford CT (06492) ***(G-4801)***
Rowley Biochemical Institute.....978 739-4883
10 Electronics Ave Danvers MA (01923) ***(G-10253)***
Rowley Concrete, Rowley *Also called Rowley Ready Mix Inc* ***(G-14864)***
Rowley Ready Mix Inc.....978 948-2544
84 Central St Rowley MA (01969) ***(G-14864)***
Rowley Spring & Stamping Corp.....860 582-8175
210 Redstone Hill Rd # 2 Bristol CT (06010) ***(G-610)***
Roxanne L Tardie.....207 540-4945
918 Presque Isle Rd Ashland ME (04732) ***(G-5540)***
Roy E Amey.....603 538-6913
191 Tabor Rd Pittsburg NH (03592) ***(G-19495)***
Royal Adhesives & Sealants LLC.....860 788-3380
63 Epping St Raymond NH (03077) ***(G-19644)***
Royal Consumer Products LLC (HQ).....203 847-8500
108 Main St Ste 3 Norwalk CT (06851) ***(G-3234)***
Royal Diversified Products.....401 245-6900
287 Market St Warren RI (02885) ***(G-21304)***
Royal Furniture Mfg Co Inc.....978 632-1301
1 S Main St Gardner MA (01440) ***(G-11125)***
Royal Harvest Foods, Springfield *Also called Suffield Poultry Inc* ***(G-15510)***
Royal Ice Cream Company Inc (PA).....860 649-5358
27 Warren St Manchester CT (06040) ***(G-2043)***
Royal Label Co Inc.....617 825-6050
50 Park St Ste 3 Boston MA (02122) ***(G-8828)***
Royal Machine and Tool Corp.....860 828-6555
4 Willow Brook Dr Berlin CT (06037) ***(G-108)***
Royal Screw Machine Pdts Co.....860 845-8920
409 Lake Ave Bristol CT (06010) ***(G-611)***
Royal Stamp Works Inc.....978 531-5555
19 Centennial Dr Peabody MA (01960) ***(G-14367)***
Royal Welding LLC.....860 232-5255
50 Francis Ave Ste 4 Hartford CT (06106) ***(G-1867)***
Royale Limousines, Haverhill *Also called Cabot Coach Builders Inc* ***(G-11412)***
Roymal Inc.....603 863-2410
475 Sunapee St Newport NH (03773) ***(G-19357)***
Roytoy, East Machias *Also called Bruce Dennison* ***(G-5983)***
Rozelle Inc.....802 744-2270
4260 Loop Rd Westfield VT (05874) ***(G-22627)***
RP Abrasives & Machine Inc.....603 335-2132
20 Spaulding Ave Unit 2 Rochester NH (03868) ***(G-19685)***
Rph Enterprises Inc.....508 238-3351
50 Earls Way Franklin MA (02038) ***(G-11076)***
RPI Printing, Fall River *Also called Ramsbottom Printing Inc* ***(G-10752)***
RPM Technologies Inc.....413 583-3385
100 State St Ludlow MA (01056) ***(G-12477)***
RPM Wood Finishes Group Inc.....413 562-9655
221 Union St Westfield MA (01085) ***(G-16724)***
Rpp, Lawrence *Also called Emerson Process Management* ***(G-12022)***
Rpt Holdings LLC.....877 997-3674
30 Log Bridge Rd Bldg 200 Middleton MA (01949) ***(G-13099)***
RR Design.....203 792-3419
13 Hearthstone Dr Bethel CT (06801) ***(G-176)***
Rrk Walker Inc.....508 541-8100
22 Park St Mendon MA (01756) ***(G-12995)***
Rrt of Springfield Mass Inc, Springfield *Also called Waste Mgmt Inc* ***(G-15523)***
RS Nazarian Inc.....617 723-3040
333 Washington St Ste 625 Boston MA (02108) ***(G-8829)***
RSA Corp.....203 790-8100
36 Old Sherman Tpke Danbury CT (06810) ***(G-980)***
Rsa Security LLC (HQ).....781 515-5000
174 Middlesex Tpke Bedford MA (01730) ***(G-8007)***
Rscc Aerospace & Defense, Manchester *Also called Marmon Aerospace & Defense LLC* ***(G-18867)***
Rscc Wire & Cable LLC.....603 622-3500
680 Hayward St Manchester NH (03103) ***(G-18912)***
Rscc Wire & Cable LLC (HQ).....860 653-8300
20 Bradley Park Rd East Granby CT (06026) ***(G-1143)***
RSI Metal Fabrication LLC.....603 382-8367
213 Haverhill Rd Bldg 9 East Kingston NH (03827) ***(G-18091)***
Rsj LLC.....508 695-5555
52 Orne St North Attleboro MA (02760) ***(G-13777)***
Rsl Fiber Systems LLC.....860 282-4930
473 Silver Ln East Hartford CT (06118) ***(G-1218)***
Rss Enterprises LLC.....203 736-6220
101 Elizabeth St Ste 7 Derby CT (06418) ***(G-1078)***
Rsv Management.....207 255-8608
9 Valley View Rd Machias ME (04654) ***(G-6394)***
Rtas Systems, Bedford *Also called Sudbury Systems Inc* ***(G-8010)***
RTC Mfg Co Inc.....800 888-3701
1094 Echo Lake Rd Watertown CT (06795) ***(G-5022)***
RTD Technologies Inc.....603 692-5978
360 Route 108 Somersworth NH (03878) ***(G-19848)***
Rtr Technologies Inc (PA).....413 298-0025
48 Main St Stockbridge MA (01262) ***(G-15551)***
RTS Packaging LLC.....207 883-8921
16 Washington Ave Scarborough ME (04074) ***(G-6938)***
Rubb Building Systems, Sanford *Also called Rubb Inc* ***(G-6892)***
Rubb Inc.....207 324-2877
1 Rubb Ln Sanford ME (04073) ***(G-6892)***
Rubber Group, The, Rochester *Also called Humphreys Industrial Pdts Inc* ***(G-19671)***
Rubber Labels USA LLC.....203 713-8059
500 Bic Dr Bldg 2 Milford CT (06461) ***(G-2357)***
Rubber Right Rollers Inc.....617 466-1447
120 Eastern Ave Ste 3 Chelsea MA (02150) ***(G-9965)***
Rubber Supplies Company Inc.....203 736-9995
1 Park Ave Ste 1 # 1 Derby CT (06418) ***(G-1079)***
Rubberright Rollers Inc.....617 387-6060
101 Tileston St Everett MA (02149) ***(G-10629)***
Rubco Products Company.....860 496-1178
1697 E Main St Torrington CT (06790) ***(G-4597)***
Rubil Associates Inc.....978 670-7192
34 Dunham Rd Billerica MA (01821) ***(G-8292)***
Ruby Automation LLC (HQ).....860 687-5000
1 Vision Way Bloomfield CT (06002) ***(G-258)***
Ruby Electric, Worcester *Also called Dkd Solutions Inc* ***(G-17365)***
Ruby Fluid Power LLC (HQ).....860 243-7100
1 Vision Way Bloomfield CT (06002) ***(G-259)***
Ruby Industrial Tech LLC (PA).....860 687-5000
1 Vision Way Bloomfield CT (06002) ***(G-260)***
Ruby Moon LLC.....207 200-3242
7 Fieldcrest Dr Casco ME (04015) ***(G-5897)***
Ruckus Wireless Inc.....203 303-6400
15 Sterling Dr Wallingford CT (06492) ***(G-4802)***
Ruckus Wireless Inc.....508 870-1184
8 Technology Dr Ste 200 Westborough MA (01581) ***(G-16645)***
Ruckus Wireless Inc.....978 614-2900
900 Chelmsford St Lowell MA (01851) ***(G-12430)***
Rudison Routhier Engrg Co.....413 247-9341
32 West St West Hatfield MA (01088) ***(G-16485)***
Rudolph Technologies Inc (HQ).....978 253-6200
16 Jonspin Rd Wilmington MA (01887) ***(G-17042)***
Ruger Records Dept, Newport *Also called Sturm Ruger & Company Inc* ***(G-19361)***
Rugg Manufacturing Company Inc.....413 773-5471
554 Willard St Leominster MA (01453) ***(G-12185)***

Ruggles-Klingemann Mfg Co (PA) 978 232-8300
78 Water St Beverly MA (01915) ***(G-8173)***
Ruggles-Klingemann Mfg Co 603 474-8500
34 Folly Mill Rd Ste 400 Seabrook NH (03874) ***(G-19814)***
Rugsalecom LLC 860 756-0959
17 S Main St West Hartford CT (06107) ***(G-5094)***
Rule Signs 802 728-6030
792 Bear Hill Rd Randolph VT (05060) ***(G-22302)***
Rumford Falls Times, Rumford *Also called James Newspapers Inc* ***(G-6836)***
Runamok Maple LLC 802 849-7943
293 Fletcher Rd Fairfax VT (05454) ***(G-21978)***
Runtal North America Inc 800 526-2621
187 Neck Rd Haverhill MA (01835) ***(G-11469)***
Rupe Slate Co 802 287-9692
54 New Boston Rd Poultney VT (05764) ***(G-22276)***
Rusco Steel Company 401 732-0548
25 Bleachery Ct Warwick RI (02886) ***(G-21418)***
Russ Walter Publishing, Manchester *Also called Secret Guide To Computers* ***(G-18920)***
Russard Inc 781 986-4545
160 Pleasant St Rockland MA (02370) ***(G-14823)***
Russelectric Inc (HQ) 781 749-6000
99 Industrial Park Rd Hingham MA (02043) ***(G-11509)***
Russell Amy Kahn (PA) 203 438-2133
225 S Salem Rd Ridgefield CT (06877) ***(G-3680)***
Russell Brands LLC 413 735-1400
489 Whitney Ave Ste 301 Holyoke MA (01040) ***(G-11653)***
Russell Group 781 648-0302
56 College Ave Arlington MA (02474) ***(G-7636)***
Russell Optics, West Rutland *Also called Jack Russell* ***(G-22617)***
Russell Organics LLC 203 285-6633
329 Main St Ste 208 Wallingford CT (06492) ***(G-4803)***
Russell Partition Co Inc 203 239-5749
20 Dodge Ave North Haven CT (06473) ***(G-3059)***
Russell Precision 603 524-3772
252 Hillcrest Dr Laconia NH (03246) ***(G-18584)***
Russian Information Services 802 223-4955
88 Grandview Ter Montpelier VT (05602) ***(G-22160)***
Russos Inc 781 233-1737
329 Main St Saugus MA (01906) ***(G-14995)***
Russound/Fmp Inc 603 659-5170
1 Forbes Rd Ste 1 # 1 Newmarket NH (03857) ***(G-19338)***
Rustic Crust, Pittsfield *Also called Ever Better Eating Inc* ***(G-19499)***
Rustic Marlin Designs LLC 508 376-1004
389 Columbia Rd Ste 40 Hanover MA (02339) ***(G-11350)***
Rustic Renditions, Meredith *Also called Tucker Mountain Homes Inc* ***(G-18981)***
Rustoleum Attleboro Plant 508 222-3710
113 Olive St Attleboro MA (02703) ***(G-7791)***
Rusty D Inc 802 888-8838
442 Worcester Rdg Elmore VT (05661) ***(G-21922)***
Rutland Business Journal, Rutland *Also called Creative Marketing Services* ***(G-22327)***
Rutland City Band 802 775-5378
129 Cannon Dr Rutland VT (05701) ***(G-22349)***
Rutland Herald, Rutland *Also called Herald Association Inc* ***(G-22338)***
Rutland Plywood Corp 802 747-4000
92 Park St Ste 1 Rutland VT (05701) ***(G-22350)***
Rutland Printing Co Inc 802 775-1948
267 Lincoln Ave Rutland VT (05701) ***(G-22351)***
Ruwac Inc 413 532-4030
54 Winter St Holyoke MA (01040) ***(G-11654)***
Rvs & Co 401 231-8200
387 George Waterman Rd Johnston RI (02919) ***(G-20539)***
RWK Tool Inc 860 635-0116
200 Corporate Row Cromwell CT (06416) ***(G-860)***
Rwo Inc 802 497-1563
251 Pinehurst Dr Shelburne VT (05482) ***(G-22423)***
Rwt Corporation 203 245-2731
32 New Rd Madison CT (06443) ***(G-1973)***
Rwwi Holdings LLC 781 239-0700
55 William St Ste 240 Wellesley MA (02481) ***(G-16384)***
Rx Analytic Inc 203 733-0837
6 Bob Hill Rd Ridgefield CT (06877) ***(G-3681)***
Rx Green Solutions LLC 603 769-3450
873 Page St Fl 2 Manchester NH (03109) ***(G-18913)***
RXI, Marlborough *Also called Phio Pharmaceuticals Corp* ***(G-12807)***
Ry KY Inc 781 235-4581
21 Cunningham Rd Wellesley MA (02481) ***(G-16385)***
Ryan & Wood Distillery 978 281-2282
15 Great Republic Dr # 2 Gloucester MA (01930) ***(G-11208)***
Ryan Iron Works Inc 508 821-2058
1830 Broadway Raynham MA (02767) ***(G-14729)***
Ryan Tool Co Inc 508 822-6576
336 Weir St 2 Taunton MA (02780) ***(G-15781)***
Ryca Inc 978 851-3265
1768 Main St Ste 2 Tewksbury MA (01876) ***(G-15833)***
Ryco Trimming Inc 401 725-1779
25 Carrington St Lincoln RI (02865) ***(G-20595)***
Rymsa Micro Communications (PA) 603 429-0800
15 Caron St Merrimack NH (03054) ***(G-19026)***
Rynel Inc (HQ) 207 882-0200
11 Twin Rivers Dr Wiscasset ME (04578) ***(G-7287)***
Rypos Inc (PA) 508 429-4552
40 Kenwood Cir Ste 8 Franklin MA (02038) ***(G-11077)***
Ryszard A Kokosinski 508 943-2700
75 Oxford Ave Dudley MA (01571) ***(G-10383)***
S & A Trombley Corporation 802 888-2394
76 Houle Ave Morrisville VT (05661) ***(G-22176)***
S & D Rubber Co Div, Hanover *Also called Standard Rubber Products Inc* ***(G-11353)***
S & D Sheet Metal Inc 207 777-7338
945 Washington St N Auburn ME (04210) ***(G-5596)***
S & D Spinning Mill Inc 508 865-2267
190 W Main St Millbury MA (01527) ***(G-13175)***
S & E Fuels Inc 617 407-9977
113 Dean St Taunton MA (02780) ***(G-15782)***
S & F Machine Co Inc 978 374-1552
1405 River St Haverhill MA (01832) ***(G-11470)***
S & H Engineering Inc 978 256-7231
248 Mill Rd Ste 4 Chelmsford MA (01824) ***(G-9929)***
S & H Precision Mfg Co Inc (PA) 603 659-8323
10 Forbes Rd Newmarket NH (03857) ***(G-19339)***
S & M Enameling Co Inc 401 272-0333
70 South St Providence RI (02903) ***(G-21118)***
S & M Fuels Inc 508 746-1495
86 Sandwich St Plymouth MA (02360) ***(G-14581)***
S & M Swiss Products Inc 860 283-4020
135 S Main St Ste 7 Thomaston CT (06787) ***(G-4513)***
S & P Heat Treating Inc 401 737-9272
16a Dewey Ave Warwick RI (02886) ***(G-21419)***
S & P Metallurgy Service, Warwick *Also called S & P Heat Treating Inc* ***(G-21419)***
S & Q Printers Inc 603 654-2888
Howard St Wilton NH (03086) ***(G-19987)***
S & R Tool & Die Inc 781 447-8446
24 Commercial Waye Hanson MA (02341) ***(G-11368)***
S & S Computer Imaging Inc 413 536-0117
252 Open Square Way # 415 Holyoke MA (01040) ***(G-11655)***
S & S Fabric Products, Portsmouth *Also called Black Dog Corporation* ***(G-20920)***
S & S Machine and Welding Inc 413 743-5714
128 Windsor Rd Savoy MA (01256) ***(G-15003)***
S & S Machine Company Inc 781 319-9882
65 Commerce Way Marshfield MA (02050) ***(G-12867)***
S & S Machine LLC 603 204-5542
11 Caldwell Dr Ste 4 Amherst NH (03031) ***(G-17587)***
S & S Publications Inc 781 925-9266
41 Highland Ave Hull MA (02045) ***(G-11830)***
S & S Sealcoating LLC 203 284-0054
5 Barker Dr Wallingford CT (06492) ***(G-4804)***
S & S Statuary 978 535-5837
8 Patricia Rd Peabody MA (01960) ***(G-14368)***
S & T Global Inc 781 376-1774
470 Wildwood Ave Ste 3 Woburn MA (01801) ***(G-17287)***
S & T Precision Plate Cutting 781 447-1084
205 Commercial St Rear Whitman MA (02382) ***(G-16928)***
S A Candelora Enterprises 203 484-2863
250 Totoket Rd North Branford CT (06471) ***(G-2975)***
S A N Inc (PA) 978 686-3875
92 S Broadway Lawrence MA (01843) ***(G-12073)***
S and Z Graphics LLC 203 783-9675
415 Boston Post Rd Ste 7 Milford CT (06460) ***(G-2358)***
S B E Inc (PA) 802 476-4146
81 Parker Rd Barre VT (05641) ***(G-21638)***
S C T, Norwalk *Also called Sound Control Technologies* ***(G-3248)***
S Camerota & Sons Inc 603 228-9343
865 Route 3a Bow NH (03304) ***(G-17730)***
S Camerota & Sons Inc 203 782-0360
166 Universal Dr Unit 2 North Haven CT (06473) ***(G-3060)***
S D & D Inc 860 357-2603
99 Clark Dr 1 East Berlin CT (06023) ***(G-1107)***
S H P, Wilton *Also called Special Hermetic Products* ***(G-19989)***
S I Howard Glass Company Inc 508 753-8146
379 Sw Cutoff Worcester MA (01604) ***(G-17461)***
S K Machine Co Inc 508 993-6387
83 Harding Rd Fairhaven MA (02719) ***(G-10647)***
S Karger Publishers Inc 860 675-7834
26 W Avon Rd Unionville CT (06085) ***(G-4661)***
S Kyle Equipment Llc 978 422-8448
7 Crowley Rd Sterling MA (01564) ***(G-15543)***
S Lane John & Son Incorporated (PA) 413 568-8986
730 E Mountain Rd Westfield MA (01085) ***(G-16725)***
S Lane John & Son Incorporated 508 987-3959
Off Clara Barton Oxford MA (01540) ***(G-14273)***
S M B Machine Co 978 948-7624
79 Boxford Rd Rowley MA (01969) ***(G-14865)***
S M Churyk Iron Works Inc 860 355-1777
539 Danbury Rd New Milford CT (06776) ***(G-2826)***
S M D, Stamford *Also called Surface Mount Devices LLC* ***(G-4336)***
S M Engineering Co Inc 508 699-4484
83 Chestnut St North Attleboro MA (02760) ***(G-13778)***
S M Lorusso & Sons Inc (PA) 508 668-2600
331 West St Walpole MA (02081) ***(G-16010)***

S M Lorusso & Sons Inc 781 337-6770
611 Pleasant St East Weymouth MA (02189) ***(G-10546)***
S M Lorusso & Sons Inc 617 323-6380
10 Grove St Boston MA (02132) ***(G-8830)***
S M Lorusso & Sons Inc 508 384-3587
128 East St Wrentham MA (02093) ***(G-17528)***
S M O C, Framingham *Also called PIP Foundation Inc* ***(G-10995)***
S M Services Inc 603 883-3381
14 Progress Ave Nashua NH (03062) ***(G-19256)***
S M T Graphics LLC 802 897-5231
260 Shacksboro Rd Shoreham VT (05770) ***(G-22433)***
S P, East Windsor *Also called Specialty Printing LLC* ***(G-1303)***
S P & G, Stamford *Also called Speed Printing & Graphics Inc* ***(G-4328)***
S P Holt Corporation 207 866-4867
20 Water St Orono ME (04473) ***(G-6558)***
S P I, Haverhill *Also called Specialized Plating Inc* ***(G-11473)***
S Ralph Cross and Sons Inc 508 865-8112
68 Providence Rd Sutton MA (01590) ***(G-15691)***
S S Fabrications Inc 860 974-1910
82 County Rd Eastford CT (06242) ***(G-1314)***
S T White Concrete Forms 781 982-9116
12 Central St Abington MA (02351) ***(G-7329)***
S W Keats Company 781 935-4282
85 Libby Ave Reading MA (01867) ***(G-14742)***
S White Fuel Stop 802 293-5804
1187 Us Route 7 Danby VT (05739) ***(G-21894)***
S&E Specialty Polymers LLC 978 537-8261
140 Leominster Shirley Rd # 100 Lunenburg MA (01462) ***(G-12483)***
S&S Excavation and Logging LLC 207 312-5590
447 Danville Corner Rd Auburn ME (04210) ***(G-5597)***
S&S Industries Inc (PA) 914 885-1500
1551 Central St Stoughton MA (02072) ***(G-15619)***
S2s Surgical LLC 401 398-1933
1503 S County Trl East Greenwich RI (02818) ***(G-20378)***
S3 Digital Publishing Inc 207 351-8006
60a Capital Ave Lisbon Falls ME (04252) ***(G-6372)***
SA Feole Masonry Svcs Inc 401 273-2766
80 Angell Ave Cranston RI (02920) ***(G-20282)***
SA Photonics Inc 781 861-1430
450 Bedford St Lexington MA (02420) ***(G-12260)***
Saar Corporation 860 674-9440
81 Spring Ln Farmington CT (06032) ***(G-1511)***
Saatva Inc 877 672-2882
8 Wright St Ste 108 Westport CT (06880) ***(G-5228)***
Saba Software Inc 781 238-6730
25 Burlington Mall Rd Burlington MA (01803) ***(G-9331)***
Sabar Graphics LLC (PA) 203 467-3016
330 Main St East Haven CT (06512) ***(G-1260)***
Sabatino North America LLC (PA) 718 328-4120
135 Front Ave West Haven CT (06516) ***(G-5144)***
Sabbow and Co Inc 603 444-6724
390 Highland Ave Littleton NH (03561) ***(G-18665)***
Saber Line Club, Providence *Also called Patrick T Conley Atty* ***(G-21087)***
Saber Machine Design Corp 603 870-8190
50 Northwestern Dr Ste 9b Salem NH (03079) ***(G-19764)***
Sabian Ltd 506 272-2199
91 Airport Dr Houlton ME (04730) ***(G-6210)***
Sabic US Holdings LP 413 448-7110
1 Plastics Ave Pittsfield MA (01201) ***(G-14506)***
Sabon Industries Inc 203 255-8880
150 Jennie Ln Fairfield CT (06824) ***(G-1453)***
Sabr Enterprises LLC 978 264-0499
6 Eastern Rd Acton MA (01720) ***(G-7382)***
Sabra Foods, Norwood *Also called International Food Products* ***(G-14166)***
Sacar Enterprises LLC 978 834-6494
12 Oakland St Ste 220 Amesbury MA (01913) ***(G-7506)***
Saccuzzo Company Inc 860 665-1101
149 Louis St Newington CT (06111) ***(G-2900)***
Saco Bay Millwork Co 207 929-8400
20 Tory Hill Dr Buxton ME (04093) ***(G-5860)***
Saco Manufacturing & Wdwkg 207 284-6613
39 Lincoln St Saco ME (04072) ***(G-6857)***
Sadlak Industries LLC 860 742-0227
712 Bread And Milk St A9 Coventry CT (06238) ***(G-838)***
Sadlak Innovative Design, Coventry *Also called Mike Sadlak* ***(G-835)***
Sadlak Manufacturing LLC 860 742-0227
712 Bread And Milk St # 7 Coventry CT (06238) ***(G-839)***
Saeilo Inc 508 799-9809
130 Goddard Memorial Dr Worcester MA (01603) ***(G-17462)***
Saeilo Manufacturing Inds, Worcester *Also called SMI Ma Inc* ***(G-17476)***
Saeilo USA Inc 508 795-3919
130 Goddard Memorial Dr Worcester MA (01603) ***(G-17463)***
Saes Memry, Bethel *Also called Memry Corporation* ***(G-170)***
Saf Industries LLC 203 729-4900
106 Evansville Ave Meriden CT (06451) ***(G-2127)***
Saf Industries LLC (HQ) 203 729-4900
106 Evansville Ave Meriden CT (06451) ***(G-2128)***
Safari Books Online LLC 617 426-8600
2 Avenue De Lafayette 6 Boston MA (02111) ***(G-8831)***
Safariland LLC 413 684-3104
401 South St Dalton MA (01226) ***(G-10183)***
Safe and Secure Fou A NJ Non 848 992-3623
448 Henry Gould Rd Perkinsville VT (05151) ***(G-22257)***
Safe Approach Inc 207 345-9900
206 Mechanic Falls Rd Poland ME (04274) ***(G-6597)***
Safe Conveyor Incorporated 774 688-9109
1658 Gar Hwy Ste 2 Swansea MA (02777) ***(G-15714)***
Safe Guard Signs 401 725-9090
211 Weeden St Pawtucket RI (02860) ***(G-20894)***
Safe Harbour Products Inc 203 295-8377
1 Selleck St Ste 3e Norwalk CT (06855) ***(G-3235)***
Safe Hydrogen LLC 781 861-7016
30 York St Lexington MA (02420) ***(G-12261)***
Safe Hydrogen LLC 781 861-7252
4 Bates Rd Lexington MA (02421) ***(G-12262)***
Safe Laser Therapy LLC 203 261-4400
1747 Summer St Ste 4 Stamford CT (06905) ***(G-4308)***
Safe Process Systems Inc 508 285-5109
54 S Washington St Norton MA (02766) ***(G-14087)***
Safe T Cut Inc 413 267-9984
97 Main St Monson MA (01057) ***(G-13211)***
Safe Water 203 732-4806
371 Roosevelt Dr Seymour CT (06483) ***(G-3764)***
Safe-T-Tank Corp 203 237-6320
25 Powers Dr Meriden CT (06451) ***(G-2129)***
Safecor Health LLC 781 933-8780
317 New Boston St Ste 100 Woburn MA (01801) ***(G-17288)***
Safety & Gloves Inc 800 221-0570
100 Foxborough Blvd # 240 Foxboro MA (02035) ***(G-10900)***
Safety 1st, Foxboro *Also called Dorel Juvenile Group Inc* ***(G-10881)***
Safety Bags Inc 203 242-0727
2 Corporate Dr Ste 250 Shelton CT (06484) ***(G-3867)***
Safety Dispatch Inc 203 885-5722
57 Jefferson Dr Ridgefield CT (06877) ***(G-3682)***
Safety Flag Company, Central Falls *Also called Vogue Industries Ltd Partnr* ***(G-20128)***
Safety Seals, Peabody *Also called North Shore Laboratories Corp* ***(G-14358)***
Safety-Kleen Systems Inc 508 481-3116
50a Brigham St Marlborough MA (01752) ***(G-12823)***
Safeworld International, Canton *Also called Spectrowax Corporation* ***(G-9784)***
Saffron Group Inc (PA) 401 245-3725
601 Metacom Ave Warren RI (02885) ***(G-21305)***
Saft America Inc 203 234-8333
3 Powdered Metal Rd North Haven CT (06473) ***(G-3061)***
Safve Inc 781 545-3546
24 Ladds Way Scituate MA (02066) ***(G-15011)***
Saga Packaging Machinery Div, Southbridge *Also called A & M Tool & Die Company Inc* ***(G-15374)***
Sage Envirotech Drlg Svcs Inc 401 723-9900
172 Armistice Blvd Pawtucket RI (02860) ***(G-20895)***
Sage Therapeutics Inc (PA) 617 299-8380
215 1st St Cambridge MA (02142) ***(G-9640)***
Sahara Heaters Mfg Co 603 888-7351
22 Pinehurst Ave Nashua NH (03062) ***(G-19257)***
Sahara Heating Systems, Nashua *Also called Sahara Heaters Mfg Co* ***(G-19257)***
Sailmaking Support Systems, Greenland *Also called Anson Sailmakers Inc* ***(G-18220)***
Saint Josephs Wood Pdts LLC 203 787-5746
80 Middletown Ave New Haven CT (06513) ***(G-2732)***
Saint Thecla Retreat House, Billerica *Also called Daughters of St Paul Inc* ***(G-8235)***
Saint-Gobain Abrasives Inc (HQ) 508 795-5000
1 New Bond St Worcester MA (01606) ***(G-17464)***
Saint-Gobain Abrasives Inc 603 673-7560
47 Powers St Milford NH (03055) ***(G-19074)***
Saint-Gobain Ceramic Materials, Worcester *Also called Saint-Gobain Ceramics Plas Inc* ***(G-17465)***
Saint-Gobain Ceramics Plas Inc 508 795-5000
1 New Bond St Worcester MA (01606) ***(G-17465)***
Saint-Gobain Ceramics Plas Inc 508 795-5000
351 Stores St Worcester MA (01606) ***(G-17466)***
Saint-Gobain Ceramics Plas Inc 603 673-5831
33 Powers St Milford NH (03055) ***(G-19075)***
Saint-Gobain Ceramics Plas Inc 413 586-8167
175 Industrial Dr Northampton MA (01060) ***(G-14020)***
Saint-Gobain Ceramics Plas Inc 508 351-7754
9 Goddard Rd Northborough MA (01532) ***(G-14046)***
Saint-Gobain Corporation 508 351-7112
9 Goddard Rd Northborough MA (01532) ***(G-14047)***
Saint-Gobain Crystals, Milford *Also called Saint-Gobain Ceramics Plas Inc* ***(G-19075)***
Saint-Gobain Glass Corporation 603 673-7560
47 Powers St Milford NH (03055) ***(G-19076)***
Saint-Gobain Igniter Products, Milford *Also called Saint-Gobain Glass Corporation* ***(G-19076)***
Saint-Gobain Prfmce Plas Corp 603 424-9000
701 Daniel Webster Hwy Merrimack NH (03054) ***(G-19027)***
Saint-Gobain Prfmce Plas Corp 508 823-7701
700 Joseph E Warner Blvd Taunton MA (02780) ***(G-15783)***
Saint-Gobain Prfmce Plas Corp 401 253-2000
386 Metacom Ave Bristol RI (02809) ***(G-20102)***

ALPHABETIC

Saint-Gobain Prfmce Plas Corp.....508 852-3072
717 Plantation St Worcester MA (01605) *(G-17467)*
Sajawi Corporation.....978 486-9050
24 Porter Rd Littleton MA (01460) *(G-12323)*
Saklax Manufacturing Company.....860 242-2538
1346 Blue Hills Ave Ste B Bloomfield CT (06002) *(G-261)*
Salamander Designs Ltd.....860 761-9500
811 Blue Hills Ave Bloomfield CT (06002) *(G-262)*
Salamon Industries LLC.....860 612-8420
250 John Downey Dr New Britain CT (06051) *(G-2575)*
Salarius Pharmaceuticals Inc (PA).....617 874-1821
800 Boylston St Fl 24 Boston MA (02199) *(G-8832)*
Salem Beer Works, Salem *Also called Slesar Bros Brewing Co Inc (G-14943)*
Salem House Press.....978 578-9238
11 Beacon St Salem MA (01970) *(G-14940)*
Salem Metal Inc.....978 774-2100
177 N Main St Middleton MA (01949) *(G-13100)*
Salem Preferred Partners LLC (PA).....540 389-3922
200 Berkeley St Fl 3 Boston MA (02116) *(G-8833)*
Salem Press, Windham *Also called Sumner Fancy (G-20011)*
Salem Vly Farms Ice Cream Inc.....860 859-2980
20 Darling Rd Salem CT (06420) *(G-3739)*
Salems Old Fshoned Candies Inc.....978 744-3242
93 Canal St Salem MA (01970) *(G-14941)*
Salesbrief Inc.....203 216-0270
695 Atlantic Ave Boston MA (02111) *(G-8834)*
Saleschain LLC.....203 262-1611
61 Mattatuck Heights Rd # 201 Waterbury CT (06705) *(G-4951)*
Salesforcecom Inc.....857 415-3510
500 Boylston St Fl 19 Boston MA (02116) *(G-8835)*
Salgado Sand & Gravel Inc.....774 202-2626
779 Russells Mills Rd South Dartmouth MA (02748) *(G-15243)*
Salibas Rug & Upholstery Clrs.....207 947-8876
59 May St Bangor ME (04401) *(G-5658)*
Saliga Machine Co Inc.....978 562-7959
10 Bonazzoli Ave Hudson MA (01749) *(G-11814)*
Salisbury Cove Associates Inc.....207 288-2337
15 Knox Rd Bar Harbor ME (04609) *(G-5669)*
Salk Company Inc.....617 782-4030
119 Braintree St Ste 701 Allston MA (02134) *(G-7474)*
Sally Conant.....203 878-3005
454 Old Cellar Rd Orange CT (06477) *(G-3383)*
Sally Seaver.....833 322-8483
11 Makechnie Rd Burlington MA (01803) *(G-9332)*
Sallyharrold Inc.....508 258-0253
49 Corporation Rd Dennis MA (02638) *(G-10310)*
Salmon Falls Woodworks LLC.....603 740-6060
38 Littleworth Rd Dover NH (03820) *(G-18051)*
Salmon Press LLC (PA).....603 279-4516
5 Water St Meredith NH (03253) *(G-18978)*
Salmon Press LLC.....603 332-2300
4 Union St Rochester NH (03867) *(G-19686)*
Salo Bay Trading Co.....207 283-4732
40 Granite Point Rd Biddeford ME (04005) *(G-5762)*
Salon Monet.....617 425-0010
176 Newbury St Ste 400 Boston MA (02116) *(G-8836)*
Saloom Furniture Co Inc.....978 297-1901
256 Murdock Ave Winchendon MA (01475) *(G-17082)*
Sals Clothing & Fabric Restor.....617 387-6726
15 Henderson St Everett MA (02149) *(G-10630)*
Salt Marsh Canvas.....978 462-0070
10 Bittersweet Ln Newbury MA (01951) *(G-13465)*
Salt Wellfleet.....508 237-4415
55 Commercial St Wellfleet MA (02667) *(G-16402)*
Salt Woods LLC.....617 744-9401
19 Calvin Rd Watertown MA (02472) *(G-16313)*
Saltwhistle Technology LLC.....603 887-3161
96 Lane Rd Chester NH (03036) *(G-17825)*
Salty Dog Gallery.....207 244-5918
322 Main St Southwest Harbor ME (04679) *(G-7050)*
Salute Spirits LLC.....609 306-2258
52 Lee Ave Apt 1 Newport RI (02840) *(G-20678)*
Salvadore Tool & Findings Inc (PA).....401 331-6000
24 Althea St Providence RI (02907) *(G-21119)*
Sam & Ty LLC (PA).....212 840-1871
12 S Main St Ste 403 Norwalk CT (06854) *(G-3236)*
Sam Kasten Handweaver LLC.....413 637-8900
55 Pittsfield Rd Ste 12a Lenox MA (01240) *(G-12103)*
Sam Maulucci & Sons, Wethersfield *Also called Mozzicato Fmly Investments LLC (G-5259)*
Sam's & Son, Hyde Park *Also called Sams Drapery Workroom Inc (G-11878)*
Samar Co Inc.....781 297-7264
220 Cushing St Stoughton MA (02072) *(G-15620)*
Samarc Inc.....617 924-3884
28 Damrell St Ste B01 Boston MA (02127) *(G-8837)*
Same Day Dumpsters LLC.....203 676-1219
225 Quinnipiac Ave New Haven CT (06513) *(G-2733)*
Samic Mfg Company.....401 421-2400
807 Hartford Ave Johnston RI (02919) *(G-20540)*
Sammarval Co Ltd.....802 843-2637
661 Wright Orchard Rd Grafton VT (05146) *(G-21996)*
Sammel Sign Company.....802 879-3360
20 Morse Dr Ste C Essex Junction VT (05452) *(G-21958)*
Sammi Sleeping Systems LLC.....203 684-3131
5 Science Park New Haven CT (06511) *(G-2734)*
Sampco Inc (PA).....413 442-4043
56 Downing Pkwy Pittsfield MA (01201) *(G-14507)*
Samples Shipyard, Boothbay Harbor *Also called B Marine Corp (G-5782)*
Sams Drapery Workroom Inc.....617 364-9440
63 Sprague St Ste 2-3 Hyde Park MA (02136) *(G-11878)*
Sams Good News.....802 773-4040
162 N Main St Ste 8 Rutland VT (05701) *(G-22352)*
Samsara Fitness LLC.....860 895-8533
10 Denlar Dr Chester CT (06412) *(G-776)*
Samson Manufacturing Corp.....603 355-3903
32 Optical Ave Keene NH (03431) *(G-18523)*
Samsonite Company Stores LLC.....401 245-2100
95 Main St Warren RI (02885) *(G-21306)*
Samtan Engineering Corp.....781 322-7880
127 Wyllis Ave Malden MA (02148) *(G-12594)*
San Francisco Market.....781 780-3731
2 Lafayette Park Lynn MA (01902) *(G-12536)*
San-Tron Inc (PA).....978 356-1585
4 Turnpike Rd Ipswich MA (01938) *(G-11936)*
Sanchez Associates, Lawrence *Also called Aerospace Semiconductor Inc (G-11990)*
Sanchez Octavio Storage.....508 853-3309
9 Short St Worcester MA (01604) *(G-17468)*
Sancliff Inc.....508 795-0747
97 Temple St Worcester MA (01604) *(G-17469)*
Sanco Energy.....203 259-5914
41 Riders Ln Fairfield CT (06824) *(G-1454)*
Sand 9 Inc.....617 358-0957
1 Kendall Sq Ste B2305 Cambridge MA (02139) *(G-9641)*
Sandballz International LLC.....860 465-9628
832 Stafford Rd Storrs Mansfield CT (06268) *(G-4386)*
Sandberg Enterprises Inc.....401 568-1602
806 Broncos Hwy Pascoag RI (02859) *(G-20804)*
Sandberg Enterprises Inc (PA).....401 568-1602
806 Broncos Hwy Mapleville RI (02839) *(G-20614)*
Sandberg Machine, Mapleville *Also called Sandberg Enterprises Inc (G-20614)*
Sandcastle Publishing LLC.....508 398-3100
434 Route 134 South Dennis MA (02660) *(G-15266)*
Sandelin Foundation Inc.....207 725-7004
82 Old Augusta Rd Topsham ME (04086) *(G-7094)*
Sanders- A Lockheed Martin Co, Merrimack *Also called Lockheed Martin Corporation (G-19012)*
Sanderson-Macleod Incorporated.....413 283-3481
1199 S Main St Palmer MA (01069) *(G-14295)*
Sandler & Sons Co.....508 533-8282
2 Franklin St Ste 1 Medway MA (02053) *(G-12970)*
Sandstrom Carbide Pdts Corp.....401 739-5220
140 Imera Ave Warwick RI (02886) *(G-21420)*
Sandur Tool Co.....203 753-0004
853 Hamilton Ave Waterbury CT (06706) *(G-4952)*
Sandvik Heating Technogy USA, Bethel *Also called Sandvik Wire and Htg Tech Corp (G-178)*
Sandvik Pubg Interactive Inc (PA).....203 205-0188
83 Wooster Hts Ste 208 Danbury CT (06810) *(G-981)*
Sandvik Wire and Htg Tech Corp.....203 744-1440
119 Wooster St Bethel CT (06801) *(G-177)*
Sandvik Wire and Htg Tech Corp (HQ).....203 744-1440
119 Wooster St Bethel CT (06801) *(G-178)*
Sandviks Inc (PA).....866 984-0188
83 Wooster Hts Ste 110 Danbury CT (06810) *(G-982)*
Sandwich Lantern.....508 833-0515
17 Jan Sebastian Dr Ste 1 Sandwich MA (02563) *(G-14973)*
Sandy Bay Machine Inc.....978 546-1331
11 Dory Rd 2 Gloucester MA (01930) *(G-11209)*
Sandy Point Boat Works LLC.....508 878-8057
57 Cranberry Rd Carver MA (02330) *(G-9807)*
Sandys Machine.....978 970-1800
24 Towanda Rd Tewksbury MA (01876) *(G-15834)*
Sanford Manufacturing Facility, Sanford *Also called Roehm America LLC (G-6891)*
Sanford Redmond Inc.....203 351-9800
746 Riverbank Rd Stamford CT (06903) *(G-4309)*
Sangari Active Science, Greenwich *Also called Sasc LLC (G-1646)*
Sanger Equipment and Mfg.....413 625-8304
Wilder Hill Rd Conway MA (01341) *(G-10166)*
Sangstat Medical LLC.....510 789-4300
500 Kendall St Cambridge MA (02142) *(G-9642)*
Sani Tank Inc.....978 537-9784
60 Lanides Ln Leominster MA (01453) *(G-12186)*
Sanken North America Inc., Manchester *Also called Allegro Microsystems Inc (G-18776)*
Sanmina Corporation.....603 621-1800
140 Abby Rd Manchester NH (03103) *(G-18914)*
Sanmina Corporation.....207 623-6511
500 Civic Center Dr Augusta ME (04330) *(G-5618)*
Sano LLC.....617 290-3348
14 Thackeray Rd 1c Wellesley MA (02481) *(G-16386)*
Sanofi Genzyme, Framingham *Also called Genzyme Corporation (G-10954)*

Sanofi Genzyme 508 871-5871
1 The Mountain Rd Framingham MA (01701) ***(G-11001)***
Sanofi US Services Inc 617 562-4555
500 Kendall St Ste 500 # 500 Cambridge MA (02142) ***(G-9643)***
Sanova Bioscience Inc 978 429-8079
42 Nagog Park Acton MA (01720) ***(G-7383)***
Sant Bani Press Inc 603 286-3114
60 Buckley Cir Ste 3 Manchester NH (03109) ***(G-18915)***
Santa Cruz Gunlocks LLC 603 746-7740
450 Tyler Rd Webster NH (03303) ***(G-19945)***
Santa Rosa Lead Products LLC 508 893-6021
70 Bartzak Dr Holliston MA (01746) ***(G-11600)***
Santec Corporation 203 878-1379
84 Old Gate Ln Milford CT (06460) ***(G-2359)***
Santhera Pharmaceuticals usa 781 552-5145
25 Corporate Dr Burlington MA (01803) ***(G-9333)***
Santhera Phrmceuticals USA Inc 617 886-5161
40 Warren St Fl 3 Charlestown MA (02129) ***(G-9843)***
Santini Brothers Ir Works Inc 781 396-1450
28 Sycamore Ave Medford MA (02155) ***(G-12947)***
Santo C De Spirt Marble & Gran 413 786-7073
2 S Bridge Dr Agawam MA (01001) ***(G-7450)***
Santorella Publication Ltd (PA) 978 750-0566
24 Water St Danvers MA (01923) ***(G-10254)***
Santorini Breeze LLC 203 640-3431
374 E Main St Branford CT (06405) ***(G-344)***
Santoto LLC 203 984-2540
Danbury Municipal Danbury CT (06810) ***(G-983)***
Sap, Burlington *Also called Smith & Salmon Inc* ***(G-21809)***
Sap America Inc 781 852-3000
15 Wayside Rd Burlington MA (01803) ***(G-9334)***
Sap Press, Dedham *Also called Wellesley Information Svcs LLC* ***(G-10301)***
Sap Professional Journal (PA) 781 407-0360
20 Carematrix Dr Dedham MA (02026) ***(G-10297)***
Saperion Inc 781 899-1228
275 Grove St Ste 2-400 Auburndale MA (02466) ***(G-7868)***
Saphikon Inc 603 672-7221
33 Powers St Milford NH (03055) ***(G-19077)***
Saphlux Inc 475 221-8981
4 Pin Oak Dr Branford CT (06405) ***(G-345)***
Sapphire Engineering, Middleboro *Also called Idex Health & Science LLC* ***(G-13064)***
Sappi Fine Paper North America, Skowhegan *Also called Sappi North America Inc* ***(G-6986)***
Sappi Fine Paper North America, South Portland *Also called Sappi North America Inc* ***(G-7039)***
Sappi North America Inc 207 858-4201
98 North Ave Skowhegan ME (04976) ***(G-6985)***
Sappi North America Inc 207 238-3000
1329 Waterville Rd Skowhegan ME (04976) ***(G-6986)***
Sappi North America Inc 207 854-7000
179 John Roberts Rd South Portland ME (04106) ***(G-7039)***
Sappi North America Inc 207 856-4000
89 Cumberland St Westbrook ME (04092) ***(G-7205)***
Sara Campbell Ltd (PA) 617 423-3134
67 Kemble St Ste 4 Boston MA (02119) ***(G-8838)***
Sara Sassy Inc 802 864-4791
29 Myers Ct South Burlington VT (05403) ***(G-22464)***
Saratoga Salad Dressing, Canton *Also called Pearlco of Boston Inc* ***(G-9766)***
Sardine Can Giftware, Brewer *Also called Gregg Stewart* ***(G-5796)***
Sarepta Therapeutics Inc (PA) 617 274-4000
215 1st St Ste 415 Cambridge MA (02142) ***(G-9644)***
Sargeant & Wilbur Inc 401 726-0013
20 Monticello Pl Pawtucket RI (02861) ***(G-20896)***
Sargent Manufacturing Company 203 562-2151
100 Sargent Dr New Haven CT (06511) ***(G-2735)***
Sargent Quality Tools, Branford *Also called Rostra Tool Company* ***(G-343)***
Sarna Div, Canton *Also called Sika Sarnafil Inc* ***(G-9781)***
Sarnafil Services Inc 781 828-5400
100 Dan Rd Canton MA (02021) ***(G-9775)***
Sarro Manufacturing Inc 603 378-9161
6 Puzzle Ln Newton NH (03858) ***(G-19369)***
Sas Institute Inc 860 633-4119
95 Glastonbury Blvd # 301 Glastonbury CT (06033) ***(G-1577)***
Sasc LLC (PA) 203 846-2274
44 Amogerone Crossway Greenwich CT (06830) ***(G-1646)***
Sassone Labwear LLC 860 666-4484
480 Barnum Ave Ste 5 Bridgeport CT (06608) ***(G-485)***
Sat, Springfield *Also called Spirig Advanced Tech Incies* ***(G-15508)***
Satcom Division, South Deerfield *Also called Smiths Interconnect Inc* ***(G-15256)***
Satellite Aerospace Inc 860 643-2771
240 Chapel Rd Manchester CT (06042) ***(G-2044)***
Satellite Tool & Mch Co Inc 860 290-8558
185 Commerce Way Ste 1 South Windsor CT (06074) ***(G-4008)***
Sathorn Corporation 802 860-2121
581 Industrial Ave Williston VT (05495) ***(G-22689)***
Satin American Corporation 203 929-6363
40 Oliver Ter Shelton CT (06484) ***(G-3868)***
Satisfashion, East Providence *Also called Jonette Jewelry Company* ***(G-20425)***
Satori Audio LLC 203 571-6050
180 Post Rd E Ste 201 Westport CT (06880) ***(G-5229)***
Satori Nyc, Westport *Also called Satori Audio LLC* ***(G-5229)***
Sauciers Misc Metal Works LLC 860 747-4577
89 Birch St Southington CT (06489) ***(G-4075)***
Saucony Inc (HQ) 617 824-6000
500 Totten Pond Rd Ste 1 Waltham MA (02451) ***(G-16191)***
Saugatuck Kitchens LLC 203 334-1099
125 Bruce Ave Stratford CT (06615) ***(G-4442)***
Saugus Advertiser 781 233-2040
72 Cherry Hill Dr Beverly MA (01915) ***(G-8174)***
Saugy Inc 401 640-1879
43 Ralls Dr Cranston RI (02920) ***(G-20283)***
Saunders At Locke Mills LLC 207 875-2853
256 Main St Greenwood ME (04255) ***(G-6156)***
Saunders Electronics, South Portland *Also called David Saunders Inc* ***(G-7021)***
Saunders Manufacturing & Mktg, Readfield *Also called Saunders Mfg Co Inc* ***(G-6778)***
Saunders Mfg Co Inc (PA) 207 685-9860
65 Nickerson Hill Rd Readfield ME (04355) ***(G-6778)***
Savage Arms, Westfield *Also called Caliber Company* ***(G-16676)***
Savage Arms Inc (HQ) 413 642-4135
100 Springdale Rd Ste 1 Westfield MA (01085) ***(G-16726)***
Savage Companies 508 616-8772
19 Walkup Dr Westborough MA (01581) ***(G-16646)***
Savage Range Systems Inc 413 568-7001
100 Springdale Rd Westfield MA (01085) ***(G-16727)***
Savage Sports Corporation (HQ) 413 568-7001
100 Springdale Rd Westfield MA (01085) ***(G-16728)***
Savant Systems LLC (PA) 508 683-2500
45 Perseverance Way Hyannis MA (02601) ***(G-11857)***
Save Energy Systems Inc 617 564-4442
39 Blossom Ct Westborough MA (01581) ***(G-16647)***
Savetime Corporation 203 382-2991
2710 North Ave Ste 105b Bridgeport CT (06604) ***(G-486)***
Savin Products Company Inc 781 961-2743
214 High St Randolph MA (02368) ***(G-14697)***
Savory Creations International 650 638-1024
330 Lynnway Ste 401 Lynn MA (01901) ***(G-12537)***
Savron Graphics, Jaffrey *Also called Jeba Graphics LLC* ***(G-18468)***
Savron Graphics Inc (PA) 603 532-7726
4 Stratton Rd Jaffrey NH (03452) ***(G-18476)***
Savron Graphics Inc 603 924-7088
19 Wilton Rd Ste 5 Peterborough NH (03458) ***(G-19487)***
Savvy On Main 508 255-5076
50 Main St Orleans MA (02653) ***(G-14241)***
Savvy Workshop 603 792-0080
55 South Commercial St Manchester NH (03101) ***(G-18916)***
Saw Mill Brook LLC 617 332-5793
16 Sycamore Rd Newton MA (02459) ***(G-13632)***
Saw Mill Site Farm 413 665-3005
324 Wells St Greenfield MA (01301) ***(G-11274)***
Sawmill Brook Farm 508 697-7847
140 Lyman Pl Bridgewater MA (02324) ***(G-9087)***
Sawmill Park 413 569-3393
1 Saw Mill Park Southwick MA (01077) ***(G-15417)***
Sawtech Scientific Inc 603 228-1811
14 Dow Rd Unit A Bow NH (03304) ***(G-17731)***
Sawyer Bentwood Inc 802 368-2357
247 Maple Dr Whitingham VT (05361) ***(G-22647)***
Sawyer Printers, Boston *Also called Henry N Sawyer Co Inc* ***(G-8594)***
Saxon Manufacturing Inc 603 898-2499
50 Northwestern Dr Ste 9b Salem NH (03079) ***(G-19765)***
Saxony Wood Products Inc 203 869-3717
18 Beech St Greenwich CT (06830) ***(G-1647)***
Saxslab US Inc 413 237-4309
7 Pomeroy Ln Ste 3 Amherst MA (01002) ***(G-7524)***
Say It In Stitches Inc 603 224-6470
128 Hall St Ste B Concord NH (03301) ***(G-17927)***
Saybrook Press Incorporated 203 458-3637
39 Chaffinch Island Rd Guilford CT (06437) ***(G-1717)***
Sazacks Inc 860 647-8367
520 Center St Manchester CT (06040) ***(G-2045)***
Sb Development Corp 978 263-2744
17 Craig Rd Acton MA (01720) ***(G-7384)***
Sb Electronics, Barre *Also called S B E Inc* ***(G-21638)***
Sb Marketers Inc 508 943-7162
14 Mark Ave Webster MA (01570) ***(G-16350)***
Sb Signs Inc 802 879-7969
466 Shunpike Rd Williston VT (05495) ***(G-22690)***
Sbfk Inc 802 297-7665
251 West St Unit A Rutland VT (05701) ***(G-22353)***
Sbh Diagnostics Inc 508 545-0333
2 Mercer Rd Natick MA (01760) ***(G-13278)***
SBwinsor Creamery LLC 401 231-5113
58 Pine Hill Ave Johnston RI (02919) ***(G-20541)***
SC Technologies Inc 401 667-7370
342 Compass Cir Unit A2 North Kingstown RI (02852) ***(G-20738)***
Sca Pharmaceuticals LLC 501 312-2800
755 Rainbow Rd Bldg 1 Windsor CT (06095) ***(G-5359)***

ALPHABETIC

Scallop Imaging LLC 617 849-6400
18 Sewall St Marblehead MA (01945) ***(G-12692)***
Scallops Mineral & Shell Empor 603 431-7658
65 Daniel St Portsmouth NH (03801) ***(G-19617)***
Scan Tool & Mold Inc 203 459-4950
2 Trefoil Dr Trumbull CT (06611) ***(G-4631)***
Scan-Optics LLC 860 645-7878
169 Progress Dr Manchester CT (06042) ***(G-2046)***
Scandia Kitchens Inc 508 966-0300
38 Maple St Bellingham MA (02019) ***(G-8058)***
Scandia Marine Inc 401 625-5881
337 Nanaquaket Rd Tiverton RI (02878) ***(G-21262)***
Scandia Plastics Inc 603 382-6533
55 Westville Rd Plaistow NH (03865) ***(G-19523)***
Scanmix Inc 207 782-1885
36 Hogan Rd Lewiston ME (04240) ***(G-6320)***
Scannell Boiler Works Inc 978 454-5629
50 Tanner St Ste 1 Lowell MA (01852) ***(G-12431)***
Scansmart LLC 603 664-7773
66 Valentine Dr Manchester NH (03103) ***(G-18917)***
Scapa Holdings Inc (HQ) 860 688-8000
111 Great Pond Dr Windsor CT (06095) ***(G-5360)***
Scapa Tapes North America LLC (HQ) 860 688-8000
111 Great Pond Dr Windsor CT (06095) ***(G-5361)***
Scapin Sand & Gravel Inc 413 568-0091
260 Blandford Rd Russell MA (01071) ***(G-14878)***
Scarborough Faire Inc (PA) 401 724-4200
1151 Main St Pawtucket RI (02860) ***(G-20897)***
Scargo Stoneware Pottery 508 385-3894
30 Doctor Lords Rd Dennis MA (02638) ***(G-10311)***
Scarlet Letter Press, The, Salem *Also called Scarlet Ltr Press Gallery LLC* ***(G-14942)***
Scarlet Ltr Press Gallery LLC 978 741-1850
10 Colonial Rd Ste 14 Salem MA (01970) ***(G-14942)***
Scarzello & Assocs Inc 603 673-7746
3 Carol Ann Ln Amherst NH (03031) ***(G-17548)***
Scentastics, Brattleboro *Also called Green Mountain Fragrances Inc* ***(G-21731)***
Scg Signs 781 297-9400
72 Taunton St Ste 202 Plainville MA (02762) ***(G-14534)***
Schaefer Machine Company Inc 860 526-4000
200 Commercial Dr Deep River CT (06417) ***(G-1065)***
Schaefer Rolls Inc 203 910-0224
32 Bolduc Ct Wolcott CT (06716) ***(G-5455)***
Schaeferrolls Inc 603 335-1786
23 Plank Industrial Dr Farmington NH (03835) ***(G-18144)***
Schaeffler Aerospace USA Corp (HQ) 203 744-2211
200 Park Ave Danbury CT (06810) ***(G-984)***
Schaeffler Aerospace USA Corp 860 379-7558
159 Colebrook River Rd Winsted CT (06098) ***(G-5421)***
Schaeffler Group USA Inc 203 790-5474
200 Park Ave Danbury CT (06810) ***(G-985)***
Schaller Corporation 508 655-9171
857 Union St Franklin MA (02038) ***(G-11078)***
Scharn Industries 781 376-9777
9 Presidential Way Woburn MA (01801) ***(G-17289)***
Scheduling Systems Inc 508 620-0390
85 Speen St Ste 300 Framingham MA (01701) ***(G-11002)***
Schiavi Homes LLC 207 539-9600
754 Main St Oxford ME (04270) ***(G-6573)***
Schick Manufacturing Inc (HQ) 203 882-2100
10 Leighton Rd Milford CT (06460) ***(G-2360)***
Schick-Wilkinson Sword, Milford *Also called Schick Manufacturing Inc* ***(G-2360)***
Schiff Architectual Detail, Chelsea *Also called Jeff Schiff* ***(G-9956)***
Schiff Archtectural Detail LLC 617 846-6437
120 Eastern Ave Chelsea MA (02150) ***(G-9966)***
Schindler Combustion LLC 203 371-5068
159 Tahmore Dr Fairfield CT (06825) ***(G-1455)***
Schlage Lock Company LLC 781 828-6655
437 Turnpike St Canton MA (02021) ***(G-9776)***
Schleifring, Chelmsford *Also called Schleifring North America LLC* ***(G-9930)***
Schleifring North America LLC 978 677-2500
222 Mill Rd Chelmsford MA (01824) ***(G-9930)***
Schlenk Metallic Pigments, Ashland *Also called O A Both Corporation* ***(G-7666)***
Schleuniger Inc (HQ) 603 627-4860
87 Colin Dr Manchester NH (03103) ***(G-18918)***
Schlotterbeck & Foss LLC (PA) 207 772-4666
3 Ledgeview Dr Westbrook ME (04092) ***(G-7206)***
Schlumberger Technology Corp 617 768-2000
1 Hampshire St Ste 1 # 1 Cambridge MA (02139) ***(G-9645)***
Schlumberger-Doll Research, Cambridge *Also called Schlumberger Technology Corp* ***(G-9645)***
Schmidt Tool Manufacturing 203 877-8149
76 Finch St Ste D Milford CT (06461) ***(G-2361)***
Schmitt Realty Holdings Inc (PA) 203 453-4334
251 Boston Post Rd Guilford CT (06437) ***(G-1718)***
Schmitt Realty Holdings Inc 203 488-3252
746 E Main St Branford CT (06405) ***(G-346)***
Schmitt Realty Holdings Inc 203 453-4334
251 Boston Post Rd Guilford CT (06437) ***(G-1719)***
Schmitt Realty Holdings Inc 203 662-6661
1082 Post Rd Darien CT (06820) ***(G-1031)***
Schneeberger Inc (HQ) 781 271-0140
44 Sixth Rd Woburn MA (01801) ***(G-17290)***
Schneider Automation Inc 978 975-9600
800 Federal St Andover MA (01810) ***(G-7602)***
Schneider Elc Systems USA Inc 508 543-8750
38 Neponset Ave Foxboro MA (02035) ***(G-10901)***
Schneider Elc Systems USA Inc 508 543-8750
70 Mechanic St Foxboro MA (02035) ***(G-10902)***
Schneider Electric It Corp (HQ) 401 789-5735
132 Fairgrounds Rd West Kingston RI (02892) ***(G-21471)***
Schneider Electric It USA Inc (HQ) 401 789-5735
132 Fairgrounds Rd West Kingston RI (02892) ***(G-21472)***
Schneider Electric Usa Inc (HQ) 978 975-9600
201 Wshington St Ste 2700 Boston MA (02108) ***(G-8839)***
Schneider Electric Usa Inc 781 571-9677
24 Alison Way Lynn MA (01904) ***(G-12538)***
Schneider Electric Usa Inc 508 549-3385
15 Pond Ave Foxboro MA (02035) ***(G-10903)***
Schoeffel International Corp 978 256-4512
7a Stuart Rd Chelmsford MA (01824) ***(G-9931)***
Schofield Concrete Forms Inc 781 662-0796
195 Warwick Rd Melrose MA (02176) ***(G-12992)***
Schofield Printing Inc 401 728-6980
211 Weeden St Pawtucket RI (02860) ***(G-20898)***
Scholar Rock Holding Corp (PA) 857 259-3860
620 Memorial Dr Fl 2 Cambridge MA (02139) ***(G-9646)***
Scholastic Corporation 617 924-3846
1200 Soldiers Field Rd # 1 Allston MA (02134) ***(G-7475)***
Scholastic Library Pubg Inc (HQ) 203 797-3500
90 Sherman Tpke Danbury CT (06816) ***(G-986)***
School Specialty Inc 617 547-6706
625 Mount Auburn St Ste 4 Cambridge MA (02138) ***(G-9647)***
School Yourself Inc 516 729-7478
45 Longwood Ave Apt 510 Brookline MA (02446) ***(G-9219)***
Schoolsuite LLC 800 671-1905
301 State Rd Great Barrington MA (01230) ***(G-11245)***
Schott Electronic Packaging, Southbridge *Also called Schott North America Inc* ***(G-15402)***
Schott Lighting and Imaging, Southbridge *Also called Schott North America Inc* ***(G-15400)***
Schott North America Inc 508 765-3300
122 Charlton St Southbridge MA (01550) ***(G-15400)***
Schott North America Inc 508 765-9744
122 Charlton St Southbridge MA (01550) ***(G-15401)***
Schott North America Inc 508 765-7450
15 Wells St Ste 1 Southbridge MA (01550) ***(G-15402)***
Schrader Bellows 860 749-2215
80 Shaker Rd Enfield CT (06082) ***(G-1380)***
Schrafel Paperboard Converting 203 931-1700
82 W Clark St Ste 1 West Haven CT (06516) ***(G-5145)***
Schroff Inc (HQ) 763 204-7700
170 Commerce Dr Warwick RI (02886) ***(G-21421)***
Schroff Inc 401 535-4826
170 Commerce Dr Warwick RI (02886) ***(G-21422)***
Schuco International, Newington *Also called Schuco USA Lllp* ***(G-2901)***
Schuco USA Lllp (HQ) 860 666-0505
240 Pane Rd Newington CT (06111) ***(G-2901)***
Schuerch Corporation 781 982-7000
452 Randolph St Abington MA (02351) ***(G-7330)***
Schul International Co Inc 603 889-6872
34 Executive Dr Hudson NH (03051) ***(G-18367)***
Schul International Co LLC 603 889-6872
1 Industrial Park Dr # 14 Pelham NH (03076) ***(G-19446)***
Schultz Co Inc 413 568-1592
18 Coleman Ave Westfield MA (01085) ***(G-16729)***
Schuremed, Abington *Also called Schuerch Corporation* ***(G-7330)***
Schwerdtle Stamp Company 203 330-2750
41 Benham Ave Bridgeport CT (06605) ***(G-487)***
Schwing Bioset Technologies 203 744-2100
98 Mill Plain Rd Ste A Danbury CT (06811) ***(G-987)***
SCI Tech New England Molding, West Hatfield *Also called Mill Valley Molding LLC* ***(G-16484)***
Sciaps Inc (PA) 339 222-2585
7 Constitution Way Woburn MA (01801) ***(G-17291)***
Scidyne 781 293-3059
649 School St Pembroke MA (02359) ***(G-14425)***
Science Serum LLC 508 369-7733
194 John Scott Blvd Norton MA (02766) ***(G-14088)***
Scientific Alloys Inc 401 596-4947
72 Old Hopkinton Rd Westerly RI (02891) ***(G-21540)***
Scientific Instrument Facility 617 353-5056
590 Commonwealth Ave # 255 Boston MA (02215) ***(G-8840)***
Scientific Solutions Inc 978 251-4554
55 Middlesex St Unit 210 North Chelmsford MA (01863) ***(G-13910)***
Scinetx LLC 203 355-3676
1836 Long Ridge Rd Stamford CT (06903) ***(G-4310)***
Scintitech Inc 978 425-0800
1000 Mt Lurel Cir Shirley Shirley MA (01464) ***(G-15093)***
Scion Medical Techologies LLC 617 455-5186
90 Oak St 1 Newton Upper Falls MA (02464) ***(G-13658)***
Scitech Ingredients, Stamford *Also called Scitech International LLC* ***(G-4311)***

Scitech International LLC 203 967-8502
50 Soundview Dr Stamford CT (06902) *(G-4311)*
Scituate Caseworks Inc 781 534-4167
7 Sangay Ln Scituate MA (02066) *(G-15012)*
Scituate Concrete Pipe Corp 781 545-0564
1 Buckeye Ln Scituate MA (02066) *(G-15013)*
Sconset Woodman, Nantucket *Also called George A Vollans (G-13224)*
Scope Display & Box Co Inc (PA) 401 942-7150
1840 Cranston St Cranston RI (02920) *(G-20284)*
Scope Display & Box Co Inc 401 467-3910
421 Station St Providence RI (02910) *(G-21120)*
Scope Technology Inc 860 963-1141
8 Center Pkwy Plainfield CT (06374) *(G-3457)*
Score Board Enterprises, Mansfield *Also called Scoreboard Enterprises Inc (G-12657)*
Scoreboard Enterprises Inc 508 339-8113
274 Fruit St Mansfield MA (02048) *(G-12657)*
Scorebuilders 207 885-0304
6 Woodgate Rd Scarborough ME (04074) *(G-6939)*
Scorpian Printing 617 319-6114
72 Nicholas Rd Apt 23 Framingham MA (01701) *(G-11003)*
Scotia Boat Builders 781 871-2120
624 Bedford St Abington MA (02351) *(G-7331)*
Scotia Company 207 782-3824
358 Lincoln St Lewiston ME (04240) *(G-6321)*
Scotia Technology, Laconia *Also called Lakes Region Tubular Pdts Inc (G-18573)*
Scotland Hardwoods LLC 860 423-1233
117 Ziegler Rd Scotland CT (06264) *(G-3747)*
Scots Landing 860 923-0437
929 Riverside Dr Fabyan CT (06245) *(G-1410)*
Scott Brass, Cranston *Also called House of Stainless Inc (G-20237)*
Scott Docks Inc 207 647-3824
Rr 302 Bridgton ME (04009) *(G-5811)*
Scott Electronics Inc (PA) 603 893-2845
5 Industrial Way Ste 2d Salem NH (03079) *(G-19766)*
Scott G Reed Truck Svcs Inc 603 542-5032
287 Washington St Claremont NH (03743) *(G-17860)*
Scott Grusby LLC 617 538-9112
26 Jerome Ave Newton MA (02465) *(G-13633)*
Scott L Northcott 603 756-4204
103 Cheney Hill Rd Walpole NH (03608) *(G-19924)*
Scott Metal Finishing, Bristol *Also called Scotts Metal Finishing LLC (G-612)*
Scott Olson Enterprises LLC 860 482-4391
1707 E Main St Torrington CT (06790) *(G-4598)*
Scott Stanton 207 477-2956
654 County Rd Acton ME (04001) *(G-5509)*
Scott Woodford 203 245-4266
817 Boston Post Rd Madison CT (06443) *(G-1974)*
Scott's Vanilla, Lexington *Also called Walter Scott (G-12284)*
Scott-Lynn Mfg 207 784-3372
45 Hutchins St Auburn ME (04210) *(G-5598)*
Scottis Brand US, Burlington *Also called Irving Consumer Products Inc (G-9286)*
Scotts Company LLC 860 642-7591
20 Industrial Rd Lebanon CT (06249) *(G-1937)*
Scotts Company LLC 207 746-9033
100 Nicatou Industrial Ln Medway ME (04460) *(G-6427)*
Scotts Doors and Windows 401 743-2083
30 Cutler St Unit 227 Warren RI (02885) *(G-21307)*
Scotts Metal Finishing LLC 860 589-3778
310 Birch St Bristol CT (06010) *(G-612)*
Scout Out LLC 970 476-0209
18 Shipyard Dr Ste 2a-50 Hingham MA (02043) *(G-11510)*
Scp Management LLC 860 738-2600
29 Industrial Park Rd New Hartford CT (06057) *(G-2647)*
Scpharmaceuticals Inc 617 517-0730
2400 District Ave Ste 310 Burlington MA (01803) *(G-9335)*
Scrapbook Clubhouse 860 399-4443
20 Westbrook Pl Westbrook CT (06498) *(G-5162)*
Scrappin Soul Sisters 603 717-7136
3 Lawrence Street Ext Concord NH (03301) *(G-17928)*
Scratch Art Company Inc (PA) 508 583-8085
11 Robbie Rd Ste A Avon MA (02322) *(G-7895)*
Screamin Stevens, Southwick *Also called Ferrari Classics Corporation (G-15413)*
Screen Gems Inc 603 474-5353
34 Folly Mill Rd Ste 2 Seabrook NH (03874) *(G-19815)*
Screen Printed Special TS 603 622-2901
18 Lake Ave Manchester NH (03101) *(G-18919)*
Screen Printery Downeast Maine, Bar Harbor *Also called Robert Gaynor (G-5668)*
Screen Tek Printing Co Inc 203 248-6248
130 Welton St Hamden CT (06517) *(G-1782)*
Screen-Tech Inc 860 496-8016
230 Ella Grasso Ave Torrington CT (06790) *(G-4599)*
Screenco Printing Inc 978 465-1211
4 Malcolm Hoyt Dr Newburyport MA (01950) *(G-13533)*
Screencraft Tileworks LLC 401 427-2816
9 Powder Hill Rd Lincoln RI (02865) *(G-20596)*
Screening Ink LLC 860 212-0475
39 Celtic Ct Enfield CT (06082) *(G-1381)*
Screenprint, Wilmington *Also called Wtd Inc (G-17068)*
Screenprint/Dow Inc 978 657-7290
200 Research Dr Ste 6 Wilmington MA (01887) *(G-17043)*
Screw-Matic Corporation (PA) 978 356-6200
1 Chase Park Rd Seabrook NH (03874) *(G-19816)*
Screw-Matic Corporation 603 293-8850
10 Primrose Dr S Laconia NH (03246) *(G-18585)*
Screwtron Engineering Inc 508 881-1370
32 Stone Ave Ashland MA (01721) *(G-7669)*
Scrimshaw Screenprinting 508 617-7498
1587 Purchase St New Bedford MA (02740) *(G-13447)*
Scry Health Inc 203 936-8244
1 Bradley Rd Ste 404 Woodbridge CT (06525) *(G-5478)*
Scully Data Systems, Wilmington *Also called Scully Signal Company (G-17044)*
Scully Signal Company (PA) 617 692-8600
70 Industrial Way Wilmington MA (01887) *(G-17044)*
SCW Corporation 401 808-6849
126 Chestnut St Warwick RI (02888) *(G-21423)*
SDA Laboratories Inc 203 861-0005
280 Railroad Ave Ste 207 Greenwich CT (06830) *(G-1648)*
SDC Solutions Inc 603 629-4242
35 Constitution Dr Ste 99 Bedford NH (03110) *(G-17661)*
Sdl Xyenterprise LLC (PA) 781 756-4400
201 Edgewater Dr Ste 225 Wakefield MA (01880) *(G-15974)*
SDS Logging Inc 603 586-7098
180 Presidential Hwy Jefferson NH (03583) *(G-18486)*
SE Mass Devlopment LLC 401 434-3329
930 Waterman Ave East Providence RI (02914) *(G-20443)*
SE Shires Inc 508 634-6805
260 Hopping Brook Rd Holliston MA (01746) *(G-11601)*
Sea & Reef Aquaculture LLC 207 422-2422
33 Salmon Farm Rd Franklin ME (04634) *(G-6069)*
Sea Bags Inc 207 939-3679
6 Bow St Freeport ME (04032) *(G-6086)*
Sea Bags LLC (PA) 207 780-0744
25 Custom House Wharf Portland ME (04101) *(G-6724)*
Sea Fuels Marine 508 992-2323
465 N Front St New Bedford MA (02746) *(G-13448)*
Sea Hagg Distillery 603 380-4022
12 Willow Ln Hampton NH (03842) *(G-18271)*
Sea Land Energy Maine Inc 207 892-3284
6 Brookhaven Dr Windham ME (04062) *(G-7250)*
Sea Machines Robotics Inc (PA) 617 455-6266
256 Marginal St Ste 14a Boston MA (02128) *(G-8841)*
Sea Pet, Wakefield *Also called Sea Starr Animal Health (G-21275)*
Sea Point Chandlers LLC 207 703-2395
76 Brave Boat Harbor Rd Kittery Point ME (03905) *(G-6261)*
Sea Sciences Inc 781 643-1600
40 Massachusetts Ave Arlington MA (02474) *(G-7637)*
Sea Side Fuel 401 284-2636
55 State St Narragansett RI (02882) *(G-20648)*
Sea Starr Animal Health 401 783-2185
1305 Kingstown Rd B-7 Wakefield RI (02879) *(G-21275)*
Sea Street Graphics, Thomaston *Also called Seastreet Graphics (G-7088)*
Sea Street Technologies Inc 617 600-5150
779 Washington St Ste 2c Canton MA (02021) *(G-9777)*
Sea Watch International Ltd 508 984-1406
15 Antonio Costa Ave New Bedford MA (02740) *(G-13449)*
Sea-Band International Inc 401 841-5900
580 Thames St 440 Newport RI (02840) *(G-20679)*
Sea-Land Envmtl Svcs Inc 508 359-1085
18 N Meadows Rd Ste 1 Medfield MA (02052) *(G-12919)*
Sea-Lect, East Providence *Also called Bosworth Company (G-20392)*
Seaboard Flour LLC (PA) 917 928-6040
6 Liberty Sq Boston MA (02109) *(G-8842)*
Seaboard Folding Box Co Inc 401 753-7778
1 Campbell St Pawtucket RI (02860) *(G-20899)*
Seaboard Metal Finishing Co 203 933-1603
410 John Downey Dr New Britain CT (06051) *(G-2576)*
Seaboard Plating, New Britain *Also called Seaboard Metal Finishing Co (G-2576)*
Seaborn Management Inc 978 377-8366
600 Cummings Ctr Fl 2 Beverly MA (01915) *(G-8175)*
Seaborn Networks, Beverly *Also called Seaborn Management Inc (G-8175)*
Seaborn Networks Holdings LLC (PA) 978 471-3171
600 Cummings Ctr Fl 2 Beverly MA (01915) *(G-8176)*
Seabrook International, LLC, Seabrook *Also called Seabrook Medical LLC (G-19817)*
Seabrook Medical LLC 603 474-1919
15 Woodworkers Way Seabrook NH (03874) *(G-19817)*
Seabury Splash Inc 508 830-3440
10 Cordage Park Cir # 212 Plymouth MA (02360) *(G-14582)*
Seachange International Inc (PA) 978 897-0100
50 Nagog Park Acton MA (01720) *(G-7385)*
Seachange Therapeutics Inc 603 424-6009
66 Jessica Dr Merrimack NH (03054) *(G-19028)*
Seacoast Machine Company LLC 603 659-3404
80a Exeter Rd Newmarket NH (03857) *(G-19340)*
Seacoast Newspapers, Portsmouth *Also called Local Media Group Inc (G-19587)*
Seacoast Redimix Concrete LLC (PA) 603 742-4441
349 Mast Rd Dover NH (03820) *(G-18052)*

ALPHABETIC

Seacoast Screen Printing.....603 758-6398
5 Forbes Rd Newmarket NH (03857) ***(G-19341)***
Seacoast Shearwater Dev LLC.....603 427-0000
144 Washington St Portsmouth NH (03801) ***(G-19618)***
Seacoast Technologies Inc.....603 766-9800
222 International Dr # 145 Portsmouth NH (03801) ***(G-19619)***
Seafarer Canvas (PA).....203 853-2624
144 Water St Norwalk CT (06854) ***(G-3237)***
Seafood Gourmet Inc.....203 272-1544
264 Lyman Rd Apt 3-13 Wolcott CT (06716) ***(G-5456)***
Seafood Hut and Creamery.....508 993-9355
2 S Main St Acushnet MA (02743) ***(G-7406)***
Seagate Technology LLC.....508 770-3111
333 South St Shrewsbury MA (01545) ***(G-15130)***
Seahorse Bioscience Inc (HQ).....978 671-1600
121 Hartwell Ave Lexington MA (02421) ***(G-12263)***
Seahorse Labware, Lexington *Also called Seahorse Bioscience Inc* ***(G-12263)***
Seak Inc (PA).....508 548-7023
316 Gifford St Unit 2 Falmouth MA (02540) ***(G-10797)***
Seal 1 LLC.....207 965-8860
193 Davis St Brownville ME (04414) ***(G-5827)***
Sealcoating.....508 926-8080
110 Blackstone River Rd Worcester MA (01607) ***(G-17470)***
Sealed Air Corp.....508 521-5694
100 Westford Rd Ayer MA (01432) ***(G-7936)***
Sealed Air Corporation.....413 534-0231
2030 Homestead Ave Lowr Holyoke MA (01040) ***(G-11656)***
Sealed Air Corporation.....203 791-3648
10 Old Sherman Tpke Danbury CT (06810) ***(G-988)***
Sealite Usa LLC.....603 737-1310
61 Business Park Dr Tilton NH (03276) ***(G-19911)***
Sealpro LLC.....860 289-0804
721 Burnham St East Hartford CT (06108) ***(G-1219)***
Seaman Paper Company Mass Inc (PA).....978 632-1513
35 Wilkins Rd Gardner MA (01440) ***(G-11126)***
Seaman Paper Company Mass Inc.....978 544-2455
184 Gov Dukakis Dr Orange MA (01364) ***(G-14228)***
Seaman Paper Company Mass Inc.....978 939-5356
51 Main St Baldwinville MA (01436) ***(G-7945)***
Seaman Paper Warehouse.....978 632-5524
21 Industrial Rowe Gardner MA (01440) ***(G-11127)***
Seamans Media Inc.....617 773-9955
552 Adams St Ste 2 Milton MA (02186) ***(G-13200)***
Seamark International LLC.....603 546-0100
16 Celina Ave Unit 5 Nashua NH (03063) ***(G-19258)***
Sean Byrnes Welding LLC.....603 726-4315
532 Upper Mad River Rd Thornton NH (03285) ***(G-19902)***
Sean Mecesery.....203 869-2277
5 Strickland Rd Cos Cob CT (06807) ***(G-829)***
Seapoint Sensors Inc.....603 642-4921
45 Water St Frnt Exeter NH (03833) ***(G-18131)***
Seastreet Graphics.....207 594-1915
161 Main St Thomaston ME (04861) ***(G-7088)***
Seatek Wireless, Stamford *Also called Southwire Company LLC* ***(G-4326)***
Seattle Times Company.....207 623-3811
274 Western Ave Augusta ME (04330) ***(G-5619)***
Sebago Brewing Co (PA).....207 856-2537
616 Main St Gorham ME (04038) ***(G-6129)***
Sebago Brewing Co.....207 856-2537
616 Main St Gorham ME (04038) ***(G-6130)***
Sebago Converted Products Inc.....207 892-0576
15 Enterprise Dr Windham ME (04062) ***(G-7251)***
Sebago Lake Distillery LLC.....207 557-0557
463 Water St Gardiner ME (04345) ***(G-6105)***
Sebago Signworks, Limington *Also called Ssw Inc* ***(G-6349)***
Sebastian Kitchen Cabinets.....203 853-4411
4 Taft St Ste B1 Norwalk CT (06854) ***(G-3238)***
Sebasticook Lumber LLC.....207 660-1360
446 Hartland Rd Saint Albans ME (04971) ***(G-6865)***
Seceon Inc.....978 923-0040
238 Littleton Rd Ste 206 Westford MA (01886) ***(G-16791)***
Second Lac Inc (PA).....203 321-1221
401 Merritt 7 Ste 1 Norwalk CT (06851) ***(G-3239)***
Second Wind Media Limited.....203 781-3480
315 Front St New Haven CT (06513) ***(G-2736)***
Second Wind Systems Inc.....617 581-6090
15 Riverdale Ave Newton MA (02458) ***(G-13634)***
Secondaries Inc.....203 879-4633
19 Venus Dr Wolcott CT (06716) ***(G-5457)***
Secondary Operations Inc.....203 288-8241
46 Manila Ave Hamden CT (06514) ***(G-1783)***
Seconn Automation Solutions.....860 442-4325
147 Cross Rd Waterford CT (06385) ***(G-4992)***
Seconn Fabrication LLC.....860 443-0000
180 Cross Rd Waterford CT (06385) ***(G-4993)***
Secret Guide To Computers.....603 666-6644
196 Tiffany Ln Manchester NH (03104) ***(G-18920)***
Secret Sock Society.....603 443-3208
170 Beechwood Ln Franconia NH (03580) ***(G-18154)***
Securelytix Inc.....617 283-5227
2 Newton Executive Park # 104 Newton MA (02462) ***(G-13635)***
Securemark Decal Corp.....773 622-6815
20 Nutmeg Dr Trumbull CT (06611) ***(G-4632)***
Securities Software & Consulti.....860 298-4500
80 Lamberton Rd Windsor CT (06095) ***(G-5362)***
Security Devices Intl Inc.....905 582-6402
107 Audubon Rd Ste 201 Wakefield MA (01880) ***(G-15975)***
Security Systems Inc.....800 833-3211
1125 Middle St Middletown CT (06457) ***(G-2220)***
Seekonk Manufacturing Co Inc.....508 761-8284
87 Perrin Ave Seekonk MA (02771) ***(G-15036)***
SEEKONK PRECISION TOOLS, Seekonk *Also called Seekonk Manufacturing Co Inc* ***(G-15036)***
Seesmart Inc.....203 504-1111
177 Broad St Fl 12 Stamford CT (06901) ***(G-4312)***
Sefacor Inc.....617 471-0176
30 Murdock St Apt 1 Somerville MA (02145) ***(G-15214)***
Sega Ready Mix Incorporated (PA).....860 354-3969
519 Danbury Rd New Milford CT (06776) ***(G-2827)***
Sega Ready Mix Incorporated.....203 465-1052
310 Chase River Rd Waterbury CT (06704) ***(G-4953)***
Segue Manufacturing Svcs LLC.....978 970-1200
70 Industrial Ave E Lowell MA (01852) ***(G-12432)***
Segway Inc (HQ).....603 222-6000
14 Technology Dr Bedford NH (03110) ***(G-17662)***
Seica Inc (PA).....603 890-6002
110 Avco Rd Haverhill MA (01835) ***(G-11471)***
Seidel Inc.....203 757-7349
1883 Thomaston Ave Waterbury CT (06704) ***(G-4954)***
Seidel Inc.....203 757-7349
2223 Thomaston Ave Waterbury CT (06704) ***(G-4955)***
Seifert Mtm Systems, Inc., North Kingstown *Also called Seifert Systems Inc* ***(G-20739)***
Seifert Systems Inc.....401 294-6960
75 Circuit Dr North Kingstown RI (02852) ***(G-20739)***
Seize Sur Vingt, Lenox *Also called 16sur20 Management LLC* ***(G-12099)***
Sekisui Diagnostics LLC.....203 602-7777
500 West Ave Stamford CT (06902) ***(G-4313)***
Sekisui Diagnostics LLC (HQ).....781 652-7800
1 Wall St Ste 301 Burlington MA (01803) ***(G-9336)***
Select Logging.....978 386-6861
81 West Rd Ashby MA (01431) ***(G-7648)***
Select Plastics LLC.....203 866-3767
219 Liberty Sq Norwalk CT (06855) ***(G-3240)***
Selecta Biosciences Inc (PA).....617 923-1400
480 Arsenal Way Ste 1 Watertown MA (02472) ***(G-16314)***
Selectcom Mfg Co Inc.....203 879-9900
29 Nutmeg Valley Rd Wolcott CT (06716) ***(G-5458)***
Selectech Inc.....508 583-3200
33 Wales Ave Ste F Avon MA (02322) ***(G-7896)***
Selection Unlimited, South Burlington *Also called Sentar Inc* ***(G-22465)***
Selectives LLC.....860 585-1956
166 Litchfield St Thomaston CT (06787) ***(G-4514)***
Self Defense Innovations Inc.....207 991-1641
767 Acadia Hwy Orland ME (04472) ***(G-6550)***
Sellers Publishing Inc.....207 772-6833
161 John Roberts Rd Ste 1 South Portland ME (04106) ***(G-7040)***
Selvita Inc.....857 998-4075
100 Cambridge St Ste 1400 Boston MA (02114) ***(G-8843)***
Sem-Tec Inc.....508 798-8551
47 Lagrange St Worcester MA (01610) ***(G-17471)***
Semantic Objects LLC.....617 272-0955
25 Cabot St Newton MA (02458) ***(G-13636)***
Semco Instruments Inc (HQ).....661 257-2000
186 Cedar St Branford CT (06405) ***(G-347)***
Semco Instruments Inc.....661 362-6117
186 Cedar St Branford CT (06405) ***(G-348)***
Semco Machine Corp.....508 384-8303
14 High St Plainville MA (02762) ***(G-14535)***
Semco Tool Manufacturing Co.....203 723-7411
30 Naugatuck Dr Naugatuck CT (06770) ***(G-2495)***
Semicndctor Cmpnnts Inds of RI (HQ).....401 885-3600
1900 S County Trl East Greenwich RI (02818) ***(G-20379)***
Semiconductor Circuits Inc (PA).....603 893-2330
14c Industrial Way Atkinson NH (03811) ***(G-17607)***
Semiconsoft Inc.....617 388-6832
83 Pine Hill Rd Southborough MA (01772) ***(G-15364)***
Semigen Inc.....603 624-8311
54 Grenier Field Rd Londonderry NH (03053) ***(G-18735)***
Semikron Inc (HQ).....603 883-8102
11 Executive Dr Hudson NH (03051) ***(G-18437)***
Semilab USA LLC.....508 647-8400
101 Billerica Ave Bldg 5 North Billerica MA (01862) ***(G-13863)***
Seminex Corporation.....978 326-7700
100 Corporate Pl Ste 302 Peabody MA (01960) ***(G-14369)***
Semiotics LLC.....860 644-5700
1540 Pleasant Valley Rd D Manchester CT (06042) ***(G-2047)***
Semipilot, Waterbury *Also called Hotseat Chassis Inc* ***(G-4884)***
Semiprobe Inc.....802 860-7000
276 E Allen St Winooski VT (05404) ***(G-22723)***

Semitech Solutions Inc 978 589-3850
43 Nagog Park Ste 115 Acton MA (01720) ***(G-7386)***
Semivation 802 878-5153
9 Oakwood Ln Essex Junction VT (05452) ***(G-21959)***
Sempco Inc 603 889-1830
51 Lake St Ste 7 Nashua NH (03060) ***(G-19259)***
Semper FI Power Supply Inc 603 656-9729
21 W Auburn St Ste 29 Manchester NH (03101) ***(G-18921)***
Semper/Exeter Paper Company, Pawtucket *Also called Cellmark Inc* ***(G-20821)***
Semya Corp (PA) 802 875-6564
3643 Vt Route 103 N Chester VT (05143) ***(G-21849)***
Send Pymets To Washer Wizzards 413 733-2739
34 Cambridge St Springfield MA (01109) ***(G-15504)***
Seneca Machine 603 755-8900
317 Main St Farmington NH (03835) ***(G-18145)***
Senesco Marine LLC 401 295-0373
10 Macnaught St North Kingstown RI (02852) ***(G-20740)***
Senior Aerospace Connecticut, Enfield *Also called Senior Operations LLC* ***(G-1382)***
Senior Flexonics Pthwy, Lewiston *Also called Wahlcometroflex Inc* ***(G-6327)***
Senior Network Inc 203 969-2700
777 Summer St Ste 103 Stamford CT (06901) ***(G-4314)***
Senior Operations LLC 860 741-2546
4 Peerless Way Enfield CT (06082) ***(G-1382)***
Senior Operations LLC 207 784-2338
29 Lexington St Lewiston ME (04240) ***(G-6322)***
Senior Operations LLC 781 784-1400
1075 Providence Hwy Sharon MA (02067) ***(G-15056)***
Senior Operations LLC 860 741-2546
4 Peerless Way Enfield CT (06082) ***(G-1383)***
Senix Corporation 802 489-7300
10516 Route 116 Ste 300 Hinesburg VT (05461) ***(G-22030)***
Senopsys LLC 781 935-7450
800 W Cummings Park # 1500 Woburn MA (01801) ***(G-17292)***
Sens All Inc 860 628-8379
85 Water St Southington CT (06489) ***(G-4076)***
Sensarray Infrared Corporation 781 306-0338
150 George St Medford MA (02155) ***(G-12948)***
Sensata Technologies Inc (HQ) 508 236-3800
529 Pleasant St Attleboro MA (02703) ***(G-7792)***
Sensata Technologies Ind Inc (HQ) 508 236-3800
529 Pleasant St Attleboro MA (02703) ***(G-7793)***
Sensata Technologies Mass Inc (HQ) 508 236-3800
529 Pleasant St Attleboro MA (02703) ***(G-7794)***
Sensear Inc 603 589-4072
20 Trafalgar Sq Ste 472 Nashua NH (03063) ***(G-19260)***
Sensedriver Technologies LLC 978 232-3990
350 Main St Ste 31 Malden MA (02148) ***(G-12595)***
Sensing Systems Corporation 508 992-0872
7 Commerce Way Dartmouth MA (02747) ***(G-10276)***
Sensitech Inc (HQ) 978 927-7033
800 Cummings Ctr Ste 258x Beverly MA (01915) ***(G-8177)***
Sensomotoric Instruments Inc 617 557-0010
236 Lewis Wharf Boston MA (02110) ***(G-8844)***
Sensor Switch Inc (HQ) 203 265-2842
265 Church St Fl 15 New Haven CT (06510) ***(G-2737)***
Sensormatic Electronics LLC 781 466-6660
70 Westview St Ste 1 Lexington MA (02421) ***(G-12264)***
Sentar Inc 802 861-6004
102 Kimball Ave Ste 2 South Burlington VT (05403) ***(G-22465)***
Sentien Biotechnologies Inc 781 361-9031
99 Hayden Ave Ste 200 Lexington MA (02421) ***(G-12265)***
Sentinel and Enterprise, Fitchburg *Also called Medianews Group Inc* ***(G-10835)***
Sentrol Lifesafety, Framingham *Also called UTC Fire SEC Americas Corp Inc* ***(G-11009)***
Sentry Company 508 543-5391
62 Main St Foxboro MA (02035) ***(G-10904)***
Separett USA, Durham *Also called Eco Services LLC* ***(G-18076)***
Separett-Usa 603 682-0963
50 Commerce Way Barrington NH (03825) ***(G-17623)***
Sepaton Inc 508 490-7900
400 Nickerson Rd Marlborough MA (01752) ***(G-12824)***
Sepinuck Sign Co Inc 781 849-1181
130 Wood Rd Braintree MA (02184) ***(G-9036)***
Septitech Inc 207 333-6940
69 Holland St Lewiston ME (04240) ***(G-6323)***
Sequa Corporation 603 889-2500
220 Daniel Webster Hwy Merrimack NH (03054) ***(G-19029)***
Sequel Special Products LLC 203 759-1020
1 Hillside Dr Wolcott CT (06716) ***(G-5459)***
Serac Corporation (HQ) 802 527-9609
Arrwhead Indstl Bldg 110b Fairfax VT (05454) ***(G-21979)***
Seracare Life Sciences Inc (HQ) 508 244-6400
37 Birch St Milford MA (01757) ***(G-13143)***
Serafin Sulky Co 860 684-2986
65 Buckley Hwy Stafford Springs CT (06076) ***(G-4114)***
Seraph, The, Sturbridge *Also called 1817 Shoppe Inc* ***(G-15636)***
Seratis, Cambridge *Also called Divlan Inc* ***(G-9454)***
Serigraphics Unlimited 978 356-4896
108 Newburyport Tpke Rowley MA (01969) ***(G-14866)***
Serono Inc 781 681-2137
1 Technology Pl Rockland MA (02370) ***(G-14824)***
Serono Laboratories Inc 781 681-2288
1 Technology Pl Rockland MA (02370) ***(G-14825)***
Serrato Sign Co 508 756-7004
15 Dewey St Worcester MA (01609) ***(G-17472)***
Serrato Signs, Worcester *Also called Serrato Sign Co* ***(G-17472)***
Serv, Mansfield *Also called Cusa Technologies Inc* ***(G-12626)***
Servers Storage Networking LLC 203 433-0808
25 Perry Ave Norwalk CT (06850) ***(G-3241)***
Service Oriented Sales Inc 508 845-3330
775 Hartford Tpke Ste 2 Shrewsbury MA (01545) ***(G-15131)***
Service Plus Press Inc 401 461-2929
662 Warwick Ave Warwick RI (02888) ***(G-21424)***
Service Tech Inc (PA) 401 353-3664
1164 Douglas Ave North Providence RI (02904) ***(G-20774)***
Servicetune Inc 860 284-4445
107 Cider Brook Rd Avon CT (06001) ***(G-45)***
Servomotive Corporation 508 726-9222
10 Mohawk Dr Westborough MA (01581) ***(G-16648)***
SERVPRO of Portland, Westbrook *Also called Cml Services Inc* ***(G-7184)***
Set Americas Inc 413 203-6130
180 Pleasant St Ste 207 Easthampton MA (01027) ***(G-10578)***
Seth Hetherington 207 833-5400
66 Allen Point Rd South Harpswell ME (04079) ***(G-7008)***
Setma Inc 409 833-9797
458 Danbury Rd Ste A2 New Milford CT (06776) ***(G-2828)***
Setra Systems Inc 978 263-1400
159 Swanson Rd Ste 1 Boxboro MA (01719) ***(G-8954)***
Sevcon Inc (HQ) 508 281-5500
155 Northboro Rd Ste 1 Southborough MA (01772) ***(G-15365)***
Sevcon Usa Inc 508 281-5500
155 Northboro Rd Ste 1 Southborough MA (01772) ***(G-15366)***
Seven Cycles Inc 617 923-7774
125 Walnut St Ste 206 Watertown MA (02472) ***(G-16315)***
Seven Days Newspaper, Burlington *Also called Da Capo Publishing Inc* ***(G-21778)***
Seven Mist LLC 413 210-7255
1040 N Pleasant St Amherst MA (01002) ***(G-7525)***
Seven Star Inc 401 683-6222
190 Admiral Kalbfus Rd Newport RI (02840) ***(G-20680)***
Seven Star Marine Engineering, Newport *Also called Seven Star Inc* ***(G-20680)***
Seven Sweets Inc 781 631-0303
154 Atlantic Ave Marblehead MA (01945) ***(G-12693)***
Sevenoaks Biosystems 617 299-0404
1 Mifflin Pl Ste 320 Cambridge MA (02138) ***(G-9648)***
Seventh Generation Inc (HQ) 802 658-3773
60 Lake St Ste 3n Burlington VT (05401) ***(G-21808)***
Seventy Nine N Main St Prtg 978 475-4945
79 N Main St Andover MA (01810) ***(G-7603)***
Severance Foods Inc 860 724-7063
3478 Main St Hartford CT (06120) ***(G-1868)***
Severances Sugarhouse 413 498-2032
286 Capt Beers Plain Rd Northfield MA (01360) ***(G-14066)***
Sevigny, David L Supplies, Winchendon *Also called David Sevigny Inc* ***(G-17073)***
Sevignys, Brockton *Also called F B Washburn Candy Corporation* ***(G-9145)***
Sew What Embroidery 413 684-0672
385 Main St Ste 1 Dalton MA (01226) ***(G-10184)***
Sewerman, North Billerica *Also called Cleanbasins Inc* ***(G-13802)***
Sewn In America Inc (PA) 203 438-9149
54 Danbury Rd Ste 240 Ridgefield CT (06877) ***(G-3683)***
Sewrite Mfg Inc 401 334-3868
30 Martin St Ste 2a1 Cumberland RI (02864) ***(G-20342)***
Sextant Btsllc 203 500-3245
166 Route 81 Killingworth CT (06419) ***(G-1929)***
Seymour Associates Inc 978 562-1373
43 Parmenter Rd Hudson MA (01749) ***(G-11815)***
Seymour Woodworking 603 679-2055
479 Calef Hwy Epping NH (03042) ***(G-18102)***
SFE Mfg, Limestone *Also called Stainless Fdsrvice Eqp Mfg Inc* ***(G-6344)***
Sfj Pharma 781 924-1148
31 Schoosett St Pembroke MA (02359) ***(G-14426)***
Sga Components Group LLC 203 758-3702
13 Gramar Ave Prospect CT (06712) ***(G-3596)***
Sgri Inc 401 473-7320
1643 Warwick Ave Unit 164 Warwick RI (02889) ***(G-21425)***
Shackletonthomas, Bridgewater *Also called Charles Shackleton & Miranda T* ***(G-21757)***
Shade Adams & Screen Co 617 244-2188
182 Central St Framingham MA (01701) ***(G-11004)***
Shadowbrook Custom Cabinetry 413 664-9590
62 Stratton Rd Williamstown MA (01267) ***(G-16960)***
Shaeffer Plastic Mfg Corp 860 537-5524
523 Old Hartford Rd Colchester CT (06415) ***(G-808)***
Shafiis Inc (PA) 413 224-2100
50 Industrial Dr East Longmeadow MA (01028) ***(G-10492)***
Shaker Maple Farm, Starksboro *Also called Steven W Willsey* ***(G-22517)***
Shakour Publishers Inc 603 352-5250
445 West St Keene NH (03431) ***(G-18524)***
Shamrock Sheet Metal 860 537-4282
23 Briarwood Dr Colchester CT (06415) ***(G-809)***

ALPHABETIC

Shanklin Corporation (HQ) 978 487-2204
100 Westford Rd Ayer MA (01432) ***(G-7937)***
Shanklin Research Corporation 978 772-2090
100 Westford Rd Ayer MA (01432) ***(G-7938)***
Shannon Boat Company Inc 401 253-2441
19 Broadcommon Rd Bristol RI (02809) ***(G-20103)***
Shannon Drilling 207 255-6149
684 Route 1 Machias ME (04654) ***(G-6395)***
Shannon Yachts, Bristol *Also called Shannon Boat Company Inc* ***(G-20103)***
Shape Global Technologies, Sanford *Also called R&V Industries Inc* ***(G-6887)***
Shapewood, Providence *Also called Scope Display & Box Co Inc* ***(G-21120)***
Shari M Roth MD 860 676-2525
100 Simsbury Rd Ste 210 Avon CT (06001) ***(G-46)***
Sharkninja Operating LLC (HQ) 617 243-0235
89 A St Ste 100 Needham MA (02494) ***(G-13310)***
Sharon Associates 781 784-2455
7 King Phillip Rd Sharon MA (02067) ***(G-15057)***
Sharon Vacuum Co Inc 508 588-2323
69 Falmouth Ave Brockton MA (02301) ***(G-9173)***
Sharp Grinding Co Inc 413 737-8808
168 Windsor St West Springfield MA (01089) ***(G-16551)***
Sharp Manufacturing Inc 508 583-4080
415 N Elm St West Bridgewater MA (02379) ***(G-16452)***
Sharp Precision Grinding, West Springfield *Also called Sharp Grinding Co Inc* ***(G-16551)***
Sharp Services Inc 781 854-3334
222 Central St Saugus MA (01906) ***(G-14996)***
Sharp Tool Co Inc 978 568-9292
7 Bonazzoli Ave Hudson MA (01749) ***(G-11816)***
Sharpac Cutter Grinding & Sls, Bridgeport *Also called Sharpac LLC* ***(G-488)***
Sharpac LLC 203 384-0568
114 Miles St Bridgeport CT (06607) ***(G-488)***
Sharpe Hill Vineyard Inc 860 974-3549
108 Wade Rd Pomfret CT (06258) ***(G-3554)***
Sharrocks English Bakery Inc 508 997-5710
135 Potter St New Bedford MA (02740) ***(G-13450)***
Shattuck Prcsion Machining Inc 978 392-0848
2 Park Dr Ste 7 Westford MA (01886) ***(G-16792)***
Shaughnessy Seagull Inc 603 433-4680
195 Nh Ave Portsmouth NH (03801) ***(G-19620)***
Shaw & Tenney, Orono *Also called S P Holt Corporation* ***(G-6558)***
Shaw Glass Holdings LLC 508 238-0112
55 Bristol Dr Ste 1 South Easton MA (02375) ***(G-15292)***
Shaw Welding Company Inc 978 667-0197
7 Innis Dr Billerica MA (01821) ***(G-8293)***
Shaw Woodworking Inc 508 563-1242
150 Highland Ave Pocasset MA (02559) ***(G-14601)***
Shawmut Advertising Inc (PA) 978 762-7500
33 Cherry Hill Dr Danvers MA (01923) ***(G-10255)***
Shawmut Engineering Co 508 850-9500
87 West St Walpole MA (02081) ***(G-16011)***
Shawmut LLC (PA) 508 588-3300
208 Manley St West Bridgewater MA (02379) ***(G-16453)***
Shawmut Metal Products Inc 508 379-0803
1914 Gar Hwy Swansea MA (02777) ***(G-15715)***
Shawmut Printing 978 762-7500
33 Cherry Hill Dr Ste 1 Danvers MA (01923) ***(G-10256)***
Shawn Roberts Woodworking 413 477-0060
830 Lower Rd Gilbertville MA (01031) ***(G-11155)***
Shawnee Chemical 203 938-3003
429 Rock House Rd Redding CT (06896) ***(G-3652)***
Shawnee Steps, Bangor *Also called American Concrete Inds Inc* ***(G-5629)***
Shaws Pump Company Inc 860 872-6891
37 Windermere Ave Ellington CT (06029) ***(G-1339)***
Shawsheen Rubber Co Inc 978 470-1760
220 Andover St Andover MA (01810) ***(G-7604)***
Shea Concrete Products Inc (PA) 978 658-2645
87 Haverhill Rd Amesbury MA (01913) ***(G-7507)***
Shea Concrete Products Inc 978 388-1509
87 Haverhill Rd Amesbury MA (01913) ***(G-7508)***
Sheaffer Pen Corp 203 783-2894
1 Bic Way Ste 1 Shelton CT (06484) ***(G-3869)***
Shear Color Printing Inc 781 376-9607
30d 6th Rd Woburn MA (01801) ***(G-17293)***
Sheaumann Laser Inc 508 970-0600
45 Bartlett St Marlborough MA (01752) ***(G-12825)***
Shed Happens Inc (PA) 207 892-3636
509 Warren Ave Portland ME (04103) ***(G-6725)***
Shedworks Inc 413 284-1600
8 3rd St Palmer MA (01069) ***(G-14296)***
Sheehan & Sons Lumber 802 263-5545
251 Stoughton Pond Rd Perkinsville VT (05151) ***(G-22258)***
Sheet Metal Design 802 288-9700
3 Corporate Dr Essex Junction VT (05452) ***(G-21960)***
Sheffield Pharmaceuticals LLC 860 442-4451
9 Wisconsin Ave Norwich CT (06360) ***(G-3290)***
Sheffield Pharmaceuticals LLC (PA) 860 442-4451
170 Broad St New London CT (06320) ***(G-2779)***
Sheffield Plastic Division, Sheffield *Also called Plaskolite LLC* ***(G-15063)***
Sheffield Pottery Inc 413 229-7700
995 N Main St Sheffield MA (01257) ***(G-15065)***
Shegear Inc 401 619-0072
128 Long Wharf Fl 2 Newport RI (02840) ***(G-20681)***
Sheila P Patrick 203 575-1716
179 Dwight St Waterbury CT (06704) ***(G-4956)***
Shelborne Plastics, South Burlington *Also called Plastic Technologies NY LLC* ***(G-22460)***
Shelburne Corporation (PA) 802 985-3321
6221 Shelburne Rd Shelburne VT (05482) ***(G-22424)***
Shelburne Limestone Corp 802 446-2045
4792 Us Route 7 S Wallingford VT (05773) ***(G-22574)***
Shelburne Plastics, South Burlington *Also called Consolidated Container Co LLC* ***(G-22444)***
Shelburne Plastics, South Burlington *Also called Plastic Technologies MD Inc* ***(G-22459)***
Shelburne Plastics, Londonderry *Also called Consolidated Container Co LLC* ***(G-18688)***
Shelco Filters Division, Middletown *Also called Tinny Corporation* ***(G-2228)***
Sheldon Precision LLC 203 758-4441
10 Industrial Rd Waterbury CT (06712) ***(G-4957)***
Sheldon Precision LLC 203 758-4441
10 Industrial Rd Prospect CT (06712) ***(G-3597)***
Sheldon Slate Products Co Inc 207 997-3615
38 Farm Quarry Rd Monson ME (04464) ***(G-6452)***
Shelfdig LLC 617 299-6335
150 Meeting St Providence RI (02906) ***(G-21121)***
Shelfgenie, Norwalk *Also called Lookout Solutions LLC* ***(G-3187)***
Shell Shock Technologies Llc 203 557-3256
38 Owenoke Park Westport CT (06880) ***(G-5230)***
Shelpak Plastics Inc 781 305-3937
339 N Main St Middleton MA (01949) ***(G-13101)***
Shelterlogic Corp (HQ) 860 945-6442
150 Callender Rd Watertown CT (06795) ***(G-5023)***
Shelters of America LLC 203 397-1037
73 Ford Rd Woodbridge CT (06525) ***(G-5479)***
Shemin Landscape Supply Co, Lexington *Also called Shemin Nurseries Inc* ***(G-12266)***
Shemin Nurseries Inc 781 861-1111
1265 Massachusetts Ave Lexington MA (02420) ***(G-12266)***
Shenitech, Marlborough *Also called Spire Metering Technology LLC* ***(G-12829)***
Shenondah Vly Specialty Foods 203 348-0402
28 Intervale Rd Stamford CT (06905) ***(G-4315)***
Shepard & Parker Inc 978 343-3907
18 Lincoln St Fitchburg MA (01420) ***(G-10852)***
Shepard Steel Co Inc (PA) 860 525-4446
110 Meadow St Hartford CT (06114) ***(G-1869)***
Shepard Steel Co Inc 860 525-4446
55 Shepard Dr Newington CT (06111) ***(G-2902)***
Sheppard Envelope Company Inc 508 791-5588
133 Southbridge St Auburn MA (01501) ***(G-7849)***
Sherborn Market Inc 781 489-5006
29 Grantland Rd Wellesley MA (02481) ***(G-16387)***
Sheridan NH 603 643-2220
69 Lyme Rd Hanover NH (03755) ***(G-18297)***
Sherman Printing Co Inc 781 828-8855
1020 Turnpike St Ste 11 Canton MA (02021) ***(G-9778)***
Sherwin Dodge Printers Inc 603 444-6552
365 Union St Littleton NH (03561) ***(G-18666)***
Sherwood Brands of RI 401 726-4500
275 Ferris Ave Rumford RI (02916) ***(G-21195)***
Sherwood Trunks 413 687-3167
85 Mount Holyoke Dr Amherst MA (01002) ***(G-7526)***
Shewstone Publishing LLC 781 648-1251
165 Scituate St Arlington MA (02476) ***(G-7638)***
Shi Printing, Dennis *Also called Sallyharrold Inc* ***(G-10310)***
Shibumicom Inc 855 744-2864
50 Washington St Ste 302e Norwalk CT (06854) ***(G-3242)***
Shield Packaging Co Inc 508 949-0900
50 Oxford Rd Dudley MA (01571) ***(G-10384)***
Shields Mri At Umass Memorial, Worcester *Also called Umass Mem Mri Imaging Ctr LLC* ***(G-17492)***
Shiller and Company Inc 203 210-5208
258 Thunder Lake Rd Wilton CT (06897) ***(G-5303)***
Shillermath, Wilton *Also called Shiller and Company Inc* ***(G-5303)***
Shiloh Software Inc 203 272-8456
718 Cortland Cir Cheshire CT (06410) ***(G-761)***
Shiner Signs Inc 203 634-4331
38 Elm St Ste 3 Meriden CT (06450) ***(G-2130)***
Shipping Containers Neng, Alton *Also called Skmr Construction LLC* ***(G-17547)***
Shipyard Brewing Ltd Lblty Co 207 761-0807
86 Newbury St Portland ME (04101) ***(G-6726)***
Shire Inc (HQ) 781 482-9222
300 Shire Way Lexington MA (02421) ***(G-12267)***
Shire City Herbals Inc 413 344-4740
15 Commercial St Pittsfield MA (01201) ***(G-14508)***
Shire Humn Gntic Therapies Inc 781 862-1561
1100 Winter St Fl 3 Waltham MA (02451) ***(G-16192)***
Shire Humn Gntic Therapies Inc 617 349-0200
125 Binney St Cambridge MA (02142) ***(G-9649)***
Shire Humn Gntic Therapies Inc (HQ) 617 349-0200
300 Shire Way Lexington MA (02421) ***(G-12268)***

Shire Humn Gntic Therapies Inc 617 349-0200
300 Patriot Way Lexington MA (02421) *(G-12269)*
Shire Humn Gntic Therapies Inc 781 482-0883
200 Riverpark Dr North Reading MA (01864) *(G-13989)*
Shire Inc (HQ) 781 274-1248
125 Spring St Lexington MA (02421) *(G-12270)*
Shire Pharmaceuticals, Waltham *Also called Shire Humn Gntic Therapies Inc (G-16192)*
Shire Pharmaceuticals, Cambridge *Also called Shire Humn Gntic Therapies Inc (G-9649)*
Shire Pharmaceuticals, Lexington *Also called Shire US Inc (G-12272)*
Shire Pharmaceuticals, Lexington *Also called Shire Humn Gntic Therapies Inc (G-12268)*
Shire Pharmaceuticals LLC 617 349-0200
45 Hayden Ave Lexington MA (02421) *(G-12271)*
Shire Pharmaceuticals LLC 617 588-8800
650 E Kendall St Cambridge MA (02142) *(G-9650)*
Shire Rgenerative Medicine Inc (HQ) 877 422-4463
36 Church Ln Westport CT (06880) *(G-5231)*
Shire US Inc (HQ) 781 482-9222
300 Shire Way Lexington MA (02421) *(G-12272)*
Shire Viropharma Incorporated (HQ) 610 458-7300
300 Shire Way Lexington MA (02421) *(G-12273)*
Shire-NPS Pharmaceuticals Inc (HQ) 617 349-0200
300 Shire Way Lexington MA (02421) *(G-12274)*
Shirt Graphix 203 294-1656
198 Center St Wallingford CT (06492) *(G-4805)*
Shirt Out of Luck LLC 603 898-9002
45 Northwestern Dr Salem NH (03079) *(G-19767)*
Shirts Illustrated, Salem *Also called Jph Graphics LLC (G-14926)*
Shock Sock Inc LLC 860 680-7252
409 Colt Hwy Farmington CT (06032) *(G-1512)*
Shoofly, Needham *Also called Lynwood Laboratories Inc (G-13304)*
Shookus Special Tools Inc 603 895-1200
11 Center St Raymond NH (03077) *(G-19645)*
Shooters Pizza & Pub, Avon *Also called Chris Martin (G-7882)*
Shop Smart Central Inc 914 962-3871
31 Pecks Ln Newtown CT (06470) *(G-2936)*
Shop Therapy Imports 508 487-8970
20 Province Rd Provincetown MA (02657) *(G-14609)*
Shoppers Guide, Putnam *Also called Shoppers-Turnpike Corporation (G-3632)*
Shoppers-Turnpike Corporation 860 928-3040
70 Main St Putnam CT (06260) *(G-3632)*
Shore Publishing LLC 203 245-1877
724 Boston Post Rd Madison CT (06443) *(G-1975)*
Shore Therapeutics Inc 646 562-1243
177 Broad St Ste 1101 Stamford CT (06901) *(G-4316)*
Shoreline Bus Solutions Inc (HQ) 877 914-7856
275 Circuit Dr North Kingstown RI (02852) *(G-20741)*
Shoreline Coatings LLC 203 213-3471
14 Commerce Dr Ste 1 North Branford CT (06471) *(G-2976)*
Shoreline Metal Services LLC 203 466-7372
250 Dodge Ave East Haven CT (06512) *(G-1261)*
Shoreline Publications 207 646-8448
952 Post Rd Unit 10 Wells ME (04090) *(G-7165)*
Shoreline Vine 203 779-5331
724 Boston Post 105a Madison CT (06443) *(G-1976)*
Shoreside Docks, Oxford *Also called Rj Marine Industries (G-14272)*
Shoreside Organics LLC 401 267-4473
65 State St Narragansett RI (02882) *(G-20649)*
Shorey Precast Division, Harwich *Also called Acme-Shorey Precast Co Inc (G-11386)*
Short Courses 781 631-1178
16 Preston Beach Rd Marblehead MA (01945) *(G-12694)*
Short Path Distillery Inc 857 417-2396
59 Magnolia St Arlington MA (02474) *(G-7639)*
Short Path Distillery Inc 617 830-7954
71 Kelvin St Everett MA (02149) *(G-10631)*
Shotbyshop.com, Stamford *Also called Golf Research Associates (G-4201)*
Show Motion Inc 203 866-1866
1034 Bridgeport Ave Milford CT (06460) *(G-2362)*
Showhegan New Balance, Skowhegan *Also called New Balance Athletics Inc (G-6983)*
Shrewsbury Chronicle 508 842-8787
33 New York Ave Framingham MA (01701) *(G-11005)*
Shrewsbury National Press 508 756 7502
298 Boston Tpke Ste 3 Shrewsbury MA (01545) *(G-15132)*
Shrink Equipment, Ayer *Also called Shanklin Corporation (G-7937)*
Shrinkfast Marketing 603 863-7719
460 Sunapee St Newport NH (03773) *(G-19358)*
Shrut & Asch Leather Co Inc 781 460-2288
5 Cranes Ct Woburn MA (01801) *(G-17294)*
Shucks Maine Lobster LLC 207 737-4800
150 Main St Ste 4 Richmond ME (04357) *(G-6783)*
Shufro Engineering Labs, Newton *Also called Shufro Security Company Inc (G-13637)*
Shufro Security Company Inc 617 244-3355
1231 Washington St Newton MA (02460) *(G-13637)*
Shurtape Specialty Coating LLC (HQ) 860 738-2600
29 Industrial Park Rd New Hartford CT (06057) *(G-2648)*
Shutters & Sails LLC 860 331-1510
31 Water St Mystic CT (06355) *(G-2451)*
Shutters R US 978 376-0201
22 S Pond St Newbury MA (01951) *(G-13466)*

Si Group USA (usaa) LLC (HQ) 203 702-6140
4 Mountainview Ter Danbury CT (06810) *(G-989)*
Si Group USA Hldings Usha Corp (HQ) 203 702-6140
4 Mountainview Ter Danbury CT (06810) *(G-990)*
Si Tech Inc 978 887-3550
218 Boston St Ste 105 Topsfield MA (01983) *(G-15865)*
Sia, Ridgefield *Also called Sewn In America Inc (G-3683)*
Siam Valee 203 269-6888
20 Ives Rd Wallingford CT (06492) *(G-4806)*
Sibco LLC 508 520-2040
837 Upper Union St C14 Franklin MA (02038) *(G-11079)*
Sibs LLC 781 864-7498
114 Upper Mile Point Dr Meredith NH (03253) *(G-18979)*
Sick Inc (HQ) 781 302-2500
800 Technology Center Dr # 5 Stoughton MA (02072) *(G-15621)*
Sidekim LLC 781 595-3663
82 Sanderson Ave Ste 112 Lynn MA (01902) *(G-12539)*
Sidney Hutter Glass & Light 617 630-1929
225 Riverview Ave Ste B5 Auburndale MA (02466) *(G-7869)*
Sie Computing Solutions Inc 508 588-6110
10 Mupac Dr Brockton MA (02301) *(G-9174)*
Siebe Inc (HQ) 508 549-6768
33 Commercial St B51-2c Foxboro MA (02035) *(G-10905)*
Siemens Components, Essex Junction *Also called Infineon Tech Americas Corp (G-21947)*
Siemens Hlthcare Dgnostics Inc 781 551-7000
115 Norwood Park S Norwood MA (02062) *(G-14198)*
Siemens Hlthcare Dgnostics Inc 781 269-3000
2 Edgewater Dr Norwood MA (02062) *(G-14199)*
Siemens Industry Inc 508 849-6519
40 Crescent St Worcester MA (01605) *(G-17473)*
Siemens Industry Inc 401 942-2121
140 Pettaconsett Ave Cranston RI (02920) *(G-20285)*
Siemens Industry Inc 781 364-1000
40 Shawmut Rd Ste 100 Canton MA (02021) *(G-9779)*
Siemens Industry Software Inc 781 250-6800
200 5th Ave Fl 5 Waltham MA (02451) *(G-16193)*
Siemon Company (PA) 860 945-4200
101 Siemon Company Dr Watertown CT (06795) *(G-5024)*
Siemon Company 860 945-4218
101 Siemon Company Dr Watertown CT (06795) *(G-5025)*
Siemon Global Project Services, Watertown *Also called Siemon Company (G-5024)*
Sierra Nevada Corporation 775 331-0222
43 Constitution Dr # 202 Bedford NH (03110) *(G-17663)*
Sierra Press Inc 617 923-4150
713 Main St Waltham MA (02451) *(G-16194)*
Sifco Applied Srfc Cncepts LLC 860 623-6006
22 Thompson Rd Ste 2 East Windsor CT (06088) *(G-1301)*
Sifos Technologies Inc 978 975-2100
1 Tech Dr Ste 100 Andover MA (01810) *(G-7605)*
Siftex Equipment Company 860 289-8779
52 Connecticut Ave Ste D South Windsor CT (06074) *(G-4009)*
Sig Sauer Inc 603 610-3000
12 Industrial Dr Exeter NH (03833) *(G-18132)*
Sig Sauer Inc (HQ) 603 610-3000
72 Pease Blvd Newington NH (03801) *(G-19325)*
Sigco LLC 207 775-2676
600 County Rd Westbrook ME (04092) *(G-7207)*
Sigco LLC (HQ) 207 775-2676
48 Spiller Dr Westbrook ME (04092) *(G-7208)*
Sigfridson Wood Products LLC 860 774-2075
125 Fitzgerald Rd Brooklyn CT (06234) *(G-672)*
Sigg Switzerland (usa) Inc 203 321-1232
1177 High Ridge Rd Stamford CT (06905) *(G-4317)*
Siggpay Inc 203 957-8261
50 Water St Rear B Norwalk CT (06854) *(G-3243)*
Sigilon Therapeutics Inc 617 336-7540
100 Binney St Ste 600 Cambridge MA (02142) *(G-9651)*
Sigler Machine Co, Princeton *Also called Lawrence Sigler (G-14606)*
Sigler Machine Co 978 422-7868
3 Northeast Blvd Sterling MA (01564) *(G-15544)*
Sigma Systems Corp 781 688-2354
41 Hampden Rd Mansfield MA (02048) *(G-12658)*
Sigma Tankers Inc 203 662-2600
20 Glover Ave Ste 5 Norwalk CT (06850) *(G-3244)*
Sigmet, Westford Operations, Woburn *Also called Vaisala Inc (G-17311)*
Sigmund Software LLC 800 448-6975
83 Wooster Hts Ste 210 Danbury CT (06810) *(G-991)*
Sign A Rama 508 822-7533
1470 New State Hwy # 21 Raynham MA (02767) *(G-14730)*
Sign A Rama 860 443-9744
365 Broad St New London CT (06320) *(G-2780)*
Sign A Rama 203 795-5450
553 Boston Post Rd Orange CT (06477) *(G-3384)*
Sign A Rama 203 792-4091
35 Eagle Rd Danbury CT (06810) *(G-992)*
Sign Art Inc 781 322-3785
60 Sharon St Malden MA (02148) *(G-12596)*
Sign Company 508 760-5400
343 Main St Dennis Port MA (02639) *(G-10314)*

ALPHABETIC

Sign Concepts 207 699-2920
342 Warren Ave Portland ME (04103) ***(G-6727)***
Sign Connection Inc 860 870-8855
101 West St Vernon Rockville CT (06066) ***(G-4682)***
Sign Creations 203 259-8330
89 Arbor Dr Southport CT (06890) ***(G-4098)***
Sign Design Inc 508 580-0094
170 Liberty St Brockton MA (02301) ***(G-9175)***
Sign Design & Display, East Berlin *Also called S D & D Inc* ***(G-1107)***
Sign Design Inc 207 856-2600
306 Warren Ave Ste 3 Portland ME (04103) ***(G-6728)***
Sign Effects Inc 978 663-0787
29 High St North Billerica MA (01862) ***(G-13864)***
Sign Express LLC 603 606-1279
120 Edmond St Manchester NH (03102) ***(G-18922)***
Sign Factory 860 763-1085
25 Dust House Rd Enfield CT (06082) ***(G-1384)***
Sign Gallery 603 622-7212
101 West River Rd Hooksett NH (03106) ***(G-18360)***
Sign Guy Inc 207 892-5851
103 Tandberg Trl Windham ME (04062) ***(G-7252)***
Sign In Soft Inc 203 216-3046
1 Waterview Dr Shelton CT (06484) ***(G-3870)***
Sign Language LLC 203 778-2250
71 Newtown Rd Ste 6 Danbury CT (06810) ***(G-993)***
Sign Maintenance Service Co 203 336-1051
24 Wallace St Bridgeport CT (06604) ***(G-489)***
Sign Post LLC 617 469-4400
4190 Washington St Roslindale MA (02131) ***(G-14843)***
Sign Pro Inc 860 229-1812
60 Westfield Dr Plantsville CT (06479) ***(G-3539)***
Sign Professionals 860 823-1122
303 W Main St Norwich CT (06360) ***(G-3291)***
Sign Services Inc 207 296-2400
512 Wolfboro Rd Stetson ME (04488) ***(G-7066)***
Sign Shop Inc 413 562-1876
215 E Main St Ste 2 Westfield MA (01085) ***(G-16730)***
Sign Station, Wilmington *Also called J K L Corp* ***(G-17009)***
Sign Stop, Wallingford *Also called Rokap Inc* ***(G-4799)***
Sign Stop Inc 860 721-1411
657 Main St East Hartford CT (06108) ***(G-1220)***
Sign System Solutions LLC 508 497-6340
7 Sadie Ln Hopkinton MA (01748) ***(G-11735)***
Sign Systems of Maine Inc 207 775-7110
22 Free St Ste 303 Portland ME (04101) ***(G-6729)***
Sign Techniques Inc 413 594-8240
361 Chicopee St Chicopee MA (01013) ***(G-10060)***
Sign Wizard 860 525-7729
1 Union Pl Hartford CT (06103) ***(G-1870)***
Sign-A-Rama, Springfield *Also called P&G Graphic Solutions Inc* ***(G-15497)***
Sign-A-Rama, Kingston *Also called Titus & Bean Graphics Inc* ***(G-11965)***
Sign-A-Rama, Raynham *Also called Sign A Rama* ***(G-14730)***
Sign-A-Rama, Framingham *Also called Newman Enterprises Inc* ***(G-10988)***
Sign-A-Rama, South Yarmouth *Also called of Cape Cod Incorporated* ***(G-15332)***
Sign-A-Rama, North Kingstown *Also called Fine Designs Inc* ***(G-20710)***
Sign-A-Rama, Concord *Also called Signs Happen Inc* ***(G-17929)***
Sign-A-Rama, New London *Also called Sign A Rama* ***(G-2780)***
Sign-A-Rama, Orange *Also called Sign A Rama* ***(G-3384)***
Sign-A-Rama, Norwalk *Also called Jaime M Camacho* ***(G-3178)***
Sign-A-Rama, Danbury *Also called Sign A Rama* ***(G-992)***
Sign-A-Rama, South Burlington *Also called Diaco Communication Inc* ***(G-22446)***
Sign-A-Rama 978 774-0936
75 High St Danvers MA (01923) ***(G-10257)***
Sign-Grafx Group, Norwich *Also called Derrick Mason* ***(G-3278)***
Signage US, Meriden *Also called Shiner Signs Inc* ***(G-2130)***
Signal Cnstr Insul Mintainence, Revere *Also called Bellofatto Electrical* ***(G-14764)***
Signal Communications Corp 781 933-0998
4 Wheeling Ave Woburn MA (01801) ***(G-17295)***
Signal Graphics 225 617 472-1700
17 Foster St Quincy MA (02169) ***(G-14655)***
Signal Graphics Printing, Newton *Also called Task Printing Inc* ***(G-13643)***
Signal Graphics Printing, Glastonbury *Also called Empire Printing Systems LLC* ***(G-1549)***
Signal Integrity Journal, Norwood *Also called Horizon House Publications Inc* ***(G-14158)***
Signalfire Telemetry Inc 978 212-2868
140 Lock Dr Marlborough MA (01752) ***(G-12826)***
Signalquest LLC 603 448-6266
10 Water St Ste 425 Lebanon NH (03766) ***(G-18635)***
Signarama Saco 207 494-8085
872 Portland Rd Saco ME (04072) ***(G-6858)***
Signature Engrv Systems Inc 413 533-7500
120 Whiting Farms Rd Holyoke MA (01040) ***(G-11657)***
Signature Graphics & Signs, Weymouth *Also called Innovative Media Group Inc* ***(G-16892)***
Signature Press & Blue Prtg, Hooksett *Also called RB Graphics Inc* ***(G-18358)***
Signature Printing Inc 401 438-1200
5 Almeida Ave East Providence RI (02914) ***(G-20444)***
Signature Signs 508 993-8511
634 State Rd Unit F Dartmouth MA (02747) ***(G-10277)***
Signcenter LLC 800 269-2130
333 Quarry Rd Milford CT (06460) ***(G-2363)***
Signcrafters Inc 203 353-9535
874 E Main St Stamford CT (06902) ***(G-4318)***
Signeffects, North Billerica *Also called Sign Effects Inc* ***(G-13864)***
Signet Products Corporation 650 592-3575
521 Mount Hope St North Attleboro MA (02760) ***(G-13779)***
Signify North America Corp 603 645-6061
386 Commercial St Manchester NH (03101) ***(G-18923)***
Signify North America Corp 508 679-8131
631 Airport Rd Fall River MA (02720) ***(G-10761)***
Signify North America Corp 617 423-9999
3 Burlington Woods Dr # 4 Burlington MA (01803) ***(G-9337)***
Signity Americas, Cranston *Also called Swarovski North America Ltd* ***(G-20295)***
Signode Industrial Group LLC 401 438-5203
50 Taylor Dr Rumford RI (02916) ***(G-21196)***
Signs & Sites Inc 508 336-5858
20 Commerce Way Ste 10 Seekonk MA (02771) ***(G-15037)***
Signs By Anthony Inc 203 866-1744
19 Fitch St Norwalk CT (06855) ***(G-3245)***
Signs By Autografix 203 481-6502
7 Svea Ave Branford CT (06405) ***(G-349)***
Signs By CAM Inc 508 528-0766
837 Upper Union St C18 Franklin MA (02038) ***(G-11080)***
Signs By Doug 978 463-2222
213 Lafayette Rd Salisbury MA (01952) ***(G-14956)***
Signs By J Inc 617 825-9855
100 Tenean St Boston MA (02122) ***(G-8845)***
Signs By MO 207 384-2363
Railroad Avenue Ext South Berwick ME (03908) ***(G-7004)***
Signs By Russ Inc 508 580-2221
244 Liberty St Ste 9a Brockton MA (02301) ***(G-9176)***
Signs By Tomorrow, Wallingford *Also called Image360* ***(G-4755)***
Signs By Tomorrow, Newton *Also called A S P Enterprises Inc* ***(G-13551)***
Signs By Tomorrow, South Easton *Also called Jim Haluck* ***(G-15283)***
Signs Happen Inc 603 225-4081
190 Manchester St Frnt Concord NH (03301) ***(G-17929)***
Signs Now LLC 860 667-8339
2434 Berlin Tpke Ste 14 Newington CT (06111) ***(G-2903)***
Signs Now New Hampshire, Pelham *Also called Ink Outside Box Incorporated* ***(G-19435)***
Signs of All Kinds 860 649-1989
227 Progress Dr Ste A Manchester CT (06042) ***(G-2048)***
Signs of Success Inc 203 329-3374
1084 Hope St Stamford CT (06907) ***(G-4319)***
Signs On Site, Duxbury *Also called Insite Sign LLC* ***(G-10399)***
Signs Plus 508 478-5077
89 S Main St Milford MA (01757) ***(G-13144)***
Signs Plus Inc (PA) 860 653-0547
3 Turkey Hills Rd East Granby CT (06026) ***(G-1144)***
Signs Plus LLC 860 423-3048
700 Main St Willimantic CT (06226) ***(G-5269)***
Signs Solutions Unlimited 781 942-0111
53 Tamarack Rd Reading MA (01867) ***(G-14743)***
Signs To Go Inc 781 938-7700
400 W Cummings Park # 1975 Woburn MA (01801) ***(G-17296)***
Signs Unlimited Inc 203 734-7446
2 Francis St Derby CT (06418) ***(G-1080)***
Signworks Group Inc 617 924-0292
60 Arsenal St Ste 2 Watertown MA (02472) ***(G-16316)***
Signworks Inc 207 778-3822
680 Farmington Falls Rd Farmington ME (04938) ***(G-6053)***
Sigwa Company, Acton *Also called Zhang Fengling* ***(G-7395)***
Sihl, Fiskeville *Also called Arkwright Advanced Coating Inc* ***(G-20454)***
Sika Sarnafil Inc (HQ) 781 828-5400
100 Dan Rd Canton MA (02021) ***(G-9780)***
Sika Sarnafil Inc 800 451-2502
225 Dan Rd Canton MA (02021) ***(G-9781)***
Sikorsky Aircraft Corporation 203 384-7532
1201 South Ave Bridgeport CT (06604) ***(G-490)***
Sikorsky Aircraft Corporation 203 386-7861
1 Far Mill Xing Shelton CT (06484) ***(G-3871)***
Sikorsky Aircraft Corporation 516 228-2000
1 N Frontage Rd North Haven CT (06473) ***(G-3062)***
Sikorsky Aircraft Corporation 203 386-4000
1825 Main St Stratford CT (06615) ***(G-4443)***
Sikorsky Aircraft Corporation 203 386-4000
1210 South Ave Bridgeport CT (06604) ***(G-491)***
Sikorsky Aircraft Corporation (HQ) 203 386-4000
6900 Main St Stratford CT (06614) ***(G-4444)***
Sikorsky Aircraft Corporation 610 644-4430
9 Farm Springs Rd Ste 3 Farmington CT (06032) ***(G-1513)***
Sikorsky Export Corporation 203 386-4000
6900 Main St Stratford CT (06614) ***(G-4445)***
Sil-Med Corporation 508 823-7701
700 Warner Blvd Taunton MA (02780) ***(G-15784)***
Silex Microsystems Inc 617 834-7197
9 Hamilton Pl Ste 300 Boston MA (02108) ***(G-8846)***

Silgan Containers Corporation 203 975-7110
4 Landmark Sq Stamford CT (06901) ***(G-4320)***
Silgan Dispensing Systems (HQ) 401 767-2400
110 Graham Dr Slatersville RI (02876) ***(G-21206)***
Silgan Holdings Inc (PA) 203 975-7110
4 Landmark Sq Ste 400 Stamford CT (06901) ***(G-4321)***
Silgan Plastics LLC 860 526-6300
38 Bridge St Deep River CT (06417) ***(G-1066)***
Silicon Catalyst LLC 203 240-0499
258 W Mountain Rd Ridgefield CT (06877) ***(G-3684)***
Silicon Micro Display Inc 617 433-7630
1126 Beacon St Ste 2 Newton MA (02461) ***(G-13638)***
Silicon Sense Inc 603 891-4248
110 Daniel Webster Hwy # 217 Nashua NH (03060) ***(G-19261)***
Silicon Transistor Corporation 978 256-3321
27 Katrina Rd Chelmsford MA (01824) ***(G-9932)***
Silicone Casting Technologies 860 347-5227
9 Red Orange Rd Middletown CT (06457) ***(G-2221)***
Silkscreen Plus LLC 203 879-0345
413 Wolcott Rd Wolcott CT (06716) ***(G-5460)***
Silly Cow Farms LLC 802 429-2920
293 Industrial Park Rd Wells River VT (05081) ***(G-22603)***
Silpro Llc (PA) 978 772-4444
2 New England Way Ayer MA (01432) ***(G-7939)***
Silva Woodworking 508 636-0059
337 American Legion Hwy Westport MA (02790) ***(G-16846)***
Silver Bay Software LLC 800 364-2889
100 Adams St Dunstable MA (01827) ***(G-10391)***
Silver Bear Distillery LLC 413 242-4892
63 Flansburg Ave Dalton MA (01226) ***(G-10185)***
Silver City Aluminum Corp 508 824-8631
704 W Water St Taunton MA (02780) ***(G-15785)***
Silver Direct Inc 603 355-8855
351 Monadnock Hwy Swanzey NH (03446) ***(G-19889)***
Silver Eagle, Westport *Also called Precision Handling Devices* ***(G-16845)***
Silver Graphics 603 669-6955
200 Gay St Ste 1 Manchester NH (03103) ***(G-18924)***
Silver Lake Fabrication 603 630-5658
28 Gardners Grove Rd Belmont NH (03220) ***(G-17683)***
Silver Leaf Books LLC 781 799-6609
13 Temi Rd Holliston MA (01746) ***(G-11602)***
Silver Little Shop Inc 860 678-1976
23 E Main St Avon CT (06001) ***(G-47)***
Silver Mountain Graphics Inc 802 748-1170
89 Maple St Saint Johnsbury VT (05819) ***(G-22395)***
Silver Screen Design Inc 413 773-1692
324 Wells St Ste 3 Greenfield MA (01301) ***(G-11275)***
Silver Sweet Candies Co, Lawrence *Also called Silver Sweet Products Co* ***(G-12074)***
Silver Sweet Products Co 978 688-0474
522 Essex St Lawrence MA (01840) ***(G-12074)***
Silvermine Press Inc 203 847-4368
4 Van Tassell Ct Norwalk CT (06851) ***(G-3246)***
Silversmith Inc 203 869-4244
392 W Putnam Ave Greenwich CT (06830) ***(G-1649)***
Silvex Incorporated 207 761-0392
45 Thomas Dr Westbrook ME (04092) ***(G-7209)***
Simbex LLC 603 448-2367
10 Water St Ste 410 Lebanon NH (03766) ***(G-18636)***
Simfer Precision Machine Co 978 667-1138
42 Manning Rd Billerica MA (01821) ***(G-8294)***
Similarweb Inc 800 540-1086
100 Summit Dr Burlington MA (01803) ***(G-9338)***
Simkins Industries 203 787-7171
317 Foxon Rd Ste 3 East Haven CT (06513) ***(G-1262)***
Simmedtec LLC 802 872-5968
309 Highlands Dr Williston VT (05495) ***(G-22691)***
Simmonds Precision Pdts Inc (HQ) 802 877-4000
100 Panton Rd Vergennes VT (05491) ***(G-22556)***
Simmonds Precision Pdts Inc 203 797-5000
100 Wooster Hts Danbury CT (06810) ***(G-994)***
Simon & Schuster Inc 603 924-7209
20 Depot St Unit 30 Peterborough NH (03458) ***(G-19488)***
Simon Holding, Fitchburg *Also called Simonds Saw LLC* ***(G-10856)***
Simon Pearce Glass and Pottery, Windsor *Also called Simon Pearce US Inc* ***(G-22714)***
Simon Pearce PA, Windsor *Also called Simon Pearce US Inc* ***(G-22715)***
Simon Pearce US Inc (PA) 802 674-6280
109 Park Rd Windsor VT (05089) ***(G-22714)***
Simon Pearce US Inc 802 674-6280
109 Park Rd Windsor VT (05089) ***(G-22715)***
Simon Pearce US Inc 203 861-0780
125 E Putnam Ave Greenwich CT (06830) ***(G-1650)***
Simon Pearce US Inc 617 450-8388
115 Newbury St Ste 1 Boston MA (02116) ***(G-8847)***
Simonds Incorporated 508 764-3235
248 Elm St Southbridge MA (01550) ***(G-15403)***
Simonds Industries Intl 978 424-0100
135 Intervale Rd Fitchburg MA (01420) ***(G-10853)***
Simonds International LLC 978 424-0327
139 Intervale Rd Fitchburg MA (01420) ***(G-10854)***
Simonds International LLC (HQ) 978 424-0100
135 Intervale Rd Fitchburg MA (01420) ***(G-10855)***
Simonds Saw LLC (PA) 978 424-0100
135 Intervale Rd Fitchburg MA (01420) ***(G-10856)***
Simoniz Usa Inc (PA) 860 646-0172
201 Boston Tpke Bolton CT (06043) ***(G-278)***
Simons Stamps Inc 413 863-6800
320 Avenue A Turners Falls MA (01376) ***(G-15885)***
Simpatico Software Systems 401 246-1358
15 Blanding Ave Barrington RI (02806) ***(G-20055)***
Simple Syrup Glass Studio LLC 781 444-8275
60 Otis St Needham MA (02492) ***(G-13311)***
Simplex Time Recorder Co (HQ) 978 731-2500
50 Technology Drive Westminster MA (01441) ***(G-16813)***
Simplex Time Recorder LLC 802 879-6149
310 Hurricane Ln Unit 2 Williston VT (05495) ***(G-22692)***
Simpliprotected LLC 603 669-7465
50 Westminster Ln Auburn NH (03032) ***(G-17613)***
Simply Birkenstock, Concord *Also called Simply Footwear Utah LLC* ***(G-17930)***
Simply Cupcakes 802 871-5634
8 Pioneer St Essex Junction VT (05452) ***(G-21961)***
Simply Designs & Printing 508 234-3424
2236 Providence Rd Northbridge MA (01534) ***(G-14061)***
Simply Footwear Utah LLC 603 715-2259
8 S Main St Concord NH (03301) ***(G-17930)***
Simply Media Inc 781 259-8029
59 S Great Rd Lincoln MA (01773) ***(G-12289)***
Simply Originals LLC 203 273-3523
14 Crest Rd Norwalk CT (06853) ***(G-3247)***
Simply Sisters Silk Screening, Woburn *Also called Lisa Signs Inc* ***(G-17215)***
Simpson Cabinetry, Essex Junction *Also called Catamount North Cabinetry LLC* ***(G-21935)***
Simpson Strong-Tie Company Inc 860 741-8923
7 Pearson Way Enfield CT (06082) ***(G-1385)***
Sims Portex Inc 603 352-3812
10 Bowman Dr Keene NH (03431) ***(G-18525)***
Simsak Machine & Tool Co Inc 508 764-4958
28 Sandersdale Rd Ste 1 Southbridge MA (01550) ***(G-15404)***
Simsbury Precision Products 860 658-6909
11 Herman Dr Ste C Simsbury CT (06070) ***(G-3911)***
Simsoft Corp 508 366-5451
1 Butterfield Dr Westborough MA (01581) ***(G-16649)***
Simson Products Co Inc 203 265-9882
50 N Plains Industrial Rd Wallingford CT (06492) ***(G-4807)***
Simunition Operations, Avon *Also called General Dynamics Ordnance* ***(G-34)***
Sinauer Associates Inc 413 549-4300
23 Plumtree Rd Sunderland MA (01375) ***(G-15676)***
Sincere Specialty Fabrication 781 974-9580
214 Arlington St Chelsea MA (02150) ***(G-9967)***
Sinclair Manufacturing Co LLC 508 222-7440
12 S Worcester St Norton MA (02766) ***(G-14089)***
Sing Tao Newspapers NY Ltd 617 426-9642
128 Lincoln St Ste 106 Boston MA (02111) ***(G-8848)***
Singing River Publications 218 365-3498
172 Foster St Brighton MA (02135) ***(G-9106)***
Single Load LLC 860 944-7507
2056 Main St Bridgeport CT (06604) ***(G-492)***
Singularity Space Systems LLC 860 713-3626
33 Wolcott Dr Granby CT (06035) ***(G-1591)***
Sinicon Plastics Inc 413 684-5290
455 Housatonic St Dalton MA (01226) ***(G-10186)***
Sinol Usa Inc 203 470-7404
77 S Main St Newtown CT (06470) ***(G-2937)***
Sionyx LLC (PA) 978 922-0684
100 Cummings Ctr 303b Beverly MA (01915) ***(G-8178)***
Sippi/GSM Subma Antenn Joint V 774 553-6218
7 Barnabas Rd Marion MA (02738) ***(G-12703)***
Sippican Week 774 553-5250
163 Front St Marion MA (02738) ***(G-12704)***
Sir Speedy, Springfield *Also called Graphic Excellence LLC* ***(G-15471)***
Sir Speedy, Framingham *Also called Duggan Associates Inc* ***(G-10942)***
Sir Speedy, Boston *Also called Massachusetts Repro Ltd* ***(G-8686)***
Sir Speedy, Waltham *Also called Descal Inc* ***(G-16085)***
Sir Speedy, Marlborough *Also called Linmel Associates Inc* ***(G-12787)***
Sir Speedy, Bloomfield *Also called Kool Ink LLC* ***(G-238)***
Sir Speedy, Lexington *Also called Lexington Graphics* ***(G-12237)***
Sir Speedy, Portsmouth *Also called Southport Management Group LLC* ***(G-19621)***
Sir Speedy, Ashland *Also called J C Enterprises Inc* ***(G-7662)***
Sir Speedy, Orleans *Also called W S Walcott Inc* ***(G-14244)***
Sir Speedy, Boston *Also called Rj Printing LLC* ***(G-8822)***
Sir Speedy 603 625-6868
41 Elm St Manchester NH (03101) ***(G-18925)***
Sir Speedy 401 232-2000
1 Charles St Unit 1 # 1 Providence RI (02904) ***(G-21122)***
Sir Speedy Inc 508 643-1016
865 E Washington St North Attleboro MA (02760) ***(G-13780)***
Sir Speedy Printing 203 346-0716
199 Park Road Ext Ste D Middlebury CT (06762) ***(G-2158)***

Sir Speedy Printing Inc 401 781-5650
969 Park Ave Cranston RI (02910) ***(G-20286)***
Siri Manufacturing Company 860 236-5901
90 Wauregan Rd Danielson CT (06239) ***(G-1017)***
Sirius Analytical Inc 978 338-5790
10 Cook St Ste 6 Billerica MA (01821) ***(G-8295)***
Sirois Tool Company Inc (PA) 860 828-5327
169 White Oak Dr Berlin CT (06037) ***(G-109)***
SIS Ergo, Londonderry *Also called SIS-USA Inc* ***(G-18736)***
SIS-USA Inc 603 432-4495
55 Wentworth Ave Londonderry NH (03053) ***(G-18736)***
Sisson Engineering Corp 413 498-2840
330 Old Wendell Rd Northfield MA (01360) ***(G-14067)***
Sisters Salsa Inc 207 374-2170
689 Hinckley Ridge Rd Blue Hill ME (04614) ***(G-5774)***
SIT Inc 617 479-7796
41 Franklin St Quincy MA (02169) ***(G-14656)***
Site Resources LLC 401 295-4998
1 Cedar St Ste 3 Providence RI (02903) ***(G-21123)***
Siteone Landscape Supply LLC 603 425-2572
3 Aviation Park Dr Londonderry NH (03053) ***(G-18737)***
SIVS Oil Inc 508 951-0528
197 State Rd North Dartmouth MA (02747) ***(G-13925)***
Sixfurlongs LLC 203 255-8553
382 Round Hill Rd Fairfield CT (06824) ***(G-1456)***
Sjm Etronics LLC 603 512-3821
5 Clark Rd Londonderry NH (03053) ***(G-18738)***
Sjm Properties Inc 860 979-0060
164 Maple St Ellington CT (06029) ***(G-1340)***
Sjogren Industries Inc 508 987-3206
982 Southbridge St Worcester MA (01610) ***(G-17474)***
Skelmet Inc 617 396-0612
21 Drydock Ave Ste 610 Boston MA (02210) ***(G-8849)***
Skelmir LLC 617 625-1551
55 Davis Sq 2 Somerville MA (02144) ***(G-15215)***
Skew Products Incorporated 508 580-5800
4 Bert Dr Ste 6 West Bridgewater MA (02379) ***(G-16454)***
Skeyetrac LLC 603 898-8000
70 N Broadway Salem NH (03079) ***(G-19768)***
SKF Specialty Balls 860 379-8511
149 Colebrook River Rd Winsted CT (06098) ***(G-5422)***
SKF USA Inc 860 379-8511
149 Colebrook River Rd Winsted CT (06098) ***(G-5423)***
Skg Associates Inc 781 878-7250
59 Mcdonald St Dedham MA (02026) ***(G-10298)***
Ski Area Management, Woodbury *Also called Beardsley Publishing Corp* ***(G-5483)***
Skico Manufacturing Co LLC 203 230-1305
3 Industrial Cir Hamden CT (06517) ***(G-1784)***
Skidmore Co, Randolph *Also called Vent-Rite Valve Corp* ***(G-14701)***
Skillcraft Machine Tool Co 860 953-1246
255 Nutmeg Rd S South Windsor CT (06074) ***(G-4010)***
Skillsoft Corporation (HQ) 603 324-3000
300 Innovative Way # 201 Nashua NH (03062) ***(G-19262)***
Skillsoft Corporation 800 899-1038
100 River Ridge Dr # 104 Norwood MA (02062) ***(G-14200)***
Skineez Skin Care Wear, Sudbury *Also called Legends & Heroes* ***(G-15662)***
Skmr Construction LLC 603 520-0117
42 Stage Coach Rd Alton NH (03809) ***(G-17547)***
Skowhegan Machine, Skowhegan *Also called Howard P Fairfield LLC* ***(G-6976)***
Skowhegan Press, Skowhegan *Also called Bromar* ***(G-6970)***
Sky & Telescope, Cambridge *Also called Sky Publishing Corporation* ***(G-9652)***
Sky Computers Inc 978 250-2420
27 Industrial Ave Unit 1 Chelmsford MA (01824) ***(G-9933)***
Sky Mfg Company 203 439-7016
268 Sandbank Rd Cheshire CT (06410) ***(G-762)***
Sky Publishing Corporation 617 864-7360
90 Sherman St Ste D Cambridge MA (02140) ***(G-9652)***
Skybuilders.com, Cambridge *Also called Skybuildersdotcom Inc* ***(G-9653)***
Skybuildersdotcom Inc 617 876-5678
77 Huron Ave Cambridge MA (02138) ***(G-9653)***
Skydog Kites LLC 860 365-0600
220 Westchester Rd Colchester CT (06415) ***(G-810)***
Skyko International LLC (PA) 860 928-5170
243 New Sweden Rd Woodstock CT (06281) ***(G-5502)***
Skylight Jewelers, Boston *Also called Edward Spencer* ***(G-8519)***
Skylight Navigation Technology 508 655-7516
19 Peckham Hill Rd Sherborn MA (01770) ***(G-15079)***
Skyline Corporation 802 278-8222
875 S Main St Fair Haven VT (05743) ***(G-21969)***
Skyline Exhibits & Graphics 860 635-2400
362 Industrial Park Rd # 6 Middletown CT (06457) ***(G-2222)***
Skyline Productions 508 326-4982
130 Sargent St Cherry Valley MA (01611) ***(G-9977)***
Skyline Quarry 860 875-3580
110 Conklin Rd Stafford Springs CT (06076) ***(G-4115)***
Skyline Vet Pharma Inc 860 625-0424
37 Skyline Dr Groton CT (06340) ***(G-1686)***
Skyquip, Sterling *Also called S Kyle Equipment Llc* ***(G-15543)***
Skyray Instrument Inc 617 202-3879
6 Brooks Dr Braintree MA (02184) ***(G-9037)***
Skytech Machining Inc 203 378-9994
765 Woodend Rd Stratford CT (06615) ***(G-4446)***
Skytrans Mfg LLC 802 230-7783
106 Burnham Intervale Rd Contoocook NH (03229) ***(G-17948)***
Skyworks Luxembourg S.A.R.L., Woburn *Also called Skyworks Solutions Inc* ***(G-17298)***
Skyworks Solutions Inc (PA) 781 376-3000
20 Sylvan Rd Woburn MA (01801) ***(G-17297)***
Skyworks Solutions Inc 781 935-5150
20 Sylvan Rd Woburn MA (01801) ***(G-17298)***
Skyworks Solutions Inc 978 327-6850
300 Federal St 100 Andover MA (01810) ***(G-7606)***
SL Montevideo Technology Inc 978 667-5100
6 Enterprise Rd Billerica MA (01821) ***(G-8296)***
Slacktide Cafe LLC 207 467-3822
1697 Portland Rd Arundel ME (04046) ***(G-5535)***
Slater Hill Tool LLC 860 963-0415
77 Industrial Park Rd Putnam CT (06260) ***(G-3633)***
Sleep Management Solutions LLC (HQ) 888 497-5337
20 Church St Ste 900 Hartford CT (06103) ***(G-1871)***
Sleepnet Corp 603 758-6600
5 Merrill Industrial Dr Hampton NH (03842) ***(G-18272)***
Slesar Bros Brewing Co Inc 781 749-2337
18 Shipyard Dr Hingham MA (02043) ***(G-11511)***
Slesar Bros Brewing Co Inc 978 745-2337
278 Derby St Salem MA (01970) ***(G-14943)***
Slideways Inc 508 854-0799
705 Plantation St Ste 1 Worcester MA (01605) ***(G-17475)***
Slim-Fast Foods Company, Trumbull *Also called Conopco Inc* ***(G-4621)***
Slingshot Software, Dedham *Also called Celerity Solutions Inc* ***(G-10282)***
Slinky, Greenwich *Also called Poof-Alex Holdings LLC* ***(G-1638)***
Sloan MGT Review, Cambridge *Also called Massachusetts Institute Tech* ***(G-9548)***
Sloan Valve Company 617 796-9001
19 Connector Rd Ste 4 Andover MA (01810) ***(G-7607)***
Slogic Holding Corp (PA) 203 966-2800
36 Grove St New Canaan CT (06840) ***(G-2614)***
Slopeside Syrup, Williston *Also called LLC Cochran Cousins* ***(G-22679)***
Slowinski Wood Products 413 624-3415
13 Bennett Galipo Dr Colrain MA (01340) ***(G-10105)***
Slt Logic, Boston *Also called Coredge Networks Inc* ***(G-8484)***
Sluggo-Ox Corporation 508 726-8221
430 Franklin Village Dr Franklin MA (02038) ***(G-11081)***
Slush Connection Inc 508 230-3788
109 Chestnut St North Easton MA (02356) ***(G-13952)***
SM Heat Treating, North Attleboro *Also called S M Engineering Co Inc* ***(G-13778)***
SMA Inc 207 846-4112
33 Yarmouth Crossing Dr Yarmouth ME (04096) ***(G-7300)***
Smaall Beer Press 413 203-1636
150 Pleasant St Ste 306 Easthampton MA (01027) ***(G-10579)***
Small Batch Organics LLC 802 367-1054
53b Manchester Valley Rd Manchester Center VT (05255) ***(G-22090)***
Small Bites Cupcakes 603 387-6333
135 Franklin St Laconia NH (03246) ***(G-18586)***
Small Corp 413 772-0889
19 Butternut St Greenfield MA (01301) ***(G-11276)***
Smart Manufacturing 508 219-0327
55 Turnpike St Ste 7 West Bridgewater MA (02379) ***(G-16455)***
Smart Modular Technologies Inc 978 221-3513
2 Highwood Dr Ste 101 Tewksbury MA (01876) ***(G-15835)***
Smart Polishing 203 559-1541
24 Betts Ave Stamford CT (06902) ***(G-4322)***
Smart Software Inc 617 489-2743
4 Hill Rd Ste 2 Belmont MA (02478) ***(G-8081)***
Smart Textile Products LLC 401 427-1374
240 Bald Hill Rd Warwick RI (02886) ***(G-21426)***
Smartcatcher Mats, Braintree *Also called 7 Waves Inc* ***(G-8984)***
Smartco Services LLC 508 880-0816
200 Myles Standish Blvd A Taunton MA (02780) ***(G-15786)***
Smarter Living, Boston *Also called Smarter Travel Media LLC* ***(G-8850)***
Smarter Sealants LLC 860 218-2210
14 Eastern Park Rd East Hartford CT (06108) ***(G-1221)***
Smarter Travel Media LLC 617 886-5555
226 Causeway St Ste 3 Boston MA (02114) ***(G-8850)***
Smartfan, Littleton *Also called Control Resources Inc* ***(G-12297)***
Smartfuel America LLC 603 474-5005
15 Batchelder Rd Seabrook NH (03874) ***(G-19818)***
Smartlipo, Westford *Also called Cynosure Inc* ***(G-16763)***
Smartpak Equine LLC (HQ) 774 773-1100
40 Grissom Rd Ste 500 Plymouth MA (02360) ***(G-14583)***
Smartpay Solutions 860 986-7659
200 Executive Blvd Ste 3a Southington CT (06489) ***(G-4077)***
Smartstripe Software Corp 781 861-1812
21 Carriage Dr Lexington MA (02420) ***(G-12275)***
Smartware Products, Leominster *Also called F & M Tool & Plastics Inc* ***(G-12138)***
Smashfly Technologies Inc (HQ) 978 369-3932
9 Damonmill Sq Ste 3a Concord MA (01742) ***(G-10157)***

Smb LLC....802 425-2862
239 Quaker St North Ferrisburgh VT (05473) *(G-22227)*
SMC Ltd....978 422-6800
18 Independence Dr Devens MA (01434) *(G-10333)*
SMH Fine Foods Inc....617 364-1772
139 Milton Ave Hyde Park MA (02136) *(G-11879)*
SMI Ma Inc....508 799-9809
130 Goddard Memorial Dr Worcester MA (01603) *(G-17476)*
SMI Podwer Coating, Amesbury *Also called Specialty Manufacturing Inc (G-7509)*
Smiling Dog....860 344-0707
77 Arbutus St Middletown CT (06457) *(G-2223)*
Smith & Assoc....866 299-6487
581 Us Route 1 Scarborough ME (04074) *(G-6940)*
Smith & Nephew Inc....978 208-0680
100 Glenn St Lawrence MA (01843) *(G-12075)*
Smith & Nephew Inc....978 749-1000
150 Minuteman Rd Andover MA (01810) *(G-7608)*
Smith & Nephew Inc....508 261-3600
130 Forbes Blvd Mansfield MA (02048) *(G-12659)*
Smith & Nephew Inc....508 261-3600
130 Forbes Blvd Mansfield MA (02048) *(G-12660)*
Smith & Nephew Endoscopy Inc....978 749-1000
150 Minuteman Rd Andover MA (01810) *(G-7609)*
Smith & Salmon Inc....802 578-8242
110 Summit St Burlington VT (05401) *(G-21809)*
Smith & Town Printers LLC....603 752-2150
42 Main St Berlin NH (03570) *(G-17700)*
Smith Hill of Delaware Inc....860 767-7502
34 Plains Rd Essex CT (06426) *(G-1405)*
Smith River Sand & Gravel LLC....603 768-3330
289 Ragged Mountain Rd Danbury NH (03230) *(G-17965)*
SMIth&press, Newton *Also called Nahas Selim (G-13616)*
Smithfied Times....401 232-9600
543 Putnam Pike Greenville RI (02828) *(G-20475)*
Smithfield Direct LLC....413 781-5620
20 Carando Dr Springfield MA (01104) *(G-15505)*
Smithfield Foods Inc....413 781-5620
20 Carando Dr Springfield MA (01104) *(G-15506)*
Smiths Detection LLC....510 449-4197
23 Frontage Rd Andover MA (01810) *(G-7610)*
Smiths Detection Inc....401 848-7678
88 Silva Ln Ste 1 Middletown RI (02842) *(G-20632)*
Smiths Interconnect Inc....413 665-0965
5 6 North St South Deerfield MA (01373) *(G-15256)*
Smiths Intrcnnect Americas Inc....978 568-0451
16 Brent Dr Hudson MA (01749) *(G-11817)*
Smiths Medical Asd Inc....508 636-6909
47 Fallon Dr Westport MA (02790) *(G-16847)*
Smiths Medical Asd Inc....603 352-3812
Production Ave Keene NH (03431) *(G-18526)*
Smiths Medical Asd Inc....603 352-3812
10 Bowman Dr Keene NH (03431) *(G-18527)*
Smiths Medical Asd Inc....860 621-9111
201 W Queen St Southington CT (06489) *(G-4078)*
Smiths Tblar Systms-Lconia Inc....603 524-2064
93 Lexington Dr Laconia NH (03246) *(G-18587)*
Smj Metal Co Inc....413 586-3535
36 Smith St Northampton MA (01060) *(G-14021)*
Sml Inc....207 784-2961
777 Main St Lewiston ME (04240) *(G-6324)*
Smoke & Print Universe....203 540-5151
4106 Main St Bridgeport CT (06606) *(G-493)*
Smokey Mountain Chew Inc (PA)....203 656-1088
1 Center St Fl 2 Darien CT (06820) *(G-1032)*
Smoky Quartz Distillery LLC....603 601-0342
14 Kimberly Dr Seabrook NH (03874) *(G-19819)*
SMP DBA A BAND FOR BROTHERS, Attleboro *Also called Sweet Metal Finishing Inc (G-7799)*
Smpretty Inc....508 358-1639
97 Lincoln Rd Wayland MA (01778) *(G-16336)*
SMR Metal Technology....860 291-8259
524 Sullivan Ave Ste 15 South Windsor CT (06074) *(G-4011)*
SMS Machine Inc....860 829-0813
54 Clark Dr Ste A East Berlin CT (06023) *(G-1108)*
Smsc Flags and Flagpoles, Bridgeport *Also called Sign Maintenance Service Co (G-489)*
Smudge Ink Incorporated....617 242-8228
50 Terminal St Ste 21 Charlestown MA (02129) *(G-9844)*
Smurfit Stone, Wakefield *Also called Westrock Cp LLC (G-15984)*
Smurfit-Stone, Concord *Also called Graphic Packaging Intl LLC (G-17904)*
Smyth Companies LLC....800 776-1201
271 Ballardvale St Wilmington MA (01887) *(G-17045)*
Snapple Juices, Bridgeport *Also called B & E Juices Inc (G-380)*
Snapwire Innovations LLC....203 806-4773
125 Commerce Ct Ste 11 Cheshire CT (06410) *(G-763)*
Sneham Manufacturing Inc....203 610-6669
727 Honeyspot Rd Ste 99 Stratford CT (06615) *(G-4447)*
Snomatic Controls & Engrg Inc....603 795-2900
4 Britton Ln Lyme NH (03768) *(G-18756)*
Snow Economics Inc....508 655-3232
15 Mercer Rd Natick MA (01760) *(G-13279)*
Snow Farm Winery....802 372-9463
190 W Shore Rd South Hero VT (05486) *(G-22482)*
Snow Findings Company Inc....401 821-7712
14 Sheldon St West Warwick RI (02893) *(G-21509)*
Snow-Nbstedt Pwr Transmissions, Manchester *Also called Allard Nazarian Group Inc (G-18775)*
Snowathome LLC....860 584-2991
84 Napco Dr Ste 6 Terryville CT (06786) *(G-4491)*
Snowbound Software Corporation....617 607-2000
309 Waverly Oaks Rd # 401 Waltham MA (02452) *(G-16195)*
Snowman's Printing & Stamps, Hermon *Also called Armstrong Family Inds Inc (G-6183)*
Snows Nice Cream Co Inc....413 774-7438
80 School St Greenfield MA (01301) *(G-11277)*
Snowshoe Pond Mple Sgrwrks LLC....802 777-9676
431 Barnes Rd Enosburg Falls VT (05450) *(G-21927)*
Snug....207 772-6839
223 Congress St Ste 1 Portland ME (04101) *(G-6730)*
Snyder Machine Co Inc....781 233-2080
9 Thomas St Unit C9 Saugus MA (01906) *(G-14997)*
Snyders-Lance Inc....508 771-1872
100 Breeds Hill Rd Hyannis MA (02601) *(G-11858)*
So and Sew Plushies....860 916-2918
104 Elm St Meriden CT (06450) *(G-2131)*
Sobi Inc....610 228-2040
890 Winter St Ste 200 Waltham MA (02451) *(G-16196)*
Soccerscarf.com, Mattapoisett *Also called Sportsscarf LLC (G-12891)*
Social Sentinel Inc....800 628-0158
128 Lakeside Ave Ste 100 Burlington VT (05401) *(G-21810)*
Society For Marine Mammalogy....508 744-2276
290 Summer St Yarmouth Port MA (02675) *(G-17531)*
Sock Shack....207 805-1348
564 Congress St Portland ME (04101) *(G-6731)*
Socks For Siberia Inc....774 200-1617
122 Long Hill Rd Brookfield MA (01506) *(G-9192)*
Socomec Inc (HQ)....617 245-0447
9 Galen St Ste 120 Watertown MA (02472) *(G-16317)*
Soda Shoppe of Franklin....603 934-0100
901 Central St Franklin NH (03235) *(G-18164)*
Sodexo Abbott Bioresearch, Worcester *Also called Abbott Laboratories (G-17331)*
Sofrito Ponce, New Haven *Also called Louis Rodriguz (G-2708)*
Softbank Robotics America Inc....617 986-6700
55 Thomson Pl Boston MA (02210) *(G-8851)*
Softmedia Inc....978 528-3266
27 Crane Rd Walpole MA (02081) *(G-16012)*
Software Cnslting Rsources Inc....860 491-2689
9 Valcove Ct Goshen CT (06756) *(G-1587)*
Software Concepts Inc....978 584-0400
3 Survey Cir Ste 2 North Billerica MA (01862) *(G-13865)*
Software Experts Inc....978 692-5343
4 Grey Fox Ln Westford MA (01886) *(G-16793)*
Software Leverage Inc....781 894-3399
465 Waverley Oaks Rd # 103 Waltham MA (02452) *(G-16197)*
Soil Exploration Corp (PA)....978 840-0391
148 Pioneer Dr Leominster MA (01453) *(G-12187)*
Soitec Usa Inc (HQ)....978 531-2222
2 Blackburn Ctr Gloucester MA (01930) *(G-11210)*
Soja Woodworking LLC....860 345-3909
548 Killingworth Rd Higganum CT (06441) *(G-1906)*
Sojournix Inc....781 864-1111
400 Totten Pond Rd # 115 Waltham MA (02451) *(G-16198)*
Solace Therapeutics Inc....508 283-1200
135 Newbury St Ste 1 Framingham MA (01701) *(G-11006)*
Solais Lighting Inc....203 683-6222
650 West Ave Stamford CT (06902) *(G-4323)*
Solar Data Systems Inc....203 702-7189
23 Francis J Clarke Cir Bethel CT (06801) *(G-179)*
Solar Generations LLC....203 453-3920
741 Podunk Rd Guilford CT (06437) *(G-1720)*
Solar Seal, South Easton *Also called Shaw Glass Holdings LLC (G-15292)*
Solar Seal of Connecticut, Hamden *Also called Insulpane Connecticut Inc (G-1761)*
Solar Source, Keene *Also called Keebowil Inc (G-18509)*
Solar Stream, Temple *Also called Solar-Stream LLC (G-19899)*
Solar-Stream LLC....603 878-0066
184 Hill Rd Temple NH (03084) *(G-19899)*
Solarone Solutions Inc (PA)....339 225-4530
220 Reservoir St Ste 19 Needham Heights MA (02494) *(G-13344)*
Soldier Socks....203 832-2005
90 Fairfield Ave Stamford CT (06902) *(G-4324)*
Soldream Inc....860 871-6883
129 Reservoir Rd Vernon Rockville CT (06066) *(G-4683)*
Soldream Spcial Process - Wldg....860 858-5247
203 Hartford Tpke Tolland CT (06084) *(G-4552)*
Sole Proprietorship, New Bedford *Also called Blue Fleet Welding Service (G-13363)*
Solect Energy Development LLC....508 250-8358
45 South St Hopkinton MA (01748) *(G-11736)*
Solect Energy Development LLC....508 598-3511
89 Hayden Rowe St Ste E Hopkinton MA (01748) *(G-11737)*

A
L
P
H
A
B
E
T
I
C

Solectria Renewables LLC......978 683-9700
360 Merrimack St Ste 9 Lawrence MA (01843) ***(G-12076)***
Solemma LLC......415 238-2231
2 Reed Street Ct Cambridge MA (02140) ***(G-9654)***
Solenis LLC......413 536-6426
1111 Grattan St Chicopee MA (01013) ***(G-10061)***
Soleo Health Inc......781 298-3427
5 Shawmut Rd Ste 103 Canton MA (02021) ***(G-9782)***
Soleras Advanced Coatings Ltd (PA)......207 282-5699
589 Elm St Biddeford ME (04005) ***(G-5763)***
Solico, West Hartford *Also called Sorenson Lighted Controls Inc* ***(G-5095)***
Solid Access Technologies LLC......978 463-0642
6 Liberty St Newport RI (02840) ***(G-20682)***
Solid Biosciences Inc (PA)......617 337-4680
141 Portland St Fl Gr Cambridge MA (02139) ***(G-9655)***
Solid Earth Technologies Inc......603 882-5319
3 Howe Dr Ste 3 # 3 Amherst NH (03031) ***(G-17588)***
Solid Oak Inc......401 637-4855
244 Post Rd Ste 102 Westerly RI (02891) ***(G-21541)***
Solid State Heating, Westbrook *Also called Sshc Inc* ***(G-5163)***
Solidenergy Systems LLC......617 972-3412
35 Cabot Rd Woburn MA (01801) ***(G-17299)***
Solidification Pdts Intl Inc......203 484-9494
524 Forest Rd Northford CT (06472) ***(G-3092)***
Solidification Products Intl, Northford *Also called Solidification Products Intl* ***(G-3093)***
Solidification Products Intl......203 484-9494
215 Village St Northford CT (06472) ***(G-3093)***
Solidphase Inc......207 797-0211
44 Caddie Ln Portland ME (04103) ***(G-6732)***
Solidscape Inc......603 424-0590
316 Daniel Webster Hwy Merrimack NH (03054) ***(G-19030)***
Solifor Timberlands Inc......207 827-7195
1141 Main St Old Town ME (04468) ***(G-6547)***
Solla Eyelet Products Inc......860 274-5729
50 Seemar Rd Watertown CT (06795) ***(G-5026)***
Solo Cup Operating Corporation......802 524-5966
1521 Lower Newton Rd Saint Albans VT (05478) ***(G-22378)***
Solos Endoscopy Inc......617 360-9700
65 Sprague St Boston MA (02136) ***(G-8852)***
Solusoft Inc......978 375-6021
300 Willow St North Andover MA (01845) ***(G-13728)***
Solutek Corporation......617 445-5335
94 Shirley St Boston MA (02119) ***(G-8853)***
Solutia Inc......413 788-6911
730 Worcester St Springfield MA (01151) ***(G-15507)***
Solutions Atlantic Inc......617 423-2699
75 State St Ste 100bston Boston MA (02109) ***(G-8854)***
Solvent Kleene Inc......978 531-2279
119 Foster St Bldg 6 Peabody MA (01960) ***(G-14370)***
Solx Inc......978 808-6926
98 Ruddock Rd Sudbury MA (01776) ***(G-15668)***
Somatex Inc......207 487-6141
70 North Rd Detroit ME (04929) ***(G-5953)***
Somers Manufacturing Inc......860 314-1075
165 Riverside Ave Bristol CT (06010) ***(G-613)***
Somers Thin Strip, Waterbury *Also called Global Brass & Copper LLC* ***(G-4879)***
Somerset Industries Inc......978 667-3355
137 Phoenix Ave Lowell MA (01852) ***(G-12433)***
Somerset Log Yard, Skowhegan *Also called Jackman Lumber Inc* ***(G-6979)***
Somerset Plastics Company......860 635-1601
454 Timber Ridge Rd Middletown CT (06457) ***(G-2224)***
Somersets Usa LLC......617 803-6833
30 Academy St Arlington MA (02476) ***(G-7640)***
Somerville News......617 666-4010
699 Broadway Somerville MA (02144) ***(G-15216)***
Somerville Office......617 776-0738
344 Somerville Ave Somerville MA (02143) ***(G-15217)***
Somerville Ornamental Ir Works......617 666-8872
7 George St Somerville MA (02145) ***(G-15218)***
Somerville Quick Print Inc......617 492-5343
1722 Massachusetts Ave A Cambridge MA (02138) ***(G-9656)***
Somerville Science and Tech......617 628-3150
15 Ward St Somerville MA (02143) ***(G-15219)***
Something Sweet Inc (PA)......203 603-9766
724 Grand Ave New Haven CT (06511) ***(G-2738)***
Somic America Inc......207 989-1759
6 Baker Blvd Brewer ME (04412) ***(G-5801)***
Son Co Inc......508 966-2970
15 N Main St Bellingham MA (02019) ***(G-8059)***
Son-Chief Stampings, Winsted *Also called Sonchief Electrics Inc* ***(G-5424)***
Son-Co Printing & Copying, Bellingham *Also called Son Co Inc* ***(G-8059)***
Sonare Winds, Maynard *Also called Verne Q Powell Flutes Inc* ***(G-12905)***
Sonchief Electrics Inc......860 379-2741
41 Meadow St Ste 1 Winsted CT (06098) ***(G-5424)***
Sonco Worldwide Inc......401 406-3761
450 Pavilion Ave Warwick RI (02888) ***(G-21427)***
Sonesys LLC......603 423-9000
21 Continental Blvd Merrimack NH (03054) ***(G-19031)***
Song Bath LLC......800 353-0313
146 Old Kings Hwy New Canaan CT (06840) ***(G-2615)***
Song Even......603 256-6018
15 Old Brattleboro Rd Hinsdale NH (03451) ***(G-18321)***
Song Wind Industries Inc......401 245-7582
6 Stratford Rd Barrington RI (02806) ***(G-20056)***
Sonias Chocolaterie Inc......203 438-5965
6 Ascot Way Ridgefield CT (06877) ***(G-3685)***
Sonic Blue Aerospace Inc......207 776-2471
80 Exchange St Ste 36 Portland ME (04101) ***(G-6733)***
Sonic Corp......203 375-0063
1 Research Dr Stratford CT (06615) ***(G-4448)***
Sonic Manufacturing Co Inc......603 882-1020
35 Sagamore Park Rd Hudson NH (03051) ***(G-18438)***
Sonicators, Newtown *Also called Qsonica LLC* ***(G-2933)***
Sonicron Systems Corporation......413 562-5218
382 Suthampton Rd Ste 102 Westfield MA (01085) ***(G-16731)***
Sonics & Materials Inc (PA)......203 270-4600
53 Church Hill Rd Newtown CT (06470) ***(G-2938)***
Sonitek Corporation......203 878-9321
84 Research Dr Milford CT (06460) ***(G-2364)***
Sonitor Technologies Inc......727 466-4557
37 Brookside Dr Greenwich CT (06830) ***(G-1651)***
Sonnax Industries Inc (PA)......802 463-9722
1 Automatic Dr Bellows Falls VT (05101) ***(G-21654)***
Sonnys Pizza Inc......617 381-1900
3 Fox Hollow Dr Saugus MA (01906) ***(G-14998)***
Sonoco Products Company......413 536-4546
200 S Water St Holyoke MA (01040) ***(G-11658)***
Sonoco Products Company......207 487-3206
101 Industrial Dr Pittsfield ME (04967) ***(G-6591)***
Sonoco Products Company......413 493-1298
111 Mosher St Holyoke MA (01040) ***(G-11659)***
Sonoco Prtective Solutions Inc......860 928-7795
29 Park Rd Putnam CT (06260) ***(G-3634)***
Sonolite Plastics Corporation......978 281-0662
10 Fernwood Lake Ave Gloucester MA (01930) ***(G-11211)***
Sonomedescalon, Stoneham *Also called Escalon Digital Solutions Inc* ***(G-15562)***
Sonosystems N Schunk Amer Corp (HQ)......978 658-9400
250 Andover St Wilmington MA (01887) ***(G-17046)***
Sons Liberty Spirits Company......401 284-4006
1425 Kingstown Rd Wakefield RI (02879) ***(G-21276)***
Sony Dadc......617 714-5776
545 Concord Ave Ste 102 Cambridge MA (02138) ***(G-9657)***
Sophia Institute......603 641-9344
525 Greeley St Manchester NH (03102) ***(G-18926)***
Sophic Alliance Inc......508 495-3801
99 Meadow Neck Rd East Falmouth MA (02536) ***(G-10449)***
Sorby & Son Heating......603 532-7214
21 Erin Ln Jaffrey NH (03452) ***(G-18477)***
Sorenson Lighted Controls Inc (PA)......860 527-3092
100 Shield St West Hartford CT (06110) ***(G-5095)***
Sorenson Sewing Inc......617 333-6955
65 Sprague St Hyde Park MA (02136) ***(G-11880)***
Sorge Industries Inc......203 924-8900
289 Coram Rd Shelton CT (06484) ***(G-3872)***
Soro Systems Inc......802 763-2248
190 Chelsea St 9 South Royalton VT (05068) ***(G-22493)***
Sorriso Technologies Inc......978 635-3900
40 Nagog Park Ste 110 Acton MA (01720) ***(G-7387)***
Soto Holdings Inc......203 781-8020
300 East St New Haven CT (06511) ***(G-2739)***
Souhegan Management Corp......603 898-8868
99 Faltin Dr Manchester NH (03103) ***(G-18927)***
Souhegan Wood Products Inc......603 654-2311
10 Souhegan St Wilton NH (03086) ***(G-19988)***
Soulas Homemade Salsa LLC......978 314-7735
21 Stonecleave Rd Boxford MA (01921) ***(G-8978)***
Sound Construction & Engrg Co......860 242-2109
522 Cottage Grove Rd H Bloomfield CT (06002) ***(G-263)***
Sound Control Technologies......203 854-5701
22 S Smith St Norwalk CT (06855) ***(G-3248)***
Sound Manufacturing Inc......860 388-4466
1 Williams Ln Old Saybrook CT (06475) ***(G-3350)***
Sound Oasis Company, Marblehead *Also called Headwaters Inc* ***(G-12685)***
Sound Seal Holdings Inc (HQ)......413 789-1770
50 Hp Almgren Dr Agawam MA (01001) ***(G-7451)***
Soundcure Inc......408 938-5745
100 High St 28 Boston MA (02110) ***(G-8855)***
Soundings Publications LLC......860 767-8227
10 Bokum Rd Essex CT (06426) ***(G-1406)***
Soundview Paper Mills LLC (HQ)......201 796-4000
1 Sound Shore Dr Ste 203 Greenwich CT (06830) ***(G-1652)***
Soundview Vermont Holdings LLC......802 387-5571
67 Kathan Meadow Rd Putney VT (05346) ***(G-22292)***
Source Inc (PA)......203 488-6400
101 Fowler Rd North Branford CT (06471) ***(G-2977)***
Source Inc......207 729-1107
7 Industrial Pkwy Brunswick ME (04011) ***(G-5845)***

Source International Corp 508 842-5555
17 Gilmore Dr Sutton MA (01590) *(G-15692)*
Source Loudspeakers 860 918-3088
701 Nutmeg Rd N Ste 2 South Windsor CT (06074) *(G-4012)*
Source Maine, Brunswick *Also called Source Inc (G-5845)*
Source Technologies, South Windsor *Also called Source Loudspeakers (G-4012)*
Source Two Inc 413 289-1251
7 Third St Bondsville MA (01009) *(G-8325)*
Sourcing Opportunities, Shrewsbury *Also called Service Oriented Sales Inc (G-15131)*
Sousa & Demayo, Attleboro Falls *Also called Sousa Bros & Demayo Inc (G-7817)*
Sousa Bros & Demayo Inc 508 695-6800
266 John L Dietsch Blvd Attleboro Falls MA (02763) *(G-7817)*
Sousa Corp 860 523-9090
565 Cedar St Newington CT (06111) *(G-2904)*
South Bend Ethanol LLC 203 326-8132
107 Elm St Stamford CT (06902) *(G-4325)*
South Boston Today 617 268-4032
396 W 4th St Boston MA (02127) *(G-8856)*
South County Choppers 401 788-1000
22 1st St Narragansett RI (02882) *(G-20650)*
South County Steel Inc 401 789-5570
192 Waites Corner Rd West Kingston RI (02892) *(G-21473)*
South Hero Fire District 4 .... 802 372-3088
28 Hill Rd South Hero VT (05486) *(G-22483)*
South Poultney Slate 802 287-9278
376 York St Poultney VT (05764) *(G-22277)*
South River Miso Co Inc 413 369-4057
888 Shelburne Falls Rd Conway MA (01341) *(G-10167)*
South Shore Custom Prints 781 293-8300
85 Mattakeesett St Pembroke MA (02359) *(G-14427)*
South Shore Dental Labs 781 924-5382
159 Plymouth Rd Hanover MA (02339) *(G-11351)*
South Shore Dstless Blastg LLC 508 789-4575
12 Cedarhill Park Dr 1 Plymouth MA (02360) *(G-14584)*
South Shore Manufacturing Inc 781 447-9264
647 First Parish Rd Scituate MA (02066) *(G-15014)*
South Shore Meats, East Bridgewater *Also called Crocetti-Oakdale Packing Inc (G-10410)*
South Shore Meats, Brockton *Also called Crocetti-Oakdale Packing Inc (G-9135)*
South Shore Millwork Inc 508 226-5500
7 Maple St Norton MA (02766) *(G-14090)*
South Shore Plating Co Inc 617 773-8064
28 Forest Ave Quincy MA (02169) *(G-14657)*
South Shore Signs 781 834-1120
846 Webster St Ste 3 Marshfield MA (02050) *(G-12868)*
South Shore Wood Pellets Inc 781 986-7797
279 Centre St Ste 2 Holbrook MA (02343) *(G-11538)*
South Win, Leominster *Also called North/Win Ltd (G-12172)*
Southborough Villager, Marlborough *Also called Gatehouse Media Mass I Inc (G-12758)*
Southbridge News, Southbridge *Also called Stonebridge Press Inc (G-15405)*
Southbridge Shtmtl Works Inc 508 347-7800
441 Main St Sturbridge MA (01566) *(G-15647)*
Southbridge Tool & Mfg Inc 508 764-6819
181 Southbridge Rd Dudley MA (01571) *(G-10385)*
Southbury Printing Centre Inc 203 264-0102
385 Main St S Ste 107 Southbury CT (06488) *(G-4033)*
Southcoast Stoneworks Inc 774 319-5200
875 State Rd Unit 9 Westport MA (02790) *(G-16848)*
Southcoast Woodworking Inc 508 758-3184
13 Industrial Dr Unit 3 Mattapoisett MA (02739) *(G-12890)*
Southeast Railing Co Inc 781 828-7088
901 Turnpike St Unit A Canton MA (02021) *(G-9783)*
Southeastern Millwork Co Inc 508 888-6038
150 State Rd Sagamore Beach MA (02562) *(G-14887)*
Southeastern Millwork Co Inc 508 888-6038
150 State Rd Bourne MA (02532) *(G-8949)*
Southeastern Sand and Grav Inc 781 413-6884
27 Pine Hill Rd Kingston MA (02364) *(G-11964)*
Southern Berkshire Shoppers Gu 413 528-0095
141 West Ave Great Barrington MA (01230) *(G-11246)*
Southern Conn Pallet Co Inc 203 265-1313
346 Quinnipiac St Wallingford CT (06492) *(G-4808)*
Southern Maine Industries Corp 207 856 7391
68 Outlet Cove Rd Windham ME (04062) *(G-7253)*
Southern Neng Ultraviolet Co, Branford *Also called Southern Neng Ultraviolet Inc (G-350)*
Southern Neng Ultraviolet Inc 203 483-5810
55029 E Main St Branford CT (06405) *(G-350)*
Southern Redi-Mix Corporation 781 837-5353
506 Plain St Ste 105 Marshfield MA (02050) *(G-12869)*
Southern RI Newspapers (HQ) 401 789-9744
187 Main St Wakefield RI (02879) *(G-21277)*
Southfield Carton, Concord *Also called Graphic Packaging Intl LLC (G-17907)*
Southington Citizen 860 620-5960
500 S Broad St Ste 1 Meriden CT (06450) *(G-2132)*
Southington Metal Fabg Co 860 621-0149
95 Corporate Dr Southington CT (06489) *(G-4079)*
Southington Tool & Mfg Corp 860 276-0021
300 Atwater St Plantsville CT (06479) *(G-3540)*
Southington Transm Auto Repr 860 329-0381
1900 West St Southington CT (06489) *(G-4080)*
Southpack LLC 860 224-2242
1 Hartford Sq New Britain CT (06052) *(G-2577)*
Southport Brewing Co 203 874-2337
33 New Haven Ave Milford CT (06460) *(G-2365)*
Southport Brewing Company, Shelton *Also called Nutmeg Brewing Rest Group LLC (G-3843)*
Southport Management Group LLC 603 433-4664
738 Islington St Portsmouth NH (03801) *(G-19621)*
Southport Printing Company, Portsmouth *Also called Spirit Advisory LLC (G-19622)*
Southport Products LLC 860 379-0761
157 Colebrook River Rd Winsted CT (06098) *(G-5425)*
Southside Media, Hartford *Also called Gamut Publishing (G-1824)*
Southstern Mtal Fbricators Inc 781 878-1505
Air Station Industrial Pa Rockland MA (02370) *(G-14826)*
Southwest Asian Incorporated 508 753-7126
55 Millbrook St Ste 4 Worcester MA (01606) *(G-17477)*
Southwick, Haverhill *Also called Golden Fleece Mfg Group LLC (G-11439)*
Southwick & Meister Inc 203 237-0000
1455 N Colony Rd Meriden CT (06450) *(G-2133)*
Southwick Clothing LLC (HQ) 800 634-5312
25 Computer Dr Haverhill MA (01832) *(G-11472)*
Southwire Company LLC 203 324-0067
392 Pacific St Stamford CT (06902) *(G-4326)*
Southworth Intl Group Inc (PA) 207 878-0700
11 Gray Rd Falmouth ME (04105) *(G-6033)*
Southworth Products Corp (HQ) 207 878-0700
11 Gray Rd Falmouth ME (04105) *(G-6034)*
Southworth Timber Frames Inc 603 788-2619
273 Garland Rd Lancaster NH (03584) *(G-18605)*
Sovipe Food Distributors LLC 203 648-2781
87 E Liberty St Danbury CT (06810) *(G-995)*
Soya Techcom, Bar Harbor *Also called Soyatech Inc (G-5670)*
Soyatech Inc 207 288-4969
1369 State Highway 102 Bar Harbor ME (04609) *(G-5670)*
Soyaz 207 453-4911
7 Truss Ln Fairfield ME (04937) *(G-6029)*
Sp Machine Inc 978 562-2019
526 Main St Hudson MA (01749) *(G-11818)*
Space Age Electronics Inc (PA) 800 486-1723
58 Chocksett Rd Sterling MA (01564) *(G-15545)*
Space Age Electronics Inc 978 652-5421
283 Baldwinville Rd Templeton MA (01468) *(G-15805)*
Space Building Corp 508 947-7277
8 Harding St Ste 107 Lakeville MA (02347) *(G-11978)*
Space Electronics LLC 860 829-0001
81 Fuller Way Berlin CT (06037) *(G-110)*
Space Optics Research Labs LLC 978 250-8640
15 Caron St Merrimack NH (03054) *(G-19032)*
Space Swiss Manufacturing Inc 860 567-4341
428 Maple St Litchfield CT (06759) *(G-1952)*
Space Tool & Machine Co Inc 860 290-8599
130 Commerce Way Ste 1 South Windsor CT (06074) *(G-4013)*
Spadafora Slush Co 617 548-5870
195 Pearl St Malden MA (02148) *(G-12597)*
Spargo Machine Products Inc 860 583-3925
6 Gear Dr Terryville CT (06786) *(G-4492)*
Spark Vt Inc 802 985-3321
6221 Shelburne Rd Shelburne VT (05482) *(G-22425)*
Sparkman & Stephens LLC (PA) 401 847-5449
26 Washington Sq Ste 3 Newport RI (02840) *(G-20683)*
Sparrow Engineering 508 867-3984
108 North St East Brookfield MA (01515) *(G-10423)*
Sparrow, Jacob, Pittston *Also called William B Sparrow Jr (G-6593)*
Sparrows Little Tech LLC 781 799-6442
176 Mystic Valley Pkwy Winchester MA (01890) *(G-17096)*
Sparta Kefalas Organics LLC 978 810-5300
361 Central St East Bridgewater MA (02333) *(G-10420)*
Spartan Aerospace LLC 860 533-7500
41 Progress Dr Manchester CT (06042) *(G-2049)*
Spartech LLC 203 327-6010
69 Southfield Ave Stamford CT (06902) *(G-4327)*
Sparton Beckwood, Plaistow *Also called Beckwood Services Inc (G-19508)*
Sparton Beckwood LLC 603 382-3840
27 Hale Spring Rd Plaistow NH (03865) *(G-19524)*
Sparton Technology Corp 603 880-3692
8 Hampshire Dr Hudson NH (03051) *(G-18439)*
Spatter Inc 617 510-0498
21 Randolph St Newton MA (02461) *(G-13639)*
Spaulding Composites Inc (PA) 603 332-0555
55 Nadeau Dr Rochester NH (03867) *(G-19687)*
Spb LLC 207 620-7998
681 Riverside Dr Augusta ME (04330) *(G-5620)*
Spc Marcom Studio, North Springfield *Also called Springfield Printing Corp (G-22238)*
Speakeasy Ai, Old Greenwich *Also called Open Water Development LLC (G-3313)*
Spear Group Holdings 603 673-6400
48 Powers St Milford NH (03055) *(G-19078)*
Spear New Hampshire, Milford *Also called Spear Group Holdings (G-19078)*
Spear Systems, Milford *Also called Gardoc Inc (G-19056)*

A L P H A B E T I C

Spear USA Inc 513 459-1100
86 Powers St Milford NH (03055) ***(G-19079)***
Spec Lines 781 245-0044
4 Railroad Ave Ste 2 Wakefield MA (01880) ***(G-15976)***
Spec Plating Inc 203 366-3638
740 Seaview Ave Bridgeport CT (06607) ***(G-494)***
Spec Tools, West Bridgewater *Also called Skew Products Incorporated* ***(G-16454)***
Spec-Elec Plating Corp 508 347-7255
101 Colonial Dr Sturbridge MA (01566) ***(G-15648)***
Special Diversified Opp Inc 207 856-6151
52 Anderson Rd Windham ME (04062) ***(G-7254)***
Special Electronics Plating, Sturbridge *Also called Spec-Elec Plating Corp* ***(G-15648)***
Special Events Screen Prtg LLC 203 468-5453
35 Washington Ave East Haven CT (06512) ***(G-1263)***
Special Hermetic Products 603 654-2002
Riverview Mill 39 Souhgn Wilton NH (03086) ***(G-19989)***
Special Projects Group LLC 603 391-9700
221 Intervale Rd B2 Gilford NH (03249) ***(G-18192)***
Special Vhcl Developments Inc 203 272-7928
337 Blacks Rd Cheshire CT (06410) ***(G-764)***
Specialized Coating Services 978 362-0346
16 Esquire Rd Unit A North Billerica MA (01862) ***(G-13866)***
Specialized Plastics Inc 978 562-9314
567 Main St Hudson MA (01749) ***(G-11819)***
Specialized Plating Inc 978 373-8030
15 Ward Hill Ave Haverhill MA (01835) ***(G-11473)***
Specialized Turning Inc 978 977-0444
147 Summit St Ste 7 Peabody MA (01960) ***(G-14371)***
Specialty Cable Corp 203 265-7126
2 Tower Dr Wallingford CT (06492) ***(G-4809)***
Specialty Coated Products, Merrimack *Also called Nashua Corporation* ***(G-19015)***
Specialty Components Inc (PA) 203 284-9112
14 Village Ln Ste 1 Wallingford CT (06492) ***(G-4810)***
Specialty Components Inc 203 284-9112
14 Village Ln Wallingford CT (06492) ***(G-4811)***
Specialty Manufacturing Inc 978 388-1601
40 Water St Amesbury MA (01913) ***(G-7509)***
Specialty Materials, Lowell *Also called Global Materials Inc* ***(G-12376)***
Specialty Metals and Fab 203 509-5028
51 Elm St Naugatuck CT (06770) ***(G-2496)***
Specialty Minerals Inc 207 897-4492
Riley Rd Gate 15 Jay ME (04239) ***(G-6221)***
Specialty Minerals Inc 860 824-5435
30 Daisy Hill Rd Canaan CT (06018) ***(G-690)***
Specialty Packaging Inc 413 543-1814
34 Front St Ste 38 Indian Orchard MA (01151) ***(G-11895)***
Specialty Polymers Inc 203 575-5727
245 Freight St Waterbury CT (06702) ***(G-4958)***
Specialty Printing LLC 860 654-1850
15 Thompson Rd East Windsor CT (06088) ***(G-1302)***
Specialty Printing LLC (PA) 860 623-8870
4 Thompson Rd East Windsor CT (06088) ***(G-1303)***
Specialty Products Company 207 549-7232
208 Rockland Rd Whitefield ME (04353) ***(G-7218)***
Specialty Products Mfg LLC 860 621-6969
251 Captain Lewis Dr Southington CT (06489) ***(G-4081)***
Specialty Prtrs F Bush Son Co 781 585-9444
79 Upland Rd Plympton MA (02367) ***(G-14593)***
Specialty Saw Inc 860 658-4419
30 Wolcott Rd Simsbury CT (06070) ***(G-3912)***
Specialty Shop Inc 860 647-1477
18 Sanrico Dr Manchester CT (06042) ***(G-2050)***
Specialty Steel Treating Inc 860 653-0061
12 Kripes Rd East Granby CT (06026) ***(G-1145)***
Specialty Textile Products LLC 603 330-3334
1 Progress Dr Dover NH (03820) ***(G-18053)***
Specialty Tool Company USA LLC 203 874-2009
61 Erna Ave Milford CT (06461) ***(G-2366)***
Specialty Truss Inc 603 886-5523
12 Mercier Ln Nashua NH (03062) ***(G-19263)***
Specialty Wholesale Sup Corp 978 632-1472
101 Linus Allain Ave Gardner MA (01440) ***(G-11128)***
Specialty Wire & Cord Sets 203 498-2932
1 Gallagher Rd Hamden CT (06517) ***(G-1785)***
Specmatrix, Colchester *Also called Isotech North America Inc* ***(G-21868)***
Specs Tii Inc 508 618-1292
20 Cabot Blvd Ste 300 Mansfield MA (02048) ***(G-12661)***
Spectacle Eye Ware Inc 617 542-9600
544 Tremont St Boston MA (02116) ***(G-8857)***
Spectex, Dover *Also called Specialty Textile Products LLC* ***(G-18053)***
Spectex LLC 603 330-3334
1 Progress Dr Ste 1 # 1 Dover NH (03820) ***(G-18054)***
Spector Metal Products Co Inc 781 767-5600
608 South St Holbrook MA (02343) ***(G-11539)***
Spectra Analysis Inc (PA) 508 281-6232
257 Simarano Dr Ste 106 Marlborough MA (01752) ***(G-12827)***
Spectra Analysis Instrs Inc 508 281-6233
257 Simarano Dr Ste 106 Marlborough MA (01752) ***(G-12828)***
Spectral Evolution Inc 978 687-1833
26 Parkridge Rd Ste 1a Haverhill MA (01835) ***(G-11474)***
Spectral Inc 401 921-2690
50 Minnesota Ave Unit 1 Warwick RI (02888) ***(G-21428)***
Spectral LLC (PA) 860 928-7726
111 Highland Dr Putnam CT (06260) ***(G-3635)***
Spectral Products, Putnam *Also called Spectral LLC* ***(G-3635)***
Spectris Inc (HQ) 508 768-6400
117 Flanders Rd Westborough MA (01581) ***(G-16650)***
Spectro Coating Corp 978 534-6191
107 Scott Dr Leominster MA (01453) ***(G-12188)***
Spectro Coating Corp (PA) 978 534-1800
101 Scott Dr Leominster MA (01453) ***(G-12189)***
Spectro-Film, Billerica *Also called Rubil Associates Inc* ***(G-8292)***
Spectrogram Corporation 203 245-2433
287 Boston Post Rd Madison CT (06443) ***(G-1977)***
Spectros Instruments Inc 508 478-1648
17d Airport Rd Hopedale MA (01747) ***(G-11683)***
Spectrowax Corporation (PA) 617 543-0400
330 Pine St Canton MA (02021) ***(G-9784)***
Spectrum Associates Inc 203 878-4618
440 New Haven Ave Ste 1 Milford CT (06460) ***(G-2367)***
Spectrum Brands Inc 203 205-2900
44 Old Ridgebury Rd # 300 Danbury CT (06810) ***(G-996)***
Spectrum Coatings Labs Inc 401 781-4847
217 Chapman St Providence RI (02905) ***(G-21124)***
Spectrum Graphix, Milford *Also called Spectrum Press* ***(G-2368)***
Spectrum Lighting Inc 508 678-2303
994 Jefferson St Ste 5 Fall River MA (02721) ***(G-10762)***
Spectrum Litho Inc 781 575-0700
112 Will Dr Canton MA (02021) ***(G-9785)***
Spectrum Machine & Design LLC 860 386-6490
800 Old County Cir Windsor Locks CT (06096) ***(G-5400)***
Spectrum Marketing Dbalogo Loc 603 644-4800
95 Eddy Rd Ste 101 Manchester NH (03102) ***(G-18928)***
Spectrum Plastics Group 978 249-5343
764 S Athol Rd Athol MA (01331) ***(G-7694)***
Spectrum Press 203 878-9090
354 Woodmont Rd Ste 15 Milford CT (06460) ***(G-2368)***
Spectrum Press Inc 781 828-5050
112 Will Dr Canton MA (02021) ***(G-9786)***
Spectrum Services 603 635-2439
164 Jeremy Hill Rd Pelham NH (03076) ***(G-19447)***
Spectrum Thermal Proc LLC 401 808-6249
818 Wellington Ave Cranston RI (02910) ***(G-20287)***
Spectrum Virtual LLC 203 303-7540
55 Realty Dr Ste 315 Cheshire CT (06410) ***(G-765)***
Speed Mat Inc 207 294-4358
374 South St Biddeford ME (04005) ***(G-5764)***
Speed Printing & Graphics Inc 203 324-4000
330 Fairfield Ave Ste 3 Stamford CT (06902) ***(G-4328)***
Speedboard Usa Inc 978 462-2700
4 Malcolm Hoyt Dr Newburyport MA (01950) ***(G-13534)***
Speedi Sign LLC 203 775-0700
770 Federal Rd Brookfield CT (06804) ***(G-658)***
Speedway LLC 603 434-9702
50 Birch St Derry NH (03038) ***(G-17996)***
Speedway LLC 781 233-5491
240 Broadway Saugus MA (01906) ***(G-14999)***
Speedway LLC 617 244-4601
2370 Commonwealth Ave Auburndale MA (02466) ***(G-7870)***
Speedway LLC 603 798-3154
135 Dover Rd Chichester NH (03258) ***(G-17830)***
Speedway LLC 401 941-4740
473-479 Reservoir Ave Cranston RI (02910) ***(G-20288)***
Speedy Food Group USA, West Haven *Also called Sabatino North America LLC* ***(G-5144)***
Speedy Petroleum Inc 401 781-3350
95 Warwick Ave Cranston RI (02905) ***(G-20289)***
Speedy Sign-A-Rama USA 781 849-1181
130 Wood Rd Braintree MA (02184) ***(G-9038)***
Spence & Co Ltd 508 427-5577
76 Campanelli Indus Dr Brockton MA (02301) ***(G-9177)***
Spencer Industrial Painting 508 885-5406
60 Wire Village Rd Spencer MA (01562) ***(G-15436)***
Spencer Metal Finishing Inc (PA) 508 885-6477
55 Mill St Brookfield MA (01506) ***(G-9193)***
Spencer Plating Company 401 331-5923
77 Bucklin St Providence RI (02907) ***(G-21125)***
Spencer Turbine Company (HQ) 860 688-8361
600 Day Hill Rd Windsor CT (06095) ***(G-5363)***
Spencer-Johnston Co, Farmington *Also called J J Plank Corporation* ***(G-18143)***
Sperber Tool Works Inc 802 442-8839
75 Bowen Rd Bennington VT (05201) ***(G-21691)***
Sperian Protection Usa Inc (HQ) 401 232-1200
900 Douglas Pike Smithfield RI (02917) ***(G-21250)***
Sperian Protectn Instrumentatn 860 344-1079
651 S Main St Middletown CT (06457) ***(G-2225)***
Spero Devices Inc 978 849-8000
125 Nagog Park Ste 220 Acton MA (01720) ***(G-7388)***
Spero Therapeutics Inc (PA) 857 242-1600
675 Msschusetts Ave Fl 14 Flr 14 Cambridge MA (02139) ***(G-9658)***

Sperry Automatics Co Inc 203 729-4589
1372 New Haven Rd Naugatuck CT (06770) ***(G-2497)***
Sperry Product Innovation Inc 781 271-1400
12 Deangelo Dr Bedford MA (01730) ***(G-8008)***
Sperry Sails Inc 508 748-2581
11 Marconi Ln Marion MA (02738) ***(G-12705)***
Sperry Tents Inc 508 748-1792
11 Marconi Ln Marion MA (02738) ***(G-12706)***
Sperry Valve Inc 802 375-6703
181 Barney Orchard Rd East Arlington VT (05252) ***(G-21910)***
Spf, West Springfield *Also called Steel Panel Foundations LLC* ***(G-16552)***
Spidle Corp 617 448-7386
519 Main St Waltham MA (02452) ***(G-16199)***
Spike Aerospace Inc 617 338-1400
292 Newbury St Boston MA (02115) ***(G-8858)***
Spilldam Environmental Inc 508 583-7850
89 N Montello St Brockton MA (02301) ***(G-9178)***
Spillers Repro Graphics, Manchester *Also called Rgm Enterprises Inc* ***(G-18911)***
Spin Analytical Inc 207 704-0160
468 Portland St Berwick ME (03901) ***(G-5712)***
Spinal Technology Inc (PA) 508 775-0990
191 Mid Tech Dr West Yarmouth MA (02673) ***(G-16582)***
Spindle City Precious Metals 508 567-1597
161 Wilbur Ave Somerset MA (02725) ***(G-15148)***
Spindoc Inc 207 689-7010
126 Western Ave Ste 147 Augusta ME (04330) ***(G-5621)***
Spine Wave Inc 203 944-9494
3 Enterprise Dr Ste 210 Shelton CT (06484) ***(G-3873)***
Spinella Bakery 203 753-9451
53 Interstate Ln Waterbury CT (06705) ***(G-4959)***
Spinelli Bky Ravioli Pastry Sp, Boston *Also called Spinelli Ravioli Mfg Co Inc* ***(G-8859)***
Spinelli Ravioli Mfg Co Inc 617 567-1992
282 Bennington St Boston MA (02128) ***(G-8859)***
Spinlock USA 401 619-5200
11 Bowler Ln Unit A Newport RI (02840) ***(G-20684)***
Spinnaker Contract Mfg Inc 603 286-4366
95 Business Park Dr Tilton NH (03276) ***(G-19912)***
Spinner Publications Inc 508 994-4564
164 William St New Bedford MA (02740) ***(G-13451)***
Spiral Air Manufacturing Inc 603 624-6647
1 B St Derry NH (03038) ***(G-17997)***
Spiral Software, Newton *Also called Stuart Karon* ***(G-13641)***
Spire, Peabody *Also called Digipress Inc* ***(G-14331)***
Spire Corporation (PA) 978 584-3958
25 Linnell Cir Billerica MA (01821) ***(G-8297)***
Spire Express, Peabody *Also called Desk Top Graphics Inc* ***(G-14330)***
Spire Express, Portland *Also called Desk Top Graphics Inc* ***(G-6651)***
Spire Metering Technology LLC 978 263-7100
249 Cedar Hill St Marlborough MA (01752) ***(G-12829)***
Spire Solar Inc 781 275-6000
1 Patriots Park Bedford MA (01730) ***(G-8009)***
Spire Technology Solutions LLC 603 594-0005
3 Capitol St Nashua NH (03063) ***(G-19264)***
Spirent Communications Inc 774 463-0281
5 Crystal Pond Rd Southborough MA (01772) ***(G-15367)***
Spirig Advanced Tech Incies 413 788-6191
144 Oakland St Springfield MA (01108) ***(G-15508)***
Spirit Advisory LLC 603 433-4664
738 Islington St Ste C Portsmouth NH (03801) ***(G-19622)***
Spirol International Corp (HQ) 860 774-8571
30 Rock Ave Danielson CT (06239) ***(G-1018)***
Spirol Intl Holdg Corp (PA) 860 774-8571
30 Rock Ave Danielson CT (06239) ***(G-1019)***
Spiroll International Corp 617 876-8141
190 Hamilton St Cambridge MA (02139) ***(G-9659)***
Spirometrics, Gray *Also called Vuetek Scientific LLC* ***(G-6143)***
Spirus Medical LLC 781 297-7220
375 West St West Bridgewater MA (02379) ***(G-16456)***
Splash Products, Ayer *Also called Elliott Auto Supply Co Inc* ***(G-7918)***
Splash Shield Inc 781 935-8844
8 Cedar St Ste 61 Woburn MA (01801) ***(G-17300)***
Splendid Loon Studio 401 789-7879
726 Tuckertown Rd Wakefield RI (02879) ***(G-21278)***
Splice Therapeutics Inc 914 804-4136
14 Curlew St West Roxbury MA (02132) ***(G-16503)***
Spoontiques Inc 781 344-9530
111 Island St Stoughton MA (02072) ***(G-15622)***
Sportees LLC 860 440-3922
262 Boston Post Rd Unit 8 Waterford CT (06385) ***(G-4994)***
Sports Insights Inc 877 838-2853
100 Cummings Ctr Ste 226q Beverly MA (01915) ***(G-8179)***
Sports Power Drive Inc 774 233-0175
539 Fiske St Holliston MA (01746) ***(G-11603)***
Sports Products Incorporated 802 655-2620
1 East St Winooski VT (05404) ***(G-22724)***
Sports Systems Custom Bags 401 767-3770
44 Hazel St Woonsocket RI (02895) ***(G-21579)***
Sportsscarf LLC 508 758-8176
8 County Rd Ste 5 Mattapoisett MA (02739) ***(G-12891)***
Spotliteusa LLC 508 347-2627
31 Audubon Way Sturbridge MA (01566) ***(G-15649)***
Sprague & Son Maple 802 368-2776
Rr 100 Jacksonville VT (05342) ***(G-22043)***
Spragues Dairy Inc 802 728-3863
13 Weston St Ste 1 Randolph VT (05060) ***(G-22303)***
Spray Foam Distrs Neng Inc 603 745-3911
1366 Daniel Wecster Hwy Woodstock NH (03293) ***(G-20029)***
Spray Foam Outlets LLC 631 291-9355
30 Muller Ave Unit 19 Norwalk CT (06851) ***(G-3249)***
Spray Maine Inc 207 384-2273
104 Parker St Newburyport MA (01950) ***(G-13535)***
Sprayfoampolymerscom LLC 800 853-1577
134 Old Ridgefield Rd # 3 Wilton CT (06897) ***(G-5304)***
Spraying Systems Co 603 517-1854
243 Daniel Webster Hwy Merrimack NH (03054) ***(G-19033)***
Spraying Systems Co 603 471-0505
174 Route 101 Bedford NH (03110) ***(G-17664)***
Spring Air Ohio LLC 617 884-0041
124 2nd St Chelsea MA (02150) ***(G-9968)***
Spring Bnk Pharmaceuticals Inc (PA) 508 473-5993
35 Parkwood Dr Ste 210 Hopkinton MA (01748) ***(G-11738)***
Spring Break Maple & Honey 207 757-7373
3276 Us Route 2 Smyrna Mills ME (04780) ***(G-6995)***
Spring Computerized Inds LLC 860 605-9206
93 Oakwood Dr Harwinton CT (06791) ***(G-1893)***
Spring Fill 802 846-5900
1775 Williston Rd Ste 250 South Burlington VT (05403) ***(G-22466)***
Spring Manufacturing Corp 978 658-7396
2235 Main St Tewksbury MA (01876) ***(G-15836)***
Spring Water Associates USA 978 371-0138
31 Oakley Rd Watertown MA (02472) ***(G-16318)***
Springboard Retail Inc 888 347-2191
361 Newbury St Ste 500 Boston MA (02115) ***(G-8860)***
Springdale Machine & Gear Co 413 536-2976
21 Temple St Holyoke MA (01040) ***(G-11660)***
Springfield Label Tape Co Inc 413 733-6634
430 Saint James Ave Springfield MA (01109) ***(G-15509)***
Springfield Newspaper, Springfield *Also called Republican Company* ***(G-15502)***
Springfield Pallet Inc 413 593-0044
1819 Page Blvd Indian Orchard MA (01151) ***(G-11896)***
Springfield Printing Corp 802 886-2201
19 Precision Dr North Springfield VT (05150) ***(G-22238)***
Springfield Reporter Inc 802 885-2246
151 Summer St Springfield VT (05156) ***(G-22509)***
Springfield Spring Corporation (PA) 413 525-6837
311 Shaker Rd East Longmeadow MA (01028) ***(G-10493)***
Springfield Spring Corporation 860 584-6560
24 Dell Manor Dr Bristol CT (06010) ***(G-614)***
Springs Manufacturer Supply Co, Southington *Also called Northeast Carbide Inc* ***(G-4069)***
Sprinker Innovations, Seabrook *Also called Jmsc Enterprises Inc* ***(G-19808)***
Sprint Systems of Photography 401 597-5790
60 Kindergarten St Woonsocket RI (02895) ***(G-21580)***
Sproutel Inc 914 806-6514
60 Valley St Apt 29 Providence RI (02909) ***(G-21126)***
Sproutman and Co, Great Barrington *Also called Sproutman Publications* ***(G-11247)***
Sproutman Publications 413 528-5200
20 W Sheffield Rd Great Barrington MA (01230) ***(G-11247)***
Spruce Environmental Tech Inc (PA) 978 521-0901
3 Saber Way Haverhill MA (01835) ***(G-11475)***
Spruce Mountain Wind LLC 617 890-0600
549 South St Quincy MA (02169) ***(G-14658)***
Spruce Mountian Granites Inc 802 476-7474
84 Pitman Rd Barre VT (05641) ***(G-21639)***
SPS, Manchester *Also called Summit Packaging Systems Inc* ***(G-18932)***
Spv Industries LLC 860 953-5928
9 Tolles St West Hartford CT (06110) ***(G-5096)***
SPX Corporation 207 655-8100
22 Tower Rd Raymond ME (04071) ***(G-6774)***
SPX Corporation 207 655-8525
28 Tower Rd Raymond ME (04071) ***(G-6775)***
SPX Corporation 704 752-4400
595 Pleasant St Norwood MA (02062) ***(G-14201)***
Sq Innovation Inc 617 500-0121
20 Mall Rd Ste 220 Burlington MA (01803) ***(G-9339)***
Sqdm 888 993-9674
100 Tower Office Park M Woburn MA (01801) ***(G-17301)***
Square Creamery LLC 203 456-3490
7 P T Barnum Sq Bethel CT (06801) ***(G-180)***
Square Spot Publishing LLC 603 625-6003
79 Pleasant St Ste 2 Manchester NH (03101) ***(G-18929)***
Squeegee Printers Inc 802 266-3426
4067 Vt Route 102 Canaan VT (05903) ***(G-21825)***
Squeteague Sailmakers, Cataumet *Also called Cape Cod Sailmakers Inc* ***(G-9810)***
Squire Laboratories, Revere *Also called Atlantic Animal Health Inc* ***(G-14763)***
Sqz Biotechnologies Company 617 758-8672
134 Coolidge Ave Watertown MA (02472) ***(G-16319)***
SRC Liquidation Company 802 862-9932
20 Kimball Ave Ste 206 South Burlington VT (05403) ***(G-22467)***

ALPHABETIC

SRC Medical Inc......781 826-9100
263 Winter St Hanover MA (02339) ***(G-11352)***
SRC Publishing Inc......508 749-3212
23 Midstate Dr Ste 114 Auburn MA (01501) ***(G-7850)***
SRI Hermetics Inc......508 321-1023
43 Magnavista Dr Haverhill MA (01830) ***(G-11476)***
Srods LLC......207 743-6194
30 Fair St Norway ME (04268) ***(G-6525)***
SRP Sign & Awning, Somerville *Also called SRP Signs* ***(G-15220)***
SRP Signs......617 623-6222
236 Pearl St Somerville MA (02145) ***(G-15220)***
SRS Medical Corp......978 663-2800
76 Treble Cove Rd Ste 3 North Billerica MA (01862) ***(G-13867)***
SRS Medical Systems Inc (PA)......978 663-2800
76 Treble Cove Rd Ste 3 North Billerica MA (01862) ***(G-13868)***
Ss & G LLC......603 635-7400
30 Pulpit Rock Rd Pelham NH (03076) ***(G-19448)***
SS&c Holdings, Windsor *Also called SS&c Technologies Holdings Inc* ***(G-5366)***
SS&c Technologies Inc......860 930-5882
261 Broad St Windsor CT (06095) ***(G-5364)***
SS&c Technologies Inc (HQ)......860 298-4500
80 Lamberton Rd Windsor CT (06095) ***(G-5365)***
SS&c Technologies Inc......781 654-6498
3 Burlington Woods Dr Burlington MA (01803) ***(G-9340)***
SS&c Technologies Holdings Inc (PA)......860 298-4500
80 Lamberton Rd Windsor CT (06095) ***(G-5366)***
Ssb Manufacturing Company......413 789-4410
320 Bowles Rd Agawam MA (01001) ***(G-7452)***
Ssh Government Solutions Inc......781 247-2124
460 Totten Pond Rd # 460 Waltham MA (02451) ***(G-16200)***
Sshc Inc......860 399-5434
1244 Old Clinton Rd Westbrook CT (06498) ***(G-5163)***
Ssi Investments I Limited (HQ)......603 324-3000
107 Northeastern Blvd Nashua NH (03062) ***(G-19265)***
Ssi Investments II Limited......603 324-3000
107 Northeastern Blvd Nashua NH (03062) ***(G-19266)***
Ssi Manufacturing Tech Corp......860 589-8004
675 Emmett St Bristol CT (06010) ***(G-615)***
Ssidm Inc......781 871-7677
800 Hingham St Ste 200 Rockland MA (02370) ***(G-14827)***
Ssquare Detect Medical Devices......978 202-5707
108 Colonial Dr Andover MA (01810) ***(G-7611)***
SSS, Granby *Also called Singularity Space Systems LLC* ***(G-1591)***
Sst Components Inc (PA)......978 670-7300
780 Boston Rd Ste 1 Billerica MA (01821) ***(G-8298)***
Ssw Inc......207 793-4440
206 Ossipee Trl Limington ME (04049) ***(G-6349)***
St Albans Cooperative Crmry......802 524-9366
140 Federal St Saint Albans VT (05478) ***(G-22379)***
St Albans Messenger, Saint Albans *Also called Vermont Publishing Comany* ***(G-22384)***
St Cyr Inc......508 752-2222
235 Park Ave Worcester MA (01609) ***(G-17478)***
St Cyr Salon Spa, Worcester *Also called St Cyr Inc* ***(G-17478)***
St Equipment and Tech LLC......781 972-2300
101 Hampton Ave Needham MA (02494) ***(G-13312)***
St John......401 944-0159
727 Atwood Ave Cranston RI (02920) ***(G-20290)***
St Jude Medical LLC......978 657-6519
600 Research Dr Ste 1 Wilmington MA (01887) ***(G-17047)***
St Pierre Box and Lumber Co......860 413-9813
66 Lovely St Canton CT (06019) ***(G-699)***
St Pierre Chain & Wire Rope, Worcester *Also called St Pierre Manufacturing Corp* ***(G-17479)***
St Pierre Manufacturing Corp......508 853-8010
317 E Mountain St Worcester MA (01606) ***(G-17479)***
St Regis Sportswear Ltd......518 725-6767
3 Ironwood Rd North Andover MA (01845) ***(G-13729)***
STA Cruz Gun Locks, Webster *Also called Santa Cruz Gunlocks LLC* ***(G-19945)***
STA Fit For Women LLC......603 357-8880
815 Court St Keene NH (03431) ***(G-18528)***
Stabaarte Inc......401 364-8633
90 Bliss Rd Apt 1 Newport RI (02840) ***(G-20685)***
Staban Engineering Corp......203 294-1997
65 N Plains Industrial Rd Wallingford CT (06492) ***(G-4812)***
Stabil, Biddeford *Also called 32 North Corporation* ***(G-5716)***
Stabilizing Technologies LLC......978 928-4142
45 Williamsville Rd Hubbardston MA (01452) ***(G-11746)***
Stace Welding, East Windsor *Also called Stacy B Goff* ***(G-1304)***
Stacey Thomson......603 353-9700
53 Nh Route 10 Orford NH (03777) ***(G-19421)***
Stacey's Window Fashions, Lynn *Also called Staceys Shade Shop Inc* ***(G-12540)***
Staceys Shade Shop Inc (PA)......781 595-0097
20 Melvin Ave Lynn MA (01902) ***(G-12540)***
Stacis Stitches LLC......781 206-7478
761 Country Way Scituate MA (02066) ***(G-15015)***
Stackbin Corporation......401 333-1600
29 Powder Hill Rd Lincoln RI (02865) ***(G-20597)***
Stacy B Goff......860 623-2547
100 Newberry Rd East Windsor CT (06088) ***(G-1304)***
Stacys Pita Chip Company Inc......781 961-2800
1 Posturepedic Dr Randolph MA (02368) ***(G-14698)***
Stadion Publishing Co Inc......802 723-6175
135 Fitzgerald Ave Island Pond VT (05846) ***(G-22041)***
Staffall Inc......401 461-5554
1468 Elmwood Ave Cranston RI (02910) ***(G-20291)***
Stafford Manufacturing Corp......978 657-8000
256 Andover St Wilmington MA (01887) ***(G-17048)***
Stafford Manufacturing Corp......978 657-8000
91 Holbrook St Norfolk MA (02056) ***(G-13664)***
Stafford Reminder, Vernon Rockville *Also called Rmi Inc* ***(G-4681)***
Stafford Special Tool, Worcester *Also called Form Roll Die Corp* ***(G-17378)***
Stafford Wire Specialty Inc......508 799-6124
243 Stafford St Ste 1 Worcester MA (01603) ***(G-17480)***
Stag Arms LLC......860 229-9994
515 John Downey Dr New Britain CT (06051) ***(G-2578)***
Stag Arms LLC......860 229-9994
515 John Downey Dr New Britain CT (06051) ***(G-2579)***
Stage Stop Candy Ltd Inc......508 394-1791
411 Main St Dennis Port MA (02639) ***(G-10315)***
Stahl (usa) Inc (HQ)......978 968-1382
13 Corwin St Peabody MA (01960) ***(G-14372)***
Stainless Fdsrvice Eqp Mfg Inc......207 227-7747
14 Connecticut Rd Limestone ME (04750) ***(G-6344)***
Stainless Steel Coatings Inc......978 365-9828
835 Sterling Rd Lancaster MA (01523) ***(G-11985)***
Stairs Unlimited Inc......802 848-7030
484 Hardwood Hill Rd Richford VT (05476) ***(G-22310)***
Stake Company LLC......860 623-2700
22 Thompson Rd Ste 7 East Windsor CT (06088) ***(G-1305)***
Stallrgenes Greer Holdings Inc......617 588-4900
55 Cambridge Pkwy Cambridge MA (02142) ***(G-9660)***
Stamford Capital Group Inc (PA)......800 977-7837
1266 E Main St Stamford CT (06902) ***(G-4329)***
Stamford Fabricating, Stamford *Also called Wendon Technologies Inc* ***(G-4358)***
Stamford Forge & Metal Cft Inc......203 348-8290
63 Victory St Stamford CT (06902) ***(G-4330)***
Stamford Iron & Stl Works Inc......203 324-6751
347 Courtland Ave Stamford CT (06906) ***(G-4331)***
Stamford Risk Analytics LLC......203 559-0883
263 Tresser Blvd Fl 9 Stamford CT (06901) ***(G-4332)***
Stamford RPM Raceway LLC......203 323-7223
600 West Ave Stamford CT (06902) ***(G-4333)***
Stamler Publishing Company......203 488-9808
178 Thimble Island Rd Branford CT (06405) ***(G-351)***
Stamp News Publishing Inc......603 424-7556
42 Sentry Way Merrimack NH (03054) ***(G-19034)***
Stamping Technologies Inc......603 524-5958
20 Growth Rd Laconia NH (03246) ***(G-18588)***
Stan Ray Products Co......978 594-0667
8 Roslyn St Salem MA (01970) ***(G-14944)***
Stan-Allen Co., Three Rivers *Also called Millennium Die Group Inc* ***(G-15851)***
Stanadyne Intrmdate Hldngs LLC (HQ)......860 525-0821
92 Deerfield Rd Windsor CT (06095) ***(G-5367)***
Stanadyne LLC (HQ)......860 525-0821
92 Deerfield Rd Windsor CT (06095) ***(G-5368)***
Stanchfield Farms......207 943-2133
73 Medford Rd Milo ME (04463) ***(G-6448)***
Standard Bellows Co (PA)......860 623-2307
375 Ella Grasso Tpke Windsor Locks CT (06096) ***(G-5401)***
Standard Box Company Inc......617 884-2345
1 Boatswains Way Chelsea MA (02150) ***(G-9969)***
Standard Chain Co......508 695-6611
55 Access Rd Ste 500 Warwick RI (02886) ***(G-21429)***
Standard Chair Gardner Inc......978 632-1301
1 S Main St Gardner MA (01440) ***(G-11129)***
Standard Lock Washer & Mfg Co......508 757-4508
1451 Grafton St Worcester MA (01604) ***(G-17481)***
Standard Machine & Arms......603 746-3562
35 Tyler Rd Contoocook NH (03229) ***(G-17949)***
Standard Machines Inc......978 462-4999
25 Hale St Newburyport MA (01950) ***(G-13536)***
Standard Mill Machinery Corp......401 822-7871
1370c Main St West Warwick RI (02893) ***(G-21510)***
Standard Modern Company......774 425-3537
186 Duchaine Blvd New Bedford MA (02745) ***(G-13452)***
Standard Molecular Inc......617 401-3318
1 Broadway Fl 14 Cambridge MA (02142) ***(G-9661)***
Standard Pneumatic Products......203 270-1400
31 Shepard Hill Rd Newtown CT (06470) ***(G-2939)***
Standard Publishing Corp (PA)......617 457-0600
10 High St Ste 1107 Boston MA (02110) ***(G-8861)***
Standard Repair Co Division, Plymouth *Also called R B Machine Co Inc* ***(G-14578)***
Standard Rubber Products Inc......781 878-2626
64 B St Hanover MA (02339) ***(G-11353)***
Standard Times, Wakefield *Also called Southern RI Newspapers* ***(G-21277)***
Standard Times, New Bedford *Also called Local Media Group Inc* ***(G-13409)***
Standard Washer & Mat Inc......860 643-5125
299 Progress Dr Manchester CT (06042) ***(G-2051)***

Standard Welding Company Inc 860 528-9628
212 Prospect St East Hartford CT (06108) ***(G-1222)***
Standard-Knapp Inc 860 342-1100
63 Pickering St Portland CT (06480) ***(G-3575)***
Standex International Corp (PA) 603 893-9701
11 Keewaydin Dr Ste 300 Salem NH (03079) ***(G-19769)***
Standex International Corp 978 667-2771
500 Iron Horse Park North Billerica MA (01862) ***(G-13869)***
Standex International Corp 413 536-1311
939 Chicopee St Ste 3 Chicopee MA (01013) ***(G-10062)***
Standex International Corp 978 538-0808
107 Audubon Rd Wakefield MA (01880) ***(G-15977)***
Standley Brothers Mch Co Inc 978 927-0278
96 Park St Beverly MA (01915) ***(G-8180)***
Stanley Black & Decker Inc (PA) 860 225-5111
1000 Stanley Dr New Britain CT (06053) ***(G-2580)***
Stanley Black & Decker Inc 860 225-5111
100 Curtis St New Britain CT (06052) ***(G-2581)***
Stanley Black & Decker Inc 860 225-5111
65 Spot Swamp Rd Farmington CT (06032) ***(G-1514)***
Stanley Black & Decker Inc 860 225-5111
480 Myrtle St New Britain CT (06053) ***(G-2582)***
Stanley Black & Decker Inc 860 225-5111
480 Myrtle St New Britain CT (06053) ***(G-2583)***
Stanley Black & Decker Inc 401 471-4280
1 Briggs Dr East Greenwich RI (02818) ***(G-20380)***
Stanley Black and Decker, New Britain *Also called Black & Decker (us) Inc* ***(G-2514)***
Stanley Fastening Systems LP 860 225-5111
480 Myrtle St New Britain CT (06053) ***(G-2584)***
Stanley Fastening Systems LP (HQ) 401 884-2500
2 Briggs Dr East Greenwich RI (02818) ***(G-20381)***
Stanley Industrial & Auto LLC 800 800-8005
480 Myrtle St New Britain CT (06053) ***(G-2585)***
Stanley Industrial & Auto LLC 508 429-1350
106 Lowland St Holliston MA (01746) ***(G-11604)***
Stanley Tool, East Greenwich *Also called Stanley Black & Decker Inc* ***(G-20380)***
Stanley Vidmar 610 797-6600
106 Lowland St Holliston MA (01746) ***(G-11605)***
Stanley-Bostitch, New Britain *Also called Stanley Fastening Systems LP* ***(G-2584)***
Stanlok Corporation 508 757-4508
1451 Grafton St Worcester MA (01604) ***(G-17482)***
Star Engineering Inc 508 316-1492
1 Vaillancourt Dr North Attleboro MA (02763) ***(G-13781)***
Star Kitchen Cabinets Inc 508 510-3123
75 Stockwell Dr Ste H Avon MA (02322) ***(G-7897)***
Star Litho Inc 781 340-9401
360 Libbey Indus Pkwy Weymouth MA (02189) ***(G-16901)***
Star Machine Inc 603 882-1423
17 Airport Rd Ste 4 Nashua NH (03063) ***(G-19267)***
Star Pickling Corp 508 672-8535
941 Wood St Swansea MA (02777) ***(G-15716)***
Star Plating, New Bedford *Also called Plating Technology Inc* ***(G-13439)***
Star Printing Corp 508 583-9046
10 Mozzone Blvd Taunton MA (02780) ***(G-15787)***
Star Steel Structures Inc 860 763-5681
392 Four Bridges Rd Somers CT (06071) ***(G-3920)***
Star Tech Instruments Inc 203 312-0767
3 State Route 39 New Fairfield CT (06812) ***(G-2627)***
Star Vaccine Inc 617 584-5483
45 Irving St Newton MA (02459) ***(G-13640)***
Star Wind Turbines LLC 802 779-8118
95 Tesla Ln East Dorset VT (05253) ***(G-21916)***
Starboard Exchange Inc 978 810-5577
14 Exeter Rd Beverly MA (01915) ***(G-8181)***
Starburst Prtg & Graphics Inc 508 893-0900
300 Hopping Brook Rd Holliston MA (01746) ***(G-11606)***
Starc Systems Inc 844 596-1784
166 Orion St Brunswick ME (04011) ***(G-5846)***
Starchem Inc (PA) 413 967-8700
85 Beaver Rd Ware MA (01082) ***(G-16237)***
Starchem Inc 508 943-2337
420 W Main St Dudley MA (01571) ***(G-10386)***
Starcrafts Publishing LLC 603 734-5303
68a Fogg Rd Epping NH (03042) ***(G-18103)***
Starensier Inc (PA) 978 462-7311
12 Kent Way Ste 201 Byfield MA (01922) ***(G-9365)***
Starfish Storage Corporation 781 250-3000
271 Waverley Oaks Rd # 301 Waltham MA (02452) ***(G-16201)***
Starflex Inc 978 937-3889
52 Meadowcroft St Lowell MA (01852) ***(G-12434)***
Starherald Newspaper Pubg, Presque Isle *Also called Northeast Publishing Company* ***(G-6766)***
Stark Mountain Woodworking Co, New Haven *Also called Stark Mountain Woodworks Co* ***(G-22187)***
Stark Mountain Woodworks Co 802 453-5549
359 South St New Haven VT (05472) ***(G-22187)***
Starkey Welding Crane Service 603 679-2553
444 Route 125 Brentwood NH (03833) ***(G-17758)***
Starkweather Engineering Inc 978 858-3700
1615 Shawsheen St Ste 14 Tewksbury MA (01876) ***(G-15837)***
Starry Inc 617 861-8300
38 Chauncy St Ste 200 Boston MA (02111) ***(G-8862)***
Startech Environmental Corp (PA) 203 762-2499
88 Danbury Rd Ste 2b Wilton CT (06897) ***(G-5305)***
Starting Treatment Effctvly 857 544-8051
554 Washington St Boston MA (02124) ***(G-8863)***
Starwind Software Inc 617 449-7717
35 Village Rd Ste 100 Middleton MA (01949) ***(G-13102)***
Stat Products Inc 508 881-8022
200 Butterfield Dr Ste D Ashland MA (01721) ***(G-7670)***
State Awning Company 860 246-2575
100 Cedar St Hartford CT (06106) ***(G-1872)***
State Fuel 781 438-5557
74 Swanton St Winchester MA (01890) ***(G-17097)***
State House News 617 969-9175
37 Holly Rd Waban MA (02468) ***(G-15939)***
State Maine Cheese Company LLC 207 236-8895
341 Gillette Rd Hope ME (04847) ***(G-6201)***
State Military Reservation 603 225-1230
1 Minuteman Way Concord NH (03301) ***(G-17931)***
State Pattern Works 603 882-0701
3 Winn Ave Hudson NH (03051) ***(G-18440)***
State Road Cement Block Co 508 993-9473
656 State Rd North Dartmouth MA (02747) ***(G-13926)***
State Welding & Fabg Inc 203 294-4071
107 N Cherry St Wallingford CT (06492) ***(G-4813)***
State-Line Graphics Inc 617 389-1200
6 Victoria St Ste 109 Everett MA (02149) ***(G-10632)***
State-Wide Mltiple Listing Svc 401 785-3650
100 Bignall St Warwick RI (02888) ***(G-21430)***
Stateline Fuel 508 336-0665
1587 Fall River Ave Seekonk MA (02771) ***(G-15038)***
Stateline Review 603 898-2554
236 N Broadway Salem NH (03079) ***(G-19770)***
Stately Stair Co Inc 203 575-1966
3810 E Main St Waterbury CT (06705) ***(G-4960)***
Statham Woodwork 203 831-0629
38 Hemlock Pl Norwalk CT (06854) ***(G-3250)***
Static & Dynamic Tech Inc 802 859-0238
289 Leroy Rd Williston VT (05495) ***(G-22693)***
Static Clean International 781 229-7799
267 Boston Rd Ste 8 North Billerica MA (01862) ***(G-13870)***
Static Control, Rockland *Also called Static Technologies Corp* ***(G-14828)***
Static Safe Products Company 203 937-6391
8 Cook Rd Cornwall Bridge CT (06754) ***(G-820)***
Static Solutions Inc (PA) 508 480-0700
331 Boston Post Rd E # 12 Marlborough MA (01752) ***(G-12830)***
Static Technologies Corp 781 871-8962
138 Weymouth St Rockland MA (02370) ***(G-14828)***
Staticsmart Flooring, Andover *Also called Julie Industries Inc* ***(G-7560)***
Staticworx Inc 617 923-2000
4706 Waterbury-Stowe Rd Waterbury Center VT (05677) ***(G-22592)***
Statiflo International Ltd 413 684-9911
75 S Church St Ste 6f Pittsfield MA (01201) ***(G-14509)***
Statim Pharmaceuticals Inc 650 305-0657
58 Bean Rd Moultonborough NH (03254) ***(G-19098)***
Statistical Solutions Ltd 617 535-7677
1 International Pl Boston MA (02110) ***(G-8864)***
Statvideo, Edgartown *Also called Meddevice Concepts LLC* ***(G-10586)***
Stauffer Sheet Metal LLC 860 623-0518
56 Depot St Windsor CT (06006) ***(G-5369)***
Stave Puzzles Incorporated 802 295-5200
163 Olcott Dr Wilder VT (05088) ***(G-22648)***
Stay Sharp Tool Company Inc 508 699-6990
229 West St North Attleboro MA (02760) ***(G-13782)***
Std Manufacturing Inc 781 828-4400
1063 Turnpike St Stoughton MA (02072) ***(G-15623)***
Std Precision Gear & Instr Inc 508 580-0035
318 Manley St Ste 5 West Bridgewater MA (02379) ***(G-16457)***
Stealth Biologics LLC 603 643-5134
16 Cavendish Ct Rm 229 Lebanon NH (03766) ***(G-18637)***
Steam Turbine 4 U 603 465-8881
5 Demery Rd Hudson NH (03051) ***(G-18441)***
Steam Turbine Services 207 272-8664
34 Fieldstone Dr North Yarmouth ME (04097) ***(G-6519)***
Stearns Perry & Smith Co Inc 617 423-4775
33 Fayette St Ste 1 Quincy MA (02171) ***(G-14659)***
Stearns Tool Company Inc 401 351-4765
56 Sprague St Providence RI (02907) ***(G-21127)***
Stebennes Logging 802 436-3250
468 Route 12 Hartland VT (05048) ***(G-22018)***
Stedagio LLC 401 568-6228
1000 Danielle Dr Mapleville RI (02839) ***(G-20615)***
Stedt Hydraulic Crane Corp 508 366-9151
27 Washington St Westborough MA (01581) ***(G-16651)***
Steed Read Horsemans Classifie 860 859-0770
16b Mill Ln Salem CT (06420) ***(G-3740)***

A L P H A B E T I C

Steel Connections Inc......508 958-5129
101 Jefferson Rd Franklin MA (02038) ***(G-11082)***
Steel Elements Intl LLC......603 466-2500
3 Security Dr Hudson NH (03051) ***(G-18442)***
Steel Panel Foundations LLC......413 439-0218
1111 Elm St Ste 33 West Springfield MA (01089) ***(G-16552)***
Steel Pro Services, Rockland *Also called Steel-Pro Inc* ***(G-6810)***
Steel Products Corporation (PA)......508 892-4770
105 Huntoon Memorial Hwy Rochdale MA (01542) ***(G-14783)***
Steel Rule Die Corp America......860 621-5284
289 Clark Street Ext Milldale CT (06467) ***(G-2387)***
Steel-Fab Inc......978 345-1112
430 Crawford St Fitchburg MA (01420) ***(G-10857)***
Steel-It, Lancaster *Also called Stainless Steel Coatings Inc* ***(G-11985)***
Steel-Pro Inc......207 596-0061
771 Main St Rockland ME (04841) ***(G-6810)***
Steelcraft Inc......508 865-4445
115 W Main St Millbury MA (01527) ***(G-13176)***
Steele & Rowe Inc......508 993-6413
190 Chase Rd North Dartmouth MA (02747) ***(G-13927)***
Steele and Steele Inc......401 782-2278
682 Kingstown Rd Wakefield RI (02879) ***(G-21279)***
Steele Canvas Basket Corp......800 541-8929
201 Williams St Chelsea MA (02150) ***(G-9970)***
Steelfish Media LLC......312 730-8016
619 Hale St 4 Beverly MA (01915) ***(G-8182)***
Steelstone Industries, Houlton *Also called McQuade Tidd Industries* ***(G-6207)***
Steeltech Building Pdts Inc......860 290-8930
636 Nutmeg Rd N South Windsor CT (06074) ***(G-4014)***
Steelwrist Inc......225 936-1111
576 Christian Ln Berlin CT (06037) ***(G-111)***
Steerforth Press LLC......603 643-4787
25 Lebanon St Frnt Hanover NH (03755) ***(G-18298)***
Steger Power Connection Inc......508 646-0950
994 Jefferson St Ste 10 Fall River MA (02721) ***(G-10763)***
Steinerfilm Inc......413 458-9525
987 Simonds Rd Williamstown MA (01267) ***(G-16961)***
Steinerfilm USA, Williamstown *Also called Steinerfilm Inc* ***(G-16961)***
Stella Press LLC......203 661-2735
58 Brookridge Dr Greenwich CT (06830) ***(G-1653)***
Stellar Industries Corp......508 865-1668
50 Howe Ave Millbury MA (01527) ***(G-13177)***
Stellar Manufacturing Inc......978 241-9537
10 Manor Pkwy Ste A Salem NH (03079) ***(G-19771)***
Stellar Medical Publications......508 732-6767
20 North St Ste 1 Plymouth MA (02360) ***(G-14585)***
Stellar Steam, Winooski *Also called Colburntreat LLC* ***(G-22719)***
Stelray Plastic Products Inc......203 735-2331
50 Westfield Ave Ansonia CT (06401) ***(G-23)***
Stem Solutions LLC......617 826-6111
301 Edgewater Pl Ste 100 Wakefield MA (01880) ***(G-15978)***
Stencil Ease, Old Saybrook *Also called Liftline Capital LLC* ***(G-3342)***
Stencils Online LLC......603 934-5034
70 Industrial Park Dr # 7 Franklin NH (03235) ***(G-18165)***
Stenhouse Publishers......207 253-1600
282 Corporate Dr Ste 1 Portsmouth NH (03801) ***(G-19623)***
Stentech Inc (HQ)......603 505-4470
22 Manchester Rd Unit 8b Derry NH (03038) ***(G-17998)***
Stentech Photo Stencil LLC......719 287-7934
22 Manchester Rd Unit 8b Derry NH (03038) ***(G-17999)***
Step Ahead Innovations Inc......802 233-0211
6 Green Tree Dr South Burlington VT (05403) ***(G-22468)***
Step Saver Inc......860 621-6751
213 Spring St Southington CT (06489) ***(G-4082)***
Stephane Inkel Inc......802 266-8878
1780 Vt Route 102 Canaan VT (05903) ***(G-21826)***
Stephen A Burt......802 893-0600
162 Jimmo Dr Colchester VT (05446) ***(G-21880)***
Stephen C Dematrick......401 789-4712
201p Gravelly Hill Rd Narragansett RI (02879) ***(G-20651)***
Stephen E Witham......207 657-3410
31 Weymouth Rd Gray ME (04039) ***(G-6142)***
Stephen F Madden......207 827-5737
183 Greenfield Rd Cardville ME (04418) ***(G-5884)***
Stephen Gould Corporation......978 851-2500
30 Commerce Way Ste 1 Tewksbury MA (01876) ***(G-15838)***
Stephen J Russell & Co......802 869-2540
60 Atcherson Hollow Rd Chester VT (05143) ***(G-21850)***
Stephen McArthur......802 839-0371
Granger Rd Barre VT (05641) ***(G-21640)***
Stephen Plaud Inc......401 625-5909
381 State Ave Tiverton RI (02878) ***(G-21263)***
Stephens Precision Inc......802 222-9600
293 Industrial Dr Bradford VT (05033) ***(G-21705)***
Stepping Stones MBL & Gran LLC (PA)......203 854-0552
4 Taft St Ste D1 Norwalk CT (06854) ***(G-3251)***
Steralon Inc......603 296-0490
7 Perimeter Rd Ste 10 Manchester NH (03103) ***(G-18930)***
Stergis Aluminum Products Corp......508 455-0661
79 Walton St Attleboro MA (02703) ***(G-7795)***
Stergis/Alliance, Attleboro *Also called Stergis Aluminum Products Corp* ***(G-7795)***
Steris Corporation......508 393-9323
435 Whitney St Northborough MA (01532) ***(G-14048)***
Sterizign Precision Tech LLC......888 234-3074
74 Orion St Brunswick ME (04011) ***(G-5847)***
Sterling Business Corp......603 924-9401
206 Concord St Peterborough NH (03458) ***(G-19489)***
Sterling Business Print & Mail, Peterborough *Also called Sterling Business Corp* ***(G-19489)***
Sterling Concrete Corp......978 422-8282
194 Worcester Rd Sterling MA (01564) ***(G-15546)***
Sterling Custom Cabinetry LLC......203 335-5151
323 North Ave Bridgeport CT (06606) ***(G-495)***
Sterling Engineering Corp......860 379-3366
236 New Hartford Rd Pleasant Valley CT (06063) ***(G-3547)***
Sterling Gun Drills Inc......802 442-3525
940 Water St North Bennington VT (05257) ***(G-22213)***
Sterling Hydraulics, Haverhill *Also called Runtal North America Inc* ***(G-11469)***
Sterling Jewelers Inc......860 644-7207
194 Buckland Hills Dr # 1 Manchester CT (06042) ***(G-2052)***
Sterling Machine Company Inc......781 593-3000
23 Farrar St Lynn MA (01901) ***(G-12541)***
Sterling Machine Division, Enfield *Also called Senior Operations LLC* ***(G-1383)***
Sterling Manufacturing Co Inc......978 368-8733
640 Sterling St Lancaster MA (01523) ***(G-11986)***
Sterling Materials LLC......203 315-6619
17 Tanglewood Dr Branford CT (06405) ***(G-352)***
Sterling Name Tape Company......860 379-5142
9 Willow St Winsted CT (06098) ***(G-5426)***
Sterling Peat & Loam, Sterling *Also called Sterling Peat Inc* ***(G-15547)***
Sterling Peat Inc......978 422-8294
64 Greenland Rd Sterling MA (01564) ***(G-15547)***
Sterling Power Usa LLC......207 226-3500
406 Harold L Dow Hwy # 6 Eliot ME (03903) ***(G-6010)***
Sterling Precision Inc......978 365-4999
90 Parker St Clinton MA (01510) ***(G-10093)***
Sterling Precision Machining......860 564-4043
112 Industrial Park Rd Sterling CT (06377) ***(G-4372)***
Sterling Rope Company Inc......207 885-0033
26 Morin St Biddeford ME (04005) ***(G-5765)***
Sterling Sand and Gravel LLC......860 774-3985
485 Saw Mill Hill Rd Sterling CT (06377) ***(G-4373)***
Sterling Screw Machine Div, Milford *Also called Alinabal Inc* ***(G-2242)***
Sterling Screw Machine Pdts, Kensington *Also called Alinabal Inc* ***(G-1917)***
Sterling Technologies Inc......802 888-4753
320 Wilkins St Morrisville VT (05661) ***(G-22177)***
Sterlingwear of Boston Inc (PA)......617 567-2100
175 Wlliam F Mcclllan Hwy Boston MA (02128) ***(G-8865)***
Sterlingwear of Boston Inc......617 567-6465
175 William F Mcclellan H Boston MA (02128) ***(G-8866)***
Sterngold Dental LLC......508 226-5660
23 Frank Mossberg Dr Attleboro MA (02703) ***(G-7796)***
Stetco, Westborough *Also called Stedt Hydraulic Crane Corp* ***(G-16651)***
Stetson Brewing Co Inc......860 643-0257
22 Fleming Rd Manchester CT (06042) ***(G-2053)***
Steve Leighton......603 664-2378
801 Province Rd Barnstead NH (03218) ***(G-17617)***
Stevells Jewelry Inc......401 521-1930
181 Macklin St Cranston RI (02920) ***(G-20292)***
Steven Sprott......774 276-6534
121 Cottage St 1 Whitinsville MA (01588) ***(G-16918)***
Steven Tedesco......978 777-4070
100 Newbury St Ste A Danvers MA (01923) ***(G-10258)***
Steven W Willsey......802 434-5353
2047 Shaker Hill Rd Starksboro VT (05487) ***(G-22517)***
Stevens Company Incorporated......860 283-8201
1085 Waterbury Rd 1 Thomaston CT (06787) ***(G-4515)***
Stevens Electric Pump Service......207 933-2143
18 Berry Rd Monmouth ME (04259) ***(G-6451)***
Stevens Kiln Drying LLC......802 472-5013
289 Marsh Rd Wolcott VT (05680) ***(G-22732)***
Stevens Linen Associates Inc......508 943-0813
137 Schofield Ave Ste 5 Dudley MA (01571) ***(G-10387)***
Stevens Manufacturing Co Inc......203 878-2328
220 Rock Ln Milford CT (06460) ***(G-2369)***
Stevens Publishing Inc......401 821-2216
1049 Main St Coventry RI (02816) ***(G-20165)***
Stevenson Learning Skills Inc......774 233-0457
220 Marked Tree Rd Holliston MA (01746) ***(G-11607)***
Steves Publication Svc......508 671-9192
80 Thompson Rd Webster MA (01570) ***(G-16351)***
Steves Sports......413 746-1696
94 Front St West Springfield MA (01089) ***(G-16553)***
Stewart Efi LLC (PA)......860 283-8213
45 Old Waterbury Rd Thomaston CT (06787) ***(G-4516)***
Stewart Efi LLC......860 283-2523
332 Reynolds Bridge Rd Thomaston CT (06787) ***(G-4517)***
Stewart Efi Connecticut LLC......860 283-8213
45 Old Waterbury Rd Thomaston CT (06787) ***(G-4518)***

Stickler Machine Company LLC 860 267-8246
4 N Main St Ste 1 East Hampton CT (06424) ***(G-1165)***
Stiebel Eltron Inc 413 535-1734
242 Suffolk St Holyoke MA (01040) ***(G-11661)***
Stihl Incorporated 203 929-8488
2 Patriot Way Oxford CT (06478) ***(G-3425)***
Stik-II Products, Easthampton *Also called Adhesive Applications Inc* ***(G-10553)***
Stiles & Hart Brick Company 508 697-6928
127 Cook St Bridgewater MA (02324) ***(G-9088)***
Stiletto Cupcakes 207 212-9788
21 Donna Dr Lisbon ME (04250) ***(G-6365)***
Stilisti 617 262-2234
116 Newbury St Fl 2 Boston MA (02116) ***(G-8867)***
Still Water Design Inc 617 308-5820
1 Winnisimmet St Ste 1 # 1 Chelsea MA (02150) ***(G-9971)***
Stillpoint International Inc 603 756-9281
17 Eastridge Dr Peterborough NH (03458) ***(G-19490)***
STILLPOINT PUBLISHING, Peterborough *Also called Stillpoint International Inc* ***(G-19490)***
Stillwater Fasteners LLC 508 763-8044
25 Gurney Rd East Freetown MA (02717) ***(G-10460)***
Stillwater Graphics Inc 802 433-9898
71 Depot St Williamstown VT (05679) ***(G-22651)***
Stingray Manufacturing LLC 603 642-8987
187c Route 125 Unit C5 Brentwood NH (03833) ***(G-17759)***
Stingray Optics LLC 603 358-5577
17a Bradco St Keene NH (03431) ***(G-18529)***
Stirrings LLC 508 324-9800
1 West St Unit 2 Fall River MA (02720) ***(G-10764)***
Stirrings Better Cocktails, Fall River *Also called Stirrings LLC* ***(G-10764)***
Stitch This 603 774-0736
11 White Tail Ln Dunbarton NH (03046) ***(G-18074)***
Stitchers Hideaway LLC 860 268-4741
172 Birch St Manchester CT (06040) ***(G-2054)***
Stitches By Kayo Inc 603 965-0158
44 Nashua Rd Unit 11 Londonderry NH (03053) ***(G-18739)***
Stitchs Custom Embroidery LLC 401 943-5900
554 Killingly St Johnston RI (02919) ***(G-20542)***
Stmc, Plantsville *Also called Southington Tool & Mfg Corp* ***(G-3540)***
Sto Corp 802 775-4117
251 Quality Ln Rutland VT (05701) ***(G-22354)***
Stockley Storage, Landaff *Also called Stockley Trucking Inc* ***(G-18609)***
Stockley Trucking Inc 603 838-2860
405 S Main St Landaff NH (03585) ***(G-18609)***
Stokes Woodworking Co Inc (PA) 508 481-0414
12 Bonazzoli Ave Hudson MA (01749) ***(G-11820)***
Stolberger Incorporated 401 724-8800
1211 High St Central Falls RI (02863) ***(G-20126)***
Stone Bridge Restaurant, Tiverton *Also called Stonebridge Restaurant Inc* ***(G-21264)***
Stone Company 413 442-1447
2 Westview Rd Pittsfield MA (01201) ***(G-14510)***
Stone Decor Galleria Inc 781 937-9377
15 Normac Rd Woburn MA (01801) ***(G-17302)***
Stone Design Marble & Gran Co 781 331-3000
1235 Main St South Weymouth MA (02190) ***(G-15322)***
Stone House Farm Inc 978 352-2323
276 Washington St West Boxford MA (01885) ***(G-16408)***
Stone Image Custom Concrete 860 668-2434
1186 Old Coach Xing Suffield CT (06078) ***(G-4468)***
Stone Machine Co Inc 603 887-4287
45 E Derry Rd Chester NH (03036) ***(G-17826)***
Stone Soup Concrete 413 203-5600
122 Pleasant St Ste B Easthampton MA (01027) ***(G-10580)***
Stone Surfaces Inc 781 270-4600
275 Salem St Ste 2 Woburn MA (01801) ***(G-17303)***
Stone Systems New England LLC 401 766-3603
9 Steel St North Smithfield RI (02896) ***(G-20796)***
Stone Vault Co 603 863-2720
57 Main St Apt 1 Newport NH (03773) ***(G-19359)***
Stone Workshop LLC 203 362-1144
1108 Railroad Ave Bridgeport CT (06605) ***(G-496)***
Stoneage LLC 203 926-1133
36 Narragansett Trl Shelton CT (06484) ***(G-3874)***
Stonebridge Press Inc (PA) 508 764-4325
25 Elm St Southbridge MA (01550) ***(G-15405)***
Stonebridge Restaurant Inc 401 625-5780
25 Russell Dr Tiverton RI (02878) ***(G-21264)***
Stonegate Capital Group 860 899-1181
100 Pearl St Fl 12 Hartford CT (06103) ***(G-1873)***
Stonehouse Fine Cakes 203 235-5091
61 N 1st St Meriden CT (06451) ***(G-2134)***
Stoneman Custom Jewelers 603 352-0811
82 Washington St Ste 2 Keene NH (03431) ***(G-18530)***
Stoneridge Inc 781 830-0340
300 Dan Rd Canton MA (02021) ***(G-9787)***
Stonewall Cable Inc 603 536-1601
126 Hawkensen Dr Rumney NH (03266) ***(G-19698)***
Stonewall Kitchen LLC 860 648-9215
400 Evergreen Way # 408 South Windsor CT (06074) ***(G-4015)***
Stonewall Kitchen LLC 603 356-3342
Settlers Grn Green North Conway NH (03860) ***(G-19379)***
Stonewall Kitchen LLC (PA) 207 351-2713
2 Stonewall Ln York ME (03909) ***(G-7316)***
Stoney Industries Inc 508 845-6731
89 School St Shrewsbury MA (01545) ***(G-15133)***
Stonington Vineyards Inc 860 535-1222
523 Taugwonk Rd Stonington CT (06378) ***(G-4378)***
Stony Creek Quarry Corporation 203 483-3904
7 Business Park Dr Ste A Branford CT (06405) ***(G-353)***
Stonybrook Fine Arts LLC 617 799-3644
24 Porter St Jamaica Plain MA (02130) ***(G-11950)***
Stonybrook Water Company LLC 978 865-9899
11 Beach St Unit 1 Manchester MA (01944) ***(G-12607)***
Stora Enso N Amercn Sls Inc (HQ) 203 541-5178
201 Broad St Stamford CT (06901) ***(G-4334)***
Storage and Repair, East Blue Hill *Also called Webbers Cove Boat Yard Inc* ***(G-5975)***
Storage and Workplace Systems, Holliston *Also called Stanley Vidmar* ***(G-11605)***
Storage Concepts 603 752-1111
1 Francis St Berlin NH (03570) ***(G-17701)***
Storage With Style, Danville *Also called Post Woodworking Inc* ***(G-17969)***
Stored Solar J&We LLC 207 434-6500
Rr Box 1a Jonesboro ME (04648) ***(G-6225)***
Storey Publishing LLC (HQ) 413 346-2100
210 Mass Moca Way North Adams MA (01247) ***(G-13685)***
Storm Duds Raingear, Attleboro *Also called Mr Idea Inc* ***(G-7770)***
Stoughton Steel Company Inc 781 826-6496
347 Circuit St Hanover MA (02339) ***(G-11354)***
Stowaway Sweets, Marblehead *Also called Seven Sweets Inc* ***(G-12693)***
Stowe Woodward Co-Div SW Ind, Concord *Also called Stowe Woodward LLC* ***(G-17932)***
Stowe Woodward LLC 603 224-6300
60 Old Turnpike Rd Concord NH (03301) ***(G-17932)***
STP Bindery Services Inc 860 528-1430
265 Prestige Park Rd # 2 East Hartford CT (06108) ***(G-1223)***
STP Products Manufacturing Co (HQ) 203 205-2900
44 Old Ridgebury Rd # 300 Danbury CT (06810) ***(G-997)***
Str Grinnell GP Holding LLC 978 731-2500
50 Technology Dr Westminster MA (01441) ***(G-16814)***
Str Holdings Inc (PA) 860 272-4235
1559 King St Enfield CT (06082) ***(G-1386)***
Strafello Precast Inc 774 501-2628
250 Cape Hwy Ste 12 East Taunton MA (02718) ***(G-10518)***
Strafford Machine Inc 603 664-9758
385 Province Rd Strafford NH (03884) ***(G-19866)***
Strafford Organic Creamery, Strafford *Also called Ebws LLC* ***(G-22526)***
Straightline Excavation Corp 978 858-0800
86 Lee St Tewksbury MA (01876) ***(G-15839)***
Strain Measurement Devices Inc 203 294-5800
55 Barnes Park Rd N Wallingford CT (06492) ***(G-4814)***
Stran & Company Inc (PA) 617 822-6950
2 Heritage Dr Ste 600 Quincy MA (02171) ***(G-14660)***
Stran Promotional Solutions, Quincy *Also called Stran & Company Inc* ***(G-14660)***
Strange Famous Inc 310 254-8974
2 Meadowbrook Dr North Smithfield RI (02896) ***(G-20797)***
Strange Planet Printing 508 857-1816
1041 Pearl St Brockton MA (02301) ***(G-9179)***
Stratabond Co Inc 802 747-4000
92 Park St Rutland VT (05701) ***(G-22355)***
Strategic Bio Solutions, Windham *Also called Special Diversified Opp Inc* ***(G-7254)***
Stratford Publishing Services 802 254-6073
70 Landmark Hill Dr Brattleboro VT (05301) ***(G-21747)***
Stratford Steel LLC 203 612-7350
185 Masarik Ave Stratford CT (06615) ***(G-4449)***
Straton Industries Inc 203 375-4488
180 Surf Ave Stratford CT (06615) ***(G-4450)***
Stratosphere Inc 207 351-8011
611 Us Route 1 York ME (03909) ***(G-7317)***
Straumann Usa LLC (HQ) 978 747-2500
60 Minuteman Rd Andover MA (01810) ***(G-7612)***
Strawberry Hill Farms LLC 207 474-5262
279 Back Rd Skowhegan ME (04976) ***(G-6987)***
Strawberry Ridge Vineyard Inc 860 868-0730
23 Strawbery Ridge Rd Cornwall Bridge CT (06754) ***(G-821)***
Strawbrry Hl Grnd Delights LLC 617 319-3557
39 Emerson Rd Ste 104 Waltham MA (02451) ***(G-16202)***
Streak Media LLC 617 242-9460
109 Kingston St Fl 2 Boston MA (02111) ***(G-8868)***
Streamline Plastics Co Inc 718 401-4000
35 Industrial Dr East Longmeadow MA (01028) ***(G-10494)***
Streamline Press 203 484-9799
21 Commerce Dr Ste 2 North Branford CT (06471) ***(G-2978)***
Streamline Press LLC 203 484-9799
21 Commerce Dr Ste 2 North Branford CT (06471) ***(G-2979)***
Streamware, Dedham *Also called Crane Mdsg Systems Inc* ***(G-10284)***
Streetscan Inc 617 399-8236
151 S Bedford St Ste 2 Burlington MA (01803) ***(G-9341)***
Strem Chemicals Incorporated 978 499-1600
7 Mulliken Way Newburyport MA (01950) ***(G-13537)***
Strescon of New England 781 221-2153
25 Mall Rd Ste 104 Burlington MA (01803) ***(G-9342)***

ALPHABETIC

Stretch Products Corp 401 722-0400
392 Pine St Pawtucket RI (02860) ***(G-20900)***
Strickland K Wheelock 508 265-2896
46 Pleasant St Uxbridge MA (01569) ***(G-15930)***
Stride Inc 203 758-8307
80 Turnpike Dr Ste 1 Middlebury CT (06762) ***(G-2159)***
Strolid Inc 978 655-8550
8 Fletcher Rd Windham NH (03087) ***(G-20010)***
Stromatec Inc 802 425-2700
3050 Fuller Mt Rd North Ferrisburgh VT (05473) ***(G-22228)***
Strong Electric 855 709-0701
100 Country Club Dr Tewksbury MA (01876) ***(G-15840)***
Strong Group Inc (PA) 978 281-3300
39 Grove St Gloucester MA (01930) ***(G-11212)***
Strong H J G Bros Grav Corp 603 487-5551
143 Riverdale Rd New Boston NH (03070) ***(G-19298)***
Strong Leather Co, Gloucester *Also called Strong Group Inc* ***(G-11212)***
Strong Wood Products Inc 207 778-4063
156 Cummings Hill Rd Temple ME (04984) ***(G-7080)***
Stroud International Ltd 781 631-8806
123 Pleasant St Ste 300 Marblehead MA (01945) ***(G-12695)***
Strout Custom Millwork, Broad Brook *Also called Strouts Woodworking* ***(G-630)***
Strouts Woodworking 860 623-8445
45 Plantation Rd Broad Brook CT (06016) ***(G-630)***
Structural Stone LLC 401 667-4969
285 Smith St North Kingstown RI (02852) ***(G-20742)***
Structured Solutions II LLC 203 972-5717
55 Saint Johns Pl Ste 201 New Canaan CT (06840) ***(G-2616)***
Stryker Biotech, Hopkinton *Also called Stryker Corporation* ***(G-11739)***
Stryker Corporation 860 528-1111
155 Founders Plz East Hartford CT (06108) ***(G-1224)***
Stryker Corporation 508 416-5200
35 South St Ste C Hopkinton MA (01748) ***(G-11739)***
Stuart Allyn Co Inc 413 443-7306
17 Taconic Park Dr Ste 2 Pittsfield MA (01201) ***(G-14511)***
Stuart Hardwood Corp 203 376-0036
32 Old Amity Rd New Haven CT (06524) ***(G-2740)***
Stuart Karon 802 649-1911
248 Park St Newton MA (02458) ***(G-13641)***
Stuart Marine Corp Inc 207 594-5515
38 Gordon Dr Rockland ME (04841) ***(G-6811)***
Stuart Sports Specialties Inc 413 543-1524
34 Front St Ste 6 Indian Orchard MA (01151) ***(G-11897)***
Stuart Townsend Carr, Limington *Also called Townsend Cabinet Makers Inc* ***(G-6350)***
Stuart Xlan, New Haven *Also called Stuart Hardwood Corp* ***(G-2740)***
Studio 2, Monson *Also called Christmas Studio* ***(G-13203)***
Studio 24 Graphix & Prtg Inc 617 296-2058
1182 Blue Hill Ave Mattapan MA (02126) ***(G-12884)***
Studio 4 RI LLC 401 578-5419
122 Manton Ave Ste 1 Providence RI (02909) ***(G-21128)***
Studio of Engaging Learning 617 975-0268
167 Corey Rd Ste 209 Brighton MA (02135) ***(G-9107)***
Studio Print, Portland *Also called East Shore Production* ***(G-6657)***
Studio Steel Inc 860 868-7305
159 New Milford Tpke New Preston CT (06777) ***(G-2835)***
Studley Press Inc 413 684-0441
151 E Housatonic St Dalton MA (01226) ***(G-10187)***
Stuffed Foods LLC 978 203-0370
14 Jewel Dr Ste 3 Wilmington MA (01887) ***(G-17049)***
Stultz Electric, Portland *Also called Timken Motor & Crane Svcs LLC* ***(G-6740)***
Stump City Cider 603 234-6288
52 Bernard Rd Rochester NH (03868) ***(G-19688)***
Stupell Industries Ltd Inc 401 831-5640
14 Industrial Ln Johnston RI (02919) ***(G-20543)***
Stur-Dee Boat Co 401 624-9373
1117 Bulgarmarsh Rd Tiverton RI (02878) ***(G-21265)***
Sturbridge Associates III LLC (PA) 401 943-8600
185 Union Ave Providence RI (02909) ***(G-21129)***
Sturdibuilt Storage Bldgs LLC 207 757-7877
2587 Us Route 2 Smyrna Mills ME (04780) ***(G-6996)***
Sturm Ruger & Company Inc 603 863-2000
411 Sunapee St Newport NH (03773) ***(G-19360)***
Sturm Ruger & Company Inc 603 865-2424
529 Sunapee St Newport NH (03773) ***(G-19361)***
Sturm Ruger & Company Inc (PA) 203 259-7843
1 Lacey Pl Southport CT (06890) ***(G-4099)***
Sturm Ruger & Company Inc 603 863-3300
411 Sunapee St Newport NH (03773) ***(G-19362)***
Sturtevant Inc (PA) 781 829-6501
348 Circuit St Ste 1 Hanover MA (02339) ***(G-11355)***
Sturtevant Mill Company, Hanover *Also called Sturtevant Inc* ***(G-11355)***
Stylair LLC 860 747-4588
161 Woodford Ave Plainville CT (06062) ***(G-3515)***
Style and Grace LLC 917 751-2043
101 Franklin St Ste 3 Westport CT (06880) ***(G-5232)***
Style ME Pretty, Wayland *Also called Smpretty Inc* ***(G-16336)***
Stylecraft Inc 401 463-9944
1510 Pontiac Ave Cranston RI (02920) ***(G-20293)***
Styletech Company 978 537-0711
28 Jytek Rd Leominster MA (01453) ***(G-12190)***
Stysil Enterprises Ltd 781 834-7279
38 Indian Rd 200 Marshfield MA (02050) ***(G-12870)***
Subatomic Digital LLC 802 857-4864
151 Blair Park Rd Williston VT (05495) ***(G-22694)***
Subcom LLC 603 436-6100
100 Piscataqua Dr Newington NH (03801) ***(G-19326)***
Subcom Cable Systems LLC 603 436-6100
100 Piscataqua Dr Newington NH (03801) ***(G-19327)***
Subcon Technology, Leominster *Also called M & K Industries Inc* ***(G-12164)***
Subimods LLC 860 291-0015
9 Old Windsor Rd Ste B Bloomfield CT (06002) ***(G-264)***
Subinas USA LLC 860 298-0401
4 Market Cir Windsor CT (06095) ***(G-5370)***
Submarine Research Labs 781 749-0900
Porters Cove Is Hingham MA (02043) ***(G-11512)***
Subsalve USA LLC 401 884-8801
51 Circuit Dr North Kingstown RI (02852) ***(G-20743)***
Suburban Machine 978 392-9100
69 Broadway St Westford MA (01886) ***(G-16794)***
Suburban News Dealers LLC 508 962-9807
19 Shaw St Carver MA (02330) ***(G-9808)***
Suburban Publishing Corp 978 818-6300
2 1st Ave Ste 103 Peabody MA (01960) ***(G-14373)***
Suburban Real Estate News, Peabody *Also called Suburban Publishing Corp* ***(G-14373)***
Suburban Shopper Inc 781 821-2590
780 Washington St Canton MA (02021) ***(G-9788)***
Suburban Voices Publishing LLC 203 934-6397
840 Boston Post Rd Ste 2 West Haven CT (06516) ***(G-5146)***
Subx Inc 207 775-0808
428 Fore St Unit 4 Portland ME (04101) ***(G-6734)***
Success Printing & Mailing Inc 203 847-1112
10 Pearl St Norwalk CT (06850) ***(G-3252)***
Sud-Chemie Protech Inc 781 444-5188
32 Fremont St Ste 1 Needham Heights MA (02494) ***(G-13345)***
Sudbury Granite & Marble Inc (PA) 508 478-3976
12 Rosenfeld Dr Hopedale MA (01747) ***(G-11684)***
Sudbury Systems Inc 800 876-8888
200 Great Rd Ste 211 Bedford MA (01730) ***(G-8010)***
Suddekor LLC (HQ) 413 821-9000
240 Bowles Rd Agawam MA (01001) ***(G-7453)***
Suddekor LLC 413 525-4070
82 Deer Park Dr East Longmeadow MA (01028) ***(G-10495)***
Sue's Shirt Creations, Somers *Also called Wink Ink LLC* ***(G-3922)***
Suez Wts Services Usa Inc 860 291-9660
405 School St East Hartford CT (06108) ***(G-1225)***
Suffield Poultry Inc 413 737-8392
90 Avocado St Springfield MA (01104) ***(G-15510)***
Suflex, Somersworth *Also called Regal Sleeving & Tubing LLC* ***(G-19847)***
Sugar Mountain Farm LLC 802 439-6462
252 Riddle Pond Rd West Topsham VT (05086) ***(G-22624)***
Sugar Shack On Roaring Branch 802 375-6747
Rr Box 7a Arlington VT (05250) ***(G-21600)***
Sugar Shack, The, Montpelier *Also called Morse Farm Inc* ***(G-22156)***
Sugarbakers Maple Syrup 802 773-7731
940 Middle Rd North Clarendon VT (05759) ***(G-22221)***
Sugarbush Farm Inc 802 457-1757
591 Sugarbush Farm Rd Woodstock VT (05091) ***(G-22739)***
Sugarhill Containers, Turners Falls *Also called Hillside Plastics Inc* ***(G-15879)***
Suisman & Blumenthal, Hartford *Also called Aerospace Metals Inc* ***(G-1803)***
Sukesha, Manchester *Also called Chuckles Inc* ***(G-18798)***
Suleys Soccer Center 603 668-7227
1525 S Willow St Unit 3 Manchester NH (03103) ***(G-18931)***
Sullivan Apple Cider 781 233-7090
34 Prospect St Saugus MA (01906) ***(G-15000)***
Sullivan Associates, East Boothbay *Also called Williams Partners Ltd* ***(G-5981)***
Sullivan Industries LLC 802 229-1909
1 Deerfield Dr Montpelier VT (05602) ***(G-22161)***
Sullivan JW 781 275-5818
244 South Rd Bedford MA (01730) ***(G-8011)***
Sullivan Manufacturing Company 781 982-1550
41 Accord Park Dr Norwell MA (02061) ***(G-14112)***
Sullivan Paper Company Inc (PA) 413 827-7030
42 Progress Ave West Springfield MA (01089) ***(G-16554)***
Sullivan Tire, Norwell *Also called Sullivan Manufacturing Company* ***(G-14112)***
Sulzer Pump Solutions US Inc (PA) 203 238-2700
140 Pond View Dr Meriden CT (06450) ***(G-2135)***
Sum Machine & Tool Co Inc 860 742-6827
156 Mark Dr Coventry CT (06238) ***(G-840)***
Sumake North America LLC 603 402-2924
10 Northern Blvd Ste 13 Amherst NH (03031) ***(G-17589)***
Sumal Enterprises LLC 860 945-3337
620 Main St Watertown CT (06795) ***(G-5027)***
Summer Infant Inc (PA) 401 671-6550
1275 Park East Dr Woonsocket RI (02895) ***(G-21581)***
Summer Infant Inc 401 671-6550
1275 Park East Dr Woonsocket RI (02895) ***(G-21582)***

Summer Infant (usa) Inc 401 671-6551
1275 Park East Dr Woonsocket RI (02895) ***(G-21583)***
Summer Ink Inc 617 714-0263
258 Harvard St Brookline MA (02446) ***(G-9220)***
Summer Street Press LLC 203 978-0098
460 Summer St Stamford CT (06901) ***(G-4335)***
Summerwind Jewelers Goldsmiths, Portsmouth *Also called Melvin Reisz* ***(G-19594)***
Summit Corporation of America 860 283-4391
1430 Waterbury Rd Thomaston CT (06787) ***(G-4519)***
Summit Finishing Division, Thomaston *Also called Summit Corporation of America* ***(G-4519)***
Summit Forms 508 853-6838
456 W Boylston St Worcester MA (01606) ***(G-17483)***
Summit Metal Fabricators Inc 603 328-2211
144a Main St Plaistow NH (03865) ***(G-19525)***
Summit Mfg Corp 401 723-6272
248 Pine St Pawtucket RI (02860) ***(G-20901)***
Summit Orthopedic Tech Inc 203 693-2727
294 Quarry Rd Milford CT (06460) ***(G-2370)***
Summit Packaging Systems Inc (PA) 603 669-5410
400 Gay St Manchester NH (03103) ***(G-18932)***
Summit Press Inc (PA) 617 889-3991
63 6th St Chelsea MA (02150) ***(G-9972)***
Summit Printing LLC 401 732-7848
155 Jefferson Blvd Ste 3 Warwick RI (02888) ***(G-21431)***
Summit Screw Machine Corp 203 693-2727
49 Research Dr Ste 3 Milford CT (06460) ***(G-2371)***
Summit Springs, Watertown *Also called Spring Water Associates USA* ***(G-16318)***
Summit Stair Co Inc 203 778-2251
101 Wooster St Bethel CT (06801) ***(G-181)***
Summit Therapeutics Inc 617 225-4455
1 Broadway Fl 14 Cambridge MA (02142) ***(G-9662)***
Sumner Communications Inc 203 748-2050
24 Stony Hill Rd Ste 5 Bethel CT (06801) ***(G-182)***
Sumner Fancy 603 893-3081
12 Telo Rd Windham NH (03087) ***(G-20011)***
Sumner Printing Inc 603 692-7424
433 Route 108 Somersworth NH (03878) ***(G-19849)***
Sumo Steel Corp 978 927-4950
6 Dearborn Ave Beverly MA (01915) ***(G-8183)***
Sun & Moon Originals, Shelburne Falls *Also called Brian Summer* ***(G-15066)***
Sun Corp 860 567-0817
27 Anderson Road Ext Morris CT (06763) ***(G-2432)***
Sun Country Foods Inc (HQ) 855 824-7645
1 Edgewater Dr Ste 200 Norwood MA (02062) ***(G-14202)***
Sun Diagnostics LLC 207 926-1125
60 Pinelnd Dr Auburn Hl New Gloucester ME (04260) ***(G-6472)***
Sun Farm Corporation 203 882-8000
75 Woodmont Rd Milford CT (06460) ***(G-2372)***
Sun Gro Holdings Inc 413 786-4343
770 Silver St Agawam MA (01001) ***(G-7454)***
Sun Gro Horticulture Dist Inc 800 732-8667
770 Silver St Agawam MA (01001) ***(G-7455)***
Sun Gro Horticulture Proc, Agawam *Also called Sun Gro Horticulture Dist Inc* ***(G-7455)***
Sun Hing Noodle Co, Boston *Also called United Foods Incorporated* ***(G-8898)***
Sun Journal, Lewiston *Also called Lewiston Daily Sun* ***(G-6299)***
Sun Journal, Lewiston *Also called Lewiston Daily Sun* ***(G-6300)***
Sun Journal Newspaper, Rumford *Also called Lewiston Daily Sun* ***(G-6837)***
Sun Ray Bakery 978 922-1941
240 Rantoul St Beverly MA (01915) ***(G-8184)***
Sun Ray Technologies Inc 802 422-8680
80 Weathervane Dr Killington VT (05751) ***(G-22056)***
Sunborne Energy Holding, Cambridge *Also called Sunborne Energy Technologies* ***(G-9663)***
Sunborne Energy Technologies 617 234-7000
20 University Rd Ste 450 Cambridge MA (02138) ***(G-9663)***
Sunburst Electronic Manufactur (PA) 508 580-1881
70 Pleasant St West Bridgewater MA (02379) ***(G-16458)***
Sunburst Ems, West Bridgewater *Also called Sunburst Electronic Manufactur* ***(G-16458)***
Suncook Valley Sun Inc 603 435-6291
21 Broadway St Pittsfield NH (03263) ***(G-19505)***
Sundance Screenprints 978 281-6006
14a Whittemore St Gloucester MA (01930) ***(G-11213)***
Sundance Sign & Design 603 742-1517
89 Oak St Dover NH (03820) ***(G-18055)***
Sundance/Newbridge LLC (HQ) 800 343-8204
33 Boston Post Rd W # 440 Marlborough MA (01752) ***(G-12831)***
Sunday River Brewing Co Inc 207 824-4253
320 D St Unit 426 Boston MA (02127) ***(G-8869)***
Sunderland Printing, Hyannis *Also called Instant Offset Press Inc* ***(G-11843)***
Sundial Wire LLC 413 582-6909
296 Nonotuck St Florence MA (01062) ***(G-10869)***
Sundrum Solar Inc 508 740-6256
15 Hillside Rd Northborough MA (01532) ***(G-14049)***
Sunfield Solar 508 885-3300
22 Treadwell Dr Spencer MA (01562) ***(G-15437)***
Sungard, Boston *Also called Fis Systems International LLC* ***(G-8548)***
Sungard, Burlington *Also called Fis Financial Systems LLC* ***(G-9274)***
Sungard Insurance Systems Inc 603 641-3636
250 Commercial St # 4004 Manchester NH (03101) ***(G-18933)***

Sunjas Oriental Foods Inc 802 244-7644
40 Foundry St Ste 1a Waterbury VT (05676) ***(G-22585)***
Sunny Sky Products LLC 802 861-6004
102 Kimball Ave Ste 1 South Burlington VT (05403) ***(G-22469)***
Sunny Young LLC 917 667-0528
150 Causeway St Boston MA (02114) ***(G-8870)***
Sunnyside Maples 603 848-7091
130 Asby Rd Canterbury NH (03224) ***(G-17786)***
Sunnyside Maples Inc 603 783-9961
554 Meadow Pond Rd Gilmanton NH (03237) ***(G-18194)***
Sunopta Ingredients Inc 781 276-5100
25 Wiggins Ave Bedford MA (01730) ***(G-8012)***
Sunovion Pharmaceuticals Inc (HQ) 508 481-6700
84 Waterford Dr Marlborough MA (01752) ***(G-12832)***
Sunovion Respiratory Dev, Marlborough *Also called Sunovion Pharmaceuticals Inc* ***(G-12832)***
Sunray Bakery, Beverly *Also called Sun Ray Bakery* ***(G-8184)***
Sunrise, Pembroke *Also called Apple Mill Holding Company Inc* ***(G-14392)***
Sunrise Composting 207 483-4081
444 E Side Rd Addison ME (04606) ***(G-5511)***
Sunrise Foods Incorporated 603 772-4420
25 Pine St Brentwood NH (03833) ***(G-17760)***
Sunrise Guide LLC 207 221-3450
503 Woodford St Portland ME (04103) ***(G-6735)***
Sunrise Home Inc 207 839-8801
324 Gorham Rd Scarborough ME (04074) ***(G-6941)***
Sunrise Printing & Graphics 207 892-3534
89 Tandberg Trl Windham ME (04062) ***(G-7255)***
Sunrise Prosthetics Orthotics 508 473-9943
2 S Main St Milford MA (01757) ***(G-13145)***
Sunrise Prosthetics Orthotics (PA) 508 753-4738
10 Harvard St Worcester MA (01609) ***(G-17484)***
Sunrise Systems Elec Co Inc (PA) 781 826-9706
720 Washington St Pembroke MA (02359) ***(G-14428)***
Sunrise Technologies LLC 508 884-9732
54 Commercial St Ste 2 Raynham MA (02767) ***(G-14731)***
Suns International LLC 978 349-2329
127 Riverneck Rd Chelmsford MA (01824) ***(G-9934)***
Sunset Engravers 978 687-1111
678 Lowell St Methuen MA (01844) ***(G-13045)***
Sunset Hill Vineyard 860 598-9427
5 Elys Ferry Rd Lyme CT (06371) ***(G-1956)***
Sunset Tool Inc 603 355-2246
58 Optical Ave Keene NH (03431) ***(G-18531)***
Sunsetter Products Ltd Partnr 781 321-9600
184 Charles St Malden MA (02148) ***(G-12598)***
Sunshine Scoops LLC 603 668-0992
210 Lowell St Manchester NH (03104) ***(G-18770)***
Sunshine Sign Company Inc 508 839-5588
121 Westboro Rd North Grafton MA (01536) ***(G-13965)***
Sunu Inc 617 980-9807
245 Main St Fl 2 Cambridge MA (02142) ***(G-9664)***
Suominen Nonwoven, East Windsor *Also called Windsor Locks Nonwovens Inc* ***(G-1311)***
Suominen US Holding Inc (HQ) 860 386-8001
1 Hartfield Blvd Ste 101 East Windsor CT (06088) ***(G-1306)***
Super Brush LLC 413 543-1442
800 Worcester St Springfield MA (01151) ***(G-15511)***
Super Dup'r Instant Printing, Marlborough *Also called Jordan Enterprises Inc* ***(G-12781)***
Super Faraday Labs, Waltham *Also called Spidle Corp* ***(G-16199)***
Super Seal Corp 203 378-5015
45 Seymour St Stratford CT (06615) ***(G-4451)***
Super Sport Screen Printing 781 397-8166
910 Eastern Ave Malden MA (02148) ***(G-12599)***
Super Thin Saws, Waterbury *Also called T S S Inc* ***(G-22586)***
Super-Temp Wire & Cable Inc 802 655-4211
104 Bowdoin St South Burlington VT (05403) ***(G-22470)***
Superconductivity Inc (HQ) 608 831-5773
114 E Main St Ayer MA (01432) ***(G-7940)***
Superior Baking Co Inc 508 586-6601
176 N Warren Ave Brockton MA (02301) ***(G-9180)***
Superior Bindery Inc 781 303-0022
1 Federal Dr Braintree MA (02184) ***(G-9039)***
Superior Cake Products Inc 508 764-3276
94 Ashland Ave Southbridge MA (01550) ***(G-15406)***
Superior Concrete Products LLC 860 342-0186
830 Portland Cobalt Rd Portland CT (06480) ***(G-3576)***
Superior Die & Stamping Inc 774 203-3674
96 County St Attleboro MA (02703) ***(G-7797)***
Superior Docks, Ellsworth *Also called Superior Wldg Fabrication Inc* ***(G-6022)***
Superior Elc Holdg Group LLC (HQ) 860 582-9561
1 Cowles Rd Plainville CT (06062) ***(G-3516)***
Superior Fire Services, Fairfield *Also called J & M Enterprises Inc* ***(G-6027)***
Superior Fuel Co 203 337-1213
154 Admiral St Bridgeport CT (06605) ***(G-497)***
Superior Glass, East Providence *Also called Jmh Industries Inc* ***(G-20423)***
Superior Ice Cream Eqp LLC 603 225-4207
155 River Rd Unit 9 Bow NH (03304) ***(G-17732)***
Superior Kitchen Designs Inc 978 632-5072
166 Mill St Gardner MA (01440) ***(G-11130)***

ALPHABETIC

Superior Manufacturing Corp 508 677-0100
1 Ace St Unit 12 Fall River MA (02720) *(G-10765)*
Superior Novelty Equipment 603 225-4207
155 River Rd Unit 12 Bow NH (03304) *(G-17733)*
Superior Nut Company Inc 800 251-6060
225 Monsignor Obrien Hwy Cambridge MA (02141) *(G-9665)*
Superior Packaging & Finishing, Braintree *Also called Superior Bindery Inc (G-9039)*
Superior Plas Extrusion Co Inc 860 234-1864
154 West St Cromwell CT (06416) *(G-861)*
Superior Plas Extrusion Co Inc (PA) 860 963-1976
5 Highland Dr Putnam CT (06260) *(G-3636)*
Superior Plating Company 203 255-1501
2 Lacey Pl Southport CT (06890) *(G-4100)*
Superior Power Systems, Attleboro *Also called Power Equipment Co Inc (G-7781)*
Superior Power Systems 508 226-3400
7 Franklin R Mckay Rd Attleboro MA (02703) *(G-7798)*
Superior Printing Ink Co Inc 203 281-1921
750 Sherman Ave Hamden CT (06514) *(G-1786)*
Superior Printing Ink Co Inc 508 481-8250
255 E Main St Marlborough MA (01752) *(G-12833)*
Superior Sheet Metal LLC 603 577-8620
14 Flagstone Dr Hudson NH (03051) *(G-18443)*
Superior Steel Fabricators Inc 603 673-7509
46 Route 13 Brookline NH (03033) *(G-17773)*
Superior Tchncal Ceramics Corp 802 527-7726
600 Industrial Park Rd Saint Albans VT (05478) *(G-22380)*
Superior Technology Corp (PA) 203 255-1501
Lacey Pl Southport CT (06890) *(G-4101)*
Superior Trawl, Wakefield *Also called Jonathan Knight (G-21273)*
Superior Wldg Fabrication Inc 207 664-2121
420 Christian Ridge Rd Ellsworth ME (04605) *(G-6022)*
Superlative Printing Inc 781 341-9000
4 Cabot Pl Ste 3 Stoughton MA (02072) *(G-15624)*
Supermedia LLC 781 849-7670
186 Forbes Rd Braintree MA (02184) *(G-9040)*
Supermedia LLC 401 468-1500
300 Jefferson Blvd # 201 Warwick RI (02888) *(G-21432)*
Supermedia LLC 207 828-6100
600 Sthborough Dr Ste 100 South Portland ME (04106) *(G-7041)*
Supernova Diagnostics Inc 301 792-4345
36 Richmond Hill Rd New Canaan CT (06840) *(G-2617)*
Superpedestrian Inc 617 945-1892
84 Hamilton St Cambridge MA (02139) *(G-9666)*
Supervisor of Shipbuilding 207 442-2520
574 Washington St Bath ME (04530) *(G-5681)*
Supfina Machine Co Inc 401 294-6600
181 Circuit Dr North Kingstown RI (02852) *(G-20744)*
Supper Time USA, Peabody *Also called Palaka Corp (G-14359)*
Supplies Unlimited 207 563-7010
47 School St Damariscotta ME (04543) *(G-5940)*
Supreme Brass & Alum Castings 413 737-4433
210 Windsor St West Springfield MA (01089) *(G-16555)*
Supreme Painting Company, Assonet *Also called Joseph Nachado (G-7682)*
Supreme Storm Services LLC 860 201-0642
49 Depaolo Dr Southington CT (06489) *(G-4083)*
Supreme-Lake Mfg Inc 860 621-8911
455 Atwater St Plantsville CT (06479) *(G-3541)*
Suraci Corp 203 624-1345
90 River St Ste 2 New Haven CT (06513) *(G-2741)*
Suraci Metal Finishing LLC 203 624-1345
90 River St Ste 2 New Haven CT (06513) *(G-2742)*
Suraci Paint & Powder Coating, New Haven *Also called Suraci Corp (G-2741)*
Sure Industries Inc 860 289-2522
122 Park Ave Ste C East Hartford CT (06108) *(G-1226)*
Surell Accessories Inc 603 242-7784
198 N Main St Troy NH (03465) *(G-19914)*
Surelock Division, Shelton *Also called Inline Plastics Corp (G-3819)*
Surf Metal Co Inc 203 375-2211
460 Lordship Blvd Stratford CT (06615) *(G-4452)*
Surface Coatings Div, Providence *Also called Westwell Industries Inc (G-21154)*
Surface Mount Devices LLC 203 322-8290
16 Acre View Dr Stamford CT (06903) *(G-4336)*
Surface Plate Co 860 652-8905
23 Pearl St Glastonbury CT (06033) *(G-1578)*
Surfaceworx, West Bridgewater *Also called CCS Marine Inc (G-16434)*
Surfari Inc 978 704-9051
210 Main St Gloucester MA (01930) *(G-11214)*
Surgibox Inc 617 982-3908
8 Juniper St Apt 18 Brookline MA (02445) *(G-9221)*
Surgical Devices, New Haven *Also called Covidien LP (G-2680)*
Surgical Devices, North Haven *Also called Covidien LP (G-3021)*
Surgical Specialties Corp (HQ) 781 751-1000
247 Station Dr Ste Ne1 Westwood MA (02090) *(G-16876)*
Surgiquest Inc 203 799-2400
488 Wheelers Farms Rd # 3 Milford CT (06461) *(G-2373)*
Surplus Solutions LLC 401 526-0055
2010 Diamond Hill Rd Woonsocket RI (02895) *(G-21584)*
Surry Licensing LLC 603 354-7000
7 Corporate Dr Keene NH (03431) *(G-18532)*
Surtan Manufacturing Co 508 394-4099
1198 Route 28 Unit E South Yarmouth MA (02664) *(G-15334)*
Surys Inc 203 333-5503
20 Nutmeg Dr Trumbull CT (06611) *(G-4633)*
Susan M Rexford Title Examiner 978 827-3015
6 Hillandale Rd Ashburnham MA (01430) *(G-7645)*
Susan Martovich 203 881-1848
118 Bowers Hill Rd Oxford CT (06478) *(G-3426)*
Suse Linux, Cambridge *Also called Suse LLC (G-9667)*
Suse LLC 617 613-2000
10 Canal Park Ste 200 Cambridge MA (02141) *(G-9667)*
Suse LLC 617 613-2111
150 Cambridgepark Dr # 10 Cambridge MA (02140) *(G-9668)*
Susie BZ Natural Lip Balm 603 529-7083
17 Fieldstone Cir Weare NH (03281) *(G-19940)*
Suspect Technologies Inc 843 318-8278
618 Cambridge St Cambridge MA (02141) *(G-9669)*
Sutherland Welles Ltd 802 635-2700
123 Locke Ave Hyde Park VT (05655) *(G-22038)*
Suture Concepts Inc 978 969-0070
100 Cummings Ctr Ste 414g Beverly MA (01915) *(G-8185)*
Suzhou-Chem Inc 781 433-8618
396 Washington St Ste 318 Wellesley MA (02481) *(G-16388)*
SW Boatworks 207 667-7427
358 Douglas Hwy Lamoine ME (04605) *(G-6264)*
Swaffield Enterprises Inc 603 569-3017
26 Mill St Wolfeboro NH (03894) *(G-20025)*
Swagnificent Ent LLC 203 449-0124
79 Sage Ave Bridgeport CT (06610) *(G-498)*
Swampscott Fuel Inc 781 592-1065
197 Essex St Swampscott MA (01907) *(G-15700)*
Swampscott Fuel Inc 781 251-0993
69 Peartree Dr Westwood MA (02090) *(G-16877)*
Swampscott Reporter, Beverly *Also called Gatehouse Media Mass I Inc (G-8136)*
Swan Dyeing and Printing Corp 508 674-4611
372 Stevens St Fall River MA (02721) *(G-10766)*
Swan Fabrics, Fall River *Also called Swan Dyeing and Printing Corp (G-10766)*
Swan Finishing Company Inc (PA) 508 674-4611
372 Stevens St Fall River MA (02721) *(G-10767)*
Swan Valley Cheese Vermont LLC 802 868-7181
11 Jonergin Dr Swanton VT (05488) *(G-22537)*
Swanhart Woodworking 203 746-1184
5 Bayberry Ln New Fairfield CT (06812) *(G-2628)*
Swans Island, Northport *Also called Atlantic Blanket Company Inc (G-6520)*
Swanson Moore Dental Mfg, Hanover *Also called South Shore Dental Labs (G-11351)*
Swanson Tool Manufacturing Inc 860 953-1641
71 Custer St West Hartford CT (06110) *(G-5097)*
Swansons Die Co Inc 603 623-3832
141 Queen City Ave Manchester NH (03101) *(G-18934)*
Swap Buy Sell Guide, Presque Isle *Also called A & D Print Shop (G-6751)*
Swaponz Inc 508 650-4456
190 N Main St Ste 1 Natick MA (01760) *(G-13280)*
Swarovski Digital Business USA 888 207-9873
1 Kenney Dr Cranston RI (02920) *(G-20294)*
Swarovski Gallery Store, Boston *Also called Swarovski North America Ltd (G-8871)*
Swarovski North America Ltd 617 578-0705
800 Boylston St Spc 160 Boston MA (02199) *(G-8871)*
Swarovski North America Ltd 203 462-3357
100 Greyrock Pl Stamford CT (06901) *(G-4337)*
Swarovski North America Ltd 401 732-0794
400 Bald Hill Rd Warwick RI (02886) *(G-21433)*
Swarovski North America Ltd 203 372-0336
5065 Main St Trumbull CT (06611) *(G-4634)*
Swarovski North America Ltd (HQ) 401 463-6400
1 Kenney Dr Cranston RI (02920) *(G-20295)*
Swarovski US Holding Limited (HQ) 401 463-6400
1 Kenney Dr Cranston RI (02920) *(G-20296)*
Swarovski US Holding Limited 978 531-4582
210 Andover St Peabody MA (01960) *(G-14374)*
SWC, Hamden *Also called Specialty Wire & Cord Sets (G-1785)*
Swedish News Inc 203 299-0380
268 Fillow St Norwalk CT (06850) *(G-3253)*
Sweeney Manufacturing 603 814-4127
103 Ledge Rd Unit 11 Seabrook NH (03874) *(G-19820)*
Sweeney Metal Fabricators Inc 603 881-8720
15 Progress Ave Nashua NH (03062) *(G-19268)*
Sweeney Ridge 207 482-0499
186 River Rd Edgecomb ME (04556) *(G-6004)*
Sweenors Chocolates Inc (PA) 401 783-4433
21 Charles St Wakefield RI (02879) *(G-21280)*
Sweet Country Roads LLC 860 537-0069
180 Mcdonald Rd Colchester CT (06415) *(G-811)*
Sweet Creations 781 246-0836
23 Water St Ste R Wakefield MA (01880) *(G-15979)*
Sweet Grass Farm, Greenland *Also called Deborah Ludington (G-18223)*
Sweet Leaf Tea Company (HQ) 203 863-0263
900 Long Ridge Rd Bldg 2 Stamford CT (06902) *(G-4338)*
Sweet Metal Finishing Inc 508 226-4359
28 John Williams St Attleboro MA (02703) *(G-7799)*

Sweet Peet North America Inc......860 361-6444
3 West St Ste 3 Litchfield CT (06759) *(G-1953)*
Sweet Tree Holdings 1 LLC......802 723-6753
1 Sweet Tree Ln Island Pond VT (05846) *(G-22042)*
Sweetheart Flute Company LLC......860 749-8514
32 S Maple St Enfield CT (06082) *(G-1387)*
Sweethearts Candy Co LLC......781 485-4500
135 American Legion Hwy Revere MA (02151) *(G-14776)*
Sweethearts Three Inc......781 784-5193
24 Pond St Sharon MA (02067) *(G-15058)*
Swenson Granite Company LLC (HQ)......603 225-4322
369 N State St Concord NH (03301) *(G-17933)*
Swenson Granite Company LLC......802 476-7021
54 Willey St Barre VT (05641) *(G-21641)*
Swg Promotions LLC......401 272-6050
6 Robin St Providence RI (02908) *(G-21130)*
Swh Inc......207 538-6666
186 Drews Mills Rd Linneus ME (04730) *(G-6363)*
Swift Innovations LLC......860 572-8322
800 Flanders Rd Bldg 5 Mystic CT (06355) *(G-2452)*
Swift River Wood Products......603 323-3317
358 White Mountain Hwy Chocorua NH (03817) *(G-17832)*
Swift Textile Metalizing LLC (PA)......860 243-1122
23 Britton Dr Bloomfield CT (06002) *(G-265)*
Swift-Cut Automation Usa Inc......888 572-1160
212 S Meadow Rd Ste 6 Plymouth MA (02360) *(G-14586)*
Swimex Inc......508 646-1600
390 Airport Rd Ste 3 Fall River MA (02720) *(G-10768)*
Swing By Swing Golf Inc......310 922-8023
80 State House Sq # 158 Hartford CT (06123) *(G-1874)*
Swing Center Factory Outlet, Billerica *Also called April Twenty One Corporation* *(G-8213)*
Swing Labels Inc......978 425-0855
81 Fitzgerald Dr Jaffrey NH (03452) *(G-18478)*
Swiss Ace Manufacturing Inc......978 860-3199
36 School St Leominster MA (01453) *(G-12191)*
Swiss Concept Inc......781 894-1281
77 Felton St Waltham MA (02453) *(G-16203)*
Swiss Precision Products Inc (HQ)......508 987-8003
627 Main St North Oxford MA (01537) *(G-13975)*
Swiss Precision Turning Inc......802 257-1935
74 Cotton Mill Hl A108 Brattleboro VT (05301) *(G-21748)*
Swiss Technology New England, Plainville *Also called Gaskin Manufacturing Corp* *(G-14519)*
Swisset Tool Company Inc......603 524-0082
32 Eastgate Park Dr Belmont NH (03220) *(G-17684)*
Swissline Precision LLC......401 333-8888
23 Ashton Pkwy Unit A Cumberland RI (02864) *(G-20343)*
Swissline Precision Mfg Inc......401 333-8888
23 Ashton Park Way Unit A Cumberland RI (02864) *(G-20344)*
Swissline Products Inc......401 333-8888
23 Ashton Park Way Unit A Cumberland RI (02864) *(G-20345)*
Swisstronics, Woburn *Also called Fraen Machining Corporation* *(G-17186)*
Swissturn/Usa Inc......508 987-6211
21 Dana Rd Oxford MA (01540) *(G-14274)*
Switchback Beerworks Inc......802 651-4114
160 Flynn Ave Burlington VT (05401) *(G-21811)*
Switchback Brewing Co, Burlington *Also called Switchback Beerworks Inc* *(G-21811)*
Swivel Machine Works Inc......203 270-6343
11 Monitor Hill Rd Newtown CT (06470) *(G-2940)*
Swizzles of Greenwhich......917 662-0080
207 E Putnam Ave Cos Cob CT (06807) *(G-830)*
Swm......413 772-2564
53 Silvio O Conte Dr Greenfield MA (01301) *(G-11278)*
Swm International......413 774-3772
49 Greenfield St Greenfield MA (01301) *(G-11279)*
Sword-Agencyport, Farmington *Also called Agencyport Software Corp* *(G-1464)*
Swpc Plastics LLC......860 526-3200
12 Bridge St Deep River CT (06417) *(G-1067)*
Swr & Son Logging......603 237-4158
597 Noyes Rd Stewartstown NH (03576) *(G-19864)*
Sx Industries, Stoughton *Also called Timco Corporation* *(G 15626)*
Sx Industries Inc (PA)......781 828-7111
1551 Central St Stoughton MA (02072) *(G-15625)*
Syam Software Inc......603 598-9575
12 Lantern Ln Londonderry NH (03053) *(G-18740)*
Sycast Inc......860 308-2122
148 Bartholomew Ave Hartford CT (06106) *(G-1875)*
Sychron Inc......860 953-8157
683 N Mountain Rd Newington CT (06111) *(G-2905)*
Sydenstricker Galleries Inc (PA)......508 385-3272
490 Main St Brewster MA (02631) *(G-9058)*
Sydenstricker Glass, Brewster *Also called Sydenstricker Galleries Inc* *(G-9058)*
Syferlock Technology Corp......203 292-5441
917 Bridgeport Ave Ste 5 Shelton CT (06484) *(G-3875)*
Sykes Hollow Innovations Ltd......802 549-4671
315 Tennis Way East Dorset VT (05253) *(G-21917)*
Syl Ver Logging Inc......207 398-3158
206 Allagash Rd Allagash ME (04774) *(G-5520)*
Sylvan R Shemitz Designs LLC......203 934-3441
114 Boston Post Rd West Haven CT (06516) *(G-5147)*
Sylvan Software, White River Junction *Also called Richard Akerboom* *(G-22642)*
Sylvester Products Division, Marlborough *Also called Gregory Engineering Corp* *(G-12765)*
Sylvesters Sales, Marlborough *Also called Credit Card Supplies Corp* *(G-12743)*
Sylvia Wyler Pottery Inc (PA)......207 729-1321
150 Maine St Brunswick ME (04011) *(G-5848)*
Syman Machine LLC......860 747-8337
161 Woodford Ave Ste 5b Plainville CT (06062) *(G-3517)*
Symantec, Cambridge *Also called Nortonlifelock Inc* *(G-9584)*
Symantec, Glastonbury *Also called Nortonlifelock Inc* *(G-1568)*
Symbol Mattress of New England......860 779-3112
312 Lake Rd Dayville CT (06241) *(G-1053)*
Symbotic LLC......978 284-2800
200 Research Dr Wilmington MA (01887) *(G-17050)*
Symetrica Inc......508 718-5610
4 Lyberty Way A Westford MA (01886) *(G-16795)*
Symmetry Medical Inc......508 998-1104
61 John Vertente Blvd New Bedford MA (02745) *(G-13453)*
Symmetry Medical Manufacturing, Manchester *Also called Poly-Vac Inc* *(G-18903)*
Symmetry Products, Lincoln *Also called Lance Industries Inc* *(G-20578)*
Symmons Industries Inc (PA)......781 848-2250
31 Brooks Dr Braintree MA (02184) *(G-9041)*
Symmons Industries Inc......781 664-5236
11 Brooks Dr Braintree MA (02184) *(G-9042)*
Symphony Talent LLC......781 275-2716
209 Burlington Rd Bedford MA (01730) *(G-8013)*
Symptllgnce Med Infrmatics LLC......617 755-0576
73 Stone Ridge Rd Franklin MA (02038) *(G-11083)*
Syn-Mar Products Inc......860 872-8505
5 Nutmeg Dr Ellington CT (06029) *(G-1341)*
Synap Inc......888 572-1150
77 Fourth St Dover NH (03820) *(G-18056)*
Synapse Ic Llc......802 881-4028
50 Main St Unit 157 Winooski VT (05404) *(G-22725)*
Synchrgnix Info Strategies Inc......302 892-4800
238 Main St Ste 317 Cambridge MA (02142) *(G-9670)*
Synchro Stars Sst......603 493-4762
17 Mahogany Dr Nashua NH (03062) *(G-19269)*
Synchroneuron Inc......617 538-5688
130 Tobey Garden St Duxbury MA (02332) *(G-10402)*
Syndax Pharmaceuticals Inc (PA)......781 419-1400
35 Gatehouse Dr Fl 3 Waltham MA (02451) *(G-16204)*
Syndax Securities Corporation......781 472-2985
35 Gatehouse Dr Waltham MA (02451) *(G-16205)*
Synectic Engineering Inc......203 877-8488
60 Commerce Park Ste 1 Milford CT (06460) *(G-2374)*
Syner-G Pharma Consulting LLC......508 460-9700
371 Trnpike Rd 2 Pk Cntl Southborough MA (01772) *(G-15368)*
Synergy Solutions LLC......203 762-1153
276 Newtown Tpke Wilton CT (06897) *(G-5306)*
Syneron Candela, Marlborough *Also called Candela Corporation* *(G-12734)*
Synertide Pharmaceuticals Inc......801 671-1329
88 Kingsbury St Wellesley MA (02481) *(G-16389)*
Synlogic Inc (PA)......617 401-9975
301 Binney St Ste 3 Cambridge MA (02142) *(G-9671)*
Synopsys Inc......508 870-6500
1800 W Park Dr Ste 410 Westborough MA (01581) *(G-16652)*
Synostics Inc......781 248-5699
3 Old Coach Rd Weston MA (02493) *(G-16832)*
Synqor Holdings LLC......978 849-0600
155 Swanson Rd Boxborough MA (01719) *(G-8970)*
Synqor Inc (PA)......978 849-0600
155 Swanson Rd Boxborough MA (01719) *(G-8971)*
Syntac Coated Products, New Hartford *Also called Scp Management LLC* *(G-2647)*
Syntech Microwave Inc......603 880-9767
8 Rebel Rd Hudson NH (03051) *(G-18444)*
Syntegratech Incorporated......603 225-4008
33 Tonga Dr Bow NH (03304) *(G-17734)*
Syntel, Framingham *Also called CCL Label Inc* *(G-10932)*
Synthetic Labs Inc......978 957-2919
24 Victory Ln Dracut MA (01826) *(G-10368)*
Synthetic Surfaces Inc......781 593-0860
638 Summer St Lynn MA (01905) *(G-12542)*
Syphers Monument DBA Affordabl......603 468-3033
255 Lafayette Rd Seabrook NH (03874) *(G-19821)*
Syqwest Inc......401 432-7129
30 Kenney Dr Ste 1 Cranston RI (02920) *(G-20297)*
Syratech Acquisition Corp (HQ)......781 539-0100
22 Blake St Medford MA (02155) *(G-12949)*
Syros Pharmaceuticals Inc (PA)......617 744-1340
35 Cambridgepark Dr Fl 4 Cambridge MA (02140) *(G-9672)*
Sysaid Technologies Inc......800 686-7047
128 Chestnut St Newton MA (02465) *(G-13642)*
Sysdyne Technologies LLC......203 327-3649
9 Riverbend Dr S Stamford CT (06907) *(G-4339)*
Systamedic Inc......860 912-6101
1084 Shennecossett Rd Groton CT (06340) *(G-1687)*

System Intgrtion Cnsulting LLC.....203 926-9599
1000 Bridgeport Ave 1-3 Shelton CT (06484) *(G-3876)*
Systematics Inc.....860 721-0706
1275 Cromwell Ave Ste B1 Rocky Hill CT (06067) *(G-3729)*
Systematics Inc.....401 253-0050
26 Burnside St Bristol RI (02809) *(G-20104)*
Systems and Tech Intl Inc.....860 871-0401
24 Goose Ln Ste 5 Tolland CT (06084) *(G-4553)*
Systems Limited, Hingham *Also called Submarine Research Labs (G-11512)*
Syzygy Halthcare Solutions LLC.....203 226-4449
33 Cannon Rd Wilton CT (06897) *(G-5307)*
Szr Fuel LLC.....978 649-2409
46 Anderson Dr Tyngsboro MA (01879) *(G-15901)*
T & J Manufacturing LLP.....860 632-8655
1385 Newfield St Middletown CT (06457) *(G-2226)*
T & J Screw Machine Pdts LLC.....860 417-3801
27 Main St Oakville CT (06779) *(G-3303)*
T & M Enterprises Inc.....802 447-0601
251 Church St Shaftsbury VT (05262) *(G-22406)*
T & T Anodizing Inc.....978 454-9631
35 Maple St Lowell MA (01852) *(G-12435)*
T & T Anodizing Incorporated.....978 454-9631
35 Maple St Ste 8 Lowell MA (01852) *(G-12436)*
T & T Anonizing & Indus Spray, Lowell *Also called T & T Anodizing Inc (G-12435)*
T & T Automation Inc.....860 683-8788
88 Pierson Ln Windsor CT (06095) *(G-5371)*
T & T Machine Products Inc.....781 878-3861
254 Beech St Rockland MA (02370) *(G-14829)*
T B Lincoln Logging Inc.....802 276-3172
64 Bakers Pond Rd Brookfield VT (05036) *(G-21765)*
T C M Trucking & Logging, South Paris *Also called Harold C Moore II (G-7011)*
T D F Metal Finishing Co Inc.....978 223-4292
9 Electronics Ave Danvers MA (01923) *(G-10259)*
T D I Enterprises LLC.....203 630-1268
22 Gypsy Ln Meriden CT (06451) *(G-2136)*
T D L, Canton *Also called Tdl Inc (G-9789)*
T E M, Buxton *Also called Tem Inc (G-5861)*
T G G Inc.....978 777-5010
3 Birch Rd Middleton MA (01949) *(G-13103)*
T G Industries Inc.....203 235-3239
361 S Colony St Ste 1 Meriden CT (06451) *(G-2137)*
T H Grogan & Associates Inc.....978 266-9548
12 Woodchester Dr Acton MA (01720) *(G-7389)*
T H M, Attleboro *Also called Techncal Hrdfcing McHining Inc (G-7801)*
T Henri Inc.....207 244-7787
1 Apple Ln Southwest Harbor ME (04679) *(G-7051)*
T I S Software Corp.....508 528-9027
9 Noon Hill Ave Norfolk MA (02056) *(G-13665)*
T J Bark Mulch Inc.....413 569-2400
25 Sam West Rd Southwick MA (01077) *(G-15418)*
T J Holmes Co Inc.....508 222-1723
301 W Main St Chartley MA (02712) *(G-9858)*
T K Machining, Waterboro *Also called TK Machining Inc (G-7152)*
T K O Printing Inc.....603 332-0511
189 Wakefield St Rochester NH (03867) *(G-19689)*
T Keefe and Sons.....203 457-0267
1790 Little Meadow Rd Guilford CT (06437) *(G-1721)*
T L S Design & Manufacturing.....860 439-1414
100 Blinman St New London CT (06320) *(G-2781)*
T Lex Inc.....617 731-8606
105 Babcock St Brookline MA (02446) *(G-9222)*
T M C, Durham *Also called Technical Manufacturing Corp (G-1094)*
T M F, Wallingford *Also called Technical Metal Finishing Inc (G-4815)*
T M Industries Inc.....860 828-0344
134 Commerce St East Berlin CT (06023) *(G-1109)*
T M Morris Productions Inc.....401 331-7780
11 Peck St Providence RI (02903) *(G-21131)*
T N Dickinson Company.....860 267-2279
31 E High St East Hampton CT (06424) *(G-1166)*
T N T Precision, Hudson *Also called Dennis Thompson (G-18384)*
T O C Finishing Corp.....617 623-3310
22 Clifton St Somerville MA (02144) *(G-15221)*
T O Nam Sausage.....401 941-9620
444 Wellington Ave Cranston RI (02910) *(G-20298)*
T P Engineering, Danbury *Also called TP Cycle & Engineering Inc (G-1000)*
T R & H Inc.....207 743-8981
186 Ashton Rd Norway ME (04268) *(G-6526)*
T R D Specialities, Pine Meadow *Also called Trd Specialties Inc (G-3446)*
T R Sign Design Inc.....207 856-2600
306 Warren Ave Ste 3 Portland ME (04103) *(G-6736)*
T Raymond Forest Products Inc.....207 738-2313
260 Arab Rd Lee ME (04455) *(G-6266)*
T Roy Inc.....207 834-6385
2356 St John Rd St John Plt ME (04743) *(G-7059)*
T S S Inc.....802 244-8101
80 Commercial Dr Ste 5 Waterbury VT (05676) *(G-22586)*
T S X Products Corporation.....781 769-1800
100 Lowder Brook Dr # 2500 Westwood MA (02090) *(G-16878)*
T Shirt Gallery, Burlington *Also called Amalgamated Culture Work Inc (G-21766)*
T Stop, Wakefield *Also called All City Screen Printing Inc (G-15940)*
T Tech Machine Inc.....401 732-3590
11 Knight St Bldg A Warwick RI (02886) *(G-21434)*
T Woodward Stair Building LLC.....860 664-0515
10 Bailey Dr North Branford CT (06471) *(G-2980)*
T&J Manufacturing, Middletown *Also called T & J Manufacturing LLP (G-2226)*
T&R Flagg Log Sons & Daughters.....207 897-5212
68 Lake Rd Livermore ME (04253) *(G-6377)*
T-S Display Systems Inc.....203 964-0575
76 Progress Dr Stamford CT (06902) *(G-4340)*
T-Shirt Station, West Springfield *Also called Imprinted Sportswear Inc (G-16525)*
T-Shirts N Jeans Inc.....781 279-4220
3 Southside Rd 2 Danvers MA (01923) *(G-10260)*
T2 Biosystems Inc (PA).....781 761-4646
101 Hartwell Ave Lexington MA (02421) *(G-12276)*
Ta Instruments-Waters LLC (PA).....781 233-1717
107 Audubon Rd Ste 140 Wakefield MA (01880) *(G-15980)*
Ta Update Inc (PA).....802 479-4040
47 N Main St Ste 200 Barre VT (05641) *(G-21642)*
Table Talk Pies Inc (PA).....508 438-1556
120 Washington St Ste 1 Worcester MA (01610) *(G-17485)*
Tables of Stone (PA).....603 424-7577
759 Daniel Webster Hwy Merrimack NH (03054) *(G-19035)*
Tac Inc (HQ).....978 470-0555
1 High St Andover MA (01810) *(G-7613)*
TAC Life Systems LLC.....617 719-8797
44 Heritage Dr Walpole MA (02081) *(G-16013)*
Tachwa Enterprises Inc.....203 691-5772
4 Industrial Cir Hamden CT (06517) *(G-1787)*
Tack-Tiles Braille Systems LLC.....603 382-1904
97 Forrest St Plaistow NH (03865) *(G-19526)*
Taco Inc (PA).....401 942-8000
1160 Cranston St Cranston RI (02920) *(G-20299)*
Taco Inc.....508 675-7300
583 Bedford St Fall River MA (02720) *(G-10769)*
Taco Comfort Solutions, Cranston *Also called Taco Inc (G-20299)*
Taco Electronic Solutions Inc.....401 942-8000
1160 Cranston St Cranston RI (02920) *(G-20300)*
Taco Fasteners Inc.....860 747-5597
71 Northwest Dr Plainville CT (06062) *(G-3518)*
Taconic Wire, North Branford *Also called S A Candelora Enterprises (G-2975)*
Tafa Incorporated (HQ).....603 224-9585
146 Pembroke Rd Ste 1 Concord NH (03301) *(G-17934)*
Taft Sound.....508 476-2662
3 Carrier Ln Sutton MA (01590) *(G-15693)*
Tafts Milk Maple Farm.....802 434-2727
1470 Taft Rd Huntington VT (05462) *(G-22034)*
Tag Promotions Inc.....800 909-4011
500 Purdy Hill Rd Ste 9 Monroe CT (06468) *(G-2417)*
Tagetik North America LLC.....203 391-7520
9 W Broad St Ste 400 Stamford CT (06902) *(G-4341)*
Taggart Ice Inc.....603 888-4630
8 Taggart Dr Nashua NH (03060) *(G-19270)*
Tagteam.com, Maynard *Also called Longwood Software Inc (G-12900)*
Tahoe Jewelry Inc.....401 435-4114
20 J Medeiros Way East Providence RI (02914) *(G-20445)*
Tailor Vintage, Norwalk *Also called Sam & Ty LLC (G-3236)*
Tak Systems, Wareham *Also called Cataki International Inc (G-16243)*
Takasago Electric Inc.....508 983-1434
1900 W Park Dr Ste 280 Westborough MA (01581) *(G-16653)*
Takasago Fluidic Systems, Westborough *Also called Takasago Electric Inc (G-16653)*
Take 2 Dough Productions Inc.....207 490-6502
79 Emery St Ste B Sanford ME (04073) *(G-6893)*
Take Cake LLC.....203 453-1896
2458 Boston Post Rd Ste 2 Guilford CT (06437) *(G-1722)*
Takeda Building 35 5.....617 444-4352
35 Landsdowne St Cambridge MA (02139) *(G-9673)*
Takeda Pharmaceuticals.....617 441-6930
300 Massachusetts Ave Cambridge MA (02139) *(G-9674)*
Takeda Pharmaceuticals USA Inc.....781 837-1528
38 Deerpath Trl N Duxbury MA (02332) *(G-10403)*
Takeda Pharmaceuticals USA Inc (HQ).....617 349-0200
95 Hayden Ave Lexington MA (02421) *(G-12277)*
Takeda Pharmaceuticals USA Inc.....617 444-1348
40 Landsdowne St Cambridge MA (02139) *(G-9675)*
Takeda Vaccines Inc.....970 672-4918
40 Landsdowne St Cambridge MA (02139) *(G-9676)*
Taklite LLC.....508 298-8331
8 Shire Dr Ste 3 Norfolk MA (02056) *(G-13666)*
Talalay Global, Shelton *Also called Latex Foam Intl Holdings Inc (G-3826)*
Talaria Company LLC.....207 244-5572
130 Shore Rd Southwest Harbor ME (04679) *(G-7052)*
Talaria Company LLC (PA).....401 683-7100
1 Lil Hrbr Landing Prt Portsmouth RI (02871) *(G-20940)*
Talaria Company LLC.....207 667-1891
40 Industrial Way Trenton ME (04605) *(G-7102)*
Talaria Company LLC.....401 683-7280
1 Little Harbor Lndg # 1 Portsmouth RI (02871) *(G-20941)*

Talcott Mountain Engineering 860 651-3141
22 Talcott Mountain Rd Simsbury CT (06070) ***(G-3913)***
Talient Action Group, Manchester *Also called Printers Square Inc* ***(G-18905)***
Talient Action Group 603 703-0795
105 Faltin Dr Manchester NH (03103) ***(G-18935)***
Talin Bookbindery 508 362-8144
947 Route 6a Yarmouth Port MA (02675) ***(G-17532)***
Tall Oak Printing LLC 207 251-4138
1237 Tatnic Rd Wells ME (04090) ***(G-7166)***
Tall Ship Distillery LLC 603 842-0098
32 Crosby Rd Ste 5 Dover NH (03820) ***(G-18057)***
Tallon Lumber Inc 860 824-0733
2 Tallon Dr Canaan CT (06018) ***(G-691)***
Talon Engineering 978 465-5571
65 Parker St Ste 9 Newburyport MA (01950) ***(G-13538)***
Tam Communications Inc 203 425-8777
37 North Ave Ste 208 Norwalk CT (06851) ***(G-3254)***
Tamale Software Inc (HQ) 617 443-1033
201 South St Ste 3 Boston MA (02111) ***(G-8872)***
Tamboo Bistro 508 584-8585
252 Main St Brockton MA (02301) ***(G-9181)***
Tamer Industries Inc 508 677-0900
185 Riverside Ave Somerset MA (02725) ***(G-15149)***
Tamor Plastics, Leominster *Also called Home Pdts Intl - N Amer Inc* ***(G-12152)***
Tandem Kross LLC 603 369-7060
490 S Stark Hwy Weare NH (03281) ***(G-19941)***
Tandemkross, Weare *Also called Tandem Kross LLC* ***(G-19941)***
Tangen Biosciences Inc 203 433-4045
20 Commercial St Branford CT (06405) ***(G-354)***
Tango Modem LLC 203 421-2245
303 Race Hill Rd Madison CT (06443) ***(G-1978)***
Tango Seaport 857 277-1191
200 Seaport Blvd Boston MA (02210) ***(G-8873)***
Tangoe Us Inc 203 859-9300
1 Waterview Dr Ste 200 Shelton CT (06484) ***(G-3877)***
Tangoe Us Inc (HQ) 973 257-0300
1 Waterview Dr Ste 200 Shelton CT (06484) ***(G-3878)***
Tanorama Suntanning Center 603 742-1600
827 Central Ave Dover NH (03820) ***(G-18058)***
Tanscript Newspapers, Sharon *Also called Gatehouse Media Mass I Inc* ***(G-15050)***
Tantar Corp 508 643-1017
865 E Washington St North Attleboro MA (02760) ***(G-13783)***
Tantor Media Incorporated 860 395-1155
6 Business Park Rd Old Saybrook CT (06475) ***(G-3351)***
Tanury Industries Inc 800 428-6213
6 New England Way Lincoln RI (02865) ***(G-20598)***
Tanyx Measurements Inc 978 671-0183
505 Middlesex Tpke Unit 9 Billerica MA (01821) ***(G-8299)***
Tap Lab, The, Cambridge *Also called Work Play Sleep Inc* ***(G-9703)***
Tap Printing Inc 401 247-2188
628 Metacom Ave Unit 6 Warren RI (02885) ***(G-21308)***
Tap Technologies Inc 860 333-7834
23 Sachem Rd Narragansett RI (02882) ***(G-20652)***
Tapecoat Company 781 332-0700
295 University Ave Westwood MA (02090) ***(G-16879)***
Tapestry Inc 413 243-4897
100 Premium Outlets Blvd Lee MA (01238) ***(G-12096)***
Tapestry Inc 617 723-1777
S Market Building Boston MA (02109) ***(G-8874)***
Tapestry Press Ltd 978 486-0200
19 Nashoba Rd Littleton MA (01460) ***(G-12324)***
Tapped Apple Winery 401 637-4946
37 High St Westerly RI (02891) ***(G-21542)***
Taproot 802 472-1617
49 Fox St Portland ME (04101) ***(G-6737)***
Taps, Barrington *Also called Turbocam Atmted Prod Systems I* ***(G-17626)***
Taran Bros Inc (PA) 802 287-5853
Rr 30 Poultney VT (05764) ***(G-22278)***
Taran Bros Inc 802 287-9308
2522 Vermont Route 30 N Poultney VT (05764) ***(G-22279)***
Target Custom Manufacturing Co 860 388-5848
164 Old Boston Post Rd Old Saybrook CT (06475) ***(G-3352)***
Target Flavors Inc 203 775-4727
7 Del Mar Dr Brookfield CT (06804) ***(G-659)***
Target Machine Inc 978 356-7373
36 Mitchell Rd Unit C Ipswich MA (01938) ***(G-11937)***
Target Machines Inc 860 675-1539
713 George Wash Tpke Burlington CT (06013) ***(G-680)***
Target Marketing Assoc Inc 860 571-7294
35 Cold Spring Rd Ste 224 Rocky Hill CT (06067) ***(G-3730)***
Target Marketing Group Inc 508 252-6575
72 Rocky Hill Rd Rehoboth MA (02769) ***(G-14761)***
Target Therapeutics Inc (HQ) 508 683-4000
300 Boston Scientific Way Marlborough MA (01752) ***(G-12834)***
Taris Biomedical LLC 781 676-7750
113 Hartwell Ave Lexington MA (02421) ***(G-12278)***
Tark Inc 978 663-8074
35 Dunham Rd Ste 7 Billerica MA (01821) ***(G-8300)***
Taroli Chris, New Canaan *Also called Eastern Inc* ***(G-2597)***
Tarpon Biosystems Inc 978 979-4222
197 Boston Post Rd W M Marlborough MA (01752) ***(G-12835)***
Tarry Manufacturing, Danbury *Also called Tarry Medical Products Inc* ***(G-998)***
Tarry Medical Products Inc 203 794-1438
22 Shelter Rock Ln Unit 7 Danbury CT (06810) ***(G-998)***
Tarveda Therapeutics Inc 617 923-4100
134 Coolidge Ave Watertown MA (02472) ***(G-16320)***
Tasco Engineering, North Dighton *Also called Taunton Stove Company Inc* ***(G-13937)***
Task Printing Inc 617 332-4414
441 Centre St Newton MA (02458) ***(G-13643)***
Tasman Industries Inc 207 938-4491
9 Main St Hartland ME (04943) ***(G-6179)***
Tata Harper Labratory, Whiting *Also called Tatas Natural Alchemy LLC* ***(G-22646)***
Tata Harper Skincare, Whiting *Also called Tatas Natural Alchemy LLC* ***(G-22645)***
Tatas Natural Alchemy LLC (PA) 802 462-3814
1135 Wooster Rd Whiting VT (05778) ***(G-22645)***
Tatas Natural Alchemy LLC 802 462-3958
1136 Wooster Rd Whiting VT (05778) ***(G-22646)***
Tate Lyle Ingrdnts Amricas LLC 207 532-9523
48 Morningstar Rd Houlton ME (04730) ***(G-6211)***
Tate Lyle Ingrdnts Amricas LLC 508 366-8322
30 Walkup Dr Westborough MA (01581) ***(G-16654)***
Tate Woodworking, Dorset *Also called Tates Building & Woodworking* ***(G-21909)***
Tates Building & Woodworking 802 867-4082
414 Scarlet Dr Dorset VT (05251) ***(G-21909)***
Tattersall Machining Inc 508 529-2300
190 Milford St Upton MA (01568) ***(G-15910)***
Taughton Daily Gazette, Taunton *Also called Gatehouse Media LLC* ***(G-15752)***
Taunton Inc 203 426-8171
63 S Main St Newtown CT (06470) ***(G-2941)***
Taunton Aluminum Foundry Inc 508 822-4141
632 Berkley St Berkley MA (02779) ***(G-8089)***
Taunton MA 774 226-0681
155 Myles Standish Blvd Taunton MA (02780) ***(G-15788)***
Taunton Press, Newtown *Also called Taunton Inc* ***(G-2941)***
Taunton Press Inc 203 426-8171
191 S Main St Newtown CT (06470) ***(G-2942)***
Taunton Stove Company Inc 508 823-0786
490 Somerset Ave Ste 490 # 490 North Dighton MA (02764) ***(G-13937)***
Taunton Venetian Blind Inc 508 822-7548
27 Main St Taunton MA (02780) ***(G-15789)***
Tauten Inc 978 961-3272
100 Cummings Ctr Ste 215f Beverly MA (01915) ***(G-8186)***
Tavisca LLC 203 956-1000
6 High Ridge Park Stamford CT (06905) ***(G-4342)***
Taylor & Fenn Company 860 219-9393
22 Deerfield Rd Windsor CT (06095) ***(G-5372)***
Taylor & Stevens Cabinetry 603 880-2022
1 Industrial Park Dr # 24 Pelham NH (03076) ***(G-19449)***
Taylor Box Company 401 245-5900
293 Child St Warren RI (02885) ***(G-21309)***
Taylor Bryson Inc 207 838-0961
199 New County Rd Saco ME (04072) ***(G-6859)***
Taylor Coml Foodservice Inc 336 245-6400
3 Farm Glen Blvd Ste 301 Farmington CT (06032) ***(G-1515)***
Taylor Communications Inc 508 584-0102
81 Uraco Way Avon MA (02322) ***(G-7898)***
Taylor Communications Inc 401 738-0257
2346 Post Rd Ste 101 Warwick RI (02886) ***(G-21435)***
Taylor Communications Inc 781 843-0250
400 Washington St Braintree MA (02184) ***(G-9043)***
Taylor Communications Inc 860 290-6851
800 Connecticut Blvd East Hartford CT (06108) ***(G-1227)***
Taylor Egg Products Inc 603 742-1050
242 Littleworth Rd Madbury NH (03823) ***(G-18761)***
Taylor Made Cabinets LLC 978 840-0100
139 Central St Leominster MA (01453) ***(G-12192)***
Taylor Rental Center 413 525-2576
200 Shaker Rd East Longmeadow MA (01028) ***(G-10496)***
Taylor Rentl Ctr E Longmeadows, East Longmeadow *Also called Taylor Rental Center* ***(G-10496)***
Taza Chocolate, Somerville *Also called Whitmore Family Entps LLC* ***(G-15232)***
Tbd Brands LLC 603 775-7772
7 Beech Hill Rd Exeter NH (03833) ***(G-18133)***
Tbs Technologies LLC 508 429-3111
68 Briarcliff Ln Holliston MA (01746) ***(G-11608)***
Tc Design Works Inc 978 768-0034
94 Hart St Beverly MA (01915) ***(G-8187)***
Tcc Multi Kargo 203 803-1462
349 Dr Mrtin L King Jr Dr Norwalk CT (06854) ***(G-3255)***
Tcg Green Technologies Inc 860 364-4694
1 Skiff Mountain Rd Sharon CT (06069) ***(G-3770)***
TCI, Seekonk *Also called Telco Communications Inc* ***(G-15041)***
TCI America Inc 508 336-6633
21 Industrial Ct Seekonk MA (02771) ***(G-15039)***
TCI Press Inc 508 336-6633
21 Industrial Ct Seekonk MA (02771) ***(G-15040)***
Tdf Incorporated 207 631-4325
63 Water St Howland ME (04448) ***(G-6214)***

Tdf Metal Finishing Co Inc...978 223-4292
6 Electronics Ave Danvers MA (01923) ***(G-10261)***
Tdi, Torrington *Also called Torrington Distributors Inc* ***(G-4604)***
Tdl Inc...781 828-3366
550 Turnpike St Canton MA (02021) ***(G-9789)***
Tdr Co Inc...508 226-1221
503 Tiffany St Attleboro MA (02703) ***(G-7800)***
Tdy Industries LLC...860 259-6346
33 John St Ste 39 New Britain CT (06051) ***(G-2586)***
Te Connctvity Phenix Optix Inc...401 637-4600
15 Gray Ln Ste 301 Ashaway RI (02804) ***(G-20041)***
Te Connectivity Corporation...860 684-8000
15 Tyco Dr Stafford Springs CT (06076) ***(G-4116)***
Te Connectivity Corporation...781 278-5273
62 Nahatan St Norwood MA (02062) ***(G-14203)***
Te Connectivity Corporation...401 432-8200
76 Commercial Way East Providence RI (02914) ***(G-20446)***
Te Connectivity Corporation...717 592-4299
125 Goddard Memorial Dr Worcester MA (01603) ***(G-17486)***
Tea Forte Inc...978 369-7777
5 Mill Main Pl Ste 05211 Maynard MA (01754) ***(G-12904)***
Teachers Publishing Group, Portsmouth *Also called Stenhouse Publishers* ***(G-19623)***
Team Bes, Plainville *Also called Building Envelope Systems LLC* ***(G-14516)***
Team Destination Inc...203 235-6000
477 S Broad St Ste 14 Meriden CT (06450) ***(G-2138)***
Team Solutions Machining Inc...978 420-2389
17 Gigante Dr Hampstead NH (03841) ***(G-18250)***
Team-At-Work...978 448-8562
20 Whiley Rd Ste 101 Groton MA (01450) ***(G-11295)***
Teameda Inc...603 656-5200
1001 Elm St 305 Manchester NH (03101) ***(G-18936)***
TEC Engineering Corp...508 987-0231
31 Town Forest Rd Oxford MA (01540) ***(G-14275)***
TEC Mark Plating, Norwood *Also called Remtec Incorporated* ***(G-14194)***
Teca-Print USA Corp...781 369-1084
2a Lowell Ave Winchester MA (01890) ***(G-17098)***
Tech Air, Naugatuck *Also called Airgas Usa LLC* ***(G-2459)***
Tech Circuits, Wallingford *Also called Apct-Wallingford Inc* ***(G-4703)***
Tech Fab Inc...413 532-9022
1 W Main St Ste B South Hadley MA (01075) ***(G-15311)***
Tech Nh Inc (PA)...603 424-4404
8 Continental Blvd Merrimack NH (03054) ***(G-19036)***
Tech Ridge Inc...978 256-5741
190 Hunt Rd Chelmsford MA (01824) ***(G-9935)***
Tech, The, Cambridge *Also called Massachusetts Institute Tech* ***(G-9545)***
Tech-Air Incorporated...860 848-1287
152 Route 163 Uncasville CT (06382) ***(G-4649)***
Tech-Etch Inc (PA)...508 747-0300
45 Aldrin Rd Plymouth MA (02360) ***(G-14587)***
Tech-Etch Inc...508 675-5757
100 Riggenbach Rd Fall River MA (02720) ***(G-10770)***
Tech180 Corp...413 203-6123
180 Pleasant St Ste 211 Easthampton MA (01027) ***(G-10581)***
Tech180 System, Easthampton *Also called Tech180 Corp* ***(G-10581)***
Techfilm Services Inc...978 531-3300
103 Foster St Peabody MA (01960) ***(G-14375)***
Techflex Enterprises Inc...413 592-2800
717 Fuller Rd Chicopee MA (01020) ***(G-10063)***
Techlaw Inc...617 918-8612
7 Technology Dr Ste 202 North Chelmsford MA (01863) ***(G-13911)***
Techlok Inc...617 902-0322
125 Ray St Manchester NH (03104) ***(G-18937)***
Techncal Hrdfcing McHining Inc...508 223-2900
35 Extension St Attleboro MA (02703) ***(G-7801)***
Techni-Products Inc...413 525-6321
126 Industrial Dr East Longmeadow MA (01028) ***(G-10497)***
Technic Inc (PA)...401 781-6100
47 Molter St Cranston RI (02910) ***(G-20301)***
Technic Inc...401 781-6100
55 Maryland Ave Pawtucket RI (02860) ***(G-20902)***
Technic Inc...401 769-7000
300 Park East Dr Woonsocket RI (02895) ***(G-21585)***
Technic Inc Equipment Division, Pawtucket *Also called Technic Inc* ***(G-20902)***
Technical Communications Corp (PA)...978 287-5100
100 Domino Dr Concord MA (01742) ***(G-10158)***
Technical Enterprises Inc...781 603-9402
40 Country Club Dr Bridgewater MA (02324) ***(G-9089)***
Technical Industries Inc (PA)...860 489-2160
336 Pinewoods Rd Torrington CT (06790) ***(G-4600)***
Technical Machine Components...603 880-0444
4 Security Dr Hudson NH (03051) ***(G-18445)***
Technical Manufacturing Corp (HQ)...978 532-6330
15 Centennial Dr Peabody MA (01960) ***(G-14376)***
Technical Manufacturing Corp...860 349-1735
645 New Haven Rd Durham CT (06422) ***(G-1094)***
Technical Metal Fabricators...508 473-2223
134 Uxbridge Rd Mendon MA (01756) ***(G-12996)***
Technical Metal Finishing Inc...203 284-7825
29 Capital Dr Wallingford CT (06492) ***(G-4815)***
Technical Publications Inc...781 899-0263
45 Calvary St Waltham MA (02453) ***(G-16206)***
Technical Sales & Svc of Neng...207 946-5506
170 N Daggett Hill Rd Greene ME (04236) ***(G-6151)***
Technical Services Inc...781 389-8342
263 South St E Raynham MA (02767) ***(G-14732)***
Technicoil LLC...603 569-3100
775 Route 16 Ossipee NH (03864) ***(G-19422)***
Technipower Systems Inc (HQ)...203 748-7001
57 Commerce Dr Brookfield CT (06804) ***(G-660)***
Technique Printers Inc...860 669-2516
36 Old Post Rd Clinton CT (06413) ***(G-795)***
Technisonic Research Inc...203 368-3600
328 Commerce Dr Fairfield CT (06825) ***(G-1457)***
Technlogy Dev Cllaborative LLC...781 933-6116
3r Green St Ste B Woburn MA (01801) ***(G-17304)***
Techno Bloc...774 449-8400
70 E Brookfield Rd North Brookfield MA (01535) ***(G-13882)***
Techno Mtal Post Watertown LLC...203 755-6403
88 Meadowbrook Dr Waterbury CT (06706) ***(G-4961)***
Technodic Inc...401 467-6660
245 Carolina Ave Providence RI (02905) ***(G-21132)***
Technologies 'n Typography, Merrimac *Also called Technologies/Typography* ***(G-13006)***
Technologies 2010 Inc...508 482-0164
45 Pond St 2 Milford MA (01757) ***(G-13146)***
Technologies/Typography...978 346-4867
8 Church St Merrimac MA (01860) ***(G-13006)***
Technology Organization Inc...617 623-4488
76 Highland Ave Somerville MA (02143) ***(G-15222)***
Technology Plastics LLC...806 583-1590
75 Napco Dr Terryville CT (06786) ***(G-4493)***
Technology Review Inc...617 475-8000
1 Main St Ste 7 Cambridge MA (02142) ***(G-9677)***
Technolutions Inc...203 404-4835
234 Church St Fl 15 New Haven CT (06510) ***(G-2743)***
Technomad Associates LLC...413 665-6704
37 Harvard St Ste 2 South Deerfield MA (01373) ***(G-15257)***
Technomad Associates LLC (PA)...413 665-6704
5 Tina Dr South Deerfield MA (01373) ***(G-15258)***
Techprecision Corporation (PA)...978 874-0591
1 Bella Dr Westminster MA (01473) ***(G-16815)***
Techprint Inc...978 975-1245
137 Marston St Lawrence MA (01841) ***(G-12077)***
Techtrade Inc...781 724-7878
964 Great Plain Ave Needham MA (02492) ***(G-13313)***
Techtrak LLC...401 397-3983
2435 Nsneck Hl Rd Ste A1b Coventry RI (02816) ***(G-20166)***
Teclens LLC...919 824-5224
9 Riverbend Dr S Ste C Stamford CT (06907) ***(G-4343)***
Tecnau Inc (HQ)...978 608-0356
4 Suburban Park Dr Billerica MA (01821) ***(G-8301)***
Tecogen Inc (PA)...781 622-1120
45 1st Ave Waltham MA (02451) ***(G-16207)***
Tecomet Inc...978 642-2400
301 Ballardvale St Ste 3 Wilmington MA (01887) ***(G-17051)***
Tecomet Inc (PA)...978 642-2400
115 Eames St Wilmington MA (01887) ***(G-17052)***
Tecomet Inc...781 782-6400
170 New Boston St Woburn MA (01801) ***(G-17305)***
Ted Best...617 361-7258
1205 Hyde Park Ave Hyde Park MA (02136) ***(G-11881)***
Ted Ondrick Company LLC (PA)...413 592-2565
58 Industry Rd Chicopee MA (01020) ***(G-10064)***
Teddie Peanut Butter, Everett *Also called Leavitt Corporation* ***(G-10616)***
Teddys Tees Inc...603 226-2762
9 Perley St Concord NH (03301) ***(G-17935)***
Tedor Pharma Inc...401 658-5219
400 Highland Corporate Dr Cumberland RI (02864) ***(G-20346)***
Tee Enterprises...603 447-5662
Rr 16 Conway NH (03818) ***(G-17958)***
Tee-It-Up LLC...203 949-9455
21 N Plains Industrial Rd Wallingford CT (06492) ***(G-4816)***
Teed Off Publishing Inc...561 266-0872
48 Nicholas Ave Greenwich CT (06831) ***(G-1654)***
TEEN INK, Newton *Also called Young Authors Foundation Inc* ***(G-13655)***
Tees & More LLC...860 244-2224
306 Murphy Rd Hartford CT (06114) ***(G-1876)***
Tees Plus...800 782-8337
850 Main St Fl 6 Bridgeport CT (06604) ***(G-499)***
Teesmile Inc...781 325-8587
15 New England Exec Park Burlington MA (01803) ***(G-9343)***
Tego Inc...781 547-5680
460 Totten Pond Rd # 720 Waltham MA (02451) ***(G-16208)***
Tegos Technology Inc...617 571-5077
81 Pemberton St Cambridge MA (02140) ***(G-9678)***
Tegra Medical LLC (HQ)...508 541-4200
9 Forge Pkwy Franklin MA (02038) ***(G-11084)***
Tei, Bridgewater *Also called Technical Enterprises Inc* ***(G-9089)***
Tei Biosciences Inc...617 268-1616
7 Elkins St Boston MA (02127) ***(G-8875)***

Tek Arms Inc 860 748-6289
282 Jagger Ln Hebron CT (06248) *(G-1898)*
Tek Industries Inc 860 870-0001
48 Hockanum Blvd Unit 1 Vernon CT (06066) *(G-4673)*
Tek Scientific Division, Malden *Also called P & K Custom Acrylics Inc (G-12585)*
Tek-Air Systems Inc 203 791-1400
600 Pepper St Monroe CT (06468) *(G-2418)*
Tekcast Industries RI, Warwick *Also called Conley Casting Supply Corp (G-21345)*
Tekkware Inc 603 380-4257
11 Dory Rd Gloucester MA (01930) *(G-11215)*
Tekni-Plex Inc 508 881-2440
150 Homer Ave Ashland MA (01721) *(G-7671)*
Teknicote Inc 401 724-2230
10 New Rd Unit 4 Rumford RI (02916) *(G-21197)*
Teknikor Automtn & Contrls Inc 508 679-9474
595 Airport Rd Fall River MA (02720) *(G-10771)*
Teknor Apex Co, Pawtucket *Also called Teknor Color Company (G-20904)*
Teknor Apex Co 802 524-7704
300 Industrial Park Rd Saint Albans VT (05478) *(G-22381)*
Teknor Apex Company (PA) 401 725-8000
505 Central Ave Pawtucket RI (02861) *(G-20903)*
Teknor Apex Elastomers Inc 978 466-5344
31 Fuller St Leominster MA (01453) *(G-12193)*
Teknor Color Company 401 725-8000
505 Central Ave Pawtucket RI (02861) *(G-20904)*
Teknor Prfmce Elastomers Inc 401 725-8000
505 Central Ave Pawtucket RI (02861) *(G-20905)*
Tekscan Inc 617 464-4500
307 W 1st St Ste 1 Boston MA (02127) *(G-8876)*
Tektron Inc 978 887-0091
424 Boston St Ste B Topsfield MA (01983) *(G-15866)*
Tel -Tuk Enterprises LLC 603 267-1966
4 Dearborn St Belmont NH (03220) *(G-17685)*
Tel Epion Inc 978 436-2300
900 Middlesex Tpke 6-1 Billerica MA (01821) *(G-8302)*
Tel-Tuk Construction, Belmont *Also called Tel -Tuk Enterprises LLC (G-17685)*
Telco Communications Inc 508 336-6633
21 Industrial Ct Seekonk MA (02771) *(G-15041)*
Telco Systems Inc (HQ) 508 339-1516
15 Berkshire Rd Mansfield MA (02048) *(G-12662)*
Telco Systems/Integrol Sytems, Mansfield *Also called Telco Systems Inc (G-12662)*
Tele-Spot Systems, Stamford *Also called T-S Display Systems Inc (G-4340)*
Teleboardusa.com, Putnam *Also called Uniboard Corp (G-3637)*
Telecast Fiber Systems, Worcester *Also called Belden Inc (G-17347)*
Teledyne Benthos, North Falmouth *Also called Teledyne Instruments Inc (G-13955)*
Teledyne Benthos Inc (HQ) 508 563-1000
49 Edgerton Dr North Falmouth MA (02556) *(G-13954)*
Teledyne D.G. O Brien, Hampton *Also called Teledyne Instruments Inc (G-18273)*
Teledyne D.G. O'Brien, Portsmouth *Also called Teledyne Instruments Inc (G-19624)*
Teledyne Dgital Imaging US Inc (HQ) 978 670-2000
700 Technology Park Dr # 2 Billerica MA (01821) *(G-8303)*
Teledyne Instrs Leeman Labs 603 521-3299
110 Lowell Rd Hudson NH (03051) *(G-18446)*
Teledyne Instruments Inc 508 563-1000
49 Edgerton Dr North Falmouth MA (02556) *(G-13955)*
Teledyne Instruments Inc 603 886-8400
110 Lowell Rd Hudson NH (03051) *(G-18447)*
Teledyne Instruments Inc 603 474-5571
162 Corporate Dr Ste 100 Portsmouth NH (03801) *(G-19624)*
Teledyne Instruments Inc 508 563-1000
49 Edgerton Dr North Falmouth MA (02556) *(G-13956)*
Teledyne Instruments Inc 508 548-2077
49 Edgerton Dr North Falmouth MA (02556) *(G-13957)*
Teledyne Instruments Inc 603 474-5571
1 Lafayette Rd Unit 1 # 1 Hampton NH (03842) *(G-18273)*
Teledyne Lecroy Inc 508 748-0103
513 Mill St Marion MA (02738) *(G-12707)*
Teledyne Webb Research, North Falmouth *Also called Teledyne Instruments Inc (G-13957)*
Teleflex, Chelmsford *Also called Arrow Interventional Inc (G-9872)*
Teleflex Incorporated 617 577-2200
1 Kendall Sq 14101 Cambridge MA (02139) *(G-9679)*
Teleflex Incorporated 603 532-7706
50 Plantation Dr Jaffrey NH (03452) *(G-18479)*
Teleflex Incorporated 860 742-8821
1295 Main St Coventry CT (06238) *(G-841)*
Teleflex Medical, Chelmsford *Also called Arrow International Inc (G-9871)*
Teleflex Medical Incorporated 800 474-0178
375 Forbes Blvd Mansfield MA (02048) *(G-12663)*
Telefluent Communications Inc 508 393-0005
104 Otis St Ste 22 Northborough MA (01532) *(G-14050)*
Telefunken Elektro Acoustic, South Windsor *Also called Telefunken USA LLC (G-4016)*
Telefunken USA LLC 860 882-5919
300 Pleasant Valley Rd E South Windsor CT (06074) *(G-4016)*
Telegram & Gazette, Worcester *Also called Hearst Communications Inc (G-17389)*
Telegraph Publishing LLC 802 875-2703
3008 Popple Dungeon Rd Chester VT (05143) *(G-21851)*
Telegraph Publishing Company (HQ) 603 594-6472
110 Main St 1 Nashua NH (03060) *(G-19271)*
Telegraph, The, Nashua *Also called Telegraph Publishing Company (G-19271)*
Telegraph, The, Nashua *Also called Ogden Newspapers NH LLC (G-19222)*
Telemed Systems Inc 978 567-9033
8 Kane Industrial Dr Hudson MA (01749) *(G-11821)*
Telenity Inc 203 445-2000
755 Main St Ste 7 Monroe CT (06468) *(G-2419)*
Telescada, Canton *Also called Advanced Control Systems Corp (G-9711)*
Teletrak Envmtl Systems Inc (PA) 508 949-2430
2 Sutton Rd Webster MA (01570) *(G-16352)*
Teletypesetting Company Inc 617 542-6220
10 Post Office Sq 800s Boston MA (02109) *(G-8877)*
Televeh Inc 857 400-1938
132 Charles St Ste 201 Auburndale MA (02466) *(G-7871)*
Telke Tool & Die Mfg Co 860 828-9955
47 Cambridge Hts Kensington CT (06037) *(G-1921)*
Tell Tool Inc 413 568-1671
35 Turnpike Industrial Rd Westfield MA (01085) *(G-16732)*
Tell Tool Acquisition Inc (HQ) 413 568-1671
35 Turnpike Industrial Rd Westfield MA (01085) *(G-16733)*
Tellus Technology Inc (PA) 646 265-7960
10 Corbin Dr Ste 210 Darien CT (06820) *(G-1033)*
Telome Inc 617 383-7565
1393 Main St Waltham MA (02451) *(G-16209)*
Teltron Engineering Inc 508 543-6600
131 Morse St Ste 9 Foxboro MA (02035) *(G-10906)*
Tem Inc 207 929-8700
8 Pierce Dr Buxton ME (04093) *(G-5861)*
Temco Tool Company Inc 603 622-6989
800 Holt Ave Manchester NH (03109) *(G-18938)*
Temp-Flex LLC 508 839-3120
26 Milford Rd South Grafton MA (01560) *(G-15299)*
Temp-Pro Incorporated 413 584-3165
200 Industrial Dr Northampton MA (01060) *(G-14022)*
Tempron Products Corp 508 473-5880
21 Maple St Milford MA (01757) *(G-13147)*
Tempshield, Trenton *Also called Ad M Holdings LLC (G-7096)*
Temptronic Corporation (HQ) 781 688-2300
41 Hampden Rd Mansfield MA (02048) *(G-12664)*
Temtec, Billerica *Also called Precision Dynamics Corporation (G-8276)*
Ten Bamboo Studio, West Kennebunk *Also called William Arthur Inc (G-7174)*
Ten West Trunk Shows 508 755-7547
10 West St Beverly MA (01915) *(G-8188)*
Tena Group LLC 207 893-2920
2 Plaza Dr Windham ME (04062) *(G-7256)*
Tender Corporation (PA) 603 444-5464
944 Industrial Park Rd Littleton NH (03561) *(G-18667)*
Tennis Loft 508 228-9228
12 Straight Wharf Nantucket MA (02554) *(G-13231)*
Tensor Communications Systems 603 938-5206
159 Day Pond Rd Bradford NH (03221) *(G-17742)*
Tent Connection Inc 508 234-8746
1682 Providence Rd Northbridge MA (01534) *(G-14062)*
Tentsmith, Conway *Also called Peter Marques (G-17957)*
Teradiode Inc 978 988-1040
30 Upton Dr Wilmington MA (01887) *(G-17053)*
Teradyne Inc (PA) 978 370-2700
600 Riverpark Dr North Reading MA (01864) *(G-13990)*
Teradyne Inc 978 370-2700
36 Cabot Rd Woburn MA (01801) *(G-17306)*
Teradyne Inc 617 482-2700
9 Crosby Dr Bedford MA (01730) *(G-8014)*
Teradyne Inc 978 370-2700
500 Riverpark Dr North Reading MA (01864) *(G-13991)*
Terarecon Inc 978 274-0461
42 Nagog Park Ste 202 Acton MA (01720) *(G-7390)*
Terason Ultrasound, Burlington *Also called Teratech Corporation (G-9344)*
Teratech Corporation 781 270-4143
77 Terrace Hall Ave Burlington MA (01803) *(G-9344)*
Tercat Tool and Die Co Inc 401 421-3371
31 Delaine St Providence RI (02909) *(G-21133)*
Terecon Corp (PA) 508 791-1875
55 Carter Rd Worcester MA (01609) *(G-17487)*
Teresa Burgess 207 848-5697
11 Bond Rd Bangor ME (04401) *(G-5659)*
Terex Corporation (PA) 203 222-7170
200 Nyala Farms Rd Ste 2 Westport CT (06880) *(G-5233)*
Terex Environmental Equipment, Newton *Also called Terex Usa LLC (G-19370)*
Terex Usa LLC 603 382-0556
22 Whittier St Newton NH (03858) *(G-19370)*
Terex Usa LLC (HQ) 203 222-7170
200 Nyala Farms Rd Westport CT (06880) *(G-5234)*
Terex Utilities Inc 860 436-3700
61 Arrow Rd Ste 12 Hartford CT (06109) *(G-1877)*
Terra Americana, Southwick *Also called Julie Cecchini (G-15414)*
Terracon Corporation 508 429-9950
1376 W Central St Ste 130 Franklin MA (02038) *(G-11085)*
Terracotta Pasta Co (PA) 603 749-2288
1 Washington St Ste 206 Dover NH (03820) *(G-18059)*

ALPHABETIC

Terrafugia Inc...781 491-0812
23 Rainin Rd Ste 2 Woburn MA (01801) ***(G-17307)***
Terrasonics LLC...978 692-3274
91 Depot St Westford MA (01886) ***(G-16796)***
Terraverdae Bioworks Inc...978 712-0220
100 Cummings Ctr Ste 235c Beverly MA (01915) ***(G-8189)***
Terrence L Hayford...207 357-0142
74 Moses Young Rd Hartford ME (04220) ***(G-6178)***
Terroir Coffee, Acton *Also called George Howell Coffee Co LLC* ***(G-7358)***
Terroir Wines LLC...508 329-1626
134 Flanders Rd Westborough MA (01581) ***(G-16655)***
Tesaro Inc (HQ)...339 970-0900
1000 Winter St Ste 3300 Waltham MA (02451) ***(G-16210)***
Tesaro Securities Corporation...339 970-0900
1000 Winter St Waltham MA (02451) ***(G-16211)***
Tesco Associates Inc...978 649-5527
500 Businema Pk Dr Unit 1 Tyngsboro MA (01879) ***(G-15902)***
Tesco Resources Inc...203 754-3900
170 Freight St Waterbury CT (06702) ***(G-4962)***
Tessier Machine Company, Hudson *Also called Sp Machine Inc* ***(G-11818)***
Tessolar Inc...508 479-9818
10 State St Ste 1b Woburn MA (01801) ***(G-17308)***
Test Evolution Corporation...508 377-5757
102 South St Hopkinton MA (01748) ***(G-11740)***
Test Logic Inc...860 347-8378
17 Kenneth Dooley Dr Middletown CT (06457) ***(G-2227)***
Test Msrment Instrmntation Inc...603 882-8610
1 Chestnut St Ste 40 Nashua NH (03060) ***(G-19272)***
Test Rep Associates Inc...978 692-8000
319 Littleton Rd Ste 104 Westford MA (01886) ***(G-16797)***
Testing Machines Inc...302 613-5600
1658 Gar Hwy Ste 6 Swansea MA (02777) ***(G-15717)***
TET Mfg Co Inc...860 349-1004
2 Old Indian Trl Middlefield CT (06455) ***(G-2166)***
Tet Mfg Co/Machine Shop, Middlefield *Also called TET Mfg Co Inc* ***(G-2166)***
Teta Activewear By Custom...203 879-4420
14 Town Line Rd Ste 1 Wolcott CT (06716) ***(G-5461)***
Teta Actvwear By Cstm Sprtwear, Wolcott *Also called Custom Sportswear Mfg* ***(G-5437)***
Tetco Inc...860 747-1280
4 Northwest Dr Plainville CT (06062) ***(G-3519)***
Tetherx Inc...508 308-7845
41 Darlene Dr Southborough MA (01772) ***(G-15369)***
Tetragenetics Inc...617 500-7471
91 Mystic St Arlington MA (02474) ***(G-7641)***
Tetraphase Pharmaceuticals Inc (PA)...617 715-3600
480 Arsenal Way Ste 2 Watertown MA (02472) ***(G-16321)***
Tetrault & Sons Inc...860 872-9187
75 Tetrault Rd Stafford Springs CT (06076) ***(G-4117)***
Teufelberger Fiber Rope Corp...508 678-8200
848 Airport Rd Fall River MA (02720) ***(G-10772)***
Teva Pharmaceuticals...617 252-6586
700 Technology Sq Cambridge MA (02139) ***(G-9680)***
Tevtech LLC...978 667-4557
100 Billerica Ave North Billerica MA (01862) ***(G-13871)***
Tewksbury Welding Inc...978 851-7401
285 Beech St Tewksbury MA (01876) ***(G-15841)***
Tewksbury Welding Service, Tewksbury *Also called Tewksbury Welding Inc* ***(G-15841)***
Tex Apps 1 LLC...781 375-6975
38 Chauncy St Boston MA (02111) ***(G-8878)***
Tex Elm Inc...860 873-9715
136 Town St East Haddam CT (06423) ***(G-1153)***
Tex Flock Inc...401 765-2340
200 Founders Dr Woonsocket RI (02895) ***(G-21586)***
Tex Tech Industries, Portland *Also called Tex-Tech Industries Inc* ***(G-6738)***
Tex-Tech Industries Inc...207 933-4404
105 N Main St North Monmouth ME (04265) ***(G-6512)***
Tex-Tech Industries Inc (PA)...207 756-8606
1 City Ctr Ste 11 Portland ME (04101) ***(G-6738)***
Texas Dip Molding Coating Inc (PA)...508 533-6101
24 Jayar Rd Medway MA (02053) ***(G-12971)***
Texas Instruments Incorporated...508 236-3800
529 Pleasant St Attleboro MA (02703) ***(G-7802)***
Texas Instruments Incorporated...603 222-8500
50 Phillippe Cote St # 100 Manchester NH (03101) ***(G-18939)***
Texas Instruments Incorporated...603 429-6079
7 Continental Blvd Merrimack NH (03054) ***(G-19037)***
Texcel Inc...401 727-2113
18 Meeting St Cumberland RI (02864) ***(G-20347)***
Texcel Industries Inc...401 727-2113
18 Meeting St Cumberland RI (02864) ***(G-20348)***
Textcafe...508 654-8520
325 Speen St Apt 602 Natick MA (01760) ***(G-13281)***
Textech Inc...802 254-6073
70 Landmark Hill Dr Brattleboro VT (05301) ***(G-21749)***
Texthelp Inc...781 503-0421
600 Unicorn Park Dr Ste 2 Woburn MA (01801) ***(G-17309)***
Textile Buff & Wheel Co Inc...617 241-8100
511 Medford St Ste 1 Boston MA (02129) ***(G-8879)***
Textile Engineering & Mfg, Woonsocket *Also called E A M T Inc* ***(G-21558)***
Textile Waste Supply LLC...617 241-8100
511 Medford St Boston MA (02129) ***(G-8880)***
Textiles Coated Incorporated...603 296-2221
200 Bouchard St Manchester NH (03103) ***(G-18940)***
Textiles Coated Incorporated (PA)...603 296-2221
6 George Ave Londonderry NH (03053) ***(G-18741)***
Textiles Coated International, Londonderry *Also called Textiles Coated Incorporated* ***(G-18741)***
Textnology Corp...603 465-8398
15 Trafalgar Sq Ste 203 Nashua NH (03063) ***(G-19273)***
Textron Aviation Inc...203 262-9366
288 Christian St Oxford CT (06478) ***(G-3427)***
Textron Defense Systems, Wilmington *Also called Textron Systems Corporation* ***(G-17054)***
Textron Inc (PA)...401 421-2800
40 Westminster St Providence RI (02903) ***(G-21134)***
Textron Lycoming Corp (HQ)...401 421-2800
40 Westminster St Providence RI (02903) ***(G-21135)***
Textron Systems Corporation (HQ)...978 657-5111
201 Lowell St Wilmington MA (01887) ***(G-17054)***
TFC Enterprises LLC...866 996-2701
4 Beeton Path Westborough MA (01581) ***(G-16656)***
Tfi Technologies, Greenfield *Also called Thin Film Imaging Technologies* ***(G-11280)***
Tfx Medical Incorporated...603 532-7706
50 Plantation Dr Jaffrey NH (03452) ***(G-18480)***
Tgs Cables...203 668-6568
290 Pratt St Meriden CT (06450) ***(G-2139)***
TH Glennon Co Inc...978 465-7222
25 Fanaras Dr Salisbury MA (01952) ***(G-14957)***
Th Logging...603 787-6235
2000 Briar Hill Rd North Haverhill NH (03774) ***(G-19390)***
Thadieo LLC...860 621-4500
405 Queen St Ste M Southington CT (06489) ***(G-4084)***
Thai Noodle Bar...617 689-8847
501 Washington St Quincy MA (02169) ***(G-14661)***
Thames Glass Inc...401 846-0576
139 Old Beach Rd Newport RI (02840) ***(G-20686)***
Thames Shipyard & Repair Co...860 442-5349
50 Farnsworth St New London CT (06320) ***(G-2782)***
That Corporation (PA)...508 478-9200
45 Sumner St Milford MA (01757) ***(G-13148)***
Thavenet Machine Company Inc...860 599-4495
12 Chase St Ste 14 Pawcatuck CT (06379) ***(G-3442)***
Thayer Industries Inc...401 789-8825
100 Brook Farm Rd N Wakefield RI (02879) ***(G-21281)***
Thayer Machine Shop...603 646-3261
8000 Cummings Hall Hanover NH (03755) ***(G-18299)***
Thayer Wood Products Inc...401 789-8825
100 Brook Farm Rd N Narragansett RI (02879) ***(G-20653)***
Thayermahan Inc...860 785-9994
120b Leonard Dr Groton CT (06340) ***(G-1688)***
Thayers Natural Remedies, Easton *Also called Henry Thayer Company* ***(G-1319)***
The Bee Publishing Company (PA)...203 426-8036
5 Church Hill Rd Newtown CT (06470) ***(G-2943)***
The Bee Publishing Company...203 426-0178
17 Commerce Rd Newtown CT (06470) ***(G-2944)***
The Cape Cod Sandal, South Yarmouth *Also called Surtan Manufacturing Co* ***(G-15334)***
The Childsplay, East Longmeadow *Also called Reminder Publications* ***(G-10491)***
The Connecticut Law Tribune, Hartford *Also called Alm Media LLC* ***(G-1805)***
The Cricket System Inc...617 905-1420
5 Perkins Way Ste 2 Newburyport MA (01950) ***(G-13539)***
The Daily Times & Chronicle, Reading *Also called Daily Woburn Times Inc* ***(G-14733)***
The E J Davis Company...203 239-5391
10 Dodge Ave North Haven CT (06473) ***(G-3063)***
THE FRY COMPANY J. M., Canton *Also called Fry Company J M* ***(G-9734)***
The Great N Woods Assoc/ Blind...603 490-9877
23 Gould St Colebrook NH (03576) ***(G-17876)***
the Installation Station, Rutland *Also called Wireless For Less* ***(G-22361)***
The Keeney Manufacturing Co (PA)...603 239-6371
1170 Main St Newington CT (06111) ***(G-2906)***
The Keeney Manufacturing Co...603 239-6371
75 Plumb Pak Dr Winchester NH (03470) ***(G-19996)***
The L C Doane Company (PA)...860 767-8295
110 Pond Meadow Rd Ivoryton CT (06442) ***(G-1909)***
The L Suzio Concrete Co Inc (PA)...203 237-8421
975 Westfield Rd Meriden CT (06450) ***(G-2140)***
The Lane Press Inc...802 863-5555
87 Meadowland Dr South Burlington VT (05403) ***(G-22471)***
The Merrill Anderson Co Inc...203 377-4996
1166 Barnum Ave Stratford CT (06614) ***(G-4453)***
The Orion Society Inc...413 528-4422
187 Main St Ste 1 Great Barrington MA (01230) ***(G-11248)***
The Quick Print Color Center, Saco *Also called Quick Print Color Center* ***(G-6856)***
The Real Estate Book, Guilford *Also called Donnin Publishing Inc* ***(G-1702)***
The Recorder, Greenfield *Also called Newspapers of Massachusetts* ***(G-11270)***
The Ruggles-Klingemann Company, Beverly *Also called Ruggles-Klingemann Mfg Co* ***(G-8173)***
The Rumford Falls Times, Norway *Also called James Newspapers Inc* ***(G-6523)***

The Smith Worthington Sad Co 860 527-9117
275 Homestead Ave Hartford CT (06112) *(G-1878)*
The Sonus Company, Auburn *Also called Yankee Craftsman Inc (G-17614)*
The Stone Depot, Chester *Also called Semya Corp (G-21849)*
Theam, Brunswick *Also called Westcon Mfg Inc (G-5851)*
Theatre Stricken Apparel LLC 978 325-2335
246 Theresa Rd Bellingham MA (02019) *(G-8060)*
Thebeamer LLC 860 212-5071
87 Church St East Hartford CT (06108) *(G-1228)*
Theis Precision Steel USA Inc (HQ) 860 589-5511
300 Broad St Bristol CT (06010) *(G-616)*
Thelemic Printshop 860 383-4014
13 West Pkwy Plainfield CT (06374) *(G-3458)*
Theme Merchandise Inc 508 226-4717
53 County St Attleboro MA (02703) *(G-7803)*
Then & Now Publishing 781 378-2013
421 1st St Paris Rd Scituate MA (02066) *(G-15016)*
Theodore Wolf Inc 508 457-0667
494 Thomas B Landers Rd East Falmouth MA (02536) *(G-10450)*
Theodores 508 409-1421
4 County St Taunton MA (02780) *(G-15790)*
Theological Threads Inc 978 927-7031
48 Park St Beverly MA (01915) *(G-8190)*
Theracycle, Franklin *Also called Xthera Corporation (G-11100)*
Theragenics Corporation 978 528-4307
19 Sterling Rd Ste 4 North Billerica MA (01862) *(G-13872)*
Therapedic of New England LLC 508 559-9944
135 Spark St Brockton MA (02302) *(G-9182)*
Therapeutic Innovations Inc 347 754-0252
13 Dexter St Unit 7 North Attleboro MA (02760) *(G-13784)*
Therastat LLC 781 373-1865
44 Kings Grant Rd Weston MA (02493) *(G-16833)*
Therese Rose Manufacturing 508 586-5812
59 Pleasant St 69 Brockton MA (02301) *(G-9183)*
Theriault Jr Peter Inc 207 446-9441
264 Calais Rd Danforth ME (04424) *(G-5943)*
Therma-Flow Inc 617 924-3877
191 Arlington St Watertown MA (02472) *(G-16322)*
Therma-Scan Inc 860 872-9770
43 Claire Rd Vernon Rockville CT (06066) *(G-4684)*
Thermacell Corporation 816 510-9428
26 Crosby Dr Bedford MA (01730) *(G-8015)*
Thermacell Repellents Inc 781 541-6900
26 Crosby Dr Bedford MA (01730) *(G-8016)*
Thermacut Inc 603 543-0585
153 Charlestown Rd Claremont NH (03743) *(G-17861)*
Thermadyne, West Lebanon *Also called Thermal Dynamics Corporation (G-19963)*
Thermaglo, Uncasville *Also called Northeast Wood Products LLC (G-4647)*
Thermal Arc Inc 800 462-2782
82 Benning St West Lebanon NH (03784) *(G-19962)*
Thermal Circuits Inc 978 745-1162
1 Technology Way Salem MA (01970) *(G-14945)*
Thermal Dynamics Corporation (HQ) 603 298-5711
82 Benning St West Lebanon NH (03784) *(G-19963)*
Thermal Dynamix Inc 413 562-1266
15 E Silver St Westfield MA (01085) *(G-16734)*
Thermal Fab Inc 207 926-5212
405 Tobey Rd New Gloucester ME (04260) *(G-6473)*
Thermal Fluids Inc 508 238-9660
93 Kevins Way South Easton MA (02375) *(G-15293)*
Thermal Printing Solutions 978 562-1329
80 Priest St Hudson MA (01749) *(G-11822)*
Thermal Seal Insulating GL Inc 508 278-4243
47 Industrial Dr Uxbridge MA (01569) *(G-15931)*
Thermal Solutions, Hampton *Also called Tsi Group Inc (G-18275)*
Thermal Technic Inc 978 270-5674
13a Tremont St Newburyport MA (01950) *(G-13540)*
Thermalogic Corporation 800 343-4492
22 Kane Industrial Dr Hudson MA (01749) *(G-11823)*
Thermatool Corp (HQ) 203 468-4100
31 Commerce St East Haven CT (06512) *(G-1264)*
Thermatron Engineering Inc 978 687-8844
687 Lowell St Methuen MA (01844) *(G-13046)*
Thermaxx LLC (PA) 203 672-1021
14 Farwell St West Haven CT (06516) *(G-5148)*
Thermedetec Inc 508 520-0430
21 Hickory Dr 4 Waltham MA (02451) *(G-16212)*
Thermo Conductor Services Inc 203 758-6611
3 Industrial Rd Prospect CT (06712) *(G-3598)*
Thermo Craft Engineering Corp 781 599-4023
701 Western Ave Lynn MA (01905) *(G-12543)*
Thermo Detection, Waltham *Also called Thermedetec Inc (G-16212)*
Thermo Electron, Franklin *Also called Thermo Process Instruments LP (G-11089)*
Thermo Electron Karlsruhe GMBH 978 513-3724
2 Radcliff Rd Tewksbury MA (01876) *(G-15842)*
Thermo Envmtl Instrs LLC (HQ) 508 520-0430
27 Forge Pkwy Franklin MA (02038) *(G-11086)*
Thermo Fisher Scientific, Newington *Also called Owl Separation Systems LLC (G-19323)*
Thermo Fisher Scientific Inc (PA) 781 622-1000
168 3rd Ave Waltham MA (02451) *(G-16213)*
Thermo Fisher Scientific Inc 603 433-7676
23 Hampton St Portsmouth NH (03801) *(G-19625)*
Thermo Fisher Scientific Inc 413 577-2600
710 N Pleasant St Amherst MA (01003) *(G-7527)*
Thermo Fisher Scientific Inc 401 294-1234
1130 Ten Rod Rd North Kingstown RI (02852) *(G-20745)*
Thermo Fisher Scientific Inc 978 735-3091
1455 Concord St Framingham MA (01701) *(G-11007)*
Thermo Fisher Scientific Inc 978 250-7000
22 Alpha Rd Chelmsford MA (01824) *(G-9936)*
Thermo Fisher Scientific Inc 781 622-1000
2 Radcliff Rd Tewksbury MA (01876) *(G-15843)*
Thermo Fisher Scientific Inc 781 280-5600
35 Wiggins Ave Bedford MA (01730) *(G-8017)*
Thermo Fisher Scientific Inc 603 595-0505
22 Friars Dr Hudson NH (03051) *(G-18448)*
Thermo Fisher Scientific Inc 603 431-8410
6 Post Rd Portsmouth NH (03801) *(G-19626)*
Thermo Fisher Scientific Inc 978 275-0800
200 Research Dr Ste 3 Wilmington MA (01887) *(G-17055)*
Thermo Fisher Scientific Inc 978 667-4016
9 Andover Rd Billerica MA (01821) *(G-8304)*
Thermo Fisher Scientific Inc 508 520-0430
27 Forge Pkwy Franklin MA (02038) *(G-11087)*
Thermo Fisher Scientific Inc 978 223-1540
99 Rosewood Dr Ste 220 Danvers MA (01923) *(G-10262)*
Thermo Instrument Systems Inc 781 622-1000
81 Wyman St Waltham MA (02451) *(G-16214)*
Thermo Keytek, Wilmington *Also called Thermo Fisher Scientific Inc (G-17055)*
Thermo Keytek LLC 978 275-0800
2 Radcliff Rd Tewksbury MA (01876) *(G-15844)*
Thermo Neslab LLC 603 436-9444
25 Nimble Hill Rd Newington NH (03801) *(G-19328)*
Thermo Optek Corporation 508 553-5100
27 Forge Pkwy Franklin MA (02038) *(G-11088)*
Thermo Orion Inc (HQ) 800 225-1480
22 Alpha Rd Chelmsford MA (01824) *(G-9937)*
Thermo Process Instruments LP 508 553-6913
27 Forge Pkwy Franklin MA (02038) *(G-11089)*
Thermo Products 413 279-1980
2341 Boston Rd Ste A120b Wilbraham MA (01095) *(G-16943)*
Thermo Scientific Portable Ana 978 670-7460
900 Middlesex Tpke 8-1 Billerica MA (01821) *(G-8305)*
Thermo Scntfic Prtble Anlytcal (HQ) 978 657-5555
2 Radcliff Rd Tewksbury MA (01876) *(G-15845)*
Thermo Vision Corp (HQ) 508 520-0083
8 Forge Pkwy Ste 4 Franklin MA (02038) *(G-11090)*
Thermo Wave Technologies LLC 800 733-9615
12 Garden St Danvers MA (01923) *(G-10263)*
Thermo-Fab Corporation 978 425-2311
76 Walker Rd Shirley MA (01464) *(G-15094)*
Thermoceramix Inc 978 425-0404
241 A St Ste 300 Boston MA (02210) *(G-8881)*
Thermocermet 978 425-0404
4 Lomar Park Pepperell MA (01463) *(G-14446)*
Thermoformed Plastics Neng LLC 207 286-1775
362 Hill St Biddeford ME (04005) *(G-5766)*
Thermokinetics 978 459-6073
25 Tobey Rd U55 Dracut MA (01826) *(G-10369)*
Thermonics Inc 408 542-5900
41 Hampden Rd Mansfield MA (02048) *(G-12665)*
Thermoplastics Co Inc 508 754-4668
24 Woodward St Worcester MA (01610) *(G-17488)*
Thermopol Inc 603 692-6300
13 Interstate Dr Somersworth NH (03878) *(G-19850)*
Thermospas Hot Tub Products 203 303-0005
10 Research Pkwy Ste 300 Wallingford CT (06492) *(G-4817)*
Thh Associates LLC 603 536-3600
800 Eastside Rd North Woodstock NH (03262) *(G-19399)*
Thibault Fuel Oil 413 782-9577
215 Albany St Springfield MA (01105) *(G-15512)*
Thibco Inc 603 623-3011
41 Alpheus St Manchester NH (03103) *(G-18941)*
Thibodeau Logging & Excav LLC 603 953-5983
6 Partridge Dr Wolfeboro NH (03894) *(G-20026)*
Thin Film Division, Attleboro *Also called Mini-Systems Inc (G-7768)*
Thin Film Imaging Technologies 413 774-6692
11 Blanker Ln Greenfield MA (01301) *(G-11280)*
Thin Line Defense LLC 774 696-5285
28 Town Forest Rd Webster MA (01570) *(G-16353)*
Think Ahead Software LLC (PA) 860 463-9786
30 Wardwell Rd West Hartford CT (06107) *(G-5098)*
Thinkflood Inc 617 299-2000
295 Reservoir St Needham MA (02494) *(G-13314)*
Thinklite LLC 617 500-6689
117 W Central St Ste 201 Natick MA (01760) *(G-13282)*
Thinkmd Inc 802 734-7993
210 Colchester Ave Burlington VT (05405) *(G-21812)*

ALPHABETIC

Third Wave Technologies Inc (HQ) 608 273-8933
250 Campus Dr Marlborough MA (01752) *(G-12836)*
This Old House Ventures LLC 475 209-8665
2 Harbor Dr Stamford CT (06902) *(G-4344)*
Thl-Nortek Investors LLC (PA) 617 227-1050
100 Federal St Ste 3100 Boston MA (02110) *(G-8882)*
Thomas & Thomas Rodmakers 413 475-3840
627 Barton Rd Ste 1 Greenfield MA (01301) *(G-11281)*
Thomas B Fullen 978 534-5255
225 Viscoloid Ave Ste 1 Leominster MA (01453) *(G-12194)*
Thomas Barn Equipment, Brooks *Also called Dale A Thomas and Sons Inc (G-5823)*
Thomas Bernhard Building Sys 203 925-0414
281 Pequot Ave Southport CT (06890) *(G-4102)*
THOMAS CONWAY, DBA NORTH BRIDGE WOODWORKING, Pepperell *Also called North Bridge Woodworking (G-14443)*
Thomas Design Group LLC 203 588-1910
360 Fairfield Ave Stamford CT (06902) *(G-4345)*
Thomas Drake 802 655-0990
46 Troy Ave Colchester VT (05446) *(G-21881)*
Thomas Engineering 401 822-1235
9 Morin Ave Coventry RI (02816) *(G-20167)*
Thomas Enterprises Inc 207 342-5001
72 Lime Kiln Rd Searsmont ME (04973) *(G-6946)*
Thomas H Conner 603 778-0322
120 Exeter Rd Newfields NH (03856) *(G-19320)*
Thomas Higgins 978 930-0573
66 Shawsheen Rd Billerica MA (01821) *(G-8306)*
Thomas Hooker Brewing Co LLC 860 242-3111
16 Tobey Rd Rear Bloomfield CT (06002) *(G-266)*
Thomas Instruments Inc 603 363-4500
1453 Route 9 Spofford NH (03462) *(G-19858)*
Thomas J Doane 978 821-2361
59 Ward Rd Orange MA (01364) *(G-14229)*
Thomas J Lipton, Trumbull *Also called Conopco Inc (G-4620)*
Thomas J Lipton Inc 206 381-3500
75 Merritt Blvd Trumbull CT (06611) *(G-4635)*
Thomas Jewelry Design Inc 603 372-6102
11 Cross St Newport NH (03773) *(G-19363)*
Thomas La Ganga 860 489-0920
612 S Main St Torrington CT (06790) *(G-4601)*
Thomas Machine Works Inc 978 462-7182
9 New Pasture Rd Newburyport MA (01950) *(G-13541)*
Thomas Michaels Designers Inc 207 236-2708
11 Elm St Camden ME (04843) *(G-5870)*
Thomas Michaels USA, Camden *Also called Thomas Michaels Designers Inc (G-5870)*
Thomas Products Ltd 860 621-9101
987 West St Southington CT (06489) *(G-4085)*
Thomas S Klise Co 860 536-4200
42 Denison Ave Mystic CT (06355) *(G-2453)*
Thomas Spring Co of Connenicut 203 874-7030
29 Seemans Ln Milford CT (06460) *(G-2375)*
Thomas W Raftery Inc 860 278-9870
1055 Broad St Hartford CT (06106) *(G-1879)*
Thomastn-Mdtown Screw Mch Pdts 860 283-9796
550 N Main St Thomaston CT (06787) *(G-4520)*
Thomaston Express, The Div, Torrington *Also called Bristol Press (G-4568)*
Thomaston Industries Inc 860 283-4358
41 Electric Ave Thomaston CT (06787) *(G-4521)*
Thomaston Swiss, Thomaston *Also called Tyler Automatics Incorporated (G-4523)*
Thommen, Harry Co, Bridgeport *Also called Harry Thommen Company (G-424)*
Thompson & Anderson Inc 207 854-2905
53 Seavey St Westbrook ME (04092) *(G-7210)*
Thompson Aerospace LLC 860 516-0472
220 Business Park Dr Bristol CT (06010) *(G-617)*
Thompson Brands LLC 203 235-2541
80 S Vine St Meriden CT (06451) *(G-2141)*
Thompson Candy Company 203 235-2541
80 S Vine St Meriden CT (06451) *(G-2142)*
Thompson Family Enterprises 802 456-7421
2280 E Hill Rd Woodbury VT (05681) *(G-22734)*
Thompson Lumber, Hopkinton *Also called James Thompson Native Lumber (G-20487)*
Thompson Press, Franklin *Also called Thomson National Press Company (G-11091)*
Thompson Printing, Brewer *Also called L H Thompson Inc (G-5797)*
Thompson Printing Inc 802 362-1140
4995 Main St Manchester Center VT (05255) *(G-22091)*
Thompson SCI, Derry *Also called Neuraxis LLC (G-17991)*
Thompson Timber Harvesting 207 227-6290
46 Cross Rd Washburn ME (04786) *(G-7147)*
Thompson Trucking Inc 207 794-6101
725 Enfield Rd Lincoln ME (04457) *(G-6360)*
Thompson/Center Arms Co Inc 603 332-2394
400 N Main St Rochester NH (03867) *(G-19690)*
Thompson/Center Arms Co Inc (HQ) 800 331-0852
2100 Roosevelt Ave Springfield MA (01104) *(G-15513)*
Thompsons Printing Inc 508 255-0099
51 Finlay Rd Orleans MA (02653) *(G-14242)*
Thomson National Press Company (PA) 508 528-2000
842 Union St Ste 1 Franklin MA (02038) *(G-11091)*
Thomson Reuters Corporation 203 466-5055
250 Dodge Ave East Haven CT (06512) *(G-1265)*
Thomson Reuters US LLC (HQ) 203 539-8000
1 Station Pl Ste 6 Stamford CT (06902) *(G-4346)*
Thomson Timber Harvstg & Trckg, Orford *Also called Stacey Thomson (G-19421)*
Thoratec Corporation 781 272-0139
168 Middlesex Tpke Burlington MA (01803) *(G-9345)*
Thoratec Corporation 781 272-0139
23 4th Ave Ste 2 Burlington MA (01803) *(G-9346)*
Thorn Industries Inc 413 737-2464
732 Cottage St Springfield MA (01104) *(G-15514)*
Thorndike Corporation 508 378-9797
680 N Bedford St Ste 1 East Bridgewater MA (02333) *(G-10421)*
Thorndike Mills, Palmer *Also called TMI Industries Inc (G-14297)*
Thorne Diagnostics Inc 978 299-1727
100 Cummings Ctr Ste 465e Beverly MA (01915) *(G-8191)*
Thornton and Company Inc 860 628-6771
132 Main St Ste 2a 3 Southington CT (06489) *(G-4086)*
Thos Moser Cabinetmakers Inc (PA) 207 753-9834
72 Wrights Lndg Auburn ME (04210) *(G-5599)*
Thos Moser Cabinetmakers Inc 207 865-4519
149 Main St Freeport ME (04032) *(G-6087)*
Thos Moser Cabinetmakers Inc 617 224-1245
19 Arlington St Ste 1 Boston MA (02116) *(G-8883)*
Thought Industries Inc 617 669-7725
3 Post Office Sq Ste 400 Boston MA (02109) *(G-8884)*
Thought One LLC 408 623-3278
194 Gray St North Andover MA (01845) *(G-13730)*
Thread Rolling Inc 860 528-1515
41 Cedar St East Hartford CT (06108) *(G-1229)*
Threadhead Inc 508 778-6516
38 Plant Rd Hyannis MA (02601) *(G-11859)*
Threads of Evidence LLC 203 929-5209
52 Oronoque Trl Shelton CT (06484) *(G-3879)*
Three Fays Power LLC 413 427-2665
189 River Rd Ware MA (01082) *(G-16238)*
Three Finger Seabrook Firewrks, Seabrook *Also called Americ An Novelty Inc (G-19792)*
Three Jakes 781 706-6886
116 Long Pond Rd Plymouth MA (02360) *(G-14588)*
Three Jakes Screenprinting, Plymouth *Also called Three Jakes (G-14588)*
Three Kings Products LLC 860 945-5294
1021 Echo Lake Rd Watertown CT (06795) *(G-5028)*
Three Night Delivery Inc 603 595-6230
4 Industrial Park Dr # 30 Pelham NH (03076) *(G-19450)*
Three Ring Binders 617 354-4084
11 Miller St Ste 205a Somerville MA (02143) *(G-15223)*
Three Sons Provision, Barrington *Also called Whitestone Provision Sup Corp (G-20057)*
Three Suns Ltd 860 233-7658
157 Robin Rd Hartford CT (06119) *(G-1880)*
Three Twins Productions Inc 617 926-0377
18 Bridge St Watertown MA (02472) *(G-16323)*
Threshold, Unionville *Also called Data Management Incorporated (G-4655)*
Thriftco Printing, Peabody *Also called Thriftco Speedi-Print Center (G-14377)*
Thriftco Speedi-Print Center 978 531-5546
56 Pulaski St Unit 7 Peabody MA (01960) *(G-14377)*
Thrislington Cubicles, Boston *Also called European Cubicles LLC (G-8529)*
Thrive Bioscience Inc 978 720-8048
11 Audubon Rd Wakefield MA (01880) *(G-15981)*
Thrombolytic Science LLC 617 661-1107
763d Concord Ave Cambridge MA (02138) *(G-9681)*
Thrombolytic Science Intl, Cambridge *Also called Thrombolytic Science LLC (G-9681)*
Thryv Inc 972 453-7000
201 Jones Rd Ste 1 Waltham MA (02451) *(G-16215)*
Tht Inc 203 226-6408
33 Riverside Ave Ste 506 Westport CT (06880) *(G-5235)*
Thule Inc (HQ) 203 881-9600
42 Silvermine Rd Seymour CT (06483) *(G-3765)*
Thule Holding Inc (HQ) 203 881-9600
42 Silvermine Rd Seymour CT (06483) *(G-3766)*
Thunderbolt Innovation LLC 888 335-6234
53 Washington St Ste 300 Dover NH (03820) *(G-18060)*
Thurston Sails Inc 401 254-0970
112 Tupelo St Bristol RI (02809) *(G-20105)*
Tiara Enterprises Inc 401 521-2988
299 Carpenter St Unit 209 Providence RI (02909) *(G-21136)*
Tibbetts Logging and Trucking, Livermore *Also called Darrel L Tibbetts (G-6374)*
Tibby's Electric Motor Service, Bethel *Also called Cudzilo Enterprises Inc (G-139)*
Tibbys Electric Motor Service 203 748-4694
40 Taylor Ave Bethel CT (06801) *(G-183)*
Tibco Software Inc 617 859-6800
281 Summer St Fl 3 Boston MA (02210) *(G-8885)*
Tick Box Technology Corp 203 852-7171
15 Chapel St Norwalk CT (06850) *(G-3256)*
Ticked Off Inc 603 742-0925
97 Spruce Ln Dover NH (03820) *(G-18061)*
Tide Mill Enterprises 207 733-4425
40 Tide Mill Rd Edmunds Twp ME (04628) *(G-6006)*
Tidestone Solutions 207 761-2133
30 Milk St Ste 3 Portland ME (04101) *(G-6739)*

Tidland Corporation 603 352-1696
11 Bradco St Keene NH (03431) ***(G-18533)***
Tien Vo Corp 781 340-7245
311 North St Weymouth MA (02191) ***(G-16902)***
Tier 7 Communications 978 425-9543
41 Holden Rd Shirley MA (01464) ***(G-15095)***
Tier One LLC 203 426-3030
31 Pecks Ln Ste 1 Newtown CT (06470) ***(G-2945)***
Tiffany Printing Company 401 828-5514
952 Tiogue Ave Coventry RI (02816) ***(G-20168)***
Tiger Enterprises Inc 860 621-9155
379 Summer St Plantsville CT (06479) ***(G-3542)***
Tiger-Sul Products LLC 251 202-3850
4 Armstrong Rd Ste 220 Shelton CT (06484) ***(G-3880)***
Tighitco Inc 860 828-0298
245 Old Brickyard Ln Berlin CT (06037) ***(G-112)***
Tilbury House Publishers 800 582-1899
12 Star St Thomaston ME (04861) ***(G-7089)***
Tilcon Arthur Whitcomb Inc (HQ) 603 352-0101
28 Old Homestead Hwy North Swanzey NH (03431) ***(G-19393)***
Tilcon Bituminous Concrete, Portland *Also called Tilcon Connecticut Inc* ***(G-3577)***
Tilcon Connecticut Inc 860 342-6157
231 Airline Ave Portland CT (06480) ***(G-3577)***
Tilcon Connecticut Inc 860 756-8016
301 Harford Ave Unit 301 Newington CT (06111) ***(G-2907)***
Tilcon Connecticut Inc 860 342-1096
Black Rock Ave Portland CT (06480) ***(G-3578)***
Tilcon Connecticut Portland, Portland *Also called Tilcon Connecticut Inc* ***(G-3578)***
Tillett's, Sheffield *Also called Dek Tillett Ltd* ***(G-15059)***
Tillotson Corporation (PA) 781 402-1731
1539 Fall River Ave Ste 1 Seekonk MA (02771) ***(G-15042)***
Tillotson Rubber Co Inc 781 402-1731
1539 Fall River Ave Seekonk MA (02771) ***(G-15043)***
Tim Gratuski 978 466-9000
136 Pond St Leominster MA (01453) ***(G-12195)***
Tim Kat Inc 207 784-9675
4 Gendron Dr Unit 5 Lewiston ME (04240) ***(G-6325)***
Tim Meiklejohn Logging 413 652-1223
499 East Rd Clarksburg MA (01247) ***(G-10076)***
Tim Poloski 860 508-6566
38 Risley Rd Vernon Rockville CT (06066) ***(G-4685)***
Tim Prentice 860 672-6728
129 Lake Rd West Cornwall CT (06796) ***(G-5047)***
Tim Robinson Logging 978 355-4287
199 Wauwinet Rd Barre MA (01005) ***(G-7951)***
Tim Welding 203 488-3486
107 W Pond Rd North Branford CT (06471) ***(G-2981)***
Timber Frame Barn Conversions 860 219-0519
226 Rollingbrook Windsor CT (06095) ***(G-5373)***
Timber Leasing, Spencer *Also called Godin Land Clearing* ***(G-15431)***
Timber-Top Inc 860 274-6706
210 Hopkins Rd Watertown CT (06795) ***(G-5029)***
Timberchic, Millinocket *Also called Maine Heritage Timber LLC* ***(G-6442)***
Timbercraft LLC 860 355-5538
70 S End Plz New Milford CT (06776) ***(G-2829)***
Timberlake and Compny, Bethel *Also called Mayville House* ***(G-5715)***
Timberland Company, The, Stratham *Also called Timberland LLC* ***(G-19876)***
Timberland LLC (HQ) 603 772-9500
200 Domain Dr Stratham NH (03885) ***(G-19876)***
Timbernest, Williston *Also called Static & Dynamic Tech Inc* ***(G-22693)***
Timberpeg, Claremont *Also called WH Silverstein Inc* ***(G-17864)***
Timberpeg East Inc (PA) 603 542-7762
61 Plains Rd Claremont NH (03743) ***(G-17862)***
Timco Corporation 781 821-1041
1551 Central St Stoughton MA (02072) ***(G-15626)***
Timco Instruments Div, Guilford *Also called Fitzhugh Electrical Corp* ***(G-1704)***
Time Plating Incorporated 401 943-3020
30 Libera St Cranston RI (02920) ***(G-20302)***
Time4printing Inc 207 838-1496
588 Roosevelt Trl Windham ME (04062) ***(G-7257)***
Timelinx Software LLC 978 662-1171
800 Turnpike St Ste 300 North Andover MA (01845) ***(G-13731)***
Timer Digest Publishing Inc 203 629-2589
268 Round Hill Rd Greenwich CT (06831) ***(G-1655)***
Times Community News Group 860 437-1150
47 Eugene Oneill Dr New London CT (06320) ***(G-2783)***
Times Fiber Communications Inc (HQ) 203 265-8500
358 Hall Ave Wallingford CT (06492) ***(G-4818)***
Times Microwave Systems Inc (HQ) 203 949-8400
358 Hall Ave Wallingford CT (06492) ***(G-4819)***
Times Publishing LLC 860 349-8532
491 Main St Middlefield CT (06455) ***(G-2167)***
Times Record Main Ofc 207 729-3311
3 Business Pkwy Brunswick ME (04011) ***(G-5849)***
Times Wire and Cable Company (HQ) 203 949-8400
358 Hall Ave Wallingford CT (06492) ***(G-4820)***
Timet, East Windsor *Also called Titanium Metals Corporation* ***(G-1307)***
Timex Group Usa Inc (HQ) 203 346-5000
555 Christian Rd Middlebury CT (06762) ***(G-2160)***
Timken Arospc Drv Systems LLC 860 649-0000
586 Hilliard St Manchester CT (06042) ***(G-2055)***
Timken Company 860 652-4630
701 Hebron Ave Ste 2 Glastonbury CT (06033) ***(G-1579)***
Timken Company 603 443-5281
336 Mechanic St Lebanon NH (03766) ***(G-18638)***
Timken Motor & Crane Svcs LLC 207 699-2501
190 Riverside St Unit 4a Portland ME (04103) ***(G-6740)***
Timken Super Precision, Keene *Also called Mpb Corporation* ***(G-18518)***
Timmons Machine & Fabricating, Windham *Also called Robert Timmons Jr* ***(G-7249)***
Timna Manufacturing Inc 203 265-4656
204 N Plains Indus Rd Wallingford CT (06492) ***(G-4821)***
Timothy Sills 781 635-8193
64 Summer St Rockland MA (02370) ***(G-14830)***
Tims Sign & Lighting Service 203 634-8840
38 Elm St Ste 2 Meriden CT (06450) ***(G-2143)***
Tin Can Alley 508 487-1648
269 Commercial St Provincetown MA (02657) ***(G-14610)***
Tin Can Sally 207 651-6188
50 Russell Rd Eliot ME (03903) ***(G-6011)***
Tin Man Fabrication Inc 401 822-4509
161 Pilgrim Ave Coventry RI (02816) ***(G-20169)***
Tincanpally LLC 732 485-5636
84 Miller St Belfast ME (04915) ***(G-5697)***
Tinny Corporation 860 854-6121
100 Bradley St Middletown CT (06457) ***(G-2228)***
Tinsley GROup-Ps&w Inc (HQ) 919 742-5832
1 Eastern Steel Rd Milford CT (06460) ***(G-2376)***
Tiny-Clutch, Clinton *Also called Helander Products Inc* ***(G-788)***
Tinytown Gazette (PA) 781 383-9115
172 S Main St Cohasset MA (02025) ***(G-10102)***
Tisbury Printer Inc 508 693-4222
39 Lagoon Pond Rd Vineyard Haven MA (02568) ***(G-15935)***
Tisco, Sudbury *Also called Information Server Co* ***(G-15658)***
Titalist and Footjoy Worldwide, Brockton *Also called Acushnet Company* ***(G-9115)***
Titan Advnced Enrgy Sltons Inc 561 654-5558
35 Congress St Ste 2251 Salem MA (01970) ***(G-14946)***
Titan Chain & Welding 207 465-4144
15 Sportsmans Trl Oakland ME (04963) ***(G-6535)***
Titanium Advisors 508 528-3120
9 Summer St Unit 303 Franklin MA (02038) ***(G-11092)***
Titanium Industries Inc 860 870-3939
362 Mile Hill Rd Tolland CT (06084) ***(G-4554)***
Titanium Metals Corporation 860 627-7051
7 Craftsman Rd East Windsor CT (06088) ***(G-1307)***
Titeflex Aerospace, Laconia *Also called Smiths Tblar Systms-Lconia Inc* ***(G-18587)***
Titeflex Commercial Inc 413 739-5631
603 Hendee St Springfield MA (01104) ***(G-15515)***
Titeflex Corporation (HQ) 413 739-5631
603 Hendee St Springfield MA (01104) ***(G-15516)***
Titeflex Corporation 413 781-0008
603 Hendee St Springfield MA (01104) ***(G-15517)***
Titeflex Corporation 603 524-2064
93 Lexington Dr Laconia NH (03246) ***(G-18589)***
Titeflex Teflon & Metal Hose, Springfield *Also called Titeflex Corporation* ***(G-15517)***
Titleist, New Bedford *Also called Acushnet Company* ***(G-13351)***
Titleist, Brockton *Also called Acushnet Company* ***(G-9116)***
Titleist & Footjoy Worldwide, New Bedford *Also called Acushnet Company* ***(G-13349)***
Titus & Bean Graphics Inc 781 585-1355
62 Main St Ste 107 Kingston MA (02364) ***(G-11965)***
Titus Engraving & Stonesetting 508 695-6842
44 Washington St Unit 1 Plainville MA (02762) ***(G-14536)***
Tivoli Audio, Boston *Also called Fargo Ta LLC* ***(G-8537)***
Tivoly Inc 802 873-3106
434 Baxter Ave Derby Line VT (05830) ***(G-21906)***
Tivorsan Pharmaceuticals Inc 410 419-2171
3 Davol Sq Ste A301 Providence RI (02903) ***(G-21137)***
Tizra 401 935-5317
9 Catalpa Rd Providence RI (02906) ***(G-21138)***
Tj Mold and Tool Company Inc 802 748-1390
61 Lewis Ct Saint Johnsbury VT (05819) ***(G-22396)***
Tjl Industries LLC 203 250-2187
19 Willow St Cheshire CT (06410) ***(G-766)***
Tk Cups-Sorg's, Fitchburg *Also called Birch Point Paper Products Inc* ***(G-10811)***
TK Machining Inc 207 247-3114
4 Dyer Ln Waterboro ME (04087) ***(G-7152)***
TK&k Services LLC 770 844-8710
719 Hale St Ste 3 Beverly MA (01915) ***(G-8192)***
Tl Sports Sales Inc 603 577-1931
20 Clarke Farm Rd Windham NH (03087) ***(G-20012)***
Tl Woodworking 203 787-9661
299 Welton St Hamden CT (06517) ***(G-1788)***
TLC Media LLC 203 980-1361
900 Mix Ave Apt 22 Hamden CT (06514) ***(G-1789)***
TLC Ultrasound Inc 860 354-6333
143 West St Ste V New Milford CT (06776) ***(G-2830)***
TLC Vision (usa) Corporation 978 531-4114
201 Andover St Peabody MA (01960) ***(G-14378)***

A L P H A B E T I C

Tld Ace Corporation 860 602-3300
805 Bloomfield Ave Windsor CT (06095) ***(G-5374)***
Tli Group Ltd 508 866-9825
35 Kennedy Dr Carver MA (02330) ***(G-9809)***
Tls International LLC 781 449-4454
76 Brewster Dr Needham MA (02492) ***(G-13315)***
Tls Printing LLC 508 234-2344
84 Tyler Rd Townsend MA (01469) ***(G-15874)***
Tm & Tm, Livermore Falls *Also called Tm and Tm Inc* ***(G-6382)***
Tm and Tm Inc 207 897-3442
49 Gilbert St Livermore Falls ME (04254) ***(G-6382)***
Tm Custom 401 226-2173
510 Victory Hwy West Greenwich RI (02817) ***(G-21466)***
TM Electronics Inc 978 772-0970
68 Barnum Rd Devens MA (01434) ***(G-10334)***
Tm Ward Co of Connecticut LLC 203 866-9203
5 Wilbur St Norwalk CT (06854) ***(G-3257)***
Tmax Publishing LLC 603 505-7693
85 Lowell Rd Salem NH (03079) ***(G-19772)***
TMC Books LLC 603 447-5589
731 Tasker Hill Rd Conway NH (03818) ***(G-17959)***
TMC Rhode Island Company Inc 401 596-2816
36 Beach St Westerly RI (02891) ***(G-21543)***
Tmcs, Peabody *Also called Technical Manufacturing Corp* ***(G-14376)***
Tme Co Inc 860 354-0686
315 Cole Ave Providence RI (02906) ***(G-21139)***
Tmf Incorporated 203 267-7364
1266 Main St S Ste 3 Southbury CT (06488) ***(G-4034)***
Tmh Machining & Welding Corp 508 580-6899
124 Turnpike St Ste 15 West Bridgewater MA (02379) ***(G-16459)***
TMI, Nashua *Also called Test Msrment Instrmntation Inc* ***(G-19272)***
TMI Industries Inc 413 283-9021
25 Ware St Palmer MA (01069) ***(G-14297)***
Tms International LLC 203 629-8383
165 W Putnam Ave Greenwich CT (06830) ***(G-1656)***
Tnco Inc 781 447-6661
61 John Vertente Blvd New Bedford MA (02745) ***(G-13454)***
Tnd Inc 603 595-4795
4 Industrial Park Dr # 30 Pelham NH (03076) ***(G-19451)***
Tne, Greene *Also called Technical Sales & Svc of Neng* ***(G-6151)***
Tnemec East Inc 978 988-9500
11 Upton Dr Wilmington MA (01887) ***(G-17056)***
TNT Manufacturing LLC 413 562-0690
988 Southampton Rd Ste B Westfield MA (01085) ***(G-16735)***
To Give Is Better 860 261-5443
139 Center St Ste 5007 Bristol CT (06010) ***(G-618)***
Toast Inc (PA) 617 682-0225
401 Park Dr Ste 801 Boston MA (02215) ***(G-8886)***
Toby Leary Fine Wdwkg Inc 508 957-2281
135 Barnstable Rd Ste A Hyannis MA (02601) ***(G-11860)***
Todd Enterprises, Cranston *Also called Chem-Tainer Industries Inc* ***(G-20196)***
Todd's Salsa, Glenburn *Also called Todds Originals LLC* ***(G-6108)***
Todds Originals LLC 844 328-7257
51 Aa Landing Rd Glenburn ME (04401) ***(G-6108)***
Todrin Industries Inc 508 946-3600
305 Kenneth Welch Dr Lakeville MA (02347) ***(G-11979)***
Toff Industry Inc 860 378-0532
323 Clark St Milldale CT (06467) ***(G-2388)***
Toggle-Aire, Smithfield *Also called Joraco Inc* ***(G-21234)***
Tokay Software Incorporated 508 788-0896
237 Belknap Rd Framingham MA (01701) ***(G-11008)***
Tolerx Inc 617 354-8100
300 Technology Sq Ste 4 Cambridge MA (02139) ***(G-9682)***
Tolland Machine Company LLC 860 872-4863
1050 Hartford Tpke Vernon CT (06066) ***(G-4674)***
Tolles Communications Corp 603 627-9500
103 Bay St Manchester NH (03104) ***(G-18942)***
Tollman Spring Company Inc 860 583-4856
560 Birch St Bristol CT (06010) ***(G-619)***
Tom and Sallys Handmade Choco 800 289-8783
59 Tom Harvey Rd Westerly RI (02891) ***(G-21544)***
Tom Berkowitz Trucking Inc (PA) 508 234-2920
279 Douglas Rd Whitinsville MA (01588) ***(G-16919)***
Tom James Company 603 601-6944
4 Merrill Industrial Dr Hampton NH (03842) ***(G-18274)***
Tom Knows Salsa LLC 802 793-5079
445 White Rd Eden VT (05652) ***(G-21921)***
Tom Raredon Metal Work, Florence *Also called Raredon Resources Inc* ***(G-10868)***
Tom Snyder Productions Inc (HQ) 617 600-2145
100 Talcott Ave Ste 6 Watertown MA (02472) ***(G-16324)***
Tom Stebbins DBA Kite Ene 802 878-9650
745 Woods Hollow Rd Westford VT (05494) ***(G-22629)***
Tom Waters Golf Shop 978 526-7311
153 School St Manchester MA (01944) ***(G-12608)***
Tom's Natural Soap, Kennebunk *Also called Toms of Maine Inc* ***(G-6242)***
Tomandtim Enterprises LLC 508 380-5550
75 W Main St Northborough MA (01532) ***(G-14051)***
Tomkins Corporation 508 528-2000
117 Dean Ave Franklin MA (02038) ***(G-11093)***
Tommila Brothers Inc 603 242-7774
487 Nh Fitzwilliam NH (03447) ***(G-18153)***
Tommy Hilfiger Footwear Inc 617 824-6000
191 Spring St Fl 4 Lexington MA (02421) ***(G-12279)***
Tommy LLC Sock It 860 688-2019
4 Walters Way Windsor CT (06095) ***(G-5375)***
Tommy Tape, Berlin *Also called Midsun Specialty Products Inc* ***(G-96)***
Tomophase Corporation 781 229-5700
1 North Ave Ste A Burlington MA (01803) ***(G-9347)***
Tomra Mass LLC 203 395-3484
969 Shawmut Ave New Bedford MA (02746) ***(G-13455)***
Toms of Maine Inc 802 387-2393
148 Banning Rd Putney VT (05346) ***(G-22293)***
Toms of Maine Inc 207 985-2944
1 Trackside Dr Kennebunk ME (04043) ***(G-6241)***
Toms of Maine Inc (HQ) 207 985-2944
2 Storer St Ste 302 Kennebunk ME (04043) ***(G-6242)***
Toms of Maine Inc 207 985-2944
27 Community Dr Sanford ME (04073) ***(G-6894)***
Tomtec 203 795-5030
607 Harborview Rd Orange CT (06477) ***(G-3385)***
Tomtec Inc 203 281-6790
1000 Sherman Ave Hamden CT (06514) ***(G-1790)***
Tomz Corporation 860 829-0670
47 Episcopal Rd Berlin CT (06037) ***(G-113)***
Toner Plastics Inc 413 789-1300
35 Industrial Dr East Longmeadow MA (01028) ***(G-10498)***
Tonlino & Sons LLC 413 329-8083
1678 Monterey Rd Otis MA (01253) ***(G-14250)***
Tonmar LLC 860 974-3714
56 Babbitt Hill Rd Pomfret Center CT (06259) ***(G-3559)***
Tony's Trains Exchange, Essex Junction *Also called Charter Dev & Consulting Corp* ***(G-21936)***
Tool 2000 ....860 620-0020
327 Captain Lewis Dr Southington CT (06489) ***(G-4087)***
Tool Factory Inc 802 375-6549
3336 Sunderland Hill Rd Arlington VT (05250) ***(G-21601)***
Tool Logistics II 203 855-9754
46 Chestnut St Norwalk CT (06854) ***(G-3258)***
Tool Specialties Mfg Co LLC 603 652-9346
343 Farmington Rd Milton NH (03851) ***(G-19088)***
Tool Technology Inc 978 777-5006
Riverview Indl Pk 3 Middleton MA (01949) ***(G-13104)***
Tool The Somma Company 203 753-2114
109 Scott Rd Waterbury CT (06705) ***(G-4963)***
Tooling Research Inc (PA) 508 668-1950
81 Diamond St Walpole MA (02081) ***(G-16014)***
Tooling Tech Center, Northfield *Also called Freudenberg-Nok General Partnr* ***(G-19401)***
Toollab Inc 401 461-2110
65 Manchester St West Warwick RI (02893) ***(G-21511)***
Toolmax Designing Tooling Inc 860 871-7265
69 Industrial Park Rd E A Tolland CT (06084) ***(G-4555)***
Toolmex Indus Solutions Inc (PA) 508 653-5110
34 Talbot Rd Northborough MA (01532) ***(G-14052)***
Toolsgroup Inc 617 263-0080
75 Federal St Ste 920 Boston MA (02110) ***(G-8887)***
Top Dead Center Apparel, Wells River *Also called Green Mountain Monogram Inc* ***(G-22601)***
Top Flight Machine Tool LLC 860 747-4726
90 Robert Jackson Way Plainville CT (06062) ***(G-3520)***
Top Kayaker Geo Odyssey Llc 603 651-1036
1805 Route 16 Center Ossipee NH (03814) ***(G-17806)***
Top Notch Mill Work 508 432-4976
245 County Rd Bourne MA (02532) ***(G-8950)***
Top Shelf Installations 508 697-1550
400 Walnut St Bridgewater MA (02324) ***(G-9090)***
Top Shell LLC 401 726-7890
55 Conduit St Unit 1 Central Falls RI (02863) ***(G-20127)***
Top Shop Inc 802 658-1351
87 Ethan Allen Dr South Burlington VT (05403) ***(G-22472)***
Top Source Inc 203 753-6490
490 S Main St Waterbury CT (06706) ***(G-4964)***
Top Stitch Embroidery Inc 603 448-2931
233 Mascoma St Lebanon NH (03766) ***(G-18639)***
Topaz Enterprise Sand Pubg 203 449-1903
304 Main Ave Norwalk CT (06851) ***(G-3259)***
Topek LLC 603 863-2400
131 Yankee Barn Rd Grantham NH (03753) ***(G-18217)***
Topex Inc 203 748-5918
10 Precision Rd Fl 2 Danbury CT (06810) ***(G-999)***
Toppan Photomasks Inc 203 775-9001
246 Federal Rd Ste C22 Brookfield CT (06804) ***(G-661)***
Tops Manufacturing Co Inc (PA) 203 655-9367
83 Salisbury Rd Darien CT (06820) ***(G-1034)***
Topsall Machine Tool Co Inc 508 755-0332
33 Bullard Ave Worcester MA (01605) ***(G-17489)***
Topsham Woodworking LLC 207 751-1032
3 Rex Rd Topsham ME (04086) ***(G-7095)***
Topside Canvas Upholstery 860 399-4845
768 Boston Post Rd Westbrook CT (06498) ***(G-5164)***

Tornik Inc 860 282-6081
16 Old Forge Rd B Rocky Hill CT (06067) *(G-3731)*
Torqmaster Inc 203 326-5945
200 Harvard Ave Stamford CT (06902) *(G-4347)*
Torqmaster International, Stamford *Also called Torqmaster Inc (G-4347)*
Torque Specialties, Windsor *Also called AKO Inc (G-5317)*
Torrefaction Tech USA LLC 207 775-2464
2 Market St Ste 500 Portland ME (04101) *(G-6741)*
Torrey S Crane Company 860 628-4778
492 Summer St Plantsville CT (06479) *(G-3543)*
Torrington Brush Works Inc 860 482-3517
63 Avenue A Torrington CT (06790) *(G-4602)*
Torrington Diesel Corporation 860 496-9948
287 Old Winsted Rd Torrington CT (06790) *(G-4603)*
Torrington Distributors Inc (PA) 860 482-4464
43 Norfolk St Torrington CT (06790) *(G-4604)*
Torrington Lumber Company 860 482-3529
281 Church St Torrington CT (06790) *(G-4605)*
Torromeo Industries Inc 603 642-5564
18 Dorre Rd Kingston NH (03848) *(G-18546)*
Tortilleria Pachanga 207 797-9700
1 Industrial Way Portland ME (04103) *(G-6742)*
Tory Inc 401 766-4502
481 2nd Ave Woonsocket RI (02895) *(G-21587)*
Toscana European Day Spa 401 658-5277
3460 Mendon Rd Unit 4 Cumberland RI (02864) *(G-20349)*
Toshiba America Electronic 508 481-0034
290 Donald Lynch Blvd # 201 Marlborough MA (01752) *(G-12837)*
Toshiba International Corp 781 273-9000
2400 District Ave Ste 130 Burlington MA (01803) *(G-9348)*
Tot-Lot Child Care Products, West Greenwich *Also called John Carlevale (G-21459)*
Total Air Supply Inc 603 889-0100
171 E Hollis St Nashua NH (03060) *(G-19274)*
Total Communications Inc (PA) 860 282-9999
333 Burnham St East Hartford CT (06108) *(G-1230)*
Total Concept Tool Inc 203 483-1130
2 Research Dr Ste 1 Branford CT (06405) *(G-355)*
Total Control Inc 203 269-4749
130 S Turnpike Rd Wallingford CT (06492) *(G-4822)*
Total Fab LLC 475 238-8176
140 Commerce St East Haven CT (06512) *(G-1266)*
Total Food Service, Greenwich *Also called Ida Publishing Co Inc (G-1621)*
Total Packaging Concepts Inc 603 432-4651
115 Franklin Street Ext Derry NH (03038) *(G-18000)*
Total Parts Services LLC 203 263-5619
97 S Pomperaug Ave Woodbury CT (06798) *(G-5490)*
Total Plastics Resources LLC 401 463-3090
1518 Pontiac Ave Cranston RI (02920) *(G-20303)*
Total Power International Inc 978 453-7272
418 Bridge St Ste 206 Lowell MA (01850) *(G-12437)*
Total Ptrchemicals Ref USA Inc 203 375-0668
125 Ontario St Stratford CT (06615) *(G-4454)*
Total Recoil Magnetics Inc 508 429-9600
84 October Hill Rd Ste 6a Holliston MA (01746) *(G-11609)*
Total Register Inc 860 210-0465
180 Sunny Valley Rd Ste 1 New Milford CT (06776) *(G-2831)*
Total Temp Inc 508 947-8628
22 Cambridge St Ste C Middleboro MA (02346) *(G-13078)*
Total Temperature Control, Middleboro *Also called Total Temp Inc (G-13078)*
Totally Maine Lobster, Bucksport *Also called Central Maine Cold Storage (G-5854)*
Toto LLC 203 776-6000
27 Whitney Ave New Haven CT (06510) *(G-2744)*
Toto USA Holdings Inc 617 227-1321
123 N Washington St Boston MA (02114) *(G-8888)*
Toucanect Inc 617 437-1400
14 Hancock St Boston MA (02114) *(G-8889)*
Touch Ahead Software LLC 866 960-9301
2 Liberty Sq Ste 700 Boston MA (02109) *(G-8890)*
Touch Bionics 774 719-2199
35 Hampden Rd Mansfield MA (02048) *(G-12666)*
Touch Inc 781 894-8133
27 Spring St Waltham MA (02451) *(G-16216)*
Touchfight Games LLC 802 753-7360
545 Twitchell Hill Rd Shaftsbury VT (05262) *(G-22407)*
Touchpoint Software Corp 978 443-0094
490 Boston Post Rd Ste 5 Sudbury MA (01776) *(G-15669)*
Tough End Logging Corp 207 455-8016
320 High Meadow Rd Perham ME (04766) *(G-6582)*
Tova Industries Inc 413 569-5688
10 Hudson Dr Southwick MA (01077) *(G-15419)*
Towbandit, Rutland *Also called First Place Welding Inc (G-14881)*
Tower Brands, Centerbrook *Also called Tower Laboratories Ltd (G-704)*
Tower Laboratories Ltd 860 669-7078
7 Heritage Park Rd Clinton CT (06413) *(G-796)*
Tower Laboratories Ltd (PA) 860 767-2127
8 Industrial Park Rd Centerbrook CT (06409) *(G-704)*
Tower Manufacturing Corp 401 467-7550
25 Reservoir Ave Providence RI (02907) *(G-21140)*
Tower Optical Company Inc 203 866-4535
275 East Ave Fl 2 Norwalk CT (06855) *(G-3260)*
Towle Manufacturing Company (HQ) 781 539-0100
22 Blake St Medford MA (02155) *(G-12950)*
Towle Silversmiths, Medford *Also called Towle Manufacturing Company (G-12950)*
Town & Country, Conway *Also called John J Marr (G-17954)*
Town & Country Cleaners & Tlrs, Watertown *Also called Sumal Enterprises LLC (G-5027)*
Town & Country Fine Jwly Group 617 345-4771
25 Union St Chelsea MA (02150) *(G-9973)*
Town & Country Reprographics 603 225-9521
230 N Main St Concord NH (03301) *(G-17936)*
Town & Country Sheds 802 888-7012
2175 N Wolcott Rd Wolcott VT (05680) *(G-22733)*
Town and Country Cabinets Inc 207 839-2709
420 Fort Hill Rd Gorham ME (04038) *(G-6131)*
Town Bookbindery Inc 508 763-2713
154 County Rd East Freetown MA (02717) *(G-10461)*
Town Common Inc 978 948-8696
77 Wethersfield St Rowley MA (01969) *(G-14867)*
Town Crier, Wilmington *Also called Daily Woburn Times Inc (G-16993)*
Town Crier Publications Inc 508 529-7791
48 Mechanic St Upton MA (01568) *(G-15911)*
Town Crier, The, Pittsfield *Also called New England Newspapers Inc (G-14496)*
Town Fair Tire Centers Inc 860 646-2807
328 Middle Tpke W Manchester CT (06040) *(G-2056)*
Town Line 207 445-2234
16 Jones Brook Xing South China ME (04358) *(G-7007)*
Town of Brimfield 413 245-4103
34b Wales Rd Brimfield MA (01010) *(G-9111)*
Town of Burlington 781 270-1680
62 Winter St Burlington MA (01803) *(G-9349)*
Town of Gorham (PA) 207 222-1610
75 South St Ste 1 Gorham ME (04038) *(G-6132)*
Town of Gorham 207 839-5555
270 Main St Gorham ME (04038) *(G-6133)*
Town of Hartford 802 295-9425
812 Va Cutoff Rd White River Junction VT (05001) *(G-22643)*
Town of Montville 860 848-3830
83 Pink Row Uncasville CT (06382) *(G-4650)*
Town of North Reading 978 664-6027
235 North St North Reading MA (01864) *(G-13992)*
Town of Putnam, Putnam *Also called Superior Plas Extrusion Co Inc (G-3636)*
Town of Uxbridge 508 278-2887
80 River Rd Uxbridge MA (01569) *(G-15932)*
Town of Vernon 860 870-3545
100 Windsorville Rd Vernon CT (06066) *(G-4675)*
Town of Vernon 860 870-3699
5 Park St Fl 2 Vernon Rockville CT (06066) *(G-4686)*
Town of Westminster 978 874-2313
7 South St Westminster MA (01473) *(G-16816)*
Town of Wilton 203 563-0152
238 Danbury Rd Wilton CT (06897) *(G-5308)*
Town Planner, Gorham *Also called Town of Gorham (G-6133)*
Town Times, Meriden *Also called Record-Journal Newspaper (G-2124)*
Town Times, Watertown *Also called Prime Publishers Inc (G-5018)*
Town Tribune LLC 203 648-6085
10 Sleepy Hollow Rd New Fairfield CT (06812) *(G-2629)*
Townie Frozen Desserts LLC 781 925-6095
46 G St Hull MA (02045) *(G-11831)*
Townsend Cabinet Makers Inc 207 793-7086
1 Malloy Mountain Rd Limington ME (04049) *(G-6350)*
Townsend Systems, Barrington *Also called Richard Townsend (G-17622)*
Toy Pallet 860 803-9838
11 Rothe Ln Ellington CT (06029) *(G-1342)*
Tozier Group Inc 207 838-7939
185 Mountain Rd Falmouth ME (04105) *(G-6035)*
Tozier Group, The, Falmouth *Also called Tozier Group Inc (G-6035)*
TP Cycle & Engineering Inc 203 744-4960
4 Finance Dr Danbury CT (06810) *(G-1000)*
Tpe Solutions Inc (PA) 978 425-3033
3 Patterson Rd Ste 2 Shirley MA (01464) *(G-15096)*
Tpi Inc 401 247-4010
373 Market St Unit B Warren RI (02885) *(G-21310)*
Tpi Composites, Warren *Also called Tpi Inc (G-21310)*
Tpi Composites Inc 401 247-4010
373 Market St Warren RI (02885) *(G-21311)*
Tpi Industries LLC 508 588-3300
208 Manley St West Bridgewater MA (02379) *(G-16460)*
Tpi Solutions Ink, Waltham *Also called Technical Publications Inc (G-16206)*
Tpni, Norwood *Also called Pulse Network Inc (G-14189)*
Tps Acquisition LLC (PA) 860 589-5511
151 Sharon Rd Waterbury CT (06705) *(G-4965)*
Tr Dillon Logging Inc 207 696-8137
144 Main St Madison ME (04950) *(G-6407)*
Tr Flag Logging, Livermore *Also called T&R Flagg Log Sons & Daughters (G-6377)*
Tr Landworks LLC 860 402-6177
36 Kensington Acres Rd East Hartland CT (06027) *(G-1240)*

ALPHABETIC

Tracer Technologies Inc...617 776-6410
20 Assembly Square Dr Somerville MA (02145) ***(G-15224)***
Tracey Gear Inc...401 725-3920
740 York Ave Pawtucket RI (02861) ***(G-20906)***
Tracey Gear & Precision Shaft, Pawtucket *Also called Tracey Gear Inc* ***(G-20906)***
Track180 LLC...203 605-3540
900 Chapel St Fl 10 New Haven CT (06510) ***(G-2745)***
Tracksmith Corporation...781 235-0037
285 Newbury St Boston MA (02115) ***(G-8891)***
Tracs Chillers LLC...603 707-2241
790 Route 16 Ossipee NH (03864) ***(G-19423)***
Tracy J Morrison...207 683-2371
26 Wellington Rd Harmony ME (04942) ***(G-6172)***
Tracy Joseph Woodworks...207 244-0004
Rr 102 Box 447 Mount Desert ME (04660) ***(G-6457)***
Trade Labels Inc...860 535-4828
28 Cottrell St Ste 28e Mystic CT (06355) ***(G-2454)***
Trademark Print Inc...781 829-0209
300 Oak St Ste 1925 Pembroke MA (02359) ***(G-14429)***
Tradern Fine Woodworking Inc...617 393-3733
175 California St Newton MA (02458) ***(G-13644)***
Tradewinds...203 723-6966
274 Bethany Rd Beacon Falls CT (06403) ***(G-65)***
Tradewinds...203 324-2994
1010 Washington Blvd # 3 Stamford CT (06901) ***(G-4348)***
Traditional Breads Inc...781 598-4451
161 Pleasant St Lynn MA (01901) ***(G-12544)***
Traditional Wood Works Inc...207 676-9668
27 Commercial Dr Berwick ME (03901) ***(G-5713)***
Traditional Woodworking LLC...603 272-9324
164 River Rd Piermont NH (03779) ***(G-19493)***
Trafalgar Square Farm Inc...802 457-1911
388 Howe Hill Rd North Pomfret VT (05053) ***(G-22235)***
Traffic Signs & Safety Inc...401 396-9840
70 Ballou Blvd Bristol RI (02809) ***(G-20106)***
Trailheads, Kent *Also called Indigo Coast Inc* ***(G-1922)***
Trailjournals LLC...978 358-7536
64 Carter St Apt 2 Newburyport MA (01950) ***(G-13542)***
Trailspace, Rome *Also called Macleay Interactive Design Inc* ***(G-6828)***
Trajan Scientific Americas Inc...203 830-4910
21 Berkshire Blvd Bethel CT (06801) ***(G-184)***
Trajan Scientific and Medical, Bethel *Also called Trajan Scientific Americas Inc* ***(G-184)***
Trane Inc...203 866-7115
145 Main St Norwalk CT (06851) ***(G-3261)***
Trane Inc...860 437-6208
178 Wallace St New Haven CT (06511) ***(G-2746)***
Trane Inc...978 737-3900
181 Ballardvale St # 201 Wilmington MA (01887) ***(G-17057)***
Trane Supply, New Haven *Also called Trane Inc* ***(G-2746)***
Trane US Inc...207 773-0637
860 Spring St 1 Westbrook ME (04092) ***(G-7211)***
Trane US Inc...860 437-6208
571 Broad St New London CT (06320) ***(G-2784)***
Trane US Inc...860 470-3901
135 South Rd Ste 1 Farmington CT (06032) ***(G-1516)***
Trane US Inc...401 434-3146
10 Hemingway Dr Riverside RI (02915) ***(G-21176)***
Trane US Inc...860 541-1721
485 Ledyard St Hartford CT (06114) ***(G-1881)***
Tranquilitees...207 441-8058
139 Northern Ave Augusta ME (04330) ***(G-5622)***
Trans Form Plastics Corp...978 777-1440
45 Prince St Danvers MA (01923) ***(G-10264)***
Trans Mag Corp...978 458-1487
250 Jackson St Lowell MA (01852) ***(G-12438)***
Trans Metrics Division, Watertown *Also called United Electric Controls Co* ***(G-16327)***
Trans Metrics Inc (HQ)...617 926-1000
180 Dexter Ave Watertown MA (02472) ***(G-16325)***
Trans-Mate LLC...800 867-9274
13 Sterling Rd North Billerica MA (01862) ***(G-13873)***
Trans-Tek Inc...860 872-8351
10 Industrial Dr Ellington CT (06029) ***(G-1343)***
Trans-Tex LLC...401 331-8483
117 Pettaconsett Ave Cranston RI (02920) ***(G-20304)***
Transact Technologies Inc (PA)...203 859-6800
2319 Whitney Ave Ste 3b Hamden CT (06518) ***(G-1791)***
Transamerica Printing Corp...781 821-6166
2 Appletree Ln Natick MA (01760) ***(G-13283)***
Transcon Technologies Inc...413 562-7684
53 Mainline Dr Westfield MA (01085) ***(G-16736)***
Transcript, The, Morrisville *Also called News and Citizen Inc* ***(G-22175)***
Transene Company Inc...978 777-7860
10 Electronics Ave Danvers MA (01923) ***(G-10265)***
Transfer Technologies, Campton *Also called Brn Corporation* ***(G-17775)***
Transformer Technology Inc...860 349-1061
60 Commerce Cir Durham CT (06422) ***(G-1095)***
Transfusion Boat Works Inc...401 348-5878
67a Tom Harvey Rd Westerly RI (02891) ***(G-21545)***
Transit Systems Inc...860 747-3669
161 Woodford Ave Ste 34 Plainville CT (06062) ***(G-3521)***
Transition Automation Inc...978 670-5500
101 Billerica Ave Bldg 5 North Billerica MA (01862) ***(G-13874)***
Translational Sciences Corp...617 331-4014
1 Mifflin Pl Ste 400 Cambridge MA (02138) ***(G-9683)***
Transmedics Inc (PA)...978 552-0443
200 Minuteman Rd Ste 302 Andover MA (01810) ***(G-7614)***
Transmedics Group Inc...978 552-0900
200 Minuteman Rd Andover MA (01810) ***(G-7615)***
Transmille Calibration Inc...802 846-7582
158 Brentwood Dr Ste 4 Colchester VT (05446) ***(G-21882)***
Transmode USA, North Branford *Also called Transmonde USa Inc* ***(G-2982)***
Transmonde USa Inc...203 484-1528
100 Shaw Rd North Branford CT (06471) ***(G-2982)***
Transom Scopes Inc...413 562-3606
33 Airport Rd Westfield MA (01085) ***(G-16737)***
Transparent Audio Inc...207 284-1100
47 Industrial Park Rd Saco ME (04072) ***(G-6860)***
Transportation Conn Dept...860 342-5996
263 Freestone Ave Portland CT (06480) ***(G-3579)***
Trap Rock Quarry...203 263-2195
236 Roxbury Rd Southbury CT (06488) ***(G-4035)***
Trassig Corp...203 659-0456
65 Redding Rd Unit 874 Georgetown CT (06829) ***(G-1533)***
Travel Medicine Inc...413 584-0381
369 Pleasant St Northampton MA (01060) ***(G-14023)***
Travel Wear, Norwalk *Also called Business Journals Inc* ***(G-3117)***
Travelbrains Inc...603 471-0127
14 Tether Rd Bedford NH (03110) ***(G-17665)***
Traveling Vineyard, Ipswich *Also called Phoenix Vintners LLC* ***(G-11934)***
Traver Electric Motor Co Inc...203 753-5103
151 Homer St Waterbury CT (06704) ***(G-4966)***
Travers Printing Inc...978 632-0530
32 Mission St Gardner MA (01440) ***(G-11131)***
Travis M Bonnett...802 524-1890
6 Rublee St Saint Albans VT (05478) ***(G-22382)***
Travis Worster...207 738-3792
528 Brown Rd Carroll Plt ME (04487) ***(G-5894)***
Traxon Technologies...201 508-1570
200 Ballardvale St # 300 Wilmington MA (01887) ***(G-17058)***
Trd Specialties Inc...860 738-4505
8 Wickett St Pine Meadow CT (06061) ***(G-3446)***
Tre Olive LLC...617 680-0096
180 Shaker Rd East Longmeadow MA (01028) ***(G-10499)***
Treadwell Corporation...860 283-7600
341 Railroad St Thomaston CT (06787) ***(G-4522)***
Treasury & Risk Management, Shelton *Also called Wicks Business Information LLC* ***(G-3889)***
Tree Co Inc...508 432-7529
239 Great Western Rd South Dennis MA (02660) ***(G-15267)***
Tree Enterprises...207 233-6479
1697 North Rd Parsonsfield ME (04047) ***(G-6577)***
Treehouse Hardwoods & Mill Sp, South Burlington *Also called Jenson Enterprises LLC* ***(G-22451)***
Treeline Timber...603 586-7725
11 Nevers Ln Jefferson NH (03583) ***(G-18487)***
Trees Ltd A Partnr Consisting...207 547-3168
2506 Middle Rd Sidney ME (04330) ***(G-6965)***
Treetop, South Easton *Also called Case Assembly Solutions Inc* ***(G-15273)***
Trego Inc...508 291-3816
5 Little Brook Rd Wareham MA (02571) ***(G-16255)***
Treif USA Inc...203 929-9930
50 Waterview Dr Ste 130 Shelton CT (06484) ***(G-3881)***
Trellborg Pipe Sals Mlford Inc (HQ)...800 626-2180
250 Elm St Milford NH (03055) ***(G-19080)***
Trellborg Pipe Sals Mlford Inc...603 673-8680
279 Riverway W Milford NH (03055) ***(G-19081)***
Trelleborg Ctd Systems US Inc...203 468-0342
30 Lenox St New Haven CT (06513) ***(G-2747)***
Trelleborg Offshore Boston Inc...774 719-1400
24 Teed Dr Randolph MA (02368) ***(G-14699)***
Trellis Structures Inc...888 285-4624
25 N Main St East Templeton MA (01438) ***(G-10521)***
Tremcar USA...978 556-5330
89 Newark St Haverhill MA (01832) ***(G-11477)***
Tremco Police Products, Billerica *Also called Tremco Products Inc* ***(G-8307)***
Tremco Products Inc...781 275-7692
34 Sullivan Rd Unit 17 Billerica MA (01821) ***(G-8307)***
Trems Inc...207 596-6989
19 Merrill Dr Rockland ME (04841) ***(G-6812)***
Trento Group LLC...860 623-1361
32 North Rd East Windsor CT (06088) ***(G-1308)***
Trevi Therapeutics Inc...203 304-2499
195 Church St Fl 14 New Haven CT (06510) ***(G-2748)***
Trew Corp (PA)...413 665-4051
Amherst Rd Sunderland MA (01375) ***(G-15677)***
Trew Corp...413 773-9798
901 River Rd Deerfield MA (01342) ***(G-10304)***

Trexel Inc 781 932-0202
100 Research Dr Ste 1 Wilmington MA (01887) ***(G-17059)***
Tri LLC 203 353-8418
34 Crescent St Apt 1i Stamford CT (06906) ***(G-4349)***
Tri C Manufacturing Inc 603 642-8448
33 Haverhill Rd East Kingston NH (03827) ***(G-18092)***
Tri C Tool & Die 802 864-7144
228 Elmwood Ave Burlington VT (05401) ***(G-21813)***
Tri Cast Inc (PA) 603 692-2480
23 Interstate Dr Somersworth NH (03878) ***(G-19851)***
Tri Mar Manufacturing Compan 860 628-4791
191 Captain Lewis Dr Southington CT (06489) ***(G-4088)***
Tri Med Group, Peterborough *Also called Tri-Med Inc* ***(G-19491)***
Tri Source Inc 203 924-7030
84 Platt Rd Shelton CT (06484) ***(G-3882)***
Tri Star Printing & Graphics 617 666-4480
33 Park St Somerville MA (02143) ***(G-15225)***
Tri Star Sheet Metal Company 207 225-2043
1817 Auburn Rd Turner ME (04282) ***(G-7110)***
Tri State Choppers LLC 860 210-1854
30 Old Route 7 Plz New Milford CT (06776) ***(G-2832)***
Tri State Maintenance Svcs LLC 203 691-1343
356 Old Maple Ave North Haven CT (06473) ***(G-3064)***
Tri State Precision Inc 413 498-2961
1 Ashuelot Rd Northfield MA (01360) ***(G-14068)***
Tri Town Discount Liquors 781 828-8393
100 Washington St Ste A Canton MA (02021) ***(G-9790)***
Tri Town Precision Plastics, Deep River *Also called Swpc Plastics LLC* ***(G-1067)***
Tri Town Transcript 978 887-4146
152 Sylvan St Danvers MA (01923) ***(G-10266)***
Tri-Angle Metal Fab, Milton *Also called Milton Vermont Sheet Metal Inc* ***(G-22134)***
Tri-Bro Tool Company 401 781-6323
1370 Elmwood Ave Cranston RI (02910) ***(G-20305)***
Tri-Mack Plastics Mfg Corp 401 253-2140
55 Broadcommon Rd 1 Bristol RI (02809) ***(G-20107)***
Tri-Med Inc 603 924-7211
305 Union St Peterborough NH (03458) ***(G-19491)***
Tri-Star Industries Inc 860 828-7570
101 Massirio Dr Berlin CT (06037) ***(G-114)***
Tri-Star Machine Inc 978 683-2600
55 Chase St Ste 1 Methuen MA (01844) ***(G-13047)***
Tri-Star Molding 207 783-5820
555 Lincoln St Lewiston ME (04240) ***(G-6326)***
Tri-Star Sportswear Inc 508 799-4117
1051 Millbury St Ste A Worcester MA (01607) ***(G-17490)***
Tri-State Iron Works Inc 603 228-0020
24 Industrial Park Dr Concord NH (03301) ***(G-17937)***
Tri-State Led Inc 203 813-3791
255 Mill St Greenwich CT (06830) ***(G-1657)***
Tri-State Mfg Solutions LLC 508 769-2891
124 Kennard Rd Nottingham NH (03290) ***(G-19417)***
Triad Inc 508 695-2247
44 Washington St Plainville MA (02762) ***(G-14537)***
Triad Designs 978 952-0136
35 Crosswinds Dr Groton MA (01450) ***(G-11296)***
Triangle Engineering Inc 781 878-1500
6 Industrial Way Hanover MA (02339) ***(G-11356)***
Triangle Sheet Metal Inc 603 393-6770
170 Waukewan St Meredith NH (03253) ***(G-18980)***
Triatic Incorporated 860 236-2298
22 Grassmere Ave West Hartford CT (06110) ***(G-5099)***
Tribal Wear 203 637-7884
27 Summit Rd Riverside CT (06878) ***(G-3691)***
Tribe Mediterranean Foods Inc 774 961-0000
110 Prince Henry Dr Taunton MA (02780) ***(G-15791)***
Triboro Supply, North Attleboro *Also called Peter Thrasher* ***(G-13771)***
Tribuna Newspaper LLC 203 730-0457
32 Farview Ave 3 Danbury CT (06810) ***(G-1001)***
Tricab (usa) Inc 508 421-4680
15 Coppage Dr Worcester MA (01603) ***(G-17491)***
Trickett Woodworks Company, Auburn *Also called Forest Manufacturing Corp* ***(G-17609)***
Trico Millworks Inc 207 637-2711
300 Hardscrabble Rd Limington ME (04049) ***(G-6351)***
Trico Specialty Films LLC 401 294-7022
310 Compass Cir North Kingstown RI (02852) ***(G-20746)***
Trico Welding Company LLC 203 720-3782
84 Feldspar Ave Beacon Falls CT (06403) ***(G-66)***
Trident Alloys Inc 413 737-1477
181 Abbe Ave Springfield MA (01107) ***(G-15518)***
Tridyne Process Systems Inc 802 863-6873
80 Allen Rd South Burlington VT (05403) ***(G-22473)***
Triem Industries LLC 203 888-1212
105 Napco Dr Terryville CT (06786) ***(G-4494)***
Trigila Construction Inc 860 828-8444
30 And A Half Ripple Ct Berlin CT (06037) ***(G-115)***
Trijay Inc 978 692-6104
149 Groton Rd Westford MA (01886) ***(G-16798)***
Trikinetics Inc 781 891-6110
56 Emerson Rd Waltham MA (02451) ***(G-16217)***
Trilap Company Inc 978 453-2205
649 Lawrence St Ste 1 Lowell MA (01852) ***(G-12439)***
Trillium Valves USA, Ipswich *Also called Fr Flow Ctrl Vlves US Bdco Inc* ***(G-11920)***
Trimaran Pharma Inc 508 577-7110
115 Hawthorne Village Rd Nashua NH (03062) ***(G-19275)***
Trimble Inc 508 381-5800
200 Nickerson Rd Ste 175 Marlborough MA (01752) ***(G-12838)***
Trimed Media Group Inc 401 919-5165
235 Promenade St Rm 298 Providence RI (02908) ***(G-21141)***
Trine Access Technology Inc 203 730-1756
2 Park Lawn Dr Bethel CT (06801) ***(G-185)***
Trinity Heating & Air Inc 508 291-0007
20 Pattersons Brook Rd West Wareham MA (02576) ***(G-16577)***
Trinity Mobile Networks Inc 301 332-6401
770 Chapel St Ste 2 New Haven CT (06510) ***(G-2749)***
Trinity Press Inc 508 998-1072
199 Pine Island Rd North Dartmouth MA (02747) ***(G-13928)***
Trinity Solar Systems, West Wareham *Also called Trinity Heating & Air Inc* ***(G-16577)***
Trinseo LLC 860 447-7298
1761 Route 12 Bldg 21 Gales Ferry CT (06335) ***(G-1528)***
Trio Software Corp 207 942-6222
56 Banair Rd Bangor ME (04401) ***(G-5660)***
Tripbuilder Media, Westport *Also called Community Brands Holdings LLC* ***(G-5185)***
Triple A Spring Ltd Partnr 860 589-3231
95 Valley St Ste 1 Bristol CT (06010) ***(G-620)***
Triple Clover Products LLC 475 558-9503
4 Smith Ridge Ln New Canaan CT (06840) ***(G-2618)***
Triple Crown Cbnets Mllwk Corp 508 833-6500
12b Jan Sebastian Dr Sandwich MA (02563) ***(G-14974)***
Triple D Transportation Inc 860 243-5057
129 W Dudley Town Rd Bloomfield CT (06002) ***(G-267)***
Triple P Packg & Ppr Pdts Inc 508 588-0444
20 Burke Dr Brockton MA (02301) ***(G-9184)***
Triple Play Sports 860 417-2877
16 Straits Tpke Watertown CT (06795) ***(G-5030)***
Triple S Machine Inc 978 774-0354
19 Warren St Danvers MA (01923) ***(G-10267)***
Triple Seat Software LLC 978 635-0615
6 Ashwood Rd Acton MA (01720) ***(G-7391)***
Triple Stitch Sportswear, Prospect *Also called TSS & A Inc* ***(G-3599)***
Tripoli Bakery Inc 978 682-7754
106 Common St Ste 6 Lawrence MA (01840) ***(G-12078)***
Trireme Manufacturing Co Inc 978 887-2132
245 Boston St Topsfield MA (01983) ***(G-15867)***
Tritex Corporation 203 756-7441
1500 Meriden Rd Waterbury CT (06705) ***(G-4967)***
Triton Thalassic Tech Inc (PA) 203 438-0633
241 Ethan Allen Hwy Ridgefield CT (06877) ***(G-3686)***
Triumph Actuation Systems - Co (HQ) 860 687-5412
175 Addison Rd Ste 4 Windsor CT (06095) ***(G-5376)***
Triumph Eng Ctrl Systems LLC 860 236-0651
1 Charter Oak Blvd West Hartford CT (06110) ***(G-5100)***
Triumph Eng Ctrl Systems LLC 860 236-0651
1 Talcott Rd West Hartford CT (06110) ***(G-5101)***
Triumph Group Inc 860 726-9378
1395 Blue Hills Ave Bloomfield CT (06002) ***(G-268)***
Triumph Manufacturing Co Inc 860 635-8811
422 Timber Ridge Rd Middletown CT (06457) ***(G-2229)***
Trivak Inc 978 453-7123
280 Howard St Lowell MA (01852) ***(G-12440)***
Trividia Mfg Solutions (HQ) 603 788-2848
89 Bridge St Lancaster NH (03584) ***(G-18606)***
Trividia Mfg Solutions 603 788-4952
248 Main St Lancaster NH (03584) ***(G-18607)***
Troemner 978 655-3377
1600 Osgood St Ste E213 North Andover MA (01845) ***(G-13732)***
Trombley Industries Inc 207 328-4503
849 Access Hwy Limestone ME (04750) ***(G-6345)***
Trombley Redi-Mix Inc (PA) 207 551-3770
221 Parsons Rd Presque Isle ME (04769) ***(G-6770)***
Tronica Circuits Inc 978 372-7224
26 Parkridge Rd Haverhill MA (01835) ***(G-11478)***
Tronox Incorporated (HQ) 203 705-3800
1 Stamford Plz Stamford CT (06901) ***(G-4350)***
Tronox Limited 203 705-3800
1 Stamford Plz Stamford CT (06901) ***(G-4351)***
Tronox LLC (PA) 203 705-3800
263 Tresser Blvd Ste 1100 Stamford CT (06901) ***(G-4352)***
Tropax Precision Manufacturing 203 794-0733
10 Precision Rd Danbury CT (06810) ***(G-1002)***
Tropical Products Inc 978 740-5665
220 Highland Ave Salem MA (01970) ***(G-14947)***
Tropical Smoothie of Bristol 508 636-1424
14 Eliza Ln Dartmouth MA (02747) ***(G-10278)***
Tropicana Products Inc 508 821-2056
305 Constitution Dr Ste 2 Taunton MA (02780) ***(G-15792)***
Trow & Holden Co Inc 802 476-7221
45 S Main St Ste 57 Barre VT (05641) ***(G-21643)***
Troy City Woodworking, Fall River *Also called Brendan C Kinnane Inc* ***(G-10672)***

ALPHABETIC

Troy Industries Inc....413 788-4288
151 Capital Dr West Springfield MA (01089) ***(G-16556)***
Troy Micro Five Inc....802 524-0076
79 Walnut St Saint Albans VT (05478) ***(G-22383)***
Troy Minerals Inc....802 878-5103
180 Fire Hill Rd Florence VT (05744) ***(G-21992)***
Troy Minerals Co....802 878-5103
312 Village Dr Colchester VT (05446) ***(G-21883)***
Troy Voisine Logging Inc....207 794-6301
60 N Chester Rd Chester ME (04457) ***(G-5906)***
Troy Winger....207 667-1815
22 Old Brewer Farm Rd Trenton ME (04605) ***(G-7103)***
Trp Logging....207 263-6425
9 Dike Gaddis Loop East Machias ME (04630) ***(G-5984)***
Tru Chocolate Inc....855 878-2462
610 Kenoza St Haverhill MA (01830) ***(G-11479)***
Tru Hitch Inc....860 379-7772
16 W West Hill Rd Pleasant Valley CT (06063) ***(G-3548)***
Tru Technologies Inc....978 532-0775
245 Lynnfield St Peabody MA (01960) ***(G-14379)***
Truck Buyer Inc....413 273-9993
33 Oakdale St Springfield MA (01104) ***(G-15519)***
True Colors Print & Design, North Woodstock *Also called Thh Associates LLC* ***(G-19399)***
True Grit Abrasive Inc....508 636-2008
46 Westlook Ln Westport MA (02790) ***(G-16849)***
True Guilford Inc....207 876-3331
9 Oak St Guilford ME (04443) ***(G-6162)***
True Machine Co Inc....508 379-0329
2222 Gar Hwy Swansea MA (02777) ***(G-15718)***
True North Networks LLC....603 624-6777
15 Business Center Dr Swanzey NH (03446) ***(G-19890)***
True Position Mfg LLC....860 291-2987
40 Sandra Dr Ste 3 South Windsor CT (06074) ***(G-4017)***
True Precision Inc....413 788-4226
17 Allston Ave West Springfield MA (01089) ***(G-16557)***
True Precision Industries Inc....413 788-4226
17 Allston Ave West Springfield MA (01089) ***(G-16558)***
True Publishing Company....203 272-5316
125 Grandview Ave Wallingford CT (06492) ***(G-4823)***
True Technology....978 352-8701
2c Moulton St Georgetown MA (01833) ***(G-11151)***
True Words Tortillas Inc....508 255-3338
136 Rt 6a Orleans MA (02653) ***(G-14243)***
Trueform Runner, Chester *Also called Samsara Fitness LLC* ***(G-776)***
Trueline Corporation....203 757-0344
196 Mill St Ste 1 Waterbury CT (06706) ***(G-4968)***
Trueline Publishing LLC....207 510-4099
561 Congress St Portland ME (04101) ***(G-6743)***
Truelove & Maclean Inc....860 274-9600
57 Callender Rd Watertown CT (06795) ***(G-5031)***
Truex Machine Co Inc....781 826-6875
25 Pond St Hanover MA (02339) ***(G-11357)***
Trumbull Printing, Trumbull *Also called Hersam Acorn Cmnty Pubg LLC* ***(G-4624)***
Trumbull Printing Inc....203 261-2548
205 Spring Hill Rd Trumbull CT (06611) ***(G-4636)***
Trumbull Recreation Supply Co....860 429-6604
148 River Rd Willington CT (06279) ***(G-5271)***
Trumpf Inc (HQ)....860 255-6000
111 Hyde Rd Farmington CT (06032) ***(G-1517)***
Trumpf Inc....860 255-6000
3 Johnson Ave Plainville CT (06062) ***(G-3522)***
Trumpf Inc....860 255-6000
1 Johnson Ave Farmington CT (06032) ***(G-1518)***
Trumpf Photonics Inc....860 255-6000
111 Hyde Rd Farmington CT (06032) ***(G-1519)***
Trumpit Inc (PA)....617 650-9292
13 Briarwood Ln Winchester MA (01890) ***(G-17099)***
Truss Engineering Corporation....413 543-1298
181 Goodwin St Indian Orchard MA (01151) ***(G-11898)***
Truss Manufacturing Inc....860 665-0000
97 Stanwell Rd Newington CT (06111) ***(G-2908)***
Truss Worthy Truss....207 532-3200
217 Lincoln Rd Hodgdon ME (04730) ***(G-6194)***
Trussco Inc....401 295-0669
25 Bonneau Rd North Kingstown RI (02852) ***(G-20747)***
Trustees of Boston College....617 552-2844
22 Stone Ave Chestnut Hill MA (02467) ***(G-9993)***
Trustees of Boston University....617 353-3081
10 Lenox St Fl 3 Brookline MA (02446) ***(G-9223)***
Trustees of Tufts College....617 628-5000
520 Boston Ave Medford MA (02155) ***(G-12951)***
Truth Trckg Expedited Svcs LLC....860 306-5630
2015 Main St Hartford CT (06120) ***(G-1882)***
TRW Fastening Systems, Westminster *Also called ZF Active Safety & Elec US LLC* ***(G-16821)***
Trycycle Data Systems US Inc....860 558-1148
400 Farmington Ave # 1844 Farmington CT (06032) ***(G-1520)***
Tryon Manufacturing Company....203 929-0464
30 Oliver Ter Shelton CT (06484) ***(G-3883)***
TSC, Cambridge *Also called Translational Sciences Corp* ***(G-9683)***

Tshb Inc....978 465-8950
11 Malcolm Hoyt Dr Newburyport MA (01950) ***(G-13543)***
Tsi Group Inc (HQ)....603 964-0296
94 Tide Mill Rd Hampton NH (03842) ***(G-18275)***
Tsl Snowshoes LLC....802 660-8232
73 Armand Ln Williston VT (05495) ***(G-22695)***
TSS & A Inc....800 633-3536
115 Waterbury Rd Prospect CT (06712) ***(G-3599)***
Tte Lab Services, Hopkinton *Also called Tte Laboratories Inc* ***(G-11741)***
Tte Laboratories Inc....800 242-6022
77 Main St Hopkinton MA (01748) ***(G-11741)***
Ttm Printed Circuit Group Inc....860 684-8000
15 Industrial Park Dr Stafford Springs CT (06076) ***(G-4118)***
Ttm Technologies Inc....860 684-5881
4 Old Monson Rd Stafford Springs CT (06076) ***(G-4119)***
Ttm Technologies Inc....860 684-8000
20 Industrial Park Dr Stafford Springs CT (06076) ***(G-4120)***
Tub's & Stuff Plumbing Supply, Ansonia *Also called Kensco Inc* ***(G-20)***
Tube Chassis Designz....781 293-5005
1484 Main St Hanson MA (02341) ***(G-11369)***
Tube Hollows International....844 721-8823
39 Enterprise Dr Ste 2 Windham ME (04062) ***(G-7258)***
Tubodyne Company....401 438-2540
4 Industrial Way Riverside RI (02915) ***(G-21177)***
Tubular Automotive & Engrg....781 878-9875
248 Weymouth St Rockland MA (02370) ***(G-14831)***
Tucci Lumber Co LLC....203 956-6181
227 Wilson Ave Norwalk CT (06854) ***(G-3262)***
Tucel Industries Inc....802 247-6824
2014 Forest Dale Rd Forest Dale VT (05745) ***(G-21993)***
Tucker Engineering Inc....978 532-5900
4 5th St Peabody MA (01960) ***(G-14380)***
Tucker Mountain Homes Inc....603 279-4320
26 Tucker Mountain Rd Meredith NH (03253) ***(G-18981)***
Tuckerman Stl Fabricators Inc....617 569-8373
256 Marginal St Ste 2 Boston MA (02128) ***(G-8892)***
Tudor Converted Products Inc (PA)....203 304-1875
22 Main St Unit 1b Newtown CT (06470) ***(G-2946)***
Tudor House Furniture Co Inc....203 288-8451
929 Sherman Ave Hamden CT (06514) ***(G-1792)***
Tuff Crete Corporation....603 485-1969
84 Exeter Rd South Hampton NH (03827) ***(G-19857)***
Tuff Parts Inc....207 767-1063
33 Haskell Ave South Portland ME (04106) ***(G-7042)***
Tufin Software North Amer Inc....781 685-4940
2 Oliver St Boston MA (02109) ***(G-8893)***
Tufpak Inc....603 539-4126
698 Browns Ridge Rd Ossipee NH (03864) ***(G-19424)***
Tuftane Eti, Fall River *Also called Tuftane Extrusion Tech Inc* ***(G-10773)***
Tuftane Extrusion Tech Inc....978 921-8200
96 Wordell St Fall River MA (02721) ***(G-10773)***
Tufts Daily, Medford *Also called Trustees of Tufts College* ***(G-12951)***
Tug Hollow Firearms, Wakefield *Also called Thayer Industries Inc* ***(G-21281)***
Tukey Brothers Inc....207 465-3570
460 Smithfield Rd Belgrade ME (04917) ***(G-5700)***
Tulco Inc....978 772-4412
9 Bishop Rd Ayer MA (01432) ***(G-7941)***
Tulip Interfaces Inc (PA)....833 468-8547
561 Windsor St B402 Somerville MA (02143) ***(G-15226)***
Tune-Bot, Lawrence *Also called Overtone Labs Inc* ***(G-12070)***
Tunstall Corporation (PA)....413 594-8695
118 Exchange St Chicopee MA (01013) ***(G-10065)***
Turbine Controls Inc (PA)....860 242-0448
5 Old Windsor Rd Bloomfield CT (06002) ***(G-269)***
Turbine Kinetics Inc....860 633-8520
60 Sequin Dr Ste 2 Glastonbury CT (06033) ***(G-1580)***
Turbine Specialists LLC....207 947-9327
55 Baker Blvd Brewer ME (04412) ***(G-5802)***
Turbine Technologies Inc (PA)....860 678-1642
126 Hyde Rd Farmington CT (06032) ***(G-1521)***
Turbocam Inc....603 905-0200
38 Redemption Rd Barrington NH (03825) ***(G-17624)***
Turbocam Inc (PA)....603 905-0200
607 Calef Hwy Ste 200 Barrington NH (03825) ***(G-17625)***
Turbocam Atmted Prod Systems I (HQ)....603 905-0220
607 Calef Hwy Ste 100 Barrington NH (03825) ***(G-17626)***
Turbocam Automated Production....603 905-0240
5 Faraday Dr Dover NH (03820) ***(G-18062)***
Turbocam Energy Solutions LLC....603 905-0200
5 Faraday Dr Dover NH (03820) ***(G-18063)***
Turbocam International, Barrington *Also called Turbocam Inc* ***(G-17625)***
Turley Publications Inc....413 786-7747
14 Southwick St Feeding Hills MA (01030) ***(G-10804)***
Turley Publications Inc (PA)....800 824-6548
24 Water St Palmer MA (01069) ***(G-14298)***
Turley Publications Inc....413 967-3505
80 Main St Ware MA (01082) ***(G-16239)***
Turley Publications Inc....978 355-4000
5 Exchange St Fl 1 Barre MA (01005) ***(G-7952)***

Turmax Printing Services, Winooski *Also called Chester Brothers* ***(G-22718)***
Turmoil Inc 603 352-0053
735 W Swanzey Rd West Swanzey NH (03469) ***(G-19969)***
Turmoil Manufacturing, West Swanzey *Also called RMA Manufacturing LLC* ***(G-19968)***
Turn Key Lumber Inc 978 798-1370
305 Leominster Shirley Rd Lunenburg MA (01462) ***(G-12484)***
Turn Wright Machine Work 508 394-0724
791 Main St West Dennis MA (02670) ***(G-16476)***
Turnaround Letter, The, Boston *Also called New Generation Research Inc* ***(G-8734)***
Turner Publishing Inc 207 225-2076
5 Fern St Turner ME (04282) ***(G-7111)***
Turning Acquisitions LLC 207 336-2400
46 John Ellingwood Rd Buckfield ME (04220) ***(G-5853)***
Turning Memories Into Memois, Lisbon *Also called Memoir Network* ***(G-6364)***
Turning Point Industry FL 239 340-1942
160 Corporate Park Dr Pembroke MA (02359) ***(G-14430)***
Turning Stone Sand & Grav LLC 413 519-1560
128 Moody Rd Enfield CT (06082) ***(G-1388)***
Turnstone Inc 203 625-0000
154 Prospect St Greenwich CT (06830) ***(G-1658)***
Turq LLC 203 344-1257
123 Lockwood Rd Riverside CT (06878) ***(G-3692)***
Turtle Clan Global, Sharon *Also called Tcg Green Technologies Inc* ***(G-3770)***
Turtle Skin, New Ipswich *Also called Warwick Mills Inc* ***(G-19311)***
Tutti Frutti 508 695-7795
999 S Washington St North Attleboro MA (02760) ***(G-13785)***
Tuttle Law Print Inc 802 773-9171
414 Quality Ln 453 Rutland VT (05701) ***(G-22356)***
Tuttle Printing & Engraving, Rutland *Also called Tuttle Law Print Inc* ***(G-22356)***
Tuttle Publishing, North Clarendon *Also called Charles E Tuttle Co Inc* ***(G-22214)***
TW Clark Pulp & Logging LLC 207 368-4766
607 Elm St Newport ME (04953) ***(G-6487)***
TW Lighting Incorporated (PA) 617 830-6755
396 Washington St 277 Wellesley MA (02481) ***(G-16390)***
TWC Trans World Consulting 860 668-5108
383 S Main St Windsor Locks CT (06096) ***(G-5402)***
Twd Inc 508 279-2650
75 Hale St Bridgewater MA (02324) ***(G-9091)***
Twd Surfaces, Bridgewater *Also called Twd Inc* ***(G-9091)***
Tweave LLC 508 285-6701
1450 Brayton Ave Fall River MA (02721) ***(G-10774)***
Twentieth Century Casting 401 728-6836
11 Webb St Pawtucket RI (02860) ***(G-20907)***
Twenty First Century Foods, Boston *Also called 21st Century Foods Inc* ***(G-8327)***
Twenty Five Commerce Inc 203 866-0540
25 Commerce St Norwalk CT (06850) ***(G-3263)***
Twentyfrst Cntury Bchmcals Inc 508 303-8222
260 Cedar Hill St Marlborough MA (01752) ***(G-12839)***
Twin City Machining Inc 978 874-1940
4 Curtis Rd Westminster MA (01473) ***(G-16817)***
Twin City Times 207 795-5017
10 Valley View Dr Gorham ME (04038) ***(G-6134)***
Twin Coast Metrology Inc 508 517-4508
6 Eastern Rd Acton MA (01720) ***(G-7392)***
Twin Creeks Technologies Inc 978 777-0846
1 Industrial Dr Unit 1 # 1 Danvers MA (01923) ***(G-10268)***
Twin Cy Upholstering & Mat Co 781 843-1780
476 Quincy Ave Braintree MA (02184) ***(G-9044)***
Twin Leather Co Inc 508 583-3485
24 Jason Way West Bridgewater MA (02379) ***(G-16461)***
Twin Rivers Paper Company Corp 207 523-2350
82 Bridge Ave Madawaska ME (04756) ***(G-6402)***
Twin Rivers Paper Company LLC 207 523-2350
707 Sable Oaks Dr Ste 100 South Portland ME (04106) ***(G-7043)***
Twin Rivers Paper Company LLC (PA) 207 728-3321
82 Bridge Ave Madawaska ME (04756) ***(G-6403)***
Twin Rivers Tech Holdings Inc 617 472-9200
780 Washington St Quincy MA (02169) ***(G-14662)***
Twin Rivers Tech Ltd Partnr 617 472-9200
780 Washington St Quincy MA (02169) ***(G-14663)***
Twin Rivers Tech Mfg Corp 888 929-8780
780 Washington St Quincy MA (02169) ***(G-14664)***
Twin Rivers Technologies U.S., Quincy *Also called Twin Rivers Tech Holdings Inc* ***(G-14662)***
Twin State Signs Inc 802 872-8949
14 Gauthier Dr Essex Junction VT (05452) ***(G-21962)***
Twincraft Inc (PA) 802 655-2200
2 Tigan St Winooski VT (05404) ***(G-22726)***
Twincraft Soap, Winooski *Also called Twincraft Inc* ***(G-22726)***
Twisted 207 942-9530
663 Stillwater Ave Bangor ME (04401) ***(G-5661)***
Two C Pack, Nashua *Also called Autajon Packg - Boston Corp* ***(G-19118)***
Two Go Drycleaning Inc 802 658-9469
1233 Shelburne Rd Ste 190 South Burlington VT (05403) ***(G-22474)***
Two Hands Inc 401 785-2727
7 Ninigret Ave Providence RI (02907) ***(G-21142)***
Two In One Manufacturing Inc 603 595-8212
51 Lake St Ste 4 Nashua NH (03060) ***(G-19276)***
Two Islands Corporation 207 469-3600
583 Acadia Hwy Orland ME (04472) ***(G-6551)***
Two Old Broads 207 255-6561
41 Broadway Machias ME (04654) ***(G-6396)***
Two Rivers Pet Products Inc 207 225-3965
469 N Parish Rd Turner ME (04282) ***(G-7112)***
Two Saints Inc 401 490-5500
81 Western Industrial Dr B Cranston RI (02921) ***(G-20306)***
Txc Inc 603 893-4999
8 Industrial Way Ste C7 Salem NH (03079) ***(G-19773)***
Txv Aerospace Composites LLC 425 785-0883
55 Broadcommon Rd Unit 2 Bristol RI (02809) ***(G-20108)***
Tyca Corporation (PA) 978 612-0002
470 Main St Clinton MA (01510) ***(G-10094)***
Tyco Acquisition Corp. Xxv NV, Westminster *Also called Simplex Time Recorder Co* ***(G-16813)***
Tyco Adhesives 508 918-1600
25 Forge Pkwy Franklin MA (02038) ***(G-11094)***
Tyco Elec Identification, East Providence *Also called Te Connectivity Corporation* ***(G-20446)***
Tyco Fire Products LP 508 583-8447
27 Doherty Ave Avon MA (02322) ***(G-7899)***
Tyco Fire Protection Products, Avon *Also called Tyco Fire Products LP* ***(G-7899)***
Tyco International MGT Co LLC 508 261-6200
15 Hampshire St Mansfield MA (02048) ***(G-12667)***
Tyco Safety Products Us Inc 800 435-3192
91 Technology Dr Westminster MA (01441) ***(G-16818)***
Tyger Tool Inc 203 375-4344
45 Sperry Ave Stratford CT (06615) ***(G-4455)***
Tylaska Marine Hardware, Mystic *Also called Vector Engineering Inc* ***(G-2455)***
Tyler Automatics Incorporated 860 283-5878
437 S Main St Thomaston CT (06787) ***(G-4523)***
Tyler R Hews 207 272-9273
309 Fort Fairfield Rd Caribou ME (04736) ***(G-5891)***
Tyler Technologies Inc 603 578-6745
10 Al Paul Ln Ste 202 Merrimack NH (03054) ***(G-19038)***
Tyler Technologies Inc 207 781-2260
1 Tyler Dr Yarmouth ME (04096) ***(G-7301)***
Tyler Technologies Inc 800 288-8167
307 Highlander Way Manchester NH (03103) ***(G-18943)***
Tyler Technologies Inc 207 781-4606
1 Tyler Dr Yarmouth ME (04096) ***(G-7302)***
Tylergraphics Inc 603 524-6625
14 Lexington Dr Ste 2 Laconia NH (03246) ***(G-18590)***
Tylers Sheet Metal Shop Inc 207 929-6912
1126 Long Plains Rd Ir3 Buxton ME (04093) ***(G-5862)***
Tyne Plastics LLC (PA) 860 673-7100
252 Spielman Hwy Ste B Burlington CT (06013) ***(G-681)***
Type Is Right The, Moosup *Also called Typeisright* ***(G-2428)***
Typeisright 860 564-0537
11 E Main St Moosup CT (06354) ***(G-2428)***
Typesafe Inc 617 622-2200
1 Brattle Sq Cambridge MA (02138) ***(G-9684)***
U M S, Bow *Also called Unique Mechanical Services Inc* ***(G-17735)***
U S A Trains, Malden *Also called Charles Ro Mfg Co Inc* ***(G-12565)***
U S Artistic Embroidery Inc 603 929-0505
416 High St Hampton NH (03842) ***(G-18276)***
U S Bells, Prospect Harbor *Also called Richard Fisher* ***(G-6771)***
U S Felt Company Inc 207 324-0063
61 Industrial Ave Sanford ME (04073) ***(G-6895)***
U S Fluids Inc 413 525-0660
198 Benton Dr 202 East Longmeadow MA (01028) ***(G-10500)***
U S Made Co Inc 978 777-8383
76 Newbury St Danvers MA (01923) ***(G-10269)***
U S Product Labels Inc 603 894-6020
8c Industrial Way Salem NH (03079) ***(G-19774)***
U S Stucco LLC 860 667-1935
28 Costello Pl Newington CT (06111) ***(G-2909)***
U S Synthetics Corp 978 345-0176
158 Airport Rd Fitchburg MA (01420) ***(G-10858)***
U T Z 860 383-4266
140 Route 32 North Franklin CT (06254) ***(G-2992)***
U Haul Co of Massachusetts 508 668-2242
1 Production Rd Walpole MA (02081) ***(G-16015)***
U-Sealusa LLC 860 667-0911
56 Fenn Rd Newington CT (06111) ***(G-2910)***
U-Tech Wire Rope & Supply LLC 203 865-8885
222 Universal Dr Bldg 9 North Haven CT (06473) ***(G-3065)***
U.s Surgical, New Haven *Also called United States Surgical Corp* ***(G-2750)***
Ua, Naugatuck *Also called United Avionics Inc* ***(G-2499)***
Uav - America Inc 603 389-6364
240 Stage Rd Nottingham NH (03290) ***(G-19418)***
Ubio Inc 401 541-9172
1603 Plainfield Pike B5 Johnston RI (02919) ***(G-20544)***
Ubm LLC 203 662-6501
330 Post Rd Fl 2 Darien CT (06820) ***(G-1035)***
Ufp Technologies Inc (PA) 978 352-2200
100 Hale St Newburyport MA (01950) ***(G-13544)***
Ufp Technologies Inc 978 352-2200
175 Ward Hill Ave Haverhill MA (01835) ***(G-11480)***

ALPHABETIC

Ugly Dog Hunting Co 802 482-7054
1067 Silver St Hinesburg VT (05461) ***(G-22031)***
Uh Motor Sports, Monroe *Also called New Age Motorsports LLC* ***(G-2410)***
Ulbrich of Georgia Inc 203 239-4481
153 Washington Ave North Haven CT (06473) ***(G-3066)***
Ulbrich Stainless Steels 203 269-2507
1 Dudley Ave Wallingford CT (06492) ***(G-4824)***
Ulbrich Steel, Wallingford *Also called Ulbrich Stainless Steels* ***(G-4824)***
Ulbrich Stnless Stels Spcial M (PA) 203 239-4481
153 Washington Ave North Haven CT (06473) ***(G-3067)***
Ullman Devices Corporation 203 438-6577
664 Danbury Rd Ridgefield CT (06877) ***(G-3687)***
Uls of New England LLC 978 683-7390
65 Manchester St Lawrence MA (01841) ***(G-12079)***
Ultimate Glass Services LLC 603 642-3375
17 Route 125 Unit 12 Kingston NH (03848) ***(G-18547)***
Ultimate Industries 617 923-1568
6 Clark Rd Kennebunkport ME (04046) ***(G-6248)***
Ultimate Ink LLC 203 762-0602
681 Danbury Rd Ste 1 Wilton CT (06897) ***(G-5309)***
Ultimate Wireforms Inc 860 582-9111
200 Central St Bristol CT (06010) ***(G-621)***
Ultra Clean Equipment Inc 860 669-1354
112 Nod Rd Ste 9 Clinton CT (06413) ***(G-797)***
Ultra Elec Measurement Systems, Wallingford *Also called Measurement Systems Inc* ***(G-4772)***
Ultra Elec Ocean Systems Inc 781 848-3400
115 Bay State Dr Braintree MA (02184) ***(G-9045)***
Ultra Filtronics Ltd 781 961-4775
91 York Ave Randolph MA (02368) ***(G-14700)***
Ultra Food and Fuel 860 223-2005
788 W Main St New Britain CT (06053) ***(G-2587)***
Ultra Precision Machining, Smithfield *Also called D Simpson Inc* ***(G-21217)***
Ultra Sonic Seal Co, Newtown *Also called Sonics & Materials Inc* ***(G-2938)***
Ultraclad Corporation 978 358-7945
10 Perry Way Newburyport MA (01950) ***(G-13545)***
Ultragenyx Pharmaceutical Inc 617 949-4010
840 Memorial Dr Cambridge MA (02139) ***(G-9685)***
Ultramar Inc 603 788-2771
440 Glen Ave Lancaster NH (03584) ***(G-18608)***
Ultramatic West 203 745-4688
87 Beechwood Ave Hamden CT (06514) ***(G-1793)***
Ultrasonic Systems Inc 978 521-0095
135 Ward Hill Ave Haverhill MA (01835) ***(G-11481)***
Ultron LLC 207 832-4502
948 Back Cove Rd Waldoboro ME (04572) ***(G-7137)***
Umaco Inc 978 453-8881
60 Newhall St Rear Lowell MA (01852) ***(G-12441)***
Umami Noodle 207 947-9991
1 Main St Bangor ME (04401) ***(G-5662)***
Umass Extention Book Store, Amherst *Also called University Massachusetts Inc* ***(G-7529)***
Umass Mem Mri Imaging Ctr LLC 508 756-7300
214 Shrewsbury St Worcester MA (01604) ***(G-17492)***
Umech Technologies LLC 617 923-2942
25 Clarendon St Watertown MA (02472) ***(G-16326)***
Umicore Precious Mtls USA Inc 401 450-0907
300 Wampanoag Trl Ste A Riverside RI (02915) ***(G-21178)***
Unadilla Antennas Mfgco 978 975-2711
8 Marblehead St Ste B North Andover MA (01845) ***(G-13733)***
Unarco Material Handling Inc 603 772-2070
1 Hampton Rd Unit 106 Exeter NH (03833) ***(G-18134)***
Unas Grinding Corporation 860 289-1538
28 Cherry St East Hartford CT (06108) ***(G-1231)***
Uncle Bill's Tweezers, West Hartford *Also called El Mar Inc* ***(G-5068)***
Uncle Wileys Inc 203 256-9313
1220 Post Rd Ste 2 Fairfield CT (06824) ***(G-1458)***
Under Cover Inc 508 997-7600
138 Hatch St New Bedford MA (02745) ***(G-13456)***
Under Pressure LLC 508 641-0421
1 Apple House Rd Lakeville MA (02347) ***(G-11980)***
Underground Press 603 323-2022
516 Huckins Rd Freedom NH (03836) ***(G-18171)***
Uneco Manufacturing Inc 413 594-2700
330 Fuller Rd Chicopee MA (01020) ***(G-10066)***
Unerectors Inc 617 436-8333
82 Crescent Ave Boston MA (02125) ***(G-8894)***
Unetixs Vascular Inc 401 583-0089
125 Commerce Park Rd North Kingstown RI (02852) ***(G-20748)***
Unger Enterprises LLC 203 366-4884
425 Asylum St Bridgeport CT (06610) ***(G-500)***
Unger Industrial LLC 203 336-3344
425 Asylum St Bridgeport CT (06610) ***(G-501)***
Unholtz-Dickie Corporation (PA) 203 265-9875
6 Brookside Dr Wallingford CT (06492) ***(G-4825)***
UNI Pac, Holyoke *Also called UNI-Pac Inc* ***(G-11662)***
UNI-Cast LLC 603 625-5761
11 Industrial Dr Londonderry NH (03053) ***(G-18742)***
UNI-Pac Inc 413 534-5284
150 Middle Water St Holyoke MA (01040) ***(G-11662)***
UNI-SIM, Windham *Also called Windham Millwork Inc* ***(G-7260)***
Uniboard Corp 860 428-5979
570 River Rd Putnam CT (06260) ***(G-3637)***
Unicast Development Co., New Haven *Also called Joshua LLC* ***(G-2699)***
Unicom Engineering Inc (HQ) 781 332-1000
25 Dan Rd Canton MA (02021) ***(G-9791)***
Unicor, Danbury *Also called Federal Prison Industries* ***(G-919)***
Unicore LLC 413 284-9995
6 Chamber Rd Palmer MA (01069) ***(G-14299)***
Unicorr Group, North Haven *Also called Connecticut Container Corp* ***(G-3018)***
Unicus Pharmaceuticals LLC 508 659-7002
30 Robert W Boyden Rd Taunton MA (02780) ***(G-15793)***
Unified2 Globl Packg Group LLC 508 865-1155
223 Wrcster Prvdence Tpke Sutton MA (01590) ***(G-15694)***
Unilever Ascc AG 203 381-2482
3 Corporate Dr Shelton CT (06484) ***(G-3884)***
Unilever Bestfoods North Amer 802 775-4986
69 Park St Rutland VT (05701) ***(G-22357)***
Unilever Foods Chill, Trumbull *Also called Thomas J Lipton Inc* ***(G-4635)***
Unilever Home and Per Care NA 203 502-0086
75 Merritt Blvd Trumbull CT (06611) ***(G-4637)***
Unilever Hpc NA, Trumbull *Also called Unilever Home and Per Care NA* ***(G-4637)***
Unilever Hpc USA, Trumbull *Also called Unilever Trumbull RES Svcs Inc* ***(G-4639)***
Unilever Hpc USA 203 381-3311
45 Commerce Dr Trumbull CT (06611) ***(G-4638)***
Unilever Trumbull RES Svcs Inc (HQ) 203 502-0086
40 Merritt Blvd Trumbull CT (06611) ***(G-4639)***
Unimacts Global LLC (PA) 410 415-6070
2 Sedge Rd Lexington MA (02420) ***(G-12280)***
Unimark Plastics, East Wilton *Also called Jarden LLC* ***(G-5987)***
Unimation 203 792-3412
102 Wooster St Ste 4a Bethel CT (06801) ***(G-186)***
Unimetal Surface Finishing LLC 203 729-8244
15 E Waterbury Rd Naugatuck CT (06770) ***(G-2498)***
Unimetal Surface Finishing LLC (PA) 860 283-0271
135 S Main St Thomaston CT (06787) ***(G-4524)***
Unimin Lime Corporation (HQ) 203 966-8880
258 Elm St New Canaan CT (06840) ***(G-2619)***
Uninsred Alttude Cnnection Inc 860 333-1461
330 Day St Brooklyn CT (06234) ***(G-673)***
Union Biometrica Inc (PA) 508 893-3115
84 October Hill Rd Ste 12 Holliston MA (01746) ***(G-11610)***
Union Bookbinding Company Inc (PA) 508 676-8580
649 Alden St Fall River MA (02723) ***(G-10775)***
Union Bookbinding II LLC 508 676-8580
649 Alden St Fall River MA (02723) ***(G-10776)***
Union Etchants International 978 777-7860
10 Electronics Ave Danvers MA (01923) ***(G-10270)***
Union Group , The, Fall River *Also called Union Bookbinding Company Inc* ***(G-10775)***
Union Group, The, Fall River *Also called Union Bookbinding II LLC* ***(G-10776)***
Union Leader Corporation (PA) 603 668-4321
100 William Loeb Dr Manchester NH (03109) ***(G-18944)***
Union Machine Company Lynn Inc (PA) 978 521-5100
6 Federal Way Groveland MA (01834) ***(G-11304)***
Union Miniere 617 960-5900
12 Channel St Ste 702 Boston MA (02210) ***(G-8895)***
Union Products, Fitchburg *Also called Cado Products Inc* ***(G-10817)***
Union Specialties Inc 978 465-1717
3 Malcolm Hoyt Dr Newburyport MA (01950) ***(G-13546)***
Unipoint Technologies 617 952-4244
275 Grove St Auburndale MA (02466) ***(G-7872)***
Uniprise International Inc 860 589-7262
50 Napco Dr Terryville CT (06786) ***(G-4495)***
Uniprise Sales, Terryville *Also called Uniprise International Inc* ***(G-4495)***
Unique Extrusions Incorporated 860 632-1314
10 Countyline Dr Cromwell CT (06416) ***(G-862)***
Unique Mechanical Services Inc 603 856-0057
162 W Main St Bow NH (03304) ***(G-17735)***
Unique Plating Co 401 943-7366
66 Mill St Johnston RI (02919) ***(G-20545)***
Unique Spiral Stairs Inc 207 437-2415
117 Benton Rd Albion ME (04910) ***(G-5513)***
Unique Woodworking, East Weymouth *Also called L D G Corporation* ***(G-10545)***
Unisite LLC 781 926-7135
116 Huntington Ave # 1750 Boston MA (02116) ***(G-8896)***
Unistar Corporation 603 323-9327
Junction Of Rtes 25 113 E Tamworth NH (03886) ***(G-19895)***
Unistress Corp 413 499-1441
550 Cheshire Rd Pittsfield MA (01201) ***(G-14512)***
Unit Tool Co 401 781-2647
101 Venturi Ave Frnt 1 Warwick RI (02888) ***(G-21436)***
Unit4 Business Software Inc (HQ) 877 704-5974
3 Burlington Woods Dr # 201 Burlington MA (01803) ***(G-9350)***
Unitarian Universalist Assn 617 742-2110
41 Mount Vernon St Boston MA (02108) ***(G-8897)***
Unitec Engineering Inc 978 764-0553
10 Collins Brook Rd Windham NH (03087) ***(G-20013)***

United Abrasives Inc (PA)......860 456-7131
185 Boston Post Rd North Windham CT (06256) ***(G-3084)***
United Aero Group, Shelton *Also called Gelder Aerospace LLC* ***(G-3804)***
United Avionics Inc......203 723-1404
38 Great Hill Rd Naugatuck CT (06770) ***(G-2499)***
United Citrus Products Co......800 229-7300
195 Constitution Dr Taunton MA (02780) ***(G-15794)***
United Comb & Novelty Corp (PA)......978 537-2096
33 Patriots Cir Leominster MA (01453) ***(G-12196)***
United Communications Corp......508 222-7000
34 S Main St Attleboro MA (02703) ***(G-7804)***
United Curtain Co Inc (PA)......508 588-4100
91 Wales Ave Ste 1 Avon MA (02322) ***(G-7900)***
United Electric Controls Co......203 877-2795
340 Woodmont Rd Milford CT (06460) ***(G-2377)***
United Electric Controls Co......617 926-1000
180 Dexter Ave Watertown MA (02472) ***(G-16327)***
United Fbrcnts Strainrite Corp (HQ)......207 376-1600
65 First Flight Dr Auburn ME (04210) ***(G-5600)***
United Foods Incorporated (PA)......617 482-9879
170 Lincoln St Boston MA (02111) ***(G-8898)***
United Gear & Machine Co Inc......860 623-6618
1087 East St S Suffield CT (06078) ***(G-4469)***
United Glass To Metal Sealing......978 327-5880
15 Union St Ste G30 Lawrence MA (01840) ***(G-12080)***
United Global Supply, Middleboro *Also called United Shoe Machinery Corp* ***(G-13079)***
United Industrial Tex Pdts Inc (PA)......413 737-0095
321 Main St West Springfield MA (01089) ***(G-16559)***
United Industrial Tex Pdts Inc......413 737-0095
136 Bliss St West Springfield MA (01089) ***(G-16560)***
United Innovations Inc......413 533-7500
120 Whiting Farms Rd # 2 Holyoke MA (01040) ***(G-11663)***
United Lens Company Inc......508 765-5421
259 Worcester St Southbridge MA (01550) ***(G-15407)***
United Marble Fabricators Inc......617 926-6226
10 Munroe Ave Watertown MA (02472) ***(G-16328)***
United Mch & Tl Design Co Inc......603 642-3601
18 River Rd Fremont NH (03044) ***(G-18181)***
United Metal Fabricators Inc......508 754-1800
1021 Southbridge St Worcester MA (01610) ***(G-17493)***
United Ophthalmics LLC......203 745-8399
430 Smith St Meriden CT (06451) ***(G-2144)***
United Photonics LLC......617 752-2073
42 Diane Dr Vernon Rockville CT (06066) ***(G-4687)***
United Pioneer Company, Stamford *Also called Corinth Acquisition Corp* ***(G-4174)***
United Plastic Fabricating Inc (PA)......978 975-4520
165 Flagship Dr North Andover MA (01845) ***(G-13734)***
United Plastics, Leominster *Also called United Comb & Novelty Corp* ***(G-12196)***
United Plastics Technologies......860 224-1110
163 John Downey Dr New Britain CT (06051) ***(G-2588)***
United Plating Inc......401 461-5857
2 2nd Ave Cranston RI (02910) ***(G-20307)***
United Prosthetics Inc......617 773-7140
300 Congress St Ste 404a Quincy MA (02169) ***(G-14665)***
United Publications Inc......207 846-0600
106 Lafayette St Yarmouth ME (04096) ***(G-7303)***
United Puett Starting Gate......802 463-3440
7668 Us Route 5 Ste B Westminster VT (05158) ***(G-22631)***
United Screw Machine Products......508 865-7295
34 Howe Ave Millbury MA (01527) ***(G-13178)***
United Seating & Mobility LLC (PA)......860 761-0700
1111 Cromwell Ave Rocky Hill CT (06067) ***(G-3732)***
United Sensor Corp......603 672-0909
3 Northern Blvd Ste B2 Amherst NH (03031) ***(G-17590)***
United Shoe Machinery Corp......508 923-6001
3 Abbey Ln Ste B Middleboro MA (02346) ***(G-13079)***
United Sign Co Inc......978 927-9346
33 Tozer Rd Ste 3 Beverly MA (01915) ***(G-8193)***
United States Associates LLC......401 272-7760
1205 Westminster St Providence RI (02909) ***(G-21143)***
United States Chemical Corp......860 621-6831
609 Old Turnpike Rd Plantsville CT (06479) ***(G-3544)***
United States Dept of Navy......860 694-3524
33 Grayback Ave Bldg 33 Groton CT (06349) ***(G-1689)***
United States Dept of Navy......207 438-2714
Portsmouth Naval Shr Portsmouth NH (03804) ***(G-19627)***
United States Fire Arms Mfg Co......860 296-7441
445 Ledyard St Ste 453 Hartford CT (06114) ***(G-1883)***
United States Surgical Corp (HQ)......203 845-1000
555 Long Wharf Dr Fl 4 New Haven CT (06511) ***(G-2750)***
United Steel Inc......860 289-2323
164 School St East Hartford CT (06108) ***(G-1232)***
United Stretch Design Corp......978 562-7781
11 Bonazzoli Ave Hudson MA (01749) ***(G-11824)***
United Stts Sgn & Fbrction......203 601-1000
1 Trefoil Dr Ste 2 Trumbull CT (06611) ***(G-4640)***
United Technical Coating Inc......978 521-2779
115 Hale St Ste 1 Haverhill MA (01830) ***(G-11482)***
United Technologies Corp, North Berwick *Also called Pratt & Whitney Engine Svcs* ***(G-6510)***
United Technologies Corp (PA)......860 728-7000
10 Farm Springs Rd Farmington CT (06032) ***(G-1522)***
United Technologies Corp......860 565-4321
400 Main St East Hartford CT (06118) ***(G-1233)***
United Technologies Corp......508 942-8883
30 Robert W Boyden Rd 1200a Taunton MA (02780) ***(G-15795)***
United Technologies Corp......860 565-7622
400 Main St East Hartford CT (06108) ***(G-1234)***
United Technologies Corp......860 727-2200
Governors Hwy South Windsor CT (06074) ***(G-4018)***
United Technologies Corp......860 767-9592
10 Curiosity Ln Essex CT (06426) ***(G-1407)***
United Technologies Corp......954 485-6501
9 Farm Springs Rd Ste 3 Farmington CT (06032) ***(G-1523)***
United Technologies Corp......860 565-4321
400 Main St East Hartford CT (06108) ***(G-1235)***
United Technologies Corp......860 565-4321
400 Main St East Hartford CT (06118) ***(G-1236)***
United Technologies Corp......860 292-3270
200 Signature Way East Granby CT (06026) ***(G-1146)***
United Technologies Corp......860 610-7000
411 Silver Ln East Hartford CT (06118) ***(G-1237)***
United Technologies Corp......860 557-3333
400 Main St East Hartford CT (06108) ***(G-1238)***
United Thread Rolling LLC......860 290-9349
25 Rosenthal St East Hartford CT (06108) ***(G-1239)***
United Tool & Machine Corp......978 658-5500
98 Eames St Wilmington MA (01887) ***(G-17060)***
United Tool & Stamping Co Inc......603 352-2585
6 Ben Molesky Dr Alstead NH (03602) ***(G-17543)***
United Tool and Die Company (PA)......860 246-6531
1 Carney Rd West Hartford CT (06110) ***(G-5102)***
United Wire & Cable Corp (PA)......508 757-3872
425 Shrewsbury St Worcester MA (01604) ***(G-17494)***
United-County Industries Corp......508 865-5885
32 Howe Ave Millbury MA (01527) ***(G-13179)***
Unitex Textile Rental Service, Hartford *Also called A & P Coat Apron & Lin Sup Inc* ***(G-1799)***
Unitrode Corporation (HQ)......603 222-8500
50 Phillippe Cote St # 100 Manchester NH (03101) ***(G-18945)***
Unity Scientific LLC......203 740-2999
113 Cedar St Ste S3 Milford MA (01757) ***(G-13149)***
Universal Auto Service, Norwood *Also called Universal Carburetor Inc* ***(G-14204)***
Universal Bath Systems, Holyoke *Also called Universal Plastics Corporation* ***(G-11664)***
Universal Body & Eqp Co LLC......860 274-7541
17 Di Nunzio Rd Oakville CT (06779) ***(G-3304)***
Universal Building Contrls Inc......203 235-1530
170 Research Pkwy Ste 1 Meriden CT (06450) ***(G-2145)***
Universal Business Forms Inc......508 852-5520
759 Salisbury St Worcester MA (01609) ***(G-17495)***
Universal Carburetor Inc......781 762-3771
544 Pleasant St Norwood MA (02062) ***(G-14204)***
Universal Color Corp Inc......978 658-2300
377 Ballardvale St Unit 1 Wilmington MA (01887) ***(G-17061)***
Universal Component Corp......203 481-8787
193 Silver Sands Rd East Haven CT (06512) ***(G-1267)***
Universal Foam Products LLC......860 216-3015
101 W Dudley Town Rd Bloomfield CT (06002) ***(G-270)***
Universal Hardwood Flooring......617 783-2307
85 Arlington St Boston MA (02135) ***(G-8899)***
Universal Hinge Corp (PA)......603 935-9848
18 Newton Rd Westminster MA (01473) ***(G-16819)***
Universal Hinge Corp......603 935-9848
114 Bay St Ste 100 Manchester NH (03104) ***(G-18946)***
Universal Machine & Design......978 343-4688
323 Princeton Rd Fitchburg MA (01420) ***(G-10859)***
Universal Pharma Tech LLC......978 975-7216
70 Flagship Dr Ste 3 North Andover MA (01845) ***(G-13735)***
Universal Plastics Corporation (PA)......413 592-4791
75 Whiting Farms Rd Holyoke MA (01040) ***(G-11664)***
Universal Plating Co Inc......401 861-3530
25 River Ave Providence RI (02908) ***(G-21144)***
Universal Precision Mfg......203 374-9809
21 Leffert Rd Trumbull CT (06611) ***(G-4641)***
Universal Relay Company, Bridgeport *Also called Park Distributories Inc* ***(G-463)***
Universal Screening Studio Inc......617 387-1832
175 Ferry St Everett MA (02149) ***(G-10633)***
Universal Specialty Awards......401 272-7760
1205 Westminster St Providence RI (02909) ***(G-21145)***
Universal Systems USA Inc......603 222-9070
21 W Auburn St Ste 22 Manchester NH (03101) ***(G-18947)***
Universal Tag Inc......508 949-2411
36 Hall Rd Dudley MA (01571) ***(G-10388)***
Universal Thread Grinding Co......203 336-1849
30 Chambers St Fairfield CT (06825) ***(G-1459)***
Universal Tipping Co Inc......781 826-5135
11 Parker Rd Pembroke MA (02359) ***(G-14431)***
Universal Tool Co Inc......413 732-4807
33 Rose Pl Springfield MA (01104) ***(G-15520)***
Universal Voltronics Corp......203 740-8555
57 Commerce Dr Brookfield CT (06804) ***(G-662)***

ALPHABETIC

Universal Wilde Inc 508 429-5515
201 Summer St Holliston MA (01746) ***(G-11611)***
Universal Wilde Inc 781 251-2700
403 Vfw Dr Rockland MA (02370) ***(G-14832)***
Universal Wilde Inc (PA) 781 251-2700
26 Dartmouth St Ste 1 Westwood MA (02090) ***(G-16880)***
Universal Wilde Inc 978 658-0800
26 Dartmouth St Ste 1 Westwood MA (02090) ***(G-16881)***
Universal Window and Door LLC 508 481-2850
303 Mechanic St Marlborough MA (01752) ***(G-12840)***
Universe Publishing Co LLC 203 283-5201
167 Cherry St Ste 261 Milford CT (06460) ***(G-2378)***
University Hlth Pubg Group LLC 203 791-0101
6 Trowbridge Dr Ste 1 Bethel CT (06801) ***(G-187)***
University Massachusetts Inc 413 545-2217
671 N Pleasant St Amherst MA (01003) ***(G-7528)***
University Massachusetts Inc 413 545-2682
40 Campus Center Way Amherst MA (01003) ***(G-7529)***
University of Maine System 207 581-2843
5755 Nutting Hall Orono ME (04469) ***(G-6559)***
University of Maine System 207 581-1273
5748 Memorial Un Orono ME (04469) ***(G-6560)***
University of Massachusetts 413 545-3500
113 Campus Ctr Amherst MA (01003) ***(G-7530)***
University of Massachusetts 413 545-2718
151 Whitmore University F Flr 1 Amherst MA (01003) ***(G-7531)***
University Opticians, Dayville *Also called University Optics LLC* ***(G-1054)***
University Optics LLC 860 779-6123
791 Hartford Pike Dayville CT (06241) ***(G-1054)***
University Wine Shop Inc 617 547-4258
1737 Massachusetts Ave Cambridge MA (02138) ***(G-9686)***
Univex Corporation 603 893-6191
3 Old Rockingham Rd Salem NH (03079) ***(G-19775)***
Uniweld Inc 978 352-8008
36 Jackman St Unit 7 Georgetown MA (01833) ***(G-11152)***
Uniworld Bus Publications Inc 201 384-4900
35 Kensett Ln Darien CT (06820) ***(G-1036)***
Unlimited Fuel Heating Inc 508 543-1043
11 Maple Pl Foxboro MA (02035) ***(G-10907)***
Unlimited Manufacturing Svc 978 835-4915
20 Foot Of Crosby St Lowell MA (01852) ***(G-12442)***
Unlimited Plant Care Service, Waltham *Also called Marie Deprofio* ***(G-16147)***
Uno Foods Inc (HQ) 617 323-9200
100 Charles Park Rd Boston MA (02132) ***(G-8900)***
Uno Foods Inc 508 580-1561
180 Spark St Brockton MA (02302) ***(G-9185)***
Unruly Studios Inc 857 327-5080
2 Avenue De Lafayette Boston MA (02111) ***(G-8901)***
Untha Shredding Tech Amer, Newburyport *Also called Untha Shredding Tech Amer Inc* ***(G-13547)***
Untha Shredding Tech Amer Inc 978 465-0083
10 Perry Way Newburyport MA (01950) ***(G-13547)***
UNUM Therapeutics Inc 617 945-5576
200 Cmbrdge Pk Dr Ste 310 Cambridge MA (02140) ***(G-9687)***
Unwrapped Inc 978 441-0242
95 Rock St Fl 1 Lowell MA (01854) ***(G-12443)***
Up Country Inc 401 431-2940
76 Boyd Ave East Providence RI (02914) ***(G-20447)***
Up North Corp Inc 207 834-6178
185 Pleasant St Fort Kent ME (04743) ***(G-6068)***
Up With Paper 203 453-3300
34 York St Ste 3 Guilford CT (06437) ***(G-1723)***
UPACO ADHESIVES, Nashua *Also called Worthen Industries Inc* ***(G-19288)***
Upc LLC 877 466-1137
170 Research Pkwy Meriden CT (06450) ***(G-2146)***
Upcycle Solutions Inc 603 809-6843
7 Delta Dr Londonderry NH (03053) ***(G-18743)***
Upnovr Inc 603 625-8639
31 Pulpit Rock Rd Unit A Pelham NH (03076) ***(G-19452)***
Uppababy, Hingham *Also called Monahan Products LLC* ***(G-11506)***
Upper Access Book Publishers, Hinesburg *Also called Upper Access Inc* ***(G-22032)***
Upper Access Inc 802 482-2988
87 Upper Access Rd Hinesburg VT (05461) ***(G-22032)***
Upper Pass Beer Co LLC 802 889-3421
37 Ordway Rd Tunbridge VT (05077) ***(G-22544)***
Upper Valley Mold LLC 860 489-8282
481 Guerdat Rd Torrington CT (06790) ***(G-4606)***
Upper Valley Press Inc 603 787-7000
446 Benton Rd North Haverhill NH (03774) ***(G-19391)***
Uppermark LLC 413 303-9653
147 Coolidge St Brookline MA (02446) ***(G-9224)***
UPS Scs Pratt & Whitney 860 565-0353
52 Pettengill Rd Londonderry NH (03053) ***(G-18744)***
Upstairs 207 799-2217
251 Us Route 1 Ste 11 Falmouth ME (04105) ***(G-6036)***
Uptite Co Inc 603 401-3856
1 Timothy Ln Salem NH (03079) ***(G-19776)***
Uptite Company Inc 978 377-0451
1001 Hilldale Ave Haverhill MA (01832) ***(G-11483)***
Uptodate Inc (HQ) 781 392-2000
230 3rd Ave Ste 1000 Waltham MA (02451) ***(G-16218)***
Upton & Mendon Town Crier, Upton *Also called Town Crier Publications Inc* ***(G-15911)***
Uraseal Inc 603 749-1004
1 Washington St Ste 5126 Dover NH (03820) ***(G-18064)***
Urban Mnshine Natural Pdts LLC 802 862-6233
1 Mill St Ste 101 Burlington VT (05401) ***(G-21814)***
Uretek, New Haven *Also called Trelleborg Ctd Systems US Inc* ***(G-2747)***
Urethane Solutions LLC 207 284-5400
52 Spring Hill Rd Saco ME (04072) ***(G-6861)***
Urg Graphics Inc (PA) 860 928-0835
12 Fox Hill Dr Stafford Springs CT (06076) ***(G-4121)***
Urolaze Inc 413 374-5006
192 Worcester St Wellesley Hills MA (02481) ***(G-16400)***
Urquhart Family LLC 978 632-3600
205 School St Ste 203 Gardner MA (01440) ***(G-11132)***
Ursa Major LLC 802 560-7116
1 Stowe St Waterbury VT (05676) ***(G-22587)***
Ursa Navigation Solutions Inc 781 538-5299
85 Rangeway Rd Ste 110 North Billerica MA (01862) ***(G-13875)***
Ursanav, North Billerica *Also called Ursa Navigation Solutions Inc* ***(G-13875)***
Urschel Tool Co 401 944-0600
43 Navaho St Cranston RI (02907) ***(G-20308)***
US Athletic Equipment, Waterford *Also called Jaypro Sports LLC* ***(G-4986)***
US Avionics, South Windsor *Also called US Avionics Inc / Superabr* ***(G-4019)***
US Avionics Inc / Superabr 860 528-1114
1265 John Fitch Blvd # 3 South Windsor CT (06074) ***(G-4019)***
US Bedding Inc 508 678-6988
451 Quarry St Fall River MA (02723) ***(G-10777)***
US Biofuels Inc 706 291-4829
225 Franklin St Ste 2320 Boston MA (02110) ***(G-8902)***
US Bronze Foundry & Mch Inc 781 871-1420
145 Webster St Ste J Hanover MA (02339) ***(G-11358)***
US Button Corporation 860 928-2707
328 Kennedy Dr Putnam CT (06260) ***(G-3638)***
US Chemicals Inc 203 655-8878
280 Elm St New Canaan CT (06840) ***(G-2620)***
US Cutting Chain Mfg Co Inc 508 588-0322
95 Spark St Brockton MA (02302) ***(G-9186)***
US Discount Products LLC 877 841-5782
354 West St Ste 4 West Bridgewater MA (02379) ***(G-16462)***
US Extruders Inc 401 584-4710
87 Tom Harvey Rd Westerly RI (02891) ***(G-21546)***
US Firearms Manufacturing Co 860 296-7441
453 Ledyard St Hartford CT (06114) ***(G-1884)***
US Flag Manufacturing Inc 781 383-6607
166 King St Ste 5 Cohasset MA (02025) ***(G-10103)***
US Games Systems Inc 203 353-8400
179 Ludlow St Stamford CT (06902) ***(G-4353)***
US Gold and Diamond Exch LLC (PA) 603 300-8888
64 Crystal Ave Derry NH (03038) ***(G-18001)***
US Highway Products Inc 203 336-0332
500 Bostwick Ave Bridgeport CT (06605) ***(G-502)***
US Sheetmetal Inc 508 427-0500
420 West St West Bridgewater MA (02379) ***(G-16463)***
US Sign, Trumbull *Also called United Stts Sgn & Fbrction* ***(G-4640)***
US Smokeless Tobacco Co LLC 203 661-1100
6 High Ridge Park Bldg A Stamford CT (06905) ***(G-4354)***
US Standard Brands Inc 617 719-8796
44 Heritage Dr Walpole MA (02081) ***(G-16016)***
US Tsubaki Automotive LLC 413 593-1100
152 Apremont Way Westfield MA (01085) ***(G-16738)***
US Tsubaki Automotive LLC (HQ) 413 593-1100
106 Lonczak St Chicopee MA (01022) ***(G-10067)***
US Tsubaki Power Transm LLC 413 536-1576
821 Main St Holyoke MA (01040) ***(G-11665)***
Us-Malabar Company Inc 203 226-1773
25 Timber Mill Ln Weston CT (06883) ***(G-5174)***
USA Circuits LLC 203 364-1378
114 Lakeview Ter Sandy Hook CT (06482) ***(G-3746)***
USA Notepads, West Haven *Also called Panagrafix Inc* ***(G-5139)***
USA Renewable LLC 617 319-7237
22 Considine Rd Newton MA (02459) ***(G-13645)***
USA Wood Incorporated 203 238-4285
998 N Colony Rd Meriden CT (06450) ***(G-2147)***
Usaccess Inc 207 541-9421
57 Lemon Stream Rd New Portland ME (04961) ***(G-6475)***
Usc Technologies LLC 203 378-9622
175 Garfield Ave Stratford CT (06615) ***(G-4456)***
User-Friendly Recycling LLC 781 269-5021
186 Tosca Dr Stoughton MA (02072) ***(G-15627)***
Uses Mfg Inc 860 443-8737
152 Old Colchester Rd Quaker Hill CT (06375) ***(G-3644)***
USI Education & Government Sls, Madison *Also called New Precision Technology LLC* ***(G-1969)***
Usmdumpsters 774 218-2822
35 E Main St Middleboro MA (02346) ***(G-13080)***
Uspack Inc 978 466-9700
300 Whitney St Leominster MA (01453) ***(G-12197)***

Uspack Inc......978 562-8522
14 Brent Dr Hudson MA (01749) ***(G-11825)***
Usquepaugh Baking Co LLC......401 782-6907
87 Old Usquepaugh Rd West Kingston RI (02892) ***(G-21474)***
UST......203 661-1100
100 W Putnam Ave Greenwich CT (06830) ***(G-1659)***
UST LLC (HQ)......203 817-3000
6 High Ridge Park Bldg A Stamford CT (06905) ***(G-4355)***
UTC, Farmington *Also called United Technologies Corp* ***(G-1522)***
UTC, Haverhill *Also called United Technical Coating Inc* ***(G-11482)***
UTC Aerospace, Vergennes *Also called Goodrich Corporation* ***(G-22553)***
UTC Aerospace Systems, Danbury *Also called Simmonds Precision Pdts Inc* ***(G-994)***
UTC Aerospace Systems, Peabody *Also called Goodrich Corporation* ***(G-14336)***
UTC Aerospace Systems, Windsor Locks *Also called Hamilton Sundstrand Corp* ***(G-5397)***
UTC Climate Controls & SEC, Farmington *Also called United Technologies Corp* ***(G-1523)***
UTC Fire SEC Americas Corp Inc......203 426-1180
16 Commerce Rd Newtown CT (06470) ***(G-2947)***
UTC Fire SEC Americas Corp Inc......508 620-4773
945 Concord St Ste 220 Framingham MA (01701) ***(G-11009)***
Uti Holding Company......978 570-6900
100 Fordham Rd Bldg C Wilmington MA (01887) ***(G-17062)***
Utility Cloud, Salem *Also called Advanced Entp Systems Corp* ***(G-19703)***
Utility Mfg Co, Wilbraham *Also called Frank L Reed Inc* ***(G-16937)***
Utility Systems Inc......401 351-6681
123 King Philip St Johnston RI (02919) ***(G-20546)***
Utitec Inc (HQ)......860 945-0605
169 Callender Rd Watertown CT (06795) ***(G-5032)***
Utitec Holdings Inc (PA)......860 945-0601
169 Callender Rd Watertown CT (06795) ***(G-5033)***
Utrc, East Hartford *Also called United Technologies Corp* ***(G-1237)***
Utz Quality Foods Inc......978 342-6038
759 Water St Fitchburg MA (01420) ***(G-10860)***
Uv III Systems Inc......508 883-4881
59 Cedarvale Est Alburg VT (05440) ***(G-21593)***
Uva Lidkoping Inc......508 634-4301
4 Industrial Rd Ste 4 # 4 Milford MA (01757) ***(G-13150)***
Uvex Distribution Inc......401 232-1200
900 Douglas Pike Ste 100 Smithfield RI (02917) ***(G-21251)***
Uvex Safety Manufacturing Ltd......401 232-1200
10 Thurber Blvd Smithfield RI (02917) ***(G-21252)***
Uvtech Systems Inc......978 440-7282
490 Boston Post Rd Sudbury MA (01776) ***(G-15670)***
Uxbridge Dpw Dept, Uxbridge *Also called Town of Uxbridge* ***(G-15932)***
V & G Iron Works Inc......978 851-9191
1500 Shawsheen St Tewksbury MA (01876) ***(G-15846)***
V & V Woodworking LLC......203 740-9494
107 Wooster St Bethel CT (06801) ***(G-188)***
V J Electronix Inc......631 589-8800
19 Alpha Rd Chelmsford MA (01824) ***(G-9938)***
V M F, Seymour *Also called Vernier Metal Fabricating Inc* ***(G-3767)***
V P E Inc......802 263-9474
22 Kendricks Corner Rd Perkinsville VT (05151) ***(G-22259)***
V P M S, Springfield *Also called Vermont Precision Machine Svcs* ***(G-22511)***
V Power Equipment LLC......508 273-7596
297 Charge Pond Rd Wareham MA (02571) ***(G-16256)***
V&S Taunton Galvanizing LLC......508 828-9499
585 John Hancock Rd Taunton MA (02780) ***(G-15796)***
V-Tron Electronics Corp......508 761-9100
10 Venus Way Attleboro MA (02703) ***(G-7805)***
Vab Inc......860 793-0246
49 Johnson Ave Plainville CT (06062) ***(G-3523)***
Vacca Architectural Woodworkin......860 599-3677
9 Coggswell St Pawcatuck CT (06379) ***(G-3443)***
Vacca Sign & Awning Service, Newton *Also called Vacca Sign Service Inc* ***(G-13646)***
Vacca Sign Service Inc......617 332-3111
69 Adams St Rear Newton MA (02458) ***(G-13646)***
Vaccine Technologies Inc (PA)......781 489-3388
15 S Woodside Ave Wellesley MA (02482) ***(G-16391)***
Vaccon Company Inc......508 359-7200
9 Industrial Park Rd Medway MA (02053) ***(G-12972)***
Vacutherm Inc......802 496-4241
2535 Airport Rd Warren VT (05674) ***(G-22579)***
Vacuum Barrier Corporation......781 933-3570
4 Barten Ln Woburn MA (01801) ***(G-17310)***
Vacuum Plus Manufacturing Inc......978 441-3100
80 Turnpike Rd Chelmsford MA (01824) ***(G-9939)***
Vacuum Pressing Systems Inc......207 725-0935
553 River Rd Brunswick ME (04011) ***(G-5850)***
Vacuum Process Technology LLC......508 732-7200
70 Industrial Park Rd Plymouth MA (02360) ***(G-14589)***
Vacuum Processing Systems LLC......401 397-8578
9 Mcgraw Ct East Greenwich RI (02818) ***(G-20382)***
Vacuum Technology Associates......781 740-8600
110 Industrial Park Rd Hingham MA (02043) ***(G-11513)***
Vacuum Technology Inc......510 333-6562
15 Great Republic Dr Gloucester MA (01930) ***(G-11216)***
Vae, Providence *Also called Veterans Assembled Elec LLC* ***(G-21150)***
Vaillancourt Folk Art Inc......508 476-3601
9 Main St Ste 1h Sutton MA (01590) ***(G-15695)***
Vaisala Inc......617 467-1500
15 Riverdale Ave Newton MA (02458) ***(G-13647)***
Vaisala Inc......508 574-1163
10d Gill St Woburn MA (01801) ***(G-17311)***
Vaisala Inc......781 933-4500
10d Gill St Woburn MA (01801) ***(G-17312)***
Valco Precision Machine Inc......508 559-9009
800 W Chestnut St Brockton MA (02301) ***(G-9187)***
Valcom Division, Walpole *Also called Tooling Research Inc* ***(G-16014)***
Valde Systems Inc......603 577-1728
4 Hobart Hill Rd Brookline NH (03033) ***(G-17774)***
Valente Backhoe Service LLC......508 754-7013
1 Temple Ct Shrewsbury MA (01545) ***(G-15134)***
Valentine & Company Inc......207 774-4769
90 Bridge St Ste 206 Westbrook ME (04092) ***(G-7212)***
Valentine Plating Company Inc......413 732-0009
155 Allston Ave West Springfield MA (01089) ***(G-16561)***
Valentine Tool & Stamping Inc......508 285-6911
171 W Main St Norton MA (02766) ***(G-14091)***
Valeritas Inc......774 239-2498
293 Boston Post Rd W # 330 Marlborough MA (01752) ***(G-12841)***
Valhalla Circuits Corp......603 854-3300
77 Gould Rd Weare NH (03281) ***(G-19942)***
Valiant Industries Inc......978 388-3792
12 Merrill Ave Amesbury MA (01913) ***(G-7510)***
Valid Mfg Inc......603 880-0948
13 Hampshire Dr Ste 3 Hudson NH (03051) ***(G-18449)***
Validity Inc......978 635-3400
1300 Mamaachsts Ave 205 Boxboro MA (01719) ***(G-8955)***
Validus DC Systems LLC......203 448-3600
50 Pocono Rd Brookfield CT (06804) ***(G-663)***
Valkyrie Company Inc (PA)......508 756-3633
60 Fremont St Worcester MA (01603) ***(G-17496)***
Valkyrie Company Inc......508 756-3633
60 Fremont St Worcester MA (01603) ***(G-17497)***
Valley Advocate......413 584-0003
115 Conz St Ste 2 Northampton MA (01060) ***(G-14024)***
Valley Breeze, Lincoln *Also called Breeze Publications Inc* ***(G-20559)***
Valley Container Inc......203 368-6546
850 Union Ave Bridgeport CT (06607) ***(G-503)***
Valley Independent Sentinel......203 446-2335
158 Main St Ansonia CT (06401) ***(G-24)***
Valley News, Concord *Also called Newspapers New England Inc* ***(G-17917)***
Valley of Mexico, Stamford *Also called Shenondah Vly Specialty Foods* ***(G-4315)***
Valley Plating Inc 8-1-80......413 788-7375
412 Albany St Springfield MA (01105) ***(G-15521)***
Valley Press Inc......860 651-4700
540 1/2 Hopmeadow St Simsbury CT (06070) ***(G-3914)***
Valley Printing Company......508 892-9818
31 Redfield Rd Cherry Valley MA (01611) ***(G-9978)***
Valley Publishing Company Inc......203 735-6696
7 Francis St Derby CT (06418) ***(G-1081)***
Valley Reporter Inc......802 496-3607
5222 Main St Ste 2 Waitsfield VT (05673) ***(G-22569)***
Valley Signs......603 252-1977
22 Fairview Ave Lebanon NH (03766) ***(G-18640)***
Valley Steel Stamp Inc......413 773-8200
15 Greenfield St Greenfield MA (01301) ***(G-11282)***
Valley Times, Derby *Also called Valley Publishing Company Inc* ***(G-1081)***
Valley Tool and Mfg LLC (HQ)......203 799-8800
22 Prindle Hill Rd Orange CT (06477) ***(G-3386)***
Valley Truckstop, Waterbury *Also called John Hychko* ***(G-4893)***
Valley View Orchard Pies, Oxford *Also called C J Cranam Inc* ***(G-6564)***
Valley Welding & Fabg Inc......603 465-3266
261 Proctor Hill Rd Hollis NH (03049) ***(G-18340)***
Vallum Corporation......603 577-1989
61 Spit Brook Rd Ste 200 Nashua NH (03060) ***(G-19277)***
Valmet Inc......207 377-6909
30 Summer St Ste G Winthrop ME (04364) ***(G-7283)***
Valmet Inc......207 202-1521
516 Alfred St Biddeford ME (04005) ***(G-5767)***
Valmet Inc (HQ)......603 882-2711
1 Cellu Dr Nashua NH (03063) ***(G-19278)***
Valmont Inc......413 583-8351
656 Chapin St Ludlow MA (01056) ***(G-12478)***
Valora Technologies Inc......781 229-2265
101 Great Rd Bedford MA (01730) ***(G-8018)***
Valore Inc......203 854-4799
2 Academy St Norwalk CT (06850) ***(G-3264)***
Value Print Incorporated......203 265-1371
34 Mellor Dr Wallingford CT (06492) ***(G-4826)***
Valve Components Division, Worcester *Also called Standard Lock Washer & Mfg Co* ***(G-17481)***
Vampfangs / 321fx Studios LLC......781 799-5048
100 Cummings Ctr Ste 245g Beverly MA (01915) ***(G-8194)***
Van & Company Inc......401 722-9829
547 Weeden St Pawtucket RI (02860) ***(G-20908)***

ALPHABETIC

Van Alstyne Family Farm Inc 802 763-7036
330 Walker Hill Rd South Royalton VT (05068) ***(G-22494)***
Van Alstyne Farm and Mill, South Royalton *Also called Van Alstyne Family Farm Inc* ***(G-22494)***
Van Benten Joseph Furn Makers 617 738-6575
823 Boylston St Chestnut Hill MA (02467) ***(G-9994)***
Van Deusen & Levitt Assoc Inc 203 445-6244
14 Wood Hill Rd Weston CT (06883) ***(G-5175)***
Van Dorn and Curtiss 603 542-3081
178 Broad St Claremont NH (03743) ***(G-17863)***
Van Dusen Racing Boats, Concord *Also called Composite Engineering Inc* ***(G-10122)***
Van Heusen, Chatham *Also called Pvh Corp* ***(G-9863)***
Van Leer Jodi 603 643-3034
38 Goodfellow Rd Hanover NH (03755) ***(G-18300)***
Van Pelt Capital Precision Inc 413 527-1204
69 Ferry St Ste 10 Easthampton MA (01027) ***(G-10582)***
Van Stry Design Inc 781 388-9998
420 Pearl St Ste 2 Malden MA (02148) ***(G-12600)***
Van Wal Machine Inc 508 966-0733
97 Depot St Bellingham MA (02019) ***(G-8061)***
Van-Go Graphics 508 865-7300
94 Fitzpatrick Rd Grafton MA (01519) ***(G-11225)***
Vanderbilt Chemicals LLC 203 744-3900
31 Taylor Ave Bethel CT (06801) ***(G-189)***
Vanderbilt Chemicals LLC (HQ) 203 295-2141
30 Winfield St Norwalk CT (06855) ***(G-3265)***
Vanderbilt Minerals LLC (HQ) 203 295-2140
33 Winfield St Norwalk CT (06855) ***(G-3266)***
Vangor Engineering Corporation 203 267-4377
115 Hurley Rd Ste 7f Oxford CT (06478) ***(G-3428)***
Vanguard Plastics Corporation 860 628-4736
100 Robert Porter Rd Southington CT (06489) ***(G-4089)***
Vanguard Products Corporation 203 744-7265
87 Newtown Rd Danbury CT (06810) ***(G-1003)***
Vanguard Solar Inc 508 361-1463
365 Boston Post Rd # 303 Sudbury MA (01776) ***(G-15671)***
Vangy Tool Company Inc 508 754-2669
621 Millbury St Worcester MA (01607) ***(G-17498)***
Vanity World Inc 508 668-1800
348 Turnpike St Ste 1 Canton MA (02021) ***(G-9792)***
Vans Inc 781 229-7700
75 Middlesex Tpke # 1303 Burlington MA (01803) ***(G-9351)***
Vanson Leathers Inc 508 678-2000
951 Broadway Ste 1 Fall River MA (02724) ***(G-10778)***
Vantage Graphics, Norwood *Also called BBCg LLC* ***(G-14137)***
Vantage Printing, Auburn *Also called Norman Ellis* ***(G-7845)***
Vantage Reporting Inc 212 750-2256
3 Allied Dr Ste 303 Dedham MA (02026) ***(G-10299)***
Vantage Software, Dedham *Also called Vantage Reporting Inc* ***(G-10299)***
Vantastic Inc 603 524-1419
94 Primrose Dr N Laconia NH (03246) ***(G-18591)***
Vanu Inc 617 864-1711
81 Hartwell Ave Ste 4 Lexington MA (02421) ***(G-12281)***
Vapco Inc 978 975-0302
360 Merrimack St Ste 23 Lawrence MA (01843) ***(G-12081)***
Vaporizer LLC 860 564-7225
245 Main St Moosup CT (06354) ***(G-2429)***
Vapotherm Inc (PA) 603 658-0011
100 Domain Dr Ste 102 Exeter NH (03833) ***(G-18135)***
Varian Semicdtr Eqp Assoc Inc 978 463-1500
4 Stanley Tucker Dr Newburyport MA (01950) ***(G-13548)***
Variation Btechnologies US Inc 617 830-3031
222 3rd St Ste 2241 Cambridge MA (02142) ***(G-9688)***
Varitrade, Waldoboro *Also called Ultron LLC* ***(G-7137)***
Varitron Hudson, Hudson *Also called Varitron Technologies USA Inc* ***(G-18450)***
Varitron Technologies USA Inc 603 577-8855
12 Executive Dr Ste 2 Hudson NH (03051) ***(G-18450)***
Varney Bros Concrete, Bellingham *Also called Varney Bros Sand & Gravel Inc* ***(G-8062)***
Varney Bros Sand & Gravel Inc 508 966-1313
79 Hartford Ave Bellingham MA (02019) ***(G-8062)***
Varnum Enterprises LLC 203 743-4443
11 Trowbridge Dr Bethel CT (06801) ***(G-190)***
Varpro Inc 203 227-6876
4 Shadbush Ln Pmb 2224 Westport CT (06880) ***(G-5236)***
Varsity Imprints 203 354-4371
22 Roller Ter Milford CT (06461) ***(G-2379)***
Varstreet Inc 781 273-3979
66 Charles St Boston MA (02114) ***(G-8903)***
Vartanian Custom Cabinets 413 283-3438
10 2nd St Palmer MA (01069) ***(G-14300)***
Vas Integrated LLC 860 748-4058
600 Four Rod Rd Ste 9 Berlin CT (06037) ***(G-116)***
Vasca Inc 978 640-0431
3 Highwood Dr Tewksbury MA (01876) ***(G-15847)***
Vascular Technology Inc 603 594-9700
12 Murphy Dr Unit C Nashua NH (03062) ***(G-19279)***
Vasotech Inc 617 686-2770
55 Plainfield Ave Shrewsbury MA (01545) ***(G-15135)***
Vater Percussion Inc 781 767-1877
270 Centre St Unit D Holbrook MA (02343) ***(G-11540)***
Vaughan W C Co Ltd Inc 781 848-0308
55 Messina Dr Braintree MA (02184) ***(G-9046)***
Vaughn Thermal Corporation 978 462-6683
26 Old Elm St Salisbury MA (01952) ***(G-14958)***
Vaultive Inc 212 875-1210
470 Atlantic Ave Fl 12 Boston MA (02210) ***(G-8904)***
Vbi Vaccines 617 714-3451
222 3rd St Ste 2242 Cambridge MA (02142) ***(G-9689)***
Vbi Vaccines Inc 617 830-3031
222 3rd St Ste 2241 Cambridge MA (02142) ***(G-9690)***
Vblearning LLC 617 527-9999
109 Oak St Ste 203 Newton MA (02464) ***(G-13648)***
Vbrick Systems Inc 203 265-0044
1743 Washington St Canton MA (02021) ***(G-9793)***
Vc News Daily, Arlington *Also called Massinvestor Incorporated* ***(G-7629)***
Vc Print 207 492-1919
9 Vesta Dr Caribou ME (04736) ***(G-5892)***
VCA Inc 413 587-2750
209 Earle St Northampton MA (01060) ***(G-14025)***
Vce, Franklin *Also called EMC Corporation* ***(G-11042)***
Vck Best Machining LLC 603 880-8858
4 Townsend W Ste 8 Nashua NH (03063) ***(G-19280)***
Vcs Group LLC 203 413-6500
411 W Putnam Ave Fl 2 Greenwich CT (06830) ***(G-1660)***
Vdc Research Group Inc (PA) 508 653-9000
679 Worcester St Ste 2 Natick MA (01760) ***(G-13284)***
Ve Interactive LLC 857 284-7000
580 Harrison Ave Ste 400 Boston MA (02118) ***(G-8905)***
Vector 5 Collaborative LLC 978 348-2997
198 Summer St Lunenburg MA (01462) ***(G-12485)***
Vector Contrls & Automtn Group, Bethel *Also called Vector Controls LLC* ***(G-191)***
Vector Controls LLC (PA) 203 749-0883
17 Francis J Clarke Cir Bethel CT (06801) ***(G-191)***
Vector Engineering Inc 860 572-0422
800 Flanders Rd Unit 1-4 Mystic CT (06355) ***(G-2455)***
Vector Tool & Die Corporation 413 562-1616
317 Northwest Rd Westfield MA (01085) ***(G-16739)***
Vectura Incorporated 508 573-5700
371 Turnpike Rd Ste 120 Southborough MA (01772) ***(G-15370)***
Veeam Software Corporation 781 592-0752
45 New Ocean St Swampscott MA (01907) ***(G-15701)***
Veeder-Root Company (HQ) 860 651-2700
125 Powder Forest Dr Fl 1 Weatogue CT (06089) ***(G-5045)***
Vega Food Industries Inc 401 942-0620
1 Financial Plz Fl 26 Providence RI (02903) ***(G-21146)***
Vegan Publishers LLC 857 364-4344
6 Moore Cir Danvers MA (01923) ***(G-10271)***
Vegware Us Inc 860 779-7970
90 Wauregan Rd Danielson CT (06239) ***(G-1020)***
Vehicle Wash Systems, Portland *Also called Maintenance Tech Inc* ***(G-6691)***
Veho Tech Inc 617 909-6026
13 Greene St North Reading MA (01864) ***(G-13993)***
Velcro Inc (HQ) 603 669-4880
95 Sundial Ave Manchester NH (03103) ***(G-18948)***
Velcro USA Inc (HQ) 603 669-4880
95 Sundial Ave Manchester NH (03103) ***(G-18949)***
Velex Corporation 617 440-4948
215 Western Ave Cambridge MA (02139) ***(G-9691)***
Vellano Corporation 401 434-1030
124 Reservoir Ave Unit 1 Pawtucket RI (02860) ***(G-20909)***
Vellumoid Inc 508 853-2500
54 Rockdale St Worcester MA (01606) ***(G-17499)***
Velocity Manufacturing Inc 603 773-2386
41 Industrial Dr Ste 1 Exeter NH (03833) ***(G-18136)***
Velocity Print Solution, Middlebury *Also called JMS Graphics Inc* ***(G-2155)***
Velocity Print Solutions, Middleton *Also called Northern Graphics Inc* ***(G-13097)***
Veloxint Corporation 774 777-3369
125 Newbury St Ste 200 Framingham MA (01701) ***(G-11010)***
Veloxity One LLC 855 844-5060
51 Middlesex St Unit 110 North Chelmsford MA (01863) ***(G-13912)***
Velux America LLC 207 216-4500
85 Spencer Dr Unit A Wells ME (04090) ***(G-7167)***
Vemployee 888 471-1982
47 Taylor Rd Portsmouth RI (02871) ***(G-20942)***
Vemuri International LLC 401 723-4200
402 Walcott St Pawtucket RI (02860) ***(G-20910)***
Venda Ravioli Inc 401 421-9105
150 Royal Little Dr Providence RI (02904) ***(G-21147)***
Venda Ravioli Inc (PA) 401 421-9105
265 Atwells Ave Ste 1 Providence RI (02903) ***(G-21148)***
Vendituoli Limited Company 802 535-4319
44 W Main St Vergennes VT (05491) ***(G-22557)***
Vendome Guide 401 849-8025
28 Pelham St Newport RI (02840) ***(G-20687)***
Veneer Division, Presque Isle *Also called Columbia Forest Products Inc* ***(G-6757)***
Veneer Services Unlimited, Kennebunk *Also called John Costin Studio* ***(G-6237)***

Venlo Company 781 826-0485
125 Church St Unit 90-411 Pembroke MA (02359) *(G-14432)*
Venmill Industries Inc 508 363-0410
36 Town Forest Rd Oxford MA (01540) *(G-14276)*
Venom Imaging, Manchester *Also called JCP Trading Inc (G-18849)*
Vent-Rite Valve Corp (PA) 781 986-2000
300 Pond St Randolph MA (02368) *(G-14701)*
Ventech Industries Inc 207 439-0069
384 Harold L Dw Hwy Eliot ME (03903) *(G-6012)*
Vention Medical, Marlborough *Also called Nordson Med Design & Dev Inc (G-12797)*
Vention Medical, Salem *Also called Nordson Medical (nh) Inc (G-19756)*
Ventricom Wireless Tech 603 226-0025
58 Mandevilla Ln Concord NH (03301) *(G-17938)*
Venture Print Unlimited Inc 603 536-2410
44 Main St Plymouth NH (03264) *(G-19531)*
Venture Publishing, Andover *Also called Gwb Corporation (G-7554)*
Venture Tape, Rockland *Also called Gta-Nht Inc (G-14804)*
Venture Tool and Manufacturing 860 267-9647
12 Summit St East Hampton CT (06424) *(G-1167)*
Ventures LLC DOT Com LLC 203 930-8972
35-31 Tlcottville Rd 23 Vernon CT (06066) *(G-4676)*
Venu Magazine LLC 203 259-2075
840 Reef Rd Fairfield CT (06824) *(G-1460)*
Venus Wafers Inc 781 740-1002
100 Research Rd Hingham MA (02043) *(G-11514)*
Veoci.com, New Haven *Also called Grey Wall Software LLC (G-2693)*
Veolia NA Regeneration Srvcs (HQ) 312 552-2800
53 State St Boston MA (02109) *(G-8906)*
Veoneer Lowell, Lowell *Also called Veoneer Us Inc (G-12446)*
Veoneer Roadscape Auto Inc 978 656-2500
1011 Pawtucket Blvd Lowell MA (01854) *(G-12444)*
Veoneer Roadscape Auto Inc (HQ) 978 656-2500
1011 Pawtucket Blvd Lowell MA (01854) *(G-12445)*
Veoneer Roadscape Lowell, Lowell *Also called Veoneer Roadscape Auto Inc (G-12444)*
Veoneer Us Inc 978 674-6500
1001 Pawtucket Blvd Lowell MA (01854) *(G-12446)*
Vera Bradley Designs Inc 781 794-9860
250 Granite St Ste 131 Braintree MA (02184) *(G-9047)*
Vera Roasting Company 603 969-7970
99 Bow St Ste 100e Portsmouth NH (03801) *(G-19628)*
Verastem Inc (PA) 781 292-4200
117 Kendrick St Ste 500 Needham MA (02494) *(G-13316)*
Verax Biomedical Incorporated 508 755-7029
148 Bartlett St Marlborough MA (01752) *(G-12842)*
Verde LLC 617 955-2402
95 Suomi Rd Quincy MA (02169) *(G-14666)*
Vericel Corporation 857 600-8191
64 Sidney St Cambridge MA (02139) *(G-9692)*
Vericel Corporation (PA) 800 556-0311
64 Sidney St Cambridge MA (02139) *(G-9693)*
Verico Technology LLC 413 539-9111
749 New Ludlow Rd South Hadley MA (01075) *(G-15312)*
Verico Technology LLC (HQ) 800 492-7286
230 Shaker Rd Enfield CT (06082) *(G-1389)*
Verico Technology LLC 603 402-7573
200 Innovative Way Nashua NH (03062) *(G-19281)*
Verifacts 781 337-1717
1285 Washington St Ste 1 Weymouth MA (02189) *(G-16903)*
Verify LLC 513 285-7258
62 Whittemore Ave Cambridge MA (02140) *(G-9694)*
Verionix Inc 978 682-5671
251 Granville Ln North Andover MA (01845) *(G-13736)*
Veritas Medicine Inc 617 234-1500
11 Cambridge Ctr Cambridge MA (02142) *(G-9695)*
Verizon, Warwick *Also called Supermedia LLC (G-21432)*
Verizon Business, Merrimack *Also called Rymsa Micro Communications (G-19026)*
Verizon Communications Inc 508 647-4008
1245 Worcester St Natick MA (01760) *(G-13285)*
Vermilion Software 617 279-0799
50 Congress St Ste 500 Boston MA (02109) *(G-8907)*
Vermont Aerospace Inds LLC 802 748-8705
966 Industrial Pkwy Lyndonville VT (05851) *(G-22073)*
Vermont Art Studio Inc 802 747-7446
175 Woodstock Ave Rutland VT (05701) *(G-22358)*
Vermont Awards and Engrv Inc 802 862-3000
566 Hercules Dr Colchester VT (05446) *(G-21884)*
Vermont Base Waters LLC 802 893-2131
156 Brentwood Dr Colchester VT (05446) *(G-21885)*
Vermont Beef Jerky Co 802 754-9412
348 Industrial Park Ln Orleans VT (05860) *(G-22252)*
Vermont Beer Shapers Ltd 802 376-0889
100 River St Springfield VT (05156) *(G-22510)*
Vermont Birch Syrup Co 802 249-0574
440 Clark Rd Glover VT (05839) *(G-21995)*
Vermont Business Magazine, South Burlington *Also called Boutin McQuiston Inc (G-22439)*
Vermont Canvas Products 802 773-7311
259 Woodstock Ave Rutland VT (05701) *(G-22359)*
Vermont Center Wreaths Inc 802 334-6432
44 Kimberly Ln Newport Center VT (05857) *(G-22208)*
Vermont Christmas Company 802 893-1670
24 Clapper Rd Milton VT (05468) *(G-22139)*
Vermont Compost Company Inc 802 223-6049
1996 Main St Montpelier VT (05602) *(G-22162)*
Vermont Container Div, Bennington *Also called K&H Group Inc (G-21677)*
Vermont Country Soap Corp 802 388-4302
183 Industrial Ave Middlebury VT (05753) *(G-22119)*
Vermont Creamery LLC 802 479-9371
40 Pitman Rd Websterville VT (05678) *(G-22598)*
Vermont Culinary Islands LLC 802 246-2277
22 Browne Ct Unit 115 Brattleboro VT (05301) *(G-21750)*
Vermont Custom Cabinetry, North Walpole *Also called J H Dunning Corporation (G-19394)*
Vermont Custom Cabinetry, North Walpole *Also called Vermont Custom Wood Products (G-19396)*
Vermont Custom Gage LLC 802 868-0104
180 Commercial Ln Lyndonville VT (05851) *(G-22074)*
Vermont Custom Tool Box Inc 802 863-9798
5 Ethan Allen Dr South Burlington VT (05403) *(G-22475)*
Vermont Custom Wood Products 802 463-9930
5 Dunning Dr North Walpole NH (03609) *(G-19396)*
Vermont Distillers Inc 802 464-2003
7627 Route 9 E West Marlboro VT (05363) *(G-22609)*
Vermont Eco Floors 802 425-7737
3222 Greenbush Rd Charlotte VT (05445) *(G-21835)*
Vermont Farm Table LLC (PA) 888 425-8838
206 College St Burlington VT (05401) *(G-21815)*
Vermont Fire Technologies, Williamstown *Also called American Rural Fire Apparatus (G-22649)*
Vermont Flannel Co 802 457-4111
13 Elm St Woodstock VT (05091) *(G-22740)*
Vermont Flexible Tubing Inc 802 626-5723
75 Smiths Rd Lyndonville VT (05851) *(G-22075)*
Vermont Forgings Inc 802 446-3900
41 Cook Dr Wallingford VT (05773) *(G-22575)*
Vermont Furn Hardwoods Inc 802 875-2550
386 Depot St Chester VT (05143) *(G-21852)*
Vermont Furniture Designs Inc 802 655-6568
4 Tigan St Winooski VT (05404) *(G-22727)*
Vermont Gage, Swanton *Also called Vermont Precision Tools Inc (G-22538)*
Vermont Gage, Swanton *Also called Vermont Thread Gage LLC (G-22539)*
Vermont Glass, North Walpole *Also called Woodstone Company Inc (G-19397)*
Vermont Hand Crafters Inc 802 434-5044
855 Bolton Vly Access Rd Waterbury VT (05676) *(G-22588)*
Vermont Handcrafters, Waterbury *Also called Vermont Hand Crafters Inc (G-22588)*
Vermont Hard Cider Company LLC (HQ) 802 388-0700
1321 Exchange St Middlebury VT (05753) *(G-22120)*
Vermont Hardwoods, Chester *Also called Vermont Furn Hardwoods Inc (G-21852)*
Vermont Heritage Spring Water 802 334-2528
3662 N Derby Rd Derby VT (05829) *(G-21904)*
Vermont Independent Media Inc 802 246-6397
139 Main St Rm 604 Brattleboro VT (05301) *(G-21751)*
Vermont Indexable Tooling Inc 802 752-2002
331b Bryce Blvd Fairfax VT (05454) *(G-21980)*
Vermont Islands, Brattleboro *Also called Vermont Culinary Islands LLC (G-21750)*
Vermont Islands Culinary LLC 802 387-8591
22 Browne Ct Unit 115 Brattleboro VT (05301) *(G-21752)*
Vermont Islands Kitchens Bars, Brattleboro *Also called Vermont Islands Culinary LLC (G-21752)*
Vermont Journalism Trust Ltd 802 225-6224
97 State St Ste 1 Montpelier VT (05602) *(G-22163)*
Vermont Juvenile Furn Mfg Inc 802 438-2231
192 Sheldon Ave West Rutland VT (05777) *(G-22620)*
Vermont Lvstk Slghter Proc LLC 802 877-3421
76 Depot Rd Ferrisburgh VT (05456) *(G-21990)*
Vermont Made Scents, Saint Albans *Also called Travis M Bonnett (G-22382)*
Vermont Maple Direct 802 793-3326
233 Emery Rd Washington VT (05675) *(G-22581)*
Vermont Maple Sug Makers Assoc 802 498-7767
248 Maggies Way Waterbury Center VT (05677) *(G-22593)*
Vermont Maple Sug Makers Assoc 802 763-7435
189 Vt Route 15 Jericho VT (05465) *(G-22048)*
Vermont Maple Sugar Co Inc (PA) 802 888-3491
37 Industrial Park Dr Morrisville VT (05661) *(G-22178)*
Vermont Maple Sugar Co Inc 802 635-7483
31 Main St Johnson VT (05656) *(G-22052)*
Vermont Maturity, Williston *Also called Williston Pubg Promotions LLC (G-22699)*
Vermont MBL Gran Slate Spstone 802 468-8800
1565 Main St Castleton VT (05735) *(G-21830)*
Vermont Media Corp 802 464-5757
797 Vt Route 100 N Wilmington VT (05363) *(G-22705)*
Vermont Microtechnologies, Barnet *Also called Vermont Mold & Tool Corp (G-21605)*
Vermont Mold & Tool Corp 802 633-2300
4693 Garland Hl Barnet VT (05821) *(G-21605)*
Vermont News Guide, Manchester Center *Also called Hersam Acorn Newspapers LLC (G-22087)*
Vermont Nut Free Choclat Inc 802 372-4654
146 Brentwood Dr Colchester VT (05446) *(G-21886)*

A L P H A B E T I C

Vermont Olde Tyme Kettle Corn, Newport *Also called Quirion Luc* ***(G-22205)***
Vermont Optechs Inc....802 425-2040
3195 Ethan Allen Hwy Charlotte VT (05445) ***(G-21836)***
Vermont Originals, Morrisville *Also called Washburn Company Inc* ***(G-22179)***
Vermont Packinghouse LLC....802 886-8688
25 Fairbanks Rd North Springfield VT (05150) ***(G-22239)***
Vermont Pallet & Skid Shop....860 822-6949
104 Baltic Rd Norwich CT (06360) ***(G-3292)***
Vermont Pie and Pasta Co....802 334-7770
4278 Us Rte 5 Derby VT (05829) ***(G-21905)***
Vermont Plastics Specialties....802 879-0072
209 Blair Park Rd Williston VT (05495) ***(G-22696)***
Vermont Platting, Rutland *Also called Deermont Corpopration* ***(G-22329)***
Vermont Powder Coating Sy....802 862-0061
57 Commerce Ave Ste 5 South Burlington VT (05403) ***(G-22476)***
Vermont Precision Machine Svcs....802 885-8291
280 Clinton St Springfield VT (05156) ***(G-22511)***
Vermont Precision Tools Inc (PA)....802 868-4246
10 Precision Ln Swanton VT (05488) ***(G-22538)***
Vermont Probiotica....802 279-4998
162 Pine Hill Dr Northfield VT (05663) ***(G-22245)***
Vermont Pub Brewry Burlington....802 865-0500
144 College St Burlington VT (05401) ***(G-21816)***
Vermont Publishing Comany....802 524-9771
281 N Main St Saint Albans VT (05478) ***(G-22384)***
Vermont Quarries Corp....802 775-1065
1591 Us Route 4 Rutland VT (05701) ***(G-22360)***
Vermont Rolling Pins....802 658-3733
68 East Ter South Burlington VT (05403) ***(G-22477)***
Vermont Ski Safety Equipment....802 899-4738
1 Sand Hill Rd Underhill VT (05489) ***(G-22549)***
Vermont Smoke and Cure, Hinesburg *Also called VSC Holdings Inc* ***(G-22033)***
Vermont Soap, Middlebury *Also called Vermont Country Soap Corp* ***(G-22119)***
Vermont Soapstone Inc....802 263-5577
248 Stoughton Pond Rd Perkinsville VT (05151) ***(G-22260)***
Vermont Soy LLC....802 472-8500
180 Junction Rd Hardwick VT (05843) ***(G-22014)***
Vermont Speciality Slate Inc....802 247-6615
855 North St Brandon VT (05733) ***(G-21714)***
Vermont Sportswear Emboridery....802 863-0237
34 Princess Ann Dr Colchester VT (05446) ***(G-21887)***
Vermont Stone Art LLC....802 238-1498
21 Metro Way Ste 1 Barre VT (05641) ***(G-21644)***
Vermont Stoneworks....802 885-6535
100 River St Springfield VT (05156) ***(G-22512)***
Vermont Structural Slate Co (PA)....802 265-4933
3 Prospect St Fair Haven VT (05743) ***(G-21970)***
Vermont Sweet Maple Inc....802 398-2776
1197 Exchange St Ste 3 Middlebury VT (05753) ***(G-22121)***
Vermont Sweetwater Bottling Co....800 974-9877
2087 Hillside Rd Poultney VT (05764) ***(G-22280)***
Vermont Syrup Company LLC....802 309-8861
406 Johnny Bull Hl Fairfield VT (05455) ***(G-21985)***
Vermont Systems Inc....802 879-6993
12 Market Pl Essex Junction VT (05452) ***(G-21963)***
Vermont Teddy Bear Co Inc....802 985-1319
6655 Shelburne Rd Shelburne VT (05482) ***(G-22426)***
Vermont Teddy Bear Company, Shelburne *Also called Hibernation Holding Co Inc* ***(G-22419)***
Vermont Thinstone Assoc LLC....802 448-3000
4211 Roosevelt Hwy Colchester VT (05446) ***(G-21888)***
Vermont Thread Gage LLC....802 868-4246
10 Precision Ln Swanton VT (05488) ***(G-22539)***
Vermont Times Vox, Middlebury *Also called New Market Press Inc* ***(G-22115)***
Vermont Toner Recharge Inc....802 864-7637
12 Claire Dr Essex Junction VT (05452) ***(G-21964)***
Vermont TS Inc....802 875-2091
354 Elm St Chester VT (05143) ***(G-21853)***
Vermont Unfading Green Slate (PA)....802 265-3200
963 S Main St Fair Haven VT (05743) ***(G-21971)***
Vermont Verde Antique Intl....802 767-4421
2561 Sugar Hollow Rd Pittsford VT (05763) ***(G-22265)***
Vermont Ware Inc....802 482-4426
157 Barber Rd A St George VT (05495) ***(G-22514)***
Vermont Wireform Inc....802 889-3200
Rr 110 Chelsea VT (05038) ***(G-21840)***
Vermont Woman Newspaper....802 861-6200
4 Laurel Hill Dr Ste 5 South Burlington VT (05403) ***(G-22478)***
Vermont Wood Pellet Co LLC....802 747-1093
1105 Route 7b Central North Clarendon VT (05759) ***(G-22222)***
Vermonter, The, Putney *Also called H L Handy Company Inc* ***(G-22289)***
Vermonts Northland Journal LLC....802 334-5920
2180 Pine Hill Rd Newport VT (05855) ***(G-22206)***
Vermonts Original LLC....802 626-3610
91 Williams St Lyndonville VT (05851) ***(G-22076)***
Verne Q Powell Flutes Inc....978 461-6111
1 Mill And Main Pl # 300 Maynard MA (01754) ***(G-12905)***
Vernier Metal Fabricating Inc....203 881-3133
26 Progress Ave Seymour CT (06483) ***(G-3767)***
Vernon Printing Co Inc....860 872-1826
352 Hartford Tpke Ste 9 Vernon Rockville CT (06066) ***(G-4688)***
Verosound Inc....978 440-7898
128 Powder Mill Rd Sudbury MA (01776) ***(G-15672)***
Verotec Inc....603 821-9921
473e Washington Ave North Haven CT (06473) ***(G-3068)***
Verpol Plant, Florence *Also called Omya Inc* ***(G-21991)***
Verrillon Inc....508 890-7100
15 Centennial Dr North Grafton MA (01536) ***(G-13966)***
Versatile Printing....781 221-2112
18 Lisa St Burlington MA (01803) ***(G-9352)***
Versatile Subcontracting LLC....603 286-8081
200 Tilton Rd Unit A Northfield NH (03276) ***(G-19409)***
Verso Paper Holding LLC....207 897-3431
300 Riley Rd Jay ME (04239) ***(G-6222)***
Verso Paper Holding LLC....207 897-3431
21 Riley Rd Jay ME (04239) ***(G-6223)***
Vertal US Inc....603 490-1711
18a French Cross Rd Madbury NH (03823) ***(G-18762)***
Vertex Pharmaceuticals Inc....617 201-4171
1 Harbor St Boston MA (02210) ***(G-8908)***
Vertex Pharmaceuticals Inc (PA)....617 341-6100
50 Northern Ave Boston MA (02210) ***(G-8909)***
Vertex Tool & Die Co....508 763-4749
11 Quanapoag Rd East Freetown MA (02717) ***(G-10462)***
Vertica Systems LLC....617 386-4400
150 Cambridgepark Dr Cambridge MA (02140) ***(G-9696)***
Vertical Dreams....603 943-7571
25 E Otterson St Nashua NH (03060) ***(G-19282)***
Vertiv, Walpole *Also called High Voltage Maintenance Corp* ***(G-15993)***
Vertiv Corporation....203 294-6020
8 Fairfield Blvd Ste 4 Wallingford CT (06492) ***(G-4827)***
Vervain Mill....207 774-5744
35 Buttonwood Ln Portland ME (04102) ***(G-6744)***
Verve Inc....401 351-6415
498 Pine St Providence RI (02907) ***(G-21149)***
Veryfine Products Inc (HQ)....978 486-0812
20 Harvard Rd Littleton MA (01460) ***(G-12325)***
Verzatec Inc....860 628-0511
119 Sabina Dr Southington CT (06489) ***(G-4090)***
Vesper Technologies Inc....617 315-9144
77 Summer St Ste 801 Boston MA (02110) ***(G-8910)***
Vespoli Usa Inc....203 773-0311
385 Clinton Ave New Haven CT (06513) ***(G-2751)***
Veteran Software Solutions LLC....508 330-4553
209 Vega Rd Marlborough MA (01752) ***(G-12843)***
Veterans Affairs US Dept....774 240-6764
144 Winthrop St Fall River MA (02721) ***(G-10779)***
Veterans Assembled Elec LLC (PA)....401 228-6165
40 Fountain St Fl 8 Providence RI (02903) ***(G-21150)***
Veterinary Medical Associates....860 693-0214
60 Lovely St Canton CT (06019) ***(G-700)***
Veto Pro Pac LLC....203 847-0297
3 Morgan Ave Ste 4 Norwalk CT (06851) ***(G-3267)***
Vette North American Power Div, Pelham *Also called Vette Thermal Solutions LLC* ***(G-19453)***
Vette Thermal Solutions LLC (HQ)....603 635-2800
14 Manchester Sq Portsmouth NH (03801) ***(G-19629)***
Vette Thermal Solutions LLC....603 635-2800
33 Bridge St Pelham NH (03076) ***(G-19453)***
Vew Do Balance Boards, Manchester Center *Also called Balance Designs Inc* ***(G-22080)***
Vf Outdoor Inc....508 651-7676
1245 Worcester St # 4016 Natick MA (01760) ***(G-13286)***
VH Blackinton & Co Inc....508 699-4436
221 John L Dietsch Blvd Attleboro Falls MA (02763) ***(G-7818)***
Vhp Flight Systems LLC....508 229-2615
36 Clifford Rd Southborough MA (01772) ***(G-15371)***
Via Science Inc (PA)....857 600-2171
100 Dover St Somerville MA (02144) ***(G-15227)***
Viabella Holdings LLC....800 688-9998
9 Kendrick Rd Wareham MA (02571) ***(G-16257)***
Viacell Inc (HQ)....617 914-3400
940 Winter St Waltham MA (02451) ***(G-16219)***
Viacomcbs Inc....508 620-3342
10 California Ave Framingham MA (01701) ***(G-11011)***
Viacord, Waltham *Also called Viacell Inc* ***(G-16219)***
Viamed Corp....508 238-0220
15d Plymouth Dr D South Easton MA (02375) ***(G-15294)***
Viamet Phrmctcals Holdings LLC....919 467-8539
124 Washington St Ste 101 Foxboro MA (02035) ***(G-10908)***
Viant AS&o Holdings LLC....866 899-1392
100 Fordham Rd Wilmington MA (01887) ***(G-17063)***
Viasat Inc....508 229-6500
300 Nickerson Rd Ste 100 Marlborough MA (01752) ***(G-12844)***
Vibco Inc (PA)....401 539-2392
75 Stilson Rd Wyoming RI (02898) ***(G-21591)***
Vibrac LLC (PA)....603 882-6777
1050 Perimeter Rd Ste 600 Manchester NH (03103) ***(G-18950)***
Vibram Corporation (HQ)....508 867-6494
18 School St North Brookfield MA (01535) ***(G-13883)***

Vibram Corporation (HQ)....978 318-0000
9 Damonmill Sq Fl 2 Concord MA (01742) ***(G-10159)***
Vibram USA Inc., Concord *Also called Vibram Corporation* ***(G-10159)***
Vibrascience Inc....203 483-6113
186 N Main St Branford CT (06405) ***(G-356)***
Vibration & Shock Tech LLC....781 281-0721
13 Arbella Dr Beverly MA (01915) ***(G-8195)***
Vic Firth Company....207 368-4358
77 High St Newport ME (04953) ***(G-6488)***
Vic Firth Gourmet, Newport *Also called Vic Firth Manufacturing Inc* ***(G-6489)***
Vic Firth Manufacturing Inc....207 368-4358
77 High St Newport ME (04953) ***(G-6489)***
Vicor Corporation....603 623-3222
540 N Coml St Ste 210 Manchester NH (03101) ***(G-18951)***
Vicor Corporation (PA)....978 470-2900
25 Frontage Rd Andover MA (01810) ***(G-7616)***
Vicor Corporation....978 470-2900
400 Federal St Andover MA (01810) ***(G-7617)***
Victaulic Company....508 406-3220
145 Plymouth St Ste A Mansfield MA (02048) ***(G-12668)***
Victor Microwave Inc....781 245-4472
38 W Water St Wakefield MA (01880) ***(G-15982)***
Victor Tool Co Inc....203 634-8113
290 Pratt St Ste 7 Meriden CT (06450) ***(G-2148)***
Victoria Ann Varga Inc....207 781-4050
21 Foreside Rd Cumberland Foreside ME (04110) ***(G-5933)***
Victoria Brand, Boston *Also called Mutual Beef Co Inc* ***(G-8717)***
Victoria H Bradshaw....508 992-1702
686 Belleville Ave New Bedford MA (02745) ***(G-13457)***
Victory Fuel LLC....860 585-0532
248 Main St Terryville CT (06786) ***(G-4496)***
Victory Productions Inc....508 755-0051
55 Linden St Ste 2 Worcester MA (01609) ***(G-17500)***
Video Automation Systems Inc....203 312-0152
13 Arrow Meadow Rd New Fairfield CT (06812) ***(G-2630)***
Videoiq Inc....781 222-3069
450 Artisan Way Ste 200 Somerville MA (02145) ***(G-15228)***
Videology Imging Solutions Inc (PA)....401 949-5332
37 Lark Industrial Pkwy M Greenville RI (02828) ***(G-20476)***
Vientek LLC (PA)....915 225-1309
373 Market St Warren RI (02885) ***(G-21312)***
Vier Eck Machine and Tool Inc....603 860-1616
277 W Bay Rd Freedom NH (03836) ***(G-18172)***
VIESTE ROSA, Johnston *Also called AG & G Inc* ***(G-20498)***
Vietaz Inc....617 322-1933
2288 Dorchester Ave Dorchester MA (02124) ***(G-10349)***
View, The, Dedham *Also called Sap Professional Journal* ***(G-10297)***
Viewpoint Sign & Awning, Northborough *Also called Expansion Opportunities Inc* ***(G-14033)***
Vigilant Incoporated....603 285-0400
85 Industrial Park Dover NH (03820) ***(G-18065)***
Vigiroda Enterprises Inc....203 268-6117
104 Garwood Rd Trumbull CT (06611) ***(G-4642)***
Vijon Stdios Stined GL Sup Ctr, Old Saybrook *Also called Vijon Studios Inc* ***(G-3354)***
Vijon Studios Inc....860 399-7440
97a Spencer Plain Rd Old Saybrook CT (06475) ***(G-3353)***
Vijon Studios Inc....860 399-7440
97 Spencer Plain Rd Ste A Old Saybrook CT (06475) ***(G-3354)***
Viken Detection Corporation....617 467-5526
21 North Ave Burlington MA (01803) ***(G-9353)***
Viking Corporation....508 594-1800
60 Maple St Ste 3 Mansfield MA (02048) ***(G-12669)***
Viking Enterprises Inc....860 440-0728
41 Millstone Rd Waterford CT (06385) ***(G-4995)***
Viking Industrial Products....508 481-4600
3 Brigham St Marlborough MA (01752) ***(G-12845)***
Viking Platinum LLC....203 574-7979
46 Municipal Rd Waterbury CT (06708) ***(G-4969)***
Viking Tool Company....203 929-1457
435 Access Rd Shelton CT (06484) ***(G-3885)***
Viking Wldg & Fabrication LLC....603 394-7887
243 Amesbury Rd Ste 1 Kensington NH (03833) ***(G-18537)***
Villa Machine Associates Inc....781 326-5969
61 Mcdonald St Dedham MA (02026) ***(G-10300)***
Village Cabinets, Bristol *Also called Belmont Corporation* ***(G-532)***
Village Candle Inc....207 251-4800
90 Spencer Dr Wells ME (04090) ***(G-7168)***
Village Forge Inc....617 361-2591
51 Industrial Dr Boston MA (02136) ***(G-8911)***
Village Industrial Power Inc....802 522-8584
330 Industrial Dr Bradford VT (05033) ***(G-21706)***
Village Netmedia Inc (PA)....207 594-4401
91 Camden St Ste 403 Rockland ME (04841) ***(G-6813)***
Village Netmedia Inc....617 846-3700
39 Putnam St Winthrop MA (02152) ***(G-17101)***
Village Netmedia Inc....207 594-4401
91 Camden St Ste 403 Rockland ME (04841) ***(G-6814)***
Village Netmedia Inc....207 338-3333
156 High St Belfast ME (04915) ***(G-5698)***
Village of Orleans....802 754-8584
1 Memorial Sq Orleans VT (05860) ***(G-22253)***
Village Press Inc....401 434-8130
331 N Broadway Rumford RI (02916) ***(G-21198)***
Village Printer, Ridgefield *Also called Economy Printing & Copy Center* ***(G-3666)***
Village Printer....802 463-9697
5 Canal St Bellows Falls VT (05101) ***(G-21655)***
Village Sports....508 672-4284
737 State Rd Westport MA (02790) ***(G-16850)***
Village West Publishing Inc....603 528-4285
Village W Cntry Clb 403 Laconia NH (03246) ***(G-18592)***
Villager Newspapers....860 928-1818
107 Providence St Putnam CT (06260) ***(G-3639)***
Villagesoup, Rockland *Also called Village Netmedia Inc* ***(G-6814)***
Villanti & Sons Printers Inc....802 864-0723
15 Catamount Dr Milton VT (05468) ***(G-22140)***
Villanti Printers, Milton *Also called Villanti & Sons Printers Inc* ***(G-22140)***
Villarina Pasta & Fine Foods (PA)....203 917-4463
22 Shelter Rock Ln Unit 4 Danbury CT (06810) ***(G-1004)***
Ville Swiss Automatics Inc....203 756-2825
205 Cherry St Waterbury CT (06702) ***(G-4970)***
Villeroy & Boch Usa Inc....207 439-6440
360 Us Route 1 Kittery ME (03904) ***(G-6259)***
Vincent Enterprises, Feeding Hills *Also called Michael Vincent* ***(G-10801)***
Vincent Metals Corporation....401 737-4167
33 Plan Way Bldg 3c Warwick RI (02886) ***(G-21437)***
Vindor Music Inc....617 984-9831
12 Salisbury Rd Newton MA (02458) ***(G-13649)***
Vinegar Hill LLC....781 233-3190
20 Main St Saugus MA (01906) ***(G-15001)***
Vinegar Syndrome LLC....212 722-9755
100 Congress St Bridgeport CT (06604) ***(G-504)***
Vineyard At Strawberry Ridge, Cornwall Bridge *Also called Strawberry Ridge Vineyard Inc* ***(G-821)***
Vineyard Gazette LLC (PA)....508 627-4311
34 S Summer St Edgartown MA (02539) ***(G-10588)***
Vingtech, Biddeford *Also called American Rhnmetall Systems LLC* ***(G-5718)***
Vintage Boat Restorations LLC....860 582-0774
201 Terryville Rd Ste 1 Bristol CT (06010) ***(G-622)***
Vintage Maine Kitchen LLC....207 317-2536
491 Us Route 1 Ste 10 Freeport ME (04032) ***(G-6088)***
Vintage Millwork Corporation....978 957-1400
19 School St Dracut MA (01826) ***(G-10370)***
Vintners Cellar Winery....603 356-9463
1857 White Mountain Hwy North Conway NH (03860) ***(G-19380)***
Vinyl Approach....508 755-5279
12 Walnut St Paxton MA (01612) ***(G-14303)***
Vinyl Technologies Inc....978 342-9800
195 Industrial Rd Fitchburg MA (01420) ***(G-10861)***
Viola Associates Inc....508 771-3457
110 Rosary Ln Ste A Hyannis MA (02601) ***(G-11861)***
Viola Audio Laboratories Inc....203 772-0435
446a Blake St Ste 220 New Haven CT (06515) ***(G-2752)***
Vipi, Auburn *Also called Milor Corporation Inc* ***(G-5581)***
Virginia Industries Inc (PA)....860 571-3600
1022 Elm St Rocky Hill CT (06067) ***(G-3733)***
Virginia Stainless....508 880-5498
700 W Water St Taunton MA (02780) ***(G-15797)***
Virginia Stainless Div....508 823-1747
20 Water St Cambridge MA (02141) ***(G-9697)***
Viricor Inc....508 733-5537
98 Ruddock Rd Sudbury MA (01776) ***(G-15673)***
Viridis Diagnostics Inc....802 316-0894
6 Depot St Underhill VT (05489) ***(G-22550)***
Viridis3d LLC....781 305-4961
10 Roessler Rd Woburn MA (01801) ***(G-17313)***
Virogen Corp....617 926-9167
200 Dexter Ave Watertown MA (02472) ***(G-16329)***
Viropharma Biologics Inc....610 458-7300
300 Shire Way Lexington MA (02421) ***(G-12282)***
Virostat Inc....207 856-6620
8 Spiller Dr Westbrook ME (04092) ***(G-7213)***
Virtual Cove Inc....781 354-0492
6 Kelsey Rd Natick MA (01760) ***(G-13287)***
Virtual Publishing LLC....603 627-9500
103 Bay St Manchester NH (03104) ***(G-18952)***
Virtual Software Systems Inc....774 270-1207
1500 District Ave Burlington MA (01803) ***(G-9354)***
Visco Products Inc....401 831-1665
7 Victory Ave Johnston RI (02919) ***(G-20547)***
Vishay Americas Inc (HQ)....203 452-5648
1 Greenwich Pl Shelton CT (06484) ***(G-3886)***
Vishay Electrofilm, Warwick *Also called Vishay Sprague Inc* ***(G-21438)***
Vishay Hirel Systems LLC....603 742-4375
140 Crosby Rd Dover NH (03820) ***(G-18066)***
Vishay Sprague Inc....401 738-9150
111 Gilbane St Warwick RI (02886) ***(G-21438)***
Vishay Ultrasource, Hollis *Also called Dale Vishay Electronics LLC* ***(G-18328)***

A L P H A B E T I C

Visible Electrophysiology LLC 802 847-4539
197 Moonlight Rdg Colchester VT (05446) *(G-21889)*
Visible Good, Newburyport *Also called The Cricket System Inc (G-13539)*
Visible Light Inc 603 926-6049
24 Stickney Ter Ste 6 Hampton NH (03842) *(G-18277)*
Visible Light Inc 603 926-6049
6 Merrill Industrial Dr # 11 Hampton NH (03842) *(G-18278)*
Visible Measures Corp (PA) 617 482-0222
745 Atlantic Ave Fl 9 Boston MA (02111) *(G-8912)*
Visible Record Systems, Shelton *Also called Inform Inc (G-3818)*
Visimark Inc 508 832-3471
200 Southbridge St Auburn MA (01501) *(G-7851)*
Visimark Inc (PA) 866 344-7721
33 Arctic St Ste 2 Worcester MA (01604) *(G-17501)*
Vision Consulting Group Inc 508 314-5378
104 Fairview St Holliston MA (01746) *(G-11612)*
Vision Designs LLC 203 778-9898
1120 Federal Rd Ste 2 Brookfield CT (06804) *(G-664)*
Vision Dynamics LLC 203 271-1944
799 W Boylston St Ste 1 Worcester MA (01606) *(G-17502)*
Vision Machining Inc 413 247-5678
9 West St West Hatfield MA (01088) *(G-16486)*
Vision Technical Molding, Manchester *Also called Advance Mold & Mfg Inc (G-1983)*
Vision Technical Molding 860 783-5050
20 Utopia Rd Manchester CT (06042) *(G-2057)*
Vision Wine & Spirits LLC 781 278-2000
540 N Coml St Ste 311 Manchester NH (03101) *(G-18953)*
Visionaid Inc 508 295-3300
11 Kendrick Rd Wareham MA (02571) *(G-16258)*
Visionquest Holdings LLC 978 776-9518
305 Foster St Ste 204 Littleton MA (01460) *(G-12326)*
Visit WEI 603 893-0900
43 Northwestern Dr Salem NH (03079) *(G-19777)*
Visitor Guide Publishing Inc 617 542-5283
19 Jacobs Ter Newton MA (02459) *(G-13650)*
Visitor Printing Co 401 272-1010
1 Cathedral Sq Providence RI (02903) *(G-21151)*
Visitrend LLC 857 919-2372
80 Hope Ave Apt 402 Waltham MA (02453) *(G-16220)*
Visterra Inc 617 498-1070
275 2nd Ave Waltham MA (02451) *(G-16221)*
Visual Creations Inc 401 588-5151
500 Narragansett Park Dr Pawtucket RI (02861) *(G-20911)*
Visual Departures Ltd 413 229-2272
48 Sheffield Business Par Ashley Falls MA (01222) *(G-7675)*
Visual Impact LLC 203 790-9650
12 Finance Dr Danbury CT (06810) *(G-1005)*
Visual Inspection Products 603 929-4414
7 Kershaw Ave Ste 3 Hampton NH (03842) *(G-18279)*
Visual Magnetics Ltd 508 381-2400
1 Emerson St Mendon MA (01756) *(G-12997)*
Visual Magnetics Ltd Partnr 508 381-2400
1 Emerson St Mendon MA (01756) *(G-12998)*
Visual Polymer Tech LLC 603 488-5064
91 Brick Mill Rd Bedford NH (03110) *(G-17666)*
Vita Pasta Inc 860 395-1452
225 Elm St Old Saybrook CT (06475) *(G-3355)*
Vita-Crete Inc 508 473-1799
12 S Free St Ste 1 Milford MA (01757) *(G-13151)*
Vital Health Publishing Inc 203 438-3229
149 Old Branchville Rd Ridgefield CT (06877) *(G-3688)*
Vital Signs 617 645-3946
44 Joseph Rd Newton MA (02460) *(G-13651)*
Vital Stretch LLC 203 847-4477
112 Main St Norwalk CT (06851) *(G-3268)*
Vital Wood Products Inc 508 673-7976
218 Shove St Fall River MA (02724) *(G-10780)*
Vitalsensors Technologies LLC 978 635-0450
29 Glenwood Ave Newton MA (02459) *(G-13652)*
Vitaminsea LLC 207 671-0955
369 Beech Plain Rd Buxton ME (04093) *(G-5863)*
Vitec Industries Inc 978 282-7700
1 Blackburn Ctr Gloucester MA (01930) *(G-11217)*
Vitec Production Solutions Inc (HQ) 203 929-1100
14 Progress Dr Shelton CT (06484) *(G-3887)*
Vitek Research Corporation 203 735-1813
33 Sheridan Dr Naugatuck CT (06770) *(G-2500)*
Vito Wheel Music More 781 241-9476
105 Thornton St Revere MA (02151) *(G-14777)*
Vitri Forms Inc 802 254-5235
675 Thomashill Rd West Halifax VT (05358) *(G-22608)*
Vitriesse Glass Studio 802 645-9800
1258 Betts Bridge Rd West Pawlet VT (05775) *(G-22613)*
Vitro Technology Ltd 203 783-9566
205 Research Dr Ste 12 Milford CT (06460) *(G-2380)*
Vitta Corporation 203 790-8155
7 Trowbridge Dr Ste 2 Bethel CT (06801) *(G-192)*
Vittamed Corporation (PA) 617 977-4536
25 Kirsi Cir Westford MA (01886) *(G-16799)*
Vivagene Biotech Inc 617 302-4398
2 Eustis St Quincy MA (02170) *(G-14667)*
Vivantio Inc 617 982-0390
200 Portland St Ste 500 Boston MA (02114) *(G-8913)*
Vivaproducts Inc 978 952-6868
521 Great Rd Littleton MA (01460) *(G-12327)*
Vivid Engineering 508 842-0165
415 Boston Tpke Ste 305 Shrewsbury MA (01545) *(G-15136)*
Vivid Technologies Inc 781 939-3986
10 Commerce Way Woburn MA (01801) *(G-17314)*
Vivido Natural LLC 617 630-0131
22 Keefe Ave Ste 1 Newton MA (02464) *(G-13653)*
Vivox Inc (HQ) 508 650-3571
40 Speen St Ste 305 Framingham MA (01701) *(G-11012)*
Viz-Pro LLC 860 379-0055
120 Colebrook River Rd Winsted CT (06098) *(G-5427)*
Vizient Inc 781 271-0980
209 Burlington Rd Ste 111 Bedford MA (01730) *(G-8019)*
VMS Software Inc 978 451-0110
580 Main St Ste 7 Bolton MA (01740) *(G-8324)*
Vmt LLC 802 633-3900
477 W Main St Barnet VT (05821) *(G-21606)*
Vn Machine Co 860 666-8797
57 Maselli Rd Newington CT (06111) *(G-2911)*
Vocero Hispano Newspaper Inc 508 792-1942
44 Hamilton St Southbridge MA (01550) *(G-15408)*
Vogel Capital Inc (HQ) 508 481-5944
85 Hayes Memorial Dr Marlborough MA (01752) *(G-12846)*
Vogel Printing Company Inc 978 682-6828
300 Canal St Lawrence MA (01840) *(G-12082)*
Vogform Tool & Die Co Inc 413 737-6947
56 Doty Cir West Springfield MA (01089) *(G-16562)*
Vogue Industries Ltd Partnr 401 722-0900
82 Hadwin St Central Falls RI (02863) *(G-20128)*
Voice Express Corp 203 221-7799
1525 Kings Hwy Ste 1 Fairfield CT (06824) *(G-1461)*
Voice Glance LLC 800 260-3025
12 Roosevelt Ave Mystic CT (06355) *(G-2456)*
Voicescript Technologies 401 524-2246
193 Crestwood Rd Warwick RI (02886) *(G-21439)*
Voisine & Son Logging Inc 207 794-3336
1094 N Chester Rd Chester ME (04457) *(G-5907)*
Volcano Corporation 978 439-3560
1 Fortune Dr Billerica MA (01821) *(G-8308)*
Volicon Inc 781 221-7400
99 S Bedford St Ste 209 Burlington MA (01803) *(G-9355)*
Volk Packaging Corporation 207 282-6151
11 Morin St Biddeford ME (04005) *(G-5768)*
Volo Aero Mro Inc 413 525-7211
140 Industrial Dr East Longmeadow MA (01028) *(G-10501)*
Volpe Cable Corporation 203 623-1818
201 Linden Ave Branford CT (06405) *(G-357)*
Volpe Tool & Die Incorporated 508 528-8103
290 Beaver St Franklin MA (02038) *(G-11095)*
Voltarc, Orange *Also called Lcd Lighting Inc (G-3370)*
Voltree Power Inc 781 858-4939
34 Mohawk Rd Canton MA (02021) *(G-9794)*
Vortex Inc 978 535-8721
4 Dearborn Rd Peabody MA (01960) *(G-14381)*
Vortex Manufacturing 860 749-9769
60 Sunshine Farms Dr Somers CT (06071) *(G-3921)*
Vox Communications Group LLC 781 239-8018
70 Walnut St Wellesley MA (02481) *(G-16392)*
Voxel8 Inc 916 396-3714
21 Rev Nazareno Properzi Somerville MA (02143) *(G-15229)*
Voyager Therapeutics Inc (PA) 857 259-5340
75 Sidney St Fl 4 Cambridge MA (02139) *(G-9698)*
Voyteks Inc 860 967-6558
7 Thompson Rd East Windsor CT (06088) *(G-1309)*
Vpt Components, Billerica *Also called Sst Components Inc (G-8298)*
Vr Industries Inc 401 732-6800
333 Strawberry Field Rd # 6 Warwick RI (02886) *(G-21440)*
VSC Holdings Inc 802 482-4666
10516 Route 116 Ste 200 Hinesburg VT (05461) *(G-22033)*
Vsea Inc 978 282-2000
35 Dory Rd Gloucester MA (01930) *(G-11218)*
VSR Video, Underhill *Also called Vermont Ski Safety Equipment (G-22549)*
Vss, Greenfield *Also called Valley Steel Stamp Inc (G-11282)*
VT Adirondack 802 496-9271
1358 German Flats Rd Waitsfield VT (05673) *(G-22570)*
Vtdigger.org, Montpelier *Also called Vermont Journalism Trust Ltd (G-22163)*
Vtfolkus 802 246-1410
51 Main St Ste 1 Brattleboro VT (05301) *(G-21753)*
Vuetek Scientific LLC 207 657-6565
22 Shaker Rd Gray ME (04039) *(G-6143)*
Vulcan Company Inc (PA) 781 337-5970
51 Sharp St Hingham MA (02043) *(G-11515)*
Vulcan Electric Company (PA) 207 625-3231
28 Endfield St Porter ME (04068) *(G-6605)*

Vulcan Flex Circuit Corp 603 883-1500
28 Endfield St Porter ME (04068) *(G-6606)*
Vulcan Industries Inc 860 683-2005
651 Day Hill Rd Windsor CT (06095) *(G-5377)*
Vulcan Industries Inc 413 525-8846
16 Deer Park Dr East Longmeadow MA (01028) *(G-10502)*
Vulcan Tool Mfg, Hingham *Also called Vulcan Company Inc (G-11515)*
Vulplex Incorporated 508 996-6787
305 Nash Rd New Bedford MA (02746) *(G-13458)*
Vw Quality Coating 617 963-6503
62 Cross St Norton MA (02766) *(G-14092)*
Vxe, Lexington *Also called Realtime Dx Inc (G-12259)*
Vxi Corporation 603 742-2888
900 Chelmsford St # 313 Lowell MA (01851) *(G-12447)*
Vynorius Companies, The, Salisbury *Also called Vynorius Prestress Inc (G-14959)*
Vynorius Prestress Inc 978 462-7765
150 Elm St Salisbury MA (01952) *(G-14959)*
Vytek, Fitchburg *Also called Vinyl Technologies Inc (G-10861)*
W & G Gas Services LLC 617 327-2515
103 Mount Hope St Roslindale MA (02131) *(G-14844)*
W A M, South Windham *Also called Windham Automated Machines Inc (G-3929)*
W A Mitchell Chair Makers, Farmington *Also called W A Mitchell Inc (G-6054)*
W A Mitchell Inc 207 778-5212
710 Wilton Rd Farmington ME (04938) *(G-6054)*
W and D Enterprise Inc 508 883-4811
159 Lincoln St Millville MA (01529) *(G-13188)*
W and G Machine Company Inc 203 288-8772
4 Hamden Park Dr Hamden CT (06517) *(G-1794)*
W B Machine Inc 978 372-5396
40 Middlesex St Haverhill MA (01835) *(G-11484)*
W C Canniff & Sons Inc (PA) 617 323-3690
531 Cummins Hwy Boston MA (02131) *(G-8914)*
W C Canniff & Sons Inc 617 323-3690
531 Cummins Hwy Roslindale MA (02131) *(G-14845)*
W C Vaughn, Braintree *Also called Vaughan W C Co Ltd Inc (G-9046)*
W Canning Inc 203 575-5727
245 Freight St Waterbury CT (06702) *(G-4971)*
W Craig Washburn 603 237-8403
45 Diamond Pond Rd Colebrook NH (03576) *(G-17877)*
W D C Holdings Inc 508 699-4412
200 John J Dietsch Blvd Attleboro MA (02703) *(G-7806)*
W E Richards Co Inc 508 226-1036
40 John Williams St Attleboro MA (02703) *(G-7807)*
W F Young Incorporated (PA) 800 628-9653
302 Benton Dr East Longmeadow MA (01028) *(G-10503)*
W G Fry Corp 413 747-2551
28 Sylvan Ln Florence MA (01062) *(G-10870)*
W G Machine Works Inc 508 883-4903
140 Suffolk St Ste 140 # 140 Bellingham MA (02019) *(G-8063)*
W H Bagshaw Co Inc 603 883-7758
1 Pine Street Ext Ste 135 Nashua NH (03060) *(G-19283)*
W H M Industries Inc 603 835-6015
Hemlock Rd Charlestown NH (03603) *(G-17820)*
W J Roberts Co Inc 781 233-8176
181 Central St Saugus MA (01906) *(G-15002)*
W K Hillquist Inc 603 595-7790
37 Executive Dr Hudson NH (03051) *(G-18451)*
W L Fuller 401 467-2900
7 Cypress St Warwick RI (02888) *(G-21441)*
W M G and Sons Inc 860 584-0143
8 Summerberry Rd Bristol CT (06010) *(G-623)*
W M Gulliksen Mfg Co Inc (PA) 617 323-5750
30 Fairway Lndg South Weymouth MA (02190) *(G-15323)*
W P Moore Co Inc 781 878-9566
249 High St Norwell MA (02061) *(G-14113)*
W R Cobb Company (PA) 401 438-7000
800 Waterman Ave East Providence RI (02914) *(G-20448)*
W R Grace & Co 617 876-1400
91 Hartwell Ave Ste 2 Lexington MA (02421) *(G-12283)*
W R H Industries Ltd 508 674-2444
957 Airport Rd Fall River MA (02720) *(G-10781)*
W R Hartigan & Son Inc 860 673-9203
10 Spielman Hwy Burlington CT (06013) *(G-682)*
W S Bessett Inc 207 324-9232
1923 Main St Sanford ME (04073) *(G-6896)*
W S Emerson Company Inc (PA) 207 989-3410
15 Acme Rd Brewer ME (04412) *(G-5803)*
W S Packaging 603 654-6131
1 Riverside Way Wilton NH (03086) *(G-19990)*
W S Polymers 203 268-1557
93 Calhoun Ave Trumbull CT (06611) *(G-4643)*
W S Sign Design Corp 413 241-6916
884 Alden St Springfield MA (01109) *(G-15522)*
W S Walcott Inc 508 240-0882
180 Hilltop Plz Rr 6 Orleans MA (02653) *(G-14244)*
W&R Manufacturing Inc 203 877-5955
230 Woodmont Rd Ste U Milford CT (06460) *(G-2381)*
W2w Partners LLC 781 424-7824
65 Acorn Street Duxbury Duxbury MA (02332) *(G-10404)*
W5 Circuits LLC 603 964-6780
27 Hobbs Rd North Hampton NH (03862) *(G-19388)*
WA Logging LLC 207 694-2921
634 White Settlement Rd Hodgdon ME (04730) *(G-6195)*
Wabash Technologies Inc (HQ) 260 355-4100
529 Pleasant St Attleboro MA (02703) *(G-7808)*
Wachusett Brewing Company Inc 978 874-9965
175 State Rd E Westminster MA (01473) *(G-16820)*
Wachusett Molding LLC 508 459-0477
3 Cutting Ave Auburn MA (01501) *(G-7852)*
Wachusett Precast Inc 978 422-3311
74 Pratts Junction Rd Sterling MA (01564) *(G-15548)*
Wackerbarth Box Mfg Co 413 357-8816
383 Granby Rd Granville MA (01034) *(G-11231)*
Wackerbarth Box Shop, Granville *Also called Wackerbarth Box Mfg Co (G-11231)*
Wad Inc 860 828-3331
100 Clark Dr East Berlin CT (06023) *(G-1110)*
Waddington Group Inc 201 610-6728
6 Stuart Rd Chelmsford MA (01824) *(G-9940)*
Waddington North America Inc 978 256-6551
6 Stuart Rd Chelmsford MA (01824) *(G-9941)*
Wadsworth Medical Tech Inc 508 789-6531
5 Harvest Way Westborough MA (01581) *(G-16657)*
Wafer LLC 978 304-3821
54 Cherry Hill Dr Danvers MA (01923) *(G-10272)*
Wafer Inspection Services Inc 508 944-2851
Woodland Dr Orleans MA (02653) *(G-14245)*
Wagner Instruments, Riverside *Also called Weigh & Test Systems Inc (G-3693)*
Wagner Lifescience LLC 978 539-8102
136 N Main St Middleton MA (01949) *(G-13105)*
Wagz Inc (PA) 603 570-6015
230 Commerce Way Ste 325 Portsmouth NH (03801) *(G-19630)*
Wagz Inc 203 553-9336
1 Landmark Sq Ste 505 Stamford CT (06901) *(G-4356)*
Wahlcometroflex Inc 207 784-2338
29 Lexington St Lewiston ME (04240) *(G-6327)*
Wainwright USA LLC 413 717-4211
964 S Main St Ste 5 Great Barrington MA (01230) *(G-11249)*
Waiteco Machine Inc 978 772-5535
18 Saratoga Blvd Ayer MA (01434) *(G-7942)*
Waja Associates Inc 508 543-6050
38 Forge Pkwy Franklin MA (02038) *(G-11096)*
Wakefeld Thermal Solutions Inc (HQ) 603 635-2800
33 Bridge St Pelham NH (03076) *(G-19454)*
Wakefield Daily Item, Wakefield *Also called Wakefield Item Co (G-15983)*
Wakefield Investments Inc 978 582-0261
1000 Reservoir Rd Lunenburg MA (01462) *(G-12486)*
Wakefield Item Co 781 245-0080
26 Albion St Wakefield MA (01880) *(G-15983)*
Wakefield-Vette, Pelham *Also called Wakefeld Thermal Solutions Inc (G-19454)*
Wakefield-Vette, Portsmouth *Also called Vette Thermal Solutions LLC (G-19629)*
Walch Publishing, Portland *Also called J Weston Walch Publisher (G-6676)*
Walden Services Inc 781 642-7653
3 Roseanna Park Dr Waltham MA (02452) *(G-16222)*
Wales Copy Center, Boston *Also called Andrew T Johnson Company Inc (G-8366)*
Walker Industries LLC 860 455-3554
464 Zaicek Rd Ashford CT (06278) *(G-28)*
Walker Machine 508 867-8097
1290 W Brookfield Rd New Braintree MA (01531) *(G-13461)*
Walker Magnetics Group Inc (HQ) 508 853-3232
600 Day Hill Rd Windsor CT (06095) *(G-5378)*
Walker Magnetics Group Inc 774 670-1423
60 Solferino St Ste A Worcester MA (01604) *(G-17503)*
Walker Products Incorporated 860 659-3781
80 Commerce St Ste C Glastonbury CT (06033) *(G-1581)*
Walkers VT Pure Mple Syrup LLC 802 899-3088
75 Sand Hill Rd Underhill VT (05489) *(G-22551)*
Wall Industries Inc 603 778-2300
37 Industrial Dr Ste 3 Exeter NH (03833) *(G-18137)*
Wall Street Journal 800 369-5663
84 2nd Ave Chicopee MA (01020) *(G-10068)*
Wallace Building Products Corp 603 768-5402
40 Wallace Ln Danbury NH (03230) *(G-17966)*
Wallach Surgical Devices Inc (PA) 203 799-2000
75 Corporate Dr Trumbull CT (06611) *(G-4644)*
Wallach Surgical Devices Inc 800 243-2463
95 Corporate Dr Trumbull CT (06611) *(G-4645)*
Wallaston Foundry and Machine, Taunton *Also called Wollaston Foundry (G-15800)*
Wallgoldfinger Inc 802 483-4200
706 Garvey Hill Rd Northfield VT (05663) *(G-22246)*
Wallingford Industries Inc 203 481-0359
31 Business Park Dr Ste 3 Branford CT (06405) *(G-358)*
Wallingford Prtg Bus Forms Inc 203 481-1911
758 E Main St Branford CT (06405) *(G-359)*
Walnut Bottom Inc 603 224-6606
30 Terrill Park Dr Concord NH (03301) *(G-17939)*
Walpole Cabinetry 603 826-4100
5 Lambro Ln Walpole NH (03608) *(G-19925)*

ALPHABETIC

Walpole Creamery Ltd..........603 445-5700
532 Main St Walpole NH (03608) ***(G-19926)***
Walpole Fence Company, Ridgefield *Also called Walpole Woodworkers Inc* ***(G-3689)***
Walpole Outdoors, Westport *Also called Walpole Woodworkers Inc* ***(G-5237)***
Walpole Print Works Inc..........508 668-0247
430 High Plain St Walpole MA (02081) ***(G-16017)***
Walpole Times Inc..........508 668-0243
1 Speen St Ste 200 Framingham MA (01701) ***(G-11013)***
Walpole Woodworkers Inc..........207 368-4302
88 Main St Detroit ME (04929) ***(G-5954)***
Walpole Woodworkers Inc..........508 668-2800
346 Ethan Allen Hwy Ridgefield CT (06877) ***(G-3689)***
Walpole Woodworkers Inc..........508 540-0300
958 E Falmouth Hwy East Falmouth MA (02536) ***(G-10451)***
Walpole Woodworkers Inc..........781 681-9099
183 Washington St Norwell MA (02061) ***(G-14114)***
Walpole Woodworkers Inc..........978 658-3373
168 Lowell St Wilmington MA (01887) ***(G-17064)***
Walpole Woodworkers Inc..........203 255-9010
1835 Post Rd E Ste 6 Westport CT (06880) ***(G-5237)***
Walpole Woodworkers Inc..........207 794-2248
235 N Chester Rd Chester ME (04457) ***(G-5908)***
Walrus Enterprises LLC..........413 387-4387
30 Aldrich St Northampton MA (01060) ***(G-14026)***
Walsh Claim Services..........203 481-0680
6 Enterprise Dr North Branford CT (06471) ***(G-2983)***
Walston Inc..........203 453-5929
131 Nut Plains Rd Guilford CT (06437) ***(G-1724)***
Walter A Furman Co Inc..........508 674-7751
180 Liberty St Fall River MA (02724) ***(G-10782)***
Walter Buckwold Logging..........603 523-9626
34 Cross Rd Orange NH (03741) ***(G-19419)***
Walter De Gruyter Inc..........857 284-7073
121 High St Fl 3 Boston MA (02110) ***(G-8915)***
Walter Drake Inc (PA)..........413 536-5463
85 Sargeant St Holyoke MA (01040) ***(G-11666)***
Walter Scott..........781 862-4893
16 S Rindge Ave Lexington MA (02420) ***(G-12284)***
Waltham Fuel..........617 364-2890
295 Eastern Ave Chelsea MA (02150) ***(G-9974)***
Walts Machine Shop..........207 864-5083
560 Rumford Rd Oquossoc ME (04964) ***(G-6548)***
Walz & Krenzer Inc (PA)..........203 267-5712
91 Willenbrock Rd Ste B4 Oxford CT (06478) ***(G-3429)***
Walz & Krenzer Inc..........203 267-5712
91 Willenbrock Rd Ste B4 Oxford CT (06478) ***(G-3430)***
Wanderer Communications Inc..........508 758-9055
55 County Rd Mattapoisett MA (02739) ***(G-12892)***
Waniewski Farms Inc..........413 786-1182
409 S Westfield St Feeding Hills MA (01030) ***(G-10805)***
Ward Cedar Log Homes, Houlton *Also called Wlhc Inc* ***(G-6212)***
Ward Fabrication Inc..........603 382-9700
7 Beechwood Rd Sandown NH (03873) ***(G-19788)***
Ward Leonard CT LLC (HQ)..........860 283-5801
401 Watertown Rd Thomaston CT (06787) ***(G-4525)***
Ward Leonard CT LLC..........860 283-2294
401 Watertown Rd Thomaston CT (06787) ***(G-4526)***
Ward Process Inc..........508 429-1165
311 Hopping Brook Rd Holliston MA (01746) ***(G-11613)***
Wards Woodworking Inc..........603 642-7300
16 Route 125 Kingston NH (03848) ***(G-18548)***
Wardwell Piping Inc..........207 892-0034
194 Roosevelt Trl Windham ME (04062) ***(G-7259)***
Ware Rite Distributors Inc..........508 690-2145
40 Industrial Dr East Bridgewater MA (02333) ***(G-10422)***
Ware Sportswear, Ware *Also called Joseph Lotuff Sr* ***(G-16234)***
Wareham Courier, Wareham *Also called Gatehouse Media Mass I Inc* ***(G-16247)***
Warehouse, Westwood *Also called Cambridge Soundworks Inc* ***(G-16859)***
Warehouse, Newburyport *Also called Rochester Electronics LLC* ***(G-13532)***
Warehouse Cables LLC..........401 737-5677
1303 Jefferson Blvd Warwick RI (02886) ***(G-21442)***
Warick Management Company Inc..........603 538-7112
10 Farr Rd Pittsburg NH (03592) ***(G-19496)***
Waring Products Division, Torrington *Also called Conair Corporation* ***(G-4572)***
Warm Water Sales Group..........413 567-0750
24 Knollwood Dr Ste 78 Longmeadow MA (01106) ***(G-12338)***
Warmup Inc..........203 791-0072
52 Federal Rd Ste 1b Danbury CT (06810) ***(G-1006)***
Warner Electric..........781 917-0600
300 Granite St Ste 201 Braintree MA (02184) ***(G-9048)***
Warner Graphics Inc..........207 236-2065
22 Washington St Camden ME (04843) ***(G-5871)***
Warner Power Acquisition LLC (HQ)..........603 456-3111
40 Depot St Warner NH (03278) ***(G-19930)***
Warner Power Conversion LLC..........603 456-3111
40 Depot St Warner NH (03278) ***(G-19931)***
Warren Chair Works Inc..........401 247-0426
30 Cutler St Unit 220 Warren RI (02885) ***(G-21313)***
Warren Environmental Inc (PA)..........508 947-8539
137 Pine St Middleboro MA (02346) ***(G-13081)***
Warren River Boatworks Inc..........401 245-6949
66 Church St B Warren RI (02885) ***(G-21314)***
Warwick Group Inc..........401 438-9451
8 Burke Rd Bristol RI (02809) ***(G-20109)***
Warwick Hanger Company, Westerly *Also called Cramik Enterprises Inc* ***(G-21521)***
Warwick Ice Cream Company..........401 821-8403
743 Bald Hill Rd Warwick RI (02886) ***(G-21443)***
Warwick Mills Inc (PA)..........603 291-1000
301 Turnpike Rd New Ipswich NH (03071) ***(G-19311)***
Wasco Products, Wells *Also called Velux America LLC* ***(G-7167)***
Washburn & Doughty Assoc Inc..........207 633-6517
7 Enterprise St East Boothbay ME (04544) ***(G-5980)***
Washburn Boat & Auto Body..........802 863-1383
4989 Williston Rd Williston VT (05495) ***(G-22697)***
Washburn Company Inc..........802 888-3032
320 Wilkins St Morrisville VT (05661) ***(G-22179)***
Washburn Vault Company Inc..........802 254-9150
795 Meadowbrook Rd Brattleboro VT (05301) ***(G-21754)***
Washer Tech Inc..........203 886-0054
956 Old Colony Rd Meriden CT (06451) ***(G-2149)***
Washington ABC Imaging Inc..........857 753-4241
274 Summer St Boston MA (02210) ***(G-8916)***
Washington Copper Works Inc..........860 868-7637
49 South St Washington CT (06793) ***(G-4831)***
Washington Mills Ceramic Corp (HQ)..........508 839-6511
20 N Main St North Grafton MA (01536) ***(G-13967)***
Washington Mills N Grafton Inc (HQ)..........508 839-6511
20 N Main St North Grafton MA (01536) ***(G-13968)***
Wasik Associates Inc..........978 454-9787
29 Diana Ln Dracut MA (01826) ***(G-10371)***
Wasp Archery Products Inc..........860 283-0246
707 Main St Plymouth CT (06782) ***(G-3549)***
Waste Mgmt Inc..........413 747-9294
84 Birnie Ave Springfield MA (01107) ***(G-15523)***
Waste Resource Recovery Inc (PA)..........860 287-3332
505 Exeter Rd Lebanon CT (06249) ***(G-1938)***
Waste To Green Fuel LLC..........203 536-5855
1376 Chopsey Hill Rd Bridgeport CT (06606) ***(G-505)***
Waste Water Evaporators Inc..........978 256-3259
6 Marion St Wilmington MA (01887) ***(G-17065)***
Water Analytics Inc..........978 749-9949
100 School St Andover MA (01810) ***(G-7618)***
Water Pollution Control Dept, Vernon Rockville *Also called Town of Vernon* ***(G-4686)***
Water Street Printing LLC..........603 595-1444
97 Main St Nashua NH (03060) ***(G-19284)***
Water Street Woodworking..........401 245-1921
332 Water St Frnt Warren RI (02885) ***(G-21315)***
Water Structures LLC..........603 474-0615
60 Stard Rd Seabrook NH (03874) ***(G-19822)***
Water Treatment Plant, Vernon *Also called Town of Vernon* ***(G-4675)***
Water Treatment Plant, Chicopee *Also called City of Chicopee* ***(G-10013)***
Water Works..........203 546-6000
60 Backus Ave Danbury CT (06810) ***(G-1007)***
Water Works Supply Corp..........781 322-1238
220 Old Sandown Rd Chester NH (03036) ***(G-17827)***
Waterbury Button Company, Cheshire *Also called Ogs Technologies Inc* ***(G-749)***
Waterbury Leatherworks Co..........203 755-7789
1691 Thomaston Ave Ste 3 Waterbury CT (06704) ***(G-4972)***
Waterbury Plating, Waterbury *Also called Halco Inc* ***(G-4881)***
Waterbury Printing, Waterbury *Also called Master Engrv & Printery Inc* ***(G-4911)***
Waterbury Rolling Mills Inc..........203 597-5000
215 Piedmont St Waterbury CT (06706) ***(G-4973)***
Waterbury Screw Machine..........203 756-8084
319 Thomaston Ave Waterbury CT (06702) ***(G-4974)***
Waterbury Screw Mch Pdts Co..........203 756-8084
311 Thomaston Ave Ste 319 Waterbury CT (06702) ***(G-4975)***
Waterbury Swiss Automatics..........203 573-8584
43 Mattatuck Heights Rd Waterbury CT (06705) ***(G-4976)***
Waterfront Graphics & Prtg LLC..........207 799-3519
104 Ocean St South Portland ME (04106) ***(G-7044)***
Waterfront Printing Company..........617 345-9711
12 Channel St Ste 7 Boston MA (02210) ***(G-8917)***
Waterlac Coating Inc..........573 885-2506
142 Starr Ave Lowell MA (01852) ***(G-12448)***
Waterrower Inc..........800 852-2210
560 Metacom Ave Warren RI (02885) ***(G-21316)***
Waters Corp USA, Milford *Also called Waters Corporation* ***(G-13152)***
Waters Corporation..........508 478-0208
34 Maple St Milford MA (01757) ***(G-13152)***
Waters Corporation (PA)..........508 478-2000
34 Maple St Milford MA (01757) ***(G-13153)***
Waters Technologies Corp..........508 482-5223
177 Robert Treat Paine Dr Taunton MA (02780) ***(G-15798)***
Waters Technologies Corp (HQ)..........508 478-2000
34 Maple St Milford MA (01757) ***(G-13154)***
Waters Technologies Corp..........978 927-7468
100 Cummings Ctr Ste 407n Beverly MA (01915) ***(G-8196)***

Waters Technologies Corp....508 482-4807
210 Grove St Franklin MA (02038) **(G-11097)**
Waterseed Wooden Bird Feeders, Burlington *Also called Koss Industries Inc* **(G-21791)**
Waterside Vending LLC....860 399-6039
643 Old Clinton Rd Westbrook CT (06498) **(G-5165)**
Watertech International....781 592-8224
12 Alfred St Ste 300 Woburn MA (01801) **(G-17315)**
Watertown Canvas and Awng LLC....860 274-0933
98 Falls Ave Oakville CT (06779) **(G-3305)**
Watertown Cremation Products, Whitman *Also called Watertown Engineering Corp* **(G-16929)**
Watertown Engineering Corp....781 857-2555
1200 Auburn St Whitman MA (02382) **(G-16929)**
Watertown Ironworks Inc....781 491-0229
47 Henshaw St Woburn MA (01801) **(G-17316)**
Watertown Jig Bore Service Inc....860 274-5898
29 New Wood Rd Watertown CT (06795) **(G-5034)**
Watertown Plastics Inc....860 274-7535
830 Echo Lake Rd Watertown CT (06795) **(G-5035)**
Watertown Printers Inc....781 893-9400
21 Mcgrath Hwy Ste 3 Somerville MA (02143) **(G-15230)**
Waterwear Inc....603 654-5344
24 Howard St Wilton NH (03086) **(G-19991)**
Waterwood Corporation....413 572-1010
77 Servistar Indus Way Westfield MA (01085) **(G-16740)**
Waterworks....207 941-8306
25 Dowd Rd Bangor ME (04401) **(G-5663)**
Watson Brothers Inc....978 774-7677
6 Birch Rd Middleton MA (01949) **(G-13106)**
Watson LLC (HQ)....203 932-3000
301 Heffernan Dr West Haven CT (06516) **(G-5149)**
Watson Printing Co Inc....781 237-1336
118 Cedar St Ste 2 Wellesley MA (02481) **(G-16393)**
Watson-Marlow/Bredel Pumps, Wilmington *Also called Marlow Watson Inc* **(G-17020)**
Watts Regulator Co (HQ)....978 689-6000
815 Chestnut St North Andover MA (01845) **(G-13737)**
Watts Regulator Co....603 934-5110
583 S Main St Franklin NH (03235) **(G-18166)**
Watts Regulator Co....978 688-1811
1600 Osgood St North Andover MA (01845) **(G-13738)**
Watts Water Technologies Inc....603 934-1369
583 S Main St Franklin NH (03235) **(G-18167)**
Watts Water Technologies Inc (PA)....978 688-1811
815 Chestnut St North Andover MA (01845) **(G-13739)**
Watts Water Technologies Inc....603 934-1367
20 Industrial Park Dr Franklin NH (03235) **(G-18168)**
Waughs Mountainview Elec....207 545-2421
246 Roxbury Rd Mexico ME (04257) **(G-6430)**
Wauregan Machine Shop....860 774-0686
51 S Walnut St Wauregan CT (06387) **(G-5040)**
Wavefront Semiconductor, Cumberland *Also called Alesis LP* **(G-20313)**
Waveguide Corporation....617 892-9700
85 Bolton St Ste 153 Cambridge MA (02140) **(G-9699)**
Wavelink LLC....603 606-7489
800 Holt Ave Manchester NH (03109) **(G-18954)**
Wavesense Inc....917 488-9677
444 Somerville Ave Somerville MA (02143) **(G-15231)**
Way Out Wax Inc....802 730-8069
76 Deer Run Ln North Hyde Park VT (05665) **(G-22233)**
Waybest Foods Inc....860 289-7948
1510 John Fitch Blvd South Windsor CT (06074) **(G-4020)**
Wayland Millwork Corporation....508 485-4172
344 Boston Post Rd E # 1 Marlborough MA (01752) **(G-12847)**
Wayland Sudbury Septage....508 358-7328
490 Boston Post Rd Wayland MA (01778) **(G-16337)**
Wayne Horn....860 491-3315
308 Cedar Ln New Hartford CT (06057) **(G-2649)**
Wayne Kerr Electronics Inc....781 938-8390
165l New Boston St Woburn MA (01801) **(G-17317)**
Wayne Manufacturing Inds LLC....978 416-0899
13 Prescott Rd Brentwood NH (03833) **(G-17761)**
Wayne Peters Phill....207 736-4191
24 Medway Rd Mattawamkeag ME (04459) **(G-6416)**
Waynes Sheet Metal Inc....508 431-8057
157 Tremont St Rehoboth MA (02769) **(G-14762)**
Waypoint Distillery....860 519-5390
410 Woodland Ave Bloomfield CT (06002) **(G-271)**
Wayside Fences, Brattleboro *Also called George L Martin* **(G-21729)**
Wayside Publishing....888 302-2519
262 Us Route 1 Ste 2 Freeport ME (04032) **(G-6089)**
WB Engineering Inc....508 952-4000
50 Commerce Way Norton MA (02766) **(G-14093)**
WB Engineering Inc (HQ)....207 878-0700
11 Gray Rd Falmouth ME (04105) **(G-6037)**
Wbc Extrusion Products Inc (HQ)....978 469-0668
60 Fondi Rd Haverhill MA (01832) **(G-11485)**
Wbmx Mix 985 Tweeter Cntr....508 339-1296
885 S Main St Mansfield MA (02048) **(G-12670)**
Wces Inc....203 573-1325
225 S Leonard St Waterbury CT (06708) **(G-4977)**
Wdss Corporation....203 854-5930
7 Old Well Ct Norwalk CT (06855) **(G-3269)**
Wdw Machine Inc....603 329-9604
17 Gigante Dr Ste 1 Hampstead NH (03841) **(G-18251)**
We Cork Enterprises Inc....603 778-8558
16 Kingston Rd Unit 6 Exeter NH (03833) **(G-18138)**
We Dream In Colur LLC....978 768-0168
31 Forest Ave Essex MA (01929) **(G-10598)**
We Love Construction....978 239-1308
1 Arrowhead Trl Ipswich MA (01938) **(G-11938)**
We Make Paint, Stratford *Also called Grafted Coatings Inc* **(G-4416)**
We Palmer Co, Boston *Also called Harry Miller Co Inc* **(G-8589)**
We Print Today LLC....781 585-6021
66 Summer St Kingston MA (02364) **(G-11966)**
Wealth2kcom Inc....781 989-5200
75 Arlington St Ste 5000 Boston MA (02116) **(G-8918)**
Weather Build Inc....617 460-5556
486 Green St Cambridge MA (02139) **(G-9700)**
Weatherend Estate Furniture, Rockland *Also called Imagineering Inc* **(G-6798)**
Weatherford International LLC....203 294-0190
8 Enterprise Rd Wallingford CT (06492) **(G-4828)**
Web Closeout....413 222-8302
360 El Paso St Springfield MA (01104) **(G-15524)**
Web Converting Inc....508 879-4442
160 Fountain St Framingham MA (01702) **(G-11014)**
Web Die Cutters Etc Inc....413 552-3100
265 Main St Agawam MA (01001) **(G-7456)**
Web Handling Equipment, West Bridgewater *Also called Double E Company LLC* **(G-16438)**
Web Home Phoenix Fabrication....781 424-8076
106 Wapping Rd Kingston MA (02364) **(G-11967)**
Web Industries Hartford Inc (HQ)....860 779-3197
20 Louisa Viens Dr Dayville CT (06241) **(G-1055)**
Web Industries Inc (PA)....508 898-2988
700 Nickerson Rd Ste 250 Marlborough MA (01752) **(G-12848)**
Webb-Mason Inc....781 272-5530
50 Mall Rd Ste 207 Burlington MA (01803) **(G-9356)**
Webbers Cove Boat Yard Inc....207 374-2841
Morgan Bay Rd East Blue Hill ME (04629) **(G-5975)**
Webbers Truck Service Inc....860 623-4554
27 Depot Hill Rd East Windsor CT (06088) **(G-1310)**
Webco, Dudley *Also called Starchem Inc* **(G-10386)**
Webco Engineering Inc....508 303-0500
155 Northboro Rd Ste 20 Southborough MA (01772) **(G-15372)**
Webport Global LLC....617 385-5058
2 Seaport Ln Fl 9 Boston MA (02210) **(G-8919)**
Webster Printing Company Inc (PA)....781 447-5484
1069 W Washington St Hanson MA (02341) **(G-11370)**
Webteamwork....781 344-8373
25 Pondview Ln Stoughton MA (02072) **(G-15628)**
Wecare Environmental LLC....508 480-9922
856 Boston Post Rd E Marlborough MA (01752) **(G-12849)**
Wedgerock....207 793-2289
34 Business Park Rd Limerick ME (04048) **(G-6338)**
Wee Forest Folk Inc....978 369-0286
887 Bedford Rd Carlisle MA (01741) **(G-9800)**
Weeden Street Associates LLC....401 725-2610
173 Weeden St Pawtucket RI (02860) **(G-20912)**
Weekly Packet, The, Blue Hill *Also called Penobscot Bay Press Inc* **(G-5772)**
Weekly Sentinel, The, Wells *Also called Shoreline Publications* **(G-7165)**
Weetabix Company Inc....978 422-2905
12 Industrial Dr Sterling MA (01564) **(G-15549)**
Wehr Industries Inc....401 732-6565
14 Minnesota Ave Warwick RI (02888) **(G-21444)**
Wei Inc (PA)....401 781-3904
33 Webb St Cranston RI (02920) **(G-20309)**
Wei Inc....401 781-3904
25 Webb St Cranston RI (02920) **(G-20310)**
Weidner Services LLC....603 532-4833
5 Saw Mill Dr Jaffrey NH (03452) **(G-18481)**
Weigh & Test Systems Inc....203 698-9681
17 Wilmot Ln Ste 2 Riverside CT (06878) **(G-3693)**
Weil McLain....508 485-8050
313 Boston Post Rd W # 125 Marlborough MA (01752) **(G-12850)**
Weimann Brothers Mfg Co....203 735-3311
247 Roosevelt Dr Derby CT (06418) **(G-1082)**
Weirs Publishing Company Inc....888 308-8463
515 Endicott St N Laconia NH (03246) **(G-18593)**
Weirs Times, Laconia *Also called Weirs Publishing Company Inc* **(G-18593)**
Weiss Sheet Metal Inc....508 583-8300
105 Bodwell St Avon MA (02322) **(G-7901)**
Welch Fluorocarbon Inc....603 742-0164
113 Crosby Rd Ste 10 Dover NH (03820) **(G-18067)**
Welch Foods Inc A Cooperative (HQ)....978 371-1000
575 Virginia Rd Concord MA (01742) **(G-10160)**
Welch Foods Inc A Cooperative....978 371-3762
300 Baker Ave Ste 101 Concord MA (01742) **(G-10161)**
Welch Welding and Trck Eqp Inc....978 251-8726
164 Middlesex St North Chelmsford MA (01863) **(G-13913)**

ALPHABETIC

Welch Welding and Truck Eqp, North Chelmsford *Also called Welch Welding and Trck Eqp Inc* ***(G-13913)***
Welch Welding Inc....978 251-8726
162 Middlesex St North Chelmsford MA (01863) ***(G-13914)***
Welch's, Concord *Also called Welch Foods Inc A Cooperative* ***(G-10160)***
Weld Engineering Co Inc....508 842-2224
34 Fruit St Shrewsbury MA (01545) ***(G-15137)***
Weld Rite....617 524-9747
3371 Washington St Jamaica Plain MA (02130) ***(G-11951)***
Weld-All Inc....860 621-3156
987 West St Southington CT (06489) ***(G-4091)***
Welder Repair & Rental Svc Inc....203 238-9284
37 Commerce Cir Durham CT (06422) ***(G-1096)***
Welding Craftsmen Co Inc....508 230-7878
63 Norfolk Ave South Easton MA (02375) ***(G-15295)***
Welding Works, Madison *Also called Rwt Corporation* ***(G-1973)***
Weldship Industries Inc....508 898-0100
75 E Main St Fl 2 Westborough MA (01581) ***(G-16658)***
Welfab Inc....978 667-0180
100 Rangeway Rd North Billerica MA (01862) ***(G-13876)***
Wellcoin Inc....617 512-8617
11 Drumlin Rd Newton MA (02459) ***(G-13654)***
Weller E E Co Inc/MCS Finshg....401 461-4275
253 Georgia Ave Providence RI (02905) ***(G-21152)***
Wellesley Information Svcs LLC (HQ)....781 407-0360
20 Carematrix Dr Dedham MA (02026) ***(G-10301)***
Wellesley Townsman, Randolph *Also called Gatehouse Media Mass I Inc* ***(G-14683)***
Wellfleet Pharmaceuticals Inc....617 767-6264
121 Mount Vernon St Boston MA (02108) ***(G-8920)***
Wellinks Inc....650 704-0714
770 Chapel St Ste 2d New Haven CT (06510) ***(G-2753)***
Wellman Engineering Inc....617 484-8338
35 Louise Rd Belmont MA (02478) ***(G-8082)***
Wellpet LLC (PA)....877 869-2971
200 Ames Pond Dr Ste 200 # 200 Tewksbury MA (01876) ***(G-15848)***
Wells Tool Company....413 773-3465
106 Hope St Greenfield MA (01301) ***(G-11283)***
Wells Wood Turning & Finishing, Buckfield *Also called Turning Acquisitions LLC* ***(G-5853)***
Wellumina Health Inc....978 777-1854
300 Rosewood Dr Ste 107 Danvers MA (01923) ***(G-10273)***
Welmold Tool & Die Inc....401 738-0505
40 Fairfield Dr North Kingstown RI (02852) ***(G-20749)***
Welog Inc....603 237-8277
11 Skyline Dr Colebrook NH (03576) ***(G-17878)***
Wenaumet Bluffs Boat Works Inc....888 224-9942
239 Barlows Landing Rd Pocasset MA (02559) ***(G-14602)***
Wenco Molding Inc....401 781-2600
90 Narragansett Ave Providence RI (02907) ***(G-21153)***
Wendi C Smith....508 362-4595
89 Willow St Yarmouth Port MA (02675) ***(G-17533)***
Wendon Company Inc....203 348-6272
17 Irving Ave Stamford CT (06902) ***(G-4357)***
Wendon Technologies Inc....203 348-6271
17 Irving Ave Stamford CT (06902) ***(G-4358)***
Wenstrom Metalworks....207 215-0651
268 N Howe Rd Whitefield ME (04353) ***(G-7219)***
Wentworth Laboratories Inc (PA)....203 775-0448
1087 Federal Rd Ste 4 Brookfield CT (06804) ***(G-665)***
Wentworth Laboratories Inc....203 775-9311
500 Federal Rd Brookfield CT (06804) ***(G-666)***
Wentworth Manufacturing LLC....860 205-6437
623 E Main St New Britain CT (06051) ***(G-2589)***
Wentworth Manufacturing LLC (PA)....860 423-4575
1102 Windham Rd South Windham CT (06266) ***(G-3928)***
Wepco, Westfield *Also called Westfield Electroplating Co* ***(G-16743)***
Wepco Plastics Inc....860 349-3407
27 Indstrial Pk Access Rd Middlefield CT (06455) ***(G-2168)***
Were Tops Inc....802 660-8677
90 Adams Dr Ste 10 Williston VT (05495) ***(G-22698)***
Werfen USA LLC....781 861-0710
180 Hartwell Rd Bedford MA (01730) ***(G-8020)***
Werner Precision Machine Corp....603 524-0570
60 Bay St Ste 1 Laconia NH (03246) ***(G-18594)***
Werner Publishing Corporation....310 820-1500
25 Braintree Hill Park # 404 Braintree MA (02184) ***(G-9049)***
Wes Press, Middletown *Also called Wesleyan University* ***(G-2230)***
Wesco Building & Design Inc....781 279-0490
271 Main St Ste G01 Stoneham MA (02180) ***(G-15572)***
Wesco Manufacturing, Westfield *Also called Schultz Co Inc* ***(G-16729)***
Wescon Corp of Conn....860 599-2500
Elmata Ave Pawcatuck CT (06379) ***(G-3444)***
Wesconn Stairs Inc....203 792-7367
2 Mill Plain Rd Danbury CT (06811) ***(G-1008)***
Wescor Ltd....617 731-3963
77 Avenue Louis Pasteur Boston MA (02115) ***(G-8921)***
Wescor Ltd....781 938-8686
5 Conn St Woburn MA (01801) ***(G-17318)***
Wescor Ltd (PA)....781 279-0490
271 Main St Ste G01 Stoneham MA (02180) ***(G-15573)***
Wesley Lash....207 832-7807
31 Harbor Rd Friendship ME (04547) ***(G-6094)***
Wesleyan University....860 685-2980
110 Mount Vernon St Middletown CT (06457) ***(G-2230)***
Wesmac Custom Boats Inc (PA)....207 667-4822
158 Blue Hill Rd Surry ME (04684) ***(G-7077)***
Wesmac Custom Boats Inc....207 667-4822
Rr 172 Surry ME (04684) ***(G-7078)***
Wesmac Customs Bulds, Surry *Also called Wesmac Custom Boats Inc* ***(G-7078)***
Wesport Signs....203 286-7710
17 Linden St Norwalk CT (06851) ***(G-3270)***
Wess Tool & Die Company Inc....203 237-5277
140 Research Pkwy Ste 2 Meriden CT (06450) ***(G-2150)***
Wessmark NH LLC....603 974-2932
2 Red Oak Dr Plaistow NH (03865) ***(G-19527)***
West and Package, Middletown *Also called Risha Rishi LLC* ***(G-2219)***
West Bay Printing, Providence *Also called Women & Infants Hospital* ***(G-21156)***
West Bay Welding & Fabrication, Warwick *Also called Westbay Welding & Fabrication* ***(G-21445)***
West County Winery....413 624-3481
248 Greenfield Rd Colrain MA (01340) ***(G-10106)***
West End Auto Parts....203 453-9009
797 Foxon Rd North Branford CT (06471) ***(G-2984)***
West End Strollers....617 720-6020
1 Faneuil Hall Market Pl Boston MA (02109) ***(G-8922)***
West Gardiner Beef Inc....207 724-3378
10 Gilley Dr West Gardiner ME (04345) ***(G-7173)***
West Hartford Stone Mulch LLC....860 461-7616
154 Reed Ave West Hartford CT (06110) ***(G-5103)***
West Haven Voice, West Haven *Also called Suburban Voices Publishing LLC* ***(G-5146)***
West Hrtford Stirs Cbinets Inc....860 953-9151
17 Main St Newington CT (06111) ***(G-2912)***
West Minot Millwork Inc....207 966-3200
296 W Minot Rd West Minot ME (04288) ***(G-7175)***
West Mont Group....203 931-1033
14 Gilbert St Ste 202 West Haven CT (06516) ***(G-5150)***
West Park Stamping Co Inc....508 399-7488
84 Lord St Attleboro MA (02703) ***(G-7809)***
West Roxbury Crushed Stone Div, Boston *Also called S M Lorusso & Sons Inc* ***(G-8830)***
West Shore Metals LLC....860 749-8013
28 W Shore Dr Enfield CT (06082) ***(G-1390)***
West Side Metal Door Corp....413 589-0945
190 Moody St Ludlow MA (01056) ***(G-12479)***
West Springfield Record Inc....413 736-1587
516 Main St West Springfield MA (01089) ***(G-16563)***
West St Intrmdate Hldings Corp (PA)....781 434-5051
195 West St Waltham MA (02451) ***(G-16223)***
West Warwick Screw Products Co....401 821-4729
21 Factory St West Warwick RI (02893) ***(G-21512)***
West Warwick Welding Inc....401 822-8200
970 Main St West Warwick RI (02893) ***(G-21513)***
West Wearham Pine....508 763-4108
10 Long Pond Rd East Freetown MA (02717) ***(G-10463)***
West-Conn Tool and Die Inc....203 538-5081
128 Long Hill Cross Rd Shelton CT (06484) ***(G-3888)***
Westbay Welding & Fabrication....401 737-2357
19 Locust Ave Warwick RI (02886) ***(G-21445)***
Westbrook Con Block Co Inc....860 399-6201
Cold Spring Brook Ind Par Westbrook CT (06498) ***(G-5166)***
Westbrook Products LLC....860 205-6437
623 E Main St New Britain CT (06051) ***(G-2590)***
Westchester Book Group, Danbury *Also called Westchester Pubg Svcs LLC* ***(G-1009)***
Westchester Forge Inc....914 584-2429
28 Benedict Hill Rd New Canaan CT (06840) ***(G-2621)***
Westchester Industries Inc....203 661-0055
485 W Putnam Ave Greenwich CT (06830) ***(G-1661)***
Westchester Pet Vaccines....860 267-4554
111 Loomis Rd Ste 1 Colchester CT (06415) ***(G-812)***
Westchester Pubg Svcs LLC (PA)....203 791-0080
4 Old Newtown Rd Danbury CT (06810) ***(G-1009)***
Westchster Bk/Rnsford Type Inc....203 791-0080
4 Old Newtown Rd Danbury CT (06810) ***(G-1010)***
Westcon Mfg Inc....207 725-5537
22 Bibber Pkwy Brunswick ME (04011) ***(G-5851)***
Westconn Orthopedic Laboratory....203 743-4420
52 Federal Rd Ste 2 Danbury CT (06810) ***(G-1011)***
Westcott Baking Company Inc....401 821-8007
30 Newell St West Warwick RI (02893) ***(G-21514)***
Westek Architectural Wdwkg Inc....413 562-6363
97 Servistar Indus Way Westfield MA (01085) ***(G-16741)***
Westerbeke Corporation (PA)....508 977-4273
150 John Hancock Rd Taunton MA (02780) ***(G-15799)***
Westerbeke Corporation....508 823-7677
41 Ledin Dr Avon Indus Pa Avon Industrial Park Avon MA (02322) ***(G-7902)***
Westerly Sun....401 348-1000
99 Mechanic St Ste C Pawcatuck CT (06379) ***(G-3445)***
Western Bronze Inc....413 737-1319
54 Western Ave West Springfield MA (01089) ***(G-16564)***

Western Conn Craftsmen LLC 203 312-8167
246 Pine Hill Rd New Fairfield CT (06812) *(G-2631)*
Western Maine Timberlands 207 925-1138
278 Mcneil Rd Fryeburg ME (04037) *(G-6103)*
Western Maine Welding & Piping 207 652-2327
513 Pond Rd Strong ME (04983) *(G-7074)*
Western Managment Co, Newport *Also called Vendome Guide (G-20687)*
Western Mass Copying Prtg Inc 413 734-2679
138 Memorial Ave Ste 1 West Springfield MA (01089) *(G-16565)*
Western Mass Rendering Co Inc 413 569-6265
94 Foster Rd Southwick MA (01077) *(G-15420)*
Western Mass Truss, Westfield *Also called Nu-Truss Inc (G-16708)*
Western Polymer Corporation 207 472-1250
145 Presque Isle St Fort Fairfield ME (04742) *(G-6057)*
Western Progress, Bristol *Also called McIntire Company (G-580)*
Westfalia Inc 860 314-2920
625 Middle St Bristol CT (06010) *(G-624)*
Westfall Manufacturing Co 401 253-3799
15 Broadcommon Rd Bristol RI (02809) *(G-20110)*
Westfield - Pipe, Westfield *Also called Cemex Materials LLC (G-16677)*
Westfield Concrete Inc 413 562-4814
403 Paper Mill Rd Westfield MA (01085) *(G-16742)*
Westfield Electroplating Co (PA) 413 568-3716
68 N Elm St Westfield MA (01085) *(G-16743)*
Westfield Evening News, Westfield *Also called Westfield News Publishing Inc (G-16746)*
Westfield Grinding Wheel Co 413 568-8634
135 Apremont Way Westfield MA (01085) *(G-16744)*
Westfield News Group LLC 413 562-4181
62 School St Westfield MA (01085) *(G-16745)*
Westfield News Publishing Inc (HQ) 413 562-4181
64 School St Westfield MA (01085) *(G-16746)*
Westfield Ready-Mix Inc 413 594-4700
652 Prospect St Chicopee MA (01020) *(G-10069)*
Westfield Tool & Die Inc 413 562-2393
55 Arnold St Ste 101 Westfield MA (01085) *(G-16747)*
Westfield Whip Mfg Co 413 568-8244
360 Elm St Westfield MA (01085) *(G-16748)*
Westford Chemical Corporation 978 392-0689
98 Concord Rd Westford MA (01886) *(G-16800)*
Westford Hill Distillers LLC 860 429-0464
196 Chatey Rd Ashford CT (06278) *(G-29)*
Westfort Construction Corp 860 833-7970
3000 Whitney Ave Hamden CT (06518) *(G-1795)*
Westminster Fire Department, Westminster *Also called Town of Westminster (G-16816)*
Westminster Millwork Corp 978 665-9200
310 Broad St Fitchburg MA (01420) *(G-10862)*
Westminster Tool Inc 860 564-6966
5 East Pkwy Plainfield CT (06374) *(G-3459)*
Westmor Industries LLC 207 989-0100
42 Coffin Ave Brewer ME (04412) *(G-5804)*
Westmount Group LLC 203 931-1033
14b Gilbert St M202 West Haven CT (06516) *(G-5151)*
Weston Communications, Hingham *Also called Weston Corporation (G-11516)*
Weston Corporation 781 749-0936
45 Industrial Park Rd Hingham MA (02043) *(G-11516)*
Weston Island Logging Inc 802 824-3708
25 Johnson Hill Rd Londonderry VT (05148) *(G-22058)*
Weston Medical Publishing LLC 781 899-2702
470 Boston Post Rd Weston MA (02493) *(G-16834)*
Weston Papers, Dalton *Also called Crane & Co Inc (G-10177)*
Westport Envmtl Systems LP 508 636-8811
251 Forge Rd Westport MA (02790) *(G-16851)*
Westport Group Ltd 617 489-6581
29 Oliver Rd Belmont MA (02478) *(G-8083)*
Westport Magazine, Westport *Also called Moffly Publications Inc (G-5215)*
Westport Precision LLC 203 378-2175
280 Hathaway Dr Stratford CT (06615) *(G-4457)*
Westrex International Inc 617 254-1200
25 Denby Rd Boston MA (02134) *(G-8923)*
Westrock - Southern Cont LLC 978 772-5050
84 State St Boston MA (02109) *(G-8924)*
Westrock Commercial LLC 203 595-3130
1635 Coining Dr Stamford CT (06902) *(G-4359)*
Westrock Container LLC 413 733-2211
320 Parker St Springfield MA (01129) *(G-15525)*
Westrock Converting Company 802 933-7733
369 Mill St Sheldon Springs VT (05485) *(G-22430)*
Westrock Cp LLC 781 245-8600
365 Audubon Rd Wakefield MA (01880) *(G-15984)*
Westrock Cp LLC 770 448-2193
47 Maple St Mansfield MA (02048) *(G-12671)*
Westrock Cp LLC 860 848-1500
125 Depot Rd Uncasville CT (06382) *(G-4651)*
Westrock Cp LLC 508 337-0400
60 Maple St Mansfield MA (02048) *(G-12672)*
Westrock Cp LLC 413 543-2311
320 Parker St Springfield MA (01129) *(G-15526)*
Westrock Cp LLC 802 933-7733
369 Mill St Sheldon Springs VT (05485) *(G-22431)*
Westrock Mwv LLC 413 736-7211
2001 Roosevelt Ave Springfield MA (01104) *(G-15527)*
WESTROCK RKT COMPANY, Bethel *Also called Westrock Rkt Company (G-193)*
Westrock Rkt Company 413 543-7300
320 Parker St Springfield MA (01129) *(G-15528)*
Westrock Rkt Company 203 739-0318
2 Research Dr Bethel CT (06801) *(G-193)*
Westside Finishing Co Inc 413 533-4909
15 Samosett St Holyoke MA (01040) *(G-11667)*
Westwell Industries Inc 401 467-2992
26 Plymouth St Providence RI (02907) *(G-21154)*
Westwood Mills Corp 781 335-4466
55 Sharp St Ste 6 Hingham MA (02043) *(G-11517)*
Westwood Press 781 433-8354
33 New York Ave Framingham MA (01701) *(G-11015)*
Westwood Products Inc 860 379-9401
167 Torrington Rd Winsted CT (06098) *(G-5428)*
Westwood Systems Inc 781 821-1117
80 Hudson Rd Ste 200 Canton MA (02021) *(G-9795)*
Westwood Youth Softball Inc 781 762-5185
6 Winter Ter Westwood MA (02090) *(G-16882)*
Wetech 781 320-8646
44 Trenton Rd Dedham MA (02026) *(G-10302)*
Wethersfield Offset Inc 860 721-8236
1795 Silas Deane Hwy Rocky Hill CT (06067) *(G-3734)*
Wethersfield Printing Co Inc 860 721-8236
1795 Silas Deane Hwy Rocky Hill CT (06067) *(G-3735)*
Weymouth Braided Rug Co Inc 508 987-8525
5 Clara Barton Rd North Oxford MA (01537) *(G-13976)*
Weymouth News 781 337-1944
15 Pacella Park Dr # 120 Randolph MA (02368) *(G-14702)*
Weymouths Inc 207 426-3211
121 Mutton Ln Clinton ME (04927) *(G-5917)*
Wezenski Woodworking 203 488-3255
214 Crosswoods Rd Branford CT (06405) *(G-360)*
Wf Holdings Inc (PA) 603 888-5443
3 E Spit Brook Rd Nashua NH (03060) *(G-19285)*
Wfs Earth Materialsi LLC 203 488-2055
11 Business Park Dr Branford CT (06405) *(G-361)*
Wgi Inc 413 569-9444
34 Hudson Dr Southwick MA (01077) *(G-15421)*
Wh Property Service LLC 802 257-8566
287 Locust Hill Rd Guilford VT (05301) *(G-22008)*
WH Silverstein Inc 603 542-5418
61 Plains Rd Claremont NH (03743) *(G-17864)*
Whale Water Systems Inc 802 367-1091
91 Manchstr Vly Bldg E Manchester VT (05254) *(G-22079)*
Whaling City Graphics Inc 508 998-3511
352 Main St Acushnet MA (02743) *(G-7407)*
Whalley Glass Company (PA) 203 735-9388
72 Chapel St Derby CT (06418) *(G-1083)*
Whalley Precision Inc 413 569-1400
28 Hudson Dr Southwick MA (01077) *(G-15422)*
Wharf Industries Printing Inc 603 421-2566
3 Lexington Rd Unit 2 Windham NH (03087) *(G-20014)*
What Woodworking 617 429-2461
163 Reynolds Ave Warwick RI (02889) *(G-21446)*
Wheel House Designs Inc 802 888-8552
559 Harrel St Apt A Morrisville VT (05661) *(G-22180)*
Wheelchair Recycler Custm & R 978 760-4444
54 Linda Cir Marlborough MA (01752) *(G-12851)*
Wheeler Avenue LLC 401 714-0996
999 Pontiac Ave Unit A Cranston RI (02920) *(G-20311)*
Wheeler Hill Logging Inc 207 639-2391
37 Wheeler Hill Rd Phillips ME (04966) *(G-6587)*
Wheelock Textile, Uxbridge *Also called Strickland K Wheelock (G-15930)*
Wheeltrak Inc 800 296-1326
3622 Main Rd Tiverton RI (02878) *(G-21266)*
Wheg.fm, Portsmouth *Also called Iheartcommunications Inc (G-19577)*
Whelen Engineering Co 860 526-9504
99 Ceda Rd Charlestown NH (03603) *(G-17821)*
Whelen Engineering Company Inc (PA) 860 526-9504
51 Winthrop Rd Chester CT (06412) *(G-777)*
Whelen Engineering Company Inc 860 526-9504
Rr 145 Chester CT (06412) *(G-778)*
When Words Count Press LLC 802 767-4372
1764 Marsh Brook Rd Rochester VT (05767) *(G-22321)*
Where Inc 617 502-3100
1 International Pl # 315 Boston MA (02110) *(G-8925)*
Whetstone Workshop LLC 401 368-7410
41 Dexter Rd East Providence RI (02914) *(G-20449)*
Whico, Winterport *Also called Derek White (G-7277)*
Whiffle Tree Candle, Billerica *Also called Whiffletree Cntry Str Gift Sp (G-8309)*
Whiffletree Cntry Str Gift Sp 978 663-6346
101 Andover Rd Billerica MA (01821) *(G-8309)*
Whip City Jerky LLC 413 568-2050
271 Elm St Westfield MA (01085) *(G-16749)*
Whip City Tool & Die Corp 413 569-5528
813 College Hwy Southwick MA (01077) *(G-15423)*

ALPHABETIC

Whisper Hills....802 296-7627
5573 Woodstock Rd Quechee VT (05059) ***(G-22295)***
Whisper Tree, Newport *Also called Bumwraps Inc* ***(G-22190)***
Whistlekick LLC....802 225-6676
2030 Jones Brook Rd Montpelier VT (05602) ***(G-22164)***
Whistlepig LLC (PA)....802 897-7700
2139 Quiet Valley Rd Shoreham VT (05770) ***(G-22434)***
Whitco Ameritest, Johnston *Also called Fueling Services LLC* ***(G-20513)***
Whitcombs Forest Harvesting....207 234-2351
440 Chapman Rd Newburgh ME (04444) ***(G-6481)***
Whitcraft LLC (PA)....860 974-0786
76 County Rd Eastford CT (06242) ***(G-1315)***
Whitcraft Scrborough/Tempe LLC....763 780-0060
28 Pond View Dr Scarborough ME (04074) ***(G-6942)***
Whitcraft Scrborough/Tempe LLC (HQ)....860 974-0786
76 County Rd Eastford CT (06242) ***(G-1316)***
White Birch Brewing LLC....603 402-4444
460 Amherst St Ste 2 Nashua NH (03063) ***(G-19286)***
White Birch Paper Company, Greenwich *Also called Brant Industries Inc* ***(G-1601)***
White Dog Press, Fall River *Also called A Bismark Company* ***(G-10648)***
White Dog Printing Inc....978 630-1091
35 Parker St Gardner MA (01440) ***(G-11133)***
White Dog Woodworking LLC....860 482-3776
199 W Pearl Rd Torrington CT (06790) ***(G-4607)***
White Hills Tool....203 590-3143
8 Maple Dr Monroe CT (06468) ***(G-2420)***
White Knight Studio....781 799-0569
70 North St Grafton MA (01519) ***(G-11226)***
White Mountain Biodiesel LLC....603 444-0335
83 Elm St Littleton NH (03561) ***(G-18668)***
White Mountain Cupcakery LLC....603 730-5140
2 Common Ct Unit D52 North Conway NH (03860) ***(G-19381)***
White Mountain Distillery LLC....603 391-1306
2072 Elm St Manchester NH (03104) ***(G-18955)***
White Mountain Imaging....603 228-2630
46 Chenell Dr Concord NH (03301) ***(G-17940)***
White Mountain Plowing....603 817-0913
67 Glen St Farmington NH (03835) ***(G-18146)***
White Oak Farms....603 887-2233
343 Main St Sandown NH (03873) ***(G-19789)***
White Publishing, West Hartford *Also called Life Publications* ***(G-5083)***
White Welding Company Inc....203 753-1197
44 N Elm St Waterbury CT (06702) ***(G-4978)***
White's Logging & Chipping, Shapleigh *Also called Norman White Inc* ***(G-6958)***
Whitecap Composites Inc....978 278-5718
147 Summit St Peabody MA (01960) ***(G-14382)***
Whitefield Dry Kiln Inc....207 549-5470
45 Mills Rd Whitefield ME (04353) ***(G-7220)***
Whitegate Features Syndicate, Providence *Also called Whitegate International Corp* ***(G-21155)***
Whitegate International Corp....401 274-2149
71 Faunce Dr Providence RI (02906) ***(G-21155)***
Whiteledge Inc....860 647-1883
134 Pine St Manchester CT (06040) ***(G-2058)***
Whites Welding Co Inc....603 926-2261
6 Kershaw Ave Hampton NH (03842) ***(G-18280)***
Whitestone Provision Sup Corp (PA)....401 245-1346
4 Woodmont Ct Barrington RI (02806) ***(G-20057)***
Whitewater LLC....413 237-5032
15 West St West Hatfield MA (01088) ***(G-16487)***
Whitewater Plastics Inc....413 237-5032
15 West St West Hatfield MA (01088) ***(G-16488)***
Whitewood Encrytion....617 419-1800
100 High St Fl 28 Boston MA (02110) ***(G-8926)***
Whiting & Davis LLC....508 699-4412
171 Commonwealth Ave # 2 Attleboro Falls MA (02763) ***(G-7819)***
Whiting & Davis Safety, Attleboro *Also called W D C Holdings Inc* ***(G-7806)***
Whitman Castings Inc (PA)....781 447-4417
40 Raynor Ave Whitman MA (02382) ***(G-16930)***
Whitman Communications Inc....603 448-2600
10 Water St Lebanon NH (03766) ***(G-18641)***
Whitman Company Inc....781 447-2422
356 South Ave Ste 1 Whitman MA (02382) ***(G-16931)***
Whitman Controls LLC....800 233-4401
201 Dolphin Rd Bristol CT (06010) ***(G-625)***
Whitman Products Company Inc....978 975-0502
96 Powder House Ave Haverhill MA (01830) ***(G-11486)***
Whitman Tool and Die Co Inc....781 447-0421
72 Raynor Ave Whitman MA (02382) ***(G-16932)***
Whitman's Feed Store, North Bennington *Also called Poulin Grain Inc* ***(G-22212)***
Whitmor Company Inc (PA)....781 284-8000
15 Whitmore Rd Revere MA (02151) ***(G-14778)***
Whitmore Family Entps LLC....617 623-0804
561 Windsor St Ste B206 Somerville MA (02143) ***(G-15232)***
Whitney & Son Inc....978 343-6353
95 Kelly Ave Fitchburg MA (01420) ***(G-10863)***
Whitney Bros Co....603 352-2610
93 Railroad St Keene NH (03431) ***(G-18534)***
Whitney Learning Materials, Keene *Also called Whitney Bros Co* ***(G-18534)***
Whitney Originals Inc....207 255-3392
600 Us Route 1 Whitneyville ME (04654) ***(G-7222)***
Whitney Vgas Architectural Pdts....781 449-1351
56 Coulton Park Needham MA (02492) ***(G-13317)***
Whittemore Company Inc....978 681-8833
30 Glenn St Lawrence MA (01843) ***(G-12083)***
Whittet-Higgins Company....401 728-0700
33 Higginson Ave Central Falls RI (02863) ***(G-20129)***
Whole Earth Hat Co Inc....508 672-7033
394 Kilburn St Fall River MA (02724) ***(G-10783)***
Whole German Breads LLC....203 507-0663
85 Willow St New Haven CT (06511) ***(G-2754)***
Wholesale Poster Frames, Derby *Also called M & B Enterprise LLC* ***(G-1075)***
Wholesale Printing Inc....781 937-3357
2 Cedar St Ste 2 # 2 Woburn MA (01801) ***(G-17319)***
Wholesale Printing Specialists, Lawrence *Also called Business Cards Overnight Inc* ***(G-11999)***
Wholistic Pet Organics LLC....603 472-8300
341 Route 101 Bedford NH (03110) ***(G-17667)***
Whoop Inc....617 670-1074
1325 Boylston St Ste 401 Boston MA (02215) ***(G-8927)***
Whyco Finishing Tech LLC....860 283-5826
670 Waterbury Rd Thomaston CT (06787) ***(G-4527)***
Whyte Electric LLC....781 348-6239
95 Shaw St Braintree MA (02184) ***(G-9050)***
Wicare, Cambridge *Also called Worldwide Innvtive Hlthcare In* ***(G-9705)***
Wicked Cornhole....978 851-7600
1875 Main St Ste 5 Tewksbury MA (01876) ***(G-15849)***
Wicks Business Information LLC (PA)....203 334-2002
4 Research Dr Ste 402 Shelton CT (06484) ***(G-3889)***
Wicor Americas Inc (HQ)....802 751-3404
1 Gordon Mills Way Saint Johnsbury VT (05819) ***(G-22397)***
Wide Angle Marketing Inc....978 928-5400
27d Old Colony Rd Hubbardston MA (01452) ***(G-11747)***
Widham Wood Corporation....781 932-8572
13 Cranes Ct Rear Woburn MA (01801) ***(G-17320)***
Wielock Farms, Dudley *Also called John F Wielock* ***(G-10378)***
Wiesner Chain, Warwick *Also called Wiesner Manufacturing Company* ***(G-21447)***
Wiesner Manufacturing Company....401 421-2406
55 Access Rd Ste 700 Warwick RI (02886) ***(G-21447)***
Wiffle Ball Incorporated....203 924-4643
275 Bridgeport Ave Shelton CT (06484) ***(G-3890)***
Wiggin Means Precast Co Inc....508 564-6776
79 Barlows Landing Rd Pocasset MA (02559) ***(G-14603)***
Wiggin Precast Corp....508 564-6776
79 Barlows Landing Rd Pocasset MA (02559) ***(G-14604)***
Wikifoods, Boston *Also called Incredible Foods Inc* ***(G-8614)***
Wikoff Color Corporation....603 864-6456
4 Hampshire Dr Hudson NH (03051) ***(G-18452)***
Wilbert Swans Vault Co....207 854-5324
674 Bridgton Rd Westbrook ME (04092) ***(G-7214)***
Wilbur Technical Services LLC....603 880-7100
97 S Main St Mont Vernon NH (03057) ***(G-19094)***
Wilcom Inc....603 524-2622
73 Daniel Webster Hwy Belmont NH (03220) ***(G-17686)***
Wilcox Industries Corp (PA)....603 431-1331
25 Piscataqua Dr Newington NH (03801) ***(G-19329)***
Wild Apple Graphics Ltd....802 457-3003
2513 W Woodstock Rd Woodstock VT (05091) ***(G-22741)***
Wild Apples Inc....978 456-9616
38 Eldridge Rd Harvard MA (01451) ***(G-11385)***
Wild Blue Yonder Foods....978 532-3400
65 Tedesco St Marblehead MA (01945) ***(G-12696)***
Wild Card Golf LLC....860 296-1661
222 Murphy Rd Hartford CT (06114) ***(G-1885)***
Wild Cow Creamery LLC....207 907-0301
28 Broad St Bangor ME (04401) ***(G-5664)***
Wild Duck Boat Works LLC....207 837-2920
1444 Harpswell Neck Rd Harpswell ME (04079) ***(G-6175)***
Wild Farm Maple....802 362-1656
670 Bentley Hill Rd Arlington VT (05250) ***(G-21602)***
Wild Fibers Magazine....207 594-9455
20 Elm St Rockland ME (04841) ***(G-6815)***
Wild Hart Distillery....802 489-5067
26 Sage Ct Shelburne VT (05482) ***(G-22427)***
Wild Ocean Aquaculture LLC....207 458-6288
72 Commercial St 15 Portland ME (04101) ***(G-6745)***
Wild Rver Cstm Screen Prtg LLC....203 426-1500
3 Simm Ln Ste 2e1 Newtown CT (06470) ***(G-2948)***
Wild Wood Acres Alpacas Inc....802 365-7053
8 Wildwood Acres Rd Newfane VT (05345) ***(G-22188)***
Wildflour Cupcakes Sweets LLC....203 828-6576
18 Bank St Seymour CT (06483) ***(G-3768)***
Wildlife Acoustics Inc....978 369-5225
3 Mill And Main Pl # 210 Maynard MA (01754) ***(G-12906)***
Wildtree Inc....401 732-1856
15 Wellington Rd Lincoln RI (02865) ***(G-20599)***
Wilevco Inc....978 667-0400
10 Fortune Dr Billerica MA (01821) ***(G-8310)***

Wilex Inc 617 492-3900
100 Acorn Park Dr Fl 6 Cambridge MA (02140) ***(G-9701)***
Wilkins Lumber Co Inc 603 673-2545
495 Mont Vernon Rd Milford NH (03055) ***(G-19082)***
Wilkinson Tool & Die Co 860 599-5821
55 Stillman Rd North Stonington CT (06359) ***(G-3077)***
Wilkscraft Creative Printing, Beverly *Also called Wilkscraft Inc* ***(G-8197)***
Wilkscraft Inc 978 922-1855
59 Park St Beverly MA (01915) ***(G-8197)***
Will Kirkpatricks Decoy Shop 978 562-7841
124 Forest Ave Hudson MA (01749) ***(G-11826)***
Will-Mor Manufacturing Inc 603 474-8971
153 Batchelder Rd Seabrook NH (03874) ***(G-19823)***
Willard J Stearns & Sons Inc 860 423-9289
50 Stearns Rd Storrs Mansfield CT (06268) ***(G-4387)***
Willard S Hanington & Son Inc 207 456-7511
1619 Military Rd Reed Plt ME (04497) ***(G-6780)***
Willard's Concrete, Springfield *Also called Bill Willard Inc* ***(G-15453)***
Willett Institute of Finance 617 247-3030
16 Red Gate Ln Reading MA (01867) ***(G-14744)***
William A Day Jr & Sons Inc 207 625-8181
28 Wild Turkey Ln Porter ME (04068) ***(G-6607)***
William Arthur Inc 413 684-2600
7 Alewive Park Rd West Kennebunk ME (04094) ***(G-7174)***
William B Sparrow Jr 207 582-5731
414 Whitefield Rd Pittston ME (04345) ***(G-6593)***
William Blanchard Co Inc 781 245-8050
486 Main St Wakefield MA (01880) ***(G-15985)***
William Chadburn 802 695-8166
980 Willson Rd North Concord VT (05858) ***(G-22223)***
William Clements 978 663-3103
18 Mount Pleasant St North Billerica MA (01862) ***(G-13877)***
William Clements Boatbuilder, North Billerica *Also called William Clements* ***(G-13877)***
William Connell LLC 508 785-1292
2 Mill St Dover MA (02030) ***(G-10353)***
William Crosby 978 371-1111
53 Bradford St Concord MA (01742) ***(G-10162)***
William J Devaney 603 436-7603
230 Lafayette Rd Ste 2 Portsmouth NH (03801) ***(G-19631)***
William McCaskie Inc 508 636-8845
197 Forge Rd Westport MA (02790) ***(G-16852)***
William N Lamarre Con Pdts Inc 603 878-1340
87 Adams Hill Rd Greenville NH (03048) ***(G-18230)***
William R Raap 802 660-3508
128 Intervale Rd Burlington VT (05401) ***(G-21817)***
William S Haynes Co Inc 978 268-0600
68 Nonset Path Acton MA (01720) ***(G-7393)***
William Sever Inc 617 651-2483
61 Sever St Worcester MA (01609) ***(G-17504)***
William Smith Enterprises Inc 207 549-3103
5 Thistle Ln Sidney ME (04330) ***(G-6966)***
Williams & Co Mining Inc 802 263-5404
248 Stoughton Pond Rd Perkinsville VT (05151) ***(G-22261)***
Williams & Hussey Mch Co Inc 603 732-0219
105 State Route 101a # 4 Amherst NH (03031) ***(G-17591)***
Williams Lea Boston 617 371-2300
260 Franklin St Ste 730 Boston MA (02110) ***(G-8928)***
Williams Machine 781 762-1342
20 Railroad Ave Norwood MA (02062) ***(G-14205)***
Williams Partners Ltd 207 633-3111
29 Lincoln St East Boothbay ME (04544) ***(G-5981)***
Williams Printing Group LLC 860 423-8779
387 Tuckie Rd Ste G North Windham CT (06256) ***(G-3085)***
Williams Sign Erection Inc 978 658-3787
20 Lowell St Wilmington MA (01887) ***(G-17066)***
Williams Stone Co Inc 413 269-4544
1158 Lee Westfield Rd East Otis MA (01029) ***(G-10504)***
Williamsburg Blacksmiths Inc 413 268-7341
26 Williams St Williamsburg MA (01096) ***(G-16953)***
Williamson Corporation 978 369-9607
70 Domino Dr Concord MA (01742) ***(G-10163)***
Williamson Ncng Elc Mtr Svc 617 884-9200
25 Griffin Way Chelsea MA (02150) ***(G-9975)***
Williamsville Products, Sudbury *Also called R G J Associates Inc* ***(G-15667)***
Willie's Superbrew, Providence *Also called Farmer Willies Inc* ***(G-21011)***
Willies Welding Inc 203 237-6235
313 Spring St Meriden CT (06451) ***(G-2151)***
Willigent Corporation 617 663-5707
275 Grove St Ste 2-400 Auburndale MA (02466) ***(G-7873)***
Willigent Technologies, Auburndale *Also called Willigent Corporation* ***(G-7873)***
Willimantic, CT Plant, Willimantic *Also called General Cable Industries Inc* ***(G-5264)***
Willimatic Instant Print, Willimantic *Also called Gulemo Inc* ***(G-5265)***
Willis & Pham LLC 603 893-6029
3 Scotts Ter Salem NH (03079) ***(G-19778)***
Willis & Sons Inc 207 288-4935
69 Main St 73 Bar Harbor ME (04609) ***(G-5671)***
Willis Wood 802 263-5547
1482 Weathersfield Ctr Rd Springfield VT (05156) ***(G-22513)***
Williston Pubg Promotions LLC 802 872-9000
300 Cornerstone Dr # 330 Williston VT (05495) ***(G-22699)***
Willoughby's Coffee & Tea, Branford *Also called B & B Ventures Ltd Lblty Co* ***(G-294)***
Willowtoys 603 367-4657
196 E Madison Rd Madison NH (03849) ***(G-18765)***
Willson Manufacturing of Conn 860 643-8182
71 Batson Dr Manchester CT (06042) ***(G-2059)***
Willson Road Woodworking, North Concord *Also called William Chadburn* ***(G-22223)***
Wilmington Compliance Week 888 519-9200
77 N Washington St Boston MA (02114) ***(G-8929)***
Wilmington Partners LP 978 658-6111
100 Research Dr Ste 2 Wilmington MA (01887) ***(G-17067)***
Wilmington Research & Dev Corp 978 499-0100
50 Parker St Ste 3 Newburyport MA (01950) ***(G-13549)***
Wilshire Manufacturing Co., Framingham *Also called American Lighting Fixture Corp* ***(G-10920)***
Wilson Anchor Bolt Sleeve 203 516-5260
259 Roosevelt Dr Derby CT (06418) ***(G-1084)***
Wilson Arms Company 203 488-7297
97 Leetes Island Rd 101 Branford CT (06405) ***(G-362)***
Wilson Partitions Inc 203 316-8033
120 Viaduct Rd Stamford CT (06907) ***(G-4360)***
Wilson Woodworks Inc 860 870-2500
100 Lamberton Rd Windsor CT (06095) ***(G-5379)***
Wilsonart Intl Holdings LLC 978 664-5230
29 Concord St North Reading MA (01864) ***(G-13994)***
Wilt Pruf Products Inc 860 767-7033
132 River Rd Essex CT (06426) ***(G-1408)***
Wilton Art Framing, Wilton *Also called Rockwell Art & Framing LLC* ***(G-5302)***
Wilton Pressed Metals 603 863-1488
488 Oak St Newport NH (03773) ***(G-19364)***
Win Enterprises Inc 978 688-2000
300 Willow St Ste 2 North Andover MA (01845) ***(G-13740)***
Win-Pressor LLC 207 948-4800
336 Stagecoach Rd Unity ME (04988) ***(G-7119)***
Winchester Fishing Inc 978 282-0679
54 Cherry St Gloucester MA (01930) ***(G-11219)***
Winchester Industries Inc 860 379-5336
106 Groppo Dr Winsted CT (06098) ***(G-5429)***
Winchester Interconnect Corp 978 532-0775
245 Lynnfield St Peabody MA (01960) ***(G-14383)***
Winchester Interconnect Corp 978 717-2543
101 Constitution Blvd Franklin MA (02038) ***(G-11098)***
Winchester Interconnect Corp 978 532-0775
245 Lynnfield St Peabody MA (01960) ***(G-14384)***
Winchester Interconnect Corp (HQ) 203 741-5400
68 Water St Norwalk CT (06854) ***(G-3271)***
Winchester Precision Tech Ltd 603 239-6326
41 Hildreth St Winchester NH (03470) ***(G-19997)***
Winchester Products Inc 860 379-8590
22 Lanson Dr Winsted CT (06098) ***(G-5430)***
Winchester Systems Inc (PA) 781 265-0200
305 Foster St Littleton MA (01460) ***(G-12328)***
Winchester Woodworks LLC 860 379-9875
12 Munro St Winsted CT (06098) ***(G-5431)***
Winchster Interconnect Rf Corp (HQ) 978 532-0775
245 Lynnfield St Peabody MA (01960) ***(G-14385)***
Wincor Inc 860 589-5530
47 Race St Bristol CT (06010) ***(G-626)***
Wind Corporation 203 778-1001
30 Pecks Ln Newtown CT (06470) ***(G-2949)***
Wind Hardware & Engineering, Newtown *Also called Wind Corporation* ***(G-2949)***
Wind River Systems Inc 603 897-2000
10 Tara Blvd Ste 130 Nashua NH (03062) ***(G-19287)***
Wind Tunnel Heating & AC LLC 978 977-7783
20 State St Peabody MA (01960) ***(G-14386)***
Windgap Medical Inc 617 440-3311
200 Dexter Ave Ste 2 Watertown MA (02472) ***(G-16330)***
Windham Automated Machines Inc 860 208-5297
1102 Windham Rd South Windham CT (06266) ***(G-3929)***
Windham Container Corporation 860 928-7934
30 Park Rd Putnam CT (06260) ***(G-3640)***
Windham Millwork Inc 207 892-3238
4 Architectural Dr Windham ME (04062) ***(G-7260)***
Windham Sand and Stone Inc 860 643-5578
60 Adams St S Manchester CT (06040) ***(G-2060)***
Windham Weaponry Inc 207 893-2223
999 Roosevelt Trl Ste 22 Windham ME (04062) ***(G-7261)***
Windham Wood Interiors Inc 781 932-8572
13 Cranes Ct Woburn MA (01801) ***(G-17321)***
Windhover Information Inc (HQ) 203 838-4401
383 Main Ave Norwalk CT (06851) ***(G-3272)***
Windhver Rvw-Emerging Med Vent, Norwalk *Also called Windhover Information Inc* ***(G-3272)***
Winding Drive Corporation 203 263-6961
744 Main St S Woodbury CT (06798) ***(G-5491)***
Windle Industries Inc 508 865-5773
94 Singletary Ave Sutton MA (01590) ***(G-15696)***
Windmill Associates Inc 401 732-4700
112 Knight St Warwick RI (02886) ***(G-21448)***

ALPHABETIC

Window Quilt, Brattleboro *Also called Blw LLC* ***(G-21719)***
Windsor Architectural Wdwkg, Malden *Also called Kabinet Korner Inc* ***(G-12574)***
Windsor Chairmakers, Lincolnville *Also called Jim Brown* ***(G-6362)***
Windsor Locks Nonwovens Inc (HQ)....860 292-5600
1 Hartfield Blvd Ste 101 East Windsor CT (06088) ***(G-1311)***
Windsor Press Inc....781 235-0265
356 Washington St Wellesley MA (02481) ***(G-16394)***
Windstream Enrgy Solutions LLC....781 333-5450
10g Roessler Rd Ste 524 Woburn MA (01801) ***(G-17322)***
Wine Well Chiller Comp Inc....203 878-2465
301 Brewster Rd Ste 3 Milford CT (06460) ***(G-2382)***
Winer Woodworking....508 695-5871
54 Walnut St Plainville MA (02762) ***(G-14538)***
Winfield Brooks Company Inc....781 933-5300
70 Conn St Woburn MA (01801) ***(G-17323)***
Winfield Woodworking Inc....508 429-4320
1278 Washington St Holliston MA (01746) ***(G-11614)***
Winfrey's Fudge & Candy, Rowley *Also called Winfreys Olde English Fdge Inc* ***(G-14868)***
Winfreys Olde English Fdge Inc (PA)....978 948-7448
40 Newburyport Tpke Ste 1 Rowley MA (01969) ***(G-14868)***
Wingate Sales Associates LLC....603 303-7189
2 College Rd Unit 1142 Stratham NH (03885) ***(G-19877)***
Wingbrace LLC....617 480-8737
6 Evergreen Ln Hingham MA (02043) ***(G-11518)***
Wink Ink LLC....860 202-8709
154 Main St Somers CT (06071) ***(G-3922)***
Winkir Instant Printing Inc....508 398-9748
23 Whites Path Ste R South Yarmouth MA (02664) ***(G-15335)***
Winkler Group Ltd (PA)....401 272-2885
54 Taylor Dr Rumford RI (02916) ***(G-21199)***
Winkler Group Ltd....401 751-6120
54 Taylor Dr Rumford RI (02916) ***(G-21200)***
Winkler USA, Shelton *Also called Bakery Engineering/Winkler Inc* ***(G-3779)***
Winkumpaugh Line Construction....207 667-2962
233 Thorsen Rd Ellsworth ME (04605) ***(G-6023)***
Winnepesaukee Forge Inc....603 279-5492
5 Winona Rd Meredith NH (03253) ***(G-18982)***
Winning Moves Inc....978 777-7464
75 Sylvan St Ste C104 Danvers MA (01923) ***(G-10274)***
Winning Moves Games, Danvers *Also called Winning Moves Inc* ***(G-10274)***
Winning Solutions Inc....978 525-2813
66 Summer St Ste 2 Manchester MA (01944) ***(G-12609)***
Winninghoff Boats Inc....978 948-2314
55 Warehouse Ln Rowley MA (01969) ***(G-14869)***
Winnisquam Printing Inc....603 524-2803
71 Beacon St W A Laconia NH (03246) ***(G-18595)***
Winnisquam Printing & Copying, Laconia *Also called Winnisquam Printing Inc* ***(G-18595)***
Winooski Press LLC....802 655-1611
10 Stevens St Winooski VT (05404) ***(G-22728)***
Winslow Automatics Inc....860 225-6321
23 Saint Claire Ave New Britain CT (06051) ***(G-2591)***
Winslow Manufacturing Inc....203 269-1977
68 N Plains Indus Hwy Wallingford CT (06492) ***(G-4829)***
Winsted Precision Ball, Winsted *Also called Schaeffler Aerospace USA Corp* ***(G-5421)***
Winsupply of Warwick, Warwick *Also called Winwholesale Inc* ***(G-21450)***
Wintech Intl Corp - Nk....401 383-3307
36 Bellair Ave Warwick RI (02886) ***(G-21449)***
Winterport Winery Inc....207 223-4500
279 S Main St Winterport ME (04496) ***(G-7278)***
Wintersteiger Inc....802 496-6166
3489 Main St Waitsfield VT (05673) ***(G-22571)***
Winthrop Tool LLC....860 526-9079
55 Plains Rd Essex CT (06426) ***(G-1409)***
Wintriss Controls Group LLC....978 268-2700
100 Discovery Way Ste 110 Acton MA (01720) ***(G-7394)***
Winwholesale Inc....401 732-1585
289 Kilvert St Warwick RI (02886) ***(G-21450)***
Wire Belt Company of America (PA)....603 644-2500
154 Harvey Rd Londonderry NH (03053) ***(G-18745)***
Wire Journal Inc....203 453-2777
71 Bradley Rd Unit 9 Madison CT (06443) ***(G-1979)***
Wire Rope Div, Pomfret *Also called Loos & Co Inc* ***(G-3552)***
Wire Tech LLC....860 945-9473
1094 Echo Lake Rd Watertown CT (06795) ***(G-5036)***
Wire Winders, Milford *Also called Wirewinders Inc* ***(G-19083)***
Wirecraft Products, West Brookfield *Also called Quirk Wire Co Inc* ***(G-16473)***
Wired Informatics LLC....646 623-7459
265 Franklin St Ste 1702 Boston MA (02110) ***(G-8930)***
Wireless Construction Inc....207 642-5751
40 Blake Rd Standish ME (04084) ***(G-7064)***
Wireless For Less....802 786-0918
161 S Main St Rutland VT (05701) ***(G-22361)***
Wiremold Company (HQ)....860 233-6251
60 Woodlawn St West Hartford CT (06110) ***(G-5104)***
Wiremold Company....860 263-3115
21 Railroad Pl West Hartford CT (06110) ***(G-5105)***
Wiremold Legrand Co Centerex....877 295-3472
60 Woodlawn St West Hartford CT (06110) ***(G-5106)***
Wireover Co....617 308-7993
323 Commonwealth Ave Boston MA (02115) ***(G-8931)***
Wiretek Inc....860 242-9473
48 E Newberry Rd Bloomfield CT (06002) ***(G-272)***
Wireway/Husky Corp....978 422-6716
Pratts Junction Rd Sterling MA (01564) ***(G-15550)***
Wirewinders Inc....603 673-1763
151 Mont Vernon Rd Milford NH (03055) ***(G-19083)***
Wiscasset Music Publishing Co....617 492-5720
10 Mason St Cambridge MA (02138) ***(G-9702)***
Wiscasset Newspaper, Boothbay Harbor *Also called Maine-OK Enterprises Inc* ***(G-5784)***
Wisdom Publications Inc (PA)....617 776-7416
199 Elm St Somerville MA (02144) ***(G-15233)***
Wise Mouth Inc....508 345-2559
84 Bank St North Attleboro MA (02760) ***(G-13786)***
Wise-Acre Inc....207 374-5400
9 Tradewinds Ln Blue Hill ME (04614) ***(G-5775)***
Wiseguide, The, Parsonsfield *Also called Tree Enterprises* ***(G-6577)***
Wiseman & Spaulding Designs....207 862-3513
12 Shaw Hill Rd Hampden ME (04444) ***(G-6169)***
Wish Designs Inc (PA)....978 566-1232
15 Union St Ste 209 Lawrence MA (01840) ***(G-12084)***
Witches Almanac....401 847-3388
32 Halsey St Newport RI (02840) ***(G-20688)***
Withrow Inc....603 898-8868
9 Hemlock Ln Salem NH (03079) ***(G-19779)***
Witkowsky John....203 483-0152
73 Branford Rd North Branford CT (06471) ***(G-2985)***
Witricity Corporation (PA)....617 926-2700
57 Water St Watertown MA (02472) ***(G-16331)***
Wittmann Battenfeld Inc (HQ)....860 496-9603
1 Technology Park Dr Torrington CT (06790) ***(G-4608)***
Wizard Too LLC....203 984-7180
34 Little Fox Ln Westport CT (06880) ***(G-5238)***
WJ Kettleworks LLC....203 377-5000
55 Sperry Ave Stratford CT (06615) ***(G-4458)***
Wlhc Inc (PA)....207 532-6531
37 Bangor St Houlton ME (04730) ***(G-6212)***
Wmb Industries LLC....203 927-2822
62 Pool Rd North Haven CT (06473) ***(G-3069)***
Wna, Chelmsford *Also called Waddington North America Inc* ***(G-9941)***
Wohrles Foods Inc (PA)....413 442-1518
1619 East St Pittsfield MA (01201) ***(G-14513)***
Wold Tool Engineering Inc....860 564-8338
7 Commonway Dr Brooklyn CT (06234) ***(G-674)***
Wolf Colorprint, Newington *Also called Flow Resources Inc* ***(G-2864)***
Wollaston Alloys Inc....781 848-3333
205 Wood Rd Braintree MA (02184) ***(G-9051)***
Wollaston Foundry....508 884-3400
36 Allison Ave Taunton MA (02780) ***(G-15800)***
Wolters Kluwer Fincl Svcs Inc....978 263-1212
130 Turner St Bldg 34 Waltham MA (02453) ***(G-16224)***
Women & Infants Hospital....401 453-7600
79 Plain St Providence RI (02903) ***(G-21156)***
Wonder Tablitz Corporation....508 660-0011
4 Walpole Park S Ste 3 Walpole MA (02081) ***(G-16018)***
Wonderland Smoke Shop Inc....401 823-3134
666 East Ave Warwick RI (02886) ***(G-21451)***
Wood & Signs Ltd....802 362-2386
2036 Vermont Rte 7 East Dorset VT (05253) ***(G-21918)***
Wood & Wood Inc....413 772-0889
19 Butternut St Greenfield MA (01301) ***(G-11284)***
Wood & Wood Inc....802 496-3000
98 Carroll Rd Waitsfield VT (05673) ***(G-22572)***
Wood & Wood Sign Systems, Waitsfield *Also called Wood & Wood Inc* ***(G-22572)***
Wood Cider Mill, Springfield *Also called Willis Wood* ***(G-22513)***
Wood Decor Inc....781 826-4954
300 Oak St Pembroke MA (02359) ***(G-14433)***
Wood Dynamics Corporation (PA)....802 457-3970
4120 Pomfret Rd South Pomfret VT (05067) ***(G-22489)***
Wood Geek Inc....508 858-5282
685 Orchard St New Bedford MA (02744) ***(G-13459)***
Wood Group Component Repair, Wallingford *Also called Ethosenergy Component Repr LLC* ***(G-4738)***
Wood Mill LLC....978 683-2901
250 Merrimack St Lawrence MA (01843) ***(G-12085)***
Wood N Excellence Cab Refacing, Higganum *Also called N Excellence Wood Inc* ***(G-1904)***
Wood Products Unlimited Inc....978 687-7449
60 Hidden Rd Methuen MA (01844) ***(G-13048)***
Wood Science/Technology, Orono *Also called University of Maine System* ***(G-6559)***
Wood St Wood Co....508 947-6886
225 Wood St Middleboro MA (02346) ***(G-13082)***
Wood St Woodworkers....401 253-8257
274 Wood St Bristol RI (02809) ***(G-20111)***
Wood Visions Inc....603 595-9663
66b Old Derry Rd Hudson NH (03051) ***(G-18453)***
Wood Works....603 436-3805
855 Islington St Ste 123 Portsmouth NH (03801) ***(G-19632)***

Wood-Mizer Holdings Inc 207 645-2072
541 Borough Rd Chesterville ME (04938) *(G-5909)*
Woodard & Curran Inc 508 487-5474
200 Route 6 Provincetown MA (02657) *(G-14611)*
Woodards Sugar House LLC 603 358-3321
1200 Route 12a Surry NH (03431) *(G-19883)*
Woodbury Golf Course, Woodbury *Also called Thompson Family Enterprises (G-22734)*
Woodbury Pewterers Inc 203 263-2668
860 Main St S Woodbury CT (06798) *(G-5492)*
Woodcraft Designers Bldrs LLC 508 584-4200
45 North St Canton MA (02021) *(G-9796)*
Wooden Things Inc 207 712-4654
85 Egypt Rd Gray ME (04039) *(G-6144)*
Woodenboat Publications Inc 207 359-4651
41 Wooden Boat Ln Brooklin ME (04616) *(G-5822)*
Woodex Bearing Company Inc 207 371-2210
216 Bay Point Rd Georgetown ME (04548) *(G-6107)*
Woodforms Inc 508 543-9417
131 Morse St Ste 10 Foxboro MA (02035) *(G-10909)*
Woodfree Crating Systems Inc 203 759-1799
150 Mattatuck Heights Rd Waterbury CT (06705) *(G-4979)*
Woodlan Tool and Machine Co 802 463-4597
9 Spencer Dr Bellows Falls VT (05101) *(G-21656)*
Woodland Power Products Inc 888 531-7253
72 Acton St West Haven CT (06516) *(G-5152)*
Woodland Pulp LLC (PA) 207 427-3311
144 Main St Baileyville ME (04694) *(G-5627)*
Woodland Studios Inc 207 667-3286
406 State St Ellsworth ME (04605) *(G-6024)*
Woodman Precision Engineering 978 538-9544
119 Foster St Peabody MA (01960) *(G-14387)*
Woods End Inc 203 226-6303
11 Lilac Ln Weston CT (06883) *(G-5176)*
Woods Vermont Syrup Company 802 565-0309
780 Hebard Rd Randolph VT (05060) *(G-22304)*
Woodshop At Acdia Weathervanes, Trenton *Also called Woodshop Cupolas Inc (G-7104)*
Woodshop Cupolas Inc 207 667-6331
749 Bar Harbor Rd Trenton ME (04605) *(G-7104)*
Woodshop News Magazine, Essex *Also called Soundings Publications LLC (G-1406)*
Woodsmiths Inc 508 548-8343
168 Stevens St Ste 2c Fall River MA (02721) *(G-10784)*
Woodsound Studio 207 596-7407
1103 Commercial St Rockport ME (04856) *(G-6827)*
Woodstock Grnola Trail Mix LLC 802 457-3149
112 Pomfret Rd Woodstock VT (05091) *(G-22742)*
Woodstock Line Co 860 928-6557
91 Canal St Putnam CT (06260) *(G-3641)*
Woodstone Company Inc (PA) 802 722-9217
17 Morse Brook Rd Westminster VT (05158) *(G-22632)*
Woodstone Company Inc 603 445-2449
1164 Main St North Walpole NH (03609) *(G-19397)*
Woodway Print Inc 203 323-6423
48 Union St Ste 21 Stamford CT (06906) *(G-4361)*
Woodwork Specialties Inc 860 583-4848
123 New St Bristol CT (06010) *(G-627)*
Woodworkers Club LLC 203 847-9663
215 Westport Ave Norwalk CT (06851) *(G-3273)*
Woodworkers Heaven Inc 203 333-2778
955 Conn Ave Ste 4106 Bridgeport CT (06607) *(G-506)*
Woodworking Machinery Services 978 663-8488
11 Esquire Rd Ste 2 North Billerica MA (01862) *(G-13878)*
Woodworking Plus LLC 203 393-1967
375 Bethmour Rd Bethany CT (06524) *(G-125)*
Woodworks Architectural Mllwk 603 432-4050
16 N Wentworth Ave Londonderry NH (03053) *(G-18746)*
Wool Felt Division, Easthampton *Also called National Nonwovens Inc (G-10569)*
Woolrich Inc 857 263-7554
299 Newbury St Ste 1 Boston MA (02115) *(G-8932)*
Woolwich Ice Cream Inc 207 442-8830
35 Main St Woolwich ME (04579) *(G-7291)*
Woolworks Ltd 860 963-1228
154 Main St B Putnam CT (06260) *(G-3642)*
Worcester Business Journal, Worcester *Also called New England Business Media LLC (G-17429)*
Worcester Chrome Furniture, Worcester *Also called Worcester Manufacturing Inc (G-17505)*
Worcester Envelope Company 508 832-5394
22 Millbury St Auburn MA (01501) *(G-7853)*
Worcester Indus Rbr Sup Co Inc 508 853-2332
172 Doyle Rd Holden MA (01520) *(G-11551)*
Worcester Manufacturing Inc 508 756-0301
35 New St Worcester MA (01605) *(G-17505)*
Worcester Publishing 508 749-3166
101 Water St Worcester MA (01604) *(G-17506)*
Worcester Sun LLC 774 364-0553
20 Cook St Holden MA (01520) *(G-11552)*
Worcester Tlegram Gazette Corp (HQ) 508 793-9100
100 Front St Fl 20 Worcester MA (01608) *(G-17507)*
Worcester Tlegram Gazette Corp 978 368-0176
100 Front St Fl 20 Worcester MA (01608) *(G-17508)*
Worcester Tlegram Gazette Corp 508 764-2519
39 Elm St Ste 2 Southbridge MA (01550) *(G-15409)*
Wordstream Inc 617 963-0555
101 Huntington Ave Fl 7 Boston MA (02199) *(G-8933)*
Work and Tactical Gear, Woburn *Also called Black Diamond Group Inc (G-17133)*
Work Play Sleep Inc 617 902-0827
222 3rd St Ste 4000 Cambridge MA (02142) *(G-9703)*
Work Technology Corporation (PA) 617 625-5888
1 Mercer Cir Cambridge MA (02138) *(G-9704)*
Workday Inc 617 936-1100
33 Arch St Ste 2200 Boston MA (02110) *(G-8934)*
Works In Progress Inc (PA) 802 658-3797
20 Farrell St Ste 103 South Burlington VT (05403) *(G-22479)*
Worksafe Traffic Ctrl Inds Inc (PA) 802 223-8948
115 Industrial Ln Barre VT (05641) *(G-21645)*
Workscape 508 861-5500
500 Old Connecticut Path Framingham MA (01701) *(G-11016)*
Workscape Inc (HQ) 508 573-9000
313 Boston Post Rd W # 210 Marlborough MA (01752) *(G-12852)*
Workwise LLC 802 881-8178
121 S Pinnacle Ridge Rd Waterbury VT (05676) *(G-22589)*
World Asset Management LLC 617 889-7300
225 Franklin St Ste 2320 Boston MA (02110) *(G-8935)*
World Cord Sets Inc 860 763-2100
210 Moody Rd Enfield CT (06082) *(G-1391)*
World Cuisine Concepts LLC 603 676-8591
43 Pine St White River Junction VT (05001) *(G-22644)*
World Energy Biox Biofuels LLC (PA) 617 889-7300
225 Franklin St Ste 2320 Boston MA (02110) *(G-8936)*
World Harbors Inc 207 786-3200
176 First Flight Dr Auburn ME (04210) *(G-5601)*
World Journal Chinese Daily 617 542-1230
216 Lincoln St Boston MA (02111) *(G-8937)*
World News Firm Inc 781 335-0113
87 Knollwood Cir Weymouth MA (02188) *(G-16904)*
World Publications Inc 508 880-5555
455 Somerset Ave North Dighton MA (02764) *(G-13938)*
World Publications Inc 802 479-2582
403 Us Route 302 Barre VT (05641) *(G-21646)*
World Satellite Media, Ashfield *Also called Eratech Inc (G-7650)*
World Sleep Products Inc 978 667-6648
12 Esquire Rd North Billerica MA (01862) *(G-13879)*
World Stone 617 293-4373
142 Hancock St Everett MA (02149) *(G-10634)*
World Trophies Company Inc 401 272-5846
275 Silver Spring St Providence RI (02904) *(G-21157)*
World, The, Barre *Also called World Publications Inc (G-21646)*
Worldscreen Inc 860 274-9218
843 Echo Lake Rd Watertown CT (06795) *(G-5037)*
Worldwide Antenna Systems LLC 781 275-1147
42 Elm St Ste 3 Kingston MA (02364) *(G-11968)*
Worldwide Information Inc 888 273-3260
100 Cummings Ctr Ste 235m Beverly MA (01915) *(G-8198)*
Worldwide Innvtive Hlthcare In 646 694-2273
217 Thorndike St Apt 207 Cambridge MA (02141) *(G-9705)*
Worldwide Tooling LLC 401 334-9806
1 Christopher Dr Lincoln RI (02865) *(G-20600)*
Wormtown Atomic Propulsion 781 487-7777
303 Bear Hill Rd Waltham MA (02451) *(G-16225)*
Worsted Spinning Neng LLC 207 324-5622
5 Water St Springvale ME (04083) *(G-7056)*
Worthen Industries Inc (HQ) 603 888-5443
3 E Spit Brook Rd Nashua NH (03060) *(G-19288)*
Worthen Industries Inc 978 365-6345
530 Main St Clinton MA (01510) *(G-10095)*
Worthen Industries Inc 603 886-0973
34 Cellu Dr Nashua NH (03063) *(G-19289)*
Worthington Assembly Inc 413 397-8265
14 Industrial Dr E Unit 2 South Deerfield MA (01373) *(G-15259)*
Wotech Associates 781 935-3787
26 Mayflower Rd Woburn MA (01801) *(G-17324)*
WR Sharples Co Inc 508 695-5656
211 John L Dietsch Sq North Attleboro MA (02763) *(G-13787)*
Wrabacon Inc 207 465-2068
150 Old Waterville Rd Oakland ME (04963) *(G-6536)*
Wrd Innovative Controls, Newburyport *Also called Wilmington Research & Dev Corp (G-13549)*
Wrentham Quarry Div, Walpole *Also called S M Lorusso & Sons Inc (G-16010)*
Wrentham Tool Group LLC 508 966-2332
155 Farm St Bellingham MA (02019) *(G-8064)*
Wright Architectural Mllwk Corp 413 586-3528
115 Industrial Dr Northampton MA (01060) *(G-14027)*
Wright Electric Motors, Hooksett *Also called Chase Electric Motors LLC (G-18346)*
Wright G F Steel & Wire Co 508 363-2718
243 Stafford St Worcester MA (01603) *(G-17509)*
Wright Industrial Products Co 508 695-3924
45 Industrial Rd Cumberland RI (02864) *(G-20350)*
Wright Line LLC (HQ) 508 852-4300
160 Gold Star Blvd Worcester MA (01606) *(G-17510)*

ALPHABETIC

Wright Maintenance Inc 802 365-9253
151 Vt Route 30 Newfane VT (05345) **(G-22189)**
Wright Trailers Inc 508 336-8530
1825 Fall River Ave Seekonk MA (02771) **(G-15044)**
Wright Wire, Worcester *Also called Wright G F Steel & Wire Co* **(G-17509)**
Wristies Inc 978 937-9500
650 Suffolk St Lowell MA (01854) **(G-12449)**
Write Way Signs & Design Inc 860 482-8893
73 Migeon Ave Torrington CT (06790) **(G-4609)**
Writing Company 207 370-8078
2 Portland Fish Pier # 213 Portland ME (04101) **(G-6746)**
Wrobel Engineering Co Inc 508 586-8338
154 Bodwell St Ste A Avon MA (02322) **(G-7903)**
WS Anderson Associates Inc 508 832-5550
303 Washington St 313 Auburn MA (01501) **(G-7854)**
WS Badger Company Inc 603 357-2958
768 Route 10 Gilsum NH (03448) **(G-18196)**
Ws Dennison Cabinets Inc 603 224-8434
779 Silver Hills Dr Pembroke NH (03275) **(G-19464)**
Wtd Inc (PA) 978 658-8200
271 Ballardvale St Wilmington MA (01887) **(G-17068)**
Wti Systems, Pembroke *Also called Datanational Corporation* **(G-14397)**
Wtm Company 860 283-5871
135 S Main St Ste 12 Thomaston CT (06787) **(G-4528)**
Wuersch Time Inc 401 828-2525
10 Monroe Dr Coventry RI (02816) **(G-20170)**
Wurszt Inc 413 599-4900
2460 Boston Rd Wilbraham MA (01095) **(G-16944)**
Wwas, Kingston *Also called Worldwide Antenna Systems LLC* **(G-11968)**
Www.lapelpinplanet.com, Coventry *Also called Jim Clift Design Inc* **(G-20150)**
Www.sand9.com, Cambridge *Also called Sand 9 Inc* **(G-9641)**
Www.sluggo-Ox.com, Franklin *Also called Sluggo-Ox Corporation* **(G-11081)**
Wyatt Engineering LLC (PA) 401 334-1170
6 Blackstone Valley Pl # 401 Lincoln RI (02865) **(G-20601)**
Wyebot Inc 508 481-2603
2 Mount Royal Ave Ste 310 Marlborough MA (01752) **(G-12853)**
Wyeth Biopharma Division, Andover *Also called Wyeth Pharmaceuticals LLC* **(G-7619)**
Wyeth Pharmaceuticals LLC 978 475-9214
1 Burtt Rd Andover MA (01810) **(G-7619)**
Wyler Gallery, Brunswick *Also called Sylvia Wyler Pottery Inc* **(G-5848)**
Wyman-Gordon Company (HQ) 508 839-8252
244 Worcester St North Grafton MA (01536) **(G-13969)**
Wyman-Gordon Company 508 839-8253
80 Hermon St Worcester MA (01610) **(G-17511)**
Wyman-Gordon Company 603 934-6630
35 Industrial Park Dr Franklin NH (03235) **(G-18169)**
Wyrmwood Inc 508 837-0057
144 W Britannia St Taunton MA (02780) **(G-15801)**
Wyz Machine Co Inc 413 786-6816
95 Industrial Ln Agawam MA (01001) **(G-7457)**
X Cafe, Portland *Also called Kerry Inc* **(G-6677)**
X Press In Stowe Inc 802 253-9788
73 Pond Ln Stowe VT (05672) **(G-22525)**
X Sonix 978 266-2106
159 Swanson Rd Boxborough MA (01719) **(G-8972)**
X-4 Tool Div, North Billerica *Also called Gear/Tronics Industries Inc* **(G-13820)**
X4 Pharmaceuticals Inc (PA) 857 529-8300
955 Mssachusetts Ave Fl 4 Flr 4 Cambridge MA (02139) **(G-9706)**
Xam Online Inc (PA) 781 662-9268
25 1st St Cambridge MA (02141) **(G-9707)**
Xamax Industries Inc 203 888-7200
63 Silvermine Rd Seymour CT (06483) **(G-3769)**
Xavier Corporation 603 668-8892
124 Plymouth St Manchester NH (03102) **(G-18956)**
Xcalibur Communications 603 625-9555
95 Charlotte St Manchester NH (03103) **(G-18957)**
XCEL Fuel 203 481-4510
501 Main St Branford CT (06405) **(G-363)**
Xcerra Corporation (HQ) 781 461-1000
825 University Ave Norwood MA (02062) **(G-14206)**
Xcerra Corporation 781 461-1000
825 University Ave Norwood MA (02062) **(G-14207)**
Xcerra Corporation 781 461-1000
825 University Ave Norwood MA (02062) **(G-14208)**
Xemplar Pharmaceuticals, Fall River *Also called Exemplar Laboratories LLC* **(G-10692)**
Xenetic Biosciences Inc 781 778-7720
40 Speen St Ste 102 Framingham MA (01701) **(G-11017)**
Xenics Usa Inc 978 969-1706
600 Cummings Ctr Ste 166y Beverly MA (01915) **(G-8199)**
Xenon Corporation (PA) 978 661-9033
37 Upton Dr Ste 2 Wilmington MA (01887) **(G-17069)**
Xenotherapeutics LLC 617 750-1907
21 Drydock Ave Ste 610e Boston MA (02210) **(G-8938)**
Xerox Corporation (HQ) 203 968-3000
201 Merritt 7 Norwalk CT (06851) **(G-3274)**
Xg Industries LLC 475 282-4643
53 Hancock St Stratford CT (06615) **(G-4459)**
Xijet Corp 203 397-2800
8 Lunar Dr Ste 3 New Haven CT (06525) **(G-2755)**
Xilectric Inc 617 312-5678
151 Martine St Rm 125 Fall River MA (02723) **(G-10785)**
Xilinx Inc 603 891-1096
10 Tara Blvd Ste 410 Nashua NH (03062) **(G-19290)**
Xintekidel Inc 203 348-9229
56 W Broad St Stamford CT (06902) **(G-4362)**
Xl Adhesives North LLC 508 675-0528
63 Water St Fall River MA (02721) **(G-10786)**
Xl Fleet, Brighton *Also called Xl Hybrids Inc* **(G-9108)**
Xl Hybrids Inc (PA) 617 718-0329
145 Newton St Brighton MA (02135) **(G-9108)**
Xma Corporation 603 222-2256
7 Perimeter Rd Ste 2 Manchester NH (03103) **(G-18958)**
Xmi Corporation 800 838-0424
140 Greenwich Ave Greenwich CT (06830) **(G-1662)**
Xmix, Tyngsboro *Also called Dj Wholesale Club Inc* **(G-15888)**
Xos Digital, Wilmington *Also called Xos Technologies Inc* **(G-17070)**
Xos Technologies Inc (HQ) 978 447-5220
181 Ballardvale St Ste 2 Wilmington MA (01887) **(G-17070)**
Xp Comdel, Gloucester *Also called Xp Power LLC* **(G-11220)**
Xp Power LLC 978 282-0620
11 Kondelin Rd Gloucester MA (01930) **(G-11220)**
Xphotonics LLC 978 952-2568
32 Surrey Rd Littleton MA (01460) **(G-12329)**
Xponent Global Inc 978 562-3485
30 Tower St Hudson MA (01749) **(G-11827)**
Xpress Copy Services, Portland *Also called Xpress of Maine* **(G-6747)**
Xpress of Maine (PA) 207 775-2444
17 Westfield St Ste A Portland ME (04102) **(G-6747)**
Xpression Prints 401 413-6930
31 Hayward St Ste I1 Franklin MA (02038) **(G-11099)**
Xtalic Corporation 508 485-9730
260 Cedar Hill St Ste 4 Marlborough MA (01752) **(G-12854)**
Xthera Corporation 508 528-3100
31 Hayward St Ste B1 Franklin MA (02038) **(G-11100)**
Xtralis Inc 800 229-4434
175 Bodwell St Ste 2 Avon MA (02322) **(G-7904)**
Xtreme Screen & Sportswear LLC 207 857-9200
937 Main St Westbrook ME (04092) **(G-7215)**
Xtreme Seal LLC 508 933-1894
67 Sharp St Hingham MA (02043) **(G-11519)**
Xuare LLC 860 383-8863
471 N Main St Norwich CT (06360) **(G-3293)**
Xuron Corp 207 283-1401
62 Industrial Park Rd Saco ME (04072) **(G-6862)**
Xybol Interlynks Inc 978 356-0750
89 Turnpike Rd Ste 204 Ipswich MA (01938) **(G-11939)**
Xylem Inc 978 778-1010
100 Cummings Ctr Ste 535n Beverly MA (01915) **(G-8200)**
Xylem Water Solutions USA Inc 781 935-6515
78 Olympia Ave Woburn MA (01801) **(G-17325)**
Xylem Water Solutions USA Inc 203 450-3715
1000 Bridgeport Ave # 402 Shelton CT (06484) **(G-3891)**
XYZ Sheet Metal Inc 781 878-1419
281 Washington St Abington MA (02351) **(G-7332)**
Yacht Club Bottling Works Inc 401 231-9290
2239 Mineral Spring Ave North Providence RI (02911) **(G-20775)**
Yale Alumni Publications Inc 203 432-0645
149 York St Fl 2 New Haven CT (06511) **(G-2756)**
Yale Commercial Locks & Hdwr, Berlin *Also called Yale Security Inc* **(G-117)**
Yale Cordage Inc 207 282-3396
77 Industrial Park Rd Saco ME (04072) **(G-6863)**
Yale Daily News, New Haven *Also called Yale University* **(G-2760)**
Yale Daily News Publishing Co 203 432-2400
212 York St New Haven CT (06511) **(G-2757)**
Yale Herald, New Haven *Also called Yale University* **(G-2762)**
Yale Security Inc 865 986-7511
225 Episcopal Rd Berlin CT (06037) **(G-117)**
Yale University 203 432-2880
149 York St New Haven CT (06511) **(G-2758)**
Yale University 203 432-3916
225 Prospect St Rm 1 New Haven CT (06511) **(G-2759)**
Yale University 203 432-2424
202 York St New Haven CT (06511) **(G-2760)**
Yale University 203 432-6320
285 Mansfield St New Haven CT (06511) **(G-2761)**
Yale University 203 432-7494
305 Crown St New Haven CT (06511) **(G-2762)**
Yamaha Unfied Cmmnications Inc (HQ) 978 610-4040
144 North Rd Ste 3250 Sudbury MA (01776) **(G-15674)**
Yankee Barn Home, Grantham *Also called Topek LLC* **(G-18217)**
Yankee Barn Homes Inc 603 863-4545
61 Plains Rd Claremont NH (03743) **(G-17865)**
Yankee Candle Company Inc (HQ) 413 665-8306
16 Yankee Candle Way South Deerfield MA (01373) **(G-15260)**
Yankee Candle Investments LLC (HQ) 413 665-8306
16 Yankee Candle Way South Deerfield MA (01373) **(G-15261)**
Yankee Casting Co Inc 860 749-6171
243 Shaker Rd Enfield CT (06082) **(G-1392)**

Yankee Corporation 802 527-0177
125 Yankee Park Rd Fairfax VT (05454) *(G-21981)*
Yankee Crafters Wampum Jewelry 508 394-0575
48 N Main St South Yarmouth MA (02664) *(G-15336)*
Yankee Craftsman Inc 603 483-5900
261 Old Candia Rd Auburn NH (03032) *(G-17614)*
Yankee Electrical Mfg Co 413 596-8256
600 Main St Wilbraham MA (01095) *(G-16945)*
Yankee Glass Blower Inc 978 369-7545
117 Robbins Dr Carlisle MA (01741) *(G-9801)*
Yankee Hardwoods LLC 207 459-7779
Lincoln St Sanford ME (04073) *(G-6897)*
Yankee Hill Machine Co Inc 413 584-1400
412 Main St Easthampton MA (01027) *(G-10583)*
Yankee Holding Corp (HQ) 413 665-8306
16 Yankee Candle Way South Deerfield MA (01373) *(G-15262)*
Yankee Insulation, New Boston *Also called Yankee Shutter Co (G-19299)*
Yankee Machine Inc 207 627-4277
1300 Poland Spring Rd # 11 Casco ME (04015) *(G-5898)*
Yankee Magazine, Dublin *Also called Yankee Publishing Incorporated (G-18069)*
Yankee Marina and Billiards, Yarmouth *Also called Yankee Marina Inc (G-7304)*
Yankee Marina Inc 207 846-9120
142 Lafayette St Yarmouth ME (04096) *(G-7304)*
Yankee Metals LLC 203 612-7470
76 Knowlton St Bridgeport CT (06608) *(G-507)*
Yankee Pennysaver Inc 203 775-9122
246 Federal Rd Ste D15 Brookfield CT (06804) *(G-667)*
Yankee Pride Fisheries Inc 401 783-9647
81 Point Ave Wakefield RI (02879) *(G-21282)*
Yankee Printing Group Inc 413 532-9513
630 New Ludlow Rd South Hadley MA (01075) *(G-15313)*
Yankee Publishing Incorporated (PA) 603 563-8111
1121 Main St Dublin NH (03444) *(G-18069)*
Yankee Screen Printing 203 924-9926
15 Kings Ct Derby CT (06418) *(G-1085)*
Yankee Shopper 508 943-8784
168 Gore Rd Webster MA (01570) *(G-16354)*
Yankee Shutter Co 603 487-2400
480 Bedford Rd New Boston NH (03070) *(G-19299)*
Yankee Soldering Technology, Westerly *Also called Donald G Lockard (G-21523)*
Yankee Steel Service LLC 203 879-5707
9 Venus Dr Wolcott CT (06716) *(G-5462)*
Yankee Trader Seafood Ltd 781 829-4350
1610 Corporate Park Pembroke MA (02359) *(G-14434)*
Yard Stick Decore 203 330-0360
145 Hart St # 1 Bridgeport CT (06606) *(G-508)*
Yarde Metals Inc (HQ) 860 406-6061
45 Newell St Southington CT (06489) *(G-4092)*
Yarmouth Printing & Graphics, Yarmouth *Also called Csg Inc (G-7293)*
Yarra Design & Fabrication LLC 603 224-6880
1 Tallwood Dr Bow NH (03304) *(G-17736)*
Yarrington Weaving Studio, New Haven *Also called Lynn Yarrington (G-22185)*
Yaskawa - Solectria Solar, Lawrence *Also called Solectria Renewables LLC (G-12076)*
Yates Lumber Inc 207 738-2331
137 Winn Rd Lee ME (04455) *(G-6267)*
Yblank 857 544-9991
766 Cambridge St Cambridge MA (02141) *(G-9708)*
Ycc Holdings LLC 413 665-8306
16 Yankee Candle Way South Deerfield MA (01373) *(G-15263)*
Ydc Precision Machine Inc 603 934-6200
518 North Rd Franklin NH (03235) *(G-18170)*
Yellowfin Holdings Inc 866 341-0979
160 West Rd Ellington CT (06029) *(G-1344)*
Yesco Sign and Ltg Concord 603 238-6988
322 W Main St Ste 127 Tilton NH (03276) *(G-19913)*
Yeuell Name Plate & Label, Woburn *Also called E V Yeuell Inc (G-17171)*
Yield10 Bioscience Inc (PA) 617 583-1700
19 Presidential Way # 201 Woburn MA (01801) *(G-17326)*
YKK (usa) Inc 978 458-3200
5 Mount Royal Ave Ste 3 Marlborough MA (01752) *(G-12855)*
Ymaa Publication Center Inc 603 569-7988
51 Mill St Unit 4 Wolfeboro NH (03894) *(G-20027)*
Ymittos Candle Mfg Co, Lowell *Also called Battalion Co Inc (G-12352)*
Ymittos Candle Mfg Co 978 453-2824
279 Dutton St Lowell MA (01852) *(G-12450)*
Yoc 207 363-9322
21 Railroad Ave York ME (03909) *(G-7318)*
Yodil, Boston *Also called Duck Creek Technologies LLC (G-8512)*
Yoffa Woodworking 401 846-7659
62 Halsey St Unit I Newport RI (02840) *(G-20689)*
Yoga For Daily Living 978 448-3751
104 Mill St Groton MA (01450) *(G-11297)*
Yogapipe Inc 844 964-2747
800 Hingham St Ste 200n Rockland MA (02370) *(G-14833)*
Yoghund, Exeter *Also called Tbd Brands LLC (G-18133)*
Yogibo LLC (PA) 603 595-0207
16 Celina Ave Unit 13 Nashua NH (03063) *(G-19291)*
Yolanda Dubose Records and 203 823-6699
105 W Prospect St West Haven CT (06516) *(G-5153)*
York County Coast Star Inc 207 985-5901
39 Main St Kennebunk ME (04043) *(G-6243)*
York Harbor Brewing Company 207 703-8060
8 Blueberry Ln Kittery ME (03904) *(G-6260)*
York Hill Farm 207 778-9741
257 York Hill Rd New Sharon ME (04955) *(G-6479)*
York Hill Trap Rock Quarry Co 203 237-8421
975 Westfield Rd Meriden CT (06450) *(G-2152)*
York Manufacturing Inc 207 324-1300
43 Community Dr Sanford ME (04073) *(G-6898)*
York Marine Inc 207 596-7400
11 Gordon Dr Rockland ME (04841) *(G-6816)*
York Millwork LLC 203 698-3460
210 Sound Beach Ave Old Greenwich CT (06870) *(G-3314)*
York Street Studio Inc 203 266-9000
143 West St Ste Y New Milford CT (06776) *(G-2833)*
York's Sign Shop, Skowhegan *Also called Yorks Signs (G-6988)*
Yorks Signs 207 474-9331
127 Waterville Rd Skowhegan ME (04976) *(G-6988)*
Yorkstreet.com, New Milford *Also called York Street Studio Inc (G-2833)*
Yost Manufacturing & Supply 860 447-9678
1018 Hartford Tpke Waterford CT (06385) *(G-4996)*
You Know Solutions, Belgrade *Also called Ron Lavallee (G-5699)*
Young & Constantin N River GL (PA) 413 625-6422
Deerfield Ave Shelburne Falls MA (01370) *(G-15076)*
Young Authors Foundation Inc 617 964-6800
437 Newtonville Ave Ste 1 Newton MA (02460) *(G-13655)*
Young Furniture Mfg Inc 603 224-8830
161 River Rd Bow NH (03304) *(G-17737)*
Young Writers Project Inc 802 324-9537
47 Maple St Ste 216 Burlington VT (05401) *(G-21818)*
Youngs Communications Inc 860 347-8567
182 Court St Middletown CT (06457) *(G-2231)*
Youngs Printing, Middletown *Also called Youngs Communications Inc (G-2231)*
Your Heaven LLC 401 273-7076
172 Congdon St Providence RI (02906) *(G-21158)*
Your Membership.com, Groton *Also called Yourmembershipcom Inc (G-1690)*
Your Oil Tools LLC 701 645-8665
78 Londonderry Tpke D5 Hooksett NH (03106) *(G-18361)*
Yourmembershipcom Inc 860 271-7241
541 Eastern Point Rd Groton CT (06340) *(G-1690)*
Yourplayingcards.com, Londonderry *Also called Camera Works Inc (G-18683)*
Yoway LLC 617 505-5158
1376 Beacon St Brookline MA (02446) *(G-9225)*
Yoway LLC (PA) 508 459-0611
395 Park Ave Ste 2 Worcester MA (01610) *(G-17512)*
Ysnc Fuel Inc 508 436-2716
64 N Montello St Brockton MA (02301) *(G-9188)*
Yuen Ho Bakery Inc 617 426-8320
54 Beach St Ste 1 Boston MA (02111) *(G-8939)*
Yuma Therapeutics Corporaiton 617 953-4618
10 Linnaean St Cambridge MA (02138) *(G-9709)*
Yumearth, Stamford *Also called Yummyearth LLC (G-4363)*
Yummyearth LLC (PA) 203 276-1259
9 W Broad St Ste 440 Stamford CT (06902) *(G-4363)*
Yvon, Russel, South Hadley *Also called Quality Loose Leaf Co (G-15310)*
Yvons Valvoline Express Care 207 777-3600
698 Main St Lewiston ME (04240) *(G-6328)*
Yxlon International, Shelton *Also called Comet Technologies USA Inc (G-3790)*
Z & W Machine Tool Company, Guild *Also called Frank Wiggins (G-18235)*
Z M Weapons High Performance 802 777-8964
1958 Wes White Hl Richmond VT (05477) *(G-22313)*
Z Magazine, Dedham *Also called Institute For Scial Cltral Cmm (G-10293)*
Z-Flex (us) Inc 603 669-5136
20 Commerce Park North # 107 Bedford NH (03110) *(G-17668)*
Z-Loda Systems Inc 203 359-2991
111 Prospect St Stamford CT (06901) *(G-4364)*
Z-Tech LLC 603 228-1305
56 Dow Rd Bow NH (03304) *(G-17738)*
Zachary Shuster Hrmswoth Agncy 617 262-2400
545 Boylston St Ste 1103 Boston MA (02116) *(G-8940)*
Zackin Publications Inc 203 262-4670
100 Willenbrock Rd Oxford CT (06478) *(G-3431)*
Zafgen Inc 617 622-4003
13 Center Plz Boston MA (02108) *(G-8941)*
Zag Machine & Tool Co, New Britain *Also called Adam Z Golas (G-2504)*
Zajac LLC 207 286-9100
92 Industrial Park Rd Saco ME (04072) *(G-6864)*
Zampell Refractories Inc 207 786-2400
192 First Flight Dr Auburn ME (04210) *(G-5602)*
Zampini Industrial Group LLC 401 305-7997
85 Industrial Cir # 2211 Lincoln RI (02865) *(G-20602)*
Zappix Inc 781 214-8124
25 Mall Rd Burlington MA (01803) *(G-9357)*
Zatec LLC 508 880-3388
620 Spring St North Dighton MA (02764) *(G-13939)*
Zato Health, Springfield *Also called Zato Inc (G-15529)*

ALPHABETIC

Zato Inc....617 834-8105
1350 Main St Ste 502 Springfield MA (01103) ***(G-15529)***
Zatorski Coating Company Inc....860 267-9889
77 Wopowog Rd East Hampton CT (06424) ***(G-1168)***
Zavarella Woodworking Inc....860 666-6969
48 Commerce Ct Newington CT (06111) ***(G-2913)***
Zax Signage Corp....603 319-6178
6 Autumn Pond Park Greenland NH (03840) ***(G-18225)***
ZB Ceramic....413 512-0879
61 Taylor St Chicopee MA (01020) ***(G-10070)***
Zd USA Holdings Inc (PA)....508 998-4000
744 Belleville Ave New Bedford MA (02745) ***(G-13460)***
Zeeco Inc....860 479-0999
80 Spring Ln Plainville CT (06062) ***(G-3524)***
Zeevee Inc....978 467-1395
295 Foster St Ste 2 Littleton MA (01460) ***(G-12330)***
Zekes Sheet Metal....207 883-3877
2 Washington Ave Scarborough ME (04074) ***(G-6943)***
Zen Art & Design Inc....800 215-6010
119 Rocky Hill Rd Hadley MA (01035) ***(G-11312)***
Zen Bakery, MA, Milford *Also called Pin Hsiao & Associates LLC* ***(G-13138)***
Zen Bear Honey Tea LLC....207 449-1553
114 Old Brunswick Rd Bath ME (04530) ***(G-5682)***
Zenith Die Cutting Inc....508 877-8811
2 Watson Pl Bldg 3 Framingham MA (01701) ***(G-11018)***
Zenith Hearing Aid, New Haven *Also called Zenith-Omni Hearing Center* ***(G-2763)***
Zenith-Omni Hearing Center (PA)....203 624-9857
111 Park St Ste 1k New Haven CT (06511) ***(G-2763)***
Zenna Noodle Bar....781 883-8624
1374 Beacon St Brookline MA (02446) ***(G-9226)***
Zephyr Designs Ltd....802 254-2788
129 Main St Brattleboro VT (05301) ***(G-21755)***
Zephyr Lock LLC....866 937-4971
30 Pecks Ln Newtown CT (06470) ***(G-2950)***
Zephyr Press, Brookline *Also called Aspect Inc* ***(G-9194)***
Zepkas Antigues....413 782-2964
121 Wildwood Ave Springfield MA (01118) ***(G-15530)***
Zerious Electronic Pubg Corp....978 922-4990
93 Park St Ste 1 Beverly MA (01915) ***(G-8201)***
Zero Balla....978 735-2015
67 Payne St Lowell MA (01851) ***(G-12451)***
Zero Check LLC....860 283-5629
297 Reynolds Bridge Rd Thomaston CT (06787) ***(G-4529)***
Zero Discharge....413 593-5470
2096 Westover Rd Chicopee MA (01022) ***(G-10071)***
Zero Hazard LLC....860 561-9879
38 Pembroke Hl Farmington CT (06032) ***(G-1524)***
Zero Porosity Casting Inc....781 373-1951
411 Waverley Oaks Rd Waltham MA (02452) ***(G-16226)***
Zeus Packing Inc....978 281-6900
27 Harbor Loop 29 Gloucester MA (01930) ***(G-11221)***
Zexen Technology LLC....508 786-9928
238 Cherry St Ste C Shrewsbury MA (01545) ***(G-15138)***
ZF Active Safety & Elec US LLC....978 874-0151
180 State Rd E Westminster MA (01473) ***(G-16821)***
Zhang Fengling....978 289-8606
20 Main St Acton MA (01720) ***(G-7395)***
Zibra Corporation....508 636-6606
640 American Legion Hwy Westport MA (02790) ***(G-16853)***
Ziemke Glass Blowing Studio....802 244-6126
3033 Rte 100 N Waterbury Center VT (05677) ***(G-22594)***
Ziga Media LLC....203 656-0076
5 Overbrook Ln Darien CT (06820) ***(G-1037)***
Ziggy Woodworking....781 335-5218
60 Charles St East Weymouth MA (02189) ***(G-10547)***
Zillion Group Inc....203 810-5400
501 Merritt 7 Norwalk CT (06851) ***(G-3275)***
Zingon LLC....716 491-0000
100 Exchange St Unit 1207 Providence RI (02903) ***(G-21159)***
Zinn Graphics Inc....802 254-6742
1012 Western Ave Brattleboro VT (05301) ***(G-21756)***
Ziopharm Oncology Inc....617 259-1970
1 1st Ave Charlestown MA (02129) ***(G-9845)***
Ziprint Centers Inc....781 963-2250
217 N Main St Randolph MA (02368) ***(G-14703)***
Zipwall LLC (PA)....781 648-8808
37 Broadway Ste 2 Arlington MA (02474) ***(G-7642)***
Zlink Inc....978 309-3628
141 Parker St Ste 311 Maynard MA (01754) ***(G-12907)***
Zmetra Clarspan Structures LLC....508 943-0940
2 Old Worcester Rd Webster MA (01570) ***(G-16355)***
Zoiray Technologies Inc....617 358-6003
8 Saint Marys St Ste 611 Boston MA (02215) ***(G-8942)***
Zolikon Inc....978 689-4789
55 Chase St Ste 17 Methuen MA (01844) ***(G-13049)***
Zolin Technologies Inc....978 794-4300
300 Canal St Bldg 12nd Lawrence MA (01840) ***(G-12086)***
Zoll Medical, Pawtucket *Also called Bio-Detek Incorporated* ***(G-20816)***
Zoll Medical Corporation (HQ)....978 421-9655
269 Mill Rd Chelmsford MA (01824) ***(G-9942)***
Zone & Co Sftwr Consulting LLC....617 307-7068
800 Boylston St Fl 16 Boston MA (02199) ***(G-8943)***
Zoneup Inc....802 868-2300
2396 Highgate Rd Saint Albans VT (05478) ***(G-22385)***
Zoom Information LLC (HQ)....781 693-7500
170 Data Dr Waltham MA (02451) ***(G-16227)***
Zoom Telephonics Inc (PA)....617 423-1072
99 High St Ste 2801 Boston MA (02110) ***(G-8944)***
Zoran Corporation....408 523-6500
1 Wall St Ste 10 Burlington MA (01803) ***(G-9358)***
Zp Couture LLC....888 697-7239
410 State St Rm 6 North Haven CT (06473) ***(G-3070)***
Zrc Worldwide, Marshfield *Also called Norfolk Corporation* ***(G-12864)***
Zuckerman Hrpsichords Intl LLC....860 535-1715
65 Cutler St Stonington CT (06378) ***(G-4379)***
Zuerner Design LLC....401 324-9490
376 Dry Bridge Rd G3 North Kingstown RI (02852) ***(G-20750)***
Zuse Inc....203 458-3295
727 Boston Post Rd Ste 1 Guilford CT (06437) ***(G-1725)***
Zycal Bioceuticals Mfg LLC....888 779-9225
3 Turning Leaf Cir Shrewsbury MA (01545) ***(G-15139)***
Zygo Corporation (HQ)....860 347-8506
21 Laurel Brook Rd Middlefield CT (06455) ***(G-2169)***
Zygo Corporation....508 541-1268
13 Main St Franklin MA (02038) ***(G-11101)***
Zyno Medical LLC....508 650-2008
177 Pine St Natick MA (01760) ***(G-13288)***

PRODUCT INDEX

• **Product categories are listed in alphabetical order.**

INDEX

B

C

D

E

F

G

H

J

K

L

M

INDEX

Q

R

S

T

U

V

W

X

Y

PRODUCT SECTION

4-digit SIC number & description

HQ=Headquarters
DH=Division Headquarters
PA=Parent Company

2033 Canned Fruits, Vegetables & Preserves

Blount Seafood Corporation	Warren	RI	D	401 245-8800	22984
Gerardo Gourmet Frz Foods Corp	Agawam	MA	E	413 737-0183	8378
Cathay Food Corp (HQ)	Boston	MA	F	617 427-1507	9350

Employment codes
A = Over 500 employees
B = 251-500 C = 101-250
D = 51-100 E = 20-50
F = 10-19 G = 3-9

Alpha Section entry number where full company information appears.

Business phone

See footnotes for symbols and codes identification.

- The SIC codes in this section are from the latest Standard Industrial Classification manual published by the U.S. Government's Office of Management and Budget. For more information regarding SICs, see the Explanatory Notes.
- Companies may be listed under multiple classifications.

ABRASIVES

	CITY	ST	EMP	PHONE	ENTRY #
Ahlstrom-Munksjo Nonwovens LLC **(DH)**	Windsor Locks	CT	B	860 654-8300	5382
Chessco Industries Inc **(PA)**	Westport	CT	E	203 255-2804	5183
Pressure Blast Mfg Co Inc	South Windsor	CT	F	800 722-5278	4004
Tcg Green Technologies Inc	Sharon	CT	F	860 364-4694	3770
3M Company	Haverhill	MA	G	978 420-0001	11403
Chas G Allen Realty LLC	Barre	MA	D	978 355-2911	7950
Diamond Plated Technology Inc	Taunton	MA	G	508 823-2711	15743
Ewm Corp **(PA)**	Middleton	MA	G	978 774-1191	13088
Mosher Company Inc	Chicopee	MA	F	413 598-8341	10047
New England Abrasives	Holliston	MA	G	508 893-9540	11589
Olsen & Silk Abrasives	Salem	MA	G	978 744-4720	14933
Saint-Gobain Ceramics Plas Inc	Worcester	MA	D	508 795-5000	17465
Vogel Capital Inc **(HQ)**	Marlborough	MA	E	508 481-5944	12846
Best Machine Inc	Fremont	NH	G	603 895-4018	18174
Johnson Abrasives Co Inc	Jaffrey	NH	E	603 532-4434	18469
Peg Kearsarge Co Inc	Bartlett	NH	G	603 374-2341	17627
RP Abrasives & Machine Inc	Rochester	NH	F	603 335-2132	19685
Bates Abrasive Products Inc	Lincoln	RI	E	773 586-8700	20558
Marvel Abrasives Products LLC	Lincoln	RI	F	800 621-0673	20582
Meister Abrasives Usa Inc	North Kingstown	RI	F	401 294-4503	20727
Dessureau Machines Inc	Barre	VT	F	802 476-4561	21613

ABRASIVES: Artificial

Triatic Incorporated	West Hartford	CT	F	860 236-2298	5099

ABRASIVES: Coated

Precision Dip Coating LLC	Waterbury	CT	G	203 805-4564	4943
General Abrasives Inc	Sharon	VT	F	802 763-7264	22409

ABRASIVES: Grains

Micro Abrasives Corporation	Westfield	MA	E	413 562-3641	16704
Washington Mills N Grafton Inc **(HQ)**	North Grafton	MA	D	508 839-6511	13968

ABRASIVES: Synthetic

Eastwind Lapidary Inc	Windsor	VT	G	802 674-5427	22707

ACCELERATION INDICATORS & SYSTEM COMPONENTS: Aerospace

Accuturn Mfg Co LLC	South Windsor	CT	F	860 289-6355	3931
Carl Perry	Middletown	CT	G	860 834-4459	2181
Eaton Aerospace LLC	Bethel	CT	E	203 796-6000	150
Hermtech Inc	East Windsor	CT	G	860 758-7528	1285
Kaman Corporation	Middletown	CT	C	860 632-1000	2196
Kaman Precision Products Inc	Middletown	CT	E	860 632-1000	2197
Saf Industries LLC **(HQ)**	Meriden	CT	E	203 729-4900	2128
Parts Tool and Die Inc	Agawam	MA	E	413 821-9718	7445
Hunting Dearborn Inc	Fryeburg	ME	C	207 935-2171	6099
ARC Technology Solutions LLC	Nashua	NH	E	603 883-3027	19117

ACCELEROMETERS

Whoop Inc	Boston	MA	F	617 670-1074	8927

ACIDS

Chute Chemical Agency	Houlton	ME	G	207 532-4370	6204

ACIDS: Hydrofluoric

New Haven Chlor-Alkali LLC	New Haven	CT	D	203 772-3350	2714

ACIDS: Inorganic

Metamorphic Materials Inc	Winsted	CT	F	860 738-8638	5417

ACIDS: Sulfuric, Oleum

Veolia NA Regeneration Srvcs **(DH)**	Boston	MA	G	312 552-2800	8906

ACOUSTICAL BOARD & TILE

Eckel Industries Inc **(PA)**	Ayer	MA	F	978 772-0840	7917

ACRYLIC RESINS

Pinnacle Polymers LLC	Ridgefield	CT	G	203 313-4116	3677
Optical Polymers Lab Corp	Pawtucket	RI	F	401 722-0710	20870

ACTUATORS: Indl, NEC

Hamilton Sundstrand Corp **(HQ)**	Windsor Locks	CT	A	860 654-6000	5397
Asahi/America Inc **(HQ)**	Lawrence	MA	C	781 321-5409	11995
Rexa Inc	West Bridgewater	MA	D	508 584-1199	16451

ADDITIVE BASED PLASTIC MATERIALS: Plasticizers

	CITY	ST	EMP	PHONE	ENTRY #
Gxt Green Inc	Billerica	MA	E	978 735-4367	8253
Image Polymers Company **(DH)**	Wakefield	MA	G	978 296-0194	15955

ADHESIVES

Advanced Adhesive Systems Inc	Newington	CT	E	860 953-4100	2838
Apcm Manufacturing LLC	Plainfield	CT	G	860 564-7817	3448
Converting McHy Adhesives LLC	Newington	CT	G	860 561-0226	2856
Ctech Adhesives	New Hartford	CT	G	860 482-5947	2634
Edison Coatings Inc	Plainville	CT	F	860 747-2220	3484
Henkel Loctite Corporation **(DH)**	Rocky Hill	CT	E	860 571-5100	3714
Henkel of America Inc **(HQ)**	Rocky Hill	CT	B	860 571-5100	3715
Henkel US Operations Corp **(DH)**	Rocky Hill	CT	B	860 571-5100	3716
Hexcel Corporation **(PA)**	Stamford	CT	E	203 969-0666	4213
Permatex Inc **(PA)**	Hartford	CT	E	860 543-7500	1856
Shurtape Specialty Coating LLC **(DH)**	New Hartford	CT	E	860 738-2600	2648
3M Company	Rockland	MA	F	781 871-1400	14788
Adhesive Applications Inc	Easthampton	MA	G	413 527-7120	10552
Adhesive Applications Inc	Easthampton	MA	E	413 527-7120	10553
Aerospace Adhsive Bonding Tech	Chicopee	MA	G	413 315-9349	9997
Allcoat Technology Inc	Wilmington	MA	E	978 988-0880	16971
American Adhesive Coatings LLC **(PA)**	Lawrence	MA	E	978 688-7400	11992
AP Plastics LLC	Peabody	MA	G	800 222-1117	14313
Bacon Industries Inc	Wrentham	MA	F	508 384-0780	17515
Bemis Associates Inc **(PA)**	Shirley	MA	C	978 425-6761	15081
Bemis Associates Inc	Shirley	MA	C	978 425-6761	15082
Bostik Inc	Middleton	MA	C	978 777-0100	13085
Coatings Adhesives Inks	Georgetown	MA	E	978 352-7273	11140
Creative Materials Inc	Ayer	MA	F	978 391-4700	7916
Diemat Inc	Byfield	MA	F	978 499-0900	9362
Elite Adhesives LLC	Haverhill	MA	G	978 852-8269	11431
FDM Adhesives LLC	Haverhill	MA	G	978 423-3553	11433
Flexcon Company Inc **(PA)**	Spencer	MA	A	508 885-8200	15429
Functional Coatings LLC	Newburyport	MA	D	978 462-0746	13493
Innovative Chem Pdts Group LLC **(PA)**	Andover	MA	E	978 623-9980	7558
ITW Devcon Inc	Danvers	MA	E	978 777-1100	10227
Key Polymer Holdings LLC	Lawrence	MA	E	978 683-9411	12043
L H C Inc **(PA)**	Lynn	MA	E	781 592-6444	12520
Mace Adhesives Coatings Co Inc	Dudley	MA	E	508 943-9052	10380
Olympic Adhesives Inc **(PA)**	Norwood	MA	E	800 829-1871	14186
Resin Designs LLC **(HQ)**	Woburn	MA	E	781 935-3133	17284
Saint-Gobain Corporation	Northborough	MA	E	508 351-7112	14047
Synthetic Surfaces Inc	Lynn	MA	F	781 593-0860	12542
Tyco Adhesives	Franklin	MA	G	508 918-1600	11094
Xl Adhesives North LLC	Fall River	MA	G	508 675-0528	10786
Exact Dispensing Systems	Newcastle	ME	G	207 563-2299	6482
Adhesive Innovations LLC	Dover	NH	G	877 589-0544	18003
Bond Adhesives & Coatings Corp	Seabrook	NH	G	603 474-3811	19795
Protavic America Inc	Londonderry	NH	G	603 623-8624	18733
Wf Holdings Inc **(PA)**	Nashua	NH	G	603 888-5443	19285
Worthen Industries Inc **(HQ)**	Nashua	NH	D	603 888-5443	19288
Worthen Industries Inc	Nashua	NH	F	603 886-0973	19289
Atom Adhesives	Providence	RI	G	401 413-9902	20962
Brandywine Materials LLC	Woonsocket	RI	G	781 281-2746	21553
Fri Resins Holding Company	Cranston	RI	F	401 946-5564	20228
Jmt Epoxy	Cranston	RI	G	401 331-9730	20245
Morton International LLC	Providence	RI	G	401 274-7258	21072
Mylan Technologies Inc **(DH)**	Saint Albans	VT	C	802 527-7792	22373

ADHESIVES & SEALANTS

Chessco Industries Inc **(PA)**	Westport	CT	E	203 255-2804	5183
Cunningham Tech LLC **(PA)**	New Hartford	CT	G	860 738-8759	2635
Five Star Products Inc	Shelton	CT	E	203 336-7900	3802
Incure Inc	New Britain	CT	G	860 748-2979	2540
Metamorphic Materials Inc	Winsted	CT	F	860 738-8638	5417
Panacol-Usa Inc	Torrington	CT	F	860 738-7449	4592
S & S Sealcoating LLC	Wallingford	CT	G	203 284-0054	4804
Vanderbilt Chemicals LLC	Bethel	CT	E	203 744-3900	189
Xg Industries LLC	Stratford	CT	F	475 282-4643	4459
3M Company	Haverhill	MA	G	978 420-0001	11403
Acton Research Corporation	Acton	MA	E	941 556-2601	7334
C L Hauthaway & Sons Corp	Lynn	MA	E	781 592-6444	12495
Falmer	Lynn	MA	G	781 593-0088	12507

	CITY	ST	EMP	PHONE	ENTRY #
Illinois Tool Works Inc	Danvers	MA	E	978 777-1100	10225
Illinois Tool Works Inc	Rockland	MA	D	781 878-7015	14808
Mussel Bound LLC	Brewster	MA	G	774 212-5488	9054
Ngac LLC	Burlington	MA	E	781 258-0008	9309
Parker-Hannifin Corporation	Woburn	MA	B	781 935-4850	17257
Stahl (usa) Inc **(DH)**	Peabody	MA	E	978 968-1382	14372
Standard Rubber Products Inc	Hanover	MA	E	781 878-2626	11353
Transene Company Inc	Danvers	MA	F	978 777-7860	10265
Tulco Inc	Ayer	MA	G	978 772-4412	7941
Union Specialties Inc	Newburyport	MA	E	978 465-1717	13546
Winfield Brooks Company Inc	Woburn	MA	F	781 933-5300	17323
Adhesive Engineering & Supply	Seabrook	NH	G	603 895-4028	19790
Aqua Tite Innovative Solutions	Hampton	NH	G	603 431-5555	18254
Hampshire Chemical Corp **(DH)**	Nashua	NH	E	603 888-2320	19176
Henkel Locktite	Seabrook	NH	G	603 474-5541	19805
Ipn Industries Inc	Londonderry	NH	G	603 623-8626	18705
Royal Adhesives & Sealants LLC	Raymond	NH	G	860 788-3380	19644
Schul International Co Inc	Hudson	NH	G	603 889-6872	18367
Trellborg Pipe Sals Mlford Inc **(DH)**	Milford	NH	C	800 626-2180	19080
All Star Adhesive Products	Warren	RI	G	401 247-1866	21283
Epoxies Inc	Cranston	RI	F	401 946-5564	20219
Gurit (usa) Inc	Bristol	RI	E	401 396-5008	20083

ADHESIVES: Adhesives, plastic

	CITY	ST	EMP	PHONE	ENTRY #
Indusol Inc	Sutton	MA	E	508 865-9516	15683
Polymer Technologies LLC	Nashua	NH	G	603 883-4002	19235

ADHESIVES: Epoxy

	CITY	ST	EMP	PHONE	ENTRY #
Anchor-Seal Inc	Gloucester	MA	G	978 515-6004	11159
Arcor Epoxy Inc	Harwich	MA	F	508 385-5598	11388
Epoxy Technology Inc **(PA)**	Billerica	MA	E	978 667-3805	8248
Techfilm Services Inc	Peabody	MA	G	978 531-3300	14375
Enterprise Castings LLC	Lewiston	ME	G	207 782-5511	6288
Mereco Technologies Group Inc **(HQ)**	Londonderry	NH	E	401 822-9300	18720
Schul International Co LLC	Pelham	NH	F	603 889-6872	19446
Alfa International Corp	Woonsocket	RI	G	401 765-0503	21548

ADVERTISING AGENCIES

	CITY	ST	EMP	PHONE	ENTRY #
Automotive Coop Couponing Inc	Weston	CT	G	203 227-2722	5169
2 Cool Promos	Westborough	MA	G	508 351-9700	16583
Carnegie Communications LLC	Westford	MA	E	978 692-5092	16760
Carnegie Dartlet LLC **(PA)**	Westford	MA	G	978 692-5092	16761
Crain Communications Inc	Boston	MA	G	617 357-9090	8486
Madison Group Inc	Revere	MA	G	781 853-0029	14771
RMS Media Group Inc	Andover	MA	E	978 623-8020	7600
Ve Interactive LLC	Boston	MA	G	857 284-7000	8905
Vocero Hispano Newspaper Inc	Southbridge	MA	G	508 792-1942	15408
Printers Square Inc	Manchester	NH	F	603 623-0802	18905
Upper Valley Press Inc	North Haverhill	NH	D	603 787-7000	19391
Scarborough Faire Inc **(PA)**	Pawtucket	RI	E	401 724-4200	20897

ADVERTISING AGENCIES: Consultants

	CITY	ST	EMP	PHONE	ENTRY #
Applied Advertising Inc	Danbury	CT	F	860 640-0800	872
Venture Print Unlimited Inc	Plymouth	NH	F	603 536-2410	19531

ADVERTISING CURTAINS

	CITY	ST	EMP	PHONE	ENTRY #
Screencraft Tileworks LLC	Lincoln	RI	G	401 427-2816	20596

ADVERTISING DISPLAY PRDTS

	CITY	ST	EMP	PHONE	ENTRY #
Connecticut Components Inc	Tolland	CT	G	860 633-0277	4541
Tag Promotions Inc	Monroe	CT	G	800 909-4011	2417
Elite Sem Inc	Medfield	MA	G	508 955-0414	12914
Stran & Company Inc **(PA)**	Quincy	MA	E	617 822-6950	14660
Affordable Exhibit Displays	Auburn	ME	G	207 782-6175	5547
Scope Display & Box Co Inc **(PA)**	Cranston	RI	D	401 942-7150	20284

ADVERTISING MATERIAL DISTRIBUTION

	CITY	ST	EMP	PHONE	ENTRY #
Liberty Publishing Inc	Beverly	MA	E	978 777-8200	8148

ADVERTISING REPRESENTATIVES: Electronic Media

	CITY	ST	EMP	PHONE	ENTRY #
Ve Interactive LLC	Boston	MA	G	857 284-7000	8905

ADVERTISING REPRESENTATIVES: Magazine

	CITY	ST	EMP	PHONE	ENTRY #
Sixfurlongs LLC	Fairfield	CT	G	203 255-8553	1456

ADVERTISING REPRESENTATIVES: Media

	CITY	ST	EMP	PHONE	ENTRY #
Hearst Communications Inc	Worcester	MA	C	508 793-9100	17389

ADVERTISING REPRESENTATIVES: Newspaper

	CITY	ST	EMP	PHONE	ENTRY #
Eagle-Tribune Publishing Co	Haverhill	MA	E	978 374-0321	11430
Local Media Group Inc	New Bedford	MA	B	508 997-7411	13409
Vocero Hispano Newspaper Inc	Southbridge	MA	G	508 792-1942	15408
Northeast Publishing Company	Dover Foxcroft	ME	G	207 564-8355	5961
Two Old Broads	Machias	ME	G	207 255-6561	6396
North Eastern Publishing Co	Bennington	VT	E	802 447-7567	21686
Springfield Reporter Inc	Springfield	VT	G	802 885-2246	22509

ADVERTISING REPRESENTATIVES: Radio

	CITY	ST	EMP	PHONE	ENTRY #
Iheartcommunications Inc	Colchester	VT	E	802 655-0093	21866

ADVERTISING SPECIALTIES, WHOLESALE

	CITY	ST	EMP	PHONE	ENTRY #
McWeeney Marketing Group Inc	Orange	CT	G	203 891-8100	3373
R & B Apparel Plus LLC	Groton	CT	G	860 333-1757	1685
2 Cool Promos	Westborough	MA	G	508 351-9700	16583
Ad-A-Day Company Inc	Taunton	MA	E	508 824-8676	15719
Color Media Group LLC	Boston	MA	F	617 620-0229	8480
Elite Sem Inc	Medfield	MA	G	508 955-0414	12914
George Guertin Trophy Inc	Auburn	MA	G	508 832-4001	7836
Heritage Press Inc	Sandwich	MA	G	508 888-2111	14969
Shawmut Advertising Inc **(PA)**	Danvers	MA	E	978 762-7500	10255
E Print Inc	Hudson	NH	G	603 594-0009	18388
Powerplay Management LLC	Portsmouth	NH	E	603 436-3030	19609

ADVERTISING SVCS: Direct Mail

	CITY	ST	EMP	PHONE	ENTRY #
Automotive Coop Couponing Inc	Weston	CT	G	203 227-2722	5169
L P Macadams Company Inc	Bridgeport	CT	D	203 366-3647	442
Life Study Fllwship Foundation	Darien	CT	E	203 655-1436	1028
R R Donnelley & Sons Company	Manchester	CT	F	860 649-5570	2040
Transmonde USa Inc	North Branford	CT	D	203 484-1528	2982
Billard Corporation	Sandwich	MA	G	508 888-4964	14961
Carnegie Communications LLC	Westford	MA	E	978 692-5092	16760
Carnegie Dartlet LLC **(PA)**	Westford	MA	G	978 692-5092	16761
Communication Ink Inc	Peabody	MA	F	978 977-4595	14324
Owl Stamp Company Inc	Lowell	MA	G	978 452-4541	12418
Quad/Graphics Inc	East Longmeadow	MA	C	413 525-8552	10490
Rivkind Associates Inc **(PA)**	South Easton	MA	F	781 269-2415	15291
Shawmut Advertising Inc **(PA)**	Danvers	MA	E	978 762-7500	10255
Tom Snyder Productions Inc **(HQ)**	Watertown	MA	D	617 600-2145	16324
Turner Publishing Inc	Turner	ME	F	207 225-2076	7111
Puritan Press Inc **(PA)**	Hollis	NH	E	603 889-4500	18339
ABS Printing Inc	West Warwick	RI	G	401 826-0870	21475
Villanti & Sons Printers Inc	Milton	VT	D	802 864-0723	22140

ADVERTISING SVCS: Display

	CITY	ST	EMP	PHONE	ENTRY #
Resavue Inc	Orange	CT	F	203 878-0944	3381
Valley Container Inc	Bridgeport	CT	E	203 368-6546	503
Carnegie Communications LLC	Westford	MA	E	978 692-5092	16760
Carnegie Dartlet LLC **(PA)**	Westford	MA	G	978 692-5092	16761
Reid Publication Inc	Portsmouth	NH	G	603 433-2200	19614
Parsonskellogg LLC	East Providence	RI	E	401 438-0650	20439

ADVERTISING SVCS: Outdoor

	CITY	ST	EMP	PHONE	ENTRY #
Lane Printing Co Inc	Holbrook	MA	F	781 767-4450	11529
Dales Paint n Place Inc	Newport	NH	G	603 863-5050	19344

ADVERTISING SVCS: Transit

	CITY	ST	EMP	PHONE	ENTRY #
Applied Advertising Inc	Danbury	CT	F	860 640-0800	872

AERIAL WORK PLATFORMS

	CITY	ST	EMP	PHONE	ENTRY #
Capewell Aerial Systems LLC **(PA)**	South Windsor	CT	D	860 610-0700	3947

AEROSOLS

	CITY	ST	EMP	PHONE	ENTRY #
M J Gordon Company Inc	Pittsfield	MA	G	413 448-6066	14487
Shield Packaging Co Inc	Dudley	MA	D	508 949-0900	10384

AGRICULTURAL DISINFECTANTS

	CITY	ST	EMP	PHONE	ENTRY #
Healthy Harvest Inc	Madison	CT	G	203 245-3786	1963

AGRICULTURAL EQPT: BARN, SILO, POULTRY, DAIRY/LIVESTOCK MACH

	CITY	ST	EMP	PHONE	ENTRY #
American Calan Inc	Northwood	NH	G	603 942-7711	19410
Feed Commodities Intl Inc	Newport	VT	G	802 334-2942	22197
Heritage Post & Beam	Barre	VT	F	802 223-6319	21621

AGRICULTURAL EQPT: Fertilizng, Sprayng, Dustng/Irrigatn Mach

	CITY	ST	EMP	PHONE	ENTRY #
Hayden Manufacturing Co Inc	West Wareham	MA	G	508 295-0497	16574

AGRICULTURAL EQPT: Grade, Clean & Sort Machines, Fruit/Veg

	CITY	ST	EMP	PHONE	ENTRY #
Harold Haines Inc	Presque Isle	ME	F	207 762-1411	6758

AGRICULTURAL EQPT: Haying Mach, Mowers, Rakes, Stackers, Etc

	CITY	ST	EMP	PHONE	ENTRY #
Hubbard Rake Co	Jonesport	ME	G	207 497-5949	6226

AGRICULTURAL EQPT: Irrigation Eqpt, Self-Propelled

	CITY	ST	EMP	PHONE	ENTRY #
Larchmont Engineering Inc	Manchester	NH	G	603 622-8825	18860

AGRICULTURAL EQPT: Spreaders, Fertilizer

	CITY	ST	EMP	PHONE	ENTRY #
Grassroots of New England	Cumberland	RI	G	401 333-1963	20323

AGRICULTURAL LIMESTONE: Ground

	CITY	ST	EMP	PHONE	ENTRY #
Allyndale Corporation	East Canaan	CT	F	860 824-7959	1111

AIR CLEANING SYSTEMS

	CITY	ST	EMP	PHONE	ENTRY #
Novaerus US Inc **(PA)**	Stamford	CT	F	813 304-2468	4262
Nq Industries Inc	Rocky Hill	CT	G	860 258-3466	3725
Planet Technologies Inc	Ridgefield	CT	F	800 255-3749	3678
Weld Engineering Co Inc	Shrewsbury	MA	E	508 842-2224	15137

AIR CONDITIONERS, AUTOMOTIVE: Wholesalers

	CITY	ST	EMP	PHONE	ENTRY #
Koda Industries Indiana LLC	Waltham	MA	D	781 891-3066	16140

AIR CONDITIONERS: Motor Vehicle

	CITY	ST	EMP	PHONE	ENTRY #
Koda Industries Indiana LLC	Waltham	MA	D	781 891-3066	16140

AIR CONDITIONING & VENTILATION EQPT & SPLYS: Wholesales

	CITY	ST	EMP	PHONE	ENTRY #
Outland Engineering Inc	Milford	CT	F	800 797-3709	2329

AIR CONDITIONING EQPT

	CITY	ST	EMP	PHONE	ENTRY #
Alvest (usa) Inc **(HQ)**	Windsor	CT	E	860 602-3400	5320
Carrier Corporation	Farmington	CT	G	860 728-7000	1471
Dp2 LLC Head	Darien	CT	F	203 655-0747	1022
Engineered Assembly & Services	Marshfield	MA	G	781 834-9085	12860
Northeast Twr Svc	Uxbridge	MA	G	508 533-1620	15927
Maine Market Refrigeration LLC **(PA)**	Fayette	ME	E	207 685-3504	6055

AIR CONDITIONING EQPT, WHOLE HOUSE: Wholesalers

	CITY	ST	EMP	PHONE	ENTRY #
Total Air Supply Inc	Nashua	NH	E	603 889-0100	19274

AIR CONDITIONING REPAIR SVCS

	CITY	ST	EMP	PHONE	ENTRY #
Tecogen Inc **(PA)**	Waltham	MA	E	781 622-1120	16207

AIR CONDITIONING UNITS: Complete, Domestic Or Indl

	CITY	ST	EMP	PHONE	ENTRY #
Dasco Supply LLC	Stamford	CT	G	203 388-0095	4185
Nanocap Technologies LLC **(PA)**	Hartford	CT	G	860 521-9743	1849
Trane Inc	Norwalk	CT	D	203 866-7115	3261
Tecogen Inc **(PA)**	Waltham	MA	E	781 622-1120	16207

AIR COOLERS: Metal Plate

	CITY	ST	EMP	PHONE	ENTRY #
Mastercraft Tool and Mch Co	Southington	CT	F	860 628-5551	4064
Tracs Chillers LLC	Ossipee	NH	G	603 707-2241	19423

AIR CURTAINS

	CITY	ST	EMP	PHONE	ENTRY #
Air Control Industries Inc	Windsor	ME	G	207 445-2518	7262

AIR MATTRESSES: Plastic

	CITY	ST	EMP	PHONE	ENTRY #
E F Inc	Gardner	MA	F	978 630-3800	11113

AIR PURIFICATION EQPT

	CITY	ST	EMP	PHONE	ENTRY #
Clean Air Group Inc	Fairfield	CT	E	203 335-3700	1420
Treadwell Corporation	Thomaston	CT	E	860 283-7600	4522
Koch Separation Solutions Inc **(DH)**	Wilmington	MA	C	978 694-7000	17013
Vacuum Technology Inc	Gloucester	MA	G	510 333-6562	11216
Pollution Research & Dev Corp **(PA)**	Newport	NH	F	603 863-7553	19353

AIRCRAFT & AEROSPACE FLIGHT INSTRUMENTS & GUIDANCE SYSTEMS

	CITY	ST	EMP	PHONE	ENTRY #
Higgs Energy LLC	Norwich	CT	G	860 213-5561	3282
Msj Investments Inc	Stafford Springs	CT	F	860 684-9956	4113
Adcole Corporation **(HQ)**	Marlborough	MA	C	508 485-9100	12710
Altair Avionics Corporation	Norwood	MA	E	781 762-8600	14125
Ametek Arospc Pwr Holdings Inc **(HQ)**	Wilmington	MA	C	978 988-4771	16974
Craig AAR	North Andover	MA	G	978 691-0024	13696
General Dynamics Corporation	Pittsfield	MA	G	413 494-2313	14470
Spike Aerospace Inc	Boston	MA	F	617 338-1400	8858
Aero Defense International LLC	Manchester	NH	G	603 644-0305	18773
Allard Nazarian Group Inc **(PA)**	Manchester	NH	C	603 668-1900	18774
Allard Nazarian Group Inc	Manchester	NH	F	603 314-0017	18775
American Ir Solutions LLC	Hudson	NH	G	662 626-2477	18373
Lewis and Saunders	Laconia	NH	G	603 528-1871	18574
Kearflex Engineering Company	Warwick	RI	F	401 781-4900	21382
BF Goodrich Aerspce Aircrft In	Vergennes	VT	G	802 877-2911	22552
Liquid Measurement Systems Inc	Milton	VT	E	802 528-8100	22133

AIRCRAFT & HEAVY EQPT REPAIR SVCS

	CITY	ST	EMP	PHONE	ENTRY #
Doncasters Inc **(HQ)**	Groton	CT	D	860 449-1603	1671
Sign Maintenance Service Co	Bridgeport	CT	G	203 336-1051	489
Skico Manufacturing Co LLC	Hamden	CT	G	203 230-1305	1784
Ricks Truck & Trailer Repair	Hillsborough	NH	G	603 464-3636	18318

AIRCRAFT ASSEMBLY PLANTS

	CITY	ST	EMP	PHONE	ENTRY #
Amco Precision Tools Inc **(PA)**	Berlin	CT	E	860 828-5640	70
Avolon Aerospace New York Inc	Stamford	CT	G	203 663-5490	4146
Edac Nd Inc	Glastonbury	CT	D	860 633-9474	1548
Embraer Executive Jet Svcs LLC	Windsor Locks	CT	G	860 804-4600	5392
Gulfstream Aerospace Corp	New Milford	CT	G	860 210-1469	2803
Gulfstream Aerospace Corp	East Granby	CT	G	912 965-3000	1129
Hartford Jet Center LLC	Hartford	CT	G	860 548-9334	1835
Kaman Aerospace Corporation **(DH)**	Bloomfield	CT	A	860 242-4461	230
Kaman Aerospace Corporation	Bloomfield	CT	D	860 242-4461	232
Kaman Aerospace Group Inc **(HQ)**	Bloomfield	CT	F	860 243-7100	233
MB Aerospace	East Granby	CT	G	860 653-0569	1133
New England Airfoil Pdts Inc	Farmington	CT	E	860 677-1376	1498
Santoto LLC	Danbury	CT	G	203 984-2540	983
Sikorsky Aircraft Corporation	North Haven	CT	F	516 228-2000	3062
Sikorsky Aircraft Corporation	Bridgeport	CT	C	203 386-4000	491
Stonegate Capital Group	Hartford	CT	G	860 899-1181	1873
Target Marketing Assoc Inc	Rocky Hill	CT	G	860 571-7294	3730
Textron Aviation Inc	Oxford	CT	A	203 262-9366	3427
United Technologies Corp **(PA)**	Farmington	CT	B	860 728-7000	1522
Aerovironment Inc	Burlington	MA	E	805 520-8350	9230
Arise Air Inc	Plympton	MA	E	888 359-2747	14590
Ascent Aerosystems LLC	Tewksbury	MA	G	330 554-6334	15806
Aurora Flight Sciences Corp	Cambridge	MA	F	617 500-4800	9397
C & H Air Inc	Plymouth	MA	G	508 746-5511	14546
Goodrich Corporation	Westford	MA	F	978 303-6700	16770
Gulfstream Aerospace Corp	Westfield	MA	E	413 562-5866	16686
Legion Flying Club Inc	Granby	MA	G	413 467-7844	11229
Liquiglide Inc	Cambridge	MA	E	617 901-0700	9538
Plane Fantasy	Chestnut Hill	MA	G	617 734-4950	9990
Terrafugia Inc	Woburn	MA	F	781 491-0812	17307
Wingbrace LLC	Hingham	MA	G	617 480-8737	11518
Sonic Blue Aerospace Inc	Portland	ME	G	207 776-2471	6733
Lagasse & Lewis LLC	Plaistow	NH	G	603 382-5898	19519
Mercury Systems Inc	Hudson	NH	G	203 792-7474	18366
Uav - America Inc	Nottingham	NH	G	603 389-6364	19418
Lockheed Martin Global Inc	Middletown	RI	F	401 849-3703	20625
Textron Inc **(PA)**	Providence	RI	B	401 421-2800	21134

AIRCRAFT CONTROL SYSTEMS:

	CITY	ST	EMP	PHONE	ENTRY #
Triumph Eng Ctrl Systems LLC	West Hartford	CT	F	860 236-0651	5101
Triumph Eng Ctrl Systems LLC	West Hartford	CT	A	860 236-0651	5100

AIRCRAFT CONTROL SYSTEMS: Electronic Totalizing Counters

	CITY	ST	EMP	PHONE	ENTRY #
Dynamic Controls Hs Inc	Windsor Locks	CT	G	860 654-6000	5391

AIRCRAFT DEALERS

	CITY	ST	EMP	PHONE	ENTRY #
Sikorsky Aircraft Corporation **(HQ)**	Stratford	CT	A	203 386-4000	4444

AIRCRAFT ELECTRICAL EQPT REPAIR SVCS

	CITY	ST	EMP	PHONE	ENTRY #
Electro-Methods Inc **(PA)**	South Windsor	CT	C	860 289-8661	3962

AIRCRAFT ENGINES & ENGINE PARTS: Airfoils

	CITY	ST	EMP	PHONE	ENTRY #
General Electric Company **(PA)**	Boston	MA	A	617 443-3000	8558

AIRCRAFT ENGINES & ENGINE PARTS: Cooling Systems

	CITY	ST	EMP	PHONE	ENTRY #
Evans Cooling Systems Inc **(PA)**	Suffield	CT	G	860 668-1114	4462

AIRCRAFT ENGINES & ENGINE PARTS: Mount Parts

	CITY	ST	EMP	PHONE	ENTRY #
Bolducs Machine Works Inc	North Windham	CT	G	860 455-1232	3078
Precision Components Group	West Springfield	MA	G	413 333-4184	16547
Pratt & Whitney Engine Svcs	North Berwick	ME	B	207 676-4100	6510

AIRCRAFT ENGINES & ENGINE PARTS: Pumps

	CITY	ST	EMP	PHONE	ENTRY #
Columbia Manufacturing Inc	Columbia	CT	D	860 228-2259	817
Northeast Fuel Systems LLC	Merrimack	NH	G	603 365-4103	19017

AIRCRAFT ENGINES & ENGINE PARTS: Research & Development, Mfr

	CITY	ST	EMP	PHONE	ENTRY #
Pratt & Whitney Eng Svcs Inc	East Hartford	CT	C	860 610-2631	1213
Fountain Plating Company Inc	West Springfield	MA	D	413 781-4651	16521
General Electric Company	Westborough	MA	F	508 870-5200	16619

AIRCRAFT ENGINES & PARTS

	CITY	ST	EMP	PHONE	ENTRY #
A-1 Machining Co	New Britain	CT	D	860 223-6420	2501
Absolute Precision Co	Southbury	CT	G	203 767-9066	4021
Accupaulo Holding Corporation **(PA)**	Bristol	CT	E	860 666-5621	511
Acmt Inc	Manchester	CT	D	860 645-0592	1982
Aero Component Services LLC	East Hartford	CT	G	860 291-0417	1171
AGC Acquisition LLC	Meriden	CT	C	203 639-7125	2075
Alloy Specialties Incorporated	Manchester	CT	E	860 646-4587	1985
American Design & Mfg Inc	South Windsor	CT	E	860 282-2719	3935
American Unmanned Systems LLC	Stamford	CT	G	203 406-7611	4136
ATI Ladish Machining Inc **(DH)**	East Hartford	CT	D	860 688-3688	1174
ATI Ladish Machining Inc	South Windsor	CT	D	860 688-3688	3939
ATI Ladish Machining Inc	East Hartford	CT	D	860 688-3688	1175
Barnes Group Inc **(PA)**	Bristol	CT	B	860 583-7070	526
Barnes Group Inc	Windsor	CT	A	860 298-7740	5322
Barnes Group Inc	Bristol	CT	A	513 759-3503	528
Beacon Group Inc **(PA)**	Newington	CT	C	860 594-5200	2846
Birken Manufacturing Company	Bloomfield	CT	D	860 242-2211	209
Birotech Inc	Stamford	CT	G	203 968-5080	4150
Cambridge Specialty Co Inc	Berlin	CT	D	860 828-3579	80
CBS Manufacturing Company	East Granby	CT	E	860 653-8100	1120
Chromalloy Component Svcs Inc	Windsor	CT	C	860 688-7798	5325
Chromalloy Gas Turbine LLC	Windsor	CT	D	860 688-7798	5326
D & M Tool Company Inc	West Hartford	CT	G	860 236-6037	5064
Deburring House Inc	East Berlin	CT	E	860 828-0889	1098
Demusz Mfg Co Inc	East Hartford	CT	E	860 528-9845	1186
Drt Aerospace LLC	Meriden	CT	E	203 781-8020	2092
Dynamic Controls Hs Inc	Windsor Locks	CT	G	860 654-6000	5391
Edac Technologies LLC	East Windsor	CT	F	860 789-2511	1283
Edac Technologies LLC **(HQ)**	Cheshire	CT	C	203 806-2090	728
Electro-Methods Inc **(PA)**	South Windsor	CT	C	860 289-8661	3962
Electro-Methods Inc	South Windsor	CT	D	860 289-8661	3963
Engine Alliance LLC	Glastonbury	CT	B	860 565-2239	1550
First Aviation Services Inc **(PA)**	Westport	CT	G	203 291-3300	5192
First Equity Group Inc **(PA)**	Westport	CT	F	203 291-7700	5193
Fredericks Jf Aero LLC	Farmington	CT	D	860 677-2646	1483
GKN Aerospace Newington LLC	Newington	CT	G	800 667-8502	2866
GKN Aerospace Newington LLC **(DH)**	Newington	CT	C	860 667-8502	2867
GKN Arspace Svcs Strctures LLC	Cromwell	CT	C	860 613-0236	853
Global Trbine Cmpnent Tech LLC	South Windsor	CT	E	860 528-4722	3973
Honeywell International Inc	Northford	CT	D	203 484-7161	3087
Honeywell International Inc	Northford	CT	B	203 484-7161	3088
Honeywell International Inc	Northford	CT	B	203 484-6202	3089
Honeywell International Inc	North Branford	CT	A	203 484-7161	2967
Honeywell International Inc	Northford	CT	E	203 484-7161	3090
Horst Engrg De Mexico LLC	East Hartford	CT	E	860 289-8209	1199
Hsb Aircraft Components LLC	New Britain	CT	F	860 505-7349	2539
I & J Machine Tool Company	Milford	CT	F	203 877-5376	2298
Iae International Aero Engs AG	East Hartford	CT	C	860 565-1773	1201
International Aero Engines LLC	East Hartford	CT	E	860 565-5515	1203
Intlaero Beta Corp	East Hartford	CT	G	317 821-2000	1204
Kaman Aerospace Corporation	Bloomfield	CT	D	860 242-4461	232
Kaman Aerospace Group Inc **(HQ)**	Bloomfield	CT	F	860 243-7100	233
Kamatics Corporation **(DH)**	Bloomfield	CT	E	860 243-9704	235
Lighthouse International LLC	South Windsor	CT	E	860 528-4722	3990
Morning Star Tool LLC	Milford	CT	G	203 878-6026	2316
Msj Investments Inc	Stafford Springs	CT	F	860 684-9956	4113
N & B Manufacturing Co Inc	Newington	CT	G	860 667-3204	2885
New England Airfoil Pdts Inc	Farmington	CT	E	860 677-1376	1498
Numet Machining Techniques LLC	Orange	CT	E	203 375-4995	3376
Pdq Inc **(PA)**	Rocky Hill	CT	E	860 529-9051	3727
Pinnacle Aerospace Mfg LLC	Greenwich	CT	F	203 258-3398	1637
Point Machine Company	Berlin	CT	E	860 828-6901	102
Polar Corporation	New Britain	CT	E	860 223-7891	2564
Pratt & Whitney Company Inc **(HQ)**	East Hartford	CT	C	860 565-4321	1212
Pratt & Whitney Engine Svcs	North Haven	CT	B	203 934-2806	3053
Pratt & Whitney Engine Svcs	East Hartford	CT	E	860 565-4321	1214
Pratt & Whitney Engine Svcs	Middletown	CT	B	860 344-4000	2212
Pratt & Whitney Services Inc	East Hartford	CT	E	860 565-5489	1215

	CITY	ST	EMP	PHONE	ENTRY #
Precision Speed Mfg LLC	Middletown	CT	E	860 635-8811	2213
Saar Corporation	Farmington	CT	F	860 674-9440	1511
Schaefer Rolls Inc	Wolcott	CT	G	203 910-0224	5455
Sikorsky Aircraft Corporation	Stratford	CT	A	203 386-4000	4443
Simmonds Precision Pdts Inc	Danbury	CT	E	203 797-5000	994
Soto Holdings Inc	New Haven	CT	E	203 781-8020	2739
Spartan Aerospace LLC	Manchester	CT	D	860 533-7500	2049
Specialty Tool Company USA LLC	Milford	CT	F	203 874-2009	2366
Tdy Industries LLC	New Britain	CT	G	860 259-6346	2586
Timken Arospc Drv Systems LLC	Manchester	CT	C	860 649-0000	2055
Triumph Eng Ctrl Systems LLC	West Hartford	CT	A	860 236-0651	5100
Turbine Kinetics Inc	Glastonbury	CT	F	860 633-8520	1580
Turbine Technologies Inc **(PA)**	Farmington	CT	D	860 678-1642	1521
United Technologies Corp **(PA)**	Farmington	CT	B	860 728-7000	1522
United Technologies Corp	East Hartford	CT	G	860 565-4321	1233
United Technologies Corp	South Windsor	CT	B	860 727-2200	4018
United Technologies Corp	East Hartford	CT	D	860 565-4321	1235
United Technologies Corp	East Hartford	CT	G	860 565-4321	1236
United Tool and Die Company **(PA)**	West Hartford	CT	C	860 246-6531	5102
Wentworth Manufacturing LLC	New Britain	CT	G	860 205-6437	2589
Westbrook Products LLC	New Britain	CT	G	860 205-6437	2590
Winslow Automatics Inc	New Britain	CT	D	860 225-6321	2591
325 Silver Street Inc	Agawam	MA	E	413 789-1800	7415
Actronics Incorporated	Waltham	MA	F	781 890-7030	16024
Aero - Bond Corp	Springfield	MA	F	413 734-2224	15441
Ametek Arospc Pwr Holdings Inc **(HQ)**	Wilmington	MA	C	978 988-4771	16974
Curtil North America LLC	Pittsfield	MA	G	661 294-0030	14468
Enjet Aero Danvers LLC **(HQ)**	Danvers	MA	E	978 777-1980	10216
GE Aviation	Lynn	MA	E	513 552-3272	12510
General Electric Company	Lynn	MA	D	781 598-7303	12511
General Electric Company	Lynn	MA	A	781 594-0100	12512
Goodrich Corporation	Westford	MA	A	978 303-6700	16771
Honeywell International Inc	Canton	MA	A	781 298-2700	9740
Honeywell International Inc	Southborough	MA	C	508 490-7100	15361
Honeywell Robert Warner	Newburyport	MA	G	978 358-8080	13498
Hutchinson Arospc & Indust Inc **(DH)**	Hopkinton	MA	B	508 417-7000	11718
Jet Industries Inc	Agawam	MA	E	413 786-2010	7435
LKM Industries Inc	Woburn	MA	D	781 935-9210	17216
Magellan Arospc Haverhill Inc	Haverhill	MA	C	978 774-6000	11452
Materials Development Corp	Andover	MA	F	781 391-0400	7568
Mer+ge	Chestnut Hill	MA	G	512 665-2266	9987
Palmer Manufacturing Co Llc **(DH)**	Malden	MA	C	781 321-0480	12586
Palmer Manufacturing Co LLC	Peabody	MA	G	781 321-0480	14360
Paradigm Prcision Holdings LLC	Peabody	MA	F	978 278-7100	14361
Parker-Hannifin Corporation	Devens	MA	C	978 784-1200	10329
Sterling Machine Company Inc	Lynn	MA	E	781 593-3000	12541
Tell Tool Inc	Westfield	MA	D	413 568-1671	16732
Tell Tool Acquisition Inc **(HQ)**	Westfield	MA	G	413 568-1671	16733
Union Machine Company Lynn Inc **(PA)**	Groveland	MA	E	978 521-5100	11304
United Technologies Corp	Taunton	MA	B	508 942-8883	15795
Van Pelt Capital Precision Inc	Easthampton	MA	F	413 527-1204	10582
Wgi Inc	Southwick	MA	C	413 569-9444	15421
C&L Engine Solutions LLC	Bangor	ME	G	307 217-6050	5634
Honeywell International Inc	Yarmouth	ME	A	207 846-3350	7296
Tem Inc	Buxton	ME	E	207 929-8700	5861
Aeroweld Inc	Laconia	NH	F	603 524-8121	18553
General Electric Company	Hooksett	NH	A	603 666-8300	18351
GKN Aerospace New England Inc	Charlestown	NH	D	603 542-5135	17814
Pratt & Whitney	Londonderry	NH	G	800 742-5877	18731
Titeflex Corporation	Laconia	NH	F	603 524-2064	18589
Avco Corporation **(DH)**	Providence	RI	C	401 421-2800	20965
Honeywell International Inc	Smithfield	RI	C	401 757-2560	21231
Honeywell International Inc	Warwick	RI	G	973 455-2000	21371
Textron Inc **(PA)**	Providence	RI	B	401 421-2800	21134
Textron Lycoming Corp **(HQ)**	Providence	RI	E	401 421-2800	21135
Aeroparts Plus Inc	South Burlington	VT	G	802 489-5023	22435
General Electric Company	Rutland	VT	A	802 775-9842	22335
Honeywell International Inc	Williston	VT	G	877 841-2840	22674
Simmonds Precision Pdts Inc **(DH)**	Vergennes	VT	A	802 877-4000	22556
Superior Tchncal Ceramics Corp	Saint Albans	VT	C	802 527-7726	22380

AIRCRAFT EQPT & SPLYS WHOLESALERS

Connecticut Advanced Products	Glastonbury	CT	G	860 659-2260	1545

AIRCRAFT FLIGHT INSTRUMENTS

Agilynx Inc	Billerica	MA	G	617 314-6463	8206
Radenna LLC	Westford	MA	G	781 248-8826	16787

AIRCRAFT LIGHTING

B/E Aerospace Inc	Rockport	MA	G	978 546-1331	14834
B/E Aerospace Inc	Hampton	NH	G	603 926-5700	18256

AIRCRAFT MAINTENANCE & REPAIR SVCS

Gulfstream Aerospace Corp	New Milford	CT	G	860 210-1469	2803
Sikorsky Aircraft Corporation **(HQ)**	Stratford	CT	A	203 386-4000	4444
Turbine Controls Inc **(PA)**	Bloomfield	CT	D	860 242-0448	269

AIRCRAFT PARTS & AUX EQPT: Panel Assy/Hydro Prop Test Stands

Electro-Methods Inc **(PA)**	South Windsor	CT	C	860 289-8661	3962

AIRCRAFT PARTS & AUXILIARY EQPT: Accumulators, Propeller

Saf Industries LLC	Meriden	CT	E	203 729-4900	2127

AIRCRAFT PARTS & AUXILIARY EQPT: Ailerons

Pas Technologies Inc	Manchester	CT	E	860 649-2727	2037

AIRCRAFT PARTS & AUXILIARY EQPT: Assys, Subassemblies/Parts

	CITY	ST	EMP	PHONE	ENTRY #
A G C Incorporated **(PA)**	Meriden	CT	C	203 235-3361	2072
All Power Manufacturing Co **(HQ)**	Oxford	CT	C	562 802-2640	3389
Athens Industries Inc	Plantsville	CT	G	860 621-8957	3527
B&N Aerospace Inc	Newington	CT	E	860 665-0134	2845
Budney Aerospace Inc	Berlin	CT	D	860 828-0585	78
Connecticut Tool & Mfg Co LLC	Plainville	CT	D	860 846-0800	3478
Edac Nd Inc	Glastonbury	CT	D	860 633-9474	1548
Flanagan Brothers Inc	Glastonbury	CT	G	860 633-3558	1551
Jarvis Airfoil Inc	Portland	CT	D	860 342-5000	3568
Metallon Inc	Thomaston	CT	E	860 283-8265	4509
Paradigm Manchester Inc **(DH)**	Manchester	CT	B	860 646-4048	2031
Pcx Aerostructures LLC **(PA)**	Newington	CT	C	860 666-2471	2893
Pratt & Whitney Engine Svcs	Middletown	CT	B	860 344-4000	2212
Precision Metals and Plastics	Winsted	CT	G	860 238-4320	5419
Richard Manufacturing Co Inc	Milford	CT	E	203 874-3617	2350
Saf Industries LLC **(HQ)**	Meriden	CT	E	203 729-4900	2128
Tachwa Enterprises Inc	Hamden	CT	G	203 691-5772	1787
Whitcraft Scrborough/Tempe LLC	Scarborough	ME	C	763 780-0060	6942
Screw-Matic Corporation	Laconia	NH	F	603 293-8850	18585

AIRCRAFT PARTS & AUXILIARY EQPT: Body & Wing Assys & Parts

Triumph Eng Ctrl Systems LLC	West Hartford	CT	A	860 236-0651	5100
Opalala Inc	Fall River	MA	F	508 646-0950	10743
Steger Power Connection Inc	Fall River	MA	F	508 646-0950	10763
Insource Design & Mfg Tech LLC	Merrimack	NH	G	603 718-8228	19007

AIRCRAFT PARTS & AUXILIARY EQPT: Body Assemblies & Parts

Airborne Industries Inc	Branford	CT	F	203 315-0200	286
I & J Machine Tool Company	Milford	CT	F	203 877-5376	2298
Timken Arospc Drv Systems LLC	Manchester	CT	C	860 649-0000	2055
United Technologies Corp	East Hartford	CT	D	860 557-3333	1238

AIRCRAFT PARTS & AUXILIARY EQPT: Countermeasure Dispensers

Bae Systems Info & Elec Sys	Nashua	NH	G	603 885-3770	19124

AIRCRAFT PARTS & AUXILIARY EQPT: Deicing Eqpt

Integrated Deicing Svcs LLC **(DH)**	Manchester	NH	B	603 647-1717	18843
Integrated Deicing Svcs LLC	Manchester	NH	C	603 647-1717	18844

AIRCRAFT PARTS & AUXILIARY EQPT: Dusting & Spraying Eqpt

Pressue Techniques	North Andover	MA	G	978 686-2211	13725

AIRCRAFT PARTS & AUXILIARY EQPT: Gears, Power Transmission

Aero Gear Incorporated	Windsor	CT	C	860 688-0888	5316
Hamilton Sundstrand Corp **(HQ)**	Windsor Locks	CT	A	860 654-6000	5397
Perry Technology Corporation	New Hartford	CT	D	860 738-2525	2644

AIRCRAFT PARTS & AUXILIARY EQPT: Lighting/Landing Gear Assy

Straton Industries Inc	Stratford	CT	D	203 375-4488	4450
Goodrich Corporation	Peabody	MA	C	978 532-2350	14336

AIRCRAFT PARTS & AUXILIARY EQPT: Military Eqpt & Armament

Faille Precision Machining	Baltic	CT	G	860 822-1964	49
Morning Star Tool LLC	Milford	CT	G	203 878-6026	2316
Boniface Tool & Die Inc	Dudley	MA	E	508 764-3248	10373
General Dynamics-Ots Inc	Saco	ME	E	207 283-3611	6847
Granite Mountain Inds LLC	South Portland	ME	G	978 369-0014	7028
Exothermics Inc	Amherst	NH	F	603 821-5660	17560
General Dynamics-Ots Inc	Williston	VT	G	802 662-7000	22670

AIRCRAFT PARTS & AUXILIARY EQPT: Oxygen Systems

Hamilton Standard Space	Windsor Locks	CT	E	860 654-6000	5396

AIRCRAFT PARTS & AUXILIARY EQPT: Research & Development, Mfr

Delta-Ray Industries Inc	Bridgeport	CT	F	203 367-9903	404

AIRCRAFT PARTS & EQPT, NEC

A-1 Machining Co	New Britain	CT	D	860 223-6420	2501
Acmt Inc	Manchester	CT	D	860 645-0592	1982
Advanced Def Slutions Tech LLC	Bloomfield	CT	G	860 243-1122	199
Aero Tube Technologies LLC	South Windsor	CT	E	860 289-2520	3932
Aerocision LLC	Chester	CT	D	860 526-9700	767
Air-Lock Incorporated	Milford	CT	E	203 878-4691	2238
Alexis Aerospace Inds LLC	Canton	CT	G	860 516-4602	695
Alinabal Inc **(HQ)**	Milford	CT	C	203 877-3241	2242
Anderson Manufacturing Company	Woodbury	CT	G	203 263-2318	5481
Arrow Diversified Tooling Inc	Ellington	CT	E	860 872-9072	1329
Avalon Advanced Tech Repr Inc	East Windsor	CT	E	860 254-5442	1277
B/E Aerospace Inc	Stratford	CT	G	203 380-5000	4394
Beacon Industries Inc	Newington	CT	C	860 594-5200	2847
Birken Manufacturing Company	Bloomfield	CT	D	860 242-2211	209
Brandstrom Instruments Inc	Ridgefield	CT	E	203 544-9341	3661
Bryka Skystocks LLC	Newington	CT	G	845 507-8200	2850
C & W Manufacturing Co Inc	Glastonbury	CT	E	860 633-4631	1542
C V Tool Company Inc **(PA)**	Southington	CT	E	978 353-7901	4042
Cambridge Specialty Co Inc	Berlin	CT	D	860 828-3579	80
CBS Manufacturing Company	East Granby	CT	E	860 653-8100	1120
Connecticut Advanced Products	Glastonbury	CT	G	860 659-2260	1545
Continental Machine Tl Co Inc	New Britain	CT	D	860 223-2896	2522
Crane Aerospace Inc **(DH)**	Stamford	CT	C	203 363-7300	4176
Crane Co **(PA)**	Stamford	CT	D	203 363-7300	4177
Dell Acquisition LLC	Plainville	CT	E	860 677-8545	3480
Doncasters Inc **(HQ)**	Groton	CT	D	860 449-1603	1671
Drt Aerospace LLC	Winsted	CT	F	860 379-0783	5408
Dynamic Flight Systems	Monroe	CT	G	203 449-7211	2401

	CITY	ST	EMP	PHONE	ENTRY #
Edac Technologies LLC	Newington	CT	C	860 667-2134	2860
Enjet Aero New Britain LLC	New Britain	CT	C	860 356-0330	2531
Evoaero Inc	South Windsor	CT	D	860 289-2520	3967
First Aviation Services Inc **(PA)**	Westport	CT	G	203 291-3300	5192
Flight Enhancements Corp	Oxford	CT	G	912 257-0440	3401
Flight Support Inc	North Haven	CT	E	203 562-1415	3028
Forrest Machine Inc	Berlin	CT	D	860 563-1796	84
Gelder Aerospace LLC	Shelton	CT	G	203 283-9524	3804
GKN Aerospace Newington LLC **(DH)**	Newington	CT	C	860 667-8502	2867
Global Trbine Cmpnent Tech LLC	South Windsor	CT	E	860 528-4722	3973
Glyne Manufacturing Co Inc	Stratford	CT	F	203 375-4495	4415
Goodrich Corporation	Danbury	CT	B	203 797-5000	927
H & B Tool & Engineering Co	South Windsor	CT	E	860 528-9341	3976
Hexcel Corporation **(PA)**	Stamford	CT	E	203 969-0666	4213
Hexcel Pottsville Corporation	Stamford	CT	G	203 969-0666	4214
Isr (ntllgnce Srvllance Reconn	Danbury	CT	G	203 797-5000	936
Ithaco Space Systems Inc	Danbury	CT	D	607 272-7640	937
Jobin Machine Inc	West Hartford	CT	E	860 953-1631	5079
Jonal Labs Logistics LLC	Meriden	CT	G	203 634-4444	2097
Kaman Aerospace Corporation **(DH)**	Bloomfield	CT	A	860 242-4461	230
Kaman Aerospace Corporation	Bloomfield	CT	E	860 242-4461	231
Kaman Aerospace Group Inc **(HQ)**	Bloomfield	CT	F	860 243-7100	233
Kaman Corporation **(PA)**	Bloomfield	CT	D	860 243-7100	234
Kamatics Corporation **(DH)**	Bloomfield	CT	E	860 243-9704	235
L M Gill Welding and Mfr LLC	Manchester	CT	E	860 647-9931	2018
Lee Company **(PA)**	Westbrook	CT	A	860 399-6281	5157
LM Gill Welding & Mfg LLC	Manchester	CT	E	860 647-9931	2020
McMellon Bros Incorporated	Stratford	CT	E	203 375-5685	4431
Mtm Corporation	Andover	CT	G	860 742-9600	3
Naiad Dynamics Us Inc **(HQ)**	Shelton	CT	E	203 929-6355	3836
Nelson Tool & Machine Co Inc	Bristol	CT	G	860 589-8004	586
Overhaul Support Services LLC	East Granby	CT	G	860 653-1980	1140
Overhaul Support Services LLC **(PA)**	East Granby	CT	E	860 264-2101	1141
Paradigm Manchester Inc	Manchester	CT	D	860 646-4048	2029
Paradigm Manchester Inc	Manchester	CT	C	860 646-4048	2030
Paragon Tool Company Inc	Manchester	CT	G	860 647-9935	2035
Polamer Precision Inc	New Britain	CT	C	860 259-6200	2563
Polar Corporation	New Britain	CT	E	860 223-7891	2564
Precision Aerospace Inc	Seymour	CT	E	203 888-3022	3762
Precision Speed Mfg LLC	Middletown	CT	E	860 635-8811	2213
Ramar-Hall Inc	Middlefield	CT	E	860 349-1081	2165
Rotair Aerospace Corporation	Bridgeport	CT	E	203 576-6545	484
Rotating Composite Tech LLC	Kensington	CT	G	860 829-6809	1920
Saklax Manufacturing Company	Bloomfield	CT	G	860 242-2538	261
Satellite Tool & Mch Co Inc	South Windsor	CT	E	860 290-8558	4008
Senior Operations LLC	Enfield	CT	D	860 741-2546	1382
Simmonds Precision Pdts Inc	Danbury	CT	E	203 797-5000	994
Sky Mfg Company	Cheshire	CT	G	203 439-7016	762
Susan Martovich	Oxford	CT	G	203 881-1848	3426
Thompson Aerospace LLC	Bristol	CT	F	860 516-0472	617
Triumph Actuation Systems - Co **(HQ)**	Windsor	CT	D	860 687-5412	5376
Triumph Group Inc	Bloomfield	CT	G	860 726-9378	268
United Avionics Inc	Naugatuck	CT	E	203 723-1404	2499
Valley Tool and Mfg LLC **(HQ)**	Orange	CT	D	203 799-8800	3386
W and G Machine Company Inc	Hamden	CT	E	203 288-8772	1794
W&R Manufacturing Inc	Milford	CT	G	203 877-5955	2381
Whitcraft LLC **(PA)**	Eastford	CT	C	860 974-0786	1315
Whitcraft Scrborough/Tempe LLC **(HQ)**	Eastford	CT	C	860 974-0786	1316
325 Silver Street Inc	Agawam	MA	E	413 789-1800	7415
Actronics Incorporated	Waltham	MA	F	781 890-7030	16024
Advanced Aerostructures Inc **(PA)**	Chicopee	MA	G	413 315-9284	9996
Aerobond Composites LLC	Springfield	MA	E	413 734-2224	15442
B & E Tool Company Inc	Southwick	MA	D	413 569-5585	15411
B/E Aerospace Inc	Rockport	MA	G	978 546-1331	14834
Demars	Amesbury	MA	G	978 388-2349	7484
Drt Aerospace LLC	Agawam	MA	E	413 789-1800	7428
General Airmotive Pwr Pdts LLC	Fall River	MA	G	508 674-6400	10702
Goodrich Corporation	Westford	MA	A	978 303-6700	16771
Ground Support Products Corp	Pembroke	MA	G	860 491-3348	14407
Hardric Laboratories Inc	North Chelmsford	MA	E	978 251-1702	13895
Jet Industries Inc	Agawam	MA	E	413 786-2010	7435
MSC Manufacturing Inc	Rockland	MA	G	781 888-8587	14816
Parker-Hannifin Corporation	Devens	MA	C	978 784-1200	10329
Parts Tool and Die Inc	Agawam	MA	E	413 821-9718	7445
Precision Components Group	West Springfield	MA	G	413 333-4184	16547
Raytheon Company	Marlborough	MA	C	508 490-1000	12814
Rodney Hunt-Fontaine Inc **(DH)**	Orange	MA	C	978 544-2511	14227
Sibco LLC	Franklin	MA	G	508 520-2040	11079
Union Machine Company Lynn Inc **(PA)**	Groveland	MA	E	978 521-5100	11304
Wyman-Gordon Company **(DH)**	North Grafton	MA	B	508 839-8252	13969
C & L Aviation Group **(PA)**	Bangor	ME	E	207 217-6050	5633
Elmet Technologies LLC	Lewiston	ME	C	207 333-6100	6287
Albany Safran Composites LLC **(HQ)**	Rochester	NH	E	603 330-5800	19657
Atco-Aircraft Technical Co	Newington	NH	G	603 433-0081	19321
B/E Aerospace Inc	Hampton	NH	G	603 926-5700	18256
Bae Systems Info & Elec Sys	Merrimack	NH	B	603 885-4321	18990
Brazonics Inc **(DH)**	Hampton	NH	D	603 758-6237	18259
Continental Cable LLC	Hinsdale	NH	D	800 229-5131	18319
General Electric Company	Hooksett	NH	A	603 666-8300	18351
Lakes Region Tubular Pdts Inc	Laconia	NH	E	603 528-2838	18573
Lanair Research & Development	Portsmouth	NH	G	603 433-6134	19584
Matrix Aerospace Corp	Claremont	NH	D	603 542-0191	17854
Screw-Matic Corporation **(PA)**	Seabrook	NH	E	978 356-6200	19816
Sierra Nevada Corporation	Bedford	NH	B	775 331-0222	17663
Avco Corporation **(DH)**	Providence	RI	C	401 421-2800	20965
Magnetic Seal Corp	Warren	RI	E	401 247-2800	21298
Textron Inc **(PA)**	Providence	RI	B	401 421-2800	21134
Textron Lycoming Corp **(HQ)**	Providence	RI	E	401 421-2800	21135
Goodrich Corporation	Vergennes	VT	E	802 877-4000	22553
Liquid Measurement Systems Inc	Milton	VT	E	802 528-8100	22133
Sathorn Corporation	Williston	VT	E	802 860-2121	22689
Simmonds Precision Pdts Inc **(DH)**	Vergennes	VT	A	802 877-4000	22556

AIRCRAFT PARTS WHOLESALERS

James J Scott LLC	Rocky Hill	CT	G	860 571-9200	3719

AIRCRAFT PARTS/AUX EQPT: Airframe Assy, Exc Guided Missiles

Kaman Aerospace Corporation	Bloomfield	CT	D	860 242-4461	232

AIRCRAFT PROPELLERS & PARTS

Leading Edge Concepts Inc	Bethel	CT	G	203 797-1200	168

AIRCRAFT SEATS

Torrington Distributors Inc **(PA)**	Torrington	CT	E	860 482-4464	4604
B/E Aerospace Inc	Rockport	MA	G	978 546-1331	14834
B/E Aerospace Inc	Hampton	NH	G	603 926-5700	18256

AIRCRAFT SERVICING & REPAIRING

Integrated Deicing Svcs LLC **(DH)**	Manchester	NH	B	603 647-1717	18843

AIRCRAFT TURBINES

Ethosenergy Component Repr LLC	Wallingford	CT	E	203 949-8144	4738
Aero Turbine Components Inc	Worcester	MA	G	508 755-2121	17335

AIRCRAFT: Airplanes, Fixed Or Rotary Wing

Boeing Company	Concord	MA	A	978 369-9522	10117
Raytheon Sutheast Asia Systems **(HQ)**	Billerica	MA	E	978 470-5000	8289

AIRCRAFT: Motorized

Ambrose D Cedrone Lodge 1069	Newton	MA	G	617 460-4664	13561
American Drone Solutions LLC	West Bridgewater	MA	E	413 306-9427	16428
D Cedrone Inc	Framingham	MA	G	508 405-4260	10939
Echelon Industries Corporation	Westfield	MA	E	413 562-6659	16681
Vhp Flight Systems LLC	Southborough	MA	G	508 229-2615	15371

AIRCRAFT: Nonmotorized & Lighter-Than-air

Aquiline Drones LLC	Hartford	CT	F	860 361-7958	1807
BF Goodrich Aerspce Aircrft In	Vergennes	VT	G	802 877-2911	22552

AIRCRAFT: Research & Development, Manufacturer

Straton Industries Inc	Stratford	CT	D	203 375-4488	4450
Attleboro Scholarship Co	Attleboro	MA	G	508 226-4414	7709
Greensight Agronomics Inc	Boston	MA	G	617 633-4919	8580
Infotrends Research Group	Weymouth	MA	E	781 616-2100	16891
Spike Aerospace Inc	Boston	MA	F	617 338-1400	8858

AIRFRAME ASSEMBLIES: Guided Missiles

Entwistle Company **(HQ)**	Hudson	MA	C	508 481-4000	11772
Raytheon International Inc **(PA)**	Waltham	MA	G	781 522-3000	16185
Wgi Inc	Southwick	MA	C	413 569-9444	15421

AIRPORTS, FLYING FIELDS & SVCS

United Technologies Corp	East Granby	CT	F	860 292-3270	1146

ALARMS: Burglar

Alarm One	North Haven	CT	G	203 239-1714	3004
UTC Fire SEC Americas Corp Inc	Newtown	CT	C	203 426-1180	2947
Alarmsafe Inc	Chelmsford	MA	E	978 658-6717	9868
Keltron Corporation **(HQ)**	Waltham	MA	E	781 894-8710	16137
Shufro Security Company Inc	Newton	MA	G	617 244-3355	13637
UTC Fire SEC Americas Corp Inc	Framingham	MA	G	508 620-4773	11009

ALARMS: Fire

King Fisher Co Inc	Lowell	MA	E	978 596-0214	12389
L W Bills Co	Georgetown	MA	E	978 352-6660	11144
Simplex Time Recorder Co **(DH)**	Westminster	MA	C	978 731-2500	16813
Space Age Electronics Inc **(PA)**	Sterling	MA	E	800 486-1723	15545
Space Age Electronics Inc	Templeton	MA	E	978 652-5421	15805

ALCOHOL, GRAIN: For Beverage Purposes

Mr Boston Brands LLC **(HQ)**	Lewiston	ME	E	207 783-1433	6308

ALKALIES & CHLORINE

International Dioxcide Inc	North Kingstown	RI	E	401 295-8800	20718

ALLERGENS & ALLERGENIC EXTRACTS

Hooke Laboratories Inc	Lawrence	MA	D	617 475-5114	12036
Elution Technologies LLC	Colchester	VT	G	802 540-0296	21862

ALLOYS: Additive, Exc Copper Or Made In Blast Furnaces

Alent USA Holding Inc	Waterbury	CT	B	203 575-5727	4839
Fit America Inc	Southborough	MA	G	309 839-1695	15357

ALTERNATORS & GENERATORS: Battery Charging

Liquidsky Technologies Inc **(PA)**	Norwood	MA	F	857 389-9893	14175

ALTERNATORS: Automotive

Gauss Corporation	Scarborough	ME	F	207 883-4121	6918

ALUMINUM

Arconic Inc	Winsted	CT	G	860 379-3314	5404
Wilson Partitions Inc	Stamford	CT	F	203 316-8033	4360
Gear/Tronics Inc	North Billerica	MA	E	781 933-1400	13819
Putnam Rf Machining LLC	Manchester	NH	G	603 623-0700	18769
Bill Lztte Archtctural GL Alum	Riverside	RI	F	401 383-9535	21164

ALUMINUM PRDTS

	CITY	ST	EMP	PHONE	ENTRY #
Narragansett Screw Co	Winsted	CT	F	860 379-4059	5418
Unique Extrusions Incorporated	Cromwell	CT	E	860 632-1314	862
Atrenne Cmpt Solutions LLC **(DH)**	Brockton	MA	B	508 588-6110	9121
Atrenne Cmpt Solutions LLC	Brockton	MA	G	508 588-6110	9122
Cycle-TEC	Bellingham	MA	G	508 966-0066	8036
Mair-Mac Machine Company Inc	Brockton	MA	F	508 895-9001	9164
Silver City Aluminum Corp	Taunton	MA	D	508 824-8631	15785

ALUMINUM: Pigs

	CITY	ST	EMP	PHONE	ENTRY #
All Steel LLC	Ellington	CT	G	860 871-6023	1328

ALUMINUM: Rolling & Drawing

	CITY	ST	EMP	PHONE	ENTRY #
Acme Monaco Corporation **(PA)**	New Britain	CT	C	860 224-1349	2503
Alpha-Core Inc	Shelton	CT	E	203 954-0050	3773
Echo Industries Inc	Orange	MA	E	978 544-7000	14215
Joseph Freedman Co Inc	Springfield	MA	E	413 781-4444	15482

AMMONIUM NITRATE OR AMMONIUM SULFATE

	CITY	ST	EMP	PHONE	ENTRY #
Gac Chemical Corporation **(PA)**	Searsport	ME	D	207 548-2525	6951

AMMUNITION

	CITY	ST	EMP	PHONE	ENTRY #
Ensign-Bickford Industries Inc	Simsbury	CT	E	860 658-4411	3905
Cadillac Gage Textron Inc **(HQ)**	Wilmington	MA	G	978 657-5111	16986
Chamberlain Manufacturing Corp	New Bedford	MA	B	508 996-5621	13370

AMMUNITION: Bombs & Parts

	CITY	ST	EMP	PHONE	ENTRY #
Gun F X Tactical Development **(PA)**	Portland	ME	G	207 797-8200	6667

AMMUNITION: Cartridges Case, 30 mm & Below

	CITY	ST	EMP	PHONE	ENTRY #
Shell Shock Technologies Llc	Westport	CT	G	203 557-3256	5230
Green Mtn Rifle Barrel Co Inc	Conway	NH	F	603 447-1095	17953

AMMUNITION: Components

	CITY	ST	EMP	PHONE	ENTRY #
Textron Systems Corporation **(DH)**	Wilmington	MA	E	978 657-5111	17054

AMMUNITION: Pellets & BB's, Pistol & Air Rifle

	CITY	ST	EMP	PHONE	ENTRY #
Ammo and Bullet Manufacturing	Arundel	ME	G	978 807-7681	5527

AMMUNITION: Small Arms

	CITY	ST	EMP	PHONE	ENTRY #
General Dynamics Ordnance	Avon	CT	F	860 404-0162	34
Illinois Tool Works Inc	Waterbury	CT	C	203 574-2119	4887
Jkb Daira Inc **(PA)**	Norwalk	CT	G	203 642-4824	3182
Executive Force Protection LLC	Cambridge	MA	F	617 470-9230	9476
Green Mountain Risk MGT LLC	Dover	NH	F	802 683-8586	18024
Green Mountain Risk MGT Inc	Strafford	VT	G	802 763-7773	22527

AMPLIFIERS

	CITY	ST	EMP	PHONE	ENTRY #
Ki Inc	Orange	CT	E	203 641-5492	3368
Krell Industries LLC	Orange	CT	F	203 298-4000	3369
Fishman Transducers Inc	Andover	MA	D	978 988-9199	7549
Taft Sound	Sutton	MA	G	508 476-2662	15693

AMPLIFIERS: Parametric

	CITY	ST	EMP	PHONE	ENTRY #
Beta Dyne Inc	Bridgewater	MA	F	508 697-1993	9064
Copley Controls Corporation **(DH)**	Canton	MA	B	781 828-8090	9722

AMPLIFIERS: RF & IF Power

	CITY	ST	EMP	PHONE	ENTRY #
Advanced Receiver Research	Harwinton	CT	G	860 485-0310	1886
Axiom Microdevices Inc	Woburn	MA	G	781 376-3000	17124

AMUSEMENT & RECREATION SVCS: Amusement Mach Rental, Coin-Op

	CITY	ST	EMP	PHONE	ENTRY #
Happy House Amusement Inc	Goffstown	NH	E	603 497-4151	18203

AMUSEMENT & RECREATION SVCS: Art Gallery, Commercial

	CITY	ST	EMP	PHONE	ENTRY #
Herbert Mosher	Nashua	NH	G	603 882-4357	19177

AMUSEMENT & RECREATION SVCS: Gun & Hunting Clubs

	CITY	ST	EMP	PHONE	ENTRY #
Northeast Outdoors Inc	Paxton	MA	F	508 752-8762	14302

AMUSEMENT & RECREATION SVCS: Physical Fitness Instruction

	CITY	ST	EMP	PHONE	ENTRY #
Safe Laser Therapy LLC	Stamford	CT	G	203 261-4400	4308
Breed Nutrition Inc	Rehoboth	MA	G	508 840-3888	14747

AMUSEMENT & RECREATION SVCS: Tourist Attraction, Commercial

	CITY	ST	EMP	PHONE	ENTRY #
Cg Roxane LLC	Moultonborough	NH	E	603 476-8844	19095

AMUSEMENT MACHINES: Coin Operated

	CITY	ST	EMP	PHONE	ENTRY #
Rlp Inc	Stamford	CT	G	203 359-2504	4303
Happy House Amusement Inc	Goffstown	NH	E	603 497-4151	18203

AMUSEMENT PARK DEVICES & RIDES

	CITY	ST	EMP	PHONE	ENTRY #
EA Patten Co LLC	Manchester	CT	D	860 649-2851	2004
A & D Tool Co	Indian Orchard	MA	G	413 543-3166	11883
Agis Inc	Plymouth	MA	G	508 591-8400	14540
Pearson Machine Company LLC	Stoughton	MA	G	781 341-9416	15614
Precision Assemblies	Malden	MA	G	781 324-9054	12591
R M Machine LLC	Chicopee	MA	G	413 331-0576	10056
S W Keats Company	Reading	MA	G	781 935-4282	14742
Play To Win Inc	Manchester	NH	G	603 669-6770	18901
Skytrans Mfg LLC	Contoocook	NH	F	802 230-7783	17948

AMUSEMENT PARK DEVICES & RIDES: Carnival Mach & Eqpt, NEC

	CITY	ST	EMP	PHONE	ENTRY #
Marenna Amusements LLC	Orange	CT	F	203 623-4386	3372
Bumper Boats Inc	Newport	RI	G	401 841-8200	20658

ANALYZERS: Blood & Body Fluid

	CITY	ST	EMP	PHONE	ENTRY #
Biomerieux Inc	Boston	MA	G	617 879-8000	8411

ANALYZERS: Moisture

	CITY	ST	EMP	PHONE	ENTRY #
Vacuum Technology Inc	Gloucester	MA	G	510 333-6562	11216

ANALYZERS: Network

	CITY	ST	EMP	PHONE	ENTRY #
Anova Data Inc	Westford	MA	G	978 577-6600	16753
Context Labs Inc	Cambridge	MA	E	617 902-0932	9442
Xcalibur Communications	Manchester	NH	G	603 625-9555	18957

ANALYZERS: Respiratory

	CITY	ST	EMP	PHONE	ENTRY #
Covidien LP **(HQ)**	Mansfield	MA	A	763 514-4000	12622

ANESTHESIA EQPT

	CITY	ST	EMP	PHONE	ENTRY #
Annovation Biopharma Inc	Wayland	MA	G	617 724-0343	16332
Draeger Medical Systems Inc	Andover	MA	C	800 437-2437	7545
Hallowell Engrg & Mfg Corp	Pittsfield	MA	G	413 445-4263	14475
Vascular Technology Inc	Nashua	NH	E	603 594-9700	19279

ANESTHETICS: Bulk Form

	CITY	ST	EMP	PHONE	ENTRY #
Airgas Usa LLC	East Greenwich	RI	G	401 884-0201	20351

ANIMAL BASED MEDICINAL CHEMICAL PRDTS

	CITY	ST	EMP	PHONE	ENTRY #
Ticked Off Inc	Dover	NH	G	603 742-0925	18061

ANIMAL FEED & SUPPLEMENTS: Livestock & Poultry

	CITY	ST	EMP	PHONE	ENTRY #
Channel Fish Co Inc	Boston	MA	D	617 569-3200	8467
Designing Health Inc	East Longmeadow	MA	E	661 257-1705	10472
Tropicana Products Inc	Taunton	MA	E	508 821-2056	15792
Kent Nutrition Group Inc	Windham	ME	G	207 892-9411	7239
Trividia Mfg Solutions **(DH)**	Lancaster	NH	C	603 788-2848	18606
Trividia Mfg Solutions	Lancaster	NH	G	603 788-4952	18607
Dittmar & McNeil CPA S Inc	Warwick	RI	G	401 921-2600	21352
Kent Nutrition Group Inc	Brandon	VT	E	802 247-9599	21709
Poulin Grain Inc	Swanton	VT	F	802 868-3323	22534

ANIMAL FEED: Wholesalers

	CITY	ST	EMP	PHONE	ENTRY #
Dittmar & McNeil CPA S Inc	Warwick	RI	G	401 921-2600	21352
Feed Commodities Intl Inc	Newport	VT	G	802 334-2942	22197

ANIMAL FOOD & SUPPLEMENTS: Dog

	CITY	ST	EMP	PHONE	ENTRY #
A L C Inovators Inc	Milford	CT	G	203 877-8526	2232
Bravo LLC **(PA)**	Manchester	CT	F	866 922-9222	1988
Bravo LLC	Vernon	CT	E	860 896-1899	4664
2 Dogs Treats LLC	Dorchester	MA	G	617 286-4844	10339
Tbd Brands LLC	Exeter	NH	G	603 775-7772	18133

ANIMAL FOOD & SUPPLEMENTS: Dog & Cat

	CITY	ST	EMP	PHONE	ENTRY #
Blue Buffalo Company Ltd **(DH)**	Wilton	CT	B	203 762-9751	5279
Fine Pets LLC	Greenwich	CT	G	203 833-1517	1611
Channel Fish Co Inc	Boston	MA	D	617 569-3200	8467
Mars Incorporated	Bellingham	MA	G	508 966-0022	8047
Polka Dog Designs LLC **(PA)**	Boston	MA	F	617 338-5155	8784
Wellpet LLC **(PA)**	Tewksbury	MA	D	877 869-2971	15848
Pure Pup Love Inc	Scarborough	ME	G	207 588-8111	6936
Kent Nutrition Group Inc	Londonderry	NH	F	603 437-3400	18708
Wholistic Pet Organics LLC	Bedford	NH	G	603 472-8300	17667

ANIMAL FOOD & SUPPLEMENTS: Feed Concentrates

	CITY	ST	EMP	PHONE	ENTRY #
Q A S	Boston	MA	G	617 345-3000	8802
Savory Creations International	Lynn	MA	F	650 638-1024	12537

ANIMAL FOOD & SUPPLEMENTS: Feed Premixes

	CITY	ST	EMP	PHONE	ENTRY #
Lucerne Farms	Fort Fairfield	ME	E	207 488-2520	6056

ANIMAL FOOD & SUPPLEMENTS: Feed Supplements

	CITY	ST	EMP	PHONE	ENTRY #
A L C Inovators Inc	Milford	CT	G	203 877-8526	2232
ALC Sales Company LLC **(PA)**	Milford	CT	G	203 877-8526	2239
Earth Animal Ventures Inc	Stamford	CT	G	717 271-6393	4190
Source Inc **(PA)**	North Branford	CT	G	203 488-6400	2977
Euroduna Americas Inc	Plymouth	MA	G	508 888-2710	14556
N2bm Nutrition Inc	Salisbury	MA	G	978 241-2851	14954
Smartpak Equine LLC **(DH)**	Plymouth	MA	D	774 773-1100	14583
Northern Tack	Calais	ME	G	207 217-7584	5865
Source Inc	Brunswick	ME	G	207 729-1107	5845
Wholistic Pet Organics LLC	Bedford	NH	G	603 472-8300	17667
Nutra-Blend LLC	North Troy	VT	G	802 988-4474	22241

ANIMAL FOOD & SUPPLEMENTS: Livestock

	CITY	ST	EMP	PHONE	ENTRY #
Kent Nutrition Group Inc	Londonderry	NH	F	603 437-3400	18708
Kent Nutrition Group Inc	Richford	VT	D	802 848-7718	22308
Phoenix Feeds Organix LLC	New Haven	VT	E	802 453-6684	22186
Poulin Grain Inc	North Bennington	VT	E	802 681-1605	22212

ANIMAL FOOD & SUPPLEMENTS: Pet, Exc Dog & Cat, Canned

	CITY	ST	EMP	PHONE	ENTRY #
Blue Buffalo Pet Products Inc **(HQ)**	Wilton	CT	E	203 762-9751	5280

ANIMAL FOOD & SUPPLEMENTS: Poultry

	CITY	ST	EMP	PHONE	ENTRY #
HJ Baker & Bro LLC **(PA)**	Shelton	CT	E	203 682-9200	3812
Kent Nutrition Group Inc	Augusta	ME	F	207 622-1530	5611

ANODIZING EQPT

	CITY	ST	EMP	PHONE	ENTRY #
Reliable	Winchendon	MA	G	978 230-2689	17081

ANODIZING SVC

	CITY	ST	EMP	PHONE	ENTRY #
Aluminum Finishing Company Inc	Bridgeport	CT	E	203 333-1690	371
Anomatic Corporation	Naugatuck	CT	G	203 720-2367	2461

	CITY	ST	EMP	PHONE	ENTRY #
Chemical-Electric Corporation	Danbury	CT	G	203 743-5131	888
Light Metals Coloring Co Inc	Southington	CT	D	860 621-0145	4062
Anomet Products Inc	Shrewsbury	MA	E	508 842-0174	15102
Central Metal Finishing Inc	North Andover	MA	C	978 291-0500	13694
CIL Electroplating Inc	Lawrence	MA	D	978 683-2082	12008
Cil Inc	Lawrence	MA	D	978 685-8300	12009
Poly-Metal Finishing Inc	Springfield	MA	D	413 781-4535	15498
Qc Industries Inc **(PA)**	Mansfield	MA	D	781 344-1000	12653
T & T Anodizing Inc	Lowell	MA	E	978 454-9631	12435
T & T Anodizing Incorporated	Lowell	MA	F	978 454-9631	12436
Jmd Industries Inc	Hudson	NH	E	603 882-3198	18404
Technodic Inc	Providence	RI	E	401 467-6660	21132

ANTENNAS: Radar Or Communications

	CITY	ST	EMP	PHONE	ENTRY #
Meriden Electronics Corp.	Meriden	CT	G	203 237-8811	2103
Antenna Associates Inc	Brockton	MA	E	508 583-3241	9120
Hxi LLC	Harvard	MA	F	978 772-7774	11379
Magnetic Sciences Inc	Acton	MA	G	978 266-9355	7372
Megawave Corporation	Worcester	MA	G	978 615-7200	17412
Sippi/GSM Subma Antenn Joint V	Marion	MA	G	774 553-6218	12703

ANTENNAS: Receiving

	CITY	ST	EMP	PHONE	ENTRY #
Magnetic Sciences Inc	Acton	MA	G	978 266-9355	7372
Micro Metal Components Inc	Deerfield	NH	G	603 463-5986	17970

ANTI-OXIDANTS

	CITY	ST	EMP	PHONE	ENTRY #
Si Group USA (usaa) LLC **(DH)**	Danbury	CT	C	203 702-6140	989
Si Group USA Hldings Usha Corp **(HQ)**	Danbury	CT	E	203 702-6140	990
Polnox Corporation	Lowell	MA	G	978 735-4438	12423

ANTIBIOTICS

	CITY	ST	EMP	PHONE	ENTRY #
Microbiotix Inc	Worcester	MA	E	508 757-2800	17416
Tetraphase Pharmaceuticals Inc **(PA)**	Watertown	MA	D	617 715-3600	16321
Biodesign International Inc	Saco	ME	E	207 283-6500	6843

ANTIFREEZE

	CITY	ST	EMP	PHONE	ENTRY #
Prestone Products Corporation	Danbury	CT	E	203 731-7880	975
Aspen Products Group Inc	Marlborough	MA	G	508 481-5058	12722
Camco Manufacturing Inc	Leominster	MA	F	978 537-6777	12123
Cristy Corporation	Fitchburg	MA	F	978 343-4330	10822

ANTIQUE FURNITURE RESTORATION & REPAIR

	CITY	ST	EMP	PHONE	ENTRY #
Craft Interiors	Malden	MA	G	781 321-8695	12566

ANTIQUE SHOPS

	CITY	ST	EMP	PHONE	ENTRY #
Grant Larkin	Richmond	MA	G	413 698-2599	14779

ANTISEPTICS, MEDICINAL

	CITY	ST	EMP	PHONE	ENTRY #
Aplicare Products LLC **(HQ)**	Meriden	CT	C	203 630-0500	2077

APPAREL DESIGNERS: Commercial

	CITY	ST	EMP	PHONE	ENTRY #
Sara Campbell Ltd **(PA)**	Boston	MA	F	617 423-3134	8838

APPAREL FILLING MATERIALS: Cotton Waste, Kapok/Related Matl

	CITY	ST	EMP	PHONE	ENTRY #
Cornell Online LLC	Burlington	VT	E	802 448-3281	21776

APPAREL: Hand Woven

	CITY	ST	EMP	PHONE	ENTRY #
Lynn Yarrington	New Haven	VT	G	802 453-4221	22185

APPLIANCE CORDS: Household Electrical Eqpt

	CITY	ST	EMP	PHONE	ENTRY #
Naugatuck Elec Indus Sup LLC	Naugatuck	CT	G	203 723-1082	2486
World Cord Sets Inc	Enfield	CT	G	860 763-2100	1391
Grove Labs Inc	Somerville	MA	F	703 608-8178	15179

APPLIANCES, HOUSEHOLD: Drycleaning Machines, Incl Coin-Op

	CITY	ST	EMP	PHONE	ENTRY #
Easy Way Dry Cleaners Inc	Woburn	MA	G	781 933-1473	17173

APPLIANCES, HOUSEHOLD: Kitchen, Major, Exc Refrigs & Stoves

	CITY	ST	EMP	PHONE	ENTRY #
Clarke Distribution Corp	Norwalk	CT	G	203 838-9385	3126
Conair Corporation **(PA)**	Stamford	CT	B	203 351-9000	4171
Euro-Pro Holdco LLC	Needham Heights	MA	D	617 243-0235	13330
Sharkninja Operating LLC **(HQ)**	Needham	MA	E	617 243-0235	13310
Vaughn Thermal Corporation	Salisbury	MA	E	978 462-6683	14958
Vermont Islands Culinary LLC	Brattleboro	VT	F	802 387-8591	21752

APPLIANCES, HOUSEHOLD: Refrigs, Mechanical & Absorption

	CITY	ST	EMP	PHONE	ENTRY #
Medelco Inc	Bridgeport	CT	G	203 275-8070	449
General Electric Company	Westborough	MA	F	508 870-5200	16619
Raytheon Sutheast Asia Systems **(HQ)**	Billerica	MA	E	978 470-5000	8289

APPLIANCES, HOUSEHOLD: Sewing Machines & Attchmnts, Domestic

	CITY	ST	EMP	PHONE	ENTRY #
Alco Technology	Fall River	MA	G	508 678-7449	10651
Dan-Ray Machine Co Inc	Haverhill	MA	G	978 374-7611	11423
W S Bessett Inc	Sanford	ME	F	207 324-9232	6896

APPLIANCES: Household, Refrigerators & Freezers

	CITY	ST	EMP	PHONE	ENTRY #
General Electric Company **(PA)**	Boston	MA	A	617 443-3000	8558
Gbo Inc	Portland	ME	G	207 772-0302	6665

APPLIANCES: Major, Cooking

	CITY	ST	EMP	PHONE	ENTRY #
Conair Corporation **(PA)**	Stamford	CT	B	203 351-9000	4171
General Electric Company **(PA)**	Boston	MA	A	617 443-3000	8558
Cooking Solutions Group Inc **(HQ)**	Salem	NH	G	603 893-9701	19719
GS Blodgett Corporation	Essex Junction	VT	G	802 871-3287	21943
GS Blodgett Corporation **(HQ)**	Essex Junction	VT	C	802 860-3700	21944

APPLIANCES: Small, Electric

	CITY	ST	EMP	PHONE	ENTRY #
Conair Corporation	Torrington	CT	D	800 492-7464	4572
Conair Corporation **(PA)**	Stamford	CT	B	203 351-9000	4171
Dampits LLC	Wilton	CT	G	203 210-7946	5287
Jarden LLC	Norwalk	CT	E	203 845-5300	3179
McIntire Company **(HQ)**	Bristol	CT	F	860 585-8559	580
Convectronics Inc	Haverhill	MA	F	978 374-7714	11419
Gillette Company **(HQ)**	Boston	MA	A	617 421-7000	8561
Reach Distribution Inc	Boston	MA	G	617 542-6466	8811
Sharon Associates	Sharon	MA	G	781 784-2455	15057
Thl-Nortek Investors LLC **(PA)**	Boston	MA	D	617 227-1050	8882

APPLICATIONS SOFTWARE PROGRAMMING

	CITY	ST	EMP	PHONE	ENTRY #
Connected Automotive	South Easton	MA	E	508 238-5855	15274
VMS Software Inc	Bolton	MA	G	978 451-0110	8324

AQUARIUMS & ACCESS: Plastic

	CITY	ST	EMP	PHONE	ENTRY #
Governor Supply Co	Lancaster	MA	G	978 870-6888	11983

ARCHERY & SHOOTING RANGES

	CITY	ST	EMP	PHONE	ENTRY #
Sig Sauer Inc **(DH)**	Newington	NH	C	603 610-3000	19325

ARCHITECTURAL PANELS OR PARTS: Porcelain Enameled

	CITY	ST	EMP	PHONE	ENTRY #
Insulpane Connecticut Inc	Hamden	CT	D	800 922-3248	1761
Bnz Materials Inc	North Billerica	MA	E	978 663-3401	13796

ARCHITECTURAL SVCS

	CITY	ST	EMP	PHONE	ENTRY #
Faverco Inc	Boston	MA	G	617 247-1440	8540
Zlink Inc	Maynard	MA	G	978 309-3628	12907
Saco Manufacturing & Wdwkg	Saco	ME	G	207 284-6613	6857
Northern Design Precast Inc	Loudon	NH	E	603 783-8989	18751
Herrick & White Ltd	Cumberland	RI	D	401 658-0440	20324

ARCHITECTURAL SVCS: Engineering

	CITY	ST	EMP	PHONE	ENTRY #
Unerectors Inc	Boston	MA	F	617 436-8333	8894

ARGILLITE: Dimension

	CITY	ST	EMP	PHONE	ENTRY #
Taran Bros Inc	Poultney	VT	G	802 287-9308	22279

ARMATURE REPAIRING & REWINDING SVC

	CITY	ST	EMP	PHONE	ENTRY #
Maxon Precision Motors Inc **(HQ)**	Taunton	MA	E	508 677-0520	15763

ARMOR PLATES

	CITY	ST	EMP	PHONE	ENTRY #
Armor Holdings Protech Div	Pittsfield	MA	G	413 445-4000	14454

ART & ORNAMENTAL WARE: Pottery

	CITY	ST	EMP	PHONE	ENTRY #
Company of Craftsmen	Mystic	CT	G	860 536-4189	2436
Conversation Concepts LLC	Fitchburg	MA	F	978 342-1414	10820
Mudpie Potters	Leverett	MA	E	413 548-3939	12198
Sylvia Wyler Pottery Inc **(PA)**	Brunswick	ME	G	207 729-1321	5848
Clayground	East Greenwich	RI	G	401 884-4888	20358
Beth Mueller Inc	Barre	VT	G	802 476-3582	21609
Romulus Craft	Washington	VT	G	802 685-3869	22580

ART DESIGN SVCS

	CITY	ST	EMP	PHONE	ENTRY #
Gloucester Graphics Inc **(PA)**	Gloucester	MA	F	978 281-4500	11188
Master Printing & Signs	Somerville	MA	G	617 623-8270	15196
E Print Inc	Hudson	NH	G	603 594-0009	18388

ART GALLERY, NONCOMMERCIAL

	CITY	ST	EMP	PHONE	ENTRY #
Exit Five Gallery	West Barnstable	MA	G	508 375-1011	16407

ART GOODS, WHOLESALE

	CITY	ST	EMP	PHONE	ENTRY #
Arthur H Gaebel Inc	Boxborough	MA	G	978 263-4401	8958

ART NEEDLEWORK, MADE FROM PURCHASED MATERIALS

	CITY	ST	EMP	PHONE	ENTRY #
Apparel 2000 LLC	Rockland	MA	G	781 740-6204	14790
Premier Services Inc	Weymouth	MA	G	781 335-9305	16898

ART SPLY STORES

	CITY	ST	EMP	PHONE	ENTRY #
Renaissance Glassworks Inc	Nashua	NH	G	603 882-1779	19249
Zephyr Designs Ltd	Brattleboro	VT	G	802 254-2788	21755

ARTIST'S MATERIALS & SPLYS

	CITY	ST	EMP	PHONE	ENTRY #
Color Craft Ltd	East Granby	CT	F	800 509-6563	1121

ARTISTS' AGENTS & BROKERS

	CITY	ST	EMP	PHONE	ENTRY #
Kirchoff Wohlberg Inc	Madison	CT	F	212 644-2020	1967
Witricity Corporation **(PA)**	Watertown	MA	F	617 926-2700	16331

ARTISTS' MATERIALS, WHOLESALE

	CITY	ST	EMP	PHONE	ENTRY #
Color Craft Ltd	East Granby	CT	F	800 509-6563	1121
Canson Inc	South Hadley	MA	D	413 538-9250	15300

ARTISTS' MATERIALS: Canvas, Prepared On Frames

	CITY	ST	EMP	PHONE	ENTRY #
Henry J Montville	Auburn	MA	G	508 832-6111	7837

ARTISTS' MATERIALS: Frames, Artists' Canvases

	CITY	ST	EMP	PHONE	ENTRY #
Exit Five Gallery	West Barnstable	MA	G	508 375-1011	16407
Wood & Wood Inc	Waitsfield	VT	G	802 496-3000	22572

ARTISTS' MATERIALS: Ink, Drawing, Black & Colored

	CITY	ST	EMP	PHONE	ENTRY #
Colors Ink	Wallingford	CT	G	203 269-4000	4722
Screening Ink LLC	Enfield	CT	G	860 212-0475	1381

ARTWORK: Framed

	CITY	ST	EMP	PHONE	ENTRY #
Alpine Management Group LLC	Westport	CT	G	954 531-1692	5180
K F Machining	East Windsor	CT	G	860 292-6466	1289
Picture This Hartford Inc	East Hartford	CT	G	860 528-1409	1210

	CITY	ST	EMP	PHONE	ENTRY #
Asian Art Society New England	Sherborn	MA	G	781 250-6311	15077
Small Corp	Greenfield	MA	G	413 772-0889	11276

ASBESTOS PRODUCTS

	CITY	ST	EMP	PHONE	ENTRY #
Zero Hazard LLC	Farmington	CT	G	860 561-9879	1524
Atc Group Services LLC	Williston	VT	G	802 862-1980	22656

ASBESTOS REMOVAL EQPT

	CITY	ST	EMP	PHONE	ENTRY #
D P Engineering Inc	Madison	CT	G	203 421-7965	1959
Untha Shredding Tech Amer Inc	Newburyport	MA	G	978 465-0083	13547

ASH TRAYS: Stamped Metal

	CITY	ST	EMP	PHONE	ENTRY #
No Butts Bin Company Inc	Madison	CT	G	203 245-5924	1970

ASPHALT & ASPHALT PRDTS

	CITY	ST	EMP	PHONE	ENTRY #
AEN Asphalt Inc	Bozrah	CT	G	860 885-0500	279
Betkoski Brothers LLC	Beacon Falls	CT	G	203 723-8262	55
L Suzio Asphalt Co Inc	Meriden	CT	F	203 237-8421	2098
T D I Enterprises LLC	Meriden	CT	G	203 630-1268	2136
Wescon Corp of Conn	Pawcatuck	CT	G	860 599-2500	3444
Westchester Industries Inc	Greenwich	CT	F	203 661-0055	1661
Granger Lynch Corp	Millbury	MA	E	508 756-6244	13165
Heffron Asphalt Corp **(PA)**	North Reading	MA	G	781 935-1455	13984
Lorusso Corp **(PA)**	Plainville	MA	E	508 668-6520	14527
Norfolk Asphalt Company Inc	Plainville	MA	E	508 668-3100	14531
Oxford Asphalt Inc	Oxford	MA	G	508 987-0321	14271
Ted Ondrick Company LLC **(PA)**	Chicopee	MA	F	413 592-2565	10064
McBreairty Ransford	Woodland	ME	G	207 498-3182	7288
Trombley Industries Inc	Limestone	ME	G	207 328-4503	6345

ASPHALT COATINGS & SEALERS

	CITY	ST	EMP	PHONE	ENTRY #
Driveway Medics LLC	Seekonk	MA	G	508 761-6921	15021
Omg Inc **(DH)**	Agawam	MA	B	413 789-0252	7443
Newmont Slate Co Inc **(PA)**	West Pawlet	VT	E	802 645-0203	22612
Quarry Slate Industries Inc	Poultney	VT	D	802 287-9701	22274
Vermont Structural Slate Co **(PA)**	Fair Haven	VT	E	802 265-4933	21970

ASPHALT MINING & BITUMINOUS STONE QUARRYING SVCS

	CITY	ST	EMP	PHONE	ENTRY #
Galasso Materials LLC	East Granby	CT	C	860 527-1825	1128
Brox Industries Inc **(PA)**	Dracut	MA	D	978 454-9105	10355

ASPHALT PLANTS INCLUDING GRAVEL MIX TYPE

	CITY	ST	EMP	PHONE	ENTRY #
Advanced Concepts & Engrg LLC	Dexter	ME	G	207 270-3025	5955
County Concrete & Cnstr Co	Columbia Falls	ME	E	207 483-4409	5919
Hudson Terminal Corp **(PA)**	Providence	RI	F	401 274-2200	21033
Hudson Terminal Corp	Cranston	RI	G	401 941-0500	20239

ASSEMBLING SVC: Clocks

	CITY	ST	EMP	PHONE	ENTRY #
Cape Cod Wind Wther Indicators	Harwich Port	MA	G	508 432-9475	11398
Electric Time Company Inc	Medfield	MA	E	508 359-4396	12913
Wuersch Time Inc	Coventry	RI	G	401 828-2525	20170

ASSEMBLING SVC: Plumbing Fixture Fittings, Plastic

	CITY	ST	EMP	PHONE	ENTRY #
Plastic Assembly Systems LLC	Bethany	CT	F	203 393-0639	123
P A G Industries Inc	North Chelmsford	MA	F	978 265-5610	13906
Plumbers of RI	Providence	RI	G	401 919-0980	21091

ASSOCIATIONS: Business

	CITY	ST	EMP	PHONE	ENTRY #
Chief Executive Group LLC **(PA)**	Stamford	CT	F	785 832-0303	4164
Ram Belting Company Inc	New Britain	CT	G	860 438-7029	2568
Pittsfield Gazette Inc	Pittsfield	MA	G	413 443-2010	14499
Technology Organization Inc	Somerville	MA	G	617 623-4488	15222
Our Town Publishing Inc	Center Barnstead	NH	G	603 776-2500	17790
Mill Publishing Inc	Williston	VT	G	802 862-4109	22682

ASSOCIATIONS: Scientists'

	CITY	ST	EMP	PHONE	ENTRY #
American Mteorological Soc Inc **(PA)**	Boston	MA	D	617 227-2425	8361

ASSOCIATIONS: Trade

	CITY	ST	EMP	PHONE	ENTRY #
National Shooting Sports Found	Newtown	CT	E	203 426-1320	2929

ATOM SMASHER (Particle Accelerators)

	CITY	ST	EMP	PHONE	ENTRY #
Nhv America Inc	Methuen	MA	F	978 682-4900	13040

ATOMIZERS

	CITY	ST	EMP	PHONE	ENTRY #
Norfolk Industries LLC	Greenwich	CT	G	860 618-8822	1635
O & G Industries Inc	Harwinton	CT	C	860 485-6600	1891
O & G Industries Inc	Beacon Falls	CT	C	203 881-5192	63
Solidification Pdts Intl Inc	Northford	CT	G	203 484-9494	3092
EMD Millipore Corporation **(DH)**	Burlington	MA	A	781 533-6000	9262
Hci Cleaning Products LLC	Burlington	MA	G	508 864-5510	9281
Red Hawk Fire & Security LLC	Holyoke	MA	G	413 568-4709	11650
T J Holmes Co Inc	Chartley	MA	E	508 222-1723	9858
Thought Industries Inc	Boston	MA	G	617 669-7725	8884
Mobilerobots Inc	Amherst	NH	E	603 881-7960	17576
Valid Mfg Inc	Hudson	NH	F	603 880-0948	18449
Cas Acquisition Co LLC	North Smithfield	RI	F	401 884-8556	20783

ATTENUATORS

	CITY	ST	EMP	PHONE	ENTRY #
Anaren Ceramics Inc	Salem	NH	D	603 898-2883	19706
IDS Highway Safety Inc	Cumberland	RI	G	401 333-0740	20328

AUDIO & VIDEO EQPT, EXC COMMERCIAL

	CITY	ST	EMP	PHONE	ENTRY #
Harman Becker Automotive Syste	Stamford	CT	G	203 328-3501	4205
Impact Sales & Marketing LLC	West Hartford	CT	G	860 523-5366	5077
Insight Plus Technology LLC	Bristol	CT	G	860 930-4763	571
Microphase Corporation	Shelton	CT	E	203 866-8000	3833
PMC Technologies LLC	Weston	CT	G	203 222-0000	5172
Whelen Engineering Company Inc **(PA)**	Chester	CT	B	860 526-9504	777
Xintekidel Inc	Stamford	CT	G	203 348-9229	4362
Artel Video Systems Corp	Westford	MA	E	978 263-5775	16755
Courtsmart Digital Systems Inc	North Chelmsford	MA	E	978 251-3300	13891
Cue Inc	South Easton	MA	F	617 591-9500	15275
Mini-Systems Inc **(PA)**	North Attleboro	MA	C	508 695-1420	13765
Outlaw Audio LLC	Norton	MA	F	508 286-4110	14085
Venmill Industries Inc	Oxford	MA	E	508 363-0410	14276
Viking Industrial Products	Marlborough	MA	E	508 481-4600	12845
Volicon Inc	Burlington	MA	D	781 221-7400	9355
Connectivity Works Inc	Holden	ME	G	207 843-0854	6196
Cc1 Inc	Portsmouth	NH	E	603 319-2000	19548
Nel-Tech Labs Incorporated	Derry	NH	F	603 425-1096	17990
Videology Imging Solutions Inc **(PA)**	Greenville	RI	E	401 949-5332	20476

AUDIO COMPONENTS

	CITY	ST	EMP	PHONE	ENTRY #
Harman International Inds Inc **(DH)**	Stamford	CT	B	203 328-3500	4207
Harman International Inds Inc	Stamford	CT	G	203 328-3500	4208
Harman KG Holding LLC **(DH)**	Stamford	CT	F	203 328-3500	4210
Redco Audio Inc	Stratford	CT	F	203 502-7600	4441
Bose Corporation **(PA)**	Framingham	MA	A	508 879-7330	10928
Bose Corporation	Framingham	MA	E	508 766-1265	10929
Cambridge Soundworks Inc	Hanover	MA	G	781 829-8818	11332
Basis Audio Inc	Hollis	NH	G	603 889-4776	18326

AUDIO ELECTRONIC SYSTEMS

	CITY	ST	EMP	PHONE	ENTRY #
Harman Consumer Inc	Stamford	CT	G	203 328-3500	4206
Proxtalkercom LLC **(PA)**	Waterbury	CT	G	203 721-6074	4947
Alto Technologies Corporation **(PA)**	Sterling	MA	F	978 422-9071	15534
Cambridge Soundworks Inc	Westwood	MA	G	781 329-2777	16859
Fargo Ta LLC	Boston	MA	E	617 345-0066	8537
Hevc Advance LLC	Boston	MA	F	617 367-4802	8597
Premium Sund Slutions Amer LLC **(PA)**	Wakefield	MA	F	781 968-5511	15972
Rf Venue Inc	Ashland	MA	G	800 795-0817	7668
Savant Systems LLC **(PA)**	Hyannis	MA	D	508 683-2500	11857
Yamaha Unfied Cmmnications Inc **(HQ)**	Sudbury	MA	D	978 610-4040	15674
Transparent Audio Inc	Saco	ME	E	207 284-1100	6860

AUDIO-VISUAL PROGRAM PRODUCTION SVCS

	CITY	ST	EMP	PHONE	ENTRY #
Play-It Productions Inc	Colchester	CT	F	212 695-6530	805

AUDIOLOGICAL EQPT: Electronic

	CITY	ST	EMP	PHONE	ENTRY #
Medrhythms Inc	Gorham	ME	G	207 447-2177	6121
Qesidyne Inc	Hudson	NH	G	603 883-3116	18431

AUTO & HOME SUPPLY STORES: Automotive Access

	CITY	ST	EMP	PHONE	ENTRY #
J G Performance Inc	Abington	MA	G	781 871-1404	7325

AUTO & HOME SUPPLY STORES: Automotive parts

	CITY	ST	EMP	PHONE	ENTRY #
Peter Thrasher	North Attleboro	MA	G	-	13771
Scott G Reed Truck Svcs Inc	Claremont	NH	F	603 542-5032	17860
Scarborough Faire Inc **(PA)**	Pawtucket	RI	E	401 724-4200	20897
A C Performance Center Ltd	Colchester	VT	G	802 862-6074	21855

AUTO & HOME SUPPLY STORES: Speed Shops, Incl Race Car Splys

	CITY	ST	EMP	PHONE	ENTRY #
Reliable Welding & Speed LLC	Enfield	CT	G	860 749-3977	1379

AUTO & HOME SUPPLY STORES: Truck Eqpt & Parts

	CITY	ST	EMP	PHONE	ENTRY #
Lo Stocco Motors	Danbury	CT	G	203 797-9618	949
S Camerota & Sons Inc	North Haven	CT	G	203 782-0360	3060
Middlesex Truck & Auto Bdy Inc	Boston	MA	E	617 442-3000	8705
S Camerota & Sons Inc	Bow	NH	G	603 228-9343	17730

AUTO SPLYS & PARTS, NEW, WHSLE: Exhaust Sys, Mufflers, Etc

	CITY	ST	EMP	PHONE	ENTRY #
J-A Industries Incorporated	North Easton	MA	G	508 297-1648	13948

AUTOMATIC REGULATING CNTRLS: Liq Lvl, Residential/Comm Heat

	CITY	ST	EMP	PHONE	ENTRY #
Center For Discovery	Southport	CT	E	203 955-1381	4095

AUTOMATIC REGULATING CONTROL: Building Svcs Monitoring, Auto

	CITY	ST	EMP	PHONE	ENTRY #
Clarios	Meriden	CT	D	678 297-4040	2086
Universal Building Contrls Inc	Meriden	CT	F	203 235-1530	2145
Johnson Controls Inc	Wrentham	MA	E	508 384-0018	17524
Tac Inc **(DH)**	Andover	MA	C	978 470-0555	7613
Ene Systems of Nh Inc	Bow	NH	G	603 856-0330	17711
Granite 3 LLC	Temple	NH	G	603 566-0339	19897
Avtech Software Inc **(PA)**	Warren	RI	E	401 628-1600	21287
Energy MGT & Ctrl Svcs Inc	Cranston	RI	F	401 946-1440	20217

AUTOMATIC REGULATING CONTROLS: AC & Refrigeration

	CITY	ST	EMP	PHONE	ENTRY #
Siemens Industry Inc	Worcester	MA	D	508 849-6519	17473
Degree Controls Inc **(PA)**	Milford	NH	E	603 672-8900	19055
Dijitized Communications Inc	Middleton	NH	G	603 473-2144	19039
RMA Manufacturing LLC	West Swanzey	NH	E	603 352-0053	19968
Turmoil Inc	West Swanzey	NH	E	603 352-0053	19969
R H Travers Company	Warren	VT	G	802 496-5205	22578

AUTOMATIC REGULATING CONTROLS: Elect Air Cleaner, Automatic

	CITY	ST	EMP	PHONE	ENTRY #
Bluezone Products Inc	Woburn	MA	G	781 937-0202	17134

AUTOMATIC REGULATING CONTROLS: Electric Heat

	CITY	ST	EMP	PHONE	ENTRY #
Engineered Assembly & Services	Marshfield	MA	G	781 834-9085	12860

AUTOMATIC REGULATING CONTROLS: Energy Cutoff, Residtl/Comm

	CITY	ST	EMP	PHONE	ENTRY #
Johnson Controls Inc	Windsor	CT	C	860 688-7151	5341
Clarios	Lynnfield	MA	C	781 213-3463	12547

AUTOMATIC REGULATING CONTROLS: Hardware, Environmental Reg

	CITY	ST	EMP	PHONE	ENTRY #
Pardi Mfg Inc	West Boylston	MA	G	508 835-7887	16426
Lyco Enterprises Inc	Nashua	NH	G	603 888-2640	19201

AUTOMATIC REGULATING CONTROLS: Humidity, Air-Conditioning

	CITY	ST	EMP	PHONE	ENTRY #
Siebe Inc **(DH)**	Foxboro	MA	G	508 549-6768	10905

AUTOMATIC REGULATING CONTROLS: Hydronic Pressure Or Temp

	CITY	ST	EMP	PHONE	ENTRY #
J & B Service Company LLC	Bethel	CT	G	203 743-9357	163

AUTOMATIC REGULATING CONTROLS: Incinerator, Residential/Comm

	CITY	ST	EMP	PHONE	ENTRY #
Falmouth Products Inc	East Falmouth	MA	G	508 548-6686	10442
Sud-Chemie Protech Inc	Needham Heights	MA	E	781 444-5188	13345

AUTOMATIC REGULATING CONTROLS: Limit, Heating, Residtl/Comm

	CITY	ST	EMP	PHONE	ENTRY #
Emme E2ms LLC	Bristol	CT	F	860 845-8810	554

AUTOMATIC REGULATING CONTROLS: Refrig/Air-Cond Defrost

	CITY	ST	EMP	PHONE	ENTRY #
Belimo Aircontrols (usa) Inc **(HQ)**	Danbury	CT	C	800 543-9038	879
Belimo Automation AG	Danbury	CT	F	203 749-3319	880
Belimo Customization USA Inc	Danbury	CT	G	203 791-9915	881

AUTOMATIC REGULATING CONTROLS: Refrigeration, Pressure

	CITY	ST	EMP	PHONE	ENTRY #
Mv3 LLC	Buzzards Bay	MA	G	617 658-4420	9361

AUTOMATIC REGULATING CONTROLS: Sequencing, Electric Heat

	CITY	ST	EMP	PHONE	ENTRY #
Molecular Health Inc	Boston	MA	E	832 482-3898	8709

AUTOMATIC REGULATING CONTROLS: Static Pressure

	CITY	ST	EMP	PHONE	ENTRY #
Static Solutions Inc **(PA)**	Marlborough	MA	F	508 480-0700	12830
Static Technologies Corp	Rockland	MA	F	781 871-8962	14828

AUTOMATIC REGULATING CTRLS: Damper, Pneumatic Or Electric

	CITY	ST	EMP	PHONE	ENTRY #
Senior Operations LLC	Lewiston	ME	D	207 784-2338	6322
Wahlcometroflex Inc	Lewiston	ME	B	207 784-2338	6327

AUTOMATIC REGULATING CTRLS: Elec Heat Proportion, Modultg

	CITY	ST	EMP	PHONE	ENTRY #
Lee Electric Inc	Danvers	MA	C	978 777-0070	10231
Sigma Systems Corp	Mansfield	MA	E	781 688-2354	12658

AUTOMATIC TELLER MACHINES

	CITY	ST	EMP	PHONE	ENTRY #
Marinero Express 809 East	Stamford	CT	G	203 487-0636	4244
AAA Atm Services	Amesbury	MA	G	603 841-5615	7476
Arck Enterprises Inc	Danvers	MA	G	978 777-9166	10196
Atlantic Atm LLC	Ipswich	MA	G	978 356-4051	11903
Danversbank	South Hamilton	MA	G	978 468-2243	15314
Atlas Atm Corp	Providence	RI	F	401 421-4183	20960

AUTOMOBILE RECOVERY SVCS

	CITY	ST	EMP	PHONE	ENTRY #
GAP Promotions LLC	Gloucester	MA	F	978 281-0335	11185
Thought Industries Inc	Boston	MA	G	617 669-7725	8884

AUTOMOBILES & OTHER MOTOR VEHICLES WHOLESALERS

	CITY	ST	EMP	PHONE	ENTRY #
New Haven Companies Inc	East Haven	CT	F	203 469-6421	1257
Tel Epion Inc	Billerica	MA	E	978 436-2300	8302

AUTOMOBILES: Off-Road, Exc Recreational Vehicles

	CITY	ST	EMP	PHONE	ENTRY #
Moody Investments LLC	Exeter	RI	G	401 423-0121	20453

AUTOMOTIVE & TRUCK GENERAL REPAIR SVC

	CITY	ST	EMP	PHONE	ENTRY #
All Tech Auto/Truck Electric	Danbury	CT	G	203 790-8990	868
Raymond Spinazzola	Ashland	MA	G	508 881-3089	7667
Universal Carburetor Inc	Norwood	MA	G	781 762-3771	14204
J O Brown & Son Inc	North Haven	ME	G	207 867-4621	6511

AUTOMOTIVE BODY SHOP

	CITY	ST	EMP	PHONE	ENTRY #
Giroux Body Shop Inc	Hinesburg	VT	F	802 482-2162	22025
Washburn Boat & Auto Body	Williston	VT	G	802 863-1383	22697

AUTOMOTIVE BODY, PAINT & INTERIOR REPAIR & MAINTENANCE SVC

	CITY	ST	EMP	PHONE	ENTRY #
Special Projects Group LLC	Gilford	NH	G	603 391-9700	18192

AUTOMOTIVE COLLISION SHOPS

	CITY	ST	EMP	PHONE	ENTRY #
Mbw Tractor Sales LLC	Berwick	ME	F	207 384-2001	5711

AUTOMOTIVE EXTERIOR REPAIR SVCS

	CITY	ST	EMP	PHONE	ENTRY #
Middlesex Truck & Auto Bdy Inc	Boston	MA	E	617 442-3000	8705
Bri-Weld Industries LLC	Auburn	NH	F	603 622-9480	17608

AUTOMOTIVE PAINT SHOP

	CITY	ST	EMP	PHONE	ENTRY #
Marketing Worldwide Corp **(PA)**	Rockland	ME	G	631 444-8090	6804

AUTOMOTIVE PARTS, ACCESS & SPLYS

	CITY	ST	EMP	PHONE	ENTRY #
Airpot Corporation	Norwalk	CT	E	800 848-7681	3097
Armored Autogroup Inc **(DH)**	Danbury	CT	D	203 205-2900	874
Armored Autogroup Sales Inc	Danbury	CT	C	203 205-2900	876
Beacon Group Inc **(PA)**	Newington	CT	C	860 594-5200	2846
Cambridge Specialty Co Inc	Berlin	CT	D	860 828-3579	80
Cheshire Manufacturing Co Inc	Cheshire	CT	G	203 272-3586	721
Clayton Offroad Manufacturer	East Haven	CT	G	475 238-8251	1245
Competition Engineering Inc	Guilford	CT	C	203 453-5200	1697
Continental Machine Tl Co Inc	New Britain	CT	D	860 223-2896	2522
Expressway Lube Centers	Danbury	CT	F	203 744-2511	915
Fram Group Operations LLC	Danbury	CT	E	203 830-7800	922
International Automobile Entps **(PA)**	New Britain	CT	F	860 224-0253	2543
International Automobile Entps	New Britain	CT	F	860 224-0253	2544
Jk Motorsports	Fairfield	CT	G	203 255-9120	1438
Jobin Machine Inc	West Hartford	CT	E	860 953-1631	5079
King of Covers Inc **(PA)**	Winsted	CT	G	860 379-2427	5415
Lee Company **(PA)**	Westbrook	CT	A	860 399-6281	5157
Nickson Industries Inc	Plainville	CT	E	860 747-1671	3509
Nucap US Inc **(DH)**	Wolcott	CT	E	203 879-1423	5450
Platt-Labonia of N Haven Inc	North Haven	CT	D	203 239-5681	3052
Pratt & Whitney Engine Svcs	Middletown	CT	B	860 344-4000	2212
S Camerota & Sons Inc	North Haven	CT	G	203 782-0360	3060
Spectrum Brands Inc	Danbury	CT	G	203 205-2900	996
Turbine Technologies Inc **(PA)**	Farmington	CT	D	860 678-1642	1521
Vulcan Industries Inc	Windsor	CT	C	860 683-2005	5377
Araces Incorporated	Pittsfield	MA	G	413 499-9997	14453
Blendco Systems LLC	Holyoke	MA	E	800 537-7797	11619
Blue Magic Inc	Marblehead	MA	G	781 639-8428	12678
Boston Steel & Mfg Co	Haverhill	MA	E	781 324-3000	11409
Clearmotion Inc	Wilmington	MA	G	617 313-0822	16987
Clearmotion Inc **(PA)**	Billerica	MA	F	617 313-0822	8231
Creative Services	East Longmeadow	MA	G	413 525-4993	10470
Curtis Industries LLC **(PA)**	West Boylston	MA	F	508 853-2200	16413
General Electric Company	Lynn	MA	D	781 598-7303	12511
Geoorbital Inc	Somerville	MA	F	617 651-1102	15178
Gtb Innovative Solutions Inc	Westfield	MA	F	413 733-0146	16685
H&H Propeller Shop Inc **(PA)**	Salem	MA	E	978 744-3806	14918
Hewlett Packard HP Autonomy So	Southborough	MA	D	508 476-0000	15360
Hi-Tech Inc	Attleboro	MA	F	401 454-4086	7746
High Voltage Engineering Corp	Wakefield	MA	F	781 224-1001	15954
Jnc Rebuilders Inc	Ipswich	MA	G	978 356-2996	11925
Lfr Chassis Inc	Shrewsbury	MA	G	508 425-3117	15121
North Shore Laboratories Corp	Peabody	MA	F	978 531-5954	14358
Thermokinetics	Dracut	MA	F	978 459-6073	10369
Xl Hybrids Inc **(PA)**	Brighton	MA	E	617 718-0329	9108
Distance Racing Products	Fairfield	ME	G	207 453-2644	6026
Electrnic Mobility Contrls LLC	Augusta	ME	F	207 512-8009	5607
Irish Inc **(PA)**	Turner	ME	G	207 224-7605	7108
Marketing Worldwide Corp **(PA)**	Rockland	ME	G	631 444-8090	6804
Nichols Portland LLC **(PA)**	Portland	ME	B	207 774-6121	6702
Somic America Inc	Brewer	ME	D	207 989-1759	5801
Freudenberg-Nok General Partnr	Northfield	NH	D	603 286-1600	19401
Freudenberg-Nok General Partnr	Northfield	NH	E	603 286-1600	19402
General Electric Company	Hooksett	NH	A	603 666-8300	18351
Larry Dingee	Cornish	NH	G	603 542-9682	17962
Osram Sylvania Inc	Hillsborough	NH	B	603 464-7235	18317
Bear Hydraulics Inc	Warwick	RI	G	401 732-5832	21335
Kennedy Incorporated	North Kingstown	RI	F	401 295-7800	20720
Autotech Inc	Winooski	VT	G	802 497-2482	22716
General Electric Company	Rutland	VT	A	802 775-9842	22335
JBM Sherman Carmel Inc	Bennington	VT	E	802 442-5115	21675
Rennline Inc	Milton	VT	G	802 893-7366	22138
Safe and Secure Fou A NJ Non	Perkinsville	VT	G	848 992-3623	22257

AUTOMOTIVE PARTS: Plastic

	CITY	ST	EMP	PHONE	ENTRY #
Jor Services LLC	New Canaan	CT	G	203 594-7774	2602
Lawrence Holdings Inc **(PA)**	Wallingford	CT	F	203 949-1600	4764
Atlantic Auto & Trck Parts LLC	Peabody	MA	G	978 535-6777	14314
Clean Products LLC	Fall River	MA	G	508 676-9355	10675
Harpoon Productions	Cohasset	MA	G	781 383-0500	10099
Illinois Tool Works Inc	Westminster	MA	C	978 874-0151	16805
Larkin Motors LLC	Bridgewater	MA	G	508 807-1333	9082
Deflex Innovations Inc	Berlin	NH	G	603 215-6738	17695
Mrp Manufacturing LLC	Pittsfield	NH	G	603 435-5337	19503
Scarborough Faire Inc **(PA)**	Pawtucket	RI	E	401 724-4200	20897

AUTOMOTIVE PRDTS: Rubber

	CITY	ST	EMP	PHONE	ENTRY #
Hutchinson Sealing Systems Inc	Newfields	NH	C	603 772-3771	19317

AUTOMOTIVE REPAIR SHOPS: Carburetor Repair

	CITY	ST	EMP	PHONE	ENTRY #
Universal Carburetor Inc	Norwood	MA	G	781 762-3771	14204

AUTOMOTIVE REPAIR SHOPS: Catalytic Conversion

	CITY	ST	EMP	PHONE	ENTRY #
J-A Industries Incorporated	North Easton	MA	G	508 297-1648	13948

AUTOMOTIVE REPAIR SHOPS: Engine Rebuilding

	CITY	ST	EMP	PHONE	ENTRY #
A & M Auto Machine Inc	Meriden	CT	G	203 237-3502	2071

AUTOMOTIVE REPAIR SHOPS: Engine Repair, Exc Diesel

	CITY	ST	EMP	PHONE	ENTRY #
Melton Sales and Service Inc	Hallowell	ME	F	207 623-8895	6163

AUTOMOTIVE REPAIR SHOPS: Machine Shop

	CITY	ST	EMP	PHONE	ENTRY #
A & M Auto Machine Inc	Meriden	CT	G	203 237-3502	2071
Accu-Mill Technologies LLC	Plainville	CT	G	860 747-3921	3462
M & B Automotive Machine Shop	Stamford	CT	G	203 348-6134	4242
Centerline Machine Company Inc	Beverly	MA	F	978 524-8842	8115
Days Auto Body Inc	Medway	ME	G	207 746-5310	6423
Hagan Design and Machine Inc	Newmarket	NH	G	603 292-1101	19335

AUTOMOTIVE REPAIR SHOPS: Powertrain Components Repair Svcs

	CITY	ST	EMP	PHONE	ENTRY #
Rhode Island Driveshaft Sup Co	Warwick	RI	G	401 941-0210	21412

AUTOMOTIVE REPAIR SHOPS: Trailer Repair

	CITY	ST	EMP	PHONE	ENTRY #
Boston Trailer Manufacturing	Walpole	MA	E	508 668-2242	15990
U-Haul Co of Massachusetts	Walpole	MA	F	508 668-2242	16015
Wright Trailers Inc	Seekonk	MA	F	508 336-8530	15044
Ricks Truck & Trailer Repair	Hillsborough	NH	G	603 464-3636	18318

	CITY	ST	EMP	PHONE	ENTRY#
AUTOMOTIVE REPAIR SHOPS: Truck Engine Repair, Exc Indl					
Lo Stocco Motors	Danbury	CT	G	203 797-9618	949
Jon Shafts & Stuff	Manchester	NH	G	603 518-5033	18851
Ralph L Osgood Inc	Claremont	NH	F	603 543-1703	17859
Scott G Reed Truck Svcs Inc	Claremont	NH	F	603 542-5032	17860
AUTOMOTIVE REPAIR SHOPS: Turbocharger & Blower Repair					
Kent Pearce	East Wareham	MA	G	508 295-3791	10531
AUTOMOTIVE REPAIR SVC					
Taylor Rental Center	East Longmeadow	MA	G	413 525-2576	10496
Auto Electric Service LLC	Brentwood	NH	G	603 642-5990	17746
AUTOMOTIVE SPLYS & PARTS, NEW, WHOL: Auto Servicing Eqpt					
Connected Automotive	South Easton	MA	E	508 238-5855	15274
AUTOMOTIVE SPLYS & PARTS, NEW, WHOLESALE: Engines/Eng Parts					
Drt Aerospace LLC	Winsted	CT	F	860 379-0783	5408
AUTOMOTIVE SPLYS & PARTS, NEW, WHOLESALE: Splys					
Blendco Systems LLC	Holyoke	MA	E	800 537-7797	11619
AUTOMOTIVE SPLYS & PARTS, NEW, WHOLESALE: Trailer Parts					
Kensington Welding & Trlr Co	Kensington	CT	G	860 828-3564	1918
AUTOMOTIVE SPLYS & PARTS, WHOLESALE, NEC					
Scarborough Faire Inc **(PA)**	Pawtucket	RI	E	401 724-4200	20897
Wheeltrak Inc	Tiverton	RI	E	800 296-1326	21266
AUTOMOTIVE SVCS, EXC REPAIR & CARWASHES: Customizing					
Larkin Motors LLC	Bridgewater	MA	G	508 807-1333	9082
AUTOMOTIVE SVCS, EXC REPAIR & CARWASHES: Lubrication					
Yvons Valvoline Express Care	Lewiston	ME	G	207 777-3600	6328
AUTOMOTIVE SVCS, EXC REPAIR & CARWASHES: Maintenance					
J G Performance Inc	Abington	MA	G	781 871-1404	7325
Wheeltrak Inc	Tiverton	RI	E	800 296-1326	21266
AUTOMOTIVE SVCS, EXC REPAIR & CARWASHES: Trailer Maintenance					
Standard Welding Company Inc	East Hartford	CT	G	860 528-9628	1222
AUTOMOTIVE SVCS, EXC RPR/CARWASHES: High Perf Auto Rpr/Svc					
Melton Sales and Service Inc	Hallowell	ME	F	207 623-8895	6163
AUTOMOTIVE WELDING SVCS					
Burton Frame and Trailer Inc	Pepperell	MA	G	978 433-2051	14437
Larkin Motors LLC	Bridgewater	MA	G	508 807-1333	9082
Raymond Spinazzola	Ashland	MA	G	508 881-3089	7667
Caron Fabrication LLC	Groveton	NH	G	603 631-0025	18231
AUTOMOTIVE: Bodies					
Mirak Building Trust	Arlington	MA	G	781 643-8000	7631
AUTOMOTIVE: Seating					
Clarios	Ledyard	CT	D	860 886-9021	1940
Clarios	Meriden	CT	D	678 297-4040	2086
Johnson Controls Inc	Rocky Hill	CT	G	860 571-3300	3720
Johnson Controls Inc	Boston	MA	D	617 992-2073	8636
Clarios	Portland	ME	G	603 222-2400	6638
Clarios	Manchester	NH	G	603 222-2400	18799
AUTOTRANSFORMERS: Electric					
General Electric Company	Westborough	MA	F	508 870-5200	16619
Moveras LLC	Salem	NH	E	603 685-0404	19753
AVIATION PROPELLER & BLADE REPAIR SVCS					
Amk Welding Inc **(HQ)**	South Windsor	CT	E	860 289-5634	3937
AWNING REPAIR SHOP					
Leavitt & Parris Inc	Portland	ME	F	207 797-0100	6679
AWNINGS & CANOPIES					
Niantic Awning Company	Niantic	CT	G	860 739-0161	2954
Plymouth Awning Co	Plymouth	MA	G	508 746-3740	14574
Railings Unlimited	Fall River	MA	G	508 679-5678	10751
Futureguard Building Pdts Inc **(PA)**	Auburn	ME	D	800 858-5818	5565
L F Pease Co	East Providence	RI	F	401 438-2850	20428
Durasol Systems Inc	Middlebury	VT	E	802 388-7309	22109
AWNINGS & CANOPIES: Awnings, Fabric, From Purchased Matls					
B and G Enterprise LLC **(PA)**	New Haven	CT	G	203 562-7232	2663
Fitzgerald-Norwalk Awning Co	Norwalk	CT	G	203 847-5858	3153
State Awning Company	Hartford	CT	G	860 246-2575	1872
Tetrault & Sons Inc	Stafford Springs	CT	G	860 872-9187	4117
Toff Industry Inc	Milldale	CT	G	860 378-0532	2388
Cheyne Awning & Sign Co	Pittsfield	MA	G	413 442-4742	14464
Da Costa Awnings & Canvas Spc	Taunton	MA	G	508 822-4944	15739
Dartmouth Awning Co Inc	Westport	MA	G	508 636-6838	16838
Expansion Opportunities Inc	Northborough	MA	E	508 303-8200	14033
Harry Miller Co Inc	Boston	MA	E	617 427-2300	8589
Harry Miller Co LLC **(PA)**	Boston	MA	E	617 427-2300	8590
Lyman Conrad **(PA)**	South Hadley	MA	E	413 538-8200	15306
MM Reif Ltd	Boston	MA	D	617 442-9500	8708
Moderne Rug Inc	Fitchburg	MA	G	978 343-3210	10840
R H M Group Inc	Beverly	MA	G	978 745-4710	8169
Readys Window Products Inc	Tewksbury	MA	G	978 851-3963	15832
Sunsetter Products Ltd Partnr	Malden	MA	D	781 321-9600	12598
William Blanchard Co Inc	Wakefield	MA	F	781 245-8050	15985
Canvasworks Inc	Kennebunk	ME	G	207 985-2419	6230
Collabric	Veazie	ME	F	207 945-5095	7126
Leavitt & Parris Inc	Portland	ME	F	207 797-0100	6679
Lewiston-Auburn Tent & Awng Co	Lewiston	ME	G	207 784-7353	6301
McDonald Duvall Design Inc	Rockland	ME	G	207 596-7940	6805
Image Awnings Inc	Wolfeboro	NH	G	603 569-6680	20020
Just Right Awnings & Signs	Dover	NH	G	603 740-8416	18033
Yarra Design & Fabrication LLC	Bow	NH	F	603 224-6880	17736
Awning Guy LLC	Providence	RI	G	401 787-0097	20966
Kinder Industries Inc	Bristol	RI	F	401 253-7076	20087
AWNINGS & CANOPIES: Canopies, Fabric, From Purchased Matls					
Federal Specialties Inc	West Springfield	MA	G	413 782-6900	16520
Durasol Systems Inc	Williston	VT	E	802 864-3009	22663
AWNINGS & CANOPIES: Fabric					
Genvario Awning Co	Norwalk	CT	G	203 847-5858	3161
Maple Leaf Cpitl Ventures Corp **(PA)**	Medford	MA	G	781 569-6311	12939
Signs By J Inc	Boston	MA	G	617 825-9855	8845
L F Pease Co	East Providence	RI	F	401 438-2850	20428
Green Mountain Awning Inc	West Rutland	VT	G	802 438-2951	22615
AWNINGS: Fiberglass					
Signs Unlimited Inc	Derby	CT	G	203 734-7446	1080
Lyman Conrad **(PA)**	South Hadley	MA	E	413 538-8200	15306
New England Signs & Awngs LLC	Hudson	NH	G	603 235-7205	18420
AWNINGS: Metal					
Tetrault & Sons Inc	Stafford Springs	CT	G	860 872-9187	4117
High Grade Shade & Screen Co	Lynn	MA	F	781 592-5027	12516
Lyman Conrad **(PA)**	South Hadley	MA	E	413 538-8200	15306
Taunton Venetian Blind Inc	Taunton	MA	G	508 822-7548	15789
Green Mountain Awning Inc	West Rutland	VT	G	802 438-2951	22615
AXES & HATCHETS					
Lewmar Inc **(DH)**	Guilford	CT	E	203 458-6200	1708
Camelot Tools LLC	Holden	MA	G	508 981-7443	11542
BABY PACIFIERS: Rubber					
Mayborn Usa Inc	Stamford	CT	F	781 269-7490	4245
Dorel Juvenile Group Inc	Foxboro	MA	D	800 544-1108	10881
BACKHOES					
Valente Backhoe Service LLC	Shrewsbury	MA	G	508 754-7013	15134
BADGES: Identification & Insignia					
GA Rel Manufacturing Company	Providence	RI	E	401 331-5455	21019
Ira Green Inc	Providence	RI	C	800 663-7487	21040
BAGS & CONTAINERS: Textile, Exc Sleeping					
Uninsred Alttude Cnnection Inc	Brooklyn	CT	G	860 333-1461	673
Fleming Industries Inc	Chicopee	MA	D	413 593-3300	10026
Sorenson Sewing Inc	Hyde Park	MA	G	617 333-6955	11880
Lapoint Industries Inc **(PA)**	Auburn	ME	D	207 777-3100	5575
Enviro-Tote Inc	Londonderry	NH	E	603 647-7171	18696
BAGS & SACKS: Shipping & Shopping					
Accurate Services Inc	Fall River	MA	E	508 674-5773	10650
BAGS: Canvas					
CB Sports Inc	Malden	MA	G	781 322-0307	12564
Steele Canvas Basket Corp	Chelsea	MA	E	800 541-8929	9970
BAGS: Cellophane					
Eastern Packaging Inc	Lawrence	MA	D	978 685-7723	12020
BAGS: Duffle, Canvas, Made From Purchased Materials					
Nancy Lawrence	Portland	ME	G	207 774-7276	6697
BAGS: Food Storage & Trash, Plastic					
Inteplast Engineered Films Inc	Westborough	MA	D	508 366-8884	16626
BAGS: Garment, Plastic Film, Made From Purchased Materials					
Flashbags LLC	Burlington	VT	G	802 999-8981	21782
BAGS: Laundry, From Purchased Materials					
Almont Company Inc	East Weymouth	MA	E	617 269-8244	10534
BAGS: Laundry, Garment & Storage					
Unwrapped Inc	Lowell	MA	D	978 441-0242	12443
BAGS: Paper					
Accutech Packaging Inc	Foxboro	MA	D	508 543-3800	10873
Maine Potato Growers Inc	Caribou	ME	E	207 764-3131	5886
Sappi North America Inc	Skowhegan	ME	A	207 238-3000	6986
Sappi North America Inc	South Portland	ME	D	207 854-7000	7039
Pak 2000 Inc	Lancaster	NH	D	603 569-3700	18603
Mason Box Company	Pawtucket	RI	E	800 842-9526	20857
BAGS: Paper, Made From Purchased Materials					
Northeast Packaging Co **(PA)**	Presque Isle	ME	E	207 764-6271	6763
BAGS: Plastic					
Amgraph Packaging Inc	Baltic	CT	C	860 822-2000	48

	CITY	ST	EMP	PHONE	ENTRY #
Armin Innovative Products Inc	Dighton	MA	E	508 822-4629	10335
Cold River Mining Inc	Greenfield	MA	G	413 219-3315	11256
Extrafresh LLC	Longmeadow	MA	G	413 567-8995	12333
Mettler Packaging LLC	Raynham	MA	G	508 738-2201	14719
R & P Plastics LLC	Winchendon	MA	G	978 297-1115	17079
Northeast Packaging Co	Caribou	ME	G	207 496-3141	5888
Admiral Packaging Inc	Providence	RI	D	401 274-5588	20945
Liftbag Usa Inc	North Kingstown	RI	F	401 884-8801	20722
Subsalve USA LLC	North Kingstown	RI	F	401 884-8801	20743

BAGS: Plastic & Pliofilm

	CITY	ST	EMP	PHONE	ENTRY #
Pakpro Inc	Andover	MA	G	978 474-5018	7580
Pak 2000 Inc	Lancaster	NH	D	603 569-3700	18603

BAGS: Plastic, Made From Purchased Materials

	CITY	ST	EMP	PHONE	ENTRY #
Safety Bags Inc	Shelton	CT	G	203 242-0727	3867
Ace-Lon Corporation	Malden	MA	E	781 322-7121	12556
Crown Poly Inc	Norton	MA	G	781 883-4979	14075
Hi-De Liners Inc	Orange	MA	E	978 544-7801	14218
Jannel Manufacturing Inc	Holbrook	MA	E	781 767-0666	11527
Laddawn Inc **(HQ)**	Devens	MA	D	800 446-3639	10322
Northeast Packaging Co **(PA)**	Presque Isle	ME	E	207 764-6271	6763
Tufpak Inc	Ossipee	NH	E	603 539-4126	19424
Monument Industries Inc	Bennington	VT	E	802 442-8187	21684

BAGS: Rubber Or Rubberized Fabric

	CITY	ST	EMP	PHONE	ENTRY #
Ponn Machine Cutting Co	Woburn	MA	F	781 937-3373	17267

BAGS: Textile

	CITY	ST	EMP	PHONE	ENTRY #
Dayton Bag & Burlap Co	East Granby	CT	G	860 653-8191	1125
Dow Cover Company Incorporated	New Haven	CT	D	203 469-5394	2683
Smiling Dog	Middletown	CT	G	860 344-0707	2223
Clarkie Industries	North Attleboro	MA	F	508 404-0202	13753
Fall River Apparel Inc	Fall River	MA	G	508 677-1975	10694
Hosokawa Micron International	Northborough	MA	F	508 655-1123	14037
MM Reif Ltd	Boston	MA	D	617 442-9500	8708
Pacheco Gear Inc	East Freetown	MA	G	508 763-5709	10456
Under Cover Inc	New Bedford	MA	F	508 997-7600	13456
United Industrial Tex Pdts Inc **(PA)**	West Springfield	MA	E	413 737-0095	16559
United Industrial Tex Pdts Inc	West Springfield	MA	G	413 737-0095	16560
Unwrapped Inc	Lowell	MA	D	978 441-0242	12443
Byer Manufacturing Company	Orono	ME	E	207 866-2171	6552
C B P Corp **(PA)**	Arundel	ME	F	207 985-9767	5529
Baileyworks Inc	Newmarket	NH	G	603 292-6485	19330
Curator	Walpole	NH	G	603 756-3888	19919
J B A Products	Effingham	NH	G	603 539-5034	18095
Absorbent Specialty Pdts LLC	Cumberland	RI	F	401 722-1177	20312
Sports Systems Custom Bags	Woonsocket	RI	D	401 767-3770	21579

BAGS: Trash, Plastic Film, Made From Purchased Materials

	CITY	ST	EMP	PHONE	ENTRY #
Maine Cleaners Supply Inc	North Yarmouth	ME	G	207 657-3166	6517

BAGS: Wardrobe, Closet Access, Made From Purchased Materials

	CITY	ST	EMP	PHONE	ENTRY #
Re-Style Your Closets LLC	Simsbury	CT	G	860 658-9450	3910
Convanta Holliston	Holliston	MA	G	508 429-9750	11564

BAKERIES, COMMERCIAL: On Premises Baking Only

	CITY	ST	EMP	PHONE	ENTRY #
Amodios Inc **(PA)**	Waterbury	CT	F	203 573-1229	4843
Atticus Bakery LLC	New Haven	CT	C	203 562-9007	2661
Better Baking By Beth	Torrington	CT	G	860 482-4706	4564
Big Purple Cupcake LLC	Branford	CT	G	203 483-8738	297
Boston Model Bakery	New Haven	CT	E	203 562-9491	2671
Freihofer Charles Baking Co	Naugatuck	CT	G	203 729-4545	2474
Hardcore Sweet Cupcakes LLC	Waterbury	CT	G	203 808-5547	4882
I and U LLC	Waterbury	CT	G	860 803-1491	4886
Katona Bakery LLC	Fairfield	CT	E	203 337-5349	1440
Pastry Shop	Meriden	CT	G	203 238-0483	2115
Red Rose Desserts	Colchester	CT	G	860 603-2670	807
Riverside Baking Company LLC	Fairfield	CT	G	203 451-0331	1452
Spinella Bakery	Waterbury	CT	F	203 753-9451	4959
Thadieo LLC	Southington	CT	G	860 621-4500	4084
Watson LLC **(DH)**	West Haven	CT	B	203 932-3000	5149
Whole German Breads LLC	New Haven	CT	G	203 507-0663	2754
Wildflour Cupcakes Sweets LLC	Seymour	CT	G	203 828-6576	3768
Arts International Wholesale	Raynham	MA	G	508 822-7181	14705
Bakery To Go Inc	Boston	MA	G	617 482-1015	8388
Bbu Inc	Chicopee	MA	E	413 593-2700	10000
Bimbo Bakeries Usa Inc	Medford	MA	F	781 306-0221	12922
Bollywood Delights Inc	Southborough	MA	G	508 740-1908	15350
Budiproducts	Boston	MA	G	617 470-3086	8448
Buttergirl Baking Co	Lexington	MA	G	857 891-6625	12210
Buzzworthy Baking LLC	Concord	MA	G	978 254-5910	10119
C Q P Bakery	Lawrence	MA	E	978 557-5626	12000
Concord Teacakes Etcetera Inc	Concord	MA	F	978 369-7644	10123
Cupcake Town	Mansfield	MA	G	774 284-4667	12625
Duva Distributors Inc	Shrewsbury	MA	E	508 841-8182	15109
Elie Baking Corporation	Brockton	MA	F	508 584-4890	9143
Forge Baking Company Inc	Arlington	MA	G	617 764-5365	7627
G H Bent Company	Milton	MA	E	617 322-9287	13192
George Weston Bakeries	Pittsfield	MA	G	413 443-6095	14473
Ginsco Inc	North Dartmouth	MA	F	508 990-3350	13921
Jacquelines Wholesale Bky Inc	Salem	MA	D	978 744-8600	14923
Meyers Gluten Free Baking LLC	Beverly	MA	G	978 381-9629	8152
Middle East Bakery Inc **(PA)**	Lawrence	MA	D	978 688-2221	12057
Montiones Biscotti **(PA)**	Norton	MA	F	508 285-7004	14083
Multigrains Inc	Lawrence	MA	C	978 691-6100	12060
N B Baking Co	New Bedford	MA	G	508 992-5413	13419
Old San Juan Bakery Inc	Holyoke	MA	F	413 534-5555	11646
Pipe Dream Cupcakes LLC	North Andover	MA	G	978 397-6470	13724
Spinelli Ravioli Mfg Co Inc	Boston	MA	E	617 567-1992	8859
B&G Foods Inc	Portland	ME	C	207 772-8341	6616
Bimbo Bakeries Usa Inc	Scarborough	ME	G	207 883-5252	6911
Freihofer Baking Co	Bangor	ME	G	207 947-2387	5646
Labrees Inc	Old Town	ME	B	207 827-6121	6543
Lepage Bakeries Park St LLC **(HQ)**	Auburn	ME	E	207 783-9161	5577
Little Gottage Baking	Sanford	ME	G	207 432-2930	6880
Little Notch Bakery	Southwest Harbor	ME	G	207 244-4043	7048
Moonbat City Baking Co LLC	Belfast	ME	G	207 323-4955	5695
Out Sweet Tooth Cupcakes	South Portland	ME	G	207 272-4363	7035
Stiletto Cupcakes	Lisbon	ME	G	207 212-9788	6365
A Sweet As Sugar Life-Cupcakes	Londonderry	NH	G	603 591-8957	18669
Cupcake Rowe LLC	Milford	NH	G	603 673-0489	19054
Gone Baking LLC	Bedford	NH	G	603 305-6026	17643
Happy Bird Baking Company LLC	Peterborough	NH	G	603 759-0714	19471
Lepage Bakeries Park St LLC	Hudson	NH	E	603 880-4446	18410
Small Bites Cupcakes	Laconia	NH	G	603 387-6333	18586
White Mountain Cupcakery LLC	North Conway	NH	G	603 730-5140	19381
Calise & Sons Bakery Inc **(PA)**	Lincoln	RI	C	401 334-3444	20560
Cavanagh Company	Greenville	RI	E	401 949-4000	20464
Frostbite Cupcakes	Chepachet	RI	G	508 801-6706	20134
Jojoscupcakes LLC	Coventry	RI	G	401 297-4900	20151
Usquepaugh Baking Co LLC	West Kingston	RI	G	401 782-6907	21474
Bakers Dozen Inc	Colchester	VT	F	802 879-4001	21857
Capitol Cupcake Company LLC	Montpelier	VT	G	802 522-3576	22147
Fudge Factory Inc	Manchester Center	VT	F	888 669-7425	22085
Harringtons In Vermont Inc **(PA)**	Richmond	VT	F	802 434-7500	22312
Simply Cupcakes	Essex Junction	VT	G	802 871-5634	21961

BAKERIES: On Premises Baking & Consumption

	CITY	ST	EMP	PHONE	ENTRY #
Capricorn Investors II LP	Greenwich	CT	A	203 861-6600	1602
Lupis Inc	New Haven	CT	E	203 562-9491	2710
Milite Bakery	Waterbury	CT	G	203 753-9451	4916
Concord Teacakes Etcetera Inc	Concord	MA	F	978 369-7644	10123
G H Bent Company	Milton	MA	E	617 322-9287	13192
Harbar LLC	Canton	MA	C	781 828-0848	9735
Nantucket Bake Shop Inc	Nantucket	MA	G	508 228-2797	13228
Spinelli Ravioli Mfg Co Inc	Boston	MA	E	617 567-1992	8859
Tripoli Bakery Inc	Lawrence	MA	E	978 682-7754	12078
Lepage Bakeries Park St LLC	Auburn	ME	E	207 783-9161	5576
Lepage Bakeries Park St LLC **(HQ)**	Auburn	ME	E	207 783-9161	5577
Fudge Factory Inc	Manchester Center	VT	F	888 669-7425	22085

BAKERY FOR HOME SVC DELIVERY

	CITY	ST	EMP	PHONE	ENTRY #
Arnold Bakeries	Bass River	MA	G	508 398-6588	7953

BAKERY MACHINERY

	CITY	ST	EMP	PHONE	ENTRY #
C H Babb Co Inc	Raynham	MA	E	508 977-0600	14706
Somerset Industries Inc	Lowell	MA	E	978 667-3355	12433

BAKERY PRDTS: Bagels, Fresh Or Frozen

	CITY	ST	EMP	PHONE	ENTRY #
Bagel Boys Inc **(PA)**	Glastonbury	CT	F	860 657-4400	1539
Bagel Boy Inc	Lawrence	MA	D	978 682-8646	11998
Boston Bagel Inc	Hyde Park	MA	E	617 364-6900	11863
Frozen Batters Inc	North Andover	MA	D	508 683-1414	13706
Ginsco Inc	Fall River	MA	F	508 677-4767	10703
Ginsco Inc **(PA)**	Fall River	MA	F	508 677-4767	10704
Korner Bagel Partnership	Seekonk	MA	E	508 336-5204	15025

BAKERY PRDTS: Bakery Prdts, Partially Cooked, Exc frozen

	CITY	ST	EMP	PHONE	ENTRY #
Haylons Market LLC	Niantic	CT	G	860 739-9509	2951
Lepage Bakeries Park St LLC	Belmont	NH	F	603 524-9104	17677

BAKERY PRDTS: Bread, All Types, Fresh Or Frozen

	CITY	ST	EMP	PHONE	ENTRY #
Bricins Inc	Torrington	CT	F	860 482-0250	4567
Krafty Kakes Inc	Wallingford	CT	G	203 284-0299	4762
Lupis Inc	New Haven	CT	E	203 562-9491	2710
Milite Bakery	Waterbury	CT	G	203 753-9451	4916
Bernardinos Bakery Inc **(PA)**	Chicopee	MA	D	413 592-1944	10001
Cohens United Baking Inc	Worcester	MA	G	508 754-0232	17357
Gold Medal Bakery Inc **(PA)**	Fall River	MA	B	508 674-5766	10705
Newly Weds Foods Inc	Watertown	MA	D	617 926-7600	16303
Piantedosi Baking Co Inc **(PA)**	Malden	MA	C	781 321-3400	12590
Pittsfield Rye Bakery Inc	Pittsfield	MA	E	413 443-9141	14501
Lepage Bakeries Park St LLC	Lewiston	ME	D	207 783-9161	6298
Mathews Bakery Inc	Portland	ME	E	207 773-9647	6693
Westcott Baking Company Inc	West Warwick	RI	F	401 821-8007	21514

BAKERY PRDTS: Cakes, Bakery, Exc Frozen

	CITY	ST	EMP	PHONE	ENTRY #
Bimbo Bakeries Usa Inc	Orange	CT	D	203 932-1000	3360
Izzi BS Allergy Free LLC	Norwalk	CT	G	203 810-4378	3177
3 Little Figs LLC	Somerville	MA	G	617 623-3447	15150
Little Delights Bakery	Lowell	MA	G	978 455-0040	12396
Margies Sweet Surrender	Hull	MA	G	781 925-2271	11828
Morais Marizete	Marlborough	MA	G	508 460-8200	12795
New Brand Sebsatians LLC	Boston	MA	G	617 624-7999	8729
Superior Cake Products Inc	Southbridge	MA	D	508 764-3276	15406
Betty Reez Whoopiez	Freeport	ME	G	207 865-1735	6072
Cakes For All Seasons LLC	Biddeford	ME	G	207 432-9192	5724
ME and Ollies	Portsmouth	NH	G	603 319-1561	19592

BAKERY PRDTS: Cakes, Bakery, Frozen

	CITY	ST	EMP	PHONE	ENTRY #
Something Sweet Inc **(PA)**	New Haven	CT	E	203 603-9766	2738
Somerville Office	Somerville	MA	G	617 776-0738	15217
C J Cranam Inc	Oxford	ME	E	207 739-1016	6564

	CITY	ST	EMP	PHONE	ENTRY #
Crazy Russian Girls Whole	Bennington	VT	G	802 681-3983	21667

BAKERY PRDTS: Cones, Ice Cream

Wild Cow Creamery LLC	Bangor	ME	G	207 907-0301	5664
Lincoln Creamery Inc	Lincoln	RI	F	401 724-1050	20579

BAKERY PRDTS: Cookies

Bimbo Bakeries Usa Inc	Orange	CT	D	203 932-1000	3360
R & K Cookies LLC	Cromwell	CT	G	860 613-2893	858
Boston Chipyard The Inc	Boston	MA	F	617 742-9537	8428
Concord Teacakes Etcetera Inc	Concord	MA	F	978 369-7644	10123
Ho Toy Noodles Inc **(PA)**	Stoughton	MA	F	617 426-0247	15596
Julie Cecchini	Southwick	MA	F	413 562-2042	15414
Keebler Company	Franklin	MA	D	508 520-7223	11060
Murray Biscuit Company LLC	Canton	MA	G	781 760-0220	9758
Peggy Lawton Kitchens Inc	East Walpole	MA	E	508 668-1215	10528
Snyders-Lance Inc	Hyannis	MA	G	508 771-1872	11858
Sweet Creations	Wakefield	MA	E	781 246-0836	15979
Daddys Private Stock LLC	Canaan	ME	G	207 399-7154	5872
Moms Organic Munchies	Freeport	ME	G	207 869-4078	6084
Homefree LLC	Windham	NH	E	603 898-0172	20008
Sherwood Brands of RI	Rumford	RI	E	401 726-4500	21195

BAKERY PRDTS: Cookies & crackers

Beldotti Bakeries	Stamford	CT	F	203 348-9029	4148
Bob The Baker LLC	Brookfield	CT	F	203 775-1032	635
Barbaras Bakery Inc **(DH)**	Marlborough	MA	E	800 343-0590	12725
Nantucket Bake Shop Inc	Nantucket	MA	G	508 228-2797	13228
Maine Crisp Company LLC **(PA)**	Waterville	ME	G	207 213-9296	7158
Catanzaro Food Products Inc	Pawtucket	RI	G	401 255-1700	20820
Dr Lucys LLC	Rutland	VT	E	757 233-9495	22330
Harringtons In Vermont Inc **(PA)**	Richmond	VT	F	802 434-7500	22312

BAKERY PRDTS: Crackers

G H Bent Company	Milton	MA	E	617 322-9287	13192
Venus Wafers Inc	Hingham	MA	E	781 740-1002	11514

BAKERY PRDTS: Doughnuts, Exc Frozen

Daybrake Donuts Inc	Bridgeport	CT	F	203 368-4962	401
Donut Stop	Shelton	CT	G	203 924-7133	3797
Hartford Cpl Co-Op Inc	Hartford	CT	C	860 296-5636	1833
Massconn Distribute Cpl	South Windsor	CT	D	860 882-0717	3992
Pops Donuts	Milford	CT	G	203 876-1210	2335
Jumbo Donuts	Uxbridge	MA	F	508 278-9977	15922
Junes Place	Medway	MA	G	508 533-5037	12964
Holy Donut	Scarborough	ME	G	207 303-0137	6924
Limerick Dough Boy	Limerick	ME	G	207 793-4145	6336
Lafayette Distributors Cpl Inc	Hampton	NH	E	603 430-9405	18266
Lasalle Donuts Inc	Providence	RI	G	401 272-9773	21049

BAKERY PRDTS: Dry

Cherise Cpl LLC	Meriden	CT	G	203 238-3482	2085
Foundry Foods Inc	Norwalk	CT	G	314 982-3204	3154
Harsha Inc	Waterford	CT	G	860 439-1466	4985
Sharrocks English Bakery Inc	New Bedford	MA	G	508 997-5710	13450
Chase S Daily LLC	Belfast	ME	G	207 338-0555	5687

BAKERY PRDTS: Frozen

Cooper Marketing Group Inc	Danbury	CT	G	203 797-9386	893
Rich Products Corporation	New Britain	CT	A	866 737-8884	2570
Rich Products Corporation	New Britain	CT	A	800 356-7094	2571
Bimbo Bakeries Usa Inc	Rehoboth	MA	C	508 336-7735	14745
Diannes Fine Desserts Inc **(PA)**	Newburyport	MA	C	978 463-3832	13482
Diannes Fine Desserts Inc	Newburyport	MA	C	978 463-3881	13483
Ocean State Cpl Inc	East Providence	RI	C	401 431-0153	20438
Cosmic Bakers of Vermont LLC	Saint Albans	VT	F	802 524-0800	22366
Harringtons In Vermont Inc **(PA)**	Richmond	VT	F	802 434-7500	22312

BAKERY PRDTS: Pastries, Exc Frozen

Take Cake LLC	Guilford	CT	G	203 453-1896	1722
Jean Charles Blondine	Roxbury	MA	G	857 247-9369	14873

BAKERY PRDTS: Pies, Bakery, Frozen

Aristocrat Products Inc	Upton	MA	G	508 529-3471	15904
New England Country Pies LLC	Lynn	MA	F	781 596-0176	12528
Peppercorn Food Service Inc	Marblehead	MA	E	781 639-6035	12690
Stone House Farm Inc	West Boxford	MA	G	978 352-2323	16408

BAKERY PRDTS: Pretzels

New England Prtzel Popcorn Inc	Lawrence	MA	G	978 687-0342	12064
Twisted	Bangor	ME	G	207 942-9530	5661

BAKERY PRDTS: Rolls, Bread Type, Fresh Or Frozen

Tm and Tm Inc	Livermore Falls	ME	F	207 897-3442	6382
Homestead Baking Co	Rumford	RI	D	401 434-0551	21186

BAKERY PRDTS: Wholesalers

Fudge Factory Inc	Manchester Center	VT	F	888 669-7425	22085
Koffee Kup Bakery Inc **(PA)**	Colchester	VT	D	802 863-2696	21870

BAKERY: Wholesale Or Wholesale & Retail Combined

Artisan Bread & Products LLC	Norwalk	CT	G	914 843-4401	3103
Beans Inc	Watertown	CT	G	860 945-9234	4999
Beldotti Bakeries	Stamford	CT	F	203 348-9029	4148
Bimbo Bakeries Usa Inc	Portland	CT	E	860 691-1180	3564
Dl Distributors LLC	West Haven	CT	G	203 931-1724	5117
Gracie Maes Kitchen LLC	Griswold	CT	G	860 885-8250	1663
Northeast Foods Inc	Dayville	CT	D	860 779-1117	1049
Stonehouse Fine Cakes	Meriden	CT	F	203 235-5091	2134
Alves Baking Co	Fall River	MA	G	508 673-8003	10654
Athans Inc	Brighton	MA	F	617 783-0313	9095
Berkshire Mtn Bky Pizza Cafe	Pittsfield	MA	G	413 464-9394	14458
Beth Veneto	Quincy	MA	G	617 472-4729	14615
Bimbo Bakeries Usa Inc	Middleboro	MA	F	508 923-1023	13055
Bimbo Bakeries Usa Inc	Wilbraham	MA	G	413 543-5328	16933
Boston Baking Inc	Boston	MA	E	617 364-6900	8421
Cakewalk Bakers LLC	Boston	MA	G	617 903-4352	8454
Concord Teacakes Etcetera Inc **(PA)**	Concord	MA	E	978 369-2409	10124
Hole In One	Eastham	MA	E	508 255-5359	10549
Iggys Bread Ltd	Watertown	MA	E	617 491-7600	16291
Mrs Macks Bakery Inc	Worcester	MA	G	508 753-0610	17426
Pain DAvignon II Inc	Hyannis	MA	E	508 771-9771	11853
Piantedosi Baking Co	Malden	MA	G	781 321-3400	12589
Pin Hsiao & Associates LLC	Milford	MA	D	206 818-0155	13138
Sun Ray Bakery	Beverly	MA	G	978 922-1941	8184
Sweet Creations	Wakefield	MA	E	781 246-0836	15979
Traditional Breads Inc	Lynn	MA	E	781 598-4451	12544
Yuen Ho Bakery Inc	Boston	MA	G	617 426-8320	8939
Italian Bakery Products Co	Lewiston	ME	F	207 782-8312	6293
Lepage Bakeries Park St LLC	Auburn	ME	E	207 783-9161	5576
Barbara Brownie LLC	Hampton	NH	G	603 601-2886	18257
Bimbo Bakeries Usa Inc	Hooksett	NH	E	603 626-7405	18343
Bimbo Bakeries Usa Inc	Lebanon	NH	F	603 448-4227	18615
Fredericks Pastries **(PA)**	Amherst	NH	G	603 882-7725	17563
Harveys Bakeries	Dover	NH	G	603 749-5149	18027
Koffee Kup Bakery Inc	Bow	NH	G	603 225-6149	17720
Catanzaro Food Products Inc	Pawtucket	RI	G	401 255-1700	20820
La Casona Restaurant Inc	Central Falls	RI	G	401 727-0002	20118
Against Grn Gourmet Foods LLC	Brattleboro	VT	G	802 258-3838	21716
Bimbo Bakeries Usa Inc	Saint Johnsbury	VT	G	802 748-1389	22386
Delicate Decadence LLC	Barre	VT	G	802 479-7948	21612
Greniers Garden & Bakery	Waterbury Center	VT	G	802 244-8057	22591
Koffee Kup Bakery Inc **(PA)**	Colchester	VT	D	802 863-2696	21870
Unilever Bestfoods North Amer	Rutland	VT	G	802 775-4986	22357

BALCONIES: Metal

Colonial Ornamental Iron Works	Peabody	MA	G	978 531-1474	14323

BALLASTS: Lighting

Omni Measurement Systems Inc	Colchester	VT	E	802 497-2253	21875

BALLOONS: Toy & Advertising, Rubber

Nordson Medical (nh) Inc **(HQ)**	Salem	NH	C	603 327-0600	19756

BALLS: Steel

Abbott Ball Company	West Hartford	CT	D	860 236-5901	5050
Ball Supply Corporation	Avon	CT	G	860 673-3364	32
Hartford Technologies Inc	Rocky Hill	CT	E	860 571-3602	3712
Schaeffler Aerospace USA Corp	Winsted	CT	D	860 379-7558	5421
Schaeffler Aerospace USA Corp **(DH)**	Danbury	CT	B	203 744-2211	984
Trd Specialties Inc	Pine Meadow	CT	G	860 738-4505	3446
Sem-Tec Inc	Worcester	MA	E	508 798-8551	17471

BANNERS: Fabric

Banner Works	Oakville	CT	G	203 597-9999	3297
Brewer Banner Designs	New Bedford	MA	G	508 996-6006	13364
Cyr Sign & Banner Company	Medford	MA	G	781 395-7297	12928
Faverco Inc	Boston	MA	G	617 247-1440	8540
Custom Banner & Graphics LLC	Rochester	NH	G	603 332-2067	19666

BAR

Lost Nation Brewing LLC	Morrisville	VT	F	802 851-8041	22171
Vermont Pub Brewry Burlington	Burlington	VT	D	802 865-0500	21816

BAR FIXTURES: Wood

American Custom Displays	Hanover	MA	G	781 829-0585	11326

BAR JOISTS & CONCRETE REINFORCING BARS: Fabricated

Dominion Rebar Company	Pawtucket	RI	E	401 724-9200	20834
Rusco Steel Company	Warwick	RI	D	401 732-0548	21418

BARBECUE EQPT

Kenyon International Inc	Clinton	CT	E	860 664-4906	789
Vigiroda Enterprises Inc	Trumbull	CT	G	203 268-6117	4642
Kettlepizza LLC	North Andover	MA	G	888 205-1931	13714

BARRELS: Shipping, Metal

Mass Engineering & Tank Inc	Middleboro	MA	E	508 947-8669	13068
Roche Bros Barrel & Drum Co	Lowell	MA	E	978 454-9135	12428
Roche Manufacturing Inc	Lowell	MA	F	978 454-9135	12429

BARRETTES

Barrette Mechanical	Brooklyn	CT	G	860 774-0499	670

BARRICADES: Metal

K-Tech International	Torrington	CT	E	860 489-9399	4584

BARS & BAR SHAPES: Steel, Hot-Rolled

Natale Co Safetycare LL	Woburn	MA	G	781 933-7205	17237

BARS, COLD FINISHED: Steel, From Purchased Hot-Rolled

Channel Alloys	Norwalk	CT	G	203 975-1404	3123

BARS, PLATES & SHEETS: Zinc & Zinc Alloy Bars, Plates, Etc

Jarden LLC	East Wilton	ME	C	207 645-2574	5987

BARS: Concrete Reinforcing, Fabricated Steel

	CITY	ST	EMP	PHONE	ENTRY #
Barker Steel LLC	South Windsor	CT	E	860 282-1860	3943
Eastern Metal Works Inc	Milford	CT	E	203 878-6995	2281
Nucor Steel Connecticut Inc	Wallingford	CT	C	203 265-0615	4780
Barker Steel LLC	Westfield	MA	E	413 568-7803	16671
Building Envelope Systems LLC	Plainville	MA	D	508 381-0429	14516
Rebars & Mesh Inc	Haverhill	MA	E	978 374-2244	11467
Barker Steel LLC	Scarborough	ME	G	207 883-3444	6907
Newbama Steel Inc	East Kingston	NH	G	603 382-2261	18089
Audette Group LLC	Providence	RI	E	401 667-5884	20963
Cuivre & Co LLC	East Greenwich	RI	G	401 965-4569	20359
Heavy Metal Corp	Providence	RI	F	401 944-2002	21027

BATH SHOPS

	CITY	ST	EMP	PHONE	ENTRY #
Enefco International Inc **(PA)**	Auburn	ME	D	207 514-7218	5561

BATHMATS, COTTON

	CITY	ST	EMP	PHONE	ENTRY #
Textile Waste Supply LLC	Boston	MA	E	617 241-8100	8880

BATHROOM ACCESS & FITTINGS: Vitreous China & Earthenware

	CITY	ST	EMP	PHONE	ENTRY #
Water Works	Danbury	CT	G	203 546-6000	1007
Kenney Manufacturing Company **(PA)**	Warwick	RI	B	401 739-2200	21383
Summer Infant Inc **(PA)**	Woonsocket	RI	D	401 671-6550	21581
Summer Infant Inc	Woonsocket	RI	G	401 671-6550	21582

BATHROOM FIXTURES: Plastic

	CITY	ST	EMP	PHONE	ENTRY #
Roma Marble Inc	Ludlow	MA	E	413 583-5017	12476
Toto USA Holdings Inc	Boston	MA	G	617 227-1321	8888

BATHTUBS: Concrete

	CITY	ST	EMP	PHONE	ENTRY #
Amazing Glaze	Norton	MA	G	508 285-7234	14070

BATTERIES, EXC AUTOMOTIVE: Wholesalers

	CITY	ST	EMP	PHONE	ENTRY #
A123 Systems LLC	Waltham	MA	C	617 778-5700	16020

BATTERIES: Alkaline, Cell Storage

	CITY	ST	EMP	PHONE	ENTRY #
Duracell Company **(HQ)**	Bethel	CT	E	203 796-4000	144
Duracell US Holding LLC **(HQ)**	Bethel	CT	F	203 796-4000	148
Evercel Inc **(PA)**	Stamford	CT	D	781 741-8800	4195

BATTERIES: Dry

	CITY	ST	EMP	PHONE	ENTRY #
Duracell Manufacturing LLC	Bethel	CT	C	203 796-4000	147
Energizer Manufacturing Inc	Bennington	VT	E	802 442-6301	21669

BATTERIES: Lead Acid, Storage

	CITY	ST	EMP	PHONE	ENTRY #
Clarios	Meriden	CT	D	678 297-4040	2086
American Battery Company LLC	Norwood	MA	G	781 440-0325	14127
Mega-Power Inc	Newton	MA	G	800 982-4339	13613

BATTERIES: Rechargeable

	CITY	ST	EMP	PHONE	ENTRY #
Nofet LLC	New Haven	CT	F	203 848-9064	2719
Battery Resourcers LLC	Worcester	MA	G	206 948-6325	17346
Lionano Inc	Woburn	MA	G	607 216-8156	17214
Titan Advnced Enrgy Sltons Inc	Salem	MA	F	561 654-5558	14946

BATTERIES: Storage

	CITY	ST	EMP	PHONE	ENTRY #
B S T Systems Inc	Plainfield	CT	D	860 564-4078	3451
Duracell Company	Bethel	CT	A	203 796-4000	145
Duracell Manufacturing Inc	Bethel	CT	G	203 796-4000	146
Hbl America Inc **(HQ)**	Rocky Hill	CT	G	860 257-9800	3713
Saft America Inc	North Haven	CT	E	203 234-8333	3061
24m Technologies Inc	Cambridge	MA	G	617 553-1012	9366
A123 Systems LLC	Waltham	MA	C	617 778-5700	16020
Advanced Battery Systems Inc	Halifax	MA	G	508 378-2284	11313
Boston-Power Inc **(PA)**	Westborough	MA	D	508 366-0885	16595
Fastcap Systems Corporation	Boston	MA	F	857 239-7500	8539
Integer Holdings Corporation	Canton	MA	C	781 830-5800	9744
L3 Technologies Inc	Foxboro	MA	G	617 895-6841	10891
Power Solutions LLC **(PA)**	Swansea	MA	F	800 876-9373	15713
Rolls Battery of New England	Salem	MA	G	978 745-3333	14939
Solidenergy Systems LLC	Woburn	MA	E	617 972-3412	17299
Thermacell Corporation	Bedford	MA	F	816 510-9428	8015
Tracer Technologies Inc	Somerville	MA	E	617 776-6410	15224
Xilectric Inc	Fall River	MA	G	617 312-5678	10785
Tim Kat Inc	Lewiston	ME	G	207 784-9675	6325
Casanna Designs	Tiverton	RI	G	401 835-4029	21255
Eaglepicher Technologies LLC	East Greenwich	RI	F	401 471-6580	20363
Ener-Tek International Inc	East Greenwich	RI	C	401 471-6580	20366

BATTERIES: Wet

	CITY	ST	EMP	PHONE	ENTRY #
B S T Systems Inc	Plainfield	CT	D	860 564-4078	3451
Vitec Production Solutions Inc **(HQ)**	Shelton	CT	D	203 929-1100	3887
Electrochem Solutions Inc	Raynham	MA	C	781 575-0800	14714
Integer Holdings Corporation	Canton	MA	C	781 830-5800	9744
Ener-Tek International Inc	East Greenwich	RI	C	401 471-6580	20366

BATTERY CASES: Plastic Or Plastics Combination

	CITY	ST	EMP	PHONE	ENTRY #
GP Industries	Taftville	CT	G	860 859-9938	4470

BATTERY CHARGERS

	CITY	ST	EMP	PHONE	ENTRY #
Charge Solutions Inc	Milford	CT	G	203 871-7282	2264
Crystal Tool LLC	Old Saybrook	CT	G	860 510-0113	3333
Digatron Power Electronics Inc	Shelton	CT	E	203 446-8000	3796
Williamson Neng Elc Mtr Svc	Chelsea	MA	G	617 884-9200	9975
Sterling Power Usa LLC	Eliot	ME	G	207 226-3500	6010
Aak Power Supply Corporation	Plaistow	NH	F	603 382-2222	19506

BATTERY CHARGING GENERATORS

	CITY	ST	EMP	PHONE	ENTRY #
Blackburn Energy Inc	Amesbury	MA	G	800 342-9194	7480
Pellion Technologies Inc	Arlington	MA	E	617 547-3191	7632
Ev Launchpad LLC	Portsmouth	NH	F	603 828-2919	19561

BEADS: Unassembled

	CITY	ST	EMP	PHONE	ENTRY #
Buick LLC	Hope Valley	RI	E	401 539-2432	20481
Splendid Loon Studio	Wakefield	RI	G	401 789-7879	21278

BEARINGS

	CITY	ST	EMP	PHONE	ENTRY #
A Papish Incorporated **(PA)**	Danbury	CT	E	203 744-0323	863
American Sleeve Bearing LLC	Stafford Springs	CT	E	860 684-8060	4104
Ball & Roller Bearing Co LLC	New Milford	CT	F	860 355-4161	2787
Virginia Industries Inc **(PA)**	Rocky Hill	CT	G	860 571-3600	3733

BEARINGS & PARTS Ball

	CITY	ST	EMP	PHONE	ENTRY #
Abek LLC	Bristol	CT	F	860 314-3905	510
Buswell Manufacturing Co Inc	Bridgeport	CT	F	203 334-6069	392
Fag Bearings LLC **(DH)**	Danbury	CT	D	203 790-5474	916
FAg Holding Corporation **(DH)**	Danbury	CT	F	203 790-5474	917
Gwilliam Company Inc	New Milford	CT	F	860 354-2884	2804
Rbc Bearings Incorporated **(PA)**	Oxford	CT	B	203 267-7001	3421
Schaeffler Aerospace USA Corp **(DH)**	Danbury	CT	B	203 744-2211	984
Schaeffler Aerospace USA Corp	Winsted	CT	D	860 379-7558	5421
Mpb Corporation **(HQ)**	Keene	NH	A	603 352-0310	18518
Mpb Corporation	Lebanon	NH	B	603 448-3000	18630
New Hmpshire Ball Bearings Inc	Laconia	NH	B	603 524-0004	18577
New Hmpshire Ball Bearings Inc	Peterborough	NH	E	603 924-3311	19479

BEARINGS: Ball & Roller

	CITY	ST	EMP	PHONE	ENTRY #
Ball & Roller Bearing Co LLC	New Milford	CT	F	860 355-4161	2787
C & S Engineering Inc	Meriden	CT	E	203 235-5727	2082
Hartford Technologies Inc	Rocky Hill	CT	E	860 571-3602	3712
K A F Manufacturing Co Inc	Stamford	CT	E	203 324-3012	4234
Kamatics Corporation	Bloomfield	CT	G	860 243-7230	236
Kamatics Corporation **(DH)**	Bloomfield	CT	E	860 243-9704	235
Rbc Linear Precision Pdts Inc	Fairfield	CT	G	203 255-1511	1450
Roller Bearing Co Amer Inc	Oxford	CT	E	203 267-7001	3424
SKF Specialty Balls	Winsted	CT	G	860 379-8511	5422
SKF USA Inc	Winsted	CT	E	860 379-8511	5423
Timken Company	Glastonbury	CT	F	860 652-4630	1579
Virginia Industries Inc **(PA)**	Rocky Hill	CT	G	860 571-3600	3733
Mpb Corporation	Lebanon	NH	G	603 448-3000	18631
New Hmpshire Ball Bearings Inc **(DH)**	Peterborough	NH	B	603 924-3311	19478
Timken Company	Lebanon	NH	A	603 443-5281	18638

BEARINGS: Plastic

	CITY	ST	EMP	PHONE	ENTRY #
Asti Company Inc	Torrington	CT	G	860 482-2675	4563
Pobco Inc	Worcester	MA	E	508 791-6376	17442
Slideways Inc	Worcester	MA	E	508 854-0799	17475

BEARINGS: Railroad Car Journal

	CITY	ST	EMP	PHONE	ENTRY #
Savage Companies	Westborough	MA	G	508 616-8772	16646

BEARINGS: Roller & Parts

	CITY	ST	EMP	PHONE	ENTRY #
Del-Tron Precision Inc	Bethel	CT	E	203 778-2727	143
Roller Bearing Co Amer Inc **(HQ)**	Oxford	CT	C	203 267-7001	3423
Schaeffler Group USA Inc	Danbury	CT	B	203 790-5474	985

BEARINGS: Wooden

	CITY	ST	EMP	PHONE	ENTRY #
Pobco Inc	Worcester	MA	E	508 791-6376	17442
Woodex Bearing Company Inc	Georgetown	ME	E	207 371-2210	6107

BEAUTY & BARBER SHOP EQPT

	CITY	ST	EMP	PHONE	ENTRY #
Ace Beauty Supply Inc	Branford	CT	G	203 488-2416	284
Bridgeport Proc & Mfg LLC	Bridgeport	CT	G	203 612-7733	389
Components For Mfg LLC	Groton	CT	G	860 572-1671	1668
Conair Corporation **(PA)**	Stamford	CT	B	203 351-9000	4171
Grohe Manufacturing	Ansonia	CT	G	203 516-5536	17
Hannes Precision Industry Inc	Norwalk	CT	F	203 853-7276	3166
Kent Billings LLC	Glastonbury	CT	G	860 659-1104	1561
Thomaston Industries Inc	Thomaston	CT	F	860 283-4358	4521
Cotuit Works	Cotuit	MA	G	508 428-3971	10169
Freestyle Systems LLC	Shrewsbury	MA	G	508 845-4911	15113
Inverness Corporation **(DH)**	Attleboro	MA	E	774 203-1130	7752
Manomet Manufacturing Inc	New Bedford	MA	G	508 997-1795	13415
Neo Green Technology Corp	Woburn	MA	G	617 500-7103	17239
Salon Monet	Boston	MA	G	617 425-0010	8836
Three Fays Power LLC	Ware	MA	G	413 427-2665	16238
Zycal Bioceuticals Mfg LLC	Shrewsbury	MA	E	888 779-9225	15139
Cellblock Fcs LLC	Standish	ME	F	603 276-5785	7061
Marca Manufacturing LLC	Gorham	ME	F	207 854-8471	6120
Pike Industries Inc	Dover Foxcroft	ME	G	207 564-8444	5963
Village Candle Inc	Wells	ME	C	207 251-4800	7168
Enviromart Industries Inc	Plaistow	NH	G	603 378-0154	19513
GKN Aerospace New England Inc	Charlestown	NH	D	603 542-5135	17814
Key Industries	New Ipswich	NH	G	603 369-9634	19306

BEAUTY SALONS

	CITY	ST	EMP	PHONE	ENTRY #
Prostrong Inc	Pembroke	MA	G	781 829-0000	14422
Stilisti	Boston	MA	G	617 262-2234	8867

BED SHEETING, COTTON

	CITY	ST	EMP	PHONE	ENTRY #
Maine Heritage Weavers	Monmouth	ME	F	207 933-2605	6449

BEDDING & BEDSPRINGS STORES

	CITY	ST	EMP	PHONE	ENTRY #
US Bedding Inc	Fall River	MA	F	508 678-6988	10777

BEDDING, BEDSPREAD, BLANKET/SHEET: Pillowcase, Purchd Mtrl

	CITY	ST	EMP	PHONE	ENTRY #
Two Rivers Pet Products Inc	Turner	ME	E	207 225-3965	7112

BEDDING, BEDSPREADS, BLANKETS & SHEETS

	CITY	ST	EMP	PHONE	ENTRY #
Thomas W Raftery Inc	Hartford	CT	E	860 278-9870	1879
PDk Worldwide Entps Inc **(PA)**	Fall River	MA	E	508 676-2155	10746
Therapedic of New England LLC	Brockton	MA	G	508 559-9944	9182
Cleanbrands LLC	Warwick	RI	F	877 215-7378	21342
Heart of Vermont Inc	Barre	VT	G	802 476-3098	21620

BEDDING, FROM SILK OR MANMADE FIBER

	CITY	ST	EMP	PHONE	ENTRY #
US Bedding Inc	Fall River	MA	F	508 678-6988	10777

BEDS & ACCESS STORES

	CITY	ST	EMP	PHONE	ENTRY #
Drive-O-Rama Inc	Dennis Port	MA	D	508 394-0028	10312

BEDS: Institutional

	CITY	ST	EMP	PHONE	ENTRY #
Kingston Krafts	Cranston	RI	G	401 272-0292	20248

BEDSPREADS, FROM SILK OR MANMADE FIBER

	CITY	ST	EMP	PHONE	ENTRY #
Natco Home Fashions Inc	West Warwick	RI	F	401 828-0300	21501
Natco Home Fashions Inc	West Warwick	RI	F	401 828-0300	21502
Natco Home Fashions Inc **(PA)**	West Warwick	RI	F	401 828-0300	21503

BEEKEEPERS' SPLYS: Bee Smokers

	CITY	ST	EMP	PHONE	ENTRY #
G&R Industries Inc	Goffstown	NH	G	603 626-3071	18202

BEER & ALE WHOLESALERS

	CITY	ST	EMP	PHONE	ENTRY #
A & I Concentrate LLC	Shelton	CT	F	203 447-1938	3771

BEER & ALE, WHOLESALE: Beer & Other Fermented Malt Liquors

	CITY	ST	EMP	PHONE	ENTRY #
Matias Importing & Distrg Corp	Newington	CT	G	860 666-5544	2880

BEER, WINE & LIQUOR STORES

	CITY	ST	EMP	PHONE	ENTRY #
Old Creamery Grocery Store	Cummington	MA	G	413 634-5560	10173
Sunday River Brewing Co Inc	Boston	MA	D	207 824-4253	8869
University Wine Shop Inc	Cambridge	MA	G	617 547-4258	9686

BEER, WINE & LIQUOR STORES: Beer, Packaged

	CITY	ST	EMP	PHONE	ENTRY #
Longmeadow Package Store Inc	Longmeadow	MA	G	413 567-3201	12335
Mass Bay Brewing Company Inc **(PA)**	Boston	MA	C	617 574-9551	8682
Discount Beverages Plus Cig	Center Conway	NH	G	603 356-8844	17794
Mbbc Vermont LLC	Windsor	VT	D	802 674-5491	22712

BEER, WINE & LIQUOR STORES: Wine

	CITY	ST	EMP	PHONE	ENTRY #
Bartlett Maine Estate Winery	Gouldsboro	ME	G	207 546-2408	6135

BEER, WINE & LIQUOR STORES: Wine & Beer

	CITY	ST	EMP	PHONE	ENTRY #
Alvarium Beer Company LLC	New Britain	CT	G	860 306-3857	2508

BEESWAX PROCESSING

	CITY	ST	EMP	PHONE	ENTRY #
Woods End Inc	Weston	CT	G	203 226-6303	5176

BELLOWS

	CITY	ST	EMP	PHONE	ENTRY #
Standard Bellows Co **(PA)**	Windsor Locks	CT	E	860 623-2307	5401
John Crane Sealol Inc **(DH)**	Warwick	RI	C	401 732-0715	21381
Metal-Flex Welded Bellows Inc	Newport	VT	E	802 334-5550	22201

BELLOWS ASSEMBLIES: Missiles, Metal

	CITY	ST	EMP	PHONE	ENTRY #
Cliflex Bellows Corporation	Boston	MA	E	617 268-5774	8477

BELLS: Electric

	CITY	ST	EMP	PHONE	ENTRY #
Bevin Bros Manufacturing Co	East Hampton	CT	E	860 267-4431	1158

BELTING: Fabric

	CITY	ST	EMP	PHONE	ENTRY #
Albany International Corp **(PA)**	Rochester	NH	D	603 330-5850	19655

BELTING: Rubber

	CITY	ST	EMP	PHONE	ENTRY #
Dresco Belting Co Inc	East Weymouth	MA	G	781 335-1350	10541

BELTS & BELT PRDTS

	CITY	ST	EMP	PHONE	ENTRY #
Kemper Manufacturing Corp	West Haven	CT	E	203 934-1600	5128

BELTS: Chain

	CITY	ST	EMP	PHONE	ENTRY #
Belt Technologies Inc **(PA)**	Agawam	MA	E	413 786-9922	7422

BELTS: Conveyor, Made From Purchased Wire

	CITY	ST	EMP	PHONE	ENTRY #
Habasit Abt Inc	Middletown	CT	C	860 632-2211	2188
Alvin Johnson	East Longmeadow	MA	G	413 525-6334	10465
Custom Convyrs Fabrication Inc	North Oxford	MA	F	508 922-0283	13971
Den Technologies Corp	Boylston	MA	E	401 263-7579	8979
O/K Machinery Corporation	Marlborough	MA	E	508 303-8286	12799
Wire Belt Company of America **(PA)**	Londonderry	NH	D	603 644-2500	18745
Qbm New York Inc	Providence	RI	F	716 821-1475	21102

BENCHES, WORK : Factory

	CITY	ST	EMP	PHONE	ENTRY #
General Woodworking Inc **(PA)**	Lowell	MA	F	978 458-6625	12373
General Woodworking Inc	Lowell	MA	E	978 251-4070	12374
Hendrick Manufacturing Corp **(PA)**	Salem	MA	F	781 631-4400	14919
R W Hatfield Company Inc **(PA)**	Haverhill	MA	E	978 521-2600	11466
Stackbin Corporation	Lincoln	RI	E	401 333-1600	20597

BENTONITE MINING

	CITY	ST	EMP	PHONE	ENTRY #
Vanderbilt Minerals LLC **(HQ)**	Norwalk	CT	E	203 295-2140	3266

BEVERAGE BASES & SYRUPS

	CITY	ST	EMP	PHONE	ENTRY #
Flavrz Organic Beverages LLC	Darien	CT	G	203 716-8082	1026
Focus Now Solutions LLC	Fairfield	CT	G	203 247-9038	1432
Jmf Group LLC	East Windsor	CT	D	860 627-7003	1288
Keurig Dr Pepper Inc **(PA)**	Burlington	MA	D	781 418-7000	9292
Powell and Mahoney LLC	Salem	MA	G	978 745-4332	14936
Walter Scott	Lexington	MA	G	781 862-4893	12284

BEVERAGE PRDTS: Brewers' Grain

	CITY	ST	EMP	PHONE	ENTRY #
Kent Falls Brewing Company	Kent	CT	G	860 398-9645	1923
Cape Cod Beer Inc	Barnstable	MA	F	508 790-4200	7947
Neighborhood Beer Company Inc	Stratham	NH	G	603 418-7124	19875
Upper Pass Beer Co LLC	Tunbridge	VT	G	802 889-3421	22544

BEVERAGE PRDTS: Malt, Barley

	CITY	ST	EMP	PHONE	ENTRY #
Blue Ox Malthouse LLC	Lisbon Falls	ME	G	207 649-0018	6367

BEVERAGE, NONALCOHOLIC: Iced Tea/Fruit Drink, Bottled/Canned

	CITY	ST	EMP	PHONE	ENTRY #
Sweet Leaf Tea Company **(DH)**	Stamford	CT	F	203 863-0263	4338
Wise Mouth Inc	North Attleboro	MA	G	508 345-2559	13786

BEVERAGES, ALCOHOLIC: Ale

	CITY	ST	EMP	PHONE	ENTRY #
A&S Brewing Collaborative LLC	Boston	MA	G	617 368-5000	8333
American Craft Brewery LLC **(DH)**	Boston	MA	G	617 368-5000	8359
Cambridge Brewing Co Inc	Cambridge	MA	E	617 494-1994	9426
Mayflower Brewing Company LLC	Plymouth	MA	E	508 746-2674	14562
Ashleigh Inc **(PA)**	Kennebunk	ME	E	207 967-4311	6228
Shipyard Brewing Ltd Lblty Co	Portland	ME	E	207 761-0807	6726
Craft Brew Alliance Inc	Portsmouth	NH	D	603 430-8600	19555
Revival Brewing Company	Providence	RI	F	401 372-7009	21110

BEVERAGES, ALCOHOLIC: Applejack

	CITY	ST	EMP	PHONE	ENTRY #
Downeast Cider House LLC	Boston	MA	G	857 301-8881	8509

BEVERAGES, ALCOHOLIC: Beer

	CITY	ST	EMP	PHONE	ENTRY #
Beerd Brewing Co LLC	Stonington	CT	F	585 771-7428	4375
East Rock Brewing Company LLC	New Haven	CT	G	203 530-3484	2684
Easton Brewing Company LLC	Easton	CT	G	203 921-7263	1317
Front Porch Brewing	Wallingford	CT	G	203 679-1096	4747
Guinness America Inc	Norwalk	CT	G	203 229-2100	3165
New England Brewing Co LLC	Woodbridge	CT	G	203 387-2222	5473
Nutmeg Brewing Rest Group LLC	Shelton	CT	E	203 256-2337	3843
Southport Brewing Co	Milford	CT	E	203 874-2337	2365
Thomas Hooker Brewing Co LLC	Bloomfield	CT	E	860 242-3111	266
Amherst Brewing Co Inc	Amherst	MA	E	413 253-4400	7511
Atlas Distributing Inc	Auburn	MA	C	508 791-6221	7828
Barrel House Z LLC	Weymouth	MA	G	339 207-7888	16885
Berkshire Brewing Company Inc **(PA)**	South Deerfield	MA	F	413 665-6600	15246
Boston Beer Company Inc	Boston	MA	F	617 368-5080	8422
Boston Beer Company Inc **(PA)**	Boston	MA	B	617 368-5000	8423
Boston Beer Corporation **(DH)**	Boston	MA	C	617 368-5000	8424
Brewmasters Brewing Svcs LLC	Williamsburg	MA	G	413 268-2199	16947
British Beer Company Inc	Westford	MA	E	978 577-6034	16758
Buzzards Bay Brewing Inc	Westport	MA	G	508 636-2288	16836
Cape Ann Brewing Company Inc	Gloucester	MA	F	978 281-4782	11169
Castle Island Brewing Co LLC	Norwood	MA	E	781 951-2029	14140
Cisco Brewers Inc	Nantucket	MA	E	508 325-5929	13222
Common Crossing Inc	Berkley	MA	G	508 822-8225	8084
Crue Brew Brewery LLC	Raynham	MA	G	508 272-6090	14708
Downeast Cider House LLC	Boston	MA	G	857 301-8881	8509
Essex County Brewing Co LLC	Peabody	MA	G	978 587-2254	14334
Independent Fermentations	Plymouth	MA	G	508 789-9940	14561
John Harvards Brewhouse Llc	Framingham	MA	D	508 875-2337	10974
Lamplighter Brewing Co LLC	Cambridge	MA	G	207 650-3325	9531
Lord Hobo Brewing Company LLC	Woburn	MA	F	781 281-0809	17218
Mass Bay Brewing Company Inc **(PA)**	Boston	MA	C	617 574-9551	8682
Massachusetts Bev Aliance LLC	Bellingham	MA	F	617 701-6238	8048
Mercury Brewing & Dist Co	Ipswich	MA	F	978 356-3329	11930
Paragraph 11 LLC	Woburn	MA	G	781 281-1143	17254
Pioneer Brewing Company LLC	Fiskdale	MA	G	508 347-7500	10808
Redemption Rock Brewery Co	Worcester	MA	G	978 660-5526	17454
Slesar Bros Brewing Co Inc	Hingham	MA	E	781 749-2337	11511
Slesar Bros Brewing Co Inc	Salem	MA	E	978 745-2337	14943
Sullivan Apple Cider	Saugus	MA	G	781 233-7090	15000
Wachusett Brewing Company Inc	Westminster	MA	D	978 874-9965	16820
Allagash Brewing Company	Portland	ME	D	207 878-5385	6611
Belfast Bay Brewing Company	Belfast	ME	G	866 338-5722	5686
Maine Beer Company LLC	Freeport	ME	F	207 221-5711	6082
Salisbury Cove Associates Inc	Bar Harbor	ME	E	207 288-2337	5669
Sebago Brewing Co	Gorham	ME	E	207 856-2537	6130
7th Settlement Brewery LLC	Dover	NH	E	603 534-5292	18002
Capitol Distributors Inc	Concord	NH	G	603 224-3348	17890
Hobbs Tavern & Brewing Co LLC	West Ossipee	NH	E	603 539-2000	19966
Incredibrew Inc	Nashua	NH	G	603 891-2477	19187
Oddball Brewing Co	Pembroke	NH	G	603 210-5654	19461
Coastal Extreme Brewing Co LLC	Newport	RI	G	401 849-5232	20660
D & H Inc	Middletown	RI	G	401 847-6690	20618
Linesider Brewing Company LLC	East Greenwich	RI	F	401 398-7700	20371
Long Live Beerworks Inc	Providence	RI	G	203 980-0121	21056
14th Star Brewing LLC	Saint Albans	VT	G	802 528-5988	22362
Alchemy Canning Ltd	Stowe	VT	E	802 244-7744	22519
Bullock & Block Ltd	Rutland	VT	F	802 773-3350	22326
Frost Beer Works LLC	Hinesburg	VT	F	949 945-4064	22024
Long Trail Brewing Company 21758	Bridgewater Corners	VT	D	802 672-5011	
Lost Nation Brewing LLC	Morrisville	VT	F	802 851-8041	22171
Magic Hat Brewing Company & Pe	South Burlington	VT	D	802 658-2739	22453
Mbbc Vermont LLC	Windsor	VT	D	802 674-5491	22712
Otter Creek Brewing Co LLC	Middlebury	VT	E	802 388-0727	22118
Switchback Beerworks Inc	Burlington	VT	E	802 651-4114	21811
Vermont Pub Brewry Burlington	Burlington	VT	D	802 865-0500	21816

BEVERAGES, ALCOHOLIC: Beer & Ale

	CITY	ST	EMP	PHONE	ENTRY #
Bear Hands Brewing Company	Central Village	CT	G	860 576-5374	705
Breakaway Brew Haus LLC	Bolton	CT	G	860 647-9811	275
Brook Broad Brewing LLC	East Windsor	CT	F	860 623-1000	1280
Cold Brew Coffee Company LLC	Cheshire	CT	G	860 250-4410	723
Diageo Investment Corporation	Norwalk	CT	F	203 229-2100	3137
Hamden Brewing Company LLC	Shelton	CT	G	203 247-4677	3807
Stetson Brewing Co Inc	Manchester	CT	G	860 643-0257	2053
Swagnificent Ent LLC	Bridgeport	CT	G	203 449-0124	498
3cross Brewing Company	Worcester	MA	F	508 615-8195	17328
Basement LLC	Worcester	MA	G	508 762-9080	17345
Bent Water Brewing Co	Lynn	MA	G	781 780-9948	12492
Cody Brewing Company	Amesbury	MA	G	978 387-4329	7482
Craft Beer Guild Distrg VT LLC **(PA)**	Kingston	MA	E	781 585-5165	11956
Deja Brew Inc	Shrewsbury	MA	G	508 842-8991	15107
Endurance Brewing Company LLC	Boston	MA	G	617 725-0256	8525
Riverwalk Brewing	Newburyport	MA	F	978 499-2337	13530
Sunday River Brewing Co Inc	Boston	MA	D	207 824-4253	8869
One Eye Open Brewing Co LLC	Portland	ME	G	207 536-4176	6706
Sebago Brewing Co **(PA)**	Gorham	ME	E	207 856-2537	6129
York Harbor Brewing Company	Kittery	ME	G	207 703-8060	6260
Big Daddy Brews LLC	East Kingston	NH	G	603 569-5647	18084
Great Rhythm Brewing Co LLC	Portsmouth	NH	G	603 300-8588	19569
White Birch Brewing LLC	Nashua	NH	F	603 402-4444	19286
Brewers Supply Group Inc	Providence	RI	G	401 275-4920	20974
Farm Coast Brewery LLC	Tiverton	RI	G	401 816-5021	21258
Sons Liberty Spirits Company	Wakefield	RI	G	401 284-4006	21276
Black Flannel Brewing Co LLC	Essex Junction	VT	G	802 488-0089	21931
Foam Brewers	Burlington	VT	G	802 399-2511	21783
Independent Brewers Untd Corp **(DH)**	Burlington	VT	F	802 862-6114	21789
Maple Leaf Malt & Brewing	Wilmington	VT	G	802 464-9900	22703
Northshire Brewery Inc	Bennington	VT	G	802 681-0201	21687

BEVERAGES, ALCOHOLIC: Brandy

	CITY	ST	EMP	PHONE	ENTRY #
Mr Boston Brands LLC **(HQ)**	Lewiston	ME	E	207 783-1433	6308

BEVERAGES, ALCOHOLIC: Cocktails

	CITY	ST	EMP	PHONE	ENTRY #
Stirrings LLC	Fall River	MA	E	508 324-9800	10764

BEVERAGES, ALCOHOLIC: Cordials

	CITY	ST	EMP	PHONE	ENTRY #
Diageo North America Inc **(HQ)**	Norwalk	CT	A	203 229-2100	3138

BEVERAGES, ALCOHOLIC: Distilled Liquors

	CITY	ST	EMP	PHONE	ENTRY #
Asylum Distillery	Southport	CT	G	203 209-0146	4093
Diageo PLC	Norwalk	CT	D	203 229-2100	3139
Hartford Flavor Company LLC	Hartford	CT	G	860 604-9767	1834
Millbrook Distillery LLC	Cos Cob	CT	G	203 637-2231	828
Mine Hill Distillery	Roxbury	CT	G	860 210-1872	3736
Modern Distillery Age	Norwalk	CT	G	203 971-8710	3200
Waypoint Distillery	Bloomfield	CT	G	860 519-5390	271
Westford Hill Distillers LLC	Ashford	CT	G	860 429-0464	29
Berkshire Mountain Distlrs Inc	Great Barrington	MA	G	413 229-0219	11234
Bradford Distillery LLC **(PA)**	Scituate	MA	G	781 378-2491	15006
Bradford Distillery LLC	Hingham	MA	G	781 385-7145	11494
Bully Boy Distillers	Roxbury	MA	G	617 442-6000	14870
Deacon Giles Inc	Salem	MA	G	781 883-8256	14905
Mad River Distillers	Boston	MA	G	617 262-1990	8679
Pirate Dog Brand LLC	Salem	MA	G	978 745-4786	14935
Powerhouse Botanic Distillery	Newbury	MA	G	978 930-8281	13464
Ryan & Wood Distillery	Gloucester	MA	G	978 281-2282	11208
Short Path Distillery Inc	Arlington	MA	G	857 417-2396	7639
Short Path Distillery Inc	Everett	MA	G	617 830-7954	10631
Silver Bear Distillery LLC	Dalton	MA	G	413 242-4892	10185
Backwash Brew Holdings LLC	Brewer	ME	F	207 659-2300	5794
Doom Forest Distillery LLC	Pittston	ME	G	207 462-1990	6592
Maine Distilleries LLC	Freeport	ME	G	207 865-4828	6083
New England Distilling Co	Portland	ME	G	207 878-9759	6701
Sebago Lake Distillery LLC	Gardiner	ME	G	207 557-0557	6105
Sea Hagg Distillery	Hampton	NH	G	603 380-4022	18271
Smoky Quartz Distillery LLC	Seabrook	NH	G	603 601-0342	19819
Tall Ship Distillery LLC	Dover	NH	G	603 842-0098	18057
White Mountain Distillery LLC	Manchester	NH	G	603 391-1306	18955
Appalachian Gap Distillery Inc	Middlebury	VT	G	802 989-7359	22099
Backus Distillery LLC	Westfield	VT	G	802 999-2255	22626
Champlain Distilleries	South Hero	VT	G	802 378-5059	22480
Green Mountain Distillers LLC	Morrisville	VT	G	802 498-4848	22168
Mad River Distillers	Warren	VT	G	802 496-6973	22577
Old Route Two Spirits Inc	Barre	VT	G	802 424-4864	21633
Vermont Distillers Inc	West Marlboro	VT	G	802 464-2003	22609
Vermont Hard Cider Company LLC **(HQ)**	Middlebury	VT	D	802 388-0700	22120
Wild Hart Distillery	Shelburne	VT	G	802 489-5067	22427

BEVERAGES, ALCOHOLIC: Gin

	CITY	ST	EMP	PHONE	ENTRY #
Caledonia Spirits Inc	Hardwick	VT	E	802 472-8000	22010

BEVERAGES, ALCOHOLIC: Liquors, Malt

	CITY	ST	EMP	PHONE	ENTRY #
861 Corp	Boston	MA	G	617 268-8855	8330
Tri Town Discount Liquors	Canton	MA	G	781 828-8393	9790

BEVERAGES, ALCOHOLIC: Near Beer

	CITY	ST	EMP	PHONE	ENTRY #
Alvarium Beer Company LLC	New Britain	CT	G	860 306-3857	2508
Dorchester Beer Holdings LLC	Boston	MA	G	617 869-7092	8508
Medusa Brewing Company Inc	Hudson	MA	G	978 310-1933	11791
Hill Farmstead LLC	Greensboro Bend	VT	F	802 533-7450	22004
Vermont Beer Shapers Ltd	Springfield	VT	G	802 376-0889	22510

BEVERAGES, ALCOHOLIC: Neutral Spirits, Fruit

	CITY	ST	EMP	PHONE	ENTRY #
Citizen Cider LLC	Burlington	VT	F	802 448-3278	21774

BEVERAGES, ALCOHOLIC: Rum

	CITY	ST	EMP	PHONE	ENTRY #
Privateer International LLC	Ipswich	MA	F	978 356-0477	11935

BEVERAGES, ALCOHOLIC: Rye Whiskey

	CITY	ST	EMP	PHONE	ENTRY #
Goamericago Beverages LLC	Shoreham	VT	G	802 897-7700	22432
Whistlepig LLC **(PA)**	Shoreham	VT	F	802 897-7700	22434

BEVERAGES, ALCOHOLIC: Vodka

	CITY	ST	EMP	PHONE	ENTRY #
Cylinder Vodka Inc	Stamford	CT	G	203 979-0792	4182

BEVERAGES, ALCOHOLIC: Wines

	CITY	ST	EMP	PHONE	ENTRY #
Arrigoni Winery	Portland	CT	G	860 342-1999	3562
Brooke Taylor Winery LLC **(PA)**	Woodstock	CT	G	860 974-1263	5495
Cocchia Norwalk Grape Co	Norwalk	CT	F	203 855-7911	3127
Connecticut Valley Winery LLC	New Hartford	CT	G	860 489-9463	2633
Crush Club LLC	Wallingford	CT	G	203 626-9545	4729
Edwards Wines LLC	North Stonington	CT	G	860 535-0202	3073
Land of Nod Winery LLC	East Canaan	CT	G	860 824-5225	1112
Miranda Vineyard LLC	Goshen	CT	G	860 491-9906	1586
Paradise Hlls Vnyrd Winery LLC	Wallingford	CT	G	203 284-0123	4782
Pozzi Fmly Wine & Spirits LLC	Stamford	CT	G	646 422-9134	4289
Preston Ridge Vineyard LLC	Preston	CT	G	860 383-4278	3582
Sharpe Hill Vineyard Inc	Pomfret	CT	E	860 974-3549	3554
Stonington Vineyards Inc	Stonington	CT	G	860 535-1222	4378
Strawberry Ridge Vineyard Inc	Cornwall Bridge	CT	G	860 868-0730	821
Three Suns Ltd	Hartford	CT	G	860 233-7658	1880
1634 Meadery	Ipswich	MA	G	508 517-4058	11899
21st Century Foods Inc	Boston	MA	G	617 522-7595	8327
59 Beecher Street LLC	Southbridge	MA	G	631 734-6200	15373
Archer Roose Inc	Boston	MA	G	646 283-4152	8373
Balderdash Cellars	Pittsfield	MA	G	413 464-4629	14455
Boston Winery LLC	Dorchester	MA	G	617 265-9463	10341
Cape Cod Winery	East Falmouth	MA	F	508 457-5592	10438
Clos De La Tech	East Falmouth	MA	G	508 648-2505	10439
Constellation Brands Inc	Quincy	MA	G	617 249-5082	14619
E & J Gallo Winery	Wakefield	MA	E	781 213-5050	15951
Eno Massachusetts	Stoughton	MA	G	781 297-7331	15587
Grove Street Enterprises Inc	Richmond	MA	F	413 698-3301	14780
Hardwickvmeyard & Winery	Hardwick	MA	G	413 967-7763	11372
Longmeadow Package Store Inc	Longmeadow	MA	G	413 567-3201	12335
Marthas Seastreak Vineyard LLC	New Bedford	MA	G	617 896-0293	13416
Mount Warner Vineyards LLC	Hadley	MA	G	413 531-4046	11311
Nashoba Valley Spirits Limited	Bolton	MA	E	978 779-5521	8321
Nemerever Vineyards LLC	Chestnut Hill	MA	G	617 320-6994	9989
Oak Barrel Imports LLC	Beverly	MA	G	617 286-2524	8162
Phoenix Vintners LLC	Ipswich	MA	F	877 340-9869	11934
Plymouth Bay Winery	Plymouth	MA	G	508 746-2100	14575
Queen Bee Vineyard Inc	Monson	MA	G	413 267-9329	13210
Red Oak Winnery LLC	Saugus	MA	G	781 558-1702	14994
University Wine Shop Inc	Cambridge	MA	G	617 547-4258	9686
West County Winery	Colrain	MA	G	413 624-3481	10106
Bartlett Maine Estate Winery	Gouldsboro	ME	G	207 546-2408	6135
Cellar Door Winery **(PA)**	Lincolnville	ME	G	207 763-4478	6361
Maine Craft Distilling LLC	Portland	ME	G	207 798-2528	6685
Winterport Winery Inc	Winterport	ME	G	207 223-4500	7278
Executive Wine & Spirits Inc	Manchester	NH	E	603 647-8048	18820
Flag Hill Distillery LLC	Lee	NH	G	603 659-2949	18643
Flag Hill Winery & Vinyrd LLC	Lee	NH	G	603 659-2949	18644
Hermit Woods Inc	Meredith	NH	G	603 253-7968	18974
Moonlight Meadery LLC	Londonderry	NH	F	603 216-2162	18724
Vintners Cellar Winery	North Conway	NH	G	603 356-9463	19380
Douglas Wine & Spirits Inc	North Providence	RI	F	401 353-6400	20757
Nickle Creek Vineyard LLC	Foster	RI	G	401 369-3694	20458
Tapped Apple Winery	Westerly	RI	G	401 637-4946	21542
Boyden Valley Winery LLC	Cambridge	VT	G	802 644-8151	21822
Grand View Winery Co LLC	Plainfield	VT	F	802 456-8810	22267
Honora Winery & Vineyard Inc	Brattleboro	VT	G	802 368-2930	21732
Independent Brewers Untd Corp **(DH)**	Burlington	VT	F	802 862-6114	21789
Neshobe River Winery	Brandon	VT	G	802 247-8002	21710
Putney Mountain Winery	Putney	VT	G	802 387-5925	22291
Snow Farm Winery	South Hero	VT	F	802 372-9463	22482

BEVERAGES, BEER & ALE, WHOLESALE: Ale

	CITY	ST	EMP	PHONE	ENTRY #
Revival Brewing Company	Providence	RI	F	401 372-7009	21110

BEVERAGES, MALT

	CITY	ST	EMP	PHONE	ENTRY #
Outer Light Brewing Co LLC	Groton	CT	G	475 201-9972	1681
Life Force Beverages LLC	Boston	MA	G	551 265-9482	8665

BEVERAGES, NONALCOHOLIC: Bottled & canned soft drinks

	CITY	ST	EMP	PHONE	ENTRY #
B & E Juices Inc	Bridgeport	CT	E	203 333-1802	380
Bombadils Spirit Shop Inc	Mansfield Center	CT	G	860 423-9661	2062
Cell Nique	Weston	CT	G	888 417-9343	5170
Coca-Cola Company	Waterford	CT	G	860 443-2816	4983
Company of Coca-Cola Bottling	East Hartford	CT	D	860 569-0037	1183
Company of Coca-Cola Bottling	Stamford	CT	D	203 905-3900	4169
Foundry Foods Inc	Norwalk	CT	G	314 982-3204	3154
Niagara Bottling LLC	Bloomfield	CT	G	909 226-7353	245
Red Bull LLC	Bloomfield	CT	G	860 519-1018	255
Sigg Switzerland (usa) Inc	Stamford	CT	G	203 321-1232	4317
Adams Redemption Center	Adams	MA	G	413 743-7691	7408
Better Bottling Solutions LLC	Newton	MA	G	219 308-5616	13567
Coca-Cola Bottling Company	Sandwich	MA	D	508 888-0001	14965
Coca-Cola Bottling Company	Lowell	MA	D	978 459-9378	12360

	CITY	ST	EMP	PHONE	ENTRY #
Coca-Cola Refreshments USA Inc	Northampton	MA	D	413 586-8450	13999
Coca-Cola Refreshments USA Inc	Greenfield	MA	C	413 772-2617	11255
Company of Coca-Cola Bottling	Waltham	MA	E	781 672-8624	16073
Company of Coca-Cola Bottling	Waltham	MA	G	617 622-5400	16074
Company of Coca-Cola Bottling	Westborough	MA	E	508 836-5200	16606
Company of Coca-Cola Bottling	Greenfield	MA	E	413 448-8296	11257
Company of Coca-Cola Bottling	Needham Heights	MA	D	781 449-4300	13322
Company of Coca-Cola Bottling	Northampton	MA	D	413 586-8450	14000
Katalyst Kombucha LLC	Greenfield	MA	G	413 773-9700	11265
Nixie Sparkling Water LLC	Chatham	MA	G	617 784-8671	9861
Tropicana Products Inc	Taunton	MA	E	508 821-2056	15792
Coca-Cola Bottling Company	Bangor	ME	D	207 942-5546	5637
Coca-Cola Bottling Company	South Portland	ME	C	207 773-5505	7020
Coca-Cola Bottling Company	Presque Isle	ME	E	207 764-4481	6756
Farmington Coca Cola Btlg Dstr	Farmington	ME	E	207 778-4733	6047
Maine Pure	Fryeburg	ME	G	207 256-8111	6100
Maine Soft Drink Association	South Portland	ME	D	207 773-5505	7032
Roopers Redemption & Bev Ctr	Lewiston	ME	F	207 782-1482	6319
Coca-Cola Bottling Company	Manchester	NH	D	603 623-6033	18800
Coca-Cola Bottling Company	Seabrook	NH	E	603 926-0404	19796
Coca-Cola Bottling Company	Londonderry	NH	D	603 437-3530	18685
Coca-Cola Bottling Company	Belmont	NH	D	603 267-8834	17672
Discount Beverages Plus Cig	Center Conway	NH	G	603 356-8844	17794
North Country Hard Cider LLC	Rollinsford	NH	G	603 834-9915	19694
Surry Licensing LLC	Keene	NH	G	603 354-7000	18532
Coca-Cola Refreshments USA Inc	Providence	RI	B	401 331-1981	20986
L & B Beverage Inc	East Providence	RI	G	401 434-9991	20427
Coca-Cola Bottling Company	Colchester	VT	D	802 654-3800	21860
Smith & Salmon Inc	Burlington	VT	G	802 578-8242	21809

BEVERAGES, NONALCOHOLIC: Carbonated

	CITY	ST	EMP	PHONE	ENTRY #
Pepsi-Cola Btlg of Wrcster Inc	Dayville	CT	E	860 774-4007	1050
Pepsi-Cola Metro Btlg Co Inc	Stratford	CT	B	203 375-2484	4439
Pepsi-Cola Metro Btlg Co Inc	Uncasville	CT	E	860 848-1231	4648
Pepsi-Cola Metro Btlg Co Inc	Windsor	CT	C	860 688-6281	5353
Pepsico	New Haven	CT	F	203 974-8912	2723
Pepsi	Randolph	MA	G	781 986-5249	14692
Pepsi Bottling Group Inc	Ayer	MA	G	978 772-2340	7933
Pepsi-Cola Btlg of Wrcster Inc **(PA)**	Holden	MA	D	508 829-6551	11549
Pepsico	Foxboro	MA	G	508 216-1681	10897
Pepsico Inc	Boylston	MA	G	508 869-1000	8982
Pepsico Inc	Randolph	MA	C	781 767-6622	14693
Pepsi Cola Bottling Aroostook	Presque Isle	ME	E	207 760-3000	6769
Pepsi-Cola Metro Btlg Co Inc	Augusta	ME	D	207 623-1313	5616
Pepsi-Cola Metro Btlg Co Inc	Hampden	ME	D	207 973-2217	6167
Pepsi-Cola Metro Btlg Co Inc	Portland	ME	C	207 773-4258	6707
Pepsi-Cola Metro Btlg Co Inc	Manchester	NH	D	603 625-5764	18899
Organic Studio 13 LLC	Pawtucket	RI	G	770 369-0756	20871
Yacht Club Bottling Works Inc	North Providence	RI	G	401 231-9290	20775
Leader Dist Systems Inc	Brattleboro	VT	D	802 254-6093	21736
Pepsi Cola Bottling Co	Brattleboro	VT	C	802 254-6093	21743

BEVERAGES, NONALCOHOLIC: Carbonated, Canned & Bottled, Etc

	CITY	ST	EMP	PHONE	ENTRY #
Als Beverage Company Inc	East Windsor	CT	E	860 627-7003	1276
Castle Beverages Inc	Ansonia	CT	G	203 732-0883	8
New England Beverages LLC	Branford	CT	G	203 208-4517	332
Simply Originals LLC	Norwalk	CT	G	203 273-3523	3247
Enterade USA	Norwood	MA	F	781 352-5450	14149
Epic Enterprises Inc	Ayer	MA	D	978 772-2340	7919
Flavrz Beverage Corporation	Gloucester	MA	G	978 879-4567	11182
Goodbev Inc	Lynn	MA	G	617 545-5240	12514
Keurig Green Mountain Inc	Burlington	MA	D	781 246-3466	9293
Market Square Beverage Co Inc	Lynn	MA	G	781 593-2150	12525
Mocktail Beverages Inc	Wenham	MA	G	855 662-5824	16403
Refresco Beverages US Inc	East Freetown	MA	G	508 763-3515	10458
Thomas H Conner	Newfields	NH	G	603 778-0322	19320
Vermont Sweetwater Bottling Co	Poultney	VT	G	800 974-9877	22280

BEVERAGES, NONALCOHOLIC: Cider

	CITY	ST	EMP	PHONE	ENTRY #
Mountain Cider LLC	N Chittenden	VT	G	802 483-2270	22183
Willis Wood	Springfield	VT	G	802 263-5547	22513

BEVERAGES, NONALCOHOLIC: Flavoring extracts & syrups, nec

	CITY	ST	EMP	PHONE	ENTRY #
American Distilling Inc	Marlborough	CT	G	860 267-4444	2063
American Distilling Inc **(PA)**	East Hampton	CT	D	860 267-4444	1156
Brookside Flvors Ingrdents LLC **(HQ)**	Stamford	CT	D	203 595-4520	4152
Carrubba Incorporated	Milford	CT	D	203 878-0605	2262
Herbasway Laboratories LLC	Wallingford	CT	E	203 269-6991	4750
Osf Flavors Inc **(PA)**	Windsor	CT	F	860 298-8350	5352
Scitech International LLC	Stamford	CT	G	203 967-8502	4311
Watson LLC **(DH)**	West Haven	CT	B	203 932-3000	5149
Drink Maple Inc	Sudbury	MA	G	978 610-6408	15656
Northice	Plymouth	MA	F	781 985-5225	14569
B&G Foods Inc	Portland	ME	C	207 772-8341	6616
FMC Corporation	Rockland	ME	C	207 594-3200	6795
Luces Pure Maple Syrup	Anson	ME	G	207 696-3732	5525
Sunrise Foods Incorporated	Brentwood	NH	F	603 772-4420	17760
Fountain Dispensers Co Inc	Providence	RI	G	401 461-8400	21014
Rhode Island Distrg Co LLC	West Greenwich	RI	E	401 822-6400	21465
Maple Grove Farms Vermont Inc **(HQ)**	Saint Johnsbury	VT	D	802 748-5141	22391
Runamok Maple LLC	Fairfax	VT	G	802 849-7943	21978

BEVERAGES, NONALCOHOLIC: Fruit Drnks, Under 100% Juice, Can

	CITY	ST	EMP	PHONE	ENTRY #
Harvest Hill Holdings LLC **(PA)**	Stamford	CT	F	203 914-1620	4211
Veryfine Products Inc **(DH)**	Littleton	MA	D	978 486-0812	12325

BEVERAGES, NONALCOHOLIC: Lemonade, Bottled & Canned, Etc

	CITY	ST	EMP	PHONE	ENTRY #
Newmans Own Inc **(PA)**	Westport	CT	E	203 222-0136	5218

BEVERAGES, NONALCOHOLIC: Soft Drinks, Canned & Bottled, Etc

	CITY	ST	EMP	PHONE	ENTRY #
Averys Beverage LLC	New Britain	CT	G	860 224-0830	2511
Foxon Park Beverages Inc	East Haven	CT	G	203 467-7874	1250
Light Rock Spring Water Co	Danbury	CT	F	203 743-2251	948
Pepsi-Cola Metro Btlg Co Inc	North Haven	CT	C	203 234-9014	3050
Reeds Inc	Norwalk	CT	E	203 890-0557	3228
Coca Cola Btlg Co of Cape Cod	Sandwich	MA	D	508 888-0001	14964
Ginseng Up Corporation **(PA)**	Worcester	MA	G	508 799-6178	17383
Keurig Dr Pepper Inc	Canton	MA	D	781 575-4033	9750
Keurig Dr Pepper Inc **(PA)**	Burlington	MA	D	781 418-7000	9292
Polar Corp **(PA)**	Worcester	MA	A	508 753-6383	17443
Dr Pepper Bottling Co Portland	Portland	ME	G	207 773-4258	6654
Pepsi-Cola Metro Btlg Co Inc	Auburn	ME	C	207 784-5791	5588
Pepsi-Cola Metro Btlg Co Inc	Cranston	RI	D	401 468-3221	20270
Pepsi-Cola Metro Btlg Co Inc	Cranston	RI	C	401 468-3300	20271
Aqua Vitea LLC	Middlebury	VT	G	802 453-8590	22100

BEVERAGES, NONALCOHOLIC: Tea, Iced, Bottled & Canned, Etc

	CITY	ST	EMP	PHONE	ENTRY #
Northeast Hot-Fill Co-Op Inc	Ayer	MA	E	978 772-2338	7930

BEVERAGES, WINE & DISTILLED ALCOHOLIC, WHOLESALE: Wine

	CITY	ST	EMP	PHONE	ENTRY #
Matias Importing & Distrg Corp	Newington	CT	G	860 666-5544	2880
Bartlett Maine Estate Winery	Gouldsboro	ME	G	207 546-2408	6135

BEVERAGES, WINE/DISTILLED ALCOHOLIC, WHOL: Bttlg Wine/Liquor

	CITY	ST	EMP	PHONE	ENTRY #
Cellar Door Winery **(PA)**	Lincolnville	ME	G	207 763-4478	6361

BICYCLES WHOLESALERS

	CITY	ST	EMP	PHONE	ENTRY #
Columbia Manufacturing Inc	Westfield	MA	D	413 562-3664	16679

BICYCLES, PARTS & ACCESS

	CITY	ST	EMP	PHONE	ENTRY #
Avalanche Downhill Racing Inc	Colchester	CT	G	860 537-4306	799
Cycling Sports Group Inc **(HQ)**	Wilton	CT	D	608 268-8916	5286
Crimsonbikes LLC	Cambridge	MA	E	617 958-1727	9445
Lifestyle Hq LLC	Amherst	MA	G	310 741-8489	7517
Parlee Cycles Inc	Beverly	MA	G	978 998-4880	8164
Seven Cycles Inc	Watertown	MA	E	617 923-7774	16315
Bike & Ski Touring Ctr of Neng	Middlebury	VT	G	802 388-6666	22102

BILLFOLD INSERTS: Plastic

	CITY	ST	EMP	PHONE	ENTRY #
Aline Systems Inc	Marblehead	MA	G	781 990-1462	12673

BILLIARD & POOL TABLES & SPLYS

	CITY	ST	EMP	PHONE	ENTRY #
Pfd Studios	Marlborough	CT	G	860 295-8500	2068
Cuesport Inc	Southfield	MA	G	413 229-6626	15410
Great American Recrtl Eqp	Cranston	RI	E	401 463-5587	20233

BILLIARD EQPT & SPLYS WHOLESALERS

	CITY	ST	EMP	PHONE	ENTRY #
Happy House Amusement Inc	Goffstown	NH	E	603 497-4151	18203

BILLING & BOOKKEEPING SVCS

	CITY	ST	EMP	PHONE	ENTRY #
Numeric Inc	West Springfield	MA	F	413 732-6544	16536
Outer Limits Publishing LLC	Killington	VT	F	802 422-2399	22055

BINDING SVC: Books & Manuals

	CITY	ST	EMP	PHONE	ENTRY #
Adkins Printing Company	New Britain	CT	E	800 228-9745	2506
Allied Printing Services Inc **(PA)**	Manchester	CT	B	860 643-1101	1984
E R Hitchcock Company	New Britain	CT	E	860 229-2024	2529
Eccles-Lehman Inc	Easton	CT	G	203 268-0605	1318
Elm Press Incorporated	Terryville	CT	E	860 583-3600	4477
Falcon Press	Enfield	CT	G	860 763-2293	1362
G & R Enterprises Incorporated	Hartford	CT	G	860 549-6120	1822
Imperial Grphic Cmmnctions Inc	Milford	CT	E	203 650-3478	2301
Jerrys Printing & Graphics LLC	Bridgeport	CT	G	203 384-0015	435
Joseph Merritt & Company Inc	Danbury	CT	G	203 743-6734	940
Kool Ink LLC	Bloomfield	CT	F	860 242-0303	238
Master Engrv & Printery Inc **(PA)**	Waterbury	CT	G	203 723-2779	4911
Palmisano Printing LLC	Bristol	CT	G	860 582-6883	590
Paul Dewitt	Danbury	CT	F	203 792-5610	965
Phoenix Press Inc	New Haven	CT	E	203 865-5555	2726
Prosperous Printing LLC	Wilton	CT	G	203 834-1962	5300
Step Saver Inc	Southington	CT	E	860 621-6751	4082
Vernon Printing Co Inc	Vernon Rockville	CT	G	860 872-1826	4688
Alliance Book Mfg Co Inc	Pembroke	MA	G	781 294-0802	14390
American Prtg & Envelope Inc	Auburn	MA	E	508 832-6100	7825
Andrew T Johnson Company Inc **(PA)**	Boston	MA	E	617 742-1610	8366
Apb Enterprises Inc	Marlborough	MA	G	508 481-0966	12715
Belmont Printing Company	Belmont	MA	E	617 484-0833	8066
Bill Martel	Somerville	MA	G	617 776-1040	15158
Business Cards Overnight Inc	Lawrence	MA	G	978 974-9271	11999
Chaco Inc	Norwood	MA	G	781 769-5557	14141
Color Images Inc	Methuen	MA	G	978 688-4994	13015
Coprico Inc	Chelsea	MA	G	617 889-0520	9951
D & L Associates Inc	Needham Heights	MA	G	781 400-5068	13326
D S Graphics Inc **(PA)**	Lowell	MA	C	978 970-1359	12365
Ddfhklt Inc	West Springfield	MA	F	413 733-7441	16515
Dmr Print Inc **(PA)**	Concord	MA	E	617 876-3688	10128
Elbonais Incorporated	Framingham	MA	G	508 626-2318	10945
Flagship Press Inc	North Andover	MA	C	978 975-3100	13704
Generation Four Inc	Waltham	MA	G	781 899-3180	16119
Ghp Media Inc	North Adams	MA	D	413 663-3771	13675
Graphic Fllfillment Finshg Inc	Holbrook	MA	G	781 727-8845	11525
Hf Group LLC	Charlestown	MA	G	617 242-1100	9836

	CITY	ST	EMP	PHONE	ENTRY #
J C Enterprises Inc	Ashland	MA	G	508 881-7228	7662
J T Gardner Inc **(PA)**	Westborough	MA	E	800 540-4993	16627
J T Gardner Inc	Worcester	MA	G	508 751-6600	17396
Keating Communication Group	Canton	MA	G	781 828-9030	9749
Kirkwood Holdings Inc **(PA)**	Wilmington	MA	C	978 658-4200	17012
Laplume & Sons Printing Inc	Lawrence	MA	E	978 683-1009	12045
Linmel Associates Inc	Marlborough	MA	F	508 481-6699	12787
LPI Printing and Graphic Inc	Stoneham	MA	E	781 438-5400	15566
Marcus Company Inc	Holyoke	MA	E	413 534-3303	11637
Massachusetts Repro Ltd	Boston	MA	F	617 227-2237	8686
McDermott Pallotta Inc	Watertown	MA	G	617 924-2318	16300
Miles Press Inc	Auburn	MA	F	508 752-6430	7843
Minuteman Press	Newburyport	MA	G	978 465-2242	13515
Minuteman Press	Fitchburg	MA	G	978 345-0818	10839
Minuteman Printing Corp	Concord	MA	F	978 369-2808	10141
Modus Media Inc	Waltham	MA	E	781 663-5000	16153
Northern Graphics Inc	Middleton	MA	F	978 646-9925	13097
Picken Printing Inc	North Chelmsford	MA	E	978 251-0730	13907
PIP Itsa Inc	Beverly	MA	G	978 927-5717	8165
Power Graphics Printing	Tewksbury	MA	G	978 851-8988	15827
Printing Place Inc	Melrose	MA	G	781 272-7209	12988
Professional Lithography Inc	South Hadley	MA	E	413 532-9473	15309
Pyramid Printing and Advg Inc	Weymouth	MA	E	781 337-7609	16899
R & H Communications Inc **(PA)**	Waltham	MA	F	781 893-6221	16181
Robert Murphy	Salem	MA	E	978 745-7170	14938
Rogers Printing Co Inc	Leominster	MA	E	978 537-9791	12184
S A N Inc **(PA)**	Lawrence	MA	G	978 686-3875	12073
Sherman Printing Co Inc	Canton	MA	E	781 828-8855	9778
Ted Best	Hyde Park	MA	G	617 361-7258	11881
Three Ring Binders	Somerville	MA	G	617 354-4084	15223
Universal Wilde Inc	Westwood	MA	C	978 658-0800	16881
Yankee Printing Group Inc	South Hadley	MA	E	413 532-9513	15313
Bruce A Pettengill	Leeds	ME	G	207 933-2578	6268
Davic Inc	Portland	ME	F	207 774-0093	6649
Penmor Lithographers Inc	Lewiston	ME	E	207 784-1341	6316
Quick Print Color Center	Saco	ME	G	207 282-6480	6856
R & W Engraving Inc	Biddeford	ME	G	207 286-3020	5760
Xpress of Maine **(PA)**	Portland	ME	G	207 775-2444	6747
Capitol Copy Inc	Concord	NH	G	603 226-2679	17889
Channelbind International Corp **(PA)**	Concord	NH	E	864 579-7072	17892
Custom Die Cut Inc	Windham	NH	G	603 437-3090	20003
Letterman Press LLC	West Lebanon	NH	G	603 543-0500	19956
New England Printing Corp	Portsmouth	NH	F	603 431-0142	19599
RB Graphics Inc	Hooksett	NH	G	603 624-4025	18358
Walnut Bottom Inc	Concord	NH	G	603 224-6606	17939
A & H Composition and Prtg Inc	East Providence	RI	G	401 438-1200	20383
Dome Enterprises Trust **(PA)**	Warwick	RI	G	401 738-7900	21353
Rag and Bone Bindery Ltd	Pawtucket	RI	F	401 728-0762	20889
Warwick Group Inc	Bristol	RI	F	401 438-9451	20109
Darwin A Lewis Inc	Hartland	VT	G	802 457-4521	22015
L Brown and Sons Printing Inc	Barre	VT	E	802 476-3164	21627
Queen City Printers Inc	Burlington	VT	E	802 864-4566	21804
Villanti & Sons Printers Inc	Milton	VT	D	802 864-0723	22140

BINDING SVC: Trade

	CITY	ST	EMP	PHONE	ENTRY #
Jackson Bookbinding Co Inc	Greenville	RI	F	401 231-0800	20469

BINDINGS: Bias, Made From Purchased Materials

	CITY	ST	EMP	PHONE	ENTRY #
Brand & Oppenheimer Co Inc	Bedford	MA	E	781 271-0000	7965

BINOCULARS

	CITY	ST	EMP	PHONE	ENTRY #
Tower Optical Company Inc	Norwalk	CT	G	203 866-4535	3260
S I Howard Glass Company Inc	Worcester	MA	E	508 753-8146	17461

BINS: Prefabricated, Metal Plate

	CITY	ST	EMP	PHONE	ENTRY #
Linvar LLC	Rocky Hill	CT	G	860 951-3818	3721

BIOLOGICAL PRDTS: Exc Diagnostic

	CITY	ST	EMP	PHONE	ENTRY #
Axiomx Inc	Branford	CT	E	203 208-1034	293
Charles River Laboratories Inc	Voluntown	CT	E	860 376-1240	4689
Coopersurgical Inc	Guilford	CT	E	203 453-1700	1699
Evotec (us) Inc	Branford	CT	E	650 228-1400	314
Genx International Inc **(PA)**	Guilford	CT	E	203 453-1700	1705
Oncosynergy Inc	Greenwich	CT	G	617 755-9156	1636
Phoenixsongs Biologicals Inc	Branford	CT	G	203 433-4329	337
Vegware Us Inc	Danielson	CT	G	860 779-7970	1020
3dm Inc	Cambridge	MA	G	617 875-6204	9367
Acceleron Pharma Inc **(PA)**	Cambridge	MA	C	617 649-9200	9370
ACS Division Biochemical Tech	Boston	MA	F	617 216-6144	8338
Agenus Inc **(PA)**	Lexington	MA	C	781 674-4400	12204
Akebia Therapeutics Inc **(PA)**	Cambridge	MA	D	617 871-2098	9379
Allena Pharmaceuticals Inc **(PA)**	Newton	MA	E	617 467-4577	13558
Ambergen Inc **(PA)**	Watertown	MA	F	617 923-9990	16268
Amgen Inc	Cambridge	MA	E	617 444-5000	9388
Aqua Bio Compliance Corp	Worcester	MA	G	508 798-2966	17341
Ariad Pharmaceuticals Inc	Cambridge	MA	B	617 494-0400	9392
Beverly Qiagen Inc	Beverly	MA	D	978 927-7027	8109
Bioanalytix Inc	Cambridge	MA	G	857 829-3200	9408
Biogen Inc **(PA)**	Cambridge	MA	B	617 679-2000	9409
Biogen MA Inc **(HQ)**	Cambridge	MA	C	617 679-2000	9410
Biohelix Corporation	Beverly	MA	F	978 927-5056	8111
Bittid LLC	Winchester	MA	G	781 570-2077	17083
Boston Biochem Inc	Cambridge	MA	G	617 241-7072	9415
Capralogics Inc	Gilbertville	MA	G	413 477-6866	11153
Cellaria Biosciences LLC	Boxford	MA	G	617 981-4208	8974
Curis Inc **(PA)**	Lexington	MA	E	617 503-6500	12217
Cytocure LLC	Beverly	MA	G	978 232-1243	8122
Diagnosys LLC **(PA)**	Lowell	MA	E	978 458-1600	12367
Dicerna Pharmaceuticals Inc	Lexington	MA	E	617 621-8097	12219
Diversified Biotech Inc	Dedham	MA	F	781 326-6709	10288
Editas Medicine Inc	Cambridge	MA	D	617 401-9000	9458
Elicio Therapeutics Inc	Cambridge	MA	G	617 945-2077	9463
Endogen Inc	Woburn	MA	D	617 225-0055	17177
Excelimmune Inc	Beverly	MA	G	617 262-8055	8129
Excelimmune Inc **(PA)**	Lexington	MA	G	781 262-8055	12224
Extend Biosciences Inc	Newton	MA	G	732 599-8580	13591
Genocea Biosciences Inc	Cambridge	MA	D	617 876-8191	9488
Genzyme Corporation **(DH)**	Cambridge	MA	A	617 252-7500	9489
Ginkgo Bioworks Inc	Boston	MA	C	814 422-5362	8565
Global Lf Scnces Sltons USA LL	Marlborough	MA	D	508 480-9235	12761
Heka Instruments Incorporated	Holliston	MA	G	516 882-1155	11576
Helixbind Inc	Marlborough	MA	F	508 460-1028	12767
Intellia Therapeutics Inc **(PA)**	Cambridge	MA	D	857 285-6200	9517
Jounce Therapeutics Inc **(PA)**	Cambridge	MA	D	857 259-3840	9522
Joyn Bio LLC	Boston	MA	E	978 549-3723	8641
Kaleido Biosciences Inc **(PA)**	Lexington	MA	D	617 674-9000	12234
Kiniksa Pharmaceuticals Corp	Lexington	MA	G	781 431-9100	12236
Koan Biotherapeutics Inc	Waban	MA	G	617 968-7882	15937
Lariat Biosciences Inc	Chelsea	MA	G	603 244-9657	9960
Logicbio Therapeutics Inc	Cambridge	MA	E	617 230-0399	9540
Microbot Medical Inc **(PA)**	Hingham	MA	G	781 875-3605	11505
Moderna Inc **(PA)**	Cambridge	MA	E	617 714-6500	9564
Moderna LLC **(HQ)**	Cambridge	MA	G	617 714-6500	9565
Organogenesis Inc **(HQ)**	Canton	MA	B	781 575-0775	9764
Pierce Biotechnology Inc	Woburn	MA	E	781 622-1000	17264
Primmbiotech Inc	West Roxbury	MA	G	617 308-8135	16500
Project Plasma Holdings Corp **(DH)**	Milford	MA	G	508 244-6400	13139
Puretech Health LLC **(PA)**	Boston	MA	D	617 482-2333	8799
Repligen Corporation **(PA)**	Waltham	MA	B	781 250-0111	16187
Replimune Group Inc	Woburn	MA	D	781 995-2443	17283
Rowley Biochemical Institute	Danvers	MA	G	978 739-4883	10253
Scholar Rock Holding Corp **(PA)**	Cambridge	MA	G	857 259-3860	9646
Solid Biosciences Inc **(PA)**	Cambridge	MA	D	617 337-4680	9655
Twentyfrst Cntury Bchmcals Inc	Marlborough	MA	E	508 303-8222	12839
Variation Btechnologies US Inc	Cambridge	MA	E	617 830-3031	9688
Vericel Corporation	Cambridge	MA	G	857 600-8191	9692
Vericel Corporation **(PA)**	Cambridge	MA	C	800 556-0311	9693
Vivagene Biotech Inc	Quincy	MA	G	617 302-4398	14667
Voyager Therapeutics Inc **(PA)**	Cambridge	MA	D	857 259-5340	9698
X4 Pharmaceuticals Inc **(PA)**	Cambridge	MA	F	857 529-8300	9706
Gulf of Maine Inc	Pembroke	ME	G	207 726-4620	6580
Lobster Rx	Orono	ME	G	207 949-2028	6555
Lohmann Animal Health Intl Inc	Winslow	ME	C	207 873-3989	7270
Lonza Rockland Inc	Rockland	ME	D	207 594-3400	6802
McWilliams Inc	North Berwick	ME	G	207 676-7639	6509
Opco Inc	Edgecomb	ME	G	207 882-6783	6003
Aurora Biosystems LLC	Portsmouth	NH	G	603 766-1947	19540
Avitide Inc	Lebanon	NH	E	603 965-2100	18613
Lyophilization Svcs Neng Inc **(PA)**	Manchester	NH	F	603 626-5763	18866
Lyophilization Svcs Neng Inc	Bedford	NH	E	603 668-5763	17651
Lyophilization Svcs Neng Inc	Bedford	NH	F	603 626-9559	17652
Amgen Inc	West Greenwich	RI	D	401 392-1200	21452
Colloidal Science Solutions	West Warwick	RI	G	401 826-3641	21487
Tivorsan Pharmaceuticals Inc	Providence	RI	G	410 419-2171	21137

BIOLOGICAL PRDTS: Extracts

	CITY	ST	EMP	PHONE	ENTRY #
Kbioscience LLC	Beverly	MA	G	978 232-9430	8145
Nashoba Valley Extract LLC	Stow	MA	G	978 201-5245	15634
Revo Biologics Inc	Spencer	MA	E	508 370-5451	15434
Revo Biologics Inc **(DH)**	Framingham	MA	D	508 620-9700	11000
Hightech Extracts LLC	Biddeford	ME	G	207 590-3251	5738

BIOLOGICAL PRDTS: Serums

	CITY	ST	EMP	PHONE	ENTRY #
New England Immunology Assoc	Lexington	MA	G	781 863-5774	12249
Science Serum LLC	Norton	MA	G	508 369-7733	14088
Special Diversified Opp Inc	Windham	ME	E	207 856-6151	7254

BIOLOGICAL PRDTS: Vaccines

	CITY	ST	EMP	PHONE	ENTRY #
Charles River Laboratories Inc	Storrs	CT	E	860 429-7261	4381
Protein Sciences Corporation **(HQ)**	Meriden	CT	D	203 686-0800	2119
Westchester Pet Vaccines	Colchester	CT	G	860 267-4554	812
Massbiologics	Boston	MA	C	617 474-3000	8687
Takeda Vaccines Inc	Cambridge	MA	G	970 672-4918	9676
Tetragenetics Inc	Arlington	MA	F	617 500-7471	7641
Vbi Vaccines	Cambridge	MA	G	617 714-3451	9689
Vbi Vaccines Inc	Cambridge	MA	G	617 830-3031	9690
Epivax Inc	Providence	RI	F	401 272-2123	21007

BIOLOGICAL PRDTS: Vaccines & Immunizing

	CITY	ST	EMP	PHONE	ENTRY #
Curevac Inc	Boston	MA	G	617 694-1537	8490
Star Vaccine Inc	Newton	MA	G	617 584-5483	13640
Vaccine Technologies Inc **(PA)**	Wellesley	MA	G	781 489-3388	16391
Solidphase Inc	Portland	ME	G	207 797-0211	6732
Maxi Green Inc	Colchester	VT	G	802 657-3586	21873

BIOLOGICAL PRDTS: Veterinary

	CITY	ST	EMP	PHONE	ENTRY #
Charles River Laboratories Inc	Norwich	CT	E	860 889-1389	3277
Fresenius Usa Inc	Marlborough	MA	E	508 460-1150	12757
Launchworks LLC	Beverly	MA	E	978 338-3045	8147

BLACKBOARDS: Slate

	CITY	ST	EMP	PHONE	ENTRY #
High Standard Inc	Jaffrey	NH	G	603 532-8000	18466

BLADES: Knife

	CITY	ST	EMP	PHONE	ENTRY #
Colonial Cutlery Intl Inc	North Kingstown	RI	C	401 737-0024	20697
Famars USA LLC	Richmond	RI	G	401 397-5500	21161

BLADES: Saw, Hand Or Power

	CITY	ST	EMP	PHONE	ENTRY #
Blackstone Industries LLC	Bethel	CT	D	203 792-8622	133
Specialty Saw Inc	Simsbury	CT	E	860 658-4419	3912
LS Starrett Company **(PA)**	Athol	MA	A	978 249-3551	7689
Malco Saw Co Inc	Cranston	RI	G	401 942-7380	20258

BLANKBOOKS

	CITY	ST	EMP	PHONE	ENTRY #
Eureka Lab Book Inc	Holyoke	MA	F	413 534-5671	11625

BLANKBOOKS & LOOSELEAF BINDERS

	CITY	ST	EMP	PHONE	ENTRY #
Atlantic Bookbinders Inc	South Lancaster	MA	G	978 365-4524	15315
Nettwerk Music Group LLC	Cambridge	MA	G	617 497-8200	9576
Union Bookbinding II LLC	Fall River	MA	E	508 676-8580	10776
W G Fry Corp	Florence	MA	E	413 747-2551	10870
Bank & Business Forms Inc	Keene	NH	G	603 357-0567	18495
Allied Group Inc **(PA)**	Cranston	RI	C	401 461-1700	20177

BLANKBOOKS: Account

	CITY	ST	EMP	PHONE	ENTRY #
Data Management Incorporated	Unionville	CT	E	860 677-8586	4655

BLANKBOOKS: Albums, Record

	CITY	ST	EMP	PHONE	ENTRY #
Yolanda Dubose Records and	West Haven	CT	F	203 823-6699	5153
Strange Famous Inc	North Smithfield	RI	G	310 254-8974	20797

BLANKBOOKS: Scrapbooks

	CITY	ST	EMP	PHONE	ENTRY #
Grannys Got It	Wolcott	CT	G	203 879-0042	5443
Scrapbook Clubhouse	Westbrook	CT	F	860 399-4443	5162
Fabricate LLC	Bar Harbor	ME	G	207 288-5113	5665
Scrappin Soul Sisters	Concord	NH	G	603 717-7136	17928

BLANKETING, FROM MANMADE FIBER

	CITY	ST	EMP	PHONE	ENTRY #
Peristere LLC	Manchester	CT	G	860 783-5301	2038

BLANKETS & BLANKETING, COTTON

	CITY	ST	EMP	PHONE	ENTRY #
Maine Woolens LLC	Brunswick	ME	E	207 725-7900	5841

BLANKS: Textile Machinery Access, Wood

	CITY	ST	EMP	PHONE	ENTRY #
Lawson Hemphill Inc	Swansea	MA	G	508 679-5364	15706

BLASTING SVC: Sand, Metal Parts

	CITY	ST	EMP	PHONE	ENTRY #
South Shore Dstless Blastg LLC	Plymouth	MA	G	508 789-4575	14584

BLINDS & SHADES: Mini

	CITY	ST	EMP	PHONE	ENTRY #
Kenney Manufacturing Company **(PA)**	Warwick	RI	B	401 739-2200	21383

BLINDS & SHADES: Porch, Wood Slat

	CITY	ST	EMP	PHONE	ENTRY #
Niantic Awning Company	Niantic	CT	G	860 739-0161	2954
L F Pease Co	East Providence	RI	F	401 438-2850	20428

BLINDS & SHADES: Vertical

	CITY	ST	EMP	PHONE	ENTRY #
Decorator Services Inc	Bridgeport	CT	E	203 384-8144	402
Kilcourse Specialty Products	New Milford	CT	G	860 210-2075	2810
Landmark Window Fashions Inc	Holbrook	MA	E	781 767-3535	11528
New England Blinds	Sterling	MA	G	508 868-5399	15542
Custom Window Decorators	Lewiston	ME	G	207 784-4113	6282
Vertical Dreams	Nashua	NH	G	603 943-7571	19282
Gordons Window Decor Inc **(PA)**	Williston	VT	F	802 655-7777	22671

BLINDS : Window

	CITY	ST	EMP	PHONE	ENTRY #
Porter Preston Inc	Waterbury	CT	E	203 753-1113	4941
Roto-Frank of America Inc	Chester	CT	C	860 526-4996	775
Marjorie Royer Interiors Inc	Middleton	MA	G	978 774-0533	13095
TLC Vision (usa) Corporation	Peabody	MA	E	978 531-4114	14378

BLOCKS & BRICKS: Concrete

	CITY	ST	EMP	PHONE	ENTRY #
Messiah Development LLC	Bridgeport	CT	G	203 368-2405	450
J & O Construction Inc	Brockton	MA	G	508 586-4900	9157
Stiles & Hart Brick Company	Bridgewater	MA	E	508 697-6928	9088

BLOCKS: Landscape Or Retaining Wall, Concrete

	CITY	ST	EMP	PHONE	ENTRY #
Greener Group LLC	Lowell	MA	D	978 441-3900	12378

BLOCKS: Paving, Asphalt, Not From Refineries

	CITY	ST	EMP	PHONE	ENTRY #
Cruz Construction Company Inc	Cumberland	RI	F	401 727-3770	20316

BLOCKS: Paving, Cut Stone

	CITY	ST	EMP	PHONE	ENTRY #
Connecticut Stone Supplies Inc **(PA)**	Milford	CT	D	203 882-1000	2270

BLOCKS: Standard, Concrete Or Cinder

	CITY	ST	EMP	PHONE	ENTRY #
Connecticut Concrete Form Inc	Farmington	CT	F	860 674-1314	1474
Kobyluck Ready-Mix Inc	Waterford	CT	F	860 444-9604	4987
New Milford Block & Supply	New Milford	CT	F	860 355-1101	2816
Westbrook Con Block Co Inc	Westbrook	CT	E	860 399-6201	5166
Adolf Jandris & Sons Inc	Gardner	MA	E	978 632-0089	11102
Hi-Way Concrete Pdts Co Inc	Wareham	MA	E	508 295-0834	16249
Ideal Concrete Block Co **(PA)**	Westford	MA	E	978 692-3076	16773
Johns Building Supply Co Inc	Pittsfield	MA	F	413 442-7846	14478
Kingston Block Co Inc	Kingston	MA	G	781 585-6400	11960
Oldcastle Apg Northeast Inc	Holbrook	MA	D	781 506-9473	11535
P & M Brick & Block Inc	Watertown	MA	G	617 924-6020	16304
R Ducharme Inc	Chicopee	MA	G	413 534-4516	10055
State Road Cement Block Co	North Dartmouth	MA	G	508 993-9473	13926
Gagne & Son Con Blocks Inc	Auburn	ME	G	207 495-3313	5566
Tilcon Arthur Whitcomb Inc **(HQ)**	North Swanzey	NH	F	603 352-0101	19393
Anchor Concrete	Cranston	RI	E	401 942-4800	20182
Anthony Corrado Inc	Lincoln	RI	G	401 723-7600	20556
Ferreira Concrete Forms Inc	East Providence	RI	F	401 639-0931	20413

BLOOD RELATED HEALTH SVCS

	CITY	ST	EMP	PHONE	ENTRY #
New England Ctr For Hring Rhab	Hampton	CT	G	860 455-1404	1798

BLOWERS & FANS

	CITY	ST	EMP	PHONE	ENTRY #
Adk Pressure Equipment Corp **(DH)**	Bristol	CT	G	860 585-0050	514
Anderson Technologies Inc	Killingworth	CT	G	860 663-2100	1924
Nidec America Corporation	East Granby	CT	F	860 653-2144	1136
Stylair LLC	Plainville	CT	F	860 747-4588	3515
Heat Fab Inc	Turners Falls	MA	D	413 863-2242	15878
Impolit Envmtl Ctrl Corp	Beverly	MA	E	978 927-4619	8140
Munters Corporation **(DH)**	Amesbury	MA	C	978 241-1100	7498
Northern Air Inc	Raynham	MA	G	508 823-4900	14721
Pall Northborough **(DH)**	Northborough	MA	G	978 263-9888	14043
Parker-Hannifin Corporation	Haverhill	MA	C	978 858-0505	11457
Pioneer Consolidated Corp	North Oxford	MA	E	508 987-8438	13973
Riley Power Inc	Marlborough	MA	C	508 852-7100	12817
Spruce Environmental Tech Inc **(PA)**	Haverhill	MA	D	978 521-0901	11475
Westport Envmtl Systems LP	Westport	MA	D	508 636-8811	16851
Brailsford & Company Inc	Antrim	NH	E	603 588-2880	17593
Electrocraft New Hampshire Inc **(DH)**	Dover	NH	E	603 742-3330	18021

BLOWERS & FANS

	CITY	ST	EMP	PHONE	ENTRY #
McIntire Company **(HQ)**	Bristol	CT	F	860 585-8559	580
Nauset Engineer Equipment	Mansfield	MA	G	508 339-2662	12648

BLOWERS, TURBO: Indl

	CITY	ST	EMP	PHONE	ENTRY #
Mechancal Engnered Systems LLC	New Canaan	CT	G	203 400-4658	2606
Spencer Turbine Company **(HQ)**	Windsor	CT	C	860 688-8361	5363

BLUEPRINTING SVCS

	CITY	ST	EMP	PHONE	ENTRY #
Andrew T Johnson Company Inc **(PA)**	Boston	MA	E	617 742-1610	8366
Weston Corporation	Hingham	MA	F	781 749-0936	11516
Central Street Corporation	Bangor	ME	F	207 947-8049	5635
Xpress of Maine **(PA)**	Portland	ME	G	207 775-2444	6747
Capitol Copy Inc	Concord	NH	G	603 226-2679	17889
RB Graphics Inc	Hooksett	NH	G	603 624-4025	18358

BOAT & BARGE COMPONENTS: Metal, Prefabricated

	CITY	ST	EMP	PHONE	ENTRY #
Kw Steel Structures LLC	Walpole	MA	G	857 342-7838	15998
Down Wind Dockside Svcs LLC	Newport	RI	G	401 619-1990	20663

BOAT BUILDING & REPAIR

	CITY	ST	EMP	PHONE	ENTRY #
Dutch Wharf Boat Yard & Marina	Branford	CT	F	203 488-9000	310
Hbi Boat LLC	Groton	CT	G	860 536-7776	1677
Kiwanis Fndtion Middletown Inc	Middletown	CT	G	860 638-8135	2198
A To Z Boatworks Inc	Scituate	MA	G	781 545-6632	15004
Boston Family Boat Building	Jamaica Plain	MA	G	617 522-5366	11941
Cooper Eldred Boat Builders	Falmouth	MA	G	508 540-7130	10788
Hazard Marine A Div Ltd Inds	Webster	MA	G	508 943-7531	16342
Howard Boats LLC	Barnstable	MA	G	508 362-6859	7948
Inriver Tank & Boat Inc	Concord	MA	G	978 287-9534	10136
Karls Boat Shop Inc	Harwich	MA	F	508 432-4488	11395
Pease Boat Works & Marine Rlwy	Chatham	MA	G	508 945-7800	9862
Pleasant Bay Boat Spar Co LLC	Orleans	MA	G	508 240-0058	14240
Sandy Point Boat Works LLC	Carver	MA	G	508 878-8057	9807
Sperry Sails Inc	Marion	MA	G	508 748-2581	12705
Still Water Design Inc	Chelsea	MA	G	617 308-5820	9971
Wenaumet Bluffs Boat Works Inc	Pocasset	MA	G	888 224-9942	14602
Whitecap Composites Inc	Peabody	MA	G	978 278-5718	14382
William Clements	North Billerica	MA	G	978 663-3103	13877
Winninghoff Boats Inc	Rowley	MA	F	978 948-2314	14869
Alley Road LLC	Boothbay Harbor	ME	E	207 633-3171	5781
B Marine Corp	Boothbay Harbor	ME	F	207 633-3171	5782
Belmont Boatworks LLC	Belmont	ME	F	207 342-2885	5701
Benjamin River Marine Inc	Brooklin	ME	G	207 359-2244	5814
Billings Diesel & Marine Svc	Stonington	ME	E	207 367-2328	7069
Blevins Company	Edgecomb	ME	G	207 882-6396	5999
Carpenters Boat Shop Inc	Pemaquid	ME	G	207 677-2614	6579
Clark Island Boat Works	South Thomaston	ME	G	207 594-4112	7045
Classic Boat Shop Inc	Bernard	ME	G	207 244-3374	5706
Dana Robes Boat Builders	Round Pond	ME	G	207 529-2433	6829
Danas Boat Shop	Westport Island	ME	G	207 882-7205	7216
Dark Harbor Boatyard Corp	Islesboro	ME	F	207 734-2246	6215
Edgecomb Boat Works	Edgecomb	ME	G	207 882-5038	6002
Ellis Boat Co Inc	Southwest Harbor	ME	F	207 244-9221	7046
Flowers Boat Works Inc	Walpole	ME	G	207 563-7404	7141
French Webb & Co Inc	Belfast	ME	F	207 338-6706	5689
Hodgdon Shipbuilding LLC	Damariscotta	ME	G	207 563-7033	5936
Hodgdon Yachts Inc	Richmond	ME	G	207 737-2802	6782
Hollands Boat Shop Inc	Belfast	ME	G	207 338-3155	5690
J O Brown & Son Inc	North Haven	ME	G	207 867-4621	6511
James H Rich Boatyard	Bernard	ME	G	207 244-3208	5707
Johansons Boatworks	Rockland	ME	F	207 596-7060	6800
Libbys Boat Shop	Beals	ME	G	207 497-5487	5684
Lyman Morse Boatbuilding Inc	Thomaston	ME	D	207 354-6904	7086
Padebco Custom Boats Inc	Round Pond	ME	G	207 529-5106	6832
Rockport Marine Inc	Rockport	ME	E	207 236-9651	6826
Stuart Marine Corp Inc	Rockland	ME	G	207 594-5515	6811
Talaria Company LLC	Trenton	ME	C	207 667-1891	7102
Washburn & Doughty Assoc Inc	East Boothbay	ME	D	207 633-6517	5980
Wesmac Custom Boats Inc **(PA)**	Surry	ME	F	207 667-4822	7077
Wesmac Custom Boats Inc	Surry	ME	G	207 667-4822	7078
Wild Duck Boat Works LLC	Harpswell	ME	G	207 837-2920	6175
York Marine Inc	Rockland	ME	G	207 596-7400	6816

	CITY	ST	EMP	PHONE	ENTRY #
American Marine Products Inc	Charlestown	NH	E	954 782-1400	17810
Juliet Marine Systems Inc	Portsmouth	NH	G	603 319-8412	19582
Special Projects Group LLC	Gilford	NH	G	603 391-9700	18192
Viking Wldg & Fabrication LLC	Kensington	NH	G	603 394-7887	18537
American Boat Builders	Newport	RI	E	401 236-2466	20654
Aquidneck Cstm Composites Inc	Bristol	RI	G	401 254-6911	20063
Berthon Usa Inc	Newport	RI	G	401 846-8404	20657
Bristol Cushions Inc	Bristol	RI	F	401 247-4499	20065
C & C Fiberglass Components	Bristol	RI	F	401 254-4342	20067
C R Scott Marine Wdwkg Co	Newport	RI	G	401 849-0715	20659
Chem-Tainer Industries Inc	Cranston	RI	D	401 467-2750	20196
Clark Boat-Yard	Jamestown	RI	G	401 423-3625	20488
Dur A Flex Motor Sports	Warwick	RI	G	401 739-0202	21356
East Passage Boatwrights Inc	Bristol	RI	G	401 253-5535	20074
Jamestown Boat Yard Inc	Jamestown	RI	E	401 423-0600	20492
Morris Yachts LLC	Portsmouth	RI	G	207 667-2499	20929
Narragansett Shipwrights Inc	Newport	RI	G	401 846-3312	20674
Rhode Northsales Island Inc	Portsmouth	RI	E	401 683-7997	20939
Talaria Company LLC **(PA)**	Portsmouth	RI	F	401 683-7100	20940
Talaria Company LLC	Portsmouth	RI	C	401 683-7280	20941
Transfusion Boat Works Inc	Westerly	RI	G	401 348-5878	21545
Warren River Boatworks Inc	Warren	RI	G	401 245-6949	21314
Darling Boatworks Inc	Charlotte	VT	G	802 425-2004	21833
Fiberglass Plus Inc	North Hero	VT	G	802 878-2066	22230
Washburn Boat & Auto Body	Williston	VT	G	802 863-1383	22697

BOAT BUILDING & REPAIRING: Dinghies

	CITY	ST	EMP	PHONE	ENTRY #
Portland Pudgy Inc	Portland	ME	G	207 761-2428	6712

BOAT BUILDING & REPAIRING: Fiberglass

	CITY	ST	EMP	PHONE	ENTRY #
Chester Boatworks	Deep River	CT	G	860 526-2227	1059
New England Fiberglass Repair **(PA)**	Norwalk	CT	G	203 866-1690	3207
Vespoli Usa Inc	New Haven	CT	E	203 773-0311	2751
Vintage Boat Restorations LLC	Bristol	CT	G	860 582-0774	622
Beetle Inc	Wareham	MA	G	508 295-8585	16241
Boston Boatworks LLC	Charlestown	MA	E	617 561-9111	9825
Charr Custom Boat Company	Yarmouth Port	MA	G	508 375-0028	17529
Cutlass Marine Inc	East Weymouth	MA	G	781 740-1260	10540
Danalevi Corp	Belchertown	MA	G	413 626-8120	8023
E M Crosby Boat Works	West Barnstable	MA	G	508 362-7100	16406
Fiberglas Fabrications	Orleans	MA	G	508 255-9409	14233
Fortier Boats Inc	Somerset	MA	G	508 673-5253	15144
Intercept Boat Corp	Pembroke	MA	G	781 294-8100	14411
Marshall Marine Corp	South Dartmouth	MA	F	508 994-0414	15240
Atlantic Boat Company	Brooklin	ME	E	207 664-2900	5813
Bridges Point Boat Yard Inc	Brooklin	ME	G	207 359-2713	5815
C B Boatworks Inc	Peru	ME	G	207 562-8849	6584
Custom Composite Technologies	Bath	ME	G	207 442-7007	5675
D N Hylan Associates Inc	Brooklin	ME	G	207 359-9807	5819
Downeast Boats & Composites	Penobscot	ME	G	207 326-9400	6581
Farrins Boat Shop	Walpole	ME	G	207 563-5510	7140
Johns Bay Boat Co	South Bristol	ME	G	207 644-8261	7005
Johnsons Boatyard Inc	Long Island	ME	G	207 766-3319	6383
Malcolm L Pettegrow Inc	Southwest Harbor	ME	F	207 244-3514	7049
North End Composites LLC	Rockland	ME	C	207 594-8427	6806
Otis Enterprises Marine Corp	Searsport	ME	G	207 548-6362	6953
Spb LLC	Augusta	ME	G	207 620-7998	5620
SW Boatworks	Lamoine	ME	G	207 667-7427	6264
Webbers Cove Boat Yard Inc	East Blue Hill	ME	G	207 374-2841	5975
Wesley Lash	Friendship	ME	G	207 832-7807	6094
Eastern Boats Inc	Milton	NH	E	603 652-9213	19084
Anchorage Inc	Warren	RI	F	401 245-3300	21285
Blount Boats Inc	Warren	RI	D	401 245-8300	21289
Element Industries Inc	Bristol	RI	F	401 253-8802	20075
Midland Co Inc	Coventry	RI	G	401 397-4425	20156
Naiad Inflatables Newport Inc	Newport	RI	F	401 683-6700	20673
Outerlmits Offshore Powerboats	Bristol	RI	F	401 253-7300	20096
Stur-Dee Boat Co	Tiverton	RI	G	401 624-9373	21265
Adirondack Guide Boat	North Ferrisburgh	VT	G	802 425-3926	22224
Martin Custom Boat Works LLC	North Ferrisburgh	VT	G	802 318-7882	22226

BOAT BUILDING & REPAIRING: Motorboats, Inboard Or Outboard

	CITY	ST	EMP	PHONE	ENTRY #
General Marine Inc	Biddeford	ME	G	207 284-7517	5737

BOAT BUILDING & REPAIRING: Motorized

	CITY	ST	EMP	PHONE	ENTRY #
Eric Dow Boatbuilder	Brooklin	ME	G	207 359-2277	5820
Chisletts Boating & Design LLC	Dover	NH	F	603 755-6815	18013
Pearson Composites LLC	Warren	RI	F	401 245-1200	21301

BOAT BUILDING & REPAIRING: Rowboats

	CITY	ST	EMP	PHONE	ENTRY #
Peinert Boatworks Inc	Mattapoisett	MA	G	508 758-3020	12889

BOAT BUILDING & REPAIRING: Yachts

	CITY	ST	EMP	PHONE	ENTRY #
Jennings Yacht Services	Mystic	CT	G	860 625-1368	2440
CW Hood Yachts Inc	Marblehead	MA	F	781 631-0192	12680
Heritage Wharf Company LLC	Dartmouth	MA	G	508 990-1011	10275
Brion Rieff Boatbuilder Inc	Brooklin	ME	G	207 359-4455	5816
Brooklin Boat Yard Inc **(PA)**	Brooklin	ME	D	207 359-2236	5817
C W Paine Yacht Design Inc	Camden	ME	G	207 236-2166	5866
Hodgdon Shipbuilding LLC **(HQ)**	East Boothbay	ME	F	207 633-4194	5976
Lyman Morse Boatbuilding Inc **(PA)**	Thomaston	ME	D	207 354-6904	7085
Maine Cat Co Inc	Bremen	ME	F	207 529-6500	5792
Talaria Company LLC	Southwest Harbor	ME	C	207 244-5572	7052
New England Nautical LLC	Portsmouth	NH	G	603 601-3166	19598
Alden Yachts Corporation	Bristol	RI	D	401 683-4200	20060
Eric Goetz Custom Sailboats	Bristol	RI	E	401 253-2670	20077
Hunt Boatbuilders Inc	Portsmouth	RI	G	401 324-4205	20924
Hunt Yachts LLC	Portsmouth	RI	D	401 324-4201	20925
International Yacht Restoratio	Newport	RI	F	401 846-2587	20666
Jon Barrett Associates Inc	Newport	RI	G	401 846-8226	20669
Shannon Boat Company Inc	Bristol	RI	E	401 253-2441	20103
Sparkman & Stephens LLC **(PA)**	Newport	RI	F	401 847-5449	20683

BOAT BUILDING & RPRG: Fishing, Small, Lobster, Crab, Oyster

	CITY	ST	EMP	PHONE	ENTRY #
Newbury Port Meritown Society	Amesbury	MA	G	978 834-0050	7501
Scotia Boat Builders	Abington	MA	G	781 871-2120	7331
H & H Marine Inc	Steuben	ME	F	207 546-7477	7067
Hodgdon Yachts Inc **(PA)**	East Boothbay	ME	C	207 737-2802	5977
Hampton North Fisheries Inc	Nottingham	NH	G	603 463-5874	19414
F V Sea Breeze LLC	Wakefield	RI	G	401 792-0188	21270

BOAT DEALERS

	CITY	ST	EMP	PHONE	ENTRY #
F L Tripp & Sons Inc	Westport Point	MA	E	508 636-4058	16854
Karls Boat Shop Inc	Harwich	MA	F	508 432-4488	11395
Downeast Boats & Composites	Penobscot	ME	G	207 326-9400	6581
Eric Dow Boatbuilder	Brooklin	ME	G	207 359-2277	5820
Navigator Publishing LLC	Portland	ME	E	207 822-4350	6698
Wesmac Custom Boats Inc **(PA)**	Surry	ME	F	207 667-4822	7077
Eastern Boats Inc	Milton	NH	E	603 652-9213	19084
Berthon Usa Inc	Newport	RI	G	401 846-8404	20657
International Yacht Restoratio	Newport	RI	F	401 846-2587	20666

BOAT DEALERS: Marine Splys & Eqpt

	CITY	ST	EMP	PHONE	ENTRY #
Hadley Propeller Inc	Hadley	MA	G	413 585-0500	11306
Hercules Slr (us) Inc **(PA)**	New Bedford	MA	F	508 993-0010	13394

BOAT DEALERS: Sails & Eqpt

	CITY	ST	EMP	PHONE	ENTRY #
Vespoli Usa Inc	New Haven	CT	E	203 773-0311	2751
Cape Cod Sailmakers Inc	Cataumet	MA	G	508 563-3080	9810

BOAT REPAIR SVCS

	CITY	ST	EMP	PHONE	ENTRY #
Rokap Inc	Wallingford	CT	G	203 265-6895	4799
Hazard Marine A Div Ltd Inds	Webster	MA	G	508 943-7531	16342
B Marine Corp	Boothbay Harbor	ME	F	207 633-3171	5782

BOAT YARD: Boat yards, storage & incidental repair

	CITY	ST	EMP	PHONE	ENTRY #
Nu Line Design LLC	Wallingford	CT	G	203 949-0726	4779
Cape Cod Shipbuilding Co	Wareham	MA	F	508 295-3550	16242
Marshall Marine Corp	South Dartmouth	MA	F	508 994-0414	15240
Bridges Point Boat Yard Inc	Brooklin	ME	G	207 359-2713	5815
Brooklin Boat Yard Inc **(PA)**	Brooklin	ME	D	207 359-2236	5817
Dark Harbor Boatyard Corp	Islesboro	ME	F	207 734-2246	6215
Ellis Boat Co Inc	Southwest Harbor	ME	F	207 244-9221	7046
J O Brown & Son Inc	North Haven	ME	G	207 867-4621	6511
James H Rich Boatyard	Bernard	ME	G	207 244-3208	5707
Paul E Luke Inc	East Boothbay	ME	G	207 633-4971	5979
Webbers Cove Boat Yard Inc	East Blue Hill	ME	G	207 374-2841	5975
Yankee Marina Inc	Yarmouth	ME	E	207 846-9120	7304

BOATS & OTHER MARINE EQPT: Plastic

	CITY	ST	EMP	PHONE	ENTRY #
Big Rock Oyster Company Inc	Harwich	MA	G	774 408-7951	11389
Creative Canvas	Boothbay	ME	G	207 633-2056	5776
Coastal Inflatables LLC	Newmarket	NH	G	603 490-7606	19332

BODIES: Truck & Bus

	CITY	ST	EMP	PHONE	ENTRY #
Rj 15 Inc	Bristol	CT	F	860 585-0111	607
Bart Truck Equipment LLC	West Springfield	MA	G	413 737-2766	16511
Boston Trailer Manufacturing	Walpole	MA	E	508 668-2242	15990
Nashua Fabrication Co Inc	Hudson	NH	F	603 889-2181	18418

BODY PARTS: Automobile, Stamped Metal

	CITY	ST	EMP	PHONE	ENTRY #
Inertia Dynamics Inc	New Hartford	CT	F	860 379-1252	2640
Subimods LLC	Bloomfield	CT	G	860 291-0015	264
Auto Body Supplies and Paint	Worcester	MA	G	508 791-4111	17343
Energy Release LLC	Hudson	MA	G	978 466-9700	11771
Great Barrington Auto Sup Inc	Great Barrington	MA	G	413 528-0838	11238
Illinois Tool Works Inc	Westminster	MA	C	978 874-0151	16805
Acton Custom Enterprises	Holderness	NH	G	603 279-0241	18322
Albert Kemperle Inc	Warwick	RI	E	401 826-5111	21321

BOILER & HEATING REPAIR SVCS

	CITY	ST	EMP	PHONE	ENTRY #
Industrial Stl Boiler Svcs Inc	Chicopee	MA	E	413 532-7788	10032

BOILER REPAIR SHOP

	CITY	ST	EMP	PHONE	ENTRY #
Bri Metal Works Inc	Bridgeport	CT	G	203 368-1649	386
Bellingham Metal Works LLC	Franklin	MA	G	617 519-5958	11025

BOILERS & BOILER SHOP WORK

	CITY	ST	EMP	PHONE	ENTRY #
Vent-Rite Valve Corp **(PA)**	Randolph	MA	E	781 986-2000	14701
Weil McLain	Marlborough	MA	G	508 485-8050	12850

BOILERS: Low-Pressure Heating, Steam Or Hot Water

	CITY	ST	EMP	PHONE	ENTRY #
Advanced Burner Solutions Corp	Medway	MA	G	508 400-3289	12953
H B Smith Company Inc	Westfield	MA	E	413 568-3148	16687
Stiebel Eltron Inc	Holyoke	MA	G	413 535-1734	11661

BOLTS: Handle, Wooden, Hewn

	CITY	ST	EMP	PHONE	ENTRY #
Pride Manufacturing Co LLC **(PA)**	Burnham	ME	C	207 487-3322	5855
Pride Manufacturing Co LLC	Guilford	ME	F	207 876-2719	6159

BOLTS: Metal

	CITY	ST	EMP	PHONE	ENTRY #
Ametek Inc	Wallingford	CT	C	203 265-6731	4699
Click Bond Inc	Watertown	CT	E	860 274-5435	5003
Industrial Prssure Washers LLC	Wethersfield	CT	G	860 608-6153	5249
American Bolt & Nut Co Inc	Chelsea	MA	G	617 884-3331	9944

	CITY	ST	EMP	PHONE	ENTRY #
Gaynor Industries Corporation	Wilmington	MA	G	978 658-5500	17003
Robbins Manufacturing Co Inc	Fall River	MA	E	508 675-2555	10760

BONDERIZING: Bonderizing, Metal Or Metal Prdts

	CITY	ST	EMP	PHONE	ENTRY #
Polymetallurgical LLC	North Attleboro	MA	E	508 695-9312	13773

BOOK STORES

	CITY	ST	EMP	PHONE	ENTRY #
Circlet Press Inc	Cambridge	MA	G	617 864-0663	9438
Exact Change	Cambridge	MA	G	617 492-5405	9475
Young Authors Foundation Inc	Newton	MA	G	617 964-6800	13655
Sellers Publishing Inc	South Portland	ME	E	207 772-6833	7040

BOOK STORES: Religious

	CITY	ST	EMP	PHONE	ENTRY #
Deveney & White Inc	Boston	MA	G	617 288-3080	8501
Fred F Waltz Co Inc	North Smithfield	RI	F	401 769-4900	20786

BOOKS, WHOLESALE

	CITY	ST	EMP	PHONE	ENTRY #
Scholastic Library Pubg Inc **(HQ)**	Danbury	CT	A	203 797-3500	986
Courier Companies Inc **(PA)**	North Chelmsford	MA	E	978 251-6000	13888
Horizon House Publications Inc **(PA)**	Norwood	MA	D	781 769-9750	14158
O E M Health Information Inc	Beverly	MA	G	978 921-7300	8161
Redwheel/Weiser LLC **(PA)**	Newburyport	MA	G	978 465-0504	13527
Robert Bentley Inc	Cambridge	MA	E	617 547-4170	9636
Storey Publishing LLC **(HQ)**	North Adams	MA	E	413 346-2100	13685
Sundance/Newbridge LLC **(HQ)**	Marlborough	MA	G	800 343-8204	12831
Trafalgar Square Farm Inc	North Pomfret	VT	F	802 457-1911	22235

BOOTS: Men's

	CITY	ST	EMP	PHONE	ENTRY #
C & J Clark America Inc **(DH)**	Waltham	MA	B	617 964-1222	16054
C & J Clark Latin America	Waltham	MA	F	617 243-4100	16055
Peter Limmer & Sons Inc	Intervale	NH	G	603 356-5378	18455
Timberland LLC **(HQ)**	Stratham	NH	B	603 772-9500	19876

BOOTS: Women's

	CITY	ST	EMP	PHONE	ENTRY #
Cecelia New York LLC	Darien	CT	G	917 392-4536	1021
Peter Limmer & Sons Inc	Intervale	NH	G	603 356-5378	18455

BORING MILL

	CITY	ST	EMP	PHONE	ENTRY #
National Screw Manufacturing	East Haven	CT	F	203 469-7109	1256

BOTTLE CAPS & RESEALERS: Plastic

	CITY	ST	EMP	PHONE	ENTRY #
Berry Plastics Corp	Easthampton	MA	F	413 529-2183	10556
Pourer Fedora LLC	Boston	MA	G	617 267-0333	8786
Covalnce Spcalty Adhesives LLC	Bristol	RI	C	401 253-2595	20071

BOTTLE EXCHANGES

	CITY	ST	EMP	PHONE	ENTRY #
Ambrose G McCarthy Jr	Skowhegan	ME	E	207 474-8837	6968

BOTTLED WATER DELIVERY

	CITY	ST	EMP	PHONE	ENTRY #
Averys Beverage LLC	New Britain	CT	G	860 224-0830	2511
Craft Beer Guild Distrg VT LLC **(PA)**	Kingston	MA	E	781 585-5165	11956

BOTTLES: Plastic

	CITY	ST	EMP	PHONE	ENTRY #
Ansa Company Inc	Norwalk	CT	F	203 687-1664	3101
Green Egg Design LLC	Hartford	CT	G	860 541-5411	1828
Mayborn Usa Inc	Stamford	CT	F	781 269-7490	4245
Packaging Concepts Assoc LLC	Torrington	CT	G	860 489-0480	4591
Silgan Holdings Inc **(PA)**	Stamford	CT	C	203 975-7110	4321
Camco Manufacturing Inc	Leominster	MA	F	978 537-6777	12123
Maine Container LLC	Poland	ME	E	603 888-1315	6594
Quality Containers of Neng	Yarmouth	ME	G	207 846-5420	7299
Carr Management Inc **(PA)**	Nashua	NH	F	603 888-1315	19131
Devtech Pet Inc **(PA)**	Amherst	NH	E	603 889-8311	17556
Foxx Life Sciences LLC	Salem	NH	F	603 890-3699	19736
Plastic Industries Inc **(HQ)**	Nashua	NH	D	603 888-1315	19234
Preforms Plus	Nashua	NH	G	603 889-8311	19101
Plastic Technologies MD Inc	South Burlington	VT	G	802 658-6588	22459
Plastic Technologies NY LLC	South Burlington	VT	G	802 658-6588	22460

BOULDER: Crushed & Broken

	CITY	ST	EMP	PHONE	ENTRY #
Tonlino & Sons LLC	Otis	MA	G	413 329-8083	14250

BOUTIQUE STORES

	CITY	ST	EMP	PHONE	ENTRY #
American Meadows Inc	Shelburne	VT	F	802 862-6560	22410

BOXES & CRATES: Rectangular, Wood

	CITY	ST	EMP	PHONE	ENTRY #
Pith Products LLC	Ashford	CT	F	860 487-4859	26
St Pierre Box and Lumber Co	Canton	CT	G	860 413-9813	699
Woodfree Crating Systems Inc	Waterbury	CT	F	203 759-1799	4979
Nefab Packaging North East LLC	Bellingham	MA	F	800 258-4692	8053
Central Maine Crate Inc	Oakland	ME	G	207 873-5880	6531
Brentwood Box Company Inc	Raymond	NH	G	603 895-0829	19637
Koss Industries Inc	Burlington	VT	G	802 863-5004	21791

BOXES & SHOOK: Nailed Wood

	CITY	ST	EMP	PHONE	ENTRY #
Coastal Pallet Corporation	Bridgeport	CT	E	203 333-1892	398
Nefab Packaging North East LLC	Bellingham	MA	F	800 258-4692	8053
Unified2 Globl Packg Group LLC	Sutton	MA	A	508 865-1155	15694
Index Packaging Inc	Milton	NH	C	603 350-0018	19086
Poultney Pallet Inc	Fair Haven	VT	G	802 265-4444	21968

BOXES: Chests & Trunks, Wood

	CITY	ST	EMP	PHONE	ENTRY #
D Mac Consulting LLC **(PA)**	North Kingstown	RI	G	401 500-3879	20701

BOXES: Corrugated

	CITY	ST	EMP	PHONE	ENTRY #
AP Disposition LLC	Norwich	CT	D	860 889-1344	3276
Champlin-Packrite Inc	Manchester	CT	E	860 951-9217	1993
Colonial Corrugated Pdts Inc	Waterbury	CT	E	203 597-1707	4860
Connecticut Container Corp **(PA)**	North Haven	CT	C	203 248-2161	3018
Danbury Square Box Company	Danbury	CT	E	203 744-4611	899
General Packaging Products Inc	Norwalk	CT	G	203 846-1340	3160
HI-Tech Packaging Inc	Stratford	CT	E	203 378-2700	4420
Holm Corrugated Container Inc	Southington	CT	E	860 628-5559	4058
Jackson Corrugated Cont Corp	Essex	CT	E	860 767-3373	1399
Knapp Container Inc	Beacon Falls	CT	G	203 888-0511	59
Merrill Industries Inc	Ellington	CT	E	860 871-1888	1336
Merrill Industries LLC	Ellington	CT	E	860 871-1888	1337
Nutmeg Container Corporation **(HQ)**	Putnam	CT	D	860 963-6727	3622
R & R Corrugated Container Inc	Bristol	CT	D	860 584-1194	601
Rand-Whitney Group LLC	Newtown	CT	D	203 426-5871	2934
Windham Container Corporation	Putnam	CT	E	860 928-7934	3640
Abbott-Action Inc **(PA)**	Attleboro	MA	E	401 722-2100	7699
Commonwealth Packaging Corp	Chicopee	MA	D	413 593-1482	10015
Corrugated Packaging Inc	Fitchburg	MA	F	978 342-6076	10821
Corrugated Stitcher Service	Berkley	MA	G	508 823-2844	8085
Craft Corrugated Box Inc	New Bedford	MA	F	508 998-2115	13374
Friend Box Company Inc	Danvers	MA	D	978 774-0240	10218
Horn Corporation **(PA)**	Lancaster	MA	E	800 832-7020	11984
Ideal Box Company	Lawrence	MA	G	978 683-2802	12037
Interstate Cont Lowell LLC **(DH)**	Lowell	MA	D	978 458-4555	12383
Kerrigan Paper Products Inc	Haverhill	MA	G	978 374-4797	11445
Kraft Group LLC **(PA)**	Foxboro	MA	C	508 384-4230	10890
Massachusetts Container Corp	Marlborough	MA	C	508 481-1100	12793
Mount Tom Box Company Inc	West Springfield	MA	E	413 781-5300	16531
New England Wooden Ware Corp **(PA)**	Gardner	MA	E	978 632-3600	11122
Packaging Corporation America	Chelmsford	MA	E	978 256-4586	9920
Packaging Corporation America	Northampton	MA	D	413 584-6132	14017
Packaging Corporation America	Westfield	MA	G	413 562-0610	16710
Phillips Packaging	Palmer	MA	G	413 289-1070	14292
Rand-Whitney Container LLC **(DH)**	Worcester	MA	C	508 890-7000	17450
Rand-Whitney Group LLC **(HQ)**	Worcester	MA	C	508 791-2301	17452
Romanow Inc **(PA)**	Westwood	MA	C	781 320-9200	16874
Romanow Packaging LLC	Westwood	MA	C	781 320-8309	16875
Triple P Packg & Ppr Pdts Inc	Brockton	MA	D	508 588-0444	9184
Westrock Container LLC	Springfield	MA	D	413 733-2211	15525
Westrock Cp LLC	Wakefield	MA	D	781 245-8600	15984
Westrock Cp LLC	Mansfield	MA	C	770 448-2193	12671
Westrock Cp LLC	Springfield	MA	C	413 543-2311	15526
Volk Packaging Corporation	Biddeford	ME	D	207 282-6151	5768
Aegis Holdings LLC	Milford	NH	E	603 673-8900	19042
Environmental Science Tech Inc	Plaistow	NH	F	603 378-0809	19516
Mills Industries Inc	Laconia	NH	F	603 528-4217	18576
Rand-Whitney Container LLC	Dover	NH	C	603 822-7300	18049
Total Packaging Concepts Inc	Derry	NH	F	603 432-4651	18000
Custom & Miller Box Company	East Providence	RI	E	401 431-9007	20401
Hope-Bffnton Pckging Group LLC	Central Falls	RI	F	401 725-3646	20116
Key Container Corporation **(PA)**	Pawtucket	RI	C	401 723-2000	20851
Miller Corrugated Box Co	Warwick	RI	E	401 739-7020	21391
Mount Tom Box Co Inc	Pawtucket	RI	G	413 781-5300	20861
K&H Group Inc	Bennington	VT	E	802 442-5455	21677

BOXES: Filing, Paperboard Made From Purchased Materials

	CITY	ST	EMP	PHONE	ENTRY #
Westrock Rkt Company	Springfield	MA	G	413 543-7300	15528
Taylor Box Company	Warren	RI	E	401 245-5900	21309

BOXES: Hard Rubber

	CITY	ST	EMP	PHONE	ENTRY #
Apothecary Products LLC	North Attleboro	MA	E	508 695-0727	13745

BOXES: Mail Or Post Office, Collection/Storage, Sheet Metal

	CITY	ST	EMP	PHONE	ENTRY #
Post Mortem Services LLC	Farmington	CT	G	860 675-1103	1508

BOXES: Packing & Shipping, Metal

	CITY	ST	EMP	PHONE	ENTRY #
Case Future Corporation Inc	Johnston	RI	E	401 944-0402	20503
Jewel Case Corporation	Providence	RI	B	401 943-1400	21044

BOXES: Paperboard, Folding

	CITY	ST	EMP	PHONE	ENTRY #
Agi-Shorewood Group Us LLC	Stamford	CT	A	203 324-4839	4132
B-P Products Inc	Hamden	CT	E	203 288-0200	1733
Clondalkin Pharma & Healthcare	Portland	CT	E	860 342-1987	3565
Curtis Corporation A Del Corp	Sandy Hook	CT	C	203 426-5861	3742
Curtis Packaging Corporation	Sandy Hook	CT	C	203 426-5861	3743
Keystone Paper & Box Co Inc	South Windsor	CT	D	860 291-0027	3988
Rice Packaging Inc	Ellington	CT	D	860 870-7057	1338
Accutech Packaging Inc	Foxboro	MA	D	508 543-3800	10873
Americraft Carton Inc	Lowell	MA	C	978 459-9328	12343
Boutwell Owens & Co Inc **(PA)**	Fitchburg	MA	C	978 343-3067	10813
Dusobox Co Inc	Haverhill	MA	E	978 372-7192	11426
Fuller Box Co Inc **(PA)**	North Attleboro	MA	D	508 695-2525	13756
Gooby Industries Corp	Methuen	MA	C	978 689-0100	13024
Harvard Folding Box Co Inc	Lawrence	MA	G	978 683-2802	12030
Hub Folding Box Company Inc	Mansfield	MA	B	508 339-0005	12636
Packaging Specialties Inc	Newburyport	MA	D	978 462-1300	13520
Pioneer Packaging Inc **(PA)**	Chicopee	MA	D	413 378-6930	10050
Rand-Whitney Group LLC **(HQ)**	Worcester	MA	C	508 791-2301	17452
Standard Box Company Inc	Chelsea	MA	G	617 884-2345	9969
UNI-Pac Inc	Holyoke	MA	D	413 534-5284	11662
RTS Packaging LLC	Scarborough	ME	D	207 883-8921	6938
Volk Packaging Corporation	Biddeford	ME	D	207 282-6151	5768
Autajon Packg - Boston Corp	Nashua	NH	D	603 595-0700	19118
Graphic Packaging Intl LLC	Concord	NH	D	603 224-2333	17907
Graphic Packaging Intl LLC	Concord	NH	C	603 230-5100	17904
Kimark Specialty Box Company	Manchester	NH	E	603 668-1336	18855
Foxon Company	Providence	RI	E	401 421-2386	21015
Northeast Buffinton Group Inc	Riverside	RI	F	401 434-1107	21174
Numaco Packaging LLC	East Providence	RI	F	401 438-4952	20436
Seaboard Folding Box Co Inc	Pawtucket	RI	G	401 753-7778	20899

BOXES: Paperboard, Set-Up

	CITY	ST	EMP	PHONE	ENTRY #
Agi-Shorewood Group Us LLC	Stamford	CT	A	203 324-4839	4132
Millen Industries Inc **(PA)**	Norwalk	CT	G	203 847-8500	3198
Rice Packaging Inc	Ellington	CT	D	860 870-7057	1338
Rondo America Incorporated	Naugatuck	CT	C	203 723-5831	2494
Egoh Packaging Inc	Marlborough	MA	E	508 460-6683	12752
Friend Box Company Inc	Danvers	MA	D	978 774-0240	10218
Packaging Specialties Inc	Newburyport	MA	D	978 462-1300	13520
Quality Packaging & Graphics	Westfield	MA	G	413 568-1923	16722
Specialty Packaging Inc	Indian Orchard	MA	G	413 543-1814	11895
UNI-Pac Inc	Holyoke	MA	D	413 534-5284	11662
Westrock Cp LLC	Mansfield	MA	C	770 448-2193	12671
Volk Packaging Corporation	Biddeford	ME	D	207 282-6151	5768
C & O Box & Printing Company	Hooksett	NH	G	508 881-1760	18345
Graphic Packaging Intl LLC	Concord	NH	D	603 230-5100	17906
Graphic Packaging Intl LLC	Concord	NH	C	603 230-5100	17904
Fuller Box Co Inc	Central Falls	RI	D	401 725-4300	20113
Hope Buffinton Packaging Inc	Central Falls	RI	E	401 725-3646	20115

BOXES: Plastic

	CITY	ST	EMP	PHONE	ENTRY #
Althor Products LLC	Windsor Locks	CT	G	860 386-6700	5385
Mills Industries Inc	Laconia	NH	F	603 528-4217	18576
Morris Transparent Box Co	East Providence	RI	E	401 438-6116	20433

BOXES: Solid Fiber

	CITY	ST	EMP	PHONE	ENTRY #
Common Sense Engineered Pdts	Beacon Falls	CT	G	203 888-8695	56
RTS Packaging LLC	Scarborough	ME	D	207 883-8921	6938
Foxon Company	Providence	RI	E	401 421-2386	21015

BOXES: Stamped Metal

	CITY	ST	EMP	PHONE	ENTRY #
Durham Manufacturing Company **(PA)**	Durham	CT	D	860 349-3427	1090

BOXES: Wooden

	CITY	ST	EMP	PHONE	ENTRY #
Colonial Wood Products Inc	West Haven	CT	F	203 932-9003	5112
Merrill Industries Inc	Ellington	CT	E	860 871-1888	1336
St Pierre Box and Lumber Co	Canton	CT	G	860 413-9813	699
Vermont Pallet & Skid Shop	Norwich	CT	G	860 822-6949	3292
Westwood Products Inc	Winsted	CT	F	860 379-9401	5428
Atlas Box and Crating Co Inc **(PA)**	Sutton	MA	C	508 865-1155	15679
D A Mfg Co LLC	Winchendon	MA	G	978 297-1059	17072
Kelley Wood Products Inc	Fitchburg	MA	F	978 345-7531	10830
E B Frye & Son Inc	Wilton	NH	G	603 654-6581	19979
Granite State Forest Products	Henniker	NH	G	603 428-7890	18306
J H Dunning Corporation	North Walpole	NH	E	603 445-5591	19394
Greene Industries Inc	East Greenwich	RI	G	401 884-7530	20369

BRAKES & BRAKE PARTS

	CITY	ST	EMP	PHONE	ENTRY #
King Kalipers Inc	Peabody	MA	E	978 977-4994	14347
Ryca Inc	Tewksbury	MA	G	978 851-3265	15833
Tremco Products Inc	Billerica	MA	G	781 275-7692	8307

BRAKES: Electromagnetic

	CITY	ST	EMP	PHONE	ENTRY #
Carlyle Johnson Machine Co LLC **(PA)**	Bolton	CT	E	860 643-1531	276
Inertia Dynamics LLC	New Hartford	CT	C	860 379-1252	2639
Altra Industrial Motion Corp **(PA)**	Braintree	MA	B	781 917-0600	8986
Warner Electric	Braintree	MA	G	781 917-0600	9048

BRAKES: Metal Forming

	CITY	ST	EMP	PHONE	ENTRY #
Eyelet Tech LLC	Wolcott	CT	E	203 879-5306	5442
Altra Industrial Motion Corp **(PA)**	Braintree	MA	B	781 917-0600	8986
Armadillo Noise Vibration LLC	Acushnet	MA	G	774 992-7156	7399
Warner Electric	Braintree	MA	G	781 917-0600	9048

BRAKES: Press

	CITY	ST	EMP	PHONE	ENTRY #
J D & Associates	Canterbury	CT	G	860 546-2112	693

BRASS & BRONZE PRDTS: Die-casted

	CITY	ST	EMP	PHONE	ENTRY #
Industrial Foundry Corporation	Uxbridge	MA	G	508 278-5523	15920
Kingston Aluminum Foundry Inc	Kingston	MA	G	781 585-6631	11959
Hebert Manufacturing Company **(PA)**	Laconia	NH	D	603 524-2065	18567

BRAZING SVCS

	CITY	ST	EMP	PHONE	ENTRY #
D B F Industries Inc	New Britain	CT	E	860 827-8283	2525
Parama Corp	Bethel	CT	F	203 790-8155	174
Aero Brazing Corp	Woburn	MA	F	781 933-7511	17114
Aero Manufacturing Corp	Beverly	MA	D	978 720-1000	8096
Brazen Innovations Inc	Marlow	NH	G	603 446-7919	18966

BRAZING: Metal

	CITY	ST	EMP	PHONE	ENTRY #
Accurate Brazing Corporation	Manchester	CT	F	860 432-1840	1981
Bodycote Thermal Proc Inc	South Windsor	CT	E	860 282-1371	3944
Bodycote Thermal Proc Inc	Ipswich	MA	E	978 356-3818	11906
United-County Industries Corp	Millbury	MA	E	508 865-5885	13179
Accurate Brazing Corporation **(HQ)**	Goffstown	NH	E	603 945-3750	18197
Brazen Innovations Inc	Marlow	NH	G	603 446-7919	18966
Tsi Group Inc **(DH)**	Hampton	NH	E	603 964-0296	18275
Trow & Holden Co Inc	Barre	VT	F	802 476-7221	21643

BREAD WRAPPERS: Waxed Or Laminated, Made From Purchased Matl

	CITY	ST	EMP	PHONE	ENTRY #
Koster Keunen LLC **(PA)**	Watertown	CT	F	860 945-3333	5013
Admiral Packaging Inc	Providence	RI	D	401 274-5588	20945

BRICK, STONE & RELATED PRDTS WHOLESALERS

	CITY	ST	EMP	PHONE	ENTRY #
Dan Beard Inc	Shelton	CT	F	203 924-4346	3794
Alfred J Cavallaro Inc	Andover	MA	G	978 475-2466	7536
Colonial Landscape Corp	Groton	MA	G	978 448-3329	11287
International Stone Inc	Woburn	MA	D	781 937-3300	17206
Stacey Thomson	Orford	NH	G	603 353-9700	19421

BRICKS & BLOCKS: Structural

	CITY	ST	EMP	PHONE	ENTRY #
Redi-Mix Services Incorporated	Taunton	MA	G	508 823-0771	15778
Ventech Industries Inc	Eliot	ME	G	207 439-0069	6012

BRICKS: Clay

	CITY	ST	EMP	PHONE	ENTRY #
Stiles & Hart Brick Company	Bridgewater	MA	E	508 697-6928	9088

BRICKS: Concrete

	CITY	ST	EMP	PHONE	ENTRY #
Vynorius Prestress Inc	Salisbury	MA	F	978 462-7765	14959
Rjf - Morin Brick LLC	Auburn	ME	D	207 784-9375	5595
Gorham Brick & Block Inc	Berlin	NH	G	603 752-3631	17696

BRIDGE COMPONENTS: Bridge sections, prefabricated, highway

	CITY	ST	EMP	PHONE	ENTRY #
Spector Metal Products Co Inc	Holbrook	MA	F	781 767-5600	11539

BRIEFCASES

	CITY	ST	EMP	PHONE	ENTRY #
Baby Briefcase LLC	Milton	MA	G	617 696-7668	13189
David King & Co Inc	Boston	MA	G	617 482-6950	8496
Code Briefcase	New Boston	NH	G	603 487-2381	19292

BROACHING MACHINES

	CITY	ST	EMP	PHONE	ENTRY #
Mini-Broach Machine Co Inc	Ashby	MA	G	978 386-7959	7647

BROADCASTING & COMMS EQPT: Antennas, Transmitting/Comms

	CITY	ST	EMP	PHONE	ENTRY #
Jk Antennas Inc	Brookfield	CT	G	845 228-8700	649
Radio Frequency Systems Inc **(DH)**	Meriden	CT	E	203 630-3311	2122
Antenna Research Assoc Inc	Pembroke	MA	E	781 829-4740	14391
CPI Radant Tech Div Inc	Clinton	MA	F	978 562-3866	10078
Fractal Antenna Systems Inc	Bedford	MA	F	781 290-5308	7977
Infinite Electronics Intl Inc	North Billerica	MA	G	978 459-8800	13827
Linx Consulting LLC	Webster	MA	F	508 461-6333	16347
Alaris Usa LLC	Windham	ME	F	207 517-5304	7228
SPX Corporation	Raymond	ME	C	207 655-8100	6774
Metz Communication Corporation	Laconia	NH	G	603 528-2590	18575
Research In Motion Rf Inc **(HQ)**	Nashua	NH	E	603 598-8880	19250

BROADCASTING & COMMS EQPT: Rcvr-Transmitter Unt, Transceiver

	CITY	ST	EMP	PHONE	ENTRY #
Aqyr Technologies Inc	Nashua	NH	E	603 402-6099	19116

BROADCASTING & COMMS EQPT: Trnsmttng TV Antennas/Grndng Eqpt

	CITY	ST	EMP	PHONE	ENTRY #
Submarine Research Labs	Hingham	MA	G	781 749-0900	11512

BROADCASTING & COMMUNICATION EQPT: Transmit-Receiver, Radio

	CITY	ST	EMP	PHONE	ENTRY #
Ashcroft Inc **(DH)**	Stratford	CT	B	203 378-8281	4392
Big Pond Wireless LLC	North Reading	MA	G	781 593-2321	13979

BROADCASTING & COMMUNICATIONS EQPT: Cellular Radio Tele-phone

	CITY	ST	EMP	PHONE	ENTRY #
Ei-Envrnmental Integration LLC	Shelburne Falls	MA	G	413 219-9547	15070
Mlc Services LLC	Holliston	MA	G	781 366-1132	11587
Laird Technologies Inc	Manchester	NH	F	603 627-7877	18858

BROADCASTING & COMMUNICATIONS EQPT: Transmitting, Radio/TV

	CITY	ST	EMP	PHONE	ENTRY #
Video Automation Systems Inc	New Fairfield	CT	G	203 312-0152	2630
Nautel Maine Inc	Bangor	ME	C	207 947-8200	5654
Rymsa Micro Communications **(PA)**	Merrimack	NH	E	603 429-0800	19026

BROADCASTING STATIONS, RADIO: Educational

	CITY	ST	EMP	PHONE	ENTRY #
Sundance/Newbridge LLC **(HQ)**	Marlborough	MA	G	800 343-8204	12831
GS Inc	Rockland	ME	G	207 593-7730	6797

BROKERS & DEALERS: Securities

	CITY	ST	EMP	PHONE	ENTRY #
New Generation Research Inc	Boston	MA	F	617 573-9550	8734
Monahan Associates	Portland	ME	G	207 771-0900	6694

BROKERS' SVCS

	CITY	ST	EMP	PHONE	ENTRY #
TMI Industries Inc	Palmer	MA	E	413 283-9021	14297

BROKERS: Business

	CITY	ST	EMP	PHONE	ENTRY #
First Equity Group Inc **(PA)**	Westport	CT	F	203 291-7700	5193

BROKERS: Food

	CITY	ST	EMP	PHONE	ENTRY #
Dahlicious Holdings LLC	Leominster	MA	F	978 401-2103	12131

BROKERS: Printing

	CITY	ST	EMP	PHONE	ENTRY #
Prints Charming Printers Inc	Boothbay	ME	G	207 633-6663	5780

BROKERS: Yacht

	CITY	ST	EMP	PHONE	ENTRY #
Alden Yachts Corporation	Bristol	RI	D	401 683-4200	20060
Sparkman & Stephens LLC **(PA)**	Newport	RI	F	401 847-5449	20683

BRONZE FOUNDRY, NEC

	CITY	ST	EMP	PHONE	ENTRY #
Michael Healy Designs Inc	Manville	RI	G	401 597-5900	20610

BRONZE ROLLING & DRAWING

	CITY	ST	EMP	PHONE	ENTRY #
Waterbury Rolling Mills Inc	Waterbury	CT	D	203 597-5000	4973

BROOMS

	CITY	ST	EMP	PHONE	ENTRY #
Butler Home Products LLC **(DH)**	Hudson	MA	F	508 597-8000	11761
Tucel Industries Inc	Forest Dale	VT	F	802 247-6824	21993

BROOMS & BRUSHES

	CITY	ST	EMP	PHONE	ENTRY #
Loos & Co Inc	Pomfret	CT	F	860 928-6681	3553
Torrington Brush Works Inc	Torrington	CT	G	860 482-3517	4602
Angel Guard Products Inc	Worcester	MA	G	508 791-1073	17339
Cardinal Comb & Brush Mfg Corp	Leominster	MA	E	978 537-6330	12125
Felton Brush	Londonderry	NH	F	603 425-0200	18698
ACS Industries Inc **(PA)**	Lincoln	RI	E	401 769-4700	20552

BROOMS & BRUSHES: Household Or Indl

	CITY	ST	EMP	PHONE	ENTRY #
Goode Brush Company	Nahant	MA	G	781 581-0280	13215
Felton Inc	Londonderry	NH	D	603 425-0200	18697

BROOMS & BRUSHES: Paintbrushes

	CITY	ST	EMP	PHONE	ENTRY #
Liftline Capital LLC	Old Saybrook	CT	F	860 395-0150	3342
Jen Mfg Inc	Millbury	MA	E	508 753-1076	13168
American Brush Company Inc	Claremont	NH	F	603 542-9951	17834

BROOMS & BRUSHES: Street Sweeping, Hand Or Machine

	CITY	ST	EMP	PHONE	ENTRY #
R&R Sweeping Services Inc	East Bridgewater	MA	G	508 586-5705	10419
Howard P Fairfield LLC **(DH)**	Skowhegan	ME	E	207 474-9836	6976

BRUSH BLOCKS: Carbon Or Molded Graphite

	CITY	ST	EMP	PHONE	ENTRY #
High Prfmce Composites Ltd	Providence	RI	G	401 274-8560	21030

BRUSHES

	CITY	ST	EMP	PHONE	ENTRY #
Sanderson-Macleod Incorporated	Palmer	MA	C	413 283-3481	14295

BUCKETS: Plastic

	CITY	ST	EMP	PHONE	ENTRY #
Mauser Packg Solutions Holdg	Leominster	MA	C	978 728-5000	12165
Plastican Inc	Leominster	MA	A	978 728-5000	12176

BUCKLES & PARTS

	CITY	ST	EMP	PHONE	ENTRY #
Buckleguycom LLC	Newburyport	MA	G	978 213-9989	13475

BUFFING FOR THE TRADE

	CITY	ST	EMP	PHONE	ENTRY #
Baron & Young Co Inc	Bristol	CT	G	860 589-3235	529
D D M Metal Finishing Co Inc	Tolland	CT	G	860 872-4683	4542
Deburring House Inc	East Berlin	CT	E	860 828-0889	1098
J M Compounds Inc	Meriden	CT	G	203 376-9854	2095
R J Brass Inc	Plainville	CT	F	860 793-2336	3513

BUILDING & STRUCTURAL WOOD MBRS: Timbers, Struct, Lam Lumber

	CITY	ST	EMP	PHONE	ENTRY #
Timber Frame Barn Conversions	Windsor	CT	G	860 219-0519	5373
Benson Woodworking Company Inc	Walpole	NH	D	603 756-3600	19917
Saxon Manufacturing Inc	Salem	NH	F	603 898-2499	19765
Southworth Timber Frames Inc	Lancaster	NH	G	603 788-2619	18605
Old Timers Timber Frames	Saxtons River	VT	G	802 376-9529	22401

BUILDING & STRUCTURAL WOOD MEMBERS

	CITY	ST	EMP	PHONE	ENTRY #
Country Carpenters Inc	Hebron	CT	G	860 228-2276	1896
Eastern Company **(PA)**	Naugatuck	CT	E	203 729-2255	2471
Architectural Timber Mllwk Inc	Hadley	MA	F	413 586-3045	11305
Caliper Woodworking Corp	Malden	MA	E	781 322-9760	12563
Reliable Truss & Components In	Mansfield	MA	G	508 339-8020	12655
Atlantic Prefab Inc **(PA)**	Wilton	NH	G	603 668-2648	19975
Energy Smart Building Inc	Starksboro	VT	E	802 453-4438	22515
Granville Manufacturing Co	Granville	VT	G	802 767-4747	22003

BUILDING & STRUCTURAL WOOD MEMBERS: Arches, Laminated Lumber

	CITY	ST	EMP	PHONE	ENTRY #
Perkins Brothers Corp	Stoughton	MA	E	781 858-3031	15615

BUILDING CLEANING & MAINTENANCE SVCS

	CITY	ST	EMP	PHONE	ENTRY #
Lps Enterprises Inc	East Freetown	MA	E	508 763-3830	10455
Maine Turnpike Authority	Cumberland Center	ME	F	207 829-4531	5929

BUILDING COMPONENTS: Structural Steel

	CITY	ST	EMP	PHONE	ENTRY #
All Phase Steel Works LLC	New Haven	CT	D	203 375-8881	2654
Pisani Steel Fabrication Inc	Naugatuck	CT	G	203 720-0679	2490
Qsr Steel Corporation LLC	Hartford	CT	E	860 548-0248	1863
Shepard Steel Co Inc **(PA)**	Hartford	CT	D	860 525-4446	1869
State Welding & Fabg Inc	Wallingford	CT	G	203 294-4071	4813
T Keefe and Sons	Guilford	CT	G	203 457-0267	1721
All Steel Fabricating Inc	North Grafton	MA	E	508 839-4471	13958
Auciello Iron Works Inc **(PA)**	Hudson	MA	E	978 568-8382	11758
Boston Steel Fabricators Inc	Holbrook	MA	G	781 767-1540	11522
D Cronins Welding Service	Lawrence	MA	G	978 664-4488	12014
Diamond Stl & Fabrication LLC	Wakefield	MA	G	781 245-3255	15950
Dublin Steel Corporation	Palmer	MA	E	413 289-1218	14286
First Fabricators Co Inc	Ipswich	MA	G	978 356-2901	11919
Lally Column Corp	Stoughton	MA	G	508 828-5997	15602
Package Steel Systems Inc	Sutton	MA	E	508 865-5871	15689
PEC Detailing Co Inc	Walpole	MA	G	508 660-8954	16006
Uniweld Inc	Georgetown	MA	G	978 352-8008	11152
Belanger Welding & Fabrication	New Gloucester	ME	G	207 657-5558	6464
Fournier Steel Fabrication	West Bath	ME	G	207 443-6404	7169
Newport Indus Fabrication Inc	Newport	ME	E	207 368-4344	6485
Canam Bridges US Inc	Claremont	NH	E	603 542-5202	17839
Novel Iron Works Inc	Greenland	NH	C	603 436-7950	18224
Powerfab Inc	Merrimack	NH	G	603 424-3900	19023
Quality Components Rp	Pelham	NH	G	603 864-8196	19443
Radius Mfg & Fabrication Inc	Weare	NH	G	603 529-0801	19939
Farber Industrial Fabricating	Pawtucket	RI	G	401 725-2492	20837
Frontier Welding & Fabrication	Woonsocket	RI	G	401 769-0271	21565

BUILDING ITEM REPAIR SVCS, MISCELLANEOUS

	CITY	ST	EMP	PHONE	ENTRY #
Otis Elevator Company **(HQ)**	Farmington	CT	B	860 674-3000	1503
Barlo Signs International Inc	Hudson	NH	D	603 880-8949	18377

BUILDING MAINTENANCE SVCS, EXC REPAIRS

	CITY	ST	EMP	PHONE	ENTRY #
Qba Inc	Woodstock	CT	G	860 963-9438	5500

BUILDING PRDTS & MATERIALS DEALERS

	CITY	ST	EMP	PHONE	ENTRY #
Homewood Cabinet Co Inc	Pawcatuck	CT	G	860 599-2441	3437
Moores Sawmill Inc	Bloomfield	CT	G	860 242-3003	244
Baxter Sand & Gravel Inc	Chicopee	MA	E	413 536-3370	9999
Brightman Corp	Assonet	MA	E	508 644-2620	7678
Builders Supply of Cape Cod	Sandwich	MA	G	508 888-0444	14963
Da Costa Awnings & Canvas Spc	Taunton	MA	G	508 822-4944	15739
Federal Specialties Inc	West Springfield	MA	G	413 782-6900	16520
Hampton Door Company Inc	Westfield	MA	G	413 568-5730	16688
Rebars & Mesh Inc	Haverhill	MA	E	978 374-2244	11467
Sika Sarnafil Inc **(HQ)**	Canton	MA	C	781 828-5400	9780
Southeastern Millwork Co Inc	Bourne	MA	F	508 888-6038	8949
Turn Key Lumber Inc	Lunenburg	MA	E	978 798-1370	12484
Great Brook Lumber Inc	Lebanon	ME	G	207 457-1063	6265
Moose Creek Home Center Inc	Turner	ME	G	207 224-7497	7109
N C Hunt Inc	Damariscotta	ME	E	207 563-8503	5937
Beech River Mill	Center Ossipee	NH	G	603 539-2636	17802
Goss Lumber Co Inc	Henniker	NH	G	603 428-3363	18305
Granite State Log Homes Inc **(PA)**	Campton	NH	F	603 536-4949	17777
Kimballs Lumber Center LLC **(PA)**	Wolfeboro	NH	G	603 569-2477	20021
Koss Industries Inc	Burlington	VT	G	802 863-5004	21791
M B Heath & Sons Lumber Inc	North Hyde Park	VT	G	802 635-2538	22232
Mill River Lumber Ltd	North Clarendon	VT	D	802 775-0032	22220

BUILDING PRDTS: Concrete

	CITY	ST	EMP	PHONE	ENTRY #
Direct Sales LLC **(PA)**	Fairfield	CT	G	203 371-2373	1426
Byrne Sand & Gravel Co Inc	Middleboro	MA	F	508 947-0724	13058
Northeast Building Supply LLC	Hanson	MA	G	781 294-0400	11367
Turn Key Lumber Inc	Lunenburg	MA	E	978 798-1370	12484

BUILDING PRDTS: Stone

	CITY	ST	EMP	PHONE	ENTRY #
Mark Dzidzk	Plainville	CT	E	860 793-2767	3504
Nickerson Stonecrafters of Cao	Orleans	MA	G	508 255-8600	14238
Phillip Ippolito	Seekonk	MA	F	508 336-9616	15033
Vermont Thinstone Assoc LLC	Colchester	VT	G	802 448-3000	21888

BUILDING STONE, ARTIFICIAL: Concrete

	CITY	ST	EMP	PHONE	ENTRY #
West Hartford Stone Mulch LLC	West Hartford	CT	G	860 461-7616	5103

BUILDINGS & COMPONENTS: Prefabricated Metal

	CITY	ST	EMP	PHONE	ENTRY #
Illinois Tool Works Inc	Waterbury	CT	C	203 574-2119	4887
Morin Corporation **(DH)**	Bristol	CT	D	860 584-0900	584
Shelters of America LLC	Woodbridge	CT	G	203 397-1037	5479
Walpole Woodworkers Inc	Ridgefield	CT	E	508 668-2800	3689
Isun International Group LLC	West Boylston	MA	G	508 835-9000	16418
Morton Buildings Inc	Westfield	MA	F	413 562-7028	16706
The Cricket System Inc	Newburyport	MA	G	617 905-1420	13539
Walpole Woodworkers Inc	Wilmington	MA	F	978 658-3373	17064
Walpole Woodworkers Inc	East Falmouth	MA	F	508 540-0300	10451
Walpole Woodworkers Inc	Norwell	MA	G	781 681-9099	14114
Maine Micro Furnace Inc	Portland	ME	G	207 329-9207	6687
Walpole Woodworkers Inc	Detroit	ME	E	207 368-4302	5954
Walpole Woodworkers Inc	Chester	ME	E	207 794-2248	5908
Concrete Systems Inc	Hudson	NH	D	603 886-5472	18380
Concrete Systems Inc	Londonderry	NH	F	603 432-1840	18686
Inofab LLC	Pittsfield	NH	G	603 435-5082	19501

BUILDINGS: Farm & Utility

	CITY	ST	EMP	PHONE	ENTRY #
Jf2 LLC	Holliston	MA	D	508 429-1022	11581

BUILDINGS: Portable

	CITY	ST	EMP	PHONE	ENTRY #
Mobile Mini Inc	Suffield	CT	E	860 668-1888	4465
Membrane Structure Solutions	Hingham	MA	E	908 520-0112	11503
Mobile Mini Inc	Salisbury	MA	E	866 344-4092	14953
Mobile Mini Inc	West Bridgewater	MA	F	508 427-5395	16446
Package Industries Inc	Sutton	MA	E	508 865-5871	15688
Space Building Corp	Lakeville	MA	E	508 947-7277	11978
Ekto Manufacturing Corp	Sanford	ME	E	207 324-4427	6874
Sturdibuilt Storage Bldgs LLC	Smyrna Mills	ME	G	207 757-7877	6996
Konrad Prefab LLC	Springfield	VT	G	802 885-6780	22504
Sperber Tool Works Inc	Bennington	VT	G	802 442-8839	21691

BUILDINGS: Prefabricated, Metal

	CITY	ST	EMP	PHONE	ENTRY #
Rubb Inc	Sanford	ME	D	207 324-2877	6892

BUILDINGS: Prefabricated, Wood

	CITY	ST	EMP	PHONE	ENTRY #
Country Carpenters Inc	Hebron	CT	G	860 228-2276	1896
Trigila Construction Inc	Berlin	CT	E	860 828-8444	115
Walpole Woodworkers Inc	Ridgefield	CT	E	508 668-2800	3689
Walpole Woodworkers Inc	Westport	CT	G	203 255-9010	5237
Architectural Timber Mllwk Inc	Hadley	MA	F	413 586-3045	11305
Chapins Wood Products Inc **(PA)**	Halifax	MA	G	781 294-0758	11316
Jarica Inc	Woburn	MA	F	781 935-1907	17210
Jobart Inc **(PA)**	Methuen	MA	F	978 689-4414	13029
Walpole Woodworkers Inc	Wilmington	MA	F	978 658-3373	17064
Walpole Woodworkers Inc	East Falmouth	MA	F	508 540-0300	10451
Walpole Woodworkers Inc	Norwell	MA	G	781 681-9099	14114
Kbs Building Systems Inc	South Paris	ME	G	207 739-2222	7012
Walpole Woodworkers Inc	Detroit	ME	E	207 368-4302	5954
Walpole Woodworkers Inc	Chester	ME	E	207 794-2248	5908

	CITY	ST	EMP	PHONE	ENTRY #
Benson Woodworking Company Inc	Walpole	NH	D	603 756-3600	19917
L & M Sheds LLC	Epping	NH	G	603 679-5243	18100
Southworth Timber Frames Inc	Lancaster	NH	G	603 788-2619	18605
Serac Corporation **(HQ)**	Fairfax	VT	F	802 527-9609	21979

BUILDINGS: Prefabricated, Wood

	CITY	ST	EMP	PHONE	ENTRY #
American Prefab Wood Pdts Co	Bloomfield	CT	G	860 242-5468	200
Bond-Bilt Garages Inc	Wallingford	CT	G	203 269-3375	4711
Carefree Building Co Inc **(PA)**	Colchester	CT	F	860 267-7600	800
Post Woodworking Inc	Danville	NH	E	603 382-4951	17969
Reeds Ferry Small Buildings	Hudson	NH	D	603 883-1362	18434
Wallace Building Products Corp	Danbury	NH	E	603 768-5402	17966
Yankee Barn Homes Inc	Claremont	NH	D	603 863-4545	17865

BULLETPROOF VESTS

	CITY	ST	EMP	PHONE	ENTRY #
Safariland LLC	Dalton	MA	D	413 684-3104	10183
Gaffco Ballistics LLC	South Londonderry	VT	G	802 824-9899	22486

BUOYS: Plastic

	CITY	ST	EMP	PHONE	ENTRY #
Island Mooring Supplies LLC	Prudence Island	RI	F	401 447-5387	21160

BURGLAR ALARM MAINTENANCE & MONITORING SVCS

	CITY	ST	EMP	PHONE	ENTRY #
Grayfin Security LLC	Madison	CT	G	203 800-6760	1961
AES Corporation	Peabody	MA	D	978 535-7310	14308

BURIAL VAULTS: Concrete Or Precast Terrazzo

	CITY	ST	EMP	PHONE	ENTRY #
Bridgeport Burial Vault Co	Stratford	CT	G	203 375-7375	4399
Elm-Cap Industries Inc	West Hartford	CT	E	860 953-1060	5070
DAngelo Burial Vaults	Franklin	MA	G	508 528-0385	11036
Derek Ciccone	East Douglas	MA	G	508 476-2105	10426
Flagg Palmer Precast Inc	Oxford	MA	G	508 987-3400	14261
Green Burial Massachusetts	Gill	MA	G	413 863-4634	11156
Hardy Doric Inc	Chelmsford	MA	G	978 250-1113	9903
Keating Wilbert Vault Company	Wilbraham	MA	F	413 543-1226	16939
Montachsett Tcci Burial Vaults	Leominster	MA	G	978 537-6190	12169
Precast Vault Co Inc	North Dighton	MA	G	508 252-4886	13933
Precast Vault Co Inc **(PA)**	Braintree	MA	G	508 252-4886	9031
Quintal Burial Vaults	Dighton	MA	F	508 669-5717	10338
Watertown Engineering Corp	Whitman	MA	E	781 857-2555	16929
Elm Street Vault Inc	Biddeford	ME	G	207 284-4855	5731
Wilbert Swans Vault Co	Westbrook	ME	E	207 854-5324	7214
New England Vlts Monuments LLC	Milan	NH	G	603 449-2165	19041
Sabbow and Co Inc	Littleton	NH	F	603 444-6724	18665
D G Robertson Inc	South Burlington	VT	G	802 864-6027	22445
Washburn Vault Company Inc	Brattleboro	VT	G	802 254-9150	21754

BURIAL VAULTS: Stone

	CITY	ST	EMP	PHONE	ENTRY #
Quintal Burial Vaults	Dighton	MA	F	508 669-5717	10338
Stone Vault Co	Newport	NH	G	603 863-2720	19359

BURNERS: Gas, Domestic

	CITY	ST	EMP	PHONE	ENTRY #
Mainline Energy Systems Inc	Northbridge	MA	G	860 429-9663	14057

BURNERS: Gas, Indl

	CITY	ST	EMP	PHONE	ENTRY #
Carlin Combustion Tech Inc **(HQ)**	North Haven	CT	D	203 680-9401	3014
Hamworthy Peabody Combustn Inc **(DH)**	Shelton	CT	E	203 922-1199	3808
Preferred Utilities Mfg Corp **(HQ)**	Danbury	CT	D	203 743-6741	974
Pumc Holding Corporation **(PA)**	Danbury	CT	E	203 743-6741	976
Zeeco Inc	Plainville	CT	G	860 479-0999	3524
Maxon Corporation	Acton	MA	G	978 795-1285	7373

BURNERS: Oil, Domestic Or Indl

	CITY	ST	EMP	PHONE	ENTRY #
John Zink Company LLC	Shelton	CT	D	203 925-0380	3821

BURNT WOOD ARTICLES

	CITY	ST	EMP	PHONE	ENTRY #
Northeast Wood Products LLC	Uncasville	CT	E	860 862-6350	4647

BUS BARS: Electrical

	CITY	ST	EMP	PHONE	ENTRY #
Schneider Electric Usa Inc **(DH)**	Boston	MA	A	978 975-9600	8839
Schneider Electric Usa Inc	Foxboro	MA	G	508 549-3385	10903

BUSHINGS & BEARINGS

	CITY	ST	EMP	PHONE	ENTRY #
Quality Babbitting Services	East Kingston	NH	G	603 642-7147	18090

BUSHINGS: Rubber

	CITY	ST	EMP	PHONE	ENTRY #
HI Tech Profiles Inc	Ashaway	RI	E	401 377-2040	20037

BUSINESS ACTIVITIES: Non-Commercial Site

	CITY	ST	EMP	PHONE	ENTRY #
Actimus Inc	Cromwell	CT	D	617 438-9968	843
Alternate Energy Futures	Danbury	CT	G	917 745-7097	870
API Wizard LLC	Ridgefield	CT	G	914 764-5726	3655
Art of Wellbeing LLC	Stamford	CT	G	917 453-3009	4144
Biofibers Capital Group LLC	Ashford	CT	G	203 561-6133	25
Connecticut Trade Company Inc	Fairfield	CT	G	203 368-0398	1424
Donali Systems Integration Inc	Guilford	CT	G	860 715-5432	1701
Indigo Coast Inc	Kent	CT	G	860 592-0088	1922
Mindtrainr LLC	Stamford	CT	G	914 799-1515	4251
Nofet LLC	New Haven	CT	F	203 848-9064	2719
Perosphere Inc	Danbury	CT	F	203 885-1111	966
Single Load LLC	Bridgeport	CT	G	860 944-7507	492
Target Machines Inc	Burlington	CT	G	860 675-1539	680
Triple Clover Products LLC	New Canaan	CT	G	475 558-9503	2618
Uniworld Bus Publications Inc	Darien	CT	G	201 384-4900	1036
Us-Malabar Company Inc	Weston	CT	G	203 226-1773	5174
Westfort Construction Corp	Hamden	CT	G	860 833-7970	1795
Yolanda Dubose Records and	West Haven	CT	F	203 823-6699	5153
3wyc Inc	Newton	MA	G	617 584-7767	13550
7 Waves Inc	Braintree	MA	G	781 519-9389	8984
Actifio Federal Inc	Needham	MA	F	781 795-9182	13290
Alepack LLC	Mashpee	MA	G	508 274-5792	12874
Alphamed Incorporated	Wrentham	MA	G	774 571-9415	17514
Amalgamated Titanium Intl Corp	Cambridge	MA	F	617 395-7700	9386
Amazon Fruit Corp	Ludlow	MA	G	774 244-2820	12453
Anexis LLC	Beverly	MA	G	978 921-6293	8100
Atlas Devices LLC	Boston	MA	G	617 415-1657	8383
Beagle Learning Inc	Boston	MA	G	617 784-3817	8396
Biophysical Devices Inc	Somerville	MA	G	617 629-0304	15159
Boston Sports Journal LLC	Medway	MA	G	617 306-0166	12957
Bring Up Inc	Cambridge	MA	G	617 803-4248	9422
Crue Brew Brewery LLC	Raynham	MA	G	508 272-6090	14708
Davriel Jewelers Inc	East Longmeadow	MA	G	413 525-4975	10471
Day Zero Diagnostics Inc	Allston	MA	G	857 770-1125	7463
Drizly Inc	Boston	MA	G	972 234-1033	8510
Egyptian Cotton Tshirts LLC	Burlington	MA	G	781 272-7922	9261
Emri Systems LLP	Cambridge	MA	G	617 417-9798	9465
Firejudge Worldwide Inc	Haverhill	MA	G	978 604-0009	11434
Floc LLC	Pembroke	MA	G	617 823-5798	14405
Greenbrier Games LLP	Marlborough	MA	G	978 618-8442	12764
Greener 3000 LLC	Boston	MA	G	781 589-5777	8579
Healersource	Allston	MA	G	212 464-7748	7467
Hergon Design Inc	Revere	MA	G	781 286-0663	14766
Infinite Knot LLC	Whitinsville	MA	G	617 372-0707	16914
Innovative Publishing Co LLC	Edgartown	MA	F	267 266-8876	10585
Intelon Optics Inc	Lexington	MA	G	310 980-3087	12232
Klypper Inc	Chelmsford	MA	G	978 987-8548	9909
Leaderclips Inc	Wellesley	MA	G	248 808-1093	16370
Lennys Screen Printing	Braintree	MA	G	781 267-5977	9022
Lifeady Inc	Watertown	MA	G	781 632-1296	16295
Lincoln Learning Solutions LLC	Lincoln	MA	G	781 259-9696	12287
Medisight Corporation	Cambridge	MA	G	415 205-2764	9550
Mg2 Technologies LLC	Danvers	MA	G	978 739-1068	10241
Mobilesuites Inc	Cambridge	MA	G	302 593-3055	9563
Mocktail Beverages Inc	Wenham	MA	G	855 662-5824	16403
Mp Optical Communications Inc **(PA)**	Harvard	MA	G	978 456-7728	11382
Neurasense Inc	Cambridge	MA	G	618 917-4686	9577
North Shore Laboratories Corp	Peabody	MA	F	978 531-5954	14358
Paperpile LLC	Cambridge	MA	G	617 682-9250	9606
Portela Soni Medical LLC	Attleboro	MA	G	508 818-2727	7780
Preventiy Inc	Cambridge	MA	G	617 981-0920	9618
Rhine Inc	Weston	MA	G	781 710-7121	16831
Righthand Robotics Inc	Somerville	MA	G	617 501-0085	15210
Semantic Objects LLC	Newton	MA	F	617 272-0955	13636
Smpretty Inc	Wayland	MA	G	508 358-1639	16336
Sqz Biotechnologies Company	Watertown	MA	G	617 758-8672	16319
Surgibox Inc	Brookline	MA	G	617 982-3908	9221
Symptllgnce Med Infrmatics LLC	Franklin	MA	G	617 755-0576	11083
Textcafe	Natick	MA	G	508 654-8520	13281
Theatre Stricken Apparel LLC	Bellingham	MA	G	978 325-2335	8060
Therapeutic Innovations Inc	North Attleboro	MA	G	347 754-0252	13784
Veloxint Corporation	Framingham	MA	E	774 777-3369	11010
Virtual Cove Inc	Natick	MA	G	781 354-0492	13287
Wingbrace LLC	Hingham	MA	G	617 480-8737	11518
Xilectric Inc	Fall River	MA	G	617 312-5678	10785
Zato Inc	Springfield	MA	G	617 834-8105	15529
Connectivity Works Inc	Holden	ME	G	207 843-0854	6196
Coursestorm Inc	Orono	ME	G	207 866-0328	6553
Globeco Maine LLC	Scarborough	ME	G	207 809-2671	6921
Granite Mountain Inds LLC	South Portland	ME	G	978 369-0014	7028
In Your Own Words LLC	Greene	ME	G	207 946-5049	6149
Lilypad LLC	Cape Elizabeth	ME	G	207 200-0221	5877
Limmer Education LLC	Kennebunk	ME	G	207 482-0622	6238
Macleay Interactive Design Inc	Rome	ME	G	207 495-2208	6828
Martin Forest Products	Caribou	ME	G	207 498-6723	5887
Rockstep Solutions Inc	Portland	ME	G	844 800-7625	6723
Seal 1 LLC	Brownville	ME	G	207 965-8860	5827
William B Sparrow Jr	Pittston	ME	G	207 582-5731	6593
2d Material Technologies LLC	New London	NH	G	603 763-4791	19312
A B Excavating Inc	Lancaster	NH	E	603 788-5110	18596
Bavec LLC	Dover	NH	G	603 290-5285	18007
Beta Acquisition Inc	Thornton	NH	G	603 726-7500	19900
Chemcage US LLC	East Kingston	NH	G	617 504-9548	18085
Cogent Mfg Solutions LLC	Atkinson	NH	G	603 898-3212	17603
Granite 3 LLC	Temple	NH	G	603 566-0339	19897
Lbry Inc	Manchester	NH	G	267 210-4292	18863
Micro Weld Fabtec Corp	Windham	NH	G	603 234-6531	20009
Pyromate Inc	Peterborough	NH	G	603 924-4251	19485
Secret Guide To Computers	Manchester	NH	G	603 666-6644	18920
Simpliprotected LLC	Auburn	NH	G	603 669-7465	17613
Stencils Online LLC	Franklin	NH	G	603 934-5034	18165
Synap Inc	Dover	NH	G	888 572-1150	18056
Wagz Inc **(PA)**	Portsmouth	NH	F	603 570-6015	19630
Ocean State Software LLC	East Greenwich	RI	G	202 695-8049	20375
Philippine Pot Partners LLC	Lincoln	RI	G	401 789-7372	20590
Rhode Island Family Guide	Barrington	RI	G	401 247-0850	20053
Shelfdig LLC	Providence	RI	G	617 299-6335	21121
Vacuum Processing Systems LLC	East Greenwich	RI	G	401 397-8578	20382
Your Heaven LLC	Providence	RI	G	401 273-7076	21158
Bindery Solutions Inc **(PA)**	Grand Isle	VT	G	802 372-3492	21997
Chittenden Environmental	Williston	VT	G	802 578-0194	22660
Forward Inc	Shelburne	VT	G	802 585-1098	22417
Hi-Vue Maples LLC	Richford	VT	G	802 752-8888	22306
Old Timers Timber Frames	Saxtons River	VT	G	802 376-9529	22401
Roger Reed	Sheldon	VT	G	802 933-2535	22429
Touchfight Games LLC	Shaftsbury	VT	G	802 753-7360	22407

PRODUCT

Employee Codes: A=Over 500 employees, B=251-500
C=101-250, D=51-100 E=20-50, F=10-19, G=3-9

	CITY	ST	EMP	PHONE	ENTRY #
Twincraft Inc **(PA)**	Winooski	VT	C	802 655-2200	22726
Wild Farm Maple	Arlington	VT	G	802 362-1656	21602

BUSINESS FORMS WHOLESALERS

	CITY	ST	EMP	PHONE	ENTRY #
Brady Business Forms Inc	Lowell	MA	G	978 458-2585	12355
Massachusetts Envelope Co Inc **(PA)**	Somerville	MA	E	617 623-8000	15195
Kelley Solutions Inc	Portsmouth	NH	G	603 431-3881	19583
Choice Printing & Product LLC	Rumford	RI	F	401 438-3838	21182

BUSINESS FORMS: Printed, Manifold

	CITY	ST	EMP	PHONE	ENTRY #
Mlk Business Forms Inc	New Haven	CT	F	203 624-6304	2712
Taylor Communications Inc	East Hartford	CT	F	860 290-6851	1227
Wallingford Prtg Bus Forms Inc	Branford	CT	F	203 481-1911	359
Belmont Printing Company	Belmont	MA	E	617 484-0833	8066
BFI Print Communications Inc **(PA)**	Boston	MA	D	781 447-1199	8405
Regal Press Incorporated **(PA)**	Norwood	MA	C	781 769-3900	14192
Taylor Communications Inc	Avon	MA	F	508 584-0102	7898
Taylor Communications Inc	Braintree	MA	F	781 843-0250	9043
Bank & Business Forms Inc	Keene	NH	G	603 357-0567	18495

BUSINESS MACHINE REPAIR, ELECTRIC

	CITY	ST	EMP	PHONE	ENTRY #
Agissar Corporation	Stratford	CT	D	203 375-8662	4389
Neopost USA Inc **(DH)**	Milford	CT	C	203 301-3400	2319
Xerox Corporation **(HQ)**	Norwalk	CT	B	203 968-3000	3274
Encore Images Inc	Marblehead	MA	F	781 631-4568	12681

BUSINESS SUPPORT SVCS

	CITY	ST	EMP	PHONE	ENTRY #
Heat-Flo Inc	Uxbridge	MA	G	508 278-2400	15919
Mbm Building Systems Ltd	Boston	MA	F	617 478-3466	8690
Sally Seaver	Burlington	MA	G	833 322-8483	9332
Aqua Systems Inc **(PA)**	Hampton Falls	NH	G	603 778-8796	18281

BUSINESS TRAINING SVCS

	CITY	ST	EMP	PHONE	ENTRY #
Larson Worldwide Inc	Norwell	MA	G	781 659-2115	14105
Management Roundtable Inc	Newton	MA	G	781 891-8080	13612
Cafe Refugee Inc	Claremont	NH	G	603 499-7415	17838

BUTTER WHOLESALERS

	CITY	ST	EMP	PHONE	ENTRY #
Casco Bay Butter Company LLC	Portland	ME	G	207 712-9148	6632

BUTTONS

	CITY	ST	EMP	PHONE	ENTRY #
Ogs Technologies Inc	Cheshire	CT	E	203 271-9055	749
US Button Corporation	Putnam	CT	C	860 928-2707	3638

CABINETS & CASES: Show, Display & Storage, Exc Wood

	CITY	ST	EMP	PHONE	ENTRY #
Bull Metal Products Inc	Middletown	CT	E	860 346-9691	2180
Platt-Labonia of N Haven Inc	North Haven	CT	D	203 239-5681	3052
Rogers Cabinets	Norwood	MA	G	781 762-5700	14197
Stanley Vidmar	Holliston	MA	G	610 797-6600	11605
PCL Fixtures Inc	Rumford	RI	G	401 334-4646	21193
Stabaarte Inc	Newport	RI	G	401 364-8633	20685
Konrad Prefab LLC	Springfield	VT	G	802 885-6780	22504
Town & Country Sheds	Wolcott	VT	G	802 888-7012	22733

CABINETS: Bathroom Vanities, Wood

	CITY	ST	EMP	PHONE	ENTRY #
Christopoulos Designs Inc	Bridgeport	CT	F	203 576-1110	397
Kingswood Kitchens Co Inc	Danbury	CT	D	203 792-8700	945
Knb Design LLC	New Haven	CT	G	203 777-6661	2701
Martin Cabinet Inc	Bristol	CT	D	860 747-5769	579
Sebastian Kitchen Cabinets	Norwalk	CT	G	203 853-4411	3238
Hamlin Cabinets Corp	Norfolk	MA	G	508 384-8371	13662
Milford Woodworking Company	Milford	MA	F	508 473-2335	13128
Vanity World Inc	Canton	MA	G	508 668-1800	9792
Crown Point Realty Corp Inc	Claremont	NH	D	603 543-1208	17846
Vermont Custom Wood Products	North Walpole	NH	F	802 463-9930	19396
Young Furniture Mfg Inc	Bow	NH	E	603 224-8830	17737
Kitchen Center RI Inc	Pawtucket	RI	G	401 640-6514	20852
Catamount North Cabinetry LLC	Essex Junction	VT	F	802 264-9009	21935
Knight Industries Inc	North Clarendon	VT	E	802 773-8777	22219

CABINETS: Entertainment

	CITY	ST	EMP	PHONE	ENTRY #
Belmont Corporation	Bristol	CT	E	860 589-5700	532
Custom Ktchens By Chmpagne Inc	Franklin	MA	E	508 528-7919	11034
Superior Kitchen Designs Inc	Gardner	MA	E	978 632-5072	11130
VCA Inc	Northampton	MA	E	413 587-2750	14025
Crown Point Realty Corp Inc	Claremont	NH	D	603 543-1208	17846

CABINETS: Entertainment Units, Household, Wood

	CITY	ST	EMP	PHONE	ENTRY #
Hilltop Wood Crafts	Auburn	MA	G	508 754-3915	7838

CABINETS: Factory

	CITY	ST	EMP	PHONE	ENTRY #
Curtiss Woodworking Inc	Prospect	CT	F	203 527-9305	3586
Liberty Garage Inc	Danbury	CT	G	203 778-0222	947
River Mill Co	Clinton	CT	F	860 669-5915	794
Westmount Group LLC	West Haven	CT	G	203 931-1033	5151
JS International Inc	Fall River	MA	E	508 675-4722	10718
Stanley Industrial & Auto LLC	Holliston	MA	B	508 429-1350	11604
Coast To Coast Ff & E Installa	Greenland	NH	F	603 433-0164	18222
Storage Concepts	Berlin	NH	G	603 752-1111	17701

CABINETS: Kitchen, Metal

	CITY	ST	EMP	PHONE	ENTRY #
CT Acquisitions LLC	Wallingford	CT	E	888 441-0537	4730
Coastal N Counters Inc	Mashpee	MA	F	508 539-3500	12879

CABINETS: Kitchen, Wood

	CITY	ST	EMP	PHONE	ENTRY #
A S J Specialties LLC	Wallingford	CT	G	203 284-8650	4692
American Refacing Cstm Cab LLC	Manchester	CT	G	860 647-0868	1986
Bailey Avenue Kitchens	Ridgefield	CT	G	203 438-4868	3656
Belmont Corporation	Bristol	CT	E	860 589-5700	532
Bergan Architectural Wdwkg Inc	Middletown	CT	E	860 346-0869	2177
Bonito Manufacturing Inc	North Haven	CT	D	203 234-8786	3011
BP Countertop Design Co LLC	Derby	CT	G	203 732-1620	1069
C J Brand & Son	Mystic	CT	G	860 536-9266	2435
Cabinet Harward Specialti	West Hartford	CT	G	860 231-1192	5056
Cabinet Resources Ct Inc	Canton	CT	G	860 352-2030	696
Chris Cross LLC	Stratford	CT	G	203 386-8426	4404
Connecticut Solid Surface LLC	Plainville	CT	E	860 410-9800	3477
Conway Hardwood Products LLC	Gaylordsville	CT	E	860 355-4030	1530
Custom Furniture & Design LLC	Litchfield	CT	F	860 567-3519	1947
Custom Interiors	Winchester Center	CT	G	860 738-8754	5310
Cyr Woodworking Inc	Newington	CT	G	860 232-1991	2858
Dante Ltd	Jewett City	CT	G	860 376-0204	1911
Domestic Kitchens Inc	Fairfield	CT	E	203 368-1651	1427
East Hartford Lamination Co	Glastonbury	CT	G	860 633-4637	1547
Forest Remodeling	Somers	CT	G	413 222-7953	3918
Greenhaven Cabinetry & Millwor	Stonington	CT	G	860 535-1106	4376
Gridiron Capital LLC **(PA)**	New Canaan	CT	D	203 972-1100	2599
H & B Woodworking Co	Plainville	CT	G	860 793-6991	3495
Hanford Cabinet & Wdwkg Co	Old Saybrook	CT	G	860 388-5055	3337
Heartwood Cabinetry	Marlborough	CT	G	860 295-0304	2065
Homewood Cabinet Co Inc	Pawcatuck	CT	G	860 599-2441	3437
Hope Kit Cbinets Stone Sup LLC **(PA)**	Bridgeport	CT	G	203 610-6147	427
Industrial Wood Product Co	Shelton	CT	G	203 735-2374	3817
John June Custom Cabinetry LLC	Bridgeport	CT	G	203 334-1720	436
John M Kriskey Carpentry	Greenwich	CT	G	203 531-0194	1625
Kitchen Cab Resurfacing LLC	Bridgeport	CT	F	203 334-2857	441
Kitchen Kraftsmen	Windsor	CT	G	860 616-1240	5343
Legere Group Ltd	Avon	CT	C	860 674-0392	37
Leos Kitchen & Stair Corp	New Britain	CT	G	860 225-7363	2548
Luchon Cabinet Woodwork	Stafford Springs	CT	G	860 684-5037	4112
Martin Cabinet Inc **(PA)**	Plainville	CT	E	860 747-5769	3505
N Excellence Wood Inc	Higganum	CT	G	860 345-2050	1904
New England Kitchen Design Ctr	Monroe	CT	G	203 268-2626	2411
Northeast Cabinet Design	Ridgefield	CT	G	203 438-1709	3674
P L Woodworking	Sherman	CT	G	860 354-6855	3895
Peacock Cabinetry	Norwalk	CT	G	203 862-9333	3216
Porta Door Co	Seymour	CT	E	203 888-6191	3761
Prescott Cabinet Co	Pawcatuck	CT	G	860 495-0176	3441
Quality Woodworks LLC	Ansonia	CT	G	203 736-9200	22
Rj Cabinetry LLC	Westport	CT	G	203 515-8401	5226
Robert L Lovallo	Stamford	CT	G	203 324-6655	4304
Song Bath LLC	New Canaan	CT	G	800 353-0313	2615
Specialty Shop Inc	Manchester	CT	G	860 647-1477	2050
Sterling Custom Cabinetry LLC	Bridgeport	CT	G	203 335-5151	495
West Hrtford Stirs Cbinets Inc	Newington	CT	D	860 953-9151	2912
West Mont Group	West Haven	CT	G	203 931-1033	5150
28 Kitchen Cabinet LLC	Auburn	MA	G	774 321-6099	7820
About-Face Kitchens Inc	Peabody	MA	G	978 532-0212	14305
Alcides D Fortes D/B/A Custom	East Bridgewater	MA	G	508 378-7815	10405
Ancom Custom Cabinets	Ayer	MA	G	978 456-7780	7908
Anthony Manufacturing Co Inc	Medford	MA	F	781 396-1400	12921
Architectural Kitchens Inc	Wellesley	MA	G	781 239-9750	16360
Ashland Cabinet Corp	Southborough	MA	G	508 303-8100	15343
Avon Cabinet Company	Avon	MA	G	508 587-9122	7877
B & G Cabinet	Newburyport	MA	F	978 465-6455	13471
Builders Choice Kitchen & Bath	Southwick	MA	G	413 569-9802	15412
Cabinet House LLC	Norwell	MA	G	781 424-2259	14099
Cabinet Warehouse LLC **(PA)**	Marlborough	MA	G	508 281-2077	12732
Camio Custom Cabinetry Inc	Canton	MA	F	781 562-1573	9720
Classic Kitchen Design Inc	Hyannis	MA	F	508 775-3075	11837
Classic Woodworks Inc	Cataumet	MA	G	508 563-9922	9811
Clever Green Cabinets LLC	Waltham	MA	G	508 963-6776	16070
Coastal N Counters Inc	Mashpee	MA	F	508 539-3500	12879
Colonial Village Refinishing	Hingham	MA	G	781 740-8844	11496
Cope & Scribe Incorporated	West Brookfield	MA	G	508 410-7100	16467
Counter Productions Inc	Brockton	MA	F	508 587-0416	9133
Counterra LLC	Canton	MA	F	781 821-2100	9723
Craig F Bradford	Northampton	MA	G	413 586-4500	14003
Creative Kitchen & Bath Inc	Mashpee	MA	G	508 477-3347	12880
Cronin Cabinet Marine LLP	Charlton	MA	G	508 248-7026	9847
Custom Ktchens By Chmpagne Inc	Franklin	MA	E	508 528-7919	11034
Detail Woodworking Ltd	Billerica	MA	G	617 323-8100	8236
Diakosmisis Corporation	Somerville	MA	G	617 776-7714	15169
Dixon Bros Millwork Inc	Abington	MA	G	781 261-9962	7323
Dracut Kitchen & Bath	Dracut	MA	G	978 453-3869	10359
Eastern Cabinet Shop Inc	Boston	MA	G	617 361-7575	8517
European Cabinet Design Inc	Norwood	MA	G	781 769-7100	14151
Fallon Fine Cabinetry	Needham Heights	MA	F	781 453-6988	13331
Furniture Design Services Inc	Peabody	MA	F	978 531-3250	14335
Glenwood Kitchens USA	Framingham	MA	G	508 875-1180	10960
Heartwood Cabinetmakers LLC	Uxbridge	MA	G	508 634-2004	15918
Holland Woodworking Inc	Marlborough	MA	G	508 481-2990	12768
Ideal Kitchens of Palmer **(PA)**	Chicopee	MA	G	413 532-2253	10030
Ipswich Cabinetry Inc	Ipswich	MA	G	978 356-1123	11922
J & M Cabinet Shop Inc	Walpole	MA	F	508 660-6660	15996
J Dana Design Inc	Hardwick	MA	G	413 477-6844	11374
JC Clocks Company Inc	North Dartmouth	MA	E	508 998-8442	13922
Jim Lovejoy Cabinetmaker	Sheffield	MA	G	413 229-9008	15061
Joe Batson	Lawrence	MA	G	978 689-0072	12041
Joel Cassidy	Medway	MA	G	508 533-5887	12963
JS International Inc	Fall River	MA	E	508 675-4722	10718
Kitchens & Bath of Norwood	Norwood	MA	G	781 255-1448	14171
Kitchens R US Inc	East Bridgewater	MA	G	508 378-7474	10415
Kochman Reidt & Haigh Inc	Stoughton	MA	E	781 573-1500	15601

	CITY	ST	EMP	PHONE	ENTRY #
Landmark Finish Inc	Andover	MA	G	978 470-2040	7564
Macdonald Cabinet &	South Easton	MA	G	508 346-3221	15285
Mascaros Woodcraft Co Inc **(PA)**	Chicopee	MA	G	413 594-4255	10040
Mass Cabinets Inc	Methuen	MA	E	978 738-0600	13034
Mediterranean Custom Cabinets	West Bridgewater	MA	G	508 588-5498	16445
Metropolitan Cab Distrs Corp	Natick	MA	G	508 651-8950	13267
Metropolitan Cab Distrs Corp **(PA)**	Norwood	MA	G	781 949-8900	14178
Miller H C Wood Working Inc	Holliston	MA	G	508 429-4220	11586
Modern Woodworks Co	Foxboro	MA	G	508 543-9830	10892
Munro Woodworking	Bellingham	MA	G	508 966-2654	8052
Ne Choice Cabinet	Wakefield	MA	G	781 245-3800	15964
Norfolk Factory Direct Kitchen	Braintree	MA	G	781 848-5333	9027
Northast Cab Cntrtop Dstrs Inc	Braintree	MA	G	617 296-2100	9028
Pridemaxx Fine Wood Cabinetry	Walpole	MA	G	508 527-8700	16007
R F Mc Manus Company Inc	Charlestown	MA	F	617 241-8081	9842
Rgc Millwork Incorporated	Lowell	MA	G	978 275-9529	12427
Richards Dean Custom Wdwkg	Essex	MA	G	978 768-7104	10597
Rosario Cabinets Inc	Dedham	MA	G	781 329-0639	10296
Scandia Kitchens Inc	Bellingham	MA	E	508 966-0300	8058
Shadowbrook Custom Cabinetry	Williamstown	MA	G	413 664-9590	16960
Star Kitchen Cabinets Inc	Avon	MA	G	508 510-3123	7897
Stokes Woodworking Co Inc **(PA)**	Hudson	MA	G	508 481-0414	11820
Superior Kitchen Designs Inc	Gardner	MA	E	978 632-5072	11130
Taylor Made Cabinets LLC	Leominster	MA	G	978 840-0100	12192
Triple Crown Cbnets Mllwk Corp	Sandwich	MA	G	508 833-6500	14974
Vartanian Custom Cabinets	Palmer	MA	F	413 283-3438	14300
Watson Brothers Inc	Middleton	MA	F	978 774-7677	13106
Winfield Woodworking Inc	Holliston	MA	G	508 429-4320	11614
Atlantic Wood & Cabinet Works	Scarborough	ME	F	207 885-0767	6905
Bench Dogs	Washington	ME	G	207 845-2084	7148
Black Cove Cabinetry	Scarborough	ME	F	207 883-8901	6912
Kennebec Cabinetry Inc	Bath	ME	F	207 442-0813	5678
Kennebec Company	Bath	ME	E	207 443-2131	5679
Lauzon Gilles	Biddeford	ME	G	207 286-0600	5743
Lawrence Parson	Brownfield	ME	G	207 935-3737	5825
Mike Guillemette & Sons	Lyman	ME	G	207 324-6221	6391
Naheks Inc	Hermon	ME	G	207 848-7770	6191
Northport LLC	East Waterboro	ME	G	207 247-7600	5985
Ridgetop Cabinetry	Boothbay Harbor	ME	G	207 563-8249	5786
Topsham Woodworking LLC	Topsham	ME	G	207 751-1032	7095
Town and Country Cabinets Inc	Gorham	ME	G	207 839-2709	6131
Trico Millworks Inc	Limington	ME	E	207 637-2711	6351
West Minot Millwork Inc	West Minot	ME	G	207 966-3200	7175
Advanced Custom Cabinets Inc	Brentwood	NH	E	603 772-6211	17743
Cabinet Masters Inc	Derry	NH	G	603 425-6428	17975
Cabinets For Less LLC	Manchester	NH	G	603 935-7551	18794
Counter Pro Inc	Manchester	NH	F	603 647-2444	18807
Crown Point Cabinetry Corp	Claremont	NH	D	603 542-1273	17845
Custom Woodworking Brentwood	Chester	NH	G	603 887-6766	17824
Evergreen Cabinetry LLC	Milton	NH	G	603 833-6881	19085
Exeter Cabinet Company Inc	Exeter	NH	G	603 778-8113	18120
Jensen Cabinet Co	Milford	NH	G	603 554-8363	19067
Kimballs Lumber Center LLC **(PA)**	Wolfeboro	NH	G	603 569-2477	20021
King & Co Architectural Wdwkg	Marlborough	NH	G	603 876-4900	18961
Mark Allen Cabinetry LLC	Amherst	NH	G	603 491-7570	17573
Mark Allen Cabinetry LLC **(PA)**	Brookline	NH	G	603 321-3163	17772
Northeast Cabinet Designs LLC	Hampstead	NH	G	603 329-3465	18246
Northeast Woodworking Products	Raymond	NH	G	603 895-4271	19642
Nutfield Cabinetry LLC	Derry	NH	G	603 498-6252	17992
Oakwood Cabinetry	Concord	NH	G	603 927-4713	17920
Plaistow Cabinet Co Inc	Plaistow	NH	F	603 382-1098	19520
Purewood Cabinetry	Newton	NH	G	603 378-2001	19368
Taylor & Stevens Cabinetry	Pelham	NH	G	603 880-2022	19449
Walpole Cabinetry	Walpole	NH	F	603 826-4100	19925
Ws Dennison Cabinets Inc	Pembroke	NH	G	603 224-8434	19464
Cabinet Assembly Systems Corp	East Greenwich	RI	F	401 884-8556	20355
European Custom Casework Inc	North Smithfield	RI	G	401 356-0400	20785
Gary Eldridge	Woonsocket	RI	G	401 769-0026	21566
Hardwood Design Inc	Exeter	RI	E	401 294-2235	20450
Imperia Corporation	Barrington	RI	E	508 894-3000	20046
Joe Martin	West Warwick	RI	G	401 823-1860	21497
Mycabinetsonline	Lincoln	RI	G	401 722-3863	20587
Riley Kitchen & Bath Co Inc	Bristol	RI	G	401 253-2205	20100
Tm Custom	West Greenwich	RI	G	401 226-2173	21466
Water Street Woodworking	Warren	RI	G	401 245-1921	21315
Jericho Woodworking	White River Junction	VT	G	802 295-9399	22640
Killington Cabinets	Killington	VT	G	802 773-3960	22054
William Chadburn	North Concord	VT	G	802 695-8166	22223

CABINETS: Office, Metal

	CITY	ST	EMP	PHONE	ENTRY #
Nutmeg Architectural Wdwrk Inc	Stamford	CT	E	203 325-4434	4264
L D G Corporation	East Weymouth	MA	G	781 337-7155	10545

CABINETS: Office, Wood

	CITY	ST	EMP	PHONE	ENTRY #
Clay Furniture Industries Inc	Manchester	CT	F	860 643-7580	1995
G Woodcraft	Norwalk	CT	G	203 846-4168	3156
Gregory Woodworks LLC	Bethel	CT	G	203 794-0726	157
Statham Woodwork	Norwalk	CT	G	203 831-0629	3250
Gill Metal Fab Inc	Brockton	MA	E	508 580-4445	9151
Imperia Corporation	Barrington	RI	E	508 894-3000	20046

CABINETS: Show, Display, Etc, Wood, Exc Refrigerated

	CITY	ST	EMP	PHONE	ENTRY #
Lingard Cabinet Co LLC	Manchester	CT	G	860 647-9886	2019
New England Cabinet Co Inc	New Britain	CT	F	860 747-9995	2555
B&B Micro Manufacturing Inc	Adams	MA	E	413 281-9431	7410

	CITY	ST	EMP	PHONE	ENTRY #
Baranowski Woodworking Co Inc	East Bridgewater	MA	G	508 690-1515	10407
Custom Ktchens By Chmpagne Inc	Franklin	MA	E	508 528-7919	11034
Diakosmisis Corporation	Somerville	MA	G	617 776-7714	15169
Eagle Woodworking Inc	Lawrence	MA	F	978 681-6194	12019
Jules A Gourdeau Inc	Beverly	MA	G	978 922-0102	8144
Kochman Reidt & Haigh Inc	Stoughton	MA	E	781 573-1500	15601
Norwood Woodworking Inc	Norwood	MA	G	781 762-8367	14185
Padco Inc	Worcester	MA	F	508 753-8486	17438
Pbd Productions LLC	Hopedale	MA	F	508 482-9300	11679
Tozier Group Inc	Falmouth	ME	E	207 838-7939	6035
Advanced Custom Cabinets Inc	Brentwood	NH	E	603 772-6211	17743
Cole Cabinet Co Inc	Cranston	RI	F	401 467-4343	20199
Laminated Products Inc	Woonsocket	RI	G	401 762-0711	21573

CABLE & OTHER PAY TELEVISION DISTRIBUTION

	CITY	ST	EMP	PHONE	ENTRY #
Ripley Tools LLC **(PA)**	Cromwell	CT	E	860 635-2200	859

CABLE TELEVISION

	CITY	ST	EMP	PHONE	ENTRY #
Burns Industries Incorporated	Hollis	NH	G	603 881-8336	18327

CABLE TELEVISION PRDTS

	CITY	ST	EMP	PHONE	ENTRY #
RFS Americas	Meriden	CT	G	203 630-3311	2125

CABLE: Coaxial

	CITY	ST	EMP	PHONE	ENTRY #
A J R Inc	Bridgeport	CT	F	203 384-0400	365
Times Fiber Communications Inc **(HQ)**	Wallingford	CT	D	203 265-8500	4818
Volpe Cable Corporation	Branford	CT	C	203 623-1818	357
Dynawave Cable Incorporated	Haverhill	MA	G	978 469-9448	11428
James Monroe Wire & Cable Corp **(PA)**	South Lancaster	MA	D	978 368-0131	15318
Amphenol Corporation	Nashua	NH	B	603 879-3000	19114
Cable Assemblies Inc	Amherst	NH	F	603 889-4090	17553

CABLE: Fiber

	CITY	ST	EMP	PHONE	ENTRY #
Nca Inc	Abington	CT	G	860 974-2310	1
Photonic Systems Inc	Billerica	MA	F	978 670-4990	8275

CABLE: Fiber Optic

	CITY	ST	EMP	PHONE	ENTRY #
Ensign-Bickford Industries Inc	Weatogue	CT	C	860 843-2000	5042
ABB Installation Products Inc	Hopkinton	MA	C	508 435-0101	11686
Linden Photonics Inc	Westford	MA	G	978 392-7985	16776
Maine Fiber Company LLC	Portland	ME	G	207 699-4550	6686
Fiberoptic Resale Corp	Nashua	NH	G	603 496-1258	19157
Microspec Corporation	Peterborough	NH	E	603 924-4300	19477
Subcom Cable Systems LLC	Newington	NH	B	603 436-6100	19327

CABLE: Noninsulated

	CITY	ST	EMP	PHONE	ENTRY #
Armored Shield Technologies	Redding	CT	F	714 848-5796	3646
Redco Audio Inc	Stratford	CT	F	203 502-7600	4441
Axiom Wire and Cable	Attleboro	MA	G	508 498-8899	7711
Saint-Gobain Prfmce Plas Corp	Worcester	MA	E	508 852-3072	17467
Amphenol Corporation	Nashua	NH	B	603 879-3000	19114
Continental Cable LLC	Hinsdale	NH	D	800 229-5131	18319
Ametek Scp Inc **(HQ)**	Westerly	RI	D	401 596-6658	21515

CABLE: Ropes & Fiber

	CITY	ST	EMP	PHONE	ENTRY #
Orion Ropeworks Inc **(PA)**	Winslow	ME	E	207 877-2224	7273
Marmon Utility	Milford	NH	G	603 249-1302	19068
Two In One Manufacturing Inc	Nashua	NH	E	603 595-8212	19276
Lrv Properties LLC	Providence	RI	G	401 714-7001	21058

CABLE: Steel, Insulated Or Armored

	CITY	ST	EMP	PHONE	ENTRY #
Custom House LLC	East Haddam	CT	F	860 873-1259	1150
Federal Prison Industries	Danbury	CT	F	203 743-6471	919
Lex Products LLC **(PA)**	Shelton	CT	C	203 363-3738	3828
Rscc Wire & Cable LLC **(DH)**	East Granby	CT	B	860 653-8300	1143
Specialty Cable Corp	Wallingford	CT	D	203 265-7126	4809
Alliance Cable Corp	Taunton	MA	E	508 824-5896	15724
Electroweave Inc	Worcester	MA	G	508 752-8932	17371
Heat Trace Products LLC	Leominster	MA	E	978 534-2810	12151
James Monroe Wire & Cable Corp **(PA)**	South Lancaster	MA	D	978 368-0131	15318
Temp-Flex LLC	South Grafton	MA	D	508 839-3120	15299
Micro Wire Transm Systems Inc	Essex Junction	VT	F	802 876-7901	21951

CAFES

	CITY	ST	EMP	PHONE	ENTRY #
Berkshire Mtn Bky Pizza Cafe	Pittsfield	MA	G	413 464-9394	14458

CAGES: Wire

	CITY	ST	EMP	PHONE	ENTRY #
Excel Spring & Stamping LLC	Bristol	CT	G	860 585-1495	559
Innovive LLC	Billerica	MA	G	617 500-1691	8257
Scott-Lynn Mfg	Auburn	ME	G	207 784-3372	5598

CALCAREOUS TUFA: Dimension

	CITY	ST	EMP	PHONE	ENTRY #
Vermont Verde Antique Intl	Pittsford	VT	G	802 767-4421	22265

CALCULATING & ACCOUNTING EQPT

	CITY	ST	EMP	PHONE	ENTRY #
Blackwold Inc	Chester	CT	D	860 526-0800	768

CALENDARS, WHOLESALE

	CITY	ST	EMP	PHONE	ENTRY #
Noah Publications	Brooklin	ME	G	207 359-2131	5821

CALIBRATING SVCS, NEC

	CITY	ST	EMP	PHONE	ENTRY #
Bay State Scale & Systems Inc	Burlington	MA	G	781 993-9035	9239
N E M T R LLC	Shutesbury	MA	G	413 259-1444	15140

CAMERA & PHOTOGRAPHIC SPLYS STORES

	CITY	ST	EMP	PHONE	ENTRY #
27th Exposure LLC	Littleton	NH	G	603 444-5800	18653

CAMERA & PHOTOGRAPHIC SPLYS STORES: Cameras

	CITY	ST	EMP	PHONE	ENTRY #
Lyfeshot LLC	Acton	MA	G	978 451-4662	7370

Employee Codes: A=Over 500 employees, B=251-500
C=101-250, D=51-100 E=20-50, F=10-19, G=3-9

CAMERA CARRYING BAGS

	CITY	ST	EMP	PHONE	ENTRY #
Porta-Brace Inc	Bennington	VT	D	802 442-8171	21689

CAMERAS & RELATED EQPT: Photographic

	CITY	ST	EMP	PHONE	ENTRY #
Vitec Production Solutions Inc **(HQ)**	Shelton	CT	D	203 929-1100	3887
Glidecam Industries Inc	Kingston	MA	F	781 585-7900	11957
Scallop Imaging LLC	Marblehead	MA	E	617 849-6400	12692
Xenics Usa Inc	Beverly	MA	G	978 969-1706	8199
Flir Systems Inc	Nashua	NH	C	603 324-7783	19161
Hyndsight Vision Systems Inc	Peterborough	NH	G	603 924-1334	19473

CAMERAS: Microfilm

	CITY	ST	EMP	PHONE	ENTRY #
Ebeam Film LLC	Shelton	CT	F	203 926-0100	3798

CAMPERS: Truck Mounted

	CITY	ST	EMP	PHONE	ENTRY #
Bear Country Powersports LLC	Errol	NH	G	603 482-3370	18109

CAMSHAFTS

	CITY	ST	EMP	PHONE	ENTRY #
Westfalia Inc	Bristol	CT	E	860 314-2920	624

CANDLE SHOPS

	CITY	ST	EMP	PHONE	ENTRY #
Colton Hollow Candle Company	Monson	MA	G	413 267-3986	13205
Country Candle Co Inc **(PA)**	Millbury	MA	E	508 865-6061	13160
Mole Hollow Candles Limited	Worcester	MA	E	508 756-7415	17423
Pilgrim Candle Company Inc **(PA)**	Westfield	MA	E	413 562-2635	16715
Yankee Candle Company Inc **(DH)**	South Deerfield	MA	C	413 665-8306	15260
Yankee Candle Investments LLC **(DH)**	South Deerfield	MA	G	413 665-8306	15261
Ycc Holdings LLC	South Deerfield	MA	A	413 665-8306	15263

CANDLES

	CITY	ST	EMP	PHONE	ENTRY #
Crystal Journey Candles LLC	Branford	CT	E	203 433-4735	307
Battalion Co Inc **(PA)**	Lowell	MA	G	978 453-2824	12352
Colton Hollow Candle Company	Monson	MA	G	413 267-3986	13205
Country Candle Co Inc **(PA)**	Millbury	MA	E	508 865-6061	13160
Farm Table At Kringle Candle	Bernardston	MA	G	413 648-5200	8093
Hmh Religious Mfg Inc	Plainville	MA	F	508 699-9464	14522
Mole Hollow Candles Limited	Worcester	MA	E	508 756-7415	17423
NV Candles LLC	Auburn	MA	G	774 234-6895	7846
Partylite Inc **(HQ)**	Plymouth	MA	D	203 661-1926	14572
Partylite Worldwide LLC **(DH)**	Norwell	MA	C	888 999-5706	14110
Pilgrim Candle Company Inc **(PA)**	Westfield	MA	E	413 562-2635	16715
Whiffletree Cntry Str Gift Sp	Billerica	MA	G	978 663-6346	8309
Yankee Candle Company Inc **(DH)**	South Deerfield	MA	C	413 665-8306	15260
Yankee Candle Investments LLC **(DH)**	South Deerfield	MA	G	413 665-8306	15261
Yankee Holding Corp **(DH)**	South Deerfield	MA	G	413 665-8306	15262
Ycc Holdings LLC	South Deerfield	MA	A	413 665-8306	15263
Ymittos Candle Mfg Co	Lowell	MA	G	978 453-2824	12450
Danica Design Inc **(PA)**	Rockport	ME	G	207 236-3060	6819
Maine Made Stuffcom	Lexington Twp	ME	G	207 628-3160	6329
RFI Industries	Dexter	ME	G	443 255-8767	5956
Sea Point Chandlers LLC	Kittery Point	ME	G	207 703-2395	6261
Alene Candles LLC **(PA)**	Milford	NH	C	603 673-5050	19046
Marklin Candle Design LLC	Contoocook	NH	F	603 746-2211	17946
Aunt Sadies Inc	Lunenburg	VT	F	802 892-5267	22066
Travis M Bonnett	Saint Albans	VT	F	802 524-1890	22382
Way Out Wax Inc	North Hyde Park	VT	F	802 730-8069	22233

CANDLES: Wholesalers

	CITY	ST	EMP	PHONE	ENTRY #
Colton Hollow Candle Company	Monson	MA	G	413 267-3986	13205
Mole Hollow Candles Limited	Worcester	MA	E	508 756-7415	17423
Partylite Inc **(HQ)**	Plymouth	MA	D	203 661-1926	14572

CANDY & CONFECTIONS: Cake Ornaments

	CITY	ST	EMP	PHONE	ENTRY #
Samarc Inc	Boston	MA	G	617 924-3884	8837

CANDY & CONFECTIONS: Candy Bars, Including Chocolate Covered

	CITY	ST	EMP	PHONE	ENTRY #
Hebert Retail LLC	Shrewsbury	MA	D	508 845-8051	15116
Gartland Distributors LLC	Biddeford	ME	G	207 282-9456	5736

CANDY & CONFECTIONS: Chocolate Candy, Exc Solid Chocolate

	CITY	ST	EMP	PHONE	ENTRY #
Bb Walpole Liquidation NH Inc	Boston	MA	G	617 303-0113	8394
Bb Walpole Liquidation NH Inc **(PA)**	Walpole	NH	D	603 756-3701	19916
McCains Vermont Products Inc	Bennington	VT	G	802 447-2610	21682

CANDY & CONFECTIONS: Fudge

	CITY	ST	EMP	PHONE	ENTRY #
Winfreys Olde English Fdge Inc **(PA)**	Rowley	MA	F	978 948-7448	14868

CANDY & CONFECTIONS: Nuts, Candy Covered

	CITY	ST	EMP	PHONE	ENTRY #
H L Handy Company Inc	Putney	VT	G	802 387-4040	22289

CANDY & CONFECTIONS: Popcorn Balls/Other Trtd Popcorn Prdts

	CITY	ST	EMP	PHONE	ENTRY #
Mini Pops Inc	Sharon	MA	G	781 436-5864	15053
Quirion Luc **(PA)**	Newport	VT	G	802 673-8386	22205

CANDY, NUT & CONFECTIONERY STORE: Popcorn, Incl Caramel Corn

	CITY	ST	EMP	PHONE	ENTRY #
Quirion Luc **(PA)**	Newport	VT	G	802 673-8386	22205

CANDY, NUT & CONFECTIONERY STORES: Candy

	CITY	ST	EMP	PHONE	ENTRY #
Thompson Brands LLC	Meriden	CT	D	203 235-2541	2141
Thompson Candy Company	Meriden	CT	D	203 235-2541	2142
Bb Walpole Liquidation NH Inc	Cambridge	MA	E	617 491-4340	9406
Ben & Bills Chocolate Emporium	Falmouth	MA	F	508 548-7878	10787
Ben & Blls Chclat Emporium Inc **(PA)**	Northampton	MA	F	413 584-5695	13997
Dorothy Coxs Candies Inc	Wareham	MA	E	774 678-0654	16245
Furlongs Cottage Candies	Norwood	MA	F	781 762-4124	14154
Gowell Candy Shop Inc	Brockton	MA	G	508 583-2521	9152
Hilliards House Candy Inc **(PA)**	North Easton	MA	D	508 238-6231	13947
Levaggis Candies	South Weymouth	MA	G	781 335-1231	15321
Russos Inc	Saugus	MA	F	781 233-1737	14995
Seven Sweets Inc	Marblehead	MA	F	781 631-0303	12693
Stage Stop Candy Ltd Inc	Dennis Port	MA	G	508 394-1791	10315
Sweethearts Three Inc	Sharon	MA	G	781 784-5193	15058
Bavarian Chocolate Haus Inc	North Conway	NH	G	603 356-2663	19372
Fredericks Pastries **(PA)**	Amherst	NH	G	603 882-7725	17563
Lindt & Sprungli (usa) Inc **(HQ)**	Stratham	NH	C	603 778-8100	19871
Sweenors Chocolates Inc **(PA)**	Wakefield	RI	E	401 783-4433	21280
Tom and Sallys Handmade Choco	Westerly	RI	F	800 289-8783	21544
Fudge Factory Inc	Manchester Center	VT	F	888 669-7425	22085

CANDY, NUT & CONFECTIONERY STORES: Confectionery

	CITY	ST	EMP	PHONE	ENTRY #
Chip In A Bottle LLC	New Haven	CT	G	203 460-0665	2676
Nichols Candies Inc	Gloucester	MA	F	978 283-9850	11197
Len Libbys Inc	Scarborough	ME	E	207 883-4897	6931

CANDY, NUT & CONFECTIONERY STORES: Produced For Direct Sale

	CITY	ST	EMP	PHONE	ENTRY #
Harbor Candy Shop Inc	Ogunquit	ME	E	207 646-8078	6537
Hauser Foods Inc	Westerly	RI	E	401 596-8866	21526

CANDY: Chocolate From Cacao Beans

	CITY	ST	EMP	PHONE	ENTRY #
Sweethearts Three Inc	Sharon	MA	G	781 784-5193	15058
Champlain Chocolate Company	Williston	VT	G	802 864-1808	22659

CANDY: Hard

	CITY	ST	EMP	PHONE	ENTRY #
Lollipop Kids LLC	Redding	CT	G	203 664-1799	3649
Yummyearth LLC **(PA)**	Stamford	CT	G	203 276-1259	4363
F B Washburn Candy Corporation	Brockton	MA	E	508 588-0820	9145

CANDY: Soft

	CITY	ST	EMP	PHONE	ENTRY #
Seven Sweets Inc	Marblehead	MA	F	781 631-0303	12693

CANNED SPECIALTIES

	CITY	ST	EMP	PHONE	ENTRY #
Cushs Homegrown LLC	Old Lyme	CT	G	860 739-7373	3318
Shenondah Vly Specialty Foods	Stamford	CT	G	203 348-0402	4315
New England Country Foods LLC	Cambridge	MA	G	617 682-3650	9580
R Walters Foods	Danvers	MA	D	978 646-8950	10249
Stonewall Kitchen LLC **(PA)**	York	ME	C	207 351-2713	7316

CANOE BUILDING & REPAIR

	CITY	ST	EMP	PHONE	ENTRY #
Composite Engineering Inc	Concord	MA	G	978 371-3132	10122
Johnson Otdoors Watercraft Inc **(HQ)**	Old Town	ME	E	207 827-5513	6541
Northwood Canoe Co	Atkinson	ME	G	207 564-3667	5544

CANS: Aluminum

	CITY	ST	EMP	PHONE	ENTRY #
CCL Industries Corporation **(DH)**	Shelton	CT	D	203 926-1253	3785
CCL Label Inc	Shelton	CT	C	203 926-1253	3786
CCL Label Inc **(HQ)**	Framingham	MA	D	508 872-4511	10932

CANS: Composite Foil-Fiber, Made From Purchased Materials

	CITY	ST	EMP	PHONE	ENTRY #
Globe Composite Solutions LLC	Stoughton	MA	E	781 871-3700	15593
R F Consulting LLC **(PA)**	Freeport	ME	G	207 233-8846	6085
Txv Aerospace Composites LLC	Bristol	RI	E	425 785-0883	20108
Precision Composites VT LLC	Lyndonville	VT	F	802 626-5900	22072

CANS: Garbage, Stamped Or Pressed Metal

	CITY	ST	EMP	PHONE	ENTRY #
Bearicuda Inc	Litchfield	CT	G	860 361-6860	1945

CANS: Metal

	CITY	ST	EMP	PHONE	ENTRY #
Silgan Containers Corporation	Stamford	CT	F	203 975-7110	4320
Leaktite Corporation **(PA)**	Leominster	MA	D	978 537-8000	12160
MIW Corp	Fall River	MA	E	508 672-4029	10736
Van Dorn and Curtiss	Claremont	NH	G	603 542-3081	17863

CANS: Tin

	CITY	ST	EMP	PHONE	ENTRY #
Tin Can Alley	Provincetown	MA	G	508 487-1648	14610
Tin Can Sally	Eliot	ME	G	207 651-6188	6011
Tincanpally LLC	Belfast	ME	G	732 485-5636	5697

CANVAS PRDTS

	CITY	ST	EMP	PHONE	ENTRY #
Custom Marine Canvas LLC	Groton	CT	G	860 572-9547	1669
Dimension-Polyant Inc	Putnam	CT	E	860 928-8300	3610
New Haven Companies Inc	East Haven	CT	F	203 469-6421	1257
Seafarer Canvas **(PA)**	Norwalk	CT	F	203 853-2624	3237
Second Lac Inc **(PA)**	Norwalk	CT	G	203 321-1221	3239
Topside Canvas Upholstery	Westbrook	CT	G	860 399-4845	5164
Watertown Canvas and Awng LLC	Oakville	CT	G	860 274-0933	3305
Canvas Link Inc	Westborough	MA	G	508 366-3323	16600
Canvasmith	Fairhaven	MA	G	207 379-2121	10641
Columbia ASC Inc	Lawrence	MA	F	978 683-2205	12012
Katherine McAloon	Gloucester	MA	G	978 525-2223	11194
Leisure Time Canvas	West Springfield	MA	G	413 785-5500	16528
Peaks Tarps	Clinton	MA	G	978 365-5555	10088
Sperry Tents Inc	Marion	MA	G	508 748-1792	12706
Steele Canvas Basket Corp	Chelsea	MA	E	800 541-8929	9970
Tim Gratuski	Leominster	MA	G	978 466-9000	12195
United Industrial Tex Pdts Inc **(PA)**	West Springfield	MA	E	413 737-0095	16559
United Industrial Tex Pdts Inc	West Springfield	MA	G	413 737-0095	16560
Byer Manufacturing Company	Orono	ME	E	207 866-2171	6552
C B P Corp **(PA)**	Arundel	ME	F	207 985-9767	5529
Custom Canvas & Upholstery LLC	Lewiston	ME	F	207 241-8518	6281
Nancy Lawrence	Portland	ME	G	207 774-7276	6697
Seth Hetherington	South Harpswell	ME	G	207 833-5400	7008
American Canvas Company LLC	Kingston	NH	G	603 642-6665	18539
Enviro-Tote Inc	Londonderry	NH	E	603 647-7171	18696
Corrados Canvas & Cushions Inc	Bristol	RI	G	401 253-5511	20070

	CITY	ST	EMP	PHONE	ENTRY #
Fit N Stitch Inc	North Kingstown	RI	G	401 294-3492	20711
Stupell Industries Ltd Inc	Johnston	RI	F	401 831-5640	20543
Durasol Systems Inc	Middlebury	VT	E	802 388-7309	22109
Vermont Canvas Products	Rutland	VT	G	802 773-7311	22359

CANVAS PRDTS, WHOLESALE

	CITY	ST	EMP	PHONE	ENTRY #
American Canvas Company LLC	Kingston	NH	G	603 642-6665	18539

CANVAS PRDTS: Air Cushions & Mattresses

	CITY	ST	EMP	PHONE	ENTRY #
Fortune Inc **(PA)**	Portland	ME	F	207 878-5760	6663

CANVAS PRDTS: Convertible Tops, Car/Boat, Fm Purchased Mtrl

	CITY	ST	EMP	PHONE	ENTRY #
Oakum Bay Sail Co	Marblehead	MA	G	781 631-8983	12689
Nilsen Canvas Products	Portland	ME	G	207 797-4863	6703
Cloth N Canvas Recovery Inc	Colchester	VT	G	802 658-6826	21859

CAPACITORS & CONDENSERS

	CITY	ST	EMP	PHONE	ENTRY #
AVX Tantalum Corporation	Biddeford	ME	C	207 282-5111	5720
Desco Industries Inc	Rochester	NH	G	603 332-0717	19667

CAPACITORS: AC, Motors Or Fluorescent Lamp Ballasts

	CITY	ST	EMP	PHONE	ENTRY #
Vishay Sprague Inc	Warwick	RI	A	401 738-9150	21438

CAPACITORS: Fixed Or Variable

	CITY	ST	EMP	PHONE	ENTRY #
S B E Inc **(PA)**	Barre	VT	E	802 476-4146	21638

CAPACITORS: NEC

	CITY	ST	EMP	PHONE	ENTRY #
Electronic Film Capacitors	Waterbury	CT	E	203 755-5629	4869
Newco Condenser Inc	Shelton	CT	G	475 882-4000	3839
Fortiming Corporation	Marlborough	MA	G	508 281-5980	12756
Philips Medical Systems Hsg **(PA)**	Andover	MA	E	978 687-1501	7583
Steinerfilm Inc	Williamstown	MA	C	413 458-9525	16961
Tdl Inc	Canton	MA	E	781 828-3366	9789
AVX Tantalum Corporation	Biddeford	ME	C	207 282-5111	5720
Standex International Corp **(PA)**	Salem	NH	E	603 893-9701	19769
Polyrack North America Corp	Cumberland	RI	G	401 770-1500	20340
S B E Inc **(PA)**	Barre	VT	E	802 476-4146	21638

CAPS & TOPS: Bottle, Stamped Metal

	CITY	ST	EMP	PHONE	ENTRY #
Kinex Cappers LLC **(PA)**	Amherst	NH	F	603 883-2400	17571

CAPS: Plastic

	CITY	ST	EMP	PHONE	ENTRY #
Bprex Halthcare Brookville Inc	Waterbury	CT	C	203 754-4141	4851
Summit Packaging Systems Inc **(PA)**	Manchester	NH	B	603 669-5410	18932
Silgan Dispensing Systems **(DH)**	Slatersville	RI	C	401 767-2400	21206

CAR WASH EQPT

	CITY	ST	EMP	PHONE	ENTRY #
RPM Technologies Inc	Ludlow	MA	G	413 583-3385	12477
Maintenance Tech Inc	Portland	ME	G	207 797-7233	6691
Yvons Valvoline Express Care	Lewiston	ME	G	207 777-3600	6328

CARBIDES

	CITY	ST	EMP	PHONE	ENTRY #
Carbide Solutions LLC	Windsor	CT	G	860 515-8665	5324
Carbide Technology Inc	Southington	CT	G	860 621-8981	4043
Benchmark Carbide	Springfield	MA	G	800 523-8570	15451
Cutting Edge Carbide Tech Inc	Leominster	MA	G	888 210-9670	12130
Sharp Tool Co Inc	Hudson	MA	E	978 568-9292	11816

CARBON & GRAPHITE PRDTS, NEC

	CITY	ST	EMP	PHONE	ENTRY #
Carbon Products Inc	Somersville	CT	G	860 749-0614	3923
Graphite Die Mold Inc	Durham	CT	G	860 349-4444	1091
Joshua LLC **(PA)**	New Haven	CT	E	203 624-0080	2699
Minteq International Inc	Canaan	CT	C	860 824-5435	689
Rain Carbon Inc **(HQ)**	Stamford	CT	G	203 406-0535	4296
Across Usa Inc	Everett	MA	G	617 678-0350	10599
Advanced Diamond Solutions Inc	Cambridge	MA	G	617 291-3497	9374
Applied Nnstrctred Sltions LLC	Billerica	MA	E	978 670-6959	8211
Carbon Composites Inc	Leominster	MA	F	978 840-0707	12124
Geonautics Manufacturing Inc	Newburyport	MA	E	978 462-7161	13494
2d Material Technologies LLC	New London	NH	G	603 763-4791	19312
Clear Carbon & Components Inc	Bristol	RI	F	401 254-5085	20068

CARBON BLACK

	CITY	ST	EMP	PHONE	ENTRY #
Cabot Corporation **(PA)**	Boston	MA	C	617 345-0100	8452
Cabot Corporation	Billerica	MA	E	978 671-4000	8230
Cabot Corporation	Haverhill	MA	C	978 556-8400	11413

CARBON PAPER & INKED RIBBONS

	CITY	ST	EMP	PHONE	ENTRY #
Avcarb LLC	Lowell	MA	D	978 452-8961	12347

CARBON SPECIALTIES Electrical Use

	CITY	ST	EMP	PHONE	ENTRY #
Hyperion Catalysis Intl Inc **(PA)**	Cambridge	MA	E	617 354-9678	9509
Nanolab Inc	Waltham	MA	G	781 609-2722	16156

CARBURETORS

	CITY	ST	EMP	PHONE	ENTRY #
Universal Carburetor Inc	Norwood	MA	G	781 762-3771	14204

CARDIOVASCULAR SYSTEM DRUGS, EXC DIAGNOSTIC

	CITY	ST	EMP	PHONE	ENTRY #
Boehringer Ingelheim Pharma **(DH)**	Ridgefield	CT	A	203 798-9988	3658
Sanofi US Services Inc	Cambridge	MA	E	617 562-4555	9643
Bentley Pharmaceuticals Inc **(HQ)**	Exeter	NH	F	603 658-6100	18113

CARDS, PLASTIC, UNPRINTED, WHOLESALE

	CITY	ST	EMP	PHONE	ENTRY #
Abcorp NA Inc	Boston	MA	B	617 325-9600	8335

CARDS: Beveled

	CITY	ST	EMP	PHONE	ENTRY #
JS McCarthy Co Inc **(PA)**	Augusta	ME	D	207 622-6241	5609

CARDS: Color

	CITY	ST	EMP	PHONE	ENTRY #
American Banknote Corporation **(PA)**	Stamford	CT	G	203 941-4090	4135

CARDS: Greeting

	CITY	ST	EMP	PHONE	ENTRY #
Caspari Inc **(PA)**	Seymour	CT	F	203 888-1100	3750
Joy Carole Creations Inc	Danbury	CT	G	203 794-1401	942
Smiling Dog	Middletown	CT	G	860 344-0707	2223
Caspi Cards and Art	Newton	MA	G	617 964-8888	13574
Expressive Design Group Inc	Holyoke	MA	E	413 315-6296	11626
Fein Things	Centerville	MA	G	508 778-5200	9815
Good Cause Greetings Inc	Wilbraham	MA	G	413 543-1515	16938
New England Business Svc Inc **(HQ)**	Groton	MA	D	978 448-6111	11291
Viabella Holdings LLC	Wareham	MA	F	800 688-9998	16257
Borealis Press Inc	Blue Hill	ME	G	207 370-6020	5771
In Your Own Words LLC	Greene	ME	G	207 946-5049	6149
Patricks Inc	Bangor	ME	G	207 990-9303	5657
Renaissance Greeting Cards Inc	Sanford	ME	C	207 324-4153	6888
William Arthur Inc	West Kennebunk	ME	C	413 684-2600	7174
Be Youneeq LLC	Raymond	NH	G	603 244-3933	19635
Gloria Jean Photography	Pembroke	NH	G	603 485-7176	19457
Pen & Inc	Bow	NH	G	603 225-7522	17726
Oatmeal Studios Inc	Rochester	VT	F	802 967-8014	22320
Vermont Christmas Company	Milton	VT	G	802 893-1670	22139

CARDS: Identification

	CITY	ST	EMP	PHONE	ENTRY #
Connecticut Laminating Co Inc	New Haven	CT	D	203 787-2184	2677
Idemia Identity & SEC USA LLC	Rocky Hill	CT	G	860 529-2559	3717
Andrew Rolden PC	Ayer	MA	G	978 391-4655	7909
Budgetcard Inc	Attleboro Falls	MA	F	508 695-8762	7811
Idemia America Corp **(DH)**	Billerica	MA	B	978 215-2400	8255
Jewelry Creations	Norton	MA	G	508 285-4230	14079
Precision Dynamics Corporation	Burlington	MA	D	888 202-3684	9321
Precision Dynamics Corporation	Billerica	MA	D	800 528-8005	8276
Reeves Coinc	Attleboro	MA	E	508 222-2877	7785

CARPET & RUG CLEANING PLANTS

	CITY	ST	EMP	PHONE	ENTRY #
Moderne Rug Inc	Fitchburg	MA	G	978 343-3210	10840

CARPETS & RUGS: Tufted

	CITY	ST	EMP	PHONE	ENTRY #
Mohawk Industries Inc	Danbury	CT	C	203 739-0260	956
Mohawk Industries Inc	Torrington	CT	G	706 629-7721	4588
Mohawk Industries Inc	Walpole	MA	C	508 660-8935	16003
East Providence Mohawks	East Providence	RI	G	401 829-1411	20409

CARPETS, RUGS & FLOOR COVERING

	CITY	ST	EMP	PHONE	ENTRY #
Apricot Home LLC	Greenwich	CT	G	203 552-1791	1593
New Haven Companies Inc	East Haven	CT	F	203 469-6421	1257
Bentley Mills Inc	Boston	MA	G	617 439-0405	8401
Cape Cod Drmats of Distinction	Hyannis	MA	E	508 790-0070	11836
Delaware Valley Corp	Tewksbury	MA	E	978 459-6932	15814
Julie Industries Inc **(PA)**	Andover	MA	G	978 276-0820	7660
Medallion Gallery Inc	Boston	MA	G	617 236-8283	8692
Merida LLC	Fall River	MA	E	508 675-6572	10731
Sam Kasten Handweaver LLC	Lenox	MA	G	413 637-8900	12103
Stevens Linen Associates Inc	Dudley	MA	D	508 943-0813	10387

CARPETS: Hand & Machine Made

	CITY	ST	EMP	PHONE	ENTRY #
Holland & Sherry Inc **(PA)**	Norwalk	CT	F	212 628-1950	3169

CARPETS: Textile Fiber

	CITY	ST	EMP	PHONE	ENTRY #
Natco Products Corporation **(PA)**	West Warwick	RI	B	401 828-0300	21504

CARRIAGES: Horse Drawn

	CITY	ST	EMP	PHONE	ENTRY #
Serafin Sulky Co	Stafford Springs	CT	G	860 684-2986	4114
Places To Go LLC	New Bedford	MA	G	774 202-7756	13438

CARRIERS: Infant, Textile

	CITY	ST	EMP	PHONE	ENTRY #
Summer Infant Inc **(PA)**	Woonsocket	RI	D	401 671-6550	21581
Summer Infant Inc	Woonsocket	RI	G	401 671-6550	21582
Summer Infant (usa) Inc	Woonsocket	RI	C	401 671-6551	21583

CARRYING CASES, WHOLESALE

	CITY	ST	EMP	PHONE	ENTRY #
David King & Co Inc	Boston	MA	G	617 482-6950	8496

CARS: Electric

	CITY	ST	EMP	PHONE	ENTRY #
Flexcar	Cambridge	MA	G	617 995-4231	9479

CASEIN PRDTS

	CITY	ST	EMP	PHONE	ENTRY #
Armor Box Company LLC	Bloomfield	CT	G	860 242-9981	203

CASEMENTS: Aluminum

	CITY	ST	EMP	PHONE	ENTRY #
Cusson Sash Company	Glastonbury	CT	G	860 659-0354	1546
Far Industries Inc	Assonet	MA	F	508 644-3122	7679

CASES, WOOD

	CITY	ST	EMP	PHONE	ENTRY #
W R Hartigan & Son Inc	Burlington	CT	G	860 673-9203	682

CASES: Attache'

	CITY	ST	EMP	PHONE	ENTRY #
Case Concepts Intl LLC **(PA)**	Stamford	CT	F	203 883-8602	4157

CASES: Carrying

	CITY	ST	EMP	PHONE	ENTRY #
Armor Box Company LLC	Bloomfield	CT	G	860 242-9981	203
Calzone Ltd **(PA)**	Bridgeport	CT	E	203 367-5766	394
Fabrique Ltd	Branford	CT	F	203 481-5400	315
A T S Cases Inc	Northborough	MA	G	508 393-9110	14028
Union Bookbinding Company Inc **(PA)**	Fall River	MA	E	508 676-8580	10775
Van & Company Inc	Pawtucket	RI	F	401 722-9829	20908

CASES: Carrying, Clothing & Apparel

	CITY	ST	EMP	PHONE	ENTRY #
Baileyworks Inc	Newmarket	NH	G	603 292-6485	19330

CASES: Jewelry

	CITY	ST	EMP	PHONE	ENTRY #
Fuller Box Co Inc **(PA)**	North Attleboro	MA	D	508 695-2525	13756
Jewel Case Corporation	Providence	RI	B	401 943-1400	21044
Numaco Packaging LLC	East Providence	RI	F	401 438-4952	20436

CASES: Packing, Nailed Or Lock Corner, Wood

	CITY	ST	EMP	PHONE	ENTRY #
Champlin-Packrite Inc	Manchester	CT	E	860 951-9217	1993
Barton Corporation Salisbury	Seabrook	NH	G	603 760-2669	19793

CASES: Plastic

	CITY	ST	EMP	PHONE	ENTRY #
Incase Inc	Holden	MA	G	508 478-6500	11545
Hcp Packaging Usa Inc	Hinsdale	NH	C	603 256-3141	18320
Case Hard	Little Compton	RI	G	401 635-8201	20604

CASES: Sample Cases

	CITY	ST	EMP	PHONE	ENTRY #
Pelican Products Inc	East Longmeadow	MA	G	413 525-3990	10485

CASES: Shipping, Nailed Or Lock Corner, Wood

	CITY	ST	EMP	PHONE	ENTRY #
Manning Brothers Wood Products	Northfield	NH	G	603 286-4896	19405

CASH REGISTER REPAIR SVCS

	CITY	ST	EMP	PHONE	ENTRY #
NCR Corporation	Newton	MA	C	617 558-2000	13617
Dgf Indstrial Innvations Group	Gilford	NH	F	603 528-6591	18185
Hd Supply Construction Supply	West Lebanon	NH	G	603 298-6072	19952

CASH REGISTERS & PARTS

	CITY	ST	EMP	PHONE	ENTRY #
NCR Corporation	Newton	MA	C	617 558-2000	13617

CASINGS: Sheet Metal

	CITY	ST	EMP	PHONE	ENTRY #
Brouillette Hvac & Shtmtl Inc	East Taunton	MA	G	508 822-4800	10511
Churchill Corporation	Melrose	MA	E	781 665-4700	12978

CASINGS: Storage, Missile & Missile Components

	CITY	ST	EMP	PHONE	ENTRY #
Geonautics Manufacturing Inc	Newburyport	MA	E	978 462-7161	13494
Massmicro LLC	Canton	MA	F	781 828-6110	9756

CASKETS & ACCESS

	CITY	ST	EMP	PHONE	ENTRY #
Dignified Endings LLC	East Hartford	CT	D	860 291-0575	1187
Cambium Corp	Athol	MA	F	978 249-7557	7685
Florence Casket Company	Florence	MA	D	413 584-4244	10866
Colony Casket Inc	Providence	RI	G	401 831-7100	20987

CAST STONE: Concrete

	CITY	ST	EMP	PHONE	ENTRY #
Dawn Enterprises LLC	Manchester	CT	G	860 646-8200	1999
Stone Image Custom Concrete	Suffield	CT	G	860 668-2434	4468

CASTERS

	CITY	ST	EMP	PHONE	ENTRY #
Vulcan Industries Inc	East Longmeadow	MA	G	413 525-8846	10502
Caster Crative Photography LLC	Charlestown	RI	G	401 364-3545	20131

CASTINGS GRINDING: For The Trade

	CITY	ST	EMP	PHONE	ENTRY #
A D Grinding	Plainville	CT	F	860 747-6630	3460
JEM Precision Grinding Inc	Glastonbury	CT	G	860 633-0152	1560
Unas Grinding Corporation	East Hartford	CT	E	860 289-1538	1231
Arm Centerless Grinding	Georgetown	MA	G	978 352-2410	11136
Daily Grind	Bridgewater	MA	G	508 279-9952	9070
Form Centerless Grinding Inc	Franklin	MA	F	508 520-0900	11046
Precision Machinists Co Inc	Franklin	MA	F	508 528-2325	11073
Marshall Specialty Grinding	Chelsea	ME	G	207 623-3700	5901
Monadnock Grinding LLC	Fitzwilliam	NH	G	603 585-7275	18151
Grind	Cranston	RI	G	401 223-1212	20235
Precision Cutter Grinding Inc	Hartland	VT	F	802 436-2039	22017

CASTINGS: Aerospace Investment, Ferrous

	CITY	ST	EMP	PHONE	ENTRY #
Doncasters US Hldings 2018 Inc	Groton	CT	F	860 677-1376	1672
Hexcel Corporation	South Windsor	CT	D	925 520-3232	3979
Jl Aerotech Inc	South Windsor	CT	G	860 248-8628	3985
Parts Tool and Die Inc	Agawam	MA	E	413 821-9718	7445
Tecomet Inc	Wilmington	MA	D	978 642-2400	17051
Wyman-Gordon Company **(DH)**	North Grafton	MA	B	508 839-8252	13969
PCC Structurals Groton	Franklin	NH	G	603 286-4301	18162

CASTINGS: Aerospace, Aluminum

	CITY	ST	EMP	PHONE	ENTRY #
Accu-Mill Technologies LLC	Plainville	CT	G	860 747-3921	3462
Aerocess Inc	Berlin	CT	F	860 357-2451	67
Integra-Cast Inc	New Britain	CT	D	860 225-7600	2541
Arcam Cad To Metal Inc	Woburn	MA	F	781 281-1718	17121
Industrial Biomedical Sensors	Waltham	MA	F	781 891-4201	16132
Parts Tool and Die Inc	Agawam	MA	E	413 821-9718	7445
Tecomet Inc	Wilmington	MA	D	978 642-2400	17051
UPS Scs Pratt & Whitney	Londonderry	NH	G	860 565-0353	18744

CASTINGS: Aerospace, Nonferrous, Exc Aluminum

	CITY	ST	EMP	PHONE	ENTRY #
Carrier Manufacturing Inc	New Britain	CT	G	860 223-2264	2517
Consoldted Inds Acqsition Corp	Cheshire	CT	D	203 272-5371	724
Parts Tool and Die Inc	Agawam	MA	E	413 821-9718	7445
Tecomet Inc	Wilmington	MA	D	978 642-2400	17051
Component Technologies Corpora	Barrington	RI	G	401 965-2699	20044

CASTINGS: Aluminum

	CITY	ST	EMP	PHONE	ENTRY #
Us-Malabar Company Inc	Weston	CT	G	203 226-1773	5174
Amesbury Foundry Co	Amesbury	MA	G	978 388-0830	7477
Bulcast LLC	Chestnut Hill	MA	G	617 901-6836	9983
Marlborough Foundry Inc	Marlborough	MA	E	508 485-2848	12791
Supreme Brass & Alum Castings	West Springfield	MA	G	413 737-4433	16555
Taunton Aluminum Foundry Inc	Berkley	MA	G	508 822-4141	8089
Diamond Casting and Mch Co Inc	Hollis	NH	E	603 465-2263	18330
Granite State Casting	Mason	NH	G	603 878-2759	18967
Nu-Cast Inc	Londonderry	NH	C	603 432-1600	18729

CASTINGS: Brass, Bronze & Copper

	CITY	ST	EMP	PHONE	ENTRY #
Kt Acquisition LLC	Worcester	MA	D	508 853-4500	17402
Western Bronze Inc	West Springfield	MA	F	413 737-1319	16564
Paul King Foundry Inc	Johnston	RI	G	401 231-3120	20528

CASTINGS: Brass, NEC, Exc Die

	CITY	ST	EMP	PHONE	ENTRY #
Supreme Brass & Alum Castings	West Springfield	MA	G	413 737-4433	16555

CASTINGS: Bronze, NEC, Exc Die

	CITY	ST	EMP	PHONE	ENTRY #
Amesbury Foundry Co	Amesbury	MA	G	978 388-0830	7477
Atlas Brass & Aluminum Co	Westfield	MA	G	413 732-4604	16668
Mystic Valley Foundry Inc	Somerville	MA	G	617 547-1819	15201
Sincere Specialty Fabrication	Chelsea	MA	G	781 974-9580	9967
Taunton Aluminum Foundry Inc	Berkley	MA	G	508 822-4141	8089
Bronze Craft Corporation	Nashua	NH	D	603 883-7747	19130
Granite State Casting	Mason	NH	G	603 878-2759	18967

CASTINGS: Commercial Investment, Ferrous

	CITY	ST	EMP	PHONE	ENTRY #
Howmet Castings & Services Inc	Winsted	CT	B	860 379-3314	5413
Howmet Corporation	Branford	CT	B	203 481-3451	325
Sturm Ruger & Company Inc **(PA)**	Southport	CT	B	203 259-7843	4099
A Young Casting	Attleboro	MA	F	508 222-8188	7697
Kervick Family Foundation Inc	Worcester	MA	G	508 853-4500	17399
New England Castings LLC	Standish	ME	E	207 642-3029	7063
Leemar Casting Company Inc	Johnston	RI	G	401 276-2844	20517

CASTINGS: Die, Aluminum

	CITY	ST	EMP	PHONE	ENTRY #
Advanced Prcsion Castings Corp	Milford	CT	G	203 736-9452	2237
Arrow Diversified Tooling Inc	Ellington	CT	E	860 872-9072	1329
Custom Metal Crafters Inc	Newington	CT	D	860 953-4210	2857
Atlas Brass & Aluminum Co	Westfield	MA	G	413 732-4604	16668
Atlas Founders Inc	Agawam	MA	F	413 786-4210	7420
Bulcast LLC	Chestnut Hill	MA	G	617 901-6836	9983
Diecast Connections Co Inc	Plymouth	MA	C	413 592-8444	14552
Kingston Aluminum Foundry Inc	Kingston	MA	G	781 585-6631	11959
Mascon Inc	Woburn	MA	E	781 938-5800	17223
Meteor Globl Mfg Solutions Inc	Monson	MA	G	617 733-6506	13209
Mystic Valley Foundry Inc	Somerville	MA	G	617 547-1819	15201
Pace Industries LLC	North Billerica	MA	C	978 667-8400	13852
Connectcut Prcsion Cstings Inc	Claremont	NH	G	603 542-3373	17843
Diamond Casting and Mch Co Inc	Hollis	NH	E	603 465-2263	18330
Hebert Manufacturing Company **(PA)**	Laconia	NH	D	603 524-2065	18567
Hitchiner Manufacturing Co Inc	Milford	NH	D	603 673-1100	19061
Hitchiner Manufacturing Co Inc	Milford	NH	B	603 673-1100	19063
Wyman-Gordon Company	Franklin	NH	E	603 934-6630	18169

CASTINGS: Die, Copper & Copper Alloy

	CITY	ST	EMP	PHONE	ENTRY #
Meteor Globl Mfg Solutions Inc	Monson	MA	G	617 733-6506	13209

CASTINGS: Die, Nonferrous

	CITY	ST	EMP	PHONE	ENTRY #
Custom Metal Crafters Inc	Newington	CT	D	860 953-4210	2857
Integra-Cast Inc	New Britain	CT	D	860 225-7600	2541
Narragansett Screw Co	Winsted	CT	F	860 379-4059	5418
PCC Structurals Groton **(DH)**	Groton	CT	C	860 405-3700	1682
Atlas Founders Inc	Agawam	MA	F	413 786-4210	7420
Medalco Metals Inc **(PA)**	South Hadley	MA	F	413 586-6010	15307
Diamond Casting and Mch Co Inc	Hollis	NH	E	603 465-2263	18330
Watts Regulator Co	Franklin	NH	A	603 934-5110	18166
Fielding Manufacturing Inc	Cranston	RI	E	401 461-0400	20226
Miniature Casting Corporation	Cranston	RI	F	401 463-5090	20264
Rona Incorporated	Warwick	RI	G	401 737-4388	21417
Rvs & Co	Johnston	RI	F	401 231-8200	20539
New England Precision Inc	Randolph	VT	D	800 293-4112	22299

CASTINGS: Die, Zinc

	CITY	ST	EMP	PHONE	ENTRY #
Fall River Tool & Die Co Inc	Fall River	MA	F	508 674-4621	10699
Pace Industries LLC	North Billerica	MA	C	978 667-8400	13852
Fielding Mfg Zinc Diecasting	Cranston	RI	D	401 461-0400	20227
Ridco Casting Co	Pawtucket	RI	D	401 724-0400	20893

CASTINGS: Ductile

	CITY	ST	EMP	PHONE	ENTRY #
G & W Foundry Corp	Millbury	MA	E	508 581-8719	13164
Kadant Inc **(PA)**	Westford	MA	B	978 776-2000	16774

CASTINGS: Gray Iron

	CITY	ST	EMP	PHONE	ENTRY #
Taylor & Fenn Company	Windsor	CT	D	860 219-9393	5372
Henry Perkins Company	Bridgewater	MA	F	508 697-6978	9076
Whitman Castings Inc **(PA)**	Whitman	MA	E	781 447-4417	16930
Millincket Fabrication Mch Inc **(PA)**	Millinocket	ME	E	207 723-9733	6443
Nashua Foundries Inc	Nashua	NH	E	603 882-4811	19213
Cumberland Foundry Co Inc	Cumberland	RI	E	401 658-3300	20317
Fairmount Foundry Inc	Woonsocket	RI	F	401 769-1585	21561

CASTINGS: Lead

	CITY	ST	EMP	PHONE	ENTRY #
Gary Kellner	Westwood	MA	G	781 329-0404	16866

CASTINGS: Machinery, Nonferrous, Exc Die or Aluminum Copper

	CITY	ST	EMP	PHONE	ENTRY #
Accent On Industrial Metal Inc	Springfield	MA	F	413 785-1654	15439

CASTINGS: Precision

	CITY	ST	EMP	PHONE	ENTRY #
B H S Industries Ltd	Wallingford	CT	G	203 284-9764	4708
Sycast Inc	Hartford	CT	G	860 308-2122	1875
Yankee Casting Co Inc	Enfield	CT	D	860 749-6171	1392

	CITY	ST	EMP	PHONE	ENTRY #
Kervick Family Foundation Inc	Worcester	MA	G	508 853-4500	17399
Al CU Met Inc	Londonderry	NH	E	603 432-6220	18674
Providence Casting Inc	North Providence	RI	G	401 231-0860	20773
CASTINGS: Rubber					
Fastcast Consortium Inc	Worcester	MA	C	508 853-4500	17373
CASTINGS: Steel					
Frank Roth Co Inc	Stratford	CT	D	203 377-2155	4413
Silicone Casting Technologies	Middletown	CT	G	860 347-5227	2221
Trident Alloys Inc	Springfield	MA	E	413 737-1477	15518
Wollaston Alloys Inc	Braintree	MA	C	781 848-3333	9051
CASTINGS: Titanium					
Tighitco Inc	Berlin	CT	C	860 828-0298	112
Oerlikon Blzers Cating USA Inc	Agawam	MA	E	413 786-9380	7442
CASTINGS: Zinc					
Castechnologies Inc	Attleboro	MA	F	508 222-2915	7716
Graphicast Inc	Jaffrey	NH	E	603 532-4481	18465
Bayview Marine Inc	Warwick	RI	G	401 737-3111	21333
CATALOG & MAIL-ORDER HOUSES					
Partylite Worldwide LLC **(DH)**	Norwell	MA	C	888 999-5706	14110
Storey Publishing LLC **(HQ)**	North Adams	MA	E	413 346-2100	13685
Noah Publications	Brooklin	ME	G	207 359-2131	5821
Top Kayaker Geo Odyssey Llc	Center Ossipee	NH	G	603 651-1036	17806
J H Breakell & Company Inc	Newport	RI	F	401 849-3522	20667
Koss Industries Inc	Burlington	VT	G	802 863-5004	21791
Stephen McArthur	Barre	VT	G	802 839-0371	21640
Vermont Christmas Company	Milton	VT	G	802 893-1670	22139
CATALOG SALES					
Connecticut Advanced Products	Glastonbury	CT	G	860 659-2260	1545
Renovators Supply Inc	Millers Falls	MA	E	413 423-3300	13181
CATALYSTS: Chemical					
Joshua LLC **(PA)**	New Haven	CT	E	203 624-0080	2699
Menon Laboratories Inc	Somerville	MA	G	339 224-2787	15198
CATAPULTS					
Entwistle Company **(HQ)**	Hudson	MA	C	508 481-4000	11772
CATERERS					
Bakery To Go Inc	Boston	MA	G	617 482-1015	8388
Spinelli Ravioli Mfg Co Inc	Boston	MA	E	617 567-1992	8859
Delicate Decadence LLC	Barre	VT	G	802 479-7948	21612
New England Smoked Seafood	Rutland	VT	G	802 773-4628	22346
CAULKING COMPOUNDS					
Ensign-Bickford Industries Inc	Weatogue	CT	C	860 843-2000	5042
CEILING SYSTEMS: Luminous, Commercial					
C Cowles & Company **(PA)**	North Haven	CT	D	203 865-3117	3012
Asd Lighting Corp	Canton	MA	F	781 739-3977	9717
Genlyte Group Incorporated	Andover	MA	A	781 418-7900	7550
Genlyte Thomas Group LLC	Andover	MA	C	978 659-3732	7551
CELLULOSE DERIVATIVE MATERIALS					
Macgregor Bay Corporation	Belchertown	MA	E	413 283-8747	8025
CEMENT, EXC LINOLEUM & TILE					
Babcock & King Incorporated **(PA)**	Fairfield	CT	G	203 336-7989	1415
CEMENT: High Temperature, Refractory, Nonclay					
Coleman Manufacturing Co Inc	Everett	MA	G	617 389-0380	10607
LMI Liquidation Corporation	Lynn	MA	G	781 593-2561	12521
CEMENT: Hydraulic					
Beard Concrete Co Derby Inc	Derby	CT	F	203 735-4641	1068
Lafarge North America Inc	New Haven	CT	G	203 468-6068	2704
McInnis USA Inc	Stamford	CT	E	203 890-9950	4246
Dragon Products Company LLC	Thomaston	ME	C	207 594-5555	7083
Conproco Corp	Bow	NH	G	603 743-5800	17710
CEMENT: Portland					
Andrews Holdings Inc	Ayer	MA	F	978 772-4444	7910
Dragon Products Company LLC **(DH)**	South Portland	ME	E	207 774-6355	7022
Lehigh Cement Company	Providence	RI	G	800 833-4157	21051
CEMETERY MEMORIAL DEALERS					
American Stonecrafters Inc	Wallingford	CT	G	203 514-9725	4698
Pistritto Marble Imports Inc	Hartford	CT	G	860 296-5263	1857
Santo C De Spirt Marble & Gran	Agawam	MA	G	413 786-7073	7450
Frederick Wieninger Monuments	Milbridge	ME	G	207 546-2356	6432
Ripano Stoneworks Ltd	Nashua	NH	E	603 886-6655	19254
Stone Vault Co	Newport	NH	G	603 863-2720	19359
Kinfolk Memorials Inc	East Barre	VT	G	802 479-1423	21912
Swenson Granite Company LLC	Barre	VT	E	802 476-7021	21641
CERAMIC FIBER					
International Crmic Engrg Corp **(PA)**	Worcester	MA	E	508 853-4700	17394
Ceramco Inc	Center Conway	NH	E	603 447-2090	17793
CESSPOOL CLEANING SVCS					
Bayview Marine Inc	Warwick	RI	G	401 737-3111	21333
CHAIN: Welded, Made From Purchased Wire					
St Pierre Manufacturing Corp	Worcester	MA	E	508 853-8010	17479
CHAIN: Wire					
Hale Brothers Inc	Seabrook	NH	G	603 474-2511	19802
CHAINS: Forged					
Jackman Equipment	Norridgewock	ME	G	207 858-0690	6497
CHAMBERS & CAISSONS					
Herb Chambers Brookline Inc	Brookline	MA	C	617 278-3920	9202
CHANGE MAKING MACHINES					
Crane Payment Solutions Inc **(HQ)**	Bedford	NH	E	603 685-6999	17637
CHARCOAL: Activated					
Carbtrol Corporation	Stratford	CT	E	203 337-4340	4403
CHASSIS: Motor Vehicle					
Chassis Dynamics Inc	Oxford	CT	G	203 262-6272	3396
Prfrred Lancaster Partners LLC	Boston	MA	C	717 299-0782	8795
Rod Jakes Shop LLC	Bridgton	ME	G	207 595-0677	5810
Costello/April Design Inc	Dover	NH	E	603 749-6755	18015
CHEESE WHOLESALERS					
Mozzicato Fmly Investments LLC	Wethersfield	CT	G	860 296-0426	5259
Ndr Liuzzi Inc	Hamden	CT	E	203 287-8477	1774
Agri-Mark Inc	Hingham	MA	G	781 740-0090	11489
Albert Capone **(PA)**	Somerville	MA	G	617 629-2296	15151
Sunrise Foods Incorporated	Brentwood	NH	F	603 772-4420	17760
Cabot Creamery Cooperative Inc	Waitsfield	VT	B	978 552-5500	22562
CHEMICAL ELEMENTS					
Designing Element	Norwalk	CT	G	203 849-3076	3134
Element One LLC	Norwalk	CT	G	203 344-1553	3149
Fitness Elemnet	New Britain	CT	G	860 670-2855	2534
Meb Enterprises Inc	Meriden	CT	G	203 599-0273	2102
Perennial Elements LLC	Mystic	CT	G	860 536-8593	2448
Distinct Element	Mattapan	MA	G	617 322-3979	12883
Element Brainerd LLC	Allston	MA	G	617 487-8114	7465
Element Precision LLC	Southbridge	MA	G	774 318-1777	15381
Elements East LLC	Franklin	MA	G	508 528-1902	11040
Four Elements Salon & Spa	Westport	MA	G	508 672-3111	16839
Mindful Elements LLC	Shrewsbury	MA	G	508 845-2833	15123
Element All Stars	Lewiston	ME	G	207 576-6931	6286
Elemental Energies	Wells	ME	G	207 641-5070	7162
All Natures Elements	Fremont	NH	G	603 427-3535	18173
Element Hanover - Lebanon	Lebanon	NH	G	603 646-8108	18621
Element Metal Arts	North Kingstown	RI	G	631 896-9683	20708
Element Marketing	Waitsfield	VT	G	802 448-4252	22566
Elemental Development LLC	Hinesburg	VT	G	802 318-1041	22023
CHEMICAL INDICATORS					
Bioenergy International LLC	Quincy	MA	D	617 657-5200	14616
Solvent Kleene Inc	Peabody	MA	F	978 531-2279	14370
CHEMICAL PROCESSING MACHINERY & EQPT					
Lamor USA Corporation	Shelton	CT	G	203 888-7700	3823
Artisan Industries Inc	Stoughton	MA	D	781 893-6800	15581
Celeros Inc	Newton	MA	E	248 478-2800	13576
Hosokawa Micron International	Northborough	MA	F	508 655-1123	14037
Jgp Enterprises Inc	Andover	MA	E	978 691-2737	7559
Sturtevant Inc **(PA)**	Hanover	MA	E	781 829-6501	11355
Ultrasonic Systems Inc	Haverhill	MA	E	978 521-0095	11481
White Mountain Imaging	Concord	NH	F	603 228-2630	17940
Environmental Ctrl Systems Inc	East Providence	RI	F	401 437-8612	20410
CHEMICAL SPLYS FOR FOUNDRIES					
Cabot Specialty Chemicals Inc **(HQ)**	Boston	MA	G	617 345-0100	8453
CHEMICAL: Sodm Compnds/Salts, Inorg, Exc Rfnd Sodm Chloride					
Tronox Incorporated **(DH)**	Stamford	CT	C	203 705-3800	4350
Chemtrade Chemicals US LLC	Hampton	NH	F	603 926-0191	18261
International Dioxcide Inc	North Kingstown	RI	E	401 295-8800	20718
CHEMICALS & ALLIED PRDTS WHOLESALERS, NEC					
Cloverdale Inc	West Cornwall	CT	G	860 672-0216	5046
Hydrochemical Techniques Inc	Hartford	CT	G	860 527-6350	1836
Miyoshi America Inc **(HQ)**	Dayville	CT	D	860 779-3990	1046
Miyoshi America Inc	Dayville	CT	F	860 779-3990	1047
Miyoshi America Inc	Dayville	CT	G	860 779-3990	1048
Vanderbilt Chemicals LLC **(HQ)**	Norwalk	CT	D	203 295-2141	3265
Coleman Manufacturing Co Inc	Everett	MA	G	617 389-0380	10607
Fisher Scientific Intl LLC **(HQ)**	Waltham	MA	C	781 622-1000	16107
Guardian Indus Pdts Inc Mass	Norfolk	MA	G	508 384-0060	13660
Lubrizol Global Management	Wilmington	MA	D	978 642-5051	17019
Savin Products Company Inc	Randolph	MA	F	781 961-2743	14697
Starchem Inc **(PA)**	Ware	MA	G	413 967-8700	16237
Gac Chemical Corporation **(PA)**	Searsport	ME	D	207 548-2525	6951
Medical Isotopes Inc	Pelham	NH	G	603 635-2255	19439
Electrolizing Inc	Providence	RI	E	401 861-5900	21004
Seventh Generation Inc **(DH)**	Burlington	VT	C	802 658-3773	21808
CHEMICALS & ALLIED PRDTS, WHOL: Chemicals, Swimming Pool/Spa					
Accu-Care Supply Inc	Rumford	RI	E	401 438-7110	21179
CHEMICALS & ALLIED PRDTS, WHOLESALE: Acids					
US Chemicals Inc	New Canaan	CT	G	203 655-8878	2620

PRODUCT

CHEMICALS & ALLIED PRDTS, WHOLESALE: Aerosols

	CITY	ST	EMP	PHONE	ENTRY #
Shield Packaging Co Inc	Dudley	MA	D	508 949-0900	10384

CHEMICALS & ALLIED PRDTS, WHOLESALE: Chemicals, Indl

	CITY	ST	EMP	PHONE	ENTRY #
Pressure Techniques Intl Corp	Haverhill	MA	G	978 686-2211	11460

CHEMICALS & ALLIED PRDTS, WHOLESALE: Detergent/Soap

	CITY	ST	EMP	PHONE	ENTRY #
MD Stetson Company Inc	Randolph	MA	E	781 986-6161	14689

CHEMICALS & ALLIED PRDTS, WHOLESALE: Essential Oils

	CITY	ST	EMP	PHONE	ENTRY #
Cape Ann Olive Oil Company	Gloucester	MA	G	978 281-1061	11170

CHEMICALS & ALLIED PRDTS, WHOLESALE: Plastics Film

	CITY	ST	EMP	PHONE	ENTRY #
Orafol Americas Inc	Avon	CT	C	860 676-7100	41
Web Industries Hartford Inc **(HQ)**	Dayville	CT	E	860 779-3197	1055
Epv Plastics Corporation	Oxford	MA	G	508 987-2595	14259
Web Industries Inc **(PA)**	Marlborough	MA	G	508 898-2988	12848

CHEMICALS & ALLIED PRDTS, WHOLESALE: Plastics Materials, NEC

	CITY	ST	EMP	PHONE	ENTRY #
Edco Industries Inc	Bridgeport	CT	F	203 333-8982	410

CHEMICALS & ALLIED PRDTS, WHOLESALE: Plastics Prdts, NEC

	CITY	ST	EMP	PHONE	ENTRY #
Brighton & Hove Mold Ltd	Oxford	CT	G	203 264-3013	3392
Thornton and Company Inc	Southington	CT	F	860 628-6771	4086
Seventh Generation Inc **(DH)**	Burlington	VT	C	802 658-3773	21808

CHEMICALS & ALLIED PRDTS, WHOLESALE: Plastics Sheets & Rods

	CITY	ST	EMP	PHONE	ENTRY #
Morris Transparent Box Co	East Providence	RI	E	401 438-6116	20433

CHEMICALS & ALLIED PRDTS, WHOLESALE: Resins

	CITY	ST	EMP	PHONE	ENTRY #
Neu Spclty Engineered Mtls LLC	North Haven	CT	F	203 239-9629	3043
DSM Coating Resins Inc	Wilmington	MA	C	800 458-0014	16996

CHEMICALS & ALLIED PRDTS, WHOLESALE: Resins, Plastics

	CITY	ST	EMP	PHONE	ENTRY #
Polymer Corporation **(HQ)**	Rockland	MA	D	781 871-4606	14819
Konneco International LLC	North Smithfield	RI	G	401 767-3690	20788

CHEMICALS & ALLIED PRDTS, WHOLESALE: Rubber, Synthetic

	CITY	ST	EMP	PHONE	ENTRY #
Auburn Manufacturing Company	Middletown	CT	E	860 346-6677	2173

CHEMICALS & ALLIED PRDTS, WHOLESALE: Sealants

	CITY	ST	EMP	PHONE	ENTRY #
Redi-Mix Services Incorporated	Taunton	MA	G	508 823-0771	15778

CHEMICALS & ALLIED PRDTS, WHOLESALE: Spec Clean/Sanitation

	CITY	ST	EMP	PHONE	ENTRY #
A W Chesterton Company **(PA)**	Groveland	MA	E	781 438-7000	11298

CHEMICALS & ALLIED PRDTS, WHOLESALE: Syn Resin, Rub/Plastic

	CITY	ST	EMP	PHONE	ENTRY #
Clariant Plas Coatings USA LLC	Lewiston	ME	E	207 784-0733	6280
QST Inc	Saint Albans	VT	E	802 524-7704	22377

CHEMICALS: Agricultural

	CITY	ST	EMP	PHONE	ENTRY #
Lanxess Solutions US Inc	Naugatuck	CT	D	203 723-2237	2483
Macdermid AG Solutions Inc	Waterbury	CT	F	203 575-5727	4903
P2 Science Inc	Woodbridge	CT	G	203 821-7457	5475
Wilt Pruf Products Inc	Essex	CT	G	860 767-7033	1408
Monsanto Company	Cambridge	MA	D	617 551-7200	9570
Shield Packaging Co Inc	Dudley	MA	D	508 949-0900	10384
Coast Maine Organic Pdts Inc **(PA)**	Portland	ME	F	207 879-0002	6640
Sunrise Composting	Addison	ME	G	207 483-4081	5511

CHEMICALS: Aluminum Sulfate

	CITY	ST	EMP	PHONE	ENTRY #
Gac Chemical Corporation **(PA)**	Searsport	ME	D	207 548-2525	6951
General Alum New England Corp	Searsport	ME	D	207 548-2525	6952

CHEMICALS: Ammonium Compounds, Exc Fertilizers, NEC

	CITY	ST	EMP	PHONE	ENTRY #
Twin Rivers Tech Mfg Corp	Quincy	MA	G	888 929-8780	14664

CHEMICALS: Calcium & Calcium Compounds

	CITY	ST	EMP	PHONE	ENTRY #
Specialty Minerals Inc	Jay	ME	F	207 897-4492	6221
Omya Inc	Florence	VT	E	802 459-3311	21991
Omya Inc	Proctor	VT	F	802 459-3311	22287

CHEMICALS: Caustic Potash & Potassium Hydroxide

	CITY	ST	EMP	PHONE	ENTRY #
Driscolls Restaurant	Mansfield	MA	F	508 261-1574	12629

CHEMICALS: Fire Retardant

	CITY	ST	EMP	PHONE	ENTRY #
Command Chemical Corporation	Fairfield	CT	G	203 319-1857	1422
Great Lakes Chemical Corp **(DH)**	Shelton	CT	E	203 573-2000	3806
Lanxess Solutions US Inc **(DH)**	Shelton	CT	E	203 573-2000	3824
Avtec Industries Inc	Wellesley	MA	G	978 562-2300	16362
Westford Chemical Corporation	Westford	MA	G	978 392-0689	16800

CHEMICALS: Fuel Tank Or Engine Cleaning

	CITY	ST	EMP	PHONE	ENTRY #
Ouellette Sand & Gravel Inc	South China	ME	G	207 445-4131	7006

CHEMICALS: High Purity Grade, Organic

	CITY	ST	EMP	PHONE	ENTRY #
Bi Medical LLC	Coventry	RI	G	866 246-3301	20139

CHEMICALS: High Purity, Refined From Technical Grade

	CITY	ST	EMP	PHONE	ENTRY #
Americanbio Inc	Canton	MA	E	508 655-4336	9713
Concept Chemicals Inc	Hingham	MA	F	781 740-0711	11497
Monahan Associates	Portland	ME	G	207 771-0900	6694

CHEMICALS: Hydrogen Peroxide

	CITY	ST	EMP	PHONE	ENTRY #
Peroxygen Systems Inc	Lowell	MA	G	248 835-9026	12420

CHEMICALS: Inorganic, NEC

	CITY	ST	EMP	PHONE	ENTRY #
CCL Industries Corporation **(DH)**	Shelton	CT	D	203 926-1253	3785
Chromatics Inc	Bethel	CT	F	203 743-6868	137
Elements LLC	West Hartford	CT	G	860 231-8011	5069
Greek Elements LLC	New Canaan	CT	G	203 594-2022	2598
H Krevit and Company Inc	New Haven	CT	E	203 772-3350	2694
Innophase Corp	Westbrook	CT	G	860 399-2269	5156
Kwant Elements Intl LLC	Cos Cob	CT	G	203 625-5553	827
Solidification Pdts Intl Inc	Northford	CT	G	203 484-9494	3092
Solidification Products Intl	Northford	CT	F	203 484-9494	3093
Specialty Minerals Inc	Canaan	CT	C	860 824-5435	690
Vanderbilt Chemicals LLC **(HQ)**	Norwalk	CT	D	203 295-2141	3265
Vanderbilt Chemicals LLC	Bethel	CT	E	203 744-3900	189
A W Chesterton Company	Groveland	MA	B	781 438-7000	11299
Bruker Detection Corporation	Billerica	MA	F	978 663-3660	8225
Div Cabot Road LLC	Medford	MA	F	781 396-3122	12931
Dow Chemical Company	Marlborough	MA	E	508 229-7676	12750
E I Du Pont De Nemours & Co	North Billerica	MA	E	978 663-7113	13811
Element LLC	West Dennis	MA	G	508 394-3032	16475
Fiberlock Technologies Inc	Andover	MA	F	978 623-9987	7548
Gcp Applied Technologies Inc **(PA)**	Cambridge	MA	B	617 876-1400	9486
Hgi Incorporated	Amesbury	MA	G	978 388-2808	7490
Holland Company Inc	Adams	MA	E	413 743-1292	7413
MD Stetson Company Inc	Randolph	MA	E	781 986-6161	14689
Metallium Inc	Watertown	MA	G	508 728-9074	16301
Metalor USA Refining Corp **(DH)**	North Attleboro	MA	C	508 699-8800	13764
Omnova Solutions Inc	Fitchburg	MA	E	978 342-5831	10845
Qsa Global Inc **(HQ)**	Burlington	MA	D	781 272-2000	9325
Rohm Haas Electronic Mtls LLC **(DH)**	Marlborough	MA	A	508 481-7950	12820
S & T Global Inc	Woburn	MA	F	781 376-1774	17287
Saint-Gobain Ceramics Plas Inc	Worcester	MA	G	508 795-5000	17466
Strem Chemicals Incorporated	Newburyport	MA	D	978 499-1600	13537
Sud-Chemie Protech Inc	Needham Heights	MA	E	781 444-5188	13345
Transene Company Inc	Danvers	MA	F	978 777-7860	10265
Trelleborg Offshore Boston Inc	Randolph	MA	D	774 719-1400	14699
Union Etchants International	Danvers	MA	G	978 777-7860	10270
JM Huber Corporation	Easton	ME	C	207 488-2051	5990
Plasmine Technology Inc	Portland	ME	G	207 797-5009	6710
Hampshire Chemical Corp **(DH)**	Nashua	NH	E	603 888-2320	19176
Medical Isotopes Inc	Pelham	NH	G	603 635-2255	19439
Pure Element	Derry	NH	G	603 235-4373	17995
Saint-Gobain Ceramics Plas Inc	Milford	NH	D	603 673-5831	19075
Z-Tech LLC	Bow	NH	E	603 228-1305	17738
Cal Chemical Corporation	Coventry	RI	E	401 821-0320	20140
Prosys Finishing Tech Inc	Cranston	RI	G	401 781-1011	20275
Matrixchem Inc	Cambridgeport	VT	G	347 727-6886	21824
O M Y A Inc	Proctor	VT	G	802 499-8131	22286

CHEMICALS: Isotopes, Radioactive

	CITY	ST	EMP	PHONE	ENTRY #
Alphamed Incorporated	Wrentham	MA	G	774 571-9415	17514

CHEMICALS: Medicinal

	CITY	ST	EMP	PHONE	ENTRY #
Nzymsys Inc	Manchester	CT	G	877 729-4190	2028
Anexis LLC	Beverly	MA	G	978 921-6293	8100
Flo Chemical Corp	Ashburnham	MA	G	978 827-5101	7644
Fulcrum Thrptics Scrities Corp	Cambridge	MA	G	617 651-8851	9483
Johnson Matthey Phrm Mtls Inc	North Andover	MA	E	978 784-5000	13713

CHEMICALS: Medicinal, Organic, Uncompounded, Bulk

	CITY	ST	EMP	PHONE	ENTRY #
Corden Pharma Intl Inc	Braintree	MA	G	781 305-3332	8996

CHEMICALS: Metal Compounds Or Salts, Inorganic, NEC

	CITY	ST	EMP	PHONE	ENTRY #
W R Grace & Co	Lexington	MA	B	617 876-1400	12283

CHEMICALS: NEC

	CITY	ST	EMP	PHONE	ENTRY #
All Power Manufacturing Co **(HQ)**	Oxford	CT	C	562 802-2640	3389
Armored Autogroup Parent Inc **(DH)**	Danbury	CT	G	203 205-2900	875
Brand-Nu Laboratories Inc **(PA)**	Meriden	CT	E	203 235-7989	2080
Chemotex Protective Coatings **(PA)**	Durham	CT	F	860 349-0144	1088
Chessco Industries Inc **(PA)**	Westport	CT	E	203 255-2804	5183
Cytec Industries Inc	Stamford	CT	D	203 321-2200	4183
Element Solutions Inc	Waterbury	CT	E	203 575-5850	4870
Five Star Products Inc	Shelton	CT	E	203 336-7900	3802
Flottec International Sls Corp	Westport	CT	G	973 588-4717	5195
Henkel of America Inc **(HQ)**	Rocky Hill	CT	B	860 571-5100	3715
Henkel US Operations Corp **(DH)**	Rocky Hill	CT	B	860 571-5100	3716
Intersurface Dynamics Inc	Bethel	CT	F	203 778-9995	161
Lonza Wood Protection	Norwalk	CT	G	203 229-2900	3186
Macdermid Acumen Inc	Waterbury	CT	G	203 575-5700	4902
Macdermid Enthone Inc **(HQ)**	West Haven	CT	C	203 934-8611	5132
Macdermid Overseas Asia Ltd **(HQ)**	Waterbury	CT	G	203 575-5799	4906
Macdermid Printing Solutions	Waterbury	CT	G	203 575-5727	4907
OMI International Corporation	West Haven	CT	G	203 575-5727	5138
Permatex Inc **(PA)**	Hartford	CT	E	860 543-7500	1856
Purification Technologies LLC **(DH)**	Chester	CT	F	860 526-7801	774
REM Chemicals Inc **(PA)**	Southington	CT	F	860 621-6755	4074
W Canning Inc	Waterbury	CT	G	203 575-5727	4971
A W Chesterton Company	Groveland	MA	B	781 438-7000	11299
Adaptive Surface Tech Inc	Cambridge	MA	G	617 360-7080	9373
Alden Medical LLC **(PA)**	West Springfield	MA	G	413 747-9717	16507
Amastan Technologies Inc	North Andover	MA	F	978 258-1645	13689
Arrakis Therapeutics Inc	Waltham	MA	G	617 913-0348	16037
Ashland LLC	Assonet	MA	E	508 235-7164	7676
Baker Petrolite LLC	Braintree	MA	C	781 849-9699	8989
Barclay Water Management Inc	Newton	MA	D	617 926-3400	13565
Biosolve Company	Dracut	MA	G	781 482-7900	10354

COMPANY	CITY	ST	EMP	PHONE	ENTRY #
Bolger & OHearn Inc	Fall River	MA	E	508 676-1518	10670
Cabot Corporation	Billerica	MA	E	978 671-4000	8230
Cold Chain Technologies Inc **(PA)**	Franklin	MA	D	508 429-1395	11030
Conseal International Inc	Norwood	MA	G	781 278-0010	14142
Creative Materials Inc	Ayer	MA	F	978 391-4700	7916
Dropwise Technologies Corp	Cambridge	MA	G	617 945-5180	9457
Emco Services Inc	Fall River	MA	G	508 674-5504	10688
Gcp Applied Technologies Inc **(PA)**	Cambridge	MA	B	617 876-1400	9486
Holland Company Inc	Adams	MA	E	413 743-1292	7413
Katahdin Industries Inc **(PA)**	Hudson	MA	E	781 329-1420	11781
Kayaku Advanced Materials Inc **(PA)**	Westborough	MA	E	617 965-5511	16629
Kayaku Advanced Materials Inc	Newton	MA	F	617 965-5511	13607
Key Polymer Corporation	Lawrence	MA	E	978 683-9411	12042
Lubrizol Global Management	Wilmington	MA	D	978 642-5051	17019
MD Chemicals LLC	Holliston	MA	G	508 314-9664	11584
MD Stetson Company Inc	Randolph	MA	E	781 986-6161	14689
Mexichem Spcalty Compounds Inc **(HQ)**	Leominster	MA	C	978 537-8071	12166
Rectorseal Corporation	Fall River	MA	G	508 673-7561	10755
Terecon Corp **(PA)**	Worcester	MA	G	508 791-1875	17487
Terraverdae Bioworks Inc	Beverly	MA	G	978 712-0220	8189
Transene Company Inc	Danvers	MA	F	978 777-7860	10265
FMC Corporation	Rockland	ME	C	207 594-3200	6795
Diversified Enterprises-ADT	Claremont	NH	G	603 543-0038	17847
Hampshire Chemical Corp **(DH)**	Nashua	NH	E	603 888-2320	19176
Performance Chemicals LLC	Franklin	NH	F	603 228-1200	18163
Aspen Aerogels RI LLC	East Providence	RI	F	401 432-2612	20389
Cranston Print Works Company **(PA)**	Cranston	RI	E	401 943-4800	20202
Dryvit Holdings Inc **(DH)**	Providence	RI	G	401 822-4100	20998
Dryvit Systems Inc **(DH)**	West Warwick	RI	D	401 822-4100	21491
International Dioxcide Inc	North Kingstown	RI	E	401 295-8800	20718

CHEMICALS: Organic, NEC

COMPANY	CITY	ST	EMP	PHONE	ENTRY #
Brian Safa	Cheshire	CT	G	203 271-3499	716
Dymax Corporation	Torrington	CT	G	860 626-7006	4575
Dymax Materials Inc **(HQ)**	Torrington	CT	G	860 482-1010	4576
Dymax Oligomers & Coatings	Torrington	CT	F	860 626-7006	4577
Greenleaf Bfuels New Haven LLC	New Haven	CT	F	203 672-9028	2692
H Krevit and Company Inc	New Haven	CT	E	203 772-3350	2694
Hajan LLC	New Britain	CT	G	860 223-2005	2538
Hampford Research Inc **(PA)**	Stratford	CT	E	203 375-1137	4417
Lanxess Solutions US Inc **(DH)**	Shelton	CT	E	203 573-2000	3824
Nalas Engineering Services	Norwich	CT	D	860 861-3691	3286
Sanco Energy	Fairfield	CT	F	203 259-5914	1454
Vanderbilt Chemicals LLC **(HQ)**	Norwalk	CT	D	203 295-2141	3265
Vanderbilt Chemicals LLC	Bethel	CT	E	203 744-3900	189
C5bio	Cambridge	MA	G	617 955-4626	9424
Cambridge Isotope Labs Inc **(DH)**	Tewksbury	MA	D	978 749-8000	15810
Continuus Pharmaceuticals Inc	Woburn	MA	F	781 281-0226	17153
Epoxy Technology Inc **(PA)**	Billerica	MA	E	978 667-3805	8248
Kalion Inc	Milton	MA	G	617 698-2113	13193
Liquiglide Inc	Cambridge	MA	E	617 901-0700	9538
Myriant Lake Providence Inc	Quincy	MA	E	617 657-5200	14641
Nutrasweet Company	Waltham	MA	E	706 303-5600	16163
Pttgc Innovation America Corp **(HQ)**	Woburn	MA	E	617 657-5234	17271
Purposeenergy Inc **(PA)**	Woburn	MA	G	617 202-9156	17274
Rohm Haas Electronic Mtls LLC	Marlborough	MA	E	978 689-1503	12821
Rohm Haas Electronic Mtls LLC **(DH)**	Marlborough	MA	A	508 481-7950	12820
Stabilizing Technologies LLC	Hubbardston	MA	G	978 928-4142	11746
World Asset Management LLC	Boston	MA	F	617 889-7300	8935
World Energy Biox Biofuels LLC **(PA)**	Boston	MA	F	617 889-7300	8936
Yield10 Bioscience Inc **(PA)**	Woburn	MA	D	617 583-1700	17326
FMC Corporation	Rockland	ME	C	207 594-3200	6795
Inland Technologies	Portland	ME	G	207 761-6951	6674
Stored Solar J&We LLC	Jonesboro	ME	E	207 434-6500	6225
Americ An Novelty Inc	Seabrook	NH	G	401 785-9850	19792
Hampshire Chemical Corp **(DH)**	Nashua	NH	E	603 888-2320	19176
Medical Isotopes Inc	Pelham	NH	G	603 635-2255	19439
Z-Tech LLC	Bow	NH	E	603 228-1305	17738
Cal Chemical Corporation	Coventry	RI	E	401 821-0320	20140
Epoxies Inc	Cranston	RI	F	401 946-5564	20219
Fri Resins Holding Company	Cranston	RI	F	401 946-5564	20228
C E Bradley Laboratories **(PA)**	Brattleboro	VT	E	802 257-1122	21722

CHEMICALS: Reagent Grade, Refined From Technical Grade

COMPANY	CITY	ST	EMP	PHONE	ENTRY #
Instrumentation Laboratory Co **(DH)**	Bedford	MA	A	781 861-0710	7982
Magellan Diagnostics Inc **(HQ)**	Chelmsford	MA	D	978 250-7000	9915
Thermal Fluids Inc	South Easton	MA	G	508 238-9660	15293
Twin Rivers Tech Holdings Inc	Quincy	MA	C	617 472-9200	14662

CHEMICALS: Silica Compounds

COMPANY	CITY	ST	EMP	PHONE	ENTRY #
Nyacol Nano Technologies Inc	Ashland	MA	E	508 881-2220	7665

CHEMICALS: Silica Gel

COMPANY	CITY	ST	EMP	PHONE	ENTRY #
Jordi Labs LLC	Mansfield	MA	E	508 719-8543	12639

CHEMICALS: Silica, Amorphous

COMPANY	CITY	ST	EMP	PHONE	ENTRY #
Cabot Corporation **(PA)**	Boston	MA	C	617 345-0100	8452
Cabot Corporation	Haverhill	MA	C	978 556-8400	11413

CHEMICALS: Silver Compounds Or Salts, Inorganic

COMPANY	CITY	ST	EMP	PHONE	ENTRY #
Arzol Corp	Keene	NH	G	603 352-5242	18493

CHEMICALS: Sodium Bicarbonate

COMPANY	CITY	ST	EMP	PHONE	ENTRY #
Genesis Alkali LLC	Stamford	CT	D	215 299-6773	4198

CHEMICALS: Sulfur, Incl Rcvrd/Refined, Fm Sour Natural Gas

COMPANY	CITY	ST	EMP	PHONE	ENTRY #
Tiger-Sul Products LLC	Shelton	CT	E	251 202-3850	3880

CHEMICALS: Water Treatment

COMPANY	CITY	ST	EMP	PHONE	ENTRY #
Globe Environmental Corp	Branford	CT	F	203 481-5586	320
Gotham Chemical Company Inc	Norwalk	CT	D	203 854-6644	3163
Suez Wts Services Usa Inc	East Hartford	CT	E	860 291-9660	1225
Duraflow LLC	Tewksbury	MA	F	978 851-7439	15815
Ecochlor Inc	Maynard	MA	G	978 298-1463	12898
Solenis LLC	Chicopee	MA	E	413 536-6426	10061
Town of Burlington	Burlington	MA	G	781 270-1680	9349
Aquarion Water Company	Westerly	RI	G	401 596-2847	21516
Atlantic Water Management	Coventry	RI	G	401 397-8200	20137
Bardon Industries Inc	East Greenwich	RI	F	401 884-1814	20353
Burrillville Town of Inc	Oakland	RI	G	401 568-6296	20798
Everett M Windover Inc	Colchester	VT	E	802 865-0000	21863

CHEWING GUM

COMPANY	CITY	ST	EMP	PHONE	ENTRY #
Verve Inc	Providence	RI	G	401 351-6415	21149

CHICKEN SLAUGHTERING & PROCESSING

COMPANY	CITY	ST	EMP	PHONE	ENTRY #
Advancepierre Foods Inc	Portland	ME	E	207 541-2800	6610

CHILDREN'S & INFANTS' CLOTHING STORES

COMPANY	CITY	ST	EMP	PHONE	ENTRY #
Chuck Roast Equipment Inc **(PA)**	Conway	NH	E	603 447-5492	17951

CHIMNEYS & FITTINGS

COMPANY	CITY	ST	EMP	PHONE	ENTRY #
North American Supaflu Systems	Scarborough	ME	F	207 883-1155	6935

CHINA & GLASS REPAIR SVCS

COMPANY	CITY	ST	EMP	PHONE	ENTRY #
Designer Stained Glass	Acushnet	MA	G	508 763-3255	7401

CHINA COOKWARE

COMPANY	CITY	ST	EMP	PHONE	ENTRY #
International Event Products	Stoughton	MA	G	781 341-0929	15598
Butternuts Good Dishes Inc	Wolfeboro	NH	G	603 569-6869	20016

CHIPPER MILL

COMPANY	CITY	ST	EMP	PHONE	ENTRY #
Carrier Chipping Inc	Skowhegan	ME	F	207 858-4277	6971
Jordan Family Chipping Inc	Kezar Falls	ME	G	207 625-8890	6249
Robert W Libby	Porter	ME	G	207 625-8285	6604

CHIROPRACTORS' OFFICES

COMPANY	CITY	ST	EMP	PHONE	ENTRY #
Respond Systems	Branford	CT	F	203 481-2810	341

CHLORINE

COMPANY	CITY	ST	EMP	PHONE	ENTRY #
Kuehne New Haven LLC	New Haven	CT	E	203 508-6703	2703

CHOCOLATE, EXC CANDY FROM BEANS: Chips, Powder, Block, Syrup

COMPANY	CITY	ST	EMP	PHONE	ENTRY #
Divine Treasure	Manchester	CT	G	860 643-2552	2001
Mantrose-Haeuser Co Inc **(HQ)**	Westport	CT	E	203 454-1800	5212
Thompson Brands LLC	Meriden	CT	D	203 235-2541	2141
Cambridge Brands Mfg Inc	Cambridge	MA	C	617 491-2500	9425
Dorothy Coxs Candies Inc	Wareham	MA	E	774 678-0654	16245
Gowell Candy Shop Inc	Brockton	MA	G	508 583-2521	9152
Hilliards House Candy Inc **(PA)**	North Easton	MA	D	508 238-6231	13947
Phillips Candy House Inc	Boston	MA	E	617 282-2090	8778
Russos Inc	Saugus	MA	F	781 233-1737	14995
Samarc Inc	Boston	MA	G	617 924-3884	8837
Sweethearts Candy Co LLC	Revere	MA	B	781 485-4500	14776
Winfreys Olde English Fdge Inc **(PA)**	Rowley	MA	F	978 948-7448	14868
Bixby & Co LLC	Rockland	ME	G	207 691-1778	6785
Harbor Candy Shop Inc	Ogunquit	ME	E	207 646-8078	6537
Lady Ann Candies	Warwick	RI	E	401 738-4321	21384
Birnn Chocolates Vermont Inc	South Burlington	VT	F	802 860-1047	22438
Sentar Inc	South Burlington	VT	E	802 861-6004	22465
Sunny Sky Products LLC	South Burlington	VT	E	802 861-6004	22469
Vermont Nut Free Choclat Inc	Colchester	VT	F	802 372-4654	21886

CHOCOLATE, EXC CANDY FROM PURCH CHOC: Chips, Powder, Block

COMPANY	CITY	ST	EMP	PHONE	ENTRY #
Chip In A Bottle LLC	New Haven	CT	G	203 460-0665	2676
Nel Group LLC	Windsor	CT	F	860 683-0190	5350
Bb Walpole Liquidation NH Inc	Cambridge	MA	E	617 491-4340	9406
Beacon Hill Chocolates	Boston	MA	G	617 725-1900	8395
Chilmark Chocolates Inc	Chilmark	MA	F	508 645-3013	10072
Chocolate Therapy	Framingham	MA	F	508 875-1571	10933
Godiva Chocolatier Inc	Braintree	MA	F	781 843-0466	9011
Green Mountain Chocolate Co **(PA)**	Hopedale	MA	G	508 473-9060	11673
Heavenly Chocolate	Northampton	MA	E	413 586-0038	14008
Levaggis Candies	South Weymouth	MA	G	781 335-1231	15321
Tru Chocolate Inc	Haverhill	MA	G	855 878-2462	11479
Whitmore Family Entps LLC	Somerville	MA	F	617 623-0804	15232
Lindt & Sprungli (usa) Inc **(HQ)**	Stratham	NH	C	603 778-8100	19871
Barry Callebaut USA LLC	Saint Albans	VT	D	802 524-9711	22364

CHRISTMAS NOVELTIES, WHOLESALE

COMPANY	CITY	ST	EMP	PHONE	ENTRY #
Ambrose G McCarthy Jr	Skowhegan	ME	E	207 474-8837	6968

CHROMATOGRAPHY EQPT

COMPANY	CITY	ST	EMP	PHONE	ENTRY #
Waters Corporation	Milford	MA	G	508 478-0208	13152
Waters Corporation **(PA)**	Milford	MA	C	508 478-2000	13153
Waters Technologies Corp	Taunton	MA	F	508 482-5223	15798
Waters Technologies Corp	Beverly	MA	F	978 927-7468	8196
Waters Technologies Corp **(HQ)**	Milford	MA	A	508 478-2000	13154

CHUCKS

COMPANY	CITY	ST	EMP	PHONE	ENTRY #
Miracle Instruments Co	Lebanon	CT	F	860 642-7745	1936
O S Walker Company Inc **(DH)**	Windsor	CT	D	508 853-3232	5351
Royal Machine and Tool Corp	Berlin	CT	E	860 828-6555	108

	CITY	ST	EMP	PHONE	ENTRY #
Double E Company LLC **(PA)**	West Bridgewater	MA	C	508 588-8099	16438
Leavitt Machine Co	Orange	MA	G	978 544-3872	14220
Mechanical Specialties Inc	Wyoming	RI	G	401 267-4410	21589

CIGAR STORES

	CITY	ST	EMP	PHONE	ENTRY #
Foundation Cigar Company LLC	Windsor	CT	F	203 738-9377	5334

CIGARETTE & CIGAR PRDTS & ACCESS

	CITY	ST	EMP	PHONE	ENTRY #
King Gt Inc	Canton	MA	G	781 562-1554	9751

CIGARETTE LIGHTERS

	CITY	ST	EMP	PHONE	ENTRY #
Bic Corporation **(HQ)**	Shelton	CT	A	203 783-2000	3782
Bic USA Inc **(DH)**	Shelton	CT	C	203 783-2000	3783

CIRCUIT BOARD REPAIR SVCS

	CITY	ST	EMP	PHONE	ENTRY #
Microboard Processing Inc	Seymour	CT	C	203 881-4300	3757
AC Electric Corp **(PA)**	Auburn	ME	E	207 784-7341	5545

CIRCUIT BOARDS, PRINTED: Television & Radio

	CITY	ST	EMP	PHONE	ENTRY #
Apct-Wallingford Inc	Wallingford	CT	E	203 269-3311	4703
Microboard Processing Inc	Seymour	CT	C	203 881-4300	3757
Power Trans Co Inc	Oxford	CT	G	203 881-0314	3419
Precise Circuit Company Inc	Shelton	CT	E	203 924-2512	3858
An Electronic Instrumentation	Methuen	MA	D	978 208-4555	13011
Azores Corp **(DH)**	Wilmington	MA	F	978 253-6200	16977
Imi Inc	Haverhill	MA	E	978 373-9190	11442
Zolin Technologies Inc	Lawrence	MA	F	978 794-4300	12086
Alternative Manufacturing Inc	Winthrop	ME	D	207 377-9377	7279
Circuit Connect Inc	Nashua	NH	E	603 880-7447	19133
Finite Surface Mount Tech LLC	Merrimack	NH	G	603 423-0300	19000
Gorilla Circuits	Nashua	NH	F	603 864-0283	19170
Ncab Group Usa Inc **(PA)**	Hampstead	NH	E	603 329-4551	18245
Willis & Pham LLC	Salem	NH	G	603 893-6029	19778

CIRCUIT BOARDS: Wiring

	CITY	ST	EMP	PHONE	ENTRY #
Murata Power Solutions Inc **(DH)**	Westborough	MA	C	508 339-3000	16637
Valhalla Circuits Corp	Weare	NH	G	603 854-3300	19942

CIRCUIT BREAKERS

	CITY	ST	EMP	PHONE	ENTRY #
Bass Products LLC	Bristol	CT	G	860 585-7923	530
Carling Technologies Inc **(PA)**	Plainville	CT	C	860 793-9281	3473
GE Grid Solutions LLC	Windsor	CT	G	425 250-2695	5335
Schneider Electric Usa Inc **(DH)**	Boston	MA	A	978 975-9600	8839
Schneider Electric Usa Inc	Foxboro	MA	G	508 549-3385	10903
General Electric Company	Auburn	ME	B	207 786-5100	5567

CIRCUIT BREAKERS: Air

	CITY	ST	EMP	PHONE	ENTRY #
EC Holdings Inc	Norwalk	CT	G	203 846-1651	3147

CIRCUITS, INTEGRATED: Hybrid

	CITY	ST	EMP	PHONE	ENTRY #
Hi-Rel Group LLC	Essex	CT	G	860 767-9031	1397
Hi-Rel Products LLC	Essex	CT	E	860 767-9031	1398
Aerospace Semiconductor Inc	Lawrence	MA	F	978 688-1299	11990
API Technologies Corporation	Marlborough	MA	D	508 485-0336	12718
Mini-Systems Inc **(PA)**	North Attleboro	MA	C	508 695-1420	13765
Raytheon Company	Quincy	MA	B	781 522-3000	14653
Stellar Industries Corp	Millbury	MA	E	508 865-1668	13177
Impellimax Inc	Nashua	NH	F	603 886-9569	19185
Micro-Precision Tech Inc	Salem	NH	E	603 893-7600	19752
Texas Instruments Incorporated	Merrimack	NH	C	603 429-6079	19037

CIRCUITS, INTEGRATED: Monolithic, Solid State

	CITY	ST	EMP	PHONE	ENTRY #
Eta Devices Inc	Cambridge	MA	E	617 577-8300	9473
Melexis Inc	Nashua	NH	E	603 223-2362	19206

CIRCUITS: Electronic

	CITY	ST	EMP	PHONE	ENTRY #
AB Electronics Inc	Brookfield	CT	E	203 740-2793	632
Arccos Golf LLC	Stamford	CT	E	844 692-7226	4143
Bead Industries Inc **(PA)**	Milford	CT	E	203 301-0270	2251
Cable Electronics Inc	Hartford	CT	G	860 953-0300	1809
Electro-Tech Inc	Cheshire	CT	E	203 271-1976	729
General Electro Components	Glastonbury	CT	G	860 659-3573	1554
Goodrich Corporation	Danbury	CT	B	505 345-9031	926
Imperial Elctrnic Assembly Inc	Brookfield	CT	D	203 740-8425	647
Kbc Electronics Inc	Milford	CT	F	203 298-9654	2306
Osda Contract Services Inc	Milford	CT	E	203 878-2155	2327
Osda Inc	Milford	CT	G	203 878-2155	2328
Park Distributories Inc	Bridgeport	CT	F	203 366-7200	464
Protronix Inc	Wallingford	CT	F	203 269-5858	4791
Qtran Inc	Milford	CT	E	203 367-8777	2344
Sean Mecesery	Cos Cob	CT	G	203 869-2277	829
Tgs Cables	Meriden	CT	G	203 668-6568	2139
USA Circuits LLC	Sandy Hook	CT	G	203 364-1378	3746
Verotec Inc	North Haven	CT	G	603 821-9921	3068
Americansub	Dudley	MA	E	508 949-2320	10372
Aved Electronics LLC	North Billerica	MA	D	978 453-6393	13794
Bae Systems Info & Elec Sys	Lexington	MA	B	603 885-4321	12208
Biophysical Devices Inc	Somerville	MA	G	617 629-0304	15159
Carlo Gavazzi Incorporated	Brockton	MA	G	508 588-6110	9126
Case Assembly Solutions Inc	South Easton	MA	E	508 238-5665	15273
Cullinan Manufacturing Inc	Topsfield	MA	E	978 465-1110	15855
Datacon Inc	Burlington	MA	E	781 273-5800	9253
Datel Inc	Mansfield	MA	E	508 964-5131	12627
Designers Metalcraft	East Bridgewater	MA	G	508 378-0404	10412
DI Technology LLC	Haverhill	MA	F	978 374-6451	11425
East West Boston LLC	Boston	MA	D	617 598-3000	8516
Embr Labs Inc	Charlestown	MA	G	413 218-0629	9834
Esmail Riyaz	Andover	MA	G	978 689-3837	7547
Etc Components Usa Inc	Worcester	MA	G	508 353-7075	17372
Excelitas Technologies Corp **(DH)**	Waltham	MA	E	781 522-5910	16104
Fraen Corporation **(PA)**	Reading	MA	C	781 205-5300	14734
Hdm Systems Corporation	Brighton	MA	F	617 562-4054	9101
K V A Electronics	Billerica	MA	G	978 262-2264	8260
Kernco Inc	Danvers	MA	F	978 777-1956	10229
Keystone Precision Inc	Pepperell	MA	G	978 433-8484	14441
Liberty Engineering Inc	Newton	MA	E	617 965-6644	13609
M & G Metal Inc	Clarksburg	MA	G	413 664-4057	10073
Massmicro LLC	Canton	MA	F	781 828-6110	9756
Massmicroelectronics LLC	Canton	MA	F	781 828-6110	9757
Matthew Associates Inc	Waban	MA	G	617 965-6126	15938
Micrometal Technologies Inc **(PA)**	Newburyport	MA	F	978 462-3600	13513
Midas Technology Inc	Woburn	MA	E	781 938-0069	17232
Minarik Corporation	Franklin	MA	G	781 329-2700	11067
Mioe Inc	Andover	MA	G	978 494-9460	7572
Murata Power Solutions Inc **(DH)**	Westborough	MA	C	508 339-3000	16637
N&N Manufacturing Inc **(PA)**	Topsfield	MA	F	978 465-1110	15862
Nanosemi Inc	Waltham	MA	E	781 472-2832	16157
New England Cm Inc	Franklin	MA	G	508 541-1307	11069
Orion Industries Incorporated	Ayer	MA	E	978 772-0020	7932
Paricon Technologies Corp	Taunton	MA	F	508 823-0876	15771
Parisi Associates LLC	Chelmsford	MA	F	978 667-8700	9921
Photonis Scientific Inc **(DH)**	Sturbridge	MA	D	508 347-4000	15646
Polyonics Corporation	Newburyport	MA	F	978 462-3600	13522
Port Electronics Corporation	Lawrence	MA	F	800 253-8510	12072
Protek Power North America Inc	Hudson	MA	G	978 567-9615	11808
Raytheon Arabian Systems Co	Billerica	MA	G	978 858-4547	8283
Raytheon European MGT Systems	Billerica	MA	G	978 858-4547	8284
Raytheon Intl Support Co	Billerica	MA	G	978 858-4547	8285
Raytheon Korean Support Co	Billerica	MA	F	978 858-4547	8286
Raytheon Middle E Systems Co	Billerica	MA	G	978 858-4547	8287
Raytheon Radar Ltd	Billerica	MA	G	978 858-4547	8288
Raytheon Tchnical ADM Svcs Ltd	Billerica	MA	G	978 858-4547	8290
Sensata Technologies Inc **(HQ)**	Attleboro	MA	A	508 236-3800	7792
Sensata Technologies Mass Inc **(DH)**	Attleboro	MA	D	508 236-3800	7794
Sie Computing Solutions Inc	Brockton	MA	D	508 588-6110	9174
Skyworks Solutions Inc	Woburn	MA	B	781 935-5150	17298
Star Engineering Inc	North Attleboro	MA	E	508 316-1492	13781
Texas Instruments Incorporated	Attleboro	MA	E	508 236-3800	7802
That Corporation **(PA)**	Milford	MA	E	508 478-9200	13148
Toshiba America Electronic	Marlborough	MA	G	508 481-0034	12837
Voltree Power Inc	Canton	MA	G	781 858-4939	9794
Advance Electronic Concepts	Portland	ME	G	207 797-9825	6609
Artel Inc	Westbrook	ME	E	207 854-0860	7180
Chip Component Electronx	Limington	ME	G	207 510-7608	6347
603 Manufacturing LLC	Hudson	NH	G	603 578-9876	18368
Aavid Corporation	Laconia	NH	A	603 528-3400	18549
Accelerator Systems Inc	Atkinson	NH	G	603 898-6010	17602
Additive Circuits Inc	Laconia	NH	G	603 366-1578	18552
Amphenol Printed Circuits Inc	Nashua	NH	A	603 324-4500	19115
Asia Direct LLC	Plaistow	NH	B	603 382-9485	19507
Bae Systems Info & Elec Sys	Hudson	NH	A	603 885-4321	18376
Bae Systems Info & Elec Sys	Merrimack	NH	B	603 885-4321	18990
Data Electronic Devices Inc	Salem	NH	C	603 893-2047	19720
Finite Surface Mount Tech LLC	Merrimack	NH	G	603 423-0300	19000
Gill Design Inc	Windham	NH	G	603 890-1237	20006
Janco Electronics Inc	Rollinsford	NH	D	603 742-1581	19692
Long Range LLC	Franklin	NH	G	603 934-3009	18159
Microfab Inc	Manchester	NH	G	603 621-9522	18872
Miltronics Mfg Svcs Inc	Keene	NH	F	603 352-3333	18516
Odhner Holographics	Amherst	NH	G	603 673-8651	17580
Pd & E Electronics LLC	North Hampton	NH	G	603 964-3165	19386
Pgc Wire & Cable LLC	Hudson	NH	F	603 821-7300	18426
Phoenix Resources	Goshen	NH	G	603 863-9096	18215
Princeton Technology Corp	Hudson	NH	D	603 595-1987	18428
Provencal Manufacturing Inc **(PA)**	Newfields	NH	G	603 772-6716	19319
Remcon-North Corporation	Meredith	NH	D	603 279-7091	18977
Sonesys LLC	Merrimack	NH	F	603 423-9000	19031
Stellar Manufacturing Inc	Salem	NH	E	978 241-9537	19771
W5 Circuits LLC	North Hampton	NH	G	603 964-6780	19388
Andon Electronics Corporation	Lincoln	RI	E	401 333-0388	20555
Charter Industries Inc	Warren	RI	G	401 245-0850	21293
Cooliance Inc	Warwick	RI	F	401 921-6500	21346
Federal Electronics Inc	Cranston	RI	D	401 944-6200	20225
Kearney-National Inc	North Kingstown	RI	E	401 943-2686	20719
Narragansett Imaging Usa LLC	North Smithfield	RI	E	401 762-3800	20791
Raytheon Company	Portsmouth	RI	D	401 847-8000	20938
Staffall Inc	Cranston	RI	E	401 461-5554	20291
Veterans Assembled Elec LLC **(PA)**	Providence	RI	G	401 228-6165	21150
Aviatron Inc (us)	South Burlington	VT	F	802 865-9318	22437
Moscow Mills Incorporated	Stowe	VT	F	802 253-2036	22524
Necsel Intllctual Property Inc	Vergennes	VT	E	802 877-6432	22554
Prom Software Inc	South Burlington	VT	F	802 862-7500	22462
Sammarval Co Ltd	Grafton	VT	G	802 843-2637	21996

CLAMPS: Ground, Electric-Wiring Devices

	CITY	ST	EMP	PHONE	ENTRY #
Opalala Inc	Fall River	MA	F	508 646-0950	10743
Steger Power Connection Inc	Fall River	MA	F	508 646-0950	10763

CLAMPS: Metal

	CITY	ST	EMP	PHONE	ENTRY #
Lassy Tools Inc	Plainville	CT	G	860 747-2748	3500
Mitee-Bite Products LLC	Center Ossipee	NH	F	603 539-4538	17804
Vincent Metals Corporation	Warwick	RI	G	401 737-4167	21437

CLAY MINING

	CITY	ST	EMP	PHONE	ENTRY #
Lumacera Innovative Mtls Inc	Pepperell	MA	G	978 302-6475	14442

CLAY MINING, COMMON

Sheffield Pottery Inc	Sheffield	MA	E	413 229-7700	15065

CLEANING & DESCALING SVC: Metal Prdts

E & J Parts Cleaning Inc	Waterbury	CT	F	203 757-1716	4866
Preventative Maintenance Corp	Poquonock	CT	F	860 683-1180	3560

CLEANING & DYEING PLANTS, EXC RUGS

Easy Way Dry Cleaners Inc	Woburn	MA	G	781 933-1473	17173

CLEANING EQPT: Commercial

Jfj Services LLC	Old Saybrook	CT	G	860 395-1922	3340
Present Arms Inc	Indian Orchard	MA	G	413 575-4656	11894
Uvtech Systems Inc	Sudbury	MA	G	978 440-7282	15670
Hubscrub Co Inc	Manchester	NH	G	603 624-4243	18839
SC Technologies Inc	North Kingstown	RI	E	401 667-7370	20738
Vacuum Processing Systems LLC	East Greenwich	RI	G	401 397-8578	20382
Industrial Safety Products LLC	Colchester	VT	G	802 338-9035	21867

CLEANING EQPT: Floor Washing & Polishing, Commercial

J & M Enterprises Inc	Fairfield	ME	G	207 968-2729	6027

CLEANING EQPT: High Pressure

Under Pressure LLC	Lakeville	MA	G	508 641-0421	11980
Landa Pressure Washers of RI	Cranston	RI	G	401 463-8303	20250

CLEANING OR POLISHING PREPARATIONS, NEC

Grill Daddy Brush Company	Old Greenwich	CT	E	888 840-7552	3310
Hydrochemical Techniques Inc	Hartford	CT	G	860 527-6350	1836
Macdermid Incorporated **(HQ)**	Waterbury	CT	C	203 575-5700	4900
Nature Plus Inc	Stratford	CT	G	203 380-0316	4432
Simoniz Usa Inc **(PA)**	Bolton	CT	C	860 646-0172	278
Brady Enterprises Inc **(PA)**	East Weymouth	MA	D	781 682-6280	10538
Chemco Corporation	Lawrence	MA	E	978 687-9000	12006
Connoisseurs Products Corp **(PA)**	Woburn	MA	D	800 851-5333	17148
Lamco Chemical Company Inc	Chelsea	MA	G	617 884-8470	9959
Perma Incorporated	Bedford	MA	F	978 667-5161	8000
Savin Products Company Inc	Randolph	MA	F	781 961-2743	14697
Winfield Brooks Company Inc	Woburn	MA	F	781 933-5300	17323
GM Specialties Inc	Scarborough	ME	G	207 883-8300	6922

CLEANING PRDTS: Ammonia, Household

Wonder Tablitz Corporation	Walpole	MA	G	508 660-0011	16018

CLEANING PRDTS: Automobile Polish

Armored Autogroup Parent Inc **(DH)**	Danbury	CT	G	203 205-2900	875

CLEANING PRDTS: Disinfectants, Household Or Indl Plant

Concept Chemicals Inc	Hingham	MA	F	781 740-0711	11497
Aqua Tite Innovative Solutions	Hampton	NH	G	603 431-5555	18254

CLEANING PRDTS: Drain Pipe Solvents Or Cleaners

D J Bass Inc	New Bedford	MA	G	508 678-4499	13376
Allens Environmental Svcs Inc	Presque Isle	ME	G	207 764-9336	6752

CLEANING PRDTS: Floor Waxes

Koster Keunen LLC **(PA)**	Watertown	CT	F	860 945-3333	5013
Maine Cleaners Supply Inc	North Yarmouth	ME	G	207 657-3166	6517

CLEANING PRDTS: Furniture Polish Or Wax

R G J Associates Inc	Sudbury	MA	G	978 443-7642	15667

CLEANING PRDTS: Laundry Preparations

Uls of New England LLC	Lawrence	MA	D	978 683-7390	12079

CLEANING PRDTS: Leather Dressings & Finishes

Maranatha Industries Inc **(PA)**	Wakefield	MA	F	781 245-0038	15960
House of Laurila	Hopkinton	NH	G	603 224-8123	18363

CLEANING PRDTS: Polishing Preparations & Related Prdts

Cape Cod Polish Company Inc	Dennis	MA	G	508 385-5099	10306

CLEANING PRDTS: Rug, Upholstery/Dry Clng Detergents/Spotters

Roll Tide of Nh LLC	Nashua	NH	G	603 417-2498	19255

CLEANING PRDTS: Sanitation Preparations

Roeblc Laboratories Inc **(PA)**	Orange	CT	C	203 795 1283	3382

CLEANING PRDTS: Sanitation Preps, Disinfectants/Deodorants

Great Lakes Chemical Corp **(DH)**	Shelton	CT	E	203 573-2000	3806
Lanxess Solutions US Inc **(DH)**	Shelton	CT	E	203 573-2000	3824
Global Biotechnologies Inc	Scarborough	ME	G	800 755-8420	6920

CLEANING PRDTS: Specialty

Cloverdale Inc	West Cornwall	CT	G	860 672-0216	5046
Comanche Clean Energy Corp	Stamford	CT	G	203 326-4570	4167
Korner Kare	Goshen	CT	G	860 491-3731	1584
Micro Care Corporation **(PA)**	New Britain	CT	F	860 827-0626	2554
Odd Jobs Handyman Service LLC	Woodbridge	CT	G	203 397-5275	5474
Alpha Chemical Services Inc	Stoughton	MA	E	781 344-8688	15579
Buckeye International Inc	East Weymouth	MA	G	617 827-2137	10539
MD Stetson Company Inc	Randolph	MA	E	781 986-6161	14689
Powerwash Co	Raynham	MA	G	508 823-9274	14726
Spectrowax Corporation **(PA)**	Canton	MA	D	617 543-0400	9784
Cml Services Inc	Westbrook	ME	G	207 772-5032	7184
Kicteam Inc	Auburn	ME	E	207 514-7030	5574
Chem Quest Inc	Hampton	NH	G	207 856-2993	18260
Brown Country Services LLC	West Dover	VT	G	802 464-5200	22606

CLEANING PRDTS: Stain Removers

Amodex Products Inc	Bridgeport	CT	E	203 335-1255	375

CLEANING SVCS

Albarrie Technical Fabrics Inc	Auburn	ME	G	207 786-0424	5549

CLEANING SVCS: Industrial Or Commercial

E & J Parts Cleaning Inc	Waterbury	CT	F	203 757-1716	4866

CLIPS & FASTENERS, MADE FROM PURCHASED WIRE

Royal Diversified Products	Warren	RI	D	401 245-6900	21304

CLOSURES: Closures, Stamped Metal

Orca Inc	New Britain	CT	E	860 223-4180	2558

CLOSURES: Plastic

Aptargroup Inc	Stratford	CT	B	203 377-8100	4391

CLOTHES HANGERS, WHOLESALE

American Keder Inc **(PA)**	Rindge	NH	G	603 899-3233	19646

CLOTHING & ACCESS, WHOLESALE: Leather & Sheep Lined

Kerr Leathers Inc	Salem	MA	E	978 852-0660	14927

CLOTHING & ACCESS, WOMEN, CHILD & INFANT, WHSLE: Sportswear

Image Factory	Pocasset	MA	G	508 295-3876	14598

CLOTHING & ACCESS, WOMEN, CHILDREN & INFANT, WHOL: Handbags

Samsonite Company Stores LLC	Warren	RI	F	401 245-2100	21306

CLOTHING & ACCESS, WOMEN, CHILDREN & INFANT, WHOL: Uniforms

Action Apparel Inc **(PA)**	Stoneham	MA	F	781 224-0777	15552
Collegiate Uniforms Inc	Medford	MA	G	781 219-4952	12927
Officers Equipment Co	Providence	RI	E	703 221-1912	21082

CLOTHING & ACCESS: Costumes, Masquerade

Vampfangs / 321fx Studios LLC	Beverly	MA	G	781 799-5048	8194
Masquerade	Salem	NH	F	603 275-0717	19749

CLOTHING & ACCESS: Handicapped

Savvy On Main	Orleans	MA	G	508 255-5076	14241

CLOTHING & ACCESS: Handkerchiefs, Exc Paper

New York Accessory Group Inc	Bristol	RI	D	401 245-6096	20095

CLOTHING & ACCESS: Men's Miscellaneous Access

De Muerte Usa LLC	Hartford	CT	G	860 331-7085	1817
Malabar Bay LLC	Stamford	CT	G	203 359-9714	4243
Matrix Apparel Group LLC	New Fairfield	CT	G	203 740-7837	2625
Style and Grace LLC	Westport	CT	G	917 751-2043	5232
Gava Group Inc	Hanover	MA	G	781 878-9889	11338

CLOTHING & ACCESS: Suspenders

Chaucer Accessories Inc	Haverhill	MA	F	978 373-1566	11416

CLOTHING & APPAREL STORES: Custom

Logo Sportswear Inc	Wallingford	CT	G	203 678-4700	4767
Team Destination Inc	Meriden	CT	G	203 235-6000	2138
Cloak & Dagger Creations	Littleton	MA	G	978 486-4414	12296
Theatre Stricken Apparel LLC	Bellingham	MA	G	978 325-2335	8060
Vermont Teddy Bear Co Inc	Shelburne	VT	C	802 985-1319	22426
Vermont TS Inc	Chester	VT	G	802 875-2091	21853

CLOTHING & FURNISHINGS, MEN'S & BOYS', WHOLESALE: Gloves

Gima LLC	Hartford	CT	E	860 296-4441	1826

CLOTHING & FURNISHINGS, MEN'S & BOYS', WHOLESALE: Outerwear

Woodland Studios Inc	Ellsworth	ME	F	207 667-3286	6024

CLOTHING & FURNISHINGS, MEN'S & BOYS', WHOLESALE: Uniforms

Collegiate Uniforms Inc	Medford	MA	G	781 219-4952	12927

CLOTHING STORES, NEC

Malabar Bay LLC	Stamford	CT	G	203 359-9714	4243

CLOTHING STORES: Caps & Gowns

Therese Rose Manufacturing	Brockton	MA	G	508 586-5812	9183

CLOTHING STORES: Designer Apparel

Jak Designs LLC	Kennebunk	ME	E	330 689-6849	6236
Jak Designs LLC **(PA)**	Kennebunkport	ME	F	207 204-0396	6245

CLOTHING STORES: Formal Wear

Our Place - Shop For Men Inc **(PA)**	North Providence	RI	G	401 231-2370	20769

CLOTHING STORES: Leather

L & J Leathers Manufacturing	Revere	MA	G	781 289-6466	14770

PRODUCT

Employee Codes: A=Over 500 employees, B=251-500
C=101-250, D=51-100 E=20-50, F=10-19, G=3-9

CLOTHING STORES: T-Shirts, Printed, Custom

	CITY	ST	EMP	PHONE	ENTRY #
Garrett Printing & Graphics	Bristol	CT	G	860 589-6710	567
Yankee Screen Printing	Derby	CT	G	203 924-9926	1085
Itg Group Inc	Medway	MA	G	508 645-4994	12962
Follenderwerks Inc	Barre	VT	G	802 362-0911	21615
Precision Print and Copy Inc	Vergennes	VT	G	802 877-3711	22555

CLOTHING STORES: Work

	CITY	ST	EMP	PHONE	ENTRY #
Air Tool Sales & Service Co **(PA)**	Unionville	CT	G	860 673-2714	4652

CLOTHING: Access

	CITY	ST	EMP	PHONE	ENTRY #
Ricco Vishnu	Bridgeport	CT	G	203 449-0124	482
Bravo Maslow LLC	Quincy	MA	G	912 580-0044	14618
Image Factory	Pocasset	MA	G	508 295-3876	14598
Marblehead Weather Gmts LLC	Marblehead	MA	G	781 639-1060	12688

CLOTHING: Access, Women's & Misses'

	CITY	ST	EMP	PHONE	ENTRY #
Kathy Clark	Natick	MA	G	508 655-3666	13263
Solid Oak Inc	Westerly	RI	G	401 637-4855	21541

CLOTHING: Aprons, Exc Rubber/Plastic, Women, Misses, Junior

	CITY	ST	EMP	PHONE	ENTRY #
Ideal Bias Binding Corp	Marion	MA	G	508 748-2712	12698

CLOTHING: Aprons, Harness

	CITY	ST	EMP	PHONE	ENTRY #
1947 LLC	Portsmouth	RI	G	401 293-5500	20916

CLOTHING: Aprons, Work, Exc Rubberized & Plastic, Men's

	CITY	ST	EMP	PHONE	ENTRY #
Ideal Bias Binding Corp	Marion	MA	G	508 748-2712	12698

CLOTHING: Athletic & Sportswear, Men's & Boys'

	CITY	ST	EMP	PHONE	ENTRY #
Custom Sportswear Mfg	Wolcott	CT	G	203 879-4420	5437
Cycling Sports Group Inc **(HQ)**	Wilton	CT	D	608 268-8916	5286
Gg Sportswear Inc	Hartford	CT	E	860 296-4441	1825
Gima LLC	Hartford	CT	E	860 296-4441	1826
Turq LLC	Riverside	CT	G	203 344-1257	3692
16sur20 Management LLC	Lenox	MA	F	413 637-5061	12099
Custom Sports Sleeves LLC	Leominster	MA	G	508 344-9749	12129
Fieldston Clothes Inc **(HQ)**	Fall River	MA	G	508 646-2900	10700
Golden Fleece Mfg Group LLC **(HQ)**	Haverhill	MA	B	978 686-3833	11439
M & M Garment Manufacturing	Everett	MA	F	617 389-7787	10620
Madewell Manufacturing Co Inc	New Bedford	MA	G	508 997-0768	13414
Perfect Curve Inc **(PA)**	Boston	MA	G	617 224-1600	8774
Pop Tops Company Inc	South Easton	MA	E	508 580-2580	15286
Robert H Thoms	Cambridge	MA	G	617 876-0662	9637
Saucony Inc **(DH)**	Waltham	MA	C	617 824-6000	16191
Tracksmith Corporation	Boston	MA	F	781 235-0037	8891
Chuck Roast Equipment Inc **(PA)**	Conway	NH	E	603 447-5492	17951
Dartmouth Undying Inc	Hanover	NH	G	603 643-2143	18287
Legacy Global Sports LP	Portsmouth	NH	G	603 373-7262	19585
Bogner of America Inc **(DH)**	Burlington	VT	E	802 861-6900	21769
Louis Garneau USA Inc	Derby	VT	D	802 334-5885	21901

CLOTHING: Athletic & Sportswear, Women's & Girls'

	CITY	ST	EMP	PHONE	ENTRY #
Custom Sportswear Mfg	Wolcott	CT	G	203 879-4420	5437
Cloak & Dagger Creations	Littleton	MA	G	978 486-4414	12296
Perfect Curve Inc **(PA)**	Boston	MA	G	617 224-1600	8774
Pop Tops Company Inc	South Easton	MA	E	508 580-2580	15286
Salt Wellfleet	Wellfleet	MA	G	508 237-4415	16402
Saucony Inc **(DH)**	Waltham	MA	C	617 824-6000	16191
Tracksmith Corporation	Boston	MA	F	781 235-0037	8891
Chuck Roast Equipment Inc **(PA)**	Conway	NH	E	603 447-5492	17951
Mat Game Set	Lyme	NH	G	603 277-9763	18755

CLOTHING: Baker, Barber, Lab/Svc Ind Apparel, Washable, Men

	CITY	ST	EMP	PHONE	ENTRY #
Theatre Stricken Apparel LLC	Bellingham	MA	G	978 325-2335	8060

CLOTHING: Belts

	CITY	ST	EMP	PHONE	ENTRY #
Dooney & Bourke Inc **(PA)**	Norwalk	CT	E	203 853-7515	3142
Cape Cod Manufacturing	Mashpee	MA	G	508 477-1188	12878
Chaucer Accessories Inc	Haverhill	MA	F	978 373-1566	11416
Contemporary Apparel Inc	Mansfield	MA	G	508 339-3523	12619
Dick Muller Designer/Craftsman	Shelburne Falls	MA	G	413 625-0016	15068
Mackenzie Couture ACC Inc	Lynnfield	MA	G	781 334-2805	12552
Surtan Manufacturing Co	South Yarmouth	MA	G	508 394-4099	15334

CLOTHING: Bibs, Waterproof, From Purchased Materials

	CITY	ST	EMP	PHONE	ENTRY #
Gonco Inc **(PA)**	Sandwich	MA	G	508 833-3900	14968
Ideal Bias Binding Corp	Marion	MA	G	508 748-2712	12698

CLOTHING: Blouses, Women's & Girls'

	CITY	ST	EMP	PHONE	ENTRY #
Fyc Apparel Group LLC	East Haven	CT	E	203 466-6525	1252
Fyc Apparel Group LLC **(PA)**	Branford	CT	D	203 481-2420	319
American Power Source Inc **(PA)**	Fall River	MA	C	508 672-8847	10657
Contemporary Apparel Inc	Mansfield	MA	G	508 339-3523	12619
Counterwerks Inc	Bellingham	MA	G	508 553-9600	8035
LJL Enterprises Inc	Peabody	MA	G	781 639-2714	14353
Shop Therapy Imports	Provincetown	MA	G	508 487-8970	14609
Imeldas Fabrics & Designs	New Sharon	ME	G	207 778-0665	6476

CLOTHING: Blouses, Womens & Juniors, From Purchased Mtrls

	CITY	ST	EMP	PHONE	ENTRY #
A Personal Touch Inc **(PA)**	Hanson	MA	G	781 447-0467	11360
Pvh Corp	Wrentham	MA	F	508 384-0070	17527

CLOTHING: Body Stockings, Knit

	CITY	ST	EMP	PHONE	ENTRY #
Legends & Heroes	Sudbury	MA	E	617 571-6990	15662

CLOTHING: Brassieres

	CITY	ST	EMP	PHONE	ENTRY #
Valmont Inc	Ludlow	MA	F	413 583-8351	12478

CLOTHING: Caps, Baseball

	CITY	ST	EMP	PHONE	ENTRY #
Athletic Emblem & Lettering Co	Springfield	MA	F	413 734-0415	15449

CLOTHING: Children & Infants'

	CITY	ST	EMP	PHONE	ENTRY #
Agawam Novelty Company Inc	Agawam	MA	G	413 536-0471	7418
Ideal Bias Binding Corp	Marion	MA	G	508 748-2712	12698

CLOTHING: Children's, Girls'

	CITY	ST	EMP	PHONE	ENTRY #
One Kid LLC **(PA)**	Westport	CT	G	203 254-9978	5219
Accurate Services Inc	Fall River	MA	E	508 674-5773	10650
Charles River Apparel Inc	Sharon	MA	D	781 793-5300	15047
E-I-E-I-o Incorporated	Fall River	MA	G	508 324-9311	10684
Precision Sportswear Inc	Fall River	MA	E	508 674-3034	10748
Shop Therapy Imports	Provincetown	MA	G	508 487-8970	14609
Imeldas Fabrics & Designs	New Sharon	ME	G	207 778-0665	6476
Richardson Mfg Co Inc	Silver Lake	NH	G	603 367-9018	19825

CLOTHING: Clergy Vestments

	CITY	ST	EMP	PHONE	ENTRY #
Theological Threads Inc	Beverly	MA	G	978 927-7031	8190
CM Almy & Son Inc	Pittsfield	ME	C	207 487-3232	6589

CLOTHING: Coats & Jackets, Leather & Sheep-Lined

	CITY	ST	EMP	PHONE	ENTRY #
Leprechaun Sheepskin Company	Charlemont	MA	G	413 339-4355	9820
Timberland LLC **(HQ)**	Stratham	NH	B	603 772-9500	19876

CLOTHING: Coats & Suits, Men's & Boys'

	CITY	ST	EMP	PHONE	ENTRY #
Sassone Labwear LLC	Bridgeport	CT	G	860 666-4484	485
Charles River Apparel Inc	Sharon	MA	D	781 793-5300	15047
Sterlingwear of Boston Inc **(PA)**	Boston	MA	D	617 567-2100	8865
Woolrich Inc	Boston	MA	G	857 263-7554	8932

CLOTHING: Coats, Hunting & Vests, Men's

	CITY	ST	EMP	PHONE	ENTRY #
Ugly Dog Hunting Co	Hinesburg	VT	G	802 482-7054	22031

CLOTHING: Coats, Leatherette, Oiled Fabric, Etc, Mens & Boys

	CITY	ST	EMP	PHONE	ENTRY #
Timberland LLC **(HQ)**	Stratham	NH	B	603 772-9500	19876

CLOTHING: Coats, Overcoats & Vests

	CITY	ST	EMP	PHONE	ENTRY #
Corinth Acquisition Corp **(PA)**	Stamford	CT	G	203 504-6260	4174

CLOTHING: Costumes

	CITY	ST	EMP	PHONE	ENTRY #
Costume Works Inc	Somerville	MA	F	617 623-7510	15167
Dynasty Production	Boston	MA	G	617 361-5297	8513
Peko Creations Ltd	Pawtucket	RI	F	401 722-6661	20878
Tiara Enterprises Inc	Providence	RI	G	401 521-2988	21136

CLOTHING: Down-Filled, Men's & Boys'

	CITY	ST	EMP	PHONE	ENTRY #
Richardson Mfg Co Inc	Silver Lake	NH	G	603 367-9018	19825

CLOTHING: Dresses

	CITY	ST	EMP	PHONE	ENTRY #
Fyc Apparel Group LLC **(PA)**	Branford	CT	D	203 481-2420	319
Fall River Apparel Inc	Fall River	MA	G	508 677-1975	10694
Kathy Clark	Natick	MA	G	508 655-3666	13263
LJL Enterprises Inc	Peabody	MA	G	781 639-2714	14353

CLOTHING: Dresses & Skirts

	CITY	ST	EMP	PHONE	ENTRY #
Babtech Inc	Rockland	ME	G	207 594-7106	6784

CLOTHING: Furs

	CITY	ST	EMP	PHONE	ENTRY #
Surell Accessories Inc	Troy	NH	F	603 242-7784	19914

CLOTHING: Garments, Indl, Men's & Boys

	CITY	ST	EMP	PHONE	ENTRY #
A Gerber Corp	Stamford	CT	G	203 918-1913	4123
Nitefighter International	Silver Lake	NH	G	603 367-4741	19824

CLOTHING: Hats & Caps, NEC

	CITY	ST	EMP	PHONE	ENTRY #
Whole Earth Hat Co Inc	Fall River	MA	F	508 672-7033	10783

CLOTHING: Hats & Headwear, Knit

	CITY	ST	EMP	PHONE	ENTRY #
Ahead LLC	New Bedford	MA	B	508 985-9898	13354

CLOTHING: Hosiery, Pantyhose & Knee Length, Sheer

	CITY	ST	EMP	PHONE	ENTRY #
Footsox Inc	Gloucester	MA	G	800 338-0833	11183

CLOTHING: Hospital, Men's

	CITY	ST	EMP	PHONE	ENTRY #
Sassone Labwear LLC	Bridgeport	CT	G	860 666-4484	485

CLOTHING: Jackets, Field, Military

	CITY	ST	EMP	PHONE	ENTRY #
Niche Inc	New Bedford	MA	E	508 990-4202	13427
Alcor-Usa Llc	Alton	NH	G	603 398-1564	17544

CLOTHING: Jackets, Overall & Work

	CITY	ST	EMP	PHONE	ENTRY #
Outlast Uniform Corporation	Chelsea	MA	G	617 889-0510	9962
Tyca Corporation **(PA)**	Clinton	MA	E	978 612-0002	10094

CLOTHING: Jeans, Men's & Boys'

	CITY	ST	EMP	PHONE	ENTRY #
Guess Inc	Braintree	MA	E	781 843-3147	9014

CLOTHING: Leather

	CITY	ST	EMP	PHONE	ENTRY #
U S Made Co Inc	Danvers	MA	E	978 777-8383	10269

CLOTHING: Leather & Sheep-Lined

	CITY	ST	EMP	PHONE	ENTRY #
S & S Computer Imaging Inc	Holyoke	MA	G	413 536-0117	11655

CLOTHING: Leather & sheep-lined clothing

	CITY	ST	EMP	PHONE	ENTRY #
Vanson Leathers Inc	Fall River	MA	D	508 678-2000	10778
Surell Accessories Inc	Troy	NH	F	603 242-7784	19914
Bren Corporation	Johnston	RI	E	401 943-8200	20501

	CITY	ST	EMP	PHONE	ENTRY #
CLOTHING: Lounge, Bed & Leisurewear					
Tamboo Bistro	Brockton	MA	G	508 584-8585	9181
CLOTHING: Maternity					
Luca	Warren	RI	G	401 289-2251	21297
CLOTHING: Men's & boy's clothing, nec					
176 Willow Avenue LLC	Little Compton	RI	G	401 635-2329	20603
CLOTHING: Men's & boy's underwear & nightwear					
L L Bean Inc	Brunswick	ME	B	207 725-0300	5840
CLOTHING: Mens & Boys Jackets, Sport, Suede, Leatherette					
Tribal Wear	Riverside	CT	G	203 637-7884	3691
New Balance Athletics Inc **(HQ)**	Boston	MA	B	617 783-4000	8727
Tyca Corporation **(PA)**	Clinton	MA	E	978 612-0002	10094
CLOTHING: Neckwear					
Xmi Corporation	Greenwich	CT	G	800 838-0424	1662
Foster-Miller Inc	Devens	MA	D	781 684-4000	10320
New York Accessory Group Inc	Bristol	RI	D	401 245-6096	20095
Btl Holdings LLC	Middlebury	VT	E	917 596-3660	22105
CLOTHING: Outerwear, Knit					
River Falls Manufacturing Co	Fall River	MA	D	508 646-2900	10759
Russell Brands LLC	Holyoke	MA	G	413 735-1400	11653
CLOTHING: Outerwear, Lthr, Wool/Down-Filled, Men, Youth/Boy					
Vf Outdoor Inc	Natick	MA	F	508 651-7676	13286
Fat Hat Clothing Co	Quechee	VT	F	802 296-6646	22294
CLOTHING: Outerwear, Women's & Misses' NEC					
Accurate Services Inc	Fall River	MA	E	508 674-5773	10650
Charles River Apparel Inc	Sharon	MA	D	781 793-5300	15047
Fashions Inc **(PA)**	Boston	MA	G	617 338-0163	8538
Fieldston Clothes Inc **(HQ)**	Fall River	MA	G	508 646-2900	10700
LJL Enterprises Inc	Peabody	MA	G	781 639-2714	14353
Northeast Knitting Mills Inc **(PA)**	Fall River	MA	E	508 678-7553	10741
Tyca Corporation **(PA)**	Clinton	MA	E	978 612-0002	10094
Two Islands Corporation	Orland	ME	G	207 469-3600	6551
St John	Cranston	RI	G	401 944-0159	20290
Geiger of Austria Inc	Middlebury	VT	E	802 388-3156	22112
Johnson Woolen Mills LLC	Johnson	VT	E	802 635-2271	22050
CLOTHING: Overcoats & Topcoats, Men/Boy, Purchased Materials					
Sterlingwear of Boston Inc	Boston	MA	C	617 567-6465	8866
CLOTHING: Pants, Leather					
L & J Leathers Manufacturing	Revere	MA	G	781 289-6466	14770
CLOTHING: Raincoats, Exc Vulcanized Rubber, Purchased Matls					
Mr Idea Inc	Attleboro	MA	E	508 222-0155	7770
Neptune Garment Company	Boston	MA	D	617 482-3980	8722
CLOTHING: Robes & Dressing Gowns					
Graduation Solutions LLC	Greenwich	CT	E	914 934-5991	1617
L L Bean Inc	Brunswick	ME	B	207 725-0300	5840
CLOTHING: Shirts					
16sur20 Management LLC	Lenox	MA	F	413 637-5061	12099
Acme Merchandise and AP Inc	Gloucester	MA	E	978 282-4800	11158
Kathy Clark	Natick	MA	G	508 655-3666	13263
Shop Therapy Imports	Provincetown	MA	G	508 487-8970	14609
Imeldas Fabrics & Designs	New Sharon	ME	G	207 778-0665	6476
Timberland LLC **(HQ)**	Stratham	NH	B	603 772-9500	19876
CLOTHING: Shirts & T-Shirts, Knit					
Blvd Graphix	Limestone	ME	G	207 325-2583	6339
CLOTHING: Shirts, Dress, Men's & Boys'					
Pickwick	Scituate	MA	G	781 545-0884	15010
Pvh Corp	Wrentham	MA	F	508 384-0070	17527
Pvh Corp	Chatham	MA	G	508 945-4063	9863
CLOTHING: Shirts, Sports & Polo, Men's & Boys'					
New Balance Athletics Inc **(HQ)**	Boston	MA	B	617 783-4000	8727
Halbro America Inc	East Providence	RI	G	401 438-2727	20418
CLOTHING: Ski Suits, Knit					
Kneebinding Inc	Stowe	VT	G	802 760-3026	22522
CLOTHING: Skirts					
A Personal Touch Inc **(PA)**	Hanson	MA	G	781 447-0467	11360
CLOTHING: Socks					
Shock Sock Inc LLC	Farmington	CT	G	860 680-7252	1512
Soldier Socks	Stamford	CT	G	203 832-2005	4324
Tommy LLC Sock It	Windsor	CT	G	860 688-2019	5375
Lost Sock Corporation	North Reading	MA	G	978 664-0730	13986
Mvk Silt Sock	Rowley	MA	G	978 204-9483	14860
Socks For Siberia Inc	Brookfield	MA	G	774 200-1617	9192
Sock Shack	Portland	ME	G	207 805-1348	6731
Secret Sock Society	Franconia	NH	G	603 443-3208	18154
Eurosocks North America Inc	Warwick	RI	G	401 739-6500	21362
CLOTHING: Sportswear, Women's					
Gg Sportswear Inc	Hartford	CT	E	860 296-4441	1825
Teta Activewear By Custom	Wolcott	CT	G	203 879-4420	5461
Dek Tillett Ltd	Sheffield	MA	G	413 229-8764	15059
M & M Garment Manufacturing	Everett	MA	F	617 389-7787	10620
Madewell Manufacturing Co Inc	New Bedford	MA	G	508 997-0768	13414
New Balance Athletics Inc **(HQ)**	Boston	MA	B	617 783-4000	8727
Pashi Inc	Everett	MA	G	617 304-2742	10624
Pellys Sports	Indian Orchard	MA	G	413 301-0889	11893
Tango Seaport	Boston	MA	G	857 277-1191	8873
Legacy Global Sports LP	Portsmouth	NH	G	603 373-7262	19585
Lululemon USA Inc	Portsmouth	NH	G	603 431-0871	19591
Bogner of America Inc **(DH)**	Burlington	VT	E	802 861-6900	21769
Gsg Inc	Shelburne	VT	G	802 828-6221	22418
Louis Garneau USA Inc	Derby	VT	D	802 334-5885	21901
CLOTHING: Suits & Skirts, Women's & Misses'					
Fyc Apparel Group LLC **(PA)**	Branford	CT	D	203 481-2420	319
CLOTHING: Suits, Men's & Boys', From Purchased Materials					
Bayer Clothing Group Inc **(PA)**	Greenwich	CT	D	203 661-4140	1599
Ja Apparel Corp	New Bedford	MA	G	580 990-4580	13399
Joseph Abboud Mfg Corp **(DH)**	New Bedford	MA	B	508 999-1301	13401
Joseph Abboud Mfg Corp	New Bedford	MA	G	508 961-1726	13402
Southwick Clothing LLC **(HQ)**	Haverhill	MA	C	800 634-5312	11472
Tom James Company	Hampton	NH	F	603 601-6944	18274
CLOTHING: Sweaters & Sweater Coats, Knit					
Kielo America Inc	Ridgefield	CT	G	203 431-3999	3671
Alps Sportswear Mfg Co Inc	Natick	MA	E	978 685-5159	13233
Evergreen Enterprises Inc	Berkley	MA	G	508 823-2377	8086
Northeast Knitting Mills Inc **(PA)**	Fall River	MA	E	508 678-7553	10741
Pvh Corp	Wrentham	MA	F	508 384-0070	17527
CLOTHING: Sweatshirts & T-Shirts, Men's & Boys'					
MB Sport LLC **(PA)**	New Canaan	CT	F	203 966-1985	2605
Mountain Tops Custom T-Shirts **(PA)**	Arundel	ME	G	207 985-1919	5534
Ibex Outdoor Clothing LLC	White River Junction	VT	E	802 359-4239	22639
CLOTHING: Swimwear, Men's & Boys'					
Everest Isles LLC	Wallingford	CT	G	203 561-5128	4739
Waterwear Inc	Wilton	NH	E	603 654-5344	19991
CLOTHING: Swimwear, Women's & Misses'					
Waterwear Inc	Wilton	NH	E	603 654-5344	19991
CLOTHING: T-Shirts & Tops, Knit					
Egyptian Cotton Tshirts LLC	Burlington	MA	G	781 272-7922	9261
New England Shirt Co LLC	Fall River	MA	G	508 672-2223	10739
Hanesbrands Inc	Merrimack	NH	F	603 424-6737	19006
Mountain Corporation	Marlborough	NH	D	603 876-3630	18963
Mountain Corporation **(PA)**	Keene	NH	C	603 355-2272	18517
Shirt Out of Luck LLC	Salem	NH	G	603 898-9002	19767
Mister Sister	Providence	RI	G	401 421-6969	21069
CLOTHING: T-Shirts & Tops, Women's & Girls'					
Acme Merchandise and AP Inc	Gloucester	MA	E	978 282-4800	11158
CLOTHING: Ties, Neck & Bow, Men's & Boys'					
Grande Brothers Inc	West Roxbury	MA	G	617 323-6169	16496
CLOTHING: Trousers & Slacks, Men's & Boys'					
16sur20 Management LLC	Lenox	MA	F	413 637-5061	12099
American Power Source Inc **(PA)**	Fall River	MA	C	508 672-8847	10657
Timberland LLC **(HQ)**	Stratham	NH	B	603 772-9500	19876
CLOTHING: Tuxedos, From Purchased Materials					
Our Place - Shop For Men Inc **(PA)**	North Providence	RI	G	401 231-2370	20769
CLOTHING: Underwear, Women's & Children's					
LJL Enterprises Inc	Peabody	MA	G	781 639-2714	14353
L L Bean Inc	Brunswick	ME	B	207 725-0300	5840
CLOTHING: Uniforms, Ex Athletic, Women's, Misses' & Juniors'					
Collegiate Uniforms Inc	Medford	MA	G	781 219-4952	12927
Nitefighter International	Silver Lake	NH	G	603 367-4741	19824
Professional Images Inc	Pawtucket	RI	G	401 725-7000	20884
CLOTHING: Uniforms, Firemen's, From Purchased Materials					
Sperian Protection Usa Inc **(DH)**	Smithfield	RI	E	401 232-1200	21250
CLOTHING: Uniforms, Men's & Boys'					
Neptune Garment Company	Boston	MA	D	617 482-3980	8722
Professional Images Inc	Pawtucket	RI	G	401 725-7000	20884
CLOTHING: Uniforms, Military, Men/Youth, Purchased Materials					
Creative Apparel Assoc LLC	Dover Foxcroft	ME	E	207 564-0235	5960
CLOTHING: Uniforms, Policemen's, From Purchased Materials					
Gerard R Davis Ltd	North Smithfield	RI	G	401 766-8760	20787
CLOTHING: Uniforms, Team Athletic					
Nomis Enterprises	Wallingford	CT	G	631 821-3120	4778
Collegiate Uniforms Inc	Medford	MA	G	781 219-4952	12927
Custom Crafted Enterprises	North Attleboro	MA	G	508 695-2878	13754
Precision Sportswear Inc	Fall River	MA	E	508 674-3034	10748
H R P Products Inc	Farmington	NH	F	603 330-3757	18142
Hilco Athletic & Graphics Inc	West Warwick	RI	F	401 822-1775	21495
CLOTHING: Uniforms, Work					
Cintas Corporation	Cheshire	CT	F	203 272-2036	722
Cintas Corporation	Bangor	ME	G	207 307-2448	5636

CLOTHING: Warm Weather Knit Outerwear, Including Beachwear

	CITY	ST	EMP	PHONE	ENTRY #
Douglas DK Company Incorporate	Longmeadow	MA	G	413 567-8572	12332

CLOTHING: Waterproof Outerwear

	CITY	ST	EMP	PHONE	ENTRY #
Sterlingwear of Boston Inc **(PA)**	Boston	MA	D	617 567-2100	8865
Sterlingwear of Boston Inc	Boston	MA	C	617 567-6465	8866
Wristies Inc	Lowell	MA	G	978 937-9500	12449
Log House Designs Inc **(PA)**	Chatham	NH	E	603 694-3373	17822

CLOTHING: Work Apparel, Exc Uniforms

	CITY	ST	EMP	PHONE	ENTRY #
Ad M Holdings LLC	Trenton	ME	F	207 667-9696	7096

CLOTHING: Work, Men's

	CITY	ST	EMP	PHONE	ENTRY #
G&K Services LLC	Hartford	CT	G	860 856-4400	1823
Sewn In America Inc **(PA)**	Ridgefield	CT	D	203 438-9149	3683
Madewell Manufacturing Co Inc	New Bedford	MA	G	508 997-0768	13414
Salk Company Inc	Allston	MA	E	617 782-4030	7474
W D C Holdings Inc	Attleboro	MA	D	508 699-4412	7806
Izzy Industries Inc	Pembroke	NH	F	603 219-0596	19458
Labonville Inc	Gorham	NH	E	603 752-3221	18214
Codet-Newport Corporation **(HQ)**	Newport	VT	F	802 334-5811	22192

CLUTCHES, EXC VEHICULAR

	CITY	ST	EMP	PHONE	ENTRY #
Carlyle Johnson Machine Co LLC **(PA)**	Bolton	CT	E	860 643-1531	276
Helander Products Inc	Clinton	CT	F	860 669-7953	788
Inertia Dynamics LLC	New Hartford	CT	C	860 379-1252	2639
Rollease Acmeda Inc **(PA)**	Stamford	CT	D	203 964-1573	4305
Hersey Clutch Co	Orleans	MA	F	508 255-2533	14235
Magnetic Technologies Ltd	Oxford	MA	F	508 987-3303	14268

COAL MINING SERVICES

	CITY	ST	EMP	PHONE	ENTRY #
Coronado Group LLC **(PA)**	Wilton	CT	G	203 761-1291	5284
Tronox LLC **(PA)**	Stamford	CT	E	203 705-3800	4352

COAL MINING: Bituminous & Lignite Surface

	CITY	ST	EMP	PHONE	ENTRY #
Rhino Energy Holdings LLC	Greenwich	CT	A	203 862-7000	1642

COAL MINING: Bituminous Underground

	CITY	ST	EMP	PHONE	ENTRY #
Rhino Energy Holdings LLC	Greenwich	CT	A	203 862-7000	1642

COAL, MINERALS & ORES, WHOLESALE: Sulfur

	CITY	ST	EMP	PHONE	ENTRY #
HJ Baker & Bro LLC **(PA)**	Shelton	CT	E	203 682-9200	3812

COATED OR PLATED PRDTS

	CITY	ST	EMP	PHONE	ENTRY #
Applied Diamond Coatings LLC	Durham	CT	G	860 349-3133	1086
Scp Management LLC	New Hartford	CT	E	860 738-2600	2647
Primetals Technologies USA LLC	Worcester	MA	F	508 755-6111	17447

COATERS: High Vacuum, Metal Plate

	CITY	ST	EMP	PHONE	ENTRY #
Sharon Vacuum Co Inc	Brockton	MA	F	508 588-2323	9173

COATING COMPOUNDS: Tar

	CITY	ST	EMP	PHONE	ENTRY #
Neyra Industries Inc	South Windsor	CT	G	860 289-4359	3995

COATING OR WRAPPING SVC: Steel Pipe

	CITY	ST	EMP	PHONE	ENTRY #
Defense Manufacturers Inc	Somersworth	NH	G	603 332-4186	19834

COATING SVC

	CITY	ST	EMP	PHONE	ENTRY #
Clear & Colored Coatings LLC **(PA)**	Wolcott	CT	G	203 879-1379	5435
Tim Poloski	Vernon Rockville	CT	G	860 508-6566	4685
Churchill Coatings Corporation	South Yarmouth	MA	G	508 394-6573	15327
Custom Coatings	Hyannis	MA	G	508 771-8830	11838
Pike Powder Coating LLC	Allston	MA	G	617 779-7311	7473
Vw Quality Coating	Norton	MA	F	617 963-6503	14092
Northeast Coatings Inc	Warren	RI	G	401 649-1552	21300
Shoreline Coatings LLC	North Branford	CT	G	203 213-3471	2976
Vitek Research Corporation	Naugatuck	CT	F	203 735-1813	2500
Amex Inc	Boston	MA	E	617 569-5630	8364
Anjen Finishing	Marlborough	MA	G	508 251-1532	12713
Berkshire Custom Coating Inc	Pittsfield	MA	E	413 442-3757	14457
Central Mass Powdr Coating Inc	Clinton	MA	G	978 365-1700	10077
Coating Application Tech	Woburn	MA	F	781 491-0699	17146
Coatings and Coverings	Harwich	MA	G	774 237-0882	11392
Collt Mfg Inc	Millis	MA	E	508 376-2525	13183
Falmer Associates Inc	Salem	MA	G	978 745-4000	14911
Feeleys Company Inc	Quincy	MA	G	617 773-1711	14625
G T R Finishing Corporation	Brockton	MA	E	508 588-3240	9147
Manning Way Cpitl Partners LLC	Bellingham	MA	E	508 966-4800	8044
New England Indus Coatings	Worcester	MA	G	508 754-1066	17430
North East Indus Coatings Inc	Ipswich	MA	G	978 356-1200	11932
Pace Industries LLC	North Billerica	MA	C	978 667-8400	13852
Paratronix Inc	Westborough	MA	F	508 222-8979	16642
Powder Pro Powder Coating Inc	New Bedford	MA	G	508 991-5999	13441
Precision Coating Co Inc **(HQ)**	Hudson	MA	D	781 329-1420	11805
Precision Coating Co Inc	Hudson	MA	E	978 562-7561	11806
RPM Wood Finishes Group Inc	Westfield	MA	F	413 562-9655	16724
Spencer Metal Finishing Inc **(PA)**	Brookfield	MA	F	508 885-6477	9193
Westside Finishing Co Inc	Holyoke	MA	E	413 533-4909	11667
Xtalic Corporation	Marlborough	MA	E	508 485-9730	12854
Cianbro Fbrcation Coating Corp	Pittsfield	ME	C	207 487-3311	6588
Northeast Coating Tech Inc	Kennebunk	ME	E	207 985-3232	6239
Atkinson Thin Film Systems	Hampstead	NH	G	603 329-7322	18236
Good Hues Custom Powdr Coating	Derry	NH	G	603 434-8034	17980
Omni Metals Company Inc	Somersworth	NH	E	603 692-6664	19845
Pf Pro Fnshg Silkscreening Inc	Hampstead	NH	G	603 329-8344	18248
Difruscia Industries Inc	Cranston	RI	E	401 943-9900	20210
Me-92 Operations Inc	Providence	RI	E	401 831-9200	21065
Metal Spraying Co Inc	Central Falls	RI	G	401 725-2722	20120
Providence Metallizing Co Inc **(PA)**	Pawtucket	RI	D	401 722-5300	20886
Quality Spraying Stenciling Co	Providence	RI	D	401 861-2413	21103
Ellison Surface Tech Inc	North Clarendon	VT	D	802 775-9300	22215
R&B Powder Coating LLC	Poultney	VT	G	802 287-2300	22275
Vermont Ware Inc	St George	VT	G	802 482-4426	22514

COATING SVC: Aluminum, Metal Prdts

	CITY	ST	EMP	PHONE	ENTRY #
Gybenorth Industries LLC	Milford	CT	F	203 876-9876	2295
Superior Wldg Fabrication Inc	Ellsworth	ME	F	207 664-2121	6022
G S P Coatings Inc	Brattleboro	VT	F	802 257-5858	21726

COATING SVC: Electrodes

	CITY	ST	EMP	PHONE	ENTRY #
Chase Corp Inc	Westwood	MA	G	781 332-0700	16860
Chase Corporation **(PA)**	Westwood	MA	G	781 332-0700	16861
Chase Corporation	Oxford	MA	F	508 731-2710	14256
Chase Corporation	Westwood	MA	F	781 329-3259	16862

COATING SVC: Hot Dip, Metals Or Formed Prdts

	CITY	ST	EMP	PHONE	ENTRY #
Marjan Inc	Waterbury	CT	F	203 573-1742	4910
Paint & Powder Works LLC	New Britain	CT	F	860 225-2019	2560

COATING SVC: Metals & Formed Prdts

	CITY	ST	EMP	PHONE	ENTRY #
American Metallizing	South Windsor	CT	G	860 289-1677	3936
Cametoid Technologies Inc	Manchester	CT	F	860 646-4667	1991
Central Connecticut Coating	East Hartford	CT	F	860 528-8281	1180
Chem-Tron Pntg Pwdr Cating Inc	Danbury	CT	G	203 743-5131	887
Colonial Coatings Inc	Milford	CT	E	203 783-9933	2265
Competitive Edge Coatings LLC	South Windsor	CT	G	860 882-0762	3952
Connecticut Plasma Tech LLC	South Windsor	CT	F	860 289-5500	3953
Covalent Coating Tech LLC	East Hartford	CT	G	860 214-6452	1184
Engineered Coatings Inc	Litchfield	CT	E	860 567-5556	1948
Integrity Cylinder Sales LLC	East Hampton	CT	G	860 267-6667	1160
K & G Corp	Manchester	CT	F	860 643-1133	2015
Metallizing Service Co Inc **(PA)**	Hartford	CT	E	860 953-1144	1848
Plas-TEC Coatings Inc	South Windsor	CT	F	860 289-6029	4000
Praxair Inc **(HQ)**	Danbury	CT	B	203 837-2000	971
Praxair Surface Tech Inc	Manchester	CT	D	860 646-0700	2039
Pti Industries Inc **(HQ)**	Enfield	CT	E	800 318-8438	1376

COATING SVC: Metals, With Plastic Or Resins

	CITY	ST	EMP	PHONE	ENTRY #
American Roller Company LLC	Middlebury	CT	F	203 598-3100	2154
Donwell Company	Manchester	CT	E	860 649-5374	2002
Mitchell-Bate Company	Waterbury	CT	E	203 233-0862	4918
Plastonics Inc	Hartford	CT	E	860 249-5455	1859
Applied Plastics Co Inc	Norwood	MA	E	781 762-1881	14133
Central Coating Tech Inc	West Boylston	MA	D	508 835-6225	16411
DSM Coating Resins Inc	Wilmington	MA	C	800 458-0014	16996
East Coast Plastics Inc	Framingham	MA	G	508 429-8080	10944
Indepenent Plating Co	Worcester	MA	E	508 756-0301	17391
Innovative Coatings Inc	Medway	MA	F	508 533-6101	12961
Parker-Hannifin Corporation	Hudson	NH	C	603 880-4807	18425
Development Associates Inc	North Kingstown	RI	F	401 884-1350	20702
Teknicote Inc	Rumford	RI	D	401 724-2230	21197
Gds Manufacturing Company	Williston	VT	G	802 862-7610	22669

COATING SVC: Rust Preventative

	CITY	ST	EMP	PHONE	ENTRY #
Praxair Surface Tech Inc	Biddeford	ME	D	207 282-3787	5757

COATINGS: Air Curing

	CITY	ST	EMP	PHONE	ENTRY #
Tcg Green Technologies Inc	Sharon	CT	F	860 364-4694	3770
L H C Inc **(PA)**	Lynn	MA	E	781 592-6444	12520
Norfolk Corporation	Marshfield	MA	F	781 319-0400	12864
Carroll Coatings Company Inc **(PA)**	Providence	RI	F	401 781-4942	20980
Spectrum Coatings Labs Inc	Providence	RI	F	401 781-4847	21124

COATINGS: Epoxy

	CITY	ST	EMP	PHONE	ENTRY #
A W Chesterton Company **(PA)**	Groveland	MA	E	781 438-7000	11298
Cast Coat Inc	West Bridgewater	MA	G	508 587-4502	16433
Creative Stone Systems Inc	Buzzards Bay	MA	F	866 608-7625	9360
Duromar Inc	Pembroke	MA	G	781 826-2525	14401
Novolac Epoxy Technologies Inc **(PA)**	Harwich	MA	G	508 385-5598	11396
Warren Environmental Inc **(PA)**	Middleboro	MA	G	508 947-8539	13081
Northern Industries Inc **(PA)**	Coventry	RI	G	401 769-4305	20160

COATINGS: Polyurethane

	CITY	ST	EMP	PHONE	ENTRY #
C L Hauthaway & Sons Corp	Lynn	MA	E	781 592-6444	12495
Urethane Solutions LLC	Saco	ME	G	207 284-5400	6861

COCKTAIL LOUNGE

	CITY	ST	EMP	PHONE	ENTRY #
E M K Inc	Skowhegan	ME	F	207 474-2666	6973

COFFEE MAKERS: Electric

	CITY	ST	EMP	PHONE	ENTRY #
Casa Antigua	Lynn	MA	G	781 584-8240	12496
Mrs Mitchells Kitchen Inc	Holyoke	MA	G	413 322-8816	11641

COIL WINDING SVC

	CITY	ST	EMP	PHONE	ENTRY #
Jan Manufacturing Inc	Wolcott	CT	G	203 879-0580	5445
Wirewinders Inc	Milford	NH	G	603 673-1763	19083

COILS & TRANSFORMERS

	CITY	ST	EMP	PHONE	ENTRY #
Bicron Electronics Company **(PA)**	Torrington	CT	D	860 482-2524	4566
Cable Technology Inc	Willington	CT	E	860 429-7889	5270
Coils Plus Inc	Wolcott	CT	E	203 879-0755	5436
Future Manufacturing Inc	Bristol	CT	E	860 584-0685	565
Microphase Corporation	Shelton	CT	E	203 866-8000	3833
Microtech Inc	Cheshire	CT	D	203 272-3234	745
Qtran Inc	Milford	CT	E	203 367-8777	2344

	CITY	ST	EMP	PHONE	ENTRY #
Excelitas Technologies Corp	Salem	MA	C	800 775-6786	14910
M V Mason Elec Inc	Walpole	MA	G	508 668-6200	15999
Microwave Engineering Corp	North Andover	MA	D	978 685-2776	13718
GE Energy Management Svcs Inc	Somersworth	NH	C	603 692-2100	19838
Pd & E Electronics LLC	North Hampton	NH	G	603 964-3165	19386
Technicoil LLC	Ossipee	NH	F	603 569-3100	19422
Kearney-National Inc	North Kingstown	RI	E	401 943-2686	20719
Dynapower Company LLC **(PA)**	South Burlington	VT	C	802 860-7200	22447

COILS: Electric Motors Or Generators

	CITY	ST	EMP	PHONE	ENTRY #
Autac Incorporated	Branford	CT	F	203 481-3444	292
Coils Plus Inc	Wolcott	CT	E	203 879-0755	5436

COILS: Pipe

	CITY	ST	EMP	PHONE	ENTRY #
JFd Tube & Coil Products Inc	Hamden	CT	E	203 288-6941	1763

COINS & TOKENS: Non-Currency

	CITY	ST	EMP	PHONE	ENTRY #
Jim Carr Inc	Pelham	NH	G	603 635-2821	19437

COINS, WHOLESALE

	CITY	ST	EMP	PHONE	ENTRY #
Jim Carr Inc	Pelham	NH	G	603 635-2821	19437

COKE: Calcined Petroleum, Made From Purchased Materials

	CITY	ST	EMP	PHONE	ENTRY #
Rain Cii Carbon LLC	Stamford	CT	F	203 406-0535	4297

COKE: Petroleum

	CITY	ST	EMP	PHONE	ENTRY #
Ultron LLC	Waldoboro	ME	G	207 832-4502	7137

COLLEGE, EXC JUNIOR

	CITY	ST	EMP	PHONE	ENTRY #
President Fllows Hrvard Cllege	Cambridge	MA	G	617 495-2020	9615
President Fllows Hrvard Cllege	Cambridge	MA	C	617 495-4043	9617
Trustees of Boston College	Chestnut Hill	MA	F	617 552-2844	9993
Trustees of Tufts College	Medford	MA	E	617 628-5000	12951

COLOR PIGMENTS

	CITY	ST	EMP	PHONE	ENTRY #
Hudson Color Concentrates LLC	Leominster	MA	D	978 537-3538	12153

COLORS IN OIL, EXC ARTISTS'

	CITY	ST	EMP	PHONE	ENTRY #
Raymond Agler	Gloucester	MA	G	978 281-5048	11206

COLORS: Pigments, Inorganic

	CITY	ST	EMP	PHONE	ENTRY #
Clariant Plas Coatings USA LLC	Holden	MA	D	508 829-6321	11543
Color Change Technology Inc	North Andover	MA	G	978 377-0050	13695
F & D Plastics Inc **(PA)**	Leominster	MA	E	978 668-5140	12136
Engelhard Corp Scales	Eastport	ME	G	207 853-2501	5994
Ecc Holdings Inc **(HQ)**	Providence	RI	E	401 331-9000	21002

COLORS: Pigments, Organic

	CITY	ST	EMP	PHONE	ENTRY #
Ecc Holdings Inc **(HQ)**	Providence	RI	E	401 331-9000	21002

COLUMNS: Concrete

	CITY	ST	EMP	PHONE	ENTRY #
Essex Column Corp	Georgetown	MA	F	978 352-7670	11141
Portland Stone Ware Co Inc **(PA)**	Dracut	MA	E	978 459-7272	10367

COMBS: Plastic

	CITY	ST	EMP	PHONE	ENTRY #
Apothecary Products LLC	North Attleboro	MA	E	508 695-0727	13745
Jumbo Plastics Inc	Leominster	MA	F	978 537-7835	12157
Krest Products Corp	Leominster	MA	E	978 537-1244	12159

COMFORTERS & QUILTS, FROM MANMADE FIBER OR SILK

	CITY	ST	EMP	PHONE	ENTRY #
Rosscommon Quilts Inc	Dorchester	MA	G	617 436-5848	10348

COMMERCIAL & OFFICE BUILDINGS RENOVATION & REPAIR

	CITY	ST	EMP	PHONE	ENTRY #
Lockheed Window Corp	Pascoag	RI	D	401 568-3061	20802

COMMERCIAL ART & GRAPHIC DESIGN SVCS

	CITY	ST	EMP	PHONE	ENTRY #
Garrett Printing & Graphics	Bristol	CT	G	860 589-6710	567
Gerber Scientific LLC **(PA)**	Tolland	CT	C	860 871-8082	4548
Print Source Ltd	Milford	CT	G	203 876-1822	2341
S and Z Graphics LLC	Milford	CT	G	203 783-9675	2358
Success Printing & Mailing Inc	Norwalk	CT	F	203 847-1112	3252
Zp Couture LLC	North Haven	CT	G	888 697-7239	3070
Accela Graphics Neng Inc	Westborough	MA	G	508 366-5999	16586
Argosy Publishing Inc **(PA)**	Newton	MA	E	617 527-9999	13562
Clayton LLC	Woburn	MA	E	617 250-8500	17144
Congruity 360 LLC	Fall River	MA	D	508 689-9516	10679
Desk Top Graphics Inc **(HQ)**	Peabody	MA	E	617 832-1927	14330
Digital Graphics Inc	North Billerica	MA	E	781 270-3670	13809
Publishers Design & Prod Svcs	Sagamore Beach	MA	F	508 833-8300	14886
Designtex Group Inc	Portland	ME	E	207 774-2689	6650
Lynne Bailey	York	ME	G	207 363-7999	7310
Savvy Workshop	Manchester	NH	G	603 792-0080	18916
Textnology Corp	Nashua	NH	F	603 465-8398	19273
T M Morris Productions Inc	Providence	RI	G	401 331-7780	21131
Balance Designs Inc	Manchester Center	VT	G	802 362-2893	22080

COMMERCIAL ART & ILLUSTRATION SVCS

	CITY	ST	EMP	PHONE	ENTRY #
Weston Corporation	Hingham	MA	F	781 749-0936	11516
Graphic Consumer Services Inc	Candia	NH	G	603 483-5355	17785

COMMERCIAL CONTAINERS WHOLESALERS

	CITY	ST	EMP	PHONE	ENTRY #
Quality Containers of Neng	Yarmouth	ME	G	207 846-5420	7299

COMMERCIAL EQPT WHOLESALERS, NEC

	CITY	ST	EMP	PHONE	ENTRY #
Treif USA Inc	Shelton	CT	F	203 929-9930	3881
Fitness Em LLC	Uxbridge	MA	E	508 278-3209	15916
Industrial Safety Products LLC	Colchester	VT	G	802 338-9035	21867

COMMERCIAL EQPT, WHOLESALE: Coffee Brewing Eqpt & Splys

	CITY	ST	EMP	PHONE	ENTRY #
Saccuzzo Company Inc	Newington	CT	G	860 665-1101	2900

COMMERCIAL EQPT, WHOLESALE: Display Eqpt, Exc Refrigerated

	CITY	ST	EMP	PHONE	ENTRY #
Ardent Inc **(PA)**	East Hartford	CT	E	860 528-6000	1173

COMMERCIAL EQPT, WHOLESALE: Scales, Exc Laboratory

	CITY	ST	EMP	PHONE	ENTRY #
Public Scales	Lewiston	ME	F	207 784-9466	6317

COMMERCIAL LAUNDRY EQPT

	CITY	ST	EMP	PHONE	ENTRY #
Naugatuck Recovery Inc **(HQ)**	Naugatuck	CT	E	203 723-1122	2487

COMMERCIAL PRINTING & NEWSPAPER PUBLISHING COMBINED

	CITY	ST	EMP	PHONE	ENTRY #
Bristol Press	Torrington	CT	D	860 584-0501	4568
Chronicle Printing Company	Willimantic	CT	D	860 423-8466	5262
Day Publishing Company **(HQ)**	New London	CT	B	860 701-4200	2770
Gatehouse Media Conn Holdings	Norwich	CT	E	860 887-9211	3281
GPA	Plainville	CT	G	860 410-0624	3494
Green Manor Corporation **(PA)**	Manchester	CT	B	860 643-8111	2007
Hersam Publishing Company	New Canaan	CT	B	203 966-9541	2601
Hillside Capital Inc De Corp **(HQ)**	Stamford	CT	F	203 618-0202	4217
New Haven Register LLC	New Haven	CT	A	203 789-5200	2716
Printed Communications	South Windsor	CT	G	860 436-9619	4005
Record-Journal Newspaper **(PA)**	Meriden	CT	C	203 235-1661	2124
Shore Publishing LLC	Madison	CT	E	203 245-1877	1975
The Bee Publishing Company **(PA)**	Newtown	CT	E	203 426-8036	2943
Villager Newspapers	Putnam	CT	G	860 928-1818	3639
2 Cool Promos	Westborough	MA	G	508 351-9700	16583
Bh Media Inc **(HQ)**	Braintree	MA	D	617 426-3000	8990
Boston Globe LLC	Boston	MA	A	617 929-2684	8431
Boston Neighborhood News Inc	Boston	MA	G	617 436-1222	8435
East Boston Times Inc	Boston	MA	E	617 567-9600	8515
Enterprise Newsmedia LLC **(HQ)**	Quincy	MA	G	585 598-0030	14623
Enterprise Publishing Co LLC	Fall River	MA	A	585 598-0030	10689
Families and Wealth LLC	Newton	MA	G	617 558-5800	13592
Gatehouse Media Mass I Inc **(HQ)**	Beverly	MA	A	585 598-0030	8135
Gatehouse Media Mass I Inc	Somerville	MA	G	617 629-3381	15176
Gatehouse Media Mass I Inc	Lexington	MA	G	781 861-9110	12227
Gatehouse Media Mass I Inc	Beverly	MA	G	781 639-4800	8136
Gatehouse Media Mass I Inc	Weymouth	MA	G	781 682-4850	16889
Hopkinton Crier	Framingham	MA	G	508 626-3939	10963
Infotrak National Data Service	Needham	MA	F	781 276-1711	13301
Inquirer and Mirror Inc	Nantucket	MA	F	508 228-0001	13226
Jewish Advocate Pubg Corp	Boston	MA	F	617 523-6232	8629
Jewish Journal	Salem	MA	F	978 745-4111	14925
Journal Register Company	Fall River	MA	F	508 678-3844	10717
Leominster Champion	Leominster	MA	G	978 534-6006	12161
Metro Boston LLC	Boston	MA	E	617 210-7905	8701
Middlesex News	Framingham	MA	G	508 626-3800	10985
Sing Tao Newspapers NY Ltd	Boston	MA	E	617 426-9642	8848
Stonebridge Press Inc **(PA)**	Southbridge	MA	E	508 764-4325	15405
Target Marketing Group Inc	Rehoboth	MA	G	508 252-6575	14761
Technology Organization Inc	Somerville	MA	G	617 623-4488	15222
Turley Publications Inc **(PA)**	Palmer	MA	C	800 824-6548	14298
Valley Advocate	Northampton	MA	G	413 584-0003	14024
Vineyard Gazette LLC **(PA)**	Edgartown	MA	E	508 627-4311	10588
Westfield News Group LLC	Westfield	MA	E	413 562-4181	16745
Bangor Publishing Company **(PA)**	Bangor	ME	C	207 990-8000	5632
Beacon Press Inc	Biddeford	ME	E	207 282-1535	5722
Forecaster Publishing Inc	South Portland	ME	F	207 781-3661	7027
Franklin Group	Farmington	ME	E	207 778-2075	6048
Lewiston Daily Sun **(PA)**	Lewiston	ME	C	207 784-3555	6299
Lewiston Daily Sun	Lewiston	ME	G	207 784-5411	6300
Mtm Oldco Inc **(PA)**	Portland	ME	B	207 791-6650	6696
RH Rosenfield Co	Sanford	ME	E	207 324-1798	6889
Two Old Broads	Machias	ME	G	207 255-6561	6396
Caledonian Record Pubg Co Inc	Littleton	NH	G	603 444-7141	18656
Country News Club Inc	North Conway	NH	E	603 356-2999	19376
Eagle Publications Inc	Claremont	NH	E	603 543-3100	17849
Fosters Daily Dmcrat Fstrs Sun	Portsmouth	NH	G	603 431-4888	19565
Keene Publishing Corporation	Keene	NH	D	603 352-1234	18511
Local Media Group Inc	Portsmouth	NH	C	603 436-1800	19587
News & Sentinel Inc	Colebrook	NH	F	603 237-5501	17874
Newspapers New England Inc **(PA)**	Concord	NH	G	603 224-5301	17917
Salmon Press LLC **(PA)**	Meredith	NH	F	603 279-4516	18978
Telegraph Publishing Company **(HQ)**	Nashua	NH	C	603 594-6472	19271
Union Leader Corporation **(PA)**	Manchester	NH	B	603 668-4321	18944
Kent County Daily Times	West Warwick	RI	E	401 789-9744	21498
Lmg Rhode Island Holdings Inc **(HQ)**	Providence	RI	G	585 598-0030	21054
Phoenix-Times Publishing Co	Bristol	RI	D	401 253-6000	20098
Providence Journal Company	Providence	RI	B	401 277-7000	21096
Rhode Island Media Group	Woonsocket	RI	E	401 762-3000	21578
Herald of Randolph	Randolph	VT	F	802 728-3232	22297
New Market Press Inc	Middlebury	VT	F	802 388-6397	22115
News and Citizen Inc	Morrisville	VT	E	802 888-2212	22175
Other Paper	South Burlington	VT	G	802 864-6670	22455
Ta Update Inc **(PA)**	Barre	VT	D	802 479-4040	21642

COMMODITY CONTRACT TRADING COMPANIES

	CITY	ST	EMP	PHONE	ENTRY #
US Gold and Diamond Exch LLC **(PA)**	Derry	NH	G	603 300-8888	18001

COMMON SAND MINING

	CITY	ST	EMP	PHONE	ENTRY #
Dunning Sand & Gravel Company	Farmington	CT	F	860 677-1616	1478
Kacerguis Farms Inc	Bethlehem	CT	G	203 405-1202	197
Kobyluck Sand and Gravel Inc	Waterford	CT	F	860 444-9600	4988
Laurelbrook Ntral Rsources LLC	East Canaan	CT	F	860 824-5843	1113
Aggregate Inds - Northeast Reg	Ashland	MA	E	508 881-1430	7655

PRODUCT

	CITY	ST	EMP	PHONE	ENTRY #
Chick Trucking Inc	Newmarket	NH	G	603 659-3566	19331
Tilcon Arthur Whitcomb Inc **(HQ)**	North Swanzey	NH	F	603 352-0101	19393

COMMUNICATION HEADGEAR: Telephone

	CITY	ST	EMP	PHONE	ENTRY #
Holase Incorporated	Portsmouth	NH	G	603 397-0038	19575
Sensear Inc	Nashua	NH	G	603 589-4072	19260

COMMUNICATIONS EQPT & SYSTEMS, NEC

	CITY	ST	EMP	PHONE	ENTRY #
IBC Communications Inc	North Chelmsford	MA	G	978 455-9692	13896
Saltwhistle Technology LLC	Chester	NH	G	603 887-3161	17825

COMMUNICATIONS EQPT WHOLESALERS

	CITY	ST	EMP	PHONE	ENTRY #
Fenton Corp	Westport	CT	F	203 221-2788	5191
Socomec Inc **(DH)**	Watertown	MA	F	617 245-0447	16317
Sensear Inc	Nashua	NH	G	603 589-4072	19260

COMMUNICATIONS EQPT: Microwave

	CITY	ST	EMP	PHONE	ENTRY #
Microphase Corporation	Shelton	CT	E	203 866-8000	3833
Scinetx LLC	Stamford	CT	G	203 355-3676	4310
Comtech PST Corp	Topsfield	MA	F	978 887-5754	15854
Hxi LLC	Harvard	MA	F	978 772-7774	11379
Microwave Video Systems LLC	Melrose	MA	G	781 665-6600	12985
Victor Microwave Inc	Wakefield	MA	F	781 245-4472	15982
Tensor Communications Systems	Bradford	NH	G	603 938-5206	17742

COMMUNICATIONS EQPT: Radio, Marine

	CITY	ST	EMP	PHONE	ENTRY #
Raytheon Sutheast Asia Systems **(HQ)**	Billerica	MA	E	978 470-5000	8289

COMMUNICATIONS SVCS

	CITY	ST	EMP	PHONE	ENTRY #
Acacia Communications Inc **(PA)**	Maynard	MA	C	978 938-4896	12894

COMMUNICATIONS SVCS: Cellular

	CITY	ST	EMP	PHONE	ENTRY #
James G Hachey Inc	Peabody	MA	G	781 229-6400	14344

COMMUNICATIONS SVCS: Data

	CITY	ST	EMP	PHONE	ENTRY #
Everbridge Inc **(PA)**	Burlington	MA	C	818 230-9700	9271
MTI Unified Communications LLC	South Yarmouth	MA	G	774 352-1110	15331
Holase Incorporated	Portsmouth	NH	G	603 397-0038	19575

COMMUNICATIONS SVCS: Facsimile Transmission

	CITY	ST	EMP	PHONE	ENTRY #
Canalside Printing	Monument Beach	MA	G	508 759-4141	13214
Courier Printing Inc	Pittsfield	MA	G	413 442-3242	14465
Rgp Corp	Milford	MA	G	508 478-8511	13141
Northeast Publishing Company	Dover Foxcroft	ME	G	207 564-8355	5961
Allegra Print & Imaging	East Greenwich	RI	G	401 884-9280	20352
Sir Speedy	Providence	RI	G	401 232-2000	21122
ASC Duplicating Inc	Montpelier	VT	G	802 229-0660	22145
Zinn Graphics Inc	Brattleboro	VT	G	802 254-6742	21756

COMMUNICATIONS SVCS: Internet Connectivity Svcs

	CITY	ST	EMP	PHONE	ENTRY #
Battilana & Associates	Woodstock	VT	G	802 457-3375	22736

COMMUNICATIONS SVCS: Internet Host Svcs

	CITY	ST	EMP	PHONE	ENTRY #
20/20 Software Inc	Stamford	CT	G	203 316-5500	4122

COMMUNICATIONS SVCS: Online Svc Providers

	CITY	ST	EMP	PHONE	ENTRY #
Streak Media LLC	Boston	MA	G	617 242-9460	8868
Technologies 2010 Inc	Milford	MA	G	508 482-0164	13146
Grolen Communications Inc	Manchester	NH	G	603 645-0101	18831

COMMUNICATIONS SVCS: Telegraph Cable, Land Or Submarine

	CITY	ST	EMP	PHONE	ENTRY #
Seaborn Management Inc	Beverly	MA	F	978 377-8366	8175

COMMUNICATIONS SVCS: Telephone Or Video

	CITY	ST	EMP	PHONE	ENTRY #
MTI Unified Communications LLC	South Yarmouth	MA	G	774 352-1110	15331

COMMUNICATIONS SVCS: Telephone, Voice

	CITY	ST	EMP	PHONE	ENTRY #
Mirion Tech Canberra Inc **(HQ)**	Meriden	CT	B	203 238-2351	2109

COMMUTATORS: Electronic

	CITY	ST	EMP	PHONE	ENTRY #
Sysdyne Technologies LLC	Stamford	CT	F	203 327-3649	4339
Intellisense Software Corp	Lynnfield	MA	E	781 933-8098	12550

COMPACT DISC PLAYERS

	CITY	ST	EMP	PHONE	ENTRY #
Color Film Media Group LLC **(PA)**	Norwalk	CT	G	203 202-2929	3129

COMPACT DISCS OR CD'S, WHOLESALE

	CITY	ST	EMP	PHONE	ENTRY #
Forced Exposure Inc	Arlington	MA	E	781 321-0320	7626

COMPACT LASER DISCS: Prerecorded

	CITY	ST	EMP	PHONE	ENTRY #
Harvey Bravman	Roslindale	MA	G	617 323-9969	14838
Image Software Services Inc	Shirley	MA	E	978 425-3600	15087

COMPARATORS: Optical

	CITY	ST	EMP	PHONE	ENTRY #
Macro Systems Inc	Shelton	CT	G	203 225-6266	3830
Vermont Precision Machine Svcs	Springfield	VT	G	802 885-8291	22511

COMPOST

	CITY	ST	EMP	PHONE	ENTRY #
Collins Compost	Enfield	CT	G	860 749-3416	1350
Curbside Compost LLC	Ridgefield	CT	G	914 646-6890	3664
New Milford Farms Inc	New Milford	CT	F	860 210-0250	2818
360 Recycling LLC	Westfield	MA	F	413 562-0193	16659
Black Earth Compost LLC	Gloucester	MA	F	262 227-1067	11166
Infinite Compost	Hyde Park	MA	G	617 922-6419	11870
Martins Farm Recycling	Greenfield	MA	G	413 774-5631	11269
Massachusetts Natural Fert Inc	Westminster	MA	G	978 874-0744	16808
North Shore Compost LLC	Lynn	MA	G	781 581-3489	12529
Offbeet Composting Llc	Lowell	MA	G	603 568-2756	12415
Ideal Compost Company	Peterborough	NH	G	603 924-5050	19474
Green Mountain Compost	Williston	VT	G	802 660-4949	22672
Queen City Soil & Stone DBA	Burlington	VT	G	802 318-2411	21805
Vermont Compost Company Inc	Montpelier	VT	G	802 223-6049	22162
William R Raap	Burlington	VT	G	802 660-3508	21817

COMPRESSORS: Air & Gas

	CITY	ST	EMP	PHONE	ENTRY #
Afcon Products Inc	Bethany	CT	F	203 393-9301	118
Bauer Compressors Inc	Monroe	CT	G	203 445-9514	2394
Norwalk Compreseer Company	Stratford	CT	E	203 386-1234	4433
Norwalk Compressor Inc	Stratford	CT	G	203 386-1234	4434
Standard Pneumatic Products	Newtown	CT	G	203 270-1400	2939
Stylair LLC	Plainville	CT	F	860 747-4588	3515
Air Energy Group LLC	South Easton	MA	E	508 230-9445	15269
Anver Corporation	Hudson	MA	D	978 568-0221	11755
Atlas Copco Compressors LLC	Westfield	MA	E	518 765-3344	16669
Atlas Copco Compressors LLC	West Springfield	MA	F	413 493-7290	16510
Ebara Technologies Inc	Newburyport	MA	G	978 465-1983	13485
Edwards Vacuum LLC	Chelmsford	MA	G	978 262-7565	9896
Guardair Corporation	Chicopee	MA	E	413 594-4400	10028
Oscomp Systems Inc **(PA)**	Boston	MA	G	617 418-4640	8761
V Power Equipment LLC	Wareham	MA	F	508 273-7596	16256
General Electric Company	Bangor	ME	B	207 941-2500	5648
Compressor Energy Services LLC	Bedford	NH	G	603 491-2200	17636

COMPRESSORS: Air & Gas, Including Vacuum Pumps

	CITY	ST	EMP	PHONE	ENTRY #
P&G Metal Components Corp	Bloomfield	CT	F	860 243-2220	248
Dr Guilbeault Air Comprsr LLC	Hudson	NH	E	603 598-0891	18386

COMPRESSORS: Wholesalers

	CITY	ST	EMP	PHONE	ENTRY #
Spencer Turbine Company **(HQ)**	Windsor	CT	C	860 688-8361	5363

COMPUTER & COMPUTER SOFTWARE STORES

	CITY	ST	EMP	PHONE	ENTRY #
Laser Lightning LLC **(PA)**	East Douglas	MA	G	508 476-0138	10428
Valora Technologies Inc	Bedford	MA	E	781 229-2265	8018
Electronics For Imaging Inc	West Lebanon	NH	B	603 279-6800	19949
Glacier Computer LLC	Amherst	NH	F	603 882-1560	17564
Robert Veinot	Merrimack	NH	G	603 424-1799	19025
Quantifacts Inc	Riverside	RI	G	401 421-8300	21175

COMPUTER & COMPUTER SOFTWARE STORES: Peripheral Eqpt

	CITY	ST	EMP	PHONE	ENTRY #
Mimoco Inc	Needham Heights	MA	F	617 783-1100	13339

COMPUTER & COMPUTER SOFTWARE STORES: Printers & Plotters

	CITY	ST	EMP	PHONE	ENTRY #
Hartford Toner & Cartridge Inc **(PA)**	Broad Brook	CT	G	860 292-1280	629

COMPUTER & COMPUTER SOFTWARE STORES: Software & Access

	CITY	ST	EMP	PHONE	ENTRY #
Beyondtrust Software Inc	Andover	MA	F	978 206-3700	7540

COMPUTER & COMPUTER SOFTWARE STORES: Software, Bus/Non-Game

	CITY	ST	EMP	PHONE	ENTRY #
Cunningham Industries Inc	Stamford	CT	G	203 324-2942	4180
David Corporation **(PA)**	Wakefield	MA	E	781 587-3008	15948
Quinn Curtis Inc	Medfield	MA	G	508 359-6639	12918

COMPUTER & DATA PROCESSING EQPT REPAIR & MAINTENANCE

	CITY	ST	EMP	PHONE	ENTRY #
Bull Hn Info Systems Inc	Chelmsford	MA	G	978 256-1033	9883

COMPUTER & OFFICE MACHINE MAINTENANCE & REPAIR

	CITY	ST	EMP	PHONE	ENTRY #
Frontier Vision Tech Inc	Rocky Hill	CT	E	860 953-0240	3709
Mackenzie Mch & Mar Works Inc	East Haven	CT	G	203 777-3479	1254
Modern Electronic Fax & Cmpt	Fairfield	CT	G	203 292-6520	1445
Bull Data Systems Inc **(DH)**	Chelmsford	MA	G	978 294-6000	9882
Cybtek Inc	Peabody	MA	G	978 532-7110	14327
Deerwalk Inc **(PA)**	Lexington	MA	B	781 325-1775	12218
Di An Enterprises Inc	Chestnut Hill	MA	F	617 469-0819	9986
Sdl Xyenterprise LLC **(PA)**	Wakefield	MA	C	781 756-4400	15974
Valora Technologies Inc	Bedford	MA	E	781 229-2265	8018
Tyler Technologies Inc	Yarmouth	ME	B	207 781-4606	7302
Robert Veinot	Merrimack	NH	G	603 424-1799	19025

COMPUTER FACILITIES MANAGEMENT SVCS

	CITY	ST	EMP	PHONE	ENTRY #
Executive Force Protection LLC	Cambridge	MA	F	617 470-9230	9476
Research Cmpt Consulting Svcs **(PA)**	Canton	MA	G	781 821-1221	9774

COMPUTER FORMS

	CITY	ST	EMP	PHONE	ENTRY #
American Health Resources Inc	North Easton	MA	G	508 588-7700	13941
D B S Industries Inc	Haverhill	MA	D	978 373-4748	11421
Stat Products Inc	Ashland	MA	E	508 881-8022	7670
Wolters Kluwer Fincl Svcs Inc	Waltham	MA	B	978 263-1212	16224
J A Black Company	Belfast	ME	G	207 338-4040	5691
Allied Group Inc **(PA)**	Cranston	RI	C	401 461-1700	20177

COMPUTER GRAPHICS SVCS

	CITY	ST	EMP	PHONE	ENTRY #
Anderson Publishing Inc	Nantucket	MA	G	508 228-3866	13219
Desk Top Graphics Inc **(HQ)**	Peabody	MA	E	617 832-1927	14330
Homeportfolio Inc	Newton	MA	D	617 559-1197	13602
Textnology Corp	Nashua	NH	F	603 465-8398	19273
Valley Signs	Lebanon	NH	G	603 252-1977	18640

COMPUTER HARDWARE REQUIREMENTS ANALYSIS

	CITY	ST	EMP	PHONE	ENTRY #
Advanced Decisions Inc	Orange	CT	F	203 402-0603	3357
Automatech Inc **(PA)**	Plymouth	MA	G	508 830-0088	14544

COMPUTER INTERFACE EQPT: Indl Process

	CITY	ST	EMP	PHONE	ENTRY #
Aci Technology Inc	Woburn	MA	F	781 937-9888	17107
Agency Systems Group	Sterling	MA	G	978 422-8479	15531
Cognex Corporation **(PA)**	Natick	MA	B	508 650-3000	13246
Cognex International Inc **(HQ)**	Natick	MA	F	508 650-3000	13249

	CITY	ST	EMP	PHONE	ENTRY #
Cybertools Inc	Boston	MA	G	978 772-9200	8493
Got Interface	Waltham	MA	F	781 547-5700	16121
Infolibria Inc	Waltham	MA	D	781 392-2200	16134
Invensense Inc **(PA)**	Boston	MA	F	857 268-4400	8619
Magmotor Technologies Inc	Worcester	MA	F	508 835-4305	17411
Wintriss Controls Group LLC	Acton	MA	E	978 268-2700	7394
Dutile Glines & Higgins Inc	Hooksett	NH	F	603 622-0452	18348
Neo Markets Inc	Portsmouth	NH	F	603 766-8716	19597

COMPUTER PERIPHERAL EQPT REPAIR & MAINTENANCE

	CITY	ST	EMP	PHONE	ENTRY #
Transact Technologies Inc **(PA)**	Hamden	CT	C	203 859-6800	1791
Xerox Corporation **(HQ)**	Norwalk	CT	B	203 968-3000	3274
Encore Images Inc	Marblehead	MA	F	781 631-4568	12681

COMPUTER PERIPHERAL EQPT, NEC

	CITY	ST	EMP	PHONE	ENTRY #
Braxton Manufacturing Co Inc	Watertown	CT	C	860 274-6781	5000
Cadesk Company LLC **(PA)**	Trumbull	CT	G	203 268-8083	4617
Computer Express LLC	Berlin	CT	F	860 829-1310	82
Contek International Corp	New Canaan	CT	G	203 972-3406	2594
Contek International Corp	New Canaan	CT	F	203 972-7330	2595
Data Technology Inc	Tolland	CT	E	860 871-8082	4545
Dictaphone Corporation **(HQ)**	Stratford	CT	C	203 381-7000	4409
Ellipson Data LLC	Westport	CT	G	203 227-5520	5190
Hint Peripherals Corp	Meriden	CT	G	203 634-4468	2094
Measurement Systems Inc	Wallingford	CT	E	203 949-3500	4772
Morse Watchmans Inc	Oxford	CT	E	203 264-1108	3415
O E M Controls Inc **(PA)**	Shelton	CT	C	203 929-8431	3845
Ortronics Inc **(DH)**	New London	CT	D	860 445-3900	2776
Ortronics Inc	West Hartford	CT	G	877 295-3472	5088
Ortronics Legrand	Ivoryton	CT	G	860 767-3515	1908
Syferlock Technology Corp	Shelton	CT	G	203 292-5441	3875
Xerox Corporation **(HQ)**	Norwalk	CT	B	203 968-3000	3274
3M Touch Systems Inc **(HQ)**	Methuen	MA	B	978 659-9000	13008
3M Touch Systems Inc	Methuen	MA	B	978 659-9000	13009
3M Touch Systems Inc	Westborough	MA	C	508 871-1840	16584
Adaptive Optics Associates Inc **(DH)**	Devens	MA	D	978 757-9600	10317
Aereo Inc	Hopedale	MA	E	617 861-8287	11669
Apem Inc **(HQ)**	Haverhill	MA	E	978 372-1602	11404
Bull Data Systems Inc **(DH)**	Chelmsford	MA	G	978 294-6000	9882
Bull Hn Info Systems Inc	Chelmsford	MA	G	978 256-1033	9883
C S I Keyboards Inc	Peabody	MA	E	978 532-8181	14318
Circle Twelve Inc	Framingham	MA	G	508 620-5360	10934
Corero Network Security Inc	Marlborough	MA	E	978 212-1500	12741
Cortron Inc	Lowell	MA	E	978 975-5445	12362
Csp Inc **(PA)**	Lowell	MA	D	978 954-5038	12364
Decitek Corp	Westborough	MA	G	508 366-1011	16614
Di An Enterprises Inc	Chestnut Hill	MA	F	617 469-0819	9986
Divya Marigowda	Lexington	MA	G	781 863-5189	12220
EMC Corporation	Southborough	MA	G	508 382-7556	15356
EMC Corporation **(HQ)**	Hopkinton	MA	B	508 435-1000	11706
EMC International Holdings Inc **(DH)**	Hopkinton	MA	G	508 435-1000	11710
Encore Images Inc	Marblehead	MA	F	781 631-4568	12681
G4s Technology Software	Chelmsford	MA	D	781 457-0700	9901
Grandstream Networks Inc **(PA)**	Boston	MA	E	617 566-9300	8576
Grey Force Cooling	Rochester	MA	G	508 441-1753	14787
Humanscale Corporation	Boston	MA	F	617 338-0077	8611
INTEL Network Systems Inc **(HQ)**	Hudson	MA	C	978 553-4000	11778
Intellitech International Inc	Hudson	MA	F	978 212-7200	11779
Inteset Technologies LLC	Hanover	MA	G	781 826-1560	11342
Iva Corporation	Sudbury	MA	G	978 443-5800	15661
Kamel Peripherals Inc **(PA)**	Hopkinton	MA	E	508 435-7771	11724
Kemp Technologies Inc	Rochdale	MA	G	631 418-8407	14781
Kentron Technologies Inc	Wilmington	MA	E	978 988-9100	17011
L-Com Inc **(DH)**	North Andover	MA	D	978 682-6936	13715
M8trix Tech LLC	Canton	MA	G	617 925-7030	9753
Mack Technologies Inc **(HQ)**	Westford	MA	C	978 392-5500	16777
Macraigor Systems LLC **(PA)**	Brookline	MA	G	617 264-4459	9208
Madison Cable Corporation	Worcester	MA	C	508 752-2884	17410
Metroblity Optical Systems Inc	North Billerica	MA	D	781 255-5300	13843
Milford Manufacturing Svcs LLC	Hopedale	MA	D	508 478-8544	11678
Mimoco Inc	Needham Heights	MA	F	617 783-1100	13339
Nemonix Engineering Inc	Bolton	MA	G	508 393-7700	8322
Network Equipment Tech Inc **(DH)**	Westford	MA	E	510 713-7300	16780
New England Technology Group	Cambridge	MA	F	617 864-5551	9581
Onset Computer Corporation	Bourne	MA	C	508 759-9500	8948
Parallel Systems Corp	Georgetown	MA	F	978 352-7100	11148
Power Systems Integrity Inc	Northborough	MA	G	508 393-1655	14045
Precision Handling Devices **(PA)**	Westport	MA	F	508 679-5282	16845
Project Resources Inc	Wareham	MA	F	508 295-7444	16254
Psjl Corporation **(PA)**	Billerica	MA	D	978 313-2500	8279
Riverbed Technology Inc	Cambridge	MA	G	617 250-5300	9635
Rsa Security LLC **(DH)**	Bedford	MA	A	781 515-5000	8007
Sap America Inc	Burlington	MA	E	781 852-3000	9334
Servomotive Corporation	Westborough	MA	G	508 726-9222	16648
Silicon Micro Display Inc	Newton	MA	G	617 433-7630	13638
Sky Computers Inc	Chelmsford	MA	F	978 250-2420	9933
Smart Modular Technologies Inc	Tewksbury	MA	G	978 221-3513	15835
Sunny Young LLC	Boston	MA	E	917 667-0528	8870
Teledyne Dgital Imaging US Inc **(HQ)**	Billerica	MA	E	978 670-2000	8303
Terarecon Inc	Acton	MA	D	978 274-0461	7390
Vitec Industries Inc	Gloucester	MA	G	978 282-7700	11217
Vivid Engineering	Shrewsbury	MA	G	508 842-0165	15136
Whitewood Encrytion	Boston	MA	G	617 419-1800	8926
Winchester Systems Inc **(PA)**	Littleton	MA	E	781 265-0200	12328
Wright Line LLC **(HQ)**	Worcester	MA	C	508 852-4300	17510
Zoom Telephonics Inc **(PA)**	Boston	MA	E	617 423-1072	8944
Allen Datagraph Systems Inc	Salem	NH	E	603 216-6344	19705
Allied Telesis Inc	Portsmouth	NH	G	603 334-6058	19534
Bantry Components Inc	Manchester	NH	E	603 668-3210	18785
Dutile Glines & Higgins Inc	Hooksett	NH	F	603 622-0452	18348
Enterasys Networks Inc **(HQ)**	Salem	NH	D	603 952-5000	19725
Kaycee Group	Londonderry	NH	G	603 505-5754	18707
Memtec Corporation	Salem	NH	E	603 893-8080	19751
Nel-Tech Labs Incorporated	Derry	NH	F	603 425-1096	17990
Psjl Corporation	Exeter	NH	D	978 313-2550	18129
Seamark International LLC	Nashua	NH	F	603 546-0100	19258
Unarco Material Handling Inc	Exeter	NH	E	603 772-2070	18134
Electro Standards Lab Inc	Cranston	RI	D	401 946-1390	20215
Warehouse Cables LLC	Warwick	RI	G	401 737-5677	21442
Alken Inc	Colchester	VT	E	802 655-3159	21856
Fulcrum Design	Bennington	VT	F	802 442-6441	21670
Gvh Studio Inc	Bennington	VT	G	802 379-1135	21671
Image Tek Mfg Inc	Springfield	VT	E	802 885-6208	22502
Mack Group Inc **(PA)**	Arlington	VT	B	802 375-2511	21597
Mack Molding Company Inc **(HQ)**	Arlington	VT	C	802 375-2511	21598

COMPUTER PERIPHERAL EQPT, WHOLESALE

	CITY	ST	EMP	PHONE	ENTRY #
W R Hartigan & Son Inc	Burlington	CT	G	860 673-9203	682
Macraigor Systems LLC **(PA)**	Brookline	MA	G	617 264-4459	9208
Mimoco Inc	Needham Heights	MA	F	617 783-1100	13339
Morgan Scientific Inc **(PA)**	Haverhill	MA	F	978 521-4440	11454
Warehouse Cables LLC	Warwick	RI	G	401 737-5677	21442

COMPUTER PERIPHERAL EQPT: Graphic Displays, Exc Terminals

	CITY	ST	EMP	PHONE	ENTRY #
Frontier Vision Tech Inc	Rocky Hill	CT	E	860 953-0240	3709
Resavue Inc	Orange	CT	F	203 878-0944	3381
Mobile Monitor Tech LLC	Newton Centre	MA	G	617 965-5057	13656

COMPUTER PERIPHERAL EQPT: Input Or Output

	CITY	ST	EMP	PHONE	ENTRY #
Cyclone Pcie Systems LLC	Hamden	CT	G	203 786-5536	1742
Multi Touch Surface Inc	Somerville	MA	E	408 634-9224	15200
Pison Technology Inc	Brookline	MA	G	540 394-0998	9215

COMPUTER PERIPHERAL EQPT: Output To Microfilm Units

	CITY	ST	EMP	PHONE	ENTRY #
Ebeam Film LLC	Shelton	CT	F	203 926-0100	3798

COMPUTER PROGRAMMING SVCS

	CITY	ST	EMP	PHONE	ENTRY #
Kimchuk Incorporated **(PA)**	Danbury	CT	F	203 790-7800	943
Peerless Systems Corporation **(DH)**	Stamford	CT	F	203 350-0040	4281
Able Software Corp **(PA)**	Lexington	MA	F	781 862-2804	12200
Aclara Technologies LLC	Wellesley	MA	E	781 694-3300	16357
Aries Systems Corporation	North Andover	MA	E	978 975-7570	13691
Bitflow Inc	Woburn	MA	F	781 932-2900	17132
C2c Systems Inc	Westborough	MA	F	508 870-2205	16597
Canvas Link Inc	Westborough	MA	G	508 366-3323	16600
CLC Bio LLC **(PA)**	Beverly	MA	F	617 945-0178	8117
Cosmic Software Inc	Billerica	MA	F	978 667-2556	8234
Cybertools Inc	Boston	MA	G	978 772-9200	8493
Diacritech Inc	Boston	MA	F	617 236-7500	8502
Divya Marigowda	Lexington	MA	G	781 863-5189	12220
EMC Corporation	Southborough	MA	G	508 382-7556	15356
EMC Corporation **(HQ)**	Hopkinton	MA	B	508 435-1000	11706
Fis Financial Systems LLC	Burlington	MA	G	952 935-3300	9274
Intac International Inc	Woburn	MA	E	781 272-4494	17204
JM Software Inc	Dracut	MA	G	978 957-9105	10361
Kewill Inc **(DH)**	Chelmsford	MA	D	978 482-2500	9908
Microsemi Frequency Time Corp	Beverly	MA	D	978 232-0040	8155
Modus Media Inc	Waltham	MA	E	781 663-5000	16153
Monotype Imaging Inc **(DH)**	Woburn	MA	D	781 970-6000	17234
Para Research Inc	Gloucester	MA	F	978 282-1100	11201
Pmweb Inc	Wakefield	MA	D	617 207-7080	15970
Progress Software Corporation **(PA)**	Bedford	MA	B	781 280-4000	8003
Rockstar New England Inc	Andover	MA	E	978 409-6272	7601
Sea Sciences Inc	Arlington	MA	G	781 643-1600	7637
Skybuildersdotcom Inc	Cambridge	MA	G	617 876-5678	9653
Solusoft Inc	North Andover	MA	E	978 375-6021	13728
Sophic Alliance Inc	East Falmouth	MA	G	508 495-3801	10449
Tom Snyder Productions Inc **(HQ)**	Watertown	MA	D	617 600-2145	16324
Zlink Inc	Maynard	MA	G	978 309-3628	12907
Tyler Technologies Inc	Yarmouth	ME	B	207 781-4606	7302
CNi Corp	Milford	NH	G	603 249-5075	19050
Infinizone Corp	Hollis	NH	F	603 465-2917	18333
Profitkey International Inc	Salem	NH	E	603 898-9800	19760
Smiths Detection Inc	Middletown	RI	F	401 848-7678	20632
Mediware/Synergy Human & Socia	Essex Junction	VT	D	802 878-8514	21949
Natworks Inc	Northfield	VT	F	802 485-6818	22244
Vermont Systems Inc	Essex Junction	VT	D	802 879-6993	21963

COMPUTER PROGRAMMING SVCS: Custom

	CITY	ST	EMP	PHONE	ENTRY #
Gerber Technology LLC **(HQ)**	Tolland	CT	B	860 871-8082	4549
SS&c Technologies Inc **(HQ)**	Windsor	CT	C	860 298-4500	5365
SS&c Technologies Holdings Inc **(PA)**	Windsor	CT	D	860 298-4500	5366
Raytheon Company	Marlborough	MA	C	508 490-1000	12814

COMPUTER RELATED MAINTENANCE SVCS

	CITY	ST	EMP	PHONE	ENTRY #
Modus Media Inc	Waltham	MA	E	781 663-5000	16153
Oneview Commerce Inc	Boston	MA	F	617 292-0400	8750
Research Cmpt Consulting Svcs **(PA)**	Canton	MA	G	781 821-1221	9774

COMPUTER SOFTWARE DEVELOPMENT

	CITY	ST	EMP	PHONE	ENTRY #
Desrosier of Greenwich Inc	Greenwich	CT	F	203 661-2334	1608
Presco Incorporated	Woodbridge	CT	F	203 397-8722	5477
Scholastic Library Pubg Inc **(HQ)**	Danbury	CT	A	203 797-3500	986

	CITY	ST	EMP	PHONE	ENTRY #
Human Resource Dev Press **(PA)**	Pelham	MA	E	413 253-3488	14388
Kemp Technologies Inc	Rochdale	MA	G	631 418-8407	14781
King Fisher Co Inc	Lowell	MA	E	978 596-0214	12389
Macraigor Systems LLC **(PA)**	Brookline	MA	G	617 264-4459	9208
Meta Software Corporation **(PA)**	Burlington	MA	F	781 238-0293	9302
MTI Systems Inc	West Springfield	MA	E	413 733-1972	16532
Renaissance International	Newburyport	MA	G	978 465-5111	13529
Research Applications and	Cambridge	MA	G	800 939-7238	9630
Seachange International Inc **(PA)**	Acton	MA	C	978 897-0100	7385
Sepaton Inc	Marlborough	MA	D	508 490-7900	12824
Superpedestrian Inc	Cambridge	MA	G	617 945-1892	9666
Avtech Software Inc **(PA)**	Warren	RI	E	401 628-1600	21287

COMPUTER SOFTWARE DEVELOPMENT & APPLICATIONS

	CITY	ST	EMP	PHONE	ENTRY #
Betx LLC	New Hartford	CT	G	860 459-1681	2632
Broadstripes LLC	New Haven	CT	G	203 350-9824	2672
Cantata Media LLC	Norwalk	CT	F	203 951-9885	3118
Fergtech Inc **(PA)**	Darien	CT	G	203 656-1139	1025
Fidelux Lighting LLC **(HQ)**	Hartford	CT	F	860 436-5000	1821
Ladrdefense LLC	Plantsville	CT	G	860 637-8488	3536
W R Hartigan & Son Inc	Burlington	CT	G	860 673-9203	682
Expertek Systems Inc	Marlborough	MA	F	508 624-0006	12754
G4s Technology Software	Chelmsford	MA	D	781 457-0700	9901
Grove Labs Inc	Somerville	MA	F	703 608-8178	15179
Hottinger Bldwin Msrements Inc **(DH)**	Marlborough	MA	D	508 624-4500	12775
Neuromotion Inc	Boston	MA	F	415 676-9326	8726
Novolac Epoxy Technologies Inc **(PA)**	Harwich	MA	G	508 385-5598	11396
Sdl Xyenterprise LLC **(PA)**	Wakefield	MA	C	781 756-4400	15974
Voxel8 Inc	Somerville	MA	F	916 396-3714	15229
Xos Technologies Inc **(HQ)**	Wilmington	MA	E	978 447-5220	17070
Myturncom Pbc	Lebanon	NH	G	206 552-8488	18632
Sungard Insurance Systems Inc	Manchester	NH	G	603 641-3636	18933
Thinkmd Inc	Burlington	VT	G	802 734-7993	21812

COMPUTER SOFTWARE SYSTEMS ANALYSIS & DESIGN: Custom

	CITY	ST	EMP	PHONE	ENTRY #
Dataprep Inc	Orange	CT	E	203 795-2095	3364
Grayfin Security LLC	Madison	CT	G	203 800-6760	1961
Innovation Group	Farmington	CT	E	860 674-2900	1486
Iet Solutions LLC **(DH)**	Canton	MA	E	818 838-0606	9743
Nemonix Engineering Inc	Bolton	MA	G	508 393-7700	8322
Origo Automation Inc	Lowell	MA	G	877 943-5677	12417
Waters Corporation **(PA)**	Milford	MA	C	508 478-2000	13153
Garmin International Inc	Yarmouth	ME	C	800 561-5105	7294
Sproutel Inc	Providence	RI	G	914 806-6514	21126

COMPUTER SOFTWARE WRITERS

	CITY	ST	EMP	PHONE	ENTRY #
Picis Clinical Solutions Inc **(DH)**	Wakefield	MA	C	336 397-5336	15969
Prom Software Inc	South Burlington	VT	F	802 862-7500	22462

COMPUTER STORAGE DEVICES, NEC

	CITY	ST	EMP	PHONE	ENTRY #
EMC Corporation	Fairfield	CT	D	203 418-4500	1429
Emc7 LLC	Fairfield	CT	G	203 429-4355	1430
Kaman Aerospace Corporation	Middletown	CT	C	860 632-1000	2195
Pexagon Technology Inc	Branford	CT	E	203 458-3364	336
Quantum Bpower Southington LLC	Southington	CT	G	860 201-0621	4071
Quantum Circuits Inc	New Haven	CT	F	203 891-6216	2729
Systematics Inc	Rocky Hill	CT	F	860 721-0706	3729
Cambex Corporation	Southborough	MA	G	508 217-4508	15352
Cambex Corporation **(PA)**	Westborough	MA	F	508 983-1200	16598
Em &M Builders LLC	Hopkinton	MA	G	508 497-3446	11703
EMC Corporation	Hopkinton	MA	D	508 249-5883	11704
EMC Corporation	Southborough	MA	G	508 382-7556	15356
EMC Corporation	Hopkinton	MA	E	508 346-2900	11705
EMC Corporation **(HQ)**	Hopkinton	MA	B	508 435-1000	11706
EMC Corporation	Bellingham	MA	G	508 613-2022	8038
EMC Corporation	Newton	MA	C	617 618-3400	13587
EMC Corporation	Hopkinton	MA	F	508 435-0369	11707
EMC Corporation	Hopkinton	MA	F	800 445-2588	11708
EMC Corporation	Franklin	MA	D	508 435-1000	11041
EMC Corporation	Franklin	MA	D	508 528-2546	11042
EMC Corporation	Milford	MA	B	508 634-2774	13116
EMC Corporation	Franklin	MA	D	866 438-3622	11043
EMC Corporation	Franklin	MA	D	800 275-8777	11044
EMC Global Holdings Company	Hopkinton	MA	G	508 544-2852	11709
EMC International Holdings Inc **(DH)**	Hopkinton	MA	G	508 435-1000	11710
EMC Investment Corporation	Hopkinton	MA	G	508 435-1000	11711
Fidelis EMC	North Andover	MA	G	978 655-3390	13703
Interactive Media Corp	Millis	MA	E	508 376-4245	13184
Kaminario Inc **(PA)**	Needham Heights	MA	E	877 982-2555	13335
Paul Parrino	East Walpole	MA	G	508 668-2936	10527
Raid Inc	Andover	MA	E	978 683-6444	7591
Seagate Technology LLC	Shrewsbury	MA	C	508 770-3111	15130
Sepaton Inc	Marlborough	MA	D	508 490-7900	12824
Sudbury Systems Inc	Bedford	MA	E	800 876-8888	8010
Unicom Engineering Inc **(HQ)**	Canton	MA	B	781 332-1000	9791
Winchester Systems Inc **(PA)**	Littleton	MA	E	781 265-0200	12328
Zerious Electronic Pubg Corp	Beverly	MA	G	978 922-4990	8201
Blue Dawg Pwr Wash Southern NH	Hampstead	NH	G	603 498-9473	18238
Visit WEI	Salem	NH	G	603 893-0900	19777
Solid Access Technologies LLC	Newport	RI	G	978 463-0642	20682
Quantum Corporation LLC	Worcester	VT	G	802 505-5088	22743

COMPUTER STORAGE UNITS: Auxiliary

	CITY	ST	EMP	PHONE	ENTRY #
Mini LLC	Naugatuck	CT	G	203 464-5495	2484

COMPUTER SYSTEM SELLING SVCS

	CITY	ST	EMP	PHONE	ENTRY #
Minuteman Software Associates	Arlington	MA	G	781 643-4918	7630

COMPUTER SYSTEMS ANALYSIS & DESIGN

	CITY	ST	EMP	PHONE	ENTRY #
Custom Computer Systems Inc	Northborough	MA	G	508 393-8899	14032
Diacritech Inc	Boston	MA	F	617 236-7500	8502
Cafe Refugee Inc	Claremont	NH	G	603 499-7415	17838

COMPUTER TERMINALS

	CITY	ST	EMP	PHONE	ENTRY #
Omega Engineering Inc **(HQ)**	Norwalk	CT	C	203 359-1660	3211
Actuality Systems Inc	Arlington	MA	G	617 325-9230	7622
Igt Global Solutions Corp	Braintree	MA	F	781 849-5642	9019
New England Keyboard Inc	Fitchburg	MA	E	978 345-8332	10843
Verizon Communications Inc	Natick	MA	F	508 647-4008	13285
American Business Service	Lee	NH	G	603 659-2912	18642
Assured Computing Technologies	Bedford	NH	G	603 627-8728	17631
Igt Global Solutions Corp	West Greenwich	RI	E	401 392-7025	21456

COMPUTER-AIDED DESIGN SYSTEMS SVCS

	CITY	ST	EMP	PHONE	ENTRY #
Kubotek Usa Inc	Marlborough	MA	E	508 229-2020	12785
Phoenix Resources	Goshen	NH	G	603 863-9096	18215

COMPUTER-AIDED ENGINEERING SYSTEMS SVCS

	CITY	ST	EMP	PHONE	ENTRY #
Exa Corporation **(DH)**	Burlington	MA	D	781 564-0200	9272

COMPUTERS, NEC

	CITY	ST	EMP	PHONE	ENTRY #
American Railway Technologies	East Hartford	CT	G	860 291-1170	1172
Black Rock Tech Group LLC	Bridgeport	CT	F	203 916-7200	384
Glacier Computer LLC **(PA)**	New Milford	CT	G	860 355-7552	2800
Hg Tech LLC	Naugatuck	CT	G	203 632-5946	2477
Kimchuk Incorporated	Danbury	CT	C	203 798-0799	944
Modern Electronic Fax & Cmpt	Fairfield	CT	G	203 292-6520	1445
Abaco Systems Technology Corp	Billerica	MA	E	256 382-8115	8202
Acbel (usa) Polytech Inc	Hopkinton	MA	G	508 625-1768	11687
Biscom Inc	Westford	MA	D	978 250-1800	16757
Bull Data Systems Inc **(DH)**	Chelmsford	MA	G	978 294-6000	9882
Cape Setups LLC	West Barnstable	MA	G	508 375-6444	16405
Comark LLC **(PA)**	Milford	MA	D	508 359-8161	13110
Embedded Now Inc	Holliston	MA	G	508 246-8196	11569
General Dynamics Mission	Dedham	MA	B	781 410-9635	10291
General Dynamics Mission	Taunton	MA	A	508 880-4000	15754
Industrial Biomedical Sensors	Waltham	MA	F	781 891-4201	16132
Kinetic Systems Inc	Boston	MA	E	617 522-8700	8649
Mack Technologies Inc **(HQ)**	Westford	MA	C	978 392-5500	16777
Onset Computer Corporation	Bourne	MA	C	508 759-9500	8948
Power Systems Integrity Inc	Northborough	MA	G	508 393-1655	14045
Scidyne	Pembroke	MA	F	781 293-3059	14425
Sie Computing Solutions Inc	Brockton	MA	D	508 588-6110	9174
Thinkflood Inc	Needham	MA	G	617 299-2000	13314
Veloxity One LLC	North Chelmsford	MA	G	855 844-5060	13912
Ron Lavallee	Belgrade	ME	G	248 705-3231	5699
Dutile Glines & Higgins Inc	Hooksett	NH	F	603 622-0452	18348
Elite Manufacturing Svcs Corp	Salem	NH	F	978 688-6150	19724
Ezenia Inc **(PA)**	Salem	NH	F	603 589-7600	19727
Grolen Communications Inc	Manchester	NH	G	603 645-0101	18831
Lexington Data Incorporated	Rindge	NH	G	603 899-5673	19650
Monarch International Inc	Amherst	NH	E	603 883-3390	17577
Robert Veinot	Merrimack	NH	G	603 424-1799	19025
Wagz Inc **(PA)**	Portsmouth	NH	F	603 570-6015	19630
Taco Electronic Solutions Inc	Cranston	RI	G	401 942-8000	20300

COMPUTERS, NEC, WHOLESALE

	CITY	ST	EMP	PHONE	ENTRY #
Inteset Technologies LLC	Hanover	MA	G	781 826-1560	11342
Robert Veinot	Merrimack	NH	G	603 424-1799	19025
Vermont Systems Inc	Essex Junction	VT	D	802 879-6993	21963

COMPUTERS, PERIPHERALS & SOFTWARE, WHOLESALE: Printers

	CITY	ST	EMP	PHONE	ENTRY #
Westrex International Inc	Boston	MA	F	617 254-1200	8923

COMPUTERS, PERIPHERALS & SOFTWARE, WHOLESALE: Software

	CITY	ST	EMP	PHONE	ENTRY #
Richard Breault	Milford	CT	G	203 876-2707	2349
Sign In Soft Inc	Shelton	CT	G	203 216-3046	3870
Syferlock Technology Corp	Shelton	CT	G	203 292-5441	3875
American Well Corporation	Boston	MA	B	617 204-3500	8363
Dynatrace Holdings LLC **(HQ)**	Waltham	MA	C	781 530-1000	16094
Iva Corporation	Sudbury	MA	G	978 443-5800	15661
New England Business Svc Inc **(HQ)**	Groton	MA	D	978 448-6111	11291
Quinn Curtis Inc	Medfield	MA	G	508 359-6639	12918
Thought Industries Inc	Boston	MA	G	617 669-7725	8884
Mach 7 Technologies Inc	South Burlington	VT	F	802 861-7745	22452

COMPUTERS: Indl, Process, Gas Flow

	CITY	ST	EMP	PHONE	ENTRY #
Cidra Oilsands Inc **(HQ)**	Wallingford	CT	G	203 265-0035	4721
Environics Inc	Tolland	CT	E	860 872-1111	4547

COMPUTERS: Mainframe

	CITY	ST	EMP	PHONE	ENTRY #
Bull Hn Info Systems Inc	Chelmsford	MA	G	978 256-1033	9883
Glacier Computer LLC	Amherst	NH	F	603 882-1560	17564

COMPUTERS: Mini

	CITY	ST	EMP	PHONE	ENTRY #
Oracle America Inc	Stamford	CT	D	203 703-3000	4273

COMPUTERS: Personal

	CITY	ST	EMP	PHONE	ENTRY #
Cyclone Microsystems Inc	Hamden	CT	E	203 786-5536	1741
Interactive Marketing Corp	North Haven	CT	G	203 248-5324	3032
HP Inc	Littleton	MA	A	650 857-1501	12307
HP Inc	Littleton	MA	D	800 222-5547	12308
Oram Corporate Advisors	Newton	MA	G	617 701-7430	13622
Win Enterprises Inc	North Andover	MA	E	978 688-2000	13740
Cad Management Resources Inc	New Gloucester	ME	G	207 221-2911	6465

	CITY	ST	EMP	PHONE	ENTRY #
Dell Inc	Nashua	NH	C	603 579-9630	19143
Marspec-Abernaqui-America	North Hampton	NH	G	603 964-4063	19384
Battilana & Associates	Woodstock	VT	G	802 457-3375	22736
Robillards Apple Crisp	Saint Johnsbury	VT	G	802 748-4451	22394

CONCENTRATES, DRINK

	CITY	ST	EMP	PHONE	ENTRY #
Coca-Cola Refreshments USA Inc	Northampton	MA	D	413 586-8450	13999
Mrp Trading Innovations LLC	Beverly	MA	F	978 762-3900	8157
Aqua Vitea LLC	Salisbury	VT	G	802 352-1049	22398

CONCENTRATES, FLAVORING, EXC DRINK

	CITY	ST	EMP	PHONE	ENTRY #
Target Flavors Inc	Brookfield	CT	F	203 775-4727	659

CONCRETE BUILDING PRDTS WHOLESALERS

	CITY	ST	EMP	PHONE	ENTRY #
Lemac Iron Works Inc	West Hartford	CT	G	860 232-7380	5081
Wachusett Precast Inc	Sterling	MA	G	978 422-3311	15548
Washburn Vault Company Inc	Brattleboro	VT	G	802 254-9150	21754

CONCRETE CURING & HARDENING COMPOUNDS

	CITY	ST	EMP	PHONE	ENTRY #
Concrete Supplement Co	Litchfield	CT	G	860 567-5556	1946

CONCRETE MIXERS

	CITY	ST	EMP	PHONE	ENTRY #
Bonsal American Inc	Oxford	MA	E	508 987-8188	14254

CONCRETE PLANTS

	CITY	ST	EMP	PHONE	ENTRY #
Advanced Concrete Tech Inc-NH	Greenland	NH	G	603 431-5661	18219

CONCRETE PRDTS

	CITY	ST	EMP	PHONE	ENTRY #
Bonsal American Inc	Canaan	CT	G	860 824-7733	684
Bonsal American Inc	Canaan	CT	E	860 824-7733	685
Oldcastle Infrastructure Inc	Avon	CT	E	860 673-3291	40
Bonsal American Inc	Millbury	MA	G	508 791-6366	13157
Bonsal American Inc	Oxford	MA	E	508 987-8188	14254
Bonsal American Inc	Lee	MA	E	413 243-0053	12090
Cement Well Concrete Products	Palmer	MA	G	413 283-8450	14284
Diversitech Corporation	Taunton	MA	G	800 699-0453	15744
Environmental Improvements **(PA)**	Abington	MA	G	781 857-2375	7324
Fireslate 2 Inc	East Wareham	MA	F	508 273-0047	10530
Fletcher Granite LLC **(DH)**	Westford	MA	G	978 692-1312	16767
Forterra Pipe & Precast LLC	Ashland	MA	A	508 881-2000	7659
Lorusso Corp **(PA)**	Plainville	MA	E	508 668-6520	14527
Nantucket Pavers Inc	Rehoboth	MA	F	508 336-5800	14753
Oldcastle Apg Northeast Inc	Holbrook	MA	D	781 506-9473	11535
Oldcastle Precast Inc	Rehoboth	MA	E	508 867-8312	14757
Schofield Concrete Forms Inc	Melrose	MA	G	781 662-0796	12992
Umaco Inc	Lowell	MA	G	978 453-8881	12441
Williams Stone Co Inc	East Otis	MA	E	413 269-4544	10504
Ferraiolo Construction Inc	Rockland	ME	E	207 582-6162	6792
Mattingly Products Company	North Anson	ME	E	207 635-2719	6504
Concrete Systems Inc	Londonderry	NH	F	603 432-1840	18686
Conproco Corp **(PA)**	Somersworth	NH	F	603 743-5800	19831
E-Z Crete LLC	Harrisville	NH	G	603 313-6462	18301
N H Central Concrete Corp	Henniker	NH	F	603 428-7900	18308
Quikrete Companies LLC	Brentwood	NH	E	603 778-2123	17756
Anchor Concrete	Cranston	RI	E	401 942-4800	20182
Artcrete Enterprises Inc	Providence	RI	G	401 270-0700	20958
Cardi Materials LLC **(PA)**	Warwick	RI	E	401 739-8300	21340
Joseph P Carrara & Sons Inc	Middlebury	VT	D	802 388-6363	22113

CONCRETE PRDTS, PRECAST, NEC

	CITY	ST	EMP	PHONE	ENTRY #
Concrete Products	North Windham	CT	G	860 423-4144	3081
Eastern Precast Company Inc	Brookfield	CT	E	203 775-0230	643
Essex Concrete Products Inc	Essex	CT	F	860 767-1768	1396
Forterra Pipe & Precast LLC	Wauregan	CT	F	860 564-9000	5039
New Milford Block & Supply	New Milford	CT	F	860 355-1101	2816
Acme-Shorey Precast Co Inc **(PA)**	Harwich	MA	F	508 432-0530	11386
County Concrete Corp **(PA)**	Dalton	MA	E	413 499-3359	10175
David Sevigny Inc	Winchendon	MA	G	978 297-2775	17073
J and R Pre Cast Inc	Berkley	MA	F	508 822-3311	8087
Means Pre-Cast Co Inc	Braintree	MA	G	781 843-1909	9025
Pavestone LLC	Middleboro	MA	D	508 947-6001	13075
Popular Precast Products	Bellingham	MA	G	508 966-4622	8057
Precast Specialties Corp	Abington	MA	E	781 878-7220	7328
Ray Scituate Precast Con Corp	Marshfield	MA	E	781 837-1747	12866
Wachusett Precast Inc	Sterling	MA	G	978 422-3311	15548
Wiggin Means Precast Co Inc	Pocasset	MA	G	508 564-6776	14603
Wiggin Precast Corp	Pocasset	MA	F	508 564-6776	14604
American Concrete Inds Inc **(PA)**	Auburn	ME	E	207 947-8334	5550
American Concrete Inds Inc	Bangor	ME	D	207 947-8334	5629
Gagne & Son Con Blocks Inc	Auburn	ME	G	207 495-3313	5566
Nicmar Industries	Alfred	ME	E	207 324-6571	5516
Conproco Corp	Bow	NH	G	603 743-5800	17710
East Coast Concrete Pdts LLC	Amherst	NH	G	603 883-3042	17558
Eldorado Stone	Rochester	NH	G	617 947-6722	19669
Newstress Inc	Epsom	NH	E	603 736-9000	18107
Northern Design Precast Inc	Loudon	NH	E	603 783-8989	18751
Tuff Crete Corporation	South Hampton	NH	G	603 485-1969	19857
Durastone Corporation	Lincoln	RI	F	401 723-7100	20569
Fernandes Precast Company	Smithfield	RI	G	401 349-4907	21223
Caledonia Inc **(PA)**	Saint Johnsbury	VT	F	802 748-2319	22388

CONCRETE: Bituminous

	CITY	ST	EMP	PHONE	ENTRY #
Tilcon Connecticut Inc	Portland	CT	G	860 342-6157	3577
Aggregate Inds - Northeast Reg	Saugus	MA	G	781 941-7200	14975
Massachusetts Broken Stone Co **(PA)**	Berlin	MA	G	978 838-9999	8091
Trew Corp **(PA)**	Sunderland	MA	G	413 665-4051	15677

CONCRETE: Ready-Mixed

	CITY	ST	EMP	PHONE	ENTRY #
Aiudi Concrete Inc	Westbrook	CT	G	860 399-9289	5155
Armed & Ready Alarm System	Waterbury	CT	F	203 596-0327	4846
B&R Sand and Gravel	Gales Ferry	CT	G	860 464-5099	1525
Barnes Concrete Co Inc	Putnam	CT	E	860 928-7242	3602
Beard Concrete Co Derby Inc **(PA)**	Milford	CT	G	203 874-2533	2252
Bonsal American Inc	Canaan	CT	E	860 824-7733	685
Builders Concrete East LLC	North Windham	CT	E	860 456-4111	3079
Century Acquisition	Canaan	CT	G	518 758-7229	686
Enfield Transit Mix Inc	Enfield	CT	F	860 763-0864	1357
Essex Concrete Products Inc	Essex	CT	F	860 767-1768	1396
Federici Brands LLC	Wilton	CT	F	203 762-7667	5289
Five Star Products Inc	Shelton	CT	E	203 336-7900	3802
Mohican Valley Concrete Corp	Fairfield	CT	E	203 254-7133	1446
Mohican Vly Sand & Grav Corp	Fairfield	CT	F	203 254-7133	1447
O & G Industries Inc	Bridgeport	CT	E	203 366-4586	459
O & G Industries Inc	Danbury	CT	E	203 748-5694	963
Pick & Mix Corp	West Hartford	CT	G	860 521-1521	5091
Sega Ready Mix Incorporated **(PA)**	New Milford	CT	F	860 354-3969	2827
Sega Ready Mix Incorporated	Waterbury	CT	G	203 465-1052	4953
Sterling Materials LLC	Branford	CT	G	203 315-6619	352
The L Suzio Concrete Co Inc **(PA)**	Meriden	CT	E	203 237-8421	2140
Tilcon Connecticut Inc	Portland	CT	G	860 342-1096	3578
Windham Sand and Stone Inc	Manchester	CT	D	860 643-5578	2060
Aggregate Inds - Northeast Reg	Waltham	MA	F	781 893-7562	16026
Aggregate Inds - Northeast Reg	Stoughton	MA	G	781 344-1100	15574
Aggregate Inds - Northeast Reg	South Dennis	MA	G	508 398-8865	15264
Aggregate Inds - Northeast Reg	Watertown	MA	G	617 924-8550	16264
Aggregate Inds - Northeast Reg	Dennis	MA	G	508 398-8865	10305
Aggregate Inds - Northeast Reg	Saugus	MA	G	781 941-7200	14975
Aggregate Industries	Lunenburg	MA	E	978 582-0261	12480
Aggregate Industries - Mwr Inc	Saugus	MA	E	781 941-7200	14976
Aggregate Industries - Mwr Inc	Saugus	MA	D	781 231-3400	14977
Aggregate Industries - Mwr Inc	East Weymouth	MA	E	781 337-2304	10533
Aggregate Industries - Mwr Inc	Stoughton	MA	E	781 344-1100	15575
Aggregate Industries - Mwr Inc	Shrewsbury	MA	G	508 754-4709	15098
Aggregate Industries - Mwr Inc	Saugus	MA	E	781 941-3108	14978
Attleboro Sand & Gravel Corp	Attleboro	MA	G	508 222-2870	7708
Banas Sand & Gravel Co Inc	Ludlow	MA	F	413 583-8321	12456
Berkshire Concrete Corp **(HQ)**	Pittsfield	MA	C	413 443-4734	14456
Bill Willard Inc	Springfield	MA	G	413 584-1054	15453
Bonded Concrete Inc	Ashley Falls	MA	G	413 229-2075	7672
Boro Sand & Stone Corp **(PA)**	North Attleboro	MA	E	508 699-2911	13750
Boro Sand & Stone Corp	South Easton	MA	G	508 238-7222	15271
Boston Sand & Gravel Company **(PA)**	Boston	MA	E	617 227-9000	8440
Boston Sand & Gravel Company	Charlestown	MA	C	617 242-5540	9826
Boston Sand & Gravel Company	Sandwich	MA	F	508 888-8002	14962
Boucher Con Foundation Sups	Middleboro	MA	G	508 947-4279	13056
Cape Cod Ready Mix Inc	Orleans	MA	E	508 255-4600	14231
Cemex Materials LLC	Westfield	MA	E	413 562-3647	16677
Chicopee Foundations Inc **(PA)**	Chicopee	MA	E	413 536-3370	10007
Chicopee Foundations Inc	Chicopee	MA	E	413 594-4700	10008
Concrete & Mortar Packg LLC	Milford	MA	G	508 473-1799	13111
Crh Americas Inc	Leominster	MA	G	978 840-1176	12127
Cs-Ma LLC	Wilbraham	MA	E	413 733-6631	16934
Dauphinais & Son Inc	North Grafton	MA	G	508 839-9258	13959
Dauphinais & Son Inc	Wilbraham	MA	F	413 596-3964	16935
Dmjl Consulting LLC	Methuen	MA	F	978 989-0790	13018
Fall River Ready-Mix Con LLC	Fall River	MA	G	508 675-7540	10698
Falmouth Ready Mix Inc	East Falmouth	MA	F	508 548-6100	10443
Fuccillo Ready Mix Inc	East Falmouth	MA	F	508 540-2821	10444
GP Aggregate Corp	Gloucester	MA	G	978 283-5318	11190
Graziano Redi-Mix Inc	Bridgewater	MA	E	508 697-8350	9074
Hyde Park Concrete Inc	Hyde Park	MA	G	617 364-5485	11869
J G Maclellan Con Co Inc **(PA)**	Lowell	MA	D	978 458-1223	12385
L & S Industries Inc **(PA)**	New Bedford	MA	E	508 995-4654	13407
L & S Industries Inc	Acushnet	MA	E	508 998-7900	7403
McCabe Sand & Gravel Co Inc	Taunton	MA	E	508 823-0771	15764
Mix	Vineyard Haven	MA	G	508 693-8240	15934
Mix and Company Ltd	Wellesley	MA	F	781 235-0028	16373
Morse Ready Mix LLC	Plainville	MA	E	508 809-4644	14529
Morse Sand & Gravel Corp	Attleboro	MA	E	508 809-4644	7769
Preferred Concrete Corp	East Freetown	MA	F	508 763-5500	10457
Ragged Hill Incorporated	East Templeton	MA	E	978 939-5712	10520
Ready 4	Cambridge	MA	G	857 233-5455	9627
Redi-Mix Services Incorporated	Taunton	MA	G	508 823-0771	15778
Rosenfeld Concrete Corp **(HQ)**	Hopedale	MA	E	508 473-7200	11682
Rowley Ready Mix Inc	Rowley	MA	F	978 948-2544	14864
Southern Redi-Mix Corporation	Marshfield	MA	E	781 837-5353	12869
Sterling Concrete Corp	Sterling	MA	F	978 422-8282	15546
Varney Bros Sand & Gravel Inc	Bellingham	MA	E	508 966-1313	8062
Vita-Crete Inc	Milford	MA	G	508 473-1799	13151
Wakefield Investments Inc	Lunenburg	MA	D	978 582-0261	12486
Wbmx Mix 985 Tweeter Cntr	Mansfield	MA	G	508 339-1296	12670
Westfield Concrete Inc	Westfield	MA	E	413 562-4814	16742
Westfield Ready-Mix Inc	Chicopee	MA	E	413 594-4700	10069
County Concrete & Cnstr Co	Columbia Falls	ME	E	207 483-4409	5919
Dayton Sand & Gravel Inc	Dayton	ME	D	207 499-2306	5944
Dragon Products Company Inc	Portland	ME	F	207 879-2328	6655
Dragon Products Company LLC **(DH)**	South Portland	ME	E	207 774-6355	7022
Dragon Products Company LLC	Thomaston	ME	C	207 594-5555	7083
F R Carroll Inc	Limerick	ME	E	207 793-8615	6334
Haley Construction Inc	Farmington	ME	G	207 778-9990	6049
Lees Concrete Inc	Bangor	ME	G	207 974-4936	5653
Mattingly Products Company	North Anson	ME	E	207 635-2719	6504
R A Cummings Inc	Auburn	ME	E	207 777-7100	5594

	CITY	ST	EMP	PHONE	ENTRY #
R Pepin & Sons Inc	Sanford	ME	E	207 324-6125	6886
Scanmix Inc	Lewiston	ME	G	207 782-1885	6320
Trombley Industries Inc	Limestone	ME	G	207 328-4503	6345
Trombley Redi-Mix Inc **(PA)**	Presque Isle	ME	G	207 551-3770	6770
Aggregate Industries - Mwr Inc	Portsmouth	NH	E	603 427-1137	19533
Aggregate Industries - Mwr Inc	Raymond	NH	F	603 243-3554	19633
Alvin J Coleman & Son Inc	Albany	NH	E	603 447-3056	17534
Boston Sand & Gravel Company	Rochester	NH	C	603 330-3999	19662
Carroll Concrete Co Inc	Newport	NH	F	603 863-1765	19343
Coleman Concrete Inc	Albany	NH	E	603 447-5936	17536
Granite State Concrete Co Inc	Milford	NH	E	603 673-3327	19057
In The Mix	Nashua	NH	G	603 557-2078	19186
LE Weed & Son LLC **(PA)**	Newport	NH	F	603 863-1540	19349
Michie Corporation	Henniker	NH	D	603 428-7426	18307
Newport Concrete Block Co	Newport	NH	F	603 863-1540	19351
Newport Sand & Gravel Co Inc **(PA)**	Newport	NH	F	603 298-0199	19352
Newport Sand & Gravel Co Inc	Peterborough	NH	G	603 924-1999	19480
Newport Sand & Gravel Co Inc	Charlestown	NH	G	603 826-4444	17817
Oldcastle Materials Inc	Manchester	NH	G	603 669-2373	18893
Redimix Companies Inc **(DH)**	Belmont	NH	E	603 524-4434	17682
Seacoast Redimix Concrete LLC **(PA)**	Dover	NH	F	603 742-4441	18052
Tilcon Arthur Whitcomb Inc **(HQ)**	North Swanzey	NH	F	603 352-0101	19393
Torromeo Industries Inc	Kingston	NH	E	603 642-5564	18546
Adamsdale Concrete & Pdts Co	Pawtucket	RI	G	401 722-6725	20808
Consolidated Concrete Corp **(PA)**	East Providence	RI	G	401 438-4700	20399
Consolidated Concrete Corp	Coventry	RI	G	401 828-4700	20143
Greenville Ready Mix Inc	Ashaway	RI	G	401 539-2333	20035
Heritage Concrete Corp	Exeter	RI	F	401 294-1524	20451
Lehigh Cement Company LLC	Providence	RI	G	401 467-6750	21052
Material Concrete Corp	North Smithfield	RI	F	401 765-0204	20790
Mix Marketing Corp	Narragansett	RI	G	401 954-6121	20642
Pawtucket Hot Mix	Pawtucket	RI	F	401 722-4488	20876
Rhode Island Ready Mix LLC	Wyoming	RI	F	401 539-8222	21590
Carroll Concrete Co	Barre	VT	G	802 229-0191	21611
Dailey Precast LLC	Shaftsbury	VT	G	802 442-4418	22402
Gray Rock Concrete	Milton	VT	F	802 379-5393	22130
Harrison Redi-Mix Corp	Fairfax	VT	F	802 849-6688	21976
Joseph P Carrara & Sons Inc	Middlebury	VT	D	802 388-6363	22113
Joseph P Carrara & Sons Inc **(PA)**	North Clarendon	VT	E	802 775-2301	22216
Newport Sand & Gravel Co Inc	Swanton	VT	G	802 868-4119	22532
Newport Sand & Gravel Co Inc	Randolph	VT	G	802 728-5055	22300
Newport Sand & Gravel Co Inc	Guildhall	VT	G	802 328-3384	22006
Newport Sand & Gravel Co Inc	Newport	VT	F	802 334-2000	22204
Woodstock Grnola Trail Mix LLC	Woodstock	VT	G	802 457-3149	22742

CONDENSERS & CONDENSING UNITS: Air Conditioner

Broadstone Industries	Lowell	MA	G	978 691-2790	12356

CONDENSERS: Barometric

Heat Exchanger Products Corp	Hingham	MA	G	781 749-0220	11499

CONDENSERS: Refrigeration

Filtrine Manufacturing Co Inc **(PA)**	Keene	NH	D	603 352-5500	18503

CONDUITS & FITTINGS: Electric

Bridgeport Fittings LLC	Stratford	CT	C	203 377-5944	4400

CONFECTIONERY PRDTS WHOLESALERS

Frito-Lay North America Inc	Wilmington	MA	C	978 657-8344	17002
Granite State Candy Shoppe LLC **(PA)**	Concord	NH	F	603 225-2591	17903

CONFECTIONS & CANDY

Mantrose-Haeuser Co Inc **(HQ)**	Westport	CT	E	203 454-1800	5212
Pez Candy Inc **(HQ)**	Orange	CT	D	203 795-0531	3379
Pez Manufacturing Corp	Orange	CT	D	203 795-0531	3380
Reeds Inc	Norwalk	CT	E	203 890-0557	3228
Sonias Chocolaterie Inc	Ridgefield	CT	F	203 438-5965	3685
Thompson Brands LLC	Meriden	CT	D	203 235-2541	2141
Thompson Candy Company	Meriden	CT	D	203 235-2541	2142
Belgiums Chocolate Source Inc	Milton	MA	G	781 283-5787	13190
Ben & Bills Chocolate Emporium	Falmouth	MA	F	508 548-7878	10787
Ben & Blls Chclat Emporium Inc **(PA)**	Northampton	MA	F	413 584-5695	13997
Boston Pretzel Bakery Inc	Boston	MA	F	617 522-9494	8438
Cambridge Brands Mfg Inc	Cambridge	MA	C	617 491-2500	9425
Dante Confection	North Billerica	MA	G	978 262-2242	13806
Dorothy Coxs Candies Inc	Wareham	MA	E	774 678-0654	16245
Eaton Farm Confectioners Inc	Worcester	MA	G	508 865-5235	17369
Furlongs Cottage Candies	Norwood	MA	F	781 762-4124	14154
Hilliards House Candy Inc **(PA)**	North Easton	MA	D	508 238-6231	13947
Hilltop Candies	Brockton	MA	G	508 583-0895	9154
McCrea Capital Advisors Inc	Hyde Park	MA	G	617 276-3388	11874
Melville Candy Corporation	Randolph	MA	E	800 638-8063	14690
Nafp Inc	Methuen	MA	D	978 682-1855	13038
Nichols Candies Inc	Gloucester	MA	F	978 283-9850	11197
Phillips Candy House Inc	Boston	MA	E	617 282-2090	8778
Russos Inc	Saugus	MA	F	781 233-1737	14995
Salems Old Fshoned Candies Inc	Salem	MA	F	978 744-3242	14941
Silver Sweet Products Co	Lawrence	MA	G	978 688-0474	12074
Stage Stop Candy Ltd Inc	Dennis Port	MA	G	508 394-1791	10315
Strawbrry Hl Grnd Delights LLC	Waltham	MA	G	617 319-3557	16202
Sweethearts Candy Co LLC	Revere	MA	B	781 485-4500	14776
Bixby & Co LLC	Rockland	ME	G	207 691-1778	6785
Harbor Candy Shop Inc	Ogunquit	ME	E	207 646-8078	6537
Len Libbys Inc	Scarborough	ME	E	207 883-4897	6931
Bavarian Chocolate Haus Inc	North Conway	NH	G	603 356-2663	19372
Bb Walpole Liquidation NH Inc	Walpole	NH	G	603 756-2882	19915
Bens Sugar Shack	Temple	NH	G	603 924-3177	19896
Fredericks Pastries **(PA)**	Amherst	NH	G	603 882-7725	17563
Granite State Candy Shoppe LLC **(PA)**	Concord	NH	F	603 225-2591	17903
Grist For Mill LLC	Bristol	NH	F	603 744-0405	17767
Kellerhaus Inc	Laconia	NH	E	603 366-4466	18569
Original Gourmet Food Co LLC	Salem	NH	G	603 894-1200	19759
Pollys Pancake Parlor	Sugar Hill	NH	G	603 823-5575	19878
B Fresh	Greenville	RI	G	401 349-0001	20463
Hauser Foods Inc	Westerly	RI	E	401 596-8866	21526
Lady Ann Candies	Warwick	RI	E	401 738-4321	21384
Sherwood Brands of RI	Rumford	RI	E	401 726-4500	21195
Sweenors Chocolates Inc **(PA)**	Wakefield	RI	E	401 783-4433	21280
Tom and Sallys Handmade Choco	Westerly	RI	F	800 289-8783	21544
Fudge Factory Inc	Manchester Center	VT	F	888 669-7425	22085
Maple Grove Farms Vermont Inc **(HQ)**	Saint Johnsbury	VT	D	802 748-5141	22391
Runamok Maple LLC	Fairfax	VT	G	802 849-7943	21978
Tafts Milk Maple Farm	Huntington	VT	G	802 434-2727	22034

CONFINEMENT SURVEILLANCE SYS MAINTENANCE & MONITORING SVCS

Videoiq Inc	Somerville	MA	E	781 222-3069	15228
Assured Computing Technologies	Bedford	NH	G	603 627-8728	17631

CONNECTORS & TERMINALS: Electrical Device Uses

Amphenol Corporation **(PA)**	Wallingford	CT	D	203 265-8900	4700
Hubbell Incorporated	Newtown	CT	E	203 426-2555	2926
Ark-Les Connectors Corporation	East Taunton	MA	F	781 297-6324	10510
Atlee Delaware Incorporated	Melrose	MA	F	978 681-1003	12975
Konnext Inc	Hudson	MA	G	978 567-0800	11782
Teradyne Inc **(PA)**	North Reading	MA	B	978 370-2700	13990
Teradyne Inc	Woburn	MA	C	978 370-2700	17306
Winchster Interconnect Rf Corp **(HQ)**	Peabody	MA	D	978 532-0775	14385
Amphenol Corporation	Nashua	NH	B	603 879-3000	19114
Burndy LLC	Londonderry	NH	C	603 647-5000	18681
Burndy LLC **(DH)**	Manchester	NH	B	603 647-5000	18793
Hubbell Incorporated	Londonderry	NH	D	800 346-4175	18703
Hubbell Incorporated	Manchester	NH	C	603 647-5000	18838
Quick Fitting Inc	Warwick	RI	D	401 734-9500	21408

CONNECTORS: Cord, Electric

Gold Line Connector Inc **(PA)**	Redding	CT	E	203 938-2588	3648

CONNECTORS: Electrical

Amphenol Nexus Technologies	Stamford	CT	D	203 327-7300	4139
Siemon Company **(PA)**	Watertown	CT	A	860 945-4200	5024
Southport Products LLC	Winsted	CT	G	860 379-0761	5425
Dorn Equipment Corp	Melrose	MA	F	781 662-9300	12981
T & T Machine Products Inc	Rockland	MA	F	781 878-3861	14829
Burndy LLC	Londonderry	NH	C	603 647-5119	18682
Burndy LLC	Lincoln	NH	G	603 745-8114	18646

CONNECTORS: Electronic

Amphenol Corporation	Danbury	CT	C	203 743-9272	871
Amphenol Corporation **(PA)**	Wallingford	CT	D	203 265-8900	4700
Amphenol Corporation	Hamden	CT	D	203 287-2272	1732
Amphenol International Ltd **(HQ)**	Wallingford	CT	G	203 265-8900	4701
Bead Industries Inc **(PA)**	Milford	CT	E	203 301-0270	2251
Burndy LLC	Bethel	CT	D	203 792-1115	134
Component Concepts Inc	West Hartford	CT	G	860 523-4066	5062
Electro-Tech Inc	Cheshire	CT	E	203 271-1976	729
Hubbell Incorporated **(PA)**	Shelton	CT	D	475 882-4000	3813
Microtech Inc	Cheshire	CT	D	203 272-3234	745
Phoenix Company of Chicago Inc **(PA)**	Naugatuck	CT	D	630 595-2300	2489
Radiall Usa Inc	Wallingford	CT	C	203 776-2813	4794
RC Connectors LLC	Weatogue	CT	G	860 413-2196	5044
Surface Mount Devices LLC	Stamford	CT	G	203 322-8290	4336
Times Microwave Systems Inc **(HQ)**	Wallingford	CT	B	203 949-8400	4819
Winchester Interconnect Corp **(HQ)**	Norwalk	CT	E	203 741-5400	3271
Amphenol Alden Products Co **(HQ)**	Brockton	MA	C	508 427-7000	9118
Anderson Power Products Inc **(HQ)**	Sterling	MA	D	978 422-3600	15535
Atlee Delaware Incorporated	Melrose	MA	F	978 681-1003	12975
C & K Components LLC **(PA)**	Waltham	MA	D	617 969-3700	16056
Component Sources Intl	Westborough	MA	F	508 986-2300	16607
Cristek Interconnects Inc	Lowell	MA	G	978 735-2161	12363
Delta Electronics Mfg Corp	Beverly	MA	C	978 927-1060	8125
Electro-Term Inc	Springfield	MA	D	413 734-6469	15468
Elpakco Inc **(PA)**	Westford	MA	E	978 392-0400	16765
Global Interconnect Inc	Pocasset	MA	D	508 563-6306	14595
Ideal Industries Inc	Sterling	MA	C	978 422-3600	15540
Ksaria Corporation **(PA)**	Methuen	MA	D	866 457-2742	13030
L-Com Inc **(DH)**	North Andover	MA	D	978 682-6936	13715
Microwave Engineering Corp	North Andover	MA	D	978 685-2776	13718
Nabson Inc	Taunton	MA	G	617 323-1101	15767
Paricon Technologies Corp	Taunton	MA	F	508 823-0876	15771
Reinforced Structures For Elec	Worcester	MA	E	508 754-5316	17457
San-Tron Inc **(PA)**	Ipswich	MA	D	978 356-1585	11936
Te Connectivity Corporation	Norwood	MA	B	781 278-5273	14203
Te Connectivity Corporation	Worcester	MA	B	717 592-4299	17486
Texas Instruments Incorporated	Attleboro	MA	E	508 236-3800	7802
Trego Inc	Wareham	MA	G	508 291-3816	16255
Tru Technologies Inc	Peabody	MA	C	978 532-0775	14379
Winchester Interconnect Corp	Peabody	MA	D	978 532-0775	14383
Winchester Interconnect Corp	Peabody	MA	D	978 532-0775	14384
Winchester Interconnect Corp	Franklin	MA	F	978 717-2543	11098
Winchster Interconnect Rf Corp **(HQ)**	Peabody	MA	D	978 532-0775	14385
Wotech Associates	Woburn	MA	G	781 935-3787	17324
Xybol Interlynks Inc	Ipswich	MA	F	978 356-0750	11939

	CITY	ST	EMP	PHONE	ENTRY #
Alpha Technologies Group Inc	Pelham	NH	B	603 635-2800	19428
Amphenol Corporation	Nashua	NH	B	603 879-3000	19114
Amphenol Printed Circuits Inc	Nashua	NH	A	603 324-4500	19115
Burndy LLC	Littleton	NH	C	603 444-6781	18655
Electronics Aid Inc	Marlborough	NH	G	603 876-4161	18959
Hubbell Incorporated	Manchester	NH	C	603 647-5000	18838
Incon Inc	Hudson	NH	E	603 595-0550	18398
Q A Technology Company Inc	Hampton	NH	D	603 926-1193	18269
Special Hermetic Products	Wilton	NH	E	603 654-2002	19989
Teledyne Instruments Inc	Portsmouth	NH	C	603 474-5571	19624
Wavelink LLC	Manchester	NH	F	603 606-7489	18954
Xma Corporation	Manchester	NH	E	603 222-2256	18958
Advanced Interconnections Corp	West Warwick	RI	D	401 823-5200	21476
Ametek Scp Inc **(HQ)**	Westerly	RI	D	401 596-6658	21515
Atec	Wakefield	RI	G	401 782-6950	21267
Photonic Marketing Corporation	Lincoln	RI	G	401 333-3538	20591
Precision Trned Cmponents Corp	Smithfield	RI	D	401 232-3377	21244

CONNECTORS: Power, Electric

Skyko International LLC **(PA)**	Woodstock	CT	G	860 928-5170	5502

CONNECTORS: Solderless, Electric-Wiring Devices

Electro-Term Inc	Springfield	MA	D	413 734-6469	15468

CONSTRUCTION & MINING MACHINERY WHOLESALERS

Bell Power Systems LLC	Essex	CT	D	860 767-7502	1393
Knm Holdings LLC	Marlborough	MA	G	508 229-1400	12783
North Country Tractor Inc	Sanford	ME	F	207 324-5646	6884
North Country Tractor Inc	Dover	NH	F	603 742-5488	18041
Siteone Landscape Supply LLC	Londonderry	NH	G	603 425-2572	18737

CONSTRUCTION & ROAD MAINTENANCE EQPT: Drags, Road

Town of Wilton	Wilton	CT	G	203 563-0152	5308

CONSTRUCTION EQPT REPAIR SVCS

J J Plank Corporation	Farmington	NH	G	920 733-4479	18143

CONSTRUCTION EQPT: Attachments

Steelwrist Inc	Berlin	CT	G	225 936-1111	111
Stoughton Steel Company Inc	Hanover	MA	E	781 826-6496	11354

CONSTRUCTION EQPT: Attachments, Backhoe Mounted, Hyd Pwrd

Indeco North America Inc	Milford	CT	E	203 713-1030	2302

CONSTRUCTION EQPT: Attachments, Snow Plow

Industrial Stl Boiler Svcs Inc	Chicopee	MA	E	413 532-7788	10032

CONSTRUCTION EQPT: Backhoes, Tractors, Cranes & Similar Eqpt

J C B Leasing Inc	Weare	NH	D	603 529-7974	19934

CONSTRUCTION EQPT: Blade, Grader, Scraper, Dozer/Snow Plow

Howard P Fairfield LLC **(DH)**	Skowhegan	ME	E	207 474-9836	6976
Rebtek Diamnd Blades Bits LLC	Barre	VT	G	802 476-6520	21637

CONSTRUCTION EQPT: Buckets, Excavating, Clamshell, Etc

Maine Dock & Dredge LLC	Woolwich	ME	G	207 660-5577	7290

CONSTRUCTION EQPT: Cranes

Bay Crane Service Conn Inc	North Haven	CT	G	203 785-8000	3010
Terex Corporation **(PA)**	Westport	CT	F	203 222-7170	5233
Williams Sign Erection Inc	Wilmington	MA	G	978 658-3787	17066
Somatex Inc	Detroit	ME	E	207 487-6141	5953
Ordway Electric & Machine	Graniteville	VT	G	802 476-8011	22001

CONSTRUCTION EQPT: Finishers & Spreaders

J J Plank Corporation	Farmington	NH	G	920 733-4479	18143

CONSTRUCTION EQPT: Grapples, Rock, Wood, Etc

Champlain Construction Co Inc	Middlebury	VT	F	802 388-2652	22108

CONSTRUCTION EQPT: Hammer Mills, Port, Incl Rock/Ore Crush

Numa Tool Company **(PA)**	Thompson	CT	D	860 923-9551	4537

CONSTRUCTION EQPT: Rakes, Land Clearing, Mechanical

Davis Village Solutions LLC	New Ipswich	NH	G	603 878-3662	19304

CONSTRUCTION EQPT: Roofing Eqpt

Metal Plus LLC	Winsted	CT	G	860 379-1327	5416
JP Obelisk Inc	Bridgewater	MA	G	508 942-6248	9079
Metal Solutions LLC	Millbury	MA	G	774 276-0096	13171
Rugg Manufacturing Company Inc	Leominster	MA	F	413 773-5471	12185
Santa Rosa Lead Products LLC	Holliston	MA	F	508 893-6021	11600

CONSTRUCTION EQPT: Spreaders, Aggregates

Ace Torwel Inc **(HQ)**	Framingham	MA	F	888 878-0898	10916

CONSTRUCTION EQPT: Tunneling

Wintersteiger Inc	Waitsfield	VT	G	802 496-6166	22571

CONSTRUCTION MATERIALS, WHOLESALE: Aggregate

Morning Star Marble & Gran Inc	Topsham	ME	F	207 725-7309	7091

CONSTRUCTION MATERIALS, WHOLESALE: Awnings

Federal Specialties Inc	West Springfield	MA	G	413 782-6900	16520
Readys Window Products Inc	Tewksbury	MA	G	978 851-3963	15832

CONSTRUCTION MATERIALS, WHOLESALE: Block, Concrete & Cinder

New Milford Block & Supply	New Milford	CT	F	860 355-1101	2816
Ideal Concrete Block Co **(PA)**	Westford	MA	E	978 692-3076	16773

CONSTRUCTION MATERIALS, WHOLESALE: Building Stone

Connecticut Stone Supplies Inc **(PA)**	Milford	CT	D	203 882-1000	2270
LH Gault & Son Incorporated	Westport	CT	D	203 227-5181	5209
Skyline Quarry	Stafford Springs	CT	E	860 875-3580	4115
Portland Stone Ware Co Inc **(PA)**	Dracut	MA	E	978 459-7272	10367

CONSTRUCTION MATERIALS, WHOLESALE: Building Stone, Granite

Mkl Stone LLC	Everett	MA	G	781 844-9811	10622
Stone Decor Galleria Inc	Woburn	MA	G	781 937-9377	17302
Sudbury Granite & Marble Inc **(PA)**	Hopedale	MA	E	508 478-3976	11684
Tables of Stone **(PA)**	Merrimack	NH	G	603 424-7577	19035

CONSTRUCTION MATERIALS, WHOLESALE: Building Stone, Marble

American Stonecrafters Inc	Wallingford	CT	G	203 514-9725	4698
Pauls Marble Depot LLC	Stamford	CT	F	203 978-0669	4279
Pistritto Marble Imports Inc	Hartford	CT	G	860 296-5263	1857
Aldrich Marble & Granite Co	Norwood	MA	E	781 762-6111	14124
Louis W Mian Inc **(PA)**	Boston	MA	E	617 241-7900	8672
Stone Design Marble & Gran Co	South Weymouth	MA	G	781 331-3000	15322
Wingate Sales Associates LLC	Stratham	NH	G	603 303-7189	19877
Vermont Quarries Corp	Rutland	VT	F	802 775-1065	22360

CONSTRUCTION MATERIALS, WHOLESALE: Building, Exterior

Moose Creek Home Center Inc	Turner	ME	G	207 224-7497	7109
Kimballs Lumber Center LLC **(PA)**	Wolfeboro	NH	G	603 569-2477	20021

CONSTRUCTION MATERIALS, WHOLESALE: Cement

Lafarge North America Inc	New Haven	CT	G	203 468-6068	2704

CONSTRUCTION MATERIALS, WHOLESALE: Concrete Mixtures

Babcock & King Incorporated **(PA)**	Fairfield	CT	G	203 336-7989	1415

CONSTRUCTION MATERIALS, WHOLESALE: Drywall Materials

Alco Construction Inc	Hudson	NH	G	603 305-8493	18372

CONSTRUCTION MATERIALS, WHOLESALE: Eavestroughing, Part/Sply

Custom Seamless Gutters Inc	Pawtucket	RI	G	401 726-3137	20831

CONSTRUCTION MATERIALS, WHOLESALE: Flue Linings

North American Supaflu Systems	Scarborough	ME	F	207 883-1155	6935

CONSTRUCTION MATERIALS, WHOLESALE: Glass

Liberty Glass and Met Inds Inc	North Grosvenordale	CT	E	860 923-3623	2997
New Milford Block & Supply	New Milford	CT	F	860 355-1101	2816

CONSTRUCTION MATERIALS, WHOLESALE: Gravel

Dauphinais & Son Inc	Wilbraham	MA	F	413 596-3964	16935
R Pepin & Sons Inc	Sanford	ME	E	207 324-6125	6886

CONSTRUCTION MATERIALS, WHOLESALE: Hardboard

Keiver Willard-Lumber Corp	Newburyport	MA	D	978 462-7193	13503

CONSTRUCTION MATERIALS, WHOLESALE: Masons' Materials

State Road Cement Block Co	North Dartmouth	MA	G	508 993-9473	13926
Rjf - Morin Brick LLC	Auburn	ME	D	207 784-9375	5595
Tilcon Arthur Whitcomb Inc **(HQ)**	North Swanzey	NH	F	603 352-0101	19393

CONSTRUCTION MATERIALS, WHOLESALE: Millwork

Brockway-Smith Company	West Hatfield	MA	D	413 247-9674	16482
New England Shrlines Companies	Pembroke	MA	F	781 826-0140	14418
Tommila Brothers Inc	Fitzwilliam	NH	F	603 242-7774	18153
Cas Acquisition Co LLC	North Smithfield	RI	F	401 884-8556	20783

CONSTRUCTION MATERIALS, WHOLESALE: Molding, All Materials

Stelray Plastic Products Inc	Ansonia	CT	E	203 735-2331	23
Fine Line Woodworking Inc	Boxboro	MA	G	978 263-4322	8952
Woodsmiths Inc	Fall River	MA	G	508 548-8343	10784

CONSTRUCTION MATERIALS, WHOLESALE: Prefabricated Structures

Town & Country Sheds	Wolcott	VT	G	802 888-7012	22733

CONSTRUCTION MATERIALS, WHOLESALE: Roofing & Siding Material

Dfs In-Home Services	Danbury	CT	G	845 405-6464	900
Qba Inc	Woodstock	CT	G	860 963-9438	5500

CONSTRUCTION MATERIALS, WHOLESALE: Sand

Rawson Development Inc	Putnam	CT	F	860 928-4536	3629
Aggregate Inds - Northeast Reg	Waltham	MA	F	781 893-7562	16026
Boro Sand & Stone Corp **(PA)**	North Attleboro	MA	E	508 699-2911	13750
Heffron Asphalt Corp **(PA)**	North Reading	MA	G	781 935-1455	13984
McCabe Sand & Gravel Co Inc	Taunton	MA	E	508 823-0771	15764
Torromeo Industries Inc	Kingston	NH	E	603 642-5564	18546

CONSTRUCTION MATERIALS, WHOLESALE: Septic Tanks

Elm Street Vault Inc	Biddeford	ME	G	207 284-4855	5731
Gagne & Son Con Blocks Inc	Auburn	ME	G	207 495-3313	5566

CONSTRUCTION MATERIALS, WHOLESALE: Stone, Crushed Or Broken

Aggregate Inds - Northeast Reg	Taunton	MA	F	508 821-9508	15720
B R S Inc	Bridgewater	MA	E	508 697-5448	9061

	CITY	ST	EMP	PHONE	ENTRY #
S Lane John & Son Incorporated	Oxford	MA	F	508 987-3959	14273

CONSTRUCTION MATERIALS, WHOLESALE: Windows

	CITY	ST	EMP	PHONE	ENTRY #
Beacon Sales Acquisition Inc	Salem	NH	G	207 797-7950	19712
Custom Seamless Gutters Inc	Pawtucket	RI	G	401 726-3137	20831

CONSTRUCTION MATL, WHOLESALE: Structural Assy, Prefab, Wood

	CITY	ST	EMP	PHONE	ENTRY #
Architectural Timber Mllwk Inc	Hadley	MA	F	413 586-3045	11305

CONSTRUCTION MATLS, WHOL: Lumber, Rough, Dressed/Finished

	CITY	ST	EMP	PHONE	ENTRY #
River Mill Co	Clinton	CT	F	860 669-5915	794
F C Hammond & Son Lbr Co Inc	Canaan	NH	F	603 523-4353	17778
A Johnson Co	Bristol	VT	D	802 453-4884	21760
N W P Inc	Pownal	VT	G	802 442-4749	22282

CONSTRUCTION MATLS, WHOLESALE: Soil Erosion Cntrl Fabrics

	CITY	ST	EMP	PHONE	ENTRY #
Lindon Group Inc	East Providence	RI	G	401 272-2081	20430

CONSTRUCTION MATLS, WHOLESALE: Struct Assy, Prefab, Non-Wood

	CITY	ST	EMP	PHONE	ENTRY #
Architectural Timber Mllwk Inc	Hadley	MA	F	413 586-3045	11305

CONSTRUCTION SAND MINING

	CITY	ST	EMP	PHONE	ENTRY #
Baxter Sand & Gravel Inc	Chicopee	MA	E	413 536-3370	9999
Boston Sand & Gravel Company **(PA)**	Boston	MA	E	617 227-9000	8440
Brox Industries Inc **(PA)**	Dracut	MA	D	978 454-9105	10355
Lorusso Corp **(PA)**	Plainville	MA	E	508 668-6520	14527
Ossipee Aggregates Corporation **(HQ)**	Boston	MA	G	617 227-9000	8762
Rosenfeld Concrete Corp **(HQ)**	Hopedale	MA	E	508 473-7200	11682
S Lane John & Son Incorporated **(PA)**	Westfield	MA	F	413 568-8986	16725
S M Lorusso & Sons Inc **(PA)**	Walpole	MA	E	508 668-2600	16010
Fuller Sand & Gravel Inc	Danby	VT	G	802 293-5700	21893

CONSTRUCTION SITE PREPARATION SVCS

	CITY	ST	EMP	PHONE	ENTRY #
Brox Industries Inc **(PA)**	Dracut	MA	D	978 454-9105	10355
Cook Forest Products Inc	Upton	MA	E	508 634-3300	15906
Heyes Forest Products Inc	Orange	MA	G	978 544-8801	14217
Robert W Libby	Porter	ME	G	207 625-8285	6604
DH Hardwick & Sons Inc	Bennington	NH	E	603 588-6618	17688
Monadnock Land Clearing	Greenville	NH	G	603 878-2803	18227
Green Mountain Chipping Inc **(PA)**	Underhill	VT	G	802 899-1239	22548
T B Lincoln Logging Inc	Brookfield	VT	G	802 276-3172	21765

CONSTRUCTION: Athletic & Recreation Facilities

	CITY	ST	EMP	PHONE	ENTRY #
Tucker Mountain Homes Inc	Meredith	NH	G	603 279-4320	18981

CONSTRUCTION: Commercial & Institutional Building

	CITY	ST	EMP	PHONE	ENTRY #
Central Construction Inds LLC	Putnam	CT	E	860 963-8902	3604
Ada Fabricators Inc	Wilmington	MA	E	978 262-9900	16965
Lewicki & Sons Excavating Inc	Plainville	MA	G	508 695-0122	14526
Space Building Corp	Lakeville	MA	E	508 947-7277	11978

CONSTRUCTION: Commercial & Office Building, New

	CITY	ST	EMP	PHONE	ENTRY #
Kafa Group LLC	Bridgeport	CT	G	475 275-0090	438
O & G Industries Inc	Danbury	CT	E	203 748-5694	963
O & G Industries Inc	Beacon Falls	CT	F	203 729-4529	64
O & G Industries Inc	New Milford	CT	D	860 354-4438	2820
O & G Industries Inc	Bridgeport	CT	E	203 366-4586	459
Acton Woodworks Inc	Acton	MA	G	978 263-0222	7335
Days Auto Body Inc	Medway	ME	G	207 746-5310	6423
Dexter Sign Co	East Providence	RI	E	401 434-1100	20406
Robert B Evans Inc	Westerly	RI	G	401 596-2719	21538

CONSTRUCTION: Dam

	CITY	ST	EMP	PHONE	ENTRY #
Absorbent Specialty Pdts LLC	Cumberland	RI	F	401 722-1177	20312

CONSTRUCTION: Dams, Waterways, Docks & Other Marine

	CITY	ST	EMP	PHONE	ENTRY #
Chas G Allen Realty LLC	Barre	MA	D	978 355-2911	7950
Louie and Teds Blacktop Inc	Swansea	MA	F	508 678-4948	15707

CONSTRUCTION: Drainage System

	CITY	ST	EMP	PHONE	ENTRY #
LH Gault & Son Incorporated	Westport	CT	D	203 227-5181	5209
A B Excavating Inc	Lancaster	NH	E	603 788-5110	18596

CONSTRUCTION: Factory

	CITY	ST	EMP	PHONE	ENTRY #
Executive Force Protection LLC	Cambridge	MA	F	617 470-9230	9476

CONSTRUCTION: Food Prdts Manufacturing or Packing Plant

	CITY	ST	EMP	PHONE	ENTRY #
Core Concepts Inc	Franklin	MA	E	508 528-0070	11032
Elution Technologies LLC	Colchester	VT	G	802 540-0296	21862

CONSTRUCTION: Guardrails, Highway

	CITY	ST	EMP	PHONE	ENTRY #
Atlas Industrial Services LLC	Branford	CT	E	203 315-4538	290
Fall River Ready-Mix Con LLC	Fall River	MA	G	508 675-7540	10698

CONSTRUCTION: Heavy Highway & Street

	CITY	ST	EMP	PHONE	ENTRY #
Liddell Brothers Inc	Norwell	MA	E	781 293-2100	14106
R A Thomas Logging Inc	Guilford	ME	G	207 876-2722	6161
A B Excavating Inc	Lancaster	NH	E	603 788-5110	18596
Stacey Thomson	Orford	NH	G	603 353-9700	19421

CONSTRUCTION: Indl Building & Warehouse

	CITY	ST	EMP	PHONE	ENTRY #
Airmar Technology Corp	Milford	NH	F	603 673-9570	19045

CONSTRUCTION: Indl Building, Prefabricated

	CITY	ST	EMP	PHONE	ENTRY #
Space Building Corp	Lakeville	MA	E	508 947-7277	11978

CONSTRUCTION: Indl Buildings, New, NEC

	CITY	ST	EMP	PHONE	ENTRY #
Kafa Group LLC	Bridgeport	CT	G	475 275-0090	438

CONSTRUCTION: Indl Plant

	CITY	ST	EMP	PHONE	ENTRY #
Raytheon Sutheast Asia Systems **(HQ)**	Billerica	MA	E	978 470-5000	8289

CONSTRUCTION: Land Preparation

	CITY	ST	EMP	PHONE	ENTRY #
Wright Maintenance Inc	Newfane	VT	G	802 365-9253	22189

CONSTRUCTION: Marine

	CITY	ST	EMP	PHONE	ENTRY #
Burnham Associates Inc	Salem	MA	F	978 745-1788	14899
Dock Doctors LLC	Ferrisburgh	VT	E	802 877-6756	21988

CONSTRUCTION: Multi-Family Housing

	CITY	ST	EMP	PHONE	ENTRY #
Space Building Corp	Lakeville	MA	E	508 947-7277	11978

CONSTRUCTION: Paper & Pulp Mill

	CITY	ST	EMP	PHONE	ENTRY #
Acuren Inspection Inc	Auburn	ME	F	207 786-7884	5546

CONSTRUCTION: Pharmaceutical Manufacturing Plant

	CITY	ST	EMP	PHONE	ENTRY #
EMD Millipore Corporation **(DH)**	Burlington	MA	A	781 533-6000	9262

CONSTRUCTION: Power Plant

	CITY	ST	EMP	PHONE	ENTRY #
Tecomet Inc	Woburn	MA	D	781 782-6400	17305

CONSTRUCTION: Residential, Nec

	CITY	ST	EMP	PHONE	ENTRY #
Connectcut Shreline Developers	Clinton	CT	G	860 669-4424	781
Interntonal MBL Gran Entps Inc	Hartford	CT	G	860 296-0741	1838
J H Faddens & Sons	North Woodstock	NH	G	603 745-2406	19398

CONSTRUCTION: Retaining Wall

	CITY	ST	EMP	PHONE	ENTRY #
Dauphinais & Son Inc	Wilbraham	MA	F	413 596-3964	16935

CONSTRUCTION: Single-Family Housing

	CITY	ST	EMP	PHONE	ENTRY #
C J Brand & Son	Mystic	CT	G	860 536-9266	2435
Central Construction Inds LLC	Putnam	CT	E	860 963-8902	3604
Country Carpenters Inc	Hebron	CT	G	860 228-2276	1896
Country Log Homes Inc	Goshen	CT	F	413 229-8084	1582
Eastern Electric Cnstr Co	Harwinton	CT	G	860 485-1100	1889
Hanford Cabinet & Wdwkg Co	Old Saybrook	CT	G	860 388-5055	3337
Chicopee Foundations Inc	Chicopee	MA	E	413 594-4700	10008
Schiavi Homes LLC	Oxford	ME	E	207 539-9600	6573
Cabinet Masters Inc	Derry	NH	G	603 425-6428	17975
Timberpeg East Inc **(PA)**	Claremont	NH	E	603 542-7762	17862

CONSTRUCTION: Single-family Housing, New

	CITY	ST	EMP	PHONE	ENTRY #
Post & Beam Homes Inc	East Hampton	CT	G	860 267-2060	1163
Acton Woodworks Inc	Acton	MA	G	978 263-0222	7335
Wlhc Inc **(PA)**	Houlton	ME	G	207 532-6531	6212
Robert B Evans Inc	Westerly	RI	G	401 596-2719	21538

CONSTRUCTION: Steel Buildings

	CITY	ST	EMP	PHONE	ENTRY #
D Cronins Welding Service	Lawrence	MA	G	978 664-4488	12014

CONSTRUCTION: Street Surfacing & Paving

	CITY	ST	EMP	PHONE	ENTRY #
Aggregate Inds - Northeast Reg	Raynham	MA	G	508 822-7120	14704
Heffron Asphalt Corp **(PA)**	North Reading	MA	G	781 935-1455	13984
Rochester Bituminous Products	West Wareham	MA	G	508 295-8001	16576
County Concrete & Cnstr Co	Columbia Falls	ME	E	207 483-4409	5919
Perry Paving	Warwick	RI	G	401 732-1730	21403
Black Beauty Driveway Sealing	Colchester	VT	G	802 860-7113	21858

CONSTRUCTION: Swimming Pools

	CITY	ST	EMP	PHONE	ENTRY #
Fairfield Pool & Equipment Co **(PA)**	Fairfield	CT	G	203 334-3600	1431
Group Works	Wilton	CT	G	203 834-7905	5290

CONSTRUCTION: Telephone & Communication Line

	CITY	ST	EMP	PHONE	ENTRY #
Charles Curtis LLC	Danville	VT	G	802 274-0060	21895

CONSTRUCTION: Waste Water & Sewage Treatment Plant

	CITY	ST	EMP	PHONE	ENTRY #
Alexander Moles	Taunton	MA	G	508 823-8864	15723

CONSTRUCTION: Water & Sewer Line

	CITY	ST	EMP	PHONE	ENTRY #
Ecosystem Consulting Svc Inc	Coventry	CT	G	860 742-0744	833
A B Excavating Inc	Lancaster	NH	E	603 788-5110	18596

CONSULTING SVC: Actuarial

	CITY	ST	EMP	PHONE	ENTRY #
Computer Prgrm & Systems Inc **(PA)**	Stamford	CT	G	203 324-9203	4170

CONSULTING SVC: Business, NEC

	CITY	ST	EMP	PHONE	ENTRY #
Anderson David C & Assoc LLC **(PA)**	Enfield	CT	F	860 749-7547	1346
Childrens Health Market Inc	Wilton	CT	G	203 762-2938	5283
Video Automation Systems Inc	New Fairfield	CT	G	203 312-0152	2630
Bauer Associates Inc	Natick	MA	G	508 310-0201	13236
Corden Pharma Intl Inc	Braintree	MA	G	781 305-3332	8996
Environmental Svcs Group Inc	Medway	MA	E	508 533-7683	12959
Jobsmart Inc	Ashfield	MA	F	724 272-3448	7652
Larson Worldwide Inc	Norwell	MA	G	781 659-2115	14105
Moseley Corporation	Franklin	MA	E	508 520-4004	11068
Patricia Seybold Group Inc	Brighton	MA	F	617 742-5200	9103
Union Etchants International	Danvers	MA	G	978 777-7860	10270
Cad Management Resources Inc	New Gloucester	ME	G	207 221-2911	6465
R F Consulting LLC **(PA)**	Freeport	ME	G	207 233-8846	6085
Cafe Refugee Inc	Claremont	NH	G	603 499-7415	17838
Creative Digital Inc	Cranston	RI	G	401 942-0771	20204
Hope & Main	Warren	RI	G	401 245-7400	21295
Nestor Traffic Systems Inc **(PA)**	Pawtucket	RI	E	401 714-7781	20864
Green Mountain Honey Farms	Ferrisburg	VT	G	802 877-3396	21986
Stephen McArthur	Barre	VT	G	802 839-0371	21640

CONSULTING SVC: Chemical

	CITY	ST	EMP	PHONE	ENTRY #
Innophase Corp	Westbrook	CT	G	860 399-2269	5156

CONSULTING SVC: Computer

	CITY	ST	EMP	PHONE	ENTRY #
Information Tech Intl Corp	Manchester	CT	G	860 648-2570	2012
Management Software Inc	Ledyard	CT	G	860 536-5177	1942
Oracle America Inc	Stamford	CT	D	203 703-3000	4273
Woods End Inc	Weston	CT	G	203 226-6303	5176
Expertek Systems Inc	Marlborough	MA	F	508 624-0006	12754
Kenexa Brassring Inc	Littleton	MA	C	781 530-5000	12312
Logmein Inc **(PA)**	Boston	MA	C	781 638-9050	8671
M8trix Tech LLC	Canton	MA	G	617 925-7030	9753
Ntt Data Inc	Boston	MA	C	617 241-9200	8744
Pathai Inc	Boston	MA	G	617 543-5250	8767
Renaissance International	Newburyport	MA	G	978 465-5111	13529
Technologies 2010 Inc	Milford	MA	G	508 482-0164	13146
Westrex International Inc	Boston	MA	F	617 254-1200	8923
Zerious Electronic Pubg Corp	Beverly	MA	G	978 922-4990	8201
Cafe Refugee Inc	Claremont	NH	G	603 499-7415	17838
Dijitized Communications Inc	Middleton	NH	G	603 473-2144	19039
Lcm Group Inc	Nashua	NH	G	603 888-1248	19198
Profitkey International Inc	Salem	NH	E	603 898-9800	19760
Purchasing & Inventory Cons	Windsor	VT	F	802 674-2620	22713

CONSULTING SVC: Data Processing

	CITY	ST	EMP	PHONE	ENTRY #
Advanced Sonics LLC	Oxford	CT	G	203 266-4440	3387
Shiloh Software Inc	Cheshire	CT	G	203 272-8456	761

CONSULTING SVC: Educational

	CITY	ST	EMP	PHONE	ENTRY #
Bunting & Lyon Inc	Cheshire	CT	G	203 272-4623	718
Stevenson Learning Skills Inc	Holliston	MA	G	774 233-0457	11607
Educational Directions Inc	Portsmouth	RI	G	401 683-3523	20922
Miravia LLC **(PA)**	Charlotte	VT	G	802 425-6483	21834

CONSULTING SVC: Engineering

	CITY	ST	EMP	PHONE	ENTRY #
Doctor Stuff LLC	Wallingford	CT	G	203 785-8475	4735
TP Cycle & Engineering Inc	Danbury	CT	E	203 744-4960	1000
Enginred Plas Sltons Group Inc	Norwood	MA	G	781 762-3913	14148
Exergen Corporation	Watertown	MA	D	617 923-9900	16284
Phadean Engineering Co Inc	Shrewsbury	MA	G	888 204-0900	15128
Quality Engineering Assoc Inc	Billerica	MA	F	978 528-2034	8280
Star Engineering Inc	North Attleboro	MA	E	508 316-1492	13781
TK&k Services LLC	Beverly	MA	C	770 844-8710	8192
Bath Iron Works Corporation **(HQ)**	Bath	ME	B	207 443-3311	5674
Aeration Technologies Inc	Londonderry	NH	G	603 434-3539	18673
Haigh-Farr Inc	Bedford	NH	F	603 644-6170	17644
Tech Nh Inc **(PA)**	Merrimack	NH	D	603 424-4404	19036
Metallurgical Solutions Inc	Providence	RI	F	401 941-2100	21066

CONSULTING SVC: Financial Management

	CITY	ST	EMP	PHONE	ENTRY #
Smith & Assoc	Scarborough	ME	G	866 299-6487	6940

CONSULTING SVC: Management

	CITY	ST	EMP	PHONE	ENTRY #
Ca Inc	East Windsor	CT	E	800 225-5224	1281
Chief Executive Group LLC **(PA)**	Stamford	CT	F	785 832-0303	4164
Chief Executive Group LP **(PA)**	Stamford	CT	E	203 930-2700	4165
Computer Prgrm & Systems Inc **(PA)**	Stamford	CT	G	203 324-9203	4170
Enginuity Plm LLC **(HQ)**	Milford	CT	F	203 218-7225	2286
Ensign-Bickford Industries Inc	Simsbury	CT	E	860 658-4411	3905
Forecast International Inc	Newtown	CT	D	203 426-0800	2922
Varpro Inc	Westport	CT	E	203 227-6876	5236
Beacon Application Svcs Corp **(PA)**	Framingham	MA	E	508 663-4433	10926
Cape Cod Life LLC	Mashpee	MA	F	508 419-7381	12877
City Pblcations Greater Boston	Wayland	MA	G	617 549-7622	16335
Front Run Organx Inc	Ipswich	MA	G	978 356-7133	11921
M R P Group Inc (de)	Lawrence	MA	G	978 687-7979	12049
Network World Inc	Framingham	MA	C	800 622-1108	10986
North River Press Pubg Corp	Great Barrington	MA	F	413 528-0034	11243
Synchrgnix Info Strategies Inc	Cambridge	MA	G	302 892-4800	9670
Vdc Research Group Inc **(PA)**	Natick	MA	E	508 653-9000	13284
Cafe Refugee Inc	Claremont	NH	G	603 499-7415	17838
Centric Software Inc	Lebanon	NH	G	603 448-3009	18618
Durastone Corporation	Lincoln	RI	F	401 723-7100	20569
Vermont Ski Safety Equipment	Underhill	VT	G	802 899-4738	22549

CONSULTING SVC: Marketing Management

	CITY	ST	EMP	PHONE	ENTRY #
Ihs Herold Inc **(DH)**	Norwalk	CT	D	203 857-0215	3171
Intersec LLC	Rocky Hill	CT	G	860 985-3158	3718
The Merrill Anderson Co Inc	Stratford	CT	F	203 377-4996	4453
Alpha Tech Pet Inc	Littleton	MA	F	978 486-3690	12291
Blanchard Press Inc	Winchester	MA	F	617 426-6690	17084
Dahl Group	Boxford	MA	G	978 887-2598	8976
Innovative Chem Pdts Group LLC **(PA)**	Andover	MA	E	978 623-9980	7558
John Latka & Co Inc	Westfield	MA	G	413 562-4374	16694
Pioneer Vly Milk Mktg Coop Inc	Greenfield	MA	G	413 772-2332	11272
Ve Interactive LLC	Boston	MA	G	857 284-7000	8905
Vocero Hispano Newspaper Inc	Southbridge	MA	G	508 792-1942	15408
R2b Inc	Portland	ME	F	207 797-0019	6719
Eco Services LLC	Durham	NH	G	603 682-0963	18076
Powerplay Management LLC	Portsmouth	NH	E	603 436-3030	19609
Trimed Media Group Inc	Providence	RI	F	401 919-5165	21141

CONSULTING SVC: Online Technology

	CITY	ST	EMP	PHONE	ENTRY #
Datanyze Inc **(DH)**	Waltham	MA	E	415 237-3434	16080
Intelligent Bus Entrmt Inc	Watertown	MA	F	617 519-4172	16292
Textcafe	Natick	MA	G	508 654-8520	13281

CONSULTING SVC: Sales Management

	CITY	ST	EMP	PHONE	ENTRY #
Silicon Sense Inc	Nashua	NH	G	603 891-4248	19261

CONSULTING SVC: Telecommunications

	CITY	ST	EMP	PHONE	ENTRY #
Horizon House Publications Inc **(PA)**	Norwood	MA	D	781 769-9750	14158

CONSULTING SVCS, BUSINESS: Communications

	CITY	ST	EMP	PHONE	ENTRY #
Tensor Communications Systems	Bradford	NH	G	603 938-5206	17742

CONSULTING SVCS, BUSINESS: Energy Conservation

	CITY	ST	EMP	PHONE	ENTRY #
New Resources Group Inc	Bridgeport	CT	G	203 366-1000	457
National Resource MGT Inc **(PA)**	Canton	MA	E	781 828-8877	9759

CONSULTING SVCS, BUSINESS: Environmental

	CITY	ST	EMP	PHONE	ENTRY #
Ecosystem Consulting Svc Inc	Coventry	CT	G	860 742-0744	833
Rain Cii Carbon LLC	Stamford	CT	F	203 406-0535	4297
E Paint Company	East Falmouth	MA	F	508 540-4412	10441
Kerfoot Technologies Inc	Mashpee	MA	F	508 539-3002	12881

CONSULTING SVCS, BUSINESS: Publishing

	CITY	ST	EMP	PHONE	ENTRY #
Ubm LLC	Darien	CT	G	203 662-6501	1035
Nsight Inc	Andover	MA	E	781 273-6300	7579

CONSULTING SVCS, BUSINESS: Sys Engnrg, Exc Computer/Prof

	CITY	ST	EMP	PHONE	ENTRY #
High Voltage Outsourcing LLC	Danbury	CT	G	203 456-3101	932
Sophic Alliance Inc	East Falmouth	MA	G	508 495-3801	10449

CONSULTING SVCS, BUSINESS: Systems Analysis & Engineering

	CITY	ST	EMP	PHONE	ENTRY #
Advanced Electronic Design Inc	Attleboro Falls	MA	F	508 699-0249	7810
Applied Science Group Inc	Billerica	MA	E	781 275-4000	8212
River City Software LLC	Exeter	NH	G	603 686-5525	18130

CONSULTING SVCS, BUSINESS: Systems Analysis Or Design

	CITY	ST	EMP	PHONE	ENTRY #
Solectria Renewables LLC	Lawrence	MA	C	978 683-9700	12076
Phoenix Resources	Goshen	NH	G	603 863-9096	18215

CONSULTING SVCS: Oil

	CITY	ST	EMP	PHONE	ENTRY #
Daniel Johnston & Co Inc	Hancock	NH	G	603 525-9330	18284

CONSULTING SVCS: Scientific

	CITY	ST	EMP	PHONE	ENTRY #
Scry Health Inc	Woodbridge	CT	F	203 936-8244	5478
Sophic Alliance Inc	East Falmouth	MA	G	508 495-3801	10449

CONSUMER ELECTRONICS STORE: Video & Disc Recorder/Player

	CITY	ST	EMP	PHONE	ENTRY #
Amb Signs Inc **(PA)**	Dover Foxcroft	ME	G	207 564-3633	5959

CONTACT LENSES

	CITY	ST	EMP	PHONE	ENTRY #
Wilmington Partners LP	Wilmington	MA	C	978 658-6111	17067
Blanchard Contact Lens Inc	Manchester	NH	F	800 367-4009	18788

CONTACTS: Electrical

	CITY	ST	EMP	PHONE	ENTRY #
Deringer-Ney Inc **(PA)**	Bloomfield	CT	C	860 242-2281	217
Checon Corporation **(PA)**	North Attleboro	MA	C	508 643-0940	13752
Pep Industries LLC	Attleboro	MA	A	508 226-5600	7776
Precision Engineered Pdts LLC **(DH)**	Attleboro	MA	G	508 226-5600	7782

CONTAINERS, GLASS: Food

	CITY	ST	EMP	PHONE	ENTRY #
Calyx Containers LLC	Allston	MA	E	617 249-6870	7461
Saint-Gobain Corporation	Northborough	MA	E	508 351-7112	14047

CONTAINERS, GLASS: Medicine Bottles

	CITY	ST	EMP	PHONE	ENTRY #
Matthew Fisel ND	Guilford	CT	G	203 453-0122	1709

CONTAINERS: Cargo, Wood & Metal Combination

	CITY	ST	EMP	PHONE	ENTRY #
Tcc Multi Kargo	Norwalk	CT	G	203 803-1462	3255

CONTAINERS: Corrugated

	CITY	ST	EMP	PHONE	ENTRY #
Cascades Holding US Inc	Newtown	CT	D	203 426-5871	2918
Kapstone Paper and Packg Corp	Putnam	CT	G	860 928-2211	3619
Rice Packaging Inc	Ellington	CT	D	860 870-7057	1338
Westrock Rkt Company	Bethel	CT	F	203 739-0318	193
Atlas Box and Crating Co Inc **(PA)**	Sutton	MA	C	508 865-1155	15679
Buy Boxescom LLC	Boston	MA	G	617 305-7865	8451
New England Business Svc Inc **(HQ)**	Groton	MA	D	978 448-6111	11291
Newcorr Packaging Inc	Northborough	MA	D	508 393-9256	14040
Rand-Whitney Container LLC	Worcester	MA	G	774 420-2425	17451
Unified2 Globl Packg Group LLC	Sutton	MA	A	508 865-1155	15694
Westrock - Southern Cont LLC	Boston	MA	F	978 772-5050	8924
Wood Products Unlimited Inc	Methuen	MA	G	978 687-7449	13048
Fuller Box Co Inc	Central Falls	RI	D	401 725-4300	20113
Ljm Packaging Co Inc	North Kingstown	RI	D	401 295-2660	20724
Mason Box Company	Pawtucket	RI	E	800 842-9526	20857
Rand-Whitney Container LLC	Pawtucket	RI	E	401 729-7900	20890
Poultney Pallet Inc	Fair Haven	VT	G	802 265-4444	21968

CONTAINERS: Food & Beverage

	CITY	ST	EMP	PHONE	ENTRY #
Silgan Holdings Inc **(PA)**	Stamford	CT	C	203 975-7110	4321

CONTAINERS: Frozen Food & Ice Cream

	CITY	ST	EMP	PHONE	ENTRY #
Menchies Frozen Yogurt	Hingham	MA	F	781 740-1245	11504

CONTAINERS: Glass

	CITY	ST	EMP	PHONE	ENTRY #
Emhart Glass Manufacturing Inc **(DH)**	Windsor	CT	E	860 298-7340	5332
Glass By Petze	Osterville	MA	F	508 428-0971	14248
Yankee Glass Blower Inc	Carlisle	MA	G	978 369-7545	9801
Erie Scientific LLC **(DH)**	Portsmouth	NH	B	603 430-6859	19560

CONTAINERS: Laminated Phenolic & Vulcanized Fiber

	CITY	ST	EMP	PHONE	ENTRY #
Barrday Corporation **(HQ)**	Millbury	MA	D	508 581-2100	13156

CONTAINERS: Liquid Tight Fiber, From Purchased Materials

	CITY	ST	EMP	PHONE	ENTRY #
Echo Industries Inc	Orange	MA	E	978 544-7000	14215

	CITY	ST	EMP	PHONE	ENTRY #
Lapoint Industries Inc **(PA)**	Auburn	ME	D	207 777-3100	5575

CONTAINERS: Metal

	CITY	ST	EMP	PHONE	ENTRY #
Architectural Supplements LLC	Waterbury	CT	F	203 591-5505	4845
Champlin-Packrite Inc	Manchester	CT	E	860 951-9217	1993
Connecticut Container Corp **(PA)**	North Haven	CT	C	203 248-2161	3018
Clarks Steel Drum Company	Medford	MA	G	781 396-1109	12926
Cold Chain Technologies Inc **(PA)**	Franklin	MA	D	508 429-1395	11030
Index Packaging Inc	Milton	NH	C	603 350-0018	19086
Modern Metal Solutions LLC	Hudson	NH	G	603 402-3022	18415
Van Leer Jodi	Hanover	NH	G	603 643-3034	18300
Rand-Whitney Container LLC	Pawtucket	RI	E	401 729-7900	20890

CONTAINERS: Plastic

	CITY	ST	EMP	PHONE	ENTRY #
Architectural Supplements LLC	Waterbury	CT	F	203 591-5505	4845
CKS Packaging Inc	Naugatuck	CT	D	203 729-0716	2466
Clearly Clean Products LLC **(PA)**	South Windsor	CT	F	860 646-1040	3950
Cool-It LLC	Wallingford	CT	G	203 284-4848	4727
Jarden Corporation	Oxford	CT	G	203 264-9717	3410
Jarden LLC	Norwalk	CT	E	203 845-5300	3179
Select Plastics LLC	Norwalk	CT	G	203 866-3767	3240
Silgan Holdings Inc **(PA)**	Stamford	CT	C	203 975-7110	4321
Silgan Plastics LLC	Deep River	CT	C	860 526-6300	1066
Upc LLC	Meriden	CT	G	877 466-1137	2146
Air-Tite Holders Inc	North Adams	MA	F	413 664-2730	13667
Americad Technology Corporat	Norwood	MA	E	781 551-8220	14126
Berry Global Inc	Franklin	MA	C	508 918-1715	11026
Berry Global Inc	Easthampton	MA	C	812 424-2904	10555
Berry Global Inc	Nantucket	MA	G	508 325-0004	13221
Bway Corporation	Leominster	MA	F	978 537-4911	12121
CDF Corporation **(PA)**	Plymouth	MA	D	508 747-5858	14550
Consolidated Cont Holdings LLC	Marlborough	MA	F	508 485-2109	12740
Consolidated Container Co LLC	Franklin	MA	B	508 520-8800	11031
Covalnce Spcalty Adhesives LLC	Franklin	MA	C	812 424-2904	11033
Donahue Industries Inc	Shrewsbury	MA	E	508 845-6501	15108
Dupont Packaging Inc	Holyoke	MA	F	413 552-0048	11622
Fraen Corporation **(PA)**	Reading	MA	C	781 205-5300	14734
Grainpro Inc **(PA)**	Concord	MA	G	978 371-7118	10133
Hillside Plastics Inc	Turners Falls	MA	C	413 863-2222	15879
Hytex Industries Inc	Randolph	MA	E	781 963-4400	14686
John F Wielock	Dudley	MA	G	508 943-5366	10378
Leaktite Corporation **(PA)**	Leominster	MA	D	978 537-8000	12160
N P Medical Inc	Clinton	MA	E	978 365-9721	10084
New England Business Svc Inc **(HQ)**	Groton	MA	D	978 448-6111	11291
Onebin	Boston	MA	G	617 851-6402	8748
Pep Industries LLC	Attleboro	MA	A	508 226-5600	7776
Precision Engineered Pdts LLC **(DH)**	Attleboro	MA	G	508 226-5600	7782
Seabury Splash Inc	Plymouth	MA	E	508 830-3440	14582
Clark Island Boat Works	South Thomaston	ME	G	207 594-4112	7045
Consolidated Container Co LLC	Portland	ME	F	207 772-7468	6642
Jarden LLC	East Wilton	ME	C	207 645-2574	5987
Consolidated Container Co LLC	Londonderry	NH	E	603 329-6747	18687
Consolidated Container Co LLC	Londonderry	NH	E	603 624-6055	18688
Aspects Inc	Warren	RI	E	401 247-1854	21286
Berry Global Inc	Bristol	RI	C	401 254-0600	20064
C & W Co Inc	Providence	RI	G	401 941-6311	20977
Custom Design Incorporated	North Kingstown	RI	E	401 294-0200	20700
Consolidated Container Co LLC	South Burlington	VT	E	802 658-6588	22444
Questech Corporation **(PA)**	Rutland	VT	E	802 773-1228	22347

CONTAINERS: Plywood & Veneer, Wood

	CITY	ST	EMP	PHONE	ENTRY #
Aspects Inc	Warren	RI	E	401 247-1854	21286

CONTAINERS: Shipping, Bombs, Metal Plate

	CITY	ST	EMP	PHONE	ENTRY #
Skmr Construction LLC	Alton	NH	G	603 520-0117	17547

CONTAINERS: Shipping, Wood

	CITY	ST	EMP	PHONE	ENTRY #
Champlin-Packrite Inc	Manchester	CT	E	860 951-9217	1993
Abbott-Action Inc	Canton	MA	E	781 702-5710	9710
Hardigg Industries Inc	Northampton	MA	G	413 665-2163	14007

CONTAINERS: Wood

	CITY	ST	EMP	PHONE	ENTRY #
Vermont Pallet & Skid Shop	Norwich	CT	G	860 822-6949	3292
Westwood Products Inc	Winsted	CT	F	860 379-9401	5428
Dartmouth Feeders & Traps Inc	South Dartmouth	MA	G	774 202-6594	15237
E G W Bradbury Enterprises	Bridgewater	ME	F	207 429-8141	5805
Index Packaging Inc	Milton	NH	C	603 350-0018	19086
Ljm Packaging Co Inc	North Kingstown	RI	D	401 295-2660	20724
Granville Manufacturing Co	Granville	VT	G	802 767-4747	22003

CONTAINMENT VESSELS: Reactor, Metal Plate

	CITY	ST	EMP	PHONE	ENTRY #
Fiba Technologies Inc **(PA)**	Littleton	MA	C	508 887-7100	12305

CONTRACT FOOD SVCS

	CITY	ST	EMP	PHONE	ENTRY #
Sidekim LLC	Lynn	MA	E	781 595-3663	12539

CONTRACTORS: Access Control System Eqpt

	CITY	ST	EMP	PHONE	ENTRY #
Citiworks Corp	Attleboro	MA	F	508 761-7400	7720
Celestial Monitoring Corp **(HQ)**	Narragansett	RI	E	401 782-1045	20635

CONTRACTORS: Acoustical & Ceiling Work

	CITY	ST	EMP	PHONE	ENTRY #
Procoat Products Inc	Holbrook	MA	G	781 767-2270	11536

CONTRACTORS: Asphalt

	CITY	ST	EMP	PHONE	ENTRY #
O & G Industries Inc	Bridgeport	CT	E	203 366-4586	459
Louie and Teds Blacktop Inc	Swansea	MA	F	508 678-4948	15707

CONTRACTORS: Awning Installation

	CITY	ST	EMP	PHONE	ENTRY #
Fitzgerald-Norwalk Awning Co	Norwalk	CT	G	203 847-5858	3153
Tetrault & Sons Inc	Stafford Springs	CT	G	860 872-9187	4117
DCB Welding and Fabrication	Lowell	MA	G	978 587-3883	12366
Just Right Awnings & Signs	Dover	NH	G	603 740-8416	18033
Yarra Design & Fabrication LLC	Bow	NH	F	603 224-6880	17736

CONTRACTORS: Blasting, Exc Building Demolition

	CITY	ST	EMP	PHONE	ENTRY #
Coleman Drilling & Blasting	Voluntown	CT	G	860 376-3813	4690

CONTRACTORS: Boiler Maintenance Contractor

	CITY	ST	EMP	PHONE	ENTRY #
Riley Power Inc	Marlborough	MA	C	508 852-7100	12817

CONTRACTORS: Boiler Setting

	CITY	ST	EMP	PHONE	ENTRY #
Helfrich Bros Boiler Works Inc	Lawrence	MA	E	978 975-2464	12033

CONTRACTORS: Building Eqpt & Machinery Installation

	CITY	ST	EMP	PHONE	ENTRY #
Atlantic Eqp Installers Inc	Wallingford	CT	E	203 284-0402	4705
Chas G Allen Realty LLC	Barre	MA	D	978 355-2911	7950
Hillman Enterprises **(PA)**	Attleboro	MA	G	508 761-6967	7747
Coast To Coast Ff & E Installa	Greenland	NH	F	603 433-0164	18222
Bmco Industries Inc	East Greenwich	RI	G	401 781-6884	20354
Custom Iron Works Inc	Coventry	RI	F	401 826-3310	20144

CONTRACTORS: Building Front Installation, Metal

	CITY	ST	EMP	PHONE	ENTRY #
All Phase Steel Works LLC	New Haven	CT	D	203 375-8881	2654

CONTRACTORS: Building Sign Installation & Mntnce

	CITY	ST	EMP	PHONE	ENTRY #
Adamsahern Sign Solutions Inc	Hartford	CT	F	860 523-8835	1802
Derrick Mason **(PA)**	Norwich	CT	G	413 527-4282	3278
Tims Sign & Lighting Service	Meriden	CT	G	203 634-8840	2143
Wad Inc	East Berlin	CT	E	860 828-3331	1110
Graphic Impact Signs Inc	Pittsfield	MA	E	413 499-0382	14474
Mass Sign & Decal Inc	Rockland	MA	G	781 878-7446	14812
Speedy Sign-A-Rama USA	Braintree	MA	G	781 849-1181	9038
Visimark Inc	Auburn	MA	F	508 832-3471	7851
Bailey Sign Inc	Westbrook	ME	E	207 774-2843	7181
Sign Services Inc	Stetson	ME	F	207 296-2400	7066
Valley Signs	Lebanon	NH	G	603 252-1977	18640
Twin State Signs Inc	Essex Junction	VT	G	802 872-8949	21962

CONTRACTORS: Cable Laying

	CITY	ST	EMP	PHONE	ENTRY #
Connectivity Works Inc	Holden	ME	G	207 843-0854	6196

CONTRACTORS: Caisson Drilling

	CITY	ST	EMP	PHONE	ENTRY #
Wireless Construction Inc	Standish	ME	E	207 642-5751	7064

CONTRACTORS: Carpentry Work

	CITY	ST	EMP	PHONE	ENTRY #
Pine Baker Inc	Tewksbury	MA	G	978 851-1215	15826
Owen Gray & Son	Brewer	ME	G	207 989-3575	5800
Advanced Custom Cabinets Inc	Brentwood	NH	E	603 772-6211	17743
Donald A Jhnson Fine Wdwkg LLC	Intervale	NH	G	603 356-9080	18454

CONTRACTORS: Carpentry, Cabinet & Finish Work

	CITY	ST	EMP	PHONE	ENTRY #
Industrial Wood Product Co	Shelton	CT	G	203 735-2374	3817
Joe Batson	Lawrence	MA	G	978 689-0072	12041
Mr Sandless Central Mass	Worcester	MA	G	508 864-6517	17425
Procraft Corporation	New Boston	NH	F	603 487-2080	19296
Thibco Inc	Manchester	NH	E	603 623-3011	18941

CONTRACTORS: Carpentry, Cabinet Building & Installation

	CITY	ST	EMP	PHONE	ENTRY #
Custom Crft Ktchns By Rizio BR	Monroe	CT	F	203 268-0271	2400

CONTRACTORS: Carpet Laying

	CITY	ST	EMP	PHONE	ENTRY #
Industrial Floor Covering Inc	North Billerica	MA	G	978 362-8655	13826

CONTRACTORS: Chimney Construction & Maintenance

	CITY	ST	EMP	PHONE	ENTRY #
North American Supaflu Systems	Scarborough	ME	F	207 883-1155	6935

CONTRACTORS: Closed Circuit Television Installation

	CITY	ST	EMP	PHONE	ENTRY #
Command Corporation	East Granby	CT	F	800 851-6012	1122

CONTRACTORS: Coating, Caulking & Weather, Water & Fire

	CITY	ST	EMP	PHONE	ENTRY #
United Glass To Metal Sealing	Lawrence	MA	F	978 327-5880	12080

CONTRACTORS: Commercial & Office Building

	CITY	ST	EMP	PHONE	ENTRY #
J & O Construction Inc	Brockton	MA	G	508 586-4900	9157
Wesco Building & Design Inc	Stoneham	MA	E	781 279-0490	15572
Wescor Ltd **(PA)**	Stoneham	MA	F	781 279-0490	15573
D M G Enterprises	Edmunds Twp	ME	G	207 726-4603	6005
Northrup & Gibson Entps LLC	Jamestown	RI	G	401 423-2152	20493

CONTRACTORS: Communications Svcs

	CITY	ST	EMP	PHONE	ENTRY #
General Datacomm Inc **(HQ)**	Oxford	CT	E	203 729-0271	3404
Exacom Inc	Concord	NH	E	603 228-0706	17900

CONTRACTORS: Computer Power Conditioning Svcs

	CITY	ST	EMP	PHONE	ENTRY #
Atrex Energy Inc **(PA)**	Walpole	MA	E	781 461-8251	15988

CONTRACTORS: Computerized Controls Installation

	CITY	ST	EMP	PHONE	ENTRY #
McGuire & Co Inc	Falmouth	ME	G	207 797-3323	6032

CONTRACTORS: Concrete

	CITY	ST	EMP	PHONE	ENTRY #
J J Concrete Foundations	Bethel	CT	G	203 798-8310	164
Caya Construction Co	Northbridge	MA	G	508 234-5082	14054
P J Albert Inc	Fitchburg	MA	E	978 345-7828	10847
Relevant Energy Concepts Inc	Springfield	MA	G	413 733-7692	15501
Days Auto Body Inc	Medway	ME	G	207 746-5310	6423
F R Carroll Inc	Limerick	ME	E	207 793-8615	6334

	CITY	ST	EMP	PHONE	ENTRY #
Bjorklund Corp	Providence	RI	G	401 944-6400	20970

CONTRACTORS: Construction Caulking

	CITY	ST	EMP	PHONE	ENTRY #
Jaeger Usa Inc	Rochester	NH	F	603 332-5816	19674

CONTRACTORS: Construction Site Cleanup

	CITY	ST	EMP	PHONE	ENTRY #
J & M Plumbing & Cnstr LLC	Norwich	CT	F	860 319-3082	3284

CONTRACTORS: Construction Site Metal Structure Coating

	CITY	ST	EMP	PHONE	ENTRY #
Nsa Industries LLC **(PA)**	Saint Johnsbury	VT	C	802 748-5007	22393

CONTRACTORS: Countertop Installation

	CITY	ST	EMP	PHONE	ENTRY #
Custom Crft Ktchns By Rizio BR	Monroe	CT	F	203 268-0271	2400
Jarica Inc	Woburn	MA	F	781 935-1907	17210
Ripano Stoneworks Ltd	Nashua	NH	E	603 886-6655	19254
Stone Systems New England LLC	North Smithfield	RI	C	401 766-3603	20796

CONTRACTORS: Directional Oil & Gas Well Drilling Svc

	CITY	ST	EMP	PHONE	ENTRY #
Millbrae Energy LLC **(PA)**	Greenwich	CT	F	203 742-2800	1631

CONTRACTORS: Drywall

	CITY	ST	EMP	PHONE	ENTRY #
Alco Construction Inc	Hudson	NH	G	603 305-8493	18372

CONTRACTORS: Electric Power Systems

	CITY	ST	EMP	PHONE	ENTRY #
Ac/DC Industrial Electric LLC	Yantic	CT	G	860 886-2232	5506
Electrcal Instllations Inc Eii	Moultonborough	NH	E	603 253-4525	19097

CONTRACTORS: Electrical

	CITY	ST	EMP	PHONE	ENTRY #
American Railway Technologies	East Hartford	CT	G	860 291-1170	1172
E-J Electric T & D LLC	Wallingford	CT	D	203 626-9625	4737
Eastern Electric Cnstr Co	Harwinton	CT	G	860 485-1100	1889
Eastside Electric Inc	Harwinton	CT	F	860 485-0700	1890
Modern Electronic Fax & Cmpt	Fairfield	CT	G	203 292-6520	1445
Andrus Power Solutions Inc	Lee	MA	F	413 243-0043	12087
Brewer Electric & Utilities In	South Yarmouth	MA	E	508 771-2040	15325
George A Vollans	Nantucket	MA	G	508 257-6241	13224
L T X International Inc	Norwood	MA	D	781 461-1000	14173
Markarian Electric LLC	Watertown	MA	G	617 393-9700	16297
Whyte Electric LLC	Braintree	MA	G	781 348-6239	9050
Energy MGT & Ctrl Svcs Inc	Cranston	RI	F	401 946-1440	20217
Newport Electric Corporation	Portsmouth	RI	F	401 293-0527	20930

CONTRACTORS: Energy Management Control

	CITY	ST	EMP	PHONE	ENTRY #
Universal Building Contrls Inc	Meriden	CT	F	203 235-1530	2145

CONTRACTORS: Excavating

	CITY	ST	EMP	PHONE	ENTRY #
Brox Industries Inc **(PA)**	Dracut	MA	D	978 454-9105	10355
Days Auto Body Inc	Medway	ME	G	207 746-5310	6423
John Khiel III Log Chpping Inc	Denmark	ME	E	207 452-2157	5949
Garland Lumber Company Inc	Center Conway	NH	E	603 356-5636	17798
J C B Leasing Inc	Weare	NH	D	603 529-7974	19934
Laurence Sharpe	Alexandria	NH	G	603 744-8175	17537
Max Roads LLC	Raymond	NH	G	603 895-5200	19640
Michie Corporation	Henniker	NH	D	603 428-7426	18307
Peter Pierce	Belmont	NH	G	603 524-8312	17679
R L Cook Timber Harvesting	Winchester	NH	G	603 239-6424	19994
Stacey Thomson	Orford	NH	G	603 353-9700	19421
Welog Inc	Colebrook	NH	F	603 237-8277	17878
Champlain Construction Co Inc	Middlebury	VT	F	802 388-2652	22108
Dale E Percy Inc	Stowe	VT	F	802 253-8503	22521
Wright Maintenance Inc	Newfane	VT	G	802 365-9253	22189

CONTRACTORS: Excavating Slush Pits & Cellars Svcs

	CITY	ST	EMP	PHONE	ENTRY #
Copp Excavating Inc	Durham	ME	F	207 926-4988	5970
Dig Rite Company Inc	Cranston	RI	G	401 862-5895	20211

CONTRACTORS: Fence Construction

	CITY	ST	EMP	PHONE	ENTRY #
Citiworks Corp	Attleboro	MA	F	508 761-7400	7720
Dogwatch Inc **(PA)**	Natick	MA	F	508 650-0600	13252
Feeney Fence Inc	Hyde Park	MA	G	617 364-1407	11866
Custom Iron Works Inc	Coventry	RI	F	401 826-3310	20144

CONTRACTORS: Fire Detection & Burglar Alarm Systems

	CITY	ST	EMP	PHONE	ENTRY #
Americansub	Dudley	MA	E	508 949-2320	10372
Shufro Security Company Inc	Newton	MA	G	617 244-3355	13637

CONTRACTORS: Fire Escape Installation

	CITY	ST	EMP	PHONE	ENTRY #
John Carter Fire Escape Svcs	Boston	MA	G	617 990-7387	8633

CONTRACTORS: Fire Sprinkler System Installation Svcs

	CITY	ST	EMP	PHONE	ENTRY #
Tyco International MGT Co LLC	Mansfield	MA	G	508 261-6200	12667
R R Sprinkler Inc	Swanton	VT	G	802 868-2423	22535

CONTRACTORS: Floor Laying & Other Floor Work

	CITY	ST	EMP	PHONE	ENTRY #
Interntonal MBL Gran Entps Inc	Hartford	CT	G	860 296-0741	1838

CONTRACTORS: Flooring

	CITY	ST	EMP	PHONE	ENTRY #
J & O Construction Inc	Brockton	MA	G	508 586-4900	9157

CONTRACTORS: Foundation & Footing

	CITY	ST	EMP	PHONE	ENTRY #
Sandelin Foundation Inc	Topsham	ME	F	207 725-7004	7094
Joseph P Carrara & Sons Inc **(PA)**	North Clarendon	VT	E	802 775-2301	22216

CONTRACTORS: Foundation Building

	CITY	ST	EMP	PHONE	ENTRY #
Richard A Tibbetts	Oxford	ME	G	207 539-5073	6571

CONTRACTORS: Gas Detection & Analysis Svcs

	CITY	ST	EMP	PHONE	ENTRY #
On-Site Analysis Inc	Marlborough	MA	E	508 460-7778	12802
Orono Spectral Solutions Inc	Hermon	ME	G	866 269-8007	6192

CONTRACTORS: Gas Field Svcs, NEC

	CITY	ST	EMP	PHONE	ENTRY #
Maple Road Service Station	Longmeadow	MA	G	413 567-6233	12336
W & G Gas Services LLC	Roslindale	MA	G	617 327-2515	14844

CONTRACTORS: General Electric

	CITY	ST	EMP	PHONE	ENTRY #
Louis Electric Co Inc	Wolcott	CT	G	203 879-5483	5447
Tri State Maintenance Svcs LLC	North Haven	CT	F	203 691-1343	3064
Giner Elx Inc	Auburndale	MA	F	781 392-0300	7862
Pretorius Electric	West Bridgewater	MA	G	508 326-9492	16450
Bob Walker Inc	Standish	ME	F	207 642-2083	7060
Dexter Sign Co	East Providence	RI	E	401 434-1100	20406

CONTRACTORS: Glass, Glazing & Tinting

	CITY	ST	EMP	PHONE	ENTRY #
Kensington Glass and Frmng Co	Berlin	CT	G	860 828-9428	91
Liberty Glass and Met Inds Inc	North Grosvenordale	CT	E	860 923-3623	2997
Contract Glass Service Inc	Billerica	MA	E	978 262-1323	8233
New England Stained Glass	North Attleboro	MA	G	508 699-6965	13769
Prestige Custom Mirror & Glass	Waltham	MA	F	781 647-0878	16177
Bill Lztte Archtctural GL Alum	Riverside	RI	F	401 383-9535	21164

CONTRACTORS: Grouting Work

	CITY	ST	EMP	PHONE	ENTRY #
Mr Sandless Central Mass	Worcester	MA	G	508 864-6517	17425

CONTRACTORS: Gutters & Downspouts

	CITY	ST	EMP	PHONE	ENTRY #
Clark & Sons Seamless Gutter	Chicopee	MA	G	413 732-3934	10014
Minuteman Seamless Gutters	Hudson	MA	F	978 562-1744	11794
Mr Gutter Inc	Holyoke	MA	G	413 536-7451	11640
Gutter Wholesalers Inc	Raymond	ME	G	207 655-7407	6773

CONTRACTORS: Heating & Air Conditioning

	CITY	ST	EMP	PHONE	ENTRY #
Brideau Shtmtl & Fabrication	Leominster	MA	F	978 537-3372	12119
Harrington Air Systems LLC	Watertown	MA	E	781 341-1999	16290
Total Temp Inc	Middleboro	MA	G	508 947-8628	13078
Century Sheet Metal Inc	Riverside	RI	G	401 433-1380	21166

CONTRACTORS: Highway & Street Construction, General

	CITY	ST	EMP	PHONE	ENTRY #
Worksafe Traffic Ctrl Inds Inc **(PA)**	Barre	VT	F	802 223-8948	21645

CONTRACTORS: Highway & Street Paving

	CITY	ST	EMP	PHONE	ENTRY #
Westchester Industries Inc	Greenwich	CT	F	203 661-0055	1661
Aggregate Inds - Northeast Reg	Saugus	MA	G	781 941-7200	14975
Brox Industries Inc **(PA)**	Dracut	MA	D	978 454-9105	10355
P J Albert Inc	Fitchburg	MA	E	978 345-7828	10847
Ted Ondrick Company LLC **(PA)**	Chicopee	MA	F	413 592-2565	10064
M & L Asphalt Services LLC	Swanzey	NH	G	603 355-1230	19884

CONTRACTORS: Highway Sign & Guardrail Construction & Install

	CITY	ST	EMP	PHONE	ENTRY #
Jutras Signs Inc	Bedford	NH	E	603 622-2344	17648

CONTRACTORS: Hydraulic Eqpt Installation & Svcs

	CITY	ST	EMP	PHONE	ENTRY #
B L C Investments Inc	Milford	CT	G	203 877-1888	2249
Stedt Hydraulic Crane Corp	Westborough	MA	F	508 366-9151	16651
Seven Star Inc	Newport	RI	G	401 683-6222	20680

CONTRACTORS: Indl Building Renovation, Remodeling & Repair

	CITY	ST	EMP	PHONE	ENTRY #
Helfrich Bros Boiler Works Inc	Lawrence	MA	E	978 975-2464	12033

CONTRACTORS: Insulation Installation, Building

	CITY	ST	EMP	PHONE	ENTRY #
Ecologic Energy Solutions LLC	Stamford	CT	E	203 889-0505	4191
Zampell Refractories Inc	Auburn	ME	E	207 786-2400	5602

CONTRACTORS: Kitchen & Bathroom Remodeling

	CITY	ST	EMP	PHONE	ENTRY #
Roman Woodworking	New Britain	CT	G	860 490-5989	2574
About-Face Kitchens Inc	Peabody	MA	G	978 532-0212	14305

CONTRACTORS: Kitchen Cabinet Installation

	CITY	ST	EMP	PHONE	ENTRY #
Holland Woodworking Inc	Marlborough	MA	G	508 481-2990	12768

CONTRACTORS: Lead Burning

	CITY	ST	EMP	PHONE	ENTRY #
Gary Kellner	Westwood	MA	G	781 329-0404	16866

CONTRACTORS: Machinery Dismantling

	CITY	ST	EMP	PHONE	ENTRY #
Robert Russell Co Inc	Rehoboth	MA	G	508 226-4140	14760

CONTRACTORS: Machinery Installation

	CITY	ST	EMP	PHONE	ENTRY #
Nsa Industries LLC **(PA)**	Saint Johnsbury	VT	C	802 748-5007	22393

CONTRACTORS: Marble Installation, Interior

	CITY	ST	EMP	PHONE	ENTRY #
Colonial Marble Co Inc	Everett	MA	G	617 389-1130	10608
Louis W Mian Inc **(PA)**	Boston	MA	E	617 241-7900	8672
Morning Star Marble & Gran Inc	Topsham	ME	F	207 725-7309	7091

CONTRACTORS: Masonry & Stonework

	CITY	ST	EMP	PHONE	ENTRY #
Colonial Landscape Corp	Groton	MA	G	978 448-3329	11287
Rmi Titanium Company LLC	Burlington	MA	F	781 272-5967	9330
Ted Ondrick Company LLC **(PA)**	Chicopee	MA	F	413 592-2565	10064
Conproco Corp	Bow	NH	G	603 743-5800	17710

CONTRACTORS: Mechanical

	CITY	ST	EMP	PHONE	ENTRY #
Dean Paige Welding Inc	Baldwinville	MA	G	978 939-8187	7943

CONTRACTORS: Millwrights

	CITY	ST	EMP	PHONE	ENTRY #
Oliver Barrette Millwrights	Providence	RI	G	401 421-3750	21083

CONTRACTORS: Office Furniture Installation

	CITY	ST	EMP	PHONE	ENTRY #
Superior Manufacturing Corp	Fall River	MA	G	508 677-0100	10765
Nouveau Interiors LLC	Manchester	NH	G	603 398-1732	18889

CONTRACTORS: Oil & Gas Well Drilling Svc

	CITY	ST	EMP	PHONE	ENTRY #
Coleman Drilling & Blasting	Voluntown	CT	G	860 376-3813	4690
Eows Midland Inc	Stamford	CT	E	203 358-5705	4194
Louis E Allyn Sons Inc	Norfolk	CT	G	860 542-5741	2958
Mercuria Energy Trading Inc	Greenwich	CT	G	203 413-3355	1630
Soil Exploration Corp **(PA)**	Leominster	MA	G	978 840-0391	12187
Jeff Cummings Services LLC	Warner	NH	G	603 456-3706	19927

CONTRACTORS: Oil & Gas Well Flow Rate Measurement Svcs

	CITY	ST	EMP	PHONE	ENTRY #
Sensing Systems Corporation	Dartmouth	MA	F	508 992-0872	10276

CONTRACTORS: Oil & Gas Wells Pumping Svcs

	CITY	ST	EMP	PHONE	ENTRY #
Weymouths Inc	Clinton	ME	G	207 426-3211	5917

CONTRACTORS: Oil & Gas Wells Svcs

	CITY	ST	EMP	PHONE	ENTRY #
Schlumberger Technology Corp	Cambridge	MA	C	617 768-2000	9645

CONTRACTORS: Oil Field Lease Tanks: Erectg, Clng/Rprg Svcs

	CITY	ST	EMP	PHONE	ENTRY #
Palmieri Industries Inc	Bridgeport	CT	D	203 384-6020	462
Cleanbasins Inc	North Billerica	MA	G	978 670-5838	13802
Commtank Cares Inc	Wakefield	MA	G	781 224-1021	15946
Modern Tractor & Truck Service	Seekonk	MA	G	508 761-4425	15029
Sea-Land Envmtl Svcs Inc	Medfield	MA	G	508 359-1085	12919
Hamco Tank Systems LLC	Mason	NH	G	603 878-0585	18968

CONTRACTORS: Oil Sampling Svcs

	CITY	ST	EMP	PHONE	ENTRY #
Cyn Oil Corporation	Stoughton	MA	D	781 341-8074	15585

CONTRACTORS: Oil/Gas Well Construction, Rpr/Dismantling Svcs

	CITY	ST	EMP	PHONE	ENTRY #
Alliance Energy LLC	New Haven	CT	G	203 933-2511	2655
Alterio Tractor Pulling LLC	Oxford	CT	G	203 305-9812	3390
Buon Appetito From Italy LLC	New London	CT	G	860 437-3668	2767
Connectcut Shreline Developers	Clinton	CT	G	860 669-4424	781
J & M Plumbing & Cnstr LLC	Norwich	CT	F	860 319-3082	3284
Kafa Group LLC	Bridgeport	CT	G	475 275-0090	438
My Slide Lines LLC	Norwalk	CT	G	203 324-1642	3202
Tri State Maintenance Svcs LLC	North Haven	CT	F	203 691-1343	3064
W M G and Sons Inc	Bristol	CT	G	860 584-0143	623
Acheson Company LLC	Williamsburg	MA	G	413 268-0246	16946
Biszko Contracting Corp	Fall River	MA	E	508 679-0518	10668
Kenyon Composites	Gloucester	MA	G	617 803-3198	11195
Liberty Construction Svcs LLC	Roxbury	MA	D	617 602-4001	14874
RCO Renovations Inc	South Walpole	MA	G	508 668-5524	15320
Wireless Construction Inc	Standish	ME	E	207 642-5751	7064
Doggie Passport	Manchester	NH	G	603 315-8243	18812
Maillet Construction	Mason	NH	G	603 582-2810	18969

CONTRACTORS: On-Site Welding

	CITY	ST	EMP	PHONE	ENTRY #
Alloy Welding & Mfg Co Inc	Bristol	CT	F	860 582-3638	518
Hamden Sheet Metal Inc	Hamden	CT	G	203 776-1472	1757
J T Fantozzi Co Inc	Meriden	CT	G	203 238-7018	2096
Allied Fabrication Inc	North Billerica	MA	G	978 667-5901	13791
D Cronins Welding Service	Lawrence	MA	G	978 664-4488	12014
Dean Paige Welding Inc	Baldwinville	MA	G	978 939-8187	7943
Franklin County Fabricators	Greenfield	MA	G	413 774-3518	11261
Jam Plastics Inc	Leominster	MA	E	978 537-2570	12156
Lizotte Welding	East Freetown	MA	G	508 763-8784	10454
Marios Welding	Fall River	MA	G	508 646-1038	10727
Starkweather Engineering Inc	Tewksbury	MA	F	978 858-3700	15837
Dennis Welding & Marine Inc	Beals	ME	G	207 497-5998	5683
ME Tomacelli Inc	Boothbay	ME	G	207 633-7553	5779
Bri-Weld Industries LLC	Auburn	NH	F	603 622-9480	17608
Custom Welding & Fabrications	West Nottingham	NH	F	603 942-5170	19964
East Coast Metal Works Co Inc	Kingston	NH	G	603 642-9600	18543
LAD Welding & Fabrication	Concord	NH	F	603 228-6617	17911
Champlin Welding Inc	Narragansett	RI	G	401 782-4099	20636
Ducharme Machine Shop Inc	Graniteville	VT	G	802 476-6575	21999
Milton Vermont Sheet Metal Inc	Milton	VT	D	802 893-1581	22134
Vermont Indexable Tooling Inc	Fairfax	VT	G	802 752-2002	21980

CONTRACTORS: Ornamental Metal Work

	CITY	ST	EMP	PHONE	ENTRY #
Lundys Company Inc	Lynn	MA	F	781 595-8639	12522
Southeast Railing Co Inc	Canton	MA	F	781 828-7088	9783

CONTRACTORS: Painting, Commercial, Exterior

	CITY	ST	EMP	PHONE	ENTRY #
Metal Magic Inc	Trenton	ME	G	207 667-8519	7100

CONTRACTORS: Painting, Commercial, Interior

	CITY	ST	EMP	PHONE	ENTRY #
J & O Construction Inc	Brockton	MA	G	508 586-4900	9157

CONTRACTORS: Patio & Deck Construction & Repair

	CITY	ST	EMP	PHONE	ENTRY #
Tetrault & Sons Inc	Stafford Springs	CT	G	860 872-9187	4117
Integrity Composites LLC	Biddeford	ME	F	207 571-0743	5740

CONTRACTORS: Petroleum Storage Tank Install, Underground

	CITY	ST	EMP	PHONE	ENTRY #
Foleys Pump Service Inc	Danbury	CT	E	203 792-2236	921

CONTRACTORS: Plumbing

	CITY	ST	EMP	PHONE	ENTRY #
J & M Plumbing & Cnstr LLC	Norwich	CT	F	860 319-3082	3284
Benson Enterprises Inc	North Easton	MA	F	508 583-5401	13943
R I Baker Co Inc **(PA)**	Clarksburg	MA	E	413 663-3791	10075
Days Auto Body Inc	Medway	ME	G	207 746-5310	6423
Weymouths Inc	Clinton	ME	G	207 426-3211	5917

CONTRACTORS: Prefabricated Window & Door Installation

	CITY	ST	EMP	PHONE	ENTRY #
All-Time Manufacturing Co Inc	Montville	CT	F	860 848-9258	2421
Cusson Sash Company	Glastonbury	CT	G	860 659-0354	1546
Westminster Millwork Corp	Fitchburg	MA	F	978 665-9200	10862

CONTRACTORS: Process Piping

	CITY	ST	EMP	PHONE	ENTRY #
Process Cooling Systems Inc	Leominster	MA	E	978 537-1996	12177
Wardwell Piping Inc	Windham	ME	F	207 892-0034	7259

CONTRACTORS: Pulpwood, Engaged In Cutting

	CITY	ST	EMP	PHONE	ENTRY #
Bernard Ginn and Sons Inc	Winterport	ME	G	207 234-2187	7276
Colin Bartlett & Sons Inc	Amity	ME	E	207 532-2214	5523
Edward Bernard Inc	West Enfield	ME	F	207 732-3987	7170
Herbert C Haynes Inc **(PA)**	Winn	ME	E	207 736-3412	7264
Paul N Foulkes Inc	Williamsburg Twp	ME	G	207 965-9481	7223
Up North Corp Inc	Fort Kent	ME	E	207 834-6178	6068

CONTRACTORS: Rigging, Theatrical

	CITY	ST	EMP	PHONE	ENTRY #
Show Motion Inc	Milford	CT	E	203 866-1866	2362
Link Enterprises Corp	Northampton	MA	G	413 585-9869	14010

CONTRACTORS: Roofing

	CITY	ST	EMP	PHONE	ENTRY #
J & O Construction Inc	Brockton	MA	G	508 586-4900	9157
Sarnafil Services Inc	Canton	MA	C	781 828-5400	9775
Keebowil Inc **(PA)**	Keene	NH	D	603 352-4232	18509
Maillet Construction	Mason	NH	G	603 582-2810	18969

CONTRACTORS: Roustabout Svcs

	CITY	ST	EMP	PHONE	ENTRY #
Ace Servicing Co Inc	Orange	CT	G	203 795-1400	3356
Loanworks Servicing LLC	Shelton	CT	G	203 402-7304	3829

CONTRACTORS: Safety & Security Eqpt

	CITY	ST	EMP	PHONE	ENTRY #
Q-Lane Turnstiles LLC	Sandy Hook	CT	F	860 410-1801	3745
Tyco International MGT Co LLC	Mansfield	MA	G	508 261-6200	12667

CONTRACTORS: Sandblasting Svc, Building Exteriors

	CITY	ST	EMP	PHONE	ENTRY #
Frederick Wieninger Monuments	Milbridge	ME	G	207 546-2356	6432

CONTRACTORS: Seismograph Survey Svcs

	CITY	ST	EMP	PHONE	ENTRY #
Geosonics Inc	Cheshire	CT	F	203 271-2504	735

CONTRACTORS: Septic System

	CITY	ST	EMP	PHONE	ENTRY #
Acme Precast Co Inc	West Falmouth	MA	E	508 548-9607	16477
Clivus New England Inc	Lawrence	MA	G	978 794-9400	12011
Oldcastle Infrastructure Inc	Rehoboth	MA	D	508 336-7600	14756
Earl W Gerrish & Sons Inc	Brownville	ME	F	207 965-2171	5826
Maillet Construction	Mason	NH	G	603 582-2810	18969
Wright Maintenance Inc	Newfane	VT	G	802 365-9253	22189

CONTRACTORS: Sheet Metal Work, NEC

	CITY	ST	EMP	PHONE	ENTRY #
Redco Audio Inc	Stratford	CT	F	203 502-7600	4441
Tech-Air Incorporated	Uncasville	CT	E	860 848-1287	4649
Crocker Architectural Shtmtl	North Oxford	MA	E	508 987-9900	13970
Modern Sheetmetal Inc	Worcester	MA	G	508 798-6665	17422
Oliver Welding & Fabricating	Ipswich	MA	G	978 356-4488	11933
Phoenix Sheet Metal	South Dartmouth	MA	G	508 994-4046	15242
Eastern Metals Inc	Londonderry	NH	G	603 818-8639	18693

CONTRACTORS: Single-family Home General Remodeling

	CITY	ST	EMP	PHONE	ENTRY #
Cusson Sash Company	Glastonbury	CT	G	860 659-0354	1546
Deschenes & Cooper Architectur	Pawcatuck	CT	G	860 599-2481	3434
Trigila Construction Inc	Berlin	CT	E	860 828-8444	115
Fine Line Woodworking Inc	Boxboro	MA	G	978 263-4322	8952
Jan Woodworks Renovation	Westfield	MA	G	413 563-2534	16691

CONTRACTORS: Store Fixture Installation

	CITY	ST	EMP	PHONE	ENTRY #
Alco Construction Inc	Hudson	NH	G	603 305-8493	18372

CONTRACTORS: Structural Steel Erection

	CITY	ST	EMP	PHONE	ENTRY #
Colonial Iron Shop Inc	Enfield	CT	G	860 763-0659	1351
New Canaan Forge LLC **(PA)**	New Canaan	CT	G	203 966-3858	2610
Steeltech Building Pdts Inc	South Windsor	CT	D	860 290-8930	4014
United Steel Inc	East Hartford	CT	C	860 289-2323	1232
D Cronins Welding Service	Lawrence	MA	G	978 664-4488	12014
DCB Welding and Fabrication	Lowell	MA	G	978 587-3883	12366
Hillman Enterprises **(PA)**	Attleboro	MA	G	508 761-6967	7747
James A McBrady Inc	Scarborough	ME	E	207 883-4176	6928
New Hampshire Stl Erectors Inc	Goffstown	NH	E	603 668-3464	18207
Frontier Welding & Fabrication	Woonsocket	RI	G	401 769-0271	21565

CONTRACTORS: Svc Station Eqpt Installation, Maint & Repair

	CITY	ST	EMP	PHONE	ENTRY #
Millers Petroleum Systems Inc	Pittsfield	MA	G	413 499-2134	14490

CONTRACTORS: Svc Well Drilling Svcs

	CITY	ST	EMP	PHONE	ENTRY #
Marks Wells & Pumps Inc	Bellingham	MA	G	508 528-1741	8046
High Pine Well Drilling Inc	Buxton	ME	G	207 929-4122	5857

CONTRACTORS: Tile Installation, Ceramic

	CITY	ST	EMP	PHONE	ENTRY #
Atlantic MBL & Gran Group Inc	East Falmouth	MA	G	508 540-9770	10436

CONTRACTORS: Ventilation & Duct Work

	CITY	ST	EMP	PHONE	ENTRY #
Betlan Corporation	Newtown	CT	F	203 270-7898	2916
L & L Mechanical LLC	Goshen	CT	F	860 491-4007	1585

CONTRACTORS: Wall Covering

	CITY	ST	EMP	PHONE	ENTRY #
Marjorie Royer Interiors Inc	Middleton	MA	G	978 774-0533	13095

CONTRACTORS: Warm Air Heating & Air Conditioning

	CITY	ST	EMP	PHONE	ENTRY #
Hamden Sheet Metal Inc	Hamden	CT	G	203 776-1472	1757
J & B Service Company LLC	Bethel	CT	G	203 743-9357	163
DSM Metal Fabrication Inc	Biddeford	ME	E	207 282-6740	5729

CONTRACTORS: Water Intake Well Drilling Svc

	CITY	ST	EMP	PHONE	ENTRY #
Pine State Drilling Inc	Athens	ME	G	207 654-2771	5543

	CITY	ST	EMP	PHONE	ENTRY #
NA Manosh Inc	Morrisville	VT	E	802 888-5722	22174

CONTRACTORS: Water Well Drilling

	CITY	ST	EMP	PHONE	ENTRY #
Pine State Drilling Inc	Athens	ME	G	207 654-2771	5543

CONTRACTORS: Waterproofing

	CITY	ST	EMP	PHONE	ENTRY #
Conproco Corp	Bow	NH	G	603 743-5800	17710

CONTRACTORS: Window Treatment Installation

	CITY	ST	EMP	PHONE	ENTRY #
Marjorie Royer Interiors Inc	Middleton	MA	G	978 774-0533	13095

CONTRACTORS: Windows & Doors

	CITY	ST	EMP	PHONE	ENTRY #
Tetrault & Sons Inc	Stafford Springs	CT	G	860 872-9187	4117
National Service Systems Inc	Stoughton	MA	G	781 344-6504	15609
Lockheed Window Corp	Pascoag	RI	D	401 568-3061	20802

CONTRACTORS: Wood Floor Installation & Refinishing

	CITY	ST	EMP	PHONE	ENTRY #
L S Hardwood Floor	Dorchester	MA	G	617 288-0339	10346

CONTRACTORS: Wrecking & Demolition

	CITY	ST	EMP	PHONE	ENTRY #
Stacey Thomson	Orford	NH	G	603 353-9700	19421

CONTROL CIRCUIT DEVICES

	CITY	ST	EMP	PHONE	ENTRY #
Richmond Contract Mfg	Bowdoinham	ME	E	207 737-4385	5790

CONTROL EQPT: Buses Or Trucks, Electric

	CITY	ST	EMP	PHONE	ENTRY #
Sevcon Usa Inc	Southborough	MA	F	508 281-5500	15366

CONTROL EQPT: Electric

	CITY	ST	EMP	PHONE	ENTRY #
Altek Electronics Inc	Torrington	CT	C	860 482-7626	4558
CET Inc	Milford	CT	G	203 882-8057	2263
Delta Elevator Service Corp **(DH)**	Canton	CT	E	860 676-6152	697
Kimchuk Incorporated **(PA)**	Danbury	CT	F	203 790-7800	943
New Haven Companies Inc	East Haven	CT	F	203 469-6421	1257
P-Q Controls Inc **(PA)**	Bristol	CT	E	860 583-6994	589
T & T Automation Inc	Windsor	CT	F	860 683-8788	5371
AC General Inc	Hudson	MA	G	978 568-8229	11749
Airloc Corporation	Franklin	MA	G	508 528-0022	11020
ITT Corporation	Woburn	MA	F	781 932-5665	17207
Massa Products Corporation	Hingham	MA	D	781 749-3120	11501
Omni Control Technology Inc	Whitinsville	MA	E	508 234-9121	16917
Performance Motion Devices Inc	Westford	MA	E	978 266-1210	16783
Safe Process Systems Inc	Norton	MA	G	508 285-5109	14087
Waja Associates Inc	Franklin	MA	F	508 543-6050	11096
P-Q Controls Inc	Dover Foxcroft	ME	G	207 564-7141	5962
Hollis Controls Inc **(PA)**	Nashua	NH	G	603 595-2482	19179
Ie Chemical Systems Inc	Nashua	NH	F	603 888-4777	19183
L3harris Technologies Inc	Nashua	NH	E	603 689-1450	19196
Cooper Lighting Inc	Essex Junction	VT	F	800 767-3674	21937
Intergrated Control Systems	South Burlington	VT	G	802 658-6385	22449

CONTROL EQPT: Noise

	CITY	ST	EMP	PHONE	ENTRY #
Bell Rubber	Abington	MA	G	781 400-7262	7321
Control Resources Inc	Littleton	MA	E	978 486-4160	12297

CONTROL PANELS: Electrical

	CITY	ST	EMP	PHONE	ENTRY #
Accutron Inc	Windsor	CT	C	860 683-8300	5315
B & A Design Inc	Vernon Rockville	CT	G	860 871-0134	4679
Connecticut Valley Inds LLC	Old Saybrook	CT	G	860 388-0822	3332
Corotec Corp	Farmington	CT	F	860 678-0038	1475
Industrial Cnnctons Sltons LLC	Plainville	CT	E	860 747-7677	3497
La Chance Controls	Portland	CT	G	860 342-2212	3569
Precision Graphics Inc	East Berlin	CT	E	860 828-6561	1106
Ayan Electric Inc	Lowell	MA	G	978 256-6306	12349
Control 7 Inc	Bridgewater	MA	E	508 697-3197	9068
Dike Corporation **(PA)**	Lawrence	MA	G	978 208-7046	12018
Doranco Inc	Attleboro	MA	G	508 236-0290	7727
McStowe Engineering & Met Pdts	East Bridgewater	MA	F	508 378-7400	10417
Microtek Inc	Chicopee	MA	C	413 593-1025	10046
Tektron Inc	Topsfield	MA	F	978 887-0091	15866
Electrcal Instllations Inc Eii	Moultonborough	NH	E	603 253-4525	19097
Hycon Inc	Manchester	NH	G	603 644-1414	18841
Provencal Manufacturing Inc **(PA)**	Newfields	NH	G	603 772-6716	19319
Wei Inc **(PA)**	Cranston	RI	E	401 781-3904	20309
Wei Inc	Cranston	RI	F	401 781-3904	20310

CONTROLS & ACCESS: Indl, Electric

	CITY	ST	EMP	PHONE	ENTRY #
Alinabal Inc **(HQ)**	Milford	CT	C	203 877-3241	2242
Clarktron Products Inc	Fairfield	CT	G	203 333-6517	1419
Devar Inc	Bridgeport	CT	E	203 368-6751	405
Gordon Products Incorporated	Brookfield	CT	E	203 775-4501	646
Measurement Systems Inc	Wallingford	CT	E	203 949-3500	4772
O E M Controls Inc **(PA)**	Shelton	CT	C	203 929-8431	3845
Control Technology Corporation **(PA)**	Hopkinton	MA	E	508 435-9596	11697
Manufctring Resource Group Inc	Norwood	MA	C	781 440-9700	14176
Rockwell Automation Inc	Chelmsford	MA	C	978 441-9500	9928
Tomkins Corporation	Franklin	MA	E	508 528-2000	11093
Wilmington Research & Dev Corp	Newburyport	MA	G	978 499-0100	13549
Antrim Controls & Systems	Bennington	NH	G	603 588-6297	17687
Hampshire Controls Corporation	Dover	NH	F	603 749-9424	18026
Kusa LLC	Salem	NH	G	603 912-5325	19745
Regent Controls Inc	Greenville	RI	F	203 732-6200	20473

CONTROLS & ACCESS: Motor

	CITY	ST	EMP	PHONE	ENTRY #
Advanced Control Systems Corp	Canton	MA	G	781 829-9228	9711
Backseat Gorilla Applications	Wilmington	MA	G	978 658-6161	16980
SL Montevideo Technology Inc	Billerica	MA	E	978 667-5100	8296
Viking Industrial Products	Marlborough	MA	E	508 481-4600	12845

CONTROLS: Adjustable Speed Drive

	CITY	ST	EMP	PHONE	ENTRY #
Advanced Micro Controls Inc	Terryville	CT	E	860 585-1254	4473
Gefran Inc **(DH)**	North Andover	MA	E	781 729-5249	13707
McGuire & Co Inc	Falmouth	ME	G	207 797-3323	6032
Wei Inc **(PA)**	Cranston	RI	E	401 781-3904	20309
Wei Inc	Cranston	RI	F	401 781-3904	20310

CONTROLS: Air Flow, Refrigeration

	CITY	ST	EMP	PHONE	ENTRY #
Emme Controls LLC	Bristol	CT	G	503 793-3792	553
7ac Technologies Inc	Beverly	MA	F	781 574-1348	8094
Munters Corporation **(DH)**	Amesbury	MA	C	978 241-1100	7498
Save Energy Systems Inc	Westborough	MA	G	617 564-4442	16647

CONTROLS: Automatic Temperature

	CITY	ST	EMP	PHONE	ENTRY #
Food Atmtn - Svc Tchniques Inc **(PA)**	Stratford	CT	C	203 377-4414	4412
Grove Systems Inc	Deep River	CT	G	860 663-2555	1061
Omega Engineering Inc	Norwalk	CT	D	714 540-4914	3212
Burnell Controls Inc	Danvers	MA	G	978 646-9992	10204
Control Resources Inc	Littleton	MA	E	978 486-4160	12297
Contronautics Incorporated	Hudson	MA	G	978 568-8883	11766
Nanmac Corp	Holliston	MA	E	508 872-4811	11588
Spirig Advanced Tech Incies	Springfield	MA	G	413 788-6191	15508
Hansa Consult North Amer LLC	Portsmouth	NH	F	603 422-8833	19572
Goldline Controls Inc **(HQ)**	North Kingstown	RI	D	401 583-1100	20713

CONTROLS: Electric Motor

	CITY	ST	EMP	PHONE	ENTRY #
ABB Enterprise Software Inc	Danbury	CT	E	203 798-6210	864
Digatron Power Electronics Inc	Shelton	CT	E	203 446-8000	3796
Ward Leonard CT LLC **(DH)**	Thomaston	CT	C	860 283-5801	4525

CONTROLS: Environmental

	CITY	ST	EMP	PHONE	ENTRY #
Alloy Engineering Co Inc **(PA)**	Bridgeport	CT	E	203 366-5253	369
Graywolf Sensing Solutions LLC **(PA)**	Shelton	CT	G	203 402-0477	3805
Hamilton Standard Space	Windsor Locks	CT	E	860 654-6000	5396
Hamilton Sundstrand Corp **(HQ)**	Windsor Locks	CT	A	860 654-6000	5397
Mission Allergy Inc	Hawleyville	CT	G	203 364-1570	1894
Tek-Air Systems Inc	Monroe	CT	E	203 791-1400	2418
Whitman Controls LLC	Bristol	CT	F	800 233-4401	625
Bbhs Thermal Solutions Corp	Malden	MA	G	781 718-2352	12562
Demandq Inc	Watertown	MA	G	617 401-2165	16277
Irrigation Automtn Systms Inc	Whitinsville	MA	G	800 549-4551	16915
Kidde-Fenwal Inc **(HQ)**	Ashland	MA	A	508 881-2000	7663
Massachusetts Clean Energy Ctr	Boston	MA	E	617 315-9355	8684
Mestek Inc	Westfield	MA	B	413 568-9571	16702
Mettler-Toledo Process Analyti	Billerica	MA	D	781 301-8800	8265
Product Resources LLC	Newburyport	MA	E	978 524-8500	13523
Sensitech Inc **(DH)**	Beverly	MA	D	978 927-7033	8177
Hampshire Controls Corporation	Dover	NH	F	603 749-9424	18026
Nooney Controls Corporation **(PA)**	North Kingstown	RI	E	401 294-6000	20730
Taco Inc **(PA)**	Cranston	RI	B	401 942-8000	20299

CONTROLS: Marine & Navy, Auxiliary

	CITY	ST	EMP	PHONE	ENTRY #
Naiad Dynamics Us Inc **(HQ)**	Shelton	CT	E	203 929-6355	3836
Hydroid Inc **(PA)**	Pocasset	MA	C	508 563-6565	14596

CONTROLS: Nuclear Reactor

	CITY	ST	EMP	PHONE	ENTRY #
Drs Naval Power Systems Inc	Danbury	CT	B	203 798-3000	905

CONTROLS: Numerical

	CITY	ST	EMP	PHONE	ENTRY #
Ben Franklin Design Mfg Co Inc	Agawam	MA	F	413 786-4220	7423
Intelligent Platforms LLC	Hadley	MA	G	413 586-7884	11308

CONTROLS: Positioning, Electric

	CITY	ST	EMP	PHONE	ENTRY #
Invetech Inc	Boxborough	MA	D	508 475-3400	8964

CONTROLS: Relay & Ind

	CITY	ST	EMP	PHONE	ENTRY #
Altek Company	Torrington	CT	C	860 482-7626	4557
Asea Brown Boveri Inc **(DH)**	Norwalk	CT	G	203 750-2200	3105
Belimo Aircontrols (usa) Inc **(HQ)**	Danbury	CT	C	800 543-9038	879
Belimo Customization USA Inc	Danbury	CT	G	203 791-9915	881
Conntrol International Inc	Putnam	CT	F	860 928-0567	3607
Everlast Products LLC	Cheshire	CT	G	203 250-7111	731
Gems Sensors Inc **(HQ)**	Plainville	CT	B	860 747-3000	3491
General Electric Company	Bridgeport	CT	D	203 396-1572	418
Independence Park	Madison	CT	G	203 421-9396	1965
Minarik Corporation	Bloomfield	CT	C	860 687-5000	243
P/A Industries Inc **(PA)**	Bloomfield	CT	E	860 243-8306	249
Park Distributories Inc **(PA)**	Bridgeport	CT	G	203 579-2140	463
Park Distributories Inc	Bridgeport	CT	F	203 366-7200	464
Quality Name Plate Inc	East Glastonbury	CT	D	860 633-9495	1114
Sound Construction & Engrg Co	Bloomfield	CT	E	860 242-2109	263
United Electric Controls Co	Milford	CT	D	203 877-2795	2377
Contronautics Incorporated	Hudson	MA	G	978 568-8883	11766
Cordmaster Engineering Co Inc	North Adams	MA	E	413 664-9371	13671
Dolan-Jenner Industries Inc	Boxborough	MA	E	978 263-1400	8961
Dynisco Instruments LLC **(HQ)**	Franklin	MA	C	508 541-9400	11037
Electro Switch Corp	Weymouth	MA	C	781 607-3306	16887
Fluigent Inc	Lowell	MA	G	978 934-5283	12371
GE Infrastructure Sensing LLC **(DH)**	Billerica	MA	A	978 437-1000	8249
General Dynamics Def	Pittsfield	MA	A	413 494-1110	14471
Horlick Company Inc	Randolph	MA	G	781 963-0090	14685
Ics Corp	Tyngsboro	MA	G	978 362-0057	15889
Iwaki America Incorporated **(HQ)**	Holliston	MA	D	508 429-1440	11579
Jnc Rebuilders Inc	Ipswich	MA	G	978 356-2996	11925
Keene Bradford Esq PC	Lynnfield	MA	G	781 246-4545	12551
Kidde-Fenwal Inc **(HQ)**	Ashland	MA	A	508 881-2000	7663
L3 Technologies Inc	Northampton	MA	A	413 586-2330	14009

PRODUCT

Employee Codes: A=Over 500 employees, B=251-500
C=101-250, D=51-100 E=20-50, F=10-19, G=3-9

	CITY	ST	EMP	PHONE	ENTRY #
Magnetic Technologies Ltd	Oxford	MA	F	508 987-3303	14268
Maxon Precision Motors Inc **(HQ)**	Taunton	MA	E	508 677-0520	15763
Murata Power Solutions Inc **(DH)**	Westborough	MA	C	508 339-3000	16637
Potomac Electric Corp	Boston	MA	E	617 364-0400	8785
Radar Technology Inc	Newburyport	MA	E	978 463-6064	13526
Rockwell Automation Inc	Marlborough	MA	D	508 357-8400	12819
Schneider Electric Usa Inc **(DH)**	Boston	MA	A	978 975-9600	8839
Schneider Electric Usa Inc	Foxboro	MA	G	508 549-3385	10903
Scully Signal Company **(PA)**	Wilmington	MA	C	617 692-8600	17044
Setra Systems Inc	Boxboro	MA	F	978 263-1400	8954
Sick Inc **(DH)**	Stoughton	MA	F	781 302-2500	15621
Tektron Inc	Topsfield	MA	F	978 887-0091	15866
Texas Instruments Incorporated	Attleboro	MA	E	508 236-3800	7802
Electrnic Mobility Contrls LLC	Augusta	ME	F	207 512-8009	5607
Illinois Tool Works Inc	Mechanic Falls	ME	E	207 998-5140	6420
Montalvo Corporation	Gorham	ME	E	207 856-2501	6122
Southworth Intl Group Inc **(PA)**	Falmouth	ME	D	207 878-0700	6033
Beckwood Services Inc	Plaistow	NH	D	603 382-3840	19508
Dmi Technology Corp **(PA)**	Dover	NH	F	603 742-3330	18019
Electrocraft Inc **(HQ)**	Stratham	NH	E	855 697-7966	19867
Electrocraft New Hampshire Inc **(DH)**	Dover	NH	E	603 742-3330	18021
Mercury Systems Inc	Hudson	NH	G	203 792-7474	18366
Kearflex Engineering Company	Warwick	RI	F	401 781-4900	21382
Kearney-National Inc	North Kingstown	RI	E	401 943-2686	20719
Raytheon Company	Portsmouth	RI	D	401 847-8000	20938
Dynapower Company LLC **(PA)**	South Burlington	VT	C	802 860-7200	22447

CONTROLS: Remote, Boat

American Unmanned Systems LLC	Stamford	CT	G	203 406-7611	4136

CONTROLS: Resistance Welder

Ewald Instruments Corp	Bristol	CT	F	860 491-9042	558

CONTROLS: Thermostats

Rich Plastic Products Inc	Meriden	CT	G	203 235-4241	2126
Honeywell International Inc	Danvers	MA	D	978 774-3007	10223

CONTROLS: Thermostats, Exc Built-in

Xavier Corporation	Manchester	NH	G	603 668-8892	18956

CONVENTION & TRADE SHOW SVCS

Information Today Inc	Wilton	CT	F	203 761-1466	5291
Affordable Exhibit Displays	Auburn	ME	G	207 782-6175	5547

CONVERTERS: Data

Cisco Systems Inc	Norwalk	CT	E	203 229-2300	3125
Cisco Systems Inc	Farmington	CT	A	860 284-5500	1472
Spectrum Virtual LLC	Cheshire	CT	G	203 303-7540	765
Camiant Inc	Marlborough	MA	D	508 486-9996	12733
Cisco Systems Inc	Scituate	MA	G	978 936-1246	15008
Cisco Systems Inc	Boxborough	MA	A	408 526-4000	8960
MTI Unified Communications LLC	South Yarmouth	MA	G	774 352-1110	15331
Dasan Zhone Solutions Inc	Portsmouth	NH	E	510 777-7000	19557
Document Archives Imaging LLC	Manchester	NH	G	603 656-5209	18811
Simpliprotected LLC	Auburn	NH	G	603 669-7465	17613
Retromedia Inc	Smithfield	RI	G	401 349-4640	21246

CONVERTERS: Frequency

Hamilton Sundstrand Corp **(HQ)**	Windsor Locks	CT	A	860 654-6000	5397
Data Electronic Devices Inc	Salem	NH	C	603 893-2047	19720
Wall Industries Inc	Exeter	NH	E	603 778-2300	18137

CONVERTERS: Phase Or Rotary, Electrical

Sjm Etronics LLC	Londonderry	NH	G	603 512-3821	18738

CONVERTERS: Power, AC to DC

GE Enrgy Pwr Cnversion USA Inc	Fairfield	CT	G	203 373-2211	1434
High Voltage Outsourcing LLC	Danbury	CT	G	203 456-3101	932
Assurance Technology Corp	Chelmsford	MA	D	978 250-8060	9875
Atrex Energy Inc **(PA)**	Walpole	MA	E	781 461-8251	15988
Bel Power Inc	Westborough	MA	D	508 870-9775	16593
Murata Power Solutions Inc **(DH)**	Westborough	MA	C	508 339-3000	16637
Vicor Corporation	Andover	MA	F	978 470-2900	7617
Hollis Controls Inc **(PA)**	Nashua	NH	G	603 595-2482	19179
Milpower Source Inc	Belmont	NH	D	603 267-8865	17678
Warner Power Conversion LLC	Warner	NH	C	603 456-3111	19931
Schneider Electric It Corp **(DH)**	West Kingston	RI	A	401 789-5735	21471
Northern Power Systems Inc **(HQ)**	Barre	VT	D	802 461-2955	21631

CONVERTERS: Torque, Exc Auto

Hersey Clutch Co	Orleans	MA	F	508 255-2533	14235

CONVEYOR SYSTEMS

Alvest (usa) Inc **(HQ)**	Windsor	CT	E	860 602-3400	5320
JR Grady Company LLC	North Chelmsford	MA	G	978 458-3662	13898
Luck Industrial Sales Inc	Watertown	MA	G	617 924-0728	16296
Magnemotion Inc	Devens	MA	D	978 757-9100	10323

CONVEYOR SYSTEMS: Belt, General Indl Use

Ashworth Bros Inc **(PA)**	Fall River	MA	G	508 674-4693	10663

CONVEYOR SYSTEMS: Bucket Type

Maine Barrel & Display Company	Lewiston	ME	E	207 784-6700	6303

CONVEYOR SYSTEMS: Bulk Handling

Orbetron LLC	Cumberland	RI	G	651 983-2872	20337

CONVEYOR SYSTEMS: Robotic

International Robotics Inc	Stamford	CT	F	914 630-1060	4228
R & I Manufacturing Co	Terryville	CT	F	860 589-6364	4489
Unimation	Bethel	CT	G	203 792-3412	186
Ascend Robotics LLC	Cambridge	MA	F	978 451-0170	9393
Barrett Technology Inc	Cambridge	MA	G	617 252-9000	9402
Softbank Robotics America Inc	Boston	MA	E	617 986-6700	8851
Fabworx Solutions Inc	Concord	NH	G	603 224-9679	17901

CONVEYORS & CONVEYING EQPT

Affordable Conveyors Svcs LLC	Bristol	CT	F	860 582-1800	516
CT Conveyor LLC	Bristol	CT	G	860 637-2926	545
Goldslager Conveyor Company	Hamden	CT	G	203 795-9886	1751
National Conveyors Company Inc	East Granby	CT	E	860 653-0374	1135
Roller Bearing Co Amer Inc	Middlebury	CT	E	203 758-8272	2157
Walker Magnetics Group Inc **(HQ)**	Windsor	CT	E	508 853-3232	5378
Z-Loda Systems Inc	Stamford	CT	G	203 359-2991	4364
AMA Engineering Smartmove	Westport	MA	F	508 636-7740	16835
Anaconda Usa Inc	Natick	MA	F	800 285-5721	13234
Belt Technologies Inc **(PA)**	Agawam	MA	E	413 786-9922	7422
Chelsea Industries Inc **(HQ)**	Newton	MA	G	617 232-6060	13578
Conveytrex LLC	Swansea	MA	G	508 812-4333	15704
Conviber Inc	Oxford	MA	G	724 274-6300	14257
Dg Marshall Associates Inc	Webster	MA	E	508 943-2394	16341
Kleenline LLC	Newburyport	MA	D	978 463-0827	13504
Northeast Equipment Design Inc	Hingham	MA	E	781 740-0007	11508
Omtec Corp	Marlborough	MA	F	508 481-3322	12801
Precision Handling Devices **(PA)**	Westport	MA	F	508 679-5282	16845
Safe Conveyor Incorporated	Swansea	MA	G	774 688-9109	15714
TEC Engineering Corp	Oxford	MA	F	508 987-0231	14275
Eltec Industries Inc **(PA)**	Freeport	ME	G	207 541-9085	6077
Maine Conveyor Inc **(PA)**	Gorham	ME	G	207 854-5661	6118
Plastic Techniques Inc	Goffstown	NH	E	603 622-5570	18209
Action Conveyor Tech Inc	Smithfield	RI	F	401 722-2300	21207
Bmco Industries Inc	East Greenwich	RI	G	401 781-6884	20354
Bindery Solutions Inc **(PA)**	Grand Isle	VT	G	802 372-3492	21997

CONVEYORS: Overhead

Production Equipment Company	Meriden	CT	E	800 758-5697	2118
Acorn Overhead Door	Quincy	MA	G	508 378-0441	14613
Nikotrack LLC	Portsmouth	RI	G	401 683-7525	20932

COOKING & FOOD WARMING EQPT: Commercial

Motion Technology Inc	Northborough	MA	E	508 460-9800	14039
Colburntreat LLC	Winooski	VT	F	802 654-8603	22719

COOKING & FOODWARMING EQPT: Coffee Brewing

Crystal Rock Holdings Inc **(HQ)**	Watertown	CT	E	860 945-0661	5005
Bay State Espresso	Haverhill	MA	G	978 686-5049	11408
Crane Mdsg Systems Inc	Dedham	MA	F	781 501-5800	10284

COOKING & FOODWARMING EQPT: Commercial

Continental Metal Pdts Co Inc	Woburn	MA	E	781 935-4400	17151
Den Mar Corporation	North Dartmouth	MA	F	508 999-3295	13918
GS Blodgett Corporation	Bow	NH	B	603 225-5688	17715
Pitco Frialator Inc **(HQ)**	Bow	NH	B	603 225-6684	17727
Pitco Frialator Inc	Pembroke	NH	E	603 225-6684	19462
Pitco Frialator Inc	Concord	NH	G	603 225-6684	17923
GS Blodgett Corporation	Essex Junction	VT	E	802 860-3700	21945
GS Blodgett Corporation **(HQ)**	Essex Junction	VT	C	802 860-3700	21944
Mfi Corp	Burlington	VT	D	802 658-6600	21797

COOKING & FOODWARMING EQPT: Microwave Ovens, Commercial

Thermo Wave Technologies LLC	Danvers	MA	G	800 733-9615	10263
Micronetixx Technologies LLC	Lewiston	ME	G	207 786-2000	6306

COOKING EQPT, HOUSEHOLD: Stoves, Disk

Taunton Stove Company Inc	North Dighton	MA	E	508 823-0786	13937

COOLING TOWERS: Metal

SPX Corporation	Norwood	MA	F	704 752-4400	14201
Fluid Eqp Solutions Neng LLC	Exeter	NH	G	855 337-6633	18121

COPPER ORES

Baobab Asset Management LLC	Greenwich	CT	G	203 340-5700	1597
Quantum Discoveries Inc	Boston	MA	G	857 272-9998	8803

COPPER PRDTS: Smelter, Primary

Browns Greens	Brooksville	ME	G	207 326-4636	5824
Materion Technical Mtls Inc	Lincoln	RI	C	401 333-1700	20583

COPPER: Rolling & Drawing

Global Brass & Copper LLC **(PA)**	Waterbury	CT	G	203 597-5000	4879
Data Guide Cable Corporation	Gardner	MA	D	978 632-0900	11111
Pep Industries LLC	Attleboro	MA	A	508 226-5600	7776
Precision Engineered Pdts LLC **(DH)**	Attleboro	MA	G	508 226-5600	7782
Sanderson-Macleod Incorporated	Palmer	MA	C	413 283-3481	14295
Advanced Building Products Inc	Sanford	ME	F	207 490-2306	6870
York Manufacturing Inc	Sanford	ME	F	207 324-1300	6898
Aetna Insulated Wire LLC	Milford	NH	C	757 460-3381	19043
AT Wall Company **(HQ)**	Warwick	RI	E	401 739-0740	21329
Millard Wire Company **(PA)**	Warwick	RI	D	401 737-9330	21389

COPY MACHINES WHOLESALERS

Hosokawa Micron International	Northborough	MA	F	508 655-1123	14037

CORD & TWINE

Detotec North America Inc	Moosup	CT	G	860 230-0078	2425

	CITY	ST	EMP	PHONE	ENTRY #
Detotec North America Inc	Sterling	CT	G	860 564-1012	4366
Loos & Co Inc **(PA)**	Pomfret	CT	B	860 928-7981	3552
Heinrich LLC	Waltham	MA	G	781 891-9591	16125
Its A Corker	Winchester	MA	G	781 729-9630	17089
Julius Koch USA Inc	Mattapoisett	MA	D	508 995-9565	12887
Link Enterprises Corp	Northampton	MA	G	413 585-9869	14010
Pepperell Braiding Company Inc **(PA)**	Pepperell	MA	E	978 433-2133	14444
Teufelberger Fiber Rope Corp	Fall River	MA	C	508 678-8200	10772
Auburn Manufacturing Inc **(PA)**	Mechanic Falls	ME	E	207 345-8271	6418
David Bird LLC	Waldoboro	ME	F	207 832-0569	7132
Rope Co LLC	Spruce Head	ME	G	207 838-4358	7057
Jonathan Knight	Wakefield	RI	G	401 263-3671	21273

CORD: Braided

	CITY	ST	EMP	PHONE	ENTRY #
Woodstock Line Co	Putnam	CT	F	860 928-6557	3641
Artcraft Braid Co LLC	Hudson	MA	E	401 831-9077	11757
Frank B Struzik Inc	Woonsocket	RI	F	401 766-6880	21563

CORES: Magnetic

	CITY	ST	EMP	PHONE	ENTRY #
Alpha-Core Inc	Shelton	CT	E	203 954-0050	3773
Bridgeport Magnetics Group Inc	Shelton	CT	E	203 954-0050	3784

CORK & CORK PRDTS

	CITY	ST	EMP	PHONE	ENTRY #
Cork Technologies LLC	Lawrence	MA	G	978 687-9500	12013
We Cork Enterprises Inc	Exeter	NH	G	603 778-8558	18138

CORK & CORK PRDTS: Tiles

	CITY	ST	EMP	PHONE	ENTRY #
New England Tile & Stone Inc	Stamford	CT	F	914 481-4488	4256

CORRECTION FLUID

	CITY	ST	EMP	PHONE	ENTRY #
Bic Consumer Products Mfg Co	Milford	CT	C	203 783-2000	2254
Bic Corporation **(HQ)**	Shelton	CT	A	203 783-2000	3782
Bic USA Inc **(DH)**	Shelton	CT	C	203 783-2000	3783
Gillette Company	Bethel	CT	G	203 796-4000	155
Blank Industries Inc	Hudson	MA	F	855 887-3123	11759
Gillette Company	Andover	MA	A	781 662-9600	7552
Gillette Company **(HQ)**	Boston	MA	A	617 421-7000	8561

CORRECTIONAL INSTITUTIONS

	CITY	ST	EMP	PHONE	ENTRY #
Federal Prison Industries	Danbury	CT	F	203 743-6471	919

CORRESPONDENCE SCHOOLS

	CITY	ST	EMP	PHONE	ENTRY #
Cortina Learning Intl Inc **(PA)**	Wilton	CT	F	800 245-2145	5285

COSMETIC PREPARATIONS

	CITY	ST	EMP	PHONE	ENTRY #
Albea Thomaston Inc	Thomaston	CT	B	860 283-2000	4497
Amodex Products Inc	Bridgeport	CT	E	203 335-1255	375
Casaro Labs Ltd	Stamford	CT	G	203 353-8500	4156
CCL Industries Corporation **(DH)**	Shelton	CT	D	203 926-1253	3785
Ecometics Inc	Norwalk	CT	E	203 853-7856	3148
Innarah Inc	Stratford	CT	G	203 873-0015	4423
Judith Jackson Inc	Old Greenwich	CT	G	203 698-3011	3311
Milbar Labs Inc	East Haven	CT	F	203 467-1577	1255
Miyoshi America Inc **(HQ)**	Dayville	CT	D	860 779-3990	1046
Russell Organics LLC	Wallingford	CT	G	203 285-6633	4803
Elma & Sana LLC	Littleton	MA	G	617 529-4532	12304
Harrison Specialty Co Inc **(PA)**	Canton	MA	E	781 828-8180	9736
Harrison Specialty Co Inc	Canton	MA	E	781 828-8180	9737
Pride India Inc **(PA)**	Brighton	MA	F	617 202-9659	9105
St Cyr Inc	Worcester	MA	E	508 752-2222	17478
Fizz Time	Salem	NH	F	603 870-0000	19734
Maybrook Inc	Salem	NH	F	603 898-0811	19750
Riverview Labs Inc	Bow	NH	G	603 715-2759	17729
Rozelle Inc	Westfield	VT	E	802 744-2270	22627
Tatas Natural Alchemy LLC **(PA)**	Whiting	VT	E	802 462-3814	22645
Toms of Maine Inc	Putney	VT	C	802 387-2393	22293

COSMETICS & TOILETRIES

	CITY	ST	EMP	PHONE	ENTRY #
Blessed Creek	Suffield	CT	G	860 416-3692	4460
Carrubba Incorporated	Milford	CT	D	203 878-0605	2262
Harjani Hitesh	Waterford	CT	G	860 913-6032	4984
High Ridge Brands Co **(HQ)**	Stamford	CT	D	203 674-8080	4215
Miyoshi America Inc	Dayville	CT	F	860 779-3990	1047
Miyoshi America Inc	Dayville	CT	G	860 779-3990	1048
Rjtb Group LLC	Greenwich	CT	G	203 531-7216	1644
T N Dickinson Company	East Hampton	CT	F	860 267-2279	1166
Unilever Trumbull RES Svcs Inc **(HQ)**	Trumbull	CT	G	203 502-0086	4639
Commonwlth Soap Toiletries Inc **(PA)**	Fall River	MA	D	508 676-9355	10678
Conopco Inc	Foxboro	MA	F	508 543-6767	10880
Elemental Scents LLC	Auburndale	MA	G	617 504-2559	7860
Elizabeth Arden Inc	Wrentham	MA	G	508 384-9018	17519
European Cubicles LLC	Boston	MA	G	617 681-6700	8529
Gillette Company	Boston	MA	D	617 268-1363	8562
Novagenesis	Sharon	MA	E	781 784-1149	15054
Rare Beauty Brands Inc	Norwood	MA	D	888 243-0646	14191
Rougeluxe Apothecary Inc	Oak Bluffs	MA	G	508 696-0900	14211
Brickell Brands LLC	Portland	ME	E	877 598-0060	6626
Fabula Nebulae LLC	Holden	ME	G	917 545-9049	6197
J R Liggett Ltd Inc	Cornish	NH	G	603 675-2055	17961
Just Naturals & Company LLC	Bedford	NH	G	603 471-0944	17647
Trividia Mfg Solutions **(DH)**	Lancaster	NH	C	603 788-2848	18606
Trividia Mfg Solutions	Lancaster	NH	G	603 788-4952	18607
Aidance Skincare & Topical Sol	Woonsocket	RI	F	401 432-7750	21547
Frueii	Providence	RI	G	401 499-5887	21017
Java Worx International LLC	Saunderstown	RI	G	866 609-3258	21202
Toscana European Day Spa	Cumberland	RI	G	401 658-5277	20349
Autumn Harp Inc	Bristol	VT	G	802 453-4807	21761
Autumn-Harp Inc	Essex Junction	VT	C	802 857-4600	21930
Tatas Natural Alchemy LLC	Whiting	VT	D	802 462-3958	22646
Ursa Major LLC	Waterbury	VT	G	802 560-7116	22587

COSMETOLOGIST

	CITY	ST	EMP	PHONE	ENTRY #
St Cyr Inc	Worcester	MA	E	508 752-2222	17478

COSTUME JEWELRY & NOVELTIES: Apparel, Exc Precious Metals

	CITY	ST	EMP	PHONE	ENTRY #
Lenn Arts Inc	Attleboro	MA	E	508 223-3400	7759
American Ring Co Inc **(PA)**	East Providence	RI	E	401 438-9060	20385

COSTUME JEWELRY & NOVELTIES: Bracelets, Exc Precious Metals

	CITY	ST	EMP	PHONE	ENTRY #
Mystic Knotwork LLC	Mystic	CT	F	860 889-3793	2444
Barnstable Bracelet	West Barnstable	MA	G	508 362-1630	16404

COSTUME JEWELRY & NOVELTIES: Costume Novelties

	CITY	ST	EMP	PHONE	ENTRY #
American Biltrite Inc **(PA)**	Wellesley	MA	G	781 237-6655	16359
Barrington Manufacturing Inc	Warren	RI	F	401 245-1737	21288
Gloria Duchin Inc	Rumford	RI	D	401 431-5016	21185

COSTUME JEWELRY & NOVELTIES: Earrings, Exc Precious Metals

	CITY	ST	EMP	PHONE	ENTRY #
AB Group Inc	Attleboro	MA	F	508 222-1404	7698
Reed Allison Group Inc	Providence	RI	D	617 846-1237	21107

COSTUME JEWELRY & NOVELTIES: Exc Semi & Precious

	CITY	ST	EMP	PHONE	ENTRY #
Adina Inc **(PA)**	Norwood	MA	E	781 762-4477	14119
Ashworth Assoc Mfg Whl Jewelers	North Attleboro	MA	F	508 695-1900	13747
J & K Sales Company Inc	Rehoboth	MA	E	508 252-6235	14751
Newpro Designs Inc **(HQ)**	Norwood	MA	E	781 762-4477	14183
Sweet Metal Finishing Inc	Attleboro	MA	E	508 226-4359	7799
Victoria Ann Varga Inc	Cumberland Foreside	ME	G	207 781-4050	5933
Accu-Tool Inc	Pawtucket	RI	G	401 725-5350	20806
Aetna Manufacturing Company	Providence	RI	G	401 751-3260	20948
AG & G Inc **(PA)**	Johnston	RI	E	401 946-4330	20498
Amsco Ltd Inc	Cranston	RI	G	401 785-2860	20181
Barlow Designs Inc	East Providence	RI	G	401 438-7925	20390
Bazar Group Inc **(PA)**	East Providence	RI	E	401 434-2595	20391
Decor Craft Inc	Providence	RI	E	401 621-2324	20996
Dina Inc	Cranston	RI	G	401 942-9633	20212
Esposito Jewelry Inc	Providence	RI	F	401 943-1900	21008
Gennaro Inc	Cranston	RI	F	401 632-4100	20232
Jewelry Holding Co Inc	West Warwick	RI	G	401 826-7934	21496
Jim Clift Design Inc	Coventry	RI	G	401 823-9680	20150
Jji International Inc	Cranston	RI	E	401 780-8668	20244
Jonette Jewelry Company	East Providence	RI	D	401 438-1941	20425
Kennedy Incorporated	North Kingstown	RI	F	401 295-7800	20720
Llmage Inc	Johnston	RI	E	401 369-7141	20518
Mag Jewelry Co Inc	Cranston	RI	E	401 942-1840	20257
Michael Healy Designs Inc	Manville	RI	G	401 597-5900	20610
Pauley Co	Warwick	RI	F	401 467-2930	21400
Rolyn Inc **(PA)**	Cranston	RI	E	401 944-0844	20281
Stylecraft Inc	Cranston	RI	D	401 463-9944	20293
Two Hands Inc	Providence	RI	E	401 785-2727	21142
Ubio Inc	Johnston	RI	E	401 541-9172	20544
Winkler Group Ltd **(PA)**	Rumford	RI	C	401 272-2885	21199
Winkler Group Ltd	Rumford	RI	E	401 751-6120	21200
Baked Beads Inc	Waitsfield	VT	F	802 496-2440	22560

COSTUME JEWELRY & NOVELTIES: Keychains, Exc Precious Metal

	CITY	ST	EMP	PHONE	ENTRY #
K W Bristol Co Inc	North Attleboro	MA	G	508 699-4742	13760

COSTUME JEWELRY & NOVELTIES: Necklaces, Exc Precious Metals

	CITY	ST	EMP	PHONE	ENTRY #
Nano-Ice LLC	Brookline	MA	G	617 512-8811	9212

COSTUME JEWELRY & NOVELTIES: Ornament, Exc Precious Mtl/Gem

	CITY	ST	EMP	PHONE	ENTRY #
A Capela Do Santo Antonio Inc	New London	CT	G	860 447-3329	2764

COSTUME JEWELRY & NOVELTIES: Pins, Exc Precious Metals

	CITY	ST	EMP	PHONE	ENTRY #
Conversation Concepts LLC	Fitchburg	MA	F	978 342-1414	10820

COSTUME JEWELRY & NOVELTIES: Rosaries & Sm Religious Items

	CITY	ST	EMP	PHONE	ENTRY #
Bliss Manufacturing Co Inc	Pawtucket	RI	E	401 729-1690	20818

COSTUME JEWELRY STORES

	CITY	ST	EMP	PHONE	ENTRY #
Carole Sousa Jewelry	Boston	MA	G	617 232-4087	8460

COUGH MEDICINES

	CITY	ST	EMP	PHONE	ENTRY #
Gsk Innovations	East Walpole	MA	G	508 566-5212	10523

COUNTER & SINK TOPS

	CITY	ST	EMP	PHONE	ENTRY #
Custom Crft Ktchns By Rizio BR	Monroe	CT	F	203 268-0271	2400
Pro Counters New England LLC	Ansonia	CT	G	203 347-8663	21
Specialty Shop Inc	Manchester	CT	G	860 647-1477	2050
Carriage Hse Developments LLC	Winchester	MA	G	339 221-4253	17085
Dorie Enterprises Inc	Attleboro	MA	G	508 761-7588	7728
Metropolitan Cab Distrs Corp	Natick	MA	G	508 651-8950	13267
Metropolitan Cab Distrs Corp **(PA)**	Norwood	MA	G	781 949-8900	14178
Rau Brothers Inc	Winchendon	MA	G	978 297-1381	17080
Twd Inc	Bridgewater	MA	E	508 279-2650	9091
Ware Rite Distributors Inc	East Bridgewater	MA	D	508 690-2145	10422
K & D Millworks Inc	Windham	ME	E	207 892-5188	7238
Portland Stone Works Inc	Portland	ME	F	207 878-6832	6713
Daniel Preston	Hudson	NH	G	603 579-0525	18383
Just Counters	Goffstown	NH	G	603 627-2027	18205
Artisan Surfaces Inc	Springfield	VT	E	802 885-8677	22499
Vermont MBL Gran Slate Spstone	Castleton	VT	G	802 468-8800	21830

PRODUCT

COUNTERS & COUNTING DEVICES

	CITY	ST	EMP	PHONE	ENTRY #
Alinabal Holdings Corporation **(PA)**	Milford	CT	B	203 877-3241	2243
Aclara Technologies LLC	Wellesley	MA	E	781 694-3300	16357
Block Mems LLC	Southborough	MA	F	508 251-3100	15349
Dff Corp	Agawam	MA	C	413 786-8880	7427
Schleifring North America LLC	Chelmsford	MA	F	978 677-2500	9930
Setra Systems Inc	Boxboro	MA	F	978 263-1400	8954
Verify LLC	Cambridge	MA	F	513 285-7258	9694

COUNTERS OR COUNTER DISPLAY CASES, EXC WOOD

	CITY	ST	EMP	PHONE	ENTRY #
American Stonecrafters Inc	Wallingford	CT	G	203 514-9725	4698
C Mather Company Inc	South Windsor	CT	G	860 528-5667	3946
Top Shop Inc	South Burlington	VT	F	802 658-1351	22472

COUNTERS OR COUNTER DISPLAY CASES, WOOD

	CITY	ST	EMP	PHONE	ENTRY #
Counter Tech Inc	Keene	NH	G	603 352-1882	18498
Elmwood Countertop Inc	Cranston	RI	G	401 785-1677	20216
Jenson Enterprises LLC	South Burlington	VT	G	802 497-3530	22451
Top Shop Inc	South Burlington	VT	F	802 658-1351	22472

COUNTERS: Mechanical

	CITY	ST	EMP	PHONE	ENTRY #
Denominator Company Inc	Woodbury	CT	F	203 263-3210	5485

COUNTING DEVICES: Controls, Revolution & Timing

	CITY	ST	EMP	PHONE	ENTRY #
Kongsberg Dgtal Simulation Inc	Groton	CT	F	860 405-2300	1678
Druck LLC **(HQ)**	Billerica	MA	C	978 437-1000	8238

COUNTING DEVICES: Electromechanical

	CITY	ST	EMP	PHONE	ENTRY #
Bidwell Industrial Group Inc **(PA)**	Middletown	CT	E	860 346-9283	2178
Lq Mechatronics Inc	Branford	CT	G	203 433-4430	328
Connexus Manufacturing LLC	Hudson	MA	G	978 568-1831	11764

COUNTING DEVICES: Tachometer, Centrifugal

	CITY	ST	EMP	PHONE	ENTRY #
Faria Beede Instruments Inc	North Stonington	CT	C	860 848-9271	3074
Monarch International Inc	Amherst	NH	E	603 883-3390	17577

COUNTING DEVICES: Vehicle Instruments

	CITY	ST	EMP	PHONE	ENTRY #
Ametek Arizona Instrument LLC	Middleboro	MA	C	508 946-6200	13051

COUPLINGS, EXC PRESSURE & SOIL PIPE

	CITY	ST	EMP	PHONE	ENTRY #
Saf Industries LLC	Meriden	CT	E	203 729-4900	2127
Axenics Inc **(PA)**	Middleton	MA	E	978 774-9393	13084
Scully Signal Company **(PA)**	Wilmington	MA	C	617 692-8600	17044

COUPLINGS: Hose & Tube, Hydraulic Or Pneumatic

	CITY	ST	EMP	PHONE	ENTRY #
Hosetech Plus More Inc	Ludlow	MA	G	413 385-0035	12467

COUPLINGS: Pipe

	CITY	ST	EMP	PHONE	ENTRY #
Queen City Sounds Inc	Manchester	NH	G	603 668-4306	18908

COUPLINGS: Shaft

	CITY	ST	EMP	PHONE	ENTRY #
Lovejoy Curtis LLC	Springfield	MA	E	413 737-0281	15485
Naugler Co Inc	Newburyport	MA	G	978 463-9199	13517
Renbrandt Inc	Gloucester	MA	F	617 445-8910	11207
Stafford Manufacturing Corp	Wilmington	MA	E	978 657-8000	17048
Tracey Gear Inc	Pawtucket	RI	E	401 725-3920	20906

COVERS: Automobile Seat

	CITY	ST	EMP	PHONE	ENTRY #
Pb & J Discoveries LLC	Newton	MA	G	617 903-7253	13624

COVERS: Automotive, Exc Seat & Tire

	CITY	ST	EMP	PHONE	ENTRY #
Power Cover Usa LLC	Waterbury	CT	G	203 755-2687	4942

COVERS: Book, Fabric

	CITY	ST	EMP	PHONE	ENTRY #
Arlington Sample Book Co Inc **(PA)**	Sunapee	NH	G	603 763-9082	19879

COVERS: Canvas

	CITY	ST	EMP	PHONE	ENTRY #
Pioneer Consolidated Corp	North Oxford	MA	E	508 987-8438	13973

COVERS: Slip Made Of Fabric, Plastic, Etc.

	CITY	ST	EMP	PHONE	ENTRY #
Craft Interiors	Malden	MA	G	781 321-8695	12566

CRACKED CASTING REPAIR SVCS

	CITY	ST	EMP	PHONE	ENTRY #
Harris Tool & Die Company Inc	Fitchburg	MA	G	978 479-1842	10828
Housatonic Welding Company	Housatonic	MA	G	413 274-6631	11742

CRADLES: Boat

	CITY	ST	EMP	PHONE	ENTRY #
Brownell Boat Stands Inc	Mattapoisett	MA	F	508 758-3671	12885

CRANE & AERIAL LIFT SVCS

	CITY	ST	EMP	PHONE	ENTRY #
Tims Sign & Lighting Service	Meriden	CT	G	203 634-8840	2143
Franklin County Fabricators	Greenfield	MA	G	413 774-3518	11261
Serrato Sign Co	Worcester	MA	G	508 756-7004	17472
Somatex Inc	Detroit	ME	E	207 487-6141	5953
Starkey Welding Crane Service	Brentwood	NH	G	603 679-2553	17758
Dexter Enterprises Corp	East Providence	RI	G	401 434-2300	20404
Dexter Sign Co	East Providence	RI	E	401 434-1100	20406

CRANES: Indl Plant

	CITY	ST	EMP	PHONE	ENTRY #
Central Maine Crane Inc	Oakland	ME	G	207 465-2229	6530

CRANES: Indl Truck

	CITY	ST	EMP	PHONE	ENTRY #
Stedt Hydraulic Crane Corp	Westborough	MA	F	508 366-9151	16651

CRANES: Overhead

	CITY	ST	EMP	PHONE	ENTRY #
Production Equipment Company	Meriden	CT	E	800 758-5697	2118
Altec Northeast LLC	Sterling	MA	F	508 320-9041	15533
American Crane and Hoist Corp	Boston	MA	C	617 482-8383	8360
Dearborn Crane and Engrg Co	Woburn	MA	G	781 897-4100	17166

CRANKSHAFTS & CAMSHAFTS: Machining

	CITY	ST	EMP	PHONE	ENTRY #
Lawrence Crankshaft Inc	Haverhill	MA	G	978 372-0504	11447
Nuforj LLC	Springfield	MA	F	413 530-0349	15495
Horizon Manufacturing & Design	Westminster W	VT	G	802 384-3715	22634

CRATING SVCS: Shipping

	CITY	ST	EMP	PHONE	ENTRY #
Eimskip USA Inc	Portland	ME	G	207 221-5268	6660

CRAYONS

	CITY	ST	EMP	PHONE	ENTRY #
Eco-Kids LLC	Portland	ME	G	207 899-2752	6659

CREATIVE SVCS: Advertisers, Exc Writers

	CITY	ST	EMP	PHONE	ENTRY #
Lane Printing Co Inc	Holbrook	MA	F	781 767-4450	11529
Maineline Graphics LLC	Antrim	NH	G	603 588-3177	17596

CREDIT UNIONS: Federally Chartered

	CITY	ST	EMP	PHONE	ENTRY #
Mpb Corporation **(HQ)**	Keene	NH	A	603 352-0310	18518

CROCKERY

	CITY	ST	EMP	PHONE	ENTRY #
Hendersons Redware	Bangor	ME	G	207 942-9013	5649

CROWNS & CLOSURES

	CITY	ST	EMP	PHONE	ENTRY #
Eyelet Design Inc	Waterbury	CT	D	203 754-4141	4872
Dental Studios of Western Mass	South Hadley	MA	G	413 787-9920	15301
M2 Inc	Winooski	VT	G	802 655-2364	22722

CRUCIBLES

	CITY	ST	EMP	PHONE	ENTRY #
Osram Sylvania Inc **(HQ)**	Wilmington	MA	A	978 570-3000	17036

CRUDE PETROLEUM & NATURAL GAS PRODUCTION

	CITY	ST	EMP	PHONE	ENTRY #
Spotliteusa LLC	Sturbridge	MA	G	508 347-2627	15649

CRUDE PETROLEUM & NATURAL GAS PRODUCTION

	CITY	ST	EMP	PHONE	ENTRY #
Alternate Energy Futures	Danbury	CT	G	917 745-7097	870
CCI Robinsons Bend LLC	Stamford	CT	G	203 564-8571	4160
Dietze & Associates LLC	Wilton	CT	F	203 762-3500	5288
Merrill Oil LLC	Woodbridge	CT	G	203 387-1130	5472
Outpost Exploration LLC	Wilton	CT	G	203 762-7206	5297
Promise Propane	Newington	CT	G	860 685-0676	2894
River Valley Oil Service LLC	Portland	CT	G	860 342-5670	3574
Landfil Gas Prodcrs of Plnvlle	Plainville	MA	G	508 695-3252	14525
MRC Global (us) Inc	Bellingham	MA	E	508 966-3205	8051
MRC Global (us) Inc	South Portland	ME	F	207 767-3861	7033
Liberty Enrgy Utilities NH Corp **(DH)**	Londonderry	NH	D	905 287-2061	18713
Your Oil Tools LLC	Hooksett	NH	G	701 645-8665	18361

CRUDE PETROLEUM PRODUCTION

	CITY	ST	EMP	PHONE	ENTRY #
El Paso Prod Oil Gas Texas LP	Hartford	CT	F	860 293-1990	1819
Bradley Oil Company	Rehoboth	MA	G	508 336-4400	14746
Exxonmobil Oil Corporation	Randolph	MA	G	781 963-7252	14679
Hess Corporation	West Bridgewater	MA	F	508 580-6530	16441
Speedway LLC	Saugus	MA	D	781 233-5491	14999
Speedway LLC	Auburndale	MA	G	617 244-4601	7870
Speedway LLC	Derry	NH	F	603 434-9702	17996
Speedway LLC	Chichester	NH	D	603 798-3154	17830
Speedway LLC	Cranston	RI	G	401 941-4740	20288
Kcm Oil	Shaftsbury	VT	G	802 447-7371	22403

CRYOGENIC COOLING DEVICES: Infrared Detectors, Masers

	CITY	ST	EMP	PHONE	ENTRY #
Vette Thermal Solutions LLC **(HQ)**	Portsmouth	NH	F	603 635-2800	19629

CRYSTAL GOODS, WHOLESALE

	CITY	ST	EMP	PHONE	ENTRY #
Swarovski US Holding Limited **(HQ)**	Cranston	RI	G	401 463-6400	20296

CRYSTALS

	CITY	ST	EMP	PHONE	ENTRY #
Crystal Fairfield Tech LLC	New Milford	CT	F	860 354-2111	2795

CRYSTALS: Piezoelectric

	CITY	ST	EMP	PHONE	ENTRY #
Ebl Products Inc	East Hartford	CT	F	860 290-3737	1190
Piezo Systems Inc	Woburn	MA	G	781 933-4850	17265

CULTURE MEDIA

	CITY	ST	EMP	PHONE	ENTRY #
Hockey12com	Billerica	MA	G	781 910-2877	8254
Pathfire Inc	Needham Heights	MA	G	972 581-2000	13343
Program LLC	Marlborough	MA	G	781 281-0751	12810
Sports Insights Inc	Beverly	MA	G	877 838-2853	8179
Northeast Laboratory Svcs Inc **(PA)**	Winslow	ME	D	207 873-7711	7272

CULVERTS: Sheet Metal

	CITY	ST	EMP	PHONE	ENTRY #
Contech Engnered Solutions LLC	Scarborough	ME	E	207 885-9830	6915
Hancor Inc	Springfield	VT	E	802 886-8403	22501

CUPOLAS: Metal Plate

	CITY	ST	EMP	PHONE	ENTRY #
Cape Cod Cupola Co Inc	North Dartmouth	MA	G	508 994-2119	13916
John J Marr	Conway	NH	F	603 939-2698	17954

CUPS & PLATES: Foamed Plastics

	CITY	ST	EMP	PHONE	ENTRY #
Georgia-Pacific LLC	Leominster	MA	C	978 537-4701	12144
Waddington North America Inc	Chelmsford	MA	C	978 256-6551	9941
Providence Spillproof Cntrs	Providence	RI	G	401 723-4900	21099

CUPS: Paper

	CITY	ST	EMP	PHONE	ENTRY #
Harrison Enterprise LLC	Bridgeport	CT	G	914 665-8348	423

CUPS: Plastic Exc Polystyrene Foam

	CITY	ST	EMP	PHONE	ENTRY #
Little Kids Inc	Seekonk	MA	E	401 454-7600	15026

CURBING: Granite Or Stone

	CITY	ST	EMP	PHONE	ENTRY #
Central Marble & Granite LLC	Ansonia	CT	G	203 734-4644	9

	CITY	ST	EMP	PHONE	ENTRY #
Granite & Kitchen Studio LLC	South Windsor	CT	G	860 290-4444	3975
Granite LLC	Newington	CT	G	860 586-8132	2868
New England Gran Cabinets LLC	West Hartford	CT	G	860 310-2981	5087
Escountertops LLC	West Springfield	MA	G	413 732-8128	16519
Williams Stone Co Inc	East Otis	MA	E	413 269-4544	10504
Global Values VT LLC	Barre	VT	E	802 476-8000	21616
Memorial Sandblast Inc	Barre	VT	G	802 476-7086	21629

CURTAIN & DRAPERY FIXTURES: Poles, Rods & Rollers

	CITY	ST	EMP	PHONE	ENTRY #
Ahlstrom-Munksjo Nonwovens LLC **(DH)**	Windsor Locks	CT	B	860 654-8300	5382
Ben Baena & Son	Bridgeport	CT	G	203 334-8568	382
Rollease Acmeda Inc **(PA)**	Stamford	CT	D	203 964-1573	4305
Thomas W Raftery Inc	Hartford	CT	E	860 278-9870	1879
Cdi LLC A Valley Forge Co	Brockton	MA	C	508 587-7000	9128
Craft Interiors	Malden	MA	G	781 321-8695	12566
Kings Draperies Inc	Brockton	MA	G	508 230-0055	9159
Lundys Company Inc	Lynn	MA	F	781 595-8639	12522
Winnepesaukee Forge Inc	Meredith	NH	G	603 279-5492	18982
Bristol Cushions Inc	Bristol	RI	F	401 247-4499	20065
Decorators Sewing Shoppe Inc	Johnston	RI	G	401 453-3500	20507
Dometic Uk Blind Systems Ltd	Manchester Center	VT	E	802 362-5258	22082

CURTAINS: Cottage Sets, From Purchased Materials

	CITY	ST	EMP	PHONE	ENTRY #
Salo Bay Trading Co	Biddeford	ME	G	207 283-4732	5762

CURTAINS: Window, From Purchased Materials

	CITY	ST	EMP	PHONE	ENTRY #
R L Fisher Inc	Hartford	CT	D	860 951-8110	1865
A L Ellis Inc	Fall River	MA	D	508 672-4799	10649
Bloom & Company Inc	Watertown	MA	F	617 923-1526	16273
Curtain Manufacturers Plus	Fall River	MA	E	508 675-8680	10681
Natco Home Fashions Inc	West Warwick	RI	F	401 828-0300	21501
Natco Home Fashions Inc	West Warwick	RI	F	401 828-0300	21502
Natco Home Fashions Inc **(PA)**	West Warwick	RI	F	401 828-0300	21503

CUSHIONS & PILLOWS

	CITY	ST	EMP	PHONE	ENTRY #
Sammi Sleeping Systems LLC	New Haven	CT	G	203 684-3131	2734
Brian Summer	Shelburne Falls	MA	G	413 625-9990	15066
Klear-Vu Corporation **(PA)**	Fall River	MA	D	508 674-5723	10721
Boston Billows Inc	Nashua	NH	G	603 598-1200	19129
Lucci Corp	Peterborough	NH	F	603 567-4301	19475

CUSHIONS & PILLOWS: Bed, From Purchased Materials

	CITY	ST	EMP	PHONE	ENTRY #
Ksg Enterprises Inc	Peabody	MA	F	978 977-7357	14349
Lulla Smith	Camden	ME	G	207 230-0832	5867

CUSHIONS & PILLOWS: Boat

	CITY	ST	EMP	PHONE	ENTRY #
Bristal Cushion & ACC LLC	Warren	RI	F	401 247-4499	21291
Bristol Cushions Inc	Bristol	RI	F	401 247-4499	20065
Moore Company	Westerly	RI	C	401 596-2816	21532
Garflex Inc	Brattleboro	VT	D	802 257-5256	21728

CUSHIONS: Carpet & Rug, Foamed Plastics

	CITY	ST	EMP	PHONE	ENTRY #
HI-Tech Packaging Inc	Stratford	CT	E	203 378-2700	4420
Future Foam Inc	Mansfield	MA	F	508 339-0354	12633
Innocor Foam Technical	Newburyport	MA	F	978 462-5400	13500

CUSTOM COMPOUNDING OF RUBBER MATERIALS

	CITY	ST	EMP	PHONE	ENTRY #
Avon Custom Mixing Svcs Inc	Holbrook	MA	E	781 767-0511	11521
Teknor Apex Company **(PA)**	Pawtucket	RI	B	401 725-8000	20903

CUT STONE & STONE PRODUCTS

	CITY	ST	EMP	PHONE	ENTRY #
American Stonecrafters Inc	Wallingford	CT	G	203 514-9725	4698
Architectural Stone Group LLC	Bridgeport	CT	G	203 494-5451	377
Connecticut Solid Surface LLC	Plainville	CT	E	860 410-9800	3477
Dan Beard Inc	Shelton	CT	F	203 924-4346	3794
Interntonal MBL Gran Entps Inc	Hartford	CT	G	860 296-0741	1838
Tri LLC	Stamford	CT	G	203 353-8418	4349
B R S Inc	Bridgewater	MA	E	508 697-5448	9061
Bonsal American Inc	Lee	MA	E	413 243-0053	12090
Colonial Landscape Corp	Groton	MA	G	978 448-3329	11287
Counterra LLC	Canton	MA	F	781 821-2100	9723
Fletcher Granite LLC **(DH)**	Westford	MA	G	978 692-1312	16767
Hi-Way Concrete Pdts Co Inc	Wareham	MA	E	508 295-0834	16249
International Stone Inc	Woburn	MA	D	781 937-3300	17206
McC Materials Inc	North Adams	MA	G	860 309-9491	13680
Quarry Brothers Incorporated	Rehoboth	MA	G	508 252-9922	14758
Roma Stone	Harwich	MA	G	508 430-1200	11397
Stone Surfaces Inc	Woburn	MA	F	781 270-4600	17303
Dragon Products Company LLC **(DH)**	South Portland	ME	E	207 774-6355	7022
Sheldon Slate Products Co Inc	Monson	ME	F	207 997-3615	6452
Trombley Industries Inc	Limestone	ME	G	207 328-4503	6345
Conproco Corp	Bow	NH	G	603 743-5800	17710
Galleria Stone	Merrimack	NH	G	603 424-2884	19001
Structural Stone LLC	North Kingstown	RI	F	401 667-4969	20742
Family Memorials Inc	Barre	VT	G	802 476-7831	21614
Paul Thomas	Chester	VT	G	802 875-4004	21848
Vermont Soapstone Inc	Perkinsville	VT	F	802 263-5577	22260
Vermont Stone Art LLC	Barre	VT	G	802 238-1498	21644
Vermont Stoneworks	Springfield	VT	G	802 885-6535	22512

CUTLERY

	CITY	ST	EMP	PHONE	ENTRY #
Donahue Industries Inc	Shrewsbury	MA	E	508 845-6501	15108
Georgia-Pacific LLC	Leominster	MA	C	978 537-4701	12144
JH Smith Co Inc **(PA)**	Greenfield	MA	F	413 772-0191	11264
Khalsa Jot	Millis	MA	G	508 376-6206	13185
Longcap Lamson Products LLC	Westfield	MA	F	413 642-8135	16697
R Murphy Company Inc	Ayer	MA	F	978 772-3481	7935
Lifetime Brands Inc	Pawtucket	RI	G	401 333-2040	20854
Perry Blackburne Inc	North Providence	RI	E	401 231-7200	20771
Wood Dynamics Corporation **(PA)**	South Pomfret	VT	G	802 457-3970	22489

CUTLERY: Table, Exc Metal Handled

	CITY	ST	EMP	PHONE	ENTRY #
Lamson and Goodnow Mfg Co	Shelburne Falls	MA	E	413 625-6311	15074

CUTOUTS: Distribution

	CITY	ST	EMP	PHONE	ENTRY #
Dow Div of UTC	Windsor	CT	G	860 683-7340	5329

CUTTING EQPT: Milling

	CITY	ST	EMP	PHONE	ENTRY #
Keo Milling Cutters LLC	Athol	MA	B	800 523-5233	7688
Lovejoy Tool Company Inc	Springfield	VT	E	802 885-2194	22506

CUTTING SVC: Paper, Exc Die-Cut

	CITY	ST	EMP	PHONE	ENTRY #
Visual Inspection Products	Hampton	NH	G	603 929-4414	18279

CYLINDER & ACTUATORS: Fluid Power

	CITY	ST	EMP	PHONE	ENTRY #
Airpot Corporation	Norwalk	CT	E	800 848-7681	3097
Wedgerock	Limerick	ME	G	207 793-2289	6338
Parker & Harper Companies Inc **(PA)**	Raymond	NH	D	603 895-4761	19643
Quality Controls Inc	Northfield	NH	E	603 286-3321	19408
Watts Regulator Co	Franklin	NH	A	603 934-5110	18166

CYLINDERS: Pressure

	CITY	ST	EMP	PHONE	ENTRY #
PSI Plus Inc	East Hampton	CT	F	860 267-6667	1164
Larson Tool & Stamping Company	Attleboro	MA	D	508 222-0897	7758

CYLINDERS: Pump

	CITY	ST	EMP	PHONE	ENTRY #
Essential Life Solutions Ltd	Stoughton	MA	G	781 341-7240	15589

DAIRY EQPT

	CITY	ST	EMP	PHONE	ENTRY #
Engineering Services & Pdts Co **(PA)**	South Windsor	CT	D	860 528-1119	3965

DAIRY PRDTS STORE: Butter

	CITY	ST	EMP	PHONE	ENTRY #
Cabot Creamery Cooperative Inc	Waitsfield	VT	B	978 552-5500	22562

DAIRY PRDTS STORE: Cheese

	CITY	ST	EMP	PHONE	ENTRY #
Agri-Mark Inc	Hingham	MA	G	781 740-0090	11489

DAIRY PRDTS STORE: Ice Cream, Packaged

	CITY	ST	EMP	PHONE	ENTRY #
Hilliards House Candy Inc **(PA)**	North Easton	MA	D	508 238-6231	13947
Russos Inc	Saugus	MA	F	781 233-1737	14995
Walpole Creamery Ltd	Walpole	NH	G	603 445-5700	19926
Newport Creamery LLC	Cranston	RI	B	401 946-4000	20268

DAIRY PRDTS STORES

	CITY	ST	EMP	PHONE	ENTRY #
Big Dipper	Somersworth	NH	E	603 742-7075	19829

DAIRY PRDTS WHOLESALERS: Fresh

	CITY	ST	EMP	PHONE	ENTRY #
Guida-Seibert Dairy Company **(PA)**	New Britain	CT	C	860 224-2404	2537
Longfords Ice Cream Ltd	Stamford	CT	F	914 935-9469	4239
Getchell Bros Inc	Sanford	ME	E	207 490-0809	6877

DAIRY PRDTS: Butter

	CITY	ST	EMP	PHONE	ENTRY #
Grass Roots Creamery	Granby	CT	G	860 653-6303	1589
Redding Creamery LLC	Redding	CT	G	203 938-2766	3651
Square Creamery LLC	Bethel	CT	G	203 456-3490	180
Agri-Mark Inc	West Springfield	MA	D	413 732-4168	16506
Captain Bonneys Creamery	Rochester	MA	G	774 218-3586	14784
Maple Valley Creamery	Hadley	MA	G	413 588-4881	11310
Seafood Hut and Creamery	Acushnet	MA	G	508 993-9355	7406
Casco Bay Butter Company LLC	Portland	ME	G	207 712-9148	6632
Kates Homemade Butter Inc	Kennebunkport	ME	G	207 934-5134	6246
SBwinsor Creamery LLC	Johnston	RI	G	401 231-5113	20541
Cabot Creamery	Middlebury	VT	G	888 792-2268	22106
Co Op Creamery	Saint Albans	VT	G	802 524-6581	22365
Gammelgarden Creamery	Pownal	VT	G	802 823-5757	22281

DAIRY PRDTS: Cheese

	CITY	ST	EMP	PHONE	ENTRY #
Chris & Zack LLC	Orange	CT	G	203 298-0742	3361
Mozzicato Fmly Investments LLC	Wethersfield	CT	G	860 296-0426	5259
Ndr Liuzzi Inc	Hamden	CT	E	203 287-8477	1774
Red Apple Cheese LLC **(PA)**	Watertown	CT	G	203 755-5579	5021
Agri-Mark Inc	Hingham	MA	G	781 740-0090	11489
Agri-Mark Inc **(PA)**	Andover	MA	D	978 552-5500	7535
Emga Foods LLC	Peabody	MA	G	978 532-0000	14333
Tribe Mediterranean Foods Inc	Taunton	MA	D	774 961-0000	15791
Crooked Face Creamery LLC	Norridgewock	ME	G	207 858-5096	6496
Pine Land Farm Cheese Factory	New Gloucester	ME	G	207 688-6400	6470
Garfields Smokehouse Inc	Meriden	NH	G	603 469-3225	18983
Agri-Mark Inc	Middlebury	VT	C	802 388-6731	22098
Agri-Mark Inc	Waitsfield	VT	D	802 496-1200	22559

DAIRY PRDTS: Cheese, Cottage

	CITY	ST	EMP	PHONE	ENTRY #
Garelick Farms LLC	Franklin	MA	C	508 528-9000	11050

DAIRY PRDTS: Cream, Sweet

	CITY	ST	EMP	PHONE	ENTRY #
HP Hood LLC **(PA)**	Lynnfield	MA	C	617 887-8441	12549
Houlton Farms Dairy Inc **(PA)**	Houlton	ME	F	207 532-3170	6206

DAIRY PRDTS: Cream, Whipped

	CITY	ST	EMP	PHONE	ENTRY #
Johnsons Food Products Corp	Boston	MA	F	617 265-3400	8637

DAIRY PRDTS: Dairy Based Desserts, Frozen

	CITY	ST	EMP	PHONE	ENTRY #
Gelato Giuliana LLC	New Haven	CT	G	203 772-0607	2690
Poppys LLC	Hartford	CT	F	860 778-9044	1860
A Baileys LLC	Barrington	RI	G	401 252-6002	20042

DAIRY PRDTS: Dietary Supplements, Dairy & Non-Dairy Based

	CITY	ST	EMP	PHONE	ENTRY #
Natures First Inc **(PA)**	Orange	CT	G	203 795-8400	3374
Ajinomoto Cambrooke Inc **(DH)**	Ayer	MA	E	508 782-2300	7906
Breed Nutrition Inc	Rehoboth	MA	G	508 840-3888	14747
Dmi Nutraceuticals Inc	Bedford	MA	G	617 999-7219	7971
Meganutra Inc **(PA)**	Norwood	MA	G	781 762-9600	14177
Partylite Inc **(HQ)**	Plymouth	MA	D	203 661-1926	14572
Prescientpharma LLC	Canton	MA	G	617 955-0490	9772
Salarius Pharmaceuticals Inc **(PA)**	Boston	MA	E	617 874-1821	8832
Human Body Recon Company	Nottingham	NH	G	603 895-2920	19415
Naked Nutrient By Deseo LLC	Derry	NH	G	646 809-4943	17989
Bariatrix Nutrition Corp	Fairfax	VT	E	802 527-2500	21972
Canadian American Resources	Montpelier	VT	G	802 223-2271	22146
Nutragenesis LLC	Brattleboro	VT	G	802 257-5345	21741
Vermont Base Waters LLC	Colchester	VT	G	802 893-2131	21885

DAIRY PRDTS: Dried Milk

	CITY	ST	EMP	PHONE	ENTRY #
St Albans Cooperative Crmry	Saint Albans	VT	D	802 524-9366	22379

DAIRY PRDTS: Evaporated Milk

	CITY	ST	EMP	PHONE	ENTRY #
Nestle Usa Inc	Pomfret Center	CT	C	860 928-0082	3558
Nestle Usa Inc	Wilmington	MA	C	978 988-2030	17028

DAIRY PRDTS: Farmers' Cheese

	CITY	ST	EMP	PHONE	ENTRY #
Main Street Cheese LLC	Hancock	NH	G	603 525-3300	18285

DAIRY PRDTS: Frozen Desserts & Novelties

	CITY	ST	EMP	PHONE	ENTRY #
Chip In A Bottle LLC	New Haven	CT	G	203 460-0665	2676
Dari-Farms Ice Cream Co Inc	Tolland	CT	F	860 872-8313	4544
Greg Robbins and Associates	Branford	CT	G	888 699-8876	321
HP Hood LLC	Suffield	CT	C	860 623-4435	4463
J Foster Ice Cream	Simsbury	CT	G	860 651-1499	3907
Kan Pak LLC	Southbury	CT	G	203 933-6631	4029
Longfords Ice Cream Ltd	Stamford	CT	F	914 935-9469	4239
Rbf Frozen Desserts LLC	West Hartford	CT	F	516 474-6488	5092
Rich Products Corporation	New Britain	CT	B	860 827-8000	2572
Captain Dustys Ice Cream	Salem	MA	G	978 744-0777	14901
Dads	Charlton	MA	G	508 248-9774	9848
HP Hood LLC **(PA)**	Lynnfield	MA	C	617 887-8441	12549
Ice Treat Inc	Chelsea	MA	G	617 889-0300	9954
Incredible Foods Inc	Boston	MA	E	617 491-6600	8614
Mixx Frozen Yogurt Inc **(PA)**	Allston	MA	F	617 782-6499	7470
Puritan Ice Cream Co of Boston	Boston	MA	G	617 524-3580	8801
Puritan Icecream Inc	Roslindale	MA	G	617 524-7500	14842
Rainbow Shack	Adams	MA	G	413 743-4031	7414
Russos Inc	Saugus	MA	F	781 233-1737	14995
HP Hood LLC	Portland	ME	D	207 774-9861	6672
Mount Desert Island Ice Cream	Bar Harbor	ME	G	207 460-5515	5666
Round Top Ice Cream Inc	Damariscotta	ME	E	207 563-5307	5939
Woolwich Ice Cream Inc	Woolwich	ME	G	207 442-8830	7291
Big Dipper	Somersworth	NH	E	603 742-7075	19829
Kellerhaus Inc	Laconia	NH	E	603 366-4466	18569
Soda Shoppe of Franklin	Franklin	NH	F	603 934-0100	18164
Walpole Creamery Ltd	Walpole	NH	G	603 445-5700	19926
Newport Creamery LLC	Cranston	RI	B	401 946-4000	20268
Nutricopia Inc	Montpelier	VT	G	808 832-2080	22158

DAIRY PRDTS: Ice Cream & Ice Milk

	CITY	ST	EMP	PHONE	ENTRY #
Reeds Inc	Norwalk	CT	E	203 890-0557	3228
Royal Ice Cream Company Inc **(PA)**	Manchester	CT	F	860 649-5358	2043
Puleos Dairy	Salem	MA	G	978 590-7611	14937
Rhino Foods Inc **(PA)**	Burlington	VT	C	802 862-0252	21807

DAIRY PRDTS: Ice Cream, Bulk

	CITY	ST	EMP	PHONE	ENTRY #
Abbydabby	West Hartford	CT	G	860 586-8832	5051
B-Sweet LLC	Monroe	CT	G	203 452-0499	2393
Ben & Jerrys Homemade Inc	Newington	CT	G	203 488-9666	2848
Bucks Spumoni Company Inc	Milford	CT	F	203 874-2007	2257
Pralines Inc	Wallingford	CT	F	203 284-8847	4786
Pralines of Plainville	Plainville	CT	G	860 410-1151	3512
Ritas of Milford	Milford	CT	F	203 301-4490	2353
Salem Vly Farms Ice Cream Inc	Salem	CT	G	860 859-2980	3739
County Street Ice Cream Corp	Somerset	MA	G	508 674-3357	15143
Gone Troppo Inc **(PA)**	Brookline	MA	G	617 739-7995	9201
J P Licks Homemade Ice Cream	Dedham	MA	G	781 329-9100	10294
Philip RS Sorbets	Winchester	MA	F	781 721-6330	17095
Richardsons Ice Cream	Reading	MA	G	781 944-9121	14740
Snows Nice Cream Co Inc	Greenfield	MA	G	413 774-7438	11277
Giffords Dairy Inc	Skowhegan	ME	E	207 474-9821	6975
Gorgeous Gelato LLC	Portland	ME	G	207 699-4309	6666
Stephen E Witham	Gray	ME	G	207 657-3410	6142
Morano Gelato Inc	Hanover	NH	G	603 643-4233	18295
Sunshine Scoops LLC	Manchester	NH	G	603 668-0992	18770
Ice Cream Machine Co	Cumberland	RI	F	401 333-5053	20327
Warwick Ice Cream Company	Warwick	RI	E	401 821-8403	21443

DAIRY PRDTS: Ice Cream, Packaged, Molded, On Sticks, Etc.

	CITY	ST	EMP	PHONE	ENTRY #
Conopco Inc	Trumbull	CT	E	708 606-0540	4620
Thomas J Lipton Inc	Trumbull	CT	A	206 381-3500	4635
Berry Twist	Boston	MA	G	857 362-7455	8402
Protein Holdings Inc **(PA)**	Portland	ME	F	207 771-0965	6717

DAIRY PRDTS: Milk & Cream, Cultured & Flavored

	CITY	ST	EMP	PHONE	ENTRY #
A B Munroe Dairy Inc	East Providence	RI	D	401 438-4450	20384
Green Mtn Organic Crmry LLC	Hinesburg	VT	G	802 482-6455	22026
Spragues Dairy Inc	Randolph	VT	G	802 728-3863	22303

DAIRY PRDTS: Milk, Fluid

	CITY	ST	EMP	PHONE	ENTRY #
HP Hood LLC	Newtown	CT	B	203 304-9151	2925
Kohler Mix Specialties LLC	Newington	CT	C	860 666-1511	2876
Willard J Stearns & Sons Inc	Storrs Mansfield	CT	E	860 423-9289	4387
HP Hood LLC	Agawam	MA	C	413 786-2178	7431
HP Hood LLC	Feeding Hills	MA	B	413 789-8194	10800
HP Hood LLC	Peabody	MA	F	978 535-3385	14342
HP Hood LLC	Portland	ME	D	207 774-9861	6672
Agri-Mark Inc	Middlebury	VT	C	802 388-6731	22098
Duhamel Family Farm LLC	Highgate Center	VT	G	802 868-4954	22019
Ebws LLC	Strafford	VT	G	802 765-4180	22526
St Albans Cooperative Crmry	Saint Albans	VT	D	802 524-9366	22379
Tafts Milk Maple Farm	Huntington	VT	G	802 434-2727	22034

DAIRY PRDTS: Milk, Processed, Pasteurized, Homogenized/Btld

	CITY	ST	EMP	PHONE	ENTRY #
Guida-Seibert Dairy Company **(PA)**	New Britain	CT	C	860 224-2404	2537
Agri-Mark Inc **(PA)**	Andover	MA	D	978 552-5500	7535
Agri-Mark Inc	West Springfield	MA	D	413 732-4168	16506
Garelick Farms LLC **(DH)**	Franklin	MA	A	508 528-9000	11049
Garelick Farms LLC	Haverhill	MA	F	781 599-1300	11438
Pioneer Vly Milk Mktg Coop Inc	Greenfield	MA	G	413 772-2332	11272
Puleos Dairy	Salem	MA	G	978 590-7611	14937
Protein Holdings Inc **(PA)**	Portland	ME	F	207 771-0965	6717
Agri-Mark Inc	Waitsfield	VT	D	802 496-1200	22559

DAIRY PRDTS: Natural Cheese

	CITY	ST	EMP	PHONE	ENTRY #
Elm City Cheese Company Inc	Hamden	CT	F	203 865-5768	1746
Orange Cheese Company	Orange	CT	G	917 603-4378	3377
Extra Virgin Foods Inc	Watertown	MA	G	617 407-9161	16285
Julima Cheese Inc	Baldwinville	MA	G	978 939-8800	7944
Martins Cheese Co Inc	Westport	MA	G	508 636-2357	16843
State Maine Cheese Company LLC	Hope	ME	G	207 236-8895	6201
York Hill Farm	New Sharon	ME	G	207 778-9741	6479
Cabot Creamery Cooperative Inc	Waitsfield	VT	B	978 552-5500	22562
Crowley Cheese Incorporated	Mount Holly	VT	G	802 259-2340	22181
Grafton Village Cheese Co LLC	Brattleboro	VT	E	802 843-2221	21730
Sugarbush Farm Inc	Woodstock	VT	G	802 457-1757	22739
Swan Valley Cheese Vermont LLC	Swanton	VT	E	802 868-7181	22537
Vermont Creamery LLC	Websterville	VT	E	802 479-9371	22598

DAIRY PRDTS: Processed Cheese

	CITY	ST	EMP	PHONE	ENTRY #
HP Hood LLC **(PA)**	Lynnfield	MA	C	617 887-8441	12549
Kraft Heinz Foods Company	Woburn	MA	C	781 933-2800	17212
Mondelez Global LLC	Hanover	MA	G	781 878-0103	11348
Mountain Mozzarella LLC	North Bennington	VT	E	802 440-9950	22210

DAIRY PRDTS: Sour Cream

	CITY	ST	EMP	PHONE	ENTRY #
Tribe Mediterranean Foods Inc	Taunton	MA	D	774 961-0000	15791

DAIRY PRDTS: Yogurt, Exc Frozen

	CITY	ST	EMP	PHONE	ENTRY #
Peachwave of Watertown	Watertown	CT	G	203 942-4949	5015
R & D Services LLC	Southington	CT	G	860 628-5205	4072
Swizzles of Greenwhich	Cos Cob	CT	G	917 662-0080	830
Dahlicious Holdings LLC	Leominster	MA	F	978 401-2103	12131
Dahlicious LLC	Leominster	MA	E	505 200-0396	12132
Frozen Cups LLC	Lawrence	MA	G	978 918-1872	12026
Lets Yo Yogurt	East Longmeadow	MA	G	413 525-4002	10482
Pinkberry	Cambridge	MA	G	617 547-0573	9611
Postdoc Ventures LLC	Cambridge	MA	G	617 492-3555	9613
Tutti Frutti	North Attleboro	MA	G	508 695-7795	13785
Yoway LLC	Brookline	MA	G	617 505-5158	9225
Yoway LLC **(PA)**	Worcester	MA	G	508 459-0611	17512

DAIRY PRDTS: Yogurt, Frozen

	CITY	ST	EMP	PHONE	ENTRY #
Bruce Luong DBA Pure Froyo	Lowell	MA	G	978 996-7800	12357
Masonry & More Inc	Framingham	MA	G	508 740-8537	10981
SA Feole Masonry Svcs Inc	Cranston	RI	G	401 273-2766	20282

DATA ENTRY SVCS

	CITY	ST	EMP	PHONE	ENTRY #
Xpress of Maine **(PA)**	Portland	ME	G	207 775-2444	6747

DATA PROCESSING & PREPARATION SVCS

	CITY	ST	EMP	PHONE	ENTRY #
Shibumicom Inc	Norwalk	CT	F	855 744-2864	3242
Spectrum Virtual LLC	Cheshire	CT	G	203 303-7540	765
Xerox Corporation **(HQ)**	Norwalk	CT	B	203 968-3000	3274
Akamai Technologies Inc **(PA)**	Cambridge	MA	B	617 444-3000	9378
Carbonite Inc **(PA)**	Boston	MA	C	617 587-1100	8458
Diacritech Inc	Boston	MA	F	617 236-7500	8502
Lexington Press Inc	Lexington	MA	G	781 862-8900	12238
Research Cmpt Consulting Svcs **(PA)**	Canton	MA	G	781 821-1221	9774
Scully Signal Company **(PA)**	Wilmington	MA	C	617 692-8600	17044
Zlink Inc	Maynard	MA	G	978 309-3628	12907
Oracle Systems Corporation	Nashua	NH	B	603 897-3000	19225

DATA PROCESSING SVCS

	CITY	ST	EMP	PHONE	ENTRY #
Campus Yellow Pages LLC	West Hartford	CT	G	860 523-9909	5057
Dataprep Inc	Orange	CT	E	203 795-2095	3364

DATABASE INFORMATION RETRIEVAL SVCS

	CITY	ST	EMP	PHONE	ENTRY #
Windhover Information Inc **(DH)**	Norwalk	CT	E	203 838-4401	3272
Worldwide Information Inc	Beverly	MA	G	888 273-3260	8198

DECORATIVE WOOD & WOODWORK

	CITY	ST	EMP	PHONE	ENTRY #
C N C Router Technologies	Danbury	CT	G	203 744-6651	883
Clint S Custom Woodworkin	Jewett City	CT	G	860 887-1476	1910
Company of Craftsmen	Mystic	CT	G	860 536-4189	2436
Desjardins Woodworking Inc	Goshen	CT	G	860 491-9972	1583

	CITY	ST	EMP	PHONE	ENTRY #
Elm City Manufacturing LLC	North Haven	CT	F	203 248-1969	3024
Finishing Solutions LLC	Colchester	CT	G	860 705-8231	803
John M Kriskey Carpentry	Greenwich	CT	G	203 531-0194	1625
Legere Group Ltd	Avon	CT	C	860 674-0392	37
New England Joinery Works Inc	Essex	CT	G	860 767-3377	1404
Strouts Woodworking	Broad Brook	CT	G	860 623-8445	630
Vacca Architectural Woodworkin	Pawcatuck	CT	G	860 599-3677	3443
Butler Architectural Wdwkg Inc	New Bedford	MA	F	508 985-9980	13368
Eagle Woodworking Inc	Lawrence	MA	F	978 681-6194	12019
Holland Woodworking	Southampton	MA	G	413 527-6588	15339
J Carvalho LLC	New Bedford	MA	G	774 206-1435	13398
Joe Batson	Lawrence	MA	G	978 689-0072	12041
Mark Gauvin	Mattapoisett	MA	G	508 758-2324	12888
Michael Humphries Wdwkg Inc	Northfield	MA	G	413 498-0018	14064
North Bridge Woodworking	Pepperell	MA	G	978 433-0148	14443
Pine Baker Inc	Tewksbury	MA	G	978 851-1215	15826
Pridecraft Inc	North Andover	MA	G	978 685-2831	13726
Scott Grusby LLC	Newton	MA	G	617 538-9112	13633
South Shore Millwork Inc	Norton	MA	D	508 226-5500	14090
Watson Brothers Inc	Middleton	MA	F	978 774-7677	13106
Wescor Ltd	Woburn	MA	G	781 938-8686	17318
Coastal Woodworking Inc	Nobleboro	ME	E	207 563-1072	6492
Finest Kind	Dayton	ME	G	207 499-7176	5945
Maine Heritage Timber LLC	Millinocket	ME	E	207 723-9200	6442
Anthony Galluzzo Corp	Londonderry	NH	E	603 432-2681	18676
Barlow Architectural Mllwk LLC	Hampstead	NH	E	603 329-6026	18237
Jensen Cabinet Co	Milford	NH	G	603 554-8363	19067
Mike Sequore	Marlborough	NH	G	603 876-4634	18962
Seymour Woodworking	Epping	NH	G	603 679-2055	18102
Vigilant Incoporated	Dover	NH	E	603 285-0400	18065
Stupell Industries Ltd Inc	Johnston	RI	F	401 831-5640	20543
Stark Mountain Woodworks Co	New Haven	VT	F	802 453-5549	22187
Wood Dynamics Corporation **(PA)**	South Pomfret	VT	G	802 457-3970	22489

DEFENSE SYSTEMS & EQPT

Amius Partners LLC	New Haven	CT	G	203 526-5926	2656
Hard-Core Self Defense	Shelton	CT	G	203 231-2344	3809
Ladrdefense LLC	Plantsville	CT	G	860 637-8488	3536
Northmen Defense LLC	Oakdale	CT	G	860 908-9308	3294
United States Dept of Navy	Groton	CT	G	860 694-3524	1689
Americas Best Defense	Shrewsbury	MA	G	774 745-5809	15101
Asymmetrical Defense LLC	Townsend	MA	G	978 597-6078	15868
Cormiers Self Defense Aca	Holliston	MA	G	508 596-7326	11565
Defense Integration	Brockton	MA	G	617 515-2470	9138
Defense Support Solutions LLC	Lawrence	MA	G	978 989-9460	12016
Emergent Biodefense Ops	Canton	MA	G	718 302-3000	9731
Perspecta Svcs & Solutions Inc **(DH)**	Waltham	MA	E	781 684-4000	16173
Raytheon Company **(PA)**	Waltham	MA	B	781 522-3000	16184
Raytheon Company	Pittsfield	MA	G	413 494-8042	14505
Raytheon Company	Chelmsford	MA	C	978 256-6054	9925
Raytheon Company	Framingham	MA	C	508 877-5231	10999
Raytheon Company	Marlborough	MA	E	310 647-9438	12813
Raytheon Company	Andover	MA	D	978 470-6922	7596
Raytheon Company	North Billerica	MA	G	978 313-0201	13858
Raytheon Systems Support Co **(HQ)**	Tewksbury	MA	G	978 851-2134	15831
Thin Line Defense LLC	Webster	MA	G	774 696-5285	16353
Self Defense Innovations Inc	Orland	ME	G	207 991-1641	6550
Custom Manufacturing Svcs Inc	Nashua	NH	E	603 883-1355	19141
Micro-Precision Inc **(PA)**	Sunapee	NH	E	603 763-2394	19882
Online Defense Products LLC	Hudson	NH	G	603 845-3211	18423
Patriot Cyber Defense LLC	Rochester	NH	G	603 231-7000	19682
Resurrection Defense LLC	Winchester	NH	G	603 313-1040	19995
Advanced Self Defense	Chepachet	RI	G	401 486-8135	20132
Beechcraft Defense Co LLC	Providence	RI	G	401 457-2485	20968
November Defense LLC	Coventry	RI	G	401 662-7902	20161
Raytheon Company	Portsmouth	RI	D	401 847-8000	20938

DEGREASING MACHINES

A B Engineering & Co	Oxford	MA	G	508 987-0318	14251
Degreasing Devices Co	Southbridge	MA	G	508 765-0045	15379
Safety-Kleen Systems Inc	Marlborough	MA	F	508 481-3116	12823
Greco Bros Inc	Providence	RI	F	401 421-9306	21023

DEHUMIDIFIERS: Electric

Munters Corporation	Amesbury	MA	E	978 241-1100	7496

DEHYDRATION EQPT

Q-Jet DSI Inc	North Haven	CT	G	203 230-4700	3056
Sharp Services Inc	Saugus	MA	G	781 854-3334	14996

DELAY LINES

Rf Logic LLC **(PA)**	Hudson	NH	E	603 578-9876	18435

DENTAL EQPT

Centrix Inc	Shelton	CT	C	203 929-5582	3788
J S Dental Manufacturing Inc	Ridgefield	CT	G	203 438-8832	3669
Kinetic Instruments Inc	Bethel	CT	E	203 743-0080	167
Nova Dental LLC **(PA)**	North Haven	CT	G	203 234-3900	3044
Benco Dental	Hopkinton	MA	E	508 435-3000	11693
Bicon LLC **(PA)**	Boston	MA	E	617 524-4443	8406
Tekscan Inc	Boston	MA	D	617 464-4500	8876
Bausch Articulating Papers Inc	Nashua	NH	G	603 883-2155	19125

DENTAL EQPT & SPLYS

Aero-Med Ltd	South Windsor	CT	G	860 659-2270	3933
Palmero Healthcare LLC	Stratford	CT	F	203 377-6424	4438
Pickadent Inc	Ridgefield	CT	G	203 431-8716	3675
Ultimate Wireforms Inc	Bristol	CT	D	860 582-9111	621
Winslow Automatics Inc	New Britain	CT	D	860 225-6321	2591
3d Diagnostix Inc	Allston	MA	G	617 820-5279	7458
Apogent Technologies Inc	Waltham	MA	A	781 622-1300	16035
Boston M4 Tech LLC	Woburn	MA	G	617 279-3172	17136
Cataki International Inc	Wareham	MA	E	508 295-9630	16243
Cendres+metaux USA Inc	Attleboro	MA	G	508 316-0962	7717
Convergent Dental Inc	Needham Heights	MA	E	508 500-5656	13323
Dentovations Inc	Boston	MA	F	617 737-1199	8500
Dillon Laboratories Inc	Abington	MA	F	781 871-2333	7322
Encore Crown & Bridge Inc	Plymouth	MA	E	508 746-6025	14555
Ergonomic Products Inc	Fall River	MA	E	508 636-2263	10691
Independent Product Service **(PA)**	Amesbury	MA	G	978 352-8887	7491
Jacobs Precision Corp	Avon	MA	G	508 588-2121	7888
Pulpdent Corporation	Watertown	MA	D	617 926-6666	16308
South Shore Dental Labs	Hanover	MA	G	781 924-5382	11351
Sterngold Dental LLC	Attleboro	MA	E	508 226-5660	7796
New England Denture Cntr Bangr **(PA)**	Bangor	ME	F	207 941-6550	5655

DENTAL EQPT & SPLYS WHOLESALERS

Dentovations Inc	Boston	MA	F	617 737-1199	8499

DENTAL EQPT & SPLYS: Alloys, For Amalgams

Jensen Industries Inc **(PA)**	North Haven	CT	D	203 285-1402	3033

DENTAL EQPT & SPLYS: Dental Materials

Custom Atmated Prosthetics LLC **(DH)**	Stoneham	MA	G	781 279-2771	15559
Prosthetic Design Inc	Fitchburg	MA	G	978 345-2588	10850
Dutchmen Dental LLC	Tiverton	RI	G	401 624-9177	21257

DENTAL EQPT & SPLYS: Enamels

Anna M Chisilenco-Raho	Milford	CT	G	203 877-0377	2244
Scott Woodford	Madison	CT	G	203 245-4266	1974
Dental Dreams LLC	Brockton	MA	G	508 583-2256	9139
Keystone Dental Inc **(PA)**	Burlington	MA	D	781 328-3300	9294
William J Devaney	Portsmouth	NH	G	603 436-7603	19631

DENTAL EQPT & SPLYS: Orthodontic Appliances

Acme Monaco Corporation **(PA)**	New Britain	CT	C	860 224-1349	2503
A2z Dental LLC	Marlborough	MA	G	844 442-5587	12708

DENTAL EQPT & SPLYS: Teeth, Artificial, Exc In Dental Labs

North East Ceramic Studio Inc	Bow	NH	G	603 225-9310	17724

DENTISTS' OFFICES & CLINICS

Ultimate Wireforms Inc	Bristol	CT	D	860 582-9111	621
Dental Studios of Western Mass	South Hadley	MA	G	413 787-9920	15301

DEODORANTS: Personal

Unilever Hpc USA	Trumbull	CT	G	203 381-3311	4638
Procter & Gamble Company	Auburn	ME	C	207 753-4000	5593
Toms of Maine Inc	Kennebunk	ME	C	207 985-2944	6241
Toms of Maine Inc **(HQ)**	Kennebunk	ME	D	207 985-2944	6242
Toms of Maine Inc	Sanford	ME	C	207 985-2944	6894

DEPARTMENT STORES

Wonderland Smoke Shop Inc	Warwick	RI	G	401 823-3134	21451

DEPARTMENT STORES: Country General

Sugar Shack On Roaring Branch	Arlington	VT	G	802 375-6747	21600

DEPOLISHING SVC: Metal

Automated Finishing Co Inc	Attleboro	MA	E	508 222-6262	7710

DERMATOLOGICALS

Kinderma LLC	Glastonbury	CT	G	860 796-5503	1562
New England Drmtlgcal Soc Bret	New Haven	CT	G	203 432-0092	2713
Conseal International Inc	Norwood	MA	G	781 278-0010	14142
Medical Asthtics Assoc Neng PC	Acton	MA	G	978 263-5376	7374
Sanova Bioscience Inc	Acton	MA	G	978 429-8079	7383
Naturally Maine	Biddeford	ME	G	207 423-6443	5751
Tender Corporation **(PA)**	Littleton	NH	D	603 444-5464	18667
Agape Dermatology	Providence	RI	G	401 396-2227	20949
Meadham Inc	Ferrisburgh	VT	G	802 878-1236	21989
Mylan Technologies Inc **(DH)**	Saint Albans	VT	C	802 527-7792	22373
Mylan Technologies Inc	Saint Albans	VT	G	802 527-7792	22374

DERRICKS

Altec Northeast LLC	Sterling	MA	F	508 320-9041	15533

DESIGN SVCS, NEC

20/20 Software Inc	Stamford	CT	G	203 316-5500	4122
Century Tool and Design Inc	Milldale	CT	F	860 621-6748	2383
John Oldham Studios Inc	Wethersfield	CT	E	860 529-3331	5251
Presco Incorporated	Woodbridge	CT	F	203 397-8722	5477
West Mont Group	West Haven	CT	G	203 931-1033	5150
Carriage Hse Developments LLC	Winchester	MA	G	339 221-4253	17085
Iva Corporation	Sudbury	MA	G	978 443-5800	15661
Tanyx Measurements Inc	Billerica	MA	E	978 671-0183	8299
Thomas Michaels Designers Inc	Camden	ME	G	207 236-2708	5870
Indaba Holdings Corp	Auburn	NH	F	603 437-1200	17611
Geotec Inc	Warwick	RI	E	401 228-7395	21366
Paroline/Wright Design Inc	Pawtucket	RI	F	401 781-5300	20875
Trussco Inc	North Kingstown	RI	E	401 295-0669	20747
Leo D Bernstein & Sons Inc	Shaftsbury	VT	D	802 442-8029	22404

DESIGN SVCS: Commercial & Indl

Kimchuk Incorporated **(PA)**	Danbury	CT	F	203 790-7800	943

PRODUCT

	CITY	ST	EMP	PHONE	ENTRY #
Architects of Packaging Inc	Westfield	MA	G	413 568-3187	16667
Microwave Development Labs Inc	Needham Heights	MA	D	781 292-6600	13337
Nypro Inc **(HQ)**	Clinton	MA	A	978 365-8100	10086
Sampco Inc **(PA)**	Pittsfield	MA	C	413 442-4043	14507
Wilmington Research & Dev Corp	Newburyport	MA	G	978 499-0100	13549

DESIGN SVCS: Computer Integrated Systems

	CITY	ST	EMP	PHONE	ENTRY #
Insys Micro Inc	Norwalk	CT	G	917 566-5045	3175
Kimchuk Incorporated **(PA)**	Danbury	CT	F	203 790-7800	943
Aclara Technologies LLC	Wellesley	MA	E	781 694-3300	16357
Cape Setups LLC	West Barnstable	MA	G	508 375-6444	16405
Csp Inc **(PA)**	Lowell	MA	D	978 954-5038	12364
Kronos Acquisition Corporation **(HQ)**	Lowell	MA	G	978 250-9800	12391
Kronos Incorporated **(DH)**	Lowell	MA	C	978 250-9800	12392
Kronos Parent Corporation **(PA)**	Lowell	MA	G	978 250-9800	12394
L T X International Inc	Norwood	MA	D	781 461-1000	14173
Milford Manufacturing Svcs LLC	Hopedale	MA	D	508 478-8544	11678
Rsa Security LLC **(DH)**	Bedford	MA	A	781 515-5000	8007
Securelytix Inc	Newton	MA	G	617 283-5227	13635
Sophic Alliance Inc	East Falmouth	MA	G	508 495-3801	10449
Superpedestrian Inc	Cambridge	MA	G	617 945-1892	9666
Xcerra Corporation	Norwood	MA	E	781 461-1000	14208
Sign Systems of Maine Inc	Portland	ME	G	207 775-7110	6729
Ezenia Inc **(PA)**	Salem	NH	F	603 589-7600	19727
Pep Central Inc	Warwick	RI	A	401 732-3770	21402

DESIGN SVCS: Hand Tools

	CITY	ST	EMP	PHONE	ENTRY #
Tool 2000	Southington	CT	G	860 620-0020	4087

DETECTION APPARATUS: Electronic/Magnetic Field, Light/Heat

	CITY	ST	EMP	PHONE	ENTRY #
J W Fishers Mfg Inc	East Taunton	MA	F	508 822-7330	10514
Vacuum Barrier Corporation	Woburn	MA	E	781 933-3570	17310

DETECTIVE & ARMORED CAR SERVICES

	CITY	ST	EMP	PHONE	ENTRY #
Executive Force Protection LLC	Cambridge	MA	F	617 470-9230	9476

DETECTORS: Water Leak

	CITY	ST	EMP	PHONE	ENTRY #
Gutermann Inc	Newmarket	NH	G	603 200-0340	19334
Progeo Group Inc	Tilton	NH	G	603 286-1942	19910

DETONATORS & DETONATING CAPS

	CITY	ST	EMP	PHONE	ENTRY #
Dyno Nobel Inc	Simsbury	CT	C	860 843-2000	3900
Ensign-Bickford Arospc Def Co **(HQ)**	Simsbury	CT	B	860 843-2289	3903
Ensign-Bickford Company **(HQ)**	Simsbury	CT	G	860 843-2001	3904

DETONATORS: Detonators, high explosives

	CITY	ST	EMP	PHONE	ENTRY #
Ensign-Bickford Industries Inc	Weatogue	CT	C	860 843-2000	5042
Ensign-Bickford Industries Inc	Waltham	MA	G	781 693-1870	16098

DIAGNOSTIC SUBSTANCES

	CITY	ST	EMP	PHONE	ENTRY #
Bioarray Genetics Inc	Farmington	CT	G	508 577-0205	1468
Branford Open Mri & Diagnostic	Branford	CT	G	203 481-7800	299
Charles River Laboratories Inc	Storrs	CT	E	860 429-7261	4381
Abpro Corporation	Woburn	MA	E	617 225-0808	17105
Akrivis Technologies LLC	Cambridge	MA	G	617 233-4097	9380
Alere US Holdings LLC	Waltham	MA	G	781 647-3900	16028
Associates of Cape Cod Inc **(PA)**	East Falmouth	MA	D	508 540-3444	10435
Axis-Shield Poc As	Norton	MA	E	508 285-4870	14071
Bionostics Inc	Devens	MA	D	978 772-7070	10319
Bluejay Diagnostics Inc	Acton	MA	G	978 631-0152	7345
Catalyst Medical LLC	Belmont	MA	G	857 928-8817	8068
Cellay LLC	Cambridge	MA	F	617 995-1307	9434
Daktari Diagnostics Inc	Cambridge	MA	F	617 336-3299	9449
Detectogen Inc	Westborough	MA	G	508 330-1709	16615
Endogen Inc	Woburn	MA	D	617 225-0055	17177
Genzyme Corporation	Boston	MA	C	617 779-3100	8559
Glycozym Usa Inc	Beverly	MA	G	425 985-2556	8137
Hypoxyprobe Inc	Burlington	MA	G	781 272-6888	9283
Instrumentation Laboratory Co **(DH)**	Bedford	MA	A	781 861-0710	7982
Lantheus Holdings Inc **(PA)**	North Billerica	MA	E	978 671-8001	13831
Moderna LLC **(HQ)**	Cambridge	MA	G	617 714-6500	9565
Nanobiosym Inc	Cambridge	MA	E	781 391-7979	9574
Nanobiosym Inc	Medford	MA	F	781 391-7979	12944
New England Immunology Assoc	Lexington	MA	G	781 863-5774	12249
Ninth Sense Inc	Boston	MA	G	617 835-4472	8738
Oxford Immunotec Inc **(DH)**	Marlborough	MA	D	508 481-4648	12804
Phoenix Diagnostics Inc	Natick	MA	F	508 655-8310	13272
Pierce Biotechnology Inc	Woburn	MA	E	781 622-1000	17264
Quidel Corporation	Beverly	MA	G	866 800-5458	8168
Regenocell Therapeutics Inc	Natick	MA	G	508 651-1598	13277
Sangstat Medical LLC	Cambridge	MA	B	510 789-4300	9642
Seracare Life Sciences Inc **(DH)**	Milford	MA	C	508 244-6400	13143
Third Wave Technologies Inc **(HQ)**	Marlborough	MA	E	608 273-8933	12836
Abbott Dgnstics Scrborough Inc **(DH)**	Scarborough	ME	D	207 730-5750	6901
Alere Inc	Scarborough	ME	G	207 730-5714	6903
Bioprocessing Inc	Portland	ME	F	207 457-0025	6623
Idexx Distribution Inc	Westbrook	ME	D	207 556-0637	7190
Solidphase Inc	Portland	ME	G	207 797-0211	6732
C&S Chmcal Sprtons Sensors LLC	Pembroke	NH	G	603 491-9511	19456
Viridis Diagnostics Inc	Underhill	VT	G	802 316-0894	22550

DIAGNOSTIC SUBSTANCES OR AGENTS: Blood Derivative

	CITY	ST	EMP	PHONE	ENTRY #
Capricorn Products LLC	Portland	ME	E	207 321-0014	6630

DIAGNOSTIC SUBSTANCES OR AGENTS: Enzyme & Isoenzyme

	CITY	ST	EMP	PHONE	ENTRY #
Genzyme Corporation	Framingham	MA	G	508 271-3631	10950
Genzyme Corporation **(DH)**	Cambridge	MA	A	617 252-7500	9489
Genzyme Corporation	Cambridge	MA	D	508 271-2919	9490
Genzyme Corporation	Natick	MA	C	617 768-9292	13258
Genzyme Corporation	Waltham	MA	D	781 487-5728	16120
Sano LLC	Wellesley	MA	G	617 290-3348	16386

DIAGNOSTIC SUBSTANCES OR AGENTS: In Vitro

	CITY	ST	EMP	PHONE	ENTRY #
Aldatu Biosciences Inc	Watertown	MA	G	978 705-1036	16266
Amag Pharmaceuticals Inc **(PA)**	Waltham	MA	B	617 498-3300	16032
Cellanyx Diagnostics LLC	Beverly	MA	G	571 212-9991	8114
Confer Health Inc	Charlestown	MA	G	617 433-8810	9830
Creatics LLC	Braintree	MA	F	781 843-2202	8997
Jane Diagnostics Inc	Brookline	MA	G	617 651-2295	9206
Sbh Diagnostics Inc	Natick	MA	G	508 545-0333	13278
T2 Biosystems Inc **(PA)**	Lexington	MA	C	781 761-4646	12276
Telome Inc	Waltham	MA	G	617 383-7565	16209
Therastat LLC	Weston	MA	G	781 373-1865	16833
Thorne Diagnostics Inc	Beverly	MA	G	978 299-1727	8191
Werfen USA LLC	Bedford	MA	C	781 861-0710	8020
Cape Technologies LLC	South Portland	ME	G	207 741-2995	7018
Maine Biotechnology Svcs Inc	Portland	ME	E	207 797-5454	6683
Sun Diagnostics LLC	New Gloucester	ME	G	207 926-1125	6472
Virostat Inc	Westbrook	ME	G	207 856-6620	7213

DIAGNOSTIC SUBSTANCES OR AGENTS: In Vivo

	CITY	ST	EMP	PHONE	ENTRY #
Lam Therapeutics Inc	Guilford	CT	F	203 458-7100	1707
USA Renewable LLC	Newton	MA	G	617 319-7237	13645

DIAGNOSTIC SUBSTANCES OR AGENTS: Microbiology & Virology

	CITY	ST	EMP	PHONE	ENTRY #
Abclonal-Neo Inc	Woburn	MA	F	617 412-1176	17104
Amasa Technologies Inc	Andover	MA	G	617 899-8223	7537
Asimov Inc	Cambridge	MA	E	425 750-4182	9395
Preceding Inc	Natick	MA	G	617 953-6173	13273
Qteros LLC	Amherst	MA	G	413 531-6884	7523
Reservoir Genomics Inc	Cambridge	MA	G	412 304-5063	9631
Rootpath Genomics	Cambridge	MA	G	857 209-1060	9638
Rootpath Genomics Inc	Boston	MA	G	501 258-0969	8827
O E M Concepts **(HQ)**	Saco	ME	G	207 283-6500	6854

DIAGNOSTIC SUBSTANCES OR AGENTS: Radioactive

	CITY	ST	EMP	PHONE	ENTRY #
Cardinal Health 414 LLC	East Hartford	CT	G	860 291-9135	1179
Petnet Solutions Inc	Woburn	MA	G	865 218-2000	17261
Qsa Global Inc **(HQ)**	Burlington	MA	D	781 272-2000	9325

DIAGNOSTIC SUBSTANCES OR AGENTS: Veterinary

	CITY	ST	EMP	PHONE	ENTRY #
Veterinary Medical Associates	Canton	CT	G	860 693-0214	700
Immucell Corporation **(PA)**	Portland	ME	E	207 878-2770	6673

DIAMONDS, GEMS, WHOLESALE

	CITY	ST	EMP	PHONE	ENTRY #
Town & Country Fine Jwly Group	Chelsea	MA	A	617 345-4771	9973

DIAMONDS: Cutting & Polishing

	CITY	ST	EMP	PHONE	ENTRY #
Diamond Express Inc	Wilmington	MA	E	781 284-9402	16994

DIAPERS: Disposable

	CITY	ST	EMP	PHONE	ENTRY #
Capricorn Investors II LP	Greenwich	CT	A	203 861-6600	1602
American Disposables Inc	Hardwick	MA	E	413 967-6201	11371

DICE & DICE CUPS

	CITY	ST	EMP	PHONE	ENTRY #
Koplow Games Inc	Boston	MA	F	617 482-4011	8654

DIE CUTTING SVC: Paper

	CITY	ST	EMP	PHONE	ENTRY #
C & T Print Finishing Inc	South Windsor	CT	F	860 282-0616	3945
Agawam Novelty Company Inc	Agawam	MA	G	413 536-0471	7418
Zenith Die Cutting Inc	Framingham	MA	G	508 877-8811	11018
New England Paper Tube Co Inc	Pawtucket	RI	E	401 725-2610	20868

DIE SETS: Presses, Metal Stamping

	CITY	ST	EMP	PHONE	ENTRY #
Globe Tool & Met Stampg Co Inc	Southington	CT	E	860 621-6807	4054
P&G Metal Components Corp	Bloomfield	CT	F	860 243-2220	248
Connell Limited Partnership **(PA)**	Boston	MA	F	617 737-2700	8481
GA Rel Manufacturing Company	Providence	RI	E	401 331-5455	21019

DIES & TOOLS: Special

	CITY	ST	EMP	PHONE	ENTRY #
Accurate Tool & Die Inc	Stamford	CT	E	203 967-1200	4127
All Five Tool Co Inc	Berlin	CT	E	860 583-1693	69
Anderson Tool Company Inc	New Haven	CT	G	203 777-4153	2657
Arrow Diversified Tooling Inc	Ellington	CT	E	860 872-9072	1329
B & L Tool and Machine Company	Plainville	CT	G	860 747-2721	3468
B & P Plating Equipment LLC	Bristol	CT	F	860 589-5799	523
Bremser Technologies Inc	Stratford	CT	F	203 378-8486	4398
Bridgeport Tl & Stamping Corp	Bridgeport	CT	E	203 336-2501	390
Bristol Tool & Die Company	Bristol	CT	E	860 582-2577	539
Candlewood Tool & Machine Shop	Gaylordsville	CT	F	860 355-1892	1529
Carnegie Tool Inc	Norwalk	CT	F	203 866-0744	3119
Cgl Inc	Watertown	CT	F	860 945-6166	5002
Diecraft Compacting Tool Inc	Wolcott	CT	G	203 879-3019	5439
E & E Tool & Manufacturing Co	Winsted	CT	F	860 738-8577	5409
Fad Tool Company LLC	Bristol	CT	E	860 582-7890	560
G P Tool Co Inc	Danbury	CT	F	203 744-0310	924
Highland Manufacturing Inc	Manchester	CT	E	860 646-5142	2009
Hobson and Motzer Incorporated **(PA)**	Durham	CT	C	860 349-1756	1092
Jovek Tool and Die	Bristol	CT	G	860 261-5020	573
Lassy Tools Inc	Plainville	CT	G	860 747-2748	3500
Laurel Tool & Manufacturing	Norwich	CT	G	860 889-5354	3285
Lou-Jan Tool & Die Inc	Cheshire	CT	F	203 272-3536	742
Lyons Tool and Die Company	Meriden	CT	E	203 238-2689	2100
Manchester Molding and Mfg Co	Manchester	CT	E	860 643-2141	2023
Marc Tool & Die Inc	Prospect	CT	G	203 758-5933	3588
Mastercraft Tool and Mch Co	Southington	CT	F	860 628-5551	4064

	CITY	ST	EMP	PHONE	ENTRY #
Michaud Tool Co Inc	Terryville	CT	G	860 582-6785	4486
Mid-State Manufacturing Inc	Milldale	CT	F	860 621-6855	2386
Northeast Carbide Inc	Southington	CT	F	860 628-2515	4069
Paragon Tool Company Inc	Manchester	CT	G	860 647-9935	2035
Plainville Machine & Tl Co Inc	Bristol	CT	F	860 589-5595	594
Preferred Tool & Die Inc **(PA)**	Shelton	CT	D	203 925-8525	3861
Quality Wire Edm Inc	Bristol	CT	G	860 583-9867	600
R A Tool Co	Milford	CT	G	203 877-2998	2346
Ramar-Hall Inc	Middlefield	CT	E	860 349-1081	2165
Ray Machine Corporation	Terryville	CT	E	860 582-8202	4490
Reliable Tool & Die Inc	Milford	CT	E	203 877-3264	2348
Reynolds Carbide Die Co Inc	Thomaston	CT	E	860 283-8246	4512
Richards Machine Tool Co Inc	Newington	CT	F	860 436-2938	2899
Rintec Corporation	Oakville	CT	F	860 274-3697	3302
Sandur Tool Co	Waterbury	CT	G	203 753-0004	4952
Skico Manufacturing Co LLC	Hamden	CT	G	203 230-1305	1784
Skillcraft Machine Tool Co	South Windsor	CT	F	860 953-1246	4010
Spartan Aerospace LLC	Manchester	CT	D	860 533-7500	2049
Steel Rule Die Corp America	Milldale	CT	G	860 621-5284	2387
Straton Industries Inc	Stratford	CT	D	203 375-4488	4450
Taco Fasteners Inc	Plainville	CT	F	860 747-5597	3518
Telke Tool & Die Mfg Co	Kensington	CT	G	860 828-9955	1921
Total Concept Tool Inc	Branford	CT	G	203 483-1130	355
Victor Tool Co Inc	Meriden	CT	G	203 634-8113	2148
Watertown Jig Bore Service Inc	Watertown	CT	F	860 274-5898	5034
Weimann Brothers Mfg Co	Derby	CT	F	203 735-3311	1082
Wess Tool & Die Company Inc	Meriden	CT	G	203 237-5277	2150
West-Conn Tool and Die Inc	Shelton	CT	F	203 538-5081	3888
Wilkinson Tool & Die Co	North Stonington	CT	G	860 599-5821	3077
A Luongo & Sons Incorporated	Bridgewater	MA	G	508 226-0788	9059
Abco Tool & Die Inc	Hyannis	MA	E	508 771-3225	11832
Accudie Inc	Worcester	MA	G	508 756-8482	17334
Adt/Diversity Inc	Attleboro	MA	G	508 222-9601	7701
B & D Precision Inc	Stoneham	MA	G	781 438-8644	15555
Big 3 Precision Products Inc	Holliston	MA	F	508 429-4774	11559
Btd Precision Inc	Chicopee	MA	F	413 594-2783	10002
Built-Rite Tool and Die Inc	Leominster	MA	F	978 751-8432	12120
Built-Rite Tool and Die Inc	Lancaster	MA	F	978 365-3867	11981
C & M Tool and Die LLC	Waltham	MA	G	781 893-1880	16057
Columbia ASC Inc	Lawrence	MA	F	978 683-2205	12012
Cycle Engineering Inc	Ware	MA	G	413 967-3818	16231
Diecutting Tooling Svcs Inc **(PA)**	Chicopee	MA	F	413 331-3500	10018
Fiore Machine Inc	Indian Orchard	MA	G	413 543-5767	11886
Fort Hill Sign Products Inc	Hopedale	MA	G	781 321-4320	11672
G&F Precision Molding Inc **(PA)**	Fiskdale	MA	D	508 347-9132	10807
Interstate Design Company Inc	Agawam	MA	F	413 786-7730	7432
Interstate Manufacturing Co	Agawam	MA	G	413 789-8674	7433
J I Morris Company	Southbridge	MA	G	508 764-4394	15388
Jls Tool & Die Inc	Middleton	MA	G	978 304-3111	13091
Micon Die Corporation	West Springfield	MA	G	413 478-5029	16530
Millennium Die Group Inc	Three Rivers	MA	E	413 283-3500	15851
Orchard Tool Die Inc	Indian Orchard	MA	G	413 433-1233	11892
PCC Specialty Products Inc	Auburn	MA	D	508 753-6530	7847
Raynham Tool & Die Inc	Raynham	MA	G	508 822-4489	14728
Sancliff Inc	Worcester	MA	F	508 795-0747	17469
Skg Associates Inc	Dedham	MA	G	781 878-7250	10298
Superior Die & Stamping Inc	Attleboro	MA	G	774 203-3674	7797
Tech Ridge Inc	Chelmsford	MA	E	978 256-5741	9935
Ultraclad Corporation	Newburyport	MA	G	978 358-7945	13545
Vector Tool & Die Corporation	Westfield	MA	G	413 562-1616	16739
Volpe Tool & Die Incorporated	Franklin	MA	G	508 528-8103	11095
W M Gulliksen Mfg Co Inc **(PA)**	South Weymouth	MA	E	617 323-5750	15323
Westfield Tool & Die Inc	Westfield	MA	F	413 562-2393	16747
Whip City Tool & Die Corp	Southwick	MA	E	413 569-5528	15423
Whitman Tool and Die Co Inc	Whitman	MA	E	781 447-0421	16932
WR Sharples Co Inc	North Attleboro	MA	E	508 695-5656	13787
Kennebec Technologies	Augusta	ME	D	207 626-0188	5610
Northeast Tool & Die Co Inc	Norway	ME	G	207 743-7273	6524
Atlantic Microtool	Salem	NH	G	603 898-3212	19710
Berube Tool & Die Inc	Plaistow	NH	G	603 382-2224	19509
Hamilton Precision LLC	Belmont	NH	G	603 524-7622	17673
New England Industries Inc	Lebanon	NH	E	603 448-5330	18633
North East Cutting Die Corp	Dover	NH	E	603 436-8952	18042
RTD Technologies Inc	Somersworth	NH	G	603 692-5978	19848
Sunset Tool Inc	Keene	NH	E	603 355-2246	18531
Swansons Die Co Inc	Manchester	NH	E	603 623-3832	18934
Temco Tool Company Inc	Manchester	NH	E	603 622-6989	18938
Guill Tool & Engrg Co Inc	West Warwick	RI	D	401 822-8186	21493
Ldc Inc	East Providence	RI	F	401 861-4667	20429
Mono Die Cutting Co Inc	Riverside	RI	F	401 434-1274	21173
Newport Tool & Die Inc	Middletown	RI	F	401 847-6711	20628
Pep Central Inc	Warwick	RI	A	401 732-3770	21402
Rol-Flo Engineering Inc	Westerly	RI	E	401 596-0060	21539
Stearns Tool Company Inc	Providence	RI	G	401 351-4765	21127
North Hartland Tool Corp	North Hartland	VT	D	802 295-3196	22229
Tri C Tool & Die	Burlington	VT	G	802 864-7144	21813
Vermont Mold & Tool Corp	Barnet	VT	G	802 633-2300	21605

DIES: Cutting, Exc Metal

	CITY	ST	EMP	PHONE	ENTRY #
Bessette Holdings Inc	East Hartford	CT	E	860 289-6000	1176
Interstate Specialty Pdts Inc	Sutton	MA	E	800 984-1811	15685
Quality Die Cutting Inc **(PA)**	Haverhill	MA	F	978 374-8027	11465
Irwin Industrial Tool Company	Gorham	ME	C	207 856-6111	6115
Swansons Die Co Inc	Manchester	NH	E	603 623-3832	18934

DIES: Extrusion

	CITY	ST	EMP	PHONE	ENTRY #
Richard D Johnson & Son Inc	Ashaway	RI	G	401 377-4312	20040
Raymond Gadues Inc	Swanton	VT	E	802 868-2033	22536

DIES: Plastic Forming

	CITY	ST	EMP	PHONE	ENTRY #
Aba-PGT Inc **(PA)**	Manchester	CT	C	860 649-4591	1980
Acson Tool Company	Bridgeport	CT	F	203 334-8050	367
Bermer Tool & Die Inc	Southbridge	MA	E	508 764-2521	15377
Fall River Tool & Die Co Inc	Fall River	MA	F	508 674-4621	10699
Moldmaster Engineering Inc	Pittsfield	MA	E	413 442-5793	14492

DIES: Steel Rule

	CITY	ST	EMP	PHONE	ENTRY #
B-P Products Inc	Hamden	CT	E	203 288-0200	1733
Bessette Holdings Inc	East Hartford	CT	E	860 289-6000	1176
Apple Steel Rule Die Co Inc	Springfield	MA	E	414 353-2444	15447
Barnard Die Inc	Wakefield	MA	F	781 246-3117	15942
Csw Inc **(PA)**	Ludlow	MA	E	413 589-1311	12461
Ditech	Byfield	MA	G	978 463-0665	9363
Pearl Die Cutting & Finishing	Woburn	MA	F	781 721-6900	17259
Kimark Specialty Box Company	Manchester	NH	E	603 668-1336	18855

DIGESTERS: Process, Metal Plate

	CITY	ST	EMP	PHONE	ENTRY #
Bio Green	Portsmouth	NH	G	603 570-6159	19544

DIODES & RECTIFIERS

	CITY	ST	EMP	PHONE	ENTRY #
Excelitas Technologies Corp **(DH)**	Waltham	MA	E	781 522-5910	16104
Ipg Photonics Corporation **(PA)**	Oxford	MA	B	508 373-1100	14263
Microsemi Corp- Massachusetts	Lawrence	MA	G	978 794-1666	12052
Gpd Optoelectronics Corp	Salem	NH	E	603 894-6865	19739
Two In One Manufacturing Inc	Nashua	NH	E	603 595-8212	19276

DIODES: Light Emitting

	CITY	ST	EMP	PHONE	ENTRY #
Ray Green Corp	Greenwich	CT	F	707 544-2662	1640
Revolution Lighting **(HQ)**	Stamford	CT	G	203 504-1111	4299
Revolution Lighting Tech Inc **(PA)**	Stamford	CT	C	203 504-1111	4300
Optomistic Products Inc	Leominster	MA	F	207 865-9181	12175
4382412 Canada Inc	Williston	VT	G	802 225-5911	22652
Leddynamics Inc	Randolph	VT	D	802 728-4533	22298

DIODES: Solid State, Germanium, Silicon, Etc

	CITY	ST	EMP	PHONE	ENTRY #
Microsemi Corporation	Lawrence	MA	D	781 665-1071	12055
Microsemi Nes Inc	Lawrence	MA	C	978 794-1666	12056

DIRECT SELLING ESTAB: Coffee, Soda/Beer, Etc, Door-To-Door

	CITY	ST	EMP	PHONE	ENTRY #
Alvarium Beer Company LLC	New Britain	CT	G	860 306-3857	2508

DIRECT SELLING ESTABLISHMENTS, NEC

	CITY	ST	EMP	PHONE	ENTRY #
Bluecatbio MA Inc	Concord	MA	G	978 405-2533	10116

DIRECT SELLING ESTABLISHMENTS: Clothing, House-To-House

	CITY	ST	EMP	PHONE	ENTRY #
Theatre Stricken Apparel LLC	Bellingham	MA	G	978 325-2335	8060

DIRECT SELLING ESTABLISHMENTS: Encyclopedias, House-To-House

	CITY	ST	EMP	PHONE	ENTRY #
Scholastic Library Pubg Inc **(HQ)**	Danbury	CT	A	203 797-3500	986

DIRECT SELLING ESTABLISHMENTS: Food Svcs

	CITY	ST	EMP	PHONE	ENTRY #
Sidekim LLC	Lynn	MA	E	781 595-3663	12539

DIRECT SELLING ESTABLISHMENTS: Telemarketing

	CITY	ST	EMP	PHONE	ENTRY #
Taunton Inc	Newtown	CT	A	203 426-8171	2941
North Sails Group LLC	Newport	RI	D	401 849-7997	20675

DISCS & TAPE: Optical, Blank

	CITY	ST	EMP	PHONE	ENTRY #
Adaptive Optics Associates Inc **(DH)**	Devens	MA	D	978 757-9600	10317

DISHWASHING EQPT: Commercial

	CITY	ST	EMP	PHONE	ENTRY #
Auto-Chlor System NY Cy Inc	Foxboro	MA	E	508 543-6767	10876

DISINFECTING & DEODORIZING SVCS

	CITY	ST	EMP	PHONE	ENTRY #
Able Pest Control Service	Brockton	MA	G	508 559-7987	9114

DISK & DRUM DRIVES & COMPONENTS: Computers

	CITY	ST	EMP	PHONE	ENTRY #
Persistor Instruments Inc	Marstons Mills	MA	G	508 420-1600	12873
Primearray Systems Inc	Burlington	MA	G	978 455-9488	9322
Boulder Technologies LLC	Dover	NH	G	603 740-8402	18010

DISKETTE DUPLICATING SVCS

	CITY	ST	EMP	PHONE	ENTRY #
Computer Tech Express LLC	Norwalk	CT	G	203 810-4932	3130

DISKETTE OR KEY-DISK EQPT

	CITY	ST	EMP	PHONE	ENTRY #
Mumm Engineering Inc	Monroe	CT	G	203 445-9777	2409

DISPENSERS: Soap

	CITY	ST	EMP	PHONE	ENTRY #
Highland Labs Inc	Holliston	MA	E	508 429-2918	11577

DISPENSING EQPT & PARTS, BEVERAGE: Beer

	CITY	ST	EMP	PHONE	ENTRY #
Bsg Handcraft	Providence	RI	E	508 636-5154	20975

DISPENSING EQPT & PARTS, BEVERAGE: Coolers, Milk/Water, Elec

	CITY	ST	EMP	PHONE	ENTRY #
Four Seasons Cooler Eqp LLC	Woodbury	CT	G	203 263-0705	5488
Process Cooling Systems Inc	Leominster	MA	E	978 537-1996	12177

DISPENSING EQPT & PARTS, BEVERAGE: Fountain/Other Beverage

	CITY	ST	EMP	PHONE	ENTRY #
Beer Saver USA	Kennebunk	ME	F	207 299-2826	6229

DISPLAY FIXTURES: Wood

	CITY	ST	EMP	PHONE	ENTRY #
W R Hartigan & Son Inc	Burlington	CT	G	860 673-9203	682
Armco Woodworking & Display	Worcester	MA	G	508 831-0990	17342

	CITY	ST	EMP	PHONE	ENTRY #
Franklin Fixtures Inc **(PA)**	West Wareham	MA	E	508 291-1475	16573
Phillips Enterprises Inc	Northampton	MA	F	413 586-5860	14018
Jsi Store Fixtures Inc **(PA)**	Milo	ME	C	207 943-5203	6446
Maine Barrel & Display Company	Lewiston	ME	E	207 784-6700	6303
Custom Design Incorporated	North Kingstown	RI	E	401 294-0200	20700
Elliott Sales Group Inc	Providence	RI	D	401 944-0002	21005
Kenney Manufacturing Company **(PA)**	Warwick	RI	B	401 739-2200	21383

DISPLAY ITEMS: Corrugated, Made From Purchased Materials

Corr/Dis Incorporated	Norwalk	CT	G	203 838-6075	3132
Skyline Exhibits & Graphics	Middletown	CT	F	860 635-2400	2222
E Ink Corporation	Billerica	MA	D	617 499-6000	8242
Contempo Card Co Inc **(PA)**	Providence	RI	D	401 272-4210	20990
Elmco/Mpc Tool Company LLC **(PA)**	Bristol	RI	G	401 253-3611	20076
Packaging Company LLC **(PA)**	Johnston	RI	D	401 943-5040	20527

DISPLAY LETTERING SVCS

Modern Marking Products Inc	Bridgewater	MA	G	508 697-6066	9085

DISPLAY STANDS: Merchandise, Exc Wood

Present Arms Inc	Indian Orchard	MA	G	413 575-4656	11894
Green Mountain Gazebo	Westminster	VT	G	802 869-1212	22630

DISTILLERS DRIED GRAIN & SOLUBLES

American Distilling Inc	Marlborough	CT	G	860 267-4444	2063
American Distilling Inc **(PA)**	East Hampton	CT	D	860 267-4444	1156

DOCK EQPT & SPLYS, INDL

CCI Cyrus River Terminal LLC	Stamford	CT	G	203 761-8000	4159
Readydock Inc	Avon	CT	G	860 523-9980	44
Dock Doctors LLC	Ferrisburgh	VT	E	802 877-6756	21988
Hazelett Strip-Casting Corp	Colchester	VT	G	802 951-6846	21865

DOCK OPERATION SVCS, INCL BLDGS, FACILITIES, OPERS & MAINT

Scott Docks Inc	Bridgton	ME	G	207 647-3824	5811
Dock Doctors LLC	Ferrisburgh	VT	E	802 877-6756	21988

DOCKS: Floating, Wood

Scott Docks Inc	Bridgton	ME	G	207 647-3824	5811

DOCKS: Prefabricated Metal

Readydock Inc	Avon	CT	G	860 523-9980	44
Great Northern Docks Inc **(PA)**	Naples	ME	G	207 693-3770	6461
Dyer S Docking Systems Corp	West Nottingham	NH	F	603 942-5122	19965

DOLLIES: Industrial

Steele Canvas Basket Corp	Chelsea	MA	E	800 541-8929	9970

DOLLIES: Mechanics'

Hostar Mar Trnspt Systems Inc	Wareham	MA	E	508 295-2900	16250

DOOR FRAMES: Wood

Red Barn Woodworkers	Winsted	CT	G	860 379-3158	5420
River Mill Co	Clinton	CT	F	860 669-5915	794
Kelley Bros New England LLC	Westbrook	ME	G	207 517-4100	7192
Kelley Bros New England LLC	Nashua	NH	G	603 748-0274	19193
Kelley Bros New England LLC **(HQ)**	Hudson	NH	F	603 881-5559	18406
Kelley Bros New England LLC	Williston	VT	F	802 865-5133	22675

DOOR MATS: Rubber

Cape Cod Drmats of Distinction	Hyannis	MA	E	508 790-0070	11836

DOOR OPERATING SYSTEMS: Electric

Miracle Instruments Co	Lebanon	CT	F	860 642-7745	1936
Assa Abloy Entrance Sys US Inc	Auburn	MA	E	508 368-2600	7827
Ekeys4 Cars	North Andover	MA	G	978 655-3135	13701
Dual Control Inc	Londonderry	NH	G	603 627-4114	18692

DOORS & WINDOWS WHOLESALERS: All Materials

Advanced Window Systems LLC	Cromwell	CT	F	800 841-6544	844
Specialty Wholesale Sup Corp	Gardner	MA	E	978 632-1472	11128
H Hirschmann Ltd	West Rutland	VT	F	802 438-4447	22616

DOORS & WINDOWS: Screen & Storm

Ld Assoc LLC	Monroe	CT	G	203 452-9393	2406
William Connell LLC	Dover	MA	G	508 785-1292	10353

DOORS & WINDOWS: Storm, Metal

All-Time Manufacturing Co Inc	Montville	CT	F	860 848-9258	2421
Centco Architectural Metals	East Bridgewater	MA	F	508 456-1888	10408
Diamond Windows Doors Mfg Inc	Boston	MA	E	617 282-1688	8503
Harvey Industries Inc	Woburn	MA	E	781 935-7990	17197

DOORS: Fiberglass

Hexcel Corporation **(PA)**	Stamford	CT	E	203 969-0666	4213
Fiberglass Building Pdts Inc	Halifax	MA	G	847 650-3045	11318

DOORS: Folding, Plastic Or Plastic Coated Fabric

Albany International Corp **(PA)**	Rochester	NH	D	603 330-5850	19655
Flexi-Door Corporation	Epping	NH	G	603 679-2286	18099

DOORS: Garage, Overhead, Metal

American Overhead Ret Div Inc	Middletown	CT	G	860 876-4552	2171
E I J Inc	Tunbridge	VT	F	802 889-3432	22543

DOORS: Garage, Overhead, Wood

American Overhead Ret Div Inc	Middletown	CT	G	860 876-4552	2171
New England Standard Corp	Milford	CT	G	203 876-7733	2320
Ridgefield Overhead Door LLC	Ridgefield	CT	G	203 431-3667	3679

DOORS: Glass

Prestige Custom Mirror & Glass	Waltham	MA	F	781 647-0878	16177

DOORS: Rolling, Indl Building Or Warehouse, Metal

National Service Systems Inc	Stoughton	MA	G	781 344-6504	15609

DOORS: Wooden

Deschenes & Cooper Architectur	Pawcatuck	CT	G	860 599-2481	3434
Architectural Openings Inc	Somerville	MA	F	617 776-9223	15155
Baranowski Woodworking Co Inc	East Bridgewater	MA	G	508 690-1515	10407
Dixon Bros Millwork Inc	Abington	MA	G	781 261-9962	7323
J P Moriarty & Co Inc	Somerville	MA	G	617 628-3000	15187
Miller H C Wood Working Inc	Holliston	MA	G	508 429-4220	11586
Sb Development Corp	Acton	MA	G	978 263-2744	7384
Wright Architectural Mllwk Corp	Northampton	MA	E	413 586-3528	14027
Little Harbor Window Co Inc	Berwick	ME	E	207 698-1332	5710
Topsham Woodworking LLC	Topsham	ME	G	207 751-1032	7095
AP Dley Cstm Laminating Corp	Windham	NH	E	603 437-6666	20000
Procraft Corporation	New Boston	NH	F	603 487-2080	19296
H Hirschmann Ltd	West Rutland	VT	F	802 438-4447	22616
Jeld-Wen Inc	Ludlow	VT	D	802 228-2020	22064
Jeld-Wen Inc	North Springfield	VT	C	802 886-1728	22237
Woodstone Company Inc **(PA)**	Westminster	VT	F	802 722-9217	22632

DOWELS & DOWEL RODS

Saco Manufacturing & Wdwkg	Saco	ME	G	207 284-6613	6857

DOWNSPOUTS: Sheet Metal

Custom Seamless Gutters Inc	Pawtucket	RI	G	401 726-3137	20831

DRAFTING SVCS

Insource Design & Mfg Tech LLC	Merrimack	NH	G	603 718-8228	19007

DRAINAGE PRDTS: Concrete

Atlantic Pipe Corporation	Plainville	CT	D	860 747-5557	3466
R B L Holdings Inc	Coventry	RI	F	401 821-2200	20163

DRAINBOARDS, PLASTIC LAMINATED

R B L Holdings Inc	Coventry	RI	F	401 821-2200	20163

DRAPERIES & CURTAINS

Dominics Decorating Inc	Norwalk	CT	G	203 838-1827	3141
Tetrault & Sons Inc	Stafford Springs	CT	G	860 872-9187	4117
Threads of Evidence LLC	Shelton	CT	G	203 929-5209	3879
Yard Stick Decore	Bridgeport	CT	F	203 330-0360	508
Angies Work Room Inc	Attleboro	MA	F	508 761-5636	7705
Davids Drapery	Braintree	MA	G	781 849-9499	8999
Dra-Cor Industries Inc	Brockton	MA	E	508 580-3770	9140
Fall River Apparel Inc	Fall River	MA	G	508 677-1975	10694
Ksg Enterprises Inc	Peabody	MA	F	978 977-7357	14349
Quest Drape	Woburn	MA	G	781 859-0300	17278
Reliable Fabrics Inc	Everett	MA	E	617 387-5321	10626
Sam Kasten Handweaver LLC	Lenox	MA	G	413 637-8900	12103
Staceys Shade Shop Inc **(PA)**	Lynn	MA	G	781 595-0097	12540
United Curtain Co Inc **(PA)**	Avon	MA	F	508 588-4100	7900
Dirigo Stitching Inc	Skowhegan	ME	E	207 474-8421	6972
Gordons Window Decor Inc **(PA)**	Williston	VT	F	802 655-7777	22671

DRAPERIES & DRAPERY FABRICS, COTTON

Contract Decor Intl Inc	Brockton	MA	D	508 587-7000	9132
Kings Draperies Inc	Brockton	MA	G	508 230-0055	9159
Marjorie Royer Interiors Inc	Middleton	MA	G	978 774-0533	13095
Staceys Shade Shop Inc **(PA)**	Lynn	MA	G	781 595-0097	12540
Gordons Window Decor Inc **(PA)**	Williston	VT	F	802 655-7777	22671

DRAPERIES: Plastic & Textile, From Purchased Materials

Byron Lord Inc	Old Lyme	CT	G	203 287-9881	3315
Decorator Services Inc	Bridgeport	CT	E	203 384-8144	402
Thomas W Raftery Inc	Hartford	CT	E	860 278-9870	1879
Craft Interiors	Malden	MA	G	781 321-8695	12566
Drape It Inc	Waltham	MA	F	781 209-1912	16091
Huot Enterprises Inc	Ludlow	MA	G	413 589-7422	12468
Mohawk Shade & Blind Co Inc	Cambridge	MA	G	617 868-6000	9568
Sams Drapery Workroom Inc	Hyde Park	MA	F	617 364-9440	11878
J & R Langley Co Inc	Manchester	NH	F	603 622-9653	18847
Perfect Fit Industries LLC	Allenstown	NH	G	603 485-7161	17540
Marion Mfg Co	Providence	RI	F	401 331-4343	21060
Chrisandras Interiors Inc	Ludlow	VT	G	802 228-2075	22062

DRAPERY & UPHOLSTERY STORES: Curtains

Beverly Shade Shoppe	Beverly	MA	G	978 922-0374	8110

DRAPERY & UPHOLSTERY STORES: Draperies

Reliable Fabrics Inc	Everett	MA	E	617 387-5321	10626
Staceys Shade Shop Inc **(PA)**	Lynn	MA	G	781 595-0097	12540
Custom Window Decorators	Lewiston	ME	G	207 784-4113	6282
Marion Mfg Co	Providence	RI	F	401 331-4343	21060
Chrisandras Interiors Inc	Ludlow	VT	G	802 228-2075	22062

DRILLING MACHINERY & EQPT: Oil & Gas

Rmi Titanium Company LLC	Burlington	MA	F	781 272-5967	9330

DRILLING MACHINERY & EQPT: Water Well

Kyle Equipment Co Inc	Sterling	MA	G	978 422-8448	15541
Shannon Drilling	Machias	ME	G	207 255-6149	6395
Northeast Drill Supply	Greenville	NH	G	603 878-0998	18228

DRILLS & DRILLING EQPT: Mining

Company	CITY	ST	EMP	PHONE	ENTRY #
Numa Tool Company **(PA)**	Thompson	CT	D	860 923-9551	4537
P2 Science Inc	Woodbridge	CT	G	203 821-7457	5475

DRINK MIXES, NONALCOHOLIC: Cocktail

Company	CITY	ST	EMP	PHONE	ENTRY #
Brady Enterprises Inc **(PA)**	East Weymouth	MA	D	781 682-6280	10538
Diageo North America Inc	Mansfield	MA	G	508 324-9800	12628
Stirrings LLC	Fall River	MA	E	508 324-9800	10764

DRINKING PLACES: Alcoholic Beverages

Company	CITY	ST	EMP	PHONE	ENTRY #
Amherst Brewing Co Inc	Amherst	MA	E	413 253-4400	7511
Phillips Candy House Inc	Boston	MA	E	617 282-2090	8778
Sunday River Brewing Co Inc	Boston	MA	D	207 824-4253	8869
Ashleigh Inc **(PA)**	Kennebunk	ME	E	207 967-4311	6228

DRINKING PLACES: Bars & Lounges

Company	CITY	ST	EMP	PHONE	ENTRY #
Swagnificent Ent LLC	Bridgeport	CT	G	203 449-0124	498

DRINKING PLACES: Tavern

Company	CITY	ST	EMP	PHONE	ENTRY #
Chris Martin **(PA)**	Avon	MA	G	508 580-0069	7882
Hobbs Tavern & Brewing Co LLC	West Ossipee	NH	E	603 539-2000	19966

DRINKING WATER COOLERS WHOLESALERS: Mechanical

Company	CITY	ST	EMP	PHONE	ENTRY #
United Fbrcnts Strainrite Corp **(HQ)**	Auburn	ME	D	207 376-1600	5600

DRIVE SHAFTS

Company	CITY	ST	EMP	PHONE	ENTRY #
Capeway Bearing & Machine Inc	Plymouth	MA	G	508 747-2800	14548
Jon Shafts & Stuff	Manchester	NH	G	603 518-5033	18851
Rhode Island Driveshaft Sup Co	Warwick	RI	G	401 941-0210	21412

DRONES: Target, Used By Ships, Metal

Company	CITY	ST	EMP	PHONE	ENTRY #
Lockheed Martin Sippican Inc **(HQ)**	Marion	MA	B	508 748-3399	12699

DRUG TESTING KITS: Blood & Urine

Company	CITY	ST	EMP	PHONE	ENTRY #
Onsite Drug Testing Neng	Concord	NH	G	603 226-3858	17921

DRUGS & DRUG PROPRIETARIES, WHOL: Biologicals/Allied Prdts

Company	CITY	ST	EMP	PHONE	ENTRY #
McWilliams Inc	North Berwick	ME	G	207 676-7639	6509
O E M Concepts **(HQ)**	Saco	ME	G	207 283-6500	6854

DRUGS & DRUG PROPRIETARIES, WHOLESALE

Company	CITY	ST	EMP	PHONE	ENTRY #
Genzyme Corporation **(DH)**	Cambridge	MA	A	617 252-7500	9489
Sea-Band International Inc	Newport	RI	G	401 841-5900	20679

DRUGS & DRUG PROPRIETARIES, WHOLESALE: Antiseptics

Company	CITY	ST	EMP	PHONE	ENTRY #
Beiersdorf Inc	Norwalk	CT	B	203 854-8000	3110
Beiersdorf North America Inc **(DH)**	Wilton	CT	F	203 563-5800	5277

DRUGS & DRUG PROPRIETARIES, WHOLESALE: Medicinals/Botanicals

Company	CITY	ST	EMP	PHONE	ENTRY #
GE Healthcare Inc **(DH)**	Marlborough	MA	B	800 526-3593	12759

DRUGS & DRUG PROPRIETARIES, WHOLESALE: Pharmaceuticals

Company	CITY	ST	EMP	PHONE	ENTRY #
Frederick Purdue Company Inc **(PA)**	Stamford	CT	B	203 588-8000	4197
Pharmaceutical RES Assoc Inc **(HQ)**	Stamford	CT	G	203 588-8000	4284
PRA Holdings Inc	Stamford	CT	G	203 853-0123	4290
Purdue Pharma LP **(PA)**	Stamford	CT	B	203 588-8000	4294
Sheffield Pharmaceuticals LLC **(PA)**	New London	CT	C	860 442-4451	2779
Beigene Usa Inc **(HQ)**	Cambridge	MA	G	781 801-1887	9407
Central Admxture Phrm Svcs Inc	Woburn	MA	E	781 376-0032	17142
MBL International Corporation **(DH)**	Woburn	MA	F	781 939-6964	17225
Sobi Inc	Waltham	MA	E	610 228-2040	16196
Windgap Medical Inc	Watertown	MA	G	617 440-3311	16330
Surplus Solutions LLC	Woonsocket	RI	F	401 526-0055	21584

DRUGS ACTING ON THE CENTRAL NERVOUS SYSTEM & SENSE ORGANS

Company	CITY	ST	EMP	PHONE	ENTRY #
Biohaven Phrm Holdg Co Ltd	New Haven	CT	E	203 404-0410	2667
Neurohydrate LLC	Bridgeport	CT	G	203 799-7900	455
Alseres Pharmaceuticals Inc	Auburndale	MA	G	508 497-2360	7855
Amorsa Therapeutics Inc	Southborough	MA	G	508 571-8240	15342
Cerevance Inc **(PA)**	Boston	MA	G	408 220-5722	8465
Civitas Therapeutics Inc	Chelsea	MA	D	617 884-3004	9949
Eyemax LLC	Weston	MA	G	781 424-9281	16825
Ptc Therapeutics Gt Inc	Cambridge	MA	G	781 799-9179	9619
Rhenovia Incorporated	Cambridge	MA	G	310 382-4079	9632
Shire-NPS Pharmaceuticals Inc **(DH)**	Lexington	MA	A	617 349-0200	12274

DRUGS: Parasitic & Infective Disease Affecting

Company	CITY	ST	EMP	PHONE	ENTRY #
Idenix Pharmaceuticals Inc **(HQ)**	Cambridge	MA	E	617 995-9800	9510
Amgen Inc	West Greenwich	RI	D	401 392-1200	21452

DRUMS: Shipping, Metal

Company	CITY	ST	EMP	PHONE	ENTRY #
Mobile Mini Inc	Suffield	CT	E	860 668-1888	4465
John H Collins & Son Co	Pawtucket	RI	G	401 722-0775	20849

DRYCLEANING & LAUNDRY SVCS: Commercial & Family

Company	CITY	ST	EMP	PHONE	ENTRY #
Sally Conant	Orange	CT	F	203 878-3005	3383

DRYCLEANING EQPT & SPLYS: Commercial

Company	CITY	ST	EMP	PHONE	ENTRY #
Rema Dri-Vac Corp	Norwalk	CT	F	203 847-2464	3231

DRYERS & REDRYERS: Indl

Company	CITY	ST	EMP	PHONE	ENTRY #
Dri-Air Industries Inc	East Windsor	CT	E	860 627-5110	1282
Valmet Inc	Biddeford	ME	C	207 282-1521	5767

DUCTING: Metal Plate

Company	CITY	ST	EMP	PHONE	ENTRY #
L & L Mechanical LLC	Goshen	CT	F	860 491-4007	1585
New Haven Sheet Metal Co	New Haven	CT	G	203 468-0341	2717

DUCTING: Plastic

Company	CITY	ST	EMP	PHONE	ENTRY #
Siftex Equipment Company	South Windsor	CT	E	860 289-8779	4009

DUCTS: Sheet Metal

Company	CITY	ST	EMP	PHONE	ENTRY #
General Sheet Metal Works Inc	Bridgeport	CT	F	203 333-6111	419
Manufacturers Service Co Inc	Woodbridge	CT	G	203 389-9595	5471
Brideau Shtmtl & Fabrication	Leominster	MA	F	978 537-3372	12119
Carl Fisher Co Inc	Springfield	MA	E	413 736-3661	15458
Duc-Pac Corporation	East Longmeadow	MA	E	413 525-3302	10474
Integrated Dynamic Metals Corp	Marlborough	MA	F	508 624-7271	12777
Belanger Sheet Metal Inc	Skowhegan	ME	G	207 474-8990	6969
Tylers Sheet Metal Shop Inc	Buxton	ME	G	207 929-6912	5862
Spiral Air Manufacturing Inc	Derry	NH	G	603 624-6647	17997

DUMPSTERS: Garbage

Company	CITY	ST	EMP	PHONE	ENTRY #
All Phase Dumpsters LLC	Bethel	CT	G	203 778-9104	127
CT Dumpster LLC	Milford	CT	G	203 521-0779	2271
Same Day Dumpsters LLC	New Haven	CT	G	203 676-1219	2733
All In One Dumpster Service	Millbury	MA	G	508 735-8979	13155
Big Dog Disposal Inc	Seekonk	MA	G	508 695-9539	15019
Haulaway Dumpster Disposal	Rockland	MA	G	781 871-1234	14806
Mr Dumpster	Boston	MA	G	781 233-3006	8715
Usmdumpsters	Middleboro	MA	G	774 218-2822	13080
Bear Pond Dumpster LLC	Turner	ME	G	207 224-0337	7105
Ne Dumpster	Nashua	NH	G	603 438-6402	19214
Recycling Mechanical Neng LLC	Allenstown	NH	F	603 268-8028	17541

DURABLE GOODS WHOLESALERS, NEC

Company	CITY	ST	EMP	PHONE	ENTRY #
Pbuttri LLC	Pawtucket	RI	G	401 996-5583	20877

DUST OR FUME COLLECTING EQPT: Indl

Company	CITY	ST	EMP	PHONE	ENTRY #
Hendrick Manufacturing Corp **(PA)**	Salem	MA	F	781 631-4400	14919
Toollab Inc	West Warwick	RI	G	401 461-2110	21511

DYEING & FINISHING: Wool Or Similar Fibers

Company	CITY	ST	EMP	PHONE	ENTRY #
Custom Banner & Graphics LLC	Rochester	NH	G	603 332-2067	19666

DYES & PIGMENTS: Organic

Company	CITY	ST	EMP	PHONE	ENTRY #
Primary Colors Inc	North Grafton	MA	E	508 839-3202	13964
Rowley Biochemical Institute	Danvers	MA	G	978 739-4883	10253
U S Synthetics Corp	Fitchburg	MA	G	978 345-0176	10858
Walrus Enterprises LLC	Northampton	MA	G	413 387-4387	14026
Clariant Plas Coatings USA LLC	Lewiston	ME	E	207 784-0733	6280
Teknor Color Company	Pawtucket	RI	D	401 725-8000	20904

DYES: Synthetic Organic

Company	CITY	ST	EMP	PHONE	ENTRY #
Polymer Solutions Inc	Pawtucket	RI	G	401 423-1638	20881

DYNAMOMETERS

Company	CITY	ST	EMP	PHONE	ENTRY #
Kahn Industries Inc	Wethersfield	CT	E	860 529-8643	5252

EATING PLACES

Company	CITY	ST	EMP	PHONE	ENTRY #
Baltasar & Sons Inc	Naugatuck	CT	G	203 723-0425	2462
Fine Food Services Inc	Groton	CT	E	860 445-5276	1676
Sharpe Hill Vineyard Inc	Pomfret	CT	E	860 974-3549	3554
Southport Brewing Co	Milford	CT	E	203 874-2337	2365
Amherst Brewing Co Inc	Amherst	MA	E	413 253-4400	7511
Cambridge Brewing Co Inc	Cambridge	MA	E	617 494-1994	9426
Dads	Charlton	MA	G	508 248-9774	9848
G H Bent Company	Milton	MA	E	617 322-9287	13192
Gerard Farms Inc	Framingham	MA	G	781 858-1013	10959
Korner Bagel Partnership	Seekonk	MA	E	508 336-5204	15025
Lolas Italian Harvest LLC	Natick	MA	G	508 651-0524	13265
Neovii Biotech Na Inc	Lexington	MA	F	781 966-3830	12247
Nolas Fresh Foods LLC	Roslindale	MA	G	617 283-2644	14840
Paramount South Boston	Boston	MA	G	617 269-9999	8765
Phillips Candy House Inc	Boston	MA	E	617 282-2090	8778
Piantedosi Baking Co Inc **(PA)**	Malden	MA	C	781 321-3400	12590
Plymouth Bay Winery	Plymouth	MA	G	508 746-2100	14575
Quarterly Review of Wines	Quincy	MA	E	781 721-0525	14650
Slesar Bros Brewing Co Inc	Salem	MA	E	978 745-2337	14943
Sunday River Brewing Co Inc	Boston	MA	D	207 824-4253	8869
Tamboo Bistro	Brockton	MA	G	508 584-8585	9181
Ashleigh Inc **(PA)**	Kennebunk	ME	E	207 967-4311	6228
Bennington Potters Inc **(PA)**	Bennington	VT	E	800 205-8033	21664
Lost Nation Brewing LLC	Morrisville	VT	F	802 851-8041	22171
Vermont Pub Brewry Burlington	Burlington	VT	D	802 865-0500	21816

ECCLESIASTICAL WARE, PLATED, ALL METALS

Company	CITY	ST	EMP	PHONE	ENTRY #
Alviti Creations Inc	Attleboro	MA	G	508 222-4030	7703

EDITING SVCS

Company	CITY	ST	EMP	PHONE	ENTRY #
Nsight Inc	Andover	MA	E	781 273-6300	7579

EDITING SVCS: Motion Picture Production

Company	CITY	ST	EMP	PHONE	ENTRY #
Community of Jesus Inc **(PA)**	Orleans	MA	D	508 255-1094	14232
Paraclete Press Inc	Brewster	MA	G	508 255-4685	9056

EDUCATIONAL SVCS

Company	CITY	ST	EMP	PHONE	ENTRY #
Executive Force Protection LLC	Cambridge	MA	F	617 470-9230	9476
Willett Institute of Finance	Reading	MA	G	617 247-3030	14744
Mathemtics Problem Solving LLC	Portland	ME	G	207 772-2846	6692
Center For Northern Woodlands	Lyme	NH	G	802 439-6292	18753
Nippon American Limited	East Greenwich	RI	F	401 885-7353	20374
Learning Materials Workshop	Burlington	VT	G	802 862-0112	21793

EFFERVESCENT SALTS

	CITY	ST	EMP	PHONE	ENTRY #
Tower Laboratories Ltd **(PA)**	Centerbrook	CT	D	860 767-2127	704

ELASTIC BRAID & NARROW WOVEN FABRICS

	CITY	ST	EMP	PHONE	ENTRY #
Dial Fabrics Co Inc	Taunton	MA	E	508 822-5333	15742
RI Knitting Co Inc	Taunton	MA	E	508 822-5333	15780
United Stretch Design Corp	Hudson	MA	E	978 562-7781	11824
North East Knitting Inc	Pawtucket	RI	C	401 727-0500	20869
Providence Braid Company	Pawtucket	RI	E	401 722-2120	20885

ELASTOMERS

	CITY	ST	EMP	PHONE	ENTRY #
Origyn Inc	Boston	MA	G	781 888-8834	8759
TAC Life Systems LLC	Walpole	MA	G	617 719-8797	16013

ELECTRIC MOTOR & GENERATOR AUXILIARY PARTS

	CITY	ST	EMP	PHONE	ENTRY #
ACS Group Inc	Everett	MA	F	617 381-0822	10600

ELECTRIC MOTOR REPAIR SVCS

	CITY	ST	EMP	PHONE	ENTRY #
Aparos Electric Motor Service	Southington	CT	G	860 276-2044	4039
Central Electric Inc	Dayville	CT	G	860 774-3054	1041
Cudzilo Enterprises Inc	Bethel	CT	G	203 748-4694	139
Electric Enterprise Inc	Stratford	CT	F	203 378-7311	4410
Palmers Elc Mtrs & Pumps Inc	Norwalk	CT	G	203 348-7378	3214
Precision Devices Inc **(PA)**	Wallingford	CT	F	203 265-9308	4788
Tibbys Electric Motor Service	Bethel	CT	G	203 748-4694	183
Total Control Inc	Wallingford	CT	G	203 269-4749	4822
Traver Electric Motor Co Inc	Waterbury	CT	E	203 753-5103	4966
Bay State Electric Motor Co	Methuen	MA	G	978 686-7089	13012
Delta Elc Mtr Repr Sls & Svc	Medford	MA	G	781 395-0551	12930
First Electric Motor Svc Inc	Woburn	MA	E	781 491-1100	17181
Hancock Electric Mtr Svcs Inc	Quincy	MA	G	617 472-5789	14631
Kalman Electric Motors Inc	Stoughton	MA	G	781 341-4900	15600
Morse Electric Motors Co Inc	Gardner	MA	G	978 632-3733	11120
Reliance Electric Service	Holyoke	MA	G	413 533-3557	11651
Shepard & Parker Inc	Fitchburg	MA	G	978 343-3907	10852
Stearns Perry & Smith Co Inc	Quincy	MA	G	617 423-4775	14659
AC Electric Corp	Bangor	ME	F	207 945-9487	5628
Moir Company Inc	Denmark	ME	F	207 452-2000	5951
Prime Electric Motors	Gorham	ME	F	207 591-7800	6128
Timken Motor & Crane Svcs LLC	Portland	ME	F	207 699-2501	6740
Algers Leo NH Elc Mtrs	Laconia	NH	G	603 524-3729	18555
Chase Electric Motors LLC	Hooksett	NH	G	603 669-2565	18346
Lawrence Fay	Manchester	NH	G	603 668-3811	18862
Pioneer Motors and Drives Inc	South Burlington	VT	E	802 651-0114	22458

ELECTRIC POWER GENERATION: Fossil Fuel

	CITY	ST	EMP	PHONE	ENTRY #
GE Steam Power Inc **(HQ)**	Windsor	CT	A	866 257-8664	5336

ELECTRIC POWER, COGENERATED

	CITY	ST	EMP	PHONE	ENTRY #
GE Steam Power Inc **(HQ)**	Windsor	CT	A	866 257-8664	5336

ELECTRIC SVCS, NEC: Power Generation

	CITY	ST	EMP	PHONE	ENTRY #
Tecomet Inc	Woburn	MA	D	781 782-6400	17305
Simon Pearce US Inc **(PA)**	Windsor	VT	C	802 674-6280	22714

ELECTRIC TOOL REPAIR SVCS

	CITY	ST	EMP	PHONE	ENTRY #
Air Tool Sales & Service Co **(PA)**	Unionville	CT	G	860 673-2714	4652
Kalman Electric Motors Inc	Stoughton	MA	G	781 341-4900	15600

ELECTRICAL APPARATUS & EQPT WHOLESALERS

	CITY	ST	EMP	PHONE	ENTRY #
Asea Brown Boveri Inc **(DH)**	Norwalk	CT	G	203 750-2200	3105
EC Holdings Inc	Norwalk	CT	G	203 846-1651	3147
Lighting Edge Inc	Essex	CT	G	860 767-8968	1402
Pathway Lighting Products Inc	Old Saybrook	CT	D	860 388-6881	3347
Precision Devices Inc **(PA)**	Wallingford	CT	F	203 265-9308	4788
Deerfield Corporation	Framingham	MA	G	508 877-0143	10941
Epropelled Inc **(PA)**	Lowell	MA	G	978 703-1350	12369
Period Lighting Fixtures Inc	Clarksburg	MA	F	413 664-7141	10074
Phoenix Electric Corp	Canton	MA	E	781 821-0200	9767
Polytec Inc	Hudson	MA	F	508 417-1040	11803
Schneider Electric Usa Inc **(DH)**	Boston	MA	A	978 975-9600	8839
Schneider Electric Usa Inc	Foxboro	MA	G	508 549-3385	10903
Soitec Usa Inc **(HQ)**	Gloucester	MA	F	978 531-2222	11210
Enercon **(PA)**	Gray	ME	C	207 657-7000	6139
Enercon	Auburn	ME	E	207 657-7001	5562
Burndy Americas Inc **(HQ)**	Manchester	NH	G	603 647-5000	18791
Burndy Americas Intl Holdg LLC	Manchester	NH	A	603 647-5000	18792
Hubbell Incorporated	Londonderry	NH	D	800 346-4175	18703
Sun Ray Technologies Inc	Killington	VT	G	802 422-8680	22056

ELECTRICAL APPLIANCES, TELEVISIONS & RADIOS WHOLESALERS

	CITY	ST	EMP	PHONE	ENTRY #
Conair Corporation	Torrington	CT	D	800 492-7464	4572
Stonewall Kitchen LLC **(PA)**	York	ME	C	207 351-2713	7316

ELECTRICAL CURRENT CARRYING WIRING DEVICES

	CITY	ST	EMP	PHONE	ENTRY #
ABB Enterprise Software Inc	Plainville	CT	A	860 747-7111	3461
Allied Controls Inc	Stamford	CT	F	860 628-8443	4134
American Specialty Pdts LLC	Vernon	CT	G	860 871-2279	4662
Bead Industries Inc **(PA)**	Milford	CT	E	203 301-0270	2251
Burndy LLC	Bethel	CT	D	203 792-1115	134
Dicon Connections Inc	North Branford	CT	E	203 481-8080	2961
Eaton Aerospace LLC	Bethel	CT	E	203 796-6000	150
Eaton Corporation	Bethel	CT	E	203 796-6000	151
Ek-Ris Cable Company Inc	New Britain	CT	E	860 223-4327	2530
Everlast Products LLC	Cheshire	CT	G	203 250-7111	731
Faria Beede Instruments Inc	North Stonington	CT	C	860 848-9271	3074
Gordon Products Incorporated	Brookfield	CT	E	203 775-4501	646
Hubbell Incorporated Delaware	Shelton	CT	C	475 882-4800	3814
Hubbell Incorporated Delaware **(HQ)**	Shelton	CT	D	475 882-4000	3815
Hubbell Wiring Device	Milford	CT	F	203 882-4800	2297
Legrand Holding Inc **(DH)**	West Hartford	CT	E	860 233-6251	5080
Lex Products LLC **(PA)**	Shelton	CT	C	203 363-3738	3828
Old Cambridge Products Corp	Bloomfield	CT	G	860 243-1761	247
Old Ni Incorporated	Stamford	CT	G	203 327-7300	4267
Oslo Switch Inc	Cheshire	CT	E	203 272-2794	750
Ripley Tools LLC **(PA)**	Cromwell	CT	E	860 635-2200	859
Siemon Company	Watertown	CT	E	860 945-4218	5025
Spectrum Associates Inc	Milford	CT	F	203 878-4618	2367
Thomas Products Ltd	Southington	CT	E	860 621-9101	4085
Times Wire and Cable Company **(HQ)**	Wallingford	CT	G	203 949-8400	4820
United Electric Controls Co	Milford	CT	D	203 877-2795	2377
Wiremold Company **(DH)**	West Hartford	CT	A	860 233-6251	5104
World Cord Sets Inc	Enfield	CT	G	860 763-2100	1391
Anderson Power Products Inc **(HQ)**	Sterling	MA	D	978 422-3600	15535
Anomet Products Inc	Shrewsbury	MA	E	508 842-0174	15102
Artisan Industries Inc	Stoughton	MA	D	781 893-6800	15581
C & K Components LLC **(PA)**	Waltham	MA	D	617 969-3700	16056
C S I Keyboards Inc	Peabody	MA	E	978 532-8181	14318
Caton Connector Corp	Kingston	MA	E	781 585-4315	11955
Component Sources Intl	Westborough	MA	F	508 986-2300	16607
Cooper Interconnect Inc	Chelsea	MA	D	617 389-7080	9950
Cordmaster Engineering Co Inc	North Adams	MA	E	413 664-9371	13671
Dynawave Incorporated	Haverhill	MA	D	978 469-0555	11429
Electro Switch Corp	Weymouth	MA	C	781 607-3306	16887
Electroweave Inc	Worcester	MA	G	508 752-8932	17371
First Electronics Corporation	Dorchester	MA	D	617 288-2430	10342
General Electric Company	Newton	MA	C	617 608-6008	13595
General Wire Products Inc	Worcester	MA	E	508 752-8260	17381
Ideal Industries Inc	Sterling	MA	C	978 422-3600	15540
Intersense Incorporated	Billerica	MA	E	781 541-6330	8258
Kidde-Fenwal Inc **(HQ)**	Ashland	MA	A	508 881-2000	7663
Madison Cable Corporation	Worcester	MA	C	508 752-2884	17410
Mini-Systems Inc	Plainville	MA	E	508 695-2000	14528
Osram Sylvania Inc **(HQ)**	Wilmington	MA	A	978 570-3000	17036
Phoenix Electric Corp	Canton	MA	E	781 821-0200	9767
Quabbin Wire & Cable Co Inc **(PA)**	Ware	MA	D	413 967-6281	16236
San-Tron Inc **(PA)**	Ipswich	MA	D	978 356-1585	11936
Schott North America Inc	Southbridge	MA	D	508 765-7450	15402
Segue Manufacturing Svcs LLC	Lowell	MA	D	978 970-1200	12432
Te Connectivity Corporation	Worcester	MA	B	717 592-4299	17486
Texas Instruments Incorporated	Attleboro	MA	E	508 236-3800	7802
Tru Technologies Inc	Peabody	MA	C	978 532-0775	14379
W J Roberts Co Inc	Saugus	MA	E	781 233-8176	15002
Bcr Technology Center	Scarborough	ME	G	207 885-9700	6910
General Electric Company	Auburn	ME	B	207 786-5100	5567
Burndy Americas Inc **(HQ)**	Manchester	NH	G	603 647-5000	18791
Burndy Americas Intl Holdg LLC	Manchester	NH	A	603 647-5000	18792
Burndy LLC	Lincoln	NH	C	603 745-8114	18645
Burndy LLC	Littleton	NH	C	603 444-6781	18655
Fci Electrical-Brundy Products	Littleton	NH	G	603 444-6781	18659
Jr Hinds Const Serv	Tilton	NH	G	603 496-2344	19907
O Brien D G Inc	Seabrook	NH	F	603 474-5571	19812
Osram Sylvania Inc	Exeter	NH	D	603 772-4331	18127
Parker & Harper Companies Inc **(PA)**	Raymond	NH	D	603 895-4761	19643
Q A Technology Company Inc	Hampton	NH	D	603 926-1193	18269
Spire Technology Solutions LLC	Nashua	NH	F	603 594-0005	19264
Teledyne Instruments Inc	Portsmouth	NH	C	603 474-5571	19624
Ametek Scp Inc **(HQ)**	Westerly	RI	D	401 596-6658	21515
Leviton Manufacturing Co Inc	Providence	RI	F	401 273-4875	21053
Precision Trned Cmponents Corp	Smithfield	RI	D	401 232-3377	21244
Cooper Lighting Inc	Essex Junction	VT	F	800 767-3674	21937
Duelmark Aerospace Corporation	Cambridge	VT	G	802 644-2603	21823

ELECTRICAL DISCHARGE MACHINING, EDM

	CITY	ST	EMP	PHONE	ENTRY #
Arcade Technology LLC	Bridgeport	CT	E	203 366-3871	376
Cgl Inc	Watertown	CT	F	860 945-6166	5002
Michaud Tool Co Inc	Terryville	CT	G	860 582-6785	4486
Pw Precision Machine LLC	Higganum	CT	G	203 889-8615	1905
Quality Wire Edm Inc	Bristol	CT	G	860 583-9867	600
Wire Tech LLC	Watertown	CT	G	860 945-9473	5036
Tektron Inc	Topsfield	MA	F	978 887-0091	15866
Hagan Design and Machine Inc	Newmarket	NH	G	603 292-1101	19335
Newport Tool & Die Inc	Middletown	RI	F	401 847-6711	20628

ELECTRICAL EQPT & SPLYS

	CITY	ST	EMP	PHONE	ENTRY #
Alent Inc	Waterbury	CT	D	203 575-5727	4838
Alent USA Holding Inc	Waterbury	CT	B	203 575-5727	4839
Brookfield Industries Inc	Thomaston	CT	E	860 283-6211	4500
Carey Manufacturing Co Inc **(PA)**	Cromwell	CT	E	860 829-1803	850
Carey Manufacturing Co Inc	Cromwell	CT	E	860 829-1803	851
DC & D Inc	Broad Brook	CT	G	860 623-2941	628
E-J Electric T & D LLC	Wallingford	CT	D	203 626-9625	4737
Eagle Electric Service LLC	Bethlehem	CT	F	860 868-9898	194
Eastern Electric Cnstr Co	Harwinton	CT	G	860 485-1100	1889
Eastside Electric Inc	Harwinton	CT	F	860 485-0700	1890
Electro Mech Specialists LLC	Bozrah	CT	G	860 887-2613	280
Electrodes Incorporated	Milford	CT	E	203 878-7400	2284
Evse Llc	Enfield	CT	G	860 745-2433	1361
Fuelcell Energy Inc	Torrington	CT	E	860 496-1111	4579
Hubbell Incorporated **(PA)**	Shelton	CT	D	475 882-4000	3813
Iemct	Milford	CT	G	203 683-4382	2300
Jamieson Laser LLC	Litchfield	CT	G	860 482-3375	1950

	CITY	ST	EMP	PHONE	ENTRY #
Jared Manufacturing Co Inc	Norwalk	CT	F	203 846-1732	3180
Newco Condenser Inc	Shelton	CT	G	475 882-4000	3839
Presco Incorporated	Woodbridge	CT	F	203 397-8722	5477
Trine Access Technology Inc	Bethel	CT	F	203 730-1756	185
United Technologies Corp **(PA)**	Farmington	CT	B	860 728-7000	1522
Accutronics Inc	Chelmsford	MA	E	978 250-9144	9866
Asco Power Technologies LP	Marlborough	MA	G	508 624-0466	12720
Azz Inc	Medway	MA	E	774 854-0700	12956
Cordmaster Engineering Co Inc	North Adams	MA	E	413 664-9371	13671
Cortron Inc	Lowell	MA	E	978 975-5445	12362
Degreasing Devices Co	Southbridge	MA	G	508 765-0045	15379
Diamond Solar Group LLC	Topsfield	MA	E	978 808-9288	15856
Diamond-Roltran LLC	Littleton	MA	F	978 486-0039	12302
Digital Vdeo Cmmunications Inc	Woburn	MA	G	781 932-6882	17168
Distribution & Control Product	Malden	MA	G	781 324-0070	12568
Electrical Safety Products LLC	Woburn	MA	G	781 249-5007	17174
Exatel Visual Systems Inc	Burlington	MA	F	781 221-7400	9273
Excel Dryer Inc	East Longmeadow	MA	E	413 525-4531	10475
GE Infrastructure Sensing LLC **(DH)**	Billerica	MA	A	978 437-1000	8249
Giner Elx Inc	Auburndale	MA	F	781 392-0300	7862
Hardric Laboratories Inc	North Chelmsford	MA	E	978 251-1702	13895
Hutchinson Arospc & Indust Inc	Hopkinton	MA	E	508 417-7000	11720
Living Power Systems Inc	Cambridge	MA	G	617 496-8328	9539
Lumina Power Inc	Haverhill	MA	E	978 241-8260	11450
Markarian Electric LLC	Watertown	MA	G	617 393-9700	16297
Matec Instrument Companies Inc **(PA)**	Northborough	MA	E	508 393-0155	14038
Mc10 Inc	Lexington	MA	E	617 234-4448	12242
Meddevice Concepts LLC	Edgartown	MA	G	617 834-7420	10586
Mettler-Toledo Process Analyti	Billerica	MA	D	781 301-8800	8265
Nextek Inc	Westford	MA	E	978 577-6214	16781
Optowares Incorporated	Woburn	MA	F	781 427-7106	17251
Photonwares Corporation **(PA)**	Woburn	MA	G	781 935-1200	17263
Polar Controls Inc	Shirley	MA	G	978 425-2233	15092
Precision Dynamics Corporation	Billerica	MA	D	800 528-8005	8276
Product Resources LLC	Newburyport	MA	E	978 524-8500	13523
Schneider Automation Inc	Andover	MA	D	978 975-9600	7602
Seica Inc **(PA)**	Haverhill	MA	G	603 890-6002	11471
Sluggo-Ox Corporation	Franklin	MA	G	508 726-8221	11081
Socomec Inc **(DH)**	Watertown	MA	F	617 245-0447	16317
Spirig Advanced Tech Incies	Springfield	MA	G	413 788-6191	15508
Static Clean International	North Billerica	MA	F	781 229-7799	13870
Stellar Industries Corp	Millbury	MA	E	508 865-1668	13177
Stoneridge Inc	Canton	MA	B	781 830-0340	9787
Tel Epion Inc	Billerica	MA	E	978 436-2300	8302
Teledyne Instruments Inc	North Falmouth	MA	E	508 548-2077	13957
Urquhart Family LLC	Gardner	MA	G	978 632-3600	11132
W J Roberts Co Inc	Saugus	MA	E	781 233-8176	15002
Whyte Electric LLC	Braintree	MA	G	781 348-6239	9050
Zero Balla	Lowell	MA	G	978 735-2015	12451
Eami Inc	Biddeford	ME	F	207 283-3001	5730
Electrotech Inc	Rockland	ME	F	207 596-0556	6791
Enercon **(PA)**	Gray	ME	C	207 657-7000	6139
Kritzer Industries Inc	Scarborough	ME	F	207 883-4141	6930
Waughs Mountainview Elec	Mexico	ME	F	207 545-2421	6430
Albert Langin	Pelham	NH	G	603 635-3560	19426
Auger Electric LLC	Rochester	NH	G	603 335-5633	19661
Auto Electric Service LLC	Brentwood	NH	G	603 642-5990	17746
Beckwood Services Inc	Plaistow	NH	D	603 382-3840	19508
Brailsford & Company Inc	Antrim	NH	E	603 588-2880	17593
Burns Industries Incorporated	Hollis	NH	G	603 881-8336	18327
Electronics Aid Inc	Marlborough	NH	G	603 876-4161	18959
On Board Solutions LLC	Portsmouth	NH	F	603 373-6500	19603
Spinnaker Contract Mfg Inc	Tilton	NH	D	603 286-4366	19912
Teledyne Instruments Inc	Portsmouth	NH	C	603 474-5571	19624
Warner Power Acquisition LLC **(HQ)**	Warner	NH	C	603 456-3111	19930
Wilcox Industries Corp **(PA)**	Newington	NH	C	603 431-1331	19329
Bear Hydraulics Inc	Warwick	RI	G	401 732-5832	21335
Endiprev Usa LLC	Providence	RI	D	401 519-3600	21006
Instantron Co Inc	Riverside	RI	G	401 433-6800	21170
Newport Electric Corporation	Portsmouth	RI	F	401 293-0527	20930
Nordson Efd LLC **(HQ)**	East Providence	RI	C	401 431-7000	20435
Ritec Inc	Warwick	RI	F	401 738-3660	21413
Ask-Inttag LLC	Essex Junction	VT	E	802 288-7210	21929
Macdermid Incorporated	Springfield	VT	F	802 885-8089	22507
Omni Measurement Systems Inc	Colchester	VT	E	802 497-2253	21875

ELECTRICAL EQPT FOR ENGINES

	CITY	ST	EMP	PHONE	ENTRY #
All Tech Auto/Truck Electric	Danbury	CT	G	203 790-8990	868
Beede Electrical Instr Co Inc	North Stonington	CT	C	603 753-6362	3071
Electrocraft New Hampshire Inc **(DH)**	Dover	NH	E	603 742-3330	18021
Rickss Motorsport Electrics	Hampstead	NH	G	603 329-9901	18249

ELECTRICAL EQPT REPAIR & MAINTENANCE

	CITY	ST	EMP	PHONE	ENTRY #
Conair Corporation	Torrington	CT	D	800 492-7464	4572
Integrated Packg Systems Inc	East Windsor	CT	G	860 623-2623	1287
Genelec Inc	Natick	MA	F	508 652-0900	13257
J F OMalley Welding Co	Worcester	MA	G	508 791-8671	17395
Rl Controls LLC	Woburn	MA	E	781 932-3349	17286
Ersa Inc	Westerly	RI	E	401 348-4000	21524

ELECTRICAL EQPT REPAIR SVCS: High Voltage

	CITY	ST	EMP	PHONE	ENTRY #
Wasik Associates Inc	Dracut	MA	F	978 454-9787	10371

ELECTRICAL EQPT: Automotive, NEC

	CITY	ST	EMP	PHONE	ENTRY #
West End Auto Parts	North Branford	CT	G	203 453-9009	2984
Jnc Rebuilders Inc	Ipswich	MA	G	978 356-2996	11925
Mobile Specialties	Lawrence	MA	G	978 416-0107	12059

	CITY	ST	EMP	PHONE	ENTRY #
Taylor Rental Center	East Longmeadow	MA	G	413 525-2576	10496
Veoneer Roadscape Auto Inc	Lowell	MA	G	978 656-2500	12444
Veoneer Roadscape Auto Inc **(DH)**	Lowell	MA	G	978 656-2500	12445
Veoneer Us Inc	Lowell	MA	C	978 674-6500	12446
Hubbell Incorporated	Manchester	NH	C	603 647-5000	18838
Kinne Electric Service Company	Manchester	NH	G	603 622-0441	18856
Antaya Inc	Warwick	RI	E	401 941-7050	21324
Antaya Technologies Corp	Warwick	RI	C	401 921-3197	21325
Wicor Americas Inc **(HQ)**	Saint Johnsbury	VT	F	802 751-3404	22397

ELECTRICAL EQPT: Household

	CITY	ST	EMP	PHONE	ENTRY #
Abisee Inc	Acton	MA	F	978 637-2900	7333

ELECTRICAL GOODS, WHOL: Antennas, Receiving/Satellite Dishes

	CITY	ST	EMP	PHONE	ENTRY #
Big Pond Wireless LLC	North Reading	MA	G	781 593-2321	13979

ELECTRICAL GOODS, WHOLESALE: Burglar Alarm Systems

	CITY	ST	EMP	PHONE	ENTRY #
Alarm One	North Haven	CT	G	203 239-1714	3004

ELECTRICAL GOODS, WHOLESALE: Connectors

	CITY	ST	EMP	PHONE	ENTRY #
Phoenix Company of Chicago Inc **(PA)**	Naugatuck	CT	D	630 595-2300	2489
Nabson Inc	Taunton	MA	G	617 323-1101	15767

ELECTRICAL GOODS, WHOLESALE: Electrical Entertainment Eqpt

	CITY	ST	EMP	PHONE	ENTRY #
Philips Holding USA Inc **(HQ)**	Andover	MA	C	978 687-1501	7582

ELECTRICAL GOODS, WHOLESALE: Electronic Parts

	CITY	ST	EMP	PHONE	ENTRY #
Component Concepts Inc	West Hartford	CT	G	860 523-4066	5062
Cudzilo Enterprises Inc	Bethel	CT	G	203 748-4694	139
Park Distributories Inc **(PA)**	Bridgeport	CT	G	203 579-2140	463
Servers Storage Networking LLC	Norwalk	CT	G	203 433-0808	3241
Cipem USA Inc	Melrose	MA	G	347 642-1106	12979
Psjl Corporation **(PA)**	Billerica	MA	D	978 359-4310	8279
Rbd Electronics Inc **(PA)**	Dalton	MA	F	413 442-1111	10182
Rochester Electronics LLC **(PA)**	Newburyport	MA	C	978 462-9332	13531

ELECTRICAL GOODS, WHOLESALE: Fire Alarm Systems

	CITY	ST	EMP	PHONE	ENTRY #
Citiworks Corp	Attleboro	MA	F	508 761-7400	7720

ELECTRICAL GOODS, WHOLESALE: Garbage Disposals

	CITY	ST	EMP	PHONE	ENTRY #
Tom Berkowitz Trucking Inc **(PA)**	Whitinsville	MA	E	508 234-2920	16919

ELECTRICAL GOODS, WHOLESALE: Generators

	CITY	ST	EMP	PHONE	ENTRY #
Ac/DC Industrial Electric LLC	Yantic	CT	G	860 886-2232	5506
Delta Elc Mtr Repr Sls & Svc	Medford	MA	G	781 395-0551	12930
Giltron Inc	North Dighton	MA	G	508 359-4310	13931
Hamilton Ferris Co Inc	Bourne	MA	G	508 743-9901	8946
Chase Electric Motors LLC	Hooksett	NH	G	603 669-2565	18346

ELECTRICAL GOODS, WHOLESALE: High Fidelity Eqpt

	CITY	ST	EMP	PHONE	ENTRY #
Aerial Acoustics Corporation	Wilmington	MA	F	978 988-1600	16968

ELECTRICAL GOODS, WHOLESALE: Lighting Fixtures, Comm & Indl

	CITY	ST	EMP	PHONE	ENTRY #
Point Lighting Corporation	Bloomfield	CT	E	860 243-0600	253

ELECTRICAL GOODS, WHOLESALE: Motors

	CITY	ST	EMP	PHONE	ENTRY #
Aparos Electric Motor Service	Southington	CT	G	860 276-2044	4039
Cudzilo Enterprises Inc	Bethel	CT	G	203 748-4694	139
Electric Enterprise Inc	Stratford	CT	F	203 378-7311	4410
Palmers Elc Mtrs & Pumps Inc	Norwalk	CT	G	203 348-7378	3214
Hancock Electric Mtr Svcs Inc	Quincy	MA	G	617 472-5789	14631
Kalman Electric Motors Inc	Stoughton	MA	G	781 341-4900	15600
Morse Electric Motors Co Inc	Gardner	MA	G	978 632-3733	11120
Shepard & Parker Inc	Fitchburg	MA	G	978 343-3907	10852
Toolmex Indus Solutions Inc **(PA)**	Northborough	MA	D	508 653-5110	14052
AC Electric Corp **(PA)**	Auburn	ME	E	207 784-7341	5545
Algers Leo NH Elc Mtrs	Laconia	NH	G	603 524-3729	18555
Lawrence Fay	Manchester	NH	G	603 668-3811	18862

ELECTRICAL GOODS, WHOLESALE: Security Control Eqpt & Systems

	CITY	ST	EMP	PHONE	ENTRY #
Grayfin Security LLC	Madison	CT	G	203 800-6760	1961
C3i Inc	Exeter	NH	E	603 929-9989	18115
Klein Marine Systems Inc	Salem	NH	D	603 893-6131	19744

ELECTRICAL GOODS, WHOLESALE: Semiconductor Devices

	CITY	ST	EMP	PHONE	ENTRY #
Advance Data Technology Inc	Topsfield	MA	F	978 801-4376	15852

ELECTRICAL GOODS, WHOLESALE: Sound Eqpt

	CITY	ST	EMP	PHONE	ENTRY #
Vibrascience Inc	Branford	CT	G	203 483-6113	356

ELECTRICAL GOODS, WHOLESALE: Telephone & Telegraphic Eqpt

	CITY	ST	EMP	PHONE	ENTRY #
Esmail Riyaz	Andover	MA	G	978 689-3837	7547

ELECTRICAL GOODS, WHOLESALE: Telephone Eqpt

	CITY	ST	EMP	PHONE	ENTRY #
Total Communications Inc **(PA)**	East Hartford	CT	D	860 282-9999	1230

ELECTRICAL GOODS, WHOLESALE: Transformer & Transmission Eqpt

	CITY	ST	EMP	PHONE	ENTRY #
Carlyle Johnson Machine Co LLC **(PA)**	Bolton	CT	E	860 643-1531	276

ELECTRICAL GOODS, WHOLESALE: Transformers

	CITY	ST	EMP	PHONE	ENTRY #
Warner Power Acquisition LLC **(HQ)**	Warner	NH	C	603 456-3111	19930

ELECTRICAL GOODS, WHOLESALE: Wire & Cable

	CITY	ST	EMP	PHONE	ENTRY #
Autac Incorporated **(PA)**	Branford	CT	G	203 481-3444	291
Rel-Tech Electronics Inc	Milford	CT	D	203 877-8770	2347
Specialty Cable Corp	Wallingford	CT	D	203 265-7126	4809

	CITY	ST	EMP	PHONE	ENTRY #
James Monroe Wire & Cable Corp **(PA)**	South Lancaster	MA	D	978 368-0131	15318
Burndy LLC **(DH)**	Manchester	NH	B	603 647-5000	18793
Warehouse Cables LLC	Warwick	RI	G	401 737-5677	21442
Duelmark Aerospace Corporation	Cambridge	VT	G	802 644-2603	21823

ELECTRICAL GOODS, WHOLESALE: Wire & Cable, Electronic

	CITY	ST	EMP	PHONE	ENTRY #
Advanced Product Solutions LLC	Hamden	CT	G	203 745-4225	1730
Phoenix Company of Chicago Inc **(PA)**	Naugatuck	CT	D	630 595-2300	2489
Times Wire and Cable Company **(HQ)**	Wallingford	CT	G	203 949-8400	4820

ELECTRICAL SPLYS

	CITY	ST	EMP	PHONE	ENTRY #
Traver Electric Motor Co Inc	Waterbury	CT	E	203 753-5103	4966
Keene Bradford Esq PC	Lynnfield	MA	G	781 246-4545	12551

ELECTRICAL SUPPLIES: Porcelain

	CITY	ST	EMP	PHONE	ENTRY #
Coorstek Inc	East Granby	CT	E	860 653-8071	1124
Accumet Engineering Corp	Hudson	MA	E	978 568-8311	11750
Coorstek Inc	Worcester	MA	B	774 317-2600	17360
Idex Health & Science LLC	Middleboro	MA	C	774 213-0200	13064
Ceramco Inc	Center Conway	NH	E	603 447-2090	17793
Coorstek Inc	Milford	NH	D	603 673-7560	19052
J Yeager Inc **(PA)**	Manchester	VT	G	802 362-0810	22077
Superior Tchncal Ceramics Corp	Saint Albans	VT	C	802 527-7726	22380

ELECTRICAL WIRING TOOLS: Fish Wire

	CITY	ST	EMP	PHONE	ENTRY #
Intellihome of Vermont L L C	Wilmington	VT	F	802 464-2499	22701

ELECTRODES: Thermal & Electrolytic

	CITY	ST	EMP	PHONE	ENTRY #
Electrodes Incorporated	Worcester	MA	G	508 757-2295	17370

ELECTROMEDICAL EQPT

	CITY	ST	EMP	PHONE	ENTRY #
Atlantic Inertial Systems Inc	Cheshire	CT	A	203 250-3500	714
Bio-Med Devices Inc	Guilford	CT	D	203 458-0202	1693
Epicurean Feast Medtron O	North Haven	CT	G	203 492-5000	3025
Hobbs Medical Inc	Stafford Springs	CT	E	860 684-5875	4111
Philips Ultrasound Inc	Waterbury	CT	D	203 753-5215	4938
Respironics Novametrix LLC	Wallingford	CT	C	203 697-6475	4796
Walker Magnetics Group Inc **(HQ)**	Windsor	CT	E	508 853-3232	5378
Abiomed Cardiovascular Inc	Danvers	MA	D	978 777-5410	10190
Alip Corporation	Brighton	MA	G	857 234-6073	9092
Ashametrics Inc	Cambridge	MA	G	617 694-1428	9394
Balancetek	Boston	MA	G	617 320-4340	8389
Biosensics LLC	Newton	MA	G	888 589-6213	13569
Blink Neurotech Corp	Brighton	MA	G	917 767-6829	9096
Boston Scientific Corporation **(PA)**	Marlborough	MA	B	508 683-4000	12727
Cambridge Heart Inc **(PA)**	Foxborough	MA	E	978 654-7600	10912
Cardiofocus Inc	Marlborough	MA	E	508 658-7200	12735
Cerenova Inc	Cambridge	MA	G	715 212-2595	9435
Csa Medical Inc	Lexington	MA	D	443 921-8053	12215
Delsys Inc	Natick	MA	F	508 545-8200	13251
Diagnosys LLC **(PA)**	Lowell	MA	E	978 458-1600	12367
Docbox Inc	Waltham	MA	F	978 987-2569	16089
Eldersafe Technologies Inc	Harvard	MA	F	617 852-3018	11375
Electrosonics Medical Inc	Boston	MA	G	216 357-3310	8524
Ergosuture Inc	Arlington	MA	G	339 234-6289	7625
General Electric Company **(PA)**	Boston	MA	A	617 443-3000	8558
Haemonetics Asia Incorporated **(HQ)**	Braintree	MA	G	781 848-7100	9015
Haemonetics Corporation **(PA)**	Braintree	MA	A	781 848-7100	9016
Heartlander Surgical Inc	Westwood	MA	G	781 320-9601	16868
Highland Instruments	Sharon	MA	G	617 504-6031	15051
L3 Technologies Inc	Northampton	MA	A	413 586-2330	14009
Lake Region Manufacturing Inc **(HQ)**	Wilmington	MA	A	952 361-2515	17015
Lantos Technologies Inc	Wilmington	MA	G	781 443-7633	17017
Lockheed Martin Sippican Inc **(HQ)**	Marion	MA	B	508 748-3399	12699
Lumicell Inc	Newton	MA	G	617 404-1001	13611
Luxcath LLC	Boston	MA	G	617 419-1800	8674
M R Resources Inc	Fitchburg	MA	E	978 696-3060	10831
Medicametrix Inc	Lowell	MA	G	617 694-1713	12407
Medtronic Inc	Danvers	MA	F	978 739-3080	10239
Medtronic Inc	Danvers	MA	F	978 777-0042	10240
Mettler-Toledo Process Analyti	Billerica	MA	D	781 301-8800	8265
Micro-Leads Inc	Somerville	MA	G	617 299-0295	15199
Myolex Inc	Brookline	MA	G	888 382-8656	9210
Neurasense Inc	Cambridge	MA	G	618 917-4686	9577
Nihon Khden Innovation Ctr Inc	Cambridge	MA	G	617 318-5904	9582
Omnimedics	Melrose	MA	G	617 527-4590	12986
Opko Diagnostics LLC	Woburn	MA	G	781 933-8012	17249
Pendar Technologies LLC **(PA)**	Cambridge	MA	G	617 588-2128	9608
Perkinelmer Inc **(PA)**	Waltham	MA	C	781 663-6900	16171
Precision Optics Corp Inc **(PA)**	Gardner	MA	E	978 630-1800	11123
Proven Process Med Dvcs Inc	Mansfield	MA	D	508 261-0800	12652
Quanterix Corporation **(PA)**	Billerica	MA	C	617 301-9400	8281
Radiation Monitoring Dvcs Inc **(HQ)**	Watertown	MA	E	617 668-6800	16310
Respiratory Motion Inc	Watertown	MA	E	508 954-2706	16311
Reviveflow Inc	Chelmsford	MA	G	978 621-9466	9927
Sensomotoric Instruments Inc	Boston	MA	G	617 557-0010	8844
Smith & Nephew Endoscopy Inc	Andover	MA	D	978 749-1000	7609
Soundcure Inc	Boston	MA	G	408 938-5745	8855
Sparrows Little Tech LLC	Winchester	MA	G	781 799-6442	17096
Telemed Systems Inc	Hudson	MA	E	978 567-9033	11821
Thermo Envmtl Instrs LLC **(HQ)**	Franklin	MA	C	508 520-0430	11086
Thermo Fisher Scientific Inc	Wilmington	MA	D	978 275-0800	17055
Thermo Fisher Scientific Inc **(PA)**	Waltham	MA	C	781 622-1000	16213
Thoratec Corporation	Burlington	MA	C	781 272-0139	9345
Thoratec Corporation	Burlington	MA	D	781 272-0139	9346
Tomophase Corporation	Burlington	MA	G	781 229-5700	9347
Translational Sciences Corp	Cambridge	MA	G	617 331-4014	9683
Transmedics Inc **(PA)**	Andover	MA	C	978 552-0443	7614
Transmedics Group Inc	Andover	MA	D	978 552-0900	7615
Vasotech Inc	Shrewsbury	MA	G	617 686-2770	15135
Volcano Corporation	Billerica	MA	G	978 439-3560	8308
Artel Inc	Westbrook	ME	E	207 854-0860	7180
David Saunders Inc	South Portland	ME	E	207 228-1888	7021
Electrnic Mobility Contrls LLC	Augusta	ME	F	207 512-8009	5607
Fhc Inc **(PA)**	Bowdoin	ME	D	207 666-8190	5787
Physician Engineered Products	Fryeburg	ME	G	207 935-1256	6101
Vuetek Scientific LLC	Gray	ME	F	207 657-6565	6143
Memtec Corporation	Salem	NH	E	603 893-8080	19751
Monarch International Inc	Amherst	NH	E	603 883-3390	17577
Sleepnet Corp	Hampton	NH	E	603 758-6600	18272
Azulite Inc	Providence	RI	G	916 801-8528	20967
Bio-Detek Incorporated	Pawtucket	RI	C	401 729-1400	20816
Criticare Technologies Inc	North Kingstown	RI	E	401 667-3837	20699
Hanna Instruments Inc **(PA)**	Woonsocket	RI	E	401 765-7500	21567
Natus Medical Incorporated	Warwick	RI	G	401 732-5251	21395
Lionheart Technologies Inc **(PA)**	Winooski	VT	C	802 655-4040	22721
Raj Communications Ltd	Williston	VT	F	802 658-4961	22687

ELECTROMETALLURGICAL PRDTS

	CITY	ST	EMP	PHONE	ENTRY #
H C Starck Inc **(HQ)**	Newton	MA	C	617 630-5800	13598
Purecoat International LLC	Belmont	MA	E	561 844-0100	8079

ELECTRON BEAM: Cutting, Forming, Welding

	CITY	ST	EMP	PHONE	ENTRY #
Integral Technologies Inc **(DH)**	Enfield	CT	G	860 741-2281	1366
Arcam Cad To Metal Inc	Woburn	MA	F	781 281-1718	17121

ELECTRON TUBES

	CITY	ST	EMP	PHONE	ENTRY #
Conklin-Sherman Company Incthe	Beacon Falls	CT	G	203 881-0190	57
Connecticut Coining Inc	Bethel	CT	D	203 743-3861	138
Whelen Engineering Company Inc **(PA)**	Chester	CT	B	860 526-9504	777
Adaptas Solutions **(PA)**	Palmer	MA	D	413 284-9975	14277
Bridge 12 Technologies Inc	Framingham	MA	G	617 674-2766	10930
Photonis Scientific Inc **(DH)**	Sturbridge	MA	D	508 347-4000	15646
Osram Sylvania Inc	Exeter	NH	D	603 772-4331	18127
Narragansett Imaging Usa LLC	North Smithfield	RI	E	401 762-3800	20791

ELECTRON TUBES: Cathode Ray

	CITY	ST	EMP	PHONE	ENTRY #
Jem Electronics Inc	Franklin	MA	C	508 520-3105	11057

ELECTRON TUBES: Parts

	CITY	ST	EMP	PHONE	ENTRY #
Remtec Incorporated **(PA)**	Norwood	MA	E	781 762-9191	14194

ELECTRONIC COMPONENTS

	CITY	ST	EMP	PHONE	ENTRY #
Insys Micro Inc	Norwalk	CT	G	917 566-5045	3175
Preferred PDT & Mktg Group LLC	Shelton	CT	G	203 567-0221	3860
Allston Power LLC	Brighton	MA	F	617 562-4054	9093
Audio Video Designs	Nantucket	MA	G	508 325-9989	13220
Noeveon Inc	Wilmington	MA	G	978 642-5004	17031
SRI Hermetics Inc	Haverhill	MA	G	508 321-1023	11476
Theodores	Taunton	MA	G	508 409-1421	15790
Hammamatsu Corporation	Hudson	NH	G	603 883-3888	18397

ELECTRONIC DETECTION SYSTEMS: Aeronautical

	CITY	ST	EMP	PHONE	ENTRY #
Aero Surveillance Inc	North Andover	MA	G	978 691-5832	13688
Atk Space Systems Inc	Hopkinton	MA	G	508 497-9457	11692
Raytheon Company	Andover	MA	C	978 470-5000	7594

ELECTRONIC DEVICES: Solid State, NEC

	CITY	ST	EMP	PHONE	ENTRY #
Servers Storage Networking LLC	Norwalk	CT	G	203 433-0808	3241
Aetruim Incorporated	Billerica	MA	E	651 773-4200	8205
Apple Mill Holding Company Inc	Pembroke	MA	F	781 826-9706	14392
Atlas Devices LLC	Boston	MA	G	617 415-1657	8383
Forward Photonics LLC	Woburn	MA	F	617 767-3519	17184
Sevcon Inc **(HQ)**	Southborough	MA	E	508 281-5500	15365
Sunrise Systems Elec Co Inc **(PA)**	Pembroke	MA	G	781 826-9706	14428
Yankee Electrical Mfg Co	Wilbraham	MA	G	413 596-8256	16945

ELECTRONIC EQPT REPAIR SVCS

	CITY	ST	EMP	PHONE	ENTRY #
Doosan Fuel Cell America Inc **(HQ)**	South Windsor	CT	C	860 727-2200	3956
Modern Electronic Fax & Cmpt	Fairfield	CT	G	203 292-6520	1445
Nct Inc	Newington	CT	F	860 666-8424	2886
T-S Display Systems Inc	Stamford	CT	G	203 964-0575	4340
Genrad Inc	Westford	MA	A	978 589-7000	16768
L T X International Inc	Norwood	MA	D	781 461-1000	14173
Xcerra Corporation	Norwood	MA	E	781 461-1000	14208
Burns Industries Incorporated	Hollis	NH	G	603 881-8336	18327

ELECTRONIC LOADS & POWER SPLYS

	CITY	ST	EMP	PHONE	ENTRY #
Hartford Electric Sup Co Inc	Rocky Hill	CT	F	860 760-4887	3711
Topex Inc	Danbury	CT	F	203 748-5918	999
Advanced Electronic Controls	West Springfield	MA	G	413 736-3625	16505
Drs Power Technology Inc	Fitchburg	MA	C	978 343-9719	10823
Dsk Engineering and Technology	Waltham	MA	G	413 289-6485	16092
Starboard Exchange Inc	Beverly	MA	G	978 810-5577	8181
Vicor Corporation **(PA)**	Andover	MA	B	978 470-2900	7616
Ritronics Inc	Warwick	RI	F	401 732-8175	21414
Village of Orleans	Orleans	VT	G	802 754-8584	22253

ELECTRONIC PARTS & EQPT WHOLESALERS

	CITY	ST	EMP	PHONE	ENTRY #
Radio Frequency Systems Inc **(DH)**	Meriden	CT	E	203 630-3311	2122
Systems and Tech Intl Inc	Tolland	CT	G	860 871-0401	4553
Anderson Power Products Inc **(HQ)**	Sterling	MA	D	978 422-3600	15535
Electrochem Solutions Inc	Raynham	MA	C	781 575-0800	14714
Elpakco Inc **(PA)**	Westford	MA	E	978 392-0400	16765
Ideal Industries Inc	Sterling	MA	C	978 422-3600	15540

	CITY	ST	EMP	PHONE	ENTRY #
Keene Bradford Esq PC	Lynnfield	MA	G	781 246-4545	12551
Power Solutions LLC **(PA)**	Swansea	MA	F	800 876-9373	15713
Static Clean International	North Billerica	MA	F	781 229-7799	13870
Tdl Inc	Canton	MA	E	781 828-3366	9789
Wayne Kerr Electronics Inc	Woburn	MA	G	781 938-8390	17317
Wotech Associates	Woburn	MA	G	781 935-3787	17324
Comnav Engineering Inc	Portland	ME	E	207 221-8524	6641
Insulectro	Londonderry	NH	E	603 629-4403	18704
Rme Filters Inc	Amherst	NH	F	603 595-4573	17585
Andon Electronics Corporation	Lincoln	RI	E	401 333-0388	20555
Atec	Wakefield	RI	G	401 782-6950	21267

ELECTRONIC SHOPPING

	CITY	ST	EMP	PHONE	ENTRY #
Magnetic Sciences Inc	Acton	MA	G	978 266-9355	7372
Mountain Corporation **(PA)**	Keene	NH	C	603 355-2272	18517
Stencils Online LLC	Franklin	NH	G	603 934-5034	18165

ELECTRONIC TRAINING DEVICES

	CITY	ST	EMP	PHONE	ENTRY #
Outsource Electronic Mfg	North Kingstown	RI	G	401 615-0705	20732

ELECTROPLATING & PLATING SVC

	CITY	ST	EMP	PHONE	ENTRY #
Chromalloy Component Svcs Inc	Shelton	CT	G	203 924-1666	3789
Gybenorth Industries LLC	Milford	CT	F	203 876-9876	2295
Jarvis Precision Polishing	Bristol	CT	F	860 589-5822	572
M & Z Engineering Inc	Torrington	CT	G	860 496-0282	4585
National Integrated Inds Inc **(PA)**	Farmington	CT	C	860 677-7995	1495
Sifco Applied Srfc Cncepts LLC	East Windsor	CT	G	860 623-6006	1301
Usc Technologies LLC	Stratford	CT	G	203 378-9622	4456
Bay State Plating Inc	Holyoke	MA	G	413 533-6927	11618
Fountain Plating Company Inc	West Springfield	MA	D	413 781-4651	16521

ELEVATORS & EQPT

	CITY	ST	EMP	PHONE	ENTRY #
Ascend Elevator Inc	Bloomfield	CT	C	215 703-0358	205
International Elevator Corp	Cos Cob	CT	G	203 302-1023	826
K-Tech International	Torrington	CT	E	860 489-9399	4584
Otis Elevator Company **(HQ)**	Farmington	CT	B	860 674-3000	1503
Otis Elevator Company	Farmington	CT	G	860 290-3318	1504
United Technologies Corp **(PA)**	Farmington	CT	B	860 728-7000	1522
Bay State Elevator Company Inc **(PA)**	Agawam	MA	E	413 786-7000	7421
Draper Metal Fabrication Inc	Holbrook	MA	G	781 961-3146	11524
Hamilton Elevator Interiors	Saugus	MA	F	781 233-9540	14984
Armanni Usa Inc	Windham	ME	G	207 893-0557	7229

ELEVATORS: Installation & Conversion

	CITY	ST	EMP	PHONE	ENTRY #
Otis Elevator Company **(HQ)**	Farmington	CT	B	860 674-3000	1503
Bay State Elevator Company Inc **(PA)**	Agawam	MA	E	413 786-7000	7421

EMBALMING FLUID

	CITY	ST	EMP	PHONE	ENTRY #
Dodge Company Inc **(PA)**	Billerica	MA	G	800 443-6343	8237

EMBLEMS: Embroidered

	CITY	ST	EMP	PHONE	ENTRY #
All American Embroidery Inc	Wilmington	MA	G	978 657-0414	16970
Athletic Emblem & Lettering Co	Springfield	MA	F	413 734-0415	15449
Coastal Image Inc	Harwich	MA	G	508 430-7870	11391
G & G Silk Screening	Plymouth	MA	G	508 830-1075	14559
T Henri Inc	Southwest Harbor	ME	G	207 244-7787	7051
Woodland Studios Inc	Ellsworth	ME	F	207 667-3286	6024
Better Life LLC	Manchester	NH	G	603 647-0077	18787

EMBOSSING SVC: Paper

	CITY	ST	EMP	PHONE	ENTRY #
West Park Stamping Co Inc	Attleboro	MA	G	508 399-7488	7809
Custom Die Cut Inc	Windham	NH	G	603 437-3090	20003

EMBROIDERING & ART NEEDLEWORK FOR THE TRADE

	CITY	ST	EMP	PHONE	ENTRY #
American Stitch & Print Inc	North Haven	CT	G	203 239-5383	3006
Grand Embroidery Inc	Oxford	CT	F	203 888-7484	3406
Guidera Marketing Services	Pawcatuck	CT	E	860 599-8880	3436
Initial Step Monogramming	West Hartford	CT	G	860 665-0542	5078
J & D Embroidering Co	Baltic	CT	G	860 822-9777	50
Mad Sportswear LLC	West Haven	CT	G	203 932-4868	5133
R F H Company Inc	Norwalk	CT	F	203 853-2863	3226
Stitchers Hideaway LLC	Manchester	CT	G	860 268-4741	2054
All City Screen Printing Inc	Wakefield	MA	G	781 665-0000	15940
Avon Cstm EMB & Screenprinting	Avon	MA	F	781 341-4663	7878
Camelot Enterprises Inc **(PA)**	Stoughton	MA	F	781 341-9100	15583
Copy Caps	Wellfleet	MA	G	508 349-1300	16401
Custom Stitch	Wilmington	MA	G	978 988-1344	16991
E S Sports Corporation	Holyoke	MA	D	413 534-5634	11623
Elegant Stitches Inc	Pittsfield	MA	G	413 447-9452	14469
Embroider-Ism LLC	Centerville	MA	G	508 375-6461	9814
Embroidery Clinic LLC	Braintree	MA	G	781 843-5293	9004
Embroidery Place	Shrewsbury	MA	G	508 842-5311	15110
ESP Solutions Services LLC	Taunton	MA	E	508 285-0017	15749
Haiti Projects Inc	Hanover	MA	C	978 969-1064	11341
Inter-All Corporation	Granby	MA	E	413 467-7181	11228
Jph Graphics LLC	Salem	MA	G	978 744-7873	14926
Marcott Designs	Attleboro	MA	G	508 226-2680	7762
Olde Village Monogramming Inc	Great Barrington	MA	G	413 528-3904	11244
Pro Am Enterprises Inc	Melrose	MA	G	781 662-8888	12989
Sew What Embroidery	Dalton	MA	G	413 684-0672	10184
Universal Screening Studio Inc	Everett	MA	G	617 387-1832	10633
Black Bear Graphics	Kingfield	ME	G	207 265-4593	6252
Creative Embroidery LLC	Auburn	ME	G	207 777-6300	5556
D R Designs Inc	Manchester	ME	G	207 622-3303	6409
Michael V Morin	Sanford	ME	G	207 459-1200	6883
Nes Embroidery Inc	Tilton	NH	F	603 293-4664	19908
New England Embroidery Company	Conway	NH	G	603 447-3878	17956
Stitches By Kayo Inc	Londonderry	NH	G	603 965-0158	18739
U S Artistic Embroidery Inc	Hampton	NH	G	603 929-0505	18276
Cool Air Creations Inc	Smithfield	RI	E	401 830-5780	21216
Bennington Army and Navy Inc	Bennington	VT	F	802 447-0020	21663
Green Mountain Monogram Inc	Wells River	VT	F	802 757-2553	22601
J C Image Inc	Saint Albans	VT	G	802 527-1557	22369
Pumpkin Harbor Designs Inc	Jeffersonville	VT	G	802 644-6588	22047
Squeegee Printers Inc	Canaan	VT	G	802 266-3426	21825

EMBROIDERING SVC

	CITY	ST	EMP	PHONE	ENTRY #
Bruce Park Sports EMB LLC	Norwalk	CT	G	203 853-4488	3115
Expert Embroidery	Wallingford	CT	F	203 269-9675	4741
Gg Sportswear Inc	Hartford	CT	E	860 296-4441	1825
Monogramit LLC	Brooklyn	CT	G	860 779-0694	671
Rainbow Graphics Inc	Manchester	CT	G	860 646-8997	2042
Rss Enterprises LLC	Derby	CT	G	203 736-6220	1078
Shirt Graphix	Wallingford	CT	G	203 294-1656	4805
Tee-It-Up LLC	Wallingford	CT	G	203 949-9455	4816
TSS & A Inc	Prospect	CT	F	800 633-3536	3599
Abra-Cadabra Promotional AP	Lakeville	MA	G	508 821-2002	11970
Corporate Image Apparel Inc	Fall River	MA	E	508 676-3099	10680
Embroidery Loft	Methuen	MA	G	978 681-1155	13020
Fosters Promotional Goods	Marblehead	MA	F	781 631-3824	12683
Gemini Screenprinting & EMB Co	Brockton	MA	G	508 586-8223	9149
Gonco Inc **(PA)**	Sandwich	MA	G	508 833-3900	14968
Great Threads	Belchertown	MA	G	413 323-9402	8024
Lisa Signs Inc	Woburn	MA	G	781 935-1821	17215
Matouk Textile Works Inc	Fall River	MA	E	508 997-3444	10728
Threadhead Inc	Hyannis	MA	F	508 778-6516	11859
Tri-Star Sportswear Inc	Worcester	MA	G	508 799-4117	17490
B & B Embroidery Inc	Oakland	ME	G	207 465-2846	6529
BBH Apparrel	Boothbay Harbor	ME	F	207 633-0601	5783
Commercial Screenprint EMB Inc	Bangor	ME	G	207 942-2862	5639
Maine Coast Marketing	Portland	ME	G	207 781-9801	6684
Perfect Stitch Emroidery Inc	South Paris	ME	G	207 743-2830	7016
Creative Threads LLC	Gorham	NH	G	603 466-2752	18211
Evergreen Embroidery	Campton	NH	F	603 726-4271	17776
First Impressions Embroidery	Hooksett	NH	G	603 606-1400	18350
Martin D Marguerite	Londonderry	NH	G	603 421-9654	18718
Say It In Stitches Inc	Concord	NH	G	603 224-6470	17927
Silver Graphics	Manchester	NH	G	603 669-6955	18924
Top Stitch Embroidery Inc	Lebanon	NH	G	603 448-2931	18639
Classic Embroidery Co	East Providence	RI	E	401 434-9632	20397
Sewrite Mfg Inc	Cumberland	RI	G	401 334-3868	20342
Stitchs Custom Embroidery LLC	Johnston	RI	G	401 943-5900	20542
Brett Lewis Threads Ltd	Shelburne	VT	G	802 985-1166	22414
Bumwraps Inc **(PA)**	Montgomery Center	VT	G	802 326-4080	22141
Bumwraps Inc	Newport	VT	G	802 326-4080	22190
Initial Ideas Inc **(PA)**	Rutland	VT	F	802 773-6310	22339
New Hrizons EMB Screenprinting	Essex Junction	VT	G	802 651-9801	21952
Vermont Sportswear Emboridery	Colchester	VT	G	802 863-0237	21887
Vermont TS Inc	Chester	VT	G	802 875-2091	21853

EMBROIDERING SVC: Schiffli Machine

	CITY	ST	EMP	PHONE	ENTRY #
Inter-All Corporation	Granby	MA	E	413 467-7181	11228

EMBROIDERING: Swiss Loom

	CITY	ST	EMP	PHONE	ENTRY #
Embrodery By Evrything Per LLC	Littleton	NH	G	603 444-0130	18658

EMBROIDERY ADVERTISING SVCS

	CITY	ST	EMP	PHONE	ENTRY #
Nomis Enterprises	Wallingford	CT	G	631 821-3120	4778
R & B Apparel Plus LLC	Groton	CT	G	860 333-1757	1685
Imprinted Sportswear Inc	West Springfield	MA	G	413 732-5271	16525
Itg Group Inc	Medway	MA	G	508 645-4994	12962
Three Twins Productions Inc	Watertown	MA	F	617 926-0377	16323
BBH Apparrel	Boothbay Harbor	ME	F	207 633-0601	5783
Parsonskellogg LLC	East Providence	RI	E	401 438-0650	20439

EMBROIDERY KITS

	CITY	ST	EMP	PHONE	ENTRY #
Callenstitch LLC	Concord	MA	E	978 369-9080	10120
Image Factory LLC	Raymond	NH	G	603 895-3024	19639

EMERGENCY ALARMS

	CITY	ST	EMP	PHONE	ENTRY #
Endoto Corp	East Hartford	CT	G	860 289-8033	1193
Lumentum Operations LLC	Bloomfield	CT	G	408 546-5483	242
Nutmeg Utility Products Inc **(PA)**	Cheshire	CT	E	203 250-8802	748
United Technologies Corp **(PA)**	Farmington	CT	B	860 728-7000	1522
Eas Holdings LLC **(DH)**	Needham Heights	MA	G	781 449-3056	13329
Electro-Mechanical Tech Co	Hudson	MA	G	978 562-7898	11770
Fall Prevention Alarms Inc	Southbridge	MA	G	508 765-5050	15382
General Dynamics Mission	Needham Heights	MA	A	954 846-3000	13334
Lifeline Systems Company **(DH)**	Framingham	MA	A	508 988-1000	10977
Lifeline Systems Company	Framingham	MA	C	508 988-3000	10978
Multec Communications	Rockland	MA	G	781 294-4992	14817
Philips Hlthcare Infrmtics Inc	Framingham	MA	F	508 988-1000	10993
Signal Communications Corp	Woburn	MA	E	781 933-0998	17295
Lifeline Systems Company	Lewiston	ME	C	207 777-8827	6302
Lifeline Systems Company	Lebanon	NH	G	603 653-1610	18627

EMPLOYMENT AGENCY SVCS

	CITY	ST	EMP	PHONE	ENTRY #
ABB Enterprise Software Inc	Plainville	CT	A	860 747-7111	3461
Symphony Talent LLC	Bedford	MA	F	781 275-2716	8013

EMPLOYMENT SVCS: Teachers' Registry

	CITY	ST	EMP	PHONE	ENTRY #
Bunting & Lyon Inc	Cheshire	CT	G	203 272-4623	718

ENAMELING SVC: Jewelry

	CITY	ST	EMP	PHONE	ENTRY #
Epoxalot Jewelry	North Attleboro	MA	G	508 699-0767	13755
Jack Hodgdon	Attleboro	MA	G	508 223-9990	7754
S & M Enameling Co Inc	Providence	RI	G	401 272-0333	21118

ENAMELING SVC: Metal Prdts, Including Porcelain

	CITY	ST	EMP	PHONE	ENTRY #
Hartford Industrial Finshg Co	Bloomfield	CT	G	860 243-2040	224
Sunset Engravers	Methuen	MA	G	978 687-1111	13045
Unerectors Inc	Boston	MA	F	617 436-8333	8894
Weller E E Co Inc/MCS Finshg	Providence	RI	E	401 461-4275	21152

ENCLOSURES: Electronic

	CITY	ST	EMP	PHONE	ENTRY #
Barber Elc Enclosures Mfg Inc	North Attleboro	MA	E	508 699-4872	13749
Norpin Mfg Co Inc	Wilbraham	MA	F	413 599-1628	16941
Powerbox (usa) Inc	Bedford	NH	G	303 439-7211	17660
Schroff Inc **(HQ)**	Warwick	RI	B	763 204-7700	21421
Schroff Inc	Warwick	RI	D	401 535-4826	21422

ENCLOSURES: Screen

	CITY	ST	EMP	PHONE	ENTRY #
Connecticut Screen Works Inc	Wallingford	CT	G	203 269-4499	4726
High Grade Shade & Screen Co	Lynn	MA	F	781 592-5027	12516

ENCODERS: Digital

	CITY	ST	EMP	PHONE	ENTRY #
Mango Dsp Inc	Norwalk	CT	E	203 857-4008	3190
Digital Image Fidelity LLC	Whitman	MA	G	508 577-8496	16922
Zeevee Inc	Littleton	MA	E	978 467-1395	12330
Warner Graphics Inc	Camden	ME	G	207 236-2065	5871

ENCRYPTION EQPT & DEVICES

	CITY	ST	EMP	PHONE	ENTRY #
Technical Communications Corp **(PA)**	Concord	MA	E	978 287-5100	10158

ENERGY MEASUREMENT EQPT

	CITY	ST	EMP	PHONE	ENTRY #
General Electric Company	Norwalk	CT	D	518 385-7164	3159
Uses Mfg Inc	Quaker Hill	CT	G	860 443-8737	3644

ENGINEERING SVCS

	CITY	ST	EMP	PHONE	ENTRY #
American Specialty Pdts LLC	Vernon	CT	G	860 871-2279	4662
Asea Brown Boveri Inc **(DH)**	Norwalk	CT	G	203 750-2200	3105
Connecticut Analytical Corp	Bethany	CT	F	203 393-9666	119
DC & D Inc	Broad Brook	CT	G	860 623-2941	628
Electric Boat Corporation	Groton	CT	D	860 433-3000	1674
Electric Boat Corporation **(HQ)**	Groton	CT	A	860 433-3000	1675
GE Steam Power Inc **(HQ)**	Windsor	CT	A	866 257-8664	5336
Henkel Loctite Corporation **(DH)**	Rocky Hill	CT	E	860 571-5100	3714
John Zink Company LLC	Shelton	CT	D	203 925-0380	3821
Mike Sadlak	Coventry	CT	G	860 742-0227	835
Vector Engineering Inc	Mystic	CT	F	860 572-0422	2455
Accellent LLC **(DH)**	Wilmington	MA	C	978 570-6900	16963
ARINC Incorporated	Lexington	MA	D	781 863-0711	12207
Bluecatbio MA Inc	Concord	MA	G	978 405-2533	10116
Dale Engineering & Son Inc	Bedford	MA	F	781 541-6055	7969
Final Forge LLC	Plymouth	MA	G	857 244-0764	14557
Kinemetrics Inc	Harvard	MA	G	978 772-4774	11381
Marblehead Engineering	Essex	MA	F	978 432-1386	10595
Medsource Tech Holdings LLC **(DH)**	Wilmington	MA	F	978 570-6900	17021
Nypro Inc **(HQ)**	Clinton	MA	A	978 365-8100	10086
Pridecraft Inc	North Andover	MA	G	978 685-2831	13726
Product Resources LLC	Newburyport	MA	E	978 524-8500	13523
Radio Engineering Assoc Inc	Townsend	MA	G	978 597-0010	15873
Schneider Elc Systems USA Inc	Foxboro	MA	F	508 543-8750	10901
Teledyne Dgital Imaging US Inc **(HQ)**	Billerica	MA	E	978 670-2000	8303
Teradyne Inc	Bedford	MA	C	617 482-2700	8014
Triangle Engineering Inc	Hanover	MA	F	781 878-1500	11356
Vacuum Process Technology LLC	Plymouth	MA	E	508 732-7200	14589
Xp Power LLC	Gloucester	MA	D	978 282-0620	11220
Cascades Auburn Fiber Inc	Auburn	ME	E	207 753-5300	5552
Comnav Engineering Inc	Portland	ME	E	207 221-8524	6641
Enercon **(PA)**	Gray	ME	C	207 657-7000	6139
Knowlton Machine Company	Gorham	ME	E	207 854-8471	6117
Nichols Portland LLC **(PA)**	Portland	ME	B	207 774-6121	6702
4power LLC	Salem	NH	G	617 299-0068	19701
Fronek Anchor Darling Entp	Laconia	NH	F	603 528-1931	18564
Gill Design Inc	Windham	NH	G	603 890-1237	20006
Insource Design & Mfg Tech LLC	Merrimack	NH	G	603 718-8228	19007
Net Results In Cad Inc	Amherst	NH	G	603 249-9995	17578
Phoenix Resources	Goshen	NH	G	603 863-9096	18215
Simbex LLC	Lebanon	NH	E	603 448-2367	18636
Texas Instruments Incorporated	Merrimack	NH	C	603 429-6079	19037
Two In One Manufacturing Inc	Nashua	NH	E	603 595-8212	19276
Aspen Aerogels Inc	East Providence	RI	F	401 432-2612	20388
Eagle Industries Inc	Ashaway	RI	E	401 596-8111	20033
Electric Boat Corporation	North Kingstown	RI	D	401 268-2410	20707
Ersa Inc	Westerly	RI	E	401 348-4000	21524
Palmer Industries Inc	North Providence	RI	F	800 398-9676	20770
Konrad Prefab LLC	Springfield	VT	G	802 885-6780	22504

ENGINEERING SVCS: Aviation Or Aeronautical

	CITY	ST	EMP	PHONE	ENTRY #
Goodrich Corporation	Danbury	CT	B	505 345-9031	926
Greensight Agronomics Inc	Boston	MA	G	617 633-4919	8580
ARC Technology Solutions LLC	Nashua	NH	E	603 883-3027	19117
As Liquidation I Company Inc **(PA)**	Amherst	NH	D	603 879-0205	17552
Astronics Aerosat Corporation	Manchester	NH	D	603 879-0205	18782

ENGINEERING SVCS: Building Construction

	CITY	ST	EMP	PHONE	ENTRY #
Arnitex LLC	Cos Cob	CT	G	203 869-1406	822

ENGINEERING SVCS: Civil

	CITY	ST	EMP	PHONE	ENTRY #
Holase Incorporated	Portsmouth	NH	G	603 397-0038	19575

ENGINEERING SVCS: Construction & Civil

	CITY	ST	EMP	PHONE	ENTRY #
Louie and Teds Blacktop Inc	Swansea	MA	F	508 678-4948	15707

ENGINEERING SVCS: Electrical Or Electronic

	CITY	ST	EMP	PHONE	ENTRY #
AB Electronics Inc	Brookfield	CT	E	203 740-2793	632
High Voltage Outsourcing LLC	Danbury	CT	G	203 456-3101	932
Tornik Inc	Rocky Hill	CT	C	860 282-6081	3731
Dsk Engineering and Technology	Waltham	MA	G	413 289-6485	16092
Design Consultants Associates	Hampstead	NH	F	603 329-4541	18239
Sproutel Inc	Providence	RI	G	914 806-6514	21126
Veterans Assembled Elec LLC **(PA)**	Providence	RI	G	401 228-6165	21150

ENGINEERING SVCS: Energy conservation

	CITY	ST	EMP	PHONE	ENTRY #
Honeywell International Inc	Danvers	MA	D	978 774-3007	10223
National Resource MGT Inc **(PA)**	Canton	MA	E	781 828-8877	9759

ENGINEERING SVCS: Industrial

	CITY	ST	EMP	PHONE	ENTRY #
Invensys Systems Argentina	Foxboro	MA	E	508 543-8750	10889
Schneider Elc Systems USA Inc	Foxboro	MA	F	508 543-8750	10902
Senior Operations LLC	Lewiston	ME	D	207 784-2338	6322
Wahlcometroflex Inc	Lewiston	ME	B	207 784-2338	6327
Zajac LLC	Saco	ME	E	207 286-9100	6864

ENGINEERING SVCS: Machine Tool Design

	CITY	ST	EMP	PHONE	ENTRY #
Ceda Company Inc	Newington	CT	G	860 666-1593	2853
Johnson Gage Company	Bloomfield	CT	E	860 242-5541	229
Prospect Machine Products Inc	Prospect	CT	E	203 758-4448	3593
T L S Design & Manufacturing	New London	CT	G	860 439-1414	2781
Polyneer Inc	New Bedford	MA	E	508 998-5225	13440

ENGINEERING SVCS: Marine

	CITY	ST	EMP	PHONE	ENTRY #
RI Waterjet LLC	Newport	RI	G	781 801-2500	20676

ENGINEERING SVCS: Mechanical

	CITY	ST	EMP	PHONE	ENTRY #
109 Design LLC **(PA)**	New Haven	CT	G	203 941-1812	2650
Atp Industries LLC **(PA)**	Plainville	CT	F	860 479-5007	3467
Technical Enterprises Inc	Bridgewater	MA	G	781 603-9402	9089
Oizero9 Inc	Sanford	ME	F	207 324-3582	6885
Hycon Inc	Manchester	NH	G	603 644-1414	18841

ENGINEERING SVCS: Pollution Control

	CITY	ST	EMP	PHONE	ENTRY #
Hosokawa Micron International	Northborough	MA	F	508 655-1123	14037

ENGINEERING SVCS: Professional

	CITY	ST	EMP	PHONE	ENTRY #
Alstom Power Co	Windsor	CT	F	860 688-1911	5318

ENGINEERING SVCS: Structural

	CITY	ST	EMP	PHONE	ENTRY #
PEC Detailing Co Inc	Walpole	MA	G	508 660-8954	16006
Celestial Monitoring Corp **(HQ)**	Narragansett	RI	E	401 782-1045	20635

ENGINES & ENGINE PARTS: Guided Missile, Research & Develpt

	CITY	ST	EMP	PHONE	ENTRY #
Exothermics Inc	Amherst	NH	F	603 821-5660	17560

ENGINES: Diesel & Semi-Diesel Or Duel Fuel

	CITY	ST	EMP	PHONE	ENTRY #
Jacobs Vehicle Systems Inc	Bloomfield	CT	B	860 243-5222	227
Growth I M33 L P	Boston	MA	E	617 877-0046	8584

ENGINES: Gasoline, NEC

	CITY	ST	EMP	PHONE	ENTRY #
Westerbeke Corporation	Avon	MA	E	508 823-7677	7902

ENGINES: Internal Combustion, NEC

	CITY	ST	EMP	PHONE	ENTRY #
Liquidpiston Inc	Bloomfield	CT	F	860 838-2677	241
Smith Hill of Delaware Inc	Essex	CT	E	860 767-7502	1405
Cummins Inc	Springfield	MA	G	413 737-2659	15464
Cummins Northeast LLC	Dedham	MA	G	781 329-1750	10285
Melton Sales and Service Inc	Hallowell	ME	F	207 623-8895	6163
Davis Village Solutions LLC	New Ipswich	NH	G	603 878-3662	19304

ENGINES: Jet Propulsion

	CITY	ST	EMP	PHONE	ENTRY #
CAM Group LLC	Manchester	CT	F	860 646-2378	1990
Kco Numet Inc	Orange	CT	F	203 375-4995	3367
Andy Collazzo	Danvers	MA	G	978 539-8962	10194

ENGINES: Marine

	CITY	ST	EMP	PHONE	ENTRY #
Westerbeke Corporation **(PA)**	Taunton	MA	E	508 977-4273	15799
Vitaminsea LLC	Buxton	ME	G	207 671-0955	5863

ENGINES: Steam

	CITY	ST	EMP	PHONE	ENTRY #
Green Mountain Fly Wheeler	Montpelier	VT	G	802 223-1595	22148
Village Industrial Power Inc	Bradford	VT	F	802 522-8584	21706

ENGRAVING SVC, NEC

	CITY	ST	EMP	PHONE	ENTRY #
Baron Technology Inc	Trumbull	CT	E	203 452-0515	4614
Eccles-Lehman Inc	Easton	CT	G	203 268-0605	1318
Tex Elm Inc	East Haddam	CT	F	860 873-9715	1153
Colonial Key & Engraving	Salem	MA	G	978 745-8237	14902
Elite	Watertown	MA	G	617 407-9300	16281
International Laser Systems	Holyoke	MA	G	413 533-4372	11634
L & J of New England Inc	Worcester	MA	E	508 756-8080	17403
Paul Thomas	Chester	VT	G	802 875-4004	21848

ENGRAVING SVC: Jewelry & Personal Goods

	CITY	ST	EMP	PHONE	ENTRY #
F J Weidner Inc	East Haven	CT	G	203 469-4202	1249
Robert Audette **(PA)**	Cheshire	CT	G	203 872-3119	760
Silversmith Inc	Greenwich	CT	G	203 869-4244	1649
Bertoldo Inc	Wakefield	MA	G	781 324-9145	15944

	CITY	ST	EMP	PHONE	ENTRY #
Brothers Inc	Harwich Port	MA	E	508 222-7234	11399
ll Sign Products Inc	Hopedale	MA	G	781 321-4320	11672
ingham Engraving Co	Framingham	MA	G	508 877-7867	10946
s Engraving & Stonesetting	Plainville	MA	E	508 695-6842	14536
ehr Industries Inc	Warwick	RI	E	401 732-6565	21444

ENGRAVING SVCS

	CITY	ST	EMP	PHONE	ENTRY #
A D Perkins Company	New Haven	CT	G	203 777-3456	2651
Ann S Davis	Lebanon	CT	F	860 642-7228	1932
Robert Audette **(PA)**	Cheshire	CT	G	203 872-3119	760
Rokap Inc	Wallingford	CT	G	203 265-6895	4799
Northeast Stamp & Engraving	Milford	MA	G	508 473-5818	13132
Owl Stamp Company Inc	Lowell	MA	G	978 452-4541	12418
All Seasons Printing & Awards	Pelham	NH	G	603 881-7106	19427
Anything Printed LLC	Woodstock	VT	G	802 457-3414	22735
Vermont Awards and Engrv Inc	Colchester	VT	G	802 862-3000	21884

ENGRAVING: Bank Note

	CITY	ST	EMP	PHONE	ENTRY #
Crane Currency Us LLC	Boston	MA	G	617 648-3710	8488

ENGRAVINGS: Plastic

	CITY	ST	EMP	PHONE	ENTRY #
Bertoldo Inc	Wakefield	MA	G	781 324-9145	15944
Ezra J Leboff Co Inc	Brighton	MA	G	617 783-4200	9098
Fort Hill Sign Products Inc	Hopedale	MA	G	781 321-4320	11672
ID Graphics Group Inc	South Easton	MA	E	508 238-8500	15279

ENTERTAINERS & ENTERTAINMENT GROUPS

	CITY	ST	EMP	PHONE	ENTRY #
Russian Information Services	Montpelier	VT	G	802 223-4955	22160

ENTERTAINMENT SVCS

	CITY	ST	EMP	PHONE	ENTRY #
Yolanda Dubose Records and	West Haven	CT	F	203 823-6699	5153

ENVELOPES

	CITY	ST	EMP	PHONE	ENTRY #
Cenveo Inc	Stamford	CT	A	203 595-3000	4161
Cenveo Enterprises Inc **(PA)**	Stamford	CT	G	203 595-3000	4162
Cenveo Worldwide Limited **(DH)**	Stamford	CT	F	203 595-3000	4163
Cwl Enterprises Inc **(HQ)**	Stamford	CT	G	303 790-8023	4181
Accutech Packaging Inc	Foxboro	MA	D	508 543-3800	10873
American Prtg & Envelope Inc	Auburn	MA	E	508 832-6100	7825
Classic Envelope Inc	East Douglas	MA	D	508 731-6747	10425
Jannel Manufacturing Inc	Holbrook	MA	E	781 767-0666	11527
Sheppard Envelope Company Inc	Auburn	MA	E	508 791-5588	7849
Westrock Mwv LLC	Springfield	MA	A	413 736-7211	15527
Worcester Envelope Company	Auburn	MA	C	508 832-5394	7853
Tufpak Inc	Ossipee	NH	E	603 539-4126	19424
Fred F Waltz Co Inc	North Smithfield	RI	F	401 769-4900	20786
Leahy Press Inc	Montpelier	VT	E	802 223-2100	22153

ENVELOPES WHOLESALERS

	CITY	ST	EMP	PHONE	ENTRY #
Massachusetts Envelope Co Inc	Hartford	CT	E	860 727-9100	1845
Fred F Waltz Co Inc	North Smithfield	RI	F	401 769-4900	20786

ENZYMES

	CITY	ST	EMP	PHONE	ENTRY #
Alcresta Therapeutics Inc	Newton	MA	E	617 431-3600	13557
Bio-Catalytic Enterprises Inc	Springfield	MA	E	413 739-9148	15454
Bbi Enzymes USA Ltd	Portland	ME	G	608 709-5270	6621
Alltech Inc	Saint Albans	VT	G	802 524-7460	22363

EPOXY RESINS

	CITY	ST	EMP	PHONE	ENTRY #
Hexcel Corporation **(PA)**	Stamford	CT	E	203 969-0666	4213
Barrday Corporation **(HQ)**	Millbury	MA	D	508 581-2100	13156
Novolac Epoxy Technologies Inc **(PA)**	Harwich	MA	G	508 385-5598	11396
Eastern Resins Corp	Woonsocket	RI	E	401 769-6700	21559
Rbc Industries Inc	Warwick	RI	D	401 941-3000	21410

EQUIPMENT: Pedestrian Traffic Control

	CITY	ST	EMP	PHONE	ENTRY #
Onsite Services Inc	Clinton	CT	F	860 669-3988	792
Q-Lane Turnstiles LLC	Sandy Hook	CT	F	860 410-1801	3745
Nestor Inc **(PA)**	Providence	RI	F	401 274-5345	21076

EQUIPMENT: Rental & Leasing, NEC

	CITY	ST	EMP	PHONE	ENTRY #
Welder Repair & Rental Svc Inc	Durham	CT	G	203 238-9284	1096
Advantcraft Inc	Upton	MA	G	508 498-4644	15903
Giltron Inc	North Dighton	MA	G	508 359-4310	13931
Lyn-Lad Group Ltd **(PA)**	Lynn	MA	F	781 598-6010	12523
Modern Tractor & Truck Service	Seekonk	MA	G	508 761-4425	15029
Wafer Inspection Services Inc	Orleans	MA	G	508 944-2851	14245
Whitney & Son Inc	Fitchburg	MA	E	978 343-6353	10863
Wilevco Inc	Billerica	MA	F	978 667-0400	8310

ESCROW INSTITUTIONS: Other Than Real Estate

	CITY	ST	EMP	PHONE	ENTRY #
Creative Success Alliance Corp	Rockland	MA	E	781 878-7114	14796

ETCHING & ENGRAVING SVC

	CITY	ST	EMP	PHONE	ENTRY #
Metamorphic Materials Inc	Winsted	CT	F	860 738-8638	5417
Acralube Inc	Westfield	MA	G	413 562-5019	16663
Ariston Engraving & Machine Co	Woburn	MA	G	781 935-2328	17122
Automated Finishing Co Inc	Attleboro	MA	E	508 222-6262	7710
Focal Point Technologies	Plymouth	MA	G	508 830-9716	14558
Jr Chemical Coatings LLC	Harwich	MA	G	508 896-3383	11394
Mass Coating Corp	East Walpole	MA	G	347 325-0001	10526
N2 Biomedical LLC	Bedford	MA	E	781 275-6001	7993
New England Etching Co Inc	Holyoke	MA	E	413 532-9482	11643
Tech-Etch Inc **(PA)**	Plymouth	MA	B	508 747-0300	14587
Futureguard Building Pdts Inc **(PA)**	Auburn	ME	D	800 858-5818	5565
Advanced Polymerics Inc	Salem	NH	G	603 328-8177	19704
American Trophy & Supply Co	East Providence	RI	G	401 438-3060	20386
Etched Image LLC	North Providence	RI	G	401 225-6095	20760
GA Rel Manufacturing Company	Providence	RI	E	401 331-5455	21019
PM Colors Inc	Johnston	RI	G	401 521-7280	20530
JBM Carmel LLC	Bennington	VT	E	802 442-9110	21674

ETCHING SVC: Metal

	CITY	ST	EMP	PHONE	ENTRY #
Conard Corporation	Glastonbury	CT	E	860 659-0591	1544
Summit Corporation of America	Thomaston	CT	D	860 283-4391	4519
Elenel Industries Inc **(PA)**	Milford	MA	E	508 478-2025	13115
Industrial Etching Inc	East Longmeadow	MA	F	413 525-4110	10479
Photofabrication Engrg Inc **(HQ)**	Milford	MA	E	508 478-2025	13137
International Etching Inc	Providence	RI	F	401 781-6800	21038

ETCHING SVC: Photochemical

	CITY	ST	EMP	PHONE	ENTRY #
Chemart Company	Lincoln	RI	E	401 333-9200	20562
Chemart Company **(PA)**	Lincoln	RI	D	401 333-9200	20563

ETHERS

	CITY	ST	EMP	PHONE	ENTRY #
Westwood Youth Softball Inc	Westwood	MA	G	781 762-5185	16882

ETHYLENE-PROPYLENE RUBBERS: EPDM Polymers

	CITY	ST	EMP	PHONE	ENTRY #
Aardvark Polymers	Woodstock	CT	G	609 483-1013	5493
Si Group USA (usaa) LLC **(DH)**	Danbury	CT	C	203 702-6140	989
Specialty Polymers Inc	Waterbury	CT	G	203 575-5727	4958
Advanced Frp Systems Inc	Weymouth	MA	G	508 927-6915	16883
Allcoat Technology Inc	Wilmington	MA	E	978 988-0880	16971
American Prfmce Polymers LLC	Manchester	MA	G	603 237-8001	12603

EXCAVATING MACHINERY & EQPT WHOLESALERS

	CITY	ST	EMP	PHONE	ENTRY #
Merrick Services	Millbury	MA	G	508 802-3751	13170
Dig Rite Company Inc	Cranston	RI	G	401 862-5895	20211

EXERCISE EQPT STORES

	CITY	ST	EMP	PHONE	ENTRY #
Full Circle Padding Inc	Norton	MA	F	508 285-2500	14077

EXHAUST SYSTEMS: Eqpt & Parts

	CITY	ST	EMP	PHONE	ENTRY #
Bm Undercar Warehouse	Chelsea	MA	G	516 736-0476	9946
Davico Inc	New Bedford	MA	F	508 998-1150	13377
Peter Thrasher	North Attleboro	MA	G	-	13771
Tubular Automotive & Engrg	Rockland	MA	G	781 878-9875	14831

EXPLOSIVES

	CITY	ST	EMP	PHONE	ENTRY #
Austin Powder Company	Sterling	CT	E	860 564-5466	4365
Ensign-Bickford Industries Inc	Simsbury	CT	E	860 658-4411	3905
Maxam Initiation Systems LLC	Sterling	CT	F	860 774-3507	4368
Maxam North America Inc	Sterling	CT	G	860 774-2333	4369

EXTRACTS, FLAVORING

	CITY	ST	EMP	PHONE	ENTRY #
America Extract Corporation	East Hampton	CT	F	860 267-4444	1155
Charles Boggini Company LLC	Coventry	CT	G	860 742-2652	832
Schlotterbeck & Foss LLC **(PA)**	Westbrook	ME	E	207 772-4666	7206
Finlay EXT Ingredients USA Inc **(DH)**	Lincoln	RI	D	800 288-6272	20574

EYEGLASSES

	CITY	ST	EMP	PHONE	ENTRY #
Encore Optics	South Windsor	CT	F	860 282-0082	3964
Lenses Only LLC	Bloomfield	CT	F	860 769-2020	239
Pilla Inc	Ridgefield	CT	G	203 894-3265	3676
Precision Optical Co	East Hartford	CT	E	860 289-6023	1216
University Optics LLC	Dayville	CT	G	860 779-6123	1054
Chicopee Vision Center Inc	Springfield	MA	F	413 796-7570	15460
Claris Vision LLC	North Dartmouth	MA	G	508 994-1400	13917
Eyes On Europe LLC	Milton	MA	G	617 696-9311	13191
Focal Point Opticians Inc **(PA)**	Newton	MA	G	617 965-2770	13593
Menicon America Inc	North Billerica	MA	G	781 609-2042	13842
Nauset Optical	Orleans	MA	G	508 255-6394	14237
Skelmet Inc	Boston	MA	G	617 396-0612	8849
McLeod Optical Company Inc	Augusta	ME	F	207 623-3841	5614

EYEGLASSES: Sunglasses

	CITY	ST	EMP	PHONE	ENTRY #
Cashon	Groton	CT	G	786 325-4144	1666
Worldscreen Inc	Watertown	CT	G	860 274-9218	5037
Jcptrading Inc	Manchester	NH	G	603 880-7042	18767

EYELASHES, ARTIFICIAL

	CITY	ST	EMP	PHONE	ENTRY #
Eyelash Extensions and More	West Hartford	CT	F	860 951-9355	5071

EYES & HOOKS Screw

	CITY	ST	EMP	PHONE	ENTRY #
Reed & Prince Mfg Corp	Leominster	MA	E	978 466-6903	12181
Hindley Manufacturing Co Inc	Cumberland	RI	D	401 722-2550	20325

FABRIC STORES

	CITY	ST	EMP	PHONE	ENTRY #
E W Winship Ltd Inc	Nantucket	MA	G	508 228-1908	13223
North East Knitting Inc	Pawtucket	RI	C	401 727-0500	20869
Chrisandras Interiors Inc	Ludlow	VT	G	802 228-2075	22062
Simon Pearce US Inc **(PA)**	Windsor	VT	C	802 674-6280	22714

FABRICATED METAL PRODUCTS, NEC

	CITY	ST	EMP	PHONE	ENTRY #
Independent Metalworx Inc	Ansonia	CT	G	203 520-4089	19
Royal Welding LLC	Hartford	CT	G	860 232-5255	1867
Specialty Metals and Fab	Naugatuck	CT	G	203 509-5028	2496
A B Metal Fabricators	Lakeville	MA	G	508 947-5577	11969
Alliance Sheet Metal	Avon	MA	G	508 587-0314	7875
Bolger Products	Barre	MA	G	978 355-2226	7949
Dans Machine	Easthampton	MA	G	413 529-9635	10559
Noyes Sheet Metal	Milford	MA	F	508 482-9302	13134
Minuteman Metal LLC	Wilton	ME	G	207 217-8908	7226
Three Night Delivery Inc	Pelham	NH	G	603 595-6230	19450
Bb Metal Fabrication Inc	Fair Haven	VT	G	802 265-8375	21965
Moscow Mills Inc	Barre	VT	G	802 253-2036	21630

FABRICS & CLOTHING: Rubber Coated

	CITY	ST	EMP	PHONE	ENTRY #
Tillotson Corporation **(PA)**	Seekonk	MA	F	781 402-1731	15042
Worthen Industries Inc	Clinton	MA	E	978 365-6345	10095

FABRICS & YARN: Plastic Coated

	CITY	ST	EMP	PHONE	ENTRY #
Deitsch Plastic Company Inc	West Haven	CT	D	203 934-6601	5115
Pascale Industries Inc	Fall River	MA	E	508 673-3307	10745

FABRICS: Alpacas, Mohair, Woven

	CITY	ST	EMP	PHONE	ENTRY #
Wild Wood Acres Alpacas Inc	Newfane	VT	G	802 365-7053	22188

FABRICS: Apparel & Outerwear, Broadwoven

	CITY	ST	EMP	PHONE	ENTRY #
Johnson Woolen Mills LLC	Johnson	VT	E	802 635-2271	22050

FABRICS: Apparel & Outerwear, Cotton

	CITY	ST	EMP	PHONE	ENTRY #
Moore Company	Westerly	RI	C	401 596-2816	21534
Oshea Mary Lynn Weaving Studio	Middlebury	VT	G	802 545-2090	22117

FABRICS: Apparel & Outerwear, From Manmade Fiber Or Silk

	CITY	ST	EMP	PHONE	ENTRY #
Sally Conant	Orange	CT	F	203 878-3005	3383
Phoenix Trading Co Inc **(PA)**	Framingham	MA	G	617 794-8368	10994
Oshea Mary Lynn Weaving Studio	Middlebury	VT	G	802 545-2090	22117

FABRICS: Bird's-Eye Diaper Cloth, Cotton

	CITY	ST	EMP	PHONE	ENTRY #
Parrot The & Bird Emporium	Feeding Hills	MA	G	413 569-5555	10803

FABRICS: Blankets & Blanketing, Wool Or Similar Fibers

	CITY	ST	EMP	PHONE	ENTRY #
Joseph Lotuff Sr	Ware	MA	E	413 967-5964	16234
Atlantic Blanket Company Inc	Northport	ME	E	207 338-9691	6520

FABRICS: Bonded-Fiber, Exc Felt

	CITY	ST	EMP	PHONE	ENTRY #
Insulsafe Textiles Inc	Lewiston	ME	E	207 782-7011	6292

FABRICS: Broad Woven, Goods, Cotton

	CITY	ST	EMP	PHONE	ENTRY #
A Lyons & Company Inc	Manchester	MA	F	978 526-4244	12601

FABRICS: Broadwoven, Cotton

	CITY	ST	EMP	PHONE	ENTRY #
138 Barrows Street Realty Inc	Norton	MA	D	508 285-2904	14069
Brand & Oppenheimer Co Inc	Bedford	MA	E	781 271-0000	7965
Dawn Auger	Brockton	MA	G	508 587-0363	9137
E W Winship Ltd Inc	Nantucket	MA	G	508 228-1908	13223
Green Solar LLC	Springfield	MA	G	413 552-4114	15473
Kravet Inc	Boston	MA	G	617 428-0370	8655
Stevens Linen Associates Inc	Dudley	MA	D	508 943-0813	10387
Insulsafe Textiles Inc	Lewiston	ME	E	207 782-7011	6292
P & B Fabrics Inc	Pawtucket	RI	F	800 351-9087	20872
Rihm Management Inc	Manchester Center	VT	G	802 867-5325	22089

FABRICS: Broadwoven, Synthetic Manmade Fiber & Silk

	CITY	ST	EMP	PHONE	ENTRY #
Deer Creek Fabrics Inc	Stamford	CT	G	203 964-0922	4188
Deitsch Plastic Company Inc	West Haven	CT	D	203 934-6601	5115
Dimension-Polyant Inc	Putnam	CT	E	860 928-8300	3610
G Thomas and Sons Inc	North Grosvenordale	CT	G	860 935-5174	2995
Nextec Applications Inc **(PA)**	Greenwich	CT	G	203 661-1484	1634
Second Lac Inc **(PA)**	Norwalk	CT	G	203 321-1221	3239
Swift Textile Metalizing LLC **(PA)**	Bloomfield	CT	D	860 243-1122	265
138 Barrows Street Realty Inc	Norton	MA	D	508 285-2904	14069
Anglo Silver Liner Co	Webster	MA	F	508 943-1440	16339
Astenjohnson Inc	Springfield	MA	C	413 733-6603	15448
Avcarb LLC	Lowell	MA	D	978 452-8961	12347
Brand & Oppenheimer Co Inc	Bedford	MA	E	781 271-0000	7965
E W Winship Ltd Inc	Nantucket	MA	G	508 228-1908	13223
Kravet Inc	Boston	MA	G	617 428-0370	8655
Pwh Corporation	Haverhill	MA	E	978 373-9111	11463
Sanderson-Macleod Incorporated	Palmer	MA	C	413 283-3481	14295
Steele Canvas Basket Corp	Chelsea	MA	E	800 541-8929	9970
Auburn Manufacturing Inc **(PA)**	Mechanic Falls	ME	E	207 345-8271	6418
Duvaltex (us) Inc **(DH)**	Guilford	ME	C	207 873-3331	6157
Tex-Tech Industries Inc	North Monmouth	ME	C	207 933-4404	6512
Tex-Tech Industries Inc **(PA)**	Portland	ME	C	207 756-8606	6738
Booth Felt Co Inc	Dover	NH	G	603 330-3334	18009
Cramer Fabrics Inc	Dover	NH	E	603 742-3838	18016
Rosco Laboratories Inc	Central Falls	RI	G	401 725-6765	20124
Astenjohnson Inc	Williston	VT	D	802 658-2040	22655

FABRICS: Broadwoven, Wool

	CITY	ST	EMP	PHONE	ENTRY #
E W Winship Ltd Inc	Nantucket	MA	G	508 228-1908	13223
Kravet Inc	Boston	MA	G	617 428-0370	8655
New England Fleece Company	Fall River	MA	G	508 678-5550	10738
Richmand Textiles Inc	South Grafton	MA	F	508 839-6600	15298
Ramblers Way Farm Inc	Kennebunk	ME	E	888 793-9665	6240
Ramblers Way Farm Inc	Portland	ME	G	207 699-4600	6720
Ramblers Way Farm Inc	Portsmouth	NH	G	603 319-5141	19612
Brand & Oppenheimer Co Inc **(PA)**	Portsmouth	RI	D	401 293-5500	20921

FABRICS: Canvas

	CITY	ST	EMP	PHONE	ENTRY #
Custom Marine Canvas LLC	Groton	CT	G	860 572-9547	1669
Bass River Marine Canvas LLC	South Dennis	MA	G	781 856-5145	15265
Lifecanvas Technologies Inc	Cambridge	MA	G	404 274-1953	9536
Salt Marsh Canvas	Newbury	MA	G	978 462-0070	13465
C B P Corp **(PA)**	Arundel	ME	F	207 985-9767	5529
Kinder Industries Inc	Bristol	RI	F	401 253-7076	20087

FABRICS: Card Roll, Cotton

	CITY	ST	EMP	PHONE	ENTRY #
Arnitex LLC	Cos Cob	CT	G	203 869-1406	822

FABRICS: Chemically Coated & Treated

	CITY	ST	EMP	PHONE	ENTRY #
Jaeger Usa Inc	Rochester	NH	F	603 332-5816	
Textiles Coated Incorporated	Manchester	NH	C	603 296-2221	18

FABRICS: Cloth, Waxing

	CITY	ST	EMP	PHONE	ENTRY #
Leo D Bernstein and Sons Inc	Shaftsbury	VT	C	212 337-9578	22405

FABRICS: Coated Or Treated

	CITY	ST	EMP	PHONE	ENTRY #
Advanced Def Slutions Tech LLC	Bloomfield	CT	G	860 243-1122	199
Nextec Applications Inc **(PA)**	Greenwich	CT	G	203 661-1484	1634
Second Lac Inc **(PA)**	Norwalk	CT	G	203 321-1221	3239
Bennett Goding & Cooper Inc	Waltham	MA	G	978 682-8868	16046
Gta-Nht Inc **(HQ)**	Rockland	MA	C	781 331-5900	14804
Majilite Corporation	Dracut	MA	D	978 441-6800	10363
Middlesex Research Mfg Co Inc	Hudson	MA	E	978 562-3697	11793
Sika Sarnafil Inc **(HQ)**	Canton	MA	C	781 828-5400	9780
Whitecap Composites Inc	Peabody	MA	G	978 278-5718	14382
Auburn Manufacturing Inc **(PA)**	Mechanic Falls	ME	E	207 345-8271	6418
Junora Ltd	Biddeford	ME	G	207 284-4900	5741
Regal Sleeving & Tubing LLC	Somersworth	NH	E	603 659-5555	19847
Textiles Coated Incorporated **(PA)**	Londonderry	NH	D	603 296-2221	18741
Wf Holdings Inc **(PA)**	Nashua	NH	G	603 888-5443	19285
Worthen Industries Inc	Nashua	NH	F	603 886-0973	19289
Bruin Plastics Co Inc	Glendale	RI	E	401 568-3081	20459
Cooley Incorporated **(HQ)**	Pawtucket	RI	C	401 724-9000	20825
Cooley Incorporated	Cranston	RI	E	401 721-6374	20200
Kenyon Industries Inc	Kenyon	RI	B	401 364-7761	20548
Tex Flock Inc	Woonsocket	RI	E	401 765-2340	21586

FABRICS: Cords

	CITY	ST	EMP	PHONE	ENTRY #
Global Engineered Mtls Corp	Manville	RI	G	401 725-2100	20608

FABRICS: Felts, Blanketing & Upholstery, Wool

	CITY	ST	EMP	PHONE	ENTRY #
Bouckaert Industrial Textiles	Woonsocket	RI	E	401 769-5474	21552
Brookline Textiles Inc	Lower Waterford	VT	G	802 748-1933	22060

FABRICS: Fiberglass, Broadwoven

	CITY	ST	EMP	PHONE	ENTRY #
Claremont Sales Corporation	Durham	CT	E	860 349-4499	1089
Whitecap Composites Inc	Peabody	MA	G	978 278-5718	14382
Amatex Corporation	Laconia	NH	E	603 524-2552	18556
Duro-Fiber Co Inc	Hudson	NH	F	603 881-4200	18387
Pro Design & Manufacturing	Newton	NH	G	603 819-4131	19367
Saint-Gobain Abrasives Inc	Milford	NH	B	603 673-7560	19074
Crww Specialty Composites Inc	Hope Valley	RI	F	401 539-8555	20483

FABRICS: Fringes, Woven

	CITY	ST	EMP	PHONE	ENTRY #
Fringe Factory	New Bedford	MA	G	508 992-7563	13389

FABRICS: Fur-Type, From Manmade Fiber

	CITY	ST	EMP	PHONE	ENTRY #
Furs By Prezioso Ltd	Hamden	CT	G	203 230-2930	1750

FABRICS: Ginghams

	CITY	ST	EMP	PHONE	ENTRY #
Gingham Ventures LLC **(PA)**	Boston	MA	G	617 206-1197	8564

FABRICS: Glass & Fiberglass, Broadwoven

	CITY	ST	EMP	PHONE	ENTRY #
Noreaster Yachts Inc	Milford	CT	G	203 877-4339	2322

FABRICS: Hand Woven

	CITY	ST	EMP	PHONE	ENTRY #
Lenis Inc	Canton	MA	G	781 401-3273	9752

FABRICS: Lace & Lace Prdts

	CITY	ST	EMP	PHONE	ENTRY #
Maguire Lace & Warping Inc	Coventry	RI	G	401 821-1290	20154

FABRICS: Lace, Knit, NEC

	CITY	ST	EMP	PHONE	ENTRY #
Leavers Lace Corporation **(PA)**	West Greenwich	RI	F	401 397-5555	21461
Midland Co Inc	Coventry	RI	G	401 397-4425	20156

FABRICS: Laminated

	CITY	ST	EMP	PHONE	ENTRY #
Brookwood Laminating Inc	Wauregan	CT	D	860 774-5001	5038
Bradford Coatings Inc	Lowell	MA	D	978 459-4100	12354
Dela Incorporated **(PA)**	Haverhill	MA	E	978 372-7783	11424
Flame Laminating Corporation **(PA)**	North Andover	MA	F	978 725-9527	13705
Hardwick Laminators Inc	Gilbertville	MA	G	413 477-6600	11154
Laminating Coating Tech Inc	Monson	MA	D	413 267-4808	13208
Shawmut LLC **(PA)**	West Bridgewater	MA	C	508 588-3300	16453
Starensier Inc **(PA)**	Byfield	MA	F	978 462-7311	9365
Tpi Industries LLC	West Bridgewater	MA	G	508 588-3300	16460

FABRICS: Lining, From Manmade Fiber Or Silk

	CITY	ST	EMP	PHONE	ENTRY #
Harodite Industries Inc **(PA)**	Taunton	MA	D	508 824-6961	15757

FABRICS: Manmade Fiber, Narrow

	CITY	ST	EMP	PHONE	ENTRY #
Avila Textiles Inc	North Dighton	MA	G	508 828-5882	13929
Moore Company **(PA)**	Westerly	RI	C	401 596-2816	21531
Moore Company	Westerly	RI	C	401 596-2816	21532
Garflex Inc	Brattleboro	VT	D	802 257-5256	21728

FABRICS: Metallized

	CITY	ST	EMP	PHONE	ENTRY #
Swift Textile Metalizing LLC **(PA)**	Bloomfield	CT	D	860 243-1122	265
Custom Metal Fabrication	Leeds	MA	G	413 584-8200	12098
Polar Focus Inc	South Deerfield	MA	G	413 665-2044	15253

FABRICS: Nonwoven

	CITY	ST	EMP	PHONE	ENTRY #
Lydall Inc **(PA)**	Manchester	CT	E	860 646-1233	2021
Lydall Thermal Acoustical Inc	Manchester	CT	G	860 646-1233	2022
New England Nonwovens LLC	West Haven	CT	F	203 891-0851	5137
Suominen US Holding Inc **(HQ)**	East Windsor	CT	F	860 386-8001	1306
Swift Textile Metalizing LLC **(PA)**	Bloomfield	CT	D	860 243-1122	265

	CITY	ST	EMP	PHONE	ENTRY #
Windsor Locks Nonwovens Inc **(DH)**	East Windsor	CT	E	860 292-5600	1311
Xamax Industries Inc	Seymour	CT	E	203 888-7200	3769
Delaware Valley Corp	Tewksbury	MA	E	978 459-6932	15814
Draper Knitting Company Inc	Canton	MA	E	781 828-0029	9728
Hollingsworth & Vose Company **(PA)**	East Walpole	MA	C	508 850-2000	10524
National Nonwovens Inc **(PA)**	Easthampton	MA	D	413 527-3445	10568
National Nonwovens Inc	Easthampton	MA	E	413 527-3445	10570
Neenah Technical Materials	Pittsfield	MA	G	413 684-7488	14494
Nonwovens Inc	North Chelmsford	MA	F	978 251-8612	13905
Pwh Corporation	Haverhill	MA	E	978 373-9111	11463
Vulplex Incorporated	New Bedford	MA	E	508 996-6787	13458
Scotia Company	Lewiston	ME	G	207 782-3824	6321
Booth Felt Co Inc	Dover	NH	G	603 330-3334	18009
Cramer Fabrics Inc	Dover	NH	E	603 742-3838	18016
Northeastern Nonwovens Inc	Rochester	NH	E	603 332-5900	19680
Rontex America Inc	Amherst	NH	E	603 883-5076	17586
E A M T Inc	Woonsocket	RI	E	401 762-1500	21558

FABRICS: Paper, Broadwoven

	CITY	ST	EMP	PHONE	ENTRY #
Albany International Corp **(PA)**	Rochester	NH	D	603 330-5850	19655
Albany International Corp	Rochester	NH	G	603 330-5993	19656

FABRICS: Parachute Fabrics

	CITY	ST	EMP	PHONE	ENTRY #
Brand & Oppenheimer Co Inc **(PA)**	Portsmouth	RI	D	401 293-5500	20921

FABRICS: Pile, Circular Knit

	CITY	ST	EMP	PHONE	ENTRY #
Draper Knitting Company Inc	Canton	MA	E	781 828-0029	9728

FABRICS: Pile, Cotton

	CITY	ST	EMP	PHONE	ENTRY #
Cesyl Mills Inc	Millbury	MA	D	508 865-6129	13159

FABRICS: Poplin, Cotton

	CITY	ST	EMP	PHONE	ENTRY #
Brand & Oppenheimer Co Inc **(PA)**	Portsmouth	RI	D	401 293-5500	20921

FABRICS: Print, Cotton

	CITY	ST	EMP	PHONE	ENTRY #
All American Embroidery Inc	Wilmington	MA	G	978 657-0414	16970

FABRICS: Resin Or Plastic Coated

	CITY	ST	EMP	PHONE	ENTRY #
Au New Haven LLC	New Haven	CT	C	203 468-0342	2662
Park Advnced Cmposite Mtls Inc	Waterbury	CT	D	203 755-1344	4936
Trelleborg Ctd Systems US Inc	New Haven	CT	C	203 468-0342	2747
Allied Resin Technologies LLC	Leominster	MA	G	978 401-2267	12112
Foamtech LLC	Fitchburg	MA	F	978 343-4022	10827
Haartz Corporation **(PA)**	Acton	MA	B	978 264-2600	7359
Industrial Polymers & Chem Inc **(PA)**	Shrewsbury	MA	E	508 845-6112	15117
Ipac Fabrics Inc	Shrewsbury	MA	G	508 845-6112	15119
Teknor Apex Elastomers Inc	Leominster	MA	D	978 466-5344	12193

FABRICS: Rubberized

	CITY	ST	EMP	PHONE	ENTRY #
Allan Ponn	Stoneham	MA	G	781 438-4338	15553
Haartz Corporation **(PA)**	Acton	MA	B	978 264-2600	7359

FABRICS: Sail Cloth

	CITY	ST	EMP	PHONE	ENTRY #
Dimension-Polyant Inc	Putnam	CT	E	860 928-8300	3610
North Sails Group LLC **(DH)**	Milford	CT	D	203 874-7548	2323
Center Harbor Sails LLC	Brooklin	ME	G	207 359-2003	5818

FABRICS: Specialty Including Twisted Weaves, Broadwoven

	CITY	ST	EMP	PHONE	ENTRY #
Green Mountain Knitting Inc	Milton	VT	E	800 361-1190	22131

FABRICS: Stretch, Cotton

	CITY	ST	EMP	PHONE	ENTRY #
American Woolen Company Inc	Stafford Springs	CT	G	860 684-2766	4105

FABRICS: Trimmings

	CITY	ST	EMP	PHONE	ENTRY #
Advanced Graphics Inc	Stratford	CT	E	203 378-0471	4388
Allied Printing Services Inc **(PA)**	Manchester	CT	B	860 643-1101	1984
Concordia Ltd	North Branford	CT	G	203 483-0221	2960
Hi-Tech Fabricating Inc	Cheshire	CT	E	203 284-0894	737
Jornik Man Corp	Stamford	CT	F	203 969-0500	4232
Kinamor Incorporated	Wallingford	CT	E	203 269-0380	4760
Quality Name Plate Inc	East Glastonbury	CT	D	860 633-9495	1114
R F H Company Inc	Norwalk	CT	F	203 853-2863	3226
Second Lac Inc **(PA)**	Norwalk	CT	G	203 321-1221	3239
Argosy Publishing Inc **(PA)**	Newton	MA	E	617 527-9999	13562
E V Yeuell Inc	Woburn	MA	E	781 933-2984	17171
Gemini Screenprinting & EMB Co	Brockton	MA	G	508 586-8223	9149
Ghp Media Inc	North Adams	MA	D	413 663-3771	13675
Light Metal Platers LLC	Waltham	MA	E	781 899-8855	16145
Nrz Companies Inc	Worcester	MA	G	508 856-7237	17435
Serigraphics Unlimited	Rowley	MA	G	978 356-4896	14866
Silver Screen Design Inc	Greenfield	MA	F	413 773-1692	11275
Specialty Manufacturing Inc	Amesbury	MA	E	978 388-1601	7509
Sunset Engravers	Methuen	MA	G	978 687-1111	13045
Atlantic Sportswear Inc	Portland	ME	E	207 797-5028	6612
Black Bear Graphics	Kingfield	ME	G	207 265-4593	6252
DVE Manufacturing Inc	Lewiston	ME	E	207 783-9895	6284
Liberty Graphics Inc	Liberty	ME	E	207 589-4596	6331
Liquid Blue Inc	Derry	NH	D	401 333-6200	17987
Mountain Corporation	Marlborough	NH	D	603 876-3630	18963
Mrp Manufacturing LLC	Pittsfield	NH	G	603 435-5337	19503
Printed Matter Inc	Newfields	NH	E	603 778-2990	19318
Rapid Finishing Corp	Nashua	NH	E	603 889-4234	19244

FABRICS: Upholstery, Cotton

	CITY	ST	EMP	PHONE	ENTRY #
Dominics Decorating Inc	Norwalk	CT	G	203 838-1827	3141
New England Worldwide Export	Quincy	MA	G	617 472-0251	14642
Alfreds Upholstering & Custom	Alfred	ME	F	207 536-5565	5514

FABRICS: Upholstery, Wool

	CITY	ST	EMP	PHONE	ENTRY #
Dominics Decorating Inc	Norwalk	CT	G	203 838-1827	3141
Robinson Manufacturing Co **(PA)**	Oxford	ME	F	207 539-4481	6572

FABRICS: Wall Covering, From Manmade Fiber Or Silk

	CITY	ST	EMP	PHONE	ENTRY #
Deco Interior Finishes Inc	New Bedford	MA	G	508 994-9436	13378

FABRICS: Warp & Flat Knit Prdts

	CITY	ST	EMP	PHONE	ENTRY #
Charbert Inc	Chestnut Hill	MA	C	401 364-7751	9984

FABRICS: Warp Knit, Lace & Netting

	CITY	ST	EMP	PHONE	ENTRY #
Novelty Textile Mills LLC	Waterford	CT	G	860 774-5000	4990
Leavers Lace Corporation	West Warwick	RI	F	401 828-8117	21499

FABRICS: Waterproofed, Exc Rubberized

	CITY	ST	EMP	PHONE	ENTRY #
Clark Hammerbeam Corporation	Dedham	MA	E	781 461-1946	10283

FABRICS: Weft Or Circular Knit

	CITY	ST	EMP	PHONE	ENTRY #
Swift Textile Metalizing LLC **(PA)**	Bloomfield	CT	D	860 243-1122	265
Nfa Corp	Cumberland	RI	B	401 333-8990	20334

FABRICS: Wool, Broadwoven

	CITY	ST	EMP	PHONE	ENTRY #
138 Barrows Street Realty Inc	Norton	MA	D	508 285-2904	14069
Swan Finishing Company Inc **(PA)**	Fall River	MA	C	508 674-4611	10767

FABRICS: Woven Wire, Made From Purchased Wire

	CITY	ST	EMP	PHONE	ENTRY #
Albany International Corp **(PA)**	Rochester	NH	D	603 330-5850	19655

FABRICS: Woven, Narrow Cotton, Wool, Silk

	CITY	ST	EMP	PHONE	ENTRY #
H-O Products Corporation	Winsted	CT	E	860 379-9875	5412
138 Barrows Street Realty Inc	Norton	MA	D	508 285-2904	14069
Chase Corporation	Randolph	MA	E	781 963-2600	14673
E W Winship Ltd Inc	Nantucket	MA	G	508 228-1908	13223
Gta-Nht Inc **(HQ)**	Rockland	MA	C	781 331-5900	14804
Julius Koch USA Inc	Mattapoisett	MA	D	508 995-9565	12887
Massasoit/Tackband Inc	Chicopee	MA	E	413 593-6731	10041
MM Reif Ltd	Boston	MA	D	617 442-9500	8708
Pepperell Braiding Company Inc **(PA)**	Pepperell	MA	E	978 433-2133	14444
Revolution Composites LLC	Norwood	MA	G	781 255-1111	14196
Sam Kasten Handweaver LLC	Lenox	MA	G	413 637-8900	12103
Tweave LLC	Fall River	MA	E	508 285-6701	10774
Vulplex Incorporated	New Bedford	MA	E	508 996-6787	13458
Auburn Manufacturing Inc **(PA)**	Mechanic Falls	ME	E	207 345-8271	6418
Sml Inc	Lewiston	ME	E	207 784-2961	6324
Conrad-Jarvis Corp	Pawtucket	RI	D	401 722-8700	20824
Nfa Corp	Cumberland	RI	E	401 333-8990	20332
Stretch Products Corp	Pawtucket	RI	E	401 722-0400	20900

FABRICS: Yarn-Dyed, Cotton

	CITY	ST	EMP	PHONE	ENTRY #
Stacis Stitches LLC	Scituate	MA	G	781 206-7478	15015

FACILITIES SUPPORT SVCS

	CITY	ST	EMP	PHONE	ENTRY #
Clarios	Meriden	CT	D	678 297-4040	2086
Pitney Bowes Inc **(PA)**	Stamford	CT	A	203 356-5000	4285
Pitney Bowes Inc	Shelton	CT	E	203 356-5000	3855
Milk Street Press Inc	Boston	MA	F	617 742-7900	8706
G C Management Corp **(PA)**	Southwest Harbor	ME	G	207 244-5363	7047

FACSIMILE COMMUNICATION EQPT

	CITY	ST	EMP	PHONE	ENTRY #
Pitney Bowes Inc **(PA)**	Stamford	CT	A	203 356-5000	4285
Pitney Bowes Inc	Shelton	CT	E	203 356-5000	3855

FAMILY CLOTHING STORES

	CITY	ST	EMP	PHONE	ENTRY #
Fyc Apparel Group LLC **(PA)**	Branford	CT	D	203 481-2420	319
Image Factory	Pocasset	MA	G	508 295-3876	14598
Bennington Army and Navy Inc	Bennington	VT	F	802 447-0020	21663
Johnson Woolen Mills LLC	Johnson	VT	E	802 635-2271	22050

FANS, BLOWING: Indl Or Commercial

	CITY	ST	EMP	PHONE	ENTRY #
APA LLC	Canton	MA	E	781 986-5900	9714

FANS, EXHAUST: Indl Or Commercial

	CITY	ST	EMP	PHONE	ENTRY #
Kennedy Gustafson and Cole Inc	Berlin	CT	E	860 828-2594	90

FANS, VENTILATING: Indl Or Commercial

	CITY	ST	EMP	PHONE	ENTRY #
Measured Air Performance LLC	Manchester	NH	G	603 606-8350	18870

FARM & GARDEN MACHINERY WHOLESALERS

	CITY	ST	EMP	PHONE	ENTRY #
Stihl Incorporated	Oxford	CT	E	203 929-8488	3425
Oesco Inc	Conway	MA	E	413 369-4335	10164
Giddings Manufacturing Co Inc	Pittsford	VT	G	802 483-2292	22263

FARM SPLY STORES

	CITY	ST	EMP	PHONE	ENTRY #
Kent Nutrition Group Inc	Augusta	ME	F	207 622-1530	5611

FARM SPLYS, WHOLESALE: Feed

	CITY	ST	EMP	PHONE	ENTRY #
HJ Baker & Bro LLC **(PA)**	Shelton	CT	E	203 682-9200	3812

FARM SPLYS, WHOLESALE: Garden Splys

	CITY	ST	EMP	PHONE	ENTRY #
Sun Gro Holdings Inc	Agawam	MA	A	413 786-4343	7454
Mill River Lumber Ltd	North Clarendon	VT	D	802 775-0032	22220

FARM SPLYS, WHOLESALE: Greenhouse Eqpt & Splys

	CITY	ST	EMP	PHONE	ENTRY #
Rimol Greenhouse Systems Inc	Hooksett	NH	F	603 629-9004	18359

FARM SPLYS, WHOLESALE: Hay

	CITY	ST	EMP	PHONE	ENTRY #
Maple Heights Farm	Northfield	NH	G	603 286-7942	19406

FARM SPLYS, WHOLESALE: Soil, Potting & Planting

	CITY	ST	EMP	PHONE	ENTRY #
Grillo Services LLC	Milford	CT	E	203 877-5070	2294
Sunrise Composting	Addison	ME	G	207 483-4081	5511

FASTENERS WHOLESALERS

	CITY	ST	EMP	PHONE	ENTRY #
East Coast Lightning Eqp Inc	Winsted	CT	E	860 379-9072	5410
Timber-Top Inc	Watertown	CT	G	860 274-6706	5029

FASTENERS: Metal

	CITY	ST	EMP	PHONE	ENTRY #
Timber-Top Inc	Watertown	CT	G	860 274-6706	5029

FASTENERS: Metal

	CITY	ST	EMP	PHONE	ENTRY #
Engineered Inserts & Systems **(PA)**	Milford	CT	F	203 301-3334	2285
Norse Inc	Torrington	CT	G	860 482-1532	4589
Wtm Company	Thomaston	CT	G	860 283-5871	4528
Anderson Components Corp	Malden	MA	F	781 324-0350	12558
Device Technologies Inc	Southborough	MA	E	508 229-2000	15354
McStowe Engineering & Met Pdts	East Bridgewater	MA	F	508 378-7400	10417
Gripnail Corporation	East Providence	RI	E	401 431-1791	20416

FASTENERS: Notions, Hooks & Eyes

	CITY	ST	EMP	PHONE	ENTRY #
Metalform Acquisition LLC **(PA)**	New Britain	CT	E	860 224-2630	2553

FASTENERS: Notions, NEC

	CITY	ST	EMP	PHONE	ENTRY #
ITW Powertrain Fastening	Naugatuck	CT	G	203 720-1676	2480
Manchester Tl & Design ADP LLC	Hartford	CT	G	860 296-6541	1843
Paneloc Corporation	Farmington	CT	E	860 677-6711	1505
Rome Fastener Corporation	Milford	CT	E	203 874-6719	2354
Rome Fastener Sales Corp	Milford	CT	F	203 874-6719	2355
Timber-Top Inc	Watertown	CT	G	860 274-6706	5029
Briscon Electric Mfg Corp	Auburn	MA	F	508 832-3481	7830
M C Machine Co Inc	Hopedale	MA	G	508 473-3642	11677
Allied Endeavers Inc	Waldoboro	ME	G	207 832-0511	7130

FASTENERS: Notions, Snaps

	CITY	ST	EMP	PHONE	ENTRY #
Lord & Hodge Inc	Middletown	CT	F	860 632-7006	2201
Rings Wire Inc **(PA)**	Milford	CT	E	203 874-6719	2352

FASTENERS: Notions, Zippers

	CITY	ST	EMP	PHONE	ENTRY #
Bees Knees Zipper Wax LLC	Berlin	CT	G	203 521-5727	75
Bees Knees Zipper Wax LLC	Fall River	MA	G	203 521-5727	10667
YKK (usa) Inc	Marlborough	MA	G	978 458-3200	12855

FATTY ACID ESTERS & AMINOS

	CITY	ST	EMP	PHONE	ENTRY #
Henkel of America Inc **(HQ)**	Rocky Hill	CT	B	860 571-5100	3715
Waste Resource Recovery Inc **(PA)**	Lebanon	CT	G	860 287-3332	1938
Twin Rivers Tech Ltd Partnr	Quincy	MA	D	617 472-9200	14663

FAUCETS & SPIGOTS: Metal & Plastic

	CITY	ST	EMP	PHONE	ENTRY #
Symmons Industries Inc **(PA)**	Braintree	MA	C	781 848-2250	9041

FEATHERS & FEATHER PRODUCTS

	CITY	ST	EMP	PHONE	ENTRY #
Prysm Inc	Concord	MA	E	408 586-1100	10152

FELT PARTS

	CITY	ST	EMP	PHONE	ENTRY #
National Nonwovens Inc	Easthampton	MA	E	413 527-3445	10569
Best Felts Inc	Thomaston	ME	F	207 596-0566	7081
American Bacon Boston Felt Inc	Rochester	NH	E	603 332-7000	19658
Booth Felt Co Inc	Dover	NH	G	603 330-3334	18009
Carbon Felt Inc	Claremont	NH	F	603 542-0202	17840

FELT, WHOLESALE

	CITY	ST	EMP	PHONE	ENTRY #
U S Felt Company Inc	Sanford	ME	E	207 324-0063	6895

FELT: Acoustic

	CITY	ST	EMP	PHONE	ENTRY #
Specialty Textile Products LLC	Dover	NH	F	603 330-3334	18053

FENCES & FENCING MATERIALS

	CITY	ST	EMP	PHONE	ENTRY #
Merchants Metals LLC	Chicopee	MA	F	413 562-9981	10044

FENCES OR POSTS: Ornamental Iron Or Steel

	CITY	ST	EMP	PHONE	ENTRY #
Burdon Enterprises LLC	Higganum	CT	G	860 345-4882	1902
Colonial Blacksmith	Sandwich	MA	G	508 420-5326	14966
Larkin Iron Works Inc	Hyde Park	MA	G	617 333-9710	11873
Needham Certified Welding Corp	Needham Heights	MA	G	781 444-7470	13340
Somerville Ornamental Ir Works	Somerville	MA	G	617 666-8872	15218
Blackthorne Forge Ltd	Marshfield	VT	G	802 426-3369	22092

FENCING DEALERS

	CITY	ST	EMP	PHONE	ENTRY #
Walpole Woodworkers Inc	Ridgefield	CT	E	508 668-2800	3689
Walpole Woodworkers Inc	Westport	CT	G	203 255-9010	5237
Graney John F Metal Design LLC	Sheffield	MA	G	413 528-6744	15060
RD Contractors Inc	North Billerica	MA	F	978 667-6545	13859
Walpole Woodworkers Inc	East Falmouth	MA	F	508 540-0300	10451
Walpole Woodworkers Inc	Norwell	MA	G	781 681-9099	14114
Walpole Woodworkers Inc	Detroit	ME	E	207 368-4302	5954
Walpole Woodworkers Inc	Chester	ME	E	207 794-2248	5908
Chasco Inc	Portsmouth	NH	F	603 436-2141	19552
Cedar Craft Fence Co	Coventry	RI	G	401 397-7765	20141

FENCING MATERIALS: Docks & Other Outdoor Prdts, Wood

	CITY	ST	EMP	PHONE	ENTRY #
April Twenty One Corporation	Billerica	MA	G	978 667-8472	8213
A-Po-G Inc	Portland	ME	G	207 774-7606	6608
Woodshop Cupolas Inc	Trenton	ME	G	207 667-6331	7104
Chasco Inc	Portsmouth	NH	F	603 436-2141	19552
Wood Visions Inc	Hudson	NH	G	603 595-9663	18453

FENCING MATERIALS: Snow Fence, Wood

	CITY	ST	EMP	PHONE	ENTRY #
Brattleworks Company Inc	Gardner	MA	G	978 410-5078	11105

FENCING MATERIALS: Wood

	CITY	ST	EMP	PHONE	ENTRY #
Pleasant Valley Fence Co Inc	Pleasant Valley	CT	F	860 379-0088	3546
Walpole Woodworkers Inc	Ridgefield	CT	E	508 668-2800	3689
Walpole Woodworkers Inc	Westport	CT	G	203 255-9010	5237
Cape Cod Fence Co	South Yarmouth	MA	F	508 398-2293	15326
New England Fencewrights Inc	New Bedford	MA	G	508 999-3337	13423
Pine and Baker Mfg Inc	Tewksbury	MA	F	978 851-1215	15825
RD Contractors Inc	North Billerica	MA	F	978 667-6545	13859
Walpole Woodworkers Inc	East Falmouth	MA	F	508 540-0300	10451
Walpole Woodworkers Inc	Norwell	MA	G	781 681-9099	14114
Walpole Woodworkers Inc	Wilmington	MA	F	978 658-3373	17064
Frost Cedar Products Inc	North Anson	ME	G	207 566-5912	6501
Katahdin Forest Products Co **(PA)**	Oakfield	ME	D	800 845-4533	6527
Walpole Woodworkers Inc	Detroit	ME	E	207 368-4302	5954
Walpole Woodworkers Inc	Chester	ME	E	207 794-2248	5908
Cedar Craft Fence Co	Coventry	RI	G	401 397-7765	20141
George L Martin	Brattleboro	VT	G	802 254-5838	21729

FENCING: Chain Link

	CITY	ST	EMP	PHONE	ENTRY #
Master-Halco Inc	West Bridgewater	MA	E	508 583-7474	16444

FERTILIZERS: NEC

	CITY	ST	EMP	PHONE	ENTRY #
Scotts Company LLC	Lebanon	CT	D	860 642-7591	1937
Garden World Inc	Saugus	MA	G	781 233-9510	14982
Ocean Crest Seafoods Inc **(PA)**	Gloucester	MA	E	978 281-0232	11199
Sun Gro Horticulture Dist Inc	Agawam	MA	E	800 732-8667	7455
Wecare Environmental LLC	Marlborough	MA	G	508 480-9922	12849
Rx Green Solutions LLC	Manchester	NH	F	603 769-3450	18913
Naturcom Enterprises LLC	Bradford	VT	G	802 222-4277	21704
Northeast Agricultural Sls Inc **(PA)**	Lyndonville	VT	F	802 626-3351	22070

FERTILIZERS: Nitrogenous

	CITY	ST	EMP	PHONE	ENTRY #
Agrium Advanced Tech US Inc	Sterling	MA	G	978 422-3331	15532

FIBER & FIBER PRDTS: Organic, Noncellulose

	CITY	ST	EMP	PHONE	ENTRY #
Casco Bay Fibers	Freeport	ME	G	207 869-5429	6073

FIBER & FIBER PRDTS: Polyester

	CITY	ST	EMP	PHONE	ENTRY #
Fairfield Processing Corp **(PA)**	Danbury	CT	C	203 744-2090	918
Conform Gissing Intl LLC	Auburn	ME	C	207 784-1118	5555
Detroit Technologies Inc	Auburn	ME	A	207 784-1118	5560

FIBER & FIBER PRDTS: Protein

	CITY	ST	EMP	PHONE	ENTRY #
Proteus Industries Inc	Gloucester	MA	G	978 281-9545	11205

FIBER & FIBER PRDTS: Synthetic Cellulosic

	CITY	ST	EMP	PHONE	ENTRY #
Global Materials Inc	Lowell	MA	E	978 322-1900	12376
Casco Bay Fibers	Freeport	ME	G	207 869-5429	6073
Conform Gissing Intl LLC	Auburn	ME	C	207 784-1118	5555
Detroit Technologies Inc	Auburn	ME	A	207 784-1118	5560

FIBER OPTICS

	CITY	ST	EMP	PHONE	ENTRY #
Fluid Coating Technology Inc	Putnam	CT	G	860 963-2505	3612
Nufern	East Granby	CT	D	860 408-5000	1137
O E M Controls Inc **(PA)**	Shelton	CT	C	203 929-8431	3845
Pioneer Optics Company Inc	Bloomfield	CT	F	860 286-0071	251
Diamond USA Inc **(HQ)**	North Billerica	MA	E	978 256-6544	13807
Ipg Photonics Corporation **(PA)**	Oxford	MA	B	508 373-1100	14263
Mp Optical Communications Inc **(PA)**	Harvard	MA	G	978 456-7728	11382
Myriad Fiber Imaging Tech Inc	Dudley	MA	F	508 949-3000	10382
Schott North America Inc	Southbridge	MA	C	508 765-3300	15400
Schott North America Inc	Southbridge	MA	D	508 765-9744	15401
T & T Machine Products Inc	Rockland	MA	F	781 878-3861	14829
New Hampshire Optical Sys Inc	Nashua	NH	G	603 391-2909	19215
Brantner and Associates Inc	Ashaway	RI	G	401 326-9368	20032
Te Connctvity Phenix Optix Inc	Ashaway	RI	E	401 637-4600	20041

FIBER: Vulcanized

	CITY	ST	EMP	PHONE	ENTRY #
Conform Gissing Intl LLC	Auburn	ME	C	207 784-1118	5555
Detroit Technologies Inc	Auburn	ME	A	207 784-1118	5560

FIBERS: Carbon & Graphite

	CITY	ST	EMP	PHONE	ENTRY #
Hexcel Corporation **(PA)**	Stamford	CT	E	203 969-0666	4213
N12 Technologies Inc	Foxboro	MA	G	857 259-6622	10893
Nextchar LLC	Amherst	MA	G	877 582-1825	7520
Composite Energy Tech Inc	Bristol	RI	E	401 253-2670	20069
Graphene Composites Usa Inc	Providence	RI	G	401 261-5811	21022

FILE FOLDERS

	CITY	ST	EMP	PHONE	ENTRY #
Ames Safety Envelope Company **(DH)**	Somerville	MA	D	617 684-1000	15154
Elbe-Cesco Inc	Fall River	MA	D	508 676-8531	10687
Neci LLC	Canton	MA	E	781 828-4883	9761

FILLERS & SEALERS: Putty

	CITY	ST	EMP	PHONE	ENTRY #
H F Staples & Co Inc	Merrimack	NH	G	603 889-8600	19005

FILLERS & SEALERS: Wood

	CITY	ST	EMP	PHONE	ENTRY #
Kretetek Industries LLC	Hudson	NH	F	603 402-3073	18408

FILM & SHEET: Unsuppported Plastic

	CITY	ST	EMP	PHONE	ENTRY #
American Polyfilm Inc **(PA)**	Branford	CT	G	203 483-9797	289
Apogee Corporation **(PA)**	Putnam	CT	D	860 963-1976	3601
Apogee Corporation	Cromwell	CT	D	860 632-3550	846
Brushfoil LLC	Guilford	CT	F	203 453-7403	1696
Filmx Technologies	Dayville	CT	G	860 779-3403	1044

	CITY	ST	EMP	PHONE	ENTRY #
Flagship Converters Inc	Danbury	CT	D	203 792-0034	920
Spartech LLC	Stamford	CT	C	203 327-6010	4327
Str Holdings Inc **(PA)**	Enfield	CT	F	860 272-4235	1386
Avery Dennison Corporation	Westborough	MA	C	508 948-3500	16591
Berry Global Films LLC	Danvers	MA	C	978 532-2000	10202
CDF Corporation **(PA)**	Plymouth	MA	D	508 747-5858	14550
Chase Corporation	Randolph	MA	E	781 963-2600	14673
Coorstek Inc	Worcester	MA	B	774 317-2600	17360
Covestro LLC	South Deerfield	MA	D	412 777-2000	15248
Danafilms Corp	Westborough	MA	G	508 366-8884	16612
Eastern Etching and Mfg Co	Chicopee	MA	E	413 594-6601	10022
Inteplast Group Corporation	North Dighton	MA	F	508 880-7640	13932
K2w LLC	Waltham	MA	G	617 818-2613	16136
Micron Plastics Inc	Ayer	MA	F	978 772-6900	7926
New England Plastics Corp	New Bedford	MA	E	508 995-7334	13424
Sika Sarnafil Inc **(HQ)**	Canton	MA	C	781 828-5400	9780
Dewal Industries LLC	Narragansett	RI	C	401 789-9736	20637
Astenjohnson Inc	Williston	VT	D	802 658-2040	22655

FILM DEVELOPING SVCS

	CITY	ST	EMP	PHONE	ENTRY #
27th Exposure LLC	Littleton	NH	G	603 444-5800	18653

FILM PROCESSING & FINISHING LABORATORY

	CITY	ST	EMP	PHONE	ENTRY #
Amb Signs Inc **(PA)**	Dover Foxcroft	ME	G	207 564-3633	5959

FILTER ELEMENTS: Fluid & Hydraulic Line

	CITY	ST	EMP	PHONE	ENTRY #
Avenger Inc	Ipswich	MA	F	978 356-7311	11904

FILTERS

	CITY	ST	EMP	PHONE	ENTRY #
3M Purification Inc **(HQ)**	Meriden	CT	B	203 237-5541	2070
Isopur Fluid Technologies Inc	North Stonington	CT	F	860 599-1872	3076
Mott Corporation **(PA)**	Farmington	CT	C	860 793-6333	1493
Armstrong Machine Co Inc	Beverly	MA	F	978 232-9466	8102
East Coast Filter Inc	Wrentham	MA	G	716 649-2326	17518
East Coast Filter Corp	Blackstone	MA	G	508 883-7744	8311
Filtrex Corp	Attleboro	MA	G	508 226-7711	7735
General Electric Company	Harwich	MA	C	617 444-8777	11393
Isp Freetown Fine Chem Inc	Assonet	MA	D	508 672-0634	7681
Mestek Inc	Westfield	MA	D	413 564-5530	16701
Parker-Hannifin Corporation	Haverhill	MA	C	978 858-0505	11457
Rypos Inc **(PA)**	Franklin	MA	E	508 429-4552	11077
Vivaproducts Inc	Littleton	MA	F	978 952-6868	12327
Comnav Engineering Inc	Portland	ME	E	207 221-8524	6641
Mikrolar Inc	Hampton	NH	G	603 617-2508	18267
Rob Geoffroy	Londonderry	NH	G	603 425-2517	18734
Bioprocessh2o LLC	Portsmouth	RI	E	401 683-5400	20919
Filters Inc	Pawtucket	RI	G	401 722-8999	20840
Filcorp Industries Inc	Milton	VT	G	802 893-1882	22127

FILTERS & SOFTENERS: Water, Household

	CITY	ST	EMP	PHONE	ENTRY #
Evoqua Water Technologies LLC	South Windsor	CT	E	860 528-6512	3968
Guardian Envmtl Tech Inc	New Milford	CT	F	860 350-2200	2802
Safe Water	Seymour	CT	G	203 732-4806	3764
Diamond Water Systems Inc	Chicopee	MA	E	413 536-8186	10017
Duraflow LLC	Tewksbury	MA	F	978 851-7439	15815
Safve Inc	Scituate	MA	G	781 545-3546	15011
Advanced Radon Mitigation Inc	Hooksett	NH	G	603 644-1207	18341
Aquawave of New England LLC	Portsmouth	NH	F	603 431-8975	19538
Pentair Rsdntial Fltration LLC	Dover	NH	F	603 749-1610	18045

FILTERS: Air

	CITY	ST	EMP	PHONE	ENTRY #
Guardian Envmtl Tech Inc	New Milford	CT	F	860 350-2200	2802
Lydall Inc **(PA)**	Manchester	CT	E	860 646-1233	2021
7ac Technologies Inc	Beverly	MA	F	781 574-1348	8094
Gremarco Industries Inc	West Brookfield	MA	F	508 867-5244	16470
Airex Corporation	Hudson	NH	E	603 821-3065	18371
Creative Filtration Systems	Tamworth	NH	F	603 323-2000	19891

FILTERS: Air Intake, Internal Combustion Engine, Exc Auto

	CITY	ST	EMP	PHONE	ENTRY #
Accutrol LLC	Danbury	CT	E	203 445-9991	866
Filter Fab Inc	Somers	CT	G	860 749-6381	3917
Melton Sales and Service Inc	Hallowell	ME	F	207 623-8895	6163

FILTERS: Gasoline, Internal Combustion Engine, Exc Auto

	CITY	ST	EMP	PHONE	ENTRY #
Porogen Corporation **(DH)**	Woburn	MA	E	781 491-0807	17268

FILTERS: General Line, Indl

	CITY	ST	EMP	PHONE	ENTRY #
Applied Porous Tech Inc	Tariffville	CT	F	860 408-9793	4472
Pallflex Products Company	Putnam	CT	E	860 928-7761	3625
Tinny Corporation	Middletown	CT	E	860 854-6121	2228
Evoqua Water Technologies LLC	Tewksbury	MA	E	978 863-4600	15817
Filter-Kleen Manufacturing Co	Westford	MA	F	978 692-5137	16766
Munters Corporation **(DH)**	Amesbury	MA	C	978 241-1100	7498
Pall Corporation	Westborough	MA	B	508 871-5394	16641
Plating Supplies Intl Inc	Agawam	MA	G	413 786-2020	7446
Polytech Filtration Systems	Hudson	MA	F	978 562-7700	11804
Albarrie Technical Fabrics Inc	Auburn	ME	G	207 786-0424	5549
Lapoint Industries Inc **(PA)**	Auburn	ME	D	207 777-3100	5575
National Filter Media Corp	Winthrop	ME	F	207 377-2626	7281
National Filter Media Corp	Winthrop	ME	D	207 377-2626	7282
United Fbrcnts Strainrite Corp **(HQ)**	Auburn	ME	D	207 376-1600	5600
Micronics Filtration LLC **(HQ)**	Portsmouth	NH	C	603 433-1299	19596
R F Hunter Co Inc	Dover	NH	G	603 742-9565	18048
Essex Manufacturing Co	Williston	VT	G	802 864-4584	22665

FILTERS: Motor Vehicle

	CITY	ST	EMP	PHONE	ENTRY #
Lydall Inc **(PA)**	Manchester	CT	E	860 646-1233	2021
Phillips Fuel Systems	Bridgeport	CT	G	203 908-3323	468

FILTERS: Oil, Internal Combustion Engine, Exc Auto

	CITY	ST	EMP	PHONE	ENTRY #
Dynamic Bldg Enrgy Sltions LLC **(PA)**	North Stonington	CT	F	860 599-1872	3072
Expressway Lube Centers	Danbury	CT	F	203 744-2511	915

FILTRATION DEVICES: Electronic

	CITY	ST	EMP	PHONE	ENTRY #
3M Purification Inc	Stafford Springs	CT	C	860 684-8628	4103
Able Coil and Electronics Co	Bolton	CT	E	860 646-5686	273
Aer Control Systems LLC	North Haven	CT	G	203 772-4700	3003
JB Filtration LLC	Essex	CT	G	860 333-7962	1400
New England Filter Company Inc **(PA)**	Greenwich	CT	G	203 531-0500	1633
Purfx Inc	Westbrook	CT	G	860 399-4045	5161
Atrex Energy Inc **(PA)**	Walpole	MA	E	781 461-8251	15988
Degreasing Devices Co	Southbridge	MA	G	508 765-0045	15379
Modular Air Filtration Systems	Raynham	MA	E	508 823-4900	14720
Orbital Biosciences LLC **(PA)**	Topsfield	MA	G	978 887-5077	15864
Chemrock Corporation	Thomaston	ME	G	207 594-8225	7082
Porvair Filtration Group Inc	Caribou	ME	G	207 493-3027	5890
Jmk Inc	Amherst	NH	E	603 886-4100	17569
Rme Filters Inc	Amherst	NH	F	603 595-4573	17585
Bio Holdings Inc	Portsmouth	RI	F	401 683-5400	20918
Schneider Electric It Corp **(DH)**	West Kingston	RI	A	401 789-5735	21471

FINDINGS & TRIMMINGS Fabric, NEC

	CITY	ST	EMP	PHONE	ENTRY #
Ryco Trimming Inc	Lincoln	RI	F	401 725-1779	20595

FINDINGS & TRIMMINGS: Fabric

	CITY	ST	EMP	PHONE	ENTRY #
Byron Lord Inc	Old Lyme	CT	G	203 287-9881	3315

FINGERPRINT EQPT

	CITY	ST	EMP	PHONE	ENTRY #
Validity Inc	Boxboro	MA	F	978 635-3400	8955

FINISHING AGENTS

	CITY	ST	EMP	PHONE	ENTRY #
Unimetal Surface Finishing LLC **(PA)**	Thomaston	CT	E	860 283-0271	4524
Peg Kearsarge Co Inc	Bartlett	NH	G	603 374-2341	17627

FINISHING AGENTS: Leather

	CITY	ST	EMP	PHONE	ENTRY #
Union Specialties Inc	Newburyport	MA	E	978 465-1717	13546

FINISHING SVCS

	CITY	ST	EMP	PHONE	ENTRY #
Bradford Finshg Powdr Coat Inc	Haverhill	MA	G	978 469-9965	11410
J & M Machining Inc	Skowhegan	ME	F	207 474-7300	6978

FIRE ARMS, SMALL: Guns Or Gun Parts, 30 mm & Below

	CITY	ST	EMP	PHONE	ENTRY #
Colts Manufacturing Co LLC **(DH)**	West Hartford	CT	C	860 236-6311	5061
Gunworks International L L C	Old Saybrook	CT	G	860 388-4591	3336
Jkb Daira Inc **(PA)**	Norwalk	CT	G	203 642-4824	3182
Kinetic Development Group LLC	Seymour	CT	G	203 888-4321	3754
New Designz Inc	Cheshire	CT	F	860 384-1809	747
Davinci Arms LLC	Ludlow	MA	G	413 583-4327	12462
Kahr Arms Inc	Worcester	MA	E	508 635-1414	17398
Present Arms Inc	Indian Orchard	MA	G	413 575-4656	11894
American Outdoor Brands Sls Co	Houlton	ME	D	207 532-7966	6202
Windham Weaponry Inc	Windham	ME	D	207 893-2223	7261
Brigade Tactical Corp	Manchester	NH	G	603 682-7063	18790
Grip Pod Systems Intl LLC	Dover	NH	G	239 233-3694	18025
Sturm Ruger & Company Inc	Newport	NH	A	603 863-2000	19360
Sturm Ruger & Company Inc	Newport	NH	B	603 865-2424	19361
Thayer Industries Inc	Wakefield	RI	G	401 789-8825	21281
Caspian Arms Ltd	Wolcott	VT	G	802 472-6454	22729
Z M Weapons High Performance	Richmond	VT	G	802 777-8964	22313

FIRE ARMS, SMALL: Machine Guns/Machine Gun Parts, 30mm/below

	CITY	ST	EMP	PHONE	ENTRY #
Colt Defense LLC **(HQ)**	West Hartford	CT	B	860 232-4489	5060
Continental Machine Tl Co Inc	New Britain	CT	D	860 223-2896	2522

FIRE ARMS, SMALL: Pellet & BB guns

	CITY	ST	EMP	PHONE	ENTRY #
Scott Olson Enterprises LLC	Torrington	CT	G	860 482-4391	4598

FIRE ARMS, SMALL: Pistols Or Pistol Parts, 30 mm & below

	CITY	ST	EMP	PHONE	ENTRY #
Sturm Ruger & Company Inc **(PA)**	Southport	CT	B	203 259-7843	4099
Thompson/Center Arms Co Inc **(HQ)**	Springfield	MA	E	800 331-0852	15513
Sturm Ruger & Company Inc	Newport	NH	C	603 863-3300	19362
Thompson/Center Arms Co Inc	Rochester	NH	F	603 332-2394	19690
Foster Industries Inc	Wolcott	VT	E	802 472-6147	22730

FIRE ARMS, SMALL: Revolvers Or Revolver Parts, 30 mm & Below

	CITY	ST	EMP	PHONE	ENTRY #
US Firearms Manufacturing Co	Hartford	CT	G	860 296-7441	1884

FIRE ARMS, SMALL: Rifles Or Rifle Parts, 30 mm & below

	CITY	ST	EMP	PHONE	ENTRY #
Mike Sadlak	Coventry	CT	G	860 742-0227	835
Stag Arms LLC	New Britain	CT	G	860 229-9994	2578
Stag Arms LLC	New Britain	CT	G	860 229-9994	2579
Wilson Arms Company	Branford	CT	F	203 488-7297	362
Caliber Company **(PA)**	Westfield	MA	F	413 642-4260	16676
Savage Arms Inc **(DH)**	Westfield	MA	C	413 642-4135	16726
Savage Sports Corporation **(HQ)**	Westfield	MA	F	413 568-7001	16728
Green Mtn Rifle Barrel Co Inc	Conway	NH	F	603 447-1095	17953

FIRE ARMS, SMALL: Shotguns Or Shotgun Parts, 30 mm & Below

	CITY	ST	EMP	PHONE	ENTRY #
Dewey J Manufacturing Company	Oxford	CT	G	203 264-3064	3399
Mossberg Corporation **(PA)**	North Haven	CT	G	203 230-5300	3042
O F Mossberg & Sons Inc **(HQ)**	North Haven	CT	C	203 230-5300	3045

FIRE DETECTION SYSTEMS

	CITY	ST	EMP	PHONE	ENTRY #
United Technologies Corp	Farmington	CT	B	954 485-6501	1523
Kidde-Fenwal Inc **(HQ)**	Ashland	MA	A	508 881-2000	7663
Protectowire Co Inc	Pembroke	MA	E	781 826-3878	14423
Tyco International MGT Co LLC	Mansfield	MA	G	508 261-6200	12667

Employee Codes: A=Over 500 employees, B=251-500
C=101-250, D=51-100 E=20-50, F=10-19, G=3-9

	CITY	ST	EMP	PHONE	ENTRY #
Voltree Power Inc	Canton	MA	G	781 858-4939	9794
Fireye Inc **(DH)**	Derry	NH	C	603 432-4100	17979

FIRE ESCAPES

	CITY	ST	EMP	PHONE	ENTRY #
S M Churyk Iron Works Inc	New Milford	CT	G	860 355-1777	2826
Weld Rite	Jamaica Plain	MA	G	617 524-9747	11951

FIRE EXTINGUISHER CHARGES

	CITY	ST	EMP	PHONE	ENTRY #
Eagle Fire Safety Inc	Chelmsford	MA	G	978 256-3777	9894
King Fisher Co Inc	Lowell	MA	E	978 596-0214	12389
Tli Group Ltd	Carver	MA	F	508 866-9825	9809

FIRE EXTINGUISHER SVC

	CITY	ST	EMP	PHONE	ENTRY #
Fire Defenses New England LLC	Danvers	MA	F	978 304-1506	10217

FIRE EXTINGUISHERS, WHOLESALE

	CITY	ST	EMP	PHONE	ENTRY #
Eagle Fire Safety Inc	Chelmsford	MA	G	978 256-3777	9894

FIRE EXTINGUISHERS: Portable

	CITY	ST	EMP	PHONE	ENTRY #
Fire Prevention Services	Norwalk	CT	F	203 866-6357	3152
Fire Defenses New England LLC	Danvers	MA	F	978 304-1506	10217
Hydro-Test Products Inc	Stow	MA	F	978 897-4647	15632
Mooneytunco Inc	Weymouth	MA	G	781 331-4445	16894
Tyco International MGT Co LLC	Mansfield	MA	G	508 261-6200	12667
Wheel House Designs Inc	Morrisville	VT	G	802 888-8552	22180

FIRE OR BURGLARY RESISTIVE PRDTS

	CITY	ST	EMP	PHONE	ENTRY #
Plansee USA LLC **(DH)**	Franklin	MA	D	508 553-3800	11071
Viking Corporation	Mansfield	MA	G	508 594-1800	12669
Holase Incorporated	Portsmouth	NH	G	603 397-0038	19575

FIRE PROTECTION EQPT

	CITY	ST	EMP	PHONE	ENTRY #
McIntire Brass Works Inc	Somerville	MA	G	617 547-1819	15197
Town of Westminster	Westminster	MA	E	978 874-2313	16816
Alert Fire Protection Inc	Cranston	RI	G	401 261-8836	20173
American Rural Fire Apparatus	Williamstown	VT	G	802 433-1554	22649

FIREARMS & AMMUNITION, EXC SPORTING, WHOLESALE

	CITY	ST	EMP	PHONE	ENTRY #
Barile Printers LLC	New Britain	CT	G	860 224-0127	2513
Gems Sensors Inc	Plainville	CT	F	800 378-1600	3492

FIREARMS: Large, Greater Than 30mm

	CITY	ST	EMP	PHONE	ENTRY #
Tek Arms Inc	Hebron	CT	G	860 748-6289	1898

FIREARMS: Small, 30mm or Less

	CITY	ST	EMP	PHONE	ENTRY #
Deburring House Inc	East Berlin	CT	E	860 828-0889	1098
Maverick Arms Inc	North Haven	CT	G	203 230-5300	3038
United States Fire Arms Mfg Co	Hartford	CT	E	860 296-7441	1883
Accudyne Machine Tool Inc	Bellingham	MA	G	508 966-3110	8027
Saeilo USA Inc	Worcester	MA	E	508 795-3919	17463
Q LLC	Portsmouth	NH	G	603 294-0047	19611
Sig Sauer Inc	Exeter	NH	D	603 610-3000	18132
Sig Sauer Inc **(DH)**	Newington	NH	C	603 610-3000	19325
Tandem Kross LLC	Weare	NH	G	603 369-7060	19941

FIREBRICK: Clay

	CITY	ST	EMP	PHONE	ENTRY #
Bnz Materials Inc	North Billerica	MA	E	978 663-3401	13796

FIREFIGHTING APPARATUS

	CITY	ST	EMP	PHONE	ENTRY #
Hydro-Test Products Inc	Stow	MA	F	978 897-4647	15632
King Fisher Co Inc	Lowell	MA	E	978 596-0214	12389
Northast Emrgncy Apparatus LLC	Auburn	ME	F	207 753-0080	5584

FIREPLACE & CHIMNEY MATERIAL: Concrete

	CITY	ST	EMP	PHONE	ENTRY #
J & D Associates Corp	Milford	MA	G	508 478-9770	13120

FIREPLACES: Concrete

	CITY	ST	EMP	PHONE	ENTRY #
TFC Enterprises LLC	Westborough	MA	G	866 996-2701	16656
Livingstone Studios	Lincoln	RI	G	401 475-1145	20580

FIREWOOD, WHOLESALE

	CITY	ST	EMP	PHONE	ENTRY #
Eylward Timber Co	Wallingford	CT	G	203 265-4276	4742
Bolstridge Logging LLC	New Durham	NH	G	603 859-8241	19300
Ossipee Mountain Land Co LLC	Tamworth	NH	E	603 323-7677	19894

FIREWORKS

	CITY	ST	EMP	PHONE	ENTRY #
Atlas Pyrovision Entertainment **(PA)**	Jaffrey	NH	E	603 532-8324	18457
D C Speeney Sons Pyrotechnics	Jaffrey	NH	G	603 532-9323	18458

FISH & SEAFOOD PROCESSORS: Canned Or Cured

	CITY	ST	EMP	PHONE	ENTRY #
Christhopher Dinatale	Marshfield	MA	G	781 834-4248	12857
Kneeland Bros Inc	Rowley	MA	F	978 948-3919	14855
Cherry Point Products Inc	Milbridge	ME	D	207 546-0930	6431
Looks Gourmet Food Co Inc **(HQ)**	Whiting	ME	E	207 259-3341	7221

FISH & SEAFOOD PROCESSORS: Fresh Or Frozen

	CITY	ST	EMP	PHONE	ENTRY #
Rich Products Corporation	New Britain	CT	C	609 589-3049	2573
Big G Seafood Inc	New Bedford	MA	G	508 994-5113	13361
Blount Fine Foods Corp **(PA)**	Fall River	MA	C	774 888-1300	10669
Bluemoon Oyster Co Lcc	Duxbury	MA	G	781 585-6000	10393
Channel Fish Co Inc	Boston	MA	D	617 569-3200	8467
Cold Atlantic Seafood Inc	New Bedford	MA	G	508 996-3352	13373
Gortons Inc **(DH)**	Gloucester	MA	B	978 283-3000	11189
Higson Inc	Fall River	MA	G	508 678-4970	10714
Hunts Seafood Inc	Salisbury	MA	G	978 255-2636	14951
Jordan Bros Seafood Co Inc	Boston	MA	F	508 583-9797	8638
Northern Pelagic Group LLC	New Bedford	MA	E	508 979-1171	13430
Ocean Crest Seafood Inc	Gloucester	MA	F	978 281-0232	11198
Ocean Crest Seafoods Inc **(PA)**	Gloucester	MA	E	978 281-0232	11199
Raw Sea Foods Inc	Fall River	MA	C	508 673-0111	10753
Sea Watch International Ltd	New Bedford	MA	D	508 984-1406	13449
Spence & Co Ltd	Brockton	MA	E	508 427-5577	9177
Zeus Packing Inc	Gloucester	MA	E	978 281-6900	11221
Bristol Seafood LLC	Portland	ME	D	207 761-4251	6627
Danny Boy Fisheries Inc	North Yarmouth	ME	G	207 829-6622	6516
Ducktrap River of Maine LLC	Belfast	ME	C	207 338-6280	5688
Maine Coast Nordic	Machiasport	ME	F	207 255-6714	6398
Ocean Premier Seafood Inc	Manchester	NH	G	603 206-4787	18892
Blount Fine Foods Corp	Warren	RI	D	401 245-8800	21290
Galilean Seafood Inc	Bristol	RI	D	401 253-3030	20081
Ocean State Shellfish Coop	Narragansett	RI	G	401 789-2065	20643
Yankee Pride Fisheries Inc	Wakefield	RI	G	401 783-9647	21282

FISH & SEAFOOD WHOLESALERS

	CITY	ST	EMP	PHONE	ENTRY #
Hunts Seafood Inc	Salisbury	MA	G	978 255-2636	14951
Jordan Bros Seafood Co Inc	Boston	MA	F	508 583-9797	8638
Looks Gourmet Food Co Inc **(HQ)**	Whiting	ME	E	207 259-3341	7221
North Atlantic Inc	Portland	ME	G	207 774-6025	6704

FISH FOOD

	CITY	ST	EMP	PHONE	ENTRY #
CMS Enterprise Inc	New Bedford	MA	G	508 995-2372	13371
Finicky Pet Food Inc	New Bedford	MA	E	508 991-8448	13386
Offshore Marine Outfitters	York	ME	G	207 363-8862	7314

FISHING EQPT: Lures

	CITY	ST	EMP	PHONE	ENTRY #
A & S Tackle Corp	Swansea	MA	G	508 679-8122	15702
Hogy Lure Company LLC	Falmouth	MA	G	617 699-5157	10791
Outrageous Lures LLC	Plymouth	MA	G	347 509-8610	14571
Stuart Sports Specialties Inc	Indian Orchard	MA	G	413 543-1524	11897
Austin Merrill	Scarborough	ME	G	207 219-0593	6906
Plantes Lobster Escape Vents	Somerville	ME	G	207 549-7204	6999
Gibbs Lures Inc	Cumberland	RI	G	401 726-2277	20321

FISHING EQPT: Nets & Seines

	CITY	ST	EMP	PHONE	ENTRY #
Tauten Inc	Beverly	MA	G	978 961-3272	8186

FITTINGS & ASSEMBLIES: Hose & Tube, Hydraulic Or Pneumatic

	CITY	ST	EMP	PHONE	ENTRY #
Fluid Dynamics LLC **(PA)**	Manchester	CT	G	860 791-6325	2006
Funkhouser Industrial Products	East Granby	CT	G	860 653-1972	1127
Ruby Fluid Power LLC **(HQ)**	Bloomfield	CT	E	860 243-7100	259
Landry Enterprises Inc	Franklin	MA	G	508 528-9122	11063

FITTINGS: Pipe

	CITY	ST	EMP	PHONE	ENTRY #
Crane Co **(PA)**	Stamford	CT	D	203 363-7300	4177
Larad Equipment Corp	Hopedale	MA	G	508 473-2700	11676
Newstamp Lighting Corp	North Easton	MA	F	508 238-7073	13949
Guill Tool & Engrg Co Inc	West Warwick	RI	D	401 822-8186	21493
Vellano Corporation	Pawtucket	RI	G	401 434-1030	20909

FITTINGS: Pipe, Fabricated

	CITY	ST	EMP	PHONE	ENTRY #
Virginia Stainless Div	Cambridge	MA	G	508 823-1747	9697

FIXTURES & EQPT: Kitchen, Porcelain Enameled

	CITY	ST	EMP	PHONE	ENTRY #
Rock Bottom Stone Factory Outl	Milford	MA	G	508 634-9300	13142

FIXTURES: Bank, Metal, Ornamental

	CITY	ST	EMP	PHONE	ENTRY #
Mfb Holdings LLC	Dover	NH	E	603 742-0104	18036

FLAGPOLES

	CITY	ST	EMP	PHONE	ENTRY #
Flagraphics Inc	Somerville	MA	E	617 776-7549	15172
Mass Sign & Decal Inc	Rockland	MA	G	781 878-7446	14812
Sunsetter Products Ltd Partnr	Malden	MA	D	781 321-9600	12598
Flag-Works Over America LLC	Concord	NH	G	603 225-2530	17902

FLAGS: Fabric

	CITY	ST	EMP	PHONE	ENTRY #
Flag & Gift Store Ltd	Seekonk	MA	G	508 675-6400	15022
Flagraphics Inc	Somerville	MA	E	617 776-7549	15172
Mass Sign & Decal Inc	Rockland	MA	G	781 878-7446	14812
US Flag Manufacturing Inc	Cohasset	MA	G	781 383-6607	10103
Flag-Works Over America LLC	Concord	NH	G	603 225-2530	17902

FLAGSTONES

	CITY	ST	EMP	PHONE	ENTRY #
Flagstone Inc	Mapleton	ME	G	207 227-5883	6411

FLAT GLASS: Construction

	CITY	ST	EMP	PHONE	ENTRY #
Custom Glass and Alum Co Inc	Tewksbury	MA	G	978 640-5800	15813

FLAT GLASS: Laminated

	CITY	ST	EMP	PHONE	ENTRY #
LTI Smart Glass Inc	Pittsfield	MA	D	413 637-5001	14486
Protective Armored Systems Inc	Lee	MA	E	413 637-1060	12095

FLAT GLASS: Optical, Transparent, Exc Lenses

	CITY	ST	EMP	PHONE	ENTRY #
Guild Optical Associates Inc	Amherst	NH	F	603 889-6247	17567

FLAT GLASS: Window, Clear & Colored

	CITY	ST	EMP	PHONE	ENTRY #
All Pro Tint	New Bedford	MA	G	508 992-8468	13355
American Tinter	Windham	NH	G	603 458-6379	19999

FLATWARE: Silver

	CITY	ST	EMP	PHONE	ENTRY #
Towle Manufacturing Company **(DH)**	Medford	MA	G	781 539-0100	12950

FLAVORS OR FLAVORING MATERIALS: Synthetic

	CITY	ST	EMP	PHONE	ENTRY #
Bedoukian Research Inc **(PA)**	Danbury	CT	E	203 830-4000	877

FLOCKING METAL PRDTS

	CITY	ST	EMP	PHONE	ENTRY #
Numaco Packaging LLC	East Providence	RI	F	401 438-4952	20436

FLOCKING SVC: Fabric

Company	CITY	ST	EMP	PHONE	ENTRY #
Tex Flock Inc	Woonsocket	RI	E	401 765-2340	21586

FLOOR COVERING STORES

Company	CITY	ST	EMP	PHONE	ENTRY #
Robin Industries Inc	Bristol	RI	D	401 253-8350	20101

FLOOR COVERING STORES: Carpets

Company	CITY	ST	EMP	PHONE	ENTRY #
Holland & Sherry Inc **(PA)**	Norwalk	CT	F	212 628-1950	3169
Weymouth Braided Rug Co Inc	North Oxford	MA	G	508 987-8525	13976

FLOOR COVERING STORES: Floor Tile

Company	CITY	ST	EMP	PHONE	ENTRY #
Aldrich Marble & Granite Co	Norwood	MA	E	781 762-6111	14124

FLOOR COVERING STORES: Rugs

Company	CITY	ST	EMP	PHONE	ENTRY #
Rugsalecom LLC	West Hartford	CT	G	860 756-0959	5094
Cape Cod Braided Rug Co Inc	Marstons Mills	MA	F	508 432-3133	12872
Moderne Rug Inc	Fitchburg	MA	G	978 343-3210	10840
TMI Industries Inc	Palmer	MA	E	413 283-9021	14297

FLOOR COVERING: Plastic

Company	CITY	ST	EMP	PHONE	ENTRY #
Selectech Inc	Avon	MA	G	508 583-3200	7896
Bike Track Inc	Woodstock	VT	G	802 457-3275	22737
Staticworx Inc	Waterbury Center	VT	G	617 923-2000	22592

FLOOR COVERINGS: Asphalted-Felt Base, Linoleum Or Carpet

Company	CITY	ST	EMP	PHONE	ENTRY #
Natco Products Corporation **(PA)**	West Warwick	RI	B	401 828-0300	21504

FLOOR COVERINGS: Textile Fiber

Company	CITY	ST	EMP	PHONE	ENTRY #
Rugsalecom LLC	West Hartford	CT	G	860 756-0959	5094
ICP Construction Inc	Andover	MA	G	508 829-0035	7557

FLOOR COVERINGS: Twisted Paper, Grass, Reed, Coir, Etc

Company	CITY	ST	EMP	PHONE	ENTRY #
Aj Mfg	Thompson	CT	G	860 963-7622	4530

FLOORING: Hard Surface

Company	CITY	ST	EMP	PHONE	ENTRY #
Conformis Inc	Wallingford	CT	G	203 793-7178	4724
Industrial Floor Covering Inc	North Billerica	MA	G	978 362-8655	13826
Hampshire Hardwoods LLC	Laconia	NH	G	603 434-1144	18565

FLOORING: Hardwood

Company	CITY	ST	EMP	PHONE	ENTRY #
Conway Hardwood Products LLC	Gaylordsville	CT	E	860 355-4030	1530
Tallon Lumber Inc	Canaan	CT	E	860 824-0733	691
Wilson Woodworks Inc	Windsor	CT	F	860 870-2500	5379
Hydronics Manufacturing Inc	North Billerica	MA	G	978 528-4335	13825
L S Hardwood Floor	Dorchester	MA	G	617 288-0339	10346
Mr Sandless Central Mass	Worcester	MA	G	508 864-6517	17425
Universal Hardwood Flooring	Boston	MA	G	617 783-2307	8899
Kelly Lumber Sales Inc	Old Town	ME	F	207 435-4950	6542
Moosewood Millworks LLC	Ashland	ME	F	207 435-4950	5537
Dycem Corporation **(DH)**	Smithfield	RI	E	401 738-4420	21222
Appalchian Engineered Flrg Inc	North Troy	VT	F	802 988-1073	22240
Emery Floor Inc	Johnson	VT	G	802 635-7652	22049

FLOORING: Rubber

Company	CITY	ST	EMP	PHONE	ENTRY #
Dhf LLC	Brentwood	NH	G	603 778-2440	17748
Nora Systems Inc **(DH)**	Salem	NH	D	603 894-1021	19755

FLOORING: Tile

Company	CITY	ST	EMP	PHONE	ENTRY #
Figulo Corporation	Boston	MA	G	617 269-0807	8543

FLORISTS

Company	CITY	ST	EMP	PHONE	ENTRY #
Wendi C Smith	Yarmouth Port	MA	F	508 362-4595	17533

FLORISTS' ARTICLES: Pottery

Company	CITY	ST	EMP	PHONE	ENTRY #
Central Garden & Pet Company	Taunton	MA	E	508 884-5426	15735

FLORISTS' SPLYS, WHOLESALE

Company	CITY	ST	EMP	PHONE	ENTRY #
Raymond J Bykowski	Cheshire	CT	G	203 271-2385	758

FLOWERS & FLORISTS' SPLYS WHOLESALERS

Company	CITY	ST	EMP	PHONE	ENTRY #
Shemin Nurseries Inc	Lexington	MA	F	781 861-1111	12266

FLOWERS, FRESH, WHOLESALE

Company	CITY	ST	EMP	PHONE	ENTRY #
Maple Heights Farm	Northfield	NH	G	603 286-7942	19406

FLOWERS: Artificial & Preserved

Company	CITY	ST	EMP	PHONE	ENTRY #
Raymond J Bykowski	Cheshire	CT	G	203 271-2385	758
G H Allen Associates Inc	Ayer	MA	G	978 772-4010	7920

FLUES & PIPES: Stove Or Furnace

Company	CITY	ST	EMP	PHONE	ENTRY #
Heat Fab Inc	Turners Falls	MA	D	413 863-2242	15878

FLUID METERS & COUNTING DEVICES

Company	CITY	ST	EMP	PHONE	ENTRY #
Gems Sensors Inc **(HQ)**	Plainville	CT	B	860 747-3000	3491
Habco Industries LLC	Glastonbury	CT	E	860 682-6800	1556
Data Industrial Corporation	Mattapoisett	MA	E	508 758-6390	12886
High Voltage Engineering Corp	Wakefield	MA	F	781 224-1001	15954
Cei Flowmaster Products LLC	Hudson	NH	G	603 880-0094	18379
Digital Devices Inc	Wilton	NH	G	603 654-6240	19978
Unarco Material Handling Inc	Exeter	NH	E	603 772-2070	18134
Orbetron LLC	Cumberland	RI	G	651 983-2872	20337

FLUID POWER PUMPS & MOTORS

Company	CITY	ST	EMP	PHONE	ENTRY #
Hamilton Sundstrand Corp **(HQ)**	Windsor Locks	CT	A	860 654-6000	5397
Navtec Rigging Solutions Inc	Clinton	CT	E	203 458-3163	790
Hostar Mar Trnspt Systems Inc	Wareham	MA	E	508 295-2900	16250
Parker Hannifin Corpora	Merrimac	MA	G	978 346-0578	13005
Stedt Hydraulic Crane Corp	Westborough	MA	F	508 366-9151	16651

FLUID POWER VALVES & HOSE FITTINGS

Company	CITY	ST	EMP	PHONE	ENTRY #
Atp Industries LLC **(PA)**	Plainville	CT	F	860 479-5007	3467
Enfield Technologies LLC	Shelton	CT	F	203 375-3100	3801
Parker-Hannifin Corporation	New Britain	CT	C	860 827-2300	2561
Conant Controls Inc	Woburn	MA	F	781 395-2240	17147
Guardair Corporation	Chicopee	MA	E	413 594-4400	10028
Op USA Inc	Acton	MA	G	978 658-5135	7376
Portland Valve LLC **(HQ)**	Warren	MA	E	704 289-6511	16261
Portland Valve LLC	Warren	MA	G	978 284-4000	16262
Ballistic Fluid Technologies **(PA)**	Lyndeborough	NH	G	603 654-3065	18757
Parker-Hannifin Corporation	Hollis	NH	C	603 595-1500	18336
Parker-Hannifin Corporation	Hollis	NH	E	973 575-4844	18337
Quality Controls Inc	Northfield	NH	E	603 286-3321	19408

FLUMES: Metal Plate

Company	CITY	ST	EMP	PHONE	ENTRY #
Helfrich Construction Svcs LLC	Lawrence	MA	E	978 683-7244	12034

FLUXES

Company	CITY	ST	EMP	PHONE	ENTRY #
Alent USA Holding Inc	Waterbury	CT	B	203 575-5727	4839
Inventec Prfmce Chem USA LLC	Deep River	CT	E	860 526-8300	1063
Bay State Galvanizing Inc	Everett	MA	F	617 389-0671	10604
Morgan Advanced Ceramics Inc	New Bedford	MA	C	508 995-1725	13418
Carrier Wldg & Fabrication LLC	Wilton	ME	G	207 645-3100	7225
Continental Braze Supply LLC	Rochester	NH	G	603 948-1016	19664

FOAM CHARGE MIXTURES

Company	CITY	ST	EMP	PHONE	ENTRY #
Foam Pro Inc	Bangor	ME	G	207 212-9657	5645
American Foam Technologies Inc	Newport	RI	E	304 497-3000	20655

FOAM RUBBER

Company	CITY	ST	EMP	PHONE	ENTRY #
Latex Foam International LLC **(HQ)**	Shelton	CT	D	203 924-0700	3825
New England Foam Products LLC **(PA)**	Hartford	CT	E	860 524-0121	1851
Reilly Foam Corp	Bloomfield	CT	E	860 243-8200	256
Bosal Foam and Fiber **(PA)**	Limerick	ME	E	207 793-2245	6332

FOAMS & RUBBER, WHOLESALE

Company	CITY	ST	EMP	PHONE	ENTRY #
Bosal Foam and Fiber **(PA)**	Limerick	ME	E	207 793-2245	6332

FOIL & LEAF: Metal

Company	CITY	ST	EMP	PHONE	ENTRY #
Dexmet Corporation	Wallingford	CT	D	203 294-4440	4734
Foilmark Inc	Bloomfield	CT	F	860 243-0343	220
PPG Industries Inc	Wallingford	CT	D	203 294-4440	4785
Avery Dennison Corporation	Westborough	MA	C	508 948-3500	16591
Foilmark Inc **(HQ)**	Newburyport	MA	D	978 225-8200	13490

FOIL: Laminated To Paper Or Other Materials

Company	CITY	ST	EMP	PHONE	ENTRY #
Hazen Paper Company **(PA)**	Holyoke	MA	C	413 538-8204	11631

FOOD CONTAMINATION TESTING OR SCREENING KITS

Company	CITY	ST	EMP	PHONE	ENTRY #
Airy Technology Inc	Stoughton	MA	G	781 341-1850	15576
Charm Sciences Inc **(PA)**	Lawrence	MA	C	978 687-9200	12005

FOOD PRDTS, BREAKFAST: Cereal, Granola & Muesli

Company	CITY	ST	EMP	PHONE	ENTRY #
Wild Blue Yonder Foods	Marblehead	MA	G	978 532-3400	12696
Small Batch Organics LLC	Manchester Center	VT	F	802 367-1054	22090

FOOD PRDTS, BREAKFAST: Cereal, Oatmeal

Company	CITY	ST	EMP	PHONE	ENTRY #
Garden of Light Inc	East Hartford	CT	D	860 895-6622	1197
Munk Pack Inc	Greenwich	CT	F	203 769-5005	1632

FOOD PRDTS, CANNED OR FRESH PACK: Fruit Juices

Company	CITY	ST	EMP	PHONE	ENTRY #
Guida-Seibert Dairy Company **(PA)**	New Britain	CT	C	860 224-2404	2537
National Grape Coop Assn Inc	Concord	MA	G	978 371-1000	10145
Odwalla Inc	Brookline	MA	E	336 877-1634	9213
Welch Foods Inc A Cooperative **(HQ)**	Concord	MA	B	978 371-1000	10160

FOOD PRDTS, CANNED, NEC

Company	CITY	ST	EMP	PHONE	ENTRY #
Phat Thai	Burlington	VT	G	802 863-8827	21802

FOOD PRDTS, CANNED: Baby Food

Company	CITY	ST	EMP	PHONE	ENTRY #
Foundry Foods Inc	Norwalk	CT	G	314 982-3204	3154

FOOD PRDTS, CANNED: Barbecue Sauce

Company	CITY	ST	EMP	PHONE	ENTRY #
Kens Foods Inc **(PA)**	Marlborough	MA	B	508 229-1100	12782
Denny Mikes cue Stuff Inc **(PA)**	Westbrook	ME	G	207 591-5084	7187

FOOD PRDTS, CANNED: Beans, Baked Without Meat

Company	CITY	ST	EMP	PHONE	ENTRY #
Au Soleil	Boston	MA	G	617 535-6040	8386

FOOD PRDTS, CANNED: Ethnic

Company	CITY	ST	EMP	PHONE	ENTRY #
Drews LLC	Woburn	MA	G	781 935-6045	17170
Garan Enterprises Inc	Chicopee	MA	F	413 594-4991	10027
Sunjas Oriental Foods Inc	Waterbury	VT	G	802 244-7644	22585
Vermont Probiotica	Northfield	VT	G	802 279-4998	22245

FOOD PRDTS, CANNED: Fruit Juices, Concentrated

Company	CITY	ST	EMP	PHONE	ENTRY #
Old Dutch Mustard Co Inc	Greenville	NH	D	516 466-0522	18229

FOOD PRDTS, CANNED: Fruit Juices, Fresh

Company	CITY	ST	EMP	PHONE	ENTRY #
Graystone Limited LLC **(PA)**	North Easton	MA	G	855 356-1027	13946
Farm Truck Institute	Dresden	ME	G	207 400-2242	5966

FOOD PRDTS, CANNED: Fruits

Company	CITY	ST	EMP	PHONE	ENTRY #
Ocean Spray (europe) Ltd	Middleboro	MA	F	508 946-1000	13071
Cherryfield Foods Inc **(DH)**	Cherryfield	ME	D	207 546-7573	5902
Jasper Wyman & Son	Deblois	ME	E	207 638-2201	5946
Jasper Wyman & Son	Milbridge	ME	G	207 546-2311	6434
Jasper Wyman & Son **(PA)**	Milbridge	ME	G	207 546-3800	6433
Maine Wild Blueberry Company **(DH)**	Machias	ME	D	207 255-8364	6392

	CITY	ST	EMP	PHONE	ENTRY #
Cala Fruit Distributors Inc	Pawtucket	RI	F	401 725-8189	20819

FOOD PRDTS, CANNED: Fruits

	CITY	ST	EMP	PHONE	ENTRY #
Cosmos Food Products Inc	West Haven	CT	E	800 942-6766	5114
Country Pure Foods Inc	Ellington	CT	C	330 753-2293	1331
Fruitbud Juice LLC	Danbury	CT	E	203 790-8200	923
Company of Coca-Cola Bottling	Northampton	MA	D	413 586-8450	14000
Decas Cranberry Co Inc **(PA)**	Carver	MA	G	508 866-8506	9803
HP Hood LLC	Agawam	MA	C	413 786-2178	7431
Ocean Spray Cranberries Inc	South Carver	MA	G	508 866-5306	15235
Tropicana Products Inc	Taunton	MA	E	508 821-2056	15792
Welch Foods Inc A Cooperative	Concord	MA	C	978 371-3762	10161
B&G Foods Inc	Portland	ME	C	207 772-8341	6616
Jasper Wyman & Son	Cherryfield	ME	E	207 546-3381	5903
Jasper Wyman & Son	Cherryfield	ME	E	207 546-3381	5904
Maine Wild Blueberry Company	Machias	ME	D	207 255-8364	6393
McCain Foods Usa Inc	Easton	ME	B	207 488-2561	5991
Todds Originals LLC	Glenburn	ME	G	844 328-7257	6108

FOOD PRDTS, CANNED: Fruits & Fruit Prdts

	CITY	ST	EMP	PHONE	ENTRY #
Gebelein Group Inc	Hyde Park	MA	F	617 361-6611	11867
Ocean Spray Cranberries Inc **(PA)**	Middleboro	MA	B	508 946-1000	13072
Ocean Spray Cranberries Inc	Middleboro	MA	C	508 947-4940	13073
Ocean Spray International Inc **(HQ)**	Middleboro	MA	D	508 946-1000	13074
Ocean Spray Intl Svcs Inc **(HQ)**	Lakeville	MA	E	508 946-1000	11977

FOOD PRDTS, CANNED: Italian

	CITY	ST	EMP	PHONE	ENTRY #
A S Fine Foods	Stamford	CT	D	203 322-3899	4124
Lolas Italian Harvest LLC	Natick	MA	G	508 651-0524	13265
Rachels Table LLC	Greenville	RI	G	401 949-5333	20472

FOOD PRDTS, CANNED: Jams, Including Imitation

	CITY	ST	EMP	PHONE	ENTRY #
Jam & Jelly Chatham	West Chatham	MA	G	508 945-3052	16474

FOOD PRDTS, CANNED: Jams, Jellies & Preserves

	CITY	ST	EMP	PHONE	ENTRY #
Sweet Country Roads LLC	Colchester	CT	G	860 537-0069	811
Clives Jams LLC	Everett	MA	G	617 294-9766	10606
Pembertons Food Inc	Gray	ME	G	207 657-6446	6141
Stonewall Kitchen LLC **(PA)**	York	ME	C	207 351-2713	7316
Stonewall Kitchen LLC	North Conway	NH	D	603 356-3342	19379

FOOD PRDTS, CANNED: Jellies, Edible, Including Imitation

	CITY	ST	EMP	PHONE	ENTRY #
Willis Wood	Springfield	VT	G	802 263-5547	22513

FOOD PRDTS, CANNED: Marmalade

	CITY	ST	EMP	PHONE	ENTRY #
Winding Drive Corporation	Woodbury	CT	G	203 263-6961	5491

FOOD PRDTS, CANNED: Mexican, NEC

	CITY	ST	EMP	PHONE	ENTRY #
494 Amherst St LLC	Nashua	NH	G	470 430-4608	19102
Hume Specialties Inc	Chester	VT	E	802 875-3117	21843

FOOD PRDTS, CANNED: Mushrooms

	CITY	ST	EMP	PHONE	ENTRY #
Sabatino North America LLC **(PA)**	West Haven	CT	E	718 328-4120	5144
Oyster Creek Mushrooms Company	Damariscotta	ME	G	207 563-1076	5938

FOOD PRDTS, CANNED: Seasonings, Tomato

	CITY	ST	EMP	PHONE	ENTRY #
Howard Foods Inc **(PA)**	Danvers	MA	G	978 774-6207	10224

FOOD PRDTS, CANNED: Soups

	CITY	ST	EMP	PHONE	ENTRY #
Great Soups Inc	Bristol	RI	F	401 253-3200	20082

FOOD PRDTS, CANNED: Soups, Exc Seafood

	CITY	ST	EMP	PHONE	ENTRY #
Kettle Cuisine LLC **(PA)**	Lynn	MA	C	617 409-1100	12519

FOOD PRDTS, CANNED: Spaghetti & Other Pasta Sauce

	CITY	ST	EMP	PHONE	ENTRY #
Conopco Inc	Trumbull	CT	E	708 606-0540	4620
Onofrios Ultimate Foods Inc	New Haven	CT	F	203 469-4014	2721
Ragozzino Foods Inc **(PA)**	Meriden	CT	F	203 238-2553	2123
Thomas J Lipton Inc	Trumbull	CT	A	206 381-3500	4635
Catanzaro Food Products Inc	Pawtucket	RI	G	401 255-1700	20820
Boves of Vermont Inc	Milton	VT	G	802 862-7235	22125
Dellamore Enterprises Inc	Colchester	VT	G	802 655-6264	21861

FOOD PRDTS, CANNED: Spanish

	CITY	ST	EMP	PHONE	ENTRY #
Louis Rodriguz	New Haven	CT	G	203 777-6937	2708

FOOD PRDTS, CANNED: Tomato Sauce.

	CITY	ST	EMP	PHONE	ENTRY #
Marias Food Products Inc	Medford	MA	G	781 396-4110	12940
Spinelli Ravioli Mfg Co Inc	Boston	MA	E	617 567-1992	8859

FOOD PRDTS, CANNED: Vegetables

	CITY	ST	EMP	PHONE	ENTRY #
Sisters Salsa Inc	Blue Hill	ME	G	207 374-2170	5774

FOOD PRDTS, CANNED: Vegetables

	CITY	ST	EMP	PHONE	ENTRY #
Jens & Marie Inc	Providence	RI	G	401 475-9991	21043

FOOD PRDTS, CONFECTIONERY, WHOLESALE: Candy

	CITY	ST	EMP	PHONE	ENTRY #
Thompson Brands LLC	Meriden	CT	D	203 235-2541	2141
Stage Stop Candy Ltd Inc	Dennis Port	MA	G	508 394-1791	10315
Fredericks Pastries **(PA)**	Amherst	NH	G	603 882-7725	17563
Tom and Sallys Handmade Choco	Westerly	RI	F	800 289-8783	21544

FOOD PRDTS, DAIRY, WHOLESALE: Frozen Dairy Desserts

	CITY	ST	EMP	PHONE	ENTRY #
Rich Products Corporation	New Britain	CT	B	860 827-8000	2572

FOOD PRDTS, FISH & SEAFOOD, WHOLESALE: Fresh

	CITY	ST	EMP	PHONE	ENTRY #
Ocean Crest Seafoods Inc **(PA)**	Gloucester	MA	E	978 281-0232	11199
Wohrles Foods Inc **(PA)**	Pittsfield	MA	E	413 442-1518	14513
Bristol Seafood LLC	Portland	ME	D	207 761-4251	6627

FOOD PRDTS, FISH & SEAFOOD, WHOLESALE: Seafood

	CITY	ST	EMP	PHONE	ENTRY #
Coastal Seafoods Inc **(PA)**	Fairfield	CT	F	203 431-0453	1421
North Coast Sea-Foods Corp **(PA)**	Boston	MA	C	617 345-4400	8740
Bayley Quality Seafood Inc	Scarborough	ME	G	207 883-4581	6909

FOOD PRDTS, FISH & SEAFOOD: Broth, Canned, Jarred, Etc

	CITY	ST	EMP	PHONE	ENTRY #
Ecohouse LLC	Bremen	ME	G	207 529-2700	5791

FOOD PRDTS, FISH & SEAFOOD: Canned & Jarred, Etc

	CITY	ST	EMP	PHONE	ENTRY #
Greenport Foods LLC	Westport	CT	F	203 221-2673	5199
Ditusa Corporation	Gloucester	MA	E	978 335-5259	11178
Gortons Inc **(DH)**	Gloucester	MA	B	978 283-3000	11189
IQF Custom Packing LLC	Fall River	MA	G	508 646-0400	10715
Wild Ocean Aquaculture LLC	Portland	ME	G	207 458-6288	6745

FOOD PRDTS, FISH & SEAFOOD: Chowders, Frozen

	CITY	ST	EMP	PHONE	ENTRY #
Seafood Gourmet Inc	Wolcott	CT	F	203 272-1544	5456

FOOD PRDTS, FISH & SEAFOOD: Crab cakes, Frozen

	CITY	ST	EMP	PHONE	ENTRY #
Coastal Seafoods Inc **(PA)**	Fairfield	CT	F	203 431-0453	1421
Saugatuck Kitchens LLC	Stratford	CT	G	203 334-1099	4442

FOOD PRDTS, FISH & SEAFOOD: Fish, Fresh, Prepared

	CITY	ST	EMP	PHONE	ENTRY #
M F Fley Incrprtd-New Bdford	New Bedford	MA	E	508 997-0773	13413
Sea & Reef Aquaculture LLC	Franklin	ME	G	207 422-2422	6069

FOOD PRDTS, FISH & SEAFOOD: Fish, Smoked

	CITY	ST	EMP	PHONE	ENTRY #
Boston Smoked Fish Company LLC	Boston	MA	G	617 819-5476	8442
Spence & Co Ltd	Brockton	MA	E	508 427-5577	9177
Ducktrap River of Maine LLC	Belfast	ME	C	207 338-6280	5688

FOOD PRDTS, FISH & SEAFOOD: Fresh, Prepared

	CITY	ST	EMP	PHONE	ENTRY #
Georges Bank LLC	Boston	MA	F	617 423-3474	8560
North Coast Sea-Foods Corp **(PA)**	Boston	MA	C	617 345-4400	8740
North Coast Sea-Foods Corp	New Bedford	MA	E	508 997-0766	13428
Bayley Quality Seafood Inc	Scarborough	ME	G	207 883-4581	6909
North Atlantic Inc	Portland	ME	G	207 774-6025	6704
Shucks Maine Lobster LLC	Richmond	ME	F	207 737-4800	6783

FOOD PRDTS, FISH & SEAFOOD: Fresh/Frozen Chowder, Soup/Stew

	CITY	ST	EMP	PHONE	ENTRY #
Central Maine Cold Storage	Bucksport	ME	G	419 215-7955	5854

FOOD PRDTS, FISH & SEAFOOD: Prepared Cakes & Sticks

	CITY	ST	EMP	PHONE	ENTRY #
Harmons Clam Cakes	Portland	ME	G	207 967-4100	6669

FOOD PRDTS, FISH & SEAFOOD: Sardines, Canned, Jarred, Etc

	CITY	ST	EMP	PHONE	ENTRY #
L Ray Packing Company	Milbridge	ME	G	207 546-2355	6435

FOOD PRDTS, FISH & SEAFOOD: Seafood, Frozen, Prepared

	CITY	ST	EMP	PHONE	ENTRY #
Bonamar Corp	Newton	MA	F	617 965-3400	13571
High Liner Foods USA Inc	Peabody	MA	C	978 977-5305	14341
Kyler Seafood Inc	New Bedford	MA	D	508 984-5150	13406
Maine Seafood Ventures LLC	Saco	ME	G	207 303-0165	6853

FOOD PRDTS, FROZEN, WHOLESALE: Vegetables & Fruit Prdts

	CITY	ST	EMP	PHONE	ENTRY #
Jens & Marie Inc	Providence	RI	G	401 475-9991	21043

FOOD PRDTS, FROZEN: Breakfasts, Packaged

	CITY	ST	EMP	PHONE	ENTRY #
Just Breakfast & Things	Lisbon	CT	G	860 376-4040	1943
Paramount South Boston	Boston	MA	G	617 269-9999	8765
Slacktide Cafe LLC	Arundel	ME	G	207 467-3822	5535

FOOD PRDTS, FROZEN: Ethnic Foods, NEC

	CITY	ST	EMP	PHONE	ENTRY #
Chinamerica Food Manufacture	Boston	MA	F	617 426-1818	8469
Putney Pasta Company Inc	Brattleboro	VT	E	802 257-4800	21746

FOOD PRDTS, FROZEN: Fruit Juice, Concentrates

	CITY	ST	EMP	PHONE	ENTRY #
Quality Kitchen Corp Delaware	Danbury	CT	G	203 744-2000	977
Ocean Spray Cranberries Inc **(PA)**	Middleboro	MA	B	508 946-1000	13072
Ocean Spray International Inc **(HQ)**	Middleboro	MA	D	508 946-1000	13074
Ocean Spray Intl Svcs Inc **(HQ)**	Lakeville	MA	E	508 946-1000	11977

FOOD PRDTS, FROZEN: Fruits

	CITY	ST	EMP	PHONE	ENTRY #
Allens Blueberry Freezer Inc **(PA)**	Ellsworth	ME	E	207 667-5561	6013
G M Allen & Son Inc	Orland	ME	G	207 469-7060	6549
Jasper Wyman & Son **(PA)**	Milbridge	ME	G	207 546-3800	6433
Jasper Wyman & Son	Milbridge	ME	G	207 546-2311	6434
Maine Wild Blueberry Company **(DH)**	Machias	ME	D	207 255-8364	6392

FOOD PRDTS, FROZEN: Fruits & Vegetables

	CITY	ST	EMP	PHONE	ENTRY #
McCain Foods Usa Inc	Easton	ME	B	207 488-2561	5991
Purbeck Isle Inc **(PA)**	Augusta	ME	E	207 623-5119	5617

FOOD PRDTS, FROZEN: Fruits, Juices & Vegetables

	CITY	ST	EMP	PHONE	ENTRY #
Conopco Inc	Trumbull	CT	D	203 381-3557	4621
Fruitbud Juice LLC	Danbury	CT	E	203 790-8200	923
Santorini Breeze LLC	Branford	CT	G	203 640-3431	344
Ocean Spray Cranberries Inc	Middleboro	MA	C	508 947-4940	13073
Tropicana Products Inc	Taunton	MA	E	508 821-2056	15792
Welch Foods Inc A Cooperative **(HQ)**	Concord	MA	B	978 371-1000	10160
Maine Wild Blueberry Company	Machias	ME	D	207 255-8364	6393
Merrill Blueberry Farms Inc	Hancock	ME	F	207 667-2541	6170

FOOD PRDTS, FROZEN: NEC

	CITY	ST	EMP	PHONE	ENTRY #
Kohler Mix Specialties LLC	Newington	CT	C	860 666-1511	2876
Ragozzino Foods Inc **(PA)**	Meriden	CT	F	203 238-2553	2123
Villarina Pasta & Fine Foods **(PA)**	Danbury	CT	G	203 917-4463	1004
Mama Rosies Co Inc	Boston	MA	E	617 242-4300	8680
Marias Food Products Inc	Medford	MA	G	781 396-4110	12940

	CITY	ST	EMP	PHONE	ENTRY #
Nestle	Taunton	MA	G	508 828-3954	15768
Stuffed Foods LLC	Wilmington	MA	E	978 203-0370	17049
Waterwood Corporation	Westfield	MA	E	413 572-1010	16740
Bafs Inc **(PA)**	Bangor	ME	F	207 942-5226	5630
Barber Foods	Portland	ME	E	207 772-1934	6620
Maine Meal LLC	Skowhegan	ME	G	207 779-4185	6980
McCain Foods Usa Inc	Easton	ME	B	207 488-2561	5991
Wise-Acre Inc	Blue Hill	ME	G	207 374-5400	5775
A B Munroe Dairy Inc	East Providence	RI	D	401 438-4450	20384

FOOD PRDTS, FROZEN: Pizza

	CITY	ST	EMP	PHONE	ENTRY #
Uno Foods Inc	Brockton	MA	E	508 580-1561	9185
Orono House of Pizza	Orono	ME	G	207 866-5505	6557
Take 2 Dough Productions Inc	Sanford	ME	F	207 490-6502	6893

FOOD PRDTS, FROZEN: Potato Prdts

	CITY	ST	EMP	PHONE	ENTRY #
McCain Foods Usa Inc	Easton	ME	A	207 488-2561	5992
Penobscot McCrum LLC	Belfast	ME	C	207 338-4360	5696

FOOD PRDTS, FROZEN: Snack Items

	CITY	ST	EMP	PHONE	ENTRY #
Orange Cheese Company	Orange	CT	G	917 603-4378	3377
Bobby OS Foods LLC	Salem	NH	G	603 458-2502	19714

FOOD PRDTS, FROZEN: Soups

	CITY	ST	EMP	PHONE	ENTRY #
Blount Fine Foods Corp **(PA)**	Fall River	MA	C	774 888-1300	10669
Plenus Group Inc	Lowell	MA	E	978 970-3832	12422
Blount Fine Foods Corp	Warren	RI	D	401 245-8800	21290

FOOD PRDTS, FRUITS & VEGETABLES, FRESH, WHOLESALE: Fruits

	CITY	ST	EMP	PHONE	ENTRY #
Amazon Fruit Corp	Ludlow	MA	G	774 244-2820	12453

FOOD PRDTS, MEAT & MEAT PRDTS, WHOLESALE: Cured Or Smoked

	CITY	ST	EMP	PHONE	ENTRY #
Manchester Packing Company Inc	Manchester	CT	D	860 646-5000	2024

FOOD PRDTS, MEAT & MEAT PRDTS, WHOLESALE: Fresh

	CITY	ST	EMP	PHONE	ENTRY #
Wohrles Foods Inc **(PA)**	Pittsfield	MA	E	413 442-1518	14513
Lincoln Packing Co	Cranston	RI	E	401 943-0878	20255

FOOD PRDTS, MEAT & MEAT PRDTS, WHOLESALE: Lard

	CITY	ST	EMP	PHONE	ENTRY #
Vermont Packinghouse LLC	North Springfield	VT	F	802 886-8688	22239

FOOD PRDTS, POULTRY, WHOLESALE: Poultry Prdts, NEC

	CITY	ST	EMP	PHONE	ENTRY #
Suffield Poultry Inc	Springfield	MA	G	413 737-8392	15510

FOOD PRDTS, WHOLESALE: Beverage Concentrates

	CITY	ST	EMP	PHONE	ENTRY #
Keurig Dr Pepper Inc **(PA)**	Burlington	MA	D	781 418-7000	9292

FOOD PRDTS, WHOLESALE: Chocolate

	CITY	ST	EMP	PHONE	ENTRY #
Nel Group LLC	Windsor	CT	F	860 683-0190	5350
Granite State Candy Shoppe LLC **(PA)**	Concord	NH	F	603 225-2591	17903
Lindt & Sprungli (usa) Inc **(HQ)**	Stratham	NH	C	603 778-8100	19871
Birnn Chocolates Vermont Inc	South Burlington	VT	F	802 860-1047	22438

FOOD PRDTS, WHOLESALE: Coffee & Tea

	CITY	ST	EMP	PHONE	ENTRY #
New England Partnership Inc	Norwood	MA	C	800 225-3537	14182
Carpe Diem Coffee Roasting Co	North Berwick	ME	G	207 676-2233	6505
Mills Coffee Roasting Co	Providence	RI	F	401 781-7860	21068

FOOD PRDTS, WHOLESALE: Coffee, Green Or Roasted

	CITY	ST	EMP	PHONE	ENTRY #
George Howell Coffee Co LLC	Acton	MA	F	978 635-9033	7358
Gone Troppo Inc **(PA)**	Brookline	MA	G	617 739-7995	9201

FOOD PRDTS, WHOLESALE: Condiments

	CITY	ST	EMP	PHONE	ENTRY #
Omar Coffee Company	Newington	CT	E	860 667-8889	2888
Mange LLC	Somerville	MA	G	917 880-2104	15194

FOOD PRDTS, WHOLESALE: Dog Food

	CITY	ST	EMP	PHONE	ENTRY #
Tbd Brands LLC	Exeter	NH	G	603 775-7772	18133

FOOD PRDTS, WHOLESALE: Flavorings & Fragrances

	CITY	ST	EMP	PHONE	ENTRY #
Saccuzzo Company Inc	Newington	CT	G	860 665-1101	2900

FOOD PRDTS, WHOLESALE: Health

	CITY	ST	EMP	PHONE	ENTRY #
Edesia Industries LLC	North Kingstown	RI	D	401 272-5521	20706

FOOD PRDTS, WHOLESALE: Juices

	CITY	ST	EMP	PHONE	ENTRY #
Guida-Seibert Dairy Company **(PA)**	New Britain	CT	C	860 224-2404	2537

FOOD PRDTS, WHOLESALE: Organic & Diet

	CITY	ST	EMP	PHONE	ENTRY #
Herbasway Laboratories LLC	Wallingford	CT	E	203 269-6991	4750

FOOD PRDTS, WHOLESALE: Pasta & Rice

	CITY	ST	EMP	PHONE	ENTRY #
Vita Pasta Inc	Old Saybrook	CT	G	860 395-1452	3355
Albert Capone **(PA)**	Somerville	MA	G	617 629-2296	15151
Pasta Bene Inc	Brockton	MA	F	508 583-1515	9170

FOOD PRDTS, WHOLESALE: Salad Dressing

	CITY	ST	EMP	PHONE	ENTRY #
R & N Inc	Unity	ME	G	207 948-2613	7118

FOOD PRDTS, WHOLESALE: Sauces

	CITY	ST	EMP	PHONE	ENTRY #
Cape Ann Olive Oil Company	Gloucester	MA	G	978 281-1061	11170

FOOD PRDTS, WHOLESALE: Specialty

	CITY	ST	EMP	PHONE	ENTRY #
Boyajian Inc	Canton	MA	F	781 828-9966	9718
Nasoya Foods Inc	Ayer	MA	D	978 772-6880	7927
Granny Blossom Specialty	Wells	VT	G	802 645-0507	22599
Runamok Maple LLC	Fairfax	VT	G	802 849-7943	21978

FOOD PRDTS, WHOLESALE: Spices & Seasonings

	CITY	ST	EMP	PHONE	ENTRY #
A Lot Bakery Products Inc	Boston	MA	G	617 561-1122	8332
Stonewall Kitchen LLC **(PA)**	York	ME	C	207 351-2713	7316

FOOD PRDTS, WHOLESALE: Tea

	CITY	ST	EMP	PHONE	ENTRY #
Finlay EXT Ingredients USA Inc **(DH)**	Lincoln	RI	D	800 288-6272	20574

FOOD PRDTS, WHOLESALE: Water, Mineral Or Spring, Bottled

	CITY	ST	EMP	PHONE	ENTRY #
G C Management Corp **(PA)**	Southwest Harbor	ME	G	207 244-5363	7047

FOOD PRDTS, WHOLESALE: Wine Makers' Eqpt & Splys

	CITY	ST	EMP	PHONE	ENTRY #
Cocchia Norwalk Grape Co	Norwalk	CT	F	203 855-7911	3127

FOOD PRDTS: Almond Pastes

	CITY	ST	EMP	PHONE	ENTRY #
City Fresh Foods Inc	Roxbury	MA	D	617 606-7123	14871
Modernist Pantry LLC	Eliot	ME	G	207 200-3817	6008

FOOD PRDTS: Animal & marine fats & oils

	CITY	ST	EMP	PHONE	ENTRY #
Baker Commodities Inc	Warwick	RI	G	401 821-3003	21331
Baker Commodities Inc	Williston	VT	G	802 658-0721	22657

FOOD PRDTS: Box Lunches, For Sale Off Premises

	CITY	ST	EMP	PHONE	ENTRY #
City Fresh Foods Inc	Roxbury	MA	D	617 606-7123	14872
Sidekim LLC	Lynn	MA	E	781 595-3663	12539

FOOD PRDTS: Bread Crumbs, Exc Made In Bakeries

	CITY	ST	EMP	PHONE	ENTRY #
A Lot Bakery Products Inc	Boston	MA	G	617 561-1122	8332
Sun Country Foods Inc **(HQ)**	Norwood	MA	E	855 824-7645	14202
Olivias Croutons Company Inc	Brandon	VT	G	802 465-8245	21713

FOOD PRDTS: Breakfast Bars

	CITY	ST	EMP	PHONE	ENTRY #
Attleboro Pancakes Inc	Attleboro	MA	G	508 399-8189	7707
Barbaras Bakery Inc **(DH)**	Marlborough	MA	E	800 343-0590	12725

FOOD PRDTS: Cereals

	CITY	ST	EMP	PHONE	ENTRY #
Kellogg Company	Newington	CT	A	860 665-9920	2875
Barbaras Bakery Inc **(DH)**	Marlborough	MA	E	800 343-0590	12725
Kraft Heinz Foods Company	Mansfield	MA	D	508 763-3311	12640
Old Creamery Grocery Store	Cummington	MA	G	413 634-5560	10173
Weetabix Company Inc	Sterling	MA	G	978 422-2905	15549

FOOD PRDTS: Cheese Curls & Puffs

	CITY	ST	EMP	PHONE	ENTRY #
Barbaras Bakery Inc **(DH)**	Marlborough	MA	E	800 343-0590	12725

FOOD PRDTS: Chicken, Processed, Fresh

	CITY	ST	EMP	PHONE	ENTRY #
Npc Processing Inc	Shelburne	VT	E	802 660-0496	22420

FOOD PRDTS: Chocolate Bars, Solid

	CITY	ST	EMP	PHONE	ENTRY #
Dark Matter Chocolate LLC	Cambridge	MA	G	303 718-3835	9451
Nibmor Inc	Biddeford	ME	G	207 502-7540	5752

FOOD PRDTS: Chocolate, Baking

	CITY	ST	EMP	PHONE	ENTRY #
La Creme Chocolat Inc	Standish	ME	G	443 841-2458	7062

FOOD PRDTS: Cocoa & Cocoa Prdts

	CITY	ST	EMP	PHONE	ENTRY #
Cape Cod Sweets LLC	Pocasset	MA	F	508 564-5840	14594

FOOD PRDTS: Cocoa, Instant

	CITY	ST	EMP	PHONE	ENTRY #
Silly Cow Farms LLC	Wells River	VT	E	802 429-2920	22603

FOOD PRDTS: Cocoa, Powdered

	CITY	ST	EMP	PHONE	ENTRY #
CSC Cocoa LLC	New Canaan	CT	G	203 846-5611	2596

FOOD PRDTS: Coffee

	CITY	ST	EMP	PHONE	ENTRY #
Als Beverage Company Inc	East Windsor	CT	E	860 627-7003	1276
Fjb America LLC	Westport	CT	G	203 682-2424	5194
Foundry Foods Inc	Norwalk	CT	G	314 982-3204	3154
Oasis Coffee Corp	Norwalk	CT	E	203 847-0554	3210
Batian Peak Coffee	Lowell	MA	G	978 663-2305	12351
Birds & Beans LLC	South Dartmouth	MA	G	857 233-2722	15236
George Howell Coffee Co LLC	Acton	MA	F	978 635-9033	7358
Jnp Coffee LLC	Shrewsbury	MA	G	858 518-7437	15120
Red 23 Holdings Inc	Portsmouth	NH	F	603 433-3011	19613
Vera Roasting Company	Portsmouth	NH	G	603 969-7970	19628
Farmer Willies Inc	Providence	RI	G	401 441-2997	21011

FOOD PRDTS: Coffee Extracts

	CITY	ST	EMP	PHONE	ENTRY #
Kerry Inc	Portland	ME	E	207 775-7060	6677
Finlay EXT Ingredients USA Inc **(DH)**	Lincoln	RI	D	800 288-6272	20574

FOOD PRDTS: Coffee Roasting, Exc Wholesale Grocers

	CITY	ST	EMP	PHONE	ENTRY #
B & B Ventures Ltd Lblty Co	Branford	CT	E	203 481-1700	294
Omar Coffee Company	Newington	CT	E	860 667-8889	2888
Saccuzzo Company Inc	Newington	CT	G	860 665-1101	2900
Tm Ward Co of Connecticut LLC	Norwalk	CT	G	203 866-9203	3257
Atomic Cafe **(PA)**	Salem	MA	F	978 910-0489	14895
Kraft Heinz Foods Company	Woburn	MA	C	781 933-2800	17212
New England Partnership Inc	Norwood	MA	C	800 225-3537	14182
Carpe Diem Coffee Roasting Co	North Berwick	ME	G	207 676-2233	6505
Finlay EXT Ingredients USA Inc	Woonsocket	RI	G	401 769-5490	21562
Mills Coffee Roasting Co	Providence	RI	F	401 781-7860	21068

FOOD PRDTS: Coffee, Ground, Mixed With Grain Or Chicory

	CITY	ST	EMP	PHONE	ENTRY #
Reily Foods Company	Malden	MA	G	504 524-6131	12593

FOOD PRDTS: Cole Slaw, Bulk

	CITY	ST	EMP	PHONE	ENTRY #
R & N Inc	Unity	ME	G	207 948-2613	7118

	CITY	ST	EMP	PHONE	ENTRY #

FOOD PRDTS: Cooking Oils, Refined Vegetable, Exc Corn

American Enrgy Indpendence LLC	Pittsfield	NH	G	603 228-3611	19498

FOOD PRDTS: Dessert Mixes & Fillings

Cherrybrook Kitchen LLC	Burlington	MA	G	781 272-0400	9248
Concord Foods LLC	Brockton	MA	C	508 580-1700	9131

FOOD PRDTS: Desserts, Ready-To-Mix

Island Desserts LLC	Walpole	MA	D	508 660-2200	15995

FOOD PRDTS: Dips, Exc Cheese & Sour Cream Based

Guasa Salsa Vzla	Norwalk	CT	G	203 981-7011	3164
Soulas Homemade Salsa LLC	Boxford	MA	G	978 314-7735	8978
Tribe Mediterranean Foods Inc	Taunton	MA	D	774 961-0000	15791
Galaxie Salsa Co	Buxton	ME	G	207 939-3392	5856
Drews LLC **(HQ)**	Chester	VT	E	802 875-1184	21842
Tom Knows Salsa LLC	Eden	VT	G	802 793-5079	21921

FOOD PRDTS: Dough, Pizza, Prepared

Michele Schiano Di Cola Inc	Wallingford	CT	G	203 265-5301	4773
Itllbe LLC	Scarborough	ME	G	207 730-7301	6927
Management Controls LLC	Auburn	ME	G	207 753-6844	5579
Pro Dough Inc	Manchester	NH	F	603 623-6844	18906

FOOD PRDTS: Doughs & Batters

Pillsbury Company LLC	Chelsea	MA	D	617 884-9800	9964

FOOD PRDTS: Doughs, Frozen Or Refrig From Purchased Flour

Rhino Foods Inc **(PA)**	Burlington	VT	C	802 862-0252	21807

FOOD PRDTS: Dressings, Salad, Raw & Cooked Exc Dry Mixes

Da Silva Klanko Ltd	Waterbury	CT	G	203 756-4932	4863
Kerry R Wood	Westport	CT	G	203 221-7780	5205
Newmans Own Inc **(PA)**	Westport	CT	E	203 222-0136	5218
Thomas J Lipton Inc	Trumbull	CT	A	206 381-3500	4635
Pearlco of Boston Inc	Canton	MA	E	781 821-1010	9766
World Harbors Inc	Auburn	ME	E	207 786-3200	5601
Drews LLC **(HQ)**	Chester	VT	E	802 875-1184	21842

FOOD PRDTS: Dried & Dehydrated Fruits, Vegetables & Soup Mix

Decas Cranberry Products Inc	Carver	MA	E	508 866-8506	9804
Good To-Go LLC	Kittery	ME	F	207 451-9060	6256
Maine Wild Blueberry Company	Machias	ME	D	207 255-8364	6393

FOOD PRDTS: Edible fats & oils

Baker Commodities Inc	North Billerica	MA	D	978 454-8811	13795
Felicia Winkfield	Newport	RI	G	401 849-3029	20665

FOOD PRDTS: Eggs, Processed

Pete and Gerrys Organics LLC	Monroe	NH	E	603 638-2827	19091

FOOD PRDTS: Eggs, Processed, Canned

Taylor Egg Products Inc	Madbury	NH	E	603 742-1050	18761

FOOD PRDTS: Emulsifiers

White Oak Farms	Sandown	NH	G	603 887-2233	19789

FOOD PRDTS: Fish Oil

Marine Bioproducts	Quincy	MA	G	617 847-1426	14638

FOOD PRDTS: Flavored Ices, Frozen

Ice Effects	Rockland	MA	G	781 871-7070	14807
Richies King Slush Mfg Co Inc	Everett	MA	F	800 287-5874	10627
Slush Connection Inc	North Easton	MA	G	508 230-3788	13952
Spadafora Slush Co	Malden	MA	G	617 548-5870	12597

FOOD PRDTS: Flour

Bay State Milling Company **(PA)**	Quincy	MA	E	617 328-4423	14614
Seaboard Flour LLC **(PA)**	Boston	MA	G	917 928-6040	8842

FOOD PRDTS: Flour & Other Grain Mill Products

Channel Alloys	Norwalk	CT	G	203 975-1404	3123
Pelletier Millwrights LLC	Danielson	CT	G	860 564-8936	1016
Ardent Mills LLC	Ayer	MA	E	978 772-6337	7911
Biena LLC	Boston	MA	G	617 202-5210	8407

FOOD PRDTS: Flour Mixes & Doughs

Watson LLC **(DH)**	West Haven	CT	B	203 932-3000	5149
Concord Foods LLC	Brockton	MA	C	508 580-1700	9131
Ever Better Eating Inc	Pittsfield	NH	D	603 435-5119	19499
Pollys Pancake Parlor	Sugar Hill	NH	G	603 823-5575	19878

FOOD PRDTS: Frankfurters, Poultry

Saugy Inc	Cranston	RI	G	401 640-1879	20283

FOOD PRDTS: Fruit Juices

Fruta Juice Bar LLC	Bridgeport	CT	G	203 690-9168	416
Bevovations LLC **(PA)**	Leominster	MA	F	978 227-5469	12118
Local Juice Inc	Hyannis	MA	G	508 813-9282	11846

FOOD PRDTS: Fruits & Vegetables, Pickled

Star Pickling Corp	Swansea	MA	F	508 672-8535	15716
Stonewall Kitchen LLC **(PA)**	York	ME	C	207 351-2713	7316
Vega Food Industries Inc	Providence	RI	F	401 942-0620	21146

FOOD PRDTS: Fruits, Dehydrated Or Dried

American Nut & Chocolate Inc	Boston	MA	G	617 427-1510	8362
Arcade Industries Inc	Auburn	MA	F	508 832-6300	7826
Peeled Inc	Cumberland	RI	F	212 706-2001	20338

FOOD PRDTS: Fruits, Dried Or Dehydrated, Exc Freeze-Dried

Ocean Spray Cranberries Inc **(PA)**	Middleboro	MA	B	508 946-1000	13072
Ocean Spray International Inc **(HQ)**	Middleboro	MA	D	508 946-1000	13074
Ocean Spray Intl Svcs Inc **(HQ)**	Lakeville	MA	E	508 946-1000	11977

FOOD PRDTS: Granola & Energy Bars, Nonchocolate

Maple Nut Kitchen LLC	Keene	NH	G	603 354-3219	18514
Paleo Products LLC	Pawtucket	RI	G	401 305-3473	20873
Gorilla Bars Inc	Montgomery Center	VT	G	802 309-4997	22143
Small Batch Organics LLC	Manchester Center	VT	F	802 367-1054	22090

FOOD PRDTS: Honey

Green Mountain Honey Farms	Ferrisburg	VT	G	802 877-3396	21986

FOOD PRDTS: Ice, Blocks

East Bay Ice Co Inc	East Providence	RI	G	401 434-7485	20408

FOOD PRDTS: Ice, Cubes

Dee Zee Ice LLC	Southington	CT	F	860 276-3500	4046
Twenty Five Commerce Inc	Norwalk	CT	G	203 866-0540	3263
Natural Rocks Spring Water Ice	Eliot	ME	G	207 451-2110	6009
Pier Ice Plant Inc	Narragansett	RI	G	401 789-6090	20645

FOOD PRDTS: Instant Coffee

Riseandshine Corporation **(PA)**	Stamford	CT	F	917 599-7541	4302
Mojo Cold Brewed Coffee Inc	Beverly	MA	G	617 877-2997	8156

FOOD PRDTS: Macaroni Prdts, Dry, Alphabet, Rings Or Shells

Venda Ravioli Inc	Providence	RI	E	401 421-9105	21147
Venda Ravioli Inc **(PA)**	Providence	RI	C	401 421-9105	21148

FOOD PRDTS: Macaroni, Noodles, Spaghetti, Pasta, Etc

Carlas Pasta Inc	South Windsor	CT	C	860 436-4042	3949
Oasis Coffee Corp	Norwalk	CT	E	203 847-0554	3210
Villarina Pasta & Fine Foods **(PA)**	Danbury	CT	G	203 917-4463	1004
Albert Capone **(PA)**	Somerville	MA	G	617 629-2296	15151
Chinese Spaghetti Factory	Boston	MA	G	617 542-0224	8470
Spinelli Ravioli Mfg Co Inc	Boston	MA	E	617 567-1992	8859
Pasta Patch Inc	East Greenwich	RI	F	401 884-1234	20376

FOOD PRDTS: Margarine-Butter Blends

Genuine Jamaican	Barnet	VT	G	802 633-2676	21604

FOOD PRDTS: Marshmallow Creme

Durkee-Mower Inc	Lynn	MA	E	781 593-8007	12503

FOOD PRDTS: Mixes, Bread & Roll From Purchased Flour

Wilevco Inc	Billerica	MA	F	978 667-0400	8310

FOOD PRDTS: Mixes, Pancake From Purchased Flour

Bouchard Family Farm Products	Fort Kent	ME	G	207 834-3237	6058
Maple Grove Farms Vermont Inc **(HQ)**	Saint Johnsbury	VT	D	802 748-5141	22391

FOOD PRDTS: Mixes, Salad Dressings, Dry

Avon Food Company LLC	Stoughton	MA	F	781 341-4981	15582

FOOD PRDTS: Mustard, Prepared

Howard Foods Inc **(PA)**	Danvers	MA	G	978 774-6207	10224
Rayes Mustard Mill	Eastport	ME	G	207 853-4451	5996
Old Dutch Mustard Co Inc	Greenville	NH	D	516 466-0522	18229

FOOD PRDTS: Nuts & Seeds

Arcade Industries Inc	Auburn	MA	F	508 832-6300	7826

FOOD PRDTS: Olive Oil

New Canaan Olive Oil LLC	Stamford	CT	G	845 240-3294	4255
Olive Capizzano Oils & Vinegar	Pawcatuck	CT	G	860 495-2187	3439
Olive Chiappetta Oil LLC	Stamford	CT	G	203 223-3655	4268
Olive Nutmeg Oil	New Milford	CT	G	860 354-7300	2821
Olive Oils and Balsamics LLC	Rocky Hill	CT	G	860 563-0105	3726
Olive Sabor Oil Co	Somers	CT	G	860 922-7483	3919
Shoreline Vine	Madison	CT	G	203 779-5331	1976
Andaluna Enterprises Inc	West Newbury	MA	G	617 335-3204	16489
Bogaris Corporation	Brookline	MA	G	617 505-6696	9196
Branch Olive Oil Company LLC	Peabody	MA	G	781 775-8788	14317
Cape Ann Olive Oil Company	Gloucester	MA	G	978 281-1061	11170
Extra Virgin Foods Inc	Watertown	MA	G	617 407-9161	16285
Little Shop of Olive Oils Inc	Medway	MA	G	508 533-5522	12965
New England Olive Oil Company	Concord	MA	G	978 610-6776	10146
Olive Mannys Oil Inc	Wilbraham	MA	G	413 233-2532	16942
Olive Newburyport Oil	Newburyport	MA	G	978 462-7700	13519
Olive Northampton Oil Co	Northampton	MA	G	413 537-7357	14014
Omega Olive Oil Inc	Kingston	MA	G	781 585-3179	11962
Tre Olive LLC	East Longmeadow	MA	G	617 680-0096	10499
Fiore Artisan Olive Oils	Bangor	ME	G	207 801-8549	5644
Lakonia Greek Products LLC	Biddeford	ME	G	207 282-4002	5742
Olive Fiore Oils & Vinegars	Rockland	ME	G	207 596-0276	6807
Olive Wildrose Oil	South Berwick	ME	G	603 767-0597	7003
North Conway Olive Oil Company	North Conway	NH	G	603 307-1066	19377
Olive Lakonian Oil LLC	Manchester	NH	G	603 264-5025	18894
Allavita	Montpelier	VT	G	802 225-6526	22144
Olives Oil	Colchester	VT	G	802 864-4908	21874

FOOD PRDTS: Onion Fries

Denny S Sweet Onion Rings	Lynn	MA	G	781 598-5317	12501

FOOD PRDTS: Pasta, Rice/Potatoes, Uncooked, Pkgd

	CITY	ST	EMP	PHONE	ENTRY #
Nuovo Pasta Productions Ltd	Stratford	CT	C	203 380-4090	4437
Albert Capone **(PA)**	Somerville	MA	G	617 629-2296	15151
Precision Pasta Dies Inc	Hyannis	MA	G	978 866-7720	11854
Terracotta Pasta Co **(PA)**	Dover	NH	G	603 749-2288	18059
Stonebridge Restaurant Inc	Tiverton	RI	E	401 625-5780	21264

FOOD PRDTS: Pasta, Uncooked, Packaged With Other Ingredients

	CITY	ST	EMP	PHONE	ENTRY #
Durantes Pasta Inc	West Haven	CT	G	203 387-5560	5118
Fine Food Services Inc	Groton	CT	E	860 445-5276	1676
Mastriani Gourmet Food LLC	Bridgeport	CT	G	203 368-9556	448
Vita Pasta Inc	Old Saybrook	CT	G	860 395-1452	3355
Josephs Gourmet Pasta Company	Haverhill	MA	B	978 521-1718	11443
Pasta Bene Inc	Brockton	MA	F	508 583-1515	9170
Vermont Pie and Pasta Co	Derby	VT	G	802 334-7770	21905

FOOD PRDTS: Peanut Butter

	CITY	ST	EMP	PHONE	ENTRY #
Peanut Butter and Jelly	Stamford	CT	G	203 504-2280	4280
Leavitt Corporation **(HQ)**	Everett	MA	C	617 389-2600	10616
Superior Nut Company Inc	Cambridge	MA	E	800 251-6060	9665
Edesia Industries LLC	North Kingstown	RI	D	401 272-5521	20706
Pbuttri LLC	Pawtucket	RI	G	401 996-5583	20877
Protein Plus Peanut Butter Co	Lincoln	RI	G	401 996-5583	20593

FOOD PRDTS: Pectin

	CITY	ST	EMP	PHONE	ENTRY #
Cleverfoodies Inc	Burlington	VT	G	888 938-7984	21775

FOOD PRDTS: Pizza Doughs From Purchased Flour

	CITY	ST	EMP	PHONE	ENTRY #
Dough Connection Corporation	Woburn	MA	G	877 693-6844	17169

FOOD PRDTS: Pizza, Refrigerated

	CITY	ST	EMP	PHONE	ENTRY #
Sonnys Pizza Inc	Saugus	MA	F	617 381-1900	14998
Uno Foods Inc **(DH)**	Boston	MA	F	617 323-9200	8900
Top Shell LLC	Central Falls	RI	F	401 726-7890	20127

FOOD PRDTS: Popcorn, Popped

	CITY	ST	EMP	PHONE	ENTRY #
New England Prtzel Popcorn Inc	Lawrence	MA	G	978 687-0342	12064
Micheles Sweet Shoppe LLC	Londonderry	NH	G	603 425-2946	18722

FOOD PRDTS: Popcorn, Unpopped

	CITY	ST	EMP	PHONE	ENTRY #
New England Prtzel Popcorn Inc	Lawrence	MA	G	978 687-0342	12064

FOOD PRDTS: Potato & Corn Chips & Similar Prdts

	CITY	ST	EMP	PHONE	ENTRY #
Frito-Lay North America Inc	Dayville	CT	A	860 412-1000	1045
Mediterranean Snack Fd Co LLC	Stamford	CT	F	973 402-2644	4248
U T Z	North Franklin	CT	G	860 383-4266	2992
3 Potato 4 LLC	Salem	MA	G	978 744-0948	14888
Frito-Lay North America Inc	Wilmington	MA	C	978 657-8344	17002
Frito-Lay North America Inc	Braintree	MA	F	781 348-1500	9008
Regco Corporation	Haverhill	MA	E	978 521-4370	11468
Sacar Enterprises LLC	Amesbury	MA	G	978 834-6494	7506
Stacys Pita Chip Company Inc	Randolph	MA	D	781 961-2800	14698
Vintage Maine Kitchen LLC	Freeport	ME	G	207 317-2536	6088
Gringo Kitchens LLC	Manchester Center	VT	F	802 362-0836	22086

FOOD PRDTS: Potato Chips & Other Potato-Based Snacks

	CITY	ST	EMP	PHONE	ENTRY #
Plant Snacks LLC	Needham	MA	G	617 480-6265	13308
Utz Quality Foods Inc	Fitchburg	MA	E	978 342-6038	10860
Smith & Assoc	Scarborough	ME	G	866 299-6487	6940

FOOD PRDTS: Poultry Sausage, Lunch Meats/Other Poultry Prdts

	CITY	ST	EMP	PHONE	ENTRY #
Waybest Foods Inc	South Windsor	CT	G	860 289-7948	4020

FOOD PRDTS: Poultry, Processed, Frozen

	CITY	ST	EMP	PHONE	ENTRY #
Barber Foods **(DH)**	Portland	ME	E	207 482-5500	6619

FOOD PRDTS: Poultry, Processed, NEC

	CITY	ST	EMP	PHONE	ENTRY #
Suffield Poultry Inc	Springfield	MA	G	413 737-8392	15510
Barber Foods	Portland	ME	E	207 772-1934	6620

FOOD PRDTS: Preparations

	CITY	ST	EMP	PHONE	ENTRY #
Entrees Made Easy	Monroe	CT	G	203 261-5777	2402
Frescobene Foods LLC	Fairfield	CT	G	203 610-4688	1433
Global Palate Foods LLC	Westport	CT	G	203 543-3028	5198
Hummel Bros Inc	New Haven	CT	D	203 787-4113	2697
Ikigai Foods LLC	Shelton	CT	G	203 954-8083	3816
Kohler Mix Specialties LLC	Newington	CT	C	860 666-1511	2876
Lesser Evil	Danbury	CT	G	203 529-3555	946
Malta Food Pantry Inc	Hartford	CT	G	860 725-0944	1842
Maple Craft Foods LLC	Sandy Hook	CT	G	203 913-7066	3744
Old Castle Foods LLC	Newtown	CT	G	203 426-1344	2932
Paridise Foods LLC	Milford	CT	G	203 283-3903	2331
Podunk Popcorn	South Windsor	CT	G	860 648-9565	4002
Premiere Packg Partners LLC	Waterbury	CT	E	203 694-0003	4944
Source Inc **(PA)**	North Branford	CT	G	203 488-6400	2977
Sovipe Food Distributors LLC	Danbury	CT	G	203 648-2781	995
Supreme Storm Services LLC	Southington	CT	G	860 201-0642	4083
A To Z Foods Inc	Arlington	MA	G	781 413-0221	7621
Alexis Foods Inc **(PA)**	Holden	MA	G	508 829-9111	11541
Alexis Foods Inc	Littleton	MA	G	978 952-6777	12290
Blitz Foods LLC	Boston	MA	G	617 243-7446	8414
Boyajian Inc	Canton	MA	F	781 828-9966	9718
Breakwater Foods LLC	Lynn	MA	G	617 335-6475	12493
Brozzian LLC	Whitinsville	MA	G	774 280-9338	16911
Chef Creations LLC	Lynn	MA	D	407 228-0069	12497
Chinamerica Food Manufacture	Boston	MA	F	617 426-1818	8469
Choice Foods	Bellingham	MA	G	508 332-2442	8034
Cocomama Foods Inc	Boston	MA	G	978 621-2126	8479
Cuizina Foods Company	Lynn	MA	E	425 486-7000	12498
Dough Connection Corporation	Woburn	MA	G	877 693-6844	17169
Fedhal Foods Inc	Worcester	MA	G	508 595-9178	17374
Fogg Flavor Labs LLC	West Newbury	MA	G	978 808-1732	16491
Franklin Area Survival Center	Turners Falls	MA	F	413 863-9549	15877
Freeda S Foods LLC	Stoneham	MA	G	781 662-6474	15564
Gillians Foods Inc	Salem	MA	E	781 586-0086	14915
Good Wives Inc	Lynn	MA	G	781 596-0070	12513
Goose Valley Natural Foods LLC	Boston	MA	G	617 914-0126	8574
Jbnj Foods Incorporated	Hanson	MA	G	781 293-0912	11364
Kayjay Foods Inc	East Templeton	MA	G	978 833-0728	10519
Km Foods Inc	Waltham	MA	G	781 894-7616	16138
Lillys Gastronomia Italian	Everett	MA	F	617 387-9666	10617
Longrun LLC	Belmont	MA	G	617 758-8674	8077
Navarrete Foods Inc	Charlestown	MA	G	508 735-7319	9839
Newly Weds Foods Inc	Watertown	MA	D	617 926-7600	16303
Nolas Fresh Foods LLC	Roslindale	MA	G	617 283-2644	14840
Pride India Inc **(PA)**	Brighton	MA	F	617 202-9659	9105
Puratos Corporation	Norwood	MA	G	781 688-8560	14190
Richelieu Foods Inc **(DH)**	Braintree	MA	E	781 786-6800	9034
Shire City Herbals Inc	Pittsfield	MA	F	413 344-4740	14508
Sunopta Ingredients Inc	Bedford	MA	G	781 276-5100	8012
United Citrus Products Co	Taunton	MA	G	800 229-7300	15794
Vivido Natural LLC	Newton	MA	F	617 630-0131	13653
Walter Scott	Lexington	MA	G	781 862-4893	12284
Yankee Trader Seafood Ltd	Pembroke	MA	F	781 829-4350	14434
Barney & Co California LLC	Cape Elizabeth	ME	G	559 442-1752	5874
Cherry Point Products Inc	Milbridge	ME	D	207 546-0930	6431
Lukas Foods Inc	Biddeford	ME	E	207 284-7052	5744
Maine Medicinals Inc	Dresden	ME	G	207 737-8717	5967
Reginaspices	Portland	ME	G	207 632-5544	6721
Schlotterbeck & Foss LLC **(PA)**	Westbrook	ME	E	207 772-4666	7206
Discerning Palate LLC **(PA)**	Meredith	NH	G	603 279-8600	18973
Little Acre Gourmet Foods	Dover	NH	G	603 749-7227	18035
Manna Mix	Newport	NH	G	213 519-0719	19350
Msn Corporation	Manchester	NH	D	603 623-3528	18879
Popzup LLC	Dover	NH	G	978 502-1737	18046
Stump City Cider	Rochester	NH	G	603 234-6288	19688
Cocofuel	Cranston	RI	G	401 209-8099	20198
Marilu Foods Inc	Westerly	RI	G	401 348-2858	21529
Stedagio LLC	Mapleville	RI	G	401 568-6228	20615
Bonneaus Vermont Maple	Lowell	VT	G	802 744-2742	22059
Bread & Chocolate Inc	Wells River	VT	G	802 429-2920	22600
Drinkmaple	Saint Albans	VT	G	802 528-5279	22367
Granny Blossom Specialty	Wells	VT	G	802 645-0507	22599
Harmonized Cookery	Montpelier	VT	G	802 598-9206	22149
Lunch Bundles Inc	Bristol	VT	G	802 272-3051	21764
Potter Family Maple	Bakersfield	VT	G	802 578-0937	21603
Rhapsody Natural Foods Inc	Cabot	VT	G	802 563-2172	21820
Sbfk Inc	Rutland	VT	G	802 297-7665	22353
Vermont Maple Direct	Washington	VT	G	802 793-3326	22581
Vermont Maple Sug Makers Assoc	Waterbury Center	VT	G	802 498-7767	22593
Vermont Soy LLC	Hardwick	VT	G	802 472-8500	22014
Vermont Syrup Company LLC	Fairfield	VT	G	802 309-8861	21985
World Cuisine Concepts LLC	White River Junction	VT	G	603 676-8591	22644

FOOD PRDTS: Prepared Sauces, Exc Tomato Based

	CITY	ST	EMP	PHONE	ENTRY #
Kettle Cuisine LLC **(PA)**	Lynn	MA	C	617 409-1100	12519
Great Soups Inc	Bristol	RI	F	401 253-3200	20082

FOOD PRDTS: Relishes, Fruit & Vegetable

	CITY	ST	EMP	PHONE	ENTRY #
RE Kimball & Co Inc	Amesbury	MA	G	978 388-1826	7505

FOOD PRDTS: Salads

	CITY	ST	EMP	PHONE	ENTRY #
Kerry R Wood	Westport	CT	G	203 221-7780	5205
Boston Salads and Provs Inc	Boston	MA	E	617 307-6340	8439
Hans Kissle Company LLC	Haverhill	MA	C	978 556-4500	11440
International Food Products	Norwood	MA	G	781 769-6666	14166
Jims Salad Co	Unity	ME	G	207 948-2613	7116
Hannah International Foods Inc	Seabrook	NH	D	603 474-5805	19803
Riverside Specialty Foods Inc	Seabrook	NH	G	603 474-5805	19813

FOOD PRDTS: Sandwiches

	CITY	ST	EMP	PHONE	ENTRY #
Burnside Supermarket LLC	East Hartford	CT	G	860 291-9965	1178
Greencore Oars LLC	Brockton	MA	D	508 586-8418	9153

FOOD PRDTS: Sauerkraut, Bulk

	CITY	ST	EMP	PHONE	ENTRY #
Morses Sauerkraut	Waldoboro	ME	F	207 832-5569	7135

FOOD PRDTS: Seasonings & Spices

	CITY	ST	EMP	PHONE	ENTRY #
Uncle Wileys Inc	Fairfield	CT	F	203 256-9313	1458
Beyond Shaker LLC	Woburn	MA	G	617 461-6608	17131
Brady Enterprises Inc **(PA)**	East Weymouth	MA	D	781 682-6280	10538
Brady Enterprises Inc	Weymouth	MA	F	781 337-7057	16886
Custom Seasonings Inc	Gloucester	MA	E	978 762-6300	11176
Wildtree Inc	Lincoln	RI	D	401 732-1856	20599

FOOD PRDTS: Sorbets, Non-dairy Based

	CITY	ST	EMP	PHONE	ENTRY #
Blue Moon Foods Inc	White River Junction	VT	G	802 295-1165	22635

FOOD PRDTS: Soup Mixes

	CITY	ST	EMP	PHONE	ENTRY #
Conopco Inc	Trumbull	CT	E	708 606-0540	4620
Thomas J Lipton Inc	Trumbull	CT	A	206 381-3500	4635

FOOD PRDTS: Soy Sauce

	CITY	ST	EMP	PHONE	ENTRY #
Onofrios Ultimate Foods Inc	New Haven	CT	F	203 469-4014	2721

FOOD PRDTS: Soybean Protein Concentrates & Isolates

	CITY	ST	EMP	PHONE	ENTRY #
Feldhaus Consulting LLC	Belmont	MA	G	603 276-0508	8073
Protein Products Inc	North Andover	MA	G	508 954-6020	13727

FOOD PRDTS: Spices, Including Ground

	CITY	ST	EMP	PHONE	ENTRY #
Amodios Inc **(PA)**	Waterbury	CT	F	203 573-1229	4843

FOOD PRDTS: Starch, Potato

	CITY	ST	EMP	PHONE	ENTRY #
Western Polymer Corporation	Fort Fairfield	ME	E	207 472-1250	6057

FOOD PRDTS: Sugar

	CITY	ST	EMP	PHONE	ENTRY #
Mainely Maple LLC	Norridgewock	ME	G	207 634-3073	6498
Vervain Mill	Portland	ME	G	207 774-5744	6744

FOOD PRDTS: Sugar, Cane

	CITY	ST	EMP	PHONE	ENTRY #
Jenkins Sugar Group Inc	Norwalk	CT	F	203 853-3000	3181
Roger Reed	Sheldon	VT	G	802 933-2535	22429

FOOD PRDTS: Sugar, Maple, Indl

	CITY	ST	EMP	PHONE	ENTRY #
Balsam Woods Farm	Stafford Springs	CT	G	860 265-1800	4106
Allagash Maple Products Inc	Skowhegan	ME	G	207 431-1481	6967
Jackson Sgrhuse Vgtable Stands	Oxford	ME	G	207 539-4613	6568
Pollys Pancake Parlor	Sugar Hill	NH	G	603 823-5575	19878
Woodards Sugar House LLC	Surry	NH	G	603 358-3321	19883
Branon Shady Maples Inc	Fairfield	VT	G	802 827-6605	21983
Dominion & Grimm USA	Fairfax	VT	G	802 524-9625	21974
Vermont Maple Sug Makers Assoc	Jericho	VT	G	802 763-7435	22048

FOOD PRDTS: Sugar, Powdered Cane

	CITY	ST	EMP	PHONE	ENTRY #
New England Sugars LLC	Worcester	MA	G	508 792-3801	17433

FOOD PRDTS: Syrup, Maple

	CITY	ST	EMP	PHONE	ENTRY #
Brothers & Sons Sugar House	Torrington	CT	G	860 489-2719	4569
Rivers Edge Sugar House	Ashford	CT	G	860 429-1510	27
Double Diamond Sugar House	Dover	MA	G	508 479-4950	10350
Holiday Farm Inc	Dalton	MA	G	413 684-0444	10178
Mary Ann Caproni	North Adams	MA	G	413 663-7330	13679
Pauls Sugar House	Haydenville	MA	G	413 268-3544	11487
Spring Break Maple & Honey	Smyrna Mills	ME	G	207 757-7373	6995
Strawberry Hill Farms LLC	Skowhegan	ME	G	207 474-5262	6987
Tyler R Hews	Caribou	ME	G	207 272-9273	5891
Four Saps Sugar Shack Corp	Lyndeborough	NH	G	603 858-5159	18758
J H Faddens & Sons	North Woodstock	NH	G	603 745-2406	19398
Maple Guys LLC	Wilton	NH	G	603 654-2415	19982
Maple Heights Farm	Northfield	NH	G	603 286-7942	19406
Sunnyside Maples	Canterbury	NH	G	603 848-7091	17786
Sunnyside Maples Inc	Gilmanton	NH	G	603 783-9961	18194
Branon Family Maple Orchards	Fairfield	VT	G	802 827-3914	21982
Browns River Maple	Essex Junction	VT	G	802 878-2880	21933
Burgess Sugarhouse LLC	Underhill	VT	G	802 899-5228	22546
Cabot Hills Maple LLC	Cabot	VT	G	802 426-3463	21819
Cold Corners Mapleworks LLC	Fairfield	VT	G	802 551-2270	21984
Country Shop Robb Fmly Ltd	Brattleboro	VT	G	802 258-9087	21725
Green Mtn Maple Sug Ref Co Inc	Belvidere Center	VT	E	802 644-2625	21659
Hi-Vue Maples LLC	Richford	VT	G	802 752-8888	22306
Highland Sugarworks Inc	Websterville	VT	F	802 479-1747	22597
Kendle Enterprises	South Woodstock	VT	F	802 457-3015	22498
Laraway Mountain Maple	Waterville	VT	G	802 644-5433	22595
Lehouillier Maple Orchard	Hyde Park	VT	G	802 888-6465	22036
LLC Cochran Cousins	Williston	VT	G	802 222-0440	22679
Maple Grove Farms Vermont Inc **(HQ)**	Saint Johnsbury	VT	D	802 748-5141	22391
Maple On Tap	Montpelier	VT	G	802 498-4477	22154
Matts Maple Syrup	Brattleboro	VT	G	802 464-9788	21738
Mitchs Maples Sugar House	Chester	VT	G	802 875-5240	21845
Morse Farm Inc	Montpelier	VT	G	802 223-2740	22156
Mountain Road Farm	Jeffersonville	VT	G	802 644-5138	22046
Mystic Mountain Maples LLC	Saint Albans	VT	G	802 524-6163	22375
Pure Gold Sugaring LLC	Sutton	VT	G	802 467-3921	22528
Runamok Maple LLC	Fairfax	VT	G	802 849-7943	21978
Sprague & Son Maple	Jacksonville	VT	G	802 368-2776	22043
Steven W Willsey	Starksboro	VT	G	802 434-5353	22517
Sugar Shack On Roaring Branch	Arlington	VT	G	802 375-6747	21600
Sugarbakers Maple Syrup	North Clarendon	VT	G	802 773-7731	22221
Sugarbush Farm Inc	Woodstock	VT	G	802 457-1757	22739
Sweet Tree Holdings 1 LLC	Island Pond	VT	E	802 723-6753	22042
Tafts Milk Maple Farm	Huntington	VT	G	802 434-2727	22034
Vermont Birch Syrup Co	Glover	VT	G	802 249-0574	21995
Vermont Maple Sugar Co Inc **(PA)**	Morrisville	VT	E	802 888-3491	22178
Vermont Maple Sugar Co Inc	Johnson	VT	D	802 635-7483	22052
Walkers VT Pure Mple Syrup LLC	Underhill	VT	G	802 899-3088	22551
Wh Property Service LLC	Guilford	VT	F	802 257-8566	22008
Woods Vermont Syrup Company	Randolph	VT	G	802 565-0309	22304

FOOD PRDTS: Syrups

	CITY	ST	EMP	PHONE	ENTRY #
Carriage House Companies Inc	Manchester	CT	B	860 647-1909	1992
Unilever Ascc AG	Shelton	CT	B	203 381-2482	3884
Dufresnes Sugar House	Williamsburg	MA	G	413 268-7509	16950
Severances Sugarhouse	Northfield	MA	F	413 498-2032	14066

FOOD PRDTS: Tea

	CITY	ST	EMP	PHONE	ENTRY #
Conopco Inc	Trumbull	CT	E	708 606-0540	4620
Herbasway Laboratories LLC	Wallingford	CT	E	203 269-6991	4750
RC Bigelow Inc **(PA)**	Fairfield	CT	C	888 244-3569	1451
Thomas J Lipton Inc	Trumbull	CT	A	206 381-3500	4635
Fuel For Fire Inc	Natick	MA	F	508 975-4573	13256
Reily Foods Company	Malden	MA	G	504 524-6131	12593
Tea Forte Inc	Maynard	MA	E	978 369-7777	12904
Zen Bear Honey Tea LLC	Bath	ME	G	207 449-1553	5682
Forgotten Traditions LLC	Tilton	NH	G	603 344-2231	19905

FOOD PRDTS: Tofu, Exc Frozen Desserts

	CITY	ST	EMP	PHONE	ENTRY #
21st Century Foods Inc	Boston	MA	G	617 522-7595	8327
Chang Shing Tofu Inc	Cambridge	MA	G	617 868-8878	9436
Nasoya Foods Inc	Ayer	MA	D	978 772-6880	7927
Nasoya Foods Usa LLC	Ayer	MA	C	978 772-6880	7928

FOOD PRDTS: Tortilla Chips

	CITY	ST	EMP	PHONE	ENTRY #
Severance Foods Inc	Hartford	CT	E	860 724-7063	1868

FOOD PRDTS: Tortillas

	CITY	ST	EMP	PHONE	ENTRY #
Harbar LLC	Canton	MA	C	781 828-0848	9735
Local Tortilla LLC	Hadley	MA	G	413 387-7140	11309
True Words Tortillas Inc	Orleans	MA	G	508 255-3338	14243
Montecito Roadhouse Inc	Westbrook	ME	G	207 856-6811	7197
Tortilleria Pachanga	Portland	ME	G	207 797-9700	6742

FOOD PRDTS: Vegetable Oil Mills, NEC

	CITY	ST	EMP	PHONE	ENTRY #
Baker Commodities Inc	North Billerica	MA	D	978 454-8811	13795

FOOD PRDTS: Vegetable Oil, Refined, Exc Corn

	CITY	ST	EMP	PHONE	ENTRY #
Catania-Spagna Corporation	Ayer	MA	E	978 772-7900	7914

FOOD PRDTS: Vegetables, Pickled

	CITY	ST	EMP	PHONE	ENTRY #
CHI Foods LLC	Providence	RI	G	310 309-1186	20983

FOOD PRDTS: Vinegar

	CITY	ST	EMP	PHONE	ENTRY #
Vinegar Syndrome LLC	Bridgeport	CT	G	212 722-9755	504
Gustare Oils & Vinegars **(PA)**	Chatham	MA	G	508 945-4505	9859
Mange LLC	Somerville	MA	G	917 880-2104	15194
Vinegar Hill LLC	Saugus	MA	G	781 233-3190	15001
Gourmet Oils and Vinegars Neng	Center Barnstead	NH	G	603 269-2271	17789
Old Dutch Mustard Co Inc	Greenville	NH	D	516 466-0522	18229

FOOD PRDTS: Yeast

	CITY	ST	EMP	PHONE	ENTRY #
Tekkware Inc	Gloucester	MA	G	603 380-4257	11215

FOOD PRODUCTS MACHINERY

	CITY	ST	EMP	PHONE	ENTRY #
A & I Concentrate LLC	Shelton	CT	F	203 447-1938	3771
Amt Micropure Inc	Weston	CT	G	203 226-7938	5168
Conair Corporation	Torrington	CT	D	800 492-7464	4572
Penco Corporation	Middletown	CT	C	860 347-7271	2209
Treif USA Inc	Shelton	CT	F	203 929-9930	3881
Alfa Laval Inc	Newburyport	MA	E	978 465-5777	13468
Electrolyzer Corp	West Newbury	MA	G	978 363-5349	16490
Gruenewald Mfg Co Inc	Danvers	MA	F	978 777-0200	10219
Maxant Industries Inc	Devens	MA	F	978 772-0576	10324
Pearce Processing Systems	Gloucester	MA	G	978 283-3800	11202
Westport Envmtl Systems LP	Westport	MA	D	508 636-8811	16851
Burlodge USA Inc	Litchfield	NH	F	336 776-1010	18651
Univex Corporation	Salem	NH	D	603 893-6191	19775
Leader Evaporator Co Inc **(PA)**	Swanton	VT	D	802 868-5444	22531

FOOD STORES: Convenience, Independent

	CITY	ST	EMP	PHONE	ENTRY #
Old Creamery Grocery Store	Cummington	MA	G	413 634-5560	10173

FOOD STORES: Grocery, Independent

	CITY	ST	EMP	PHONE	ENTRY #
Mellos North End Mfg Co Inc	Fall River	MA	G	508 673-2320	10729

FOOD STORES: Supermarkets

	CITY	ST	EMP	PHONE	ENTRY #
Burnside Supermarket LLC	East Hartford	CT	G	860 291-9965	1178

FOOD WARMING EQPT: Commercial

	CITY	ST	EMP	PHONE	ENTRY #
Creative Mobile Systems Inc	Manchester	CT	G	860 649-6272	1997

FOOTHOLDS: Rubber Or Rubber Soled Fabric

	CITY	ST	EMP	PHONE	ENTRY #
Biltrite Corporation	Chelsea	MA	E	617 884-3124	9945

FOOTWEAR, WHOLESALE: Athletic

	CITY	ST	EMP	PHONE	ENTRY #
Rhine Inc	Weston	MA	G	781 710-7121	16831

FOOTWEAR, WHOLESALE: Boots

	CITY	ST	EMP	PHONE	ENTRY #
Northern Tack	Calais	ME	G	207 217-7584	5865

FOOTWEAR, WHOLESALE: Shoes

	CITY	ST	EMP	PHONE	ENTRY #
C & J Clark America Inc **(DH)**	Waltham	MA	B	617 964-1222	16054
C & J Clark Latin America	Waltham	MA	F	617 243-4100	16055
Kerr Leathers Inc	Salem	MA	E	978 852-0660	14927

FOOTWEAR: Cut Stock

	CITY	ST	EMP	PHONE	ENTRY #
Macneill Engineering Co Inc	Westborough	MA	E	508 481-8830	16633
Rhine Inc	Weston	MA	G	781 710-7121	16831
Enefco International Inc **(PA)**	Auburn	ME	D	207 514-7218	5561
Jones & Vining Incorporated	Lewiston	ME	E	207 784-3547	6295

FORGINGS

	CITY	ST	EMP	PHONE	ENTRY #
Bourdon Forge Co Inc	Middletown	CT	C	860 632-2740	2179
Bristol Instrument Gears Inc	Bristol	CT	F	860 583-1395	537
Carlton Forge Works	Moodus	CT	E	860 873-9730	2424
Cunningham Industries Inc	Stamford	CT	G	203 324-2942	4180
East Shore Wire Rope	East Haven	CT	G	203 469-5204	1247
J J Ryan Corporation	Plantsville	CT	C	860 628-0393	3534
OEM Sources LLC	Milford	CT	G	203 283-5415	2325
Paradigm Manchester Inc	Manchester	CT	C	860 649-2888	2032

	CITY	ST	EMP	PHONE	ENTRY #
Perry Technology Corporation	New Hartford	CT	D	860 738-2525	2644
Roller Bearing Co Amer Inc	Middlebury	CT	E	203 758-8272	2157
Acorn Manufacturing Co Inc	Mansfield	MA	E	508 339-4500	12611
Doncasters Inc	Springfield	MA	D	413 785-1801	15467
Engineered Pressure Systems Inc	Haverhill	MA	F	978 469-8280	11432
Kervick Family Foundation Inc	Worcester	MA	G	508 853-4500	17399
Paradigm Prcision Holdings LLC	Malden	MA	F	781 321-0480	12587
Wyman-Gordon Company **(DH)**	North Grafton	MA	B	508 839-8252	13969
Wyman-Gordon Company	Worcester	MA	D	508 839-8253	17511
Ball and Chain Forge	Portland	ME	G	207 878-2217	6617
ME Industries	Biddeford	ME	G	207 286-2030	5749
New Hampshire Forge Inc	Keene	NH	E	603 357-5692	18520
Greystone of Lincoln Inc **(PA)**	Lincoln	RI	C	401 333-0444	20576
Perry Blackburne Inc	North Providence	RI	E	401 231-7200	20771
Wiesner Manufacturing Company	Warwick	RI	E	401 421-2406	21447

FORGINGS: Aircraft

Wyman-Gordon Company **(DH)**	North Grafton	MA	B	508 839-8252	13969

FORGINGS: Aircraft, Ferrous

Consoldted Inds Acqsition Corp	Cheshire	CT	D	203 272-5371	724

FORGINGS: Anchors

American Earth Anchors Inc	Franklin	MA	G	508 520-8511	11023

FORGINGS: Armor Plate, Iron Or Steel

Incident Control Systems LLC	New Bedford	MA	G	508 984-8820	13397

FORGINGS: Automotive & Internal Combustion Engine

Turbocam Atmted Prod Systems I **(HQ)**	Barrington	NH	E	603 905-0220	17626
Turbocam Automated Production	Dover	NH	G	603 905-0240	18062

FORGINGS: Construction Or Mining Eqpt, Ferrous

J C B Leasing Inc	Weare	NH	D	603 529-7974	19934

FORGINGS: Iron & Steel

J J Ryan Corporation	Plantsville	CT	C	860 628-0393	3534
Scientific Alloys Inc	Westerly	RI	G	401 596-4947	21540

FORGINGS: Machinery, Nonferrous

Smiths Tblar Systms-Lconia Inc	Laconia	NH	B	603 524-2064	18587

FORGINGS: Metal , Ornamental, Ferrous

Vermont Forgings Inc	Wallingford	VT	G	802 446-3900	22575

FORGINGS: Nonferrous

Kervick Family Foundation Inc	Worcester	MA	G	508 853-4500	17399
Sullivan JW	Bedford	MA	G	781 275-5818	8011
Wyman-Gordon Company	Worcester	MA	D	508 839-8253	17511
Tem Inc	Buxton	ME	E	207 929-8700	5861

FORGINGS: Ordnance, Ferrous

Geneve Holdings Inc **(PA)**	Stamford	CT	G	203 358-8000	4199

FORGINGS: Plumbing Fixture, Nonferrous

Winwholesale Inc	Warwick	RI	G	401 732-1585	21450

FORMS HANDLING EQPT

Energy Saving Products and Sls	Burlington	CT	E	860 675-6443	678

FORMS: Concrete, Sheet Metal

Peri Formwork Systems Inc	Boston	MA	G	857 524-5182	8775
S T White Concrete Forms	Abington	MA	G	781 982-9116	7329
Gagne & Son Con Blocks Inc	Auburn	ME	G	207 495-3313	5566
Advance Concrete Form Inc	Manchester	NH	G	603 669-4496	18771
Hd Supply Construction Supply	West Lebanon	NH	G	603 298-6072	19952

FOUNDRIES: Aluminum

Burlington Foundry Co Inc	Burlington	MA	G	781 272-1182	9242
Consoldted Precision Pdts Corp	Braintree	MA	C	781 848-3333	8995
Industrial Foundry Corporation	Uxbridge	MA	G	508 278-5523	15920
Kingston Aluminum Foundry Inc	Kingston	MA	G	781 585-6631	11959
Mystic Valley Foundry Inc	Somerville	MA	G	617 547-1819	15201
Pace Industries LLC	North Billerica	MA	C	978 667-8400	13852
Prue Foundry Inc	Dennis	MA	G	508 385-3011	10309
Bronze Craft Corporation	Nashua	NH	D	603 883-7747	19130
Patriot Foundry & Castings LLC	Franklin	NH	F	603 934-3919	18161
UNI-Cast LLC	Londonderry	NH	C	603 625-5761	18742
Friends Foundry Inc	Woonsocket	RI	F	401 769-0160	21564
Michael Healy Designs Inc	Manville	RI	G	401 597-5900	20610

FOUNDRIES: Brass, Bronze & Copper

American Sleeve Bearing LLC	Stafford Springs	CT	E	860 684-8060	4104
Mystic River Foundry LLC	Mystic	CT	G	860 536-7634	2445
Spirol International Corp **(HQ)**	Danielson	CT	C	860 774-8571	1018
Alloy Castings Co Inc	East Bridgewater	MA	F	508 378-2541	10406
D W Clark Inc **(PA)**	East Bridgewater	MA	E	508 378-4014	10411
Palmer Foundry Inc	Palmer	MA	D	413 283-2976	14291
Hebert Foundry & Machine Inc	Laconia	NH	E	603 524-2065	18566
New Hmpshire Ball Bearings Inc	Laconia	NH	B	603 524-0004	18577
New England Precision Inc	Randolph	VT	D	800 293-4112	22299

FOUNDRIES: Gray & Ductile Iron

Neenah Foundry Company	Stoughton	MA	G	781 344-1711	15610
Anvil International LLC **(HQ)**	Exeter	NH	E	603 418-2800	18110

FOUNDRIES: Iron

G & W Foundry Corp	Millbury	MA	E	508 581-8719	13164
Rodney Hunt-Fontaine Inc **(DH)**	Orange	MA	C	978 544-2511	14227

FOUNDRIES: Nonferrous

Custom Metal Crafters Inc	Newington	CT	D	860 953-4210	2857
Doncasters Inc	Groton	CT	D	860 446-4803	1670
D W Clark Inc **(PA)**	East Bridgewater	MA	E	508 378-4014	10411
Edson Corporation	Taunton	MA	G	508 822-0100	15747
Glines Rhodes Inc	Brewster	MA	G	508 385-8828	9053
Langstrom Metals Inc	North Grafton	MA	G	508 839-5224	13962
Mack Prototype Inc	Gardner	MA	E	978 632-3700	11119
Merrimac Vly Alum Brass Fndry	Amesbury	MA	G	978 388-0830	7495
Pace Industries LLC	North Billerica	MA	C	978 667-8400	13852
Trident Alloys Inc	Springfield	MA	E	413 737-1477	15518
Whitman Castings Inc **(PA)**	Whitman	MA	E	781 447-4417	16930
Wollaston Alloys Inc	Braintree	MA	C	781 848-3333	9051
Hawk Motors Inc	York	ME	G	207 363-4716	7308
Bomar Inc	Charlestown	NH	D	603 826-5781	17811
Diamond Casting and Mch Co Inc	Hollis	NH	E	603 465-2263	18330
PCC Structurals Groton	Northfield	NH	C	603 286-4301	19407
Fielding Manufacturing Inc	Cranston	RI	E	401 461-0400	20226
Optical Polymers Lab Corp	Pawtucket	RI	F	401 722-0710	20870
Osram Sylvania Inc	Central Falls	RI	B	401 723-1378	20122
Ridco Casting Co	Pawtucket	RI	D	401 724-0400	20893
Smb LLC	North Ferrisburgh	VT	G	802 425-2862	22227

FOUNDRIES: Steel

Polstal Corporation	Wilton	CT	G	203 849-7788	5299
D W Clark Inc **(PA)**	East Bridgewater	MA	E	508 378-4014	10411
Doncasters Inc	Springfield	MA	D	413 785-1801	15467

FOUNDRIES: Steel Investment

Doncasters Inc	Groton	CT	D	860 446-4803	1670
Dundee Holding Inc **(DH)**	Farmington	CT	G	860 677-1376	1477
Integra-Cast Inc	New Britain	CT	D	860 225-7600	2541
Miller Castings Inc	North Franklin	CT	C	860 822-9991	2989
Tps Acquisition LLC **(PA)**	Waterbury	CT	G	860 589-5511	4965
Consoldted Precision Pdts Corp	Braintree	MA	C	781 848-3333	8995
Hitchiner Manufacturing Co Inc **(PA)**	Milford	NH	A	603 673-1100	19060
Hitchiner Manufacturing Co Inc	Milford	NH	D	603 673-1100	19061
Hitchiner Manufacturing Co Inc	Milford	NH	C	603 732-1935	19062
Hitchiner Manufacturing Co Inc	Milford	NH	B	603 673-1100	19063
Sturm Ruger & Company Inc	Newport	NH	B	603 865-2424	19361
Sturm Ruger & Company Inc	Newport	NH	C	603 863-3300	19362
Tidland Corporation	Keene	NH	D	603 352-1696	18533

FOUNDRY MACHINERY & EQPT

Gerber Technology LLC **(HQ)**	Tolland	CT	B	860 871-8082	4549
Arcast Inc	Oxford	ME	G	207 539-9638	6563
Fab Braze Corp **(PA)**	Nashua	NH	G	781 893-6777	19153

FRACTIONATION PRDTS OF CRUDE PETROLEUM, HYDROCARBONS, NEC

Burtco Inc	Westminster Station	VT	F	802 722-3358	22633

FRAMES: Chair, Metal

V & G Iron Works Inc	Tewksbury	MA	F	978 851-9191	15846
Whetstone Workshop LLC	East Providence	RI	G	401 368-7410	20449

FRANCHISES, SELLING OR LICENSING

Gordon Industries Inc **(PA)**	Boston	MA	E	857 401-1114	8575
Discovery Map Intl Inc	Waitsfield	VT	G	802 316-4060	22564

FREIGHT TRANSPORTATION ARRANGEMENTS

Armada Logistics Inc	Somerville	MA	G	855 727-6232	15156

FRICTION MATERIAL, MADE FROM POWDERED METAL

Torqmaster Inc	Stamford	CT	E	203 326-5945	4347
Capstan Atlantic	Wrentham	MA	C	508 384-3100	17517
Veloxint Corporation	Framingham	MA	E	774 777-3369	11010
Elmet Technologies LLC	Lewiston	ME	C	207 333-6100	6287

FRUIT & VEGETABLE MARKETS

Nashoba Valley Spirits Limited	Bolton	MA	E	978 779-5521	8321

FUEL ADDITIVES

Armored Autogroup Parent Inc **(DH)**	Danbury	CT	G	203 205-2900	875

FUEL CELLS: Solid State

Doosan Fuel Cell America Inc **(HQ)**	South Windsor	CT	C	860 727-2200	3956
Fuelcell Energy Inc	Torrington	CT	E	860 496-1111	4579
Merrick Services	Millbury	MA	G	508 802-3751	13170

FUEL DEALERS: Wood

Gaylord West	Franklin	VT	G	802 285-6438	21994

FUEL OIL DEALERS

Weymouths Inc	Clinton	ME	G	207 426-3211	5917

FUELS: Diesel

Greener 3000 LLC	Boston	MA	G	781 589-5777	8579
Homeland Fuels Company LLC	Canton	MA	F	781 737-1892	9739
Maine Bio-Fuel Inc	Portland	ME	F	207 878-3001	6682
Smartfuel America LLC	Seabrook	NH	G	603 474-5005	19818
White Mountain Biodiesel LLC	Littleton	NH	G	603 444-0335	18668

FUELS: Ethanol

Advanced Fuel Co LLC	North Franklin	CT	G	860 642-4817	2986
Alternative Fuel & Energy LLC	Colchester	CT	G	860 537-5345	798

	CITY	ST	EMP	PHONE	ENTRY #
Anthony s Fuel	Shelton	CT	G	203 513-7400	3776
Bestway Food and Fuel	Waterford	CT	G	860 447-0729	4981
Cobal-USA Altrnative Fuels LLC	Ansonia	CT	G	203 751-1974	10
Crossroads Deli & Fuel LLC	Falls Village	CT	G	860 824-8474	1462
CTS Services LLC	Shelton	CT	G	203 268-5865	3791
Deep River Fuel Terminals LLC	Portland	CT	G	860 342-4619	3566
E&S Automotive Operations LLC	Bridgeport	CT	G	203 332-4555	409
Extra Fuel	Bridgeport	CT	G	203 330-0613	412
Falls Fuel LLC	Bethel	CT	G	203 744-3835	153
Firehouse Discount Oil LLC **(PA)**	Unionville	CT	G	860 404-1827	4656
Fuel First	Ansonia	CT	G	203 735-5097	16
Fuel For Humanity Inc	Westport	CT	G	203 255-5913	5196
Fuel Lab	Farmington	CT	G	860 677-4987	1485
Galaxy Fuel LLC	Milford	CT	G	203 878-8173	2292
Hitbro Realty LLC	Canaan	CT	G	860 824-1370	687
Husky Fuel	Oxford	CT	G	203 783-0783	3408
Miller Fuel LLC	Burlington	CT	G	860 675-6121	679
New England Fuels & Energy LLC	Terryville	CT	G	860 585-5917	4487
Power Fuels LLC	Cheshire	CT	G	203 699-0099	754
Priced Right Fuel LLC	Norwalk	CT	G	203 856-7031	3224
Pucks Putters & Fuel LLC	Milford	CT	F	203 877-5457	2343
Pucks Putters & Fuel LLC **(PA)**	Shelton	CT	G	203 494-3952	3864
Superior Fuel Co	Bridgeport	CT	G	203 337-1213	497
Ultra Food and Fuel	New Britain	CT	G	860 223-2005	2587
Victory Fuel LLC	Terryville	CT	G	860 585-0532	4496
Waste To Green Fuel LLC	Bridgeport	CT	G	203 536-5855	505
XCEL Fuel	Branford	CT	G	203 481-4510	363
All Seasonal Fuel Inc	Dedham	MA	G	781 329-7800	10279
Amal Fuel Inc	Chelmsford	MA	G	978 934-9704	9870
Belco Fuel Company Inc	Pembroke	MA	G	781 331-6521	14393
Bio Energy Inc	Boston	MA	G	617 822-1220	8409
Cannan Fuels	Mansfield	MA	G	508 339-3317	12616
Chapman Fuel	Lowell	MA	G	978 452-9656	12358
Coelho Fuel Inc	Lowell	MA	G	978 458-8252	12361
Commonwealth Biofuel	Newburyport	MA	G	978 881-0478	13479
Commonwealth Fuel Corp	Waltham	MA	G	617 884-5444	16071
Dems Fuel Inc	Chelmsford	MA	G	978 660-0018	9892
E J White Fuel	Rockland	MA	G	781 878-0802	14798
Felicia Oil Co Inc	Gloucester	MA	G	978 283-3808	11181
Fuel America	Brighton	MA	G	617 782-0999	9099
Fuel First Elm Inc	West Springfield	MA	G	413 732-5732	16523
Fuel Gym LLC	Wakefield	MA	G	781 315-8001	15953
Fuel Magazine	Hatfield	MA	G	413 247-5579	11400
Fuel Source Inc	Norwood	MA	G	781 469-8449	14153
Fuel Training Studio LLC	Newburyport	MA	G	617 694-5489	13492
H I Five Renewables	Merrimac	MA	G	978 384-8032	13001
Homeland Fuels Company LLC	Canton	MA	F	781 737-1892	9739
Inversant Inc	Boston	MA	F	617 423-0331	8620
James Devaney Fuel Co	Dedham	MA	G	781 326-7608	10295
Khoury Fuel Inc	Melrose	MA	G	781 251-0993	12984
Kinetic Fuel LLC	Walpole	MA	G	508 668-8278	15997
Lawrence Fuel Inc	Lawrence	MA	G	978 984-5255	12046
Lisha & Nirali Fuel LLC	Middleton	MA	G	908 433-6504	13094
McCarthy Bros Fuel Co Inc	West Brookfield	MA	G	508 867-5515	16471
Miami Heat Discount Fuel	Fairhaven	MA	G	508 991-2875	10642
MK Fuel Inc	Brimfield	MA	G	413 245-7507	9110
Northeast Biodiesel LLC	Greenfield	MA	G	413 772-8891	11271
Novogy Inc	Cambridge	MA	F	617 674-5800	9594
Paul M Depalma Fuel LLC	Weymouth	MA	G	781 812-0156	16896
Perley Burrill Fuel	Lynnfield	MA	G	781 593-9292	12554
Polar Fuel Inc	Foxboro	MA	G	508 543-5200	10898
Powersure Fuel Rcndtioning LLC	Andover	MA	G	978 886-2476	7587
Pure Energy Corporation **(PA)**	Burlington	MA	F	201 843-8100	9324
Rachad Fuel Inc	Burlington	MA	G	781 273-0292	9328
S & E Fuels Inc	Taunton	MA	G	617 407-9977	15782
S & M Fuels Inc	Plymouth	MA	G	508 746-1495	14581
Sea Fuels Marine	New Bedford	MA	G	508 992-2323	13448
Sherborn Market Inc	Wellesley	MA	G	781 489-5006	16387
State Fuel	Winchester	MA	G	781 438-5557	17097
Stateline Fuel	Seekonk	MA	G	508 336-0665	15038
Swampscott Fuel Inc	Swampscott	MA	G	781 592-1065	15700
Swampscott Fuel Inc	Westwood	MA	G	781 251-0993	16877
Szr Fuel LLC	Tyngsboro	MA	G	978 649-2409	15901
TK&k Services LLC	Beverly	MA	C	770 844-8710	8192
Unlimited Fuel Heating Inc	Foxboro	MA	G	508 543-1043	10907
US Biofuels Inc	Boston	MA	F	706 291-4829	8902
Waltham Fuel	Chelsea	MA	G	617 364-2890	9974
Ysnc Fuel Inc	Brockton	MA	G	508 436-2716	9188
D & J Fuels LLC	Wells	ME	G	207 646-5561	7161
Grenier Fuels LLC	Saco	ME	G	207 602-1400	6848
Hometown Fuel DBA Hometo	Limestone	ME	G	207 325-4411	6341
J S Wholesale Fuels	Manchester	ME	G	207 622-4332	6410
Jessicas Discount Fuel	Pownal	ME	G	207 310-1966	6749
John Seavey Acadia Fuel	Trenton	ME	G	207 664-6050	7099
Land & Sea Fuel	Lubec	ME	G	207 733-0005	6386
M A Haskell & Sons LLC	China	ME	F	207 993-2265	5910
MA Haskell Fuel Co LLC	China	ME	G	207 993-2265	5911
Maine Bio-Fuel Inc	Portland	ME	F	207 878-3001	6682
Milford Fuel	Milford	ME	G	207 827-2701	6436
Offshore Fuel	Gouldsboro	ME	G	207 963-7068	6137
R H Foster Inc	Van Buren	ME	G	207 868-2983	7123
Yoc	York	ME	G	207 363-9322	7318
A F Fuels	Brookline	NH	G	603 672-7010	17769
Alternative Fuel Systems E LLC	Dunbarton	NH	G	603 231-1942	18072
Energex Pellet Fuel Inc	West Lebanon	NH	G	603 298-7007	19950
Favorite Fuels LLC	Hampton Falls	NH	G	603 967-4889	18282
Howards Fuel Co Inc	Manchester	NH	G	603 635-9955	18837
L R Fuel Systems	Gilmanton	NH	G	603 848-3835	18193
Nas Fuels LLC	Rye	NH	G	603 964-6967	19699
Racing Mart Fuels LLC	Nashua	NH	G	508 878-7664	19243
Aurora Fuel Company Inc	West Warwick	RI	G	401 345-5996	21481
Aurora Fuel Company Inc	West Warwick	RI	G	401 821-5996	21482
Fuel Co	Providence	RI	G	401 467-8773	21018
Hirst Fuel LLC	Wakefield	RI	G	401 789-6376	21271
Quality Fuel	West Warwick	RI	G	401 822-9482	21507
Reliable Fuel Incorporated	Tiverton	RI	G	401 624-2903	21261
Sea Side Fuel	Narragansett	RI	G	401 284-2636	20648
Abba Fuels Inc	Underhill	VT	G	802 878-8095	22545
Accordant Energy LLC	Rutland	VT	G	802 772-7368	22322
Brosseau Fuels LLC	Morrisville	VT	G	802 888-9209	22165
Jam Fuel LLC	Windsor	VT	G	802 345-6118	22710
McAllister Fuels Inc	Richford	VT	G	802 782-5293	22309
S White Fuel Stop	Danby	VT	G	802 293-5804	21894

FUELS: Gas, Liquefied

	CITY	ST	EMP	PHONE	ENTRY #
Blue Rhino of Ne	Springfield	MA	G	413 781-3694	15455
Paul E Wentworth	Vassalboro	ME	G	207 923-3547	7125

FUELS: Kerosene

	CITY	ST	EMP	PHONE	ENTRY #
CN Brown Company	Windham	ME	G	207 892-5955	7231

FUELS: Oil

	CITY	ST	EMP	PHONE	ENTRY #
Leclaire Fuel Oil LLC	Shelton	CT	G	203 922-1512	3827
STP Products Manufacturing Co **(DH)**	Danbury	CT	F	203 205-2900	997
Thibault Fuel Oil	Springfield	MA	G	413 782-9577	15512
Kenoco Inc	Farmingdale	ME	G	207 620-7260	6039
Baycorp Holdings Ltd **(PA)**	Portsmouth	NH	F	603 294-4850	19542

FUNDRAISING SVCS

	CITY	ST	EMP	PHONE	ENTRY #
Safve Inc	Scituate	MA	G	781 545-3546	15011
TCI America Inc	Seekonk	MA	E	508 336-6633	15039

FUNERAL HOMES & SVCS

	CITY	ST	EMP	PHONE	ENTRY #
Dignified Endings LLC	East Hartford	CT	D	860 291-0575	1187

FUR: Apparel

	CITY	ST	EMP	PHONE	ENTRY #
Varpro Inc	Westport	CT	E	203 227-6876	5236

FURNACE CASINGS: Sheet Metal

	CITY	ST	EMP	PHONE	ENTRY #
Advanced Air Systems Inc	Abington	MA	F	781 878-5733	7319

FURNACES & OVENS: Indl

	CITY	ST	EMP	PHONE	ENTRY #
David Weisman LLC	Stamford	CT	G	203 322-9978	4187
Earth Engineered Systems	Derby	CT	G	203 231-4614	1070
Furnace Source LLC	Terryville	CT	F	860 582-4201	4479
Hamworthy Peabody Combustn Inc **(DH)**	Shelton	CT	E	203 922-1199	3808
HI Heat Company Inc	South Windsor	CT	G	860 528-9315	3981
Jad LLC	South Windsor	CT	E	860 289-1551	3983
Modean Industries Inc	Easton	CT	G	203 371-6625	1321
Noble Fire Brick Company Inc **(PA)**	East Windsor	CT	G	860 623-9256	1297
Preferred Utilities Mfg Corp **(HQ)**	Danbury	CT	D	203 743-6741	974
Sandvik Wire and Htg Tech Corp	Bethel	CT	D	203 744-1440	177
Duc-Pac Corporation	East Longmeadow	MA	E	413 525-3302	10474
H B Smith Company Inc	Westfield	MA	E	413 568-3148	16687
S M Engineering Co Inc	North Attleboro	MA	F	508 699-4484	13778
Arcast Inc	Oxford	ME	G	207 539-9638	6562
Onix Corporation	Caribou	ME	E	866 290-5362	5889
Ebner Furnaces	Londonderry	NH	G	603 552-3806	18694
Hollis Line Machine Co Inc **(PA)**	Hollis	NH	E	603 465-2251	18332
Infra Red Technology Inc	Laconia	NH	G	603 524-1177	18568
Mellen Company Inc **(PA)**	Concord	NH	E	603 228-2929	17914
Sahara Heaters Mfg Co	Nashua	NH	G	603 888-7351	19257
Gasbarre Products Inc	Cranston	RI	F	401 467-5200	20230
Rettig USA Inc	Colchester	VT	G	802 654-7500	21879

FURNACES & OVENS: Vacuum

	CITY	ST	EMP	PHONE	ENTRY #
Envax Products Inc	Oxford	CT	G	203 264-8181	3400
Avs Incorporated	Ayer	MA	D	978 772-0710	7912
Tevtech LLC	North Billerica	MA	F	978 667-4557	13871
Centorr/Vacuum Industries LLC **(PA)**	Nashua	NH	E	603 595-7233	19132
CVI Group Inc **(PA)**	Nashua	NH	G	603 595-7233	19100
Gtat Corporation	Nashua	NH	G	603 883-5200	19173
Gtat Corporation **(HQ)**	Hudson	NH	C	603 883-5200	18396
Materials Research Frncs Inc	Allenstown	NH	F	603 485-2394	17539

FURNITURE & CABINET STORES: Cabinets, Custom Work

	CITY	ST	EMP	PHONE	ENTRY #
B H Davis Co	Thompson	CT	G	860 923-2771	4531
Berger Corporation	Orleans	MA	G	508 255-3267	14230
F A Wilnauer Woodwork Inc	South Berwick	ME	G	207 384-4824	7002
Cole Cabinet Co Inc	Cranston	RI	F	401 467-4343	20199

FURNITURE & FIXTURES Factory

	CITY	ST	EMP	PHONE	ENTRY #
October Company Inc **(PA)**	Easthampton	MA	C	413 527-9380	10572
Higgins Fabrication LLC	Bangor	ME	G	719 930-6437	5650
Holmris US Inc	Manchester	NH	G	603 232-3490	18836
Green Mountain Vista Inc	Williston	VT	G	802 862-0159	22673

FURNITURE COMPONENTS: Porcelain Enameled

	CITY	ST	EMP	PHONE	ENTRY #
Intellgent Office Intriors LLC	Wilmington	MA	G	978 808-7884	17006

FURNITURE PARTS: Metal

	CITY	ST	EMP	PHONE	ENTRY #
October Company Inc **(PA)**	Easthampton	MA	C	413 527-9380	10572
October Company Inc	Easthampton	MA	E	413 529-0718	10573
Production Basics Inc	Billerica	MA	E	617 926-8100	8278

FURNITURE REFINISHING SVCS

Company	CITY	ST	EMP	PHONE	ENTRY #
Colonial Village Refinishing	Hingham	MA	G	781 740-8844	11496

FURNITURE STOCK & PARTS: Carvings, Wood

Company	CITY	ST	EMP	PHONE	ENTRY #
Blue Hill Cabinet & Woodwork	Blue Hill	ME	G	207 374-2260	5770
F & S Wood Products	Jamestown	RI	G	401 423-1048	20490
Charron Wood Products Inc	Windsor	VT	G	802 369-0166	22706

FURNITURE STOCK & PARTS: Dimension Stock, Hardwood

Company	CITY	ST	EMP	PHONE	ENTRY #
Pine and Baker Mfg Inc	Tewksbury	MA	F	978 851-1215	15825
Robes Dana Wood Craftsmen **(PA)**	Hanover	NH	G	603 643-9355	18296

FURNITURE STOCK & PARTS: Hardwood

Company	CITY	ST	EMP	PHONE	ENTRY #
Oak Gallery Inc **(PA)**	Littleton	MA	G	978 486-9846	12314
Elkins & Co Inc	Boothbay	ME	F	207 633-0109	5777

FURNITURE STOCK & PARTS: Squares, Hardwood

Company	CITY	ST	EMP	PHONE	ENTRY #
Ernest R Palmer Lumber Co Inc	Sangerville	ME	G	207 876-2725	6899

FURNITURE STOCK & PARTS: Turnings, Wood

Company	CITY	ST	EMP	PHONE	ENTRY #
Pride Manufacturing Co LLC	Guilford	ME	F	207 876-2719	6159
Turning Acquisitions LLC	Buckfield	ME	E	207 336-2400	5853
Vic Firth Company	Newport	ME	G	207 368-4358	6488
Vic Firth Manufacturing Inc	Newport	ME	C	207 368-4358	6489
Scott L Northcott	Walpole	NH	G	603 756-4204	19924

FURNITURE STORES

Company	CITY	ST	EMP	PHONE	ENTRY #
Cerrito Furniture Inds Inc	Branford	CT	F	203 481-2580	304
Domino Media Group Inc	Westport	CT	E	877 223-7844	5188
Ethan Allen Interiors Inc **(PA)**	Danbury	CT	C	203 743-8000	914
Nap Brothers Parlor Frame Inc	Glastonbury	CT	F	860 633-9998	1565
Porta Door Co	Seymour	CT	E	203 888-6191	3761
Acton Woodworks Inc	Acton	MA	G	978 263-0222	7335
Charles Webb Inc **(PA)**	Woburn	MA	E	781 569-0444	17143
CJ Sprong & Co Inc	Williamsburg	MA	G	413 628-4410	16948
Custom Woods Designs M Marion	Hampden	MA	G	413 566-8230	11320
Ecin Industries Inc	Fall River	MA	E	508 675-6920	10686
Eustis Enterprises Inc	Cambridge	MA	G	978 827-3103	9474
Oak Gallery Inc **(PA)**	Littleton	MA	G	978 486-9846	12314
Ralph Curcio Co Inc	Gardner	MA	G	978 632-1120	11124
Twin Cy Upholstering & Mat Co	Braintree	MA	F	781 843-1780	9044
Higgins Fabrication LLC	Bangor	ME	G	719 930-6437	5650
Huston & Company Wood Design	Arundel	ME	G	207 967-2345	5532
Mayville House	Bethel	ME	G	207 824-6545	5715
Northeastern Rustic Furni	Smyrna Mills	ME	G	207 757-8300	6994
Portland Mattress Makers Inc **(PA)**	Biddeford	ME	F	207 772-2276	5756
Town and Country Cabinets Inc	Gorham	ME	G	207 839-2709	6131
Borroughs Corporation	Raymond	NH	G	603 895-3991	19636
Holmris US Inc	Manchester	NH	G	603 232-3490	18836
Beeken/Parsons Inc	Shelburne	VT	G	802 985-2913	22413

FURNITURE STORES: Custom Made, Exc Cabinets

Company	CITY	ST	EMP	PHONE	ENTRY #
1817 Shoppe Inc **(PA)**	Sturbridge	MA	G	508 347-2241	15636
Country Bed Shop Inc	Ashby	MA	G	978 386-7550	7646
Graney John F Metal Design LLC	Sheffield	MA	G	413 528-6744	15060

FURNITURE STORES: Outdoor & Garden

Company	CITY	ST	EMP	PHONE	ENTRY #
Walpole Woodworkers Inc	Ridgefield	CT	E	508 668-2800	3689
Walpole Woodworkers Inc	Westport	CT	G	203 255-9010	5237
Jobart Inc **(PA)**	Methuen	MA	F	978 689-4414	13029
Walpole Woodworkers Inc	Wilmington	MA	F	978 658-3373	17064
Walpole Woodworkers Inc	East Falmouth	MA	F	508 540-0300	10451
Walpole Woodworkers Inc	Norwell	MA	G	781 681-9099	14114
Walpole Woodworkers Inc	Detroit	ME	E	207 368-4302	5954
Walpole Woodworkers Inc	Chester	ME	E	207 794-2248	5908
Cedar Craft Fence Co	Coventry	RI	G	401 397-7765	20141

FURNITURE STORES: Unfinished

Company	CITY	ST	EMP	PHONE	ENTRY #
Chilton Paint Co Inc ME	Freeport	ME	G	207 865-4443	6074

FURNITURE WHOLESALERS

Company	CITY	ST	EMP	PHONE	ENTRY #
J Dana Design Inc	Hardwick	MA	G	413 477-6844	11374
Knoll Inc	Boston	MA	E	617 695-0220	8653
Higgins Fabrication LLC	Bangor	ME	G	719 930-6437	5650
Jackson Caldwell	Oxford	ME	G	207 539-2325	6567

FURNITURE, BARBER & BEAUTY SHOP

Company	CITY	ST	EMP	PHONE	ENTRY #
Formatron Ltd	Farmington	CT	F	860 676-0227	1482

FURNITURE, GARDEN: Concrete

Company	CITY	ST	EMP	PHONE	ENTRY #
Concretebenchmolds LLC	Framingham	MA	G	800 242-1809	10936
Lunaform LLC	North Sullivan	ME	G	207 422-3306	6514

FURNITURE, HOUSEHOLD: Wholesalers

Company	CITY	ST	EMP	PHONE	ENTRY #
CB Seating Etc LLC **(PA)**	Norwalk	CT	G	203 359-3880	3120

FURNITURE, MATTRESSES: Wholesalers

Company	CITY	ST	EMP	PHONE	ENTRY #
Drive-O-Rama Inc	Dennis Port	MA	D	508 394-0028	10312

FURNITURE, OFFICE: Wholesalers

Company	CITY	ST	EMP	PHONE	ENTRY #
McKearney Associates Inc **(PA)**	Boston	MA	G	617 269-7600	8691
Mkind Inc	Manchester	NH	G	603 493-6882	18877

FURNITURE, OUTDOOR & LAWN: Wholesalers

Company	CITY	ST	EMP	PHONE	ENTRY #
Baldwin Lawn Furniture LLC	Middletown	CT	F	860 347-1306	2176

FURNITURE, WHOLESALE: Beds & Bedding

Company	CITY	ST	EMP	PHONE	ENTRY #
Cleanbrands LLC	Warwick	RI	F	877 215-7378	21342

FURNITURE, WHOLESALE: Racks

Company	CITY	ST	EMP	PHONE	ENTRY #
Di-Cor Industries Inc	Bristol	CT	F	860 585-5583	549
Thule Inc **(DH)**	Seymour	CT	C	203 881-9600	3765

FURNITURE: Altars, Cut Stone

Company	CITY	ST	EMP	PHONE	ENTRY #
Morning Star Marble & Gran Inc	Topsham	ME	F	207 725-7309	7091

FURNITURE: Bed Frames & Headboards, Wood

Company	CITY	ST	EMP	PHONE	ENTRY #
Charles Shackleton & Miranda T	Bridgewater	VT	E	802 672-5175	21757

FURNITURE: Bedroom, Wood

Company	CITY	ST	EMP	PHONE	ENTRY #
Ethan Allen Interiors Inc **(PA)**	Danbury	CT	C	203 743-8000	914
Woodforms Inc	Foxboro	MA	G	508 543-9417	10909
Healthy Homeworks	Portland	ME	G	207 415-4245	6670

FURNITURE: Bookcases & Stereo Cabinets, Metal

Company	CITY	ST	EMP	PHONE	ENTRY #
M J Industries Inc	Georgetown	MA	E	978 352-6190	11145

FURNITURE: Box Springs, Assembled

Company	CITY	ST	EMP	PHONE	ENTRY #
Leggett & Platt Incorporated	Oxford	MA	E	508 987-8706	14265
Vital Wood Products Inc	Fall River	MA	F	508 673-7976	10780

FURNITURE: Buffets

Company	CITY	ST	EMP	PHONE	ENTRY #
Vermont Culinary Islands LLC	Brattleboro	VT	F	802 246-2277	21750

FURNITURE: Cabinets & Vanities, Medicine, Metal

Company	CITY	ST	EMP	PHONE	ENTRY #
Advanced Prototype Development	Southbury	CT	G	203 267-1262	4022

FURNITURE: Camp, Wood

Company	CITY	ST	EMP	PHONE	ENTRY #
Byer Manufacturing Company	Orono	ME	E	207 866-2171	6552

FURNITURE: Chair & Couch Springs, Assembled

Company	CITY	ST	EMP	PHONE	ENTRY #
Massage Chairs For Less	Nashua	NH	G	603 882-7580	19205

FURNITURE: Chairs, Bentwood

Company	CITY	ST	EMP	PHONE	ENTRY #
Sawyer Bentwood Inc	Whitingham	VT	E	802 368-2357	22647

FURNITURE: Chairs, Household Wood

Company	CITY	ST	EMP	PHONE	ENTRY #
CB Seating Etc LLC **(PA)**	Norwalk	CT	G	203 359-3880	3120
Oomph LLC	New Canaan	CT	G	203 216-9848	2612
Peter Galbert	Roslindale	MA	G	978 660-5580	14841
R H Le Mieur Corp	Templeton	MA	F	978 939-8741	15804
Ralph Curcio Co Inc	Gardner	MA	G	978 632-1120	11124
Royal Furniture Mfg Co Inc	Gardner	MA	G	978 632-1301	11125
Standard Chair Gardner Inc	Gardner	MA	D	978 632-1301	11129
Jim Brown	Lincolnville	ME	F	207 789-5188	6362
Warren Chair Works Inc	Warren	RI	F	401 247-0426	21313

FURNITURE: Chests, Cedar

Company	CITY	ST	EMP	PHONE	ENTRY #
Cedar Chest Inc	Northampton	MA	F	413 584-3860	13998

FURNITURE: Club Room, Household, Metal

Company	CITY	ST	EMP	PHONE	ENTRY #
Patrick T Conley Atty	Providence	RI	G	-	21087

FURNITURE: Couches, Sofa/Davenport, Upholstered Wood Frames

Company	CITY	ST	EMP	PHONE	ENTRY #
Barclay Furniture Associates	Holyoke	MA	G	413 536-8084	11617

FURNITURE: Cut Stone

Company	CITY	ST	EMP	PHONE	ENTRY #
Stone Decor Galleria Inc	Woburn	MA	G	781 937-9377	17302
Ripano Stoneworks Ltd	Nashua	NH	E	603 886-6655	19254

FURNITURE: Desks, Household, Wood

Company	CITY	ST	EMP	PHONE	ENTRY #
Vermont Custom Wood Products	North Walpole	NH	F	802 463-9930	19396

FURNITURE: Desks, Metal

Company	CITY	ST	EMP	PHONE	ENTRY #
Custom Office Furn Boston Inc	Woburn	MA	F	781 933-9970	17158
Desco Industries Inc	Canton	MA	E	781 821-8370	9726

FURNITURE: Desks, Wood

Company	CITY	ST	EMP	PHONE	ENTRY #
Custom Office Furn Boston Inc	Woburn	MA	F	781 933-9970	17158
Desco Industries Inc	Canton	MA	E	781 821-8370	9726

FURNITURE: End Tables, Wood

Company	CITY	ST	EMP	PHONE	ENTRY #
Christopoulos Designs Inc	Bridgeport	CT	F	203 576-1110	397

FURNITURE: Foundations & Platforms

Company	CITY	ST	EMP	PHONE	ENTRY #
J J Concrete Foundations	Bethel	CT	G	203 798-8310	164
Steel Panel Foundations LLC	West Springfield	MA	G	413 439-0218	16552

FURNITURE: Frames, Box Springs Or Bedsprings, Metal

Company	CITY	ST	EMP	PHONE	ENTRY #
Leggett & Platt Incorporated	Oxford	MA	E	508 987-8706	14265

FURNITURE: Game Room, Wood

Company	CITY	ST	EMP	PHONE	ENTRY #
Winning Solutions Inc	Manchester	MA	G	978 525-2813	12609

FURNITURE: Hotel

Company	CITY	ST	EMP	PHONE	ENTRY #
Wingate Sales Associates LLC	Stratham	NH	G	603 303-7189	19877
Cricket Radio LLC	Burlington	VT	G	802 825-8368	21777

FURNITURE: Household, Metal

Company	CITY	ST	EMP	PHONE	ENTRY #
Durham Manufacturing Company **(PA)**	Durham	CT	D	860 349-3427	1090
Modern Objects Inc	Norwalk	CT	G	203 378-5785	3201
Salamander Designs Ltd	Bloomfield	CT	E	860 761-9500	262
Graney John F Metal Design LLC	Sheffield	MA	G	413 528-6744	15060
Raredon Resources Inc	Florence	MA	F	413 586-0941	10868
Sincere Specialty Fabrication	Chelsea	MA	G	781 974-9580	9967
Winnepesaukee Forge Inc	Meredith	NH	G	603 279-5492	18982
Cobble Mountain Inc	East Corinth	VT	G	802 439-5232	21913

FURNITURE: Household, NEC

	CITY	ST	EMP	PHONE	ENTRY #
Ace Result LLC	Norwood	MA	G	612 559-3838	14118

FURNITURE: Household, Upholstered On Metal Frames

	CITY	ST	EMP	PHONE	ENTRY #
Allegheny River Group Inc	Milford	MA	E	508 634-0181	13107

FURNITURE: Household, Upholstered, Exc Wood Or Metal

	CITY	ST	EMP	PHONE	ENTRY #
Northeastern Rustic Furni	Smyrna Mills	ME	G	207 757-8300	6994
Yogibo LLC **(PA)**	Nashua	NH	E	603 595-0207	19291
Vermont Farm Table LLC **(PA)**	Burlington	VT	G	888 425-8838	21815

FURNITURE: Household, Wood

	CITY	ST	EMP	PHONE	ENTRY #
American Wood Products	North Haven	CT	G	203 248-4433	3007
Andre Furniture Industries	South Windsor	CT	G	860 528-8826	3938
Bonito Manufacturing Inc	North Haven	CT	D	203 234-8786	3011
Cherner Chair Company LLC	Ridgefield	CT	G	203 894-4702	3662
Connecticut Solid Surface LLC	Plainville	CT	E	860 410-9800	3477
Custom Furniture & Design LLC	Litchfield	CT	F	860 567-3519	1947
Industrial Wood Product Co	Shelton	CT	G	203 735-2374	3817
Lookout Solutions LLC	Norwalk	CT	G	203 750-0307	3187
Madigan Millwork Inc	Unionville	CT	G	860 673-7601	4658
Nap Brothers Parlor Frame Inc	Glastonbury	CT	F	860 633-9998	1565
Salamander Designs Ltd	Bloomfield	CT	E	860 761-9500	262
Tudor House Furniture Co Inc	Hamden	CT	E	203 288-8451	1792
USA Wood Incorporated	Meriden	CT	G	203 238-4285	2147
Walpole Woodworkers Inc	Westport	CT	G	203 255-9010	5237
Walpole Woodworkers Inc	Ridgefield	CT	E	508 668-2800	3689
Woodworkers Heaven Inc	Bridgeport	CT	F	203 333-2778	506
Abcrosby & Company Inc	Ashburnham	MA	G	978 827-6064	7643
Acton Woodworks Inc	Acton	MA	G	978 263-0222	7335
Bellecraft Woodworking Inc	Winchendon	MA	E	978 297-2672	17071
Charles Webb Inc **(PA)**	Woburn	MA	E	781 569-0444	17143
Connors Design Ltd	Marlborough	MA	G	508 481-1930	12739
Country Bed Shop Inc	Ashby	MA	G	978 386-7550	7646
Countryside Woodcraft	Russell	MA	F	413 862-3276	14877
Cove Woodworking Inc	Gloucester	MA	G	978 704-9773	11175
Craig F Bradford	Northampton	MA	G	413 586-4500	14003
Custom Ktchens By Chmpagne Inc	Franklin	MA	E	508 528-7919	11034
Custom Woods Designs M Marion	Hampden	MA	G	413 566-8230	11320
Damark Woodcraft Inc	Haverhill	MA	G	978 373-6670	11422
David Lefort	Halifax	MA	E	781 826-9033	11317
Drive-O-Rama Inc	Dennis Port	MA	D	508 394-0028	10312
Eustis Enterprises Inc	Cambridge	MA	G	978 827-3103	9474
Fabrizio Corporation	Medford	MA	E	781 396-1400	12933
Field Pendleton	Jefferson	MA	G	508 829-2470	11953
Fine Line Woodworking Inc	Boxboro	MA	G	978 263-4322	8952
Fox Brothers Furniture Studio	Newburyport	MA	G	978 462-7726	13491
Klein Design Inc	Gloucester	MA	G	978 281-5276	11196
M1 Project LLC	Boston	MA	G	617 906-6032	8676
Modu Form Inc **(PA)**	Fitchburg	MA	D	978 345-7942	10841
Pridecraft Inc	North Andover	MA	G	978 685-2831	13726
Robert Kowalski	Spencer	MA	G	508 885-5392	15435
Sincere Specialty Fabrication	Chelsea	MA	G	781 974-9580	9967
Thos Moser Cabinetmakers Inc	Boston	MA	G	617 224-1245	8883
Van Benten Joseph Furn Makers	Chestnut Hill	MA	G	617 738-6575	9994
VCA Inc	Northampton	MA	E	413 587-2750	14025
Walpole Woodworkers Inc	Wilmington	MA	F	978 658-3373	17064
Walpole Woodworkers Inc	East Falmouth	MA	F	508 540-0300	10451
Walpole Woodworkers Inc	Norwell	MA	G	781 681-9099	14114
Huston & Company Wood Design	Arundel	ME	G	207 967-2345	5532
Imagineering Inc	Rockland	ME	E	207 596-6483	6798
Jackson Caldwell	Oxford	ME	G	207 539-2325	6567
Mayville House	Bethel	ME	G	207 824-6545	5715
Mystic Woodworks	Warren	ME	G	207 273-3937	7145
Premium Log Yards Inc **(PA)**	Rumford	ME	F	207 364-7500	6842
Shed Happens Inc **(PA)**	Portland	ME	G	207 892-3636	6725
Thos Moser Cabinetmakers Inc **(PA)**	Auburn	ME	D	207 753-9834	5599
Thos Moser Cabinetmakers Inc	Freeport	ME	G	207 865-4519	6087
Town and Country Cabinets Inc	Gorham	ME	G	207 839-2709	6131
Townsend Cabinet Makers Inc	Limington	ME	G	207 793-7086	6350
Tracy Joseph Woodworks	Mount Desert	ME	G	207 244-0004	6457
Walpole Woodworkers Inc	Detroit	ME	E	207 368-4302	5954
Walpole Woodworkers Inc	Chester	ME	E	207 794-2248	5908
Waterworks	Bangor	ME	F	207 941-8306	5663
Wooden Things Inc	Gray	ME	G	207 712-4654	6144
Anthony Galluzzo Corp	Londonderry	NH	E	603 432-2681	18676
Chatham Furn Reproductions	South Hampton	NH	E	603 394-0089	19855
Cherry Pond Designs Inc	Jefferson	NH	F	603 586-7795	18482
Janice Miller	Manchester	NH	G	603 629-9995	18848
Kimballs Lumber Center LLC **(PA)**	Wolfeboro	NH	G	603 569-2477	20021
Maynard & Maynard Furn Makers	South Acworth	NH	G	603 835-2969	19853
Michael Perra Inc	Manchester	NH	F	603 644-2110	18871
Swift River Wood Products	Chocorua	NH	G	603 323-3317	17832
Bess Home Fashions Inc	West Warwick	RI	F	401 828-0300	21484
Joe Martin	West Warwick	RI	G	401 823-1860	21497
Stephen Plaud Inc	Tiverton	RI	F	401 625-5909	21263
Studio 4 RI LLC	Providence	RI	G	401 578-5419	21128
Two Saints Inc	Cranston	RI	F	401 490-5500	20306
Beeken/Parsons Inc	Shelburne	VT	G	802 985-2913	22413
Carris Financial Corp **(PA)**	Proctor	VT	F	802 773-9111	22283
Dock Doctors LLC	Ferrisburgh	VT	E	802 877-6756	21988
Gaylord West	Franklin	VT	G	802 285-6438	21994
Greenrange Furniture Company	Hinesburg	VT	G	802 747-8564	22027
Lyndon Woodworking Inc **(PA)**	Saint Johnsbury	VT	E	802 748-0100	22390
Merle Schloff	Salisbury	VT	G	802 352-4246	22399
New England Woodcraft Inc	Brandon	VT	C	802 247-8211	21712
Newport Furniture Parts Corp	Newport	VT	D	802 334-5428	22203
Static & Dynamic Tech Inc	Williston	VT	G	802 859-0238	22693
Vermont Furniture Designs Inc	Winooski	VT	E	802 655-6568	22727
William Chadburn	North Concord	VT	G	802 695-8166	22223

FURNITURE: Institutional, Exc Wood

	CITY	ST	EMP	PHONE	ENTRY #
Gallivan Company Inc	Foxboro	MA	G	508 543-5233	10883
Production Basics Inc	Billerica	MA	E	617 926-8100	8278
Ry KY Inc	Wellesley	MA	G	781 235-4581	16385
VCA Inc	Northampton	MA	E	413 587-2750	14025
Dci Inc **(PA)**	Lisbon	NH	D	603 838-6544	18648
Nhrpa	Concord	NH	G	603 340-5583	17919
New England Woodcraft Inc	Brandon	VT	C	802 247-8211	21712

FURNITURE: Juvenile, Metal

	CITY	ST	EMP	PHONE	ENTRY #
Summer Infant Inc **(PA)**	Woonsocket	RI	D	401 671-6550	21581
Summer Infant Inc	Woonsocket	RI	G	401 671-6550	21582

FURNITURE: Juvenile, Wood

	CITY	ST	EMP	PHONE	ENTRY #
Cedarworks of Maine Inc **(PA)**	Rockport	ME	E	207 596-1010	6817
Whitney Bros Co	Keene	NH	E	603 352-2610	18534

FURNITURE: Kitchen & Dining Room

	CITY	ST	EMP	PHONE	ENTRY #
Bostoncounters LLC	Woburn	MA	G	781 281-1622	17138
Zuerner Design LLC	North Kingstown	RI	G	401 324-9490	20750

FURNITURE: Kitchen & Dining Room, Metal

	CITY	ST	EMP	PHONE	ENTRY #
Stonewall Kitchen LLC	South Windsor	CT	C	860 648-9215	4015
Bostoncounters LLC	Woburn	MA	G	781 281-1622	17138
GKS Service Company Inc	Candia	NH	G	603 483-2122	17784

FURNITURE: Laboratory

	CITY	ST	EMP	PHONE	ENTRY #
Jeio Tech Inc	Billerica	MA	G	781 376-0700	8259
Lab Frnture Instlltons Sls Inc	Middleton	MA	F	978 646-0600	13093

FURNITURE: Lawn & Garden, Except Wood & Metal

	CITY	ST	EMP	PHONE	ENTRY #
CJ Sprong & Co Inc	Williamsburg	MA	G	413 628-4410	16948

FURNITURE: Lawn, Wood

	CITY	ST	EMP	PHONE	ENTRY #
Baldwin Lawn Furniture LLC	Middletown	CT	F	860 347-1306	2176
Carefree Building Co Inc **(PA)**	Colchester	CT	F	860 267-7600	800
SIT Inc	Quincy	MA	G	617 479-7796	14656
Richardson-Allen Inc	Biddeford	ME	F	207 284-8402	5761
L & M Sheds LLC	Epping	NH	G	603 679-5243	18100
Cedar Craft Fence Co	Coventry	RI	G	401 397-7765	20141

FURNITURE: Living Room, Upholstered On Wood Frames

	CITY	ST	EMP	PHONE	ENTRY #
Tudor House Furniture Co Inc	Hamden	CT	E	203 288-8451	1792
1817 Shoppe Inc **(PA)**	Sturbridge	MA	G	508 347-2241	15636
Twin Cy Upholstering & Mat Co	Braintree	MA	F	781 843-1780	9044
VT Adirondack	Waitsfield	VT	G	802 496-9271	22570

FURNITURE: Mattresses & Foundations

	CITY	ST	EMP	PHONE	ENTRY #
Symbol Mattress of New England	Dayville	CT	B	860 779-3112	1053
Ecin Industries Inc	Fall River	MA	E	508 675-6920	10686
US Bedding Inc	Fall River	MA	F	508 678-6988	10777

FURNITURE: Mattresses, Box & Bedsprings

	CITY	ST	EMP	PHONE	ENTRY #
A&S Innersprings Usa LLC	Windsor	CT	G	860 298-0401	5313
Ramdial Parts and Services LLC	Hartford	CT	G	860 296-5175	1866
Saatva Inc	Westport	CT	E	877 672-2882	5228
Kendall Productions	Cambridge	MA	G	617 661-0402	9525
Leggett & Platt Incorporated	Woburn	MA	B	336 956-5000	17213
Mockingbird Studios Inc	Mansfield	MA	G	508 339-6755	12646
Therapedic of New England LLC	Brockton	MA	G	508 559-9944	9182

FURNITURE: Mattresses, Innerspring Or Box Spring

	CITY	ST	EMP	PHONE	ENTRY #
Blue Bell Mattress Company LLC	East Windsor	CT	C	860 292-6372	1278
Restopedic Inc	Bethany	CT	G	203 393-1520	124
Subinas USA LLC	Windsor	CT	F	860 298-0401	5370
Gardner Mattress Corporation **(PA)**	Salem	MA	F	978 744-1810	14914
Spring Air Ohio LLC	Chelsea	MA	E	617 884-0041	9968
Ssb Manufacturing Company	Agawam	MA	C	413 789-4410	7452
Twin Cy Upholstering & Mat Co	Braintree	MA	F	781 843-1780	9044
World Sleep Products Inc	North Billerica	MA	D	978 667-6648	13879
Daly Bros Bedding Co Inc	Biddeford	ME	G	207 282-9583	5727
Bourdons Institutional Sls Inc	Claremont	NH	E	603 542-8709	17836

FURNITURE: NEC

	CITY	ST	EMP	PHONE	ENTRY #
42 Design Fab Studio Inc	Indian Orchard	MA	G	413 203-4948	11882
Bunzl Maine	Portland	ME	G	207 772-9825	6629

FURNITURE: Office Panel Systems, Exc Wood

	CITY	ST	EMP	PHONE	ENTRY #
Ais Group Holdings LLC **(PA)**	Hudson	MA	G	978 562-7500	11753
Ais Holdings Corp **(DH)**	Leominster	MA	G	978 562-7500	12110
Cano Corporation **(PA)**	Fitchburg	MA	E	978 342-0953	10818

FURNITURE: Office Panel Systems, Wood

	CITY	ST	EMP	PHONE	ENTRY #
Knoll Inc	Old Saybrook	CT	E	860 395-2093	3341
Neiss Corp	Vernon	CT	F	860 872-8528	4671
Cano Corporation **(PA)**	Fitchburg	MA	E	978 342-0953	10818
NS Converters LLC	Sudbury	MA	G	508 628-1501	15664

FURNITURE: Office, Exc Wood

	CITY	ST	EMP	PHONE	ENTRY #
Bonito Manufacturing Inc	North Haven	CT	D	203 234-8786	3011
Conco Wood Working Inc	West Haven	CT	G	203 934-9665	5113
Durham Manufacturing Company **(PA)**	Durham	CT	D	860 349-3427	1090
One and Co Inc	Norwich	CT	F	860 892-5180	3288
Sabon Industries Inc	Fairfield	CT	G	203 255-8880	1453

	CITY	ST	EMP	PHONE	ENTRY #
Static Safe Products Company	Cornwall Bridge	CT	F	203 937-6391	820
Affordable Intr Systems Inc **(DH)**	Leominster	MA	D	978 562-7500	12108
Flex-Rest Inc	Worcester	MA	G	508 797-4046	17376
Krueger International Inc	Boston	MA	G	617 542-4043	8656
Modu Form Inc	Fitchburg	MA	G	978 345-7942	10842
Modu Form Inc **(PA)**	Fitchburg	MA	D	978 345-7942	10841
Production Basics Inc	Billerica	MA	E	617 926-8100	8278
Wright Line LLC **(HQ)**	Worcester	MA	C	508 852-4300	17510
Mkind Inc	Manchester	NH	G	603 493-6882	18877
Nouveau Interiors LLC	Manchester	NH	G	603 398-1732	18889
SIS-USA Inc	Londonderry	NH	F	603 432-4495	18736
William Chadburn	North Concord	VT	G	802 695-8166	22223

FURNITURE: Office, Wood

	CITY	ST	EMP	PHONE	ENTRY #
Belmont Corporation	Bristol	CT	E	860 589-5700	532
Bergan Architectural Wdwkg Inc	Middletown	CT	E	860 346-0869	2177
Bloomfield Wood & Melamine Inc	Bloomfield	CT	F	860 243-3226	211
Bold Wood Interiors LLC	New Haven	CT	F	203 907-4077	2670
Conco Wood Working Inc	West Haven	CT	G	203 934-9665	5113
Cyr Woodworking Inc	Newington	CT	G	860 232-1991	2858
Lesro Industries Inc	Bloomfield	CT	D	800 275-7545	240
Salamander Designs Ltd	Bloomfield	CT	E	860 761-9500	262
Charles Webb Inc **(PA)**	Woburn	MA	E	781 569-0444	17143
Contemporary Cabinet Designs	Norwood	MA	G	781 769-7979	14143
Fox Brothers Furniture Studio	Newburyport	MA	G	978 462-7726	13491
JC Clocks Company Inc	North Dartmouth	MA	E	508 998-8442	13922
Knoll Inc	Boston	MA	E	617 695-0220	8653
McKearney Associates Inc **(PA)**	Boston	MA	G	617 269-7600	8691
Modern Woodworks Co	Foxboro	MA	G	508 543-9830	10892
Modu Form Inc **(PA)**	Fitchburg	MA	D	978 345-7942	10841
Modu Form Inc	Fitchburg	MA	G	978 345-7942	10842
Wright Line LLC **(HQ)**	Worcester	MA	C	508 852-4300	17510
Cabinet Assembly Systems Corp	East Greenwich	RI	F	401 884-8556	20355
Neudorfer Inc	Waterbury	VT	F	802 244-5338	22584
New England Woodcraft Inc	Brandon	VT	C	802 247-8211	21712
William Chadburn	North Concord	VT	G	802 695-8166	22223

FURNITURE: Outdoor, Wood

	CITY	ST	EMP	PHONE	ENTRY #
Parish Associates Inc	Fairfield	CT	G	203 335-4100	1448
Burger-Roy Inc	Madison	ME	D	207 696-3978	6404

FURNITURE: Restaurant

	CITY	ST	EMP	PHONE	ENTRY #
General Seating Solutions LLC	South Windsor	CT	F	860 242-3307	3971
Cove Woodworking Inc	Gloucester	MA	G	978 704-9773	11175

FURNITURE: School

	CITY	ST	EMP	PHONE	ENTRY #
Columbia Manufacturing Inc	Westfield	MA	D	413 562-3664	16679
Whitney Bros Co	Keene	NH	E	603 352-2610	18534

FURNITURE: Storage Chests, Household, Wood

	CITY	ST	EMP	PHONE	ENTRY #
Wood Geek Inc	New Bedford	MA	G	508 858-5282	13459
Kenney Manufacturing Company **(PA)**	Warwick	RI	B	401 739-2200	21383

FURNITURE: Studio Couches

	CITY	ST	EMP	PHONE	ENTRY #
Vijon Studios Inc	Old Saybrook	CT	G	860 399-7440	3353

FURNITURE: Table Tops, Marble

	CITY	ST	EMP	PHONE	ENTRY #
Creative Stone LLC	East Haven	CT	F	203 624-1882	1246
East Coast Marble & Gran Corp	Lynn	MA	G	781 760-0207	12504
Vanity World Inc	Canton	MA	G	508 668-1800	9792

FURNITURE: Tables & Table Tops, Wood

	CITY	ST	EMP	PHONE	ENTRY #
Saloom Furniture Co Inc	Winchendon	MA	D	978 297-1901	17082

FURNITURE: Tables, Office, Wood

	CITY	ST	EMP	PHONE	ENTRY #
Lorimer Studios LLC	North Kingstown	RI	F	401 714-0014	20725

FURNITURE: Television, Wood

	CITY	ST	EMP	PHONE	ENTRY #
Christopoulos Designs Inc	Bridgeport	CT	F	203 576-1110	397
Frame My Tvcom LLC	Haverhill	MA	G	978 912-7200	11435

FURNITURE: Theater

	CITY	ST	EMP	PHONE	ENTRY #
New England Scenic LLC	Canton	MA	G	781 562-1792	9762

FURNITURE: Unfinished, Wood

	CITY	ST	EMP	PHONE	ENTRY #
Western Conn Craftsmen LLC	New Fairfield	CT	G	203 312-8167	2631

FURNITURE: Upholstered

	CITY	ST	EMP	PHONE	ENTRY #
Cerrito Furniture Inds Inc	Branford	CT	F	203 481-2580	304
Clark Manner Marguarite	New London	CT	G	860 444-7679	2769
Ethan Allen Interiors Inc **(PA)**	Danbury	CT	C	203 743-8000	914
Alliance Upholstery Inc	Springfield	MA	G	413 731-7857	15444
Charles Webb Inc **(PA)**	Woburn	MA	E	781 569-0444	17143
David Lefort	Halifax	MA	E	781 826-9033	11317
Huot Enterprises Inc	Ludlow	MA	G	413 589-7422	12468
Jerrys Custom Upholstery	Bridgewater	MA	G	508 697-2183	9078
Alfreds Upholstering & Custom	Alfred	ME	F	207 536-5565	5514
Custom Canvas & Upholstery LLC	Lewiston	ME	F	207 241-8518	6281
Jackson Caldwell	Oxford	ME	G	207 539-2325	6567
Hwang Bishop Designs Ltd	Warren	RI	G	401 245-9557	21296
New England Woodcraft Inc	Brandon	VT	C	802 247-8211	21712

FURNITURE: Wall Cases, Office, Exc Wood

	CITY	ST	EMP	PHONE	ENTRY #
Peristere LLC	Manchester	CT	G	860 783-5301	2038

GAMES & TOYS: Automobiles & Trucks

	CITY	ST	EMP	PHONE	ENTRY #
Mwb Toy Company LLC	Danbury	CT	G	212 598-4500	958

GAMES & TOYS: Baby Carriages & Restraint Seats

	CITY	ST	EMP	PHONE	ENTRY #
Monahan Products LLC	Hingham	MA	E	781 413-3000	11506

GAMES & TOYS: Blocks

	CITY	ST	EMP	PHONE	ENTRY #
Poof-Alex Holdings LLC **(PA)**	Greenwich	CT	G	203 930-7711	1638
Green Mountain Blocks	Danville	VT	G	802 748-1341	21896

GAMES & TOYS: Board Games, Children's & Adults'

	CITY	ST	EMP	PHONE	ENTRY #
Winning Solutions Inc	Manchester	MA	G	978 525-2813	12609
Hasbro Inc **(PA)**	Pawtucket	RI	A	401 431-8697	20845

GAMES & TOYS: Carriages, Baby

	CITY	ST	EMP	PHONE	ENTRY #
West End Strollers	Boston	MA	G	617 720-6020	8922

GAMES & TOYS: Chessmen & Chessboards

	CITY	ST	EMP	PHONE	ENTRY #
Massachusetts Chess Assn **(PA)**	Lexington	MA	G	781 862-3799	12241

GAMES & TOYS: Craft & Hobby Kits & Sets

	CITY	ST	EMP	PHONE	ENTRY #
Essex Wood Products Inc	Colchester	CT	E	860 537-3451	802
Gail Wilson Designs	South Acworth	NH	G	603 835-6551	19852
Hasbro Inc	Providence	RI	F	401 280-2127	21026
Homespun Samplar	Harrisville	RI	G	401 732-3181	20480
Learning Materials Workshop	Burlington	VT	G	802 862-0112	21793
Vermont Hand Crafters Inc	Waterbury	VT	G	802 434-5044	22588

GAMES & TOYS: Doll Clothing

	CITY	ST	EMP	PHONE	ENTRY #
Marcias Dollclothes	North Scituate	RI	G	401 742-3654	20780

GAMES & TOYS: Dollhouses & Furniture

	CITY	ST	EMP	PHONE	ENTRY #
Real Good Toys Inc	Montpelier	VT	G	802 479-2217	22159

GAMES & TOYS: Dolls, Exc Stuffed Toy Animals

	CITY	ST	EMP	PHONE	ENTRY #
Bonnies Bundles Dolls	Chester	VT	G	802 875-2114	21841
R John Wright Dolls Inc	Bennington	VT	E	802 447-7072	21690

GAMES & TOYS: Electronic

	CITY	ST	EMP	PHONE	ENTRY #
Enterplay LLC	Guilford	CT	F	203 458-1128	1703
Greenbrier Games LLP	Marlborough	MA	G	978 618-8442	12764
Hitpoint Inc **(PA)**	Springfield	MA	F	508 314-6070	15476
Neuromotion Inc	Boston	MA	F	415 676-9326	8726

GAMES & TOYS: Erector Sets

	CITY	ST	EMP	PHONE	ENTRY #
Lego Systems Inc **(DH)**	Enfield	CT	A	860 749-2291	1368

GAMES & TOYS: Kits, Science, Incl Microscopes/Chemistry Sets

	CITY	ST	EMP	PHONE	ENTRY #
Voltree Power Inc	Canton	MA	G	781 858-4939	9794
Delta Education LLC	Nashua	NH	B	800 258-1302	19144

GAMES & TOYS: Marbles

	CITY	ST	EMP	PHONE	ENTRY #
Infinity Stone Inc	Waterbury	CT	F	203 575-9484	4888

GAMES & TOYS: Models, Airplane, Toy & Hobby

	CITY	ST	EMP	PHONE	ENTRY #
Paul K Guillow Inc	Wakefield	MA	E	781 245-5255	15967

GAMES & TOYS: Models, Boat & Ship, Toy & Hobby

	CITY	ST	EMP	PHONE	ENTRY #
Bluejacket Inc	Searsport	ME	F	207 548-9970	6947

GAMES & TOYS: Models, Railroad, Toy & Hobby

	CITY	ST	EMP	PHONE	ENTRY #
Zepkas Antigues	Springfield	MA	G	413 782-2964	15530

GAMES & TOYS: Puzzles

	CITY	ST	EMP	PHONE	ENTRY #
Ceaco Inc	Newton	MA	G	617 926-8080	13575
Edaron Inc **(PA)**	Holyoke	MA	C	413 533-7159	11624
Ferrari Classics Corporation	Southwick	MA	G	413 569-6179	15413
Leap Year Publishing LLC	North Andover	MA	F	978 688-9900	13717
Zen Art & Design Inc	Hadley	MA	F	800 215-6010	11312
Elms Puzzles Inc	Harrison	ME	F	207 583-6262	6176
Puzzle House	Jaffrey	NH	F	603 532-4442	18475
Stave Puzzles Incorporated	Wilder	VT	E	802 295-5200	22648

GAMES & TOYS: Trains & Eqpt, Electric & Mechanical

	CITY	ST	EMP	PHONE	ENTRY #
Ross Curtis Product Inc	Norwich	CT	G	860 886-6800	3289
Charles Ro Mfg Co Inc	Malden	MA	G	781 322-6084	12565

GARAGES: Portable, Prefabricated Metal

	CITY	ST	EMP	PHONE	ENTRY #
Mdm Products LLC	Milford	CT	F	203 877-7070	2314

GARBAGE CONTAINERS: Plastic

	CITY	ST	EMP	PHONE	ENTRY #
Big Dog Disposal Inc	Seekonk	MA	G	508 695-9539	15019
Billy Hill Tubs LLC	Sterling	MA	G	978 422-8800	15536
Edward F Briggs Disposal Inc	East Greenwich	RI	G	401 294-6391	20365

GARBAGE DISPOSALS: Household

	CITY	ST	EMP	PHONE	ENTRY #
Maciel John	Maynard	MA	G	978 897-5865	12901

GARMENT: Pressing & cleaners' agents

	CITY	ST	EMP	PHONE	ENTRY #
Sally Conant	Orange	CT	F	203 878-3005	3383

GAS & OIL FIELD EXPLORATION SVCS

	CITY	ST	EMP	PHONE	ENTRY #
El Paso Prod Oil Gas Texas LP	Hartford	CT	F	860 293-1990	1819
Maine Power Express LLC	Greenwich	CT	G	203 661-0055	1628
Vab Inc	Plainville	CT	G	860 793-0246	3523
Als Oil Service	Shrewsbury	MA	G	508 853-2539	15099
Greener 3000 LLC	Boston	MA	G	781 589-5777	8579
Nuvera Fuel Cells LLC	Billerica	MA	D	617 245-7500	8269
Quantum Discoveries Inc	Boston	MA	G	857 272-9998	8803
Schlumberger Technology Corp	Cambridge	MA	C	617 768-2000	9645
SIVS Oil Inc	North Dartmouth	MA	G	508 951-0528	13925
Stroud International Ltd	Marblehead	MA	G	781 631-8806	12695

	CITY	ST	EMP	PHONE	ENTRY #
Hunting Dearborn Inc	Fryeburg	ME	C	207 935-2171	6099
D F Richard Inc	Dover	NH	D	603 742-2020	18017
Energy Today Inc	Manchester	NH	G	603 425-8933	18816
Dionne & Sons Piping Dynamics	Coventry	RI	G	401 821-9266	20145

GAS & OIL FIELD SVCS, NEC

	CITY	ST	EMP	PHONE	ENTRY #
Home Heating Services Corp	Somerville	MA	E	617 625-8255	15183
Msr Utility	Dunstable	MA	G	978 649-0002	10390
North End Oil Service Co Inc	Springfield	MA	G	413 734-7057	15493
Dysarts	Hermon	ME	G	207 947-8649	6185

GASES: Carbon Dioxide

	CITY	ST	EMP	PHONE	ENTRY #
Praxair Distribution Inc	Slatersville	RI	E	401 767-3450	21205

GASES: Helium

	CITY	ST	EMP	PHONE	ENTRY #
A Helium Plus Balloons LLC	Wethersfield	CT	G	860 833-1761	5239
Helium Plus Inc	Newtown	CT	G	203 304-1880	2923

GASES: Hydrogen

	CITY	ST	EMP	PHONE	ENTRY #
Hydrogen Highway LLC	North Branford	CT	G	203 871-1000	2968
Electrochem Inc	Woburn	MA	F	781 938-5300	17175
Hydrogen Energy California LLC	Concord	MA	E	978 287-9529	10134
Safe Hydrogen LLC	Lexington	MA	G	781 861-7016	12261
Safe Hydrogen LLC	Lexington	MA	G	781 861-7252	12262
Verde LLC	Quincy	MA	G	617 955-2402	14666

GASES: Indl

	CITY	ST	EMP	PHONE	ENTRY #
Airgas Usa LLC	Naugatuck	CT	G	203 729-2159	2459
Aldlab Chemicals LLC	North Haven	CT	G	203 589-4934	3005
Praxair Inc	Wallingford	CT	E	203 793-1200	4787
Praxair Inc	Naugatuck	CT	E	203 720-2477	2491
Praxair Inc	Suffield	CT	D	860 292-5400	4466
Praxair Inc **(HQ)**	Danbury	CT	B	203 837-2000	971
Praxair Distribution Inc	Durham	CT	E	860 349-0305	1093
Praxair Distribution Inc **(DH)**	Danbury	CT	F	203 837-2000	972
Praxair Distribution Inc	Danbury	CT	F	203 837-2162	973
Airgas Usa LLC	Billerica	MA	E	978 439-1344	8207
Boc Gases	Boston	MA	G	617 878-2090	8418
Boc Gasses At Mit	Cambridge	MA	G	617 374-9992	9413
Messer LLC	Bellingham	MA	F	508 966-3148	8050
Praxair Distribution Inc	Auburn	MA	E	203 837-2000	7848
Weldship Industries Inc	Westborough	MA	G	508 898-0100	16658
Edwards Ltd	Kittery	ME	G	207 439-2400	6255
Matheson Tri-Gas Inc	Westbrook	ME	F	207 775-0515	7195
Hanna Instruments Inc **(PA)**	Woonsocket	RI	E	401 765-7500	21567
Messer LLC	Essex Junction	VT	E	802 878-6339	21950

GASES: Neon

	CITY	ST	EMP	PHONE	ENTRY #
New England Ortho Neuro LLC	Hamden	CT	G	203 200-7228	1776
Neon Goose	Hull	MA	G	781 925-5118	11829
Neon Pipe	Corinth	ME	G	207 285-7420	5924

GASES: Nitrogen

	CITY	ST	EMP	PHONE	ENTRY #
Linde Gas North America LLC	Marlborough	MA	F	508 229-8118	12786
Messer LLC	Kittery	ME	E	207 475-3102	6257

GASES: Oxygen

	CITY	ST	EMP	PHONE	ENTRY #
Air Products and Chemicals Inc	Hopkinton	MA	E	508 435-3428	11688
Hydro-Test Products Inc	Stow	MA	F	978 897-4647	15632
Messer LLC	Attleboro	MA	E	508 236-0222	7767
Messer LLC	Stoughton	MA	F	781 341-4575	15607
Airgas Usa LLC	East Greenwich	RI	G	401 884-0201	20351

GASKET MATERIALS

	CITY	ST	EMP	PHONE	ENTRY #
Auburn Manufacturing Company	Middletown	CT	E	860 346-6677	2173
Hollingsworth & Vose Company **(PA)**	East Walpole	MA	C	508 850-2000	10524

GASKETS

	CITY	ST	EMP	PHONE	ENTRY #
Chas W House & Sons Inc	Unionville	CT	D	860 673-2518	4654
Corru Seals Inc	Wallingford	CT	F	203 284-0319	4728
Lydall Inc **(PA)**	Manchester	CT	E	860 646-1233	2021
Parker-Hannifin Corporation	North Haven	CT	D	203 239-3341	3049
Rubber Supplies Company Inc	Derby	CT	G	203 736-9995	1079
Spirol International Corp **(HQ)**	Danielson	CT	C	860 774-8571	1018
Standard Washer & Mat Inc	Manchester	CT	E	860 643-5125	2051
Vanguard Products Corporation	Danbury	CT	D	203 744-7265	1003
A W Chesterton Company **(PA)**	Groveland	MA	E	781 438-7000	11298
Acushnet Rubber Company Inc	New Bedford	MA	B	508 998-4000	13352
Atlantic Rubber Company Inc	Littleton	MA	F	800 882-3666	12294
B G Peck Company Inc	Lawrence	MA	E	978 686-4181	11997
D V Die Cutting Inc	Danvers	MA	E	978 777-0300	10210
Eastern Industrial Products	Pembroke	MA	F	781 826-9511	14403
I G Marston Company	Holbrook	MA	F	781 767-2894	11526
Interstate Gasket Company Inc	Sutton	MA	F	508 234-5500	15684
Vellumoid Inc	Worcester	MA	E	508 853-2500	17499

GASKETS & SEALING DEVICES

	CITY	ST	EMP	PHONE	ENTRY #
American Seal and Engrg Co Inc **(DH)**	Orange	CT	E	203 789-8819	3358
Derby Cellular Products Inc	Shelton	CT	C	203 735-4661	3795
H-O Products Corporation	Winsted	CT	E	860 379-9875	5412
SKF USA Inc	Winsted	CT	E	860 379-8511	5423
Boston Atlantic Corp	Worcester	MA	F	508 754-4076	17350
Parker-Hannifin Corporation	Woburn	MA	B	781 939-4278	17255
Saint-Gobain Prfmce Plas Corp	Worcester	MA	E	508 852-3072	17467
Xtreme Seal LLC	Hingham	MA	G	508 933-1894	11519
Woodex Bearing Company Inc	Georgetown	ME	E	207 371-2210	6107
Ferrotec (usa) Corporation **(HQ)**	Bedford	NH	D	603 472-6800	17640
Trellborg Pipe Sals Mlford Inc **(DH)**	Milford	NH	C	800 626-2180	19080

	CITY	ST	EMP	PHONE	ENTRY #
John Crane Inc	Warwick	RI	D	401 463-8700	21380

GASOLINE FILLING STATIONS

	CITY	ST	EMP	PHONE	ENTRY #
Old Creamery Grocery Store	Cummington	MA	G	413 634-5560	10173

GASTROINTESTINAL OR GENITOURINARY SYSTEM DRUGS

	CITY	ST	EMP	PHONE	ENTRY #
Cristcot LLC	Concord	MA	G	978 212-6380	10126
Deciphera Pharmaceuticals LLC	Waltham	MA	G	781 209-6400	16081
Sobi Inc	Waltham	MA	E	610 228-2040	16196
Global Biotechnologies Inc	Scarborough	ME	G	800 755-8420	6920

GATES: Dam, Metal Plate

	CITY	ST	EMP	PHONE	ENTRY #
Rodney Hunt-Fontaine Inc **(DH)**	Orange	MA	C	978 544-2511	14227
Steel-Fab Inc	Fitchburg	MA	E	978 345-1112	10857

GATES: Ornamental Metal

	CITY	ST	EMP	PHONE	ENTRY #
Artistic Iron Works LLC	Norwalk	CT	G	203 838-9200	3104
Deangelis Iron Work Inc	South Easton	MA	E	508 238-4310	15276
Graney John F Metal Design LLC	Sheffield	MA	G	413 528-6744	15060
Mezzanine Safeti Gates Inc	Essex	MA	G	978 768-3000	10596

GAUGE BLOCKS

	CITY	ST	EMP	PHONE	ENTRY #
Great Neck Saw Mfrs Inc	Millbury	MA	E	508 865-4482	13166

GAUGES

	CITY	ST	EMP	PHONE	ENTRY #
All Five Tool Co Inc	Berlin	CT	E	860 583-1693	69
D & M Tool Company Inc	West Hartford	CT	G	860 236-6037	5064
E and S Gage Inc	Tolland	CT	F	860 872-5917	4546
Hartford Gauge Co	West Hartford	CT	G	860 233-9619	5075
Highland Manufacturing Inc	Manchester	CT	E	860 646-5142	2009
LLC Dow Gage	Berlin	CT	E	860 828-5327	92
Lyons Tool and Die Company	Meriden	CT	E	203 238-2689	2100
Meyer Gage Co Inc	South Windsor	CT	F	860 528-6526	3993
Moore Tool Company Inc **(HQ)**	Bridgeport	CT	D	203 366-3224	453
Precision Punch + Tooling Corp	Berlin	CT	G	860 225-4159	104
Q Alpha Inc	Colchester	CT	E	860 357-7340	806
Sirois Tool Company Inc **(PA)**	Berlin	CT	D	860 828-5327	109
Victor Tool Co Inc	Meriden	CT	G	203 634-8113	2148
Zero Check LLC	Thomaston	CT	G	860 283-5629	4529
Comtorgage Corporation	Slatersville	RI	E	401 765-0900	21203
Vermont Custom Gage LLC	Lyndonville	VT	G	802 868-0104	22074

GAUGES: Pressure

	CITY	ST	EMP	PHONE	ENTRY #
Ashcroft Inc **(DH)**	Stratford	CT	B	203 378-8281	4392
Mija Industries Inc	Rockland	MA	E	781 871-5629	14814

GEARS

	CITY	ST	EMP	PHONE	ENTRY #
United Gear & Machine Co Inc	Suffield	CT	F	860 623-6618	4469
Boulevard Machine & Gear Inc	Springfield	MA	E	413 788-6466	15456
Lampin Corporation **(PA)**	Uxbridge	MA	E	508 278-2422	15923

GEARS & GEAR UNITS: Reduction, Exc Auto

	CITY	ST	EMP	PHONE	ENTRY #
Onvio Servo LLC	Salem	NH	E	603 685-0404	19758

GEARS: Power Transmission, Exc Auto

	CITY	ST	EMP	PHONE	ENTRY #
Cunningham Industries Inc	Stamford	CT	G	203 324-2942	4180
Bendon Gear & Machine Inc	Rockland	MA	E	781 878-8100	14793
Commercial Gear Sprocket Inc	East Walpole	MA	F	508 668-1073	10522
Custom Machine & Tool Co Inc	Hanover	MA	F	781 924-1003	11334
Martin Sprocket & Gear Inc	Milford	MA	G	508 634-3990	13125
Std Precision Gear & Instr Inc	West Bridgewater	MA	E	508 580-0035	16457
Allard Nazarian Group Inc **(PA)**	Manchester	NH	C	603 668-1900	18774

GEMSTONE & INDL DIAMOND MINING SVCS

	CITY	ST	EMP	PHONE	ENTRY #
North East Materials Group LLC	Graniteville	VT	F	802 479-7004	22000

GENERAL MERCHANDISE, NONDURABLE, WHOLESALE

	CITY	ST	EMP	PHONE	ENTRY #
Ira Green Inc	Providence	RI	C	800 663-7487	21040

GENERATING APPARATUS & PARTS: Electrical

	CITY	ST	EMP	PHONE	ENTRY #
Afcon Products Inc	Bethany	CT	F	203 393-9301	118
Polaris Management Inc	Easton	CT	G	203 261-6399	1322
Raymond Thibault	Walpole	MA	G	508 281-5500	16008
Powerdyne International Inc	Cranston	RI	G	401 739-3300	20273

GENERATION EQPT: Electronic

	CITY	ST	EMP	PHONE	ENTRY #
Acceleron Inc	East Granby	CT	E	860 651-9333	1115
Advanced Sonics LLC	Oxford	CT	G	203 266-4440	3387
B S T Systems Inc	Plainfield	CT	D	860 564-4078	3451
Parmaco LLC	Glastonbury	CT	G	860 573-7118	1570
Acumentrics Rups LLC	Walpole	MA	E	617 932-7877	15987
Asco Power Technologies LP	Marlborough	MA	G	508 624-0466	12720
Cipem USA Inc	Melrose	MA	G	347 642-1106	12979
Helix Power Corporation	Somerville	MA	G	781 718-7282	15182
Phoenix Electric Corp	Canton	MA	E	781 821-0200	9767
Southwest Asian Incorporated	Worcester	MA	G	508 753-7126	17477
Superconductivity Inc **(HQ)**	Ayer	MA	D	608 831-5773	7940
Thermo Fisher Scientific Inc	Wilmington	MA	D	978 275-0800	17055
Thermo Fisher Scientific Inc **(PA)**	Waltham	MA	C	781 622-1000	16213
Thinklite LLC	Natick	MA	G	617 500-6689	13282
Wafer LLC	Danvers	MA	G	978 304-3821	10272
Zexen Technology LLC	Shrewsbury	MA	G	508 786-9928	15138
Elecyr Corporation	Portsmouth	NH	G	617 905-6800	19558
Pyromate Inc	Peterborough	NH	G	603 924-4251	19485
Vicor Corporation	Manchester	NH	F	603 623-3222	18951
International Technologies Inc	Warwick	RI	F	401 467-6907	21376
Veterans Assembled Elec LLC **(PA)**	Providence	RI	G	401 228-6165	21150
Charter Dev & Consulting Corp	Essex Junction	VT	G	802 878-5005	21936

Employee Codes: A=Over 500 employees, B=251-500
C=101-250, D=51-100 E=20-50, F=10-19, G=3-9

	CITY	ST	EMP	PHONE	ENTRY #
White Oak Farms	Sandown	NH	G	603 887-2233	19789

	CITY	ST	EMP	PHONE	ENTRY #
Genuine Jamaican	Barnet	VT	G	802 633-2676	21604

	CITY	ST	EMP	PHONE	ENTRY #
Durkee-Mower Inc	Lynn	MA	E	781 593-8007	12503

GENERATOR REPAIR SVCS

	CITY	ST	EMP	PHONE	ENTRY #
Afcon Products Inc	Bethany	CT	F	203 393-9301	118
Chase Electric Motors LLC	Hooksett	NH	G	603 669-2565	18346

GENERATOR SETS: Motor

	CITY	ST	EMP	PHONE	ENTRY #
Horlick Company Inc	Randolph	MA	G	781 963-0090	14685

GENERATORS SETS: Steam

	CITY	ST	EMP	PHONE	ENTRY #
Asea Brown Boveri Inc **(DH)**	Norwalk	CT	G	203 750-2200	3105
PJ Schwalbenberg & Assoc	Cushing	ME	G	207 354-0700	5934

GENERATORS: Automotive & Aircraft

	CITY	ST	EMP	PHONE	ENTRY #
Merl Inc	Meriden	CT	G	203 237-8811	2106

GENERATORS: Electric

	CITY	ST	EMP	PHONE	ENTRY #
Ac/DC Industrial Electric LLC	Yantic	CT	G	860 886-2232	5506
Drs Naval Power Systems Inc	Bridgeport	CT	B	203 366-5211	407
Drs Naval Power Systems Inc	Bridgeport	CT	E	203 366-5211	408
Ward Leonard CT LLC	Thomaston	CT	D	860 283-2294	4526
Andrus Power Solutions Inc	Lee	MA	F	413 243-0043	12087
Dzi	Easthampton	MA	F	413 527-4500	10560
Raven Technology LLC	Brunswick	ME	F	207 729-7904	5844
Generator Power Solutions Neng	Nashua	NH	G	603 577-1766	19166

GENERATORS: Electrochemical, Fuel Cell

	CITY	ST	EMP	PHONE	ENTRY #
Ballard Unmanned Systems Inc	Southborough	MA	F	508 687-4970	15344
El-Op US Inc	Merrimack	NH	B	603 889-2500	18998
KMC Systems Inc	Merrimack	NH	D	866 742-0442	19010
Kollsman Inc **(DH)**	Merrimack	NH	A	603 889-2500	19011

GENERATORS: Gas

	CITY	ST	EMP	PHONE	ENTRY #
Angstrom Advanced Inc	Stoughton	MA	D	781 519-4765	15580
New England Gen-Connect LLC	Hingham	MA	G	617 571-6884	11507
Peak Scientific Instruments	North Billerica	MA	E	978 262-1384	13854
Thermal Dynamix Inc	Westfield	MA	G	413 562-1266	16734

GENERATORS: Ultrasonic

	CITY	ST	EMP	PHONE	ENTRY #
Rinco Ultrasonics USA Inc	Danbury	CT	G	203 744-4500	978

GIFT SHOP

	CITY	ST	EMP	PHONE	ENTRY #
Bovano Industries Incorporated	Cheshire	CT	F	203 272-3208	715
Nel Group LLC	Windsor	CT	F	860 683-0190	5350
Colonial Key & Engraving	Salem	MA	G	978 745-8237	14902
Country Candle Co Inc **(PA)**	Millbury	MA	E	508 865-6061	13160
Vaillancourt Folk Art Inc	Sutton	MA	E	508 476-3601	15695
Whiffletree Cntry Str Gift Sp	Billerica	MA	G	978 663-6346	8309
Harbor Candy Shop Inc	Ogunquit	ME	E	207 646-8078	6537
E B Frye & Son Inc	Wilton	NH	G	603 654-6581	19979
Kellerhaus Inc	Laconia	NH	E	603 366-4466	18569
Next Event Corporation	Portsmouth	RI	G	401 683-0070	20931
Johnson Marble and Granite	Proctor	VT	G	802 459-3303	22285
Lake Champlain Trnsp Co	Burlington	VT	C	802 660-3495	21792

GIFT, NOVELTY & SOUVENIR STORES: Artcraft & carvings

	CITY	ST	EMP	PHONE	ENTRY #
Company of Craftsmen	Mystic	CT	G	860 536-4189	2436

GIFT, NOVELTY & SOUVENIR STORES: Trading Cards, Sports

	CITY	ST	EMP	PHONE	ENTRY #
Jim Carr Inc	Pelham	NH	G	603 635-2821	19437

GIFTS & NOVELTIES: Wholesalers

	CITY	ST	EMP	PHONE	ENTRY #
Concord Industries Inc	Norwalk	CT	E	203 750-6060	3131
Executive Greetings Inc **(HQ)**	New Hartford	CT	B	860 379-9911	2636
Nel Group LLC	Windsor	CT	F	860 683-0190	5350
Ketcham Traps	New Bedford	MA	G	508 997-4787	13404
Mooneytunco Inc	Weymouth	MA	G	781 331-4445	16894
Mystic Industries Corp	Wakefield	MA	F	781 245-1950	15962
Wheel House Designs Inc	Morrisville	VT	G	802 888-8552	22180

GIFTWARE: Brass

	CITY	ST	EMP	PHONE	ENTRY #
B & J Manufacturing Corp	Taunton	MA	D	508 822-1990	15730
Artvac Corporation	Lincoln	RI	E	401 333-6120	20557
Hex Design Inc **(PA)**	Bennington	VT	G	802 442-3309	21672

GLASS & GLASS CERAMIC PRDTS, PRESSED OR BLOWN: Tableware

	CITY	ST	EMP	PHONE	ENTRY #
Periodic Tableware LLC	Shelton	CT	F	310 428-4250	3850
Sydenstricker Galleries Inc **(PA)**	Brewster	MA	F	508 385-3272	9058

GLASS FABRICATORS

	CITY	ST	EMP	PHONE	ENTRY #
Baron Technology Inc	Trumbull	CT	E	203 452-0515	4614
Flabeg Technical Glass US Corp	Naugatuck	CT	E	203 729-5227	2473
Acton Research Corporation	Acton	MA	E	941 556-2601	7334
Diamond Windows Doors Mfg Inc	Boston	MA	E	617 282-1688	8503
Fibertec Inc	Bridgewater	MA	D	508 697-5100	9073
Glass By Petze	Osterville	MA	F	508 428-0971	14248
Glass Dimension Inc	Essex	MA	E	978 768-7984	10593
Hardric Laboratories Inc	North Chelmsford	MA	E	978 251-1702	13895
Idex Health & Science LLC	Middleboro	MA	C	774 213-0200	13064
LTI Smart Glass Inc	Pittsfield	MA	D	413 637-5001	14486
Mini-Systems Inc	Plainville	MA	E	508 695-2000	14528
Modern Mfg Inc Worcester	Worcester	MA	E	508 791-7151	17421
Omni Glass Inc	North Billerica	MA	G	978 667-6664	13850
Patriot Armored Systems LLC	Lenox Dale	MA	E	413 637-1060	12104
Protective Armored Systems Inc	Lee	MA	E	413 637-1060	12095
T J Holmes Co Inc	Chartley	MA	E	508 222-1723	9858
Brass Foundry	West Rockport	ME	G	207 236-3200	7178
McDonald Stain Glass Ltd	Boothbay Harbor	ME	G	207 633-4815	5785
Baker Salmon Christopher	Antrim	NH	G	603 588-4000	17592
Erie Scientific LLC **(DH)**	Portsmouth	NH	B	603 430-6859	19560
Glass Pro Inc	Brentwood	NH	G	603 436-2882	17750
Ultimate Glass Services LLC	Kingston	NH	G	603 642-3375	18547
Swarovski North America Ltd **(DH)**	Cranston	RI	A	401 463-6400	20295
Brass Butterfly Inc	Poultney	VT	G	802 287-9818	22270
Vitriesse Glass Studio	West Pawlet	VT	G	802 645-9800	22613

GLASS PRDTS, FROM PURCHASED GLASS: Art

	CITY	ST	EMP	PHONE	ENTRY #
Dan Dailey Inc	Kensington	NH	F	603 778-2303	18536

GLASS PRDTS, FROM PURCHASED GLASS: Enameled

	CITY	ST	EMP	PHONE	ENTRY #
Bovano Industries Incorporated	Cheshire	CT	F	203 272-3208	715

GLASS PRDTS, FROM PURCHASED GLASS: Glass Beads, Reflecting

	CITY	ST	EMP	PHONE	ENTRY #
AMS Glass Bead Cabinets	Hampden	MA	E	413 566-0037	11319
Printguard Inc	Millbury	MA	F	508 890-8822	13173

GLASS PRDTS, FROM PURCHASED GLASS: Glassware

	CITY	ST	EMP	PHONE	ENTRY #
Glass Industries America LLC	Wallingford	CT	F	203 269-6700	4749

GLASS PRDTS, FROM PURCHASED GLASS: Insulating

	CITY	ST	EMP	PHONE	ENTRY #
Sigco LLC	Westbrook	ME	E	207 775-2676	7207
Sigco LLC **(DH)**	Westbrook	ME	C	207 775-2676	7208

GLASS PRDTS, FROM PURCHASED GLASS: Mirrored

	CITY	ST	EMP	PHONE	ENTRY #
Canner Incorporated	West Groton	MA	F	978 448-3063	16479

GLASS PRDTS, FROM PURCHASED GLASS: Novelties, Fruit, Etc

	CITY	ST	EMP	PHONE	ENTRY #
Swarovski US Holding Limited **(HQ)**	Cranston	RI	G	401 463-6400	20296

GLASS PRDTS, PRESSED OR BLOWN: Bowls

	CITY	ST	EMP	PHONE	ENTRY #
Anchor Bend Glassworks LLC **(PA)**	North Kingstown	RI	G	401 667-7338	20690

GLASS PRDTS, PRESSED OR BLOWN: Bulbs, Electric Lights

	CITY	ST	EMP	PHONE	ENTRY #
Atlas Global Ltg Solutions Inc **(PA)**	Boston	MA	G	617 304-3264	8384
Beon Home Inc	North Easton	MA	G	617 600-8329	13944

GLASS PRDTS, PRESSED OR BLOWN: Furnishings & Access

	CITY	ST	EMP	PHONE	ENTRY #
Magic Industries Inc	Bozrah	CT	F	860 949-8380	281
Whalley Glass Company **(PA)**	Derby	CT	D	203 735-9388	1083
Vaillancourt Folk Art Inc	Sutton	MA	E	508 476-3601	15695
Church & Maple Glass Studio	Burlington	VT	G	802 863-3880	21773
Simon Pearce US Inc	Windsor	VT	D	802 674-6280	22715

GLASS PRDTS, PRESSED OR BLOWN: Glass Fibers, Textile

	CITY	ST	EMP	PHONE	ENTRY #
Fiberoptics Technology Inc	Pomfret	CT	D	860 928-0443	3551
Ward Process Inc	Holliston	MA	D	508 429-1165	11613

GLASS PRDTS, PRESSED OR BLOWN: Glassware, Art Or Decorative

	CITY	ST	EMP	PHONE	ENTRY #
Fritz Glass	Dennis Port	MA	G	508 394-0441	10313
Glass Dimension Inc	Essex	MA	E	978 768-7984	10593
Pgc Acquisition LLC	Reading	MA	F	508 888-2344	14738
Herrmann Pepi Crystal Inc	Gilford	NH	G	603 528-1020	18188
Thames Glass Inc	Newport	RI	F	401 846-0576	20686
Crest Studios	Townshend	VT	F	802 365-4200	22541
Penelope Wurr Glass	Putney	VT	G	802 387-5607	22290

GLASS PRDTS, PRESSED OR BLOWN: Glassware, Novelty

	CITY	ST	EMP	PHONE	ENTRY #
McDonald Stain Glass Ltd	Boothbay Harbor	ME	G	207 633-4815	5785

GLASS PRDTS, PRESSED OR BLOWN: Optical

	CITY	ST	EMP	PHONE	ENTRY #
Flabeg Technical Glass US Corp	Naugatuck	CT	E	203 729-5227	2473
Avian Technologies LLC	New London	NH	G	603 526-2420	19313

GLASS PRDTS, PRESSED OR BLOWN: Ornaments, Christmas Tree

	CITY	ST	EMP	PHONE	ENTRY #
Pams Wreaths	Harpswell	ME	G	207 751-7234	6174

GLASS PRDTS, PRESSED OR BLOWN: Reflector, Lighting Eqpt

	CITY	ST	EMP	PHONE	ENTRY #
Hosokawa Alpine American Inc	Northborough	MA	F	508 655-1123	14036

GLASS PRDTS, PRESSED OR BLOWN: Scientific Glassware

	CITY	ST	EMP	PHONE	ENTRY #
Apogent Technologies Inc	Waltham	MA	A	781 622-1300	16035
G Finkenbeiner Inc	Waltham	MA	G	781 899-3138	16117

GLASS PRDTS, PRESSED OR BLOWN: Stationers Glassware

	CITY	ST	EMP	PHONE	ENTRY #
Incjet Inc	Norwich	CT	F	860 823-3090	3283

GLASS PRDTS, PRESSED OR BLOWN: Yarn, Fiberglass

	CITY	ST	EMP	PHONE	ENTRY #
Woolworks Ltd	Putnam	CT	G	860 963-1228	3642

GLASS PRDTS, PRESSED/BLOWN: Glassware, Art, Decor/Novelty

	CITY	ST	EMP	PHONE	ENTRY #
Ed Branson	Ashfield	MA	G	413 625-2933	7649
Young & Constantin N River GL **(PA)**	Shelburne Falls	MA	G	413 625-6422	15076

GLASS PRDTS, PURCHASED GLASS: Insulating, Multiple-Glazed

	CITY	ST	EMP	PHONE	ENTRY #
Jmh Industries Inc	East Providence	RI	G	401 438-2500	20423

GLASS PRDTS, PURCHSD GLASS: Ornamental, Cut, Engraved/Décor

	CITY	ST	EMP	PHONE	ENTRY #
Daniel Wheeler	Gilford	NH	G	603 528-6363	18184
Kheops International Inc **(PA)**	Stewartstown	NH	E	603 237-8188	19862

GLASS STORE: Leaded Or Stained

	CITY	ST	EMP	PHONE	ENTRY #
Vijon Studios Inc	Old Saybrook	CT	G	860 399-7440	3354

GLASS STORES

	CITY	ST	EMP	PHONE	ENTRY #
Designer Stained Glass	Acushnet	MA	G	508 763-3255	7401

GLASS: Fiber

	CITY	ST	EMP	PHONE	ENTRY #
Vitro Technology Ltd	Milford	CT	G	203 783-9566	2380
Sound Seal Holdings Inc **(HQ)**	Agawam	MA	G	413 789-1770	7451

GLASS: Flat

	CITY	ST	EMP	PHONE	ENTRY #
Nantucket Glass & Mirror Inc	Nantucket	MA	G	508 228-3713	13229
Shaw Glass Holdings LLC	South Easton	MA	C	508 238-0112	15292
Erie Scientific LLC **(DH)**	Portsmouth	NH	B	603 430-6859	19560
Renaissance Glassworks Inc	Nashua	NH	G	603 882-1779	19249
Robert Cairns Company LLC	Plaistow	NH	G	603 382-0044	19522
Jmh Industries Inc	East Providence	RI	G	401 438-2500	20423

GLASS: Indl Prdts

	CITY	ST	EMP	PHONE	ENTRY #
Liberty Glass and Met Inds Inc	North Grosvenordale	CT	E	860 923-3623	2997
Yankee Glass Blower Inc	Carlisle	MA	G	978 369-7545	9801

GLASS: Insulating

	CITY	ST	EMP	PHONE	ENTRY #
Insulpane Connecticut Inc	Hamden	CT	D	800 922-3248	1761
Contract Glass Service Inc	Billerica	MA	E	978 262-1323	8233
Thermal Seal Insulating GL Inc	Uxbridge	MA	F	508 278-4243	15931
Green Mountain Glass LLC	Charlestown	NH	G	603 826-4660	17815

GLASS: Pressed & Blown, NEC

	CITY	ST	EMP	PHONE	ENTRY #
Bovano Industries Incorporated	Cheshire	CT	F	203 272-3208	715
G Schoepferinc	Cheshire	CT	F	203 250-7794	734
Medelco Inc	Bridgeport	CT	G	203 275-8070	449
Schaeffler Aerospace USA Corp	Winsted	CT	D	860 379-7558	5421
Simon Pearce US Inc	Greenwich	CT	G	203 861-0780	1650
Tops Manufacturing Co Inc **(PA)**	Darien	CT	G	203 655-9367	1034
Brook Heath Studio	Heath	MA	G	413 337-5736	11488
Fused Fiberoptics LLC	Southbridge	MA	F	508 765-1652	15383
Josh Smpson Cntemporary GL Inc	Shelburne Falls	MA	F	413 625-6145	15072
Mini-Systems Inc	Plainville	MA	E	508 695-2000	14528
Omni Glass Inc	North Billerica	MA	G	978 667-6664	13850
Pegasus Glassworks Inc	Sturbridge	MA	F	508 347-5656	15644
Simon Pearce US Inc	Boston	MA	G	617 450-8388	8847
Simple Syrup Glass Studio LLC	Needham	MA	G	781 444-8275	13311
Stiles & Hart Brick Company	Bridgewater	MA	E	508 697-6928	9088
Corning Incorporated	Kennebunk	ME	D	207 985-3111	6231
Corning Incorporated	Keene	NH	C	603 357-7662	18497
Erie Scientific LLC **(DH)**	Portsmouth	NH	B	603 430-6859	19560
M & M Glass Blowing Co Inc	Nashua	NH	G	603 598-8195	19202
Robert Cairns Company LLC	Plaistow	NH	G	603 382-0044	19522
Saint-Gobain Prfmce Plas Corp	Bristol	RI	C	401 253-2000	20102
Jack Russell	West Rutland	VT	G	802 438-5213	22617
Little River Hotglass Studio	Stowe	VT	G	802 253-0889	22523
Vitri Forms Inc	West Halifax	VT	G	802 254-5235	22608
Ziemke Glass Blowing Studio	Waterbury Center	VT	G	802 244-6126	22594

GLASS: Safety

	CITY	ST	EMP	PHONE	ENTRY #
American Marine Products Inc	Charlestown	NH	E	954 782-1400	17810

GLASS: Stained

	CITY	ST	EMP	PHONE	ENTRY #
Vijon Studios Inc	Old Saybrook	CT	G	860 399-7440	3354
Artigiano Stained Glass	Newton	MA	G	617 244-0141	13563
Designer Stained Glass	Acushnet	MA	G	508 763-3255	7401
Guarducci Stained GL Studios	Great Barrington	MA	G	413 528-6287	11239
New England Stained Glass	North Attleboro	MA	G	508 699-6965	13769
Sidney Hutter Glass & Light	Auburndale	MA	G	617 630-1929	7869
Renaissance Glassworks Inc	Nashua	NH	G	603 882-1779	19249

GLASSWARE STORES

	CITY	ST	EMP	PHONE	ENTRY #
Pgc Acquisition LLC	Reading	MA	F	508 888-2344	14738
Simon Pearce US Inc **(PA)**	Windsor	VT	C	802 674-6280	22714

GLASSWARE WHOLESALERS

	CITY	ST	EMP	PHONE	ENTRY #
Whalley Glass Company **(PA)**	Derby	CT	D	203 735-9388	1083
Pgc Acquisition LLC	Reading	MA	F	508 888-2344	14738
Swarovski North America Ltd **(DH)**	Cranston	RI	A	401 463-6400	20295

GLASSWARE, NOVELTY, WHOLESALE

	CITY	ST	EMP	PHONE	ENTRY #
Pgc Acquisition LLC	Reading	MA	F	508 888-2344	14738

GLASSWARE: Cut & Engraved

	CITY	ST	EMP	PHONE	ENTRY #
American Crystal Works	North Conway	NH	G	603 356-7879	19371

GLASSWARE: Laboratory

	CITY	ST	EMP	PHONE	ENTRY #
Periodic Tableware LLC	Shelton	CT	F	310 428-4250	3850

GLOBAL POSITIONING SYSTEMS & EQPT

	CITY	ST	EMP	PHONE	ENTRY #
Wagz Inc	Stamford	CT	G	203 553-9336	4356
Easy Locate LLC	Arlington	MA	G	617 216-3654	7624

GLOVES: Fabric

	CITY	ST	EMP	PHONE	ENTRY #
Acushnet Company **(DH)**	Fairhaven	MA	A	508 979-2000	10635
Cold River Stitching LLC	Fryeburg	ME	G	207 515-0039	6096

GLOVES: Leather, Dress Or Semidress

	CITY	ST	EMP	PHONE	ENTRY #
Damascus Worldwide Inc	Rutland	VT	G	802 775-6062	22328

GLOVES: Safety

	CITY	ST	EMP	PHONE	ENTRY #
Playtex Products LLC **(HQ)**	Shelton	CT	D	203 944-5500	3856
Safety & Gloves Inc	Foxboro	MA	G	800 221-0570	10900
Tillotson Rubber Co Inc	Seekonk	MA	G	781 402-1731	15043
W D C Holdings Inc	Attleboro	MA	D	508 699-4412	7806
Healthco International LLC	Colebrook	NH	F	603 255-3771	17871

GLUE

	CITY	ST	EMP	PHONE	ENTRY #
Adhesive Technologies Inc **(PA)**	Hampton	NH	E	603 926-1616	18252

GOLD BULLION PRODUCTION

	CITY	ST	EMP	PHONE	ENTRY #
US Gold and Diamond Exch LLC **(PA)**	Derry	NH	G	603 300-8888	18001

GOLD ORE MINING

	CITY	ST	EMP	PHONE	ENTRY #
Lion Gold Mining Llc	Malden	MA	G	617 785-2345	12577

GOLF DRIVING RANGES

	CITY	ST	EMP	PHONE	ENTRY #
Hollrock Engineering Inc	Hadley	MA	F	413 586-2256	11307

GOLF EQPT

	CITY	ST	EMP	PHONE	ENTRY #
Brampton Technology Ltd	Newington	CT	G	860 667-7689	2849
Golf Galaxy LLC	Norwalk	CT	G	203 855-0500	3162
Acushnet Holdings Corp **(HQ)**	Fairhaven	MA	E	800 225-8500	10636
Hollrock Engineering Inc	Hadley	MA	F	413 586-2256	11307
Paradigm Sports Inc	Amesbury	MA	G	978 687-6687	7502
Tom Waters Golf Shop	Manchester	MA	G	978 526-7311	12608
Dennco Inc	Salem	NH	E	603 898-0004	19721

GOLF GOODS & EQPT

	CITY	ST	EMP	PHONE	ENTRY #
Golf Galaxy LLC	Norwalk	CT	G	203 855-0500	3162

GOURMET FOOD STORES

	CITY	ST	EMP	PHONE	ENTRY #
Boyajian Inc	Canton	MA	F	781 828-9966	9718
Jam & Jelly Chatham	West Chatham	MA	G	508 945-3052	16474
Bread & Chocolate Inc	Wells River	VT	G	802 429-2920	22600
Willis Wood	Springfield	VT	G	802 263-5547	22513

GRAIN & FIELD BEANS WHOLESALERS

	CITY	ST	EMP	PHONE	ENTRY #
Poulin Grain Inc	Swanton	VT	F	802 868-3323	22534

GRANITE: Crushed & Broken

	CITY	ST	EMP	PHONE	ENTRY #
Skyline Quarry	Stafford Springs	CT	E	860 875-3580	4115
Stone Company	Pittsfield	MA	G	413 442-1447	14510
Tables of Stone **(PA)**	Merrimack	NH	G	603 424-7577	19035
McCullough Crushing Inc **(PA)**	Middlesex	VT	E	802 223-5693	22122

GRANITE: Cut & Shaped

	CITY	ST	EMP	PHONE	ENTRY #
Granitech LLC	Plantsville	CT	G	860 620-1733	3532
Stone Workshop LLC	Bridgeport	CT	G	203 362-1144	496
Stoneage LLC	Shelton	CT	G	203 926-1133	3874
Surface Plate Co	Glastonbury	CT	G	860 652-8905	1578
Atlantic MBL & Gran Group Inc	East Falmouth	MA	G	508 540-9770	10436
Cassa Floor Design Inc	Shrewsbury	MA	F	508 845-0600	15106
Continental Stone MBL Gran Inc	Sterling	MA	E	978 422-8700	15538
David P Deveney Memorial Co	Medford	MA	G	781 396-7772	12929
Deveney & White Inc	Boston	MA	G	617 288-3080	8501
Divine Stoneworks LLC	Ashland	MA	G	774 221-6006	7657
Earthworks Granite & Marble	Braintree	MA	G	781 356-3544	9002
Foxrock Granite LLC	Quincy	MA	G	617 249-8015	14626
Majestic Marble & Granite Inc	Canton	MA	G	781 830-1020	9755
Ricciardi Marble and Granite	Hyannis	MA	G	508 790-2734	11855
United Marble Fabricators Inc	Watertown	MA	G	617 926-6226	16328
Barre Tile Inc	Lebanon	NH	F	802 476-0912	18614
Swenson Granite Company LLC **(DH)**	Concord	NH	E	603 225-4322	17933
Stone Systems New England LLC	North Smithfield	RI	C	401 766-3603	20796
Adams Granite Company Inc	Websterville	VT	D	802 476-5281	22596
Buttura & Sons Inc	Barre	VT	E	802 476-6646	21610
Gandin Brothers Inc	South Ryegate	VT	F	802 584-3521	22496
Granite Industries Vermont Inc	Barre	VT	D	800 451-3236	21618
Hillside Solid Surfaces	Barre	VT	F	802 479-2508	21622
Joes Custom Polishing	East Barre	VT	G	802 479-9266	21911
Kinfolk Memorials Inc	East Barre	VT	G	802 479-1423	21912
La Perle & Sons Granite Co	Barre	VT	G	802 476-6463	21628
Peerless Granite Co Inc	Barre	VT	F	802 476-3061	21634
Rock of Ages Corporation	Graniteville	VT	F	802 476-3119	22002
Spruce Mountian Granites Inc	Barre	VT	E	802 476-7474	21639

GRANITE: Dimension

	CITY	ST	EMP	PHONE	ENTRY #
Armetta LLC	Middletown	CT	E	860 788-2369	2172
Stony Creek Quarry Corporation	Branford	CT	G	203 483-3904	353
Fletcher Granite LLC **(DH)**	Westford	MA	G	978 692-1312	16767
Le Masurier Granite Quarry	North Chelmsford	MA	G	978 251-3841	13900
Sudbury Granite & Marble Inc **(PA)**	Hopedale	MA	E	508 478-3976	11684
Old York Quarry Inc	York	ME	G	603 772-6061	7315
Swenson Granite Company LLC **(DH)**	Concord	NH	E	603 225-4322	17933
Rock of Ages Corporation	Graniteville	VT	F	802 476-3119	22002
Semya Corp **(PA)**	Chester	VT	G	802 875-6564	21849

GRANITE: Dimension

	CITY	ST	EMP	PHONE	ENTRY #
Academy Marble & Granite LLC **(PA)**	Bethel	CT	G	203 791-2956	126
LH Gault & Son Incorporated	Westport	CT	D	203 227-5181	5209
Precision Stone Works Inc	Shrewsbury	MA	G	774 261-4420	15129
Flat Rock Tile and Stone	Claremont	NH	G	603 542-0678	17850
Georgia Stone Industries Inc **(HQ)**	Smithfield	RI	G	401 232-2040	21227
Julian Materials LLC	Chester	VT	F	802 875-6564	21844

GRAPHIC ARTS & RELATED DESIGN SVCS

	CITY	ST	EMP	PHONE	ENTRY #
Arteffects Incorporated	Bloomfield	CT	E	860 242-0031	204
P C I Group	Stamford	CT	F	203 327-0410	4276
Play-It Productions Inc	Colchester	CT	F	212 695-6530	805
Print Shop of Wolcott LLC	Wolcott	CT	G	203 879-3353	5453
R R Donnelley & Sons Company	Manchester	CT	F	860 649-5570	2040
Schwerdtle Stamp Company	Bridgeport	CT	E	203 330-2750	487
BBCg LLC	Norwood	MA	G	617 796-8800	14137
Blanchard Press Inc	Winchester	MA	F	617 426-6690	17084

	CITY	ST	EMP	PHONE	ENTRY #
Creative Publishing Corp Amer **(PA)**	Peabody	MA	E	978 532-5880	14326
Economy Coupon & Printing Inc	Peabody	MA	G	781 279-8555	14332
Impressions Plus Inc	Quincy	MA	F	617 479-5777	14633
Modern Graphics Inc	Quincy	MA	F	781 331-5000	14640
Printing & Graphic Services	Billerica	MA	G	978 667-6950	8277
Silver Screen Design Inc	Greenfield	MA	F	413 773-1692	11275
Insty-Prints of Bedford Inc	Bedford	NH	G	603 622-3821	17646
My-T-Man Screen Printing Inc	Manchester	NH	F	603 622-7740	18881
P2k Printing LLC	North Conway	NH	G	603 356-2010	19378
Fine Line Graphics Inc **(PA)**	Smithfield	RI	E	401 349-3300	21226
Platinum Recognition LLC **(PA)**	North Providence	RI	G	401 305-6700	20772
Garlic Press Inc	Williston	VT	F	802 864-0670	22667
Oatmeal Studios Inc	Rochester	VT	F	802 967-8014	22320
Stillwater Graphics Inc	Williamstown	VT	F	802 433-9898	22651
Thompson Printing Inc	Manchester Center	VT	F	802 362-1140	22091

GRATINGS: Tread, Fabricated Metal

	CITY	ST	EMP	PHONE	ENTRY #
B & T Millworks	Gorham	ME	G	207 591-5740	6109

GRAVEL & PEBBLE MINING

	CITY	ST	EMP	PHONE	ENTRY #
Northeast Aggregate Corp	Saint Albans	VT	G	802 524-2627	22376

GRAVEL MINING

	CITY	ST	EMP	PHONE	ENTRY #
Dedham Recycled Gravel Inc	Dedham	MA	F	781 329-1044	10287
S M Lorusso & Sons Inc	Boston	MA	E	617 323-6380	8830
Dwight R Mills Inc	Porter	ME	G	207 625-3965	6602
Gravel Electric Inc	Harrisville	RI	G	401 265-6041	20479

GREENHOUSES: Prefabricated Metal

	CITY	ST	EMP	PHONE	ENTRY #
Star Steel Structures Inc	Somers	CT	G	860 763-5681	3920
Rimol Greenhouse Systems Inc	Hooksett	NH	F	603 629-9004	18359
Serac Corporation **(HQ)**	Fairfax	VT	F	802 527-9609	21979

GREENSTONE: Dimension

	CITY	ST	EMP	PHONE	ENTRY #
Williams Stone Co Inc	East Otis	MA	E	413 269-4544	10504

GREETING CARD SHOPS

	CITY	ST	EMP	PHONE	ENTRY #
McClelland Press Inc **(PA)**	Williamstown	MA	F	413 663-5750	16958
Renaissance Greeting Cards Inc	Sanford	ME	C	207 324-4153	6888
Paper Packaging and Panache	Bristol	RI	G	401 253-2273	20097

GREETING CARDS WHOLESALERS

	CITY	ST	EMP	PHONE	ENTRY #
Executive Greetings Inc **(HQ)**	New Hartford	CT	B	860 379-9911	2636
Expressive Design Group Inc	Holyoke	MA	E	413 315-6296	11626

GRILLS & GRILLWORK: Woven Wire, Made From Purchased Wire

	CITY	ST	EMP	PHONE	ENTRY #
Wireway/Husky Corp	Sterling	MA	E	978 422-6716	15550

GRINDING BALLS: Ceramic

	CITY	ST	EMP	PHONE	ENTRY #
Prematech LLC	Worcester	MA	E	508 791-9549	17445

GRINDING SVC: Precision, Commercial Or Indl

	CITY	ST	EMP	PHONE	ENTRY #
Advanced Machine Services LLC **(PA)**	Waterbury	CT	G	203 888-6600	4836
Nct Inc	Newington	CT	F	860 666-8424	2886
White Hills Tool	Monroe	CT	G	203 590-3143	2420
Idex Health & Science LLC	Middleboro	MA	C	774 213-0200	13064
True Machine Co Inc	Swansea	MA	G	508 379-0329	15718
Nikel Precision Group LLC	Biddeford	ME	D	207 282-6080	5753

GRINDING SVCS: Ophthalmic Lens, Exc Prescription

	CITY	ST	EMP	PHONE	ENTRY #
Bomas Machine Specialties Inc	Somerville	MA	F	617 628-3831	15160

GRITS: Crushed & Broken

	CITY	ST	EMP	PHONE	ENTRY #
Galasso Materials LLC	East Granby	CT	C	860 527-1825	1128
Joe Passarelli & Co	Milford	CT	G	203 877-1434	2304
Aggregate Inds - Northeast Reg	Wrentham	MA	E	508 384-3161	17513
Aggregate Inds - Northeast Reg	Taunton	MA	F	508 821-9508	15720
Isp Freetown Fine Chem Inc	Assonet	MA	D	508 672-0634	7681

GROCERIES WHOLESALERS, NEC

	CITY	ST	EMP	PHONE	ENTRY #
Durantes Pasta Inc	West Haven	CT	G	203 387-5560	5118
Jmf Group LLC	East Windsor	CT	D	860 627-7003	1288
Supreme Storm Services LLC	Southington	CT	G	860 201-0642	4083
Buzzards Bay Brewing Inc	Westport	MA	G	508 636-2288	16836
Coca-Cola Bottling Company	Sandwich	MA	D	508 888-0001	14965
Coca-Cola Refreshments USA Inc	Greenfield	MA	C	413 772-2617	11255
Incredibrew Inc	Nashua	NH	G	603 891-2477	19187
Coca-Cola Refreshments USA Inc	Providence	RI	B	401 331-1981	20986
Vermont Sweetwater Bottling Co	Poultney	VT	G	800 974-9877	22280

GROCERIES, GENERAL LINE WHOLESALERS

	CITY	ST	EMP	PHONE	ENTRY #
Wohrles Foods Inc **(PA)**	Pittsfield	MA	E	413 442-1518	14513
Roopers Redemption & Bev Ctr	Lewiston	ME	F	207 782-1482	6319
Portion Meat Associates Inc	Providence	RI	F	401 421-2438	21092

GROMMETS: Rubber

	CITY	ST	EMP	PHONE	ENTRY #
Lord & Hodge Inc	Middletown	CT	F	860 632-7006	2201

GUARDRAILS

	CITY	ST	EMP	PHONE	ENTRY #
Atlas Industrial Services LLC	Branford	CT	E	203 315-4538	290
Highway Safety Corp **(PA)**	Glastonbury	CT	D	860 659-4330	1558

GUARDS: Machine, Sheet Metal

	CITY	ST	EMP	PHONE	ENTRY #
Noise Reduction Products Inc	Langdon	NH	G	603 835-6400	18611

GUARDS: Metal Pipe

	CITY	ST	EMP	PHONE	ENTRY #
Burtco Inc	Westminster Station	VT	F	802 722-3358	22633

GUIDANCE SYSTEMS & EQPT: Space Vehicle

	CITY	ST	EMP	PHONE	ENTRY #
Farsounder Inc	Warwick	RI	G	401 784-6700	21363

GUIDED MISSILES & SPACE VEHICLES

	CITY	ST	EMP	PHONE	ENTRY #
Electron Solutions Inc	Lexington	MA	F	781 674-2440	12222
Raytheon Company	Tewksbury	MA	C	978 858-5000	15829

GUIDED MISSILES & SPACE VEHICLES: Research & Development

	CITY	ST	EMP	PHONE	ENTRY #
Raytheon Company **(PA)**	Waltham	MA	B	781 522-3000	16184
Raytheon Company	Marlborough	MA	E	310 647-9438	12813
Raytheon Company	North Billerica	MA	G	978 313-0201	13858
Raytheon Lgstics Spport Trning **(HQ)**	Bedford	MA	F	310 647-9438	8005

GUIDED MISSILES/SPACE VEHICLE PARTS/AUX EQPT: Research/Devel

	CITY	ST	EMP	PHONE	ENTRY #
Fiber Materials Inc **(HQ)**	Biddeford	ME	E	207 282-5911	5733
Superior Tchncal Ceramics Corp	Saint Albans	VT	C	802 527-7726	22380

GUN SIGHTS: Optical

	CITY	ST	EMP	PHONE	ENTRY #
Brightsight Llc	Woodstock	CT	G	860 208-0222	5494
Opto-Line International Inc	Wilmington	MA	F	978 658-7255	17035
Bulzeyepro	Augusta	ME	G	207 626-0000	5604

GUN STOCKS: Wood

	CITY	ST	EMP	PHONE	ENTRY #
South Shore Wood Pellets Inc	Holbrook	MA	G	781 986-7797	11538

GUN SVCS

	CITY	ST	EMP	PHONE	ENTRY #
Seal 1 LLC	Brownville	ME	G	207 965-8860	5827

GUTTERS

	CITY	ST	EMP	PHONE	ENTRY #
Dfs In-Home Services	Danbury	CT	G	845 405-6464	900
Savetime Corporation	Bridgeport	CT	F	203 382-2991	486
R B L Holdings Inc	Coventry	RI	F	401 821-2200	20163

GUTTERS: Sheet Metal

	CITY	ST	EMP	PHONE	ENTRY #
U-Sealusa LLC	Newington	CT	D	860 667-0911	2910
Yost Manufacturing & Supply	Waterford	CT	F	860 447-9678	4996
Clark & Sons Seamless Gutter	Chicopee	MA	G	413 732-3934	10014
Minuteman Seamless Gutters	Hudson	MA	F	978 562-1744	11794
Mr Gutter Inc	Holyoke	MA	G	413 536-7451	11640
On The Spot	West Bridgewater	MA	G	508 583-6070	16448
Gutter Wholesalers Inc	Raymond	ME	G	207 655-7407	6773

GYPSUM PRDTS

	CITY	ST	EMP	PHONE	ENTRY #
Georgia-Pacific LLC	Norwood	MA	G	781 440-3600	14155

GYROSCOPES

	CITY	ST	EMP	PHONE	ENTRY #
Ais Global Holdings LLC	Cheshire	CT	A	203 250-3500	709
Atlantic Inertial Systems Inc **(DH)**	Cheshire	CT	B	203 250-3500	713
Atlantic Inertial Systems Inc	Cheshire	CT	A	203 250-3500	714

HAIR & HAIR BASED PRDTS

	CITY	ST	EMP	PHONE	ENTRY #
National Fiber Technology LLC	Lawrence	MA	G	978 686-2964	12062

HAIR CARE PRDTS

	CITY	ST	EMP	PHONE	ENTRY #
Golden Sun Inc	Stamford	CT	F	800 575-7960	4200
Concept Chemicals Inc	Hingham	MA	F	781 740-0711	11497
LAvant Garde Inc	Newburyport	MA	G	805 522-0045	13508
Chuckles Inc	Manchester	NH	E	603 669-4228	18798
Kanu Inc	Londonderry	NH	G	603 437-6311	18706

HAIR CARE PRDTS: Hair Coloring Preparations

	CITY	ST	EMP	PHONE	ENTRY #
Continental Fragrances Ltd	Stamford	CT	F	800 542-5903	4173

HAIR CURLERS: Beauty Shop

	CITY	ST	EMP	PHONE	ENTRY #
Creative Strands	Sutton	MA	G	508 865-1141	15681

HAIR DRYERS: Beauty Shop

	CITY	ST	EMP	PHONE	ENTRY #
Stilisti	Boston	MA	G	617 262-2234	8867

HALL EFFECT DEVICES

	CITY	ST	EMP	PHONE	ENTRY #
Cyclones Arena	Hudson	NH	F	603 880-4424	18381

HAND TOOLS, NEC: Wholesalers

	CITY	ST	EMP	PHONE	ENTRY #
Kell-Strom Tool Intl Inc	Wethersfield	CT	E	860 529-6851	5254

HANDBAG STORES

	CITY	ST	EMP	PHONE	ENTRY #
Dick Muller Designer/Craftsman	Shelburne Falls	MA	G	413 625-0016	15068
Sea Bags LLC **(PA)**	Portland	ME	E	207 780-0744	6724

HANDBAGS

	CITY	ST	EMP	PHONE	ENTRY #
Leatherby	Weatogue	CT	G	860 658-6166	5043
Bagrout Inc	Ware	MA	G	413 949-0743	16229
Brahmin Leather Works LLC	Fairhaven	MA	G	509 994-4000	10638
W D C Holdings Inc	Attleboro	MA	D	508 699-4412	7806
Nancy Lawrence	Portland	ME	G	207 774-7276	6697
Bren Corporation	Johnston	RI	E	401 943-8200	20501

HANDBAGS: Men's

	CITY	ST	EMP	PHONE	ENTRY #
Boccelli	Uncasville	CT	G	860 862-9300	4646

HANDBAGS: Women's

	CITY	ST	EMP	PHONE	ENTRY #
Coach Inc	Trumbull	CT	F	203 372-0208	4619
Dooney & Bourke Inc **(PA)**	Norwalk	CT	E	203 853-7515	3142
Dick Muller Designer/Craftsman	Shelburne Falls	MA	G	413 625-0016	15068
Surtan Manufacturing Co	South Yarmouth	MA	G	508 394-4099	15334
Tapestry Inc	Boston	MA	G	617 723-1777	8874
Vera Bradley Designs Inc	Braintree	MA	G	781 794-9860	9047

HANDCUFFS & LEG IRONS

	CITY	ST	EMP	PHONE	ENTRY #
Peerless Handcuff Co Inc	West Springfield	MA	G	413 732-2156	16541

HANGERS: Garment, Plastic

	CITY	ST	EMP	PHONE	ENTRY #
National Hanger Company Inc	North Bennington	VT	D	800 426-4377	22211

HARD RUBBER PRDTS, NEC

	CITY	ST	EMP	PHONE	ENTRY #
Standard Rubber Products Inc	Hanover	MA	E	781 878-2626	11353
Maine Industrial P & R Corp	Newcastle	ME	G	207 563-5532	6484

HARDBOARD & FIBERBOARD PRDTS

	CITY	ST	EMP	PHONE	ENTRY #
Designer Board Specialties	Braintree	MA	G	781 794-9413	9000

HARDWARE

	CITY	ST	EMP	PHONE	ENTRY #
Ador Inc	Bristol	CT	G	860 583-2367	515
Air-Lock Incorporated	Milford	CT	E	203 878-4691	2238
Brookfield Industries Inc	Thomaston	CT	E	860 283-6211	4500
Composite McHining Experts LLC	North Haven	CT	G	203 624-0664	3017
D & M Screw Machine Pdts LLC	Plainville	CT	G	860 410-9781	3479
Hicks and Otis Prints Inc	Norwalk	CT	E	203 846-2087	3168
Industrial Shipg Entps MGT LLC	Stamford	CT	G	203 504-5800	4222
Lewmar Inc **(DH)**	Guilford	CT	E	203 458-6200	1708
Mc Kinney Products Company	Berlin	CT	C	800 346-7707	95
Oslo Switch Inc	Cheshire	CT	E	203 272-2794	750
Outland Engineering Inc	Milford	CT	F	800 797-3709	2329
Paradigm Manchester Inc	Manchester	CT	C	860 649-2888	2032
Pemko Manufacturing Co	New Haven	CT	G	901 365-2160	2722
Perry Technology Corporation	New Hartford	CT	D	860 738-2525	2644
Roller Bearing Co Amer Inc	Middlebury	CT	E	203 758-8272	2157
Stanley Black & Decker Inc	New Britain	CT	D	860 225-5111	2581
Stanley Industrial & Auto LLC	New Britain	CT	E	800 800-8005	2585
Tiger Enterprises Inc	Plantsville	CT	E	860 621-9155	3542
Unger Industrial LLC	Bridgeport	CT	G	203 336-3344	501
Vector Engineering Inc	Mystic	CT	F	860 572-0422	2455
Wind Corporation	Newtown	CT	E	203 778-1001	2949
Atlantic RES Mktg Systems Inc	West Bridgewater	MA	F	508 584-7816	16429
Atrenne Cmpt Solutions LLC **(DH)**	Brockton	MA	B	508 588-6110	9121
Craft Inc	Attleboro	MA	E	508 761-7917	7725
Delaware Valley Corp	Tewksbury	MA	E	978 459-6932	15814
Dorel Juvenile Group Inc	Foxboro	MA	D	800 544-1108	10881
Hostar Mar Trnspt Systems Inc	Wareham	MA	E	508 295-2900	16250
Molly Merchandising Unlimited	Holden	MA	G	508 829-2544	11548
Newstamp Lighting Corp	North Easton	MA	F	508 238-7073	13949
Rolls-Royce Marine North Amer **(DH)**	Walpole	MA	C	508 668-9610	16009
Taunton Stove Company Inc	North Dighton	MA	E	508 823-0786	13937
Universal Hinge Corp **(PA)**	Westminster	MA	F	603 935-9848	16819
W J Roberts Co Inc	Saugus	MA	E	781 233-8176	15002
Xcerra Corporation **(HQ)**	Norwood	MA	C	781 461-1000	14206
Edgar Clark & Son Inc	Readfield	ME	G	207 685-4568	6776
Richard Fisher	Prospect Harbor	ME	G	207 963-7184	6771
Anvil International LLC **(HQ)**	Exeter	NH	E	603 418-2800	18110
Bomar Inc	Charlestown	NH	D	603 826-5781	17811
Bronze Craft Corporation	Nashua	NH	D	603 883-7747	19130
United Mch & Tl Design Co Inc	Fremont	NH	E	603 642-3601	18181
Universal Hinge Corp	Manchester	NH	G	603 935-9848	18946
Fulford Manufacturing Company **(PA)**	Riverside	RI	F	401 431-2000	21168
Groov-Pin Corporation **(PA)**	Smithfield	RI	D	770 251-5054	21230
Hindley Manufacturing Co Inc	Cumberland	RI	D	401 722-2550	20325

HARDWARE & BUILDING PRDTS: Plastic

	CITY	ST	EMP	PHONE	ENTRY #
AA & B Co	West Haven	CT	G	203 933-9110	5107
Hosokawa Micron Intl Inc	Berlin	CT	E	860 828-0541	89
Fibertec Inc	Bridgewater	MA	D	508 697-5100	9073
Flagraphics Inc	Somerville	MA	E	617 776-7549	15172
Korolath of New England Inc **(HQ)**	Woburn	MA	G	781 933-6004	17211
Korolath of New England Inc	Hudson	MA	F	978 562-7366	11783
LD Plastics Inc	Brockton	MA	E	508 584-7651	9161
Millennium Plastics Inc	Groveland	MA	F	978 372-4822	11302
Multifab Plastics Inc	Dorchester	MA	F	617 287-1411	10347
Pexco LLC	Athol	MA	C	978 249-5343	7692
Plastic Concepts Inc	North Billerica	MA	E	978 663-7996	13856
Saint-Gobain Prfmce Plas Corp	Bristol	RI	C	401 253-2000	20102
Carris Financial Corp **(PA)**	Proctor	VT	F	802 773-9111	22283
Carris Reels Inc **(HQ)**	Proctor	VT	C	802 773-9111	22284

HARDWARE CLOTH: Woven Wire, Made From Purchased Wire

	CITY	ST	EMP	PHONE	ENTRY #
Ferguson Perforating Company **(DH)**	Providence	RI	D	401 941-8876	21013

HARDWARE STORES

	CITY	ST	EMP	PHONE	ENTRY #
F W Webb Company	New Haven	CT	F	203 865-6124	2688
Lyn-Lad Group Ltd **(PA)**	Lynn	MA	F	781 598-6010	12523
Renovators Supply Inc	Millers Falls	MA	E	413 423-3300	13181
Pine State Drilling Inc	Athens	ME	G	207 654-2771	5543

HARDWARE STORES: Pumps & Pumping Eqpt

	CITY	ST	EMP	PHONE	ENTRY #
Proflow Inc	North Haven	CT	E	203 230-4700	3055
Sulzer Pump Solutions US Inc **(PA)**	Meriden	CT	E	203 238-2700	2135

HARDWARE STORES: Tools

	CITY	ST	EMP	PHONE	ENTRY #
Swanson Tool Manufacturing Inc	West Hartford	CT	E	860 953-1641	5097
Safe T Cut Inc	Monson	MA	F	413 267-9984	13211
Vacuum Pressing Systems Inc	Brunswick	ME	G	207 725-0935	5850

HARDWARE STORES: Tools, Power

	CITY	ST	EMP	PHONE	ENTRY #
Zampini Industrial Group LLC	Lincoln	RI	G	401 305-7997	20602

HARDWARE WHOLESALERS

	CITY	ST	EMP	PHONE	ENTRY #
Steeltech Building Pdts Inc	South Windsor	CT	D	860 290-8930	4014

HARDWARE, WHOLESALE: Builders', NEC

	CITY	ST	EMP	PHONE	ENTRY #
Prescott Cabinet Co	Pawcatuck	CT	G	860 495-0176	3441

HARDWARE, WHOLESALE: Furniture, NEC

	CITY	ST	EMP	PHONE	ENTRY #
Bloomfield Wood & Melamine Inc	Bloomfield	CT	F	860 243-3226	211

HARDWARE, WHOLESALE: Power Tools & Access

	CITY	ST	EMP	PHONE	ENTRY #
Air Tool Sales & Service Co **(PA)**	Unionville	CT	G	860 673-2714	4652
Express Assemblyproducts LLC	Amherst	NH	F	603 424-5590	17561

HARDWARE, WHOLESALE: Screws

	CITY	ST	EMP	PHONE	ENTRY #
Allesco Industries Inc **(PA)**	Cranston	RI	C	401 943-0680	20176
Eastern Screw Company	Cranston	RI	C	401 943-0680	20214

HARDWARE: Aircraft

	CITY	ST	EMP	PHONE	ENTRY #
D & B Tool Co LLC	Milford	CT	G	203 878-6026	2272
Hartford Aircraft Products	Bloomfield	CT	E	860 242-8228	223
James Ippolito & Co Conn Inc	Bridgeport	CT	E	203 366-3840	433
Kell-Strom Tool Co Inc **(PA)**	Wethersfield	CT	E	860 529-6851	5253
Kell-Strom Tool Intl Inc	Wethersfield	CT	E	860 529-6851	5254
Morning Star Tool LLC	Milford	CT	G	203 878-6026	2316
Paneloc Corporation	Farmington	CT	E	860 677-6711	1505
Albany Safran Composites LLC **(HQ)**	Rochester	NH	E	603 330-5800	19657

HARDWARE: Builders'

	CITY	ST	EMP	PHONE	ENTRY #
Colonial Bronze Company	Torrington	CT	D	860 489-9233	4570
Stanley Black & Decker Inc **(PA)**	New Britain	CT	C	860 225-5111	2580
Stanley Black & Decker Inc	New Britain	CT	E	860 225-5111	2583
Stanley Black & Decker Inc	New Britain	CT	C	860 225-5111	2582
Acorn Manufacturing Co Inc	Mansfield	MA	E	508 339-4500	12611
Dormakaba USA Inc	Randolph	MA	E	781 963-0182	14676
Qc Industries Inc **(PA)**	Mansfield	MA	D	781 344-1000	12653
Renovators Supply Inc	Millers Falls	MA	E	413 423-3300	13181
Turning Point Industry FL	Pembroke	MA	G	239 340-1942	14430

HARDWARE: Cabinet

	CITY	ST	EMP	PHONE	ENTRY #
Halls Edge Inc	Stamford	CT	G	203 653-2281	4204
Horton Brasses Inc	Cromwell	CT	G	860 635-4400	855
AMS Glass Bead Cabinets	Hampden	MA	E	413 566-0037	11319
Boston Garage	Hanover	MA	F	339 788-9580	11330
Kingslide USA Inc	Andover	MA	G	978 475-0120	7562
Nantucket Beadboard Co Inc	Rochester	NH	F	603 330-3338	19679

HARDWARE: Casket

	CITY	ST	EMP	PHONE	ENTRY #
Eastern Cast Hardware Co Inc	West Springfield	MA	G	413 733-7690	16517

HARDWARE: Door Opening & Closing Devices, Exc Electrical

	CITY	ST	EMP	PHONE	ENTRY #
Connecticut Greenstar Inc	Fairfield	CT	G	203 368-1522	1423
Connecticut Trade Company Inc	Fairfield	CT	G	203 368-0398	1424
Vaughan W C Co Ltd Inc	Braintree	MA	G	781 848-0308	9046

HARDWARE: Furniture, Builders' & Other Household

	CITY	ST	EMP	PHONE	ENTRY #
Panza Woodwork & Supply LLC	West Haven	CT	G	203 934-3430	5140
York Street Studio Inc	New Milford	CT	G	203 266-9000	2833
Grant Larkin	Richmond	MA	G	413 698-2599	14779
Lighthouse Woodworks LLC	Boston	MA	G	781 223-4302	8666
Williamsburg Blacksmiths Inc	Williamsburg	MA	G	413 268-7341	16953

HARDWARE: Parachute

	CITY	ST	EMP	PHONE	ENTRY #
Bourdon Forge Co Inc	Middletown	CT	C	860 632-2740	2179
Crrc LLC	Cromwell	CT	D	860 635-2200	852

HARDWARE: Plastic

	CITY	ST	EMP	PHONE	ENTRY #
Cpk Manufacturing LLC	Augusta	ME	E	207 622-6229	5606
Bayhead Products Corporation	Dover	NH	E	603 742-3000	18008

HARNESS ASSEMBLIES: Cable & Wire

	CITY	ST	EMP	PHONE	ENTRY #
Data Signal Corporation	Milford	CT	E	203 882-5393	2273
Electronic Connection Corp	Waterbury	CT	E	860 243-3356	4868
Lq Mechatronics Inc	Branford	CT	G	203 433-4430	328
Power Trans Co Inc	Oxford	CT	G	203 881-0314	3419
Precision Electronic Assembly	Monroe	CT	F	203 452-1839	2413
Rel-Tech Electronics Inc	Milford	CT	D	203 877-8770	2347
Robert Warren LLC **(PA)**	Westport	CT	E	203 247-3347	5227
Siemon Company **(PA)**	Watertown	CT	A	860 945-4200	5024
Technical Manufacturing Corp	Durham	CT	E	860 349-1735	1094
Tornik Inc	Rocky Hill	CT	C	860 282-6081	3731
Cooper Interconnect Inc	Chelsea	MA	D	617 389-7080	9950
Desco Electronics Inc	Plainville	MA	F	508 643-1950	14517
Electronic Assemblies Mfg Inc	Methuen	MA	E	978 374-6840	13019
First Electronics Corporation	Dorchester	MA	D	617 288-2430	10342
General Manufacturing Corp	North Billerica	MA	E	978 667-5514	13822
Global Interconnect Inc	Pocasset	MA	D	508 563-6306	14595
Interface Prcsion Bnchwrks Inc	Orange	MA	G	978 544-8866	14219
Ksaria Corporation **(PA)**	Methuen	MA	D	866 457-2742	13030
Meehan Electronics Corporation	North Adams	MA	F	413 664-9371	13681
Microtek Inc	Chicopee	MA	C	413 593-1025	10046
Sunburst Electronic Manufactur **(PA)**	West Bridgewater	MA	D	508 580-1881	16458
V-Tron Electronics Corp	Attleboro	MA	D	508 761-9100	7805
Advanced Design & Mfg Inc	Portsmouth	NH	E	603 430-7573	19532
Custom Manufacturing Svcs Inc	Nashua	NH	E	603 883-1355	19141
Electronics Aid Inc	Marlborough	NH	G	603 876-4161	18959
Metz Electronics Corp	Gilford	NH	E	603 524-8806	18191
Scott Electronics Inc **(PA)**	Salem	NH	D	603 893-2845	19766
Velocity Manufacturing Inc	Exeter	NH	E	603 773-2386	18136

	CITY	ST	EMP	PHONE	ENTRY #
Versatile Subcontracting LLC	Northfield	NH	G	603 286-8081	19409
Image Tek Mfg Inc	Springfield	VT	E	802 885-6208	22502

HARNESSES, HALTERS, SADDLERY & STRAPS

	CITY	ST	EMP	PHONE	ENTRY #
The Smith Worthington Sad Co	Hartford	CT	G	860 527-9117	1878
Niche Inc	New Bedford	MA	E	508 990-4202	13427
Mitch Rosen Extraordinary Gunl	Manchester	NH	F	603 647-2971	18876

HAT BOXES

	CITY	ST	EMP	PHONE	ENTRY #
Specialty Packaging Inc	Indian Orchard	MA	G	413 543-1814	11895

HEADPHONES: Radio

	CITY	ST	EMP	PHONE	ENTRY #
Porta Phone Co Inc	Narragansett	RI	E	401 789-8700	20646

HEADS-UP DISPLAY & HUD SYSTEMS Aeronautical

	CITY	ST	EMP	PHONE	ENTRY #
Modeltronix	Upton	MA	G	508 529-3567	15909
Sensedriver Technologies LLC	Malden	MA	G	978 232-3990	12595

HEALTH & ALLIED SERVICES, NEC

	CITY	ST	EMP	PHONE	ENTRY #
American Health Resources Inc	North Easton	MA	G	508 588-7700	13941

HEALTH AIDS: Exercise Eqpt

	CITY	ST	EMP	PHONE	ENTRY #
Aqua Massage International Inc	Mystic	CT	F	860 536-3735	2434
Brewers Ledge Inc	Randolph	MA	G	781 961-5200	14671
Cybex International Inc	Medway	MA	C	508 533-4167	12958
Duane Smith	Attleboro	MA	G	508 222-9541	7729
Power Gripps Usa Inc	Sorrento	ME	G	207 422-2051	7000
Advanced Fitnes Components LLC	Hudson	NH	F	603 595-1967	18370

HEALTH FOOD & SUPPLEMENT STORES

	CITY	ST	EMP	PHONE	ENTRY #
Breed Nutrition Inc	Rehoboth	MA	G	508 840-3888	14747
Vera Roasting Company	Portsmouth	NH	G	603 969-7970	19628

HEARING AID REPAIR SVCS

	CITY	ST	EMP	PHONE	ENTRY #
Zenith-Omni Hearing Center **(PA)**	New Haven	CT	G	203 624-9857	2763

HEARING AIDS

	CITY	ST	EMP	PHONE	ENTRY #
Advanced Hearing Solutions LLC	Avon	CT	F	860 674-8558	31
New England Ctr For Hring Rhab	Hampton	CT	G	860 455-1404	1798
Zenith-Omni Hearing Center **(PA)**	New Haven	CT	G	203 624-9857	2763
Hearing Armor LLC	Needham	MA	F	781 789-5017	13300
Finetone Hearing Instruments	Windham	ME	G	207 893-2922	7233
Tena Group LLC	Windham	ME	G	207 893-2920	7256

HEAT EMISSION OPERATING APPARATUS

	CITY	ST	EMP	PHONE	ENTRY #
Design Architectural Heating	Lewiston	ME	F	207 784-0309	6283

HEAT EXCHANGERS

	CITY	ST	EMP	PHONE	ENTRY #
Geo Knight & Co Inc	Brockton	MA	E	508 588-0186	9150
Therma-Flow Inc	Watertown	MA	E	617 924-3877	16322
Chester H Chapman	Porter	ME	G	207 625-3349	6600

HEAT EXCHANGERS: After Or Inter Coolers Or Condensers, Etc

	CITY	ST	EMP	PHONE	ENTRY #
Mp Systems Inc	East Granby	CT	F	860 687-3460	1134
Alfa Laval Inc	Newburyport	MA	E	978 465-5777	13468
Taco Inc **(PA)**	Cranston	RI	B	401 942-8000	20299

HEAT TREATING: Metal

	CITY	ST	EMP	PHONE	ENTRY #
A G C Incorporated **(PA)**	Meriden	CT	C	203 235-3361	2072
Advance Heat Treating Co	Bridgeport	CT	G	203 380-8898	368
American Heat Treating Inc	Monroe	CT	E	203 268-1750	2390
Amk Welding Inc **(HQ)**	South Windsor	CT	E	860 289-5634	3937
Anderson Specialty Company	West Hartford	CT	G	860 953-6630	5053
Beehive Heat Treating Svcs Inc	Fairfield	CT	G	203 866-1635	1416
Bodycote Thermal Proc Inc	Berlin	CT	E	860 225-7691	76
Eastern Metal Treating Inc	Enfield	CT	F	860 763-4311	1356
General Heat Treating Co	Waterbury	CT	G	203 755-5441	4878
Johnstone Company Inc	North Haven	CT	E	203 239-5834	3036
Nelson Heat Treating Co Inc	Waterbury	CT	F	203 754-0670	4925
New Britain Heat Treating Corp	Enfield	CT	F	860 223-0684	1371
O W Heat Treat Inc	South Glastonbury	CT	G	860 430-6709	3924
Paradigm Manchester Inc	Manchester	CT	C	860 649-2888	2032
Sousa Corp	Newington	CT	F	860 523-9090	2904
Specialty Steel Treating Inc	East Granby	CT	E	860 653-0061	1145
Bodycote Imt Inc **(DH)**	Andover	MA	D	978 470-0876	7542
Bodycote Thermal Proc Inc	Worcester	MA	E	508 754-1724	17349
Fireball Heat Treating Co Inc	Attleboro	MA	G	508 222-2617	7737
Heatbath Corporation **(HQ)**	Indian Orchard	MA	E	413 452-2000	11887
Hy-Temp Inc	Attleboro	MA	F	508 222-6626	7748
Industrial Heat Treating Inc	North Quincy	MA	E	617 328-1010	13977
Materials Development Corp	Andover	MA	F	781 391-0400	7568
Metal Processing Co Inc	Tyngsboro	MA	G	978 649-1289	15896
Norking Company Inc	Attleboro	MA	E	508 222-3100	7773
Northeast Metals Tech LLC	Rowley	MA	G	978 948-2633	14861
S M Engineering Co Inc	North Attleboro	MA	F	508 699-4484	13778
Thermal Technic Inc	Newburyport	MA	G	978 270-5674	13540
Enterprise Castings LLC	Lewiston	ME	G	207 782-5511	6288
Bodycote Thermal Proc Inc	Laconia	NH	E	603 524-7886	18559
Brazecom Industries LLC	Weare	NH	G	603 529-2080	19933
Ionbond LLC	Portsmouth	NH	E	603 610-4460	19580
Mushield Company Inc	Londonderry	NH	E	603 666-4433	18726
Smiths Tblar Systms-Lconia Inc	Laconia	NH	B	603 524-2064	18587
Turbocam Energy Solutions LLC	Dover	NH	E	603 905-0200	18063
Induplate Inc **(PA)**	North Providence	RI	D	401 231-5770	20765
Metallurgical Solutions Inc	Providence	RI	F	401 941-2100	21066
Microweld Co Inc	Riverside	RI	G	401 438-5985	21172
R I Heat Treating Co Inc	Providence	RI	G	401 467-9200	21105
S & P Heat Treating Inc	Warwick	RI	F	401 737-9272	21419
Spectrum Thermal Proc LLC	Cranston	RI	F	401 808-6249	20287

HEATERS: Room & Wall, Including Radiators

	CITY	ST	EMP	PHONE	ENTRY #
AAA Radiator	Melrose	MA	G	781 662-7203	12973

HEATERS: Space, Exc Electric

	CITY	ST	EMP	PHONE	ENTRY #
Dp2 LLC Head	Darien	CT	F	203 655-0747	1022

HEATERS: Swimming Pool, Oil Or Gas

	CITY	ST	EMP	PHONE	ENTRY #
Kerigans Fuel Inc	Bridgeport	CT	G	203 334-3646	439
Marios Oil Corp	Everett	MA	G	617 202-8259	10621

HEATING & AIR CONDITIONING UNITS, COMBINATION

	CITY	ST	EMP	PHONE	ENTRY #
All Phase Htg Coolg Contr LLC	East Haddam	CT	G	860 873-9680	1147
Comfortable Environments	Milford	CT	G	203 876-2140	2266
7ac Technologies Inc	Beverly	MA	F	781 574-1348	8094
Harris Envmtl Systems Inc	Andover	MA	D	978 470-8600	7555
Heat-Flo Inc	Uxbridge	MA	G	508 278-2400	15919

HEATING APPARATUS: Steam

	CITY	ST	EMP	PHONE	ENTRY #
Tunstall Corporation **(PA)**	Chicopee	MA	E	413 594-8695	10065

HEATING EQPT & SPLYS

	CITY	ST	EMP	PHONE	ENTRY #
Carlin Combustion Tech Inc	North Haven	CT	G	413 525-7700	3013
CP Solar Thermal LLC	Bristol	CT	G	860 877-2238	544
Fives N Amercn Combustn Inc	East Lyme	CT	G	860 739-3466	1270
Fives N Amercn Combustn Inc	Southington	CT	E	216 271-6000	4051
Jad LLC	South Windsor	CT	E	860 289-1551	3983
Lewis R Martino	Oxford	CT	G	203 463-4430	3412
Macristy Industries Inc **(PA)**	Newington	CT	C	860 225-4637	2879
McIntire Company **(HQ)**	Bristol	CT	F	860 585-8559	580
Omega Engineering Inc **(HQ)**	Norwalk	CT	C	203 359-1660	3211
Schindler Combustion LLC	Fairfield	CT	G	203 371-5068	1455
Cunniff Corp **(PA)**	East Falmouth	MA	G	508 540-6232	10440
Heatmaker Parts & Service	Reading	MA	G	617 930-0036	14737
Integrated Clean Tech Inc	Pittsfield	MA	G	413 281-2555	14477
Neutrasafe Corporation	Stoughton	MA	G	781 616-3951	15611
Riley Power Inc	Worcester	MA	C	508 852-7100	17459
Runtal North America Inc	Haverhill	MA	E	800 526-2621	11469
Sundrum Solar Inc	Northborough	MA	G	508 740-6256	14049
Taco Inc	Fall River	MA	D	508 675-7300	10769
Thermal Circuits Inc	Salem	MA	C	978 745-1162	14945
Thermo Products	Wilbraham	MA	G	413 279-1980	16943
Warm Water Sales Group	Longmeadow	MA	G	413 567-0750	12338
American Solartechnics LLC	Stockton Springs	ME	G	207 548-1122	7068
Jotul North America Inc	Gorham	ME	D	207 797-5912	6116
Mestek Inc	Clinton	ME	C	207 426-2351	5916
Onix Corporation	Caribou	ME	E	866 290-5362	5889
Bbt North America Corporation	Londonderry	NH	G	603 552-1100	18679
Bradford White Corp	Rochester	NH	G	603 332-0116	19663
Efficiency Plus	Center Ossipee	NH	G	603 539-8125	17803
Granite 3 LLC	Temple	NH	G	603 566-0339	19897
Osram Sylvania Inc	Exeter	NH	D	603 772-4331	18127
Taco Inc **(PA)**	Cranston	RI	B	401 942-8000	20299

HEATING EQPT: Complete

	CITY	ST	EMP	PHONE	ENTRY #
Novy International Inc	Danbury	CT	G	203 743-7720	962
Alpha Instruments Inc	Acton	MA	G	978 264-2966	7339
Backer Hotwatt Inc	Danvers	MA	G	978 777-0000	10201
Massachusetts Control Ctr Inc	Tyngsboro	MA	G	978 649-1128	15895
Mestek Inc **(PA)**	Westfield	MA	E	470 898-4533	16700
Thermoceramix Inc	Boston	MA	G	978 425-0404	8881
Lyme Green Heat	Lyme	NH	G	603 359-8837	18754
Amtrol Inc **(DH)**	West Warwick	RI	B	401 884-6300	21477
Davidon Industries Inc	Warwick	RI	F	401 737-8380	21349

HEATING EQPT: Dielectric

	CITY	ST	EMP	PHONE	ENTRY #
Dielectric Products	Watertown	MA	G	617 924-5688	16278

HEATING EQPT: Induction

	CITY	ST	EMP	PHONE	ENTRY #
East Coast Induction Inc	Brockton	MA	F	508 587-2800	9141
Giltron Inc	North Dighton	MA	G	508 359-4310	13931
Radio Frequency Company Inc	Millis	MA	E	508 376-9555	13186
Rettig USA Inc	Williston	VT	F	802 654-7500	22688

HEATING SYSTEMS: Radiant, Indl Process

	CITY	ST	EMP	PHONE	ENTRY #
Calorique LLC	West Wareham	MA	F	508 291-2000	16567
Runtal North America Inc	Haverhill	MA	E	800 526-2621	11469

HEATING UNITS & DEVICES: Indl, Electric

	CITY	ST	EMP	PHONE	ENTRY #
Birk Manufacturing Inc	East Lyme	CT	D	800 531-2070	1269
Duralite Incorporated	Riverton	CT	F	860 379-3113	3694
Industrial Heater Corp	Cheshire	CT	D	203 250-0500	740
Manufacturers Coml Fin LLC	West Hartford	CT	E	860 242-6287	5084
Sshc Inc	Westbrook	CT	F	860 399-5434	5163
Warmup Inc	Danbury	CT	F	203 791-0072	1006
Dalton Electric Heating Co Inc	Ipswich	MA	E	978 356-9844	11915
I V I Corp	Pembroke	MA	F	781 826-3195	14410
Infinity	Worcester	MA	G	508 753-1981	17392
Reheat Co Inc	Danvers	MA	F	978 777-4441	10251
Sentry Company	Foxboro	MA	G	508 543-5391	10904
Vulcan Electric Company **(PA)**	Porter	ME	D	207 625-3231	6605
Sargeant & Wilbur Inc	Pawtucket	RI	F	401 726-0013	20896

HEATING UNITS: Gas, Infrared

	CITY	ST	EMP	PHONE	ENTRY #
Creative Hydronics Intl Inc	Sagamore Beach	MA	G	508 524-3535	14885
R Filion Manufacturing Inc	Newport	NH	F	603 865-1893	19355

Employee Codes: A=Over 500 employees, B=251-500
C=101-250, D=51-100 E=20-50, F=10-19, G=3-9

	CITY	ST	EMP	PHONE	ENTRY #
HELICOPTERS					
Kaman Aerospace Corporation	Bloomfield	CT	E	860 242-4461	231
Kaman Corporation **(PA)**	Bloomfield	CT	D	860 243-7100	234
Sikorsky Aircraft Corporation	Bridgeport	CT	B	203 384-7532	490
Sikorsky Aircraft Corporation	Shelton	CT	A	203 386-7861	3871
Sikorsky Aircraft Corporation **(HQ)**	Stratford	CT	A	203 386-4000	4444
Sikorsky Aircraft Corporation	Farmington	CT	E	610 644-4430	1513
Sikorsky Export Corporation	Stratford	CT	B	203 386-4000	4445
Boston Executive Helicopters	Norwood	MA	G	781 603-6186	14138
Bell Helicopter Korea Inc	Providence	RI	G	401 421-2800	20969
HELMETS: Athletic					
Final Forge LLC	Plymouth	MA	G	857 244-0764	14557
Old Bh Inc **(PA)**	Exeter	NH	C	603 430-2111	18126
HELMETS: Steel					
Government Surplus Sales Inc	Hartford	CT	G	860 247-7787	1827
Galvion Ballistics Ltd	Newport	VT	D	802 334-2774	22198
HIGHWAY SIGNALS: Electric					
T-S Display Systems Inc	Stamford	CT	G	203 964-0575	4340
HISTORICAL SOCIETY					
American Lighthouse Foundation	Owls Head	ME	G	207 594-4174	6561
HOBBY & CRAFT SPLY STORES					
Grannys Got It	Wolcott	CT	G	203 879-0042	5443
HOBBY GOODS, WHOLESALE					
Jim Carr Inc	Pelham	NH	C	603 635-2821	19437
HOBBY, TOY & GAME STORES: Arts & Crafts & Splys					
Vermont Hand Crafters Inc	Waterbury	VT	G	802 434-5044	22588
HOBBY, TOY & GAME STORES: Children's Toys & Games, Exc Dolls					
Learning Materials Workshop	Burlington	VT	G	802 862-0112	21793
HOISTS					
St Pierre Manufacturing Corp	Worcester	MA	E	508 853-8010	17479
Somatex Inc	Detroit	ME	E	207 487-6141	5953
HOISTS: Aircraft Loading					
Entwistle Company **(HQ)**	Hudson	MA	C	508 481-4000	11772
HOLDING COMPANIES: Investment, Exc Banks					
Kco Numet Inc	Orange	CT	F	203 375-4995	3367
Legrand Holding Inc **(DH)**	West Hartford	CT	E	860 233-6251	5080
Polymedex Discovery Group Inc **(PA)**	Putnam	CT	F	860 928-4102	3627
Connell Limited Partnership **(PA)**	Boston	MA	F	617 737-2700	8481
Euro-Pro Holdco LLC	Needham Heights	MA	D	617 243-0235	13330
Lund Precision Products Inc	Hyannis	MA	G	617 413-0236	11848
Rf1 Holding Company **(PA)**	Marlborough	MA	F	855 294-3800	12816
Capricorn Products LLC	Portland	ME	E	207 321-0014	6630
Kullson Holding Company Inc	Lewiston	ME	E	207 783-3442	6296
Bce Acquisition Us Inc **(HQ)**	Exeter	NH	G	603 430-2111	18112
Mack Group Inc **(PA)**	Arlington	VT	B	802 375-2511	21597
HOLLOWARE, SILVER					
J H Breakell & Company Inc	Newport	RI	F	401 849-3522	20667
HOME CENTER STORES					
Thomas Bernhard Building Sys	Southport	CT	E	203 925-0414	4102
Hosetech Plus More Inc	Ludlow	MA	G	413 385-0035	12467
HOME ENTERTAINMENT EQPT: Electronic, NEC					
Viola Audio Laboratories Inc	New Haven	CT	G	203 772-0435	2752
HOME FURNISHINGS WHOLESALERS					
Lifetime Brands Inc	Pawtucket	RI	G	401 333-2040	20854
G Scatchard Ltd	Westford	VT	G	802 899-2181	22628
HOME IMPROVEMENT & RENOVATION CONTRACTOR AGENCY					
This Old House Ventures LLC	Stamford	CT	E	475 209-8665	4344
HOMEBUILDERS & OTHER OPERATIVE BUILDERS					
Crown Properties & HM Sls LLC	North Hampton	NH	G	603 964-2005	19382
HOMEFURNISHING STORE: Bedding, Sheet, Blanket,Spread/Pillow					
Sammi Sleeping Systems LLC	New Haven	CT	G	203 684-3131	2734
HOMEFURNISHING STORES: Cookware, Exc Aluminum					
Sheffield Pottery Inc	Sheffield	MA	E	413 229-7700	15065
HOMEFURNISHING STORES: Lighting Fixtures					
Acme Sign Co **(PA)**	Stamford	CT	F	203 324-2263	4128
Washington Copper Works Inc	Washington	CT	G	860 868-7637	4831
HOMEFURNISHING STORES: Mirrors					
Kensington Glass and Frmng Co	Berlin	CT	G	860 828-9428	91
Mirror Polishing & Pltg Co Inc	Waterbury	CT	E	203 574-5400	4917
HOMEFURNISHING STORES: Pictures & Mirrors					
Picture This Hartford Inc	East Hartford	CT	G	860 528-1409	1210
HOMEFURNISHING STORES: Pottery					
Potting Shed Inc	Concord	MA	G	617 899-6290	10151
Scargo Stoneware Pottery	Dennis	MA	G	508 385-3894	10311
Darmariscotta Pottery Inc	Damariscotta	ME	G	207 563-8843	5935
Georgetown Pottery	Georgetown	ME	G	207 371-2801	6106
Rackliffe Pottery Inc	Blue Hill	ME	G	207 374-2297	5773
Sylvia Wyler Pottery Inc **(PA)**	Brunswick	ME	G	207 729-1321	5848
Romulus Craft	Washington	VT	G	802 685-3869	22580
HOMEFURNISHING STORES: Venetian Blinds					
Arrow Window Shade Mfg Co Mrdn	Wethersfield	CT	F	860 563-4035	5241
Beverly Shade Shoppe	Beverly	MA	G	978 922-0374	8110
J & R Langley Co Inc	Manchester	NH	F	603 622-9653	18847
HOMEFURNISHING STORES: Window Furnishings					
Reliable Fabrics Inc	Everett	MA	E	617 387-5321	10626
Staceys Shade Shop Inc **(PA)**	Lynn	MA	G	781 595-0097	12540
HOMEFURNISHING STORES: Window Shades, NEC					
Arrow Window Shade Mfg Co	Wethersfield	CT	G	860 956-3570	5240
HOMEFURNISHINGS & SPLYS, WHOLESALE: Decorative					
Modern Objects Inc	Norwalk	CT	G	203 378-5785	3201
Partylite Inc **(HQ)**	Plymouth	MA	D	203 661-1926	14572
Stupell Industries Ltd Inc	Johnston	RI	F	401 831-5640	20543
HOMEFURNISHINGS, WHOLESALE: Bedspreads					
Dci Inc **(PA)**	Lisbon	NH	D	603 838-6544	18648
HOMEFURNISHINGS, WHOLESALE: Blinds, Venetian					
J & R Langley Co Inc	Manchester	NH	F	603 622-9653	18847
HOMEFURNISHINGS, WHOLESALE: Carpets					
Holland & Sherry Inc **(PA)**	Norwalk	CT	F	212 628-1950	3169
HOMEFURNISHINGS, WHOLESALE: Draperies					
New England Drapery Assoc Inc	Woburn	MA	G	781 944-7536	17241
HOMEFURNISHINGS, WHOLESALE: Kitchenware					
Glass Industries America LLC	Wallingford	CT	F	203 269-6700	4749
Petermans Boards and Bowls Inc	Gill	MA	E	413 863-2116	11157
R2b Inc	Portland	ME	F	207 797-0019	6719
Dee Kay Designs Inc **(PA)**	Hope Valley	RI	D	401 539-2400	20484
HOMEFURNISHINGS, WHOLESALE: Pottery					
Sylvia Wyler Pottery Inc **(PA)**	Brunswick	ME	G	207 729-1321	5848
Bennington Potters Inc **(PA)**	Bennington	VT	E	800 205-8033	21664
HOMEFURNISHINGS, WHOLESALE: Rugs					
Natco Products Corporation **(PA)**	West Warwick	RI	B	401 828-0300	21504
HOMEFURNISHINGS, WHOLESALE: Window Covering Parts & Access					
Green Mountain Vista Inc	Williston	VT	G	802 862-0159	22673
HOMEFURNISHINGS, WHOLESALE: Wood Flooring					
Ben Barretts LLC	Thompson	CT	G	860 928-9373	4532
Cabinets For Less LLC	Manchester	NH	G	603 935-7551	18794
HOMES, MODULAR: Wooden					
Fox Modular Homes Inc	Lee	MA	F	413 243-1950	12092
Habitat Post & Beam Inc	South Deerfield	MA	E	413 665-4006	15250
Home Kore Mfg Co Mass Inc	Lakeville	MA	G	508 947-0000	11976
Modulease Corporation	North Attleboro	MA	G	508 695-4145	13766
Leland Boggs II	Warren	ME	G	207 273-2610	7143
Modular Fun I Inc	South Paris	ME	C	207 739-2400	7014
New England Bldg Solutions LLC	Scarborough	ME	G	207 323-0012	6934
Schiavi Homes LLC	Oxford	ME	E	207 539-9600	6573
HOMES: Log Cabins					
Country Log Homes Inc	Goshen	CT	F	413 229-8084	1582
Post & Beam Homes Inc	East Hampton	CT	G	860 267-2060	1163
Katahdin Forest Products Co **(PA)**	Oakfield	ME	D	800 845-4533	6527
Moose Creek Home Center Inc	Turner	ME	G	207 224-7497	7109
Moosehead Country Log Homes	Greenville	ME	E	207 695-3730	6153
Moosehead Wood Components Inc	Greenville Junction	ME	F	207 695-3730	6154
Wlhc Inc **(PA)**	Houlton	ME	G	207 532-6531	6212
Coventry Log Homes	Woodsville	NH	E	603 747-8177	20030
Granite State Log Homes Inc **(PA)**	Campton	NH	F	603 536-4949	17777
Log Cabin Bldg Co & Sawmill	Lancaster	NH	G	603 788-3036	18601
Monadnock Log Home Svcs LLC	Jaffrey	NH	F	603 876-4800	18474
Timberpeg East Inc **(PA)**	Claremont	NH	E	603 542-7762	17862
Tucker Mountain Homes Inc	Meredith	NH	G	603 279-4320	18981
WH Silverstein Inc	Claremont	NH	E	603 542-5418	17864
Authentic Log Homes Inc	Hardwick	VT	G	802 472-5096	22009
Gilcris Enterprises Inc	Proctorsville	VT	F	802 226-7764	22288
Goodridge Lumber	Albany	VT	G	802 755-6298	21592
Groton Timberworks of Vermont	Groton	VT	G	802 584-4446	22005
Jamaica Cottage Shop Inc	South Londonderry	VT	E	802 297-3760	22487
Moosehead Cedar Log Homes	Wilmington	VT	G	802 464-7609	22704
HONES					
Hones LLC	Hanover	NH	G	603 643-4223	18289
HONEYCOMB CORE & BOARD: Made From Purchased Materials					
Pactiv Corporation	North Haven	CT	E	203 288-7722	3047
HOPPERS: Metal Plate					
Merchants Fabrication Inc **(PA)**	Southbridge	MA	G	508 784-6700	15396
HORSE & PET ACCESSORIES: Textile					
Puppy Hugger	Greenwich	CT	G	203 661-4858	1639
Lupine Inc	Center Conway	NH	D	603 356-7371	17801

	CITY	ST	EMP	PHONE	ENTRY #

HORSE ACCESS: Harnesses & Riding Crops, Etc, Exc Leather

Equinature LLC	Northbridge	MA	G	774 217-8057	14055

HORSE DRAWN VEHICLE REPAIR SVCS

Serafin Sulky Co	Stafford Springs	CT	G	860 684-2986	4114

HORSESHOES

St Pierre Manufacturing Corp	Worcester	MA	E	508 853-8010	17479

HOSE: Fire, Rubber

Diversified Industrial Sup LLC	Charlestown	MA	F	800 244-3647	9831

HOSE: Flexible Metal

East Coast Metal Hose Inc	Naugatuck	CT	G	203 723-7459	2470
Senior Operations LLC	Enfield	CT	D	860 741-2546	1383
Senior Operations LLC	Sharon	MA	C	781 784-1400	15056
Titeflex Corporation **(HQ)**	Springfield	MA	B	413 739-5631	15516
Niantic Seal Inc	Lincoln	RI	E	401 334-6870	20588

HOSE: Garden, Rubber

Seven Mist LLC	Amherst	MA	G	413 210-7255	7525
Teknor Apex Company **(PA)**	Pawtucket	RI	B	401 725-8000	20903

HOSE: Plastic

Titeflex Corporation **(HQ)**	Springfield	MA	B	413 739-5631	15516
Contitech Thermopol LLC	Somersworth	NH	G	603 692-6300	19832
Contitech Thermopol LLC	Rochester	NH	D	603 692-6300	19665
Contitech Thermopol LLC **(HQ)**	Somersworth	NH	G	603 692-6300	19833

HOSE: Pneumatic, Rubber Or Rubberized Fabric, NEC

Flexaust Company Inc	Newburyport	MA	G	978 465-0445	13489
Techflex Enterprises Inc	Chicopee	MA	G	413 592-2800	10063

HOSE: Rubber

Rubco Products Company	Torrington	CT	G	860 496-1178	4597
Samar Co Inc	Stoughton	MA	D	781 297-7264	15620

HOSES & BELTING: Rubber & Plastic

Kongsberg Actuation **(HQ)**	Suffield	CT	G	860 668-1285	4464
Ram Belting Company Inc	New Britain	CT	G	860 438-7029	2568
Flexaust Inc	Amesbury	MA	G	978 388-1005	7485
Guardair Corporation	Chicopee	MA	E	413 594-4400	10028
Titeflex Commercial Inc	Springfield	MA	F	413 739-5631	15515
Advanced Flexible Composites	Bennington	VT	G	802 681-7121	21662

HOT TUBS

Thermospas Hot Tub Products	Wallingford	CT	E	203 303-0005	4817
Maine Cedar Hot Tubs Inc	Madison	ME	G	207 474-0953	6406

HOUSEHOLD APPLIANCE STORES: Air Cond Rm Units, Self-Contnd

Massachusetts Control Ctr Inc	Tyngsboro	MA	G	978 649-1128	15895

HOUSEHOLD APPLIANCE STORES: Electric Household, Major

Clarke Distribution Corp	Norwalk	CT	G	203 838-9385	3126

HOUSEHOLD ARTICLES, EXC FURNITURE: Cut Stone

Williams & Co Mining Inc	Perkinsville	VT	F	802 263-5404	22261

HOUSEHOLD ARTICLES, EXC KITCHEN: Pottery

Gare Incorporated	Haverhill	MA	E	978 373-9131	11437
Simon Pearce US Inc **(PA)**	Windsor	VT	C	802 674-6280	22714

HOUSEHOLD ARTICLES: Metal

J OConnor LLC	Newington	CT	F	860 665-7702	2873
Hampden Fence Supply Inc	Agawam	MA	F	413 786-4390	7430
Custom Mtal Fabricators VT LLC	Hyde Park	VT	G	802 888-0033	22035
S & A Trombley Corporation	Morrisville	VT	E	802 888-2394	22176

HOUSEHOLD FURNISHINGS, NEC

Hills Point Industries LLC **(PA)**	Westport	CT	G	917 515-8650	5200
Latex Foam International LLC **(HQ)**	Shelton	CT	D	203 924-0700	3825
R L Fisher Inc	Hartford	CT	D	860 951-8110	1865
Beantown Bedding LLC	Hingham	MA	F	781 608-9915	11493
Berkshire Corporation **(HQ)**	Great Barrington	MA	E	413 528-2602	11233
Fall River Apparel Inc	Fall River	MA	G	508 677-1975	10694
Dirigo Stitching Inc	Skowhegan	ME	E	207 474-8421	6972
Maine Balsam Fir Prodcts	West Paris	ME	F	207 674-5090	7176
North Country Comforters	Great Pond	ME	G	207 584-2196	6145
Rsv Management	Machias	ME	G	207 255-8608	6394
Masquerade	Salem	NH	F	603 275-0717	19749

HOUSEWARE STORES

Ralph Curcio Co Inc	Gardner	MA	G	978 632-1120	11124

HOUSEWARES, ELECTRIC, EXC COOKING APPLIANCES & UTEN-SILS

Headwaters Inc	Marblehead	MA	G	781 715-6404	12685
Qci Inc	Seekonk	MA	F	508 399-8983	15035
1911 Office LLC	Keene	NH	G	603 352-2448	18488

HOUSEWARES, ELECTRIC: Air Purifiers, Portable

Celios Corporation	Portsmouth	NH	G	978 877-2044	19549

HOUSEWARES, ELECTRIC: Appliances, Personal

Bedjet LLC	Newport	RI	G	401 404-5250	20656

HOUSEWARES, ELECTRIC: Blowers, Portable

Crrc LLC	Cromwell	CT	D	860 635-2200	852

HOUSEWARES, ELECTRIC: Bottle Warmers

Mayborn Usa Inc	Stamford	CT	F	781 269-7490	4245

HOUSEWARES, ELECTRIC: Broilers

Bkmfg Corp	Winsted	CT	E	860 738-2200	5405

HOUSEWARES, ELECTRIC: Cooking Appliances

Black & Decker (us) Inc	New Britain	CT	G	860 225-5111	2514
Black & Decker (us) Inc **(HQ)**	New Britain	CT	G	860 225-5111	2515
Vaughn Thermal Corporation	Salisbury	MA	E	978 462-6683	14958

HOUSEWARES, ELECTRIC: Fans, Exhaust & Ventilating

Betlan Corporation	Newtown	CT	F	203 270-7898	2916
Ecovent Corp	Charlestown	MA	F	620 983-6863	9832
Spruce Environmental Tech Inc **(PA)**	Haverhill	MA	D	978 521-0901	11475

HOUSEWARES, ELECTRIC: Heating Units, Electric Appliances

Eichenauer Inc	Newport	NH	E	603 863-1454	19345

HOUSEWARES, ELECTRIC: Heating, Bsbrd/Wall, Radiant Heat

Mestek Inc **(PA)**	Westfield	MA	E	470 898-4533	16700
Sahara Heaters Mfg Co	Nashua	NH	G	603 888-7351	19257

HOUSEWARES, ELECTRIC: Massage Machines, Exc Beauty/Barber

Infinite Creative Entps Inc	Seabrook	NH	G	603 910-5000	19807

HOUSEWARES: Can Openers, Exc Electric

R2b Inc	Portland	ME	F	207 797-0019	6719

HOUSEWARES: Dishes, China

Wainwright USA LLC	Great Barrington	MA	G	413 717-4211	11249

HOUSEWARES: Dishes, Earthenware

JH Smith Co Inc **(PA)**	Greenfield	MA	F	413 772-0191	11264
Waddington North America Inc	Chelmsford	MA	C	978 256-6551	9941

HOUSEWARES: Dishes, Plastic

American Marketing & Sales	Leominster	MA	G	978 514-8929	12113
Broadstone Industries	Lowell	MA	G	978 691-2790	12356
Dorel Juvenile Group Inc	Foxboro	MA	D	800 544-1108	10881
Home Pdts Intl - N Amer Inc	Leominster	MA	C	978 534-6536	12152
Lamson and Goodnow LLC	Shelburne Falls	MA	E	413 625-0201	15073
Newell Brands Inc	East Longmeadow	MA	B	413 526-5150	10484
Questech Tile LLC	Rutland	VT	G	802 773-1228	22348

HOUSEWARES: Food Dishes & Utensils, Pressed & Molded Pulp

Solo Cup Operating Corporation	Saint Albans	VT	F	802 524-5966	22378

HOUSEWARES: Pots & Pans, Glass

Catamount Glassware Co Inc	Bennington	VT	E	802 442-5438	21666

HOUSEWARES: Toothpicks, Wood

Strong Wood Products Inc	Temple	ME	F	207 778-4063	7080

HOUSING COMPONENTS: Prefabricated, Concrete

Concrete Pdts of Londonderry	Wilmington	MA	G	978 658-2645	16988
Shea Concrete Products Inc **(PA)**	Amesbury	MA	E	978 658-2645	7507
Shea Concrete Products Inc	Amesbury	MA	E	978 388-1509	7508
Jamaica Cottage Shop Inc	South Londonderry	VT	E	802 297-3760	22487

HOUSINGS: Pressure

Northbridge Companies	Burlington	MA	F	781 272-2424	9311
Core Assemblies Inc	Gilford	NH	F	603 293-0270	18183

HUB CAPS: Automobile, Stamped Metal

Distinctive Steering Wheels	Watertown	CT	G	860 274-9087	5007

HUMIDIFIERS & DEHUMIDIFIERS

Munters Corporation **(DH)**	Amesbury	MA	C	978 241-1100	7498
Pool Environments Inc	Gorham	ME	F	207 839-8225	6126

HYDRAULIC EQPT REPAIR SVC

Power-Dyne LLC	Middletown	CT	E	860 346-9283	2211

HYDRAULIC FLUIDS: Synthetic Based

Ai Divestitures Inc	Waterbury	CT	G	203 575-5727	4837
Element Solutions Inc	Waterbury	CT	E	203 575-5850	4870
Houston Macdermid Inc	Waterbury	CT	G	203 575-5700	4885
Macdermid Anion Inc	Waterbury	CT	G	203 575-5700	4904
Macdermid Brazil Inc	Waterbury	CT	G	203 575-5700	4905
Macdermid South America Inc	Waterbury	CT	G	203 575-5700	4908
Macdermid South Atlantic Inc	Waterbury	CT	G	203 575-5700	4909

Hard Rubber & Molded Rubber Prdts

Cooper Crouse-Hinds LLC	Windsor	CT	D	860 683-4300	5327
Simons Stamps Inc	Turners Falls	MA	F	413 863-6800	15885

ICE

Leonard F Brooks **(PA)**	Bridgeport	CT	G	203 335-4934	445
Olde Burnside Brewing Co LLC	East Hartford	CT	G	860 528-2200	1208
Vaporizer LLC	Moosup	CT	E	860 564-7225	2429
American Dry Ice Corporation **(PA)**	Palmer	MA	F	413 283-9906	14279
Brewster Ice Co	Brewster	MA	G	508 896-3593	9052
Cape Pond Ice Company **(PA)**	Gloucester	MA	E	978 283-0174	11172
Cape Pond Ice Company	Lawrence	MA	G	978 688-2300	12002
Cape Pond Ice Company	Peabody	MA	G	978 531-4853	14320
Crystal Ice Co Inc	New Bedford	MA	F	508 997-7522	13375
Eastern Ice Company Inc	Fall River	MA	E	508 672-1800	10685
Got Ice LLC	Nantucket	MA	G	508 228-1156	13225

	CITY	ST	EMP	PHONE	ENTRY #
JP Lillis Enterprises Inc **(PA)**	Sandwich	MA	F	508 888-8394	14970
Leominster Ice Company Inc	Leominster	MA	G	978 537-5322	12162
Getchell Bros Inc	Sanford	ME	E	207 490-0809	6877
Taggart Ice Inc	Nashua	NH	F	603 888-4630	19270

ICE CREAM & ICES WHOLESALERS

Spadafora Slush Co	Malden	MA	G	617 548-5870	12597

ICE CREAM TRUCK VENDORS

Walpole Creamery Ltd	Walpole	NH	G	603 445-5700	19926

ICE WHOLESALERS

Taggart Ice Inc	Nashua	NH	F	603 888-4630	19270

IDENTIFICATION PLATES

Northeast Stamp & Engraving	Milford	MA	G	508 473-5818	13132
Endur Id Inc	Hampton	NH	G	603 758-1488	18262

IDENTIFICATION TAGS, EXC PAPER

Ann S Davis	Lebanon	CT	F	860 642-7228	1932
Apothecary Products LLC	North Attleboro	MA	E	508 695-0727	13745
Currys Leather Shop Inc	Randolph	MA	F	781 963-0679	14675

IGNEOUS ROCK: Crushed & Broken

Nu-Stone Mfg & Distrg LLC	Sterling	CT	G	860 564-6555	4370
Aggregate Inds - Northeast Reg	Saugus	MA	G	781 941-7200	14975
Massachusetts Broken Stone Co **(PA)**	Berlin	MA	G	978 838-9999	8091
Concord Sand and Gravel Inc	Loudon	NH	G	603 435-6787	18747
Marcou Construction Company	Dunbarton	NH	G	603 774-6511	18073

IGNITION APPARATUS & DISTRIBUTORS

Tanyx Measurements Inc	Billerica	MA	E	978 671-0183	8299

IGNITION CONTROLS: Gas Appliance

Ssidm Inc	Rockland	MA	G	781 871-7677	14827

IGNITION SYSTEMS: High Frequency

Simmonds Precision Pdts Inc	Danbury	CT	E	203 797-5000	994
Simmonds Precision Pdts Inc **(DH)**	Vergennes	VT	A	802 877-4000	22556

INCENSE

Three Kings Products LLC	Watertown	CT	G	860 945-5294	5028
Quality Incense	Cambridge	MA	G	339 224-0655	9620
Paine Products Inc	Auburn	ME	F	207 782-0931	5585

INDL & PERSONAL SVC PAPER WHOLESALERS

Birch Point Paper Products Inc	Fitchburg	MA	E	978 422-1447	10811
Diamond Water Systems Inc	Chicopee	MA	E	413 536-8186	10017

INDL & PERSONAL SVC PAPER, WHOL: Bags, Paper/Disp Plastic

Pakpro Inc	Andover	MA	G	978 474-5018	7580
K&H Group Inc	Bennington	VT	E	802 442-5455	21677

INDL & PERSONAL SVC PAPER, WHOL: Paper, Wrap/Coarse/Prdts

Expressive Design Group Inc	Holyoke	MA	E	413 315-6296	11626
Desnoyers Enterprises Inc	Harrisville	RI	G	800 922-4445	20478

INDL & PERSONAL SVC PAPER, WHOLESALE: Disposable

Admiral Packaging Inc	Providence	RI	D	401 274-5588	20945

INDL & PERSONAL SVC PAPER, WHOLESALE: Fiber Cans & Drums

Dusobox Co Inc	Haverhill	MA	E	978 372-7192	11426

INDL & PERSONAL SVC PAPER, WHOLESALE: Sanitary Food

Bees Wrap LLC	Middlebury	VT	E	802 643-2132	22101

INDL & PERSONAL SVC PAPER, WHOLESALE: Shipping Splys

IR Industries Inc	Bethel	CT	F	203 790-8273	162
Horn Corporation **(PA)**	Lancaster	MA	E	800 832-7020	11984

INDL DIAMONDS WHOLESALERS

Diamondsharp Corporation	Walpole	NH	G	603 445-2224	19920

INDL EQPT SVCS

Afcon Products Inc	Bethany	CT	F	203 393-9301	118
Hydro Service & Supplies Inc	Middletown	CT	G	203 265-3995	2190
Nemtec Inc	Cheshire	CT	G	203 272-0788	746
American Water Systems LLC	Canton	MA	D	781 830-9722	9712
Brooks Automation Inc **(PA)**	Chelmsford	MA	B	978 262-2400	9880
Woodworking Machinery Services	North Billerica	MA	G	978 663-8488	13878
Macy Industries Inc	Hooksett	NH	E	603 623-5568	18353

INDL GASES WHOLESALERS

Connecticut Analytical Corp	Bethany	CT	F	203 393-9666	119
Airgas Usa LLC	Billerica	MA	E	978 439-1344	8207

INDL MACHINERY & EQPT WHOLESALERS

A F M Engineering Corp	Brooklyn	CT	G	860 774-7518	668
Anderson Technologies Inc	Killingworth	CT	G	860 663-2100	1924
Beardsworth Group Inc	Thomaston	CT	G	860 283-4014	4498
Bernell Tool & Mfg Co	Waterbury	CT	G	203 756-4405	4849
Bjm Pumps LLC	Old Saybrook	CT	E	860 399-5937	3329
Bremser Technologies Inc	Stratford	CT	F	203 378-8486	4398
Cable Electronics Inc	Hartford	CT	G	860 953-0300	1809
Del-Tron Precision Inc	Bethel	CT	E	203 778-2727	143
Devar Inc	Bridgeport	CT	E	203 368-6751	405
Finishers Technology Corp	East Berlin	CT	F	860 829-1000	1101
Gems Sensors Inc **(HQ)**	Plainville	CT	B	860 747-3000	3491
Hall Machine Systems Inc **(HQ)**	North Branford	CT	G	203 481-4275	2965
Helander Products Inc	Clinton	CT	F	860 669-7953	788
Interface Devices Incorporated	Milford	CT	G	203 878-4648	2303
Jovil Universal LLC	Danbury	CT	E	203 792-6700	941
L M Gill Welding and Mfr LLC **(PA)**	Manchester	CT	F	860 647-9931	2017
Novo Precision LLC	Bristol	CT	E	860 583-0517	587
Richard Dahlen	Bristol	CT	G	860 584-8226	606
Royal Machine and Tool Corp	Berlin	CT	E	860 828-6555	108
Viking Tool Company	Shelton	CT	E	203 929-1457	3885
Wittmann Battenfeld Inc **(DH)**	Torrington	CT	D	860 496-9603	4608
Acme-Shorey Precast Co Inc **(PA)**	Harwich	MA	F	508 432-0530	11386
Anver Corporation	Hudson	MA	D	978 568-0221	11755
Auburn Systems LLC	Beverly	MA	G	978 777-2460	8105
Baker Parts Inc	New Bedford	MA	G	508 636-3121	13360
Black Diamond Drill Grinders	Shrewsbury	MA	F	978 465-3799	15104
Circor Naval Solutions LLC **(HQ)**	Warren	MA	D	413 436-7711	16260
Degreasing Devices Co	Southbridge	MA	G	508 765-0045	15379
Dynisco Instruments LLC **(HQ)**	Franklin	MA	C	508 541-9400	11037
GE Infrastructure Sensing LLC **(DH)**	Billerica	MA	A	978 437-1000	8249
Giltron Inc	North Dighton	MA	G	508 359-4310	13931
Gorman Machine Corp	Middleboro	MA	E	508 923-9462	13063
Hydro Quip Inc **(PA)**	Seekonk	MA	G	508 399-5771	15024
Jeio Tech Inc	Billerica	MA	G	781 376-0700	8259
Kadant Inc	Auburn	MA	C	508 791-8171	7840
Luster-On Products Inc	Springfield	MA	F	413 739-2541	15486
M E Baker Company **(PA)**	Framingham	MA	F	508 620-5304	10979
Metso Usa Inc **(HQ)**	Boston	MA	G	617 369-7850	8703
Mettler-Toledo Thornton Inc	Billerica	MA	D	978 262-0210	8266
Omtec Corp	Marlborough	MA	F	508 481-3322	12801
Polytech Filtration Systems	Hudson	MA	F	978 562-7700	11804
Prazi USA Inc	Plymouth	MA	G	508 747-1490	14577
Romax Inc	Hudson	MA	G	502 327-8555	11813
Sanger Equipment and Mfg	Conway	MA	G	413 625-8304	10166
Toolmex Indus Solutions Inc **(PA)**	Northborough	MA	D	508 653-5110	14052
Trans Metrics Inc **(HQ)**	Watertown	MA	F	617 926-1000	16325
Vaccon Company Inc	Medway	MA	E	508 359-7200	12972
Wafer Inspection Services Inc	Orleans	MA	G	508 944-2851	14245
Whitmor Company Inc **(PA)**	Revere	MA	F	781 284-8000	14778
Whitney & Son Inc	Fitchburg	MA	E	978 343-6353	10863
ECB Motor Company Inc	Lyman	ME	G	508 717-5441	6389
HMC Corporation **(PA)**	Hopkinton	NH	E	603 746-3399	18362
Donald G Lockard	Westerly	RI	G	401 965-3182	21523
Rbc Industries Inc	Warwick	RI	D	401 941-3000	21410
Fellows Corporation	Windsor	VT	C	802 674-6500	22708
Worksafe Traffic Ctrl Inds Inc **(PA)**	Barre	VT	F	802 223-8948	21645

INDL MACHINERY REPAIR & MAINTENANCE

Arico Engineering Inc	North Franklin	CT	G	860 642-7040	2987
H G Steinmetz Machine Works	Bethel	CT	F	203 794-1880	158
Quick Machine Services LLC	Meriden	CT	G	203 634-8822	2121
Thomas La Ganga	Torrington	CT	G	860 489-0920	4601
Brodeur Machine Company Bus Tr	New Bedford	MA	D	508 995-2662	13367
Giltron Inc	North Dighton	MA	G	508 359-4310	13931
Leo Coons Jr	Acushnet	MA	G	508 995-3300	7404
New Bedford Scale Co Inc	New Bedford	MA	G	508 997-6730	13421
Pearce Processing Systems	Gloucester	MA	G	978 283-3800	11202
Thermoplastics Co Inc	Worcester	MA	E	508 754-4668	17488
Webco Engineering Inc	Southborough	MA	F	508 303-0500	15372
Machinery Service Co Inc	Wiscasset	ME	G	207 882-6788	7285
M & A Advnced Design Cnstr Inc **(PA)**	Hampstead	NH	G	603 329-9515	18242
Nexvac Inc **(PA)**	Sandown	NH	F	603 887-0015	19786

INDL PATTERNS: Foundry Cores

Roehr Tool Corp	Leominster	MA	F	978 562-4488	12183

INDL PATTERNS: Foundry Patternmaking

Bradley Goodwin Pattern Co	Providence	RI	F	401 461-5220	20973

INDL PROCESS INSTR: Transmit, Process Variables

Wilcom Inc	Belmont	NH	E	603 524-2622	17686

INDL PROCESS INSTRUMENTS: Absorp Analyzers, Infrared, X-Ray

Buck Scientific Inc	Norwalk	CT	D	203 853-9444	3116
Bedrock Automtn Platforms Inc	Mansfield	MA	G	781 821-0280	12615

INDL PROCESS INSTRUMENTS: Analyzers

Pid Analyzers LLC	Sandwich	MA	F	774 413-5281	14972

INDL PROCESS INSTRUMENTS: Control

Bristol Inc **(HQ)**	Watertown	CT	B	860 945-2200	5001
Gordon Engineering Corp	Brookfield	CT	F	203 775-4501	645
Micromod Automation & Controls	Wallingford	CT	F	585 321-9209	4774
Assembly Guidance Systems Inc	Chelmsford	MA	F	978 244-1166	9874
Bel Legacy Corporation	Boston	MA	C	508 923-5000	8400
Dynisco Parent Inc	Billerica	MA	E	978 667-5301	8241
Honeywell Data Instruments Inc	Acton	MA	B	978 264-9550	7361
Instrumentation & Control Tech	Waltham	MA	F	781 273-5052	16135
Massmicro LLC	Canton	MA	F	781 828-6110	9756
Rigaku Analytical Devices Inc	Wilmington	MA	E	781 328-1024	17041
Electrochemical Devices Inc **(PA)**	Lincoln	RI	G	401 333-6112	20571
Orbetron LLC	Cumberland	RI	G	651 983-2872	20337
Systematics Inc	Bristol	RI	G	401 253-0050	20104

INDL PROCESS INSTRUMENTS: Controllers, Process Variables

Louis Electric Co Inc	Wolcott	CT	G	203 879-5483	5447
Prime Technology LLC	North Branford	CT	C	203 481-5721	2974
Quad/Graphics Inc	North Haven	CT	A	203 288-2468	3057
Applewood Controls Inc	Littleton	MA	G	978 486-9220	12292

	CITY	ST	EMP	PHONE	ENTRY #
Iwaki America Incorporated **(HQ)**	Holliston	MA	D	508 429-1440	11579
Mettler-Toledo Thornton Inc	Billerica	MA	D	978 262-0210	8266
National Resource MGT Inc **(PA)**	Canton	MA	E	781 828-8877	9759
Schneider Electric Usa Inc **(DH)**	Boston	MA	A	978 975-9600	8839
Schneider Electric Usa Inc	Foxboro	MA	G	508 549-3385	10903
Scully Signal Company **(PA)**	Wilmington	MA	C	617 692-8600	17044
Qesidyne Inc	Hudson	NH	G	603 883-3116	18431

INDL PROCESS INSTRUMENTS: Data Loggers

	CITY	ST	EMP	PHONE	ENTRY #
Datapaq Inc	Derry	NH	E	603 537-2680	17977

INDL PROCESS INSTRUMENTS: Digital Display, Process Variables

	CITY	ST	EMP	PHONE	ENTRY #
Kapcom LLC	East Haven	CT	G	203 891-5112	1253
Precision Digital Corporation	Hopkinton	MA	E	508 655-7300	11733
Shawmut Advertising Inc **(PA)**	Danvers	MA	E	978 762-7500	10255
Astonish Results LP	Warwick	RI	F	401 921-6220	21328

INDL PROCESS INSTRUMENTS: Fluidic Devices, Circuit & Systems

	CITY	ST	EMP	PHONE	ENTRY #
Diba Industries Inc **(HQ)**	Danbury	CT	C	203 744-0773	901
Lee Company **(PA)**	Westbrook	CT	A	860 399-6281	5157
Lee Company	Essex	CT	C	860 399-6281	1401
Parker-Hannifin Corporation	Hollis	NH	C	603 595-1500	18336

INDL PROCESS INSTRUMENTS: Indl Flow & Measuring

	CITY	ST	EMP	PHONE	ENTRY #
C F D Engineering Company	Waterbury	CT	F	203 754-2807	4853
Cidra Corporate Services Inc	Wallingford	CT	D	203 265-0035	4718
Cidra Corporation	Wallingford	CT	D	203 265-0035	4719
Proflow Inc	North Haven	CT	E	203 230-4700	3055
Auburn International Inc	Beverly	MA	F	978 777-2460	8104
Auburn Systems LLC	Beverly	MA	G	978 777-2460	8105
Tte Laboratories Inc	Hopkinton	MA	F	800 242-6022	11741
Airgas Usa LLC	East Greenwich	RI	G	401 884-0201	20351

INDL PROCESS INSTRUMENTS: Manometers

	CITY	ST	EMP	PHONE	ENTRY #
Rosemount Inc	Mansfield	MA	G	508 261-2928	12656

INDL PROCESS INSTRUMENTS: Moisture Meters

	CITY	ST	EMP	PHONE	ENTRY #
Laticrete Supercap LLC	Bethany	CT	G	203 393-4558	122
GE Infrastructure Sensing LLC **(DH)**	Billerica	MA	A	978 437-1000	8249

INDL PROCESS INSTRUMENTS: On-Stream Gas Or Liquid Analysis

	CITY	ST	EMP	PHONE	ENTRY #
Lynn Products Co	Lynn	MA	E	781 593-2500	12524

INDL PROCESS INSTRUMENTS: Temperature

	CITY	ST	EMP	PHONE	ENTRY #
Jad LLC	South Windsor	CT	E	860 289-1551	3983
Kidde-Fenwal Inc **(HQ)**	Ashland	MA	A	508 881-2000	7663
Temp-Pro Incorporated	Northampton	MA	E	413 584-3165	14022
United Electric Controls Co	Watertown	MA	D	617 926-1000	16327
Digitry Company Inc **(PA)**	Portland	ME	G	207 774-0300	6652
Paper Thermometer Co Inc	Manchester	NH	G	603 547-2034	18897

INDL PROCESS INSTRUMENTS: Thermistors

	CITY	ST	EMP	PHONE	ENTRY #
Advanced Thermal Solutions Inc **(PA)**	Norwood	MA	E	781 769-2800	14123

INDL PROCESS INSTRUMENTS: Water Quality Monitoring/Cntrl Sys

	CITY	ST	EMP	PHONE	ENTRY #
Danaher Tool Group	Wallingford	CT	F	203 284-7000	4732
Aqua Solutions Inc	Middleboro	MA	G	508 947-5777	13053
Atlantic Metalcraft Co	Middleboro	MA	G	781 447-9900	13054
City of Chicopee	Chicopee	MA	G	413 594-1870	10013
E Gs Gauging Incorporated	Wilmington	MA	G	978 663-2300	16999
Ecochlor Inc	Maynard	MA	G	978 298-1463	12898
Evoqua Water Technologies LLC	Tewksbury	MA	E	978 863-4600	15817
Water Analytics Inc	Andover	MA	F	978 749-9949	7618
Watertech International	Woburn	MA	G	781 592-8224	17315
Aqua Specialties	Northwood	NH	G	603 942-5671	19411
Northern RI Conservation Dst	Johnston	RI	G	401 934-0840	20526

INDL SALTS WHOLESALERS

	CITY	ST	EMP	PHONE	ENTRY #
Blank Industries Inc	Hudson	MA	F	855 887-3123	11759

INDL SPLYS WHOLESALERS

	CITY	ST	EMP	PHONE	ENTRY #
Automation Inc	West Hartford	CT	F	860 236-5991	5054
Barker Steel LLC	South Windsor	CT	E	860 282-1860	3943
Dayton Bag & Burlap Co	East Granby	CT	G	860 653-8191	1125
Kell-Strom Tool Intl Inc	Wethersfield	CT	E	860 529-6851	5254
Ruby Automation LLC **(HQ)**	Bloomfield	CT	C	860 687-5000	258
Ruby Industrial Tech LLC **(PA)**	Bloomfield	CT	D	860 687-5000	260
Spectrum Associates Inc	Milford	CT	F	203 878-4618	2307
Sperry Automatics Co Inc	Naugatuck	CT	E	203 729-4589	2497
Stanley Black & Decker Inc	New Britain	CT	E	860 225-5111	2583
A1a Steel LLC	East Falmouth	MA	G	774 763-2503	10432
Airgas Usa LLC	Billerica	MA	E	978 439-1344	8207
Esco Technologies Inc	Holliston	MA	E	508 429-4441	11570
Joma Diamond Tool Company	East Longmeadow	MA	F	413 525-0760	10481
Kinefac Corporation	Worcester	MA	D	508 754-6901	17401
M E Baker Company **(PA)**	Framingham	MA	F	508 620-5304	10979
AC Electric Corp	Bangor	ME	F	207 945-9487	5628
Deepwater Buoyancy Inc	Biddeford	ME	F	207 468-2565	5728
Micronics Filtration LLC **(HQ)**	Portsmouth	NH	C	603 433-1299	19596
New Hmpshire Ball Bearings Inc	Peterborough	NH	E	603 924-3311	19479
Ar-Ro Engineering Company Inc **(PA)**	North Smithfield	RI	G	401 766-6669	20781
W L Fuller	Warwick	RI	E	401 467-2900	21441

INDL SPLYS, WHOL: Fasteners, Incl Nuts, Bolts, Screws, Etc

	CITY	ST	EMP	PHONE	ENTRY #
Spirol International Corp **(HQ)**	Danielson	CT	C	860 774-8571	1018
Standard Lock Washer & Mfg Co	Worcester	MA	E	508 757-4508	17481

INDL SPLYS, WHOLESALE: Abrasives

	CITY	ST	EMP	PHONE	ENTRY #
Meister Abrasives Usa Inc	North Kingstown	RI	F	401 294-4503	20727

INDL SPLYS, WHOLESALE: Bearings

	CITY	ST	EMP	PHONE	ENTRY #
Kaman Aerospace Corporation	Bloomfield	CT	E	860 242-4461	231
Kaman Corporation **(PA)**	Bloomfield	CT	D	860 243-7100	234
Capeway Bearing & Machine Inc	Plymouth	MA	G	508 747-2800	14548

INDL SPLYS, WHOLESALE: Drums, New Or Reconditioned

	CITY	ST	EMP	PHONE	ENTRY #
Clarks Steel Drum Company	Medford	MA	G	781 396-1109	12926

INDL SPLYS, WHOLESALE: Electric Tools

	CITY	ST	EMP	PHONE	ENTRY #
Kalman Electric Motors Inc	Stoughton	MA	G	781 341-4900	15600

INDL SPLYS, WHOLESALE: Filters, Indl

	CITY	ST	EMP	PHONE	ENTRY #
Tinny Corporation	Middletown	CT	E	860 854-6121	2228
Lapoint Industries Inc **(PA)**	Auburn	ME	D	207 777-3100	5575

INDL SPLYS, WHOLESALE: Gaskets

	CITY	ST	EMP	PHONE	ENTRY #
Boston Atlantic Corp	Worcester	MA	F	508 754-4076	17350

INDL SPLYS, WHOLESALE: Gaskets & Seals

	CITY	ST	EMP	PHONE	ENTRY #
Worcester Indus Rbr Sup Co Inc	Holden	MA	G	508 853-2332	11551

INDL SPLYS, WHOLESALE: Power Transmission, Eqpt & Apparatus

	CITY	ST	EMP	PHONE	ENTRY #
Altra Industrial Motion Corp **(PA)**	Braintree	MA	B	781 917-0600	8986
Warner Electric	Braintree	MA	G	781 917-0600	9048

INDL SPLYS, WHOLESALE: Rubber Goods, Mechanical

	CITY	ST	EMP	PHONE	ENTRY #
Applied Rubber & Plastics Inc	Windsor	CT	F	860 987-9018	5321
Gordon Rubber and Pkg Co Inc	Derby	CT	E	203 735-7441	1072
Opac Inc **(PA)**	Smithfield	RI	G	401 231-3552	21242

INDL SPLYS, WHOLESALE: Seals

	CITY	ST	EMP	PHONE	ENTRY #
Dichtomatik Americas LP	Manchester	NH	G	603 628-7030	18809
Niantic Seal Inc	Lincoln	RI	E	401 334-6870	20588

INDL SPLYS, WHOLESALE: Signmaker Eqpt & Splys

	CITY	ST	EMP	PHONE	ENTRY #
US Highway Products Inc	Bridgeport	CT	F	203 336-0332	502

INDL SPLYS, WHOLESALE: Springs

	CITY	ST	EMP	PHONE	ENTRY #
Lee Spring Company LLC	Bristol	CT	E	860 584-0991	576
Leggett & Platt Incorporated	Oxford	MA	E	508 987-8706	14265

INDL SPLYS, WHOLESALE: Tools

	CITY	ST	EMP	PHONE	ENTRY #
Mrse	West Brookfield	MA	F	508 867-5083	16472
Vacuum Pressing Systems Inc	Brunswick	ME	G	207 725-0935	5850
Zampini Industrial Group LLC	Lincoln	RI	G	401 305-7997	20602

INDL SPLYS, WHOLESALE: Tools, NEC

	CITY	ST	EMP	PHONE	ENTRY #
Nelson Apostle Inc	Hartford	CT	G	860 953-4633	1850
Safe T Cut Inc	Monson	MA	F	413 267-9984	13211

INDL SPLYS, WHOLESALE: Valves & Fittings

	CITY	ST	EMP	PHONE	ENTRY #
Carlyle Johnson Machine Co LLC **(PA)**	Bolton	CT	E	860 643-1531	276
Crosby Valve & Gage Intl Inc	Mansfield	MA	D	508 384-3121	12624
L & B Associates Inc	Saint Albans	VT	G	802 868-5210	22371

INDL TOOL GRINDING SVCS

	CITY	ST	EMP	PHONE	ENTRY #
M & M Carbide Inc	Southington	CT	G	860 628-2002	4063

INDUCTORS

	CITY	ST	EMP	PHONE	ENTRY #
Henkel Loctite Corporation **(DH)**	Rocky Hill	CT	E	860 571-5100	3714
Rcd Components LLC **(HQ)**	Manchester	NH	D	603 666-4627	18909

INERTIAL GUIDANCE SYSTEMS

	CITY	ST	EMP	PHONE	ENTRY #
Qualtre Inc **(HQ)**	Sudbury	MA	E	508 658-8360	15666

INFORMATION RETRIEVAL SERVICES

	CITY	ST	EMP	PHONE	ENTRY #
Ebsco Publishing Inc **(HQ)**	Ipswich	MA	A	978 356-6500	11917
Homeportfolio Inc	Newton	MA	D	617 559-1197	13602
Research Cmpt Consulting Svcs **(PA)**	Canton	MA	G	781 821-1221	9774
Ellsworth American Inc	Ellsworth	ME	D	207 667-2576	6018
Grolen Communications Inc	Manchester	NH	G	603 645-0101	18831
Caledonian Record Pubg Co Inc **(PA)**	Saint Johnsbury	VT	D	802 748-8121	22389

INFRARED OBJECT DETECTION EQPT

	CITY	ST	EMP	PHONE	ENTRY #
Brandstrom Instruments Inc	Ridgefield	CT	E	203 544-9341	3661
Sensor Switch Inc **(DH)**	New Haven	CT	E	203 265-2842	2737
Flir Systems Boston Inc **(HQ)**	North Billerica	MA	B	978 901 8000	13815
Sensarray Infrared Corporation	Medford	MA	G	781 306-0338	12948

INK OR WRITING FLUIDS

	CITY	ST	EMP	PHONE	ENTRY #
American Ink & Oil Corporation	Norwood	MA	G	781 762-0026	14129
Dispersion Services LLC	Nashua	NH	G	603 577-9520	19146

INK: Gravure

	CITY	ST	EMP	PHONE	ENTRY #
Gem Gravure Co Inc **(PA)**	Hanover	MA	D	781 878-0456	11339

INK: Lithographic

	CITY	ST	EMP	PHONE	ENTRY #
Gotham Ink of New England Inc	Marlborough	MA	G	508 485-7911	12762

INK: Printing

	CITY	ST	EMP	PHONE	ENTRY #
Hubergroup Usa Inc	Windsor	CT	F	860 687-1617	5338
Superior Printing Ink Co Inc	Hamden	CT	E	203 281-1921	1786
A I C Inc **(PA)**	Georgetown	MA	E	978 352-4510	11135
Actega North America Inc	Shrewsbury	MA	G	508 845-6600	15097
Brian Leopold	Carver	MA	G	508 465-0345	9802
Coatings Adhesives Inks	Georgetown	MA	E	978 352-7273	11140

	CITY	ST	EMP	PHONE	ENTRY #
Flint Group US LLC	Rockland	MA	F	781 763-0600	14803
Fry Company J M	Canton	MA	G	781 575-1520	9734
Keystone Printing Ink Co	Norwood	MA	G	781 762-6974	14170
RPM Wood Finishes Group Inc	Westfield	MA	F	413 562-9655	16724
Superior Printing Ink Co Inc	Marlborough	MA	E	508 481-8250	12833
Universal Color Corp Inc	Wilmington	MA	F	978 658-2300	17061
Graphic Utilities Incorporated	Limestone	ME	F	207 370-9178	6340
Ink Mill Corp	Belmont	NH	F	603 217-4144	17674
Wikoff Color Corporation	Hudson	NH	F	603 864-6456	18452

INSECT LAMPS: Electric

	CITY	ST	EMP	PHONE	ENTRY #
Armatron International Inc **(PA)**	Malden	MA	D	781 321-2300	12559

INSECTICIDES

	CITY	ST	EMP	PHONE	ENTRY #
Chemtura Receivables LLC	Waterbury	CT	G	203 573-3327	4856
Lynwood Laboratories Inc	Needham	MA	G	781 449-6776	13304

INSECTICIDES & PESTICIDES

	CITY	ST	EMP	PHONE	ENTRY #
Bedoukian Research Inc **(PA)**	Danbury	CT	E	203 830-4000	877
Tick Box Technology Corp	Norwalk	CT	G	203 852-7171	3256
Munters Moisture Control Svcs	Amesbury	MA	G	978 388-4900	7499
Northern Turf Prfessionals Inc	Brunswick	ME	G	207 522-8598	5843
Pine State Pest Solutions Inc	Auburn	ME	G	207 795-1100	5590
Bio-Concept Laboratories Inc	Salem	NH	E	603 437-4990	19713
Tender Corporation **(PA)**	Littleton	NH	D	603 444-5464	18667

INSPECTION & TESTING SVCS

	CITY	ST	EMP	PHONE	ENTRY #
Eastern Connecticut	Willimantic	CT	F	860 423-1972	5263
Accumet Engineering Corp	Hudson	MA	E	978 568-8311	11750
Aetruim Incorporated	Billerica	MA	E	651 773-4200	8205
Etec Inc	West Roxbury	MA	E	617 477-4308	16495
Massachusetts Mtls Tech LLC **(PA)**	Weston	MA	G	617 500-8325	16827
Massachusetts Mtls Tech LLC	Cambridge	MA	G	617 502-5636	9549
Sst Components Inc **(PA)**	Billerica	MA	E	978 670-7300	8298
Wafer Inspection Services Inc	Orleans	MA	G	508 944-2851	14245
B and R Modern Hand Tool Inc	Portland	ME	G	207 773-6706	6615
Fiber Materials Inc **(HQ)**	Biddeford	ME	E	207 282-5911	5733

INSTRUMENT DIALS: Painted

	CITY	ST	EMP	PHONE	ENTRY #
Envirocare Corporation **(PA)**	North Andover	MA	G	978 658-0123	13702

INSTRUMENTS & ACCESSORIES: Surveying

	CITY	ST	EMP	PHONE	ENTRY #
Data Technology Inc	Tolland	CT	E	860 871-8082	4545

INSTRUMENTS & METERS: Measuring, Electric

	CITY	ST	EMP	PHONE	ENTRY #
Altek Electronics Inc	Torrington	CT	C	860 482-7626	4558
Omega Engineering Inc	Norwalk	CT	D	714 540-4914	3212
Axiam Inc **(PA)**	Gloucester	MA	G	978 281-3550	11163
B C Ames Incorporated	Framingham	MA	G	781 893-0095	10924
Inventronics Inc	Tyngsboro	MA	G	978 649-9040	15891
Krohn-Hite Corporation	Brockton	MA	F	508 580-1660	9160
Magnos Incorporated	Hudson	MA	G	978 562-1173	11790
Ocean Industries LLC	Hudson	NH	G	603 622-2481	18421
Red Nun Instrument Corporation	Bridport	VT	G	802 758-6000	21759

INSTRUMENTS, LAB: Spectroscopic/Optical Properties Measuring

	CITY	ST	EMP	PHONE	ENTRY #
Block Engineering LLC	Southborough	MA	E	508 480-9643	15348
Boston Piezo-Optics Inc	Bellingham	MA	F	508 966-4988	8032
EMD Millipore Corporation	Taunton	MA	B	781 533-5754	15748
Rigaku Analytical Devices Inc	Wilmington	MA	E	781 328-1024	17041
Hindsight Imaging Inc	Freeport	ME	G	607 793-3762	6080
Hindsight Imaging Inc	Manchester	NH	G	607 793-3762	18833

INSTRUMENTS, LABORATORY: Amino Acid Analyzers

	CITY	ST	EMP	PHONE	ENTRY #
Biochrom Us Inc	Holliston	MA	G	508 893-8999	11560

INSTRUMENTS, LABORATORY: Analyzers, Automatic Chemical

	CITY	ST	EMP	PHONE	ENTRY #
Millennium Research Labs Inc	Woburn	MA	G	781 935-0790	17233
American Healthcare	Scarborough	ME	F	888 567-7733	6904

INSTRUMENTS, LABORATORY: Analyzers, Thermal

	CITY	ST	EMP	PHONE	ENTRY #
Hamilton Sndstrnd Space	Windsor Locks	CT	A	860 654-6000	5395
Biomass Commodities Corp	Williamstown	MA	G	413 458-5326	16955
Spectris Inc **(HQ)**	Westborough	MA	F	508 768-6400	16650
Ta Instruments-Waters LLC **(PA)**	Wakefield	MA	F	781 233-1717	15980

INSTRUMENTS, LABORATORY: Blood Testing

	CITY	ST	EMP	PHONE	ENTRY #
General Fluidics Corporation	Waltham	MA	G	617 543-3114	16118
Nova Biomedical Corporation **(PA)**	Waltham	MA	A	781 894-0800	16162
Siemens Hlthcare Dgnostics Inc	Norwood	MA	C	781 269-3000	14199
Idexx Laboratories Inc **(PA)**	Westbrook	ME	A	207 556-0300	7191

INSTRUMENTS, LABORATORY: Dust Sampling & Analysis

	CITY	ST	EMP	PHONE	ENTRY #
Wafer Inspection Services Inc	Orleans	MA	G	508 944-2851	14245

INSTRUMENTS, LABORATORY: Infrared Analytical

	CITY	ST	EMP	PHONE	ENTRY #
Cam2 Technologies LLC	Danbury	CT	G	203 456-3025	884
Long Life Saunas	Bowdoinham	ME	G	802 349-0501	5789

INSTRUMENTS, LABORATORY: Integrators, Mathematical

	CITY	ST	EMP	PHONE	ENTRY #
Studio of Engaging Learning	Brighton	MA	G	617 975-0268	9107

INSTRUMENTS, LABORATORY: Liquid Chromatographic

	CITY	ST	EMP	PHONE	ENTRY #
Cohesive Technologies Inc **(HQ)**	Franklin	MA	E	508 528-7989	11028

INSTRUMENTS, LABORATORY: Magnetic/Elec Properties Measuring

	CITY	ST	EMP	PHONE	ENTRY #
Madison Technology Intl	Mystic	CT	G	860 245-0245	2442
M R Resources Inc	Fitchburg	MA	E	978 696-3060	10831

INSTRUMENTS, LABORATORY: Mass Spectrometers

	CITY	ST	EMP	PHONE	ENTRY #
New Objective Inc	Woburn	MA	F	781 933-9560	17244

INSTRUMENTS, LABORATORY: Mass Spectroscopy

	CITY	ST	EMP	PHONE	ENTRY #
Czitek LLC	Danbury	CT	G	888 326-8186	896
Real-Time Analyzers Inc	Middletown	CT	G	860 635-9800	2218
Viken Detection Corporation	Burlington	MA	E	617 467-5526	9353

INSTRUMENTS, LABORATORY: Measuring, Specific Ion

	CITY	ST	EMP	PHONE	ENTRY #
Dewetron Inc	East Greenwich	RI	F	401 284-3750	20360

INSTRUMENTS, LABORATORY: Protein Analyzers

	CITY	ST	EMP	PHONE	ENTRY #
Bone Biologics Corporation **(PA)**	Boston	MA	G	732 661-2224	8420
Mtoz Biolabs Inc	Cambridge	MA	E	617 401-8103	9571
President Fllows Hrvard Cllege	Cambridge	MA	C	617 495-4043	9617
Elution Technologies LLC	Colchester	VT	G	802 540-0296	21862

INSTRUMENTS, LABORATORY: Spectrometers

	CITY	ST	EMP	PHONE	ENTRY #
Bruker Axs Inc	Billerica	MA	F	978 663-3660	8221
Bruker Daltonics Inc	Billerica	MA	G	978 663-2548	8224
Bruker Optics Inc **(HQ)**	Billerica	MA	E	978 901-1528	8227
Bruker Scientific LLC **(HQ)**	Billerica	MA	C	978 667-9580	8228
Minuteman Laboratories Inc	Chelmsford	MA	F	978 263-2632	9917
Spectros Instruments Inc	Hopedale	MA	G	508 478-1648	11683
Teledyne Instruments Inc	Hudson	NH	D	603 886-8400	18447

INSTRUMENTS, LABORATORY: Ultraviolet Analytical

	CITY	ST	EMP	PHONE	ENTRY #
Honle Uv America Inc	Marlborough	MA	G	508 229-7774	12773

INSTRUMENTS, MEASURING & CNTRG: Plotting, Drafting/Map Rdg

	CITY	ST	EMP	PHONE	ENTRY #
United Innovations Inc	Holyoke	MA	F	413 533-7500	11663

INSTRUMENTS, MEASURING & CNTRL: Auto Turnstiles

	CITY	ST	EMP	PHONE	ENTRY #
Q-Lane Turnstiles LLC	Sandy Hook	CT	F	860 410-1801	3745

INSTRUMENTS, MEASURING & CNTRL: Geophysical & Meteorological

	CITY	ST	EMP	PHONE	ENTRY #
Pmd Scientific Inc	Bloomfield	CT	G	860 242-8177	252
Doble Engineering Company	Hinesburg	VT	C	802 482-2255	22022

INSTRUMENTS, MEASURING & CNTRL: Geophysical/Meteorological

	CITY	ST	EMP	PHONE	ENTRY #
Nortekusa Inc	Boston	MA	G	617 205-5750	8739

INSTRUMENTS, MEASURING & CNTRL: Radiation & Testing, Nuclear

	CITY	ST	EMP	PHONE	ENTRY #
Mirion Tech Canberra Inc **(HQ)**	Meriden	CT	B	203 238-2351	2109
Princeton Security Tech Inc **(HQ)**	Franklin	MA	G	609 924-7310	11074
Princton Gamma-Tech Instrs Inc	Franklin	MA	F	609 924-7310	11075
Radiation Monitoring Dvcs Inc **(HQ)**	Watertown	MA	E	617 668-6800	16310
Raywatch Inc	West Roxbury	MA	G	401 338-2211	16502
Motorway Engineering Inc	Manchester	NH	F	603 668-6315	18878

INSTRUMENTS, MEASURING & CNTRL: Tester, Acft Hydc Ctrl Test

	CITY	ST	EMP	PHONE	ENTRY #
American Design & Mfg Inc	South Windsor	CT	E	860 282-2719	3935

INSTRUMENTS, MEASURING & CNTRL: Testing, Abrasion, Etc

	CITY	ST	EMP	PHONE	ENTRY #
Electro-Methods Inc **(PA)**	South Windsor	CT	C	860 289-8661	3962
Chauvin Arnoux Inc	Foxboro	MA	F	508 698-2115	10878
Illinois Tool Works Inc	Norwood	MA	B	781 828-2500	14160
Lawrence Instron Corporation	Norwood	MA	C	781 828-2500	14174
Chauvin Arnoux Inc **(PA)**	Dover	NH	E	603 749-6434	18012
Nexus Technology Inc	Nashua	NH	F	877 595-8116	19216

INSTRUMENTS, MEASURING & CNTRLG: Aircraft & Motor Vehicle

	CITY	ST	EMP	PHONE	ENTRY #
Bauer Inc	Bristol	CT	D	860 583-9100	531
Harcosemco LLC	Branford	CT	C	203 483-3700	322
Simmonds Precision Pdts Inc	Danbury	CT	E	203 797-5000	994
Foster-Miller Inc	Devens	MA	D	781 684-4000	10320
Allard Nazarian Group Inc **(PA)**	Manchester	NH	C	603 668-1900	18774
ARC Technology Solutions LLC	Nashua	NH	E	603 883-3027	19117
Textron Inc **(PA)**	Providence	RI	B	401 421-2800	21134
Simmonds Precision Pdts Inc **(DH)**	Vergennes	VT	A	802 877-4000	22556

INSTRUMENTS, MEASURING & CNTRLG: Chronometers, Electronic

	CITY	ST	EMP	PHONE	ENTRY #
Nix Inc	Allston	MA	G	617 458-9407	7472

INSTRUMENTS, MEASURING & CNTRLG: Detectors, Scintillation

	CITY	ST	EMP	PHONE	ENTRY #
Scintitech Inc	Shirley	MA	G	978 425-0800	15093

INSTRUMENTS, MEASURING & CNTRLG: Thermometers/Temp Sensors

	CITY	ST	EMP	PHONE	ENTRY #
Semco Instruments Inc **(DH)**	Branford	CT	C	661 257-2000	347
Advanced Mechanical Tech Inc **(PA)**	Watertown	MA	E	617 923-4174	16263
Auburn Filtersense LLC	Beverly	MA	E	978 777-2460	8103
Insense Medical LLC	Hopkinton	MA	G	518 316-4759	11722
Spectris Inc **(HQ)**	Westborough	MA	F	508 768-6400	16650

INSTRUMENTS, MEASURING & CNTRLNG: Levels & Tapes, Surveying

	CITY	ST	EMP	PHONE	ENTRY #
Miracle Instruments Co	Lebanon	CT	F	860 642-7745	1936

INSTRUMENTS, MEASURING & CNTRLNG: Nuclear Instrument Modules

	CITY	ST	EMP	PHONE	ENTRY #
Judge Tool & Gage Inc	Stratford	CT	G	800 214-5990	4426
Advanced Measurement Tech Inc	Woburn	MA	D	781 938-7800	17111

INSTRUMENTS, MEASURING & CNTRLNG: Press & Vac Ind, Acft Eng

	CITY	ST	EMP	PHONE	ENTRY #
Kearflex Engineering Company	Warwick	RI	F	401 781-4900	21382

INSTRUMENTS, MEASURING & CNTRLNG: Wind Direction Indicators

	CITY	ST	EMP	PHONE	ENTRY #
Cape Cod Wind Wther Indicators	Harwich Port	MA	G	508 432-9475	11398

INSTRUMENTS, MEASURING & CONTROLLING: Gas Detectors

	CITY	ST	EMP	PHONE	ENTRY #
Sperian Protectn Instrumentatn	Middletown	CT	C	860 344-1079	2225
Environmental Svcs Group Inc	Medway	MA	E	508 533-7683	12959
Ion Track Instruments LLC	Wilmington	MA	D	978 658-3767	17007

INSTRUMENTS, MEASURING & CONTROLLING: Ion Chambers

	CITY	ST	EMP	PHONE	ENTRY #
Axcelis Technologies Inc **(PA)**	Beverly	MA	C	978 787-4000	8106

INSTRUMENTS, MEASURING & CONTROLLING: Leak Detection, Liquid

	CITY	ST	EMP	PHONE	ENTRY #
On Grade USA	Northborough	MA	G	508 351-9480	14042

INSTRUMENTS, MEASURING & CONTROLLING: Magnetometers

	CITY	ST	EMP	PHONE	ENTRY #
Magnetic Sciences Inc	Acton	MA	G	978 266-9355	7372

INSTRUMENTS, MEASURING & CONTROLLING: Reactor Controls, Aux

	CITY	ST	EMP	PHONE	ENTRY #
Quantek Instruments	Grafton	MA	G	508 839-0108	11224
Thermo Process Instruments LP	Franklin	MA	C	508 553-6913	11089

INSTRUMENTS, MEASURING & CONTROLLING: Spectrometers

	CITY	ST	EMP	PHONE	ENTRY #
Waters Corporation **(PA)**	Milford	MA	C	508 478-2000	13153
Waters Technologies Corp **(HQ)**	Milford	MA	A	508 478-2000	13154

INSTRUMENTS, MEASURING & CONTROLLING: Surveying & Drafting

	CITY	ST	EMP	PHONE	ENTRY #
Ocean Data Equipment Corp	Warwick	RI	F	401 454-1810	21397

INSTRUMENTS, MEASURING & CONTROLLING: Ultrasonic Testing

	CITY	ST	EMP	PHONE	ENTRY #
Technisonic Research Inc	Fairfield	CT	G	203 368-3600	1457
TLC Ultrasound Inc	New Milford	CT	G	860 354-6333	2830
CTS Valpey Corporation **(HQ)**	Hopkinton	MA	E	508 435-6831	11699
Spire Metering Technology LLC	Marlborough	MA	F	978 263-7100	12829
Proteq Solutions LLC	Nashua	NH	F	603 888-6630	19241

INSTRUMENTS, MEASURING & CONTROLLING: Weather Tracking

	CITY	ST	EMP	PHONE	ENTRY #
Rainwise Inc	Trenton	ME	E	800 762-5723	7101
Wuersch Time Inc	Coventry	RI	G	401 828-2525	20170
Alken Inc	Colchester	VT	E	802 655-3159	21856

INSTRUMENTS, MEASURING/CNTRL: Gauging, Ultrasonic Thickness

	CITY	ST	EMP	PHONE	ENTRY #
Power-Dyne LLC	Middletown	CT	E	860 346-9283	2211
Ade Technologies Inc **(HQ)**	Westwood	MA	D	781 467-3500	16857

INSTRUMENTS, MEASURING/CNTRL: Hydrometers, Exc Indl Process

	CITY	ST	EMP	PHONE	ENTRY #
Kerfoot Technologies Inc	Mashpee	MA	F	508 539-3002	12881

INSTRUMENTS, MEASURING/CNTRLG: Fire Detect Sys, Non-Electric

	CITY	ST	EMP	PHONE	ENTRY #
Bojak Company	Milford	CT	G	203 378-5086	2255

INSTRUMENTS, MEASURING/CNTRLG: Pulse Analyzers, Nuclear Mon

	CITY	ST	EMP	PHONE	ENTRY #
Anova Data Inc	Westford	MA	G	978 577-6600	16753

INSTRUMENTS, MEASURING/CNTRLNG: Med Diagnostic Sys, Nuclear

	CITY	ST	EMP	PHONE	ENTRY #
Biotech Diagnostics	Newton	MA	G	617 332-8787	13570
G T C Falcon Inc	Plymouth	MA	F	508 746-0200	14560
IDS Imaging Dev Systems Inc	Stoneham	MA	F	781 787-0048	15565
Newton-Wellesley Health Care	Newton	MA	F	617 726-2142	13618
Microvision Inc	Seabrook	NH	E	603 474-5566	19810

INSTRUMENTS, OPTICAL: Boards, Plot, Spot/Gun Fire Adjust

	CITY	ST	EMP	PHONE	ENTRY #
Semigen Inc	Londonderry	NH	E	603 624-8311	18735

INSTRUMENTS, OPTICAL: Borescopes

	CITY	ST	EMP	PHONE	ENTRY #
Instrument Technology Inc	Westfield	MA	E	413 562-3512	16690
Zibra Corporation	Westport	MA	F	508 636-6606	16853

INSTRUMENTS, OPTICAL: Contour Projectors

	CITY	ST	EMP	PHONE	ENTRY #
Lenco Inc	Rutland	VT	E	802 775-2505	22344

INSTRUMENTS, OPTICAL: Elements & Assemblies, Exc Ophthalmic

	CITY	ST	EMP	PHONE	ENTRY #
Adaptive Optics Associates Inc	East Hartford	CT	F	860 282-4401	1170
Nano Beam Technologies	Lexington	MA	G	617 548-9495	12246
Opticraft Inc	Woburn	MA	E	781 938-0456	17250
Transom Scopes Inc	Westfield	MA	E	413 562-3606	16737
Chroma Technology Corp	Bellows Falls	VT	C	802 428-2500	21650

INSTRUMENTS, OPTICAL: Gratings, Diffraction

	CITY	ST	EMP	PHONE	ENTRY #
Plymouth Grating Lab Inc	Carver	MA	F	508 465-2274	9806

INSTRUMENTS, OPTICAL: Lenses, All Types Exc Ophthalmic

	CITY	ST	EMP	PHONE	ENTRY #
Optical Research Technologies	Wilton	CT	G	203 762-9063	5296
Orafol Americas Inc	Avon	CT	C	860 676-7100	41
Retina Systems Inc	Seymour	CT	E	203 881-1311	3763
Adaptive Optics Associates Inc	Devens	MA	F	978 757-9600	10316
Adaptive Optics Associates Inc **(DH)**	Devens	MA	D	978 757-9600	10317
AMF Optical Solutions LLC	Woburn	MA	G	781 933-6125	17118
Bern Optics Inc	Westfield	MA	E	413 568-6800	16674
Eidolon Corporation	Natick	MA	G	781 400-0586	13253
J P Mfg Inc	Southbridge	MA	E	508 764-2538	15389
Newport Corporation	Wilmington	MA	D	978 296-1306	17030
Opco Laboratory Inc	Fitchburg	MA	E	978 345-2522	10846
Optometrics Corporation	Littleton	MA	E	978 772-1700	12316
Bond Optics LLC	Lebanon	NH	E	603 448-2300	18616
General Dynamics Mission	Nashua	NH	C	603 864-6300	19165
Janos Technology LLC	Keene	NH	C	603 757-0070	18508
Silicon Sense Inc	Nashua	NH	G	603 891-4248	19261

INSTRUMENTS, OPTICAL: Magnifying, NEC

	CITY	ST	EMP	PHONE	ENTRY #
Scope Technology Inc	Plainfield	CT	F	860 963-1141	3457

INSTRUMENTS, OPTICAL: Mirrors

	CITY	ST	EMP	PHONE	ENTRY #
Flabeg Technical Glass US Corp	Naugatuck	CT	E	203 729-5227	2473
Hardric Laboratories Inc	North Chelmsford	MA	E	978 251-1702	13895

INSTRUMENTS, OPTICAL: Prisms

	CITY	ST	EMP	PHONE	ENTRY #
Guild Optical Associates Inc	Amherst	NH	F	603 889-6247	17567

INSTRUMENTS, OPTICAL: Reflectors

	CITY	ST	EMP	PHONE	ENTRY #
Nanoptek Corporation	Shirley	MA	G	978 460-7107	15091

INSTRUMENTS, OPTICAL: Test & Inspection

	CITY	ST	EMP	PHONE	ENTRY #
4 D Technology Corporation	East Hampton	CT	G	860 365-0420	1154
Abet Technologies Inc	Milford	CT	G	203 540-9990	2234
Enos Engineering LLC	Acton	MA	G	978 654-6522	7353
KLA Corporation	Williston	VT	F	802 318-9100	22677

INSTRUMENTS, SURGICAL & MED: Needles & Syringes, Hypodermic

	CITY	ST	EMP	PHONE	ENTRY #
Becton Dickinson and Company	Canaan	CT	B	860 824-5487	683
Connecticut Hypodermics Inc	Wallingford	CT	D	203 265-4881	4725
Medical Instrument Technology	Hyannis	MA	G	508 775-8682	11849
Cadence Science Inc	Cranston	RI	C	401 942-1031	20193

INSTRUMENTS, SURGICAL & MED: Otoscopes, Exc Electromedical

	CITY	ST	EMP	PHONE	ENTRY #
Firefly Global	Belmont	MA	G	781 835-6548	8074

INSTRUMENTS, SURGICAL & MEDI: Knife Blades/Handles, Surgical

	CITY	ST	EMP	PHONE	ENTRY #
Microspecialities Inc	Middletown	CT	F	203 874-1832	2205
Beaver-Visitec Intl Inc **(HQ)**	Waltham	MA	C	781 906-8080	16044
Beaver-Visitec Intl Inc	Waltham	MA	G	847 739-3219	16045

INSTRUMENTS, SURGICAL & MEDICAL: Biopsy

	CITY	ST	EMP	PHONE	ENTRY #
Lorad Corporation	Danbury	CT	C	203 790-5544	950
Intact Medical Corporation	Framingham	MA	E	508 655-7820	10969

INSTRUMENTS, SURGICAL & MEDICAL: Blood & Bone Work

	CITY	ST	EMP	PHONE	ENTRY #
E M M Inc	Madison	CT	E	203 245-0306	1960
Furnace Source LLC	Terryville	CT	F	860 582-4201	4479
Newmark Medical Components Inc	Waterbury	CT	F	203 753-1158	4928
Cheetah Medical Inc **(PA)**	Newton	MA	E	617 964-0613	13577
Conformis Inc **(PA)**	Billerica	MA	C	781 345-9001	8232
David Clark Company Inc **(PA)**	Worcester	MA	C	508 756-6216	17362
Etex Corporation	Braintree	MA	E	617 577-7270	9006
Haemonetics Asia Incorporated **(HQ)**	Braintree	MA	G	781 848-7100	9015
Haemonetics Corporation **(PA)**	Braintree	MA	A	781 848-7100	9016
Hemedex Inc	Waltham	MA	F	617 577-1759	16126
Hightech American Indus Labs	Lexington	MA	E	781 862-9884	12229
Hologic Inc	Marlborough	MA	C	508 263-2900	12769
Hologic Inc **(PA)**	Marlborough	MA	C	508 263-2900	12771
Isolux LLC	Danvers	MA	G	978 774-9136	10226
Medical Cmpression Systems Inc	Concord	MA	G	800 377-5804	10140
Photo Diagnostic Systems Inc	Boxborough	MA	E	978 266-0420	8966
SRS Medical Corp	North Billerica	MA	G	978 663-2800	13867
Stryker Corporation	Hopkinton	MA	B	508 416-5200	11739
Insphero Inc	Brunswick	ME	G	800 779-7558	5838
Biomedical Structures LLC	Warwick	RI	E	401 223-0990	21336

INSTRUMENTS, SURGICAL & MEDICAL: Blood Pressure

	CITY	ST	EMP	PHONE	ENTRY #
Cas Medical Systems Inc	Branford	CT	G	203 315-6953	301

INSTRUMENTS, SURGICAL & MEDICAL: Blood Transfusion

	CITY	ST	EMP	PHONE	ENTRY #
Novatek Medical Inc	Stamford	CT	G	203 356-0156	4263
Medtronic Inc	Danvers	MA	F	978 739-3080	10239
Medtronic Inc	Danvers	MA	F	978 777-0042	10240

INSTRUMENTS, SURGICAL & MEDICAL: Catheters

	CITY	ST	EMP	PHONE	ENTRY #
Synectic Engineering Inc	Milford	CT	F	203 877-8488	2374
Cardiofocus Inc	Marlborough	MA	E	508 658-7200	12735
Clinical Instruments Intl	Burlington	MA	F	781 221-2266	9251
Medtrnic Intrvntnal Vsclar Inc	Danvers	MA	A	978 777-0042	10238
Portela Soni Medical LLC	Attleboro	MA	G	508 818-2727	7780
Viamed Corp	South Easton	MA	F	508 238-0220	15294
Microcatheter Components LLC	Jaffrey	NH	G	603 532-0345	18473

INSTRUMENTS, SURGICAL & MEDICAL: Hemodialysis

	CITY	ST	EMP	PHONE	ENTRY #
Fresenius Med Care Rnal Thrpie	Waltham	MA	G	781 699-9000	16111
Mds Nxstage Corporation **(DH)**	Lawrence	MA	E	866 697-8243	12050
Human Biomed Inc	South Burlington	VT	G	802 556-1394	22448

INSTRUMENTS, SURGICAL & MEDICAL: Holders, Surgical Needle

	CITY	ST	EMP	PHONE	ENTRY #
Dale Medical Products Inc **(PA)**	Franklin	MA	C	508 695-9316	11035

INSTRUMENTS, SURGICAL & MEDICAL: IV Transfusion

	CITY	ST	EMP	PHONE	ENTRY #
Smiths Medical Asd Inc	Southington	CT	B	860 621-9111	4078
Ivenix Inc	North Andover	MA	E	978 775-8050	13711

INSTRUMENTS, SURGICAL & MEDICAL: Inhalators

	CITY	ST	EMP	PHONE	ENTRY #
Convexity Scientific LLC	Fairfield	CT	G	949 637-1216	1425
Therapeutic Innovations Inc	North Attleboro	MA	G	347 754-0252	13784

INSTRUMENTS, SURGICAL & MEDICAL: Knives

	CITY	ST	EMP	PHONE	ENTRY #
Nu-Lustre Finishing Corp	Providence	RI	D	401 521-7800	21079

INSTRUMENTS, SURGICAL & MEDICAL: Lasers, Surgical

	CITY	ST	EMP	PHONE	ENTRY #
Aroma Spa & Laser Center Inc	Westford	MA	G	978 685-8883	16754
Legacy Medical Solutions LLC	Tyngsboro	MA	G	978 655-6007	15893
Palomar Medical Tech LLC **(DH)**	Burlington	MA	E	781 993-2330	9317
Atlantic Laser Clinic	York	ME	G	207 854-8200	7305

INSTRUMENTS, SURGICAL & MEDICAL: Muscle Exercise, Ophthalmic

	CITY	ST	EMP	PHONE	ENTRY #
STA Fit For Women LLC	Keene	NH	G	603 357-8880	18528

INSTRUMENTS, SURGICAL & MEDICAL: Needles, Suture

	CITY	ST	EMP	PHONE	ENTRY #
Needletech Products Inc	North Attleboro	MA	C	508 431-4000	13767
Surgical Specialties Corp **(HQ)**	Westwood	MA	C	781 751-1000	16876
Precision Electrolysis Needles	Barrington	RI	F	401 246-1155	20052

INSTRUMENTS, SURGICAL & MEDICAL: Ophthalmic

	CITY	ST	EMP	PHONE	ENTRY #
Avedro Inc **(HQ)**	Waltham	MA	D	781 768-3400	16040
Beaver-Visitec Intl Holdings **(PA)**	Waltham	MA	F	847 739-3219	16043
Deerfield Corporation	Framingham	MA	G	508 877-0143	10941
Integrated Ophthalmic Sys	Woburn	MA	G	617 571-8238	17205
Intelon Optics Inc	Lexington	MA	G	310 980-3087	12232

INSTRUMENTS, SURGICAL & MEDICAL: Physiotherapy, Electrical

	CITY	ST	EMP	PHONE	ENTRY #
Arctic Holdings LLC	West Harwich	MA	G	978 535-5351	16480
Functional Assessment Tech Inc	North Billerica	MA	F	978 663-2800	13817
SRS Medical Systems Inc **(PA)**	North Billerica	MA	E	978 663-2800	13868
Luv2bu Inc	Cranston	RI	G	401 612-9585	20256

INSTRUMENTS, SURGICAL & MEDICAL: Retractors

	CITY	ST	EMP	PHONE	ENTRY #
Plenoptika Inc **(PA)**	Cambridge	MA	G	617 862-2203	9612

INSTRUMENTS, SURGICAL & MEDICAL: Stapling Devices, Surgical

	CITY	ST	EMP	PHONE	ENTRY #
Southington Tool & Mfg Corp	Plantsville	CT	E	860 276-0021	3540

INSTRUMENTS, SURGICAL & MEDICAL: Suction Therapy

	CITY	ST	EMP	PHONE	ENTRY #
Worldwide Innvtive Hlthcare In	Cambridge	MA	G	646 694-2273	9705

INSTRUMENTS, SURGICAL/MED: Bronchoscopes, Exc Electromedical

	CITY	ST	EMP	PHONE	ENTRY #
Lenses Only LLC	Bloomfield	CT	F	860 769-2020	239
Eyenetra Inc	Cambridge	MA	G	973 229-3341	9477

INSTRUMENTS, SURGICAL/MED: Microsurgical, Exc Electromedical

	CITY	ST	EMP	PHONE	ENTRY #
Ceek Enterprises Inc	Melrose	MA	G	919 522-4837	12976
Qesidyne Inc	Hudson	NH	G	603 883-3116	18431

INSTRUMENTS: Airspeed

	CITY	ST	EMP	PHONE	ENTRY #
Mtu Aero Engines N Amer Inc	Rocky Hill	CT	G	860 258-9700	3724

INSTRUMENTS: Analytical

	CITY	ST	EMP	PHONE	ENTRY #
Alpha 1c LLC	Sherman	CT	G	860 354-7979	3892
Applied Biosystems LLC	Norwalk	CT	G	781 271-0045	3102
Buck Scientific Inc	Norwalk	CT	D	203 853-9444	3116
Carestream Health Molecular	New Haven	CT	E	888 777-2072	2674
Connecticut Analytical Corp	Bethany	CT	F	203 393-9666	119
Designs & Prototypes Ltd	Simsbury	CT	G	860 658-0458	3899
Energy Beam Sciences Inc	East Granby	CT	F	860 653-0411	1126
Idex Health & Science LLC	Bristol	CT	C	860 314-2880	570
Ihs Herold Inc **(DH)**	Norwalk	CT	D	203 857-0215	3171
Industrial Analytics Corp	Madison	CT	G	203 245-0380	1966
K A F Manufacturing Co Inc	Stamford	CT	E	203 324-3012	4234
Owlstone Inc **(PA)**	Westport	CT	G	203 908-4848	5221
Perkinelmer Inc	Shelton	CT	G	203 925-4600	3851
Perkinelmer Hlth Sciences Inc	Shelton	CT	C	203 925-4600	3852
Spectral LLC **(PA)**	Putnam	CT	G	860 928-7726	3635
Tomtec Inc	Hamden	CT	D	203 281-6790	1790
Trajan Scientific Americas Inc	Bethel	CT	G	203 830-4910	184
Wentworth Laboratories Inc	Brookfield	CT	G	203 775-9311	666
AB Sciex LLC	Framingham	MA	G	508 383-7300	10914
AB Sciex Sales LP	Framingham	MA	D	508 383-7700	10915
Acton Research Corporation	Acton	MA	E	941 556-2601	7334
Advanced Instruments LLC **(PA)**	Norwood	MA	D	781 320-9000	14122
Advanced Thermal Solutions Inc **(PA)**	Norwood	MA	E	781 769-2800	14123
Amnis Corporation	Billerica	MA	G	206 374-7000	8208
Andor Technology Inc	Concord	MA	E	978 405-1116	10109
Antec (usa) LLC	Boston	MA	G	888 572-0012	8367
Applied Biosystems LLC	Bedford	MA	F	781 271-0045	7958
Applied Biosystems LLC	Framingham	MA	G	508 877-1307	10922
Autogen Inc	Holliston	MA	E	508 429-5965	11557
Balaji International Inc	North Easton	MA	G	508 472-1953	13942
Behavioral Research Tools	Boston	MA	G	802 578-4874	8399
Bel Legacy Corporation	Boston	MA	C	508 923-5000	8400
Biomerieux Inc	Boston	MA	G	617 879-8000	8411
Bruker Biospin Mri Inc	Billerica	MA	F	978 667-9580	8222
Bruker Corporation **(PA)**	Billerica	MA	C	978 663-3660	8223
Bruker Enrgy Supercon Tech Inc **(HQ)**	Billerica	MA	G	978 901-7550	8226
Caliper Life Sciences Inc **(DH)**	Hopkinton	MA	C	203 954-9442	11694
Cape Bioresearch Inc	East Falmouth	MA	G	413 658-5426	10437
Covaris Inc **(PA)**	Woburn	MA	E	781 932-3959	17154
Day Zero Diagnostics Inc	Allston	MA	G	857 770-1125	7463
Doble Engineering Company **(HQ)**	Watertown	MA	F	617 926-4900	16279
Duke River Engineering Co	Newton	MA	G	617 965-7255	13586
EMD Millipore Corporation	Burlington	MA	B	800 854-3417	9263
EMD Millipore Corporation	Burlington	MA	D	978 715-4321	9264
EMD Millipore Corporation	Bedford	MA	C	781 533-6000	7973
EMD Millipore Corporation	Bedford	MA	C	781 533-6000	7974
EMD Millipore Corporation	Danvers	MA	E	978 762-5100	10215
Eyepoint Pharmaceuticals Inc **(PA)**	Watertown	MA	E	617 926-5000	16287
Fluid Management Systems Inc	Watertown	MA	E	617 393-2396	16288
Galvanic Applied Sciences	North Billerica	MA	F	978 848-2701	13818
Genomic Solutions Inc	Holliston	MA	E	734 975-4800	11572
Gnr USA Instruments LLC	Foxboro	MA	G	508 698-3816	10884
Harvard Bioscience Inc **(PA)**	Holliston	MA	C	508 893-8999	11575
Headwall Photonics Inc **(PA)**	Fitchburg	MA	F	978 353-4040	10829
High Voltage Engineering Corp	Wakefield	MA	F	781 224-1001	15954
Illinois Tool Works Inc	Norwood	MA	B	781 828-2500	14160
Imaging W Varex Holdings Inc	Waltham	MA	G	781 663-6900	16129
International Light Tech Inc	Peabody	MA	E	978 818-6180	14343
Ionsense Inc	Saugus	MA	F	781 231-1739	14987
Izon Science US Ltd	Medford	MA	G	617 945-5936	12937
Janis Research Company Inc **(PA)**	Woburn	MA	D	781 491-0888	17208
Janis Research Company LLC	Woburn	MA	D	781 491-0888	17209
Jeol Usa Inc **(HQ)**	Peabody	MA	C	978 535-5900	14345
Jsi Medical Systems Corp	Boston	MA	G	917 472-5022	8643
Krohn-Hite Corporation	Brockton	MA	F	508 580-1660	9160
Kt Assocs Inc	Cambridge	MA	G	617 547-3737	9529
Leica Biosystems	Danvers	MA	F	978 471-0625	10232
Life Technologies Corporation	Framingham	MA	F	508 383-7700	10976
Listen Inc	Boston	MA	F	617 556-4104	8668
Magellan Diagnostics Inc **(HQ)**	Chelmsford	MA	D	978 250-7000	9915
Magellan Diagnostics Inc	North Billerica	MA	E	978 856-2345	13838
Matec Instrument Companies Inc **(PA)**	Northborough	MA	E	508 393-0155	14038
Mettler-Toledo Intl Inc	Newton	MA	G	800 472-4646	13614
Nanosurf Inc	Woburn	MA	G	781 549-7361	17235
New England Photoconductor	Norton	MA	F	508 285-5561	14084
Nova Instruments LLC **(PA)**	Wakefield	MA	G	781 897-1200	15966
Omniprobe Inc	Concord	MA	E	214 572-6800	10148
On-Site Analysis Inc **(DH)**	Chelmsford	MA	G	561 775-5756	9918
Organomation Associates Inc	Berlin	MA	F	978 838-7300	8092
Particles Plus Inc **(PA)**	Stoughton	MA	F	781 341-6898	15613
Pelagic Electronics	East Falmouth	MA	G	508 540-1200	10446
Perkinelmer Inc	Cambridge	MA	G	617 577-7744	9609
Perkinelmer Inc	Hopkinton	MA	F	508 435-9500	11731
Perkinelmer Inc	Arlington	MA	G	617 350-9440	7633
Perkinelmer Inc	Boston	MA	E	617 596-9909	8776
Perkinelmer Hlth Sciences Inc	North Billerica	MA	E	617 350-9024	13855
Perkinelmer Holdings Inc **(HQ)**	Wellesley	MA	G	781 663-6900	16380
Philips North America LLC	Natick	MA	C	508 647-1130	13271
Photonics N Picoquant Amer Inc	West Springfield	MA	G	413 562-6161	16542
Photonis Scientific Inc **(DH)**	Sturbridge	MA	D	508 347-4000	15646
Precision Systems Inc	Natick	MA	E	508 655-7010	13274
Proveris Scientific Corp	Hudson	MA	E	508 460-8822	11809
Resonance Research Inc	Billerica	MA	E	978 671-0811	8291
Schoeffel International Corp	Chelmsford	MA	E	978 256-4512	9931
Sciaps Inc **(PA)**	Woburn	MA	E	339 222-2585	17291
Semilab USA LLC	North Billerica	MA	F	508 647-8400	13863
Sirius Analytical Inc	Billerica	MA	G	978 338-5790	8295
Skyray Instrument Inc	Braintree	MA	F	617 202-3879	9037
Specs Tii Inc	Mansfield	MA	G	508 618-1292	12661
Spectra Analysis Inc **(PA)**	Marlborough	MA	F	508 281-6232	12827
Spectra Analysis Instrs Inc	Marlborough	MA	F	508 281-6233	12828
Spectral Evolution Inc	Haverhill	MA	G	978 687-1833	11474
Thermo Envmtl Instrs LLC **(HQ)**	Franklin	MA	C	508 520-0430	11086
Thermo Fisher Scientific Inc **(PA)**	Waltham	MA	C	781 622-1000	16213
Thermo Fisher Scientific Inc	Amherst	MA	B	413 577-2600	7527
Thermo Fisher Scientific Inc	Framingham	MA	G	978 735-3091	11007
Thermo Fisher Scientific Inc	Chelmsford	MA	F	978 250-7000	9936
Thermo Fisher Scientific Inc	Tewksbury	MA	G	781 622-1000	15843
Thermo Fisher Scientific Inc	Bedford	MA	C	781 280-5600	8017
Thermo Fisher Scientific Inc	Billerica	MA	E	978 667-4016	8304
Thermo Fisher Scientific Inc	Franklin	MA	F	508 520-0430	11087
Thermo Fisher Scientific Inc	Danvers	MA	G	978 223-1540	10262
Thermo Keytek LLC	Tewksbury	MA	D	978 275-0800	15844
Thermo Orion Inc **(HQ)**	Chelmsford	MA	E	800 225-1480	9937
Thermo Scntfic Prtble Anlytcal **(HQ)**	Tewksbury	MA	C	978 657-5555	15845
Thoratec Corporation	Burlington	MA	D	781 272-0139	9346
Thrive Bioscience Inc	Wakefield	MA	G	978 720-8048	15981
Union Biometrica Inc **(PA)**	Holliston	MA	E	508 893-3115	11610
Verosound Inc	Sudbury	MA	G	978 440-7898	15672
Virogen Corp	Watertown	MA	G	617 926-9167	16329
Waters Technologies Corp	Franklin	MA	E	508 482-4807	11097
Waveguide Corporation	Cambridge	MA	G	617 892-9700	9699
Williamson Corporation	Concord	MA	E	978 369-9607	10163
Allan Fuller	Benton	ME	G	603 886-5555	5703
Artel Inc	Westbrook	ME	E	207 854-0860	7180
Bio RAD Lab	Portland	ME	G	207 615-0571	6622
Dirigo Analytics LLC	Kennebunk	ME	G	978 376-5522	6232
Fhc Inc **(PA)**	Bowdoin	ME	D	207 666-8190	5787
Fluid Imaging Technologies Inc	Scarborough	ME	E	207 289-3200	6917
Idexx Distribution Inc	Westbrook	ME	D	207 556-0637	7190
Allen Datagraph Systems Inc	Salem	NH	E	603 216-6344	19705
Diversified Enterprises-ADT	Claremont	NH	G	603 543-0038	17847
EMD Millipore Corporation	Jaffrey	NH	B	603 532-8711	18462
Flir Systems Inc	Nashua	NH	G	866 636-4487	19162
Hiden Analytical Inc **(DH)**	Peterborough	NH	G	603 924-5008	19472
Integra Biosciences Corp	Hudson	NH	F	603 578-5800	18401

	CITY	ST	EMP	PHONE	ENTRY #
Labsphere Inc	North Sutton	NH	C	603 927-4266	19392
M Braun Inc	Stratham	NH	D	603 773-9333	19872
Metavac LLC	Portsmouth	NH	E	631 207-2344	19595
Microelectrodes Inc	Bedford	NH	G	603 668-0692	17654
Opti-Sciences Inc	Hudson	NH	G	603 883-4400	18424
Poly-Vac Inc	Manchester	NH	C	603 647-7822	18903
Teledyne Instrs Leeman Labs	Hudson	NH	D	603 521-3299	18446
Thermo Fisher Scientific Inc	Portsmouth	NH	B	603 433-7676	19625
Thermo Fisher Scientific Inc	Hudson	NH	G	603 595-0505	18448
Thermo Fisher Scientific Inc	Portsmouth	NH	G	603 431-8410	19626
Hanna Instruments Inc **(PA)**	Woonsocket	RI	E	401 765-7500	21567
Thermo Fisher Scientific Inc	North Kingstown	RI	G	401 294-1234	20745
Biotek Instruments Inc **(HQ)**	Winooski	VT	D	802 655-4040	22717
Living Systems Instrumentation	Burlington	VT	G	802 863-5547	21794
Med Associates Inc **(PA)**	Fairfax	VT	D	802 527-2343	21977

INSTRUMENTS: Analyzers, Radio Apparatus, NEC

	CITY	ST	EMP	PHONE	ENTRY #
Gold Line Connector Inc **(PA)**	Redding	CT	E	203 938-2588	3648

INSTRUMENTS: Analyzers, Spectrum

	CITY	ST	EMP	PHONE	ENTRY #
Spectrum Services	Pelham	NH	G	603 635-2439	19447

INSTRUMENTS: Colonoscopes, Electromedical

	CITY	ST	EMP	PHONE	ENTRY #
Door Step Prep LLC	West Hartford	CT	G	860 550-0460	5066
Cape Colon Hydrotherapy	East Sandwich	MA	G	508 833-9855	10505
Colonic Connection	Peterborough	NH	G	603 924-4449	19470

INSTRUMENTS: Combustion Control, Indl

	CITY	ST	EMP	PHONE	ENTRY #
Global Fire Products Inc	Boston	MA	G	617 750-1125	8567

INSTRUMENTS: Digital Panel Meters, Electricity Measuring

	CITY	ST	EMP	PHONE	ENTRY #
Analogic Corporation	Peabody	MA	F	978 977-3000	14312
Brewer Electric & Utilities In	South Yarmouth	MA	E	508 771-2040	15325

INSTRUMENTS: Drafting

	CITY	ST	EMP	PHONE	ENTRY #
Spiroll International Corp	Cambridge	MA	G	617 876-8141	9659

INSTRUMENTS: Electrocardiographs

	CITY	ST	EMP	PHONE	ENTRY #
Infobionic Inc	Waltham	MA	E	978 674-8304	16133

INSTRUMENTS: Electroencephalographs

	CITY	ST	EMP	PHONE	ENTRY #
Axio Inc	Leeds	MA	G	413 552-8355	12097
Emri Systems LLP	Cambridge	MA	G	617 417-9798	9465
Hydrodot Inc	Acton	MA	G	978 399-0206	7362
Mindsciences Inc	Worcester	MA	G	516 658-2985	17418
Neuroelectrics Corporation	Cambridge	MA	G	617 390-6447	9579

INSTRUMENTS: Electrolytic Conductivity, Laboratory

	CITY	ST	EMP	PHONE	ENTRY #
Prospect Products Incorporated	Newington	CT	E	860 666-0323	2896

INSTRUMENTS: Electron Test Tube

	CITY	ST	EMP	PHONE	ENTRY #
Fitzhugh Electrical Corp	Guilford	CT	G	203 453-3171	1704
Iworx Systems Inc	Dover	NH	F	603 742-2492	18030

INSTRUMENTS: Electronic, Analog-Digital Converters

	CITY	ST	EMP	PHONE	ENTRY #
ARS Products LLC	Plainfield	CT	E	860 564-0208	3449
Durridge Company Inc	Billerica	MA	F	978 667-9556	8239
Pitman An AGFA Company	Andover	MA	G	800 526-5441	7584
Hoyt Elec Instr Works Inc	Concord	NH	D	603 753-6321	17909
Omni Measurement Systems Inc	Colchester	VT	E	802 497-2253	21875
Synapse Ic Llc	Winooski	VT	G	802 881-4028	22725

INSTRUMENTS: Endoscopic Eqpt, Electromedical

	CITY	ST	EMP	PHONE	ENTRY #
American Dream Unlimited LLC	Andover	CT	G	860 742-5055	2
American Optics Limited	Wellesley Hills	MA	F	905 631-5377	16395
Myriad Fiber Imaging Tech Inc	Dudley	MA	F	508 949-3000	10382
Photonview Technologies	Newton	MA	G	781 366-4836	13626
Solos Endoscopy Inc	Boston	MA	G	617 360-9700	8852

INSTRUMENTS: Eye Examination

	CITY	ST	EMP	PHONE	ENTRY #
United Ophthalmics LLC	Meriden	CT	G	203 745-8399	2144
Cognex Germany Inc	Natick	MA	C	508 650-3000	13248
M R P Group Inc (de)	Lawrence	MA	G	978 687-7979	12049
Robert Tyszko Od Pllc	Peterborough	NH	G	603 924-9591	19486

INSTRUMENTS: Flow, Indl Process

	CITY	ST	EMP	PHONE	ENTRY #
Cidra Chemical Management Inc **(HQ)**	Wallingford	CT	D	203 265-0035	4717
Cidra Mineral Processing Inc	Wallingford	CT	D	203 265-0035	4720
Accusonic Technologies **(DH)**	New Bedford	MA	F	508 495-6600	13348
CDI Meters Inc	Woburn	MA	G	508 867-3178	17141
Data Industrial Corporation	Mattapoisett	MA	E	508 758-6390	12886
Teledyne Instruments Inc	Hampton	NH	D	603 474-5571	18273

INSTRUMENTS: Frequency Meters, Electrical, Mech & Electronic

	CITY	ST	EMP	PHONE	ENTRY #
CTS Valpey Corporation **(HQ)**	Hopkinton	MA	E	508 435-6831	11699

INSTRUMENTS: Humidity, Indl Process

	CITY	ST	EMP	PHONE	ENTRY #
Edgetech Instruments Inc	Hudson	MA	F	508 263-5900	11769

INSTRUMENTS: Indicating, Electric

	CITY	ST	EMP	PHONE	ENTRY #
Oslo Switch Inc	Cheshire	CT	E	203 272-2794	750

INSTRUMENTS: Indl Process Control

	CITY	ST	EMP	PHONE	ENTRY #
AKO Inc	Windsor	CT	E	860 298-9765	5317
Alloy Engineering Co Inc **(PA)**	Bridgeport	CT	E	203 366-5253	369
Ametek Inc	Wallingford	CT	C	203 265-6731	4699
Appleton Grp LLC	East Granby	CT	E	860 653-1603	1117
Clinton Instrument Company	Clinton	CT	E	860 669-7548	780
Devar Inc	Bridgeport	CT	E	203 368-6751	405
Differential Pressure Plus	Branford	CT	G	203 481-2545	309
Faria Beede Instruments Inc	North Stonington	CT	C	860 848-9271	3074
Fleet Management LLC	Enfield	CT	G	800 722-6654	1363
GE Steam Power Inc **(HQ)**	Windsor	CT	A	866 257-8664	5336
H & B Tool & Engineering Co	South Windsor	CT	E	860 528-9341	3976
Haydon Kerk Mtion Slutions Inc	Waterbury	CT	C	203 756-7441	4883
Idex Health & Science LLC	Bristol	CT	C	860 314-2880	570
Innovative Components LLC	Plantsville	CT	G	860 621-7220	3533
Johnson Gage Company	Bloomfield	CT	E	860 242-5541	229
Kaman Aerospace Corporation	Middletown	CT	C	860 632-1000	2195
Lee Company	Westbrook	CT	E	860 399-6281	5158
Lq Mechatronics Inc	Branford	CT	G	203 433-4430	328
Minteq International Inc	Canaan	CT	C	860 824-5435	689
National Magnetic Sensors Inc	Plantsville	CT	G	860 621-6816	3537
Omega Engineering Inc	Stamford	CT	G	203 359-7922	4269
Projects Inc	Glastonbury	CT	C	860 633-4615	1574
RA Smythe LLC	Middletown	CT	G	860 398-5764	2216
Sperian Protectn Instrumentatn	Middletown	CT	C	860 344-1079	2225
Tek-Air Systems Inc	Monroe	CT	E	203 791-1400	2418
Veeder-Root Company **(HQ)**	Weatogue	CT	D	860 651-2700	5045
Vertiv Corporation	Wallingford	CT	F	203 294-6020	4827
Wentworth Laboratories Inc	Brookfield	CT	G	203 775-9311	666
Adcole Corporation **(HQ)**	Marlborough	MA	C	508 485-9100	12710
Ametek Arizona Instrument LLC	Middleboro	MA	C	508 946-6200	13051
Amphenol Advanced Sensors	Billerica	MA	G	978 294-8300	8209
B C Ames Incorporated	Framingham	MA	G	781 893-0095	10924
Bae Systems Info & Elec Sys	Lexington	MA	B	603 885-4321	12208
Big Belly Solar Inc	Needham Heights	MA	E	888 820-0300	13319
Cape Cod Wind Wther Indicators	Harwich Port	MA	G	508 432-9475	11398
Chemtrac Systems	Groton	MA	G	978 448-0061	11286
Cimetrics Inc	Boston	MA	D	617 350-7550	8475
Cognex Corporation	Natick	MA	G	508 650-3044	13247
D 2 Incorporated	Bourne	MA	G	508 329-2046	8945
Dolan-Jenner Industries Inc	Boxborough	MA	E	978 263-1400	8961
Druck LLC **(HQ)**	Billerica	MA	C	978 437-1000	8238
Dynisco Instruments LLC **(HQ)**	Franklin	MA	C	508 541-9400	11037
Emerson Electric Co	Mansfield	MA	G	774 266-4136	12632
Emerson Process Management	Lawrence	MA	C	978 689-2800	12022
Entegris Inc	Billerica	MA	F	978 436-6500	8247
Finesse Solutions Inc	Newburyport	MA	G	978 255-1296	13488
GE Panametrics Inc	Billerica	MA	G	978 670-6454	8250
Gefran Isi Inc	North Andover	MA	E	781 729-0842	13708
Hamilton Storage Tech Inc **(DH)**	Franklin	MA	E	508 544-7000	11051
High Voltage Maintenance Corp	Walpole	MA	F	508 668-9205	15993
Impolit Envmtl Ctrl Corp	Beverly	MA	E	978 927-4619	8140
Industrial Biomedical Sensors	Waltham	MA	F	781 891-4201	16132
Instrument & Valve Services Co	Shrewsbury	MA	G	508 842-7000	15118
Invensys Systems Argentina	Foxboro	MA	E	508 543-8750	10889
Invetech Inc	Boxborough	MA	D	508 475-3400	8964
Jowa Usa Inc	Littleton	MA	E	978 486-9800	12311
Kadant Fibergen Inc **(HQ)**	Bedford	MA	F	781 275-3600	7986
KPM Analytics North Amer Corp **(PA)**	Milford	MA	E	508 473-9901	13123
Liquid Metronics Incorporated	Acton	MA	C	978 263-9800	7369
LS Starrett Company **(PA)**	Athol	MA	A	978 249-3551	7689
M & K Industries Inc	Leominster	MA	E	978 514-9850	12164
Mettler-Toledo Intl Inc	Newton	MA	G	800 472-4646	13614
Mks Instruments Inc	Andover	MA	E	978 738-3721	7576
Mks Instruments Inc	Lawrence	MA	C	978 975-2350	12058
Nova Instruments Corporation **(PA)**	Woburn	MA	G	781 897-1200	17247
Onset Computer Corporation	Bourne	MA	C	508 759-9500	8948
Patriot Worldwide Inc	Holliston	MA	G	800 786-4669	11595
Performance Motion Devices Inc	Westford	MA	E	978 266-1210	16783
Phoenix Electric Corp	Canton	MA	E	781 821-0200	9767
Schneider Elc Systems USA Inc	Foxboro	MA	F	508 543-8750	10901
Schneider Elc Systems USA Inc	Foxboro	MA	F	508 543-8750	10902
Sensitech Inc **(DH)**	Beverly	MA	D	978 927-7033	8177
Set Americas Inc	Easthampton	MA	G	413 203-6130	10578
Setra Systems Inc	Boxboro	MA	F	978 263-1400	8954
Tecomet Inc	Woburn	MA	D	781 782-6400	17305
Teknikor Automtn & Contrls Inc	Fall River	MA	F	508 679-9474	10771
Test Evolution Corporation	Hopkinton	MA	G	508 377-5757	11740
Thermedetec Inc	Waltham	MA	A	508 520-0430	16212
Thermo Envmtl Instrs LLC **(HQ)**	Franklin	MA	C	508 520-0430	11086
Thermo Fisher Scientific Inc **(PA)**	Waltham	MA	C	781 622-1000	16213
Thermo Fisher Scientific Inc	Wilmington	MA	D	978 275-0800	17055
Thermo Optek Corporation	Franklin	MA	A	508 553-5100	11088
Thermo Orion Inc **(HQ)**	Chelmsford	MA	E	800 225-1480	9937
Thermo Process Instruments LP	Franklin	MA	C	508 553-6913	11089
Verify LLC	Cambridge	MA	F	513 285-7258	9694
Walker Magnetics Group Inc	Worcester	MA	F	774 670-1423	17503
Wilmington Research & Dev Corp	Newburyport	MA	G	978 499-0100	13549
David Saunders Inc	South Portland	ME	E	207 228-1888	7021
Montalvo Corporation	Gorham	ME	E	207 856-2501	6122
Bantry Components Inc	Manchester	NH	E	603 668-3210	18785
Ellab Inc	Nashua	NH	G	603 417-3363	19148
Jewell Instruments LLC **(PA)**	Manchester	NH	C	603 669-5121	18850
L3harris Technologies Inc	Nashua	NH	E	603 689-1450	19195
Madgetech Inc **(PA)**	Warner	NH	E	603 456-2011	19928
Memtec Corporation	Salem	NH	E	603 893-8080	19751
Monarch International Inc	Amherst	NH	E	603 883-3390	17577
Nelson Robotics Corp	Concord	NH	G	603 856-7421	17915
Pneucleus Technologies LLC	Hollis	NH	G	603 921-5300	18338
Praecis Inc	West Lebanon	NH	G	603 277-9288	19959
Unarco Material Handling Inc	Exeter	NH	E	603 772-2070	18134
Valde Systems Inc	Brookline	NH	G	603 577-1728	17774
Coldstash Inc	West Greenwich	RI	G	617 780-5603	21453

PRODUCT

	CITY	ST	EMP	PHONE	ENTRY #
Crest Manufacturing Company	Lincoln	RI	E	401 333-1350	20566
E H Benz Co Inc	Providence	RI	G	401 331-5650	20999
Hanna Instruments Inc **(PA)**	Woonsocket	RI	E	401 765-7500	21567
Hexagon Holdings Inc **(DH)**	North Kingstown	RI	G	401 886-2000	20715
Hexagon Metrology Inc **(DH)**	North Kingstown	RI	B	401 886-2000	20716
Honeywell International Inc	Woonsocket	RI	E	401 769-7274	21570
Sgri Inc	Warwick	RI	G	401 473-7320	21425
Doble Engineering Company	Hinesburg	VT	C	802 482-2255	22022
Isotech North America Inc	Colchester	VT	G	802 863-8050	21868
Lord Corporation **(DH)**	Williston	VT	D	802 862-6629	22680
Senix Corporation	Hinesburg	VT	F	802 489-7300	22030
Vermont Precision Tools Inc **(PA)**	Swanton	VT	C	802 868-4246	22538

INSTRUMENTS: Infrared, Indl Process

	CITY	ST	EMP	PHONE	ENTRY #
Singularity Space Systems LLC	Granby	CT	G	860 713-3626	1591
Flir Systems-Boston Inc **(HQ)**	North Billerica	MA	B	978 901-8000	13815

INSTRUMENTS: Laser, Scientific & Engineering

	CITY	ST	EMP	PHONE	ENTRY #
Albrayco Technologies Inc	Cromwell	CT	G	860 635-3369	845
Corindus Inc	Waltham	MA	E	508 653-3335	16076
Park Bio Services LLC	Groveland	MA	G	978 794-8500	11303
Pvd Products Inc	Wilmington	MA	F	978 694-9455	17040
Coherent Inc	Salem	NH	F	603 685-0900	19716
Kentek Corporation	Pittsfield	NH	E	603 223-4900	19502
Wilbur Technical Services LLC	Mont Vernon	NH	G	603 880-7100	19094

INSTRUMENTS: Liquid Analysis, Indl Process

	CITY	ST	EMP	PHONE	ENTRY #
Step Ahead Innovations Inc	South Burlington	VT	F	802 233-0211	22468

INSTRUMENTS: Liquid Level, Indl Process

	CITY	ST	EMP	PHONE	ENTRY #
Madison Company **(PA)**	Branford	CT	E	203 488-4477	329

INSTRUMENTS: Measurement, Indl Process

	CITY	ST	EMP	PHONE	ENTRY #
Advanced Control Systems Corp	Canton	MA	G	781 829-9228	9711
Michell Instruments Inc	Rowley	MA	G	978 484-0005	14857
Mj Research Inc **(HQ)**	Waltham	MA	C	510 724-7000	16152
Technlogy Dev Cllaborative LLC	Woburn	MA	G	781 933-6116	17304
Extech Instruments Corporation	Nashua	NH	D	887 439-8324	19152
Fluke Electronics Corporation	Salem	NH	G	603 537-2680	19735
Industrial Marine Elec Inc	Manchester	NH	F	603 434-2309	18842

INSTRUMENTS: Measuring & Controlling

	CITY	ST	EMP	PHONE	ENTRY #
Ai-Tek Instruments LLC	Cheshire	CT	E	203 271-6927	708
Clinton Instrument Company	Clinton	CT	E	860 669-7548	780
Comet Technologies USA Inc **(DH)**	Shelton	CT	E	203 447-3200	3790
Edmunds Manufacturing Company **(PA)**	Farmington	CT	D	860 677-2813	1480
Gems Sensors Inc	Plainville	CT	F	800 378-1600	3492
Gold Line Connector Inc **(PA)**	Redding	CT	E	203 938-2588	3648
Habco Industries LLC	Glastonbury	CT	E	860 682-6800	1556
Hitachi Aloka Medical Ltd	Wallingford	CT	D	203 269-5088	4752
Hitachi Aloka Medical Amer Inc	Wallingford	CT	D	203 269-5088	4753
Image Insight Inc	East Hartford	CT	G	860 528-9806	1202
Jurman Metrics Inc	Monroe	CT	F	203 261-9388	2405
Lex Products LLC **(PA)**	Shelton	CT	C	203 363-3738	3828
Luxpoint Inc	Rocky Hill	CT	G	860 982-9588	3722
Megasonics Inc	New Canaan	CT	G	203 966-3404	2607
Mistras Group Inc	Waterford	CT	E	860 447-2474	4989
Owlstone Inc **(PA)**	Westport	CT	G	203 908-4848	5221
Pratt Whtney Msurement Systems	Bloomfield	CT	E	860 286-8181	254
Preferred Utilities Mfg Corp **(HQ)**	Danbury	CT	D	203 743-6741	974
Semco Instruments Inc	Branford	CT	G	661 362-6117	348
Soldream Inc	Vernon Rockville	CT	E	860 871-6883	4683
Specialty Components Inc	Wallingford	CT	G	203 284-9112	4811
Strain Measurement Devices Inc	Wallingford	CT	E	203 294-5800	4814
Tek-Air Systems Inc	Monroe	CT	E	203 791-1400	2418
Trans-Tek Inc	Ellington	CT	E	860 872-8351	1343
Weigh & Test Systems Inc	Riverside	CT	F	203 698-9681	3693
Abbess Instrs & Systems Inc	Holliston	MA	F	508 429-0002	11555
Accusonic Technologies **(DH)**	New Bedford	MA	F	508 495-6600	13348
Aclara Technologies LLC	Wellesley	MA	E	781 694-3300	16357
Adaptive Wreless Solutions LLC	Hudson	MA	F	978 875-6000	11751
Admet Inc	Norwood	MA	G	781 769-0850	14120
Advanced Thermal Solutions Inc **(PA)**	Norwood	MA	E	781 769-2800	14123
Aja International Inc	Scituate	MA	E	781 545-7365	15005
Ametek Inc	Wilmington	MA	D	978 988-4101	16973
Anderson Power Products Inc **(HQ)**	Sterling	MA	D	978 422-3600	15535
Associated Envmtl Systems Inc **(PA)**	Acton	MA	C	978 772-0022	7342
Barrett Technology LLC	Newton	MA	E	617 252-9000	13566
Blueline NDT LLC	Bedford	MA	G	781 791-9511	7963
Bmi Surplus Inc	Hanover	MA	G	781 871-8868	11328
Capacitec Inc **(PA)**	Ayer	MA	F	978 772-6033	7913
Control Resources Inc	Littleton	MA	E	978 486-4160	12297
Doble Engineering Company **(HQ)**	Watertown	MA	F	617 926-4900	16279
Dynisco Instruments LLC	Billerica	MA	D	978 215-3401	8240
Dynisco Instruments LLC **(HQ)**	Franklin	MA	C	508 541-9400	11037
Dynisco LLC **(HQ)**	Franklin	MA	D	508 541-3195	11038
Electro-Fix Inc	Plainville	MA	E	508 695-0228	14518
Fitbit Inc	Boston	MA	G	857 277-0594	8549
Gefran Isi Inc	North Andover	MA	E	781 729-0842	13708
Grozier Technical Systems Inc	Westwood	MA	G	781 762-4446	16867
Hamilton Thorne Inc **(PA)**	Beverly	MA	E	978 921-2050	8138
Hawk Measurement America LLC **(PA)**	Lawrence	MA	G	978 304-3000	12031
Hefring LLC	Boston	MA	G	617 206-5750	8593
Hitec Products Inc	Pepperell	MA	F	978 772-6963	14438
Ideal Industries Inc	Sterling	MA	C	978 422-3600	15540
Instron Japan Company Ltd	Norwood	MA	B	781 828-2500	14165
Integrated Dynamics Engrg Inc **(HQ)**	Randolph	MA	E	781 326-5700	14687
Intelligent Medical Dvcs Inc	Foxboro	MA	G	617 871-6401	10888
International Light Tech Inc	Peabody	MA	E	978 818-6180	14343
ITW Instron	Norwood	MA	G	781 762-3216	14167
Johnson Controls Inc	Wrentham	MA	E	508 384-0018	17524
Krohn-Hite Corporation	Brockton	MA	F	508 580-1660	9160
Live Cell Technologies LLC	Boston	MA	G	646 662-4157	8669
M R Resources Inc	Fitchburg	MA	E	978 696-3060	10831
Matec Instrument Companies Inc **(PA)**	Northborough	MA	E	508 393-0155	14038
Microsense LLC **(HQ)**	Lowell	MA	E	978 843-7670	12411
Millimeter Wave Systems LLC	Amherst	MA	G	413 345-6467	7519
Mistras Group Inc	Auburn	MA	E	508 832-5500	7844
Mks Instruments Inc	Lawrence	MA	C	978 975-2350	12058
Neotron Inc	Wellesley	MA	G	781 239-3461	16376
On Line Controls Inc	Hudson	MA	G	978 562-5353	11798
Onto Innovation Inc **(PA)**	Wilmington	MA	B	978 253-6200	17032
Oxford Instrs Msrement Systems	Concord	MA	D	978 369-9933	10149
Photonis Scientific Inc **(DH)**	Sturbridge	MA	D	508 347-4000	15646
Pinpoint Laser Systems Inc	Peabody	MA	E	978 532-8001	14362
Prior Scientific Inc **(HQ)**	Rockland	MA	F	781 878-8442	14820
Quadtech Inc	Marlborough	MA	E	978 461-2100	12811
Quality Engineering Assoc Inc	Billerica	MA	F	978 528-2034	8280
Redshift Bioanalytics Inc	Burlington	MA	G	781 345-7300	9329
Rmd Instruments Corp	Watertown	MA	E	617 668-6900	16312
Rotek Instrument Corp	Waltham	MA	E	781 899-4611	16190
Rudolph Technologies Inc **(HQ)**	Wilmington	MA	B	978 253-6200	17042
Schneeberger Inc **(DH)**	Woburn	MA	G	781 271-0140	17290
Schoeffel International Corp	Chelmsford	MA	E	978 256-4512	9931
Sea Machines Robotics Inc **(PA)**	Boston	MA	G	617 455-6266	8841
Second Wind Systems Inc	Newton	MA	F	617 581-6090	13634
Semiconsoft Inc	Southborough	MA	F	617 388-6832	15364
Technical Manufacturing Corp **(HQ)**	Peabody	MA	D	978 532-6330	14376
Teledyne Instruments Inc	North Falmouth	MA	E	508 563-1000	13956
Thermo Electron Karlsruhe GMBH	Tewksbury	MA	G	978 513-3724	15842
Thermo Envmtl Instrs LLC **(HQ)**	Franklin	MA	C	508 520-0430	11086
Thermo Instrument Systems Inc	Waltham	MA	G	781 622-1000	16214
TM Electronics Inc	Devens	MA	F	978 772-0970	10334
Toolmex Indus Solutions Inc **(PA)**	Northborough	MA	D	508 653-5110	14052
Trimble Inc	Marlborough	MA	G	508 381-5800	12838
Vaisala Inc	Newton	MA	D	617 467-1500	13647
Vaisala Inc	Woburn	MA	E	781 933-4500	17312
Verify LLC	Cambridge	MA	F	513 285-7258	9694
Viricor Inc	Sudbury	MA	G	508 733-5537	15673
Wildlife Acoustics Inc	Maynard	MA	G	978 369-5225	12906
X Sonix	Boxborough	MA	G	978 266-2106	8972
Abbott Dgnstics Scrborough Inc **(DH)**	Scarborough	ME	D	207 730-5750	6901
Ibcontrols	Windham	ME	E	207 893-0080	7237
Idexx Distribution Inc	Westbrook	ME	D	207 556-0637	7190
Illinois Tool Works Inc	Mechanic Falls	ME	E	207 998-5140	6420
Intelligent Controls Inc **(HQ)**	Saco	ME	E	207 571-1123	6849
McGuire & Co Inc	Falmouth	ME	G	207 797-3323	6032
Airmar Technology Corp **(PA)**	Milford	NH	B	603 673-9570	19044
Avid Corp	Portsmouth	NH	F	603 559-9700	19541
Cc1 Inc	Portsmouth	NH	E	603 319-2000	19548
Enertrac Inc	Portsmouth	NH	F	603 821-0003	19559
Geophysical Survey Systems Inc **(DH)**	Nashua	NH	D	603 893-1109	19167
Guidewire Technologies Inc	Salem	NH	E	603 894-4399	19740
Hampshire Controls Corporation	Dover	NH	F	603 749-9424	18026
Kimball Physics Inc	Wilton	NH	E	603 878-1616	19981
National Aperture Inc	Salem	NH	F	603 893-7393	19754
Oztek Corp	Merrimack	NH	F	603 546-0090	19018
RDF Corporation	Hudson	NH	D	603 882-5195	18432
Thomas Instruments Inc	Spofford	NH	G	603 363-4500	19858
United Sensor Corp	Amherst	NH	F	603 672-0909	17590
Vibrac LLC **(PA)**	Manchester	NH	F	603 882-6777	18950
Aspects Inc	Warren	RI	E	401 247-1854	21286
Astronova Inc **(PA)**	West Warwick	RI	B	401 828-4000	21479
Atec	Wakefield	RI	G	401 782-6950	21267
Calibrators Inc	Cumberland	RI	G	401 769-0333	20315
Crest Manufacturing Company	Lincoln	RI	E	401 333-1350	20566
Eppley Laboratory Inc	Newport	RI	F	401 847-1020	20664
Honeywell International Inc	Woonsocket	RI	C	401 769-7274	21568
Lindon Group Inc	East Providence	RI	G	401 272-2081	20430
Raytheon Company	Portsmouth	RI	D	401 847-8000	20938
Bowles Corporation	North Ferrisburgh	VT	F	802 425-3447	22225
Ion Science LLC	Waterbury	VT	G	802 244-5153	22583
Microstrain Inc	Williston	VT	F	802 862-6629	22681

INSTRUMENTS: Measuring Electricity

	CITY	ST	EMP	PHONE	ENTRY #
Ashcroft Inc	Stratford	CT	E	203 378-8281	4393
Clinton Instrument Company	Clinton	CT	E	860 669-7548	780
Dictaphone Corporation **(HQ)**	Stratford	CT	C	203 381-7000	4409
Faria Beede Instruments Inc	North Stonington	CT	C	860 848-9271	3074
Habco Industries LLC	Glastonbury	CT	E	860 682-6800	1556
Nutmeg Utility Products Inc **(PA)**	Cheshire	CT	E	203 250-8802	748
Wentworth Laboratories Inc **(PA)**	Brookfield	CT	D	203 775-0448	665
Aclara Technologies LLC	Wellesley	MA	E	781 694-3300	16357
Agilent Technologies Inc	Andover	MA	A	978 794-3664	7534
Agilent Technologies Inc	Chicopee	MA	F	413 593-2900	9998
Agilent Technologies Inc	Lexington	MA	C	781 861-7200	12205
Ametek Inc	Wilmington	MA	D	978 988-4101	16973
Analogic Corporation **(HQ)**	Peabody	MA	A	978 326-4000	14311
Cape Cod Wind Wther Indicators	Harwich Port	MA	G	508 432-9475	11398
Dynisco Instruments LLC **(HQ)**	Franklin	MA	C	508 541-9400	11037
Engement Company Inc	Topsfield	MA	G	978 561-3008	15857
Flintec Inc	Hudson	MA	E	978 562-4548	11774
Ghg Electronic Services	Medford	MA	G	781 391-1147	12934

	CITY	ST	EMP	PHONE	ENTRY #
Gold Line Connector Inc	New Bedford	MA	F	508 999-5656	13391
Hampden Engineering Corp	East Longmeadow	MA	D	413 525-3981	10478
Honeywell Data Instruments Inc	Acton	MA	B	978 264-9550	7361
Ineoquest Technologies Inc **(PA)**	Westwood	MA	C	508 339-2497	16870
Ion Track Instruments LLC	Wilmington	MA	D	978 658-3767	17007
Keysight Technologies Inc	Andover	MA	G	800 829-4444	7561
Kidde-Fenwal Inc **(HQ)**	Ashland	MA	A	508 881-2000	7663
Laser Labs Inc	Pembroke	MA	G	781 826-4138	14415
Lynn Products Co	Lynn	MA	E	781 593-2500	12524
Magcap Engineering LLC	Canton	MA	F	781 821-2300	9754
Magellan Diagnostics Inc **(HQ)**	Chelmsford	MA	D	978 250-7000	9915
Matec Instrument Companies Inc **(PA)**	Northborough	MA	E	508 393-0155	14038
Microsemi Frequency Time Corp	Beverly	MA	D	978 232-0040	8155
Mini-Systems Inc	Plainville	MA	E	508 695-2000	14528
Mks Instruments Inc	Lawrence	MA	C	978 975-2350	12058
Mti-Milliren Technologies Inc	Newburyport	MA	E	978 465-6064	13516
Nanomoleculardx	Pittsfield	MA	F	518 588-7815	14493
Novotechnik US Inc	Southborough	MA	G	508 485-2244	15363
Power Systems Integrity Inc	Northborough	MA	G	508 393-1655	14045
Qorvo Inc	Chelmsford	MA	G	978 770-2158	9923
Relevant Energy Concepts Inc	Springfield	MA	G	413 733-7692	15501
Scully Signal Company **(PA)**	Wilmington	MA	C	617 692-8600	17044
Seahorse Bioscience Inc **(HQ)**	Lexington	MA	E	978 671-1600	12263
Spirent Communications Inc	Southborough	MA	G	774 463-0281	15367
Teledyne Lecroy Inc	Marion	MA	E	508 748-0103	12707
Teradyne Inc	Bedford	MA	C	617 482-2700	8014
Thermo Orion Inc **(HQ)**	Chelmsford	MA	E	800 225-1480	9937
Thermo Scientific Portable Ana	Billerica	MA	C	978 670-7460	8305
Wayne Kerr Electronics Inc	Woburn	MA	G	781 938-8390	17317
Aclara Technologies LLC	Somersworth	NH	F	603 749-8376	19826
Bantry Components Inc	Manchester	NH	E	603 668-3210	18785
Eagle Test Systems Inc	Bedford	NH	F	603 624-5757	17639
Electri-Temp Corporation	Pelham	NH	G	603 422-2509	19432
Electrocraft New Hampshire Inc **(DH)**	Dover	NH	E	603 742-3330	18021
Everett Charles Tech LLC	Hudson	NH	G	603 882-2621	18389
H6 Systems Incorporated	Nashua	NH	G	603 880-4190	19175
Ion Physics Corp	Fremont	NH	G	603 895-5100	18177
Martel Electronics Corp	Derry	NH	E	603 434-6033	17988
Optical Fiber Systems Inc	New Ipswich	NH	G	603 291-0345	19309
Physical Measurement Tech	Marlborough	NH	G	603 876-9990	18964
Calibrators Inc	Cumberland	RI	G	401 769-0333	20315
Everett Charles Tech LLC	Lincoln	RI	F	401 739-7310	20572
Interplex Industries Inc **(DH)**	Rumford	RI	F	718 961-6212	21188
Transmille Calibration Inc	Colchester	VT	G	802 846-7582	21882

INSTRUMENTS: Measuring, Current, NEC

	CITY	ST	EMP	PHONE	ENTRY #
High Voltage Engineering Corp	Wakefield	MA	F	781 224-1001	15954

INSTRUMENTS: Measuring, Electrical Energy

	CITY	ST	EMP	PHONE	ENTRY #
Extech Instruments Corporation	Nashua	NH	D	887 439-8324	19152

INSTRUMENTS: Measuring, Electrical Power

	CITY	ST	EMP	PHONE	ENTRY #
Space Electronics LLC	Berlin	CT	E	860 829-0001	110
Doble Engineering Company **(HQ)**	Watertown	MA	F	617 926-4900	16279
Everett Charles Tech LLC	Nashua	NH	E	603 882-2621	19151
Hanna Instruments Inc **(PA)**	Woonsocket	RI	E	401 765-7500	21567

INSTRUMENTS: Medical & Surgical

	CITY	ST	EMP	PHONE	ENTRY #
109 Design LLC **(PA)**	New Haven	CT	G	203 941-1812	2650
Abbott Associates Inc	Milford	CT	F	203 878-2370	2233
Acme Monaco Corporation **(PA)**	New Britain	CT	C	860 224-1349	2503
Auto Suture Company Australia	Norwalk	CT	G	203 845-1000	3106
Auto Suture Company UK	Norwalk	CT	B	203 845-1000	3107
Auto Suture Russia Inc	Norwalk	CT	G	203 845-1000	3108
Bio-Med Devices Inc	Guilford	CT	D	203 458-0202	1693
Boston Endo-Surgical Tech LLC	Bridgeport	CT	D	203 336-6479	385
Boston Scientific Corporation	Avon	CT	B	860 673-2500	33
C & W Manufacturing Co Inc	Glastonbury	CT	E	860 633-4631	1542
Calmare Therapeutics Inc **(PA)**	Fairfield	CT	G	203 368-6044	1417
Carwild Corporation **(PA)**	New London	CT	E	860 442-4914	2768
Cirtec Medical Corp	Enfield	CT	C	860 814-3973	1349
Clinical Dynamics Conn LLC	Plantsville	CT	G	203 269-0090	3528
Covidien Holding Inc	North Haven	CT	G	203 492-5000	3019
Covidien LP	North Haven	CT	B	203 492-6332	3020
Covidien LP	New Haven	CT	B	781 839-1722	2680
Covidien LP	North Haven	CT	A	203 492-5000	3021
Cygnus Medical LLC	Branford	CT	G	800 990-7489	308
Dcg-Pmi Inc	Bethel	CT	E	203 743-5525	142
Delfin Marketing Inc	Greenwich	CT	G	203 554-2707	1607
Eppendorf Manufacturing Corp	Enfield	CT	C	860 253-3400	1360
Frank Roth Co Inc	Stratford	CT	D	203 377-2155	4413
Gr Enterprises and Tech	Woodbridge	CT	G	203 387-1430	5467
Hitachi Aloka Medical Ltd	Wallingford	CT	D	203 269-5088	4752
Hitachi Aloka Medical Amer Inc	Wallingford	CT	D	203 269-5088	4753
Hobbs Medical Inc	Stafford Springs	CT	E	860 684-5875	4111
Hologic Inc	Danbury	CT	C	203 790-1188	933
Home Diagnostics Corp	Trumbull	CT	C	203 445-1170	4625
Kbc Electronics Inc	Milford	CT	F	203 298-9654	2306
Lambdavision Incorporated	Farmington	CT	G	860 486-6593	1489
Lee Company **(PA)**	Westbrook	CT	A	860 399-6281	5157
Lumendi LLC	Westport	CT	G	203 528-0316	5210
Marel Corporation	West Haven	CT	F	203 934-8187	5135
Medtronic Inc	North Haven	CT	E	203 492-5764	3039
Memry Corporation **(HQ)**	Bethel	CT	C	203 739-1100	170
Memry Corporation	Bethel	CT	G	203 739-1146	171
Monopol Corporation	Bristol	CT	F	860 583-3852	583
Natural Polymer Devices Inc	Farmington	CT	G	860 679-7894	1496
New Wave Surgical Corp	New Haven	CT	E	954 796-4126	2718
Oral Fluid Dynamics LLC	Farmington	CT	G	860 561-5036	1502
Orthozon Technologies LLC	Stamford	CT	G	203 989-4937	4274
Oxford Science Inc	Oxford	CT	F	203 881-3115	3417
Oxford Science Center LLC	Oxford	CT	G	203 751-1912	3418
Precision Engineered Pdts LLC	Bridgeport	CT	G	203 336-6479	473
Precision Metal Products Inc	Milford	CT	C	203 877-4258	2337
Respironics Novametrix LLC	Wallingford	CT	C	203 697-6475	4796
Saar Corporation	Farmington	CT	F	860 674-9440	1511
Sequel Special Products LLC	Wolcott	CT	E	203 759-1020	5459
Spine Wave Inc	Shelton	CT	D	203 944-9494	3873
Stryker Corporation	East Hartford	CT	F	860 528-1111	1224
Summit Orthopedic Tech Inc	Milford	CT	E	203 693-2727	2370
Surgiquest Inc	Milford	CT	D	203 799-2400	2373
Tarry Medical Products Inc	Danbury	CT	F	203 794-1438	998
Tomtec	Orange	CT	G	203 795-5030	3385
Ultimate Wireforms Inc	Bristol	CT	D	860 582-9111	621
Utitec Inc **(HQ)**	Watertown	CT	D	860 945-0605	5032
Utitec Holdings Inc **(PA)**	Watertown	CT	G	860 945-0601	5033
Wallach Surgical Devices Inc **(PA)**	Trumbull	CT	E	203 799-2000	4644
Wallach Surgical Devices Inc	Trumbull	CT	F	800 243-2463	4645
Winslow Automatics Inc	New Britain	CT	D	860 225-6321	2591
3M Company	Haverhill	MA	G	978 420-0001	11403
Accellent Holdings Corp	Wilmington	MA	A	978 570-6900	16962
Accellent LLC **(DH)**	Wilmington	MA	C	978 570-6900	16963
Acuitybio Corporation	Newton	MA	G	617 515-9671	13554
Adoneh LLC	Concord	MA	G	978 618-0389	10107
Advansource Biomaterials Corp	Wilmington	MA	F	978 657-0075	16967
Agile Devices Inc	Boston	MA	G	617 416-5495	8344
Allen Medical Systems Inc **(DH)**	Acton	MA	F	978 263-7727	7338
Angiodynamics Inc	Marlborough	MA	F	508 658-7990	12712
Anika Therapeutics Inc **(PA)**	Bedford	MA	C	781 457-9000	7957
Apogee Technology Inc **(PA)**	Norwood	MA	G	781 551-9450	14132
Applied Tissue Tech LLC	Hingham	MA	G	781 366-3848	11491
Archetype Hardware	Brighton	MA	G	707 303-6003	9094
Arrow Interventional Inc	Chelmsford	MA	E	919 433-4948	9872
Arteriocyte Med Systems Inc	Hopkinton	MA	F	508 497-9350	11690
Atc Technologies Inc **(PA)**	Wilmington	MA	F	781 939-0725	16975
Autocam Medical Inc	Plymouth	MA	E	508 830-1442	14543
AV Medical Technologies Inc	Duxbury	MA	G	612 200-0118	10392
Balancetek Corporation	Watertown	MA	G	781 910-9706	16272
Baril Corporation	Haverhill	MA	E	978 373-7910	11407
Beaver Medical LLC	Natick	MA	G	617 935-3500	13237
Becton Dickinson and Company	Andover	MA	D	978 901-7319	7539
Belmont Instrument LLC **(PA)**	Billerica	MA	E	978 663-0212	8218
Biomerieux Inc	Boston	MA	G	617 879-8000	8411
Bitome Inc	Jamaica Plain	MA	G	207 812-8099	11940
Bl Healthcare Inc	Foxboro	MA	G	508 543-4150	10877
Boston Plstic Oral Srgery Fndt	Boston	MA	G	617 355-6058	8437
Boston Scientific Corporation **(PA)**	Marlborough	MA	B	508 683-4000	12727
Boston Scientific Corporation	Bedford	MA	G	781 259-2501	7964
Boston Scientific Corporation	Marlborough	MA	B	508 382-0200	12728
Boston Scientific Corporation	Quincy	MA	B	617 689-6000	14617
Boston Scientific Corporation	Watertown	MA	B	617 972-4000	16274
Boston Scientific Intl Corp	Marlborough	MA	G	508 683-4000	12729
Boston Transtec LLC	Newton	MA	G	617 930-6088	13572
Braintree Scientific Inc	Braintree	MA	G	781 348-0768	8993
Brimfield Precision LLC	Brimfield	MA	D	413 245-7144	9109
Btl Industries Inc	Marlborough	MA	C	866 285-1656	12730
C R Bard Inc	Chelmsford	MA	B	978 441-6202	9884
Cambridge Interventional LLC	Burlington	MA	G	978 793-2674	9243
Castlewood Surgical	Groton	MA	G	978 448-3628	11285
Chmc Otlrynglgic Fundation Inc **(PA)**	Boston	MA	F	617 355-8290	8472
Cognoptix Inc	Concord	MA	G	978 263-0005	10121
Concert Medical LLC	Norwell	MA	E	781 261-7400	14100
Corindus Vascular Robotics Inc **(PA)**	Waltham	MA	E	508 653-3335	16077
Covidien LP **(HQ)**	Mansfield	MA	A	763 514-4000	12622
Cytonome/St LLC	Bedford	MA	F	617 330-5030	7968
Cytovera Inc	Chestnut Hill	MA	G	617 682-8981	9985
Davol Inc	Woburn	MA	E	781 932-5900	17165
Dentsply Ih Inc **(HQ)**	Waltham	MA	C	781 890-6800	16084
Depuy Mitek LLC	Raynham	MA	B	508 880-8100	14709
Depuy Synthes Products Inc **(DH)**	Raynham	MA	D	508 880-8100	14711
Depuy Synthes Sales Inc	Raynham	MA	G	508 880-8100	14712
Depuy Synthes Sales Inc	Bridgewater	MA	F	508 880-8100	9071
Diagnosys LLC **(PA)**	Lowell	MA	E	978 458-1600	12367
Differential Pipetting Inc	Gloucester	MA	G	978 515-3392	11177
Digilab Genomic Solutions Inc	Holliston	MA	D	508 893-3130	11568
Direx Systems Corp	Canton	MA	G	339 502-6013	9727
Eagle Vision Inc	Dennis	MA	G	508 385-2283	10307
Earlysense Inc	Woburn	MA	F	781 373-3228	17172
Endodynamix Inc	Salem	MA	F	978 740-0400	14909
Endogen Inc	Woburn	MA	D	617 225-0055	17177
Eos Imaging Inc	Cambridge	MA	F	678 564-5400	9467
Escalon Digital Solutions Inc	Stoneham	MA	F	610 688-6830	15562
Everest Hlthcare Holdings Inc **(DH)**	Waltham	MA	G	781 699-9000	16100
Everest Healthcare Texas Holdg	Waltham	MA	G	781 699-9000	16101
Exalpha Biologicals Inc	Shirley	MA	G	978 425-1370	15083
Eyepoint Pharmaceuticals Inc **(PA)**	Watertown	MA	E	617 926-5000	16287
Fci Ophthalmics Inc	Pembroke	MA	G	781 826-9060	14404
Five Star Manufacturing Inc	New Bedford	MA	D	508 998-1404	13387
Fms New York Services LLC **(DH)**	Waltham	MA	G	781 699-9000	16108
Fresenius Med Care Hldings Inc **(DH)**	Waltham	MA	A	781 699-9000	16110
Fresenius Med Care Vntures LLC **(DH)**	Waltham	MA	G	781 699-9000	16112
Fresenius Med Care W Wllow LLC	Waltham	MA	F	781 699-9000	16113
Fresenius Med Svcs Group LLC	Waltham	MA	G	781 699-9000	16114

PRODUCT

	CITY	ST	EMP	PHONE	ENTRY #
Fresenius Medical Care North **(DH)**	Waltham	MA	D	781 699-9000	16115
Fresenius USA Marketing Inc **(DH)**	Waltham	MA	F	781 699-9000	16116
Green Heron Hlth Solutions Inc	Rockport	MA	G	978 309-8118	14835
Gregory Manufacturing Inc	Holyoke	MA	D	413 536-5432	11628
Guidant Corporation	Marlborough	MA	A	508 683-4000	12766
Gyrus Acmi LLC **(DH)**	Southborough	MA	C	508 804-2600	15359
Harvard Clinical Tech Inc	Natick	MA	E	508 655-2000	13259
Highland Labs Inc	Holliston	MA	E	508 429-2918	11577
Home Intensive Care Inc	Waltham	MA	G	781 699-9000	16127
Hyalex Orthopaedics Inc	Lexington	MA	G	347 871-5850	12230
Insulet Corporation **(PA)**	Acton	MA	B	978 600-7000	7365
Intech Inc	Acton	MA	E	978 263-2210	7366
Integra Lifesciences Prod Corp	Mansfield	MA	G	781 971-5682	12637
Integra Luxtec Inc	North Billerica	MA	D	508 835-9700	13828
Invivo Thrputics Holdings Corp	Cambridge	MA	G	617 863-5500	9518
Iq Medical Devices LLC	Belmont	MA	F	617 484-3188	8076
Ives Eeg Solutions LLC	Newburyport	MA	G	978 358-8006	13502
Jacobs Precision Corp	Avon	MA	G	508 588-2121	7888
Jarvis Surgical Inc	Westfield	MA	E	413 562-6659	16692
Karl Storz Endovision Inc	Charlton	MA	B	508 248-9011	9852
Kirwan Enterprise LLC	Marshfield	MA	G	781 834-9500	12861
Lake Region Medical Inc **(HQ)**	Wilmington	MA	E	978 570-6900	17016
Laser Engineering	Milford	MA	G	508 520-2500	13124
Lemaitre Vascular Inc **(PA)**	Burlington	MA	C	781 221-2266	9297
Logan Instruments Inc	Braintree	MA	F	617 394-0601	9024
Lymol Medical Corp **(PA)**	Woburn	MA	F	781 935-0004	17219
Maruho Htsujyo Innovations Inc **(PA)**	Norwell	MA	F	617 653-1617	14107
Medcon Biolab Technologies Inc	Grafton	MA	G	508 839-4203	11223
Medical Device Bus Svcs Inc	Raynham	MA	E	508 880-8100	14717
Medical-Technical Gases Inc	North Billerica	MA	E	781 395-1946	13841
Medisight Corporation	Cambridge	MA	G	415 205-2764	9550
Medsix Inc	Jamaica Plain	MA	G	617 935-2716	11946
Medsource Tech Holdings LLC **(DH)**	Wilmington	MA	F	978 570-6900	17021
Medsource Technologies LLC **(DH)**	Wilmington	MA	F	978 570-6900	17022
Medtrnic Sofamor Danek USA Inc	Hopkinton	MA	G	508 497-0792	11727
Medtronic	Mansfield	MA	F	508 452-4203	12645
Medtronic Inc	Chicopee	MA	F	413 593-6400	10043
Merit Medical Systems Inc **(HQ)**	Rockland	MA	F	781 681-7900	14813
Microline Surgical Inc **(HQ)**	Beverly	MA	C	978 922-9810	8153
Mobius Imaging LLC	Shirley	MA	D	978 796-5068	15090
Moderna LLC **(HQ)**	Cambridge	MA	G	617 714-6500	9565
Mossman Associates Inc	Milford	MA	G	508 488-6169	13130
Most Cardio Incorporated	Salem	MA	G	978 594-1614	14930
Nellcor Puritan Bennett LLC **(DH)**	Mansfield	MA	B	508 261-8000	12649
Nelmed Corporation	North Attleboro	MA	G	508 695-8817	13768
Neurologica Corp	Danvers	MA	C	978 564-8500	10242
Neurometrix Inc **(PA)**	Waltham	MA	E	781 890-9989	16159
Newton Laboratories Inc	Belmont	MA	G	617 484-7003	8078
Newton Scientific Inc	Charlestown	MA	E	617 354-9469	9840
Nordson Med Design & Dev Inc **(HQ)**	Marlborough	MA	E	508 481-6233	12797
Northeast Ems Enterprises	Rehoboth	MA	G	508 252-6584	14755
Omarc LLC	Norwood	MA	G	781 702-6732	14187
Omnilife Science Inc	Raynham	MA	G	508 824-2444	14724
Opportunity/Discovery LLC	Wilmington	MA	G	781 301-1596	17034
Optim LLC	Sturbridge	MA	E	508 347-5100	15643
Park Bio Services LLC	Groveland	MA	G	978 794-8500	11303
Pep Industries LLC	Attleboro	MA	A	508 226-5600	7776
Phase-N Corporation	Boston	MA	G	617 737-0064	8777
Precision Biopsy Inc	Boston	MA	G	720 859-3553	8790
Precision Engineered Pdts LLC **(DH)**	Attleboro	MA	G	508 226-5600	7782
Precision Systems Inc	Natick	MA	E	508 655-7010	13274
Pressure Biosciences Inc	South Easton	MA	F	508 230-1828	15288
Primo Medical Group Inc **(PA)**	Stoughton	MA	C	781 297-5700	15617
Primrose Medical Inc	East Walpole	MA	F	508 660-8688	10529
Professnal Cntract Strlization	Taunton	MA	F	508 822-5524	15774
Radius Medical Tech Inc	Stow	MA	F	978 263-4466	15635
Ranfac Corp	Avon	MA	D	508 588-4400	7894
Rebiscan Inc	Boston	MA	F	857 600-0982	8813
Reboot Medical Inc	Lowell	MA	G	818 621-6554	12426
Rest Ensured Medical Inc	Norwood	MA	G	603 225-2860	14195
Rhealth Corporation	Bedford	MA	E	617 913-7630	8006
Sangstat Medical LLC	Cambridge	MA	B	510 789-4300	9642
Schuerch Corporation	Abington	MA	F	781 982-7000	7330
Sevenoaks Biosystems	Cambridge	MA	G	617 299-0404	9648
Sil-Med Corporation	Taunton	MA	D	508 823-7701	15784
Smith & Nephew Inc	Mansfield	MA	E	508 261-3600	12659
Smith & Nephew Inc	Mansfield	MA	E	508 261-3600	12660
Smiths Medical Asd Inc	Westport	MA	G	508 636-6909	16847
Spirus Medical LLC	West Bridgewater	MA	G	781 297-7220	16456
Sqz Biotechnologies Company	Watertown	MA	G	617 758-8672	16319
Steris Corporation	Northborough	MA	G	508 393-9323	14048
Suture Concepts Inc	Beverly	MA	G	978 969-0070	8185
T & T Machine Products Inc	Rockland	MA	F	781 878-3861	14829
T2 Biosystems Inc **(PA)**	Lexington	MA	C	781 761-4646	12276
Team-At-Work	Groton	MA	G	978 448-8562	11295
Tegra Medical LLC **(HQ)**	Franklin	MA	C	508 541-4200	11084
Teleflex Incorporated	Cambridge	MA	D	617 577-2200	9679
Telemed Systems Inc	Hudson	MA	E	978 567-9033	11821
Tetherx Inc	Southborough	MA	G	508 308-7845	15369
Uti Holding Company	Wilmington	MA	G	978 570-6900	17062
Valeritas Inc	Marlborough	MA	E	774 239-2498	12841
Vasca Inc	Tewksbury	MA	E	978 640-0431	15847
Viant AS&o Holdings LLC	Wilmington	MA	G	866 899-1392	17063
Visionquest Holdings LLC	Littleton	MA	F	978 776-9518	12326
Xenotherapeutics LLC	Boston	MA	G	617 750-1907	8938
Zyno Medical LLC	Natick	MA	F	508 650-2008	13288
Idexx Distribution Inc	Westbrook	ME	D	207 556-0637	7190
Mars Medical Products LLC	Skowhegan	ME	G	207 385-3278	6982
Special Diversified Opp Inc	Windham	ME	E	207 856-6151	7254
Sterizign Precision Tech LLC	Brunswick	ME	G	888 234-3074	5847
Accellent Endoscopy Inc	Laconia	NH	C	603 528-1211	18550
Aponos Medical Corporation	Kingston	NH	G	603 347-8229	18540
Apriomed Inc	Derry	NH	G	603 421-0875	17971
Atech Designs Inc	Dover	NH	G	603 926-8216	18006
Atrium Medical Corporation **(HQ)**	Merrimack	NH	B	603 880-1433	18986
Design Standards Corp	Charlestown	NH	D	603 826-7744	17813
Dutch Ophthalmic Usa Inc	Exeter	NH	F	603 778-6929	18119
Getinge Group Logis Ameri LLC	Merrimack	NH	A	603 880-1433	19003
Grason & Associates LLC	Rindge	NH	G	603 899-3089	19649
Gtimd LLC	Amherst	NH	F	603 880-0277	17566
Iometry Inc	Hanover	NH	G	603 643-5670	18294
KMC Systems Inc	Merrimack	NH	D	866 742-0442	19010
Lake Region Medical Inc	Laconia	NH	D	603 528-1211	18571
Maxilon Laboratories Inc	Amherst	NH	G	603 594-9300	17575
Multi-Med Inc	Keene	NH	E	603 357-8733	18519
Neuraxis LLC	Derry	NH	G	603 912-5306	17991
New England Small Tube Corp	Litchfield	NH	D	603 429-1600	18652
Prepco Inc	Colebrook	NH	G	603 237-4080	17875
Prometheus Group of NH Ltd	Dover	NH	F	800 442-2325	18047
Seacoast Technologies Inc	Portsmouth	NH	G	603 766-9800	19619
Sims Portex Inc	Keene	NH	F	603 352-3812	18525
Smiths Medical Asd Inc	Keene	NH	E	603 352-3812	18526
Smiths Medical Asd Inc	Keene	NH	E	603 352-3812	18527
Steralon Inc	Manchester	NH	G	603 296-0490	18930
Teleflex Incorporated	Jaffrey	NH	E	603 532-7706	18479
Tfx Medical Incorporated	Jaffrey	NH	B	603 532-7706	18480
Ticked Off Inc	Dover	NH	G	603 742-0925	18061
Vallum Corporation	Nashua	NH	G	603 577-1989	19277
Bi Medical LLC	Coventry	RI	G	866 246-3301	20139
Bnr Supplies	Cranston	RI	G	401 461-9132	20190
C R Bard Inc	Warwick	RI	B	401 825-8300	21338
Confluent Medical Tech Inc	Warwick	RI	G	401 223-0990	21344
Contech Medical Inc	Providence	RI	D	401 351-4890	20989
Davol Inc **(DH)**	Warwick	RI	E	401 825-8300	21350
Degania Silicone Inc **(PA)**	Smithfield	RI	G	401 349-5373	21219
Geotec Inc	Warwick	RI	E	401 228-7395	21366
Illuminoss Medical Inc	East Providence	RI	F	401 714-0008	20419
RJ Mansour Inc	Providence	RI	E	401 521-7800	21116
S2s Surgical LLC	East Greenwich	RI	G	401 398-1933	20378
Biotek Instruments Inc **(HQ)**	Winooski	VT	D	802 655-4040	22717
Eric Lawhite Co	South Royalton	VT	G	802 763-7670	22491
Lord Corporation **(DH)**	Williston	VT	D	802 862-6629	22680
PBL Incorporated	Colchester	VT	F	802 893-0111	21876
Raj Communications Ltd	Williston	VT	F	802 658-4961	22687
Stromatec Inc	North Ferrisburgh	VT	G	802 425-2700	22228

INSTRUMENTS: Meteorological

	CITY	ST	EMP	PHONE	ENTRY #
Airflo Instrument Company	Glastonbury	CT	G	860 633-9455	1536
Maximum Inc	New Bedford	MA	F	508 995-2200	13417
Beta Acquisition Inc	Thornton	NH	G	603 726-7500	19900

INSTRUMENTS: Meters, Integrating Electricity

	CITY	ST	EMP	PHONE	ENTRY #
Granite Reliable Power LLC	Marlborough	MA	G	508 251-7650	12763

INSTRUMENTS: Microwave Test

	CITY	ST	EMP	PHONE	ENTRY #
Victor Microwave Inc	Wakefield	MA	F	781 245-4472	15982
Leusin Microwave LLC	Hampstead	NH	F	603 329-7270	18241
Omega Laboratories Inc	Hampstead	NH	F	978 768-7771	18247

INSTRUMENTS: Nautical

	CITY	ST	EMP	PHONE	ENTRY #
Drs Naval Power Systems Inc	Danbury	CT	B	203 798-3000	904
E S Ritchie & Sons Inc	Pembroke	MA	E	781 826-5131	14402
Seapoint Sensors Inc	Exeter	NH	G	603 642-4921	18131

INSTRUMENTS: Optical, Analytical

	CITY	ST	EMP	PHONE	ENTRY #
Cassini Usa Inc	Burlington	MA	G	781 487-7000	9244
Eye Point Pharmac	Watertown	MA	G	617 926-5000	16286
Vacuum Process Technology LLC	Plymouth	MA	E	508 732-7200	14589

INSTRUMENTS: Photographic, Electronic

	CITY	ST	EMP	PHONE	ENTRY #
Editshare LLC	Allston	MA	G	617 782-0479	7464

INSTRUMENTS: Power Measuring, Electrical

	CITY	ST	EMP	PHONE	ENTRY #
Solar Data Systems Inc	Bethel	CT	F	203 702-7189	179

INSTRUMENTS: Pressure Measurement, Indl

	CITY	ST	EMP	PHONE	ENTRY #
Orange Research Inc	Milford	CT	D	203 877-5657	2326
PMC Engineering LLC	Danbury	CT	E	203 792-8686	968
Precision Sensors Inc	Milford	CT	E	203 877-2795	2338
United Electric Controls Co	Milford	CT	D	203 877-2795	2377
Airflow Direction Inc	Newbury	MA	G	978 462-9995	13462
Mks Instruments Inc **(PA)**	Andover	MA	B	978 645-5500	7574
Mks Instruments Inc	Wilmington	MA	C	978 284-4000	17024
Mks Instruments Inc	Andover	MA	E	978 645-5500	7575
Mks Instruments Inc	Methuen	MA	D	978 682-3512	13037
Mks Msc Inc	Wilmington	MA	A	978 284-4000	17025
Verionix Inc	North Andover	MA	G	978 682-5671	13736
X Sonix	Boxborough	MA	G	978 266-2106	8972
Celestial Monitoring Corp **(HQ)**	Narragansett	RI	E	401 782-1045	20635

INSTRUMENTS: Radar Testing, Electric

	CITY	ST	EMP	PHONE	ENTRY #
Energy Tech LLC	Haddam	CT	G	860 345-3993	1726

INSTRUMENTS: Radio Frequency Measuring

	CITY	ST	EMP	PHONE	ENTRY #
Hid Global Corporation	Newton	MA	C	617 581-6200	13601
Amphenol Corporation	Nashua	NH	B	603 879-3000	19114

INSTRUMENTS: Refractometers, Indl Process

	CITY	ST	EMP	PHONE	ENTRY #
George Baggett	Union	ME	G	207 785-5442	7113

INSTRUMENTS: Seismographs

	CITY	ST	EMP	PHONE	ENTRY #
Kinemetrics Inc	Harvard	MA	G	978 772-4774	11381

INSTRUMENTS: Signal Generators & Averagers

	CITY	ST	EMP	PHONE	ENTRY #
James G Hachey Inc	Peabody	MA	G	781 229-6400	14344

INSTRUMENTS: Standards & Calibration, Electrical Measuring

	CITY	ST	EMP	PHONE	ENTRY #
Rotek Instrument Corp	Waltham	MA	E	781 899-4611	16190
Mainely Metrology Inc	Smithfield	ME	G	207 362-5520	6989

INSTRUMENTS: Stroboscopes

	CITY	ST	EMP	PHONE	ENTRY #
Monarch International Inc	Amherst	NH	E	603 883-3390	17577

INSTRUMENTS: Surface Area Analyzers

	CITY	ST	EMP	PHONE	ENTRY #
Anova Data Inc	Westford	MA	G	978 577-6600	16753

INSTRUMENTS: Telemetering, Indl Process

	CITY	ST	EMP	PHONE	ENTRY #
Signalfire Telemetry Inc	Marlborough	MA	G	978 212-2868	12826

INSTRUMENTS: Temperature Measurement, Indl

	CITY	ST	EMP	PHONE	ENTRY #
Moeller Instrument Company Inc	Ivoryton	CT	E	800 243-9310	1907
Omega Engineering Inc **(HQ)**	Norwalk	CT	C	203 359-1660	3211
Dias Infrared Corp	West Boylston	MA	G	845 987-8152	16414
Thermonics Inc	Mansfield	MA	G	408 542-5900	12665
Optris Ir Sensing LLC	Portsmouth	NH	G	603 766-6060	19604
Wyatt Engineering LLC **(PA)**	Lincoln	RI	G	401 334-1170	20601

INSTRUMENTS: Test, Digital, Electronic & Electrical Circuits

	CITY	ST	EMP	PHONE	ENTRY #
Auriga Measurement Systems **(PA)**	Wayland	MA	G	978 452-7700	16334
Bose Corporation	Framingham	MA	E	508 766-1265	10929
Fulcrum9 Systems Inc	Acton	MA	G	978 549-3868	7357
Pharmatron Inc	Westborough	MA	F	603 645-6766	16643
Sifos Technologies Inc	Andover	MA	G	978 975-2100	7605
Digital Devices Inc	Wilton	NH	G	603 654-6240	19978

INSTRUMENTS: Test, Electrical, Engine

	CITY	ST	EMP	PHONE	ENTRY #
Test Logic Inc	Middletown	CT	F	860 347-8378	2227
Ametek Arizona Instrument LLC	Middleboro	MA	C	508 946-6200	13051
Connected Automotive	South Easton	MA	E	508 238-5855	15274

INSTRUMENTS: Test, Electronic & Electric Measurement

	CITY	ST	EMP	PHONE	ENTRY #
AKO Inc	Windsor	CT	E	860 298-9765	5317
All-Test Pro LLC **(PA)**	Old Saybrook	CT	F	860 399-4222	3327
International Contact Tech	Southbury	CT	E	203 264-5757	4028
Advanced Mechanical Tech Inc **(PA)**	Watertown	MA	E	617 923-4174	16263
Analog Devices Intl Inc **(HQ)**	Norwood	MA	F	781 329-4700	14131
Barbour Stockwell Inc	Woburn	MA	E	781 933-5200	17127
EMC Test Design LLC	Newton	MA	F	508 292-1833	13588
Genrad Inc	Westford	MA	A	978 589-7000	16768
Precise Time and Frequency LLC	Wakefield	MA	G	781 245-9090	15971
Programmed Test Sources Inc	Littleton	MA	F	978 486-3008	12320
Quadtech Inc	Marlborough	MA	E	978 461-2100	12811
Rika Denshi America Inc	Attleboro	MA	E	508 226-2080	7788
Tech180 Corp	Easthampton	MA	F	413 203-6123	10581
ARC Technology Solutions LLC	Nashua	NH	E	603 883-3027	19117
Auriga Piv Tech Inc	Merrimack	NH	G	603 402-2955	18987
Fluke Electronics Corporation	Salem	NH	G	603 537-2680	19735
Centrodyne Corp of America	South Burlington	VT	G	802 658-4715	22442

INSTRUMENTS: Test, Electronic & Electrical Circuits

	CITY	ST	EMP	PHONE	ENTRY #
Aetruim Incorporated	Billerica	MA	E	651 773-4200	8205
Analysis Tech Inc	Wakefield	MA	G	781 224-1223	15941
Electro-Fix Inc	Plainville	MA	E	508 695-0228	14518
H & W Test Products Inc	Seekonk	MA	F	508 336-3200	15023
Teradyne Inc	North Reading	MA	B	978 370-2700	13991
Eastern Time Design Inc	Candia	NH	F	603 483-5876	17781
Innovative Test Solutions LLC	Nashua	NH	G	603 288-0280	19188
Q A Technology Company Inc	Hampton	NH	D	603 926-1193	18269
Wilcom Inc	Belmont	NH	E	603 524-2622	17686

INSTRUMENTS: Testing, Semiconductor

	CITY	ST	EMP	PHONE	ENTRY #
Wentworth Laboratories Inc	Brookfield	CT	G	203 775-9311	666
Etec Inc	West Roxbury	MA	E	617 477-4308	16495
Inspectrology LLC	Sudbury	MA	E	978 212-3100	15659
L T X International Inc	Norwood	MA	D	781 461-1000	14173
Middlesex General Industries	Newburyport	MA	E	781 935-8870	13514
Origo Automation Inc	Lowell	MA	G	877 943-5677	12417
Teradyne Inc **(PA)**	North Reading	MA	B	978 370-2700	13990
Teradyne Inc	Woburn	MA	C	978 370-2700	17306
Xcerra Corporation **(HQ)**	Norwood	MA	C	781 461-1000	14206
Xcerra Corporation	Norwood	MA	C	781 461-1000	14207
Xcerra Corporation	Norwood	MA	E	781 461-1000	14208
Vermont Mold & Tool Corp	Barnet	VT	G	802 633-2300	21605

INSTRUMENTS: Thermal Conductive, Indl

	CITY	ST	EMP	PHONE	ENTRY #
Solar Generations LLC	Guilford	CT	G	203 453-3920	1720
Brooks Automation Inc **(PA)**	Chelmsford	MA	B	978 262-2400	9880
Btu Overseas Ltd **(DH)**	North Billerica	MA	G	978 667-4111	13801
Netzsch Instruments N Amer LLC **(DH)**	Burlington	MA	E	781 272-5353	9307
Temptronic Corporation **(HQ)**	Mansfield	MA	D	781 688-2300	12664
Contact Inc	Edgecomb	ME	G	207 882-6116	6001

INSTRUMENTS: Thermal Property Measurement

	CITY	ST	EMP	PHONE	ENTRY #
Exergen Corporation	Watertown	MA	D	617 923-9900	16284
Oldcastle Buildingenvelope Inc	Warwick	RI	G	866 653-2278	21398

INSTRUMENTS: Transducers, Volts, Amperes, Watts, VARs & Freq

	CITY	ST	EMP	PHONE	ENTRY #
Trans-Tek Inc	Ellington	CT	E	860 872-8351	1343
Fishman Transducers Inc	Andover	MA	D	978 988-9199	7549
Group Four Transducers Inc **(PA)**	East Longmeadow	MA	F	413 525-2705	10477
Airmar Technology Corp **(PA)**	Milford	NH	B	603 673-9570	19044
Airmar Technology Corp	Milford	NH	F	603 673-9570	19045

INSTRUMENTS: Transformers, Portable

	CITY	ST	EMP	PHONE	ENTRY #
Ftircom LLC	Benton	ME	G	603 886-5555	5705

INSTRUMENTS: Vibration

	CITY	ST	EMP	PHONE	ENTRY #
Unholtz-Dickie Corporation **(PA)**	Wallingford	CT	E	203 265-9875	4825
Kinetic Systems Inc	Boston	MA	E	617 522-8700	8649
Geokon LLC	Lebanon	NH	D	603 448-1562	18624

INSTRUMENTS: Viscometer, Indl Process

	CITY	ST	EMP	PHONE	ENTRY #
Norcross Corporation	Newton	MA	G	617 969-7020	13620

INSULATING BOARD, HARD PRESSED

	CITY	ST	EMP	PHONE	ENTRY #
Bnz Materials Inc	North Billerica	MA	E	978 663-3401	13796

INSULATING COMPOUNDS

	CITY	ST	EMP	PHONE	ENTRY #
Lydall Inc **(PA)**	Manchester	CT	E	860 646-1233	2021
Aspen Aerogels Inc **(PA)**	Northborough	MA	C	508 691-1111	14029
Albany International Corp **(PA)**	Rochester	NH	D	603 330-5850	19655
Aspen Aerogels Inc	East Providence	RI	F	401 432-2612	20388
Sto Corp	Rutland	VT	E	802 775-4117	22354

INSULATION & CUSHIONING FOAM: Polystyrene

	CITY	ST	EMP	PHONE	ENTRY #
Claremont Sales Corporation	Durham	CT	E	860 349-4499	1089
Foam Plastics New England Inc	Waterbury	CT	G	203 758-6651	4874
H-O Products Corporation	Winsted	CT	E	860 379-9875	5412
Sprayfoampolymerscom LLC	Wilton	CT	G	800 853-1577	5304
Vibrascience Inc	Branford	CT	G	203 483-6113	356
Trelleborg Offshore Boston Inc	Randolph	MA	D	774 719-1400	14699
Carlisle Construction Mtls LLC	Portland	ME	C	888 746-1114	6631
Johns Manville Corporation	Saco	ME	E	207 283-8000	6850

INSULATION MATERIALS WHOLESALERS

	CITY	ST	EMP	PHONE	ENTRY #
Vibrascience Inc	Branford	CT	G	203 483-6113	356
Harvey Industries Inc	Woburn	MA	E	781 935-7990	17197

INSULATION: Felt

	CITY	ST	EMP	PHONE	ENTRY #
Fiber Materials Inc **(HQ)**	Biddeford	ME	E	207 282-5911	5733

INSULATION: Fiberglass

	CITY	ST	EMP	PHONE	ENTRY #
Ecologic Energy Solutions LLC	Stamford	CT	E	203 889-0505	4191
Installed Building Pdts Inc	Stamford	CT	G	203 889-0505	4225
The E J Davis Company	North Haven	CT	E	203 239-5391	3063
Composite Engineering Inc	Concord	MA	G	978 371-3132	10122
Colonial Green Products LLC	Sanford	ME	G	207 614-6660	6872
Colonial Green Products LLC **(PA)**	Rindge	NH	F	603 532-7005	19648

INSULATORS & INSULATION MATERIALS: Electrical

	CITY	ST	EMP	PHONE	ENTRY #
Chase Corp Inc	Westwood	MA	G	781 332-0700	16860
Chase Corporation **(PA)**	Westwood	MA	G	781 332-0700	16861
Chase Corporation	Oxford	MA	F	508 731-2710	14256
Chase Corporation	Westwood	MA	F	781 329-3259	16862
Coolcomposites Inc	Jamaica Plain	MA	G	510 717-9125	11942
H Loeb Corporation	New Bedford	MA	E	508 996-3745	13392
Matkim Industries Inc	Oxford	MA	E	508 987-3599	14269
Isovolta Inc	Rutland	VT	E	802 775-5528	22341
Superior Tchncal Ceramics Corp	Saint Albans	VT	C	802 527-7726	22380

INSULATORS, PORCELAIN: Electrical

	CITY	ST	EMP	PHONE	ENTRY #
Newco Condenser Inc	Shelton	CT	G	475 882-4000	3839
Ceramics Grinding Co Inc	Maynard	MA	G	978 461-5935	12897

INSULIN PREPARATIONS

	CITY	ST	EMP	PHONE	ENTRY #
Albireo Pharma Inc **(PA)**	Boston	MA	E	857 254-5555	8352

INSURANCE: Agents, Brokers & Service

	CITY	ST	EMP	PHONE	ENTRY #
Boston Software Corp	Needham Heights	MA	F	781 449-8585	13320

INTEGRATED CIRCUITS, SEMICONDUCTOR NETWORKS, ETC

	CITY	ST	EMP	PHONE	ENTRY #
Alacrity Semiconductors Inc	Branford	CT	G	475 325-8435	287
Photronics Inc **(PA)**	Brookfield	CT	B	203 775-9000	654
Aceinna Inc	Andover	MA	E	978 965-3200	7532
American Power Devices Inc	Lynn	MA	E	781 592-6090	12489
Analog Devices Inc **(PA)**	Norwood	MA	A	781 329-4700	14130
Ase (us) Inc	Woburn	MA	G	781 305-5900	17123
Broadcom Corporation	Andover	MA	D	978 719-1300	7543
Composite Modules	Attleboro	MA	D	508 226-6969	7723
Contour Semiconductor Inc	North Billerica	MA	F	978 670-4100	13804
Dover Microsystems Inc	Waltham	MA	G	781 577-0300	16090
Eastwind Communications Inc	Hyannis	MA	F	508 862-8600	11840
Hittite Microwave LLC **(HQ)**	Chelmsford	MA	C	978 250-3343	9905
Kita Usa Inc	Attleboro	MA	G	774 331-2265	7756
Memsic Inc **(HQ)**	Andover	MA	G	978 738-0900	7569
Microsemi Corporation	Lowell	MA	D	978 442-5637	12410
Piconics Inc	Tyngsboro	MA	E	978 649-7501	15899
Qualcomm Incorporated	Andover	MA	B	858 587-1121	7590
Qualcomm Incorporated	Boxborough	MA	B	858 587-1121	8968
R F Integration Inc **(PA)**	North Billerica	MA	F	978 654-6770	13857

	CITY	ST	EMP	PHONE	ENTRY #
Rochester Electronics LLC **(PA)**	Newburyport	MA	C	978 462-9332	13531
Rochester Electronics LLC	Newburyport	MA	G	978 462-1248	13532
Skyworks Solutions Inc **(PA)**	Woburn	MA	A	781 376-3000	17297
Spero Devices Inc	Acton	MA	G	978 849-8000	7388
Telco Systems Inc **(HQ)**	Mansfield	MA	E	508 339-1516	12662
Tessolar Inc	Woburn	MA	G	508 479-9818	17308
Tier 7 Communications	Shirley	MA	G	978 425-9543	15095
Eyepvideo Systems LLC	Danville	NH	G	603 382-2547	17968
Paragon Electronic Systems	Manchester	NH	F	603 645-7630	18898
Qmagiq LLC	Nashua	NH	G	603 821-3092	19242
True North Networks LLC	Swanzey	NH	E	603 624-6777	19890
Veterans Assembled Elec LLC **(PA)**	Providence	RI	G	401 228-6165	21150
I C Haus Corp	Grand Isle	VT	G	802 372-8340	21998

INTERCOMMUNICATIONS SYSTEMS: Electric

	CITY	ST	EMP	PHONE	ENTRY #
Farmington River Holdings LLC	Hamden	CT	G	203 777-2130	1749
Voice Express Corp	Fairfield	CT	G	203 221-7799	1461
Bridgesat Inc	Boston	MA	G	617 419-1800	8444
Cambrdge Sund MGT Holdings LLC **(DH)**	Waltham	MA	G	781 547-7100	16059
Converdent Networks Inc	Boston	MA	D	978 262-0231	8483
Coredge Networks Inc	Boston	MA	D	617 267-5205	8484
Housing Devices Inc	Medford	MA	F	781 395-5200	12935
L3 Technologies Inc	Ayer	MA	C	978 784-1999	7925
Segue Manufacturing Svcs LLC	Lowell	MA	D	978 970-1200	12432
Starry Inc	Boston	MA	F	617 861-8300	8862
Astronics Aerosat Corporation	Manchester	NH	D	603 879-0205	18782
Custom Manufacturing Svcs Inc	Nashua	NH	E	603 883-1355	19141
Nel-Tech Labs Incorporated	Derry	NH	F	603 425-1096	17990
Nextmove Technologies LLC	Hollis	NH	G	603 654-1280	18335

INTERIOR DECORATING SVCS

	CITY	ST	EMP	PHONE	ENTRY #
Bloom & Company Inc	Watertown	MA	F	617 923-1526	16273

INTERIOR DESIGN SVCS, NEC

	CITY	ST	EMP	PHONE	ENTRY #
Kilcourse Specialty Products	New Milford	CT	G	860 210-2075	2810
Grant Larkin	Richmond	MA	G	413 698-2599	14779
Audio File Publications Inc	Portland	ME	G	207 774-7563	6614
Nouveau Interiors LLC	Manchester	NH	G	603 398-1732	18889

INTERMEDIATE CARE FACILITY

	CITY	ST	EMP	PHONE	ENTRY #
Amicus Hlthcare Lving Ctrs LLC	North Chelmsford	MA	E	978 934-0000	13884

INVERTERS: Nonrotating Electrical

	CITY	ST	EMP	PHONE	ENTRY #
Solectria Renewables LLC	Lawrence	MA	C	978 683-9700	12076

INVESTMENT ADVISORY SVCS

	CITY	ST	EMP	PHONE	ENTRY #
Baxter Bros Inc	Greenwich	CT	G	203 637-4559	1598
Timer Digest Publishing Inc	Greenwich	CT	G	203 629-2589	1655
New Frontier Advisors LLC **(PA)**	Boston	MA	G	617 482-1433	8733

INVESTMENT BANKERS

	CITY	ST	EMP	PHONE	ENTRY #
Stamford Capital Group Inc **(PA)**	Stamford	CT	A	800 977-7837	4329
Monadnock Associates Inc **(PA)**	Watertown	MA	F	617 924-7032	16302

INVESTMENT FUNDS, NEC

	CITY	ST	EMP	PHONE	ENTRY #
Kronos Acquisition Corporation **(HQ)**	Lowell	MA	G	978 250-9800	12391
Longworth Venture Partners LP **(PA)**	Norfolk	MA	E	781 663-3600	13663

INVESTMENT RESEARCH SVCS

	CITY	ST	EMP	PHONE	ENTRY #
Ihs Herold Inc **(DH)**	Norwalk	CT	D	203 857-0215	3171

INVESTORS: Real Estate, Exc Property Operators

	CITY	ST	EMP	PHONE	ENTRY #
Chapman & Wheeler Inc	Bethel	ME	G	207 824-2224	5714

IRON & STEEL PRDTS: Hot-Rolled

	CITY	ST	EMP	PHONE	ENTRY #
Ccr Products LLC	West Hartford	CT	E	860 953-0499	5058
Gerdau Ameristeel US Inc	Plainville	CT	G	860 351-9029	3493
Martells Metal Works	Attleboro	MA	G	508 226-0136	7764

IRON ORE PELLETIZING

	CITY	ST	EMP	PHONE	ENTRY #
Farrel Corporation **(DH)**	Ansonia	CT	D	203 736-5500	15

IRRADIATION EQPT: Beta Ray

	CITY	ST	EMP	PHONE	ENTRY #
Protom International Inc	Wakefield	MA	E	781 245-3964	15973

ISOCYANATES

	CITY	ST	EMP	PHONE	ENTRY #
Creative Stone Systems Inc	Buzzards Bay	MA	F	866 608-7625	9360

JACKETS: Indl, Metal Plate

	CITY	ST	EMP	PHONE	ENTRY #
Thermaxx LLC **(PA)**	West Haven	CT	G	203 672-1021	5148

JACKS: Hydraulic

	CITY	ST	EMP	PHONE	ENTRY #
Richard Dudgeon Inc	Waterbury	CT	G	203 336-4459	4950
Hostar Mar Trnspt Systems Inc	Wareham	MA	E	508 295-2900	16250

JANITORIAL EQPT & SPLYS WHOLESALERS

	CITY	ST	EMP	PHONE	ENTRY #
Edsan Chemical Company Inc	New Haven	CT	C	203 624-3123	2685
A1a Steel LLC	East Falmouth	MA	G	774 763-2503	10432
Maine Cleaners Supply Inc	North Yarmouth	ME	G	207 657-3166	6517

JARS: Plastic

	CITY	ST	EMP	PHONE	ENTRY #
Colts Plastics Company Inc	Dayville	CT	C	860 774-2277	1042
Handyaid Co	Feeding Hills	MA	G	413 786-9865	10799

JAZZ MUSIC GROUP OR ARTISTS

	CITY	ST	EMP	PHONE	ENTRY #
Grist For Mill LLC	Bristol	NH	F	603 744-0405	17767

JEWELERS' FINDINGS & MATERIALS

	CITY	ST	EMP	PHONE	ENTRY #
EF Leach & Company	Attleboro	MA	B	508 643-3309	7731
Hallmark Healy Group Inc **(DH)**	Attleboro	MA	C	508 222-9234	7744
M S Company	Attleboro	MA	D	508 222-1700	7760
ALA Casting Co Inc	Warwick	RI	E	516 371-4350	21320
APAC Tool Inc	North Providence	RI	F	401 724-6090	20753
Aro-Sac Inc	North Providence	RI	E	401 231-6655	20754
Automatic Findings	Cranston	RI	G	401 781-4810	20185
Crystal Hord Corporation	Pawtucket	RI	E	401 723-2989	20829
Dama Jewelry Technology Inc	East Providence	RI	E	401 272-6513	20402
Eagle Tool Inc	Providence	RI	F	401 421-5105	21001
Fulford Manufacturing Company **(PA)**	Riverside	RI	F	401 431-2000	21168
Geo H Fuller and Son Company	Pawtucket	RI	E	401 722-6530	20843
L & M Torsion Spring Co Inc	Providence	RI	G	401 231-5635	21048
Lees Manufacturing Co Inc	Providence	RI	E	401 275-2383	21050
Lorac Company Inc	Providence	RI	E	401 781-3330	21057
Pruefer Metalworks Inc	Warwick	RI	F	401 785-4688	21407
Salvadore Tool & Findings Inc **(PA)**	Providence	RI	E	401 331-6000	21119
Unit Tool Co	Warwick	RI	E	401 781-2647	21436
W R Cobb Company **(PA)**	East Providence	RI	C	401 438-7000	20448

JEWELERS' FINDINGS & MATERIALS: Bearings, Synthetic

	CITY	ST	EMP	PHONE	ENTRY #
Idex Health & Science LLC	Middleboro	MA	C	774 213-0200	13064
Richard H Bird & Co Inc	Waltham	MA	E	781 894-0160	16189

JEWELERS' FINDINGS & MATERIALS: Castings

	CITY	ST	EMP	PHONE	ENTRY #
FE Knight Inc **(PA)**	Franklin	MA	G	508 520-1666	11045
Creative Castings Inc	Pawtucket	RI	G	401 724-1070	20827
Natale & Sons Castings	Cranston	RI	G	401 467-4744	20266

JEWELERS' FINDINGS & MATERIALS: Parts, Unassembled

	CITY	ST	EMP	PHONE	ENTRY #
A Murphy James & Son Inc	Attleboro	MA	E	508 761-5060	7696
B & L Manufacturing Inc	Bellingham	MA	F	508 966-3066	8031
Alex and Ani LLC **(PA)**	Cranston	RI	B	401 633-1486	20175

JEWELERS' FINDINGS & MTLS: Jewel Prep, Instr, Tools, Watches

	CITY	ST	EMP	PHONE	ENTRY #
J S Ritter Jewelers Supply LLC	Portland	ME	G	207 712-4744	6675

JEWELERS' FINDINGS/MTRLS: Gem Prep, Settings, Real/Imitation

	CITY	ST	EMP	PHONE	ENTRY #
Cold River Mining Inc	Turners Falls	MA	G	413 863-5445	15876

JEWELRY & PRECIOUS STONES WHOLESALERS

	CITY	ST	EMP	PHONE	ENTRY #
AG Jewelry Designs LLC **(PA)**	Stamford	CT	G	800 643-0978	4130
Hadc	Providence	RI	G	401 274-1870	21024

JEWELRY APPAREL

	CITY	ST	EMP	PHONE	ENTRY #
Jack Hodgdon	Attleboro	MA	G	508 223-9990	7754
Jewelry Creations	Norton	MA	G	508 285-4230	14079
Michael Good Designs Inc	Rockport	ME	F	207 236-9619	6824
Creative Findings LLC	Pawtucket	RI	G	401 274-5579	20828
Racecar Jewelry Co Inc	Pawtucket	RI	G	401 475-5701	20888

JEWELRY FINDINGS & LAPIDARY WORK

	CITY	ST	EMP	PHONE	ENTRY #
A & J Tool Findings Co Inc	Plainville	MA	F	508 695-6631	14514
Alex and Ani LLC	Natick	MA	G	401 336-1397	13232
Edward Spencer	Boston	MA	G	617 426-0521	8519
Guyot Brothers Company Inc	Attleboro	MA	F	508 222-2000	7743
Ronald Pratt Company Inc	Attleboro	MA	E	508 222-9601	7790
Angelo Di Maria Inc	Providence	RI	E	401 274-0100	20954
Claire Stewart LLC	East Providence	RI	C	401 467-7400	20396
Contract Fusion Inc	East Providence	RI	E	401 438-1298	20400
Evans Findings Company Inc	East Providence	RI	E	401 434-5600	20412
Fashions By Gary Inc	Pawtucket	RI	F	401 726-1453	20838
Meloni Tool Co Inc	Johnston	RI	G	401 272-6513	20521
Roland & Whytock Company	Providence	RI	E	401 781-1234	21117
Rolyn Inc **(PA)**	Cranston	RI	E	401 944-0844	20281
Tercat Tool and Die Co Inc	Providence	RI	D	401 421-3371	21133
Tri-Bro Tool Company	Cranston	RI	F	401 781-6323	20305
Ablap Inc	Bradford	VT	G	802 748-5900	21698

JEWELRY REPAIR SVCS

	CITY	ST	EMP	PHONE	ENTRY #
Goldworks	Danbury	CT	G	203 743-9668	925
A & A Jewelers Inc	North Dartmouth	MA	G	508 992-5320	13915
Davriel Jewelers Inc	East Longmeadow	MA	G	413 525-4975	10471
Stoneman Custom Jewelers	Keene	NH	G	603 352-0811	18530

JEWELRY STORES

	CITY	ST	EMP	PHONE	ENTRY #
Goldworks	Danbury	CT	G	203 743-9668	925
Joseph A Cnte Mfg Jewelers Inc	Hamden	CT	G	203 248-9853	1764
Alexis Bittar LLC	Boston	MA	G	617 236-0505	8354
Charles Thomae & Son Inc	Attleboro	MA	E	508 222-0785	7719
Hallmark Healy Group Inc **(DH)**	Attleboro	MA	C	508 222-9234	7744
Impulse Packaging Inc	Rockport	MA	E	401 434-5588	14836
John Lewis Inc	Boston	MA	G	617 266-6665	8634
Plastic Craft Novelty Co Inc	Attleboro	MA	E	508 222-1486	7777
Daunis	Portland	ME	F	207 773-6011	6648
Pyramid Studios	Ellsworth	ME	G	207 667-3321	6020
Thomas Jewelry Design Inc	Newport	NH	D	603 372-6102	19363
Ahlers Designs Inc	Pawtucket	RI	G	401 365-1010	20811
APAC Tool Inc	North Providence	RI	F	401 724-6090	20753
Danecraft Inc **(PA)**	Providence	RI	D	401 941-7700	20993
Dina Inc	Cranston	RI	G	401 942-9633	20212
Ldc Inc	East Providence	RI	F	401 861-4667	20429
Racecar Jewelry Co Inc	Pawtucket	RI	G	401 475-5701	20888
Designed Essence Enterprise	Burlington	VT	G	802 864-4238	21780

JEWELRY STORES: Precious Stones & Precious Metals

	CITY	ST	EMP	PHONE	ENTRY #
Elm City Mfg Jewelers Inc	Hamden	CT	G	203 248-2195	1747
Silver Little Shop Inc	Avon	CT	G	860 678-1976	47
Artinian Garabet Corporation	Concord	MA	F	978 371-7110	10113

	CITY	ST	EMP	PHONE	ENTRY #
Barmakian Brothers Ltd Partnr	Boston	MA	E	617 227-3724	8392
Block Jewelers Inc	Agawam	MA	G	413 789-2940	7424
Davriel Jewelers Inc	East Longmeadow	MA	G	413 525-4975	10471
Edward Spencer	Boston	MA	G	617 426-0521	8519
Joel Goldsmith Bagnal Inc	Wellesley	MA	G	781 235-8266	16368
Precious Metals Reclaiming Svc **(PA)**	Canton	MA	G	781 326-3442	9771
Yankee Crafters Wampum Jewelry	South Yarmouth	MA	G	508 394-0575	15336
Thomas Michaels Designers Inc	Camden	ME	G	207 236-2708	5870
Willis & Sons Inc	Bar Harbor	ME	G	207 288-4935	5671
Melvin Reisz	Portsmouth	NH	G	603 436-9188	19594
Stoneman Custom Jewelers	Keene	NH	G	603 352-0811	18530
Alex and Ani LLC **(PA)**	Cranston	RI	B	401 633-1486	20175

JEWELRY STORES: Silverware

	CITY	ST	EMP	PHONE	ENTRY #
Silversmith Inc	Greenwich	CT	G	203 869-4244	1649

JEWELRY, PREC METAL: Mountings, Pens, Lthr, Etc, Gold/Silver

	CITY	ST	EMP	PHONE	ENTRY #
Goldman-Kolber Inc	Norwood	MA	E	781 769-6362	14156

JEWELRY, PRECIOUS METAL: Buttons, Precious Or Semi Or Stone

	CITY	ST	EMP	PHONE	ENTRY #
Narragasett Jewelry Inc	Providence	RI	E	401 944-2200	21075

JEWELRY, PRECIOUS METAL: Cases

	CITY	ST	EMP	PHONE	ENTRY #
Mrk Fine Arts LLC	New Canaan	CT	G	203 972-3115	2609

JEWELRY, PRECIOUS METAL: Cigar & Cigarette Access

	CITY	ST	EMP	PHONE	ENTRY #
Muhammad Choudhry	Pawtucket	RI	G	401 726-1118	20862
Emporium	Rutland	VT	G	802 773-4478	22334

JEWELRY, PRECIOUS METAL: Earrings

	CITY	ST	EMP	PHONE	ENTRY #
EF Leach & Company	Attleboro	MA	B	508 643-3309	7731
Reed Allison Group Inc	Providence	RI	D	617 846-1237	21107

JEWELRY, PRECIOUS METAL: Handbags

	CITY	ST	EMP	PHONE	ENTRY #
Whiting & Davis LLC	Attleboro Falls	MA	E	508 699-4412	7819

JEWELRY, PRECIOUS METAL: Necklaces

	CITY	ST	EMP	PHONE	ENTRY #
Jcc Residual Ltd	Woonsocket	RI	E	508 699-4401	21572

JEWELRY, PRECIOUS METAL: Pearl, Natural Or Cultured

	CITY	ST	EMP	PHONE	ENTRY #
Thomas Jewelry Design Inc	Newport	NH	D	603 372-6102	19363

JEWELRY, PRECIOUS METAL: Pins

	CITY	ST	EMP	PHONE	ENTRY #
Robbins Company	Attleboro	MA	C	508 222-2900	7789
Creative Pins By Lynne	Greenville	RI	G	401 949-3665	20465

JEWELRY, PRECIOUS METAL: Rings, Finger

	CITY	ST	EMP	PHONE	ENTRY #
Herff Jones LLC	Warwick	RI	F	401 331-1240	21370

JEWELRY, PRECIOUS METAL: Rosaries/Other Sm Religious Article

	CITY	ST	EMP	PHONE	ENTRY #
McVan Inc	Attleboro	MA	E	508 431-2400	7766
Avanti Jewelry Inc	Cranston	RI	F	401 944-9430	20186

JEWELRY, PRECIOUS METAL: Settings & Mountings

	CITY	ST	EMP	PHONE	ENTRY #
First Card Co Inc	East Providence	RI	E	401 434-6140	20414

JEWELRY, PRECIOUS METAL: Trimmings, Canes, Umbrellas, Etc

	CITY	ST	EMP	PHONE	ENTRY #
Mr Idea Inc	Attleboro	MA	E	508 222-0155	7770

JEWELRY, WHOLESALE

	CITY	ST	EMP	PHONE	ENTRY #
Elm City Mfg Jewelers Inc	Hamden	CT	G	203 248-2195	1747
American Biltrite Inc **(PA)**	Wellesley	MA	G	781 237-6655	16359
Artinian Garabet Corporation	Concord	MA	F	978 371-7110	10113
Edward Spencer	Boston	MA	G	617 426-0521	8519
Michael Vincent	Feeding Hills	MA	G	413 786-4911	10801
We Dream In Colur LLC	Essex	MA	G	978 768-0168	10598
Pyramid Studios	Ellsworth	ME	G	207 667-3321	6020
Song Even	Hinsdale	NH	G	603 256-6018	18321
Bazar Group Inc **(PA)**	East Providence	RI	E	401 434-2595	20391
Imperial-Deltah Inc	East Providence	RI	D	401 434-2597	20420
Ldc Inc	East Providence	RI	F	401 861-4667	20429
R & D Manufacturing Company	Pawtucket	RI	F	401 305-7662	20887
Baked Beads Inc	Waitsfield	VT	F	802 496-2440	22560

JEWELRY: Decorative, Fashion & Costume

	CITY	ST	EMP	PHONE	ENTRY #
Smiling Dog	Middletown	CT	G	860 344-0707	2223
Swarovski North America Ltd	Stamford	CT	G	203 462-3357	4337
Swarovski North America Ltd	Trumbull	CT	G	203 372-0336	4634
Carole Sousa Jewelry	Boston	MA	G	617 232-4087	8460
Charles Thomae & Son Inc	Attleboro	MA	E	508 222-0785	7719
Gear2succeed LLC	Duxbury	MA	G	781 733-0559	10397
Joel Goldsmith Bagnal Inc	Wellesley	MA	G	781 235-8266	16368
North Attleboro Jewelry Co	Attleboro	MA	G	508 222-4660	7774
Plastic Craft Novelty Co Inc	Attleboro	MA	E	508 222-1486	7777
Swarovski North America Ltd	Boston	MA	G	617 578-0705	8871
Swarovski US Holding Limited	Peabody	MA	G	978 531-4582	14374
Yankee Crafters Wampum Jewelry	South Yarmouth	MA	G	508 394-0575	15336
Chronomatic Inc	East Greenwich	RI	E	401 884-6361	20357
Clayton Company Inc	Providence	RI	G	401 421-2978	20984
Dama Jewelry Technology Inc	East Providence	RI	E	401 272-6513	20402
Danecraft Inc **(PA)**	Providence	RI	D	401 941-7700	20993
Fulford Manufacturing Company **(PA)**	Riverside	RI	F	401 431-2000	21168
Ira Holtz & Associates	Cranston	RI	G	401 521-8960	20241
J P I Inc	Warwick	RI	G	401 737-7433	21377
Jcc Residual Ltd	Woonsocket	RI	E	508 699-4401	21572
Josef Creations Inc **(PA)**	Chepachet	RI	E	401 421-4198	20135
Kerissa Creations Inc	Greenville	RI	E	401 949-3700	20470
Klitzner Industries Inc	Lincoln	RI	D	800 621-0161	20577
Kmb International	Bristol	RI	F	401 253-6798	20088
Modern Manufacturing Inc	Johnston	RI	F	401 944-9230	20523
Perry Blackburne Inc	North Providence	RI	E	401 231-7200	20771
R & D Manufacturing Company	Pawtucket	RI	F	401 305-7662	20887
Ramco Inc	Warwick	RI	G	401 739-4343	21409
Salvadore Tool & Findings Inc **(PA)**	Providence	RI	E	401 331-6000	21119
Swarovski Digital Business USA	Cranston	RI	G	888 207-9873	20294
Swarovski North America Ltd	Warwick	RI	G	401 732-0794	21433
Swarovski North America Ltd **(DH)**	Cranston	RI	A	401 463-6400	20295
Swarovski US Holding Limited **(HQ)**	Cranston	RI	G	401 463-6400	20296
Unit Tool Co	Warwick	RI	E	401 781-2647	21436
Wehr Industries Inc	Warwick	RI	E	401 732-6565	21444

JEWELRY: Precious Metal

	CITY	ST	EMP	PHONE	ENTRY #
AG Jewelry Designs LLC **(PA)**	Stamford	CT	G	800 643-0978	4130
Brannkey Inc	Old Saybrook	CT	E	860 510-0501	3330
Carol Ackerman Designs	Collinsville	CT	G	860 693-1013	814
Elm City Mfg Jewelers Inc	Hamden	CT	G	203 248-2195	1747
Gemma Oro Inc	Westport	CT	G	203 227-0774	5197
George S Preisner Jewelers	Wallingford	CT	G	203 265-0057	4748
Goldworks	Danbury	CT	G	203 743-9668	925
Herff Jones LLC	Stratford	CT	F	203 368-9344	4419
Joseph A Cnte Mfg Jewelers Inc	Hamden	CT	G	203 248-9853	1764
Karavas Fashions Ltd	Norwalk	CT	F	203 866-4000	3184
Kenneth R Carson	Manchester	CT	G	860 247-2707	2016
O C Tanner Company	Shelton	CT	G	203 944-5430	3844
Russell Amy Kahn **(PA)**	Ridgefield	CT	F	203 438-2133	3680
Silver Little Shop Inc	Avon	CT	G	860 678-1976	47
Silversmith Inc	Greenwich	CT	G	203 869-4244	1649
A & A Jewelers Inc	North Dartmouth	MA	G	508 992-5320	13915
AB Group Inc	Attleboro	MA	F	508 222-1404	7698
Adina Inc **(PA)**	Norwood	MA	E	781 762-4477	14119
Alan W Leavitt Company	Boston	MA	G	617 338-9335	8349
Alexis Bittar LLC	Boston	MA	G	617 236-0505	8354
Artinian Garabet Corporation	Concord	MA	F	978 371-7110	10113
Ashworth Assoc Mfg Whl Jwelers	North Attleboro	MA	F	508 695-1900	13747
Barmakian Brothers Ltd Partnr	Boston	MA	E	617 227-3724	8392
Block Jewelers Inc	Agawam	MA	G	413 789-2940	7424
Charles Thomae & Son Inc	Attleboro	MA	E	508 222-0785	7719
Design Jewelry	Belmont	MA	G	617 489-0764	8072
E A Dion Inc	Attleboro	MA	C	800 445-1007	7730
Edward Spencer	Boston	MA	G	617 426-0521	8519
Hallmark Healy Group Inc **(DH)**	Attleboro	MA	C	508 222-9234	7744
Hummingbird Productions	Aquinnah	MA	G	508 645-3030	7620
J T Inman Co Inc	Attleboro Falls	MA	E	508 226-0080	7814
Jewelry Solutions LLC	Canton	MA	G	781 821-6100	9748
John E Lepper Inc	Attleboro	MA	G	508 222-6723	7755
John Lewis Inc	Boston	MA	G	617 266-6665	8634
Khalsa Jot	Millis	MA	G	508 376-6206	13185
Lenn Arts Inc	Attleboro	MA	E	508 223-3400	7759
Lestage	Wrentham	MA	G	508 695-7038	17525
M S Company	Attleboro	MA	D	508 222-1700	7760
Marley Hall Inc	Attleboro	MA	G	508 226-2666	7763
Michael Vincent	Feeding Hills	MA	G	413 786-4911	10801
Michele Mercaldo	Boston	MA	G	617 350-7909	8704
Newpro Designs Inc **(HQ)**	Norwood	MA	E	781 762-4477	14183
North Attleboro Jewelry Co	Attleboro	MA	G	508 222-4660	7774
P&N Jewelry Inc	Chelsea	MA	G	617 889-3200	9963
Plainville Stock Company	Plainville	MA	D	508 699-4434	14533
Richline Group Inc	Attleboro	MA	C	774 203-1199	7787
RS Nazarian Inc	Boston	MA	F	617 723-3040	8829
Sweet Metal Finishing Inc	Attleboro	MA	E	508 226-4359	7799
Theme Merchandise Inc	Attleboro	MA	G	508 226-4717	7803
Touch Inc	Waltham	MA	F	781 894-8133	16216
Town & Country Fine Jwly Group	Chelsea	MA	A	617 345-4771	9973
W E Richards Co Inc	Attleboro	MA	F	508 226-1036	7807
We Dream In Colur LLC	Essex	MA	G	978 768-0168	10598
Zero Porosity Casting Inc	Waltham	MA	F	781 373-1951	16226
Daunis	Portland	ME	F	207 773-6011	6648
Gem Creations of Maine	Charlotte	ME	G	207 454-2139	5900
Pyramid Studios	Ellsworth	ME	G	207 667-3321	6020
Thomas Michaels Designers Inc	Camden	ME	G	207 236-2708	5870
Willis & Sons Inc	Bar Harbor	ME	G	207 288-4935	5671
Melvin Reisz	Portsmouth	NH	G	603 436-9188	19594
Song Even	Hinsdale	NH	G	603 256-6018	18321
Stoneman Custom Jewelers	Keene	NH	G	603 352-0811	18530
A & N Jewelry Company	North Providence	RI	G	401 431-9500	20751
A F F Inc **(PA)**	Greenville	RI	D	401 949-3000	20460
Accu-Tool Inc	Pawtucket	RI	G	401 725-5350	20806
Alviti Link All Inc	Johnston	RI	G	401 861-6656	20499
Anatolia Creations	Warwick	RI	G	401 737-4774	21323
Anatone Jewelry Co Inc	North Providence	RI	E	401 728-0490	20752
Arden Jewelry Mfg Co	Johnston	RI	E	401 274-9800	20500
Armbrust International Ltd	Providence	RI	C	401 781-3300	20957
Atamian Manufacturing Corp	Providence	RI	E	800 286-9614	20959
Bazar Group Inc **(PA)**	East Providence	RI	E	401 434-2595	20391
Bliss Manufacturing Co Inc	Pawtucket	RI	E	401 729-1690	20818
Bu Inc	Providence	RI	F	401 831-2112	20976
Carla Corp	East Providence	RI	C	401 438-7070	20395
Cellini Inc **(PA)**	Kingston	RI	D	212 594-3812	20549
Chronomatic Inc	East Greenwich	RI	E	401 884-6361	20357
D & D Model Cleaning & Casting	Johnston	RI	G	401 274-4011	20505
Damico Mfg Co	Greenville	RI	G	401 949-0023	20466
Danecraft Inc **(PA)**	Providence	RI	D	401 941-7700	20993
Danecraft Inc	Providence	RI	C	401 941-7700	20994
David Grau	Providence	RI	G	401 831-0351	20995
Edgar Modeliers	Providence	RI	E	401 781-3506	21003

PRODUCT

	CITY	ST	EMP	PHONE	ENTRY #
Esposito Jewelry Inc	Providence	RI	F	401 943-1900	21008
Fashion Accents LLC **(PA)**	Providence	RI	E	401 331-6626	21012
Fiesta Jewelry Corporation	Pawtucket	RI	G	212 564-6847	20839
Gem-Craft Inc	Cranston	RI	E	401 854-1200	20231
Geo H Fuller and Son Company	Pawtucket	RI	E	401 722-6530	20843
Grant Foster Group L P	Smithfield	RI	F	401 231-4077	21229
Hadc	Providence	RI	G	401 274-1870	21024
Herff Jones LLC	Providence	RI	E	401 331-0888	21029
Imperial-Deltah Inc	East Providence	RI	D	401 434-2597	20420
J H Breakell & Company Inc	Newport	RI	F	401 849-3522	20667
JMS Casting Inc	Providence	RI	G	401 453-5990	21045
Jomay Inc	Cranston	RI	F	401 944-5240	20246
Kennedy Incorporated	North Kingstown	RI	F	401 295-7800	20720
Klitzner Industries Inc	Lincoln	RI	D	800 621-0161	20577
Lim Jewelry	Cranston	RI	G	401 946-9656	20254
Mag Jewelry Co Inc	Cranston	RI	E	401 942-1840	20257
Marketplace Inc Corporate	East Greenwich	RI	F	401 336-3000	20372
Martins Soldering	Johnston	RI	G	401 521-2280	20520
National Chain Company **(PA)**	Warwick	RI	D	401 732-3634	21393
Paroline/Wright Design Inc	Pawtucket	RI	F	401 781-5300	20875
Pearl Comet Inc	Lincoln	RI	G	401 475-1309	20589
Quinonez Mynor	Providence	RI	G	401 751-9292	21104
Rolyn Inc **(PA)**	Cranston	RI	E	401 944-0844	20281
Snow Findings Company Inc	West Warwick	RI	G	401 821-7712	21509
Stylecraft Inc	Cranston	RI	D	401 463-9944	20293
Tahoe Jewelry Inc	East Providence	RI	E	401 435-4114	20445
Tme Co Inc	Providence	RI	E	860 354-0686	21139
Twentieth Century Casting	Pawtucket	RI	G	401 728-6836	20907
Wehr Industries Inc	Warwick	RI	E	401 732-6565	21444
Wiesner Manufacturing Company	Warwick	RI	E	401 421-2406	21447
Designed Essence Enterprise	Burlington	VT	G	802 864-4238	21780
PBL Incorporated	Colchester	VT	F	802 893-0111	21876

JIGS & FIXTURES

	CITY	ST	EMP	PHONE	ENTRY #
Apex Machine Tool Company Inc	Cheshire	CT	D	860 677-2884	711
Astro Industries Inc	Berlin	CT	G	860 828-6304	74
F J Weidner Inc	East Haven	CT	G	203 469-4202	1249
Gary Tool Company	Stratford	CT	G	203 377-3077	4414
Hartford Gauge Co	West Hartford	CT	G	860 233-9619	5075
M & R Manufacturing Inc	Newington	CT	G	860 666-5066	2878
Sirois Tool Company Inc **(PA)**	Berlin	CT	D	860 828-5327	109
Trueline Corporation	Waterbury	CT	G	203 757-0344	4968
A & M Tool & Die Company Inc	Southbridge	MA	E	508 764-3241	15374

JOB PRINTING & NEWSPAPER PUBLISHING COMBINED

	CITY	ST	EMP	PHONE	ENTRY #
Cromwell Chronicle	Rocky Hill	CT	G	860 257-8715	3705
Glastonbury Citizen Inc	Glastonbury	CT	E	860 633-4691	1555
Lakeville Journal Company LLC **(PA)**	Lakeville	CT	D	860 435-9873	1931
Middlbury Bee-Intelligencer-Ct	Middlebury	CT	G	203 577-6800	2156
Record-Journal Newspaper	Mystic	CT	G	860 536-9577	2450
Amherst College Public Affairs	Amherst	MA	F	413 542-2321	7512
Turley Publications Inc	Ware	MA	G	413 967-3505	16239
Wakefield Item Co	Wakefield	MA	E	781 245-0080	15983
Lincoln News	Lincoln	ME	F	207 794-6532	6357
Penobscot Times Inc	Old Town	ME	G	207 827-4451	6546
County Courier Inc	Enosburg Falls	VT	F	802 933-4375	21924
Journal Opinion Inc	Bradford	VT	E	802 222-5281	21702

JOINTS & COUPLINGS

	CITY	ST	EMP	PHONE	ENTRY #
Emseal Joint Systems Ltd	Westborough	MA	E	508 836-0280	16617

JOINTS: Expansion

	CITY	ST	EMP	PHONE	ENTRY #
Westwood Systems Inc	Canton	MA	F	781 821-1117	9795
Franke Associates Inc	South Paris	ME	G	207 743-6654	7010
Rbw Inc	Windham	ME	F	207 786-2446	7246
Senior Operations LLC	Lewiston	ME	D	207 784-2338	6322
Wahlcometroflex Inc	Lewiston	ME	B	207 784-2338	6327

JOINTS: Expansion, Pipe

	CITY	ST	EMP	PHONE	ENTRY #
Flue Gas Solutions Inc	Windham	ME	G	207 893-1510	7234
Fronek Anchor Darling Entp	Laconia	NH	F	603 528-1931	18564

JOINTS: Swivel & Universal, Exc Aircraft & Auto

	CITY	ST	EMP	PHONE	ENTRY #
Curtis Universal Joint Co Inc	Springfield	MA	E	413 737-0281	15465

JOISTS: Long-Span Series, Open Web Steel

	CITY	ST	EMP	PHONE	ENTRY #
Stairs Unlimited Inc	Richford	VT	G	802 848-7030	22310

KAOLIN & BALL CLAY MINING

	CITY	ST	EMP	PHONE	ENTRY #
Sandballz International LLC	Storrs Mansfield	CT	G	860 465-9628	4386

KAOLIN MINING

	CITY	ST	EMP	PHONE	ENTRY #
Imerys Kaolin Inc	South Portland	ME	G	207 741-2118	7030
Imerys Usa Inc	Skowhegan	ME	C	207 238-9267	6977

KEY-TAPE EQPT, EXC DRIVES

	CITY	ST	EMP	PHONE	ENTRY #
Fujifilm Rcrding Media USA Inc **(DH)**	Bedford	MA	D	781 271-4400	7979
Syntegratech Incorporated	Bow	NH	G	603 225-4008	17734

KEYBOARDS: Computer Or Office Machine

	CITY	ST	EMP	PHONE	ENTRY #
Precision Electronic Assembly	Monroe	CT	F	203 452-1839	2413
C S I Keyboards Inc	Peabody	MA	E	978 532-8181	14318
Cortron Inc	Lowell	MA	E	978 975-5445	12362
Imaging Solutions & More	Chicopee	MA	G	413 331-4100	10031

KIDNEY DIALYSIS CENTERS

	CITY	ST	EMP	PHONE	ENTRY #
Fresenius Med Care Hldings Inc **(DH)**	Waltham	MA	A	781 699-9000	16110
Fresenius Med Svcs Group LLC	Waltham	MA	G	781 699-9000	16114

KITCHEN & COOKING ARTICLES: Pottery

	CITY	ST	EMP	PHONE	ENTRY #
Tonmar LLC	Pomfret Center	CT	G	860 974-3714	3559
Potting Shed Inc	Concord	MA	G	617 899-6290	10151
Darmariscotta Pottery Inc	Damariscotta	ME	G	207 563-8843	5935
Georgetown Pottery	Georgetown	ME	G	207 371-2801	6106

KITCHEN ARTICLES: Coarse Earthenware

	CITY	ST	EMP	PHONE	ENTRY #
Ah Nelsen Associates LLC	Kingston	NH	G	603 716-6687	18538

KITCHEN ARTICLES: Semivitreous Earthenware

	CITY	ST	EMP	PHONE	ENTRY #
Express Cntertops Kit Flrg LLC	Orange	CT	G	203 283-4909	3365

KITCHEN CABINET STORES, EXC CUSTOM

	CITY	ST	EMP	PHONE	ENTRY #
East Hartford Lamination Co	Glastonbury	CT	G	860 633-4637	1547
Martin Cabinet Inc **(PA)**	Plainville	CT	E	860 747-5769	3505
Avon Cabinet Company	Avon	MA	G	508 587-9122	7877
Coastal N Counters Inc	Mashpee	MA	F	508 539-3500	12879

KITCHEN CABINETS WHOLESALERS

	CITY	ST	EMP	PHONE	ENTRY #
Coastal N Counters Inc	Mashpee	MA	F	508 539-3500	12879
K & D Millworks Inc	Windham	ME	E	207 892-5188	7238

KITCHEN UTENSILS: Bakers' Eqpt, Wood

	CITY	ST	EMP	PHONE	ENTRY #
Jsi Store Fixtures Inc **(PA)**	Milo	ME	C	207 943-5203	6446

KITCHEN UTENSILS: Wooden

	CITY	ST	EMP	PHONE	ENTRY #
Petermans Boards and Bowls Inc	Gill	MA	E	413 863-2116	11157
New England Wood Products LLC	West Kingston	RI	G	401 789-7474	21469
J K Adams Company Inc	Dorset	VT	E	802 362-2303	21908
John Mc Leod Ltd **(PA)**	Wilmington	VT	E	802 464-8175	22702

KITCHEN WIRE: From Purchased Wire

	CITY	ST	EMP	PHONE	ENTRY #
Macryan Inc	Poultney	VT	G	802 287-4788	22273

KITCHENWARE STORES

	CITY	ST	EMP	PHONE	ENTRY #
Cape Ann Olive Oil Company	Gloucester	MA	G	978 281-1061	11170
Petermans Boards and Bowls Inc	Gill	MA	E	413 863-2116	11157
Plastican Inc	Leominster	MA	A	978 728-5000	12176
Mystic Woodworks	Warren	ME	G	207 273-3937	7145
Lifetime Brands Inc	Pawtucket	RI	G	401 333-2040	20854
J K Adams Company Inc	Dorset	VT	E	802 362-2303	21908

KITCHENWARE: Plastic

	CITY	ST	EMP	PHONE	ENTRY #
Tops Manufacturing Co Inc **(PA)**	Darien	CT	G	203 655-9367	1034

KNIT OUTERWEAR DYEING & FINISHING, EXC HOSIERY & GLOVE

	CITY	ST	EMP	PHONE	ENTRY #
Red Fish-Blue Fish Dye Works	Somersworth	NH	F	603 692-3900	19846

KNITTING MILLS, NEC

	CITY	ST	EMP	PHONE	ENTRY #
Giral LLC	Burlington	VT	G	802 238-7852	21787

KNIVES: Agricultural Or indl

	CITY	ST	EMP	PHONE	ENTRY #
Dexter-Russell Inc	Southbridge	MA	C	800 343-6042	15380
Greenfield Silver Inc **(PA)**	Greenfield	MA	D	413 774-2774	11262
Lamson and Goodnow Mfg Co	Shelburne Falls	MA	E	413 625-6311	15074
Peterson and Nash Inc	Norwell	MA	E	781 826-9085	14111
R Murphy Company Inc	Ayer	MA	F	978 772-3481	7935

KNURLING

	CITY	ST	EMP	PHONE	ENTRY #
Form Roll Die Corp **(PA)**	Worcester	MA	E	508 755-2010	17377

LABELS: Cotton, Printed

	CITY	ST	EMP	PHONE	ENTRY #
Sterling Name Tape Company	Winsted	CT	G	860 379-5142	5426
Conntext Labels	Great Barrington	MA	G	413 528-3303	11237
Screenco Printing Inc	Newburyport	MA	G	978 465-1211	13533

LABELS: Paper, Made From Purchased Materials

	CITY	ST	EMP	PHONE	ENTRY #
Flexo Label Solutions LLC	Deep River	CT	G	860 243-9300	1060
Specialty Printing LLC **(PA)**	East Windsor	CT	D	860 623-8870	1303
Graphics Source Co	Southampton	MA	F	413 543-0700	15338
Screenprint/Dow Inc	Wilmington	MA	D	978 657-7290	17043
Smyth Companies LLC	Wilmington	MA	G	800 776-1201	17045
Lamtec Inc	Portland	ME	G	207 774-6560	6678
Computype Inc	Concord	NH	F	603 225-5500	17894
Swing Labels Inc	Jaffrey	NH	G	978 425-0855	18478
Foxon Company	Providence	RI	E	401 421-2386	21015

LABELS: Woven

	CITY	ST	EMP	PHONE	ENTRY #
Bell Manufacturing Co	Lewiston	ME	D	207 784-2961	6276

LABORATORIES, TESTING: Metallurgical

	CITY	ST	EMP	PHONE	ENTRY #
Pti Industries Inc **(HQ)**	Enfield	CT	E	800 318-8438	1376

LABORATORIES, TESTING: Product Testing

	CITY	ST	EMP	PHONE	ENTRY #
AKO Inc	Windsor	CT	E	860 298-9765	5317
Sousa Corp	Newington	CT	F	860 523-9090	2904
K S E Inc	Sunderland	MA	F	413 549-5506	15675
Microplasmic Corporation	Peabody	MA	G	978 548-9762	14355
American Iron & Metal USA Inc **(HQ)**	Cranston	RI	E	401 463-5605	20178

LABORATORIES, TESTING: Product Testing, Safety/Performance

	CITY	ST	EMP	PHONE	ENTRY #
Parker-Hannifin Corporation	Woburn	MA	B	781 939-4278	17255

LABORATORIES, TESTING: Water

	CITY	ST	EMP	PHONE	ENTRY #
Everett M Windover Inc	Colchester	VT	E	802 865-0000	21863

LABORATORIES: Biological

	CITY	ST	EMP	PHONE	ENTRY #
Genzyme Corporation **(DH)**	Cambridge	MA	A	617 252-7500	9489
Kalvista Pharmaceuticals Inc **(PA)**	Cambridge	MA	F	857 999-0075	9524

LABORATORIES: Biological Research

Company	CITY	ST	EMP	PHONE	ENTRY #
Acer Therapeutics Inc **(PA)**	Newton	MA	G	844 902-6100	13553
Agenus Inc **(PA)**	Lexington	MA	C	781 674-4400	12204
Akcea Therapeutics Inc **(HQ)**	Boston	MA	D	617 207-0202	8347
Akebia Therapeutics Inc **(PA)**	Cambridge	MA	D	617 871-2098	9379
Biogen Inc **(PA)**	Cambridge	MA	B	617 679-2000	9409
Dicerna Pharmaceuticals Inc	Lexington	MA	E	617 621-8097	12219
Dyax Corp	Lexington	MA	C	617 349-0200	12221
Moderna LLC **(HQ)**	Cambridge	MA	G	617 714-6500	9565
Synlogic Inc **(PA)**	Cambridge	MA	E	617 401-9975	9671

LABORATORIES: Biotechnology

Company	CITY	ST	EMP	PHONE	ENTRY #
Achillion Pharmaceuticals Inc	New Haven	CT	D	203 624-7000	2652
Arvinas Inc **(PA)**	New Haven	CT	F	203 535-1456	2658
Agios Pharmaceuticals Inc **(PA)**	Cambridge	MA	C	617 649-8600	9377
Aileron Therapeutics Inc	Watertown	MA	E	774 444-0704	16265
Alkermes Inc **(HQ)**	Waltham	MA	B	781 609-6000	16029
Alnylam Pharmaceuticals Inc **(PA)**	Cambridge	MA	C	617 551-8200	9384
Arqule Inc **(PA)**	Burlington	MA	E	781 994-0300	9234
Cambridge Polymer Group Inc	Boston	MA	F	617 629-4400	8456
Enanta Pharmaceuticals Inc	Watertown	MA	D	617 607-0800	16282
Epizyme Inc	Cambridge	MA	C	617 229-5872	9469
Helixbind Inc	Marlborough	MA	F	508 460-1028	12767
Mersana Therapeutics Inc **(PA)**	Cambridge	MA	D	617 498-0020	9552
Microbot Medical Inc **(PA)**	Hingham	MA	G	781 875-3605	11505
Restorbio Inc	Boston	MA	E	857 315-5521	8818
Solid Biosciences Inc **(PA)**	Cambridge	MA	D	617 337-4680	9655
USA Renewable LLC	Newton	MA	G	617 319-7237	13645
Vertex Pharmaceuticals Inc **(PA)**	Boston	MA	B	617 341-6100	8909
Voyager Therapeutics Inc **(PA)**	Cambridge	MA	D	857 259-5340	9698
Wagner Lifescience LLC	Middleton	MA	G	978 539-8102	13105
X4 Pharmaceuticals Inc **(PA)**	Cambridge	MA	F	857 529-8300	9706
Amgen Inc	West Greenwich	RI	D	401 392-1200	21452

LABORATORIES: Commercial Nonphysical Research

Company	CITY	ST	EMP	PHONE	ENTRY #
Angel Guard Products Inc	Worcester	MA	G	508 791-1073	17339
Idg Corporate Services Group	Framingham	MA	F	508 875-5000	10967
Raytheon Company	Lexington	MA	G	781 862-6800	12258

LABORATORIES: Dental

Company	CITY	ST	EMP	PHONE	ENTRY #
Dillon Laboratories Inc	Abington	MA	F	781 871-2333	7322

LABORATORIES: Dental, Crown & Bridge Production

Company	CITY	ST	EMP	PHONE	ENTRY #
Encore Crown & Bridge Inc	Plymouth	MA	E	508 746-6025	14555

LABORATORIES: Electronic Research

Company	CITY	ST	EMP	PHONE	ENTRY #
Connecticut Analytical Corp	Bethany	CT	F	203 393-9666	119
Madison Technology Intl	Mystic	CT	G	860 245-0245	2442
Videoiq Inc	Somerville	MA	E	781 222-3069	15228
David Saunders Inc	South Portland	ME	E	207 228-1888	7021

LABORATORIES: Environmental Research

Company	CITY	ST	EMP	PHONE	ENTRY #
Ion Physics Corp	Fremont	NH	G	603 895-5100	18177

LABORATORIES: Medical

Company	CITY	ST	EMP	PHONE	ENTRY #
Biomerieux Inc	Boston	MA	G	617 879-8000	8411
Massbiologics	Boston	MA	C	617 474-3000	8687

LABORATORIES: Physical Research, Commercial

Company	CITY	ST	EMP	PHONE	ENTRY #
Cara Therapeutics Inc	Stamford	CT	E	203 406-3700	4155
Charles River Laboratories Inc	Storrs	CT	E	860 429-7261	4381
Cytec Industries Inc	Stamford	CT	D	203 321-2200	4183
Hampford Research Inc **(PA)**	Stratford	CT	E	203 375-1137	4417
Henkel Loctite Corporation **(DH)**	Rocky Hill	CT	E	860 571-5100	3714
Herbasway Laboratories LLC	Wallingford	CT	E	203 269-6991	4750
Jet Process Corporation	North Haven	CT	G	203 985-6000	3035
Spectrogram Corporation	Madison	CT	G	203 245-2433	1977
Thayermahan Inc	Groton	CT	E	860 785-9994	1688
Adaptive Optics Associates Inc **(DH)**	Devens	MA	D	978 757-9600	10317
Barrett Technology LLC	Newton	MA	E	617 252-9000	13566
Electron Solutions Inc	Lexington	MA	F	781 674-2440	12222
Endogen Inc	Woburn	MA	D	617 225-0055	17177
Flintec Inc	Hudson	MA	E	978 562-4548	11774
Infinity Pharmaceuticals Inc **(PA)**	Cambridge	MA	D	617 453-1000	9515
Instrumentation Laboratory Co **(DH)**	Bedford	MA	A	781 861-0710	7982
Ironwood Pharmaceuticals Inc **(PA)**	Boston	MA	C	617 621-7722	8622
Jounce Therapeutics Inc **(PA)**	Cambridge	MA	D	857 259-3840	9522
Lyne Laboratories Inc	Brockton	MA	D	508 583-8700	9163
Micro Magnetics Inc	Fall River	MA	F	508 672-4489	10732
New Balance Athletics Inc	Lawrence	MA	B	978 685-8400	12063
Scientific Solutions Inc	North Chelmsford	MA	F	978 251-4554	13910
Teradyne Inc	Bedford	MA	C	617 482-2700	8014
Ultraclad Corporation	Newburyport	MA	G	978 358-7945	13545
Biodesign International Inc	Saco	ME	E	207 283-6500	6843
At Comm Corp	Manchester	NH	F	603 624-4424	18783
Bae Systems Info & Elec Sys	Hudson	NH	A	603 885-4321	18376
Exothermics Inc	Amherst	NH	F	603 821-5660	17560
Oracle Systems Corporation	Nashua	NH	B	603 897-3000	19225
Simbex LLC	Lebanon	NH	E	603 448-2367	18636
Bioprocessh2o LLC	Portsmouth	RI	E	401 683-5400	20919

LABORATORIES: Testing

Company	CITY	ST	EMP	PHONE	ENTRY #
Acuren Inspection Inc **(HQ)**	Danbury	CT	A	203 702-8740	867
Magellan Diagnostics Inc	North Billerica	MA	E	978 856-2345	13838
Magellan Diagnostics Inc **(HQ)**	Chelmsford	MA	D	978 250-7000	9915
Enginuity Plm LLC **(HQ)**	Milford	CT	F	203 218-7225	2286
Barbour Stockwell Inc	Woburn	MA	E	781 933-5200	17127
Cambridge Polymer Group Inc	Boston	MA	F	617 629-4400	8456
Gentest Corporation	Woburn	MA	E	781 935-5115	17191
Jordi Labs LLC	Mansfield	MA	E	508 719-8543	12639
Netzsch Instruments N Amer LLC **(DH)**	Burlington	MA	E	781 272-5353	9307
Teledyne Dgital Imaging US Inc **(HQ)**	Billerica	MA	E	978 670-2000	8303
Northeast Laboratory Svcs Inc **(PA)**	Winslow	ME	D	207 873-7711	7272
Everett Charles Tech LLC	Hudson	NH	G	603 882-2621	18389
Smiths Tblar Systms-Lconia Inc	Laconia	NH	B	603 524-2064	18587
Allstate Drilling Co	Riverside	RI	G	401 434-7458	21163

LABORATORY APPARATUS & FURNITURE

Company	CITY	ST	EMP	PHONE	ENTRY #
Fmp Products	Greenwich	CT	G	203 422-0686	1615
Idex Health & Science LLC	Bristol	CT	C	860 314-2880	570
Mark V Laboratory Inc	East Granby	CT	G	860 653-7201	1132
Proteowise Inc	Branford	CT	G	203 430-4187	340
Tomtec Inc	Hamden	CT	D	203 281-6790	1790
Aja International Inc	Scituate	MA	E	781 545-7365	15005
Bluecatbio MA Inc	Concord	MA	G	978 405-2533	10116
Digilab Inc	Hopkinton	MA	D	508 305-2410	11700
Harvard Bioscience Inc **(PA)**	Holliston	MA	C	508 893-8999	11575
Idex Health & Science LLC	Middleboro	MA	C	774 213-0200	13064
Inert Corporation	Amesbury	MA	E	978 462-4415	7492
Kinetic Systems Inc	Boston	MA	E	617 522-8700	8649
Labtech Inc **(PA)**	Hopkinton	MA	G	508 435-5500	11726
Lc Technology Solutions Inc	Salisbury	MA	G	978 255-1620	14952
Microfluidics Intl Corp	Westwood	MA	E	617 969-5452	16873
Parallel Systems Corp	Georgetown	MA	F	978 352-7100	11148
Perkinelmer Hlth Sciences Inc **(DH)**	Waltham	MA	C	781 663-6900	16172
Pharyx Inc	Woburn	MA	G	617 792-0524	17262
Troemner	North Andover	MA	G	978 655-3377	13732
Wright Line LLC **(HQ)**	Worcester	MA	C	508 852-4300	17510
Baker Company Inc **(PA)**	Sanford	ME	C	207 324-8773	6871
Emerson Apparatus Company	Gorham	ME	F	207 856-0055	6111
Colonial Medical Supply Co Inc	Windham	NH	G	603 328-5130	20002
Erie Scientific LLC **(DH)**	Portsmouth	NH	B	603 430-6859	19560
Materials Research Frncs Inc	Allenstown	NH	F	603 485-2394	17539
Owl Separation Systems LLC	Newington	NH	E	603 559-9297	19323
Thermo Neslab LLC	Newington	NH	C	603 436-9444	19328
Omichron Corp	South Londonderry	VT	F	802 824-3136	22488
Raj Communications Ltd	Williston	VT	F	802 658-4961	22687

LABORATORY APPARATUS & FURNITURE: Worktables

Company	CITY	ST	EMP	PHONE	ENTRY #
Bnz Materials Inc	North Billerica	MA	E	978 663-3401	13796

LABORATORY APPARATUS, EXC HEATING & MEASURING

Company	CITY	ST	EMP	PHONE	ENTRY #
M/K Systems Inc	Peabody	MA	G	978 857-9228	14354

LABORATORY APPARATUS: Calibration Tapes, Phy Testing Mach

Company	CITY	ST	EMP	PHONE	ENTRY #
Environics Inc	Tolland	CT	E	860 872-1111	4547
Instron Applications Lab	Norwood	MA	G	800 564-8378	14164
Spectris Inc **(HQ)**	Westborough	MA	F	508 768-6400	16650

LABORATORY APPARATUS: Calorimeters

Company	CITY	ST	EMP	PHONE	ENTRY #
Blacktrace Inc	Norwell	MA	G	617 848-1211	14097
Microcal LLC	Northampton	MA	G	413 586-7720	14012

LABORATORY APPARATUS: Evaporation

Company	CITY	ST	EMP	PHONE	ENTRY #
Vacuum Technology Inc	Gloucester	MA	G	510 333-6562	11216

LABORATORY APPARATUS: Freezers

Company	CITY	ST	EMP	PHONE	ENTRY #
Hamilton Storage Tech Inc	Franklin	MA	G	508 544-7000	11052

LABORATORY APPARATUS: Heating

Company	CITY	ST	EMP	PHONE	ENTRY #
Apogent Technologies Inc	Waltham	MA	A	781 622-1300	16035
R D Webb Co Inc	Natick	MA	G	508 650-0110	13276

LABORATORY APPARATUS: Laser Beam Alignment Device

Company	CITY	ST	EMP	PHONE	ENTRY #
Pinpoint Laser Systems Inc	Peabody	MA	E	978 532-8001	14362

LABORATORY APPARATUS: Physics, NEC

Company	CITY	ST	EMP	PHONE	ENTRY #
Kimball Physics Inc	Wilton	NH	E	603 878-1616	19981

LABORATORY APPARATUS: Shakers & Stirrers

Company	CITY	ST	EMP	PHONE	ENTRY #
Eppendorf Holding Inc **(DH)**	Enfield	CT	E	860 253-3417	1359

LABORATORY CHEMICALS: Organic

Company	CITY	ST	EMP	PHONE	ENTRY #
Dragonlab LLC	Rocky Hill	CT	G	860 436-9221	3708
Yale University	New Haven	CT	G	203 432-3916	2759
Avantgarde Molecular LLC	Maynard	MA	G	617 549-2238	12895
Fisher Scientific Intl LLC **(HQ)**	Waltham	MA	C	781 622-1000	16107
Giner Life Sciences Inc	Auburndale	MA	G	781 529-0576	7863
Glixx Laboratories Inc	Hopkinton	MA	G	781 333-5348	11716
Strem Chemicals Incorporated	Newburyport	MA	D	978 499-1600	13537

LABORATORY EQPT, EXC MEDICAL: Wholesalers

Company	CITY	ST	EMP	PHONE	ENTRY #
Fisher Scientific Intl LLC **(HQ)**	Waltham	MA	C	781 622-1000	16107
Jeio Tech Inc	Billerica	MA	G	781 376-0700	8259
M R Resources Inc	Fitchburg	MA	E	978 696-3060	10831
Advanced Concepts & Engrg LLC	Dexter	ME	G	207 270-3025	5955
Opti-Sciences Inc	Hudson	NH	G	603 883-4400	18424
Raj Communications Ltd	Williston	VT	F	802 658-4961	22687

LABORATORY EQPT: Balances

Company	CITY	ST	EMP	PHONE	ENTRY #
CFM Test & Balance Corp	Bethel	CT	G	203 778-1900	136
Setra Systems Inc	Boxboro	MA	F	978 263-1400	8954

LABORATORY EQPT: Centrifuges

	CITY	ST	EMP	PHONE	ENTRY #
Dragonlab LLC	Rocky Hill	CT	G	860 436-9221	3708

LABORATORY EQPT: Chemical

	CITY	ST	EMP	PHONE	ENTRY #
Novamont North America Inc	Shelton	CT	F	203 744-8801	3842

LABORATORY EQPT: Clinical Instruments Exc Medical

	CITY	ST	EMP	PHONE	ENTRY #
Bioclinica Inc	New London	CT	G	860 701-0082	2766
Andrew Alliance Usa Inc	Waltham	MA	G	617 797-9071	16033
Openclinica LLC	Waltham	MA	E	617 621-8585	16167
Pharmask Inc	Medfield	MA	G	508 359-6700	12916
Primevigilance Inc	Waltham	MA	G	781 703-5540	16178
Unity Scientific LLC	Milford	MA	E	203 740-2999	13149
Xylem Inc	Beverly	MA	E	978 778-1010	8200
Maine Mlclar Qulty Contrls Inc	Saco	ME	E	207 885-1072	6852

LABORATORY EQPT: Distilling

	CITY	ST	EMP	PHONE	ENTRY #
Pall Northborough **(DH)**	Northborough	MA	G	978 263-9888	14043

LABORATORY EQPT: Measuring

	CITY	ST	EMP	PHONE	ENTRY #
Mettler-Toledo Intl Inc	Newton	MA	G	800 472-4646	13614
Rochester USA	Rochester	NH	G	603 332-0717	19683

LABORATORY EQPT: Sterilizers

	CITY	ST	EMP	PHONE	ENTRY #
Mayborn Usa Inc	Stamford	CT	F	781 269-7490	4245

LACQUERING SVC: Metal Prdts

	CITY	ST	EMP	PHONE	ENTRY #
Baron & Young Co Inc	Bristol	CT	G	860 589-3235	529
Spray Maine Inc	Newburyport	MA	F	207 384-2273	13535

LADDERS: Metal

	CITY	ST	EMP	PHONE	ENTRY #
St Pierre Manufacturing Corp	Worcester	MA	E	508 853-8010	17479

LADDERS: Wood

	CITY	ST	EMP	PHONE	ENTRY #
Lyn-Lad Group Ltd **(PA)**	Lynn	MA	F	781 598-6010	12523

LAMINATED PLASTICS: Plate, Sheet, Rod & Tubes

	CITY	ST	EMP	PHONE	ENTRY #
Beckson Manufacturing Inc **(PA)**	Bridgeport	CT	E	203 366-3644	381
CT Composites & Marine Svc LLC	South Windsor	CT	G	860 282-0100	3955
Diba Industries Inc **(HQ)**	Danbury	CT	C	203 744-0773	901
Panolam Industries Inc **(HQ)**	Shelton	CT	E	203 925-1556	3848
Pioneer Plastics Corporation **(HQ)**	Shelton	CT	D	203 925-1556	3853
Polymedex Discovery Group Inc **(PA)**	Putnam	CT	F	860 928-4102	3627
Quality Name Plate Inc	East Glastonbury	CT	D	860 633-9495	1114
The E J Davis Company	North Haven	CT	E	203 239-5391	3063
3M Company	Chelmsford	MA	C	978 256-3911	9865
Fort Hill Sign Products Inc	Hopedale	MA	G	781 321-4320	11672
Insultab Inc	Woburn	MA	D	781 935-0800	17203
M M Newman Corporation	Marblehead	MA	F	781 631-7100	12687
October Company Inc	Easthampton	MA	E	413 529-0718	10573
Samar Co Inc	Stoughton	MA	D	781 297-7264	15620
United Plastic Fabricating Inc **(PA)**	North Andover	MA	D	978 975-4520	13734
Panolam Industries Intl Inc	Auburn	ME	E	207 784-9111	5586
Pioneer Plastics Corporation	Auburn	ME	B	207 784-9111	5592
Nordson Medical (nh) Inc **(HQ)**	Salem	NH	C	603 327-0600	19756
Scandia Plastics Inc	Plaistow	NH	E	603 382-6533	19523
Spaulding Composites Inc **(PA)**	Rochester	NH	D	603 332-0555	19687
Teleflex Incorporated	Jaffrey	NH	E	603 532-7706	18479
Tfx Medical Incorporated	Jaffrey	NH	B	603 532-7706	18480
Nelipak Corporation **(PA)**	Cranston	RI	D	401 946-2699	20267
Tpi Inc	Warren	RI	D	401 247-4010	21310
Tpi Composites Inc	Warren	RI	G	401 247-4010	21311
Kaman Composites - Vermont Inc	Bennington	VT	C	802 442-9964	21678

LAMINATING MATERIALS

	CITY	ST	EMP	PHONE	ENTRY #
Middlesex Research Mfg Co Inc	Hudson	MA	E	978 562-3697	11793
Rogers Corporation	Kingston	MA	G	508 746-3311	11963

LAMINATING SVCS

	CITY	ST	EMP	PHONE	ENTRY #
Flagship Converters Inc	Danbury	CT	D	203 792-0034	920
AP Dley Cstm Laminating Corp	Windham	NH	E	603 437-6666	20000

LAMP & LIGHT BULBS & TUBES

	CITY	ST	EMP	PHONE	ENTRY #
Whelen Engineering Company Inc **(PA)**	Chester	CT	B	860 526-9504	777
Acera Inc	Beverly	MA	G	978 998-4281	8095
Dolan-Jenner Industries Inc	Boxborough	MA	E	978 263-1400	8961
International Light Tech Inc	Peabody	MA	E	978 818-6180	14343
Osram Sylvania Inc	Wilmington	MA	B	978 750-3900	17037
Osram Sylvania Inc	Beverly	MA	C	978 750-1529	8163
Osram Sylvania Inc **(HQ)**	Wilmington	MA	A	978 570-3000	17036
Partylite Inc **(HQ)**	Plymouth	MA	D	203 661-1926	14572
Philips Holding USA Inc **(HQ)**	Andover	MA	C	978 687-1501	7582
Traxon Technologies	Wilmington	MA	F	201 508-1570	17058
Luminescent Systems Inc	Lebanon	NH	C	603 643-7766	18629
Osram Sylvania Inc	Exeter	NH	D	603 772-4331	18127
Osram Sylvania Inc	Hillsborough	NH	B	603 464-7235	18317
Brownlie Lamar Design Group	Warren	RI	G	401 714-9371	21292
Global Value Lighting LLC **(PA)**	West Warwick	RI	F	401 535-4002	21492
Osram Sylvania Inc	Central Falls	RI	B	401 723-1378	20122

LAMP BULBS & TUBES, ELECTRIC: For Specialized Applications

	CITY	ST	EMP	PHONE	ENTRY #
Southern Neng Ultraviolet Inc	Branford	CT	G	203 483-5810	350

LAMP BULBS & TUBES, ELECTRIC: Health, Infrared/Ultraviolet

	CITY	ST	EMP	PHONE	ENTRY #
Osram Sylvania Inc	Exeter	NH	C	603 669-5350	18128

LAMP BULBS & TUBES, ELECTRIC: Light, Complete

	CITY	ST	EMP	PHONE	ENTRY #
Revolution Lighting **(HQ)**	Stamford	CT	G	203 504-1111	4299
Revolution Lighting Tech Inc **(PA)**	Stamford	CT	C	203 504-1111	4300

LAMP BULBS & TUBES/PARTS, ELECTRIC: Generalized Applications

	CITY	ST	EMP	PHONE	ENTRY #
Lcd Lighting Inc	Orange	CT	C	203 799-7877	3370
General Electric Company	Westborough	MA	F	508 870-5200	16619

LAMP FIXTURES: Ultraviolet

	CITY	ST	EMP	PHONE	ENTRY #
Incure Inc	New Britain	CT	G	860 748-2979	2540
Uv III Systems Inc	Alburg	VT	F	508 883-4881	21593

LAMP REPAIR & MOUNTING SVCS

	CITY	ST	EMP	PHONE	ENTRY #
Blanche P Field LLC	Boston	MA	E	617 423-0714	8413

LAMP STORES

	CITY	ST	EMP	PHONE	ENTRY #
Keeling Company Inc	Old Lyme	CT	G	860 349-0916	3324
Vijon Studios Inc	Old Saybrook	CT	G	860 399-7440	3354

LAMPS: Ultraviolet

	CITY	ST	EMP	PHONE	ENTRY #
Light Sources Inc **(PA)**	Orange	CT	C	203 799-7877	3371
Triton Thalassic Tech Inc **(PA)**	Ridgefield	CT	G	203 438-0633	3686
First Light Technologies Inc	Poultney	VT	D	802 287-4195	22271

LAND SUBDIVIDERS & DEVELOPERS: Residential

	CITY	ST	EMP	PHONE	ENTRY #
Fox Modular Homes Inc	Lee	MA	F	413 243-1950	12092

LAND SUBDIVISION & DEVELOPMENT

	CITY	ST	EMP	PHONE	ENTRY #
Wesco Building & Design Inc	Stoneham	MA	E	781 279-0490	15572
Wescor Ltd **(PA)**	Stoneham	MA	F	781 279-0490	15573

LANTERNS

	CITY	ST	EMP	PHONE	ENTRY #
Nauset Lantern Shop	Orleans	MA	G	508 255-1009	14236
Heritage Lanterns	Windham	ME	F	207 893-1134	7236
John J Marr	Conway	NH	F	603 939-2698	17954

LAPIDARY WORK & DIAMOND CUTTING & POLISHING

	CITY	ST	EMP	PHONE	ENTRY #
Eastwind Lapidary Inc	Windsor	VT	G	802 674-5427	22707

LAPIDARY WORK: Jewel Cut, Drill, Polish, Recut/Setting

	CITY	ST	EMP	PHONE	ENTRY #
Davriel Jewelers Inc	East Longmeadow	MA	G	413 525-4975	10471

LAPIDARY WORK: Jewelry Polishing, For The Trade

	CITY	ST	EMP	PHONE	ENTRY #
Jmt Epoxy	Providence	RI	G	401 331-9730	21046

LASER SYSTEMS & EQPT

	CITY	ST	EMP	PHONE	ENTRY #
Advanced Photonics Intl Inc	Fairfield	CT	G	203 259-0437	1413
Coherent-Deos LLC	Bloomfield	CT	C	860 243-9557	216
Total Register Inc	New Milford	CT	F	860 210-0465	2831
Convergent - Photonics LLC	Chicopee	MA	D	413 598-5200	10016
Excel Technology Inc **(HQ)**	Bedford	MA	D	781 266-5700	7976
Ipg Photonics Corporation **(PA)**	Oxford	MA	B	508 373-1100	14263
Ipg Photonics Corporation	Marlborough	MA	F	508 229-2130	12778
Ipg Photonics Corporation	Marlborough	MA	F	508 506-2812	12779
Iradion Laser Inc	Uxbridge	MA	G	401 762-5100	15921
Novanta Corporation **(HQ)**	Bedford	MA	B	781 266-5700	7995
Novanta Inc **(PA)**	Bedford	MA	C	781 266-5700	7996
Polytec Inc	Hudson	MA	F	508 417-1040	11803
Rofin-Baasel Inc **(DH)**	Devens	MA	E	978 635-9100	10332
Sancliff Inc	Worcester	MA	F	508 795-0747	17469
Teradiode Inc	Wilmington	MA	D	978 988-1040	17053
Urolaze Inc	Wellesley Hills	MA	G	413 374-5006	16400
Davco	Danbury	NH	G	603 768-3517	17963
Faro Technologies Inc	Hudson	NH	G	603 893-6200	18390
I R Sources Inc	Brookline	NH	G	603 672-0582	17771
Ipg Photonics Corporation	Nashua	NH	E	603 518-3200	19191
JP Sercel Associates Inc	Manchester	NH	D	603 595-7048	18852
Laser Advantage LLC	Nashua	NH	F	603 886-9464	19197
Laser Light Engines Inc	Salem	NH	F	603 952-4550	19746
Laser Projection Technologies	Londonderry	NH	E	603 421-0209	18712
Prophotonix Limited **(PA)**	Salem	NH	E	603 893-8778	19761
Laser Fare Inc **(PA)**	Smithfield	RI	D	401 231-4400	21235
Laservall North America LLC	Pawtucket	RI	G	401 724-0076	20853

LASERS: Welding, Drilling & Cutting Eqpt

	CITY	ST	EMP	PHONE	ENTRY #
Cadence Ct Inc	Suffield	CT	D	860 370-9780	4461
Varnum Enterprises LLC	Bethel	CT	F	203 743-4443	190
Green Brothers Fabricating	Taunton	MA	E	508 880-3608	15756
Litron LLC	Agawam	MA	D	413 789-0700	7437
Lfi Inc **(PA)**	Smithfield	RI	D	401 231-4400	21236
Maley Laser Processing Inc	Warwick	RI	F	401 732-8400	21386

LATEX: Foamed

	CITY	ST	EMP	PHONE	ENTRY #
Ktt Enterprises LLC	Hamden	CT	G	203 288-7883	1765
Latex Foam Intl Holdings Inc **(PA)**	Shelton	CT	C	203 924-0700	3826
Universal Foam Products LLC	Bloomfield	CT	F	860 216-3015	270

LATH: Snow Fence

	CITY	ST	EMP	PHONE	ENTRY #
Sonco Worldwide Inc	Warwick	RI	F	401 406-3761	21427

LATHES

	CITY	ST	EMP	PHONE	ENTRY #
F W Derbyshire Inc	Blackstone	MA	G	508 883-2385	8312
Ramco Machine LLC	Rowley	MA	E	978 948-3778	14863

LAUNDRY EQPT: Commercial

	CITY	ST	EMP	PHONE	ENTRY #
Sumal Enterprises LLC	Watertown	CT	G	860 945-3337	5027

LAUNDRY EQPT: Household

	CITY	ST	EMP	PHONE	ENTRY #
Instinctive Works LLC	Westport	CT	G	203 434-8094	5204

LAUNDRY SVC: Safety Glove Sply

	CITY	ST	EMP	PHONE	ENTRY #
Sperian Protection Usa Inc **(DH)**	Smithfield	RI	E	401 232-1200	21250

LAUNDRY SVCS: Indl

	CITY	ST	EMP	PHONE	ENTRY #
A & P Coat Apron & Lin Sup Inc	Hartford	CT	D	914 840-3200	1799

LAWN & GARDEN EQPT

	CITY	ST	EMP	PHONE	ENTRY #
Greenscape of Clinton LLC	Clinton	CT	G	860 669-1880	787
Woodland Power Products Inc	West Haven	CT	E	888 531-7253	5152
Armatron International Inc **(PA)**	Malden	MA	D	781 321-2300	12559
Douglas Dynamics LLC	Rockland	ME	C	207 701-4200	6790
Eastman Industries **(PA)**	Portland	ME	E	207 878-5353	6658
Eschdale Lawn & Grdn Pdts LLC	Smyrna Mills	ME	G	207 757-7268	6991
Genest Landscape Masonry	Windham	ME	G	207 892-3778	7235
Maine Barrel & Display Company	Lewiston	ME	E	207 784-6700	6303
Oldcastle Lawn & Garden Inc	Poland	ME	E	207 998-5580	6595
North Country Tractor Inc	Dover	NH	F	603 742-5488	18041
Little House By Andre Inc	Colchester	VT	G	802 878-8733	21872
Vermont Ware Inc	St George	VT	G	802 482-4426	22514
Zoneup Inc	Saint Albans	VT	G	802 868-2300	22385

LAWN & GARDEN EQPT: Tractors & Eqpt

	CITY	ST	EMP	PHONE	ENTRY #
R I Baker Co Inc **(PA)**	Clarksburg	MA	E	413 663-3791	10075
Machining Innovations Inc	Oakland	ME	G	207 465-2500	6534

LEAD

	CITY	ST	EMP	PHONE	ENTRY #
Alent USA Holding Inc	Waterbury	CT	B	203 575-5727	4839

LEAD PENCILS & ART GOODS

	CITY	ST	EMP	PHONE	ENTRY #
Bic Corporation **(HQ)**	Shelton	CT	A	203 783-2000	3782
Jen Mfg Inc	Millbury	MA	E	508 753-1076	13168
Pucker Gallery Inc	Somerville	MA	F	617 261-1817	15207
Scratch Art Company Inc **(PA)**	Avon	MA	F	508 583-8085	7895
Garland Industries Inc	Coventry	RI	E	401 821-1450	20147

LEAF TOBACCO WHOLESALERS

	CITY	ST	EMP	PHONE	ENTRY #
Nuway Tobacco Company	South Windsor	CT	D	860 289-6414	3996

LEASING & RENTAL SVCS: Cranes & Aerial Lift Eqpt

	CITY	ST	EMP	PHONE	ENTRY #
Baxter Inc	West Yarmouth	MA	G	508 228-8136	16578
Energy Smart Building Inc	Starksboro	VT	E	802 453-4438	22515

LEASING & RENTAL SVCS: Oil Field Eqpt

	CITY	ST	EMP	PHONE	ENTRY #
P2 Science Inc	Woodbridge	CT	G	203 821-7457	5475

LEASING & RENTAL: Boats & Ships

	CITY	ST	EMP	PHONE	ENTRY #
Alden Yachts Corporation	Bristol	RI	D	401 683-4200	20060

LEASING & RENTAL: Construction & Mining Eqpt

	CITY	ST	EMP	PHONE	ENTRY #
Richard Dudgeon Inc	Waterbury	CT	G	203 336-4459	4950

LEASING & RENTAL: Trucks, Without Drivers

	CITY	ST	EMP	PHONE	ENTRY #
Standard Welding Company Inc	East Hartford	CT	G	860 528-9628	1222
U-Haul Co of Massachusetts	Walpole	MA	F	508 668-2242	16015

LEASING: Residential Buildings

	CITY	ST	EMP	PHONE	ENTRY #
Ambrose G McCarthy Jr	Skowhegan	ME	E	207 474-8837	6968

LEASING: Shipping Container

	CITY	ST	EMP	PHONE	ENTRY #
Mobile Mini Inc	Suffield	CT	E	860 668-1888	4465

LEATHER & CUT STOCK WHOLESALERS

	CITY	ST	EMP	PHONE	ENTRY #
Tasman Industries Inc	Hartland	ME	E	207 938-4491	6179

LEATHER GOODS, EXC FOOTWEAR, GLOVES, LUGGAGE/BELTING, WHOL

	CITY	ST	EMP	PHONE	ENTRY #
Strong Group Inc **(PA)**	Gloucester	MA	E	978 281-3300	11212

LEATHER GOODS: Belting & Strapping

	CITY	ST	EMP	PHONE	ENTRY #
Brockway Ferry Corporation **(PA)**	Essex	CT	G	860 767-8231	1394
Safe Approach Inc	Poland	ME	F	207 345-9900	6597
Page Belting Company Inc	Boscawen	NH	E	603 796-2463	17705

LEATHER GOODS: Boxes

	CITY	ST	EMP	PHONE	ENTRY #
Jaeger Usa Inc	Rochester	NH	F	603 332-5816	19674

LEATHER GOODS: Cigarette & Cigar Cases

	CITY	ST	EMP	PHONE	ENTRY #
Ecoflik LLC	Old Lyme	CT	G	860 460-4419	3322

LEATHER GOODS: Corners, Luggage

	CITY	ST	EMP	PHONE	ENTRY #
Craftmens Corner	Springfield	MA	G	413 782-3783	15462

LEATHER GOODS: Cosmetic Bags

	CITY	ST	EMP	PHONE	ENTRY #
Putu LLC	New Canaan	CT	G	203 594-9700	2613

LEATHER GOODS: Garments

	CITY	ST	EMP	PHONE	ENTRY #
A X M S Inc	Woodbury	CT	G	203 263-5046	5480
Hague Textiles Inc	Fall River	MA	E	508 678-7556	10711
Venlo Company	Pembroke	MA	G	781 826-0485	14432
Justleathercom	Wells	ME	G	207 641-8313	7163
Maineline Industries Inc	Lewiston	ME	G	207 782-6622	6304
Perfect Fit	Corinna	ME	F	207 278-3333	5923
Bellows Inc	Forestdale	RI	G	401 766-5331	20455

LEATHER GOODS: Harnesses Or Harness Parts

	CITY	ST	EMP	PHONE	ENTRY #
Lirakis Safety Harness Inc	Newport	RI	G	401 846-5356	20671

LEATHER GOODS: Holsters

	CITY	ST	EMP	PHONE	ENTRY #
Currys Leather Shop Inc	Randolph	MA	F	781 963-0679	14675
Hague Textiles Inc **(PA)**	Fall River	MA	G	508 678-7556	10710
Safariland LLC	Dalton	MA	D	413 684-3104	10183
Strong Group Inc **(PA)**	Gloucester	MA	E	978 281-3300	11212

LEATHER GOODS: Personal

	CITY	ST	EMP	PHONE	ENTRY #
Brockway Ferry Corporation **(PA)**	Essex	CT	G	860 767-8231	1394
Dooney & Bourke Inc **(PA)**	Norwalk	CT	E	203 853-7515	3142
Mayan Corporation	Norwalk	CT	F	203 854-4711	3192
Waterbury Leatherworks Co	Waterbury	CT	F	203 755-7789	4972
Alliance Leather Finishing	Peabody	MA	F	978 531-6771	14309
Brahmin Leather Works LLC	Fairhaven	MA	G	509 994-4000	10638
Charles Thomae & Son Inc	Attleboro	MA	E	508 222-0785	7719
Hague Textiles Inc	Fall River	MA	E	508 678-7556	10711
HI Operating LLC **(DH)**	Mansfield	MA	E	508 851-1400	12635
Miles Kedex Co Inc	Westminster	MA	E	978 874-1403	16810
Montello Heel Mfg Inc	Brockton	MA	E	508 586-0603	9167
Niche Inc	New Bedford	MA	E	508 990-4202	13427
Strong Group Inc **(PA)**	Gloucester	MA	E	978 281-3300	11212
Valkyrie Company Inc	Worcester	MA	D	508 756-3633	17497
Maineline Industries Inc	Lewiston	ME	G	207 782-6622	6304
Perfect Fit	Corinna	ME	F	207 278-3333	5923
Appalachian Stitching Co LLC **(PA)**	Littleton	NH	E	603 444-4422	18654
Bren Corporation	Johnston	RI	E	401 943-8200	20501
Perry Blackburne Inc	North Providence	RI	E	401 231-7200	20771

LEATHER GOODS: Safety Belts

	CITY	ST	EMP	PHONE	ENTRY #
Kerr Leathers Inc	Salem	MA	E	978 852-0660	14927

LEATHER GOODS: Wallets

	CITY	ST	EMP	PHONE	ENTRY #
Leatherby	Weatogue	CT	G	860 658-6166	5043
Dick Muller Designer/Craftsman	Shelburne Falls	MA	G	413 625-0016	15068
Surtan Manufacturing Co	South Yarmouth	MA	G	508 394-4099	15334
Valkyrie Company Inc **(PA)**	Worcester	MA	D	508 756-3633	17496

LEATHER GOODS: Whips

	CITY	ST	EMP	PHONE	ENTRY #
Westfield Whip Mfg Co	Westfield	MA	F	413 568-8244	16748

LEATHER TANNING & FINISHING

	CITY	ST	EMP	PHONE	ENTRY #
MGI usa Inc	Danbury	CT	G	203 312-1200	954
Alliance Leather Finishing	Peabody	MA	F	978 531-6771	14309
Hawtan Leathers LLC	Newburyport	MA	C	978 465-3791	13496

LEATHER, LEATHER GOODS & FURS, WHOLESALE

	CITY	ST	EMP	PHONE	ENTRY #
Hawtan Leathers LLC	Newburyport	MA	C	978 465-3791	13496

LEATHER: Accessory Prdts

	CITY	ST	EMP	PHONE	ENTRY #
Patricia Poke	New Milford	CT	G	860 354-4193	2823
Brettunsvillagecom	Lewiston	ME	F	207 782-7863	6278

LEATHER: Artificial

	CITY	ST	EMP	PHONE	ENTRY #
Coaters Inc	New Bedford	MA	E	508 996-5700	13372
Miles Kedex Co Inc	Westminster	MA	E	978 874-1403	16810
Vulplex Incorporated	New Bedford	MA	E	508 996-6787	13458
Braided Products Company	Riverside	RI	G	401 434-0300	21165

LEATHER: Bag

	CITY	ST	EMP	PHONE	ENTRY #
Veto Pro Pac LLC	Norwalk	CT	G	203 847-0297	3267

LEATHER: Belting

	CITY	ST	EMP	PHONE	ENTRY #
Barbour Plastics Inc **(HQ)**	Brockton	MA	E	508 583-8200	9125

LEATHER: Embossed

	CITY	ST	EMP	PHONE	ENTRY #
Malik Embossing Corp	Salem	MA	G	978 745-6060	14928
Twin Leather Co Inc	West Bridgewater	MA	G	508 583-3485	16461

LEATHER: Finished

	CITY	ST	EMP	PHONE	ENTRY #
Broleco Inc **(PA)**	North Andover	MA	G	978 689-3200	13693

LEATHER: Shoe

	CITY	ST	EMP	PHONE	ENTRY #
Cuero Operating	Westport	CT	G	203 253-8651	5187

LECTURE BUREAU

	CITY	ST	EMP	PHONE	ENTRY #
Art New England Magazine	Boston	MA	G	617 259-1040	8376

LEGAL OFFICES & SVCS

	CITY	ST	EMP	PHONE	ENTRY #
Real Data Corp	Boston	MA	G	603 669-3822	8812
Seak Inc **(PA)**	Falmouth	MA	G	508 548-7023	10797
T Lex Inc	Brookline	MA	G	617 731-8606	9222
Tremco Products Inc	Billerica	MA	G	781 275-7692	8307
Wolters Kluwer Fincl Svcs Inc	Waltham	MA	B	978 263-1212	16224

LEGAL SVCS: General Practice Attorney or Lawyer

	CITY	ST	EMP	PHONE	ENTRY #
Keene Bradford Esq PC	Lynnfield	MA	G	781 246-4545	12551
Marks Printing House Inc	Belfast	ME	G	207 338-5460	5692

LENS COATING: Ophthalmic

	CITY	ST	EMP	PHONE	ENTRY #
General Dynamics Mission	Nashua	NH	C	603 864-6300	19165
McLeod Optical Company Inc **(PA)**	Warwick	RI	E	401 467-3000	21388

LENSES: Plastic, Exc Optical

	CITY	ST	EMP	PHONE	ENTRY #
Fusion Optix Inc	Woburn	MA	E	781 995-0805	17189

LICENSE TAGS: Automobile, Stamped Metal

	CITY	ST	EMP	PHONE	ENTRY #
Historic Map Works	Portland	ME	G	207 756-5215	6671

LIFE RAFTS: Rubber

	CITY	ST	EMP	PHONE	ENTRY #
Givens Marine Survival Svc Co	Tiverton	RI	F	617 441-5400	21259

LIFESAVING & SURVIVAL EQPT, EXC MEDICAL, WHOLESALE

	CITY	ST	EMP	PHONE	ENTRY #
Life+gear Inc	Wellesley Hills	MA	E	858 755-2099	16398

LIGHT SENSITIVE DEVICES

	CITY	ST	EMP	PHONE	ENTRY #
AMS Qi Inc	Cambridge	MA	G	617 797-4709	9389
Dolan-Jenner Industries Inc	Boxborough	MA	E	978 263-1400	8961

LIGHTING EQPT: Flashlights

	CITY	ST	EMP	PHONE	ENTRY #
Brite-Strike Technologies Inc	Duxbury	MA	F	781 585-3525	10394

LIGHTING EQPT: Locomotive & Railroad Car Lights

	CITY	ST	EMP	PHONE	ENTRY #
Ridge View Associates Inc	Milford	CT	D	203 878-8560	2351

LIGHTING EQPT: Motor Vehicle, Dome Lights

	CITY	ST	EMP	PHONE	ENTRY #
Light Fantastic Realty Inc	West Haven	CT	C	203 934-3441	5131

LIGHTING EQPT: Motor Vehicle, Headlights

	CITY	ST	EMP	PHONE	ENTRY #
Osram Sylvania Inc **(HQ)**	Wilmington	MA	A	978 570-3000	17036

LIGHTING EQPT: Motor Vehicle, NEC

	CITY	ST	EMP	PHONE	ENTRY #
Whelen Engineering Company Inc **(PA)**	Chester	CT	B	860 526-9504	777

LIGHTING EQPT: Motorcycle Lamps

	CITY	ST	EMP	PHONE	ENTRY #
Hightechspeed LLC	Groveland	MA	G	978 600-8222	11300

LIGHTING EQPT: Outdoor

	CITY	ST	EMP	PHONE	ENTRY #
Dave Ross	Brookfield	CT	G	203 775-4327	640
Pennsylvania Globe Gaslight Co	North Branford	CT	E	203 484-7749	2971
Point Lighting Corporation	Bloomfield	CT	E	860 243-0600	253
Excelitas Technologies Corp **(DH)**	Waltham	MA	E	781 522-5910	16104
Genlyte Thomas Group LLC	Andover	MA	C	978 659-3732	7551
Genlyte Thomas Group LLC	Burlington	MA	C	781 418-7900	9279
Grabber Construction Pdts Inc	Windham	NH	F	603 890-0455	20007

LIGHTING FIXTURES WHOLESALERS

	CITY	ST	EMP	PHONE	ENTRY #
Pennsylvania Globe Gaslight Co	North Branford	CT	E	203 484-7749	2971
Washington Copper Works Inc	Washington	CT	G	860 868-7637	4831
Current Ltg Employeeco LLC	Boston	MA	A	216 266-2906	8491
Wafer Inspection Services Inc	Orleans	MA	G	508 944-2851	14245
Hubbardton Forge LLC	Castleton	VT	C	802 468-3090	21828

LIGHTING FIXTURES, NEC

	CITY	ST	EMP	PHONE	ENTRY #
Astralite Inc	Brookfield	CT	G	203 775-0172	634
Elc Acquisition Corporation	Bethel	CT	G	203 743-4059	152
Fidelux Lighting LLC **(HQ)**	Hartford	CT	F	860 436-5000	1821
Macris Industries Inc	Mystic	CT	G	860 514-7003	2441
Malco Inc	Terryville	CT	F	860 584-0446	4485
Moonlighting LLC	Brookfield	CT	G	203 740-8964	653
Pathway Lighting Products Inc	Old Saybrook	CT	D	860 388-6881	3347
Rsl Fiber Systems LLC	East Hartford	CT	F	860 282-4930	1218
Sensor Switch Inc **(DH)**	New Haven	CT	E	203 265-2842	2737
Solais Lighting Inc	Stamford	CT	F	203 683-6222	4323
Sorenson Lighted Controls Inc **(PA)**	West Hartford	CT	D	860 527-3092	5095
Studio Steel Inc	New Preston	CT	G	860 868-7305	2835
Whelen Engineering Company Inc **(PA)**	Chester	CT	B	860 526-9504	777
York Street Studio Inc	New Milford	CT	G	203 266-9000	2833
Acton Research Corporation	Acton	MA	E	941 556-2601	7334
Bloom Boss LLC	Natick	MA	G	774 777-5208	13238
Current Ltg Employeeco LLC	Boston	MA	A	216 266-2906	8491
Cyalume Technologies Inc **(DH)**	West Springfield	MA	C	888 451-4885	16514
Dolan-Jenner Industries Inc	Boxborough	MA	E	978 263-1400	8961
Dorel Juvenile Group Inc	Foxboro	MA	D	800 544-1108	10881
Eclipse Mfg Inc	Ware	MA	E	920 457-2311	16233
Excelitas Tech Holdg Corp	Waltham	MA	F	781 522-5914	16102
Excelitas Tech Holdings LLC **(PA)**	Waltham	MA	F	781 522-5900	16103
Genlyte Group Incorporated	Andover	MA	A	781 418-7900	7550
Nedap Inc	Burlington	MA	F	844 876-3327	9305
Northast Green Enrgy Group Inc	Merrimac	MA	G	978 478-8425	13004
Northern Outdoor Lighting	Westford	MA	G	978 987-9845	16782
Pelican Products Inc	South Deerfield	MA	E	413 665-2163	15251
Period Lighting Fixtures Inc	Clarksburg	MA	F	413 664-7141	10074
Reflek Corp	Fall River	MA	G	508 603-6807	10756
Solarone Solutions Inc **(PA)**	Needham Heights	MA	F	339 225-4530	13344
Taklite LLC	Norfolk	MA	G	508 298-8331	13666
TW Lighting Incorporated **(PA)**	Wellesley	MA	G	617 830-6755	16390
Xenon Corporation **(PA)**	Wilmington	MA	E	978 661-9033	17069
Gates Moore Lighting	Hillsborough	NH	G	203 847-3231	18315
Luminescent Systems Inc	Lebanon	NH	C	603 643-7766	18629
Visible Light Inc	Hampton	NH	G	603 926-6049	18278
Atomic Led Inc	Greenville	RI	G	401 265-0222	20462
Emissive Energy Corp	North Kingstown	RI	D	401 294-2030	20709
Cooper Lighting Inc	Essex Junction	VT	F	800 767-3674	21937

LIGHTING FIXTURES: Airport

	CITY	ST	EMP	PHONE	ENTRY #
Airflo Instrument Company	Glastonbury	CT	G	860 633-9455	1536
Connecticut Valley Inds LLC	Old Saybrook	CT	G	860 388-0822	3332
Cooper Crouse-Hinds LLC	Windsor	CT	D	860 683-4300	5327
Eaton Electric Holdings LLC	Windsor	CT	F	860 683-4300	5330
Integro LLC	New Britain	CT	E	860 832-8960	2542

LIGHTING FIXTURES: Decorative Area

	CITY	ST	EMP	PHONE	ENTRY #
Electrix LLC	New Haven	CT	D	203 776-5577	2686

LIGHTING FIXTURES: Fluorescent, Commercial

	CITY	ST	EMP	PHONE	ENTRY #
Newco Lighting Inc **(HQ)**	Shelton	CT	G	475 882-4000	3840
Litecontrol Corporation	Plympton	MA	C	781 294-0100	14592
SCW Corporation	Warwick	RI	E	401 808-6849	21423

LIGHTING FIXTURES: Indl & Commercial

	CITY	ST	EMP	PHONE	ENTRY #
3t Lighting Inc	Brookfield	CT	G	203 775-1805	631
Green Ray Led Intl LLC **(PA)**	Greenwich	CT	G	203 485-1435	1618
Innovative ARC Tubes Corp	Bridgeport	CT	E	203 333-1031	430
Lcd Lighting Inc	Orange	CT	C	203 799-7877	3370
Lighting Edge Inc	Essex	CT	G	860 767-8968	1402
Nutron Manufacturing Inc	Norwich	CT	E	860 887-4550	3287
Pathway Lighting Products Inc	Old Saybrook	CT	D	860 388-6881	3347
Pegasus Capital Advisors LP **(PA)**	Stamford	CT	E	203 869-4400	4282
Prolume Inc	Monroe	CT	G	203 268-7778	2415
Seesmart Inc	Stamford	CT	E	203 504-1111	4312
Sylvan R Shemitz Designs LLC	West Haven	CT	C	203 934-3441	5147
The L C Doane Company **(PA)**	Ivoryton	CT	F	860 767-8295	1909
Tri-State Led Inc	Greenwich	CT	F	203 813-3791	1657
Whelen Engineering Company Inc	Chester	CT	F	860 526-9504	778
Whelen Engineering Company Inc **(PA)**	Chester	CT	B	860 526-9504	777
American Lighting Fixture Corp	Framingham	MA	C	508 824-1970	10920
Architectural Star Ltg LLC	Fall River	MA	F	508 678-1900	10662
Asd-Lighting Corp	Norwood	MA	G	781 739-3977	14135
Atlantic Lighting Inc	Fall River	MA	E	508 678-5411	10665
Cdiled LLC	Palmer	MA	G	413 530-2921	14283
Dion Signs and Service Inc	New Bedford	MA	F	401 724-4459	13379
Genlyte Thomas Group LLC	Burlington	MA	C	781 418-7900	9279
International Light Tech Inc	Peabody	MA	E	978 818-6180	14343
Janna Ugone & Associates Inc	Easthampton	MA	F	413 527-5530	10566
Jlc Tech LLC	Pembroke	MA	E	781 826-8162	14412
Light Engines LLC	Sturbridge	MA	G	508 347-3647	15640
Loto Lighting LLc	Somerville	MA	G	617 776-3115	15191
Lumenpulse Lighting Corp	Boston	MA	E	617 307-5700	8673
Mg2 Technologies LLC	Danvers	MA	G	978 739-1068	10241
Newstamp Lighting Corp	North Easton	MA	F	508 238-7073	13949
O C White Company	Thorndike	MA	E	413 289-1751	15850
Osram Sylvania Inc **(HQ)**	Wilmington	MA	A	978 570-3000	17036
Renovators Supply Inc	Millers Falls	MA	E	413 423-3300	13181
Rpt Holdings LLC	Middleton	MA	E	877 997-3674	13099
Signify North America Corp	Fall River	MA	B	508 679-8131	10761
Signify North America Corp	Burlington	MA	B	617 423-9999	9337
Spec Lines	Wakefield	MA	G	781 245-0044	15976
Spectrum Lighting Inc	Fall River	MA	D	508 678-2303	10762
Lighting Solutions Inc	Falmouth	ME	G	207 772-2738	6031
Affinity Led Light LLC	Dover	NH	G	978 378-5338	18004
Plastic Techniques Inc	Goffstown	NH	E	603 622-5570	18209
Signify North America Corp	Manchester	NH	C	603 645-6061	18923
Lexington Lighting Group LLC	Rumford	RI	E	860 564-4512	21192
Lumetta Inc	Warwick	RI	E	401 691-3994	21385
Mastro Lighting Mfg Co Inc **(PA)**	Providence	RI	G	401 467-7700	21063
Orion Ret Svcs & Fixturing Inc	Smithfield	RI	D	401 334-5000	21243
PMC Lighting Inc	Warwick	RI	E	401 738-7266	21404
Renova Lighting Systems Inc	Warwick	RI	E	800 635-6682	21411
Authentic Designs Inc	West Rupert	VT	F	802 394-7715	22614
Cooper Lighting Inc	Essex Junction	VT	F	800 767-3674	21937

LIGHTING FIXTURES: Marine

	CITY	ST	EMP	PHONE	ENTRY #
Cornell-Carr Co Inc	Monroe	CT	E	203 261-2529	2399
The L C Doane Company **(PA)**	Ivoryton	CT	F	860 767-8295	1909

LIGHTING FIXTURES: Motor Vehicle

	CITY	ST	EMP	PHONE	ENTRY #
Cape Strobe Emergency Lighting	Harwich	MA	G	508 776-0911	11390

LIGHTING FIXTURES: Residential

	CITY	ST	EMP	PHONE	ENTRY #
3t Lighting Inc	Brookfield	CT	G	203 775-1805	631
E-Lite Technologies Inc	Trumbull	CT	F	203 371-2070	4623
Keeling Company Inc	Old Lyme	CT	G	860 349-0916	3324
Light Fantastic Realty Inc	West Haven	CT	C	203 934-3441	5131
Light Sources Inc	Milford	CT	C	203 799-7877	2309
Premier Mfg Group Inc	Shelton	CT	D	203 924-6617	3863
Seesmart Inc	Stamford	CT	E	203 504-1111	4312
Washington Copper Works Inc	Washington	CT	G	860 868-7637	4831
Atlantic Lighting Inc	Fall River	MA	E	508 678-5411	10665
Blanche P Field LLC	Boston	MA	E	617 423-0714	8413
Genlyte Group Incorporated	Andover	MA	A	781 418-7900	7550
Genlyte Thomas Group LLC	Andover	MA	C	978 659-3732	7551
Genlyte Thomas Group LLC	Burlington	MA	C	781 418-7900	9279
Global Light Co LLC	Cambridge	MA	G	617 620-2084	9495
Janna Ugone & Associates Inc	Easthampton	MA	F	413 527-5530	10566
Newstamp Lighting Corp	North Easton	MA	F	508 238-7073	13949
Norwell Mfg Co Inc	East Taunton	MA	E	508 822-2831	10516
Period Lighting Fixtures Inc	Clarksburg	MA	F	413 664-7141	10074
Renovators Supply Inc	Millers Falls	MA	E	413 423-3300	13181
Sandwich Lantern	Sandwich	MA	G	508 833-0515	14973
Lighting Solutions Inc	Falmouth	ME	G	207 772-2738	6031
Collins Lighting & Assoc LLC	Salem	NH	G	603 893-1106	19717
Creative Ltg Designs Decor LLC	Lebanon	NH	G	603 448-2066	18620
Gates Moore Lighting	Hillsborough	NH	G	203 847-3231	18315
Visible Light Inc	Hampton	NH	G	603 926-6049	18277
Brownlie Lamar Design Group	Warren	RI	G	401 714-9371	21292
Lexington Lighting Group LLC	Rumford	RI	E	860 564-4512	21192
Mastro Lighting Mfg Co Inc **(PA)**	Providence	RI	G	401 467-7700	21063
SCW Corporation	Warwick	RI	E	401 808-6849	21423
Authentic Designs Inc	West Rupert	VT	F	802 394-7715	22614
Hubbardton Forge LLC	Castleton	VT	C	802 468-3090	21828
Light Logic Inc	Hyde Park	VT	E	802 888-7984	22037

LIGHTING FIXTURES: Street

	CITY	ST	EMP	PHONE	ENTRY #
Pegasus Capital Advisors LP **(PA)**	Stamford	CT	E	203 869-4400	4282
Sunrise Technologies LLC	Raynham	MA	F	508 884-9732	14731

	CITY	ST	EMP	PHONE	ENTRY#
Prism Streetlights Inc	Wakefield	RI	G	401 792-9900	21274

LIGHTING FIXTURES: Swimming Pool

	CITY	ST	EMP	PHONE	ENTRY#
Aquacomfort Solutions LLC	Cheshire	CT	G	407 831-1941	712

LIME

	CITY	ST	EMP	PHONE	ENTRY#
Bonsal American Inc	Lee	MA	E	413 243-0053	12090
Dragon Products Company LLC **(DH)**	South Portland	ME	E	207 774-6355	7022

LIMESTONE: Crushed & Broken

	CITY	ST	EMP	PHONE	ENTRY#
Specialty Minerals Inc	Canaan	CT	C	860 824-5435	690
Trap Rock Quarry	Southbury	CT	G	203 263-2195	4035
S Lane John & Son Incorporated	Oxford	MA	F	508 987-3959	14273
Dragon Products Company LLC	Thomaston	ME	C	207 594-5555	7083
Dragon Products Company LLC **(DH)**	South Portland	ME	E	207 774-6355	7022
Conklin Limestone Company	Lincoln	RI	G	401 334-2330	20565
Shelburne Limestone Corp	Wallingford	VT	G	802 446-2045	22574

LIMESTONE: Dimension

	CITY	ST	EMP	PHONE	ENTRY#
Coccomo Brothers Drilling LLC	Berlin	CT	F	860 828-1632	81

LINEN SPLY SVC: Coat

	CITY	ST	EMP	PHONE	ENTRY#
Joseph Nachado	Assonet	MA	G	508 644-3404	7682

LINEN SPLY SVC: Uniform

	CITY	ST	EMP	PHONE	ENTRY#
A & P Coat Apron & Lin Sup Inc	Hartford	CT	D	914 840-3200	1799

LINENS & TOWELS WHOLESALERS

	CITY	ST	EMP	PHONE	ENTRY#
Mr Idea Inc	Attleboro	MA	E	508 222-0155	7770

LINENS: Table & Dresser Scarves, From Purchased Materials

	CITY	ST	EMP	PHONE	ENTRY#
Bess Home Fashions Inc	West Warwick	RI	F	401 828-0300	21484

LINENS: Tablecloths, From Purchased Materials

	CITY	ST	EMP	PHONE	ENTRY#
Rihm Management Inc	Manchester Center	VT	G	802 867-5325	22089

LINERS & COVERS: Fabric

	CITY	ST	EMP	PHONE	ENTRY#
Commercial Sewing Inc	Torrington	CT	C	860 482-5509	4571
Custom Covers	Clinton	CT	G	860 669-4169	784

LINERS & LINING

	CITY	ST	EMP	PHONE	ENTRY#
Bath Systems Massachusetts Inc	West Bridgewater	MA	F	508 521-2700	16432

LINIMENTS

	CITY	ST	EMP	PHONE	ENTRY#
W F Young Incorporated **(PA)**	East Longmeadow	MA	E	800 628-9653	10503

LININGS: Apparel, Made From Purchased Materials

	CITY	ST	EMP	PHONE	ENTRY#
Sam & Ty LLC **(PA)**	Norwalk	CT	G	212 840-1871	3236

LININGS: Fabric, Apparel & Other, Exc Millinery

	CITY	ST	EMP	PHONE	ENTRY#
Theatre Stricken Apparel LLC	Bellingham	MA	G	978 325-2335	8060
Fuller Box Co Inc	Central Falls	RI	D	401 725-4300	20113

LIP BALMS

	CITY	ST	EMP	PHONE	ENTRY#
Mad Gabs Inc	Yarmouth	ME	G	207 854-1679	7298
Susie BZ Natural Lip Balm	Weare	NH	G	603 529-7083	19940

LOCKERS

	CITY	ST	EMP	PHONE	ENTRY#
Top Shelf Installations	Bridgewater	MA	G	508 697-1550	9090

LOCKS

	CITY	ST	EMP	PHONE	ENTRY#
Assa Inc	New Haven	CT	G	800 235-7482	2660
Eastern Company **(PA)**	Naugatuck	CT	E	203 729-2255	2471
Fsb Inc	Berlin	CT	F	203 404-4700	86
Pro-Lock USA LLC	Monroe	CT	G	203 382-3428	2414
Sargent Manufacturing Company	New Haven	CT	A	203 562-2151	2735
Specialty Products Mfg LLC	Southington	CT	G	860 621-6969	4081
Yale Security Inc	Berlin	CT	B	865 986-7511	117
Zephyr Lock LLC	Newtown	CT	F	866 937-4971	2950
G S Davidson Co Inc	North Reading	MA	G	617 389-4000	13982
Inner-Tite Corp	Holden	MA	D	508 829-6361	11546
Relcor Inc	East Sandwich	MA	G	561 844-8335	10508
Schlage Lock Company LLC	Canton	MA	E	781 828-6655	9776

LOCKSMITHS

	CITY	ST	EMP	PHONE	ENTRY#
All Security Co Inc	New Bedford	MA	F	508 993-4271	13356
Ekeys4 Cars	North Andover	MA	G	978 655-3135	13701

LOCOMOTIVES & PARTS

	CITY	ST	EMP	PHONE	ENTRY#
Motive Power	Boston	MA	G	857 350-3765	8713

LOG SPLITTERS

	CITY	ST	EMP	PHONE	ENTRY#
Built Rite Manufacturing Inc	Ludlow	VT	F	802 228-7293	22061

LOGGING

	CITY	ST	EMP	PHONE	ENTRY#
B&B Logging LLC	Higganum	CT	G	860 982-2425	1900
Brad Kettle	Canterbury	CT	G	860 546-9929	692
Clover Hill Forest LLC	Cornwall	CT	G	860 672-0394	819
Cold River Logging LLC	North Windham	CT	G	860 334-9506	3080
Industrial Forrest Products LL	Greenwich	CT	G	203 863-9486	1622
James Callahan	Ridgefield	CT	G	914 641-2852	3670
James M Munch	Sherman	CT	G	802 353-3114	3894
Limb-It-Less Logging LLC	Essex	CT	G	860 227-0987	1403
Witkowsky John	North Branford	CT	G	203 483-0152	2985
Anderson Logging and Lumber	Westminster	MA	G	978 874-2751	16802
Fisher Logging	Northfield	MA	G	413 498-2615	14063
Forward Enterprises Inc	Oakham	MA	G	508 882-0265	14212
Godin Land Clearing	Spencer	MA	G	508 885-9666	15431
Lashway Logging Inc	Williamsburg	MA	F	413 268-3600	16952
Mike Orzel Logging	Northampton	MA	G	413 320-3367	14013
Norton Land Clearing and Log	Ayer	MA	G	978 391-4029	7931
OConnell Logging LLC	Hudson	MA	G	978 568-9740	11796
Paul R Hicks	Charlemont	MA	G	413 625-2623	9822
Roberts Brothers Lumber Co	Ashfield	MA	E	413 628-3333	7654
Select Logging	Ashby	MA	G	978 386-6861	7648
Thomas J Doane	Orange	MA	G	978 821-2361	14229
Tim Meiklejohn Logging	Clarksburg	MA	G	413 652-1223	10076
Tim Robinson Logging	Barre	MA	F	978 355-4287	7951
Tree Co Inc	South Dennis	MA	G	508 432-7529	15267
A S & C B Gould & Sons Inc	Cornville	ME	E	207 474-3930	5926
Alan Stevens	Sidney	ME	G	207 547-3840	6961
Ambrose G McCarthy Jr	Skowhegan	ME	E	207 474-8837	6968
Anderson Family Tree Farm Inc	Crystal	ME	G	207 463-2843	5928
B & R Bartlett Enterprises	Amity	ME	F	207 448-7060	5522
Ben Jordan Logging LLC	Millinocket	ME	G	207 694-2011	6439
Ben Savage Logging Inc	Sebec	ME	G	207 735-6699	6955
Bolduc Brothers Log & Shipg	Lisbon Falls	ME	G	207 353-5990	6368
Brochu Logging Inc	Benton	ME	G	207 453-2982	5704
Brook Wiles Logging Inc	Allagash	ME	G	207 398-4105	5518
Bruce C Smith Logging	Machiasport	ME	G	207 255-3259	6397
C T L Land Management Inc	Washington	ME	G	207 845-2841	7149
CB Logging	New Canada	ME	G	207 231-4952	6462
Charles Lane Inc	Sherman Mills	ME	G	207 365-4606	6960
Chopper One Inc	Eagle Lake	ME	G	207 444-5476	5973
Clinton G Bradbury Inc	Rumford	ME	G	207 562-8014	6833
Corey Madden Logging Inc	Greenbush	ME	G	207 827-1632	6146
D F Moody LLC	Cornville	ME	G	207 474-6029	5927
D M G Enterprises	Edmunds Twp	ME	G	207 726-4603	6005
Dana Hardy	Dyer Brook	ME	G	207 757-8445	5972
Darrel L Tibbetts	Livermore	ME	G	207 897-4932	6374
Dennis Frigon	Caratunk	ME	F	207 672-4076	5881
Ellen McLaughlin	Medway	ME	E	207 746-3398	6424
Fogg Lumbering Inc	Lowell	ME	G	207 732-4087	6385
Gammon Milam	Rumford	ME	G	207 364-2889	6834
Gary M Pomeroy Logging Inc	Hermon	ME	F	207 848-3171	6187
Harold C Moore II	South Paris	ME	G	207 595-5683	7011
Hartland Inc	Rockport	ME	G	207 785-4350	6823
Hellgren Logging LLC	Temple	ME	G	207 778-0401	7079
Herbert C Haynes Inc	Hermon	ME	G	207 848-5930	6188
Herbert L Hardy and Son Inc	Smyrna Mills	ME	G	207 757-8550	6992
Highland Logging Inc	Wallagrass	ME	G	207 436-1113	7139
Humphrey Mh & Sons Inc	Parsonsfield	ME	F	207 625-4965	6575
J C Logging Inc	Lincoln	ME	G	207 794-4349	6354
J Voisine & Son Logging Inc	Fort Kent	ME	G	207 436-0932	6061
Jackman Lumber Inc	Skowhegan	ME	G	207 858-0321	6979
Jacob Burdin Logging	Sebec	ME	G	207 564-3384	6957
James H Carville	Lisbon Falls	ME	G	207 353-2625	6370
James M Dunn	Hebron	ME	G	207 212-2963	6180
Jmk Logging LLC	Mapleton	ME	G	207 227-2964	6413
Jordan Millworks Inc	Lincoln	ME	G	207 794-6178	6356
K B Logging Inc	Smyrna Mills	ME	F	207 757-8818	6993
Lakewood Logging Inc	Madison	ME	G	207 431-4052	6405
Leslie W Robertson	Newry	ME	G	207 824-2764	6491
Madtown Logging LLC	Madawaska	ME	G	207 728-6260	6400
Maine Custom Woodlands LLC	Durham	ME	F	207 353-9020	5971
Martin Forest Products	Caribou	ME	G	207 498-6723	5887
McCafferty Logging LLC	Buckfield	ME	G	207 212-8600	5852
MJB Logging Inc	Fort Kent	ME	G	207 231-1376	6062
Mk Logging	Frenchville	ME	G	207 436-1809	6091
North Shore Logging Inc	Saint Francis	ME	G	207 398-4173	6867
Olson S Logging LLC	Canaan	ME	G	207 474-8835	5873
Paul H Warren Forest Products	Smithfield	ME	G	207 362-3681	6990
PFC Logging Inc	Danforth	ME	G	207 448-7998	5942
Premium Log Yards Inc **(PA)**	Rumford	ME	F	207 364-7500	6842
R B Logging Inc	Saint Francis	ME	G	207 398-3176	6868
Regan S Pingree	Phillips	ME	F	207 639-5706	6586
Reginold D Ricker	Newburgh	ME	G	207 234-4811	6480
Richard A Tibbetts	Oxford	ME	G	207 539-5073	6571
Rickie D Osgood Sr	Greenwood	ME	G	207 674-3529	6155
Robert Babb & Sons	Windham	ME	G	207 892-9692	7248
Robert W Carr & Sons Inc	Limington	ME	G	207 637-2885	6348
Roland Levesque	Fort Kent	ME	G	207 834-6244	6067
S&S Excavation and Logging LLC	Auburn	ME	G	207 312-5590	5597
Swh Inc	Linneus	ME	G	207 538-6666	6363
T Roy Inc	St John Plt	ME	G	207 834-6385	7059
Teresa Burgess	Bangor	ME	G	207 848-5697	5659
Terrence L Hayford	Hartford	ME	G	207 357-0142	6178
Theriault Jr Peter Inc	Danforth	ME	G	207 446-9441	5943
Tide Mill Enterprises	Edmunds Twp	ME	G	207 733-4425	6006
Tough End Logging Corp	Perham	ME	G	207 455-8016	6582
Travis Worster	Carroll Plt	ME	G	207 738-3792	5894
TW Clark Pulp & Logging LLC	Newport	ME	G	207 368-4766	6487
WA Logging LLC	Hodgdon	ME	G	207 694-2921	6195
Wayne Peters Phill	Mattawamkeag	ME	G	207 736-4191	6416
Western Maine Timberlands	Fryeburg	ME	F	207 925-1138	6103
Wheeler Hill Logging Inc	Phillips	ME	G	207 639-2391	6587
William A Day Jr & Sons Inc	Porter	ME	E	207 625-8181	6607
William B Sparrow Jr	Pittston	ME	G	207 582-5731	6593
Yankee Hardwoods LLC	Sanford	ME	G	207 459-7779	6897
3d Logging Co Inc	Berlin	NH	F	603 915-3020	17690
Adam E Mock and Son Logging An	Webster	NH	G	603 648-2444	19943
B Hall & Sons Logging Inc	Errol	NH	G	603 482-7741	18108
B P Logging	Stewartstown	NH	G	603 237-4131	19860
Bolstridge Logging LLC	New Durham	NH	G	603 859-8241	19300
Bunnell Rocky Log & Forest Mgt	Monroe	NH	G	603 638-4983	19089

	CITY	ST	EMP	PHONE	ENTRY #
Butch Eaton Logging & Trucki	East Wakefield	NH	G	603 522-3894	18094
C W Mock Logging	Bradford	NH	G	603 938-6096	17740
CCM Logging Land Clearing LLC	New London	NH	G	603 387-1853	19314
Chuck Rose Inc	Contoocook	NH	F	603 746-2311	17942
Cmd Logging	Center Barnstead	NH	G	603 986-5055	17788
Copp Logging LLC	Fremont	NH	G	603 479-4828	18175
Dale E Crawford	Sanbornville	NH	G	603 473-2738	19782
David R Burl	Goffstown	NH	G	603 235-2661	18199
G M L of NH Inc	Colebrook	NH	G	603 237-5231	17868
G&S Logging	Colebrook	NH	G	603 237-4929	17869
Garrett G Gilpatric	Bristol	NH	G	603 744-3286	17765
Haffordlogging	Hillsboro	NH	G	603 478-0142	18313
HB Logging LLC	Monroe	NH	G	603 638-4983	19090
Jason S Landry	Loudon	NH	G	603 783-1154	18749
John C Whyte	Salisbury	NH	G	603 530-1168	19781
Jon Strong Low Impact Log LLC	New Boston	NH	G	603 487-5298	19293
Kel Log Inc **(PA)**	Milan	NH	E	603 752-2000	19040
Kel Log Inc	Gorham	NH	E	603 752-2000	18213
Magoon Logging LLC	Loudon	NH	G	603 435-9918	18750
Mark Welch	Walpole	NH	G	603 835-6347	19923
On The Ball Cutnhaul	Laconia	NH	G	603 851-3283	18578
Phils Tree Service and Log	Keene	NH	G	603 352-0202	18521
Pine River Logging	Effingham	NH	G	603 833-1340	18096
R L Cook Timber Harvesting	Winchester	NH	G	603 239-6424	19994
Rancloes Logging LLC	Stewartstown	NH	G	603 237-4474	19863
SDS Logging Inc	Jefferson	NH	G	603 586-7098	18486
Stacey Thomson	Orford	NH	G	603 353-9700	19421
Stockley Trucking Inc	Landaff	NH	G	603 838-2860	18609
Swr & Son Logging	Stewartstown	NH	G	603 237-4158	19864
Th Logging	North Haverhill	NH	G	603 787-6235	19390
Thibodeau Logging & Excav LLC	Wolfeboro	NH	G	603 953-5983	20026
Treeline Timber	Jefferson	NH	G	603 586-7725	18487
W Craig Washburn	Colebrook	NH	G	603 237-8403	17877
Warick Management Company Inc	Pittsburg	NH	G	603 538-7112	19496
James Thompson Native Lumber	Hopkinton	RI	F	401 377-2837	20487
Miller Firewood & Logging Inc	Exeter	RI	G	401 539-7707	20452
Basin Timber LLC	Belvidere Center	VT	G	802 343-4694	21658
Calvin Johnson	Chelsea	VT	G	802 685-3205	21837
Ceylon R Morehouse Logging	Concord	VT	G	802 695-4660	21890
Chris Clark	Vershire	VT	G	802 356-0044	22558
Chris J Seamans	Middletown Springs	VT	G	802 287-9399	22123
Cobb Lumber Inc	South Londonderry	VT	G	802 824-5228	22484
Codling Brothers Logging	Plainfield	VT	G	802 454-7177	22266
Corbin & Son Logging Inc	Reading	VT	G	802 484-3329	22305
Dennis Ducharme	Marshfield	VT	G	802 426-3796	22094
Fontaine Logging	Hardwick	VT	G	802 472-6140	22011
La Foe Brian	Orleans	VT	G	802 754-8837	22249
Leavitt Logging LLC	Belvidere Center	VT	G	802 644-1440	21660
Marc J Riendeau	Danville	VT	G	802 748-6252	21897
Mike Lowell Logging & Wood	Wolcott	VT	G	802 279-6993	22731
New Life Logging	Rochester	VT	G	802 767-9142	22319
Paul A Morse	Newport Center	VT	G	802 334-9160	22207
Reginald J Riendeau	Orleans	VT	G	802 754-6003	22251
Rusty D Inc	Elmore	VT	G	802 888-8838	21922
Stephane Inkel Inc	Canaan	VT	G	802 266-8878	21826
Thompson Family Enterprises	Woodbury	VT	G	802 456-7421	22734
Weston Island Logging Inc	Londonderry	VT	G	802 824-3708	22058

LOGGING CAMPS & CONTRACTORS

	CITY	ST	EMP	PHONE	ENTRY #
Bryan Heavens Logging & Firewo	Harwinton	CT	G	860 485-1712	1887
C & C Logging	Windsor	CT	G	860 683-0071	5323
Wayne Horn	New Hartford	CT	G	860 491-3315	2649
Ezequelle Logging Inc	Sandisfield	MA	G	413 258-0265	14960
George A Vollans	Nantucket	MA	G	508 257-6241	13224
Gmo Threshold Logging II LLC	Boston	MA	G	617 330-7500	8569
Gmo Threshold Logging LLC	Boston	MA	G	617 330-7500	8570
Gmo Thrshold Tmber Hldings LLC	Boston	MA	G	617 330-7500	8571
Albert M M Johnston IV	Hermon	ME	G	207 848-2561	6181
Andrew Irish Logging	Peru	ME	F	207 562-8839	6583
Ashley & Harmon Logging Inc	East Machias	ME	F	207 259-2043	5982
Berry Logging/R A Berry & Sons	Norridgewock	ME	G	207 634-4808	6495
BP Logging	Saint Francis	ME	G	207 398-4457	6866
Chapman & Wheeler Inc	Bethel	ME	G	207 824-2224	5714
Chipping & Logging	Porter	ME	G	207 625-4056	6601
Darrell C McGuire & Sons Inc	Houlton	ME	F	207 532-0511	6205
Day Bros	Oxford	ME	G	207 743-0508	6565
Ducas Logging Inc	Wallagrass	ME	G	207 834-5506	7138
E J Carrier Inc	Jackman	ME	D	207 668-4457	6216
G J Logging	Mapleton	ME	G	207 764-3826	6412
G R Logging Inc	Van Buren	ME	G	207 868-2692	7120
Gary Green Trucking Logging	Turner	ME	G	207 225-3433	7107
Gca Logging Inc	Avon	ME	G	207 639-3941	5623
Gerard Poulin & Sons Logging	Readfield	ME	F	207 246-3537	6777
Glenn S Viles & Sons Inc	North Anson	ME	G	207 635-2493	6502
Gloria J Gordon Logging	Strong	ME	G	207 684-4462	7071
Guimond Logging	Fort Kent	ME	G	207 834-6329	6060
H Arthur York Logging Inc **(PA)**	Medway	ME	E	207 746-5883	6425
H Arthur York Logging Inc	Medway	ME	G	207 746-5912	6426
Hanington Bros Inc	Macwahoc Plt	ME	E	207 765-2681	6399
Hanington Timberlands	Reed Plt	ME	F	207 456-7003	6779
Hickey Logging	West Gardiner	ME	G	207 724-3648	7172
J & M Logging Inc	Sidney	ME	F	207 622-6353	6962
J & S Logging	Rangeley	ME	G	207 864-5617	6772
Jackman Lumber Inc **(PA)**	Jackman	ME	E	207 668-4407	6217
John Khiel III Log Chpping Inc	Denmark	ME	E	207 452-2157	5949
Johnny H Castonguay	Livermore	ME	G	207 897-5945	6375
Jordan Family Chipping Inc	Kezar Falls	ME	G	207 625-8890	6249
K M Morin Logging Inc	Clinton	ME	G	207 399-8835	5915
L E Taylor and Sons Inc	Porter	ME	G	207 625-4056	6603
Luce Dirt Excavation	Union	ME	G	207 785-3478	7114
M B Eastman Logging Inc	Parsonsfield	ME	G	207 625-8020	6576
Madden Timberlands Inc	Old Town	ME	E	207 827-0112	6544
Mainely Trees Inc	Strong	ME	G	207 684-3301	7073
Mc Crossins Logging Inc	Cardville	ME	G	207 826-2225	5883
Morris Logging	Fort Kent	ME	G	207 834-6210	6064
Nadeau Logging Inc	Fort Kent	ME	F	207 834-6338	6065
Nicols Brothers Inc	Rumford	ME	E	207 364-7032	6840
Nicols Brothers Logging Inc	Mexico	ME	F	207 364-8685	6428
Norman White Inc	Shapleigh	ME	G	207 636-1636	6958
Pelletier & Pelletier	Fort Kent	ME	E	207 834-2296	6066
R H Wales & Son Inc	Fryeburg	ME	G	207 925-1363	6102
R&R Logging Forest Management	Addison	ME	G	207 483-4612	5510
Rich Logging	Mexico	ME	G	207 357-7863	6429
Robert Daigle & Sons Inc	New Canada	ME	G	207 834-3676	6463
Robert W Libby	Porter	ME	G	207 625-8285	6604
Roland H Tyler Logging Inc	Dixfield	ME	G	207 562-7282	5958
Ron Ledger Son Logging	Amity	ME	G	207 532-2423	5524
Roussel Logging Inc	Madawaska	ME	G	207 728-3250	6401
Stephen F Madden	Cardville	ME	F	207 827-5737	5884
Syl Ver Logging Inc	Allagash	ME	G	207 398-3158	5520
T Raymond Forest Products Inc	Lee	ME	E	207 738-2313	6266
T&R Flagg Log Sons & Daughters	Livermore	ME	G	207 897-5212	6377
Tdf Incorporated	Howland	ME	G	207 631-4325	6214
Thompson Trucking Inc	Lincoln	ME	E	207 794-6101	6360
Tr Dillon Logging Inc	Madison	ME	F	207 696-8137	6407
Tracy J Morrison	Harmony	ME	G	207 683-2371	6172
Trees Ltd A Partnr Consisting	Sidney	ME	G	207 547-3168	6965
Troy Voisine Logging Inc	Chester	ME	G	207 794-6301	5906
Trp Logging	East Machias	ME	G	207 263-6425	5984
Voisine & Son Logging Inc	Chester	ME	G	207 794-3336	5907
Whitcombs Forest Harvesting	Newburgh	ME	G	207 234-2351	6481
Willard S Hanington & Son Inc	Reed Plt	ME	E	207 456-7511	6780
A B Excavating Inc	Lancaster	NH	E	603 788-5110	18596
Adam Burtt Tree and Log LLC	Center Barnstead	NH	G	603 269-2019	17787
Bliss Logging	Meredith	NH	G	603 279-5674	18971
Dans Logging & Construction	Colebrook	NH	G	603 237-4040	17867
DH Hardwick & Sons Inc	Bennington	NH	E	603 588-6618	17688
Fadden Chipping & Logging Inc	Center Conway	NH	F	603 939-2462	17797
Forrest P Hicks II	Jefferson	NH	G	603 586-9819	18483
Fred C Weld Inc	Cornish	NH	G	603 675-6147	17960
Gagne & Sons Logging Co LLC	Dummer	NH	G	603 449-2255	18070
Garland Lumber Company Inc	Center Conway	NH	E	603 356-5636	17798
Garland Transportation Corp	Center Conway	NH	G	603 356-5636	17799
Gilles Champagne	Colebrook	NH	G	603 237-5272	17870
Huntington Logging	Piermont	NH	G	603 272-9322	19492
J R Logging Inc	Colebrook	NH	G	603 237-8010	17872
Lance Williams & Son Logging &	Center Tuftonboro	NH	G	603 569-3349	17808
Laurence Sharpe	Alexandria	NH	G	603 744-8175	17537
Lemire R & Sons LLC	Antrim	NH	G	603 588-3718	17595
Lessard & Sons Logging Inc	Berlin	NH	G	603 752-5767	17699
Margaret Quint Logging	Conway	NH	G	603 447-3957	17955
Moose Mountain Logging Inc	Tamworth	NH	G	603 491-3667	19893
Nadeau Logging	Lyndeborough	NH	G	603 654-2594	18759
Ossipee Mountain Land Co LLC	Tamworth	NH	E	603 323-7677	19894
Pat Gagne Logging	Dummer	NH	G	603 449-2479	18071
Peter Pierce	Belmont	NH	G	603 524-8312	17679
Richard Dupuis Logging Inc	Groveton	NH	G	603 636-2986	18234
Roy E Amey	Pittsburg	NH	G	603 538-6913	19495
Steve Leighton	Barnstead	NH	G	603 664-2378	17617
Walter Buckwold Logging	Orange	NH	G	603 523-9626	19419
Welog Inc	Colebrook	NH	F	603 237-8277	17878
Edwoods Firewood & Logging	Mapleville	RI	G	401 568-6585	20613
J Tefft Logging & Firewoo	Hope Valley	RI	G	401 539-9838	20485
AMP Timber Harvesting Inc	West Townshend	VT	G	802 874-7260	22625
Black Bear Tree Svc	Brandon	VT	G	802 345-2815	21707
Bruce Waite Logging Inc	Dorset	VT	G	802 867-2213	21907
Canopy Timber Alternatives	Middlebury	VT	G	802 388-1548	22107
Chief Logging & Cnstr Inc	South Ryegate	VT	F	802 584-3868	22495
Dave and Jeff Logging & Firewd	Barton	VT	G	802 355-0465	21649
Derrick Clifford Logging LLC	Orwell	VT	G	802 948-2798	22254
E&M Logging & Land Clearing LL	Wardsboro	VT	G	802 896-6091	22576
Greg Manning Logging LLC	Corinth	VT	G	802 439-6255	21891
Lafoe Logging LLC	Orleans	VT	G	802 754-8837	22250
Mahar Excavating & Logging	Bennington	VT	G	802 442-2954	21681
Norm Brown Logging	Benson	VT	G	802 537-4474	21692
Otterman Logging & Excavating	West Topsham	VT	G	802 439-5714	22623
P and L Trucking	Chester	VT	G	802 875-2819	21847
Pjf Trucking and Logging LLC	Bellows Falls	VT	G	802 463-3343	21653
Stebennes Logging	Hartland	VT	G	802 436-3250	22018
T B Lincoln Logging Inc	Brookfield	VT	G	802 276-3172	21765
Wright Maintenance Inc	Newfane	VT	G	802 365-9253	22189

LOGGING: Fuel Wood Harvesting

	CITY	ST	EMP	PHONE	ENTRY #
Lenox Lumber Co	Pittsfield	MA	F	413 637-2744	14484
Jordan Tree Harvesters Inc **(PA)**	Kezar Falls	ME	G	207 625-4378	6250
High Tech Harvesting LLC	Loudon	NH	G	603 229-0750	18748

LOGGING: Skidding Logs

	CITY	ST	EMP	PHONE	ENTRY #
Cranes Contract Cutting Inc	Lamoine	ME	G	207 667-9008	6263

LOGGING: Stumping For Turpentine Or Powder Manufacturing

	CITY	ST	EMP	PHONE	ENTRY #
Hillside Stone Products Inc	Barre	VT	F	802 479-2508	21623

LOGGING: Timber, Cut At Logging Camp

	CITY	ST	EMP	PHONE	ENTRY #
Tr Landworks LLC	East Hartland	CT	G	860 402-6177	1240

LOGGING: Wood Chips, Produced In The Field

	CITY	ST	EMP	PHONE	ENTRY #
Honey Hill Farm	Millers Falls	MA	G	413 659-3141	13180
Daniel L Dunnells Logging Inc	Parsonsfield	ME	G	207 793-2901	6574
Farmington Chipping Enterprise	Farmington	ME	G	207 778-4888	6046
Forest Chester Products Inc	Lincoln	ME	E	207 794-2303	6353
Monadnock Land Clearing	Greenville	NH	G	603 878-2803	18227
Green Mountain Chipping Inc **(PA)**	Underhill	VT	G	802 899-1239	22548

LOGGING: Wooden Logs

	CITY	ST	EMP	PHONE	ENTRY #
Brightman Corp	Assonet	MA	E	508 644-2620	7678
R A Thomas Logging Inc	Guilford	ME	G	207 876-2722	6161
Mark Goodwin Wooden Bowls	Foster	RI	G	866 478-4065	20457
Authentic Log Homes Inc	Hardwick	VT	G	802 472-5096	22009
Longto Tree Service	Bradford	VT	G	802 274-9308	21703

LOOMS

	CITY	ST	EMP	PHONE	ENTRY #
Macomber Looms	York	ME	G	207 363-2808	7311
Harrisville Designs Inc **(PA)**	Harrisville	NH	G	603 827-3333	18302

LOOSELEAF BINDERS

	CITY	ST	EMP	PHONE	ENTRY #
American CT Rng Bnder Index &	Washington	CT	F	860 868-7900	4830
Elbe-Cesco Inc	Fall River	MA	D	508 676-8531	10687
Quality Loose Leaf Co	South Hadley	MA	G	413 534-5891	15310
Union Bookbinding Company Inc **(PA)**	Fall River	MA	E	508 676-8580	10775
Jackson Bookbinding Co Inc	Greenville	RI	F	401 231-0800	20469

LOTIONS OR CREAMS: Face

	CITY	ST	EMP	PHONE	ENTRY #
Beiersdorf Inc **(DH)**	Wilton	CT	G	203 563-5800	5276
Beiersdorf Inc	Norwalk	CT	B	203 854-8000	3110
Beiersdorf North America Inc **(DH)**	Wilton	CT	F	203 563-5800	5277
Bunsen Rush Laboratories Inc	Woodbridge	CT	G	203 397-0820	5463
Conopco Inc	Clinton	CT	B	860 669-8601	783
Durol Laboratories LLC	West Haven	CT	F	866 611-9694	5119
Jolen Cream Bleach Corp	Fairfield	CT	F	203 259-8779	1439
Lady Anne Cosmetics Inc	Trumbull	CT	G	203 372-6972	4626
Peninsula Skincare Labs Inc	Boston	MA	G	650 339-4299	8773
Tropical Products Inc	Salem	MA	E	978 740-5665	14947
WS Badger Company Inc	Gilsum	NH	E	603 357-2958	18196
Ogee Inc	Burlington	VT	G	802 540-8082	21800

LOTIONS: SHAVING

	CITY	ST	EMP	PHONE	ENTRY #
Edgewell Per Care Brands LLC **(HQ)**	Shelton	CT	B	203 944-5500	3799

LOUDSPEAKERS

	CITY	ST	EMP	PHONE	ENTRY #
Source Loudspeakers	South Windsor	CT	G	860 918-3088	4012
Genelec Inc	Natick	MA	F	508 652-0900	13257
Loud Technologies Inc	Whitinsville	MA	C	508 234-6158	16916
Technomad Associates LLC	South Deerfield	MA	G	413 665-6704	15257
Technomad Associates LLC **(PA)**	South Deerfield	MA	G	413 665-6704	15258

LOZENGES: Pharmaceutical

	CITY	ST	EMP	PHONE	ENTRY #
Henry Thayer Company	Easton	CT	G	203 226-0940	1319

LUBRICANTS: Corrosion Preventive

	CITY	ST	EMP	PHONE	ENTRY #
Ro 59 Inc	Stoughton	MA	G	781 341-1222	15618

LUBRICATING EQPT: Indl

	CITY	ST	EMP	PHONE	ENTRY #
Automation Inc	West Hartford	CT	F	860 236-5991	5054
Location Lube Inc	West Yarmouth	MA	G	508 888-5000	16579

LUBRICATING OIL & GREASE WHOLESALERS

	CITY	ST	EMP	PHONE	ENTRY #
Artech Packaging LLC	Bethel	CT	G	845 858-8558	128
Fuchs Lubricants Co	East Haven	CT	E	203 469-2336	1251
Seal 1 LLC	Brownville	ME	G	207 965-8860	5827

LUBRICATING SYSTEMS: Centralized

	CITY	ST	EMP	PHONE	ENTRY #
Lubrite LLC	Hanover	MA	G	781 871-1420	11346

LUBRICATORS: Grease Guns

	CITY	ST	EMP	PHONE	ENTRY #
Seal 1 LLC	Brownville	ME	G	207 965-8860	5827

LUGGAGE & BRIEFCASES

	CITY	ST	EMP	PHONE	ENTRY #
Commercial Sewing Inc	Torrington	CT	C	860 482-5509	4571
Marc Johnson	Danielson	CT	G	860 774-3315	1015
Brahmin Leather Works LLC	Fairhaven	MA	G	509 994-4000	10638
Case Technology Inc	Ipswich	MA	G	978 356-6011	11910
Byer Manufacturing Company	Orono	ME	E	207 866-2171	6552
C B P Corp **(PA)**	Arundel	ME	F	207 985-9767	5529
L L Bean Inc	Brunswick	ME	B	207 725-0300	5840
Nancy Lawrence	Portland	ME	G	207 774-7276	6697
Sea Bags Inc	Freeport	ME	G	207 939-3679	6086
Samsonite Company Stores LLC	Warren	RI	F	401 245-2100	21306

LUGGAGE & LEATHER GOODS STORES

	CITY	ST	EMP	PHONE	ENTRY #
Leatherby	Weatogue	CT	G	860 658-6166	5043
Surtan Manufacturing Co	South Yarmouth	MA	G	508 394-4099	15334

LUGGAGE & LEATHER GOODS STORES: Leather, Exc Luggage & Shoes

	CITY	ST	EMP	PHONE	ENTRY #
Dick Muller Designer/Craftsman	Shelburne Falls	MA	G	413 625-0016	15068

LUGGAGE & LEATHER GOODS STORES: Luggage, Exc Footlckr/Trunk

	CITY	ST	EMP	PHONE	ENTRY #
Sea Bags Inc	Freeport	ME	G	207 939-3679	6086

LUGGAGE REPAIR SHOP

	CITY	ST	EMP	PHONE	ENTRY #
Junction Frame Shop Inc	White River Junction	VT	G	802 296-2121	22641

LUGGAGE: Wardrobe Bags

	CITY	ST	EMP	PHONE	ENTRY #
Hartmann Incorporated	Mansfield	MA	D	508 851-1400	12634
HI Operating LLC **(DH)**	Mansfield	MA	E	508 851-1400	12635

LUMBER & BLDG MATLS DEALERS, RET: Energy Conservation Prdts

	CITY	ST	EMP	PHONE	ENTRY #
Allearth Renewables Inc	Williston	VT	E	802 872-9600	22654

LUMBER & BLDG MATRLS DEALERS, RET: Bath Fixtures, Eqpt/Sply

	CITY	ST	EMP	PHONE	ENTRY #
Kensco Inc **(PA)**	Ansonia	CT	F	203 734-8827	20

LUMBER & BLDG MTRLS DEALERS, RET: Doors, Storm, Wood/Metal

	CITY	ST	EMP	PHONE	ENTRY #
Cusson Sash Company	Glastonbury	CT	G	860 659-0354	1546
High Grade Shade & Screen Co	Lynn	MA	F	781 592-5027	12516

LUMBER & BLDG MTRLS DEALERS, RET: Planing Mill Prdts/Lumber

	CITY	ST	EMP	PHONE	ENTRY #
Anderson Logging and Lumber	Westminster	MA	G	978 874-2751	16802
Ernest R Palmer Lumber Co Inc	Sangerville	ME	G	207 876-2725	6899
Tukey Brothers Inc	Belgrade	ME	F	207 465-3570	5700
Harold Estey Lumber Inc	Londonderry	NH	G	603 432-5184	18701
Wilkins Lumber Co Inc	Milford	NH	G	603 673-2545	19082
M Piette & Sons Lumber Inc	Irasburg	VT	F	802 754-8876	22040

LUMBER & BUILDING MATERIAL DEALERS, RETAIL: Roofing Material

	CITY	ST	EMP	PHONE	ENTRY #
Little House By Andre Inc	Colchester	VT	G	802 878-8733	21872

LUMBER & BUILDING MATERIALS DEALER, RET: Door & Window Prdts

	CITY	ST	EMP	PHONE	ENTRY #
Leek Building Products Inc	Norwalk	CT	E	203 853-3883	3185
Millwork Masters Ltd **(PA)**	Keene	NH	F	603 358-3038	18515
H Hirschmann Ltd	West Rutland	VT	F	802 438-4447	22616

LUMBER & BUILDING MATERIALS DEALER, RET: Masonry Matls/Splys

	CITY	ST	EMP	PHONE	ENTRY #
Beard Concrete Co Derby Inc	Derby	CT	F	203 735-4641	1068
Colonial Landscape Corp	Groton	MA	G	978 448-3329	11287
Johns Building Supply Co Inc	Pittsfield	MA	F	413 442-7846	14478
Oldcastle Precast Inc	Rehoboth	MA	E	508 867-8312	14757
Phillip Ippolito	Seekonk	MA	F	508 336-9616	15033
Shea Concrete Products Inc	Amesbury	MA	E	978 388-1509	7508
American Concrete Inds Inc	Bangor	ME	D	207 947-8334	5629
Gagne & Son Con Blocks Inc	Auburn	ME	G	207 495-3313	5566
Rjf - Morin Brick LLC	Auburn	ME	D	207 784-9375	5595
Northern Design Precast Inc	Loudon	NH	E	603 783-8989	18751

LUMBER & BUILDING MATERIALS DEALERS, RET: Sash, Wood/Metal

	CITY	ST	EMP	PHONE	ENTRY #
J B Sash & Door Company Inc	Chelsea	MA	E	617 884-8940	9955
Saco Manufacturing & Wdwkg	Saco	ME	G	207 284-6613	6857

LUMBER & BUILDING MATERIALS DEALERS, RETAIL: Brick

	CITY	ST	EMP	PHONE	ENTRY #
P & M Brick & Block Inc	Watertown	MA	G	617 924-6020	16304

LUMBER & BUILDING MATERIALS DEALERS, RETAIL: Countertops

	CITY	ST	EMP	PHONE	ENTRY #
Barre Tile Inc	Lebanon	NH	F	802 476-0912	18614

LUMBER & BUILDING MATERIALS DEALERS, RETAIL: Flooring, Wood

	CITY	ST	EMP	PHONE	ENTRY #
Ben Barretts LLC	Thompson	CT	G	860 928-9373	4532
Weymouth Braided Rug Co Inc	North Oxford	MA	G	508 987-8525	13976
Trussco Inc	North Kingstown	RI	E	401 295-0669	20747

LUMBER & BUILDING MATERIALS DEALERS, RETAIL: Paving Stones

	CITY	ST	EMP	PHONE	ENTRY #
Rowley Ready Mix Inc	Rowley	MA	F	978 948-2544	14864

LUMBER & BUILDING MATERIALS DEALERS, RETAIL: Sand & Gravel

	CITY	ST	EMP	PHONE	ENTRY #
LH Gault & Son Incorporated	Westport	CT	D	203 227-5181	5209
Rawson Development Inc	Putnam	CT	F	860 928-4536	3629
Berkshire Concrete Corp **(HQ)**	Pittsfield	MA	C	413 443-4734	14456
Dauphinais & Son Inc	Wilbraham	MA	F	413 596-3964	16935
Morse Sand & Gravel Corp	Attleboro	MA	E	508 809-4644	7769
DH Hardwick & Sons Inc	Bennington	NH	E	603 588-6618	17688

LUMBER & BUILDING MATERIALS DEALERS, RETAIL: Siding

	CITY	ST	EMP	PHONE	ENTRY #
Beacon Sales Acquisition Inc	Salem	NH	G	207 797-7950	19712

LUMBER & BUILDING MATERIALS DEALERS, RETAIL: Tile, Ceramic

	CITY	ST	EMP	PHONE	ENTRY #
La Pietra Thinstone Veneer	Brookfield	CT	G	203 775-6162	650
Louis W Mian Inc **(PA)**	Boston	MA	E	617 241-7900	8672
Cabinets For Less LLC	Manchester	NH	G	603 935-7551	18794

LUMBER & BUILDING MATERIALS RET DEALERS: Millwork & Lumber

	CITY	ST	EMP	PHONE	ENTRY #
Bonito Manufacturing Inc	North Haven	CT	D	203 234-8786	3011
Lingard Cabinet Co LLC	Manchester	CT	G	860 647-9886	2019
Woodsmiths Inc	Fall River	MA	G	508 548-8343	10784
Mike Sequore	Marlborough	NH	G	603 876-4634	18962
Tommila Brothers Inc	Fitzwilliam	NH	F	603 242-7774	18153

LUMBER & BUILDING MATLS DEALERS, RET: Concrete/Cinder Block

	CITY	ST	EMP	PHONE	ENTRY #
New Milford Block & Supply	New Milford	CT	F	860 355-1101	2816
Kellogg Bros Inc	Southwick	MA	G	413 569-6029	15415
Wilbert Swans Vault Co	Westbrook	ME	E	207 854-5324	7214
Seacoast Redimix Concrete LLC **(PA)**	Dover	NH	F	603 742-4441	18052

LUMBER: Box

	CITY	ST	EMP	PHONE	ENTRY #
Interstate + Lakeland Lbr Corp	Greenwich	CT	F	203 531-8050	1623

LUMBER: Furniture Dimension Stock, Softwood

	CITY	ST	EMP	PHONE	ENTRY #
Harold Estey Lumber Inc	Londonderry	NH	G	603 432-5184	18701

LUMBER: Hardboard

	CITY	ST	EMP	PHONE	ENTRY #
Speedboard Usa Inc	Newburyport	MA	G	978 462-2700	13534

LUMBER: Hardwood Dimension

	CITY	ST	EMP	PHONE	ENTRY #
Stake Company LLC	East Windsor	CT	G	860 623-2700	1305
Bear Paw Lumber Corp **(PA)**	Fryeburg	ME	F	207 935-3052	6095
Lovell Lumber Co Inc	Lovell	ME	E	207 925-6455	6384

LUMBER: Hardwood Dimension & Flooring Mills

	CITY	ST	EMP	PHONE	ENTRY #
Ben Barretts LLC	Thompson	CT	G	860 928-9373	4532
E R Hinman & Sons Inc	Burlington	CT	G	860 673-9170	677
Kellogg Hardwoods Inc	Bethel	CT	G	203 797-1992	166
Architectural Timber Mllwk Inc	Hadley	MA	F	413 586-3045	11305
Bannish Lumber Inc	Chester	MA	F	413 354-2279	9980
Canner Incorporated	West Groton	MA	F	978 448-3063	16479
Roberts Brothers Lumber Co	Ashfield	MA	E	413 628-3333	7654
Stiles & Hart Brick Company	Bridgewater	MA	E	508 697-6928	9088
Columbia Forest Products Inc	Presque Isle	ME	C	207 760-3800	6757
K B Logging Inc	Smyrna Mills	ME	F	207 757-8818	6993
Precision Lumber Inc	Wentworth	NH	D	603 764-9450	19947
Swift River Wood Products	Chocorua	NH	G	603 323-3317	17832
Tommila Brothers Inc	Fitzwilliam	NH	F	603 242-7774	18153
A Johnson Co	Bristol	VT	D	802 453-4884	21760
Columbia Forest Products Inc	Newport	VT	B	802 334-6711	22193
Dci Inc	South Royalton	VT	F	802 763-7847	22490
Dennis Ducharme	Marshfield	VT	G	802 426-3796	22094
G W Lumber & Millwork Inc **(PA)**	Williston	VT	G	802 860-7370	22666
Granville Manufacturing Co	Granville	VT	G	802 767-4747	22003
N W P Inc	Pownal	VT	G	802 442-4749	22282

LUMBER: Kiln Dried

	CITY	ST	EMP	PHONE	ENTRY #
Cersosimo Lumber Company Inc	Hardwick	MA	F	413 477-6258	11373
Leon M Fiske Company Inc	Greenfield	MA	G	413 772-6833	11268
Whitefield Dry Kiln Inc	Whitefield	ME	G	207 549-5470	7220
Precision Lumber Inc	Wentworth	NH	D	603 764-9450	19947
Blackstone Valley Prestain	Mapleville	RI	G	401 568-9745	20611
Colton Enterprises Inc	Pittsfield	VT	G	802 746-8033	22262

LUMBER: Piles, Foundation & Marine Construction, Treated

	CITY	ST	EMP	PHONE	ENTRY #
Techno Mtal Post Watertown LLC	Waterbury	CT	G	203 755-6403	4961

LUMBER: Plywood, Hardwood

	CITY	ST	EMP	PHONE	ENTRY #
Bergan Architectural Wdwkg Inc	Middletown	CT	E	860 346-0869	2177
Thomas Bernhard Building Sys	Southport	CT	E	203 925-0414	4102
Bear Paw Lumber Corp **(PA)**	Fryeburg	ME	F	207 935-3052	6095
Columbia Forest Products Inc	Presque Isle	ME	C	207 760-3800	6757
Herrick Mill Work Inc	Contoocook	NH	E	603 746-5092	17945
Columbia Forest Products Inc	Newport	VT	B	802 334-6711	22193
Columbia Forest Products Inc	Newport	VT	C	802 334-3600	22194
Mariah Group LLC	Rutland	VT	D	802 747-4000	22345
Stratabond Co Inc	Rutland	VT	G	802 747-4000	22355

LUMBER: Plywood, Hardwood or Hardwood Faced

	CITY	ST	EMP	PHONE	ENTRY #
Rutland Plywood Corp	Rutland	VT	G	802 747-4000	22350

LUMBER: Treated

	CITY	ST	EMP	PHONE	ENTRY #
Bestway of New England Inc	South Lancaster	MA	F	978 368-7667	15316
Northeast Treaters Inc **(PA)**	Belchertown	MA	E	413 323-7811	8026
Integrity Composites LLC	Biddeford	ME	F	207 571-0743	5740
University of Maine System	Orono	ME	F	207 581-2843	6559

MACHINE PARTS: Stamped Or Pressed Metal

	CITY	ST	EMP	PHONE	ENTRY #
Addamo Manufacturing Inc	Newington	CT	G	860 667-2601	2837
Alfro Custom Manufacturing Co	Southbury	CT	G	203 264-6246	4023
Astro Industries Inc	Berlin	CT	G	860 828-6304	74
Consulting Engrg Dev Svcs Inc	Oxford	CT	D	203 828-6528	3398
Forrest Machine Inc	Berlin	CT	D	860 563-1796	84
Hoyt Manufacturing Co Inc	Southington	CT	G	860 628-2050	4059
Joval Machine Co Inc	Yalesville	CT	E	203 284-0082	5505
Leelynd Corp	Waterbury	CT	G	203 753-9137	4897
Meriden Manufacturing Inc	Meriden	CT	D	203 237-7481	2104
Midconn Precision Mfg LLC	Bristol	CT	G	860 584-1340	581
Paradigm Prcision Holdings LLC	Manchester	CT	G	860 649-2888	2034
Pressure Blast Mfg Co Inc	South Windsor	CT	F	800 722-5278	4004
Schaeffler Aerospace USA Corp **(DH)**	Danbury	CT	B	203 744-2211	984
Tyger Tool Inc	Stratford	CT	F	203 375-4344	4455
Amkor Industrial Products Inc	Worcester	MA	E	508 799-4970	17336
Brodeur Machine Company Bus Tr	New Bedford	MA	D	508 995-2662	13367
Bruce Barrowclough	Beverly	MA	G	978 524-0022	8113
Cunningham Machine Co Inc	Chelmsford	MA	G	978 256-7541	9890
Dakin Road Investments Inc	Littleton	MA	F	978 443-4020	12299
Hd Bennett Machine Co Inc	North Brookfield	MA	G	508 867-0154	13881
Lee Tool Co Inc	Ludlow	MA	F	413 583-8750	12471
Micrometals Tech Corp	Worcester	MA	F	508 792-1615	17417
Pocasset Machine Corporation	Pocasset	MA	E	508 563-5572	14600
Quinn Manufacturing Inc	Danvers	MA	G	978 524-0310	10248
Sp Machine Inc	Hudson	MA	E	978 562-2019	11818
Techncal Hrdfcing McHining Inc	Attleboro	MA	F	508 223-2900	7801
Technical Enterprises Inc	Bridgewater	MA	G	781 603-9402	9089
Unlimited Manufacturing Svc	Lowell	MA	G	978 835-4915	12442
Howard Tool Company	Bangor	ME	E	207 942-1203	5651
Maine Toolroom Inc	Scarborough	ME	G	207 883-2455	6933
Tuff Parts Inc	South Portland	ME	G	207 767-1063	7042
Alan T Seeler Inc	New Hampton	NH	F	603 744-3736	19301
Ameriforge Group Inc	Newport	NH	E	603 863-1270	19342
Cobra Precision Machining Corp	Hooksett	NH	G	603 434-8424	18347
Samson Manufacturing Corp	Keene	NH	E	603 355-3903	18523
Amt Acquisition Inc	Warren	RI	F	401 247-1680	21284
Everett J Prescott Inc	Lincoln	RI	G	401 333-8588	20573
Hl Tech Mch & Fabrication LLC	Ashaway	RI	E	866 972-2077	20036
Masiello Enterprises Inc	Coventry	RI	E	401 826-1883	20155
Production Machine Sales & Svc	Cranston	RI	F	401 461-6830	20274
Cold Hollow Precision Inc	Enosburg Falls	VT	G	802 933-5542	21923

MACHINE SHOPS

	CITY	ST	EMP	PHONE	ENTRY #
A & M Auto Machine Inc	Meriden	CT	G	203 237-3502	2071
AJ Tuck Company	Brookfield	CT	E	203 775-1234	633
Altek Electronics Inc	Torrington	CT	C	860 482-7626	4558
Bracone Metal Spinning Inc	Southington	CT	E	860 628-5927	4041
Bristol Tool & Die Company	Bristol	CT	E	860 582-2577	539
Budrad Engineering Co LLC	Monroe	CT	G	203 452-7310	2397
Carnegie Tool Inc	Norwalk	CT	F	203 866-0744	3119
Continuity Engine Inc	New Haven	CT	G	866 631-5556	2678
El Mar Inc	West Hartford	CT	G	860 729-7232	5068
Faille Precision Machining	Baltic	CT	G	860 822-1964	49
Integral Technologies Inc **(DH)**	Enfield	CT	G	860 741-2281	1366
Interface Devices Incorporated	Milford	CT	G	203 878-4648	2303
Jeff Manufacturing Co Inc	Torrington	CT	F	860 482-8845	4582
Mj Tool & Manufacturing Inc	Simsbury	CT	G	860 352-2688	3908
Mrh Tool LLC	Milford	CT	G	203 878-3359	2317
Naiad Dynamics Us Inc **(HQ)**	Shelton	CT	E	203 929-6355	3836
New England Traveling Wire LLC	New Britain	CT	G	860 223-6297	2557
Stacy B Goff	East Windsor	CT	G	860 623-2547	1304
Straton Industries Inc	Stratford	CT	D	203 375-4488	4450
Voyteks Inc	East Windsor	CT	G	860 967-6558	1309
Wallingford Industries Inc	Branford	CT	F	203 481-0359	358
Axis Cnc Incorporated	Ware	MA	F	413 967-6803	16228
Gill Metal Fab Inc	Brockton	MA	E	508 580-4445	9151
H & T Specialty Co Inc	Waltham	MA	F	781 893-3866	16123
Heron Machine & Engrg Inc	Ludlow	MA	G	413 547-6308	12466
J & L Welding & Machine Co	Gloucester	MA	E	978 283-3388	11193
M-Tech	Tyngsboro	MA	G	978 649-4563	15894
Magnat-Fairview LLC	Chicopee	MA	F	413 593-5742	10039
Mj Machine Inc	Bridgewater	MA	G	508 697-5329	9084
Opteon Corporation	Cambridge	MA	G	617 520-6658	9601
Patten Machine Inc	Hudson	MA	F	978 562-9847	11801
R L Hachey Company	Waltham	MA	G	781 891-4237	16182
Ranor Inc	Westminster	MA	D	978 874-0591	16812
Sp Machine Inc	Hudson	MA	E	978 562-2019	11818
Sterling Machine Company Inc	Lynn	MA	E	781 593-3000	12541
T O C Finishing Corp	Somerville	MA	F	617 623-3310	15221
Technical Enterprises Inc	Bridgewater	MA	G	781 603-9402	9089
Techprecision Corporation **(PA)**	Westminster	MA	G	978 874-0591	16815
Teletrak Envmtl Systems Inc **(PA)**	Webster	MA	G	508 949-2430	16352
Unimacts Global LLC **(PA)**	Lexington	MA	E	410 415-6070	12280
United Metal Fabricators Inc	Worcester	MA	F	508 754-1800	17493
Valco Precision Machine Inc	Brockton	MA	G	508 559-9009	9187
Elmet Technologies LLC	Lewiston	ME	C	207 333-6100	6287
Justin Jordan	New Portland	ME	G	207 628-4123	6474
Kennebec Marine Company	Scarborough	ME	G	207 773-0392	6929
Maine Machine Products Company	South Paris	ME	C	207 743-6344	7013
Millincket Fabrication Mch Inc **(PA)**	Millinocket	ME	E	207 723-9733	6443
Montalvo Corporation	Gorham	ME	E	207 856-2501	6122
Northeast Doran Inc	Skowhegan	ME	G	207 474-2000	6984
OBrien Consolidated Inds	Lewiston	ME	F	207 783-8543	6312
Robert Timmons Jr	Windham	ME	G	207 892-3366	7249
Ameriforge Group Inc	Newport	NH	E	603 863-1270	19342
Burbak Companies	Wilton	NH	D	603 654-2291	19976
Cnc Design & Counsulting LLC	Kingston	NH	G	603 686-5437	18542
Core Assemblies Inc	Gilford	NH	F	603 293-0270	18183
Davis Village Solutions LLC	New Ipswich	NH	G	603 878-3662	19304
Dennis Trudel	Pelham	NH	G	603 635-7208	19430
Insource Design & Mfg Tech LLC	Merrimack	NH	G	603 718-8228	19007
Linear & Metric Co	Londonderry	NH	E	603 432-1700	18714
Mikros Manufacturing Inc	Claremont	NH	E	603 690-2020	17855
Pro Star Prcsion Machining LLC	Londonderry	NH	G	603 518-8570	18732
Sunset Tool Inc	Keene	NH	E	603 355-2246	18531
Tsi Group Inc **(DH)**	Hampton	NH	E	603 964-0296	18275
Turbocam Inc	Barrington	NH	G	603 905-0200	17624
Turbocam Inc **(PA)**	Barrington	NH	C	603 905-0200	17625
Winchester Precision Tech Ltd	Winchester	NH	F	603 239-6326	19997
Contract Fusion Inc	East Providence	RI	E	401 438-1298	20400
Dag Machine and Tool Inc	Pawtucket	RI	G	401 724-0450	20833

	CITY	ST	EMP	PHONE	ENTRY #
Guill Tool & Engrg Co Inc	West Warwick	RI	D	401 822-8186	21493
Hitachi Cable America Inc	Ashaway	RI	C	401 315-5100	20038
Joraco Inc	Smithfield	RI	F	401 232-1710	21234
Rosco Manufacturing Llc	Central Falls	RI	E	401 228-0120	20125
Seven Star Inc	Newport	RI	G	401 683-6222	20680
Menard Manufacturing	West Rutland	VT	G	802 438-5173	22619

MACHINE TOOL ACCESS: Arbors

	CITY	ST	EMP	PHONE	ENTRY #
Arborjet Inc	Woburn	MA	E	781 935-9070	17120

MACHINE TOOL ACCESS: Balancing Machines

	CITY	ST	EMP	PHONE	ENTRY #
Sjm Properties Inc	Ellington	CT	G	860 979-0060	1340
Space Electronics LLC	Berlin	CT	E	860 829-0001	110

MACHINE TOOL ACCESS: Broaches

	CITY	ST	EMP	PHONE	ENTRY #
Center Broach & Machine Co	Meriden	CT	G	203 235-6329	2084
Eastern Broach Inc	Plainville	CT	F	860 828-4800	3483
Lapointe Hudson Broach Co Inc	Hudson	MA	E	978 562-7943	11784
New England Broach Co Inc	Whately	MA	F	413 665-7064	16907
Pilot Precision Properties LLC	South Deerfield	MA	G	413 350-5200	15252

MACHINE TOOL ACCESS: Cutting

	CITY	ST	EMP	PHONE	ENTRY #
Alden Corporation	Wolcott	CT	D	203 879-8830	5432
Alden Tool Company Inc	Berlin	CT	E	860 828-3556	68
Brass City Technologies LLC **(PA)**	Naugatuck	CT	G	203 723-7021	2463
Drill Rite Carbide Tool Co	Terryville	CT	G	860 583-3200	4476
Ewald Instruments Corp	Bristol	CT	F	860 491-9042	558
Guhring Inc	Bloomfield	CT	C	860 216-5948	222
Kinetic Tool Co Inc	East Windsor	CT	F	860 627-5882	1292
M & M Carbide Inc	Southington	CT	G	860 628-2002	4063
M & R Manufacturing Inc	Newington	CT	G	860 666-5066	2878
Marena Industries Inc	East Hartford	CT	F	860 528-9701	1205
Nelson Apostle Inc	Hartford	CT	G	860 953-4633	1850
Powerhold Inc	Middlefield	CT	E	860 349-1044	2163
Tool The Somma Company	Waterbury	CT	E	203 753-2114	4963
Universal Precision Mfg	Trumbull	CT	G	203 374-9809	4641
Berkshire Precision Tool LLC	Pittsfield	MA	E	413 499-3875	14459
Custom Carbide Corp	Springfield	MA	F	413 732-7470	15466
Esco Technologies Inc	Holliston	MA	E	508 429-4441	11570
Industrial Cutting Tools Inc	Westfield	MA	G	413 562-2996	16689
Kennametal Inc	Greenfield	MA	B	802 626-3331	11267
L Hardy Company Inc **(PA)**	Worcester	MA	F	508 757-3480	17406
New England Carbide Inc	Topsfield	MA	F	978 887-0313	15863
North East Form Engineering	Lowell	MA	G	978 454-5290	12414
Quabbin Inc	Orange	MA	F	978 544-3872	14223
Razor Tool Inc	Woburn	MA	G	781 654-1582	17281
Richards Micro-Tool LLC	Plymouth	MA	E	508 746-6900	14580
Safe T Cut Inc	Monson	MA	F	413 267-9984	13211
Simonds Industries Intl	Fitchburg	MA	E	978 424-0100	10853
Simonds Saw LLC **(PA)**	Fitchburg	MA	E	978 424-0100	10856
Tnco Inc	New Bedford	MA	D	781 447-6661	13454
Wellman Engineering Inc	Belmont	MA	G	617 484-8338	8082
Cutting Tool Technologies Inc	Wilton	NH	G	603 654-2550	19977
R & J Tool Inc **(PA)**	Laconia	NH	G	603 366-4925	18581
Swisset Tool Company Inc	Belmont	NH	G	603 524-0082	17684
RI Carbide Tool Co	Smithfield	RI	E	401 231-1020	21248
Mark Hunter	Lyndonville	VT	G	802 626-8407	22069
Sterling Gun Drills Inc	North Bennington	VT	F	802 442-3525	22213
Trow & Holden Co Inc	Barre	VT	F	802 476-7221	21643

MACHINE TOOL ACCESS: Diamond Cutting, For Turning, Etc

	CITY	ST	EMP	PHONE	ENTRY #
M T S Tool LLC	Oakville	CT	G	860 945-0875	3299
R&R Tool & Die LLC	East Windsor	CT	G	860 627-9197	1299
Bruce Diamond Corporation	Attleboro	MA	E	508 222-3755	7715
Cutting Edge Carbide Tech Inc	Leominster	MA	G	888 210-9670	12130
Joma Diamond Tool Company	East Longmeadow	MA	F	413 525-0760	10481
Magwen Diamond Pdts Inc	Yarmouth Port	MA	G	508 375-9152	17530
Ned Acquisition Corp	Worcester	MA	E	508 798-8546	17427
Poly-Tech Diamond Co Inc	North Attleboro	MA	F	508 695-3561	13772
Saint-Gobain Abrasives Inc **(DH)**	Worcester	MA	A	508 795-5000	17464
Diamondsharp Corporation	Walpole	NH	G	603 445-2224	19920

MACHINE TOOL ACCESS: Drills

	CITY	ST	EMP	PHONE	ENTRY #
W L Fuller	Warwick	RI	E	401 467-2900	21441

MACHINE TOOL ACCESS: End Mills

	CITY	ST	EMP	PHONE	ENTRY #
Microcut Inc	Plymouth	MA	G	781 582-8090	14566

MACHINE TOOL ACCESS: Honing Heads

	CITY	ST	EMP	PHONE	ENTRY #
Vogel Capital Inc **(HQ)**	Marlborough	MA	E	508 481-5944	12846

MACHINE TOOL ACCESS: Knives, Metalworking

	CITY	ST	EMP	PHONE	ENTRY #
Ephesian Arms Inc	Fall River	MA	G	508 674-7030	10690
Trilap Company Inc	Lowell	MA	G	978 453-2205	12439

MACHINE TOOL ACCESS: Shaping Tools

	CITY	ST	EMP	PHONE	ENTRY #
Dienes Corporation	Spencer	MA	E	508 885-6301	15428

MACHINE TOOL ACCESS: Threading Tools

	CITY	ST	EMP	PHONE	ENTRY #
Swanson Tool Manufacturing Inc	West Hartford	CT	E	860 953-1641	5097
Reed Machinery Inc **(PA)**	Worcester	MA	F	508 595-9090	17456

MACHINE TOOL ACCESS: Tool Holders

	CITY	ST	EMP	PHONE	ENTRY #
Byron Lord Inc	Old Lyme	CT	G	203 287-9881	3315
Micro Insert Inc	Milldale	CT	G	860 621-5789	2385

MACHINE TOOL ACCESS: Tools & Access

	CITY	ST	EMP	PHONE	ENTRY #
Comex Machinery	Bridgeport	CT	G	203 334-2196	399
J F Tool Inc	Rockfall	CT	G	860 349-3063	3697
James J Scott LLC	Rocky Hill	CT	G	860 571-9200	3719
Meadow Manufacturing Inc	Kensington	CT	F	860 357-3785	1919
Pine Meadow Machine Co Inc	Windsor Locks	CT	G	860 623-4494	5398
Southwick & Meister Inc	Meriden	CT	C	203 237-0000	2133
Ely Tool Inc	Springfield	MA	E	413 732-2347	15469
Giltron Inc	North Dighton	MA	G	508 359-4310	13931
Michael Brisebois	Easthampton	MA	F	413 527-9590	10567
Tri State Precision Inc	Northfield	MA	G	413 498-2961	14068
Van Wal Machine Inc	Bellingham	MA	F	508 966-0733	8061
Tel -Tuk Enterprises LLC	Belmont	NH	G	603 267-1966	17685
Ar-Ro Engineering Company Inc **(PA)**	North Smithfield	RI	G	401 766-6669	20781
Fielding Mfg Zinc Diecasting	Cranston	RI	D	401 461-0400	20227
R & D Tl Engrg Four-Slide Prod	Cranston	RI	G	401 942-9710	20276

MACHINE TOOL ATTACHMENTS & ACCESS

	CITY	ST	EMP	PHONE	ENTRY #
Accu-Rite Tool & Mfg Co	Tolland	CT	F	860 688-4844	4538
Century Tool and Design Inc	Milldale	CT	F	860 621-6748	2383
Danjon Manufacturing Corp	Cheshire	CT	F	203 272-7258	727
Edrive Actuators Inc	Newington	CT	G	860 953-0588	2861
Pmt Group Inc **(PA)**	Bridgeport	CT	C	203 367-8675	471
Walker Magnetics Group Inc **(HQ)**	Windsor	CT	E	508 853-3232	5378
Thomas Machine Works Inc	Newburyport	MA	G	978 462-7182	13541
Vogform Tool & Die Co Inc	West Springfield	MA	F	413 737-6947	16562
Mestek Inc	Clinton	ME	C	207 426-2351	5916
Mid State Machine Products **(PA)**	Winslow	ME	C	207 873-6136	7271
Precise Products Company	Lincoln	RI	F	401 724-7190	20592

MACHINE TOOLS & ACCESS

	CITY	ST	EMP	PHONE	ENTRY #
Aircraft Forged Tool Company	Rockfall	CT	G	860 347-3778	3696
AKO Inc	Windsor	CT	E	860 298-9765	5317
American Grippers Inc	Trumbull	CT	E	203 459-8345	4611
Coastal Group Inc	Killingworth	CT	G	860 452-4148	1925
Edmunds Manufacturing Company **(PA)**	Farmington	CT	D	860 677-2813	1480
Fletcher-Terry Company LLC **(PA)**	East Berlin	CT	D	860 828-3400	1102
H & B Tool & Engineering Co	South Windsor	CT	E	860 528-9341	3976
Hgh Industries LLC	South Windsor	CT	G	860 644-1150	3980
J J Industries Conn Inc	Southington	CT	F	860 628-4655	4060
Jet Tool & Cutter Mfg Inc	Southington	CT	E	860 621-5381	4061
Mid-State Manufacturing Inc	Milldale	CT	F	860 621-6855	2386
Moon Cutter Co Inc	Hamden	CT	E	203 288-9249	1773
Paradigm Prcision Holdings LLC	East Berlin	CT	D	860 829-3663	1105
Perry Technology Corporation	New Hartford	CT	D	860 738-2525	2644
Preferred Utilities Mfg Corp **(HQ)**	Danbury	CT	D	203 743-6741	974
Producto Corporation **(HQ)**	Bridgeport	CT	F	203 366-3224	476
Viking Tool Company	Shelton	CT	E	203 929-1457	3885
Ade Technologies Inc **(HQ)**	Westwood	MA	D	781 467-3500	16857
American Saw & Mfg Company Inc	East Longmeadow	MA	D	413 525-3961	10466
Automec Inc	Waltham	MA	E	781 893-3403	16039
Columbia ASC Inc	Lawrence	MA	F	978 683-2205	12012
Coorstek Inc	Worcester	MA	B	774 317-2600	17360
Dmt Export Inc	Marlborough	MA	E	508 481-5944	12748
Dynisco Instruments LLC **(HQ)**	Franklin	MA	C	508 541-9400	11037
Form Roll Die Corp **(PA)**	Worcester	MA	E	508 755-2010	17377
Hutchinson Arospc & Indust Inc	Hopkinton	MA	C	508 417-7000	11719
LS Starrett Company	Athol	MA	G	978 249-3551	7690
Niagara Cutter Athol Inc	Athol	MA	E	978 249-2788	7691
PCC Specialty Products Inc	Auburn	MA	D	508 753-6530	7847
Pedros Inc	Haverhill	MA	G	978 657-7101	11458
Picture Frame Products Inc	Arlington	MA	G	781 648-7719	7634
Prism Products LLC	Lynn	MA	G	781 581-1740	12534
Standex International Corp	Wakefield	MA	G	978 538-0808	15977
Toolmex Indus Solutions Inc **(PA)**	Northborough	MA	D	508 653-5110	14052
US Cutting Chain Mfg Co Inc	Brockton	MA	G	508 588-0322	9186
Vulcan Company Inc **(PA)**	Hingham	MA	D	781 337-5970	11515
Enercon **(PA)**	Gray	ME	C	207 657-7000	6139
Irwin Industrial Tool Company	Gorham	ME	C	207 856-6111	6115
Michael Good Designs Inc	Rockport	ME	F	207 236-9619	6824
Peavey Manufacturing Company	Eddington	ME	E	207 843-7861	5997
Xuron Corp	Saco	ME	E	207 283-1401	6862
Boudrieau Tool & Die Inc	Rindge	NH	G	603 899-5795	19647
Cobra Precision Machining Corp	Hooksett	NH	G	603 434-8424	18347
Jarvis Cutting Tools Inc	Rochester	NH	D	603 332-9000	19676
Durant Tool Company Inc	North Kingstown	RI	E	401 781-7800	20703
Estate Agency Inc	Cranston	RI	G	401 946-5380	20222
Hexagon Holdings Inc **(DH)**	North Kingstown	RI	G	401 886-2000	20715
Mouldcam Inc	Bristol	RI	G	401 396-5522	20094
Numaco Packaging LLC	East Providence	RI	F	401 438-4952	20436
Rol-Flo Engineering Inc	Westerly	RI	E	401 596-0060	21539
Wei Inc **(PA)**	Cranston	RI	E	401 781-3904	20309
Tivoly Inc	Derby Line	VT	C	802 873-3106	21906
Vermont Thread Gage LLC	Swanton	VT	G	802 868-4246	22539
Woodlan Tool and Machine Co	Bellows Falls	VT	E	802 463-4597	21656
Yankee Corporation	Fairfax	VT	D	802 527-0177	21981

MACHINE TOOLS, METAL CUTTING: Drilling

	CITY	ST	EMP	PHONE	ENTRY #
Chas G Allen Realty LLC	Barre	MA	D	978 355-2911	7950
Nanospire Inc	Buxton	ME	G	207 929-6226	5859

MACHINE TOOLS, METAL CUTTING: Electrochemical Milling

	CITY	ST	EMP	PHONE	ENTRY #
Nova Analytics Corporation	Beverly	MA	G	781 897-1208	8160

MACHINE TOOLS, METAL CUTTING: Exotic, Including Explosive

	CITY	ST	EMP	PHONE	ENTRY #
B & L Tool and Machine Company	Plainville	CT	G	860 747-2721	3468
Connecticut Tool & Cutter Co	Bristol	CT	E	860 314-1740	543
Gary Tool Company	Stratford	CT	G	203 377-3077	4414
Moore Tool Company Inc **(HQ)**	Bridgeport	CT	D	203 366-3224	453

	CITY	ST	EMP	PHONE	ENTRY #
Pmt Group Inc **(PA)**	Bridgeport	CT	C	203 367-8675	471
B & D Precision Inc	Stoneham	MA	G	781 438-8644	15555

MACHINE TOOLS, METAL CUTTING: Grind, Polish, Buff, Lapp

	CITY	ST	EMP	PHONE	ENTRY #
Supfina Machine Co Inc	North Kingstown	RI	E	401 294-6600	20744

MACHINE TOOLS, METAL CUTTING: Home Workshop

	CITY	ST	EMP	PHONE	ENTRY #
Accutech Machine Inc	Danvers	MA	F	978 922-7271	10192
President Fllows Hrvard Cllege	Cambridge	MA	G	617 495-2020	9615

MACHINE TOOLS, METAL CUTTING: Jig, Boring & Grinding

	CITY	ST	EMP	PHONE	ENTRY #
Ceda Company Inc	Newington	CT	G	860 666-1593	2853
N E M T R LLC	Shutesbury	MA	G	413 259-1444	15140

MACHINE TOOLS, METAL CUTTING: Plasma Process

	CITY	ST	EMP	PHONE	ENTRY #
Ark Plasma	Alfred	ME	G	207 332-6999	5515
Centricut Manufacturing LLC	West Lebanon	NH	E	603 298-6191	19948
Thermacut Inc	Claremont	NH	E	603 543-0585	17861
Thermal Dynamics Corporation **(DH)**	West Lebanon	NH	B	603 298-5711	19963

MACHINE TOOLS, METAL CUTTING: Saws, Power

	CITY	ST	EMP	PHONE	ENTRY #
Hendrick Manufacturing Corp **(PA)**	Salem	MA	F	781 631-4400	14919

MACHINE TOOLS, METAL CUTTING: Screw & Thread

	CITY	ST	EMP	PHONE	ENTRY #
L C M Tool Co	Waterbury	CT	G	203 757-1575	4896

MACHINE TOOLS, METAL CUTTING: Tool Replacement & Rpr Parts

	CITY	ST	EMP	PHONE	ENTRY #
Nemtec Inc	Cheshire	CT	G	203 272-0788	746
Sadlak Industries LLC	Coventry	CT	E	860 742-0227	838
A N C Tool and Manufacturing	Worcester	MA	G	508 757-0224	17329
Component Sources Intl	Westborough	MA	F	508 986-2300	16607
J T Machine Co Inc	East Douglas	MA	E	508 476-1508	10427
Mardon Manufacturing Company	Rowley	MA	G	978 948-7040	14856
Thomas Enterprises Inc	Searsmont	ME	G	207 342-5001	6946
Valmet Inc	Winthrop	ME	F	207 377-6909	7283
Fremont Machine & Tool Co Inc	Fremont	NH	G	603 895-9445	18176
Piatek Machine Company Inc	Pawtucket	RI	F	401 728-9930	20880

MACHINE TOOLS, METAL CUTTING: Ultrasonic

	CITY	ST	EMP	PHONE	ENTRY #
Sonitek Corporation	Milford	CT	E	203 878-9321	2364

MACHINE TOOLS, METAL CUTTING: Vertical Turning & Boring

	CITY	ST	EMP	PHONE	ENTRY #
Atp Industries LLC **(PA)**	Plainville	CT	F	860 479-5007	3467
Charter Oak Automation LLC	Wallingford	CT	G	203 562-0699	4716

MACHINE TOOLS, METAL FORMING: Bending

	CITY	ST	EMP	PHONE	ENTRY #
Accubend LLC	Plantsville	CT	G	860 378-0303	3525
Sonolite Plastics Corporation	Gloucester	MA	F	978 281-0662	11211

MACHINE TOOLS, METAL FORMING: Die Casting & Extruding

	CITY	ST	EMP	PHONE	ENTRY #
Ace Finishing Co LLC	Bristol	CT	G	860 582-4600	513

MACHINE TOOLS, METAL FORMING: Forging Machinery & Hammers

	CITY	ST	EMP	PHONE	ENTRY #
Kt Acquisition LLC	Worcester	MA	D	508 853-4500	17402

MACHINE TOOLS, METAL FORMING: Forming, Metal Deposit

	CITY	ST	EMP	PHONE	ENTRY #
Proiron LLC	West Haven	CT	G	203 934-7967	5143

MACHINE TOOLS, METAL FORMING: Marking

	CITY	ST	EMP	PHONE	ENTRY #
A G Russell Company Inc	Hartford	CT	G	860 247-9093	1800

MACHINE TOOLS, METAL FORMING: Mechanical, Pneumatic Or Hyd

	CITY	ST	EMP	PHONE	ENTRY #
Laser Fare Inc **(PA)**	Smithfield	RI	D	401 231-4400	21235

MACHINE TOOLS, METAL FORMING: Plasma Jet Spray

	CITY	ST	EMP	PHONE	ENTRY #
Thermocermet	Pepperell	MA	G	978 425-0404	14446
Praxair Surface Tech Inc	Concord	NH	D	603 224-9585	17924
Tafa Incorporated **(DH)**	Concord	NH	E	603 224-9585	17934

MACHINE TOOLS, METAL FORMING: Presses, Hyd & Pneumatic

	CITY	ST	EMP	PHONE	ENTRY #
Greenerd Press & Mch Co LLC **(PA)**	Nashua	NH	E	603 889-4101	19172
Durant Tool Company Inc	North Kingstown	RI	E	401 781-7800	20703
Joraco Inc	Smithfield	RI	F	401 232-1710	21234

MACHINE TOOLS, METAL FORMING: Rebuilt

	CITY	ST	EMP	PHONE	ENTRY #
Fenn LLC	East Berlin	CT	E	860 259-6600	1100
L R Brown Manufacturing Co	Wallingford	CT	G	203 265-5639	4763

MACHINE TOOLS, METAL FORMING: Spinning, Spline Rollg/Windg

	CITY	ST	EMP	PHONE	ENTRY #
Advanced Machine Services LLC **(PA)**	Waterbury	CT	G	203 888-6600	4836

MACHINE TOOLS, METAL FORMING: Spring Winding & Forming

	CITY	ST	EMP	PHONE	ENTRY #
L M Gill Welding and Mfr LLC **(PA)**	Manchester	CT	F	860 647-9931	2017

MACHINE TOOLS, METAL FORMING: Stretching

	CITY	ST	EMP	PHONE	ENTRY #
Vital Stretch LLC	Norwalk	CT	G	203 847-4477	3268

MACHINE TOOLS: Metal Cutting

	CITY	ST	EMP	PHONE	ENTRY #
Bernell Tool & Mfg Co	Waterbury	CT	G	203 756-4405	4849
Book Automation Inc	New Milford	CT	G	860 354-7900	2788
Branson Ultrasonics Corp **(DH)**	Danbury	CT	B	203 796-0400	882
C V Tool Company Inc **(PA)**	Southington	CT	E	978 353-7901	4042
Denco Counter-Bore LLC	Southington	CT	G	860 276-0782	4047
Edac Technologies LLC	East Windsor	CT	F	860 789-2511	1283
Edac Technologies LLC **(HQ)**	Cheshire	CT	C	203 806-2090	728
Emhart Teknologies LLC	Danbury	CT	E	203 790-5000	908
Enginering Components Pdts LLC	Plainville	CT	G	860 747-6222	3486
Fletcher-Terry Company LLC **(PA)**	East Berlin	CT	D	860 828-3400	1102
Gmn Usa LLC	Bristol	CT	F	800 686-1679	568
Hata Hi-Tech Machining LLC	Ansonia	CT	E	203 333-9139	18
JL Lucas Machinery Co Inc	Waterbury	CT	F	203 597-1300	4891
Laser Tool Company Inc	Thomaston	CT	F	860 283-8284	4508
Max-Tek LLC	Wallingford	CT	F	860 372-4900	4771
Microbest Inc	Waterbury	CT	C	203 597-0355	4915
Mid-State Manufacturing Inc	Milldale	CT	F	860 621-6855	2386
Moon Cutter Co Inc	Hamden	CT	E	203 288-9249	1773
New England Plasma Dev Corp	Putnam	CT	F	860 928-6561	3621
New England Tooling Inc	Killingworth	CT	F	800 866-5105	1928
Nowak Products Inc	Newington	CT	G	860 666-9685	2887
P-A-R Precision Inc	Wolcott	CT	E	860 491-4181	5451
Producto Corporation **(HQ)**	Bridgeport	CT	F	203 366-3224	476
Ramdy Corporation	Oakville	CT	E	860 274-3713	3301
Ready Tool Company **(HQ)**	West Hartford	CT	E	860 524-7811	5093
Relx Inc	Windsor	CT	G	860 219-0733	5358
Secondary Operations Inc	Hamden	CT	F	203 288-8241	1783
Sperry Automatics Co Inc	Naugatuck	CT	E	203 729-4589	2497
Syman Machine LLC	Plainville	CT	G	860 747-8337	3517
United Tool and Die Company **(PA)**	West Hartford	CT	C	860 246-6531	5102
Viking Tool Company	Shelton	CT	E	203 929-1457	3885
Acp Waterjet Inc	Woburn	MA	E	800 951-5127	17108
Amherst Machine Co	Amherst	MA	F	413 549-4551	7513
Babin Machine Inc	Brockton	MA	G	508 588-9189	9123
C and M Micro-Tool Inc	South Easton	MA	E	508 230-3535	15272
Central MA Waterjet Inc	Millbury	MA	G	508 769-4308	13158
Desktop Metal Inc **(PA)**	Burlington	MA	C	978 224-1244	9254
Dexter Innvative Solutions LLC	Orange	MA	G	978 544-2751	14214
Donahue Industries Inc	Shrewsbury	MA	E	508 845-6501	15108
E T Duval & Son Inc	Leominster	MA	G	978 537-7596	12134
Frank E Lashua Inc **(PA)**	Worcester	MA	G	508 552-0023	17379
Iniram Precision Mch Tl LLC	Middleton	MA	G	978 854-3037	13089
Kinefac Corporation	Worcester	MA	D	508 754-6901	17401
Leavitt Machine Co	Orange	MA	G	978 544-3872	14220
Leo Coons Jr	Acushnet	MA	G	508 995-3300	7404
Merit Machine Manufacturing	Fitchburg	MA	F	978 342-7677	10836
Mrse	West Brookfield	MA	F	508 867-5083	16472
Newtron Inc	Auburndale	MA	G	617 969-1100	7866
PCC Specialty Products Inc	Auburn	MA	D	508 753-6530	7847
Peterson and Nash Inc	Norwell	MA	E	781 826-9085	14111
Phoenix Inc	Seekonk	MA	E	508 399-7100	15034
Precision Pcb Products Inc	Whitman	MA	G	508 966-9484	16926
Production Tool & Grinding	Athol	MA	F	978 544-8206	7693
Prof Tool Grind Inc	South Easton	MA	E	508 230-3535	15289
Professional Tl Grinding Inc **(PA)**	South Easton	MA	E	508 230-3535	15290
Swift-Cut Automation Usa Inc	Plymouth	MA	G	888 572-1160	14586
Toolmex Indus Solutions Inc **(PA)**	Northborough	MA	D	508 653-5110	14052
Uva Lidkoping Inc	Milford	MA	G	508 634-4301	13150
Coastal Industrial Distrs	Saco	ME	F	207 286-3319	6845
Helical Solutions LLC	Gorham	ME	G	866 543-5422	6113
J D Paulsen	Bridgton	ME	G	207 647-5679	5808
OBrien Consolidated Inds	Lewiston	ME	F	207 783-8543	6312
Speed Mat Inc	Biddeford	ME	G	207 294-4358	5764
Airmar Technology Corp **(PA)**	Milford	NH	B	603 673-9570	19044
Ametek Precitech Inc **(HQ)**	Keene	NH	D	603 357-2510	18491
Elmo Motion Control Inc	Nashua	NH	F	603 821-9979	19149
Express Assemblyproducts LLC	Amherst	NH	F	603 424-5590	17561
Hyertherm Inc	West Lebanon	NH	F	603 643-3441	19953
Hypertherm Inc **(PA)**	Hanover	NH	A	603 643-3441	18290
Hypertherm Inc	Hanover	NH	F	603 643-3441	18291
Hypertherm Inc	Hanover	NH	G	603 643-3441	18292
Jarvis Company Inc **(PA)**	Rochester	NH	D	603 332-9000	19675
Trellborg Pipe Sals Mlford Inc **(DH)**	Milford	NH	C	800 626-2180	19080
Williams & Hussey Mch Co Inc	Amherst	NH	F	603 732-0219	17591
J & J Machining	Coventry	RI	G	401 397-2782	20149
Malco Saw Co Inc	Cranston	RI	G	401 942-7380	20258
RI Waterjet LLC	Newport	RI	G	781 801-2500	20676
McCormacks Machine Co Inc	West Rutland	VT	G	802 438-2345	22618
Yankee Corporation	Fairfax	VT	D	802 527-0177	21981

MACHINE TOOLS: Metal Forming

	CITY	ST	EMP	PHONE	ENTRY #
American Actuator Corporation	Redding	CT	F	203 324-6334	3645
Arrow Diversified Tooling Inc	Ellington	CT	E	860 872-9072	1329
Deringer-Ney Inc **(PA)**	Bloomfield	CT	C	860 242-2281	217
Grant Manufacturing & Mch Co	Bridgeport	CT	E	203 366-4557	421
Joshua LLC **(PA)**	New Haven	CT	E	203 624-0080	2699
Lou-Jan Tool & Die Inc	Cheshire	CT	F	203 272-3536	742
Merritt Extruder Corp	Hamden	CT	E	203 230-8100	1770
Okay Industries Inc	Berlin	CT	G	860 225-8707	99
Oxford General Industries Inc	Prospect	CT	F	203 758-4467	3590
Raymon Tool LLC	Hamden	CT	F	203 248-2199	1779
Richard Dahlen	Bristol	CT	G	860 584-8226	606
Riveting Systems USA LLC	Bridgeport	CT	G	203 366-4557	483
Sandviks Inc **(PA)**	Danbury	CT	G	866 984-0188	982
Sirois Tool Company Inc **(PA)**	Berlin	CT	D	860 828-5327	109
Ab-Wey Machine & Die Co Inc	Pembroke	MA	F	781 294-8031	14389
ATI Flowform Products LLC	Billerica	MA	E	978 667-0202	8215
Babin Machine Inc	Brockton	MA	G	508 588-9189	9123
Form Roll Die Corp	Worcester	MA	F	508 755-5302	17378
Kinefac Corporation	Worcester	MA	D	508 754-6901	17401
Niagara Cutter Athol Inc	Athol	MA	E	978 249-2788	7691
PCC Specialty Products Inc	Auburn	MA	D	508 753-6530	7847
Roche Tool & Die	Marlborough	MA	G	508 485-6460	12818
Simsak Machine & Tool Co Inc	Southbridge	MA	G	508 764-4958	15404
Thomson National Press Company **(PA)**	Franklin	MA	G	508 528-2000	11091
Valentine Tool & Stamping Inc	Norton	MA	F	508 285-6911	14091
Westfield Tool & Die Inc	Westfield	MA	F	413 562-2393	16747

	CITY	ST	EMP	PHONE	ENTRY #
Whitman Castings Inc **(PA)**	Whitman	MA	E	781 447-4417	16930
Nbr Diamond Tool Corp	South Hampton	NH	G	603 394-2113	19856
Solidscape Inc	Merrimack	NH	E	603 424-0590	19030
Automated Industrial Mch Inc	Smithfield	RI	F	401 232-1710	21210
Gasbarre Products Inc	Cranston	RI	F	401 467-5200	20230
Samic Mfg Company	Johnston	RI	G	401 421-2400	20540
Thomas Drake	Colchester	VT	G	802 655-0990	21881

MACHINERY & EQPT, AGRICULTURAL, WHOLESALE: Landscaping Eqpt

Alfred J Cavallaro Inc	Andover	MA	G	978 475-2466	7536

MACHINERY & EQPT, AGRICULTURAL, WHOLESALE: Poultry Eqpt

Engineering Services & Pdts Co **(PA)**	South Windsor	CT	D	860 528-1119	3965

MACHINERY & EQPT, INDL, WHOL: Brewery Prdts Mfrg, Commercial

Cocchia Norwalk Grape Co	Norwalk	CT	F	203 855-7911	3127

MACHINERY & EQPT, INDL, WHOL: Controlling Instruments/Access

Jad LLC	South Windsor	CT	E	860 289-1551	3983

MACHINERY & EQPT, INDL, WHOLESALE: Chemical Process

Gac Chemical Corporation **(PA)**	Searsport	ME	D	207 548-2525	6951

MACHINERY & EQPT, INDL, WHOLESALE: Conveyor Systems

TEC Engineering Corp	Oxford	MA	F	508 987-0231	14275

MACHINERY & EQPT, INDL, WHOLESALE: Countersinks

Barre Tile Inc	Lebanon	NH	F	802 476-0912	18614

MACHINERY & EQPT, INDL, WHOLESALE: Cranes

Stedt Hydraulic Crane Corp	Westborough	MA	F	508 366-9151	16651
Somatex Inc	Detroit	ME	E	207 487-6141	5953

MACHINERY & EQPT, INDL, WHOLESALE: Drilling, Exc Bits

Jeff Cummings Services LLC	Warner	NH	G	603 456-3706	19927

MACHINERY & EQPT, INDL, WHOLESALE: Engines & Parts, Diesel

Melton Sales and Service Inc	Hallowell	ME	F	207 623-8895	6163

MACHINERY & EQPT, INDL, WHOLESALE: Fans

Nauset Engineer Equipment	Mansfield	MA	G	508 339-2662	12648

MACHINERY & EQPT, INDL, WHOLESALE: Hoists

St Pierre Manufacturing Corp	Worcester	MA	E	508 853-8010	17479

MACHINERY & EQPT, INDL, WHOLESALE: Hydraulic Systems

Spectrum Associates Inc	Milford	CT	F	203 878-4618	2367

MACHINERY & EQPT, INDL, WHOLESALE: Indl Machine Parts

F & W Rentals Inc	Orange	CT	F	203 795-0591	3366

MACHINERY & EQPT, INDL, WHOLESALE: Instruments & Cntrl Eqpt

Armadillo Noise Vibration LLC	Acushnet	MA	G	774 992-7156	7399
Calibrators Inc	Cumberland	RI	G	401 769-0333	20315

MACHINERY & EQPT, INDL, WHOLESALE: Lift Trucks & Parts

Southworth Products Corp **(HQ)**	Falmouth	ME	E	207 878-0700	6034

MACHINERY & EQPT, INDL, WHOLESALE: Machine Tools & Access

JL Lucas Machinery Co Inc	Waterbury	CT	F	203 597-1300	4891
Harvard Products Inc	Harvard	MA	F	978 772-0309	11378
Jarvis Company Inc **(PA)**	Rochester	NH	D	603 332-9000	19675
Moore Nntechnology Systems LLC **(DH)**	Swanzey	NH	D	603 352-3030	19886

MACHINERY & EQPT, INDL, WHOLESALE: Machine Tools & Metalwork

Manufacturing Service Corp	Millbury	MA	G	508 865-2550	13169

MACHINERY & EQPT, INDL, WHOLESALE: Measure/Test, Electric

Testing Machines Inc	Swansea	MA	G	302 613-5600	15717
Auriga Piv Tech Inc	Merrimack	NH	G	603 402-2955	18987
Martel Electronics Corp	Derry	NH	E	603 434-6033	17988

MACHINERY & EQPT, INDL, WHOLESALE: Packaging

Millwood Inc	North Haven	CT	F	203 248-7902	3041

MACHINERY & EQPT, INDL, WHOLESALE: Paper Manufacturing

Johncton Dandy Company	Holyoke	MA	F	413 315-4596	11635

MACHINERY & EQPT, INDL, WHOLESALE: Paper, Sawmill & Woodwork

Downeast Machine & Engrg Inc	Mechanic Falls	ME	F	207 345-8111	6419
Ashe America Inc	Brattleboro	VT	D	802 254-0200	21718

MACHINERY & EQPT, INDL, WHOLESALE: Plastic Prdts Machinery

Thermoplastics Co Inc	Worcester	MA	E	508 754-4668	17488

MACHINERY & EQPT, INDL, WHOLESALE: Pneumatic Tools

Air Tool Sales & Service Co **(PA)**	Unionville	CT	G	860 673-2714	4652

MACHINERY & EQPT, INDL, WHOLESALE: Processing & Packaging

BEE International Inc	South Easton	MA	E	508 238-5558	15270
Oizero9 Inc	Sanford	ME	F	207 324-3582	6885

MACHINERY & EQPT, INDL, WHOLESALE: Safety Eqpt

East Coast Sign and Supply Inc	Bethel	CT	G	203 791-8326	149
Mezzanine Safeti Gates Inc	Essex	MA	G	978 768-3000	10596
Vogue Industries Ltd Partnr	Central Falls	RI	E	401 722-0900	20128

MACHINERY & EQPT, INDL, WHOLESALE: Sewing

Superior Manufacturing Corp	Fall River	MA	G	508 677-0100	10765

MACHINERY & EQPT, INDL, WHOLESALE: Smelting

Enterprise Castings LLC	Lewiston	ME	G	207 782-5511	6288

MACHINERY & EQPT, INDL, WHOLESALE: Threading Tools

Swanson Tool Manufacturing Inc	West Hartford	CT	E	860 953-1641	5097

MACHINERY & EQPT, INDL, WHOLESALE: Water Pumps

Rema Dri-Vac Corp	Norwalk	CT	F	203 847-2464	3231

MACHINERY & EQPT, INDL, WHOLESALE: Woodworking

Goodspeed Machine Company	Winchendon	MA	G	978 297-0296	17076
US Cutting Chain Mfg Co Inc	Brockton	MA	G	508 588-0322	9186

MACHINERY & EQPT, TEXTILE: Fabric Forming

Micrex Corporation	Walpole	MA	F	508 660-1900	16002

MACHINERY & EQPT, WHOLESALE: Construction & Mining, Ladders

Lyn-Lad Group Ltd **(PA)**	Lynn	MA	F	781 598-6010	12523

MACHINERY & EQPT, WHOLESALE: Construction, General

D P Engineering Inc	Madison	CT	G	203 421-7965	1959
Numa Tool Company **(PA)**	Thompson	CT	D	860 923-9551	4537

MACHINERY & EQPT, WHOLESALE: Masonry

Genest Landscape Masonry	Windham	ME	G	207 892-3778	7235

MACHINERY & EQPT: Electroplating

Tecomet Inc	Woburn	MA	D	781 782-6400	17305
Danglers Inc	Johnston	RI	G	401 274-7742	20506
Technic Inc	Pawtucket	RI	E	401 781-6100	20902
Technic Inc **(PA)**	Cranston	RI	C	401 781-6100	20301
Technic Inc	Woonsocket	RI	E	401 769-7000	21585

MACHINERY & EQPT: Farm

Comex Machinery	Bridgeport	CT	G	203 334-2196	399
Oesco Inc	Conway	MA	E	413 369-4335	10164
Scituate Caseworks Inc	Scituate	MA	G	781 534-4167	15012
US Discount Products LLC	West Bridgewater	MA	G	877 841-5782	16462
Dale A Thomas and Sons Inc	Brooks	ME	G	207 722-3505	5823
Innovasea Systems Inc	Morrill	ME	G	207 322-3219	6454
Maine Blueberry Equipment Co	Columbia	ME	G	207 483-4156	5918
Ocean Farm Technologies Inc	Morrill	ME	G	207 322-4322	6456
AGCO Corporation	Charlestown	NH	G	603 826-4664	17809
CPM Acquisition Corp	Merrimack	NH	E	319 232-8444	18994
CPM Acquisition Corp	Merrimack	NH	E	603 423-6300	18995
Hutchinson Machine	Atkinson	NH	G	603 329-9545	17604
Siteone Landscape Supply LLC	Londonderry	NH	G	603 425-2572	18737
Coastal Aquacultural Supply	Cranston	RI	G	401 467-9370	20197
Leader Evaporator Co Inc **(PA)**	Swanton	VT	D	802 868-5444	22531
Leader Evaporatorinc	Rutland	VT	E	802 775-5411	22343
Vermont Farm Table LLC **(PA)**	Burlington	VT	G	888 425-8838	21815

MACHINERY & EQPT: Gas Producers, Generators/Other Rltd Eqpt

Hamilton Standard Space	Windsor Locks	CT	E	860 654-6000	5396
Proton Energy Systems Inc	Wallingford	CT	D	203 678-2000	4790

MACHINERY & EQPT: Liquid Automation

Alstom Power Co	Windsor	CT	F	860 688-1911	5318
Environmantal Systems Cor	Hartford	CT	F	860 953-5167	1820
Qsonica LLC	Newtown	CT	G	203 426-0101	2933
Sonics & Materials Inc **(PA)**	Newtown	CT	D	203 270-4600	2938
St Equipment and Tech LLC	Needham	MA	G	781 972-2300	13312

MACHINERY & EQPT: Metal Finishing, Plating Etc

PYC Deborring LLC F/K/A C &	Berlin	CT	G	860 828-6806	106
Bay State Plating Inc	Holyoke	MA	G	413 533-6927	11618
Black Oxide Co Inc	Worcester	MA	G	508 757-0340	17348
M E Baker Company **(PA)**	Framingham	MA	F	508 620-5304	10979
Purecoat International LLC	Belmont	MA	E	561 844-0100	8079
Mid Cape Restoration	Hollis Center	ME	F	207 929-4759	6200
B & M Plastics Inc	Pawtucket	RI	G	401 728-0404	20815
Impreglon Inc	Woonsocket	RI	F	401 766-3353	21571

MACHINERY & EQPT: Petroleum Refinery

Millers Petroleum Systems Inc	Pittsfield	MA	G	413 499-2134	14490
Fueling Services LLC	Johnston	RI	F	401 764-0711	20513

MACHINERY BASES

Airpot Corporation	Norwalk	CT	E	800 848-7681	3097
Dcg-Pmi Inc	Bethel	CT	E	203 743-5525	142
Oxford General Industries Inc	Prospect	CT	F	203 758-4467	3590
Payne Engrg Fabrication Co Inc	Canton	MA	E	781 828-9046	9765

MACHINERY, COMMERCIAL LAUNDRY & Drycleaning: Ironers

Two Go Drycleaning Inc	South Burlington	VT	E	802 658-9469	22474

MACHINERY, COMMERCIAL LAUNDRY: Dryers, Incl Coin-Operated

American Dryer Corporation	Fall River	MA	C	508 678-9000	10656
Jason Santelli Enterprises LLC	Jamaica Plain	MA	G	617 942-2205	11944

MACHINERY, COMMERCIAL LAUNDRY: Washing, Incl Coin-Operated

Edro Corporation	East Berlin	CT	E	860 828-0311	1099

MACHINERY, EQPT & SUPPLIES: Parking Facility

	CITY	ST	EMP	PHONE	ENTRY #
Snapwire Innovations LLC	Cheshire	CT	G	203 806-4773	763
Northeast Time Trak Systems	Westbrook	ME	G	207 774-2336	7200
Parkmatic Car Prkg Systems LLC	Shelburne	VT	G	802 495-0903	22421

MACHINERY, FOOD PRDTS: Beverage

	CITY	ST	EMP	PHONE	ENTRY #
Cimbali Usa Inc	Fairfield	CT	G	203 254-6046	1418
Stonybrook Water Company LLC	Manchester	MA	G	978 865-9899	12607

MACHINERY, FOOD PRDTS: Confectionery

	CITY	ST	EMP	PHONE	ENTRY #
Jimsan Enterprises Inc	West Bridgewater	MA	G	508 587-3666	16442

MACHINERY, FOOD PRDTS: Distillery

	CITY	ST	EMP	PHONE	ENTRY #
Grandten Distilling LLC	Boston	MA	G	617 269-0497	8577
Aquaback Technologies Inc	Salem	NH	F	978 863-1000	19709
Distillery Network Inc	Manchester	NH	G	603 997-6786	18810

MACHINERY, FOOD PRDTS: Food Processing, Smokers

	CITY	ST	EMP	PHONE	ENTRY #
Green Mountain Smokehouse	Windsor	VT	G	802 674-6653	22709

MACHINERY, FOOD PRDTS: Homogenizing, Dairy, Fruit/Vegetable

	CITY	ST	EMP	PHONE	ENTRY #
Pro Scientific Inc	Oxford	CT	F	203 267-4600	3420

MACHINERY, FOOD PRDTS: Mills, Food

	CITY	ST	EMP	PHONE	ENTRY #
Sun Farm Corporation	Milford	CT	G	203 882-8000	2372

MACHINERY, FOOD PRDTS: Mixers, Commercial

	CITY	ST	EMP	PHONE	ENTRY #
EMI Inc	Clinton	CT	G	860 669-1199	786
Bematek Systems Inc	Salem	MA	G	978 744-5816	14897
Wilevco Inc	Billerica	MA	F	978 667-0400	8310
Admix Inc	Londonderry	NH	E	603 627-2340	18671

MACHINERY, FOOD PRDTS: Mixers, Feed, Exc Agricultural

	CITY	ST	EMP	PHONE	ENTRY #
Sonic Corp	Stratford	CT	F	203 375-0063	4448

MACHINERY, FOOD PRDTS: Ovens, Bakery

	CITY	ST	EMP	PHONE	ENTRY #
Bakery Engineering/Winkler Inc	Shelton	CT	F	203 929-8630	3779
Baker Parts Inc	New Bedford	MA	G	508 636-3121	13360
Adjacent Bakery LLC	Scarborough	ME	G	207 252-6722	6902
Cooking Solutions Group Inc **(HQ)**	Salem	NH	G	603 893-9701	19719

MACHINERY, FOOD PRDTS: Presses, Cheese, Beet, Cider & Sugar

	CITY	ST	EMP	PHONE	ENTRY #
Oesco Inc	Conway	MA	E	413 369-4335	10164

MACHINERY, FOOD PRDTS: Roasting, Coffee, Peanut, Etc.

	CITY	ST	EMP	PHONE	ENTRY #
Ventures LLC DOT Com LLC	Vernon	CT	G	203 930-8972	4676

MACHINERY, LUBRICATION: Automatic

	CITY	ST	EMP	PHONE	ENTRY #
Azelis Americas LLC	Leominster	MA	G	212 915-8178	12115

MACHINERY, MAILING: Address Labeling

	CITY	ST	EMP	PHONE	ENTRY #
Chauncey Wings Sons Inc	Greenfield	MA	G	413 772-6611	11253

MACHINERY, MAILING: Mailing

	CITY	ST	EMP	PHONE	ENTRY #
Agissar Corporation	Stratford	CT	D	203 375-8662	4389
Hasler Inc	Shelton	CT	G	203 301-3400	3810
Pitney Bowes Inc **(PA)**	Stamford	CT	A	203 356-5000	4285
Pitney Bowes Inc	Shelton	CT	E	203 356-5000	3855

MACHINERY, MAILING: Postage Meters

	CITY	ST	EMP	PHONE	ENTRY #
Neopost USA Inc **(DH)**	Milford	CT	C	203 301-3400	2319
Pitney Bowes Inc	Stamford	CT	E	203 356-5000	4286
Pitney Bowes Inc	Shelton	CT	E	203 922-4000	3854
Pitney Bowes Inc	Portland	ME	E	207 773-2345	6709
Pitney Bowes Inc	Keene	NH	E	603 352-7766	18522
Pitney Bowes Inc	East Providence	RI	E	401 435-8500	20442

MACHINERY, METALWORKING: Assembly, Including Robotic

	CITY	ST	EMP	PHONE	ENTRY #
Adamczyk Enterprises Inc	Enfield	CT	G	860 745-9830	1345
Clear Automation LLC	Southington	CT	E	860 621-2955	4044
Te Connectivity Corporation	Stafford Springs	CT	C	860 684-8000	4116
Vangor Engineering Corporation	Oxford	CT	G	203 267-4377	3428
Automec Inc	Waltham	MA	E	781 893-3403	16039
Flir Unmnned Grund Systems Inc **(DH)**	Chelmsford	MA	D	978 769-9333	9899
Milara Inc	Milford	MA	D	508 533-5322	13127
Quiet Logistics	Devens	MA	F	978 391-4439	10331
Symbotic LLC	Wilmington	MA	G	978 284-2800	17050
Assembly Specialists Inc	Manchester	NH	F	603 624-9563	18780
High Speed Technologies Inc	Bow	NH	E	603 483-0333	17716
J-Tech Automation LLC	North Scituate	RI	G	401 934-2435	20779

MACHINERY, METALWORKING: Coil Winding, For Springs

	CITY	ST	EMP	PHONE	ENTRY #
Jovil Universal LLC	Danbury	CT	E	203 792-6700	941
Gorman Machine Corp	Middleboro	MA	E	508 923-9462	13063

MACHINERY, METALWORKING: Coiling

	CITY	ST	EMP	PHONE	ENTRY #
P/A Industries Inc **(PA)**	Bloomfield	CT	E	860 243-8306	249
Broomfield Laboratories Inc	Bolton	MA	E	978 779-6600	8318

MACHINERY, METALWORKING: Cutting & Slitting

	CITY	ST	EMP	PHONE	ENTRY #
NC Converting Inc	Seekonk	MA	G	508 336-6510	15031
New England Water Jet Cutting	New Bedford	MA	G	508 993-9235	13425

MACHINERY, OFFICE: Dictating

	CITY	ST	EMP	PHONE	ENTRY #
Dictaphone Corporation **(HQ)**	Stratford	CT	C	203 381-7000	4409
AM Technologies Inc	Watertown	MA	G	617 926-7920	16267
Sudbury Systems Inc	Bedford	MA	E	800 876-8888	8010

MACHINERY, OFFICE: Duplicating

	CITY	ST	EMP	PHONE	ENTRY #
Bidwell Industrial Group Inc **(PA)**	Middletown	CT	E	860 346-9283	2178
C P Bourg Inc **(PA)**	New Bedford	MA	D	508 998-2171	13369

MACHINERY, OFFICE: Paper Handling

	CITY	ST	EMP	PHONE	ENTRY #
Bell and Howell LLC	Deep River	CT	E	860 526-9561	1058
Xerox Corporation **(HQ)**	Norwalk	CT	B	203 968-3000	3274

MACHINERY, OFFICE: Pencil Sharpeners

	CITY	ST	EMP	PHONE	ENTRY #
Acme United Corporation **(PA)**	Fairfield	CT	C	203 254-6060	1412

MACHINERY, OFFICE: Stapling, Hand Or Power

	CITY	ST	EMP	PHONE	ENTRY #
Stanley Fastening Systems LP	New Britain	CT	G	860 225-5111	2584
Acme Staple Company Inc	Franklin	NH	F	603 934-2320	18155
Stanley Fastening Systems LP **(HQ)**	East Greenwich	RI	D	401 884-2500	20381

MACHINERY, OFFICE: Time Clocks &Time Recording Devices

	CITY	ST	EMP	PHONE	ENTRY #
Accu-Time Systems Inc **(DH)**	Ellington	CT	E	860 870-5000	1324
Pyramid Time Systems LLC	Meriden	CT	E	203 238-0550	2120
Accu-Time Systems Inc	Boston	MA	G	860 870-5000	8336
Str Grinnell GP Holding LLC	Westminster	MA	E	978 731-2500	16814
Simplex Time Recorder LLC	Williston	VT	D	802 879-6149	22692

MACHINERY, PACKAGING: Aerating, Beverages

	CITY	ST	EMP	PHONE	ENTRY #
Hydration Labs Incorporated	Charlestown	MA	G	617 333-8191	9837

MACHINERY, PACKAGING: Carton Packing

	CITY	ST	EMP	PHONE	ENTRY #
Econocorp Inc	Randolph	MA	E	781 986-7500	14677

MACHINERY, PACKAGING: Packing & Wrapping

	CITY	ST	EMP	PHONE	ENTRY #
PDC International Corp **(PA)**	Norwalk	CT	D	203 853-1516	3215
Staban Engineering Corp	Wallingford	CT	F	203 294-1997	4812
Illinois Tool Works Inc	Hopkinton	MA	E	508 520-0083	11721
Nova Packaging Systems Inc	Leominster	MA	D	978 537-8534	12174
Package Machinery Company Inc	Holyoke	MA	G	413 315-3801	11648
Tooling Research Inc **(PA)**	Walpole	MA	F	508 668-1950	16014

MACHINERY, PAPER INDUSTRY: Coating & Finishing

	CITY	ST	EMP	PHONE	ENTRY #
Zatorski Coating Company Inc	East Hampton	CT	F	860 267-9889	1168

MACHINERY, PAPER INDUSTRY: Converting, Die Cutting & Stampng

	CITY	ST	EMP	PHONE	ENTRY #
Bar-Plate Manufacturing Co	Hamden	CT	F	203 397-0033	1734
Jen-Coat Inc **(DH)**	Westfield	MA	C	413 875-9855	16693
Thomson National Press Company **(PA)**	Franklin	MA	G	508 528-2000	11091
Spectex LLC	Dover	NH	F	603 330-3334	18054

MACHINERY, PAPER INDUSTRY: Paper Forming

	CITY	ST	EMP	PHONE	ENTRY #
Snyder Machine Co Inc	Saugus	MA	F	781 233-2080	14997

MACHINERY, PAPER INDUSTRY: Paper Mill, Plating, Etc

	CITY	ST	EMP	PHONE	ENTRY #
Tecnau Inc **(DH)**	Billerica	MA	E	978 608-0356	8301
Johnston Dandy Company **(PA)**	Lincoln	ME	E	207 794-6571	6355
Bfmc LLC	Berlin	NH	E	603 752-4550	17693

MACHINERY, PAPER INDUSTRY: Pulp Mill

	CITY	ST	EMP	PHONE	ENTRY #
Barton Rice Corporation	Oxford	MA	G	508 966-2194	14253
Montague Industries Inc	Turners Falls	MA	E	413 863-4301	15882
GL&v USA Inc	Nashua	NH	D	603 882-2711	19169
J J Plank Corporation	Farmington	NH	G	920 733-4479	18143
Tidland Corporation	Keene	NH	D	603 352-1696	18533

MACHINERY, PRINTING TRADES: Bookbinding Machinery

	CITY	ST	EMP	PHONE	ENTRY #
G P 2 Technologies Inc	Bow	NH	G	603 226-0336	17714

MACHINERY, PRINTING TRADES: Bronzing Or Dusting

	CITY	ST	EMP	PHONE	ENTRY #
Hosokawa Micron International	Northborough	MA	F	508 655-1123	14037

MACHINERY, PRINTING TRADES: Lithographic Stones

	CITY	ST	EMP	PHONE	ENTRY #
Asml Us LLC	Wilton	CT	A	203 761-4000	5275

MACHINERY, PRINTING TRADES: Mats, Advertising & Newspaper

	CITY	ST	EMP	PHONE	ENTRY #
Net Vantage Point Inc	Lexington	MA	G	781 860-9158	12248

MACHINERY, PRINTING TRADES: Plates

	CITY	ST	EMP	PHONE	ENTRY #
Verico Technology LLC **(HQ)**	Enfield	CT	E	800 492-7286	1389
Presstek Overseas Corp **(DH)**	Nashua	NH	G	603 595-7000	19238
Verico Technology LLC	Nashua	NH	C	603 402-7573	19281
Fine Line Graphics Inc **(PA)**	Smithfield	RI	E	401 349-3300	21226

MACHINERY, PRINTING TRADES: Plates, Engravers' Metal

	CITY	ST	EMP	PHONE	ENTRY #
Honorcraft LLC	Stoughton	MA	E	781 341-0410	15597

MACHINERY, PRINTING TRADES: Presses, Gravure

	CITY	ST	EMP	PHONE	ENTRY #
Gem Gravure Co Inc **(PA)**	Hanover	MA	D	781 878-0456	11339
Austrian Machine Corp	Cranston	RI	F	401 946-4090	20184

MACHINERY, PRINTING TRADES: Printing Trade Parts & Attchts

	CITY	ST	EMP	PHONE	ENTRY #
Arico Engineering Inc	North Franklin	CT	G	860 642-7040	2987
Alden and Broden Corporation	Westford	MA	G	603 882-0330	16752
Blade Tech Systems Inc	Plymouth	MA	G	508 830-9506	14545
Dasko Identification Products	East Providence	RI	F	401 435-6500	20403

MACHINERY, SEWING: Buttonhole/Eyelet Mach/Attachments, Indl

	CITY	ST	EMP	PHONE	ENTRY #
Edward Segal Inc	Thomaston	CT	E	860 283-5821	4502

MACHINERY, SEWING: Hat Making & Renovating

	CITY	ST	EMP	PHONE	ENTRY #
Capesym Inc	Natick	MA	G	508 653-7100	13242

MACHINERY, SEWING: Sewing & Hat & Zipper Making

	CITY	ST	EMP	PHONE	ENTRY #
Bausch Advanced Tech Inc **(PA)**	Clinton	CT	E	860 669-7380	779

MACHINERY, TEXTILE: Braiding

	CITY	ST	EMP	PHONE	ENTRY #
Stolberger Incorporated	Central Falls	RI	E	401 724-8800	20126
Windmill Associates Inc	Warwick	RI	G	401 732-4700	21448

MACHINERY, TEXTILE: Embroidery

	CITY	ST	EMP	PHONE	ENTRY #
Ultramatic West	Hamden	CT	G	203 745-4688	1793
All Seasons	Nashua	NH	G	603 560-7777	19109

MACHINERY, TEXTILE: Finishing

	CITY	ST	EMP	PHONE	ENTRY #
Maine Stitching Spc LLC	Skowhegan	ME	F	207 812-5207	6981

MACHINERY, TEXTILE: Reeds, Loom

	CITY	ST	EMP	PHONE	ENTRY #
Reed Gowdey Company	Central Falls	RI	G	401 723-6114	20123

MACHINERY, TEXTILE: Rope & Cordage

	CITY	ST	EMP	PHONE	ENTRY #
Orion Ropeworks LLC	Winslow	ME	D	207 877-2224	7274

MACHINERY, TEXTILE: Silk Screens

	CITY	ST	EMP	PHONE	ENTRY #
Screen-Tech Inc	Torrington	CT	G	860 496-8016	4599
Gemini Screenprinting & EMB Co	Brockton	MA	G	508 586-8223	9149
Jaf Corporation	Webster	MA	G	508 943-8519	16344
Olde Village Monogramming Inc	Great Barrington	MA	G	413 528-3904	11244
Richmond Graphic Products Inc	Providence	RI	F	401 233-2700	21115

MACHINERY, TEXTILE: Warping

	CITY	ST	EMP	PHONE	ENTRY #
Maguire Lace & Warping Inc	Coventry	RI	G	401 821-1290	20154

MACHINERY, TEXTILE: Winders

	CITY	ST	EMP	PHONE	ENTRY #
Standard Mill Machinery Corp	West Warwick	RI	G	401 822-7871	21510

MACHINERY, WOODWORKING: Bandsaws

	CITY	ST	EMP	PHONE	ENTRY #
Boston Wood Art	Natick	MA	G	508 353-4129	13240

MACHINERY, WOODWORKING: Box Making, For Wooden Boxes

	CITY	ST	EMP	PHONE	ENTRY #
Enchanted World Boxes Inc	Cambridge	MA	G	617 492-6941	9466

MACHINERY, WOODWORKING: Cabinet Makers'

	CITY	ST	EMP	PHONE	ENTRY #
Homestead Kitchen Centre LLC	Kingston	NH	G	603 642-8022	18544

MACHINERY, WOODWORKING: Jointers

	CITY	ST	EMP	PHONE	ENTRY #
Walsh Claim Services	North Branford	CT	G	203 481-0680	2983

MACHINERY, WOODWORKING: Press, Partclbrd, Hrdbrd, Plywd, Etc

	CITY	ST	EMP	PHONE	ENTRY #
Vacuum Pressing Systems Inc	Brunswick	ME	G	207 725-0935	5850

MACHINERY/EQPT, INDL, WHOL: Cleaning, High Press, Sand/Steam

	CITY	ST	EMP	PHONE	ENTRY #
Northeastern Metals Corp	Stamford	CT	G	203 348-8088	4261

MACHINERY: Ammunition & Explosives Loading

	CITY	ST	EMP	PHONE	ENTRY #
Lyman Products Corporation **(PA)**	Middletown	CT	D	860 632-2020	2202
Lyman Products Corporation	Middletown	CT	E	860 632-2020	2203
Bisco Environmental Inc	Danvers	MA	E	508 738-5100	10203
Bc Nichols Machine LLC	Hampton	NH	G	603 926-2333	18258

MACHINERY: Assembly, Exc Metalworking

	CITY	ST	EMP	PHONE	ENTRY #
A F M Engineering Corp	Brooklyn	CT	G	860 774-7518	668
Arthur G Russell Company Inc	Bristol	CT	D	860 583-4109	521
Mid State Assembly & Packg Inc	Meriden	CT	G	203 634-8740	2107
Naiad Dynamics Us Inc **(HQ)**	Shelton	CT	E	203 929-6355	3836
Packard Inc	Prospect	CT	E	203 758-6219	3591
Rondo America Incorporated	Naugatuck	CT	C	203 723-5831	2494
Schaefer Machine Company Inc	Deep River	CT	G	860 526-4000	1065
Illinois Tool Works Inc	Hopkinton	MA	E	508 520-0083	11721
Op USA Inc	Acton	MA	G	978 658-5135	7376
Portuamerica Inc	Ludlow	MA	G	413 589-0095	12475
Precision Feeding Systems Inc	East Longmeadow	MA	G	413 525-9200	10488
Oizero9 Inc	Sanford	ME	F	207 324-3582	6885
Innovative Products & Eqp Inc	Hudson	NH	E	603 246-5858	18399
Interconnect Technology Inc	Hudson	NH	F	603 883-3116	18402
Schleuniger Inc **(DH)**	Manchester	NH	E	603 627-4860	18918
Kalow Technologies LLC	North Clarendon	VT	D	802 775-4633	22217

MACHINERY: Automobile Garage, Frame Straighteners

	CITY	ST	EMP	PHONE	ENTRY #
North American Auto Equipment	Plainville	MA	G	866 607-4022	14532

MACHINERY: Automotive Maintenance

	CITY	ST	EMP	PHONE	ENTRY #
Land and Sea Inc	Concord	NH	D	603 226-3966	17912
MTS Associates Londonderry LLC	Londonderry	NH	G	603 425-2562	18725

MACHINERY: Automotive Related

	CITY	ST	EMP	PHONE	ENTRY #
Day Machine Systems Inc	New Britain	CT	F	860 229-3440	2526
Evans Cooling Systems Inc **(PA)**	Suffield	CT	G	860 668-1114	4462
Windham Automated Machines Inc	South Windham	CT	F	860 208-5297	3929
Automotive Mach Shop Sup	West Bridgewater	MA	G	508 586-6706	16430
Uspack Inc	Leominster	MA	E	978 466-9700	12197
Uspack Inc	Hudson	MA	E	978 562-8522	11825
Eltec Industries Inc **(PA)**	Freeport	ME	G	207 541-9085	6077
Micro-Precision Inc **(PA)**	Sunapee	NH	E	603 763-2394	19882
Wheeltrak Inc	Tiverton	RI	E	800 296-1326	21266

MACHINERY: Bag & Envelope Making

	CITY	ST	EMP	PHONE	ENTRY #
Garlock Prtg & Converting Corp **(PA)**	Gardner	MA	D	978 630-1028	11117

MACHINERY: Banking

	CITY	ST	EMP	PHONE	ENTRY #
Idemia America Corp **(DH)**	Billerica	MA	B	978 215-2400	8255

MACHINERY: Betting

	CITY	ST	EMP	PHONE	ENTRY #
Interlott Technologies Inc	West Greenwich	RI	C	401 463-6392	21458

MACHINERY: Blasting, Electrical

	CITY	ST	EMP	PHONE	ENTRY #
Pressure Blast Mfg Co Inc	South Windsor	CT	F	800 722-5278	4004
Thomas Instruments Inc	Spofford	NH	G	603 363-4500	19858

MACHINERY: Bottling & Canning

	CITY	ST	EMP	PHONE	ENTRY #
JCB Inc	North Grafton	MA	G	508 839-5550	13961

MACHINERY: Centrifugal

	CITY	ST	EMP	PHONE	ENTRY #
PSI Water Systems Inc **(PA)**	Hooksett	NH	E	603 624-5110	18356

MACHINERY: Concrete Prdts

	CITY	ST	EMP	PHONE	ENTRY #
Saint-Gobain Abrasives Inc **(DH)**	Worcester	MA	A	508 795-5000	17464

MACHINERY: Construction

	CITY	ST	EMP	PHONE	ENTRY #
Bagela Usa LLC	Shelton	CT	G	203 944-0525	3777
Conair Corporation	Torrington	CT	D	800 492-7464	4572
Ezflow Limited Partnership **(DH)**	Old Saybrook	CT	E	860 577-7064	3334
H Barber & Sons Inc	Naugatuck	CT	E	203 729-9000	2476
Rawson Manufacturing Inc **(PA)**	Putnam	CT	F	860 928-4458	3630
Spray Foam Outlets LLC	Norwalk	CT	E	631 291-9355	3249
Terex Utilities Inc	Hartford	CT	G	860 436-3700	1877
Tinsley GROup-Ps&w Inc **(HQ)**	Milford	CT	D	919 742-5832	2376
American Crane and Hoist Corp	Boston	MA	C	617 482-8383	8360
Bertram & Leithner Inc	Lowell	MA	G	978 459-7474	12353
Gckm Machines	Newton	MA	G	617 584-6266	13594
Ghm Industries Inc **(PA)**	Charlton	MA	F	508 248-3941	9850
Leading Edge Attachments Inc **(PA)**	Jefferson	MA	G	508 829-4855	11954
Omg Inc	Agawam	MA	C	413 786-0516	7444
Omg Inc **(DH)**	Agawam	MA	B	413 789-0252	7443
Prazi USA Inc	Plymouth	MA	G	508 747-1490	14577
Rockland Equipment Company LLC	Rockland	MA	F	781 871-4400	14822
Shemin Nurseries Inc	Lexington	MA	F	781 861-1111	12266
US Discount Products LLC	West Bridgewater	MA	G	877 841-5782	16462
Douglas Dynamics LLC	Rockland	ME	C	207 701-4200	6790
Kevin Call	Levant	ME	G	207 884-7786	6271
North E Wldg & Fabrication Inc	Auburn	ME	E	207 786-2446	5583
Admix Inc	Londonderry	NH	E	603 627-2340	18671
Tel -Tuk Enterprises LLC	Belmont	NH	G	603 267-1966	17685
Tri-State Mfg Solutions LLC	Nottingham	NH	G	508 769-2891	19417
Howard P Fairfield LLC	Morrisville	VT	G	802 888-2092	22170
Jason Patenaude Excavating Inc	Derby	VT	G	802 766-4567	21900

MACHINERY: Cryogenic, Industrial

	CITY	ST	EMP	PHONE	ENTRY #
Saf Industries LLC	Meriden	CT	E	203 729-4900	2127
Accudyne Machine Tool Inc	Bellingham	MA	G	508 966-3110	8027
Atlas Machine Tool Inc	Gloucester	MA	G	508 284-3542	11161
Brooks Automation Inc	Chelmsford	MA	B	978 262-2795	9879
DH Industries USA Inc	Burlington	MA	G	781 229-5814	9255
Vacuum Barrier Corporation	Woburn	MA	E	781 933-3570	17310

MACHINERY: Custom

	CITY	ST	EMP	PHONE	ENTRY #
Darly Custom Technology Inc	Windsor	CT	F	860 298-7966	5328
Durstin Machine & Mfg	Harwinton	CT	G	860 485-1257	1888
Fryer Corporation	Oxford	CT	G	203 888-9944	3402
L R Brown Manufacturing Co	Wallingford	CT	G	203 265-5639	4763
M & Z Engineering Inc	Torrington	CT	G	860 496-0282	4585
Manchester Tl & Design ADP LLC	Hartford	CT	G	860 296-6541	1843
My Tool Company Inc	Waterbury	CT	G	203 755-2333	4920
Pilot Machine Designers Inc	Norwalk	CT	G	203 866-2227	3220
T L S Design & Manufacturing	New London	CT	G	860 439-1414	2781
Vortex Manufacturing	Somers	CT	G	860 749-9769	3921
Anver Corporation	Hudson	MA	D	978 568-0221	11755
Berkshire Group Ltd	Westfield	MA	G	413 562-7200	16673
Bossonnet Inc	Westborough	MA	G	508 986-2308	16594
C M G Precision	Ludlow	MA	G	413 547-8124	12457
Dalton Manufacturing Company	Amesbury	MA	F	978 388-2227	7483
Enos Engineering LLC	Acton	MA	G	978 654-6522	7353
Eyesaver International Inc	Hanover	MA	D	781 829-0808	11337
Falcon Precision Machine Co	Ludlow	MA	G	413 583-2117	12465
Harvard Products Inc	Harvard	MA	F	978 772-0309	11378
Holyoke Machine Company **(PA)**	Holyoke	MA	E	413 534-5612	11633
Innovative Tooling Company Inc	Lenox	MA	F	413 637-1031	12101
Kensol-Franklin Inc	Franklin	MA	G	508 528-2000	11061
Lander Inc	Pittsfield	MA	F	413 448-8734	14481
Markforged Inc **(PA)**	Watertown	MA	C	866 496-1805	16298
Markforged Inc	Billerica	MA	E	617 666-1935	8264
Markforged Inc	Watertown	MA	D	617 666-1935	16299
Mass Automation Corporation	Bourne	MA	G	508 759-0770	8947
Micro Tech Mfg Inc	Worcester	MA	F	508 752-5212	17415
Midas Technology Inc	Woburn	MA	E	781 938-0069	17232
Psjl Corporation **(PA)**	Billerica	MA	D	978 313-2500	8279
Q6 Integration Inc	Northbridge	MA	G	508 266-0638	14059
Regional Industries Inc	Danvers	MA	E	978 750-8787	10250
Trikinetics Inc	Waltham	MA	G	781 891-6110	16217
Vinyl Technologies Inc	Fitchburg	MA	E	978 342-9800	10861
Zipwall LLC **(PA)**	Arlington	MA	G	781 648-8808	7642
Zoiray Technologies Inc	Boston	MA	G	617 358-6003	8942
Down East Inc	Bridgton	ME	F	207 647-5443	5807
Eltec Industries Inc **(PA)**	Freeport	ME	G	207 541-9085	6077
Kennebec Technologies	Augusta	ME	D	207 626-0188	5610
Nikel Precision Group LLC	Biddeford	ME	D	207 282-6080	5753
Soleras Advanced Coatings Ltd **(PA)**	Biddeford	ME	E	207 282-5699	5763
Aeration Technologies Inc	Londonderry	NH	G	603 434-3539	18673
Allard Nazarian Group Inc **(PA)**	Manchester	NH	C	603 668-1900	18774

PRODUCT

	CITY	ST	EMP	PHONE	ENTRY #
Dgf Indstrial Innvations Group	Gilford	NH	F	603 528-6591	18185
Erimar System Integration	Candia	NH	G	603 483-4000	17782
Intec Automation Inc	Rochester	NH	F	603 332-7733	19673
M J C Machine Inc	Nashua	NH	F	603 889-0300	19203
Sawtech Scientific Inc	Bow	NH	G	603 228-1811	17731
Vertal US Inc	Madbury	NH	G	603 490-1711	18762
B & M Plastics Inc	Pawtucket	RI	G	401 728-0404	20815
Chase Machine Co Inc	West Warwick	RI	E	401 821-8879	21486
Cobra Precision Products Inc	North Smithfield	RI	G	401 766-3333	20784
Dynamic Converting Systems	Lincoln	RI	G	401 333-4363	20570
HMC Holding Corporation **(PA)**	Bristol	RI	G	401 253-5501	20084
Abacus Automation Inc	Bennington	VT	E	802 442-3662	21661
Gloucester Associates Inc	Barre	VT	E	802 479-1088	21617

MACHINERY: Deburring

	CITY	ST	EMP	PHONE	ENTRY #
Precision Deburring Inc	Bristol	CT	G	860 583-4662	596

MACHINERY: Desalination Eqpt

	CITY	ST	EMP	PHONE	ENTRY #
Oasys Water Inc	Foxboro	MA	E	617 963-0450	10895

MACHINERY: Die Casting

	CITY	ST	EMP	PHONE	ENTRY #
OEM Sources LLC	Milford	CT	G	203 283-5415	2325
Diecast Manufacturer **(PA)**	North Billerica	MA	G	978 667-6784	13808

MACHINERY: Electrical Discharge Erosion

	CITY	ST	EMP	PHONE	ENTRY #
New England Die Co Inc	Waterbury	CT	F	203 574-5140	4927

MACHINERY: Electronic Component Making

	CITY	ST	EMP	PHONE	ENTRY #
B & A Design Inc	Vernon Rockville	CT	G	860 871-0134	4679
Omega Engineering Inc	Norwalk	CT	D	714 540-4914	3212
Cipem USA Inc	Melrose	MA	G	347 642-1106	12979
Csi Mfg Inc	Westborough	MA	E	508 986-2300	16611
OK Engineering Inc	Hudson	MA	G	978 562-1010	11797
Onyx Spectrum Technology	Lawrence	MA	G	978 686-7000	12068
Witricity Corporation **(PA)**	Watertown	MA	F	617 926-2700	16331
CET Technology LLC	Windham	NH	F	603 894-6100	20001
Pica Mfg Solutions Inc	Derry	NH	E	603 845-3258	17993

MACHINERY: Extruding

	CITY	ST	EMP	PHONE	ENTRY #
Meloni Tool Co Inc	Johnston	RI	G	401 272-6513	20521

MACHINERY: Fiber Optics Strand Coating

	CITY	ST	EMP	PHONE	ENTRY #
Merritt Extruder Corp	Hamden	CT	E	203 230-8100	1770
New England Alpaca Fiber Pool	Westport	MA	G	508 672-6032	16844
Sancliff Inc	Worcester	MA	F	508 795-0747	17469

MACHINERY: Folding

	CITY	ST	EMP	PHONE	ENTRY #
Press Tech Company Inc	Ashaway	RI	G	401 377-4800	20039

MACHINERY: Gas Producers

	CITY	ST	EMP	PHONE	ENTRY #
Praxair Inc **(HQ)**	Danbury	CT	B	203 837-2000	971

MACHINERY: Gas Separators

	CITY	ST	EMP	PHONE	ENTRY #
ACS Industries Inc **(PA)**	Lincoln	RI	E	401 769-4700	20552
Airgas Usa LLC	East Greenwich	RI	G	401 884-0201	20351

MACHINERY: Gear Cutting & Finishing

	CITY	ST	EMP	PHONE	ENTRY #
Fellows Corporation	Windsor	VT	C	802 674-6500	22708
Gear Works Inc	Springfield	VT	E	802 885-5039	22500

MACHINERY: General, Industrial, NEC

	CITY	ST	EMP	PHONE	ENTRY #
M P Robinson Production	Redding	CT	E	203 938-1336	3650
North Haven Eqp & Lsg LLC	Orange	CT	G	203 795-9494	3375
Red Barn Innovations	Prospect	CT	G	203 393-0778	3595
Foster-Miller Inc	Devens	MA	D	781 684-4000	10320
Methods 3d Inc	Sudbury	MA	F	978 443-5388	15663
Wollaston Foundry	Taunton	MA	G	508 884-3400	15800
Environmental Energy & Finance	Newry	ME	F	978 807-0027	6490

MACHINERY: Glassmaking

	CITY	ST	EMP	PHONE	ENTRY #
Emhart Glass Inc **(DH)**	Windsor	CT	D	860 298-7340	5331
Quest Plastics Inc	Torrington	CT	F	860 489-1404	4595
Hub Consolidated Inc	Orwell	VT	G	802 948-2209	22255

MACHINERY: Grinding

	CITY	ST	EMP	PHONE	ENTRY #
Finishers Technology Corp	East Berlin	CT	F	860 829-1000	1101
Magcor Inc	Monroe	CT	G	203 445-0302	2408
Marena Industries Inc	East Hartford	CT	F	860 528-9701	1205
Tetco Inc	Plainville	CT	F	860 747-1280	3519
US Avionics Inc / Superabr	South Windsor	CT	G	860 528-1114	4019
Sharp Grinding Co Inc	West Springfield	MA	G	413 737-8808	16551
Cnc North Inc	Claremont	NH	G	603 542-3361	17842
Terex Usa LLC	Newton	NH	D	603 382-0556	19370

MACHINERY: Ice Cream

	CITY	ST	EMP	PHONE	ENTRY #
Taylor Coml Foodservice Inc	Farmington	CT	A	336 245-6400	1515
Acana Northeast Inc	Pembroke	NH	F	800 922-2629	19455
L E Jackson Corporation	North Haverhill	NH	G	603 787-6036	19389
Superior Ice Cream Eqp LLC	Bow	NH	F	603 225-4207	17732
Superior Novelty Equipment	Bow	NH	G	603 225-4207	17733

MACHINERY: Ice Making

	CITY	ST	EMP	PHONE	ENTRY #
Croteau Development Group Inc	Stafford Springs	CT	G	860 684-3605	4107

MACHINERY: Ice Resurfacing

	CITY	ST	EMP	PHONE	ENTRY #
Farmer Brown Service Inc	Acton	MA	G	978 897-7550	7355

MACHINERY: Industrial, NEC

	CITY	ST	EMP	PHONE	ENTRY #
American Metallizing	South Windsor	CT	G	860 289-1677	3936
Broadstripes LLC	New Haven	CT	G	203 350-9824	2672
Wdss Corporation	Norwalk	CT	F	203 854-5930	3269
Banacek Invstgtons Srch Recove	Sharon	MA	G	781 784-1400	15046
Legacy Machine & Mfg LLC	Amesbury	MA	G	978 388-0956	7493
New England Water Jet Cutting	New Bedford	MA	G	508 993-9235	13425
Tdr Co Inc	Attleboro	MA	G	508 226-1221	7800
Larry Balchen	Jonesport	ME	G	207 497-5621	6227
AMG-Awetis Mfg Group Corp	Gilford	NH	F	603 286-1645	18182
Gaffco Ballistics LLC	South Londonderry	VT	G	802 824-9899	22486

MACHINERY: Jack Screws

	CITY	ST	EMP	PHONE	ENTRY #
National Filter Media Corp	Wallingford	CT	E	203 741-2225	4777

MACHINERY: Jewelers

	CITY	ST	EMP	PHONE	ENTRY #
Medelco Inc	Bridgeport	CT	G	203 275-8070	449
Conley Casting Supply Corp **(PA)**	Warwick	RI	E	401 461-4710	21345

MACHINERY: Kilns

	CITY	ST	EMP	PHONE	ENTRY #
Brick Kiln Place LLC	Medford	MA	G	781 826-6027	12924
Mason Industries Inc	Marlborough	MA	G	508 485-8494	12792
Once Upon A Kiln	Bellingham	MA	G	508 657-1739	8055
Mountain Firewood Kiln	Littleton	NH	G	603 444-6954	18663
Province Kiln Dried Firewood	Belmont	NH	G	603 524-4447	17681
Cask & Kiln Kitchen LLC	Wilmington	VT	G	802 464-2275	22700
Stevens Kiln Drying LLC	Wolcott	VT	G	802 472-5013	22732

MACHINERY: Kilns, Lumber

	CITY	ST	EMP	PHONE	ENTRY #
Vacutherm Inc	Warren	VT	G	802 496-4241	22579

MACHINERY: Knitting

	CITY	ST	EMP	PHONE	ENTRY #
Lamb Knitting Machine Corp	Chicopee	MA	G	413 592-2501	10037

MACHINERY: Labeling

	CITY	ST	EMP	PHONE	ENTRY #
Computype Inc	Concord	NH	F	603 225-5500	17894
Njm Packaging LLC **(HQ)**	Lebanon	NH	F	603 448-0300	18634
Te Connectivity Corporation	East Providence	RI	E	401 432-8200	20446

MACHINERY: Lamp Making, Incandescent

	CITY	ST	EMP	PHONE	ENTRY #
Herb Con Machine Company Inc	Saugus	MA	G	781 233-2755	14985

MACHINERY: Logging Eqpt

	CITY	ST	EMP	PHONE	ENTRY #
Blue Ox Enterprise Inc	Saint Johnsbury	VT	G	802 274-4494	22387
Wood Dynamics Corporation **(PA)**	South Pomfret	VT	G	802 457-3970	22489

MACHINERY: Marking, Metalworking

	CITY	ST	EMP	PHONE	ENTRY #
C & G Precisions Products Inc	Wolcott	CT	G	203 879-6989	5433
Foilmark Inc **(HQ)**	Newburyport	MA	D	978 225-8200	13490

MACHINERY: Metalworking

	CITY	ST	EMP	PHONE	ENTRY #
Alpha-Core Inc	Shelton	CT	E	203 954-0050	3773
Charter Oak Automation LLC	Wallingford	CT	G	203 562-0699	4716
Fletcher-Terry Company LLC **(PA)**	East Berlin	CT	D	860 828-3400	1102
Foilmark Inc	Bloomfield	CT	F	860 243-0343	220
Hall Machine Systems Inc **(HQ)**	North Branford	CT	G	203 481-4275	2965
Herrick & Cowell Company Inc	Hamden	CT	G	203 288-2578	1759
L M Gill Welding and Mfr LLC **(PA)**	Manchester	CT	F	860 647-9931	2017
Merritt Extruder Corp	Hamden	CT	E	203 230-8100	1770
MGS Manufacturing Inc	North Branford	CT	G	203 481-4275	2970
Tmf Incorporated	Southbury	CT	G	203 267-7364	4034
True Position Mfg LLC	South Windsor	CT	G	860 291-2987	4017
Tyger Tool Inc	Stratford	CT	F	203 375-4344	4455
Classic Engineering LLC	Gloucester	MA	G	978 526-9003	11174
Kamrowski Metal Refinishing	Boston	MA	G	508 877-0367	8646
Ktron Inc	Marlborough	MA	E	508 229-0919	12784
Lawrence Sigler	Princeton	MA	G	978 464-2027	14606
Mestek Inc **(PA)**	Westfield	MA	E	470 898-4533	16700
Mestek Inc	Westfield	MA	B	413 568-9571	16702
Micro Electronics Inc	Seekonk	MA	F	508 761-9161	15027
Op USA Inc	Acton	MA	G	978 658-5135	7376
S & H Engineering Inc	Chelmsford	MA	E	978 256-7231	9929
Sandys Machine	Tewksbury	MA	G	978 970-1800	15834
Seymour Associates Inc	Hudson	MA	G	978 562-1373	11815
Shanklin Research Corporation	Ayer	MA	G	978 772-2090	7938
Precision Depaneling Mchs LLC	Fremont	NH	F	540 248-1381	18178
Sawtech Scientific Inc	Bow	NH	G	603 228-1811	17731
Standex International Corp **(PA)**	Salem	NH	E	603 893-9701	19769
Durant Tool Company Inc	North Kingstown	RI	E	401 781-7800	20703
Gasbarre Products Inc	Cranston	RI	F	401 467-5200	20230
Abacus Automation Inc	Bennington	VT	E	802 442-3662	21661

MACHINERY: Milling

	CITY	ST	EMP	PHONE	ENTRY #
Turbine Controls Inc **(PA)**	Bloomfield	CT	D	860 242-0448	269
Watertown Jig Bore Service Inc	Watertown	CT	F	860 274-5898	5034
True Machine Co Inc	Swansea	MA	G	508 379-0329	15718

MACHINERY: Mining

	CITY	ST	EMP	PHONE	ENTRY #
Oldenburg Group Inc	Claremont	NH	C	603 542-9548	17856
Oldenburg Group Incorporated	Claremont	NH	E	603 542-9548	17857

MACHINERY: Optical Lens

	CITY	ST	EMP	PHONE	ENTRY #
Berkshire Photonics LLC	Washington Depot	CT	G	860 868-0412	4832

MACHINERY: Packaging

	CITY	ST	EMP	PHONE	ENTRY #
B & B Equipment LLC	Portland	CT	G	860 342-5773	3563
Beardsworth Group Inc	Thomaston	CT	G	860 283-4014	4498
Gtrpet Smf LLC	Cos Cob	CT	G	203 661-1229	825
Integrated Packg Systems Inc	East Windsor	CT	G	860 623-2623	1287
Millwood Inc	North Haven	CT	F	203 248-7902	3041

	CITY	ST	EMP	PHONE	ENTRY #
OEM Sources LLC	Milford	CT	G	203 283-5415	2325
Packard Inc	Prospect	CT	E	203 758-6219	3591
Sanford Redmond Inc	Stamford	CT	G	203 351-9800	4309
Standard-Knapp Inc	Portland	CT	D	860 342-1100	3575
Accutech Packaging Inc	Foxboro	MA	D	508 543-3800	10873
Alepack LLC	Mashpee	MA	G	508 274-5792	12874
Butler Automatic Inc **(PA)**	Middleboro	MA	D	508 923-0544	13057
Energy Sciences Inc	Wilmington	MA	E	978 694-9000	17001
Epic Technologies Inc	Woburn	MA	F	781 932-7870	17178
Maruho Htsujyo Innovations Inc **(PA)**	Norwell	MA	F	617 653-1617	14107
Mrsi Systems LLC	North Billerica	MA	E	978 667-9449	13847
O/K Machinery Corporation	Marlborough	MA	E	508 303-8286	12799
Ohlson Packaging LLC **(DH)**	Taunton	MA	F	508 977-0004	15770
Packaging Devices Inc **(PA)**	Teaticket	MA	F	508 548-0224	15802
Picture Frame Products Inc	Arlington	MA	G	781 648-7719	7634
Shanklin Corporation **(HQ)**	Ayer	MA	C	978 487-2204	7937
Sperry Product Innovation Inc	Bedford	MA	F	781 271-1400	8008
Eami Inc	Biddeford	ME	F	207 283-3001	5730
Oizero9 Inc	Sanford	ME	F	207 324-3582	6885
Paul Israelson	Biddeford	ME	G	512 574-4737	5754
Wrabacon Inc	Oakland	ME	F	207 465-2068	6536
Zajac LLC	Saco	ME	E	207 286-9100	6864
Flex-Print-Labels	Hampton	NH	E	603 929-3088	18263
Folder-Glr Techl Svs Grp LLC	Pelham	NH	G	603 635-7400	19433
George Gordon Associates Inc	Merrimack	NH	F	603 424-5204	19002
ID Technology LLC	Nashua	NH	G	603 598-1553	19182
Ss & G LLC	Pelham	NH	G	603 635-7400	19448
Naepac	Williston	VT	G	802 497-3654	22684
Nestech Machine Systems Inc	Hinesburg	VT	G	802 482-4575	22029

MACHINERY: Paint Making

	CITY	ST	EMP	PHONE	ENTRY #
Highland Labs Inc	Holliston	MA	E	508 429-2918	11577

MACHINERY: Paper Industry Miscellaneous

	CITY	ST	EMP	PHONE	ENTRY #
Andritz Shw Inc	Torrington	CT	E	860 496-8888	4561
Sonic Corp	Stratford	CT	F	203 375-0063	4448
Butler Automatic Inc **(PA)**	Middleboro	MA	D	508 923-0544	13057
Functional Coatings LLC	Newburyport	MA	D	978 462-0746	13493
GL&v USA Inc	Lenox	MA	C	413 637-2424	12100
Holyoke Machine Company **(PA)**	Holyoke	MA	E	413 534-5612	11633
Johnston Dandy Company	Holyoke	MA	F	413 315-4596	11635
Kadant Inc	Auburn	MA	C	508 791-8171	7840
Kadant Inc **(PA)**	Westford	MA	B	978 776-2000	16774
Kadant Inc	Auburn	MA	C	508 791-8171	7841
Magnat-Fairview LLC	Chicopee	MA	F	413 593-5742	10039
Metso Usa Inc **(HQ)**	Boston	MA	G	617 369-7850	8703
Micrex Corporation	Walpole	MA	F	508 660-1900	16002
Mitchell Machine Incorporated **(PA)**	Springfield	MA	E	413 739-9693	15490
Rudison Routhier Engrg Co	West Hatfield	MA	G	413 247-9341	16485
Webco Engineering Inc	Southborough	MA	F	508 303-0500	15372
Southworth Intl Group Inc **(PA)**	Falmouth	ME	D	207 878-0700	6033
Valmet Inc	Biddeford	ME	C	207 282-1521	5767
GL&v USA Inc **(HQ)**	Nashua	NH	B	603 882-2711	19168
Valmet Inc **(HQ)**	Nashua	NH	G	603 882-2711	19278
Maxson Automatic Machinery Co **(PA)**	Westerly	RI	E	401 596-0162	21530
Stearns Tool Company Inc	Providence	RI	G	401 351-4765	21127
Ashe America Inc	Brattleboro	VT	D	802 254-0200	21718

MACHINERY: Pharmaciutical

	CITY	ST	EMP	PHONE	ENTRY #
Cotter Brothers Corporation	Danvers	MA	E	978 777-5001	10206
EMD Millipore Corporation **(DH)**	Burlington	MA	A	781 533-6000	9262
Healthstar Inc	Braintree	MA	E	781 428-3696	9017
Microfluidics Intl Corp	Westwood	MA	E	617 969-5452	16873
Overlook Industries Inc	Easthampton	MA	F	413 527-4344	10574
Rapid Micro Biosystems Inc **(PA)**	Lowell	MA	D	978 349-3200	12425
Synchroneuron Inc	Duxbury	MA	G	617 538-5688	10402
Universal Pharma Tech LLC	North Andover	MA	F	978 975-7216	13735

MACHINERY: Plastic Working

	CITY	ST	EMP	PHONE	ENTRY #
Davis-Standard Holdings Inc **(PA)**	Pawcatuck	CT	B	860 599-1010	3433
Crosby Machine Company Inc	West Brookfield	MA	G	508 867-3121	16468
Gloucester Engineering Co Inc **(DH)**	Gloucester	MA	D	978 281-1800	11186
Gloucester Engineering Co Inc	Gloucester	MA	G	978 515-7008	11187
Lacerta Group Inc	Mansfield	MA	G	508 339-3312	12641
Lacerta Group Inc **(PA)**	Mansfield	MA	D	508 339-3312	12642
Mitchell Machine Incorporated **(PA)**	Springfield	MA	E	413 739-9693	15490
Reifenhauser Incorporated	Danvers	MA	G	847 669-9972	10252
Rocheleau Tool and Die Co Inc	Fitchburg	MA	D	978 345-1723	10851
Roger Tool and Die Company Inc	Worcester	MA	G	508 853-3757	17460
Sonicron Systems Corporation	Westfield	MA	E	413 562-5218	16731
TEC Engineering Corp	Oxford	MA	F	508 987-0231	14275
Thermoplastics Co Inc	Worcester	MA	E	508 754-4668	17488
Topsall Machine Tool Co Inc	Worcester	MA	G	508 755-0332	17489
Hycon Inc	Manchester	NH	G	603 644-1414	18841
US Extruders Inc	Westerly	RI	F	401 584-4710	21546

MACHINERY: Polishing & Buffing

	CITY	ST	EMP	PHONE	ENTRY #
Flow Grinding Corp **(PA)**	Woburn	MA	G	781 933-5300	17182
Gary Blake Car Buffs	Exeter	NH	G	603 778-0563	18122

MACHINERY: Printing Presses

	CITY	ST	EMP	PHONE	ENTRY #
Aurora Imaging Technology Inc	Wellesley	MA	G	617 522-6900	16361
Nes Worldwide Inc	Westfield	MA	E	413 485-5038	16707
Manroland Goss Web Systems AMR **(DH)**	Durham	NH	B	603 750-6600	18078

MACHINERY: Recycling

	CITY	ST	EMP	PHONE	ENTRY #
Startech Environmental Corp **(PA)**	Wilton	CT	F	203 762-2499	5305
User-Friendly Recycling LLC	Stoughton	MA	G	781 269-5021	15627
Waste Mgmt Inc	Springfield	MA	E	413 747-9294	15523

MACHINERY: Riveting

	CITY	ST	EMP	PHONE	ENTRY #
Alcoa Global Fasteners Inc	Stoughton	MA	E	412 553-4545	15578

MACHINERY: Road Construction & Maintenance

	CITY	ST	EMP	PHONE	ENTRY #
Boston and Maine Corporation **(HQ)**	North Billerica	MA	C	978 663-1130	13797
PJ Keating Company	Acushnet	MA	G	508 992-3542	7405
Town of Brimfield	Brimfield	MA	G	413 245-4103	9111

MACHINERY: Robots, Molding & Forming Plastics

	CITY	ST	EMP	PHONE	ENTRY #
Wittmann Battenfeld Inc **(DH)**	Torrington	CT	D	860 496-9603	4608
Nypro Inc **(HQ)**	Clinton	MA	A	978 365-8100	10086
Ranger Automation Systems Inc	Millbury	MA	E	508 842-6500	13174
Lanco Assembly Systems Inc **(PA)**	Westbrook	ME	D	207 773-2060	7193

MACHINERY: Rubber Working

	CITY	ST	EMP	PHONE	ENTRY #
Farrel Corporation **(DH)**	Ansonia	CT	D	203 736-5500	15
M I R Inc	Beacon Falls	CT	F	203 888-2541	61
Castaldo Products Mfg Co Inc	Franklin	MA	G	508 520-1666	11027

MACHINERY: Saw & Sawing

	CITY	ST	EMP	PHONE	ENTRY #
Intech Inc	Acton	MA	E	978 263-2210	7366

MACHINERY: Screening Eqpt, Electric

	CITY	ST	EMP	PHONE	ENTRY #
Lambient Technologies LLC	Cambridge	MA	G	857 242-3963	9530

MACHINERY: Semiconductor Manufacturing

	CITY	ST	EMP	PHONE	ENTRY #
Emhart Teknologies LLC	Danbury	CT	G	877 364-2781	907
Jet Process Corporation	North Haven	CT	G	203 985-6000	3035
Prospect Products Incorporated	Newington	CT	E	860 666-0323	2896
Toppan Photomasks Inc	Brookfield	CT	E	203 775-9001	661
A & D Tool Co	Indian Orchard	MA	G	413 543-3166	11883
Axcelis Technologies Inc **(PA)**	Beverly	MA	C	978 787-4000	8106
Boston Process Tech Inc	Peabody	MA	F	978 854-5579	14316
Brooks Automation Inc **(PA)**	Chelmsford	MA	B	978 262-2400	9880
Btu International Inc **(HQ)**	North Billerica	MA	C	978 667-4111	13800
Cotuit Works	Cotuit	MA	G	508 428-3971	10169
Gt Advanced Technologies	Danvers	MA	D	508 954-8249	10220
Innopad Inc	Newton	MA	G	978 253-4204	13605
Mediatek USA Inc	Woburn	MA	D	781 503-8000	17227
Varian Semicdtr Eqp Assoc Inc	Newburyport	MA	C	978 463-1500	13548
Semigen Inc	Londonderry	NH	E	603 624-8311	18735
Advanced Illumination Inc	Rochester	VT	E	802 767-3830	22315

MACHINERY: Separation Eqpt, Magnetic

	CITY	ST	EMP	PHONE	ENTRY #
Walker Magnetics Group Inc **(HQ)**	Windsor	CT	E	508 853-3232	5378
Mushield Company Inc	Londonderry	NH	E	603 666-4433	18726

MACHINERY: Service Industry, NEC

	CITY	ST	EMP	PHONE	ENTRY #
Edwards Vacuums Inc	Tewksbury	MA	G	978 753-3647	15816
Pequod Inc	New Bedford	MA	G	508 858-5123	13437
Salibas Rug & Upholstery Clrs	Bangor	ME	G	207 947-8876	5658
Bering Technology Inc	Waitsfield	VT	E	408 364-6500	22561

MACHINERY: Sheet Metal Working

	CITY	ST	EMP	PHONE	ENTRY #
Trumpf Inc **(DH)**	Farmington	CT	B	860 255-6000	1517
Trumpf Inc	Plainville	CT	B	860 255-6000	3522
Trumpf Inc	Farmington	CT	B	860 255-6000	1518
Unitec Engineering Inc	Windham	NH	F	978 764-0553	20013

MACHINERY: Snow Making

	CITY	ST	EMP	PHONE	ENTRY #
Snowathome LLC	Terryville	CT	G	860 584-2991	4491
Larchmont Engineering Inc	Chelmsford	MA	G	978 250-1177	9912
Snow Economics Inc	Natick	MA	G	508 655-3232	13279
Fisher Engineering	Rockland	ME	C	207 701-4200	6794
Larchmont Engineering Inc	Manchester	NH	G	603 622-8825	18860
Snomatic Controls & Engrg Inc	Lyme	NH	G	603 795-2900	18756
Omichron Corp	South Londonderry	VT	F	802 824-3136	22488

MACHINERY: Specialty

	CITY	ST	EMP	PHONE	ENTRY #
Lynch Corp	Greenwich	CT	G	203 452-3007	1627
Willigent Corporation	Auburndale	MA	G	617 663-5707	7873
Torrefaction Tech USA LLC	Portland	ME	G	207 775-2464	6741

MACHINERY: Stone Working

	CITY	ST	EMP	PHONE	ENTRY #
Edmund Carr	Braintree	MA	G	781 817-5616	9003
Maxant Industries Inc	Devens	MA	F	978 772-0576	10324
Whitney & Son Inc	Fitchburg	MA	E	978 343-6353	10863
McCormacks Machine Co Inc	West Rutland	VT	G	802 438-2345	22618
Trow & Holden Co Inc	Barre	VT	F	802 476-7221	21643

MACHINERY: Textile

	CITY	ST	EMP	PHONE	ENTRY #
Reynolds Carbide Die Co Inc	Thomaston	CT	E	860 283-8246	4512
Sonic Corp	Stratford	CT	F	203 375-0063	4448
Holyoke Machine Company **(PA)**	Holyoke	MA	E	413 534-5612	11633
Romax Inc	Hudson	MA	G	502 327-8555	11813
J D Paulsen	Bridgton	ME	G	207 647-5679	5808
Cove Metal Company Inc **(PA)**	Pawtucket	RI	F	401 724-3500	20826
James L Gallagher Inc	Little Compton	RI	F	508 758-3102	20605
Texcel Inc	Cumberland	RI	F	401 727-2113	20347

MACHINERY: Thread Rolling

	CITY	ST	EMP	PHONE	ENTRY #
Cole S Crew Machine Products	North Haven	CT	E	203 723-1418	3016

	CITY	ST	EMP	PHONE	ENTRY #

MACHINERY: Tire Shredding

Northeast Data Destruction LLC	Mansfield	MA	G	800 783-6766	12650

MACHINERY: Tobacco Prdts

Single Load LLC	Bridgeport	CT	G	860 944-7507	492

MACHINERY: Wire Drawing

Entwistle Company **(HQ)**	Hudson	MA	C	508 481-4000	11772
Gear/Tronics Industries Inc	North Billerica	MA	D	781 933-1400	13820
Applitek Technologies Corp	Providence	RI	G	401 467-0007	20956
Cove Metal Company Inc **(PA)**	Pawtucket	RI	F	401 724-3500	20826

MACHINERY: Woodworking

United Abrasives Inc **(PA)**	North Windham	CT	B	860 456-7131	3084
A & A Architectural Wdwkg Inc	Westfield	MA	G	413 568-9914	16661
Goodspeed Machine Company	Winchendon	MA	G	978 297-0296	17076
Lawrence Sigler	Princeton	MA	G	978 464-2027	14606
Simonds International LLC	Fitchburg	MA	G	978 424-0327	10854
Simonds International LLC **(HQ)**	Fitchburg	MA	B	978 424-0100	10855
Woodworking Machinery Services	North Billerica	MA	G	978 663-8488	13878
Maxym Technologies Inc	Biddeford	ME	G	207 283-8601	5747
W A Mitchell Inc	Farmington	ME	G	207 778-5212	6054
Sawtech Scientific Inc	Bow	NH	G	603 228-1811	17731
Williams & Hussey Mch Co Inc	Amherst	NH	F	603 732-0219	17591
McCormacks Machine Co Inc	West Rutland	VT	G	802 438-2345	22618

MACHINES: Forming, Sheet Metal

Rader Industries Inc	Bridgeport	CT	G	203 334-6739	478
Aero Manufacturing Corp	Beverly	MA	D	978 720-1000	8096
Eckel Industries Inc **(PA)**	Ayer	MA	F	978 772-0840	7917
Roland Gatchell	Georgetown	MA	G	978 352-6132	11150

MACHINISTS' TOOLS & MACHINES: Measuring, Metalworking Type

Tool Technology Inc	Middleton	MA	E	978 777-5006	13104

MACHINISTS' TOOLS: Measuring, Precision

Hermann Schmidt Company Inc	South Windsor	CT	F	860 289-3347	3978
Harvard Manufacturing Inc	Shirley	MA	G	978 425-5375	15085
Lee Tool Co Inc	Ludlow	MA	F	413 583-8750	12471
LS Starrett Company **(PA)**	Athol	MA	A	978 249-3551	7689
Tektron Inc	Topsfield	MA	F	978 887-0091	15866
Onvio LLC	Salem	NH	G	603 685-0404	19757
Hexagon Metrology Inc **(DH)**	North Kingstown	RI	B	401 886-2000	20716

MACHINISTS' TOOLS: Precision

Apex Machine Tool Company Inc	Cheshire	CT	D	860 677-2884	711
Blue Chip Tool	Tolland	CT	G	860 875-7999	4540
Hart Tool & Engineering	Oxford	CT	G	203 264-9776	3407
Integral Industries Inc	Newington	CT	F	860 953-0686	2872
Johnson Gage Company	Bloomfield	CT	E	860 242-5541	229
Mrh Tool LLC	Milford	CT	G	203 878-3359	2317
Preferred Tool & Die Inc	Shelton	CT	E	203 925-8525	3862
Ray Machine Corporation	Terryville	CT	E	860 582-8202	4490
Skico Manufacturing Co LLC	Hamden	CT	G	203 230-1305	1784
Trueline Corporation	Waterbury	CT	G	203 757-0344	4968
White Hills Tool	Monroe	CT	G	203 590-3143	2420
Armset LLC	Middleton	MA	G	978 774-0035	13083
Ben Franklin Design Mfg Co Inc	Agawam	MA	F	413 786-4220	7423
D & R Products Co Inc	Hudson	MA	E	978 562-4137	11767
Dff Corp	Agawam	MA	C	413 786-8880	7427
Drc Precision Machining Co	Stoneham	MA	G	781 438-4500	15560
Hoppe Technologies Inc	Chicopee	MA	D	413 592-9213	10029
Hugard Inc	Westborough	MA	G	508 986-2300	16625
Mk Services Corp	Middleton	MA	E	978 777-2196	13096
Nortek Inc	West Springfield	MA	E	413 781-4777	16535
Rajessa LLC	East Falmouth	MA	F	508 540-4420	10447
Ametek Precitech Inc **(HQ)**	Keene	NH	D	603 357-2510	18491
Bocra Industries Inc	Seabrook	NH	E	603 474-3598	19794
Russell Precision	Laconia	NH	G	603 524-3772	18584
Team Solutions Machining Inc	Hampstead	NH	G	978 420-2389	18250
Will-Mor Manufacturing Inc	Seabrook	NH	D	603 474-8971	19823
Vermont Precision Tools Inc **(PA)**	Swanton	VT	C	802 868-4246	22538

MACHINISTS' TOOLS: Scales, Measuring, Precision

Bay State Scale & Systems Inc	Burlington	MA	G	781 993-9035	9239
Maine Scale LLC	Auburn	ME	F	207 777-9500	5578

MAGNESIUM

Magnesium Interactive LLC	Westport	CT	G	917 609-1306	5211

MAGNETIC INK & OPTICAL SCANNING EQPT

Gerber Scientific LLC **(PA)**	Tolland	CT	C	860 871-8082	4548
Verico Technology LLC **(HQ)**	Enfield	CT	E	800 492-7286	1389
Data Translation Inc **(PA)**	Norton	MA	D	508 481-3700	14076

MAGNETIC RESONANCE IMAGING DEVICES: Nonmedical

Bitome Inc	Jamaica Plain	MA	G	207 812-8099	11940
Copious Imaging LLC	Lexington	MA	F	617 921-0485	12214
Intelicoat Technologies	West Springfield	MA	G	413 536-7800	16526
Umass Mem Mri Imaging Ctr LLC	Worcester	MA	E	508 756-7300	17492

MAGNETIC SHIELDS, METAL

Kenney Manufacturing Company **(PA)**	Warwick	RI	B	401 739-2200	21383

MAGNETIC TAPE, AUDIO: Prerecorded

Porter Music Box Company Inc	Randolph	VT	G	802 728-9694	22301

MAGNETS: Permanent

Aster Enterprises Inc	Acton	MA	G	978 264-0499	7343
Sabr Enterprises LLC	Acton	MA	G	978 264-0499	7382

MAGNIFIERS

Lets Go Technology Inc **(PA)**	Worcester	MA	F	508 853-8200	17407
Vision Dynamics LLC	Worcester	MA	G	203 271-1944	17502

MAIL-ORDER HOUSE, NEC

Atlantic RES Mktg Systems Inc	West Bridgewater	MA	F	508 584-7816	16429
Travel Medicine Inc	Northampton	MA	G	413 584-0381	14023
E B Frye & Son Inc	Wilton	NH	G	603 654-6581	19979

MAIL-ORDER HOUSES: Arts & Crafts Eqpt & Splys

Color Craft Ltd	East Granby	CT	F	800 509-6563	1121

MAIL-ORDER HOUSES: Books, Exc Book Clubs

Scholastic Library Pubg Inc **(HQ)**	Danbury	CT	A	203 797-3500	986

MAIL-ORDER HOUSES: Cheese

Sugarbush Farm Inc	Woodstock	VT	G	802 457-1757	22739

MAIL-ORDER HOUSES: Clothing, Exc Women's

Del Arbour LLC	Milford	CT	F	203 882-8501	2274

MAIL-ORDER HOUSES: Collectibles & Antiques

Vijon Studios Inc	Old Saybrook	CT	G	860 399-7440	3354

MAIL-ORDER HOUSES: Computer Software

Cogz Systems LLC	Woodbury	CT	F	203 263-7882	5484

MAIL-ORDER HOUSES: Electronic Kits & Parts

Period Lighting Fixtures Inc	Clarksburg	MA	F	413 664-7141	10074

MAIL-ORDER HOUSES: Fitness & Sporting Goods

Bachar Samawi Innovations LLC **(PA)**	West Dover	VT	G	802 464-0440	22605

MAIL-ORDER HOUSES: Food

Butcher Block Inc	Claremont	NH	E	800 258-4304	17837
Granite State Candy Shoppe LLC **(PA)**	Concord	NH	F	603 225-2591	17903
Lady Ann Candies	Warwick	RI	E	401 738-4321	21384

MAIL-ORDER HOUSES: Furniture & Furnishings

Cherry Pond Designs Inc	Jefferson	NH	F	603 586-7795	18482

MAIL-ORDER HOUSES: General Merchandise

Nauset Lantern Shop	Orleans	MA	G	508 255-1009	14236

MAIL-ORDER HOUSES: Jewelry

We Dream In Colur LLC	Essex	MA	G	978 768-0168	10598

MAIL-ORDER HOUSES: Novelty Merchandise

David W Wallace	Shelburne Falls	MA	G	413 625-6523	15067
Hendrickson Advertising Inc	Sterling	MA	G	978 422-8087	15539
Forward Merch LLC	Dover	NH	G	603 742-4377	18022

MAIL-ORDER HOUSES: Order Taking Office Only

Ngraver Company	Bozrah	CT	G	860 823-1533	283

MAIL-ORDER HOUSES: Record & Tape, Music Or Video Club

Forced Exposure Inc	Arlington	MA	E	781 321-0320	7626

MAILING SVCS, NEC

American Rubber Stamp Company	Cheshire	CT	G	203 755-1135	710
Brescias Printing Services Inc	East Hartford	CT	G	860 528-4254	1177
Oddo Print Shop Inc	Torrington	CT	G	860 489-6585	4590
Technique Printers Inc	Clinton	CT	G	860 669-2516	795
Lexington Press Inc	Lexington	MA	G	781 862-8900	12238
Massachusetts Envelope Co Inc **(PA)**	Somerville	MA	E	617 623-8000	15195
Red Mill Graphics Incorporated	Chelmsford	MA	F	978 251-4081	9926
Echo Communications Inc	New London	NH	E	603 526-6006	19316
Sterling Business Corp	Peterborough	NH	G	603 924-9401	19489
L Brown and Sons Printing Inc	Barre	VT	E	802 476-3164	21627
Paw Prints Press Inc	South Burlington	VT	G	802 865-2872	22456

MANAGEMENT CONSULTING SVCS: Automation & Robotics

Origo Automation Inc	Lowell	MA	G	877 943-5677	12417

MANAGEMENT CONSULTING SVCS: Business

Automotive Coop Couponing Inc	Weston	CT	G	203 227-2722	5169
Brian Leopold	Carver	MA	G	508 465-0345	9802
Inventronics Inc	Tyngsboro	MA	G	978 649-9040	15891

MANAGEMENT CONSULTING SVCS: Business Planning & Organiz-ing

Innovative Publishing Co LLC	Edgartown	MA	F	267 266-8876	10585

MANAGEMENT CONSULTING SVCS: Construction Project

Konrad Prefab LLC	Springfield	VT	G	802 885-6780	22504

MANAGEMENT CONSULTING SVCS: Food & Beverage

Foundry Foods Inc	Norwalk	CT	G	314 982-3204	3154

MANAGEMENT CONSULTING SVCS: Industrial & Labor

Anderson David C & Assoc LLC **(PA)**	Enfield	CT	F	860 749-7547	1346
R & J Tool Inc **(PA)**	Laconia	NH	G	603 366-4925	18581

MANAGEMENT CONSULTING SVCS: Industry Specialist

Optical Energy Technologies	Stamford	CT	G	203 357-0626	4272

	CITY	ST	EMP	PHONE	ENTRY #
PRA Holdings Inc	Stamford	CT	G	203 853-0123	4290
Relocation Information Svc Inc	Norwalk	CT	E	203 855-1234	3229
Geotec Inc	Warwick	RI	E	401 228-7395	21366

MANAGEMENT CONSULTING SVCS: Information Systems

	CITY	ST	EMP	PHONE	ENTRY #
Patricia Seybold Group Inc	Brighton	MA	F	617 742-5200	9103

MANAGEMENT CONSULTING SVCS: Manufacturing

	CITY	ST	EMP	PHONE	ENTRY #
Epic Technologies Inc	Woburn	MA	F	781 932-7870	17178

MANAGEMENT SERVICES

	CITY	ST	EMP	PHONE	ENTRY #
Conair Corporation	Torrington	CT	D	800 492-7464	4572
Elot Inc **(PA)**	Old Greenwich	CT	G	203 388-1808	3308
General Dynamics Ordnance	Avon	CT	F	860 404-0162	34
Sleep Management Solutions LLC **(HQ)**	Hartford	CT	F	888 497-5337	1871
SS&c Technologies Inc **(HQ)**	Windsor	CT	C	860 298-4500	5365
Invensys Systems Argentina	Foxboro	MA	E	508 543-8750	10889
Linx Consulting LLC	Webster	MA	F	508 461-6333	16347
Massachusetts Envelope Co Inc **(PA)**	Somerville	MA	E	617 623-8000	15195
NCR Corporation	Newton	MA	C	617 558-2000	13617
Schneider Elc Systems USA Inc	Foxboro	MA	F	508 543-8750	10901
Rsv Management	Machias	ME	G	207 255-8608	6394
Coca-Cola Bottling Company	Belmont	NH	D	603 267-8834	17672
Ener-Tek International Inc	East Greenwich	RI	C	401 471-6580	20366

MANAGEMENT SVCS, FACILITIES SUPPORT: Environ Remediation

	CITY	ST	EMP	PHONE	ENTRY #
Supreme Storm Services LLC	Southington	CT	G	860 201-0642	4083

MANAGEMENT SVCS: Business

	CITY	ST	EMP	PHONE	ENTRY #
Douglas Wine & Spirits Inc	North Providence	RI	F	401 353-6400	20757

MANAGEMENT SVCS: Financial, Business

	CITY	ST	EMP	PHONE	ENTRY #
Rain Cii Carbon LLC	Stamford	CT	F	203 406-0535	4297

MANGANESE ORES MINING

	CITY	ST	EMP	PHONE	ENTRY #
Africa China Mining Corp	Braintree	MA	G	617 921-5500	8985

MANHOLES & COVERS: Metal

	CITY	ST	EMP	PHONE	ENTRY #
Ej Usa Inc	Brockton	MA	F	508 586-3130	9142

MANHOLES COVERS: Concrete

	CITY	ST	EMP	PHONE	ENTRY #
L & L Concrete Products Inc	Oxford	MA	F	508 987-8175	14264
Concrete Systems Inc	Hudson	NH	D	603 886-5472	18380

MANICURE PREPARATIONS

	CITY	ST	EMP	PHONE	ENTRY #
Kims Nail Corporation	Stratford	CT	G	203 380-8608	4428
Prostrong Inc	Pembroke	MA	G	781 829-0000	14422

MANIFOLDS: Pipe, Fabricated From Purchased Pipe

	CITY	ST	EMP	PHONE	ENTRY #
Vas Integrated LLC	Berlin	CT	G	860 748-4058	116

MANNEQUINS

	CITY	ST	EMP	PHONE	ENTRY #
Leo D Bernstein and Sons Inc	Shaftsbury	VT	C	212 337-9578	22405

MANUFACTURING INDUSTRIES, NEC

	CITY	ST	EMP	PHONE	ENTRY #
210 Innovations	Groton	CT	G	860 445-0210	1664
283 Industries Inc	Ridgefield	CT	G	203 276-8956	3653
Additive Experts LLC	New Britain	CT	G	860 351-3324	2505
Advanced Specialist LLC	Watertown	CT	G	860 945-9125	4997
Aero Precision Mfg LLC	Wallingford	CT	G	203 675-7625	4694
American Hydrogen Northeast	Bridgeport	CT	E	203 449-4614	373
Apiject Systems Corp **(PA)**	Stamford	CT	G	203 461-7121	4141
Atech Industries LLC	Orange	CT	G	203 887-4900	3359
Biological Industries	Cromwell	CT	G	860 316-5197	848
Blackbird Manufacturing and De	Coventry	CT	G	860 331-3477	831
Cad/CAM Dntl Stdio Mil Ctr Inc	Newtown	CT	G	203 733-3069	2917
Classic Tool & Mfg LLC	Waterbury	CT	G	203 755-6313	4858
Components For Mfg LLC **(PA)**	Mystic	CT	G	860 245-5326	2437
Connecticut Metal Industries	Ansonia	CT	G	203 736-0790	11
Customized Foods Mfg LLC	Waterbury	CT	G	203 759-1645	4862
Cyro Industries	Orange	CT	G	203 269-4481	3363
Delcon Industries	Trumbull	CT	G	203 371-5711	4622
Delcon Industries LLC	Bridgeport	CT	G	203 331-9720	403
Delta-Source LLC	West Hartford	CT	F	860 461-1600	5065
Diversified Manufact	Ansonia	CT	G	203 734-0379	13
East Coast Precision Mfg	Chester	CT	G	860 322-4624	771
Ellis Manufacturing LLC	Plainville	CT	G	865 518-0531	3485
Ensign Bickford Industries	Simsbury	CT	F	203 843-2126	3901
Four Twenty Industries LLC	Berlin	CT	G	860 818-3334	85
G A Industries	Bristol	CT	G	860 261-5484	566
Garbeck Airflow Industries	Middletown	CT	G	860 301-5032	2186
Go Green Industries LLC	New Milford	CT	G	914 772-0026	2801
Hpi Manufacturing Inc	Hamden	CT	G	203 777-5395	1760
Isaac Industries	Danbury	CT	G	203 778-3239	935
J&P Mfg LLC	Plainville	CT	G	860 747-4790	3499
Jfs Industries	Thomaston	CT	G	203 592-0754	4506
JS Industries	Thompson	CT	G	860 928-0786	4534
Manufacturing Productivi	Windsor	CT	G	860 916-8189	5346
Martin Mfg Services LLC	Killingworth	CT	G	860 663-1465	1927
MLS Acq Inc	East Windsor	CT	F	860 386-6878	1296
Motive Industries LLC	North Windham	CT	G	860 423-2064	3083
Oak Tree Moulding LLC	Woodstock	CT	G	860 455-3056	5499
Precision Express Mfg LLC	Bristol	CT	F	860 584-2627	597
Qds LLC	Shelton	CT	G	203 338-9668	3865
Sadlak Manufacturing LLC	Coventry	CT	E	860 742-0227	839
Simkins Industries	East Haven	CT	G	203 787-7171	1262
Spv Industries LLC	West Hartford	CT	G	860 953-5928	5096
Three Kings Products LLC	Watertown	CT	G	860 945-5294	5028
Tjl Industries LLC	Cheshire	CT	G	203 250-2187	766
Wmb Industries LLC	North Haven	CT	G	203 927-2822	3069
99degrees Custom Inc	Lawrence	MA	G	978 655-3362	11988
Accurate Composites LLC	East Falmouth	MA	D	508 457-9097	10433
Acushnet Mfg Hom	Acushnet	MA	G	508 763-2074	7398
Advanced CAM Manufacturing LLC	Hudson	MA	G	978 562-2825	11752
Advanced Electronic Technology	Ayer	MA	G	978 846-6487	7905
Ait Manufacturing LLC	Lawrence	MA	G	978 655-7257	11991
Alpha Fierce LLC	Merrimac	MA	G	781 518-3311	12999
Anthony Industries Inc	Woburn	MA	G	781 305-3750	17119
Ats Finishing Inc	North Andover	MA	G	978 975-0957	13692
B & B Mfg Co	Provincetown	MA	G	508 487-0858	14607
Barber Walters Industries LLC	Wellesley	MA	G	781 241-5433	16363
CIM Industries Inc	Bridgewater	MA	G	800 543-3458	9067
Compound Manufacturing LLC	Greenfield	MA	G	413 773-8909	11258
Constant Velocity Mfg LLC	Spencer	MA	G	508 735-3399	15427
Cory Manufacturing Inc	West Bridgewater	MA	G	508 680-2111	16435
Davis Precision Mfg LLC	Lawrence	MA	G	978 794-0042	12015
Diamondhead USA Inc	West Springfield	MA	G	413 537-4806	16516
E R S Resources	Worcester	MA	G	508 421-3434	17368
Fire-1 Manufacturing Inc	Mendon	MA	G	508 478-8473	12993
G F L Industries	Leominster	MA	G	978 728-4800	12142
Go Green Industries Inc	Westford	MA	G	978 496-1881	16769
Go Green Mfg Inc	Gardner	MA	G	978 928-4333	11118
Harvard Double Reeds	Harvard	MA	G	978 772-1898	11376
Hedge Hog Industries	Springfield	MA	G	413 363-2528	15475
Inspeedcom LLC	Sudbury	MA	G	978 397-6813	15660
Jab Industries Inc	Attleboro	MA	G	401 447-9668	7753
Keith Industrial Group Inc	Clinton	MA	G	978 365-5555	10082
Kodiak Industries LLC	Billerica	MA	G	617 839-1298	8261
Lavoie Industries Llc	Fall River	MA	G	508 542-1062	10722
Luv Manufacturing	Malden	MA	G	857 277-3573	12578
Lzj Holdings Inc	Andover	MA	G	978 409-1091	7566
Magpie Industries LLC	Somerville	MA	G	617 623-3330	15193
McF Electronic Services Inc	Lowell	MA	G	603 718-2256	12406
Milani Industries Inc	Stoughton	MA	G	781 344-3377	15608
MS Industries Inc	Lunenburg	MA	G	978 582-1492	12482
Olimpia Industries Incorporate	Bellingham	MA	G	508 966-3392	8054
PEI Realty Trust	Milford	MA	E	508 478-2025	13136
Pha Industries Inc	Orange	MA	F	978 544-8770	14222
R T Clark Manufacturing Inc	Clinton	MA	G	800 921-4330	10092
Sandler & Sons Co	Medway	MA	G	508 533-8282	12970
Scharn Industries	Woburn	MA	F	781 376-9777	17289
Sjogren Industries Inc	Worcester	MA	F	508 987-3206	17474
Std Manufacturing Inc	Stoughton	MA	G	781 828-4400	15623
Stoney Industries Inc	Shrewsbury	MA	G	508 845-6731	15133
Swiss Ace Manufacturing Inc	Leominster	MA	G	978 860-3199	12191
US Standard Brands Inc	Walpole	MA	G	617 719-8796	16016
Barringer Industries LLC	Scarborough	ME	G	207 730-7125	6908
Gardner Chipmills Millinocket	Chester	ME	F	207 794-2223	5905
Gerrish Global Industries LLC	Naples	ME	G	207 595-2150	6460
Lockwood Mfg Inc	Presque Isle	ME	F	207 764-4196	6760
New Gen Industries	Cumberland Center	ME	G	207 400-1928	5930
Ultimate Industries	Kennebunkport	ME	G	617 923-1568	6248
Armstrong Industries Inc	Amherst	NH	G	715 629-1632	17551
Auto-Lock Broadhead Co LLC	Raymond	NH	G	603 895-0502	19634
Hannan Technologies LLC	Danbury	NH	G	603 768-5656	17964
Hlf Industries	Sandown	NH	G	603 303-2425	19785
Huntley Benard Industries Inc	Nashua	NH	G	603 943-7813	19180
Imed Mfg	Hampstead	NH	G	603 489-5184	18240
Ingu LLC	Portsmouth	NH	F	603 770-5969	19579
Integrity Laser Inc	Nashua	NH	G	603 930-1413	19189
Keyspin Manufacturing	Merrimack	NH	G	603 420-8508	19009
Porter Manufacturing	New Ipswich	NH	G	603 303-6846	19310
Ricor Usa Inc	Salem	NH	G	603 718-8903	19763
Sweeney Manufacturing	Seabrook	NH	G	603 814-4127	19820
C&M Mfg Co Inc	Chepachet	RI	G	401 232-9633	20133
Dawn Industries Inc	West Warwick	RI	G	401 884-8175	21490
Lance Industries	North Providence	RI	G	401 654-5394	20766
Mjh Crawford Industries I	Lincoln	RI	G	401 728-3443	20585
Recognition Awards	Johnston	RI	G	401 365-1265	20535
Hyzer Industries	Montpelier	VT	G	802 223-8277	22150
Sullivan Industries LLC	Montpelier	VT	G	802 229-1909	22161

MAPMAKING SVCS

	CITY	ST	EMP	PHONE	ENTRY #
Edgewater Marine Inds LLC	New Bedford	MA	E	508 992-6555	13383
Streetscan Inc	Burlington	MA	F	617 399-8236	9341

MAPS

	CITY	ST	EMP	PHONE	ENTRY #
Harbor Publications Inc	Madison	CT	G	203 245-8009	1962
Map of Month	Providence	RI	G	401 274-4288	21059
Discovery Map Intl Inc	Waitsfield	VT	G	802 316-4060	22564

MARBLE BOARD

	CITY	ST	EMP	PHONE	ENTRY #
Central Marble & Granite LLC	Ansonia	CT	G	203 734-4644	9
Stepping Stones MBL & Gran LLC **(PA)**	Norwalk	CT	G	203 854-0552	3251
Colonial Marble Co Inc	Everett	MA	G	617 389-1130	10608

MARBLE, BUILDING: Cut & Shaped

	CITY	ST	EMP	PHONE	ENTRY #
Eastern Marble & Granite LLC	Milford	CT	F	203 882-8221	2280
La Pietra Thinstone Veneer	Brookfield	CT	G	203 775-6162	650
Pistritto Marble Imports Inc	Hartford	CT	G	860 296-5263	1857
Aldrich Marble & Granite Co	Norwood	MA	E	781 762-6111	14124
Ital Marble Co Inc	Lynn	MA	F	781 595-4859	12517
Louis W Mian Inc **(PA)**	Boston	MA	E	617 241-7900	8672
Mkl Stone LLC	Everett	MA	G	781 844-9811	10622

	CITY	ST	EMP	PHONE	ENTRY #
Progressive Marble Fabrication	Randolph	MA	G	781 963-6029	14694
Santo C De Spirt Marble & Gran	Agawam	MA	G	413 786-7073	7450
Steven Tedesco	Danvers	MA	G	978 777-4070	10258
Stone Design Marble & Gran Co	South Weymouth	MA	G	781 331-3000	15322
Arens Stoneworks Inc	Greenland	NH	F	603 436-8000	18221
Johnson Marble and Granite	Proctor	VT	G	802 459-3303	22285

MARBLE: Crushed & Broken

K & B Rock Crushing LLC	Auburn	NH	G	603 622-1188	17612
Martin R L & W B Inc	East Corinth	VT	G	802 439-5797	21914

MARBLE: Dimension

Infinity Stone Inc	Waterbury	CT	F	203 575-9484	4888
Vermont Quarries Corp	Rutland	VT	F	802 775-1065	22360

MARINAS

F L Tripp & Sons Inc	Westport Point	MA	E	508 636-4058	16854
Alden Yachts Corporation	Bristol	RI	D	401 683-4200	20060
Lenmarine Inc **(PA)**	Bristol	RI	E	401 253-2200	20089

MARINE HARDWARE

Beckson Manufacturing Inc **(PA)**	Bridgeport	CT	E	203 366-3644	381
C Sherman Johnson Company	East Haddam	CT	F	860 873-8697	1149
Cornell-Carr Co Inc	Monroe	CT	E	203 261-2529	2399
Dwyer Aluminum Mast Company	North Branford	CT	F	203 484-0419	2962
Walz & Krenzer Inc **(PA)**	Oxford	CT	F	203 267-5712	3429
Hancock Marine Inc	Fall River	MA	G	508 678-0301	10712
Ketcham Traps	New Bedford	MA	G	508 997-4787	13404
Rj Marine Industries	Oxford	MA	G	508 248-9933	14272
Submarine Research Labs	Hingham	MA	G	781 749-0900	11512
Knight Underwater Bearing Llc	Cape Neddick	ME	G	207 251-0001	5880
Paul E Luke Inc	East Boothbay	ME	G	207 633-4971	5979
T Henri Inc	Southwest Harbor	ME	G	207 244-7787	7051
Elemental Innovation Inc	Newton	NH	F	603 259-4400	19365
Pompanette LLC **(PA)**	Charlestown	NH	D	717 569-2300	17819
Ocean Link Inc	Portsmouth	RI	G	401 683-4434	20935

MARINE RELATED EQPT

Dp Marine LLC	Riverside	CT	G	917 705-7435	3690
Maretron LLP	Plainville	CT	F	602 861-1707	3503
Naiad Dynamics Us Inc **(HQ)**	Shelton	CT	E	203 929-6355	3836
Ecochlor Inc	Acton	MA	G	978 263-5478	7352
Hercules Slr (us) Inc **(PA)**	New Bedford	MA	F	508 993-0010	13394
Hydroid Inc **(PA)**	Pocasset	MA	C	508 563-6565	14596
Sea Sciences Inc	Arlington	MA	G	781 643-1600	7637

MARINE RELATED EQPT: Winches, Ship

Kennebec Marine Company	Scarborough	ME	G	207 773-0392	6929
Marine Hydraulic Engrg Co **(PA)**	Rockland	ME	G	207 594-9525	6803

MARINE SPLY DEALERS

Newbury Port Meritown Society	Amesbury	MA	G	978 834-0050	7501
Dark Harbor Boatyard Corp	Islesboro	ME	F	207 734-2246	6215
J O Brown & Son Inc	North Haven	ME	G	207 867-4621	6511
Aramid Rigging Inc	Portsmouth	RI	G	401 683-6966	20917
Lightship Group LLC **(PA)**	North Kingstown	RI	E	401 294-3341	20723

MARINE SPLYS WHOLESALERS

Dawid Manufacturing Inc	Ansonia	CT	G	203 734-1800	12
Hercules Slr (us) Inc **(PA)**	New Bedford	MA	F	508 993-0010	13394
Kennebec Marine Company	Scarborough	ME	G	207 773-0392	6929

MARINE SVC STATIONS

Dark Harbor Boatyard Corp	Islesboro	ME	F	207 734-2246	6215

MARKING DEVICES

Schwerdtle Stamp Company	Bridgeport	CT	E	203 330-2750	487
United Stts Sgn & Fbrctlon	Trumbull	CT	E	203 601-1000	4640
AA White Company	Uxbridge	MA	F	508 779-0821	15913
Duncan M Gillies Co Inc	West Boylston	MA	G	508 835-4445	16415
G3 Incorporated **(PA)**	Lowell	MA	E	978 805-5001	12372
Holmes Stamp Company	Salem	MA	G	978 744-1051	14922
Rofin-Baasel Inc **(DH)**	Devens	MA	E	978 635-9100	10332
Titus & Bean Graphics Inc	Kingston	MA	F	781 585-1355	11965
Valley Steel Stamp Inc	Greenfield	MA	E	413 773-8200	11282
Visimark Inc **(PA)**	Worcester	MA	E	866 344-7721	17501
Armstrong Family Inds Inc	Hermon	ME	E	207 848-7300	6183
Anco Signs & Stamps Inc	Manchester	NH	G	603 669-3779	18779
Global Rfid Systems N Amer LLC	Narragansett	RI	G	401 783-3818	20640
Henry A Evers Corp Inc	Providence	RI	F	401 781-4767	21028

MARKING DEVICES: Date Stamps, Hand, Rubber Or Metal

American Rubber Stamp Company	Cheshire	CT	G	203 755-1135	710
Lincoln Press Co Inc	Fall River	MA	E	508 673-3241	10723

MARKING DEVICES: Embossing Seals & Hand Stamps

A D Perkins Company	New Haven	CT	G	203 777-3456	2651
D R S Desings	Bethel	CT	G	203 744-2858	140
Logan Stamp Works Inc	Boston	MA	G	617 569-2121	8670
Making Your Mark Inc	Quincy	MA	G	617 479-0999	14637
Opsec Security Inc	Boston	MA	F	617 226-3000	8756
Royal Stamp Works Inc	Peabody	MA	G	978 531-5555	14367
Granite State Stamps Inc	Manchester	NH	F	603 669-9322	18829

MARKING DEVICES: Embossing Seals, Corporate & Official

Idemia America Corp **(DH)**	Billerica	MA	B	978 215-2400	8255
Owl Stamp Company Inc	Lowell	MA	G	978 452-4541	12418

MARKING DEVICES: Irons, Marking Or Branding

Van Deusen & Levitt Assoc Inc	Weston	CT	E	203 445-6244	5175

MARKING DEVICES: Pads, Inking & Stamping

Gutkin Enterprises LLC	Hamden	CT	G	203 777-5510	1752

MARKING DEVICES: Printing Dies, Marking Mach, Rubber/Plastic

A G Russell Company Inc	Hartford	CT	G	860 247-9093	1800

MARKING DEVICES: Textile Making Stamps, Hand, Rubber/Metal

Acme Sign Co **(PA)**	Stamford	CT	F	203 324-2263	4128

MASTIC ROOFING COMPOSITION

Westfort Construction Corp	Hamden	CT	G	860 833-7970	1795

MASTS: Cast Aluminum

Dwyer Aluminum Mast Company	North Branford	CT	F	203 484-0419	2962

MATCHES & MATCH BOOKS

D D Bean & Sons Co **(PA)**	Jaffrey	NH	D	603 532-8311	18459

MATERIAL GRINDING & PULVERIZING SVCS NEC

Hamden Grinding	Hamden	CT	G	203 288-2906	1753
K and R Precision Grinding	New Britain	CT	G	860 505-8030	2547
ACS Auxiliaries Group Inc	Attleboro	MA	G	508 399-3018	7700
Omni Components Corp **(PA)**	Hudson	NH	D	603 882-4467	18422

MATERIALS HANDLING EQPT WHOLESALERS

Linvar LLC	Rocky Hill	CT	G	860 951-3818	3721

MATS OR MATTING, NEC: Rubber

Interstate Mat Corporation	South Easton	MA	G	508 238-0116	15282

MATS, MATTING & PADS: Bathmats & Sets, Textile

American Veteran Textile LLC	Ansonia	CT	G	203 583-0576	6

MATS: Table, Plastic & Textile

Agawam Novelty Company Inc	Agawam	MA	G	413 536-0471	7418

MATTRESS PROTECTORS, EXC RUBBER

Perfect Fit Industries LLC	Allenstown	NH	G	603 485-7161	17540

MATTRESS STORES

Daly Bros Bedding Co Inc	Biddeford	ME	G	207 282-9583	5727

MEAT & FISH MARKETS: Food & Freezer Plans, Meat

Martin Rosols Inc	New Britain	CT	E	860 223-2707	2551

MEAT & FISH MARKETS: Freezer Provisioners, Meat

Ice Cream Machine Co	Cumberland	RI	F	401 333-5053	20327

MEAT & MEAT PRDTS WHOLESALERS

Chicopee Provision Company Inc	Chicopee	MA	E	413 594-4765	10009
Lisbon Sausage Co Inc	New Bedford	MA	F	508 993-7645	13408

MEAT CUTTING & PACKING

E & J Andrychowski Farms	Windham	CT	G	860 423-4124	5311
Grote & Weigel Inc **(PA)**	Bloomfield	CT	E	860 242-8528	221
Manchester Packing Company Inc	Manchester	CT	D	860 646-5000	2024
Martin Rosols Inc	New Britain	CT	E	860 223-2707	2551
Maurices Country Meat Mkt LLC	Canterbury	CT	G	860 546-9588	694
A Arena & Sons Inc	Hopkinton	MA	G	508 435-3673	11685
Chicopee Provision Company Inc	Chicopee	MA	E	413 594-4765	10009
Crocetti-Oakdale Packing Inc **(PA)**	East Bridgewater	MA	E	508 587-0035	10410
Demakes Enterprises Inc	Lynn	MA	C	781 586-0212	12500
Kayem Foods Inc **(PA)**	Chelsea	MA	B	781 933-3115	9957
Mutual Beef Co Inc	Boston	MA	F	617 442-3238	8717
Robbins Beef Co Inc	Boston	MA	F	617 269-1826	8824
Smithfield Direct LLC	Springfield	MA	B	413 781-5620	15505
Smithfield Foods Inc	Springfield	MA	A	413 781-5620	15506
Bubiers Meats	Greene	ME	G	207 946-7761	6148
Castonguay Meats Inc	Livermore	ME	G	207 897-4989	6373
West Gardiner Beef Inc	West Gardiner	ME	G	207 724-3378	7173
Lincoln Packing Co	Cranston	RI	E	401 943-0878	20255
Rjb Meat Processing	Warwick	RI	G	401 781-5315	21415
Vermont Lvstk Slghter Proc LLC	Ferrisburgh	VT	F	802 877-3421	21990
Vermont Packinghouse LLC	North Springfield	VT	F	802 886-8688	22239

MEAT MARKETS

Manchester Packing Company Inc	Manchester	CT	D	860 646-5000	2024
Chair City Meats Inc	Gardner	MA	F	978 630-1050	11108
Whip City Jerky LLC	Westfield	MA	G	413 568-2050	16749

MEAT PRDTS: Beef Stew, From Purchased Meat

Green Mountain Marinades	Bristol	NH	G	802 434-3731	17766

MEAT PRDTS: Bologna, From Purchased Meat

Martin Rosols Inc	New Britain	CT	E	860 223-2707	2551

MEAT PRDTS: Cured Meats, From Purchased Meat

Whitestone Provision Sup Corp **(PA)**	Barrington	RI	G	401 245-1346	20057

MEAT PRDTS: Dried Beef, From Purchased Meat

Whip City Jerky LLC	Westfield	MA	G	413 568-2050	16749
Vermont Beef Jerky Co	Orleans	VT	E	802 754-9412	22252

MEAT PRDTS: Frozen

Home Market Foods Inc **(PA)**	Norwood	MA	C	781 948-1500	14157

MEAT PRDTS: Ham, Smoked, From Purchased Meat

	CITY	ST	EMP	PHONE	ENTRY #
Harringtons In Vermont Inc **(PA)**	Richmond	VT	F	802 434-7500	22312

MEAT PRDTS: Lamb, From Slaughtered Meat

	CITY	ST	EMP	PHONE	ENTRY #
Boston Lamb & Veal Co Inc	Boston	MA	D	617 442-3644	8433

MEAT PRDTS: Pork, Cured, From Purchased Meat

	CITY	ST	EMP	PHONE	ENTRY #
Sugar Mountain Farm LLC	West Topsham	VT	G	802 439-6462	22624

MEAT PRDTS: Pork, From Slaughtered Meat

	CITY	ST	EMP	PHONE	ENTRY #
Pig + Poet Restaurant	Camden	ME	G	207 236-3391	5869

MEAT PRDTS: Pork, Salted, From Purchased Meat

	CITY	ST	EMP	PHONE	ENTRY #
Brava Enterprises LLC	Lewiston	ME	G	207 241-2420	6277

MEAT PRDTS: Prepared Beef Prdts From Purchased Beef

	CITY	ST	EMP	PHONE	ENTRY #
Custom Food Pdts Holdings LLC	Greenwich	CT	D	310 637-0900	1605
Newport Creamery LLC	Cranston	RI	B	401 946-4000	20268

MEAT PRDTS: Prepared Pork Prdts, From Purchased Meat

	CITY	ST	EMP	PHONE	ENTRY #
Hilltown Pork Inc	Granville	MA	F	413 357-6661	11230

MEAT PRDTS: Roast Beef, From Purchased Meat

	CITY	ST	EMP	PHONE	ENTRY #
Carando Gourmet Foods Corp **(PA)**	Agawam	MA	E	413 737-0183	7426

MEAT PRDTS: Sausage Casings, Natural

	CITY	ST	EMP	PHONE	ENTRY #
Massachusetts Importing Co	Medford	MA	G	781 395-1210	12942

MEAT PRDTS: Sausages & Related Prdts, From Purchased Meat

	CITY	ST	EMP	PHONE	ENTRY #
Janik Sausage Co Inc	Enfield	CT	G	860 749-4661	1367
Chair City Meats Inc	Gardner	MA	F	978 630-1050	11108
Diluigis Inc	Danvers	MA	D	978 750-9900	10213
Angostura International Ltd	Auburn	ME	G	207 786-3200	5551
Daniele International Inc	Pascoag	RI	D	401 568-6228	20800
Daniele International Inc	Pascoag	RI	C	401 568-6228	20801
Daniele International Inc **(PA)**	Mapleville	RI	C	401 568-6228	20612

MEAT PRDTS: Sausages, From Purchased Meat

	CITY	ST	EMP	PHONE	ENTRY #
Hummel Bros Inc	New Haven	CT	D	203 787-4113	2697
Lamberti Packing Company	New Haven	CT	G	203 562-0436	2705
Alden Acoreana Realty Trust **(PA)**	Fall River	MA	G	508 678-2098	10652
Gaspars Sausage Co Inc	North Dartmouth	MA	E	508 998-2012	13920
Lisbon Sausage Co Inc	New Bedford	MA	F	508 993-7645	13408
Marias Food Products Inc	Medford	MA	G	781 396-4110	12940
Mellos North End Mfg Co Inc	Fall River	MA	G	508 673-2320	10729
New Bedford Salchicharia Inc **(PA)**	New Bedford	MA	G	508 992-6257	13420
Smithfield Direct LLC	Springfield	MA	B	413 781-5620	15505
Waniewski Farms Inc	Feeding Hills	MA	F	413 786-1182	10805
Central Falls Provision Co	Central Falls	RI	G	401 725-7020	20112
Lincoln Packing Co	Cranston	RI	E	401 943-0878	20255
Rhode Island Provision Co Inc	Johnston	RI	F	401 831-0815	20537
T O Nam Sausage	Cranston	RI	G	401 941-9620	20298
Fortunas Sausage Co LLC	Sandgate	VT	G	802 375-0200	22400

MEAT PRDTS: Smoked

	CITY	ST	EMP	PHONE	ENTRY #
Kayem Foods Inc **(PA)**	Chelsea	MA	B	781 933-3115	9957
New England Smoked Seafood	Rutland	VT	G	802 773-4628	22346

MEAT PRDTS: Snack Sticks, Incl Jerky, From Purchased Meat

	CITY	ST	EMP	PHONE	ENTRY #
Mister BS Jerky Co	Meriden	CT	G	203 631-2758	2110
Hopps Company	Quincy	MA	G	617 481-1379	14632
Newport Jerky Company	Carver	MA	G	347 913-6882	9805
Heidi Jos LLC	Derry	NH	G	603 774-5375	17982

MEAT PROCESSED FROM PURCHASED CARCASSES

	CITY	ST	EMP	PHONE	ENTRY #
Baltasar & Sons Inc	Naugatuck	CT	G	203 723-0425	2462
Capitol Sausage & Provs Inc	Hartford	CT	G	860 527-5510	1811
Deyulio Sausage Company LLC	Bridgeport	CT	F	203 348-1863	406
Grote & Weigel Inc **(PA)**	Bloomfield	CT	E	860 242-8528	221
Longhini LLC	New Haven	CT	E	212 219-1230	2707
Manchester Packing Company Inc	Manchester	CT	D	860 646-5000	2024
Maurices Country Meat Mkt LLC	Canterbury	CT	G	860 546-9588	694
Amazon Fruit Corp	Ludlow	MA	G	774 244-2820	12453
Boston Lamb & Veal Co Inc	Boston	MA	D	617 442-3644	8433
Chicopee Provision Company Inc	Chicopee	MA	E	413 594-4765	10009
Crocetti-Oakdale Packing Inc **(PA)**	East Bridgewater	MA	E	508 587-0035	10410
Crocetti-Oakdale Packing Inc	Brockton	MA	E	508 941-0458	9135
Demakes Enterprises Inc **(PA)**	Lynn	MA	C	701 417-1100	12499
Demakes Enterprises Inc	Lynn	MA	C	781 586-0212	12500
Genoa Sausage Co Inc	Woburn	MA	D	781 933-3115	17190
Kraft Heinz Foods Company	Woburn	MA	C	781 933-2800	17212
Miranda Brothers Inc	Fall River	MA	G	508 672-0982	10735
Old Neighborhood Foods	Lynn	MA	G	781 595-1557	12531
Pig Rock Sausages LLC	Milton	MA	G	617 851-9422	13198
Wohrles Foods Inc **(PA)**	Pittsfield	MA	E	413 442-1518	14513
Noon Family Sheep Farm	Springvale	ME	G	207 324-3733	7055
Butcher Block Inc	Claremont	NH	E	800 258-4304	17837
Garfields Smokehouse Inc	Meriden	NH	G	603 469-3225	18983
Msn Corporation	Manchester	NH	D	603 623-3528	18879
Daniele Inc	Pascoag	RI	E	401 568-6228	20799
Kinderwagon Company	Newport	RI	G	617 256-7599	20670
Marcello Sausage Co	Cranston	RI	F	401 275-1952	20259
Portion Meat Associates Inc	Providence	RI	F	401 421-2438	21092
Npc Processing Inc	Shelburne	VT	E	802 660-0496	22420
Plumrose Usa Inc	Swanton	VT	D	802 868-7314	22533
VSC Holdings Inc	Hinesburg	VT	D	802 482-4666	22033

MECHANICAL INSTRUMENT REPAIR SVCS

	CITY	ST	EMP	PHONE	ENTRY #
E H Benz Co Inc	Providence	RI	G	401 331-5650	20999

MECHANISMS: Coin-Operated Machines

	CITY	ST	EMP	PHONE	ENTRY #
Blackwold Inc	Chester	CT	D	860 526-0800	768
Eastern Company	Chester	CT	D	860 526-0800	772
Interntonal Totalizing Systems **(PA)**	Bedford	MA	E	978 521-8867	7983

MEDIA BUYING AGENCIES

	CITY	ST	EMP	PHONE	ENTRY #
Chief Executive Group LLC **(PA)**	Stamford	CT	F	785 832-0303	4164

MEDIA: Magnetic & Optical Recording

	CITY	ST	EMP	PHONE	ENTRY #
BEI Holdings Inc	Wallingford	CT	F	203 741-9300	4709
Dictaphone Corporation **(HQ)**	Stratford	CT	C	203 381-7000	4409
ER Enterprises LLC	Newton	MA	G	617 296-9140	13590
Go2 Media Inc	Boston	MA	F	617 457-7870	8572
Media Scope International Inc	North Attleboro	MA	G	508 643-2988	13762
Sony Dadc	Cambridge	MA	G	617 714-5776	9657

MEDICAL & HOSPITAL EQPT WHOLESALERS

	CITY	ST	EMP	PHONE	ENTRY #
Tarry Medical Products Inc	Danbury	CT	F	203 794-1438	998
Brownmed Inc **(PA)**	Boston	MA	E	857 317-3354	8447
Philips Holding USA Inc **(HQ)**	Andover	MA	C	978 687-1501	7582
Tri-Med Inc	Peterborough	NH	G	603 924-7211	19491
Confluent Medical Tech Inc	Warwick	RI	G	401 223-0990	21344
Surplus Solutions LLC	Woonsocket	RI	F	401 526-0055	21584

MEDICAL & HOSPITAL SPLYS: Radiation Shielding Garments

	CITY	ST	EMP	PHONE	ENTRY #
Nuclead Incorporated	Cambridge	MA	G	508 583-2699	9595
The Great N Woods Assoc/ Blind	Colebrook	NH	G	603 490-9877	17876

MEDICAL & SURGICAL SPLYS: Absorbent Cotton, Sterilized

	CITY	ST	EMP	PHONE	ENTRY #
Barnhardt Manufacturing Co	Colrain	MA	E	413 624-3471	10104

MEDICAL & SURGICAL SPLYS: Bandages & Dressings

	CITY	ST	EMP	PHONE	ENTRY #
Beiersdorf Inc	Norwalk	CT	B	203 854-8000	3110
Beiersdorf North America Inc **(DH)**	Wilton	CT	F	203 563-5800	5277
Hermell Products Inc	Bloomfield	CT	E	860 242-6550	225
GF Health Products Inc	Warwick	RI	E	401 738-1500	21368

MEDICAL & SURGICAL SPLYS: Braces, Elastic

	CITY	ST	EMP	PHONE	ENTRY #
Eddies Wheels Inc	Shelburne Falls	MA	F	413 625-0033	15069

MEDICAL & SURGICAL SPLYS: Braces, Orthopedic

	CITY	ST	EMP	PHONE	ENTRY #
Cornell Orthotics Prosthetics **(PA)**	Beverly	MA	F	978 922-2866	8121
Oped Inc	Sudbury	MA	G	781 891-6733	15665
Pro-Tech Orthopedics Inc	Raynham	MA	F	508 821-9600	14727
Spinal Technology Inc **(PA)**	West Yarmouth	MA	D	508 775-0990	16582
Kisers Ortho Prosthetic Serv **(PA)**	Keene	NH	G	603 357-7666	18513
Carlow Orthpd & Prosthetic Inc **(PA)**	Cranston	RI	G	203 483-8488	20195
Custom Composite Mfg Inc	Cranston	RI	G	401 275-2230	20206

MEDICAL & SURGICAL SPLYS: Clothing, Fire Resistant & Protect

	CITY	ST	EMP	PHONE	ENTRY #
Ctl Corporation	West Simsbury	CT	G	860 651-9173	5154
David Clark Company Inc **(PA)**	Worcester	MA	C	508 756-6216	17362
Salk Company Inc	Allston	MA	E	617 782-4030	7474
Globe Manufacturing Co LLC **(DH)**	Pittsfield	NH	B	603 435-8323	19500
Labonville Inc	Gorham	NH	E	603 752-3221	18214
Cintas Corporation No 2	Pawtucket	RI	G	401 723-7300	20823

MEDICAL & SURGICAL SPLYS: Colostomy Appliances

	CITY	ST	EMP	PHONE	ENTRY #
Austin Medical Products Inc	Center Conway	NH	G	603 356-7004	17792

MEDICAL & SURGICAL SPLYS: Cosmetic Restorations

	CITY	ST	EMP	PHONE	ENTRY #
Sals Clothing & Fabric Restor	Everett	MA	E	617 387-6726	10630

MEDICAL & SURGICAL SPLYS: Crutches & Walkers

	CITY	ST	EMP	PHONE	ENTRY #
Kelly Manufacturing Company	Rumney	NH	G	603 786-9933	19697

MEDICAL & SURGICAL SPLYS: Ear Plugs

	CITY	ST	EMP	PHONE	ENTRY #
Sperian Protection Usa Inc **(DH)**	Smithfield	RI	E	401 232-1200	21250

MEDICAL & SURGICAL SPLYS: Foot Appliances, Orthopedic

	CITY	ST	EMP	PHONE	ENTRY #
Allied Orthotic Inc	Londonderry	NH	G	603 434-7722	18675
AF Group Inc	Lincoln	RI	C	401 757-3910	20553
Atlantic Footcare Inc	North Smithfield	RI	D	401 568-4918	20782

MEDICAL & SURGICAL SPLYS: Grafts, Artificial

	CITY	ST	EMP	PHONE	ENTRY #
Comprhnsive Prsthetic Svcs LLC	Branford	CT	G	203 315-1400	305
Orteoponix LLC	Storrs	CT	G	203 804-9775	4382

MEDICAL & SURGICAL SPLYS: Ligatures

	CITY	ST	EMP	PHONE	ENTRY #
Ethicon Inc	Southington	CT	B	860 621-9111	4048

MEDICAL & SURGICAL SPLYS: Limbs, Artificial

	CITY	ST	EMP	PHONE	ENTRY #
Biometrics Inc **(PA)**	Trumbull	CT	G	203 261-1162	4615
New England Orthotic & Prost	Meriden	CT	G	203 634-7566	2112
Stride Inc	Middlebury	CT	F	203 758-8307	2159
Advanced Orthopedic Services **(PA)**	Hyannis	MA	G	508 771-5050	11833
American Prosthetics Inc **(PA)**	Braintree	MA	G	617 328-0606	8987
Bethcare Inc	Boston	MA	G	617 997-1069	8404
Hanger Prsthetcs & Ortho Inc	Leominster	MA	G	978 466-7400	12150
Hayes Prosthetic Inc	West Springfield	MA	G	413 733-2287	16524
Liberating Technologies Inc	Holliston	MA	G	508 893-6363	11582
Lower Limb Technology	Auburndale	MA	G	617 916-1650	7864
Orthotic and Prosthetic Center	Braintree	MA	G	508 775-2570	9029
Orthotics Prosthetics Labs Inc	Northampton	MA	G	413 585-8622	14015
Orthotics West Inc	Holyoke	MA	G	413 736-3000	11647

	CITY	ST	EMP	PHONE	ENTRY #
Pioneer Vly Orthtics Prsthtics	West Springfield	MA	G	413 788-9655	16545
Hanger Prosthetics & Orthotics	Waterville	ME	F	207 872-8779	7156
Hanger Prsthetcs & Ortho Inc	Augusta	ME	G	207 622-9792	5608
Hanger Prsthetcs & Ortho Inc	Auburn	ME	G	207 782-6907	5571
Maine Artfl Limb Orthotics Co	Portland	ME	F	207 773-4963	6681
P C Northern Prosthetics	Presque Isle	ME	G	207 768-5348	6768
Fdr Center For Prost	Nashua	NH	G	603 595-9255	19155
New Hampshire Prosthetics LLC	Portsmouth	NH	G	603 294-0010	19600
Rhode Island Limb Co **(PA)**	Cranston	RI	G	401 941-6230	20279
Rhode Island Limb Co	Pawtucket	RI	G	401 475-3501	20892

MEDICAL & SURGICAL SPLYS: Models, Anatomical

	CITY	ST	EMP	PHONE	ENTRY #
Chamberlain Group LLC	Great Barrington	MA	F	413 528-7744	11236

MEDICAL & SURGICAL SPLYS: Orthopedic Appliances

	CITY	ST	EMP	PHONE	ENTRY #
Avitus Orthopaedics Inc	Farmington	CT	F	860 637-9922	1466
Cranial Technologies Inc	Madison	CT	F	203 318-8739	1958
Wellinks Inc	New Haven	CT	G	650 704-0714	2753
Westconn Orthopedic Laboratory	Danbury	CT	G	203 743-4420	1011
Brownmed Inc **(PA)**	Boston	MA	E	857 317-3354	8447
Fleming Industries Inc	Chicopee	MA	D	413 593-3300	10026
Lower Limb Technology LLC	West Yarmouth	MA	F	508 775-0990	16580
Medsix Inc	Jamaica Plain	MA	G	617 935-2716	11946
Mike Murphy	Milford	MA	G	508 473-9943	13126
Myomo Inc	Cambridge	MA	E	617 996-9058	9573
New England Orthotic & Prost	Worcester	MA	G	508 890-8808	17431
O & P Iam Inc	Woburn	MA	G	781 239-3331	17248
Omni Life Science Inc **(HQ)**	Raynham	MA	E	508 824-2444	14723
Orthotic Solutions Inc	Plymouth	MA	G	774 205-2278	14570
Prosthtic Orthtic Slutions LLC	West Springfield	MA	G	413 785-4047	16549
Rogerson Orthopedic Appls Inc	Boston	MA	F	617 268-1135	8826
Rph Enterprises Inc	Franklin	MA	D	508 238-3351	11076
Sunrise Prosthetics Orthotics **(PA)**	Worcester	MA	G	508 753-4738	17484
Pine Tree Orthopedic Lab Inc	Livermore Falls	ME	F	207 897-5558	6381
Capital Orthtics Prsthtics LLC	Manchester	NH	G	603 425-0106	18795
Capital Orthtics Prsthtics LLC **(PA)**	Concord	NH	G	603 226-0106	17888
Corflex Inc **(PA)**	Manchester	NH	E	603 623-3344	18806
New England Brace Co Inc **(PA)**	Concord	NH	F	508 588-6060	17916
Poly-Vac Inc	Manchester	NH	C	603 647-7822	18903
Ocean Orthopedic Services Inc **(PA)**	North Providence	RI	F	401 725-5240	20768

MEDICAL & SURGICAL SPLYS: Personal Safety Eqpt

	CITY	ST	EMP	PHONE	ENTRY #
Elvex Corporation	Shelton	CT	F	203 743-2488	3800
Safety Dispatch Inc	Ridgefield	CT	G	203 885-5722	3682
Angel Guard Products Inc	Worcester	MA	G	508 791-1073	17339
Honeywell Data Instruments Inc	Acton	MA	B	978 264-9550	7361
Bavec LLC	Dover	NH	G	603 290-5285	18007
Grabber Construction Pdts Inc	Windham	NH	F	603 890-0455	20007
Holase Incorporated	Portsmouth	NH	G	603 397-0038	19575
Summer Infant Inc **(PA)**	Woonsocket	RI	D	401 671-6550	21581
Summer Infant Inc	Woonsocket	RI	G	401 671-6550	21582
Revision Military JV	Essex Junction	VT	B	802 879-7002	21957

MEDICAL & SURGICAL SPLYS: Prosthetic Appliances

	CITY	ST	EMP	PHONE	ENTRY #
Alternative Prosthetic Svcs	Bridgeport	CT	G	203 367-1212	370
Hanger Prsthetcs & Ortho Inc	Stratford	CT	G	203 377-8820	4418
Leona Corp	Wethersfield	CT	G	860 257-3840	5256
Boston Artificial Limb Co	Burlington	MA	G	781 272-3132	9240
Boston Brace International Inc **(PA)**	Avon	MA	E	508 588-6060	7880
Freudenberg Medical LLC	Gloucester	MA	E	978 281-2023	11184
Hanger Prosthethics & Orthotic	South Easton	MA	G	508 238-6760	15278
Hanger Prsthetcs & Ortho Inc	Methuen	MA	G	978 683-5509	13026
Occlusion Prosthetics	Hyannis	MA	G	508 827-4377	11851
Orthotic & Prosthetic Ctrs LLC	West Yarmouth	MA	G	508 775-7151	16581
Panther Therapeutics Inc	Cambridge	MA	G	857 413-1698	9605
Precision Orthot & Prosthetics	New Bedford	MA	G	508 991-5577	13443
Sunrise Prosthetics Orthotics	Milford	MA	G	508 473-9943	13145
Boston Ocular Prosthetics Inc	Searsport	ME	G	800 824-2492	6948
Hanger Prsthetcs & Ortho Inc	Somersworth	NH	G	603 742-0334	19839
Monoplex Eye Prosthetics LLC	Bedford	NH	G	603 622-5200	17655
Next Step Bnics Prsthetics Inc **(PA)**	Manchester	NH	F	603 668-3831	18886
Jahrling Ocular Prosthetics	Cranston	RI	G	401 454-4168	20243
New England Orthopedics Inc **(PA)**	Warwick	RI	G	401 739-9838	21396
Nunnery Orthtic Prosthetic LLC	North Kingstown	RI	G	401 294-4210	20731

MEDICAL & SURGICAL SPLYS: Respiratory Protect Eqpt, Personal

	CITY	ST	EMP	PHONE	ENTRY #
Contemporary Products LLC	Middletown	CT	E	860 346-9283	2182
Praxair Inc	Danbury	CT	D	800 772-9247	970
Louis M Gerson Co Inc **(PA)**	Middleboro	MA	E	508 947-4000	13065
Louis M Gerson Co Inc	Middleboro	MA	E	508 947-4000	13066
Ops-Core Inc	Boston	MA	F	617 670-3547	8755

MEDICAL & SURGICAL SPLYS: Splints, Pneumatic & Wood

	CITY	ST	EMP	PHONE	ENTRY #
Apothecary Products LLC	North Attleboro	MA	E	508 695-0727	13745

MEDICAL & SURGICAL SPLYS: Sponges

	CITY	ST	EMP	PHONE	ENTRY #
American Surgical Company LLC	Salem	MA	E	781 592-7200	14891

MEDICAL & SURGICAL SPLYS: Stretchers

	CITY	ST	EMP	PHONE	ENTRY #
Brickyard Enterprises Inc	Ferrisburgh	VT	G	802 338-7267	21987

MEDICAL & SURGICAL SPLYS: Suits, Firefighting, Asbestos

	CITY	ST	EMP	PHONE	ENTRY #
Globe Footwear LLC **(HQ)**	Auburn	ME	G	207 784-9186	5569

MEDICAL & SURGICAL SPLYS: Supports, Abdominal, Ankle, Etc

	CITY	ST	EMP	PHONE	ENTRY #
A-T Surgical Mfg Co Inc	Holyoke	MA	E	413 532-4551	11615

MEDICAL & SURGICAL SPLYS: Sutures, Non & Absorbable

	CITY	ST	EMP	PHONE	ENTRY #
Surgical Specialties Corp **(HQ)**	Westwood	MA	C	781 751-1000	16876
Ashaway Line & Twine Mfg Co	Ashaway	RI	D	401 377-2221	20031

MEDICAL & SURGICAL SPLYS: Tape, Adhesive, Non/Medicated

	CITY	ST	EMP	PHONE	ENTRY #
Ict Business	Stamford	CT	G	203 595-9452	4219

MEDICAL & SURGICAL SPLYS: Technical Aids, Handicapped

	CITY	ST	EMP	PHONE	ENTRY #
Prospect Designs Inc	New Hartford	CT	G	860 379-7858	2645
Adaptive Mobility Equipment	Seekonk	MA	G	508 336-2556	15017
Advanced Research Development	North Andover	MA	G	781 285-8721	13687
Touch Bionics	Mansfield	MA	G	774 719-2199	12666

MEDICAL & SURGICAL SPLYS: Traction Apparatus

	CITY	ST	EMP	PHONE	ENTRY #
Babac Inc	Winslow	ME	F	207 872-0889	7267

MEDICAL & SURGICAL SPLYS: Trusses, Orthopedic & Surgical

	CITY	ST	EMP	PHONE	ENTRY #
Arcam Cad To Metal Inc	Woburn	MA	F	781 281-1718	17121

MEDICAL & SURGICAL SPLYS: Walkers

	CITY	ST	EMP	PHONE	ENTRY #
Rrk Walker Inc	Mendon	MA	G	508 541-8100	12995

MEDICAL & SURGICAL SPLYS: Welders' Hoods

	CITY	ST	EMP	PHONE	ENTRY #
Fire & Iron	West Haven	CT	G	203 934-3756	5123
Web Home Phoenix Fabrication	Kingston	MA	G	781 424-8076	11967
Silver Lake Fabrication	Belmont	NH	G	603 630-5658	17683

MEDICAL EQPT REPAIR SVCS, NON-ELECTRIC

	CITY	ST	EMP	PHONE	ENTRY #
Inert Corporation	Amesbury	MA	E	978 462-4415	7492
Pioneer Vly Orthtics Prsthtics	West Springfield	MA	G	413 788-9655	16545

MEDICAL EQPT: Cardiographs

	CITY	ST	EMP	PHONE	ENTRY #
Mobile Sense Technologies Inc	Darien	CT	G	203 914-5375	1029

MEDICAL EQPT: Defibrillators

	CITY	ST	EMP	PHONE	ENTRY #
Defibtech LLC **(PA)**	Guilford	CT	D	866 333-4248	1700
Integer Holdings Corporation	Canton	MA	C	781 830-5800	9744
Sb Marketers Inc	Webster	MA	G	508 943-7162	16350
Zoll Medical Corporation **(HQ)**	Chelmsford	MA	A	978 421-9655	9942

MEDICAL EQPT: Diagnostic

	CITY	ST	EMP	PHONE	ENTRY #
Biorasis Inc	Storrs	CT	G	860 429-3592	4380
Cas Medical Systems Inc **(HQ)**	Branford	CT	D	203 488-6056	302
Catachem Inc	Oxford	CT	G	203 262-0330	3394
Hamilton Sndstrnd Space	Windsor Locks	CT	A	860 654-6000	5395
M G M Instruments Inc **(PA)**	Hamden	CT	E	203 248-4008	1768
Perosphere Technologies Inc	Danbury	CT	G	475 218-4600	967
Sekisui Diagnostics LLC	Stamford	CT	G	203 602-7777	4313
Sleep Management Solutions LLC **(HQ)**	Hartford	CT	F	888 497-5337	1871
Supernova Diagnostics Inc	New Canaan	CT	G	301 792-4345	2617
Tangen Biosciences Inc	Branford	CT	E	203 433-4045	354
149 Medical Inc	Bolton	MA	G	617 410-8123	8316
Aurora Imaging Technology Inc **(PA)**	Danvers	MA	E	877 975-7530	10198
Becton Dickinson and Company	Woburn	MA	B	781 935-5115	17128
Biodirection Inc	Southborough	MA	E	508 599-2400	15345
Biostage Inc	Holliston	MA	E	774 233-7300	11561
Cambridge Heart Inc **(PA)**	Foxborough	MA	E	978 654-7600	10912
Collaborative Med Concept LLC	Newton	MA	G	603 494-6056	13581
Cristcot Inc	Concord	MA	G	978 212-6380	10125
Cytyc Corporation **(HQ)**	Marlborough	MA	B	508 263-2900	12744
Cytyc Corporation	Marlborough	MA	C	508 303-4746	12745
Diamond Diagnostics Inc **(PA)**	Holliston	MA	D	508 429-0450	11567
Digital Cognition Tech Inc	Waltham	MA	E	617 433-1777	16087
Hamilton Thorne Inc **(PA)**	Beverly	MA	E	978 921-2050	8138
Image Stream Medical Inc	Littleton	MA	D	978 486-8494	12309
Image Stream Medical LLC	Harvard	MA	G	978 456-9087	11380
Instrumentation Laboratory Co **(DH)**	Bedford	MA	A	781 861-0710	7982
KS Manufacturing Inc	Allston	MA	D	508 427-5727	7468
Lantheus Medical Imaging Inc **(HQ)**	North Billerica	MA	B	800 362-2668	13832
Lantheus MI Intermediate Inc	North Billerica	MA	A	978 671-8001	13833
Mauna Kea Technologies Inc	Allston	MA	G	617 657-1550	7469
Medical Monofilament Mfg LLC	Plymouth	MA	G	508 746-7877	14565
Mindgraph Medical Inc	Andover	MA	G	508 904-2563	7571
Morgan Scientific Inc **(PA)**	Haverhill	MA	F	978 521-4440	11454
Nanoentek Inc	Waltham	MA	G	781 472-2558	16155
Ninepoint Medical Inc	Bedford	MA	G	617 250-7190	7994
Nix Inc	Allston	MA	G	617 458-9407	7472
Oxford Immunotec USA Inc	Marlborough	MA	D	833 682-6933	12805
Paradigm Biodevices Inc	Rockland	MA	G	781 982-9950	14818
Pointcare Technologies Inc	Marlborough	MA	E	508 281-6925	12808
Scion Medical Techologies LLC	Newton Upper Falls	MA	G	617 455-5186	13658
Sekisui Diagnostics LLC **(DH)**	Burlington	MA	C	781 652-7800	9336
Siemens Hlthcare Dgnostics Inc	Norwood	MA	C	781 551-7000	14198
Symptllgnce Med Infrmatics LLC	Franklin	MA	G	617 755-0576	11083
Tecomet Inc	Wilmington	MA	D	978 642-2400	17051
Tecomet Inc **(PA)**	Wilmington	MA	C	978 642-2400	17052
USA Renewable LLC	Newton	MA	G	617 319-7237	13645
Verax Biomedical Incorporated	Marlborough	MA	F	508 755-7029	12842
Windgap Medical Inc	Watertown	MA	G	617 440-3311	16330
Abbott Dgnstics Scrborough Inc **(DH)**	Scarborough	ME	D	207 730-5750	6901
Medical Resources Inc	Brunswick	ME	E	207 721-1110	5842
Physician Engineered Products	Fryeburg	ME	G	207 935-1256	6101
Spin Analytical Inc	Berwick	ME	G	207 704-0160	5712
Cytyc Corporation	Londonderry	NH	E	603 668-7688	18690
Imagene Technology Inc	Lebanon	NH	F	603 448-9940	18625
Lodestone Biomedical LLC	Lebanon	NH	G	617 686-5517	18628

	CITY	ST	EMP	PHONE	ENTRY #
American Access Care RI LLC	Providence	RI	G	401 277-9729	20952
Astronova Inc	West Warwick	RI	C	401 828-4000	21480
Unetixs Vascular Inc	North Kingstown	RI	E	401 583-0089	20748
Ascension Technology Corp	Shelburne	VT	E	802 893-6657	22411
Clarity Laboratories Inc	South Burlington	VT	G	802 658-6321	22443
Simmedtec LLC	Williston	VT	G	802 872-5968	22691

MEDICAL EQPT: Dialyzers

	CITY	ST	EMP	PHONE	ENTRY #
Nxstage Medical Inc **(DH)**	Lawrence	MA	B	978 687-4700	12067
Vasca Inc	Tewksbury	MA	E	978 640-0431	15847

MEDICAL EQPT: Electromedical Apparatus

	CITY	ST	EMP	PHONE	ENTRY #
Home Diagnostics Corp	Trumbull	CT	C	203 445-1170	4625
Novatek Medical Inc	Stamford	CT	G	203 356-0156	4263
Ram Technologies LLC	Guilford	CT	F	203 453-3916	1715
Teclens LLC	Stamford	CT	G	919 824-5224	4343
Tomtec Inc	Hamden	CT	D	203 281-6790	1790
United States Surgical Corp **(HQ)**	New Haven	CT	A	203 845-1000	2750
Abiomed Inc **(PA)**	Danvers	MA	B	978 646-1400	10189
Adherean Inc	Chestnut Hill	MA	G	617 652-0304	9981
Belmont Instrument LLC **(PA)**	Billerica	MA	E	978 663-0212	8218
Beta Bionics Inc	Boston	MA	F	949 293-2076	8403
Boston Microfluidics Inc	Cambridge	MA	E	857 239-9665	9419
Cardiovascular Instrument	Wakefield	MA	F	781 245-7799	15945
Conmed Corporation	Westborough	MA	C	508 366-3668	16608
Epidemic Solutions Inc	Westwood	MA	G	504 722-3818	16865
Excelitas Tech Holdg Corp	Waltham	MA	F	781 522-5914	16102
Micron Solutions Inc **(PA)**	Fitchburg	MA	G	978 345-5000	10838
Northeast Monitoring Inc	Maynard	MA	G	978 461-3992	12902
Pathmaker Neurosystems Inc	Boston	MA	G	617 968-3006	8768
Quanttus Inc	Newton	MA	G	617 401-2648	13628
Smith & Nephew Inc	Mansfield	MA	E	508 261-3600	12660

MEDICAL EQPT: Electrotherapeutic Apparatus

	CITY	ST	EMP	PHONE	ENTRY #
Loon Medical Inc	Tolland	CT	G	860 373-0217	4550
Cosman Medical LLC	Marlborough	MA	D	781 272-6561	12742
Obsidian Therapeutics Inc	Cambridge	MA	G	339 364-6721	9596

MEDICAL EQPT: Heart-Lung Machines, Exc Iron Lungs

	CITY	ST	EMP	PHONE	ENTRY #
Gys Tech LLC	Shirley	MA	F	530 613-9233	15084
Medtronic	Framingham	MA	G	508 739-0950	10984

MEDICAL EQPT: Laser Systems

	CITY	ST	EMP	PHONE	ENTRY #
Abbey Aesthetics LLC	Avon	CT	G	860 242-0497	30
Coherent Inc	Bloomfield	CT	E	860 243-9557	215
Dynamic Lasers LLC	New Milford	CT	G	866 731-9610	2797
Focus Medical LLC	Bethel	CT	G	203 730-8885	154
Jeffrey Gold	Hamden	CT	G	203 281-5737	1762
Pioneer Optics Company Inc	Bloomfield	CT	F	860 286-0071	251
Respond Systems	Branford	CT	F	203 481-2810	341
Safe Laser Therapy LLC	Stamford	CT	G	203 261-4400	4308
Star Tech Instruments Inc	New Fairfield	CT	G	203 312-0767	2627
149 Medical Inc	Bolton	MA	G	617 410-8123	8316
Candela Corporation **(DH)**	Marlborough	MA	C	508 969-1837	12734
Cynosure Inc **(HQ)**	Westford	MA	B	978 256-4200	16763
Novanta Inc **(PA)**	Bedford	MA	C	781 266-5700	7996
Palomar Medical Products LLC	Burlington	MA	C	781 993-2300	9316
Palomar Medical Tech LLC **(DH)**	Burlington	MA	E	781 993-2330	9317
Bmed Holding LLC	Durham	NH	G	603 868-1888	18075
Mbraun	Stratham	NH	D	603 773-9333	19874
Resonetics LLC **(PA)**	Nashua	NH	C	603 886-6772	19251

MEDICAL EQPT: MRI/Magnetic Resonance Imaging Devs, Nuclear

	CITY	ST	EMP	PHONE	ENTRY #
Eclipse Systems Inc	Branford	CT	G	203 483-0665	311
Aurora Healthcare US Corp	Danvers	MA	F	978 204-5240	10197
Bitome Inc	Jamaica Plain	MA	G	207 812-8099	11940
Centers of New England MRC	Haverhill	MA	G	978 241-8232	11414
Zhang Fengling	Acton	MA	G	978 289-8606	7395

MEDICAL EQPT: PET Or Position Emission Tomography Scanners

	CITY	ST	EMP	PHONE	ENTRY #
Caritas Pet Imaging LLC	Norwood	MA	G	508 259-8919	14139

MEDICAL EQPT: Pacemakers

	CITY	ST	EMP	PHONE	ENTRY #
Charlies Ride	Windsor Locks	CT	G	860 916-3637	5388
Pace Medical Inc	Lexington	MA	F	781 862-4242	12252

MEDICAL EQPT: Patient Monitoring

	CITY	ST	EMP	PHONE	ENTRY #
Intracranial Bioanalytics LLC	Woodbridge	CT	G	914 490-1524	5468
Ivy Biomedical Systems Inc	Branford	CT	E	203 481-4183	326
Nellcor Puritan Bennett LLC **(DH)**	Mansfield	MA	B	508 261-8000	12649
Ssquare Detect Medical Devices	Andover	MA	G	978 202-5707	7611

MEDICAL EQPT: TENS Units/Transcutaneous Elec Nerve Stimulatr

	CITY	ST	EMP	PHONE	ENTRY #
Brainwave Science LLC	Southborough	MA	G	774 760-1678	15351

MEDICAL EQPT: Ultrasonic Scanning Devices

	CITY	ST	EMP	PHONE	ENTRY #
Non-Invasive Med Systems LLC	Stamford	CT	G	914 462-0701	4260
Arteriocyte Med Systems Inc **(HQ)**	Hopkinton	MA	E	866 660-2674	11691
Axiomed Spine Corporation **(PA)**	Malden	MA	F	978 232-3990	12560
Beltronics Inc	Needham	MA	F	617 244-8696	13293
Bewell Body Scan	Chestnut Hill	MA	G	617 754-0300	9982
Bioview	Billerica	MA	G	978 670-4741	8219
Clozex Medical Inc	Wellesley	MA	G	781 237-1673	16365
Inanovate Inc	Wellesley	MA	G	617 610-1712	16367
Medcool Inc	Wellesley	MA	G	617 512-4530	16372
Neutron Therapeutics Inc	Danvers	MA	E	978 326-8999	10243
Solace Therapeutics Inc	Framingham	MA	G	508 283-1200	11006
Solx Inc	Sudbury	MA	G	978 808-6926	15668

	CITY	ST	EMP	PHONE	ENTRY #
Teratech Corporation	Burlington	MA	E	781 270-4143	9344
Vittamed Corporation **(PA)**	Westford	MA	G	617 977-4536	16799

MEDICAL EQPT: Ultrasonic, Exc Cleaning

	CITY	ST	EMP	PHONE	ENTRY #
Legnos Medical Inc	Groton	CT	F	860 446-8058	1680
Biolucent LLC	Marlborough	MA	G	508 263-2900	12726
Hologic Inc **(PA)**	Marlborough	MA	C	508 263-2900	12771
Hologic Inc	Marlborough	MA	C	508 263-2900	12769
NSM Marketing Inc	Medfield	MA	G	508 359-5297	12915

MEDICAL EQPT: X-Ray Apparatus & Tubes, Radiographic

	CITY	ST	EMP	PHONE	ENTRY #
High Energy X-Rays Intl Corp	Wallingford	CT	G	203 909-9777	4751
Lorad Corporation	Danbury	CT	C	203 790-5544	950
Qsa Global Inc **(HQ)**	Burlington	MA	D	781 272-2000	9325

MEDICAL EQPT: X-Ray Apparatus & Tubes, Therapeutic

	CITY	ST	EMP	PHONE	ENTRY #
Finch Therapeutics Inc	Somerville	MA	G	617 229-6499	15171

MEDICAL FIELD ASSOCIATION

	CITY	ST	EMP	PHONE	ENTRY #
Massachusetts Medical Society **(PA)**	Waltham	MA	B	781 893-4610	16148

MEDICAL SUNDRIES: Rubber

	CITY	ST	EMP	PHONE	ENTRY #
Cataki International Inc	Wareham	MA	E	508 295-9630	16243
Cara Incorporated	Warwick	RI	G	401 732-6535	21339

MEDICAL X-RAY MACHINES & TUBES WHOLESALERS

	CITY	ST	EMP	PHONE	ENTRY #
Aadco Medical Inc	Randolph	VT	D	802 728-3400	22296

MEDICAL, DENTAL & HOSPITAL EQPT, WHOL: Hosptl Eqpt/Furniture

	CITY	ST	EMP	PHONE	ENTRY #
Hitachi Aloka Medical Ltd	Wallingford	CT	D	203 269-5088	4752
Hitachi Aloka Medical Amer Inc	Wallingford	CT	D	203 269-5088	4753
Marel Corporation	West Haven	CT	F	203 934-8187	5135

MEDICAL, DENTAL & HOSPITAL EQPT, WHOL: Surgical Eqpt & Splys

	CITY	ST	EMP	PHONE	ENTRY #
Boston Endo-Surgical Tech LLC	Bridgeport	CT	D	203 336-6479	385
Precision Engineered Pdts LLC	Bridgeport	CT	G	203 336-6479	473
Boston Medical Products Inc	Shrewsbury	MA	E	508 898-9300	15105
Braintree Scientific Inc	Braintree	MA	G	781 348-0768	8993
Image Stream Medical Inc	Littleton	MA	D	978 486-8494	12309
Rachiotek LLC	Wellesley	MA	G	407 923-0721	16383

MEDICAL, DENTAL & HOSPITAL EQPT, WHOLESALE: Diagnostic, Med

	CITY	ST	EMP	PHONE	ENTRY #
Cellanyx Diagnostics LLC	Beverly	MA	G	571 212-9991	8114
Diamond Diagnostics Inc **(PA)**	Holliston	MA	D	508 429-0450	11567
FDA Group LLC	North Grafton	MA	F	413 330-7476	13960
M R Resources Inc	Fitchburg	MA	E	978 696-3060	10831

MEDICAL, DENTAL & HOSPITAL EQPT, WHOLESALE: Med Eqpt & Splys

	CITY	ST	EMP	PHONE	ENTRY #
Contemporary Products LLC	Middletown	CT	E	860 346-9283	2182
Bl Healthcare Inc	Foxboro	MA	G	508 543-4150	10877
Gyrus Acmi LLC **(DH)**	Southborough	MA	C	508 804-2600	15359
Inert Corporation	Amesbury	MA	E	978 462-4415	7492
Baker Company Inc **(PA)**	Sanford	ME	C	207 324-8773	6871
Austin Medical Products Inc	Center Conway	NH	G	603 356-7004	17792
White Mountain Imaging	Concord	NH	F	603 228-2630	17940

MEDICAL, DENTAL & HOSPITAL EQPT, WHOLESALE: Medical Lab

	CITY	ST	EMP	PHONE	ENTRY #
Origio Midatlantic Devices Inc	Trumbull	CT	E	856 762-2000	4629
Nanofuse Biologics LLC	Malden	MA	F	978 232-3990	12584

MELTING POTS: Glasshouse, Clay

	CITY	ST	EMP	PHONE	ENTRY #
Contact Inc	Edgecomb	ME	G	207 882-6116	6001

MEMBERSHIP ORGANIZATIONS, BUSINESS: Growers' Association

	CITY	ST	EMP	PHONE	ENTRY #
Decas Cranberry Products Inc	Carver	MA	E	508 866-8506	9804

MEMBERSHIP ORGANIZATIONS, NEC: Charitable

	CITY	ST	EMP	PHONE	ENTRY #
Pharmate Inc	Cambridge	MA	G	617 800-5804	9610
Hinesburg Record	Hinesburg	VT	F	802 482-2350	22028

MEMBERSHIP ORGANIZATIONS, PROFESSIONAL: Health Association

	CITY	ST	EMP	PHONE	ENTRY #
Massachusetts Medical Society	Boston	MA	E	617 734-9800	8685

MEMBERSHIP ORGS, RELIGIOUS: Non-Denominational Church

	CITY	ST	EMP	PHONE	ENTRY #
Community of Jesus Inc **(PA)**	Orleans	MA	D	508 255-1094	14232

MEMORIES: Solid State

	CITY	ST	EMP	PHONE	ENTRY #
Amicus Hlthcare Lving Ctrs LLC	North Chelmsford	MA	E	978 934-0000	13884

MEN'S & BOYS' CLOTHING ACCESS STORES

	CITY	ST	EMP	PHONE	ENTRY #
Baileyworks Inc	Newmarket	NH	G	603 292-6485	19330

MEN'S & BOYS' CLOTHING STORES

	CITY	ST	EMP	PHONE	ENTRY #
Evergreen Enterprises Inc	Berkley	MA	G	508 823-2377	8086
Pvh Corp	Wrentham	MA	F	508 384-0070	17527

MEN'S & BOYS' CLOTHING WHOLESALERS, NEC

	CITY	ST	EMP	PHONE	ENTRY #
Accurate Services Inc	Fall River	MA	E	508 674-5773	10650
Advanced Print Technology Inc	Fitchburg	MA	G	978 342-0093	10809
New York Accessory Group Inc	Bristol	RI	D	401 245-6096	20095

MEN'S & BOYS' SPORTSWEAR CLOTHING STORES

	CITY	ST	EMP	PHONE	ENTRY #
Sew What Embroidery	Dalton	MA	G	413 684-0672	10184
Chuck Roast Equipment Inc **(PA)**	Conway	NH	E	603 447-5492	17951

PRODUCT

MEN'S & BOYS' SPORTSWEAR WHOLESALERS

	CITY	ST	EMP	PHONE	ENTRY #
Del Arbour LLC	Milford	CT	F	203 882-8501	2274
Gg Sportswear Inc	Hartford	CT	E	860 296-4441	1825
Sew What Embroidery	Dalton	MA	G	413 684-0672	10184
Gsg Inc	Shelburne	VT	G	802 828-6221	22418

MEN'S CLOTHING STORES: Everyday, Exc Suits & Sportswear

	CITY	ST	EMP	PHONE	ENTRY #
Theatre Stricken Apparel LLC	Bellingham	MA	G	978 325-2335	8060

METAL COMPONENTS: Prefabricated

	CITY	ST	EMP	PHONE	ENTRY #
Rwt Corporation	Madison	CT	E	203 245-2731	1973
Custom Machine LLC	Woburn	MA	F	781 935-4940	17157
Green Brothers Fabricating	Taunton	MA	E	508 880-3608	15756

METAL FABRICATORS: Architechtural

	CITY	ST	EMP	PHONE	ENTRY #
Company of Craftsmen	Mystic	CT	G	860 536-4189	2436
Dyco Industries Inc	South Windsor	CT	E	860 289-4957	3958
East Windsor Metal Fabg Inc	South Windsor	CT	F	860 528-7107	3961
Eastern Metal Works Inc	Milford	CT	E	203 878-6995	2281
F & L Iron Work Inc	New Haven	CT	G	203 777-0751	2687
Ida International Inc	Derby	CT	E	203 736-9249	1074
International Pipe & Stl Corp	North Branford	CT	F	203 481-7102	2969
Jozef Custom Ironworks Inc	Bridgeport	CT	F	203 384-6363	437
Kammetal Inc **(PA)**	Naugatuck	CT	E	718 722-9991	2482
Kenneth Lynch & Sons Inc	Oxford	CT	G	203 762-8363	3411
Leed - Himmel Industries Inc	Hamden	CT	D	203 288-8484	1766
Leek Building Products Inc	Norwalk	CT	E	203 853-3883	3185
Lpg Metal Crafts LLC	Plainville	CT	G	860 982-3573	3502
Luckey LLC	New Haven	CT	F	203 285-3819	2709
Magic Industries Inc	Bozrah	CT	F	860 949-8380	281
Shepard Steel Co Inc **(PA)**	Hartford	CT	D	860 525-4446	1869
Shepard Steel Co Inc	Newington	CT	E	860 525-4446	2902
Stamford Forge & Metal Cft Inc	Stamford	CT	G	203 348-8290	4330
Susan Martovich	Oxford	CT	G	203 881-1848	3426
Boston Forging & Welding Corp	Boston	MA	G	617 567-2300	8430
Boston Retail Products Inc **(PA)**	Medford	MA	C	781 395-7417	12923
Clayton LLC	Woburn	MA	E	617 250-8500	17144
Concentric Fabrication LLC	Somerset	MA	G	774 955-5692	15142
Concentric Fabrication LLC	Middleboro	MA	F	508 672-4098	13059
G&E Steel Fabricators Inc	Salem	MA	F	978 741-0391	14913
Jeff Schiff	Chelsea	MA	G	617 887-0202	9956
Kamrowski Refinishing Co Inc	Framingham	MA	F	508 877-0367	10975
Make Architectural Metalworking	West Wareham	MA	F	508 273-7603	16575
Ninos Ironworks	Everett	MA	G	617 389-6603	10623
Pbd Productions LLC	Hopedale	MA	F	508 482-9300	11679
Period Lighting Fixtures Inc	Clarksburg	MA	F	413 664-7141	10074
Rens Welding & Fabricating	Taunton	MA	F	508 828-1702	15779
Ryan Iron Works Inc	Raynham	MA	E	508 821-2058	14729
Santini Brothers Ir Works Inc	Medford	MA	F	781 396-1450	12947
Southstern Mtal Fbricators Inc	Rockland	MA	E	781 878-1505	14826
Village Forge Inc	Boston	MA	F	617 361-2591	8911
W and D Enterprise Inc	Millville	MA	G	508 883-4811	13188
Welch Welding and Trck Eqp Inc	North Chelmsford	MA	E	978 251-8726	13913
Bradbury Mtn Metalworks LLC	Pownal	ME	G	207 688-5009	6748
Cives Corporation	Augusta	ME	C	207 622-6141	5605
Sigco LLC **(DH)**	Westbrook	ME	C	207 775-2676	7208
Sigco LLC	Westbrook	ME	E	207 775-2676	7207
Asca Inc **(PA)**	Portsmouth	NH	E	603 433-6700	19539
Custom Welding & Fabrications	West Nottingham	NH	F	603 942-5170	19964
Greenfield Industries Inc	Amherst	NH	G	603 883-6423	17565
Morris and Butler	North Hampton	NH	D	603 918-0355	19385
Plp Composite Technologies	Fitzwilliam	NH	E	603 585-9100	18152
Upnovr Inc	Pelham	NH	E	603 625-8639	19452
Providence Welding	Providence	RI	G	401 941-2700	21100
Hubbardton Forge LLC	Castleton	VT	C	802 468-3090	21828
S & A Trombley Corporation	Morrisville	VT	E	802 888-2394	22176

METAL FABRICATORS: Plate

	CITY	ST	EMP	PHONE	ENTRY #
Containment Solutions Inc	Simsbury	CT	C	860 651-4371	3898
CTI Industries Inc **(HQ)**	Orange	CT	E	203 795-0070	3362
Hi-Tech Fabricating Inc	Cheshire	CT	E	203 284-0894	737
Johnstone Company Inc	North Haven	CT	E	203 239-5834	3036
Mitchell-Bate Company	Waterbury	CT	E	203 233-0862	4918
United Steel Inc	East Hartford	CT	C	860 289-2323	1232
Vulcan Industries Inc	Windsor	CT	C	860 683-2005	5377
Advanced Materials Processing	Lowell	MA	G	978 251-3060	12339
All Metal Fabricators Inc	Acton	MA	F	978 263-3904	7337
All Steel Fabricating Inc	North Grafton	MA	E	508 839-4471	13958
Contech Engnered Solutions LLC	Woburn	MA	F	781 932-4201	17150
Contech Engnered Solutions LLC	Palmer	MA	E	413 283-7611	14285
Cotter Corporation	Danvers	MA	E	978 774-6777	10207
Credit Card Supplies Corp	Marlborough	MA	F	508 485-4230	12743
Franklin County Fabricators	Greenfield	MA	G	413 774-3518	11261
Gill Metal Fab Inc	Brockton	MA	E	508 580-4445	9151
Gregory Engineering Corp	Marlborough	MA	F	508 481-0480	12765
H & H Engineering Co Inc	Methuen	MA	F	978 682-0567	13025
Heat Fab Inc	Turners Falls	MA	D	413 863-2242	15878
Industrial Stl Boiler Svcs Inc	Chicopee	MA	E	413 532-7788	10032
Lytron Incorporated	Woburn	MA	G	781 933-7300	17220
Mass Engineering & Tank Inc	Middleboro	MA	E	508 947-8669	13068
Mass Tank Sales Corp	Middleboro	MA	E	508 947-8826	13069
Riley Power Inc	Worcester	MA	C	508 852-7100	17459
Taco Inc	Fall River	MA	D	508 675-7300	10769
Thermatron Engineering Inc	Methuen	MA	E	978 687-8844	13046
Triangle Engineering Inc	Hanover	MA	F	781 878-1500	11356
Waste Water Evaporators Inc	Wilmington	MA	G	978 256-3259	17065
Contech Engnered Solutions LLC	Scarborough	ME	E	207 885-9830	6915
Knowlton Machine Company	Gorham	ME	E	207 854-8471	6117
William Smith Enterprises Inc	Sidney	ME	G	207 549-3103	6966
Custom Welding & Fabrications	West Nottingham	NH	F	603 942-5170	19964
Gilchrist Metal Fabg Co Inc **(PA)**	Hudson	NH	E	603 889-2600	18392
Greenfield Industries Inc	Amherst	NH	G	603 883-6423	17565
Laars Heating Systems Company	Rochester	NH	C	603 335-6300	19677
Tsi Group Inc **(DH)**	Hampton	NH	E	603 964-0296	18275
Valley Welding & Fabg Inc	Hollis	NH	E	603 465-3266	18340
Vette Thermal Solutions LLC	Pelham	NH	D	603 635-2800	19453
Amtrol Intl Investments Inc **(DH)**	West Warwick	RI	G	401 884-6300	21478
Modine Manufacturing Company	West Kingston	RI	D	401 792-1231	21467
Stackbin Corporation	Lincoln	RI	E	401 333-1600	20597
Leader Evaporator Co Inc **(PA)**	Swanton	VT	D	802 868-5444	22531

METAL FABRICATORS: Sheet

	CITY	ST	EMP	PHONE	ENTRY #
A B & F Sheet Metal	Cheshire	CT	G	203 272-9340	707
A G C Incorporated **(PA)**	Meriden	CT	C	203 235-3361	2072
Advanced Sheetmetal Assoc LLC	Middlefield	CT	E	860 349-1644	2161
Advantage Sheet Metal Mfg LLC	Naugatuck	CT	E	203 720-0929	2457
Aerocor Inc	East Windsor	CT	F	860 281-9274	1275
American Cladding Technologies	East Granby	CT	G	860 413-3098	1116
American Performance Pdts LLC	Wallingford	CT	G	203 269-4468	4697
Ansonia Stl Fabrication Co Inc	Beacon Falls	CT	E	203 888-4509	53
B L C Investments Inc	Milford	CT	G	203 877-1888	2249
Bantam Sheet Metal	Bantam	CT	G	860 567-9690	52
Bull Metal Products Inc	Middletown	CT	E	860 346-9691	2180
Carlson Sheet Metal	New Milford	CT	G	860 354-4660	2791
Clemson Sheet Metal LLC	Vernon Rockville	CT	G	860 871-9369	4680
Connecticut Fabricating Co Inc	Milford	CT	G	203 878-3465	2268
Croteau Development Group Inc	Stafford Springs	CT	G	860 684-3605	4107
Custom & Precision Pdts Inc	Hamden	CT	G	203 281-0818	1740
Dasco Welded Products Inc	Waterbury	CT	F	203 754-9353	4864
Dyco Industries Inc	South Windsor	CT	E	860 289-4957	3958
Fonda Fabricating & Welding Co	Plainville	CT	G	860 793-0601	3489
Hamden Sheet Metal Inc	Hamden	CT	G	203 776-1472	1757
Hi-Tech Fabricating Inc	Cheshire	CT	E	203 284-0894	737
Illinois Tool Works Inc	Naugatuck	CT	E	203 720-1676	2479
J M Sheet Metal LLC	Plainville	CT	G	860 747-5537	3498
J OConnor LLC	Newington	CT	F	860 665-7702	2873
Labco Welding Inc	Middletown	CT	G	860 632-2625	2200
Leek Building Products Inc	Norwalk	CT	E	203 853-3883	3185
M Cubed Technologies Inc **(HQ)**	Newtown	CT	E	203 304-2940	2928
McMullin Manufacturing Corp	Brookfield	CT	E	203 740-3360	651
Midget Louver Company Inc	Milford	CT	G	203 783-1444	2315
Mrnd LLC	Enfield	CT	G	860 749-0256	1370
Progressive Sheetmetal LLC	South Windsor	CT	E	860 436-9884	4006
Reliable Welding & Speed LLC	Enfield	CT	G	860 749-3977	1379
Seconn Automation Solutions	Waterford	CT	F	860 442-4325	4992
Shoreline Metal Services LLC	East Haven	CT	G	203 466-7372	1261
Sound Manufacturing Inc	Old Saybrook	CT	D	860 388-4466	3350
Stauffer Sheet Metal LLC	Windsor	CT	G	860 623-0518	5369
Suraci Corp	New Haven	CT	D	203 624-1345	2741
Target Custom Manufacturing Co	Old Saybrook	CT	G	860 388-5848	3352
Tech-Air Incorporated	Uncasville	CT	E	860 848-1287	4649
Thomas La Ganga	Torrington	CT	G	860 489-0920	4601
Trumpf Photonics Inc	Farmington	CT	G	860 255-6000	1519
United Steel Inc	East Hartford	CT	C	860 289-2323	1232
United Stts Sgn & Fbrction	Trumbull	CT	E	203 601-1000	4640
Vernier Metal Fabricating Inc	Seymour	CT	D	203 881-3133	3767
Vulcan Industries Inc	Windsor	CT	C	860 683-2005	5377
Wendon Technologies Inc	Stamford	CT	D	203 348-6271	4358
Whitcraft LLC **(PA)**	Eastford	CT	C	860 974-0786	1315
Whitcraft Scrborough/Tempe LLC **(HQ)**	Eastford	CT	C	860 974-0786	1316
A & M Welding Fabrication Inc	East Weymouth	MA	G	781 335-9548	10532
A G Miller Company Inc	Springfield	MA	E	413 732-9297	15438
Absolute Sheet Metal	Billerica	MA	E	978 667-0236	8204
Accufab Inc	Waltham	MA	G	781 894-5737	16021
Advanced Metal Systems Corp	Holliston	MA	G	508 429-0480	11556
All Metal Fabricators Inc	Acton	MA	F	978 263-3904	7337
American Sheet Metal LLC	Salisbury	MA	E	978 578-8360	14948
Arcam Cad To Metal Inc	Woburn	MA	F	781 281-1718	17121
Auciello Iron Works Inc **(PA)**	Hudson	MA	E	978 568-8382	11758
B&J Sheet Metal	Hyde Park	MA	G	617 590-2295	11862
Bedard Sheet Metal Company	Westfield	MA	G	413 572-3774	16672
Bomco Inc	Gloucester	MA	C	978 283-9000	11167
Boston Forging & Welding Corp	Boston	MA	G	617 567-2300	8430
Bryant Sheet Metal & Cnstr	Hanover	MA	G	781 826-4113	11331
Cambridgeport	Randolph	MA	G	781 302-3347	14672
Cambridgeport Air Systems Inc	Georgetown	MA	C	978 465-8481	11139
Central Vacuum Cleaners **(PA)**	Methuen	MA	F	978 682-5294	13013
Central Vacuum Cleaners	Lawrence	MA	G	978 682-5295	12004
Chicopee Welding & Tool Inc	Charlemont	MA	F	413 598-8215	9819
Columbia ASC Inc	Lawrence	MA	F	978 683-2205	12012
Connell Limited Partnership **(PA)**	Boston	MA	F	617 737-2700	8481
Crosby Machine Company Inc	West Brookfield	MA	G	508 867-3121	16468
Cunniff Corp **(PA)**	East Falmouth	MA	G	508 540-6232	10440
Daves Sheet Metal Inc	Dracut	MA	G	978 454-3144	10357
Dimark Incorporated	Whitman	MA	E	781 447-7990	16923
E T Duval & Son Inc	Leominster	MA	G	978 537-7596	12134
Electrnic Shtmtal Crftsmen Inc	Stoughton	MA	E	781 341-3260	15586
Essex Engineering Inc	Lynn	MA	E	781 595-2114	12506
Eugene F Delfino Company Inc	Chelmsford	MA	G	978 221-6496	9897
Excell Solutions Inc	North Billerica	MA	G	978 663-6100	13813
Expansion Opportunities Inc	Northborough	MA	E	508 303-8200	14033
Far Industries Inc	Assonet	MA	F	508 644-3122	7679

	CITY	ST	EMP	PHONE	ENTRY #
First Quality Metal Products	Plympton	MA	G	781 585-5820	14591
Francer Industries Inc	East Weymouth	MA	E	781 337-2882	10542
Franklin Sheet Metal Works Inc	Franklin	MA	G	508 528-3600	11048
Gerald F Dalton & Sons Inc	North Easton	MA	G	508 238-5374	13945
Gill Metal Fab Inc	Brockton	MA	E	508 580-4445	9151
Green Brothers Fabricating	Taunton	MA	E	508 880-3608	15756
Harrington Air Systems LLC	Watertown	MA	E	781 341-1999	16290
Helfrich Bros Boiler Works Inc	Lawrence	MA	E	978 975-2464	12033
Herfco Inc	Shirley	MA	E	978 772-4758	15086
Hi-Tech Metals Inc	Bellingham	MA	D	508 966-0332	8040
Hoodco Systems Inc	Tewksbury	MA	F	978 851-7473	15818
Industrial Metal Pdts Co Inc	Sharon	MA	D	781 762-3330	15052
J & B Metal Products Company	Saugus	MA	G	781 233-7506	14988
Jay Engineering Corp	Chelmsford	MA	F	978 250-0115	9907
Kennedy Sheet Metal Inc	East Weymouth	MA	E	781 331-7764	10543
Kent Pearce	East Wareham	MA	G	508 295-3791	10531
Kevin Bonney	Pembroke	MA	G	781 826-6439	14414
Kleeberg Sheet Metal Inc	Ludlow	MA	D	413 589-1854	12470
L & L Race Cars	Tyngsboro	MA	G	978 420-7852	15892
Lehi Sheet Metal Corporation	Westborough	MA	E	508 366-8550	16632
Lyman Sheet Metal Co Inc	Southampton	MA	G	413 527-0848	15340
Malone Brothers Inc	Swansea	MA	G	508 379-3662	15708
Marblehead Engineering	Essex	MA	F	978 432-1386	10595
Mestek Inc	Westfield	MA	B	413 568-9571	16702
Metal Men	Chicopee	MA	F	413 533-0513	10045
Metal Solutions LLC	Millbury	MA	G	774 276-0096	13171
Metfab Engineering Inc	Attleboro Falls	MA	E	508 695-1007	7815
MLS Sheet Metal LLC	Bedford	MA	F	781 275-2265	7992
Modern Sheetmetal Inc	Worcester	MA	G	508 798-6665	17422
Moseley Corporation	Franklin	MA	E	508 520-4004	11068
New England Laser Inc	Peabody	MA	G	978 587-3914	14356
New England Metalform Inc	Plainville	MA	E	508 695-9340	14530
New England Sheets LLC **(PA)**	Devens	MA	F	978 487-2500	10326
New-Com Metal Products Corp	Randolph	MA	E	781 767-7520	14691
Newstamp Lighting Corp	North Easton	MA	F	508 238-7073	13949
Norwood Sheet Metal Corp	Norwood	MA	F	781 762-0720	14184
Noyes Sheet Metal	Milford	MA	F	508 482-9302	13134
Omg Inc **(DH)**	Agawam	MA	B	413 789-0252	7443
P M S Manufactured Pdts Inc	Gloucester	MA	F	978 281-2600	11200
Parker-Hannifin Corporation	Woburn	MA	B	781 935-4850	17257
Payne Engrg Fabrication Co Inc	Canton	MA	E	781 828-9046	9765
Phoenix Sheet Metal	South Dartmouth	MA	G	508 994-4046	15242
Prima North America Inc	Chicopee	MA	G	413 598-5200	10053
Quality Air Metals Inc	Holbrook	MA	E	781 986-9967	11537
Quincy Steel & Welding Co Inc	Quincy	MA	G	617 472-1180	14651
R I Baker Co Inc **(PA)**	Clarksburg	MA	E	413 663-3791	10075
R R Leduc Corp	Holyoke	MA	E	413 536-4329	11649
Ralph Seaver	Cherry Valley	MA	G	508 892-9486	9976
Rhode Island Sheet Metal	Rehoboth	MA	G	508 557-1140	14759
Ricks Sheet Metal Inc	Fall River	MA	G	774 488-9576	10758
Riverside Sheet Metal & Contg	Medford	MA	F	781 396-0070	12946
Roar Industries Inc	Holliston	MA	F	508 429-5952	11599
Roberts Enterprises Inc	Brookfield	MA	F	508 867-7640	9191
Salem Metal Inc	Middleton	MA	E	978 774-2100	13100
Standex International Corp	North Billerica	MA	D	978 667-2771	13869
Sx Industries Inc **(PA)**	Stoughton	MA	E	781 828-7111	15625
Tech-Etch Inc	Fall River	MA	D	508 675-5757	10770
Techni-Products Inc	East Longmeadow	MA	E	413 525-6321	10497
Tecomet Inc **(PA)**	Wilmington	MA	C	978 642-2400	17052
Thermo Craft Engineering Corp	Lynn	MA	E	781 599-4023	12543
Thl-Nortek Investors LLC **(PA)**	Boston	MA	D	617 227-1050	8882
Todrin Industries Inc	Lakeville	MA	F	508 946-3600	11979
US Sheetmetal Inc	West Bridgewater	MA	G	508 427-0500	16463
Vortex Inc	Peabody	MA	D	978 535-8721	14381
Waynes Sheet Metal Inc	Rehoboth	MA	G	508 431-8057	14762
Weiss Sheet Metal Inc	Avon	MA	E	508 583-8300	7901
Welch Welding and Trck Eqp Inc	North Chelmsford	MA	E	978 251-8726	13913
Weld Rite	Jamaica Plain	MA	G	617 524-9747	11951
Welding Craftsmen Co Inc	South Easton	MA	F	508 230-7878	15295
Welfab Inc	North Billerica	MA	E	978 667-0180	13876
Wireway/Husky Corp	Sterling	MA	E	978 422-6716	15550
Wrobel Engineering Co Inc	Avon	MA	D	508 586-8338	7903
Bob Walker Inc	Standish	ME	F	207 642-2083	7060
Eagle Industries Inc	Hollis Center	ME	E	207 929-3700	6199
Ekto Manufacturing Corp	Sanford	ME	E	207 324-4427	6874
Knowlton Machine Company	Gorham	ME	E	207 854-8471	6117
MC Faulkner & Sons Inc	Buxton	ME	F	207 929-4545	5858
North E Wldg & Fabrication Inc	Auburn	ME	E	207 786-2446	5583
Prescott Metal **(PA)**	Biddeford	ME	E	207 283-0115	5759
Ridlons Metal Shop	Casco	ME	G	207 655-7997	5896
S & D Sheet Metal Inc	Auburn	ME	G	207 777-7338	5596
Sweeney Ridge	Edgecomb	ME	G	207 482-0499	6004
Tri Star Sheet Metal Company	Turner	ME	F	207 225-2043	7110
William Smith Enterprises Inc	Sidney	ME	G	207 549-3103	6966
Zekes Sheet Metal	Scarborough	ME	G	207 883-3877	6943
Albert Landry	Nashua	NH	G	603 883-1919	19108
April Metalworks	Hudson	NH	G	603 883-1510	18374
Barett and Gould Inc	Hillsborough	NH	F	603 464-6400	18314
Custom Welding & Fabrications	West Nottingham	NH	F	603 942-5170	19964
D D G Fabrication	Nashua	NH	G	603 883-9292	19142
East Coast Metal Works Co Inc	Kingston	NH	G	603 642-9600	18543
Evs New Hampshire Inc	Keene	NH	D	603 352-3000	18502
Gerlach Sheet Metal	Manchester	NH	G	603 782-6136	18827
Gilchrist Metal Fabg Co Inc **(PA)**	Hudson	NH	E	603 889-2600	18392
Greenfield Industries Inc	Amherst	NH	G	603 883-6423	17565
Hi-Tech Fabricators Inc	Milford	NH	F	603 672-3766	19059
Inofab LLC	Pittsfield	NH	G	603 435-5082	19501
Jsp Fabrication Inc	Charlestown	NH	G	603 826-3868	17816
Keebowil Inc **(PA)**	Keene	NH	D	603 352-4232	18509
LAD Welding & Fabrication	Concord	NH	F	603 228-6617	17911
McNally Industries Inc	Wilton	NH	G	603 654-5361	19983
Metal Works Inc	Londonderry	NH	D	603 332-9323	18721
Profile Metal Forming Inc **(HQ)**	Newmarket	NH	E	603 659-8323	19337
Progressive Manufacturing Inc	West Lebanon	NH	F	603 298-5778	19960
Prototek Shtmtal Fbrcation LLC **(PA)**	Contoocook	NH	D	603 746-2001	17947
Rapid Group	Nashua	NH	F	603 821-7300	19245
Rapid Manufacturing Group LLC	Nashua	NH	B	603 402-4020	19246
Rapid Sheet Metal LLC	Nashua	NH	D	603 821-5300	19247
S & H Precision Mfg Co Inc **(PA)**	Newmarket	NH	E	603 659-8323	19339
Sparton Technology Corp	Hudson	NH	D	603 880-3692	18439
Standard Machine & Arms	Contoocook	NH	G	603 746-3562	17949
Superior Sheet Metal LLC	Hudson	NH	F	603 577-8620	18443
Technical Machine Components	Hudson	NH	F	603 880-0444	18445
Tnd Inc	Pelham	NH	G	603 595-4795	19451
Total Air Supply Inc	Nashua	NH	E	603 889-0100	19274
Tri C Manufacturing Inc	East Kingston	NH	G	603 642-8448	18092
Triangle Sheet Metal Inc	Meredith	NH	G	603 393-6770	18980
Tsi Group Inc **(DH)**	Hampton	NH	E	603 964-0296	18275
Upcycle Solutions Inc	Londonderry	NH	G	603 809-6843	18743
Valley Welding & Fabg Inc	Hollis	NH	E	603 465-3266	18340
Ward Fabrication Inc	Sandown	NH	G	603 382-9700	19788
Will-Mor Manufacturing Inc	Seabrook	NH	D	603 474-8971	19823
Alloy Holdings LLC	Providence	RI	E	401 353-7500	20951
Champlin Welding Inc	Narragansett	RI	G	401 782-4099	20636
Ferguson Perforating Company **(DH)**	Providence	RI	D	401 941-8876	21013
Frank J Newman & Son Inc	Johnston	RI	G	401 231-0550	20511
GA Rel Manufacturing Company	Providence	RI	E	401 331-5455	21019
Lightship Group LLC **(PA)**	North Kingstown	RI	E	401 294-3341	20723
Microweld Co Inc	Riverside	RI	G	401 438-5985	21172
Morris & Broms LLC	Cranston	RI	F	401 781-3134	20265
Providence Welding	Providence	RI	G	401 941-2700	21100
Renaissance Sheet Metal L	North Kingstown	RI	G	401 294-3703	20737
Robert B Evans Inc	Westerly	RI	G	401 596-2719	21538
Stackbin Corporation	Lincoln	RI	E	401 333-1600	20597
Gloucester Associates Inc	Barre	VT	E	802 479-1088	21617
Keebowil Inc	Rutland	VT	E	802 775-3572	22342
Kimtek Corporation	Orleans	VT	G	802 754-9000	22248
Milton Vermont Sheet Metal Inc	Milton	VT	D	802 893-1581	22134

METAL FABRICATORS: Structural, Ship

Techprecision Corporation **(PA)**	Westminster	MA	G	978 874-0591	16815

METAL FABRICATORS: Structural, Ship

New England Bridge Products	Lynn	MA	G	781 592-2444	12527
Casco Bay Steel Structures Inc	South Portland	ME	F	207 780-6722	7019

METAL FINISHING SVCS

Accurate Burring Company	Plainville	CT	F	860 747-8640	3463
Allied Metal Finishing L L C	South Windsor	CT	G	860 290-8865	3934
Anodic Incorporated	Stevenson	CT	F	203 268-9966	4374
Connecticut Anodizing Finshg	Bridgeport	CT	E	203 367-1765	400
Deburr Co	Plantsville	CT	E	860 621-6634	3529
Eyelet Crafters Inc	Waterbury	CT	D	203 757-9221	4871
J H Metal Finishing Inc **(PA)**	New Britain	CT	G	860 223-6412	2545
Lake Grinding Company	Bridgeport	CT	G	203 336-3767	444
Plainville Electro Plating Co	Hartford	CT	G	860 525-5328	1858
Quality Rolling Deburring Inc	Thomaston	CT	D	860 283-0271	4511
Reliable Plating & Polsg Co	Bridgeport	CT	E	203 366-5261	481
Scotts Metal Finishing LLC	Bristol	CT	F	860 589-3778	612
Suraci Metal Finishing LLC	New Haven	CT	E	203 624-1345	2742
Technical Metal Finishing Inc	Wallingford	CT	E	203 284-7825	4815
Accurate Metal Finishing Corp	Randolph	MA	E	781 963-7300	14668
Bob Bergeron	Georgetown	MA	G	978 352-7615	11138
Bradford Finshg Powdr Coat Inc	Haverhill	MA	G	978 469-9965	11410
Circle Metal Finishing Inc	Methuen	MA	G	978 682-4297	13014
Electropolishing Systems Inc	Plymouth	MA	E	508 830-1717	14554
Electrostat	Randolph	MA	G	781 885-2135	14678
Federal Metal Finishing Inc	Boston	MA	E	617 242-3371	8541
J & B Metal Finishing	Westminster	MA	G	978 874-5944	16806
Lsa Cleanpart LLC	Southbridge	MA	G	508 765-4848	15393
Maclellan Co	Waltham	MA	G	781 891-5462	16146
Ouellette Industries Inc	Attleboro Falls	MA	G	508 695-0964	7816
River Street Metal Finishing	Braintree	MA	G	781 843-9351	9035
Tdf Metal Finishing Co Inc	Danvers	MA	G	978 223-4292	10261
Turbine Specialists LLC	Brewer	ME	F	207 947-9327	5802
Aero-Dynamics Inc	Seabrook	NH	E	603 474-2547	19791
Finishield Corp	Londonderry	NH	E	603 641-2164	18699
A & H Duffy Polishing & Finshg	Providence	RI	D	401 785-9203	20944
Anton Enterprises Inc	Cranston	RI	F	401 781-3120	20183
Bel Air Finishing Supply Corp	North Kingstown	RI	G	401 667-7902	20693
Duralectra-Chn LLC	Woonsocket	RI	D	401 597-5000	21557
Jet Electro-Finishing Co Inc	Barrington	RI	G	401 728-5809	20047
Masbro Polishing Company Inc	Smithfield	RI	F	401 722-2227	21238
Deermont Corpopration	Rutland	VT	G	802 775-5759	22329

METAL MINING SVCS

Liberty Mtals Min Holdings LLC **(PA)**	Boston	MA	G	617 654-4374	8664
Metal Suppliers Online LLC	Hampstead	NH	G	603 329-0101	18244

METAL ORES, NEC

Wenstrom Metalworks	Whitefield	ME	G	207 215-0651	7219

METAL OXIDE SILICONE OR MOS DEVICES

	CITY	ST	EMP	PHONE	ENTRY #
Fairchild Semiconductor Corp **(DH)**	South Portland	ME	B	207 775-8100	7024
Fairchild Semiconductor W Corp	South Portland	ME	G	207 775-8100	7026
Be Semiconductor Inds USA Inc **(HQ)**	Salem	NH	E	603 626-4700	19711

METAL RESHAPING & REPLATING SVCS

	CITY	ST	EMP	PHONE	ENTRY #
Rader Industries Inc	Bridgeport	CT	G	203 334-6739	478
Michael Healy Designs Inc	Manville	RI	G	401 597-5900	20610

METAL SERVICE CENTERS & OFFICES

	CITY	ST	EMP	PHONE	ENTRY #
Alloy Specialties Incorporated	Manchester	CT	E	860 646-4587	1985
M Cubed Technologies Inc **(HQ)**	Newtown	CT	E	203 304-2940	2928
Scotts Metal Finishing LLC	Bristol	CT	F	860 589-3778	612
Titanium Metals Corporation	East Windsor	CT	F	860 627-7051	1307
Mersen USA Ep Corp **(DH)**	Newburyport	MA	D	805 351-8400	13511
Portland Stone Ware Co Inc **(PA)**	Dracut	MA	E	978 459-7272	10367
New England Small Tube Corp	Litchfield	NH	D	603 429-1600	18652

METAL SLITTING & SHEARING

	CITY	ST	EMP	PHONE	ENTRY #
Goodyfab Llc	North Branford	CT	G	203 927-3059	2964

METAL SPINNING FOR THE TRADE

	CITY	ST	EMP	PHONE	ENTRY #
American Standard Company	Southington	CT	E	860 628-9643	4037
Bracone Metal Spinning Inc	Southington	CT	E	860 628-5927	4041
Enjet Aero Malden LLC	Malden	MA	D	781 321-0366	12570
Lovallo Metalspinning	Cheshire	MA	G	413 743-3947	9979
O W Landergren Inc	Pittsfield	MA	E	413 442-5632	14497
Roland Teiner Company Inc	Everett	MA	F	617 387-7800	10628
Northeast Metal Spinning Inc	Atkinson	NH	G	603 898-2232	17606

METAL STAMPING, FOR THE TRADE

	CITY	ST	EMP	PHONE	ENTRY #
A & D Components Inc	Bristol	CT	G	860 582-9541	509
Acme Monaco Corporation **(PA)**	New Britain	CT	C	860 224-1349	2503
Alto Products Corp Al	Plainville	CT	E	860 747-2736	3465
Arcade Technology LLC	Bridgeport	CT	E	203 366-3871	376
Arrow Manufacturing Company	Bristol	CT	E	860 589-3900	520
Atlas Stamping & Mfg Corp	Newington	CT	E	860 757-3233	2844
Barlow Metal Stamping Inc	Bristol	CT	E	860 583-1387	525
Barnes Group Inc **(PA)**	Bristol	CT	B	860 583-7070	526
Bessette Holdings Inc	East Hartford	CT	E	860 289-6000	1176
Blase Manufacturing Company **(PA)**	Stratford	CT	D	203 375-5646	4397
Bml Tool & Mfg Corp	Monroe	CT	D	203 880-9485	2395
Bridgeport Tl & Stamping Corp	Bridgeport	CT	E	203 336-2501	390
Bristol Tool & Die Company	Bristol	CT	E	860 582-2577	539
C F D Engineering Company **(PA)**	Prospect	CT	E	203 758-4148	3584
Companion Industries Inc	Southington	CT	D	860 628-0504	4045
Component Engineers Inc	Wallingford	CT	D	203 269-0557	4723
Connectcut Spring Stmping Corp	Farmington	CT	B	860 677-1341	1473
Cowles Stamping Inc	North Haven	CT	E	203 865-3117	3023
Eyelet Crafters Inc	Waterbury	CT	D	203 757-9221	4871
Eyelet Design Inc	Waterbury	CT	D	203 754-4141	4872
Eyelet Toolmakers Inc	Watertown	CT	E	860 274-5423	5009
Four Star Manufacturing Co	Bristol	CT	E	860 583-1614	563
Gem Manufacturing Co Inc **(PA)**	Waterbury	CT	D	203 574-1466	4877
Gemco Manufacturing Co Inc	Southington	CT	E	860 628-5529	4052
Globe Tool & Met Stampg Co Inc	Southington	CT	E	860 621-6807	4054
H&T Waterbury Inc	Waterbury	CT	C	203 574-2240	4880
Hob Industries Inc	Wolcott	CT	E	203 879-3028	5444
Hobson and Motzer Incorporated **(PA)**	Durham	CT	C	860 349-1756	1092
Howard Engineering LLC	Naugatuck	CT	E	203 729-5213	2478
J & J Precision Eyelet Inc	Thomaston	CT	D	860 283-8243	4505
Jo Vek Tool and Die Mfg Co	Waterbury	CT	G	203 755-1884	4892
Joma Incorporated	Waterbury	CT	E	203 759-0848	4894
Lawrence Holdings Inc **(PA)**	Wallingford	CT	F	203 949-1600	4764
Lyons Tool and Die Company	Meriden	CT	E	203 238-2689	2100
Marion Manufacturing Company	Cheshire	CT	E	203 272-5376	743
Mastercraft Tool and Mch Co	Southington	CT	F	860 628-5551	4064
McM Stamping Corporation	Danbury	CT	E	203 792-3080	953
McMullin Manufacturing Corp	Brookfield	CT	E	203 740-3360	651
Metalform Acquisition LLC **(PA)**	New Britain	CT	E	860 224-2630	2553
Metallon Inc	Thomaston	CT	E	860 283-8265	4509
MJM Marga LLC	Naugatuck	CT	G	203 729-0600	2485
Mohawk Manufacturing Company	Middletown	CT	F	860 632-2345	2207
National Die Company	Wolcott	CT	G	203 879-1408	5449
National Spring & Stamping Inc	Thomaston	CT	E	860 283-0203	4510
Okay Industries Inc	Berlin	CT	G	860 225-8707	99
Oscar Jobs	Bristol	CT	G	860 583-7834	588
Owen Tool and Mfg Co Inc	Southington	CT	G	860 628-6540	4070
P&G Metal Components Corp	Bloomfield	CT	F	860 243-2220	248
Patriot Manufacturing LLC	Bristol	CT	G	860 506-2213	591
Precision Resource Inc **(PA)**	Shelton	CT	C	203 925-0012	3859
Preferred Tool & Die Inc **(PA)**	Shelton	CT	D	203 925-8525	3861
Preyco Mfg Co Inc	Waterbury	CT	G	203 574-4545	4945
Prospect Machine Products Inc	Prospect	CT	E	203 758-4448	3593
Richards Metal Products Inc	Wolcott	CT	F	203 879-2555	5454
RTC Mfg Co Inc	Watertown	CT	G	800 888-3701	5022
Satellite Aerospace Inc	Manchester	CT	E	860 643-2771	2044
Southington Tool & Mfg Corp	Plantsville	CT	E	860 276-0021	3540
Spirol International Corp **(HQ)**	Danielson	CT	C	860 774-8571	1018
Spirol Intl Holdg Corp **(PA)**	Danielson	CT	C	860 774-8571	1019
Stewart Efi LLC **(PA)**	Thomaston	CT	C	860 283-8213	4516
Taco Fasteners Inc	Plainville	CT	F	860 747-5597	3518
Target Custom Manufacturing Co	Old Saybrook	CT	G	860 388-5848	3352
Tiger Enterprises Inc	Plantsville	CT	E	860 621-9155	3542
Truelove & Maclean Inc	Watertown	CT	C	860 274-9600	5031
Weimann Brothers Mfg Co	Derby	CT	F	203 735-3311	1082
Aero Manufacturing Corp	Beverly	MA	D	978 720-1000	8096
Astron Inc **(PA)**	Pepperell	MA	E	978 433-9500	14436
B & R Metal Products Inc	Lynn	MA	G	781 593-0888	12490
C & M Tool and Mfg Inc	Waltham	MA	G	781 899-1709	16058
Carlstrom Pressed Metal Co Inc	Westborough	MA	E	508 366-4472	16601
Century-Ty Wood Mfg Inc	Holliston	MA	D	508 429-4011	11563
Charles A Richardson Inc	Mansfield	MA	F	508 339-8600	12617
Crystal Engineering Co Inc	Newburyport	MA	E	978 465-7007	13480
Deltran Inc	Attleboro Falls	MA	E	508 699-7506	7812
Echo Industries Inc	Orange	MA	E	978 544-7000	14215
Elite Metal Fabricators Inc	Ludlow	MA	G	413 547-2588	12464
Excel Tool & Die Co Inc	Quincy	MA	G	617 472-0473	14624
Fraen Corporation **(PA)**	Reading	MA	C	781 205-5300	14734
Fraen Corporation	Woburn	MA	E	781 937-8825	17185
GJM Manufacturing Inc	Attleboro	MA	G	508 222-9322	7741
Hi-Tech Inc	Attleboro	MA	F	401 454-4086	7746
International Metal Pdts Inc	Chicopee	MA	E	413 532-2411	10033
Interplex Etch Logic LLC	Attleboro	MA	E	508 399-6810	7751
Killeen Machine and Tl Co Inc	Worcester	MA	D	508 754-1714	17400
Larson Tool & Stamping Company	Attleboro	MA	D	508 222-0897	7758
Matrix Metal Products Inc	Attleboro	MA	F	508 226-2374	7765
New England Metalform Inc	Plainville	MA	E	508 695-9340	14530
Norking Company Inc	Attleboro	MA	E	508 222-3100	7773
P M S Manufactured Pdts Inc	Gloucester	MA	F	978 281-2600	11200
Paramount Tool LLC	Fall River	MA	E	508 672-0844	10744
Pep Industries LLC	Attleboro	MA	A	508 226-5600	7776
Peter Forg Manufacturing Co	Somerville	MA	F	617 625-0337	15205
Precision Engineered Pdts LLC **(DH)**	Attleboro	MA	G	508 226-5600	7782
Shawmut Engineering Co	Walpole	MA	F	508 850-9500	16011
Springfield Spring Corporation **(PA)**	East Longmeadow	MA	E	413 525-6837	10493
Stay Sharp Tool Company Inc	North Attleboro	MA	G	508 699-6990	13782
Timco Corporation	Stoughton	MA	E	781 821-1041	15626
United Tool & Machine Corp	Wilmington	MA	E	978 658-5500	17060
Universal Tool Co Inc	Springfield	MA	E	413 732-4807	15520
Valentine Tool & Stamping Inc	Norton	MA	F	508 285-6911	14091
Whitman Tool and Die Co Inc	Whitman	MA	E	781 447-0421	16932
Worcester Manufacturing Inc	Worcester	MA	E	508 756-0301	17505
Laird Technologies Inc	Manchester	NH	F	603 627-7877	18858
New England Industries Inc	Lebanon	NH	E	603 448-5330	18633
New Hampshire Stamping Co Inc	Goffstown	NH	E	603 641-1234	18206
Stamping Technologies Inc	Laconia	NH	F	603 524-5958	18588
Sunset Tool Inc	Keene	NH	E	603 355-2246	18531
Angelo Di Maria Inc	Providence	RI	E	401 274-0100	20954
Atamian Manufacturing Corp	Providence	RI	E	800 286-9614	20959
C & W Co Inc	Providence	RI	G	401 941-6311	20977
C Sjoberg & Son Inc	Cranston	RI	F	401 461-8220	20192
Crest Manufacturing Company	Lincoln	RI	E	401 333-1350	20566
Demaich Industries Inc	Johnston	RI	F	401 944-3576	20508
Diversified Metal Crafters Inc	Lincoln	RI	E	401 305-7700	20568
Etco Incorporated **(PA)**	Warwick	RI	D	401 467-2400	21361
Evans Findings Company Inc	East Providence	RI	E	401 434-5600	20412
Ferguson Perforating Company **(DH)**	Providence	RI	D	401 941-8876	21013
Interplex Industries Inc	Rumford	RI	G	401 434-6543	21189
Interplex Industries Inc **(DH)**	Rumford	RI	F	718 961-6212	21188
Interplex Metal Logic	Rumford	RI	G	401 434-6543	21190
Maros Products Incorporated	Warwick	RI	G	401 885-1788	21387
Morris & Broms LLC	Cranston	RI	F	401 781-3134	20265
Pep Central Inc	Warwick	RI	A	401 732-3770	21402
R & D Tl Engrg Four-Slide Prod	Cranston	RI	G	401 942-9710	20276
Samic Mfg Company	Johnston	RI	G	401 421-2400	20540
Tercat Tool and Die Co Inc	Providence	RI	D	401 421-3371	21133
Heb Manufacturing Company Inc	Chelsea	VT	E	802 685-4821	21838
New England Precision Inc	Randolph	VT	D	800 293-4112	22299

METAL STAMPINGS: Patterned

	CITY	ST	EMP	PHONE	ENTRY #
Robert A Collins	Fremont	NH	G	603 895-2345	18180
State Pattern Works	Hudson	NH	G	603 882-0701	18440

METAL STAMPINGS: Perforated

	CITY	ST	EMP	PHONE	ENTRY #
Excel Spring & Stamping LLC	Bristol	CT	G	860 585-1495	559
Hylie Products Incorporated	Cheshire	CT	F	203 439-8786	738
New Can Company Inc **(HQ)**	Holbrook	MA	E	781 767-1650	11533
Frank Morrow Company	Providence	RI	F	401 941-3900	21016

METAL TREATING COMPOUNDS

	CITY	ST	EMP	PHONE	ENTRY #
United States Chemical Corp	Plantsville	CT	G	860 621-6831	3544
Luster-On Products Inc	Springfield	MA	F	413 739-2541	15486
Technic Inc **(PA)**	Cranston	RI	C	401 781-6100	20301
Technic Inc	Woonsocket	RI	E	401 769-7000	21585

METALS SVC CENTERS & WHOLESALERS: Cable, Wire

	CITY	ST	EMP	PHONE	ENTRY #
Loos & Co Inc **(PA)**	Pomfret	CT	B	860 928-7981	3552

METALS SVC CENTERS & WHOLESALERS: Iron & Steel Prdt, Ferrous

	CITY	ST	EMP	PHONE	ENTRY #
Canam Bridges US Inc	Claremont	NH	E	603 542-5202	17839

METALS SVC CENTERS & WHOLESALERS: Pipe & Tubing, Steel

	CITY	ST	EMP	PHONE	ENTRY #
International Pipe & Stl Corp	North Branford	CT	F	203 481-7102	2969

METALS SVC CENTERS & WHOLESALERS: Plates, Metal

	CITY	ST	EMP	PHONE	ENTRY #
Hot Plates Company	Ashland	MA	G	508 429-1445	7661

METALS SVC CENTERS & WHOLESALERS: Steel

	CITY	ST	EMP	PHONE	ENTRY #
ATI Flat Rlled Pdts Hldngs LLC	Waterbury	CT	F	203 756-7414	4847
Bushwick Metals LLC	Meriden	CT	G	203 630-2459	2081
Eastern Metal Works Inc	Milford	CT	E	203 878-6995	2281

	CITY	ST	EMP	PHONE	ENTRY #
Magna Steel Sales Inc	Beacon Falls	CT	F	203 888-0300	62
Baxter Inc	West Yarmouth	MA	G	508 228-8136	16578
Rebars & Mesh Inc	Haverhill	MA	E	978 374-2244	11467
Barker Steel LLC	Scarborough	ME	G	207 883-3444	6907

METALS SVC CENTERS & WHOLESALERS: Strip, Metal

	CITY	ST	EMP	PHONE	ENTRY #
Ulbrich Stnless Stels Spcial M **(PA)**	North Haven	CT	D	203 239-4481	3067

METALS SVC CENTERS & WHOLESALERS: Tubing, Metal

	CITY	ST	EMP	PHONE	ENTRY #
Micro Bends Corp	Peterborough	NH	G	603 924-0022	19476
Raymond Gadues Inc	Swanton	VT	E	802 868-2033	22536

METALS SVC CTRS & WHOLESALERS: Aluminum Bars, Rods, Etc

	CITY	ST	EMP	PHONE	ENTRY #
Yarde Metals Inc **(HQ)**	Southington	CT	B	860 406-6061	4092

METALS: Honeycombed

	CITY	ST	EMP	PHONE	ENTRY #
Hexcel Corporation **(PA)**	Stamford	CT	E	203 969-0666	4213

METALS: Precious NEC

	CITY	ST	EMP	PHONE	ENTRY #
Bal International Inc	Stamford	CT	E	203 359-6775	4147
Northeastern Metals Corp	Stamford	CT	G	203 348-8088	4261
Reliable Silver Corporation	Naugatuck	CT	F	203 574-7732	2493
Metalor USA Refining Corp **(DH)**	North Attleboro	MA	C	508 699-8800	13764
Spindle City Precious Metals	Somerset	MA	G	508 567-1597	15148
Colt Refining Inc **(PA)**	Merrimack	NH	E	603 429-9966	18993
Harding Metals Inc	Northwood	NH	E	603 942-5573	19412
Advanced Chemical Company	Warwick	RI	E	401 785-3434	21318
Geib Refining Corporation	Warwick	RI	E	401 738-8560	21365
Umicore Precious Mtls USA Inc	Riverside	RI	G	401 450-0907	21178

METALS: Precious, Secondary

	CITY	ST	EMP	PHONE	ENTRY #
Viking Platinum LLC	Waterbury	CT	F	203 574-7979	4969
Precious Metals Reclaiming Svc **(PA)**	Canton	MA	G	781 326-3442	9771
Pease & Curren Incorporated	Warwick	RI	E	401 738-6449	21401

METALS: Primary Nonferrous, NEC

	CITY	ST	EMP	PHONE	ENTRY #
Aztec Industries LLC	Middletown	CT	E	860 343-1960	2175
Ulbrich Stainless Steels	Wallingford	CT	C	203 269-2507	4824
Cabot Corporation **(PA)**	Boston	MA	C	617 345-0100	8452
Cabot Corporation	Haverhill	MA	C	978 556-8400	11413
Global Advanced Metals USA Inc **(PA)**	Wellesley Hills	MA	D	781 996-7300	16397
H C Starck Inc **(HQ)**	Newton	MA	C	617 630-5800	13598
J T Inman Co Inc	Attleboro Falls	MA	E	508 226-0080	7814
Carpenter Powder Products Inc	Woonsocket	RI	F	401 769-5600	21555

METALWORK: Miscellaneous

	CITY	ST	EMP	PHONE	ENTRY #
C & S Engineering Inc	Meriden	CT	E	203 235-5727	2082
Cem Group LLC **(DH)**	Burlington	CT	F	860 675-5000	675
Met Tech Inc	Fairfield	CT	G	203 254-9319	1443
Shamrock Sheet Metal	Colchester	CT	G	860 537-4282	809
Simpson Strong-Tie Company Inc	Enfield	CT	F	860 741-8923	1385
Applied Light Manufacturing	Holyoke	MA	F	413 552-3600	11616
Artisan Industries Inc	Stoughton	MA	D	781 893-6800	15581
Bay Steel Co Inc	Bridgewater	MA	F	508 697-7083	9062
Bay Steel Co Inc **(PA)**	Halifax	MA	G	781 294-8308	11315
Cdp Manufacturing LLC	Brockton	MA	F	508 588-6400	9129
Marblehead Engineering	Essex	MA	F	978 432-1386	10595
Mill City Iron Fabricators	Dracut	MA	F	978 957-6833	10366
Santini Brothers Ir Works Inc	Medford	MA	F	781 396-1450	12947
Interrotech	New Sharon	ME	G	207 778-4907	6477
Metaphor Bronze Tileworks LLC	Morrill	ME	G	207 342-2597	6455
Ward Fabrication Inc	Sandown	NH	G	603 382-9700	19788
Scientific Alloys Inc	Westerly	RI	G	401 596-4947	21540
Adaptive Fabrication LLC	Brattleboro	VT	G	802 380-3376	21715

METALWORK: Ornamental

	CITY	ST	EMP	PHONE	ENTRY #
Connecticut Iron Works Inc	Greenwich	CT	G	203 869-0657	1603
Goodyfab Llc	North Branford	CT	G	203 927-3059	2964
Pequonnock Ironworks Inc	Bridgeport	CT	F	203 336-2178	465
United Steel Inc	East Hartford	CT	C	860 289-2323	1232
Boston Steel Fabricators Inc	Holbrook	MA	G	781 767-1540	11522
Brayton Wilson Cole Corp	Hingham	MA	G	781 803-6624	11495
Mestek Inc	Westfield	MA	G	413 568-9571	16703
Stonybrook Fine Arts LLC	Jamaica Plain	MA	G	617 799-3644	11950

METALWORKING MACHINERY WHOLESALERS

	CITY	ST	EMP	PHONE	ENTRY #
N Ferrara Inc	Somerset	MA	F	508 679-2440	15147

METERING DEVICES: Measuring, Mechanical

	CITY	ST	EMP	PHONE	ENTRY #
Veeder-Root Company **(HQ)**	Weatogue	CT	D	860 651-2700	5045

METERS: Turbine Flow, Indl Process

	CITY	ST	EMP	PHONE	ENTRY #
Hamilton Sundstrand Corp **(HQ)**	Windsor Locks	CT	A	860 654-6000	5397

METERS: Voltmeters

	CITY	ST	EMP	PHONE	ENTRY #
Murata Power Solutions Inc **(DH)**	Westborough	MA	C	508 339-3000	16637

MGMT CONSULTING SVCS: Matls, Incl Purch, Handle & Invntry

	CITY	ST	EMP	PHONE	ENTRY #
Citiworks Corp	Attleboro	MA	F	508 761-7400	7720

MICROCIRCUITS, INTEGRATED: Semiconductor

	CITY	ST	EMP	PHONE	ENTRY #
Carten-Fujikin Incorporated	Cheshire	CT	G	203 699-2134	720
ABB Enterprise Software Inc	Boston	MA	G	617 574-1130	8334
Advance Data Technology Inc	Topsfield	MA	F	978 801-4376	15852
Advanced Micro Devices Inc	Boxborough	MA	C	978 795-2500	8956
Freebird Semiconductor Corp	Haverhill	MA	G	617 955-7152	11436
HCC Aegis Inc **(DH)**	New Bedford	MA	E	508 998-3141	13393
Maxim Integrated Products Inc	North Chelmsford	MA	A	978 934-7600	13903
Raysolution LLC	Andover	MA	G	765 714-0645	7593
Masimo Semiconductor Inc	Hudson	NH	E	603 595-8900	18413
Unitrode Corporation **(HQ)**	Manchester	NH	B	603 222-8500	18945
Xilinx Inc	Nashua	NH	F	603 891-1096	19290
Semicndctor Cmpnnts Inds of RI **(DH)**	East Greenwich	RI	A	401 885-3600	20379

MICROPHONES

	CITY	ST	EMP	PHONE	ENTRY #
Telefunken USA LLC	South Windsor	CT	F	860 882-5919	4016
Acoustic Magic Inc	Sudbury	MA	G	978 440-9384	15651
Vesper Technologies Inc	Boston	MA	F	617 315-9144	8910
Gentex Corporation	Manchester	NH	C	603 657-1200	18826

MICROPROCESSORS

	CITY	ST	EMP	PHONE	ENTRY #
Oracle America Inc	Stamford	CT	D	203 703-3000	4273
Intel Massachusetts Inc	Hudson	MA	A	978 553-4000	11777
Sparton Beckwood LLC	Plaistow	NH	D	603 382-3840	19524
Texas Instruments Incorporated	Manchester	NH	F	603 222-8500	18939

MICROSCOPES: Electron & Proton

	CITY	ST	EMP	PHONE	ENTRY #
E F Jeld Co Inc	North Billerica	MA	G	978 667-1416	13810
Kirstein Per	Upton	MA	G	508 473-9673	15908
Raj Communications Ltd	Williston	VT	F	802 658-4961	22687
Vermont Optechs Inc	Charlotte	VT	G	802 425-2040	21836

MICROWAVE COMPONENTS

	CITY	ST	EMP	PHONE	ENTRY #
Ens Microwave LLC	Danbury	CT	G	203 794-7940	911
Times Microwave Systems Inc **(HQ)**	Wallingford	CT	B	203 949-8400	4819
Accellent Holdings Corp	Wilmington	MA	A	978 570-6900	16962
API Technologies Corporation	Marlborough	MA	D	508 485-0336	12718
API Technologies Corporation	Marlborough	MA	D	508 251-6400	12719
Chassis Engineering LLC	Rowley	MA	F	978 948-0826	14850
Cmt Filters Inc	Marlborough	MA	E	508 258-6400	12738
Cuming Microwave Corporation **(HQ)**	Avon	MA	D	508 521-6700	7884
Currier Engineering	Needham	MA	G	781 449-7706	13298
Delta Electronics Mfg Corp	Beverly	MA	C	978 927-1060	8125
Diamond Rf LLC	Littleton	MA	G	978 486-0039	12301
Dss Circuits Inc	Worcester	MA	G	508 852-8061	17367
Dynawave Cable Incorporated	Haverhill	MA	G	978 469-9448	11428
Dynawave Incorporated	Haverhill	MA	D	978 469-0555	11429
Graytron Inc	Ashfield	MA	G	413 625-2456	7651
H & T Specialty Co Inc	Waltham	MA	F	781 893-3866	16123
Herley Industries Inc	Woburn	MA	C	781 729-9450	17199
Hxi LLC	Harvard	MA	F	978 772-7774	11379
L3 Technologies Inc	Burlington	MA	C	781 270-2100	9295
Macom Technology Solutions Inc	Lowell	MA	G	978 656-2500	12402
Macom Technology Solutions Inc **(HQ)**	Lowell	MA	B	978 656-2500	12403
Microsorb Technologies Inc	Franklin	MA	G	401 767-2269	11065
Microwave Cmpnents Systems Inc	Westborough	MA	F	508 466-8400	16636
Microwave Engineering Corp	North Andover	MA	D	978 685-2776	13718
REA Associates Inc	North Billerica	MA	G	209 521-2727	13860
Smiths Intrcnnect Americas Inc	Hudson	MA	C	978 568-0451	11817
Thorndike Corporation	East Bridgewater	MA	F	508 378-9797	10421
Tru Technologies Inc	Peabody	MA	C	978 532-0775	14379
Victor Microwave Inc	Wakefield	MA	F	781 245-4472	15982
Micronetixx Microwave LLC	Lewiston	ME	F	207 786-2000	6305
Cobham Exeter Inc	Exeter	NH	B	603 775-5200	18117
Ferrite Microwave Tech LLC	Nashua	NH	E	603 881-5234	19156
Monzite Corporation **(HQ)**	Nashua	NH	F	617 429-7050	19209
RH Laboratories Inc	Nashua	NH	E	603 459-5900	19252
Precision Trned Cmponents Corp	Smithfield	RI	D	401 232-3377	21244

MILITARY INSIGNIA

	CITY	ST	EMP	PHONE	ENTRY #
Bryant Group Inc	Contoocook	NH	F	603 746-1166	17941
Graco Awards Manufacturing Inc	Providence	RI	E	281 255-2161	21021
International Insignia Corp	Providence	RI	D	401 784-0000	21039
Officers Equipment Co	Providence	RI	E	703 221-1912	21082
Urschel Tool Co	Cranston	RI	F	401 944-0600	20308

MILITARY INSIGNIA, TEXTILE

	CITY	ST	EMP	PHONE	ENTRY #
Airborne Industries Inc	Branford	CT	F	203 315-0200	286
Niche Inc	New Bedford	MA	E	508 990-4202	13427

MILL PRDTS: Structural & Rail

	CITY	ST	EMP	PHONE	ENTRY #
Boudreaus Welding Co Inc	Dayville	CT	E	860 774-2771	1040
Draper Metals	West Bridgewater	MA	G	508 584-4617	16439
Avilite Corp	Merrimack	NH	G	603 626-4388	18988

MILLING: Cereal Flour, Exc Rice

	CITY	ST	EMP	PHONE	ENTRY #
KPM Analytics Inc **(PA)**	Milford	MA	G	774 462-6700	13122

MILLING: Rice

	CITY	ST	EMP	PHONE	ENTRY #
Saw Mill Site Farm	Greenfield	MA	G	413 665-3005	11274

MILLWORK

	CITY	ST	EMP	PHONE	ENTRY #
Alvarado Custom Cabinetry LLC	Norwalk	CT	F	203 831-0181	3099
Arbon Equipment Corporation	Bloomfield	CT	G	410 796-5902	202
Atlantic Woodcraft Inc	Enfield	CT	F	860 749-4887	1347
Axels Custom Woodworking LLC	Greenwich	CT	G	203 869-1317	1595
B H Davis Co	Thompson	CT	G	860 923-2771	4531
Bergan Architectural Wdwkg Inc	Middletown	CT	E	860 346-0869	2177
Birkett Woodworking LLC	Morris	CT	G	860 361-9142	2431
Breakfast Woodworks Inc	Guilford	CT	G	203 458-8888	1694
Byrne Woodworking Inc	Bridgeport	CT	G	203 953-3205	393
C J S Millwork Inc	Stamford	CT	F	203 708-0080	4153
Clancy Woodworking LLC	Sherman	CT	G	860 355-3655	3893
Colonial Wood Products Inc	West Haven	CT	F	203 932-9003	5112
Connecticut Carpentry LLC	Meriden	CT	E	203 639-8585	2088
Connecticut Millwork Inc	Vernon	CT	G	860 875-2860	4665

	CITY	ST	EMP	PHONE	ENTRY #
CT Woodworking LLC	North Franklin	CT	G	860 884-9586	2988
Curtiss Woodworking Inc	Prospect	CT	F	203 527-9305	3586
Custom Design Woodworks LLC	Old Lyme	CT	G	860 434-0515	3319
Dalbergia LLC **(PA)**	Tolland	CT	G	860 870-2500	4543
Dlz Architectural Mill Work	Hartford	CT	G	860 883-7562	1818
Fairfield County Millwork	Bethany	CT	F	203 393-9751	120
Fairfield Woodworks LLC	Stratford	CT	F	203 380-9842	4411
G M F Woodworking LLC	Norwalk	CT	G	203 788-8979	3155
Griffin Green	Bethlehem	CT	G	203 266-5727	195
H & S Woodworks L T D	New Milford	CT	G	914 391-3926	2805
Indars Stairs LLC	Lebanon	CT	G	860 208-3826	1935
Jacobsen Woodworking Co Inc	Greenwich	CT	G	203 531-9050	1624
John M Kriskey Carpentry	Greenwich	CT	G	203 531-0194	1625
Johnson Millwork Inc	East Hampton	CT	G	860 267-4693	1161
Legacy Woodworking LLC	Meriden	CT	G	203 440-9710	2099
Legere Group Ltd	Avon	CT	C	860 674-0392	37
Lingard Cabinet Co LLC	Manchester	CT	G	860 647-9886	2019
Luckey LLC	New Haven	CT	F	203 285-3819	2709
Mars Architectural Millwork	Bridgeport	CT	G	203 579-2632	447
Millwork Shop LLC	Torrington	CT	G	860 489-8848	4587
Modern Woodcrafts LLC	Plainville	CT	D	860 677-7371	3508
New England Cabinet Co Inc	New Britain	CT	F	860 747-9995	2555
New England Fine Woodworking	Chester	CT	G	860 526-5799	773
New England Joinery Works Inc	Essex	CT	G	860 767-3377	1404
Nichols Woodworking LLC **(PA)**	Washington Depot	CT	G	860 350-4223	4833
Northeast Stair Company LLC	Tolland	CT	G	860 875-3358	4551
Orion Manufacturing LLC	Mystic	CT	G	860 572-2921	2447
Paco Assensio Woodworking LLC	Norwalk	CT	G	203 536-2608	3213
Petrunti Design & Wdwkg LLC	West Hartford	CT	G	860 953-5332	5090
Porta Door Co	Seymour	CT	E	203 888-6191	3761
Prescott Cabinet Co	Pawcatuck	CT	G	860 495-0176	3441
R Woodworking Larson Inc	Manchester	CT	E	860 646-7904	2041
Roman Woodworking	New Britain	CT	G	860 490-5989	2574
Saxony Wood Products Inc	Greenwich	CT	G	203 869-3717	1647
Soja Woodworking LLC	Higganum	CT	G	860 345-3909	1906
Swanhart Woodworking	New Fairfield	CT	G	203 746-1184	2628
Tl Woodworking	Hamden	CT	G	203 787-9661	1788
V & V Woodworking LLC	Bethel	CT	G	203 740-9494	188
Wezenski Woodworking	Branford	CT	G	203 488-3255	360
White Dog Woodworking LLC	Torrington	CT	G	860 482-3776	4607
Winchester Woodworks LLC	Winsted	CT	G	860 379-9875	5431
Woodwork Specialties Inc	Bristol	CT	G	860 583-4848	627
Woodworkers Club LLC	Norwalk	CT	G	203 847-9663	3273
Woodworking Plus LLC	Bethany	CT	G	203 393-1967	125
York Millwork LLC	Old Greenwich	CT	G	203 698-3460	3314
Zavarella Woodworking Inc	Newington	CT	G	860 666-6969	2913
A & P Woodworking Inc	Boston	MA	G	617 459-4664	8331
Abbas Shahrestanaki	Norwood	MA	G	617 548-0986	14116
Advanced Woodworking Technolog	Lowell	MA	G	978 937-1400	12340
Al Woodworking	Rutland	MA	G	508 886-2883	14879
Allen Woodworking LLC	Bellingham	MA	G	617 306-6479	8029
Architectural Elements Inc	Boxboro	MA	G	978 263-2482	8951
Architectural Timber Mllwk Inc	Hadley	MA	F	413 586-3045	11305
Bancroft Custom Woodworks	Williamstown	MA	G	413 738-7001	16954
Bay State Partition & Fix Co	Boston	MA	G	617 782-1113	8393
Berger Corporation	Orleans	MA	G	508 255-3267	14230
Blue Anchor Woodworks Inc	Marblehead	MA	G	781 631-2390	12677
Boston Sash & Millwork Inc	North Dighton	MA	F	508 880-8808	13930
Boston Turning Works	Watertown	MA	G	617 924-4747	16275
Botelho Wood Working	Fall River	MA	G	774 240-7235	10671
Brendan C Kinnane Inc	Fall River	MA	G	508 679-8479	10672
Brockway-Smith Company	West Hatfield	MA	D	413 247-9674	16482
Brogans Custom Woodworking	Westminster	MA	G	978 502-8013	16803
Bwi of MA LLC	Leominster	MA	G	978 534-4065	12122
Caliper Woodworking Corp	Malden	MA	E	781 322-9760	12563
Chebli Architectural Woodwork	Waltham	MA	G	781 642-0733	16066
Choice Woodworking Inc	North Reading	MA	G	978 207-0289	13980
Contemporary Cabinet Designs	Norwood	MA	G	781 769-7979	14143
Continental Woodcraft Inc **(PA)**	Worcester	MA	E	508 581-9560	17359
Craig F Bradford	Northampton	MA	G	413 586-4500	14003
Dbi Woodworks Inc	Avon	MA	G	781 739-2060	7885
DH Custom Woodworks	Sharon	MA	G	781 784-5951	15049
Ebano Woodworks Inc	Lawrence	MA	G	978 879-7206	12021
Everett Custom Woodworking	Hopkinton	MA	G	508 435-7675	11712
General Woodworking Inc **(PA)**	Lowell	MA	F	978 458-6625	12373
George Dawe	Amesbury	MA	G	978 388-5565	7486
Georgia-Pacific LLC	Norwood	MA	G	781 440-3600	14155
Glenns Gardening & Woodworking	Boston	MA	G	617 548-7977	8566
Hawkes & Huberdeau Woodworking	Amesbury	MA	G	978 388-7747	7489
Horner Millwork Corp	Pembroke	MA	E	781 826-7770	14408
Jan Woodworks Renovation	Westfield	MA	G	413 563-2534	16691
JC Clocks Company Inc	North Dartmouth	MA	E	508 998-8442	13922
Johncarlo Woodworking Inc	Westfield	MA	F	413 562-4002	16695
Joinery Shop Inc	Charlestown	MA	G	617 242-4718	9838
Kabinet Korner Inc	Malden	MA	E	781 324-9600	12574
Keiver Willard-Lumber Corp	Newburyport	MA	D	978 462-7193	13503
Kenyon Woodworking Inc	Jamaica Plain	MA	F	617 524-6883	11945
Kevin Cradock Woodworking Inc	Hyde Park	MA	G	617 524-2405	11872
Kevins Woodworks LLC	Fall River	MA	G	508 989-8692	10720
Leveillee Archtctral Mllwk Inc	Spencer	MA	F	508 885-9731	15432
Lloyds Woodworking Inc	Hudson	MA	G	978 562-9007	11787
Louis Richards	Webster	MA	G	508 671-9017	16348
Mark Gauvin	Mattapoisett	MA	G	508 758-2324	12888
Mark Richey Wdwkg & Design Inc	Newburyport	MA	D	978 499-3800	13510
Meridian Custom Woodworking In	Brockton	MA	G	508 587-4400	9165
Michael Humphries Woodworking	Northfield	MA	G	413 498-2187	14065
Mitton Millworks	Andover	MA	G	978 475-7761	7573
Modern Heritage LLC	Rowley	MA	G	781 913-8261	14859
Moore Woodworking Inc	Nantucket	MA	G	508 364-7338	13227
Munro Woodworking	Bellingham	MA	G	508 966-2654	8052
Nelson & Power Inc	Woburn	MA	G	781 933-0679	17238
New England Custom Wood Wkg	New Bedford	MA	G	508 991-8038	13422
New England Shrlines Companies	Pembroke	MA	F	781 826-0140	14418
Olde Bostonian	Boston	MA	G	617 282-9300	8746
P A W Inc	Ludlow	MA	G	413 589-0399	12474
Precision Woodworking	Quincy	MA	G	617 479-7604	14647
R P Woodworking Inc	North Oxford	MA	G	508 987-3722	13974
Ran Woodworking	Charlton	MA	G	508 248-4818	9855
Rex Lumber Company **(PA)**	Acton	MA	D	800 343-0567	7378
Rgc Millwork Incorporated	Lowell	MA	G	978 275-9529	12427
Richard Cantwell Woodworking	New Bedford	MA	G	508 984-7921	13445
Rjd Woodworking LLC	Fairhaven	MA	G	508 984-4315	10646
Ronald F Birrell	Becket	MA	G	413 219-6729	7954
Shaw Woodworking Inc	Pocasset	MA	G	508 563-1242	14601
Shawn Roberts Woodworking	Gilbertville	MA	G	413 477-0060	11155
South Shore Millwork Inc	Norton	MA	D	508 226-5500	14090
Southcoast Woodworking Inc	Mattapoisett	MA	G	508 758-3184	12890
Southeastern Millwork Co Inc	Sagamore Beach	MA	F	508 888-6038	14887
Southeastern Millwork Co Inc	Bourne	MA	F	508 888-6038	8949
Specialty Wholesale Sup Corp	Gardner	MA	E	978 632-1472	11128
Stokes Woodworking Co Inc **(PA)**	Hudson	MA	G	508 481-0414	11820
Thl-Nortek Investors LLC **(PA)**	Boston	MA	D	617 227-1050	8882
Toby Leary Fine Wdwkg Inc	Hyannis	MA	F	508 957-2281	11860
Top Notch Mill Work	Bourne	MA	G	508 432-4976	8950
Valiant Industries Inc	Amesbury	MA	E	978 388-3792	7510
VCA Inc	Northampton	MA	E	413 587-2750	14025
Vintage Millwork Corporation	Dracut	MA	G	978 957-1400	10370
Walter A Furman Co Inc	Fall River	MA	D	508 674-7751	10782
Watson Brothers Inc	Middleton	MA	F	978 774-7677	13106
Wayland Millwork Corporation	Marlborough	MA	F	508 485-4172	12847
Wesco Building & Design Inc	Stoneham	MA	E	781 279-0490	15572
Wescor Ltd	Boston	MA	G	617 731-3963	8921
Wescor Ltd **(PA)**	Stoneham	MA	F	781 279-0490	15573
Westek Architectural Wdwkg Inc	Westfield	MA	F	413 562-6363	16741
Wide Angle Marketing Inc	Hubbardston	MA	E	978 928-5400	11747
Widham Wood Corporation	Woburn	MA	G	781 932-8572	17320
Windham Wood Interiors Inc	Woburn	MA	G	781 932-8572	17321
Winer Woodworking	Plainville	MA	G	508 695-5871	14538
Woodcraft Designers Bldrs LLC	Canton	MA	G	508 584-4200	9796
Woodsmiths Inc	Fall River	MA	G	508 548-8343	10784
Ziggy Woodworking	East Weymouth	MA	G	781 335-5218	10547
Bass Cabinetry and Mllwk LLC	Greene	ME	G	207 754-0087	6147
Blevins Company	Edgecomb	ME	G	207 882-6396	5999
Blue Hill Cabinet & Woodwork	Blue Hill	ME	G	207 374-2260	5770
Coastal Woodworking Inc	Nobleboro	ME	E	207 563-1072	6492
Downeast Woodworks	Freeport	ME	G	207 781-4800	6076
East Coast Woodworking Inc	Brunswick	ME	G	207 442-0025	5835
F A Wilnauer Woodwork Inc	South Berwick	ME	G	207 384-4824	7002
Georgia-Pacific LLC	Baileyville	ME	G	207 427-4077	5626
Hill Tim Fine Woodworking	Gorham	ME	G	207 854-1387	6114
JC Millwork Inc	Mount Vernon	ME	G	207 293-4204	6459
John Costin Studio	Kennebunk	ME	G	207 985-7221	6237
Jordan Millworks Inc	Lincoln	ME	G	207 794-6178	6356
Lovett & Hall Woodworks	Gray	ME	G	207 650-5139	6140
Morrison Millwork and Str Fixs	Windham	ME	G	207 892-9418	7242
New England Woodworks	Springvale	ME	G	207 324-6343	7054
P M Kelly Inc	Ashland	ME	F	207 435-6654	5539
Pickens Woodworking	Topsham	ME	G	207 725-8955	7092
Pond Cove Millwork Inc	Saco	ME	E	207 773-6819	6855
Quarter Point Woodworking LLC **(PA)**	New Gloucester	ME	G	207 926-1032	6471
Quarter Point Woodworking LLC	Windham	ME	G	207 892-7022	7245
Saco Bay Millwork Co	Buxton	ME	F	207 929-8400	5860
Traditional Wood Works Inc	Berwick	ME	G	207 676-9668	5713
West Minot Millwork Inc	West Minot	ME	G	207 966-3200	7175
Windham Millwork Inc	Windham	ME	D	207 892-3238	7260
American Custom Design Wdwkg	Tilton	NH	G	603 286-3239	19903
Anthony Galluzzo Corp	Londonderry	NH	E	603 432-2681	18676
Beech River Mill	Center Ossipee	NH	G	603 539-2636	17802
Boulia-Gorrell Lumber Co Inc	Laconia	NH	F	603 524-1300	18560
Chester Braley	Epsom	NH	G	239 841-0019	18105
Cox Woodworking Inc	Westmoreland	NH	G	603 399-7704	19970
Crossknots Woodworking	Stewartstown	NH	G	603 237-8392	19861
Depot Millworks	Littleton	NH	G	603 444-1656	18657
Dodge Woodworking LLC	East Kingston	NH	G	603 642-6188	18086
Donald A Jhnson Fine Wdwkg LLC	Intervale	NH	G	603 356-9080	18454
Dunn Woodworks	Chesterfield	NH	G	603 363-4180	17828
Fairview Millwork Inc	Seabrook	NH	G	603 929-4449	19800
Forest Manufacturing Corp	Auburn	NH	F	603 647-6991	17609
Herrick Mill Work Inc	Contoocook	NH	E	603 746-5092	17945
Jewell Woodworks LLC	Nottingham	NH	G	603 679-8025	19416
Keller Products Incorporated	Bow	NH	E	603 224-5502	17719
Kimballs Lumber Center LLC **(PA)**	Wolfeboro	NH	G	603 569-2477	20021
Kindelan Woodworking	Derry	NH	G	603 434-3253	17985
Littleton Millwork Inc	Littleton	NH	E	603 444-2677	18662
Mill City Leather Works	Manchester	NH	G	603 935-9974	18874
Millwork Masters Ltd **(PA)**	Keene	NH	F	603 358-3038	18515
NH Woodworks LLC	Milford	NH	G	603 361-4727	19071
Norteast Woodworking Inc	Raymond	NH	G	603 895-4271	19641
Pasture Hill Millwork LLC	Rochester	NH	G	603 335-4175	19681
Port-O-Lite Company Inc	West Swanzey	NH	F	603 352-3205	19967
Salmon Falls Woodworks LLC	Dover	NH	F	603 740-6060	18051
Thibco Inc	Manchester	NH	E	603 623-3011	18941

	CITY	ST	EMP	PHONE	ENTRY #
Tommila Brothers Inc	Fitzwilliam	NH	F	603 242-7774	18153
Wards Woodworking Inc	Kingston	NH	G	603 642-7300	18548
Wood Works	Portsmouth	NH	G	603 436-3805	19632
Yankee Craftsman Inc	Auburn	NH	G	603 483-5900	17614
Artisan Millwork Inc Cabi	Pawtucket	RI	G	401 721-5500	20813
Beasley Woodworks LLC	Charlestown	RI	G	401 529-5099	20130
Brouillette Realty LLC	Barrington	RI	G	401 499-4867	20043
Cas Acquisition Co LLC	North Smithfield	RI	F	401 884-8556	20783
Cloos Woodworking Inc	Johnston	RI	G	401 528-8629	20504
Design Fabricators Inc	Cranston	RI	E	401 944-5294	20209
East Coast Laminiating Company	Cumberland	RI	G	401 729-0097	20319
Grinnell Cabinet Makers Inc	Cranston	RI	E	401 781-1080	20236
Igitt Inc	Middletown	RI	F	401 841-5544	20621
Imperia Corporation	Barrington	RI	E	508 894-3000	20046
Interior Wdwkg Solutions Inc	Cranston	RI	G	401 261-6329	20240
Millwork One Inc	Cranston	RI	D	401 738-6990	20263
Mrd Woodworking LLC	West Kingston	RI	G	401 789-3933	21468
Northeast Millwork Corp	Tiverton	RI	G	401 624-7744	21260
Orion Ret Svcs & Fixturing Inc	Smithfield	RI	D	401 334-5000	21243
Stephen C Dematrick	Narragansett	RI	G	401 789-4712	20651
What Woodworking	Warwick	RI	G	617 429-2461	21446
Wood St Woodworkers	Bristol	RI	G	401 253-8257	20111
Brattleboro Kiln Dry & Milling	Brattleboro	VT	E	802 254-4528	21720
Chesters Custom Woodworking	Belmont	VT	G	802 259-3232	21657
Hawleys Fine Woodwork	Chittenden	VT	G	802 483-2575	21854
Heritage Joinery Ltd	Northfield	VT	G	802 485-6107	22243
Keen Woodworking	Mount Holly	VT	G	802 259-2963	22182
Millers Wood Working	Morrisville	VT	G	802 730-9374	22173
Tates Building & Woodworking	Dorset	VT	G	802 867-4082	21909
Vermont Furn Hardwoods Inc	Chester	VT	F	802 875-2550	21852
Wallgoldfinger Inc	Northfield	VT	E	802 483-4200	22246
William Chadburn	North Concord	VT	G	802 695-8166	22223

MINE DEVELOPMENT SVCS: Nonmetallic Minerals

Rowe Contracting Co	Melrose	MA	G	781 620-0052	12991
Ensio Resources Inc	Bow	NH	G	603 224-0221	17712

MINERAL WOOL

Leek Building Products Inc	Norwalk	CT	E	203 853-3883	3185
Bnz Materials Inc	North Billerica	MA	E	978 663-3401	13796
Johns Manville Corporation	Lewiston	ME	E	207 784-0123	6294
Booth Felt Co Inc	Dover	NH	G	603 330-3334	18009
Duxbury Composite Products	Fitzwilliam	NH	E	603 585-9100	18149
Vemployee	Portsmouth	RI	G	888 471-1982	20942

MINERAL WOOL INSULATION PRDTS

Ward Process Inc	Holliston	MA	D	508 429-1165	11613

MINERALS: Ground Or Otherwise Treated

Miyoshi America Inc	Dayville	CT	F	860 779-3990	1047
Miyoshi America Inc	Dayville	CT	G	860 779-3990	1048

MINERALS: Ground or Treated

Micro-Mech Inc	Ipswich	MA	E	978 356-2966	11931
FMC Corporation	Rockland	ME	C	207 594-3200	6795
Isovolta Inc	Rutland	VT	E	802 775-5528	22341

MINIATURE GOLF COURSES

Thompson Family Enterprises	Woodbury	VT	G	802 456-7421	22734

MINIATURES

Dakins Miniatures Inc **(PA)**	Searsport	ME	G	207 548-6084	6949

MINING EXPLORATION & DEVELOPMENT SVCS

Sage Envirotech Drlg Svcs Inc	Pawtucket	RI	G	401 723-9900	20895

MINING MACHINES & EQPT: Feeders, Ore & Aggregate

Eldred Wheeler Company	Hanover	MA	G	781 924-5067	11336

MINING MACHINES & EQPT: Pellet Mills

Northeast Pellets LLC	Ashland	ME	F	207 435-6230	5538

MINING MACHINES & EQPT: Rock Crushing, Stationary

R S Pidacks Inc	Livermore	ME	G	207 897-4622	6376

MINING SVCS, NEC: Bituminous

Buchanan Minerals LLC **(DH)**	Wilton	CT	D	304 392-1000	5281

MIRRORS: Motor Vehicle

Filters Inc	Pawtucket	RI	C	401 722-8999	20840

MISSILE GUIDANCE SYSTEMS & EQPT

Raytheon International Inc **(PA)**	Waltham	MA	G	781 522-3000	16185

MIXING EQPT

Statiflo International Ltd	Pittsfield	MA	G	413 684-9911	14509

MIXTURES & BLOCKS: Asphalt Paving

A-1 Asphalt Paving	Rocky Hill	CT	G	860 436-6085	3700
All States Asphalt Inc	Dayville	CT	G	860 774-7550	1038
E B Asphalt & Landscaping LLC	Norwich	CT	F	860 639-1921	3279
O & G Industries Inc	Stamford	CT	E	203 977-1618	4265
O & G Industries Inc	New Milford	CT	D	860 354-4438	2820
O & G Industries Inc	Bridgeport	CT	E	203 366-4586	459
Aggregate Inds - Northeast Reg	Raynham	MA	G	508 822-7120	14704
Aggregate Inds - Northeast Reg	Wrentham	MA	E	508 384-3161	17513
Aggregate Inds - Northeast Reg	Ashland	MA	E	508 881-1430	7655
Brox Industries Inc **(PA)**	Dracut	MA	D	978 454-9105	10355
Fletcher Granite LLC **(DH)**	Westford	MA	G	978 692-1312	16767
Jr & Sons Construction	Westport	MA	G	508 326-7884	16842
Kdo LLC	Taunton	MA	G	508 802-1347	15761
Massachusetts Broken Stone Co	Holden	MA	F	508 829-5353	11547
New England Emulsions Corp	Holliston	MA	G	508 429-5550	11590
Rochester Bituminous Products	West Wareham	MA	G	508 295-8001	16576
Sealcoating	Worcester	MA	G	508 926-8080	17470
Trew Corp	Deerfield	MA	F	413 773-9798	10304
A & W Paving & Sealcoating	South Paris	ME	G	207 743-6615	7009
Dayton Sand & Gravel Inc	Dayton	ME	D	207 499-2306	5944
Down E Emulsions Ltd Lblty Co	Bangor	ME	G	207 947-8624	5641
F R Carroll Inc	Limerick	ME	E	207 793-8615	6334
Mattingly Products Company	North Anson	ME	E	207 635-2719	6504
Morin Brothers	Fort Kent	ME	G	207 834-5361	6063
Asphalt Recovery Tech LLC	Brentwood	NH	G	603 778-1449	17744
M & L Asphalt Services LLC	Swanzey	NH	G	603 355-1230	19884
Recycled Asp Shingle Tech LLC	Brentwood	NH	G	603 778-1449	17757
Bjorklund Corp	Providence	RI	G	401 944-6400	20970
Driveways By R Stanley Inc	Saunderstown	RI	G	401 789-8600	21201
Hudson Liquid Asphalts Inc **(PA)**	Cranston	RI	D	401 274-2200	20238
JH Lynch & Sons Inc	East Providence	RI	C	401 434-7100	20422
Pavement Warehouse	Greenville	RI	G	401 233-3200	20471
Perry Paving	Warwick	RI	G	401 732-1730	21403
Black Beauty Driveway Sealing	Colchester	VT	G	802 860-7113	21858

MOBILE COMMUNICATIONS EQPT

Sonitor Technologies Inc	Greenwich	CT	G	727 466-4557	1651
AT&T Inc	Norwell	MA	G	781 878-8169	14095
Cellassist LLC **(PA)**	Springfield	MA	G	413 559-1256	15459
Edge Velocity Corporation	Salem	NH	G	603 912-5618	19723
Kvh Industries Inc	Middletown	RI	C	401 847-3327	20622
Kvh Industries Inc **(PA)**	Middletown	RI	C	401 847-3327	20623
Pcs Metro	East Providence	RI	G	401 574-6105	20440
Wireless For Less	Rutland	VT	G	802 786-0918	22361

MOBILE HOMES

Old Coach Home Sales	Sterling	CT	E	860 774-1379	4371
Crown Properties & HM Sls LLC	North Hampton	NH	G	603 964-2005	19382
Hilltop Cooperative	Raymond	NH	G	603 895-6476	19638
Skyline Corporation	Fair Haven	VT	C	802 278-8222	21969

MOBILE HOMES: Personal Or Private Use

Topek LLC	Grantham	NH	F	603 863-2400	18217

MODELS

Fx Models LLC	Terryville	CT	G	860 589-5279	4480

MODELS: Boat, Exc Toy

Mbm Building Systems Ltd	Boston	MA	F	617 478-3466	8690

MODELS: General, Exc Toy

Case Patterns Inc	Groton	CT	G	860 445-6722	1665
Modelvision Inc	New Milford	CT	G	860 355-3884	2814
Architectural Illusions	Boston	MA	G	617 338-8118	8374
Atlantic Industrial Models LLC	Essex	MA	E	978 768-7686	10591

MOLDED RUBBER PRDTS

Anchor Rubber Products LLC	Newington	CT	G	860 667-2628	2843
Gordon Rubber and Pkg Co Inc	Derby	CT	E	203 735-7441	1072
Hutchinson Precision Ss Inc	Danielson	CT	C	860 779-0300	1013
Bandera Acquisition LLC **(DH)**	Foxborough	MA	C	480 553-6400	10911
C H Yates Rubber Corp	Fall River	MA	G	508 674-3378	10673
Jefferson Rubber Works Inc	Worcester	MA	D	508 791-3600	17397
Polyneer Inc	New Bedford	MA	E	508 998-5225	13440
Tempron Products Corp	Milford	MA	G	508 473-5880	13147
Diacom Corporation	Amherst	NH	D	603 880-1900	17557
Humphreys Industrial Pdts Inc	Rochester	NH	D	603 692-5005	19671
Rihani Plastics Inc	Cranston	RI	F	401 942-7393	20280
Accurate Rubber Products Inc	Swanton	VT	G	802 868-3063	22529

MOLDING COMPOUNDS

Precision Dip Coating LLC	Waterbury	CT	G	203 805-4564	4943
Bi-Qem Inc	Florence	MA	G	413 584-2472	10864
Cambridge Polymer Group Inc	Boston	MA	F	617 629-4400	8456
Chemiplastica Inc	Florence	MA	E	413 584-2472	10865
Indusol Inc	Sutton	MA	E	508 865-9516	15683
Reinforced Structures For Elec	Worcester	MA	E	508 754-5316	17457
RES-Tech Corporation **(HQ)**	Hudson	MA	E	978 567-1000	11811
Unicore LLC	Palmer	MA	E	413 284-9995	14299
G & C Products LLC	Kennebunk	ME	E	207 985-9100	6234
Faber Family Associates Lpa **(PA)**	Salem	NH	G	603 681-0484	19728
Faber Industries LLC **(HQ)**	Salem	NH	F	603 681-0484	19729
Coastal Plastics Inc	Hope Valley	RI	E	401 539-2446	20482
Moore Company **(PA)**	Westerly	RI	C	401 596-2816	21531
QST Inc	Saint Albans	VT	E	802 524-7704	22377

MOLDINGS & TRIM: Metal, Exc Automobile

Watertown Engineering Corp	Whitman	MA	E	781 857-2555	16929

MOLDINGS & TRIM: Wood

Jakes Jr Lawrence	Pomfret Center	CT	E	860 974-3744	3555
Woodworks Architectural Mllwk	Londonderry	NH	E	603 432-4050	18746

MOLDINGS OR TRIM: Automobile, Stamped Metal

C Cowles & Company **(PA)**	North Haven	CT	D	203 865-3117	3012

MOLDINGS: Picture Frame

Psg Framing Inc	Somerville	MA	F	617 261-1817	15206
Herbert Mosher	Nashua	NH	G	603 882-4357	19177

PRODUCT

MOLDS: Indl

	CITY	ST	EMP	PHONE	ENTRY #
Advance Mold & Mfg Inc	Manchester	CT	C	860 432-5887	1983
American Molded Products Inc	Bridgeport	CT	F	203 333-0183	374
American Precision Mold Inc	East Hampton	CT	G	860 267-1356	1157
B & D Machine Inc	Tolland	CT	F	860 871-9226	4539
Betz Tool Company Inc	Milford	CT	G	203 878-1187	2253
Ferron Mold and Tool LLC	Dayville	CT	G	860 774-5555	1043
J & L Tool Company Inc	Wallingford	CT	E	203 265-6237	4757
Moldvision LLC	Thompson	CT	G	860 315-1025	4536
Omni Mold Systems LLC	Lisbon	CT	G	888 666-4755	1944
R&R Tool & Die LLC	East Windsor	CT	G	860 627-9197	1299
Scan Tool & Mold Inc	Trumbull	CT	E	203 459-4950	4631
Upper Valley Mold LLC	Torrington	CT	G	860 489-8282	4606
Watertown Plastics Inc	Watertown	CT	E	860 274-7535	5035
Accutech Packaging Inc	Foxboro	MA	D	508 543-3800	10873
Atco Plastics Inc	Plainville	MA	D	508 695-3573	14515
Bay State Cast Products Inc	Springfield	MA	G	413 736-1028	15450
Brenmar Molding Inc	Fitchburg	MA	G	978 343-3198	10814
Fit America Inc	Southborough	MA	G	309 839-1695	15357
Harrys Mold & Machine Inc	Bridgewater	MA	G	508 697-6432	9075
Innovative Tooling Company Inc	Lenox	MA	F	413 637-1031	12101
Lansen Mold Co Inc	Hancock	MA	F	413 443-5328	11325
Mayhew Basque Plastics LLC	Westminster	MA	F	978 537-5219	16809
Mold Makers Inc	West Bridgewater	MA	G	508 588-4212	16447
Nypromold Inc **(PA)**	Clinton	MA	D	978 365-4547	10087
Pen Ro Mold and Tool Inc	Pittsfield	MA	E	413 499-0464	14498
Pittsfield Plastics Engrg Inc	Pittsfield	MA	D	413 442-0067	14500
Pyramid Mold Inc	Pittsfield	MA	G	413 442-6198	14503
S Ralph Cross and Sons Inc	Sutton	MA	E	508 865-8112	15691
Simsak Machine & Tool Co Inc	Southbridge	MA	G	508 764-4958	15404
Stuart Allyn Co Inc	Pittsfield	MA	G	413 443-7306	14511
Whitewater LLC	West Hatfield	MA	G	413 237-5032	16487
Aluminum Castings Inc	Wilton	NH	G	603 654-9695	19974
Atlantic Sports International	Langdon	NH	G	603 835-6948	18610
Complex Mold & Machine	Plymouth	NH	G	603 536-1221	19528
Freudenberg-Nok General Partnr	Ashland	NH	C	603 968-7187	17599
Hy-Ten Die & Development Corp	Milford	NH	E	603 673-1611	19065
Jamestown Industries Inc	Northfield	NH	G	603 286-3301	19403
Jr Frank Bolton	Weare	NH	G	603 529-3633	19936
Moldpro Inc	Swanzey	NH	E	603 357-2523	19885
Whelen Engineering Co	Charlestown	NH	E	860 526-9504	17821
Ar-Ro Engineering Company Inc **(PA)**	North Smithfield	RI	G	401 766-6669	20781
Bradley Goodwin Pattern Co	Providence	RI	F	401 461-5220	20973
Choklit Mold Ltd	Lincoln	RI	G	401 725-7377	20564
Clear Carbon & Components Inc	Bristol	RI	F	401 254-5085	20068
Mtd Inc	Coventry	RI	G	401 397-5460	20158
Polyurethane Molding Inds Inc	Woonsocket	RI	E	401 765-6700	21576
Welmold Tool & Die Inc	North Kingstown	RI	G	401 738-0505	20749
G W Plastics Inc **(PA)**	Bethel	VT	B	802 234-9941	21695

MOLDS: Plastic Working & Foundry

	CITY	ST	EMP	PHONE	ENTRY #
Heise Industries Inc	East Berlin	CT	D	860 828-6538	1103
Mohawk Tool and Die Mfg Co Inc	Bridgeport	CT	F	203 367-2181	452
Mold Threads Inc	Branford	CT	G	203 483-1420	331
Plastic Design Intl Inc **(PA)**	Middletown	CT	E	860 632-2001	2210
Somerset Plastics Company	Middletown	CT	E	860 635-1601	2224
Advanced Prototypes & Molding	Leominster	MA	G	978 534-0584	12107
Alumi-Nex Mold Inc	Webster	MA	F	508 949-2200	16338
Banner Mold & Die Co Inc	Leominster	MA	E	978 534-6558	12116
Crisci Tool and Die Inc	Leominster	MA	E	978 537-4102	12128
F & M Tool & Die Co Inc	Leominster	MA	E	978 537-0290	12137
Girouard Tool & Die Inc	Leominster	MA	G	978 534-4147	12146
Harris Tool & Die Company Inc	Fitchburg	MA	G	978 479-1842	10828
Lolli Company Inc	Leominster	MA	E	978 537-8343	12163
Mar-Lee Companies Inc	Fitchburg	MA	D	978 348-1291	10834
Neu-Tool Design Inc	Wilmington	MA	E	978 658-5881	17029
Pilgrim Tool & Die Inc	Worcester	MA	G	508 753-0190	17441
Raitto Engineering & Mfg Inc	Wheelwright	MA	G	413 477-6637	16908
Maine Mold & Machine Inc	Hartford	ME	G	207 388-2732	6177
Mrpc Northeast LLC	Hudson	NH	E	603 880-3616	18417
C & W Co Inc	Providence	RI	G	401 941-6311	20977
Conley Casting Supply Corp **(PA)**	Warwick	RI	E	401 461-4710	21345
Tri-Bro Tool Company	Cranston	RI	F	401 781-6323	20305

MONOFILAMENTS: Nontextile

	CITY	ST	EMP	PHONE	ENTRY #
Astenjohnson Inc	Williston	VT	D	802 658-2040	22655

MONUMENTS & GRAVE MARKERS, EXC TERRAZZO

	CITY	ST	EMP	PHONE	ENTRY #
Monument Street Entps LLC	Concord	MA	G	781 820-1888	10142
Arthurs Memorials Inc	Center Conway	NH	G	603 356-5398	17791
Syphers Monument DBA Affordabl	Seabrook	NH	G	603 468-3033	19821
Hardrock Granite Co Inc	Barre	VT	G	802 479-3606	21619
Kinfolk Memorials Inc	East Barre	VT	G	802 479-1423	21912
Monument View Apts LP	Burlington	VT	G	802 863-8424	21798
Monumental Estates LLC	Bennington	VT	G	802 442-7339	21685

MONUMENTS: Concrete

	CITY	ST	EMP	PHONE	ENTRY #
Frederick Wieninger Monuments	Milbridge	ME	G	207 546-2356	6432
H W Dunn & Son Inc	Ellsworth	ME	G	207 667-8121	6019
Plouffs Monument Co Inc	Enosburg Falls	VT	G	802 933-4346	21926

MONUMENTS: Cut Stone, Exc Finishing Or Lettering Only

	CITY	ST	EMP	PHONE	ENTRY #
W C Canniff & Sons Inc	Roslindale	MA	F	617 323-3690	14845
International Stone Products **(PA)**	Barre	VT	D	802 476-6636	21625
Montpelier Granite Works Inc	Montpelier	VT	F	802 223-2581	22155
Pepin Granite Company Inc	Barre	VT	E	802 476-6103	21636
Riverton Memorial Inc	Riverton	VT	F	802 485-3371	22314
Swenson Granite Company LLC	Barre	VT	E	802 476-7021	21641

MOPS: Floor & Dust

	CITY	ST	EMP	PHONE	ENTRY #
Butler Home Products LLC **(DH)**	Hudson	MA	F	508 597-8000	11761

MORTAR

	CITY	ST	EMP	PHONE	ENTRY #
Conproco Corp **(PA)**	Somersworth	NH	F	603 743-5800	19831

MOTION PICTURE & VIDEO PRODUCTION SVCS

	CITY	ST	EMP	PHONE	ENTRY #
Bff Holdings Inc **(HQ)**	Old Saybrook	CT	C	860 510-0100	3328
Blue Sky Studios Inc	Greenwich	CT	C	203 992-6000	1600
Kapcom LLC	East Haven	CT	G	203 891-5112	1253
Laura Marr Productions LLC	Westbrook	ME	G	207 856-9700	7194
Take 2 Dough Productions Inc	Sanford	ME	F	207 490-6502	6893

MOTION PICTURE & VIDEO PRODUCTION SVCS: Indl

	CITY	ST	EMP	PHONE	ENTRY #
Fx Models LLC	Terryville	CT	G	860 589-5279	4480

MOTION PICTURE EQPT

	CITY	ST	EMP	PHONE	ENTRY #
Rosco Holdings Inc **(PA)**	Stamford	CT	D	203 708-8900	4306
Rosco Laboratories Inc **(HQ)**	Stamford	CT	E	203 708-8900	4307
Broadcast Pix Inc	Chelmsford	MA	E	978 600-1100	9878

MOTOR & GENERATOR PARTS: Electric

	CITY	ST	EMP	PHONE	ENTRY #
Dmi Technology Corp **(PA)**	Dover	NH	F	603 742-3330	18019
Electrocraft Inc **(HQ)**	Stratham	NH	E	855 697-7966	19867

MOTOR CONTROL CENTERS

	CITY	ST	EMP	PHONE	ENTRY #
Teknikor Automtn & Contrls Inc	Fall River	MA	F	508 679-9474	10771

MOTOR REBUILDING SVCS, EXC AUTOMOTIVE

	CITY	ST	EMP	PHONE	ENTRY #
Bemat TEC LLC	Cromwell	CT	G	860 632-0049	847
AC Electric Corp **(PA)**	Auburn	ME	E	207 784-7341	5545

MOTOR SCOOTERS & PARTS

	CITY	ST	EMP	PHONE	ENTRY #
Segway Inc **(DH)**	Bedford	NH	C	603 222-6000	17662

MOTOR VEHICLE ASSEMBLY, COMPLETE: Ambulances

	CITY	ST	EMP	PHONE	ENTRY #
Autotronics LLC **(PA)**	Frenchville	ME	G	207 543-6262	6090

MOTOR VEHICLE ASSEMBLY, COMPLETE: Autos, Incl Specialty

	CITY	ST	EMP	PHONE	ENTRY #
Abair Manufacturing Company	Waterbury	CT	F	203 757-0112	4835
Markow Race Cars	South Windsor	CT	G	860 610-0776	3991
Cabot Coach Builders Inc **(PA)**	Haverhill	MA	E	978 374-4530	11412
Mitchell Differential Inc	Shrewsbury	MA	G	508 755-3790	15124
Tube Chassis Designz	Hanson	MA	G	781 293-5005	11369

MOTOR VEHICLE ASSEMBLY, COMPLETE: Buses, All Types

	CITY	ST	EMP	PHONE	ENTRY #
American Vehicles Sales LLC	Yantic	CT	G	860 886-0327	5507
Atlantic Turtle Top Inc	South Grafton	MA	G	508 839-1711	15296
Patsys Bus Sales and Service	Concord	NH	F	603 226-2222	17922

MOTOR VEHICLE ASSEMBLY, COMPLETE: Cars, Armored

	CITY	ST	EMP	PHONE	ENTRY #
Lenco Industries Inc	Pittsfield	MA	D	413 443-7359	14483

MOTOR VEHICLE ASSEMBLY, COMPLETE: Fire Department Vehicles

	CITY	ST	EMP	PHONE	ENTRY #
Fire Emergency Maint Co LLC	Lynnfield	MA	G	781 334-3100	12548
Epping Volunteer Fire District	Columbia Falls	ME	F	207 483-2036	5920
Larry Dingee	Cornish	NH	G	603 542-9682	17962
American Rural Fire Apparatus	Williamstown	VT	G	802 433-1554	22649
Town of Hartford	White River Junction	VT	E	802 295-9425	22643

MOTOR VEHICLE ASSEMBLY, COMPLETE: Military Motor Vehicle

	CITY	ST	EMP	PHONE	ENTRY #
Wgi Inc	Southwick	MA	C	413 569-9444	15421
Loring Industries LLC	Limestone	ME	G	207 328-7005	6342

MOTOR VEHICLE ASSEMBLY, COMPLETE: Patrol Wagons

	CITY	ST	EMP	PHONE	ENTRY #
Christphrs Emrgncy Eqptmnt &	Chelmsford	MA	G	978 265-8363	9887

MOTOR VEHICLE ASSEMBLY, COMPLETE: Personnel Carriers

	CITY	ST	EMP	PHONE	ENTRY #
Cadillac Gage Textron Inc **(HQ)**	Wilmington	MA	G	978 657-5111	16986

MOTOR VEHICLE ASSEMBLY, COMPLETE: Road Oilers

	CITY	ST	EMP	PHONE	ENTRY #
Triple D Transportation Inc	Bloomfield	CT	G	860 243-5057	267

MOTOR VEHICLE ASSEMBLY, COMPLETE: Snow Plows

	CITY	ST	EMP	PHONE	ENTRY #
Structured Solutions II LLC	New Canaan	CT	G	203 972-5717	2616
Universal Body & Eqp Co LLC	Oakville	CT	F	860 274-7541	3304
Douglas Dynamics LLC	Rockland	ME	C	207 701-4200	6790
Messer Truck Equipment **(PA)**	Westbrook	ME	E	207 854-9751	7196

MOTOR VEHICLE ASSEMBLY, COMPLETE: Truck & Tractor Trucks

	CITY	ST	EMP	PHONE	ENTRY #
Dejana Trck Utility Eqp Co LLC	Smithfield	RI	E	401 231-9797	21220

MOTOR VEHICLE ASSEMBLY, COMPLETE: Trucks, Pickup

	CITY	ST	EMP	PHONE	ENTRY #
Tremcar USA	Haverhill	MA	F	978 556-5330	11477

MOTOR VEHICLE DEALERS: Automobiles, New & Used

	CITY	ST	EMP	PHONE	ENTRY #
Adaptive Mobility Equipment	Seekonk	MA	G	508 336-2556	15017

MOTOR VEHICLE PARTS & ACCESS: Bearings

	CITY	ST	EMP	PHONE	ENTRY #
Alinabal Holdings Corporation **(PA)**	Milford	CT	B	203 877-3241	2243

MOTOR VEHICLE PARTS & ACCESS: Body Components & Frames

	CITY	ST	EMP	PHONE	ENTRY #
Clarios	Meriden	CT	D	678 297-4040	2086
Cadillac Gage Textron Inc **(HQ)**	Wilmington	MA	G	978 657-5111	16986

MOTOR VEHICLE PARTS & ACCESS: Cleaners, air

Company	CITY	ST	EMP	PHONE	ENTRY #
Eco Touch Inc	Somersworth	NH	G	603 319-1762	19836

MOTOR VEHICLE PARTS & ACCESS: Electrical Eqpt

Company	CITY	ST	EMP	PHONE	ENTRY #
All Tech Auto/Truck Electric	Danbury	CT	G	203 790-8990	868
Casco Products Corporation **(HQ)**	Bridgeport	CT	F	203 922-3200	396
Armatron International Inc **(PA)**	Malden	MA	D	781 321-2300	12559
Sevcon Inc **(HQ)**	Southborough	MA	E	508 281-5500	15365
Stoneridge Inc	Canton	MA	B	781 830-0340	9787
Crescent Industries Company	Auburn	ME	G	207 777-3500	5557

MOTOR VEHICLE PARTS & ACCESS: Engines & Parts

Company	CITY	ST	EMP	PHONE	ENTRY #
Callaway Cars Inc	Old Lyme	CT	F	860 434-9002	3316
Callaway Companies Inc **(PA)**	Old Lyme	CT	F	860 434-9002	3317
Moroso Performance Pdts Inc **(PA)**	Guilford	CT	C	203 453-6571	1711
Morin Engine Services LLC	Nashua	NH	G	603 880-3009	19210
A C Performance Center Ltd	Colchester	VT	G	802 862-6074	21855

MOTOR VEHICLE PARTS & ACCESS: Engs & Trans,Factory, Rebuilt

Company	CITY	ST	EMP	PHONE	ENTRY #
S Camerota & Sons Inc	Bow	NH	G	603 228-9343	17730

MOTOR VEHICLE PARTS & ACCESS: Fifth Wheels

Company	CITY	ST	EMP	PHONE	ENTRY #
Tru Hitch Inc	Pleasant Valley	CT	F	860 379-7772	3548

MOTOR VEHICLE PARTS & ACCESS: Fuel Pumps

Company	CITY	ST	EMP	PHONE	ENTRY #
Stanadyne LLC **(DH)**	Windsor	CT	A	860 525-0821	5368

MOTOR VEHICLE PARTS & ACCESS: Fuel Systems & Parts

Company	CITY	ST	EMP	PHONE	ENTRY #
Clarcor Eng MBL Solutions LLC **(DH)**	East Hartford	CT	D	860 920-4200	1182
Stanadyne Intrmdate Hldngs LLC **(HQ)**	Windsor	CT	C	860 525-0821	5367

MOTOR VEHICLE PARTS & ACCESS: Horns

Company	CITY	ST	EMP	PHONE	ENTRY #
Nathan Airchime Inc	South Windham	CT	G	860 423-4575	3927

MOTOR VEHICLE PARTS & ACCESS: Lifting Mechanisms, Dump Truck

Company	CITY	ST	EMP	PHONE	ENTRY #
Lac Landscaping LLC	Milford	CT	F	203 807-1067	2308

MOTOR VEHICLE PARTS & ACCESS: Oil Strainers

Company	CITY	ST	EMP	PHONE	ENTRY #
JPsexton LLC	Windsor	CT	G	860 748-2048	5342

MOTOR VEHICLE PARTS & ACCESS: Pumps, Hydraulic Fluid Power

Company	CITY	ST	EMP	PHONE	ENTRY #
Dynex/Rivett Inc	Ashland	MA	G	508 881-5110	7658

MOTOR VEHICLE PARTS & ACCESS: Tie Rods

Company	CITY	ST	EMP	PHONE	ENTRY #
Alinabal Inc **(HQ)**	Milford	CT	C	203 877-3241	2242

MOTOR VEHICLE PARTS & ACCESS: Tops

Company	CITY	ST	EMP	PHONE	ENTRY #
Thule Inc **(DH)**	Seymour	CT	C	203 881-9600	3765
Thule Holding Inc **(DH)**	Seymour	CT	F	203 881-9600	3766
M & T Manufacturing Co	Peace Dale	RI	G	401 789-0472	20914

MOTOR VEHICLE PARTS & ACCESS: Transmission Housings Or Parts

Company	CITY	ST	EMP	PHONE	ENTRY #
Defeo Manufacturing Inc	Brookfield	CT	E	203 775-0254	641
Sonnax Industries Inc **(PA)**	Bellows Falls	VT	C	802 463-9722	21654

MOTOR VEHICLE PARTS & ACCESS: Transmissions

Company	CITY	ST	EMP	PHONE	ENTRY #
Dynamic Racing Transm LLC	North Branford	CT	G	203 315-0138	2963
Magmotor Technologies Inc	Worcester	MA	F	508 835-4305	17411
Allard Nazarian Group Inc	Manchester	NH	F	603 314-0017	18775

MOTOR VEHICLE PARTS & ACCESS: Universal Joints

Company	CITY	ST	EMP	PHONE	ENTRY #
Naugler Co Inc	Newburyport	MA	G	978 463-9199	13517

MOTOR VEHICLE PARTS & ACCESS: Water Pumps

Company	CITY	ST	EMP	PHONE	ENTRY #
V Power Equipment LLC	Wareham	MA	F	508 273-7596	16256

MOTOR VEHICLE PARTS & ACCESS: Wiring Harness Sets

Company	CITY	ST	EMP	PHONE	ENTRY #
Rhode Island Wiring Service	West Kingston	RI	G	401 789-1955	21470

MOTOR VEHICLE SPLYS & PARTS WHOLESALERS: New

Company	CITY	ST	EMP	PHONE	ENTRY #
Irish Inc **(PA)**	Turner	ME	G	207 224-7605	7108
Freudenberg-Nok General Partnr	Northfield	NH	D	603 286-1600	19401
Dejana Trck Utility Eqp Co LLC	Smithfield	RI	E	401 231-9797	21220

MOTOR VEHICLE: Shock Absorbers

Company	CITY	ST	EMP	PHONE	ENTRY #
Hutchinson Arospc & Indust Inc **(DH)**	Hopkinton	MA	B	508 417-7000	11718
General Kinetics LLC	Bedford	NH	G	603 627-8547	17642

MOTOR VEHICLE: Steering Mechanisms

Company	CITY	ST	EMP	PHONE	ENTRY #
NSK Steering Systems Amer Inc	Bennington	VT	B	802 442-5448	21688

MOTOR VEHICLES & CAR BODIES

Company	CITY	ST	EMP	PHONE	ENTRY #
CD Racing Products	Oxford	CT	G	203 264-7822	3395
Oshkosh Corporation	East Granby	CT	F	860 653-5548	1138
Special Vhcl Developments Inc	Cheshire	CT	G	203 272-7928	764
Ally Automotive Inc	Newton	MA	G	734 604-2257	13559
Greenwood Emrgncy Vehicles LLC **(HQ)**	North Attleboro	MA	D	508 695-7138	13758
L3 Essco Inc	Ayer	MA	D	978 568-5100	7923
Oshkosh Corporation	Burlington	MA	C	800 392-9921	9315
Needham Electric Supply LLC	Wolfeboro	NH	G	603 569-0643	20023
Denton Auto Inc	Craftsbury	VT	G	802 586-2828	21892

MOTOR VEHICLES, WHOLESALE: Commercial

Company	CITY	ST	EMP	PHONE	ENTRY #
American Vehicles Sales LLC	Yantic	CT	G	860 886-0327	5507

MOTOR VEHICLES, WHOLESALE: Fire Trucks

Company	CITY	ST	EMP	PHONE	ENTRY #
Greenwood Emrgncy Vehicles LLC **(HQ)**	North Attleboro	MA	D	508 695-7138	13758

MOTOR VEHICLES, WHOLESALE: Motorized Cycles

Company	CITY	ST	EMP	PHONE	ENTRY #
MH Rhodes Cramer LLC	South Windsor	CT	G	860 291-8402	3994

MOTORCYCLE ACCESS

Company	CITY	ST	EMP	PHONE	ENTRY #
Cat LLC	Hartford	CT	G	860 953-1807	1812
Niche Inc	New Bedford	MA	E	508 990-4202	13427
Heli Modified Inc	Cornish	ME	F	207 625-4642	5925

MOTORCYCLE DEALERS

Company	CITY	ST	EMP	PHONE	ENTRY #
Moto Tassinari Inc	West Lebanon	NH	F	603 298-6646	19957
Rowe Machine Co	Hampton	NH	F	603 926-0029	18270

MOTORCYCLE PARTS & ACCESS DEALERS

Company	CITY	ST	EMP	PHONE	ENTRY #
Government Surplus Sales Inc	Hartford	CT	G	860 247-7787	1827

MOTORCYCLE PARTS: Wholesalers

Company	CITY	ST	EMP	PHONE	ENTRY #
Kent Pearce	East Wareham	MA	G	508 295-3791	10531

MOTORCYCLES & RELATED PARTS

Company	CITY	ST	EMP	PHONE	ENTRY #
Tri State Choppers LLC	New Milford	CT	G	860 210-1854	2832
Italian Choppers LLC	Southbridge	MA	G	508 648-6816	15387
Rave Brothers LLC	South Portland	ME	G	207 773-7727	7038
Moto Tassinari Inc	West Lebanon	NH	F	603 298-6646	19957
South County Choppers	Narragansett	RI	G	401 788-1000	20650

MOTORS: Electric

Company	CITY	ST	EMP	PHONE	ENTRY #
Tritex Corporation	Waterbury	CT	C	203 756-7441	4967
Ward Leonard CT LLC **(DH)**	Thomaston	CT	C	860 283-5801	4525
Ametek Arizona Instrument LLC	Middleboro	MA	C	508 946-6200	13051
Dkd Solutions Inc	Worcester	MA	G	508 762-9114	17365
Ashland Electric Products Inc	Rochester	NH	E	603 335-1100	19659
Electrocraft New Hampshire Inc **(DH)**	Dover	NH	E	603 742-3330	18021

MOTORS: Generators

Company	CITY	ST	EMP	PHONE	ENTRY #
Cramer Company	South Windsor	CT	G	860 291-8402	3954
Fuelcell Energy Inc	Torrington	CT	E	860 496-1111	4579
GE Steam Power Inc **(HQ)**	Windsor	CT	A	866 257-8664	5336
Generators On Demand LLC	Old Lyme	CT	F	860 662-4090	3323
Hydrotec Inc	Oxford	CT	G	203 264-6700	3409
Ktcr Holding	Westport	CT	G	203 227-4115	5208
Power Strategies LLC	Fairfield	CT	G	203 254-9926	1449
Rowley Spring & Stamping Corp	Bristol	CT	C	860 582-8175	610
Sandvik Wire and Htg Tech Corp	Bethel	CT	D	203 744-1440	177
Technipower Systems Inc **(HQ)**	Brookfield	CT	G	203 748-7001	660
American Superconductor Corp **(PA)**	Ayer	MA	C	978 842-3000	7907
Ametek Inc	Wilmington	MA	D	978 988-4101	16973
Creative Motion Technology	North Reading	MA	G	978 664-6218	13981
Electra Dyne Company Inc	Plymouth	MA	G	508 746-3270	14553
Electro Switch Corp	Weymouth	MA	C	781 607-3306	16887
Epropelled Inc **(PA)**	Lowell	MA	G	978 703-1350	12369
L3 Technologies Inc	Northampton	MA	A	413 586-2330	14009
Maxon Precision Motors Inc **(HQ)**	Taunton	MA	E	508 677-0520	15763
Peak Scientific Inc **(DH)**	North Billerica	MA	E	866 647-1649	13853
Precision Electronics Corp	Marshfield	MA	F	781 834-6677	12865
Steven Sprott	Whitinsville	MA	G	774 276-6534	16918
Toshiba International Corp	Burlington	MA	G	781 273-9000	9348
Ion Physics Corp	Fremont	NH	G	603 895-5100	18177
Kearney-National Inc	North Kingstown	RI	E	401 943-2686	20719
Wei Inc **(PA)**	Cranston	RI	E	401 781-3904	20309
Hayward Tyler Inc **(DH)**	Colchester	VT	D	802 655-4444	21864
Star Wind Turbines LLC	East Dorset	VT	G	802 779-8118	21916

MOTORS: Rocket, Guided Missile

Company	CITY	ST	EMP	PHONE	ENTRY #
Blushift Aerospace Inc	Brunswick	ME	G	207 619-1703	5831

MOTORS: Torque

Company	CITY	ST	EMP	PHONE	ENTRY #
AKO Inc	Windsor	CT	E	860 298-9765	5317
Fraen Mechatronics LLC	Reading	MA	G	781 439-5934	14735
Superpedestrian Inc	Cambridge	MA	G	617 945-1892	9666
Sumake North America LLC	Amherst	NH	G	603 402-2924	17589
Teledyne Instruments Inc	Portsmouth	NH	C	603 474-5571	19624

MOUTHPIECES, PIPE & CIGARETTE HOLDERS: Rubber

Company	CITY	ST	EMP	PHONE	ENTRY #
Bite Tech Inc	Norwalk	CT	E	203 987-6898	3114

MOVEMENTS, WATCH OR CLOCK

Company	CITY	ST	EMP	PHONE	ENTRY #
Faco Metal Products Inc	Cranston	RI	F	401 943-7127	20223

MULTIPLEXERS: Telephone & Telegraph

Company	CITY	ST	EMP	PHONE	ENTRY #
General Datacomm Inds Inc **(PA)**	Oxford	CT	E	203 729-0271	3405

MUSEUMS & ART GALLERIES

Company	CITY	ST	EMP	PHONE	ENTRY #
Helmick & Schechter Inc	Newton	MA	G	617 332-2433	13600

MUSIC BOXES

Company	CITY	ST	EMP	PHONE	ENTRY #
J & J Music Boxes Inc	Pepperell	MA	F	978 433-5686	14439
Porter Music Box Company Inc	Randolph	VT	G	802 728-9694	22301

MUSIC DISTRIBUTION APPARATUS

Company	CITY	ST	EMP	PHONE	ENTRY #
Russound/Fmp Inc	Newmarket	NH	C	603 659-5170	19338

MUSIC RECORDING PRODUCER

Company	CITY	ST	EMP	PHONE	ENTRY #
Stephen McArthur	Barre	VT	G	802 839-0371	21640

	CITY	ST	EMP	PHONE	ENTRY #
MUSICAL INSTRUMENT PARTS & ACCESS, WHOLESALE					
Your Heaven LLC	Providence	RI	G	401 273-7076	21158
MUSICAL INSTRUMENTS & ACCESS: Carrying Cases					
Overtone Labs Inc	Lawrence	MA	G	978 682-1257	12070
MUSICAL INSTRUMENTS & ACCESS: NEC					
Fender Musical Instrs Corp	New Hartford	CT	G	860 379-7575	2637
Action Organ Service	Foxboro	MA	G	508 543-2161	10875
Anthem Music Group Inc	North Billerica	MA	G	978 667-3224	13793
FA Finale Inc	Boston	MA	D	617 226-7888	8536
Fishman Transducers Inc	Andover	MA	D	978 988-9199	7549
Noack Organ Company Inc	Georgetown	MA	G	978 352-6266	11147
Vindor Music Inc	Newton	MA	G	617 984-9831	13649
William S Haynes Co Inc	Acton	MA	G	978 268-0600	7393
Richard Fisher	Prospect Harbor	ME	G	207 963-7184	6771
Euphonon Co	Orford	NH	G	603 353-4882	19420
Alesis LP	Cumberland	RI	G	401 658-4032	20313
MUSICAL INSTRUMENTS & ACCESS: Pianos					
Burgett Brothers Incorporated	Haverhill	MA	E	978 374-8888	11411
MUSICAL INSTRUMENTS & ACCESS: Pipe Organs					
Broome & Company LLC	Windsor Locks	CT	G	860 623-0254	5387
C B Fisk Inc	Gloucester	MA	E	978 283-1909	11168
A David Moore Inc	North Pomfret	VT	G	802 457-3914	22234
MUSICAL INSTRUMENTS & PARTS: Brass					
SE Shires Inc	Holliston	MA	E	508 634-6805	11601
MUSICAL INSTRUMENTS & PARTS: Percussion					
Avedis Zildjian Co **(PA)**	Norwell	MA	C	781 871-2200	14096
MUSICAL INSTRUMENTS & PARTS: String					
NS Design	Nobleboro	ME	G	207 563-7705	6493
MUSICAL INSTRUMENTS & PARTS: Woodwind					
Arista Flutes LLC	Bedford	MA	G	781 275-8821	7959
MUSICAL INSTRUMENTS & SPLYS STORES					
Sweetheart Flute Company LLC	Enfield	CT	G	860 749-8514	1387
Alternate Mode Inc	East Longmeadow	MA	G	413 594-5190	10464
Woodsound Studio	Rockport	ME	G	207 596-7407	6827
MUSICAL INSTRUMENTS WHOLESALERS					
FA Finale Inc	Boston	MA	D	617 226-7888	8536
Verne Q Powell Flutes Inc	Maynard	MA	D	978 461-6111	12905
Pantheon Guitars LLC	Lewiston	ME	F	207 755-0003	6314
MUSICAL INSTRUMENTS: Electric & Electronic					
Alternate Mode Inc	East Longmeadow	MA	G	413 594-5190	10464
G Finkenbeiner Inc	Waltham	MA	G	781 899-3138	16117
Northwind Timber	Center Sandwich	NH	G	603 284-6123	17807
Your Heaven LLC	Providence	RI	G	401 273-7076	21158
MUSICAL INSTRUMENTS: Fifes & Parts					
Cooperman Fife & Drum Co	Bellows Falls	VT	G	802 463-9750	21651
MUSICAL INSTRUMENTS: Flutes & Parts					
Sweetheart Flute Company LLC	Enfield	CT	G	860 749-8514	1387
Brannen Brothers-Flutemakers	Woburn	MA	E	781 935-9522	17139
Eastman Wind Instruments Inc	Acton	MA	F	800 789-2216	7351
Verne Q Powell Flutes Inc	Maynard	MA	D	978 461-6111	12905
MUSICAL INSTRUMENTS: Guitars & Parts, Electric & Acoustic					
Pantheon Guitars LLC	Lewiston	ME	F	207 755-0003	6314
Woodsound Studio	Rockport	ME	G	207 596-7407	6827
Guitabec USA Inc	Berlin	NH	E	603 752-1432	17697
MUSICAL INSTRUMENTS: Harpsichords					
Zuckerman Hrpsichords Intl LLC	Stonington	CT	G	860 535-1715	4379
MUSICAL INSTRUMENTS: Organs					
Austin Organs Incorporated	Hartford	CT	E	860 522-8293	1808
Broome & Co LLC	East Granby	CT	G	860 653-2106	1118
Andover Organ Company Inc	Lawrence	MA	F	978 686-9600	11994
Faucher Organ Company Inc	Biddeford	ME	G	207 283-1420	5732
Stephen J Russell & Co	Chester	VT	G	802 869-2540	21850
MUSICAL INSTRUMENTS: Piccolos & Parts					
Keefe Piccolo Company Inc	Winchester	MA	G	781 369-1626	17090
MUSICAL INSTRUMENTS: Strings, Instrument					
Clear Carbon & Components Inc	Bristol	RI	F	401 254-5085	20068
MUSICAL INSTRUMENTS: Trombones & Parts					
Viz-Pro LLC	Winsted	CT	G	860 379-0055	5427
NAME PLATES: Engraved Or Etched					
American Rubber Stamp Company	Cheshire	CT	G	203 755-1135	710
Ann S Davis	Lebanon	CT	F	860 642-7228	1932
Identification Products Corp	Bridgeport	CT	F	203 334-5969	429
A S A P Engravers	Whitinsville	MA	G	508 234-6974	16909
Chemi-Graphic Inc	Ludlow	MA	E	413 589-0151	12458
E V Yeuell Inc	Woburn	MA	E	781 933-2984	17171
Eastern Etching and Mfg Co	Chicopee	MA	E	413 594-6601	10022
Modern Marking Products Inc	Bridgewater	MA	G	508 697-6066	9085
Northeast Stamp & Engraving	Milford	MA	G	508 473-5818	13132
Reid Graphics Inc	Andover	MA	D	978 474-1930	7598
Platinum Recognition LLC **(PA)**	North Providence	RI	G	401 305-6700	20772
NAMEPLATES					
Precision Graphics Inc	East Berlin	CT	E	860 828-6561	1106
Doranco Inc	Attleboro	MA	G	508 236-0290	7727
Eastern Etching and Mfg Co	Chicopee	MA	E	413 594-6601	10022
Honorcraft LLC	Stoughton	MA	E	781 341-0410	15597
Recognition Center Inc	Holliston	MA	G	508 429-5881	11598
Reeves Coinc	Attleboro	MA	E	508 222-2877	7785
NATIONAL SECURITY FORCES					
Dla Document Services	Newport	RI	G	401 841-6011	20662
NATIONAL SECURITY, GOVERNMENT: Navy					
United States Dept of Navy	Portsmouth	NH	A	207 438-2714	19627
NATURAL GAS COMPRESSING SVC, On-Site					
Consoldted Utilties Corporaion	Hudson	MA	G	978 562-3500	11765
NATURAL GAS LIQUIDS PRODUCTION					
Inov8v Energy LLC	Canaan	NH	G	603 632-7333	17779
Filters Inc	Pawtucket	RI	G	401 722-8999	20840
NATURAL GAS PRODUCTION					
Fpr Pinedale LLC	Stamford	CT	G	203 542-6000	4196
South Bend Ethanol LLC	Stamford	CT	E	203 326-8132	4325
Poweroptions Inc	Boston	MA	G	617 737-8480	8788
Revision Heat LLC	Windham	ME	F	207 221-5677	7247
NATURAL LIQUEFIED PETROLEUM GAS PRODUCTION					
Sea Land Energy Maine Inc	Windham	ME	G	207 892-3284	7250
NATURAL PROPANE PRODUCTION					
Keene Gas Corporation	Keene	NH	F	603 352-4134	18510
NAUTICAL REPAIR SVCS					
Farrar Sails Inc	New London	CT	G	860 447-0382	2772
Doyle Sailmakers Inc	South Dartmouth	MA	G	508 992-6322	15238
NAVIGATIONAL SYSTEMS & INSTRUMENTS					
Airflo Instrument Company	Glastonbury	CT	G	860 633-9455	1536
Alakai Technologies Corp	Hopkinton	MA	G	774 248-4964	11689
Entwistle Company **(HQ)**	Hudson	MA	C	508 481-4000	11772
L3 Technologies Inc	Ayer	MA	F	978 462-2400	7924
Megapulse Incorporated	Bedford	MA	E	781 538-5299	7989
Navionics Inc	Wareham	MA	E	508 291-6000	16253
Trimble Inc	Marlborough	MA	G	508 381-5800	12838
Ursa Navigation Solutions Inc	North Billerica	MA	G	781 538-5299	13875
Bae Systems Tech Sol Srvc Inc	Bath	ME	G	207 449-3577	5673
Inreach Inc	Yarmouth	ME	G	207 846-7104	7297
Bae Systems Info & Elec Sys	Nashua	NH	C	603 885-3653	19123
C-R Control Systems Inc	Lebanon	NH	G	603 727-9149	18617
C3i Inc	Exeter	NH	E	603 929-9989	18115
Kvh Industries Inc **(PA)**	Middletown	RI	C	401 847-3327	20623
NEEDLES					
Connectcut Prcsion Cmpnnts LLC	Torrington	CT	G	860 489-8621	4573
NETTING: Cargo					
International Cordage East Ltd	Colchester	CT	D	860 873-5000	804
Calling All Cargo LLC	Dover	NH	F	603 740-1900	18011
NETTING: Plastic					
Pucuda Inc	Madison	CT	F	860 526-8004	1972
NEWSPAPERS & PERIODICALS NEWS REPORTING SVCS					
Buzzafricocom	Lynn	MA	G	617 903-0152	12494
NICKEL					
Materion Technical Mtls Inc	Lincoln	RI	C	401 333-1700	20583
NICKEL ALLOY					
Norilsk Nickel USA Inc	Ridgefield	CT	G	203 730-0676	3673
If I Only Had A Nickel	Concord	NH	G	603 225-3972	17910
Nickel Corporaxion	Providence	RI	G	401 351-6555	21077
NIPPLES: Rubber					
Playtex Products LLC **(HQ)**	Shelton	CT	D	203 944-5500	3856
Tc Design Works Inc	Beverly	MA	G	978 768-0034	8187
NONAROMATIC CHEMICAL PRDTS					
Glenn LLC	Warwick	RI	G	800 521-0065	21369
NONCURRENT CARRYING WIRING DEVICES					
Chase Corporation	Woodbridge	CT	F	203 285-1244	5464
Wiremold Company	West Hartford	CT	F	860 263-3115	5105
Wiremold Legrand Co Centerex	West Hartford	CT	E	877 295-3472	5106
Chase Corporation	Randolph	MA	E	781 963-2600	14673
Reinforced Structures For Elec	Worcester	MA	E	508 754-5316	17457
Signal Communications Corp	Woburn	MA	E	781 933-0998	17295
Transene Company Inc	Danvers	MA	F	978 777-7860	10265
Baker Company Inc **(PA)**	Sanford	ME	C	207 324-8773	6871
Continental Cable LLC	Hinsdale	NH	D	800 229-5131	18319
Warehouse Cables LLC	Warwick	RI	G	401 737-5677	21442
NONFERROUS: Rolling & Drawing, NEC					
Doncasters Inc	Groton	CT	D	860 446-4803	1670
Titanium Metals Corporation	East Windsor	CT	F	860 627-7051	1307
Ulbrich Stainless Steels	Wallingford	CT	C	203 269-2507	4824

	CITY	ST	EMP	PHONE	ENTRY #
United Stts Sgn & Fbrction	Trumbull	CT	E	203 601-1000	4640
Dan-Kar Plastics Products	Woburn	MA	G	781 935-9221	17163
Echo Industries Inc	Orange	MA	E	978 544-7000	14215
H C Starck Inc **(HQ)**	Newton	MA	C	617 630-5800	13598
Sx Industries Inc **(PA)**	Stoughton	MA	E	781 828-7111	15625
Elmet Technologies LLC	Lewiston	ME	C	207 333-6100	6287
Dgf Indstrial Innvations Group	Gilford	NH	F	603 528-6591	18185
Microspec Corporation	Peterborough	NH	E	603 924-4300	19477
1st Casting Company	Johnston	RI	F	401 272-0750	20495
Callico Metals Inc	North Kingstown	RI	G	401 398-8238	20695
Lead Conversion Plus	Milton	VT	G	802 497-1557	22132

NOTEBOOKS, MADE FROM PURCHASED MATERIALS

	CITY	ST	EMP	PHONE	ENTRY #
Avery Dennison Corporation	Westborough	MA	C	508 948-3500	16591
Eureka Lab Book Inc	Holyoke	MA	F	413 534-5671	11625

NOTIONS: Pins & Needles

	CITY	ST	EMP	PHONE	ENTRY #
W H Bagshaw Co Inc	Nashua	NH	E	603 883-7758	19283

NOVELTIES

	CITY	ST	EMP	PHONE	ENTRY #
Cartamundi East Longmeadow LLC	East Longmeadow	MA	B	413 526-2000	10469
David W Wallace	Shelburne Falls	MA	G	413 625-6523	15067
Mass Logic Inc	Boxboro	MA	G	978 635-1917	8953
Sheffield Pottery Inc	Sheffield	MA	E	413 229-7700	15065
Townie Frozen Desserts LLC	Hull	MA	G	781 925-6095	11831
Initial This Inc	Veazie	ME	G	207 992-7176	7127
Imperial Ceramics	Warwick	RI	G	401 732-0500	21375
RJ Mansour Inc	Providence	RI	E	401 521-7800	21116

NOVELTIES & SPECIALTIES: Metal

	CITY	ST	EMP	PHONE	ENTRY #
JH Smith Co Inc **(PA)**	Greenfield	MA	F	413 772-0191	11264
Saunders Mfg Co Inc **(PA)**	Readfield	ME	D	207 685-9860	6778
Locked In Steel	Hudson	NH	G	603 233-8299	18365
Aspects Inc	Warren	RI	E	401 247-1854	21286
Cathedral Art Metal Co Inc	Providence	RI	E	401 273-7200	20981

NOVELTIES, DURABLE, WHOLESALE

	CITY	ST	EMP	PHONE	ENTRY #
JH Smith Co Inc **(PA)**	Greenfield	MA	F	413 772-0191	11264

NOVELTIES: Leather

	CITY	ST	EMP	PHONE	ENTRY #
Tapestry Inc	Lee	MA	F	413 243-4897	12096
Gallery Leather Co Inc	Trenton	ME	E	207 667-9474	7098

NOVELTIES: Plastic

	CITY	ST	EMP	PHONE	ENTRY #
United Plastics Technologies	New Britain	CT	F	860 224-1110	2588
Plastic Monofil Co Ltd	Medway	MA	F	732 629-7701	12969
Swaponz Inc	Natick	MA	G	508 650-4456	13280
Perry Blackburne Inc	North Providence	RI	E	401 231-7200	20771

NOVELTY SHOPS

	CITY	ST	EMP	PHONE	ENTRY #
David W Wallace	Shelburne Falls	MA	G	413 625-6523	15067
Dakins Miniatures Inc **(PA)**	Searsport	ME	G	207 548-6084	6949
Harringtons In Vermont Inc **(PA)**	Richmond	VT	F	802 434-7500	22312

NOZZLES & SPRINKLERS Lawn Hose

	CITY	ST	EMP	PHONE	ENTRY #
Boston Atmtc Sprnklr Fbrcation	Rockland	MA	G	781 681-5122	14794
Lash Lamour	Boston	MA	G	617 247-1871	8659
Viola Associates Inc	Hyannis	MA	F	508 771-3457	11861
Frank Passarella Inc	North Kingstown	RI	G	401 295-4943	20712

NOZZLES: Spray, Aerosol, Paint Or Insecticide

	CITY	ST	EMP	PHONE	ENTRY #
Bete Fog Nozzle Inc **(PA)**	Greenfield	MA	C	413 772-0846	11252
Patriot Coatings Inc	Hudson	MA	G	978 567-9006	11800
Spraying Systems Co	Merrimack	NH	E	603 517-1854	19033
Spraying Systems Co	Bedford	NH	F	603 471-0505	17664

NURSERIES & LAWN & GARDEN SPLY STORES, RETAIL: Top Soil

	CITY	ST	EMP	PHONE	ENTRY #
Grillo Services LLC	Milford	CT	E	203 877-5070	2294
Alfred J Cavallaro Inc	Andover	MA	G	978 475-2466	7536

NURSERIES & LAWN/GARDEN SPLY STORES, RET: Garden Splys/Tools

	CITY	ST	EMP	PHONE	ENTRY #
American Standard Company	Southington	CT	E	860 628-9643	4037
Northeast Agricultural Sls Inc	Detroit	ME	G	207 487-6273	5952
Mill River Lumber Ltd	North Clarendon	VT	D	802 775-0032	22220

NURSERY & GARDEN CENTERS

	CITY	ST	EMP	PHONE	ENTRY #
Bobbex Inc	Monroe	CT	G	800 792-4449	2396
Dartmouth Feeders & Traps Inc	South Dartmouth	MA	G	774 202-6594	15237
Burger-Roy Inc	Madison	ME	D	207 696-3978	6404

NURSING CARE FACILITIES: Skilled

	CITY	ST	EMP	PHONE	ENTRY #
Amicus Hlthcare Lving Ctrs LLC	North Chelmsford	MA	E	978 934-0000	13884

NUTS: Metal

	CITY	ST	EMP	PHONE	ENTRY #
Metalform Acquisition LLC **(PA)**	New Britain	CT	E	860 224-2630	2553
A1 Screw Machine Products Inc	Chicopee	MA	F	413 594-8939	9995
Donahue Industries Inc	Shrewsbury	MA	E	508 845-6501	15108
Northeast Metal Co	Indian Orchard	MA	G	413 568-1981	11891
Stanlok Corporation	Worcester	MA	E	508 757-4508	17482

NYLON RESINS

	CITY	ST	EMP	PHONE	ENTRY #
Nylon Corporation America Inc	Manchester	NH	D	603 627-5150	18890

OFFICE EQPT & ACCESSORY CUSTOMIZING SVCS

	CITY	ST	EMP	PHONE	ENTRY #
Marr Office Equipment Inc	Pawtucket	RI	G	401 725-5186	20856

OFFICE EQPT WHOLESALERS

	CITY	ST	EMP	PHONE	ENTRY #
Agissar Corporation	Stratford	CT	D	203 375-8662	4389
C P Bourg Inc **(PA)**	New Bedford	MA	D	508 998-2171	13369
MBI Graphics & Printing Corp	Southbridge	MA	F	508 765-0658	15394
Protech Digital Services LLC	Poland	ME	G	207 899-9237	6596
Relyco Sales Inc	Dover	NH	E	603 742-0999	18050

OFFICE FIXTURES: Exc Wood

	CITY	ST	EMP	PHONE	ENTRY #
Starc Systems Inc	Brunswick	ME	G	844 596-1784	5846

OFFICE FIXTURES: Wood

	CITY	ST	EMP	PHONE	ENTRY #
Premier Mfg Group Inc	Shelton	CT	D	203 924-6617	3863
Continental Woodcraft Inc **(PA)**	Worcester	MA	E	508 581-9560	17359

OFFICE MACHINES, NEC

	CITY	ST	EMP	PHONE	ENTRY #
Its New England Inc	Wallingford	CT	G	203 265-8100	4756

OFFICE SPLY & STATIONERY STORES

	CITY	ST	EMP	PHONE	ENTRY #
Eccles-Lehman Inc	Easton	CT	G	203 268-0605	1318
McClelland Press Inc **(PA)**	Williamstown	MA	F	413 663-5750	16958
Neenah Technical Materials Inc **(HQ)**	Dalton	MA	F	678 518-3343	10180
Neenah Technical Materials Inc	Pittsfield	MA	C	413 684-7874	14495

OFFICE SPLY & STATIONERY STORES: Office Forms & Splys

	CITY	ST	EMP	PHONE	ENTRY #
Adkins Printing Company	New Britain	CT	E	800 228-9745	2506
Copy Stop Inc	Hamden	CT	G	203 288-6401	1738
Hartford Business Supply Inc	Hartford	CT	E	860 233-2138	1830
Da Rosas	Oak Bluffs	MA	F	508 693-0110	14210
Encore Images Inc	Marblehead	MA	F	781 631-4568	12681
Curry Copy Center of Keene	Keene	NH	G	603 352-9542	18499
Capitol Stationery Company	Cranston	RI	G	401 943-5333	20194
Choice Printing & Product LLC	Rumford	RI	F	401 438-3838	21182
Eastern Systems Inc **(PA)**	Waitsfield	VT	G	802 496-1000	22565

OFFICE SPLYS, NEC, WHOLESALE

	CITY	ST	EMP	PHONE	ENTRY #
Adkins Printing Company	New Britain	CT	E	800 228-9745	2506
Da Rosas	Oak Bluffs	MA	F	508 693-0110	14210
State-Line Graphics Inc	Everett	MA	F	617 389-1200	10632

OFFICES & CLINICS OF DOCTORS OF MEDICINE: Dermatologist

	CITY	ST	EMP	PHONE	ENTRY #
Agape Dermatology	Providence	RI	G	401 396-2227	20949

OFFICES & CLINICS OF DOCTORS OF MEDICINE: Neurosurgeon

	CITY	ST	EMP	PHONE	ENTRY #
Cosman Medical LLC	Marlborough	MA	D	781 272-6561	12742

OFFICES & CLINICS OF DOCTORS OF MEDICINE: Ophthalmologist

	CITY	ST	EMP	PHONE	ENTRY #
Jeffrey Gold	Hamden	CT	G	203 281-5737	1762

OFFICES & CLINICS OF DOCTORS OF MEDICINE: Radiologist

	CITY	ST	EMP	PHONE	ENTRY #
Branford Open Mri & Diagnostic	Branford	CT	G	203 481-7800	299

OFFICES & CLINICS OF OPTOMETRISTS: Special, Visual Training

	CITY	ST	EMP	PHONE	ENTRY #
Lets Go Technology Inc **(PA)**	Worcester	MA	F	508 853-8200	17407
Vision Dynamics LLC	Worcester	MA	G	203 271-1944	17502

OIL & GAS FIELD MACHINERY

	CITY	ST	EMP	PHONE	ENTRY #
Numa Tool Company **(PA)**	Thompson	CT	D	860 923-9551	4537
General Electric Company **(PA)**	Boston	MA	A	617 443-3000	8558
Deepwater Buoyancy Inc	Biddeford	ME	F	207 468-2565	5728

OIL FIELD MACHINERY & EQPT

	CITY	ST	EMP	PHONE	ENTRY #
Oil Purification Systems Inc	Waterbury	CT	F	203 346-1800	4932

OIL FIELD SVCS, NEC

	CITY	ST	EMP	PHONE	ENTRY #
Cameron International Corp	Glastonbury	CT	F	860 633-0277	1543
Sigma Tankers Inc	Norwalk	CT	F	203 662-2600	3244
Weatherford International LLC	Wallingford	CT	E	203 294-0190	4828
Baker Hghes Olfld Oprtions LLC	Walpole	MA	C	508 668-0400	15989
Old Ironsides Energy LLC	Boston	MA	F	617 366-2030	8745
Cameron International Corp	Limerick	ME	F	207 793-2289	6333
Sorby & Son Heating	Jaffrey	NH	G	603 532-7214	18477

OILS & ESSENTIAL OILS

	CITY	ST	EMP	PHONE	ENTRY #
Yankee Candle Company Inc **(DH)**	South Deerfield	MA	C	413 665-8306	15260
Yankee Holding Corp **(DH)**	South Deerfield	MA	G	413 665-8306	15262
Ycc Holdings LLC	South Deerfield	MA	A	413 665-8306	15263
Americ An Novelty Inc	Seabrook	NH	G	401 785-9850	19792
Naturopatches Vermont Inc	Bellows Falls	VT	G	800 340-9083	21652

OILS & GREASES: Lubricating

	CITY	ST	EMP	PHONE	ENTRY #
Artech Packaging LLC	Bethel	CT	G	845 858-8558	128
Axel Plastics RES Labs Inc	Monroe	CT	E	718 672-8300	2392
Castrol Industrial N Amer Inc	Putnam	CT	G	860 928-5100	3603
CCL Industries Corporation **(DH)**	Shelton	CT	D	203 926-1253	3785
Permatex Inc **(PA)**	Hartford	CT	E	860 543-7500	1856
Safe Harbour Products Inc	Norwalk	CT	G	203 295-8377	3235
A W Chesterton Company	Groveland	MA	B	781 438-7000	11299
BP Lubricants USA Inc	Worcester	MA	G	508 791-3201	17351
Circuit Systems Inc **(PA)**	Westfield	MA	F	413 562-5019	16678
M J Gordon Company Inc	Pittsfield	MA	G	413 448-6066	14487
Ro 59 Inc	Stoughton	MA	G	781 341-1222	15618
Sally Seaver	Burlington	MA	G	833 322-8483	9332
Winfield Brooks Company Inc	Woburn	MA	F	781 933-5300	17323
Ed Sanders	Lancaster	NH	G	603 788-3626	18600
Battenfeld of America Inc	West Warwick	RI	G	401 823-0700	21483
Noco Energy Corp	Williston	VT	G	802 864-6626	22686

PRODUCT

OILS: Core Or Binders

	CITY	ST	EMP	PHONE	ENTRY #
Enterprise Castings LLC	Lewiston	ME	G	207 782-5511	6288

OILS: Cutting

	CITY	ST	EMP	PHONE	ENTRY #
Chessco Industries Inc **(PA)**	Westport	CT	E	203 255-2804	5183
Fuchs Lubricants Co	East Haven	CT	E	203 469-2336	1251
Homeland Fuels Company LLC	Canton	MA	F	781 737-1892	9739

OILS: Lubricating

	CITY	ST	EMP	PHONE	ENTRY #
Chessco Industries Inc **(PA)**	Westport	CT	E	203 255-2804	5183
Du-Lite Corporation	Middletown	CT	G	860 347-2505	2184

OILS: Lubricating

	CITY	ST	EMP	PHONE	ENTRY #
Macdermid Incorporated **(HQ)**	Waterbury	CT	C	203 575-5700	4900
A W Chesterton Company **(PA)**	Groveland	MA	E	781 438-7000	11298
Change Logic	Newton Upper Falls	MA	F	617 274-8661	13657
J G Performance Inc	Abington	MA	G	781 871-1404	7325
O & E High-Tech Corporation	Medford	MA	G	617 497-1108	12945
Kluber Lubric North Amercia LP	Londonderry	NH	G	603 647-4104	18709
Kluber Lubrication N Amer LP	Londonderry	NH	G	800 447-2238	18710
Kluber Lubrication NA LP **(DH)**	Londonderry	NH	D	603 647-4104	18711
Pelletier Lube Service	Barre	VT	G	802 622-0725	21635

OILS: Peppermint

	CITY	ST	EMP	PHONE	ENTRY #
Jakes Mint Chew LLC	Danvers	MA	G	978 304-0528	10228

OINTMENTS

	CITY	ST	EMP	PHONE	ENTRY #
Vermonts Original LLC	Lyndonville	VT	G	802 626-3610	22076

OLEFINS

	CITY	ST	EMP	PHONE	ENTRY #
Girouard Tool Corp	Leominster	MA	G	978 534-4147	12147

OPERATOR TRAINING, COMPUTER

	CITY	ST	EMP	PHONE	ENTRY #
Advanced Career Tech Inc **(PA)**	Boston	MA	E	508 620-5904	8341
Grolen Communications Inc	Manchester	NH	G	603 645-0101	18831

OPERATOR: Apartment Buildings

	CITY	ST	EMP	PHONE	ENTRY #
Theological Threads Inc	Beverly	MA	G	978 927-7031	8190

OPERATOR: Nonresidential Buildings

	CITY	ST	EMP	PHONE	ENTRY #
Fletcher-Terry Company LLC **(PA)**	East Berlin	CT	D	860 828-3400	1102
Macristy Industries Inc **(PA)**	Newington	CT	C	860 225-4637	2879
Lrv Properties LLC	Providence	RI	G	401 714-7001	21058

OPHTHALMIC GOODS

	CITY	ST	EMP	PHONE	ENTRY #
Coburn Technologies Inc **(PA)**	South Windsor	CT	C	860 648-6600	3951
Gerber Coburn Optical Inc **(HQ)**	South Windsor	CT	C	800 843-1479	3972
Hoya Corporation	South Windsor	CT	B	860 289-5379	3982
McLeod Optical Company Inc	Waterbury	CT	G	203 754-2187	4913
Aearo Technologies LLC	Auburn	MA	B	317 692-6645	7822
Andor Technology Ltd	Concord	MA	E	860 290-9211	10110
Bausch & Lomb Incorporated	Wilmington	MA	F	978 658-6111	16981
Beaver-Visitec Intl Inc **(HQ)**	Waltham	MA	C	781 906-8080	16044
Fosta-Tek Optics Inc **(PA)**	Leominster	MA	D	978 534-6511	12141
Gentex Optics Inc	Dudley	MA	B	508 713-5267	10375
Hilsinger Company Parent LLC **(PA)**	Plainville	MA	C	508 699-4406	14520
Hilsinger Holdings Inc	Plainville	MA	C	508 699-4406	14521
Lensmaster Optical Company	Southbridge	MA	G	508 764-4958	15392
Northeast Lens Corp	Hopkinton	MA	E	617 964-6797	11730
Prolens Inc	North Troy	VT	G	802 988-1018	22242

OPHTHALMIC GOODS WHOLESALERS

	CITY	ST	EMP	PHONE	ENTRY #
Precision Optical Co	East Hartford	CT	E	860 289-6023	1216
Avedro Inc **(HQ)**	Waltham	MA	D	781 768-3400	16040
McLeod Optical Company Inc **(PA)**	Warwick	RI	E	401 467-3000	21388
Swarovski US Holding Limited **(HQ)**	Cranston	RI	G	401 463-6400	20296

OPHTHALMIC GOODS: Eyewear, Protective

	CITY	ST	EMP	PHONE	ENTRY #
Galvion Ltd **(HQ)**	Portsmouth	NH	G	514 739-4444	19566
Sibs LLC	Meredith	NH	G	781 864-7498	18979
Honeywell Safety Products Usa	Smithfield	RI	F	401 233-0333	21233
Sperian Protection Usa Inc **(DH)**	Smithfield	RI	E	401 232-1200	21250
Uvex Distribution Inc	Smithfield	RI	F	401 232-1200	21251
Uvex Safety Manufacturing Ltd	Smithfield	RI	C	401 232-1200	21252
Galvion Ballistics Ltd	Newport	VT	F	802 334-2774	22199
Galvion Ballistics Ltd **(PA)**	Essex Junction	VT	C	802 879-7002	21940

OPHTHALMIC GOODS: Frames & Parts, Eyeglass & Spectacle

	CITY	ST	EMP	PHONE	ENTRY #
Randolph Engineering Inc	Randolph	MA	E	781 961-6070	14695
Precise Products Company	Lincoln	RI	F	401 724-7190	20592

OPHTHALMIC GOODS: Frames, Lenses & Parts, Eyeglasses

	CITY	ST	EMP	PHONE	ENTRY #
Milor Corporation Inc	Auburn	ME	G	207 783-4226	5581

OPHTHALMIC GOODS: Goggles, Sun, Safety, Indl, Etc

	CITY	ST	EMP	PHONE	ENTRY #
Paramount Corp	New Bedford	MA	E	508 999-4442	13436
Visionaid Inc	Wareham	MA	E	508 295-3300	16258
Jones Safety Equipment Company	East Providence	RI	G	401 434-4010	20424

OPHTHALMIC GOODS: Lenses, Ophthalmic

	CITY	ST	EMP	PHONE	ENTRY #
Gerber Scientific LLC **(PA)**	Tolland	CT	C	860 871-8082	4548
Essilor Industries Corp	Dudley	MA	C	787 848-4130	10374
Gentex Optics Inc **(DH)**	Dudley	MA	C	570 282-8531	10376
Accu Rx Inc	Johnston	RI	E	401 454-2920	20497

OPHTHALMIC GOODS: Protectors, Eye

	CITY	ST	EMP	PHONE	ENTRY #
Shari M Roth MD	Avon	CT	G	860 676-2525	46
Dioptics Medical Products Inc	Smithfield	RI	D	805 781-3300	21221

OPHTHALMIC GOODS: Spectacles

	CITY	ST	EMP	PHONE	ENTRY #
Spectacle Eye Ware Inc	Boston	MA	G	617 542-9600	8857

OPTICAL EQPT: Interferometers

	CITY	ST	EMP	PHONE	ENTRY #
Idealab Inc	Franklin	MA	F	508 528-9260	11054

OPTICAL GOODS STORES

	CITY	ST	EMP	PHONE	ENTRY #
Nauset Optical	Orleans	MA	G	508 255-6394	14237

OPTICAL INSTRUMENT REPAIR SVCS

	CITY	ST	EMP	PHONE	ENTRY #
Solos Endoscopy Inc	Boston	MA	G	617 360-9700	8852

OPTICAL INSTRUMENTS & APPARATUS

	CITY	ST	EMP	PHONE	ENTRY #
Conoptics Inc	Danbury	CT	F	203 743-3349	892
Amplitude Laser Inc	Boston	MA	G	617 401-2195	8365
AMS Qi Inc	Cambridge	MA	G	617 797-4709	9389
Angstrom Advanced Inc	Stoughton	MA	D	781 519-4765	15580
Atlantic Vision Inc	Shrewsbury	MA	G	508 845-8401	15103
Electro Optical Industries **(PA)**	Boston	MA	E	617 401-2196	8523
Eo Vista LLC	Acton	MA	F	978 635-8080	7354
Excel Technology Inc **(HQ)**	Bedford	MA	D	781 266-5700	7976
Excelitas Technologies Corp **(DH)**	Waltham	MA	E	781 522-5910	16104
Innovations In Optics Inc	Woburn	MA	G	781 933-4477	17202
Lexitek Inc	Watertown	MA	G	781 431-9604	16294
Ophir Optics LLC	Wilmington	MA	C	978 657-6410	17033
Precision Optics Corp Inc **(PA)**	Gardner	MA	E	978 630-1800	11123
Prior Scientific Inc **(HQ)**	Rockland	MA	F	781 878-8442	14820
Lighthouse Imaging LLC	Windham	ME	G	207 893-8233	7240
Andover Corporation	Salem	NH	E	603 893-6888	19707
Elbit Systems of America LLC	Merrimack	NH	F	603 889-2500	18999
Guidewire Technologies Inc	Salem	NH	E	603 894-4399	19740
Km Holding Inc	Hudson	NH	F	603 566-2704	18407
National Aperture Inc	Salem	NH	F	603 893-7393	19754
Optics 1 Inc **(DH)**	Bedford	NH	F	603 296-0469	17658
Robert Cairns Company LLC	Plaistow	NH	G	603 382-0044	19522
Space Optics Research Labs LLC	Merrimack	NH	F	978 250-8640	19032
Wilcox Industries Corp **(PA)**	Newington	NH	C	603 431-1331	19329
Nippon American Limited	East Greenwich	RI	F	401 885-7353	20374
Pyramid Case Co Inc	Providence	RI	A	401 273-0643	21101

OPTICAL INSTRUMENTS & LENSES

	CITY	ST	EMP	PHONE	ENTRY #
Advanced Photonics Intl Inc	Fairfield	CT	G	203 259-0437	1413
Aecc/Pearlman Buying Group LLC	Middlebury	CT	F	203 598-3200	2153
Aperture Optical Sciences Inc	Higganum	CT	G	860 301-2589	1899
Aperture Optical Sciences Inc	Meriden	CT	G	860 301-2372	2076
Argyle Optics LLC	Milford	CT	G	203 451-3320	2245
Coating Design Group Inc	Stratford	CT	E	203 878-3663	4405
Coburn Technologies Inc **(PA)**	South Windsor	CT	C	860 648-6600	3951
CT Fiberoptics Inc	Somers	CT	F	860 763-4341	3915
Data Technology Inc	Tolland	CT	E	860 871-8082	4545
Gerber Coburn Optical Inc **(HQ)**	South Windsor	CT	C	800 843-1479	3972
Karl Stetson Associates LLC	Coventry	CT	G	860 742-8414	834
Nntechnology Moore Systems LLC	Bridgeport	CT	G	203 366-3224	458
Odis Inc	Storrs Mansfield	CT	G	860 450-8407	4385
Optical Design Associates	Stamford	CT	G	203 249-6408	4271
UTC Fire SEC Americas Corp Inc	Newtown	CT	C	203 426-1180	2947
Zygo Corporation **(HQ)**	Middlefield	CT	G	860 347-8506	2169
Acton Research Corporation	Acton	MA	E	941 556-2601	7334
Adaptive Optics Associates Inc	Devens	MA	E	978 391-0000	10318
Applied Science Group Inc	Billerica	MA	E	781 275-4000	8212
Atlantic RES Mktg Systems Inc	West Bridgewater	MA	F	508 584-7816	16429
Axsun Technologies Inc	Billerica	MA	D	978 262-0049	8217
Bae Systems Info & Elec Sys	Lexington	MA	B	603 885-4321	12208
Bauer Associates Inc	Natick	MA	G	508 310-0201	13236
Boston Piezo-Optics Inc	Bellingham	MA	F	508 966-4988	8032
Cambrdge RES Instrmntation Inc	Hopkinton	MA	E	781 935-9099	11695
Chromatra LLC	Beverly	MA	G	978 473-7005	8116
Focused Resolutions Inc	Methuen	MA	G	978 794-7981	13022
Genscope Inc	East Longmeadow	MA	F	413 526-0802	10476
Gentex Optics Inc	Dudley	MA	B	508 713-5267	10375
Gtat Corporation	Salem	MA	E	978 745-0088	14917
Headwall Photonics Inc	Bolton	MA	D	978 353-4100	8319
Hilsinger Company Parent LLC **(PA)**	Plainville	MA	C	508 699-4406	14520
Hilsinger Holdings Inc	Plainville	MA	C	508 699-4406	14521
Holographix LLC	Marlborough	MA	F	978 562-4474	12772
I-Optics Corp	Burlington	MA	G	508 366-1600	9284
Incom Inc	Charlton	MA	C	508 909-2200	9851
Kinetic Systems Inc	Boston	MA	E	617 522-8700	8649
KLA Corporation	Westwood	MA	D	978 843-7670	16871
L3 Technologies Inc	Wilmington	MA	C	978 694-9991	17014
L3 Technologies Inc	Northampton	MA	A	413 586-2330	14009
Lithoptek LLC	Natick	MA	G	408 533-5847	13264
Magnolia Optical Tech Inc	Woburn	MA	G	781 376-1505	17222
Materion Prcsion Optics Thin F **(DH)**	Westford	MA	F	978 692-7513	16778
N-Vision Optics LLC	Needham	MA	G	781 505-8360	13305
Newport Corporation	Franklin	MA	D	508 553-5035	11070
Novotech Inc	Acton	MA	E	978 929-9458	7375
Optical Metrology Inc	North Andover	MA	G	978 657-6303	13721
Optimum Technologies Inc	Southbridge	MA	F	508 765-8100	15398
Optos Inc	Marlborough	MA	D	508 787-1400	12803
Orpro Vision LLC	Billerica	MA	G	617 676-1101	8271
Resident Artist Studio LLC	Boxborough	MA	G	978 635-9162	8969
Roper Scientific Inc	Acton	MA	E	978 268-0337	7381
Rubil Associates Inc	Billerica	MA	F	978 670-7192	8292
Scientific Solutions Inc	North Chelmsford	MA	F	978 251-4554	13910

	CITY	ST	EMP	PHONE	ENTRY #
Skylight Navigation Technology	Sherborn	MA	G	508 655-7516	15079
Tel Epion Inc	Billerica	MA	E	978 436-2300	8302
Thermo Vision Corp **(HQ)**	Franklin	MA	F	508 520-0083	11090
Thin Film Imaging Technologies	Greenfield	MA	F	413 774-6692	11280
Twin Coast Metrology Inc	Acton	MA	G	508 517-4508	7392
United Lens Company Inc	Southbridge	MA	C	508 765-5421	15407
Vacuum Process Technology LLC	Plymouth	MA	E	508 732-7200	14589
Zygo Corporation	Franklin	MA	E	508 541-1268	11101
American Rheinmetall Def Inc **(PA)**	Biddeford	ME	G	207 571-5850	5717
American Rhnmetall Systems LLC	Biddeford	ME	E	207 571-5850	5718
QED Optical Inc	Houlton	ME	G	207 532-6772	6209
603 Optx Inc	Keene	NH	G	603 357-4900	18489
Ametek Precitech Inc **(HQ)**	Keene	NH	D	603 357-2510	18491
Cheshire Optical Inc	Laconia	NH	G	603 352-0602	18562
Clear Align LLC	Nashua	NH	F	603 889-2116	19134
Janos Technology Inc	Keene	NH	G	603 757-0070	18507
Moore Nntechnology Systems LLC **(DH)**	Swanzey	NH	D	603 352-3030	19886
Optical Solutions Inc	Charlestown	NH	G	603 826-4411	17818
Optics 1 Inc	Bedford	NH	G	603 296-0469	17657
Prophotonix Limited **(PA)**	Salem	NH	E	603 893-8778	19761
Stingray Optics LLC	Keene	NH	F	603 358-5577	18529
Adolf Meller Company **(PA)**	Providence	RI	E	800 821-0180	20946
Adolf Meller Company	Providence	RI	E	401 331-3838	20947
Knight Optical (usa) LLC	North Kingstown	RI	G	401 521-7000	20721
89 North Inc	Williston	VT	G	802 881-0302	22653
J & L Metrology Inc	Springfield	VT	E	802 885-8291	22503
Jack Russell	West Rutland	VT	G	802 438-5213	22617
Omega Optical Incorporated	Brattleboro	VT	D	802 251-7300	21742

OPTICAL ISOLATORS

Verrillon Inc	North Grafton	MA	E	508 890-7100	13966

OPTICAL SCANNING SVCS

Ebeam Film LLC	Shelton	CT	F	203 926-0100	3798

OPTOMETRIC EQPT & SPLYS WHOLESALERS

McLeod Optical Company Inc	Augusta	ME	F	207 623-3841	5614

ORAL PREPARATIONS

Connectcut Crnial Fcial Imgery	Manchester	CT	G	860 643-2940	1996
Oraceutical LLC	Lee	MA	E	413 243-6634	12094
Cabot Hill Naturals Inc	Lancaster	NH	F	800 747-4372	18598

ORDNANCE

Ensign-Bickford Industries Inc	Simsbury	CT	E	860 658-4411	3905
Kaman Aerospace Corporation	Middletown	CT	C	860 632-1000	2195
Entwistle Company **(HQ)**	Hudson	MA	C	508 481-4000	11772
Troy Industries Inc	West Springfield	MA	D	413 788-4288	16556
Combat Weapons Development LLC	Manchester	NH	G	603 978-0244	18801

ORGAN TUNING & REPAIR SVCS

Andover Organ Company Inc	Lawrence	MA	F	978 686-9600	11994
Faucher Organ Company Inc	Biddeford	ME	G	207 283-1420	5732

ORGANIZATIONS: Medical Research

Alexion Pharma LLC **(HQ)**	New Haven	CT	E	203 272-2596	2653
Protein Sciences Corporation **(HQ)**	Meriden	CT	D	203 686-0800	2119
Alexion Pharmaceuticals Inc **(PA)**	Boston	MA	C	475 230-2596	8353
Logan Instruments Inc	Braintree	MA	F	617 394-0601	9024

ORGANIZATIONS: Religious

NRG Connecticut LLC	Hartford	CT	E	860 231-2424	1855
Stillpoint International Inc	Peterborough	NH	G	603 756-9281	19490

ORGANIZATIONS: Research Institute

Advanced Mechanical Tech Inc **(PA)**	Watertown	MA	E	617 923-4174	16263
Haigh-Farr Inc	Bedford	NH	F	603 644-6170	17644

ORGANIZATIONS: Scientific Research Agency

Cambrdge RES Instrmntation Inc	Hopkinton	MA	E	781 935-9099	11695
Longray Inc	Lexington	MA	G	781 862-5137	12240

ORGANIZERS, CLOSET & DRAWER Plastic

Bidwell Industrial Group Inc **(PA)**	Middletown	CT	E	860 346-9283	2178

ORNAMENTS: Christmas Tree, Exc Electrical & Glass

Christmas Studio	Monson	MA	G	413 267-3342	13203
Syratech Acquisition Corp **(HQ)**	Medford	MA	C	781 539-0100	12949
Christmas Cove Designs Inc	Dresden	ME	G	207 350-1035	5965
Gloria Duchin Inc	Rumford	RI	D	401 431-5016	21185

ORNAMENTS: Lawn

Createk-Stone Inc	Southbridge	MA	G	888 786-6389	15378

OSCILLATORS

Kennetron Inc	East Taunton	MA	G	508 828-9363	10515
Mti-Milliren Technologies Inc	Newburyport	MA	E	978 465-6064	13516
Rife Mltplwave Oscillators LLC	Brewster	MA	G	508 737-8468	9057

OSCILLATORS

Micronetixx Technologies LLC	Lewiston	ME	G	207 786-2000	6306

OUTBOARD MOTORS: Electric

Coherent Inc	Bloomfield	CT	E	860 243-9557	215
Enertgetic Baltic Ml	Enfield	NH	G	603 252-0804	18097

OUTLETS: Electric, Convenience

Goremote	Wrentham	MA	G	508 384-0139	17521
San Francisco Market	Lynn	MA	G	781 780-3731	12536

	CITY	ST	EMP	PHONE	ENTRY #
Corningware Corelle & More	Freeport	ME	G	207 865-3942	6075
Kirk Electronics & Plastic	Cranston	RI	G	401 467-8585	20249

OVENS: Surveillance, Powder Aging & Testing

LDB Tool and Findings Inc	Cranston	RI	G	401 944-6000	20252

OVERBURDEN REMOVAL SVCS: Nonmetallic Minerals

All American Deleading Inc	Hingham	MA	G	781 953-1673	11490

PACKAGE DESIGN SVCS

Stephen Gould Corporation	Tewksbury	MA	E	978 851-2500	15838

PACKAGED FROZEN FOODS WHOLESALERS, NEC

Wohrles Foods Inc **(PA)**	Pittsfield	MA	E	413 442-1518	14513
Getchell Bros Inc	Sanford	ME	E	207 490-0809	6877

PACKAGING & LABELING SVCS

East Coast Packaging LLC **(PA)**	Farmington	CT	G	860 675-8500	1479
Mid State Assembly & Packg Inc	Meriden	CT	G	203 634-8740	2107
Feteria Tool & Findings	Attleboro	MA	G	508 222-7788	7734
Horn Corporation **(PA)**	Lancaster	MA	E	800 832-7020	11984
Custom Die Cut Inc	Windham	NH	G	603 437-3090	20003
J-Pac LLC **(HQ)**	Somersworth	NH	D	603 692-9955	19842
Contech Medical Inc	Providence	RI	D	401 351-4890	20989

PACKAGING MATERIALS, INDL: Wholesalers

Greene Industries Inc	East Greenwich	RI	G	401 884-7530	20369

PACKAGING MATERIALS, WHOLESALE

Pactiv Corporation	North Haven	CT	E	203 288-7722	3047
Danvers Industrial Packg Corp	Beverly	MA	E	978 777-0020	8124
Liberty Packaging Co Inc	Braintree	MA	G	781 849-3355	9023
Packaging Products Corporation **(PA)**	New Bedford	MA	F	508 997-5150	13434
Packaging Specialties Inc	Newburyport	MA	D	978 462-1300	13520
Prolamina Corporation	Westfield	MA	G	413 562-2315	16718
Sealed Air Corporation	Holyoke	MA	D	413 534-0231	11656
Maine Potato Growers Inc	Caribou	ME	E	207 764-3131	5886

PACKAGING MATERIALS: Paper

Agi-Shorewood Group Us LLC	Stamford	CT	A	203 324-4839	4132
Ansel Label and Packaging Corp	Trumbull	CT	E	203 452-0311	4612
Atlas Agi Holdings LLC	Greenwich	CT	A	203 622-9138	1594
CCL Label Inc	Shelton	CT	C	203 926-1253	3786
Flagship Converters Inc	Danbury	CT	D	203 792-0034	920
Fluted Partition Inc **(PA)**	Bridgeport	CT	C	203 368-2548	414
Identification Products Corp	Bridgeport	CT	F	203 334-5969	429
Knox Enterprises Inc **(PA)**	Westport	CT	G	203 226-6408	5206
Mid State Assembly & Packg Inc	Meriden	CT	G	203 634-8740	2107
Packaging and Crating Tech LLC	Waterbury	CT	G	203 759-1799	4933
Paxxus Inc	Bloomfield	CT	E	860 242-0663	250
Polymer Films Inc	West Haven	CT	E	203 932-3000	5142
Quality Name Plate Inc	East Glastonbury	CT	D	860 633-9495	1114
Rol-Vac Limited Partnership	Dayville	CT	F	860 928-9929	1052
Sealed Air Corporation	Danbury	CT	C	203 791-3648	988
Sonoco Prtective Solutions Inc	Putnam	CT	E	860 928-7795	3634
Stora Enso N Amercn Sls Inc **(HQ)**	Stamford	CT	G	203 541-5178	4334
Tht Inc	Westport	CT	G	203 226-6408	5235
Windham Container Corporation	Putnam	CT	E	860 928-7934	3640
Adhesive Packaging Spc Inc **(DH)**	Peabody	MA	E	800 222-1117	14307
Allen-Bailey Tag & Label Inc	Whitinsville	MA	E	585 538-2324	16910
Boutwell Owens & Co Inc **(PA)**	Fitchburg	MA	C	978 343-3067	10813
CCL Label Inc **(HQ)**	Framingham	MA	D	508 872-4511	10932
Coveris Advanced Coatings	West Springfield	MA	E	413 539-5547	16513
E V Yeuell Inc	Woburn	MA	E	781 933-2984	17171
Free-Flow Packaging Intl Inc	Auburn	MA	E	508 832-5369	7835
Gta-Nht Inc **(HQ)**	Rockland	MA	C	781 331-5900	14804
Healthy Life Snack Inc	Canton	MA	G	781 575-6744	9738
Ideal Tape Co Inc	Lowell	MA	D	978 458-6833	12381
Industrial Lbling Systems Corp	Tyngsboro	MA	E	978 649-7004	15890
Jmd Manufacturing Inc	Framingham	MA	G	508 620-6563	10972
OK Durable Packaging Inc	Marlborough	MA	F	508 303-8067	12800
Opsec Security Inc	Boston	MA	F	617 226-3000	8756
Pioneer Packaging Inc **(PA)**	Chicopee	MA	D	413 378-6930	10050
Polyfiber LLC	Attleboro	MA	E	508 222-3500	7779
Reid Graphics Inc	Andover	MA	D	978 474-1930	7598
Sealed Air Corp	Ayer	MA	G	508 521-5694	7936
Sealed Air Corporation	Holyoke	MA	D	413 534-0231	11656
Vangy Tool Company Inc	Worcester	MA	G	508 754-2669	17498
Walter Drake Inc **(PA)**	Holyoke	MA	G	413 536-5463	11666
Westrock Cp LLC	Mansfield	MA	C	770 448-2193	12671
Westrock Mwv LLC	Springfield	MA	A	413 736-7211	15527
Huhtamaki Inc	Lewiston	ME	E	207 795-6000	6290
Kullson Holding Company Inc	Lewiston	ME	E	207 783-3442	6296
Penta-Tech Coated Products LLC **(PA)**	Hampden	ME	F	207 862-3105	6166
Label Tech Inc	Somersworth	NH	C	603 692-2005	19843
Pak 2000 Inc	Lancaster	NH	D	603 569-3700	18603
Roymal Inc	Newport	NH	E	603 863-2410	19357
Allied Group Inc **(PA)**	Cranston	RI	C	401 461-1700	20177
Contempo Card Co Inc **(PA)**	Providence	RI	D	401 272-4210	20990
Foxon Company	Providence	RI	E	401 421-2386	21015
Jewel Case Corporation	Providence	RI	B	401 943-1400	21044
Mason Box Company	Pawtucket	RI	E	800 842-9526	20857
Morris Transparent Box Co	East Providence	RI	E	401 438-6116	20433
Nelipak Corporation **(PA)**	Cranston	RI	D	401 946-2699	20267
Packaging Company LLC **(PA)**	Johnston	RI	D	401 943-5040	20527
Tex Flock Inc	Woonsocket	RI	E	401 765-2340	21586
Wintech Intl Corp - Nk	Warwick	RI	G	401 383-3307	21449

PACKAGING MATERIALS: Paper, Coated Or Laminated

	CITY	ST	EMP	PHONE	ENTRY #
Amgraph Packaging Inc	Baltic	CT	C	860 822-2000	48
Miami Wabash Paper LLC **(HQ)**	Norwalk	CT	E	203 847-8500	3197
Ampac Packaging LLC	Westfield	MA	G	413 572-2658	16665
Fortifiber Corporation	Attleboro	MA	E	508 222-3500	7738
Millstone Med Outsourcing LLC **(PA)**	Fall River	MA	C	508 679-8384	10733
Novacel Inc **(DH)**	Palmer	MA	E	413 283-3468	14289
Package Printing Company Inc	West Springfield	MA	E	413 736-2748	16539
Prolamina Corporation	Westfield	MA	G	413 562-2315	16718
Suddekor LLC	East Longmeadow	MA	E	413 525-4070	10495
Web Industries Inc **(PA)**	Marlborough	MA	G	508 898-2988	12848
Verso Paper Holding LLC	Jay	ME	A	207 897-3431	6222
Verso Paper Holding LLC	Jay	ME	A	207 897-3431	6223

PACKAGING MATERIALS: Paper, Thermoplastic Coated

	CITY	ST	EMP	PHONE	ENTRY #
Packaging Devices Inc **(PA)**	Teaticket	MA	F	508 548-0224	15802

PACKAGING MATERIALS: Paperboard Backs For Blister/Skin Pkgs

	CITY	ST	EMP	PHONE	ENTRY #
Stephen Gould Corporation	Tewksbury	MA	E	978 851-2500	15838

PACKAGING MATERIALS: Plastic Film, Coated Or Laminated

	CITY	ST	EMP	PHONE	ENTRY #
Bollore Inc	Dayville	CT	D	860 774-2930	1039
General Packaging Products Inc	Norwalk	CT	G	203 846-1340	3160
Polymeric Converting LLC	Enfield	CT	E	860 623-1335	1375
Hampden Papers Inc **(PA)**	Holyoke	MA	D	413 536-1000	11630
K & K Thermoforming Inc	Southbridge	MA	E	508 764-7700	15390
Ovtene Inc	Marion	MA	E	617 852-4828	12701
J-Pac LLC **(HQ)**	Somersworth	NH	D	603 692-9955	19842
Clear Choice Inc	Providence	RI	G	401 421-5275	20985
Wheeler Avenue LLC	Cranston	RI	G	401 714-0996	20311

PACKAGING MATERIALS: Polystyrene Foam

	CITY	ST	EMP	PHONE	ENTRY #
Covit America Inc	Watertown	CT	B	860 274-6791	5004
Fc Meyer Packaging LLC **(HQ)**	Norwalk	CT	D	203 847-8500	3150
General Packaging Products Inc	Norwalk	CT	G	203 846-1340	3160
Paxxus Inc	Bloomfield	CT	E	860 242-0663	250
Sealed Air Corporation	Danbury	CT	C	203 791-3648	988
Sonoco Prtective Solutions Inc	Putnam	CT	E	860 928-7795	3634
Universal Foam Products LLC	Bloomfield	CT	F	860 216-3015	270
Architects of Packaging Inc	Westfield	MA	G	413 568-3187	16667
Danvers Industrial Packg Corp	Beverly	MA	E	978 777-0020	8124
Desco Industries Inc	Canton	MA	E	781 821-8370	9726
Foam Concepts Inc	Uxbridge	MA	E	508 278-7255	15917
Horn Corporation **(PA)**	Lancaster	MA	E	800 832-7020	11984
Imanova Packaging	Leominster	MA	D	978 537-8534	12154
Lelanite Corporation **(PA)**	Webster	MA	E	508 987-2637	16346
Liberty Packaging Co Inc	Braintree	MA	G	781 849-3355	9023
Osaap America LLC	Chelmsford	MA	G	877 652-7227	9919
Packaging Products Corporation **(PA)**	New Bedford	MA	F	508 997-5150	13434
Polyfoam Corp	Northbridge	MA	D	508 234-6323	14058
Rogers Foam Corporation **(PA)**	Somerville	MA	B	617 623-3010	15212
Sealed Air Corporation	Holyoke	MA	D	413 534-0231	11656
Ufp Technologies Inc **(PA)**	Newburyport	MA	E	978 352-2200	13544
Wood Products Unlimited Inc	Methuen	MA	G	978 687-7449	13048
Rynel Inc **(DH)**	Wiscasset	ME	D	207 882-0200	7287
Langer Associates Inc	Manchester	NH	E	603 626-4388	18859
Robert A Collins	Fremont	NH	G	603 895-2345	18180
Branch River Plastics Inc	Smithfield	RI	E	401 232-0270	21214
Lance Industries Inc **(PA)**	Lincoln	RI	D	401 365-6272	20578
Spring Fill	South Burlington	VT	F	802 846-5900	22466

PACKAGING MATERIALS: Resinous Impregnated Paper

	CITY	ST	EMP	PHONE	ENTRY #
Accu Packaging Inc	Wilmington	MA	G	978 447-5590	16964

PACKAGING: Blister Or Bubble Formed, Plastic

	CITY	ST	EMP	PHONE	ENTRY #
Packaging and Crating Tech LLC	Waterbury	CT	G	203 759-1799	4933
Southpack LLC	New Britain	CT	E	860 224-2242	2577
Lacerta Group Inc	Mansfield	MA	G	508 339-3312	12641
Lacerta Group Inc **(PA)**	Mansfield	MA	D	508 339-3312	12642
Ntp/Republic Clear Thru Corp	Holyoke	MA	E	413 493-6800	11645
Walter Drake Inc **(PA)**	Holyoke	MA	G	413 536-5463	11666
Wood Products Unlimited Inc	Methuen	MA	G	978 687-7449	13048
Capco Plastics Inc **(PA)**	Providence	RI	D	401 272-3833	20978

PACKING & CRATING SVC

	CITY	ST	EMP	PHONE	ENTRY #
Abbott-Action Inc	Canton	MA	E	781 702-5710	9710
Ohlson Packaging LLC **(DH)**	Taunton	MA	F	508 977-0004	15770

PACKING & CRATING SVCS: Containerized Goods For Shipping

	CITY	ST	EMP	PHONE	ENTRY #
Horn Corporation **(PA)**	Lancaster	MA	E	800 832-7020	11984

PACKING MATERIALS: Mechanical

	CITY	ST	EMP	PHONE	ENTRY #
EMR Global Inc	East Hartford	CT	G	203 452-8166	1192
New England Braiding Co Inc	Manchester	NH	F	603 669-1987	18883

PACKING SVCS: Shipping

	CITY	ST	EMP	PHONE	ENTRY #
P2k Printing LLC	North Conway	NH	G	603 356-2010	19378
Contech Medical Inc	Providence	RI	D	401 351-4890	20989

PACKING: Rubber

	CITY	ST	EMP	PHONE	ENTRY #
Worcester Indus Rbr Sup Co Inc	Holden	MA	G	508 853-2332	11551

PADDING: Foamed Plastics

	CITY	ST	EMP	PHONE	ENTRY #
Der-Tex Corporation	Saco	ME	E	207 284-5931	6846
Wayne Manufacturing Inds LLC	Brentwood	NH	E	978 416-0899	17761
MH Stallman Company Inc **(PA)**	Providence	RI	E	401 331-5129	21067

PADS: Desk, Paper, Made From Purchased Materials

	CITY	ST	EMP	PHONE	ENTRY #
American Meadows Inc	Shelburne	VT	F	802 862-6560	22410
Oatmeal Studios Inc	Rochester	VT	F	802 967-8014	22320

PAGERS: One-way

	CITY	ST	EMP	PHONE	ENTRY #
E Z Telecom	Chelsea	MA	G	617 466-0826	9953
Hysen Technologies Inc **(PA)**	Cumberland	RI	F	401 312-6500	20326

PAILS: Shipping, Metal

	CITY	ST	EMP	PHONE	ENTRY #
3 M N Corp	Brockton	MA	G	508 586-4471	9112

PAINT STORE

	CITY	ST	EMP	PHONE	ENTRY #
Color Craft Ltd	East Granby	CT	F	800 509-6563	1121
Merrifield Paint Company Inc	Rocky Hill	CT	G	860 529-1583	3723
Durant Prfmce Coatings Inc	Revere	MA	F	781 289-1400	14765
Newbury Port Meritown Society	Amesbury	MA	G	978 834-0050	7501
Winchester Fishing Inc	Gloucester	MA	G	978 282-0679	11219
Mainline Paint Mfg Co	Pawtucket	RI	G	401 726-3650	20855

PAINTING SVC: Metal Prdts

	CITY	ST	EMP	PHONE	ENTRY #
Advanced Graphics Inc	Stratford	CT	E	203 378-0471	4388
Farrell Prcsion Mtalcraft Corp	New Milford	CT	E	860 355-2651	2799
Fonda Fabricating & Welding Co	Plainville	CT	G	860 793-0601	3489
Halco Inc	Waterbury	CT	D	203 575-9450	4881
High Grade Finishing Co LLC	Enfield	CT	G	860 749-8883	1364
Imperial Metal Finishing Inc	Stratford	CT	G	203 377-1229	4422
Jonmandy Corporation	Torrington	CT	G	860 482-2354	4583
Pauway Corp	Wallingford	CT	F	203 265-3939	4783
Cil Inc	Lawrence	MA	D	978 685-8300	12009
Jet Coating Co	Boylston	MA	G	508 869-2158	8981
L & J of New England Inc	Worcester	MA	E	508 756-8080	17403
Light Metal Platers LLC	Waltham	MA	E	781 899-8855	16145
Spencer Industrial Painting	Spencer	MA	G	508 885-5406	15436
Westfield Electroplating Co **(PA)**	Westfield	MA	C	413 568-3716	16743
Performance Products Painting	Auburn	ME	E	207 783-4222	5589
Ckm Coatings	Brentwood	NH	G	603 642-5728	17747
Rapid Finishing Corp	Nashua	NH	E	603 889-4234	19244

PAINTING: Hand, Textiles

	CITY	ST	EMP	PHONE	ENTRY #
1 Call Does It All and Then	South Deerfield	MA	G	413 584-5381	15244

PAINTS & ADDITIVES

	CITY	ST	EMP	PHONE	ENTRY #
FMI Paint & Chemical Inc	East Hartford	CT	F	860 218-2210	1196
Merrifield Paint Company Inc	Rocky Hill	CT	G	860 529-1583	3723
Benjamin Moore & Co	Milford	MA	D	508 473-8900	13108
ICP Construction Inc **(HQ)**	Andover	MA	C	978 623-9980	7556
Kirby George Jr Paint Co Inc	New Bedford	MA	G	508 997-9008	13405
Old Fashion Milk Paint Co Inc	Groton	MA	G	978 448-6336	11292
Procoat Products Inc	Holbrook	MA	G	781 767-2270	11536
Mainline Paint Mfg Co	Pawtucket	RI	G	401 726-3650	20855
Sutherland Welles Ltd	Hyde Park	VT	G	802 635-2700	22038

PAINTS & ALLIED PRODUCTS

	CITY	ST	EMP	PHONE	ENTRY #
A G C Incorporated **(PA)**	Meriden	CT	C	203 235-3361	2072
Albert Kemperle Inc	Hartford	CT	F	860 727-0933	1804
Chromalloy Component Svcs Inc	Windsor	CT	C	860 688-7798	5325
Colonial Coatings Inc	Milford	CT	E	203 783-9933	2265
Dumond Chemicals Inc	Milford	CT	G	609 655-7700	2277
Five Star Products Inc	Shelton	CT	E	203 336-7900	3802
Fougera Pharmaceuticals Inc	Wallingford	CT	D	203 265-2086	4745
Greenmaker Industries Conn LLC	West Hartford	CT	F	860 761-2830	5072
J + J Branford Inc **(PA)**	Branford	CT	G	203 488-5637	327
Jet Process Corporation	North Haven	CT	G	203 985-6000	3035
Mantrose-Haeuser Co Inc **(HQ)**	Westport	CT	E	203 454-1800	5212
Minteq International Inc	Canaan	CT	C	860 824-5435	689
PPG Industries Inc	Norwalk	CT	G	203 750-9553	3223
PPG Industries Inc	New Haven	CT	G	203 562-5173	2728
PPG Industries Inc	Danbury	CT	G	203 744-4977	969
PPG Industries Inc	Hartford	CT	G	860 522-9544	1861
Acton Research Corporation	Acton	MA	E	941 556-2601	7334
Bemis Associates Inc	Shirley	MA	C	978 425-6761	15082
C F Jameson & Co Inc	Newburyport	MA	F	978 462-4097	13476
CCS Marine Inc	West Bridgewater	MA	G	508 587-8877	16434
Clark Paint & Varnish Company	West Springfield	MA	G	413 733-3554	16512
Coveris Advanced Coatings	West Springfield	MA	E	413 539-5547	16513
DSM Coating Resins Inc	Wilmington	MA	C	800 458-0014	16996
F & D Plastics Inc **(PA)**	Leominster	MA	E	978 668-5140	12136
Franklin Paint Company Inc	Franklin	MA	E	800 486-0304	11047
Gare Incorporated	Haverhill	MA	E	978 373-9131	11437
Highland Labs Inc	Holliston	MA	E	508 429-2918	11577
Innovative Chem Pdts Group LLC	Boston	MA	F	800 393-5250	8616
Katahdin Industries Inc **(PA)**	Hudson	MA	E	781 329-1420	11781
Mantrose-Haeuser Co Inc	Attleboro	MA	D	203 454-1800	7761
Microplasmic Corporation	Peabody	MA	G	978 548-9762	14355
PPG Industries Inc	Boston	MA	E	617 268-4111	8789
Rustoleum Attleboro Plant	Attleboro	MA	G	508 222-3710	7791
Stainless Steel Coatings Inc	Lancaster	MA	F	978 365-9828	11985
Steel Products Corporation **(PA)**	Rochdale	MA	G	508 892-4770	14783
TH Glennon Co Inc	Salisbury	MA	E	978 465-7222	14957
Tnemec East Inc	Wilmington	MA	E	978 988-9500	17056
Union Specialties Inc	Newburyport	MA	E	978 465-1717	13546
Winfield Brooks Company Inc	Woburn	MA	F	781 933-5300	17323
Chilton Paint Co Inc ME	Freeport	ME	G	207 865-4443	6074
Hampshire Chemical Corp **(DH)**	Nashua	NH	E	603 888-2320	19176
Roymal Inc	Newport	NH	E	603 863-2410	19357
Development Associates Inc	North Kingstown	RI	F	401 884-1350	20702
Fri Resins Holding Company	Cranston	RI	F	401 946-5564	20228

	CITY	ST	EMP	PHONE	ENTRY #
Pg Imtech of Californ	East Providence	RI	G	401 521-2490	20441
Teknor Color Company	Pawtucket	RI	D	401 725-8000	20904
C E Bradely Lab Inc	Brattleboro	VT	D	802 257-1122	21721
PPG Industries Inc	South Burlington	VT	G	802 863-6387	22461
Sto Corp	Rutland	VT	E	802 775-4117	22354

PAINTS, VARNISHES & SPLYS WHOLESALERS

	CITY	ST	EMP	PHONE	ENTRY #
Advanced Frp Systems Inc	Weymouth	MA	G	508 927-6915	16883
Erich Husemoller Import & Expo	Easthampton	MA	G	413 585-9855	10563
Chilton Paint Co Inc ME	Freeport	ME	G	207 865-4443	6074
American-International Tl Inds	Cranston	RI	G	401 942-7855	20180
Sutherland Welles Ltd	Hyde Park	VT	G	802 635-2700	22038

PAINTS, VARNISHES & SPLYS, WHOLESALE: Paints

	CITY	ST	EMP	PHONE	ENTRY #
Color Craft Ltd	East Granby	CT	F	800 509-6563	1121
Grafted Coatings Inc	Stratford	CT	F	203 377-9979	4416

PAINTS: Lead-In-Oil

	CITY	ST	EMP	PHONE	ENTRY #
Brico LLC	Bloomfield	CT	G	860 242-7068	212

PAINTS: Marine

	CITY	ST	EMP	PHONE	ENTRY #
Dampney Company Inc	Everett	MA	E	617 389-2805	10609
E Paint Company	East Falmouth	MA	F	508 540-4412	10441

PAINTS: Oil Or Alkyd Vehicle Or Water Thinned

	CITY	ST	EMP	PHONE	ENTRY #
Durant Prfmce Coatings Inc	Revere	MA	F	781 289-1400	14765

PAINTS: Waterproof

	CITY	ST	EMP	PHONE	ENTRY #
M & D Coatings LLC	Stratford	CT	G	203 380-9466	4430
Foundation Armor LLC	Nashua	NH	F	866 306-0246	19163

PALLETS

	CITY	ST	EMP	PHONE	ENTRY #
Better Pallets Inc	Branford	CT	G	203 230-9549	296
Global Pallet Solutions LLC	New Britain	CT	G	860 826-5000	2535
Pallet Guys LLC	North Haven	CT	G	203 691-6716	3048
Pallet Inc LLC	Westport	CT	G	203 227-8148	5222
Toy Pallet	Ellington	CT	G	860 803-9838	1342
A1 Pallets Inc	Berlin	MA	G	978 838-2720	8090
Deadwood Pallets	Bellingham	MA	G	774 214-8628	8037
Groton Pallet Incorporated	Groton	MA	G	978 448-5651	11290
Nefab Packaging North East LLC	Bellingham	MA	F	800 258-4692	8053
Peco Pallet	Brighton	MA	G	845 642-2780	9104
Timothy Sills	Rockland	MA	G	781 635-8193	14830
Edgar Clark & Sons Pallet Inc	Mount Vernon	ME	G	207 685-3888	6458
Nevells Pallet Inc	Sidney	ME	G	207 547-4605	6963
Hills Pallet Company	Somersworth	NH	G	603 988-8624	19840

PALLETS & SKIDS: Wood

	CITY	ST	EMP	PHONE	ENTRY #
Acm Warehouse & Distribution	North Haven	CT	G	203 239-9557	3001
FCA LLC	Norwalk	CT	G	203 857-0825	3151
Guy Ravenelle	Central Village	CT	G	860 564-3200	706
Atlas Box and Crating Co Inc **(PA)**	Sutton	MA	C	508 865-1155	15679
Briggs Lumber Products	Gardner	MA	G	978 630-4207	11106
Fruit Basket World Division	Everett	MA	E	617 389-8989	10611
Industrial Pallet LLC	Princeton	MA	G	860 234-0962	14605
Jbm Service Inc	Templeton	MA	D	978 939-8004	15803
Pallets Recreated	Fitchburg	MA	G	978 345-5936	10848
Unified2 Globl Packg Group LLC	Sutton	MA	A	508 865-1155	15694
Isaacson Lumber Co Inc	Livermore Falls	ME	G	207 897-2115	6378
Perras Pallet LLC	Lancaster	NH	G	603 631-1169	18604
Greene Industries Inc	East Greenwich	RI	G	401 884-7530	20369
Carris Reels Inc **(HQ)**	Proctor	VT	C	802 773-9111	22284

PALLETS: Wooden

	CITY	ST	EMP	PHONE	ENTRY #
Central Pallet & Box	New Britain	CT	F	860 224-4416	2520
Coastal Pallet Corporation	Bridgeport	CT	E	203 333-1892	398
HI-Tech Packaging Inc	Stratford	CT	E	203 378-2700	4420
Industrial Pallet LLC	Eastford	CT	E	860 974-0093	1313
J J Box Co Inc	Bridgeport	CT	G	203 367-1211	432
R & R Pallet Corp	Cheshire	CT	F	203 272-2784	755
Southern Conn Pallet Co Inc	Wallingford	CT	G	203 265-1313	4808
St Pierre Box and Lumber Co	Canton	CT	G	860 413-9813	699
Vermont Pallet & Skid Shop	Norwich	CT	G	860 822-6949	3292
Westwood Products Inc	Winsted	CT	F	860 379-9401	5428
ABS Pallet	Hopedale	MA	G	508 246-1041	11668
B&D Pallet Bldg & Indus Sup	Westfield	MA	F	413 568-9624	16670
Beverly Pallet Company Inc	Ipswich	MA	G	978 356-1121	11905
Briggs Lumber Products	Rutland	MA	F	508 886-2054	14880
Conway Pallet Inc	Williamsburg	MA	F	413 268-3343	16949
Custom Pallets Inc	Brookfield	MA	G	508 867-2411	9189
Kelley Wood Products Inc	Fitchburg	MA	F	978 345-7531	10830
Lelanite Corporation	Oxford	MA	G	508 987-1771	14266
Lelanite Corporation **(PA)**	Webster	MA	E	508 987-2637	16346
Lenox Lumber Co	Pittsfield	MA	F	413 637-2744	14484
Lignetics New England Inc	Palmer	MA	G	413 284-1050	14288
Lohnes Pallet	Hanover	MA	G	781 878-6801	11345
New England Pallets Skids Inc	Ludlow	MA	F	413 583-6628	12473
Progress Pallet Inc	Middleboro	MA	E	508 923-1930	13076
Slowinski Wood Products	Colrain	MA	G	413 624-3415	10105
Springfield Pallet Inc	Indian Orchard	MA	G	413 593-0044	11896
Wackerbarth Box Mfg Co	Granville	MA	F	413 357-8816	11231
Wood Products Unlimited Inc	Methuen	MA	G	978 687-7449	13048
B & T Pallet Recycling Inc	Lewiston	ME	G	207 784-9048	6275
Gerrity Company Incorporated	Leeds	ME	E	207 933-2804	6269
Ifco Systems Us LLC	Scarborough	ME	E	207 883-0244	6926
Levesque Farm Pallets	Van Buren	ME	G	207 868-3905	7122
Mason Pallet Inc	Livermore Falls	ME	G	207 897-6270	6379
Palletone of Maine Inc	Livermore Falls	ME	C	207 897-5711	6380
Barlow Wood Products	Milford	NH	G	603 673-2642	19048
Global Pallet & Packaging LLC	Seabrook	NH	G	603 969-6660	19801
Lignetics New England Inc	Jaffrey	NH	F	603 532-4666	18471
Lignetics New England Inc	Jaffrey	NH	E	603 532-4666	18472
Atlas Barrell & Pallet Inc	Harrisville	RI	D	401 568-2900	20477
Js Pallet Co Inc	Pawtucket	RI	E	401 723-0223	20850
Carris Financial Corp **(PA)**	Proctor	VT	F	802 773-9111	22283
Hayes Recycled Pallets	Brandon	VT	E	802 247-4620	21708
Mountain View Skids	Enosburg Falls	VT	G	802 933-2623	21925

PANEL & DISTRIBUTION BOARDS & OTHER RELATED APPARATUS

	CITY	ST	EMP	PHONE	ENTRY #
Coghlin Companies Inc **(PA)**	Westborough	MA	C	508 753-2354	16604
Columbia Electrical Contrs Inc	Westborough	MA	C	508 366-8297	16605
Huber Engineered Woods LLC	Easton	ME	D	207 488-6700	5989
Bittware Inc **(DH)**	Concord	NH	E	603 226-0404	17884

PANEL & DISTRIBUTION BOARDS: Electric

	CITY	ST	EMP	PHONE	ENTRY #
Interconnect Technology Inc	Hudson	NH	F	603 883-3116	18402

PANELS, FLAT: Plastic

	CITY	ST	EMP	PHONE	ENTRY #
A A Plastic & Met Fabricators	Danvers	MA	G	978 777-0367	10188

PANELS: Building, Plastic, NEC

	CITY	ST	EMP	PHONE	ENTRY #
Nevamar Company LLC **(HQ)**	Shelton	CT	B	203 925-1556	3837
Panolam Industries Inc **(HQ)**	Shelton	CT	E	203 925-1556	3848
Panolam Industries Intl Inc **(PA)**	Shelton	CT	E	203 925-1556	3849
Kalwall Corporation **(PA)**	Manchester	NH	B	603 627-3861	18854
Kalwall Corporation	Bow	NH	D	603 224-6881	17718
Precision Letter Corporation	Manchester	NH	F	603 625-9625	18904
Clear Carbon & Components Inc	Bristol	RI	F	401 254-5085	20068

PANELS: Building, Wood

	CITY	ST	EMP	PHONE	ENTRY #
Marvic Inc	Auburn	MA	E	508 798-2600	7842
New England Homes Inc	Dover	NH	D	603 436-8830	18038
Energy Smart Building Inc	Starksboro	VT	E	802 453-4438	22515

PANELS: Electric Metering

	CITY	ST	EMP	PHONE	ENTRY #
Reactel Inc	New Haven	CT	G	203 773-0135	2730

PAPER & BOARD: Die-cut

	CITY	ST	EMP	PHONE	ENTRY #
American CT Rng Bnder Index &	Washington	CT	F	860 868-7900	4830
B-P Products Inc	Hamden	CT	E	203 288-0200	1733
Makino Inc	New Britain	CT	F	860 223-0236	2549
Walker Products Incorporated	Glastonbury	CT	F	860 659-3781	1581
B & K Enterprises Inc	Ashland	MA	G	508 881-1168	7656
H Loeb Corporation	New Bedford	MA	E	508 996-3745	13392
Merrimac Spool and Reel Co Inc	Haverhill	MA	E	978 372-7777	11453
New England Ultimate Finishing	Holyoke	MA	E	413 532-7777	11644
New England Water Jet Cutting	New Bedford	MA	G	508 993-9235	13425
Yankee Printing Group Inc	South Hadley	MA	E	413 532-9513	15313
Custom Die Cut Inc	Windham	NH	G	603 437-3090	20003
Fife Packaging LLC	Penacook	NH	E	603 753-2669	19465
Mono Die Cutting Co Inc	Riverside	RI	F	401 434-1274	21173
Mylan Technologies Inc **(DH)**	Saint Albans	VT	C	802 527-7792	22373

PAPER & PAPER PRDTS: Crepe, Made From Purchased Materials

	CITY	ST	EMP	PHONE	ENTRY #
Dennecrepe Corporation	Gardner	MA	D	978 630-8669	11112

PAPER CONVERTING

	CITY	ST	EMP	PHONE	ENTRY #
B-P Products Inc	Hamden	CT	E	203 288-0200	1733
Knox Industries Inc	Westport	CT	C	203 226-6408	5207
Mercantile Development Inc	Shelton	CT	E	203 922-8880	3832
Tudor Converted Products Inc **(PA)**	Newtown	CT	E	203 304-1875	2946
Canson Inc	South Hadley	MA	D	413 538-9250	15300
Ecological Fibers Inc **(PA)**	Lunenburg	MA	C	978 537-0003	12481
Garlock Prtg & Converting Corp	Gardner	MA	C	978 630-1028	11116
Garlock Prtg & Converting Corp **(PA)**	Gardner	MA	D	978 630-1028	11117
Mbw Incorporated	Orange	MA	C	978 544-6462	14221
Neci LLC	Canton	MA	E	781 828-4883	9761
Seaman Paper Warehouse	Gardner	MA	E	978 632-5524	11127
Sullivan Paper Company Inc **(PA)**	West Springfield	MA	C	413 827-7030	16554
W G Fry Corp	Florence	MA	E	413 747-2551	10870
Sappi North America Inc	Skowhegan	ME	A	207 238-3000	6986
Sappi North America Inc	South Portland	ME	D	207 854-7000	7039
Absorbent Specialty Pdts LLC	Cumberland	RI	F	401 722-1177	20312
Alliance Paper Company Inc	Pawtucket	RI	F	508 324-9100	20812
Arkwright Advanced Coating Inc	Fiskeville	RI	C	401 821-1000	20454

PAPER MANUFACTURERS: Exc Newsprint

	CITY	ST	EMP	PHONE	ENTRY #
Ahlstrom Windsor Locks LLC	Windsor Locks	CT	F	860 654-8629	5381
Brant Industries Inc **(PA)**	Greenwich	CT	F	203 661-3344	1601
International Paper - 16 Inc **(HQ)**	Stamford	CT	G	203 329-8544	4227
International Paper Company	Putnam	CT	C	860 928-7901	3616
Kimberly-Clark Corporation	Stratford	CT	C	973 986-8454	4427
Mafcote International Inc **(HQ)**	Norwalk	CT	F	203 644-1200	3189
Ahlstrom-Munksjo Paper Inc	Leominster	MA	F	978 342-1080	12109
Birch Point Paper Products Inc	Fitchburg	MA	E	978 422-1447	10811
Bristol Bay LLC	Salem	MA	G	978 744-4272	14898
Corona Films Inc	West Townsend	MA	G	978 597-6444	16566
Crane & Co Inc	Pittsfield	MA	F	413 684-6856	14466
Crane & Co Inc	Pittsfield	MA	C	413 684-2600	14467
Crane & Co Inc	Dalton	MA	C	413 684-2600	10177
Dennecrepe Corporation	Gardner	MA	D	978 630-8669	11112
Erving Paper Mills Inc	Erving	MA	C	413 422-2700	10590
Irving Consumer Products Inc	Burlington	MA	F	781 273-3222	9286
Kanzaki Specialty Papers Inc **(DH)**	Ware	MA	C	413 967-6204	16235
L & P Paper Inc	Charlton	MA	D	508 248-3265	9853

Company	CITY	ST	EMP	PHONE	ENTRY #
Neenah Technical Materials Inc **(HQ)**	Dalton	MA	F	678 518-3343	10180
Neenah Technical Materials Inc	Pittsfield	MA	C	413 684-7874	14495
Onyx Specialty Papers Inc	South Lee	MA	C	413 243-1231	15319
Pacothane Technologies **(PA)**	Winchester	MA	E	781 729-0927	17094
Pagell Corporation	Holliston	MA	E	508 429-2998	11594
Seaman Paper Company Mass Inc	Baldwinville	MA	D	978 939-5356	7945
Sonoco Products Company	Holyoke	MA	D	413 536-4546	11658
Cascades Auburn Fiber Inc	Auburn	ME	E	207 753-5300	5552
Georgia-Pacific LLC	Old Town	ME	B	207 827-7711	6538
Georgia-Pacific LLC	Baileyville	ME	G	207 427-4077	5626
Huhtamaki Inc	Waterville	ME	B	207 873-3351	7157
International Paper Company	Auburn	ME	C	207 784-4051	5572
ND Paper LLC	Rumford	ME	A	207 364-4521	6839
Presumpscot Water Power Co	Westbrook	ME	G	207 856-4000	7204
Sappi North America Inc	Skowhegan	ME	G	207 858-4201	6985
Sappi North America Inc	Westbrook	ME	B	207 856-4000	7205
Sappi North America Inc	Skowhegan	ME	A	207 238-3000	6986
Sappi North America Inc	South Portland	ME	D	207 854-7000	7039
Twin Rivers Paper Company Corp	Madawaska	ME	A	207 523-2350	6402
Twin Rivers Paper Company LLC	South Portland	ME	D	207 523-2350	7043
Twin Rivers Paper Company LLC **(PA)**	Madawaska	ME	E	207 728-3321	6403
Verso Paper Holding LLC	Jay	ME	A	207 897-3431	6222
Crane Security Tech Inc	Nashua	NH	E	603 881-1860	19139
Cellmark Inc	Pawtucket	RI	G	401 723-4200	20821

PAPER PRDTS: Feminine Hygiene Prdts

Company	CITY	ST	EMP	PHONE	ENTRY #
W2w Partners LLC	Duxbury	MA	G	781 424-7824	10404
Passifora Personal Products	Nashua	NH	G	603 809-6762	19227
Johnson & Johnson	Foster	RI	D	401 647-1493	20456

PAPER PRDTS: Infant & Baby Prdts

Company	CITY	ST	EMP	PHONE	ENTRY #
Alfa Nobel LLC	Milford	CT	G	203 876-2823	2241
Kimberly-Clark Corporation	New Milford	CT	A	860 210-1602	2811
Kimberly-Clark Corporation	Stratford	CT	C	973 986-8454	4427
Bumboosa LLC	Mashpee	MA	G	508 539-1373	12876
Kimberly-Clark Corporation	Franklin	MA	G	508 520-1355	11062
Kimberly-Clark Corporation	East Ryegate	VT	D	972 281-1200	21920
Seventh Generation Inc **(DH)**	Burlington	VT	C	802 658-3773	21808

PAPER PRDTS: Napkin Stock

Company	CITY	ST	EMP	PHONE	ENTRY #
Erving Industries Inc **(PA)**	Erving	MA	C	413 422-2700	10589
Soundview Vermont Holdings LLC	Putney	VT	C	802 387-5571	22292

PAPER PRDTS: Pressed & Molded Pulp & Fiber Prdts

Company	CITY	ST	EMP	PHONE	ENTRY #
Kadant Inc **(PA)**	Westford	MA	B	978 776-2000	16774

PAPER PRDTS: Sanitary

Company	CITY	ST	EMP	PHONE	ENTRY #
Dunn Paper LLC	East Hartford	CT	D	860 466-4141	1189
Soundview Paper Mills LLC **(DH)**	Greenwich	CT	G	201 796-4000	1652
Erving Industries Inc **(PA)**	Erving	MA	C	413 422-2700	10589
Essity	Palmer	MA	D	413 289-1221	14287
Irving Tissue Corporation	Burlington	MA	G	781 273-3222	9287
Milo Chip LLC	Milo	ME	G	207 943-2682	6447
Sumner Printing Inc	Somersworth	NH	E	603 692-7424	19849

PAPER PRDTS: Sanitary Tissue Paper

Company	CITY	ST	EMP	PHONE	ENTRY #
Kimberly-Clark Corporation	New Milford	CT	A	860 210-1602	2811
Georgia-Pacific LLC	Leominster	MA	C	978 537-4701	12144
Kimberly-Clark Corporation	Franklin	MA	G	508 520-1355	11062
Kimberly-Clark Corporation	East Ryegate	VT	D	972 281-1200	21920

PAPER PRDTS: Tampons, Sanitary, Made From Purchased Material

Company	CITY	ST	EMP	PHONE	ENTRY #
Edgewell Per Care Brands LLC **(HQ)**	Shelton	CT	B	203 944-5500	3799
Playtex Products LLC **(HQ)**	Shelton	CT	D	203 944-5500	3856

PAPER PRDTS: Towels, Napkins/Tissue Paper, From Purchd Mtrls

Company	CITY	ST	EMP	PHONE	ENTRY #
Maine Cleaners Supply Inc	North Yarmouth	ME	G	207 657-3166	6517

PAPER PRDTS: Wrappers, Blank, Made From Purchased Materials

Company	CITY	ST	EMP	PHONE	ENTRY #
Eagle Tissue LLC	South Windsor	CT	F	860 282-2535	3959

PAPER: Adding Machine Rolls, Made From Purchased Materials

Company	CITY	ST	EMP	PHONE	ENTRY #
Erolls Inc	Orange	MA	F	978 544-0100	14216
Nouveau Packaging LLC	Raynham	MA	G	508 880-0300	14722

PAPER: Adhesive

Company	CITY	ST	EMP	PHONE	ENTRY #
Comengs Inc	Danbury	CT	G	203 792-7306	889
Design Label Manufacturing Inc **(PA)**	Old Lyme	CT	E	860 739-6266	3321
H-O Products Corporation	Winsted	CT	E	860 379-9875	5412
Illinois Tool Works Inc	Manchester	CT	C	860 646-8153	2011
Neato Products LLC	Milford	CT	G	203 466-5170	2318
Avery Dennison Corporation	Westborough	MA	C	508 948-3500	16591
Computr Imprntble Lbl Systms	Burlington	MA	F	877 512-8763	9252
Industrial Lbling Systems Corp	Tyngsboro	MA	E	978 649-7004	15890
Pacon Corporation	Framingham	MA	E	508 370-0780	10992
Electronic Imaging Mtls Inc	Keene	NH	E	603 357-1459	18501
Trans-Tex LLC	Cranston	RI	E	401 331-8483	20304

PAPER: Bag

Company	CITY	ST	EMP	PHONE	ENTRY #
Imperial Bag and Paper	Franklin	MA	G	508 541-7220	11055

PAPER: Bank Note

Company	CITY	ST	EMP	PHONE	ENTRY #
Crane & Co Inc **(HQ)**	Boston	MA	C	617 648-3799	8487
Crane & Co Inc	Dalton	MA	G	413 684-2600	10176

PAPER: Book

Company	CITY	ST	EMP	PHONE	ENTRY #
Horizon Sales	Bolton	MA	G	978 779-0487	8320

PAPER: Bristols

Company	CITY	ST	EMP	PHONE	ENTRY #
Bristol Adult Resource Ctr Inc	Bristol	CT	E	860 583-8721	536
Doubletree	Bristol	CT	F	860 589-7766	550
LP Hometown Pizza LLC	Bristol	CT	G	860 589-1208	577
Agricltral Resources Mass Dept	Attleboro	MA	G	774 331-2818	7702
Bristol Myers Squibb	Cambridge	MA	G	781 209-2309	9423
Bristol Place Inc	Attleboro	MA	G	508 226-2300	7714
Lenmarine Inc	Somerset	MA	F	508 678-1234	15146
Tropical Smoothie of Bristol	Dartmouth	MA	G	508 636-1424	10278
Veterans Affairs US Dept	Fall River	MA	G	774 240-6764	10779
Friends Historic Bristol Inc	Bristol	RI	G	401 451-2735	20079

PAPER: Building Laminated, Made From Purchased Materials

Company	CITY	ST	EMP	PHONE	ENTRY #
3M Company	Haverhill	MA	B	978 659-9000	11402
3M Company	Methuen	MA	B	978 659-9000	13007

PAPER: Building, Insulating & Packaging

Company	CITY	ST	EMP	PHONE	ENTRY #
Honey Cell Inc **(PA)**	Bridgeport	CT	G	203 925-1818	426

PAPER: Card

Company	CITY	ST	EMP	PHONE	ENTRY #
American Banknote Corporation **(PA)**	Stamford	CT	G	203 941-4090	4135

PAPER: Cardboard

Company	CITY	ST	EMP	PHONE	ENTRY #
Lamitech	Rockland	MA	F	781 878-7708	14811
Jewel Case Corporation	Providence	RI	B	401 943-1400	21044

PAPER: Cigarette

Company	CITY	ST	EMP	PHONE	ENTRY #
UST LLC **(HQ)**	Stamford	CT	G	203 817-3000	4355

PAPER: Coated & Laminated, NEC

Company	CITY	ST	EMP	PHONE	ENTRY #
Lgl Group Inc	Greenwich	CT	G	407 298-2000	1626
Markal Finishing Co Inc	Bridgeport	CT	E	203 384-8219	446
Scapa Holdings Inc **(HQ)**	Windsor	CT	B	860 688-8000	5360
Specialty Printing LLC **(PA)**	East Windsor	CT	D	860 623-8870	1303
The E J Davis Company	North Haven	CT	E	203 239-5391	3063
Accucon Inc	Leominster	MA	G	978 840-0337	12106
American Biltrite Inc **(PA)**	Wellesley	MA	G	781 237-6655	16359
Arclin Surfaces - E Longmeadow	East Longmeadow	MA	F	678 781-5341	10467
Fortifiber Corporation	Attleboro	MA	E	508 222-3500	7738
Hampden Papers Inc **(PA)**	Holyoke	MA	D	413 536-1000	11630
Infinity Tapes LLC	Lawrence	MA	E	978 686-0632	12038
New England Ultimate Finishing	Holyoke	MA	E	413 532-7777	11644
Regal Press Incorporated **(PA)**	Norwood	MA	C	781 769-3900	14192
Shawsheen Rubber Co Inc	Andover	MA	D	978 470-1760	7604
Suddekor LLC **(DH)**	Agawam	MA	E	413 821-9000	7453
Tekni-Plex Inc	Ashland	MA	F	508 881-2440	7671
Panolam Industries Intl Inc	Auburn	ME	E	207 784-9111	5586
Quick Print Color Center	Saco	ME	G	207 282-6480	6856
R & W Engraving Inc	Biddeford	ME	G	207 286-3020	5760
Verso Paper Holding LLC	Jay	ME	A	207 897-3431	6222
Avery Dennison Corporation	Belmont	NH	E	603 217-4144	17670
Contract Mfg Tech LLC	Dover	NH	G	603 692-4488	18014
Label Tech Inc	Somersworth	NH	C	603 692-2005	19843
Nashua Corporation	Merrimack	NH	B	603 880-1110	19015
Ecological Fibers Inc	Pawtucket	RI	D	401 725-9700	20836
Neptco Incorporated **(HQ)**	Pawtucket	RI	D	401 722-5500	20863

PAPER: Coated, Exc Photographic, Carbon Or Abrasive

Company	CITY	ST	EMP	PHONE	ENTRY #
Avery Dennison Corporation	Fitchburg	MA	C	978 353-2100	10810
Hazen Paper Company **(PA)**	Holyoke	MA	C	413 538-8204	11631
Visual Magnetics Ltd	Mendon	MA	E	508 381-2400	12997
Visual Magnetics Ltd Partnr	Mendon	MA	F	508 381-2400	12998
Sappi North America Inc	Skowhegan	ME	A	207 238-3000	6986
Sappi North America Inc	South Portland	ME	D	207 854-7000	7039

PAPER: Corrugated

Company	CITY	ST	EMP	PHONE	ENTRY #
Valley Container Inc	Bridgeport	CT	E	203 368-6546	503
Westrock - Southern Cont LLC	Boston	MA	F	978 772-5050	8924

PAPER: Filter

Company	CITY	ST	EMP	PHONE	ENTRY #
Hollingsworth & Vose Company **(PA)**	East Walpole	MA	C	508 850-2000	10524

PAPER: Gift Wrap

Company	CITY	ST	EMP	PHONE	ENTRY #
Expressive Design Group Inc	Holyoke	MA	E	413 315-6296	11626

PAPER: Greeting Card

Company	CITY	ST	EMP	PHONE	ENTRY #
Up With Paper	Guilford	CT	G	203 453-3300	1723

PAPER: Insulation Siding

Company	CITY	ST	EMP	PHONE	ENTRY #
Xamax Industries Inc	Seymour	CT	E	203 888-7200	3769
Innovative Paper Tech LLC	Tilton	NH	D	603 286-4891	19906

PAPER: Kraft

Company	CITY	ST	EMP	PHONE	ENTRY #
APC Paper Company Inc **(PA)**	Claremont	NH	D	603 542-0411	17835
Weeden Street Associates LLC	Pawtucket	RI	E	401 725-2610	20912

PAPER: Metallic Covered, Made From Purchased Materials

Company	CITY	ST	EMP	PHONE	ENTRY #
AR Metallizing Ltd	Franklin	MA	D	508 541-7700	11024

PAPER: Newsprint

Company	CITY	ST	EMP	PHONE	ENTRY #
Resolute FP US Inc	Southport	CT	B	203 292-6560	4097

PAPER: Packaging

Company	CITY	ST	EMP	PHONE	ENTRY #
Packaging Specialties Inc	Newburyport	MA	D	978 462-1300	13520
Enco Container Services Inc	Plaistow	NH	G	603 382-8481	19511
Signode Industrial Group LLC	Rumford	RI	D	401 438-5203	21196

PAPER: Printer

	CITY	ST	EMP	PHONE	ENTRY #
Norcell Inc **(DH)**	Shelton	CT	F	203 254-5292	3841
Georgia-Pacific LLC	Norwood	MA	G	781 440-3600	14155
Domtar Paper Company LLC	Baileyville	ME	A	207 427-6400	5624
Ges Control Systems Inc	Dover	NH	G	905 336-5517	18023

PAPER: Specialty

	CITY	ST	EMP	PHONE	ENTRY #
Pacothane Technologies	Woburn	MA	E	781 756-3163	17253
Monadnock Paper Mills Inc **(PA)**	Bennington	NH	C	603 588-3311	17689

PAPER: Specialty Or Chemically Treated

	CITY	ST	EMP	PHONE	ENTRY #
Ahlstrom-Munksjo USA Inc **(HQ)**	Windsor Locks	CT	F	860 654-8300	5383
Boston Paper Board Corp	Boston	MA	E	617 666-1154	8436

PAPER: Tissue

	CITY	ST	EMP	PHONE	ENTRY #
McNairn Packaging Inc **(PA)**	Westfield	MA	D	413 568-1989	16699
Seaman Paper Company Mass Inc	Orange	MA	G	978 544-2455	14228

PAPER: Wallpaper

	CITY	ST	EMP	PHONE	ENTRY #
Arlington Sample Book Co Inc **(PA)**	Sunapee	NH	G	603 763-9082	19879

PAPER: Wrapping

	CITY	ST	EMP	PHONE	ENTRY #
Seaman Paper Company Mass Inc **(PA)**	Gardner	MA	E	978 632-1513	11126

PAPER: Wrapping & Packaging

	CITY	ST	EMP	PHONE	ENTRY #
H & C Sales Inc	Stoughton	MA	G	781 344-6445	15595

PAPERBOARD

	CITY	ST	EMP	PHONE	ENTRY #
Connecticut Container Corp **(PA)**	North Haven	CT	C	203 248-2161	3018
Fluted Partition Inc **(PA)**	Bridgeport	CT	C	203 368-2548	414
Graphic Packaging Intl LLC	Litchfield	CT	G	860 567-4196	1949
Metsa Board Americas Corp	Norwalk	CT	D	203 229-0037	3196
Rice Packaging Inc	Ellington	CT	D	860 870-7057	1338
Russell Partition Co Inc	North Haven	CT	G	203 239-5749	3059
Schrafel Paperboard Converting	West Haven	CT	E	203 931-1700	5145
Baird & Bartlett Coi NC	West Bridgewater	MA	G	508 588-9400	16431
Caraustar Industries Inc	Fitchburg	MA	D	978 665-2632	10819
Northeast Document Conservatio	Andover	MA	E	978 470-1010	7577
Quality Carton Converting LLC	Haverhill	MA	F	978 556-5008	11464
Rand-Whitney Container LLC **(DH)**	Worcester	MA	C	508 890-7000	17450
Rand-Whitney Group LLC **(HQ)**	Worcester	MA	C	508 791-2301	17452
Sonoco Products Company	Holyoke	MA	D	413 536-4546	11658
Sonoco Products Company	Holyoke	MA	E	413 493-1298	11659
Westrock Cp LLC	Mansfield	MA	E	508 337-0400	12672
Westrock Cp LLC	Mansfield	MA	C	770 448-2193	12671
Sonoco Products Company	Pittsfield	ME	E	207 487-3206	6591
Graphic Packaging Intl LLC	Concord	NH	E	603 230-5486	17905
Contempo Card Co Inc **(PA)**	Providence	RI	D	401 272-4210	20990
Nfa Corp	Cumberland	RI	E	401 333-8990	20332
Long Falls Paperboard LLC	Brattleboro	VT	C	802 257-0365	21737
Westrock Converting Company	Sheldon Springs	VT	G	802 933-7733	22430
Westrock Cp LLC	Sheldon Springs	VT	C	802 933-7733	22431

PAPERBOARD CONVERTING

	CITY	ST	EMP	PHONE	ENTRY #
Rand-Whitney Recycling LLC	Montville	CT	D	860 848-1900	2422
Schrafel Paperboard Converting	West Haven	CT	E	203 931-1700	5145
BBC Printing and Products Inc	Waltham	MA	G	781 647-4646	16042
Johnston Dandy Company	Holyoke	MA	F	413 315-4596	11635
RPM Technologies Inc	Ludlow	MA	G	413 583-3385	12477

PAPERBOARD PRDTS: Automobile Board

	CITY	ST	EMP	PHONE	ENTRY #
Lydall Inc **(PA)**	Manchester	CT	E	860 646-1233	2021

PAPERBOARD PRDTS: Container Board

	CITY	ST	EMP	PHONE	ENTRY #
Paper Alliance LLC	Branford	CT	G	203 315-3116	334
Georgia-Pacific LLC	Norwood	MA	G	781 440-3600	14155
Rand-Whitney Container Board L	Worcester	MA	D	860 848-1900	17449
Westrock Rkt Company	Springfield	MA	G	413 543-7300	15528
Georgia-Pacific LLC	Baileyville	ME	G	207 427-4077	5626
Graphic Packaging Intl LLC	Concord	NH	D	603 224-2333	17907

PAPERBOARD PRDTS: Folding Boxboard

	CITY	ST	EMP	PHONE	ENTRY #
Millen Industries Inc **(PA)**	Norwalk	CT	G	203 847-8500	3198
RTS Packaging LLC	Scarborough	ME	D	207 883-8921	6938
Graphic Packaging Intl LLC	Concord	NH	C	603 230-5100	17904
Rand-Whitney Container LLC	Pawtucket	RI	E	401 729-7900	20890

PAPERBOARD PRDTS: Leatherboard

	CITY	ST	EMP	PHONE	ENTRY #
Miles Kedex Co Inc	Westminster	MA	E	978 874-1403	16810

PAPERBOARD PRDTS: Packaging Board

	CITY	ST	EMP	PHONE	ENTRY #
Pact Inc	Waterbury	CT	F	203 759-1799	4934
Georgia-Pacific LLC	Leominster	MA	C	978 537-4701	12144
Signode Industrial Group LLC	Rumford	RI	D	401 438-5203	21196

PAPERBOARD PRDTS: Pressboard

	CITY	ST	EMP	PHONE	ENTRY #
Neenah Northeast LLC **(HQ)**	West Springfield	MA	C	413 533-0699	16534

PAPERBOARD PRDTS: Stencil Board

	CITY	ST	EMP	PHONE	ENTRY #
G3 Incorporated **(PA)**	Lowell	MA	E	978 805-5001	12372

PAPERBOARD: Boxboard

	CITY	ST	EMP	PHONE	ENTRY #
Action Packaging Systems Inc **(PA)**	Ellington	CT	G	860 222-9510	1325
B-P Products Inc	Hamden	CT	E	203 288-0200	1733

PAPERBOARD: Chipboard

	CITY	ST	EMP	PHONE	ENTRY #
Limlaws Pulpwood Inc	West Topsham	VT	F	802 439-3503	22622

PAPERBOARD: Coated

	CITY	ST	EMP	PHONE	ENTRY #
Hampden Papers Inc **(PA)**	Holyoke	MA	D	413 536-1000	11630

PAPERBOARD: Corrugated

	CITY	ST	EMP	PHONE	ENTRY #
Westrock Cp LLC	Uncasville	CT	C	860 848-1500	4651

PAPERBOARD: Liner Board

	CITY	ST	EMP	PHONE	ENTRY #
Westrock Mwv LLC	Springfield	MA	A	413 736-7211	15527

PARACHUTES

	CITY	ST	EMP	PHONE	ENTRY #
Cap-Tech Products Inc	Wethersfield	CT	F	860 490-5078	5243

PARTICLEBOARD

	CITY	ST	EMP	PHONE	ENTRY #
Biofibers Capital Group LLC	Ashford	CT	G	203 561-6133	25
Panolam Industries Intl Inc **(PA)**	Shelton	CT	E	203 925-1556	3849
Panolam Industries Intl Inc	Auburn	ME	E	207 784-9111	5586

PARTITIONS & FIXTURES: Except Wood

	CITY	ST	EMP	PHONE	ENTRY #
Displaycraft Inc	Plainville	CT	E	860 747-9110	3481
Durham Manufacturing Company **(PA)**	Durham	CT	D	860 349-3427	1090
Central Mass Installations	West Boylston	MA	G	508 612-3092	16412
JH Smith Co Inc **(PA)**	Greenfield	MA	F	413 772-0191	11264
New England Wire Products Inc **(PA)**	Leominster	MA	C	800 254-9473	12171
E G W Bradbury Enterprises	Bridgewater	ME	F	207 429-8141	5805
Jsi Store Fixtures Inc **(PA)**	Milo	ME	C	207 943-5203	6446
Maine Wood & Design LLC	York	ME	F	207 363-5270	7312
Alco Construction Inc	Hudson	NH	G	603 305-8493	18372
Custom Design Incorporated	North Kingstown	RI	E	401 294-0200	20700
Frank Shatz & Co	Warwick	RI	E	401 739-1822	21364
Maro Display Inc	North Kingstown	RI	E	401 294-5551	20726
Scope Display & Box Co Inc **(PA)**	Cranston	RI	D	401 942-7150	20284

PARTITIONS WHOLESALERS

	CITY	ST	EMP	PHONE	ENTRY #
Steeltech Building Pdts Inc	South Windsor	CT	D	860 290-8930	4014

PARTITIONS: Nonwood, Floor Attached

	CITY	ST	EMP	PHONE	ENTRY #
Cano Corporation **(PA)**	Fitchburg	MA	E	978 342-0953	10818

PARTITIONS: Solid Fiber, Made From Purchased Materials

	CITY	ST	EMP	PHONE	ENTRY #
Westrock Rkt Company	Springfield	MA	G	413 543-7300	15528

PARTITIONS: Wood & Fixtures

	CITY	ST	EMP	PHONE	ENTRY #
BP Countertop Design Co LLC	Derby	CT	G	203 732-1620	1069
C Mather Company Inc	South Windsor	CT	G	860 528-5667	3946
Creative Dimensions Inc	Cheshire	CT	E	203 250-6500	725
John M Kriskey Carpentry	Greenwich	CT	G	203 531-0194	1625
Modern Woodcrafts LLC	Plainville	CT	D	860 677-7371	3508
One and Co Inc	Norwich	CT	F	860 892-5180	3288
Robert L Lovallo	Stamford	CT	G	203 324-6655	4304
General Woodworking Inc **(PA)**	Lowell	MA	F	978 458-6625	12373
Jarica Inc	Woburn	MA	F	781 935-1907	17210
J H Dunning Corporation	North Walpole	NH	E	603 445-5591	19394
Herrick & White Ltd	Cumberland	RI	D	401 658-0440	20324
Orion Ret Svcs & Fixturing Inc	Smithfield	RI	D	401 334-5000	21243
Scope Display & Box Co Inc	Providence	RI	G	401 467-3910	21120
Scope Display & Box Co Inc **(PA)**	Cranston	RI	D	401 942-7150	20284

PARTITIONS: Wood, Floor Attached

	CITY	ST	EMP	PHONE	ENTRY #
Cano Corporation **(PA)**	Fitchburg	MA	E	978 342-0953	10818
Yankee Craftsman Inc	Auburn	NH	G	603 483-5900	17614

PARTS: Metal

	CITY	ST	EMP	PHONE	ENTRY #
Mimforms LLC	Norwalk	CT	G	800 445-1245	3199
SMR Metal Technology	South Windsor	CT	G	860 291-8259	4011
Alvin Johnson	East Longmeadow	MA	G	413 525-6334	10465
Atlantic Industrial Models LLC	Essex	MA	E	978 768-7686	10591
Dustin W Ciampa	Haverhill	MA	G	603 571-4325	11427
Kables and Konnector Services	Maynard	MA	G	978 897-4852	12899
Mair-Mac Machine Company Inc	Brockton	MA	F	508 895-9001	9164
McNamara Fabricating Co Inc	West Boylston	MA	F	774 243-7425	16422
HI Tech Mch & Fabrication LLC	Ashaway	RI	E	866 972-2077	20036
Burtco Inc	Westminster Station	VT	F	802 722-3358	22633

PATENT OWNERS & LESSORS

	CITY	ST	EMP	PHONE	ENTRY #
Capricorn Investors II LP	Greenwich	CT	A	203 861-6600	1602

PATTERNS: Indl

	CITY	ST	EMP	PHONE	ENTRY #
Arrow Diversified Tooling Inc	Ellington	CT	E	860 872-9072	1329
Case Patterns Inc	Groton	CT	G	860 445-6722	1665
Fitchburg Pattern and Model Co	Fitchburg	MA	G	978 342-0770	10825
Manufctrers Pattern Fndry Corp	Springfield	MA	G	413 732-8117	15487
S Ralph Cross and Sons Inc	Sutton	MA	E	508 865-8112	15691
Waiteco Machine Inc	Ayer	MA	G	978 772-5535	7942
Kestrel Tooling Company	Topsham	ME	G	207 721-0609	7090
Bomar Inc	Charlestown	NH	D	603 826-5781	17811
Clear Carbon & Components Inc	Bristol	RI	F	401 254-5085	20068
Eagle Pattern & Casting Co	Cranston	RI	G	401 943-7154	20213

PAVERS

	CITY	ST	EMP	PHONE	ENTRY #
Calvin Brown	Gales Ferry	CT	G	860 536-6178	1526
Daves Paving and Construction	Prospect	CT	G	203 753-4992	3587
LH Gault & Son Incorporated	Westport	CT	D	203 227-5181	5209
Portage Lkers Snwmbile CLB Inc	Portage	ME	F	207 415-0506	6599
All American Walls and Pavers	Concord	NH	G	603 219-0822	17882
Max Roads LLC	Raymond	NH	G	603 895-5200	19640

PRODUCT

PAVING BREAKERS

	CITY	ST	EMP	PHONE	ENTRY #
Vulcan Company Inc **(PA)**	Hingham	MA	D	781 337-5970	11515

PAVING MATERIALS: Coal Tar, Not From Refineries

	CITY	ST	EMP	PHONE	ENTRY #
Kol-Tar Inc	Abington	MA	G	781 871-0883	7326

PAVING MATERIALS: Prefabricated, Concrete

	CITY	ST	EMP	PHONE	ENTRY #
Dalton Enterprises Inc **(PA)**	Cheshire	CT	D	203 272-3221	726

PAVING MIXTURES

	CITY	ST	EMP	PHONE	ENTRY #
Addison County Asphalt Pdts	Middlebury	VT	G	802 388-2338	22096

PEAT MINING & PROCESSING SVCS

	CITY	ST	EMP	PHONE	ENTRY #
Sun Gro Horticulture Dist Inc	Agawam	MA	E	800 732-8667	7455

PEAT MINING SVCS

	CITY	ST	EMP	PHONE	ENTRY #
Sterling Peat Inc	Sterling	MA	G	978 422-8294	15547

PENCILS & PARTS: Mechanical

	CITY	ST	EMP	PHONE	ENTRY #
Derand Precision	South Londonderry	VT	G	802 874-7161	22485

PENS & PARTS: Ball Point

	CITY	ST	EMP	PHONE	ENTRY #
Bic Consumer Products Mfg Co	Milford	CT	C	203 783-2000	2254
Bic Corporation **(HQ)**	Shelton	CT	A	203 783-2000	3782
Bic USA Inc **(DH)**	Shelton	CT	C	203 783-2000	3783
EF Leach & Company	Attleboro	MA	B	508 643-3309	7731
Hub Pen Company Inc **(PA)**	Braintree	MA	D	781 535-5500	9018
Precision Handling Devices **(PA)**	Westport	MA	F	508 679-5282	16845
Riveto Manufacturing Co	Orange	MA	E	978 544-2171	14226

PENS & PENCILS: Mechanical, NEC

	CITY	ST	EMP	PHONE	ENTRY #
Gillette Company	Bethel	CT	G	203 796-4000	155
Gillette Company	Andover	MA	A	781 662-9600	7552
Gillette Company **(HQ)**	Boston	MA	A	617 421-7000	8561
Garland Industries Inc	Coventry	RI	E	401 821-1450	20147

PERFUME: Concentrated

	CITY	ST	EMP	PHONE	ENTRY #
Bedoukian Research Inc **(PA)**	Danbury	CT	E	203 830-4000	877
Green Mountain Fragrances Inc	Brattleboro	VT	G	802 490-2268	21731

PERFUME: Perfumes, Natural Or Synthetic

	CITY	ST	EMP	PHONE	ENTRY #
Chemessence Inc	New Milford	CT	G	860 355-4108	2792
Parfums De Coeur Ltd **(PA)**	Stamford	CT	E	203 655-8807	4277

PERFUMES

	CITY	ST	EMP	PHONE	ENTRY #
American Distilling Inc	Marlborough	CT	G	860 267-4444	2063
American Distilling Inc **(PA)**	East Hampton	CT	D	860 267-4444	1156

PERIODICALS, WHOLESALE

	CITY	ST	EMP	PHONE	ENTRY #
President Fllows Hrvard Cllege	Boston	MA	G	617 783-7888	8792

PERLITE: Processed

	CITY	ST	EMP	PHONE	ENTRY #
Whittemore Company Inc	Lawrence	MA	E	978 681-8833	12083
Chemrock Corporation	Thomaston	ME	G	207 594-8225	7082

PERSONAL & HOUSEHOLD GOODS REPAIR, NEC

	CITY	ST	EMP	PHONE	ENTRY #
Herbert Mosher	Nashua	NH	G	603 882-4357	19177

PEST CONTROL SVCS

	CITY	ST	EMP	PHONE	ENTRY #
Pine State Pest Solutions Inc	Auburn	ME	G	207 795-1100	5590

PESTICIDES

	CITY	ST	EMP	PHONE	ENTRY #
Able Pest Control Service	Brockton	MA	G	508 559-7987	9114
Thermacell Repellents Inc	Bedford	MA	E	781 541-6900	8016
Holy Terra Products Inc	Yarmouth	ME	G	207 846-4170	7295
Boston Fog LLC	Belmont	NH	G	888 846-4145	17671
Northeast Agricultural Sls Inc **(PA)**	Lyndonville	VT	F	802 626-3351	22070

PET & PET SPLYS STORES

	CITY	ST	EMP	PHONE	ENTRY #
Two Rivers Pet Products Inc	Turner	ME	E	207 225-3965	7112

PET ACCESS: Collars, Leashes, Etc, Exc Leather

	CITY	ST	EMP	PHONE	ENTRY #
Mackenzie Couture ACC Inc	Lynnfield	MA	G	781 334-2805	12552

PET FOOD WHOLESALERS

	CITY	ST	EMP	PHONE	ENTRY #
Blue Buffalo Company Ltd **(DH)**	Wilton	CT	B	203 762-9751	5279

PET SPLYS

	CITY	ST	EMP	PHONE	ENTRY #
A L C Inovators Inc	Milford	CT	G	203 877-8526	2232
Nano Pet Products LLC	Norwalk	CT	G	203 345-1330	3203
Pleasant Valley Fence Co Inc	Pleasant Valley	CT	F	860 379-0088	3546
Valore Inc	Norwalk	CT	G	203 854-4799	3264
Alpha Tech Pet Inc	Littleton	MA	F	978 486-3690	12291
Cape Cod Dog	Eastham	MA	G	508 255-4206	10548
Cara Armour	Waltham	MA	G	781 899-7297	16060
Champagne Tables & Pet Pdts	Southampton	MA	G	413 527-4370	15337
Four Lggers Doggie Daycare LLC	Beverly	MA	G	978 922-4182	8132
Pawsitively Yummy	Tyngsboro	MA	G	603 889-3181	15898
Fetch Inc	Portland	ME	G	207 773-5450	6662
Moore-Clark USA Inc	Westbrook	ME	F	207 591-7077	7198
Planet Ventures Inc **(PA)**	Westbrook	ME	E	207 761-1515	7203
Two Rivers Pet Products Inc	Turner	ME	E	207 225-3965	7112
Ewe Kids Inc	Candia	NH	G	603 483-0984	17783
Kevin S Boghigian	Nashua	NH	G	603 883-0236	19194
Lupine Inc	Center Conway	NH	D	603 356-7371	17801
Up Country Inc	East Providence	RI	E	401 431-2940	20447
Vermont Juvenile Furn Mfg Inc	West Rutland	VT	F	802 438-2231	22620

PET SPLYS WHOLESALERS

	CITY	ST	EMP	PHONE	ENTRY #
Alpha Tech Pet Inc	Littleton	MA	F	978 486-3690	12291
Central Garden & Pet Company	Taunton	MA	E	508 884-5426	15735
Smartpak Equine LLC **(DH)**	Plymouth	MA	D	774 773-1100	14583
Scott-Lynn Mfg	Auburn	ME	G	207 784-3372	5598

PETROLEUM & PETROLEUM PRDTS, WHOLESALE Fuel Oil

	CITY	ST	EMP	PHONE	ENTRY #
Weymouths Inc	Clinton	ME	G	207 426-3211	5917

PETROLEUM BULK STATIONS & TERMINALS

	CITY	ST	EMP	PHONE	ENTRY #
Exxonmobil Oil Corporation	Randolph	MA	G	781 963-7252	14679

PEWTER WARE

	CITY	ST	EMP	PHONE	ENTRY #
George S Preisner Jewelers	Wallingford	CT	G	203 265-0057	4748
Woodbury Pewterers Inc	Woodbury	CT	E	203 263-2668	5492

PHARMACEUTICAL PREPARATIONS: Adrenal

	CITY	ST	EMP	PHONE	ENTRY #
Fresenius Usa Inc	Marlborough	MA	E	508 460-1150	12757
Polycarbon Industries Inc **(DH)**	Newburyport	MA	D	978 462-5555	13521

PHARMACEUTICAL PREPARATIONS: Druggists' Preparations

	CITY	ST	EMP	PHONE	ENTRY #
Achillion Pharmaceuticals Inc	New Haven	CT	D	203 624-7000	2652
Boehrnger Ingelheim Roxane Inc	Ridgefield	CT	E	203 798-5555	3660
Brookfield Mdcl/Srgical Sup Inc	Brookfield	CT	F	203 775-0862	636
Cardioxyl Pharmaceuticals Inc	Wallingford	CT	G	919 869-8586	4715
Condomdepot Co	Plainville	CT	G	860 747-1338	3475
Pre -Clinical Safety Inc	East Lyme	CT	G	860 739-9797	1272
Quality Care Drg/Cntrbrook LLC	Centerbrook	CT	G	860 767-0206	702
Abbott Laboratories	Worcester	MA	A	508 849-2500	17331
Abbvie Inc	Worcester	MA	E	508 849-2500	17332
Akston Biosciences Corporation	Beverly	MA	G	978 969-3381	8097
Censa Pharmaceuticals Inc **(PA)**	Wellesley Hills	MA	F	617 225-7700	16396
Colucid Pharmaceuticals Inc	Cambridge	MA	G	857 285-6495	9439
Erytech Pharma Inc	Cambridge	MA	G	360 320-3325	9472
Ludlow Corporation **(DH)**	Mansfield	MA	G	508 261-8000	12643
Merrimack Pharmaceuticals Inc	Cambridge	MA	D	617 441-1000	9551
New England Pet Distr Ctr LLC	Woburn	MA	G	781 937-3600	17242
Nextcea Inc	Woburn	MA	G	800 225-1645	17245
Nimbus Lakshmi Inc	Cambridge	MA	G	857 999-2009	9583
Ocular Therapeutix Inc **(PA)**	Bedford	MA	E	781 357-4000	7997
Pear Tree Pharmaceuticals Inc	Auburndale	MA	G	617 500-3871	7867
Pulmatrix Inc **(PA)**	Lexington	MA	E	781 357-2333	12256
Qpharmetra LLC **(PA)**	Andover	MA	F	978 655-1943	7589
Reform Biologics LLC	Woburn	MA	F	617 871-2101	17282
Soleo Health Inc	Canton	MA	G	781 298-3427	9782
Theragenics Corporation	North Billerica	MA	G	978 528-4307	13872
Vietaz Inc	Dorchester	MA	G	617 322-1933	10349
Visterra Inc	Waltham	MA	E	617 498-1070	16221
Chemcage US LLC	East Kingston	NH	G	617 504-9548	18085

PHARMACEUTICAL PREPARATIONS: Medicines, Capsule Or Ampule

	CITY	ST	EMP	PHONE	ENTRY #
Boehringer Ingelheim Corp **(DH)**	Ridgefield	CT	A	203 798-9988	3657
Boehringer Ingelheim USA Corp **(DH)**	Ridgefield	CT	C	203 798-9988	3659
New Haven Naturopathic Center	New Haven	CT	G	203 387-8661	2715
Cellgenix USA	Portsmouth	NH	G	603 373-0408	19550
Ceres LLC **(PA)**	Burlington	VT	G	833 237-3767	21772

PHARMACEUTICAL PREPARATIONS: Pills

	CITY	ST	EMP	PHONE	ENTRY #
Boaopharma Inc	Natick	MA	G	508 315-8080	13239
Exarca Pharmaceuticals LLC	Lexington	MA	G	617 620-2776	12223
Pharmate Inc	Cambridge	MA	G	617 800-5804	9610

PHARMACEUTICAL PREPARATIONS: Powders

	CITY	ST	EMP	PHONE	ENTRY #
Alkalol Company	Boston	MA	G	617 304-3668	8357
Genzyme Corporation	Cambridge	MA	C	617 252-7500	9492
Tolerx Inc	Cambridge	MA	D	617 354-8100	9682

PHARMACEUTICAL PREPARATIONS: Proprietary Drug PRDTS

	CITY	ST	EMP	PHONE	ENTRY #
Lipid Genomics Inc	Farmington	CT	G	443 465-3495	1490
New Leaf Pharmaceutical	Newtown	CT	F	203 270-4167	2930
Abtelum Biomedical Inc	Westwood	MA	G	781 367-1696	16856
Ipsen Bioscience Inc	Cambridge	MA	E	617 679-8500	9519
Revere Pharmaceuticals Inc	Arlington	MA	G	781 718-9033	7635
Sangstat Medical LLC	Cambridge	MA	B	510 789-4300	9642

PHARMACEUTICAL PREPARATIONS: Solutions

	CITY	ST	EMP	PHONE	ENTRY #
Sca Pharmaceuticals LLC	Windsor	CT	G	501 312-2800	5359
Allergan Sales LLC	Fall River	MA	G	508 324-1481	10653
Citra Labs LLC	Braintree	MA	E	781 848-9386	8994
Cytosol Laboratories Inc	Braintree	MA	F	781 848-9386	8998
Wilmington Partners LP	Wilmington	MA	C	978 658-6111	17067
Statim Pharmaceuticals Inc	Moultonborough	NH	G	650 305-0657	19098

PHARMACEUTICAL PREPARATIONS: Tablets

	CITY	ST	EMP	PHONE	ENTRY #
Foster Delivery Science Inc	Putnam	CT	F	860 630-4515	3615
Boston Biomedical Pharma Inc	Cambridge	MA	G	617 674-6800	9416

PHARMACEUTICAL PREPARATIONS: Tranquilizers Or Mental Drug

	CITY	ST	EMP	PHONE	ENTRY #
Jfm No 3 Corp	Auburn	ME	E	207 782-2726	5573

PHARMACEUTICALS

	CITY	ST	EMP	PHONE	ENTRY #
A & S Pharmaceutical Corp	Bridgeport	CT	E	203 368-2538	364
Actimus Inc	Cromwell	CT	D	617 438-9968	843
Aeromics Inc	Branford	CT	G	216 772-1004	285
Alexion Pharma LLC **(HQ)**	New Haven	CT	E	203 272-2596	2653
Arvinas Inc **(PA)**	New Haven	CT	F	203 535-1456	2658
Avara Pharmaceutical Svcs Inc **(HQ)**	Norwalk	CT	E	203 918-1659	3109
Beta Pharma Inc	Shelton	CT	F	203 315-5062	3780

	CITY	ST	EMP	PHONE	ENTRY #
Biohaven Pharmaceuticals Inc	New Haven	CT	D	203 404-0410	2666
Biomed Health Inc	Glastonbury	CT	F	860 657-2258	1540
Bioxcel Therapeutics Inc	New Haven	CT	F	475 238-6837	2668
Cara Therapeutics Inc	Stamford	CT	E	203 406-3700	4155
Cardinal Health 414 LLC	East Hartford	CT	G	860 291-9135	1179
Carigent Therapeutics Inc	New Haven	CT	G	203 887-2873	2675
Chemin Pharma LLC	Woodbridge	CT	G	203 208-2811	5465
Evotec (us) Inc	Branford	CT	E	650 228-1400	314
Foster Delivery Science Inc **(DH)**	Putnam	CT	F	860 928-4102	3614
Frederick Purdue Company Inc **(PA)**	Stamford	CT	B	203 588-8000	4197
Frequency Therapeutics Inc	Farmington	CT	E	978 436-0704	1484
Gaia Chemical Corporation	Gaylordsville	CT	G	860 355-2730	1531
Glaxosmithkline LLC	Southbury	CT	E	203 232-5145	4026
Hoffmann-La Roche Inc	Branford	CT	A	203 871-2303	323
Innoteq Inc **(PA)**	Stratford	CT	E	203 659-4444	4424
Iterum Therapeutics Inc	Old Saybrook	CT	G	860 391-8349	3339
J & J Precision Eyelet Inc	Thomaston	CT	D	860 283-8243	4505
Kolltan Pharmaceuticals Inc **(HQ)**	New Haven	CT	E	203 773-3000	2702
Koster Keunen LLC **(PA)**	Watertown	CT	F	860 945-3333	5013
Loxo Oncology Inc **(HQ)**	Stamford	CT	E	203 653-3880	4241
MD Solarsciences Corporation	Stamford	CT	F	203 857-0095	4247
Micro Source Discovery Systems	Gaylordsville	CT	G	860 350-8078	1532
Northstar Biosciences LLC	Guilford	CT	G	203 689-5399	1713
Oncoarendi Therapeutics LLC	Madison	CT	G	609 571-0306	1971
Perosphere Inc	Danbury	CT	F	203 885-1111	966
PF Laboratories Inc **(HQ)**	Stamford	CT	C	973 256-3100	4283
Pfizer Inc	New Haven	CT	G	203 401-0100	2724
Pfizer Inc	Groton	CT	C	860 441-4100	1684
Pgxhealthholding Inc **(PA)**	New Haven	CT	C	203 786-3400	2725
Pharmaceutical RES Assoc Inc **(HQ)**	Stamford	CT	G	203 588-8000	4284
PRA Holdings Inc	Stamford	CT	G	203 853-0123	4290
Protein Sciences Corporation **(HQ)**	Meriden	CT	D	203 686-0800	2119
Purdue Pharma LP	Stamford	CT	G	203 588-8000	4293
Purdue Pharma LP **(PA)**	Stamford	CT	B	203 588-8000	4294
Renetx Bio Inc	New Haven	CT	G	203 444-6642	2731
Rx Analytic Inc	Ridgefield	CT	G	203 733-0837	3681
Sheffield Pharmaceuticals LLC	Norwich	CT	F	860 442-4451	3290
Shire Rgenerative Medicine Inc **(DH)**	Westport	CT	G	877 422-4463	5231
Shore Therapeutics Inc	Stamford	CT	G	646 562-1243	4316
Sinol Usa Inc	Newtown	CT	F	203 470-7404	2937
Systamedic Inc	Groton	CT	G	860 912-6101	1687
Syzygy Halthcare Solutions LLC	Wilton	CT	G	203 226-4449	5307
Tower Laboratories Ltd	Clinton	CT	E	860 669-7078	796
Trevi Therapeutics Inc	New Haven	CT	F	203 304-2499	2748
AA Pharmaceuticals Inc	Woburn	MA	G	617 935-1241	17103
Aastrom Biosciences Inc	Cambridge	MA	G	617 761-8642	9368
Abbott	Westford	MA	F	978 577-3467	16750
Abbvie Inc	Cambridge	MA	G	617 335-7640	9369
Abpro Corporation	Woburn	MA	E	617 225-0808	17105
Acceleron Pharma Inc **(PA)**	Cambridge	MA	C	617 649-9200	9370
Acer Therapeutics Inc **(PA)**	Newton	MA	G	844 902-6100	13553
Acusphere Inc	Cambridge	MA	G	617 577-8800	9372
Acusphere Inc **(PA)**	Lexington	MA	D	617 648-8800	12201
Adolor Corporation	Lexington	MA	D	781 860-8660	12202
Aegerion Pharmaceuticals Inc **(HQ)**	Cambridge	MA	F	877 764-3131	9375
Agentus Therapeutics Inc **(HQ)**	Lexington	MA	G	701 674-4400	12203
Agios Pharmaceuticals Inc **(PA)**	Cambridge	MA	C	617 649-8600	9377
Aileron Therapeutics Inc	Watertown	MA	E	774 444-0704	16265
Akcea Therapeutics Inc **(HQ)**	Boston	MA	D	617 207-0202	8347
Akebia Therapeutics Inc **(PA)**	Cambridge	MA	D	617 871-2098	9379
Albireo Pharma Inc	Boston	MA	G	857 415-4774	8351
Aldeyra Therapeutics Inc **(PA)**	Lexington	MA	G	781 761-4904	12206
Alexion Pharmaceuticals Inc **(PA)**	Boston	MA	C	475 230-2596	8353
Alinea Pharmaceuticals Inc	Cambridge	MA	G	617 500-7867	9381
Alkermes Inc **(HQ)**	Waltham	MA	B	781 609-6000	16029
Alkermes Cntrlled Therapeutics	Waltham	MA	D	877 706-0510	16030
Allena Labs	Sudbury	MA	G	617 467-4577	15652
Allena Pharmaceuticals Inc **(PA)**	Newton	MA	E	617 467-4577	13558
Alnara Pharmaceuticals Inc	Cambridge	MA	F	617 349-3690	9382
Alnylam Pharmaceuticals Inc	Cambridge	MA	F	617 551-8200	9383
Alnylam Pharmaceuticals Inc **(PA)**	Cambridge	MA	C	617 551-8200	9384
Alnylam US Inc	Cambridge	MA	E	617 551-8200	9385
Alopexx Pharmaceuticals LLC	Concord	MA	F	617 945-2510	10108
Alzheon Inc	Framingham	MA	G	508 861-7709	10919
Amag Pharmaceuticals Inc **(PA)**	Waltham	MA	B	617 498-3300	16032
Amplicea Therapeutics Inc	Worcester	MA	G	617 515-6755	17337
Amri Burlington Inc **(DH)**	Burlington	MA	E	781 270-7900	9233
Annovation Biopharma Inc	Wayland	MA	G	617 724-0343	16332
Anterion Therapeutics Inc	Salem	MA	G	617 240-0324	14892
Apellis Pharmaceuticals Inc **(PA)**	Waltham	MA	E	617 977-5700	16034
Appetites	Barnstable	MA	G	508 362-3623	7946
Aprea (us) Inc	Boston	MA	G	857 239-9072	8370
Aprea Therapeutics Inc	Boston	MA	F	617 463-9385	8371
Aratana Therapeutics Inc	Boston	MA	G	617 425-9226	8372
Armstrong Pharmaceuticals Inc **(HQ)**	West Roxbury	MA	D	617 323-7404	16493
Armstrong Pharmaceuticals Inc	Canton	MA	E	617 323-7404	9715
Arqule Inc **(PA)**	Burlington	MA	E	781 994-0300	9234
Avedro Inc **(HQ)**	Waltham	MA	D	781 768-3400	16040
Aveo Pharmaceuticals Inc	Cambridge	MA	F	617 299-5000	9398
Aveo Pharmaceuticals Inc **(PA)**	Cambridge	MA	F	617 588-1960	9399
Aveo Securities Corporation	Cambridge	MA	G	617 588-1960	9400
Aveta Biomics Inc	Bedford	MA	G	339 927-5994	7960
Avrobio Inc **(PA)**	Cambridge	MA	E	617 914-8420	9401
Azurity Pharmaceuticals **(PA)**	Woburn	MA	F	855 379-0382	17125
Barbaras Bakery Inc **(DH)**	Marlborough	MA	E	800 343-0590	12725
Baxalta US Inc	Cambridge	MA	F	312 656-8021	9405

	CITY	ST	EMP	PHONE	ENTRY #
Beigene Usa Inc **(HQ)**	Cambridge	MA	G	781 801-1887	9407
Benu Biopharma Inc	Sudbury	MA	G	508 208-5634	15653
Berg LLC **(PA)**	Framingham	MA	D	617 588-0083	10927
Berkshire Sterile Mfg Inc	Lee	MA	F	413 243-0330	12088
Biogen Inc **(PA)**	Cambridge	MA	B	617 679-2000	9409
Biopharma of Cape Cod Inc	Cotuit	MA	G	508 428-5823	10168
Bioverativ Inc **(DH)**	Waltham	MA	D	781 663-4400	16048
Bluefin Biomedicine Inc	Beverly	MA	E	978 712-8105	8112
Blueprint Medicines Corp **(PA)**	Cambridge	MA	C	617 374-7580	9412
Boston Biopharma LLC	Weston	MA	G	617 780-9300	16823
Boston Oncology LLC	Cambridge	MA	G	857 209-5052	9420
Bristol-Myers Squibb Company	Billerica	MA	E	978 667-9532	8220
Bryan Oncor Inc	Somerville	MA	G	617 957-9858	15162
Cadrus Therapeutics Inc	Worcester	MA	G	508 344-9719	17352
Cardurion Pharmaceuticals Inc	Cambridge	MA	G	617 863-8088	9428
Carrick Pharmaceuticals Inc	Somerville	MA	G	617 623-0525	15165
Casma Therapeutics Inc	Cambridge	MA	F	857 777-4248	9429
Catabasis Pharmaceuticals Inc	Cambridge	MA	E	617 349-1971	9430
Cedilla Therapeutics Inc	Cambridge	MA	F	617 581-9333	9431
Celgene Avilomics Research Inc	Cambridge	MA	F	857 706-1311	9432
Celgene Corporation	Amesbury	MA	G	857 225-2309	7481
Celyad Inc	Boston	MA	G	857 990-6900	8461
Central Admxture Phrm Svcs Inc	Woburn	MA	E	781 376-0032	17142
Centrexion Therapeutics Corp	Boston	MA	F	617 837-6911	8464
Chiasma Inc	Needham	MA	F	617 928-5300	13296
Cielo Therapeutics Inc	Hopkinton	MA	G	617 649-2005	11696
Clementia Pharmaceuticals USA	Auburndale	MA	G	857 226-5588	7858
Clio Designs Incorporated	Needham	MA	F	781 449-9500	13297
Cnh Technologies Inc	Woburn	MA	G	781 933-0362	17145
Coley Pharmaceutical Group Inc	Wellesley	MA	C	781 431-9000	16366
Collagen Medical LLC	Belmont	MA	G	857 928-8817	8070
Collegium Pharmaceutical Inc	Stoughton	MA	C	781 713-3699	15584
Concert Pharmaceuticals Inc **(PA)**	Lexington	MA	D	781 860-0045	12213
Constllion Phrmaceuticals Inc	Cambridge	MA	D	617 714-0555	9441
Continuus Pharmaceutical	Woburn	MA	G	781 281-0099	17152
Corbus Pharmaceuticals Inc	Norwood	MA	G	617 963-1000	14144
Corbus Phrmctcals Holdings Inc **(PA)**	Norwood	MA	E	617 963-0100	14145
Corden Pharma Intl Inc	Braintree	MA	G	781 305-3332	8996
Cordenpharma	Cambridge	MA	G	617 401-2828	9443
Courage Therapeutics Inc	Newton	MA	G	617 216-9921	13583
Cubist Pharmaceuticals LLC	Lexington	MA	D	781 860-8660	12216
Cue Biopharma Inc **(PA)**	Cambridge	MA	E	617 949-2680	9446
Curagen Corporation **(HQ)**	Needham Heights	MA	F	908 200-7500	13325
Curirx Inc	Wilmington	MA	G	978 658-2962	16990
Cutanea Life Sciences Inc	Woburn	MA	E	484 568-0100	17160
Cutispharma Inc	Wilmington	MA	F	800 461-7449	16992
Cyclerion Therapeutics Inc **(PA)**	Cambridge	MA	G	857 327-8778	9447
Cyta Therapeutics Inc	Woburn	MA	G	617 947-1416	17161
Decco	Westborough	MA	G	508 329-1391	16613
Deciphera Pharmaceuticals Inc **(PA)**	Waltham	MA	E	781 209-6400	16082
Dicerna Pharmaceuticals Inc	Lexington	MA	E	617 621-8097	12219
Djd Enterprises LLC	Cambridge	MA	G	617 803-6875	9455
Dusa Pharmaceuticals Inc **(DH)**	Wilmington	MA	D	978 657-7500	16998
Dyax Corp	Lexington	MA	C	617 349-0200	12221
Eip Pharma Inc	Cambridge	MA	G	617 945-9146	9459
Eisai Inc	Cambridge	MA	E	978 837-4616	9460
Elan Pharma	Cambridge	MA	G	415 885-6780	9461
Eli Lilly and Company	Hopkinton	MA	F	508 435-8326	11702
Eli Lilly and Company	Cambridge	MA	G	317 209-6287	9462
EMD Serono Inc	Billerica	MA	G	781 982-9000	8244
EMD Serono Inc	Burlington	MA	G	978 715-1804	9265
EMD Serono Inc **(DH)**	Rockland	MA	A	781 982-9000	14799
EMD Serono Inc	Quincy	MA	G	781 261-7500	14621
EMD Serono Biotech Center Inc	Billerica	MA	D	978 294-1100	8245
EMD Serono Biotech Center Inc **(HQ)**	Rockland	MA	D	800 283-8088	14800
EMD Serono Biotech Center Inc	Quincy	MA	E	978 294-1100	14622
EMD Serono Holding Inc	Rockland	MA	E	781 982-9000	14801
EMD Serono Research Inst Inc **(HQ)**	Rockland	MA	E	781 982-9000	14802
Enanta Pharmaceuticals Inc	Watertown	MA	D	617 607-0800	16282
Enlivity Corporation	Newton	MA	G	617 964-5237	13589
Entasis Thrputics Holdings Inc **(PA)**	Waltham	MA	G	781 810-0120	16099
Epirus Biopharmaceuticals Inc **(PA)**	Foxboro	MA	E	617 600-3497	10882
Epizyme Inc	Cambridge	MA	C	617 229-5872	9469
Epoxy Technology Inc **(PA)**	Billerica	MA	E	978 667-3805	8248
Eusa Pharma (us) LLC	Burlington	MA	F	617 584-8012	9270
Exemplar Laboratories LLC	Fall River	MA	G	508 676-6726	10692
Exemplar Pharma LLC	Fall River	MA	G	508 676-6726	10693
Eyegate Pharmaceuticals Inc **(PA)**	Waltham	MA	F	781 788-9043	16105
FDA Group LLC	North Grafton	MA	F	413 330-7476	13960
Flexion Therapeutics Inc **(PA)**	Burlington	MA	E	781 305-7777	9275
Fog Pharmaceuticals Inc	Cambridge	MA	G	617 945-9510	9480
Fog Pharmaceuticals Inc	Cambridge	MA	G	781 929-9187	9481
For Astellas Institute **(HQ)**	Marlborough	MA	E	508 756-1212	12755
Fortress Biotech Inc	Waltham	MA	F	781 652-4500	16109
Frequency Therapeutics Inc **(PA)**	Woburn	MA	F	866 389-1970	17187
Fresenius Kabi Compounding LLC	Canton	MA	E	224 358-1150	9733
Front Run Organx Inc	Ipswich	MA	G	978 356-7133	11921
Fulcrum Therapeutics Inc	Cambridge	MA	D	617 651-8851	9482
Genocea Biosciences Inc	Cambridge	MA	D	617 876-8191	9488
Gentest Corporation	Woburn	MA	E	781 935-5115	17191
Genzyme Corporation	Framingham	MA	C	508 271-2642	10951
Genzyme Corporation	Framingham	MA	D	617 252-7500	10952
Genzyme Corporation	Framingham	MA	E	508 370-9690	10953
Genzyme Corporation	Allston	MA	D	617 252-7500	7466
Genzyme Corporation	Northborough	MA	D	508 351-2699	14034
Genzyme Corporation	Westborough	MA	C	508 351-2600	16620

Employee Codes: A=Over 500 employees, B=251-500
C=101-250, D=51-100 E=20-50, F=10-19, G=3-9

	CITY	ST	EMP	PHONE	ENTRY #
Genzyme Corporation	Framingham	MA	D	508 872-8400	10954
Genzyme Corporation	Cambridge	MA	C	508 872-8400	9491
Genzyme Corporation	Cambridge	MA	B	617 494-8484	9493
Genzyme Corporation	Westborough	MA	E	508 898-9001	16621
Genzyme Corporation	Framingham	MA	C	508 872-8400	10955
Genzyme Corporation	Framingham	MA	C	508 872-8400	10956
Genzyme Corporation	Framingham	MA	C	508 872-8400	10957
Genzyme Corporation	Framingham	MA	C	508 872-8400	10958
Genzyme Corporation **(DH)**	Cambridge	MA	A	617 252-7500	9489
Genzyme Corporation	Cambridge	MA	D	508 271-2919	9490
Genzyme Corporation	Boston	MA	C	617 779-3100	8559
Genzyme Securities Corporation	Cambridge	MA	G	617 252-7500	9494
Glaxosmithkline LLC	Braintree	MA	E	617 828-9028	9010
Glaxosmithkline LLC	Topsfield	MA	E	978 853-6490	15860
Global Lf Scnces Sltons USA LL	Westborough	MA	G	508 475-2000	16622
Glsynthesis Inc	Worcester	MA	E	508 754-6700	17384
Group Artic Inc	Braintree	MA	E	781 848-2174	9013
Harbour Biomed	Cambridge	MA	F	617 682-3679	9500
Idenix Pharmaceuticals Inc	Cambridge	MA	D	617 876-5883	9511
IL Pharma Inc	Cambridge	MA	G	617 355-6910	9513
Imabiotech Corp	Billerica	MA	G	978 362-1825	8256
Immunogen Inc **(PA)**	Waltham	MA	C	781 895-0600	16130
Immunogen Securities Corp	Waltham	MA	E	617 995-2500	16131
Infinity Pharmaceuticals Inc **(PA)**	Cambridge	MA	D	617 453-1000	9515
Innovation Pharmaceuticals Inc **(PA)**	Beverly	MA	G	978 921-4125	8141
Inozyme Pharma Inc **(PA)**	Boston	MA	F	857 330-4340	8617
Ironwood Pharmaceuticals Inc **(PA)**	Boston	MA	C	617 621-7722	8622
Johnson Matthey Phrm Mtls Inc **(DH)**	Devens	MA	C	978 784-5000	10321
Johnson Matthey Phrm Mtls Inc	North Andover	MA	E	978 784-5000	13713
Juniper Pharmaceuticals Inc **(DH)**	Boston	MA	E	617 639-1500	8644
Kadmon Corporation LLC	Cambridge	MA	G	724 778-6125	9523
Kala Pharmaceuticals Inc	Watertown	MA	E	781 996-5252	16293
Kalvista Pharmaceuticals Inc **(PA)**	Cambridge	MA	F	857 999-0075	9524
Karuna Therapeutics Inc	Boston	MA	F	857 449-2244	8647
Karyopharm Therapeutics Inc **(PA)**	Newton	MA	C	617 658-0600	13606
Keryx Biopharmaceuticals Inc **(HQ)**	Cambridge	MA	D	617 871-2098	9526
Kintai Therapeutics Inc	Cambridge	MA	E	617 409-7395	9527
Kyon Pharma Inc	Boston	MA	G	617 567-2436	8657
Lantheus Holdings Inc **(PA)**	North Billerica	MA	E	978 671-8001	13831
Lantheus Medical Imaging Inc **(HQ)**	North Billerica	MA	B	800 362-2668	13832
Lantheus MI Intermediate Inc	North Billerica	MA	A	978 671-8001	13833
Leap Therapeutics Inc **(PA)**	Cambridge	MA	E	617 714-0360	9533
Lipomed Inc	Cambridge	MA	G	617 577-7222	9537
Lloyd Labs	Wakefield	MA	G	781 224-0083	15957
Lutronic USA	Billerica	MA	G	888 588-7644	8263
Luxuriance Biopharma Inc	Concord	MA	G	617 817-6679	10139
Lyne Laboratories Inc	Brockton	MA	D	508 583-8700	9163
Magenta Therapeutics Inc	Cambridge	MA	D	857 242-0170	9543
Makscientific LLC	Burlington	MA	G	781 365-0958	9300
Matrivax Research & Dev Corp	Boston	MA	G	617 385-7640	8688
MBL International Corporation **(DH)**	Woburn	MA	F	781 939-6964	17225
Merck Group	Bedford	MA	G	781 858-3284	7991
Merck Research Laboratories	Boston	MA	F	617 992-2000	8696
Merck Sharp & Dohme Corp	Lexington	MA	C	781 860-8660	12243
Merck Sharp & Dohme Corp	Boston	MA	G	617 992-2074	8697
Mersana Therapeutics Inc **(PA)**	Cambridge	MA	D	617 498-0020	9552
Metastat Inc **(PA)**	Boston	MA	G	617 531-6500	8700
Microbot Medical Inc **(PA)**	Hingham	MA	G	781 875-3605	11505
Millennium Pharmaceuticals Inc	Cambridge	MA	C	617 679-7000	9556
Millennium Pharmaceuticals Inc	Cambridge	MA	D	617 679-7000	9557
Millennium Pharmaceuticals Inc	Cambridge	MA	C	617 679-7000	9558
Millennium Pharmaceuticals Inc	Cambridge	MA	F	617 679-7000	9559
Millennium Pharmaceuticals Inc	Cambridge	MA	C	617 679-7000	9560
Minerva Neurosciences Inc **(PA)**	Waltham	MA	F	617 600-7373	16151
Moderna Inc **(PA)**	Cambridge	MA	E	617 714-6500	9564
Moderna LLC **(HQ)**	Cambridge	MA	G	617 714-6500	9565
Moderna Therapeutics Inc	Cambridge	MA	E	617 714-6500	9566
Momenta Pharmaceuticals Inc **(PA)**	Cambridge	MA	B	617 491-9700	9569
Nanofuse Biologics LLC	Malden	MA	F	978 232-3990	12584
Navitor Pharmaceuticals Inc	Cambridge	MA	F	857 285-4300	9575
Nemucore Med Innovations Inc	Wellesley	MA	G	617 943-9983	16375
Neovii Biotech Na Inc	Lexington	MA	F	781 966-3830	12247
Neuform Pharmaceuticals	Auburndale	MA	G	617 559-9822	7865
Neuro Phage Phrmaceuticals Inc	Cambridge	MA	F	617 941-7004	9578
Neurobo Pharmaceuticals Inc **(PA)**	Boston	MA	F	617 313-7331	8724
Neurobo Therapeutics Inc	Boston	MA	F	617 313-7331	8725
Neurogastrx Incorporated	Woburn	MA	G	781 730-4006	17240
New England Compounding Phrm	Boston	MA	E	800 994-6322	8730
New England Peptide Inc	Gardner	MA	E	978 630-0020	11121
Nirogyone Therapeutics LLC	Northborough	MA	G	508 439-2197	14041
Nocion Therapeutics Inc	Waltham	MA	G	781 812-6176	16160
Novartis Corporation	Cambridge	MA	G	617 871-3594	9586
Novartis Corporation	Cambridge	MA	G	617 871-8000	9587
Novartis Corporation	Cambridge	MA	D	617 871-8000	9588
Novartis Inst For Biomedical R	Cambridge	MA	E	617 871-7523	9589
Novartis Inst For Biomedical R **(HQ)**	Cambridge	MA	E	617 871-8000	9590
Novartis Vccnes Dgnostics Inc	Cambridge	MA	A	617 871-7000	9591
Novartis Vccnes Dgnostics Inc	Cambridge	MA	D	617 871-7000	9592
Novelion Therapeutics Inc	Cambridge	MA	F	877 764-3131	9593
Noxxon Pharma Inc	Weston	MA	G	617 232-0638	16828
Nuvelution Pharma Inc	Pembroke	MA	G	781 924-1148	14421
Nypro Finpack Clinton	Clinton	MA	F	978 368-6021	10085
Oasis Pharmaceuticals LLC	Lexington	MA	G	781 752-6094	12251
Olaf Pharmaceutical Inc	Worcester	MA	G	508 755-3570	17436
Oncomed Phrm Svcs MA Inc	Waltham	MA	G	781 209-5470	16166
Padlock Therapeutics Inc	Cambridge	MA	G	978 381-9601	9604

	CITY	ST	EMP	PHONE	ENTRY #
Palleon Pharma Inc	Waltham	MA	G	857 285-5904	16170
Paloma Pharmaceuticals Inc	Jamaica Plain	MA	F	617 407-6314	11947
Paratek Pharmaceuticals Inc **(PA)**	Boston	MA	G	617 807-6600	8766
Parexel International LLC	Billerica	MA	F	978 313-3435	8272
Partner Therapeutics Inc **(PA)**	Lexington	MA	G	781 727-4259	12253
Pathfinder Cell Therapy Inc	Cambridge	MA	G	617 245-0289	9607
Pfizer Inc	Westford	MA	G	978 799-8657	16784
Pfizer Inc	Andover	MA	C	978 247-1000	7581
Pharma Compliance Group LLC	Hampden	MA	G	508 377-4561	11323
Pharma Interface Analysis LLC	Groton	MA	G	978 448-6137	11294
Pharma Launcher LLC	Watertown	MA	G	508 812-0850	16307
Pharma Models LLC	Newton	MA	G	617 630-1729	13625
Pharma Models LLC	Marlborough	MA	G	617 306-2281	12806
Pharmaceutical Strtgs Stfng LL	Stoneham	MA	D	781 835-2300	15570
Pharmahealth Specialty/Lon	Fairhaven	MA	F	508 998-8000	10645
Pharmalucence Inc **(HQ)**	Billerica	MA	D	781 275-7120	8273
Phio Pharmaceuticals Corp **(PA)**	Marlborough	MA	F	508 767-3681	12807
Phio Pharmaceuticals Corp	Worcester	MA	G	508 767-3861	17440
Phosphorex Incorporated	Hopkinton	MA	F	508 435-9100	11732
Pioneer Instnl Solutions	Boston	MA	G	617 723-2277	8780
Polycarbon Industries Inc	Devens	MA	G	978 772-2111	10330
Praecis Pharmaceuticals Inc	Waltham	MA	D	781 795-4100	16176
Praktikatalyst Pharma LLC	Pittsfield	MA	G	413 442-1857	14502
Prismic Pharmaceuticals Inc	Holden	MA	G	971 506-6415	11550
Promedior Inc	Lexington	MA	F	781 538-4200	12255
Proteostasis Therapeutics Inc	Boston	MA	D	617 225-0096	8798
Ptc As LLC	Lynnfield	MA	G	339 440-5818	12555
Pulmatrix Operating Co Inc	Lexington	MA	G	781 357-2333	12257
Ra Pharmaceuticals Inc	Cambridge	MA	E	617 401-4060	9624
Radius Health Inc **(PA)**	Waltham	MA	D	617 551-4000	16183
Red Oak Sourcing LLC	Foxborough	MA	D	401 742-0701	10913
Rentschler Biopharma Inc	Milford	MA	G	508 282-5800	13140
Restorbio Inc	Boston	MA	E	857 315-5521	8818
Rhythm Pharmaceuticals Inc	Boston	MA	E	857 264-4280	8820
Riptide Synthetics Inc	Cambridge	MA	G	617 945-8832	9634
Safecor Health LLC	Woburn	MA	D	781 933-8780	17288
Sage Therapeutics Inc **(PA)**	Cambridge	MA	D	617 299-8380	9640
Sanofi Genzyme	Framingham	MA	E	508 871-5871	11001
Santhera Pharmaceuticals usa	Burlington	MA	G	781 552-5145	9333
Santhera Phrmceuticals USA Inc	Charlestown	MA	G	617 886-5161	9843
Sarepta Therapeutics Inc **(PA)**	Cambridge	MA	B	617 274-4000	9644
Scholar Rock Holding Corp **(PA)**	Cambridge	MA	G	857 259-3860	9646
Scpharmaceuticals Inc	Burlington	MA	E	617 517-0730	9335
Sefacor Inc	Somerville	MA	G	617 471-0176	15214
Selecta Biosciences Inc **(PA)**	Watertown	MA	E	617 923-1400	16314
Selvita Inc	Boston	MA	G	857 998-4075	8843
Senopsys LLC	Woburn	MA	G	781 935-7450	17292
Sentien Biotechnologies Inc	Lexington	MA	G	781 361-9031	12265
Serono Inc	Rockland	MA	F	781 681-2137	14824
Serono Laboratories Inc	Rockland	MA	D	781 681-2288	14825
Sfj Pharma	Pembroke	MA	G	781 924-1148	14426
Shire Inc **(HQ)**	Lexington	MA	C	781 482-9222	12267
Shire Humn Gntic Therapies Inc	Waltham	MA	G	781 862-1561	16192
Shire Humn Gntic Therapies Inc	Cambridge	MA	G	617 349-0200	9649
Shire Humn Gntic Therapies Inc **(HQ)**	Lexington	MA	C	617 349-0200	12268
Shire Humn Gntic Therapies Inc	Lexington	MA	G	617 349-0200	12269
Shire Humn Gntic Therapies Inc	North Reading	MA	F	781 482-0883	13989
Shire Inc **(HQ)**	Lexington	MA	E	781 274-1248	12270
Shire Pharmaceuticals LLC	Lexington	MA	G	617 349-0200	12271
Shire Pharmaceuticals LLC	Cambridge	MA	G	617 588-8800	9650
Shire US Inc **(DH)**	Lexington	MA	A	781 482-9222	12272
Shire Viropharma Incorporated **(DH)**	Lexington	MA	E	610 458-7300	12273
Sigilon Therapeutics Inc	Cambridge	MA	E	617 336-7540	9651
Sojournix Inc	Waltham	MA	G	781 864-1111	16198
Spero Therapeutics Inc **(PA)**	Cambridge	MA	E	857 242-1600	9658
Splice Therapeutics Inc	West Roxbury	MA	G	914 804-4136	16503
Spring Bnk Pharmaceuticals Inc **(PA)**	Hopkinton	MA	E	508 473-5993	11738
Sq Innovation Inc	Burlington	MA	G	617 500-0121	9339
St Jude Medical LLC	Wilmington	MA	E	978 657-6519	17047
Stallrgenes Greer Holdings Inc	Cambridge	MA	E	617 588-4900	9660
Summit Therapeutics Inc	Cambridge	MA	G	617 225-4455	9662
Sunovion Pharmaceuticals Inc **(DH)**	Marlborough	MA	A	508 481-6700	12832
Syndax Pharmaceuticals Inc **(PA)**	Waltham	MA	F	781 419-1400	16204
Syndax Securities Corporation	Waltham	MA	G	781 472-2985	16205
Syner-G Pharma Consulting LLC	Southborough	MA	G	508 460-9700	15368
Synertide Pharmaceuticals Inc	Wellesley	MA	G	801 671-1329	16389
Synlogic Inc **(PA)**	Cambridge	MA	E	617 401-9975	9671
Synostics Inc	Weston	MA	G	781 248-5699	16832
Syros Pharmaceuticals Inc **(PA)**	Cambridge	MA	D	617 744-1340	9672
Takeda Building 35 5	Cambridge	MA	G	617 444-4352	9673
Takeda Pharmaceuticals	Cambridge	MA	F	617 441-6930	9674
Takeda Pharmaceuticals USA Inc	Duxbury	MA	G	781 837-1528	10403
Takeda Pharmaceuticals USA Inc **(HQ)**	Lexington	MA	A	617 349-0200	12277
Takeda Pharmaceuticals USA Inc	Cambridge	MA	E	617 444-1348	9675
Taris Biomedical LLC	Lexington	MA	E	781 676-7750	12278
Tarpon Biosystems Inc	Marlborough	MA	G	978 979-4222	12835
Tarveda Therapeutics Inc	Watertown	MA	E	617 923-4100	16320
Tesaro Inc **(HQ)**	Waltham	MA	C	339 970-0900	16210
Tesaro Securities Corporation	Waltham	MA	A	339 970-0900	16211
Tetraphase Pharmaceuticals Inc **(PA)**	Watertown	MA	D	617 715-3600	16321
Teva Pharmaceuticals	Cambridge	MA	G	617 252-6586	9680
Thrombolytic Science LLC	Cambridge	MA	G	617 661-1107	9681
Ultragenyx Pharmaceutical Inc	Cambridge	MA	G	617 949-4010	9685
Unicus Pharmaceuticals LLC	Taunton	MA	E	508 659-7002	15793
UNUM Therapeutics Inc	Cambridge	MA	D	617 945-5576	9687
Vectura Incorporated	Southborough	MA	G	508 573-5700	15370

	CITY	ST	EMP	PHONE	ENTRY #
Verastem Inc **(PA)**	Needham	MA	D	781 292-4200	13316
Vertex Pharmaceuticals Inc	Boston	MA	F	617 201-4171	8908
Vertex Pharmaceuticals Inc **(PA)**	Boston	MA	B	617 341-6100	8909
Viacell Inc **(DH)**	Waltham	MA	E	617 914-3400	16219
Viamet Phrmctcals Holdings LLC	Foxboro	MA	E	919 467-8539	10908
Viropharma Biologics Inc	Lexington	MA	G	610 458-7300	12282
Visionaid Inc	Wareham	MA	E	508 295-3300	16258
Wellfleet Pharmaceuticals Inc	Boston	MA	G	617 767-6264	8920
West St Intrmdate Hldings Corp **(PA)**	Waltham	MA	F	781 434-5051	16223
Wilex Inc	Cambridge	MA	F	617 492-3900	9701
Wyeth Pharmaceuticals LLC	Andover	MA	B	978 475-9214	7619
Xenetic Biosciences Inc	Framingham	MA	G	781 778-7720	11017
Zafgen Inc	Boston	MA	E	617 622-4003	8941
Ziopharm Oncology Inc	Charlestown	MA	G	617 259-1970	9845
Biodesign International Inc	Saco	ME	E	207 283-6500	6843
Biotech Source Inc **(PA)**	Windham	ME	G	207 894-5690	7230
Clearh2o	Portland	ME	F	207 221-0039	6639
Dermalogix Partners Inc	Scarborough	ME	E	207 883-4103	6916
Holland Drug Inc	Farmington	ME	G	207 778-5419	6050
M Drug LLC	Brewer	ME	G	207 973-9444	5798
Maine Biotechnology Svcs Inc	Portland	ME	E	207 797-5454	6683
Pondera Pharmaceuticals Inc	Pownal	ME	G	207 688-4494	6750
Abbott Laboratories	Nashua	NH	A	603 891-3380	19103
Critical Prcess Filtration Inc **(PA)**	Nashua	NH	E	603 595-0140	19140
Icad Inc **(PA)**	Nashua	NH	C	603 882-5200	19181
Lonza Biologics Inc	Portsmouth	NH	F	603 610-4696	19588
Lonza Biologics Inc **(DH)**	Portsmouth	NH	B	603 610-4500	19589
Lyophilization Svcs Neng Inc **(PA)**	Manchester	NH	F	603 626-5763	18866
Max Pharmaceutical LLC	Bedford	NH	G	603 472-2813	17653
Msm Protein Technologies Inc	East Kingston	NH	F	617 504-9548	18088
Novo Nordisk US Bio Prod Inc	West Lebanon	NH	C	603 298-3169	19958
Seachange Therapeutics Inc	Merrimack	NH	G	603 424-6009	19028
Stealth Biologics LLC	Lebanon	NH	G	603 643-5134	18637
Trimaran Pharma Inc	Nashua	NH	G	508 577-7110	19275
Trividia Mfg Solutions **(DH)**	Lancaster	NH	C	603 788-2848	18606
Trividia Mfg Solutions	Lancaster	NH	G	603 788-4952	18607
Uptite Co Inc	Salem	NH	G	603 401-3856	19776
Denison Pharmaceuticals LLC	Lincoln	RI	C	401 723-5500	20567
Glaxosmithkline LLC	North Scituate	RI	F	401 934-2834	20778
Immunex Rhode Island Corp	West Greenwich	RI	E	401 392-1200	21457
Lockett Medical Corporation **(PA)**	Providence	RI	G	401 421-6599	21055
Mymetics Corporation	Providence	RI	G	410 216-5345	21073
Phe Investments LLC	Johnston	RI	D	401 289-2900	20529
Rhodes Pharmaceuticals LP	Coventry	RI	F	401 262-9200	20164
Sea-Band International Inc	Newport	RI	G	401 841-5900	20679
Techtrak LLC	Coventry	RI	G	401 397-3983	20166
Tedor Pharma Inc	Cumberland	RI	E	401 658-5219	20346
PBM Nutritionals LLC **(DH)**	Milton	VT	D	802 527-0521	22135

PHARMACEUTICALS: Mail-Order Svc

	CITY	ST	EMP	PHONE	ENTRY #
Designing Health Inc	East Longmeadow	MA	E	661 257-1705	10472

PHARMACEUTICALS: Medicinal & Botanical Prdts

	CITY	ST	EMP	PHONE	ENTRY #
Candlewood Stars Inc	Danbury	CT	G	203 994-8826	885
Henkel of America Inc **(HQ)**	Rocky Hill	CT	B	860 571-5100	3715
Henkel US Operations Corp **(DH)**	Rocky Hill	CT	B	860 571-5100	3716
Mantrose-Haeuser Co Inc **(HQ)**	Westport	CT	E	203 454-1800	5212
Modern Nutrition & Biotech	Ridgefield	CT	G	203 244-5830	3672
Yale University	New Haven	CT	G	203 432-6320	2761
Albany Molecular Research Inc	Waltham	MA	F	781 672-4530	16027
Cequr Corporation	Marlborough	MA	E	508 486-0010	12737
GE Healthcare Inc **(DH)**	Marlborough	MA	B	800 526-3593	12759
Ionic Pharmaceuticals LLC	Brookline	MA	G	978 509-4980	9204
Moderna LLC **(HQ)**	Cambridge	MA	G	617 714-6500	9565
Naturex-Dbs LLC	Sagamore	MA	G	774 247-0022	14884
Nitto Denko Avecia Inc **(DH)**	Milford	MA	C	508 532-2500	13131
Nova Biomedical Corporation **(PA)**	Waltham	MA	A	781 894-0800	16162
Nova Biomedical Corporation	Billerica	MA	F	781 894-0800	8268
Resilience Therapeutics Inc	Duxbury	MA	G	617 780-2375	10401
U S Fluids Inc	East Longmeadow	MA	G	413 525-0660	10500
W R Grace & Co	Lexington	MA	B	617 876-1400	12283
Yuma Therapeutics Corporaiton	Cambridge	MA	G	617 953-4618	9709
Global Biotechnologies Inc	Scarborough	ME	G	800 755-8420	6920
Mylan Technologies Inc **(DH)**	Saint Albans	VT	C	802 527-7792	22373

PHARMACIES & DRUG STORES

	CITY	ST	EMP	PHONE	ENTRY #
Soleo Health Inc	Canton	MA	G	781 298-3427	9782

PHONOGRAPH RECORDS: Prerecorded

	CITY	ST	EMP	PHONE	ENTRY #
Mosaic Records Inc	Stamford	CT	G	203 327-7111	4252
Dj Wholesale Club Inc	Tyngsboro	MA	G	978 649-2525	15888

PHOTO RECONNAISSANCE SYSTEMS

	CITY	ST	EMP	PHONE	ENTRY #
Greensight Agronomics Inc	Boston	MA	G	617 633-4919	8580

PHOTOCOPY MACHINE REPAIR SVCS

	CITY	ST	EMP	PHONE	ENTRY #
Eastern Copy Fax Inc	Gloucester	MA	G	978 768-3808	11180
Encore Images Inc	Marblehead	MA	F	781 631-4568	12681

PHOTOCOPY MACHINES

	CITY	ST	EMP	PHONE	ENTRY #
Reliance Business Systems Inc	North Haven	CT	G	203 281-4407	3058
Xerox Corporation **(HQ)**	Norwalk	CT	B	203 968-3000	3274
Eastern Copy Fax Inc	Gloucester	MA	G	978 768-3808	11180
Swaffield Enterprises Inc	Wolfeboro	NH	G	603 569-3017	20025

PHOTOCOPY SPLYS WHOLESALERS

	CITY	ST	EMP	PHONE	ENTRY #
First Step Print Shop LLC	Underhill	VT	G	802 899-2708	22547

PHOTOCOPYING & DUPLICATING SVCS

	CITY	ST	EMP	PHONE	ENTRY #
Alliance Graphics Inc	Newington	CT	F	860 666-7992	2840
Audubon Copy Shppe of Firfield	Bridgeport	CT	G	203 259-4311	378
Brescias Printing Services Inc	East Hartford	CT	G	860 528-4254	1177
Custom Printing & Copy Inc **(PA)**	Enfield	CT	F	860 290-6890	1354
Derosa Printing Company Inc	Manchester	CT	F	860 646-1698	2000
East Longmeadow Business Svcs	Enfield	CT	G	413 525-6111	1355
Economy Printing & Copy Center **(PA)**	Danbury	CT	G	203 792-5610	906
Economy Printing & Copy Center	Ridgefield	CT	G	203 438-7401	3666
G & R Enterprises Incorporated	Hartford	CT	G	860 549-6120	1822
Jerrys Printing & Graphics LLC	Bridgeport	CT	G	203 384-0015	435
Oddo Print Shop Inc	Torrington	CT	G	860 489-6585	4590
Sazacks Inc	Manchester	CT	G	860 647-8367	2045
Aleksandr S Yaskovich	Taunton	MA	G	508 822-7267	15722
Apex Press Inc	Westborough	MA	F	508 366-1110	16589
BBCg LLC	Norwood	MA	G	617 796-8800	14137
Boston Business Printing Inc	Boston	MA	F	617 482-7955	8427
Budget Printing Concord LLC	Concord	MA	G	978 369-4630	10118
Canalside Printing	Monument Beach	MA	G	508 759-4141	13214
CJ Corrado & Sons Inc	Sharon	MA	G	508 655-8434	15048
Color Images Inc	Methuen	MA	G	978 688-4994	13015
Coprico Inc	Chelsea	MA	G	617 889-0520	9951
Courier Printing Inc	Pittsfield	MA	G	413 442-3242	14465
Fasprint Inc **(PA)**	Brockton	MA	F	508 588-9961	9146
Fedex Office & Print Svcs Inc	Chelmsford	MA	G	978 275-0574	9898
Hercules Press	Boston	MA	G	617 323-1950	8596
John Karl Dietrich & Assoc	Cambridge	MA	F	617 868-4140	9521
Kreate & Print Inc	Norwood	MA	G	781 255-0505	14172
Marcus Company Inc	Holyoke	MA	E	413 534-3303	11637
Milk Street Press Inc	Boston	MA	F	617 742-7900	8706
North Shore Printing Inc	North Reading	MA	G	978 664-2609	13988
Northeast Document Conservatio	Andover	MA	E	978 470-1010	7577
Northern Graphics Inc	Middleton	MA	F	978 646-9925	13097
Paper Plus Inc	West Springfield	MA	G	413 785-1363	16540
Postal Instant Press **(PA)**	East Longmeadow	MA	G	413 525-4044	10487
Puffer International Inc	Westfield	MA	G	413 527-1069	16720
R & H Communications Inc **(PA)**	Waltham	MA	F	781 893-6221	16181
R E K Management Inc	West Harwich	MA	G	508 775-3005	16481
Rgp Corp	Milford	MA	G	508 478-8511	13141
S A N Inc **(PA)**	Lawrence	MA	G	978 686-3875	12073
Shafiis Inc **(PA)**	East Longmeadow	MA	E	413 224-2100	10492
Smudge Ink Incorporated	Charlestown	MA	G	617 242-8228	9844
Somerville Quick Print Inc	Cambridge	MA	G	617 492-5343	9656
Task Printing Inc	Newton	MA	G	617 332-4414	13643
Tri Star Printing & Graphics	Somerville	MA	G	617 666-4480	15225
We Print Today LLC	Kingston	MA	F	781 585-6021	11966
Western Mass Copying Prtg Inc	West Springfield	MA	G	413 734-2679	16565
Curry Printing & Copy Center	Portland	ME	F	207 772-5897	6645
First Choice Printing Inc	Lisbon Falls	ME	G	207 353-8006	6369
Gossamer Press	Old Town	ME	G	207 827-9881	6539
Northeast Publishing Company	Dover Foxcroft	ME	G	207 564-8355	5961
Quick Print Color Center	Saco	ME	G	207 282-6480	6856
Alpha Graph Printshop	Nashua	NH	F	603 595-1444	19111
Baker Graphics Inc	Manchester	NH	G	603 625-5427	18784
Blacksmith Prtg & Copy Ctr LLC	Wolfeboro	NH	G	603 569-6300	20015
Boles Enterprises Inc	Manchester	NH	G	603 622-4282	18789
Doolittles Print Serve Inc	Claremont	NH	G	603 543-0700	17848
Fedex Office & Print Svcs Inc	West Lebanon	NH	G	603 298-5891	19951
Hurley Ink LLC	Manchester	NH	G	603 645-0002	18840
P2k Printing LLC	North Conway	NH	G	603 356-2010	19378
Papergraphics Print & Copy	Merrimack	NH	F	603 880-1835	19019
Print Factory Inc	Nashua	NH	G	603 880-4519	19239
Ram Printing Incorporated **(PA)**	East Hampstead	NH	E	603 382-7045	18082
Southport Management Group LLC	Portsmouth	NH	G	603 433-4664	19621
Adams Printing Inc	Pawtucket	RI	G	401 722-9222	20807
Allegra Print & Imaging	East Greenwich	RI	G	401 884-9280	20352
Copy Print Company	Cranston	RI	G	401 228-3900	20201
Omo Inc	Providence	RI	G	401 421-5160	21084
Sir Speedy	Providence	RI	G	401 232-2000	21122
ASC Duplicating Inc	Montpelier	VT	G	802 229-0660	22145
Digital Press Printers LLC	Williston	VT	F	802 863-5579	22662
First Step Print Shop LLC	Underhill	VT	G	802 899-2708	22547
S M T Graphics LLC	Shoreham	VT	G	802 897-5231	22433
Zinn Graphics Inc	Brattleboro	VT	G	802 254-6742	21756

PHOTOENGRAVING SVC

	CITY	ST	EMP	PHONE	ENTRY #
Concord Photo Engraving Co	Concord	NH	F	603 225-3681	17896

PHOTOGRAPHIC EQPT & CAMERAS, WHOLESALE

	CITY	ST	EMP	PHONE	ENTRY #
IDS Imaging Dev Systems Inc	Stoneham	MA	F	781 787-0048	15565

PHOTOGRAPHIC EQPT & SPLY: Sound Recordg/Reprod Eqpt, Motion

	CITY	ST	EMP	PHONE	ENTRY #
Fujifilm North America Corp	Bedford	MA	C	781 271-4400	7978

PHOTOGRAPHIC EQPT & SPLYS

	CITY	ST	EMP	PHONE	ENTRY #
Bidwell Industrial Group Inc **(PA)**	Middletown	CT	E	860 346-9283	2178
Kenyon Laboratories LLC	Higganum	CT	G	860 345-2097	1903
Avid Technology Inc	Burlington	MA	C	978 640-3063	9236
Flir Systems Inc	North Billerica	MA	C	978 901-8000	13814
Katz Eye Optics	Greenfield	MA	G	413 743-2523	11266
Precision Dynamics Corporation	Burlington	MA	D	888 202-3684	9321
Precision Dynamics Corporation	Billerica	MA	D	800 528-8005	8276
Visual Departures Ltd	Ashley Falls	MA	G	413 229-2272	7675
Fastvision LLC	Nashua	NH	F	603 891-4317	19154
Flir Commercial Systems Inc	Nashua	NH	C	603 324-7824	19159

Employee Codes: A=Over 500 employees, B=251-500
C=101-250, D=51-100 E=20-50, F=10-19, G=3-9

	CITY	ST	EMP	PHONE	ENTRY #
Fuser Technologies Corp	Nashua	NH	G	603 886-5186	19164

PHOTOGRAPHIC EQPT & SPLYS, WHOLESALE: Identity Recorders

	CITY	ST	EMP	PHONE	ENTRY #
Bidirectional Display Inc	Acton	MA	G	617 599-8282	7344

PHOTOGRAPHIC EQPT & SPLYS, WHOLESALE: Motion Picture Camera

	CITY	ST	EMP	PHONE	ENTRY #
Abariscan Inc	Newburyport	MA	G	978 462-0284	13467

PHOTOGRAPHIC EQPT & SPLYS, WHOLESALE: Printing Apparatus

	CITY	ST	EMP	PHONE	ENTRY #
Garrett Printing & Graphics	Bristol	CT	G	860 589-6710	567

PHOTOGRAPHIC EQPT & SPLYS: Cameras, Still & Motion Pictures

	CITY	ST	EMP	PHONE	ENTRY #
Adaptive Optics Associates Inc **(DH)**	Devens	MA	D	978 757-9600	10317
Deep Sea Systems Intl Inc	Cataumet	MA	G	508 540-6732	9812
Valentine Tool & Stamping Inc	Norton	MA	F	508 285-6911	14091

PHOTOGRAPHIC EQPT & SPLYS: Developers, Not Chemical Plants

	CITY	ST	EMP	PHONE	ENTRY #
27th Exposure LLC	Littleton	NH	G	603 444-5800	18653

PHOTOGRAPHIC EQPT & SPLYS: Editing Eqpt, Motion Picture

	CITY	ST	EMP	PHONE	ENTRY #
1 Beyond Inc	Boston	MA	F	617 591-2200	8326
Avid Technology Inc **(PA)**	Burlington	MA	A	978 640-6789	9235
R & B Splicer Systems Inc	Avon	MA	G	508 580-3500	7893

PHOTOGRAPHIC EQPT & SPLYS: Film, Sensitized

	CITY	ST	EMP	PHONE	ENTRY #
AGFA Corporation	Wilmington	MA	B	978 658-5600	16969
Georgia-Pacific LLC	Leominster	MA	C	978 537-4701	12144
Dewal Industries LLC	Narragansett	RI	C	401 789-9736	20637

PHOTOGRAPHIC EQPT & SPLYS: Fixers, Not From Chemical Plnts

	CITY	ST	EMP	PHONE	ENTRY #
Evad Images	Lincoln	ME	G	207 794-2930	6352

PHOTOGRAPHIC EQPT & SPLYS: Graphic Arts Plates, Sensitized

	CITY	ST	EMP	PHONE	ENTRY #
Verico Technology LLC **(HQ)**	Enfield	CT	E	800 492-7286	1389
Progress Enterprises LLC	Westfield	MA	F	413 562-2736	16717
Verico Technology LLC	Nashua	NH	C	603 402-7573	19281

PHOTOGRAPHIC EQPT & SPLYS: Printing Eqpt

	CITY	ST	EMP	PHONE	ENTRY #
Grant John	Sheldon	VT	G	802 933-4808	22428

PHOTOGRAPHIC EQPT & SPLYS: Printing Frames

	CITY	ST	EMP	PHONE	ENTRY #
Hutchison Company Inc	North Kingstown	RI	F	401 294-3503	20717

PHOTOGRAPHIC EQPT & SPLYS: Processing Eqpt

	CITY	ST	EMP	PHONE	ENTRY #
Source Two Inc	Bondsville	MA	G	413 289-1251	8325

PHOTOGRAPHIC EQPT & SPLYS: Shutters, Camera

	CITY	ST	EMP	PHONE	ENTRY #
3derm Systems Inc	Boston	MA	G	617 237-6041	8328
Clarke Industrial Engineering **(PA)**	North Kingstown	RI	G	401 667-7880	20696

PHOTOGRAPHIC EQPT & SPLYS: Toners, Prprd, Not Chem Plnts

	CITY	ST	EMP	PHONE	ENTRY #
Laser Lightning LLC **(PA)**	East Douglas	MA	G	508 476-0138	10428

PHOTOGRAPHIC PEOCESSING CHEMICALS

	CITY	ST	EMP	PHONE	ENTRY #
Process Solutions Inc	East Longmeadow	MA	G	413 525-5870	10489
Solutek Corporation	Boston	MA	E	617 445-5335	8853
Sprint Systems of Photography	Woonsocket	RI	G	401 597-5790	21580

PHOTOGRAPHIC SENSITIZED GOODS, NEC

	CITY	ST	EMP	PHONE	ENTRY #
Advance Reproductions Corp	North Andover	MA	D	978 685-2911	13686

PHOTOGRAPHIC SVCS

	CITY	ST	EMP	PHONE	ENTRY #
Creative Digital Inc	Cranston	RI	G	401 942-0771	20204
New England Image & Print Inc	North Smithfield	RI	G	401 769-3708	20793

PHOTOGRAPHY SVCS: Commercial

	CITY	ST	EMP	PHONE	ENTRY #
Natures View Inc	Waterbury	CT	G	800 506-5307	4923
Deep Sea Systems Intl Inc	Cataumet	MA	G	508 540-6732	9812

PHOTOGRAPHY SVCS: Still Or Video

	CITY	ST	EMP	PHONE	ENTRY #
Noah Publications	Brooklin	ME	G	207 359-2131	5821

PHOTOGRAPHY: Aerial

	CITY	ST	EMP	PHONE	ENTRY #
Ebeam Film LLC	Shelton	CT	F	203 926-0100	3798

PHOTOTYPESETTING SVC

	CITY	ST	EMP	PHONE	ENTRY #
D B S Industries Inc	Haverhill	MA	D	978 373-4748	11421

PHOTOVOLTAIC Solid State

	CITY	ST	EMP	PHONE	ENTRY #
Opel Connecticut Solar LLC	Shelton	CT	E	203 612-2366	3847
Gt Advanced Technologies Inc	Salem	MA	G	978 498-4294	14916
Solect Energy Development LLC	Hopkinton	MA	G	508 250-8358	11736
Solect Energy Development LLC	Hopkinton	MA	F	508 598-3511	11737
Gt Advanced Technologies Inc **(PA)**	Hudson	NH	C	603 883-5200	18394
Gtat Corporation	Nashua	NH	G	603 883-5200	19173
Gtat Corporation **(HQ)**	Hudson	NH	C	603 883-5200	18396

PHYSICIANS' OFFICES & CLINICS: Medical doctors

	CITY	ST	EMP	PHONE	ENTRY #
Ranfac Corp	Avon	MA	D	508 588-4400	7894
Umass Mem Mri Imaging Ctr LLC	Worcester	MA	E	508 756-7300	17492
Uptodate Inc **(DH)**	Waltham	MA	D	781 392-2000	16218
Corflex Inc **(PA)**	Manchester	NH	E	603 623-3344	18806
Jahrling Ocular Prosthetics	Cranston	RI	G	401 454-4168	20243

PICTURE FRAMES: Metal

	CITY	ST	EMP	PHONE	ENTRY #
M & B Enterprise LLC	Derby	CT	F	203 298-9781	1075
Benjamin Martin Corp	Dedham	MA	F	781 326-8311	10281
Malden Intl Designs Inc	Middleboro	MA	D	508 946-2270	13067
Capco Steel Erection Company	Providence	RI	F	401 383-9388	20979
Fulford Manufacturing Company **(PA)**	Riverside	RI	F	401 431-2000	21168

PICTURE FRAMES: Wood

	CITY	ST	EMP	PHONE	ENTRY #
Alpine Management Group LLC	Westport	CT	G	954 531-1692	5180
Kensington Glass and Frmng Co	Berlin	CT	G	860 828-9428	91
Rockwell Art & Framing LLC **(PA)**	Wilton	CT	G	203 762-8311	5302
Frame Center of Norwood Inc **(PA)**	Hyannis	MA	G	781 762-2535	11841
Malden Intl Designs Inc	Middleboro	MA	D	508 946-2270	13067
Wood & Wood Inc	Greenfield	MA	E	413 772-0889	11284
Picture Frame Inc	Topsham	ME	G	207 729-7765	7093
Inkberry	Marlborough	NH	G	603 876-4880	18960
Junction Frame Shop Inc	White River Junction	VT	G	802 296-2121	22641
Zephyr Designs Ltd	Brattleboro	VT	G	802 254-2788	21755

PICTURE FRAMING SVCS, CUSTOM

	CITY	ST	EMP	PHONE	ENTRY #
Exit Five Gallery	West Barnstable	MA	G	508 375-1011	16407
Picture Frame Inc	Topsham	ME	G	207 729-7765	7093

PICTURE PROJECTION EQPT

	CITY	ST	EMP	PHONE	ENTRY #
Kinoton America Distribution	Boston	MA	G	617 562-0003	8650

PIECE GOODS & NOTIONS WHOLESALERS

	CITY	ST	EMP	PHONE	ENTRY #
Knoll Inc	Boston	MA	E	617 695-0220	8653

PIECE GOODS, NOTIONS & DRY GOODS, WHOL: Fabrics Broadwoven

	CITY	ST	EMP	PHONE	ENTRY #
Fiber Materials Inc **(HQ)**	Biddeford	ME	E	207 282-5911	5733
P & B Fabrics Inc	Pawtucket	RI	F	800 351-9087	20872

PIECE GOODS, NOTIONS & DRY GOODS, WHOLESALE: Fabrics

	CITY	ST	EMP	PHONE	ENTRY #
Bosal Foam and Fiber **(PA)**	Limerick	ME	E	207 793-2245	6332

PIECE GOODS, NOTIONS & DRY GOODS, WHOLESALE: Tape, Textile

	CITY	ST	EMP	PHONE	ENTRY #
Precision Coating Co Inc **(HQ)**	Hudson	MA	D	781 329-1420	11805

PIECE GOODS, NOTIONS & OTHER DRY GOODS, WHOL: Flags/Banners

	CITY	ST	EMP	PHONE	ENTRY #
Accent Banner LLC	Medford	MA	F	781 391-7300	12920

PIECE GOODS, NOTIONS & OTHER DRY GOODS, WHOLESALE: Cotton

	CITY	ST	EMP	PHONE	ENTRY #
Oshea Mary Lynn Weaving Studio	Middlebury	VT	G	802 545-2090	22117

PIECE GOODS, NOTIONS & OTHER DRY GOODS, WHOLESALE: Fabrics

	CITY	ST	EMP	PHONE	ENTRY #
Kravet Inc	Boston	MA	G	617 428-0370	8655
New England Fleece Company	Fall River	MA	G	508 678-5550	10738

PIECE GOODS, NOTIONS/DRY GOODS, WHOL: Fabrics, Synthetic

	CITY	ST	EMP	PHONE	ENTRY #
Thomas W Raftery Inc	Hartford	CT	E	860 278-9870	1879
Custom Banner & Graphics LLC	Rochester	NH	G	603 332-2067	19666

PIECE GOODS, NOTIONS/DRY GOODS, WHOL: Linen Piece, Woven

	CITY	ST	EMP	PHONE	ENTRY #
Patricia Spratt For Home LLC	Old Lyme	CT	F	860 434-9291	3326

PIER FOOTINGS: Prefabricated, Concrete

	CITY	ST	EMP	PHONE	ENTRY #
E-Z Crete LLC	Keene	NH	G	603 313-6462	18500

PIGMENTS, INORGANIC: Chrome Green, Chrome Yellow, Zinc Yellw

	CITY	ST	EMP	PHONE	ENTRY #
Atlantic Hardchrome Ltd	Wilton	ME	E	207 645-4300	7224

PIGMENTS, INORGANIC: Metallic & Mineral, NEC

	CITY	ST	EMP	PHONE	ENTRY #
O A Both Corporation	Ashland	MA	G	508 881-4100	7666

PILLOW FILLING MTRLS: Curled Hair, Cotton Waste, Moss

	CITY	ST	EMP	PHONE	ENTRY #
Maine Balsam Fir Prodcts	West Paris	ME	F	207 674-5090	7176

PINS

	CITY	ST	EMP	PHONE	ENTRY #
Spirol International Corp **(HQ)**	Danielson	CT	C	860 774-8571	1018
Spirol Intl Holdg Corp **(PA)**	Danielson	CT	C	860 774-8571	1019
Chen Hsi Pin	Randolph	MA	G	781 986-7900	14674
Pin Stop	Raynham	MA	G	508 824-1886	14725
Q Pin2s Billiards	West Springfield	MA	G	413 285-7971	16550
Neat As A Pin	Bedford	NH	G	603 627-3504	17628
On Pins & Needles	Manchester	NH	G	603 625-6573	18895
Bobby Pins	Cranston	RI	G	401 461-3400	20191
Vermont Rolling Pins	South Burlington	VT	G	802 658-3733	22477

PINS: Cotter

	CITY	ST	EMP	PHONE	ENTRY #
Standard Lock Washer & Mfg Co	Worcester	MA	E	508 757-4508	17481

PINS: Dowel

	CITY	ST	EMP	PHONE	ENTRY #
Horberg Industries Inc	Bridgeport	CT	F	203 334-9444	428
Rbc Prcision Pdts - Bremen Inc **(DH)**	Oxford	CT	E	203 267-7001	3422

PIPE & FITTING: Fabrication

	CITY	ST	EMP	PHONE	ENTRY #
Carli Farm & Equipment LLC	Salem	CT	G	860 908-3227	3737
Clear Water Manufacturing Corp **(PA)**	Wethersfield	CT	G	860 372-4907	5245
Diba Industries Inc **(HQ)**	Danbury	CT	C	203 744-0773	901
Farmington Mtal Fbrication LLC	Bristol	CT	G	860 404-7415	561
Long Island Pipe Supply Inc	Windsor	CT	G	860 688-1780	5345
Fiberspar Linepipe LLC	New Bedford	MA	G	281 854-2636	13385
Paterson Group Inc	Woburn	MA	C	781 935-7036	17258
Virginia Stainless	Taunton	MA	G	508 880-5498	15797
Worcester Manufacturing Inc	Worcester	MA	E	508 756-0301	17505

Company	CITY	ST	EMP	PHONE	ENTRY #
Wardwell Piping Inc	Windham	ME	F	207 892-0034	7259
Anvil International LLC **(HQ)**	Exeter	NH	E	603 418-2800	18110
Long Island Pipe Supply NH Inc	Salem	NH	F	603 685-3200	19748
Micro Weld Fabtec Corp	Windham	NH	G	603 234-6531	20009
Trellborg Pipe Sals Mlford Inc **(DH)**	Milford	NH	C	800 626-2180	19080
Anvil International LLC	North Kingstown	RI	C	401 886-3000	20691
ATW Companies Inc **(PA)**	Warwick	RI	D	401 244-1002	21330
Osram Sylvania Inc	Central Falls	RI	B	401 723-1378	20122
Tubodyne Company	Riverside	RI	G	401 438-2540	21177
L & B Associates Inc	Saint Albans	VT	G	802 868-5210	22371
Raymond Gadues Inc	Swanton	VT	E	802 868-2033	22536

PIPE & FITTINGS: Cast Iron

Company	CITY	ST	EMP	PHONE	ENTRY #
Bingham & Taylor Corp **(HQ)**	Rocky Hill	CT	G	540 825-8334	3703
Virginia Industries Inc **(PA)**	Rocky Hill	CT	G	860 571-3600	3733

PIPE & TUBES: Copper & Copper Alloy

Company	CITY	ST	EMP	PHONE	ENTRY #
Thermatron Engineering Inc	Methuen	MA	E	978 687-8844	13046

PIPE & TUBES: Seamless

Company	CITY	ST	EMP	PHONE	ENTRY #
Accellent Holdings Corp	Wilmington	MA	A	978 570-6900	16962

PIPE CLEANERS

Company	CITY	ST	EMP	PHONE	ENTRY #
Hydro-Flex Inc	Stratford	CT	G	203 269-5599	4421
UST LLC **(HQ)**	Stamford	CT	G	203 817-3000	4355

PIPE FITTINGS: Plastic

Company	CITY	ST	EMP	PHONE	ENTRY #
F F Screw Products Inc	Southington	CT	E	860 621-4567	4049
Monarch Plastic LLC	Granby	CT	F	860 653-2000	1590
Asahi/America Inc **(HQ)**	Lawrence	MA	C	781 321-5409	11995
Orion Enterprises Inc **(HQ)**	North Andover	MA	C	913 342-1653	13722

PIPE JOINT COMPOUNDS

Company	CITY	ST	EMP	PHONE	ENTRY #
A W Chesterton Company **(PA)**	Groveland	MA	E	781 438-7000	11298
Rectorseal Corporation	Fall River	MA	G	508 673-7561	10755
Piping Specialties Inc	Portland	ME	F	207 878-3955	6708
Dichtomatik Americas LP	Manchester	NH	G	603 628-7030	18809

PIPE SECTIONS, FABRICATED FROM PURCHASED PIPE

Company	CITY	ST	EMP	PHONE	ENTRY #
Lawrence Metal Forming Corp	Peabody	MA	F	978 535-1200	14351
Triangle Engineering Inc	Hanover	MA	F	781 878-1500	11356

PIPE, CAST IRON: Wholesalers

Company	CITY	ST	EMP	PHONE	ENTRY #
Water Works Supply Corp	Chester	NH	G	781 322-1238	17827

PIPE: Brass & Bronze

Company	CITY	ST	EMP	PHONE	ENTRY #
McIntire Brass Works Inc	Somerville	MA	G	617 547-1819	15197

PIPE: Concrete

Company	CITY	ST	EMP	PHONE	ENTRY #
Advanced Drainage Systems Inc	Rocky Hill	CT	E	860 529-8188	3701
Scituate Concrete Pipe Corp	Scituate	MA	E	781 545-0564	15013

PIPE: Plastic

Company	CITY	ST	EMP	PHONE	ENTRY #
Advanced Drainage Systems Inc	Rocky Hill	CT	E	860 529-8188	3701
Monarch Plastic LLC	Granby	CT	F	860 653-2000	1590
Virginia Industries Inc **(PA)**	Rocky Hill	CT	G	860 571-3600	3733
Advanced Drainage Systems Inc	Ludlow	MA	E	413 589-0515	12452
Applied Nnstrctred Sltions LLC	Billerica	MA	E	978 670-6959	8211
Asahi/America Inc **(HQ)**	Lawrence	MA	C	781 321-5409	11995
Asahi/America Inc	Lawrence	MA	G	800 343-3618	11996
Brand Dielectrics Inc	Taunton	MA	G	508 828-1200	15734
Cabot Corporation **(PA)**	Boston	MA	C	617 345-0100	8452
Cabot Corporation	Haverhill	MA	C	978 556-8400	11413
Fiberspar Spoolable Products **(PA)**	West Wareham	MA	E	508 291-9000	16572
Orion Enterprises Inc **(HQ)**	North Andover	MA	C	913 342-1653	13722
Orion Fittings Inc	North Andover	MA	G	978 689-6150	13723
Contech Engnered Solutions LLC	Scarborough	ME	E	207 885-9830	6915
Hancor Inc	Springfield	VT	E	802 886-8403	22501

PIPE: Seamless Steel

Company	CITY	ST	EMP	PHONE	ENTRY #
Wyman-Gordon Company **(DH)**	North Grafton	MA	B	508 839-8252	13969

PIPE: Sheet Metal

Company	CITY	ST	EMP	PHONE	ENTRY #
Ovl Manufacturing Inc LLC	Berlin	CT	G	860 829-0271	100
Yogapipe Inc	Rockland	MA	G	844 964-2747	14833
Thompson & Anderson Inc	Westbrook	ME	G	207 854-2905	7210

PIPELINE TERMINAL FACILITIES: Independent

Company	CITY	ST	EMP	PHONE	ENTRY #
Ethosenergy Tc Inc **(DH)**	Chicopee	MA	C	802 257-2721	10025

PIPELINES: Refined Petroleum

Company	CITY	ST	EMP	PHONE	ENTRY #
Exxonmobil Oil Corporation	Randolph	MA	G	781 963-7252	14679

PIPES & TOPS: Chimney, Clay

Company	CITY	ST	EMP	PHONE	ENTRY #
Z-Flex (us) Inc	Bedford	NH	E	603 669-5136	17668

PIPES & TUBES

Company	CITY	ST	EMP	PHONE	ENTRY #
Ldc Inc	East Providence	RI	F	401 861-4667	20429

PIPES & TUBES: Steel

Company	CITY	ST	EMP	PHONE	ENTRY #
Gordon Corporation	Southington	CT	D	860 628-4775	4055
3M Company	Chelmsford	MA	C	978 256-3911	9865
A1a Steel LLC	East Falmouth	MA	G	774 763-2503	10432
New Can Holdings Inc **(PA)**	Holbrook	MA	G	781 767-1650	11534
Thermatron Engineering Inc	Methuen	MA	E	978 687-8844	13046
Contech Engnered Solutions LLC	Scarborough	ME	E	207 885-9830	6915
Anvil International LLC **(HQ)**	Exeter	NH	E	603 418-2800	18110
Maxson Automatic Machinery Co **(PA)**	Westerly	RI	E	401 596-0162	21530
National Chimney Supply	South Burlington	VT	D	802 861-2217	22454

PIPES & TUBES: Welded

Company	CITY	ST	EMP	PHONE	ENTRY #
Unique Mechanical Services Inc	Bow	NH	G	603 856-0057	17735

PISTONS & PISTON RINGS

Company	CITY	ST	EMP	PHONE	ENTRY #
Schwing Bioset Technologies	Danbury	CT	E	203 744-2100	987

PLACEMATS: Plastic Or Textile

Company	CITY	ST	EMP	PHONE	ENTRY #
Stevens Linen Associates Inc	Dudley	MA	D	508 943-0813	10387

PLANING MILL, NEC

Company	CITY	ST	EMP	PHONE	ENTRY #
R & R Lumber Company Inc	Carmel	ME	G	207 848-3726	5893

PLANING MILLS: Millwork

Company	CITY	ST	EMP	PHONE	ENTRY #
Triple Crown Cbnets Mllwk Corp	Sandwich	MA	G	508 833-6500	14974
Index Packaging Inc	Milton	NH	C	603 350-0018	19086

PLANT HORMONES

Company	CITY	ST	EMP	PHONE	ENTRY #
Andrews Arboriculture LLC	Naugatuck	CT	G	203 565-8570	2460
Snug	Portland	ME	G	207 772-6839	6730

PLANTS: Artificial & Preserved

Company	CITY	ST	EMP	PHONE	ENTRY #
East Coast Silks Inc	Chelmsford	MA	G	978 970-5510	9895

PLAQUES: Clay, Plaster/Papier-Mache, Factory Production

Company	CITY	ST	EMP	PHONE	ENTRY #
George Guertin Trophy Inc	Auburn	MA	G	508 832-4001	7836
Nixon Company Inc	Indian Orchard	MA	E	413 543-3701	11890

PLAQUES: Picture, Laminated

Company	CITY	ST	EMP	PHONE	ENTRY #
Gutkin Enterprises LLC	Hamden	CT	G	203 777-5510	1752
George Guertin Trophy Inc	Auburn	MA	G	508 832-4001	7836
Hartnett Co Inc	Woburn	MA	F	781 935-2600	17196
Nixon Company Inc	Indian Orchard	MA	E	413 543-3701	11890
Michael Healy Designs Inc	Manville	RI	G	401 597-5900	20610

PLASMAS

Company	CITY	ST	EMP	PHONE	ENTRY #
Plasma Coatings Inc	Waterbury	CT	G	203 598-3100	4939
Plasma Technology Incorporated	South Windsor	CT	E	860 282-0659	4001
Plasma Giken Limited Company	Webster	MA	G	508 640-7708	16349

PLASTER, ACOUSTICAL: Gypsum

Company	CITY	ST	EMP	PHONE	ENTRY #
Proudfoot Company Inc	Monroe	CT	F	203 459-0031	2416

PLASTIC COLORING & FINISHING

Company	CITY	ST	EMP	PHONE	ENTRY #
Coating Design Group Inc	Stratford	CT	E	203 878-3663	4405

PLASTIC PRDTS

Company	CITY	ST	EMP	PHONE	ENTRY #
Selectives LLC	Thomaston	CT	G	860 585-1956	4514
Benoit & Company	Palmer	MA	G	413 283-8348	14280
Berry Plastics Corporation	Easthampton	MA	G	413 527-1250	10557
Elkay Plastics	Woburn	MA	G	781 932-9800	17176
Hutchison Co Advg Display	Whitinsville	MA	G	508 234-4681	16913
Matallurgical Perspectives	Wilbraham	MA	G	413 596-4283	16940
Radius Pipesystems Corp	Boston	MA	G	857 263-7161	8808
Strong Electric	Tewksbury	MA	G	855 709-0701	15840
Web Converting Inc	Framingham	MA	G	508 879-4442	11014
Panolam Surface Systems	Auburn	ME	G	203 925-1556	5587
Century Robotics LLC	Bedford	NH	G	603 540-2576	17635
Global Laminates	Portsmouth	NH	G	603 373-8081	19567
Separett-Usa	Barrington	NH	G	603 682-0963	17623
Teknor Apex Co	Saint Albans	VT	F	802 524-7704	22381

PLASTIC PRDTS REPAIR SVCS

Company	CITY	ST	EMP	PHONE	ENTRY #
Plastics Supply of Maine Inc	Biddeford	ME	G	207 775-7778	5755

PLASTICIZERS, ORGANIC: Cyclic & Acyclic

Company	CITY	ST	EMP	PHONE	ENTRY #
RSA Corp	Danbury	CT	E	203 790-8100	980
Teknor Apex Company **(PA)**	Pawtucket	RI	B	401 725-8000	20903

PLASTICS FILM & SHEET

Company	CITY	ST	EMP	PHONE	ENTRY #
Atlas Metallizing Inc	New Britain	CT	F	860 827-9777	2510
Clopay Corporation	North Haven	CT	C	203 230-9116	3015
Plastic Factory LLC	Bridgeport	CT	G	203 908-3468	470
Polymer Films Inc	West Haven	CT	E	203 932-3000	5142
Rowland Technologies Inc	Wallingford	CT	D	203 269-9500	4801
Superior Plas Extrusion Co Inc	Cromwell	CT	G	860 234-1864	861
Superior Plas Extrusion Co Inc **(PA)**	Putnam	CT	E	860 963-1976	3636
Abcorp NA Inc	Boston	MA	B	617 325-9600	8335
Applied Nnstrctred Sltions LLC	Billerica	MA	E	978 670-6959	8211
Argotec LLC **(HQ)**	Greenfield	MA	C	413 772-2564	11250
Atlantic Poly Inc	Norwood	MA	F	781 769-4260	14136
Brightec Inc	Natick	MA	G	508 647-9710	13241
Entegris Inc **(PA)**	Billerica	MA	A	978 436-6500	8246
Flexcon Company Inc **(PA)**	Spencer	MA	A	508 885-8200	15429
Glad Products Company	Braintree	MA	G	781 848-6272	9009
Hartwell Asscoiates	Cambridge	MA	G	617 686-7571	9501
New England Plastics Corp **(PA)**	Woburn	MA	E	781 933-6004	17243
Swm International	Greenfield	MA	G	413 774-3772	11279
Tel Epion Inc	Billerica	MA	E	978 436-2300	8302
Zatec LLC	North Dighton	MA	E	508 880-3388	13939
Shrinkfast Marketing	Newport	NH	D	603 863-7719	19358
Textiles Coated Incorporated **(PA)**	Londonderry	NH	D	603 296-2221	18741
Teknor Apex Company **(PA)**	Pawtucket	RI	B	401 725-8000	20903
Trico Specialty Films LLC	North Kingstown	RI	F	401 294-7022	20746
Alpa Incorporated	Essex Junction	VT	G	802 662-8401	21928

PLASTICS FILM & SHEET: Polyethylene

Company	CITY	ST	EMP	PHONE	ENTRY #
Engineering Services & Pdts Co **(PA)**	South Windsor	CT	D	860 528-1119	3965
Ensign-Bickford Industries Inc	Weatogue	CT	C	860 843-2000	5042

PRODUCT

	CITY	ST	EMP	PHONE	ENTRY #
Arlin Mfg Co Inc	Lowell	MA	F	978 454-9165	12345
Cabot Corporation **(PA)**	Boston	MA	C	617 345-0100	8452
Cabot Corporation	Haverhill	MA	C	978 556-8400	11413
Hudson Poly Bag Inc	Hudson	MA	F	978 562-7566	11776
Laddawn Inc **(HQ)**	Devens	MA	D	800 446-3639	10322
New England Extrusion Inc	Turners Falls	MA	C	413 863-3171	15884
Wbc Extrusion Products Inc **(HQ)**	Haverhill	MA	E	978 469-0668	11485

PLASTICS FILM & SHEET: Polyvinyl

	CITY	ST	EMP	PHONE	ENTRY #
Polyvinyl Films Inc	Sutton	MA	D	508 865-3558	15690
Ward Process Inc	Holliston	MA	D	508 429-1165	11613

PLASTICS FILM & SHEET: Vinyl

	CITY	ST	EMP	PHONE	ENTRY #
Grimco Inc	New Britain	CT	G	800 542-9941	2536
Orafol Americas Inc	Avon	CT	C	860 676-7100	41
Dielectrics Inc **(HQ)**	Chicopee	MA	E	413 594-8111	10019
Epv Plastics Corporation	Oxford	MA	G	508 987-2595	14259
Nordic Shield Plastic Corp	Oxford	MA	G	508 987-5361	14270

PLASTICS FINISHED PRDTS: Laminated

	CITY	ST	EMP	PHONE	ENTRY #
Alcat Incorporated	Milford	CT	E	203 878-0648	2240
Aptar Inc	Torrington	CT	G	860 489-6249	4562
Hicks and Otis Prints Inc	Norwalk	CT	E	203 846-2087	3168
General Woodworking Inc **(PA)**	Lowell	MA	F	978 458-6625	12373
Geonautics Manufacturing Inc	Newburyport	MA	E	978 462-7161	13494
High Speed Routing LLC	Haverhill	MA	G	603 527-8027	11441
Pilgrim Badge & Label Corp	Brockton	MA	D	508 436-6300	9171
Advanced Building Products Inc	Sanford	ME	F	207 490-2306	6870
York Manufacturing Inc	Sanford	ME	F	207 324-1300	6898
Plasti-Clip Corporation	Milford	NH	F	603 672-1166	19072
Riley Mountain Products Inc	Antrim	NH	F	603 588-7234	17597

PLASTICS FOAM, WHOLESALE

	CITY	ST	EMP	PHONE	ENTRY #
Sprayfoampolymerscom LLC	Wilton	CT	G	800 853-1577	5304
Jeffco Fibres Inc **(PA)**	Webster	MA	C	508 943-0440	16345

PLASTICS MATERIAL & RESINS

	CITY	ST	EMP	PHONE	ENTRY #
Allnex USA Inc	Wallingford	CT	D	203 269-4481	4695
Allread Products Co LLC	Terryville	CT	F	860 589-3566	4474
Anapo Plastics Corp	Farmington	CT	G	860 874-8174	1465
Axel Plastics RES Labs Inc	Monroe	CT	E	718 672-8300	2392
Bakelite N Sumitomo Amer Inc **(DH)**	Manchester	CT	D	860 645-3851	1987
C Mather Company Inc	South Windsor	CT	G	860 528-5667	3946
Chessco Industries Inc **(PA)**	Westport	CT	E	203 255-2804	5183
Enflo Corporation **(PA)**	Bristol	CT	E	860 589-0014	556
Engineered Polymers Inds Inc	Cheshire	CT	G	203 272-2233	730
Fimor North America Inc **(HQ)**	Cheshire	CT	E	203 272-3219	733
Henkel of America Inc **(HQ)**	Rocky Hill	CT	B	860 571-5100	3715
Henkel US Operations Corp **(DH)**	Rocky Hill	CT	B	860 571-5100	3716
Lanxess Solutions US Inc **(DH)**	Shelton	CT	E	203 573-2000	3824
Osterman & Company Inc **(PA)**	Cheshire	CT	D	203 272-2233	751
Oxford Performance Mtls Inc	South Windsor	CT	E	860 698-9300	3997
Polymer Resources Ltd **(PA)**	Farmington	CT	D	203 324-3737	1507
Polyone Corporation	Stamford	CT	G	203 327-6010	4288
Presidium USA Inc	Stamford	CT	G	203 674-9374	4291
Ravago Americas LLC	Wilton	CT	E	203 855-6000	5301
Roehm America LLC	Wallingford	CT	E	203 269-4481	4798
SMS Machine Inc	East Berlin	CT	G	860 829-0813	1108
Sonoco Prtective Solutions Inc	Putnam	CT	E	860 928-7795	3634
Spartech LLC	Stamford	CT	C	203 327-6010	4327
Total Ptrchemicals Ref USA Inc	Stratford	CT	E	203 375-0668	4454
Trinseo LLC	Gales Ferry	CT	E	860 447-7298	1528
Tyne Plastics LLC **(PA)**	Burlington	CT	G	860 673-7100	681
Aaron Industries Corp	Leominster	MA	E	978 534-6135	12105
Accurate Plastics Inc	East Falmouth	MA	E	508 457-9097	10434
Acushnet Rubber Company Inc	New Bedford	MA	B	508 998-4000	13352
Andrew Roberts Inc	Natick	MA	G	508 653-6412	13235
Argotec LLC **(HQ)**	Greenfield	MA	C	413 772-2564	11250
Atoll-Bio USA Inc	Gloucester	MA	F	978 281-4595	11162
Bagge Inc	Holliston	MA	G	508 429-8080	11558
CDF Corporation **(PA)**	Plymouth	MA	D	508 747-5858	14550
Chase Corp	Bridgewater	MA	F	508 819-4200	9066
Cold Chain Technologies Inc **(PA)**	Franklin	MA	D	508 429-1395	11030
Dj Microlaminates Inc	Sudbury	MA	G	978 261-3188	15655
Dow Chemical Company	Marlborough	MA	E	508 229-7676	12750
Enginred Syntactic Systems LLC	Attleboro	MA	G	508 226-3907	7733
Entec Polymers	Sutton	MA	G	508 865-2001	15682
Eps Polymer Distribution Inc	Shrewsbury	MA	G	508 925-5932	15111
Ernest Johnson	Marlborough	MA	G	508 259-6727	12753
Fraivillig Technologies Co	Boston	MA	G	512 784-5698	8551
Gare Incorporated	Haverhill	MA	E	978 373-9131	11437
Ineos Melamines LLC	Springfield	MA	E	413 730-3811	15478
Ineos Nova Lcc	Winchendon	MA	G	978 297-2265	17077
Isp Freetown Fine Chem Inc	Assonet	MA	D	508 672-0634	7681
Jarica Inc	Woburn	MA	F	781 935-1907	17210
Kpt Company Inc	Malden	MA	G	978 558-4009	12575
Manufacturing Service Corp	Millbury	MA	G	508 865-2550	13169
Modern Dispersions Inc **(PA)**	Leominster	MA	D	978 534-3370	12168
Omnova Solutions Inc	Fitchburg	MA	E	978 342-5831	10845
P & K Custom Acrylics Inc	Malden	MA	G	781 388-2601	12585
Pepperell International	Pepperell	MA	G	508 878-7987	14445
Plaskolite LLC	Sheffield	MA	C	800 628-5084	15062
Plaskolite LLC	Sheffield	MA	C	800 628-5084	15063
Plaskolite Massachusetts LLC	Sheffield	MA	C	413 229-8711	15064
Plastic Design Inc	North Chelmsford	MA	E	978 251-4830	13908
Poly-Mark Corp	Clinton	MA	G	978 368-1300	10090
Polyone Corporation	Littleton	MA	E	978 772-0764	12319
S&E Specialty Polymers LLC	Lunenburg	MA	D	978 537-8261	12483
Sabic US Holdings LP	Pittsfield	MA	A	413 448-7110	14506
Saint-Gobain Ceramics Plas Inc	Northborough	MA	B	508 351-7754	14046
Saint-Gobain Prfmce Plas Corp	Taunton	MA	C	508 823-7701	15783
Solutia Inc	Springfield	MA	A	413 788-6911	15507
Steel Products Corporation **(PA)**	Rochdale	MA	G	508 892-4770	14783
Styletech Company	Leominster	MA	G	978 537-0711	12190
Swm	Greenfield	MA	F	413 772-2564	11278
Swm International	Greenfield	MA	G	413 774-3772	11279
Tapecoat Company	Westwood	MA	G	781 332-0700	16879
Tpe Solutions Inc **(PA)**	Shirley	MA	G	978 425-3033	15096
Ware Rite Distributors Inc	East Bridgewater	MA	D	508 690-2145	10422
Wilsonart Intl Holdings LLC	North Reading	MA	E	978 664-5230	13994
Bosal Foam and Fiber **(PA)**	Limerick	ME	E	207 793-2245	6332
Cyro Industry	Sanford	ME	G	207 324-6000	6873
Panolam Industries Intl Inc	Auburn	ME	E	207 784-9111	5586
Roehm America LLC	Sanford	ME	C	207 324-6000	6891
Aeroplas Corp International	Hollis	NH	G	603 465-7300	18324
AP Extrusion Inc	Salem	NH	F	603 890-1086	19708
Core Elastomers	Portsmouth	NH	G	603 319-6912	19554
Dalau Incorporated	Merrimack	NH	G	603 670-1031	18997
Freudenberg-Nok General Partnr	Northfield	NH	E	603 286-1600	19402
Freudenberg-Nok General Partnr	Northfield	NH	D	603 286-1600	19401
Global Plastics LLC **(HQ)**	Manchester	NH	F	603 782-2835	18828
Itaconix Corporation	Stratham	NH	F	603 775-4400	19869
Metzger/Mcguire Inc	Bow	NH	E	603 224-6122	17722
Nyltech North America	Manchester	NH	G	603 627-5150	18891
Omni Metals Company Inc	Somersworth	NH	E	603 692-6664	19845
Plan Tech Inc	Loudon	NH	E	603 783-4767	18752
Polymer Technologies LLC	Nashua	NH	G	603 883-4002	19235
Saint-Gobain Prfmce Plas Corp	Merrimack	NH	C	603 424-9000	19027
Scandia Plastics Inc	Plaistow	NH	E	603 382-6533	19523
Textiles Coated Incorporated	Manchester	NH	C	603 296-2221	18940
Universal Systems USA Inc	Manchester	NH	F	603 222-9070	18947
Applied Plastics Tech Inc	Bristol	RI	E	401 253-0200	20062
Development Associates Inc	North Kingstown	RI	F	401 884-1350	20702
Konneco International LLC	North Smithfield	RI	G	401 767-3690	20788
Modern Plastics	Warwick	RI	G	401 732-0415	21392
Polyfoam Corporation	Cranston	RI	G	401 781-3220	20272
Polymer Solutions Inc	Pawtucket	RI	G	401 423-1638	20881
Polyworks LLC	North Smithfield	RI	E	401 769-0994	20794
Ralco Industries Inc **(PA)**	Woonsocket	RI	E	401 765-1000	21577

PLASTICS MATERIALS, BASIC FORMS & SHAPES WHOLESALERS

	CITY	ST	EMP	PHONE	ENTRY #
Nevamar Company LLC **(HQ)**	Shelton	CT	B	203 925-1556	3837
Preferred Foam Products Inc	Clinton	CT	G	860 669-3626	793
Atlantic Poly Inc	Norwood	MA	F	781 769-4260	14136
Kilder Corporation	North Billerica	MA	E	978 663-8800	13830
Manufacturing Service Corp	Millbury	MA	G	508 865-2550	13169
Millennium Plastics Inc	Groveland	MA	F	978 372-4822	11302
Plastic Concepts Inc	North Billerica	MA	E	978 663-7996	13856
Plastic Design Inc	North Chelmsford	MA	E	978 251-4830	13908

PLASTICS PROCESSING

	CITY	ST	EMP	PHONE	ENTRY #
Anderson David C & Assoc LLC **(PA)**	Enfield	CT	F	860 749-7547	1346
Design Engineering Inc	Torrington	CT	G	860 482-4120	4574
Ensign-Bickford Industries Inc	Simsbury	CT	E	860 658-4411	3905
Entegris Inc	Danbury	CT	B	800 766-2681	912
Fiberglass Engr & Design Co	Wallingford	CT	G	203 265-1644	4743
Idex Health & Science LLC	Bristol	CT	C	860 314-2880	570
Lingol Corporation	Wallingford	CT	F	203 265-3608	4766
Pel Associates LLC **(PA)**	Groton	CT	G	860 446-9921	1683
Precision Engineered Pdts LLC	Wallingford	CT	E	203 265-3299	4789
Precision Plastic Fab	Brookfield	CT	G	203 775-7047	657
Spartech LLC	Stamford	CT	C	203 327-6010	4327
C & C Thermoforming Inc	Palmer	MA	G	413 289-1900	14282
Creative Extrusion & Tech Inc	Brockton	MA	E	508 587-2290	9134
Enginred Plas Sltons Group Inc	Norwood	MA	G	781 762-3913	14148
Entegris Inc	Bedford	MA	E	978 436-6575	7975
Entegris Inc **(PA)**	Billerica	MA	A	978 436-6500	8246
Gregory Manufacturing Inc	Holyoke	MA	D	413 536-5432	11628
JMS Manufacturing Inc	Taunton	MA	F	508 675-1141	15760
Mair-Mac Machine Company Inc	Brockton	MA	F	508 895-9001	9164
MJW Mass Inc	Winchester	MA	D	781 721-0332	17092
Nevron Plastics Inc	Saugus	MA	F	781 233-1310	14991
New England Plastics Corp	New Bedford	MA	E	508 995-7334	13424
Parallel Products of Neng **(DH)**	New Bedford	MA	G	508 884-5100	13435
Phadean Engineering Co Inc	Shrewsbury	MA	G	888 204-0900	15128
Plastic Distrs Fabricators Inc	Haverhill	MA	E	978 374-0300	11459
Plastic Fabricators Corp	Woburn	MA	G	781 933-6007	17266
Poly-Cel Inc	Marlborough	MA	F	508 229-8310	12809
Worthen Industries Inc	Clinton	MA	E	978 365-6345	10095
Ecoshel Inc **(PA)**	Ashland	ME	G	207 274-3508	5536
Fbn Plastics Inc	Salem	NH	F	603 894-4326	19732
Inofab-Nnovation Infabrication	Belmont	NH	G	603 491-2946	17675
Opac Inc **(PA)**	Smithfield	RI	G	401 231-3552	21242

PLASTICS SHEET: Packing Materials

	CITY	ST	EMP	PHONE	ENTRY #
Charter Nex Films Inc	Turners Falls	MA	G	413 863-3171	15875
Gregory Manufacturing Inc	Holyoke	MA	D	413 536-5432	11628
JP Plastics Inc	Bridgewater	MA	G	508 697-4202	9080
Packaging Products Corporation **(PA)**	New Bedford	MA	F	508 997-5150	13434
Specialized Plastics Inc	Hudson	MA	E	978 562-9314	11819
Tekni-Plex Inc	Ashland	MA	F	508 881-2440	7671
Walter Drake Inc **(PA)**	Holyoke	MA	G	413 536-5463	11666
Nelipak Corporation **(PA)**	Cranston	RI	D	401 946-2699	20267

PLASTICS: Blow Molded

	CITY	ST	EMP	PHONE	ENTRY #
Plastic Forming Company Inc **(PA)**	Woodbridge	CT	E	203 397-1338	5476
Plastic Assembly Corporation	Ayer	MA	F	978 772-4725	7934
North American Plastics Ltd	Manchester	NH	E	603 644-1660	18887
B & L Plastics Inc	Pawtucket	RI	E	401 723-3000	20814

PLASTICS: Cast

	CITY	ST	EMP	PHONE	ENTRY #
Resin Systems Corporation	Amherst	NH	D	603 673-1234	17584
Mastercast Ltd	Pawtucket	RI	F	401 726-3100	20858

PLASTICS: Extruded

	CITY	ST	EMP	PHONE	ENTRY #
Cowles Products Company Inc	North Haven	CT	D	203 865-3110	3022
Davis-Standard LLC **(HQ)**	Pawcatuck	CT	B	860 599-1010	3432
Farrel Corporation **(DH)**	Ansonia	CT	D	203 736-5500	15
Merritt Extruder Corp	Hamden	CT	E	203 230-8100	1770
Bixby International Corp	Newburyport	MA	D	978 462-4100	13473
Netco Extruded Plastics Inc	Hudson	MA	E	978 562-3485	11795
Pepperell Braiding Company Inc **(PA)**	Pepperell	MA	E	978 433-2133	14444
Portuamerica Inc	Ludlow	MA	G	413 589-0095	12475
Streamline Plastics Co Inc	East Longmeadow	MA	E	718 401-4000	10494
Tuftane Extrusion Tech Inc	Fall River	MA	F	978 921-8200	10773
Xponent Global Inc	Hudson	MA	E	978 562-3485	11827
Genplex Inc	Skowhegan	ME	G	207 474-3500	6974
Dunn Industries Inc	Manchester	NH	E	603 666-4800	18814
Pbs Plastics Inc	Barrington	NH	F	603 868-1717	17620

PLASTICS: Finished Injection Molded

	CITY	ST	EMP	PHONE	ENTRY #
Accumold Technologies Inc	Bridgeport	CT	G	203 384-9256	366
Apex Machine Tool Company Inc	Cheshire	CT	D	860 677-2884	711
Brighton & Hove Mold Ltd	Oxford	CT	G	203 264-3013	3392
Doss Corporation	Wethersfield	CT	G	860 721-7384	5247
Injectech Engineering LLC **(PA)**	New Hartford	CT	G	860 379-9781	2641
Marlborough Plastics Inc	Marlborough	CT	G	860 295-9124	2066
Mbsw Inc	West Hartford	CT	D	860 243-0303	5086
Molding Technologies LLC	Old Saybrook	CT	G	860 395-3230	3345
RES-Tech Corporation	Berlin	CT	D	860 828-1504	107
Rogers Manufacturing Company	Rockfall	CT	D	860 346-8648	3699
Schaeffler Aerospace USA Corp **(DH)**	Danbury	CT	B	203 744-2211	984
Bandera Acquisition LLC **(DH)**	Foxborough	MA	C	480 553-6400	10911
Brenmar Molding Inc	Fitchburg	MA	G	978 343-3198	10814
Cardinal Comb & Brush Mfg Corp	Leominster	MA	E	978 537-6330	12125
Castle Plastics Inc	Leominster	MA	G	978 534-6220	12126
Di-MO Manufacturing Inc	Middleboro	MA	G	508 947-2200	13062
First Plastics Corp	Leominster	MA	F	978 537-0367	12139
Globe Composite Solutions Ltd	Stoughton	MA	D	781 871-3700	15594
Illinois Tool Works Inc	Raynham	MA	D	508 821-9828	14716
Industrial Production Supplies	Attleboro	MA	F	508 226-1776	7749
K and C Plastics Inc	Leominster	MA	E	978 537-0605	12158
Mill Valley Molding LLC	West Hatfield	MA	G	413 247-9313	16484
Phillips-Medisize LLC	Clinton	MA	G	978 365-1262	10089
Pilgrim Innovative Plas LLC	Plymouth	MA	F	508 732-0297	14573
Placon Corporation	West Springfield	MA	C	413 785-1553	16546
Plastic Molding Mfg Inc **(PA)**	Hudson	MA	D	978 567-1000	11802
REc Manufacturing Corp	Hopedale	MA	E	508 634-7999	11681
Super Brush LLC	Springfield	MA	D	413 543-1442	15511
United Comb & Novelty Corp **(PA)**	Leominster	MA	D	978 537-2096	12196
Web Industries Inc **(PA)**	Marlborough	MA	G	508 898-2988	12848
Maine Manufacturing LLC	Sanford	ME	D	207 324-1754	6881
Molds Plus Inc	Lewiston	ME	G	207 795-0000	6307
R&V Industries Inc	Sanford	ME	D	207 324-5200	6887
Concept Tool and Design Inc	Goffstown	NH	G	603 622-0216	18198
GI Plastek LLC	Wolfeboro	NH	B	603 569-5100	20017
Hy-Ten Die & Development Corp	Milford	NH	E	603 673-1611	19065
Precision Tool & Molding LLC	Derry	NH	D	603 437-6685	17994
Tech Nh Inc **(PA)**	Merrimack	NH	D	603 424-4404	19036
W K Hillquist Inc	Hudson	NH	E	603 595-7790	18451

PLASTICS: Injection Molded

	CITY	ST	EMP	PHONE	ENTRY #
Aba-PGT Inc **(PA)**	Manchester	CT	C	860 649-4591	1980
Aba-PGT Inc	Vernon Rockville	CT	G	860 872-2058	4677
Able Coil and Electronics Co	Bolton	CT	E	860 646-5686	273
Accurate Mold Company Inc	Cromwell	CT	G	860 301-1988	842
Ace Technical Plastics Inc	Hartford	CT	G	860 278-2444	1801
Advance Mold & Mfg Inc	Manchester	CT	C	860 432-5887	1983
Aero-Med Molding Technologies **(PA)**	Ansonia	CT	F	203 735-2331	4
American Molded Products Inc	Bridgeport	CT	F	203 333-0183	374
American Plastic Products Inc	Waterbury	CT	C	203 596-2410	4841
Better Molded Products Inc **(PA)**	Bristol	CT	C	860 589-0066	534
Betz Tool Company Inc	Milford	CT	G	203 878-1187	2253
C Cowles & Company **(PA)**	North Haven	CT	D	203 865-3117	3012
Carpin Manufacturing Inc	Waterbury	CT	D	203 574-2556	4854
Connecticut Tool Co Inc	Putnam	CT	E	860 928-0565	3606
Dymotek Corporation	Somers	CT	G	800 788-1984	3916
Dymotek Corporation	Ellington	CT	E	860 875-2868	1333
East Branch Engrg & Mfg Inc	New Milford	CT	F	860 355-9661	2798
Edco Industries Inc	Bridgeport	CT	F	203 333-8982	410
Empire Tool LLC	Derby	CT	G	203 735-7467	1071
Ensinger Prcsion Cmponents Inc	Putnam	CT	D	860 928-7911	3611
Fimor North America Inc **(HQ)**	Cheshire	CT	E	203 272-3219	733
Fluoropolymer Resources LLC **(PA)**	East Hartford	CT	G	860 423-7622	1195
Fsm Plasticoid Mfg Inc	East Windsor	CT	F	860 623-1361	1284
Hawk Integrated Plastics LLC	Columbia	CT	F	860 337-0310	818
Illinois Tool Works Inc	Lakeville	CT	E	860 435-2574	1930
Inline Plastics Corp **(PA)**	Shelton	CT	C	203 924-5933	3819
K-Tec LLC	Thomaston	CT	G	860 283-8875	4507
Kinamor Incorporated	Wallingford	CT	E	203 269-0380	4760
Lacey Manufacturing Co LLC	Bridgeport	CT	B	203 336-7427	443
Lorex Plastics Co Inc	Norwalk	CT	G	203 286-0020	3188
Manchester Molding and Mfg Co	Manchester	CT	E	860 643-2141	2023
Meriden Precision Plastics LLC	Meriden	CT	G	203 235-3261	2105
Mohawk Tool and Die Mfg Co Inc	Bridgeport	CT	F	203 367-2181	452
Mold Threads Inc	Branford	CT	G	203 483-1420	331
Orbit Design LLC	Meriden	CT	F	203 393-0171	2114
Paragon Products Inc	Old Saybrook	CT	G	860 388-1363	3346
Park-PMC Liquidation Corp	Putnam	CT	E	860 928-0401	3626
Plastic Design Intl Inc **(PA)**	Middletown	CT	E	860 632-2001	2210
Plastic Molding Technology	Seymour	CT	G	203 881-1811	3760
Plastic Solutions LLC	Bethlehem	CT	G	203 266-5675	198
Plasticoid Manufacturing Inc	East Windsor	CT	E	860 623-1361	1298
Plastics and Concepts Conn Inc	Glastonbury	CT	F	860 657-9655	1572
Polymer Engineered Pdts Inc **(PA)**	Stamford	CT	D	203 324-3737	4287
Polymold Corp	Cheshire	CT	F	203 272-2622	753
Polytronics Corporation	Windsor	CT	G	860 683-2442	5355
Precision Plastic Products Inc	Portland	CT	F	860 342-2233	3571
Prospect Products Incorporated	Newington	CT	E	860 666-0323	2896
Prototype Plastic Mold Co Inc	Middletown	CT	E	860 632-2800	2214
Quest Plastics Inc	Torrington	CT	F	860 489-1404	4595
Scan Tool & Mold Inc	Trumbull	CT	E	203 459-4950	4631
Somerset Plastics Company	Middletown	CT	E	860 635-1601	2224
Stelray Plastic Products Inc	Ansonia	CT	E	203 735-2331	23
Swpc Plastics LLC	Deep River	CT	C	860 526-3200	1067
Technical Industries Inc **(PA)**	Torrington	CT	D	860 489-2160	4600
Technology Plastics LLC	Terryville	CT	F	806 583-1590	4493
Trento Group LLC	East Windsor	CT	G	860 623-1361	1308
TWC Trans World Consulting	Windsor Locks	CT	G	860 668-5108	5402
Vanguard Plastics Corporation	Southington	CT	E	860 628-4736	4089
Vision Technical Molding	Manchester	CT	G	860 783-5050	2057
Watertown Plastics Inc	Watertown	CT	E	860 274-7535	5035
Wepco Plastics Inc	Middlefield	CT	E	860 349-3407	2168
Wilkinson Tool & Die Co	North Stonington	CT	G	860 599-5821	3077
3dfortify Inc	Boston	MA	G	978 399-4075	8329
A & J Industries LLC	Uxbridge	MA	F	508 278-4531	15912
Absolute Haitian Corporation **(PA)**	Worcester	MA	F	508 459-5372	17333
Accellent Holdings Corp	Wilmington	MA	A	978 570-6900	16962
Ace Moulding Co Inc	Monson	MA	G	413 267-4875	13201
Advance Plastics Inc	Oxford	MA	G	508 987-7235	14252
Advanced Prototypes & Molding	Leominster	MA	G	978 534-0584	12107
Agi Polymatrix LLC **(HQ)**	Pittsfield	MA	D	413 499-3550	14449
Albright Technologies Inc	Leominster	MA	F	978 466-5870	12111
Alsco Industries Inc	Sturbridge	MA	D	508 347-1199	15637
Amaray Plastics	Pittsfield	MA	F	413 499-3550	14451
Apex Resource Technologies Inc	Pittsfield	MA	D	413 442-1414	14452
Applied Plastic Technology Inc	Worcester	MA	E	508 752-5924	17340
Armstrong Mold Corporation	Hingham	MA	G	781 749-3207	11492
Atco Plastics Inc	Plainville	MA	D	508 695-3573	14515
Atom Marketing Inc **(PA)**	Hanover	MA	G	781 982-9930	11327
Axygen Bioscience Inc	Tewksbury	MA	A	978 442-2200	15808
Biomedical Polymers Inc	Sterling	MA	D	978 632-2555	15537
Built-Rite Tool and Die Inc **(PA)**	Lancaster	MA	E	978 368-7250	11982
Cado Manufacturing Inc	Fitchburg	MA	F	978 343-2989	10816
Chatham Plastic Ventures Inc	Brockton	MA	E	518 392-5761	9130
Cordmaster Engineering Co Inc	North Adams	MA	E	413 664-9371	13671
Crisci Tool and Die Inc	Leominster	MA	E	978 537-4102	12128
Double A Plastics Co Inc	Monson	MA	G	413 267-4403	13206
F & M Tool & Plastics Inc	Leominster	MA	D	978 840-1897	12138
Fall River Tool & Die Co Inc	Fall River	MA	F	508 674-4621	10699
G and W Precision	South Deerfield	MA	G	413 397-3361	15249
G and W Precision Inc	Whately	MA	G	413 665-0983	16905
G&F Medical Inc	Fiskdale	MA	E	978 560-2622	10806
G&F Precision Molding Inc **(PA)**	Fiskdale	MA	D	508 347-9132	10807
Girouard Tool & Die Inc	Leominster	MA	G	978 534-4147	12146
Great Northern Industries Inc **(PA)**	Boston	MA	C	617 262-4314	8578
Gregstrom Corporation	Woburn	MA	D	781 935-6600	17194
Grove Products Inc	Leominster	MA	F	978 534-5188	12148
Howland Tool & Machine Ltd	East Freetown	MA	G	508 763-8472	10452
Injected Solutions Inc	Lanesborough	MA	F	413 499-5800	11987
Innovative Mold Solutions Inc	Leominster	MA	E	978 840-1503	12155
Innovative Tooling Company Inc	Lenox	MA	F	413 637-1031	12101
Jam Plastics Inc	Leominster	MA	E	978 537-2570	12156
Knobby Krafters Inc	Attleboro	MA	E	508 222-7272	7757
Lakewood Industries Inc	Pittsfield	MA	D	413 499-3550	14480
Lansen Mold Co Inc	Hancock	MA	F	413 443-5328	11325
Mack Prototype Inc	Gardner	MA	E	978 632-3700	11119
Magnus Molding Inc	Pittsfield	MA	E	413 443-1192	14488
Mascon Inc	Woburn	MA	E	781 938-5800	17223
Mayhew Basque Plastics LLC	Westminster	MA	F	978 537-5219	16809
Midstate Mold & Engineering	Franklin	MA	F	508 520-0011	11066
Milacron Marketing Company LLC	Rowley	MA	E	978 238-7100	14858
Mill Valley Molding Inc	West Hatfield	MA	D	413 247-9313	16483
Modern Mold & Tool Inc **(PA)**	Pittsfield	MA	E	413 443-1192	14491
Moldmaster Engineering Inc	Pittsfield	MA	E	413 442-5793	14492
Mtd Micro Molding Inc	Charlton	MA	E	508 248-0111	9854
Naugler Mold & Engineering	Beverly	MA	F	978 922-5634	8159
Neu-Tool Design Inc	Wilmington	MA	E	978 658-5881	17029
Northeast Plastics Inc	Wakefield	MA	F	781 245-5512	15965
Northern Products Inc	Leominster	MA	F	978 840-3383	12173
Northern Tool Mfg Co Inc	Springfield	MA	F	413 732-5549	15494
Nypro Inc	Devens	MA	G	978 784-2006	10328
Nypro Inc **(HQ)**	Clinton	MA	A	978 365-8100	10086
Orbit Plastics Corp	Danvers	MA	E	978 465-5300	10245
Pen Ro Mold and Tool Inc	Pittsfield	MA	E	413 499-0464	14498
Pittsfield Plastics Engrg Inc	Pittsfield	MA	D	413 442-0067	14500

PRODUCT

	CITY	ST	EMP	PHONE	ENTRY #
Polymer Corporation	Palmer	MA	E	413 267-5524	14293
Polymer Corporation **(HQ)**	Rockland	MA	D	781 871-4606	14819
Precision Plastics Inc	Wilmington	MA	G	978 658-5345	17038
Pro Pel Plastech Inc	South Deerfield	MA	G	413 665-2282	15254
Pro Pel Plastech Inc **(PA)**	South Deerfield	MA	E	413 665-3379	15255
QEP Co Inc	Clinton	MA	G	978 368-8991	10091
Raitto Engineering & Mfg Inc	Wheelwright	MA	G	413 477-6637	16908
RES-Tech Corporation **(HQ)**	Hudson	MA	E	978 567-1000	11811
Schaller Corporation	Franklin	MA	G	508 655-9171	11078
Shelpak Plastics Inc	Middleton	MA	G	781 305-3937	13101
Sinicon Plastics Inc	Dalton	MA	E	413 684-5290	10186
SMC Ltd	Devens	MA	D	978 422-6800	10333
Sonicron Systems Corporation	Westfield	MA	E	413 562-5218	16731
Sonolite Plastics Corporation	Gloucester	MA	F	978 281-0662	11211
Spectrum Plastics Group	Athol	MA	G	978 249-5343	7694
SRC Medical Inc	Hanover	MA	D	781 826-9100	11352
Sterling Manufacturing Co Inc	Lancaster	MA	E	978 368-8733	11986
Stuart Allyn Co Inc	Pittsfield	MA	G	413 443-7306	14511
Toner Plastics Inc	East Longmeadow	MA	E	413 789-1300	10498
Trans Form Plastics Corp	Danvers	MA	E	978 777-1440	10264
Trexel Inc	Wilmington	MA	E	781 932-0202	17059
Universal Tipping Co Inc	Pembroke	MA	G	781 826-5135	14431
W R H Industries Ltd	Fall River	MA	G	508 674-2444	10781
Waddington Group Inc	Chelmsford	MA	F	201 610-6728	9940
Waddington North America Inc	Chelmsford	MA	C	978 256-6551	9941
Whitewater Plastics Inc	West Hatfield	MA	G	413 237-5032	16488
C-O Bella Rouge At Belissino	South Portland	ME	G	207 318-5214	7017
Composimold	Manchester	ME	G	888 281-2674	6408
G & G Products LLC	Kennebunk	ME	E	207 985-9100	6234
G Pro Industrial Services	Biddeford	ME	G	207 766-1671	5735
Maine Mold & Machine Inc	Hartford	ME	G	207 388-2732	6177
Molding Tooling and Design	Biddeford	ME	F	207 247-4077	5750
Plas-Tech Inc	Gorham	ME	G	207 854-8324	6125
Thermoformed Plastics Neng LLC	Biddeford	ME	F	207 286-1775	5766
Tri-Star Molding	Lewiston	ME	G	207 783-5820	6326
Advantage Mold Inc	Londonderry	NH	G	603 647-6678	18672
Advantage Plastic Products Inc	Concord	NH	E	603 227-9540	17880
Ambix Manufacturing Inc	Albany	NH	F	603 452-5247	17535
Burbak Companies	Wilton	NH	D	603 654-2291	19976
Faber Polivol LLC **(DH)**	Salem	NH	G	603 681-0484	19730
G & G Tool & Die Corp	Goffstown	NH	G	603 625-9744	18201
GI Plastek Ltd Partnership	Wolfeboro	NH	B	603 569-5100	20018
Granite State Plastics Inc	Hudson	NH	E	603 669-6715	18393
Ifg Industries LLC **(DH)**	Salem	NH	G	603 681-0484	19742
Insulfab Plastics Inc	Franklin	NH	F	603 934-2770	18158
Janco Inc **(PA)**	Rollinsford	NH	D	603 742-0043	19691
Mrpc Northeast LLC	Hudson	NH	E	603 880-3616	18417
Plan Tech Inc	Loudon	NH	E	603 783-4767	18752
Plastic Techniques Inc	Goffstown	NH	E	603 622-5570	18209
Poly-Ject Inc	Amherst	NH	E	603 882-6570	17581
Proto Part Inc	Hudson	NH	F	603 883-6531	18429
Rapid Mold Evolution	Milford	NH	G	603 673-1027	19073
Accurate Molded Products Inc	Warwick	RI	E	401 739-2400	21317
Anco Tool & Die Co Inc	East Providence	RI	F	401 438-5860	20387
Bates Plastics Inc	Cranston	RI	E	401 781-7711	20188
CPC Plastics Inc	West Warwick	RI	G	401 828-0820	21488
Eli Engineering Co Inc	Coventry	RI	G	401 822-1494	20146
Fielding Manufacturing Inc	Cranston	RI	E	401 461-0400	20226
Matrix I LLC	East Providence	RI	D	401 434-3040	20431
Total Plastics Resources LLC	Cranston	RI	E	401 463-3090	20303
Tri-Mack Plastics Mfg Corp	Bristol	RI	D	401 253-2140	20107
Wenco Molding Inc	Providence	RI	G	401 781-2600	21153
Dm Inc	Milton	VT	G	802 425-2119	22126
G W Plastics Inc **(PA)**	Bethel	VT	B	802 234-9941	21695
G W Plastics Inc	South Royalton	VT	D	802 763-2194	22492
G W Plastics Inc	Sharon	VT	G	802 233-0319	22408
K & E Plastics Inc	Bennington	VT	E	802 375-0011	21676
Mack Group Inc **(PA)**	Arlington	VT	B	802 375-2511	21597
Mack Molding Company Inc **(HQ)**	Arlington	VT	C	802 375-2511	21598
Mack Molding Company Inc	Arlington	VT	C	802 375-0500	21599
Mid-VT Molding LLC	Bethel	VT	G	802 234-9777	21696
Plastic Monofil Co Ltd	Milton	VT	G	802 893-1543	22136
Progressive Plastics Inc	Williamstown	VT	E	802 433-1563	22650
T & M Enterprises Inc	Shaftsbury	VT	G	802 447-0601	22406

PLASTICS: Molded

	CITY	ST	EMP	PHONE	ENTRY #
Advance Mold Mfg Inc	Ellington	CT	G	860 783-5024	1326
Atlas Hobbing and Tool Co Inc	Vernon Rockville	CT	F	860 870-9226	4678
Awm LLC	Windsor Locks	CT	D	860 386-1000	5386
Balfor Industries Inc	Oxford	CT	F	203 828-6473	3391
Bennice Molding Co	Meriden	CT	G	203 440-2543	2079
Bey-Low Molds	Torrington	CT	G	860 482-6561	4565
Canevari Plastics Inc	Milford	CT	G	203 878-4319	2260
Crown Molding Etc LLC	Hamden	CT	G	203 287-9424	1739
J&L Plastic Molding LLC	Wallingford	CT	G	203 265-6237	4758
Little Bits Manufacturing Inc	North Grosvenordale	CT	G	860 923-2772	2998
MPS Plastics Incorporated	Marlborough	CT	E	860 295-1161	2067
Quatum Inc	Hartford	CT	G	860 666-3464	1864
Shaeffer Plastic Mfg Corp	Colchester	CT	G	860 537-5524	808
Super Seal Corp	Stratford	CT	F	203 378-5015	4451
Alumi-Nex Mold Inc	Webster	MA	F	508 949-2200	16338
American Molding Corporation	Leominster	MA	G	978 534-0009	12114
Bacon Industries Inc	Wrentham	MA	F	508 384-0780	17515
Cmt Materials Inc	Attleboro	MA	F	508 226-3901	7721
Dan-Kar Plastics Products	Woburn	MA	G	781 935-9221	17163
Elm Industries Inc	West Springfield	MA	E	413 734-7762	16518
F & D Plastics Inc **(PA)**	Leominster	MA	E	978 668-5140	12136
Final Forge LLC	Plymouth	MA	G	857 244-0764	14557
Glass Molders Pottery Pla	Milford	MA	G	508 634-2932	13119
Mar-Lee Companies Inc	Fitchburg	MA	G	978 343-9600	10833
Restech Plastic Molding LLC **(DH)**	Hudson	MA	F	978 567-1000	11812
Sparrow Engineering	East Brookfield	MA	G	508 867-3984	10423
Texas Dip Molding Coating Inc **(PA)**	Medway	MA	G	508 533-6101	12971
Tyca Corporation **(PA)**	Clinton	MA	E	978 612-0002	10094
W M Gulliksen Mfg Co Inc **(PA)**	South Weymouth	MA	E	617 323-5750	15323
Wachusett Molding LLC	Auburn	MA	G	508 459-0477	7852
Dynamic Urethanes Inc	Gray	ME	G	207 657-3770	6138
Comstock Industries Inc	Meredith	NH	E	603 279-7045	18972
Moldpro Inc	Swanzey	NH	E	603 357-2523	19885
Paclantic Inc	Claremont	NH	G	603 542-8600	17858
Pelham Plastics Inc	Pelham	NH	D	603 886-7226	19440
PSI Molded Plastics NH Inc	Wolfeboro	NH	D	603 569-5100	20024
Scarzello & Assocs Inc	Amherst	NH	G	603 673-7746	17548
Chem-Tainer Industries Inc	Cranston	RI	D	401 467-2750	20196
Jade Engineered Plastics Inc	Bristol	RI	D	401 253-4440	20085
Mars 2000 Inc	Providence	RI	A	401 421-5275	21061
Vermont Plastics Specialties	Williston	VT	G	802 879-0072	22696

PLASTICS: Polystyrene Foam

	CITY	ST	EMP	PHONE	ENTRY #
Ansonia Plastics LLC	Ansonia	CT	D	203 736-5200	7
Duz Manufacturing Inc	Milford	CT	G	203 874-1032	2278
Gilman Corporation	Gilman	CT	E	860 887-7080	1534
Hhc LLC	Manchester	CT	E	860 456-0677	2008
Hopp Companies Inc	Newtown	CT	F	800 889-8425	2924
Hydrofera LLC	Manchester	CT	D	860 456-0677	2010
Madison Polymeric Engrg Inc	Branford	CT	E	203 488-4554	330
Merrill Industries Inc	Ellington	CT	E	860 871-1888	1336
New England Foam Products LLC **(PA)**	Hartford	CT	E	860 524-0121	1851
Plastic Forming Company Inc **(PA)**	Woodbridge	CT	E	203 397-1338	5476
Preferred Foam Products Inc	Clinton	CT	G	860 669-3626	793
Reilly Foam Corp	Bloomfield	CT	E	860 243-8200	256
Ashworth International Inc	Fall River	MA	G	508 674-4693	10664
Bbmc Inc	Hancock	MA	F	413 443-3333	11324
Concrete Block Insulating Syst	West Brookfield	MA	E	508 867-4241	16466
Flexcon Industrial LLC **(HQ)**	Spencer	MA	E	210 798-1900	15430
Fuller Box Co Inc **(PA)**	North Attleboro	MA	D	508 695-2525	13756
Geonautics Manufacturing Inc	Newburyport	MA	E	978 462-7161	13494
Insulation Technology Inc	Bridgewater	MA	G	508 697-6926	9077
Jeffco Fibres Inc **(PA)**	Webster	MA	C	508 943-0440	16345
Rogers Foam Automotive Corp	Somerville	MA	F	617 623-3010	15211
Splash Shield Inc	Woburn	MA	G	781 935-8844	17300
Trexel Inc	Wilmington	MA	E	781 932-0202	17059
Ufp Technologies Inc	Haverhill	MA	F	978 352-2200	11480
Ward Process Inc	Holliston	MA	D	508 429-1165	11613
Deepwater Buoyancy Inc	Biddeford	ME	F	207 468-2565	5728
Enefco International Inc **(PA)**	Auburn	ME	D	207 514-7218	5561
Index Packaging Inc	Milton	NH	C	603 350-0018	19086
Tex Flock Inc	Woonsocket	RI	E	401 765-2340	21586

PLASTICS: Thermoformed

	CITY	ST	EMP	PHONE	ENTRY #
Lehvoss North America LLC	Pawcatuck	CT	F	860 495-2046	3438
Newhart Plastics Inc	Milford	CT	G	203 877-5367	2321
Siemon Company **(PA)**	Watertown	CT	A	860 945-4200	5024
A Schulman Custom Compounding	Worcester	MA	C	508 756-0002	17330
Accutech Packaging Inc	Foxboro	MA	D	508 543-3800	10873
Accutech Packaging Inc	Mansfield	MA	F	508 543-3800	12610
Black Diamond Mfg & Engrg Inc	Georgetown	MA	F	978 352-6716	11137
M & A Plastics Inc	Dracut	MA	G	978 319-9930	10362
Mayfield Plastics Inc	Sutton	MA	E	508 865-8150	15687
New England Plastics Corp **(PA)**	Woburn	MA	E	781 933-6004	17243
Pioneer Packaging Inc **(PA)**	Chicopee	MA	D	413 378-6930	10050
Saint-Gobain Prfmce Plas Corp	Worcester	MA	E	508 852-3072	17467
Thermo-Fab Corporation	Shirley	MA	E	978 425-2311	15094
United Plastic Fabricating Inc **(PA)**	North Andover	MA	D	978 975-4520	13734
Universal Plastics Corporation **(PA)**	Holyoke	MA	D	413 592-4791	11664
Welch Fluorocarbon Inc	Dover	NH	E	603 742-0164	18067
Jay Packaging Group Inc **(PA)**	Warwick	RI	D	401 244-1300	21379
Mearthane Products Corporation **(PA)**	Cranston	RI	C	401 946-4400	20260
Arlington Industries Inc	Arlington	VT	E	802 375-6139	21594
Precision Composites VT LLC	Lyndonville	VT	F	802 626-5900	22072

PLATEMAKING SVC: Color Separations, For The Printing Trade

	CITY	ST	EMP	PHONE	ENTRY #
Endo Graphics Inc	Danbury	CT	G	203 778-1557	910
Four Color Ink LLC	Old Saybrook	CT	G	860 395-5471	3335
Gateway Digital Inc	Norwalk	CT	F	203 853-4929	3157
Ghp Media Inc **(PA)**	West Haven	CT	C	203 479-7500	5124
Desk Top Graphics Inc **(HQ)**	Peabody	MA	E	617 832-1927	14330
Pure Imaging	Woburn	MA	G	781 537-6992	17273

PLATEMAKING SVC: Gravure, Plates Or Cylinders

	CITY	ST	EMP	PHONE	ENTRY #
Schrader Bellows	Enfield	CT	E	860 749-2215	1380

PLATES

	CITY	ST	EMP	PHONE	ENTRY #
Baron Technology Inc	Trumbull	CT	E	203 452-0515	4614
Eccles-Lehman Inc	Easton	CT	G	203 268-0605	1318
Paul Dewitt	Danbury	CT	F	203 792-5610	965
Schmitt Realty Holdings Inc	Darien	CT	G	203 662-6661	1031
Schmitt Realty Holdings Inc	Branford	CT	E	203 488-3252	346
Success Printing & Mailing Inc	Norwalk	CT	F	203 847-1112	3252
Belmont Printing Company	Belmont	MA	E	617 484-0833	8066
Chemi-Graphic Inc	Ludlow	MA	E	413 589-0151	12458
Csw Inc **(PA)**	Ludlow	MA	C	413 589-1311	12461

	CITY	ST	EMP	PHONE	ENTRY #
Flex-O-Graphic Prtg Plate Inc	Worcester	MA	E	508 752-8100	17375
Ghp Media Inc	North Adams	MA	D	413 663-3771	13675
Hot Plates Company	Ashland	MA	G	508 429-1445	7661
ID Graphics Group Inc	South Easton	MA	E	508 238-8500	15279
J C Enterprises Inc	Ashland	MA	G	508 881-7228	7662
J T Gardner Inc **(PA)**	Westborough	MA	E	800 540-4993	16627
J T Gardner Inc	Worcester	MA	G	508 751-6600	17396
Linmel Associates Inc	Marlborough	MA	F	508 481-6699	12787
Minuteman Press	Fitchburg	MA	G	978 345-0818	10839
Prima Products	Forestdale	MA	G	508 553-8875	10872
Rogers Printing Co Inc	Leominster	MA	E	978 537-9791	12184
Rotation Dynamics Corporation	Marlborough	MA	F	508 481-0900	12822
Southern Berkshire Shoppers Gu	Great Barrington	MA	F	413 528-0095	11246
Desk Top Graphics Inc	Portland	ME	G	207 828-0041	6651
New England Printing Corp	Portsmouth	NH	F	603 431-0142	19599
Foxon Company	Providence	RI	E	401 421-2386	21015
Herald Association Inc	Rutland	VT	C	802 747-6121	22338
McClure Newspapers Inc	Burlington	VT	C	802 863-3441	21795

PLATES: Steel

	CITY	ST	EMP	PHONE	ENTRY #
Jen Col Innovations LLC	Colchester	VT	G	802 448-3053	21869

PLATFORMS: Cargo

	CITY	ST	EMP	PHONE	ENTRY #
Ada Fabricators Inc	Wilmington	MA	E	978 262-9900	16965

PLATING & FINISHING SVC: Decorative, Formed Prdts

	CITY	ST	EMP	PHONE	ENTRY #
D & S Plating Co Inc	Holyoke	MA	F	413 533-7771	11621
Jarden LLC	East Wilton	ME	C	207 645-2574	5987

PLATING & POLISHING SVC

	CITY	ST	EMP	PHONE	ENTRY #
A & A Products and Services	Windsor	CT	G	860 683-0879	5312
C & S Engineering Inc	Meriden	CT	E	203 235-5727	2082
Colonial Coatings Inc	Milford	CT	E	203 783-9933	2265
P&G Metal Components Corp	Bloomfield	CT	F	860 243-2220	248
Plasma Technology Incorporated	South Windsor	CT	E	860 282-0659	4001
Sousa Corp	Newington	CT	F	860 523-9090	2904
United States Fire Arms Mfg Co	Hartford	CT	E	860 296-7441	1883
Accumet Engineering Corp	Hudson	MA	E	978 568-8311	11750
American Metal Polishing	Shrewsbury	MA	G	978 726-7752	15100
Bay State Galvanizing Inc	Everett	MA	F	617 389-0671	10604
Berkshire Mnufactured Pdts Inc	Newburyport	MA	C	978 462-8161	13472
Katahdin Industries Inc **(PA)**	Hudson	MA	E	781 329-1420	11781
Pep Industries LLC	Attleboro	MA	A	508 226-5600	7776
Precision Engineered Pdts LLC **(DH)**	Attleboro	MA	G	508 226-5600	7782
R L Barry Inc	Attleboro	MA	F	508 226-3350	7784
Specialized Coating Services	North Billerica	MA	G	978 362-0346	13866
Spencer Metal Finishing Inc **(PA)**	Brookfield	MA	F	508 885-6477	9193
Sweet Metal Finishing Inc	Attleboro	MA	E	508 226-4359	7799
Transene Company Inc	Danvers	MA	F	978 777-7860	10265
Cobra Powder Coating	Lyman	ME	G	207 391-3060	6388
Controlled Chaos	Portland	ME	G	802 274-5321	6643
Mbw Tractor Sales LLC	Berwick	ME	F	207 384-2001	5711
Bomar Inc	Charlestown	NH	D	603 826-5781	17811
Dyna Roll Inc	Seabrook	NH	G	603 474-2547	19799
Peg Kearsarge Co Inc	Bartlett	NH	G	603 374-2341	17627
A-1 Polishing Co	Johnston	RI	G	401 751-8944	20496
Chemart Company **(PA)**	Lincoln	RI	D	401 333-9200	20563
Electrolizing Inc	Providence	RI	E	401 861-5900	21004
Interplex Engineered Pdts Inc	Rumford	RI	E	401 434-6543	21187
Polytechnic Inc	Pawtucket	RI	G	401 724-3608	20882
Precision Plsg Ornamentals Inc	Pawtucket	RI	E	401 728-9994	20883
Spencer Plating Company	Providence	RI	G	401 331-5923	21125
Alternate Finishing Inc	Hudson	MA	G	978 567-9205	11754
Aotco Metal Finishing Inc	Billerica	MA	E	781 275-0880	8210
Arborway Metal Finishing Inc	Rockland	MA	F	781 982-0137	14792
B & J Manufacturing Corp	Taunton	MA	D	508 822-1990	15730
Black Oxide Co Inc	Worcester	MA	G	508 757-0340	17348
CIL Electroplating Inc **(PA)**	Lawrence	MA	C	978 683-2082	12007
Coating Systems Inc	Lowell	MA	D	978 937-3712	12359
F M Callahan and Son Inc	Malden	MA	D	781 324-5101	12572
General Metal Finishing LLC	Attleboro	MA	D	508 222-9683	7740
Hi-Tech Plating Inc	Everett	MA	F	617 389-3400	10613
Interplex Engineered Pdts Inc **(DH)**	Attleboro	MA	D	508 399-6810	7750
L & J of New England Inc	Worcester	MA	E	508 756-8080	17403
Mueller Corporation	East Bridgewater	MA	C	508 456-4500	10418
N-Tek Inc	Lawrence	MA	G	978 687-4010	12061
New England Electropolishing	Fall River	MA	E	508 672-6616	10737
New Method Plating Co Inc	Worcester	MA	E	508 754-2671	17434
Poly Plating Inc	Chicopee	MA	F	413 593-5477	10051
Purecoat North LLC	Belmont	MA	D	617 489-2750	8080
Reliable Electro Plating Inc	Chartley	MA	G	508 222-0620	9857
Reliable Plating Co Inc	Worcester	MA	G	508 755-9434	17458
South Shore Plating Co Inc	Quincy	MA	G	617 773-8064	14657
Specialized Plating Inc	Haverhill	MA	E	978 373-8030	11473
T D F Metal Finishing Co Inc	Danvers	MA	F	978 223-4292	10259
Valentine Plating Company Inc	West Springfield	MA	E	413 732-0009	16561
Valley Plating Inc 8-1-80	Springfield	MA	D	413 788-7375	15521
Westfield Electroplating Co **(PA)**	Westfield	MA	C	413 568-3716	16743
Whitman Company Inc	Whitman	MA	E	781 447-2422	16931
Worcester Manufacturing Inc	Worcester	MA	E	508 756-0301	17505
Southern Maine Industries Corp	Windham	ME	E	207 856-7391	7253
J & E Specialty Inc	Dover	NH	G	603 742-6357	18031
Medina Plating Corp	Londonderry	NH	E	330 725-4155	18719
Accent Plating Company Inc	Pawtucket	RI	E	401 722-6306	20805
American Ring Co Inc	Cranston	RI	E	401 467-4480	20179
American Ring Co Inc **(PA)**	East Providence	RI	E	401 438-9060	20385
DFI-Ep LLC	North Providence	RI	E	401 943-9900	20756
G & A Plating & Polishing Co	North Providence	RI	E	401 351-8693	20762
G Tanury Plating Co Inc	Johnston	RI	D	401 232-2330	20514
General Plating Inc	Johnston	RI	G	401 421-0219	20515
International Chromium Pltg Co	Providence	RI	G	401 421-0205	21037
Interplex Industries Inc **(DH)**	Rumford	RI	F	718 961-6212	21188
Interplex Metals Ri Inc	Rumford	RI	D	401 732-9999	21191
Jrb Associates Inc	Cranston	RI	E	401 351-8693	20247
New Annex Plating Inc	North Providence	RI	F	401 349-0911	20767
Providence Metallizing Co Inc **(PA)**	Pawtucket	RI	D	401 722-5300	20886
Reed Allison Group Inc	Providence	RI	D	617 846-1237	21107
Tanury Industries Inc	Lincoln	RI	C	800 428-6213	20598
United Plating Inc	Cranston	RI	D	401 461-5857	20307
Universal Plating Co Inc	Providence	RI	G	401 861-3530	21144
Precision Valley Finishing	Springfield	VT	G	802 885-3150	22508

PLATING COMPOUNDS

	CITY	ST	EMP	PHONE	ENTRY #
Macdermid Incorporated	Waterbury	CT	E	203 575-5700	4901
Macdermid Incorporated **(HQ)**	Waterbury	CT	C	203 575-5700	4900
Advanced Chemical Company	Warwick	RI	E	401 785-3434	21318

PLATING SVC: Chromium, Metals Or Formed Prdts

	CITY	ST	EMP	PHONE	ENTRY #
CRC Chrome Corporation	Meriden	CT	F	203 630-1008	2090
Custom Chrome Plating	Wallingford	CT	G	203 265-5667	4731
Mirror Polishing & Pltg Co Inc	Waterbury	CT	E	203 574-5400	4917
National Chromium Company Inc	Putnam	CT	F	860 928-7965	3620
New England Chrome Plating	East Hartford	CT	G	860 528-7176	1206
Rader Industries Inc	Bridgeport	CT	G	203 334-6739	478
Pioneer Valley Plating Co	South Hadley	MA	G	413 535-1424	15308
Northeast Custom Chrome Nashua	Nashua	NH	G	603 566-6165	19218
Austin Hard Chrome	Providence	RI	G	401 421-0840	20964
Induplate Inc **(PA)**	North Providence	RI	D	401 231-5770	20765

PLATING SVC: Electro

	CITY	ST	EMP	PHONE	ENTRY #
American Electro Products Inc	Waterbury	CT	C	203 756-7051	4840
Bass Plating Company	Bloomfield	CT	E	860 243-2557	207
Danbury Metal Finishing Inc	Danbury	CT	G	203 748-5044	897
Halco Inc	Waterbury	CT	D	203 575-9450	4881
National Integrated Inds Inc	Waterbury	CT	D	203 756-7051	4922
Nylo Metal Finishing LLC	Waterbury	CT	G	203 574-5477	4930
Rayco Metal Finishing Inc	Middletown	CT	F	860 347-7434	2217
Seaboard Metal Finishing Co	New Britain	CT	E	203 933-1603	2576
Seidel Inc	Waterbury	CT	D	203 757-7349	4955
Spec Plating Inc	Bridgeport	CT	F	203 366-3638	494
Summit Corporation of America	Thomaston	CT	D	860 283-4391	4519
Superior Plating Company	Southport	CT	D	203 255-1501	4100
Superior Technology Corp **(PA)**	Southport	CT	C	203 255-1501	4101
Unimetal Surface Finishing LLC	Naugatuck	CT	E	203 729-8244	2498
Absolute Metal Finishing Inc	Norwood	MA	E	781 551-8235	14117
Acton Metal Processing Corp	Waltham	MA	E	781 893-5890	16023

PLATING SVC: Gold

	CITY	ST	EMP	PHONE	ENTRY #
Rsj LLC	North Attleboro	MA	G	508 695-5555	13777

PLATING SVC: NEC

	CITY	ST	EMP	PHONE	ENTRY #
A&R Plating Services LLC	Oakville	CT	G	860 274-9562	3295
A-1 Chrome and Polishing Corp	Newington	CT	F	860 666-4593	2836
Alpha Plating and Finishing Co	Plainville	CT	F	860 747-5002	3464
B & P Plating Equipment LLC	Bristol	CT	F	860 589-5799	523
Component Technologies Inc **(PA)**	Newington	CT	E	860 667-1065	2855
Har-Conn Chrome Company **(PA)**	West Hartford	CT	D	860 236-6801	5073
Hitech Chrome Pltg & Polsg Lc	North Windham	CT	G	860 456-8070	3082
K & K Black Oxide LLC	New Britain	CT	G	860 223-1805	2546
Marsam Metal Finishing Co	New Britain	CT	E	860 826-5489	2550
Plainville Plating Company Inc	Plainville	CT	D	860 747-1624	3511
Praxair Inc **(HQ)**	Danbury	CT	B	203 837-2000	971
Precision Finishing Svcs Inc	Windsor	CT	E	860 882-1073	5356
Prestige Metal Finishing LLC	Woodstock Valley	CT	G	860 974-1999	5504
Whyco Finishing Tech LLC	Thomaston	CT	E	860 283-5826	4527
Aerospace Support Inc	Agawam	MA	G	413 789-3103	7417
Apmar Usa Inc	Springfield	MA	G	413 781-5261	15446
Dav-Tech Plating Inc	Marlborough	MA	E	508 485-8472	12747
Five Star Plating LLC	Lawrence	MA	E	978 655-4081	12023
H Larosee and Sons Inc	Westborough	MA	E	978 562-9417	16623
H O Wire Co Inc	West Boylston	MA	F	508 243-7177	16416
Indepenent Plating Co	Worcester	MA	E	508 756-0301	17391
Light Metal Platers LLC	Waltham	MA	E	781 899-8855	16145
Millennium Plating Company Inc	Lowell	MA	G	978 454-0526	12412
Plating For Electronics Inc	Waltham	MA	E	781 893-2368	16175
Plating Technology Inc	New Bedford	MA	E	508 996-4006	13439
Spec-Elec Plating Corp	Sturbridge	MA	G	508 347-7255	15648
Silvex Incorporated	Westbrook	ME	D	207 761-0392	7209
A & F Plating Co Inc	Providence	RI	F	401 861-3597	20943
Dura Kote Technology Ltd	Johnston	RI	F	401 331-6460	20509
Ideal Plating & Polsg Co Inc	Providence	RI	F	401 455-1700	21034
Monarch Metal Finishing Co Inc	Providence	RI	E	401 785-3200	21070
Time Plating Incorporated	Cranston	RI	G	401 943-3020	20302
Unique Plating Co	Johnston	RI	G	401 943-7366	20545
Westwell Industries Inc	Providence	RI	F	401 467-2992	21154
Lawrence Lyon	Chelsea	VT	G	802 685-7790	21839

PLAYGROUND EQPT

	CITY	ST	EMP	PHONE	ENTRY #
Jammar Mfg Co Inc	Niantic	CT	G	866 848-1113	2953
Trassig Corp	Georgetown	CT	G	203 659-0456	1533
Billerica Backstage Rehearsal	Pinehurst	MA	G	978 670-1133	14447
Cedarworks of Maine Inc	Rockland	ME	E	207 596-0771	6788
Bobos Indoor Playground	Nashua	NH	G	603 718-8721	19128

	CITY	ST	EMP	PHONE	ENTRY #
Imagination Playground LLC	Providence	RI	G	678 604-7466	21035

PLEATING & STITCHING FOR THE TRADE: Appliqueing

	CITY	ST	EMP	PHONE	ENTRY #
Baa Creations	Ledyard	CT	G	860 464-1339	1939

PLEATING & STITCHING FOR THE TRADE: Decorative & Novelty

	CITY	ST	EMP	PHONE	ENTRY #
Imperial Monogram Company Inc	West Roxbury	MA	G	617 323-0100	16497

PLEATING & STITCHING FOR THE TRADE: Hemstitching

	CITY	ST	EMP	PHONE	ENTRY #
290 Industrial Stitching Inc	South Barre	MA	G	978 355-0271	15234

PLEATING & STITCHING SVC

	CITY	ST	EMP	PHONE	ENTRY #
Robert Audette **(PA)**	Cheshire	CT	G	203 872-3119	760
Zuse Inc	Guilford	CT	F	203 458-3295	1725
Callenstitch LLC	Concord	MA	E	978 369-9080	10120
Nixon Company Inc	Indian Orchard	MA	E	413 543-3701	11890
Pop Tops Company Inc	South Easton	MA	E	508 580-2580	15286
Silver Screen Design Inc	Greenfield	MA	F	413 773-1692	11275
Stitch This	Dunbarton	NH	G	603 774-0736	18074
GA Rel Manufacturing Company	Providence	RI	E	401 331-5455	21019
Ira Green Inc	Providence	RI	C	800 663-7487	21040
Kennedy Incorporated	North Kingstown	RI	F	401 295-7800	20720
Weller E E Co Inc/MCS Finshg	Providence	RI	E	401 461-4275	21152

PLUGS: Drain, Magnetic, Metal

	CITY	ST	EMP	PHONE	ENTRY #
Farmington Engineering Inc	North Haven	CT	G	800 428-7584	3027

PLUMBING & HEATING EQPT & SPLY, WHOL: Htg Eqpt/Panels, Solar

	CITY	ST	EMP	PHONE	ENTRY #
Spire Solar Inc	Bedford	MA	C	781 275-6000	8009

PLUMBING & HEATING EQPT & SPLY, WHOLESALE: Hydronic Htg Eqpt

	CITY	ST	EMP	PHONE	ENTRY #
Creative Hydronics Intl Inc	Sagamore Beach	MA	G	508 524-3535	14885
Reheat Co Inc	Danvers	MA	F	978 777-4441	10251

PLUMBING & HEATING EQPT & SPLYS WHOLESALERS

	CITY	ST	EMP	PHONE	ENTRY #
Kensco Inc **(PA)**	Ansonia	CT	F	203 734-8827	20
Pequot	Bridgeport	CT	G	800 620-1492	466
Tinny Corporation	Middletown	CT	E	860 854-6121	2228
Francer Industries Inc	East Weymouth	MA	E	781 337-2882	10542
Orion Enterprises Inc **(HQ)**	North Andover	MA	C	913 342-1653	13722
Antoine Mechanical Inc	Jay	ME	G	207 897-4100	6219

PLUMBING & HEATING EQPT & SPLYS, WHOL: Pipe/Fitting, Plastic

	CITY	ST	EMP	PHONE	ENTRY #
Jolley Precast Inc	Danielson	CT	E	860 774-9066	1014

PLUMBING & HEATING EQPT & SPLYS, WHOL: Plumbing Fitting/Sply

	CITY	ST	EMP	PHONE	ENTRY #
F W Webb Company	New Haven	CT	F	203 865-6124	2688
New Resources Group Inc	Bridgeport	CT	G	203 366-1000	457
The Keeney Manufacturing Co **(PA)**	Newington	CT	C	603 239-6371	2906
R I Baker Co Inc **(PA)**	Clarksburg	MA	E	413 663-3791	10075

PLUMBING & HEATING EQPT & SPLYS, WHOL: Plumbng/Heatng Valves

	CITY	ST	EMP	PHONE	ENTRY #
Water Works Supply Corp	Chester	NH	G	781 322-1238	17827

PLUMBING & HEATING EQPT & SPLYS, WHOL: Water Purif Eqpt

	CITY	ST	EMP	PHONE	ENTRY #
Dpc Quality Pump Service	Milford	CT	G	203 874-6877	2276
C E D Corp	Duxbury	MA	G	781 834-9312	10395
Merrimack Valley Water Assn	Lawrence	MA	G	978 975-1800	12051

PLUMBING & HEATING EQPT & SPLYS, WHOLESALE: Brass/Fittings

	CITY	ST	EMP	PHONE	ENTRY #
Neoperl Inc	Waterbury	CT	D	203 756-8891	4926

PLUMBING & HEATING EQPT & SPLYS, WHOLESALE: Oil Burners

	CITY	ST	EMP	PHONE	ENTRY #
John Zink Company LLC	Shelton	CT	D	203 925-0380	3821

PLUMBING FIXTURES

	CITY	ST	EMP	PHONE	ENTRY #
Bead Industries Inc **(PA)**	Milford	CT	E	203 301-0270	2251
Colonial Bronze Company	Torrington	CT	D	860 489-9233	4570
F W Webb Company	New Haven	CT	F	203 865-6124	2688
Fitzgerald & Wood Inc	Branford	CT	G	203 488-2553	316
Macristy Industries Inc **(PA)**	Newington	CT	C	860 225-4637	2879
Mc Guire Manufacturing Co Inc	Cheshire	CT	D	203 699-1801	744
Idex Health & Science LLC	Middleboro	MA	C	774 213-0200	13064
Orion Enterprises Inc **(HQ)**	North Andover	MA	C	913 342-1653	13722
Renovators Supply Inc	Millers Falls	MA	E	413 423-3300	13181
Turning Point Industry FL	Pembroke	MA	G	239 340-1942	14430
Eos Design LLC **(PA)**	Westbrook	ME	G	740 392-3642	7188
The Keeney Manufacturing Co	Winchester	NH	C	603 239-6371	19996
Cramik Enterprises Inc	Westerly	RI	E	401 596-8171	21521
Fulford Manufacturing Company **(PA)**	Riverside	RI	F	401 431-2000	21168
Quick Fitting Inc	Warwick	RI	D	401 734-9500	21408

PLUMBING FIXTURES: Brass, Incl Drain Cocks, Faucets/Spigots

	CITY	ST	EMP	PHONE	ENTRY #
Neoperl Inc	Waterbury	CT	D	203 756-8891	4926
The Keeney Manufacturing Co **(PA)**	Newington	CT	C	603 239-6371	2906

PLUMBING FIXTURES: Plastic

	CITY	ST	EMP	PHONE	ENTRY #
Neoperl Inc	Waterbury	CT	D	203 756-8891	4926
New Resources Group Inc	Bridgeport	CT	G	203 366-1000	457
Water Structures LLC	Seabrook	NH	G	603 474-0615	19822
Hancor Inc	Springfield	VT	E	802 886-8403	22501

PLUMBING FIXTURES: Vitreous China

	CITY	ST	EMP	PHONE	ENTRY #
Clivus Multrum Inc	Lawrence	MA	G	978 725-5591	12010
Clivus New England Inc	Lawrence	MA	G	978 794-9400	12011

POINT OF SALE DEVICES

	CITY	ST	EMP	PHONE	ENTRY #
Hopp Companies Inc	Newtown	CT	F	800 889-8425	2924
Plastics Plus Inc	Cumberland	RI	E	401 727-1447	20339

POLES & POSTS: Concrete

	CITY	ST	EMP	PHONE	ENTRY #
Techno Mtal Post Watertown LLC	Waterbury	CT	G	203 755-6403	4961
Charles Curtis LLC	Danville	VT	G	802 274-0060	21895

POLISHING SVC: Metals Or Formed Prdts

	CITY	ST	EMP	PHONE	ENTRY #
Etherington Brothers Inc	Bristol	CT	G	860 585-5624	557
Rayco Inc	New Britain	CT	G	860 357-4693	2569
Seidel Inc	Waterbury	CT	D	203 757-7349	4954
Silversmith Inc	Greenwich	CT	G	203 869-4244	1649
Smart Polishing	Stamford	CT	G	203 559-1541	4322
Dds Services Ltd	Pembroke	MA	G	781 837-3997	14398
J Crosier Mold Polishing	Florida	MA	G	413 663-6262	10871
ADI Polishing Inc	Cranston	RI	G	401 942-3955	20172
Nu-Lustre Finishing Corp	Providence	RI	D	401 521-7800	21079
R & R Polishing Co Inc	Cranston	RI	G	401 831-6335	20277
Roberts Polishing Co	Johnston	RI	G	401 946-8922	20538

POLYCARBONATE RESINS

	CITY	ST	EMP	PHONE	ENTRY #
Osterman & Company Inc	Cheshire	CT	E	203 272-2233	752

POLYESTERS

	CITY	ST	EMP	PHONE	ENTRY #
Ameramesh Technologies Inc	Fall River	MA	G	508 324-9977	10655

POLYETHYLENE RESINS

	CITY	ST	EMP	PHONE	ENTRY #
Thornton and Company Inc	Southington	CT	F	860 628-6771	4086
DSM Coating Resins Inc	Wilmington	MA	C	800 458-0014	16996
Eastern Packaging Inc	Lawrence	MA	D	978 685-7723	12020
Polyexe Corporation	Brentwood	NH	E	603 778-1143	17754

POLYPROPYLENE RESINS

	CITY	ST	EMP	PHONE	ENTRY #
Polifil Inc	Woonsocket	RI	E	401 767-2700	21575

POLYSTYRENE RESINS

	CITY	ST	EMP	PHONE	ENTRY #
Polar Industries Inc **(PA)**	Prospect	CT	E	203 758-6651	3592
Avilite Corp	Merrimack	NH	G	603 626-4388	18988
Branch River Plastics Inc	Smithfield	RI	E	401 232-0270	21214

POLYTETRAFLUOROETHYLENE RESINS

	CITY	ST	EMP	PHONE	ENTRY #
Alden and Broden Corporation	Westford	MA	G	603 882-0330	16752

POLYURETHANE RESINS

	CITY	ST	EMP	PHONE	ENTRY #
L H C Inc **(PA)**	Lynn	MA	E	781 592-6444	12520
Rynel Inc **(DH)**	Wiscasset	ME	D	207 882-0200	7287

POLYVINYL BUTYRAL RESINS

	CITY	ST	EMP	PHONE	ENTRY #
Resource Colors LLC	Leominster	MA	F	978 537-3700	12182

POLYVINYL CHLORIDE RESINS

	CITY	ST	EMP	PHONE	ENTRY #
Sykes Hollow Innovations Ltd	East Dorset	VT	G	802 549-4671	21917

PONTOONS: Plastic, Nonrigid

	CITY	ST	EMP	PHONE	ENTRY #
Liftbag Usa Inc	North Kingstown	RI	F	401 884-8801	20722
Subsalve USA LLC	North Kingstown	RI	F	401 884-8801	20743

POPCORN & SUPPLIES WHOLESALERS

	CITY	ST	EMP	PHONE	ENTRY #
Quirion Luc **(PA)**	Newport	VT	G	802 673-8386	22205

POSTERS & DECALS, WHOLESALE

	CITY	ST	EMP	PHONE	ENTRY #
Gloucester Graphics Inc **(PA)**	Gloucester	MA	F	978 281-4500	11188

POTTERY

	CITY	ST	EMP	PHONE	ENTRY #
ZB Ceramic	Chicopee	MA	G	413 512-0879	10070

POTTERY: Laboratory & Indl

	CITY	ST	EMP	PHONE	ENTRY #
Bodycote Imt Inc **(DH)**	Andover	MA	D	978 470-0876	7542
Saint-Gobain Corporation	Northborough	MA	E	508 351-7112	14047

POTTING SOILS

	CITY	ST	EMP	PHONE	ENTRY #
Grillo Services LLC	Milford	CT	E	203 877-5070	2294
Sun Gro Holdings Inc	Agawam	MA	A	413 786-4343	7454
Envirem Organics Ltd	Unity	ME	G	207 948-4500	7115

POULTRY & SMALL GAME SLAUGHTERING & PROCESSING

	CITY	ST	EMP	PHONE	ENTRY #
Chris & Zack LLC	Orange	CT	G	203 298-0742	3361
Phoenix Poultry Corporation	Enfield	CT	E	413 732-1433	1374
Puritan Food Co Inc	Boston	MA	E	617 269-5650	8800
Premium Poultry Co	Providence	RI	E	401 467-3200	21093

POULTRY, PACKAGED FROZEN: Wholesalers

	CITY	ST	EMP	PHONE	ENTRY #
Suffield Poultry Inc	Springfield	MA	G	413 737-8392	15510

POWDER: Iron

	CITY	ST	EMP	PHONE	ENTRY #
Ametek Inc	Wallingford	CT	C	203 265-6731	4699

POWDER: Metal

	CITY	ST	EMP	PHONE	ENTRY #
Allied Sinterings Incorporated	Danbury	CT	E	203 743-7502	869
Allread Products Co LLC	Terryville	CT	F	860 589-3566	4474
Conn Engineering Assoc Corp	Sandy Hook	CT	F	203 426-4733	3741
Norwalk Powdered Metals Inc	Stratford	CT	D	203 338-8000	4435
Bay State Surface Technologies	Auburn	MA	F	508 832-5035	7829
Rmi Titanium Company LLC	Burlington	MA	F	781 272-5967	9330
Powdered Metal Technology Corp	Nashua	NH	F	617 642-4135	19236
Vermont Powder Coating Sy	South Burlington	VT	G	802 862-0061	22476

POWDERS, FLAVORING, EXC DRINK

	CITY	ST	EMP	PHONE	ENTRY #
Ocean Cliff Corporation	New Bedford	MA	G	508 990-7900	13432

POWER DISTRIBUTION BOARDS: Electric

	CITY	ST	EMP	PHONE	ENTRY #
Easy Access Distribution Inc	Burlington	MA	G	781 893-3999	9260

POWER GENERATORS

	CITY	ST	EMP	PHONE	ENTRY #
A-1 Machining Co	New Britain	CT	D	860 223-6420	2501
Alstom Renewable US LLC	Windsor	CT	G	860 688-1911	5319
Energyblox Inc	Hamden	CT	G	203 230-3000	1748
Ad Hoc Energy LLC	Millis	MA	G	508 507-8005	13182
Atlantic Power GP Inc	Boston	MA	G	617 977-2400	8382
Atlantic Pwr Enrgy Svcs US LLC	Dedham	MA	G	617 977-2400	10280
Aurora Wind Project LLC	Andover	MA	E	978 409-9712	7538
Hamilton Ferris Co Inc	Bourne	MA	G	508 743-9901	8946
Hy9 Corporation	Foxboro	MA	G	508 698-1040	10886
Mt Tom Generating Company LLC	Holyoke	MA	D	413 536-9586	11642
New England Gen-Connect LLC	Hingham	MA	G	617 571-6884	11507
Power Equipment Co Inc **(PA)**	Attleboro	MA	E	508 226-3410	7781
Regen Power Systems LLC	Orange	MA	G	203 328-3045	14225
Superior Power Systems	Attleboro	MA	G	508 226-3400	7798
Viking Industrial Products	Marlborough	MA	E	508 481-4600	12845
Bear Swamp Power Company LLC	Millinocket	ME	F	207 723-4341	6438

POWER HAND TOOLS WHOLESALERS

	CITY	ST	EMP	PHONE	ENTRY #
Zampini Industrial Group LLC	Lincoln	RI	G	401 305-7997	20602

POWER SPLY CONVERTERS: Static, Electronic Applications

	CITY	ST	EMP	PHONE	ENTRY #
71 Pickett District Road LLC	New Milford	CT	G	860 350-5964	2786
Neeltran Inc	New Milford	CT	C	860 350-5964	2815
Validus DC Systems LLC	Brookfield	CT	F	203 448-3600	663
Mornsun America LLC	Milford	MA	G	978 293-3923	13129
Itech Data Services Inc	South Burlington	VT	G	802 383-1500	22450

POWER SUPPLIES: All Types, Static

	CITY	ST	EMP	PHONE	ENTRY #
Dsaencore LLC **(PA)**	Brookfield	CT	D	203 740-4200	642
Power Controls Inc	Wallingford	CT	F	203 284-0235	4784
Prime Technology LLC	North Branford	CT	C	203 481-5721	2974
Transformer Technology Inc	Durham	CT	F	860 349-1061	1095
Tri Source Inc	Shelton	CT	F	203 924-7030	3882
Acon Inc	South Easton	MA	F	508 230-8022	15268
Acumentrics Rups LLC	Walpole	MA	E	617 932-7877	15987
Excelitas Technologies Corp	Salem	MA	C	800 775-6786	14910
Power Guide Marketing Inc **(PA)**	Worcester	MA	G	508 853-7357	17444
Socomec Inc **(DH)**	Watertown	MA	F	617 245-0447	16317
Synqor Holdings LLC	Boxborough	MA	D	978 849-0600	8970
Synqor Inc **(PA)**	Boxborough	MA	C	978 849-0600	8971
Wasik Associates Inc	Dracut	MA	F	978 454-9787	10371
Wurszt Inc	Wilbraham	MA	G	413 599-4900	16944
American Power Design Inc	Windham	NH	F	603 894-4446	19998
Atc Power Systems Inc	Merrimack	NH	E	603 429-0391	18985
Semiconductor Circuits Inc **(PA)**	Atkinson	NH	F	603 893-2330	17607

POWER SUPPLIES: Transformer, Electronic Type

	CITY	ST	EMP	PHONE	ENTRY #
Magcap Engineering LLC	Canton	MA	F	781 821-2300	9754
Precision Electronics Corp	Marshfield	MA	F	781 834-6677	12865
Design Consultants Associates	Hampstead	NH	F	603 329-4541	18239
Laconia Magnetics Inc	Laconia	NH	E	603 528-2766	18570

POWER SWITCHING EQPT

	CITY	ST	EMP	PHONE	ENTRY #
Russelectric Inc **(DH)**	Hingham	MA	C	781 749-6000	11509
Total Power International Inc	Lowell	MA	F	978 453-7272	12437

POWER TOOL REPAIR SVCS

	CITY	ST	EMP	PHONE	ENTRY #
Air Tool Sales & Service Co **(PA)**	Unionville	CT	G	860 673-2714	4652

POWER TOOLS, HAND: Cartridge-Activated

	CITY	ST	EMP	PHONE	ENTRY #
Amro Tool Co	Watertown	CT	G	860 274-9766	4998

POWER TOOLS, HAND: Chain Saws, Portable

	CITY	ST	EMP	PHONE	ENTRY #
Sperber Tool Works Inc	Bennington	VT	G	802 442-8839	21691

POWER TOOLS, HAND: Drill Attachments, Portable

	CITY	ST	EMP	PHONE	ENTRY #
Alden Corporation	Wolcott	CT	D	203 879-8830	5432

POWER TOOLS, HAND: Drills & Drilling Tools

	CITY	ST	EMP	PHONE	ENTRY #
Ridge View Associates Inc	Milford	CT	D	203 878-8560	2351

POWER TOOLS, HAND: Guns, Pneumatic, Chip Removal

	CITY	ST	EMP	PHONE	ENTRY #
Guardair Corporation	Chicopee	MA	E	413 594-4400	10028

POWER TRANSMISSION EQPT WHOLESALERS

	CITY	ST	EMP	PHONE	ENTRY #
Capeway Bearing & Machine Inc	Plymouth	MA	G	508 747-2800	14548
Electrochem Solutions Inc	Raynham	MA	C	781 575-0800	14714

POWER TRANSMISSION EQPT: Mechanical

	CITY	ST	EMP	PHONE	ENTRY #
Bead Industries Inc **(PA)**	Milford	CT	E	203 301-0270	2251
Converter Consultants LLC	Naugatuck	CT	G	203 729-1031	2469
Del-Tron Precision Inc	Bethel	CT	E	203 778-2727	143
Gwilliam Company Inc	New Milford	CT	F	860 354-2884	2804
Kasheta Power Equipment	South Windsor	CT	G	860 528-8421	3987
Perry Technology Corporation	New Hartford	CT	D	860 738-2525	2644
Roller Bearing Co Amer Inc	Middlebury	CT	E	203 758-8272	2157
Altra Industrial Motion Corp **(PA)**	Braintree	MA	B	781 917-0600	8986
Datel Inc	Mansfield	MA	E	508 964-5131	12627
Martin Sprocket & Gear Inc	Milford	MA	G	508 634-3990	13125
Stafford Manufacturing Corp	Norfolk	MA	G	978 657-8000	13664
US Bronze Foundry & Mch Inc	Hanover	MA	G	781 871-1420	11358
US Tsubaki Automotive LLC	Westfield	MA	F	413 593-1100	16738
US Tsubaki Automotive LLC **(DH)**	Chicopee	MA	C	413 593-1100	10067
US Tsubaki Power Transm LLC	Holyoke	MA	C	413 536-1576	11665
Warner Electric	Braintree	MA	G	781 917-0600	9048
Wgi Inc	Southwick	MA	C	413 569-9444	15421
Mikes and Sons	Presque Isle	ME	G	207 762-6310	6762
Montalvo Corporation	Gorham	ME	E	207 856-2501	6122
Woodex Bearing Company Inc	Georgetown	ME	E	207 371-2210	6107
Ametek Precitech Inc **(HQ)**	Keene	NH	D	603 357-2510	18491
Mpb Corporation	Lebanon	NH	B	603 448-3000	18630
Tidland Corporation	Keene	NH	D	603 352-1696	18533
Whittet-Higgins Company	Central Falls	RI	E	401 728-0700	20129

POWER TRANSMISSION EQPT: Vehicle

	CITY	ST	EMP	PHONE	ENTRY #
Southington Transm Auto Repr	Southington	CT	G	860 329-0381	4080

PRECAST TERRAZZO OR CONCRETE PRDTS

	CITY	ST	EMP	PHONE	ENTRY #
Oldcastle Infrastructure Inc	Rehoboth	MA	D	508 336-7600	14756
Oldcastle Infrastructure Inc	Littleton	MA	E	978 486-9600	12315
Paul Young Precast Company	Bellingham	MA	G	508 966-4333	8056
Strafello Precast Inc	East Taunton	MA	F	774 501-2628	10518
Greenstone Precast	New Gloucester	ME	G	207 926-5704	6466
Michie Corporation	Henniker	NH	D	603 428-7426	18307
Forterra Pipe & Precast LLC	Peace Dale	RI	F	401 782-2600	20913

PRECIOUS METALS WHOLESALERS

	CITY	ST	EMP	PHONE	ENTRY #
Northeastern Metals Corp	Stamford	CT	G	203 348-8088	4261

PRECIOUS STONE MINING SVCS, NEC

	CITY	ST	EMP	PHONE	ENTRY #
Dodlin Hill Stone Company LLC	Oakland	ME	G	207 465-6463	6532

PRECIOUS STONES & METALS, WHOLESALE

	CITY	ST	EMP	PHONE	ENTRY #
Precious Metals Reclaiming Svc **(PA)**	Canton	MA	G	781 326-3442	9771
Jomay Inc	Cranston	RI	F	401 944-5240	20246
Eastwind Lapidary Inc	Windsor	VT	G	802 674-5427	22707

PRECISION INSTRUMENT REPAIR SVCS

	CITY	ST	EMP	PHONE	ENTRY #
Projects Inc	Glastonbury	CT	C	860 633-4615	1574

PRESSES

	CITY	ST	EMP	PHONE	ENTRY #
Hpm LLC	Bellingham	MA	G	508 958-5565	8041

PRESSURE COOKERS: Stamped Or Drawn Metal

	CITY	ST	EMP	PHONE	ENTRY #
Utitec Inc **(HQ)**	Watertown	CT	D	860 945-0605	5032
Utitec Holdings Inc **(PA)**	Watertown	CT	G	860 945-0601	5033

PRESTRESSED CONCRETE PRDTS

	CITY	ST	EMP	PHONE	ENTRY #
Blakeslee Prestress Inc **(PA)**	Branford	CT	B	203 315-7090	298
Acme-Shorey Precast Co Inc	South Yarmouth	MA	E	508 430-0956	15324
Stone Soup Concrete	Easthampton	MA	G	413 203-5600	10580
Strescon of New England	Burlington	MA	G	781 221-2153	9342
Unistress Corp	Pittsfield	MA	B	413 499-1441	14512
Joseph P Carrara & Sons Inc **(PA)**	North Clarendon	VT	E	802 775-2301	22216

PRIMARY METAL PRODUCTS

	CITY	ST	EMP	PHONE	ENTRY #
Lisa Lee Creations Inc	New Haven	CT	G	203 479-4462	2706
Metal Housings Enclosures	Hudson	MA	G	978 567-3324	11792
Mgi Inc	Hermon	ME	G	207 817-3280	6190
Omni Technologies Corp	Brentwood	NH	G	603 679-2211	17753

PRIMARY ROLLING MILL EQPT

	CITY	ST	EMP	PHONE	ENTRY #
Idex Mpt Inc **(HQ)**	Westwood	MA	D	630 530-3333	16869

PRINT CARTRIDGES: Laser & Other Computer Printers

	CITY	ST	EMP	PHONE	ENTRY #
Encore Images Inc	Marblehead	MA	F	781 631-4568	12681
Electronics For Imaging Inc	Londonderry	NH	F	603 279-4635	18695
Vermont Toner Recharge Inc	Essex Junction	VT	G	802 864-7637	21964

PRINTED CIRCUIT BOARDS

	CITY	ST	EMP	PHONE	ENTRY #
AB Electronics Inc	Brookfield	CT	E	203 740-2793	632
Accutron Inc	Windsor	CT	C	860 683-8300	5315
Advanced Product Solutions LLC	Hamden	CT	G	203 745-4225	1730
Altek Electronics Inc	Torrington	CT	C	860 482-7626	4558
American Backplane Inc	Morris	CT	E	860 567-2360	2430
Apct-Ct Inc	Wallingford	CT	G	203 284-1215	4702
Carlton Industries Corp	Hamden	CT	E	203 288-5605	1736
Custom Design Service Corp	Danbury	CT	G	203 748-1105	895
Cyclone Microsystems Inc	Hamden	CT	E	203 786-5536	1741
Eastern Company	Clinton	CT	E	860 669-2233	785
Electronic Spc Conn Inc	Hamden	CT	E	203 288-1707	1745
Enhanced Mfg Solutions LLC	Branford	CT	F	203 488-5796	313
Northeast Circuit Tech LLC	Glastonbury	CT	G	860 633-1967	1567
Te Connectivity Corporation	Stafford Springs	CT	C	860 684-8000	4116
Technical Manufacturing Corp	Durham	CT	E	860 349-1735	1094
Tek Industries Inc	Vernon	CT	E	860 870-0001	4673
Ttm Printed Circuit Group Inc	Stafford Springs	CT	C	860 684-8000	4118
Ttm Technologies Inc	Stafford Springs	CT	B	860 684-5881	4119
Ttm Technologies Inc	Stafford Springs	CT	D	860 684-8000	4120
Accusemble Electronics Inc	North Billerica	MA	F	978 584-0072	13789
Aerospace Semiconductor Inc	Lawrence	MA	F	978 688-1299	11990
Barry Industries Inc	Attleboro	MA	D	508 226-3350	7712
Bitflow Inc	Woburn	MA	F	781 932-2900	17132
Case Assembly Solutions Inc	South Easton	MA	E	508 238-5665	15273
Chase Corporation **(PA)**	Westwood	MA	G	781 332-0700	16861
Chase Corporation	Oxford	MA	F	508 731-2710	14256
Chase Corporation	Westwood	MA	F	781 329-3259	16862
Circuit Technology Center Inc	Haverhill	MA	E	978 374-5000	11417
Cooper Interconnect Inc	Chelsea	MA	D	617 389-7080	9950

PRODUCT

	CITY	ST	EMP	PHONE	ENTRY #
Creative Exchange Inc	Chelmsford	MA	G	978 863-9955	9889
Custom Computer Systems Inc	Northborough	MA	G	508 393-8899	14032
Darrell Wheaton	Taunton	MA	G	508 824-1669	15740
Dilla St Corp	Milford	MA	G	508 478-3419	13112
East West Boston LLC	Boston	MA	D	617 598-3000	8516
Epec LLC **(PA)**	New Bedford	MA	D	508 995-5171	13384
Frain & Associates Inc	Assonet	MA	G	508 644-3424	7680
G3 Incorporated **(PA)**	Lowell	MA	E	978 805-5001	12372
J & J Technologies Inc	Wareham	MA	D	508 291-3803	16251
Jnj Industries Inc	Franklin	MA	E	508 553-0529	11058
L-Tronics Inc	Waltham	MA	G	781 893-6672	16142
L-Tronics Inc	Waltham	MA	E	781 893-6672	16143
Lockheed Martin Sippican Inc **(HQ)**	Marion	MA	B	508 748-3399	12699
M C Test Service Inc	North Billerica	MA	F	781 218-7550	13837
Mc Assembly International LLC	North Billerica	MA	B	781 729-1073	13840
Measurement Computing Corp **(HQ)**	Norton	MA	D	508 946-5100	14081
Mercury Systems Inc **(PA)**	Andover	MA	C	978 256-1300	7570
Mfg Electronics Inc	North Billerica	MA	G	978 671-5490	13844
Micron Corporation	Norwood	MA	E	781 769-5771	14179
Milford Manufacturing Svcs LLC	Hopedale	MA	D	508 478-8544	11678
Mini-Systems Inc **(PA)**	North Attleboro	MA	C	508 695-1420	13765
New Age Ems Inc	Attleboro	MA	E	508 226-6090	7772
Parlex	Methuen	MA	F	978 946-2500	13041
Pcb Connect Inc	Sharon	MA	G	781 806-5670	15055
Photo Tool Engineering Inc	Lowell	MA	E	978 805-5000	12421
Ping Electronics Inc	Bedford	MA	G	781 275-4731	8001
Ppi/Time Zero Inc	Norwood	MA	E	508 226-6090	14188
Ppi/Time Zero Inc	Springfield	MA	G	781 881-2400	15499
Precision Circuit Corporation	Taunton	MA	G	508 479-8843	15772
Prodrive Technologies Inc	Canton	MA	G	617 475-1617	9773
Proxy Manufacturing Inc	Methuen	MA	E	978 687-3138	13044
Rbd Electronics Inc **(PA)**	Dalton	MA	F	413 442-1111	10182
Remtec Incorporated	Norwood	MA	G	781 762-5732	14193
Starflex Inc	Lowell	MA	F	978 937-3889	12434
Sunburst Electronic Manufactur **(PA)**	West Bridgewater	MA	D	508 580-1881	16458
Tech-Etch Inc **(PA)**	Plymouth	MA	B	508 747-0300	14587
Technical Services Inc	Raynham	MA	G	781 389-8342	14732
Techtrade Inc	Needham	MA	F	781 724-7878	13313
Tronica Circuits Inc	Haverhill	MA	G	978 372-7224	11478
Whitman Products Company Inc	Haverhill	MA	E	978 975-0502	11486
Worthington Assembly Inc	South Deerfield	MA	F	413 397-8265	15259
David Saunders Inc	South Portland	ME	E	207 228-1888	7021
Elscott Manufacturing LLC **(PA)**	Gouldsboro	ME	D	207 422-6747	6136
Enercon **(PA)**	Gray	ME	C	207 657-7000	6139
Enercon	Auburn	ME	E	207 657-7001	5562
Marja Corporation	Sanford	ME	F	207 324-2994	6882
Sanmina Corporation	Augusta	ME	D	207 623-6511	5618
Aci - Pcb Inc	Laconia	NH	G	603 528-7711	18551
Advanced Circuit Technolo	Nashua	NH	F	603 880-6000	19104
Amphenol Corporation	Nashua	NH	B	603 879-3000	19113
Amphenol Printed Circuits Inc	Nashua	NH	A	603 324-4500	19115
Anaren Ceramics Inc	Salem	NH	D	603 898-2883	19706
Benchmark Electronics Inc	Nashua	NH	B	603 879-7000	19126
Celestica LLC	Merrimack	NH	A	603 657-3000	18991
Circuit Express Inc	Derry	NH	G	603 537-9392	17976
Circuit Technology Inc	Merrimack	NH	D	603 424-2200	18992
Cirtronics Corporation	Milford	NH	C	603 249-9190	19049
Cogent Mfg Solutions LLC	Atkinson	NH	G	603 898-3212	17603
Colonial Electronic Mfrs Inc	Nashua	NH	E	603 881-8244	19136
Core Assemblies Inc	Gilford	NH	F	603 293-0270	18183
Custom Manufacturing Svcs Inc	Nashua	NH	E	603 883-1355	19141
Data Electronic Devices Inc	Salem	NH	C	603 893-2047	19720
Electronics Aid Inc	Marlborough	NH	G	603 876-4161	18959
Electropac Co Inc	Concord	NH	E	603 622-3711	17899
Eltek USA Inc	Manchester	NH	G	603 421-0020	18815
Ema Services Inc	Amherst	NH	E	978 251-4044	17559
Flex Technology Incorporated	Londonderry	NH	E	603 883-1500	18700
Guardian Technologies Inc	Nashua	NH	G	603 594-0430	19174
Hadco Corporation **(HQ)**	Salem	NH	B	603 421-3400	19741
Insulectro	Londonderry	NH	E	603 629-4403	18704
Manufacturing Services Group	Amherst	NH	F	603 883-1022	17572
Mass Design Inc **(PA)**	Nashua	NH	D	603 886-6460	19204
Mercury Systems Inc	Hudson	NH	C	603 883-2900	18414
Merrimack Micro LLC	Merrimack	NH	G	603 809-4183	19014
Metz Electronics Corp	Gilford	NH	E	603 524-8806	18191
Nashua Circuits Inc	Nashua	NH	E	603 882-1773	19212
Net Results In Cad Inc	Amherst	NH	G	603 249-9995	17578
Pd & E Electronics LLC	North Hampton	NH	G	603 964-3165	19386
Pica Mfg Solutions Inc	Derry	NH	E	603 845-3258	17993
Precision Placement Mchs Inc **(PA)**	Fremont	NH	F	603 895-5112	18179
Princeton Technology Corp	Hudson	NH	D	603 595-1987	18428
Qesidyne Inc	Hudson	NH	G	603 883-3116	18431
Retcomp Inc	New Boston	NH	E	603 487-5010	19297
Sanmina Corporation	Manchester	NH	C	603 621-1800	18914
Sonic Manufacturing Co Inc	Hudson	NH	E	603 882-1020	18438
Sparton Beckwood LLC	Plaistow	NH	D	603 382-3840	19524
Stellar Manufacturing Inc	Salem	NH	E	978 241-9537	19771
Test Msrment Instrmntation Inc	Nashua	NH	G	603 882-8610	19272
Two In One Manufacturing Inc	Nashua	NH	E	603 595-8212	19276
Varitron Technologies USA Inc	Hudson	NH	E	603 577-8855	18450
Wessmark NH LLC	Plaistow	NH	G	603 974-2932	19527
Ism Capital Corporation Ltd	East Providence	RI	G	401 454-8519	20421
Northeast Manufacturing Inc	Portsmouth	RI	G	401 683-2075	20934
Vr Industries Inc	Warwick	RI	E	401 732-6800	21440
Image Tek Mfg Inc	Springfield	VT	E	802 885-6208	22502
Purchasing & Inventory Cons	Windsor	VT	F	802 674-2620	22713

PRINTERS & PLOTTERS

	CITY	ST	EMP	PHONE	ENTRY #
Macdermid Incorporated **(HQ)**	Waterbury	CT	C	203 575-5700	4900
Red Rocket Site 2	Centerbrook	CT	G	860 581-8019	703
Transact Technologies Inc **(PA)**	Hamden	CT	C	203 859-6800	1791
Gforce Grafix Corporation	Leominster	MA	G	978 840-4401	12145
Imaging Data Corporation	Clinton	MA	G	978 365-9353	10081
Pt Plus At Whitney Field	Leominster	MA	G	978 534-5922	12178
Voxel8 Inc	Somerville	MA	F	916 396-3714	15229
Williams Lea Boston	Boston	MA	G	617 371-2300	8928

PRINTERS' SVCS: Folding, Collating, Etc

	CITY	ST	EMP	PHONE	ENTRY #
Xijet Corp	New Haven	CT	F	203 397-2800	2755
Arlington Swifty Printing Inc	Arlington	MA	G	781 646-8700	7623

PRINTERS: Computer

	CITY	ST	EMP	PHONE	ENTRY #
Alinabal Holdings Corporation **(PA)**	Milford	CT	B	203 877-3241	2243
Magnetec Corporation	Wallingford	CT	D	203 949-9933	4768
Omega Engineering Inc **(HQ)**	Norwalk	CT	C	203 359-1660	3211
Xijet Corp	New Haven	CT	F	203 397-2800	2755
Imaging Solutions & More	Chicopee	MA	G	413 331-4100	10031
Protech Digital Services LLC	Poland	ME	G	207 899-9237	6596
Extech Instruments Corporation	Nashua	NH	D	887 439-8324	19152
Fujifilm Dimatix Inc	Lebanon	NH	C	603 443-5300	18623
Astronova Inc **(PA)**	West Warwick	RI	B	401 828-4000	21479
Astronova Inc	West Warwick	RI	C	401 828-4000	21480
Marr Office Equipment Inc	Pawtucket	RI	G	401 725-5186	20856
Rwo Inc	Shelburne	VT	G	802 497-1563	22423

PRINTERS: Magnetic Ink, Bar Code

	CITY	ST	EMP	PHONE	ENTRY #
Yellowfin Holdings Inc	Ellington	CT	E	866 341-0979	1344

PRINTING & BINDING: Books

	CITY	ST	EMP	PHONE	ENTRY #
Ppc Books Ltd	Westport	CT	G	203 226-6644	5224
R R Donnelley & Sons Company	Manchester	CT	F	860 649-5570	2040
Dunn & Co Inc	Clinton	MA	C	978 368-8505	10080
Graphic Arts Repair	Braintree	MA	G	781 843-7954	9012
Lexington Press Inc	Lexington	MA	G	781 862-8900	12238

PRINTING & BINDING: Pamphlets

	CITY	ST	EMP	PHONE	ENTRY #
Red Sun Press Inc	Jamaica Plain	MA	F	617 524-6822	11949

PRINTING & ENGRAVING: Card, Exc Greeting

	CITY	ST	EMP	PHONE	ENTRY #
Cannelli Printing Co Inc	West Haven	CT	G	203 932-1719	5110
Shoreline Bus Solutions Inc **(DH)**	North Kingstown	RI	F	877 914-7856	20741

PRINTING & ENGRAVING: Financial Notes & Certificates

	CITY	ST	EMP	PHONE	ENTRY #
Financial Graphic Services Inc	Braintree	MA	F	617 389-0076	9007
R R Donnelley & Sons Company	Boston	MA	D	617 345-4300	8806

PRINTING & ENGRAVING: Invitation & Stationery

	CITY	ST	EMP	PHONE	ENTRY #
Ideas Inc	Milford	CT	G	203 878-9686	2299
Master Engrv & Printery Inc **(PA)**	Waterbury	CT	G	203 723-2779	4911
Designs By Lainie	Lynn	MA	G	781 592-2126	12502
Papers & Presents	Wellesley Hills	MA	G	781 235-1079	16399
Evergreen Custom Printing Inc	Auburn	ME	G	207 782-2327	5563

PRINTING & ENGRAVING: Poster & Decal

	CITY	ST	EMP	PHONE	ENTRY #
Popcorn Movie Poster Co LLC	East Hartford	CT	F	860 610-0000	1211

PRINTING & ENGRAVING: Rolls, Textile Printing

	CITY	ST	EMP	PHONE	ENTRY #
Art Swiss Corporation	New Bedford	MA	F	508 999-3281	13359

PRINTING & STAMPING: Fabric Articles

	CITY	ST	EMP	PHONE	ENTRY #
Ace Finishing Co LLC	Bristol	CT	G	860 582-4600	513
Bennettsville Holdings LLC	Hebron	CT	D	860 444-9400	1895
Rainbow Graphics Inc	Manchester	CT	G	860 646-8997	2042
Industrial Lbling Systems Corp	Tyngsboro	MA	E	978 649-7004	15890
Swan Dyeing and Printing Corp	Fall River	MA	D	508 674-4611	10766

PRINTING & WRITING PAPER WHOLESALERS

	CITY	ST	EMP	PHONE	ENTRY #
Hartford Toner & Cartridge Inc **(PA)**	Broad Brook	CT	G	860 292-1280	629
Wallingford Prtg Bus Forms Inc	Branford	CT	F	203 481-1911	359
Vemuri International LLC	Pawtucket	RI	G	401 723-4200	20910
Precision Print and Copy Inc	Vergennes	VT	G	802 877-3711	22555

PRINTING INKS WHOLESALERS

	CITY	ST	EMP	PHONE	ENTRY #
Hartford Toner & Cartridge Inc **(PA)**	Broad Brook	CT	G	860 292-1280	629
Creative Imprints Inc	Norton	MA	E	508 285-7650	14074

PRINTING MACHINERY

	CITY	ST	EMP	PHONE	ENTRY #
I Q Technology LLC	Enfield	CT	F	860 749-7255	1365
Interpro LLC	Deep River	CT	F	860 526-5869	1062
J-Teck Usa Inc	Danbury	CT	G	203 791-2121	938
Santec Corporation	Milford	CT	F	203 878-1379	2359
2l Inc	Hudson	MA	F	978 567-8867	11748
Armstrong Machine Co Inc	Beverly	MA	F	978 232-9466	8102
Art Swiss Corporation	New Bedford	MA	F	508 999-3281	13359
Butler Automatic Inc **(PA)**	Middleboro	MA	D	508 923-0544	13057
Ecrm Incorporated **(PA)**	North Andover	MA	D	800 537-3276	13700
Gillies W Technologies LLC	Worcester	MA	G	508 852-2502	17382
Inkbit LLC	Medford	MA	G	617 433-8842	12936
Integrated Web Finishing Syst	Avon	MA	E	508 580-5809	7887
Jaf Corporation	Webster	MA	G	508 943-8519	16344
Jet Graphics LLC	Avon	MA	E	508 580-5809	7889
Jnj Industries Inc	Franklin	MA	E	508 553-0529	11058
Milara Inc	Milford	MA	D	508 533-5322	13127
Rotation Dynamics Corporation	Marlborough	MA	F	508 481-0900	12822
Rudison Routhier Engrg Co	West Hatfield	MA	G	413 247-9341	16485

	CITY	ST	EMP	PHONE	ENTRY #
Signature Engrv Systems Inc	Holyoke	MA	E	413 533-7500	11657
Teca-Print USA Corp	Winchester	MA	F	781 369-1084	17098
Tooling Research Inc **(PA)**	Walpole	MA	F	508 668-1950	16014
Transition Automation Inc	North Billerica	MA	F	978 670-5500	13874
Verico Technology LLC	South Hadley	MA	C	413 539-9111	15312
Westcon Mfg Inc	Brunswick	ME	E	207 725-5537	5851
Cc1 Inc	Portsmouth	NH	E	603 319-2000	19548
Electronics For Imaging Inc	West Lebanon	NH	B	603 279-6800	19949
Prodways	Merrimack	NH	G	763 568-7966	19024
Eagle Industries Inc	Ashaway	RI	E	401 596-8111	20033
Imprint Inc	Greenville	RI	G	401 949-1177	20468
Press Tech Company Inc	Ashaway	RI	G	401 377-4800	20039
R & D Technologies Inc	North Kingstown	RI	F	401 885-6400	20734
Richard Chiovitti	Greenville	RI	G	401 949-1177	20474

PRINTING MACHINERY, EQPT & SPLYS: Wholesalers

	CITY	ST	EMP	PHONE	ENTRY #
Colors Ink	Wallingford	CT	G	203 269-4000	4722
Imprint Inc	Greenville	RI	G	401 949-1177	20468
Richard Chiovitti	Greenville	RI	G	401 949-1177	20474

PRINTING TRADES MACHINERY & EQPT REPAIR SVCS

	CITY	ST	EMP	PHONE	ENTRY #
Manroland Goss Web Systems AMR **(DH)**	Durham	NH	B	603 750-6600	18078
Imprint Inc	Greenville	RI	G	401 949-1177	20468
Richard Chiovitti	Greenville	RI	G	401 949-1177	20474

PRINTING, COMMERCIAL Newspapers, NEC

	CITY	ST	EMP	PHONE	ENTRY #
Gatehouse Media Mass I Inc	Sharon	MA	C	781 487-7200	15050
La Semana Newspaper	Boston	MA	G	617 427-6212	8658
Telegraph Publishing Company **(HQ)**	Nashua	NH	C	603 594-6472	19271

PRINTING, COMMERCIAL: Bags, Plastic, NEC

	CITY	ST	EMP	PHONE	ENTRY #
Package Printing Company Inc	West Springfield	MA	E	413 736-2748	16539

PRINTING, COMMERCIAL: Business Forms, NEC

	CITY	ST	EMP	PHONE	ENTRY #
Mlk Business Forms Inc	New Haven	CT	F	203 624-6304	2712
New Fairfield Press Inc	New Fairfield	CT	F	203 746-2700	2626
Brady Business Forms Inc	Lowell	MA	G	978 458-2585	12355
Massachusetts Envelope Co Inc **(PA)**	Somerville	MA	E	617 623-8000	15195
New England Business Svc Inc **(HQ)**	Groton	MA	D	978 448-6111	11291
Peter Young Company	Watertown	MA	G	617 923-1101	16306
Regal Press Incorporated **(PA)**	Norwood	MA	C	781 769-3900	14192
JS McCarthy Co Inc **(PA)**	Augusta	ME	D	207 622-6241	5609
Precision Direct Inc	Portland	ME	G	207 321-3677	6715
Argyle Associates Inc	Concord	NH	E	603 226-4300	17883
Bank & Business Forms Inc	Keene	NH	G	603 357-0567	18495
Taylor Communications Inc	Warwick	RI	G	401 738-0257	21435
Eastern Systems Inc **(PA)**	Waitsfield	VT	G	802 496-1000	22565

PRINTING, COMMERCIAL: Calendars, NEC

	CITY	ST	EMP	PHONE	ENTRY #
Ad-A-Day Company Inc	Taunton	MA	E	508 824-8676	15719
Leap Year Publishing LLC	North Andover	MA	F	978 688-9900	13717
Wholesale Printing Inc	Woburn	MA	F	781 937-3357	17319

PRINTING, COMMERCIAL: Cards, Visiting, Incl Business, NEC

	CITY	ST	EMP	PHONE	ENTRY #
Full Court Press	Westbrook	ME	F	207 464-0002	7189
Acara Holdings LLC	Concord	NH	F	603 434-3175	17879
CB Ventures LLC	Concord	NH	F	603 434-3175	17891

PRINTING, COMMERCIAL: Coupons, NEC

	CITY	ST	EMP	PHONE	ENTRY #
Economy Coupon & Printing Inc	Peabody	MA	G	781 279-8555	14332

PRINTING, COMMERCIAL: Decals, NEC

	CITY	ST	EMP	PHONE	ENTRY #
Eastern Etching and Mfg Co	Chicopee	MA	E	413 594-6601	10022

PRINTING, COMMERCIAL: Envelopes, NEC

	CITY	ST	EMP	PHONE	ENTRY #
Envelopes & More Inc	Newington	CT	F	860 286-7570	2862
Patriot Envelope LLC	Wethersfield	CT	G	860 529-1553	5260
Bay State Envelope Inc **(PA)**	Mansfield	MA	E	508 337-8900	12614
Classic Envelope Inc	East Douglas	MA	D	508 731-6747	10425
Quality Envelope & Printing Co	Middleboro	MA	G	508 947-8878	13077
Yankee Printing Group Inc	South Hadley	MA	E	413 532-9513	15313
Jet Service Envelope Co Inc **(PA)**	Barre	VT	F	802 229-9335	21626

PRINTING, COMMERCIAL: Imprinting

	CITY	ST	EMP	PHONE	ENTRY #
L P Macadams Company Inc	Bridgeport	CT	D	203 366-3647	442
Union Bookbinding Company Inc **(PA)**	Fall River	MA	E	508 676-8580	10775
Blue Sky Inc	Portland	ME	G	207 772-0073	6625

PRINTING, COMMERCIAL: Invitations, NEC

	CITY	ST	EMP	PHONE	ENTRY #
Ludlow Printing and Copy Ctr	Ludlow	MA	G	413 583-5220	12472
Northeast Publishing Company	Dover Foxcroft	ME	G	207 564-8355	5961
Hopkins Press	North Providence	RI	G	401 231-9654	20764
N-M Letters Inc	Barrington	RI	G	401 245-5565	20048

PRINTING, COMMERCIAL: Labels & Seals, NEC

	CITY	ST	EMP	PHONE	ENTRY #
Ad Label Inc	Brooklyn	CT	G	860 779-0513	669
Ansel Label and Packaging Corp	Trumbull	CT	E	203 452-0311	4612
CCL Label (delaware) Inc **(DH)**	Shelton	CT	G	203 926-1253	3787
Design Label Manufacturing Inc **(PA)**	Old Lyme	CT	E	860 739-6266	3321
Schmitt Realty Holdings Inc	Guilford	CT	G	203 453-4334	1719
Specialty Printing LLC **(PA)**	East Windsor	CT	D	860 623-8870	1303
Surys Inc	Trumbull	CT	C	203 333-5503	4633
Gloucester Graphics Inc **(PA)**	Gloucester	MA	F	978 281-4500	11188
Inovar Packaging Group LLC	Newburyport	MA	E	978 463-4004	13501
Label Haus Inc	Danvers	MA	G	978 777-1773	10230
Labelprint America Inc	Newburyport	MA	E	978 463-4004	13506
Reid Graphics Inc	Andover	MA	D	978 474-1930	7598
Royal Label Co Inc	Boston	MA	F	617 825-6050	8828
University of Massachusetts	Amherst	MA	F	413 545-2718	7531
Computype Inc	Concord	NH	F	603 225-5500	17894
Electronic Imaging Mtls Inc	Keene	NH	E	603 357-1459	18501
Megaprint Inc	Holderness	NH	F	603 536-2900	18323
U S Product Labels Inc	Salem	NH	G	603 894-6020	19774
Graphic Application Tech Inc	North Providence	RI	G	401 233-2100	20763
Multi-Color Corporation	North Kingstown	RI	C	401 884-7100	20729

PRINTING, COMMERCIAL: Letterpress & Screen

	CITY	ST	EMP	PHONE	ENTRY #
All American Embroidery Inc	Wilmington	MA	G	978 657-0414	16970
Morgan Enterprises Inc	Worcester	MA	G	985 377-3216	17424
Printed Matter Inc	Newfields	NH	E	603 778-2990	19318

PRINTING, COMMERCIAL: Literature, Advertising, NEC

	CITY	ST	EMP	PHONE	ENTRY #
R R Donnelley & Sons Company	Avon	CT	E	860 773-6140	43
Diversity Studio Inc	Littleton	MA	G	978 250-5553	12303
Washington ABC Imaging Inc	Boston	MA	D	857 753-4241	8916
Erin Murphy	Windham	ME	G	928 525-2056	7232

PRINTING, COMMERCIAL: Magazines, NEC

	CITY	ST	EMP	PHONE	ENTRY #
Lrp Conferences LLC	Trumbull	CT	E	203 663-0100	4627
Trimed Media Group Inc	Providence	RI	F	401 919-5165	21141

PRINTING, COMMERCIAL: Menus, NEC

	CITY	ST	EMP	PHONE	ENTRY #
BBC Printing and Products Inc	Waltham	MA	G	781 647-4646	16042

PRINTING, COMMERCIAL: Periodicals, NEC

	CITY	ST	EMP	PHONE	ENTRY #
Omega Engineering Inc **(HQ)**	Norwalk	CT	C	203 359-1660	3211
Puritan Press Inc **(PA)**	Hollis	NH	E	603 889-4500	18339
The Lane Press Inc	South Burlington	VT	C	802 863-5555	22471

PRINTING, COMMERCIAL: Promotional

	CITY	ST	EMP	PHONE	ENTRY #
Kramer Printing Company Inc	West Haven	CT	F	203 933-5416	5129
Prime Resources Corp	Bridgeport	CT	B	203 331-9100	474
Billard Corporation	Sandwich	MA	G	508 888-4964	14961
Campaignsthatwincom LLC	Worcester	MA	G	508 667-6365	17353
Data Associates Business Trust	Waltham	MA	E	781 890-0110	16079
George R King	Raynham	MA	G	508 821-3826	14715
Integrity Graphics LLC	Randolph	MA	G	339 987-5533	14688
Northpoint Printing Svcs Inc	Waltham	MA	F	781 895-1900	16161
Nova Idea Inc	Woburn	MA	G	781 281-2183	17246
Optamark LLC **(PA)**	North Attleboro	MA	G	508 643-1017	13770
D R Designs Inc	Manchester	ME	G	207 622-3303	6409
Trems Inc	Rockland	ME	G	207 596-6989	6812
AMI Graphics Inc **(PA)**	Strafford	NH	D	603 664-7174	19865
Forward Merch LLC	Dover	NH	G	603 742-4377	18022
Rgm Enterprises Inc	Manchester	NH	G	603 644-3336	18911
J Mack Studios LLC	Westerly	RI	G	401 932-8600	21528

PRINTING, COMMERCIAL: Publications

	CITY	ST	EMP	PHONE	ENTRY #
Bayard Inc **(DH)**	New London	CT	E	860 437-3012	2765
Desk Top Solutions Inc	Waltham	MA	F	781 890-7500	16086
John Brown US LLC	Boston	MA	F	617 449-4354	8632
Journal of Antq & Collectibles	Sturbridge	MA	F	508 347-1960	15639
East Shore Production	Portland	ME	G	207 775-5353	6657
James Newspapers Inc	Rumford	ME	G	207 364-7893	6836
Shoreline Publications	Wells	ME	F	207 646-8448	7165
Lighthouse Publications	Bristol	RI	G	401 396-9888	20090
National Cthlic Bthics Ctr Inc	Barrington	RI	G	401 289-0680	20049

PRINTING, COMMERCIAL: Screen

	CITY	ST	EMP	PHONE	ENTRY #
Accent Screenprinting	Wallingford	CT	G	203 284-8601	4693
Advanced Graphics Inc	Stratford	CT	E	203 378-0471	4388
American Silk Screening LLC	Berlin	CT	G	860 828-5486	71
American Stitch & Print Inc	North Haven	CT	G	203 239-5383	3006
B T S Graphics LLC	Oakville	CT	G	860 274-6422	3296
Bl Printing Shop	Bridgeport	CT	G	203 334-7779	383
Colorgraphix LLC	Oxford	CT	G	203 264-5212	3397
Concordia Ltd	North Branford	CT	G	203 483-0221	2960
Custom Tees Plus	New Haven	CT	E	203 752-1071	2681
Custom TS n More LLC	Ridgefield	CT	G	203 438-1592	3665
ECI Screen Print Inc	Watertown	CT	F	860 283-9849	5008
Ever Ready Press	Ansonia	CT	G	203 734-5157	14
Falcon Press	Enfield	CT	G	860 763-2293	1362
Integrated Print Solutions Inc	Bridgeport	CT	F	203 330-0200	431
Iovino Bros Sporting Goods	Danbury	CT	G	203 790-5966	934
Jb Muze Enterprises	New Milford	CT	G	860 355-5949	2807
Keno Graphic Services Inc	Shelton	CT	E	203 925-7722	3822
Liberty Screen Print Co LLC	Beacon Falls	CT	F	203 632-5449	60
Logo Sportswear Inc	Wallingford	CT	G	203 678-4700	4767
Lorenco Industries Inc	Bethel	CT	F	203 743-6962	169
Mad Sportswear LLC	West Haven	CT	G	203 932-4868	5133
Multiprints Inc	Meriden	CT	F	203 235-4409	2111
Novel Tees Screen Prtg EMB LLC	Manchester	CT	F	860 643-6008	2026
Novel-Tees Unlimited LLC	Manchester	CT	G	860 643-6008	2027
On Time Screen Printing & Embr	Derby	CT	F	203 874-4581	1076
Production Decorating Co Inc	Waterbury	CT	E	203 574-2975	4946
Quality Name Plate Inc	East Glastonbury	CT	D	860 633-9495	1114
R & B Apparel Plus LLC	Groton	CT	G	860 333-1757	1685
Shirt Graphix	Wallingford	CT	G	203 294-1656	4805
Signs Now LLC	Newington	CT	G	860 667-8339	2903
Silkscreen Plus LLC	Wolcott	CT	G	203 879-0345	5460
Special Events Screen Prtg LLC	East Haven	CT	G	203 468-5453	1263
Sportees LLC	Waterford	CT	G	860 440-3922	4994
Tee-It-Up LLC	Wallingford	CT	G	203 949-9455	4816
Tees Plus	Bridgeport	CT	F	800 782-8337	499

	CITY	ST	EMP	PHONE	ENTRY #
Varsity Imprints	Milford	CT	G	203 354-4371	2379
Vision Designs LLC	Brookfield	CT	F	203 778-9898	664
Yankee Screen Printing	Derby	CT	G	203 924-9926	1085
508tees Screenprinting	Acushnet	MA	G	508 717-3835	7396
Agawam Novelty Company Inc	Agawam	MA	G	413 536-0471	7418
Albert Basse Associates Inc	Stoughton	MA	E	781 344-3555	15577
All City Screen Printing Inc	Wakefield	MA	G	781 665-0000	15940
Alternative Screen Printing	Topsfield	MA	F	978 887-9927	15853
Applied Graphics Inc	Amesbury	MA	E	978 241-5300	7478
Art Shirt Co	Somerville	MA	G	617 625-2636	15157
Avon Cstm EMB & Screenprinting	Avon	MA	F	781 341-4663	7878
Basement Designs Inc	Oak Bluffs	MA	G	508 693-4442	14209
Bltees	Palmer	MA	G	413 289-0050	14281
Boostercom	Auburndale	MA	G	855 631-6850	7857
Byd Corp	Everett	MA	G	617 394-0799	10605
Comdec Incorporated	Newburyport	MA	E	978 462-3399	13478
Custom Quality Silk Screen	Rockland	MA	G	781 878-0760	14797
Diehl Graphics Co	Winchendon	MA	G	978 297-1598	17074
Elegant Stitches Inc	Pittsfield	MA	G	413 447-9452	14469
Em Screen Systems Inc	Millbury	MA	G	508 865-9995	13163
Four Seasons Trattoria Inc	South Yarmouth	MA	G	508 760-6600	15329
G & G Silk Screening	Plymouth	MA	G	508 830-1075	14559
Guertin Graphics & Awards Inc	Worcester	MA	F	508 754-0200	17386
Hendrickson Advertising Inc	Sterling	MA	G	978 422-8087	15539
Hercules Press	Boston	MA	G	617 323-1950	8596
Highland Press of Athol Inc	Athol	MA	G	978 249-6588	7687
I N I Screen Printing	New Bedford	MA	G	774 206-1341	13396
Image Factory	Pocasset	MA	G	508 295-3876	14598
Image Resolutions Inc	Norwell	MA	G	781 659-0900	14104
Industrial Etching Inc	East Longmeadow	MA	F	413 525-4110	10479
Inkify LLC	Walpole	MA	G	617 304-6642	15994
Itg Group Inc	Medway	MA	G	508 645-4994	12962
J & S Business Products Inc	Ayer	MA	G	877 425-4049	7922
Jackiestees	Beverly	MA	G	617 799-8404	8143
L & J Screen Printers Inc	Worcester	MA	G	508 791-7320	17404
Liberated Images Inc	Peabody	MA	G	978 532-1880	14352
Lisa Signs Inc	Woburn	MA	G	781 935-1821	17215
Lopesdzine	West Bridgewater	MA	G	508 857-0121	16443
M & R Screen Printing Inc	New Bedford	MA	E	508 996-0419	13412
Moonlight Ltd	Brockton	MA	G	508 584-0094	9168
New Tek Design Group Inc	West Boylston	MA	F	508 835-4544	16423
Old School Apparel	Saugus	MA	G	781 231-0753	14993
One Off Apparel Inc	West Boylston	MA	G	508 835-8883	16424
Optimum Sportswear Inc	Lawrence	MA	G	978 689-2290	12069
Pacific Printing Inc	Northampton	MA	G	413 585-5700	14016
Poputees Co	Blackstone	MA	G	401 497-6512	8314
Power Graphics Printing	Tewksbury	MA	G	978 851-8988	15827
Primary Graphics Corporation	Taunton	MA	F	781 575-0411	15773
Print Shop	Williamstown	MA	G	413 458-6039	16959
Printpro Silkscreen & EMB	Haverhill	MA	F	978 556-1695	11461
Pros Choice Inc	Agawam	MA	F	413 583-3435	7448
Puffer International Inc	Westfield	MA	G	413 527-1069	16720
Qrsts LLC	Somerville	MA	G	617 625-3335	15208
Quick Stop Printing	Worcester	MA	G	508 797-4788	17448
Red Mill Graphics Incorporated	Chelmsford	MA	F	978 251-4081	9926
S & S Computer Imaging Inc	Holyoke	MA	G	413 536-0117	11655
Sanchez Octavio Storage	Worcester	MA	G	508 853-3309	17468
Scrimshaw Screenprinting	New Bedford	MA	G	508 617-7498	13447
Silver Screen Design Inc	Greenfield	MA	F	413 773-1692	11275
Smudge Ink Incorporated	Charlestown	MA	G	617 242-8228	9844
Steves Sports	West Springfield	MA	G	413 746-1696	16553
Super Sport Screen Printing	Malden	MA	G	781 397-8166	12599
Techprint Inc	Lawrence	MA	D	978 975-1245	12077
Teesmile Inc	Burlington	MA	G	781 325-8587	9343
Three Jakes	Plymouth	MA	G	781 706-6886	14588
Three Twins Productions Inc	Watertown	MA	F	617 926-0377	16323
Triad Designs	Groton	MA	G	978 952-0136	11296
Viridis3d LLC	Woburn	MA	G	781 305-4961	17313
Whaling City Graphics Inc	Acushnet	MA	G	508 998-3511	7407
White Dog Printing Inc	Gardner	MA	G	978 630-1091	11133
Wish Designs Inc **(PA)**	Lawrence	MA	F	978 566-1232	12084
Yblank	Cambridge	MA	G	857 544-9991	9708
Action Screen Printing	Lewiston	ME	G	207 795-7786	6272
Adept Screen Prtg & Graphics	Lisbon Falls	ME	G	207 353-6094	6366
Andys Silkscreen	Bingham	ME	G	207 672-3302	5769
Artforms **(PA)**	Brunswick	ME	E	800 828-8518	5829
Atlantic Sportswear Inc	Portland	ME	E	207 797-5028	6612
Black Bear Graphics	Kingfield	ME	G	207 265-4593	6252
Black Bear Graphics Inc	Farmington	ME	G	207 778-9715	6041
Black Dog Screen Printing	Clinton	ME	G	207 426-9041	5913
Brady Screenprint Inc	Biddeford	ME	G	207 284-8531	5723
Coastal T Shirts Inc	Auburn	ME	G	207 784-4184	5553
Gossamer Press	Old Town	ME	G	207 827-9881	6539
Graphic Explosion Inc	Lewiston	ME	G	207 576-3210	6289
Identity Group Holdings Corp	Brunswick	ME	E	207 510-6800	5837
Island Approaches Inc	Sunset	ME	F	207 348-2459	7075
Liberty Graphics Inc	Liberty	ME	E	207 589-4596	6331
Lts Inc	Portland	ME	E	207 774-1104	6680
Port City Graphics Inc	Gorham	ME	G	207 450-6299	6127
Seastreet Graphics	Thomaston	ME	G	207 594-1915	7088
Tranquilitees	Augusta	ME	G	207 441-8058	5622
W S Emerson Company Inc **(PA)**	Brewer	ME	E	207 989-3410	5803
Woodland Studios Inc	Ellsworth	ME	F	207 667-3286	6024
Xtreme Screen & Sportswear LLC	Westbrook	ME	G	207 857-9200	7215
603 Screenprinting LLC	Salem	NH	G	603 505-7693	19702
All Seasons Printing & Awards	Pelham	NH	G	603 881-7106	19427

	CITY	ST	EMP	PHONE	ENTRY #
Bovie Screen Process Prtg Inc	Bow	NH	E	603 224-0651	17708
C K Productions Inc	Pelham	NH	E	603 893-5069	19429
Embrodery By Evrything Per LLC	Littleton	NH	G	603 444-0130	18658
Jembow Inc	Bow	NH	G	603 774-6055	17717
Lamprey River Screen Print	Newmarket	NH	G	603 659-9959	19336
Left-Tees Designs Bayou LLC	Derry	NH	F	603 437-6630	17986
Life Is Good **(PA)**	Hudson	NH	D	603 594-6100	18411
Loudon Screen Printing Inc	Epsom	NH	G	603 736-9420	18106
Northeast Silk Screen Inc	Nashua	NH	G	603 883-6933	19220
Northstar Direct LLC	Manchester	NH	F	603 627-3334	18888
Phoenix Screen Printing	Nashua	NH	F	603 578-9599	19233
Piches Ski Shop Inc	Belmont	NH	F	603 524-4413	17680
Red Brick Clothing Co	Hudson	NH	G	603 882-4100	18433
Savvy Workshop	Manchester	NH	G	603 792-0080	18916
Say It In Stitches Inc	Concord	NH	G	603 224-6470	17927
Screen Gems Inc	Seabrook	NH	F	603 474-5353	19815
Seacoast Screen Printing	Newmarket	NH	G	603 758-6398	19341
Sherwin Dodge Printers Inc	Littleton	NH	F	603 444-6552	18666
Spear USA Inc	Milford	NH	G	513 459-1100	19079
Spectrum Marketing Dbalogo Loc	Manchester	NH	G	603 644-4800	18928
Suleys Soccer Center	Manchester	NH	G	603 668-7227	18931
Tl Sports Sales Inc	Windham	NH	G	603 577-1931	20012
Vantastic Inc	Laconia	NH	G	603 524-1419	18591
American Trophy & Supply Co	East Providence	RI	G	401 438-3060	20386
Branding Company Inc	Westerly	RI	G	203 793-1923	21518
Cool Air Creations Inc	Smithfield	RI	E	401 830-5780	21216
Graphic Ink Incorporated	East Providence	RI	F	401 431-5081	20415
Griswold Textile Print Inc	Westerly	RI	E	401 596-2784	21525
Hilco Athletic & Graphics Inc	West Warwick	RI	F	401 822-1775	21495
Image Printing & Copying Inc	Warwick	RI	F	401 737-9311	21374
K&M/Nordic Co Inc	Riverside	RI	E	401 431-5150	21171
Moonlite Graphics Co Inc	Little Compton	RI	G	401 635-2962	20606
Park Printers	Pawtucket	RI	G	401 728-8650	20874
Quality Printing Services Inc	Rumford	RI	G	401 434-4321	21194
Schofield Printing Inc	Pawtucket	RI	E	401 728-6980	20898
Swg Promotions LLC	Providence	RI	G	401 272-6050	21130
Amalgamated Culture Work Inc **(PA)**	Burlington	VT	G	800 272-2066	21766
Bruso-Holmes Inc	Essex Junction	VT	G	802 878-8337	21934
Bumwraps Inc **(PA)**	Montgomery Center	VT	G	802 326-4080	22141
Bumwraps Inc	Newport	VT	G	802 326-4080	22190
Graphic Edge Inc	Rutland	VT	E	802 855-8840	22336
Mitchell Tees & Signs Inc	Pittsford	VT	G	802 483-6866	22264
Squeegee Printers Inc	Canaan	VT	G	802 266-3426	21825
Vermont Flannel Co	Woodstock	VT	G	802 457-4111	22740

PRINTING, COMMERCIAL: Stationery, NEC

Faux Designs	Auburndale	MA	F	617 965-0142	7861

PRINTING, COMMERCIAL: Tags, NEC

Bell Manufacturing Co	Lewiston	ME	D	207 784-2961	6276
Foxon Company	Providence	RI	E	401 421-2386	21015

PRINTING, COMMERCIAL: Tickets, NEC

Interticketcom Inc **(PA)**	Bedford	MA	G	781 275-5724	7984

PRINTING, LITHOGRAPHIC: Calendars

Ziga Media LLC	Darien	CT	G	203 656-0076	1037
Photographic Corp New England	Concord	MA	G	978 369-3002	10150

PRINTING, LITHOGRAPHIC: Calendars & Cards

Ready4 Print LLC	Bridgeport	CT	G	203 345-0376	480

PRINTING, LITHOGRAPHIC: Catalogs

LPI Printing and Graphic Inc	Stoneham	MA	E	781 438-5400	15566

PRINTING, LITHOGRAPHIC: Color

Universal Business Forms Inc	Worcester	MA	G	508 852-5520	17495
Sunrise Printing & Graphics	Windham	ME	G	207 892-3534	7255
Independent Color Press LLC	Rochester	NH	G	603 539-5959	19672

PRINTING, LITHOGRAPHIC: Decals

E V Yeuell Inc	Woburn	MA	E	781 933-2984	17171
Eastern Etching and Mfg Co	Chicopee	MA	E	413 594-6601	10022

PRINTING, LITHOGRAPHIC: Forms & Cards, Business

Narragansett Bus Forms Inc	East Providence	RI	E	401 331-2000	20434

PRINTING, LITHOGRAPHIC: Forms, Business

Inform Inc	Shelton	CT	G	203 924-9929	3818

PRINTING, LITHOGRAPHIC: Offset & photolithographic printing

Macdermid Incorporated **(HQ)**	Waterbury	CT	C	203 575-5700	4900
Jam Plastics Inc	Leominster	MA	E	978 537-2570	12156
Mbf Printing	Holliston	MA	G	774 233-0337	11583
Optamark LLC **(PA)**	North Attleboro	MA	G	508 643-1017	13770
Print Management Systems Inc	Woburn	MA	F	781 944-1041	17270

PRINTING, LITHOGRAPHIC: On Metal

Colonial Lithograph Inc	Attleboro	MA	F	508 222-1832	7722
J Joy Associates Inc	Rockland	MA	G	781 871-1569	14810
Maximus	Lowell	MA	G	978 728-8000	12404
Penmor Lithographers Inc	Lewiston	ME	E	207 784-1341	6316

PRINTING, LITHOGRAPHIC: Promotional

B N M Printing & Promotion	Boston	MA	G	617 464-1120	8387
Economy Coupon & Printing Inc	Peabody	MA	G	781 279-8555	14332

PRINTING, LITHOGRAPHIC: Publications

	CITY	ST	EMP	PHONE	ENTRY #
Arcat Inc	Fairfield	CT	G	203 929-9444	1414

PRINTING, LITHOGRAPHIC: Transfers, Decalcomania Or Dry

	CITY	ST	EMP	PHONE	ENTRY #
Brn Corporation	Campton	NH	G	603 726-3800	17775

PRINTING: Books

	CITY	ST	EMP	PHONE	ENTRY #
Center Point Inc	Knox	ME	E	207 568-3717	6262
Kensington Group Incorporated	Hampton Falls	NH	F	603 926-6742	18283

PRINTING: Books

	CITY	ST	EMP	PHONE	ENTRY #
Baikar Association Inc **(PA)**	Watertown	MA	F	617 924-4420	16271
Book-Mart Press Inc	North Chelmsford	MA	D	978 251-6000	13886
Channing Bete Company Inc **(PA)**	South Deerfield	MA	B	413 665-7611	15247
Courier Companies Inc **(PA)**	North Chelmsford	MA	E	978 251-6000	13888
Courier Intl Holdings LLC	North Chelmsford	MA	G	978 251-6000	13889
Courier New Media Inc **(DH)**	North Chelmsford	MA	E	978 251-3945	13890
Lsc Communications Inc	North Chelmsford	MA	D	978 251-6000	13902
J Weston Walch Publisher	Portland	ME	E	207 772-2846	6676
Mass Web Printing Company Inc	Providence	RI	D	508 832-5317	21062

PRINTING: Checkbooks

	CITY	ST	EMP	PHONE	ENTRY #
Deluxe Corporation	Townsend	MA	C	978 597-8715	15871
Laser Laser Inc	West Roxbury	MA	G	617 615-2292	16498
Rosencrntz Gldnstern Banknotes	Wilton	NH	F	603 654-6160	19986
Check Mate Service Line LLC	Smithfield	RI	G	401 231-7296	21215

PRINTING: Commercial, NEC

	CITY	ST	EMP	PHONE	ENTRY #
Acme Typesetting Service Co	West Hartford	CT	G	860 953-1470	5052
Allied Printing Services Inc **(PA)**	Manchester	CT	B	860 643-1101	1984
American Banknote Corporation **(PA)**	Stamford	CT	G	203 941-4090	4135
Amgraph Packaging Inc	Baltic	CT	C	860 822-2000	48
AZ Copy Center Inc	Southington	CT	G	860 621-7325	4040
B-P Products Inc	Hamden	CT	E	203 288-0200	1733
Bardell Printing Corp	East Haven	CT	G	203 469-2441	1242
Biz Wiz Print & Copy Ctr LLC **(PA)**	Rocky Hill	CT	G	860 721-0040	3704
Bread and Wine Publishing LLC	Manchester	CT	G	860 649-3109	1989
Christopher Condors	Norwalk	CT	G	203 852-8181	3124
Classic Label Inc	Woodbridge	CT	G	203 389-3535	5466
Creative Envelope Inc	Putnam	CT	G	860 963-1231	3609
Diversified Printing Solutions	Danbury	CT	G	203 826-7198	902
Doctor Stuff LLC	Wallingford	CT	G	203 785-8475	4735
Eastwood Printing Inc	Wethersfield	CT	F	860 529-6673	5248
Elm Press Incorporated	Terryville	CT	E	860 583-3600	4477
Executive Greetings Inc **(HQ)**	New Hartford	CT	B	860 379-9911	2636
Executive Office Services Inc	Bridgeport	CT	E	203 373-1333	411
G & R Enterprises Incorporated	Hartford	CT	G	860 549-6120	1822
Gateway Digital Inc	Norwalk	CT	F	203 853-4929	3157
Hat Trick Graphics LLC	Danbury	CT	G	203 748-1128	930
Hw Graphics	Windsor	CT	G	860 278-2338	5339
Image One Prtg & Graphics Inc	Monroe	CT	G	203 459-1880	2404
Imperial Grphic Cmmnctions Inc	Milford	CT	E	203 650-3478	2301
International Comm Svcs Inc	Guilford	CT	G	401 580-8888	1706
JMS Graphics Inc	Middlebury	CT	G	203 598-7555	2155
Joyce Printers Inc	Woodbridge	CT	G	203 389-4452	5469
Kool Ink LLC	Bloomfield	CT	F	860 242-0303	238
L R K Communications Inc	Fairfield	CT	G	203 372-1456	1441
McWeeney Marketing Group Inc	Orange	CT	G	203 891-8100	3373
Merrill Corporation	Hartford	CT	D	860 249-7220	1846
Mickey Herbst	Fairfield	CT	G	203 993-5879	1444
Moonlight Media LLC	Haddam	CT	G	860 345-3595	1727
Muir Envelope Plus Inc	Newington	CT	F	860 953-6847	2884
New England Printing LLC	Enfield	CT	G	860 745-3600	1372
Paul Dewitt	Danbury	CT	F	203 792-5610	965
Platt Brothers Realty II LLC	New Haven	CT	G	203 562-5112	2727
Print & Post Services	Bridgeport	CT	G	203 336-0055	475
Print Shop of Wolcott LLC	Wolcott	CT	G	203 879-3353	5453
Print Source Ltd	Milford	CT	G	203 876-1822	2341
Psd Inc	East Haven	CT	G	860 305-6346	1259
R R Donnelley & Sons Company	Manchester	CT	F	860 649-5570	2040
Rainbow Graphics Inc	Manchester	CT	G	860 646-8997	2042
Robert Audette **(PA)**	Cheshire	CT	G	203 872-3119	760
Roto-Die Company Inc	East Windsor	CT	F	860 292-7030	1300
Saybrook Press Incorporated	Guilford	CT	F	203 458-3637	1717
Schmitt Realty Holdings Inc **(PA)**	Guilford	CT	D	203 453-4334	1718
Sheila P Patrick	Waterbury	CT	G	203 575-1716	4956
Speed Printing & Graphics Inc	Stamford	CT	G	203 324-4000	4328
Visual Impact LLC	Danbury	CT	G	203 790-9650	1005
Wallingford Prtg Bus Forms Inc	Branford	CT	F	203 481-1911	359
Wink Ink LLC	Somers	CT	G	860 202-8709	3922
Abby Printing Co Inc	Easthampton	MA	G	413 536-5269	10551
Accela Graphics Neng Inc	Westborough	MA	G	508 366-5999	16586
Ad Plus Inc	Boston	MA	G	617 859-3128	8340
ADI Print Solutions Inc	Chelsea	MA	G	508 230-7024	9943
Advanced Graphics Inc	Norwood	MA	G	781 551-0550	14121
Advanced Imaging Inc	Wilmington	MA	E	978 658-7776	16966
Apex Press Inc	Westborough	MA	F	508 366-1110	16589
Appalachian Press	Westfield	MA	G	413 568-2621	16666
Archimedia Solutions Group LLC **(PA)**	Danvers	MA	G	978 774-5400	10195
Aucoins Printing	Spencer	MA	G	508 885-3595	15426
Bayview Graphics	North Weymouth	MA	G	781 878-3340	13996
Black and White Printing	Stow	MA	G	401 265-7811	15631
Boston Tag and Label Inc	Waltham	MA	G	781 893-9080	16050
Boutwell Owens & Co Inc **(PA)**	Fitchburg	MA	C	978 343-3067	10813
Business Cards Overnight Inc	Lawrence	MA	G	978 974-9271	11999
Business Resources Inc	Westborough	MA	F	508 433-4600	16596
Causeway Graphics	Framingham	MA	G	508 309-6592	10931
Coatings Adhesives Inks	Georgetown	MA	E	978 352-7273	11140
Corporate Image Apparel Inc	Fall River	MA	E	508 676-3099	10680
D & H Print Management Ltd	Pembroke	MA	G	781 829-0209	14396
Defiance Graphics Corp	Rowley	MA	F	978 948-2789	14852
Desk Top Graphics Inc **(HQ)**	Peabody	MA	E	617 832-1927	14330
Digital Graphics Inc	North Billerica	MA	E	781 270-3670	13809
Docuprint Express Ltd	West Bridgewater	MA	G	508 895-9090	16437
Docuserve Inc	Marlborough	MA	E	508 786-5820	12749
DSA Printing & Publishing Inc	Chelmsford	MA	G	978 256-3900	9893
Duckhill River Corp	Wilmington	MA	G	978 657-6186	16997
Elbe-Cesco Inc	Fall River	MA	D	508 676-8531	10687
Elbonais Incorporated	Framingham	MA	G	508 626-2318	10945
Excel Graphix	Norwood	MA	G	781 642-6736	14152
Fast Mailing	Randolph	MA	G	617 605-8693	14680
Fedex Office & Print Svcs Inc	Chelmsford	MA	G	978 275-0574	9898
First Impression Printing Inc	Stoughton	MA	G	781 344-8855	15592
Fit America Inc	Southborough	MA	G	309 839-1695	15357
Fluidform Inc	Acton	MA	G	978 287-4698	7356
Formlabs Inc **(PA)**	Somerville	MA	B	617 932-5227	15174
G B Enterprises	Amherst	MA	G	413 210-4658	7515
Gerard F Scalley	Woburn	MA	G	781 933-3009	17192
Ghp Media Inc	North Adams	MA	D	413 663-3771	13675
Hannaford & Dumas Corporation	Woburn	MA	E	781 503-0100	17195
Hillside Press	Melrose	MA	G	617 742-1922	12982
Hot Plates Company	Ashland	MA	G	508 429-1445	7661
Howarth Specialty Company	Westport	MA	G	508 674-8950	16841
Image Software Services Inc	Shirley	MA	E	978 425-3600	15087
Imaging Data Corporation	Clinton	MA	G	978 365-9353	10081
Independant Newspaper Group	Revere	MA	E	781 485-0588	14767
Instant Offset Press Inc	Hyannis	MA	F	508 790-1100	11843
Intouch Labels and Packg Inc	Lowell	MA	G	800 370-2693	12384
John Karl Dietrich & Assoc	Cambridge	MA	F	617 868-4140	9521
Kirkwood Holdings Inc **(PA)**	Wilmington	MA	C	978 658-4200	17012
Kondelin Associates Inc **(HQ)**	Peabody	MA	F	978 281-3663	14348
Kreate & Print Inc	Norwood	MA	G	781 255-0505	14172
Laplume & Sons Printing Inc	Lawrence	MA	E	978 683-1009	12045
Lennys Screen Printing	Braintree	MA	G	781 267-5977	9022
Lujean Printing Co Inc	Cotuit	MA	F	508 428-8700	10170
Madison Group Inc	Revere	MA	G	781 853-0029	14771
Marcott Designs	Attleboro	MA	G	508 226-2680	7762
McGirr Graphics Incorporated	Plymouth	MA	E	508 747-6400	14564
Medi - Print Inc	Boston	MA	G	617 566-7594	8693
Medianews Group Inc	Devens	MA	D	978 772-0777	10325
Merrill Corporation	Boston	MA	E	617 535-1500	8698
Minuteman Press	Fitchburg	MA	G	978 345-0818	10839
Nano Ops Inc	Needham	MA	G	617 543-2921	13306
Nfi LLC	New Bedford	MA	E	508 998-9021	13426
Norman Ellis	Auburn	MA	G	508 853-5833	7845
Northeast Printing & Graphics	Plymouth	MA	G	508 746-8689	14568
Northern Graphics Inc	Middleton	MA	F	978 646-9925	13097
Offset Prep Inc	Quincy	MA	G	617 472-7887	14643
On Site Printing & Copying	Needham Heights	MA	G	781 449-1871	13341
Paul H Murphy & Co Inc	Quincy	MA	F	617 472-7707	14645
Pictex Corporation	Boston	MA	G	617 375-5801	8779
PIP Itsa Inc	Beverly	MA	G	978 927-5717	8165
Precision Images Inc	North Dighton	MA	G	508 824-6200	13934
Proforma Printing & Promotion	Milton	MA	G	617 464-1120	13199
Quad/Graphics Inc	East Longmeadow	MA	C	413 525-8552	10490
Rgp Corp	Milford	MA	G	508 478-8511	13141
Sallyharrold Inc	Dennis	MA	G	508 258-0253	10310
Simply Designs & Printing	Northbridge	MA	G	508 234-3424	14061
Specialty Manufacturing Inc	Amesbury	MA	E	978 388-1601	7509
Specialty Prtrs F Bush Son Co	Plympton	MA	G	781 585-9444	14593
Taylor Communications Inc	Avon	MA	F	508 584-0102	7898
Ted Best	Hyde Park	MA	G	617 361-7258	11881
Tekni-Plex Inc	Ashland	MA	F	508 881-2440	7671
Tomandtim Enterprises LLC	Northborough	MA	G	508 380-5550	14051
Watertown Printers Inc	Somerville	MA	G	781 893-9400	15230
Bruce A Pettengill	Leeds	ME	G	207 933-2578	6268
Computech Inc	Auburn	ME	G	207 777-7468	5554
Creative Digital Imaging	Bangor	ME	E	207 973-0500	5640
Csg Inc	Yarmouth	ME	G	207 846-9567	7293
Designtex Group Inc	Portland	ME	E	207 774-2689	6650
Downeast Graphics & Prtg Inc	Ellsworth	ME	F	207 667-5582	6016
Guy Little Press Inc **(PA)**	Auburn	ME	G	207 795-0650	5570
J Weston Walch Publisher	Portland	ME	E	207 772-2846	6676
Northeast Publishing Company	Presque Isle	ME	F	207 764 4471	6765
Omni Press Inc	Portland	ME	G	207 780-6664	6705
Park Street Press Inc	South Paris	ME	G	207 743-7702	7015
Penobscot Bay Press Inc **(PA)**	Stonington	ME	F	207 367-2200	7070
Printgraphics of Maine Inc	Portland	ME	G	207 347-5700	6716
Quick Print Color Center	Saco	ME	G	207 282-6480	6856
Sunrise Printing & Graphics	Windham	ME	G	207 892-3534	7255
Waterfront Graphics & Prtg LLC	South Portland	ME	G	207 799-3519	7044
Xpress of Maine **(PA)**	Portland	ME	G	207 775-2444	6747
Camera Works Inc	Londonderry	NH	G	603 898-7175	18683
Capitol Copy Inc	Concord	NH	G	603 226-2679	17889
D M Printing Service Inc	Hudson	NH	G	603 883-1897	18382
Digital Ink Printing LLC	Somersworth	NH	G	603 692-6002	19835
Doolittles Print Serve Inc	Claremont	NH	G	603 543-0700	17848
Eagle Copy Center	Windham	NH	G	603 225-3713	20004
Electronics For Imaging Inc	Londonderry	NH	F	603 279-4635	18695
Fedex Office & Print Svcs Inc	West Lebanon	NH	G	603 298-5891	19951
Flex-Print-Labels	Hampton	NH	E	603 929-3088	18263
Letterman Press LLC	West Lebanon	NH	G	603 543-0500	19956

	CITY	ST	EMP	PHONE	ENTRY #
Liebl Printing Co	Colebrook	NH	G	603 237-8650	17873
Mg Print and Promotions	Dover	NH	G	603 343-2534	18037
Nishi Enterprises Inc	Dover	NH	G	603 749-0113	18040
Powerplay Management LLC	Portsmouth	NH	E	603 436-3030	19609
RB Graphics Inc	Hooksett	NH	G	603 624-4025	18358
Red Fish-Blue Fish Dye Works	Somersworth	NH	F	603 692-3900	19846
Silver Direct Inc	Swanzey	NH	G	603 355-8855	19889
Smith & Town Printers LLC	Berlin	NH	G	603 752-2150	17700
Spear Group Holdings	Milford	NH	E	603 673-6400	19078
Sumner Printing Inc	Somersworth	NH	E	603 692-7424	19849
T K O Printing Inc	Rochester	NH	G	603 332-0511	19689
Talient Action Group	Manchester	NH	E	603 703-0795	18935
Venture Print Unlimited Inc	Plymouth	NH	F	603 536-2410	19531
Allied Group Inc **(PA)**	Cranston	RI	C	401 461-1700	20177
Bradford Press Inc	Providence	RI	G	401 621-7195	20972
Classic Embroidery Co	East Providence	RI	E	401 434-9632	20397
Comstock Press	Westerly	RI	G	401 596-8719	21520
Davis Press	Bristol	RI	G	401 624-9331	20072
Digital Printing Concepts Inc	East Providence	RI	G	401 431-2110	20407
Mix Up Printer	Lincoln	RI	G	401 334-4291	20584
Moo Inc	Lincoln	RI	D	401 434-3561	20586
Pax Incorporated Printers	Middletown	RI	G	401 847-1157	20629
Proprint Inc	Johnston	RI	F	401 944-3855	20531
Rlcp Inc	Barrington	RI	E	401 461-6560	20054
Warwick Group Inc	Bristol	RI	F	401 438-9451	20109
Women & Infants Hospital	Providence	RI	G	401 453-7600	21156
Dawn Brainard	Newport	VT	G	802 334-2780	22196
Herald Association Inc	Rutland	VT	C	802 747-6121	22338
Leahy Press Inc	Montpelier	VT	E	802 223-2100	22153
Parent Co Applications Inc **(PA)**	Essex Junction	VT	F	802 233-3612	21953
Paw Prints Press Inc	South Burlington	VT	G	802 865-2872	22456
Pumpkin Harbor Designs Inc	Jeffersonville	VT	G	802 644-6588	22047
SRC Liquidation Company	South Burlington	VT	G	802 862-9932	22467
Tuttle Law Print Inc	Rutland	VT	D	802 773-9171	22356
Vermont Art Studio Inc	Rutland	VT	G	802 747-7446	22358

PRINTING: Engraving & Plate

	CITY	ST	EMP	PHONE	ENTRY #
Urg Graphics Inc **(PA)**	Stafford Springs	CT	E	860 928-0835	4121
Gillies W Technologies LLC	Worcester	MA	G	508 852-2502	17382

PRINTING: Fabric, Narrow

	CITY	ST	EMP	PHONE	ENTRY #
Nova Idea Inc	Woburn	MA	G	781 281-2183	17246

PRINTING: Flexographic

	CITY	ST	EMP	PHONE	ENTRY #
CCL Industries Corporation **(DH)**	Shelton	CT	D	203 926-1253	3785
CCL Label Inc	Shelton	CT	C	203 926-1253	3786
Identification Products Corp	Bridgeport	CT	F	203 334-5969	429
Privateer Ltd	Old Saybrook	CT	F	860 526-1837	3349
CCL Label Inc **(HQ)**	Framingham	MA	D	508 872-4511	10932
Design Mark Industries Inc	Wareham	MA	D	800 451-3275	16244
Garlock Prtg & Converting Corp	Gardner	MA	C	978 630-1028	11116
Garlock Prtg & Converting Corp **(PA)**	Gardner	MA	D	978 630-1028	11117
Wtd Inc **(PA)**	Wilmington	MA	D	978 658-8200	17068
Maine Poly Aquisition Corp	Greene	ME	E	207 946-7000	6150
Amherst Label Inc	Milford	NH	E	603 673-7849	19047

PRINTING: Gravure, Business Form & Card

	CITY	ST	EMP	PHONE	ENTRY #
Minike Card Care	Worcester	MA	G	508 853-4490	17419

PRINTING: Gravure, Cards, Exc Greeting

	CITY	ST	EMP	PHONE	ENTRY #
Ideas Inc	Milford	CT	G	203 878-9686	2299
Vermont Christmas Company	Milton	VT	G	802 893-1670	22139

PRINTING: Gravure, Catalogs, No Publishing On-Site

	CITY	ST	EMP	PHONE	ENTRY #
R R Donnelley & Sons Company	Manchester	CT	F	860 649-5570	2040

PRINTING: Gravure, Color

	CITY	ST	EMP	PHONE	ENTRY #
Shear Color Printing Inc	Woburn	MA	E	781 376-9607	17293

PRINTING: Gravure, Forms, Business

	CITY	ST	EMP	PHONE	ENTRY #
D B S Industries Inc	Haverhill	MA	D	978 373-4748	11421

PRINTING: Gravure, Invitations

	CITY	ST	EMP	PHONE	ENTRY #
Laplume & Sons Printing Inc	Lawrence	MA	E	978 683-1009	12045
Providence Label & Tag Co	Providence	RI	F	401 751-6677	21097

PRINTING: Gravure, Labels

	CITY	ST	EMP	PHONE	ENTRY #
Rubber Labels USA LLC	Milford	CT	G	203 713-8059	2357
Trade Labels Inc	Mystic	CT	G	860 535-4828	2454
Stat Products Inc	Ashland	MA	E	508 881-8022	7670
Label Tech Inc	Somersworth	NH	C	603 692-2005	19843
Creative Labels Vermont Inc	Winooski	VT	E	802 655-7654	22720

PRINTING: Gravure, Magazines, No Publishing On-Site

	CITY	ST	EMP	PHONE	ENTRY #
Redden Publishing Co LLC	Rockport	ME	G	207 236-0767	6825

PRINTING: Gravure, Rotogravure

	CITY	ST	EMP	PHONE	ENTRY #
Brook & Whittle Limited **(HQ)**	Guilford	CT	C	203 483-5602	1695
Massachusetts Envelope Co Inc	Hartford	CT	E	860 727-9100	1845
Naugatuck Vly Photo Engrv Inc	Waterbury	CT	G	203 756-7345	4924
Quad/Graphics Inc	North Haven	CT	A	203 288-2468	3057

PRINTING: Gravure, Stationery

	CITY	ST	EMP	PHONE	ENTRY #
Leap Year Publishing LLC	North Andover	MA	F	978 688-9900	13717
Peel People LLC	Attleboro	MA	G	773 255-9886	7775

PRINTING: Gravure, Stationery & Invitation

	CITY	ST	EMP	PHONE	ENTRY #
Capitol Stationery Company	Cranston	RI	G	401 943-5333	20194

PRINTING: Laser

	CITY	ST	EMP	PHONE	ENTRY #
Dst Output East LLC **(DH)**	South Windsor	CT	E	816 221-1234	3957
Hartford Toner & Cartridge Inc **(PA)**	Broad Brook	CT	G	860 292-1280	629
Alltec Laser Technology	Southbridge	MA	F	508 765-6666	15375
Lasercraze	North Andover	MA	E	978 689-7700	13716
M Squared Lasers Inc	Cambridge	MA	G	408 667-0553	9542
Nitor Corp	Southwick	MA	G	413 998-0510	15416
Relyco Sales Inc	Dover	NH	E	603 742-0999	18050

PRINTING: Letterpress

	CITY	ST	EMP	PHONE	ENTRY #
Clanol Systems Inc	Old Greenwich	CT	G	203 637-9909	3306
Colonial Printers of Windsor	Windsor Locks	CT	G	860 627-5433	5389
Frank Printing Co R	Wallingford	CT	G	203 265-6152	4746
Ideal Printing Co Inc	New Haven	CT	G	203 777-7626	2698
Matthews Printing Co	Wallingford	CT	F	203 265-0363	4770
Silvermine Press Inc	Norwalk	CT	G	203 847-4368	3246
Aucoins Press Inc	Spencer	MA	G	508 885-0800	15425
Barney Rabin Company Inc	Marblehead	MA	F	781 639-0593	12675
Belmont Printing Company	Belmont	MA	E	617 484-0833	8066
Blake Press Inc	Boston	MA	G	617 742-8700	8412
Cambridge Printing Co Inc	Cambridge	MA	G	617 547-0270	9427
Classic Letter Press Inc	South Yarmouth	MA	G	508 221-7496	15328
Courier Printing Inc	Pittsfield	MA	G	413 442-3242	14465
Crest Printing Co Inc	Melrose	MA	G	617 889-1171	12980
Davol/Taunton Printing Inc	Taunton	MA	F	508 824-4305	15741
Fall River Modern Printing Co	Fall River	MA	F	508 673-9421	10697
Gazette Printing Co Inc	Easthampton	MA	F	413 527-7700	10564
Golden Manet Press Inc	Quincy	MA	G	617 773-2423	14629
Green Summer	Everett	MA	G	617 387-0120	10612
Hadley Printing Company Inc	Holyoke	MA	E	413 536-8517	11629
Hitchcock Press Inc	Holyoke	MA	F	413 538-8811	11632
Lamb Printing Company Inc	North Adams	MA	G	413 662-2495	13678
Letterpress Services Inc	West Springfield	MA	G	413 732-0399	16529
Liberty Printing Co Inc	Brockton	MA	G	508 586-6810	9162
Lincoln Press Co Inc	Fall River	MA	E	508 673-3241	10723
Mc Kinnon Printing Co Inc	Revere	MA	G	781 592-3677	14773
Roberts & Sons Printing Inc	Springfield	MA	G	413 283-9356	15503
Shrewsbury National Press	Shrewsbury	MA	G	508 756-7502	15132
Thomas B Fullen	Leominster	MA	G	978 534-5255	12194
Albisons Printing Inc	Augusta	ME	G	207 622-1941	5603
Armstrong Family Inds Inc	Hermon	ME	E	207 848-7300	6183
Harbor Print Shop	Boothbay	ME	G	207 633-4176	5778
J A Black Company	Belfast	ME	G	207 338-4040	5691
C & O Box & Printing Company	Hooksett	NH	G	508 881-1760	18345
Evans Printing Co	Bow	NH	G	603 856-8238	17713
Gus & Ruby Letterpress LLC	Portsmouth	NH	G	603 319-1717	19571
Paul Revere Press Inc	Newton	NH	G	781 289-4031	19366
Sumner Fancy	Windham	NH	G	603 893-3081	20011
Swaffield Enterprises Inc	Wolfeboro	NH	G	603 569-3017	20025
Tylergraphics Inc	Laconia	NH	G	603 524-6625	18590
J B Foley Printing Company	Providence	RI	G	401 467-3616	21041
Regine Printing Co Inc	Providence	RI	G	401 943-3404	21108
Service Plus Press Inc	Warwick	RI	G	401 461-2929	21424
Rutland Printing Co Inc	Rutland	VT	G	802 775-1948	22351
Winooski Press LLC	Winooski	VT	G	802 655-1611	22728

PRINTING: Lithographic

	CITY	ST	EMP	PHONE	ENTRY #
AlphaGraphics LLC	Hamden	CT	G	203 230-0018	1731
American-Republican Inc **(PA)**	Waterbury	CT	D	203 574-3636	4842
Amgraph Packaging Inc	Baltic	CT	C	860 822-2000	48
Anderson Publishing LLC	Southington	CT	G	860 621-2192	4038
Arch Parent Inc	Willimantic	CT	G	860 336-4856	5261
BCT Reporting LLC	Plainville	CT	G	860 302-1876	3469
Bizcard Xpress LLC	Higganum	CT	G	860 324-6840	1901
Brian Berlepsch	North Branford	CT	G	203 484-9799	2959
Business Cards Tomorrow Inc	Naugatuck	CT	G	203 723-5858	2464
Byrne Group Inc	Waterbury	CT	G	203 573-0100	4852
Cadmus	Stamford	CT	G	203 595-3000	4154
Capitol Printing Co Inc	Hartford	CT	G	860 522-1547	1810
Child Evngelism Fellowship Inc	Wolcott	CT	E	203 879-2154	5434
Data-Graphics Inc	Newington	CT	D	860 667-0435	2859
Easy Graphics Inc	Greenwich	CT	G	203 622-0001	1609
Executive Office Services Inc	Bridgeport	CT	E	203 373-1333	411
Falcon Press	Enfield	CT	G	860 763-2293	1362
Financial Prtg Solutions LLC	Preston	CT	G	860 886-9931	3580
Fine Print New England Inc	Newington	CT	G	860 953-0660	2863
Franklin Print Shoppe Inc	Torrington	CT	G	860 496-9516	4578
FSNB Enterprises Inc	Monroe	CT	G	203 254-1947	2403
Fulcrum Promotions & Printing	Bridgeport	CT	G	203 909-6362	417
G & R Enterprises Incorporated	Hartford	CT	G	860 549-6120	1822
Gateway Digital Inc	Norwalk	CT	F	203 853-4929	3157
Herff Jones LLC	Bethlehem	CT	G	203 266-7170	196
Image Ink Inc	Newington	CT	G	860 665-9792	2871
J & T Printing LLC	Wethersfield	CT	G	860 529-4628	5250
Kool Ink LLC	Bloomfield	CT	F	860 242-0303	238
L P Macadams Company Inc	Bridgeport	CT	D	203 366-3647	442
Liberty Screen Print Co LLC	Beacon Falls	CT	F	203 632-5449	60
Lighthouse Printing LLC	Old Saybrook	CT	G	860 388-2677	3343
Maple Print Services Inc	Jewett City	CT	G	860 381-5470	1915
Massachusetts Envelope Co Inc	Hartford	CT	E	860 727-9100	1845
Master Engrv & Printery Inc **(PA)**	Waterbury	CT	G	203 723-2779	4911
Material Promotions Inc	Waterbury	CT	G	203 757-8900	4912
Max Productions LLC	Norwalk	CT	G	203 838-2795	3191
Melega Inc	Stamford	CT	G	203 961-8703	4249
Middletown Printing Co Inc	Middletown	CT	F	860 347-5700	2206
Minute Man Press	Hamden	CT	G	203 891-6251	1772

	CITY	ST	EMP	PHONE	ENTRY #
Minuteman Press	Wethersfield	CT	G	860 529-4628	5258
Minuteman Press of Bristol	Bristol	CT	G	860 589-1100	582
Minuteman Press of Danbury	Danbury	CT	G	203 743-6755	955
Muir Envelope Plus Inc	Newington	CT	F	860 953-6847	2884
Naugatuck Vly Photo Engrv Inc	Waterbury	CT	G	203 756-7345	4924
New Fairfield Press Inc	New Fairfield	CT	F	203 746-2700	2626
New Haven Register LLC	New Haven	CT	A	203 789-5200	2716
New London Printing Co LLC	New London	CT	G	860 701-9171	2775
Optamark CT LLC	Stamford	CT	G	203 325-1180	4270
P & M Investments LLC	Enfield	CT	G	860 745-3600	1373
P & S Printing LLC	Stamford	CT	G	203 327-9818	4275
Paw Print Pantry LLC **(PA)**	East Lyme	CT	G	860 447-8442	1271
Paw Print Pantry LLC	Niantic	CT	G	860 447-8442	2956
Pinpoint Promotions & Prtg LLC	West Haven	CT	F	203 301-4273	5141
Play-It Productions Inc	Colchester	CT	F	212 695-6530	805
Print House LLC	Glastonbury	CT	G	860 652-0803	1573
R R Donnelley & Sons Company	Avon	CT	E	860 773-6140	43
Rf Printing LLC	Wallingford	CT	G	203 265-9939	4797
S and Z Graphics LLC	Milford	CT	G	203 783-9675	2358
Sabar Graphics LLC **(PA)**	East Haven	CT	G	203 467-3016	1260
Screen Tek Printing Co Inc	Hamden	CT	G	203 248-6248	1782
Sir Speedy Printing	Middlebury	CT	E	203 346-0716	2158
Smoke & Print Universe	Bridgeport	CT	G	203 540-5151	493
Specialty Printing LLC	East Windsor	CT	F	860 654-1850	1302
Spectrum Press	Milford	CT	F	203 878-9090	2368
Step Saver Inc	Southington	CT	E	860 621-6751	4082
Team Destination Inc	Meriden	CT	G	203 235-6000	2138
Thelemic Printshop	Plainfield	CT	G	860 383-4014	3458
Toto LLC	New Haven	CT	F	203 776-6000	2744
Transmonde USa Inc	North Branford	CT	D	203 484-1528	2982
Turnstone Inc	Greenwich	CT	F	203 625-0000	1658
Typeisright	Moosup	CT	G	860 564-0537	2428
US Games Systems Inc	Stamford	CT	E	203 353-8400	4353
Vernon Printing Co Inc	Vernon Rockville	CT	G	860 872-1826	4688
Westrock Commercial LLC	Stamford	CT	G	203 595-3130	4359
Wild Rver Cstm Screen Prtg LLC	Newtown	CT	G	203 426-1500	2948
Yankee Screen Printing	Derby	CT	G	203 924-9926	1085
AA Global Printing Inc	Newton	MA	G	617 527-7629	13552
Abby Printing Co Inc	Easthampton	MA	G	413 536-5269	10551
Advanced Print Solutions Inc **(PA)**	Sharon	MA	G	508 655-8434	15045
Andrew T Johnson Company Inc **(PA)**	Boston	MA	E	617 742-1610	8366
Apb Enterprises Inc	Marlborough	MA	G	508 481-0966	12715
Arch Parent Inc	West Springfield	MA	G	413 504-1433	16508
Bassett & Cassidy Inc	Lowell	MA	G	978 452-9595	12350
BBC Printing and Products Inc	Waltham	MA	G	781 647-4646	16042
Bh Media Inc **(HQ)**	Braintree	MA	D	617 426-3000	8990
Boston Ltigation Solutions LLC	Boston	MA	F	617 933-9780	8434
Brookline Print Center	Waltham	MA	G	617 926-0300	16052
Business Cards Overnight Inc	Lawrence	MA	G	978 974-9271	11999
Cab Screen Printing	North Attleboro	MA	G	508 695-8421	13751
Castle Complements Printing Co	Chelmsford	MA	G	978 250-9122	9886
Chisholm and Hunt Printers Inc	Gloucester	MA	G	978 283-0318	11173
Cimpress USA Incorporated **(DH)**	Waltham	MA	B	866 614-8002	16067
Classic Envelope Inc	East Douglas	MA	D	508 731-6747	10425
Congruity 360 LLC	Fall River	MA	D	508 689-9516	10679
Courier Printing Inc	Pittsfield	MA	G	413 442-3242	14465
Creative Ink	Salem	MA	G	978 741-2244	14903
D B S Industries Inc	Haverhill	MA	D	978 373-4748	11421
D&P Media For Print Inc	Methuen	MA	G	978 685-2210	13017
Davis Enterprises Inc	Dedham	MA	G	781 461-8444	10286
Descal Inc	Waltham	MA	G	781 736-9400	16085
Devincentis Press Inc	Malden	MA	F	781 605-3796	12567
Digipress Inc **(PA)**	Peabody	MA	C	617 832-1927	14331
Dion Label Printing Inc	Westfield	MA	D	413 568-3713	16680
Dmr Print Inc **(PA)**	Concord	MA	E	617 876-3688	10128
Documents On Demand Inc	Worcester	MA	F	508 793-0956	17366
Docuserve Inc	Marlborough	MA	E	508 786-5820	12749
DSA Printing & Publishing Inc	Chelmsford	MA	G	978 256-3900	9893
Duggan Associates Inc	Framingham	MA	G	508 879-3277	10942
Eco2 Office Inc	Milford	MA	G	508 478-8511	13114
Elbonais Incorporated	Framingham	MA	G	508 626-2318	10945
Enon Copy Inc **(PA)**	Beverly	MA	F	978 927-8757	8128
Fenway Cmmunications Group Inc	Boston	MA	E	617 226-1900	8542
Footprint Pwr Acquisitions LLC	Salem	MA	G	978 740-8411	14912
Freedom Digital Printing LLC	Ashland	MA	F	508 881-6940	7660
G B Enterprises	Amherst	MA	G	413 210-4658	7515
Generation Four Inc	Waltham	MA	G	781 899-3180	16119
Ggs Custom Metals Inc	South Hadley	MA	F	413 315-4344	15303
Graphic Excellence LLC	Springfield	MA	G	413 733-6691	15471
Graphix Plus Inc	Fall River	MA	F	508 677-2122	10706
Greentree Marketing Inc	Framingham	MA	F	508 877-2581	10961
Grenier Print Shop Inc	Boston	MA	G	617 522-2225	8582
Guy T Piro & Sons	Somerville	MA	G	617 776-2840	15180
Henry N Sawyer Co Inc	Boston	MA	F	617 242-4610	8594
Impress Systems Inc	Chelmsford	MA	G	978 441-2022	9906
Imprint Boston Inc	Dorchester	MA	G	857 251-9383	10344
Imprint Marketing	Natick	MA	G	508 315-3433	13261
Infinite Graphic Solutions	Woburn	MA	G	781 938-6333	17201
Ingleside Corporation	Wrentham	MA	G	774 847-9386	17523
J C Enterprises Inc	Ashland	MA	G	508 881-7228	7662
J R V Smita Company LLC	Canton	MA	G	781 828-6490	9747
Jotas Corporation	Burlington	MA	G	781 273-1155	9290
Kapson Printing Service Inc	Dorchester	MA	G	617 265-2543	10345
Kondelin Associates Inc **(HQ)**	Peabody	MA	F	978 281-3663	14348
Laplume & Sons Printing Inc	Lawrence	MA	E	978 683-1009	12045
Lexington Graphics	Lexington	MA	F	781 863-9510	12237

	CITY	ST	EMP	PHONE	ENTRY #
Lincoln Press Co Inc	Fall River	MA	E	508 673-3241	10723
Linmel Associates Inc	Marlborough	MA	F	508 481-6699	12787
Lion Labels Inc	South Easton	MA	E	508 230-8211	15284
M & M Printing Rush Service	East Douglas	MA	G	508 476-4495	10429
Map Printing Inc	Fall River	MA	G	508 676-5177	10725
Marbuo Inc	North Dartmouth	MA	G	508 994-7700	13924
Massachusetts Repro Ltd	Boston	MA	F	617 227-2237	8686
McGirr Graphics Incorporated	Plymouth	MA	G	508 747-6400	14563
Medianews Group Inc	Fitchburg	MA	D	978 343-6911	10835
Merrill Corporation	Boston	MA	E	617 535-1500	8698
Mina Custom Print	Cambridge	MA	G	617 520-4797	9561
Minute Man Airfield	Stow	MA	F	978 897-3933	15633
Minuteman Press	Hyde Park	MA	G	617 361-7400	11875
Minuteman Press	Centerville	MA	G	508 775-9890	9817
Minuteman Press	Newburyport	MA	G	978 465-2242	13515
Minuteman Press	Fall River	MA	G	508 673-1407	10734
Minuteman Press	Fitchburg	MA	G	978 345-0818	10839
Minuteman Press	Seekonk	MA	G	508 336-3050	15028
Minuteman Press	Hyannis	MA	G	508 778-0220	11850
Minuteman Press Intl Inc	Newton	MA	G	617 244-7001	13615
Minuteman Press Worcester Inc	Worcester	MA	G	508 757-5450	17420
Minuteman Printing Corp	Concord	MA	F	978 369-2808	10141
Modus Media Inc	Waltham	MA	E	781 663-5000	16153
Mrf Enterprises Inc	Seekonk	MA	G	508 336-3050	15030
Neenah Technical Materials Inc **(HQ)**	Dalton	MA	F	678 518-3343	10180
Neenah Technical Materials Inc	Pittsfield	MA	C	413 684-7874	14495
New Valence Robotics Corp	Boston	MA	G	857 529-6397	8735
Newspapers of Massachusetts	Greenfield	MA	B	978 544-2118	11270
Nexus Print Group Inc	Milton	MA	G	617 429-9666	13197
North End Press Inc	Boston	MA	G	617 227-8929	8741
On Site Printing & Copying	Needham Heights	MA	G	781 449-1871	13341
Palomar Printing	West Boylston	MA	G	508 856-7237	16425
Power Graphics Printing	Tewksbury	MA	G	978 851-8988	15827
Pressed For Time Printing Inc	Boston	MA	G	617 267-4113	8793
Pretty Instant LLC	Boston	MA	G	888 551-6765	8794
Print Buyers International LLC	Chestnut Hill	MA	G	617 730-5951	9991
Print Resource	Westborough	MA	G	508 433-4660	16644
Printing Services Inc	Natick	MA	G	508 655-2535	13275
Printsake Inc	Mashpee	MA	G	508 419-7393	12882
Quad/Graphics Inc	East Longmeadow	MA	C	413 525-8552	10490
R R Donnelley & Sons Company	Hyde Park	MA	B	617 360-2000	11877
Ralph Traynham	Billerica	MA	G	978 667-0977	8282
Reid Graphics Inc	Andover	MA	D	978 474-1930	7598
Rhode Island Mktg & Prtg Inc	Attleboro	MA	G	401 351-4000	7786
Rj Printing LLC	Boston	MA	G	617 523-7656	8822
Robert Murphy	Salem	MA	E	978 745-7170	14938
Roberts & Sons Printing Inc	Springfield	MA	G	413 283-9356	15503
Seventy Nine N Main St Prtg	Andover	MA	G	978 475-4945	7603
Sir Speedy Inc	North Attleboro	MA	G	508 643-1016	13780
South Shore Custom Prints	Pembroke	MA	G	781 293-8300	14427
Standard Modern Company	New Bedford	MA	G	774 425-3537	13452
Tantar Corp	North Attleboro	MA	G	508 643-1017	13783
Taylor Communications Inc	Avon	MA	F	508 584-0102	7898
Ted Best	Hyde Park	MA	G	617 361-7258	11881
Thermal Printing Solutions	Hudson	MA	G	978 562-1329	11822
Titus & Bean Graphics Inc	Kingston	MA	F	781 585-1355	11965
Universal Wilde Inc	Rockland	MA	C	781 251-2700	14832
Van-Go Graphics	Grafton	MA	F	508 865-7300	11225
W S Walcott Inc	Orleans	MA	G	508 240-0882	14244
Wakefield Item Co	Wakefield	MA	E	781 245-0080	15983
Walpole Print Works Inc	Walpole	MA	G	508 668-0247	16017
Westfield News Publishing Inc **(DH)**	Westfield	MA	E	413 562-4181	16746
Xpression Prints	Franklin	MA	G	401 413-6930	11099
Albisons Printing Inc	Augusta	ME	G	207 622-1941	5603
Brown Fox Printing Inc **(PA)**	Scarborough	ME	G	207 883-9525	6913
Bruce A Pettengill	Leeds	ME	G	207 933-2578	6268
Charlie Horse Screen Printing/	Arundel	ME	G	207 985-3293	5530
Checksforlesscom	Portland	ME	G	800 245-5775	6636
Everlasting Images Inc	Cape Neddick	ME	G	207 351-3277	5878
Fine Print Booksellers	Kennebunkport	ME	G	207 967-9989	6244
Infinite Imaging Inc	York	ME	E	207 363-4402	7309
Lincoln County Publishing Co	Newcastle	ME	E	207 563-3171	6483
Marks Printing House Inc	Belfast	ME	G	207 338-5460	5692
Mpx	Portland	ME	E	207 774-6116	6695
Nemi Publishing Inc	Farmington	ME	E	207 778-4801	6052
Northeast Publishing Company	Dover Foxcroft	ME	G	207 564-8355	5961
Onesource Printing	Lewiston	ME	G	207 784-1538	6313
Supplies Unlimited	Damariscotta	ME	G	207 563-7010	5940
Alpha Graph Printshop	Nashua	NH	E	603 595-1444	19111
AlphaGraphics Pntshp of Future	Manchester	NH	G	603 645-0002	18778
Bam Lab LLC	Somersworth	NH	G	603 973-9388	19828
Bank & Business Forms Inc	Keene	NH	G	603 357-0567	18495
Barn Door Screen Printers	Conway	NH	G	603 447-5369	17950
Blacksmith Prtg & Copy Ctr LLC	Wolfeboro	NH	G	603 569-6300	20015
Bob Bean Company Inc	Londonderry	NH	G	603 818-4390	18680
Capitol Copy Inc	Concord	NH	G	603 226-2679	17889
Digital Printer Service	Gilford	NH	G	860 395-7942	18186
Eagle Publications Inc	Claremont	NH	E	603 543-3100	17849
Gemgraphics Inc	Keene	NH	G	603 352-7112	18504
Harrison Publishing House Inc	Littleton	NH	E	603 444-0820	18661
Infinite Imaging Inc **(PA)**	Portsmouth	NH	E	603 436-3030	19578
Insty-Prints of Bedford Inc	Bedford	NH	G	603 622-3821	17646
Itnh Inc	Manchester	NH	F	603 669-6900	18845
Minuteman Press Intl Inc	Nashua	NH	G	603 718-1439	19208
Murroneys Printing Inc	Manchester	NH	G	603 623-4677	18880
North East Printing McHy Inc	Seabrook	NH	G	603 474-7455	19811

	CITY	ST	EMP	PHONE	ENTRY #
P2k Printing LLC	North Conway	NH	G	603 356-2010	19378
Printfusion LLC	Swanzey	NH	G	603 283-0007	19888
Proforma Piper Printing	Tilton	NH	G	603 934-5055	19909
Sir Speedy	Manchester	NH	G	603 625-6868	18925
Southport Management Group LLC	Portsmouth	NH	G	603 433-4664	19621
Spirit Advisory LLC	Portsmouth	NH	G	603 433-4664	19622
Sterling Business Corp	Peterborough	NH	G	603 924-9401	19489
Teddys Tees Inc	Concord	NH	G	603 226-2762	17935
Walnut Bottom Inc	Concord	NH	G	603 224-6606	17939
Water Street Printing LLC	Nashua	NH	F	603 595-1444	19284
136 Express Printing Inc	Bristol	RI	G	401 253-0136	20059
Arch Parent Inc	Westerly	RI	G	401 388-9802	21517
Artistic Label Company Inc	Warwick	RI	G	401 737-0666	21327
B & M Printing Inc	Cumberland	RI	G	401 334-3190	20314
Camirob Corp	East Providence	RI	E	401 435-4477	20394
Choice Printing & Product LLC	Rumford	RI	F	401 438-3838	21182
Dla Document Services	Newport	RI	G	401 841-6011	20662
Fairmont Sons LLC **(PA)**	Providence	RI	G	401 351-4000	21010
Fine Line Graphics Inc	Smithfield	RI	E	401 349-3300	21225
Hopkins Press	North Providence	RI	G	401 231-9654	20764
Igt Global Solutions Corp	West Greenwich	RI	E	401 392-7025	21456
Lewis Graphics Inc	Cranston	RI	G	401 943-8300	20253
Minute Man Press	Middletown	RI	G	401 619-1650	20626
Minuteman Press of Johnston	Johnston	RI	G	401 944-0667	20522
Minuteman Press of Pawtucket	Pawtucket	RI	G	401 305-6644	20860
Mono Die Cutting Co Inc	Riverside	RI	F	401 434-1274	21173
Oberlin LLC	Providence	RI	G	401 588-8755	21080
Park Printers	Pawtucket	RI	G	401 728-8650	20874
Peak Printing Inc	Providence	RI	F	401 351-0500	21088
Perfect Print LLC	Providence	RI	E	401 347-2370	21089
Sir Speedy	Providence	RI	G	401 232-2000	21122
Sir Speedy Printing Inc	Cranston	RI	F	401 781-5650	20286
Summit Printing LLC	Warwick	RI	G	401 732-7848	21431
Warwick Group Inc	Bristol	RI	F	401 438-9451	20109
Accura Printing	Barre	VT	F	802 476-4429	21607
ASC Duplicating Inc	Montpelier	VT	G	802 229-0660	22145
Buy Monthly Publishing Inc	Waterbury Center	VT	G	802 244-6620	22590
Express Copy Inc	Manchester Center	VT	G	802 362-0501	22084
Larcoline Inc **(PA)**	Colchester	VT	F	802 864-5440	21871
Larcoline Inc	Montpelier	VT	G	802 229-0660	22152
McClure Newspapers Inc	Burlington	VT	C	802 863-3441	21795

PRINTING: Offset

	CITY	ST	EMP	PHONE	ENTRY #
A B C Printing Inc	East Haven	CT	F	203 468-1245	1241
Abbott Printing Company Inc	Hamden	CT	G	203 562-5562	1729
Academy Printing Service	Kensington	CT	G	860 828-5549	1916
Acme Press Inc	Milford	CT	G	203 334-8221	2235
Adkins Printing Company	New Britain	CT	E	800 228-9745	2506
Alliance Graphics Inc	Newington	CT	F	860 666-7992	2840
Allied Printing Services Inc **(PA)**	Manchester	CT	B	860 643-1101	1984
Ampco Publishing & Prtg Corp	Stamford	CT	G	203 325-1509	4137
Appels Printing & Mailing Bur	Hartford	CT	F	860 522-8189	1806
Audubon Copy Shppe of Firfield	Bridgeport	CT	G	203 259-4311	378
Barile Printers LLC	New Britain	CT	G	860 224-0127	2513
Bethel Printing & Graphics	Bethel	CT	G	203 748-7034	131
Brescias Printing Services Inc	East Hartford	CT	G	860 528-4254	1177
Briarwood Printing Company Inc	Plainville	CT	F	860 747-6805	3470
Brody Printing Company Inc	Bridgeport	CT	F	203 384-9313	391
Cannelli Printing Co Inc	West Haven	CT	G	203 932-1719	5110
Chase Graphics Inc	Putnam	CT	F	860 315-9006	3605
Clanol Systems Inc	Old Greenwich	CT	G	203 637-9909	3306
Colonial Printers of Windsor	Windsor Locks	CT	G	860 627-5433	5389
Copy Stop Inc	Hamden	CT	G	203 288-6401	1738
Craftsmen Printing Group Inc	Stamford	CT	G	203 327-2817	4175
Cricket Press Inc	West Hartford	CT	G	860 521-9279	5063
Custom Printing & Copy Inc **(PA)**	Enfield	CT	F	860 290-6890	1354
Data Management Incorporated	Unionville	CT	E	860 677-8586	4655
Derosa Printing Company Inc	Manchester	CT	F	860 646-1698	2000
Design Idea Printing	Ellington	CT	G	860 896-0103	1332
Docuprint & Imaging Inc	New Haven	CT	G	203 776-6000	2682
E R Hitchcock Company	New Britain	CT	E	860 229-2024	2529
East Coast Packaging LLC **(PA)**	Farmington	CT	G	860 675-8500	1479
East Longmeadow Business Svcs	Enfield	CT	G	413 525-6111	1355
Eccles-Lehman Inc	Easton	CT	G	203 268-0605	1318
Economy Printing & Copy Center **(PA)**	Danbury	CT	G	203 792-5610	906
Economy Printing & Copy Center	Ridgefield	CT	G	203 438-7401	3666
Ellington Printery Inc	Ellington	CT	G	860 875-3310	1334
Elm Press Incorporated	Terryville	CT	E	860 583-3600	4477
Empire Printing Systems LLC	Glastonbury	CT	G	860 633-3333	1549
Executive Press Inc	Plainville	CT	G	860 793-0060	3487
Executive Printing Darien LLC	Darien	CT	G	203 655-4691	1023
Flow Resources Inc **(HQ)**	Newington	CT	E	860 666-1200	2864
Garrett Printing & Graphics	Bristol	CT	G	860 589-6710	567
Ghp Media Inc **(PA)**	West Haven	CT	C	203 479-7500	5124
Goodcopy Printing Center Inc	New Haven	CT	E	203 624-0194	2691
Goulet Enterprises Inc	Pleasant Valley	CT	F	860 379-0793	3545
Graphic Image Inc	Milford	CT	E	203 877-8787	2293
Gulemo Inc	Willimantic	CT	G	860 456-1151	5265
Hartford Business Supply Inc	Hartford	CT	E	860 233-2138	1830
Harty Press Inc	New Haven	CT	D	203 562-5112	2695
Hat Trick Graphics LLC	Danbury	CT	G	203 748-1128	930
High Ridge Copy Inc	Stamford	CT	F	203 329-1889	4216
Holly Press Inc	Norwalk	CT	G	203 846-1720	3170
Ideal Printing Co Inc	New Haven	CT	G	203 777-7626	2698
Imperial Grphic Cmmnctions Inc	Milford	CT	E	203 650-3478	2301
Impression Point Inc	Stamford	CT	F	203 353-8800	4221

	CITY	ST	EMP	PHONE	ENTRY #
Integrity Graphics Inc	Simsbury	CT	D	800 343-1248	3906
Jerrys Printing & Graphics LLC	Bridgeport	CT	G	203 384-0015	435
JMS Graphics Inc	Middlebury	CT	G	203 598-7555	2155
Joseph Merritt & Company Inc	Danbury	CT	G	203 743-6734	940
JS McCarthy Co Inc	Stamford	CT	E	203 355-7600	4233
Jupiter Communications LLC	West Haven	CT	F	475 238-7082	5127
Kramer Printing Company Inc	West Haven	CT	F	203 933-5416	5129
Lithographics Inc	Farmington	CT	D	860 678-1660	1491
Magnani Press Incorporated	Hartford	CT	G	860 236-2802	1841
Marketing Sltons Unlimited LLC	West Hartford	CT	E	860 523-0670	5085
Matthews Printing Co	Wallingford	CT	F	203 265-0363	4770
Napp Printing Plate Dist Inc	Waterbury	CT	G	203 575-5727	4921
Oddo Print Shop Inc	Torrington	CT	G	860 489-6585	4590
One Source Print and Promo LLC	Cromwell	CT	G	860 635-3257	857
P C I Group	Stamford	CT	F	203 327-0410	4276
Paladin Commercial Prtrs LLC	Newington	CT	E	860 953-4900	2890
Palmisano Printing LLC	Bristol	CT	G	860 582-6883	590
Paul Dewitt	Danbury	CT	F	203 792-5610	965
Phoenix Press Inc	New Haven	CT	E	203 865-5555	2726
Prentis Printing Solutions Inc	Meriden	CT	G	203 634-1266	2117
Print Master LLC	Torrington	CT	G	860 482-8152	4593
Print Shop of Wolcott LLC	Wolcott	CT	G	203 879-3353	5453
Professional Graphics Inc	Norwalk	CT	F	203 846-4291	3225
Pronto Printer of Newington	Newington	CT	G	860 666-2245	2895
Prospect Printing LLC	Prospect	CT	F	203 758-6007	3594
Prosperous Printing LLC	Wilton	CT	G	203 834-1962	5300
Protopac Inc	Watertown	CT	G	860 274-6796	5020
Pyne-Davidson Company	Hartford	CT	E	860 522-9106	1862
Qg Printing II Corp	Enfield	CT	A	860 741-0150	1378
Quad/Graphics Inc	North Haven	CT	A	203 288-2468	3057
Quality Printers Inc	New London	CT	G	860 443-2800	2778
R R Donnelley & Sons Company	Manchester	CT	F	860 649-5570	2040
Rare Reminder Incorporated	Rocky Hill	CT	E	860 563-9386	3728
Record-Journal Newspaper **(PA)**	Meriden	CT	C	203 235-1661	2124
Rm Printing	Plantsville	CT	G	860 621-0498	3538
Rmi Inc	Vernon Rockville	CT	C	860 875-3366	4681
Rollins Printing Incorporated	Hamden	CT	G	203 248-3200	1781
Ronald Bottino	Bristol	CT	G	860 585-9505	608
Sazacks Inc	Manchester	CT	G	860 647-8367	2045
Southbury Printing Centre Inc	Southbury	CT	G	203 264-0102	4033
Speed Printing & Graphics Inc	Stamford	CT	G	203 324-4000	4328
Streamline Press	North Branford	CT	G	203 484-9799	2978
Streamline Press LLC	North Branford	CT	G	203 484-9799	2979
Success Printing & Mailing Inc	Norwalk	CT	F	203 847-1112	3252
System Intgrtion Cnsulting LLC	Shelton	CT	G	203 926-9599	3876
Technique Printers Inc	Clinton	CT	G	860 669-2516	795
Trumbull Printing Inc	Trumbull	CT	C	203 261-2548	4636
Value Print Incorporated	Wallingford	CT	F	203 265-1371	4826
Wethersfield Offset Inc	Rocky Hill	CT	G	860 721-8236	3734
Wethersfield Printing Co Inc	Rocky Hill	CT	F	860 721-8236	3735
Williams Printing Group LLC	North Windham	CT	G	860 423-8779	3085
Woodway Print Inc	Stamford	CT	G	203 323-6423	4361
Youngs Communications Inc	Middletown	CT	F	860 347-8567	2231
Accent Printing Inc	North Billerica	MA	G	781 487-9300	13788
Accucon Inc	Leominster	MA	G	978 840-0337	12106
Ad Print	Medway	MA	G	508 533-7411	12952
Adams Specialty & Printing Co	Adams	MA	G	413 743-9101	7409
Adg Printing Incorporated	North Billerica	MA	G	978 667-9285	13790
Adidas Printing Inc	Ipswich	MA	F	978 851-6337	11900
Advantage Media & Marketing	Framingham	MA	G	508 875-0011	10918
Aldam Press Inc	Pittsfield	MA	G	413 443-2800	14450
Alden Hauk Inc	Woburn	MA	F	781 281-0154	17115
Aleksandr S Yaskovich	Taunton	MA	G	508 822-7267	15722
Allegra Network LLC	Franklin	MA	G	508 528-5339	11021
Allegra Print & Imaging	Mansfield	MA	G	508 339-3555	12612
American Prtg & Envelope Inc	Auburn	MA	E	508 832-6100	7825
Apex Press Inc	Westborough	MA	F	508 366-1110	16589
Arlington Swifty Printing Inc	Arlington	MA	G	781 646-8700	7623
Artco Offset Inc	Canton	MA	D	781 830-7900	9716
Artcraft Co Inc	North Attleboro	MA	D	508 695-4042	13746
Arvest Press Inc	Waltham	MA	G	781 894-4844	16038
Atlantic Printing Co Inc	Medfield	MA	F	781 449-2700	12909
Atlas Press Worcester Inc	West Boylston	MA	G	508 835-9440	16409
Aucoins Press Inc	Spencer	MA	G	508 885-0800	15425
Austin Print	Concord	MA	G	978 369-8591	10115
Bassette Printers LLC	Belchertown	MA	D	413 781-7140	8022
Bateman & Slade Inc	Stoneham	MA	G	617 423-5556	15556
BBCg LLC	Norwood	MA	G	617 796-8800	14137
Becks Printing Co	North Adams	MA	G	413 664-7411	13668
Belmont Printing Company	Belmont	MA	E	617 484-0833	8066
Biz Tek Printing and Mktg LLC	Ware	MA	G	508 248-3377	16230
Blake Press Inc	Boston	MA	G	617 742-8700	8412
Blanchard Press Inc	Winchester	MA	F	617 426-6690	17084
Bolton Printing Co	Bolton	MA	G	978 365-4844	8317
Bond Printing Company Inc	Hanover	MA	G	781 871-3990	11329
Boston Business Printing Inc	Boston	MA	F	617 482-7955	8427
Boutwell Owens & Co Inc **(PA)**	Fitchburg	MA	C	978 343-3067	10813
Bradford & Bigelow Inc	Newburyport	MA	C	978 904-3112	13474
Brady Business Forms Inc	Lowell	MA	G	978 458-2585	12355
Braintree Printing Inc	Braintree	MA	E	781 848-5300	8992
Bridgewater Prtg Copy Ctr LLC	Bridgewater	MA	G	508 697-5227	9065
Bruno Diduca	Waltham	MA	G	781 894-5300	16053
Budget Printing Concord LLC	Concord	MA	G	978 369-4630	10118
Calendar Press Inc	Peabody	MA	E	978 531-1860	14319
Cambridge Printing Co Inc	Cambridge	MA	G	617 547-0270	9427
Canalside Printing	Monument Beach	MA	G	508 759-4141	13214

	CITY	ST	EMP	PHONE	ENTRY #
Capeway Printing & Copy Center	Rockland	MA	G	781 878-1600	14795
Cdl Print Mail LLC	Gardner	MA	G	978 410-5148	11107
Central Printing & Supply	Haverhill	MA	G	781 322-1220	11415
Chaco Inc	Norwood	MA	G	781 769-5557	14141
Choice Graphics Inc	Rowley	MA	G	978 948-2789	14851
Citius Printing & Graphics LLC	Waltham	MA	G	781 547-5550	16068
CJ Corrado & Sons Inc	Sharon	MA	G	508 655-8434	15048
Co Press	Ludlow	MA	G	413 525-6686	12459
Color Images Inc	Methuen	MA	G	978 688-4994	13015
Connolly Printing LLC	Woburn	MA	G	781 932-8885	17149
Coprico Inc	Chelsea	MA	G	617 889-0520	9951
Corporate Press	Norwood	MA	F	781 769-6656	14146
Country Press Inc	Lakeville	MA	F	508 947-4485	11975
Creative Imprints Inc	Norton	MA	E	508 285-7650	14074
Crest Printing Co Inc	Melrose	MA	G	617 889-1171	12980
Cricket Press Inc	Manchester	MA	F	978 526-7131	12604
Crockergraphics Inc	Needham Heights	MA	G	781 444-7020	13324
D & L Associates Inc	Needham Heights	MA	G	781 400-5068	13326
D S Graphics Inc **(PA)**	Lowell	MA	C	978 970-1359	12365
D-Lew Inc	Southborough	MA	G	508 481-7709	15353
Da Rosas	Oak Bluffs	MA	F	508 693-0110	14210
Daily Printing Inc	Beverly	MA	G	978 927-4630	8123
Data Print Inc	Woburn	MA	F	781 935-3350	17164
Davol/Taunton Printing Inc	Taunton	MA	F	508 824-4305	15741
Ddfhklt Inc	West Springfield	MA	F	413 733-7441	16515
Defiance Graphics Corp	Rowley	MA	F	978 948-2789	14852
Design Copy Printers Inc	Salem	MA	G	978 741-2244	14906
Desk Top Graphics Inc **(HQ)**	Peabody	MA	E	617 832-1927	14330
Digital Graphics Inc	North Billerica	MA	E	781 270-3670	13809
Dns Inc	Charlton	MA	F	508 248-5901	9849
Donnelley Financial LLC	Wilmington	MA	F	978 251-4000	16995
E D Abbott Company Inc	Boston	MA	F	617 267-5550	8514
East Coast Printing Inc	Hingham	MA	G	781 331-5635	11498
Emco/Fgs LLC	Braintree	MA	D	617 389-0076	9005
Essex Ruling & Printing Co	Methuen	MA	G	978 682-2457	13021
Excella Graphics	Malden	MA	G	781 763-7768	12571
Fall River Modern Printing Co	Fall River	MA	F	508 673-9421	10697
Farrar Press Inc	Paxton	MA	G	508 799-9874	14301
Fasprint Inc **(PA)**	Brockton	MA	F	508 588-9961	9146
Flagship Press Inc	North Andover	MA	C	978 975-3100	13704
Fleming & Son Corp	Somerville	MA	F	617 623-3047	15173
Foster Carroll Inc	Hopkinton	MA	G	508 497-0068	11715
Fowler Printing and Graphics	Randolph	MA	F	781 986-8900	14682
Full Line Graphics Inc	Taunton	MA	G	508 238-1914	15750
Gangi Printing Inc	Somerville	MA	F	617 776-6071	15175
Gatehouse Media LLC	Lexington	MA	G	781 275-7204	12226
Gateway Printing	Wareham	MA	G	508 295-0505	16248
Gazette Printing Co Inc	Easthampton	MA	F	413 527-7700	10564
Ghp Media Inc	North Adams	MA	D	413 663-3771	13675
Gmf Engineering Inc	Saugus	MA	G	781 233-0315	14983
Golden Manet Press Inc	Quincy	MA	G	617 773-2423	14629
Granite Print LLC	Quincy	MA	G	617 479-5777	14630
Graphic Developments Inc	Hanover	MA	E	781 878-2222	11340
Green Summer	Everett	MA	G	617 387-0120	10612
Hadley Printing Company Inc	Holyoke	MA	E	413 536-8517	11629
Harborside Printing Co Inc	Newburyport	MA	F	978 462-2026	13495
Harper Bros Printing Inc	North Billerica	MA	G	978 667-9459	13823
Harry B Harding & Son Inc	Whitman	MA	G	781 447-3941	16924
Harvard Instant Printing	Waltham	MA	G	781 893-2622	16124
Heritage Press Inc	Sandwich	MA	G	508 888-2111	14969
High-Speed Process Prtg Corp	Lawrence	MA	F	978 683-2766	12035
Hitchcock Press Inc	Holyoke	MA	F	413 538-8811	11632
I B A Inc	Millbury	MA	G	508 865-2507	13167
Imperial Image Inc	North Chelmsford	MA	F	978 251-0420	13897
Impressions Plus Inc	Quincy	MA	F	617 479-5777	14633
Ingleside Corporation	Norwood	MA	G	781 769-6656	14161
Ink Etcetera Corporation	Acton	MA	G	978 263-1555	7364
Inkstone Inc	Brockton	MA	E	508 587-5200	9155
Instant Offset Press Inc	Hyannis	MA	F	508 790-1100	11843
J & R Graphics Inc	Hanover	MA	F	781 871-7577	11343
J T Gardner Inc	Auburn	MA	G	508 832-2036	7839
J T Gardner Inc	Westborough	MA	G	508 366-2679	16628
J T Gardner Inc	Worcester	MA	G	508 751-6600	17396
J T Gardner Inc **(PA)**	Westborough	MA	E	800 540-4993	16627
Jen Ren Corporation	West Boylston	MA	G	508 835-3331	16419
Jet Press	Milford	MA	G	508 478-1814	13121
Jodys Quick Print	Middleton	MA	G	978 777-6114	13092
John Latka & Co Inc	Westfield	MA	G	413 562-4374	16691
John P Pow Company Inc	Boston	MA	E	617 269-6040	8635
Jordan Enterprises Inc	Marlborough	MA	F	508 481-2948	12781
Keating Communication Group	Canton	MA	G	781 828-9030	9749
Kenco Printing	Lowell	MA	G	781 391-9500	12387
Kerrin Graphics & Printing	Dudley	MA	G	508 765-1339	10379
Kervick Family Foundation Inc	Worcester	MA	G	508 853-4500	17399
King Printing Company Inc	Lowell	MA	D	978 458-2345	12390
Kirkwood Holdings Inc **(PA)**	Wilmington	MA	C	978 658-4200	17012
Kwik Print Inc	Great Barrington	MA	F	413 528-2885	11240
Lamb Printing Company Inc	North Adams	MA	G	413 662-2495	13678
Lane Printing Co Inc	Holbrook	MA	F	781 767-4450	11529
Lexington Press Inc	Lexington	MA	G	781 862-8900	12238
Liberty Printing Co Inc	Brockton	MA	G	508 586-6810	9162
Litho-Craft Inc	Winchester	MA	F	781 729-1789	17091
Lujean Printing Co Inc	Cotuit	MA	F	508 428-8700	10170
M & C Press Inc	Cambridge	MA	F	617 354-2584	9541
Mackinnon Printing Co Inc	Acton	MA	G	978 263-8435	7371
Mallard Printing Inc	Fall River	MA	F	508 675-5733	10724
Mansir Printing LLC	Holyoke	MA	F	413 536-4250	11636
Marcus Company Inc	Holyoke	MA	E	413 534-3303	11637
Maroney Associates Inc	Holbrook	MA	G	781 767-3970	11530
Mass Printing & Forms Inc	North Reading	MA	G	781 396-1970	13987
Master Printing & Signs	Somerville	MA	G	617 623-8270	15196
May Graphics & Printing Inc	Westford	MA	G	978 392-1302	16779
MBI Graphics & Printing Corp	Southbridge	MA	F	508 765-0658	15394
Mc Kinnon Printing Co Inc	Revere	MA	G	781 592-3677	14773
McClelland Press Inc **(PA)**	Williamstown	MA	F	413 663-5750	16958
McDermott Pallotta Inc	Watertown	MA	G	617 924-2318	16300
McGirr Graphics Incorporated	Plymouth	MA	E	508 747-6400	14564
Medi - Print Inc **(PA)**	Malden	MA	E	781 324-4455	12582
Medi - Print Inc	Boston	MA	G	617 566-7594	8693
Merrill Graphics Incorporated	Braintree	MA	G	781 843-0666	9026
Miano Printing Services Inc	Holliston	MA	F	617 935-2830	11585
Michael M Almeida	Taunton	MA	G	508 823-4957	15765
Miles Press Inc	Auburn	MA	F	508 752-6430	7843
Milk Street Press Inc	Boston	MA	F	617 742-7900	8706
Millennium Press Inc	Agawam	MA	E	413 821-0028	7440
Millennium Printing Corp	Weymouth	MA	G	781 337-0002	16893
Minuteman Governance Inc	Hopkinton	MA	G	508 837-3004	11729
Minuteman Implant Club Inc	Natick	MA	G	413 549-4108	13269
Monaghan Printing Company	Fairhaven	MA	F	508 991-8087	10643
My Print and Copy LLC	Beverly	MA	G	978 232-3552	8158
Mystic Parker Printing Inc	Malden	MA	G	781 321-4948	12583
Newprint Offset Inc	Lexington	MA	F	781 891-6002	12250
North River Graphics Inc	Pembroke	MA	G	781 826-6866	14420
North Shore Printing Inc	North Reading	MA	G	978 664-2609	13988
Northern Graphics Inc	Middleton	MA	F	978 646-9925	13097
Office Management Systems	Stoughton	MA	G	617 921-2966	15612
Officers Wives Club	Bedford	MA	G	781 274-8079	7998
Online Print Resources	Winthrop	MA	G	617 539-3961	17100
Ouimette Printing Inc	West Springfield	MA	G	413 736-5926	16538
Owl Stamp Company Inc	Lowell	MA	G	978 452-4541	12418
Ozzie Printing Inc	Woburn	MA	G	978 657-9400	17252
Pace Associates Inc	Wellesley	MA	G	781 433-0639	16379
Paper Plus Inc	West Springfield	MA	G	413 785-1363	16540
Parker Press Inc	Malden	MA	G	781 321-4948	12588
Partnership Resources	Chelmsford	MA	G	978 256-0499	9922
Patriot Customs Incorporated	Southbridge	MA	G	508 764-7342	15399
Picken Printing Inc	North Chelmsford	MA	E	978 251-0730	13907
Pioneer Valley Printing Co	West Springfield	MA	G	413 739-2855	16544
PIP Foundation Inc	Framingham	MA	E	508 757-0103	10995
PIP Itsa Inc	Beverly	MA	G	978 927-5717	8165
Pleasant Printing Co	Attleboro	MA	F	508 222-3366	7778
PMS Printing Inc **(PA)**	East Longmeadow	MA	G	860 563-1676	10486
Poets Corner Press Inc	Nantucket	MA	G	508 228-1051	13230
Postal Instant Press **(PA)**	East Longmeadow	MA	G	413 525-4044	10487
Potters Printing Inc	Fall River	MA	G	617 547-3161	10747
Powder Horn Press Inc **(PA)**	Plymouth	MA	G	508 746-8777	14576
President Press Inc	Quincy	MA	F	617 773-1235	14648
Pressroom Incorporated	Gloucester	MA	E	978 283-5562	11204
Print All of Boston Inc	Boston	MA	G	617 361-7400	8796
Print Synergy Solutions LLC	Brockton	MA	F	508 587-5200	9172
Print Works Inc	Hopkinton	MA	G	508 589-4626	11734
Printing & Graphic Services	Billerica	MA	G	978 667-6950	8277
Printing Place Inc	Melrose	MA	G	781 272-7209	12988
Printing Solutions Inc	Westford	MA	F	978 392-9903	16786
Puffer International Inc	Westfield	MA	G	413 562-9100	16719
Pynchon Press Co Inc	Chicopee	MA	G	413 315-8798	10054
Pyramid Printing and Advg Inc	Weymouth	MA	E	781 337-7609	16899
Qg LLC	Taunton	MA	B	508 828-4400	15776
Qg Printing Corp	Leominster	MA	C	978 534-8351	12179
Quad/Graphics Inc	Leominster	MA	A	860 741-0150	12180
Quad/Graphics Inc	Taunton	MA	B	508 692-3100	15777
Quad/Graphics Inc	Woburn	MA	C	781 231-7200	17275
Quad/Graphics Inc	Weymouth	MA	A	781 917-1601	16900
Quality Envelope & Printing Co	Middleboro	MA	G	508 947-8878	13077
Quality Printing Company Inc	Pittsfield	MA	D	413 442-4166	14504
Quick Print Ltd Inc	Chelmsford	MA	G	978 256-1822	9924
R & H Communications Inc **(PA)**	Waltham	MA	F	781 893-6221	16181
R E K Management Inc	West Harwich	MA	G	508 775-3005	16481
Ramsbottom Printing Inc	Fall River	MA	D	508 730-2220	10752
REA-Craft Press Incorporated	Foxboro	MA	F	508 543-8710	10899
Red Spot Printing	Waltham	MA	G	781 894-2211	16186
Red Sun Press Inc	Jamaica Plain	MA	F	617 524-6822	11949
Regal Press Incorporated **(PA)**	Norwood	MA	C	781 769-3900	14192
Rgp Corp	Milford	MA	C	508 478-8511	13141
Rickenbacker Resources Inc	Andover	MA	G	978 475-4520	7599
Rivkind Associates Inc **(PA)**	South Easton	MA	F	781 269-2415	15291
Rogers Printing Co Inc	Leominster	MA	E	978 537-9791	12184
S A N Inc **(PA)**	Lawrence	MA	G	978 686-3875	12073
Scorpian Printing	Framingham	MA	E	617 319-6114	11003
Screenco Printing Inc	Newburyport	MA	G	978 465-1211	13533
Shafiis Inc **(PA)**	East Longmeadow	MA	E	413 224-2100	10492
Shawmut Advertising Inc **(PA)**	Danvers	MA	E	978 762-7500	10255
Shawmut Printing	Danvers	MA	F	978 762-7500	10256
Shear Color Printing Inc	Woburn	MA	E	781 376-9607	17293
Sherman Printing Co Inc	Canton	MA	E	781 828-8855	9778
Shrewsbury National Press	Shrewsbury	MA	G	508 756-7502	15132
Sierra Press Inc	Waltham	MA	G	617 923-4150	16194
Signal Graphics 225	Quincy	MA	G	617 472-1700	14655
Skyline Productions	Cherry Valley	MA	G	508 326-4982	9977
Somerville Quick Print Inc	Cambridge	MA	G	617 492-5343	9656
Son Co Inc	Bellingham	MA	G	508 966-2970	8059
Spectrum Litho Inc	Canton	MA	G	781 575-0700	9785

	CITY	ST	EMP	PHONE	ENTRY #
Star Litho Inc	Weymouth	MA	E	781 340-9401	16901
Star Printing Corp	Taunton	MA	E	508 583-9046	15787
Starburst Prtg & Graphics Inc	Holliston	MA	F	508 893-0900	11606
State-Line Graphics Inc	Everett	MA	F	617 389-1200	10632
Strange Planet Printing	Brockton	MA	G	508 857-1816	9179
Studio 24 Graphix & Prtg Inc	Mattapan	MA	G	617 296-2058	12884
Studley Press Inc	Dalton	MA	E	413 684-0441	10187
Summit Forms	Worcester	MA	G	508 853-6838	17483
Summit Press Inc **(PA)**	Chelsea	MA	F	617 889-3991	9972
Superlative Printing Inc	Stoughton	MA	F	781 341-9000	15624
Task Printing Inc	Newton	MA	G	617 332-4414	13643
TCI Press Inc	Seekonk	MA	E	508 336-6633	15040
Technical Publications Inc	Waltham	MA	F	781 899-0263	16206
Techprint Inc	Lawrence	MA	D	978 975-1245	12077
Thomas B Fullen	Leominster	MA	G	978 534-5255	12194
Thompsons Printing Inc	Orleans	MA	F	508 255-0099	14242
Thriftco Speedi-Print Center	Peabody	MA	G	978 531-5546	14377
Tisbury Printer Inc	Vineyard Haven	MA	F	508 693-4222	15935
Trademark Print Inc	Pembroke	MA	G	781 829-0209	14429
Transamerica Printing Corp	Natick	MA	G	781 821-6166	13283
Travers Printing Inc	Gardner	MA	E	978 632-0530	11131
Tri Star Printing & Graphics	Somerville	MA	G	617 666-4480	15225
Trinity Press Inc	North Dartmouth	MA	G	508 998-1072	13928
Tshb Inc	Newburyport	MA	E	978 465-8950	13543
Universal Tag Inc	Dudley	MA	E	508 949-2411	10388
Universal Wilde Inc	Holliston	MA	C	508 429-5515	11611
Universal Wilde Inc **(PA)**	Westwood	MA	C	781 251-2700	16880
Universal Wilde Inc	Westwood	MA	C	978 658-0800	16881
Valley Printing Company	Cherry Valley	MA	G	508 892-9818	9978
Versatile Printing	Burlington	MA	G	781 221-2112	9352
Victoria H Bradshaw	New Bedford	MA	G	508 992-1702	13457
Vogel Printing Company Inc	Lawrence	MA	G	978 682-6828	12082
Waterfront Printing Company	Boston	MA	F	617 345-9711	8917
Watson Printing Co Inc	Wellesley	MA	G	781 237-1336	16393
We Print Today LLC	Kingston	MA	F	781 585-6021	11966
Webb-Mason Inc	Burlington	MA	G	781 272-5530	9356
Webster Printing Company Inc **(PA)**	Hanson	MA	E	781 447-5484	11370
Western Mass Copying Prtg Inc	West Springfield	MA	G	413 734-2679	16565
Westrex International Inc	Boston	MA	F	617 254-1200	8923
Wilkscraft Inc	Beverly	MA	F	978 922-1855	8197
Windsor Press Inc	Wellesley	MA	G	781 235-0265	16394
Winkir Instant Printing Inc	South Yarmouth	MA	G	508 398-9748	15335
Yankee Printing Group Inc	South Hadley	MA	E	413 532-9513	15313
Ziprint Centers Inc	Randolph	MA	G	781 963-2250	14703
Alliance Printers LLC	Brunswick	ME	F	207 504-8200	5828
Armstrong Family Inds Inc	Hermon	ME	E	207 848-7300	6183
Atlantic Coastal Printing Inc	Biddeford	ME	G	207 284-4328	5719
Bromar	Skowhegan	ME	G	207 474-3784	6970
Brunswick Instant Printing Inc	Brunswick	ME	G	207 729-6854	5832
Calais Press Inc	Calais	ME	G	207 454-8613	5864
Camden Printing Inc	Rockland	ME	G	207 236-4112	6787
Cardinal Printing Co Inc	Denmark	ME	G	207 452-2931	5948
Cmyk Print Services	Scarborough	ME	G	207 228-3838	6914
Computech Inc	Auburn	ME	G	207 777-7468	5554
Curry Printing & Copy Center	Portland	ME	F	207 772-5897	6645
Dale Rand Printing Inc	Portland	ME	G	207 773-8198	6647
Davic Inc	Portland	ME	F	207 774-0093	6649
Donald McIntire	Farmington	ME	G	207 778-3581	6043
Downeast Graphics & Prtg Inc	Ellsworth	ME	F	207 667-5582	6016
E I Printing Co	Portland	ME	F	207 797-4838	6656
Evergreen Custom Printing Inc	Auburn	ME	G	207 782-2327	5563
Fast Forms Printing & Paper	Hermon	ME	G	207 941-8383	6186
First Choice Printing Inc	Lisbon Falls	ME	G	207 353-8006	6369
Furbush Roberts Prtg Co Inc	Bangor	ME	G	207 945-9409	5647
Harbor Print Shop	Boothbay	ME	G	207 633-4176	5778
J A Black Company	Belfast	ME	G	207 338-4040	5691
Jiffy Print Inc	Bangor	ME	G	207 947-4490	5652
Johnson Printing & Graphics	Eliot	ME	G	207 439-2567	6007
JS McCarthy Co Inc **(PA)**	Augusta	ME	D	207 622-6241	5609
L H Thompson Inc	Brewer	ME	F	207 989-3280	5797
Laura Marr Productions LLC	Westbrook	ME	G	207 856-9700	7194
Letter Systems Inc **(PA)**	Augusta	ME	C	207 622-7126	5613
Northern Printers Inc	Presque Isle	ME	G	207 769-1231	6767
Park Street Press Inc	South Paris	ME	G	207 743-7702	7015
Partners Printing Inc	South Portland	ME	G	207 773-0439	7036
Port Printing Solutions Inc	South Portland	ME	G	207 741-5200	7037
Prints Charming Printers Inc	Boothbay	ME	G	207 633-6663	5780
Pyramid Checks & Printing	Portland	ME	D	207 878-9832	6718
Quick Print Color Center	Saco	ME	G	207 282-6480	6856
R & W Engraving Inc	Biddeford	ME	G	207 286-3020	5760
R N Haskins Printing Inc	Sidney	ME	F	207 465-2155	6964
Regal Press Inc	Ellsworth	ME	G	207 667-5227	6021
RH Rosenfield Co	Sanford	ME	E	207 324-1798	6889
Tall Oak Printing LLC	Wells	ME	G	207 251-4138	7166
Time4printing Inc	Windham	ME	G	207 838-1496	7257
Vc Print	Caribou	ME	G	207 492-1919	5892
Waterfront Graphics & Prtg LLC	South Portland	ME	G	207 799-3519	7044
Allegra Print & Imaging	Bedford	NH	G	603 622-3821	17630
American Printing Inc	Amherst	NH	F	603 880-0277	17550
Ariel Instant Printing	Keene	NH	G	603 352-3663	18492
Baker Graphics Inc	Manchester	NH	G	603 625-5427	18784
Blanchard Printing	Nashua	NH	G	603 891-1505	19127
Boles Enterprises Inc	Manchester	NH	G	603 622-4282	18789
Bridge & Byron Inc	Concord	NH	G	603 225-5221	17887
C & O Box & Printing Company	Hooksett	NH	G	508 881-1760	18345
Concord Litho Group Inc **(PA)**	Concord	NH	C	603 224-1202	17895

	CITY	ST	EMP	PHONE	ENTRY #
Curry Copy Center of Keene	Keene	NH	G	603 352-9542	18499
D M Printing Service Inc	Hudson	NH	G	603 883-1897	18382
Dr Biron Incorporated **(PA)**	Manchester	NH	F	603 622-5222	18813
E Print Inc	Hudson	NH	G	603 594-0009	18388
Eagle Copy Center	Windham	NH	G	603 225-3713	20004
Echo Communications Inc	New London	NH	E	603 526-6006	19316
Evans Printing Co	Bow	NH	G	603 856-8238	17713
Frugal Printer Inc	Salem	NH	F	603 894-6333	19737
Graphic Consumer Services Inc	Candia	NH	G	603 483-5355	17785
Hurley Ink LLC	Manchester	NH	G	603 645-0002	18840
Jeba Graphics LLC	Jaffrey	NH	G	603 532-7726	18468
Just Rewards Inc	Lebanon	NH	G	603 448-6800	18626
Kase Printing Inc	Hudson	NH	E	603 883-9223	18405
Kelley Solutions Inc	Portsmouth	NH	G	603 431-3881	19583
Kensington Group Incorporated	Hampton Falls	NH	F	603 926-6742	18283
Keystone Press LLC	Manchester	NH	F	603 622-5222	18768
Letterman Press LLC	West Lebanon	NH	G	603 543-0500	19956
Lew A Cummings Co Inc	Hooksett	NH	C	603 625-6901	18352
Liberty Press Inc	Manchester	NH	G	603 641-1991	18864
Loral Press Inc	Atkinson	NH	G	603 362-5549	17605
Mg Print and Promotions	Dover	NH	G	603 343-2534	18037
Miss Print	Meredith	NH	G	603 279-5939	18975
New England Printing Corp	Portsmouth	NH	F	603 431-0142	19599
Papergraphics Print & Copy	Merrimack	NH	F	603 880-1835	19019
Paul Revere Press Inc	Newton	NH	G	781 289-4031	19366
Print Factory Inc	Nashua	NH	G	603 880-4519	19239
Printers Square Inc	Manchester	NH	F	603 623-0802	18905
Puritan Press Inc **(PA)**	Hollis	NH	E	603 889-4500	18339
Quality Press Inc	Concord	NH	G	603 889-7211	17925
R C Brayshaw & Co Inc **(PA)**	Warner	NH	E	603 456-3101	19929
Rainville Printing Entps Inc	Pembroke	NH	G	603 485-3422	19463
Ram Printing Incorporated **(PA)**	East Hampstead	NH	E	603 382-7045	18082
Ram Printing Incorporated	East Hampstead	NH	G	603 382-3400	18083
RB Graphics Inc	Hooksett	NH	G	603 624-4025	18358
S & Q Printers Inc	Wilton	NH	G	603 654-2888	19987
Sant Bani Press Inc	Manchester	NH	F	603 286-3114	18915
Savron Graphics Inc **(PA)**	Jaffrey	NH	G	603 532-7726	18476
Savron Graphics Inc	Peterborough	NH	G	603 924-7088	19487
Shaughnessy Seagull Inc	Portsmouth	NH	G	603 433-4680	19620
Sheridan NH	Hanover	NH	G	603 643-2220	18297
Smith & Town Printers LLC	Berlin	NH	G	603 752-2150	17700
Sumner Fancy	Windham	NH	G	603 893-3081	20011
Sumner Printing Inc	Somersworth	NH	E	603 692-7424	19849
Thh Associates LLC	North Woodstock	NH	F	603 536-3600	19399
Town & Country Reprographics	Concord	NH	F	603 225-9521	17936
Txc Inc	Salem	NH	F	603 893-4999	19773
Underground Press	Freedom	NH	G	603 323-2022	18171
Upper Valley Press Inc	North Haverhill	NH	D	603 787-7000	19391
Ventricom Wireless Tech	Concord	NH	G	603 226-0025	17938
Wharf Industries Printing Inc	Windham	NH	F	603 421-2566	20014
Winnisquam Printing Inc	Laconia	NH	G	603 524-2803	18595
A & H Composition and Prtg Inc	East Providence	RI	G	401 438-1200	20383
ABS Printing Inc	West Warwick	RI	G	401 826-0870	21475
Adams Printing Inc	Pawtucket	RI	G	401 722-9222	20807
Allegra Print & Imaging	East Greenwich	RI	G	401 884-9280	20352
Allied Group Inc	Providence	RI	G	401 946-6100	20950
Barrington Print & Copy LLC	Warwick	RI	E	401 943-8300	21332
Bradford Press Inc	Providence	RI	G	401 621-7195	20972
Colonial Printing Inc **(PA)**	Warwick	RI	E	401 691-3400	21343
Colonial Printing Inc	Newport	RI	G	401 367-6690	20661
Copy Print Company	Cranston	RI	G	401 228-3900	20201
Crosstown Press Inc	Cranston	RI	F	401 941-4061	20205
Don-May of Wakefield Inc	Wakefield	RI	G	401 789-9339	21269
E&B Printing LLC	North Providence	RI	G	401 353-5777	20758
Enterprise Prtg & Pdts Corp	Rumford	RI	F	401 438-3838	21184
Formatt Printing Inc	North Providence	RI	G	401 475-6666	20761
I Copy	Kingston	RI	G	401 788-8277	20550
J B Foley Printing Company	Providence	RI	G	401 467-3616	21041
Jay Packaging Group Inc **(PA)**	Warwick	RI	D	401 244-1300	21379
Key Graphics Inc	Kingston	RI	G	401 826-2425	20551
Louis Press Inc	Johnston	RI	G	401 351-9229	20519
Mass Web Printing Company Inc	Providence	RI	D	508 832-5317	21062
Meridian Printing Inc	East Greenwich	RI	D	401 885-4882	20373
New England Image & Print Inc	North Smithfield	RI	G	401 769-3708	20793
Omo Inc	Providence	RI	G	401 421-5160	21084
Print Shops Inc	East Greenwich	RI	F	401 885-1226	20377
Printcraft Inc	Warwick	RI	G	401 739-0700	21405
Printing Plus	Westerly	RI	G	401 596-6970	21536
R J H Printing Inc	North Kingstown	RI	G	401 885-6262	20735
Realty Publishing Center Inc	Providence	RI	G	401 331-2505	21106
Regine Printing Co Inc	Providence	RI	G	401 943-3404	21108
Romano Investments Inc	Warwick	RI	E	401 691-3400	21416
Saffron Group Inc **(PA)**	Warren	RI	G	401 245-3725	21305
Service Plus Press Inc	Warwick	RI	G	401 461-2929	21424
Signature Printing Inc	East Providence	RI	D	401 438-1200	20444
Tap Printing Inc	Warren	RI	G	401 247-2188	21308
Tiffany Printing Company	Coventry	RI	G	401 828-5514	20168
Village Press Inc	Rumford	RI	F	401 434-8130	21198
Anything Printed LLC	Woodstock	VT	G	802 457-3414	22735
Buyers Digest Press Inc	Fairfax	VT	D	802 893-4214	21973
Chester Brothers	Winooski	VT	G	802 655-4159	22718
Dawn Brainard	Newport	VT	G	802 334-2780	22196
Digital Press Printers LLC	Williston	VT	F	802 863-5579	22662
E & G Graphics	Rutland	VT	G	802 773-3111	22331
Edward Group Inc	Rutland	VT	F	802 775-1029	22332
Howard Printing Inc	Brattleboro	VT	G	802 254-3550	21733

	CITY	ST	EMP	PHONE	ENTRY #
Inkspot Press	Bennington	VT	F	802 447-1768	21673
L Brown and Sons Printing Inc	Barre	VT	E	802 476-3164	21627
Leahy Press Inc	Montpelier	VT	E	802 223-2100	22153
Marus Printing	Hartland	VT	G	802 436-2044	22016
Precision Print and Copy Inc	Vergennes	VT	G	802 877-3711	22555
Queen City Printers Inc	Burlington	VT	E	802 864-4566	21804
Rutland Printing Co Inc	Rutland	VT	G	802 775-1948	22351
S M T Graphics LLC	Shoreham	VT	G	802 897-5231	22433
Silver Mountain Graphics Inc	Saint Johnsbury	VT	G	802 748-1170	22395
Springfield Printing Corp	North Springfield	VT	E	802 886-2201	22238
Stillwater Graphics Inc	Williamstown	VT	F	802 433-9898	22651
Thompson Printing Inc	Manchester Center	VT	F	802 362-1140	22091
Tuttle Law Print Inc	Rutland	VT	D	802 773-9171	22356
Vermont Publishing Comany	Saint Albans	VT	E	802 524-9771	22384
Village Printer	Bellows Falls	VT	G	802 463-9697	21655
Villanti & Sons Printers Inc	Milton	VT	D	802 864-0723	22140
Winooski Press LLC	Winooski	VT	G	802 655-1611	22728
X Press In Stowe Inc	Stowe	VT	G	802 253-9788	22525
Zinn Graphics Inc	Brattleboro	VT	G	802 254-6742	21756

PRINTING: Photo-Offset

	CITY	ST	EMP	PHONE	ENTRY #
Hamden Press Inc	Hamden	CT	G	203 624-0554	1756
American Copy Print	Norwood	MA	G	781 769-9077	14128
Cybercopy Inc	Portland	ME	G	207 775-2679	6646
Hoy Printing Corp	Biddeford	ME	G	207 284-5531	5739
Whitman Communications Inc	Lebanon	NH	E	603 448-2600	18641
Steele and Steele Inc	Wakefield	RI	G	401 782-2278	21279

PRINTING: Photogravure

	CITY	ST	EMP	PHONE	ENTRY #
Giannetti Mfg Services Inc	South Hadley	MA	G	413 532-9736	15304
Jon Goodman	Williamsburg	MA	G	413 586-9650	16951

PRINTING: Photolithographic

	CITY	ST	EMP	PHONE	ENTRY #
Central Street Corporation	Bangor	ME	F	207 947-8049	5635
First Step Print Shop LLC	Underhill	VT	G	802 899-2708	22547

PRINTING: Rotogravure

	CITY	ST	EMP	PHONE	ENTRY #
Schmitt Realty Holdings Inc	Branford	CT	E	203 488-3252	346

PRINTING: Screen, Broadwoven Fabrics, Cotton

	CITY	ST	EMP	PHONE	ENTRY #
To Give Is Better	Bristol	CT	G	860 261-5443	618
Ultimate Ink LLC	Wilton	CT	G	203 762-0602	5309
Action Apparel Inc **(PA)**	Stoneham	MA	F	781 224-0777	15552
Dasein Inc	Winchester	MA	G	781 756-0380	17086
Gonco Inc **(PA)**	Sandwich	MA	G	508 833-3900	14968
Hendrickson Advertising Inc	Sterling	MA	G	978 422-8087	15539
Pacific Printing Inc	Northampton	MA	G	413 585-5700	14016
Silver Screen Design Inc	Greenfield	MA	F	413 773-1692	11275
Gemini Firfield Screenprinting	Keene	NH	G	603 357-3847	18505
Life Is Good Wholesale Inc	Hudson	NH	D	603 594-6100	18412
Liquid Blue Inc	Derry	NH	D	401 333-6200	17987
Screen Printed Special TS	Manchester	NH	G	603 622-2901	18919
Dee Kay Designs Inc **(PA)**	Hope Valley	RI	D	401 539-2400	20484

PRINTING: Screen, Fabric

	CITY	ST	EMP	PHONE	ENTRY #
J & D Embroidering Co	Baltic	CT	G	860 822-9777	50
Zuse Inc	Guilford	CT	F	203 458-3295	1725
Advanced Print Technology Inc	Fitchburg	MA	G	978 342-0093	10809
Agawam Novelty Company Inc	Agawam	MA	G	413 536-0471	7418
E S Sports Corporation	Holyoke	MA	D	413 534-5634	11623
ESP Solutions Services LLC	Taunton	MA	E	508 285-0017	15749
First Print Inc	Winchester	MA	F	781 729-7714	17087
Fleming Industries Inc	Chicopee	MA	D	413 593-3300	10026
Gloucester Graphics Inc **(PA)**	Gloucester	MA	F	978 281-4500	11188
Imprinted Sportswear Inc	West Springfield	MA	G	413 732-5271	16525
Jph Graphics LLC	Salem	MA	G	978 744-7873	14926
Marcott Designs	Attleboro	MA	G	508 226-2680	7762
Pro Am Enterprises Inc	Melrose	MA	G	781 662-8888	12989
Sundance Screenprints	Gloucester	MA	G	978 281-6006	11213
Universal Screening Studio Inc	Everett	MA	G	617 387-1832	10633
Lynne Bailey	York	ME	G	207 363-7999	7310
Robert Gaynor	Bar Harbor	ME	G	207 288-4398	5668
Say It In Stitches Inc	Concord	NH	G	603 224-6470	17927
Vantastic Inc	Laconia	NH	G	603 524-1419	18591
Vermont TS Inc	Chester	VT	G	802 875-2091	21853

PRINTING: Screen, Manmade Fiber & Silk, Broadwoven Fabric

	CITY	ST	EMP	PHONE	ENTRY #
Tees & More LLC	Hartford	CT	G	860 244-2224	1876
Fosters Promotional Goods	Marblehead	MA	F	781 631-3824	12683
Gloucester Graphics Inc **(PA)**	Gloucester	MA	F	978 281-4500	11188
Pacific Printing Inc	Northampton	MA	G	413 585-5700	14016
Repro Craft Inc	Chicopee	MA	G	413 533-4937	10057
Serigraphics Unlimited	Rowley	MA	G	978 356-4896	14866
T-Shirts N Jeans Inc	Danvers	MA	G	781 279-4220	10260
Commercial Screenprint EMB Inc	Bangor	ME	G	207 942-2862	5639
Better Life LLC	Manchester	NH	G	603 647-0077	18787
First Impressions Embroidery	Hooksett	NH	G	603 606-1400	18350
Hammar & Sons Inc	Pelham	NH	E	603 635-2292	19434
Jembow Inc	Bow	NH	G	603 774-6055	17717
My-T-Man Screen Printing Inc	Manchester	NH	F	603 622-7740	18881
Cooley Incorporated **(HQ)**	Pawtucket	RI	C	401 724-9000	20825

PRINTING: Thermography

	CITY	ST	EMP	PHONE	ENTRY #
E & A Enterprises Inc	Wallingford	CT	E	203 250-8050	4736
Practical Automation Inc **(HQ)**	Milford	CT	D	203 882-5640	2336
Therma-Scan Inc	Vernon Rockville	CT	G	860 872-9770	4684
Imperial Image Inc	North Chelmsford	MA	F	978 251-0420	13897

	CITY	ST	EMP	PHONE	ENTRY #
Kwik Kopy Printing	Beverly	MA	G	978 232-3552	8146
Print Management Systems Inc	Woburn	MA	F	781 944-1041	17270
Professional Lithography Inc	South Hadley	MA	E	413 532-9473	15309
Van-Go Graphics	Grafton	MA	F	508 865-7300	11225

PROFESSIONAL EQPT & SPLYS, WHOLESALE: Analytical Instruments

	CITY	ST	EMP	PHONE	ENTRY #
Bruker Daltonics Inc	Billerica	MA	G	978 663-2548	8224
Bruker Scientific LLC **(HQ)**	Billerica	MA	C	978 667-9580	8228
Allan Fuller	Benton	ME	G	603 886-5555	5703
Datapaq Inc	Derry	NH	E	603 537-2680	17977
Electri-Temp Corporation	Pelham	NH	G	603 422-2509	19432

PROFESSIONAL EQPT & SPLYS, WHOLESALE: Bank

	CITY	ST	EMP	PHONE	ENTRY #
Tech180 Corp	Easthampton	MA	F	413 203-6123	10581

PROFESSIONAL EQPT & SPLYS, WHOLESALE: Engineers', NEC

	CITY	ST	EMP	PHONE	ENTRY #
Joseph Merritt & Company Inc	Danbury	CT	G	203 743-6734	940

PROFESSIONAL EQPT & SPLYS, WHOLESALE: Optical Goods

	CITY	ST	EMP	PHONE	ENTRY #
Hoya Corporation	South Windsor	CT	B	860 289-5379	3982
Sign In Soft Inc	Shelton	CT	G	203 216-3046	3870
AMF Optical Solutions LLC	Woburn	MA	G	781 933-6125	17118
Atlantic Vision Inc	Shrewsbury	MA	G	508 845-8401	15103
Boston Piezo-Optics Inc	Bellingham	MA	F	508 966-4988	8032
Gentex Optics Inc	Dudley	MA	B	508 713-5267	10375
Solos Endoscopy Inc	Boston	MA	G	617 360-9700	8852
Optical Solutions Inc	Charlestown	NH	G	603 826-4411	17818

PROFESSIONAL EQPT & SPLYS, WHOLESALE: Scientific & Engineerg

	CITY	ST	EMP	PHONE	ENTRY #
Tower Optical Company Inc	Norwalk	CT	G	203 866-4535	3260
K S E Inc	Sunderland	MA	F	413 549-5506	15675
Kayaku Advanced Materials Inc **(PA)**	Westborough	MA	E	617 965-5511	16629

PROFESSIONAL INSTRUMENT REPAIR SVCS

	CITY	ST	EMP	PHONE	ENTRY #
Timken Motor & Crane Svcs LLC	Portland	ME	F	207 699-2501	6740

PROFILE SHAPES: Unsupported Plastics

	CITY	ST	EMP	PHONE	ENTRY #
Web Industries Hartford Inc **(HQ)**	Dayville	CT	E	860 779-3197	1055
Coorstek Inc	Worcester	MA	B	774 317-2600	17360
Kilder Corporation	North Billerica	MA	E	978 663-8800	13830
Plasti-Graphics Inc	Lynn	MA	G	781 599-7766	12533
Seymour Associates Inc	Hudson	MA	G	978 562-1373	11815
David Michaud	Winthrop	ME	G	207 377-8037	7280
Teleflex Incorporated	Jaffrey	NH	E	603 532-7706	18479
Tfx Medical Incorporated	Jaffrey	NH	B	603 532-7706	18480
Hitachi Cable America Inc	Ashaway	RI	C	401 315-5100	20038

PROMOTERS OF SHOWS & EXHIBITIONS

	CITY	ST	EMP	PHONE	ENTRY #
Larson Worldwide Inc	Norwell	MA	G	781 659-2115	14105
Telco Communications Inc	Seekonk	MA	E	508 336-6633	15041

PROMOTION SVCS

	CITY	ST	EMP	PHONE	ENTRY #
Branding Company Inc	Westerly	RI	G	203 793-1923	21518

PROPELLERS: Boat & Ship, Machined

	CITY	ST	EMP	PHONE	ENTRY #
Hadley Propeller Inc	Hadley	MA	G	413 585-0500	11306
Rolls-Royce Marine North Amer **(DH)**	Walpole	MA	C	508 668-9610	16009

PROPELLERS: Ship, Nec

	CITY	ST	EMP	PHONE	ENTRY #
Flex O Fold North America Inc	Marblehead	MA	F	781 631-3190	12682

PROTECTION EQPT: Lightning

	CITY	ST	EMP	PHONE	ENTRY #
East Coast Lightning Eqp Inc	Winsted	CT	E	860 379-9072	5410
Northast Lghtning Prtction LLC	Bloomfield	CT	F	860 243-0010	246
Baystate Lightning Protection	Bridgewater	MA	G	508 697-7727	9063

PROTECTIVE FOOTWEAR: Rubber Or Plastic

	CITY	ST	EMP	PHONE	ENTRY #
Dance Paws LLC	Cambridge	MA	G	617 945-3044	9450
Klone Lab LLC	Newburyport	MA	G	978 378-3434	13505
32 North Corporation	Biddeford	ME	G	207 284-5010	5716
Simply Footwear Utah LLC	Concord	NH	G	603 715-2259	17930
Codet-Newport Corporation **(HQ)**	Newport	VT	F	802 334-5811	22192

PUBLISHERS: Art Copy

	CITY	ST	EMP	PHONE	ENTRY #
Historical Art Prints	Southbury	CT	G	203 262-6680	4027

PUBLISHERS: Art Copy & Poster

	CITY	ST	EMP	PHONE	ENTRY #
Fishing Hot Spots Inc	Nashua	NH	G	715 365-5555	19158

PUBLISHERS: Book

	CITY	ST	EMP	PHONE	ENTRY #
Bay Tact Corporation	Woodstock Valley	CT	E	860 315-7372	5503
Belvoir Publications Inc **(PA)**	Norwalk	CT	E	203 857-3100	3112
Bff Holdings Inc **(HQ)**	Old Saybrook	CT	C	860 510-0100	3328
Birdtrack Press	New Haven	CT	G	203 389-7789	2669
Carala Ventures Ltd	Stratford	CT	E	800 483-6449	4402
Connecticut Law Book Co Inc	Guilford	CT	F	203 458-8000	1698
Connecticut Parent Magazine	Branford	CT	F	203 483-1700	306
Creative Media Applications	Weston	CT	F	203 226-0544	5171
Early Advantage LLC	Fairfield	CT	F	203 259-6480	1428
Eye Ear It LLC	Woodbury	CT	F	203 487-8949	5487
Forecast International Inc	Newtown	CT	D	203 426-0800	2922
Gamut Publishing	Hartford	CT	E	860 296-6128	1824
Information Today Inc	Wilton	CT	F	203 761-1466	5291
Kieffer Associates Inc	Stamford	CT	G	203 323-3437	4235
Ppc Books Ltd	Westport	CT	G	203 226-6644	5224

PRODUCT

	CITY	ST	EMP	PHONE	ENTRY #
S Karger Publishers Inc	Unionville	CT	G	860 675-7834	4661
Sasc LLC **(PA)**	Greenwich	CT	G	203 846-2274	1646
Stamler Publishing Company	Branford	CT	G	203 488-9808	351
Summer Street Press LLC	Stamford	CT	F	203 978-0098	4335
Ubm LLC	Darien	CT	G	203 662-6501	1035
Wesleyan University	Middletown	CT	G	860 685-2980	2230
Zp Couture LLC	North Haven	CT	G	888 697-7239	3070
Acom Publishing Inc	Monson	MA	G	413 267-4999	13202
Anglo-Saxon Federation of Amer	Merrimac	MA	G	978 346-9311	13000
Anti-Phishing Wkg Group Inc	Cambridge	MA	G	404 434-7282	9390
Argosy Publishing Inc **(PA)**	Newton	MA	E	617 527-9999	13562
Berkshire Publishing Group LLC	Great Barrington	MA	F	413 528-0206	11235
Borderlines Foundation	Brookline	MA	G	617 365-9438	9197
Brown Publishing Network Inc **(PA)**	Charlestown	MA	E	781 547-7600	9828
Clp Pb LLC	Boston	MA	C	617 252-5213	8478
Courier Communications LLC **(HQ)**	North Chelmsford	MA	F	978 251-6000	13887
Courier New Media Inc **(DH)**	North Chelmsford	MA	E	978 251-3945	13890
Crawford Chandler Agency Inc	Monterey	MA	G	413 528-3035	13213
Curriculum Associates LLC	Boston	MA	G	978 313-1331	8492
Curriculum Associates LLC	Littleton	MA	E	978 313-1276	12298
Da Capo Press	Boston	MA	E	617 252-5200	8494
Ebsco Publishing Inc **(HQ)**	Ipswich	MA	A	978 356-6500	11917
Eric Carle LLC	Northampton	MA	G	413 586-2046	14006
Freeman Bedford	Boston	MA	C	617 399-4000	8554
Houghton Mifflin LLC	Boston	MA	E	617 351-5000	8602
Houghton Mifflin Co Intl Inc	Boston	MA	G	617 351-5000	8603
Houghton Mifflin Harcourt	Boston	MA	F	617 351-5000	8604
Houghton Mifflin Harcourt Co **(PA)**	Boston	MA	B	617 351-5000	8606
Information Gatekeepers Inc	Winchester	MA	G	617 782-5033	17088
International Press of Boston	Somerville	MA	G	617 623-3016	15184
Kidsbooks LLC	Boston	MA	G	617 425-0300	8648
Lama Yeshe Wisdom Archive Inc	Lincoln	MA	F	781 259-4466	12286
Massachsetts Prosecutors Guide	Milton	MA	G	617 696-6729	13195
Microtraining Assoc Inc	Hanover	MA	G	781 982-8984	11347
Page Street Publishing Company	Salem	MA	F	978 594-8758	14934
Pagoda Group LLC	Brookline	MA	G	617 833-3137	9214
Pearson Education Inc	Bedford	MA	G	781 687-8800	7999
Pearson Education Inc	Boston	MA	E	617 848-6000	8770
Pearson Education Holdings Inc	Boston	MA	D	617 671-2000	8771
Porter Sargent Publishers Inc	Westford	MA	G	617 922-0076	16785
President Fllows Hrvard Cllege	Cambridge	MA	D	617 495-9897	9616
Quarto Pubg Group USA Inc	Beverly	MA	E	978 282-9590	8166
Salem House Press	Salem	MA	E	978 578-9238	14940
Society For Marine Mammalogy	Yarmouth Port	MA	G	508 744-2276	17531
Technologies/Typography	Merrimac	MA	G	978 346-4867	13006
Vineyard Gazette LLC **(PA)**	Edgartown	MA	E	508 627-4311	10588
Wild Apples Inc	Harvard	MA	G	978 456-9616	11385
Wristies Inc	Lowell	MA	G	978 937-9500	12449
Xam Online Inc **(PA)**	Cambridge	MA	G	781 662-9268	9707
Zachary Shuster Hrmswoth Agncy	Boston	MA	G	617 262-2400	8940
Garmin International Inc	Yarmouth	ME	C	800 561-5105	7294
Herb Allure Inc	Amherst	ME	G	207 584-3550	5521
North Country Press	Unity	ME	G	207 948-2208	7117
Cafe Refugee Inc	Claremont	NH	G	603 499-7415	17838
Carrington International LLC	Candia	NH	G	603 867-8957	17780
Enfield Publishing & Dist Co	Enfield	NH	G	603 632-7377	18098
Fishing Hot Spots Inc	Nashua	NH	G	715 365-5555	19158
Greenwood Publishing Group LLC	Portsmouth	NH	E	603 431-7894	19570
Houghton Mifflin Harcourt Co	Portsmouth	NH	G	630 467-7000	19576
Stillpoint International Inc	Peterborough	NH	G	603 756-9281	19490
Alexandria Press	South Burlington	VT	G	802 497-0074	22436
Huntington Graphics	Burlington	VT	G	802 660-3605	21788
Miravia LLC **(PA)**	Charlotte	VT	G	802 425-6483	21834
Stratford Publishing Services	Brattleboro	VT	E	802 254-6073	21747

PUBLISHERS: Books, No Printing

	CITY	ST	EMP	PHONE	ENTRY #
Begell House Inc	Danbury	CT	F	203 456-6161	878
Bunting & Lyon Inc	Cheshire	CT	G	203 272-4623	718
Burns Walton	Branford	CT	G	203 422-5222	300
Cortina Learning Intl Inc **(PA)**	Wilton	CT	F	800 245-2145	5285
Graphics Press LLC	Cheshire	CT	G	203 272-9187	736
Industrial Press Inc	Norwalk	CT	F	212 889-6330	3172
Life Study Fllwship Foundation	Darien	CT	E	203 655-1436	1028
McBooks Press Inc	Guilford	CT	G	607 272-2114	1710
Millbrook Press Inc	Brookfield	CT	E	203 740-2220	652
Peninsula Publishing	Westport	CT	G	203 292-5621	5223
R G L Inc	East Granby	CT	E	860 653-7254	1142
Scholastic Library Pubg Inc **(HQ)**	Danbury	CT	A	203 797-3500	986
Tantor Media Incorporated	Old Saybrook	CT	C	860 395-1155	3351
Taunton Inc	Newtown	CT	A	203 426-8171	2941
Vital Health Publishing Inc	Ridgefield	CT	G	203 438-3229	3688
Windhover Information Inc **(DH)**	Norwalk	CT	E	203 838-4401	3272
Ziga Media LLC	Darien	CT	G	203 656-0076	1037
Artech House Inc **(HQ)**	Norwood	MA	F	781 769-9750	14134
Aspect Inc	Brookline	MA	G	617 713-2813	9194
Black Ice Publishers	Southborough	MA	G	508 481-0910	15347
Brill Usa Inc	Boston	MA	F	617 263-2323	8445
Brillacademic Publishers Inc	Boston	MA	G	617 742-5277	8446
Candlewick Press Inc	Somerville	MA	D	617 661-3330	15164
Christopher-Gordon Publishing	Foxboro	MA	F	781 762-5577	10879
Circlet Press Inc	Cambridge	MA	G	617 864-0663	9438
Council On Intl Pub Affirs Inc **(PA)**	Northampton	MA	G	212 972-9878	14002
Credo Reference Limited	Boston	MA	F	617 292-6100	8489
David R Godine Publisher Inc **(PA)**	Boston	MA	G	617 451-9600	8497
Davis Corp of Worcester Inc **(PA)**	Worcester	MA	E	508 754-7201	17363
Diacritech Inc	Boston	MA	F	617 236-7500	8502
Exact Change	Cambridge	MA	G	617 492-5405	9475
Fair Winds Press and Quiver	Beverly	MA	G	978 282-9590	8130
Greenwood Publishing Group LLC **(DH)**	Boston	MA	E	617 351-5000	8581
Hachette Book Group Inc	Boston	MA	G	617 227-0730	8587
Hackett Publishing Company	Cambridge	MA	F	617 497-6303	9499
Harvard Bus Schl Pubg Corp **(HQ)**	Brighton	MA	C	617 783-7400	9100
Hendrickson Publishers LLC	Peabody	MA	F	978 532-6546	14339
Hendrickson Publishers Inc	Peabody	MA	G	800 358-3111	14340
Hmh Publishers LLC **(DH)**	Boston	MA	G	617 351-5000	8599
Holy Cross Orthodox Press	Brookline	MA	G	800 245-0599	9203
Horizon House Publications Inc **(PA)**	Norwood	MA	D	781 769-9750	14158
Human Resource Dev Press **(PA)**	Pelham	MA	E	413 253-3488	14388
Macmillan Publishing Group LLC	Boston	MA	D	646 307-5617	8677
Massachusetts Institute Tech	Cambridge	MA	D	617 253-1000	9547
Memoirs Unlimited Inc	Beverly	MA	G	978 985-3206	8151
Merriam-Webster Incorporated **(DH)**	Springfield	MA	C	413 734-3134	15489
National Braille Press Inc	Boston	MA	D	617 425-2400	8720
Nicholas Brealey Pubg Inc	Boston	MA	G	617 523-3801	8737
North River Press Pubg Corp	Great Barrington	MA	F	413 528-0034	11243
O E M Health Information Inc	Beverly	MA	G	978 921-7300	8161
OReilly Media Inc	Boston	MA	C	617 354-5800	8758
Oriental Research Partners	Framingham	MA	G	781 642-1216	10990
Pedipress Inc	Amherst	MA	G	413 549-3918	7521
Pioneer Vly Eductl Press Inc	Northampton	MA	F	413 727-3573	14019
Planet Small Communications	Lawrence	MA	G	978 794-2201	12071
Publishing Solutions Group Inc	Woburn	MA	F	617 274-9001	17272
Quayside Publishing Group	Beverly	MA	G	978 282-9590	8167
Redwheel/Weiser LLC **(PA)**	Newburyport	MA	G	978 465-0504	13527
Robert Bentley Inc	Cambridge	MA	E	617 547-4170	9636
Robert Murphy	Salem	MA	E	978 745-7170	14938
Short Courses	Marblehead	MA	G	781 631-1178	12694
Silver Leaf Books LLC	Holliston	MA	E	781 799-6609	11602
Singing River Publications	Brighton	MA	G	218 365-3498	9106
Sproutman Publications	Great Barrington	MA	G	413 528-5200	11247
Storey Publishing LLC **(HQ)**	North Adams	MA	E	413 346-2100	13685
Tapestry Press Ltd	Littleton	MA	G	978 486-0200	12324
Textcafe	Natick	MA	G	508 654-8520	13281
Unitarian Universalist Assn	Boston	MA	E	617 742-2110	8897
Victory Productions Inc	Worcester	MA	E	508 755-0051	17500
Walter De Gruyter Inc	Boston	MA	G	857 284-7073	8915
Wellesley Information Svcs LLC **(HQ)**	Dedham	MA	D	781 407-0360	10301
Willett Institute of Finance	Reading	MA	G	617 247-3030	14744
Wisdom Publications Inc **(PA)**	Somerville	MA	G	617 776-7416	15233
Alice James Poetry Coop Inc	Farmington	ME	G	207 778-7071	6040
Child Safety Solutions Inc	Rockland	ME	G	207 226-3870	6789
Invision Inc	Brunswick	ME	G	207 725-7123	5839
Memoir Network	Lisbon	ME	G	207 353-5454	6364
Penobscot Bay Press Inc **(PA)**	Stonington	ME	F	207 367-2200	7070
Tilbury House Publishers	Thomaston	ME	G	800 582-1899	7089
Wayside Publishing	Freeport	ME	F	888 302-2519	6089
Avocus Publishing Inc	Gilsum	NH	G	603 357-0236	18195
Blue Tree LLC	Portsmouth	NH	G	603 436-0831	19545
David R Godine Publisher Inc	Jaffrey	NH	G	603 532-4100	18460
Helmers Publishing Inc	Dublin	NH	E	603 563-1631	18068
Loreto Publications Inc	Fitzwilliam	NH	G	603 239-6671	18150
Peter E Randall Publisher LLC	Portsmouth	NH	G	603 431-5667	19607
Stenhouse Publishers	Portsmouth	NH	F	207 253-1600	19623
TMC Books LLC	Conway	NH	G	603 447-5589	17959
Travelbrains Inc	Bedford	NH	G	603 471-0127	17665
Metro Inc **(PA)**	Cranston	RI	E	401 461-2200	20262
Rhode Island Family Guide	Barrington	RI	G	401 247-0850	20053
Blacklightning Publishing Inc	West Topsham	VT	G	802 439-6462	22621
Charles E Tuttle Co Inc **(DH)**	North Clarendon	VT	E	802 773-8930	22214
Chelsea Green Publishing Co	White River Junction	VT	E	802 295-6300	22636
Chooseco LLC	Waitsfield	VT	G	802 496-2595	22563
Emily Post Institute Inc	Burlington	VT	G	802 860-1814	21781
Inner Traditions International **(PA)**	Rochester	VT	E	802 767-3174	22317
Longhill Partners Inc **(PA)**	Woodstock	VT	E	802 457-4000	22738
Trafalgar Square Farm Inc	North Pomfret	VT	F	802 457-1911	22235
Upper Access Inc	Hinesburg	VT	G	802 482-2988	22032

PUBLISHERS: Comic Books, No Printing

	CITY	ST	EMP	PHONE	ENTRY #
Comicana Inc	Stamford	CT	G	203 968-0748	4168

PUBLISHERS: Directories, NEC

	CITY	ST	EMP	PHONE	ENTRY #
Campus Yellow Pages LLC	West Hartford	CT	G	860 523-9909	5057
Relocation Information Svc Inc	Norwalk	CT	E	203 855-1234	3229
Gatco Inc	Hyannis	MA	F	508 815-4910	11842
Soyatech Inc	Bar Harbor	ME	G	207 288-4969	5670
Helmers Publishing Inc	Dublin	NH	E	603 563-1631	18068

PUBLISHERS: Directories, Telephone

	CITY	ST	EMP	PHONE	ENTRY #
Northeastern Publishing Co	Holliston	MA	G	508 429-5588	11591
Supermedia LLC	Braintree	MA	B	781 849-7670	9040
Supermedia LLC	South Portland	ME	B	207 828-6100	7041
Our Town Publishing Inc	Center Barnstead	NH	G	603 776-2500	17790

PUBLISHERS: Guides

	CITY	ST	EMP	PHONE	ENTRY #
Shoppers-Turnpike Corporation	Putnam	CT	F	860 928-3040	3632
Stamford Capital Group Inc **(PA)**	Stamford	CT	A	800 977-7837	4329
Greatheart Inc	Andover	MA	G	978 475-8732	7553
Southern Berkshire Shoppers Gu	Great Barrington	MA	F	413 528-0095	11246
Visitor Guide Publishing Inc	Newton	MA	G	617 542-5283	13650
A & D Print Shop	Presque Isle	ME	G	207 764-2662	6751
Garlic Press Inc	Williston	VT	F	802 864-0670	22667

PUBLISHERS: Magazines, No Printing

	CITY	ST	EMP	PHONE	ENTRY #
Air Age Inc	Wilton	CT	E	203 431-9000	5274
American Library Association	Middletown	CT	E	860 347-6933	2170
Belvoir Media Group LLC	Norwalk	CT	G	203 857-3128	3111
Beverage Publications Inc	Hamden	CT	G	203 288-3375	1735
Bottom Line Inc **(PA)**	Stamford	CT	D	203 973-5900	4151
Chief Executive Group LLC **(PA)**	Stamford	CT	F	785 832-0303	4164
Chief Executive Group LP **(PA)**	Stamford	CT	E	203 930-2700	4165
Corporate Connecticut Mag LLC	Wethersfield	CT	G	860 257-0500	5246
Domino Media Group Inc	Westport	CT	E	877 223-7844	5188
Donnin Publishing Inc	Guilford	CT	G	203 453-8866	1702
Douglas Moss	Norwalk	CT	G	203 854-5559	3144
Fairfield County Look	Greenwich	CT	G	203 869-0077	1610
Granta USA Ltd	Danbury	CT	F	440 207-6051	928
Information Today Inc	Wilton	CT	F	203 761-1466	5291
Interstate Tax Corporation	Norwalk	CT	G	203 854-0704	3176
L M T Communications Inc	Newtown	CT	F	203 426-4568	2927
Mason Medical Communications	Westport	CT	G	203 227-9252	5213
Moffly Publications Inc	Westport	CT	F	203 222-0600	5215
Moffly Publications Inc **(PA)**	Westport	CT	E	203 222-0600	5216
National Shooting Sports Found	Newtown	CT	E	203 426-1320	2929
Penny Marketing Ltd Partnr **(PA)**	Norwalk	CT	E	203 866-6688	3217
Penny Press Inc **(PA)**	Norwalk	CT	C	203 866-6688	3218
Penny Press Inc	Milford	CT	E	203 866-6688	2332
Relocation Information Svc Inc	Norwalk	CT	E	203 855-1234	3229
Scholastic Library Pubg Inc **(HQ)**	Danbury	CT	A	203 797-3500	986
Sixfurlongs LLC	Fairfield	CT	G	203 255-8553	1456
Soundings Publications LLC	Essex	CT	E	860 767-8227	1406
Sumner Communications Inc	Bethel	CT	E	203 748-2050	182
Tam Communications Inc	Norwalk	CT	E	203 425-8777	3254
Taunton Inc	Newtown	CT	A	203 426-8171	2941
Taunton Press Inc	Newtown	CT	B	203 426-8171	2942
This Old House Ventures LLC	Stamford	CT	E	475 209-8665	4344
Timer Digest Publishing Inc	Greenwich	CT	G	203 629-2589	1655
Venu Magazine LLC	Fairfield	CT	G	203 259-2075	1460
Wicks Business Information LLC **(PA)**	Shelton	CT	F	203 334-2002	3889
Windhover Information Inc **(DH)**	Norwalk	CT	E	203 838-4401	3272
Wire Journal Inc	Madison	CT	E	203 453-2777	1979
Yale Alumni Publications Inc	New Haven	CT	G	203 432-0645	2756
Advanstar Communications Inc	Burlington	MA	E	339 298-4200	9229
Art New England Magazine	Boston	MA	G	617 259-1040	8376
Boston Critic Inc	Cambridge	MA	G	617 324-1360	9418
Boston Design Guide Inc	Sudbury	MA	F	978 443-9886	15654
Cape Cod Life LLC	Mashpee	MA	F	508 419-7381	12877
Carnegie Communications LLC	Westford	MA	E	978 692-5092	16760
Carnegie Dartlet LLC **(PA)**	Westford	MA	G	978 692-5092	16761
Cell Press Inc	Cambridge	MA	D	617 397-2800	9433
Christian Science Pubg Soc **(PA)**	Boston	MA	B	617 450-2000	8473
Cmio Magazine Publications	Newton	MA	G	617 851-6671	13580
Contact Quarterly	Northampton	MA	G	413 586-1181	14001
Davis Publications Inc	Worcester	MA	E	508 754-7201	17364
Dunfey Publishing Company Inc	Jamaica Plain	MA	G	617 522-3267	11943
Forced Exposure Inc	Arlington	MA	E	781 321-0320	7626
Gasworld Publishing LLC	Lexington	MA	G	781 862-0624	12225
Guncanco Ltd	Georgetown	MA	G	978 352-3320	11143
Harvard Lampoon Inc	Cambridge	MA	E	617 495-7801	9503
Harvard Magazine Inc	Cambridge	MA	E	617 495-5746	9504
Horn Book Inc	Boston	MA	F	617 278-0225	8601
Hotrod Hotline	North Adams	MA	G	208 562-0470	13676
Hunter Associates Inc	Saugus	MA	E	781 233-9100	14986
Idg Corporate Services Group	Framingham	MA	F	508 875-5000	10967
Information Gatekeepers Inc	Winchester	MA	G	617 782-5033	17088
Institute For Scial Cltral Cmm	Dedham	MA	G	508 548-9063	10293
Just Publications Inc	Brookline	MA	G	617 739-5878	9207
Massachusetts Medical Society	Boston	MA	E	617 734-9800	8685
Metro Corp	Boston	MA	E	617 262-9700	8702
New England Home	Boston	MA	G	617 938-3991	8731
Open Studios Press Inc	Boston	MA	G	617 778-5265	8751
Page Same Publishing Inc	Littleton	MA	G	978 486-4684	12317
Pagio Inc	Worcester	MA	G	508 756-5006	17439
Penwell	Sturbridge	MA	G	508 347-8245	15645
Provincetown Arts Press Inc **(PA)**	Provincetown	MA	G	508 487-3167	14608
Quarterly Review of Wines	Quincy	MA	E	781 721-0525	14650
Regional Spt Media Group LLC	Rockland	MA	G	781 871-9271	14821
RMS Media Group Inc	Andover	MA	E	978 623-8020	7600
Seamans Media Inc	Milton	MA	G	617 773-9955	13200
Stellar Medical Publications	Plymouth	MA	G	508 732-6767	14585
Stysil Enterprises Ltd	Marshfield	MA	G	781 834-7279	12870
Suburban Publishing Corp	Peabody	MA	F	978 818-6300	14373
Suburban Shopper Inc	Canton	MA	G	781 821-2590	9788
Trustees of Boston University	Brookline	MA	F	617 353-3081	9223
Wilmington Compliance Week	Boston	MA	E	888 519-9200	8929
Young Authors Foundation Inc	Newton	MA	G	617 964-6800	13655
Casco Bay Sbstnce Abuse Rsrces	Portland	ME	F	207 773-7993	6634
D E Enterprise Inc	Rockport	ME	D	207 594-9544	6818
Down East Enterprise Inc	Rockport	ME	E	207 594-9544	6820
Flavor Unlimited Inc	Freeport	ME	G	207 865-4432	6078
Maine Antique Digest Inc	Waldoboro	ME	E	207 832-7534	7134
Maine Bats Hrbors Publications	Camden	ME	G	207 594-8622	5868
Navigator Publishing LLC	Portland	ME	E	207 822-4350	6698
Portland Monthly Inc	Portland	ME	G	207 775-4339	6711
Soyatech Inc	Bar Harbor	ME	G	207 288-4969	5670
United Publications Inc	Yarmouth	ME	E	207 846-0600	7303
Woodenboat Publications Inc	Brooklin	ME	E	207 359-4651	5822
Common Sense Marketing	Sunapee	NH	G	603 763-2441	19880
Helmers Publishing Inc	Dublin	NH	E	603 563-1631	18068
Laser Group Publishing Inc	Manchester	NH	F	603 880-8909	18861
Paine Publishing LLC	Durham	NH	G	603 682-0735	18079
Simon & Schuster Inc	Peterborough	NH	E	603 924-7209	19488
Yankee Publishing Incorporated **(PA)**	Dublin	NH	E	603 563-8111	18069
Daily Herald Brown Inc	Providence	RI	G	401 351-3372	20992
Metro Inc **(PA)**	Cranston	RI	E	401 461-2200	20262
Newport Life Magazine Inc	Middletown	RI	G	401 841-0200	20627
Rhode Island Monthly	Providence	RI	E	401 649-4800	21112
Backcountry Magazine	Jeffersonville	VT	G	802 644-6794	22045
Dartmouth Journal Services Inc	Waterbury	VT	E	802 244-1457	22582
Eating Well Inc **(HQ)**	Shelburne	VT	G	802 425-5700	22415
Kestrel Health Information Inc	Williston	VT	G	802 482-4000	22676
Mill Publishing Inc	Williston	VT	G	802 862-4109	22682
N News LLC	Topsham	VT	G	802 439-6054	22540
Reef To Rainforest Media LLC	Shelburne	VT	G	802 985-9977	22422

PUBLISHERS: Maps

	CITY	ST	EMP	PHONE	ENTRY #
Edgewater Marine Inds LLC	New Bedford	MA	E	508 992-6555	13383
Garmin International Inc	Yarmouth	ME	C	800 561-5105	7294

PUBLISHERS: Miscellaneous

	CITY	ST	EMP	PHONE	ENTRY #
American Trade Fairs Org	Westport	CT	G	203 221-0114	5182
Arcat Inc	Fairfield	CT	G	203 929-9444	1414
Audubon Copy Shppe of Firfield	Bridgeport	CT	G	203 259-4311	378
Bay Tact Corporation	Woodstock Valley	CT	E	860 315-7372	5503
Beardsley Publishing Corp	Woodbury	CT	G	203 263-0888	5483
Bff Holdings Inc **(HQ)**	Old Saybrook	CT	C	860 510-0100	3328
Burns Walton	Branford	CT	G	203 422-5222	300
Chicken Soup For Soul LLC	Cos Cob	CT	E	203 861-4000	823
Chicken Soup For Soul Entrmt I **(HQ)**	Cos Cob	CT	G	855 398-0443	824
Childrens Health Market Inc	Wilton	CT	G	203 762-2938	5283
Connelly 3 Pubg Group Inc	Clinton	CT	G	860 664-4988	782
Debrasong Publishing LLC	Lyme	CT	G	413 204-4682	1954
Executive Greetings Inc **(HQ)**	New Hartford	CT	B	860 379-9911	2636
Freedom Press	Pawcatuck	CT	G	860 599-5390	3435
Hearst Corporation	New Canaan	CT	E	203 438-6544	2600
Hersam Publishing Company	New Canaan	CT	B	203 966-9541	2601
Hollow Frost Publishers	Woodstock	CT	G	860 974-2081	5497
Life Study Fllwship Foundation	Darien	CT	E	203 655-1436	1028
Liturgical Publications Inc	New Canaan	CT	F	203 966-6470	2603
Media Ventures Inc	Norwalk	CT	E	203 852-6570	3194
Militarylife Publishing LLC	Shelton	CT	G	203 402-7234	3834
Nancy Larson Publishers Inc	Old Lyme	CT	E	860 434-0800	3325
National Shooting Sports Found	Newtown	CT	E	203 426-1320	2929
Nelson & Miller Associates	Stamford	CT	G	203 356-9694	4253
Newsbank Inc	New Canaan	CT	G	203 966-1100	2611
Penny Publications LLC	Milford	CT	E	203 866-6688	2333
Pixels 2 Press LLC	Norwalk	CT	G	203 642-3740	3221
Portfolio Arts Group Ltd	Norwalk	CT	F	203 661-2400	3222
Publishing Dimensions LLC	Weston	CT	G	203 856-7716	5173
Publishing Directions LLC	Avon	CT	G	860 673-7650	42
Qmdi Press	North Franklin	CT	G	860 642-8074	2991
Rand Media Co LLC	Westport	CT	G	203 226-8727	5225
Sandvik Pubg Interactive Inc **(PA)**	Danbury	CT	F	203 205-0188	981
Senior Network Inc	Stamford	CT	E	203 969-2700	4314
Shiller and Company Inc	Wilton	CT	D	203 210-5208	5303
Stamler Publishing Company	Branford	CT	G	203 488-9808	351
Tam Communications Inc	Norwalk	CT	E	203 425-8777	3254
Teed Off Publishing Inc	Greenwich	CT	G	561 266-0872	1654
Thomson Reuters Corporation	East Haven	CT	F	203 466-5055	1265
Times Publishing LLC	Middlefield	CT	G	860 349-8532	2167
Topaz Enterprise Sand Pubg	Norwalk	CT	G	203 449-1903	3259
Ubm LLC	Darien	CT	G	203 662-6501	1035
Universe Publishing Co LLC	Milford	CT	G	203 283-5201	2378
University Hlth Pubg Group LLC	Bethel	CT	G	203 791-0101	187
US Games Systems Inc	Stamford	CT	E	203 353-8400	4353
Valley Press Inc	Simsbury	CT	E	860 651-4700	3914
Wizard Too LLC	Westport	CT	G	203 984-7180	5238
Ziga Media LLC	Darien	CT	G	203 656-0076	1037
A Bismark Company	Fall River	MA	G	508 675-2002	10648
Accounting Web	Woburn	MA	D	978 331-1243	17106
Ad-A-Day Company Inc	Taunton	MA	E	508 824-8676	15719
All Set Press LLC	Malden	MA	G	781 397-1993	12557
American Journal Trnsp	Plymouth	MA	G	508 927-4183	14542
Anthroposophic Press Inc	Great Barrington	MA	F	212 414-2275	11232
Artquick Corp	Wayland	MA	G	508 358-4864	16333
B V T V Inc	Marstons Mills	MA	G	508 737-7754	12871
Black Ice Publishers	Southborough	MA	G	508 481-0910	15347
Broude International Editions	Williamstown	MA	G	413 458-8131	16956
Brown Publishing Network Inc **(PA)**	Charlestown	MA	E	781 547-7600	9828
Caldwell Cmmnications Advisors	Boston	MA	G	617 425-7318	8455
Charlesbridge Publishing Inc **(PA)**	Watertown	MA	E	617 926-0329	16276
Circadian Information	Stoneham	MA	F	781 439-6326	15557
Corporate Press	Norwood	MA	F	781 769-6656	14146
Crain Communications Inc	Boston	MA	G	617 357-9090	8486
Crimson Press	Stoneham	MA	G	781 914-3111	15558
Crossed Genres	Framingham	MA	G	617 335-2101	10937
Culver Company LLC	Salisbury	MA	F	978 463-1700	14949
Daily Juice Press LLC	Cohasset	MA	G	781 261-6099	10097
Diacritech Inc	Boston	MA	F	617 236-7500	8502
Driggin Sandra DBA Extra Extra	Quincy	MA	E	617 773-6996	14620
E H Publishing Inc **(PA)**	Framingham	MA	E	508 663-1500	10943
Ebsco Publishing Inc **(HQ)**	Ipswich	MA	A	978 356-6500	11917
Eglean Inc	Boston	MA	G	617 229-5863	8520
Electronic Publishing Services	Charlestown	MA	G	508 544-1254	9833
Elsevier Inc	Cambridge	MA	D	781 663-5200	9464

PRODUCT

	CITY	ST	EMP	PHONE	ENTRY #
Fluent Technologies Inc	Woburn	MA	F	781 939-0900	17183
Fourth Street Press Inc	Beverly	MA	G	978 232-9251	8133
Frg Publications	West Springfield	MA	F	413 734-3411	16522
Gatehouse Media LLC	Fall River	MA	C	508 676-8211	10701
Gems Publishing Usa Inc	Framingham	MA	G	508 872-0066	10949
George Publishing Company	Pembroke	MA	G	781 826-4996	14406
Global Prints Inc	Hyde Park	MA	G	800 578-4278	11868
Good Tern Press Inc	Boston	MA	G	508 277-5500	8573
Groupglobalnet Corp	Boston	MA	G	857 212-4012	8583
Gtxcel Inc	Southborough	MA	F	508 804-3092	15358
Hmh Supplemental Publishers	Boston	MA	G	407 345-2000	8600
Ian Marie Inc	Newburyport	MA	E	978 463-6742	13499
Idg Paper Services	Framingham	MA	E	508 875-5000	10968
Information Gatekeepers Inc	Winchester	MA	G	617 782-5033	17088
Ink Inc Publishing Service	Cambridge	MA	G	617 576-6740	9516
Innovative Publishing Co LLC	Edgartown	MA	F	267 266-8876	10585
Interntonal Science Foundation	Somerville	MA	G	703 869-1853	15185
Jf Griffin Publishing LLC	Williamstown	MA	G	413 458-4800	16957
Kidpub Press LLC	North Attleboro	MA	G	617 407-2337	13761
Lab Publications LLC	Swampscott	MA	G	781 598-9779	15698
Laurin Publishing Co Inc **(PA)**	Pittsfield	MA	D	413 499-0514	14482
Legacy Publishing Group Inc	Clinton	MA	E	800 322-3866	10083
Lets Go Inc	Cambridge	MA	A	617 495-9659	9534
Lighthouse Publications **(PA)**	Hyannis	MA	G	508 534-9291	11845
Massachusetts Institute Tech	Cambridge	MA	E	617 253-1541	9545
Massinvestor Incorporated	Arlington	MA	G	617 620-4606	7629
Medical Arts Press Inc	Framingham	MA	G	508 253-5000	10982
Mercury Learning and Info LLC	Duxbury	MA	G	781 934-0500	10400
Merriam-Webster Incorporated **(DH)**	Springfield	MA	C	413 734-3134	15489
Microtraining Assoc Inc	Hanover	MA	G	781 982-8984	11347
Mom Central	Chestnut Hill	MA	G	617 332-6819	9988
MSP Digital Marketing	Allston	MA	G	617 868-5778	7471
Mundos Crazy Music Pubg Corp	Stoneham	MA	G	781 438-1704	15568
Myjove Corporation	Cambridge	MA	D	617 945-9051	9572
Mystockplancom Inc	Brookline	MA	F	617 734-1979	9211
Norris Enterprises Inc	Hanover	MA	G	781 982-8158	11349
Nrt Inc	Medway	MA	F	508 533-4588	12968
OBrien Publications Inc	Cohasset	MA	G	781 378-2126	10101
OReilly Media Inc	Boston	MA	C	617 354-5800	8758
Pearson Education Inc	Boston	MA	E	617 848-6000	8770
Porter Sargent Publishers Inc	Westford	MA	G	617 922-0076	16785
President Fllows Hrvard Cllege	Cambridge	MA	D	617 495-9897	9616
Press Ganey	Lexington	MA	G	800 232-8032	12254
Press-It LLC	Woburn	MA	G	781 935-0035	17269
Pure Cold Press	Brookline	MA	G	617 487-8948	9216
Quayside Publishing Group	Beverly	MA	G	978 282-9590	8167
Quinlan Publishing Co Inc **(PA)**	Boston	MA	G	617 439-0076	8805
Racemaker Press	Boston	MA	G	617 391-0911	8807
Real Data Corp	Boston	MA	G	603 669-3822	8812
Relx Inc	Cambridge	MA	D	781 663-5200	9629
Reminder Publications	East Longmeadow	MA	E	413 525-3947	10491
Rheinwerk Publishing Inc	Quincy	MA	F	781 228-5070	14654
Rockport Custom Publishing LLC	Beverly	MA	G	978 522-4316	8172
S & S Publications Inc	Hull	MA	G	781 925-9266	11830
Sandcastle Publishing LLC	South Dennis	MA	G	508 398-3100	15266
Santorella Publication Ltd **(PA)**	Danvers	MA	G	978 750-0566	10254
Scarlet Ltr Press Gallery LLC	Salem	MA	G	978 741-1850	14942
Scholastic Corporation	Allston	MA	G	617 924-3846	7475
School Specialty Inc	Cambridge	MA	D	617 547-6706	9647
Simply Media Inc	Lincoln	MA	E	781 259-8029	12289
Singing River Publications	Brighton	MA	G	218 365-3498	9106
Sky Publishing Corporation	Cambridge	MA	E	617 864-7360	9652
Smaall Beer Press	Easthampton	MA	G	413 203-1636	10579
Spectrum Press Inc	Canton	MA	G	781 828-5050	9786
SRC Publishing Inc	Auburn	MA	G	508 749-3212	7850
Steves Publication Svc	Webster	MA	G	508 671-9192	16351
Then & Now Publishing	Scituate	MA	F	781 378-2013	15016
Thryv Inc	Waltham	MA	E	972 453-7000	16215
Turley Publications Inc	Feeding Hills	MA	F	413 786-7747	10804
Turley Publications Inc **(PA)**	Palmer	MA	C	800 824-6548	14298
University Massachusetts Inc	Amherst	MA	F	413 545-2217	7528
University of Massachusetts	Amherst	MA	D	413 545-3500	7530
Vegan Publishers LLC	Danvers	MA	G	857 364-4344	10271
Veritas Medicine Inc	Cambridge	MA	F	617 234-1500	9695
Web Closeout	Springfield	MA	E	413 222-8302	15524
Westwood Press	Framingham	MA	E	781 433-8354	11015
White Knight Studio	Grafton	MA	G	781 799-0569	11226
World Publications Inc	North Dighton	MA	G	508 880-5555	13938
Almanac Publishing Co	Lewiston	ME	G	207 755-2000	6274
Bolinda Publishing Inc	Jackson	ME	G	207 722-3185	6218
Center Point Inc	Knox	ME	E	207 568-3717	6262
Central Street Corporation	Bangor	ME	F	207 947-8049	5635
Darby Pop LLC	Cape Elizabeth	ME	G	207 799-4202	5875
Downeast Networking Services	Portland	ME	G	772 485-4304	6653
Dramatic Dffrence Publications	Farmington	ME	G	207 778-9696	6044
Maine Authors Publishing	Thomaston	ME	G	207 594-0090	7087
National Poetry Foundation	Orono	ME	G	207 581-3814	6556
Noah Publications	Brooklin	ME	G	207 359-2131	5821
Original Irregular	Kingfield	ME	G	207 265-2773	6254
S3 Digital Publishing Inc	Lisbon Falls	ME	G	207 351-8006	6372
Scorebuilders	Scarborough	ME	G	207 885-0304	6939
Sellers Publishing Inc	South Portland	ME	E	207 772-6833	7040
Taylor Bryson Inc	Saco	ME	G	207 838-0961	6859
Town of Gorham **(PA)**	Gorham	ME	E	207 222-1610	6132
Town of Gorham	Gorham	ME	G	207 839-5555	6133
Valentine & Company Inc	Westbrook	ME	G	207 774-4769	7212

	CITY	ST	EMP	PHONE	ENTRY #
Writing Company	Portland	ME	G	207 370-8078	6746
Backporch Publishing	Keene	NH	G	603 357-8761	18494
Battle Road Press	Peterborough	NH	G	603 924-7600	19467
Bauhan Publishing	Peterborough	NH	G	603 567-4430	19468
Carlisle Publications	Manchester	NH	G	603 622-4056	18796
Carus Publishing	Peterborough	NH	G	603 924-7209	19466
Clark Publishing	Portsmouth	NH	G	603 431-1238	19553
Connell Communications Inc	Keene	NH	E	603 924-7271	18496
Doolittles Print Serve Inc	Claremont	NH	G	603 543-0700	17848
Hawthorn Creative Group LLC	Portsmouth	NH	E	603 610-0533	19574
Kensington Group Incorporated	Hampton Falls	NH	F	603 926-6742	18283
Leopard Snow Publishing LLC	Dover	NH	G	603 742-7714	18034
Nutfield Publishing LLC	Londonderry	NH	G	603 537-2760	18730
Ocean Publishing	Rye	NH	G	603 812-5557	19700
Paramount Publishing Inc/	Bedford	NH	G	603 472-3528	17659
Sign Express LLC	Manchester	NH	G	603 606-1279	18922
Sophia Institute	Manchester	NH	G	603 641-9344	18926
Square Spot Publishing LLC	Manchester	NH	G	603 625-6003	18929
Stamp News Publishing Inc	Merrimack	NH	G	603 424-7556	19034
Starcrafts Publishing LLC	Epping	NH	G	603 734-5303	18103
Steerforth Press LLC	Hanover	NH	G	603 643-4787	18298
Textnology Corp	Nashua	NH	F	603 465-8398	19273
Tmax Publishing LLC	Salem	NH	G	603 505-7693	19772
Top Kayaker Geo Odyssey Llc	Center Ossipee	NH	G	603 651-1036	17806
Virtual Publishing LLC	Manchester	NH	F	603 627-9500	18952
Ymaa Publication Center Inc	Wolfeboro	NH	G	603 569-7988	20027
B E Publishing	North Kingstown	RI	G	401 294-2490	20692
Cars Realty LLC	Johnston	RI	G	401 231-1389	20502
Chew Publishing Inc	Middletown	RI	G	401 808-0648	20617
CM Publications Inc	Westerly	RI	G	401 596-9358	21519
Copy Print Company	Cranston	RI	G	401 228-3900	20201
Custom Flow Solutions LLC	Providence	RI	G	401 487-2957	20991
DManielly Express	Providence	RI	G	401 490-2900	20997
Elegant Publishing Inc	Riverside	RI	G	401 245-9726	21167
Gaspee Publishing	Providence	RI	G	401 272-3668	21020
Guia Commercial Portugues Inc	East Providence	RI	G	401 438-1740	20417
Rhode Island Publications Soc	Providence	RI	G	401 273-1787	21114
Supermedia LLC	Warwick	RI	E	401 468-1500	21432
Tizra	Providence	RI	G	401 935-5317	21138
Art Licensing Intl Inc	Arlington	VT	F	802 362-3662	21595
Business Financial Pubg LLC	Williston	VT	F	802 865-9886	22658
Equinox Publishing	Shelburne	VT	G	802 497-0276	22416
Garlic Press Inc	Williston	VT	G	802 864-0670	22668
Russian Information Services	Montpelier	VT	G	802 223-4955	22160
Stadion Publishing Co Inc	Island Pond	VT	G	802 723-6175	22041
Telegraph Publishing LLC	Chester	VT	G	802 875-2703	21851
Tool Factory Inc	Arlington	VT	G	802 375-6549	21601
When Words Count Press LLC	Rochester	VT	F	802 767-4372	22321
Williston Pubg Promotions LLC	Williston	VT	F	802 872-9000	22699
Works In Progress Inc **(PA)**	South Burlington	VT	F	802 658-3797	22479

PUBLISHERS: Music Book

	CITY	ST	EMP	PHONE	ENTRY #
Yale Daily News Publishing Co	New Haven	CT	G	203 432-2400	2757
Eastgate Systems Inc	Watertown	MA	G	617 924-9044	16280
D E Enterprise Inc	Rockport	ME	D	207 594-9544	6818

PUBLISHERS: Music Book & Sheet Music

	CITY	ST	EMP	PHONE	ENTRY #
Eastern Woods Music Publishing	Sandwich	MA	G	508 238-3270	14967
Wiscasset Music Publishing Co	Cambridge	MA	G	617 492-5720	9702
Proffe Publishing	Wilton	NH	G	603 654-1070	19984

PUBLISHERS: Newsletter

	CITY	ST	EMP	PHONE	ENTRY #
Axon Communications Inc	Braintree	MA	G	781 849-6700	8988
Creative Success Alliance Corp	Rockland	MA	E	781 878-7114	14796
Early American Industries Assn	South Dartmouth	MA	G	508 439-2215	15239
Harvard Bus Schl Pubg Corp **(HQ)**	Brighton	MA	C	617 783-7400	9100
Larson Worldwide Inc	Norwell	MA	G	781 659-2115	14105
Mbo Advertising Services	Marshfield	MA	G	781 837-5897	12863
O E M Health Information Inc	Beverly	MA	G	978 921-7300	8161
Patricia Seybold Group Inc	Brighton	MA	F	617 742-5200	9103
PRI Financial Publishing	Holliston	MA	G	508 429-5949	11597
Eat Drink Lucky	Cape Elizabeth	ME	G	207 450-9060	5876
Kennedy Information LLC	Keene	NH	E	603 357-8100	18512
Mac Observer Inc	Durham	NH	G	603 868-2030	18077
Educational Directions Inc	Portsmouth	RI	G	401 683-3523	20922

PUBLISHERS: Newspaper

	CITY	ST	EMP	PHONE	ENTRY #
200 Mill Plain Road LLC	Fairfield	CT	G	203 254-0113	1411
Alm Media LLC	Hartford	CT	E	860 527-7900	1805
Bargain News Free Classified A	Stratford	CT	D	203 377-3000	4395
Cantata Media LLC	Norwalk	CT	F	203 951-9885	3118
Chromatic Press US Inc	West Hartford	CT	G	860 796-7667	5059
Efitzgerald Publishing LLC	West Hartford	CT	G	860 904-7250	5067
Freshiana LLC	Greenwich	CT	G	800 301-8071	1616
Gamut Publishing	Hartford	CT	E	860 296-6128	1824
Hartford Monthly Meeting	West Hartford	CT	G	860 232-3631	5076
Hearst Corporation	Shelton	CT	G	203 926-2080	3811
Jewish Leader Newspaper	New London	CT	G	860 442-7395	2774
Los Angles Tmes Cmmnctions LLC	Stamford	CT	C	203 965-6434	4240
M&G Berman Inc	Wilton	CT	G	203 834-8754	5293
Mkrs Corporation	Wilton	CT	G	203 762-2662	5294
Morris Communications Co LLC	Guilford	CT	D	203 458-4500	1712
Newspaper Space Buyers	Norwalk	CT	G	203 967-6452	3209
Newtown Sports Group	Newtown	CT	G	508 341-1238	2931
Quinnipiac Valley Times	Hamden	CT	G	203 675-9483	1778
Reminder Broadcaster	Vernon	CT	D	860 875-3366	4672
Stella Press LLC	Greenwich	CT	G	203 661-2735	1653

	CITY	ST	EMP	PHONE	ENTRY #
Town Tribune LLC	New Fairfield	CT	G	203 648-6085	2629
Track180 LLC	New Haven	CT	G	203 605-3540	2745
Tradewinds	Beacon Falls	CT	G	203 723-6966	65
Tradewinds	Stamford	CT	G	203 324-2994	4348
Ack Surf School LLC	Nantucket	MA	G	508 325-2589	13218
Bagdon Advertising Inc	Westborough	MA	F	508 366-5500	16592
Berkshire Totes For Tots Inc	Pittsfield	MA	G	413 442-7048	14461
Beverly Citizen	Beverly	MA	G	978 927-2777	8108
Boston Chinese News Inc	Cambridge	MA	G	617 354-4154	9417
Bridge Publishing LLC	Osterville	MA	G	508 681-8914	14246
Brookline T A B	Needham Heights	MA	G	617 566-3585	13321
Bureau of National Affairs Inc	Marshfield	MA	F	781 843-9422	12856
Burlington Union	Lexington	MA	G	781 229-0918	12209
Business West	Springfield	MA	G	413 781-8600	15457
Charlestown Bridge	Charlestown	MA	G	617 241-8500	9829
Chicopee Tribune	Chicopee	MA	G	413 552-3775	10011
Circulation	Fall River	MA	G	508 676-2526	10674
Community Newspaper	Framingham	MA	G	508 339-8977	10935
Creative Publishing Corp Amer **(PA)**	Peabody	MA	E	978 532-5880	14326
Cricket Press Inc	Manchester	MA	F	978 526-7131	12604
Dispatch	Marshfield	MA	G	781 837-8700	12859
Dispatch News	Lowell	MA	G	978 458-7100	12368
Dolan LLC	Boston	MA	G	617 451-7300	8507
Duxbury Clipper Inc	Duxbury	MA	F	781 934-2811	10396
Edic Bi Weekly	Boston	MA	G	617 918-5406	8518
Free Press	Florence	MA	E	413 585-1533	10867
Gatehouse Media Mass I Inc	Concord	MA	D	978 667-2156	10131
Greylock Press LLC	Peabody	MA	G	978 530-1740	14337
Hanson Whitman Express	Hanson	MA	G	781 293-0420	11363
Holbrook Sun Inc	Randolph	MA	F	781 767-4000	14684
I Make News	Newton	MA	G	617 864-4400	13603
Independant Newspaper Group	Revere	MA	E	781 485-0588	14767
Independent News	Shelburne Falls	MA	G	413 522-5046	15071
Jamaica Plain Porchfest Inc	Boston	MA	G	617 320-6230	8625
Journal of Commerce Inc	Boston	MA	G	617 439-7099	8640
Khmerpost USA LLC	Lowell	MA	G	978 677-7163	12388
Loop Weekly	Methuen	MA	G	978 683-8800	13033
M A D Signs	Wareham	MA	G	508 273-7887	16252
Marborough Enterprise	Marlborough	MA	G	508 485-5200	12790
Mariner Ablngton Edition	Marshfield	MA	G	781 878-4489	12862
Massachstts Med Dvcs Jurnl LLC	Boston	MA	G	617 358-5631	8683
Nantucket Chronicle LLC	Siasconset	MA	G	508 257-6683	15141
New England Runner	Norwell	MA	G	781 987-1730	14108
Retail Sales Inc	Randolph	MA	G	781 963-8169	14696
Robert Weiss Associates Inc	Boston	MA	G	617 561-4000	8825
Rosscommon Quilts Inc	Dorchester	MA	G	617 436-5848	10348
S & S Publications Inc	Hull	MA	G	781 925-9266	11830
Shewstone Publishing LLC	Arlington	MA	G	781 648-1251	7638
Shrewsbury Chronicle	Framingham	MA	G	508 842-8787	11005
Sippican Week	Marion	MA	G	774 553-5250	12704
Somerville News	Somerville	MA	G	617 666-4010	15216
State House News	Waban	MA	G	617 969-9175	15939
Streak Media LLC	Boston	MA	G	617 242-9460	8868
Tri Town Transcript	Danvers	MA	G	978 887-4146	10266
University of Massachusetts	Amherst	MA	D	413 545-3500	7530
West Springfield Record Inc	West Springfield	MA	G	413 736-1587	16563
Weymouth News	Randolph	MA	G	781 337-1944	14702
Worcester Publishing	Worcester	MA	G	508 749-3166	17506
Worcester Tlegram Gazette Corp **(HQ)**	Worcester	MA	B	508 793-9100	17507
Worcester Tlegram Gazette Corp	Worcester	MA	E	978 368-0176	17508
Worcester Tlegram Gazette Corp	Southbridge	MA	F	508 764-2519	15409
Camden Herald	Rockland	ME	G	207 236-8511	6786
Central Maine Online	Waterville	ME	G	207 872-2985	7154
Coffee News USA Inc **(PA)**	Bangor	ME	G	207 941-0860	5638
Maine Antique Digest Inc	Waldoboro	ME	E	207 832-7534	7134
Nandu Press	South Portland	ME	G	207 767-3144	7034
New England Business Media LLC	Portland	ME	F	207 761-8379	6700
Northeast Publishing Company	Dover Foxcroft	ME	G	207 564-8355	5961
Northwoods Publications LLC	West Enfield	ME	F	207 732-4880	7171
Otis Gazette	Allagash	ME	G	207 398-9001	5519
Times Record Main Ofc	Brunswick	ME	G	207 729-3311	5849
Upstairs	Falmouth	ME	G	207 799-2217	6036
Village Netmedia Inc	Rockland	ME	E	207 594-4401	6814
Village Netmedia Inc	Belfast	ME	G	207 338-3333	5698
Cardinal Communications Inc	Plaistow	NH	G	603 382-4800	19510
Constrction Summary of NH Main	Manchester	NH	G	603 627-8856	18804
Eoutreach Solutions LLC	Manchester	NH	F	603 410-5000	18817
Great Bay Gazette	Exeter	NH	C	603 703 2620	18123
Greater Manchester Sports	Manchester	NH	G	603 627-3892	18830
Mason Grapevine LLC	Mason	NH	G	603 878-4272	18970
Ogden Newspapers NH LLC	Nashua	NH	G	603 882-2741	19222
State Military Reservation	Concord	NH	G	603 225-1230	17931
Corvus Publishing LLC	Barrington	RI	G	401 595-8937	20045
Rays Newspapers	Pawtucket	RI	G	401 728-1364	20891
Stevens Publishing Inc	Coventry	RI	F	401 821-2216	20165
Visitor Printing Co	Providence	RI	F	401 272-1010	21151
Whitegate International Corp	Providence	RI	G	401 274-2149	21155
Witches Almanac	Newport	RI	G	401 847-3388	20688
Bennington Shriff GLC Slar LLC	Bennington	VT	G	802 233-3370	21665
Hardwick Gazette Print Shop	Hardwick	VT	G	802 472-6521	22013
McClure Newspapers Inc	Burlington	VT	C	802 863-3441	21795
Vtfolkus	Brattleboro	VT	G	802 246-1410	21753

PUBLISHERS: Newspapers, No Printing

	CITY	ST	EMP	PHONE	ENTRY #
21st Century Fox America Inc	Wilton	CT	G	203 563-6600	5273
Advisor	North Haven	CT	F	203 239-4121	3002
Car Buyers Market	Trumbull	CT	E	516 482-0292	4618
Catholic Transcript Inc	Bloomfield	CT	F	860 286-2828	213
CCC Media LLC	New Britain	CT	G	860 225-4601	2518
Chase Media Group	Newtown	CT	F	914 962-3871	2919
Citizen News	New Fairfield	CT	G	203 746-4669	2623
Hamlethub LLC	Ridgefield	CT	G	203 431-6400	3667
Hartford Courant Company	Avon	CT	G	860 678-1330	35
Hartford Courant Company LLC	Hartford	CT	F	860 525-5555	1832
Hispanic Communications LLC	New Haven	CT	G	203 624-8007	2696
Life Publications	West Hartford	CT	E	860 953-0444	5083
Local Media Group Inc	New Milford	CT	G	860 354-2273	2813
Minuteman Newspaper **(PA)**	Westport	CT	E	203 226-8877	5214
Northend Agents LLC	Hartford	CT	G	860 244-2445	1854
Prime Publishers Inc	Watertown	CT	G	860 274-6721	5018
Second Wind Media Limited	New Haven	CT	F	203 781-3480	2736
Swedish News Inc	Norwalk	CT	G	203 299-0380	3253
The Bee Publishing Company	Newtown	CT	G	203 426-0178	2944
Tribuna Newspaper LLC	Danbury	CT	G	203 730-0457	1001
True Publishing Company	Wallingford	CT	F	203 272-5316	4823
Valley Publishing Company Inc	Derby	CT	F	203 735-6696	1081
Wicks Business Information LLC **(PA)**	Shelton	CT	F	203 334-2002	3889
Alberto Vasallo Jr	Boston	MA	F	617 522-5060	8350
Andover Publishing Company	North Andover	MA	E	978 475-7000	13690
Baikar Association Inc **(PA)**	Watertown	MA	F	617 924-4420	16271
Brazilian Times	Somerville	MA	G	617 625-5559	15161
Bulletin Newspapers Inc	Hyde Park	MA	G	617 361-1406	11864
Bulletin Newspapers Inc **(PA)**	Hyde Park	MA	F	617 361-8400	11865
Carlisle Communications Inc	Carlisle	MA	G	978 369-7921	9797
Christian Science Pubg Soc **(PA)**	Boston	MA	B	617 450-2000	8473
Community Newspaper Company	Auburn	MA	D	508 721-5600	7832
Daily Woburn Times Inc **(PA)**	Woburn	MA	D	781 933-3700	17162
Daily Woburn Times Inc	Wilmington	MA	G	978 658-2346	16993
Diocesan Press Inc	Fall River	MA	G	508 675-3857	10683
Doncar Inc	Concord	MA	E	978 371-2442	10129
Dow Jones & Company Inc	Chicopee	MA	E	413 598-4000	10020
East Coast Publications Inc **(PA)**	Norwell	MA	E	781 878-4540	14102
Eastern Mddlsex Press Pblctons **(PA)**	Malden	MA	E	781 321-8000	12569
Easton Journal	Milford	MA	G	508 230-7964	13113
Enterprise Newsmedia LLC	Norwood	MA	F	781 769-5535	14150
Enterprise Publications **(PA)**	Falmouth	MA	E	508 548-4700	10789
Enterprise Publications	West Falmouth	MA	G	508 457-9180	16478
Ethnic Publishers Inc	Boston	MA	G	617 227-8929	8528
Gatehouse Media LLC	Norwell	MA	E	781 829-9305	14103
Grafton News Holdings LLC	Worcester	MA	G	508 839-2259	17385
Great Oak Publications Inc	North Reading	MA	F	978 664-4761	13983
Hairenik Association Inc	Watertown	MA	F	617 926-3974	16289
Harvard Crimson Inc	Cambridge	MA	G	617 576-6600	9502
Hollan Publishing Inc	Manchester	MA	G	978 704-9342	12605
Hopkinton Independent	Westborough	MA	G	508 435-5188	16624
Independent Newspaper Group	Revere	MA	E	781 485-0588	14768
Ipswich Chronicle	Ipswich	MA	G	978 356-5141	11923
Jornal Dos Sports LLC	Melrose	MA	G	857 888-9186	12983
Leader Publishing Co Inc	Everett	MA	G	617 387-4570	10615
Local Media Group Inc	Hyannis	MA	B	508 775-1200	11847
Local Media Group Inc	New Bedford	MA	B	508 997-7411	13409
Marthas Vineyard Times	Vineyard Haven	MA	F	508 693-6100	15933
Massachusetts Institute Tech	Cambridge	MA	E	617 253-1541	9545
Medford Transcript	Medford	MA	G	781 396-1982	12943
Medianews Group Inc	Fitchburg	MA	D	978 343-6911	10835
Melrose Free Press Inc	Beverly	MA	D	781 665-4000	8150
Moquin and Daley PA	Boston	MA	G	617 536-0606	8711
New England Newspapers Inc **(DH)**	Pittsfield	MA	C	413 447-7311	14496
Newspapers of Massachusetts	Greenfield	MA	B	978 544-2118	11270
North Shore Jewish Press Ltd	Salem	MA	F	978 745-4111	14932
On The Beat Inc	Cambridge	MA	G	617 491-8878	9598
Pinestream Communications Inc	Weston	MA	G	781 893-6836	16829
Pittsfield Gazette Inc	Pittsfield	MA	G	413 443-2010	14499
Profile News	West Roxbury	MA	G	617 325-1515	16501
Reminder Publications	East Longmeadow	MA	E	413 525-3947	10491
Revere Independent	Revere	MA	E	781 485-0588	14775
Suburban Publishing Corp	Peabody	MA	F	978 818-6300	14373
Town Crier Publications Inc	Upton	MA	F	508 529-7791	15911
Vocero Hispano Newspaper Inc	Southbridge	MA	G	508 792-1942	15408
Wanderer Communications Inc	Mattapoisett	MA	G	508 758-9055	12892
Advertiser-Democrat	Norway	ME	G	207 743-7011	6521
Current Publishing LLC	Falmouth	ME	E	207 854-2577	6030
Free Press Inc	Rockland	ME	E	207 594-4408	6796
James Newspapers Inc **(PA)**	Norway	ME	E	207 743-7011	6523
Kirkland Newspaper Inc	Farmington	ME	F	207 778-2075	6051
Maine-OK Enterprises Inc	Boothbay Harbor	ME	E	207 633-4620	5784
Mainely Newspapers Inc	Biddeford	ME	F	207 282-4337	5746
Penobscot Bay Press Inc **(PA)**	Stonington	ME	F	207 367-2200	7070
Penobscot Bay Press Inc	Blue Hill	ME	G	207 374-2341	5772
SMA Inc	Yarmouth	ME	F	207 846-4112	7300
Tree Enterprises	Parsonsfield	ME	G	207 233-6479	6577
Turner Publishing Inc	Turner	ME	F	207 225-2076	7111
Twin City Times	Gorham	ME	G	207 795-5017	6134
Carriage Towne News	Kingston	NH	G	603 642-4499	18541
Dartmouth Inc	Hanover	NH	E	603 646-2600	18286
Hippopress LLC **(PA)**	Manchester	NH	E	603 625-1855	18834
Independent Rowing News Inc	Hanover	NH	G	603 448-5090	18293
Lakes Region News Club Inc	Laconia	NH	G	603 527-9299	18572
McLean Communications LLC	Manchester	NH	D	603 624-1442	18869
Mount Washington Vly Mtn Ear	Lancaster	NH	G	603 447-6336	18602
Neighborhood News	Manchester	NH	E	603 206-7800	18882
New Hampshirecom	Manchester	NH	G	603 314-0447	18885

	CITY	ST	EMP	PHONE	ENTRY #
Newspapers of New Hampshire	Peterborough	NH	F	603 924-7172	19481
Salmon Press LLC	Rochester	NH	E	603 332-2300	19686
Shakour Publishers Inc	Keene	NH	E	603 352-5250	18524
Suncook Valley Sun Inc	Pittsfield	NH	G	603 435-6291	19505
Weirs Publishing Company Inc	Laconia	NH	F	888 308-8463	18593
Boston Phoenix Inc **(PA)**	Providence	RI	F	617 536-5390	20971
Breeze Publications Inc	Lincoln	RI	E	401 334-9555	20559
Manisses Inc	Block Island	RI	G	401 466-2222	20058
New England Newspapers Inc	Pawtucket	RI	D	401 722-4000	20866
Providence Business News	Providence	RI	E	401 273-2201	21095
Real Estate Journal of RI Inc	Johnston	RI	G	401 831-7778	20534
Southern RI Newspapers **(HQ)**	Wakefield	RI	E	401 789-9744	21277
Addison Press Inc	Middlebury	VT	E	802 388-4944	22097
Cohasa Publishing Inc	Bradford	VT	G	802 222-5281	21699
Creative Marketing Services	Rutland	VT	F	802 775-9500	22327
Hersam Acorn Newspapers LLC	Manchester Center	VT	G	802 362-3535	22087
Hinesburg Record	Hinesburg	VT	F	802 482-2350	22028
Islander	North Hero	VT	G	802 372-5600	22231
Its Classified Inc	Bradford	VT	G	802 222-5152	21701
Milton Independent Inc	Saint Albans	VT	G	802 893-2028	22372
North Eastern Publishing Co	Bennington	VT	E	802 447-7567	21686
Northstar Publishing LLC	Danville	VT	G	802 684-1056	21898
Outer Limits Publishing LLC	Killington	VT	F	802 422-2399	22055
Springfield Reporter Inc	Springfield	VT	G	802 885-2246	22509
Valley Reporter Inc	Waitsfield	VT	G	802 496-3607	22569

PUBLISHERS: Pamphlets, No Printing

	CITY	ST	EMP	PHONE	ENTRY #
Baikar Association Inc **(PA)**	Watertown	MA	F	617 924-4420	16271
Spinner Publications Inc	New Bedford	MA	G	508 994-4564	13451

PUBLISHERS: Patterns, Paper

	CITY	ST	EMP	PHONE	ENTRY #
P Straker Ltd	South Dartmouth	MA	G	508 996-4804	15241

PUBLISHERS: Periodical Statistical Reports, No Printing

	CITY	ST	EMP	PHONE	ENTRY #
Crane Data LLC	Westborough	MA	F	508 439-4419	16610
Vdc Research Group Inc **(PA)**	Natick	MA	E	508 653-9000	13284
Edible Green Mountains LLC	Manchester Center	VT	G	802 768-8356	22083

PUBLISHERS: Periodical, With Printing

	CITY	ST	EMP	PHONE	ENTRY #
Aapi	Monroe	CT	G	203 268-2450	2389
Premier Graphics LLC	Stratford	CT	D	800 414-1624	4440
Anderson Publishing Inc	Nantucket	MA	G	508 228-3866	13219
H O Zimman Inc	Lynn	MA	F	781 598-9230	12515
Quinlan Publishing Co Inc **(PA)**	Boston	MA	G	617 439-0076	8805
Jouve of North America Inc **(DH)**	Brattleboro	VT	G	802 254-6073	21735

PUBLISHERS: Periodicals, Magazines

	CITY	ST	EMP	PHONE	ENTRY #
Access Intelligence	Norwalk	CT	G	203 854-6730	3096
Bargain News Free Classified A	Stratford	CT	D	203 377-3000	4395
Bay Tact Corporation	Woodstock Valley	CT	E	860 315-7372	5503
Bff Holdings Inc **(HQ)**	Old Saybrook	CT	C	860 510-0100	3328
Gamut Publishing	Hartford	CT	E	860 296-6128	1824
Imani Magazine/Fmi	West Haven	CT	G	203 809-2565	5126
Informa Business Media Inc	Stamford	CT	C	203 358-9900	4224
Karger S Publishers Inc	Unionville	CT	G	860 675-7834	4657
Legal Affairs Inc	Hamden	CT	G	203 865-2520	1767
Liturgical Publications Inc	New Canaan	CT	F	203 966-6470	2603
Living Magazine	Milford	CT	G	203 283-5290	2310
Media Ventures Inc	Norwalk	CT	E	203 852-6570	3194
Motorcyclists Post	Shelton	CT	G	203 929-9409	3835
Ppc Books Ltd	Westport	CT	G	203 226-6644	5224
Relx Inc	Norwalk	CT	A	203 840-4800	3230
S Karger Publishers Inc	Unionville	CT	G	860 675-7834	4661
Ubm LLC	Darien	CT	G	203 662-6501	1035
Westchester Forge Inc	New Canaan	CT	G	914 584-2429	2621
73 75 Magazine Street LLC	Allston	MA	G	617 787-1913	7459
American Academy Arts Sciences	Cambridge	MA	G	617 491-2600	9387
Atc Information Inc	Boston	MA	G	617 723-7030	8378
Chevalier Associates Inc	Sutton	MA	G	508 770-0092	15680
Davis Corp of Worcester Inc **(PA)**	Worcester	MA	E	508 754-7201	17363
Dow Jones & Company Inc	Chicopee	MA	E	413 598-4000	10020
East Coast Publications Inc **(PA)**	Norwell	MA	E	781 878-4540	14102
Ebsco Publishing Inc **(HQ)**	Ipswich	MA	A	978 356-6500	11917
Enterprise Publications **(PA)**	Falmouth	MA	E	508 548-4700	10789
Fine Magazine	Woburn	MA	E	617 721-7372	17180
First Magazine LLC	Waban	MA	G	617 965-0504	15936
Harvard Crimson Inc	Cambridge	MA	G	617 576-6600	9502
Idg **(HQ)**	Boston	MA	G	508 875-5000	8613
J Magazine Inc	Brookline	MA	G	617 515-1822	9205
Liberty Publishing Inc	Beverly	MA	E	978 777-8200	8148
Magazine Columbiano	Revere	MA	G	617 365-3182	14772
Massachusetts Institute Tech	Cambridge	MA	D	617 253-5646	9546
Medical Publishing Assoc	Boston	MA	G	617 530-6222	8694
New Beverage Publications Inc	Boston	MA	G	617 598-1900	8728
New England RE Bulltin	Swansea	MA	F	508 675-8884	15710
Northast Prformer Publications	Somerville	MA	G	617 627-9200	15202
Now Publishers Inc	Norwell	MA	G	781 871-0245	14109
Out & About Magazine	Springfield	MA	G	413 783-6704	15496
Quarterly Update	North Falmouth	MA	G	508 540-0848	13953
Questex Brazil LLC	Framingham	MA	G	617 219-8300	10997
Relx Inc	Newton	MA	D	617 558-4925	13629
Smarter Travel Media LLC	Boston	MA	C	617 886-5555	8850
Steelfish Media LLC	Beverly	MA	G	312 730-8016	8182
The Orion Society Inc	Great Barrington	MA	F	413 528-4422	11248
Town of North Reading	North Reading	MA	E	978 664-6027	13992
Travel Medicine Inc	Northampton	MA	G	413 584-0381	14023
Turley Publications Inc	Ware	MA	G	413 967-3505	16239
Verifacts	Weymouth	MA	G	781 337-1717	16903
Weston Medical Publishing LLC	Weston	MA	G	781 899-2702	16834
Dream Spirit Publishers	Arundel	ME	G	207 283-0667	5531
Port Cy Lf Communications Inc	Cumberland Foreside	ME	G	207 781-4644	5932
Taproot	Portland	ME	G	802 472-1617	6737
Echo Communications Inc	New London	NH	E	603 526-6006	19316
Pennwell Corporation	Nashua	NH	C	603 891-9425	19228
Pennwell Corporation	Nashua	NH	C	603 891-0123	19229
Reid Publication Inc	Portsmouth	NH	G	603 433-2200	19614
Relx Inc	Portsmouth	NH	D	603 431-7894	19615
Homeland Company	East Greenwich	RI	G	401 884-2427	20370
La Bella Bride Magazine	Coventry	RI	G	401 397-5795	20152
Richardson Landscaping Corp	Jamestown	RI	G	401 423-1505	20494
Vendome Guide	Newport	RI	E	401 849-8025	20687
Boutin McQuiston Inc **(PA)**	South Burlington	VT	F	802 863-8038	22439

PUBLISHERS: Periodicals, No Printing

	CITY	ST	EMP	PHONE	ENTRY #
Baxter Bros Inc	Greenwich	CT	G	203 637-4559	1598
R G L Inc	East Granby	CT	E	860 653-7254	1142
Steed Read Horsemans Classifie	Salem	CT	G	860 859-0770	3740
Cabot Heritage Corp	Salem	MA	E	978 745-5532	14900
Harvard Bus Schl Pubg Corp **(HQ)**	Brighton	MA	C	617 783-7400	9100
Massachusetts Institute Tech	Cambridge	MA	D	617 253-1000	9547
New England Business Media LLC **(PA)**	Worcester	MA	E	508 755-8004	17429
New Generation Research Inc	Boston	MA	F	617 573-9550	8734
Seak Inc **(PA)**	Falmouth	MA	G	508 548-7023	10797
Society For Marine Mammalogy	Yarmouth Port	MA	G	508 744-2276	17531
Standard Publishing Corp **(PA)**	Boston	MA	F	617 457-0600	8861
Telco Communications Inc	Seekonk	MA	E	508 336-6633	15041
Informtion Consulting Svcs Inc	Rockland	ME	E	207 596-7783	6799

PUBLISHERS: Posters

	CITY	ST	EMP	PHONE	ENTRY #
Image Source International Inc	Pocasset	MA	E	508 801-9252	14599
Wild Apple Graphics Ltd	Woodstock	VT	E	802 457-3003	22741

PUBLISHERS: Racing Forms & Programs

	CITY	ST	EMP	PHONE	ENTRY #
R G L Inc	East Granby	CT	E	860 653-7254	1142

PUBLISHERS: Sheet Music

	CITY	ST	EMP	PHONE	ENTRY #
Mr Boltons Music Inc	Westport	CT	G	646 578-8081	5217
Performer Publications Inc	Somerville	MA	G	617 627-9200	15204

PUBLISHERS: Shopping News

	CITY	ST	EMP	PHONE	ENTRY #
Buzzafricocom	Lynn	MA	G	617 903-0152	12494
SMA Inc	Yarmouth	ME	F	207 846-4112	7300
Stevens Publishing Inc	Coventry	RI	F	401 821-2216	20165

PUBLISHERS: Technical Manuals

	CITY	ST	EMP	PHONE	ENTRY #
Business Journals Inc **(PA)**	Norwalk	CT	D	203 853-6015	3117
Guiding Channels Co	Worcester	MA	G	508 853-0781	17387

PUBLISHERS: Technical Manuals & Papers

	CITY	ST	EMP	PHONE	ENTRY #
Clearesult Consulting Inc	Westborough	MA	G	508 836-9500	16603
Megatech Corporation	Tewksbury	MA	F	978 937-9600	15822
Sap Professional Journal **(PA)**	Dedham	MA	D	781 407-0360	10297
Trustees of Boston College	Chestnut Hill	MA	F	617 552-2844	9993

PUBLISHERS: Telephone & Other Directory

	CITY	ST	EMP	PHONE	ENTRY #
Connectcut Hspnic Yellow Pages	Hartford	CT	F	860 560-8713	1815
Bergquist Family Entps Inc	Needham Heights	MA	G	781 449-9196	13318
Boxcar Media LLC	North Adams	MA	E	413 663-3384	13670
Destrail	Cambridge	MA	G	818 687-7037	9453
Russell Group	Arlington	MA	G	781 648-0302	7636
Eztousecom Directories	Bangor	ME	G	207 974-3171	5643
Connectcut Rver Vly Yllow Pges	Lebanon	NH	G	603 727-4700	18619

PUBLISHERS: Textbooks, No Printing

	CITY	ST	EMP	PHONE	ENTRY #
Kirchoff Wohlberg Inc	Madison	CT	F	212 644-2020	1967
Bedford Freeman & Worth	Boston	MA	D	617 426-7440	8398
Career Press Inc **(PA)**	Newburyport	MA	E	201 848-0310	13477
Dahlstrom & Company Inc	Holliston	MA	G	508 429-3367	11566
Gwb Corporation	Andover	MA	G	508 896-9486	7554
HM Publishing Corp	Boston	MA	A	617 251-5000	8598
Houghton Mifflin Harcourt Pubg **(HQ)**	Boston	MA	A	617 351-5000	8607
Houghton Mifflin Holdings Inc **(PA)**	Boston	MA	G	617 351-5000	8608
Jones & Bartlett Learning LLC **(PA)**	Burlington	MA	C	978 443-5000	9289
School Specialty Inc	Cambridge	MA	D	617 547-6706	9647
Sinauer Associates Inc	Sunderland	MA	E	413 549-4300	15676
Stevenson Learning Skills Inc	Holliston	MA	G	774 233-0457	11607
Sundance/Newbridge LLC **(HQ)**	Marlborough	MA	G	800 343-8204	12831
Ocean Side Publications	East Providence	RI	G	401 331-8426	20437
John Wiley & Sons Inc	Poultney	VT	D	802 287-4326	22272
Pro Lingua Associates Inc	Brattleboro	VT	G	802 257-7779	21745

PUBLISHERS: Trade journals, No Printing

	CITY	ST	EMP	PHONE	ENTRY #
Airtime Publishing Inc	Westport	CT	E	203 454-4773	5179
Business Journals Inc **(PA)**	Norwalk	CT	D	203 853-6015	3117
Ida Publishing Co Inc	Greenwich	CT	G	203 661-9090	1621
International Mktg Strategies	Stamford	CT	F	203 406-0106	4226
Zackin Publications Inc	Oxford	CT	E	203 262-4670	3431
American Mteorological Soc Inc **(PA)**	Boston	MA	D	617 227-2425	8361
Cxo Media Inc **(DH)**	Framingham	MA	C	508 766-5696	10938
Diacritech Inc	Boston	MA	F	617 236-7500	8502
Early American Industries Assn	South Dartmouth	MA	G	508 439-2215	15239
Griffin Publishing Co Inc	Duxbury	MA	F	781 829-4700	10398
Horizon House Publications Inc **(PA)**	Norwood	MA	D	781 769-9750	14158
Idg Communications Inc **(HQ)**	Framingham	MA	C	508 872-8200	10965

	CITY	ST	EMP	PHONE	ENTRY #
Idg Communications Inc	Framingham	MA	F	508 766-5300	10966
International Data Group Inc **(PA)**	Boston	MA	F	508 875-5000	8618
International Data Group Inc	Framingham	MA	E	508 766-5632	10970
International Data Group Inc	Framingham	MA	F	508 935-4719	10971
Journal of Bone Jint Srgery In	Needham	MA	E	781 449-9780	13302
Laurin Publishing Co Inc **(PA)**	Pittsfield	MA	D	413 499-0514	14482
Management Roundtable Inc	Newton	MA	G	781 891-8080	13612
McKnight Management Co Inc **(PA)**	Falmouth	MA	G	508 540-5051	10796
Municipal Market Analytics Inc **(PA)**	Concord	MA	F	978 287-0014	10143
Network World Inc	Framingham	MA	C	800 622-1108	10986
Synchrgnix Info Strategies Inc	Cambridge	MA	G	302 892-4800	9670
Compass Publications Inc	Deer Isle	ME	G	207 348-1057	5947
Connell Communications Inc	Keene	NH	E	603 924-7271	18496
Harrison Publishing House Inc	Littleton	NH	E	603 444-0820	18661
Relx Inc	Salem	NH	E	603 898-9664	19762
Ocean Side Publications	East Providence	RI	G	401 331-8426	20437
State-Wide Mltiple Listing Svc	Warwick	RI	G	401 785-3650	21430

PUBLISHING & BROADCASTING: Internet Only

	CITY	ST	EMP	PHONE	ENTRY #
Betx LLC	New Hartford	CT	G	860 459-1681	2632
Broadcastmed Inc	Farmington	CT	E	860 953-2900	1470
Gcn Publishing Inc	Norwalk	CT	F	203 665-6211	3158
Bigfoot Seo Strategies	Marblehead	MA	G	617 448-4848	12676
Boston Sports Journal LLC	Medway	MA	G	617 306-0166	12957
Cambridge Brickhouse Inc	Lawrence	MA	G	978 725-8001	12001
Datanyze Inc **(DH)**	Waltham	MA	E	415 237-3434	16080
Envie Company Inc	Stoughton	MA	G	866 700-6410	15588
Online Moderation Inc	Dover	MA	G	617 686-7737	10352
Promax Supply LLC	Melrose	MA	F	781 620-1602	12990
Roundtown Inc	Cambridge	MA	G	415 425-6891	9639
Safari Books Online LLC	Boston	MA	G	617 426-8600	8831
Smpretty Inc	Wayland	MA	G	508 358-1639	16336
Spidle Corp	Waltham	MA	G	617 448-7386	16199
TCI America Inc	Seekonk	MA	E	508 336-6633	15039
Xos Technologies Inc **(HQ)**	Wilmington	MA	E	978 447-5220	17070
Zlink Inc	Maynard	MA	G	978 309-3628	12907
Zoom Information LLC **(HQ)**	Waltham	MA	D	781 693-7500	16227
Macleay Interactive Design Inc	Rome	ME	G	207 495-2208	6828
Lbry Inc	Manchester	NH	G	267 210-4292	18863
Live Wire Marketing Corp	Manchester	NH	G	603 969-8771	18865
Alert Solutions Inc	Cranston	RI	F	401 427-2100	20174
Fuel On Line Corp	Burlington	VT	E	888 475-2552	21784

PUBLISHING & PRINTING: Book Clubs

	CITY	ST	EMP	PHONE	ENTRY #
Secret Guide To Computers	Manchester	NH	G	603 666-6644	18920

PUBLISHING & PRINTING: Books

	CITY	ST	EMP	PHONE	ENTRY #
Air Age Inc	Wilton	CT	E	203 431-9000	5274
Comicana Inc	Stamford	CT	G	203 968-0748	4168
Rocket Books Inc	Easton	CT	G	203 372-1818	1323
Charlesbridge Publishing Inc **(PA)**	Watertown	MA	E	617 926-0329	16276
Community of Jesus Inc **(PA)**	Orleans	MA	D	508 255-1094	14232
Daughters of St Paul Inc	Billerica	MA	G	617 522-2566	8235
Hachette Book Group Inc	Boston	MA	D	617 227-0730	8586
Higginson Book Company	Salem	MA	G	978 745-7170	14921
Idg Communications Inc **(HQ)**	Framingham	MA	C	508 872-8200	10965
Idg Paper Services	Framingham	MA	E	508 875-5000	10968
Maitri Learning LLC	Westhampton	MA	G	413 529-2868	16801
Meno Publishing Inc	Needham Heights	MA	G	781 209-2665	13336
Old Salt Box Publishing & Dist	Danvers	MA	G	978 750-8090	10244
Paraclete Press Inc **(HQ)**	Brewster	MA	E	508 255-4685	9055
Paraclete Press Inc	Brewster	MA	G	508 255-4685	9056
Quinlan Publishing Co Inc **(PA)**	Boston	MA	G	617 439-0076	8805
J Weston Walch Publisher	Portland	ME	E	207 772-2846	6676
Mathemtics Problem Solving LLC	Portland	ME	G	207 772-2846	6692
Earth Sky + Water LLC	Wilton	NH	G	603 654-7649	19980
Elan Publishing Company Inc	Moultonborough	NH	E	603 253-6002	19096
Mann Publishing Incorporated	Rollinsford	NH	F	603 601-0325	19693

PUBLISHING & PRINTING: Catalogs

	CITY	ST	EMP	PHONE	ENTRY #
Communication Ink Inc	Peabody	MA	F	978 977-4595	14324
Care New England Health System	Warwick	RI	G	401 739-9255	21341

PUBLISHING & PRINTING: Directories, NEC

	CITY	ST	EMP	PHONE	ENTRY #
Preferred Publications Inc	Wilmington	MA	G	978 697-4180	17039
Direct Display Publishing Inc	Bath	ME	G	207 443-4800	5676

PUBLISHING & PRINTING: Guides

	CITY	ST	EMP	PHONE	ENTRY #
Bertram Sirkin	West Hartford	CT	C	860 656 7446	5055
Allagash Guide Inc	Norridgewock	ME	G	207 634-3748	6494

PUBLISHING & PRINTING: Magazines: publishing & printing

	CITY	ST	EMP	PHONE	ENTRY #
Commerce Connect Media Inc	Westport	CT	A	800 547-7377	5184
Dulce Domum LLC	Norwalk	CT	E	203 227-1400	3145
Informa Business Media Inc	Stamford	CT	D	203 358-9900	4223
Maplegate Media Group Inc	Danbury	CT	E	203 826-7557	952
Natural Nutmeg LLC	Avon	CT	G	860 206-9500	38
Penny Publications LLC **(PA)**	Norwalk	CT	D	203 866-6688	3219
Quad/Graphics Inc	North Haven	CT	A	203 288-2468	3057
Racing Times	Wallingford	CT	E	203 298-2899	4793
Red 7 Media LLC **(HQ)**	Norwalk	CT	E	203 853-2474	3227
Atlantic Printing Co Inc	Medfield	MA	F	781 449-2700	12909
Brumberg Publications Inc	Brookline	MA	F	617 734-1979	9198
Cambridge Fund Raising Assoc	Medfield	MA	G	508 359-0019	12911
Community of Jesus Inc **(PA)**	Orleans	MA	D	508 255-1094	14232
Country Standard Time	Newton	MA	E	617 969-0331	13582
Dental Kaleidoscope Magazine	Canton	MA	G	781 821-8898	9724
Hot Stepz Magazine	Dorchester	MA	G	617 959-6403	10343
Massachusetts Review Inc	Amherst	MA	E	413 545-2689	7518
Meredith Corporation	Springfield	MA	G	413 733-4040	15488
Myrin Institute Inc	Great Barrington	MA	F	413 528-4422	11242
National Braille Press Inc	Boston	MA	D	617 425-2400	8720
New England Bride Inc	Lynnfield	MA	F	781 334-6093	12553
Northeast Outdoors Inc	Paxton	MA	F	508 752-8762	14302
Paraclete Press Inc	Brewster	MA	G	508 255-4685	9056
Prime National Publishing Corp	Weston	MA	F	781 899-2702	16830
Rhee Gold Company	Norton	MA	F	508 285-6650	14086
Robb Curtco Media LLC	Acton	MA	E	978 264-7500	7380
Technology Review Inc	Cambridge	MA	E	617 475-8000	9677
Ve Interactive LLC	Boston	MA	G	857 284-7000	8905
Werner Publishing Corporation	Braintree	MA	D	310 820-1500	9049
Audio File Publications Inc	Portland	ME	G	207 774-7563	6614
Beloit Ptry Jrnl Fundation Inc	Gorham	ME	G	207 522-1303	6110
Cremark Inc	Portland	ME	G	207 874-7720	6644
Wild Fibers Magazine	Rockland	ME	G	207 594-9455	6815
Center For Northern Woodlands	Lyme	NH	G	802 439-6292	18753
Village West Publishing Inc	Laconia	NH	F	603 528-4285	18592
CM Publications Inc	Westerly	RI	G	401 596-9358	21519
Grace Ormonde Marriage Inc	Riverside	RI	F	401 245-9726	21169
Battenkill Communications LLP	Manchester Center	VT	G	802 362-3981	22081

PUBLISHING & PRINTING: Newsletters, Business Svc

	CITY	ST	EMP	PHONE	ENTRY #
Chief Executive Group LLC **(PA)**	Stamford	CT	F	785 832-0303	4164
Custom Publishing Design Group	Rocky Hill	CT	F	860 513-1213	3706
Shop Smart Central Inc	Newtown	CT	G	914 962-3871	2936
The Merrill Anderson Co Inc	Stratford	CT	F	203 377-4996	4453
Advisor Perspectives Inc	Woburn	MA	D	781 376-0050	17113
Assoction For Grvstone Studies	Greenfield	MA	F	413 772-0836	11251
Atlantic Printing Co Inc	Medfield	MA	F	781 449-2700	12909
Curriculum Associates LLC **(PA)**	North Billerica	MA	B	978 667-8000	13805
Global Enterprises Inc	Attleboro	MA	G	508 399-8270	7742
Liberty Publishing Inc	Beverly	MA	E	978 777-8200	8148
LPI Printing and Graphic Inc	Stoneham	MA	E	781 438-5400	15566
Quality Solutions Inc **(PA)**	Newburyport	MA	E	978 465-7755	13525
Constrction Summary of NH Main	Manchester	NH	G	603 627-8856	18804

PUBLISHING & PRINTING: Newspapers

	CITY	ST	EMP	PHONE	ENTRY #
8 Times LLC	Westport	CT	G	203 227-7575	5177
American-Republican Inc **(PA)**	Waterbury	CT	D	203 574-3636	4842
American-Republican Inc	Torrington	CT	C	860 496-9301	4559
Browser Daily	Winsted	CT	G	860 469-5534	5406
Capital Cities Communications	New Haven	CT	G	203 784-8800	2673
Central Conn Cmmunications LLC	New Britain	CT	D	860 225-4601	2519
Comunidade News	Danbury	CT	G	203 730-0175	891
Conn Daily Campus	Storrs Mansfield	CT	G	860 486-3407	4384
Connecticut Newspapers Inc	Stamford	CT	G	203 964-2200	4172
Courant Specialty Products Inc	Hartford	CT	E	860 241-3795	1816
Daily Fare LLC	Bethel	CT	G	203 743-7300	141
Daily Impressions LLC	Hamden	CT	G	203 508-5305	1743
Daily Mart	Rocky Hill	CT	G	860 529-5210	3707
Disco Chick	Middletown	CT	G	860 788-6203	2183
Gatehouse Media LLC	Norwich	CT	C	860 886-0106	3280
Greenwich Gofer	Old Greenwich	CT	G	203 637-8425	3309
Greenwich Sentinel	Greenwich	CT	G	203 883-1430	1619
Greenwich Time	Stamford	CT	G	203 253-2922	4203
Hamden Journal LLC	Hamden	CT	G	203 668-6307	1754
Hamiltonbookcom LLC	Falls Village	CT	G	860 824-0275	1463
Hartford Courant Company	West Hartford	CT	F	860 560-3747	5074
Hartford Courant Company LLC **(HQ)**	Hartford	CT	A	860 241-6200	1831
Hearst Corporation	New Canaan	CT	E	203 438-6544	2600
Hearst Corporation	Norwalk	CT	E	203 625-4445	3167
Hersam Acorn Cmnty Pubg LLC	Trumbull	CT	F	203 261-2548	4624
Hersam Acorn Cmnty Pubg LLC **(HQ)**	Ridgefield	CT	F	203 438-6544	3668
Hispanic Communications LLC	Stamford	CT	G	203 674-6793	4218
India Weekly Co	Cheshire	CT	G	203 699-8419	739
Inquiring News	Bloomfield	CT	G	860 983-7587	226
Jj Portland News LLC	Middletown	CT	G	860 342-1432	2194
Journal Publishing Company Inc	Manchester	CT	A	860 646-0500	2014
Meade Daily Group LLC	Westbrook	CT	G	860 399-7342	5160
Medianews Group Inc	Norwalk	CT	F	203 333-0161	3195
My Citizens News	Waterbury	CT	G	203 729-2228	4919
New Mass Media Inc	Hartford	CT	E	860 241-3617	1852
News 12 Connecticut	Norwalk	CT	E	203 849-1321	3208
News Times	Danbury	CT	G	203 744-5100	960
Northeast Minority News Inc	Hartford	CT	G	860 249-6065	1853
NRG Connecticut LLC	Hartford	CT	E	860 231-2424	1855
Orange Democrat	Orange	CT	G	203 298-4575	3378
Our Town Crier	Westport	CT	G	203 400-5000	5220
Peaceful Daily Inc	Guilford	CT	G	203 909-2961	1714
Rhode Island Beverage Journal	Hamden	CT	G	203 288-3375	1780
Ritch Herald & Linda	Greenwich	CT	G	203 661-8634	1643
Rmi Inc	Vernon Rockville	CT	C	860 875-3366	4681
Southington Citizen	Meriden	CT	G	860 620-5960	2132
Suburban Voices Publishing LLC	West Haven	CT	G	203 934-6397	5146
Thomson Reuters US LLC **(DH)**	Stamford	CT	E	203 539-8000	4346
Times Community News Group	New London	CT	G	860 437-1150	2783
TLC Media LLC	Hamden	CT	G	203 980-1361	1789
Valley Independent Sentinel	Ansonia	CT	G	203 446-2335	24
Westerly Sun	Pawcatuck	CT	G	401 348-1000	3445
Yale Daily News Publishing Co	New Haven	CT	G	203 432-2400	2757
Yale University	New Haven	CT	G	203 432-2880	2758
Yankee Pennysaver Inc	Brookfield	CT	E	203 775-9122	667
Ack 60 Main LLC	Nantucket	MA	G	508 228-1398	13217

	CITY	ST	EMP	PHONE	ENTRY #
Advocate Newspapers **(PA)**	Everett	MA	G	617 387-2200	10601
Anchor	Fall River	MA	G	508 675-7151	10658
Antique Homes Magazine	East Douglas	MA	G	508 476-7271	10424
Arion Jrnl of Hmnties Classics	Boston	MA	G	617 353-6480	8375
Athol Press Inc	Athol	MA	E	978 249-3535	7684
Barnstable Patriot Newsppr Inc	Hyannis	MA	F	508 771-1427	11835
Boston Business Journal Inc	Boston	MA	E	617 330-1000	8426
Boston Irish Reporter	Dorchester	MA	F	617 436-1222	10340
Braintree Forum & Observer	Braintree	MA	G	781 843-2937	8991
C Newspaper Inc	Ipswich	MA	G	978 412-1800	11908
Canton Citizen Inc	Canton	MA	F	781 821-4418	9721
Canton Journal	Needham	MA	G	781 828-0006	13295
Caribe Cmmnctions Publications	Boston	MA	F	617 522-5060	8459
Changs Publishing Company	Boston	MA	G	617 542-1230	8466
Chicopee Register Newspaper	Chicopee	MA	G	413 592-3599	10010
Colonial Times Publishing	Lexington	MA	F	781 274-9997	12212
Community Newspaper Inc	Marblehead	MA	G	781 639-4800	12679
Daily Catch	Brookline	MA	G	617 734-2700	9199
Daily General Counsel Pllc	Brookline	MA	G	617 721-4342	9200
Daily Hampshire Gazette	Easthampton	MA	G	413 527-4000	10558
Daily News Tribune	Needham Heights	MA	G	781 329-5008	13327
Daily Paper	Hyannis	MA	G	508 790-8800	11839
Daily Stroll LLC	Brighton	MA	G	678 770-4531	9097
Daily Woburn Times Inc	Reading	MA	E	781 944-2200	14733
Danvers Herald	Danvers	MA	G	978 774-0505	10212
Demosthenes Greek-AM Demo	Somerville	MA	G	617 628-7766	15168
Dig Media Group Inc	Boston	MA	G	617 418-9075	8504
Dinner Daily LLC	Westford	MA	G	978 392-5887	16764
Dow Jones & Company Inc	Chicopee	MA	E	212 416-3858	10021
Driggin Sandra DBA Extra Extra	Quincy	MA	E	617 773-6996	14620
Eagle-Tribune Publishing Co **(DH)**	North Andover	MA	C	978 946-2000	13698
Eagle-Tribune Publishing Co	Haverhill	MA	E	978 374-0321	11430
Eagle-Tribune Publishing Co	North Andover	MA	D	978 946-2000	13699
Eagle-Tribune Publishing Co	Gloucester	MA	E	978 282-0077	11179
Epoch Times Boston-Chinese	Cambridge	MA	G	617 968-8019	9470
Everest Herald Ltd Partnership	Watertown	MA	G	617 744-0620	16283
Framingham Source	Framingham	MA	G	508 315-7176	10947
Gardner News Incorporated	Gardner	MA	E	978 632-8000	11114
Gatehouse Media LLC	Concord	MA	G	978 263-4736	10130
Gatehouse Media LLC	Fall River	MA	C	508 676-8211	10701
Gatehouse Media LLC	Taunton	MA	E	508 880-9000	15752
Gatehouse Media Mass I Inc	Beverly	MA	E	781 233-2040	8134
Gatehouse Media Mass I Inc	Framingham	MA	C	508 626-4412	10948
Gatehouse Media Mass I Inc	Randolph	MA	C	781 235-4000	14683
Gatehouse Media Mass I Inc	Wareham	MA	E	508 295-1190	16247
Gatehouse Media Mass I Inc	Marlborough	MA	F	508 626-3859	12758
Gatehouse Media Mass I Inc	Milford	MA	F	508 634-7522	13118
Gatehouse Media Mass I Inc	Chelmsford	MA	E	978 256-7196	9902
Gazette Publications Inc	Boston	MA	G	617 524-2626	8555
Groton Herald Inc	Groton	MA	G	978 448-6061	11289
Harbus News Corporation	Boston	MA	G	617 495-6528	8588
Harvard Press	Harvard	MA	G	978 456-3700	11377
Harwich Oracle	Orleans	MA	E	508 247-3200	14234
Hearst Communications Inc	Worcester	MA	C	508 793-9100	17389
Hyora Publications Inc	Chatham	MA	F	508 430-2700	9860
Journal Computing In Higher	Amherst	MA	G	413 549-5150	7516
Journal Infectious Diseases	Boston	MA	G	617 367-1848	8639
Journal of Interdiscplinary	Lexington	MA	G	781 862-4089	12233
JTL Falcon Title Examiner	Haverhill	MA	G	978 377-0223	11444
Lancaster Times Inc	Concord	MA	G	978 368-3393	10137
Lawyers Weekly LLC **(PA)**	Boston	MA	C	617 451-7300	8660
Limestone Communications **(PA)**	Great Barrington	MA	E	413 528-5380	11241
Lisa Jo Rudy	Falmouth	MA	G	508 540-7293	10795
Local Media Group Inc	New Bedford	MA	G	508 947-1760	13410
Lowell Sun Publishing Company **(DH)**	Lowell	MA	E	978 459-1300	12399
Lujean Printing Co Inc	Cotuit	MA	F	508 428-8700	10170
Martins News Shop	Boston	MA	G	617 267-1334	8681
Massachusetts Institute Tech	Cambridge	MA	G	617 253-7183	9548
Milton Times Inc	Milton	MA	G	617 696-7758	13196
Montague Reporter Incorporated	Turners Falls	MA	G	413 863-8666	15883
Ne Media Group Inc **(PA)**	Boston	MA	D	617 929-2000	8721
New England Business Media LLC **(PA)**	Worcester	MA	E	508 755-8004	17429
Nrt Inc	Medway	MA	F	508 533-4588	12968
Ottaway Newspapers	Hyannis	MA	G	508 775-1200	11852
Patriot-News Co	Boston	MA	G	617 345-0971	8769
President Fllows Hrvard Cllege	Boston	MA	G	617 783-7888	8792
Quincy Sun Publishing Co Inc	Quincy	MA	F	617 471-3100	14652
Republican Company **(HQ)**	Springfield	MA	A	413 788-1000	15502
Saugus Advertiser	Beverly	MA	G	781 233-2040	8174
South Boston Today	Boston	MA	G	617 268-4032	8856
Starting Treatment Effctvly	Boston	MA	G	857 544-8051	8863
Suburban News Dealers LLC	Carver	MA	G	508 962-9807	9808
Summer Ink Inc	Brookline	MA	G	617 714-0263	9220
Susan M Rexford Title Examiner	Ashburnham	MA	G	978 827-3015	7645
Taunton MA	Taunton	MA	G	774 226-0681	15788
Tinytown Gazette **(PA)**	Cohasset	MA	G	781 383-9115	10102
Town Common Inc	Rowley	MA	F	978 948-8696	14867
Trustees of Tufts College	Medford	MA	E	617 628-5000	12951
Turley Publications Inc	Barre	MA	G	978 355-4000	7952
United Communications Corp	Attleboro	MA	C	508 222-7000	7804
University Massachusetts Inc	Amherst	MA	G	413 545-2682	7529
Village Netmedia Inc	Winthrop	MA	G	617 846-3700	17101
Wall Street Journal	Chicopee	MA	G	800 369-5663	10068
Walpole Times Inc	Framingham	MA	F	508 668-0243	11013
Westfield News Publishing Inc **(DH)**	Westfield	MA	E	413 562-4181	16746
Worcester Sun LLC	Holden	MA	G	774 364-0553	11552
World Journal Chinese Daily	Boston	MA	G	617 542-1230	8937
World News Firm Inc	Weymouth	MA	G	781 335-0113	16904
Yankee Shopper	Webster	MA	F	508 943-8784	16354
Yoga For Daily Living	Groton	MA	G	978 448-3751	11297
Bangor Publishing Company	Belfast	ME	G	207 338-3034	5685
Bangor Publishing Company	Ellsworth	ME	G	207 667-9393	6014
Blethen Maine Newspapers Inc	Portland	ME	G	207 791-6650	6624
Bridgton News Corp	Bridgton	ME	F	207 647-2851	5806
Brunswick Publishing LLC	Brunswick	ME	D	207 729-3311	5833
Central Maine Morning Sentinel	Waterville	ME	G	207 873-3341	7153
Chases Daily LLC	Freedom	ME	G	207 930-0464	6070
Citizen Printers Incorporated	Albany Twp	ME	G	207 824-2444	5512
Community Advertiser	Farmingdale	ME	G	207 582-8486	6038
Ellsworth American Inc	Ellsworth	ME	D	207 667-2576	6018
Fiddlehead Focus	Fort Kent	ME	G	207 316-2243	6059
Gorham Growl	Gorham	ME	G	207 839-4795	6112
Katahdin Regional Dev Corp	Millinocket	ME	G	207 447-6913	6441
Lewiston Daily Sun	Rumford	ME	G	207 364-8728	6837
Lincoln County Publishing Co	Newcastle	ME	E	207 563-3171	6483
Maine Nwsppers In Educatn Fund	Portland	ME	G	207 791-6650	6688
Mount Desert Islander	Bar Harbor	ME	G	207 288-0556	5667
Northeast Publishing Company **(HQ)**	Presque Isle	ME	D	207 764-4471	6764
Northeast Publishing Company	Houlton	ME	G	207 532-2281	6208
Northeast Publishing Company	Presque Isle	ME	G	207 768-5431	6766
Original Irregular	Kingfield	ME	G	207 265-2773	6254
Quoddy Tides Inc	Eastport	ME	G	207 853-4806	5995
Rolling Thunder Press Inc	Newport	ME	G	207 368-2028	6486
Salty Dog Gallery	Southwest Harbor	ME	G	207 244-5918	7050
Seattle Times Company	Augusta	ME	C	207 623-3811	5619
Shoreline Publications	Wells	ME	F	207 646-8448	7165
Sunrise Guide LLC	Portland	ME	F	207 221-3450	6735
Town Line	South China	ME	G	207 445-2234	7007
University of Maine System	Orono	ME	D	207 581-1273	6560
Village Netmedia Inc **(PA)**	Rockland	ME	E	207 594-4401	6813
York County Coast Star Inc	Kennebunk	ME	F	207 985-5901	6243
Berlin Daily Sun	Berlin	NH	G	603 752-5858	17692
Concord Monitor	Contoocook	NH	G	603 224-5301	17943
Daily Fantasy Spt Rankings LLC	Dover	NH	G	609 273-8408	18018
Daily Portsmouth	Portsmouth	NH	G	603 767-1395	19556
Eagle-Tribune Publishing Co	Derry	NH	D	603 437-7000	17978
George J Foster Co Inc	Rochester	NH	G	603 332-2200	19670
Granite Quill Publishers	Hillsborough	NH	G	603 464-3388	18316
Jordan Associates	Pittsburg	NH	F	603 246-8998	19494
New Boston Bulletin	New Boston	NH	G	603 487-5200	19294
Newspapers of New Hampshire **(HQ)**	Concord	NH	C	603 224-5301	17918
Panoramic Publishing Group LLC	Wolfeboro Falls	NH	F	603 569-5257	20028
Pennysaver	Plymouth	NH	G	603 536-3160	19530
Queen City Examiner	Manchester	NH	G	603 289-6835	18907
Seacoast Shearwater Dev LLC	Portsmouth	NH	G	603 427-0000	19618
Stateline Review	Salem	NH	G	603 898-2554	19770
Tolles Communications Corp	Manchester	NH	G	603 627-9500	18942
Beacon Communications Inc **(PA)**	Warwick	RI	E	401 732-3100	21334
Bristol Phoenix	Bristol	RI	D	401 253-6000	20066
Daily Herald Brown Inc	Providence	RI	G	401 351-3372	20992
Fishermens Daily Catch LLC	Bristol	RI	G	401 252-1190	20078
International Journal of Arts	Cumberland	RI	G	401 333-1804	20329
Island News Enterprise	Jamestown	RI	G	401 423-3200	20491
Journal Roman Archaeology LLC	Portsmouth	RI	G	401 683-1955	20926
Lmg Rhode Island Holdings Inc	Middletown	RI	D	401 849-3300	20624
News Star Inc	Pascoag	RI	G	401 567-7077	20803
Outpost Journal	Providence	RI	G	401 569-1211	21086
Smithfied Times	Greenville	RI	G	401 232-9600	20475
Autism Support Daily	Shelburne	VT	G	802 985-8773	22412
Caledonian Record Pubg Co Inc **(PA)**	Saint Johnsbury	VT	D	802 748-8121	22389
Charlotte News	Charlotte	VT	G	802 425-4949	21832
Chronicle Inc	Barton	VT	E	802 525-3531	21647
Cutter & Locke Inc **(PA)**	Tunbridge	VT	G	802 889-3500	22542
Da Capo Publishing Inc	Burlington	VT	E	802 864-5684	21778
Daily Gardener	Calais	VT	G	802 223-7851	21821
Daily Rider LLC	Burlington	VT	G	802 497-1269	21779
Gannett Co Inc	Burlington	VT	D	802 863-3441	21786
Gannett River States Pubg Corp	Fairfax	VT	D	802 893-4214	21975
Herald Association Inc	Rutland	VT	C	802 747-6121	22338
Ibrattleboro	Brattleboro	VT	G	802 257-7475	21734
Journal LLC **(PA)**	Ludlow	VT	G	802 228-3600	22065
New England Newspapers Inc	Brattleboro	VT	E	802 254-2311	21740
Prison Legal News	Brattleboro	VT	G	802 257-1342	21744
Rutland City Band	Rutland	VT	G	802 775-5378	22349
Sams Good News	Rutland	VT	F	802 773-4040	22352
Vermont Independent Media Inc	Brattleboro	VT	G	802 246-6397	21751
Vermont Media Corp	Wilmington	VT	F	802 464-5757	22705
Vermont Publishing Comany	Saint Albans	VT	E	802 524-9771	22384
Vermont Woman Newspaper	South Burlington	VT	G	802 861-6200	22478
Vermonts Northland Journal LLC	Newport	VT	G	802 334-5920	22206
World Publications Inc	Barre	VT	E	802 479-2582	21646
Young Writers Project Inc	Burlington	VT	F	802 324-9537	21818

PUBLISHING & PRINTING: Pamphlets

	CITY	ST	EMP	PHONE	ENTRY #
Atlantic Printing Co Inc	Medfield	MA	F	781 449-2700	12909
Channing Bete Company Inc **(PA)**	South Deerfield	MA	B	413 665-7611	15247
Nsight Inc	Andover	MA	E	781 273-6300	7579
Kensington Group Incorporated	Hampton Falls	NH	F	603 926-6742	18283

PUBLISHING & PRINTING: Periodical Statistical Reports

	CITY	ST	EMP	PHONE	ENTRY #
Rosenoff Reports Inc	Somerville	MA	G	617 628-7783	15213

PUBLISHING & PRINTING: Posters

	CITY	ST	EMP	PHONE	ENTRY #
Image Software Services Inc	Shirley	MA	E	978 425-3600	15087

PUBLISHING & PRINTING: Racing Forms & Programs

	CITY	ST	EMP	PHONE	ENTRY #
D B S Industries Inc	Haverhill	MA	D	978 373-4748	11421

PUBLISHING & PRINTING: Shopping News

	CITY	ST	EMP	PHONE	ENTRY #
Rare Reminder Incorporated	Rocky Hill	CT	E	860 563-9386	3728
Step Saver Inc	Southington	CT	E	860 621-6751	4082
Vermont Publishing Comany	Saint Albans	VT	E	802 524-9771	22384

PUBLISHING & PRINTING: Technical Papers

	CITY	ST	EMP	PHONE	ENTRY #
Insight Media LLC	Norwalk	CT	G	203 831-8464	3174

PUBLISHING & PRINTING: Textbooks

	CITY	ST	EMP	PHONE	ENTRY #
Calculator Training	New Milford	CT	G	860 355-8255	2789
Cengage Learning Inc **(PA)**	Boston	MA	D	617 289-7918	8462
Cengage Lrng Holdings II Inc **(PA)**	Boston	MA	E	617 289-7700	8463
Curriculum Associates LLC **(PA)**	North Billerica	MA	B	978 667-8000	13805
Edward Elgar Publishing Inc	Northampton	MA	G	413 584-5551	14005
Houghton Mifflin Harcourt **(HQ)**	Boston	MA	F	617 351-5000	8605
Nahas Selim	Newton	MA	G	617 595-8808	13616
School Yourself Inc	Brookline	MA	G	516 729-7478	9219
Simon & Schuster Inc	Peterborough	NH	E	603 924-7209	19488
John Carlevale	West Greenwich	RI	E	401 392-1926	21459

PUBLISHING & PRINTING: Trade Journals

	CITY	ST	EMP	PHONE	ENTRY #
Advantage Communications LLC	New Canaan	CT	E	203 966-8390	2592
Healthcare Publishing Inc	Natick	MA	G	508 655-4489	13260
Journal Computing In Higher	Amherst	MA	G	413 549-5150	7516
Massachusetts Medical Society **(PA)**	Waltham	MA	B	781 893-4610	16148
Trailjournals LLC	Newburyport	MA	G	978 358-7536	13542
Village Netmedia Inc	Winthrop	MA	G	617 846-3700	17101
Trueline Publishing LLC	Portland	ME	E	207 510-4099	6743
Vermont Journalism Trust Ltd	Montpelier	VT	F	802 225-6224	22163

PUBLISHING & PRINTING: Yearbooks

	CITY	ST	EMP	PHONE	ENTRY #
Meno Publishing Inc	Needham Heights	MA	G	781 209-2665	13336

PULLEYS: Metal

	CITY	ST	EMP	PHONE	ENTRY #
Cascaded Purchase Holdings Inc **(PA)**	Claremont	NH	C	603 448-1090	17841
Tracey Gear Inc	Pawtucket	RI	E	401 725-3920	20906

PULP MILLS

	CITY	ST	EMP	PHONE	ENTRY #
Cellmark Pulp & Paper Inc	Norwalk	CT	F	203 299-5050	3122
Eldorado Usa Inc	Branford	CT	G	203 208-2282	312
International Paper - 16 Inc **(HQ)**	Stamford	CT	G	203 329-8544	4227
Georgia-Pacific LLC	Norwood	MA	G	781 440-3600	14155
Tomra Mass LLC	New Bedford	MA	E	203 395-3484	13455
Georgia-Pacific LLC	Baileyville	ME	G	207 427-4077	5626
ND Otm LLC	Old Town	ME	C	207 401-2879	6545
Robbins Lumber Inc	Searsmont	ME	C	207 342-5221	6945
Woodland Pulp LLC **(PA)**	Baileyville	ME	B	207 427-3311	5627
Westrock Cp LLC	Sheldon Springs	VT	C	802 933-7733	22431

PULP MILLS: Mechanical & Recycling Processing

	CITY	ST	EMP	PHONE	ENTRY #
County of Lincoln	Wiscasset	ME	G	207 882-5276	7284
Lkq Precious Metals Inc	North Smithfield	RI	C	401 762-0094	20789
Chittenden Environmental	Williston	VT	G	802 578-0194	22660

PULVERIZED EARTH

	CITY	ST	EMP	PHONE	ENTRY #
P J Albert Inc	Fitchburg	MA	E	978 345-7828	10847

PUMICE: Abrasives

	CITY	ST	EMP	PHONE	ENTRY #
Techno Bloc	North Brookfield	MA	G	774 449-8400	13882

PUMPS

	CITY	ST	EMP	PHONE	ENTRY #
Beckson Manufacturing Inc **(PA)**	Bridgeport	CT	E	203 366-3644	381
Flowserve Corporation	Milford	CT	E	203 877-4252	2290
Foleys Pump Service Inc	Danbury	CT	E	203 792-2236	921
Hamworthy Peabody Combustn Inc **(DH)**	Shelton	CT	E	203 922-1199	3808
ITT Water & Wastewater USA Inc **(HQ)**	Shelton	CT	D	262 548-8181	3820
Omega Engineering Inc	Norwalk	CT	D	714 540-4914	3212
Phillips Pump LLC	Bridgeport	CT	F	203 576-6688	469
Proflow Inc	North Haven	CT	E	203 230-4700	3055
Sonic Corp	Stratford	CT	F	203 375-0063	4448
Talcott Mountain Engineering	Simsbury	CT	F	860 651-3141	3913
Xylem Water Solutions USA Inc	Shelton	CT	E	203 450-3715	3891
A W Chesterton Company	Groveland	MA	B	781 438-7000	11299
BEE International Inc	South Easton	MA	E	508 238-5558	15270
Brooks Automation Inc	Chelmsford	MA	B	978 262-2795	9879
Circor Naval Solutions LLC **(HQ)**	Warren	MA	D	413 436-7711	16260
Clark Solutions	Hudson	MA	F	978 568-3400	11763
Flow Control LLC	Beverly	MA	E	978 281-0440	8131
Flowserve US Inc	Lawrence	MA	C	978 682-5248	12025
Fortis LLC	Northbridge	MA	G	617 600-4178	14056
Harvard Clinical Tech Inc	Natick	MA	E	508 655-2000	13259
Infutronix LLC	Natick	MA	G	508 650-2007	13262
Marlow Watson Inc **(HQ)**	Wilmington	MA	E	800 282-8823	17020
Mass Vac Inc	North Billerica	MA	E	978 667-2393	13839
Northeast Equipment Inc	Fall River	MA	E	508 324-0083	10740
Taco Inc	Fall River	MA	D	508 675-7300	10769
Tark Inc	Billerica	MA	F	978 663-8074	8300
Thermo Orion Inc **(HQ)**	Chelmsford	MA	E	800 225-1480	9937
Vaccon Company Inc	Medway	MA	E	508 359-7200	12972
Xylem Water Solutions USA Inc	Woburn	MA	G	781 935-6515	17325
Martin Carmichael	Cardville	ME	F	207 827-2858	5882
Stevens Electric Pump Service	Monmouth	ME	G	207 933-2143	6451
Larchmont Engineering Inc	Manchester	NH	G	603 622-8825	18860
Solar-Stream LLC	Temple	NH	G	603 878-0066	19899
Airgas Usa LLC	East Greenwich	RI	G	401 884-0201	20351
Aquamotion Inc	Warwick	RI	F	401 785-3000	21326
Bosworth Company	East Providence	RI	F	401 438-1110	20392
Boydco Inc **(PA)**	East Providence	RI	F	401 438-6900	20393
Taco Inc **(PA)**	Cranston	RI	B	401 942-8000	20299
Whale Water Systems Inc	Manchester	VT	F	802 367-1091	22079

PUMPS & PARTS: Indl

	CITY	ST	EMP	PHONE	ENTRY #
Bjm Pumps LLC	Old Saybrook	CT	E	860 399-5937	3329
Preferred Utilities Mfg Corp **(HQ)**	Danbury	CT	D	203 743-6741	974
Sulzer Pump Solutions US Inc **(PA)**	Meriden	CT	E	203 238-2700	2135
Boc Group Inc	Wilmington	MA	G	978 658-5410	16984
Iwaki America Incorporated **(HQ)**	Holliston	MA	D	508 429-1440	11579
Iwaki Pumps Inc **(DH)**	Holliston	MA	E	508 429-1440	11580
Netzsch USA Holdings Inc **(PA)**	Burlington	MA	G	781 272-5353	9308
Rectorseal	Fall River	MA	G	508 673-7561	10754
TNT Manufacturing LLC	Westfield	MA	G	413 562-0690	16735
Brailsford & Company Inc	Antrim	NH	E	603 588-2880	17593
Pfeiffer Vacuum Inc **(DH)**	Nashua	NH	E	603 578-6500	19231
Bsm Pump Corp	North Kingstown	RI	E	401 471-6350	20694
Mesco Corporation	Portsmouth	RI	G	401 683-2677	20928
Hayward Tyler Inc **(DH)**	Colchester	VT	D	802 655-4444	21864
Ivek Corp	North Springfield	VT	D	802 886-2238	22236
PBL Incorporated	Colchester	VT	F	802 893-0111	21876

PUMPS & PUMPING EQPT REPAIR SVCS

	CITY	ST	EMP	PHONE	ENTRY #
Chas G Allen Realty LLC	Barre	MA	D	978 355-2911	7950
Iwaki Pumps Inc **(DH)**	Holliston	MA	E	508 429-1440	11580
Mass Vac Inc	North Billerica	MA	E	978 667-2393	13839
Hayward Tyler Inc **(DH)**	Colchester	VT	D	802 655-4444	21864

PUMPS & PUMPING EQPT WHOLESALERS

	CITY	ST	EMP	PHONE	ENTRY #
Dpc Quality Pump Service	Milford	CT	G	203 874-6877	2276
Proflow Inc	North Haven	CT	E	203 230-4700	3055
Sulzer Pump Solutions US Inc **(PA)**	Meriden	CT	E	203 238-2700	2135
Delta Elc Mtr Repr Sls & Svc	Medford	MA	G	781 395-0551	12930
Iwaki America Incorporated **(HQ)**	Holliston	MA	D	508 429-1440	11579
Mass Vac Inc	North Billerica	MA	E	978 667-2393	13839
Solar-Stream LLC	Temple	NH	G	603 878-0066	19899

PUMPS, HEAT: Electric

	CITY	ST	EMP	PHONE	ENTRY #
Nyle Systems LLC	Brewer	ME	E	207 989-4335	5799

PUMPS: Domestic, Water Or Sump

	CITY	ST	EMP	PHONE	ENTRY #
Dpc Quality Pump Service	Milford	CT	G	203 874-6877	2276
Marsars Water Rescue Systems	Shelton	CT	G	203 924-7315	3831

PUMPS: Fluid Power

	CITY	ST	EMP	PHONE	ENTRY #
Kerfoot Technologies Inc	Mashpee	MA	F	508 539-3002	12881
Parker-Hannifin Corporation	Portsmouth	NH	G	603 433-6400	19605

PUMPS: Gasoline, Measuring Or Dispensing

	CITY	ST	EMP	PHONE	ENTRY #
Burlington Petroleum Equipment	South Burlington	VT	E	802 864-5155	22440

PUMPS: Hydraulic Power Transfer

	CITY	ST	EMP	PHONE	ENTRY #
Crane Co **(PA)**	Stamford	CT	D	203 363-7300	4177

PUMPS: Measuring & Dispensing

	CITY	ST	EMP	PHONE	ENTRY #
Proflow Inc	North Haven	CT	E	203 230-4700	3055
Fishman Corporation	Hopkinton	MA	F	508 435-2115	11713
Harvard Clinical Tech Inc	Natick	MA	E	508 655-2000	13259
Liquid Metronics Incorporated	Acton	MA	C	978 263-9800	7369
Sensing Systems Corporation	Dartmouth	MA	F	508 992-0872	10276
Nordson Efd LLC **(HQ)**	East Providence	RI	C	401 431-7000	20435

PUMPS: Vacuum, Exc Laboratory

	CITY	ST	EMP	PHONE	ENTRY #
Comvac Systems Inc	Enfield	CT	G	860 265-3658	1352
Artisan Industries Inc	Stoughton	MA	D	781 893-6800	15581
Brooks Automation Inc	Chelmsford	MA	B	978 262-2795	9879
Brooks Automation Inc **(PA)**	Chelmsford	MA	B	978 262-2400	9880
Mass Vac Inc	North Billerica	MA	E	978 667-2393	13839
Teletrak Envmtl Systems Inc **(PA)**	Webster	MA	G	508 949-2430	16352
Vaccon Company Inc	Medway	MA	E	508 359-7200	12972
Nexvac Inc **(PA)**	Sandown	NH	F	603 887-0015	19786

PUNCHES: Forming & Stamping

	CITY	ST	EMP	PHONE	ENTRY #
Precision Punch + Tooling Corp **(PA)**	Berlin	CT	D	860 229-9902	103
Royal Diversified Products	Warren	RI	D	401 245-6900	21304

PUPPETS & MARIONETTES

	CITY	ST	EMP	PHONE	ENTRY #
M P Robinson Production	Redding	CT	E	203 938-1336	3650
Kids On Block - Vermont Inc	Burlington	VT	G	802 860-3349	21790

PURIFICATION & DUST COLLECTION EQPT

	CITY	ST	EMP	PHONE	ENTRY #
Headwaters Inc	Marblehead	MA	G	781 715-6404	12685
K S E Inc	Sunderland	MA	F	413 549-5506	15675

PURIFIERS: Centrifugal

	CITY	ST	EMP	PHONE	ENTRY #
Ultra Filtronics Ltd	Randolph	MA	G	781 961-4775	14700

PUSHCARTS

	CITY	ST	EMP	PHONE	ENTRY #
Moseley Corporation	Franklin	MA	E	508 520-4004	11068
Steele Canvas Basket Corp	Chelsea	MA	E	800 541-8929	9970

QUARTZ CRYSTAL MINING SVCS

	CITY	ST	EMP	PHONE	ENTRY #
Mkl Stone LLC	Everett	MA	G	781 844-9811	10622

QUARTZ CRYSTALS: Electronic

	CITY	ST	EMP	PHONE	ENTRY #
Quartzite Processing Inc	Malden	MA	F	781 322-3611	12592
Infineon Tech Americas Corp	Essex Junction	VT	E	802 769-6824	21947

QUILTING SVC & SPLYS, FOR THE TRADE

	CITY	ST	EMP	PHONE	ENTRY #
Quilted Threads LLC	Henniker	NH	G	603 428-6622	18311
Long Meadow Farms Quilts	Newport	VT	G	802 334-5532	22200

RACEWAYS

	CITY	ST	EMP	PHONE	ENTRY #
Family Raceway LLC	Vernon	CT	G	860 896-0171	4667
Rhode Island Raceway LLC	Quaker Hill	CT	G	860 701-0192	3643
Roaming Raceway and RR LLC	Suffield	CT	G	413 531-3390	4467
Stamford RPM Raceway LLC	Stamford	CT	G	203 323-7223	4333
Wiremold Company **(DH)**	West Hartford	CT	A	860 233-6251	5104
8 Raceway Drive LLC	Nantucket	MA	G	508 325-0040	13216
Speedboard Usa Inc	Newburyport	MA	G	978 462-2700	13534

RACKS: Display

	CITY	ST	EMP	PHONE	ENTRY #
Di-Cor Industries Inc	Bristol	CT	F	860 585-5583	549
Mitchell-Bate Company	Waterbury	CT	E	203 233-0862	4918
Buckley Co Inc	Scituate	MA	G	781 545-7975	15007
Rack Attack USA LLP	Framingham	MA	G	508 665-4361	10998
Ronnie Marvin Enterprises	Littleton	NH	G	603 444-5017	18664

RACKS: Trash, Metal Rack

	CITY	ST	EMP	PHONE	ENTRY #
1 Call Does It All and Then	South Deerfield	MA	G	413 584-5381	15244

RADAR SYSTEMS & EQPT

	CITY	ST	EMP	PHONE	ENTRY #
Lowell Digisonde Intl LLC	Lowell	MA	G	978 735-4752	12398
Prosensing Inc	Amherst	MA	F	413 549-4402	7522
Radar Technology Inc	Newburyport	MA	E	978 463-6064	13526
Raytheon Company	Woburn	MA	C	781 933-1863	17279
Raytheon Sutheast Asia Systems **(HQ)**	Billerica	MA	E	978 470-5000	8289
Wavesense Inc	Somerville	MA	G	917 488-9677	15231
Where Inc	Boston	MA	D	617 502-3100	8925
Flir Maritime Us Inc	Nashua	NH	E	603 324-7900	19160

RADIATORS, EXC ELECTRIC

	CITY	ST	EMP	PHONE	ENTRY #
Mestek Inc	Westfield	MA	B	413 568-9571	16702

RADIO & TELEVISION COMMUNICATIONS EQUIPMENT

	CITY	ST	EMP	PHONE	ENTRY #
Commscope Technologies LLC	Prospect	CT	F	203 699-4100	3585
Comsat Inc	Southbury	CT	F	203 264-4091	4025
Cuescript Inc	Stratford	CT	G	203 763-4030	4407
Fenton Corp	Westport	CT	F	203 221-2788	5191
Frontier Vision Tech Inc	Rocky Hill	CT	E	860 953-0240	3709
Merl Inc	Meriden	CT	G	203 237-8811	2106
Microtech Inc	Cheshire	CT	D	203 272-3234	745
Adaptive Networks Inc	Needham	MA	F	781 444-4170	13291
Arris Technology Inc	Lowell	MA	F	978 614-2900	12346
Artel Video Systems Corp	Westford	MA	E	978 263-5775	16755
Asco Power Technologies LP	Marlborough	MA	G	508 624-0466	12720
Assurance Technology Corp	Chelmsford	MA	D	978 250-8060	9875
Casa Systems Inc **(PA)**	Andover	MA	C	978 688-6706	7544
Copley Controls Corporation **(DH)**	Canton	MA	B	781 828-8090	9722
G5 Scientific LLC	Burlington	MA	G	781 272-7877	9277
GE Infrastructure Sensing LLC **(DH)**	Billerica	MA	A	978 437-1000	8249
General Airmotive Pwr Pdts LLC	Fall River	MA	G	508 674-6400	10702
General Dynamics	Taunton	MA	D	508 880-4521	15753
Homeland Security Wireless Inc	Falmouth	MA	G	508 299-1404	10792
L3 Essco Inc	Ayer	MA	D	978 568-5100	7923
L3harris Technologies Inc	Chelmsford	MA	B	978 905-3500	9911
Loud Technologies Inc	Whitinsville	MA	C	508 234-6158	16916
Macom Technology Solutions Inc	Lowell	MA	G	978 656-2500	12402
Macom Technology Solutions Inc **(HQ)**	Lowell	MA	B	978 656-2500	12403
Magcap Engineering LLC	Canton	MA	F	781 821-2300	9754
Megapulse Incorporated	Bedford	MA	E	781 538-5299	7989
Microwave Engineering Corp	North Andover	MA	D	978 685-2776	13718
Motorola Mobility LLC	Marlborough	MA	D	847 523-5000	12796
Motorola Solutions Inc	Mansfield	MA	G	508 261-4502	12647
Newedge Signal Solutions LLC	Ayer	MA	G	978 425-5400	7929
Parece JP Company	Melrose	MA	G	781 662-8640	12987
Renaissnce Elec Cmmnctions LLC **(PA)**	Harvard	MA	E	978 772-7774	11383
Smiths Interconnect Inc	South Deerfield	MA	E	413 665-0965	15256
Southwest Asian Incorporated	Worcester	MA	G	508 753-7126	17477
Sunu Inc	Cambridge	MA	G	617 980-9807	9664
Unisite LLC	Boston	MA	G	781 926-7135	8896
Verizon Communications Inc	Natick	MA	F	508 647-4008	13285
Vox Communications Group LLC	Wellesley	MA	D	781 239-8018	16392
Mwave Industries LLC	Windham	ME	G	207 892-0011	7243
Aerosat Avionics LLC	Amherst	NH	D	603 943-8680	17549
Airlinx Communications Inc	New Ipswich	NH	F	603 878-1926	19302
Audio Accessories Inc	Marlow	NH	E	603 446-3335	18965
Communction Cmpnent Flters Inc **(PA)**	Seabrook	NH	G	603 294-4685	19797
County Communications	Kensington	NH	G	603 394-7070	18535
Custom Manufacturing Svcs Inc	Nashua	NH	E	603 883-1355	19141
Insource Design & Mfg Tech LLC	Merrimack	NH	G	603 718-8228	19007
Blackhawk Machine Products Inc	Smithfield	RI	E	401 232-7563	21213

RADIO & TELEVISION REPAIR

	CITY	ST	EMP	PHONE	ENTRY #
Cable Electronics Inc	Hartford	CT	G	860 953-0300	1809

RADIO BROADCASTING & COMMUNICATIONS EQPT

	CITY	ST	EMP	PHONE	ENTRY #
Atc Ponderosa B-I LLC	Boston	MA	G	617 375-7500	8379
Atc Ponderosa K LLC	Boston	MA	G	617 375-7500	8380
Burk Technology Inc	Littleton	MA	E	978 486-0086	12295
David Clark Company Inc **(PA)**	Worcester	MA	C	508 756-6216	17362
Global Tower Holdings LLC	Boston	MA	G	617 375-7500	8568
Millennial Net Inc	Lexington	MA	E	978 569-1921	12244
Pnderosa K Atc Acquisition Inc	Boston	MA	G	617 375-7500	8782
Radio Engineering Assoc Inc	Townsend	MA	G	978 597-0010	15873
Unadilla Antennas Mfgco	North Andover	MA	G	978 975-2711	13733
Worldwide Antenna Systems LLC	Kingston	MA	G	781 275-1147	11968
Maine Radio	Scarborough	ME	F	207 883-2929	6932
Haigh-Farr Inc	Bedford	NH	F	603 644-6170	17644
Iheartcommunications Inc	Colchester	VT	E	802 655-0093	21866

RADIO BROADCASTING STATIONS

	CITY	ST	EMP	PHONE	ENTRY #
Christian Science Pubg Soc **(PA)**	Boston	MA	B	617 450-2000	8473

RADIO COMMUNICATIONS: Airborne Eqpt

	CITY	ST	EMP	PHONE	ENTRY #
Auriga Measurement Systems	Chelmsford	MA	E	978 452-7700	9876
Auriga Measurement Systems **(PA)**	Wayland	MA	G	978 452-7700	16334
Qesidyne Inc	Hudson	NH	G	603 883-3116	18431

RADIO EQPT: Citizens Band

	CITY	ST	EMP	PHONE	ENTRY #
Gold Line Connector Inc **(PA)**	Redding	CT	E	203 938-2588	3648

RADIO RECEIVER NETWORKS

	CITY	ST	EMP	PHONE	ENTRY #
Iheartcommunications Inc	Portsmouth	NH	D	603 436-7300	19577

RADIO REPAIR SHOP, NEC

	CITY	ST	EMP	PHONE	ENTRY #
Sean Mecesery	Cos Cob	CT	G	203 869-2277	829
Multec Communications	Rockland	MA	G	781 294-4992	14817

RADIO, TV & CONSUMER ELECTRONICS: VCR & Access

	CITY	ST	EMP	PHONE	ENTRY #
All Security Co Inc	New Bedford	MA	F	508 993-4271	13356

RAIL & STRUCTURAL SHAPES: Aluminum rail & structural shapes

	CITY	ST	EMP	PHONE	ENTRY #
Ocean Marine Fabricating	New Bedford	MA	G	508 999-5554	13433

RAILINGS: Prefabricated, Metal

	CITY	ST	EMP	PHONE	ENTRY #
Mono Crete Step Co of CT LLC	Bethel	CT	F	203 748-8419	172
Boston Blacksmith Inc	Boston	MA	G	617 364-1499	8425
Green Brothers Fabricating	Taunton	MA	E	508 880-3608	15756
Railing Pro Inc	Hope Valley	RI	G	401 539-7998	20486
George L Martin	Brattleboro	VT	G	802 254-5838	21729

RAILROAD EQPT

	CITY	ST	EMP	PHONE	ENTRY #
James L Howard and Company Inc	Bloomfield	CT	E	860 242-3581	228
Winchester Industries Inc	Winsted	CT	G	860 379-5336	5429
N A Railrunner Inc	Lincoln	MA	G	781 860-7245	12288
Rl Controls LLC	Woburn	MA	E	781 932-3349	17286
Okonite Company	Cumberland	RI	D	401 333-3500	20336

RAILROAD EQPT & SPLYS WHOLESALERS

	CITY	ST	EMP	PHONE	ENTRY #
A & K Railroad Materials Inc	Hamden	CT	G	203 495-8790	1728

RAILROAD EQPT: Brakes, Air & Vacuum

	CITY	ST	EMP	PHONE	ENTRY #
Winslow Automatics Inc	New Britain	CT	D	860 225-6321	2591

RAILROAD EQPT: Cars & Eqpt, Interurban

	CITY	ST	EMP	PHONE	ENTRY #
Transit Systems Inc	Plainville	CT	G	860 747-3669	3521
Crrc MA Corporation	Springfield	MA	G	617 415-7190	15463

RAILROAD EQPT: Cars & Eqpt, Train, Freight Or Passenger

	CITY	ST	EMP	PHONE	ENTRY #
L T A Group Inc	South Windsor	CT	E	860 291-9911	3989
Bombardier Services Corp	Boston	MA	G	617 464-0323	8419

RAILROAD EQPT: Heating Units, Railroad Car

	CITY	ST	EMP	PHONE	ENTRY #
Rtr Technologies Inc **(PA)**	Stockbridge	MA	F	413 298-0025	15551

RAILROAD RELATED EQPT: Laying Eqpt, Rail

	CITY	ST	EMP	PHONE	ENTRY #
A & K Railroad Materials Inc	Hamden	CT	G	203 495-8790	1728

RAILROAD TIES: Wood

	CITY	ST	EMP	PHONE	ENTRY #
Tronox Incorporated **(DH)**	Stamford	CT	C	203 705-3800	4350
Gillis Lumber Inc	Danforth	ME	G	207 448-2218	5941

RAILS: Elevator, Guide

	CITY	ST	EMP	PHONE	ENTRY #
Impact Protection Systems Inc	Centerville	MA	G	508 737-8850	9816

RAILS: Steel Or Iron

	CITY	ST	EMP	PHONE	ENTRY #
Biasin Enterprises Inc	Lee	MA	G	413 243-0885	12089
Concentric Fabrication LLC	Middleboro	MA	F	508 672-4098	13059
Henrys Railings	Boston	MA	G	617 333-0535	8595
Mark Dykeman	Tewksbury	MA	G	978 691-1100	15821

RAMPS: Prefabricated Metal

	CITY	ST	EMP	PHONE	ENTRY #
Gordon Industries Inc **(PA)**	Boston	MA	E	857 401-1114	8575

RAZORS, RAZOR BLADES

	CITY	ST	EMP	PHONE	ENTRY #
Bic Corporation **(HQ)**	Shelton	CT	A	203 783-2000	3782
Bic USA Inc **(DH)**	Shelton	CT	C	203 783-2000	3783
Edgewell Per Care Brands LLC	Milford	CT	D	203 882-2300	2282
Edgewell Per Care Brands LLC **(HQ)**	Shelton	CT	B	203 944-5500	3799
Edgewell Personal Care Company	Milford	CT	E	203 882-2308	2283
Gillette Company	Bethel	CT	G	203 796-4000	155
Schick Manufacturing Inc **(HQ)**	Milford	CT	D	203 882-2100	2360
Gillette Company **(HQ)**	Boston	MA	A	617 421-7000	8561
Gillette Company	Andover	MA	A	781 662-9600	7552
A & J Grinding Service	West Burke	VT	G	802 467-3038	22604
Edgewell Per Care Brands LLC	Bennington	VT	B	802 442-5551	21668
Edgewell Per Care Brands LLC	Saint Albans	VT	C	802 524-2151	22368

RAZORS: Electric

Company	CITY	ST	EMP	PHONE	ENTRY #
Gillette De Mexico Inc	Boston	MA	A	617 421-7000	8563

REAL ESTATE AGENCIES & BROKERS

Company	CITY	ST	EMP	PHONE	ENTRY #
Multex Automation Corporation	Boston	MA	G	617 347-7278	8716
Rowe Contracting Co	Melrose	MA	G	781 620-0052	12991
Thomas Michaels Designers Inc	Camden	ME	G	207 236-2708	5870
Homeland Company	East Greenwich	RI	G	401 884-2427	20370

REAL ESTATE AGENCIES: Leasing & Rentals

Company	CITY	ST	EMP	PHONE	ENTRY #
Polytechnic Inc	Pawtucket	RI	G	401 724-3608	20882

REAL ESTATE AGENCIES: Rental

Company	CITY	ST	EMP	PHONE	ENTRY #
Malik Embossing Corp	Salem	MA	G	978 745-6060	14928

REAL ESTATE AGENTS & MANAGERS

Company	CITY	ST	EMP	PHONE	ENTRY #
Ensign-Bickford Industries Inc	Weatogue	CT	C	860 843-2000	5042
Bruno Diduca	Waltham	MA	G	781 894-5300	16053
East Coast Publications Inc **(PA)**	Norwell	MA	E	781 878-4540	14102
Greatheart Inc	Andover	MA	G	978 475-8732	7553
Just Publications Inc	Brookline	MA	G	617 739-5878	9207
Southern Berkshire Shoppers Gu	Great Barrington	MA	F	413 528-0095	11246
Ambrose G McCarthy Jr	Skowhegan	ME	E	207 474-8837	6968
Leland Boggs II	Warren	ME	G	207 273-2610	7143
Langer Associates Inc	Manchester	NH	E	603 626-4388	18859

REAL ESTATE OPERATORS, EXC DEVELOPERS: Commercial/Indl Bldg

Company	CITY	ST	EMP	PHONE	ENTRY #
Jewish Advocate Pubg Corp	Boston	MA	F	617 523-6232	8629
Sx Industries Inc **(PA)**	Stoughton	MA	E	781 828-7111	15625
Bosal Foam and Fiber **(PA)**	Limerick	ME	E	207 793-2245	6332
Leonard Philbrick Inc	Pelham	NH	G	603 635-3500	19438
North Country Engineering Inc	Derby	VT	E	802 766-5396	21902

REAL ESTATE OPERATORS, EXC DEVELOPERS: Property, Retail

Company	CITY	ST	EMP	PHONE	ENTRY #
Charles Curtis LLC	Danville	VT	G	802 274-0060	21895

REAL ESTATE OPERATORS, EXC DEVELOPERS: Retirement Hotel

Company	CITY	ST	EMP	PHONE	ENTRY #
Sawmill Park	Southwick	MA	G	413 569-3393	15417

RECEIVERS: Radio Communications

Company	CITY	ST	EMP	PHONE	ENTRY #
Nhrc LLC	Pembroke	NH	F	603 485-2248	19459

RECHROMING SVC: Automobile Bumpers

Company	CITY	ST	EMP	PHONE	ENTRY #
Nu Chrome Corp	Seekonk	MA	F	508 557-1418	15032

RECLAIMED RUBBER: Reworked By Manufacturing Process

Company	CITY	ST	EMP	PHONE	ENTRY #
Tellus Technology Inc **(PA)**	Darien	CT	G	646 265-7960	1033

RECORDERS: Sound

Company	CITY	ST	EMP	PHONE	ENTRY #
Omnicron Electronics	Putnam	CT	G	860 928-0377	3623

RECORDING HEADS: Speech & Musical Eqpt

Company	CITY	ST	EMP	PHONE	ENTRY #
Musical Playground	Centerville	MA	G	508 778-6679	9818

RECORDS & TAPES: Prerecorded

Company	CITY	ST	EMP	PHONE	ENTRY #
Bff Holdings Inc **(HQ)**	Old Saybrook	CT	C	860 510-0100	3328
Fleetwood Multi-Media Inc	Lynn	MA	F	781 599-2400	12509
Stephen McArthur	Barre	VT	G	802 839-0371	21640

RECORDS OR TAPES: Masters

Company	CITY	ST	EMP	PHONE	ENTRY #
Gateway Mastering Studios Inc	Portland	ME	F	207 828-9400	6664

RECOVERY SVC: Iron Ore, From Open Hearth Slag

Company	CITY	ST	EMP	PHONE	ENTRY #
Centritec Seals LLC	East Hartford	CT	G	860 594-7183	1181
Eastern Metals Inc	Londonderry	NH	G	603 818-8639	18693

RECOVERY SVCS: Metal

Company	CITY	ST	EMP	PHONE	ENTRY #
Greene Lyon Group Inc	Amesbury	MA	G	617 290-2276	7488

RECREATIONAL VEHICLE: Wholesalers

Company	CITY	ST	EMP	PHONE	ENTRY #
B&B Micro Manufacturing Inc	Adams	MA	E	413 281-9431	7410

RECTIFIERS: Electronic, Exc Semiconductor

Company	CITY	ST	EMP	PHONE	ENTRY #
Edal Industries Inc	East Haven	CT	E	203 467-2591	1248

RECYCLABLE SCRAP & WASTE MATERIALS WHOLESALERS

Company	CITY	ST	EMP	PHONE	ENTRY #
Colt Refining Inc **(PA)**	Merrimack	NH	E	603 429-9966	18993

RECYCLING: Paper

Company	CITY	ST	EMP	PHONE	ENTRY #
American Paper Recycling Corp **(PA)**	Mansfield	MA	E	800 422-3220	12613
Melt Cognition	Bedford	MA	G	781 275-6400	7990
ND Paper Inc	Rumford	ME	G	207 364-4521	6838
Petrofiber Corporation **(PA)**	Hopkinton	NH	G	603 627-0416	18364

REELS: Cable, Metal

Company	CITY	ST	EMP	PHONE	ENTRY #
William McCaskie Inc	Westport	MA	G	508 636-8845	16852
Carris Financial Corp **(PA)**	Proctor	VT	F	802 773-9111	22283
Carris Reels Inc **(HQ)**	Proctor	VT	C	802 773-9111	22284

REELS: Fiber, Textile, Made From Purchased Materials

Company	CITY	ST	EMP	PHONE	ENTRY #
Signode Industrial Group LLC	Rumford	RI	D	401 438-5203	21196

REELS: Wood

Company	CITY	ST	EMP	PHONE	ENTRY #
Assonet Industries Inc	Assonet	MA	G	508 644-5001	7677
Herrick Mill Work Inc	Contoocook	NH	E	603 746-5092	17945

REFINERS & SMELTERS: Aluminum

Company	CITY	ST	EMP	PHONE	ENTRY #
Connell Limited Partnership **(PA)**	Boston	MA	F	617 737-2700	8481

REFINERS & SMELTERS: Brass, Secondary

Company	CITY	ST	EMP	PHONE	ENTRY #
N Kamenske & Co Inc	Nashua	NH	G	603 888-1007	19211

REFINERS & SMELTERS: Copper

Company	CITY	ST	EMP	PHONE	ENTRY #
Ametek Inc	Wallingford	CT	C	203 265-6731	4699

REFINERS & SMELTERS: Gold

Company	CITY	ST	EMP	PHONE	ENTRY #
Hallmark Sweet/Ekru Inc	Attleboro	MA	C	508 226-9600	7745
Metalor Technologies USA Corp **(DH)**	North Attleboro	MA	C	508 699-8800	13763

REFINERS & SMELTERS: Gold, Secondary

Company	CITY	ST	EMP	PHONE	ENTRY #
Metalor Technologies USA Corp **(DH)**	North Attleboro	MA	C	508 699-8800	13763

REFINERS & SMELTERS: Lead, Secondary

Company	CITY	ST	EMP	PHONE	ENTRY #
Alent USA Holding Inc	Waterbury	CT	B	203 575-5727	4839
Surf Metal Co Inc	Stratford	CT	G	203 375-2211	4452

REFINERS & SMELTERS: Nonferrous Metal

Company	CITY	ST	EMP	PHONE	ENTRY #
5n Plus Wisconsin Inc	Trumbull	CT	F	203 384-0331	4610
Paradigm Manchester Inc	Manchester	CT	C	860 649-2888	2032
Ulbrich Stnless Stels Spcial M **(PA)**	North Haven	CT	D	203 239-4481	3067
Metalor USA Refining Corp **(DH)**	North Attleboro	MA	C	508 699-8800	13764
Polymetallurgical LLC	North Attleboro	MA	E	508 695-9312	13773
Precious Alloy Refining LLC	Stoughton	MA	G	774 296-5000	15616
Colt Refining Inc **(PA)**	Merrimack	NH	E	603 429-9966	18993
Harding Metals Inc	Northwood	NH	E	603 942-5573	19412
Sturm Ruger & Company Inc	Newport	NH	C	603 863-3300	19362
Gannon & Scott Inc	Cranston	RI	D	401 463-5550	20229
Kelley Metal Corp	East Providence	RI	F	401 434-8795	20426
Morgan Mill Metals LLC	Johnston	RI	F	401 270-9944	20524

REFINERS & SMELTERS: Platinum Group Metal Refining, Primary

Company	CITY	ST	EMP	PHONE	ENTRY #
J-A Industries Incorporated	North Easton	MA	G	508 297-1648	13948

REFINERS & SMELTERS: Platinum Group Metals, Secondary

Company	CITY	ST	EMP	PHONE	ENTRY #
Utitec Inc **(HQ)**	Watertown	CT	D	860 945-0605	5032

REFINING LUBRICATING OILS & GREASES, NEC

Company	CITY	ST	EMP	PHONE	ENTRY #
Price-Driscoll Corporation	Waterford	CT	G	860 442-3575	4991

REFINING: Petroleum

Company	CITY	ST	EMP	PHONE	ENTRY #
CCI Corpus Christi LLC	Stamford	CT	G	203 564-8100	4158
269 Walpole Street LLC	Norwood	MA	G	781 762-1128	14115
Dal-Trac Oil Company	Attleboro	MA	G	508 222-3935	7726
Exxonmobil Oil Corporation	Randolph	MA	G	781 963-7252	14679
Exxonmobil Pipeline Company	Springfield	MA	G	413 736-1881	15470
Koch Industries Inc	South Portland	ME	F	207 767-2161	7031
Prima America Corporation	Groveton	NH	E	603 631-5407	18233
Ultramar Inc	Lancaster	NH	F	603 788-2771	18608
Oxbow Creative LLC	Burlington	VT	F	802 870-0354	21801

REFRACTORIES: Brick

Company	CITY	ST	EMP	PHONE	ENTRY #
Redland Brick Inc	South Windsor	CT	C	860 528-1311	4007
LMI Liquidation Corporation	Lynn	MA	G	781 593-2561	12521

REFRACTORIES: Clay

Company	CITY	ST	EMP	PHONE	ENTRY #
Bonsal American Inc	Canaan	CT	E	860 824-7733	685
Harbisonwalker Intl Inc	West Haven	CT	G	203 934-7960	5125
Lynn Products Co	Lynn	MA	E	781 593-2500	12524
AW Perkins Company	Rutland	VT	G	802 773-3600	22323

REFRACTORIES: Graphite, Carbon Or Ceramic Bond

Company	CITY	ST	EMP	PHONE	ENTRY #
Saint-Gobain Abrasives Inc **(DH)**	Worcester	MA	A	508 795-5000	17464

REFRACTORIES: Nonclay

Company	CITY	ST	EMP	PHONE	ENTRY #
Joshua LLC **(PA)**	New Haven	CT	E	203 624-0080	2699
Specialty Minerals Inc	Canaan	CT	C	860 824-5435	690
Bay State Crucible Co	Taunton	MA	E	508 824-5121	15732
Saint-Gobain Ceramics Plas Inc	Northampton	MA	F	413 586-8167	14020
Infab Refractories Inc	Lewiston	ME	G	207 783-2075	6291
Newport Sand & Gravel Co Inc **(PA)**	Newport	NH	F	603 298-0199	19352

REFRACTORIES: Tile & Brick, Exc Plastic

Company	CITY	ST	EMP	PHONE	ENTRY #
Zampell Refractories Inc	Auburn	ME	E	207 786-2400	5602

REFRIGERATION & HEATING EQUIPMENT

Company	CITY	ST	EMP	PHONE	ENTRY #
Mechancal Engnered Systems LLC	New Canaan	CT	G	203 400-4658	2606
Tld Ace Corporation	Windsor	CT	B	860 602-3300	5374
Trane Inc	New Haven	CT	D	860 437-6208	2746
Trane US Inc	New London	CT	D	860 437-6208	2784
Trane US Inc	Farmington	CT	D	860 470-3901	1516
Trane US Inc	Hartford	CT	G	860 541-1721	1881
United Technologies Corp	East Hartford	CT	C	860 565-7622	1234
United Technologies Corp	Essex	CT	B	860 767-9592	1407
United Technologies Corp **(PA)**	Farmington	CT	B	860 728-7000	1522
Vector Controls LLC **(PA)**	Bethel	CT	F	203 749-0883	191
Airxchange Inc	Rockland	MA	D	781 871-4816	14789
Bluezone Products Inc	Woburn	MA	G	781 937-0202	17134
Cambridgeport Air Systems Inc	Georgetown	MA	C	978 465-8481	11139
Cunniff Corp **(PA)**	East Falmouth	MA	G	508 540-6232	10440
Duc-Pac Corporation	East Longmeadow	MA	E	413 525-3302	10474
Hoshizaki America Inc	Marlborough	MA	C	508 251-7060	12774
Ilios Inc	Waltham	MA	G	781 466-6481	16128
Lennox Roofing Inc	Abington	MA	G	508 328-5780	7327
Mestek Inc	Westfield	MA	D	413 564-5530	16701
Munters Corporation	Amesbury	MA	F	978 388-2666	7497
Refco Manufacturing Us Inc	Springfield	MA	G	413 746-3094	15500
Tecomet Inc	Woburn	MA	D	781 782-6400	17305

PRODUCT

	CITY	ST	EMP	PHONE	ENTRY #
Thermal Circuits Inc	Salem	MA	C	978 745-1162	14945
Thl-Nortek Investors LLC **(PA)**	Boston	MA	D	617 227-1050	8882
Total Temp Inc	Middleboro	MA	G	508 947-8628	13078
Trane Inc	Wilmington	MA	D	978 737-3900	17057
Mestek Inc	Clinton	ME	C	207 426-2351	5916
Trane US Inc	Westbrook	ME	E	207 773-0637	7211
Amtrol Intl Investments Inc **(DH)**	West Warwick	RI	G	401 884-6300	21478
Nitrotap Ltd	Warren	RI	G	401 247-2141	21299
Trane US Inc	Riverside	RI	E	401 434-3146	21176

REFRIGERATION EQPT & SPLYS WHOLESALERS

	CITY	ST	EMP	PHONE	ENTRY #
Mv3 LLC	Buzzards Bay	MA	G	617 658-4420	9361

REFRIGERATION EQPT & SPLYS, WHOLESALE: Beverage Coolers

	CITY	ST	EMP	PHONE	ENTRY #
Mp Systems Inc	East Granby	CT	F	860 687-3460	1134

REFRIGERATION EQPT: Complete

	CITY	ST	EMP	PHONE	ENTRY #
Demartino Fixture Co Inc	Wallingford	CT	E	203 269-3971	4733
Wine Well Chiller Comp Inc	Milford	CT	G	203 878-2465	2382
Ad Hoc Energy LLC	Millis	MA	G	508 507-8005	13182
Aipco Inc	Taunton	MA	E	508 823-7003	15721
Aspen Compressor LLC	Marlborough	MA	E	508 281-5322	12721
Munters USA Inc	Amesbury	MA	A	978 241-1100	7500
Standex International Corp **(PA)**	Salem	NH	E	603 893-9701	19769

REFRIGERATION REPAIR SVCS

	CITY	ST	EMP	PHONE	ENTRY #
R H Travers Company	Warren	VT	G	802 496-5205	22578

REFUSE SYSTEMS

	CITY	ST	EMP	PHONE	ENTRY #
Tomra Mass LLC	New Bedford	MA	E	203 395-3484	13455
Harding Metals Inc	Northwood	NH	E	603 942-5573	19412

REGISTERS: Air, Metal

	CITY	ST	EMP	PHONE	ENTRY #
Metalworks Inc	Burlington	VT	G	802 863-0414	21796

REGULATORS: Line Voltage

	CITY	ST	EMP	PHONE	ENTRY #
71 Pickett District Road LLC	New Milford	CT	G	860 350-5964	2786
Neeltran Inc	New Milford	CT	C	860 350-5964	2815

REGULATORS: Transmission & Distribution Voltage

	CITY	ST	EMP	PHONE	ENTRY #
Pne Energy Supply LLC	Manchester	NH	G	603 413-6602	18902

RELAYS & SWITCHES: Indl, Electric

	CITY	ST	EMP	PHONE	ENTRY #
Kenneth Crosby Co Inc	Hopkinton	MA	F	508 497-0048	11725

RELAYS: Control Circuit, Ind

	CITY	ST	EMP	PHONE	ENTRY #
Amphenol Pcd Inc **(HQ)**	Beverly	MA	D	978 921-1531	8099

RELAYS: Electric Power

	CITY	ST	EMP	PHONE	ENTRY #
Coto Technology Inc	North Kingstown	RI	B	401 943-2686	20698

RELAYS: Electronic Usage

	CITY	ST	EMP	PHONE	ENTRY #
Allied Controls Inc	Stamford	CT	F	860 628-8443	4134
Component Concepts Inc	West Hartford	CT	G	860 523-4066	5062
Computer Components Inc	East Granby	CT	F	860 653-9909	1123
General Electro Components	Glastonbury	CT	G	860 659-3573	1554
Amphenol Pcd Inc	Peabody	MA	G	978 921-1531	14310
Product Resources LLC	Newburyport	MA	E	978 524-8500	13523

RELAYS: Vacuum

	CITY	ST	EMP	PHONE	ENTRY #
Filtech Inc	Boston	MA	G	617 227-1133	8545

RELIGIOUS SPLYS WHOLESALERS

	CITY	ST	EMP	PHONE	ENTRY #
McVan Inc	Attleboro	MA	E	508 431-2400	7766

REMOVERS & CLEANERS

	CITY	ST	EMP	PHONE	ENTRY #
Clean Up Group	Meriden	CT	G	203 668-8323	2087
Handyscape LLC	Southington	CT	G	860 318-1067	4056
CJ Shaughnessy Crane Svc Inc	Avon	MA	G	781 924-1168	7883
Mr Plow	Natick	MA	G	508 207-8999	13270
Fisher LLC **(PA)**	Rockland	ME	F	207 701-4200	6793
H P Fairfield LLC	Scarborough	ME	G	207 885-4895	6923
Howard P Fairfield LLC	Scarborough	ME	G	207 885-4895	6925
White Mountain Plowing	Farmington	NH	G	603 817-0913	18146

REMOVERS: Paint

	CITY	ST	EMP	PHONE	ENTRY #
American-International Tl Inds	Cranston	RI	G	401 942-7855	20180

RENDERING PLANT

	CITY	ST	EMP	PHONE	ENTRY #
Western Mass Rendering Co Inc	Southwick	MA	E	413 569-6265	15420
Baker Commodities Inc	Vassalboro	ME	G	207 622-3505	7124

RENTAL SVCS: Business Machine & Electronic Eqpt

	CITY	ST	EMP	PHONE	ENTRY #
Neopost USA Inc **(DH)**	Milford	CT	C	203 301-3400	2319
Pitney Bowes Inc **(PA)**	Stamford	CT	A	203 356-5000	4285
Pitney Bowes Inc	Stamford	CT	E	203 356-5000	4286
Pitney Bowes Inc	Shelton	CT	E	203 922-4000	3854
Pitney Bowes Inc	Shelton	CT	E	203 356-5000	3855
Doble Engineering Company **(HQ)**	Watertown	MA	F	617 926-4900	16279
Pitney Bowes Inc	Portland	ME	E	207 773-2345	6709
Pitney Bowes Inc	Keene	NH	E	603 352-7766	18522
Pitney Bowes Inc	East Providence	RI	E	401 435-8500	20442

RENTAL SVCS: Garage Facility & Tool

	CITY	ST	EMP	PHONE	ENTRY #
Boston Garage	Hanover	MA	F	339 788-9580	11330

RENTAL SVCS: Tent & Tarpaulin

	CITY	ST	EMP	PHONE	ENTRY #
Tent Connection Inc	Northbridge	MA	G	508 234-8746	14062
Leavitt & Parris Inc	Portland	ME	F	207 797-0100	6679

RENTAL SVCS: Video Cassette Recorder & Access

	CITY	ST	EMP	PHONE	ENTRY #
Amb Signs Inc **(PA)**	Dover Foxcroft	ME	G	207 564-3633	5959

RENTAL SVCS: Work Zone Traffic Eqpt, Flags, Cones, Etc

	CITY	ST	EMP	PHONE	ENTRY #
Sonco Worldwide Inc	Warwick	RI	F	401 406-3761	21427

RENTAL: Video Tape & Disc

	CITY	ST	EMP	PHONE	ENTRY #
Cataki International Inc	Wareham	MA	E	508 295-9630	16243

REPRODUCTION SVCS: Video Tape Or Disk

	CITY	ST	EMP	PHONE	ENTRY #
Play-It Productions Inc	Colchester	CT	F	212 695-6530	805

RESEARCH & DEVELOPMENT SVCS, COMMERCIAL: Engineering Lab

	CITY	ST	EMP	PHONE	ENTRY #
Advanced Control Systems Corp	Canton	MA	G	781 829-9228	9711
Perspecta Svcs & Solutions Inc **(DH)**	Waltham	MA	E	781 684-4000	16173
Electro Standards Lab Inc	Cranston	RI	D	401 946-1390	20215

RESEARCH, DEV & TESTING SVCS, COMM: Chem Lab, Exc Testing

	CITY	ST	EMP	PHONE	ENTRY #
Creative Materials Inc	Ayer	MA	F	978 391-4700	7916
Tracer Technologies Inc	Somerville	MA	E	617 776-6410	15224
Universal Pharma Tech LLC	North Andover	MA	F	978 975-7216	13735

RESEARCH, DEVELOPMENT & TEST SVCS, COMM: Research, Exc Lab

	CITY	ST	EMP	PHONE	ENTRY #
Callaway Companies Inc **(PA)**	Old Lyme	CT	F	860 434-9002	3317
Freethink Technologies Inc	Branford	CT	F	860 237-5800	317
Healthy Harvest Inc	Madison	CT	G	203 245-3786	1963
Innophase Corp	Westbrook	CT	G	860 399-2269	5156
Polymer Technologies LLC	Nashua	NH	G	603 883-4002	19235

RESEARCH, DEVELOPMENT & TESTING SVCS, COMM: Research Lab

	CITY	ST	EMP	PHONE	ENTRY #
Beigene Usa Inc **(HQ)**	Cambridge	MA	G	781 801-1887	9407
Biogen MA Inc **(HQ)**	Cambridge	MA	C	617 679-2000	9410
McLane Research Labs Inc **(PA)**	East Falmouth	MA	G	508 495-4000	10445
Pellion Technologies Inc	Arlington	MA	E	617 547-3191	7632

RESEARCH, DEVELOPMENT & TESTING SVCS, COMMERCIAL: Business

	CITY	ST	EMP	PHONE	ENTRY #
Vitek Research Corporation	Naugatuck	CT	F	203 735-1813	2500
Continuus Pharmaceuticals Inc	Woburn	MA	F	781 281-0226	17153

RESEARCH, DEVELOPMENT & TESTING SVCS, COMMERCIAL: Education

	CITY	ST	EMP	PHONE	ENTRY #
Metacog Inc	Worcester	MA	G	508 798-6100	17413

RESEARCH, DEVELOPMENT & TESTING SVCS, COMMERCIAL: Energy

	CITY	ST	EMP	PHONE	ENTRY #
Alacrity Semiconductors Inc	Branford	CT	G	475 325-8435	287
Ebeam Film LLC	Shelton	CT	F	203 926-0100	3798
Maine Power Express LLC	Greenwich	CT	G	203 661-0055	1628
Lionano Inc	Woburn	MA	G	607 216-8156	17214
Nanoptek Corporation	Shirley	MA	G	978 460-7107	15091
Spire Solar Inc	Bedford	MA	C	781 275-6000	8009

RESEARCH, DEVELOPMENT & TESTING SVCS, COMMERCIAL: Food

	CITY	ST	EMP	PHONE	ENTRY #
Soyatech Inc	Bar Harbor	ME	G	207 288-4969	5670

RESEARCH, DEVELOPMENT & TESTING SVCS, COMMERCIAL: Medical

	CITY	ST	EMP	PHONE	ENTRY #
Home Diagnostics Corp	Trumbull	CT	C	203 445-1170	4625
Ariad Pharmaceuticals Inc	Cambridge	MA	B	617 494-0400	9392
Kaleido Biosciences Inc **(PA)**	Lexington	MA	D	617 674-9000	12234
Radius Health Inc **(PA)**	Waltham	MA	D	617 551-4000	16183
Bio-Concept Laboratories Inc	Salem	NH	E	603 437-4990	19713

RESEARCH, DEVELOPMENT & TESTING SVCS, COMMERCIAL: Opinion

	CITY	ST	EMP	PHONE	ENTRY #
Peelfly Inc	Everett	MA	G	860 608-3819	10625

RESEARCH, DEVELOPMENT & TESTING SVCS, COMMERCIAL: Physical

	CITY	ST	EMP	PHONE	ENTRY #
Beta Pharma Inc	Shelton	CT	F	203 315-5062	3780
Cambrdge RES Instrmntation Inc	Hopkinton	MA	E	781 935-9099	11695
Johnson Matthey Phrm Mtls Inc **(DH)**	Devens	MA	C	978 784-5000	10321
Johnson Matthey Phrm Mtls Inc	North Andover	MA	E	978 784-5000	13713
Millennium Pharmaceuticals Inc	Cambridge	MA	F	617 679-7000	9559
Mikros Manufacturing Inc	Claremont	NH	E	603 690-2020	17855

RESEARCH, DEVELOPMENT SVCS, COMMERCIAL: Indl Lab

	CITY	ST	EMP	PHONE	ENTRY #
Integral Technologies Inc **(DH)**	Enfield	CT	G	860 741-2281	1366

RESEARCH, DVLPT & TEST SVCS, COMM: Mkt Analysis or Research

	CITY	ST	EMP	PHONE	ENTRY #
Information Resources Inc	Norwalk	CT	D	203 845-6400	3173
Tri Source Inc	Shelton	CT	F	203 924-7030	3882
International Data Group Inc **(PA)**	Boston	MA	F	508 875-5000	8618

RESIDENTIAL REMODELERS

	CITY	ST	EMP	PHONE	ENTRY #
Tozier Group Inc	Falmouth	ME	E	207 838-7939	6035

RESIDUES

	CITY	ST	EMP	PHONE	ENTRY #
Lanxess Solutions US Inc **(DH)**	Shelton	CT	E	203 573-2000	3824

RESINS: Custom Compound Purchased

	CITY	ST	EMP	PHONE	ENTRY #
Electric Cable Compounds Inc	Naugatuck	CT	D	203 723-2590	2472
Foster Corporation **(HQ)**	Putnam	CT	D	860 928-4102	3613
Neu Spclty Engineered Mtls LLC	North Haven	CT	F	203 239-9629	3043
Performance Compounding Inc	Pawcatuck	CT	G	860 599-5616	3440
Pioneer Plastics Corporation **(HQ)**	Shelton	CT	D	203 925-1556	3853
Clariant Plas Coatings USA LLC	Holden	MA	D	508 829-6321	11543
Mexichem Spcalty Compounds Inc **(HQ)**	Leominster	MA	C	978 537-8071	12166
Shield Packaging Co Inc	Dudley	MA	D	508 949-0900	10384
Neal Specialty Compounding LLC	Lewiston	ME	D	207 777-1122	6309
Pioneer Plastics Corporation	Auburn	ME	B	207 784-9111	5592
New Hampshire Stamping Co Inc	Goffstown	NH	E	603 641-1234	18206
Visual Polymer Tech LLC	Bedford	NH	F	603 488-5064	17666
Daikin U S Corporation	Warwick	RI	G	401 738-0261	21347
Elite Custom Compounding Inc	Warwick	RI	G	401 921-2136	21359
Polymer Solutions Inc	Pawtucket	RI	G	401 423-1638	20881
Teknor Apex Company **(PA)**	Pawtucket	RI	B	401 725-8000	20903
Teknor Prfmce Elastomers Inc	Pawtucket	RI	G	401 725-8000	20905

RESISTORS

	CITY	ST	EMP	PHONE	ENTRY #
Able Coil and Electronics Co	Bolton	CT	E	860 646-5686	273
Prime Technology LLC	North Branford	CT	C	203 481-5721	2974
Vishay Americas Inc **(HQ)**	Shelton	CT	B	203 452-5648	3886
Isotek Corporation	Swansea	MA	G	508 673-2900	15705
Mini-Systems Inc **(PA)**	North Attleboro	MA	C	508 695-1420	13765
Mini-Systems Inc	Attleboro	MA	D	508 695-0203	7768
Mini-Systems Inc	Plainville	MA	E	508 695-2000	14528
Philips Medical Systems Hsg **(PA)**	Andover	MA	E	978 687-1501	7583
Phoenix Electric Corp	Canton	MA	E	781 821-0200	9767
Two In One Manufacturing Inc	Nashua	NH	E	603 595-8212	19276
Cx Thin Films LLC	Cranston	RI	F	401 461-5500	20207
Honeywell International Inc	Woonsocket	RI	D	401 762-6200	21569

RESISTORS & RESISTOR UNITS

	CITY	ST	EMP	PHONE	ENTRY #
Barry Industries Inc	Attleboro	MA	D	508 226-3350	7712
Elscott Manufacturing LLC **(PA)**	Gouldsboro	ME	D	207 422-6747	6136
Anaren Ceramics Inc	Salem	NH	D	603 898-2883	19706

RESISTORS: Networks

	CITY	ST	EMP	PHONE	ENTRY #
Bantry Components Inc	Manchester	NH	E	603 668-3210	18785
Rcd Components LLC **(HQ)**	Manchester	NH	D	603 666-4627	18909

RESORT HOTELS

	CITY	ST	EMP	PHONE	ENTRY #
Killington Ltd	Killington	VT	D	802 422-3333	22053

RESPIRATORS

	CITY	ST	EMP	PHONE	ENTRY #
Tri-Med Inc	Peterborough	NH	G	603 924-7211	19491

RESPIRATORY SYSTEM DRUGS

	CITY	ST	EMP	PHONE	ENTRY #
Infirst Healthcare Inc	Westport	CT	G	203 222-1300	5203
Calista Therapeutics Inc	Lincoln	RI	G	401 345-5979	20561

RESTAURANT EQPT: Carts

	CITY	ST	EMP	PHONE	ENTRY #
Vermont Culinary Islands LLC	Brattleboro	VT	F	802 246-2277	21750

RESTAURANT EQPT: Food Wagons

	CITY	ST	EMP	PHONE	ENTRY #
Metzys Taqueria LLC	Newburyport	MA	G	978 992-1451	13512
Chase S Daily LLC	Belfast	ME	G	207 338-0555	5687
7 South Sandwich Company LLC	Middlebury	VT	G	802 388-3354	22095

RESTAURANTS: Delicatessen

	CITY	ST	EMP	PHONE	ENTRY #
Ginsco Inc **(PA)**	Fall River	MA	F	508 677-4767	10704

RESTAURANTS: Fast Food

	CITY	ST	EMP	PHONE	ENTRY #
Orono House of Pizza	Orono	ME	G	207 866-5505	6557

RESTAURANTS:Full Svc, Ethnic Food

	CITY	ST	EMP	PHONE	ENTRY #
Slacktide Cafe LLC	Arundel	ME	G	207 467-3822	5535
Simon Pearce US Inc **(PA)**	Windsor	VT	C	802 674-6280	22714

RESTAURANTS:Full Svc, Family

	CITY	ST	EMP	PHONE	ENTRY #
La Casona Restaurant Inc	Central Falls	RI	G	401 727-0002	20118

RESTAURANTS:Full Svc, Family, Independent

	CITY	ST	EMP	PHONE	ENTRY #
E M K Inc	Skowhegan	ME	F	207 474-2666	6973
Pig + Poet Restaurant	Camden	ME	G	207 236-3391	5869
7th Settlement Brewery LLC	Dover	NH	E	603 534-5292	18002
Pollys Pancake Parlor	Sugar Hill	NH	G	603 823-5575	19878

RESTAURANTS:Full Svc, Italian

	CITY	ST	EMP	PHONE	ENTRY #
Chinese Spaghetti Factory	Boston	MA	G	617 542-0224	8470
Hole In One	Eastham	MA	E	508 255-5359	10549

RESTAURANTS:Full Svc, Mexican

	CITY	ST	EMP	PHONE	ENTRY #
Metzys Taqueria LLC	Newburyport	MA	G	978 992-1451	13512

RESTAURANTS:Full Svc, Steak

	CITY	ST	EMP	PHONE	ENTRY #
John Harvards Brewhouse Llc	Framingham	MA	D	508 875-2337	10974

RESTAURANTS:Limited Svc, Coffee Shop

	CITY	ST	EMP	PHONE	ENTRY #
Daybrake Donuts Inc	Bridgeport	CT	F	203 368-4962	401
Mrs Macks Bakery Inc	Worcester	MA	G	508 753-0610	17426
Grist For Mill LLC	Bristol	NH	F	603 744-0405	17767

RESTAURANTS:Limited Svc, Fast-Food, Independent

	CITY	ST	EMP	PHONE	ENTRY #
Song Wind Industries Inc	Barrington	RI	E	401 245-7582	20056

RESTAURANTS:Limited Svc, Hamburger Stand

	CITY	ST	EMP	PHONE	ENTRY #
Brava Enterprises LLC	Lewiston	ME	G	207 241-2420	6277

RESTAURANTS:Limited Svc, Ice Cream Stands Or Dairy Bars

	CITY	ST	EMP	PHONE	ENTRY #
J Foster Ice Cream	Simsbury	CT	G	860 651-1499	3907
Richardsons Ice Cream	Reading	MA	G	781 944-9121	14740
Spadafora Slush Co	Malden	MA	G	617 548-5870	12597
Round Top Ice Cream Inc	Damariscotta	ME	E	207 563-5307	5939

RESTAURANTS:Limited Svc, Pizzeria, Chain

	CITY	ST	EMP	PHONE	ENTRY #
Pro Dough Inc	Manchester	NH	F	603 623-6844	18906

RESTAURANTS:Limited Svc, Soda Fountain

	CITY	ST	EMP	PHONE	ENTRY #
Furlongs Cottage Candies	Norwood	MA	F	781 762-4124	14154

RESTAURANTS:Limited Svc, Soft Drink Stand

	CITY	ST	EMP	PHONE	ENTRY #
Soda Shoppe of Franklin	Franklin	NH	F	603 934-0100	18164

RESTAURANTS:Ltd Svc, Ice Cream, Soft Drink/Fountain Stands

	CITY	ST	EMP	PHONE	ENTRY #
Fudge Factory Inc	Manchester Center	VT	F	888 669-7425	22085

RETAIL BAKERY: Bagels

	CITY	ST	EMP	PHONE	ENTRY #
Driscolls Restaurant	Mansfield	MA	F	508 261-1574	12629
Ginsco Inc **(PA)**	Fall River	MA	F	508 677-4767	10704
Korner Bagel Partnership	Seekonk	MA	E	508 336-5204	15025

RETAIL BAKERY: Bread

	CITY	ST	EMP	PHONE	ENTRY #
Oasis Coffee Corp	Norwalk	CT	E	203 847-0554	3210
Iggys Bread Ltd **(PA)**	Cambridge	MA	D	617 491-7600	9512
Superior Baking Co Inc	Brockton	MA	E	508 586-6601	9180
Italian Bakery Products Co	Lewiston	ME	F	207 782-8312	6293

RETAIL BAKERY: Cookies

	CITY	ST	EMP	PHONE	ENTRY #
Boston Chipyard The Inc	Boston	MA	F	617 742-9537	8428

RETAIL BAKERY: Doughnuts

	CITY	ST	EMP	PHONE	ENTRY #
Donut Stop	Shelton	CT	G	203 924-7133	3797
Pops Donuts	Milford	CT	G	203 876-1210	2335
Hole In One	Eastham	MA	E	508 255-5359	10549
Speedway LLC	Auburndale	MA	G	617 244-4601	7870

RETAIL BAKERY: Pastries

	CITY	ST	EMP	PHONE	ENTRY #
Fredericks Pastries **(PA)**	Amherst	NH	G	603 882-7725	17563

RETAIL BAKERY: Pies

	CITY	ST	EMP	PHONE	ENTRY #
Stone House Farm Inc	West Boxford	MA	G	978 352-2323	16408

RETAIL LUMBER YARDS

	CITY	ST	EMP	PHONE	ENTRY #
A & K Railroad Materials Inc	Hamden	CT	G	203 495-8790	1728
Conway Hardwood Products LLC	Gaylordsville	CT	E	860 355-4030	1530
St Pierre Box and Lumber Co	Canton	CT	G	860 413-9813	699
Aggregate Inds - Northeast Reg	Ashland	MA	E	508 881-1430	7655
Fine Line Woodworking Inc	Boxboro	MA	G	978 263-4322	8952
Leon M Fiske Company Inc	Greenfield	MA	G	413 772-6833	11268
Theodore Wolf Inc	East Falmouth	MA	G	508 457-0667	10450
Phinney Lumber Co	Gorham	ME	E	207 839-3336	6124
Boulia-Gorrell Lumber Co Inc	Laconia	NH	F	603 524-1300	18560
Euphonon Co	Orford	NH	G	603 353-4882	19420
A Johnson Co	Bristol	VT	D	802 453-4884	21760
Goodridge Lumber	Albany	VT	G	802 755-6298	21592
Granville Manufacturing Co	Granville	VT	G	802 767-4747	22003

RETAIL STORES, NEC

	CITY	ST	EMP	PHONE	ENTRY #
US Standard Brands Inc	Walpole	MA	G	617 719-8796	16016
H W Dunn & Son Inc	Ellsworth	ME	G	207 667-8121	6019

RETAIL STORES: Alcoholic Beverage Making Eqpt & Splys

	CITY	ST	EMP	PHONE	ENTRY #
Universal Color Corp Inc	Wilmington	MA	F	978 658-2300	17061
D R Designs Inc	Manchester	ME	G	207 622-3303	6409
Opti-Sciences Inc	Hudson	NH	G	603 883-4400	18424

RETAIL STORES: Architectural Splys

	CITY	ST	EMP	PHONE	ENTRY #
Woodshop Cupolas Inc	Trenton	ME	G	207 667-6331	7104

RETAIL STORES: Artificial Limbs

	CITY	ST	EMP	PHONE	ENTRY #
Orthotics Prosthetics Labs Inc	Northampton	MA	G	413 585-8622	14015
Maine Artfl Limb Orthotics Co	Portland	ME	F	207 773-4963	6681

RETAIL STORES: Audio-Visual Eqpt & Splys

	CITY	ST	EMP	PHONE	ENTRY #
Rm Education Inc **(HQ)**	Hyannis	MA	E	508 862-0700	11856

RETAIL STORES: Awnings

	CITY	ST	EMP	PHONE	ENTRY #
Dartmouth Awning Co Inc	Westport	MA	G	508 636-6838	16838
Plymouth Awning Co	Plymouth	MA	G	508 746-3740	14574
Readys Window Products Inc	Tewksbury	MA	G	978 851-3963	15832
Image Awnings Inc	Wolfeboro	NH	G	603 569-6680	20020
Durasol Systems Inc	Williston	VT	E	802 864-3009	22663

RETAIL STORES: Canvas Prdts

	CITY	ST	EMP	PHONE	ENTRY #
Custom Canvas & Upholstery LLC	Lewiston	ME	F	207 241-8518	6281
Nancy Lawrence	Portland	ME	G	207 774-7276	6697
American Canvas Company LLC	Kingston	NH	G	603 642-6665	18539

RETAIL STORES: Christmas Lights & Decorations

	CITY	ST	EMP	PHONE	ENTRY #
Christmas Studio	Monson	MA	G	413 267-3342	13203

RETAIL STORES: Concrete Prdts, Precast

	CITY	ST	EMP	PHONE	ENTRY #
Wachusett Precast Inc	Sterling	MA	G	978 422-3311	15548

RETAIL STORES: Cosmetics

	CITY	ST	EMP	PHONE	ENTRY #
Tc Design Works Inc	Beverly	MA	G	978 768-0034	8187

PRODUCT

	CITY	ST	EMP	PHONE	ENTRY #

RETAIL STORES: Educational Aids & Electronic Training Mat

Hotseat Chassis Inc	Waterbury	CT	G	860 582-5031	4884

RETAIL STORES: Electronic Parts & Eqpt

Tech180 Corp	Easthampton	MA	F	413 203-6123	10581

RETAIL STORES: Engine & Motor Eqpt & Splys

First Electric Motor Svc Inc	Woburn	MA	E	781 491-1100	17181

RETAIL STORES: Farm Machinery, NEC

Oesco Inc	Conway	MA	E	413 369-4335	10164

RETAIL STORES: Fiberglass Materials, Exc Insulation

Fiberglass Fabricators Inc	Smithfield	RI	E	401 231-3552	21224

RETAIL STORES: Flags

Accent Banner LLC	Medford	MA	F	781 391-7300	12920
Mass Sign & Decal Inc	Rockland	MA	G	781 878-7446	14812
Flag-Works Over America LLC	Concord	NH	G	603 225-2530	17902

RETAIL STORES: Hearing Aids

Zenith-Omni Hearing Center **(PA)**	New Haven	CT	G	203 624-9857	2763

RETAIL STORES: Ice

Eastern Ice Company Inc	Fall River	MA	E	508 672-1800	10685
Leominster Ice Company Inc	Leominster	MA	G	978 537-5322	12162
Getchell Bros Inc	Sanford	ME	E	207 490-0809	6877

RETAIL STORES: Medical Apparatus & Splys

Burke Medical Equipment Inc	Chicopee	MA	E	413 592-5464	10003
Head Prone Inc	Cambridge	MA	G	617 864-0780	9506
Inert Corporation	Amesbury	MA	E	978 462-4415	7492
Solace Therapeutics Inc	Framingham	MA	G	508 283-1200	11006

RETAIL STORES: Monuments, Finished To Custom Order

Plouffs Monument Co Inc	Enosburg Falls	VT	G	802 933-4346	21926

RETAIL STORES: Motors, Electric

Aparos Electric Motor Service	Southington	CT	G	860 276-2044	4039
Palmers Elc Mtrs & Pumps Inc	Norwalk	CT	G	203 348-7378	3214
Bay State Electric Motor Co	Methuen	MA	G	978 686-7089	13012
Delta Elc Mtr Repr Sls & Svc	Medford	MA	G	781 395-0551	12930
Reliance Electric Service	Holyoke	MA	G	413 533-3557	11651
Chase Electric Motors LLC	Hooksett	NH	G	603 669-2565	18346

RETAIL STORES: Orthopedic & Prosthesis Applications

Hayes Prosthetic Inc	West Springfield	MA	G	413 733-2287	16524
Kisers Ortho Prosthetic Serv **(PA)**	Keene	NH	G	603 357-7666	18513
Rhode Island Limb Co **(PA)**	Cranston	RI	G	401 941-6230	20279

RETAIL STORES: Pet Splys

Champagne Tables & Pet Pdts	Southampton	MA	G	413 527-4370	15337
Smartpak Equine LLC **(DH)**	Plymouth	MA	D	774 773-1100	14583

RETAIL STORES: Pets

Evergreen Enterprises Inc	Berkley	MA	G	508 823-2377	8086

RETAIL STORES: Picture Frames, Ready Made

Focal Point Opticians Inc **(PA)**	Newton	MA	G	617 965-2770	13593
Frame Center of Norwood Inc **(PA)**	Hyannis	MA	G	781 762-2535	11841

RETAIL STORES: Pipe Store, Tobacco

David Sevigny Inc	Winchendon	MA	G	978 297-2775	17073

RETAIL STORES: Plumbing & Heating Splys

Kensco Inc **(PA)**	Ansonia	CT	F	203 734-8827	20
R Filion Manufacturing Inc	Newport	NH	F	603 865-1893	19355

RETAIL STORES: Posters

Picture Frame Inc	Topsham	ME	G	207 729-7765	7093

RETAIL STORES: Religious Goods

Fred F Waltz Co Inc	North Smithfield	RI	F	401 769-4900	20786

RETAIL STORES: Rubber Stamps

Academy Printing Service	Kensington	CT	G	860 828-5549	1916
Acme Sign Co **(PA)**	Stamford	CT	F	203 324-2263	4128
Modern Marking Products Inc	Bridgewater	MA	G	508 697-6066	9085
Simons Stamps Inc	Turners Falls	MA	F	413 863-6800	15885
Anco Signs & Stamps Inc	Manchester	NH	G	603 669-3779	18779

RETAIL STORES: Safety Splys & Eqpt

Sperian Protection Usa Inc **(DH)**	Smithfield	RI	E	401 232-1200	21250

RETAIL STORES: Sunglasses

Grant Foster Group L P	Smithfield	RI	F	401 231-4077	21229

RETAIL STORES: Telephone Eqpt & Systems

Connectivity Works Inc	Holden	ME	G	207 843-0854	6196

RETAIL STORES: Toilet Preparations

Eco Services LLC	Durham	NH	G	603 682-0963	18076

RETAIL STORES: Typewriters & Business Machines

McClelland Press Inc **(PA)**	Williamstown	MA	F	413 663-5750	16958

RETAIL STORES: Water Purification Eqpt

American Water Systems LLC	Canton	MA	D	781 830-9722	9712

RETAIL STORES: Welding Splys

Praxair Distribution Inc **(DH)**	Danbury	CT	F	203 837-2000	972
Praxair Distribution Inc	Slatersville	RI	E	401 767-3450	21205

REUPHOLSTERY & FURNITURE REPAIR

Bonito Manufacturing Inc	North Haven	CT	D	203 234-8786	3011
High Grade Finishing Co LLC	Enfield	CT	G	860 749-8883	1364
Canner Incorporated	West Groton	MA	F	978 448-3063	16479
Columbia ASC Inc	Lawrence	MA	F	978 683-2205	12012

REUPHOLSTERY SVCS

Ben Baena & Son	Bridgeport	CT	G	203 334-8568	382
General Seating Solutions LLC	South Windsor	CT	F	860 242-3307	3971

RIBBONS & BOWS

Charles Clay Ltd	New Canaan	CT	G	203 662-0125	2593
Hodges Badge Company Inc **(PA)**	Portsmouth	RI	C	401 682-2000	20923

RIBBONS, NEC

National Ribbon LLC	Coventry	CT	G	860 742-6966	836
Graco Awards Manufacturing Inc	Providence	RI	E	281 255-2161	21021

RIBBONS: Nonwoven

Georgia-Pacific LLC	Leominster	MA	C	978 537-4701	12144

RIVETS: Metal

Edson Manufacturing Inc	Wolcott	CT	F	203 879-1411	5441
Howard Engineering LLC	Naugatuck	CT	E	203 729-5213	2478
Nucap US Inc **(DH)**	Wolcott	CT	E	203 879-1423	5450
Alcoa Global Fasteners Inc	Stoughton	MA	E	412 553-4545	15578

ROBOTS, SERVICES OR NOVELTY, WHOLESALE

Softbank Robotics America Inc	Boston	MA	E	617 986-6700	8851

ROBOTS: Assembly Line

Balyo Inc	Woburn	MA	E	781 281-7957	17126
Barrett Technology LLC	Newton	MA	E	617 252-9000	13566
Franklin Robotics Inc	North Billerica	MA	G	617 513-7666	13816
Irobot Corporation **(PA)**	Bedford	MA	B	781 430-3000	7985
Multex Automation Corporation	Boston	MA	G	617 347-7278	8716
Persimmon Technologies Corp	Wakefield	MA	F	781 587-0677	15968
Righthand Robotics Inc	Somerville	MA	G	617 501-0085	15210
Ryan Tool Co Inc	Taunton	MA	G	508 822-6576	15781
Eltec Industries Inc **(PA)**	Freeport	ME	G	207 541-9085	6077
Wrabacon Inc	Oakland	ME	F	207 465-2068	6536
Devprotek Inc	Hollis	NH	G	603 577-5557	18329
Equipois LLC	Manchester	NH	G	603 668-1900	18818
JP Sercel Associates Inc	Manchester	NH	D	603 595-7048	18852
Mobilerobots Inc	Amherst	NH	E	603 881-7960	17576

ROCKETS: Space & Military

Blushift Aerospace Inc	Brunswick	ME	G	207 619-1703	5831

RODS: Plastic

East Coast Precision Mfg LLC	Killingworth	CT	G	978 887-5920	1926

RODS: Steel & Iron, Made In Steel Mills

CMI Specialty Products Inc	Bristol	CT	F	860 585-0409	542
Nucor Steel Connecticut Inc	Wallingford	CT	C	203 265-0615	4780
Rivinius & Sons Inc	Woburn	MA	F	781 933-5620	17285

ROLL COVERINGS: Rubber

Schaeferrolls Inc	Farmington	NH	E	603 335-1786	18144
Stowe Woodward LLC	Concord	NH	E	603 224-6300	17932

ROLL FORMED SHAPES: Custom

Ingenven Flrplymer Slutions LL	Hampton	NH	G	603 601-0877	18265

ROLLED OR DRAWN SHAPES, NEC: Copper & Copper Alloy

Aimtek Inc **(PA)**	Auburn	MA	E	508 832-5035	7823

ROLLING MILL EQPT: Picklers & Pickling Lines

Dicks Baking	Milo	ME	G	207 284-3779	6445

ROLLING MILL MACHINERY

Adam Z Golas **(PA)**	New Britain	CT	G	860 224-7178	2504
Ulbrich Stainless Steels	Wallingford	CT	C	203 269-2507	4824
Kinefac Corporation	Worcester	MA	D	508 754-6901	17401
N Ferrara Inc	Somerset	MA	F	508 679-2440	15147
CPM Acquisition Corp	Merrimack	NH	E	319 232-8444	18994
CPM Acquisition Corp	Merrimack	NH	E	603 423-6300	18995
Winchester Precision Tech Ltd	Winchester	NH	F	603 239-6326	19997
Millard Wire Company **(PA)**	Warwick	RI	D	401 737-9330	21389
Millard Wire Company	Warwick	RI	G	401 737-9330	21390

ROLLS & BLANKETS, PRINTERS': Rubber Or Rubberized Fabric

Patten Machine Inc	Hudson	MA	F	978 562-9847	11801

ROLLS & ROLL COVERINGS: Rubber

American Roller Company LLC	Middlebury	CT	F	203 598-3100	2154
Wright Industrial Products Co	Cumberland	RI	G	508 695-3924	20350

ROLLS: Rubber, Solid Or Covered

Nauta Roll Corporation	East Hampton	CT	G	860 267-2027	1162

ROOF DECKS

Jhs Restoration Inc	South Windsor	CT	F	860 757-3870	3984
A A A Sheet Metal Inc	Hanson	MA	G	781 523-1227	11359
Century Sheet Metal Inc	Riverside	RI	G	401 433-1380	21166

ROOFING MATERIALS: Asphalt

	CITY	ST	EMP	PHONE	ENTRY #
Qba Inc	Woodstock	CT	G	860 963-9438	5500
Duro-Last Inc	Ludlow	MA	E	413 631-0050	12463
Johns Manville Corporation	West Boylston	MA	C	774 261-8500	16420
Sarnafil Services Inc	Canton	MA	C	781 828-5400	9775
Sika Sarnafil Inc	Canton	MA	G	800 451-2502	9781

ROOFING MATERIALS: Sheet Metal

	CITY	ST	EMP	PHONE	ENTRY #
Northeast Panel Co LLC	Farmington	CT	G	860 678-9078	1501
Lamb & Ritchie Company Inc	Saugus	MA	E	781 941-2700	14990

ROOFING MEMBRANE: Rubber

	CITY	ST	EMP	PHONE	ENTRY #
Kevin Lyman Roofing Co	Bridgewater	MA	G	508 697-8244	9081
Cooley Incorporated **(HQ)**	Pawtucket	RI	C	401 724-9000	20825

ROPE

	CITY	ST	EMP	PHONE	ENTRY #
Highliner Rope Co LLC	Saint George	ME	G	207 372-6300	6869
Sterling Rope Company Inc	Biddeford	ME	G	207 885-0033	5765
Anacko Cordage Co	Narragansett	RI	G	401 792-3936	20634

ROTORS: Motor

	CITY	ST	EMP	PHONE	ENTRY #
Topsall Machine Tool Co Inc	Worcester	MA	G	508 755-0332	17489

RUBBER

	CITY	ST	EMP	PHONE	ENTRY #
Covestro LLC	South Deerfield	MA	D	412 777-2000	15248
Heveatex Corporation	Fall River	MA	F	508 675-0181	10713
Cri-Sil LLC	Biddeford	ME	E	207 283-6422	5726
Southworth Intl Group Inc **(PA)**	Falmouth	ME	D	207 878-0700	6033
Contitech Thermopol LLC	Somersworth	NH	G	603 692-6300	19832
Contitech Thermopol LLC	Rochester	NH	D	603 692-6300	19665
Contitech Thermopol LLC **(HQ)**	Somersworth	NH	G	603 692-6300	19833
Ipotec LLC	Exeter	NH	G	603 778-2882	18124
Conley Casting Supply Corp **(PA)**	Warwick	RI	E	401 461-4710	21345
Dryvit Holdings Inc **(DH)**	Providence	RI	G	401 822-4100	20998
QST Inc	Saint Albans	VT	E	802 524-7704	22377

RUBBER PRDTS

	CITY	ST	EMP	PHONE	ENTRY #
Plymouth Rubber Company LLC	Canton	MA	E	781 828-0220	9768
Rubber Right Rollers Inc	Chelsea	MA	F	617 466-1447	9965

RUBBER PRDTS: Appliance, Mechanical

	CITY	ST	EMP	PHONE	ENTRY #
Saint-Gobain Prfmce Plas Corp	Worcester	MA	E	508 852-3072	17467
Etco Incorporated **(PA)**	Warwick	RI	D	401 467-2400	21361
Moore Company **(PA)**	Westerly	RI	C	401 596-2816	21531
Moore Company	Westerly	RI	C	401 596-2816	21532
Garflex Inc	Brattleboro	VT	D	802 257-5256	21728

RUBBER PRDTS: Mechanical

	CITY	ST	EMP	PHONE	ENTRY #
Acmt Inc	Manchester	CT	D	860 645-0592	1982
Applied Rubber & Plastics Inc	Windsor	CT	F	860 987-9018	5321
Jem Manufacturing Inc	Wallingford	CT	G	203 250-9404	4759
Vanguard Products Corporation	Danbury	CT	D	203 744-7265	1003
Acushnet Rubber Company Inc	New Bedford	MA	B	508 998-4000	13352
Chardan Ltd	Attleboro	MA	G	508 992-0854	7718
Device Technologies Inc	Southborough	MA	E	508 229-2000	15354
Hutchinson Arospc & Indust Inc **(DH)**	Hopkinton	MA	B	508 417-7000	11718
Jefferson Rubber Works Inc	Worcester	MA	D	508 791-3600	17397
Pocasset Machine Corporation	Pocasset	MA	E	508 563-5572	14600
Jones & Vining Incorporated	Lewiston	ME	E	207 784-3547	6295
Brn Corporation	Campton	NH	G	603 726-3800	17775
Cooper Products Inc	Laconia	NH	E	603 524-3367	18563
Freudenberg-Nok General Partnr	Northfield	NH	E	603 286-1600	19402

RUBBER PRDTS: Medical & Surgical Tubing, Extrudd & Lathe-Cut

	CITY	ST	EMP	PHONE	ENTRY #
Extrusion Alternatives Inc	Portsmouth	NH	F	603 430-9600	19562

RUBBER PRDTS: Reclaimed

	CITY	ST	EMP	PHONE	ENTRY #
Meridian Operations LLC	Plainfield	CT	F	860 564-8811	3454
Rogers Corporation	Woodstock	CT	C	860 928-3622	5501
Cri-Tech Inc	Hanover	MA	E	781 826-5600	11333
Heveatex Corporation	Fall River	MA	F	508 675-0181	10713

RUBBER PRDTS: Sheeting

	CITY	ST	EMP	PHONE	ENTRY #
Biltrite Corporation	Chelsea	MA	E	617 884-3124	9945

RUBBER PRDTS: Silicone

	CITY	ST	EMP	PHONE	ENTRY #
FMI Chemical Inc	Bloomfield	CT	F	860 243-3222	219
Heaters Inc	Niantic	CT	G	860 739-5477	2952
Diversified Decorating Sales	Jaffrey	NH	G	603 532-4557	18461
Rbc Industries Inc	Warwick	RI	D	401 941-3000	21410
G W Plastics Inc	Bethel	VT	G	802 234-9941	21694

RUBBER PRDTS: Sponge

	CITY	ST	EMP	PHONE	ENTRY #
Griswold LLC	Moosup	CT	D	860 564-3321	2426
Expanded Rubber Products Inc **(PA)**	Sanford	ME	E	207 324-8226	6875

RUBBER STAMP, WHOLESALE

	CITY	ST	EMP	PHONE	ENTRY #
Simons Stamps Inc	Turners Falls	MA	F	413 863-6800	15885

RUBBER STRUCTURES: Air-Supported

	CITY	ST	EMP	PHONE	ENTRY #
Certainteed Corporation	Natick	MA	G	508 655-9731	13244
Gs Rubber Industries LLC	Fall River	MA	F	508 672-0742	10708

RUGS : Braided & Hooked

	CITY	ST	EMP	PHONE	ENTRY #
Cape Cod Braided Rug Co Inc	Marstons Mills	MA	F	508 432-3133	12872
TMI Industries Inc	Palmer	MA	E	413 283-9021	14297
Weymouth Braided Rug Co Inc	North Oxford	MA	G	508 987-8525	13976
Rhody Rug Inc	Lincoln	RI	F	401 728-5903	20594
Robin Industries Inc	Bristol	RI	D	401 253-8350	20101

RUGS : Hand & Machine Made

	CITY	ST	EMP	PHONE	ENTRY #
Flemish Master Weavers Inc	Sanford	ME	E	207 324-6600	6876
Colonial Mills Inc	Rumford	RI	D	401 724-6279	21183

RULERS: Metal

	CITY	ST	EMP	PHONE	ENTRY #
Arthur H Gaebel Inc	Boxborough	MA	G	978 263-4401	8958
LS Starrett Company **(PA)**	Athol	MA	A	978 249-3551	7689

RUST ARRESTING COMPOUNDS: Animal Or Vegetable Oil Based

	CITY	ST	EMP	PHONE	ENTRY #
Alvin Products Inc	Everett	MA	G	978 975-4580	10602

SADDLERY STORES

	CITY	ST	EMP	PHONE	ENTRY #
Northern Tack	Calais	ME	G	207 217-7584	5865

SAFE DEPOSIT BOXES

	CITY	ST	EMP	PHONE	ENTRY #
Yarde Metals Inc **(HQ)**	Southington	CT	B	860 406-6061	4092

SAFES & VAULTS: Metal

	CITY	ST	EMP	PHONE	ENTRY #
Idemia America Corp **(DH)**	Billerica	MA	B	978 215-2400	8255
Jaco Inc	Franklin	MA	C	508 553-1000	11056

SAFETY EQPT & SPLYS WHOLESALERS

	CITY	ST	EMP	PHONE	ENTRY #
Elvex Corporation	Shelton	CT	F	203 743-2488	3800

SAGGERS

	CITY	ST	EMP	PHONE	ENTRY #
Aspell Saggers LLC	North Attleboro	MA	G	508 216-3264	13748

SAILBOAT BUILDING & REPAIR

	CITY	ST	EMP	PHONE	ENTRY #
McClave Philbrick & Giblin	Mystic	CT	G	860 572-7710	2443
Cape Cod Shipbuilding Co	Wareham	MA	F	508 295-3550	16242
Knd Machine Co	Rehoboth	MA	G	508 336-5509	14752
Morris Yacht Inc **(PA)**	Bass Harbor	ME	E	207 667-6235	5672
Lenmarine Inc **(PA)**	Bristol	RI	E	401 253-2200	20089
Quarter Moon Incorporated **(PA)**	Portsmouth	RI	E	401 683-0400	20937

SAILS

	CITY	ST	EMP	PHONE	ENTRY #
Ace Sailmakers	East Lyme	CT	G	860 739-5999	1268
Farrar Sails Inc	New London	CT	G	860 447-0382	2772
Kappa Sails LLC	Gales Ferry	CT	G	860 399-8899	1527
Liberty Services LLC	Westbrook	CT	G	860 399-0077	5159
Mbm Sales	Norwalk	CT	F	203 866-3674	3193
North Sails Group LLC **(DH)**	Milford	CT	D	203 874-7548	2323
Cape Cod Sailmakers Inc	Cataumet	MA	G	508 563-3080	9810
Downs Sails	Danvers	MA	G	978 750-8140	10214
Doyle Sailmakers Inc **(PA)**	Salem	MA	E	978 740-5950	14907
Doyle Sailmakers Inc	South Dartmouth	MA	G	508 992-6322	15238
Harding Sails Inc	Marion	MA	F	508 748-0334	12697
Olsen Marine	Dennis	MA	G	508 385-2180	10308
Sperry Sails Inc	Marion	MA	G	508 748-2581	12705
Steele & Rowe Inc	North Dartmouth	MA	G	508 993-6413	13927
Center Harbor Sails LLC	Brooklin	ME	G	207 359-2003	5818
E S Bohndell & Co Inc	Rockport	ME	G	207 236-3549	6821
Maine Sailing Partners LLC	Harpswell	ME	G	207 865-0850	6173
Nathaniel S Wilson Sailmaker	East Boothbay	ME	G	207 633-5071	5978
Pope Sails and Rigging Inc	Rockland	ME	G	207 596-7293	6808
Anson Sailmakers Inc	Greenland	NH	G	603 431-6676	18220
Black Dog Corporation	Portsmouth	RI	E	401 683-5858	20920
Doyle Sailmakers Inc	East Greenwich	RI	F	401 884-4227	20361
Doyle Sails	East Greenwich	RI	G	401 884-4227	20362
Hood Sailmakers Inc **(PA)**	Middletown	RI	F	401 849-9400	20620
Jasper Aaron	Newport	RI	G	401 847-8796	20668
North Sails Group LLC	Portsmouth	RI	G	401 683-7997	20933
Rhode Northsales Island Inc	Portsmouth	RI	E	401 683-7997	20939
Thurston Sails Inc	Bristol	RI	F	401 254-0970	20105

SALES PROMOTION SVCS

	CITY	ST	EMP	PHONE	ENTRY #
Zajac LLC	Saco	ME	E	207 286-9100	6864

SALT

	CITY	ST	EMP	PHONE	ENTRY #
Salt Woods LLC	Watertown	MA	G	617 744-9401	16313
New England Salt Co LLC	Bangor	ME	G	207 262-9779	5656

SAND & GRAVEL

	CITY	ST	EMP	PHONE	ENTRY #
B & C Sand & Gravel Company	Bridgeport	CT	G	203 335-6640	379
Bethel Sand & Gravel Co	Bethel	CT	G	203 743-4469	132
Brooklyn Sand & Gravel LLC	Danielson	CT	G	860 779-3980	1012
Dan Beard Inc	Shelton	CT	F	203 924-4346	3794
Dens Sand & Gravel	Lebanon	CT	G	860 642-6470	1934
Galasso Materials LLC	East Granby	CT	C	860 527-1825	1128
John Hychko	Waterbury	CT	G	203 757-3458	4893
Pine Ridge Gravel LLC	East Haddam	CT	G	860 873-2500	1152
Rawson Development Inc	Putnam	CT	F	860 928-4536	3629
Skyline Quarry	Stafford Springs	CT	E	860 875-3580	4115
Sterling Sand and Gravel LLC	Sterling	CT	G	860 774-3985	4373
Turning Stone Sand & Grav LLC	Enfield	CT	G	413 519-1560	1388
West Hartford Stone Mulch LLC	West Hartford	CT	G	860 461-7616	5103
B R S Inc	Bridgewater	MA	E	508 697-5448	9061
Benevento Asphalt Corp	Wilmington	MA	F	978 658-5300	16982
Benevento Sand & Stone Corp	Wilmington	MA	F	978 658-4762	16983
Berkshire Concrete Corp **(HQ)**	Pittsfield	MA	C	413 443-4734	14456
Construction Source MGT LLC	Raynham	MA	G	508 484-5100	14707
FT Smith Trckg & Excvtg Inc	North Brookfield	MA	G	508 867-0400	13880
Gravel Public House	Wrentham	MA	G	508 384-0888	17522
Greylock Sand & Gravel LLC	Adams	MA	G	413 441-4967	7411
J G Maclellan Con Co Inc **(PA)**	Lowell	MA	D	978 458-1223	12385
Lakeside Management Corp	Plainville	MA	E	508 695-3252	14524

	CITY	ST	EMP	PHONE	ENTRY #
Lower Cape Sand and Gravel Inc	Eastham	MA	G	508 255-2839	10550
New England Gravel Haulers	Rehoboth	MA	G	508 922-4518	14754
New England Sand & Gravel Co	Framingham	MA	F	508 877-2460	10987
Pitcherville Sand and Gravel	Burlington	MA	G	781 365-1721	9320
S M Lorusso & Sons Inc	Wrentham	MA	G	508 384-3587	17528
Salgado Sand & Gravel Inc	South Dartmouth	MA	G	774 202-2626	15243
Sanger Equipment and Mfg	Conway	MA	G	413 625-8304	10166
Scapin Sand & Gravel Inc	Russell	MA	G	413 568-0091	14878
Southeastern Sand and Grav Inc	Kingston	MA	G	781 413-6884	11964
Wakefield Investments Inc	Lunenburg	MA	D	978 582-0261	12486
We Love Construction	Ipswich	MA	G	978 239-1308	11938
A & G Dirtworks Inc	Howland	ME	G	207 290-5054	6213
A&M Sand & Gravel LLC	Winterport	ME	G	207 223-4189	7275
Caleb Churchill	Somerville	ME	G	207 215-7949	6998
Dayton Sand & Gravel Inc	Dayton	ME	D	207 499-2306	5944
Dragon Products Company LLC	Thomaston	ME	C	207 594-5555	7083
Dragon Products Company LLC **(DH)**	South Portland	ME	E	207 774-6355	7022
Earl W Gerrish & Sons Inc	Brownville	ME	F	207 965-2171	5826
F R Carroll Inc	Limerick	ME	E	207 793-8615	6334
Gravel Doctor Midcoast Maine	Bristol	ME	G	207 633-1099	5812
Hermon Sand & Gravel LLC	Hermon	ME	G	207 848-5977	6189
J and L Sand	Lyman	ME	G	207 499-2545	6390
Jerome Martin Paul	North Sullivan	ME	G	207 422-3965	6513
K W Aggregates	Denmark	ME	G	207 452-8888	5950
McQuade Tidd Industries	Houlton	ME	D	207 532-2675	6207
Ouellette Sand & Gravel Inc	South China	ME	G	207 445-4131	7006
Penobscot Sand Grav Stone LLC	Milford	ME	G	207 827-2829	6437
Pine Tree Gravel Inc	Hampden	ME	G	207 862-4983	6168
Portland Sand & Gravel Inc	Cumberland Center	ME	G	207 829-2196	5931
A B Excavating Inc	Lancaster	NH	E	603 788-5110	18596
Big Foote Crushing LLC	Weare	NH	G	603 345-0695	19932
Brook Hollow Sand & Gravel	Bedford	NH	G	603 231-0238	17634
Cloutier Sand & Gravel	Stark	NH	G	603 636-1100	19859
Concord Sand and Gravel Inc	Loudon	NH	G	603 435-6787	18747
Gorham Sand & Gravel	Gorham	NH	E	603 466-2291	18212
Granite State Concrete Co Inc	Milford	NH	E	603 673-3327	19057
Gravel Hill Partners LLC	Hanover	NH	G	603 277-9074	18288
Hampton Sand and Gravel	Hampton	NH	G	603 601-2275	18264
Jimtown Sand and Gravel Inc	Berlin	NH	G	603 752-4622	17698
Lane Construction Corporation	East Swanzey	NH	G	603 352-2006	18093
Litchfield Sand & Gravel	Londonderry	NH	G	603 424-6515	18715
Malcolm Bradsher Co Inc	Epping	NH	G	603 679-3888	18101
Mitchell Sand & Gravel LLC	Winchester	NH	G	603 357-0881	19993
Nashua Sand & Gravel LLC	Hudson	NH	G	603 459-8662	18419
Northeast Sand & Gravel	Amherst	NH	G	603 213-6133	17579
Northeast Sand and Gravel LLC	New Ipswich	NH	G	603 305-9429	19307
Pitcherville Sand & Grav Corp	Greenville	NH	G	603 878-0035	18226
Smith River Sand & Gravel LLC	Danbury	NH	G	603 768-3330	17965
Strong H J G Bros Grav Corp	New Boston	NH	G	603 487-5551	19298
Alfred N Gravel	Woonsocket	RI	G	401 765-4432	21549
Hopkins Hill Sand & Stone LLC	Warwick	RI	G	401 739-8300	21372
Richmond Sand & Stone LLC	Richmond	RI	F	401 539-7770	21162
Calkins Rock Products Inc	Lyndonville	VT	G	802 626-5755	22067
Calkins Sand & Gravel Inc	Newport	VT	F	802 334-8418	22191
D40 Gravel LLP	Newport	VT	G	802 673-5494	22195
Dale E Percy Inc	Stowe	VT	F	802 253-8503	22521
Orwell Sand & Gravel	Benson	VT	G	802 345-6028	21693

SAND MINING

	CITY	ST	EMP	PHONE	ENTRY #
Geer Construction Co Inc	Jewett City	CT	G	860 376-5321	1912
Tilcon Connecticut Inc	Newington	CT	G	860 756-8016	2907
Tronox LLC **(PA)**	Stamford	CT	E	203 705-3800	4352
Wfs Earth Materialsi LLC	Branford	CT	G	203 488-2055	361
Indian River Sand LLC	Quincy	MA	G	413 977-0646	14634
Varney Bros Sand & Gravel Inc	Bellingham	MA	E	508 966-1313	8062
Michie Corporation	Henniker	NH	D	603 428-7426	18307
Joseph P Carrara & Sons Inc **(PA)**	North Clarendon	VT	E	802 775-2301	22216

SAND: Hygrade

	CITY	ST	EMP	PHONE	ENTRY #
Unimin Lime Corporation **(DH)**	New Canaan	CT	F	203 966-8880	2619

SANDBLASTING SVC: Building Exterior

	CITY	ST	EMP	PHONE	ENTRY #
Metal Magic Inc	Trenton	ME	G	207 667-8519	7100

SANITARY SVCS: Dumps, Operation Of

	CITY	ST	EMP	PHONE	ENTRY #
Grillo Services LLC	Milford	CT	E	203 877-5070	2294

SANITARY SVCS: Environmental Cleanup

	CITY	ST	EMP	PHONE	ENTRY #
Cloverdale Inc	West Cornwall	CT	G	860 672-0216	5046

SANITARY SVCS: Mosquito Eradication

	CITY	ST	EMP	PHONE	ENTRY #
Pine State Pest Solutions Inc	Auburn	ME	G	207 795-1100	5590

SANITARY SVCS: Oil Spill Cleanup

	CITY	ST	EMP	PHONE	ENTRY #
Spilldam Environmental Inc	Brockton	MA	F	508 583-7850	9178

SANITARY SVCS: Refuse Collection & Disposal Svcs

	CITY	ST	EMP	PHONE	ENTRY #
1 Call Does It All and Then	South Deerfield	MA	G	413 584-5381	15244

SANITARY SVCS: Waste Materials, Recycling

	CITY	ST	EMP	PHONE	ENTRY #
Ted Ondrick Company LLC **(PA)**	Chicopee	MA	F	413 592-2565	10064
Upcycle Solutions Inc	Londonderry	NH	G	603 809-6843	18743
Compost Plant L3c	Providence	RI	G	401 644-6179	20988

SANITATION CHEMICALS & CLEANING AGENTS

	CITY	ST	EMP	PHONE	ENTRY #
Citra Solv LLC	Ridgefield	CT	G	203 778-0881	3663
Edsan Chemical Company Inc	New Haven	CT	C	203 624-3123	2685
Griffith Company	Bridgeport	CT	G	203 333-5557	422
NC Brands LP	Norwalk	CT	D	203 295-2300	3204
Nci Holdings Inc **(PA)**	Norwalk	CT	E	203 295-2300	3205
3M Company	Haverhill	MA	G	978 420-0001	11403
Blendco Systems LLC	Holyoke	MA	E	800 537-7797	11619
Cape Cod Polish Company Inc	Gloucester	MA	G	800 682-4246	11171
Clint Sales & Manufacturing	Beverly	MA	G	978 927-3010	8118
Dmar Environmental LLC	Clinton	MA	G	508 331-1884	10079
Dynasol Industries Inc	Canton	MA	F	781 821-8888	9729
Elliott Auto Supply Co Inc	Ayer	MA	G	978 772-9882	7918
HI Tunes	Whately	MA	F	435 962-0405	16906
Porex Cleanroom Products Inc	Chicopee	MA	D	800 628-8606	10052
Protech Associates Inc	Newburyport	MA	G	978 462-1241	13524
Rectorseal Corporation	Fall River	MA	G	508 673-7561	10755
Shield Packaging Co Inc	Dudley	MA	D	508 949-0900	10384
Tbs Technologies LLC	Holliston	MA	G	508 429-3111	11608
Booth Felt Co Inc	Dover	NH	G	603 330-3334	18009
Hampshire Chemical Corp **(DH)**	Nashua	NH	E	603 888-2320	19176
Peg Kearsarge Co Inc	Bartlett	NH	G	603 374-2341	17627
Rochester Shoe Tree Co Inc **(PA)**	Ashland	NH	D	603 968-3301	17601
Chaudhary LLC	Pawtucket	RI	G	401 954-9695	20822
Precision Plsg Ornamentals Inc	Pawtucket	RI	E	401 728-9994	20883

SASHES: Door Or Window, Metal

	CITY	ST	EMP	PHONE	ENTRY #
Liberty Glass and Met Inds Inc	North Grosvenordale	CT	E	860 923-3623	2997

SATCHELS

	CITY	ST	EMP	PHONE	ENTRY #
Leatherby	Weatogue	CT	G	860 658-6166	5043
Currys Leather Shop Inc	Randolph	MA	F	781 963-0679	14675
L & J Leathers Manufacturing	Revere	MA	G	781 289-6466	14770

SATELLITE COMMUNICATIONS EQPT

	CITY	ST	EMP	PHONE	ENTRY #
Novelsat Inc	Newton	MA	F	617 658-1419	13621
Qualcomm Incorporated	Concord	MA	D	978 318-0650	10153
Raytheon Company **(PA)**	Waltham	MA	B	781 522-3000	16184
Raytheon Company	Marlborough	MA	E	310 647-9438	12813
Raytheon Company	North Billerica	MA	G	978 313-0201	13858
Viasat Inc	Marlborough	MA	F	508 229-6500	12844
Richard Townsend	Barrington	NH	G	603 664-5987	17622

SATELLITES: Communications

	CITY	ST	EMP	PHONE	ENTRY #
Newtec America Inc	Stamford	CT	F	203 323-0042	4258
Accelerated Media Tech Inc	Auburn	MA	E	508 459-0300	7821
Diamond Antenna Microwave Corp	Littleton	MA	D	978 486-0039	12300
Moble Internet Access Inc	Pembroke	MA	G	978 273-2390	14417
Notch Inc	Cambridge	MA	G	203 258-9141	9585
Alltraxx LLC	Portsmouth	NH	G	603 610-7179	19535
Syntech Microwave Inc	Hudson	NH	G	603 880-9767	18444

SAW BLADES

	CITY	ST	EMP	PHONE	ENTRY #
DArcy Saw LLC	Windsor Locks	CT	G	800 569-1264	5390
T S S Inc	Waterbury	VT	E	802 244-8101	22586

SAWDUST & SHAVINGS

	CITY	ST	EMP	PHONE	ENTRY #
Lmj Enterprises LLC **(PA)**	Lincoln	ME	G	207 794-3489	6358

SAWDUST, WHOLESALE

	CITY	ST	EMP	PHONE	ENTRY #
Moose Creek Home Center Inc	Turner	ME	G	207 224-7497	7109

SAWING & PLANING MILLS

	CITY	ST	EMP	PHONE	ENTRY #
Burell Bros Inc	Hampton	CT	G	860 455-9681	1796
Cedar Swamp Log & Lumber	Woodstock	CT	G	860 974-2344	5496
Charles Pike & Sons	Hampton	CT	G	860 455-9968	1797
Dalla Corte Lumber	Stafford Springs	CT	G	860 875-9480	4108
Eylward Timber Co	Wallingford	CT	G	203 265-4276	4742
John J Pawloski Lumber Inc	Bethel	CT	G	203 794-0737	165
Jordan Saw Mill L L C	Sterling	CT	F	860 774-0247	4367
Moores Sawmill Inc	Bloomfield	CT	G	860 242-3003	244
Sigfridson Wood Products LLC	Brooklyn	CT	G	860 774-2075	672
Walker Industries LLC	Ashford	CT	G	860 455-3554	28
Bannish Lumber Inc	Chester	MA	F	413 354-2279	9980
Chocorua Valley Lumber Company	Bellingham	MA	F	508 883-6878	8033
Cook Forest Products Inc	Upton	MA	E	508 634-3300	15906
Jarvenpaa & Sons	Westminster	MA	G	978 874-2231	16807
Joseph K Delano Sawmill Inc	North Dartmouth	MA	G	508 994-8752	13923
Lenox Lumber Co	Pittsfield	MA	F	413 637-2744	14484
Saw Mill Brook LLC	Newton	MA	G	617 332-5793	13632
Sawmill Brook Farm	Bridgewater	MA	G	508 697-7847	9087
Sawmill Park	Southwick	MA	G	413 569-3393	15417
Theodore Wolf Inc	East Falmouth	MA	G	508 457-0667	10450
West Wearham Pine	East Freetown	MA	G	508 763-4108	10463
Cousins Sawmill	Windsor	ME	G	207 445-2467	7263
Dimension Lumber	Peru	ME	G	207 897-9973	6585
Forest Chester Products Inc	Lincoln	ME	E	207 794-2303	6353
Fulghum Fibres Inc	Baileyville	ME	E	207 427-6560	5625
Gerrity Company Incorporated	Leeds	ME	E	207 933-2804	6269
Great Brook Lumber Inc	Lebanon	ME	G	207 457-1063	6265
Irving Woodlands LLC	Dixfield	ME	C	207 562-4400	5957
Irving Woodlands LLC **(HQ)**	St John Plt	ME	E	207 834-5767	7058
Jackman Lumber Inc **(PA)**	Jackman	ME	E	207 668-4407	6217
K B Logging Inc	Smyrna Mills	ME	F	207 757-8818	6993
K L Mason & Sons Inc	North Turner	ME	G	207 224-7628	6515
Lovell Lumber Co Inc	Lovell	ME	E	207 925-6455	6384
Maine Cedar Specialty Products	Ludlow	ME	G	207 532-4034	6387
Maine Post & Beam LLC	North Yarmouth	ME	G	207 751-6793	6518
Maine Woods Company LLC	Portage	ME	G	207 435-4393	6598

	CITY	ST	EMP	PHONE	ENTRY #
Melvin L Yoder	Corinna	ME	G	207 278-3539	5922
N C Hunt Inc	Damariscotta	ME	E	207 563-8503	5937
Palletone of Maine Inc	Livermore Falls	ME	C	207 897-5711	6380
Phinney Lumber Co	Gorham	ME	E	207 839-3336	6124
Pleasant River Lumber Company **(PA)**	Dover Foxcroft	ME	D	207 564-8520	5964
Portable Sawmill	Eddington	ME	G	207 843-7216	5998
Prl Hancock LLC	Hancock	ME	E	207 564-8520	6171
Red Mill	Casco	ME	G	207 655-7520	5895
Repose Fire Logs LLC	Sebago	ME	G	207 595-8035	6954
Sebasticook Lumber LLC	Saint Albans	ME	G	207 660-1360	6865
Tukey Brothers Inc	Belgrade	ME	F	207 465-3570	5700
Usaccess Inc	New Portland	ME	G	207 541-9421	6475
Breezy Hill Lumber Co	Barnstead	NH	F	603 496-8870	17615
Chester Forest Products Inc	Chester	NH	G	603 887-4123	17823
Contoocook River Lumber Inc	Henniker	NH	E	603 428-3636	18303
Daves Sitework and Sawmill	Fitzwilliam	NH	G	603 313-0787	18148
F C Hammond & Son Lbr Co Inc	Canaan	NH	F	603 523-4353	17778
Homegrown Lumber	Center Conway	NH	G	603 447-3800	17800
Josselyns Sawmill Inc	Jefferson	NH	G	603 586-4507	18485
Madison Lumber Mill Inc	Madison	NH	D	603 539-4145	18764
Patenaude Lumber Company Inc	Henniker	NH	E	603 428-3224	18310
Perras Lumber Co Inc	Groveton	NH	E	603 636-1830	18232
Tommila Brothers Inc	Fitzwilliam	NH	F	603 242-7774	18153
Rathbuns Sawmill Inc	West Greenwich	RI	G	401 397-3996	21464
Brattleboro Kiln Dry & Milling	Brattleboro	VT	E	802 254-4528	21720
Claire Lathrop Band Mill Inc	Bristol	VT	E	802 453-3606	21763
Cobb Lumber Inc	South Londonderry	VT	G	802 824-5228	22484
Dci Inc	South Royalton	VT	F	802 763-7847	22490
Dennis Ducharme	Marshfield	VT	G	802 426-3796	22094
Gilcris Enterprises Inc	Proctorsville	VT	F	802 226-7764	22288
Godfreys Sawmill LLC	Montgomery Center	VT	G	802 326-4868	22142
Granville Manufacturing Co	Granville	VT	G	802 767-4747	22003
Greenwood Mill Inc	Bradford	VT	F	802 626-0800	21700
Kerber Saw Mill	Guilford	VT	G	802 257-0614	22007
M B Heath & Sons Lumber Inc	North Hyde Park	VT	G	802 635-2538	22232
Manchester Lumber Inc	Johnson	VT	E	802 635-2315	22051
N W P Inc	Pownal	VT	G	802 442-4749	22282
Northeast Timber Exchange LLC **(PA)**	Chester	VT	G	802 875-1037	21846
Sheehan & Sons Lumber	Perkinsville	VT	G	802 263-5545	22258
Van Alstyne Family Farm Inc	South Royalton	VT	G	802 763-7036	22494

SAWING & PLANING MILLS: Custom

	CITY	ST	EMP	PHONE	ENTRY #
Gingras Lumber Inc	Ashley Falls	MA	G	413 229-2182	7674
Rex Lumber Company **(PA)**	Acton	MA	D	800 343-0567	7378
Hotham & Sons Lumber Inc	New Gloucester	ME	G	207 926-4231	6467
Wood-Mizer Holdings Inc	Chesterville	ME	F	207 645-2072	5909

SAWMILL MACHINES

	CITY	ST	EMP	PHONE	ENTRY #
Heyes Forest Products Inc	Orange	MA	G	978 544-8801	14217
Downeast Machine & Engrg Inc	Mechanic Falls	ME	F	207 345-8111	6419
Machinery Service Co Inc	Wiscasset	ME	G	207 882-6788	7285
HMC Corporation **(PA)**	Hopkinton	NH	E	603 746-3399	18362

SAWS: Hand, Metalworking Or Woodworking

	CITY	ST	EMP	PHONE	ENTRY #
Lie-Nielsen Toolworks Inc	Warren	ME	D	800 327-2520	7144

SCAFFOLDS: Mobile Or Stationary, Metal

	CITY	ST	EMP	PHONE	ENTRY #
Advantcraft Inc	Upton	MA	G	508 498-4644	15903
DC Scaffold Inc	West Bridgewater	MA	F	508 580-5100	16436

SCALE REPAIR SVCS

	CITY	ST	EMP	PHONE	ENTRY #
M & M Scale Company Inc	Malden	MA	F	781 321-2737	12580

SCALES & BALANCES, EXC LABORATORY

	CITY	ST	EMP	PHONE	ENTRY #
Reliable Scales & Systems LLC	Bristol	CT	G	860 380-0600	604
C & C Scale Co Inc	Lakeville	MA	G	508 947-0001	11974
Highland Labs Inc	Holliston	MA	E	508 429-2918	11577
M & M Scale Company Inc	Malden	MA	F	781 321-2737	12580
Setra Systems Inc	Boxboro	MA	F	978 263-1400	8954
Thomas Higgins	Billerica	MA	G	978 930-0573	8306
Public Scales	Lewiston	ME	F	207 784-9466	6317
Tridyne Process Systems Inc	South Burlington	VT	F	802 863-6873	22473

SCALES: Counting

	CITY	ST	EMP	PHONE	ENTRY #
Bay State Scale & Systems Inc	Burlington	MA	G	781 993-9035	9239

SCALES: Indl

	CITY	ST	EMP	PHONE	ENTRY #
Mettler-Toledo Intl Inc	Newton	MA	G	800 472-4646	13614
New Bedford Scale Co Inc	New Bedford	MA	G	508 997-6730	13421
Ocean State Scale Balance LLC	Coventry	RI	G	401 340-6622	20162

SCANNING DEVICES: Optical

	CITY	ST	EMP	PHONE	ENTRY #
Eye Ear It LLC	Woodbury	CT	F	203 487-8949	5487
Scan-Optics LLC	Manchester	CT	D	860 645-7878	2046
Abariscan Inc	Newburyport	MA	G	978 462-0284	13467
Bidirectional Display Inc	Acton	MA	G	617 599-8282	7344
Eyedeal Scanning LLC	Needham	MA	G	617 519-8696	13299
Rapiscan Systems Inc	Andover	MA	G	866 430-1913	7592

SCHOOL BUS SVC

	CITY	ST	EMP	PHONE	ENTRY #
Jarvenpaa & Sons	Westminster	MA	G	978 874-2231	16807

SCHOOLS: Vocational, NEC

	CITY	ST	EMP	PHONE	ENTRY #
Varian Semicdtr Eqp Assoc Inc	Newburyport	MA	C	978 463-1500	13548

SCIENTIFIC INSTRUMENTS WHOLESALERS

	CITY	ST	EMP	PHONE	ENTRY #
Bruker Optics Inc **(HQ)**	Billerica	MA	E	978 901-1528	8227
Edgeone LLC	West Wareham	MA	G	508 291-0960	16570
Focused Resolutions Inc	Methuen	MA	G	978 794-7981	13022
Pelagic Electronics	East Falmouth	MA	G	508 540-1200	10446
Princton Gamma-Tech Instrs Inc	Franklin	MA	F	609 924-7310	11075

SCISSORS: Hand

	CITY	ST	EMP	PHONE	ENTRY #
Acme United Corporation **(PA)**	Fairfield	CT	C	203 254-6060	1412

SCRAP & WASTE MATERIALS, WHOLESALE: Ferrous Metal

	CITY	ST	EMP	PHONE	ENTRY #
Surf Metal Co Inc	Stratford	CT	G	203 375-2211	4452

SCRAP & WASTE MATERIALS, WHOLESALE: Metal

	CITY	ST	EMP	PHONE	ENTRY #
Harding Metals Inc	Northwood	NH	E	603 942-5573	19412

SCRAP & WASTE MATERIALS, WHOLESALE: Paper

	CITY	ST	EMP	PHONE	ENTRY #
American Paper Recycling Corp **(PA)**	Mansfield	MA	E	800 422-3220	12613

SCREENS: Door, Metal Covered Wood

	CITY	ST	EMP	PHONE	ENTRY #
Complete Cvrage Wodpriming LLC	Allenstown	NH	G	603 485-1122	17538

SCREENS: Window, Metal

	CITY	ST	EMP	PHONE	ENTRY #
Connecticut Screen Works Inc	Wallingford	CT	G	203 269-4499	4726
High Grade Shade & Screen Co	Lynn	MA	F	781 592-5027	12516
Reliable Shade & Screen Co	Somerville	MA	G	617 776-9538	15209
Universal Window and Door LLC	Marlborough	MA	D	508 481-2850	12840
Beacon Sales Acquisition Inc	Salem	NH	G	207 797-7950	19712
Lockheed Window Corp	Pascoag	RI	D	401 568-3061	20802

SCREW MACHINE PRDTS

	CITY	ST	EMP	PHONE	ENTRY #
Alinabal Inc	Kensington	CT	F	860 828-9933	1917
Atp Industries LLC **(PA)**	Plainville	CT	F	860 479-5007	3467
Automatic Machine Products	Middletown	CT	G	860 346-7064	2174
B&T Screw Machine Co Inc	Bristol	CT	F	860 314-4410	524
Bar Work Manufacturing Co Inc	Waterbury	CT	F	203 753-4103	4848
Biedermann Mfg Inds Inc	Thomaston	CT	E	860 283-8268	4499
Bobken Automatics Inc	Waterbury	CT	G	203 757-5525	4850
Brass City Technologies LLC **(PA)**	Naugatuck	CT	G	203 723-7021	2463
C & A Machine Co Inc	Newington	CT	E	860 667-0605	2851
Cadcom Inc	Milford	CT	F	203 877-0640	2259
Caine Machining Inc	Winsted	CT	G	860 738-1619	5407
Cole S Crew Machine Products	North Haven	CT	E	203 723-1418	3016
Creed-Monarch Inc	New Britain	CT	B	860 225-7884	2524
Curtis Products LLC	Bristol	CT	F	203 754-4155	546
D & M Screw Machine Pdts LLC	Plainville	CT	G	860 410-9781	3479
Dacruz Manufacturing Inc	Bristol	CT	E	860 584-5315	547
David Derewianka	Manchester	CT	G	860 649-1983	1998
Day Fred A Co LLC	Bristol	CT	G	860 589-0531	548
Day Machine Systems Inc	New Britain	CT	F	860 229-3440	2526
Deco Products Inc	East Hartford	CT	G	860 528-4304	1185
Devon Precision Industries Inc	Wolcott	CT	D	203 879-1437	5438
Don S Screw Machine Pdts LLC	Thomaston	CT	G	860 283-6448	4501
Duda and Goodwin Inc	Woodbury	CT	F	203 263-4353	5486
Durco Manufacturing Co Inc	Waterbury	CT	G	203 575-0446	4865
E P M Co Inc	Bristol	CT	G	860 589-3233	552
Electro-Tech Inc	Cheshire	CT	E	203 271-1976	729
F F Screw Products Inc	Southington	CT	E	860 621-4567	4049
Fleetwood Industries Inc	Plainville	CT	G	860 747-6750	3488
Forestville Machine Co Inc	Plainville	CT	E	860 747-6000	3490
G M T Manufacturing Co Inc	Plantsville	CT	G	860 628-6757	3531
Garmac Screw Machine Inc	Naugatuck	CT	F	203 723-6911	2475
Horst Engrg De Mexico LLC	East Hartford	CT	E	860 289-8209	1199
J & R Projects	Waterbury	CT	G	203 879-2347	4890
J J Ryan Corporation	Plantsville	CT	C	860 628-0393	3534
James Wright Precision Pdts	Putnam	CT	F	860 928-7756	3618
Jay Sons Screw Mch Pdts Inc	Milldale	CT	F	860 621-0141	2384
Jeskey LLC	North Haven	CT	E	203 772-6675	3034
Kamatics Corporation **(DH)**	Bloomfield	CT	E	860 243-9704	235
Kemby Manufacturing	Terryville	CT	G	860 582-2850	4483
Leipold Inc	Windsor	CT	E	860 298-9791	5344
Mackson Mfg Co Inc	Bristol	CT	F	860 589-4035	578
Mailly Manufacturing Company	Wolcott	CT	G	203 879-1445	5448
Manufacturers Associates Inc	West Haven	CT	E	203 931-4344	5134
Mario Precision Products	Prospect	CT	G	203 758-3101	3589
Matthew Warren Inc	Seymour	CT	G	203 888-2133	3756
Microbest Inc	Waterbury	CT	C	203 597-0355	4915
OEM Sources LLC	Milford	CT	G	203 283-5415	2325
Olson Brothers Company	Plainville	CT	F	860 747-6844	3510
P-A-R Precision Inc	Wolcott	CT	E	860 491-4181	5451
Palladin Precision Pdts Inc	Waterbury	CT	E	203 574-0246	4935
Petron Automation Inc	Watertown	CT	E	860 274-9091	5016
Precision Methods Incorporated	Wolcott	CT	F	203 879-1429	5452
Prime Engineered Components Inc	Watertown	CT	G	860 274-6773	5017
Prime Screw Machine Pdts Inc **(PA)**	Watertown	CT	D	860 274-6773	5019
Pro-Manufactured Products Inc	Plainfield	CT	G	860 564-2197	3455
Quality Automatics Inc **(PA)**	Oakville	CT	E	860 945-4795	3300
Raypax Manufacturing Co Inc	Waterbury	CT	G	203 758-7416	4949
Rgd Technologies Corp	Bristol	CT	D	860 589-0756	605
Royal Screw Machine Pdts Co	Bristol	CT	E	860 845-8920	611
S & M Swiss Products Inc	Thomaston	CT	G	860 283-4020	4513
Selectcom Mfg Co Inc	Wolcott	CT	G	203 879-9900	5458
Sga Components Group LLC	Prospect	CT	G	203 758-3702	3596
Sheldon Precision LLC	Waterbury	CT	G	203 758-4441	4957
Sheldon Precision LLC	Prospect	CT	E	203 758-4441	3597
Space Swiss Manufacturing Inc	Litchfield	CT	F	860 567-4341	1952
Specialty Products Mfg LLC	Southington	CT	G	860 621-6969	4081
Sperry Automatics Co Inc	Naugatuck	CT	E	203 729-4589	2497
Sun Corp	Morris	CT	G	860 567-0817	2432

Employee Codes: A=Over 500 employees, B=251-500
C=101-250, D=51-100 E=20-50, F=10-19, G=3-9

	CITY	ST	EMP	PHONE	ENTRY #
Supreme-Lake Mfg Inc	Plantsville	CT	D	860 621-8911	3541
T & J Screw Machine Pdts LLC	Oakville	CT	G	860 417-3801	3303
Thomastn-Mdtown Screw Mch Pdts	Thomaston	CT	F	860 283-9796	4520
Thomaston Industries Inc	Thomaston	CT	F	860 283-4358	4521
Tomz Corporation	Berlin	CT	C	860 829-0670	113
Tri-Star Industries Inc	Berlin	CT	E	860 828-7570	114
Tryon Manufacturing Company	Shelton	CT	G	203 929-0464	3883
Tyler Automatics Incorporated	Thomaston	CT	E	860 283-5878	4523
Ville Swiss Automatics Inc	Waterbury	CT	F	203 756-2825	4970
Waterbury Screw Machine	Waterbury	CT	G	203 756-8084	4974
Waterbury Screw Mch Pdts Co	Waterbury	CT	E	203 756-8084	4975
Waterbury Swiss Automatics	Waterbury	CT	E	203 573-8584	4976
Whiteledge Inc	Manchester	CT	G	860 647-1883	2058
Wincor Inc	Bristol	CT	G	860 589-5530	626
Winslow Manufacturing Inc	Wallingford	CT	F	203 269-1977	4829
Wold Tool Engineering Inc	Brooklyn	CT	G	860 564-8338	674
Alpha Grainger Mfg Inc	Franklin	MA	C	508 520-4005	11022
Amkor Industrial Products Inc	Worcester	MA	E	508 799-4970	17336
Atc Screw Machine Inc	Haverhill	MA	F	781 939-0725	11406
Athol Screw Machine Products	Orange	MA	G	978 249-8072	14213
Automatic Machine Pdts Sls Co	Taunton	MA	D	508 822-4226	15728
Automatic Machine Products Co	Taunton	MA	E	508 822-4226	15729
Berkmatics Inc	North Adams	MA	F	413 664-6152	13669
Boston Centerless Inc	Avon	MA	E	508 587-3500	7881
Bourgeois Machine Co	Middleton	MA	G	978 774-6240	13086
Burlington Machine Inc	Wilmington	MA	F	978 284-6525	16985
Condon Mfg Co Inc	Springfield	MA	F	413 543-1250	15461
Device Technologies Inc	Southborough	MA	E	508 229-2000	15354
E F Inc	Gardner	MA	F	978 630-3800	11113
FC Phillips Inc	Stoughton	MA	E	781 344-9400	15591
Fisk Industries Inc	Attleboro Falls	MA	G	508 695-3661	7813
Fraen Corporation **(PA)**	Reading	MA	C	781 205-5300	14734
Fraen Machining Corporation **(PA)**	Woburn	MA	D	781 205-5400	17186
Geonautics Manufacturing Inc	Newburyport	MA	E	978 462-7161	13494
Jacobs Precision Corp	Avon	MA	G	508 588-2121	7888
Labombard Machine	Methuen	MA	G	978 688-7773	13032
Louis C Morin Company Inc	North Billerica	MA	F	978 670-1222	13836
Lutco Bearings Inc	Worcester	MA	D	508 756-6296	17408
Mansfield Machinery Co Inc	Mansfield	MA	F	508 339-7973	12644
Marver Med Inc	Stoughton	MA	F	781 341-9372	15605
Mgb Us Inc	Franklin	MA	F	774 415-0060	11064
Munsey Screw Machine Products	North Billerica	MA	G	978 667-4053	13848
North Easton Companies Inc	North Easton	MA	G	774 259-0172	13950
North Easton Machine Co Inc	North Easton	MA	F	508 238-6219	13951
R Hueter Co	Beverly	MA	G	978 927-3482	8170
Reliable Screw Mch Pdts Inc	Peabody	MA	G	978 531-0520	14364
Rosellis Machine & Mfg Co	Westfield	MA	F	413 562-4317	16723
San-Tron Inc **(PA)**	Ipswich	MA	D	978 356-1585	11936
Screwtron Engineering Inc	Ashland	MA	G	508 881-1370	7669
Specialized Turning Inc	Peabody	MA	E	978 977-0444	14371
Sterling Machine Company Inc	Lynn	MA	E	781 593-3000	12541
Swissturn/Usa Inc	Oxford	MA	D	508 987-6211	14274
United Screw Machine Products	Millbury	MA	G	508 865-7295	13178
Yankee Hill Machine Co Inc	Easthampton	MA	D	413 584-1400	10583
Arundel Machine Tool Co	Arundel	ME	D	207 985-8555	5528
David Michaud	Winthrop	ME	G	207 377-8037	7280
Newberry Enterprise	Windham	ME	G	207 892-8596	7244
Barco Manufacturing Inc	Tilton	NH	E	603 286-3324	19904
Bay State Swiss CAM Design	Alton	NH	G	603 859-7552	17545
D & E Screw Machine Pdts Inc	Colebrook	NH	F	508 658-7344	17866
Green Mountain Metals of VT	Claremont	NH	F	603 542-0005	17852
Intelitek Inc	Derry	NH	E	800 221-2763	17983
J T Manufacturing Corporation	Pelham	NH	E	603 821-5720	19436
Jtc Precision Swiss Inc	Manchester	NH	G	603 935-9830	18853
Liberty Research Co Inc **(PA)**	Rochester	NH	F	603 332-2730	19678
Link Metal Corporation	Wolfeboro	NH	G	603 569-5085	20022
New Hampshire Machine Products	Exeter	NH	G	603 772-4404	18125
Omni Components Corp **(PA)**	Hudson	NH	D	603 882-4467	18422
Parker & Harper Companies Inc **(PA)**	Raymond	NH	D	603 895-4761	19643
Precision Components Inc	Peterborough	NH	G	603 924-3597	19484
Blackhawk Machine Products Inc	Smithfield	RI	E	401 232-7563	21213
Droitcour Company	Warwick	RI	D	401 737-4646	21355
Esmond Manufacturing Company	Cranston	RI	G	401 942-9103	20220
Fasano Corp	Cranston	RI	G	401 785-9646	20224
Greystone of Lincoln Inc **(PA)**	Lincoln	RI	C	401 333-0444	20576
Groov-Pin Corporation **(PA)**	Smithfield	RI	D	770 251-5054	21230
M F Engineering Company Inc	Bristol	RI	F	401 253-6163	20092
Machinex Company Inc	Smithfield	RI	F	401 231-3230	21237
Moody Machine Products Inc	Providence	RI	G	401 941-5130	21071
Precision Trned Cmponents Corp	Smithfield	RI	D	401 232-3377	21244
Quality Screw Machine Pdts Inc	Smithfield	RI	F	401 231-8900	21245
Rhode Island Precision Co	Providence	RI	F	401 421-6661	21113
Swissline Precision LLC	Cumberland	RI	D	401 333-8888	20343
West Warwick Screw Products Co	West Warwick	RI	G	401 821-4729	21512
Lebanon Screw Products Inc	Windsor	VT	F	802 674-6347	22711

SCREW MACHINES

	CITY	ST	EMP	PHONE	ENTRY #
E H Metalcraft Company Inc	West Bridgewater	MA	G	508 580-0870	16440
LDB Tool and Findings Inc	Cranston	RI	G	401 944-6000	20252
Swissline Precision Mfg Inc	Cumberland	RI	D	401 333-8888	20344
Pad Print Machinery of Vermont	East Dorset	VT	D	802 362-0844	21915

SCREWS: Metal

	CITY	ST	EMP	PHONE	ENTRY #
Aerotech Fasteners Inc	Putnam	CT	F	860 928-6300	3600
Crescent Mnfacturing Operating	Burlington	CT	E	860 673-1921	676
L & M Manufacturing Co Inc	New Hartford	CT	E	860 379-2751	2642
Narragansett Screw Co	Winsted	CT	F	860 379-4059	5418
North East Fasteners Corp	Terryville	CT	E	860 589-3242	4488
Thread Rolling Inc	East Hartford	CT	F	860 528-1515	1229
Triem Industries LLC	Terryville	CT	E	203 888-1212	4494
Universal Thread Grinding Co	Fairfield	CT	F	203 336-1849	1459
Fall River Mfg Co Inc	Fall River	MA	D	508 675-1125	10696
Fisk Industries Inc	Attleboro Falls	MA	G	508 695-3661	7813
J I Morris Company	Southbridge	MA	G	508 764-4394	15388
Stillwater Fasteners LLC	East Freetown	MA	E	508 763-8044	10460
Merrimack Manufacturing Co	Bridgton	ME	G	207 647-3566	5809
Haydon Kerk Mtion Slutions Inc	Milford	NH	D	603 465-7227	19058
Allesco Industries Inc **(PA)**	Cranston	RI	C	401 943-0680	20176
Eastern Screw Company	Cranston	RI	C	401 943-0680	20214
MLS Screw Machine Corp	East Providence	RI	G	401 435-3850	20432
Research Engineering & Mfg Inc	Middletown	RI	F	401 841-8880	20631

SEALANTS

	CITY	ST	EMP	PHONE	ENTRY #
Grafted Coatings Inc	Stratford	CT	F	203 377-9979	4416
Sealpro LLC	East Hartford	CT	G	860 289-0804	1219
Smarter Sealants LLC	East Hartford	CT	G	860 218-2210	1221
Allied Sealant Inc	Chelmsford	MA	G	978 254-7117	9869
Dorn Equipment Corp	Melrose	MA	F	781 662-9300	12981
Emseal Joint Systems Ltd	Westborough	MA	E	508 836-0280	16617
Granger Lynch Corp	Millbury	MA	E	508 756-6244	13165
Hero Coatings Inc	Newburyport	MA	G	978 462-0746	13497
ITW Plymers Salants N Amer Inc	Rockland	MA	E	781 681-0418	14809
Absolute Rstrtion Slant Sltons	Bow	NH	G	603 518-5864	17706

SEALING COMPOUNDS: Sealing, synthetic rubber or plastic

	CITY	ST	EMP	PHONE	ENTRY #
Clint Sales & Manufacturing	Beverly	MA	G	978 927-3010	8118
JP Sealcoating Inc	Norton	MA	G	508 954-3510	14080
Nova Sports Usa Inc	Milford	MA	F	508 473-6540	13133
Saint-Gobain Abrasives Inc **(DH)**	Worcester	MA	A	508 795-5000	17464
Gripwet Inc	South Portland	ME	G	207 239-0486	7029

SEALS: Hermetic

	CITY	ST	EMP	PHONE	ENTRY #
Northeast Electronics Corp	Milford	CT	D	203 878-3511	2324
Ceramic To Metal Seals Inc	Melrose	MA	F	781 665-5002	12977
Metal Processing Co Inc	Tyngsboro	MA	G	978 649-1289	15896
Schott North America Inc	Southbridge	MA	D	508 765-7450	15402
Sinclair Manufacturing Co LLC	Norton	MA	D	508 222-7440	14089
Special Hermetic Products	Wilton	NH	E	603 654-2002	19989

SEALS: Oil, Asbestos

	CITY	ST	EMP	PHONE	ENTRY #
Parker-Hannifin Corporation	Woburn	MA	B	781 935-4850	17257

SEARCH & DETECTION SYSTEMS, EXC RADAR

	CITY	ST	EMP	PHONE	ENTRY #
Exocetus Autonomous Systems	Wallingford	CT	G	860 512-7260	4740
Advanced ID Detection LLC	Medway	MA	G	617 544-8030	12954
Analogic Corporation **(HQ)**	Peabody	MA	A	978 326-4000	14311
Bae Systems Tech Sol Srvc Inc	Sagamore	MA	G	508 833-9562	14883
Bounce Imaging Inc	Allston	MA	F	716 310-8281	7460
Chris Martin **(PA)**	Avon	MA	G	508 580-0069	7882
General Dynamics Def	Pittsfield	MA	A	413 494-1110	14471
Rigaku Analytical Devices Inc	Wilmington	MA	E	781 328-1024	17041
Bae Systems Info & Elec Sys	Nashua	NH	G	603 885-3770	19124
Skeyetrac LLC	Salem	NH	F	603 898-8000	19768

SEARCH & NAVIGATION SYSTEMS

	CITY	ST	EMP	PHONE	ENTRY #
Beacon Group Inc **(PA)**	Newington	CT	C	860 594-5200	2846
Boeing Company	East Windsor	CT	G	860 627-9393	1279
Chromalloy Component Svcs Inc	Windsor	CT	C	860 688-7798	5325
Connecticut Analytical Corp	Bethany	CT	F	203 393-9666	119
Edac Nd Inc	Glastonbury	CT	D	860 633-9474	1548
Electro-Methods Inc **(PA)**	South Windsor	CT	C	860 289-8661	3962
Gems Sensors Inc **(HQ)**	Plainville	CT	B	860 747-3000	3491
Hartford Aircraft Products	Bloomfield	CT	E	860 242-8228	223
Lee Company **(PA)**	Westbrook	CT	A	860 399-6281	5157
Meriden Manufacturing Inc	Meriden	CT	D	203 237-7481	2104
Northrop Grumman Corporation	East Hartford	CT	D	860 282-4461	1207
Passur Aerospace Inc **(PA)**	Stamford	CT	E	203 622-4086	4278
Polar Corporation	New Britain	CT	E	860 223-7891	2564
Raytheon Company	Mystic	CT	E	860 446-4900	2449
Spectrogram Corporation	Madison	CT	G	203 245-2433	1977
Sperian Protectn Instrumentatn	Middletown	CT	C	860 344-1079	2225
Thayermahan Inc	Groton	CT	E	860 785-9994	1688
AC Navigation LLC	Medfield	MA	G	508 359-5903	12908
Accusonic Technologies **(DH)**	New Bedford	MA	F	508 495-6600	13348
Ametek Inc	Wilmington	MA	D	978 988-4101	16973
API Technologies Corporation	Marlborough	MA	D	508 251-6400	12719
Bae Systems Info & Elec Sys	Burlington	MA	D	781 273-3388	9238
Cooper Interconnect Inc	Chelsea	MA	D	617 389-7080	9950
Creighton Kayla	Whitinsville	MA	G	508 612-0685	16912
Edgeone LLC	West Wareham	MA	D	508 291-0057	16571
Foster-Miller Inc	Devens	MA	D	781 684-4000	10320
General Dynamics Mission Syste	Quincy	MA	D	617 715-7000	14628
General Dynmics Mssion Systems	Pittsfield	MA	A	413 494-1110	14472
GM Merc Inc	Hopkinton	MA	G	508 878-1305	11717
Hydroid Inc **(PA)**	Pocasset	MA	C	508 563-6565	14596
L3 Technologies Inc	Northampton	MA	A	413 586-2330	14009
L3 Technologies Inc	Burlington	MA	C	781 270-2100	9295
L3harris Technologies Inc	Bellingham	MA	D	508 966-9500	8043
L3harris Technologies Inc	Bedford	MA	D	781 538-4148	7987
Laser Labs Inc	Pembroke	MA	G	781 826-4138	14415
Lockheed Martin Corp - Boston	Burlington	MA	E	781 565-1100	9298
Lockheed Martin Corporation	Chelmsford	MA	C	978 256-4113	9913
Lockheed Martin Corporation	Chelmsford	MA	A	978 256-4113	9914

	CITY	ST	EMP	PHONE	ENTRY #
Lockheed Martin Corporation	Marlborough	MA	B	508 460-0086	12788
Lockheed Martin Corporation	Lexington	MA	G	781 862-6222	12239
Lockheed Martin Corporation	Pittsfield	MA	B	413 236-3400	14485
Lockheed Martin Services LLC	Lowell	MA	E	978 275-9730	12397
Lockheed Martin Sippican Inc	Marion	MA	E	774 553-6282	12700
Magcap Engineering LLC	Canton	MA	F	781 821-2300	9754
Mettler-Toledo Thornton Inc	Billerica	MA	D	978 262-0210	8266
MSI Transducers Corp	Littleton	MA	F	978 486-0404	12313
Northrop Grumman Corporation	Devens	MA	G	978 772-0352	10327
Northrop Grumman Systems Corp	Andover	MA	G	978 247-7812	7578
Photonis Scientific Inc **(DH)**	Sturbridge	MA	D	508 347-4000	15646
Princeton Security Tech Inc **(HQ)**	Franklin	MA	G	609 924-7310	11074
Princton Gamma-Tech Instrs Inc	Franklin	MA	F	609 924-7310	11075
Raytheon Company	Andover	MA	D	781 522-3000	7595
Raytheon Italy Liaison Company	Andover	MA	D	978 684-5300	7597
Sensomotoric Instruments Inc	Boston	MA	G	617 557-0010	8844
Sensormatic Electronics LLC	Lexington	MA	C	781 466-6660	12264
Smiths Detection LLC	Andover	MA	C	510 449-4197	7610
Symetrica Inc	Westford	MA	F	508 718-5610	16795
Techlaw Inc	North Chelmsford	MA	G	617 918-8612	13911
Teledyne Benthos Inc **(HQ)**	North Falmouth	MA	C	508 563-1000	13954
Teledyne Instruments Inc	North Falmouth	MA	F	508 563-1000	13955
Tru Technologies Inc	Peabody	MA	C	978 532-0775	14379
Vaisala Inc	Woburn	MA	G	508 574-1163	17311
General Dynamics-Ots Inc	Saco	ME	E	207 283-3611	6847
Lockheed Martin Corporation	Bath	ME	E	207 442-1112	5680
Bae Systems Elctronic Solution	Nashua	NH	F	603 885-3653	19120
Bae Systems Info & Elec Sys **(DH)**	Nashua	NH	B	603 885-4321	19121
Bae Systems Info & Elec Sys	Nashua	NH	B	603 885-4321	19122
Bae Systems Info & Elec Sys	Merrimack	NH	B	603 885-4321	18989
Bae Systems Info & Elec Sys	Londonderry	NH	G	603 647-5367	18678
Bae Systems Info & Elec Sys	Hudson	NH	A	603 885-4321	18376
Cobham	Exeter	NH	G	603 418-9786	18116
Contintential Microwave	Exeter	NH	G	603 775-5200	18118
El-Op US Inc	Merrimack	NH	B	603 889-2500	18998
Fireye Inc **(DH)**	Derry	NH	C	603 432-4100	17979
Flir Systems Inc	Nashua	NH	G	866 636-4487	19162
KMC Systems Inc	Merrimack	NH	D	866 742-0442	19010
Kollsman Inc **(DH)**	Merrimack	NH	A	603 889-2500	19011
L3harris Technologies Inc	Nashua	NH	E	603 689-1450	19195
Lockheed Martin Corporation	Merrimack	NH	F	603 885-5295	19012
Lockheed Martin Corporation	Nashua	NH	B	603 885-4321	19199
Lockheed Martin Corporation	Nashua	NH	A	603 885-4321	19200
Memtec Corporation	Salem	NH	E	603 893-8080	19751
Mevatec Corp	Nashua	NH	F	603 885-4321	19207
Qesidyne Inc	Hudson	NH	G	603 883-3116	18431
Research In Motion Rf Inc **(HQ)**	Nashua	NH	E	603 598-8880	19250
Sealite Usa LLC	Tilton	NH	F	603 737-1310	19911
Sequa Corporation	Merrimack	NH	G	603 889-2500	19029
Sierra Nevada Corporation	Bedford	NH	B	775 331-0222	17663
Bae Systems Tech Sol Srvc Inc	Middletown	RI	E	401 846-5500	20616
Wei Inc **(PA)**	Cranston	RI	E	401 781-3904	20309
General Dynamics-Ots Inc	Williston	VT	G	802 662-7000	22670

SEATING: Chairs, Table & Arm

	CITY	ST	EMP	PHONE	ENTRY #
Halls Rental Service LLC	North Branford	CT	G	203 488-0383	2966

SEATING: Stadium

	CITY	ST	EMP	PHONE	ENTRY #
Hussey Corporation **(PA)**	North Berwick	ME	C	207 676-2271	6506
Hussey Seating Company	North Berwick	ME	B	207 676-2271	6507

SEATING: Transportation

	CITY	ST	EMP	PHONE	ENTRY #
Accudyne Machine Tool Inc	Bellingham	MA	G	508 966-3110	8027
Modu Form Inc	Fitchburg	MA	G	978 345-7942	10842
Modu Form Inc **(PA)**	Fitchburg	MA	D	978 345-7942	10841
Lucci Corp	Peterborough	NH	F	603 567-4301	19475

SECRETARIAL & COURT REPORTING

	CITY	ST	EMP	PHONE	ENTRY #
Publishers Design & Prod Svcs	Sagamore Beach	MA	F	508 833-8300	14886

SECRETARIAL SVCS

	CITY	ST	EMP	PHONE	ENTRY #
Sterling Business Corp	Peterborough	NH	G	603 924-9401	19489

SECURE STORAGE SVC: Document

	CITY	ST	EMP	PHONE	ENTRY #
CD Solutions Inc	Branford	CT	E	203 481-5895	303
Quintal Burial Vaults	Dighton	MA	F	508 669-5717	10338
State-Line Graphics Inc	Everett	MA	F	617 389-1200	10632

SECURITY CONTROL EQPT & SYSTEMS

	CITY	ST	EMP	PHONE	ENTRY #
Assa Inc **(HQ)**	New Haven	CT	B	203 624-5225	2659
Command Corporation	East Granby	CT	F	800 851-6012	1122
Donali Systems Integration Inc	Guilford	CT	G	860 715-5432	1701
Morse Watchmans Inc	Oxford	CT	E	203 264-1108	3415
New Line USA Inc	Coventry	CT	G	860 498-0347	837
Security Systems Inc	Middletown	CT	G	800 833-3211	2220
AES Corporation	Peabody	MA	D	978 535-7310	14308
Cogniscent Inc	Weston	MA	F	508 863-0069	16824
Dogwatch Inc **(PA)**	Natick	MA	F	508 650-0600	13252
Ion Track Instruments LLC	Wilmington	MA	D	978 658-3767	17007
Jlg Technologies LLC	Southborough	MA	G	508 424-2338	15362
Precision Dynamics Corporation	Burlington	MA	D	888 202-3684	9321
Raysecur Inc **(PA)**	Cambridge	MA	G	844 729-7328	9626
Security Devices Intl Inc	Wakefield	MA	G	905 582-6402	15975
Siemens Industry Inc	Canton	MA	D	781 364-1000	9779
T H Grogan & Associates Inc	Acton	MA	F	978 266-9548	7389
Tyco Safety Products Us Inc	Westminster	MA	E	800 435-3192	16818

SECURITY DEVICES

	CITY	ST	EMP	PHONE	ENTRY #
Aeroturn LLC	Oxford	CT	G	203 262-8309	3388
Insight Plus Technology LLC	Bristol	CT	G	860 930-4763	571
Stanley Black & Decker Inc	New Britain	CT	C	860 225-5111	2582
Stanley Black & Decker Inc **(PA)**	New Britain	CT	C	860 225-5111	2580
United Technologies Corp	Farmington	CT	B	954 485-6501	1523
United Technologies Corp	East Hartford	CT	B	860 610-7000	1237
All Security Co Inc	New Bedford	MA	F	508 993-4271	13356
Beon Home Inc	North Easton	MA	G	617 600-8329	13944
Cc-Teknologies Inc	Brockton	MA	G	508 444-8810	9127
Compu-Gard Inc	Swansea	MA	E	508 679-8845	15703
Dorel Juvenile Group Inc	Foxboro	MA	D	800 544-1108	10881
Eikon Corporation	Andover	MA	G	978 662-5200	7546
Inner-Tite Corp	Holden	MA	D	508 829-6361	11546
Interntnal Br-Tech Sltions Inc **(PA)**	Springfield	MA	F	413 739-2271	15480
Magiq Technologies Inc **(PA)**	Somerville	MA	F	617 661-8300	15192
Videoiq Inc	Somerville	MA	E	781 222-3069	15228
Alert Products	Keene	NH	G	603 357-3331	18490
Orion Entrance Control Inc	Laconia	NH	E	603 527-4187	18579
Kenney Manufacturing Company **(PA)**	Warwick	RI	B	401 739-2200	21383
Stanley Black & Decker Inc	East Greenwich	RI	C	401 471-4280	20380

SECURITY EQPT STORES

	CITY	ST	EMP	PHONE	ENTRY #
Barile Printers LLC	New Britain	CT	G	860 224-0127	2513
Framingham Engraving Co	Framingham	MA	G	508 877-7867	10946
Americ An Novelty Inc	Seabrook	NH	G	401 785-9850	19792

SECURITY PROTECTIVE DEVICES MAINTENANCE & MONITORING SVCS

	CITY	ST	EMP	PHONE	ENTRY #
Insight Plus Technology LLC	Bristol	CT	G	860 930-4763	571
Pequot	Bridgeport	CT	G	800 620-1492	466
Q-Lane Turnstiles LLC	Sandy Hook	CT	F	860 410-1801	3745
General Dynamics-Ots Inc	Williston	VT	G	802 662-7000	22670

SECURITY SYSTEMS SERVICES

	CITY	ST	EMP	PHONE	ENTRY #
Idemia America Corp **(DH)**	Billerica	MA	B	978 215-2400	8255
Connectivity Works Inc	Holden	ME	G	207 843-0854	6196

SELF-HELP ORGANIZATION, NEC

	CITY	ST	EMP	PHONE	ENTRY #
Hope Association **(PA)**	Rumford	ME	D	207 364-4561	6835

SEMICONDUCTOR CIRCUIT NETWORKS

	CITY	ST	EMP	PHONE	ENTRY #
Fiber Mountain Inc	Cheshire	CT	E	203 806-4040	732
Asm Nexx Inc	Billerica	MA	E	978 436-4600	8214
Metelics Corp	Lowell	MA	C	408 737-8197	12408
Microsemi Corp-Colorado	Lawrence	MA	D	480 941-6300	12054
Precision Pcb Inc **(PA)**	Whitman	MA	G	781 447-6285	16925
Interplex Industries Inc **(DH)**	Rumford	RI	F	718 961-6212	21188
Lrv Properties LLC	Providence	RI	G	401 714-7001	21058

SEMICONDUCTOR DEVICES: Wafers

	CITY	ST	EMP	PHONE	ENTRY #
Saphlux Inc	Branford	CT	G	475 221-8981	345
Aeroflex / Metelics Inc	Lowell	MA	G	603 641-3800	12341
Cambridge Electronics Inc	Belmont	MA	G	617 710-7013	8067
Desert Harvest Solar Farm LLC	Peabody	MA	G	978 531-2222	14329
Graphenea Inc	Cambridge	MA	F	415 568-6243	9497
Iqe Kc LLC	Taunton	MA	D	508 824-6696	15759
Kopin Corporation **(PA)**	Westborough	MA	C	508 870-5959	16630
Macom Metelics LLC	Lowell	MA	D	978 656-2500	12400
Philips Advanced Metrology Sys	Billerica	MA	G	508 647-8400	8274
Macom Tech Sltons Holdings Inc	Londonderry	NH	D	603 641-3800	18716

SEMICONDUCTORS & RELATED DEVICES

	CITY	ST	EMP	PHONE	ENTRY #
AG Semiconductor Services LLC	Stamford	CT	E	203 322-5300	4131
Asct LLC	Durham	CT	G	860 349-1121	1087
Convergent Solutions LLC	Westport	CT	G	203 293-3534	5186
Edal Industries Inc	East Haven	CT	E	203 467-2591	1248
Emosyn America Inc	Danbury	CT	E	203 794-1100	909
Gordon Products Incorporated	Brookfield	CT	E	203 775-4501	646
Micro-Probe Incorporated	Southbury	CT	G	203 267-6446	4031
Microphase Corporation	Shelton	CT	E	203 866-8000	3833
Newco Condenser Inc	Shelton	CT	G	475 882-4000	3839
Pequot	Bridgeport	CT	G	800 620-1492	466
Photronics Texas Inc	Brookfield	CT	G	203 546-3039	655
Photronics Texas I LLC	Brookfield	CT	G	203 775-9000	656
Silicon Catalyst LLC	Ridgefield	CT	G	203 240-0499	3684
United Electric Controls Co	Milford	CT	D	203 877-2795	2377
Vishay Americas Inc **(HQ)**	Shelton	CT	B	203 452-5648	3886
Acacia Communications Inc **(PA)**	Maynard	MA	C	978 938-4896	12894
Accuprobe Corporation	Salem	MA	E	978 745-7878	14889
Addilat Inc **(PA)**	Woburn	MA	G	781 258-9963	17109
Albion Beams Inc	Manchester	MA	G	978 526-4406	12602
Allegro Microsystems LLC	Marlborough	MA	C	508 853-5000	12711
American Superconductor Corp **(PA)**	Ayer	MA	C	978 842-3000	7907
Ametek Inc	New Bedford	MA	G	508 998-4335	13358
Amkor Technology Inc	Stoneham	MA	G	781 438-7800	15554
Analog Devices Intl Inc **(HQ)**	Norwood	MA	F	781 329-4700	14131
API Technologies Corp **(PA)**	Marlborough	MA	C	855 294-3800	12717
Applied Materials	Gloucester	MA	G	978 282-2917	11160
Applied Materials Inc	Boxborough	MA	E	978 795-8000	8957
Applied Nanofemto Tech LLC	Lowell	MA	G	978 761-4293	12344
Ardeo Systems Inc	Haverhill	MA	G	978 373-4680	11405
Arm Inc	Waltham	MA	G	978 264-7300	16036
Arradiance LLC	Littleton	MA	F	508 202-0593	12293
Aware Inc **(PA)**	Bedford	MA	D	781 276-4000	7962
Bae Systems Info & Elec Sys	Lexington	MA	B	603 885-4321	12208

	CITY	ST	EMP	PHONE	ENTRY #
Black Earth Technologies Inc	Dighton	MA	G	508 397-1335	10336
Boston Process Tech Inc	Peabody	MA	F	978 854-5579	14316
Cavium Inc	Marlborough	MA	F	508 357-4111	12736
Celeno Communications	Belmont	MA	G	617 500-3683	8069
Ceramic Process Systems	Taunton	MA	G	508 222-0614	15736
Component Hndng Inspctn Pckn	Peabody	MA	G	978 535-3997	14325
Control Resources Inc	Littleton	MA	E	978 486-4160	12297
Custom Mmic Design Svcs Inc	Chelmsford	MA	E	978 467-4290	9891
Digital Lumens Incorporated	Boston	MA	E	617 723-1200	8505
Drs Development LLC	Rochester	MA	G	774 271-0533	14785
Electronic Products Inds Inc	Newburyport	MA	E	978 462-8101	13486
Elpakco Inc **(PA)**	Westford	MA	E	978 392-0400	16765
Encite LLC	Burlington	MA	G	781 750-8241	9267
Entegris Inc **(PA)**	Billerica	MA	A	978 436-6500	8246
Eos Photonics Inc	Cambridge	MA	G	617 945-9137	9468
Epi II Inc	Newburyport	MA	D	978 462-1514	13487
GE Infrastructure Sensing LLC **(DH)**	Billerica	MA	A	978 437-1000	8249
Huber + Shner Platis Photonics	Bedford	MA	F	781 275-5080	7981
Ii-VI Photonics (us) Inc **(HQ)**	Woburn	MA	E	781 938-1222	17200
Immedia Semiconductor Inc	North Reading	MA	F	978 296-4950	13985
Infineon Tech Americas Corp	Tewksbury	MA	G	978 640-3893	15819
Innovion Corporation	Wilmington	MA	G	978 267-4064	17005
Isilon Systems LLC	Hopkinton	MA	G	206 315-7500	11723
Iwaki Pumps Inc **(DH)**	Holliston	MA	E	508 429-1440	11580
Ixys Intgrted Circuits Div LLC	Beverly	MA	D	978 524-6700	8142
Kcb Solutions LLC	Shirley	MA	F	978 425-0400	15088
Kopin Display Corporation **(PA)**	Westborough	MA	G	508 870-5959	16631
L T X International Inc	Norwood	MA	D	781 461-1000	14173
Lattice Semiconductor Corp	Burlington	MA	G	781 229-5819	9296
Lightmatter Inc	Boston	MA	E	857 244-0460	8667
Linear Technology LLC	North Chelmsford	MA	G	978 656-4750	13901
Macom Tech Sltons Holdings Inc **(PA)**	Lowell	MA	C	978 656-2500	12401
Massachusetts Bay Tech Inc	Stoughton	MA	F	781 344-8809	15606
Mediatek USA Inc	Woburn	MA	D	781 503-8000	17227
Mellanox Technologies Inc	Chelmsford	MA	G	978 439-5400	9916
Micro Magnetics Inc	Fall River	MA	F	508 672-4489	10732
Microchip Technology Inc	Westborough	MA	C	774 760-0087	16634
Microscale Inc	Woburn	MA	G	781 995-2245	17230
Microsemi Corp- Massachusetts	Lowell	MA	D	978 442-5600	12409
Microsemi Corp- Massachusetts	Lawrence	MA	B	978 620-2600	12053
Microsemi Corporation	Tewksbury	MA	G	978 232-3793	15823
Microsemi Corporation	Beverly	MA	G	978 232-0040	8154
Micross Express	Woburn	MA	G	781 938-0866	17231
Microtronic Inc	Edgartown	MA	E	508 627-8951	10587
Mini-Systems Inc	Plainville	MA	E	508 695-2000	14528
Murata Power Solutions Inc **(DH)**	Westborough	MA	C	508 339-3000	16637
Nano-Audio	Wellesley	MA	G	781 416-5096	16374
Nantero Inc	Woburn	MA	E	781 932-5338	17236
Nissin Ion Equipment Usa Inc	North Billerica	MA	F	978 362-2590	13849
North East Silicon Tech Inc	New Bedford	MA	D	508 999-2001	13429
Onset Computer Corporation	Bourne	MA	C	508 759-9500	8948
Optek Systems Inc	Groton	MA	G	978 448-9376	11293
Overseas Project Advancement	West Newbury	MA	F	978 255-1816	16492
Performance Motion Devices Inc	Westford	MA	E	978 266-1210	16783
Philips Holding USA Inc **(HQ)**	Andover	MA	C	978 687-1501	7582
Photronix Inc	Burlington	MA	G	781 221-0442	9319
Precision Sensing Devices Inc	Medfield	MA	G	508 359-2833	12917
Precisive LLC	Methuen	MA	G	781 850-4469	13043
Qbit Semiconductor Ltd	Littleton	MA	G	351 205-0005	12321
Quantance Inc **(PA)**	Woburn	MA	E	650 293-3300	17277
Realtime Dx Inc	Lexington	MA	G	508 479-9818	12259
Reinforced Structures For Elec	Worcester	MA	E	508 754-5316	17457
Renesas Electronics Amer Inc	Concord	MA	A	978 805-6900	10156
Rf1 Holding Company **(PA)**	Marlborough	MA	F	855 294-3800	12816
SA Photonics Inc	Lexington	MA	G	781 861-1430	12260
Sand 9 Inc	Cambridge	MA	E	617 358-0957	9641
Seminex Corporation	Peabody	MA	G	978 326-7700	14369
Semitech Solutions Inc	Acton	MA	G	978 589-3850	7386
Sheaumann Laser Inc	Marlborough	MA	G	508 970-0600	12825
Si Tech Inc	Topsfield	MA	G	978 887-3550	15865
Signet Products Corporation	North Attleboro	MA	G	650 592-3575	13779
Silex Microsystems Inc	Boston	MA	F	617 834-7197	8846
Sionyx LLC **(PA)**	Beverly	MA	F	978 922-0684	8178
Skyworks Solutions Inc	Andover	MA	C	978 327-6850	7606
Skyworks Solutions Inc	Woburn	MA	B	781 935-5150	17298
Somerville Science and Tech	Somerville	MA	G	617 628-3150	15219
Sparta Kefalas Organics LLC	East Bridgewater	MA	G	978 810-5300	10420
Sst Components Inc **(PA)**	Billerica	MA	E	978 670-7300	8298
Tego Inc	Waltham	MA	G	781 547-5680	16208
Tel Epion Inc	Billerica	MA	E	978 436-2300	8302
Teradyne Inc **(PA)**	North Reading	MA	B	978 370-2700	13990
Texas Instruments Incorporated	Attleboro	MA	E	508 236-3800	7802
That Corporation **(PA)**	Milford	MA	E	508 478-9200	13148
Transene Company Inc	Danvers	MA	F	978 777-7860	10265
Twin Creeks Technologies Inc	Danvers	MA	E	978 777-0846	10268
Union Miniere	Boston	MA	E	617 960-5900	8895
Vacuum Plus Manufacturing Inc	Chelmsford	MA	F	978 441-3100	9939
Vsea Inc	Gloucester	MA	E	978 282-2000	11218
Xcerra Corporation	Norwood	MA	E	781 461-1000	14208
Xp Power LLC	Gloucester	MA	D	978 282-0620	11220
Fairchild Energy LLC	South Portland	ME	G	207 775-8100	7023
Fairchild Semiconductor Corp	South Portland	ME	C	207 775-8100	7025
Ron Lavallee	Belgrade	ME	G	248 705-3231	5699
Advanced Consulting	Nashua	NH	G	603 882-5529	19099
Allegro Microsystems Inc	Manchester	NH	G	508 853-5000	18776
Allegro Microsystems LLC **(HQ)**	Manchester	NH	B	603 626-2300	18777
Ardent Concepts Inc	Hampton	NH	G	603 474-1760	18255
Bantry Components Inc	Manchester	NH	E	603 668-3210	18785
Boxford Designs LLC	Derry	NH	G	603 216-2399	17973
Corfin Industries LLC	Manchester	NH	D	603 893-9900	18805
Cubic Wafer Inc	Merrimack	NH	G	603 546-0600	18996
Cxe Equipment Services LLC	Seabrook	NH	G	603 437-2477	19798
Distillation Tech Pdts LLC	Manchester	NH	G	603 935-7070	18766
Dutile Glines & Higgins Inc	Hooksett	NH	F	603 622-0452	18348
Eigenlight Corporation	Newmarket	NH	E	603 692-9200	19333
Finetech	Amherst	NH	G	603 627-8989	17562
Gt Advanced Cz LLC	Merrimack	NH	G	603 883-5200	19004
Gt Advanced Technologies Ltd	Hudson	NH	G	603 883-5200	18395
Microsemi Corporation	Manchester	NH	C	978 232-3793	18873
Pd & E Electronics LLC	North Hampton	NH	G	603 964-3165	19386
Rob Geoffroy	Londonderry	NH	G	603 425-2517	18734
Saint-Gobain Glass Corporation	Milford	NH	F	603 673-7560	19076
Semikron Inc **(HQ)**	Hudson	NH	E	603 883-8102	18437
Signalquest LLC	Lebanon	NH	E	603 448-6266	18635
Silicon Sense Inc	Nashua	NH	G	603 891-4248	19261
Ampleon USA Inc	Smithfield	RI	E	401 830-5420	21209
ATW Companies Inc **(PA)**	Warwick	RI	D	401 244-1002	21330
Cherry Semiconductor Corp	East Greenwich	RI	G	401 885-3600	20356
Narragansett Imaging Usa LLC	North Smithfield	RI	E	401 762-3800	20791
Numark International Inc	Cumberland	RI	F	954 761-7550	20335
Nxp Usa Inc	Smithfield	RI	G	401 830-5410	21241
Wei Inc **(PA)**	Cranston	RI	E	401 781-3904	20309
Globalfoundries US 2 LLC	Essex Junction	VT	A	408 462-4452	21941
Mobile Semiconductor Corp	Williston	VT	G	802 399-2449	22683
Nehp Inc	Williston	VT	D	802 652-1444	22685
Semiprobe Inc	Winooski	VT	G	802 860-7000	22723
Semivation	Essex Junction	VT	G	802 878-5153	21959

SEMINARY

	CITY	ST	EMP	PHONE	ENTRY #
Crane Data LLC	Westborough	MA	F	508 439-4419	16610

SENSORS: Infrared, Solid State

	CITY	ST	EMP	PHONE	ENTRY #
Apeak Inc	Auburndale	MA	G	617 964-1709	7856
Flir Systems-Boston Inc **(HQ)**	North Billerica	MA	B	978 901-8000	13815
Spectris Inc **(HQ)**	Westborough	MA	F	508 768-6400	16650
Vitalsensors Technologies LLC	Newton	MA	F	978 635-0450	13652

SENSORS: Radiation

	CITY	ST	EMP	PHONE	ENTRY #
Radeco of Ct Inc	Plainfield	CT	F	860 564-1220	3456
Bidirectional Display Inc	Acton	MA	G	617 599-8282	7344
Charge Analytics LLC	Boxford	MA	G	978 201-7952	8975
Druck LLC **(HQ)**	Billerica	MA	C	978 437-1000	8238
Guardion Inc	Burlington	MA	G	603 769-7265	9280
Radio Act Corporation	Brookline	MA	G	617 731-6542	9218
Thought One LLC	North Andover	MA	G	408 623-3278	13730

SENSORS: Temperature, Exc Indl Process

	CITY	ST	EMP	PHONE	ENTRY #
Omega Engineering Inc	Norwalk	CT	D	714 540-4914	3212
Thermalogic Corporation	Hudson	MA	E	800 343-4492	11823
Rcd Components LLC **(HQ)**	Manchester	NH	D	603 666-4627	18909
Bachar Samawi Innovations LLC **(PA)**	West Dover	VT	G	802 464-0440	22605

SEPTIC TANKS: Concrete

	CITY	ST	EMP	PHONE	ENTRY #
Arrow Concrete Products Inc **(PA)**	Granby	CT	E	860 653-5063	1588
Connecticut Precast Corp	Monroe	CT	E	203 268-8688	2398
David Shuck	Old Lyme	CT	G	860 434-8562	3320
Jolley Precast Inc	Danielson	CT	E	860 774-9066	1014
M & M Precast Corp	Danbury	CT	F	203 743-5559	951
Superior Concrete Products LLC	Portland	CT	G	860 342-0186	3576
Benson Enterprises Inc	North Easton	MA	F	508 583-5401	13943
Kellogg Bros Inc	Southwick	MA	G	413 569-6029	15415
Kingston Block Co Inc	Kingston	MA	G	781 585-6400	11960
Pine Tree Concrete Products	Millville	MA	G	508 883-7072	13187
Sani Tank Inc	Leominster	MA	G	978 537-9784	12186
Aroostacast Inc	Presque Isle	ME	F	207 764-0077	6753
Richard Genest Inc	Sanford	ME	F	207 324-7215	6890
Sandelin Foundation Inc	Topsham	ME	F	207 725-7004	7094
Trombley Industries Inc	Limestone	ME	G	207 328-4503	6345
Andrew J Foss Company Inc	Farmington	NH	F	603 755-2515	18139
William N Lamarre Con Pdts Inc	Greenville	NH	F	603 878-1340	18230
Ashaway Cement Products Inc	Wyoming	RI	G	401 539-1010	21588

SEPTIC TANKS: Plastic

	CITY	ST	EMP	PHONE	ENTRY #
Presby Plastics Inc	Whitefield	NH	E	603 837-3826	19972
Hancor Inc	Springfield	VT	E	802 886-8403	22501

SEWAGE & WATER TREATMENT EQPT

	CITY	ST	EMP	PHONE	ENTRY #
Ecosystem Consulting Svc Inc	Coventry	CT	G	860 742-0744	833
New Milford Commission	New Milford	CT	F	860 354-3758	2817
Shaws Pump Company Inc	Ellington	CT	G	860 872-6891	1339
Town of Vernon	Vernon Rockville	CT	G	860 870-3699	4686
Alexander Moles	Taunton	MA	G	508 823-8864	15723
Change Water Labs Inc	Cambridge	MA	G	917 292-5160	9437
Emerging Cpd Trtmnt Techngy	Burlington	MA	G	617 886-7400	9266
Evoqua Water Technologies LLC	Tewksbury	MA	E	978 863-4600	15817
Evoqua Water Technologies LLC	Lowell	MA	C	978 934-9349	12370
Krofta Technologies LLC **(DH)**	Dalton	MA	G	413 236-5634	10179
M E Baker Company **(PA)**	Framingham	MA	F	508 620-5304	10979
Omni-Trol Industries Inc	Revere	MA	F	781 284-8000	14774
Pumping Systems Inc	Braintree	MA	G	508 588-6868	9033
Spilldam Environmental Inc	Brockton	MA	F	508 583-7850	9178
Wayland Sudbury Septage	Wayland	MA	G	508 358-7328	16337
Wetech	Dedham	MA	G	781 320-8646	10302

	CITY	ST	EMP	PHONE	ENTRY #
Woodard & Curran Inc	Provincetown	MA	G	508 487-5474	14611
Septitech Inc	Lewiston	ME	F	207 333-6940	6323
Dreamtech Water Solutions LLC	Nashua	NH	G	603 513-7829	19147
Siemens Industry Inc	Cranston	RI	E	401 942-2121	20285

SEWER CLEANING EQPT: Power

	CITY	ST	EMP	PHONE	ENTRY #
National Water Main Clg Co	Canton	MA	E	617 361-5533	9760

SEWING CONTRACTORS

	CITY	ST	EMP	PHONE	ENTRY #
Hilco Athletic & Graphics Inc	West Warwick	RI	F	401 822-1775	21495

SEWING MACHINE STORES

	CITY	ST	EMP	PHONE	ENTRY #
Superior Manufacturing Corp	Fall River	MA	G	508 677-0100	10765
W S Bessett Inc	Sanford	ME	F	207 324-9232	6896

SEWING MACHINES & PARTS: Household

	CITY	ST	EMP	PHONE	ENTRY #
Superior Manufacturing Corp	Fall River	MA	G	508 677-0100	10765

SEWING MACHINES & PARTS: Indl

	CITY	ST	EMP	PHONE	ENTRY #
Media One LLC	Hamden	CT	E	203 745-5825	1769
Puritan Industries Inc	Collinsville	CT	E	860 693-0791	816

SEWING, NEEDLEWORK & PIECE GOODS STORE: Needlework Gds/Sply

	CITY	ST	EMP	PHONE	ENTRY #
Optimum Sportswear Inc	Lawrence	MA	G	978 689-2290	12069
Say It In Stitches Inc	Concord	NH	G	603 224-6470	17927
Pumpkin Harbor Designs Inc	Jeffersonville	VT	G	802 644-6588	22047

SEWING, NEEDLEWORK & PIECE GOODS STORES: Knitting Splys

	CITY	ST	EMP	PHONE	ENTRY #
P Straker Ltd	South Dartmouth	MA	G	508 996-4804	15241
Harrisville Designs Inc **(PA)**	Harrisville	NH	G	603 827-3333	18302
Green Mountain Spinnery Inc	East Dummerston	VT	F	802 387-4528	21919

SEXTANTS

	CITY	ST	EMP	PHONE	ENTRY #
Sextant Btsllc	Killingworth	CT	G	203 500-3245	1929

SHADES: Lamp & Light, Residential

	CITY	ST	EMP	PHONE	ENTRY #
G Scatchard Ltd	Westford	VT	G	802 899-2181	22628

SHADES: Lamp Or Candle

	CITY	ST	EMP	PHONE	ENTRY #
Blanche P Field LLC	Boston	MA	E	617 423-0714	8413
International Light Tech Inc	Peabody	MA	E	978 818-6180	14343

SHADES: Window

	CITY	ST	EMP	PHONE	ENTRY #
Arrow Window Shade Mfg Co	Wethersfield	CT	G	860 956-3570	5240
Beverly Shade Shoppe	Beverly	MA	G	978 922-0374	8110
Mohawk Shade & Blind Co Inc	Cambridge	MA	G	617 868-6000	9568
New England Drapery Assoc Inc	Woburn	MA	G	781 944-7536	17241
Reliable Shade & Screen Co	Somerville	MA	G	617 776-9538	15209
Shade Adams & Screen Co	Framingham	MA	G	617 244-2188	11004
Staceys Shade Shop Inc **(PA)**	Lynn	MA	G	781 595-0097	12540
Blw LLC	Brattleboro	VT	G	802 246-4500	21719

SHAFTS: Flexible

	CITY	ST	EMP	PHONE	ENTRY #
Double E Company LLC **(PA)**	West Bridgewater	MA	C	508 588-8099	16438
Mass-Flex Research Inc	Medford	MA	F	781 391-3640	12941

SHAFTS: Shaft Collars

	CITY	ST	EMP	PHONE	ENTRY #
American Collars Couplings Inc	Winsted	CT	F	860 379-7043	5403
Quik Loc Inc	Lincoln	NH	G	603 745-7008	18647

SHAPES & PILINGS, STRUCTURAL: Steel

	CITY	ST	EMP	PHONE	ENTRY #
Industrial Flame Cutting Inc	Beacon Falls	CT	G	203 723-4897	58
Pequonnock Ironworks Inc	Bridgeport	CT	F	203 336-2178	465
A & G Manufacturing Co Inc	Lynn	MA	G	781 581-1892	12487
Ackles Steel & Iron Company	Waltham	MA	F	781 893-6818	16022

SHAPES: Extruded, Aluminum, NEC

	CITY	ST	EMP	PHONE	ENTRY #
Mestek Inc **(PA)**	Westfield	MA	E	470 898-4533	16700
Wakefeld Thermal Solutions Inc **(HQ)**	Pelham	NH	C	603 635-2800	19454

SHAVING PREPARATIONS

	CITY	ST	EMP	PHONE	ENTRY #
Somersets Usa LLC	Arlington	MA	G	617 803-6833	7640

SHEET METAL SPECIALTIES, EXC STAMPED

	CITY	ST	EMP	PHONE	ENTRY #
Anco Engineering Inc	Shelton	CT	D	203 925-9235	3775
Axis Laser	Wallingford	CT	G	203 284-9455	4707
Brittany Company Inc	Wallingford	CT	G	203 269-7859	4712
Chapco Inc **(PA)**	Chester	CT	D	860 526-9535	769
Ductco LLC	Bloomfield	CT	E	860 243-0350	210
Farrell Prcsion Mtalcraft Corp	New Milford	CT	E	860 355-2651	2799
Hispanic Enterprises Inc	Bridgeport	CT	E	203 588-9334	425
Jared Manufacturing Co Inc	Norwalk	CT	F	203 846-1732	3180
Jgs Properties LLC	Stratford	CT	E	203 378-7508	4425
Jones Metal Products Co Inc	South Windsor	CT	G	860 289-8023	3986
Lyon Manufacturing LLC	Milford	CT	G	203 876-7386	2311
Paradigm Manchester Inc	Manchester	CT	D	860 646-4048	2029
Paradigm Manchester Inc	Manchester	CT	C	860 646-4048	2030
Paradigm Manchester Inc	Manchester	CT	C	860 649-2888	2032
Paradigm Manchester Inc	Manchester	CT	G	860 646-4048	2033
Quality Sheet Metal Inc	Naugatuck	CT	F	203 729-2244	2492
R & D Precision Inc	Wallingford	CT	F	203 284-3396	4792
R W E Inc	Putnam	CT	E	860 974-1101	3628
R-D Mfg Inc	East Lyme	CT	F	860 739-3986	1273
Seconn Fabrication LLC	Waterford	CT	D	860 443-0000	4993
A & D Metal Inc	Westfield	MA	F	413 485-7505	16662
Aerospace Fabricators Inc	Waltham	MA	G	781 899-4535	16025
Agwey Metal Designs Inc	Plymouth	MA	G	508 747-1037	14541
Allstate Hood & Duct Inc	Westfield	MA	F	413 568-4663	16664
Apahouser Inc	Marlborough	MA	E	508 786-0309	12714
AW Airflo Industries Inc	Newburyport	MA	E	978 465-6260	13470
Better Maintenance Sheet Metal	Rowley	MA	G	978 948-7067	14846
C S H Industries Inc	Plymouth	MA	E	508 747-1990	14547
Ceric Fabrication Co Inc	Ayer	MA	E	978 772-9034	7915
Computron Metal Products Inc	Whitman	MA	F	781 447-2265	16921
Crocker Architectural Shtmtl	North Oxford	MA	E	508 987-9900	13970
Ctr Enterprises	Haverhill	MA	G	978 794-2093	11420
D J Fabricators Inc	Ipswich	MA	F	978 356-0228	11914
Doranco Inc	Attleboro	MA	G	508 236-0290	7727
Dosco Sheet Metal and Mfg	Millbury	MA	G	508 865-9998	13162
Fabco Mfg Inc	Hudson	MA	E	978 568-8519	11773
Fabtron Corporation	Waltham	MA	E	781 891-4430	16106
G T R Manufacturing Corp	Brockton	MA	D	508 588-3240	9148
Horizon Sheet Metal Inc	Springfield	MA	D	413 734-6966	15477
Howard Products Incorporated	Worcester	MA	F	508 757-2440	17390
Ideas Inc	Lowell	MA	G	978 453-6864	12382
Lectro Engineering Inc	Waltham	MA	F	781 891-9640	16144
Mc Garvin Engineering Co	Lowell	MA	F	978 454-2741	12405
Metal Tronics Inc	Georgetown	MA	E	978 659-6960	11146
Metalcrafters Inc	Methuen	MA	E	978 683-7097	13036
New England Fab Mtls Inc	Leominster	MA	E	978 466-7823	12170
P G L Industries Inc	Swansea	MA	E	508 679-8845	15712
Polaris Sheet Metal Inc	Gloucester	MA	G	978 281-5644	11203
Precise Industries Inc	Lowell	MA	E	978 453-8490	12424
Precision Engineering Inc	Uxbridge	MA	E	508 278-5700	15928
Precision Industrial Metals	Hudson	MA	G	978 562-1800	11807
Profab Metal Products Inc	Lynn	MA	E	781 599-8500	12535
Quality Metal Craft Inc	Quincy	MA	G	617 479-7374	14649
Roland Teiner Company Inc	Everett	MA	F	617 387-7800	10628
Southbridge Shtmtl Works Inc	Sturbridge	MA	E	508 347-7800	15647
Taunton Stove Company Inc	North Dighton	MA	E	508 823-0786	13937
Technical Metal Fabricators	Mendon	MA	F	508 473-2223	12996
Teltron Engineering Inc	Foxboro	MA	F	508 543-6600	10906
Trijay Inc	Westford	MA	G	978 692-6104	16798
Collins Sheet Metal Inc	Berwick	ME	F	207 384-4428	5708
Down East Shtmtl & Certif Wldg	Brewer	ME	G	207 989-3443	5795
DSM Metal Fabrication Inc	Biddeford	ME	E	207 282-6740	5729
Atlantic Air Products Mfg LLC	Bow	NH	F	603 410-3900	17707
Dgf Indstrial Innvations Group	Gilford	NH	F	603 528-6591	18185
Garvin Industries Inc	Auburn	NH	G	603 647-5410	17610
H&H Custom Metal Fabg Inc	Plaistow	NH	G	603 382-2818	19518
H&M Metals LLC	Amherst	NH	D	603 889-8320	17568
Macy Industries Inc	Hooksett	NH	E	603 623-5568	18353
Nashua Fabrication Co Inc	Hudson	NH	F	603 889-2181	18418
New Hampshire Precision Met **(PA)**	Londonderry	NH	E	603 668-6777	18727
Nhp Stratham Inc	Londonderry	NH	E	603 668-6777	18728
Omni Metals Company Inc	Somersworth	NH	E	603 692-6664	19845
Poole Sheet Metal & Wldg Inc	Brentwood	NH	G	603 679-3860	17755
Ran/All Metal Technology Inc	Hooksett	NH	G	603 668-1907	18357
Sweeney Metal Fabricators Inc	Nashua	NH	F	603 881-8720	19268
Rhode Island Ventilating Co	Cumberland	RI	F	401 723-8920	20341
Nsa Industries LLC **(PA)**	Saint Johnsbury	VT	C	802 748-5007	22393
Sheet Metal Design	Essex Junction	VT	G	802 288-9700	21960

SHEETING: Laminated Plastic

	CITY	ST	EMP	PHONE	ENTRY #
Bixby International Corp	Newburyport	MA	D	978 462-4100	13473
H Loeb Corporation	New Bedford	MA	E	508 996-3745	13392
Pioneer Plastics Corporation	Auburn	ME	C	207 784-9111	5591
Neptco Incorporated **(HQ)**	Pawtucket	RI	D	401 722-5500	20863

SHEETING: Window, Plastic

	CITY	ST	EMP	PHONE	ENTRY #
American Marine Products Inc	Charlestown	NH	E	954 782-1400	17810

SHEETS & STRIPS: Aluminum

	CITY	ST	EMP	PHONE	ENTRY #
CMI Specialty Products Inc	Bristol	CT	F	860 585-0409	542

SHEETS: Fabric, From Purchased Materials

	CITY	ST	EMP	PHONE	ENTRY #
Century-Ty Wood Mfg Inc	Holliston	MA	D	508 429-4011	11563

SHELLAC

	CITY	ST	EMP	PHONE	ENTRY #
Materials Proc Dev Group LLC	Wallingford	CT	G	203 269-6617	4769

SHELVES & SHELVING: Wood

	CITY	ST	EMP	PHONE	ENTRY #
Excalibur Shelving Systems Inc	Contoocook	NH	E	603 746-6200	17944
Herrick Mill Work Inc	Contoocook	NH	E	603 746-5092	17945

SHELVING: Office & Store, Exc Wood

	CITY	ST	EMP	PHONE	ENTRY #
Borroughs Corporation	Raymond	NH	G	603 895-3991	19636

SHIMS: Metal

	CITY	ST	EMP	PHONE	ENTRY #
Beta Shim Co	Shelton	CT	E	203 926-1150	3781
Spirol International Corp **(HQ)**	Danielson	CT	C	860 774-8571	1018
Spirol Intl Holdg Corp **(PA)**	Danielson	CT	C	860 774-8571	1019

SHIP BLDG/RPRG: Submersible Marine Robots, Manned/Unmanned

	CITY	ST	EMP	PHONE	ENTRY #
Exocetus Autonomous Systems	Wallingford	CT	G	860 512-7260	4740
Irobot Corporation **(PA)**	Bedford	MA	B	781 430-3000	7985

SHIP BUILDING & REPAIRING: Cargo Vessels

	CITY	ST	EMP	PHONE	ENTRY #
Connecticut Diesel and Marine	Milford	CT	G	203 481-1010	2267

SHIP BUILDING & REPAIRING: Cargo, Commercial

	CITY	ST	EMP	PHONE	ENTRY #
LM Gill Welding & Mfg LLC	Manchester	CT	E	860 647-9931	2020

SHIP BUILDING & REPAIRING: Combat Vessels

	CITY	ST	EMP	PHONE	ENTRY #
Bath Iron Works Corporation **(HQ)**	Bath	ME	B	207 443-3311	5674

SHIP BUILDING & REPAIRING: Ferryboats

	CITY	ST	EMP	PHONE	ENTRY #
Luscombe Ave Waiting Room	Woods Hole	MA	F	508 299-8051	17327
Lake Champlain Trnsp Co	Burlington	VT	C	802 660-3495	21792

SHIP BUILDING & REPAIRING: Fishing Vessels, Large

	CITY	ST	EMP	PHONE	ENTRY #
F L Tripp & Sons Inc	Westport Point	MA	E	508 636-4058	16854
Fv Misty Blue LLC	Bristol	RI	G	609 884-3000	20080
Relentless Inc	North Kingstown	RI	F	401 295-2585	20736

SHIP BUILDING & REPAIRING: Lighthouse Tenders

	CITY	ST	EMP	PHONE	ENTRY #
American Lighthouse Foundation	Owls Head	ME	G	207 594-4174	6561

SHIP BUILDING & REPAIRING: Military

	CITY	ST	EMP	PHONE	ENTRY #
Naiad Dynamics Us Inc **(HQ)**	Shelton	CT	E	203 929-6355	3836

SHIP BUILDING & REPAIRING: Rigging, Marine

	CITY	ST	EMP	PHONE	ENTRY #
Navtec Rigging Solutions Inc	Clinton	CT	E	203 458-3163	790
Ocean Rigging LLC	Bridgeport	CT	G	800 624-2101	460
Maloney Marine Rigging Inc	West Southport	ME	G	207 633-6788	7179
Aramid Rigging Inc	Portsmouth	RI	G	401 683-6966	20917

SHIP BUILDING & REPAIRING: Sailing Vessels, Commercial

	CITY	ST	EMP	PHONE	ENTRY #
Washburn & Doughty Assoc Inc	East Boothbay	ME	D	207 633-6517	5980

SHIP BUILDING & REPAIRING: Submarine Tenders

	CITY	ST	EMP	PHONE	ENTRY #
Hydroid LLC	Pocasset	MA	E	508 563-6565	14597

SHIP BUILDING & REPAIRING: Trawlers

	CITY	ST	EMP	PHONE	ENTRY #
Timbercraft LLC	New Milford	CT	G	860 355-5538	2829

SHIPBUILDING & REPAIR

	CITY	ST	EMP	PHONE	ENTRY #
Bridgeport Boatwork Inc **(PA)**	Bridgeport	CT	G	860 536-9651	387
Dorado Tankers Pool Inc	Norwalk	CT	E	203 662-2600	3143
Thames Shipyard & Repair Co	New London	CT	D	860 442-5349	2782
Boston Ship Repair LLC	Boston	MA	C	617 330-5045	8441
Cape Cod Sailmakers Inc	Cataumet	MA	G	508 563-3080	9810
Deep Sea Systems Intl Inc	Cataumet	MA	G	508 540-6732	9812
Ksaria Service Corporation	Methuen	MA	E	978 933-0000	13031
Northeast Ship Repair Inc **(PA)**	Boston	MA	C	617 330-5045	8743
Ocean Tug & Barge Engrg Corp	Milford	MA	G	508 473-0545	13135
Bath Iron Works Corporation	Brunswick	ME	D	207 442-1266	5830
General Dynamics Corporation	Bath	ME	E	207 442-3245	5677
Robinson-Greaves Marine Pntg	Wells	ME	G	207 313-6132	7164
Rockland Marine Corporation	Rockland	ME	E	207 594-7860	6809
Supervisor of Shipbuilding	Bath	ME	G	207 442-2520	5681
Yankee Marina Inc	Yarmouth	ME	E	207 846-9120	7304
United States Dept of Navy	Portsmouth	NH	A	207 438-2714	19627
Blount Boats Inc	Warren	RI	D	401 245-8300	21289
C R Scott Marine Wdwkg Co	Newport	RI	G	401 849-0715	20659
International Yacht Restoratio	Newport	RI	F	401 846-2587	20666
Northrup & Gibson Entps LLC	Jamestown	RI	G	401 423-2152	20493
Promet Marine Service Corp	Providence	RI	E	401 467-3730	21094
Scandia Marine Inc	Tiverton	RI	G	401 625-5881	21262
Senesco Marine LLC	North Kingstown	RI	B	401 295-0373	20740

SHOE & BOOT ACCESS

	CITY	ST	EMP	PHONE	ENTRY #
Jones & Vining Incorporated **(PA)**	Brockton	MA	E	508 232-7470	9158

SHOE & BOOT MATERIALS: Heels, Leather Or Wood

	CITY	ST	EMP	PHONE	ENTRY #
Montello Heel Mfg Inc	Brockton	MA	E	508 586-0603	9167

SHOE & BOOT MATERIALS: Soles, Exc Rubber, Plastic, NEC

	CITY	ST	EMP	PHONE	ENTRY #
Leisure Manufacturing	Haverhill	MA	F	978 373-3831	11448
Twin Leather Co Inc	West Bridgewater	MA	G	508 583-3485	16461

SHOE MAKING & REPAIRING MACHINERY

	CITY	ST	EMP	PHONE	ENTRY #
American & Schoen Machinery Co	Beverly	MA	E	978 524-0168	8098

SHOE MATERIALS: Body Parts, Outers

	CITY	ST	EMP	PHONE	ENTRY #
Vibram Corporation **(HQ)**	Concord	MA	E	978 318-0000	10159

SHOE MATERIALS: Bows

	CITY	ST	EMP	PHONE	ENTRY #
Lunder Manufacturing Inc	Saco	ME	E	207 284-5961	6851

SHOE MATERIALS: Buckles

	CITY	ST	EMP	PHONE	ENTRY #
Weller E E Co Inc/MCS Finshg	Providence	RI	E	401 461-4275	21152

SHOE MATERIALS: Counters

	CITY	ST	EMP	PHONE	ENTRY #
Catskill Gran Countertops Inc	Newington	CT	F	860 667-1555	2852
Top Source Inc	Waterbury	CT	G	203 753-6490	4964
Counter Culture	Saugus	MA	G	781 439-9810	14979
Counteredge LLC	Waltham	MA	F	781 891-0050	16078
Cohos Counters LLC	Lancaster	NH	G	603 788-4928	18599

SHOE MATERIALS: Inner Parts

	CITY	ST	EMP	PHONE	ENTRY #
North American Chemical Co	Lawrence	MA	G	978 687-9500	12066

SHOE MATERIALS: Inner Soles

	CITY	ST	EMP	PHONE	ENTRY #
International Sole & Lea Corp	South Easton	MA	F	508 588-0905	15281

SHOE MATERIALS: Ornaments

	CITY	ST	EMP	PHONE	ENTRY #
Gaynor Minden Inc	Lawrence	MA	G	212 929-0087	12027
Sx Industries Inc **(PA)**	Stoughton	MA	E	781 828-7111	15625

SHOE MATERIALS: Plastic

	CITY	ST	EMP	PHONE	ENTRY #
Macneill Engineering Co Inc	Westborough	MA	E	508 481-8830	16633
Jones & Vining Incorporated	Lewiston	ME	E	207 784-3547	6295
Genfoot America Inc	Littleton	NH	D	603 575-5114	18660

SHOE MATERIALS: Quarters

	CITY	ST	EMP	PHONE	ENTRY #
Middle Quarter Animal Hospital	Woodbury	CT	G	203 263-4772	5489
Furnished Quarters LLC	Cambridge	MA	D	212 367-9400	9484
Healthquarters Inc	Beverly	MA	G	978 922-4490	8139
McManus E Vq Gp LLC	Woburn	MA	G	781 935-2483	17226
Quarter LLC	Boston	MA	G	617 848-1249	8804
Quarter Line Drssge Unlmted	Georgetown	MA	G	978 476-6554	11149
Quarter Productions	Amesbury	MA	G	774 217-8073	7503

SHOE MATERIALS: Rands

	CITY	ST	EMP	PHONE	ENTRY #
Rand Whitney	New Milford	CT	G	860 354-6063	2825
Adra Rand	Acton	MA	G	978 274-2652	7336
Ingersoll-Rand Company	Marlborough	MA	G	508 573-1524	12776
L Hewitt Rand	North Adams	MA	G	413 664-8171	13677
Rand Barthel Treasurer	Mendon	MA	G	508 473-3305	12994
Rand Corporation	Boston	MA	G	617 338-2059	8809
Rand Grantwriting	Jamaica Plain	MA	G	617 524-5367	11948
Rand Kevin	Plainfield	VT	G	802 454-1440	22269

SHOE STORES

	CITY	ST	EMP	PHONE	ENTRY #
Cuero Operating	Westport	CT	G	203 253-8651	5187
Arrow Moccasin Company	Hudson	MA	G	978 562-7870	11756
Reebok International Ltd **(HQ)**	Boston	MA	B	781 401-5000	8816
Vibram Corporation **(HQ)**	Concord	MA	E	978 318-0000	10159
Bennington Army and Navy Inc	Bennington	VT	F	802 447-0020	21663

SHOE STORES: Athletic

	CITY	ST	EMP	PHONE	ENTRY #
Rhine Inc	Weston	MA	G	781 710-7121	16831
Pine Tree Orthopedic Lab Inc	Livermore Falls	ME	F	207 897-5558	6381

SHOE STORES: Boots, Men's

	CITY	ST	EMP	PHONE	ENTRY #
Northern Tack	Calais	ME	G	207 217-7584	5865

SHOE STORES: Men's

	CITY	ST	EMP	PHONE	ENTRY #
C & J Clark America Inc **(DH)**	Waltham	MA	B	617 964-1222	16054
C & J Clark Latin America	Waltham	MA	F	617 243-4100	16055

SHOES & BOOTS WHOLESALERS

	CITY	ST	EMP	PHONE	ENTRY #
Black Diamond Group Inc	Woburn	MA	F	781 932-4173	17133
Modern Shoe Company LLC	Hyde Park	MA	F	617 333-7470	11876

SHOES: Athletic, Exc Rubber Or Plastic

	CITY	ST	EMP	PHONE	ENTRY #
Acushnet Company **(DH)**	Fairhaven	MA	A	508 979-2000	10635
New Balance Athletics Inc	Lawrence	MA	B	978 685-8400	12063
Reebok International Ltd **(HQ)**	Boston	MA	B	781 401-5000	8816
Saucony Inc **(DH)**	Waltham	MA	C	617 824-6000	16191
Callaway Golf Ball Oprtons Inc	Richmond	ME	C	207 737-4324	6781
New Balance Athletics Inc	Norridgewock	ME	B	207 634-3033	6499
New Balance Athletics Inc	Skowhegan	ME	B	207 474-2042	6983

SHOES: Infants' & Children's

	CITY	ST	EMP	PHONE	ENTRY #
Barry Manufacturing Co Inc	Lynn	MA	E	781 598-1055	12491
Tommy Hilfiger Footwear Inc	Lexington	MA	E	617 824-6000	12279

SHOES: Men's

	CITY	ST	EMP	PHONE	ENTRY #
B H Shoe Holdings Inc **(HQ)**	Greenwich	CT	E	203 661-2424	1596
Fisher Footwear LLC	Greenwich	CT	F	203 302-2800	1612
Mbf Holdings LLC	Greenwich	CT	F	203 302-2812	1629
Pvh Corp	Wrentham	MA	F	508 384-0070	17527
Saucony Inc **(DH)**	Waltham	MA	C	617 824-6000	16191
Falcon Performance Ftwr LLC	Auburn	ME	D	207 784-9186	5564
Globe Footwear LLC	Auburn	ME	E	207 784-9186	5568
L L Bean Inc	Brunswick	ME	B	207 725-0300	5840
New Balance Athletics Inc	Norridgewock	ME	B	207 634-3033	6499

SHOES: Men's, Dress

	CITY	ST	EMP	PHONE	ENTRY #
Vcs Group LLC	Greenwich	CT	G	203 413-6500	1660
Alden Shoe Company Inc	Middleboro	MA	C	508 947-3926	13050
Reebok International Ltd **(HQ)**	Boston	MA	B	781 401-5000	8816
Rancourt & Co Shoecrafters Inc	Lewiston	ME	D	207 782-1577	6318

SHOES: Men's, Sandals

	CITY	ST	EMP	PHONE	ENTRY #
Surtan Manufacturing Co	South Yarmouth	MA	G	508 394-4099	15334

SHOES: Men's, Work

	CITY	ST	EMP	PHONE	ENTRY #
HH Brown Shoe Company Inc **(DH)**	Greenwich	CT	E	203 661-2424	1620
Footwear Specialties Inc	Biddeford	ME	F	207 284-5003	5734

SHOES: Moccasins

	CITY	ST	EMP	PHONE	ENTRY #
Arrow Moccasin Company	Hudson	MA	G	978 562-7870	11756

SHOES: Plastic Or Rubber

	CITY	ST	EMP	PHONE	ENTRY #
Black Diamond Group Inc	Woburn	MA	F	781 932-4173	17133
Macneill Engineering Co Inc	Westborough	MA	E	508 481-8830	16633
New Balance Athletics Inc	Lawrence	MA	B	978 685-8400	12063
Nike Inc	Lee	MA	E	413 243-1861	12093
Nike Inc	Burlington	MA	F	781 564-9929	9310
Twin Leather Co Inc	West Bridgewater	MA	G	508 583-3485	16461
Vans Inc	Burlington	MA	G	781 229-7700	9351
Dyeables Inc	Farmington	ME	G	207 778-9871	6045
New Balance Athletics Inc	Skowhegan	ME	B	207 474-2042	6983
New Balance Athletics Inc	Norridgewock	ME	B	207 634-3033	6499
Genfoot America Inc	Littleton	NH	D	603 575-5114	18660
Paclantic Inc	Claremont	NH	G	603 542-8600	17858
Genfoot America Inc	Milton	VT	F	802 893-4280	22129

SHOES: Plastic Or Rubber Soles With Fabric Uppers

	CITY	ST	EMP	PHONE	ENTRY #
New Balance Athletics Inc **(HQ)**	Boston	MA	B	617 783-4000	8727

SHOES: Rubber Or Rubber Soled Fabric Uppers

	CITY	ST	EMP	PHONE	ENTRY #
New Balance Licensing LLC	Brighton	MA	G	800 343-4648	9102

SHOES: Women's

	CITY	ST	EMP	PHONE	ENTRY #
Dooney & Bourke Inc **(PA)**	Norwalk	CT	E	203 853-7515	3142
Fisher Footwear LLC	Greenwich	CT	F	203 302-2800	1612
Fisher Sigerson Morrison LLC	Greenwich	CT	E	203 302-2800	1613
HH Brown Shoe Company Inc **(DH)**	Greenwich	CT	E	203 661-2424	1620
Cardinal Shoe Corporation	Lawrence	MA	E	978 686-9706	12003
Modern Shoe Company LLC	Hyde Park	MA	F	617 333-7470	11876
Saucony Inc **(DH)**	Waltham	MA	C	617 824-6000	16191
Footwear Specialties Inc	Biddeford	ME	F	207 284-5003	5734
L L Bean Inc	Brunswick	ME	B	207 725-0300	5840
New Balance Athletics Inc	Norridgewock	ME	B	207 634-3033	6499
Colby Footwear Inc	Somersworth	NH	C	603 332-2283	19830
Timberland LLC **(HQ)**	Stratham	NH	B	603 772-9500	19876

SHOES: Women's, Dress

	CITY	ST	EMP	PHONE	ENTRY #
Aj Casey LLC	Norwalk	CT	G	203 226-5961	3098
Reebok International Ltd **(HQ)**	Boston	MA	B	781 401-5000	8816

SHOES: Women's, Sandals

	CITY	ST	EMP	PHONE	ENTRY #
Surtan Manufacturing Co	South Yarmouth	MA	G	508 394-4099	15334

SHOT PEENING SVC

	CITY	ST	EMP	PHONE	ENTRY #
Aqua Blasting Corp	Bloomfield	CT	F	860 242-8855	201
Hydro Honing Laboratories Inc **(PA)**	East Hartford	CT	E	860 289-4328	1200
Metal Improvement Company LLC	Middletown	CT	E	860 635-9994	2204
Metal Improvement Company LLC	New Britain	CT	E	860 224-9148	2552
Metal Improvement Company LLC	Windsor	CT	E	860 688-6201	5349
Metal Improvement Company LLC	East Windsor	CT	D	860 523-9901	1295
P&G Metal Components Corp	Bloomfield	CT	F	860 243-2220	248
Peening Technologies Eqp LLC	East Hartford	CT	E	860 289-4328	1209
Metal Improvement Company LLC	Wakefield	MA	F	781 246-3848	15961
Metal Improvement Company LLC	Wilmington	MA	E	978 658-0032	17023

SHOWCASES & DISPLAY FIXTURES: Office & Store

	CITY	ST	EMP	PHONE	ENTRY #
Boston Retail Products Inc **(PA)**	Medford	MA	C	781 395-7417	12923
Continental Woodcraft Inc **(PA)**	Worcester	MA	E	508 581-9560	17359
Stainless Fdsrvice Eqp Mfg Inc	Limestone	ME	F	207 227-7747	6344
Atlas Fabrication Inc	Providence	RI	G	401 861-4911	20961
Herrick & White Ltd	Cumberland	RI	D	401 658-0440	20324

SHOWER STALLS: Plastic & Fiberglass

	CITY	ST	EMP	PHONE	ENTRY #
Trumbull Recreation Supply Co	Willington	CT	G	860 429-6604	5271

SHUTTERS, DOOR & WINDOW: Metal

	CITY	ST	EMP	PHONE	ENTRY #
Shutters & Sails LLC	Mystic	CT	G	860 331-1510	2451
Orange Shutter Studios	West Springfield	MA	G	413 544-8403	16537
Shutters R US	Newbury	MA	G	978 376-0201	13466

SHUTTERS: Window, Wood

	CITY	ST	EMP	PHONE	ENTRY #
Yankee Shutter Co	New Boston	NH	G	603 487-2400	19299

SIDING & STRUCTURAL MATERIALS: Wood

	CITY	ST	EMP	PHONE	ENTRY #
Decks R US	New Britain	CT	G	860 505-0726	2527
Ppk Inc	Branford	CT	G	203 376-9180	338
Heyoka Solutions LLC	Falmouth	MA	G	866 389-8578	10790
Northeast Building Products	Marlborough	MA	G	508 786-5600	12798
Turn Key Lumber Inc	Lunenburg	MA	E	978 798-1370	12484

SIDING: Plastic

	CITY	ST	EMP	PHONE	ENTRY #
Kaytec Inc	Richford	VT	D	802 848-7010	22307
Kp Building Products Inc	Williston	VT	F	866 850-4447	22678

SIDING: Sheet Metal

	CITY	ST	EMP	PHONE	ENTRY #
R G M Metals Inc	Hudson	MA	G	978 562-9773	11810

SIGN LETTERING & PAINTING SVCS

	CITY	ST	EMP	PHONE	ENTRY #
Gemini Sign Company Inc	Marlborough	MA	G	508 485-3343	12760
Bangor Neon Inc	Bangor	ME	F	207 947-2766	5631
Riverview Signs & Graphics	Westerly	RI	G	401 596-7889	21537
Diaco Communication Inc	South Burlington	VT	G	802 863-6233	22446

SIGN PAINTING & LETTERING SHOP

	CITY	ST	EMP	PHONE	ENTRY #
Century Sign LLC	Hamden	CT	G	203 230-9000	1737
Nu Line Design LLC	Wallingford	CT	G	203 949-0726	4779
Signs Unlimited Inc	Derby	CT	G	203 734-7446	1080
Dion Signs and Service Inc	New Bedford	MA	F	401 724-4459	13379
Hassan Woodcarving & Sign Co	Cohasset	MA	G	781 383-6075	10100
W S Sign Design Corp	Springfield	MA	G	413 241-6916	15522
Wish Designs Inc **(PA)**	Lawrence	MA	F	978 566-1232	12084
Caron Signs Co Inc	Hermon	ME	G	207 848-7889	6184
Hammar & Sons Inc	Pelham	NH	E	603 635-2292	19434
Twin State Signs Inc	Essex Junction	VT	G	802 872-8949	21962

SIGNALING APPARATUS: Electric

	CITY	ST	EMP	PHONE	ENTRY #
Trans-Tek Inc	Ellington	CT	E	860 872-8351	1343
I F Engineering Corp	Dudley	MA	E	860 935-0280	10377
Irrigation Automtn Systms Inc	Whitinsville	MA	G	800 549-4551	16915
L3 Technologies Inc	Burlington	MA	C	781 270-2100	9295

SIGNALS: Traffic Control, Electric

	CITY	ST	EMP	PHONE	ENTRY #
Nestor Traffic Systems Inc **(PA)**	Pawtucket	RI	E	401 714-7781	20864

SIGNALS: Transportation

	CITY	ST	EMP	PHONE	ENTRY #
Gac Inc	Glastonbury	CT	G	860 633-1768	1553
ARINC Incorporated	Lexington	MA	D	781 863-0711	12207
Bellofatto Electrical	Revere	MA	G	781 284-4164	14764
General Dynmics Mssion Systems	Pittsfield	MA	A	413 494-1110	14472
Alltraxx LLC	Portsmouth	NH	G	603 610-7179	19535
Worksafe Traffic Ctrl Inds Inc **(PA)**	Barre	VT	F	802 223-8948	21645

SIGNS & ADVERTISING SPECIALTIES

	CITY	ST	EMP	PHONE	ENTRY #
Acme Sign Co **(PA)**	Stamford	CT	F	203 324-2263	4128
Asi Sign Systems Inc	East Berlin	CT	G	860 828-3331	1097
Automotive Coop Couponing Inc	Weston	CT	G	203 227-2722	5169
Barneys Sign Service Inc	Stratford	CT	G	203 878-3763	4396
Belmeade Group LLC	West Granby	CT	G	860 413-3569	5048
Big Prints LLC	East Haven	CT	G	203 469-1100	1243
Bristol Signart Inc	Bristol	CT	G	860 582-2577	538
City Sign	Hartford	CT	G	860 232-4803	1813
Concord Industries Inc	Norwalk	CT	E	203 750-6060	3131
Connecticut Container Corp **(PA)**	North Haven	CT	C	203 248-2161	3018
Connecticut Sign Service LLC	Essex	CT	G	860 767-7446	1395
Dundorf Designs USA Inc	Salem	CT	G	860 859-2955	3738
Fastsigns	Milford	CT	G	203 298-4075	2288
Fastsigns	Bristol	CT	G	860 583-8000	562
Gerber Scientific LLC **(PA)**	Tolland	CT	C	860 871-8082	4548
Granata Signs LLC	Stamford	CT	G	203 358-0780	4202
Horizons Unlimited Inc	Willimantic	CT	F	860 423-1931	5266
Image360	Wallingford	CT	F	203 949-0726	4755
Jaime M Camacho	Norwalk	CT	G	203 846-8221	3178
Jornik Man Corp	Stamford	CT	F	203 969-0500	4232
Lewtan Industries Corporation	West Hartford	CT	D	860 278-9800	5082
Lorence Sign Works LLC	Berlin	CT	G	860 829-9999	94
McIntire Company **(HQ)**	Bristol	CT	F	860 585-8559	580
Mr Skylight LLC	New Canaan	CT	G	203 966-6005	2608
New Haven Sign Company	Northford	CT	G	203 484-2777	3091
Nomis Enterprises	Wallingford	CT	G	631 821-3120	4778
Nu Line Design LLC	Wallingford	CT	G	203 949-0726	4779
Ogs Technologies Inc	Cheshire	CT	E	203 271-9055	749
Point View Displays LLC	East Haven	CT	G	203 468-0887	1258
Prime Resources Corp	Bridgeport	CT	B	203 331-9100	474
Prokop Sign Co	Taftville	CT	G	860 889-6265	4471
Revolution Lighting **(HQ)**	Stamford	CT	G	203 504-1111	4299
Revolution Lighting Tech Inc	Stamford	CT	F	203 504-1111	4301
Revolution Lighting Tech Inc **(PA)**	Stamford	CT	C	203 504-1111	4300
Rising Sign Company Inc	Norwalk	CT	G	203 853-4155	3233
Semiotics LLC	Manchester	CT	G	860 644-5700	2047
Siam Valee	Wallingford	CT	G	203 269-6888	4806
Sign A Rama	New London	CT	G	860 443-9744	2780
Sign A Rama	Orange	CT	G	203 795-5450	3384
Sign A Rama	Danbury	CT	G	203 792-4091	992
Sign Connection Inc	Vernon Rockville	CT	G	860 870-8855	4682
Sign Factory	Enfield	CT	F	860 763-1085	1384
Sign In Soft Inc	Shelton	CT	G	203 216-3046	3870
Sign Wizard	Hartford	CT	G	860 525-7729	1870
Signcenter LLC	Milford	CT	G	800 269-2130	2363
Signs By Anthony Inc	Norwalk	CT	G	203 866-1744	3245
Signs Now LLC	Newington	CT	G	860 667-8339	2903
Signs of Success Inc	Stamford	CT	G	203 329-3374	4319
Signs Unlimited Inc	Derby	CT	G	203 734-7446	1080
Tims Sign & Lighting Service	Meriden	CT	G	203 634-8840	2143
United Stts Sgn & Fbrction	Trumbull	CT	E	203 601-1000	4640
US Highway Products Inc	Bridgeport	CT	F	203 336-0332	502
Wesport Signs	Norwalk	CT	G	203 286-7710	3270
Write Way Signs & Design Inc	Torrington	CT	G	860 482-8893	4609
A S P Enterprises Inc	Newton	MA	G	617 244-2762	13551
Accurate Graphics Inc	Lynn	MA	G	781 593-1630	12488
Ad-A-Day Company Inc	Taunton	MA	E	508 824-8676	15719
Advanced Signing LLC	Medway	MA	E	508 533-9000	12955
All American Embroidery Inc	Wilmington	MA	G	978 657-0414	16970
Allmac Signs	Harwich	MA	G	508 430-4174	11387
Apifia Inc **(PA)**	Boston	MA	E	585 506-2787	8368
B Luka Signs Inc	Taunton	MA	G	508 822-9022	15731
Back Bay Sign	Wilmington	MA	G	978 203-0570	16978
Back Street Inc	Seekonk	MA	G	508 336-6333	15018
C & D Signs Inc	Tewksbury	MA	E	978 851-2424	15809
Cheyne Awning & Sign Co	Pittsfield	MA	G	413 442-4742	14464
Clayton LLC	Woburn	MA	E	617 250-8500	17144
Cole Sign Co	Tewksbury	MA	G	978 851-5502	15811
Colonial Brass Company	Taunton	MA	G	508 947-1098	15737
Color Media Group LLC	Boston	MA	F	617 620-0229	8480
Dahl Group	Boxford	MA	G	978 887-2598	8976
Designflow Wraps Inc	Beverly	MA	G	978 729-5415	8126
E A Dion Inc	Attleboro	MA	C	800 445-1007	7730
E V Yeuell Inc	Woburn	MA	E	781 933-2984	17171
Expansion Opportunities Inc	Northborough	MA	E	508 303-8200	14033
Far Reach Graphics Inc	Needham Heights	MA	G	781 444-4889	13332
Fastsigns of Attleboro	Rehoboth	MA	G	508 699-6699	14749
GAP Promotions LLC	Gloucester	MA	F	978 281-0335	11185
Grand Image Inc	Hudson	MA	E	888 973-2622	11775
Hamilton Sign & Design Inc	Worcester	MA	G	508 459-9731	17388
Idec	Canton	MA	G	617 527-7878	9742
Insite Sign LLC	Duxbury	MA	G	781 934-5664	10399
Instant Sign Center	Norwood	MA	G	781 278-0150	14163
Jack Knight Co	Hanover	MA	G	781 340-1500	11344
JD Design LLC	Saugus	MA	G	781 941-2066	14989
Jim Haluck	South Easton	MA	G	508 230-8901	15283
Jnj Inc	Framingham	MA	G	508 620-0202	10973
JR Higgins Associates LLC	Acton	MA	E	978 266-1200	7367
Keating Communication Group	Canton	MA	G	781 828-9030	9749
Kiwi Signs & Mar Graphics LLC	Falmouth	MA	G	732 930-4121	10794

PRODUCT

	CITY	ST	EMP	PHONE	ENTRY #
Lane Printing Co Inc	Holbrook	MA	F	781 767-4450	11529
Lyons Signs Inc	Worcester	MA	G	508 754-2501	17409
Magic Printing Inc	Framingham	MA	G	413 363-1711	10980
Mark Todisco	Stoneham	MA	G	781 438-5280	15567
Merrimack Engraving & Mkg Co	Methuen	MA	G	978 683-5335	13035
Multi Sign Inc	West Springfield	MA	G	413 732-9900	16533
New England Sign Group Inc	Worcester	MA	E	508 832-3471	17432
New England Wire Products Inc **(PA)**	Leominster	MA	C	800 254-9473	12171
New England Wooden Ware Corp **(PA)**	Gardner	MA	E	978 632-3600	11122
Newman Enterprises Inc	Framingham	MA	G	508 875-7446	10988
of Cape Cod Incorporated	South Yarmouth	MA	G	508 398-9100	15332
Owl Stamp Company Inc	Lowell	MA	G	978 452-4541	12418
P&G Graphic Solutions Inc	Springfield	MA	G	413 731-9213	15497
Paint Town Inc	Palmer	MA	G	413 283-2245	14290
Paulson Electric	Watertown	MA	G	617 926-5661	16305
Pilgrim Badge & Label Corp	Brockton	MA	D	508 436-6300	9171
Pretorius Electric	West Bridgewater	MA	G	508 326-9492	16450
Quick Print Ltd Inc	Chelmsford	MA	G	978 256-1822	9924
Ready 2 Run Graphics Signs Inc	Worcester	MA	G	508 459-9977	17453
Redi-Letters Express LLC	Worcester	MA	G	508 340-3284	17455
Reid Graphics Inc	Andover	MA	D	978 474-1930	7598
Sepinuck Sign Co Inc	Braintree	MA	G	781 849-1181	9036
Sign A Rama	Raynham	MA	G	508 822-7533	14730
Sign Company	Dennis Port	MA	E	508 760-5400	10314
Sign Effects Inc	North Billerica	MA	G	978 663-0787	13864
Sign Post LLC	Roslindale	MA	G	617 469-4400	14843
Sign Shop Inc	Westfield	MA	G	413 562-1876	16730
Sign System Solutions LLC	Hopkinton	MA	F	508 497-6340	11735
Sign-A-Rama	Danvers	MA	G	978 774-0936	10257
Signature Signs	Dartmouth	MA	G	508 993-8511	10277
Signs & Sites Inc	Seekonk	MA	G	508 336-5858	15037
Signs By Doug	Salisbury	MA	G	978 463-2222	14956
Signs By J Inc	Boston	MA	G	617 825-9855	8845
Signs Solutions Unlimited	Reading	MA	G	781 942-0111	14743
Signs To Go Inc	Woburn	MA	G	781 938-7700	17296
Signworks Group Inc	Watertown	MA	F	617 924-0292	16316
Silver Screen Design Inc	Greenfield	MA	F	413 773-1692	11275
Speedy Sign-A-Rama USA	Braintree	MA	G	781 849-1181	9038
Sunshine Sign Company Inc	North Grafton	MA	C	508 839-5588	13965
Tim Gratuski	Leominster	MA	G	978 466-9000	12195
Titus & Bean Graphics Inc	Kingston	MA	F	781 585-1355	11965
United Sign Co Inc	Beverly	MA	G	978 927-9346	8193
Vacca Sign Service Inc	Newton	MA	G	617 332-3111	13646
Vinyl Approach	Paxton	MA	G	508 755-5279	14303
Vital Signs	Newton	MA	G	617 645-3946	13651
Whitney Vgas Archtectural Pdts	Needham	MA	G	781 449-1351	13317
William Crosby	Concord	MA	G	978 371-1111	10162
Affordable Exhibit Displays	Auburn	ME	G	207 782-6175	5548
Affordable Exhibit Displays	Auburn	ME	G	207 782-6175	5547
Amb Signs Inc **(PA)**	Dover Foxcroft	ME	G	207 564-3633	5959
American Nameplate	Brewer	ME	G	207 848-7187	5793
American Nameplate **(PA)**	Hermon	ME	G	207 848-7187	6182
Banner Source	Yarmouth	ME	G	207 846-0915	7292
Bishop Crown Co	Winslow	ME	G	207 873-2350	7268
Finyl Vinyl	Pittsfield	ME	G	207 487-2753	6590
Glidden Signs Inc	Scarborough	ME	F	207 396-6111	6919
Graphix Design	Old Town	ME	G	207 827-4412	6540
Minuteman Sign Centers	Belfast	ME	G	207 338-2299	5694
Pattison Sign Group (ne) Inc	Limestone	ME	A	514 856-7756	6343
R S D Graphics Inc	East Waterboro	ME	G	207 247-6430	5986
Rising Revolution Studio LLC	Shapleigh	ME	G	207 636-7136	6959
Sign Concepts	Portland	ME	F	207 699-2920	6727
Sign Guy Inc	Windham	ME	G	207 892-5851	7252
Sign Systems of Maine Inc	Portland	ME	G	207 775-7110	6729
Signarama Saco	Saco	ME	G	207 494-8085	6858
Signs By MO	South Berwick	ME	G	207 384-2363	7004
Ssw Inc	Limington	ME	G	207 793-4440	6349
T R Sign Design Inc	Portland	ME	F	207 856-2600	6736
Yorks Signs	Skowhegan	ME	G	207 474-9331	6988
Albrite Signs LLC	Gorham	NH	G	603 466-5192	18210
All Signs Steve Main	Hillsboro	NH	G	603 464-5455	18312
Big Daddys Signs Florida Inc	Laconia	NH	G	800 535-2139	18558
Courrier Graphics Inc	Manchester	NH	G	603 626-7012	18808
Dales Paint n Place Inc	Newport	NH	G	603 863-5050	19344
Fast Signs	Salem	NH	G	603 894-7446	19731
Fastrax Signs	Stratham	NH	G	603 778-4799	19868
Fastrax Signs Inc	Brentwood	NH	G	603 775-7500	17749
Gemini Signs & Design Ltd	Conway	NH	G	603 447-3336	17952
Indaba Holdings Corp	Auburn	NH	F	603 437-1200	17611
Ink Outside Box Incorporated	Pelham	NH	G	603 635-2292	19435
J H Dunning Corporation	North Walpole	NH	E	603 445-5591	19394
Loudon Screen Printing Inc	Epsom	NH	G	603 736-9420	18106
Maineline Graphics LLC	Antrim	NH	G	603 588-3177	17596
New England Signs & Awngs LLC	Hudson	NH	G	603 235-7205	18420
Northroad Wood Signs	Temple	NH	G	603 924-9330	19898
Omni Signs LLC	Meredith	NH	G	603 279-1492	18976
Powerplay Management LLC	Portsmouth	NH	E	603 436-3030	19609
Signs Happen Inc	Concord	NH	G	603 225-4081	17929
Sundance Sign & Design	Dover	NH	G	603 742-1517	18055
Valley Signs	Lebanon	NH	G	603 252-1977	18640
Yesco Sign and Ltg Concord	Tilton	NH	G	603 238-6988	19913
Zax Signage Corp	Greenland	NH	G	603 319-6178	18225
B Sign Graphics Inc	Cranston	RI	G	401 943-6941	20187
Dasko Identification Products	East Providence	RI	F	401 435-6500	20403
Dexter Enterprises Corp	East Providence	RI	G	401 434-2300	20404
Elliott Sales Group Inc	Providence	RI	D	401 944-0002	21005
Fine Designs Inc	North Kingstown	RI	G	401 886-5000	20710
Josef Creations Inc **(PA)**	Chepachet	RI	E	401 421-4198	20135
Mastercast Ltd	Pawtucket	RI	F	401 726-3100	20858
Progressive Displays Inc	Warren	RI	E	401 245-2909	21303
Riverview Signs & Graphics	Westerly	RI	G	401 596-7889	21537
Salute Spirits LLC	Newport	RI	G	609 306-2258	20678
Schofield Printing Inc	Pawtucket	RI	E	401 728-6980	20898
Anything Printed LLC	Woodstock	VT	G	802 457-3414	22735
Awesome Graphics Inc	Rutland	VT	G	802 773-6143	22324
Dexter Products Inc	Swanton	VT	G	802 868-7085	22530
Diaco Communication Inc	South Burlington	VT	G	802 863-6233	22446
Great Big Graphics Inc **(PA)**	Morrisville	VT	G	802 888-5515	22167
Green Mountain Recognition	Rutland	VT	G	802 775-7063	22337
Gvh Studio Inc	Bennington	VT	G	802 379-1135	21671
Kerins Sign Service	Montpelier	VT	F	802 223-0357	22151
Letter Barn	Springfield	VT	G	802 885-5451	22505
Sara Sassy Inc	South Burlington	VT	G	802 864-4791	22464
Wood & Wood Inc	Waitsfield	VT	G	802 496-3000	22572

SIGNS & ADVERTISING SPECIALTIES: Artwork, Advertising

	CITY	ST	EMP	PHONE	ENTRY #
Picture This Hartford Inc	East Hartford	CT	G	860 528-1409	1210
Dehaas Advertising & Design	Newburyport	MA	G	978 462-1997	13481
Dg International Holdings Corp	Needham Heights	MA	G	781 577-2016	13328
Raven Creative Inc	Marblehead	MA	G	781 476-5529	12691
Rustic Marlin Designs LLC	Hanover	MA	E	508 376-1004	11350
Ahlers Designs Inc	Pawtucket	RI	G	401 365-1010	20811

SIGNS & ADVERTISING SPECIALTIES: Letters For Signs, Metal

	CITY	ST	EMP	PHONE	ENTRY #
Lifetime Acrylic Signs Inc	Fairfield	CT	G	203 255-6751	1442
Gloucester Graphics Inc **(PA)**	Gloucester	MA	F	978 281-4500	11188
Metal Solutions LLC	Millbury	MA	G	774 276-0096	13171
Lynne Bailey	York	ME	G	207 363-7999	7310
Precision Letter Corporation	Manchester	NH	F	603 625-9625	18904
Twin State Signs Inc	Essex Junction	VT	G	802 872-8949	21962

SIGNS & ADVERTISING SPECIALTIES: Novelties

	CITY	ST	EMP	PHONE	ENTRY #
A D Perkins Company	New Haven	CT	G	203 777-3456	2651
Bay State Associates Inc	Lakeville	MA	E	508 947-6700	11973
Sew What Embroidery	Dalton	MA	G	413 684-0672	10184
Strong Group Inc **(PA)**	Gloucester	MA	E	978 281-3300	11212
Gepp LLC	Warwick	RI	F	401 808-8004	21367
Hutchison Company Inc	North Kingstown	RI	F	401 294-3503	20717
Myriad Inc	Providence	RI	G	401 855-2000	21074

SIGNS & ADVERTISING SPECIALTIES: Signs

	CITY	ST	EMP	PHONE	ENTRY #
ABC Sign Corporation	Shelton	CT	E	203 513-8110	3772
Accent Signs LLC	Stamford	CT	G	203 975-8688	4126
Arteffects Incorporated	Bloomfield	CT	E	860 242-0031	204
Compu-Signs LLC	Plainville	CT	G	860 747-1985	3474
Computer Sgns Old Saybrook LLC	Old Saybrook	CT	G	860 388-9773	3331
Derrick Mason **(PA)**	Norwich	CT	G	413 527-4282	3278
East Coast Sign and Supply Inc	Bethel	CT	G	203 791-8326	149
Jill Ghi	Canaan	CT	G	860 824-7123	688
Rokap Inc	Wallingford	CT	G	203 265-6895	4799
Sign Creations	Southport	CT	G	203 259-8330	4098
Sign Pro Inc	Plantsville	CT	F	860 229-1812	3539
Sign Professionals	Norwich	CT	G	860 823-1122	3291
Sign Stop Inc	East Hartford	CT	G	860 721-1411	1220
Signcrafters Inc	Stamford	CT	G	203 353-9535	4318
Signs By Autografix	Branford	CT	G	203 481-6502	349
Signs of All Kinds	Manchester	CT	G	860 649-1989	2048
Signs Plus Inc **(PA)**	East Granby	CT	G	860 653-0547	1144
Signs Plus LLC	Willimantic	CT	G	860 423-3048	5269
Speedi Sign LLC	Brookfield	CT	G	203 775-0700	658
Wad Inc	East Berlin	CT	E	860 828-3331	1110
Cadwell Products Company Inc	Holliston	MA	F	508 429-3100	11562
Cape Ann Sign Co Inc	Ipswich	MA	G	978 356-0960	11909
Chucks Sign Co	Chicopee	MA	G	413 592-3710	10012
Creative Signworks	Millbury	MA	G	508 865-7330	13161
Cyr Sign & Banner Company	Medford	MA	G	781 395-7297	12928
Dawns Sign Tech Incorporated	North Andover	MA	G	978 208-0012	13697
East Coast Sign Company	Stoneham	MA	G	781 858-9382	15561
Eratech Inc	Ashfield	MA	F	413 628-3219	7650
Expose Signs & Graphics Inc	Hopedale	MA	G	508 381-0941	11671
Harvey Signs Inc	Methuen	MA	G	978 794-2071	13027
Hassan Woodcarving & Sign Co	Cohasset	MA	G	781 383-6075	10100
ID Graphics Group Inc	South Easton	MA	E	508 238-8500	15279
Innovative Media Group Inc	Weymouth	MA	F	781 335-8773	16892
Intelligent Signage Inc	Longmeadow	MA	G	413 567-8399	12334
J K L Corp	Wilmington	MA	G	978 657-5575	17009
J Masse Sign	Plainville	MA	G	508 695-0534	14523
Mass Sign & Decal Inc	Rockland	MA	G	781 878-7446	14812
Mike Gath	Tewksbury	MA	G	978 851-4373	15824
Municipal Graphics Inc	Wrentham	MA	G	508 384-0925	17526
Plymouth Sign Co Inc	South Yarmouth	MA	G	508 398-2721	15333
Serrato Sign Co	Worcester	MA	G	508 756-7004	17472
Sign Art Inc	Malden	MA	F	781 322-3785	12596
Sign Design Inc	Brockton	MA	D	508 580-0094	9175
Signs By CAM Inc	Franklin	MA	G	508 528-0766	11080
Signs Plus	Milford	MA	G	508 478-5077	13144
South Shore Signs	Marshfield	MA	G	781 834-1120	12868
All Kinds of Signs LLC	Wells	ME	G	978 531-7100	7159
Banana Banners	Bowdoinham	ME	G	207 666-3951	5788
Caron Signs Co Inc	Hermon	ME	G	207 848-7889	6184
Carrot Signs	Brunswick	ME	G	207 725-0769	5834
Minuteman Sign Centers Inc **(PA)**	Augusta	ME	G	207 622-4171	5615
Plastics Supply of Maine Inc	Biddeford	ME	G	207 775-7778	5755

	CITY	ST	EMP	PHONE	ENTRY #
Advantage Signs Inc	Concord	NH	G	603 224-7446	17881
Anco Signs & Stamps Inc	Manchester	NH	G	603 669-3779	18779
Barlo Signs International Inc	Hudson	NH	D	603 880-8949	18377
Classic Signs Inc	Amherst	NH	F	603 883-0384	17555
First Sign & Corporate Image	Manchester	NH	G	603 627-0003	18822
Granite State Stamps Inc	Manchester	NH	F	603 669-9322	18829
Marvel Signs & Designs LLC	Thornton	NH	G	603 726-4111	19901
Neopa Signs	Swanzey	NH	G	603 352-3305	19887
Oakridge Sign and Graphics LLC	New Ipswich	NH	G	603 878-1183	19308
Allmark International Inc	Smithfield	RI	G	401 232-7080	21208
Finish Line Signs	Ashaway	RI	G	401 377-8454	20034
Island Reflections Corporation	Narragansett	RI	G	401 782-2744	20641
National Marker Company	North Smithfield	RI	D	401 762-9700	20792
Safe Guard Signs	Pawtucket	RI	E	401 725-9090	20894
Traffic Signs & Safety Inc	Bristol	RI	G	401 396-9840	20106
Artistic Woodworks Inc	Rochester	VT	G	802 767-3123	22316
R & W Gibson Corp	South Burlington	VT	G	802 864-4791	22463
Rule Signs	Randolph	VT	G	802 728-6030	22302
Sb Signs Inc	Williston	VT	G	802 879-7969	22690

SIGNS & ADVERTSG SPECIALTIES: Displays/Cutouts Window/Lobby

	CITY	ST	EMP	PHONE	ENTRY #
Corr/Dis Incorporated	Norwalk	CT	G	203 838-6075	3132
Displaycraft Inc	Plainville	CT	E	860 747-9110	3481
Farmington Displays Inc	Farmington	CT	E	860 677-2497	1481
John Oldham Studios Inc	Wethersfield	CT	E	860 529-3331	5251
S D & D Inc	East Berlin	CT	F	860 357-2603	1107
Acryline Inc	North Attleboro	MA	E	508 695-0060	13742
General Display Inc	Medway	MA	D	508 533-6676	12960
Mystic Scenic Studios Inc	Norwood	MA	D	781 440-0914	14180
Accent Display Corp	Cranston	RI	E	401 461-8787	20171
Orion Ret Svcs & Fixturing Inc	Smithfield	RI	D	401 334-5000	21243
Resources Unlimited Inc	Cranston	RI	F	401 369-7329	20278
Scope Display & Box Co Inc **(PA)**	Cranston	RI	D	401 942-7150	20284

SIGNS, ELECTRICAL: Wholesalers

	CITY	ST	EMP	PHONE	ENTRY #
Derrick Mason **(PA)**	Norwich	CT	G	413 527-4282	3278
Lorence Sign Works LLC	Berlin	CT	G	860 829-9999	94
Redi-Letters Express LLC	Worcester	MA	G	508 340-3284	17455

SIGNS, EXC ELECTRIC, WHOLESALE

	CITY	ST	EMP	PHONE	ENTRY #
Acme Sign Co **(PA)**	Stamford	CT	F	203 324-2263	4128
Vision Designs LLC	Brookfield	CT	F	203 778-9898	664
Fedex Office & Print Svcs Inc	Chelmsford	MA	G	978 275-0574	9898
Sign Post LLC	Roslindale	MA	G	617 469-4400	14843
Triad Designs	Groton	MA	G	978 952-0136	11296
Fedex Office & Print Svcs Inc	West Lebanon	NH	G	603 298-5891	19951

SIGNS: Electrical

	CITY	ST	EMP	PHONE	ENTRY #
420 Sign Design Inc	Norwalk	CT	G	203 852-1255	3094
Adamsahern Sign Solutions Inc	Hartford	CT	F	860 523-8835	1802
Applied Advertising Inc	Danbury	CT	F	860 640-0800	872
Camaro Signs Inc **(PA)**	Yantic	CT	G	860 886-1553	5508
Century Sign LLC	Hamden	CT	G	203 230-9000	1737
Connecticut Sign Craft Inc	Naugatuck	CT	G	203 729-0706	2468
Creative Dimensions Inc	Cheshire	CT	E	203 250-6500	725
John Rawlinson John Leary	Milford	CT	G	203 882-8484	2305
Lauretano Sign Group Inc	Terryville	CT	E	860 582-0233	4484
Pattison Sign Group Inc	Bristol	CT	G	860 583-3000	592
Shiner Signs Inc	Meriden	CT	E	203 634-4331	2130
Sign Language LLC	Danbury	CT	G	203 778-2250	993
Ace Signs Inc	Springfield	MA	F	413 739-3814	15440
Acme Sign Corporation	Peabody	MA	G	978 535-6600	14306
Agnoli Sign Company Inc	Springfield	MA	E	413 732-5111	15443
Apple Mill Holding Company Inc	Pembroke	MA	F	781 826-9706	14392
Architctral Graphics Signs Inc	Watertown	MA	G	617 924-0070	16269
Back Bay Sign LLC	Wilmington	MA	E	781 475-1001	16979
Baker Sign Works Inc	Fall River	MA	F	508 674-6600	10666
Batten Bros Inc	Wakefield	MA	F	781 245-4800	15943
Blazing Signworks Inc	Fitchburg	MA	G	800 672-4887	10812
Callahan Sign LLC	Pittsfield	MA	G	413 443-5931	14462
Design Communications Ltd **(PA)**	Avon	MA	D	617 542-9620	7886
Excel Sign & Decoration Corp	Natick	MA	G	617 479-8552	13255
Gemini Sign Company Inc	Marlborough	MA	G	508 485-3343	12760
Graphic Impact Signs Inc	Pittsfield	MA	E	413 499-0382	14474
Liddell Brothers Inc	Norwell	MA	E	781 293-2100	14106
Mediavue Systems Inc	Hingham	MA	E	781 926-0676	11502
Philadelphia Sign Co	Littleton	MA	F	978 486-0137	12318
Poyant Signs Inc **(PA)**	New Bedford	MA	E	800 544-0961	13442
Scg Signs	Plainville	MA	G	781 297-9400	14534
Sign Techniques Inc	Chicopee	MA	F	413 594-8240	10060
Signs By Russ Inc	Brockton	MA	G	508 580-2221	9176
SRP Signs	Somerville	MA	G	617 623-6222	15220
Sunrise Systems Elec Co Inc **(PA)**	Pembroke	MA	G	781 826-9706	14428
Visimark Inc	Auburn	MA	F	508 832-3471	7851
W S Sign Design Corp	Springfield	MA	G	413 241-6916	15522
Bailey Sign Inc	Westbrook	ME	E	207 774-2843	7181
Bangor Neon Inc	Bangor	ME	F	207 947-2766	5631
Blackbear Signworks Inc	Saco	ME	G	207 286-8004	6844
Northern Signs	Fairfield	ME	G	207 465-2399	6028
Scott Stanton	Acton	ME	G	207 477-2956	5509
Sign Design Inc	Portland	ME	F	207 856-2600	6728
Sign Services Inc	Stetson	ME	F	207 296-2400	7066
Signworks Inc	Farmington	ME	G	207 778-3822	6053
Assured Computing Technologies	Bedford	NH	G	603 627-8728	17631
Jutras Signs Inc	Bedford	NH	E	603 622-2344	17648
Portsmouth Sign Company	Newington	NH	G	603 436-0047	19324
Sign Gallery	Hooksett	NH	G	603 622-7212	18360

	CITY	ST	EMP	PHONE	ENTRY #
Dexter Sign Co	East Providence	RI	E	401 434-1100	20406
Hub-Federal Inc	Providence	RI	F	401 421-3400	21032
Mandeville Signs Inc	Lincoln	RI	E	401 334-9100	20581
Design Signs Inc	Essex Junction	VT	G	802 872-9906	21939
Sammel Sign Company	Essex Junction	VT	G	802 879-3360	21958

SIGNS: Neon

	CITY	ST	EMP	PHONE	ENTRY #
Sign Maintenance Service Co	Bridgeport	CT	G	203 336-1051	489
Countryside Signs	Seekonk	MA	G	508 761-9530	15020
Moren Signs Inc	Agawam	MA	G	413 786-0349	7441
Leon Merchant Signs **(PA)**	Caribou	ME	G	207 498-2475	5885
Neokraft Signs Inc	Lewiston	ME	E	207 782-9654	6310

SILICON WAFERS: Chemically Doped

	CITY	ST	EMP	PHONE	ENTRY #
Soitec Usa Inc **(HQ)**	Gloucester	MA	F	978 531-2222	11210

SILICONE RESINS

	CITY	ST	EMP	PHONE	ENTRY #
MTI Polyexe Corporation	Brentwood	NH	F	603 778-1449	17752

SILICONES

	CITY	ST	EMP	PHONE	ENTRY #
Legu Tool and Mold LLC	Sanford	ME	G	207 850-1450	6879

SILK SCREEN DESIGN SVCS

	CITY	ST	EMP	PHONE	ENTRY #
TSS & A Inc	Prospect	CT	F	800 633-3536	3599
Light Metal Platers LLC	Waltham	MA	E	781 899-8855	16145
Spray Maine Inc	Newburyport	MA	F	207 384-2273	13535
Universal Screening Studio Inc	Everett	MA	G	617 387-1832	10633
BBH Apparel	Boothbay Harbor	ME	F	207 633-0601	5783
DVE Manufacturing Inc	Lewiston	ME	E	207 783-9895	6284
Granite State Finishing Inc	Nashua	NH	G	603 880-4130	19171
Pf Pro Fnshg Silkscreening Inc	Hampstead	NH	G	603 329-8344	18248
Rapid Finishing Corp	Nashua	NH	E	603 889-4234	19244

SILO STAVES: Concrete Or Cast Stone

	CITY	ST	EMP	PHONE	ENTRY #
M G A Cast Stone Inc	Oxford	ME	E	207 926-5993	6569

SILVERSMITHS

	CITY	ST	EMP	PHONE	ENTRY #
Roger Jette Silversmiths Inc	North Attleboro	MA	G	508 695-5555	13776

SILVERWARE

	CITY	ST	EMP	PHONE	ENTRY #
Boardman Silversmiths Inc	Wallingford	CT	F	203 265-9978	4710
J T Inman Co Inc	Attleboro Falls	MA	E	508 226-0080	7814

SILVERWARE & PLATED WARE

	CITY	ST	EMP	PHONE	ENTRY #
Silversmith Inc	Greenwich	CT	G	203 869-4244	1649

SILVERWARE REPLATING & REPAIR SVCS

	CITY	ST	EMP	PHONE	ENTRY #
Rsj LLC	North Attleboro	MA	G	508 695-5555	13777

SILVERWARE, NEC

	CITY	ST	EMP	PHONE	ENTRY #
Good Taste LLC	Amesbury	MA	G	978 388-4026	7487

SILVERWARE, STERLING SILVER

	CITY	ST	EMP	PHONE	ENTRY #
Greenfield Silver Inc **(PA)**	Greenfield	MA	D	413 774-2774	11262
Syratech Acquisition Corp **(HQ)**	Medford	MA	C	781 539-0100	12949

SIMULATORS: Flight

	CITY	ST	EMP	PHONE	ENTRY #
North Andover Flight Academy	North Andover	MA	G	978 689-7600	13720

SINK TOPS, PLASTIC LAMINATED

	CITY	ST	EMP	PHONE	ENTRY #
East Hartford Lamination Co	Glastonbury	CT	G	860 633-4637	1547

SINKS: Vitreous China

	CITY	ST	EMP	PHONE	ENTRY #
Syn-Mar Products Inc	Ellington	CT	F	860 872-8505	1341

SIRENS: Vehicle, Marine, Indl & Warning

	CITY	ST	EMP	PHONE	ENTRY #
Aquatic Sensor Netwrk Tech LLC	Storrs Mansfield	CT	F	860 429-4303	4383
Navico Inc	Merrimack	NH	E	603 324-2042	19016

SKATING RINKS: Roller

	CITY	ST	EMP	PHONE	ENTRY #
Corbeil Enterprises Inc	Bristol	NH	F	603 744-2867	17762

SKIN CARE PRDTS: Suntan Lotions & Oils

	CITY	ST	EMP	PHONE	ENTRY #
Browne Hansen LLC	Wallingford	CT	G	203 269-0557	4714
Playtex Products LLC **(HQ)**	Shelton	CT	D	203 944-5500	3856

SKYLIGHTS

	CITY	ST	EMP	PHONE	ENTRY #
Architectural Skylight Co Inc	Waterboro	ME	D	207 247-6747	7150

SLATE PRDTS

	CITY	ST	EMP	PHONE	ENTRY #
Browns Quarried Slate Pdts Inc	Castleton	VT	G	802 468-2297	21827
Camara Slate Products Inc	Fair Haven	VT	E	802 265-3200	21966
J N G Hadeka Slate Flooring	West Pawlet	VT	G	802 265-3351	22611
Pedro Reese	Fair Haven	VT	G	802 265-3658	21967
Troy Minerals Co	Colchester	VT	G	802 878-5103	21883
Vermont Speciality Slate Inc	Brandon	VT	G	802 247-6615	21714
Vermont Structural Slate Co **(PA)**	Fair Haven	VT	E	802 265-4933	21970
Vermont Unfading Green Slate **(PA)**	Fair Haven	VT	F	802 265-3200	21971

SLATE: Dimension

	CITY	ST	EMP	PHONE	ENTRY #
Quarry Slate Industries Inc	Poultney	VT	D	802 287-9701	22274
South Poultney Slate	Poultney	VT	G	802 287-9278	22277
Taran Bros Inc **(PA)**	Poultney	VT	E	802 287-5853	22278

SLAUGHTERING & MEAT PACKING

	CITY	ST	EMP	PHONE	ENTRY #
Hass Bros Inc	Rehoboth	MA	G	508 336-9323	14750
Npc Processing Inc	Shelburne	VT	E	802 660-0496	22420

SLIDES & EXHIBITS: Prepared

	CITY	ST	EMP	PHONE	ENTRY #
Hemenway & Associates	West Boylston	MA	G	508 835-2859	16417

	CITY	ST	EMP	PHONE	ENTRY #
Vector 5 Collaborative LLC	Lunenburg	MA	G	978 348-2997	12485

SLINGS: Lifting, Made From Purchased Wire

	CITY	ST	EMP	PHONE	ENTRY #
Pauls Wire Rope & Sling Inc	Branford	CT	F	203 481-3469	335

SLIPCOVERS & PADS

	CITY	ST	EMP	PHONE	ENTRY #
Dominics Decorating Inc	Norwalk	CT	G	203 838-1827	3141

SLIPPERS: House

	CITY	ST	EMP	PHONE	ENTRY #
Mary Lee Harris	Castleton	VT	G	802 468-5370	21829

SNOW PLOWING SVCS

	CITY	ST	EMP	PHONE	ENTRY #
Copp Excavating Inc	Durham	ME	F	207 926-4988	5970
E Skip Grindle & Sons	Ellsworth	ME	G	207 460-0334	6017
R & R Lumber Company Inc	Carmel	ME	G	207 848-3726	5893
Scott Docks Inc	Bridgton	ME	G	207 647-3824	5811
Trp Logging	East Machias	ME	G	207 263-6425	5984
Garland Lumber Company Inc	Center Conway	NH	E	603 356-5636	17798
Dexter Service Center	East Providence	RI	G	401 438-3900	20405
Wright Maintenance Inc	Newfane	VT	G	802 365-9253	22189

SNOW REMOVAL EQPT: Residential

	CITY	ST	EMP	PHONE	ENTRY #
Lps Enterprises Inc	East Freetown	MA	E	508 763-3830	10455

SNOWMOBILE DEALERS

	CITY	ST	EMP	PHONE	ENTRY #
Northeast Agricultural Sls Inc	Detroit	ME	G	207 487-6273	5952

SNOWMOBILES

	CITY	ST	EMP	PHONE	ENTRY #
Alfred St Germain	Hiram	ME	E	207 925-1135	6193
Country Riders Snow Mobile CLB	Jay	VT	G	802 988-2255	22044
Crank Shop Inc	Essex Junction	VT	G	802 878-3615	21938

SOAPS & DETERGENTS

	CITY	ST	EMP	PHONE	ENTRY #
Henkel Consumer Goods Inc **(DH)**	Stamford	CT	A	475 210-0230	4212
Pharmacal Research Labs Inc	Waterbury	CT	E	203 755-4908	4937
Unilever Ascc AG	Shelton	CT	B	203 381-2482	3884
Unilever Home and Per Care NA	Trumbull	CT	D	203 502-0086	4637
Alpha Chemical Services Inc	Stoughton	MA	E	781 344-8688	15579
Blendco Systems LLC	Holyoke	MA	E	800 537-7797	11619
Christeyns Laundry Tech LLC	East Bridgewater	MA	F	617 203-2169	10409
Commonwealth Liquids LLC	Fall River	MA	G	508 676-9355	10677
Crazy Foam International LLC	Newton	MA	G	781 985-5048	13584
Dr Bessette Naturals	Ware	MA	G	413 277-6188	16232
Dynasol Industries Inc	Canton	MA	F	781 821-8888	9729
Ecolab Inc	Wilmington	MA	F	978 658-2423	17000
I2biomed Inc	Concord	MA	G	857 259-4410	10135
Just Soap	Ashfield	MA	G	413 625-6990	7653
Spectrowax Corporation **(PA)**	Canton	MA	D	617 543-0400	9784
Starchem Inc **(PA)**	Ware	MA	G	413 967-8700	16237
Starchem Inc	Dudley	MA	G	508 943-2337	10386
Synthetic Labs Inc	Dracut	MA	F	978 957-2919	10368
Trans-Mate LLC	North Billerica	MA	E	800 867-9274	13873
Ruby Moon LLC	Casco	ME	G	207 200-3242	5897
Deborah Ludington	Greenland	NH	G	603 766-1651	18223
Spectral Inc	Warwick	RI	G	401 921-2690	21428
Ark of Safety	West Newbury	VT	G	802 429-2537	22610
Twincraft Inc **(PA)**	Winooski	VT	C	802 655-2200	22726

SOAPSTONE MINING

	CITY	ST	EMP	PHONE	ENTRY #
Williams & Co Mining Inc	Perkinsville	VT	F	802 263-5404	22261

SOCIAL SVCS: Individual & Family

	CITY	ST	EMP	PHONE	ENTRY #
Epivax Inc	Providence	RI	F	401 272-2123	21007

SOCKETS: Electronic Tube

	CITY	ST	EMP	PHONE	ENTRY #
Surface Mount Devices LLC	Stamford	CT	G	203 322-8290	4336

SODA ASH MINING: Natural

	CITY	ST	EMP	PHONE	ENTRY #
American Natural Soda Ash Corp **(PA)**	Westport	CT	E	203 226-9056	5181

SODIUM CHLORIDE: Refined

	CITY	ST	EMP	PHONE	ENTRY #
Kuehne New Haven LLC	New Haven	CT	E	203 508-6703	2703

SOFT DRINKS WHOLESALERS

	CITY	ST	EMP	PHONE	ENTRY #
Pepsi-Cola Metro Btlg Co Inc	North Haven	CT	C	203 234-9014	3050
Company of Coca-Cola Bottling	Waltham	MA	E	781 672-8624	16073
Polar Corp **(PA)**	Worcester	MA	A	508 753-6383	17443
Coca-Cola Bottling Company	Londonderry	NH	D	603 437-3530	18685

SOFTWARE PUBLISHERS: Application

	CITY	ST	EMP	PHONE	ENTRY #
Actualmeds Corporation	East Hartford	CT	G	888 838-9053	1169
Advanced Decisions Inc	Orange	CT	F	203 402-0603	3357
Afficiency Inc	Westport	CT	G	718 496-9071	5178
Breach Intelligence Inc	Farmington	CT	E	844 312-7001	1469
Computer Tech Express LLC	Norwalk	CT	G	203 810-4932	3130
Cya Technologies Inc	Shelton	CT	E	203 513-3111	3792
Enginuity Plm LLC **(HQ)**	Milford	CT	F	203 218-7225	2286
Fergtech Inc	Darien	CT	G	203 656-1139	1024
Flexiinternational Sftwr Inc **(PA)**	Shelton	CT	E	203 925-3040	3803
Golf Research Associates	Stamford	CT	G	203 968-1608	4201
Grey Wall Software LLC	New Haven	CT	F	203 782-5944	2693
Lablite LLC	New Milford	CT	F	860 355-8817	2812
Locallive Networks Inc	Stamford	CT	G	877 355-6225	4238
Mental Canvas LLC	Madison	CT	G	475 329-0515	1968
Microsoft Corporation	Farmington	CT	E	860 678-3100	1492
Mind2mind Exchange LLC	Stamford	CT	G	203 856-0981	4250
Mindtrainr LLC	Stamford	CT	G	914 799-1515	4251
New England Computer Svcs Inc	Branford	CT	E	475 221-8200	333
Open Water Development LLC	Old Greenwich	CT	G	646 883-2062	3313
Qscend Technologies Inc	Waterbury	CT	E	203 757-6000	4948
Rindle LLC	Norwalk	CT	G	551 482-2037	3232
Sas Institute Inc	Glastonbury	CT	E	860 633-4119	1577
Satori Audio LLC	Westport	CT	G	203 571-6050	5229
Servicetune Inc	Avon	CT	G	860 284-4445	45
Swing By Swing Golf Inc	Hartford	CT	G	310 922-8023	1874
Tangoe Us Inc **(HQ)**	Shelton	CT	C	973 257-0300	3878
Telenity Inc	Monroe	CT	C	203 445-2000	2419
3derm Systems Inc	Boston	MA	G	617 237-6041	8328
AAF Microsystems Ltd	Westborough	MA	G	508 366-9100	16585
Accounttech	Bedford	MA	G	781 276-1555	7956
Acenna Data Inc	Cambridge	MA	G	443 878-9292	9371
Actifio Federal Inc	Needham	MA	F	781 795-9182	13290
Adeptis Inc	Woburn	MA	G	781 569-5996	17110
Aislebuyer Llc	Boston	MA	F	617 606-7062	8346
Akamai Technologies Inc **(PA)**	Cambridge	MA	B	617 444-3000	9378
Akumo Software Inc	Boston	MA	F	617 466-9818	8348
Alivia Capital LLC	Boston	MA	G	781 569-5212	8356
Alivia Capital LLC **(PA)**	Woburn	MA	G	781 569-5212	17116
Allure Security Technology Inc	Waltham	MA	G	877 669-8883	16031
American Well Corporation	Boston	MA	B	617 204-3500	8363
Ansys Inc	Concord	MA	G	781 229-8900	10111
Applause LLC	Framingham	MA	D	508 665-6910	10921
Architexa Inc	Cambridge	MA	G	617 500-7391	9391
Aspmd	Cambridge	MA	G	617 864-6844	9396
Aternity Inc	Westborough	MA	C	508 475-0414	16590
Atlas Devices LLC	Boston	MA	G	617 415-1657	8383
Attivio Inc	Boston	MA	D	857 226-5040	8385
Autodesk Inc	Salem	MA	E	855 646-4868	14896
Azara Healthcare LLC	Burlington	MA	G	781 365-2208	9237
Bare Bones Software Inc	North Chelmsford	MA	F	978 251-0500	13885
Basho Technologies Inc **(PA)**	Cambridge	MA	E	617 714-1700	9403
Beanstox Inc	Boston	MA	G	617 878-2102	8397
Bionetiks Co	New Bedford	MA	G	415 343-4990	13362
Biq LLC	Southborough	MA	G	508 485-9896	15346
Biscom Inc	Westford	MA	D	978 250-1800	16757
Boston Health Economics LLC	Boston	MA	F	781 290-0808	8432
Bridgeme LLC	Newton	MA	G	617 310-4801	13573
Bring Up Inc	Cambridge	MA	G	617 803-4248	9422
Cadence Design Systems Inc	Chelmsford	MA	D	978 262-6404	9885
Cambridge Semantics Inc	Boston	MA	F	617 245-0517	8457
Cerence Inc **(PA)**	Burlington	MA	D	781 565-5507	9246
Client Server Engineering Svcs	Boston	MA	E	617 338-7898	8476
Constellation Diagnostics Inc	Cambridge	MA	G	617 233-4554	9440
Crew By True Rowing Inc	Cambridge	MA	G	617 398-7480	9444
Cybtek Inc	Peabody	MA	G	978 532-7110	14327
Datanational Corporation	Pembroke	MA	F	781 826-3400	14397
Dbmaestro Inc	Concord	MA	G	508 641-6108	10127
Doorbell Inc	Cambridge	MA	G	516 375-5507	9456
Drizly Inc	Boston	MA	G	972 234-1033	8510
Elastic Cloud Gate LLC	Natick	MA	G	617 500-8284	13254
Equitrac Corporation	Burlington	MA	G	781 565-5000	9269
Etawiz LLC	Oxford	MA	G	774 823-5156	14260
Evertrue Inc	Boston	MA	E	617 460-3371	8531
Exari Group Inc **(PA)**	Boston	MA	G	617 938-3777	8533
Fis Financial Systems LLC	Burlington	MA	G	952 935-3300	9274
Floc LLC	Pembroke	MA	G	617 823-5798	14405
Fonzy Inc	Dedham	MA	G	857 342-3143	10290
Frameshift Labs Inc	Boston	MA	G	617 319-1357	8552
Galaxy Software Inc	Quincy	MA	G	617 773-7790	14627
Generative Labs Inc	Cambridge	MA	F	434 326-8061	9487
Ginger Software Inc	Newton	MA	E	617 755-0160	13596
Glogood Inc	Cambridge	MA	G	617 491-3500	9496
Good2gether	Concord	MA	G	978 371-3172	10132
Healersource	Allston	MA	G	212 464-7748	7467
Health Helm Inc	Lowell	MA	G	508 951-2156	12379
Healthedge Software Inc **(PA)**	Burlington	MA	D	781 285-1300	9282
Hubspot Inc **(PA)**	Cambridge	MA	A	888 482-7768	9508
Infinite Forest Inc	Cambridge	MA	F	617 299-1382	9514
Infinite Knot LLC	Whitinsville	MA	G	617 372-0707	16914
Informatics In Context Inc	Boston	MA	G	650 200-5110	8615
Intelycare Inc	Quincy	MA	F	617 971-8344	14636
Itrica Corp	Boston	MA	G	617 340-7777	8623
Keylium Inc	Hingham	MA	G	781 385-9178	11500
Keynectup Inc	Wellesley	MA	G	781 325-3414	16369
Kleermail LLC	Boston	MA	G	888 273-3420	8652
Klypper Inc	Chelmsford	MA	G	978 987-8548	9909
Levr Inc	Boston	MA	G	605 261-0083	8663
Lifeady Inc	Watertown	MA	G	781 632-1296	16295
Longworth Venture Partners LP **(PA)**	Norfolk	MA	E	781 663-3600	13663
Luzy Technologies LLC	Boston	MA	E	514 577-2295	8675
Measurement Computing Corp **(HQ)**	Norton	MA	D	508 946-5100	14081
Merlinone Inc **(PA)**	Quincy	MA	E	617 328-6645	14639
Microsoft Corporation	Cambridge	MA	E	781 398-4600	9554
Microsoft Corporation	Natick	MA	G	508 545-2957	13268
Microsoft Corporation	Cambridge	MA	C	857 453-6000	9555
Mixfit Inc	Salem	MA	G	617 902-8082	14929
Mobilesuites Inc	Cambridge	MA	G	302 593-3055	9563
Momedx Inc	Boston	MA	G	617 401-7780	8710
Morgan Scientific Inc **(PA)**	Haverhill	MA	F	978 521-4440	11454
Mysunbuddy Inc	Boston	MA	G	404 219-2640	8719
Netbrain Technologies Inc **(PA)**	Burlington	MA	C	781 221-7199	9306
Nuance Communications Inc **(PA)**	Burlington	MA	A	781 565-5000	9312
Oasisworks Inc	Wellesley	MA	G	617 329-5588	16378
Onecloud Labs LLC	Boston	MA	F	781 437-7966	8749

	CITY	ST	EMP	PHONE	ENTRY #
Onepin Inc	Westborough	MA	E	508 475-1000	16640
Online Marketing Solutions	Lowell	MA	F	978 937-2363	12416
Openbridge Inc	Boston	MA	G	857 234-1008	8754
Optirtc Inc	Boston	MA	F	844 678-4782	8757
Oracle Otc Subsidiary LLC	Cambridge	MA	A	617 386-1000	9603
Overtone Studio Inc	Framingham	MA	G	774 290-2900	10991
Panda Security	Burlington	MA	E	407 215-3020	9318
Paperpile LLC	Cambridge	MA	G	617 682-9250	9606
Para Research Inc	Gloucester	MA	F	978 282-1100	11201
Patheer Inc **(PA)**	Quincy	MA	G	888 968-5936	14644
Percussion Software Inc	Woburn	MA	C	781 438-9900	17260
Plataine Inc	Waltham	MA	G	336 905-0900	16174
Plynk Connect Inc	Boston	MA	G	760 815-2955	8781
Position Health Inc	Reading	MA	G	617 549-2403	14739
Preservica Inc	Boston	MA	E	617 294-6676	8791
Prevently Inc	Cambridge	MA	G	617 981-0920	9618
Promisec Holdings LLC	Boston	MA	G	781 453-1105	8797
Ptc Parametric Technology	Needham	MA	G	781 370-5699	13309
Pulse Network Inc	Norwood	MA	F	781 688-8000	14189
Red Frames Inc **(HQ)**	Boston	MA	F	617 477-8740	8814
Rejjee Inc	Cambridge	MA	G	617 283-5057	9628
Reklist LLC	Plymouth	MA	G	215 518-1637	14579
Right Submission LLC	Newton	MA	G	617 407-9076	13631
Roam Data Inc	Boston	MA	E	888 589-5885	8823
Scheduling Systems Inc	Framingham	MA	G	508 620-0390	11002
Scout Out LLC	Hingham	MA	G	970 476-0209	11510
Smashfly Technologies Inc **(HQ)**	Concord	MA	F	978 369-3932	10157
Spatter Inc	Newton	MA	G	617 510-0498	13639
Standard Molecular Inc	Cambridge	MA	G	617 401-3318	9661
Starfish Storage Corporation	Waltham	MA	G	781 250-3000	16201
Streetscan Inc	Burlington	MA	E	617 399-8236	9341
Synopsys Inc	Westborough	MA	G	508 870-6500	16652
Tex Apps 1 LLC	Boston	MA	D	781 375-6975	8878
Toast Inc **(PA)**	Boston	MA	D	617 682-0225	8886
Toucanect Inc	Boston	MA	G	617 437-1400	8889
Trumpit Inc **(PA)**	Winchester	MA	G	617 650-9292	17099
Vanu Inc	Lexington	MA	D	617 864-1711	12281
Varstreet Inc	Boston	MA	E	781 273-3979	8903
Veho Tech Inc	North Reading	MA	G	617 909-6026	13993
Veteran Software Solutions LLC	Marlborough	MA	G	508 330-4553	12843
Visible Measures Corp **(PA)**	Boston	MA	E	617 482-0222	8912
Wealth2kcom Inc	Boston	MA	F	781 989-5200	8918
Wellcoin Inc	Newton	MA	G	617 512-8617	13654
Wired Informatics LLC	Boston	MA	G	646 623-7459	8930
Wireover Co	Boston	MA	G	617 308-7993	8931
Work Play Sleep Inc	Cambridge	MA	G	617 902-0827	9703
Workscape	Framingham	MA	G	508 861-5500	11016
Zappix Inc	Burlington	MA	F	781 214-8124	9357
Zato Inc	Springfield	MA	G	617 834-8105	15529
Chimani Inc	Portland	ME	G	207 221-0266	6637
Nearpeer Inc	Portland	ME	G	207 615-0414	6699
Rockstep Solutions Inc	Portland	ME	G	844 800-7625	6723
Connexient LLC	Manchester	NH	F	603 669-1300	18803
Eversolve LLC	Windham	NH	G	603 870-9739	20005
Hopto Inc **(PA)**	Concord	NH	F	800 472-7466	17908
Hydrocad Sftwr Solutions LLC	Chocorua	NH	G	603 323-8666	17831
Interactive Systems Inc	Nashua	NH	F	603 318-7700	19190
Meetingmatrix Intl Inc	Portsmouth	NH	E	603 610-1600	19593
Paton Data Company	Merrimack	NH	G	603 598-8070	19020
Pickup Patrol LLC	Mont Vernon	NH	G	603 310-9120	19093
Synap Inc	Dover	NH	G	888 572-1150	18056
Techlok Inc	Manchester	NH	G	617 902-0322	18937
Wind River Systems Inc	Nashua	NH	E	603 897-2000	19287
Kerb Inc	Providence	RI	D	401 491-9595	21047
Voicescript Technologies	Warwick	RI	E	401 524-2246	21439
Zingon LLC	Providence	RI	G	716 491-0000	21159
Cloud Forest Solutions Inc	Bondville	VT	G	802 353-2848	21697
Gametheory Inc	Burlington	VT	G	802 779-2322	21785
Notabli Inc	Burlington	VT	F	802 448-0810	21799

SOFTWARE PUBLISHERS: Business & Professional

	CITY	ST	EMP	PHONE	ENTRY #
Ca Inc	East Windsor	CT	E	800 225-5224	1281
Channel Sources LLC	Brookfield	CT	F	203 775-6464	638
Continuity Engine Inc	New Haven	CT	G	866 631-5556	2678
Criterion Inc	Norwalk	CT	E	203 703-9000	3133
Desrosier of Greenwich Inc	Greenwich	CT	F	203 661-2334	1608
Earnix Inc	Westport	CT	F	203 557-8077	5189
Epath Learning Inc	New London	CT	E	860 444-7900	2771
Fergtech Inc **(PA)**	Darien	CT	G	203 656-1139	1025
Flagpole Software LLC	Newtown	CT	G	203 426-5166	2921
Frevvo Inc	Branford	CT	F	203 208-3117	318
Grayfin Security LLC	Madison	CT	G	203 800-6760	1961
Harpoon Acquisition Corp	Glastonbury	CT	A	860 815-5736	1557
Hypack Inc **(PA)**	Middletown	CT	F	860 635-1500	2191
Innovation Group	Farmington	CT	E	860 674-2900	1486
It Helps LLC	New Milford	CT	G	860 799-8321	2806
Jpg Consulting Inc	Wilton	CT	G	203 247-2730	5292
Kol LLC	Woodbridge	CT	E	203 393-2924	5470
Management Software Inc	Ledyard	CT	G	860 536-5177	1942
Mbsiinet Inc	Southbury	CT	F	888 466-2744	4030
Nexvue Information Systems Inc	Stamford	CT	F	203 327-0800	4259
Nortonlifelock Inc	Glastonbury	CT	D	860 652-6600	1568
Open Solutions LLC **(HQ)**	Glastonbury	CT	C	860 815-5000	1569
Oracle Corporation	Middletown	CT	B	860 632-8329	2208
Polymath Software	Willimantic	CT	G	860 423-5823	5268
Qdiscovery LLC **(HQ)**	New London	CT	E	860 271-7080	2777
Scry Health Inc	Woodbridge	CT	F	203 936-8244	5478
Shibumicom Inc	Norwalk	CT	F	855 744-2864	3242
Siggpay Inc	Norwalk	CT	G	203 957-8261	3243
Stamford Risk Analytics LLC	Stamford	CT	F	203 559-0883	4332
Tagetik North America LLC	Stamford	CT	G	203 391-7520	4341
Voice Glance LLC	Mystic	CT	F	800 260-3025	2456
128 Technology Inc **(PA)**	Burlington	MA	E	781 203-8400	9227
Able Software Corp	Billerica	MA	G	978 667-2400	8203
Accufund Inc	Needham	MA	G	781 433-0233	13289
Acquia Inc **(PA)**	Boston	MA	C	888 922-7842	8337
Adaptive Insights Inc	Framingham	MA	G	508 532-4947	10917
Affinity Project Inc	Cambridge	MA	G	202 841-4011	9376
Alfresco Software Inc **(PA)**	Wellesley	MA	D	888 317-3395	16358
Alignable Inc	Boston	MA	F	978 376-5852	8355
Alm Works Inc **(PA)**	Newton	MA	G	617 600-4369	13560
Anchor Labs Group Inc	Worcester	MA	G	508 500-9157	17338
Armada Logistics Inc	Somerville	MA	G	855 727-6232	15156
Askcody Inc	Boston	MA	G	617 455-2075	8377
Athenahealth Inc **(HQ)**	Watertown	MA	C	617 402-1000	16270
Aviation Edge LLC	Belmont	MA	G	781 405-3246	8065
Aware Inc **(PA)**	Bedford	MA	D	781 276-4000	7962
Bancware Inc **(DH)**	Boston	MA	D	617 542-2800	8391
Baramundi Software Usa Inc	Framingham	MA	G	508 861-7561	10925
Basis Technology Corporation	Cambridge	MA	G	617 386-2000	9404
Beacon Application Svcs Corp **(PA)**	Framingham	MA	E	508 663-4433	10926
Beyondtrust Software Inc	Andover	MA	F	978 206-3700	7540
Biovia Corp	Milford	MA	G	508 497-9911	13109
Blub0x Security Inc	Andover	MA	G	508 414-3517	7541
Blueconic Inc	Boston	MA	E	888 440-2583	8416
Blueday Inc	Boston	MA	G	978 461-4500	8417
Bluesnap Inc **(PA)**	Waltham	MA	E	781 790-5013	16049
Bonapp	Cambridge	MA	G	917 488-5202	9414
Botify Corporation	Cambridge	MA	G	617 576-2005	9421
Buildium LLC	Boston	MA	G	888 414-1988	8449
Casenet LLC	Bedford	MA	D	781 357-2700	7966
Cazena Inc	Waltham	MA	E	781 897-6380	16064
Celerity Solutions Inc **(PA)**	Dedham	MA	G	781 329-1900	10282
Centage Corporation	Natick	MA	D	800 366-5111	13243
Centra Software Inc **(DH)**	Lexington	MA	D	781 861-7000	12211
Cerner Corporation	Waltham	MA	D	781 434-2200	16065
Certeon Inc	Burlington	MA	E	781 425-5099	9247
CLC Bio LLC **(PA)**	Beverly	MA	F	617 945-0178	8117
Clypd Inc	Somerville	MA	E	617 800-9481	15166
Connance Inc	Auburndale	MA	G	781 577-5000	7859
Connectedview LLC	Westborough	MA	G	508 205-0243	16609
Connectrn Inc	Waltham	MA	G	781 223-2852	16075
Cura Software Solutions Co	Bedford	MA	F	781 325-7158	7967
Daedalus Software Inc	Cambridge	MA	E	617 851-5157	9448
Datadog Inc	Boston	MA	G	866 329-4466	8495
Datawatch Corporation **(HQ)**	Bedford	MA	D	978 441-2200	7970
Deerwalk Inc **(PA)**	Lexington	MA	B	781 325-1775	12218
Digital Immunity LLC	Burlington	MA	G	508 630-0321	9257
Digital Paradigms Inc	Boston	MA	G	617 723-9400	8506
Divlan Inc	Cambridge	MA	G	347 338-8843	9454
Dynamicops Inc	Burlington	MA	G	781 221-2136	9259
Eastgate Systems Inc	Watertown	MA	G	617 924-9044	16280
Elerts Corporation	Weymouth	MA	F	781 803-6362	16888
Envvisual Inc	Boston	MA	G	800 982-3221	8526
Era7 Bioinformatics Inc	Cambridge	MA	G	617 576-2005	9471
Erevnos Corporation	West Roxbury	MA	G	619 675-9536	16494
Eskill Corporation	North Chelmsford	MA	F	978 649-8010	13893
Evergage Inc	Somerville	MA	D	888 310-0589	15170
Evervest Co	Boston	MA	G	585 697-4170	8532
EZ Rater Systems Inc	Boxford	MA	G	978 887-8322	8977
Fis Systems International LLC	Boston	MA	G	617 728-7722	8548
Flimp Media	Hopkinton	MA	E	508 435-5220	11714
Geisel Software Inc	Worcester	MA	F	508 853-5310	17380
Geometric Informatics Inc	Somerville	MA	G	617 440-1078	15177
Gotuit Media Corp	Woburn	MA	E	801 592-5575	17193
Graphisoft North America Inc	Waltham	MA	E	617 485-4219	16122
Hubengage Inc	Cambridge	MA	G	877 704-6662	9507
Hycu Inc	Boston	MA	A	617 681-9100	8612
Industrial Defender Inc	Foxboro	MA	D	508 718-6777	10887
Inflight Corporation	Easthampton	MA	G	413 203-2056	10565
Infogix Inc	Burlington	MA	G	617 826-6020	9285
Infotree Inc	Acton	MA	G	978 263-8558	7363
Intelligent Bus Entrmt Inc	Watertown	MA	F	617 519-4172	16292
Intelligent Compression Tech	Quincy	MA	E	617 773-3369	14635
Irody	Boston	MA	G	781 262-0440	8621
Jrni Inc	Boston	MA	G	857 305-6477	8642
Kenexa Compensation Inc **(DH)**	Needham	MA	E	877 971-9171	13303
Kewill Inc **(DH)**	Chelmsford	MA	D	978 482-2500	9908
Kitewheel LLC	Boston	MA	E	617 447-2138	8651
Kronos Acquisition Corporation **(HQ)**	Lowell	MA	G	978 250-9800	12391
Kronos Incorporated	Waltham	MA	D	978 947-2990	16141
Kronos Parent Corporation **(PA)**	Lowell	MA	G	978 250-9800	12394
Kubotek Usa Inc	Marlborough	MA	E	508 229-2020	12785
Leading Market Technologies	Boston	MA	E	617 494-4747	8661
Leveltrigger Inc	Somerville	MA	G	650 468-1098	15190
Life Image Inc	Newton	MA	D	617 244-8411	13610
Linesider Communications Inc	Danvers	MA	E	617 671-0000	10233
Login VSI Inc	Woburn	MA	G	844 828-3693	17217
Longwood Software Inc	Maynard	MA	F	978 897-2900	12900
Macromicro LLC	Boston	MA	G	617 818-1291	8678
Medical Information Tech Inc **(PA)**	Westwood	MA	C	781 821-3000	16872
Mega Na Inc	Raynham	MA	E	781 784-7684	14718

	CITY	ST	EMP	PHONE	ENTRY #
Memento Inc	Burlington	MA	D	781 221-3030	9301
Millennial Media Inc	Boston	MA	F	617 301-4550	8707
Modkit LLC	Cambridge	MA	G	617 838-1784	9567
MTI Systems Inc	West Springfield	MA	E	413 733-1972	16532
New England Time Solutions Inc	Hampden	MA	G	888 222-3396	11322
New Frontier Advisors LLC **(PA)**	Boston	MA	G	617 482-1433	8733
Onapsis Inc **(PA)**	Boston	MA	F	617 603-9932	8747
Oneview Commerce Inc	Boston	MA	F	617 292-0400	8750
Openair Inc	Boston	MA	D	617 351-0232	8753
Oracle Corporation	Cambridge	MA	B	617 497-7713	9602
Oracle Corporation	Burlington	MA	C	781 744-0000	9314
Owncloud Inc	Foxboro	MA	E	617 515-3664	10896
Paytronix Systems Inc **(PA)**	Newton	MA	D	617 649-3300	13623
Peelfly Inc	Everett	MA	G	860 608-3819	10625
Perillon Software Inc	Acton	MA	G	978 263-0412	7377
Planon Corporation	Braintree	MA	F	781 356-0999	9030
Plumriver LLC	Wellesley	MA	E	781 431-7477	16381
Pmweb Inc	Wakefield	MA	D	617 207-7080	15970
Pointillist Inc	Boston	MA	E	617 752-2214	8783
Power Advocate Inc	Boston	MA	G	415 615-0146	8787
Profitect Inc **(HQ)**	Burlington	MA	F	781 290-0009	9323
Proximie Inc	Bedford	MA	G	617 391-6824	8004
Pxt Payments Inc	Andover	MA	G	978 247-7164	7588
Qstream Inc **(PA)**	Burlington	MA	G	781 222-2020	9327
Qualcomm Incorporated	Boxborough	MA	B	858 587-1121	8968
Quality Solutions Inc **(PA)**	Newburyport	MA	E	978 465-7755	13525
Quickdoc Inc	Brookline	MA	G	617 738-1800	9217
Rapid7 Inc **(PA)**	Boston	MA	C	617 247-1717	8810
Redi2 Technologies Inc	Boston	MA	E	617 910-3282	8815
Renaissance International	Newburyport	MA	G	978 465-5111	13529
Revulytics Inc **(PA)**	Waltham	MA	E	781 398-3400	16188
Salesforcecom Inc	Boston	MA	G	857 415-3510	8835
Saperion Inc	Auburndale	MA	C	781 899-1228	7868
Seceon Inc	Westford	MA	E	978 923-0040	16791
Semantic Objects LLC	Newton	MA	F	617 272-0955	13636
Siemens Industry Software Inc	Waltham	MA	G	781 250-6800	16193
Skelmir LLC	Somerville	MA	F	617 625-1551	15215
Smart Software Inc	Belmont	MA	E	617 489-2743	8081
Snowbound Software Corporation	Waltham	MA	D	617 607-2000	16195
Solutions Atlantic Inc	Boston	MA	G	617 423-2699	8854
Sorriso Technologies Inc	Acton	MA	E	978 635-3900	7387
Springboard Retail Inc	Boston	MA	E	888 347-2191	8860
Ssh Government Solutions Inc	Waltham	MA	G	781 247-2124	16200
Stuart Karon	Newton	MA	G	802 649-1911	13641
Symphony Talent LLC	Bedford	MA	F	781 275-2716	8013
Sysaid Technologies Inc	Newton	MA	F	800 686-7047	13642
T Lex Inc	Brookline	MA	G	617 731-8606	9222
Tegos Technology Inc	Cambridge	MA	G	617 571-5077	9678
Timelinx Software LLC	North Andover	MA	G	978 662-1171	13731
Tokay Software Incorporated	Framingham	MA	F	508 788-0896	11008
Toolsgroup Inc	Boston	MA	E	617 263-0080	8887
Touchpoint Software Corp	Sudbury	MA	F	978 443-0094	15669
Triple Seat Software LLC	Acton	MA	G	978 635-0615	7391
Tulip Interfaces Inc **(PA)**	Somerville	MA	G	833 468-8547	15226
Unicom Engineering Inc **(HQ)**	Canton	MA	B	781 332-1000	9791
Unit4 Business Software Inc **(DH)**	Burlington	MA	F	877 704-5974	9350
Uptodate Inc **(DH)**	Waltham	MA	D	781 392-2000	16218
Valora Technologies Inc	Bedford	MA	E	781 229-2265	8018
Vantage Reporting Inc	Dedham	MA	E	212 750-2256	10299
Vaultive Inc	Boston	MA	E	212 875-1210	8904
Vermilion Software	Boston	MA	G	617 279-0799	8907
Vertica Systems LLC	Cambridge	MA	C	617 386-4400	9696
Via Science Inc **(PA)**	Somerville	MA	G	857 600-2171	15227
Virtual Software Systems Inc	Burlington	MA	G	774 270-1207	9354
Weather Build Inc	Cambridge	MA	G	617 460-5556	9700
Work Technology Corporation **(PA)**	Cambridge	MA	E	617 625-5888	9704
Workscape Inc **(HQ)**	Marlborough	MA	C	508 573-9000	12852
Worldwide Information Inc	Beverly	MA	G	888 273-3260	8198
Certify Inc **(PA)**	Portland	ME	E	207 773-6100	6635
Lilypad LLC	Cape Elizabeth	ME	G	207 200-0221	5877
Spindoc Inc	Augusta	ME	G	207 689-7010	5621
Subx Inc	Portland	ME	G	207 775-0808	6734
Trio Software Corp	Bangor	ME	F	207 942-6222	5660
Akken Inc	Nashua	NH	D	866 590-6695	19105
Alignrevenue Inc	Bedford	NH	G	603 566-4117	17629
Bottomline Technologies De Inc **(PA)**	Portsmouth	NH	C	603 436-0700	19547
CCA Global Partners Inc	Manchester	NH	F	603 626-0333	18797
Connectleader LLC	Salem	NH	C	800 955-5040	19718
Crawford Sftwr Consulting Inc	Londonderry	NH	G	603 537-9630	18689
Emerlyn Software LLC	Center Conway	NH	G	603 447-6130	17795
Equinox Software Systems Inc	Westmoreland	NH	G	603 399-9970	19971
Fis Systems International LLC	Salem	NH	C	603 898-6185	19733
Ibis LLC	Bedford	NH	E	603 471-0951	17645
Inspectcheck LLC	Chichester	NH	G	603 223-0003	17829
Lanmark Controls Inc	Hudson	NH	G	978 264-0200	18409
Lcm Group Inc	Nashua	NH	G	603 888-1248	19198
Myturncom Pbc	Lebanon	NH	G	206 552-8488	18632
NWare Technologies Inc	Dover	NH	G	603 617-3760	18043
Peruse Software Inc	Nashua	NH	G	603 626-0061	19230
Protracker Software Inc	Hampton	NH	G	603 926-8085	18268
Retrieve LLC	Manchester	NH	E	603 413-0022	18910
Strolid Inc	Windham	NH	F	978 655-8550	20010
Syam Software Inc	Londonderry	NH	F	603 598-9575	18740
E Sphere Inc	Providence	RI	F	401 270-7512	21000
Ocean State Software LLC	East Greenwich	RI	G	202 695-8049	20375
Oracle Corporation	Barrington	RI	B	401 245-1110	20050
Oracle Corporation	Warwick	RI	G	401 658-3900	21399
Quantifacts Inc	Riverside	RI	G	401 421-8300	21175
Shelfdig LLC	Providence	RI	G	617 299-6335	21121
Aurora North Software Inc	Burlington	VT	E	802 540-2504	21768
Dealerpolicy LLC	Williston	VT	G	802 655-9000	22661
Faraday Inc	Middlebury	VT	G	800 442-1521	22110
Social Sentinel Inc	Burlington	VT	F	800 628-0158	21810
Vermont Systems Inc	Essex Junction	VT	D	802 879-6993	21963
Workwise LLC	Waterbury	VT	E	802 881-8178	22589

SOFTWARE PUBLISHERS: Computer Utilities

	CITY	ST	EMP	PHONE	ENTRY #
API Wizard LLC	Ridgefield	CT	G	914 764-5726	3655
Atrex Energy Inc **(PA)**	Walpole	MA	E	781 461-8251	15988
Gdm Software LLC	Boston	MA	G	617 416-6333	8556
Nortonlifelock Inc	Cambridge	MA	D	781 530-2200	9584
Solemma LLC	Cambridge	MA	G	415 238-2231	9654

SOFTWARE PUBLISHERS: Education

	CITY	ST	EMP	PHONE	ENTRY #
Becaid LLC	New Haven	CT	G	203 915-6914	2665
Hotseat Chassis Inc	Waterbury	CT	G	860 582-5031	4884
Prolink Inc	Glastonbury	CT	G	860 659-5928	1575
Thebeamer LLC	East Hartford	CT	F	860 212-5071	1228
Zillion Group Inc	Norwalk	CT	F	203 810-5400	3275
3wyc Inc	Newton	MA	G	617 584-7767	13550
Almusnet Inc	Woburn	MA	E	781 933-1846	17117
Artech House Inc **(HQ)**	Norwood	MA	F	781 769-9750	14134
Beagle Learning Inc	Boston	MA	G	617 784-3817	8396
Blackboard Inc	Brookline	MA	G	617 713-5471	9195
BRC Development LLC	Upton	MA	G	774 245-7750	15905
Ellucian	Waltham	MA	G	781 672-1800	16096
Fablevision Learning LLC	Dedham	MA	F	781 320-3225	10289
Fein Academy LLC	Swampscott	MA	G	978 495-0777	15697
Inukshukbio Interactive Inc	Falmouth	MA	G	612 916-6606	10793
Jenzabar Inc **(PA)**	Boston	MA	D	617 492-9099	8628
Leaderclips Inc	Wellesley	MA	G	248 808-1093	16370
Lexia Learning Systems LLC	Concord	MA	E	800 435-3942	10138
Lincoln Learning Solutions LLC	Lincoln	MA	G	781 259-9696	12287
Metacog Inc	Worcester	MA	G	508 798-6100	17413
Mindedge Inc	Waltham	MA	F	781 250-1805	16150
N & M Pro Solutions Inc	Lenox	MA	G	413 822-1009	12102
Peergrade Inc **(PA)**	Boston	MA	F	857 302-4023	8772
Rm Education Inc **(HQ)**	Hyannis	MA	E	508 862-0700	11856
School Yourself Inc	Brookline	MA	G	516 729-7478	9219
Skillsoft Corporation	Norwood	MA	G	800 899-1038	14200
Skybuildersdotcom Inc	Cambridge	MA	G	617 876-5678	9653
Texthelp Inc	Woburn	MA	G	781 503-0421	17309
Tom Snyder Productions Inc **(HQ)**	Watertown	MA	D	617 600-2145	16324
Vblearning LLC	Newton	MA	E	617 527-9999	13648
William Sever Inc	Worcester	MA	F	617 651-2483	17504
Bridge Education	Westbrook	ME	G	207 321-1111	7183
Coursestorm Inc	Orono	ME	G	207 866-0328	6553
Limmer Education LLC	Kennebunk	ME	G	207 482-0622	6238
Mathemtics Problem Solving LLC	Portland	ME	G	207 772-2846	6692
Powerful ME	Portland	ME	G	207 370-8830	6714
Eddefy Inc	Dover	NH	G	802 989-1934	18020
Learning Station LLC	Wilmot	NH	G	603 496-7896	19973
Regdox Solutions Inc	Nashua	NH	D	978 264-4460	19248
Skillsoft Corporation **(DH)**	Nashua	NH	C	603 324-3000	19262
Resource Engineering Inc	Waitsfield	VT	G	802 496-5888	22568

SOFTWARE PUBLISHERS: Home Entertainment

	CITY	ST	EMP	PHONE	ENTRY #
Dataprep Inc	Orange	CT	E	203 795-2095	3364
Demiurge Game Development LLC	Cambridge	MA	E	617 354-7772	9452
Homeportfolio Inc	Newton	MA	D	617 559-1197	13602
Izotope Inc **(PA)**	Cambridge	MA	D	617 577-7799	9520
Simpliprotected LLC	Auburn	NH	G	603 669-7465	17613
Touchfight Games LLC	Shaftsbury	VT	G	802 753-7360	22407

SOFTWARE PUBLISHERS: NEC

	CITY	ST	EMP	PHONE	ENTRY #
3 Story Software LLC	New Milford	CT	G	203 530-3224	2785
360alumni Inc	Weston	CT	G	203 253-5860	5167
Advanced Reasoning	Waterford	CT	G	860 437-0508	4980
Appstract Ideas	Bristol	CT	G	860 857-1123	519
Array Technologies Inc	Glastonbury	CT	G	860 657-8086	1538
Art of Wellbeing LLC	Stamford	CT	G	917 453-3009	4144
Ataccama Corp US	Stamford	CT	F	203 564-1488	4145
Automatech Inc	Unionville	CT	F	860 673-5940	4653
Blue Sky Studios Inc	Greenwich	CT	C	203 992-6000	1600
CD Solutions Inc	Branford	CT	E	203 481-5895	303
Codebridge Software Inc	West Haven	CT	G	203 535-0517	5111
Community Brands Holdings LLC	Westport	CT	F	203 227-1255	5185
Computer Prgrm & Systems Inc **(PA)**	Stamford	CT	G	203 324-9203	4170
Coss Systems Inc (not Inc)	Old Greenwich	CT	G	732 447-7724	3307
Couponz Direct LLC	Greenwich	CT	G	212 655-9615	1604
Device42 Inc	West Haven	CT	F	203 409-7242	5116
Dmt Solutions Global Corp	Danbury	CT	A	203 233-6231	903
Dreamer Software LLC	Manchester	CT	G	860 645-1240	2003
Freethink Technologies Inc	Branford	CT	F	860 237-5800	317
Gerber Scientific LLC **(PA)**	Tolland	CT	C	860 871-8082	4548
Graybark Enterprises LLC	Fairfield	CT	G	203 255-4503	1436
Horizon Software Inc	Glastonbury	CT	G	860 633-2090	1559
Information Builders Inc	Hartford	CT	F	860 249-7229	1837
Information Resources Inc	Norwalk	CT	D	203 845-6400	3173
Information Tech Intl Corp	Manchester	CT	G	860 648-2570	2012
Inner Office Inc	Moosup	CT	G	860 564-6777	2427
Innovative Software LLC	Hebron	CT	G	860 228-4144	1897
Insight Enterprises Inc	Easton	CT	G	203 374-2013	1320

	CITY	ST	EMP	PHONE	ENTRY #
Intellgent Clearing Netwrk Inc	North Haven	CT	G	203 972-0861	3031
Microtrain Inc	Newington	CT	G	860 666-7890	2882
Mpi Systems Inc	Wilton	CT	G	203 762-2260	5295
Navtech Systems Inc	Old Greenwich	CT	G	203 661-7800	3312
Neasi-Weber International	Norwalk	CT	G	203 857-4404	3206
Nuance Communications Inc	Stratford	CT	G	781 565-5000	4436
Nxtid Inc	Oxford	CT	F	203 266-2103	3416
Orisha Oracle Inc	Bridgeport	CT	G	203 612-8989	461
Pathfinder Solutions Group LLC	Wilton	CT	G	203 247-2479	5298
Peerless Systems Corporation **(DH)**	Stamford	CT	F	203 350-0040	4281
Pitney Bowes Inc **(PA)**	Stamford	CT	A	203 356-5000	4285
Private Communications Corp	Sherman	CT	F	860 355-2718	3896
Protegrity Usa Inc **(PA)**	Stamford	CT	E	203 326-7200	4292
Qualedi Inc	Shelton	CT	G	203 538-5320	3866
Qualedi Inc **(PA)**	Milford	CT	G	203 874-4334	2345
Richard Breault	Milford	CT	G	203 876-2707	2349
Saleschain LLC	Waterbury	CT	F	203 262-1611	4951
Securities Software & Consulti	Windsor	CT	G	860 298-4500	5362
Shiloh Software Inc	Cheshire	CT	G	203 272-8456	761
Sigmund Software LLC	Danbury	CT	F	800 448-6975	991
Smartpay Solutions	Southington	CT	G	860 986-7659	4077
Software Cnslting Rsources Inc	Goshen	CT	G	860 491-2689	1587
SS&c Technologies Inc	Windsor	CT	G	860 930-5882	5364
SS&c Technologies Inc **(HQ)**	Windsor	CT	C	860 298-4500	5365
SS&c Technologies Holdings Inc **(PA)**	Windsor	CT	D	860 298-4500	5366
Synergy Solutions LLC	Wilton	CT	G	203 762-1153	5306
Tangoe Us Inc	Shelton	CT	B	203 859-9300	3877
Tavisca LLC	Stamford	CT	G	203 956-1000	4342
Technolutions Inc	New Haven	CT	E	203 404-4835	2743
Think Ahead Software LLC **(PA)**	West Hartford	CT	G	860 463-9786	5098
Trinity Mobile Networks Inc	New Haven	CT	G	301 332-6401	2749
Trycycle Data Systems US Inc	Farmington	CT	G	860 558-1148	1520
Yourmembershipcom Inc	Groton	CT	G	860 271-7241	1690
Able Software Corp **(PA)**	Lexington	MA	F	781 862-2804	12200
Accord Software Inc	Methuen	MA	G	978 687-2320	13010
Acktify Inc	Melrose	MA	G	781 462-3942	12974
Aclara Software Inc	Wellesley	MA	D	781 283-9160	16356
Acronis North America Inc	Burlington	MA	F	781 782-9100	9228
Actuality Systems Inc	Arlington	MA	G	617 325-9230	7622
Actuate Corporation	Westborough	MA	G	508 870-9822	16587
Acumen Data Systems Inc	West Springfield	MA	F	413 737-4800	16504
Adanac Software Inc	Stow	MA	G	978 562-3466	15629
Adobe Systems Incorporated	Newton	MA	D	617 467-6760	13555
Advance Systems Inc	Newton	MA	F	888 238-8704	13556
Advanced Career Tech Inc **(PA)**	Boston	MA	E	508 620-5904	8341
Advantage Data Inc **(PA)**	Boston	MA	E	212 227-8870	8342
Agencyport Software Corp **(HQ)**	Boston	MA	D	866 539-6623	8343
Airworks Solutions Inc	Boston	MA	F	857 990-1060	8345
Allocation Solutions LLC	Burlington	MA	G	339 234-5695	9231
Allscrpts Hlthcare Sltions Inc	Burlington	MA	A	800 720-7351	9232
Amcs Group Inc	Boston	MA	E	610 932-4006	8358
Apifia Inc **(PA)**	Boston	MA	E	585 506-2787	8368
Applied Computer Engineering **(PA)**	Taunton	MA	G	508 824-4630	15725
Appneta Inc **(PA)**	Boston	MA	E	781 235-2470	8369
Apps Associates LLC	Acton	MA	C	978 399-0230	7341
Apriori Technologies Inc **(PA)**	Concord	MA	D	978 371-2006	10112
Aspect Software Inc	Chelmsford	MA	E	978 250-7900	9873
Asure Software Inc	Taunton	MA	G	512 437-2700	15727
Athigo	Newton	MA	G	617 410-8834	13564
Atiim Inc	Boston	MA	F	800 735-4071	8381
Atlantis Technology Corp	Concord	MA	G	978 341-0999	10114
Automatech Inc **(PA)**	Plymouth	MA	G	508 830-0088	14544
Avid Technology Inc **(PA)**	Burlington	MA	A	978 640-6789	9235
Bamboo Rose LLC	Boston	MA	G	857 284-4360	8390
Bamboo Rose LLC **(PA)**	Gloucester	MA	G	978 281-3723	11164
Battery Ventures Vi LP	Waltham	MA	A	781 577-1000	16041
Belarc Inc	Maynard	MA	F	978 461-1100	12896
Bigtincan Mobile Pty Ltd	Waltham	MA	G	617 981-7557	16047
Biobright LLC **(PA)**	Boston	MA	G	617 444-9007	8410
Biomed Software Inc	Newton	MA	G	617 513-1298	13568
Blue Cow Software Inc	Lynnfield	MA	G	781 224-2583	12546
BMC Software Inc	Needham	MA	G	781 810-4494	13294
Bombich Software Inc	Longmeadow	MA	G	413 935-2300	12331
Bonami Software Corporation	Acton	MA	G	978 264-6641	7346
Boston Software Corp	Needham Heights	MA	F	781 449-8585	13320
Boxever US Inc	Boston	MA	E	617 599-2420	8443
Bullhorn Inc **(PA)**	Boston	MA	C	617 478-9100	8450
Cadnexus Inc	Woburn	MA	G	781 281-2672	17140
Carbon Black Inc **(DH)**	Waltham	MA	B	617 393-7400	16062
Carbon Black Federal Inc	Waltham	MA	G	617 393-7400	16063
Carbonite Inc **(PA)**	Boston	MA	C	617 587-1100	8458
Cassiopae US Inc	Burlington	MA	G	435 647-9940	9245
Char Software Inc **(PA)**	Boston	MA	D	617 418-4422	8468
Check Point Software Tech Inc	Acton	MA	G	978 635-0300	7347
Cheshire Software Inc	Newton	MA	F	617 527-4000	13579
Chronologics LLC	Boston	MA	G	617 686-6770	8474
Cimcon Softwares Inc **(PA)**	Burlington	MA	D	978 692-9868	9249
City Pblcations Greater Boston	Wayland	MA	G	617 549-7622	16335
Clearway Software Corp	Medfield	MA	G	508 906-6333	12912
Computer Management Cons	Tewksbury	MA	G	603 595-0850	15812
Cosmic Software Inc	Billerica	MA	F	978 667-2556	8234
Covered Security Inc	Boston	MA	G	781 218-9894	8485
Cow Town Productions Inc	Amherst	MA	G	413 259-1350	7514
Csp Inc **(PA)**	Lowell	MA	D	978 954-5038	12364
Cyberark Software Inc **(HQ)**	Newton	MA	E	617 965-1544	13585
Data Plus Incorporated	North Chelmsford	MA	F	978 888-6300	13892

	CITY	ST	EMP	PHONE	ENTRY #
Data Translation Inc **(PA)**	Norton	MA	D	508 481-3700	14076
David Corporation **(PA)**	Wakefield	MA	E	781 587-3008	15948
Davinci Group	Wakefield	MA	G	781 391-6009	15949
Defense Logics LLC	Waltham	MA	G	781 330-9195	16083
Delve Labs Inc	Boston	MA	F	617 820-9798	8498
Digital Guardian Inc **(PA)**	Waltham	MA	E	781 788-8180	16088
Dimensional Insight Inc **(PA)**	Burlington	MA	E	781 229-9111	9258
Dmh Software	Acton	MA	G	978 263-0526	7350
Duck Creek Technologies LLC **(PA)**	Boston	MA	E	857 239-5709	8511
Duck Creek Technologies LLC	Boston	MA	G	980 613-8044	8512
Dynatrace Inc **(PA)**	Waltham	MA	G	781 530-1000	16093
Dynatrace Holdings LLC **(HQ)**	Waltham	MA	C	781 530-1000	16094
Ebsnet Inc	Groton	MA	G	978 448-9000	11288
Eclinicalworks LLC	Westborough	MA	E	508 836-2700	16616
Electra Vehicles Inc	Boston	MA	F	617 313-7848	8522
Emagine	East Taunton	MA	G	508 692-9522	10512
EMC Corporation	Southborough	MA	G	508 382-7556	15356
EMC Corporation **(HQ)**	Hopkinton	MA	B	508 435-1000	11706
EMC Corporation	Newton	MA	C	617 618-3400	13587
Endowmentsolutions LLC	Auburn	MA	G	617 308-7231	7833
Endurnce Intl Group Hldngs Inc **(PA)**	Burlington	MA	D	781 852-3200	9268
Epicenter	Westfield	MA	F	413 568-1360	16682
Erecruit Holdings LLC	Boston	MA	D	617 535-3720	8527
Everbridge Inc **(PA)**	Burlington	MA	C	818 230-9700	9271
Everteam Inc	Boston	MA	F	650 596-1800	8530
Exa Corporation **(DH)**	Burlington	MA	D	781 564-0200	9272
Exari Systems Inc	Boston	MA	E	617 938-3777	8534
Expertek Systems Inc	Marlborough	MA	F	508 624-0006	12754
Extreme Protocol Solutions Inc	Uxbridge	MA	G	508 278-3600	15915
Eze Castle Software Inc **(HQ)**	Boston	MA	C	617 316-1100	8535
Finomial Corporation **(PA)**	Cambridge	MA	G	917 488-6050	9478
Finomial Corporation	Boston	MA	G	646 820-7637	8546
Fitivity Inc	Shrewsbury	MA	G	508 308-5822	15112
Footsizer LLC	Sudbury	MA	G	617 337-3537	15657
Fundtech Corporation	Burlington	MA	E	781 993-9100	9276
G360link	Boxborough	MA	G	978 266-1500	8963
Gb and Smith Inc	Cambridge	MA	G	617 319-3563	9485
Goodrich Corporation	Westford	MA	A	978 303-6700	16771
Grid Solutions Corp	Marblehead	MA	G	781 718-4266	12684
Haystack ID	Boston	MA	G	617 422-0075	8591
Healigo Inc	Boston	MA	G	508 208-0461	8592
Heuristic Labs Inc	Westford	MA	G	347 994-0299	16772
Horizon International Inc	Belmont	MA	G	617 489-6666	8075
Hoylu Inc	Pembroke	MA	G	877 554-6958	14409
Hughes Riskapps LLC	Boston	MA	G	617 936-0301	8609
Human Care Systems Inc **(PA)**	Boston	MA	E	617 720-7838	8610
I-Pass Patient Safety Inst Inc	Framingham	MA	G	617 932-7926	10964
Iet Solutions LLC **(DH)**	Canton	MA	E	818 838-0606	9743
IMD Soft Inc **(DH)**	Dedham	MA	E	781 449-5567	10292
Information Builders Inc	Wakefield	MA	E	781 224-7660	15956
Intac International Inc	Woburn	MA	E	781 272-4494	17204
Intempo Software Inc **(PA)**	Springfield	MA	F	800 950-2221	15479
Intuit Inc	Hyannis	MA	C	508 862-1050	11844
Isubscribed Inc	Burlington	MA	E	844 378-4646	9288
Itext Software Corp	Somerville	MA	G	617 982-2646	15186
JD Software Inc	Salem	MA	G	888 419-9998	14924
Jda Software Group Inc	Boston	MA	G	857 305-8330	8626
Jedox Inc	Boston	MA	G	617 514-7300	8627
Jiminny Inc	Boston	MA	G	917 940-5886	8631
JM Software Inc	Dracut	MA	G	978 957-9105	10361
Jobsmart Inc	Ashfield	MA	F	724 272-3448	7652
Juriba Limited	Boston	MA	E	617 356-8681	8645
Kenexa Brassring Inc	Littleton	MA	C	781 530-5000	12312
Knowledge Management Assoc LLC	Waltham	MA	G	781 250-2001	16139
KPM Technologies Inc	Andover	MA	G	617 721-8770	7563
Kronos Incorporated **(DH)**	Lowell	MA	C	978 250-9800	12392
Kronos International MGT LLC	Lowell	MA	G	978 250-9800	12393
Kronos Solutions Inc **(DH)**	Lowell	MA	G	978 805-9971	12395
Ksplice Inc	Cambridge	MA	G	765 577-5423	9528
Labthink International Inc	Medford	MA	F	617 830-2190	12938
Lantiq Broadband Holdco Inc	Bedford	MA	G	781 687-0400	7988
Lattix Inc	Andover	MA	G	978 474-4332	7565
Laveem Inc	Cambridge	MA	G	617 286-6517	9532
Leftfield Software	Boston	MA	G	617 524-3842	8662
Libring Technologies Inc	Cambridge	MA	G	617 553-1015	9535
Loadspring Solutions Inc **(PA)**	Wilmington	MA	F	978 685-9715	17018
Logmein Inc **(PA)**	Boston	MA	C	781 638-9050	8671
M B S Services Inc	Wellesley	MA	G	781 431-0945	16371
Machinemetrics Inc	Northampton	MA	G	413 341-5747	14011
Magnitude Software Inc	Burlington	MA	G	781 202-3200	9299
Makemesustainable Inc	Cambridge	MA	G	617 821-1375	9544
Materialise Dental Inc	Waltham	MA	E	443 557-0121	16149
Mathworks Inc	Natick	MA	G	508 647-7000	13266
Meddata Group LLC	Danvers	MA	F	978 887-0039	10237
Meditech	Framingham	MA	G	781 821-3000	10983
Mendix Inc	Boston	MA	C	857 263-8200	8695
Mercury Systems Inc **(PA)**	Andover	MA	C	978 256-1300	7570
Meta Software Corporation **(PA)**	Burlington	MA	F	781 238-0293	9302
Micro Financial Cmpt Systems	Medway	MA	G	508 533-1233	12967
Micro Focus Software Inc	Cambridge	MA	B	617 613-2000	9553
Micros Systems Inc	Westborough	MA	F	508 655-7500	16635
Microsoft Corporation	Burlington	MA	G	781 487-6400	9303
Minuteman Software Associates	Arlington	MA	G	781 643-4918	7630
Mobilepro Corporation	Cambridge	MA	G	480 398-0909	9562
Monadnock Associates Inc **(PA)**	Watertown	MA	F	617 924-7032	16302
Monotype Imaging Inc **(DH)**	Woburn	MA	D	781 970-6000	17234

	CITY	ST	EMP	PHONE	ENTRY #
Morphisec Inc	Boston	MA	E	617 209-2552	8712
Moviri Inc	Boston	MA	G	857 233-5705	8714
Murphy Software Inc	Burlington	MA	G	781 710-8419	9304
Myinvenio US Corp	Boston	MA	G	408 464-0565	8718
Netcracker Technology Corp **(HQ)**	Waltham	MA	C	781 419-3300	16158
Netsuite	Boston	MA	G	877 638-7848	8723
North Atlantic Pubg Systems	Concord	MA	G	978 371-8989	10147
Ntt Data Inc	Boston	MA	C	617 241-9200	8744
Nuance Communications Inc	Berkley	MA	G	508 821-5954	8088
Oak Group Inc	Wellesley	MA	E	781 943-2200	16377
Oatsystems Inc	Waltham	MA	D	781 907-6100	16165
Object Management Group Inc	Needham	MA	E	781 444-0404	13307
Onshape Inc	Cambridge	MA	F	844 667-4273	9599
Open Text Inc	Boston	MA	G	617 378-3364	8752
Openeye Scientific Sftwr Inc	Cambridge	MA	G	617 374-8844	9600
Oracle America Inc	Waltham	MA	C	781 672-4280	16168
Oracle America Inc	Burlington	MA	F	781 744-0000	9313
Oracle Systems Corporation	Lynn	MA	B	781 744-0900	12532
Orbotech Inc	Billerica	MA	F	978 667-6037	8270
Osprey Compliance Software LLC	Waltham	MA	G	888 677-7394	16169
Outsystems Inc	Boston	MA	F	617 837-6840	8763
Parametric Holdings Inc	Needham Heights	MA	G	781 370-5000	13342
Parametric Technology Corp	Boston	MA	G	781 370-5000	8764
Pathai Inc	Boston	MA	G	617 543-5250	8767
Perceptive Automata Inc **(PA)**	Somerville	MA	F	617 299-1296	15203
Picis Clinical Solutions Inc **(DH)**	Wakefield	MA	C	336 397-5336	15969
Planet Small Communications	Lawrence	MA	G	978 794-2201	12071
Pongo Software LLC	Northborough	MA	G	508 393-4528	14044
Pos Center Inc	Quincy	MA	G	617 797-5026	14646
Power Object Inc	Newton	MA	E	617 630-5701	13627
Power Pros Consulting Group	South Easton	MA	G	508 238-6629	15287
Power Steering Software	Cambridge	MA	G	617 520-2100	9614
Process Dynamics Inc	Bedford	MA	G	781 271-0944	8002
Progress Software Corporation **(PA)**	Bedford	MA	B	781 280-4000	8003
Protect & Heal Children Mass	Haverhill	MA	G	978 374-8304	11462
Psyton Software	Chestnut Hill	MA	G	617 308-5058	9992
Ptc Inc	Waltham	MA	C	617 792-7622	16179
Q-Biz Solutions LLC	Watertown	MA	G	617 212-7684	16309
Quantum Simulation Tech Inc	Cambridge	MA	G	847 626-5535	9622
Quest Software Inc	Swampscott	MA	E	781 592-0752	15699
Quickbase Inc **(PA)**	Cambridge	MA	C	855 725-2293	9623
Quinn Curtis Inc	Medfield	MA	G	508 359-6639	12918
Raw Diamond Inc	Cambridge	MA	G	857 222-5601	9625
Red Hat Inc	Westford	MA	F	978 392-1000	16788
Reify Health Inc	Boston	MA	G	617 861-8261	8817
Research Applications and	Cambridge	MA	G	800 939-7238	9630
Research Cmpt Consulting Svcs **(PA)**	Canton	MA	G	781 821-1221	9774
Riffr LLC	Boston	MA	G	617 851-5989	8821
Rivermeadow Software Inc	Westford	MA	G	617 448-4990	16790
Rockstar New England Inc	Andover	MA	E	978 409-6272	7601
Rsa Security LLC **(DH)**	Bedford	MA	A	781 515-5000	8007
Rwwi Holdings LLC	Wellesley	MA	B	781 239-0700	16384
Saba Software Inc	Burlington	MA	G	781 238-6730	9331
Salesbrief Inc	Boston	MA	G	203 216-0270	8834
Schoolsuite LLC	Great Barrington	MA	G	800 671-1905	11245
Sdl Xyenterprise LLC **(PA)**	Wakefield	MA	C	781 756-4400	15974
Sea Street Technologies Inc	Canton	MA	E	617 600-5150	9777
Securelytix Inc	Newton	MA	G	617 283-5227	13635
Silver Bay Software LLC	Dunstable	MA	G	800 364-2889	10391
Similarweb Inc	Burlington	MA	F	800 540-1086	9338
Simsoft Corp	Westborough	MA	G	508 366-5451	16649
Sinauer Associates Inc	Sunderland	MA	E	413 549-4300	15676
Smartco Services LLC	Taunton	MA	E	508 880-0816	15786
Smartstripe Software Corp	Lexington	MA	G	781 861-1812	12275
Softmedia Inc	Walpole	MA	G	978 528-3266	16012
Software Concepts Inc	North Billerica	MA	F	978 584-0400	13865
Software Experts Inc	Westford	MA	F	978 692-5343	16793
Software Leverage Inc	Waltham	MA	G	781 894-3399	16197
Solusoft Inc	North Andover	MA	E	978 375-6021	13728
Sqdm	Woburn	MA	G	888 993-9674	17301
SS&c Technologies Inc	Burlington	MA	G	781 654-6498	9340
Starwind Software Inc	Middleton	MA	G	617 449-7717	13102
Statistical Solutions Ltd	Boston	MA	F	617 535-7677	8864
Suse LLC	Cambridge	MA	E	617 613-2000	9667
Suse LLC	Cambridge	MA	F	617 613-2111	9668
Suspect Technologies Inc	Cambridge	MA	G	843 318-8278	9669
T I S Software Corp	Norfolk	MA	G	508 528-9027	13665
Tamale Software Inc **(DH)**	Boston	MA	G	617 443-1033	8872
Technologies 2010 Inc	Milford	MA	G	508 482-0164	13146
Televeh Inc	Auburndale	MA	F	857 400-1938	7871
Tibco Software Inc	Boston	MA	D	617 859-6800	8885
Touch Ahead Software LLC	Boston	MA	F	866 960-9301	8890
Tufin Software North Amer Inc	Boston	MA	F	781 685-4940	8893
Typesafe Inc	Cambridge	MA	E	617 622-2200	9684
Unipoint Technologies	Auburndale	MA	G	617 952-4244	7872
Veeam Software Corporation	Swampscott	MA	G	781 592-0752	15701
Vindor Music Inc	Newton	MA	G	617 984-9831	13649
Virtual Cove Inc	Natick	MA	G	781 354-0492	13287
Vision Consulting Group Inc	Holliston	MA	F	508 314-5378	11612
Visitrend LLC	Waltham	MA	F	857 919-2372	16220
Vivantio Inc	Boston	MA	E	617 982-0390	8913
Vizient Inc	Bedford	MA	F	781 271-0980	8019
Walden Services Inc	Waltham	MA	G	781 642-7653	16222
Waters Corporation **(PA)**	Milford	MA	C	508 478-2000	13153
Webport Global LLC	Boston	MA	G	617 385-5058	8919
Webteamwork	Stoughton	MA	G	781 344-8373	15628

	CITY	ST	EMP	PHONE	ENTRY #
Westport Group Ltd	Belmont	MA	G	617 489-6581	8083
Wordstream Inc	Boston	MA	F	617 963-0555	8933
Workday Inc	Boston	MA	G	617 936-1100	8934
Wyebot Inc	Marlborough	MA	G	508 481-2603	12853
Zlink Inc	Maynard	MA	G	978 309-3628	12907
Zoll Medical Corporation **(HQ)**	Chelmsford	MA	A	978 421-9655	9942
Zone & Co Sftwr Consulting LLC	Boston	MA	G	617 307-7068	8943
Zoran Corporation	Burlington	MA	C	408 523-6500	9358
Brian D Murphy	Sebec	ME	G	207 564-2737	6956
BSD Soft Ware	Durham	ME	G	207 522-5881	5968
Carbonite Inc	Lewiston	ME	G	617 927-3521	6279
Tidestone Solutions	Portland	ME	G	207 761-2133	6739
Tyler Technologies Inc	Yarmouth	ME	C	207 781-2260	7301
Tyler Technologies Inc	Yarmouth	ME	B	207 781-4606	7302
Advanced Entp Systems Corp	Salem	NH	E	508 431-7607	19703
Akumina Inc	Nashua	NH	E	603 318-8269	19106
Alexander Lan Inc	Hollis	NH	F	603 880-8800	18325
Allen Systems Group Inc	Nashua	NH	D	239 435-2200	19110
Amber Holding Inc **(DH)**	Nashua	NH	E	603 324-3000	19112
Ansys Inc	Lebanon	NH	G	603 653-8005	18612
Assuretec Holdings Inc **(PA)**	Manchester	NH	G	603 641-8443	18781
Bid2win Software Inc	Portsmouth	NH	D	800 336-3808	19543
Brown Dog Software Inc	Danville	NH	G	603 382-2713	17967
C Sommer Software LLC	Derry	NH	G	603 432-6225	17974
Centric Software Inc	Lebanon	NH	G	603 448-3009	18618
Conest Software Systems Inc	Manchester	NH	E	603 437-9353	18802
Denali Software Inc	Nashua	NH	G	603 566-0991	19145
Episerver Inc **(DH)**	Nashua	NH	C	603 594-0249	19150
Expedience Software LLC	Manchester	NH	E	978 378-5330	18821
Infinizone Corp	Hollis	NH	F	603 465-2917	18333
Intouch Software	West Lebanon	NH	G	603 643-1952	19954
Itag LLC	Merrimack	NH	F	603 429-8436	19008
Kana Software Inc	Bedford	NH	G	650 614-8300	17649
Kentico Software LLC	Bedford	NH	E	866 328-8998	17650
Loyalty Builders Inc **(PA)**	Portsmouth	NH	F	603 610-8800	19590
Mapleleaf Software Inc	Londonderry	NH	G	603 413-0419	18717
Narrative 1 Software LLC	Plymouth	NH	G	603 968-2233	19529
Newmarket Software Systems	Portsmouth	NH	G	603 436-7500	19601
Noblespirit Entp Sftwr LLC	Pittsfield	NH	G	603 435-8218	19504
Ntp Software of Ca Inc **(PA)**	Nashua	NH	G	603 641-6937	19221
Omada Technologies LLC	Portsmouth	NH	G	603 944-7124	19602
Oracle Corporation	Manchester	NH	E	603 668-4998	18896
Oracle Systems Corporation	Nashua	NH	B	603 897-3000	19225
Perimeter Acquisition Corp **(HQ)**	Manchester	NH	F	603 645-1616	18900
Phario Solution	Nashua	NH	G	603 821-3804	19232
Premier Packaging LLC	Hooksett	NH	G	603 485-7465	18354
Professnal Sftwr For Nrses Inc	Amherst	NH	F	800 889-7627	17582
Profitkey International Inc	Salem	NH	E	603 898-9800	19760
River City Software LLC	Exeter	NH	G	603 686-5525	18130
Ssi Investments I Limited **(DH)**	Nashua	NH	G	603 324-3000	19265
Ssi Investments II Limited	Nashua	NH	A	603 324-3000	19266
Sungard Insurance Systems Inc	Manchester	NH	G	603 641-3636	18933
Teameda Inc	Manchester	NH	G	603 656-5200	18936
Thunderbolt Innovation LLC	Dover	NH	G	888 335-6234	18060
Tyler Technologies Inc	Merrimack	NH	E	603 578-6745	19038
Tyler Technologies Inc	Manchester	NH	G	800 288-8167	18943
Andera Inc	Providence	RI	D	401 621-7900	20953
Ansys Inc	Providence	RI	G	401 455-1955	20955
Avtech Software Inc **(PA)**	Warren	RI	E	401 628-1600	21287
Forensicsoft Inc	East Greenwich	RI	G	401 489-7559	20367
Igt Global Solutions Corp	West Greenwich	RI	E	401 392-7025	21456
Opal Data Technology Inc	Providence	RI	G	401 435-0033	21085
Open SRC Prjct Fr Ntwk Dt ACS	Narragansett	RI	G	401 284-1304	20644
Schneider Electric It Corp **(DH)**	West Kingston	RI	A	401 789-5735	21471
Simpatico Software Systems	Barrington	RI	F	401 246-1358	20055
Smiths Detection Inc	Middletown	RI	F	401 848-7678	20632
Tap Technologies Inc	Narragansett	RI	G	860 333-7834	20652
Bennington Microtchnlgy Center	North Bennington	VT	G	802 442-8975	22209
Concepts Eti Inc	White River Junction	VT	D	802 296-2321	22637
Concepts Nrec LLC **(PA)**	White River Junction	VT	D	802 296-2321	22638
Conix Systems **(PA)**	Pawlet	VT	G	800 332-1899	22256
Core Value Software	Norwich	VT	F	802 473-3147	22247
Gary F Girome	Milton	VT	G	802 893-7870	22128
Jamison Computer Services	Saint Albans	VT	G	802 527-9758	22370
Mach 7 Technologies Inc	South Burlington	VT	F	802 861-7745	22452
Mediware/Synergy Human & Socia	Essex Junction	VT	D	802 878-8514	21949
Natworks Inc	Northfield	VT	F	802 485-6818	22244
Piematrix Inc	Burlington	VT	F	802 318-4891	21803
Richard Akerboom	White River Junction	VT	G	802 291-6116	22642
Thinkmd Inc	Burlington	VT	G	802 734-7993	21812
Visible Electrophysiology LLC	Colchester	VT	F	802 847-4539	21889

SOFTWARE PUBLISHERS: Operating Systems

	CITY	ST	EMP	PHONE	ENTRY #
Agencyport Software Corp	Farmington	CT	G	860 674-6135	1464
Mvp Systems Software Inc	Unionville	CT	F	860 269-3112	4659
Oracle America Inc	Stamford	CT	D	203 703-3000	4273
All Around Active Co	Boxford	MA	G	978 561-1033	8973
Cusa Technologies Inc	Mansfield	MA	E	508 339-7675	12626
Dynatrace International LLC **(DH)**	Waltham	MA	G	781 530-1000	16095
Red Hat Inc	Westford	MA	F	978 692-3113	16789
Standard Machines Inc	Newburyport	MA	G	978 462-4999	13536
VMS Software Inc	Bolton	MA	G	978 451-0110	8324
SDC Solutions Inc	Bedford	NH	E	603 629-4242	17661

SOFTWARE PUBLISHERS: Publisher's

Company	CITY	ST	EMP	PHONE	ENTRY #
Radical Computing Corporation	Newington	CT	G	860 953-0240	2897
Uniworld Bus Publications Inc	Darien	CT	G	201 384-4900	1036
Aries Systems Corporation	North Andover	MA	E	978 975-7570	13691
Boston Commerce Inc	Boston	MA	G	617 782-8998	8429
Boxcar Media LLC	North Adams	MA	E	413 663-3384	13670
Dg3 Group America Inc	Woburn	MA	G	617 241-5600	17167
Nexthink Inc	Boston	MA	E	617 576-2005	8736
Quadrant LLC	Mansfield	MA	E	508 594-2700	12654
Sophic Alliance Inc	East Falmouth	MA	G	508 495-3801	10449
Teletypesetting Company Inc	Boston	MA	F	617 542-6220	8877
CNi Corp	Milford	NH	G	603 249-5075	19050
Upper Access Inc	Hinesburg	VT	G	802 482-2988	22032

SOFTWARE PUBLISHERS: Word Processing

Company	CITY	ST	EMP	PHONE	ENTRY #
Mindstorm Technologies Inc	Brookline	MA	G	781 642-1700	9209
Autovirt Inc	Nashua	NH	G	603 546-2900	19119

SOIL CONDITIONERS

Company	CITY	ST	EMP	PHONE	ENTRY #
Green Mountain Compost	Williston	VT	G	802 660-4949	22672

SOLAR CELLS

Company	CITY	ST	EMP	PHONE	ENTRY #
Fidelux Lighting LLC **(HQ)**	Hartford	CT	F	860 436-5000	1821
1366 Technologies Inc	Bedford	MA	F	781 861-1611	7955
Heila Technologies Inc	Somerville	MA	G	954 829-4839	15181
Spire Corporation **(PA)**	Billerica	MA	B	978 584-3958	8297
Vanguard Solar Inc	Sudbury	MA	G	508 361-1463	15671
4power LLC	Salem	NH	G	617 299-0068	19701
Gosolar NH LLC	Barrington	NH	E	603 948-1189	17618
Enow Inc	Warwick	RI	F	401 732-7080	21360
Powerdocks LLC	Bristol	RI	G	401 253-3103	20099
Allearth Renewables Inc	Williston	VT	E	802 872-9600	22654

SOLAR HEATING EQPT

Company	CITY	ST	EMP	PHONE	ENTRY #
Allgreenit LLC	Bristol	CT	G	860 516-4948	517
Optical Energy Technologies	Stamford	CT	G	203 357-0626	4272
New England Solar Hot Wtr Inc	Pembroke	MA	G	781 536-8633	14419
Real Goods Solar Inc	New Bedford	MA	C	508 992-1416	13444
Spire Solar Inc	Bedford	MA	C	781 275-6000	8009
Sunborne Energy Technologies	Cambridge	MA	G	617 234-7000	9663
Sunfield Solar	Spencer	MA	G	508 885-3300	15437
Trinity Heating & Air Inc	West Wareham	MA	D	508 291-0007	16577
GS Inc	Rockland	ME	G	207 593-7730	6797

SOLDERING EQPT: Electrical, Exc Handheld

Company	CITY	ST	EMP	PHONE	ENTRY #
Air-Vac Engineering Co Inc **(PA)**	Seymour	CT	E	203 888-9900	3748
Systems and Tech Intl Inc	Tolland	CT	G	860 871-0401	4553
Contact Inc	Edgecomb	ME	G	207 882-6116	6001
Donald G Lockard	Westerly	RI	G	401 965-3182	21523

SOLDERING SVC: Jewelry

Company	CITY	ST	EMP	PHONE	ENTRY #
Fisk Industries Inc	Attleboro Falls	MA	G	508 695-3661	7813

SOLDERS

Company	CITY	ST	EMP	PHONE	ENTRY #
Alent USA Holding Inc	Waterbury	CT	B	203 575-5727	4839
Torrey S Crane Company	Plantsville	CT	E	860 628-4778	3543
American Iron & Metal USA Inc **(HQ)**	Cranston	RI	E	401 463-5605	20178

SOLENOIDS

Company	CITY	ST	EMP	PHONE	ENTRY #
Able Coil and Electronics Co	Bolton	CT	E	860 646-5686	273
Bicron Electronics Company **(PA)**	Torrington	CT	D	860 482-2524	4566

SOLES, BOOT OR SHOE: Plastic

Company	CITY	ST	EMP	PHONE	ENTRY #
Polyworks LLC	North Smithfield	RI	E	401 769-0994	20794

SOLES, BOOT OR SHOE: Rubber, Composition Or Fiber

Company	CITY	ST	EMP	PHONE	ENTRY #
Vibram Corporation **(DH)**	North Brookfield	MA	C	508 867-6494	13883
Vibram Corporation **(HQ)**	Concord	MA	E	978 318-0000	10159
Hants White LLC	Mars Hill	ME	G	207 429-9786	6414

SOLVENTS

Company	CITY	ST	EMP	PHONE	ENTRY #
Purification Technologies LLC **(DH)**	Chester	CT	F	860 526-7801	774
US Chemicals Inc	New Canaan	CT	G	203 655-8878	2620
Isp Freetown Fine Chem Inc	Assonet	MA	D	508 672-0634	7681
Solvent Kleene Inc	Peabody	MA	F	978 531-2279	14370

SOLVENTS: Organic

Company	CITY	ST	EMP	PHONE	ENTRY #
C E Bradely Lab Inc	Brattleboro	VT	D	802 257-1122	21721

SONAR SYSTEMS & EQPT

Company	CITY	ST	EMP	PHONE	ENTRY #
Edgeone LLC	West Wareham	MA	G	508 291-0960	16570
Massa Products Corporation	Hingham	MA	D	781 749-3120	11501
Raytheon Company	Marlborough	MA	B	978 440-1000	12812
Raytheon Company	Tewksbury	MA	F	978 858-5000	15828
Raytheon Company	Lexington	MA	G	781 862-6800	12258
Raytheon Company	Woburn	MA	C	339 645-6000	17280
Raytheon Company	Tewksbury	MA	C	978 858-5000	15829
Raytheon Company	Marlborough	MA	C	508 490-1000	12814
Raytheon Company	Tewksbury	MA	C	978 858-4700	15830
Roche Engineering LLC	East Freetown	MA	G	508 287-1964	10459
Klein Marine Systems Inc	Salem	NH	D	603 893-6131	19744
Raytheon Company	Pelham	NH	E	603 635-6800	19444
Syqwest Inc	Cranston	RI	E	401 432-7129	20297

SOUND EQPT: Electric

Company	CITY	ST	EMP	PHONE	ENTRY #
Headwaters Inc	Marblehead	MA	G	781 715-6404	12685
Lightspeed Mfg Co LLC	Haverhill	MA	F	978 521-7676	11449
Ov Loop Inc	Danvers	MA	E	781 640-2234	10246
Thermal Circuits Inc	Salem	MA	C	978 745-1162	14945
Global Rfid Systems N Amer LLC	Narragansett	RI	G	401 783-3818	20640

SOUND EQPT: Underwater

Company	CITY	ST	EMP	PHONE	ENTRY #
McLane Research Labs Inc **(PA)**	East Falmouth	MA	G	508 495-4000	10445

SOUND REPRODUCING EQPT

Company	CITY	ST	EMP	PHONE	ENTRY #
Headwaters Inc	Marblehead	MA	G	781 715-6404	12685

SOYBEAN PRDTS

Company	CITY	ST	EMP	PHONE	ENTRY #
South River Miso Co Inc	Conway	MA	G	413 369-4057	10167

SPACE FLIGHT OPERATIONS, EXC GOVERNMENT

Company	CITY	ST	EMP	PHONE	ENTRY #
Singularity Space Systems LLC	Granby	CT	G	860 713-3626	1591

SPACE PROPULSION UNITS & PARTS

Company	CITY	ST	EMP	PHONE	ENTRY #
Wormtown Atomic Propulsion	Waltham	MA	G	781 487-7777	16225

SPACE SUITS

Company	CITY	ST	EMP	PHONE	ENTRY #
Hamilton Standard Space	Windsor Locks	CT	E	860 654-6000	5396

SPACE VEHICLE EQPT

Company	CITY	ST	EMP	PHONE	ENTRY #
Accupaulo Holding Corporation **(PA)**	Bristol	CT	E	860 666-5621	511
Aerocess Inc	Berlin	CT	F	860 357-2451	67
Braxton Manufacturing Co Inc	Watertown	CT	C	860 274-6781	5000
Edac Technologies LLC	East Windsor	CT	F	860 789-2511	1283
Edac Technologies LLC **(HQ)**	Cheshire	CT	C	203 806-2090	728
Kaman Aerospace Group Inc **(HQ)**	Bloomfield	CT	F	860 243-7100	233
Meriden Manufacturing Inc	Meriden	CT	D	203 237-7481	2104
Ramar-Hall Inc	Middlefield	CT	E	860 349-1081	2165
Spartan Aerospace LLC	Manchester	CT	D	860 533-7500	2049
Sterling Engineering Corp	Pleasant Valley	CT	C	860 379-3366	3547
United Tool and Die Company **(PA)**	West Hartford	CT	C	860 246-6531	5102
325 Silver Street Inc	Agawam	MA	E	413 789-1800	7415
L3 Technologies Inc	Burlington	MA	C	781 270-2100	9295
Raytheon Company	Tewksbury	MA	C	978 858-5000	15829
Tell Tool Inc	Westfield	MA	D	413 568-1671	16732
Tell Tool Acquisition Inc **(HQ)**	Westfield	MA	G	413 568-1671	16733
Elmet Technologies LLC	Lewiston	ME	C	207 333-6100	6287
Honeywell International Inc	Woonsocket	RI	D	401 762-6200	21569
Masiello Enterprises Inc	Coventry	RI	E	401 826-1883	20155
Swissline Products Inc	Cumberland	RI	D	401 333-8888	20345

SPACE VEHICLES

Company	CITY	ST	EMP	PHONE	ENTRY #
Singularity Space Systems LLC	Granby	CT	G	860 713-3626	1591

SPAS

Company	CITY	ST	EMP	PHONE	ENTRY #
Medical Asthtics Assoc Neng PC	Acton	MA	G	978 263-5376	7374

SPEAKER SYSTEMS

Company	CITY	ST	EMP	PHONE	ENTRY #
Aerial Acoustics Corporation	Wilmington	MA	F	978 988-1600	16968
Doranco Inc	Attleboro	MA	G	508 236-0290	7727
Inter-Ego Systems Inc **(PA)**	Hatfield	MA	F	516 576-9052	11401
Pine and Baker Mfg Inc	Tewksbury	MA	F	978 851-1215	15825

SPECIAL EVENTS DECORATION SVCS

Company	CITY	ST	EMP	PHONE	ENTRY #
Zp Couture LLC	North Haven	CT	G	888 697-7239	3070

SPECIALTY FOOD STORES: Dried Fruit

Company	CITY	ST	EMP	PHONE	ENTRY #
Modernist Pantry LLC	Eliot	ME	G	207 200-3817	6008

SPECIALTY FOOD STORES: Health & Dietetic Food

Company	CITY	ST	EMP	PHONE	ENTRY #
Designing Health Inc	East Longmeadow	MA	E	661 257-1705	10472
Drews LLC	Woburn	MA	G	781 935-6045	17170

SPECIALTY FOOD STORES: Soft Drinks

Company	CITY	ST	EMP	PHONE	ENTRY #
Harvest Hill Holdings LLC **(PA)**	Stamford	CT	F	203 914-1620	4211
Ambrose G McCarthy Jr	Skowhegan	ME	E	207 474-8837	6968
Crystal Spring Water Co Inc **(PA)**	Auburn	ME	F	207 782-1521	5558

SPECIALTY SAWMILL PRDTS

Company	CITY	ST	EMP	PHONE	ENTRY #
Cellar Crafts	Mont Vernon	NH	G	603 673-3615	19092
Carris Reels Inc **(HQ)**	Proctor	VT	C	802 773-9111	22284

SPEED CHANGERS

Company	CITY	ST	EMP	PHONE	ENTRY #
Carlyle Johnson Machine Co LLC **(PA)**	Bolton	CT	E	860 643-1531	276

SPICE & HERB STORES

Company	CITY	ST	EMP	PHONE	ENTRY #
A Lot Bakery Products Inc	Boston	MA	G	617 561-1122	8332
David W Wallace	Shelburne Falls	MA	G	413 625-6523	15067

SPINDLES: Textile

Company	CITY	ST	EMP	PHONE	ENTRY #
Advanced Machine Services LLC **(PA)**	Waterbury	CT	G	203 888-6600	4836
Ametek Precitech Inc **(HQ)**	Keene	NH	D	603 357-2510	18491

SPONGES, SCOURING: Metallic

Company	CITY	ST	EMP	PHONE	ENTRY #
ACS Industries Inc **(PA)**	Lincoln	RI	E	401 769-4700	20552

SPONGES: Bleached & Dyed

Company	CITY	ST	EMP	PHONE	ENTRY #
Jab Manufacturing LLC	Salem	NH	G	603 328-8113	19743
Blackledge Industries LLC	Pawtucket	RI	G	401 270-6779	20817

SPONGES: Plastic

Company	CITY	ST	EMP	PHONE	ENTRY #
Mdm Products LLC	Milford	CT	F	203 877-7070	2314

SPOOLS: Fiber, Made From Purchased Materials

Company	CITY	ST	EMP	PHONE	ENTRY #
Merrimac Spool and Reel Co Inc	Haverhill	MA	E	978 372-7777	11453

SPOOLS: Indl

Company	CITY	ST	EMP	PHONE	ENTRY #
Frontier Forge Inc	Kingfield	ME	E	207 265-2151	6253

	CITY	ST	EMP	PHONE	ENTRY #

SPORTING & ATHLETIC GOODS: Arrows, Archery

Wasp Archery Products Inc	Plymouth	CT	G	860 283-0246	3549

SPORTING & ATHLETIC GOODS: Bags, Golf

Pride Manufacturing Co LLC **(PA)**	Burnham	ME	C	207 487-3322	5855

SPORTING & ATHLETIC GOODS: Bags, Rosin

Hudson Poly Bag Inc	Hudson	MA	F	978 562-7566	11776
Grenade (usa) LLC	Cranston	RI	G	401 944-3960	20234

SPORTING & ATHLETIC GOODS: Balls, Baseball, Football, Etc

Acushnet Company **(DH)**	Fairhaven	MA	A	508 979-2000	10635
Acushnet Company	Brockton	MA	A	508 979-2309	9115
Acushnet Company	Brockton	MA	E	508 979-2343	9116

SPORTING & ATHLETIC GOODS: Boomerangs

Big Daddy Boomerangs LLC	Springfield	MA	G	413 297-7079	15452

SPORTING & ATHLETIC GOODS: Bows, Archery

Ace Archers Inc	Foxborough	MA	G	774 215-5292	10910
Ace Archers Inc	Foxboro	MA	G	508 697-5647	10874

SPORTING & ATHLETIC GOODS: Boxing Eqpt & Splys, NEC

Nonantum Boxing Club LLC	Newton	MA	G	617 340-3700	13619

SPORTING & ATHLETIC GOODS: Camping Eqpt & Splys

Life+gear Inc	Wellesley Hills	MA	E	858 755-2099	16398

SPORTING & ATHLETIC GOODS: Cases, Gun & Rod

Santa Cruz Gunlocks LLC	Webster	NH	G	603 746-7740	19945

SPORTING & ATHLETIC GOODS: Darts & Table Sports Eqpt & Splys

New England Spt Ventures LLC	Boston	MA	G	617 267-9440	8732

SPORTING & ATHLETIC GOODS: Decoys, Duck & Other Game Birds

Will Kirkpatricks Decoy Shop	Hudson	MA	F	978 562-7841	11826

SPORTING & ATHLETIC GOODS: Driving Ranges, Golf, Electronic

B F M Mini Golf Driving Range	North Reading	MA	F	978 664-9276	13978

SPORTING & ATHLETIC GOODS: Dumbbells & Other Weight Eqpt

Fitnow Inc	Boston	MA	E	617 699-5585	8550

SPORTING & ATHLETIC GOODS: Exercising Cycles

Xthera Corporation	Franklin	MA	G	508 528-3100	11100

SPORTING & ATHLETIC GOODS: Fencing Eqpt

International Soccer & Rugby	Southport	CT	G	203 254-1979	4096

SPORTING & ATHLETIC GOODS: Fishing Bait, Artificial

Maine Lure Company LLC	Biddeford	ME	G	413 543-1524	5745

SPORTING & ATHLETIC GOODS: Fishing Eqpt

Edgewater International LLC	Stafford Springs	CT	F	860 851-9014	4110
40 Up Tackle Company Inc	Westfield	MA	G	413 562-0385	16660
Amalgamated Titanium Intl Corp	Cambridge	MA	F	617 395-7700	9386
Neptune Inc	Attleboro	MA	G	508 222-8313	7771
Winchester Fishing Inc	Gloucester	MA	G	978 282-0679	11219
Jonathan Knight	Wakefield	RI	G	401 263-3671	21273
Northern Strike	Lyndonville	VT	G	802 427-3201	22071
Orvis Company	Manchester	VT	F	802 362-3750	22078

SPORTING & ATHLETIC GOODS: Fishing Tackle, General

Outdoor Outfitters Inc	Orleans	MA	E	508 255-0455	14239

SPORTING & ATHLETIC GOODS: Flies, Fishing, Artificial

Regal Sporting Technologies	Orange	MA	G	978 544-6571	14224

SPORTING & ATHLETIC GOODS: Gymnasium Eqpt

Velex Corporation	Cambridge	MA	G	617 440-4948	9691

SPORTING & ATHLETIC GOODS: Hockey Eqpt & Splys, NEC

Mylec Inc **(PA)**	Winchendon	MA	D	978 297-0089	17078
Bennetts Sports Inc	Cranston	RI	G	401 943-7600	20189

SPORTING & ATHLETIC GOODS: Hunting Eqpt

Extreme Dim Wildlife Calls LLC	Hampden	ME	G	207 862-2825	6165

SPORTING & ATHLETIC GOODS: Pools, Swimming, Exc Plastic

Fairfield Pool & Equipment Co **(PA)**	Fairfield	CT	G	203 334-3600	1431
Group Works	Wilton	CT	G	203 834-7905	5290
Cherry Hill Construction Corp	Pembroke	MA	G	781 826-6886	14394
Swimex Inc	Fall River	MA	E	508 646-1600	10768

SPORTING & ATHLETIC GOODS: Protective Sporting Eqpt

Ampac Enterprises Inc	Shirley	MA	D	978 425-6266	15080
Field Protection Agency LLC	Auburn	MA	G	508 832-0395	7834
JB Sports LLC	Revere	MA	G	617 930-3044	14769
H R P Products Inc	Farmington	NH	F	603 330-3757	18142
Simbex LLC	Lebanon	NH	E	603 448-2367	18636
Bacou Dalloz USA Inc	Smithfield	RI	F	401 757-2428	21211

SPORTING & ATHLETIC GOODS: Reels, Fishing

North Point Brands LLC	North Adams	MA	G	339 707-3017	13683

SPORTING & ATHLETIC GOODS: Rods & Rod Parts, Fishing

K & D Business Ventures LLC	Jewett City	CT	G	860 237-1458	1914
Reel Easy Inc	Newburyport	MA	G	978 476-7187	13528
Thomas & Thomas Rodmakers	Greenfield	MA	E	413 475-3840	11281

SPORTING & ATHLETIC GOODS: Rowing Machines

Waterrower Inc	Warren	RI	D	800 852-2210	21316
Concept2 Inc **(PA)**	Morrisville	VT	E	802 888-7971	22166
Manufacturing Solutions Inc	Morrisville	VT	E	802 888-3289	22172

SPORTING & ATHLETIC GOODS: Shafts, Golf Club

Acushnet Company	Acushnet	MA	E	508 979-2000	7397
Acushnet Company	New Bedford	MA	A	508 979-2000	13349
Acushnet Company	New Bedford	MA	E	508 979-2000	13350
Acushnet Company	New Bedford	MA	E	508 979-2156	13351

SPORTING & ATHLETIC GOODS: Shooting Eqpt & Splys, General

Robert Louis Company Inc	Newtown	CT	G	203 270-1400	2935
Savage Range Systems Inc	Westfield	MA	G	413 568-7001	16727

SPORTING & ATHLETIC GOODS: Skateboards

Rampage LLC	Trumbull	CT	F	203 930-1022	4630
Roces North America	West Lebanon	NH	G	603 298-2137	19961

SPORTING & ATHLETIC GOODS: Skates & Parts, Roller

Mearthane Products Corporation **(PA)**	Cranston	RI	C	401 946-4400	20260
Perfect Storm Sports Tech LLC	Essex Junction	VT	G	802 662-2102	21954

SPORTING & ATHLETIC GOODS: Snow Skiing Eqpt & Sply, Exc Skis

Mike Sadlak	Coventry	CT	G	860 742-0227	835
Larchmont Engineering Inc	Chelmsford	MA	G	978 250-1177	9912
E Skip Grindle & Sons	Ellsworth	ME	G	207 460-0334	6017
Atlantic Sports International	Langdon	NH	G	603 835-6948	18610
Jenex Inc	Milford	NH	G	603 672-2600	19066
Burton Corporation **(PA)**	Burlington	VT	B	802 862-4500	21770
Burton Corporation	South Burlington	VT	D	802 652-3600	22441
Red Corp	Burlington	VT	D	802 862-4500	21806
Vermont Ski Safety Equipment	Underhill	VT	G	802 899-4738	22549

SPORTING & ATHLETIC GOODS: Snow Skis

Forward Inc	Shelburne	VT	G	802 585-1098	22417

SPORTING & ATHLETIC GOODS: Snowshoes

Killington Ltd	Killington	VT	D	802 422-3333	22053
Snowshoe Pond Mple Sgrwrks LLC	Enosburg Falls	VT	G	802 777-9676	21927
Tsl Snowshoes LLC	Williston	VT	G	802 660-8232	22695

SPORTING & ATHLETIC GOODS: Strings, Tennis Racket

Ashaway Line & Twine Mfg Co	Ashaway	RI	D	401 377-2221	20031

SPORTING & ATHLETIC GOODS: Targets, Archery & Rifle Shooting

Sadlak Industries LLC	Coventry	CT	E	860 742-0227	838

SPORTING & ATHLETIC GOODS: Team Sports Eqpt

Perfect Curve Inc **(PA)**	Boston	MA	G	617 224-1600	8774
Bachar Samawi Innovations LLC **(PA)**	West Dover	VT	G	802 464-0440	22605

SPORTING & ATHLETIC GOODS: Tennis Eqpt & Splys

Tennis Loft	Nantucket	MA	G	508 228-9228	13231

SPORTING & ATHLETIC GOODS: Toboggans

Ocean Lures LLC	Rowley	MA	G	978 618-1982	14862
Pursuit Toboggan LLC	Fall River	MA	G	508 567-0550	10749

SPORTING & ATHLETIC GOODS: Trampolines & Eqpt

Aluma-Cast Corp	North Attleboro	MA	G	508 399-6650	13744

SPORTING & ATHLETIC GOODS: Treadmills

Samsara Fitness LLC	Chester	CT	F	860 895-8533	776

SPORTING & ATHLETIC GOODS: Water Sports Eqpt

Uniboard Corp	Putnam	CT	G	860 428-5979	3637
Imperial Pools Inc	Taunton	MA	F	508 339-3830	15758
North Sails Group LLC	Newport	RI	D	401 849-7997	20675

SPORTING & ATHLETIC GOODS: Winter Sports

3 Play Inc **(PA)**	Walpole	MA	G	781 205-4820	15986
Caron Alpine Technologies Inc	Tiverton	RI	G	401 624-8999	21254

SPORTING & REC GOODS, WHOLESALE: Camping Eqpt & Splys

Shelterlogic Corp **(HQ)**	Watertown	CT	C	860 945-6442	5023
Slogic Holding Corp **(PA)**	New Canaan	CT	G	203 966-2800	2614

SPORTING & RECREATIONAL GOODS & SPLYS WHOLESALERS

Jaypro Sports LLC	Waterford	CT	E	860 447-3001	4986
Fitness Em LLC	Uxbridge	MA	E	508 278-3209	15916
Outdoor Outfitters Inc	Orleans	MA	E	508 255-0455	14239
Planet Eclipse LLC	Warren	RI	G	401 247-9061	21302

SPORTING & RECREATIONAL GOODS, WHOLESALE: Athletic Goods

Ampac Enterprises Inc	Shirley	MA	D	978 425-6266	15080

SPORTING & RECREATIONAL GOODS, WHOLESALE: Bicycle Parts

Schlage Lock Company LLC	Canton	MA	E	781 828-6655	9776

SPORTING & RECREATIONAL GOODS, WHOLESALE: Boat Access & Part

Canvasmith	Fairhaven	MA	G	207 379-2121	10641
Cloth N Canvas Recovery Inc	Colchester	VT	G	802 658-6826	21859
Dock Doctors LLC	Ferrisburgh	VT	E	802 877-6756	21988

SPORTING & RECREATIONAL GOODS, WHOLESALE: Exercise

	CITY	ST	EMP	PHONE	ENTRY #
Full Circle Padding Inc	Norton	MA	F	508 285-2500	14077

SPORTING & RECREATIONAL GOODS, WHOLESALE: Fishing

	CITY	ST	EMP	PHONE	ENTRY #
Reel Easy Inc	Newburyport	MA	G	978 476-7187	13528
Thomas & Thomas Rodmakers	Greenfield	MA	E	413 475-3840	11281
Downeast Fishing Gear Inc	Trenton	ME	E	207 667-3131	7097

SPORTING & RECREATIONAL GOODS, WHOLESALE: Golf

	CITY	ST	EMP	PHONE	ENTRY #
Golf Galaxy LLC	Norwalk	CT	G	203 855-0500	3162
Wild Card Golf LLC	Hartford	CT	G	860 296-1661	1885

SPORTING & RECREATIONAL GOODS, WHOLESALE: Golf & Skiing

	CITY	ST	EMP	PHONE	ENTRY #
Hollrock Engineering Inc	Hadley	MA	F	413 586-2256	11307

SPORTING & RECREATIONAL GOODS, WHOLESALE: Watersports

	CITY	ST	EMP	PHONE	ENTRY #
Bic Corporation **(HQ)**	Shelton	CT	A	203 783-2000	3782

SPORTING GOODS

	CITY	ST	EMP	PHONE	ENTRY #
Ammunition Stor Components LLC	New Britain	CT	G	860 225-3548	2509
Bob Vess Building LLC	Cromwell	CT	G	860 729-2536	849
Dewey J Manufacturing Company	Oxford	CT	G	203 264-3064	3399
Europa Sports Products Inc	Windsor	CT	G	860 688-1110	5333
Gilman Corporation	Gilman	CT	E	860 887-7080	1534
Hamden Sports Center Inc	Hamden	CT	G	203 248-9898	1758
Homeland Fundraising	East Windsor	CT	G	860 386-6698	1286
Intersec LLC	Rocky Hill	CT	G	860 985-3158	3718
Jaypro Sports LLC	Waterford	CT	E	860 447-3001	4986
Marty Gilman Incorporated **(PA)**	Gilman	CT	D	860 889-7334	1535
Marty Gilman Incorporated	Bozrah	CT	G	860 889-7334	282
Road-Fit Enterprises LLC	Plainville	CT	G	860 371-5137	3514
Swivel Machine Works Inc	Newtown	CT	G	203 270-6343	2940
Wiffle Ball Incorporated	Shelton	CT	F	203 924-4643	3890
Wild Card Golf LLC	Hartford	CT	G	860 296-1661	1885
Al Gags	Indian Orchard	MA	G	413 285-8023	11884
Callaway Golf Company	Chicopee	MA	E	413 536-1200	10005
Cohasset Sports Complex	Cohasset	MA	G	781 383-0278	10096
Fitness Em LLC	Uxbridge	MA	E	508 278-3209	15916
Foamaction Sports LLC	Rochester	MA	G	508 887-3721	14786
Foot Locker Retail Inc	Saugus	MA	G	781 231-0142	14981
Fuji Mats LLC	Methuen	MA	G	205 419-5080	13023
Great Neck Saw Mfrs Inc	Millbury	MA	E	508 865-4482	13166
Heartbreak Hill Running Co Inc	Newton	MA	G	617 467-4487	13599
Home Grown Lacrosse LLC	North Andover	MA	G	978 208-2300	13709
Insignia Athletics LLC	Worcester	MA	G	508 756-3633	17393
Macneill Engineering Co Inc	Westborough	MA	E	508 481-8830	16633
R J Shepherd Co Inc	Whitman	MA	G	781 447-5768	16927
R R Venture	Wellesley	MA	G	781 431-6170	16382
Sports Power Drive Inc	Holliston	MA	G	774 233-0175	11603
Sportsscarf LLC	Mattapoisett	MA	G	508 758-8176	12891
Stan Ray Products Co	Salem	MA	G	978 594-0667	14944
Village Sports	Westport	MA	G	508 672-4284	16850
Chambers Leasing	Houlton	ME	G	207 532-4381	6203
Corn Snow LLC	Farmington	ME	G	603 684-2427	6042
Gregg Stewart	Brewer	ME	G	207 989-0903	5796
Athletic Innovation Inc	Rochester	NH	G	603 332-1212	19660
Bauer Hockey LLC	Exeter	NH	C	603 430-2111	18111
Bce Acquisition Us Inc **(HQ)**	Exeter	NH	G	603 430-2111	18112
Fulling Mill Fly Fishing LLC	Claremont	NH	G	603 542-5480	17851
L L Bean Inc	West Lebanon	NH	G	603 298-6975	19955
Pat Trap Inc	Henniker	NH	G	603 428-3396	18309
Pigeon Hold Targets	Merrimack	NH	G	603 420-8839	19021
Richardson Mfg Co Inc	Silver Lake	NH	G	603 367-9018	19825
East Greenwich Spine and Sport	East Greenwich	RI	F	401 886-5907	20364
Hayward Industries Inc	North Kingstown	RI	G	401 583-1150	20714
Parsonskellogg LLC	East Providence	RI	E	401 438-0650	20439
Planet Eclipse LLC	Warren	RI	G	401 247-9061	21302
Shegear Inc	Newport	RI	G	401 619-0072	20681
Balance Designs Inc	Manchester Center	VT	G	802 362-2893	22080
Burton Corporation	Burlington	VT	G	802 862-4500	21771
Gordini USA Inc **(PA)**	Essex Junction	VT	E	802 879-5211	21942
Michael Olden	Newport	VT	G	802 334-5525	22202
Sports Products Incorporated	Winooski	VT	G	802 655-2620	22724
Whistlekick LLC	Montpelier	VT	F	802 225-6676	22164
Wood Dynamics Corporation **(PA)**	South Pomfret	VT	G	802 457-3970	22489

SPORTING GOODS STORES, NEC

	CITY	ST	EMP	PHONE	ENTRY #
Avalanche Downhill Racing Inc	Colchester	CT	G	860 537-4306	799
Gunworks International L L C	Old Saybrook	CT	G	860 388-4591	3336
Iovino Bros Sporting Goods	Danbury	CT	G	203 790-5966	934
Probatter Sports LLC	Milford	CT	G	203 874-2500	2342
Swivel Machine Works Inc	Newtown	CT	G	203 270-6343	2940
April Twenty One Corporation	Billerica	MA	G	978 667-8472	8213
Budco Products Corp	Woonsocket	RI	G	401 767-2590	21554

SPORTING GOODS STORES: Baseball Eqpt

	CITY	ST	EMP	PHONE	ENTRY #
Tucci Lumber Co LLC	Norwalk	CT	G	203 956-6181	3262

SPORTING GOODS STORES: Firearms

	CITY	ST	EMP	PHONE	ENTRY #
Rosellis Machine & Mfg Co	Westfield	MA	F	413 562-4317	16723

SPORTING GOODS STORES: Fishing Eqpt

	CITY	ST	EMP	PHONE	ENTRY #
Reel Easy Inc	Newburyport	MA	G	978 476-7187	13528
Thomas & Thomas Rodmakers	Greenfield	MA	E	413 475-3840	11281
Winchester Fishing Inc	Gloucester	MA	G	978 282-0679	11219
Downeast Fishing Gear Inc	Trenton	ME	E	207 667-3131	7097

SPORTING GOODS STORES: Skating Eqpt

	CITY	ST	EMP	PHONE	ENTRY #
Del Arbour LLC	Milford	CT	F	203 882-8501	2274
Cookes Skate Supplies Inc	Wilmington	MA	G	978 657-7586	16989

SPORTING GOODS STORES: Skiing Eqpt

	CITY	ST	EMP	PHONE	ENTRY #
Bike & Ski Touring Ctr of Neng	Middlebury	VT	G	802 388-6666	22102

SPORTING GOODS STORES: Soccer Splys

	CITY	ST	EMP	PHONE	ENTRY #
Suleys Soccer Center	Manchester	NH	G	603 668-7227	18931

SPORTING GOODS STORES: Specialty Sport Splys, NEC

	CITY	ST	EMP	PHONE	ENTRY #
Pilla Inc	Ridgefield	CT	G	203 894-3265	3676

SPORTING GOODS STORES: Tennis Goods & Eqpt

	CITY	ST	EMP	PHONE	ENTRY #
Nova Sports Usa Inc	Milford	MA	F	508 473-6540	13133

SPORTING GOODS STORES: Water Sport Eqpt

	CITY	ST	EMP	PHONE	ENTRY #
3 Play Inc **(PA)**	Walpole	MA	G	781 205-4820	15986

SPORTING GOODS: Hammocks, Fabric, Made From Purchased Mat

	CITY	ST	EMP	PHONE	ENTRY #
Cobble Mountain Inc	East Corinth	VT	G	802 439-5232	21913

SPORTING GOODS: Skin Diving Eqpt

	CITY	ST	EMP	PHONE	ENTRY #
Hydro-Test Products Inc	Stow	MA	F	978 897-4647	15632
Morse Diving Inc	Rockland	MA	G	781 733-1511	14815

SPORTING GOODS: Sleeping Bags

	CITY	ST	EMP	PHONE	ENTRY #
Black Dog Corporation	Portsmouth	RI	E	401 683-5858	20920

SPORTING GOODS: Surfboards

	CITY	ST	EMP	PHONE	ENTRY #
Firejudge Worldwide Inc	Haverhill	MA	G	978 604-0009	11434
Mark Keup	Scituate	MA	G	781 544-4610	15009
Surfari Inc	Gloucester	MA	F	978 704-9051	11214
Grain Surfboards	York	ME	G	207 457-5313	7307
Maine Surfers Union	Portland	ME	G	207 771-7873	6690
Endless Wave Inc	Jamestown	RI	G	401 423-3400	20489

SPORTING/ATHLETIC GOODS: Gloves, Boxing, Handball, Etc

	CITY	ST	EMP	PHONE	ENTRY #
Damascus Worldwide Inc	Rutland	VT	G	802 775-6062	22328

SPORTS APPAREL STORES

	CITY	ST	EMP	PHONE	ENTRY #
Jph Graphics LLC	Salem	MA	G	978 744-7873	14926
Sportsscarf LLC	Mattapoisett	MA	G	508 758-8176	12891
Chuck Roast Equipment Inc **(PA)**	Conway	NH	E	603 447-5492	17951

SPRAYING & DUSTING EQPT

	CITY	ST	EMP	PHONE	ENTRY #
Praxair Surface Tech Inc	Concord	NH	D	603 224-9585	17924
Tafa Incorporated **(DH)**	Concord	NH	E	603 224-9585	17934

SPRAYING EQPT: Agricultural

	CITY	ST	EMP	PHONE	ENTRY #
Pressure Techniques Intl Corp	Haverhill	MA	G	978 686-2211	11460
Spray Foam Distrs Neng Inc	Woodstock	NH	E	603 745-3911	20029

SPRAYS: Artificial & Preserved

	CITY	ST	EMP	PHONE	ENTRY #
Jenray Products Inc	Brookfield	CT	E	914 375-5596	648

SPRINGS: Coiled Flat

	CITY	ST	EMP	PHONE	ENTRY #
Dynamic Manufacturing Company	Bristol	CT	G	860 589-2751	551
Excel Spring & Stamping LLC	Bristol	CT	G	860 585-1495	559

SPRINGS: Helical, Hot Wound, Railroad Eqpt

	CITY	ST	EMP	PHONE	ENTRY #
Solid Earth Technologies Inc	Amherst	NH	G	603 882-5319	17588

SPRINGS: Instrument, Precision

	CITY	ST	EMP	PHONE	ENTRY #
Plymouth Spring Company Inc	Bristol	CT	D	860 584-0594	595
Catalyst/Spring I Ltd Partner	Chelsea	MA	E	617 884-9410	9947
Spring Manufacturing Corp	Tewksbury	MA	F	978 658-7396	15836

SPRINGS: Mechanical, Precision

	CITY	ST	EMP	PHONE	ENTRY #
A & A Manufacturing Co Inc	North Haven	CT	E	262 786-1500	3000
Century Spring Mfg Co Inc	Bristol	CT	E	860 582-3344	540
DR Templeman Company	Plainville	CT	F	860 747-2709	3482
Lee Spring Company LLC	Bristol	CT	E	860 584-0991	576
Rowley Spring & Stamping Corp	Bristol	CT	C	860 582-8175	610
Thomas Spring Co of Connenicut	Milford	CT	G	203 874-7030	2375
Pdi International Inc	Lowell	MA	G	978 446-0840	12419

SPRINGS: Precision

	CITY	ST	EMP	PHONE	ENTRY #
Barnes Group Inc **(PA)**	Bristol	CT	B	860 583-7070	526
Dayon Manufacturing Inc	Farmington	CT	E	860 677-8561	1476
Excel Spring & Stamping LLC	Bristol	CT	G	860 585-1495	559
Matthew Warren Inc	Southington	CT	D	860 621-7358	4065
Ulbrich of Georgia Inc	North Haven	CT	G	203 239-4481	3066
Stephen A Burt	Colchester	VT	G	802 893-0600	21880

SPRINGS: Steel

	CITY	ST	EMP	PHONE	ENTRY #
Acme Monaco Corporation **(PA)**	New Britain	CT	C	860 224-1349	2503
American Specialty Co Inc	Shelton	CT	F	203 929-5324	3774
Arrow Manufacturing Company	Bristol	CT	E	860 589-3900	520
Century Spring Mfg Co Inc	Bristol	CT	E	860 582-3344	540
Connectcut Spring Stmping Corp	Farmington	CT	B	860 677-1341	1473
Dayon Manufacturing Inc	Farmington	CT	E	860 677-8561	1476
Hurley Manufacturing Company	New Hartford	CT	E	860 379-8506	2638
Lee Spring Company LLC	Bristol	CT	E	860 584-0991	576
Matthew Warren Inc	Southington	CT	D	860 621-7358	4065
Newcomb Spring Corp	Southington	CT	E	860 621-0111	4067
Oscar Jobs	Bristol	CT	G	860 583-7834	588
Rowley Spring & Stamping Corp	Bristol	CT	C	860 582-8175	610
Spring Computerized Inds LLC	Harwinton	CT	G	860 605-9206	1893

	CITY	ST	EMP	PHONE	ENTRY #
Tollman Spring Company Inc	Bristol	CT	G	860 583-4856	619
Triple A Spring Ltd Partnr	Bristol	CT	E	860 589-3231	620
Bay State Spring Corp	Jefferson	MA	G	508 829-5702	11952
Leggett & Platt Incorporated	Oxford	MA	E	508 987-8706	14265
D & W Tool Findings Inc	Pawtucket	RI	F	401 727-3030	20832

SPRINGS: Torsion Bar

	CITY	ST	EMP	PHONE	ENTRY #
Minuteman Spring Company Inc	Millbury	MA	G	508 299-6100	13172

SPRINGS: Wire

	CITY	ST	EMP	PHONE	ENTRY #
Atlantic Precision Spring Inc	Bristol	CT	E	860 583-1864	522
Barnes Group Inc	Farmington	CT	G	860 298-7740	1467
Barnes Group Inc	Bristol	CT	D	860 582-9581	527
Connectcut Spring Stmping Corp	Farmington	CT	B	860 677-1341	1473
Fourslide Spring Stamping Inc	Bristol	CT	E	860 583-1688	564
Gemco Manufacturing Co Inc	Southington	CT	E	860 628-5529	4052
National Spring & Stamping Inc	Thomaston	CT	E	860 283-0203	4510
Newcomb Spring Corp	Southington	CT	E	860 621-0111	4067
Newcomb Springs Connecticut	Southington	CT	E	860 621-0111	4068
Oscar Jobs	Bristol	CT	G	860 583-7834	588
Southington Tool & Mfg Corp	Plantsville	CT	E	860 276-0021	3540
Spring Computerized Inds LLC	Harwinton	CT	G	860 605-9206	1893
Springfield Spring Corporation	Bristol	CT	F	860 584-6560	614
Bay State Spring Corp	Jefferson	MA	G	508 829-5702	11952
Device Technologies Inc	Southborough	MA	E	508 229-2000	15354
Leggett & Platt Incorporated	Oxford	MA	E	508 987-8706	14265
Springfield Spring Corporation **(PA)**	East Longmeadow	MA	E	413 525-6837	10493
Stratosphere Inc	York	ME	D	207 351-8011	7317
D & W Tool Findings Inc	Pawtucket	RI	F	401 727-3030	20832

SPRINKLER SYSTEMS: Field

	CITY	ST	EMP	PHONE	ENTRY #
Geneisis Sprinkler Systems	Osterville	MA	G	508 428-1842	14247
Jmsc Enterprises Inc	Seabrook	NH	G	603 468-1010	19808

SPRINKLING SYSTEMS: Fire Control

	CITY	ST	EMP	PHONE	ENTRY #
Fire Technology Inc	Southington	CT	G	860 276-2181	4050
900 Industries Inc	Sutton	MA	G	508 865-9600	15678
Flexhead Industries Inc	Holliston	MA	F	508 893-9596	11571
Tyco Fire Products LP	Avon	MA	G	508 583-8447	7899
Fire Protection Team LLC	Hooksett	NH	G	603 641-2550	18349
R R Sprinkler Inc	Swanton	VT	G	802 868-2423	22535

SPROCKETS: Power Transmission

	CITY	ST	EMP	PHONE	ENTRY #
Custom Machine & Tool Co Inc	Hanover	MA	F	781 924-1003	11334
Lampin Corporation **(PA)**	Uxbridge	MA	E	508 278-2422	15923

STADIUM EVENT OPERATOR SERVICES

	CITY	ST	EMP	PHONE	ENTRY #
Cape Cod Life LLC	Mashpee	MA	F	508 419-7381	12877
Rhee Gold Company	Norton	MA	F	508 285-6650	14086

STAINLESS STEEL

	CITY	ST	EMP	PHONE	ENTRY #
ATI Flat Rlled Pdts Hldngs LLC	Waterbury	CT	F	203 756-7414	4847
Portland Slitting Co Inc	Portland	CT	G	860 342-1500	3570
Yankee Steel Service LLC	Wolcott	CT	G	203 879-5707	5462
Cutlass Marine Inc	East Weymouth	MA	G	781 740-1260	10540
Dakota Systems Inc	Dracut	MA	D	978 275-0600	10356
Ne Stainless Steel Fab	Weymouth	MA	G	781 335-0121	16895
Chase Associates Inc	Edgecomb	ME	G	207 882-7526	6000
Millincket Fabrication Mch Inc **(PA)**	Millinocket	ME	E	207 723-9733	6443

STAINLESS STEEL WARE

	CITY	ST	EMP	PHONE	ENTRY #
Dipwell Company Inc	Northampton	MA	G	413 587-4673	14004

STAINS: Wood

	CITY	ST	EMP	PHONE	ENTRY #
Hbh Prestain Inc **(PA)**	Arlington	VT	E	802 375-9723	21596

STAIRCASES & STAIRS, WOOD

	CITY	ST	EMP	PHONE	ENTRY #
Colonial Woodworking Inc	Norwalk	CT	F	203 866-5844	3128
East Coast Stairs Co Inc	South Windsor	CT	G	860 528-7096	3960
KB Custom Stair Builders Inc	North Haven	CT	G	203 234-0836	3037
Leos Kitchen & Stair Corp	New Britain	CT	G	860 225-7363	2548
Naugatuck Stair Company Inc	Naugatuck	CT	F	203 729-7134	2488
New England Stair Company Inc	Shelton	CT	E	203 924-0606	3838
Quality Stairs Inc	Bridgeport	CT	E	203 367-8390	477
Robert L Lovallo	Stamford	CT	G	203 324-6655	4304
Stately Stair Co Inc	Waterbury	CT	E	203 575-1966	4960
Summit Stair Co Inc	Bethel	CT	F	203 778-2251	181
Walston Inc	Guilford	CT	G	203 453-5929	1724
Wesconn Stairs Inc	Danbury	CT	G	203 792-7367	1008
West Hrtford Stirs Cbinets Inc	Newington	CT	D	860 953-9151	2912
AKa McHlngelo Strbuilder LLC	North Easton	MA	C	508 238-9054	13940
Unique Spiral Stairs Inc	Albion	ME	G	207 437-2415	5513
Colonial Woodworking Inc	Bradford	NH	F	603 938-5131	17741
King & Co Architectural Wdwkg	Marlborough	NH	G	603 876-4900	18961
Hardwood Design Inc	Exeter	RI	E	401 294-2235	20450
Hayley Custom Stair Co Inc	Essex Junction	VT	G	802 861-6400	21946

STAMPED ART GOODS FOR EMBROIDERING

	CITY	ST	EMP	PHONE	ENTRY #
Next Event Corporation	Portsmouth	RI	G	401 683-0070	20931
Follenderwerks Inc	Barre	VT	G	802 362-0911	21615

STAMPINGS: Automotive

	CITY	ST	EMP	PHONE	ENTRY #
3M Company	Meriden	CT	D	203 237-5541	2069
Progressive Stamping Co De Inc	Farmington	CT	E	248 299-7100	1509
Revision Automotive Inc	Providence	RI	G	401 944-4444	21109

STAMPINGS: Metal

	CITY	ST	EMP	PHONE	ENTRY #
A G Russell Company Inc	Hartford	CT	G	860 247-9093	1800
Alinabal Inc **(HQ)**	Milford	CT	C	203 877-3241	2242
Alinabal Holdings Corporation **(PA)**	Milford	CT	B	203 877-3241	2243
Anderson Manufacturing Company	Woodbury	CT	G	203 263-2318	5481
Atlantic Precision Spring Inc	Bristol	CT	E	860 583-1864	522
B & G Forming Technology Inc	Meriden	CT	G	203 235-2169	2078
Barnes Group Inc	Bristol	CT	D	860 582-9581	527
Barnes Group Inc	Farmington	CT	G	860 298-7740	1467
Ben Art Manufacturing Co Inc	Prospect	CT	G	203 758-4435	3583
Beta Shim Co	Shelton	CT	E	203 926-1150	3781
Birotech Inc	Stamford	CT	G	203 968-5080	4150
Carpin Manufacturing Inc	Waterbury	CT	D	203 574-2556	4854
Century Spring Mfg Co Inc	Bristol	CT	E	860 582-3344	540
Cgl Inc	Watertown	CT	F	860 945-6166	5002
Cheshire Manufacturing Co Inc	Cheshire	CT	G	203 272-3586	721
Cly-Del Manufacturing Company	Waterbury	CT	C	203 574-2100	4859
Demsey Manufacturing Co Inc	Watertown	CT	E	860 274-6209	5006
Deringer-Ney Inc **(PA)**	Bloomfield	CT	C	860 242-2281	217
Di-El Tool & Manufacturing	Meriden	CT	G	203 235-2169	2091
Dynamic Manufacturing Company	Bristol	CT	G	860 589-2751	551
Empire Industries Inc	Manchester	CT	E	860 647-1431	2005
Eyelet Tech LLC	Wolcott	CT	E	203 879-5306	5442
Fabor Fourslide Inc	Waterbury	CT	G	203 753-4380	4873
Ferre Form Metal Products	Oakville	CT	F	860 274-3280	3298
Fourslide Spring Stamping Inc	Bristol	CT	E	860 583-1688	564
Hessel Industries Inc	Derby	CT	G	203 736-2317	1073
Hi-Tech Fabricating Inc	Cheshire	CT	E	203 284-0894	737
Hurley Manufacturing Company	New Hartford	CT	E	860 379-8506	2638
Illinois Tool Works Inc	Naugatuck	CT	E	203 720-1676	2479
Illinois Tool Works Inc	Waterbury	CT	C	203 574-2119	4887
ITW Drawform Inc	Waterbury	CT	E	203 574-3200	4889
New Hartford Industrial Park	New Hartford	CT	E	860 379-8506	2643
Nucap US Inc **(DH)**	Wolcott	CT	E	203 879-1423	5450
OEM Sources LLC	Milford	CT	G	203 283-5415	2325
Platt Brothers & Company **(PA)**	Waterbury	CT	D	203 753-4194	4940
Pr-Mx Holdings Company LLC **(HQ)**	Shelton	CT	F	203 925-0012	3857
Pratt-Read Corporation **(PA)**	Branford	CT	F	860 625-3620	339
R A Tool Co	Milford	CT	G	203 877-2998	2346
Rowley Spring & Stamping Corp	Bristol	CT	C	860 582-8175	610
Semco Tool Manufacturing Co	Naugatuck	CT	G	203 723-7411	2495
Siemon Company **(PA)**	Watertown	CT	A	860 945-4200	5024
Solla Eyelet Products Inc	Watertown	CT	E	860 274-5729	5026
Sonchief Electrics Inc	Winsted	CT	G	860 379-2741	5424
Spartan Aerospace LLC	Manchester	CT	D	860 533-7500	2049
Stevens Company Incorporated	Thomaston	CT	D	860 283-8201	4515
Stewart Efi LLC	Thomaston	CT	E	860 283-2523	4517
Stewart Efi Connecticut LLC	Thomaston	CT	C	860 283-8213	4518
Telke Tool & Die Mfg Co	Kensington	CT	G	860 828-9955	1921
Tops Manufacturing Co Inc **(PA)**	Darien	CT	G	203 655-9367	1034
Washer Tech Inc	Meriden	CT	G	203 886-0054	2149
Wces Inc	Waterbury	CT	F	203 573-1325	4977
West Shore Metals LLC	Enfield	CT	G	860 749-8013	1390
A F Murphy Die & Mch Co Inc	Quincy	MA	G	617 328-3820	14612
A Luongo & Sons Incorporated	Bridgewater	MA	G	508 226-0788	9059
Atlee Corp	Tewksbury	MA	G	978 681-1003	15807
Atrenne Cmpt Solutions LLC **(DH)**	Brockton	MA	B	508 588-6110	9121
Automatic Specialties Inc	Marlborough	MA	E	508 481-2370	12724
B G Peck Company Inc	Lawrence	MA	E	978 686-4181	11997
Berkshire Mnufactured Pdts Inc	Newburyport	MA	C	978 462-8161	13472
Collt Mfg Inc	Millis	MA	E	508 376-2525	13183
Craft Inc	Attleboro	MA	E	508 761-7917	7725
Far Industries Inc	Assonet	MA	F	508 644-3122	7679
Fine Edge Tool Company Inc	Attleboro	MA	G	508 222-7511	7736
Gardner Tool & Stamping Co	Gardner	MA	G	978 632-0823	11115
Green Brothers Fabricating	Taunton	MA	E	508 880-3608	15756
JAS F Mullen Co Inc	Merrimac	MA	G	978 346-0045	13003
Manufctrers Pattern Fndry Corp	Springfield	MA	G	413 732-8117	15487
R H Cheney Inc	Attleboro	MA	F	508 222-7300	7783
Samtan Engineering Corp	Malden	MA	E	781 322-7880	12594
Schultz Co Inc	Westfield	MA	G	413 568-1592	16729
Skg Associates Inc	Dedham	MA	G	781 878-7250	10298
Standex International Corp	North Billerica	MA	D	978 667-2771	13869
Tech Fab Inc	South Hadley	MA	E	413 532-9022	15311
Tech-Etch Inc **(PA)**	Plymouth	MA	B	508 747-0300	14587
Tech-Etch Inc	Fall River	MA	D	508 675-5757	10770
Thermo-Fab Corporation	Shirley	MA	E	978 425-2311	15094
Thomson National Press Company **(PA)**	Franklin	MA	G	508 528-2000	11091
True Machine Co Inc	Swansea	MA	G	508 379-0329	15718
Uneco Manufacturing Inc	Chicopee	MA	E	413 594-2700	10066
ZF Active Safety & Elec US LLC	Westminster	MA	E	978 874-0151	16821
Northeast Tool & Die Co Inc	Norway	ME	G	207 743-7273	6524
Numberall Stamp & Tool Co	Sangerville	ME	F	207 876-3541	6900
Barett and Gould Inc	Hillsborough	NH	F	603 464-6400	18314
Costello/April Design Inc	Dover	NH	E	603 749-6755	18015
Design Standards Corp	Charlestown	NH	D	603 826-7744	17813
Jorgensen Tool & Stamping Inc	Belmont	NH	E	603 524-5813	17676
Mushield Company Inc	Londonderry	NH	E	603 666-4433	18726
Pioneer Metal Products Inc	Sandown	NH	G	978 372-2100	19787
United Tool & Stamping Co Inc	Alstead	NH	G	603 352-2585	17543
Wilton Pressed Metals	Newport	NH	G	603 863-1488	19364
Aro-Sac Inc	North Providence	RI	E	401 231-6655	20754
Artic Tool & Engrg Co LLC	Greenville	RI	F	401 785-2210	20461
Crystal Stamping	Pawtucket	RI	G	401 724-5880	20830
Crystal Stamping Corp	Wakefield	RI	F	401 724-5880	21268
Eastern Manufacturing Company	North Providence	RI	F	401 231-8330	20759
Evans Capacitor Company	East Providence	RI	E	401 435-3555	20411
Faco Metal Products Inc	Cranston	RI	F	401 943-7127	20223

	CITY	ST	EMP	PHONE	ENTRY #
Fulford Manufacturing Company **(PA)**	Riverside	RI	F	401 431-2000	21168
Hamilton Tool Inc	Providence	RI	E	401 421-8870	21025
Ira Green Inc	Providence	RI	C	800 663-7487	21040
Jackson Bookbinding Co Inc	Greenville	RI	F	401 231-0800	20469
Lorac Company Inc	Providence	RI	E	401 781-3330	21057
Metal Components	North Kingstown	RI	G	401 886-7979	20728
Philip Machine Company Inc	Pawtucket	RI	F	401 353-7383	20879
Precise Products Company	Lincoln	RI	F	401 724-7190	20592
Providence Mint Inc	Providence	RI	E	401 272-7760	21098
Salvadore Tool & Findings Inc **(PA)**	Providence	RI	E	401 331-6000	21119
United States Associates LLC	Providence	RI	E	401 272-7760	21143
Shelburne Corporation **(PA)**	Shelburne	VT	F	802 985-3321	22424

STAPLES

	CITY	ST	EMP	PHONE	ENTRY #
Stanley Fastening Systems LP **(HQ)**	East Greenwich	RI	D	401 884-2500	20381

STAPLES, MADE FROM PURCHASED WIRE

	CITY	ST	EMP	PHONE	ENTRY #
Briscon Electric Mfg Corp	Auburn	MA	F	508 832-3481	7830

STAPLES: Steel, Wire Or Cut

	CITY	ST	EMP	PHONE	ENTRY #
Acme Staple Company Inc	Franklin	NH	F	603 934-2320	18155
King Manufacturing Co Inc	Jaffrey	NH	F	603 532-6455	18470

STATIC ELIMINATORS: Ind

	CITY	ST	EMP	PHONE	ENTRY #
3M Company	Chelmsford	MA	C	978 256-3911	9865
Alpha Innovation Inc	Marblehead	MA	G	978 744-1100	12674
Desco Industries Inc	Canton	MA	E	781 821-8370	9725
Desco Industries Inc	Canton	MA	E	781 821-8370	9726
Illinois Tool Works Inc	Mechanic Falls	ME	E	207 998-5140	6420

STATIONARY & OFFICE SPLYS, WHOL: Computer/Photocopying Splys

	CITY	ST	EMP	PHONE	ENTRY #
Printgraphics of Maine Inc	Portland	ME	G	207 347-5700	6716

STATIONARY & OFFICE SPLYS, WHOLESALE: Data Processing Splys

	CITY	ST	EMP	PHONE	ENTRY #
Advanced Career Tech Inc **(PA)**	Boston	MA	E	508 620-5904	8341

STATIONARY & OFFICE SPLYS, WHOLESALE: Office Filing Splys

	CITY	ST	EMP	PHONE	ENTRY #
Ames Safety Envelope Company **(DH)**	Somerville	MA	D	617 684-1000	15154

STATIONARY & OFFICE SPLYS, WHOLESALE: Sales & Receipt Books

	CITY	ST	EMP	PHONE	ENTRY #
Hamco Tank Systems LLC	Mason	NH	G	603 878-0585	18968

STATIONER'S SUNDRIES: Rubber

	CITY	ST	EMP	PHONE	ENTRY #
Tory Inc	Woonsocket	RI	G	401 766-4502	21587

STATIONERY & OFFICE SPLYS WHOLESALERS

	CITY	ST	EMP	PHONE	ENTRY #
Imaging Solutions & More	Chicopee	MA	G	413 331-4100	10031
W G Fry Corp	Florence	MA	E	413 747-2551	10870
Papergraphics Print & Copy	Merrimack	NH	F	603 880-1835	19019
Relyco Sales Inc	Dover	NH	E	603 742-0999	18050
Savron Graphics Inc **(PA)**	Jaffrey	NH	G	603 532-7726	18476

STATIONERY PRDTS

	CITY	ST	EMP	PHONE	ENTRY #
American CT Rng Bnder Index &	Washington	CT	F	860 868-7900	4830
Classic Images Inc	Bloomfield	CT	G	860 243-8365	214
Pulp Paper Products Inc	Torrington	CT	G	860 806-0143	4594
William Arthur Inc	West Kennebunk	ME	C	413 684-2600	7174
Paper Packaging and Panache	Bristol	RI	G	401 253-2273	20097

STATIONERY: Made From Purchased Materials

	CITY	ST	EMP	PHONE	ENTRY #
Great Northern Industries Inc **(PA)**	Boston	MA	C	617 262-4314	8578
Viabella Holdings LLC	Wareham	MA	F	800 688-9998	16257

STATUES: Nonmetal

	CITY	ST	EMP	PHONE	ENTRY #
S & S Statuary	Peabody	MA	G	978 535-5837	14368

STEAM, HEAT & AIR CONDITIONING DISTRIBUTION SVC

	CITY	ST	EMP	PHONE	ENTRY #
P&G Metal Components Corp	Bloomfield	CT	F	860 243-2220	248

STEEL & ALLOYS: Tool & Die

	CITY	ST	EMP	PHONE	ENTRY #
Mott Corporation	Farmington	CT	C	800 289-6688	1494
National Integrated Inds Inc **(PA)**	Farmington	CT	C	860 677-7995	1495
A & R Machining Tool & Die	New Bedford	MA	G	508 985-0916	13346
New Hampshire Stamping Co Inc	Goffstown	NH	E	603 641-1234	18206
Stamping Technologics Inc	Laconia	NH	F	603 524-5958	18588

STEEL FABRICATORS

	CITY	ST	EMP	PHONE	ENTRY #
Accutron Inc	Windsor	CT	C	860 683-8300	5315
Acquisitions Controlled Svcs	Stamford	CT	G	203 327-6364	4129
All Panel Systems LLC	Branford	CT	D	203 208-3142	288
Alloy Welding & Mfg Co Inc	Bristol	CT	F	860 582-3638	518
Anco Engineering Inc	Shelton	CT	D	203 925-9235	3775
Andert Inc	Eastford	CT	G	860 974-3893	1312
Ansonia Stl Fabrication Co Inc	Beacon Falls	CT	E	203 888-4509	53
Applied Laser Solutions Inc	Danbury	CT	G	203 739-0179	873
ARC Dynamics Inc	Rocky Hill	CT	G	860 563-1006	3702
Atlantic Eqp Installers Inc	Wallingford	CT	E	203 284-0402	4705
Atlantic Fabricating Co Inc	South Windsor	CT	F	860 291-9882	3940
Atlas Metal Works LLC	South Windsor	CT	F	860 282-1030	3941
Bri Metal Works Inc	Bridgeport	CT	G	203 368-1649	386
Carpin Manufacturing Inc	Waterbury	CT	D	203 574-2556	4854
Central Construction Inds LLC	Putnam	CT	E	860 963-8902	3604
Cirillo Manufacturing Group	East Haven	CT	G	203 484-5010	1244
Coastal Steel Corporation	Waterford	CT	E	860 443-4073	4982
Colonial Iron Shop Inc	Enfield	CT	G	860 763-0659	1351
Connecticut Iron Works Inc	Greenwich	CT	G	203 869-0657	1603
Delany & Long Ltd	Greenwich	CT	G	203 532-0010	1606
Di-Cor Industries Inc	Bristol	CT	F	860 585-5583	549
Division 5 LLC	Stafford Springs	CT	G	860 752-4127	4109
Eagle Manufacturing Co Inc	Colchester	CT	F	860 537-3759	801
East Windsor Metal Fabg Inc	South Windsor	CT	F	860 528-7107	3961
Eastern Inc	New Canaan	CT	G	203 563-9535	2597
Enginering Components Pdts LLC	Plainville	CT	G	860 747-6222	3486
ES Metal Fabrications Inc	Terryville	CT	F	860 585-6067	4478
Gulf Manufacturing Inc	Rocky Hill	CT	E	860 529-8601	3710
HRF Fastener Systems Inc	Bristol	CT	E	860 589-0750	569
Iron Craft Fabricating LLC	North Grosvenordale	CT	G	860 923-9869	2996
Kinamor Incorporated	Wallingford	CT	E	203 269-0380	4760
Lemac Iron Works Inc	West Hartford	CT	G	860 232-7380	5081
LH Gault & Son Incorporated	Westport	CT	D	203 227-5181	5209
Magna Steel Sales Inc	Beacon Falls	CT	F	203 888-0300	62
Mayarc Industries Inc	Ellington	CT	G	860 871-1872	1335
Mobile Mini Inc	Suffield	CT	E	860 668-1888	4465
Mtj Manufacturing Inc	Bridgeport	CT	G	203 334-4939	454
Mystic Stainless & Alum Inc	Mystic	CT	G	860 536-2236	2446
Ovl Manufacturing Inc LLC	Berlin	CT	G	860 829-0271	100
Pcx Aerostructures LLC	Newington	CT	E	860 666-2471	2892
Platt & Labonia Company LLC	North Haven	CT	E	800 505-9099	3051
Reliable Welding & Speed LLC	Enfield	CT	G	860 749-3977	1379
Romco Contractors Inc	Bloomfield	CT	F	860 243-8872	257
Rwt Corporation	Madison	CT	E	203 245-2731	1973
Shepard Steel Co Inc	Newington	CT	E	860 525-4446	2902
Stamford Iron & Stl Works Inc	Stamford	CT	F	203 324-6751	4331
Steeltech Building Pdts Inc	South Windsor	CT	D	860 290-8930	4014
Stratford Steel LLC	Stratford	CT	E	203 612-7350	4449
Swift Innovations LLC	Mystic	CT	G	860 572-8322	2452
Thomas La Ganga	Torrington	CT	G	860 489-0920	4601
Tinsley GROup-Ps&w Inc **(HQ)**	Milford	CT	D	919 742-5832	2376
Total Fab LLC	East Haven	CT	F	475 238-8176	1266
United Steel Inc	East Hartford	CT	C	860 289-2323	1232
Varnum Enterprises LLC	Bethel	CT	F	203 743-4443	190
Vernier Metal Fabricating Inc	Seymour	CT	D	203 881-3133	3767
Viking Enterprises Inc	Waterford	CT	G	860 440-0728	4995
Yankee Metals LLC	Bridgeport	CT	G	203 612-7470	507
2l Inc	Hudson	MA	F	978 567-8867	11748
3-D Welding Inc	Attleboro	MA	F	508 222-2500	7695
A G Industries Inc	North Attleboro	MA	G	508 695-4219	13741
Accufab Iron Works Inc	Goshen	MA	F	413 268-7133	11222
All Star Fabrication Inc	Ipswich	MA	G	978 887-7617	11901
Allied Fabrication Inc	North Billerica	MA	G	978 667-5901	13791
American Metalcraft Co	East Weymouth	MA	G	781 331-8588	10535
Atlantic Steel Fabricators Inc	Wilmington	MA	G	978 657-8292	16976
Barker Steel LLC	South Deerfield	MA	E	413 665-2381	15245
Barker Steel LLC	Westfield	MA	E	413 568-7803	16671
Bay Steel Co Inc **(PA)**	Halifax	MA	G	781 294-8308	11315
Bellingham Metal Works LLC	Franklin	MA	G	617 519-5958	11025
Berkshire Bridge & Iron Co Inc	Dalton	MA	F	413 684-3182	10174
Blue Atlantic Fabricators LLC	Boston	MA	F	617 874-8503	8415
Boston Forging & Welding Corp	Boston	MA	G	617 567-2300	8430
Brayton Wilson Cole Corp	Hingham	MA	G	781 803-6624	11495
Butler Metal Fabricators Inc	Indian Orchard	MA	G	413 306-5762	11885
Capone Iron Corporation	Rowley	MA	E	978 948-8000	14848
Carl Fisher Co Inc	Springfield	MA	E	413 736-3661	15458
Composite Modules	Attleboro	MA	D	508 226-6969	7723
Custom Steel Fabrication Corp	Middleton	MA	G	978 774-4555	13087
D Clement Inc	Dunstable	MA	G	978 649-3263	10389
Danvers Engineering Co Inc	Danvers	MA	G	978 774-7501	10211
Dean Paige Welding Inc	Baldwinville	MA	G	978 939-8187	7943
Diamond Ironworks Inc	Lawrence	MA	E	978 794-4640	12017
Digital Alloys Incorporated	Burlington	MA	F	617 557-3432	9256
E T Duval & Son Inc	Leominster	MA	G	978 537-7596	12134
East Coast Fabrications	West Wareham	MA	G	508 295-1982	16569
Eastern Metal Industries Inc	Saugus	MA	F	781 231-5220	14980
Emseal Joint Systems Ltd	Westborough	MA	E	508 836-0280	16617
Environmental Improvements **(PA)**	Abington	MA	G	781 857-2375	7324
Ernest Johnson	Marlborough	MA	G	508 259-6727	12753
Fall River Boiler & Welding Co	Fall River	MA	G	508 677-4479	10695
Fitchburg Welding Co Inc	Westminster	MA	E	978 874-2911	16804
Flametech Steels Inc	Lawrence	MA	G	978 686-9518	12024
General Steel Products Co Inc	Lexington	MA	F	617 387-5400	12228
Gill Metal Fab Inc	Brockton	MA	E	508 580-4445	9151
Industrial Metal Pdts Co Inc	Sharon	MA	D	781 762-3330	15052
Industrial Stl Boiler Svcs Inc	Chicopee	MA	E	413 532-7788	10032
International Stone Inc	Woburn	MA	D	781 937-3300	17206
Ironman Inc	Mansfield	MA	G	989 386-8975	12638
Jeff Schiff	Chelsea	MA	G	617 887-0202	9956
Jlp Services Inc	Rutland	MA	G	508 667-5498	14882
Kent Fabrications Inc	Pembroke	MA	G	339 244-4533	14413
L & J Enterprises Inc	Malden	MA	G	781 233-1966	12576
Mass Metalworks LLC	Medway	MA	G	508 533-7500	12966
Mbs Fabrication Inc **(PA)**	Southbridge	MA	F	508 765-0900	15395
Metal Solutions LLC	Millbury	MA	G	774 276-0096	13171
Metrick Manufacturing Co Inc	Woburn	MA	G	781 935-1331	17228
Mill City Iron Fabricators	Dracut	MA	F	978 957-6833	10366
Moseley Corporation	Franklin	MA	E	508 520-4004	11068
Nevron Plastics Inc	Saugus	MA	F	781 233-1310	14991
New England Welding Inc	Avon	MA	F	508 580-2024	7891
North American Steel Corp	Peabody	MA	G	978 535-7587	14357
North Shore Steel Co Inc **(PA)**	Lynn	MA	E	781 598-1645	12530

PRODUCT

	CITY	ST	EMP	PHONE	ENTRY #
O W Landergren Inc	Pittsfield	MA	E	413 442-5632	14497
Payne Engrg Fabrication Co Inc	Canton	MA	E	781 828-9046	9765
Quality Laser Inc	Woburn	MA	G	617 479-7374	17276
R I Baker Co Inc **(PA)**	Clarksburg	MA	E	413 663-3791	10075
R Moody Machine & Fabrication	Deerfield	MA	G	413 773-3329	10303
Ranor Inc	Westminster	MA	D	978 874-0591	16812
Rayco Inc	Amesbury	MA	G	978 388-1039	7504
Rens Welding & Fabricating	Taunton	MA	F	508 828-1702	15779
Republic Iron Works Inc	Chicopee	MA	G	413 594-8819	10058
Robert Russell Co Inc	Rehoboth	MA	G	508 226-4140	14760
Sajawi Corporation	Littleton	MA	E	978 486-9050	12323
Scannell Boiler Works Inc	Lowell	MA	F	978 454-5629	12431
Schiff Archtectural Detail LLC	Chelsea	MA	G	617 846-6437	9966
Service Oriented Sales Inc	Shrewsbury	MA	G	508 845-3330	15131
Shawmut Metal Products Inc	Swansea	MA	E	508 379-0803	15715
Smj Metal Co Inc	Northampton	MA	E	413 586-3535	14021
Sousa Bros & Demayo Inc	Attleboro Falls	MA	E	508 695-6800	7817
Southstern Mtal Fbricators Inc	Rockland	MA	E	781 878-1505	14826
Standex International Corp	North Billerica	MA	D	978 667-2771	13869
Starkweather Engineering Inc	Tewksbury	MA	F	978 858-3700	15837
Steel Connections Inc	Franklin	MA	G	508 958-5129	11082
Stoughton Steel Company Inc	Hanover	MA	E	781 826-6496	11354
Taco Inc	Fall River	MA	D	508 675-7300	10769
Tuckerman Stl Fabricators Inc	Boston	MA	D	617 569-8373	8892
Village Forge Inc	Boston	MA	F	617 361-2591	8911
Web Industries Inc **(PA)**	Marlborough	MA	G	508 898-2988	12848
Welfab Inc	North Billerica	MA	E	978 667-0180	13876
Advanced Resources & Construct	Kingfield	ME	E	207 265-2646	6251
Brass Foundry	West Rockport	ME	G	207 236-3200	7178
Cianbro Fbrcation Coating Corp	Pittsfield	ME	C	207 487-3311	6588
Cives Corporation	Augusta	ME	C	207 622-6141	5605
Clark Metal Fabrication Inc	Turner	ME	G	207 330-6322	7106
Contech Engnered Solutions LLC	Scarborough	ME	E	207 885-9830	6915
Design Fab Inc	Auburn	ME	G	207 786-2446	5559
Floyd Baker Metal Fabrication	Oakland	ME	G	207 465-9346	6533
Glover Company Inc	Rockport	ME	F	207 236-8644	6822
Harmac Rebar & Steel Corp	Fryeburg	ME	E	207 935-3531	6098
Howies Wldg & Fabrication Inc	Jay	ME	G	207 645-2581	6220
James A McBrady Inc	Scarborough	ME	E	207 883-4176	6928
Jf Hutchinson Co	New Gloucester	ME	F	207 926-3676	6468
Jr Robert Austin	Sanford	ME	G	207 490-1500	6878
Kantahdin Welding	Patten	ME	G	207 528-2924	6578
Knowlton Machine Company	Gorham	ME	E	207 854-8471	6117
L M C Light Iron Inc	Limerick	ME	F	207 793-9957	6335
Maine Fabricators Inc	Gorham	ME	G	207 839-8555	6119
McCann Fabrication	New Gloucester	ME	E	207 926-4118	6469
ME Tomacelli Inc	Boothbay	ME	G	207 633-7553	5779
Metal Magic Inc	Trenton	ME	G	207 667-8519	7100
Mid State Sheet Metal & Wldg	Monmouth	ME	G	207 933-5603	6450
North ATL Cstm Fabrication Inc	Westbrook	ME	G	207 839-8410	7199
North E Wldg & Fabrication Inc	Auburn	ME	E	207 786-2446	5583
Prescott Metal **(PA)**	Biddeford	ME	E	207 283-0115	5759
Pro-Vac Inc	Alfred	ME	G	207 324-1846	5517
Ramsays Welding & Machine Inc	Lincoln	ME	F	207 794-8839	6359
Robert Mitchell Co Inc **(DH)**	Portland	ME	E	207 797-6771	6722
Seth Hetherington	South Harpswell	ME	G	207 833-5400	7008
Steel-Pro Inc	Rockland	ME	E	207 596-0061	6810
Thermal Fab Inc	New Gloucester	ME	G	207 926-5212	6473
Velux America LLC	Wells	ME	D	207 216-4500	7167
William Smith Enterprises Inc	Sidney	ME	G	207 549-3103	6966
Ace Welding Co Inc	Merrimack	NH	E	603 424-9936	18984
Alpine Machine Co Inc	Berlin	NH	F	603 752-1441	17691
American Steel Fabricators Inc	Greenfield	NH	E	603 547-6311	18218
Apollo Steel LLC	Jaffrey	NH	G	603 532-1156	18456
Charles Leonard Steel Svcs LLC	Concord	NH	F	603 225-0211	17893
Charles Smith Steel LLC	Boscawen	NH	G	603 753-9844	17702
Cross Machine Inc	Berlin	NH	F	603 752-6111	17694
Custom Welding & Fabrications	West Nottingham	NH	F	603 942-5170	19964
East Coast Metal Works Co Inc	Kingston	NH	G	603 642-9600	18543
Fronek Anchor Darling Entp	Laconia	NH	F	603 528-1931	18564
Fwm Inc	Hudson	NH	E	603 578-3366	18391
Gilchrist Metal Fabg Co Inc **(PA)**	Hudson	NH	E	603 889-2600	18392
Granite State Plasma Cutting	Portsmouth	NH	E	603 536-4415	19568
Greenfield Industries Inc	Amherst	NH	G	603 883-6423	17565
New Hampshire Stl Erectors Inc	Goffstown	NH	E	603 668-3464	18207
New Hmpshire Stl Fbrcators Inc	Goffstown	NH	E	603 668-3464	18208
Protective Technologies Svcs	North Hampton	NH	G	603 964-9421	19387
Quality Fabricators LLC	Barrington	NH	G	603 905-9012	17621
Smiths Tblar Systms-Lconia Inc	Laconia	NH	B	603 524-2064	18587
Steel Elements Intl LLC	Hudson	NH	G	603 466-2500	18442
Summit Metal Fabricators Inc	Plaistow	NH	D	603 328-2211	19525
Superior Steel Fabricators Inc	Brookline	NH	F	603 673-7509	17773
Tri-State Iron Works Inc	Concord	NH	E	603 228-0020	17937
Valley Welding & Fabg Inc	Hollis	NH	E	603 465-3266	18340
Viking Wldg & Fabrication LLC	Kensington	NH	G	603 394-7887	18537
Winchester Precision Tech Ltd	Winchester	NH	F	603 239-6326	19997
Amaral Custom Fabrications Inc	Rumford	RI	F	401 396-5663	21180
Blouin General Welding & Fabg	Woonsocket	RI	G	401 762-4542	21551
Blount Boats Inc	Warren	RI	D	401 245-8300	21289
Custom Iron Works Inc	Coventry	RI	F	401 826-3310	20144
Desnoyers Enterprises Inc	Harrisville	RI	G	800 922-4445	20478
Dominion Rebar Company	Pawtucket	RI	E	401 724-9200	20834
Getchell & Son Inc	Smithfield	RI	F	401 231-3850	21228
Luthers Repair Shop Inc	Bristol	RI	F	401 253-5550	20091
Metal Guy LLC	Newport	RI	G	401 474-0234	20672
New England Copperworks	Smithfield	RI	G	401 232-9899	21240
Seven Star Inc	Newport	RI	G	401 683-6222	20680
South County Steel Inc	West Kingston	RI	G	401 789-5570	21473
Westbay Welding & Fabrication	Warwick	RI	G	401 737-2357	21445
Browns Certified Welding Inc	Bristol	VT	F	802 453-3351	21762
L & G Fabricators Inc	Bennington	VT	F	802 447-0965	21679
Milton Vermont Sheet Metal Inc	Milton	VT	D	802 893-1581	22134
Nops Metal Works	Middlebury	VT	F	802 382-9300	22116
PG Adams Inc	South Burlington	VT	F	802 862-8664	22457
Reliance Steel Inc **(PA)**	Colchester	VT	F	802 655-4810	21877
Reliance Steel Vermont Inc	Colchester	VT	E	802 655-4810	21878
Rowden Bros Corporation	Wells River	VT	G	802 757-2807	22602
S & A Trombley Corporation	Morrisville	VT	E	802 888-2394	22176
Star Wind Turbines LLC	East Dorset	VT	G	802 779-8118	21916
United Puett Starting Gate	Westminster	VT	G	802 463-3440	22631
Vendituoli Limited Company	Vergennes	VT	G	802 535-4319	22557
Vermont Indexable Tooling Inc	Fairfax	VT	G	802 752-2002	21980

STEEL MILLS

	CITY	ST	EMP	PHONE	ENTRY #
Ball & Roller Bearing Co LLC	New Milford	CT	F	860 355-4161	2787
Thermo Conductor Services Inc	Prospect	CT	G	203 758-6611	3598
Tms International LLC	Greenwich	CT	G	203 629-8383	1656
Ulbrich Stainless Steels	Wallingford	CT	C	203 269-2507	4824
Ulbrich Stnless Stels Spcial M **(PA)**	North Haven	CT	D	203 239-4481	3067
Waterbury Rolling Mills Inc	Waterbury	CT	D	203 597-5000	4973
Hillman Enterprises **(PA)**	Attleboro	MA	G	508 761-6967	7747
Rudison Routhier Engrg Co	West Hatfield	MA	G	413 247-9341	16485
Harding Metals Inc	Northwood	NH	E	603 942-5573	19412
New Hmpshire Ball Bearings Inc	Laconia	NH	B	603 524-0004	18577
Capco Steel Erection Company	Providence	RI	F	401 383-9388	20979

STEEL, COLD-ROLLED: Sheet Or Strip, From Own Hot-Rolled

	CITY	ST	EMP	PHONE	ENTRY #
Bushwick Metals LLC	Meriden	CT	G	203 630-2459	2081
Kimchuk Incorporated **(PA)**	Danbury	CT	F	203 790-7800	943
Redifoils LLC	Portland	CT	F	860 342-1500	3573

STEEL, COLD-ROLLED: Strip NEC, From Purchased Hot-Rolled

	CITY	ST	EMP	PHONE	ENTRY #
Ulbrich Stnless Stels Spcial M **(PA)**	North Haven	CT	D	203 239-4481	3067
New Amtrol Holdings Inc **(DH)**	West Warwick	RI	G	614 438-3210	21505

STEEL, COLD-ROLLED: Strip Or Wire

	CITY	ST	EMP	PHONE	ENTRY #
Feroleto Steel Company Inc **(DH)**	Bridgeport	CT	D	203 366-3263	413

STEEL: Cold-Rolled

	CITY	ST	EMP	PHONE	ENTRY #
Deringer-Ney Inc **(PA)**	Bloomfield	CT	C	860 242-2281	217
Eastern Company **(PA)**	Naugatuck	CT	E	203 729-2255	2471
North East Fasteners Corp	Terryville	CT	E	860 589-3242	4488
Paradigm Manchester Inc	Manchester	CT	C	860 649-2888	2032
Sandvik Wire and Htg Tech Corp **(DH)**	Bethel	CT	D	203 744-1440	178
Sandvik Wire and Htg Tech Corp	Bethel	CT	D	203 744-1440	177
Shepard Steel Co Inc	Newington	CT	E	860 525-4446	2902
Theis Precision Steel USA Inc **(HQ)**	Bristol	CT	C	860 589-5511	616
Ulbrich Stainless Steels	Wallingford	CT	C	203 269-2507	4824
Fall River Mfg Co Inc	Fall River	MA	D	508 675-1125	10696
Frank L Reed Inc	Wilbraham	MA	E	413 596-3861	16937
Premier Roll & Tool Inc	North Attleboro	MA	G	508 695-2551	13774
Tri Cast Inc **(PA)**	Somersworth	NH	F	603 692-2480	19851

STEEL: Laminated

	CITY	ST	EMP	PHONE	ENTRY #
Alinabal Inc **(HQ)**	Milford	CT	C	203 877-3241	2242
Alinabal Holdings Corporation **(PA)**	Milford	CT	B	203 877-3241	2243

STEERING SYSTEMS & COMPONENTS

	CITY	ST	EMP	PHONE	ENTRY #
Global Steering Systems LLC **(PA)**	Watertown	CT	C	860 945-5400	5011
Lewmar Inc **(DH)**	Guilford	CT	E	203 458-6200	1708

STENCILS

	CITY	ST	EMP	PHONE	ENTRY #
Liftline Capital LLC	Old Saybrook	CT	F	860 395-0150	3342
Mbsw Inc	West Hartford	CT	D	860 243-0303	5086

STENCILS & LETTERING MATERIALS: Die-Cut

	CITY	ST	EMP	PHONE	ENTRY #
Liftline Capital LLC	Old Saybrook	CT	F	860 395-0150	3342
Stencils Online LLC	Franklin	NH	G	603 934-5034	18165
Stentech Inc **(HQ)**	Derry	NH	F	603 505-4470	17998
Stentech Photo Stencil LLC	Derry	NH	F	719 287-7934	17999

STITCHING SVCS

	CITY	ST	EMP	PHONE	ENTRY #
Agawam Novelty Company Inc	Agawam	MA	G	413 536-0471	7418
Lyman Conrad **(PA)**	South Hadley	MA	E	413 538-8200	15306

STONE: Cast Concrete

	CITY	ST	EMP	PHONE	ENTRY #
New Canaan Stone Service LLC	Johnston	RI	G	401 829-8293	20525

STONE: Crushed & Broken, NEC

	CITY	ST	EMP	PHONE	ENTRY #
Bardon Trimount Inc	Wrentham	MA	G	508 384-3161	17516

STONE: Dimension, NEC

	CITY	ST	EMP	PHONE	ENTRY #
Connecticut Stone Supplies Inc **(PA)**	Milford	CT	D	203 882-1000	2270
West Hartford Stone Mulch LLC	West Hartford	CT	G	860 461-7616	5103
Southcoast Stoneworks Inc	Westport	MA	F	774 319-5200	16848
World Stone	Everett	MA	G	617 293-4373	10634
Adams Granite Company Inc	Websterville	VT	D	802 476-5281	22596
Houle Bros Granite Co Inc	Barre	VT	E	802 476-6825	21624
International Stone Products **(PA)**	Barre	VT	D	802 476-6636	21625
Troy Minerals Inc	Florence	VT	G	802 878-5103	21992

STONE: Quarrying & Processing, Own Stone Prdts

	CITY	ST	EMP	PHONE	ENTRY #
French River Mtls Thompson LLC	North Grosvenordale	CT	G	860 450-9574	2994

	CITY	ST	EMP	PHONE	ENTRY #
Kenneth Lynch & Sons Inc	Oxford	CT	G	203 762-8363	3411
New England Materials LLC	Monroe	CT	G	203 261-5500	2412
O & G Industries Inc	Beacon Falls	CT	F	203 729-4529	64
Paul H Gesswein & Company Inc	Old Saybrook	CT	G	860 388-0652	3348
Skyline Quarry	Stafford Springs	CT	E	860 875-3580	4115
270 University Ave LLC	Westwood	MA	G	781 407-0836	16855
All Granite & Marble Inc II	Charlton	MA	G	508 434-0611	9846
Bates Bros Seam Face Gran Co	East Weymouth	MA	F	781 337-1150	10537
E W Sykes General Contractors	Athol	MA	F	978 249-7655	7686
S M Lorusso & Sons Inc	East Weymouth	MA	E	781 337-6770	10546
Newmont Slate Co Inc **(PA)**	West Pawlet	VT	E	802 645-0203	22612

STONES, SYNTHETIC: Gem Stone & Indl Use

	CITY	ST	EMP	PHONE	ENTRY #
Saphikon Inc	Milford	NH	D	603 672-7221	19077
Northeastern Importing Corp	Providence	RI	G	401 276-0654	21078

STONEWARE PRDTS: Pottery

	CITY	ST	EMP	PHONE	ENTRY #
Jill Rosenwald Ceramic Design	Boston	MA	G	617 422-0787	8630
Sheffield Pottery Inc	Sheffield	MA	E	413 229-7700	15065
Chris Davis Stoneware Pottery	York	ME	G	207 363-7561	7306
Bennington Potters Inc **(PA)**	Bennington	VT	E	800 205-8033	21664

STORE FIXTURES, EXC REFRIGERATED: Wholesalers

	CITY	ST	EMP	PHONE	ENTRY #
Jsi Store Fixtures Inc **(PA)**	Milo	ME	C	207 943-5203	6446
Leo D Bernstein & Sons Inc	Shaftsbury	VT	D	802 442-8029	22404

STORE FIXTURES: Exc Wood

	CITY	ST	EMP	PHONE	ENTRY #
In Store Experience Inc	Westport	CT	E	203 221-4777	5201

STORE FIXTURES: Wood

	CITY	ST	EMP	PHONE	ENTRY #
Anthony Manufacturing Co Inc	Medford	MA	F	781 396-1400	12921
E G W Bradbury Enterprises	Bridgewater	ME	F	207 429-8141	5805

STORES: Auto & Home Supply

	CITY	ST	EMP	PHONE	ENTRY #
International Automobile Entps **(PA)**	New Britain	CT	F	860 224-0253	2543
M & B Automotive Machine Shop	Stamford	CT	G	203 348-6134	4242

STORES: Drapery & Upholstery

	CITY	ST	EMP	PHONE	ENTRY #
Maine Stitching Spc LLC	Skowhegan	ME	F	207 812-5207	6981

STOVES: Wood & Coal Burning

	CITY	ST	EMP	PHONE	ENTRY #
Heart Quali Home Heati Produ	Morrisville	VT	D	802 888-5232	22169
L & G Fabricators Inc	Bennington	VT	F	802 447-0965	21679

STRADDLE CARRIERS: Mobile

	CITY	ST	EMP	PHONE	ENTRY #
Southworth Products Corp **(HQ)**	Falmouth	ME	E	207 878-0700	6034

STRAIN GAGES: Solid State

	CITY	ST	EMP	PHONE	ENTRY #
LLC Dow Gage	Berlin	CT	E	860 828-5327	93
Strain Measurement Devices Inc	Wallingford	CT	E	203 294-5800	4814

STRAPPING

	CITY	ST	EMP	PHONE	ENTRY #
H G Steinmetz Machine Works	Bethel	CT	F	203 794-1880	158

STRAPS: Apparel Webbing

	CITY	ST	EMP	PHONE	ENTRY #
Spectrum Marketing Dbalogo Loc	Manchester	NH	G	603 644-4800	18928

STRAPS: Beltings, Woven or Braided

	CITY	ST	EMP	PHONE	ENTRY #
Brockway Ferry Corporation **(PA)**	Essex	CT	G	860 767-8231	1394

STRAPS: Braids, Textile

	CITY	ST	EMP	PHONE	ENTRY #
Conneaut Industries Inc	West Greenwich	RI	D	401 392-1110	21454

STRAPS: Webbing, Woven

	CITY	ST	EMP	PHONE	ENTRY #
Murdock Webbing Company Inc **(PA)**	Central Falls	RI	C	401 724-3000	20121
Nfa Corp	Cumberland	RI	B	401 333-8947	20331
Nfa Corp	Cumberland	RI	B	401 333-8990	20334
Texcel Industries Inc	Cumberland	RI	E	401 727-2113	20348

STRIPS: Copper & Copper Alloy

	CITY	ST	EMP	PHONE	ENTRY #
Miller Company	Meriden	CT	E	203 235-4474	2108
House of Stainless Inc	Cranston	RI	E	800 556-3470	20237

STRUCTURAL SUPPORT & BUILDING MATERIAL: Concrete

	CITY	ST	EMP	PHONE	ENTRY #
WJ Kettleworks LLC	Stratford	CT	G	203 377-5000	4458

STUCCO

	CITY	ST	EMP	PHONE	ENTRY #
AK Stucco LLC	New Britain	CT	G	860 832-9589	2507
U S Stucco LLC	Newington	CT	G	860 667-1935	2909
Hergon Design Inc	Revere	MA	G	781 286-0663	14766

STUDIOS: Sculptor's

	CITY	ST	EMP	PHONE	ENTRY #
Vendituoli Limited Company	Vergennes	VT	G	802 535-4319	22557

SUB-LESSORS: Real Estate

	CITY	ST	EMP	PHONE	ENTRY #
Lrv Properties LLC	Providence	RI	G	401 714-7001	21058

SUBMARINE BUILDING & REPAIR

	CITY	ST	EMP	PHONE	ENTRY #
Electric Boat Corporation	Groton	CT	D	860 433-0503	1673
Electric Boat Corporation	Groton	CT	D	860 433-3000	1674
Electric Boat Corporation **(HQ)**	Groton	CT	A	860 433-3000	1675
General Dynamics Corporation	Hinsdale	MA	E	413 494-3137	11520
Portsmouth Naval Shipyard	Portsmouth	NH	G	207 438-1000	19608
Electric Boat Corporation	North Kingstown	RI	D	401 268-2410	20707

SUGAR SUBSTITUTES: Organic

	CITY	ST	EMP	PHONE	ENTRY #
Nutrasweet Company	Waltham	MA	E	706 303-5600	16164

SUITCASES

	CITY	ST	EMP	PHONE	ENTRY #
Dooney & Bourke Inc **(PA)**	Norwalk	CT	E	203 853-7515	3142

SUNDRIES & RELATED PRDTS: Medical & Laboratory, Rubber

	CITY	ST	EMP	PHONE	ENTRY #
Advent Medical Products Inc	Lincoln	MA	E	781 272-2813	12285
Hytex Industries Inc	Randolph	MA	E	781 963-4400	14686
Renco Corporation **(PA)**	Manchester	MA	G	978 526-8494	12606
Rubberright Rollers Inc	Everett	MA	G	617 387-6060	10629
Saint-Gobain Prfmce Plas Corp	Worcester	MA	E	508 852-3072	17467
Expanded Rubber Products Inc	Kennebunk	ME	G	207 985-4141	6233
Kingswood Sales Inc	Sanbornville	NH	G	603 522-6636	19783
Iselann Moss Industries Inc	Cranston	RI	F	401 463-5950	20242

SUNGLASSES, WHOLESALE

	CITY	ST	EMP	PHONE	ENTRY #
Sibs LLC	Meredith	NH	G	781 864-7498	18979

SUNROOMS: Prefabricated Metal

	CITY	ST	EMP	PHONE	ENTRY #
LLC Glass House	Pomfret Center	CT	G	860 974-1665	3556
Niantic Awning Company	Niantic	CT	G	860 739-0161	2954
Cmsr Services LLC	Auburn	MA	G	774 210-2513	7831
L F Pease Co	East Providence	RI	F	401 438-2850	20428

SUPERMARKETS & OTHER GROCERY STORES

	CITY	ST	EMP	PHONE	ENTRY #
CFM Test & Balance Corp	Bethel	CT	G	203 778-1900	136
Alden Acoreana Realty Trust **(PA)**	Fall River	MA	G	508 678-2098	10652
Biena LLC	Boston	MA	G	617 202-5210	8407
Wohrles Foods Inc **(PA)**	Pittsfield	MA	E	413 442-1518	14513

SURFACE ACTIVE AGENTS

	CITY	ST	EMP	PHONE	ENTRY #
Henkel of America Inc **(HQ)**	Rocky Hill	CT	B	860 571-5100	3715
Henkel US Operations Corp **(DH)**	Rocky Hill	CT	B	860 571-5100	3716
Lanxess Solutions US Inc **(DH)**	Shelton	CT	E	203 573-2000	3824
Isp Freetown Fine Chem Inc	Assonet	MA	D	508 672-0634	7681
Henkel Corporation	Seabrook	NH	C	508 230-1100	19804
CNc International Ltd Partnr	Woonsocket	RI	E	401 769-6100	21556

SURFACE ACTIVE AGENTS: Oils & Greases

	CITY	ST	EMP	PHONE	ENTRY #
Solidification Pdts Intl Inc	Northford	CT	G	203 484-9494	3092

SURFACERS: Concrete Grinding

	CITY	ST	EMP	PHONE	ENTRY #
Vermont Eco Floors	Charlotte	VT	G	802 425-7737	21835

SURGICAL & MEDICAL INSTRUMENTS WHOLESALERS

	CITY	ST	EMP	PHONE	ENTRY #
American Optics Limited	Wellesley Hills	MA	F	905 631-5377	16395
Lemaitre Vascular Inc **(PA)**	Burlington	MA	C	781 221-2266	9297
Idexx Laboratories Inc **(PA)**	Westbrook	ME	A	207 556-0300	7191

SURGICAL APPLIANCES & SPLYS

	CITY	ST	EMP	PHONE	ENTRY #
Bio Med Packaging Systems Inc	Norwalk	CT	E	203 846-1923	3113
Brymill Corporation **(PA)**	Ellington	CT	F	860 875-2460	1330
K W Griffen Company	Norwalk	CT	E	203 846-1923	3183
Schaeffler Aerospace USA Corp **(DH)**	Danbury	CT	B	203 744-2211	984
Arrow Interventional Inc	Chelmsford	MA	E	919 433-4948	9872
Head Prone Inc	Cambridge	MA	G	617 864-0780	9506
Steelcraft Inc	Millbury	MA	E	508 865-4445	13176
Atrium Medical Corporation **(HQ)**	Merrimack	NH	B	603 880-1433	18986
Atrium Medical Corporation	Hudson	NH	G	603 880-1433	18375

SURGICAL APPLIANCES & SPLYS

	CITY	ST	EMP	PHONE	ENTRY #
Auto Suture Company Australia	Norwalk	CT	G	203 845-1000	3106
Auto Suture Company UK	Norwalk	CT	B	203 845-1000	3107
Becton Dickinson and Company	Canaan	CT	B	860 824-5487	683
Cardiopulmonary Corp	Milford	CT	E	203 877-1999	2261
Carwild Corporation **(PA)**	New London	CT	E	860 442-4914	2768
Danbury Ortho	Danbury	CT	G	203 797-1500	898
Gordon Engineering Corp	Brookfield	CT	F	203 775-4501	645
Hanger Prsthetcs & Ortho Inc	Torrington	CT	G	860 482-5611	4581
Hanger Prsthetcs & Ortho Inc	North Haven	CT	G	203 230-0667	3029
Hanger Prsthetcs & Ortho Inc	Cromwell	CT	G	860 667-5300	854
Hanger Prsthetcs & Ortho Inc	Hartford	CT	F	860 545-9050	1829
Hanger Prsthetcs & Ortho Inc	Newington	CT	G	860 667-5370	2869
Hanger Prsthetcs & Ortho Inc	Vernon	CT	G	860 871-0905	4668
Kbc Electronics Inc	Milford	CT	F	203 298-9654	2306
Kelyniam Global Inc	Collinsville	CT	F	800 280-8192	815
Limbkeepers LLC	Lyme	CT	G	860 304-3250	1955
McIntire Company **(HQ)**	Bristol	CT	F	860 585-8559	580
McNeil Healthcare Inc	West Haven	CT	G	203 934-8187	5136
New England Shoulder Elbow Soc	Farmington	CT	G	860 679-6600	1499
Respironics Inc	Wallingford	CT	C	203 697-6490	4795
Scapa Tapes North America LLC **(DH)**	Windsor	CT	C	860 688-8000	5361
Tangen Biosciences Inc	Branford	CT	E	203 433-4045	354
Teleflex Incorporated	Coventry	CT	E	860 742-8821	841
United States Surgical Corp **(HQ)**	New Haven	CT	A	203 845-1000	2750
3M Company	Haverhill	MA	G	978 420-0001	11403
Advanced Orthopedic Svcs Inc	Hyannis	MA	G	508 771-5050	11834
Aearo Technologies LLC	Auburn	MA	B	317 692-6645	7822
Amatech Corporation **(DH)**	Acton	MA	E	978 263-5401	7340
Americal Sergical Company	Salem	MA	G	781 592-7200	14890
Bay State Elevator Company Inc **(PA)**	Agawam	MA	E	413 786-7000	7421
Bionx Medical Technologies Inc	Cambridge	MA	D	781 761-1545	9411
Bonesupport Inc	Wellesley	MA	G	781 772-1756	16364
Boston Brace International	Burlington	MA	G	781 270-3650	9241
Boston Medical Products Inc	Shrewsbury	MA	E	508 898-9300	15105
Boston Orthotics Inc	Taunton	MA	E	508 821-7655	15733
Boston Scientific Corporation **(PA)**	Marlborough	MA	B	508 683-4000	12727
Continental Metal Pdts Co Inc	Woburn	MA	E	781 935-4400	17151
Covidien France Holdings Inc	Mansfield	MA	G	508 261-8000	12620
Covidien LLC	Mansfield	MA	G	508 261-8000	12621
Covidien LP **(HQ)**	Mansfield	MA	A	763 514-4000	12622
Covidien US Holdings Inc	Mansfield	MA	G	508 261-8000	12623

	CITY	ST	EMP	PHONE	ENTRY #
Fosta-Tek Optics Inc **(PA)**	Leominster	MA	D	978 534-6511	12141
Fresenius Usa Inc	Marlborough	MA	E	508 460-1150	12757
Gentex Optics Inc **(DH)**	Dudley	MA	C	570 282-8531	10376
Genzyme Corporation **(DH)**	Cambridge	MA	A	617 252-7500	9489
Gta-Nht Inc **(HQ)**	Rockland	MA	C	781 331-5900	14804
Hanger Prosthetics & Orthotics	Leominster	MA	G	978 466-7400	12149
Hanger Prsthetcs & Ortho Inc	Springfield	MA	G	413 734-0002	15474
Jahrling Ocular Prosthetics **(PA)**	Boston	MA	G	617 523-2280	8624
Marine Polymer Tech Inc **(PA)**	Tewksbury	MA	E	781 270-3200	15820
Medical Device Bus Svcs Inc	Bridgewater	MA	G	508 828-6155	9083
Medical Device Bus Svcs Inc	Norton	MA	D	508 828-2726	14082
Medsource Technologies LLC **(DH)**	Wilmington	MA	F	978 570-6900	17022
Neogenix LLC **(PA)**	Norwood	MA	G	781 702-6732	14181
Or-6 LLC	Sandwich	MA	G	617 515-1909	14971
Palomar Medical Products LLC	Burlington	MA	C	781 993-2300	9316
Ranfac Corp	Avon	MA	D	508 588-4400	7894
Rewalk Robotics Inc	Marlborough	MA	G	508 251-1154	12815
Smith & Nephew Inc	Lawrence	MA	G	978 208-0680	12075
Teleflex Medical Incorporated	Mansfield	MA	G	800 474-0178	12663
United Prosthetics Inc	Quincy	MA	G	617 773-7140	14665
Visionaid Inc	Wareham	MA	E	508 295-3300	16258
Wadsworth Medical Tech Inc	Westborough	MA	G	508 789-6531	16657
Hanger Prsthetcs & Ortho Inc	Portland	ME	G	207 773-4963	6668
Hardwood Products Company LP	Guilford	ME	B	207 876-3311	6158
Puritan Medical Pdts Co LLC	Guilford	ME	B	207 876-3311	6160
Arzol Corp	Keene	NH	G	603 352-5242	18493
Boston Brace International	Salem	NH	G	603 772-2388	19715
Fireye Inc **(DH)**	Derry	NH	C	603 432-4100	17979
Bacou-Dalloz Safety Inc	Smithfield	RI	G	401 232-1200	21212
Honeywell Safety Pdts USA Inc	Smithfield	RI	G	800 500-4739	21232
Honeywell Safety Products Usa	Smithfield	RI	F	401 233-0333	21233
Impactwear International Lllp	Providence	RI	G	213 559-2454	21036
Johnson & Johnson	Cumberland	RI	C	401 762-6751	20330
Aadco Medical Inc	Randolph	VT	D	802 728-3400	22296
Revision Ballistics Ltd	Essex Junction	VT	E	802 879-7002	21956

SURGICAL EQPT: See Also Instruments

	CITY	ST	EMP	PHONE	ENTRY #
Aplicare Products LLC **(HQ)**	Meriden	CT	C	203 630-0500	2077
Blairden Precision Instrs Inc	Trumbull	CT	G	203 799-2000	4616
Ipsogen	Stamford	CT	G	203 504-8583	4229
Lacey Manufacturing Co LLC	Bridgeport	CT	B	203 336-7427	443
Oerlikon AM Medical Inc	Shelton	CT	D	203 712-1030	3846
United States Surgical Corp **(HQ)**	New Haven	CT	A	203 845-1000	2750
3M Company	Lexington	MA	B	651 733-1110	12199
Abiomed R&D Inc	Danvers	MA	G	978 646-1400	10191
American Optics Limited	Wellesley Hills	MA	F	905 631-5377	16395
Arrow International Inc	Chelmsford	MA	D	978 250-5100	9871
Cold Chain Technologies Inc	Franklin	MA	D	508 429-1395	11029
Cold Chain Technologies Inc **(PA)**	Franklin	MA	D	508 429-1395	11030
Five Star Surgical Inc	New Bedford	MA	D	508 998-1404	13388
Fresenius Usa Inc	Marlborough	MA	E	508 460-1150	12757
Heartware International Inc **(DH)**	Framingham	MA	E	508 739-0950	10962
Hydrocision Inc	North Billerica	MA	E	978 474-9300	13824
Jlp Machine and Welding LLC	Kingston	MA	G	781 585-1744	11958
Lab Medical Manufacturing Inc	Billerica	MA	D	978 663-2475	8262
Lake Region Manufacturing Inc **(HQ)**	Wilmington	MA	A	952 361-2515	17015
Rachiotek LLC	Wellesley	MA	G	407 923-0721	16383
Rph Enterprises Inc	Franklin	MA	D	508 238-3351	11076
Smith & Nephew Inc	Andover	MA	E	978 749-1000	7608
Smith & Nephew Endoscopy Inc	Andover	MA	D	978 749-1000	7609
Surgibox Inc	Brookline	MA	G	617 982-3908	9221
Symmetry Medical Inc	New Bedford	MA	C	508 998-1104	13453
Target Therapeutics Inc **(HQ)**	Marlborough	MA	B	508 683-4000	12834
Tei Biosciences Inc	Boston	MA	E	617 268-1616	8875
Tnco Inc	New Bedford	MA	D	781 447-6661	13454
Hmd Inc	Jaffrey	NH	E	603 532-5757	18467
Icad Inc **(PA)**	Nashua	NH	C	603 882-5200	19181
Vapotherm Inc **(PA)**	Exeter	NH	B	603 658-0011	18135

SURGICAL IMPLANTS

	CITY	ST	EMP	PHONE	ENTRY #
Brimfield Precision LLC	Brimfield	MA	D	413 245-7144	9109
Crompton Park Oral Surgery & I	Worcester	MA	G	508 799-2550	17361
Depuy Spine LLC **(HQ)**	Raynham	MA	B	508 880-8100	14710
Depuy Synthes Sales Inc	Raynham	MA	F	508 880-8100	14713
Hd Lifesciences LLC	Woburn	MA	G	866 949-5433	17198
Medtronic Inc	Danvers	MA	F	978 739-3080	10239
Medtronic Inc	Danvers	MA	F	978 777-0042	10240
Tesco Associates Inc	Tyngsboro	MA	F	978 649-5527	15902
Imcor Inc	Nashua	NH	G	603 886-4300	19184
Seabrook Medical LLC	Seabrook	NH	C	603 474-1919	19817

SURVEYING SVCS: Aerial Digital Imaging

	CITY	ST	EMP	PHONE	ENTRY #
Assured Computing Technologies	Bedford	NH	G	603 627-8728	17631

SURVEYING SVCS: Photogrammetric Engineering

	CITY	ST	EMP	PHONE	ENTRY #
Greensight Agronomics Inc	Boston	MA	G	617 633-4919	8580

SUSPENSION SYSTEMS: Acoustical, Metal

	CITY	ST	EMP	PHONE	ENTRY #
Rolls-Royce Marine North Amer **(DH)**	Walpole	MA	C	508 668-9610	16009

SVC ESTABLISHMENT EQPT & SPLYS WHOLESALERS

	CITY	ST	EMP	PHONE	ENTRY #
Ace Beauty Supply Inc	Branford	CT	G	203 488-2416	284
Blendco Systems LLC	Holyoke	MA	E	800 537-7797	11619

SVC ESTABLISHMENT EQPT, WHOL: Boot/Shoe Cut Stock/findings

	CITY	ST	EMP	PHONE	ENTRY #
Vibram Corporation **(DH)**	North Brookfield	MA	C	508 867-6494	13883

SVC ESTABLISHMENT EQPT, WHOL: Cleaning & Maint Eqpt & Splys

	CITY	ST	EMP	PHONE	ENTRY #
Griffith Company	Bridgeport	CT	G	203 333-5557	422

SVC ESTABLISHMENT EQPT, WHOL: Concrete Burial Vaults & Boxes

	CITY	ST	EMP	PHONE	ENTRY #
Keating Wilbert Vault Company	Wilbraham	MA	F	413 543-1226	16939
Quintal Burial Vaults	Dighton	MA	F	508 669-5717	10338

SVC ESTABLISHMENT EQPT, WHOL: Funeral Director's Eqpt/Splys

	CITY	ST	EMP	PHONE	ENTRY #
Dodge Company Inc **(PA)**	Billerica	MA	G	800 443-6343	8237

SVC ESTABLISHMENT EQPT, WHOLESALE: Firefighting Eqpt

	CITY	ST	EMP	PHONE	ENTRY #
Greenwood Emrgncy Vehicles LLC **(HQ)**	North Attleboro	MA	D	508 695-7138	13758

SWEEPING COMPOUNDS

	CITY	ST	EMP	PHONE	ENTRY #
Absorbent Specialty Pdts LLC	Cumberland	RI	F	401 722-1177	20312

SWIMMING POOL EQPT: Filters & Water Conditioning Systems

	CITY	ST	EMP	PHONE	ENTRY #
Accu-Care Supply Inc	Rumford	RI	E	401 438-7110	21179

SWIMMING POOL SPLY STORES

	CITY	ST	EMP	PHONE	ENTRY #
Boudrieau Tool & Die Inc	Rindge	NH	G	603 899-5795	19647

SWITCHBOARDS & PARTS: Power

	CITY	ST	EMP	PHONE	ENTRY #
Lex Products LLC **(PA)**	Shelton	CT	C	203 363-3738	3828
Whitmor Company Inc **(PA)**	Revere	MA	F	781 284-8000	14778

SWITCHES

	CITY	ST	EMP	PHONE	ENTRY #
Amphenol Corporation	Stamford	CT	D	203 327-7300	4138
Carling Technologies Inc **(PA)**	Plainville	CT	C	860 793-9281	3473
Exstar	Stoneham	MA	F	339 293-9334	15563
Membrane-Switchescom	Lynn	MA	G	508 277-2892	12526
Umech Technologies LLC	Watertown	MA	G	617 923-2942	16326
Tower Manufacturing Corp	Providence	RI	D	401 467-7550	21140

SWITCHES: Electric Power

	CITY	ST	EMP	PHONE	ENTRY #
Ashcroft Inc **(DH)**	Stratford	CT	B	203 378-8281	4392
Linemaster Switch Corporation	Woodstock	CT	C	860 630-4920	5498
High Voltage Engineering Corp	Wakefield	MA	F	781 224-1001	15954
Jena Piezosystem Inc	Hopedale	MA	G	508 634-6688	11674

SWITCHES: Electric Power, Exc Snap, Push Button, Etc

	CITY	ST	EMP	PHONE	ENTRY #
ABB Enterprise Software Inc	Plainville	CT	A	860 747-7111	3461
Control Concepts Inc **(PA)**	Putnam	CT	F	860 928-6551	3608
Oslo Switch Inc	Cheshire	CT	E	203 272-2794	750
Electro Switch Corp	Weymouth	MA	C	781 607-3306	16887
Schneider Electric Usa Inc	Lynn	MA	C	781 571-9677	12538
Vicor Corporation **(PA)**	Andover	MA	B	978 470-2900	7616

SWITCHES: Electronic

	CITY	ST	EMP	PHONE	ENTRY #
Component Concepts Inc	West Hartford	CT	G	860 523-4066	5062
Eaton Aerospace LLC	Bethel	CT	E	203 796-6000	150
Linemaster Switch Corporation	Plainfield	CT	G	860 564-7713	3453
Apem Inc **(HQ)**	Haverhill	MA	E	978 372-1602	11404
C & K Components LLC **(PA)**	Waltham	MA	D	617 969-3700	16056
Design Mark Industries Inc	Wareham	MA	D	800 451-3275	16244
Metalogic Industries LLC	Dudley	MA	F	508 461-6787	10381
Rob Geoffroy	Londonderry	NH	G	603 425-2517	18734

SWITCHES: Electronic Applications

	CITY	ST	EMP	PHONE	ENTRY #
Control Concepts Inc **(PA)**	Putnam	CT	F	860 928-6551	3608
Kc Crafts LLC	Plantsville	CT	G	860 426-9797	3535

SWITCHES: Flow Actuated, Electrical

	CITY	ST	EMP	PHONE	ENTRY #
Airflo Instrument Company	Glastonbury	CT	G	860 633-9455	1536
Thomas Products Ltd	Southington	CT	E	860 621-9101	4085
Sensata Technologies Ind Inc **(DH)**	Attleboro	MA	G	508 236-3800	7793
Wabash Technologies Inc **(DH)**	Attleboro	MA	D	260 355-4100	7808

SWITCHES: Stepping

	CITY	ST	EMP	PHONE	ENTRY #
Tritex Corporation	Waterbury	CT	C	203 756-7441	4967
High Voltage Engineering Corp	Wakefield	MA	F	781 224-1001	15954

SWITCHES: Time, Electrical Switchgear Apparatus

	CITY	ST	EMP	PHONE	ENTRY #
MH Rhodes Cramer LLC	South Windsor	CT	G	860 291-8402	3994

SWITCHGEAR & SWITCHBOARD APPARATUS

	CITY	ST	EMP	PHONE	ENTRY #
ABB Finance (usa) Inc	Norwalk	CT	G	919 856-2360	3095
Allied Controls Inc	Stamford	CT	F	860 628-8443	4134
Asea Brown Boveri Inc **(DH)**	Norwalk	CT	G	203 750-2200	3105
Ensign-Bickford Industries Inc	Simsbury	CT	E	860 658-4411	3905
Faria Beede Instruments Inc	North Stonington	CT	C	860 848-9271	3074
Gems Sensors Inc **(HQ)**	Plainville	CT	B	860 747-3000	3491
General Electro Components	Glastonbury	CT	G	860 659-3573	1554
Kilo Ampere Switch Corporation	Milford	CT	G	203 877-5994	2307
Madison Company **(PA)**	Branford	CT	E	203 488-4477	329
Newco Condenser Inc	Shelton	CT	G	475 882-4000	3839
Omega Engineering Inc	Norwalk	CT	D	714 540-4914	3212
Quality Name Plate Inc	East Glastonbury	CT	D	860 633-9495	1114
Satin American Corporation	Shelton	CT	E	203 929-6363	3868
Siemon Company **(PA)**	Watertown	CT	A	860 945-4200	5024
C & K Components LLC **(PA)**	Waltham	MA	D	617 969-3700	16056
Cgit Westboro Inc	Westborough	MA	C	508 836-4000	16602
Comtech PST Corp	Topsfield	MA	F	978 887-5754	15854
Cordmaster Engineering Co Inc	North Adams	MA	E	413 664-9371	13671
Eaton Corporation	Franklin	MA	E	508 520-2444	11039
Mettler-Toledo Thornton Inc	Billerica	MA	D	978 262-0210	8266
Pancon Corporation **(PA)**	East Taunton	MA	D	781 297-6000	10517
Power Systems Integrity Inc	Northborough	MA	G	508 393-1655	14045

Company	CITY	ST	EMP	PHONE	ENTRY #
Project Resources Inc	Wareham	MA	F	508 295-7444	16254
Teknikor Automtn & Contrls Inc	Fall River	MA	F	508 679-9474	10771
Texas Instruments Incorporated	Attleboro	MA	E	508 236-3800	7802
Viacomcbs Inc	Framingham	MA	E	508 620-3342	11011
Hoyt Elec Instr Works Inc	Concord	NH	D	603 753-6321	17909
Kearney-National Inc	North Kingstown	RI	E	401 943-2686	20719
SE Mass Devlopment LLC	East Providence	RI	G	401 434-3329	20443
Dynapower Company LLC **(PA)**	South Burlington	VT	C	802 860-7200	22447

SWITCHGEAR & SWITCHGEAR ACCESS, NEC

Company	CITY	ST	EMP	PHONE	ENTRY #
Capitol Electronics Inc	Bethel	CT	F	203 744-3300	135

SYNCHROS

Company	CITY	ST	EMP	PHONE	ENTRY #
Synchro Stars Sst	Nashua	NH	G	603 493-4762	19269

SYNTHETIC RESIN FINISHED PRDTS, NEC

Company	CITY	ST	EMP	PHONE	ENTRY #
Hiperfax Inc	Presque Isle	ME	G	207 764-4319	6759
Engineered Monofilaments Corp	Williston	VT	G	802 863-6823	22664

SYRUPS, DRINK

Company	CITY	ST	EMP	PHONE	ENTRY #
Company of Coca-Cola Bottling	Needham Heights	MA	D	781 449-4300	13322
Filtered By Forest LLC	Lynn	MA	G	978 590-3203	12508

SYRUPS, FLAVORING, EXC DRINK

Company	CITY	ST	EMP	PHONE	ENTRY #
Rhode Island Frt Syrup Co Inc	Smithfield	RI	F	401 231-0040	21247
Wild Farm Maple	Arlington	VT	G	802 362-1656	21602

SYSTEMS ENGINEERING: Computer Related

Company	CITY	ST	EMP	PHONE	ENTRY #
EMC Corporation	Milford	MA	B	508 634-2774	13116
Mediavue Systems Inc	Hingham	MA	E	781 926-0676	11502

SYSTEMS INTEGRATION SVCS

Company	CITY	ST	EMP	PHONE	ENTRY #
Frontier Vision Tech Inc	Rocky Hill	CT	E	860 953-0240	3709
Harpoon Acquisition Corp	Glastonbury	CT	A	860 815-5736	1557
Modern Electronic Fax & Cmpt	Fairfield	CT	G	203 292-6520	1445
Open Solutions LLC **(HQ)**	Glastonbury	CT	C	860 815-5000	1569
Oracle America Inc	Stamford	CT	D	203 703-3000	4273
Bull Hn Info Systems Inc	Chelmsford	MA	G	978 256-1033	9883
INTEL Network Systems Inc **(HQ)**	Hudson	MA	C	978 553-4000	11778
Kewill Inc **(DH)**	Chelmsford	MA	D	978 482-2500	9908
Nemonix Engineering Inc	Bolton	MA	G	508 393-7700	8322
Robert Veinot	Merrimack	NH	G	603 424-1799	19025

SYSTEMS INTEGRATION SVCS: Local Area Network

Company	CITY	ST	EMP	PHONE	ENTRY #
Interactive Marketing Corp	North Haven	CT	G	203 248-5324	3032
Ibcontrols	Windham	ME	E	207 893-0080	7237
Enterasys Networks Inc **(HQ)**	Salem	NH	D	603 952-5000	19725
Electro Standards Lab Inc	Cranston	RI	D	401 946-1390	20215
Lrv Properties LLC	Providence	RI	G	401 714-7001	21058

SYSTEMS INTEGRATION SVCS: Office Computer Automation

Company	CITY	ST	EMP	PHONE	ENTRY #
Management Software Inc	Ledyard	CT	G	860 536-5177	1942
Universal Building Contrls Inc	Meriden	CT	F	203 235-1530	2145

SYSTEMS SOFTWARE DEVELOPMENT SVCS

Company	CITY	ST	EMP	PHONE	ENTRY #
Desrosier of Greenwich Inc	Greenwich	CT	F	203 661-2334	1608
Enginuity Plm LLC **(HQ)**	Milford	CT	F	203 218-7225	2286
Ntt Data Inc	Boston	MA	C	617 241-9200	8744

TABLE OR COUNTERTOPS, PLASTIC LAMINATED

Company	CITY	ST	EMP	PHONE	ENTRY #
A S J Specialties LLC	Wallingford	CT	G	203 284-8650	4692
Ace Cabinet Company	New Britain	CT	G	860 225-6111	2502
Leos Kitchen & Stair Corp	New Britain	CT	G	860 225-7363	2548
Boston Fabrications	Attleboro	MA	F	781 762-9185	7713
Wilsonart Intl Holdings LLC	North Reading	MA	E	978 664-5230	13994
Bangor Millwork & Supply Inc	Portland	ME	F	207 878-8548	6618

TABLECLOTHS & SETTINGS

Company	CITY	ST	EMP	PHONE	ENTRY #
Patricia Spratt For Home LLC	Old Lyme	CT	F	860 434-9291	3326

TABLES: Lift, Hydraulic

Company	CITY	ST	EMP	PHONE	ENTRY #
Southworth Intl Group Inc **(PA)**	Falmouth	ME	D	207 878-0700	6033

TABLETS & PADS

Company	CITY	ST	EMP	PHONE	ENTRY #
Bouncepad North America Inc	Charlestown	MA	F	617 804-0110	9827
Hd Merrimack	Lawrence	MA	G	978 681-9969	12032

TABLETS & PADS: Book & Writing, Made From Purchased Material

Company	CITY	ST	EMP	PHONE	ENTRY #
Panagrafix Inc	West Haven	CT	E	203 691-5529	5139

TABLEWARE OR KITCHEN ARTICLES: Commercial, Fine Earthenware

Company	CITY	ST	EMP	PHONE	ENTRY #
Hope & Main	Warren	RI	G	401 245-7400	21295

TABLEWARE: Plastic

Company	CITY	ST	EMP	PHONE	ENTRY #
Villeroy & Boch Usa Inc	Kittery	ME	F	207 439-6440	6259

TACKS: Nonferrous Metal Or Wire

Company	CITY	ST	EMP	PHONE	ENTRY #
Ccr Products LLC	West Hartford	CT	E	860 953-0499	5058

TAGS & LABELS: Paper

Company	CITY	ST	EMP	PHONE	ENTRY #
Cenveo Inc	Stamford	CT	A	203 595-3000	4161
Cenveo Enterprises Inc **(PA)**	Stamford	CT	G	203 595-3000	4162
Cenveo Worldwide Limited **(DH)**	Stamford	CT	F	203 595-3000	4163
Cwl Enterprises Inc **(HQ)**	Stamford	CT	G	303 790-8023	4181
Royal Consumer Products LLC **(HQ)**	Norwalk	CT	E	203 847-8500	3234
Surys Inc	Trumbull	CT	C	203 333-5503	4633
D B S Industries Inc	Haverhill	MA	D	978 373-4748	11421
Dion Label Printing Inc	Westfield	MA	D	413 568-3713	16680
Tls Printing LLC	Townsend	MA	F	508 234-2344	15874
Flexogrphic Print Slutions LLC	Bedford	NH	G	603 570-6339	17641
Nashua Corporation	Merrimack	NH	B	603 880-1110	19015
Dasko Identification Products	East Providence	RI	F	401 435-6500	20403
Image Tek Mfg Inc	Springfield	VT	E	802 885-6208	22502

TAGS: Paper, Blank, Made From Purchased Paper

Company	CITY	ST	EMP	PHONE	ENTRY #
Allen-Bailey Tag & Label Inc	Whitinsville	MA	E	585 538-2324	16910
Universal Tag Inc	Dudley	MA	E	508 949-2411	10388

TALC

Company	CITY	ST	EMP	PHONE	ENTRY #
Imerys Talc America Inc	Ludlow	VT	D	802 228-6400	22063

TALC MINING

Company	CITY	ST	EMP	PHONE	ENTRY #
Troy Minerals Co	Colchester	VT	G	802 878-5103	21883

TALLOW: Animal

Company	CITY	ST	EMP	PHONE	ENTRY #
Baker Commodities Inc	North Billerica	MA	D	978 454-8811	13795

TANK REPAIR & CLEANING SVCS

Company	CITY	ST	EMP	PHONE	ENTRY #
Paul E Wentworth	Vassalboro	ME	G	207 923-3547	7125

TANKS & OTHER TRACKED VEHICLE CMPNTS

Company	CITY	ST	EMP	PHONE	ENTRY #
New England Airfoil Pdts Inc	Farmington	CT	E	860 677-1376	1498
Shawnee Chemical	Redding	CT	G	203 938-3003	3652
General Dynamics Def	Pittsfield	MA	A	413 494-1110	14471
Natgun Corporation **(HQ)**	Wakefield	MA	C	781 224-5180	15963
Negm Electric LLC	Somersworth	NH	G	603 692-4806	19844

TANKS: Concrete

Company	CITY	ST	EMP	PHONE	ENTRY #
J B Concrete Products Inc	Putnam	CT	G	860 928-9365	3617
Nteco Inc	Darien	CT	E	203 656-1154	1030
National Con Tnks / Frguard JV	Concord	MA	F	978 505-5533	10144

TANKS: For Tank Trucks, Metal Plate

Company	CITY	ST	EMP	PHONE	ENTRY #
Boston Steel & Mfg Co	Haverhill	MA	E	781 324-3000	11409
Westmor Industries LLC	Brewer	ME	E	207 989-0100	5804

TANKS: Fuel, Including Oil & Gas, Metal Plate

Company	CITY	ST	EMP	PHONE	ENTRY #
Angel Fuel LLC	Waterbury	CT	G	203 597-8759	4844
Matias Importing & Distrg Corp	Newington	CT	G	860 666-5544	2880
Safe-T-Tank Corp	Meriden	CT	G	203 237-6320	2129
Babcock Power Inc **(PA)**	Lynnfield	MA	G	978 646-3300	12545
Riley Power Inc	Marlborough	MA	C	508 852-7100	12817

TANKS: Lined, Metal

Company	CITY	ST	EMP	PHONE	ENTRY #
Boston Environmental LLC	Portsmouth	NH	F	603 334-1000	19546

TANKS: Plastic & Fiberglass

Company	CITY	ST	EMP	PHONE	ENTRY #
Terracon Corporation	Franklin	MA	F	508 429-9950	11085
Response Technologies LLC	West Warwick	RI	G	401 585-5918	21508

TANKS: Standard Or Custom Fabricated, Metal Plate

Company	CITY	ST	EMP	PHONE	ENTRY #
Tesco Resources Inc	Waterbury	CT	G	203 754-3900	4962
BE Peterson Inc	Avon	MA	D	508 436-7900	7879
Fall River Boiler & Welding Co	Fall River	MA	G	508 677-4479	10695
Flexcon Industries Inc	Randolph	MA	C	781 986-2424	14681
Millincket Fabrication Mch Inc **(PA)**	Millinocket	ME	E	207 723-9733	6443
Fiberglass Fabricators Inc	Smithfield	RI	E	401 231-3552	21224
West Warwick Welding Inc	West Warwick	RI	F	401 822-8200	21513

TANKS: Water, Metal Plate

Company	CITY	ST	EMP	PHONE	ENTRY #
Walz & Krenzer Inc	Oxford	CT	G	203 267-5712	3430

TANNERIES: Leather

Company	CITY	ST	EMP	PHONE	ENTRY #
Shrut & Asch Leather Co Inc	Woburn	MA	G	781 460-2288	17294
Tasman Industries Inc	Hartland	ME	E	207 938-4491	6179

TAPE DRIVES

Company	CITY	ST	EMP	PHONE	ENTRY #
Acbel (usa) Polytech Inc	Hopkinton	MA	G	508 625-1768	11687

TAPE MEASURES

Company	CITY	ST	EMP	PHONE	ENTRY #
Acme United Corporation **(PA)**	Fairfield	CT	C	203 254-6060	1412
LS Starrett Company **(PA)**	Athol	MA	A	978 249-3551	7689

TAPE STORAGE UNITS: Computer

Company	CITY	ST	EMP	PHONE	ENTRY #
Memtec Corporation	Salem	NH	E	603 893-8080	19751

TAPE: Rubber

Company	CITY	ST	EMP	PHONE	ENTRY #
Midsun Specialty Products Inc	Berlin	CT	E	860 378-0111	96
Plymouth Rubber Europa SA	Canton	MA	F	781 828-0220	9769

TAPES, ADHESIVE: MedicaL

Company	CITY	ST	EMP	PHONE	ENTRY #
First Aid Bandage Co Inc	New London	CT	F	860 443-8499	2773
Adhesive Tapes Intl Inc	Easthampton	MA	G	203 792-8279	10554

TAPES: Fabric

Company	CITY	ST	EMP	PHONE	ENTRY #
American Biltrite Inc **(PA)**	Wellesley	MA	G	781 237-6655	16359
Velcro Inc **(HQ)**	Manchester	NH	A	603 669-4880	18948
Velcro USA Inc **(DH)**	Manchester	NH	A	603 669-4880	18949
K & W Webbing Company Inc	Central Falls	RI	F	401 725-4441	20117
Leedon Webbing Co Inc	Central Falls	RI	E	401 722-1043	20119

TAPES: Pressure Sensitive

Company	CITY	ST	EMP	PHONE	ENTRY #
Beiersdorf Inc	Norwalk	CT	B	203 854-8000	3110
Beiersdorf North America Inc **(DH)**	Wilton	CT	F	203 563-5800	5277
3M Company	Haverhill	MA	G	978 420-0001	11403
Allen-Bailey Tag & Label Inc	Whitinsville	MA	E	585 538-2324	16910

Employee Codes: A=Over 500 employees, B=251-500
C=101-250, D=51-100 E=20-50, F=10-19, G=3-9

	CITY	ST	EMP	PHONE	ENTRY #
Gta-Nht Inc **(HQ)**	Rockland	MA	C	781 331-5900	14804
Ideal Tape Co Inc	Lowell	MA	D	978 458-6833	12381
Jaybird & Mais Inc	Lawrence	MA	E	978 686-8659	12040
Colormark Inc	Nashua	NH	F	603 595-2244	19137
W S Packaging	Wilton	NH	C	603 654-6131	19990
Dewal Industries LLC	Narragansett	RI	C	401 789-9736	20637

TAPES: Pressure Sensitive, Rubber

	CITY	ST	EMP	PHONE	ENTRY #
IR Industries Inc	Bethel	CT	F	203 790-8273	162
New England Business Svc Inc **(HQ)**	Groton	MA	D	978 448-6111	11291
Dewal Industries LLC	Narragansett	RI	C	401 789-9736	20637
Moore Company **(PA)**	Westerly	RI	C	401 596-2816	21531
Moore Company	Westerly	RI	C	401 596-2816	21532
TMC Rhode Island Company Inc	Westerly	RI	F	401 596-2816	21543
Garflex Inc	Brattleboro	VT	D	802 257-5256	21728

TAPS

	CITY	ST	EMP	PHONE	ENTRY #
J I Morris Company	Southbridge	MA	G	508 764-4394	15388
Wells Tool Company	Greenfield	MA	F	413 773-3465	11283

TARGET DRONES

	CITY	ST	EMP	PHONE	ENTRY #
Newmind Robotics LLC	North Andover	MA	G	239 322-2997	13719

TARPAULINS

	CITY	ST	EMP	PHONE	ENTRY #
Cramaro Tarpaulin Systems Inc	Northborough	MA	G	508 393-3062	14031

TAX RETURN PREPARATION SVCS

	CITY	ST	EMP	PHONE	ENTRY #
Inner Office Inc	Moosup	CT	G	860 564-6777	2427
Howarth Specialty Company	Westport	MA	G	508 674-8950	16841

TEETHING RINGS: Rubber

	CITY	ST	EMP	PHONE	ENTRY #
Hasbro Inc **(PA)**	Pawtucket	RI	A	401 431-8697	20845

TELECOMMUNICATION EQPT REPAIR SVCS, EXC TELEPHONES

	CITY	ST	EMP	PHONE	ENTRY #
General Datacomm Inc **(HQ)**	Oxford	CT	E	203 729-0271	3404
Sandy Bay Machine Inc	Gloucester	MA	E	978 546-1331	11209
Schroff Inc **(HQ)**	Warwick	RI	B	763 204-7700	21421

TELECOMMUNICATION SYSTEMS & EQPT

	CITY	ST	EMP	PHONE	ENTRY #
Arris Technology Inc	Wallingford	CT	F	678 473-8493	4704
Carrier Access - Trin Networks	Brookfield	CT	G	203 778-8222	637
Freedom Technologies LLC	Glastonbury	CT	G	860 633-0452	1552
Hubbell Premise Wiring Inc	Mystic	CT	F	860 535-8326	2439
IPC Systems Inc	Old Saybrook	CT	F	203 339-7000	3338
IPC Systems Inc	Fairfield	CT	C	860 271-4100	1437
K-Tech International	Torrington	CT	E	860 489-9399	4584
Microphase Corporation	Shelton	CT	E	203 866-8000	3833
Nutmeg Utility Products Inc **(PA)**	Cheshire	CT	E	203 250-8802	748
Radio Frequency Systems Inc **(DH)**	Meriden	CT	E	203 630-3311	2122
Total Communications Inc **(PA)**	East Hartford	CT	D	860 282-9999	1230
Adva Optical Networking North	Chelmsford	MA	C	978 674-6800	9867
Allston-Brighton Tab	Somerville	MA	G	617 629-3387	15152
Artel Video Systems Corp	Westford	MA	E	978 263-5775	16755
Avaya Inc	Billerica	MA	C	908 953-6000	8216
Biscom Inc	Westford	MA	D	978 250-1800	16757
Cambridge Electronics Laborato	Somerville	MA	G	617 629-2805	15163
Coriant America Inc **(HQ)**	Chelmsford	MA	C	978 250-2900	9888
General Dynmics Mssion Systems	Taunton	MA	G	508 880-4000	15755
Global Connector Tech Ltd	Lawrence	MA	F	978 208-1618	12028
Ruckus Wireless Inc	Westborough	MA	E	508 870-1184	16645
Ruckus Wireless Inc	Lowell	MA	D	978 614-2900	12430
Signal Communications Corp	Woburn	MA	E	781 933-0998	17295
T S X Products Corporation	Westwood	MA	G	781 769-1800	16878
SPX Corporation	Raymond	ME	E	207 655-8525	6775
At Comm Corp	Manchester	NH	F	603 624-4424	18783
Exacom Inc	Concord	NH	E	603 228-0706	17900
Extreme Networks Inc	Salem	NH	F	603 952-5000	19726
Ezenia Inc **(PA)**	Salem	NH	F	603 589-7600	19727
Nel-Tech Labs Incorporated	Derry	NH	F	603 425-1096	17990
Northeast Innovations Inc	Pembroke	NH	F	603 226-4000	19460
Subcom LLC	Newington	NH	D	603 436-6100	19326
Uraseal Inc	Dover	NH	F	603 749-1004	18064
Eartec Company Inc	Narragansett	RI	E	401 789-8700	20638
Electro Standards Lab Inc	Cranston	RI	D	401 946-1390	20215
Okonite Company	Cumberland	RI	D	401 333-3500	20336

TELECOMMUNICATIONS CARRIERS & SVCS: Wired

	CITY	ST	EMP	PHONE	ENTRY #
Ahead Communications Systems	Naugatuck	CT	D	203 720-0227	2458
James G Hachey Inc	Peabody	MA	G	781 229-6400	14344

TELECOMMUNICATIONS CARRIERS & SVCS: Wireless

	CITY	ST	EMP	PHONE	ENTRY #
Ahead Communications Systems	Naugatuck	CT	D	203 720-0227	2458
Maine Radio	Scarborough	ME	F	207 883-2929	6932

TELEMARKETING BUREAUS

	CITY	ST	EMP	PHONE	ENTRY #
Modus Media Inc	Waltham	MA	E	781 663-5000	16153
Tolles Communications Corp	Manchester	NH	G	603 627-9500	18942

TELEMETERING EQPT

	CITY	ST	EMP	PHONE	ENTRY #
L3 Secrity Dtction Systems Inc	Haverhill	MA	F	781 939-3800	11446
L3 Technologies Inc	Burlington	MA	C	781 270-2100	9295
Rennaissance Electronic Corp	Harvard	MA	E	978 772-7774	11384
Lcs Controls Inc	Rochester	VT	G	802 767-3128	22318

TELEPHONE ANSWERING SVCS

	CITY	ST	EMP	PHONE	ENTRY #
Sterling Business Corp	Peterborough	NH	G	603 924-9401	19489

TELEPHONE EQPT: Modems

	CITY	ST	EMP	PHONE	ENTRY #
Canoga Perkins Corporation	Seymour	CT	G	203 888-7914	3749
Tango Modem LLC	Madison	CT	G	203 421-2245	1978
Idg Woit Modem	Lexington	MA	G	781 861-6541	12231
Modem Srismitha	West Roxbury	MA	G	617 323-0080	16499
Zoom Telephonics Inc **(PA)**	Boston	MA	E	617 423-1072	8944

TELEPHONE EQPT: NEC

	CITY	ST	EMP	PHONE	ENTRY #
Ahead Communications Systems	Naugatuck	CT	D	203 720-0227	2458
Dac Systems Inc	Shelton	CT	F	203 924-7000	3793
Elot Inc **(PA)**	Old Greenwich	CT	G	203 388-1808	3308
General Datacomm Inc **(HQ)**	Oxford	CT	E	203 729-0271	3404
Sound Control Technologies	Norwalk	CT	G	203 854-5701	3248
Avvio Networks Inc	Bedford	MA	G	781 271-0002	7961
Genband US LLC	Billerica	MA	G	972 521-5800	8251
Opus Telecom Inc	Framingham	MA	E	508 875-4444	10989
Vbrick Systems Inc	Canton	MA	G	203 265-0044	9793
Ramtel Corporation	Johnston	RI	F	401 231-3340	20533

TELEPHONE SET REPAIR SVCS

	CITY	ST	EMP	PHONE	ENTRY #
Total Communications Inc **(PA)**	East Hartford	CT	D	860 282-9999	1230

TELEPHONE STATION EQPT & PARTS: Wire

	CITY	ST	EMP	PHONE	ENTRY #
Interntonal Totalizing Systems **(PA)**	Bedford	MA	E	978 521-8867	7983
Deborah Frost	Bedford	NH	F	603 882-3100	17638

TELEPHONE SWITCHING EQPT

	CITY	ST	EMP	PHONE	ENTRY #
Eas Holdings LLC **(DH)**	Needham Heights	MA	G	781 449-3056	13329

TELEPHONE: Fiber Optic Systems

	CITY	ST	EMP	PHONE	ENTRY #
Amphenol Corporation **(PA)**	Wallingford	CT	D	203 265-8900	4700
Communication Networks LLC	Danbury	CT	E	203 796-5300	890
Fibre Optic Plus Inc	South Windsor	CT	F	860 646-3581	3970
Opticonx Inc	Putnam	CT	E	888 748-6855	3624
Ruckus Wireless Inc	Wallingford	CT	E	203 303-6400	4802
United Photonics LLC	Vernon Rockville	CT	G	617 752-2073	4687
Em4 Inc **(DH)**	Bedford	MA	E	781 275-7501	7972
Fibertech Networks LLC	Boxborough	MA	G	978 264-6000	8962
Gsr Global Corporation	Billerica	MA	G	781 687-9191	8252
Interntonal Micro Photonix Inc	North Andover	MA	G	978 685-3800	13710
LTS Group Holdings LLC **(HQ)**	Boxborough	MA	F	978 264-6001	8965
Photon Bounce	Roxbury	MA	G	617 708-1231	14875
Photonic Systems Inc	Carlisle	MA	G	978 369-0729	9799
Sandy Bay Machine Inc	Gloucester	MA	E	978 546-1331	11209
Seaborn Management Inc	Beverly	MA	F	978 377-8366	8175
Seaborn Networks Holdings LLC **(PA)**	Beverly	MA	F	978 471-3171	8176
Xphotonics LLC	Littleton	MA	G	978 952-2568	12329
Amphenol Corporation	Nashua	NH	B	603 879-3000	19114
H&L Instruments LLC	North Hampton	NH	F	603 964-1818	19383
Maverick Photonics LLC	Manchester	NH	G	603 540-4434	18868
Ripley Odm LLC	Laconia	NH	G	603 524-8350	18583

TELEPHONE: Headsets

	CITY	ST	EMP	PHONE	ENTRY #
Gn Audio USA Inc **(DH)**	Lowell	MA	B	800 826-4656	12377
Vxi Corporation	Lowell	MA	E	603 742-2888	12447

TELEPHONE: Sets, Exc Cellular Radio

	CITY	ST	EMP	PHONE	ENTRY #
Photonex Corporation	Maynard	MA	C	978 723-2200	12903
Pagepro Wireless	Dover	NH	G	603 749-5600	18044

TELEVISION & VIDEO TAPE DISTRIBUTION

	CITY	ST	EMP	PHONE	ENTRY #
Seachange International Inc **(PA)**	Acton	MA	C	978 897-0100	7385

TELEVISION BROADCASTING & COMMUNICATIONS EQPT

	CITY	ST	EMP	PHONE	ENTRY #
Axerra Networks Inc	Woodbury	CT	G	203 906-3570	5482
Media Links Inc	Windsor	CT	F	860 206-9163	5348
Xintekidel Inc	Stamford	CT	G	203 348-9229	4362
Seachange International Inc **(PA)**	Acton	MA	C	978 897-0100	7385
Site Resources LLC	Providence	RI	G	401 295-4998	21123

TELEVISION BROADCASTING STATIONS

	CITY	ST	EMP	PHONE	ENTRY #
Christian Science Pubg Soc **(PA)**	Boston	MA	B	617 450-2000	8473
General Electric Company	Westborough	MA	F	508 870-5200	16619

TELEVISION REPAIR SHOP

	CITY	ST	EMP	PHONE	ENTRY #
Corbeil Enterprises Inc	Bristol	NH	F	603 744-2867	17762

TELEVISION: Cameras

	CITY	ST	EMP	PHONE	ENTRY #
Courtsmart Digital Systems Inc	North Chelmsford	MA	E	978 251-3300	13891

TEMPERING: Metal

	CITY	ST	EMP	PHONE	ENTRY #
Hardline Heat Treating Inc	Southbridge	MA	E	508 764-6669	15384

TEMPORARY HELP SVCS

	CITY	ST	EMP	PHONE	ENTRY #
Nsight Inc	Andover	MA	E	781 273-6300	7579

TENTS: All Materials

	CITY	ST	EMP	PHONE	ENTRY #
Shelterlogic Corp **(HQ)**	Watertown	CT	C	860 945-6442	5023
Slogic Holding Corp **(PA)**	New Canaan	CT	G	203 966-2800	2614
Tent Connection Inc	Northbridge	MA	G	508 234-8746	14062
Zmetra Clarspan Structures LLC	Webster	MA	G	508 943-0940	16355
Peter Marques	Conway	NH	G	603 447-2344	17957

TERMINAL BOARDS

	CITY	ST	EMP	PHONE	ENTRY #
Ezra J Leboff Co Inc	Brighton	MA	G	617 783-4200	9098

TERRAZZO PRECAST PRDTS

	CITY	ST	EMP	PHONE	ENTRY #
Platt Brothers & Company **(PA)**	Waterbury	CT	D	203 753-4194	4940

TEST BORING SVC: Bituminous Or Lignite Mining

	CITY	ST	EMP	PHONE	ENTRY #
New Hampshire Boring Inc	Brockton	MA	F	508 584-8201	9169

TEST BORING SVCS: Nonmetallic Minerals

	CITY	ST	EMP	PHONE	ENTRY #
New England Boring Contractors	Glastonbury	CT	F	860 633-4649	1566
Carr-Dee Corp	Medford	MA	F	781 391-4500	12925
Soil Exploration Corp **(PA)**	Leominster	MA	G	978 840-0391	12187
Allstate Drilling Co	Riverside	RI	G	401 434-7458	21163

TEST KITS: Pregnancy

	CITY	ST	EMP	PHONE	ENTRY #
Northern Berkshire Pregnancy	North Adams	MA	G	413 346-4291	13684

TESTERS: Battery

	CITY	ST	EMP	PHONE	ENTRY #
Digatron Power Electronics Inc	Shelton	CT	E	203 446-8000	3796

TESTERS: Environmental

	CITY	ST	EMP	PHONE	ENTRY #
Omega Engineering Inc **(HQ)**	Norwalk	CT	C	203 359-1660	3211
Scots Landing	Fabyan	CT	G	860 923-0437	1410
Spectrogram Corporation	Madison	CT	G	203 245-2433	1977
Atc Group Services LLC	West Springfield	MA	E	337 234-8777	16509
Fiberlock Technologies Inc	Andover	MA	F	978 623-9987	7548
Lockheed Martin Sippican Inc **(HQ)**	Marion	MA	B	508 748-3399	12699
Perkinelmer Inc **(PA)**	Waltham	MA	C	781 663-6900	16171
Sensitech Inc **(DH)**	Beverly	MA	D	978 927-7033	8177
Thermo Fisher Scientific Inc	Wilmington	MA	D	978 275-0800	17055
Envirologix Inc	Portland	ME	D	207 797-0300	6661
John Fancy Inc	Appleton	ME	G	207 785-3610	5526
Environmental Test Pdts LLC **(PA)**	Hollis	NH	G	603 924-5010	18331
Environmental Test Pdts LLC	Jaffrey	NH	G	603 593-5268	18463
GL&v USA Inc	Nashua	NH	D	603 882-2711	19169
Envirnmntal Compliance Systems	Cumberland	RI	G	401 334-0306	20320

TESTERS: Hardness

	CITY	ST	EMP	PHONE	ENTRY #
David L Ellis Company Inc **(PA)**	Acton	MA	G	978 897-1795	7349
Massachusetts Mtls Tech LLC **(PA)**	Weston	MA	G	617 500-8325	16827
Massachusetts Mtls Tech LLC	Cambridge	MA	G	617 502-5636	9549

TESTERS: Liquid, Exc Indl Process

	CITY	ST	EMP	PHONE	ENTRY #
EMD Millipore Corporation	Billerica	MA	B	978 715-4321	8243
EMD Millipore Corporation	Waltham	MA	B	781 533-5858	16097
Wellumina Health Inc	Danvers	MA	G	978 777-1854	10273

TESTERS: Physical Property

	CITY	ST	EMP	PHONE	ENTRY #
Forte Technology Inc	South Easton	MA	F	508 297-2363	15277
Lockheed Martin Sippican Inc **(HQ)**	Marion	MA	B	508 748-3399	12699
Testing Machines Inc	Swansea	MA	G	302 613-5600	15717
Triangle Engineering Inc	Hanover	MA	F	781 878-1500	11356
Northeast NDT Inc	Nashua	NH	G	603 595-4227	19219

TESTERS: Spark Plug

	CITY	ST	EMP	PHONE	ENTRY #
Forte Rts Inc	Ledyard	CT	G	860 464-5221	1941

TESTERS: Water, Exc Indl Process

	CITY	ST	EMP	PHONE	ENTRY #
Evoqua Water Technologies LLC	Tewksbury	MA	E	978 863-4600	15817
Brailsford & Company Inc	Antrim	NH	E	603 588-2880	17593

TEXTILE & APPAREL SVCS

	CITY	ST	EMP	PHONE	ENTRY #
Enefco International Inc **(PA)**	Auburn	ME	D	207 514-7218	5561
Screen Printed Special TS	Manchester	NH	G	603 622-2901	18919

TEXTILE DESIGNERS

	CITY	ST	EMP	PHONE	ENTRY #
American Woolen Company Inc	Stafford Springs	CT	G	860 684-2766	4105

TEXTILE FABRICATORS

	CITY	ST	EMP	PHONE	ENTRY #
Allen Manufacturing Inc	Lewiston	ME	E	207 333-3385	6273
Carrot Signs	Brunswick	ME	G	207 725-0769	5834

TEXTILE FINISH: Chem Coat/Treat, Fire Resist, Manmade

	CITY	ST	EMP	PHONE	ENTRY #
Auburn Manufacturing Inc	Mechanic Falls	ME	E	207 345-8271	6417
Auburn Manufacturing Inc **(PA)**	Mechanic Falls	ME	E	207 345-8271	6418

TEXTILE FINISHING: Bleaching, Broadwoven, Cotton

	CITY	ST	EMP	PHONE	ENTRY #
Cranston Print Works Company **(PA)**	Cranston	RI	E	401 943-4800	20202
Cranston Print Works Company	Cranston	RI	E	800 525-0595	20203
Cranston Print Works Company	West Greenwich	RI	E	401 397-2442	21455

TEXTILE FINISHING: Bleaching, Man Fiber & Silk, Broadwoven

	CITY	ST	EMP	PHONE	ENTRY #
Cranston Print Works Company **(PA)**	Cranston	RI	E	401 943-4800	20202
Cranston Print Works Company	Cranston	RI	E	800 525-0595	20203
Cranston Print Works Company	West Greenwich	RI	E	401 397-2442	21455

TEXTILE FINISHING: Chem Coat/Treat, Man, Broadwoven, Cotton

	CITY	ST	EMP	PHONE	ENTRY #
Nextec Applications Inc **(PA)**	Greenwich	CT	G	203 661-1484	1634
Majilite Manufacturing Inc	Dracut	MA	D	978 441-6800	10364
Starensier Inc **(PA)**	Byfield	MA	F	978 462-7311	9365

TEXTILE FINISHING: Chem Coating/Treating, Broadwoven, Cotton

	CITY	ST	EMP	PHONE	ENTRY #
Starensier Inc **(PA)**	Byfield	MA	F	978 462-7311	9365

TEXTILE FINISHING: Chemical Coating Or Treating

	CITY	ST	EMP	PHONE	ENTRY #
Emco Services Inc	Fall River	MA	G	508 674-5504	10688

TEXTILE FINISHING: Chemical Coating Or Treating, Narrow

	CITY	ST	EMP	PHONE	ENTRY #
Albany Engnered Composites Inc	Rochester	NH	D	603 330-5851	19651
Albany Engnered Composites Inc	Rochester	NH	F	603 330-5993	19652
Albany Engnered Composites Inc	Rochester	NH	E	603 330-5800	19653
Albany Engnered Composites Inc **(HQ)**	Rochester	NH	C	603 330-5800	19654

TEXTILE FINISHING: Dyeing, Broadwoven, Cotton

	CITY	ST	EMP	PHONE	ENTRY #
Swan Finishing Company Inc **(PA)**	Fall River	MA	C	508 674-4611	10767
Palisades Ltd	Peace Dale	RI	E	401 789-0295	20915

TEXTILE FINISHING: Dyeing, Finishing & Printng, Linen Fabric

	CITY	ST	EMP	PHONE	ENTRY #
Gorilla Graphics Inc	Middletown	CT	F	860 704-8208	2187
Dee Kay Designs Inc **(PA)**	Hope Valley	RI	D	401 539-2400	20484

TEXTILE FINISHING: Dyeing, Manmade Fiber & Silk, Broadwoven

	CITY	ST	EMP	PHONE	ENTRY #
Swan Finishing Company Inc **(PA)**	Fall River	MA	C	508 674-4611	10767
Kenyon Industries Inc	Kenyon	RI	B	401 364-7761	20548

TEXTILE FINISHING: Flocking, Cotton, Broadwoven

	CITY	ST	EMP	PHONE	ENTRY #
Middlesex Research Mfg Co Inc	Hudson	MA	E	978 562-3697	11793

TEXTILE: Finishing, Cotton Broadwoven

	CITY	ST	EMP	PHONE	ENTRY #
Brand & Oppenheimer Co Inc	Bedford	MA	E	781 271-0000	7965
Lawrence Textile Inc	Lawrence	MA	G	978 689-4355	12047
Majilite Corporation	Dracut	MA	D	978 441-6800	10363
Tls International LLC	Needham	MA	G	781 449-4454	13315
Tyca Corporation **(PA)**	Clinton	MA	E	978 612-0002	10094

TEXTILE: Finishing, Raw Stock NEC

	CITY	ST	EMP	PHONE	ENTRY #
Brookwood Laminating Inc	Wauregan	CT	D	860 774-5001	5038
Grand Embroidery Inc	Oxford	CT	F	203 888-7484	3406
Berkshire Corporation **(HQ)**	Great Barrington	MA	E	413 528-2602	11233
Brittany Global Tech Corp	New Bedford	MA	D	508 999-3281	13365
Stevens Linen Associates Inc	Dudley	MA	D	508 943-0813	10387
Web Industries Inc **(PA)**	Marlborough	MA	G	508 898-2988	12848
Kenyon Industries Inc	Kenyon	RI	B	401 364-7761	20548
Palisades Ltd	Peace Dale	RI	E	401 789-0295	20915

TEXTILE: Goods, NEC

	CITY	ST	EMP	PHONE	ENTRY #
Gilbride Enterprises LLC	Lowell	MA	G	978 452-0878	12375
S M Services Inc	Nashua	NH	G	603 883-3381	19256

TEXTILES

	CITY	ST	EMP	PHONE	ENTRY #
Cap-Tech Products Inc	Wethersfield	CT	F	860 490-5078	5243
Dawson Forte LLP	Westwood	MA	G	781 467-0170	16864
Warwick Mills Inc **(PA)**	New Ipswich	NH	C	603 291-1000	19311
E A M T Inc	Woonsocket	RI	E	401 762-1500	21558

TEXTILES: Crash, Linen

	CITY	ST	EMP	PHONE	ENTRY #
Advanced Linen Group	Milford	CT	F	203 877-3896	2236

TEXTILES: Flock

	CITY	ST	EMP	PHONE	ENTRY #
Spectro Coating Corp	Leominster	MA	E	978 534-6191	12188
Spectro Coating Corp **(PA)**	Leominster	MA	D	978 534-1800	12189
National Velour Corporation	Warwick	RI	E	401 737-8300	21394
Tex Flock Inc	Woonsocket	RI	E	401 765-2340	21586

TEXTILES: Linings, Carpet, Exc Felt

	CITY	ST	EMP	PHONE	ENTRY #
7 Waves Inc	Braintree	MA	G	781 519-9389	8984

TEXTILES: Mill Waste & Remnant

	CITY	ST	EMP	PHONE	ENTRY #
A & P Coat Apron & Lin Sup Inc	Hartford	CT	D	914 840-3200	1799

TEXTILES: Padding & Wadding

	CITY	ST	EMP	PHONE	ENTRY #
Full Circle Padding Inc	Norton	MA	F	508 285-2500	14077

TEXTILES: Rugbacking, Jute Or Other Fiber

	CITY	ST	EMP	PHONE	ENTRY #
Kws Inc	Waldoboro	ME	G	207 832-5095	7133

TEXTILES: Scouring & Combing

	CITY	ST	EMP	PHONE	ENTRY #
Joan Fabrics LLC	Lowell	MA	G	978 454-3777	12386
Roxanne L Tardie	Ashland	ME	G	207 540-4945	5540

TEXTILES: Slubs & Nubs

	CITY	ST	EMP	PHONE	ENTRY #
Windle Industries Inc	Sutton	MA	F	508 865-5773	15696

THEATRICAL PRODUCERS & SVCS

	CITY	ST	EMP	PHONE	ENTRY #
Mosaic Records Inc	Stamford	CT	G	203 327-7111	4252

THEATRICAL SCENERY

	CITY	ST	EMP	PHONE	ENTRY #
Global Scenic Services Inc	Bridgeport	CT	E	203 334-2130	420
Show Motion Inc	Milford	CT	E	203 866-1866	2362
Mystic Scenic Studios Inc	Norwood	MA	D	781 440-0914	14180
Advanced Animations	Stockbridge	VT	E	802 746-8974	22518

THERMISTORS, EXC TEMPERATURE SENSORS

	CITY	ST	EMP	PHONE	ENTRY #
Sensata Technologies Ind Inc **(DH)**	Attleboro	MA	G	508 236-3800	7793
Wabash Technologies Inc **(DH)**	Attleboro	MA	D	260 355-4100	7808

THERMOCOUPLES

	CITY	ST	EMP	PHONE	ENTRY #
Atlantic Sensors & Contrls LLC	Milford	CT	G	203 878-8118	2246
Projects Inc	Glastonbury	CT	C	860 633-4615	1574
Convectronics Inc	Haverhill	MA	F	978 374-7714	11419
Nanmac Corp	Holliston	MA	E	508 872-4811	11588

THERMOCOUPLES: Indl Process

	CITY	ST	EMP	PHONE	ENTRY #
Richards Arklay S Co Inc	Newton	MA	E	617 527-4385	13630

THERMOELECTRIC DEVICES: Solid State

	CITY	ST	EMP	PHONE	ENTRY #
CPS Technologies Corp	Norton	MA	C	508 222-0614	14073

THERMOMETERS: Indl

	CITY	ST	EMP	PHONE	ENTRY #
Williamson Corporation	Concord	MA	E	978 369-9607	10163

THERMOMETERS: Medical, Digital

	CITY	ST	EMP	PHONE	ENTRY #
Cooper-Atkins Corporation **(HQ)**	Middlefield	CT	C	860 349-3473	2162

THERMOPLASTIC MATERIALS

	CITY	ST	EMP	PHONE	ENTRY #
Forum Plastics LLC	Waterbury	CT	E	203 754-0777	4875
Neu Spclty Engineered Mtls LLC	North Haven	CT	F	203 239-9629	3043
Oxford Industries Conn Inc	New Britain	CT	E	860 225-3700	2559
Oxpekk Performance Mtls Inc	South Windsor	CT	F	860 698-9300	3998
W S Polymers	Trumbull	CT	G	203 268-1557	4643
Interpolymer Corporation **(DH)**	Canton	MA	E	781 828-7120	9745
Kickemuit Industries LLC	Somerset	MA	G	508 675-0594	15145
Titeflex Corporation	Springfield	MA	E	413 781-0008	15517
New Hampshire Plastics LLC	Manchester	NH	D	603 669-8523	18884
Teknor Apex Company **(PA)**	Pawtucket	RI	B	401 725-8000	20903

THERMOPLASTICS

	CITY	ST	EMP	PHONE	ENTRY #
Kalwall Corporation **(PA)**	Manchester	NH	B	603 627-3861	18854

THERMOSETTING MATERIALS

	CITY	ST	EMP	PHONE	ENTRY #
Resinall Corp **(DH)**	Stamford	CT	F	203 329-7100	4298
Textiles Coated Incorporated **(PA)**	Londonderry	NH	D	603 296-2221	18741
Epoxytech Inc	Woonsocket	RI	E	401 726-4500	21560

THIN FILM CIRCUITS

	CITY	ST	EMP	PHONE	ENTRY #
Entegris Prof Solutions Inc **(HQ)**	Danbury	CT	C	203 794-1100	913
Vulcan Flex Circuit Corp	Porter	ME	D	603 883-1500	6606
Dale Vishay Electronics LLC	Hollis	NH	D	603 881-7799	18328

THREAD: Cotton

	CITY	ST	EMP	PHONE	ENTRY #
New Bedford Thread Co Inc	Fairhaven	MA	E	508 996-8584	10644

THREAD: Embroidery

	CITY	ST	EMP	PHONE	ENTRY #
J Arnold Mittleman	Middletown	CT	E	860 346-6562	2192
Pacific Printing Inc	Northampton	MA	G	413 585-5700	14016
Hilco Athletic & Graphics Inc	West Warwick	RI	F	401 822-1775	21495

THREAD: Natural Fiber

	CITY	ST	EMP	PHONE	ENTRY #
Erich Husemoller Import & Expo	Easthampton	MA	G	413 585-9855	10563

THREAD: Thread, From Manmade Fiber

	CITY	ST	EMP	PHONE	ENTRY #
Dhm Thread Corporation	Fall River	MA	F	508 672-0032	10682

TIES, FORM: Metal

	CITY	ST	EMP	PHONE	ENTRY #
M-Fab LLC	Torrington	CT	G	860 496-0055	4586

TILE: Brick & Structural, Clay

	CITY	ST	EMP	PHONE	ENTRY #
Redland Brick Inc	South Windsor	CT	C	860 528-1311	4007
Hi-Way Concrete Pdts Co Inc	Wareham	MA	E	508 295-0834	16249
Morgan Advanced Ceramics Inc	New Bedford	MA	C	508 995-1725	13418
Rjf - Morin Brick LLC	Auburn	ME	D	207 784-9375	5595
Morgan Advanced Ceramics Inc	Hudson	NH	E	603 598-9122	18416

TILE: Clay, Drain & Structural

	CITY	ST	EMP	PHONE	ENTRY #
Eljen Corporation	East Hartford	CT	E	860 610-0426	1191

TILE: Clay, Roof

	CITY	ST	EMP	PHONE	ENTRY #
Rupe Slate Co	Poultney	VT	G	802 287-9692	22276

TILE: Fireproofing, Clay

	CITY	ST	EMP	PHONE	ENTRY #
K & G Corp	Manchester	CT	F	860 643-1133	2015

TILE: Terrazzo Or Concrete, Precast

	CITY	ST	EMP	PHONE	ENTRY #
Pauls Marble Depot LLC	Stamford	CT	F	203 978-0669	4279

TILE: Wall & Floor, Ceramic

	CITY	ST	EMP	PHONE	ENTRY #
Fit America Inc	Southborough	MA	G	309 839-1695	15357
Cabinets For Less LLC	Manchester	NH	G	603 935-7551	18794

TIMBER PRDTS WHOLESALERS

	CITY	ST	EMP	PHONE	ENTRY #
Gaylord West	Franklin	VT	G	802 285-6438	21994

TIMERS: Indl, Clockwork Mechanism Only

	CITY	ST	EMP	PHONE	ENTRY #
Lampin Corporation **(PA)**	Uxbridge	MA	E	508 278-2422	15923

TIMING DEVICES: Cycle & Program Controllers

	CITY	ST	EMP	PHONE	ENTRY #
Food Atmtn - Svc Tchniques Inc **(PA)**	Stratford	CT	C	203 377-4414	4412
AEC Engineering	Freeport	ME	F	207 865-4190	6071

TIMING DEVICES: Electronic

	CITY	ST	EMP	PHONE	ENTRY #
Idevices LLC	Avon	CT	E	860 352-5252	36
Lynx System Developers Inc	Haverhill	MA	E	978 556-9780	11451
Recall Services Healthwatch	Concord	MA	G	978 369-7253	10155
C-R Control Systems Inc	Lebanon	NH	G	603 727-9149	18617

TIN

	CITY	ST	EMP	PHONE	ENTRY #
Tien Vo Corp	Weymouth	MA	G	781 340-7245	16902
Hair Designs By Debbie Tin	Sandown	NH	G	603 887-0643	19784
Tin Man Fabrication Inc	Coventry	RI	G	401 822-4509	20169

TINSEL

	CITY	ST	EMP	PHONE	ENTRY #
Mystic Industries Corp	Wakefield	MA	F	781 245-1950	15962

TIRE & INNER TUBE MATERIALS & RELATED PRDTS

	CITY	ST	EMP	PHONE	ENTRY #
Town Fair Tire Centers Inc	Manchester	CT	F	860 646-2807	2056

TIRE CORD & FABRIC

	CITY	ST	EMP	PHONE	ENTRY #
United Abrasives Inc **(PA)**	North Windham	CT	B	860 456-7131	3084
Alvin Johnson	East Longmeadow	MA	G	413 525-6334	10465

TIRES & INNER TUBES

	CITY	ST	EMP	PHONE	ENTRY #
Gpx International Tire Corp **(PA)**	Foxboro	MA	E	781 321-3910	10885
Main Industrial Tires Ltd **(PA)**	Wakefield	MA	F	713 676-0251	15958

TIRES: Agricultural, Pneumatic

	CITY	ST	EMP	PHONE	ENTRY #
Maxam Tire North America Inc	Danvers	MA	G	844 629-2662	10235

TIRES: Auto

	CITY	ST	EMP	PHONE	ENTRY #
Ace Tire & Auto Center Inc	Ridgefield	CT	F	203 438-4042	3654
Larkin Motors LLC	Bridgewater	MA	G	508 807-1333	9082

TIRES: Cushion Or Solid Rubber

	CITY	ST	EMP	PHONE	ENTRY #
Maine Rubber International	Wakefield	MA	C	877 648-1949	15959

TITANIUM MILL PRDTS

	CITY	ST	EMP	PHONE	ENTRY #
Aerospace Metals Inc	Hartford	CT	C	860 522-3123	1803
Doncasters Inc **(HQ)**	Groton	CT	D	860 449-1603	1671
Titanium Industries Inc	Tolland	CT	G	860 870-3939	4554
Rmi Titanium Company LLC	Burlington	MA	F	781 272-5967	9330
Titanium Advisors	Franklin	MA	G	508 528-3120	11092

TITANIUM ORE MINING

	CITY	ST	EMP	PHONE	ENTRY #
Tronox Limited	Stamford	CT	G	203 705-3800	4351

TOBACCO & PRDTS, WHOLESALE: Cigarettes

	CITY	ST	EMP	PHONE	ENTRY #
Foundation Cigar Company LLC	Windsor	CT	F	203 738-9377	5334

TOBACCO LEAF PROCESSING

	CITY	ST	EMP	PHONE	ENTRY #
UST	Greenwich	CT	F	203 661-1100	1659

TOBACCO: Chewing & Snuff

	CITY	ST	EMP	PHONE	ENTRY #
Nordic American Smokeless Inc	Danbury	CT	F	203 207-9977	961
Nuway Tobacco Company	South Windsor	CT	D	860 289-6414	3996
Smokey Mountain Chew Inc **(PA)**	Darien	CT	G	203 656-1088	1032
US Smokeless Tobacco Co LLC	Stamford	CT	D	203 661-1100	4354
UST LLC **(HQ)**	Stamford	CT	G	203 817-3000	4355

TOBACCO: Cigars

	CITY	ST	EMP	PHONE	ENTRY #
F D Grave & Son Inc	North Haven	CT	G	203 239-9394	3026
Foundation Cigar Company LLC	Windsor	CT	F	203 738-9377	5334

TOBACCO: Smoking

	CITY	ST	EMP	PHONE	ENTRY #
Wonderland Smoke Shop Inc	Warwick	RI	G	401 823-3134	21451

TOILET FIXTURES: Plastic

	CITY	ST	EMP	PHONE	ENTRY #
Eco Services LLC	Durham	NH	G	603 682-0963	18076

TOILET PREPARATIONS

	CITY	ST	EMP	PHONE	ENTRY #
Gillette Company	Bethel	CT	G	203 796-4000	155
Gillette Company	Andover	MA	A	781 662-9600	7552
Gillette Company **(HQ)**	Boston	MA	A	617 421-7000	8561

TOILETRIES, COSMETICS & PERFUME STORES

	CITY	ST	EMP	PHONE	ENTRY #
Lady Anne Cosmetics Inc	Trumbull	CT	G	203 372-6972	4626
Enefco International Inc **(PA)**	Auburn	ME	D	207 514-7218	5561

TOILETRIES, WHOLESALE: Toiletries

	CITY	ST	EMP	PHONE	ENTRY #
T N Dickinson Company	East Hampton	CT	F	860 267-2279	1166

TOILETS, PORTABLE, WHOLESALE

	CITY	ST	EMP	PHONE	ENTRY #
Eco Services LLC	Durham	NH	G	603 682-0963	18076

TOMBSTONES: Cut Stone, Exc Finishing Or Lettering Only

	CITY	ST	EMP	PHONE	ENTRY #
W C Canniff & Sons Inc **(PA)**	Boston	MA	G	617 323-3690	8914

TOOL & DIE STEEL

	CITY	ST	EMP	PHONE	ENTRY #
American Standard Company	Southington	CT	E	860 628-9643	4037
Jo Vek Tool and Die Mfg Co	Waterbury	CT	G	203 755-1884	4892
Central Steel Rule Die Inc	Worcester	MA	G	508 853-2663	17354
Ludlow Tool Co	Agawam	MA	G	413 786-6415	7439
Vortex Inc	Peabody	MA	D	978 535-8721	14381
Cnc Design & Counsulting LLC	Kingston	NH	G	603 686-5437	18542
Shookus Special Tools Inc	Raymond	NH	F	603 895-1200	19645

TOOL REPAIR SVCS

	CITY	ST	EMP	PHONE	ENTRY #
Eastern Broach Inc	Plainville	CT	F	860 828-4800	3483
Sharp Tool Co Inc	Hudson	MA	E	978 568-9292	11816

TOOL STANDS: Factory

	CITY	ST	EMP	PHONE	ENTRY #
B and R Modern Hand Tool Inc	Portland	ME	G	207 773-6706	6615

TOOLS & EQPT: Used With Sporting Arms

	CITY	ST	EMP	PHONE	ENTRY #
Ludlow Tool	Agawam	MA	F	413 786-6360	7438

TOOLS: Carpenters', Including Levels & Chisels, Exc Saws

	CITY	ST	EMP	PHONE	ENTRY #
Killoran Contracting Inc	Milton	MA	G	617 298-5248	13194
Tucker Mountain Homes Inc	Meredith	NH	G	603 279-4320	18981

TOOLS: Hand

	CITY	ST	EMP	PHONE	ENTRY #
A Line Design Inc	Wallingford	CT	G	203 294-0080	4691
Ampol Tool Inc	West Haven	CT	G	203 932-3161	5109
Crrc LLC	Cromwell	CT	D	860 635-2200	852
E-Z Tools Inc	Norwalk	CT	G	203 838-2102	3146
Fletcher-Terry Company LLC **(PA)**	East Berlin	CT	D	860 828-3400	1102
Integrity Manufacturing LLC	Farmington	CT	G	860 678-1599	1487
Kell-Strom Tool Co Inc **(PA)**	Wethersfield	CT	E	860 529-6851	5253
Kell-Strom Tool Intl Inc	Wethersfield	CT	E	860 529-6851	5254
Rostra Tool Company	Branford	CT	E	203 488-8665	343
Southwire Company LLC	Stamford	CT	F	203 324-0067	4326

	CITY	ST	EMP	PHONE	ENTRY #
Stanley Black & Decker Inc	Farmington	CT	F	860 225-5111	1514
Stanley Black & Decker Inc **(PA)**	New Britain	CT	C	860 225-5111	2580
Stanley Black & Decker Inc	New Britain	CT	E	860 225-5111	2583
Tiger Enterprises Inc	Plantsville	CT	E	860 621-9155	3542
Tool 2000	Southington	CT	G	860 620-0020	4087
Toolmax Designing Tooling Inc	Tolland	CT	G	860 871-7265	4555
Trumpf Inc **(DH)**	Farmington	CT	B	860 255-6000	1517
Trumpf Inc	Farmington	CT	B	860 255-6000	1518
Trumpf Inc	Plainville	CT	B	860 255-6000	3522
Unger Enterprises LLC	Bridgeport	CT	C	203 366-4884	500
Arbortech Tools USA Corp	Norwell	MA	G	866 517-7869	14094
Art For A Cause LLC	East Weymouth	MA	E	248 645-3966	10536
Echo Industries Inc	Orange	MA	E	978 544-7000	14215
Foster-Miller Inc	Devens	MA	D	781 684-4000	10320
Hot Tools Inc	Marblehead	MA	F	781 639-1000	12686
Hyde Group Inc **(PA)**	Southbridge	MA	C	800 872-4933	15385
Hyde Tools	Southbridge	MA	G	508 764-4344	15386
Irwin Industrial Tool Company	East Longmeadow	MA	A	413 525-3961	10480
JH Smith Co Inc **(PA)**	Greenfield	MA	F	413 772-0191	11264
Lamson and Goodnow LLC	Shelburne Falls	MA	E	413 625-0201	15073
Lund Precision Products Inc	Hyannis	MA	G	617 413-0236	11848
M M Newman Corporation	Marblehead	MA	F	781 631-7100	12687
Pilgrim Badge & Label Corp	Brockton	MA	D	508 436-6300	9171
Quickpoint Corporation	Concord	MA	G	978 371-3267	10154
Riverdale Mills Corporation	Northbridge	MA	C	508 234-8715	14060
Safe T Cut Inc	Monson	MA	F	413 267-9984	13211
Seekonk Manufacturing Co Inc	Seekonk	MA	E	508 761-8284	15036
US Discount Products LLC	West Bridgewater	MA	G	877 841-5782	16462
Wrentham Tool Group LLC	Bellingham	MA	D	508 966-2332	8064
David Michaud	Winthrop	ME	G	207 377-8037	7280
Lie-Nielsen Toolworks Inc	Warren	ME	D	800 327-2520	7144
Peavey Manufacturing Company	Eddington	ME	E	207 843-7861	5997
Xuron Corp	Saco	ME	E	207 283-1401	6862
Chadwick & Trefethen Inc	Portsmouth	NH	F	603 436-2568	19551
Trellborg Pipe Sals Mlford Inc **(DH)**	Milford	NH	C	800 626-2180	19080
Joseph A Thomas Ltd	Bristol	RI	F	401 253-1330	20086
Materion Technical Mtls Inc	Lincoln	RI	C	401 333-1700	20583
Ames Companies Inc	Wallingford	VT	C	802 446-2601	22573

TOOLS: Hand, Engravers'

	CITY	ST	EMP	PHONE	ENTRY #
Ngraver Company	Bozrah	CT	G	860 823-1533	283
Pavelok	Bow	NH	G	603 225-7283	17725

TOOLS: Hand, Hammers

	CITY	ST	EMP	PHONE	ENTRY #
Mayhew Steel Products Inc **(PA)**	Turners Falls	MA	E	413 625-6351	15881

TOOLS: Hand, Ironworkers'

	CITY	ST	EMP	PHONE	ENTRY #
Conquip Systems LLC	Chester	CT	G	860 526-7883	770

TOOLS: Hand, Jewelers'

	CITY	ST	EMP	PHONE	ENTRY #
Sterling Jewelers Inc	Manchester	CT	G	860 644-7207	2052
Earths Elements Inc	Bridgewater	MA	G	508 697-2277	9072
Feteria Tool & Findings	Attleboro	MA	G	508 222-7788	7734
Fine Edge Tool Company Inc	Attleboro	MA	G	508 222-7511	7736

TOOLS: Hand, Masons'

	CITY	ST	EMP	PHONE	ENTRY #
Silpro Llc **(PA)**	Ayer	MA	E	978 772-4444	7939

TOOLS: Hand, Mechanics

	CITY	ST	EMP	PHONE	ENTRY #
An Designs Inc	Torrington	CT	G	860 618-0183	4560
Cambridge Specialty Co Inc	Berlin	CT	D	860 828-3579	80
J J Ryan Corporation	Plantsville	CT	C	860 628-0393	3534
Ullman Devices Corporation	Ridgefield	CT	D	203 438-6577	3687
Lowell Corporation	West Boylston	MA	E	508 835-2900	16421
Anthony Automotive	Gardiner	ME	G	207 582-7105	6104

TOOLS: Hand, Plumbers'

	CITY	ST	EMP	PHONE	ENTRY #
Stiebel Eltron Inc	Holyoke	MA	G	413 535-1734	11661

TOOLS: Hand, Power

	CITY	ST	EMP	PHONE	ENTRY #
Air Tool Sales & Service Co **(PA)**	Unionville	CT	G	860 673-2714	4652
Apex Machine Tool Company Inc	Cheshire	CT	D	860 677-2884	711
Black & Decker (us) Inc	Wethersfield	CT	G	860 563-5800	5242
Black & Decker (us) Inc	New Britain	CT	G	860 225-5111	2514
Black & Decker (us) Inc **(HQ)**	New Britain	CT	G	860 225-5111	2515
Blackstone Industries LLC	Bethel	CT	D	203 792-8622	133
DArcy Saw LLC	Windsor Locks	CT	G	800 569-1264	5390
Frasal Tool Co Inc	Newington	CT	F	860 666-3524	2865
HRF Fastener Systems Inc	Bristol	CT	E	860 589-0750	569
Slater Hill Tool LLC	Putnam	CT	G	860 963-0415	3633
Stanley Black & Decker Inc **(PA)**	New Britain	CT	C	860 225-5111	2580
Stanley Black & Decker Inc	New Britain	CT	E	860 225-5111	2583
Stihl Incorporated	Oxford	CT	E	203 929-8488	3425
Trumpf Inc	Plainville	CT	B	860 255-6000	3522
Trumpf Inc **(DH)**	Farmington	CT	B	860 255-6000	1517
Trumpf Inc	Farmington	CT	B	860 255-6000	1518
Universal Precision Mfg	Trumbull	CT	G	203 374-9809	4641
Aube Precision Tool Co Inc	Ludlow	MA	G	413 589-9048	12454
Black & Decker (us) Inc	East Longmeadow	MA	G	413 526-5150	10468
Black & Decker (us) Inc	Westwood	MA	G	781 329-3407	16858
Simonds Incorporated	Southbridge	MA	F	508 764-3235	15403
Vulcan Company Inc **(PA)**	Hingham	MA	D	781 337-5970	11515
Adhesive Technologies Inc **(PA)**	Hampton	NH	E	603 926-1616	18252
Black & Decker Corporation	North Conway	NH	G	603 356-7595	19373
Burndy LLC	Littleton	NH	C	603 444-6781	18655
Pneutek Inc	Hudson	NH	F	603 595-0302	18427
Malco Saw Co Inc	Cranston	RI	G	401 942-7380	20258

	CITY	ST	EMP	PHONE	ENTRY #
Textron Inc **(PA)**	Providence	RI	B	401 421-2800	21134
Zampini Industrial Group LLC	Lincoln	RI	G	401 305-7997	20602

TOOLS: Soldering

	CITY	ST	EMP	PHONE	ENTRY #
Uniprise International Inc	Terryville	CT	E	860 589-7262	4495

TOOTHPASTES, GELS & TOOTHPOWDERS

	CITY	ST	EMP	PHONE	ENTRY #
Sheffield Pharmaceuticals LLC **(PA)**	New London	CT	C	860 442-4451	2779
Dentovations Inc	Boston	MA	F	617 737-1199	8499

TOPS, DISPENSER OR SHAKER, ETC: Plastic

	CITY	ST	EMP	PHONE	ENTRY #
Mysdispensers Inc	Roslindale	MA	G	617 327-1124	14839

TOWING SVCS: Marine

	CITY	ST	EMP	PHONE	ENTRY #
Cape Cod Shipbuilding Co	Wareham	MA	F	508 295-3550	16242

TOYS

	CITY	ST	EMP	PHONE	ENTRY #
Anjar Co	Stamford	CT	G	203 321-1023	4140
Col-Lar Enterprises Inc **(PA)**	New Milford	CT	F	203 798-1786	2793
Imagine 8 LLC	Madison	CT	G	203 421-0905	1964
Mark G Cappitella **(PA)**	East Haddam	CT	G	860 873-3093	1151
Roto-Die Company Inc	East Windsor	CT	F	860 292-7030	1300
US Games Systems Inc	Stamford	CT	E	203 353-8400	4353
Burnham Associates Inc	Salem	MA	F	978 745-1788	14899
Canal Toys Usa Ltd	Westborough	MA	G	508 366-9060	16599
Charles Thomae & Son Inc	Attleboro	MA	E	508 222-0785	7719
Gemini Games	Arlington	MA	G	781 643-6965	7628
Innovative Development Inc	East Walpole	MA	G	508 668-9080	10525
Little Kids Inc	Seekonk	MA	E	401 454-7600	15026
Oyo Sportstoys Inc	Hudson	MA	D	978 264-2000	11799
Wicked Cornhole	Tewksbury	MA	G	978 851-7600	15849
Wyrmwood Inc	Taunton	MA	G	508 837-0057	15801
Bruce Dennison	East Machias	ME	G	207 255-0954	5983
Different Drummer	Solon	ME	G	207 643-2572	6997
Jwd Premium Products	Liberty	ME	G	617 429-8867	6330
Two In One Manufacturing Inc	Nashua	NH	E	603 595-8212	19276
Willowtoys	Madison	NH	G	603 367-4657	18765
Ageless Innovation LLC **(PA)**	Pawtucket	RI	G	888 569-4255	20810
Hasbro Inc	Pawtucket	RI	F	401 726-2090	20846
Hasbro Inc	Pawtucket	RI	E	401 431-8412	20847
Hasbro International Inc **(HQ)**	Pawtucket	RI	A	401 431-8697	20848
Cooperman Fife & Drum Co	Bellows Falls	VT	G	802 463-9750	21651
Maple Landmark Inc	Middlebury	VT	E	802 388-0627	22114

TOYS & HOBBY GOODS & SPLYS, WHOLESALE: Educational Toys

	CITY	ST	EMP	PHONE	ENTRY #
Unruly Studios Inc	Boston	MA	G	857 327-5080	8901
Learning Materials Workshop	Burlington	VT	G	802 862-0112	21793

TOYS & HOBBY GOODS & SPLYS, WHOLESALE: Model Kits

	CITY	ST	EMP	PHONE	ENTRY #
Bluejacket Inc	Searsport	ME	F	207 548-9970	6947

TOYS & HOBBY GOODS & SPLYS, WHOLESALE: Playing Cards

	CITY	ST	EMP	PHONE	ENTRY #
US Games Systems Inc	Stamford	CT	E	203 353-8400	4353

TOYS & HOBBY GOODS & SPLYS, WHOLESALE: Toys & Games

	CITY	ST	EMP	PHONE	ENTRY #
Leisure Learning Products Inc	Stamford	CT	F	203 325-2800	4237
Different Drummer	Solon	ME	G	207 643-2572	6997

TOYS, HOBBY GOODS & SPLYS WHOLESALERS

	CITY	ST	EMP	PHONE	ENTRY #
Lego Systems Inc **(DH)**	Enfield	CT	A	860 749-2291	1368
Ageless Innovation LLC **(PA)**	Pawtucket	RI	G	888 569-4255	20810

TOYS: Dolls, Stuffed Animals & Parts

	CITY	ST	EMP	PHONE	ENTRY #
Anjar Co	Stamford	CT	G	203 321-1023	4140
Oyo Sportstoys Inc	Hudson	MA	D	978 264-2000	11799
Verve Inc	Providence	RI	G	401 351-6415	21149

TOYS: Electronic

	CITY	ST	EMP	PHONE	ENTRY #
Gold Water Technology Inc	Walpole	MA	G	781 551-3590	15992
Sproutel Inc	Providence	RI	G	914 806-6514	21126

TOYS: Kites

	CITY	ST	EMP	PHONE	ENTRY #
Skydog Kites LLC	Colchester	CT	G	860 365-0600	810
Tom Stebbins DBA Kite Ene	Westford	VT	G	802 878-9650	22629

TRADE SHOW ARRANGEMENT SVCS

	CITY	ST	EMP	PHONE	ENTRY #
L M T Communications Inc	Newtown	CT	F	203 426-4568	2927
Information Gatekeepers Inc	Winchester	MA	G	617 782-5033	17088
International Data Group Inc **(PA)**	Boston	MA	F	508 875-5000	8618
Mystic Scenic Studios Inc	Norwood	MA	D	781 440-0914	14180

TRADERS: Commodity, Contracts

	CITY	ST	EMP	PHONE	ENTRY #
Boehringer Ingelheim Corp **(DH)**	Ridgefield	CT	A	203 798-9988	3657

TRAFFIC CONTROL FLAGGING SVCS

	CITY	ST	EMP	PHONE	ENTRY #
IDS Highway Safety Inc	Cumberland	RI	G	401 333-0740	20328
Sonco Worldwide Inc	Warwick	RI	F	401 406-3761	21427

TRAILERS & PARTS: Boat

	CITY	ST	EMP	PHONE	ENTRY #
Brownell Boat Trailers Inc	Fairhaven	MA	G	508 996-3110	10639
Brownell Trailers LLC	Fairhaven	MA	F	508 996-3110	10640
Hostar Mar Trnspt Systems Inc	Wareham	MA	E	508 295-2900	16250

TRAILERS & PARTS: Truck & Semi's

	CITY	ST	EMP	PHONE	ENTRY #
Kensington Welding & Trlr Co	Kensington	CT	G	860 828-3564	1918
Mark Karotkin	Hartford	CT	G	860 202-7821	1844
Miller Professional Trans Svc	Vernon	CT	G	860 871-6818	4669
Webbers Truck Service Inc	East Windsor	CT	F	860 623-4554	1310
Boston Trailer Manufacturing	Walpole	MA	E	508 668-2242	15990

	CITY	ST	EMP	PHONE	ENTRY #
Butlers Rv Services Corp	Oxford	MA	G	508 987-0234	14255
Lins Propane Trucks Corp	Dighton	MA	F	508 669-6665	10337
U-Haul Co of Massachusetts	Walpole	MA	F	508 668-2242	16015
On The Road Inc	Warren	ME	E	207 273-3780	7146
Pelletier Manufacturing Inc	Millinocket	ME	F	207 723-6500	6444
Granite State Cover and Canvas	Plaistow	NH	F	603 382-5462	19517
Proline Products LLC	Milton	NH	G	603 652-7337	19087
Ricks Truck & Trailer Repair	Hillsborough	NH	G	603 464-3636	18318
Scott G Reed Truck Svcs Inc	Claremont	NH	F	603 542-5032	17860
Gaines Trucking Inc	Middletown	RI	G	401 862-2993	20619

TRAILERS & TRAILER EQPT

Dolly Plow Inc	Pembroke	MA	G	781 293-9828	14400
Wright Trailers Inc	Seekonk	MA	F	508 336-8530	15044
Eimskip USA Inc	Portland	ME	G	207 221-5268	6660
Davis Village Solutions LLC	New Ipswich	NH	G	603 878-3662	19304
Proline Products LLC	Milton	NH	G	603 652-7337	19087

TRAILERS: Bodies

Alcom LLC **(PA)**	Winslow	ME	E	207 861-9800	7266

TRAILERS: Camping, Tent-Type

American Keder Inc **(PA)**	Rindge	NH	G	603 899-3233	19646

TRANSDUCERS: Electrical Properties

Ashcroft Inc **(DH)**	Stratford	CT	B	203 378-8281	4392
Flintec Inc	Hudson	MA	E	978 562-4548	11774
Hottinger Bldwin Msrements Inc **(DH)**	Marlborough	MA	D	508 624-4500	12775
Massa Products Corporation	Hingham	MA	D	781 749-3120	11501

TRANSDUCERS: Pressure

Eaton Aerospace LLC	Bethel	CT	E	203 796-6000	150
Sens All Inc	Southington	CT	G	860 628-8379	4076
Druck LLC **(HQ)**	Billerica	MA	C	978 437-1000	8238
Dynisco Parent Inc	Billerica	MA	E	978 667-5301	8241
Setra Systems Inc	Boxboro	MA	F	978 263-1400	8954
Trans Metrics Inc **(HQ)**	Watertown	MA	F	617 926-1000	16325

TRANSFORMERS: Coupling

Omnicron Electronics	Putnam	CT	G	860 928-0377	3623
Currier Engineering	Needham	MA	G	781 449-7706	13298

TRANSFORMERS: Distribution

Ethosenergy Tc Inc **(DH)**	Chicopee	MA	C	802 257-2721	10025
International Coil Inc	South Easton	MA	E	508 580-8515	15280
Magnetika East Ltd	Marlborough	MA	F	508 485-7555	12789
Regional Mfg Specialists Inc	Concord	NH	D	800 805-8991	17926

TRANSFORMERS: Electric

Bicron Electronics Company **(PA)**	Torrington	CT	D	860 482-2524	4566
Bridgeport Magnetics Group Inc	Shelton	CT	E	203 954-0050	3784
Power Trans Co Inc	Oxford	CT	G	203 881-0314	3419
Transformer Technology Inc	Durham	CT	F	860 349-1061	1095
Dsk Engineering and Technology	Waltham	MA	G	413 289-6485	16092
Schneider Electric Usa Inc **(DH)**	Boston	MA	A	978 975-9600	8839
Schneider Electric Usa Inc	Foxboro	MA	G	508 549-3385	10903
Total Recoil Magnetics Inc	Holliston	MA	F	508 429-9600	11609
Trans Mag Corp	Lowell	MA	G	978 458-1487	12438
Winkumpaugh Line Construction	Ellsworth	ME	G	207 667-2962	6023
Semper FI Power Supply Inc	Manchester	NH	F	603 656-9729	18921
Wall Industries Inc	Exeter	NH	E	603 778-2300	18137
International Innovations Inc	Plainfield	VT	G	802 454-7764	22268

TRANSFORMERS: Electronic

71 Pickett District Road LLC	New Milford	CT	G	860 350-5964	2786
Alpha Magnetics & Coils Inc	Torrington	CT	G	860 496-0122	4556
Neeltran Inc	New Milford	CT	C	860 350-5964	2815
Americansub	Dudley	MA	E	508 949-2320	10372
ATW Electronics Inc	Charlestown	MA	F	617 304-3579	9824
MV Mason Electronics Inc	Walpole	MA	G	508 668-6200	16004
Vishay Hirel Systems LLC	Dover	NH	D	603 742-4375	18066

TRANSFORMERS: Meters, Electronic

Kasalis Inc	Burlington	MA	E	781 273-6200	9291
National Meter Industries Inc	Bedford	NH	G	603 669-5790	17656

TRANSFORMERS: Power Related

ABB Enterprise Software Inc	Windsor	CT	D	860 285-0183	5314
ABB Enterprise Software Inc	Stamford	CT	F	203 329-8771	4125
ABB Inc	Danbury	CT	D	203 790-8588	865
Able Coil and Electronics Co	Bolton	CT	E	860 646-5686	273
Alpha-Core Inc	Shelton	CT	E	203 954-0050	3773
Asea Brown Boveri Inc **(DH)**	Norwalk	CT	G	203 750-2200	3105
Carling Technologies Inc **(PA)**	Plainville	CT	C	860 793-9281	3473
Emsc LLC	Stamford	CT	G	203 268-5101	4193
Superior Elc Holdg Group LLC **(HQ)**	Plainville	CT	E	860 582-9561	3516
Atrex Energy Inc **(PA)**	Walpole	MA	E	781 461-8251	15988
BP Fly Corporation **(PA)**	Tyngsboro	MA	E	978 649-9114	15886
Cgit Westboro Inc	Westborough	MA	C	508 836-4000	16602
GEC Durham Industries Inc **(PA)**	New Bedford	MA	E	508 995-2636	13390
McElroy Electronics Corp	Shirley	MA	F	978 425-4055	15089
Murata Pwr Sltons Portland LLC	Westborough	MA	G	508 339-3000	16638
Phoenix Electric Corp	Canton	MA	E	781 821-0200	9767
Precision Electronics Corp	Marshfield	MA	F	781 834-6677	12865
Brookfield Power Neng LLC	Millinocket	ME	G	207 723-4341	6440
Airex LLC	Somersworth	NH	E	603 841-2040	19827
Laconia Magnetics Inc	Laconia	NH	E	603 528-2766	18570
Russound/Fmp Inc	Newmarket	NH	C	603 659-5170	19338
Vishay Hirel Systems LLC	Dover	NH	D	603 742-4375	18066
David P Cioe	Warren	RI	G	401 247-0079	21294
Formex Inc	East Greenwich	RI	E	401 885-9800	20368
Schneider Electric It USA Inc **(DH)**	West Kingston	RI	B	401 789-5735	21472

TRANSFORMERS: Reactor

Spray Foam Distrs Neng Inc	Woodstock	NH	E	603 745-3911	20029

TRANSFORMERS: Specialty

Universal Voltronics Corp	Brookfield	CT	E	203 740-8555	662
Century Magnetics Intl	Franklin	NH	F	603 934-4931	18156
Dynapower Company LLC **(PA)**	South Burlington	VT	C	802 860-7200	22447

TRANSISTORS

API Electronics Inc	Marlborough	MA	E	508 485-6350	12716
Raytheon Sutheast Asia Systems **(HQ)**	Billerica	MA	E	978 470-5000	8289
Silicon Transistor Corporation	Chelmsford	MA	D	978 256-3321	9932
Infineon Tech Americas Corp	Essex Junction	VT	E	802 769-6824	21947

TRANSLATION & INTERPRETATION SVCS

Textnology Corp	Nashua	NH	F	603 465-8398	19273

TRANSPORTATION EPQT & SPLYS, WHOL: Aeronautical Eqpt & Splys

Valley Steel Stamp Inc	Greenfield	MA	E	413 773-8200	11282
Aeroparts Plus Inc	South Burlington	VT	G	802 489-5023	22435

TRANSPORTATION EPQT & SPLYS, WHOLESALE: Helicopter Parts

American Unmanned Systems LLC	Stamford	CT	G	203 406-7611	4136

TRANSPORTATION EPQT & SPLYS, WHOLESALE: Marine Crafts/Splys

Aerocess Inc	Berlin	CT	F	860 357-2451	67
Eaton Trap Co Inc	Woolwich	ME	G	207 443-3617	7289
Maloney Marine Rigging Inc	West Southport	ME	G	207 633-6788	7179
Dock Doctors LLC	Ferrisburgh	VT	E	802 877-6756	21988

TRANSPORTATION EQPT & SPLYS WHOLESALERS, NEC

Columbia Manufacturing Inc	Columbia	CT	D	860 228-2259	817
Textron Systems Corporation **(DH)**	Wilmington	MA	E	978 657-5111	17054

TRANSPORTATION INSPECTION SVCS

Paul E Wentworth	Vassalboro	ME	G	207 923-3547	7125

TRANSPORTATION PROGRAMS REGULATION & ADMINISTRATION SVCS

Transportation Conn Dept	Portland	CT	G	860 342-5996	3579

TRANSPORTATION SVCS, NEC

Veho Tech Inc	North Reading	MA	G	617 909-6026	13993

TRANSPORTATION SVCS: Aerial Tramways, Exc Amusement/Scenic

Skytrans Mfg LLC	Contoocook	NH	F	802 230-7783	17948

TRAP ROCK: Crushed & Broken

York Hill Trap Rock Quarry Co	Meriden	CT	F	203 237-8421	2152
S Lane John & Son Incorporated **(PA)**	Westfield	MA	F	413 568-8986	16725
Scallops Mineral & Shell Empor	Portsmouth	NH	G	603 431-7658	19617

TRAPS: Animal & Fish, Wire

Ketcham Supply Co Inc	New Bedford	MA	F	508 997-4787	13403
Downeast Fishing Gear Inc	Trenton	ME	E	207 667-3131	7097
Downeast Wire Trap Company	Jonesboro	ME	G	207 434-5791	6224
Eaton Trap Co Inc	Woolwich	ME	G	207 443-3617	7289
Ftc Inc **(PA)**	Friendship	ME	E	207 354-2545	6093

TRAPS: Animal, Iron Or Steel

Ketcham Supply Co Inc	New Bedford	MA	F	508 997-4787	13403

TRAPS: Crab, Steel

Island Lobster Supply	Vinalhaven	ME	G	207 863-4807	7128

TRAPS: Stem

CRS Steam Inc	Gardner	MA	G	978 630-2308	11110
Ruggles-Klingemann Mfg Co **(PA)**	Beverly	MA	F	978 232-8300	8173

TRAVEL AGENCIES

Smarter Travel Media LLC	Boston	MA	C	617 886-5555	8850

TRAVEL TRAILERS & CAMPERS

Fiberglass Engr & Design Co	Wallingford	CT	G	203 265-1644	4743
Keystone Rv Company	Bridgeport	CT	C	203 367-9847	440
Thule Holding Inc **(DH)**	Seymour	CT	F	203 881-9600	3766
Boston Trailer Manufacturing	Walpole	MA	E	508 668-2242	15990
Line-X Merrimack Valley LLC	Bow	NH	G	603 224-7792	17721

TRAVELER ACCOMMODATIONS, NEC

Jordan Associates	Pittsburg	NH	F	603 246-8998	19494

TRAYS: Plastic

Form-All Plastics Corporation	Meriden	CT	G	203 634-1137	2093
Detroit Forming Inc	Hudson	NH	G	603 598-2767	18385

TREAD RUBBER: Camelback For Tire Retreading

Cochin Rubbers Intl LLC **(PA)**	Mansfield	MA	G	877 289-0364	12618
Cri Rubber LLC **(HQ)**	Hopkinton	MA	G	508 657-8488	11698
Sullivan Manufacturing Company	Norwell	MA	E	781 982-1550	14112

TROPHIES, NEC

	CITY	ST	EMP	PHONE	ENTRY #
Conference Medal & Trophy Co	Buzzards Bay	MA	F	508 563-3600	9359
Greg Asselin Studios Ltd	Norton	MA	G	508 222-7361	14078
Jewelry Creations	Norton	MA	G	508 285-4230	14079
All Seasons Printing & Awards	Pelham	NH	G	603 881-7106	19427

TROPHIES, PEWTER

	CITY	ST	EMP	PHONE	ENTRY #
George Guertin Trophy Inc	Auburn	MA	G	508 832-4001	7836

TROPHIES: Metal, Exc Silver

	CITY	ST	EMP	PHONE	ENTRY #
Greco Industries Inc	Bethel	CT	G	203 798-7804	156
Conference Medal & Trophy Co	Buzzards Bay	MA	F	508 563-3600	9359
George Guertin Trophy Inc	Auburn	MA	G	508 832-4001	7836
VH Blackinton & Co Inc	Attleboro Falls	MA	C	508 699-4436	7818
American Trophy & Supply Co	East Providence	RI	G	401 438-3060	20386
World Trophies Company Inc	Providence	RI	E	401 272-5846	21157

TROPHY & PLAQUE STORES

	CITY	ST	EMP	PHONE	ENTRY #
Guertin Graphics & Awards Inc	Worcester	MA	F	508 754-0200	17386
Platinum Recognition LLC **(PA)**	North Providence	RI	G	401 305-6700	20772

TRUCK & BUS BODIES: Dump Truck

	CITY	ST	EMP	PHONE	ENTRY #
Mark D Skiest	Shrewsbury	MA	G	508 754-0639	15122

TRUCK & BUS BODIES: Garbage Or Refuse Truck

	CITY	ST	EMP	PHONE	ENTRY #
Lo Stocco Motors	Danbury	CT	G	203 797-9618	949
Tom Berkowitz Trucking Inc **(PA)**	Whitinsville	MA	E	508 234-2920	16919

TRUCK & BUS BODIES: Truck Cabs, Motor Vehicles

	CITY	ST	EMP	PHONE	ENTRY #
Sure Industries Inc	East Hartford	CT	G	860 289-2522	1226
Curtis Industries LLC **(PA)**	West Boylston	MA	F	508 853-2200	16413

TRUCK & BUS BODIES: Truck, Motor Vehicle

	CITY	ST	EMP	PHONE	ENTRY #
Universal Body & Eqp Co LLC	Oakville	CT	F	860 274-7541	3304
Altec Northeast LLC	Sterling	MA	F	508 320-9041	15533
James A Kiley Company	Somerville	MA	E	617 776-0344	15188
Middlesex Truck & Auto Bdy Inc	Boston	MA	E	617 442-3000	8705
F3 Mfg Inc	Waterville	ME	F	207 692-7178	7155
Larry Dingee	Cornish	NH	G	603 542-9682	17962

TRUCK & BUS BODIES: Utility Truck

	CITY	ST	EMP	PHONE	ENTRY #
Utility Systems Inc	Johnston	RI	F	401 351-6681	20546

TRUCK & BUS BODIES: Van Bodies

	CITY	ST	EMP	PHONE	ENTRY #
New England Wheels Inc **(PA)**	Billerica	MA	E	978 663-9724	8267

TRUCK BODIES: Body Parts

	CITY	ST	EMP	PHONE	ENTRY #
Commonwlth Ventr Funding Group **(PA)**	Waltham	MA	F	781 684-0095	16072
Cotta Truck Equipment	Bridgewater	MA	G	508 269-1960	9069
Messer Truck Equipment **(PA)**	Westbrook	ME	E	207 854-9751	7196
Dejana Trck Utility Eqp Co LLC	Smithfield	RI	E	401 231-9797	21220

TRUCK BODY SHOP

	CITY	ST	EMP	PHONE	ENTRY #
Larry Dingee	Cornish	NH	G	603 542-9682	17962

TRUCK GENERAL REPAIR SVC

	CITY	ST	EMP	PHONE	ENTRY #
Torrington Diesel Corporation	Torrington	CT	G	860 496-9948	4603
Boston Trailer Manufacturing	Walpole	MA	E	508 668-2242	15990
U-Haul Co of Massachusetts	Walpole	MA	F	508 668-2242	16015
Dexter Service Center	East Providence	RI	G	401 438-3900	20405

TRUCK PAINTING & LETTERING SVCS

	CITY	ST	EMP	PHONE	ENTRY #
Rokap Inc	Wallingford	CT	G	203 265-6895	4799
Visimark Inc	Auburn	MA	F	508 832-3471	7851
Banana Banners	Bowdoinham	ME	G	207 666-3951	5788
Advantage Signs Inc	Concord	NH	G	603 224-7446	17881
Kerins Sign Service	Montpelier	VT	F	802 223-0357	22151

TRUCK PARTS & ACCESSORIES: Wholesalers

	CITY	ST	EMP	PHONE	ENTRY #
Line-X Merrimack Valley LLC	Bow	NH	G	603 224-7792	17721

TRUCKING & HAULING SVCS: Contract Basis

	CITY	ST	EMP	PHONE	ENTRY #
Grillo Services LLC	Milford	CT	E	203 877-5070	2294
Bunnell Rocky Log & Forest Mgt	Monroe	NH	G	603 638-4983	19089

TRUCKING & HAULING SVCS: Furniture Moving & Storage, Local

	CITY	ST	EMP	PHONE	ENTRY #
G C Management Corp **(PA)**	Southwest Harbor	ME	G	207 244-5363	7047

TRUCKING & HAULING SVCS: Heavy, NEC

	CITY	ST	EMP	PHONE	ENTRY #
On The Road Inc	Warren	ME	E	207 273-3780	7146
Padebco Custom Boats Inc	Round Pond	ME	G	207 529-5106	6832

TRUCKING & HAULING SVCS: Lumber & Log, Local

	CITY	ST	EMP	PHONE	ENTRY #
Roland H Tyler Logging Inc	Dixfield	ME	G	207 562-7282	5958
Thompson Trucking Inc	Lincoln	ME	E	207 794-6101	6360
Tracy J Morrison	Harmony	ME	G	207 683-2371	6172

TRUCKING & HAULING SVCS: Lumber & Timber

	CITY	ST	EMP	PHONE	ENTRY #
Daniel L Dunnells Logging Inc	Parsonsfield	ME	G	207 793-2901	6574
Earl W Gerrish & Sons Inc	Brownville	ME	F	207 965-2171	5826
M B Eastman Logging Inc	Parsonsfield	ME	G	207 625-8020	6576

TRUCKING & HAULING SVCS: Timber, Local

	CITY	ST	EMP	PHONE	ENTRY #
P and L Trucking	Chester	VT	G	802 875-2819	21847

TRUCKING: Except Local

	CITY	ST	EMP	PHONE	ENTRY #
John F Wielock	Dudley	MA	G	508 943-5366	10378
Savage Companies	Westborough	MA	G	508 616-8772	16646
Barrup Farms Inc	Derby	VT	E	802 334-2331	21899

TRUCKING: Local, Without Storage

	CITY	ST	EMP	PHONE	ENTRY #
Darrel L Tibbetts	Livermore	ME	G	207 897-4932	6374
Sheehan & Sons Lumber	Perkinsville	VT	G	802 263-5545	22258

TRUCKS & TRACTORS: Industrial

	CITY	ST	EMP	PHONE	ENTRY #
Dri-Air Industries Inc	East Windsor	CT	E	860 627-5110	1282
Macton Corporation	Oxford	CT	D	203 267-1500	3413
New Haven Companies Inc	East Haven	CT	F	203 469-6421	1257
Terex Corporation **(PA)**	Westport	CT	F	203 222-7170	5233
Greenwood Emrgncy Vehicles LLC **(HQ)**	North Attleboro	MA	D	508 695-7138	13758
Precision Handling Devices **(PA)**	Westport	MA	F	508 679-5282	16845
WB Engineering Inc	Norton	MA	E	508 952-4000	14093
North Country Tractor Inc	Sanford	ME	F	207 324-5646	6884
Paul E Wentworth	Vassalboro	ME	G	207 923-3547	7125

TRUNKS

	CITY	ST	EMP	PHONE	ENTRY #
2 Girl A Trunk	Wilton	CT	G	203 762-0360	5272
Sherwood Trunks	Amherst	MA	G	413 687-3167	7526
Ten West Trunk Shows	Beverly	MA	G	508 755-7547	8188
Monkey-Trunks	Tamworth	NH	G	603 367-4427	19892
Budco Products Corp	Woonsocket	RI	G	401 767-2590	21554

TRUSSES: Wood, Floor

	CITY	ST	EMP	PHONE	ENTRY #
Universal Component Corp	East Haven	CT	E	203 481-8787	1267

TRUSSES: Wood, Roof

	CITY	ST	EMP	PHONE	ENTRY #
Thomas Bernhard Building Sys	Southport	CT	E	203 925-0414	4102
Truss Manufacturing Inc	Newington	CT	F	860 665-0000	2908
Nu-Truss Inc	Westfield	MA	F	413 562-3861	16708
Truss Engineering Corporation	Indian Orchard	MA	E	413 543-1298	11898
Aroostook Trusses Inc	Presque Isle	ME	E	207 768-5817	6754
Soyaz	Fairfield	ME	E	207 453-4911	6029
Truss Worthy Truss	Hodgdon	ME	G	207 532-3200	6194
Specialty Truss Inc	Nashua	NH	G	603 886-5523	19263
Trussco Inc	North Kingstown	RI	E	401 295-0669	20747

TUB CONTAINERS: Plastic

	CITY	ST	EMP	PHONE	ENTRY #
Kensco Inc **(PA)**	Ansonia	CT	F	203 734-8827	20
R H Murphy Co Inc	Amherst	NH	G	603 889-2255	17583

TUBE & TUBING FABRICATORS

	CITY	ST	EMP	PHONE	ENTRY #
Creative Rack Solutions Inc	Waterbury	CT	G	203 755-2102	4861
EA Patten Co LLC	Manchester	CT	D	860 649-2851	2004
Harry Thommen Company	Bridgeport	CT	G	203 333-3637	424
L&P Aerospace Acquisition LLC	Middletown	CT	D	860 635-8811	2199
Macristy Industries Inc **(PA)**	Newington	CT	C	860 225-4637	2879
Optinova Americas Inc	Danbury	CT	G	203 743-0908	964
Plastics and Concepts Conn Inc	Glastonbury	CT	F	860 657-9655	1572
Spencer Turbine Company **(HQ)**	Windsor	CT	C	860 688-8361	5363
Bergen Pipe Supports Inc **(HQ)**	Woburn	MA	E	781 935-9550	17130
L & R Manufacturing Co Inc	Worcester	MA	F	508 853-0562	17405
Micro Bends Corp	Peterborough	NH	G	603 924-0022	19476
New England Small Tube Corp	Litchfield	NH	D	603 429-1600	18652
Smiths Tblar Systms-Lconia Inc	Laconia	NH	B	603 524-2064	18587
Maley Laser Processing Inc	Warwick	RI	F	401 732-8400	21386

TUBES: Paper

	CITY	ST	EMP	PHONE	ENTRY #
CA J&L Enterprises Inc	Canton	MA	E	781 963-6666	9719
Ox Paper Tube and Core Inc	Holliston	MA	F	508 879-1141	11593
Hard Core Spral Tube Wnders In	Brentwood	NH	G	603 775-0230	17751
New England Paper Tube Co Inc	Pawtucket	RI	E	401 725-2610	20868
Carris Reels Inc **(HQ)**	Proctor	VT	C	802 773-9111	22284

TUBES: Vacuum

	CITY	ST	EMP	PHONE	ENTRY #
Fil-Tech Inc	Boston	MA	G	617 227-1133	8544
Filtech Inc	Boston	MA	G	617 227-1133	8545

TUBING: Flexible, Metallic

	CITY	ST	EMP	PHONE	ENTRY #
Uniprise International Inc	Terryville	CT	E	860 589-7262	4495
Vermont Flexible Tubing Inc	Lyndonville	VT	E	802 626-5723	22075

TUBING: Plastic

	CITY	ST	EMP	PHONE	ENTRY #
Cebal Americas **(PA)**	Norwalk	CT	G	203 845-6356	3121
Plastic Factory LLC	Bridgeport	CT	G	203 908-3468	470
Polymedex Discovery Group Inc **(PA)**	Putnam	CT	F	860 928-4102	3627
Putnam Plastics Corporation	Dayville	CT	C	860 774-1559	1051
Argos Corporation	Taunton	MA	F	508 828-5900	15726
Insultab Inc	Woburn	MA	D	781 935-0800	17203
Saint-Gobain Abrasives Inc **(DH)**	Worcester	MA	A	508 795-5000	17464
Samar Co Inc	Stoughton	MA	D	781 297-7264	15620
Nordson Medical (nh) Inc **(HQ)**	Salem	NH	C	603 327-0600	19756

TUBING: Rubber

	CITY	ST	EMP	PHONE	ENTRY #
Chase Corporation	Randolph	MA	E	781 963-2600	14673

TUMBLERS: Plastic

	CITY	ST	EMP	PHONE	ENTRY #
Cool Gear International LLC	Plymouth	MA	D	508 830-3440	14551

TUMBLING

	CITY	ST	EMP	PHONE	ENTRY #
HI-Tech Polishing Inc	Newington	CT	F	860 665-1399	2870
Precision Deburring Inc	Bristol	CT	G	860 583-4662	596

TURBINES & TURBINE GENERATOR SET UNITS, COMPLETE

	CITY	ST	EMP	PHONE	ENTRY #
Aeronautica Windpower LLC	Plymouth	MA	E	508 732-8945	14539
Kingston Wind Independence LLC	East Weymouth	MA	G	781 871-8200	10544

TURBINES & TURBINE GENERATOR SET UNITS: Gas, Complete

	CITY	ST	EMP	PHONE	ENTRY #
Peregrine Turbine Tech LLC	Wiscasset	ME	F	207 687-8333	7286

PRODUCT

	CITY	ST	EMP	PHONE	ENTRY #
Flexenergy Inc	Portsmouth	NH	D	603 430-7000	19563
Flexenergy Holdings LLC **(PA)**	Portsmouth	NH	D	603 430-7000	19564

TURBINES & TURBINE GENERATOR SETS

	CITY	ST	EMP	PHONE	ENTRY #
American Metal Masters LLC	Plantsville	CT	G	860 621-6911	3526
Becon Incorporated **(PA)**	Bloomfield	CT	D	860 243-1428	208
GE Engine Svcs UNC Holdg I Inc	New Haven	CT	G	518 380-0767	2689
GE Transportation Parts LLC	Fairfield	CT	G	816 650-6171	1435
Pequot	Bridgeport	CT	G	800 620-1492	466
Pw Power Systems LLC **(HQ)**	Glastonbury	CT	D	860 368-5900	1576
Altaeros Energies Inc	Somerville	MA	G	617 908-8464	15153
Camar Corp	Northborough	MA	F	508 845-9263	14030
Ethosenergy Tc Inc	Chicopee	MA	C	413 593-0500	10024
Ethosenergy Tc Inc **(DH)**	Chicopee	MA	C	802 257-2721	10025
Ethosenergy Tc Inc	Leominster	MA	F	978 353-3089	12135
Free Flow Power Corporation	Boston	MA	E	978 283-2822	8553
General Electric Company **(PA)**	Boston	MA	A	617 443-3000	8558
LKM Industries Inc	Woburn	MA	D	781 935-9210	17216
Mavel Americas Inc	Boston	MA	G	617 242-2204	8689
Northast Renewable Enrgy Group	Boston	MA	G	617 878-2063	8742
Orsted North America Inc	Boston	MA	G	857 284-1430	8760
Pivotal Aero Wind Turbines Inc	Weymouth	MA	G	781 803-2982	16897
Riley Power Inc	Marlborough	MA	C	508 852-7100	12817
Windstream Enrgy Solutions LLC	Woburn	MA	G	781 333-5450	17322
Flexor Energy Company	Orono	ME	G	207 866-3527	6554
General Electric Company	Bangor	ME	B	207 941-2500	5648
Pika Energy Inc	Westbrook	ME	F	207 887-9105	7202
Energy Resources Group Inc **(PA)**	Farmington	NH	E	603 335-2535	18141
Malagar Group LLC	Stratham	NH	G	603 778-1372	19873
Airgas Usa LLC	East Greenwich	RI	G	401 884-0201	20351
Vientek LLC **(PA)**	Warren	RI	A	915 225-1309	21312
Northern Power Systems Inc **(HQ)**	Barre	VT	D	802 461-2955	21631
Northern Power Systems Corp **(PA)**	Barre	VT	E	802 461-2955	21632
Renew Energy	Milton	VT	G	802 891-6774	22137

TURBINES & TURBINE GENERATOR SETS & PARTS

	CITY	ST	EMP	PHONE	ENTRY #
Blastech Overhaul & Repair	Bloomfield	CT	F	860 243-8811	210
Doncasters Inc **(HQ)**	Groton	CT	D	860 449-1603	1671
Jet Industries Inc	Agawam	MA	E	413 786-2010	7435
Trireme Manufacturing Co Inc	Topsfield	MA	E	978 887-2132	15867
Machining Innovations Inc	Oakland	ME	G	207 465-2500	6534
Sperry Valve Inc	East Arlington	VT	G	802 375-6703	21910

TURBINES: Steam

	CITY	ST	EMP	PHONE	ENTRY #
GE Energy Parts Intl LLC **(HQ)**	Boston	MA	G	617 443-3000	8557
General Electric Company	Westborough	MA	F	508 870-5200	16619
Steam Turbine Services	North Yarmouth	ME	G	207 272-8664	6519
Steam Turbine 4 U	Hudson	NH	G	603 465-8881	18441

TURBO-GENERATORS

	CITY	ST	EMP	PHONE	ENTRY #
Knm Holdings LLC	Marlborough	MA	G	508 229-1400	12783

TURKEY PROCESSING & SLAUGHTERING

	CITY	ST	EMP	PHONE	ENTRY #
Gerard Farms Inc	Framingham	MA	G	781 858-1013	10959

TURNKEY VENDORS: Computer Systems

	CITY	ST	EMP	PHONE	ENTRY #
Tek Industries Inc	Vernon	CT	E	860 870-0001	4673
Nestor Inc **(PA)**	Providence	RI	F	401 274-5345	21076

TURNSTILES

	CITY	ST	EMP	PHONE	ENTRY #
Hayward Turnstiles Inc	Milford	CT	G	203 877-7096	2296
Perey Turnstiles Inc	Bridgeport	CT	E	203 333-9400	467

TWINE

	CITY	ST	EMP	PHONE	ENTRY #
Brownell & Company Inc **(PA)**	Moodus	CT	F	860 873-8625	2423
Dhm Thread Corporation	Fall River	MA	F	508 672-0032	10682
John E Ruggles & Co	New Bedford	MA	G	508 992-9766	13400
Yale Cordage Inc	Saco	ME	D	207 282-3396	6863

TWINE PRDTS

	CITY	ST	EMP	PHONE	ENTRY #
Advanced Indus Solutions Inc	Waldoboro	ME	E	207 832-0569	7129

TYPESETTING SVC

	CITY	ST	EMP	PHONE	ENTRY #
Acme Typesetting Service Co	West Hartford	CT	G	860 953-1470	5052
Allied Printing Services Inc **(PA)**	Manchester	CT	B	860 643-1101	1984
Appels Printing & Mailing Bur	Hartford	CT	F	860 522-8189	1806
Birdtrack Press	New Haven	CT	G	203 389-7789	2669
Brescias Printing Services Inc	East Hartford	CT	G	860 528-4254	1177
Copy Stop Inc	Hamden	CT	G	203 288-6401	1738
E R Hitchcock Company	New Britain	CT	E	860 229-2024	2529
Eccles-Lehman Inc	Easton	CT	G	203 268-0605	1318
Elm Press Incorporated	Terryville	CT	E	860 583-3600	4477
Executive Office Services Inc	Bridgeport	CT	E	203 373-1333	411
Franklin Print Shoppe Inc	Torrington	CT	G	860 496-9516	4578
G & R Enterprises Incorporated	Hartford	CT	G	860 549-6120	1822
Gateway Digital Inc	Norwalk	CT	F	203 853-4929	3157
Jerrys Printing & Graphics LLC	Bridgeport	CT	G	203 384-0015	435
Kool Ink LLC	Bloomfield	CT	F	860 242-0303	238
Magnani Press Incorporated	Hartford	CT	G	860 236-2802	1841
Master Engrv & Printery Inc **(PA)**	Waterbury	CT	G	203 723-2779	4911
Oddo Print Shop Inc	Torrington	CT	G	860 489-6585	4590
Palmisano Printing LLC	Bristol	CT	G	860 582-6883	590
Paul Dewitt	Danbury	CT	F	203 792-5610	965
Phoenix Press Inc	New Haven	CT	E	203 865-5555	2726
Professional Graphics Inc	Norwalk	CT	F	203 846-4291	3225
Prosperous Printing LLC	Wilton	CT	G	203 834-1962	5300
Saybrook Press Incorporated	Guilford	CT	F	203 458-3637	1717
Step Saver Inc	Southington	CT	E	860 621-6751	4082
Vernon Printing Co Inc	Vernon Rockville	CT	G	860 872-1826	4688
Westchster Bk/Rnsford Type Inc	Danbury	CT	C	203 791-0080	1010
Abby Printing Co Inc	Easthampton	MA	G	413 536-5269	10551
American Prtg & Envelope Inc	Auburn	MA	E	508 832-6100	7825
Andrew T Johnson Company Inc **(PA)**	Boston	MA	E	617 742-1610	8366
Apb Enterprises Inc	Marlborough	MA	G	508 481-0966	12715
Argosy Publishing Inc **(PA)**	Newton	MA	E	617 527-9999	13562
Belmont Printing Company	Belmont	MA	E	617 484-0833	8066
Business Cards Overnight Inc	Lawrence	MA	G	978 974-9271	11999
Chaco Inc	Norwood	MA	G	781 769-5557	14141
Color Images Inc	Methuen	MA	G	978 688-4994	13015
Coprico Inc	Chelsea	MA	G	617 889-0520	9951
Creative Publishing Corp Amer **(PA)**	Peabody	MA	E	978 532-5880	14326
Crockergraphics Inc	Needham Heights	MA	G	781 444-7020	13324
Cxo Media Inc **(DH)**	Framingham	MA	C	508 766-5696	10938
D & L Associates Inc	Needham Heights	MA	G	781 400-5068	13326
D S Graphics Inc **(PA)**	Lowell	MA	C	978 970-1359	12365
Desk Top Graphics Inc **(HQ)**	Peabody	MA	E	617 832-1927	14330
Dmr Print Inc **(PA)**	Concord	MA	E	617 876-3688	10128
Elbonais Incorporated	Framingham	MA	G	508 626-2318	10945
Fasprint Inc **(PA)**	Brockton	MA	F	508 588-9961	9146
Flagship Press Inc	North Andover	MA	C	978 975-3100	13704
Generation Four Inc	Waltham	MA	G	781 899-3180	16119
Ghp Media Inc	North Adams	MA	D	413 663-3771	13675
Harvard Instant Printing	Waltham	MA	G	781 893-2622	16124
J C Enterprises Inc	Ashland	MA	G	508 881-7228	7662
J T Gardner Inc	Worcester	MA	G	508 751-6600	17396
J T Gardner Inc **(PA)**	Westborough	MA	E	800 540-4993	16627
Keating Communication Group	Canton	MA	G	781 828-9030	9749
Kirkwood Holdings Inc **(PA)**	Wilmington	MA	C	978 658-4200	17012
Laplume & Sons Printing Inc	Lawrence	MA	E	978 683-1009	12045
Linmel Associates Inc	Marlborough	MA	F	508 481-6699	12787
LPI Printing and Graphic Inc	Stoneham	MA	E	781 438-5400	15566
Marcus Company Inc	Holyoke	MA	E	413 534-3303	11637
Massachusetts Repro Ltd	Boston	MA	F	617 227-2237	8686
McDermott Pallotta Inc	Watertown	MA	G	617 924-2318	16300
Merrill Graphics Incorporated	Braintree	MA	G	781 843-0666	9026
Michael M Almeida	Taunton	MA	G	508 823-4957	15765
Minuteman Press	Newburyport	MA	G	978 465-2242	13515
Minuteman Press	Fitchburg	MA	G	978 345-0818	10839
Newspapers of Massachusetts	Greenfield	MA	B	978 544-2118	11270
Northern Graphics Inc	Middleton	MA	F	978 646-9925	13097
Picken Printing Inc	North Chelmsford	MA	E	978 251-0730	13907
PIP Itsa Inc	Beverly	MA	G	978 927-5717	8165
Postal Instant Press **(PA)**	East Longmeadow	MA	G	413 525-4044	10487
Printing Place Inc	Melrose	MA	G	781 272-7209	12988
Professional Lithography Inc	South Hadley	MA	E	413 532-9473	15309
Publishers Design & Prod Svcs	Sagamore Beach	MA	F	508 833-8300	14886
Pyramid Printing and Advg Inc	Weymouth	MA	E	781 337-7609	16899
R & H Communications Inc **(PA)**	Waltham	MA	F	781 893-6221	16181
Ramsbottom Printing Inc	Fall River	MA	D	508 730-2220	10752
Reminder Publications	East Longmeadow	MA	E	413 525-3947	10491
Rgp Corp	Milford	MA	G	508 478-8511	13141
Rogers Printing Co Inc	Leominster	MA	E	978 537-9791	12184
S A N Inc **(PA)**	Lawrence	MA	G	978 686-3875	12073
Serigraphics Unlimited	Rowley	MA	G	978 356-4896	14866
Sherman Printing Co Inc	Canton	MA	E	781 828-8855	9778
Southern Berkshire Shoppers Gu	Great Barrington	MA	F	413 528-0095	11246
Ted Best	Hyde Park	MA	G	617 361-7258	11881
Teletypesetting Company Inc	Boston	MA	F	617 542-6220	8877
Universal Wilde Inc	Westwood	MA	C	978 658-0800	16881
Weston Corporation	Hingham	MA	F	781 749-0936	11516
Yankee Printing Group Inc	South Hadley	MA	E	413 532-9513	15313
Bruce A Pettengill	Leeds	ME	G	207 933-2578	6268
Davic Inc	Portland	ME	F	207 774-0093	6649
J A Black Company	Belfast	ME	G	207 338-4040	5691
Marks Printing House Inc	Belfast	ME	G	207 338-5460	5692
Quick Print Color Center	Saco	ME	G	207 282-6480	6856
R & W Engraving Inc	Biddeford	ME	G	207 286-3020	5760
Alpha Design & Composition	Pittsfield	NH	G	603 435-8592	19497
Echo Communications Inc	New London	NH	E	603 526-6006	19316
Flash Card Inc	Manchester	NH	G	603 625-0803	18823
Graphic Consumer Services Inc	Candia	NH	G	603 483-5355	17785
Kensington Group Incorporated	Hampton Falls	NH	F	603 926-6742	18283
Letterman Press LLC	West Lebanon	NH	G	603 543-0500	19956
New England Printing Corp	Portsmouth	NH	F	603 431-0142	19599
Print Factory Inc	Nashua	NH	G	603 880-4519	19239
Puritan Press Inc **(PA)**	Hollis	NH	E	603 889-4500	18339
Ram Printing Incorporated **(PA)**	East Hampstead	NH	E	603 382-7045	18082
Smith & Town Printers LLC	Berlin	NH	G	603 752-2150	17700
Southport Management Group LLC	Portsmouth	NH	G	603 433-4664	19621
Whitman Communications Inc	Lebanon	NH	E	603 448-2600	18641
A & H Composition and Prtg Inc	East Providence	RI	G	401 438-1200	20383
Allegra Print & Imaging	East Greenwich	RI	G	401 884-9280	20352
Copy Print Company	Cranston	RI	G	401 228-3900	20201
Creative Digital Inc	Cranston	RI	G	401 942-0771	20204
Faces Typography Inc	Providence	RI	G	401 273-4455	21009
Southern RI Newspapers **(HQ)**	Wakefield	RI	E	401 789-9744	21277
T M Morris Productions Inc	Providence	RI	G	401 331-7780	21131
Warwick Group Inc	Bristol	RI	F	401 438-9451	20109
Accura Printing	Barre	VT	F	802 476-4429	21607
Asterisk Typographics Inc	Barre	VT	G	802 476-8399	21608
Dawn Brainard	Newport	VT	G	802 334-2780	22196
Herald Association Inc	Rutland	VT	C	802 747-6121	22338
L Brown and Sons Printing Inc	Barre	VT	E	802 476-3164	21627
McClure Newspapers Inc	Burlington	VT	C	802 863-3441	21795

	CITY	ST	EMP	PHONE	ENTRY #
Queen City Printers Inc	Burlington	VT	E	802 864-4566	21804
Stillwater Graphics Inc	Williamstown	VT	F	802 433-9898	22651
Stratford Publishing Services	Brattleboro	VT	E	802 254-6073	21747
Tuttle Law Print Inc	Rutland	VT	D	802 773-9171	22356
Villanti & Sons Printers Inc	Milton	VT	D	802 864-0723	22140

TYPESETTING SVC: Computer

	CITY	ST	EMP	PHONE	ENTRY #
Jupiter Communications LLC	West Haven	CT	F	475 238-7082	5127
Crane Composition Inc	East Sandwich	MA	G	774 338-5183	10506
Electronic Distribution Corp	Chicopee	MA	G	413 536-3400	10023
Modern Graphics Inc	Quincy	MA	F	781 331-5000	14640
JS McCarthy Co Inc **(PA)**	Augusta	ME	D	207 622-6241	5609
Laserwords Maine	Lewiston	ME	E	207 782-9595	6297
Scansmart LLC	Manchester	NH	G	603 664-7773	18917

TYPESETTING SVC: Hand Composition

	CITY	ST	EMP	PHONE	ENTRY #
Westchester Pubg Svcs LLC **(PA)**	Danbury	CT	G	203 791-0080	1009

TYPESETTING SVC: Linotype Composition, For Printing Trade

	CITY	ST	EMP	PHONE	ENTRY #
Red Sun Press Inc	Jamaica Plain	MA	F	617 524-6822	11949

TYPOGRAPHY

	CITY	ST	EMP	PHONE	ENTRY #
John Karl Dietrich & Assoc	Cambridge	MA	F	617 868-4140	9521
Technologies/Typography	Merrimac	MA	G	978 346-4867	13006
Textech Inc	Brattleboro	VT	G	802 254-6073	21749

ULTRASONIC EQPT: Cleaning, Exc Med & Dental

	CITY	ST	EMP	PHONE	ENTRY #
Ultra Clean Equipment Inc	Clinton	CT	G	860 669-1354	797
Branson Ultrasonics Corp	North Billerica	MA	E	978 262-9040	13798
Terrasonics LLC	Westford	MA	G	978 692-3274	16796

UNDERCOATINGS: Paint

	CITY	ST	EMP	PHONE	ENTRY #
Element 119 LLC	Thomaston	CT	F	860 358-0119	4503

UNIVERSITY

	CITY	ST	EMP	PHONE	ENTRY #
Wesleyan University	Middletown	CT	G	860 685-2980	2230
Yale University	New Haven	CT	G	203 432-2880	2758
Yale University	New Haven	CT	G	203 432-3916	2759
Yale University	New Haven	CT	G	203 432-2424	2760
Yale University	New Haven	CT	G	203 432-6320	2761
Yale University	New Haven	CT	G	203 432-7494	2762
Massachusetts Institute Tech	Cambridge	MA	D	617 253-5646	9546
Massachusetts Institute Tech	Cambridge	MA	G	617 253-7183	9548
Trustees of Boston University	Brookline	MA	F	617 353-3081	9223
University Massachusetts Inc	Amherst	MA	F	413 545-2217	7528
University Massachusetts Inc	Amherst	MA	G	413 545-2682	7529
University of Massachusetts	Amherst	MA	F	413 545-2718	7531
University of Maine System	Orono	ME	F	207 581-2843	6559
University of Maine System	Orono	ME	D	207 581-1273	6560

UNSUPPORTED PLASTICS: Floor Or Wall Covering

	CITY	ST	EMP	PHONE	ENTRY #
Guardian Indus Pdts Inc Mass	Norfolk	MA	G	508 384-0060	13660
Hytex Industries Inc	Randolph	MA	E	781 963-4400	14686

UPHOLSTERY FILLING MATERIALS

	CITY	ST	EMP	PHONE	ENTRY #
True Guilford Inc	Guilford	ME	G	207 876-3331	6162

UPHOLSTERY MATERIAL

	CITY	ST	EMP	PHONE	ENTRY #
New England Worldwide Export	Quincy	MA	G	617 472-0251	14642
Custom Canvas & Upholstery LLC	Lewiston	ME	F	207 241-8518	6281

UPHOLSTERY WORK SVCS

	CITY	ST	EMP	PHONE	ENTRY #
Alliance Upholstery Inc	Springfield	MA	G	413 731-7857	15444
Cloth N Canvas Recovery Inc	Colchester	VT	G	802 658-6826	21859

UREA

	CITY	ST	EMP	PHONE	ENTRY #
Allstar Foundation For Urea Cy	Wilmington	MA	G	978 658-5319	16972
Inspire Hope Foundtn For Urea	Braintree	MA	G	781 817-6664	9020

URNS: Cut Stone

	CITY	ST	EMP	PHONE	ENTRY #
Mackenzie Vault Inc	East Longmeadow	MA	F	413 525-8827	10483
Creative Bronze Inc	West Warwick	RI	G	401 823-7340	21489

USED CAR DEALERS

	CITY	ST	EMP	PHONE	ENTRY #
Car Buyers Market	Trumbull	CT	E	516 482-0292	4618
New Age Motorsports LLC	Monroe	CT	G	203 268-1999	2410

USED MERCHANDISE STORES

	CITY	ST	EMP	PHONE	ENTRY #
Jeff Schiff	Chelsea	MA	G	617 887-0202	9956
Maine Antique Digest Inc	Waldoboro	ME	E	207 832-7534	7134

USED MERCHANDISE STORES: Building Materials

	CITY	ST	EMP	PHONE	ENTRY #
E Skip Grindle & Sons	Ellsworth	ME	G	207 460-0334	6017

USED MERCHANDISE STORES: Computers & Access

	CITY	ST	EMP	PHONE	ENTRY #
Assured Computing Technologies	Bedford	NH	G	603 627-8728	17631

UTENSILS: Cast Aluminum, Cooking Or Kitchen

	CITY	ST	EMP	PHONE	ENTRY #
Half-Time Ventures Inc	Carlisle	MA	G	978 369-2907	9798

UTENSILS: Household, Cooking & Kitchen, Metal

	CITY	ST	EMP	PHONE	ENTRY #
Feature Products Ltd	Goffstown	NH	G	603 669-0800	18200

UTILITY TRAILER DEALERS

	CITY	ST	EMP	PHONE	ENTRY #
On The Road Inc	Warren	ME	E	207 273-3780	7146

VACUUM CLEANERS: Household

	CITY	ST	EMP	PHONE	ENTRY #
Central Vacuum Cleaners	Lawrence	MA	G	978 682-5295	12004
Headwaters Inc	Marblehead	MA	G	781 715-6404	12685
Static Solutions Inc **(PA)**	Marlborough	MA	F	508 480-0700	12830

VACUUM CLEANERS: Indl Type

	CITY	ST	EMP	PHONE	ENTRY #
Spencer Turbine Company **(HQ)**	Windsor	CT	C	860 688-8361	5363
Central Vacuum Cleaners **(PA)**	Methuen	MA	F	978 682-5294	13013
Central Vacuum Cleaners	Lawrence	MA	G	978 682-5295	12004
Cleanbasins Inc	North Billerica	MA	G	978 670-5838	13802
Filtered Air Systems Inc	Woburn	MA	G	781 491-0508	17179

VACUUM SYSTEMS: Air Extraction, Indl

	CITY	ST	EMP	PHONE	ENTRY #
Millibar Inc	Hopkinton	MA	F	508 488-9870	11728
Ruwac Inc	Holyoke	MA	F	413 532-4030	11654
Vacuum Technology Associates	Hingham	MA	D	781 740-8600	11513

VALUE-ADDED RESELLERS: Computer Systems

	CITY	ST	EMP	PHONE	ENTRY #
Grayfin Security LLC	Madison	CT	G	203 800-6760	1961
David Corporation **(PA)**	Wakefield	MA	E	781 587-3008	15948
Micro Financial Cmpt Systems	Medway	MA	G	508 533-1233	12967
Profitkey International Inc	Salem	NH	E	603 898-9800	19760

VALVE REPAIR SVCS, INDL

	CITY	ST	EMP	PHONE	ENTRY #
Knowlton Machine Company	Gorham	ME	E	207 854-8471	6117

VALVES

	CITY	ST	EMP	PHONE	ENTRY #
Carten Controls Inc	Cheshire	CT	F	203 699-2100	719
James J Scott LLC	Rocky Hill	CT	G	860 571-9200	3719
Amkor Industrial Products Inc	Worcester	MA	E	508 799-4970	17336
Conant Controls Inc	Woburn	MA	F	781 395-2240	17147
Neles USA Inc	Worcester	MA	G	508 852-0200	17428
Neles USA Inc **(DH)**	Shrewsbury	MA	C	508 852-0200	15125
Neles USA Inc	Shrewsbury	MA	G	508 852-0200	15126
Neles USA Inc	Shrewsbury	MA	F	508 852-0200	15127
Eagle America Inc	Warwick	RI	F	401 732-0333	21358

VALVES & PARTS: Gas, Indl

	CITY	ST	EMP	PHONE	ENTRY #
Broen-Lab Inc	Bedford	NH	F	205 956-9444	17633

VALVES & PIPE FITTINGS

	CITY	ST	EMP	PHONE	ENTRY #
Carten Controls Inc	Cheshire	CT	F	203 699-2100	719
Enfield Technologies LLC	Shelton	CT	F	203 375-3100	3801
Fisher Controls Intl LLC	North Stonington	CT	C	860 599-1140	3075
Houston Weber Systems Inc	Branford	CT	G	203 481-0115	324
Hydrolevel Company	North Haven	CT	F	203 776-0473	3030
Idex Health & Science LLC	Bristol	CT	C	860 314-2880	570
Automatic Machine Pdts Sls Co	Taunton	MA	D	508 822-4226	15728
Conant Controls Inc	Woburn	MA	F	781 395-2240	17147
Mks Instruments Inc **(PA)**	Andover	MA	B	978 645-5500	7574
Mks Instruments Inc	Andover	MA	E	978 645-5500	7575
Mks Msc Inc	Wilmington	MA	A	978 284-4000	17025
Portland Valve LLC **(HQ)**	Warren	MA	E	704 289-6511	16261
Rodney Hunt-Fontaine Inc **(DH)**	Orange	MA	C	978 544-2511	14227
Sem-Tec Inc	Worcester	MA	E	508 798-8551	17471
Sloan Valve Company	Andover	MA	C	617 796-9001	7607
Swiss Precision Products Inc **(DH)**	North Oxford	MA	E	508 987-8003	13975
Taco Inc	Fall River	MA	D	508 675-7300	10769
Takasago Electric Inc	Westborough	MA	G	508 983-1434	16653
Victaulic Company	Mansfield	MA	G	508 406-3220	12668
Alan T Seeler Inc	New Hampton	NH	F	603 744-3736	19301
Anvil International LLC **(HQ)**	Exeter	NH	E	603 418-2800	18110
Mem-Co Fittings Inc	Hampstead	NH	G	603 329-9633	18243
Parker & Harper Companies Inc **(PA)**	Raymond	NH	D	603 895-4761	19643
Quality Controls Inc	Northfield	NH	E	603 286-3321	19408
Everett J Prescott Inc	Lincoln	RI	G	401 333-8588	20573

VALVES & REGULATORS: Pressure, Indl

	CITY	ST	EMP	PHONE	ENTRY #
Condon Mfg Co Inc	Springfield	MA	F	413 543-1250	15461
Crosby Valve & Gage Intl Inc	Mansfield	MA	D	508 384-3121	12624
Mks Msc Inc	Wilmington	MA	A	978 284-4000	17025
Pentair Valves & Contrls US LP	Mansfield	MA	C	508 594-4410	12651
Watts Regulator Co **(HQ)**	North Andover	MA	C	978 689-6000	13737
Watts Regulator Co	North Andover	MA	A	978 688-1811	13738
Watts Water Technologies Inc **(PA)**	North Andover	MA	C	978 688-1811	13739

VALVES Solenoid

	CITY	ST	EMP	PHONE	ENTRY #
Kip Inc	Farmington	CT	C	860 677-0272	1488
Parker-Hannifin Corporation	New Britain	CT	C	860 827-2300	2561
Peter Paul Electronics Co Inc	New Britain	CT	C	860 229-4884	2562
Parker-Hannifin Corporation	Hollis	NH	E	973 575-4844	18337

VALVES: Aerosol, Metal

	CITY	ST	EMP	PHONE	ENTRY #
Aptargroup Inc	Stratford	CT	B	203 377-8100	4391
Alloy Fabricators of Neng	Randolph	MA	F	781 986-6400	14670
Summit Packaging Systems Inc **(PA)**	Manchester	NH	B	603 669-5410	18932
Champlain Precision Inc **(PA)**	New Haven	VT	G	802 453-7225	22184

VALVES: Aircraft

	CITY	ST	EMP	PHONE	ENTRY #
Nutek Aerospace Corp	New Milford	CT	G	860 355-3169	2819
Saf Industries LLC	Meriden	CT	E	203 729-4900	2127

VALVES: Aircraft, Control, Hydraulic & Pneumatic

	CITY	ST	EMP	PHONE	ENTRY #
American Metal Masters LLC	Plantsville	CT	G	860 621-6911	3526
Controls For Automation Inc	Taunton	MA	E	508 802-6005	15738
John Crane Sealol Inc **(DH)**	Warwick	RI	C	401 732-0715	21381

VALVES: Aircraft, Fluid Power

	CITY	ST	EMP	PHONE	ENTRY #
Saf Industries LLC	Meriden	CT	E	203 729-4900	2127
Wgi Inc	Southwick	MA	C	413 569-9444	15421

VALVES: Control, Automatic

Company	CITY	ST	EMP	PHONE	ENTRY #
Cr-TEC Engineering Inc	Madison	CT	G	203 318-9500	1957
Fisher Controls Intl LLC	North Stonington	CT	C	860 599-1140	3075
McGuire & Co Inc	Falmouth	ME	G	207 797-3323	6032

VALVES: Fluid Power, Control, Hydraulic & pneumatic

Company	CITY	ST	EMP	PHONE	ENTRY #
Clarcor Eng MBL Solutions LLC **(DH)**	East Hartford	CT	D	860 920-4200	1182
Crane Aerospace Inc **(DH)**	Stamford	CT	C	203 363-7300	4176
Crane Co **(PA)**	Stamford	CT	D	203 363-7300	4177
Crane Controls Inc **(DH)**	Stamford	CT	G	203 363-7300	4178
Crane Intl Holdings Inc **(HQ)**	Stamford	CT	G	203 363-7300	4179
Navtec Rigging Solutions Inc	Clinton	CT	E	203 458-3163	790
Norgren Inc	Farmington	CT	C	860 677-0272	1500
Stanadyne Intrmdate Hldngs LLC **(HQ)**	Windsor	CT	C	860 525-0821	5367

VALVES: Hard Rubber

Company	CITY	ST	EMP	PHONE	ENTRY #
David A Payne	Brockton	MA	G	508 588-7500	9136

VALVES: Indl

Company	CITY	ST	EMP	PHONE	ENTRY #
BNL Industries Inc	Vernon	CT	E	860 870-6222	4663
Contemporary Products LLC	Middletown	CT	E	860 346-9283	2182
Conval Inc	Enfield	CT	C	860 749-0761	1353
Rostra Vernatherm LLC	Bristol	CT	E	860 582-6776	609
Ruby Automation LLC **(HQ)**	Bloomfield	CT	C	860 687-5000	258
Ruby Industrial Tech LLC **(PA)**	Bloomfield	CT	D	860 687-5000	260
Asahi/America Inc **(HQ)**	Lawrence	MA	C	781 321-5409	11995
Circor International Inc **(PA)**	Burlington	MA	B	781 270-1200	9250
Clark Solutions	Hudson	MA	F	978 568-3400	11763
Conant Controls Inc	Woburn	MA	F	781 395-2240	17147
Diebolt & Company	East Longmeadow	MA	F	860 434-2222	10473
Emerson Automation Solutions	Mansfield	MA	D	508 594-4356	12630
Emerson Automation Solutions	Mansfield	MA	D	508 594-4410	12631
Mks Instruments Inc **(PA)**	Andover	MA	B	978 645-5500	7574
Mks Instruments Inc	Andover	MA	E	978 645-5500	7575
Mostmed Inc	Salem	MA	G	978 740-0400	14931
Tyco International MGT Co LLC	Mansfield	MA	G	508 261-6200	12667
Vent-Rite Valve Corp **(PA)**	Randolph	MA	E	781 986-2000	14701
Cobra Precision Machining Corp	Hooksett	NH	G	603 434-8424	18347
Quality Controls Inc	Northfield	NH	E	603 286-3321	19408
Ruggles-Klingemann Mfg Co	Seabrook	NH	G	603 474-8500	19814
Watts Regulator Co	Franklin	NH	A	603 934-5110	18166
Watts Water Technologies Inc	Franklin	NH	D	603 934-1369	18167
Watts Water Technologies Inc	Franklin	NH	E	603 934-1367	18168

VALVES: Plumbing & Heating

Company	CITY	ST	EMP	PHONE	ENTRY #
Hytek Plumbing and Heating LLC	Preston	CT	G	860 389-1122	3581
Economou Plumbing & Heating	Dracut	MA	G	978 957-6953	10360
Maxon Corporation	Acton	MA	G	978 795-1285	7373
Symmons Industries Inc **(PA)**	Braintree	MA	C	781 848-2250	9041
Symmons Industries Inc	Braintree	MA	G	781 664-5236	9042
Watts Regulator Co **(HQ)**	North Andover	MA	C	978 689-6000	13737
Watts Water Technologies Inc **(PA)**	North Andover	MA	C	978 688-1811	13739
Acme Sales	Londonderry	NH	G	603 434-8826	18670

VALVES: Regulating & Control, Automatic

Company	CITY	ST	EMP	PHONE	ENTRY #
Logic Seal LLC	Plainville	CT	G	203 598-3400	3501
Universal Building Contrls Inc	Meriden	CT	F	203 235-1530	2145

VALVES: Regulating, Process Control

Company	CITY	ST	EMP	PHONE	ENTRY #
Oventrop Corp	East Granby	CT	E	860 413-9173	1139
Saf Industries LLC	Meriden	CT	E	203 729-4900	2127

VALVES: Water Works

Company	CITY	ST	EMP	PHONE	ENTRY #
Fr Flow Ctrl Vlves US Bdco Inc **(PA)**	Ipswich	MA	D	978 744-5690	11920
Mueller Water Products Inc	Middleboro	MA	F	508 923-2870	13070
Rodney Hunt-Fontaine Inc **(DH)**	Orange	MA	C	978 544-2511	14227

VARIETY STORES

Company	CITY	ST	EMP	PHONE	ENTRY #
Sylvia Wyler Pottery Inc **(PA)**	Brunswick	ME	G	207 729-1321	5848

VASES: Pottery

Company	CITY	ST	EMP	PHONE	ENTRY #
Philippine Pot Partners LLC	Lincoln	RI	G	401 789-7372	20590

VEHICLES: Recreational

Company	CITY	ST	EMP	PHONE	ENTRY #
M & C Powersports	Leeds	ME	G	207 713-3128	6270
Rokon International Inc	Rochester	NH	F	603 335-3200	19684
Textron Inc **(PA)**	Providence	RI	B	401 421-2800	21134

VENDING MACHINES & PARTS

Company	CITY	ST	EMP	PHONE	ENTRY #
Waterside Vending LLC	Westbrook	CT	G	860 399-6039	5165
Century Food Service Inc	Acushnet	MA	F	508 995-3221	7400
Diamond Music Co	Pelham	NH	G	603 635-2083	19431
Hot Stuff RI Inc	Warwick	RI	G	401 781-7500	21373

VENETIAN BLINDS & SHADES

Company	CITY	ST	EMP	PHONE	ENTRY #
Arrow Window Shade Mfg Co Mrdn	Wethersfield	CT	F	860 563-4035	5241
High Grade Shade & Screen Co	Lynn	MA	F	781 592-5027	12516
Taunton Venetian Blind Inc	Taunton	MA	G	508 822-7548	15789

VENTILATING EQPT: Metal

Company	CITY	ST	EMP	PHONE	ENTRY #
XYZ Sheet Metal Inc	Abington	MA	F	781 878-1419	7332

VENTILATING EQPT: Sheet Metal

Company	CITY	ST	EMP	PHONE	ENTRY #
R K Solutions Inc	Agawam	MA	G	413 351-1401	7449

VETERINARY PHARMACEUTICAL PREPARATIONS

Company	CITY	ST	EMP	PHONE	ENTRY #
Skyline Vet Pharma Inc	Groton	CT	G	860 625-0424	1686
Atlantic Animal Health Inc	Revere	MA	G	781 289-9600	14763
Pp Manufacturing Corporation	Framingham	MA	F	508 766-2700	10996
Uptite Company Inc	Haverhill	MA	G	978 377-0451	11483
Vapco Inc	Lawrence	MA	G	978 975-0302	12081
Idexx Laboratories Inc **(PA)**	Westbrook	ME	A	207 556-0300	7191
Sea Starr Animal Health	Wakefield	RI	G	401 783-2185	21275

VETERINARY PRDTS: Instruments & Apparatus

Company	CITY	ST	EMP	PHONE	ENTRY #
Horsepower Technologies Inc	Lowell	MA	E	844 514-6773	12380
Swiss Precision Products Inc **(DH)**	North Oxford	MA	E	508 987-8003	13975
Blair Campbell	Rutland	VT	G	802 773-7711	22325

VIBRATORS: Concrete Construction

Company	CITY	ST	EMP	PHONE	ENTRY #
Vibco Inc **(PA)**	Wyoming	RI	D	401 539-2392	21591

VIDEO CAMERA-AUDIO RECORDERS: Household Use

Company	CITY	ST	EMP	PHONE	ENTRY #
Aquabotix Technology Corp	Fall River	MA	E	508 676-1000	10661
Industrial Video & Ctrl Co LLC	Newton	MA	E	617 467-3059	13604
Lyfeshot LLC	Acton	MA	G	978 451-4662	7370
Polycom Inc	Andover	MA	E	978 292-5000	7586

VIDEO EQPT

Company	CITY	ST	EMP	PHONE	ENTRY #
Harman International Inds Inc	Stamford	CT	C	203 328-3500	4209

VIDEO PRODUCTION SVCS

Company	CITY	ST	EMP	PHONE	ENTRY #
Stephen McArthur	Barre	VT	G	802 839-0371	21640

VIDEO TAPE PRODUCTION SVCS

Company	CITY	ST	EMP	PHONE	ENTRY #
Taunton Inc	Newtown	CT	A	203 426-8171	2941
Artech House Inc **(HQ)**	Norwood	MA	F	781 769-9750	14134
Channing Bete Company Inc **(PA)**	South Deerfield	MA	B	413 665-7611	15247
Human Resource Dev Press **(PA)**	Pelham	MA	E	413 253-3488	14388
Sinauer Associates Inc	Sunderland	MA	E	413 549-4300	15676
Invision Inc	Brunswick	ME	G	207 725-7123	5839

VINYL RESINS, NEC

Company	CITY	ST	EMP	PHONE	ENTRY #
Keller Products Incorporated	Bow	NH	E	603 224-5502	17719

VISES: Machine

Company	CITY	ST	EMP	PHONE	ENTRY #
Advanced Torque Products LLC	Newington	CT	G	860 828-1523	2839
Lord & Hodge Inc	Middletown	CT	F	860 632-7006	2201

VISUAL COMMUNICATIONS SYSTEMS

Company	CITY	ST	EMP	PHONE	ENTRY #
Essential Trading Systems Corp	Marlborough	CT	F	860 295-8100	2064
Avacea	Everett	MA	G	617 294-0261	10603
Courtsmart Digital Systems Inc	North Chelmsford	MA	E	978 251-3300	13891
Image Stream Medical Inc	Littleton	MA	D	978 486-8494	12309
Scoreboard Enterprises Inc	Mansfield	MA	G	508 339-8113	12657
Vivox Inc **(DH)**	Framingham	MA	E	508 650-3571	11012
Xtralis Inc	Avon	MA	E	800 229-4434	7904
As Liquidation I Company Inc **(PA)**	Amherst	NH	D	603 879-0205	17552

VITAMINS: Natural Or Synthetic, Uncompounded, Bulk

Company	CITY	ST	EMP	PHONE	ENTRY #
Biomed Health Inc	Glastonbury	CT	F	860 657-2258	1540
Effihealth LLC	Stamford	CT	G	888 435-3108	4192
Watson LLC **(DH)**	West Haven	CT	B	203 932-3000	5149
Country Life LLC	Norwell	MA	G	781 659-1321	14101
Designing Health Inc	East Longmeadow	MA	E	661 257-1705	10472
Indian Meadow Herbals LLC	Eastbrook	ME	G	207 565-3010	5988
Troy Micro Five Inc	Saint Albans	VT	G	802 524-0076	22383

VITAMINS: Pharmaceutical Preparations

Company	CITY	ST	EMP	PHONE	ENTRY #
Humphreys Pharmacal Inc	East Hampton	CT	F	860 267-8710	1159
Pharmavite Corp	Simsbury	CT	G	860 651-1885	3909
SDA Laboratories Inc	Greenwich	CT	G	203 861-0005	1648
Longray Inc	Lexington	MA	G	781 862-5137	12240
Suzhou-Chem Inc	Wellesley	MA	G	781 433-8618	16388
New Chapter Inc **(HQ)**	Brattleboro	VT	C	800 543-7279	21739

WALLBOARD: Gypsum

Company	CITY	ST	EMP	PHONE	ENTRY #
County Concrete & Cnstr Co	Columbia Falls	ME	E	207 483-4409	5919
Georgia-Pacific LLC	Newington	NH	C	603 433-8000	19322

WALLPAPER & WALL COVERINGS

Company	CITY	ST	EMP	PHONE	ENTRY #
Ambiance Painting LLC	Norwalk	CT	F	203 354-8689	3100
Masterwork	Woburn	MA	G	781 995-3354	17224
Len-Tex Corp	North Walpole	NH	C	603 445-2342	19395

WAREHOUSING & STORAGE FACILITIES, NEC

Company	CITY	ST	EMP	PHONE	ENTRY #
Macristy Industries Inc **(PA)**	Newington	CT	C	860 225-4637	2879
Coca-Cola Bottling Company	Colchester	VT	D	802 654-3800	21860

WAREHOUSING & STORAGE, REFRIGERATED: Cold Storage Or Re-frig

Company	CITY	ST	EMP	PHONE	ENTRY #
Supreme Storm Services LLC	Southington	CT	G	860 201-0642	4083

WAREHOUSING & STORAGE: General

Company	CITY	ST	EMP	PHONE	ENTRY #
Veoneer Roadscape Auto Inc	Lowell	MA	G	978 656-2500	12444

WAREHOUSING & STORAGE: General

Company	CITY	ST	EMP	PHONE	ENTRY #
L P Macadams Company Inc	Bridgeport	CT	D	203 366-3647	442
Pucker Gallery Inc	Somerville	MA	F	617 261-1817	15207
Ronnie Marvin Enterprises	Littleton	NH	G	603 444-5017	18664

WAREHOUSING & STORAGE: Refrigerated

Company	CITY	ST	EMP	PHONE	ENTRY #
Merrill Blueberry Farms Inc	Hancock	ME	F	207 667-2541	6170

WAREHOUSING & STORAGE: Self Storage

Company	CITY	ST	EMP	PHONE	ENTRY #
Cardinal Shoe Corporation	Lawrence	MA	E	978 686-9706	12003

WARFARE COUNTER-MEASURE EQPT

	CITY	ST	EMP	PHONE	ENTRY #
Auriga Measurement Systems **(PA)**	Wayland	MA	G	978 452-7700	16334
Lockheed Martin Sippican Inc **(HQ)**	Marion	MA	B	508 748-3399	12699
Polaris Contract Mfg Inc	Marion	MA	B	508 748-3399	12702

WARM AIR HEATING & AC EQPT & SPLYS, WHOL: Dust Collecting

	CITY	ST	EMP	PHONE	ENTRY #
Nauset Engineer Equipment	Mansfield	MA	G	508 339-2662	12648

WARM AIR HEATING & AC EQPT & SPLYS, WHOLESALE Thermostats

	CITY	ST	EMP	PHONE	ENTRY #
Energy MGT & Ctrl Svcs Inc	Cranston	RI	F	401 946-1440	20217

WARM AIR HEATING/AC EQPT/SPLY, WHOL Humidifier, Exc Portable

	CITY	ST	EMP	PHONE	ENTRY #
Belimo Aircontrols (usa) Inc **(HQ)**	Danbury	CT	C	800 543-9038	879
Belimo Customization USA Inc	Danbury	CT	G	203 791-9915	881

WARM AIR HEATING/AC EQPT/SPLYS, WHOL Warm Air Htg Eqpt/Splys

	CITY	ST	EMP	PHONE	ENTRY #
Massachusetts Control Ctr Inc	Tyngsboro	MA	G	978 649-1128	15895

WARP KNIT FABRIC FINISHING

	CITY	ST	EMP	PHONE	ENTRY #
Moore Company **(PA)**	Westerly	RI	C	401 596-2816	21531
Moore Company	Westerly	RI	C	401 596-2816	21532
Moore Company	Westerly	RI	C	401 596-0219	21533
Moore Company	Westerly	RI	C	401 596-2816	21534
Garflex Inc	Brattleboro	VT	D	802 257-5256	21728

WASHERS

	CITY	ST	EMP	PHONE	ENTRY #
Luis Pressure Washer	Waterbury	CT	G	203 706-7399	4898
Corner Washers Inc	Allston	MA	G	617 370-0350	7462
Send Pymets To Washer Wizzards	Springfield	MA	G	413 733-2739	15504

WASHERS: Leather

	CITY	ST	EMP	PHONE	ENTRY #
Twin Leather Co Inc	West Bridgewater	MA	G	508 583-3485	16461

WASHERS: Metal

	CITY	ST	EMP	PHONE	ENTRY #
Astron Inc **(PA)**	Pepperell	MA	E	978 433-9500	14436
Century-Ty Wood Mfg Inc	Holliston	MA	D	508 429-4011	11563

WASHERS: Plastic

	CITY	ST	EMP	PHONE	ENTRY #
Cultec Inc	Brookfield	CT	F	203 775-4416	639
Standard Washer & Mat Inc	Manchester	CT	E	860 643-5125	2051
I G Marston Company	Holbrook	MA	F	781 767-2894	11526

WASHERS: Rubber

	CITY	ST	EMP	PHONE	ENTRY #
Auburn Manufacturing Company	Middletown	CT	E	860 346-6677	2173
Standard Washer & Mat Inc	Manchester	CT	E	860 643-5125	2051

WASTE CLEANING SVCS

	CITY	ST	EMP	PHONE	ENTRY #
Acme Precast Co Inc	West Falmouth	MA	E	508 548-9607	16477

WATCH STRAPS, EXC METAL

	CITY	ST	EMP	PHONE	ENTRY #
Currys Leather Shop Inc	Randolph	MA	F	781 963-0679	14675

WATCHCASES

	CITY	ST	EMP	PHONE	ENTRY #
Paroline/Wright Design Inc	Pawtucket	RI	F	401 781-5300	20875

WATCHES

	CITY	ST	EMP	PHONE	ENTRY #
Morristown Star Struck LLC	Bethel	CT	E	203 778-4925	173
Timex Group Usa Inc **(DH)**	Middlebury	CT	C	203 346-5000	2160

WATER HEATERS

	CITY	ST	EMP	PHONE	ENTRY #
Eemax Inc **(DH)**	Waterbury	CT	D	203 267-7890	4867
Therma-Flow Inc	Watertown	MA	E	617 924-3877	16322

WATER PURIFICATION EQPT: Household

	CITY	ST	EMP	PHONE	ENTRY #
3M Purification Inc **(HQ)**	Meriden	CT	B	203 237-5541	2070
Kx Technologies LLC **(DH)**	West Haven	CT	F	203 799-9000	5130
American Water Systems LLC	Canton	MA	D	781 830-9722	9712
Flodesign Sonics Inc	Wilbraham	MA	E	413 596-5900	16936
Merrimack Valley Water Assn	Lawrence	MA	G	978 975-1800	12051
Fuji Clean Usa LLC	Brunswick	ME	G	207 406-2927	5836
Filtrine Manufacturing Co Inc **(PA)**	Keene	NH	D	603 352-5500	18503
Richard Arikian	Nashua	NH	G	603 881-5427	19253

WATER PURIFICATION PRDTS: Chlorination Tablets & Kits

	CITY	ST	EMP	PHONE	ENTRY #
Purdue Pharma Manufacturing LP	Stamford	CT	E	252 265-1924	4295
Bwt Pharma & Biotech Inc	Marlborough	MA	E	508 485-4291	12731

WATER SUPPLY

	CITY	ST	EMP	PHONE	ENTRY #
Evoqua Water Technologies LLC	Tewksbury	MA	E	978 863-4600	15817

WATER TREATMENT EQPT: Indl

	CITY	ST	EMP	PHONE	ENTRY #
Affordable Water Trtmnt	Mansfield Center	CT	G	860 423-3147	2061
Alliance Water Treatment Co	Stamford	CT	G	203 323-9968	4133
Aqualogic Inc	North Haven	CT	E	203 248-8959	3009
Atlas Filtri North America LLC	Wallingford	CT	F	203 284-0080	4706
Best Management Products Inc	East Haddam	CT	G	860 434-0277	1148
Brasco Technologies LLC	Northford	CT	G	203 484-4291	3086
Crane Co **(PA)**	Stamford	CT	D	203 363-7300	4177
H Krevit and Company Inc	New Haven	CT	E	203 772-3350	2694
Hydro Service & Supplies Inc	Middletown	CT	G	203 265-3995	2190
Suez Wts Services Usa Inc	East Hartford	CT	E	860 291-9660	1225
Town of Montville	Uncasville	CT	F	860 848-3830	4650
Town of Vernon	Vernon	CT	F	860 870-3545	4675
Abbey Water Treatment Inc	Sudbury	MA	G	978 443-5001	15650
Aertec	Andover	MA	G	978 475-6385	7533
Applied Water Management Inc	Fall River	MA	G	508 675-5755	10660
C E D Corp	Duxbury	MA	G	781 834-9312	10395
Emco Engineering Inc	Canton	MA	G	508 314-8305	9730
F R Mahony Associates	Townsend	MA	E	978 597-0703	15872
Hydro Quip Inc **(PA)**	Seekonk	MA	G	508 399-5771	15024
Hydrotech Services Inc	North Attleboro	MA	F	508 699-5977	13759
Keller Products Inc	North Chelmsford	MA	F	978 264-1911	13899
Kerfoot Technologies Inc	Mashpee	MA	F	508 539-3002	12881
KLA Systems Inc	Assonet	MA	G	508 359-7361	7683
L T Technologies	East Bridgewater	MA	G	508 456-0315	10416
Metro Group Inc	Woburn	MA	F	781 932-9911	17229
North Amrcn Fltration Mass Inc	Walpole	MA	F	508 660-9016	16005
Parts Per Million Inc	Cotuit	MA	G	508 479-5438	10171
Town of Uxbridge	Uxbridge	MA	G	508 278-2887	15932
Zero Discharge	Chicopee	MA	G	413 593-5470	10071
Williams Partners Ltd	East Boothbay	ME	G	207 633-3111	5981
Global Filtration Systems	Wolfeboro	NH	G	603 651-8777	20019
Itaconix LLC	Stratham	NH	G	603 775-4400	19870
Aeqrx Technologies Ltd	Warwick	RI	G	401 463-8822	21319
Benson Neptune Inc **(HQ)**	Coventry	RI	E	401 821-7140	20138
Enpure Process Systems Inc	Cranston	RI	G	401 447-3976	20218
Service Tech Inc **(PA)**	North Providence	RI	F	401 353-3664	20774
Westfall Manufacturing Co	Bristol	RI	F	401 253-3799	20110
South Hero Fire District 4	South Hero	VT	G	802 372-3088	22483
Sun Ray Technologies Inc	Killington	VT	G	802 422-8680	22056

WATER: Distilled

	CITY	ST	EMP	PHONE	ENTRY #
Perfect Infinity Inc	Milford	CT	G	203 906-0442	2334

WATER: Mineral, Carbonated, Canned & Bottled, Etc

	CITY	ST	EMP	PHONE	ENTRY #
Crystal Rock Holdings Inc **(HQ)**	Watertown	CT	E	860 945-0661	5005
Everybody Water LLC	Cohasset	MA	G	855 374-6539	10098

WATER: Pasteurized & Mineral, Bottled & Canned

	CITY	ST	EMP	PHONE	ENTRY #
Danone Holdings Inc	Stamford	CT	A	203 229-7000	4184
Crystal Spring Water Co Inc **(PA)**	Auburn	ME	F	207 782-1521	5558

WATER: Pasteurized, Canned & Bottled, Etc

	CITY	ST	EMP	PHONE	ENTRY #
Adonai Spring Water Inc	Randolph	MA	G	844 273-7672	14669
Pocahontas Spring Water Co **(PA)**	Middleton	MA	G	978 774-2690	13098
Spring Water Associates USA	Watertown	MA	G	978 371-0138	16318
G C Management Corp **(PA)**	Southwest Harbor	ME	G	207 244-5363	7047
Cg Roxane LLC	Moultonborough	NH	E	603 476-8844	19095
Vermont Heritage Spring Water	Derby	VT	G	802 334-2528	21904

WATERPROOFING COMPOUNDS

	CITY	ST	EMP	PHONE	ENTRY #
Caap Co Inc	Milford	CT	E	203 877-0375	2258
Chase Corporation	Randolph	MA	E	781 963-2600	14673
Grate Products LLC	Westport	MA	G	800 649-6140	16840
Maranatha Industries Inc **(PA)**	Wakefield	MA	F	781 245-0038	15960
CIM Industries Inc	Peterborough	NH	F	603 924-9481	19469
Northern Industries Inc **(PA)**	Coventry	RI	G	401 769-4305	20160

WAVEGUIDES & FITTINGS

	CITY	ST	EMP	PHONE	ENTRY #
Microtech Inc	Cheshire	CT	D	203 272-3234	745
Harvard Scientific Corporation	Cambridge	MA	F	617 876-5033	9505
Microwave Development Labs Inc	Needham Heights	MA	D	781 292-6600	13337

WAX REMOVERS

	CITY	ST	EMP	PHONE	ENTRY #
Head 2 Toe	Reading	MA	F	781 944-0286	14736

WAXES: Mineral, Natural

	CITY	ST	EMP	PHONE	ENTRY #
Koster Keunen Inc	Watertown	CT	G	860 945-3333	5012
Koster Keunen Mfg Inc	Watertown	CT	D	860 945-3333	5014

WAXES: Petroleum, Not Produced In Petroleum Refineries

	CITY	ST	EMP	PHONE	ENTRY #
Koster Keunen LLC **(PA)**	Watertown	CT	F	860 945-3333	5013
Trans-Mate LLC	North Billerica	MA	E	800 867-9274	13873
Speedy Petroleum Inc	Cranston	RI	G	401 781-3350	20289

WEATHER STRIP: Sponge Rubber

	CITY	ST	EMP	PHONE	ENTRY #
H-O Products Corporation	Winsted	CT	E	860 379-9875	5412

WEATHER STRIPS: Metal

	CITY	ST	EMP	PHONE	ENTRY #
Visco Products Inc	Johnston	RI	G	401 831-1665	20547

WEATHER VANES

	CITY	ST	EMP	PHONE	ENTRY #
Cape Cod Cupola Co Inc	North Dartmouth	MA	G	508 994-2119	13916

WEAVING MILL, BROADWOVEN FABRICS: Wool Or Similar Fabric

	CITY	ST	EMP	PHONE	ENTRY #
Joseph C La Fond Co Inc	Manville	RI	F	401 769-3744	20609

WEDDING CONSULTING SVCS

	CITY	ST	EMP	PHONE	ENTRY #
Grace Ormonde Marriage Inc	Riverside	RI	F	401 245-9726	21169

WEIGHING MACHINERY & APPARATUS

	CITY	ST	EMP	PHONE	ENTRY #
Orbetron LLC	Cumberland	RI	G	651 983-2872	20337

WELDING & CUTTING APPARATUS & ACCESS, NEC

	CITY	ST	EMP	PHONE	ENTRY #
Kamweld Technologies Inc	Norwood	MA	F	781 762-6922	14169
Triad Inc	Plainville	MA	G	508 695-2247	14537

WELDING EQPT

	CITY	ST	EMP	PHONE	ENTRY #
Branson Ultrasonics Corp **(DH)**	Danbury	CT	B	203 796-0400	882
Industrial Prssure Washers LLC	Wethersfield	CT	G	860 608-6153	5249
L & P Gate Company Inc	Hartford	CT	G	860 296-8009	1839
Magnatech LLC	East Granby	CT	D	860 653-2573	1131
Nelson Stud Welding Inc	Farmington	CT	G	800 635-9353	1497
Quality Welding Service LLC	Portland	CT	G	860 342-7202	3572
Sonics & Materials Inc **(PA)**	Newtown	CT	D	203 270-4600	2938

	CITY	ST	EMP	PHONE	ENTRY #
Sonitek Corporation	Milford	CT	E	203 878-9321	2364
AGM Industries Inc	Brockton	MA	E	508 587-3900	9117
Lincoln Electric Holdings Inc	Uxbridge	MA	B	508 366-7070	15925
Mitchell Machine Incorporated **(PA)**	Springfield	MA	E	413 739-9693	15490
Precision Electronics Corp	Marshfield	MA	F	781 834-6677	12865
Centricut Manufacturing LLC	West Lebanon	NH	E	603 298-6191	19948
Contract Fusion Inc	East Providence	RI	E	401 438-1298	20400
Miller Electric Mfg LLC	Coventry	RI	G	401 828-0087	20157
Nordson Efd LLC **(HQ)**	East Providence	RI	C	401 431-7000	20435

WELDING EQPT & SPLYS WHOLESALERS

	CITY	ST	EMP	PHONE	ENTRY #
Praxair Distribution Inc **(DH)**	Danbury	CT	F	203 837-2000	972
Thavenet Machine Company Inc	Pawcatuck	CT	G	860 599-4495	3442
Ashmont Welding Company Inc	Bridgewater	MA	F	508 279-1977	9060
Weld Engineering Co Inc	Shrewsbury	MA	E	508 842-2224	15137
Thermal Dynamics Corporation **(DH)**	West Lebanon	NH	B	603 298-5711	19963
Contract Fusion Inc	East Providence	RI	E	401 438-1298	20400
Praxair Distribution Inc	Slatersville	RI	E	401 767-3450	21205

WELDING EQPT & SPLYS: Arc Welders, Transformer-Rectifier

	CITY	ST	EMP	PHONE	ENTRY #
Power Systems Integrity Inc	Northborough	MA	G	508 393-1655	14045

WELDING EQPT & SPLYS: Electrode Holders, Electric Welding

	CITY	ST	EMP	PHONE	ENTRY #
Cadi Co Inc **(PA)**	Naugatuck	CT	E	203 729-1111	2465

WELDING EQPT & SPLYS: Gas

	CITY	ST	EMP	PHONE	ENTRY #
Hydro-Test Products Inc	Stow	MA	F	978 897-4647	15632
Kent Pearce	East Wareham	MA	G	508 295-3791	10531

WELDING EQPT REPAIR SVCS

	CITY	ST	EMP	PHONE	ENTRY #
Ewald Instruments Corp	Bristol	CT	F	860 491-9042	558

WELDING EQPT: Electric

	CITY	ST	EMP	PHONE	ENTRY #
Praxair Surface Tech Inc	Manchester	CT	D	860 646-0700	2039
Weld Engineering Co Inc	Shrewsbury	MA	E	508 842-2224	15137

WELDING EQPT: Electrical

	CITY	ST	EMP	PHONE	ENTRY #
Magnatech LLC	East Granby	CT	D	860 653-2573	1131
Thermal Arc Inc	West Lebanon	NH	D	800 462-2782	19962

WELDING MACHINES & EQPT: Ultrasonic

	CITY	ST	EMP	PHONE	ENTRY #
Branson Ultrasonics Corp **(DH)**	Danbury	CT	B	203 796-0400	882
Sonosystems N Schunk Amer Corp **(DH)**	Wilmington	MA	E	978 658-9400	17046

WELDING REPAIR SVC

	CITY	ST	EMP	PHONE	ENTRY #
Accurate Welding Services LLC	Windsor Locks	CT	F	860 623-9500	5380
Aerotek Welding Co Inc	North Granby	CT	G	860 653-0120	2993
Amk Welding Inc **(HQ)**	South Windsor	CT	E	860 289-5634	3937
Anderson Tool Company Inc	New Haven	CT	G	203 777-4153	2657
Ansonia Stl Fabrication Co Inc	Beacon Falls	CT	E	203 888-4509	53
B & F Machine Co Inc	New Britain	CT	D	860 225-6349	2512
C and B Welding LLC	Lebanon	CT	G	860 423-9047	1933
C V Tool Company Inc **(PA)**	Southington	CT	E	978 353-7901	4042
Cheshire Manufacturing Co Inc	Cheshire	CT	G	203 272-3586	721
City Welding	Hartford	CT	G	860 951-4714	1814
Ctr Welding	Danbury	CT	G	704 473-1587	894
Durant Machine Inc **(PA)**	Mystic	CT	G	860 536-7698	2438
Dyco Industries Inc	South Windsor	CT	E	860 289-4957	3958
East Windsor Metal Fabg Inc	South Windsor	CT	F	860 528-7107	3961
EZ Welding LLC	New Britain	CT	G	860 707-3100	2533
F & W Rentals Inc	Orange	CT	F	203 795-0591	3366
Farrell Prcsion Mtalcraft Corp	New Milford	CT	E	860 355-2651	2799
Fonda Fabricating & Welding Co	Plainville	CT	G	860 793-0601	3489
General Wldg & Fabrication Inc	Watertown	CT	F	860 274-9668	5010
Goodyfab Llc	North Branford	CT	G	203 927-3059	2964
H G Steinmetz Machine Works	Bethel	CT	F	203 794-1880	158
Harry Thommen Company	Bridgeport	CT	G	203 333-3637	424
J T Fantozzi Co Inc	Meriden	CT	G	203 238-7018	2096
Jeff Manufacturing Co Inc	Torrington	CT	F	860 482-8845	4582
Jims Welding Service LLC	Danbury	CT	G	203 744-2982	939
Joining Technologies Inc	East Granby	CT	D	860 653-0111	1130
K T I Turbo-Tech Inc	East Windsor	CT	F	860 623-2511	1290
Kell-Strom Tool Intl Inc	Wethersfield	CT	E	860 529-6851	5254
Kensington Welding & Trlr Co	Kensington	CT	G	860 828-3564	1918
Kin-Therm Inc	East Windsor	CT	F	860 623-2511	1291
KTI Bi-Metallix Inc	East Windsor	CT	F	860 623-2511	1293
KTI Inc **(HQ)**	East Windsor	CT	F	860 623-2511	1294
L M Gill Welding and Mfr LLC	Manchester	CT	E	860 647-9931	2018
Labco Welding Inc	Middletown	CT	G	860 632-2625	2200
Lemac Iron Works Inc	West Hartford	CT	G	860 232-7380	5081
LM Gill Welding & Mfg LLC	Manchester	CT	E	860 647-9931	2020
Lynn Welding Co Inc	Newington	CT	F	860 667-4400	2877
Mackenzie Mch & Mar Works Inc	East Haven	CT	G	203 777-3479	1254
Mainville Welding Co Inc	Meriden	CT	G	203 237-3103	2101
Marc Bouley	Willimantic	CT	G	860 450-1713	5267
Matias Importing & Distrg Corp	Newington	CT	G	860 666-5544	2880
Metal Industries Inc	Hartford	CT	G	860 296-6228	1847
Nct Inc	Newington	CT	F	860 666-8424	2886
New Canaan Forge LLC **(PA)**	New Canaan	CT	G	203 966-3858	2610
P & M Welding Co LLC	South Windsor	CT	G	860 528-2077	3999
Paul Welding Company Inc	Newington	CT	F	860 229-9945	2891
Phoenix Machine Inc	Seymour	CT	G	203 888-1135	3759
Quality Welding LLC	Bristol	CT	G	860 585-1121	599
Quality Welding Service LLC	Portland	CT	G	860 342-7202	3572
Recor Welding Center Inc	Southington	CT	G	860 573-1942	4073
Reliable Welding & Speed LLC	Enfield	CT	G	860 749-3977	1379
Reno Machine Company Inc	Newington	CT	D	860 666-5641	2898
S S Fabrications Inc	Eastford	CT	G	860 974-1910	1314
Sauciers Misc Metal Works LLC	Southington	CT	G	860 747-4577	4075
Somers Manufacturing Inc	Bristol	CT	G	860 314-1075	613
Sorge Industries Inc	Shelton	CT	G	203 924-8900	3872
Standard Welding Company Inc	East Hartford	CT	G	860 528-9628	1222
State Welding & Fabg Inc	Wallingford	CT	G	203 294-4071	4813
Thomas La Ganga	Torrington	CT	G	860 489-0920	4601
Tim Welding	North Branford	CT	G	203 488-3486	2981
Tinsley GROup-Ps&w Inc **(HQ)**	Milford	CT	D	919 742-5832	2376
Torrington Diesel Corporation	Torrington	CT	G	860 496-9948	4603
Total Fab LLC	East Haven	CT	F	475 238-8176	1266
Trico Welding Company LLC	Beacon Falls	CT	G	203 720-3782	66
United Steel Inc	East Hartford	CT	C	860 289-2323	1232
Weld-All Inc	Southington	CT	F	860 621-3156	4091
Welder Repair & Rental Svc Inc	Durham	CT	G	203 238-9284	1096
White Welding Company Inc	Waterbury	CT	G	203 753-1197	4978
Willies Welding Inc	Meriden	CT	G	203 237-6235	2151
A & M Welding Fabrication Inc	East Weymouth	MA	G	781 335-9548	10532
ABC Disposal Service Inc	New Bedford	MA	E	508 990-1911	13347
Advanced Welding & Design Inc	Woburn	MA	F	781 938-7644	17112
Alvin Johnson	East Longmeadow	MA	G	413 525-6334	10465
Amic Inc	Attleboro	MA	G	508 222-5300	7704
Ashmont Welding Company Inc	Bridgewater	MA	F	508 279-1977	9060
Aviation Welding	Uxbridge	MA	G	508 278-3041	15914
Baxter Inc	West Yarmouth	MA	G	508 228-8136	16578
Biasin Enterprises Inc	Lee	MA	G	413 243-0885	12089
Blue Fleet Welding Service	New Bedford	MA	F	508 997-5513	13363
Boston Forging & Welding Corp	Boston	MA	G	617 567-2300	8430
Boston Welding & Design Inc	Woburn	MA	F	781 932-0035	17137
Capeway Welding Inc	Plymouth	MA	F	508 747-6666	14549
Chicopee Welding & Tool Inc	Charlemont	MA	F	413 598-8215	9819
City Welding & Fabrication Inc	Worcester	MA	E	508 853-6000	17356
CM Murphy Welding Inc	Webster	MA	G	508 868-8511	16340
Complete Welding Services	Marshfield	MA	G	781 837-9024	12858
Composite Company Inc	Sherborn	MA	G	508 651-1681	15078
D Cronins Welding Service	Lawrence	MA	G	978 664-4488	12014
Danvers Engineering Co Inc	Danvers	MA	G	978 774-7501	10211
David Gilbert	Framingham	MA	G	508 879-1507	10940
DCB Welding and Fabrication	Lowell	MA	G	978 587-3883	12366
Diaute Bros	Braintree	MA	G	781 848-0524	9001
Dockside Repairs Inc	New Bedford	MA	F	508 993-6730	13380
East Cast Wldg Fabrication LLC	Newburyport	MA	E	978 465-2338	13484
Excalibur Welding and Piping	Rehoboth	MA	G	401 241-0548	14748
Falcon Precision Machine Co	Ludlow	MA	G	413 583-2117	12465
Feeney Fence Inc	Hyde Park	MA	G	617 364-1407	11866
First Place Welding Inc	Rutland	MA	G	508 886-4762	14881
Fitchburg Welding Co Inc	Westminster	MA	E	978 874-2911	16804
G and JW Elding Inc	East Taunton	MA	G	774 565-0223	10513
G and M Welding	Malden	MA	G	781 480-4247	12573
Gabcon Welding & Cnstr Co	Taunton	MA	D	508 822-2220	15751
Gem Welding	North Billerica	MA	G	978 362-3873	13821
Gill Metal Fab Inc	Brockton	MA	E	508 580-4445	9151
Harbor Welding	Gloucester	MA	G	978 281-5771	11192
Herb Con Machine Company Inc	Saugus	MA	G	781 233-2755	14985
Herrick Everett Welding & Mch	Holland	MA	G	413 245-7533	11553
Horacios Welding & Shtmtl Inc	New Bedford	MA	F	508 985-9940	13395
Hubb Equipment Inc	Hubbardston	MA	G	978 928-4258	11744
International Beam Wldg Corp	West Springfield	MA	F	413 781-4368	16527
J & L Welding & Machine Co	Gloucester	MA	E	978 283-3388	11193
J E Schell Welding	East Freetown	MA	G	508 763-4658	10453
J F OMalley Welding Co	Worcester	MA	G	508 791-8671	17395
K & W Machine Works	Springfield	MA	G	413 543-3329	15483
K K Welding Inc	Hyde Park	MA	G	617 361-1780	11871
Kent Pearce	East Wareham	MA	G	508 295-3791	10531
Kielb Welding Enterprises	Springfield	MA	F	413 734-4544	15484
L W Tank Repair Incorporated	North Uxbridge	MA	F	508 234-6000	13995
Ledgerock Welding and Fabg	Hudson	MA	G	978 562-6500	11785
Leo S Cavelier Inc	Acton	MA	G	978 369-2770	7368
Lima Fredy	Everett	MA	F	781 599-3055	10618
Linton Welding & Fabrication	Lawrence	MA	G	978 681-7736	12048
Lizotte Welding	East Freetown	MA	G	508 763-8784	10454
Malcom Co-Leister	Andover	MA	G	781 875-3121	7567
Marblehead Engineering	Essex	MA	F	978 432-1386	10595
McNamara Fabricating Co Inc	West Boylston	MA	F	774 243-7425	16422
Metrick Manufacturing Co Inc	Woburn	MA	G	781 935-1331	17228
Micro ARC Welding Service	Worcester	MA	G	508 852-6125	17414
Noremac Manufacturing Corp	Westborough	MA	E	508 879-7514	16639
O W Landergren Inc	Pittsfield	MA	E	413 442-5632	14497
Oleary Welding Corp	East Douglas	MA	G	508 476-9793	10431
Oliver Welding & Fabricating	Ipswich	MA	G	978 356-4488	11933
ORourke Welding Inc	Worcester	MA	G	508 755-6360	17437
Podgurski Wldg & Hvy Eqp Repr	Canton	MA	G	781 830-9901	9770
Quincy Steel & Welding Co Inc	Quincy	MA	G	617 472-1180	14651
R & M Precision Machine	Fall River	MA	G	508 678-2488	10750
R Moody Machine & Fabrication	Deerfield	MA	G	413 773-3329	10303
Rae Js	Shelburne Falls	MA	G	413 625-9228	15075
Ralph Seaver	Cherry Valley	MA	G	508 892-9486	9976
Rens Welding & Fabricating	Taunton	MA	F	508 828-1702	15779
Roar Industries Inc	Holliston	MA	F	508 429-5952	11599
Roland Teiner Company Inc	Everett	MA	F	617 387-7800	10628
Shaw Welding Company Inc	Billerica	MA	F	978 667-0197	8293
Standex International Corp	North Billerica	MA	D	978 667-2771	13869
Tewksbury Welding Inc	Tewksbury	MA	G	978 851-7401	15841
Thermo Craft Engineering Corp	Lynn	MA	E	781 599-4023	12543
Triad Inc	Plainville	MA	G	508 695-2247	14537
Trivak Inc	Lowell	MA	E	978 453-7123	12440

	CITY	ST	EMP	PHONE	ENTRY #
Union Machine Company Lynn Inc **(PA)**	Groveland	MA	E	978 521-5100	11304
Villa Machine Associates Inc	Dedham	MA	F	781 326-5969	10300
Welch Welding and Trck Eqp Inc	North Chelmsford	MA	E	978 251-8726	13913
Welch Welding Inc	North Chelmsford	MA	G	978 251-8726	13914
Weld Rite	Jamaica Plain	MA	G	617 524-9747	11951
Welding Craftsmen Co Inc	South Easton	MA	F	508 230-7878	15295
Welfab Inc	North Billerica	MA	E	978 667-0180	13876
Brooks Welding & Machining Inc	Waterboro	ME	G	207 247-4141	7151
Churchs Welding & Fab Inc	Durham	ME	G	207 353-4249	5969
Days Auto Body Inc	Medway	ME	G	207 746-5310	6423
Dennis Welding & Marine Inc	Beals	ME	G	207 497-5998	5683
Derek White	Winterport	ME	G	207 223-5746	7277
Down East Shtmtl & Certif Wldg	Brewer	ME	G	207 989-3443	5795
Espositos Wldg & Fabrication	Surry	ME	G	207 667-2442	7076
Howies Wldg & Fabrication Inc	Jay	ME	G	207 645-2581	6220
M & M Sheet Metal & Welding	Presque Isle	ME	G	207 764-6443	6761
Maine Conveyor Inc	Windham	ME	G	207 854-5661	7241
Nichols Custom Welding Inc	Wilton	ME	E	207 645-3101	7227
North E Wldg & Fabrication Inc	Auburn	ME	E	207 786-2446	5583
Praxair Surface Tech Inc	Biddeford	ME	D	207 282-3787	5757
Ramsays Welding & Machine Inc	Lincoln	ME	F	207 794-8839	6359
Titan Chain & Welding	Oakland	ME	G	207 465-4144	6535
Troy Winger	Trenton	ME	G	207 667-1815	7103
Walts Machine Shop	Oquossoc	ME	G	207 864-5083	6548
Western Maine Welding & Piping	Strong	ME	G	207 652-2327	7074
3 D Welding	Claremont	NH	G	603 543-0866	17833
Ace Welding Co Inc	Merrimack	NH	E	603 424-9936	18984
Anderson Welding LLC	Dover	NH	G	603 996-6225	18005
Andy Croteau	Portsmouth	NH	G	603 436-8919	19536
ARC Maintenance Machining	Londonderry	NH	G	603 626-8046	18677
Baron Machine Company Inc	Laconia	NH	D	603 524-6800	18557
Bocra Industries Inc	Seabrook	NH	E	603 474-3598	19794
Bri-Weld Industries LLC	Auburn	NH	F	603 622-9480	17608
Burt General Repair & Welding	Lancaster	NH	G	603 788-4821	18597
Custom Welding & Fabrications	West Nottingham	NH	F	603 942-5170	19964
D M F Machine Co Inc	Londonderry	NH	G	603 434-4945	18691
East Coast Metal Works Co Inc	Kingston	NH	G	603 642-9600	18543
East Coast Welding	Gilford	NH	G	603 293-8384	18187
Erwin Precision Inc	Manchester	NH	G	603 623-2333	18819
Hollis Line Machine Co Inc **(PA)**	Hollis	NH	E	603 465-2251	18332
J & D Welding	Grafton	NH	G	603 523-7695	18216
Mahers Welding Service Inc	Northfield	NH	G	603 286-4851	19404
Mass Chassis	Kingston	NH	F	603 642-8967	18545
Mds Welding & Fabrication	Weare	NH	G	603 660-0772	19938
Northeast Wldg Bridge Repr LLC	New Boston	NH	G	603 396-8549	19295
Ralph L Osgood Inc	Claremont	NH	F	603 543-1703	17859
Recycling Mechanical Neng LLC	Allenstown	NH	F	603 268-8028	17541
Sean Byrnes Welding LLC	Thornton	NH	G	603 726-4315	19902
Smiths Tblar Systms-Lconia Inc	Laconia	NH	B	603 524-2064	18587
Starkey Welding Crane Service	Brentwood	NH	G	603 679-2553	17758
Stone Machine Co Inc	Chester	NH	F	603 887-4287	17826
Strafford Machine Inc	Strafford	NH	G	603 664-9758	19866
Valley Welding & Fabg Inc	Hollis	NH	E	603 465-3266	18340
Weidner Services LLC	Jaffrey	NH	F	603 532-4833	18481
Whites Welding Co Inc	Hampton	NH	G	603 926-2261	18280
Will-Mor Manufacturing Inc	Seabrook	NH	D	603 474-8971	19823
Artic Tool & Engrg Co LLC	Greenville	RI	F	401 785-2210	20461
Blouin General Welding & Fabg	Woonsocket	RI	G	401 762-4542	21551
Champlin Welding Inc	Narragansett	RI	G	401 782-4099	20636
Dexter Service Center	East Providence	RI	G	401 438-3900	20405
Formex Inc	East Greenwich	RI	E	401 885-9800	20368
Frontier Welding & Fabrication	Woonsocket	RI	G	401 769-0271	21565
Goldenrod Welding Inc	Cumberland	RI	G	401 725-9248	20322
Guill Tool & Engrg Co Inc	West Warwick	RI	D	401 822-8186	21493
Laser Fare Inc **(PA)**	Smithfield	RI	D	401 231-4400	21235
Luthers Repair Shop Inc	Bristol	RI	F	401 253-5550	20091
Microweld Co Inc	Riverside	RI	G	401 438-5985	21172
Providence Welding	Providence	RI	G	401 941-2700	21100
Robert B Evans Inc	Westerly	RI	G	401 596-2719	21538
Seven Star Inc	Newport	RI	G	401 683-6222	20680
West Warwick Welding Inc	West Warwick	RI	F	401 822-8200	21513
Browns Certified Welding Inc	Bristol	VT	F	802 453-3351	21762
Cave Manufacturing Inc	Brattleboro	VT	E	802 257-9253	21723
Giroux Body Shop Inc	Hinesburg	VT	F	802 482-2162	22025
Gloucester Associates Inc	Barre	VT	E	802 479-1088	21617
Metalworks Inc	Burlington	VT	G	802 863-0414	21796
Milton Vermont Sheet Metal Inc	Milton	VT	D	802 893-1581	22134
North Country Engineering Inc	Derby	VT	E	802 766-5396	21902
PG Adams Inc	South Burlington	VT	F	802 862-8664	22457
Raymond Reynolds Welding	Essex Junction	VT	G	802 879-4650	21955
Thomas Drake	Colchester	VT	G	802 655-0990	21881

WELDING SPLYS, EXC GASES: Wholesalers

	CITY	ST	EMP	PHONE	ENTRY #
Chicopee Welding & Tool Inc	Charlemont	MA	F	413 598-8215	9819

WELDING TIPS: Heat Resistant, Metal

	CITY	ST	EMP	PHONE	ENTRY #
Performance Connection Systems	Meriden	CT	G	203 868-5517	2116
Harmony Metal Products North	Portsmouth	NH	E	603 536-6012	19573

WELDMENTS

	CITY	ST	EMP	PHONE	ENTRY #
Vitta Corporation	Bethel	CT	E	203 790-8155	192
Whitcraft LLC **(PA)**	Eastford	CT	C	860 974-0786	1315
Whitcraft Scrborough/Tempe LLC **(HQ)**	Eastford	CT	C	860 974-0786	1316
Alloy Fabricators of Neng	Randolph	MA	F	781 986-6400	14670
Green Brothers Fabricating	Taunton	MA	E	508 880-3608	15756
Steel-Fab Inc	Fitchburg	MA	E	978 345-1112	10857
United Metal Fabricators Inc	Worcester	MA	F	508 754-1800	17493

WELTING

	CITY	ST	EMP	PHONE	ENTRY #
Barbour Corporation **(PA)**	Brockton	MA	C	508 583-8200	9124
Barbour Plastics Inc **(HQ)**	Brockton	MA	E	508 583-8200	9125

WET CORN MILLING

	CITY	ST	EMP	PHONE	ENTRY #
Tate Lyle Ingrdnts Amricas LLC	Westborough	MA	G	508 366-8322	16654
Tate Lyle Ingrdnts Amricas LLC	Houlton	ME	E	207 532-9523	6211

WHEELCHAIR LIFTS

	CITY	ST	EMP	PHONE	ENTRY #
Garaventa U S A Inc	Manchester	NH	G	603 669-6553	18824

WHEELCHAIRS

	CITY	ST	EMP	PHONE	ENTRY #
Enduro Wheelchair Company	East Hartford	CT	G	860 289-0374	1194
United Seating & Mobility LLC **(PA)**	Rocky Hill	CT	G	860 761-0700	3732
A & S Transport Wheelchair Svc	Brockton	MA	G	617 701-4407	9113
Burke Medical Equipment Inc	Chicopee	MA	E	413 592-5464	10003
Easter Seals Massachusetts	New Bedford	MA	F	508 992-3128	13382
Global RES Innovation Tech Inc	Charlestown	MA	G	617 383-4748	9835
Ms Wheelchair Mass Foundation	Taunton	MA	G	774 501-1185	15766
National Seating Mobility Inc	Chicopee	MA	G	413 420-0054	10048
New England Blazers	Saugus	MA	G	617 448-3709	14992
New England Wheelchair Spt Inc	Dover	MA	G	508 785-0393	10351
New England Whlchair Athc Assn	Canton	MA	G	781 830-8751	9763
Numotion	Taunton	MA	G	401 681-2153	15769
Wheelchair Recycler Custm & R	Marlborough	MA	G	978 760-4444	12851
Allied Wheelchair	Hampton	NH	G	603 601-8174	18253
Power Chair Recyclers Neng LLC	North Kingstown	RI	G	401 294-4111	20733

WHEELS

	CITY	ST	EMP	PHONE	ENTRY #
Everything 2 Wheels LLC	New Britain	CT	G	860 225-2453	2532
Vito Wheel Music More	Revere	MA	G	781 241-9476	14777

WHEELS & PARTS

	CITY	ST	EMP	PHONE	ENTRY #
Wheeltrak Inc	Tiverton	RI	E	800 296-1326	21266

WHEELS, GRINDING: Artificial

	CITY	ST	EMP	PHONE	ENTRY #
True Grit Abrasive Inc	Westport	MA	F	508 636-2008	16849
Westfield Grinding Wheel Co	Westfield	MA	E	413 568-8634	16744
Rhode Island Centerless Inc	Johnston	RI	F	401 942-0403	20536

WHEELS: Abrasive

	CITY	ST	EMP	PHONE	ENTRY #
Avery Abrasives Inc	Trumbull	CT	E	203 372-3513	4613
Magcor Inc	Monroe	CT	G	203 445-0302	2408
Rex Cut Products Incorporated	Fall River	MA	D	508 678-1985	10757
Saint-Gobain Abrasives Inc **(DH)**	Worcester	MA	A	508 795-5000	17464
Joseph A Thomas Ltd	Bristol	RI	F	401 253-1330	20086

WHEELS: Buffing & Polishing

	CITY	ST	EMP	PHONE	ENTRY #
Textile Buff & Wheel Co Inc	Boston	MA	E	617 241-8100	8879

WINCHES

	CITY	ST	EMP	PHONE	ENTRY #
Show Motion Inc	Milford	CT	E	203 866-1866	2362
Hancock Marine Inc	Fall River	MA	G	508 678-0301	10712

WIND CHIMES

	CITY	ST	EMP	PHONE	ENTRY #
Richard Fisher	Prospect Harbor	ME	G	207 963-7184	6771
Song Wind Industries Inc	Barrington	RI	E	401 245-7582	20056

WIND TUNNELS

	CITY	ST	EMP	PHONE	ENTRY #
Wind Tunnel Heating & AC LLC	Peabody	MA	G	978 977-7783	14386

WINDINGS: Coil, Electronic

	CITY	ST	EMP	PHONE	ENTRY #
Classic Coil Company Inc	Bristol	CT	D	860 583-7600	541
Quality Coils Incorporated **(PA)**	Bristol	CT	C	860 584-0927	598
Microwave Components Inc	Dracut	MA	F	978 453-6016	10365
Transcon Technologies Inc	Westfield	MA	E	413 562-7684	16736
Ladesco Inc	Manchester	NH	C	603 623-3772	18857
Crest Manufacturing Company	Lincoln	RI	E	401 333-1350	20566

WINDMILLS: Electric Power Generation

	CITY	ST	EMP	PHONE	ENTRY #
First Wind Holdings Inc	Boston	MA	F	617 960-2888	8547
Spruce Mountain Wind LLC	Quincy	MA	G	617 890-0600	14658
Antrim Wind Energy LLC	Portsmouth	NH	G	603 570-4842	19537
Groton Wind LLC	Rumney	NH	G	603 786-2862	19696
Peaked Wind Power LLC	Portsmouth	NH	G	603 570-4842	19606

WINDOW & DOOR FRAMES

	CITY	ST	EMP	PHONE	ENTRY #
Advanced Window Systems LLC	Cromwell	CT	F	800 841 6544	844
Ckh Industries Inc	Wethersfield	CT	D	860 563-2999	5244
Lee Brown Co LLC	Riverton	CT	F	860 379-4706	3695
Architectural Glazing Systems	Avon	MA	E	508 588-4845	7876
Brunswick Enclosure Company	North Billerica	MA	G	978 670-1124	13799
ER Lewin Inc	Wrentham	MA	E	508 384-0363	17520
Modern Mfg Inc Worcester	Worcester	MA	E	508 791-7151	17421
Ron-Bet Company Inc	Kittery	ME	G	207 439-5868	6258
Win-Pressor LLC	Unity	ME	G	207 948-4800	7119
Roland J Soucy Company LLC	Pelham	NH	G	603 635-3265	19445

WINDOW BLIND REPAIR SVCS

	CITY	ST	EMP	PHONE	ENTRY #
Arrow Window Shade Mfg Co	Wethersfield	CT	G	860 956-3570	5240

WINDOW FRAMES & SASHES: Plastic

	CITY	ST	EMP	PHONE	ENTRY #
All-Time Manufacturing Co Inc	Montville	CT	F	860 848-9258	2421

WINDOW FRAMES, MOLDING & TRIM: Vinyl

	CITY	ST	EMP	PHONE	ENTRY #
Diamond Windows Doors Mfg Inc	Boston	MA	E	617 282-1688	8503
K & C Industries Inc	Franklin	MA	F	508 520-4600	11059

	CITY	ST	EMP	PHONE	ENTRY #
National Vinyl LLC	Chicopee	MA	E	413 420-0548	10049
Stergis Aluminum Products Corp	Attleboro	MA	E	508 455-0661	7795
Mathews Brothers Company **(PA)**	Belfast	ME	C	207 338-3360	5693
Sturbridge Associates III LLC **(PA)**	Providence	RI	G	401 943-8600	21129

WINDOW FURNISHINGS WHOLESALERS

	CITY	ST	EMP	PHONE	ENTRY #
Gordons Window Decor Inc **(PA)**	Williston	VT	F	802 655-7777	22671

WINDOW SASHES, WOOD

	CITY	ST	EMP	PHONE	ENTRY #
J B Sash & Door Company Inc	Chelsea	MA	E	617 884-8940	9955
Newfound Wood Works Inc **(PA)**	Bristol	NH	G	603 744-6872	17768

WINDOW TRIMMING SVCS

	CITY	ST	EMP	PHONE	ENTRY #
Design Engineering Inc	Torrington	CT	G	860 482-4120	4574

WINDOWS: Frames, Wood

	CITY	ST	EMP	PHONE	ENTRY #
Mathews Brothers Company **(PA)**	Belfast	ME	C	207 338-3360	5693

WINDOWS: Louver, Glass, Wood Framed

	CITY	ST	EMP	PHONE	ENTRY #
Woodstone Company Inc	North Walpole	NH	E	603 445-2449	19397

WINDOWS: Wood

	CITY	ST	EMP	PHONE	ENTRY #
Schuco USA Lllp **(HQ)**	Newington	CT	D	860 666-0505	2901
Andersen Corporation	Fall River	MA	G	508 235-0300	10659
Roland J Soucy Company LLC	Pelham	NH	G	603 635-3265	19445
Pella Corporation	Portsmouth	RI	B	401 662-2621	20936
Pella Corporation	Barrington	RI	B	401 247-0309	20051
Riverdale Window and Door Corp	Smithfield	RI	C	401 231-6000	21249
Scotts Doors and Windows	Warren	RI	G	401 743-2083	21307

WINDSHIELDS: Plastic

	CITY	ST	EMP	PHONE	ENTRY #
North/Win Ltd	Leominster	MA	G	978 537-5518	12172

WINE & DISTILLED ALCOHOLIC BEVERAGES WHOLESALERS

	CITY	ST	EMP	PHONE	ENTRY #
861 Corp	Boston	MA	G	617 268-8855	8330
New England Distilling Co	Portland	ME	G	207 878-9759	6701

WIRE

	CITY	ST	EMP	PHONE	ENTRY #
Accel Intl Holdings Inc	Meriden	CT	E	203 237-2700	2073
Lee Spring Company LLC	Bristol	CT	E	860 584-0991	576
Siri Manufacturing Company	Danielson	CT	E	860 236-5901	1017
Wiretek Inc	Bloomfield	CT	F	860 242-9473	272
Belden Inc	Leominster	MA	E	978 537-8911	12117
Hancock Marine Inc	Fall River	MA	G	508 678-0301	10712
James Cable LLC **(PA)**	Braintree	MA	E	781 356-8701	9021
Mersen USA Ep Corp **(DH)**	Newburyport	MA	D	805 351-8400	13511
Prysmian Cbles Systems USA LLC	North Dighton	MA	G	508 822-5444	13936
Stafford Wire Specialty Inc	Worcester	MA	G	508 799-6124	17480
Sundial Wire LLC	Florence	MA	G	413 582-6909	10869
Altenloh Brinck & Co US Inc	Bristol	RI	G	401 253-8600	20061

WIRE & CABLE: Aluminum

	CITY	ST	EMP	PHONE	ENTRY #
Omerin Usa Inc	Meriden	CT	E	475 343-3450	2113

WIRE & CABLE: Aluminum

	CITY	ST	EMP	PHONE	ENTRY #
Joseph Freedman Co Inc **(PA)**	Springfield	MA	D	888 677-7818	15481

WIRE & CABLE: Nonferrous, Aircraft

	CITY	ST	EMP	PHONE	ENTRY #
American Imex Corporation	Monroe	CT	G	203 261-5200	2391
General Airmotive Pwr Pdts LLC	Fall River	MA	G	508 674-6400	10702
Judd Wire Inc **(DH)**	Turners Falls	MA	B	413 863-9402	15880

WIRE & CABLE: Nonferrous, Automotive, Exc Ignition Sets

	CITY	ST	EMP	PHONE	ENTRY #
Autac Incorporated **(PA)**	Branford	CT	G	203 481-3444	291
General Cable Industries Inc	Lincoln	RI	C	401 333-4848	20575

WIRE & CABLE: Nonferrous, Building

	CITY	ST	EMP	PHONE	ENTRY #
Hamden Metal Service Company	Hamden	CT	F	203 281-1522	1755
Afc Cable Systems Inc	New Bedford	MA	C	508 998-8277	13353
General Wire Products Inc	Worcester	MA	E	508 752-8260	17381
Hueson Corp	South Grafton	MA	F	508 234-6372	15297
Inter-Connection Tech Inc	Lawrence	MA	F	978 975-7510	12039
Mor-Wire & Cable Inc	Lowell	MA	F	978 453-1782	12413
Prysmian Cbles Systems USA LLC	North Dighton	MA	C	508 822-5444	13935
United Wire & Cable Corp **(PA)**	Worcester	MA	G	508 757-3872	17494

WIRE & WIRE PRDTS

	CITY	ST	EMP	PHONE	ENTRY #
Acme Monaco Corporation **(PA)**	New Britain	CT	C	860 224-1349	2503
Acme Wire Products Co Inc	Mystic	CT	E	860 572-0511	2433
Apco Products	Centerbrook	CT	E	860 767-2108	701
Arrow Manufacturing Company	Bristol	CT	E	860 589-3900	520
Bes Cu Inc	Bristol	CT	G	860 582-8660	533
Bridgeport Insulated Wire Co **(PA)**	Bridgeport	CT	E	203 333-3191	388
Bridgeport Insulated Wire Co	Stratford	CT	E	203 375-9579	4401
ERA Wire Inc	West Haven	CT	F	203 933-0480	5121
General Cable Industries Inc	Willimantic	CT	C	860 456-8000	5264
Habasit America Inc	Middletown	CT	D	860 632-2211	2189
Hessel Industries Inc	Derby	CT	G	203 736-2317	1073
International Pipe & Stl Corp	North Branford	CT	F	203 481-7102	2969
Knox Enterprises Inc **(PA)**	Westport	CT	G	203 226-6408	5206
Meyer Wire & Cable Company LLC	Hamden	CT	E	203 281-0817	1771
Netsource Inc **(PA)**	Manchester	CT	D	860 649-6000	2025
Novo Precision LLC	Bristol	CT	E	860 583-0517	587
Radcliff Wire Inc	Bristol	CT	E	312 876-1754	602
Rowley Spring & Stamping Corp	Bristol	CT	C	860 582-8175	610
Tiger Enterprises Inc	Plantsville	CT	E	860 621-9155	3542
U-Tech Wire Rope & Supply LLC	North Haven	CT	G	203 865-8885	3065
Ultimate Wireforms Inc	Bristol	CT	D	860 582-9111	621
Wiremold Company **(DH)**	West Hartford	CT	A	860 233-6251	5104
Atlee Delaware Incorporated	Melrose	MA	F	978 681-1003	12975
Automatic Specialties Inc	Marlborough	MA	E	508 481-2370	12724
Dolan-Jenner Industries Inc	Boxborough	MA	E	978 263-1400	8961
Electro-Prep Inc	Wareham	MA	F	508 291-2880	16246
Frank L Reed Inc	Wilbraham	MA	E	413 596-3861	16937
General Wire Products Inc	Worcester	MA	E	508 752-8260	17381
International Metal Pdts Inc	Chicopee	MA	E	413 532-2411	10033
Lanoco Specialty Wire Pdts Inc	Sutton	MA	F	508 865-1500	15686
Micro Wire Products Inc	Brockton	MA	E	508 584-0200	9166
Polymetallurgical LLC	North Attleboro	MA	E	508 695-9312	13773
Profiles Incorporated	Palmer	MA	E	413 283-7790	14294
Quirk Wire Co Inc	West Brookfield	MA	E	508 867-3155	16473
S&S Industries Inc **(PA)**	Stoughton	MA	F	914 885-1500	15619
US Tsubaki Automotive LLC	Westfield	MA	F	413 593-1100	16738
US Tsubaki Automotive LLC **(DH)**	Chicopee	MA	C	413 593-1100	10067
Viamed Corp	South Easton	MA	F	508 238-0220	15294
W D C Holdings Inc	Attleboro	MA	D	508 699-4412	7806
Whitney & Son Inc	Fitchburg	MA	E	978 343-6353	10863
Winchester Interconnect Corp	Franklin	MA	F	978 717-2543	11098
Worcester Manufacturing Inc	Worcester	MA	E	508 756-0301	17505
Maine Cleaners Supply Inc	North Yarmouth	ME	G	207 657-3166	6517
Centroid Wire and Cable LLC	Bow	NH	G	603 227-0900	17709
Elektrisola Incorporated **(PA)**	Boscawen	NH	C	603 796-2114	17703
Felton Inc	Londonderry	NH	D	603 425-0200	18697
General Cable Industries Inc	Manchester	NH	C	603 668-1620	18825
Guidewire Technologies Inc	Salem	NH	E	603 894-4399	19740
Plasti-Clip Corporation	Milford	NH	F	603 672-1166	19072
Alloy Holdings LLC	Providence	RI	E	401 353-7500	20951
Ammeraal Beltech Inc	Warwick	RI	G	401 732-8131	21322
Electro Standards Lab Inc	Cranston	RI	D	401 946-1390	20215
Hindley Manufacturing Co Inc	Cumberland	RI	D	401 722-2550	20325
HK Chain Usa Inc	Wakefield	RI	G	401 782-0402	21272
LDB Tool and Findings Inc	Cranston	RI	G	401 944-6000	20252
Pep Central Inc	Warwick	RI	A	401 732-3770	21402
Perry Blackburne Inc	North Providence	RI	E	401 231-7200	20771
Astenjohnson Inc	Williston	VT	D	802 658-2040	22655
Brass Butterfly Inc	Poultney	VT	G	802 287-9818	22270
George L Martin	Brattleboro	VT	G	802 254-5838	21729
Vermont Wireform Inc	Chelsea	VT	F	802 889-3200	21840

WIRE CLOTH & WOVEN WIRE PRDTS, MADE FROM PURCHASED WIRE

	CITY	ST	EMP	PHONE	ENTRY #
Johnston Dandy Company	Holyoke	MA	F	413 315-4596	11635
New England Wire Products Inc **(PA)**	Leominster	MA	C	800 254-9473	12171

WIRE FABRIC: Welded Steel

	CITY	ST	EMP	PHONE	ENTRY #
Tool Logistics II	Norwalk	CT	F	203 855-9754	3258
Bergeron Machine Inc	Westford	MA	F	978 577-6235	16756

WIRE FENCING & ACCESS WHOLESALERS

	CITY	ST	EMP	PHONE	ENTRY #
Sonco Worldwide Inc	Warwick	RI	F	401 406-3761	21427

WIRE MATERIALS: Copper

	CITY	ST	EMP	PHONE	ENTRY #
Specialty Wire & Cord Sets	Hamden	CT	F	203 498-2932	1785
Frank L Reed Inc	Wilbraham	MA	E	413 596-3861	16937
Leoni Wire Inc	Chicopee	MA	D	413 593-6618	10038
Spark Vt Inc	Shelburne	VT	F	802 985-3321	22425

WIRE MATERIALS: Steel

	CITY	ST	EMP	PHONE	ENTRY #
Ametek Inc	Wallingford	CT	C	203 265-6731	4699
Bridgeport Insulated Wire Co **(PA)**	Bridgeport	CT	E	203 333-3191	388
City Data Cable Co	Stamford	CT	G	203 327-7917	4166
International Pipe & Stl Corp	North Branford	CT	F	203 481-7102	2969
Polstal Corporation	Wilton	CT	G	203 849-7788	5299
Sandvik Wire and Htg Tech Corp	Bethel	CT	D	203 744-1440	177
Wiremold Company **(DH)**	West Hartford	CT	A	860 233-6251	5104
General Wire Products Inc	Worcester	MA	E	508 752-8260	17381
Graham Whitehead & Manger Co **(PA)**	Topsfield	MA	G	203 922-9225	15861
Leoni Wire Inc	Chicopee	MA	D	413 593-6618	10038
Quirk Wire Co Inc	West Brookfield	MA	E	508 867-3155	16473
S&S Industries Inc **(PA)**	Stoughton	MA	F	914 885-1500	15619
Sanderson-Macleod Incorporated	Palmer	MA	C	413 283-3481	14295
Sumo Steel Corp	Beverly	MA	G	978 927-4950	8183
D L S Detailing	New Ipswich	NH	G	603 878-2554	19303
ACS Industries Inc **(PA)**	Lincoln	RI	E	401 769-4700	20552
Alloy Holdings LLC	Providence	RI	E	401 353-7500	20951
Dayton Superior Corporation	Warwick	RI	E	401 885-1934	21351
Sonco Worldwide Inc	Warwick	RI	F	401 406-3761	21427

WIRE PRDTS: Ferrous Or Iron, Made In Wiredrawing Plants

	CITY	ST	EMP	PHONE	ENTRY #
Housatonic Wire Co	Seymour	CT	F	203 888-9670	3752
Nutmeg Wire	Baltic	CT	F	860 822-8616	51
Accellent Holdings Corp	Wilmington	MA	A	978 570-6900	16962
Frank L Reed Inc	Wilbraham	MA	E	413 596-3861	16937
Heb Manufacturing Company Inc	Chelsea	VT	E	802 685-4821	21838

WIRE PRDTS: Steel & Iron

	CITY	ST	EMP	PHONE	ENTRY #
Microdyne Technologies	Plainville	CT	G	860 747-9473	3507
Sandvik Wire and Htg Tech Corp	Bethel	CT	D	203 744-1440	177
RSI Metal Fabrication LLC	East Kingston	NH	G	603 382-8367	18091
ACS Industries Inc **(PA)**	Lincoln	RI	E	401 769-4700	20552
Philip Machine Company Inc	Pawtucket	RI	F	401 353-7383	20879

WIRE ROPE CENTERS

	CITY	ST	EMP	PHONE	ENTRY #
I & I Sling Inc	Norwood	MA	D	781 575-0600	14159

WIRE WHOLESALERS

	CITY	ST	EMP	PHONE	ENTRY #
United Wire & Cable Corp **(PA)**	Worcester	MA	G	508 757-3872	17494
Ftc Inc **(PA)**	Friendship	ME	E	207 354-2545	6093

WIRE WINDING OF PURCHASED WIRE

	CITY	ST	EMP	PHONE	ENTRY #
Protopac Inc	Watertown	CT	G	860 274-6796	5020

WIRE: Communication

	CITY	ST	EMP	PHONE	ENTRY #
General Cable Industries Inc	Willimantic	CT	C	860 456-8000	5264
Ortronics Inc **(DH)**	New London	CT	D	860 445-3900	2776
Ortronics Inc	West Hartford	CT	G	877 295-3472	5088
Belden Inc	Worcester	MA	C	508 754-4858	17347
Mercury Wire Products Inc	Spencer	MA	C	508 885-6363	15433
Quabbin Wire & Cable Co Inc **(PA)**	Ware	MA	D	413 967-6281	16236
Eldur Corporation	Bangor	ME	E	207 942-6592	5642
Enterasys Networks Inc **(HQ)**	Salem	NH	D	603 952-5000	19725
Marmon Utility LLC **(DH)**	Milford	NH	C	603 673-2040	19069
Stonewall Cable Inc	Rumney	NH	D	603 536-1601	19698

WIRE: Magnet

	CITY	ST	EMP	PHONE	ENTRY #
American Wire Corporation	Newtown	CT	F	203 426-3133	2915
Bridgeport Magnetics Group Inc	Shelton	CT	E	203 954-0050	3784
Luvata Waterbury Inc	Waterbury	CT	D	203 753-5215	4899
Tech-Etch Inc	Fall River	MA	D	508 675-5757	10770
Elektrisola Incorporated **(PA)**	Boscawen	NH	C	603 796-2114	17703

WIRE: Mesh

	CITY	ST	EMP	PHONE	ENTRY #
Nucor Steel Connecticut Inc	Wallingford	CT	C	203 265-0615	4780
Citiworks Corp	Attleboro	MA	F	508 761-7400	7720
Riverdale Mills Corporation	Northbridge	MA	C	508 234-8715	14060
Wright G F Steel & Wire Co	Worcester	MA	E	508 363-2718	17509
Bartletts Bench and Wire Inc **(PA)**	Friendship	ME	G	207 354-0138	6092
ACS Industries Inc **(PA)**	Lincoln	RI	E	401 769-4700	20552

WIRE: Nonferrous

	CITY	ST	EMP	PHONE	ENTRY #
Algonquin Industries Inc **(HQ)**	Guilford	CT	D	203 453-4348	1692
Alpha-Core Inc	Shelton	CT	E	203 954-0050	3773
Altek Electronics Inc	Torrington	CT	C	860 482-7626	4558
American Alloy Wire Corp	Newtown	CT	G	203 426-3133	2914
Bridgeport Insulated Wire Co **(PA)**	Bridgeport	CT	E	203 333-3191	388
Bridgeport Insulated Wire Co	Stratford	CT	E	203 375-9579	4401
Cable Technology Inc	Willington	CT	E	860 429-7889	5270
Fiberoptics Technology Inc **(PA)**	Pomfret	CT	C	860 928-0443	3550
Insulated Wire Inc	Bethel	CT	F	203 791-1999	160
Loos & Co Inc **(PA)**	Pomfret	CT	B	860 928-7981	3552
Marmon Utility LLC	Seymour	CT	E	203 881-5358	3755
Multi-Cable Corp	Bristol	CT	F	860 589-9035	585
Ofs Fitel LLC	Avon	CT	B	860 678-0371	39
Platt Brothers & Company **(PA)**	Waterbury	CT	D	203 753-4194	4940
Radcliff Wire Inc	Bristol	CT	E	312 876-1754	602
REA Magnet Wire Company Inc	Guilford	CT	D	203 738-6100	1716
Rscc Wire & Cable LLC **(DH)**	East Granby	CT	B	860 653-8300	1143
Sandvik Wire and Htg Tech Corp	Bethel	CT	D	203 744-1440	177
Sandvik Wire and Htg Tech Corp **(DH)**	Bethel	CT	D	203 744-1440	178
Siemon Company **(PA)**	Watertown	CT	A	860 945-4200	5024
Specialty Cable Corp	Wallingford	CT	D	203 265-7126	4809
Times Microwave Systems Inc **(HQ)**	Wallingford	CT	B	203 949-8400	4819
Wiretek Inc	Bloomfield	CT	F	860 242-9473	272
Alliance Cable Corp	Taunton	MA	E	508 824-5896	15724
America Cable Assemblies Inc **(PA)**	Palmer	MA	G	413 283-2515	14278
Anomet Products Inc	Shrewsbury	MA	E	508 842-0174	15102
Belden Inc	Peabody	MA	C	978 573-0908	14315
Belden Inc	Leominster	MA	E	978 537-8911	12117
Brookfield Wire Company Inc **(HQ)**	West Brookfield	MA	E	508 867-6474	16465
Caton Connector Corp	Kingston	MA	E	781 585-4315	11955
Chase Corporation	Randolph	MA	E	781 963-2600	14673
Cooper Interconnect Inc	Chelsea	MA	D	617 389-7080	9950
Data Guide Cable Corporation	Gardner	MA	D	978 632-0900	11111
Draka Fibre Technology	Taunton	MA	G	508 822-0246	15745
Eis Wire & Cable Inc	South Hadley	MA	D	413 536-0152	15302
Electroweave Inc	Worcester	MA	G	508 752-8932	17371
Gavitt Wire and Cable Co Inc	West Brookfield	MA	D	508 867-6476	16469
L-Com Inc **(DH)**	North Andover	MA	D	978 682-6936	13715
Madison Cable Corporation	Worcester	MA	C	508 752-2884	17410
Milford Manufacturing Svcs LLC	Hopedale	MA	D	508 478-8544	11678
Ofs Brightwave LLC	Sturbridge	MA	G	508 347-2261	15641
Ofs Fitel LLC	Sturbridge	MA	E	508 347-2261	15642
Prysmian Cbles Systems USA LLC	Taunton	MA	G	508 822-0246	15775
Quirk Wire Co Inc	West Brookfield	MA	E	508 867-3155	16473
Saint-Gobain Prfmce Plas Corp	Worcester	MA	E	508 852-3072	17467
Segue Manufacturing Svcs LLC	Lowell	MA	D	978 970-1200	12432
Temp-Flex LLC	South Grafton	MA	D	508 839-3120	15299
Tricab (usa) Inc	Worcester	MA	E	508 421-4680	17491
V-Tron Electronics Corp	Attleboro	MA	D	508 761-9100	7805
Transparent Audio Inc	Saco	ME	E	207 284-1100	6860
Aetna Insulated Wire LLC	Milford	NH	C	757 460-3381	19043
AFL Telecommunications LLC	Belmont	NH	E	603 528-7780	17669
Amphenol Printed Circuits Inc	Nashua	NH	A	603 324-4500	19115
Burton Wire & Cable Inc	Hooksett	NH	F	603 624-2427	18344
General Cable Industries Inc	Manchester	NH	C	603 668-1620	18825
Hitachi Cable America Inc	Manchester	NH	C	603 669-4347	18835
Marmon Aerospace & Defense LLC	Manchester	NH	D	603 622-3500	18867
Marmon Utility LLC	Amherst	NH	G	603 673-2040	17574
MJM Holdings Inc **(PA)**	Lisbon	NH	G	603 838-6624	18649
New England Wire Tech Corp **(HQ)**	Lisbon	NH	B	603 838-6624	18650
Optical Fiber Systems Inc	New Ipswich	NH	G	603 291-0345	19309
Retcomp Inc	New Boston	NH	E	603 487-5010	19297
Rscc Wire & Cable LLC	Manchester	NH	D	603 622-3500	18912
Teledyne Instruments Inc	Portsmouth	NH	C	603 474-5571	19624
Electro Standards Lab Inc	Cranston	RI	D	401 946-1390	20215
Okonite Company	Cumberland	RI	D	401 333-3500	20336
Providence Cable Corporation	Johnston	RI	F	401 632-7650	20532
Phoenix Wire Inc	South Hero	VT	G	802 372-4561	22481
Super-Temp Wire & Cable Inc	South Burlington	VT	E	802 655-4211	22470

WIRE: Steel, Insulated Or Armored

	CITY	ST	EMP	PHONE	ENTRY #
Marmon Utility LLC	Seymour	CT	E	203 881-5358	3755
S A Candelora Enterprises	North Branford	CT	F	203 484-2863	2975
Lanoco Specialty Wire Pdts Inc	Sutton	MA	F	508 865-1500	15686
Larsdale Inc **(PA)**	Ipswich	MA	D	978 356-9995	11928
Precise Products Company	Lincoln	RI	F	401 724-7190	20592

WIRE: Wire, Ferrous Or Iron

	CITY	ST	EMP	PHONE	ENTRY #
Hamden Metal Service Company	Hamden	CT	F	203 281-1522	1755
Loos & Co Inc	Pomfret	CT	F	860 928-6681	3553
Loos & Co Inc **(PA)**	Pomfret	CT	B	860 928-7981	3552
Radcliff Wire Inc	Bristol	CT	E	312 876-1754	602
Brookfield Wire Company Inc **(HQ)**	West Brookfield	MA	E	508 867-6474	16465
Profiles Incorporated	Palmer	MA	E	413 283-7790	14294

WIRING DEVICES WHOLESALERS

	CITY	ST	EMP	PHONE	ENTRY #
Ripley Tools LLC **(PA)**	Cromwell	CT	E	860 635-2200	859

WOMEN'S & CHILDREN'S CLOTHING WHOLESALERS, NEC

	CITY	ST	EMP	PHONE	ENTRY #
Accurate Services Inc	Fall River	MA	E	508 674-5773	10650
Advanced Print Technology Inc	Fitchburg	MA	G	978 342-0093	10809
Shop Therapy Imports	Provincetown	MA	G	508 487-8970	14609
Imeldas Fabrics & Designs	New Sharon	ME	G	207 778-0665	6476
New York Accessory Group Inc	Bristol	RI	D	401 245-6096	20095
Cornell Online LLC	Burlington	VT	E	802 448-3281	21776

WOMEN'S & GIRLS' SPORTSWEAR WHOLESALERS

	CITY	ST	EMP	PHONE	ENTRY #
Del Arbour LLC	Milford	CT	F	203 882-8501	2274
Gg Sportswear Inc	Hartford	CT	E	860 296-4441	1825
Sew What Embroidery	Dalton	MA	G	413 684-0672	10184

WOMEN'S CLOTHING STORES

	CITY	ST	EMP	PHONE	ENTRY #
Oshea Mary Lynn Weaving Studio	Middlebury	VT	G	802 545-2090	22117

WOMEN'S CLOTHING STORES: Ready-To-Wear

	CITY	ST	EMP	PHONE	ENTRY #
Lane Printing Co Inc	Holbrook	MA	F	781 767-4450	11529
Pvh Corp	Wrentham	MA	F	508 384-0070	17527
Sew What Embroidery	Dalton	MA	G	413 684-0672	10184

WOMEN'S KNITWEAR STORES

	CITY	ST	EMP	PHONE	ENTRY #
Kielo America Inc	Ridgefield	CT	G	203 431-3999	3671
Evergreen Enterprises Inc	Berkley	MA	G	508 823-2377	8086

WOMEN'S SPECIALTY CLOTHING STORES

	CITY	ST	EMP	PHONE	ENTRY #
Joseph Lotuff Sr	Ware	MA	E	413 967-5964	16234
Sylvia Wyler Pottery Inc **(PA)**	Brunswick	ME	G	207 729-1321	5848

WOMEN'S SPORTSWEAR STORES

	CITY	ST	EMP	PHONE	ENTRY #
Chuck Roast Equipment Inc **(PA)**	Conway	NH	E	603 447-5492	17951

WOOD & WOOD BY-PRDTS, WHOLESALE

	CITY	ST	EMP	PHONE	ENTRY #
Saco Manufacturing & Wdwkg	Saco	ME	G	207 284-6613	6857

WOOD CHIPS, PRODUCED AT THE MILL

	CITY	ST	EMP	PHONE	ENTRY #
Biomass Energy LLC	Weatogue	CT	E	540 872-3300	5041
Ensign-Bckford Rnwble Enrgies	Simsbury	CT	E	860 843-2000	3902
A W Chaffee **(PA)**	Oakland	ME	G	207 465-3234	6528
A W Chaffee	Clinton	ME	E	207 426-8588	5912
Linkletter and Sons Inc	Athens	ME	E	207 654-2301	5541
R H Wales & Son Inc	Fryeburg	ME	G	207 925-1363	6102
Yates Lumber Inc	Lee	ME	F	207 738-2331	6267
Cousineau Lumber Inc	Henniker	NH	G	603 428-7155	18304
Ossipee Chipping Inc	Center Ossipee	NH	G	603 539-5097	17805
Green Mountain Forest Products	Highgate Center	VT	F	802 868-2306	22020

WOOD CHIPS, WHOLESALE

	CITY	ST	EMP	PHONE	ENTRY #
A W Chaffee **(PA)**	Oakland	ME	G	207 465-3234	6528

WOOD EXTRACT PRDTS

	CITY	ST	EMP	PHONE	ENTRY #
Sychron Inc	Newington	CT	G	860 953-8157	2905

WOOD FENCING WHOLESALERS

	CITY	ST	EMP	PHONE	ENTRY #
Fiberglass Building Pdts Inc	Halifax	MA	G	847 650-3045	11318

WOOD PRDTS

	CITY	ST	EMP	PHONE	ENTRY #
Boston Wood Art	Natick	MA	G	508 353-4129	13240
Oborain	Montague	MA	G	413 376-8854	13212
Wood Decor Inc	Pembroke	MA	G	781 826-4954	14433
La Valley Wood Inc	Van Buren	ME	F	207 316-6263	7121
Lignetics of Maine	Strong	ME	G	207 684-3457	7072
Moneysworth & Best USA Inc	Ashland	NH	E	603 968-3301	17600

WOOD PRDTS: Applicators

	CITY	ST	EMP	PHONE	ENTRY #
Carris Reels Inc	Center Rutland	VT	F	802 773-9111	21831
Kingdom Pellets LLC	North Clarendon	VT	E	802 747-1093	22218
Vermont Wood Pellet Co LLC	North Clarendon	VT	E	802 747-1093	22222

WOOD PRDTS: Barrel Heading, Sawn or split

	CITY	ST	EMP	PHONE	ENTRY #
Green Mtn Grn & Barrel LLC	Richmond	VT	G	802 324-5838	22311

WOOD PRDTS: Barrels & Barrel Parts

	CITY	ST	EMP	PHONE	ENTRY #
Bonito Manufacturing Inc	North Haven	CT	D	203 234-8786	3011

WOOD PRDTS: Baskets, Fruit & Veg, Round Stave, Till, Etc

	CITY	ST	EMP	PHONE	ENTRY #
Old Dublin Road Inc	Peterborough	NH	D	603 924-3861	19482
Daves Mrktplace Smthfield Inc	Smithfield	RI	G	401 830-5650	21218

WOOD PRDTS: Battery Separators

	CITY	ST	EMP	PHONE	ENTRY #
Hollingsworth & Vose Company **(PA)**	East Walpole	MA	C	508 850-2000	10524
Moore Company	Westerly	RI	C	401 596-2816	21532
Garflex Inc	Brattleboro	VT	D	802 257-5256	21728

WOOD PRDTS: Box Shook

	CITY	ST	EMP	PHONE	ENTRY #
Herrick Mill Work Inc	Contoocook	NH	E	603 746-5092	17945

WOOD PRDTS: Clothespins

	CITY	ST	EMP	PHONE	ENTRY #
National Clothes Pin Co Inc	Montpelier	VT	G	802 223-7332	22157

WOOD PRDTS: Engraved

	CITY	ST	EMP	PHONE	ENTRY #
Saint Josephs Wood Pdts LLC	New Haven	CT	G	203 787-5746	2732
Pierce Point Laser	Westbrook	ME	G	207 854-0133	7201

WOOD PRDTS: Flagpoles

	CITY	ST	EMP	PHONE	ENTRY #
Flagraphics Inc	Somerville	MA	E	617 776-7549	15172
Mass Sign & Decal Inc	Rockland	MA	G	781 878-7446	14812

WOOD PRDTS: Handles, Tool

	CITY	ST	EMP	PHONE	ENTRY #
Peavey Manufacturing Company	Eddington	ME	E	207 843-7861	5997
Roland & Whytock Company	Providence	RI	E	401 781-1234	21117

WOOD PRDTS: Lasts, Boot & Shoe

	CITY	ST	EMP	PHONE	ENTRY #
Jones & Vining Incorporated **(PA)**	Brockton	MA	E	508 232-7470	9158

WOOD PRDTS: Laundry

	CITY	ST	EMP	PHONE	ENTRY #
Clark Island Boat Works	South Thomaston	ME	G	207 594-4112	7045
Maine Pursuit LLC	Whitefield	ME	G	207 549-7972	7217
Maine Woods Pellet Company LLC	Athens	ME	E	207 654-2237	5542

WOOD PRDTS: Moldings, Unfinished & Prefinished

	CITY	ST	EMP	PHONE	ENTRY #
Conway Hardwood Products LLC	Gaylordsville	CT	E	860 355-4030	1530
D A Mfg Co LLC	Winchendon	MA	G	978 297-1059	17072
Forester Moulding & Lumber	Leominster	MA	F	978 840-3100	12140
Laird Woodworking Inc	Rochdale	MA	G	508 892-8877	14782
Owen Gray & Son	Brewer	ME	G	207 989-3575	5800
Boyce Highlands Furn Co Inc	Concord	NH	E	603 753-1042	17885

WOOD PRDTS: Mulch Or Sawdust

	CITY	ST	EMP	PHONE	ENTRY #
Mulch Ferris Products LLC	Danbury	CT	G	203 790-1155	957
Sweet Peet North America Inc	Litchfield	CT	G	860 361-6444	1953
Lucerne Farms	Fort Fairfield	ME	E	207 488-2520	6056

WOOD PRDTS: Mulch, Wood & Bark

	CITY	ST	EMP	PHONE	ENTRY #
Freezer Hill Mulch Company LLC	Bethany	CT	G	203 758-3725	121
Alfred J Cavallaro Inc	Andover	MA	G	978 475-2466	7536
Blank Industries Inc	Hudson	MA	F	855 887-3123	11759
Cook Forest Products Inc	Upton	MA	E	508 634-3300	15906
Granite Brook LLC	Weston	MA	G	781 788-9700	16826
Lashway Logging Inc	Williamsburg	MA	F	413 268-3600	16952
T J Bark Mulch Inc	Southwick	MA	F	413 569-2400	15418
Ingerson Transportation	Jefferson	NH	G	603 586-4335	18484
Barrup Farms Inc	Derby	VT	E	802 334-2331	21899

WOOD PRDTS: Novelties, Fiber

	CITY	ST	EMP	PHONE	ENTRY #
Essex Wood Products Inc	Colchester	CT	E	860 537-3451	802
Riley Mountain Products Inc	Antrim	NH	F	603 588-7234	17597
Brass Butterfly Inc	Poultney	VT	G	802 287-9818	22270
Hex Design Inc **(PA)**	Bennington	VT	G	802 442-3309	21672

WOOD PRDTS: Oars & Paddles

	CITY	ST	EMP	PHONE	ENTRY #
OBs Woodcrafts Inc	Swansea	MA	F	508 679-0480	15711
S P Holt Corporation	Orono	ME	G	207 866-4867	6558
Concept2 Inc **(PA)**	Morrisville	VT	E	802 888-7971	22166

WOOD PRDTS: Outdoor, Structural

	CITY	ST	EMP	PHONE	ENTRY #
Cns Outdoor Technologies LLC	Greenfield	MA	F	413 475-3840	11254
Environmental Improvements **(PA)**	Abington	MA	G	781 857-2375	7324
Gsoutfitting	Greenfield	MA	G	413 773-0247	11263
Shedworks Inc	Palmer	MA	G	413 284-1600	14296
Outdoor Enhancements LLC	Laconia	NH	G	603 524-8090	18580

WOOD PRDTS: Paint Sticks

	CITY	ST	EMP	PHONE	ENTRY #
Nottingham Wood Products	Derby	VT	G	802 766-2791	21903

WOOD PRDTS: Panel Work

	CITY	ST	EMP	PHONE	ENTRY #
Dante Ltd	Jewett City	CT	G	860 376-0204	1911

WOOD PRDTS: Planters & Window Boxes

	CITY	ST	EMP	PHONE	ENTRY #
Brattleworks Company Inc	Gardner	MA	G	978 410-5078	11105

WOOD PRDTS: Plugs

	CITY	ST	EMP	PHONE	ENTRY #
W R Hartigan & Son Inc	Burlington	CT	G	860 673-9203	682

WOOD PRDTS: Rulers & Rules

	CITY	ST	EMP	PHONE	ENTRY #
Acme United Corporation **(PA)**	Fairfield	CT	C	203 254-6060	1412

WOOD PRDTS: Shoe & Boot Prdts

	CITY	ST	EMP	PHONE	ENTRY #
New England Outerwear	Lewiston	ME	G	207 240-3069	6311

WOOD PRDTS: Shoe Trees

	CITY	ST	EMP	PHONE	ENTRY #
Rochester Shoe Tree Co Inc **(PA)**	Ashland	NH	D	603 968-3301	17601

WOOD PRDTS: Signboards

	CITY	ST	EMP	PHONE	ENTRY #
Connecticut Sign Service LLC	Essex	CT	G	860 767-7446	1395
William Crosby	Concord	MA	G	978 371-1111	10162
Maine Turnpike Authority	Cumberland Center	ME	F	207 829-4531	5929
Gemini Signs & Design Ltd	Conway	NH	G	603 447-3336	17952
Wood & Signs Ltd	East Dorset	VT	G	802 362-2386	21918
Wood & Wood Inc	Waitsfield	VT	G	802 496-3000	22572

WOOD PRDTS: Stepladders

	CITY	ST	EMP	PHONE	ENTRY #
Regional Stairs LLC	East Hartford	CT	G	860 290-1242	1217

WOOD PRDTS: Stoppers & Plugs

	CITY	ST	EMP	PHONE	ENTRY #
Peg Kearsarge Co Inc	Bartlett	NH	G	603 374-2341	17627
Souhegan Wood Products Inc	Wilton	NH	F	603 654-2311	19988

WOOD PRDTS: Trim

	CITY	ST	EMP	PHONE	ENTRY #
Advanced Trimwright Inc	East Taunton	MA	E	508 822-7745	10509
Jain America Foods Inc	Chicopee	MA	E	413 593-8883	10035
M & T Manufacturing Co	Peace Dale	RI	G	401 789-0472	20914

WOOD PRDTS: Trophy Bases

	CITY	ST	EMP	PHONE	ENTRY #
Diy Awards LLC **(PA)**	Stamford	CT	G	800 810-1216	4189
Initial Ideas Inc	Rutland	VT	G	802 775-1685	22340

WOOD PRDTS: Wrappers, Excelsior

	CITY	ST	EMP	PHONE	ENTRY #
Bees Wrap LLC	Middlebury	VT	E	802 643-2132	22101

WOOD PRODUCTS: Reconstituted

	CITY	ST	EMP	PHONE	ENTRY #
Huber Engineered Woods LLC	Easton	ME	D	207 488-6700	5989
Saunders At Locke Mills LLC	Greenwood	ME	F	207 875-2853	6156
Souhegan Wood Products Inc	Wilton	NH	F	603 654-2311	19988
Neshobe Wood Products Inc	Brandon	VT	F	802 247-3805	21711
Renewable Fuels Vermont LLC	Manchester Center	VT	F	802 362-1516	22088

WOOD TREATING: Millwork

	CITY	ST	EMP	PHONE	ENTRY #
Amerifix LLC	West Haven	CT	G	203 931-7290	5108
Wood Mill LLC	Lawrence	MA	G	978 683-2901	12085
Millwork City Internet Svcs	York	ME	G	207 370-5020	7313

WOOD TREATING: Structural Lumber & Timber

	CITY	ST	EMP	PHONE	ENTRY #
Forest Economic Advisors LLC	Littleton	MA	G	978 496-6336	12306
Oxford Timber Inc	Oxford	ME	F	207 539-9656	6570

WOOD TREATING: Wood Prdts, Creosoted

	CITY	ST	EMP	PHONE	ENTRY #
Midway United Limited	Needham Heights	MA	B	781 400-1742	13338
Thayer Wood Products Inc	Narragansett	RI	G	401 789-8825	20653
Brown Novelty Co Inc	Middlebury	VT	G	802 388-2502	22104

WOOD-BURNING STOVE STORES

	CITY	ST	EMP	PHONE	ENTRY #
John J Marr	Conway	NH	F	603 939-2698	17954

WOODWORK & TRIM: Exterior & Ornamental

	CITY	ST	EMP	PHONE	ENTRY #
Trellis Structures Inc	East Templeton	MA	F	888 285-4624	10521

WOODWORK & TRIM: Interior & Ornamental

	CITY	ST	EMP	PHONE	ENTRY #
Precision Woodcraft Inc	Canton	CT	G	860 693-3641	698
East Coast Interiors Inc	North Dartmouth	MA	F	508 995-4200	13919
Marie Deprofio	Waltham	MA	G	781 894-9793	16147
Alfreds Upholstering & Custom	Alfred	ME	F	207 536-5565	5514
Fernwood Inc **(PA)**	Cape Neddick	ME	G	207 363-7891	5879
Sunrise Home Inc	Scarborough	ME	G	207 839-8801	6941
Eastern Design Inc	Manville	RI	G	401 765-0558	20607

WOODWORK: Carved & Turned

	CITY	ST	EMP	PHONE	ENTRY #
Dundorf Designs USA Inc	Salem	CT	G	860 859-2955	3738
Fagan Design & Fabrication	West Haven	CT	G	203 937-1874	5122
Boston Turning Works	Watertown	MA	G	617 924-4747	16275
Paul White Woodcarving	East Sandwich	MA	G	508 888-1394	10507
Turning Acquisitions LLC	Buckfield	ME	E	207 336-2400	5853
Kings Cornr Woodturning Wdwkg	Weare	NH	G	603 529-0063	19937
Custom Woodturning	Tiverton	RI	G	401 625-5909	21256

WOODWORK: Interior & Ornamental, NEC

	CITY	ST	EMP	PHONE	ENTRY #
77 Mattatuck Heights LLC	Waterbury	CT	E	203 597-9338	4834
Ferraro Custom Woodwork LLC	Milford	CT	G	203 876-1280	2289
James J Licari **(PA)**	Bridgeport	CT	G	203 333-5000	434
Maddog LLC	Milford	CT	G	203 878-0147	2312
Madigan Millwork Inc	Unionville	CT	G	860 673-7601	4658
Maurer & Shepherd Joyners	Glastonbury	CT	F	860 633-2383	1563
Atlantis Woodworking Inc	Salem	MA	G	978 745-5312	14894
Builders Supply of Cape Cod	Sandwich	MA	G	508 888-0444	14963
Chilmark Archtctural Wdwkg LLC	Worcester	MA	F	508 856-9200	17355
Custom Woodworking LLC	Hubbardston	MA	G	978 928-3366	11743
K Int L Woodworking	Norwood	MA	G	781 440-0512	14168
Pomeroy & Co Inc	Charlestown	MA	E	617 241-0234	9841
Richard Pg Millwork Co Inc	Cummaquid	MA	G	508 776-2433	10172
Silva Woodworking	Westport	MA	G	508 636-0059	16846
Tradern Fine Woodworking Inc	Newton	MA	G	617 393-3733	13644
John J Marr	Conway	NH	F	603 939-2698	17954
Water Street Woodworking	Warren	RI	G	401 245-1921	21315
Yoffa Woodworking	Newport	RI	F	401 846-7659	20689

WOODWORK: Ornamental, Cornices, Mantels, Etc.

	CITY	ST	EMP	PHONE	ENTRY #
Fagan Design & Fabrication	West Haven	CT	G	203 937-1874	5122

	CITY	ST	EMP	PHONE	ENTRY #
Industrial Wood Product Co	Shelton	CT	G	203 735-2374	3817
Cape Cod Cupola Co Inc	North Dartmouth	MA	G	508 994-2119	13916
Cogworks Ltd	Antrim	NH	G	603 588-3333	17594
Traditional Woodworking LLC	Piermont	NH	G	603 272-9324	19493
Artistic Woodworks Inc	Rochester	VT	G	802 767-3123	22316

WOVEN WIRE PRDTS, NEC

	CITY	ST	EMP	PHONE	ENTRY #
Amtec Corporation	Plainfield	CT	E	860 230-0006	3447
C O Jelliff Corporation **(PA)**	Southport	CT	D	203 259-1615	4094
Gemco Manufacturing Co Inc	Southington	CT	E	860 628-5529	4052
New England Wirecloth Co LLC	Fitchburg	MA	G	978 343-4998	10844
Neptco Incorporated **(HQ)**	Pawtucket	RI	D	401 722-5500	20863
Standard Chain Co	Warwick	RI	E	508 695-6611	21429

WREATHS: Artificial

	CITY	ST	EMP	PHONE	ENTRY #
RR Design	Bethel	CT	G	203 792-3419	176
Pams Wreaths	Harpswell	ME	G	207 751-7234	6174
Whitney Originals Inc	Whitneyville	ME	D	207 255-3392	7222
Gibson Peggy Day	West Glover	VT	F	802 525-3034	22607
Vermont Center Wreaths Inc	Newport Center	VT	D	802 334-6432	22208

WRENCHES

	CITY	ST	EMP	PHONE	ENTRY #
Brimatco Corporation	Cheshire	CT	G	203 272-0044	717
Power-Dyne LLC	Middletown	CT	E	860 346-9283	2211
Skillcraft Machine Tool Co	South Windsor	CT	F	860 953-1246	4010

WRITING FOR PUBLICATION SVCS

	CITY	ST	EMP	PHONE	ENTRY #
Synchrgnix Info Strategies Inc	Cambridge	MA	G	302 892-4800	9670

X-RAY EQPT & TUBES

	CITY	ST	EMP	PHONE	ENTRY #
Bidwell Industrial Group Inc **(PA)**	Middletown	CT	E	860 346-9283	2178
Biowave Innovations LLC	Wilton	CT	C	203 982-8157	5278
Comet Technologies USA Inc **(DH)**	Shelton	CT	E	203 447-3200	3790
Hologic Inc	Danbury	CT	C	203 790-1188	933
Kub Technologies Inc	Stratford	CT	E	203 364-8544	4429
Parker Medical Inc	New Milford	CT	G	860 350-3446	2822
Precision X-Ray Inc	North Branford	CT	F	203 484-2011	2972
Precision X-Ray Inc	North Branford	CT	F	203 484-2011	2973
Remote Technologies Inc **(PA)**	Greenwich	CT	G	203 661-2798	1641
Topex Inc	Danbury	CT	F	203 748-5918	999
Biolucent LLC	Marlborough	MA	G	508 263-2900	12726
Bruker Corporation **(PA)**	Billerica	MA	C	978 663-3660	8223
Cytyc Surgical Products LLC	Marlborough	MA	D	508 263-2900	12746
Eastern Diagnostic Imaging	Taunton	MA	F	508 828-2970	15746
Grady Research Inc	Ayer	MA	G	978 772-3303	7921
Hologic Inc	Marlborough	MA	C	508 263-2900	12769
Hologic Inc	Marlborough	MA	C	508 263-2900	12770
Hologic Inc **(PA)**	Marlborough	MA	C	508 263-2900	12771
Hologic Foreign Sales Corp	Bedford	MA	A	781 999-7300	7980
Princeton Security Tech Inc **(HQ)**	Franklin	MA	G	609 924-7310	11074
Princton Gamma-Tech Instrs Inc	Franklin	MA	F	609 924-7310	11075
Saxslab US Inc	Amherst	MA	G	413 237-4309	7524
V J Electronix Inc	Chelmsford	MA	E	631 589-8800	9938
Vivid Technologies Inc	Woburn	MA	G	781 939-3986	17314
Hologic Inc	Londonderry	NH	C	603 668-7688	18702
Aadco Medical Inc	Randolph	VT	D	802 728-3400	22296

YARN & YARN SPINNING

	CITY	ST	EMP	PHONE	ENTRY #
St Regis Sportswear Ltd	North Andover	MA	G	518 725-6767	13729
Family Yarns Inc	Etna	ME	G	207 269-3852	6025
Jagger Brothers	Springvale	ME	E	207 324-5622	7053
Worsted Spinning Neng LLC	Springvale	ME	G	207 324-5622	7056
Harrisville Designs Inc **(PA)**	Harrisville	NH	G	603 827-3333	18302
Conneaut Industries Inc	West Greenwich	RI	D	401 392-1110	21454
D & T Spinning Inc	South Woodstock	VT	D	802 228-2925	22497

YARN MILLS: Texturizing, Throwing & Twisting

	CITY	ST	EMP	PHONE	ENTRY #
New England Water Jet Cutting	New Bedford	MA	G	508 993-9235	13425

YARN MILLS: Winding

	CITY	ST	EMP	PHONE	ENTRY #
Conneaut Industries Inc	West Greenwich	RI	D	401 392-1110	21454

YARN WHOLESALERS

	CITY	ST	EMP	PHONE	ENTRY #
Harrisville Designs Inc **(PA)**	Harrisville	NH	G	603 827-3333	18302

YARN: Animal Fiber, Spun

	CITY	ST	EMP	PHONE	ENTRY #
Robertson-Chase Fibers LLC	North Billerica	MA	F	978 453-2837	13862

YARN: Spinning, Spun

	CITY	ST	EMP	PHONE	ENTRY #
S & D Spinning Mill Inc	Millbury	MA	E	508 865-2267	13175

YARN: Weaving, Spun

	CITY	ST	EMP	PHONE	ENTRY #
Buffalo Industrial Fabrics Inc	Wilton	CT	G	203 553-9400	5282

YARN: Wool, Spun

	CITY	ST	EMP	PHONE	ENTRY #
Green Mountain Spinnery Inc	East Dummerston	VT	F	802 387-4528	21919

YARNS & THREADS: Non-Fabric Materials

	CITY	ST	EMP	PHONE	ENTRY #
E A M T Inc	Woonsocket	RI	E	401 762-1500	21558